Reference Guide to

AMERICAN LITERATURE

FOURTH EDITION

St. James Reference Guides

American Literature

English Literature, 3 vols.

French Literature, 2 vols.

Short Fiction

World Literature, 2 vols.

Reference Guide to

AMERICAN LITERATURE

FOURTH EDITION

Introduction by

WARREN FRENCH, JOHN ISTEL,
LEWIS LEARY, AMY LING,
LINDA WAGNER-MARTIN,
CHARLES E. MAY, MARCO PORTALES, and
A. LaVONNE BROWN RUOFF

EDITOR
THOMAS RIGGS

ST. JAMES PRESS

AN IMPRINT OF THE GALE GROUP

DETROIT • SAN FRANCISCO • LONDON
BOSTON • WOODBRIDGE, CT

Thomas Riggs, *Editor*
Terry Bain, *Associate Editor*
Sally Cobau, *Assistant Editor*
Nancy Dziedzic, Lee Esbenshade, Janice Jorgensen, Beth Judy,
Robert Rauch, Linda Tomchuck, *Contributing Editors*

Margaret Mazurkiewicz, *Project Coordinator*

Laura Standley Berger, Joann Cerrito, Dave Collins, Steve Cusack,
Nicolet V. Elert, Miranda Ferrara, Jamie FitzGerald,
Kristin Hart, Laura S. Kryhoski, Michael J. Tyrkus
St. James Press Staff

Peter M. Gareffa, *Managing Editor, St. James Press*

Dorothy Maki, *Manufacturing Manager*
Wendy Blurton, *Senior Buyer*

Cynthia Baldwin, *Product Design Manager*
Gary Leach, *Graphic Artist*

Library of Congress Cataloging-in-Publication Data

Reference guide to American literature / editor, Thomas Riggs. -- 4th ed.
    p.   cm.
    Includes bibliographical references and index.
    ISBN 1-55862-417-1
    1. American literature--Bio-bibliography Dictionaries. 2. Authors, American--Biography Dictionaries. 3. American literature Dictionaries. I. Riggs, Thomas, 1963- .
    PS129.R44 1999
    810.9′0003--dc21
    [B]   99-31376
                                                     CIP

Printed in the United States of America

St. James Press is an imprint of Gale Group
Gale Group and Design is a trademark used herein under license
10 9 8 7 6 5 4 3 2

CONTENTS

EDITOR'S NOTE

The *Reference Guide to American Literature,* now in its fourth edition, has been in print since 1983. Each edition has had the same goal: to provide biographical and bibliographic information, as well as brief critical essays, on some of the most important writers in American history.

The fourth edition has entries on 590 American writers. Of these, 311 are primarily fiction writers, 156 are poets, 74 are dramatists, and 49 are writers of nonfiction. More than 360 of the 590 entrants were deceased at the time of publication. The earliest of these is William Bradford, born in 1590, who was the governor of Plymouth Plantation and a historian of the colony. The youngest of the entrants are Kaye Gibbons and Naomi Wallace, both born in 1960. Gibbons, who grew up in North Carolina, is a novelist whose works have focused on the Southern experience of her female characters. Wallace, born in Kentucky, has written plays that explore the connection between sex, race, social class, and politics in postindustrial capitalist society.

This guide is divided into two major sections. The first section contains 590 entries, each on an American writer. These entries have the following organization:

- *Biographical data,* listing, if known, the entrant's date and place of birth, education, spouse and number of children, career, awards, and, if the entrant is deceased, the death date.

- *Bibliography,* listing the title and date of the entrant's separately published works, including short-story collections, novels, and books of plays, verse, and nonfiction. Edited and translated books are included, as well as media adaptations, theatrical activities, and manuscript collections. The bibliography ends with a selected list of critical studies about the author's work.

- *Critical essay on the entrant's work,* written by an established scholar, editor, or reviewer. Each essay ends with the contributor's byline.

The second section of the book has 138 essays, each discussing a work by one of the entrants. Of the 138 featured works, 65 are novels, 28 are poems, 17 are short stories, 15 are plays, and 13 are works of nonfiction. Some authors, such as Edgar Allan Poe, Henry David Thoreau, Edith Wharton, Ernest Hemingway, Katherine Anne Porter, and Tennessee Williams, have several works represented in this section.
St. James Press would like to thank the many people, including the advisers, who worked on this revision. The advisers' suggestions were used to select the featured writers and works and to help with other matters concerning the content and organization of the book. We would also like to thank the contributors, many of whom agreed to write for the book despite a heavy workload or prior publication commitments. Finally, we would like to express our appreciation to the living writers who provided biographical and bibliographic information for their entries.

I would personally like to thank the people who worked with me in organizing the project and editing the book: Sally Cobau, who oversaw the compilation of the biographical and bibliographic sections and helped with many day-to-day tasks; Terry Bain, who helped with commissioning writers and handled much of the correspondence with them; Robert Rauch, Nancy Dziedzic, Linda Tomchuck, Beth Judy, and Lee Esbenshade, who line edited the essays; Janice Jorgensen, who reviewed entries for last-minute problems; and Margaret Mazurkiewicz, who coordinated various in-house responsibilities, including the proofreading, and helped resolve problems with the project and with individual entries.

—Thomas Riggs

ADVISERS

Sallyann Ferguson
Warren French
Donald Hall
John Istel
Bruce King
Amy Ling
Deborah Louis

Francis O. Mattson
Charles E. May
Walter J. Meserve
Marjorie Perloff
Marco Portales
A. LaVonne-Brown Ruoff
Linda Wagner-Martin

CONTRIBUTORS

Opal Palmer Adisa
Thomas P. Adler
Joseph O. Aimone
M.J. Alexander
Sandra Carlton Alexander
Walter Allen
David D. Anderson
James Angle
Robert D. Arner
Leonard R.N. Ashley
Alvin Aubert
James C. Austin

Linda P. Bachman
Terry Bain
Jonathan Barker
Victor D.C. Bascara
John Battenburg
Brian Beatty
Peter G. Beidler
Emilio Bejel
Samuel Irving Bellman
George N. Bennett
Alice R. Bensen
Dominic J. Bisignano
Jean Frantz Blackall
Lynn Z. Bloom
Joseph Blotner
Walter Bode
B.J. Bolden
Mary Weatherspoon Bowden
Jennifer Brantley
Neville Braybrooke
Jean Bright
Lawrence R. Broer
Ashley Brown

Sharon Brown
Terry Browne
Juan Bruce-Novoa
Craig Bryson
Martin Bucco
Susan Alice Bunn
R.A. Burchell
Keith Byerman

Richard J. Calhoun
Rob Canfield
Guy A. Cardwell
Anna Carew-Miller
Brian Carpenter
Frederic I. Carpenter
Humphrey Carpenter
Thomas Cassidy
Russ Castronova
Ann Charters
Balance T.P. Chow
Karen Chow
Paul Christensen
Ed Cifelli
William Claire
Laurie Clancy
Hennig Cohen
Ruby Cohn
Clark Colahan
William J. Collins
Mary Condé
William Corbett
Neil Corcoran
Jay Ann Cox
Martha Heasley Cox
Richard H. Crowder
Eugene Current-Garcia

Tish Dace
Curtis Dahl
Frank Day
Alice Deck
Joseph Deters
Leonard J. Deutsch
Janice L. Dewey
Li Dian
Gloria Harper Dickinson
James M. Drayton
Louise Duus

Clayton L. Eichelberger
Chester E. Eisinger
Eduardo F. Elias
Patrick Evans

Charles Fanning
Ann Dahlstrom Farmer
Philip José Farmer
Pin-Chia Feng
Thomas Joseph Ferraro
M.J. Fitzgerald
Ian Fletcher
Joseph M. Flora
Edward Halsey Foster
G.S. Fraser
Warren French

Jane S. Gabin
Karen Wilkes Gainey
Sally M. Gall
Kathryn Grimm Garrett
Robert Gaspar
John C. Gerber
Donald B. Gibson
R. Barbara Gitenstein
Clarence A. Glasrud
Charlotte Margolis Goodman
Lois Gordon
Janice Gould
Sandra Y. Govan
George Grella

Paul Hadella
Janet V. Haedicke
Birgit Hans
Lisa Harper
Tomo Hattori
John Heath-Stubbs
William J. Heim
Allison Hersh
Geof Hewitt
Jack Hicks
William Higgins
Bert Hitchcock
Thomas E. Hockersmith
Jacqueline Hoefer
Daniel Hoffman
Robert Hogan
Jan Hokenson
Jonathan Holden

Janice Butler Holm
C. Hugh Holman
Arthur Horowitz
Amy E. Hudock
Robert N. Hudspeth
Jennifer A. Hynes

M. Thomas Inge
John Istel

Theresa A. James
Helen Jaskoski
Estelle C. Jelinek
Alisa Johnson
Robert K. Johnson
Andrew O. Jones
J. Sydney Jones
Lillie Jones
Nancy Carol Joyner
Catherine Judd

Zoë Coralnik Kaplan
Bruce Kellner
Bruce King
Kimball King
Keneth Kinnamon
Jerome Klinkowitz
John G. Kuhn
Chirantan Kulshrestha

Luis Leal
Lewis Leary
Hsiu-chuan Lee
Neil Andre Lester
James A. Levernier
Naomi Lewis
Bruce A. Lohof
Francisco A. Lomeli
George C. Longest
Margaret A. Loose
Deborah Louis
John Lucas
Townsend Ludington

Sheng-mei Ma
Brent MacLaine
Frank MacShane
David Madden
Tony Magistrale
Jacquelyn Marie
Suzanne Marrs
Todd Marshall
Yuko Matsukawa
Charles E. May
Mary A. McCay
Margaret B. McDowell
Robert McDowell
Howard McNaughton
Walter J. Meserve
Jordan Y. Miller
Tyrus Miller
Bruce Mills

Mozella Mitchell
Christian H. Moe
George Monteiro
Jack B. Moore
Rayburn S. Moore
Robert A. Morace
Bridget M. Morgan
Katharine M. Morsberger
Robert E. Morsberger

I.B. Nadel
Francis M. Nevins, Jr.
Joe Nordgren
Brady Nordland
Robert Lee Novak

Rafael Ocasio
Thomas F. O'Donnell
Hans Ostrom

Shirley J. Paolini
Joseph Francis Patrouch
William Peden
Tom Pendergast
Kim Pereira
Barbara M. Perkins
George Perkins
Margaret Perry
Patsy B. Perry
Joyce Pettis
John B. Pickard
Jan Pilditch
Sanford Pinsker
Helen Houser Popovich
Valerie Sweeney Prince
Ross J. Pudaloff

Peter Quartermain

Deanna E. Ramey
David Ray
Ralph Reckly, Sr.
John Q. Reed
James Reeves
Edward C. Reilly
John M. Reilly
Terry Reilly
Sylvia Lyons Render
Robert F. Richards
Robert B. Marks Ridinger
Donald A. Ringe
Salvador Rodriguez del Pino
Gary W. Rogers
Earl Rovit
James Ruppert
Glenn Richard Ruthley

Geoff Sadler
Carol Lee Saffioti
Stewart F. Sanderson
Mollie Sandock
James R. Saucerman

George Brandon Saul
John Scarry
Arnold T. Schwab
Catherine Seelye
Per Seyersted
J.N. Sharma
Allen Shepherd
David A. Shevin
David Shih
Carl R. Shirley
Paula W. Shirley
Elizabeth Shostak
Alan R. Shucard
James R. Simmons, Jr.
Amritjit Singh
Esther Marian Greenwell Smith
Larry Smith
Stan Smith
Sheila Smith-McCoy
Eric Solomon
Louis Charles Stagg
Donald E. Stanford
Michael N. Stanton
Ilan Stavans
Jane W. Stedman
Madeleine B. Stern
Dayana Stetco
Cindy Ann Stiles
David Stouck
W.J. Stuckey
James N. Stull
Claude Summers
Joseph H. Summers
Martha Sutro
Susan Swartzlander

G. Thomas Tanselle
Ann Thwaite
Rowena Tomaneng
Hector Avalos Torres
Derek A. Traversi
Richard C. Turner

George Uba

Annette Van Dyke

Linda Wagner-Martin
Marshall Walker
Mark I. Wallach
Richard Walser
Qun Wang
Carol M. Ward
Val Warner
R.J.C. Watt
Harold H. Watts
Gerald Weales
Sybil B. Weir
Marilyn C. Wesley
Perry D. Westbrook
Peter Wild
Wade Williams

Denise Wiloch
T.J. Winnifrith
Shelley Sunn Wong
Miseong Woo
James Woodress

Laura Wyrick

Thomas Daniel Young
Kenneth Young
Laura Weiss Zlogar

ALPHABETICAL LIST OF WRITERS

Henry Adams
George Ade
James Agee
Conrad Aiken
Zoë Akins
Edward Albee
Louisa May Alcott
Horatio Alger
Nelson Algren
James Lane Allen
Paula Gunn Allen
Dorothy Allison
Alurista
A.R. Ammons
Rudolfo A. Anaya
Maxwell Anderson
Robert Anderson
Sherwood Anderson
Maya Angelou
Gloria Anzaldúa
Timothy Shay Arthur
John Ashbery
Isaac Asimov
Gertrude Atherton
Louis Auchincloss

James Baldwin
Joseph G. Baldwin
Toni Cade Bambara
Nathaniel Bannister
Amiri Baraka
James Nelson Barker
Joel Barlow
Djuna Barnes
Philip Barry
John Barth
Donald Barthelme
L. Frank Baum
Ann Beattie
S.N. Behrman
David Belasco
Edward Bellamy
Saul Bellow
Ludwig Bemelmans
Robert Benchley
Stephen Vincent Benét
William Rose Benét
John Berryman
Doris Waugh Betts
Ambrose Bierce
Robert Montgomery Bird
Elizabeth Bishop

John Peale Bishop
Harold Bloom
Robert Bly
Maxwell Bodenheim
Louise Bogan
George Henry Boker
Paul Bowles
James Boyd
H.H. Boyesen
Kay Boyle
Hugh Henry Brackenridge
Ray Bradbury
Roark Bradford
William Bradford
Anne Bradstreet
Richard Brautigan
Louis Bromfield
Gwendolyn Brooks
John Brougham
Charles Brockden Brown
Rita Mae Brown
Sterling A. Brown
William Wells Brown
William Cullen Bryant
Pearl S. Buck
Ed Bullins
Carlos Bulosan
Kenneth Burke
Frances Hodgson Burnett
Edgar Rice Burroughs
William S. Burroughs
William Byrd II

James Branch Cabell
George Washington Cable
Abraham Cahan
James M. Cain
Erskine Caldwell
Hortense Calisher
S. Alice Callahan
Truman Capote
Raymond Carver
Willa Cather
Raymond Chandler
William Ellery Channing
Fray Angélico Chávez
Paddy Chayefsky
John Cheever
Charles Waddell Chesnutt
Lydia Maria Child
Alice Childress
Frank Chin

Thomas Holley Chivers
Kate Chopin
Winston Churchill
John Ciardi
Sandra Cisneros
Walter Van Tilburg Clark
Judith Ortiz Cofer
George M. Cohan
Marc Connelly
Ebenezer Cooke
John Esten Cooke
Clark Coolidge
James Fenimore Cooper
Robert Coover
James Gould Cozzens
Hart Crane
Stephen Crane
F. Marion Crawford
Robert Creeley
Harry Crews
Rachel Crothers
Countée Cullen
E.E. Cummings

Edward Dahlberg
Augustin Daly
Richard Henry Dana, Jr.
Donald Davidson
Rebecca Harding Davis
Richard Harding Davis
John William De Forest
Margaret Deland
Martin Robinson Delany
Samuel R. Delany
Don DeLillo
Floyd Dell
John Dewey
James Dickey
Emily Dickinson
Joan Didion
Annie Dillard
E.L. Doctorow
J.P. Donleavy
Ignatius Donnelly
Hilda Doolittle
Michael Anthony Dorris
John Dos Passos
Frederick Douglass
Rita Dove
Joseph Rodman Drake
Theodore Dreiser
W.E.B. Du Bois
André Dubus
Henry L. Dumas
Paul Laurence Dunbar
Robert Duncan
William Dunlap
Finley Peter Dunne
Timothy Dwight

Winnifred Eaton
Richard Eberhart

Jonathan Edwards
Edward Eggleston
T.S. Eliot
Stanley L. Elkin
Ralph Ellison
Ralph Waldo Emerson
Louise Erdrich

James T. Farrell
William Faulkner
Kenneth Fearing
Edna Ferber
Lawrence Ferlinghetti
Leslie A. Fiedler
Eugene Field
Vardis Fisher
Clyde Fitch
F. Scott Fitzgerald
John Gould Fletcher
Carolyn Forché
Richard Ford
María Irene Fornés
Hannah Foster
Stephen Collins Foster
Waldo Frank
Benjamin Franklin
Harold Frederic
Mary E. Wilkins Freeman
Philip Freneau
Robert Frost
Northrop Frye
Henry Blake Fuller

William Gaddis
Ernest J. Gaines
Zona Gale
Erle Stanley Gardner
John Gardner
Hamlin Garland
William H. Gass
Henry Louis Gates, Jr.
Kaye Gibbons
Sandra M. Gilbert and Susan Gubar
Ellen Gilchrist
William Gillette
Charlotte Perkins Gilman
Allen Ginsberg
Nikki Giovanni
Ellen Glasgow
Susan Glaspell
Louis Glück
Gail Godwin
Emma Goldman
Paul Goodman
Caroline Gordon
Paul Green
Horace Gregory
Zane Grey
John Guare
Louise Imogen Guiney
Ramon Guthrie

Jessica Tarahata Hagedorn
Donald Hall
Fitz-Greene Halleck
Dashiell Hammett
Lorraine Hansberry
Joy Harjo
Frances Ellen Watkins Harper
Michael S. Harper
Edward Harrigan
George Washington Harris
Jim Harrison
Moss Hart
Bret Harte
Robert Hass
John Hawkes
Nathaniel Hawthorne
John Hay
Robert Hayden
Paul Hamilton Hayne
Lafcadio Hearn
Ben Hecht
Robert Anson Heinlein
Lyn Hejinian
Joseph Heller
Lillian Hellman
Ernest Hemingway
O. Henry
Joseph Hergesheimer
James A. Herne
Robert Herrick
Oscar Hijuelos
Tony Hillerman
Chester Himes
Rolando Hinojosa
Charles Fenno Hoffman
Oliver Wendell Holmes
Garrett Kaoru Hongo
Johnson Jones Hooper
Francis Hopkinson
Richard Hovey
Bronson Howard
Sidney Howard
E.W. Howe
Susan Howe
William Dean Howells
Charles Hoyt
Langston Hughes
Richard Hugo
James Huneker
Zora Neale Hurston
David Henry Hwang

William Inge
Joseph Holt Ingraham
John Irving
Washington Irving
Christopher Isherwood

Helen Hunt Jackson
Shirley Jackson
Harriet Ann Jacobs
Henry James

William James
Randall Jarrell
Robinson Jeffers
Thomas Jefferson
Sarah Orne Jewett
Charles Johnson
James Weldon Johnson
Gayl Jones
James Jones

George S. Kaufman
George Kelly
John Pendleton Kennedy
Jane Kenyon
Jack Kerouac
Ken Kesey
Richard E. Kim
Stephen King
Sidney Kingsley
Barbara Kingsolver
Maxine Hong Kingston
Galway Kinnell
Joseph Kirkland
Etheridge Knight
John Knowles
Yusef Komunyakaa
Arthur Kopit
Jerzy Kosinski
Stanley Kunitz
Tony Kushner

Oliver La Farge
Louis L'Amour
Sidney Lanier
Ring Lardner
Arthur Laurents
John Howard Lawson
Elmore Leonard
Denise Levertov
Sinclair Lewis
Genny Lim
Lin Tai-Yi
Lin Yutang
Vachel Lindsay
Romulus Linney
Alain Locke
Ross Lockridge
Jack London
Henry Wadsworth Longfellow
Augustus Baldwin Longstreet
Barry Holstun Lopez
Audre Lorde
H.P. Lovecraft
Amy Lowell
James Russell Lowell
Robert Lowell
Andrew Lytle

Charles MacArthur
Ross Macdonald
Percy MacKaye
Archibald MacLeish

Haki R. Madhubuti
Norman Mailer
Bernard Malamud
David Mamet
Edwin Markham
John P. Marquand
Don Marquis
Paule Marshall
Carole Maso
Bobbie Ann Mason
Edgar Lee Masters
Cotton Mather
Mary McCarthy
Carson McCullers
Claude McKay
Terry McMillan
Larry McMurtry
D'Arcy McNickle
James Alan McPherson
Herman Melville
H.L. Mencken
Miguel Méndez M.
James Merrill
W.S. Merwin
Edna St. Vincent Millay
Arthur Miller
Henry Miller
Joaquin Miller
Janice Mirikitani
Donald Grant Mitchell
Langdon Mitchell
Margaret Mitchell
S. Weir Mitchell
Nicholasa Mohr
N. Scott Momaday
José Montoya
William Vaughn Moody
Marianne Moore
Alejandro Morales
Christopher Morley
Wright Morris
Toni Morrison
Anna Cora Mowatt
Bharati Mukherjee
Mary Noailles Murfree

Vladimir Nabokov
Petroleum V. Nasby
Ogden Nash
Gloria Naylor
John Neal
Richard Nelson
Howard Nemerov
Anaïs Nin
Frank Norris

Joyce Carol Oates
Fitz-James O'Brien
Tim O'Brien
Flannery O'Connor
Clifford Odets
Frank O'Hara

John O'Hara
Tillie Olsen
Charles Olson
Eugene O'Neill
Simon J. Ortiz
Cynthia Ozick

Thomas Nelson Page
Thomas Paine
Grace Paley
Sara Paretsky
Dorothy Parker
Francis Parkman
Suzan-Lori Parks
Kenneth Patchen
James Kirke Paulding
John Howard Payne
Walker Percy
Bob Perelman
S. J. Perelman
Ann Petry
David Graham Phillips
Jayne Anne Phillips
Robert Pinsky
Sylvia Plath
Edgar Allan Poe
Katherine Anne Porter
Estela Portillo Trambley
Ezra Pound
J.F. Powers
James Purdy
Mario Puzo
Thomas Pynchon

Ellery Queen

Ayn Rand
John Crowe Ransom
Marjorie Kinnan Rawlings
John Rechy
Saunders Redding
Ishmael Reed
Kenneth Rexroth
Elmer Rice
Adrienne Rich
Conrad Richter
Laura Riding
James Whitcomb Riley
Mary Roberts Rinehart
Tomás Rivera
Elizabeth Madox Roberts
Kenneth Roberts
Edwin Arlington Robinson
Theodore Roethke
O.E. Rølvaag
Wendy Rose
Henry Roth
Philip Roth
Mary Rowlandson
Susanna Rowson
Muriel Rukeyser
Damon Runyon

J.D. Salinger
Edgar Saltus
Ricardo Sánchez
Carl Sandburg
George Santayana
Bienvenido N. Santos
William Saroyan
May Sarton
Delmore Schwartz
Catharine Maria Sedgwick
Samuel Sewall
Anne Sexton
Ntozake Shange
Karl Shapiro
Henry Wheeler Shaw
Edward Sheldon
Sam Shepard
Robert E. Sherwood
Leslie Marmon Silko
Charles Simic
William Gilmore Simms
Neil Simon
Louis Simpson
Upton Sinclair
Isaac Bashevis Singer
Betty Smith
Lee Smith
Martin Cruz Smith
W.D. Snodgrass
Gary Snyder
Susan Sontag
Gary Soto
Elizabeth Spencer
Jean Stafford
William Stafford
Wilbur Daniel Steele
Wallace Stegner
Gertrude Stein
John Steinbeck
Gerald Stern
Wallace Stevens
Trumbull Stickney
Rex Stout
Harriet Beecher Stowe
Mark Strand
T.S. Stribling
William Styron
Ruth Suckow

Amy Tan
Booth Tarkington
Allen Tate
James Tate
Bayard Taylor
Edward Taylor
Sara Teasdale
Paul Theroux
Henry David Thoreau
Thomas Bangs Thorpe
James Thurber
Henry Timrod
Melvin B. Tolson

Jean Toomer
Albion W. Tourgée
B. Traven
Lionel Trilling
John Trumbull
Barbara W. Tuchman
Frederick Goddard Tuckerman
Mark Twain
Anne Tyler
Royall Tyler

John Updike

Mark Van Doren
John Van Druten
Carl Van Vechten
Jones Very
Gore Vidal
Alma Luz Villanueva
José Antonio Villarreal
Paula Vogel
Kurt Vonnegut, Jr.

Alice Walker
Margaret Walker
Lew Wallace
Naomi Wallace
Edward Lewis Wallant
Artemus Ward
Charles Dudley Warner
Mercy Warren
Robert Penn Warren
Booker T. Washington
Frank Waters
James Welch
Mac Wellman
Eudora Welty
Glenway Wescott
Jessamyn West
Nathanael West
Edith Wharton
Phillis Wheatley
John Wheelwright
E.B. White
Walt Whitman
John Greenleaf Whittier
John Edgar Wideman
Michael Wigglesworth
Richard Wilbur
Thornton Wilder
John A. Williams
Tennessee Williams
William Carlos Williams
Nathaniel Parker Willis
August Wilson
Edmund Wilson
Sarah Winnemucca
Yvor Winters
Owen Wister
Thomas Wolfe
Tom Wolfe, Jr.
Tobias Wolff

Constance Fenimore Woolson
James Wright
Richard Wright
Elinor Wylie

Frank Yerby
Anzia Yezierska

Louis Zukofsky

CHRONOLOGICAL LIST OF WRITERS

1590(?)-1627	William Bradford
1612/13-1672	Anne Bradstreet
1631-1705	Michael Wigglesworth
1637-1711	Mary Rowlandson
1642-1729	Edward Taylor
1652-1730	Samuel Sewall
1663-1728	Cotton Mather
1667(?)-1732(?)	Ebenezer Cooke
1674-1744	William Byrd II
1703-1758	Jonathan Edwards
1706-1790	Benjamin Franklin
1728-1814	Mercy Warren
1737-1791	Francis Hopkinson
1737-1809	Thomas Paine
1743-1826	Thomas Jefferson
1748-1816	Hugh Henry Brackenridge
1750-1831	John Trumbull
1752-1817	Timothy Dwight
1752-1832	Philip Freneau
1753/4(?)-1784	Phillis Wheatley
1754-1812	Joel Barlow
1757-1826	Royall Tyler
1758-1840	Hannah Foster
1762-1824	Susanna Rowson
1766-1839	William Dunlap
1771-1810	Charles Brockden Brown
1778-1860	James Kirke Paulding
1783-1859	Washington Irving
1784-1858	James Nelson Barker
1789-1851	James Fenimore Cooper
1789-1867	Catharine Maria Sedgwick
1790-1867	Fitz-Greene Halleck
1790-1870	Augustus Baldwin Longstreet
1791-1852	John Howard Payne
1793-1876	John Neal
1794-1878	William Cullen Bryant
1795-1820	Joseph Rodman Drake
1795-1870	John Pendleton Kennedy
1800-1884	Nathaniel Bannister
1802-1880	Lydia Maria Child
1803-1882	Ralph Waldo Emerson
1804-1864	Nathaniel Hawthorne
1806-1854	Robert Montgomery Bird
1806-1867	Nathaniel Parker Willis
1806-1870	William Gilmore Simms
1806-1884	Charles Fenno Hoffman
1807-1882	Henry Wadsworth Longfellow
1807-1892	John Greenleaf Whittier
1809-1849	Edgar Allan Poe
1809-1858	Thomas Holley Chivers
1809-1860	Joseph Holt Ingraham
1809-1885	Timothy Shay Arthur
1809-1894	Oliver Wendell Holmes
1810-1880	John Brougham
1811-1896	Harriet Beecher Stowe
1812-1885	Martin Robinson Delany
1813-1880	Jones Very
1813-1884	William Wells Brown
1813-1897	Harriet Ann Jacobs
1814-1869	George Washington Harris
1815-1862	Johnson Jones Hooper
1815-1864	Joseph G. Baldwin
1815-1878	Thomas Bangs Thorpe
1815-1882	Richard Henry Dana, Jr.
1817-1862	Henry David Thoreau
1817-1901	William Ellery Channing
1818-1885	Henry Wheeler Shaw
1818-1895	Frederick Douglass
1819-1870	Anna Cora Mowatt
1819-1891	James Russell Lowell
1819-1891	Herman Melville
1819-1892	Walt Whitman
1821-1873	Frederick Goddard Tuckerman
1822-1908	Donald Grant Mitchell
1823-1890	George Henry Boker
1823-1893	Francis Parkman
1825-1878	Bayard Taylor
1825-1911	Frances Ellen Watkins Harper
1826-1864	Stephen Collins Foster
1826-1906	John William De Forest
1827-1905	Lew Wallace
1828-1862	Fitz-James O'Brien
1828-1867	Henry Timrod
1829-1900	Charles Dudley Warner
1829-1914	S. Weir Mitchell
1830-1885	Helen Hunt Jackson
1830-1886	John Esten Cooke
1830-1886	Emily Dickinson
1830-1886	Paul Hamilton Hayne
1830-1894	Joseph Kirkland
1831-1901	Ignatius Donnelly
1831-1910	Rebecca Harding Davis
1832-1888	Louisa May Alcott
1832-1889	Horatio Alger
1833-1888	Petroleum V. Nasby
1834-1867	Artemus Ward
1835-1910	Mark Twain
1836-1902	Bret Harte
1837-1902	Edward Eggleston
1837-1920	William Dean Howells
1838-1899	Augustin Daly
1838-1905	John Hay
1838-1905	Albion W. Tourgée
1838-1918	Henry Adams
1839-1901	James A. Herne
1839-1913	Joaquin Miller
1840-1894	Constance Fenimore Woolson
1842-1881	Sidney Lanier

1842-1908	Bronson Howard
1842-1910	William James
1842-1914	Ambrose Bierce
1843-1916	Henry James
1844-1891	Sarah Winnemucca
1844-1911	Edward Harrigan
1844-1925	George Washington Cable
1848-1895	H.H. Boyesen
1849-1909	Sarah Orne Jewett
1849-1916	James Whitcomb Riley
1849-1924	Frances Hodgson Burnett
1849-1925	James Lane Allen
1850-1895	Eugene Field
1850-1898	Edward Bellamy
1850-1904	Lafcadio Hearn
1850-1922	Mary Noailles Murfree
1851-1904	Kate Chopin
1852-1930	Mary E. Wilkins Freeman
1852-1940	Edwin Markham
1853-1922	Thomas Nelson Page
1853-1931	David Belasco
1853-1937	William Gillette
1853-1937	E.W. Howe
1854-1909	F. Marion Crawford
1855-1921	Edgar Saltus
1856-1898	Harold Frederic
1856-1915	Booker T. Washington
1856-1919	L. Frank Baum
1857-1945	Margaret Deland
1857-1921	James Huneker
1857-1929	Henry Blake Fuller
1857-1948	Gertrude Atherton
1858-1932	Charles Waddell Chesnutt
1859-1900	Charles Hoyt
1859-1952	John Dewey
1860-1938	Owen Wister
1860-1939	Charlotte Perkins Gilman
1860-1940	Hamlin Garland
1860-1951	Abraham Cahan
1861-1920	Louise Imogen Guiney
1862-1910	O. Henry
1862-1935	Langdon Mitchell
1862-1937	Edith Wharton
1863-1952	George Santayana
1864-1900	Richard Hovey
1864-1916	Richard Harding Davis
1865-1909	Clyde Fitch
1866-1944	George Ade
1867-1911	David Graham Phillips
1867-1936	Finley Peter Dunne
1868-1894	S. Alice Callahan
1868-1938	Robert Herrick
1868-1950	Edgar Lee Masters
1868-1963	W.E.B. DuBois
1869-1910	William Vaughn Moody
1869-1940	Emma Goldman
1869-1946	Booth Tarkington
1870-1902	Frank Norris
1871-1900	Stephen Crane
1871-1938	James Weldon Johnson
1871-1945	Theodore Dreiser
1871-1947	Winston Churchill

1872-1906	Paul Laurence Dunbar
1872-1939	Zane Grey
1873-1945	Ellen Glasgow
1873-1947	Willa Cather
1874-1904	Trumbull Stickney
1874-1925	Amy Lowell
1874-1925	Robert Lowell
1874-1938	Zona Gale
1874-1946	Gertrude Stein
1874-1963	Robert Frost
1875-1954	Winnifred Eaton
1875-1950	Edgar Rice Burroughs
1875-1956	Percy MacKaye
1876-1916	Jack London
1876-1931	O.E. Rølvaag
1876-1941	Sherwood Anderson
1876-1958	Mary Roberts Rinehart
1878-1937	Don Marquis
1878-1942	George M. Cohan
1878-1958	Rachel Crothers
1878-1967	Carl Sandburg
1878-1968	Upton Sinclair
1879-1931	Vachel Lindsay
1879-1955	Wallace Stevens
1879-1958	James Branch Cabell
1880-1946	Damon Runyon
1880-1954	Joseph Hergesheimer
1880-1956	H.L. Mencken
1880-1964	Carl Van Vechten
1881-1941	Elizabeth Madox Roberts
1881-1965	T.S. Stribling
1882-1948	Susan Glaspell
1882-1969	B. Traven
1883-1963	William Carlos Williams
1884-1933	Sara Teasdale
1885-1928	Elinor Wylie
1885-1933	Ring Lardner
1885-1951	Sinclair Lewis
1885-1957	Kenneth Roberts
1885-1968	Edna Ferber
1885-1970	Anzia Yezierska
1885-1972	Ezra Pound
1886-1946	Edward Sheldon
1886-1950	William Rose Benét
1886-1950	John Gould Fletcher
1886-1954	Alain Locke
1886-1958	Zoë Akins
1886-1961	Hilda Doolittle
1886-1970	Wilbur Daniel Steele
1886-1975	Rex Stout
1887-1962	Robinson Jeffers
1887-1969	Floyd Dell
1887-1972	Marianne Moore
1887-1974	George Kelly
1888-1944	James Boyd
1888-1953	Eugene O'Neill
1888-1959	Maxwell Anderson
1888-1959	Raymond Chandler
1888-1965	T.S. Eliot
1888-1974	John Crowe Ransom
1889-1945	Robert Benchley
1889-1948	Claude McKay

1889-1961	George S. Kaufman
1889-1967	Waldo Frank
1889-1970	Erle Stanley Gardner
1889-1973	Conrad Aiken
1890-1937	H.P. Lovecraft
1890-1957	Christopher Morley
1890-1968	Conrad Richter
1890-1980	Marc Connelly
1890-1980	Katherine Anne Porter
1891-1939	Sidney Howard
1891-1980	Henry Miller
1892-1944	John Peale Bishop
1892-1950	Edna St. Vincent Millay
1892-1954	Maxwell Bodenheim
1892-1960	Ruth Suckow
1892-1967	Elmer Rice
1892-1973	Pearl S. Buck
1892-1977	James M. Cain
1892-1982	Djuna Barnes
1892-1982	Archibald MacLeish
1893-1960	John P. Marquand
1893-1967	Dorothy Parker
1893-1968	Donald Davidson
1893-1973	S.N. Behrman
1894-1961	Dashiell Hammett
1894-1961	James Thurber
1894-1962	E.E. Cummings
1894-1964	Ben Hecht
1894-1967	Jean Toomer
1894-1972	Mark Van Doren
1894-1977	John Howard Lawson
1894-1981	Paul Green
1895-1956	Charles MacArthur
1895-1968	Vardis Fisher
1895-1972	Edmund Wilson
1895-1976	Li Yutang
1895-1981	Caroline Gordon
1896-1940	F. Scott Fitzgerald
1896-1948	Roark Bradford
1896-1949	Philip Barry
1896-1953	Marjorie Kinnan Rawlings
1896-1955	Robert E. Sherwood
1896-1956	Louis Bromfield
1896-1970	John Dos Passos
1896-1972	Betty Smith
1896-1973	Ramon Guthrie
1897-1993	Kenneth Burke
1897-1940	John Wheelwright
1897-1962	William Faulkner
1897-1970	Louise Bogan
1897-1975	Thornton Wilder
1898-1943	Stephen Vincent Benét
1898-1962	Ludwig Bemelmans
1898-1966	Melvin B. Tolson
1898-1982	Horace Gregory
1899-1932	Hart Crane
1899-1961	Ernest Hemingway
1899-1977	Vladimir Nabokov
1899-1979	Allen Tate
1899-1985	E.B. White
1900-1938	Thomas Wolfe
1900-1949	Margaret Mitchell

1900-1968	Yvor Winters
1900-1977	Edward Dahlberg
1901-1991	Laura Riding
1901-1957	John Van Druten
1901-1960	Zora Neale Hurston
1901-1963	Oliver La Farge
1901-1987	Glenway Wescott
1901-1989	Sterling A. Brown
1902-1995	Andrew Lytle
1902-1995	Frank Waters
1902-1961	Kenneth Fearing
1902-1967	Langston Hughes
1902-1968	John Steinbeck
1902-1971	Ogden Nash
1902-1984	Jessamyn West
1902-1992	Kay Boyle
1903-1940	Nathanael West
1903-1946	Countée Cullen
1903-1977	Anaïs Nin
1903-1978	James Gould Cozzens
1903-1987	Erskine Caldwell
1904-	Richard Eberhart
1904-1991	Isaac Bashevis Singer
1904-1961	Moss Hart
1904-1977	D'Arcy McNickle
1904-1978	Louis Zukofsky
1904-1979	James T. Farrell
1904-1979	S.J. Perelman
1904-1986	Christopher Isherwood
1905-	Stanley Kunitz
1905-1970	John O'Hara
1905-1971	Manfred B. Lee (Ellery Queen)
1905-1975	Lionel Trilling
1905-1982	Frederic Dannay (Ellery Queen)
1905-1982	Ayn Rand
1905-1982	Kenneth Rexroth
1905-1984	Lillian Hellman
1905-1989	Robert Penn Warren
1906-1995	Sidney Kingsley
1906-1995	Henry Roth
1906-1963	Clifford Odets
1906-1988	Saunders Redding
1907-1988	Robert Anson Heinlein
1908-1960	Richard Wright
1908-1963	Theodore Roethke
1908-1981	William Saroyan
1908-1988	Louis L'Amour
1908-1997	Ann Petry
1909-1955	James Agee
1909-1971	Walter Van Tilburg Clark
1909-1981	Nelson Algren
1909-1984	Chester Himes
1909-1993	Wallace Stegner
1909-	Eudora Welty
1910-1970	Charles Olson
1910-1986	Paul Bowles
1910-1996	Fray Angélico Chávez
1910-1998	Wright Morris
1911-1972	Paul Goodman
1911-1972	Kenneth Patchen
1911-1979	Elizabeth Bishop
1911-1983	Tennessee Williams

1911-	Hortense Calisher
1911-	Bienvenido N. Santos
1912-1982	John Cheever
1912-1989	Barbara W. Tuchman
1912-1991	Northrop Frye
1912-1989	Mary McCarthy
1912-1995	May Sarton
1913-1966	Delmore Schwartz
1913-1973	William Inge
1913-1980	Robert Hayden
1913-1980	Muriel Rukeyser
1913-	Tillie Olsen
1913-	Karl Shapiro
1914-1948	Ross Lockridge
1914-1956	Carlos Bulosan
1914-1965	Randall Jarrell
1914-1972	John Berryman
1914-1986	Bernard Malamud
1914-1997	William S. Burroughs
1914-1994	Ralph Ellison
1914-1993	William Stafford
1915-1979	Jean Stafford
1915-1983	Ross Macdonald
1915-	Saul Bellow
1915-	Arthur Miller
1915-1998	Margaret Walker
1916-1986	John Ciardi
1916-1990	Walker Percy
1916-1991	Frank Yerby
1917-1967	Carson McCullers
1917-	Robert Anderson
1917-	Louis Auchincloss
1917-	Gwendolyn Brooks
1917-	Leslie A. Fiedler
1917-	J.F. Powers
1918-	Arthur Laurents
1919-1965	Shirley Jackson
1919-1988	Robert Duncan
1919-	Lawrence Ferlinghetti
1919-	J.D. Salinger
1920-1992	Isaac Asimov
1920-	Ray Bradbury
1920-1994	Alice Childress
1920-1991	Howard Nemerov
1920-1999	Mario Puzo
1921-1977	James Jones
1921-	Elizabeth Spencer
1921-	Richard Wilbur
1922-1969	Jack Kerouac
1922-1998	William Gaddis
1922-	Kurt Vonnegut, Jr.
1922-	Grace Paley
1923-1981	Paddy Chayefsky
1923-1982	Richard Hugo
1923-1997	James Dickey
1923-	Joseph Heller
1923-1997	Denise Levertov
1923-	Norman Mailer
1923-	James Purdy
1923-	Louis Simpson
1924-1984	Truman Capote
1924-1987	James Baldwin
1924-	William H. Gass
1924-	José Antonio Villarreal
1925-1964	Flannery O'Connor
1925-1998	John Hawkes
1925-	Tony Hillerman
1925-	Elmore Leonard
1925-	William Styron
1925-	Gore Vidal
1925-	John A. Williams
1926-1962	Edward Lewis Wallant
1926-1966	Frank O'Hara
1926-	A.R. Ammons
1926-	Robert Bly
1926-	Robert Creeley
1926-	J.P. Donleavy
1926-	John Knowles
1926-1995	James Merrill
1926-	W.D. Snodgrass
1926-	Lin Tai-yi
1927-1980	James Wright
1927-	John Ashbery
1927-	Galway Kinnell
1927-	W.S. Merwin
1927-	Neil Simon
1928-1974	Anne Sexton
1928-	Edward Albee
1928-	Maya Angelou
1928-	Cynthia Ozick
1929-	Paule Marshall
1929-	Adrienne Rich
1929-	Rolando Hinojosa
1930-1965	Lorraine Hansberry
1930-	John Barth
1930-	Harold Bloom
1930-1995	Stanley L. Elkin
1930-	María Irene Fornés
1930-	Romulus Linney
1930-	Miguel Méndez M.
1930-	Gary Snyder
1930-	Tom Wolfe, Jr.
1931-1991	Etheridge Knight
1931-1989	Donald Barthelme
1931-	E.L. Doctorow
1931-	Toni Morrison
1932-1963	Sylvia Plath
1932-	Doris Waugh Betts
1932-	Robert Coover
1932-	Richard E. Kim
1932-	José Montoya
1932-	John Updike
1933-1982	John Gardner
1933-	Ernest J. Gaines
1933-1991	Jerzy Kosinski
1933-	Philip Roth
1933-	Susan Sontag
1934-1968	Henry L. Dumas
1934-1992	Audre Lorde
1934-	Amiri Baraka
1934-	Joan Didion
1934-	N. Scott Momaday
1934-	John Rechy
1934-	Mark Strand

1935-1969	Edwin Arlington Robinson		1943-	James Alan McPherson
1935-1984	Richard Brautigan		1943-	Sam Shepard
1935-1984	Tomás Rivera		1943-	James Tate
1935-	Ed Bullins		1944-	Rita Mae Brown
1935-	Harry Crews		1944-	Richard Ford
1935-	Ellen Gilchrist		1944-	Susan Gubar
1935-	Ken Kesey		1944-	Alejandro Morales
1935-	Nicholasa Mohr		1944-	Lee Smith
1936-	Don DeLillo		1944-	Alma Luz Villanueva
1936-1999	André Dubus		1944-	Alice Walker
1936-	Sandra M. Gilbert		1945-1997	Michael Anthony Dorris
1936-	Larry McMurtry		1945-	Annie Dillard
1936-	Estela Portillo Trambley		1945-	Barry Holstun Lopez
1937-	Rudolfo A. Anaya		1945-	Mac Wellman
1937-	Jim Harrison		1945-	August Wilson
1937-	Susan Howe		1945-	Tobias Wolff
1937-	Arthur Kopit		1946-1988	Miguel Piñero
1937-	Thomas Pynchon		1946-	Genny Lim
1937-	Gerald Stern		1946-	Tim O'Brien
1938-1988	Raymond Carver		1947-1995	Jane Kenyon
1938-	John Guare		1947-	Alurista
1938-	Michael S. Harper		1947-	Ann Beattie
1938-	Joyce Carol Oates		1947-	Stephen King
1938-	Ishmael Reed		1947-	Yusef Komunyakaa
1938-	Charles Simic		1947-	David Mamet
1939-	Paula Gunn Allen		1947-	Sara Paretsky
1939-1995	Toni Cade Bambara		1947-	Bob Perelman
1939-	Clark Coolidge		1948-	Charles Johnson
1940-	Frank Chin		1948-	Wendy Rose
1940-	Maxine Hong Kingston		1948-	Ntozake Shange
1940-	Bobbie Ann Mason		1948-	Leslie Marmon Silko
1940-	Bharati Mukherjee		1949-	Dorothy Allison
1940-	Robert Pinsky		1949-	Jessica Tarahata Hagedorn
1940-	James Welch		1949-	Gayl Jones
1941-	Robert Hass		1950-	Carolyn Forché
1941-	Lyn Hejinian		1950-	Henry Louis Gates, Jr.
1941-	Simon J. Ortiz		1950-	Gloria Naylor
1941-1995	Ricardo Sánchez		1950-	Richard Nelson
1941-	Paul Theroux		1951-	Joy Harjo
1941-	Anne Tyler		1951-	Oscar Hijuelos
1941-	John Edgar Wideman		1951-	Garrett Kaoru Hongo
1942-	Gloria Anzaldúa		1951-	Terry McMillan
1942-	Samuel R. Delany		1951-	Paula Vogel
1942-	John Irving		1952-	Amy Tan
1942-	Haki R. Madhubuti		1952-	Jayne Anne Phillips
1942-	Janice Mirikitani		1955-	Barbara Kingsolver
1942-	Martin Cruz Smith		1956-	Tony Kushner
1943-	Nikki Giovanni		1960-	Kaye Gibbons
1943-	Louise Glück		1960-	Naomi Wallace

ALPHABETICAL LIST OF WORKS

Absalom, Absalom! Novel by William Faulkner, 1936.

The Adventures of Huckleberry Finn. Novel by Mark Twain, 1884.

The Adventures of Tom Sawyer. Novel by Mark Twain, 1876.

The Age of Innocence. Novel by Edith Wharton, 1920.

All the King's Men. Novel by Robert Penn Warren, 1946.

The Ambassadors. Novel by Henry James, 1903.

American Buffalo. Play by David Mamet, 1975.

Anatomy of Criticism. Criticism by Northrop Frye, 1957.

Angels in America. Play by Tony Kushner, 1991.

Annie Allen. Poems by Gwendolyn Brooks, 1970.

Ariel. Poems by Sylvia Plath, 1965.

The Assistant. Novel by Bernard Malamud, 1957.

The Autobiography of Alice B. Toklas. Memoir by Gertrude Stein, 1933.

Awake and Sing! Play by Clifford Odets, 1935.

The Awakening. Novel by Kate Chopin, 1899.

"Because I could not stop for Death." Poem by Emily Dickinson, written 1863.

Beloved. Novel by Toni Morrison, 1987.

The Big Sleep. Novel by Raymond Chandler, 1939.

"Big Two-Hearted River." Story by Ernest Hemingway, 1925.

Billy Budd. Novel by Herman Melville, 1924 (written 1888-91).

Black Elk Speaks. Autobiography by Black Elk as told to John G. Neihardt, 1932.

The Bridge. Poem by Hart Crane, 1930.

The Call of the Wild. Novel by Jack London, 1903.

The Cantos. Poems by Ezra Pound, from 1925.

Catch-22. Novel by Joseph Heller, 1961.

The Catcher in the Rye. Novel by J.D. Salinger, 1951.

The Cathedral. Poem by James Russell Lowell, 1870.

"Cathedral." Short story by Raymond Carver, 1983.

Ceremony. Novel by Leslie Marmon Silko, 1977.

"Civil Disobedience." Essay by Henry David Thoreau, 1849.

The Color Purple. Novel by Alice Walker, 1982.

Common Sense. Essay by Thomas Paine, 1776.

The Contrast. Play by Royall Tyler, 1787.

The Country of the Pointed Firs. Novel by Sarah Orne Jewett, 1896.

The Crying of Lot 49. Novel by Thomas Pynchon, 1966.

The Damnation of Theron Ware. Novel by Harold Frederic, 1896.

Darker. Poems by Mark Strand, 1968.

The Day of the Locust. Novel by Nathanael West, 1939.

Death of a Salesman. Play by Arthur Miller, 1949.

"The Death of the Hired Man." Poem by Robert Frost, 1914.

The Dream Songs. Poems by John Berryman, from 1964.

The Education of Henry Adams: An Autobiography. 1907.

"Ethan Brand." Story by Nathaniel Hawthorne, 1850.

"The Fall of the House of Usher." Story by Edgar Allan Poe, 1839.

The Federalist. Essays by Alexander Hamilton, James Madison, and John Jay, 1788.

"The Fish." Poem by Elizabeth Bishop, 1946.

"Gifts of the Magi." Story by O. Henry, 1905.

The Glass Menagerie. Play by Tennessee Williams, 1944.

Go Tell It on the Mountain. Novel by James Baldwin, 1953.

Gods Determinations. Poem by Edward Taylor, written 1680s(?).

The Grapes of Wrath. Novel by John Steinbeck, 1939.

Gravity's Rainbow. Novel by Thomas Pynchon, 1973.

The Great Gatsby. Novel by F. Scott Fitzgerald, 1925.

Herzog. Novel by Saul Bellow, 1964.

House Made of Dawn. Novel by N. Scott Momaday, 1968.

The House of Mirth. Novel by Edith Wharton, 1905.

The House on Mango Street. Stories by Sandra Cisneros, 1984.

Howl. Poem by Allen Ginsberg, 1956.

I Know Why the Caged Bird Sings. Memoir by Maya Angelou, 1970.

Invisible Man. Novel by Ralph Ellison, 1952.

John Brown's Body. Poem by Stephen Vincent Benét, 1928.

The Joy Luck Club. Novel by Amy Tan, 1989.

The Jungle. Novel by Upton Sinclair, 1906.

The Last of the Mohicans. Novel by James Fenimore Cooper, 1826.

Leaves of Grass. Poems by Walt Whitman, 1855 (and later revisions).

"The Legend of Sleepy Hollow." Story by Washington Irving, 1820.

Life Studies. Poems by Robert Lowell, 1959.

Little Women. Novel by Louisa May Alcott, 1868-69.

Lolita. Novel by Vladimir Nabokov, 1955.

Long Day's Journey into Night. Play by Eugene O'Neill, 1956.

Look Homeward, Angel. Novel by Thomas Wolfe, 1929.

Looking Backward 2000-1887. Novel by Edward Bellamy, 1888.

Losing Battles. Novel by Eudora Welty, 1970.

The Lost Son. Poem by Theodore Roethke, 1951.

Love Medicine. Novel by Louise Erdrich, 1984; expanded 1993.

"The Love Song of J. Alfred Prufrock." Poem by T.S. Eliot, 1910-11.

Main Street. Novel by Sinclair Lewis, 1920.

Main-Travelled Roads. Stories by Hamlin Garland, 1891.

The Mambo Kings Play Songs of Love. Novel by Oscar Hijuelos, 1989.

"The Man That Corrupted Hadleyburg." Story by Mark Twain, 1899.

Margaret Fleming. Play by James A. Herne, 1890.

Margret Howth. Novel by Rebecca Harding Davis, 1862.

The Maximus Poems. By Charles Olson, from 1953.

The Member of the Wedding. Novel by Carson McCullers, 1946.

Moby-Dick. Novel by Herman Melville, 1851.

Modern Chivalry. Fiction by Hugh Henry Brackenridge, 1792-1805 (and later revisions).

Murder in the Cathedral. Play by T.S. Eliot, 1935.

"The Murders in the Rue Morgue." Story by Edgar Allan Poe, 1841.

My Ántonia. Novel by Willa Cather, 1918.

The Naked and the Dead. Novel by Norman Mailer, 1948.

Native Son. Novel by Richard Wright, 1940.

Nature. Essay by Ralph Waldo Emerson, 1836.

The Octopus. Novel by Frank Norris, 1901.

"Old Mortality." Story by Katherine Anne Porter, 1938.

On the Road. Novel by Jack Kerouac, 1957.

Our Town. Play by Thornton Wilder, 1938.

Paterson. Poem by William Carlos Williams, 1946-63.

Peregrinos de Aztlán. Novel by Miguel Méndez M., 1974, English translation, 1993.

"Personal Narrative." Autobiography by Jonathan Edwards, 1765.

Picnic. Play by William Inge, 1953.

"Poetry." Poem by Marianne Moore, 1919 (and later revisions).

The Portrait of a Lady. Novel by Henry James, 1881.

A Raisin in the Sun. Play by Lorraine Hansberry, 1959.

The Red Badge of Courage. Novel by Stephen Crane, 1895.

The Rise of Silas Lapham. Novel by William Dean Howells, 1885.

The Road to Tamazunchale. Novel by Ron Arias, 1975.

The Scarlet Letter. Novel by Nathaniel Hawthorne, 1850.

"The Secret Life of Walter Mitty." Story by James Thurber, 1939.

Self-Portrait in a Convex Mirror. Poem by John Ashbery, 1975.

Ship of Fools. Novel by Katherine Anne Porter, 1962.

Sister Carrie. Novel by Theodore Dreiser, 1900.

"The Sky Is Gray." Novella by Ernest J. Gaines, 1963.

Snow-Bound. Poem by John Greenleaf Whittier, 1866.

"Somewhere i have never travelled, gladly beyond." Poem by E.E. Cummings, 1931.

Souls of Black Folk. Essays by W.E.B. Du Bois, 1903.

The Sound and the Fury. Novel by William Faulkner, 1929.

Strange Interlude. Play by Eugene O'Neill, 1928.

A Streetcar Named Desire. Play by Tennessee Williams, 1947.

The Sun Also Rises. Novel by Ernest Hemingway, 1926.

"Sunday Morning." Poem by Wallace Stevens, 1923.

"The Swimmer." Story by John Cheever, 1964.

The Tenth Muse. Poems by Anne Bradstreet, 1650.

"Thanatopsis." Poem by William Cullen Bryant, 1821.

Their Eyes Were Watching God. Novel by Zora Neale Hurston, 1937.

Three Lives. Stories by Gertrude Stein, 1909.

The Tunnel. Novel by William H. Gass, 1995.

The Turn of the Screw. Story by Henry James, 1898.

Uncle Tom's Cabin. Novel by Harriet Beecher Stowe, 1852.

U.S.A. Novels by John Dos Passos, 1930-36.

Walden. Prose by Henry David Thoreau, 1854.

The Waste Land. Poem by T.S. Eliot, 1922.

The Weary Blues. Poems by Langston Hughes, 1926.

Who's Afraid of Virginia Woolf? Play by Edward Albee, 1962.

Winesburg, Ohio. Stories by Sherwood Anderson, 1919.

Winter in the Blood. Novel by James Welch, 1974.

Wise Blood. Novel by Flannery O'Connor, 1952.

The Woman Warrior: Memories of a Girlhood among Ghosts. Autobiography by Maxine Hong Kingston, 1975.

The Wonderful Wizard of Oz. Novel by L. Frank Baum, 1900.

CHRONOLOGICAL LIST OF WORKS

The Tenth Muse. Poems by Anne Bradstreet, 1650.

Gods Determinations. Poem by Edward Taylor, written 1680s(?).

"Personal Narrative." Autobiography by Jonathan Edwards, 1765.

Common Sense. Essay by Thomas Paine, 1776.

The Contrast. Play by Royall Tyler, 1787.

The Federalist. Essays by Alexander Hamilton, James Madison, and John Jay, 1788.

Modern Chivalry. Fiction by Hugh Henry Brackenridge, 1792-1805 (and later revisions).

"The Legend of Sleepy Hollow." Story by Washington Irving, 1820.

"Thanatopsis." Poem by William Cullen Bryant, 1821.

The Last of the Mohicans. Novel by James Fenimore Cooper, 1826.

Nature. Essay by Ralph Waldo Emerson, 1836.

"The Fall of the House of Usher." Story by Edgar Allan Poe, 1839.

"The Murders in the Rue Morgue." Story by Edgar Allan Poe, 1841.

"Civil Disobedience." Essay by Henry David Thoreau, 1849.

"Ethan Brand." Story by Nathaniel Hawthorne, 1850.

The Scarlet Letter. Novel by Nathaniel Hawthorne, 1850.

Moby-Dick. Novel by Herman Melville, 1851.

Uncle Tom's Cabin. Novel by Harriet Beecher Stowe, 1852.

Walden. Prose by Henry David Thoreau, 1854.

Leaves of Grass. Poems by Walt Whitman, 1855 (and later revisions).

Margret Howth. Novel by Rebecca Harding Davis, 1862.

"Because I could not stop for Death." Poem by Emily Dickinson, written 1863.

Snow-Bound. Poem by John Greenleaf Whittier, 1866.

Little Women. Novel by Louisa May Alcott, 1868-69.

The Cathedral. Poem by James Russell Lowell, 1870.

The Adventures of Tom Sawyer. Novel by Mark Twain, 1876.

The Portrait of a Lady. Novel by Henry James, 1881.

The Adventures of Huckleberry Finn. Novel by Mark Twain, 1884.

The Rise of Silas Lapham. Novel by William Dean Howells, 1885.

Looking Backward 2000-1887. Novel by Edward Bellamy, 1888.

Billy Budd. Novel by Herman Melville, 1924 (written 1888-91).

Margaret Fleming. Play by James Herne, 1890.

Main-Travelled Roads. Stories by Hamlin Garland, 1891.

The Red Badge of Courage. Novel by Stephen Crane, 1895.

The Country of the Pointed Firs. Novel by Sarah Orne Jewett, 1896.

The Damnation of Theron Ware. Novel by Harold Frederic, 1896.

The Turn of the Screw. Story by Henry James, 1898.

The Awakening. Novel by Kate Chopin, 1899.

"The Man That Corrupted Hadleyburg." Story by Mark Twain, 1899.

Sister Carrie. Novel by Theodore Dreiser, 1900.

The Wonderful Wizard of Oz. Novel by L. Frank Baum, 1900.

The Octopus. Novel by Frank Norris, 1901.

The Ambassadors. Novel by Henry James, 1903.

The Call of the Wild. Novel by Jack London, 1903.

Souls of Black Folk. Essays by W.E.B. Du Bois, 1903.

"Gifts of the Magi." Story by O. Henry, 1905.

The House of Mirth. Novel by Edith Wharton, 1905.

The Jungle. Novel by Upton Sinclair, 1906.

The Education of Henry Adams: An Autobiography. 1907.

Three Lives. Stories by Gertrude Stein, 1909.

"The Love Song of J. Alfred Prufrock." Poem by T.S. Eliot, 1910-1911.

"The Death of the Hired Man." Poem by Robert Frost, 1914.

My Ántonia. Novel by Willa Cather, 1918.

Winesburg, Ohio. Stories by Sherwood Anderson, 1919.

"Poetry." Poem by Marianne Moore, 1919 (and later revisions).

The Age of Innocence. Novel by Edith Wharton, 1920.

Main Street. Novel by Sinclair Lewis, 1920.

The Waste Land. Poem by T.S. Eliot, 1922.

"Sunday Morning." Poem by Wallace Stevens, 1923.

"Big Two-Hearted River." Story by Ernest Hemingway, 1925.

The Cantos. Poems by Ezra Pound, from 1925.

The Great Gatsby. Novel by F. Scott Fitzgerald, 1925.

The Sun Also Rises. Novel by Ernest Hemingway, 1926.

The Weary Blues. Poems by Langston Hughes, 1926.

John Brown's Body. Poem by Stephen Vincent Benét, 1928.

Strange Interlude. Play by Eugene O'Neill, 1928.

Look Homeward, Angel. Novel by Thomas Wolfe, 1929.

The Sound and the Fury. Novel by William Faulkner, 1929.

The Bridge. Poem by Hart Crane, 1930.

U.S.A. Novels by John Dos Passos, 1930-36.

"Somewhere i have never travelled, gladly beyond." Poem by E.E. Cummings, 1931.

Black Elk Speaks. Autobiography by Black Elk as told to John G. Neihardt, 1932.

The Autobiography of Alice B. Toklas. Memoir by Gertrude Stein, 1933.

Awake and Sing! Play by Clifford Odets, 1935.

Murder in the Cathedral. Play by T. S. Eliot, 1935.

Absalom, Absalom! Novel by William Faulkner, 1936.

Their Eyes Were Watching God. Novel by Zora Neale Hurston, 1937.

"Old Mortality." Story by Katherine Anne Porter, 1938.

Our Town. Play by Thornton Wilder, 1938.

The Big Sleep. Novel by Raymond Chandler, 1939.

The Day of the Locust. Novel by Nathanael West, 1939.

The Grapes of Wrath. Novel by John Steinbeck, 1939.

The Little Foxes. Play by Lillian Hellman, 1939.

"The Secret Life of Walter Mitty." Story by James Thurber, 1939.

Native Son. Novel by Richard Wright, 1940.

The Glass Menagerie. Play by Tennessee Williams, 1944.

All the King's Men. Novel by Robert Penn Warren, 1946.

"The Fish." Poem by Elizabeth Bishop, 1946.

The Member of the Wedding. Novel by Carson McCullers, 1946.

Paterson. Poem by William Carlos Williams, 1946-63.

A Streetcar Named Desire. Play by Tennessee Williams, 1947.

The Naked and the Dead. Novel by Norman Mailer, 1948.

Death of a Salesman. Play by Arthur Miller, 1949.

Annie Allen. Poems by Gwendolyn Brook, 1950.

The Catcher in the Rye. Novel by J.D. Salinger, 1951.

The Lost Son. Poem by Theodore Roethke, 1951.

Invisible Man. Novel by Ralph Ellison, 1952.

Wise Blood. Novel by Flannery O'Connor, 1952.

Go Tell It on the Mountain. Novel by James Baldwin, 1953.

The Maximus Poems. By Charles Olson, from 1953.

Picnic. Play by William Inge, 1953.

Lolita. Novel by Vladimir Nabokov, 1955.

Howl. Poem by Allen Ginsberg, 1956.

Long Day's Journey into Night. Play by Eugene O'Neill, 1956.

Anatomy of Criticism. Criticism by Northrop Frye, 1957.

The Assistant. Novel by Bernard Malamud, 1957.

On the Road. Novel by Jack Kerouac, 1957.

Life Studies. Poems by Robert Lowell, 1959.

A Raisin in the Sun. Play by Lorraine Hansberry, 1959.

Catch-22. Novel by Joseph Heller, 1961.

Ship of Fools. Novel by Katherine Anne Porter, 1962.

Who's Afraid of Virginia Woolf? Play by Edward Albee, 1962.

"The Sky Is Gray." Novella by Ernest J. Gaines, 1963.

The Dream Songs. Poems by John Berryman, from 1964.

"The Swimmer." Story by John Cheever, 1964.

Herzog. Novel by Saul Bellow, 1964.

Ariel. Poems by Sylvia Plath, 1965.

The Crying Lost 49. Novel by Thomas Pynchon, 1966.

Darker. Poems by Mark Strand, 1968.

House Made of Dawn. Novel by N. Scott Momaday, 1968.

I Know Why the Caged Bird Sings. Memoir by Maya Angelou, 1970.

Losing Battles. Novel by Eudora Welty, 1970.

Gravity's Rainbow. Novel by Thomas Pynchon, 1973.

Peregrinos de Aztlán. Novel by Miguel Méndez M., 1974, English translation, 1993.

Winter in the Blood. Novel by James Welch, 1974.

American Buffalo. Play by David Mamet, 1975.

The Road to Tamazunchale. Novel by Ron Arias, 1975.

Self-Portrait in a Convex Mirror. Poem by John Ashbery, 1975.

The Woman Warrior: Memories of a Girlhood among Ghosts. Autobiography by Maxine Hong Kingston, 1975.

Ceremony. Novel by Leslie Marmon Silko, 1977.

The Color Purple. Novel by Alice Walker, 1982.

"Cathedral." Short story by Raymond Carver, 1983.

The House on Mango Street. Stories by Sandra Cisneros, 1984.

Love Medicine. Novel by Louise Erdrich, 1984; expanded 1993.

Beloved. Novel by Toni Morrison, 1987.

The Joy Luck Club. Novel by Amy Tan, 1989.

The Mambo Kings Play Songs of Love. Novel by Oscar Hijuelos, 1989.

Angels in America. Play by Tony Kusher, 1991.

The Tunnel. Novel by William H. Gass, 1995.

INTRODUCTION

By Lewis Leary and Warren French, with revisions and additions by John Istel, Amy Ling, Charles E. May, Marco Portales, A. LaVonne Brown Ruoff, and Linda Wagner-Martin.

The Colonial Experience: 1620-1776

From the start American literature has been shaped by the impulse to create a uniquely "American" form of expression that would rival--even surpass—the literatures settlers brought with them to this country. Literature from the geographical area that was to become the United States was first written by soldiers, missionaries, and colonists in English, Spanish, and French—the three main languages of the Europeans who explored and settled in North America. Most of the earliest such documents were published in Europe or in Mexico, as was the case with Alvar Nunez Cabeza de Vaca's wonderful *Relaciones (1542)* and Rene Goulaine de Laudonniere's *Notable histories Containing Foure Voyages Made by Certaine French Captaines unto Florida* (c.1562-1582). Other examples of American literature of the sixteenth century include the letters and travel narratives by Pedro Menendez de Aviles (1519-1574), Fray Marcos de Niza (1495?-1542?), Pedro de Castaneda (1510?-1570?), and Samuel de Champlain (1570?-1635).

Literature produced in English came later, after Stephen Day set up a printing press in Cambridge, in the Massachusetts colony, in 1638. But it took almost another century to produce the newspapers and magazines that provided a ready outlet for colonial writers. The fledging literature of the English colonies consisted mainly of adventure narratives, like Captain John Smith's account of his rescue by the Indian Princess Pocahontas. William Bradford's *Of Plimmoth Plantation* (written in the 1620s but not published until 1896), admired for its placid homespun simplicity, and Thomas Morton's *New English Canaan* (1637), a rakish account of roistering with Indians to the displeasure of his Puritan neighbors, hail from this period. Michael Wigglesworth's *The Day of Doom* (1662), the first volume of verse to be published in the colonies, was America's first best-seller. The Puritan theologian Jonathan Edwards, best remembered for his hellfire sermons like *Sinners in the Hands of an Angry God* (1741) and his logical masterwork *Freedom of the Will* (1754), laid the philosophical groundwork for the nineteenth-century Transcendentalists.

One of the most prolific writers of the period was another Puritan cleric, Cotton Mather; the bibliography of his works fills three large volumes. Mather's colossal *Magnalia Christi Americana* (1702), disregarded almost since publication, is now increasingly respected. His *Essays to Do Good* (1710) provided his young neighbor Benjamin Franklin with the essence of a practical philosophy. Franklin's "The Dogood Papers" (1721-23), published in *The New-England Courant,* became America's first series of periodical essays. Genius that he was, Franklin saw needs everywhere in the colonies: he established the first successful magazine in America (1741), and he presented in "The Speech of Polly Baker" (1747) what may be thought of as our first short story and in "Advice to a Young Man on Choosing a Mistress" (1745) our first sex manual. Much of American literature, in fact, was prompted by Franklin.

Among Franklin's eighteenth-century contemporaries were other writers who contributed to the new literature. Between 1729 and 1733 William Byrd of Virginia wrote essays like "Journey to the Land of Eden" characterized by gentle satire and stylistic skill. Coarser but more ebullient was Ebenezer Cooke of Maryland, who in *The Sot-Weed Factor*(1708) and *Sotweed Redivivus* (1730) wrote boisterous doggerel condemning sot-weed (tobacco) growers and other colonial settlers, among whom he found few honest men and chaste women.

Other new voices arose as well. As America's first black poet, Phillis Wheatley miraculously educated herself well enough to write poetry, but unfortunately in eighteenth-century America she was everywhere seen as a singular curiosity. Elizabeth Ashbridge's *Some Account of the Fore Part of the Life of Elizabeth Ashbridge. . . Wrote by Herself (1774)* is an enlightening account of her elopement at fourteen, early widowhood, experiences as an indentured servant, and eventual conversion to Quakerism.

The Epic Vision of a New Nation: 1776-1798

Literature for literature's sake, however, emerged slowly in the American colonies. The first concerted surge of activity came from young men in Philadelphia under the leadership of William Smith, provost of its college. Thomas Godfrey's *The Prince of Parthia* (1759) became the first play by an American to be performed on the professional stage. His *Juvenile Poems* (1765) were posthumously edited by his friend Nathaniel Evans, whose *Poems on Several Occasions* (1772) were in turn posthumously edited by their mentor Smith.

The first coterie to establish a theme for a national literature celebrating a newly emerged republic was another group of young writers known as "The Connecticut Wits." Their leader was John Trumbull, whose works include *The Progress of Dullness* (1772-73) and the mock-epic *M'Fingal* (1775-82), which made fun of both revolutionaries and loyalists. Though his writings long remained popular, Trumbull was too prudent to risk reputation by continued satire and turned aside from further major literary excursions. Not so his friends Timothy Dwight and Joel Barlow. Dwight's epic *The Conquest of Canaan* (1785), celebrating the leading of the Israelites to their promised land, was interpreted as an allegory (though Dwight insisted that it was not) of George Washington leading Americans to freedom. Barlow's *The Vision of Columbus* (1787) tells in cumbrous detail what the purported discoverer of the New World saw in a dream of its future. Perhaps more usefu than either of these were the spellers and readers put together by Barlow's classmate Noah Webster so that the new United States, he saic would not have to depend on English texts "to learn our children."

To harass loyalists in Boston, Mercy Warren wrote the satirical closet dramas *The Adulateur* (1773) and *The Group* (1775). But th principal scourge of the British was Philip Freneau, a young writer from Princeton who collaborated with his classmate Hugh Henr Brackenridge in writing *A Poem on the Rising Glory of America* (1772). Freneau's activities as a patriotic propagandist earned him the titl "Poet of the American Revolution." During the revolution Brackenridge wrote patriotic plays for amateur production, *The Battle of Bunkers-Hi* (1776) and *The Death of General Montgomery"* (1777). Later his failed career as a politician resulted in *Modern Chivalry* (1792-1805), a serie of quizzical adventures that reveal the shortcomings of democratic processes.

Often called America's first novel, *The Power of Sympathy* (1789) by William Hill Brown was followed in rapid succession b instructive fictions like Susanna Rowson's *Charlotte Temple: A Tale of Truth* (1791) and Hannah Foster's *The Coquette* (1797), all moral guides But America's first important novelist was not to appear until the last years of the decade.

American Gothic: 1798-1849

Charles Brockden Brown, Quaker born and bred, published essays, verse, literary criticism, and a substantial number of tales unti his death at 39. His career came to an astounding climax with *Alcuin: A Dialogue* (1798), advocating the rights of women, followed in rapi succession by the novels for which he is best remembered: *Wieland* (1798), which explores the sad consequences of religious fanaticism; *Arthu Mervyn* (1799), which details the adventures of a young man in search of himself; *Ormond* (1799), a tale of international conspiracy; and *Edga Huntly* (1799), a murder mystery, brim-filled with terror and suspense. The latter are gothic tales with proudly American settings. Admirec by Shelley and Scott and an influence on Edgar Allan Poe, his *Novels* (1827) were reprinted in Boston and were read with interest by Henr Wadsworth Longfellow and Nathaniel Hawthorne. In technique Brown was experimental, often cumbersome, but there is vigor in what he wrot and an ability to create characters that certify his writings as more than historical artifacts.

Brown's friend and biographer, William Dunlap, also began a career in the 1790s that for him would extend for almost half a century Like Franklin, he worked in a number of trades. Returning to the United States in the fall of 1787 after studying in the London atelier of th painter Benjamin West, Dunlap just missed seeing the production of Royall Tyler's *The Contrast* (1787), the first play by a U.S. citizen t be produced professionally. Tyler would produce other plays, like *May Day in Town* (1787) and *The Georgia Spec* (1797), but *The Contrast* because it was an American first, provides his claim to recognition. Dunlap's lasting contribution is in the reminiscences of people he knew in his *Diary* (1830), his *Life* (1815) of Brown, and his *A History of the American Theatre* (1832) and *A History of New York* (1837). In a remarkably good, usually unnoticed work, *Thirty Years Ago; or, The Memoirs of a Water Drinker* (1836), he provided sustenance to every historian of early American literature.

Dunlap knew and admired Washington Irving, who is best remembered for two gothic tales, "Rip Van Winkle" (1819) and "Th Legend of Sleepy Hollow" (1820), both included in *The Sketch Book of Geoffrey Crayon* (1819-20). Though most of the sketches were o English countryside and manners, they seemed to offer proof in plenty that here at last was an American who wrote with skill and grace. Bu a younger, less cautious Irving had earlier done better in his burlesque *A History of New-York (1809)*, supposed to have been the product o a crotchety Dutchman named Diedrich Knickerbocker. Irving's imitators were legion, among them John Pendleton Kennedy, Nathaniel Parke Willis, and Charles Fenno Hoffman.

James Fenimore Cooper was a different type of author who came to writing late. A former naval officer turned country squire, he never achieved felicity in prose. Among his better writings is the trilogy Satanstoe (1845), *The Chainbearer* (1845), and *The Redskins* (1846) which tells of rent wars against patroons of the Hudson River Valley. In his most popular and enduring "Leatherstocking Tales"—*The Pioneer.* (1823), *The Last of the Mohicans (1826)*, *The Prairie* (1827), *The Pathfinder* (1840), and *The Deerslayer* (1841)—he created Natty Bumppo a character who has permanently become in various avatars a part of native lore. Perhaps more important, the tales set forth in mythic term: the gradual encroachment of civilization on the wilderness and foreshadowed the loss of the frontier spirit.

The first half of the nineteenth century also saw the emergence of America's first prominent bohemian and complete man o letters—Edgar Allan Poe. Poet, essayist, editor, and a critic so severe that he was called "the tomahawk man," Poe was a pioneer in the shor story and a master of detective fiction and the mystery thriller. He liked cryptograms, puzzles, and bewilderments, reflected in tales like "Ligeia" (1838) and poems like "Ulalume" (1847) that invite a variety of interpretations, and poems like "The Raven" (1845) seem designec to create more mood than meaning. With the exception of *The Raven and Other Poems* (1845), all of his poetry was printed at his own expense He had great trouble also in finding someone to underwrite collections of his sketches and stories. *Tales of the Grotesque and Arabesque* (1840 and *Tales* (1845), however, cemented his reputation. His novel *The Narrative of Arthur Gordon Pym* (1838) is sometimes read with interes as prefiguring some elements in Melville's *Moby-Dick*.

American Renaissance: 1850-1860

Yet Poe was overshadowed by writers of less talent. Perhaps no poet writing in English has been more popular during his lifetime than Henry Wadsworth Longfellow, whose simple verse narratives were universal favorites. *Evangeline* (1847), *Hiawatha* (1855), and *The Courtship of Miles Standish* (1858) were all best-sellers. Poems like "The Village Blacksmith" (1841), "The Children's Hour" (1860), anc "Paul Revere's Ride" (1861) have long remained favorite recitation pieces. But though still remembered with affection, Longfellow is less highly regarded now. With John Greenleaf Whittier, Oliver Wendell Holmes, and James Russell Lowell, Longfellow is considered one of "the schoolroom poets"—that is, poets whose portraits once graced classrooms throughout the country.

Several other writers came to the fore during these years, though they are less widely known today. William Wells Brown (1815-1884) published the first novel written by an African American. His *Clotelle; or, The President's Daughter* (1853), in which Brown used fiction to suggest miscegenation in high places, led his British friends to purchase his freedom the following year. Brown also wrote what some consider to be the first African American play, a drama about a slave who escaped to Canada. Harriet E. Wilson (*c.* 1808-1870), an African American woman whose history has been roughly reconstructed, is now believed to have been the author of *Our Nig; Or, Sketches from the Life of a Free Black in a Two Story White House, North. Showing That Slavery's Shadows Fall Even There. By "Our Nig."* (1859). The work is part abolitionist protest writing, part sentimental fiction, and part autobiography.

John Rollin Ridge (Cherokee) was one of the few Native Americans to write fiction and poetry in the mid-nineteenth century. Ridge, who had moved from Indian Territory (present-day Oklahoma) to California during the Gold Rush, based his popular and often plagiarized *Life and Adventures of Joaquin Murieta* (1854) on accounts of a bandit known as "Joaquin." In this romance, probably the first novel published by an American Indian, Ridge depicts Murieta as a Byronic "noble outlaw" of mixed Spanish and Indian heritage.

But though Longfellow, Lowell, Holmes, and Whittier were widely admired during their lifetimes, they shared the stage with another group of writers who would ultimately supplant them in the twentieth century as the major shapers of what came to be called the American Renaissance, the title of an influential 1941 literary history by F.O. Matthiessen. Ralph Waldo Emerson may have had more influence on his and succeeding generations than any other American writer. His was the voice of independence. Rely on yourself, he counseled. Think your own thoughts. Forget the dogma of your fathers. His "The American Scholar" (1837) has been called the country's literary declaration of independence. His essay "Self Reliance" (1841) seemed to catch the buoyant spirit of the young country as it gained confidence. But essays like "Experience" in *Essays: Second Series* (1844) and "Fate" in *The Conduct of Life* (1860) showed him to be more than simply an ebullient advocate of confidence. For what purpose, he challenged, are people allowed the privilege of living? And he answered, to be themselves, to realize whatever potential they have.

As if in response or rebuttal to Emerson, there appeared in rapid succession four books that now stand high among America's masterworks. Nathaniel Hawthorne's *The Scarlet Letter* (1850) and Herman Melville's *Moby-Dick* (1851) dealt with the mischances or terrors of life. Henry David Thoreau's *Walden* (1854) and Walt Whitman's *Leaves of Grass* (1855) have been thought of as extensions or applications of Emerson's more ebullient pleas.

Until the publication of *The Scarlet Letter,* Hawthorne had been largely admired by a discriminating few. The popularity of the book, partly due to its scandalous theme, prompted him to attempt other book-length stories. *The House of the Seven Gables (1851)* owed in externals much to the pervasive influence of Charles Dickens but carried within it seeds of symbolic meaning that have borne fruit for different critical generations. But with *The Blithedale Romance* (1852), a tale that may in part be sardonic autobiography, Hawthorne's effective career was over. *The Marble Faun* (1860), a tale of Americans abroad, is perhaps more revealing of themes hidden subtly in his earlier writings than successful in its own right.

Whereas Hawthorne's reputation came to him after years of apprentice work, Melville's first fiction brought him almost instant fame. After some footloose years at sea, he wrote of his escapades in the South Seas in *Typee* (1846) and *Omoo* (1847), books that were well received. But Melville hoped to be remembered as something more than a man who had lived among savages. So in *Mardi* (1849) he put together a narrative so tangled with emblematic meanings that few in his time or since have been able to unravel them. When he published *Moby-Dick* (1851), followed by *Pierre* (1852), the critical consensus was that he was mad, for each recounted quests after great emblematic phantoms representing readers knew not what. A discouraged Melville then retreated from public exposure with two parting shots, *The Piazza Tales* (1856), which included several wonderful tales such as "Bartleby," "Benito Cereno," and "The Encantadas," and *The Confidence-Man* (1857). It was not until three decades after his death, when the manuscript of a short narrative, *Billy Budd* (1924), was discovered, that critics began to recognize his considerable accomplishments.

Even less universally appreciated during his lifetime was Henry David Thoreau. Then, as now, people were likely to admire him greatly or think him a pretentious humbug. Thoreau published only two books, *A Week on the Concord and Merrimack Rivers* (1849) and *Walden; or, Life in the Woods* (1854). He is often thought of as a hermit. But he was also a chanticleer, he said, crowing loudly to wake his neighbors from their daily stupor. Thoreau was a rebel in word and action, and his essay "Civil Disobedience" (1849) provided a rallying cry for people in rebellion, in his time and in ours.

Much the same must be said of Whitman. His one great choreographed work on America he called *Leaves of Grass.* From 1855 to 1897 this one work went through several editions while Whitman expanded and rearranged it in keeping with his changing poetics. Whitman's outspoken boldness battered through traditions of form and content and attracted many, particularly among the youth of his time; but many found him far too outspoken about matters on which respectable people do not speak. As in the cases of Emerson, Thoreau, and Melville, Whitman's poetry and prose was part of the true voice emerging out of the new nation. Their female counterpart was Emily Dickinson, a quiet recluse who published only a handful of verses during her lifetime and whose *Poems* (1890) appeared posthumously; a complete edition of her poems was not published until 1955. Dickinson spoke more about the inner personal life, and her brief, often gnomic, lines examine nature, aspiration, and other such mysteries, including death.

At midcentury the United States, in politics as in literature, was at a turning point. Civil war loomed on the horizon. Tempers flared, and indignation ran high. Thoreau went to jail rather than pay taxes to support what he saw as an unjust war against Mexico. Whittier wrote militantly in prose and verse against the injustice of slavery. Even mild Emerson was aroused. Margaret Fuller emerged as one of the more able literary critics of the nineteenth century; she never feared to correct Emerson, Thoreau, or anyone else when convinced, as she often was, that the person—usually male—was wrong. But none spoke more effectively than Harriet Beecher Stowe, whose *Uncle Tom's Cabin* (1852) exposed the evils of slavery. More than 300,000 copies were sold within a year—no American book had ever done as well. It was turned immediately into a play (in one notable season more than 300 companies were performing adaptations of Stowe's novel) and ultimately became part of American lore.

The Turn to Local Color: 1860-1870

When the Civil War ended in 1865, literature in the United States took new directions. Before 1860 it had derived almost entirely from the eastern seaboard. But after the war, as the country expanded westward, new voices rose. The new literature of the later decades of the century was largely in prose, much of it about sections of the expanding country seldom written about before.

These regions had already been heard from in humorous tales of the backwoods and frontier. Seba Smith had used rustic New England dialect in *The Life and Writings of Major Jack Downing* (1833), and James Russell Lowell had moved beyond conventional verse in *The Biglow Papers* (1848-1862), turning dialect and humor to the service of politics and reform. Augustus Baldwin Longstreet's sketches in *Georgia Scenes* (1835) had told of raucous backcountry shenanigans. None, however, was more popular than Charles Farrar Browne, who, writing as Artemus Ward, captured the fancy of the public, especially as a lecturer whose laconic humor brought both fame and fortune. It was he who prompted Mark Twain to take up the lecture circuit and produce some of the greatest classics of American humor.

Writers after the Civil War began to discover those regions that had previously been scorned by the respectable society of the Northeast as populated only by buffoons and ne'er-do-wells. Bret Harte sentimentalized the frontier tradition in stories like "The Luck of Roaring Camp" (1868) and "The Outcasts of Poker Flat" (1869), set in California's mining camps. John Hay's *Pike Country Ballads* (1871) presented dialect verse accounts of the Illinois frontier. In *Old Creole Days* (1879) and in his most powerful novel, *The Grandissimes* (1880), George Washington Cable introduced the secret tensions besetting the bilingual society of Louisiana, where the old French society resented the Yankee invaders. Joel Chandler Harris told stories of plantation life in Georgia in *Uncle Remus* (1880) and its popular sequels. Mary Noailles Murfree, as Charles Egbert Craddock, wrote of mountain people in *In the Tennessee Mountains* (1884). Thomas Nelson Page wrote sentimentally of plantation life in *In Ole Virginia* (1887). Lafcadio Hearn, a meticulous stylist, wrote descriptive sketches of urban Ohio, of New Orleans, most effectively in *Chita* (1889), then of the West Indies, and finally of Japan. New England rural life was revealed in Mary E. Wilkins Freeman's *A New England Nun* (1891) and with greater artistry in Sarah Orne Jewett's *The Country of the Pointed Firs* (1896). While many of these writers have sometimes been dismissed as mere local colorists, Jewett is almost universally recognized as an artist complete.

The writers who revealed uncommon characters in simple, often romantic situations in culturally more diverse areas not well known to ordinary readers have been called local colorists. Closely linked to them were novelists, often intent on reform, who produced uncomfortably realistic pictures of less glamorous places. A pioneer in this movement was Rebecca Harding Davis, whose *Margret Howth* (1862) exposes the sordidness of life in a northern mill town. Drab farm lives in the Midwest were realistically presented in *The Hoosier School-Master* (1871) and Edward Eggleston's other novels, but this movement did not gain momentum until after the exposure of the scandals of the Grant administration and a series of devastating financial panics, beginning in 1873, shook national confidence.

In spite of what has been called the rise of realism in the late nineteenth century, sentimentality and optimism held their own in popular reading. In *Making His Mark* (1901) and dozens of other exemplary tales, Horatio Alger, Jr., proved that indeed in America pluck and luck finally pay off. Although Timothy Shay Arthur never scored another success to equal that of his novel *Ten Nights in a Bar-Room* (1884) and its stage version, he continued to grind out fables about the triumph of virtue over demon rum. Martha Finley provided a model guide to obedience and good manners in *Elsie Dinsmore* (1868), Louisa May Alcott supported her own family with touching tales of domestic tranquility in *Little Women* (1868) and *Little Men* (1871), and Frances Hodgson Burnett produced in *Little Lord Fauntleroy* (1886) the model for the ideal young man.

The increasingly diverse narratives of the period also included an expanding body of works by African American writers. Collections of stories like *The Conjur Woman* (1899) and *The Wife of His Youth and Other Stories of the Color Line* (1899) paved the way for Charles Waddell Chestnutt's first novel, *The House Behind the Cedars* (1900), about two African Americans passing for white men. Two later novels appealed less to readers, but Chestnutt's contribution is that he was genuinely aware of the comic possibilities available to African American writers concerned with how the values and mores of white American culture affect and are reacted to by blacks. As the century ended, the works of Paul Laurence Dunbar captured the romanticized life of the old Southern plantations. In such works as *Oaks and Ivy* (1893), *Lyrics of Lowly Life* (1896), *In Old Plantation Days* (1903), and *The Heart of Happy Hollow* (1904), Dunbar gave voice to a perspective that gained him wide acclaim, although he was also criticized for rendering objectionable racial stereotypes.

The success of a play, however, depends to a degree on audiences embracing familiar stereotypes onstage. One of the ways playwrights added local color to the melodramas and comedies in the early American theater was through the Yankee character, who along with the Irish drunk and the bumbling Negro servant became a fixture of plays. Royall Tyler's late eighteenth-century *The Contrast,* considered by many as the first play in English by an American, features a Yankee character called Jonathan. Imitators soon followed, always finding the wily down-easterner outfoxing city folk in striped pants and top hat, which eventually became the emblematic Uncle Sam. One of the most noted plays in which a form of this character appeared was Anna Cora Mowatt's 1840s comedy of manners *Fashion* (Poe reviewed it for the *Broadway Journal*), which satirized Americans' attempts to emulate the British aristocracy. But perhaps the most infamous manifestation of the figure appeared as the title character in Tom Taylor's *Our American Cousin,* the play Lincoln was watching when he was assassinated at Ford's Theatre. Local color also appeared onstage in such popular entertainments as *A Glance at New York* by Benjamin A. Baker, a play that teemed with figures from street life, the most enduring of which was Mose, a loud, tough-talking fireman.

While theaters flourished not only in cities but increasingly in smaller towns, where traveling companies offered one-night stands, few memorable plays were produced during the period. Entrepreneurs found it preferable to revive imported melodramas like *The Count of Monte Cristo* or sure-fire favorites like *Uncle Tom's Cabin.* Samuel Woodworth, better known for his song "The Old Oaken Bucket" (1823), and James Nelson Barker wrote now forgotten plays with native settings, while John Howard Payne, whose major claim to fame is his nostalgic song "Home, Sweet Home" (1823), wrote equally unmemorable romantic dramas set overseas. Later in the century audiences seemed satisfied with the timely though quite undistinguished society-oriented dramas of Bronson Howard and Clyde Fitch. The slapstick comedy of the minstrel shows by both black and white performers delighted many audiences.

The Gilded Age: 1870-1890

The latter years of the nineteenth century were dominated by three writers beside whom most others seem Lilliputian indeed: Samuel Clemens, better known as Mark Twain, William Dean Howells, and Henry James. Each of these three authors continued in activity and influence into the twentieth century, when Clemens became an embittered scold and James was read with decreasing enthusiasm even though his writing continued to break new ground. Howells died esteemed as the dean of American letters.

Mark Twain was a man who seemed especially favored by fortune. Quite by chance his story "The Celebrated Jumping Frog of Calaveras County" (1865), written in California at the suggestion of Ward, took the East by storm. When the letters he wrote as a newspaper correspondent on a cruise ship to the Mediterranean were gathered as *The Innocents Abroad (1869),* his reputation was secure. He ventured first into the novel in collaboration with Charles Dudley Warner in *The Gilded Age* (1873). Then he certified himself as a novelist in his own right with *The Adventures of Tom Sawyer* (1876), *The Prince and the Pauper* (1881),and *A Connecticut Yankee in King Arthur's Court* (1889). His acknowledged masterwork is *Adventures of Huckleberry Finn* (1884). This saga of a boy and a runaway slave tells much of Clemens and his time but even more of the conditions that conscience-ridden people inevitably face.

Twain's genius exhibited itself in his control of language, colloquial and formal, and in a view of the world as a place roiled by the sometimes well-meaning misdeeds of people. As he grew older, he pointed with increasing despair at the hideous malefactions of what he called—not entirely without affection—the damned human race. His friend Howells, however, felt that people were capable of redemption, and he wrote some forty novels to demonstrate that human decency might somehow prevail. As editor of the *Atlantic Monthly* from 1871 to 1881, Howells encouraged many a younger writer. His eventual move from Boston was taken as a visible sign that New York was the new literary capital of the nation. There he continued as patron and adviser to young writers like Stephen Crane, Hamlin Garland, and Frank Norris, who ventured even further than he in realistic detail. Howells's own novels *The Rise of Silas Lapham* (1885) and *A Hazard of New Fortunes* (1889) are worthy of shelf room beside any of America's best.

To some critics Henry James is without question America's foremost writer of fiction. Each admirer will set forth his own favorites, but most will agree that *The Portrait of a Lady* (1881), *The Princess Casamassima* (1886), *The Aspern Papers* (1888), and the three novels representative of what has been called his major phase, *The Wings of the Dove* (1902), *The Ambassadors* (1903), and *The Golden Bowl* (1904), represent his supreme achievement. Each of these novels examines Americans in Europe faced with a culture different from their own. Other readers may prefer his two principal novels with American settings, *Washington Square* (1881) and *The Bostonians* (1886). Still others, however, consider James an unmitigated bore, mainly to be tolerated in his early, more simply devised stories such as *The American* (1877) and *Daisy Miller* (1878).

Naturalist Decadence and Moral Disintegration: 1890-1900

During the Gilded Age, local color writers had begun turning increasingly to the darker sides of remote places like those that George Washington Cable portrayed in his stories of New Orleans. The South in particular began to attract attention as the problems of reconstruction began to appear first in John William de Forest's *Miss Ravenel's Conversion from Secession to Loyalty* (1867) and then in Albion Tourgee's vitriolic *A Fool's Errand* (1879) and *Bricks without Straw* (1880). The Midwestern small town became a target for virulent attack in E.W. Howe's *The Story of a Country Town* (1883) and Joseph Kirkland's *Zury, the Meanest Man in Spring County* (1887), paving the way for such later works as Hamlin Garland's *Main-Travelled Roads* (1891) and, eventually, Sinclair Lewis's *Main Street* (1920). Helen Hunt Jackson attracted national attention with *Ramona* (1884), her story of the ill treatment of Native Americans in California. Harold Frederic, in *The Damnation of Theron Ware* (1896), told of the downhill trajectory of a well-intentioned but misguided young small-town minister when he abandons the church for politics. Robert Herrick began a novel-writing career that would extend for more than thirty years with *The Man Who Wins* (1897) and *The Gospel of Freedom* (1898). Ambrose Bierce leaped to prominence with short narratives of horror and suspense in *Tales of Soldiers and Civilians* (1891). Encouraged by Howells, Norwegian-born H.H. Boyesen wrote *The Golden Calf* (1892), a tale about the downfall of a young man in search of easy wealth.

Influenced by Emile Zola and encouraged by Howells, Frank Norris turned to realism of the starkest kind. He is sometimes held forth as America's first naturalistic novelist. His first attempt at fiction of this kind was *Vandover and the Brute,* a gruesome tale of moral disintegration not published until 1914, twelve years after its author's death. *McTeague* (1899) presents a more effective account of how greed and inexperience and the inexorable hand of fate can lead to the destruction of people of good intentions. Norris's brief career came to a climax with the publication of *The Octopus* (1901) and then, posthumously, *The Pit* (1903), novels that he had intended to be part of a trilogy (the final volume to be called *The Wolf*). The books centered on American agriculture and, specifically, the growing, selling, and consumption of wheat.

Younger than Norris was Stephen Crane, who brought a new dimension to the realism of his contemporaries. His novel *Maggie, A Girl of the Streets* (1893), published at his own expense, found few readers, but with it modern American fiction was born. Crane's sharp, cryptic verse, as presented in *The Black Riders* (1895) and *War Is Kind* (1899), seemed stark indeed to a generation nourished on Longfellow and Whittier. *The Red Badge of Courage* (1895) is Crane's best-known novel. Some critics have placed it beside *The Scarlet Letter, Moby-Dick,* and *The Portrait of a Lady* as among the best works produced in the nineteenth century in America. It is a story of war in which a young man faces death, first with terror but finally with acceptance of its inevitability. Crane wrote a dozen further volumes of fiction or reminiscence, none of which was completely a popular or artistic success. But his short stories "The Blue Hotel," "The Open Boat," and "The Bride Comes to Yellow Sky" identify him as a precursor of Hemingway.

The main dramatic practioner of naturalism around this time was Howells, who wrote three dozen plays between 1874 and 1911. Unfortunately, his best works were one-acts that, though incisive and realistic, found more of a following in print than in the theater. Howells championed the work of James A. Herne, often labeled the "American Ibsen." His most critically acclaimed work, *Margaret Fleming,* which was produced in Boston in 1891, considers the tragic consequences of a small-time businessman's womanizing and drinking.

Black protests had appeared only fitfully during the nineteenth century by such militant advocates of equal rights as the orator Frederick Douglass and in the form of autobiographical slave narratives written by Harriett Jacobs, Nat Turner, and William Wells Brown. Toward the end of the century, however, blacks began to become more vocal. Booker T. Washington's *The Future of the American Negro* (1899), which anticipated his better-known biographical *Up from Slavery* (1901), was regarded by many as overly optimistic. W.E.B. Du Bois, on the other hand, best known for *The Souls of Black Folk* (1903), presciently predicted that racial strife would be the most pressing American social problem of the twentieth century.

The Chinese, too, grappled with discrimination. Initially attracted by the Gold Rush, Chinese workers were hired in large numbers between 1866 and 1869 to complete the transcontinental railroad. With the economic downturn of the 1870s, however, the Chinese become scapegoats, and sinophobia swept the nation. Bret Harte's poem "Plain Language from Truthful James," popularly known as "The Heathen Chinee," added fuel to the fire. The end result was the passage of the Chinese Exclusion Act of 1882, which prohibited further immigration from China. Despite being a time of restriction and discrimination, the turn of the century also marks the beginning of Asian American literature. Edith Eaton (1865-1914), a Chinese Eurasian, published short stories in national magazines between 1894 and 1912 using the pseudonym Sui Sin Far. In 1912 her stories were collected in one volume, *Mrs. Spring Fragrance.*

The Jewish experience at the turn of the century was ably captured by Abraham Cahan in *Yekl* (1896) and *The Rise of David Levinsky* (1917), both of which have become classics. Championed by Howells, Cahan and his novels successfully served to mediate life between the Old World and the American experience for the sizeable Jewish immigrant community.

Women in general, however, did not fare well in discussions of literature in the United States before 1900. Typical was Hawthorne's memorable complaint about the "damned tribe of scribbling women." Emily Dickinson, through her own reclusiveness, remained unhonored and unknown, but the posthumous publication of her verse revived interest in poetry that was more than merely metronomically melodious. In Kate Chopin's *The Awakening* (1899), American readers were presented for the first time with a candid woman's view of the problems imposed on women by a male-dominated society. Like Flaubert's *Madame Bovary,* Chopin's novel spoke of matters that many contemporaries thought indelicate. The book shocked readers and suggested how far some American writers had drifted from the emphasis on "the smiling aspects of life" that Howells had endorsed only a few years earlier.

The Age of Innocence: 1900-1919

What has come to be called Modernism was heralded in part by novels like Theodore Dreiser's *Sister Carrie* (1900), which introduced a sensibility characterized by a feeling of the individual's isolation and alienation from an urbanized, mechanized society. Modernist writers came to see themselves as enemies of oppressive social institutions. Much of Modernist literature, in fact, describes the effort to escape from convention in general and the middle class in particular.

Except for Midwesterner Booth Tarkington, who offered indulgent criticism of the middle class in *The Magnificent Ambersons* (1918) and the Penrod stories, the novelists who flourished during the first years of the twentieth century were "muckrakers" concerned about the social consequences of corruption in high places. By far the most popular and successful of the novelists who indicted American business ethics was Upton Sinclair, whose *The Jungle* (1906) led to reforms in the meatpacking industry.

The Modernist notion of escape began to dominate American writing with the fiction of Jack London. Though presumably a socialist who predicted the return of a primitive Golden Age following a fascist revolution in *The Iron Heel* (1908), London praised the Nietzschean superman in *The Sea-Wolf* (1904). And in his most self-revelatory tale, *Martin Eden* (1909), London portrayed a hero driven at last to suicide by the personal and political problems that he vainly sought to solve. George Cabot Lodge's bleakly cynical "The Genius of the Commonplace" dramatizes the disillusionment with Boston's traditionalist Brahmin society, as does the posthumously published *The Education of Henry Adams* (1918). The collapse of the aristocrat's role as guardian of public morals finds its ultimate statement in philosopher George Santayana's novel *The Last Puritan* (1935).

The transition to Modernism was best made in the works of two distinguished women novelists who tempered their traditional conservatism with an awareness that the past was irretrievable in a changing world. In *The Age of Innocence* (1920), Edith Wharton, one of the few American writers born into the wealthy international set, symbolically provided the name for the period that ended exactly with the appearance of her novel. This work depicts the cost in human happiness of the rigid rules regulating New York Victorian society. Earlier, in *The House of Mirth* (1905), she had shown the suicidal cost of attempting to play society's games. In a different vein, *Ethan Frome* (1911) disposed of dreams of primitive virtue by showing how bad things could be in backwoods New England.

More complex is the fiction of Willa Cather, which seemed to offer fresh hope in two epic tributes to the passing frontier, O *Pioneers!* (1913) and *My Antonia* (1918). After 1922 her work, especially *A Lost Lady* (1923) and *The Professor's House* (1925), came to reflect a bitter disillusionment with contemporary materialistic society. Her increasing desire to escape into memories of a more exalted past found expression in two of her finest works, *Death Comes for the Archbishop* (1927) and *Shadows on the Rock* (1931).

The Modernist sensibility manifested itself in American poetry almost exactly at the turn of the century, when the genteel influence of New England's "fireside poets" like William Vaughn Moody, Trumbull Stickney, and George Cabot Lodge was ebbing. At first a dark new vision manifested itself through the ironic regionalism of Edwin Arlington Robinson's *The Children of the Night* (1897) and Edgar Lee Masters's *Spoon River Anthology* (1915). Robert Frost's *A Boy's Will* (1913) and *North of Boston* (1914) exhibited a wider range of sympathies. But all are unprecedented psychological probings of determined and frustrated villagers and farmers from New England and the Midwest.

The American drama made less progress than other native arts between 1900 and World War I. At the peak of its popularity, during the years before it was seriously challenged by cinema, the American theater was at a nadir. Turn-of-the-century audiences favored exotic romantic works like David Belasco's *Madame Butterfly* of 1900. Genteel longings for a theater that combined high art with high seriousness were vainly focused upon William Vaughn Moody's idealistic appeals for human dignity in *The Great Divide* (1906) and *The Faith Healer* (1909) and Percy MacKaye's spectacular historical dramas like *The Scarecrow* (1908). Almost none of the hundreds of American dramas produced between 1900 and 1915 are revived today, even as period curiosities.

The Triumph of Modernism: 1919-1929

Just as the decade of boom and bust began with the end of World War I, so 1919 also marked the Modernist breakthrough in American fiction with the publication of Sherwood Anderson's *Winesburg, Ohio* and James Branch Cabell's *Jurgen*. These works were joined the next year by Wharton's *Age of Innocence,* F. Scott Fitzgerald's *This Side of Paradise,* the first full-length plays of Eugene O'Neill, and the collected lyrics of Edna St. Vincent Millay. Above all 1920 brought Sinclair Lewis's *Main Street,* which lambasted the ugliness, complacency, and vulgarity of the small Midwestern town and satirized the death of the pioneering spirit.

Lewis became the country's most famous novelist with *Babbitt* (1922). The work provided the derogatory tag still attached to the kind of fatuous community booster it depicted. In *Arrowsmith* (1925) a genuinely idealistic doctor is driven into exile. *Elmer Gantry* (1927) dealt with hypocritical religious revivalists, and *Dodsworth* (1929) depicted a retired businessman who goes abroad to find a decent life. These confirmations of the European intelligentsia's view of the parvenu excesses of the United States led to Lewis's becoming in 1930 the first American to win the Nobel Prize for literature.

None of Lewis's novels, however, so well epitomizes the reaction of a Modernist sensibility to a demoralized United States as F. Scott Fitzgerald's *The Great Gatsby* (1925). Although he became a legendary figure himself, Fitzgerald never again wrote a novel like *The Great Gatsby.* His novel about expatriate society, *Tender Is the Night* (1934) did not find its final form, and his tale of Hollywood, *The Last Tycoon* (1941), is a collection of unfinished fragments.

Fitzgerald's reputation was also overshadowed by that of his sometime friend, often bitter foe and critic, Ernest Hemingway. Hemingway leaped to fame following the publication of *In Our Time* (1925), a collection of terse, compressed stories. He soon became the principal spokesman for the "lost generation" and became known worldwide for novels like *The Sun Also Rises* (1926), about an aimless group of American expatriates, and *A Farewell to Arms* (1929), set against the background of an Italian retreat during the war.

Like Hemingway, John Dos Passos began his literary career by serving as an ambulance driver in World War I and then becoming involved in the Spanish Civil War. His *One Man's Initiation-1917* (1920) and *Three Soldiers* (1921) rank with *A Farewell to Arms* as the classic American accounts of World War I. Dos Passos went on to develop the montage novel, producing first a cross section of the chaos of New York City life in *Manhattan Transfer* (1925) and then an epic portrait of the decay of American values in *The 42nd Parallel* (1930), *1919* (1932), and *The Big Money* (1936), the three novels constituting his U.S.A. trilogy.

The appellation "lost generation" for the morally disoriented writers who lived through World War I has been attributed to Gertrude Stein. This redoubtable avant-garde writer was at the center of the American literary community in France between the world wars. Her experimental works, from *Three Lives* (1909) through the mazes of the massive *The Making of Americans* (1925) to the mysterious *Ida* (1941), were also both thematically and formally at the very center of the Modernist tradition. Despite the range and variety of her incessant experiments, however, Stein's reputation with the general public rested on *The Autobiography of Alice B. Toklas* (1933), her account of her life with her long-time companion.

Few other expatriates or experimentalists shared Stein's fame. Djuna Barnes is known almost entirely for her stream-of-consciousness novel *Nightwood* (1936), and none of Glenway Wescott's other works enjoyed the popularity of his early *The Grandmothers* (1927), which featured a pioneering Wisconsin family as seen through the eyes of an expatriate descendant. Yet not all the uprooted writers escaped to Paris. The still mysterious B. Traven, for example, wrote social protest novels like *The Death Ship* in Mexico for initial publication in Germany.

Some writers, like Maxwell Bodenheim *(Replenishing Jessica,* 1925) and Carl Van Vechten *(Peter Whiffle,* 1922), simply fled the Midwest for Greenwich Village. There they joined poets like e.e. cummings and Edna St. Vincent Millay in turning out highly stylized and wittily cynical works about the jazz age that are valued today principally as period pieces. Van Vechten actually achieved a more enduring reputation not through his connection to the jazz age but through his association with the Harlem Renaissance, which he depicted with sympathetic realism in *Nigger Heaven* (1926).

The Harlem Renaissance of the 1920s provided the first serious opportunity for black writers to depict African American culture as it existed in urban America. Although the idea was to cultivate a black audience, their contemporary audiences were largely sympathetic white patrons. Black writers had been producing notable novels since late in the nineteenth century, but works like Chesnutt's *The Wife of His Youth* and James Weldon Johnson's *The Autobiography of an Ex-Colored Man* (1912) dealt principally with the problems of light-skinned blacks "passing" for whites. The issue was how to overcome the handicaps imposed by racial prejudices. Zora Neale Hurston published a number of works, and she was to still to publish her masterpiece, *Their Eyes Were Watching God* (1937). Encouraged, however, by the freedom of jazz age Harlem, blacks like Du Bois and Claude McKay began to produce distinguished novels about the problems of aspiring members of black communities. Most striking of these novels was the long-neglected but now much discussed *Cane* (1923) by Jean Toomer, a mysterious figure of uncertain origins. A collage of stories, songs, and plays, *Cane* dealt with the plight of blacks alienated by race and the common neglect of artists in the twentieth century.

Although Langston Hughes wrote one of the finest novels about black life, *Not without Laughter* (1930), he is best known for his stories of Simple, a black folk philosopher, and for his poetry, in which he experimented with the use of black folk song and jazz rhythms. Countee Cullen also experimented with lyrical forms in *The Ballad of the Brown Girl* (1927) and *The Black Christ* (1929), using traditional

English forms. Cullen's attitude was closely in tune with that of other respected poets of the decade, who viewed their dissolute period with dismay.

One such poet was Ezra Pound, who launched the attack against the materialism of the day in 1920 with his "Mauberley" poems. The opening stanza of *Hugh Selwyn Mauberley* epitomizes the Modernist poet's state of mind: "For three years, out of key with his time, / He strove to resuscitate the dead art / Of poetry; to maintain 'The sublime' / In the old sense. Wrong from the start—." Pound's increasing displeasure took the form of a long series of "Cantos," collages of miscellaneous erudition drawn from cultures of all times and all places mixed with rantings against modern economic and political systems.

Pound's place in the poetic hierarchy was early usurped, however unintentionally, by his major discovery, T.S. Eliot, an American expatriate in London whose *The Waste Land* (1922) became the most quoted and imitated poem of the century. It is entirely possible to take at face value the statement attributed to Eliot that to him the poem was "only the relief of a personal and wholly insignificant grouse against life" while simultaneously maintaining that it embodied "a world-view widely characteristic of thoughtful and sensitive individuals during the 1920's." Eliot's personal protest happened to give voice to the feelings of sensitive persons who lived through a generally gross age.

Yet, despite the idolization of Eliot, there were vigorous dissenters from his view. Chief among these were Hart Crane and William Carlos Williams, who could only begin to win proper recognition when Eliot's influence began to wane after World War II. Although scholars still debase the "unity" of Crane's mystical epic *The Bridge* (1930), with some finding it only a chaos of fragments like the age it mirrors, others find its vast structure a coherent reinvigoration of the lapsed tradition of Walt Whitman, which Eliot greatly mistrusted. Against Eliot's increasingly metaphysical concerns, Williams put forth a creed based on the beauty contained in physical reality. This viewpoint is best illustrated by his own epic of the commonplace, *Paterson* (1946-58), based on impressions of his home city in New Jersey. Another dissenting voice took an even bleaker view than Eliot's of the contemporary world and the entire human experience. Writing long blank-verse narratives about the forbidding California coast near Big Sur, where he lived, Robinson Jeffers shocked readers with *Tamar* (1924) and *Roan Stallion* (1925), misanthropic legends of violent, amoral people bent on self-destruction.

Although Jeffers considered protest only a bubble "in the molten mass," other poetic manifestations of discomfort with the age surfaced in Greenwich Village in the typographically eccentric satires of e.e. cummings. Another New York writer who managed to maintain a unique stability in the midst of madness was Marianne Moore, editor of the revived *The Dial* (1926-29), who persisted through the years in viewing poets as "liberators of the imagination."

A once enormously admired and now virtually forgotten poem from this period is Stephen Vincent Benet's *John Brown's Body* (1928), an epic account of the Civil War from the Union point of view. Americans have lost their taste for historical epics, for the fate of Benet's work was shared by Archibald MacLeish's narration of Cortez's conquest of Mexico, *Conquistador* (1932), though MacLeish's shorter "Ars Poetica" has continued to be regarded, perhaps wrongly, as a statement of the Modernist aesthetic, just as his much anthologized "You, Andrew Marvell" sums up a cyclical theory of destiny.

The United States developed a drama of truly international importance for the first time in the 1920s in the plays of Eugene O'Neill. His first full-length offering in New York, *Beyond the Horizon* (1920), carried off the Pulitzer Prize. O'Neill then won two more Pulitzer Prizes—for *Anna Christie* (1921) and *Strange Interlude* (1928)—and presented four other major productions in New York during the decade. While all his plays are Modernist statements of the need of individuals to escape the deadly constraints of monotonous lives or oppressive institutions, they are written in two strikingly different styles. While some are somber dramas of personal frustration in the prevailing naturalistic mode of the period (*Beyond the Horizon* and *Desire under the Elms*), others are practically the only important American examples of the European expressionist drama that sought to suggest interior states of mind through stylized sets and actions (*The Emperor Jones, The Hairy Ape,* and *The Great God Brown*). In his greatest triumph during his lifetime, the nine-act *Strange Interlude,* he combined naturalistic action with expressionist revelation through a double set of speeches that allow the audience to hear both what the characters are saying and what they are thinking.

Most of the other Pulitzer Prize-winning plays of the decade pale beside O'Neill's work. The few foreshadowings of a generally brilliant decade ahead included Sidney Howard's *The Silver Cord* (1926) and Elmer Rice's *The Adding Machine* (1923). Audiences especially enjoyed two rollicking farces that caught the bumptious pseudosophisticated tone of the decade, Maxwell Anderson and Laurence Stallings's *What Price Glory?* (1924) and Ben Hecht and Charles MacArthur's *The Front Page* (1928). But the biggest hit of all was Anne Nichols's ethnic farce *Abie's Irish Rose* (1922).

American humor generally made a great comeback during the 1920s. Since 1914 H.L. Mencken had been delighting the "smart set" with his iconoclastic attacks on the "booboisie" and his defense of American authors like Dreiser, but he and the outrageous drama critic George Jean Nathan scored their greatest successes after founding the *American Mercury* in 1923. Its cynical wit was soon overshadowed, however, by that of the *New Yorker,* founded in 1925 by editor Harold Ross. The magazine attracted the sophisticated, fun-seeking writers who became members of the Algonquin Round Table (named for the hotel where they met for lunch): James Thurber, Dorothy Parker, E.B. White, Robert Benchley, and the popular book reviewer Alexander Woollcott. But they did not have the New York scene to themselves; even more popular were the ironically comic short stories of Ring Lardner *(The Big Town,* 1921) and the poems that Don Marquis attributed to a newspaper office cockroach madly in love with a fickle cat *(Archy and Mehitabel,* 1927).

Alienation Vindicated—Depression and World War II: 1929-1945

If American writings of the 1920s were not equaled in brilliance by those of the 1930s, they were surpassed in profundity by an outpouring of moving responses to human hardship, especially that caused by the Depression and the rise to power of the authoritarian regimes that precipitated World War II. Apparently traumatized by the end of the world they had known, few established American novelists matched their earlier accomplishments after 1929. The Spanish Civil War, however, brought Hemingway out of a long slump to find a new voice in

For Whom the Bell Tolls (1940) and again in *The Old Man and the Sea* (1952).

The most enduring novelists of the 1930s, however, were those who found their inspiration rooted in their localities. John Steinbeck found his locality in the rural valleys of central California in the mystical *To a God Unknown* (1933) and the ironic *The Pastures of Heaven* (1932). After revealing a gift for humorous allegory in *Tortilla Flat* (1935) and naturalistic tragedy in *Of Mice and Men (1937),* he published what both the public and critics have acclaimed as the greatest work of American social protest since *Uncle Tom's Cabin—The Grapes of Wrath* (1939).

The long-depressed South, however, was the region that would really experience a renaissance. Beginning in 1929 with *Look Homeward, Angel,* Thomas Wolfe turned the memories of his childhood in Asheville, North Carolina, and his adult journeys throughout the United States and in Europe into epic fiction, especially in *Of Time and the River* (1935). Erskine Caldwell devastatingly satirized the rednecks of the Southern backwoods in *Tobacco Road* (1932) and *God's Little Acre* (1933), while Elizabeth Madox Roberts paid tribute to the heroically sacrificial life of the pioneers in Kentucky in *The Great Meadow* (1930).

The most important Southern author of the period, however, was William Faulkner, a writer of international stature. After an unpromising start in two jazz age novels influenced by Sherwood Anderson, Faulkner found his "little postage stamp of territory" in Yoknapatawpha County, modeled on the region where he lived in the hills of northeastern Mississippi. In *Sartoris* (1929; now published as *Flags in the Dust),* he related a late chapter in the history of the aristocratic family that became the foil for the upstart, white trash Snopeses, whose tale is told in the trilogy *The Hamlet* (1940), *The Town* (1957), and *The Mansion* (1959). Other novels and short stories, including his four supreme achievements—*The Sound and the Fury* (1929), *As I Lay Dying* (1930), *Light in August* (1932) and *Absalom, Absalom!* (1936)—fill in the story. Perhaps inspired by Faulkner's example, James Agee paid what remains the most sympathetic tribute to the hard life of Southern poor whites in *Let Us Now Praise Famous Men* (1941).

Four women novelists made especially distinguished contributions to Southern fiction, which flourished as never before. Caroline Gordon was directly associated with the influential Southern agrarian poets, and in novels from *Penhally* (1931) to *The Malefactors* (1956) she was a most outspoken critic of the region's departure from its traditional culture, as was her husband, Allen Tate, in his one novel, *The Fathers* (1938). More impressive, however, were Katherine Anne Porter's tales of her native Texas, like *Noon Wine* (1937), and of Mexico. Late during this period, the changing life of small Southern rural communities became the subject of stories by Carson McCullers and Eudora Welty. McCullers published her first novel, *The Heart Is a Lonely Hunter,* in 1940, and Welty's fantastic novelette *The Robber Bridegroom* appeared in 1942. McCullers, however, quickly reached the peak of her career with her third novel, *The Member of the Wedding* (1946), and her play version of it (1949), while Welty did not produce her most ambitious work, *Losing Battles,* until 1970. The most popular novel ever to come out of the South—Margaret Mitchell's mammoth *Gone with the Wind* (1936)—was also a product of the 1930s.

The fiction that bulked largest during the Depression years, however, was the work of the "tough guy" proletarian writers. The most prolific of these authors, James T. Farrell, was never able to equal the success of his first naturalistic stories about growing up on Chicago's South Side. Farrell, author of the *Studs Lonigan* trilogy (1932-35), and many other writers of the time, like Josephine Herbst, have been largely forgotten. Edward Dahlberg proved an exception when he developed a belated reputation for the autobiographical *Because I Was Flesh* (1964). Another exception was James M. Cain, who won a wide following for his tales of the seedy elements in glamorous southern California, *The Postman Always Rings Twice* (1934) and *Double Indemnity* (1944).

The grimmest work about decadent movieland, however, was Nathanael West's hallucinatory prediction of the destruction of Los Angeles, *The Day of the Locust* (1939). This novel followed his other powerful indictments of the American myth in A *Cool Million* (1934), a story of the self-made man, and *Miss Lonelyhearts* (1933), about the Christ complex developed by an advice-to-the-lovelorn columnist. Another cynical attack on the shoddiness of American middle-class values was John O'Hara's *Appointment in Samarra* (1934). The most infamous novels of the period were Henry Miller's *Tropic of Cancer* (1934) and *Tropic of Capricorn* (1939), melanges of turgid philosophizing and explicit pornography that were banned from the United States for decades.

A telling indictment of social injustices was Richard Wright's *Native Son* (1940), an account of the corruption and destruction of an ambitious but poorly educated black Chicago youth. Wright was the first black novelist to win major critical and public recognition, doing so not only with his novel but also with his harrowing autobiography, *Black Boy* (1945).

The poets who dominated the American academies beginning in the mid-1930s came from the South, but they were largely conservative white "fugitives" from twentieth-century urban society. The group at Vanderbilt University who had styled themselves the "Fugitives" attracted national attention when they identified themselves as "Agrarians" and called for a return to traditional values in an essay collection, *I'll Take My Stand* (1930). Although the reputation of their leader, Donald Davidson, has declined, three of the group have heavily influenced American literary culture generally. Allen Tate's "Ode to the Confederate Dead" (1926-30) overshadowed his more ambitious efforts to give a peculiarly Southern cast to T.S. Eliot's concept of the value of traditional orthodoxy. John Crowe Ransom won distinction as a poet but is best known as the theorist of the "New Criticism" that dominated American universities from the late 1930s to the 1960s. The most prominent of the group, however, was Robert Penn Warren, who won distinction not only as a poet for works like *Brother to Dragons* (1953) but also as a novelist, especially for *All the King's Men* (1946), a cautionary tale about a Southern demagogue.

Despite this Southern offensive, the center of poetic activity began during the 1930s to shift back to New England, where California-born Robert Frost—his important writing behind him—was just beginning to make his impact as a lecturer and embodiment of Yankee tradition. The most telling satirical poetry of the decade was Archibald MacLeish's *Frescoes for Mr. Rockefeller's City* (1933), inspired by the controversy over Mexican muralist Diego Rivera's designs for the Rockefellers' Radio City. MacLeish's polemics, however, have been overshadowed by those of the theorist of the "Supreme Fiction," the Hartford, Connecticut, insurance executive Wallace Stevens, whose complex and subtle work defies brief synthesis.

Drama achieved an unparalleled effectiveness in the 1930s. O'Neill no longer dominated the stage. After capping his great decade with a trilogy, *Mourning Becomes Electra* (1931), which audaciously transplanted the sole surviving Greek trilogy, the *Oresteia* of Aeschylus, to nineteenth-century New England, and after his one nostalgic comedy, *Ah, Wilderness!* (1933), O'Neill withdrew from the scene, not to be heard from again until the long, cheerless drama of the triumph of dreams over life, *The Iceman Cometh,* reached Broadway in 1946. An unprecedented number of other dramatists, however, commanded attention. Most honored at the time was Maxwell Anderson for his commercial success with a blank verse play, *Winterset* (1935), inspired by the notorious Sacco-Vanzetti case. Even more popular at the time were Robert E. Sherwood's seriocomic responses to the fascist march to European war in *Idiot's Delight* (1936) and *There Shall Be No Night* (1940). Politics also influenced the radical critique of the depravity of American bourgeois society in Clifford Odets's *Awake and Sing!* (1935) and *Golden Boy* (1937) and especially in Lillian Hellman's bitter and controversial *The Children's Hour* (1934), *The Little Foxes* (1939), and the anti-Nazi *Watch on the Rhine* (1941).

The comic collaborations of George S. Kaufman and Moss Hart, especially *You Can't Take It with You* (1936), championed individualist rejection of pressures toward social conformity in a way that delighted depression-weary Americans. William Saroyan achieved his one enduring success with *The Time of Your Life* (1939), a zany reversal of O'Neill's tragedies about defeated dreamers. The most heartening plays of the period, though, were Thornton Wilder's two internationally acclaimed meditations on the value of every moment of human experience and of the struggle to preserve the often threatened race: *Our Town* (1938) and *The Skin of Our Teeth* (1942).

The Harvest of Modernism: 1946-1957

Relatively few new writers published their first works during World War II. John Cheever published a short story collection, and Mary McCarthy, Wright Morris, Saul Bellow, and Jean Stafford, novels. But wartime paper shortages and the absence in military service and other war work of promising young writers precluded the development of a new generation of fictionists until 1946.

The prolific Gore Vidal was the first soldier-author to break into print with *Williwaw* (1946), a fictional account of his experiences on the little-known Alaskan front, but he was to become most famous for one of the first American novels to broach the forbidden subject of homosexuality in *The City and the Pillar* (1948). His works were overshadowed, however, by Norman Mailer's *The Naked and the Dead* (1948), a novel about one army squad's role in the taking of a Pacific island from the Japanese. Mailer's later work included *An American Dream* (1965) and *Why Are We in Vietnam?* (1967), hallucinatory accounts of moral disintegration in the United States. Subsequently, he temporarily abandoned fiction for journalistic nonfiction in works like *Armies of the Night* (1968), which was critical of American politics.

Another large-scale novel attacked the depravities of the American military establishment—James Jones's *From Here to Eternity* (1951)—but other subjects began to command more attention. In the novel *Other Voices, Other Rooms* (1948) and in a collection of short stories, *A Tree of Night* (1949), Truman Capote presented a South even more degenerate than Faulkner's. Capote later turned to the "nonfiction novel" with *In Cold Blood* (1966), a chilling account of the senseless murder of a family by two drifters. An appallingly grotesque picture of the South emerged in Flannery O'Conner's novels *Wise Blood* (1952) and *The Violent Bear It Away* (1960) and the short stories *A Good Man Is Hard to Find* (1955). Less gothic in its excesses but equally critical of the hypocrisy of decadent Southern aristocrats was *Lie Down in Darkness* (1951) by William Styron.

It was the still inconceivable decadence of the Nazi holocaust in Europe that accounted, at least in part, for the rise after the war of a group of Jewish-American novelists keenly aware of their people's ancient traditions and recent persecutions. Saul Bellow, winner of the Nobel Prize in 1976, first gained recognition for *The Adventures of Augie March* (1953). Bellow's cryptic *Henderson the Rain King* (1959) has attracted much speculation, but his most powerful work is *Herzog* (1964), the self-revelation of a typically alienated, overly ambitious modern man who is at last able to make peace with himself through imaginary conversations with the living and the dead.

Another in this group was Bernard Malamud, whose most impressive novel remains *The Assistant* (1957), a touching account of the relationship between an aggressive young Italian and his employer, a poor Jewish grocer. Growing to be even more respected, however, are the many works, originally written in Yiddish, by Isaac Bashevis Singer, particularly stories of life before World War I in the *shtetls* of Czarist Russia. The most troubling tale to involve recollections of a direct involvement with the Nazi persecution, however, is Edward Lewis Wallant's *The Pawnbroker* (1961).

Blacks began to win greater recognition for fiction following the war. Ralph Ellison's *Invisible Man* (1952), a brilliant bildungsroman about the transformation of a naive, ambitious Southern black boy into a sophisticated fugitive disillusioned by his experiences with both whites and other blacks, transcends racial bounds. More limited but deeply revealing of the sufferings of a sensitive young black are James Baldwin's *Go Tell It on the Mountain* (1953) and the related nonfiction work *The Fire Next Time* (1963), based on recollections of his youth in Harlem.

The most popular novel of this period, especially with young readers, however, concerns the indignities also experienced by a boy growing up during the same years as Baldwin a few miles south of Harlem in the upper-middle-class high-rise apartment district of Manhattan—J.D. Salinger's *The Catcher in the Rye* (1951). Salinger received almost hysterical adulation for the novel, a colloquial monologue about the traumatic experiences of a seventeen-year-old seeking to maintain a doomed innocence.

The Modernist sensibility remained under attack from some able traditionalists who sought the rejuvenation of nineteenth-century moral codes. John P. Marquand had begun a sentimental satire of a vanished culture in *The Late George Apley* (1937) and *Wickford Point* (1939). James Gould Cozzens, writing at the same time, did not attract great attention until his *Guard of Honor* (1948), about problems of command in a Florida training camp, won acclaim from conservative critics. Cozzens is best known for his mammoth novel *By Love Possessed* (1957); the book was hailed by critics alienated by Modernism, but its reputation faded quickly. The novels of socialite-lawyer Louis Auchincloss, like *The Rector of Justin* (1964), have continued to be well received, however, and even as late as 1977 a rabid attack on Modernist decadence, especially Southern, attracted interest in Walker Percy's austere *Lancelot*. John Steinbeck in his later works, especially his most ambitious novel, *East of Eden* (1952), also argued for a return to traditional values.

Traditional values exerted, for a time at least, a greater force in other genres than they did in fiction. Such was the case with the poetry of Robert Lowell, the main poet to emerge during those years. But other poets also became prominent, among them Theodore Roethke,

Karl Shapiro, Randall Jarrell, John Berryman, Richard Wilbur, Allen Tate, James Dickey, Robert Duncan, Richard Eberhart, Howard Nemerov, Charles Olson, and Kenneth Patchen.

The situation in post-World War II American drama was clear-cut. The stage was dominated essentially by two plays, Tennessee Williams's *A Streetcar Named Desire* (1947) and Arthur Miller's *Death of a Salesman* (1949), which are often paired in discussions of whether tragedy is possible in modern secular terms. A third playwright, William Inge, enjoyed popularity with plays like *Picnic* (1953). The ghost of Eugene O'Neill resumed in the 1950s. Through his posthumous *Long Day's Journey into Night* (1956), in which he at last faced squarely the love-hate relationships within his own family, he made his greatest contribution to the theater.

Post-Modernist Chaos and Cultural Expansion: 1957-1979

William Gaddis's *The Recognitions* (1955) is an intimidatingly long novel with many bizarre characters and plot lines that has attracted a small band of avid readers. Jack Kerouac's *On the Road* (1957), which circulated for years in manuscript until it became the best-known unpublished novel in the country, is an epic of the frenzied cross-country travels of the progenitors of the Beat Generation. Gaddis subsequently published other novels, including two more large, puzzling books, *JR* (1975) and *Carpenter's Gothic* (1985). Kerouac, too, published more books (many written during his earlier days of obscurity) before his sudden death in 1969, apparently from the ravages of high living.

The world of William S. Burroughs's *Naked Lunch* is, in fact, the most chaotic that a drugged vision could convey to paper at all. While the worlds of James Purdy (*Malcolm*), Philip Roth (*Goodbye, Columbus*), and John Updike (*The Poorhouse Fair*) are tersely mapped in better disciplined fables, they all deal with characters caught up in their own fantasies and only spasmodically in touch with the external realities of their situations (if indeed *Malcolm* has a geographical reality at all). The same can be said of the works of a number of other contemporaries. John Barth had published *The Floating Opera* in 1956 (though not in its original form until 1967), but his reputation was established by a historical fantasy (*The Sot-Weed Factor*, 1960) and an allegorical tour-de-force (*Giles Goat-Boy*, 1966). Donald Barthelme's short stories in *Come Back Dr. Caligari (1964)* and his "novel" *Snow White* (1967) presented figures from folklore and contemporary media against artificial backgrounds reminiscent of the Pop Art painting of the period. Joseph Heller's antiwar novel *Catch 22* (1961) dealt with characters whose private fantasies made more sense than the real world. Thomas Pynchon's *V.* (1963) seemed, like Vladimir Nabokov's *Lolita* (1955) and *Pale Fire* (1962), an elaborate and masterfully inventive word game that shuffled a similar deck of cards to suggest the ultimate unreality of all human action.

This tendency toward a confusion of fantasy and reality had begun to manifest itself as early as 1952 in the works of the man who was eventually to have the last word on such matters, Kurt Vonnegut, Jr. Although *Player Piano* seemed only a kind of comic strip spin-off of the science fiction that had begun to win serious attention, Vonnegut's work became increasingly serious in its portraits of paranoid self-destruction *(Mother Night,* 1962) and universal destruction *(Cat's Cradle,* 1963). *Slaughterhouse-Five* (1969) combined the historical horror of the fire raid on Dresden during World War II with science fiction fantasy to suggest that the only possible hope for humanity lay beyond our own corrupted planet, but Vonnegut returned to Earth to deliver in *Breakfast of Champions* (1973) a damning indictment of every facet of American society.

Vonnegut's erasing of the line that has conventionally existed between external and internal realities flamboyantly completes the execution of a step already taken by Nabokov, Barth, and Purdy, among others. Critics have tended to regard these writers as post-modernist. Sporadic lamentations beginning in the 1960s with the idea of "the death of the novel" appeared justified by the lack of anything to write about following the apocalypse prophesied by Thomas Pynchon in the short story "Entropy" (1960) and limned with flabbergasting erudition in *Gravity's Rainbow* (1973).

A single poem, "Howl" (1956), established Allen Ginsberg, a charter member of the Beat Generation, as the last spokesperson for a national audience in the tradition of Whitman, Hart Crane, and Sandburg. Ginsberg was one of six poets who participated at a legendary reading at San Francisco's Six Gallery in the autumn of 1955 that launched the brief San Francisco Renaissance, the last literary movement with large public support. Of Ginsberg's fellow readers—Kenneth Rexroth, Michael McClure, Philip Lamantia, Philip Whalen, and Gary Snyder—only Snyder remains almost universally respected for his deeply sensitive nature poetry inspired by his years of study of Zen Buddhism. The movement itself as a newsworthy phenomenon was exhausted by 1960, but the attack on conventional respectability that it launched has continued to affect American poetry.

Although often better regarded as a poet, James Dickey, in his novel *Deliverance* (1970), captures more vividly than his contemporaries the ambiguous feelings of those who seek to escape civilization only to find that retreat is corrupt and false. A stronger hold on the American imagination than Dickey's was achieved by Sylvia Plath, whose brief and troubled life ended in suicide before the appearance of her most remarkable works. Like Dickey, Plath complemented confessional poetry (*Ariel,* 1965) with a self-revelatory novel (*The Bell Jar,* 1963). Another poet who died tragically young, Frank O'Hara was both a leader of the New York school closely associated with young painters of the period and a hero of the gay activist movement because of his frank revelation of his homosexuality. Other talented poets have tended to develop cultist followings. Denise Levertov, Adrienne Rich, and Diane Wakoski have been strongly supported by feminists. But other poets, like W.D. Snodgrass, W.S. Merwin, James Merrill, John Ashbery, and LeRoi Jones (Amiri Baraka), have also developed coteries of devoted readers.

Like O'Neill, Edward Albee first won attention with electrifying one-act plays, *The Zoo Story* (1959) and *The American Dream* (1961). Doubts about Albee's ability to follow up these dramatic vignettes with a full-length play were triumphantly set to rest with *Who's Afraid of Virginia Woolf?* (1962), the Walpurgis night exorcism of the decadent dreams of a childless and professionally sterile American couple.

Albee is often credited with jump-starting the off-Broadway movement in the late 1950s and early 1960s. But as with other literary forms, this whole period was marked in the theater by its intense experimentation and an expansion of the definition of the theater "text" to include elements of the mise-en-scéne. Experimentalist directors and works created by acting ensembles reigned. Nevertheless, the 1960s saw an explosion of exciting new American drama, the most notable practitioner of which was Sam Shepard, whose background as a drummer in rock and roll infused his early experiments. Eventually he looked to O'Neill-like themes about fate and the family in his most enduring works, *Buried Child* and *Curse of the Starving Class*. Other playwrights of note to emerge from the off-Broadway explosion included Terrence McNally, Lanford Wilson, Maria Irene Fornes, Arthur Kopit, and David Rabe. In Chicago, David Mamet began writing naturalistic plays that were small in narrative scope but powerful in their characterization and dialogue.

Black American drama has largely failed to sustain the promise of the 1960s. Amiri Baraka scored a spectacular success with *Dutchman* (1964), a two-character play about a confrontation between a black man and a white woman on a New York subway train, but *The Toilet* (1962) and *The Slave* (1964) proved too gross for even off-Broadway audiences. Charles Gordone won a Pulitzer Prize for *No Place to Be Somebody,* and Lorraine Hansberry enjoyed both popular and critical success with her first full-length play, *A Raisin in the Sun* (1959), an inspirational drama about a Chicago black family's aspirations to own a home in a segregated suburb. Later August Wilson came to the fore with *Ma Rainey's Black Bottom* (1981), *Fences* (1985), *Joe Turner's Come and Gone* (1986), and *The Piano Lesson* (1990).

By far the most financially successful American playwright of the last third of the twentieth century was Neil Simon, whose works return to the 1930s manner of the well-made farce. Simon's most substantial achievements have been the autobiographical trilogy *Brighton Beach Memoirs* (1984), *Biloxi Blues* (1986), and *Broadway Bound* (1987) and the Pulitzer Prize-winning *Lost in Yonkers* (1992). A similar nostalgic reexamination of the past is found in the stories (and much better-known films) of Woody Allen, but this trend seems part of a larger one under way as an exhausted Modernist sensibility looks for fresh inspirations.

Fresh inspirations were indeed found through the cultural transformations of the period, largely as a result of the civil rights and feminist movements of the 1960s and 1970s. It was during this time that Asian Americans, for example, began to find their voices in larger and larger numbers. Frank Chin's play *Chickencoop Chinaman,* performed in New York in 1972, dramatized a young Chinese American man's anguished search for a viable identity. Chin's short story collection *The Chinaman Pacific & Frisco R. R. Co.* (1988) and his novel *Donald Duk* (1991) continued the quest for a Chinese American male identity. The female search for identity is vividly portrayed in Maxine Hong Kingston's *The Woman Warrior: Memoirs of a Girlhood Among Ghosts* (1975), which won the 1976 National Book Critics Award for nonfiction.

Amy Tan's best-selling *The Joy Luck Club* (1989) explores the tension between Chinese mothers and their Americanized daughters. Gish Jen examines the comic aspects of the American dream in *Typical American* (1991), while Fae Myenne Ng's *Bone* (1992) is a sensitive novel of a Chinese American family's adjustment to the suicide of one of the daughters. David Wong Louie's collection *The Pangs of Love* (1991) raises Asian American short fiction to new heights of sophistication, humor, and poignancy. Other Asian American poets and dramatists have also gained national attention through their award-winning works, among them Cathy Song (*Picture Bride,* 1983), Garrett Hongo *(River of Heaven,* 1987), and Li-young Lee (*The City in Which I Love You,* 1990). David Henry Hwang's *M. Butterfly* won the Tony Award for Best New Dramatic Play on Broadway in 1988, and Japanese-African American Velinia Hasu Houston's play *Tea* (1983) garnered awards and numerous productions nationwide.

Asians from other ethnic backgrounds have also contributed to the ever-widening stream of Asian American literature. Bharati Muhkerjee's novels *The Tiger's Daughter* (1971), *Wife* (1975), and *Jasmine* (1989) and her short story collections *Darkness (1985)* and *The Middleman and Other Stories* (1988) explore the process of acculturation for Indians and South Asians, while Tran Van Dinh in *Blue Dragon White Tiger* (1983) and Lely Hayslip in *When Heaven and Earth Changed Places* (1990) provide insider views of life in Vietnam.

The late 1960s and 1970s also brought forth a new generation of sophisticated Native American fiction writers. The first of these to achieve national recognition was N. Scott Momaday (Kiowal/Cherokee), whose *House Made of Dawn* (1968) won the Pulitzer Prize. Other notable fiction writers of the period include Leslie Marmon Silko (Laguna), author of *Ceremony* (1977), and James Welch (Blackfeet/Gros Ventre), who wrote *Winter in the Blood* (1975) and the less ethnohistorical novel *The Death of Jim Loney* (1979).

Minimalism, Reactions, Multiculturalism, and Other Developments: 1980—

Reacting against the self-reflexive tendency of such post-Modernist writers as John Barth, Robert Coover, and Donald Barthelme, a number of writers in the 1980s developed a new brand of realism, variously called "Kmart," "dirty," or "yuppie" realism, depending on whether the reference was to Bobbie Anne Mason (*Shiloh and Other Stories,* 1982), Raymond Carver (*What We Talk about When We Talk about Love,* 1981), or Ann Beattie (*Burning House,* 1982). This "return to reality," showcased more often by the short story than the novel, focused on the seemingly trivial events of everyday life in such a highly compressed way that it acquired the name "minimalism," praised by many for its focus on blue-collar life and its highly honed prose, even as it was soundly scolded by others for its emphasis on unaware characters who were "without a clue" and for its "less-is-less" language.

During the period of minimalism in the short story in the 1980s, the American novel returned to what it always did best. It seduced readers into thinking that such characters as John Updike's Rabbit Angstrom (*Rabbit Is Rich,* 1981, and *Rabbit at Rest,* 1990), Philip Roth's Nathan Zuckerman (*Anatomy Lesson,* 1983, and *The Counterlife,* 1987), and Richard Ford's Frank Bascombe (*The Sportswriter,* 1986, and *Independence Day,* 1995) were real men who could be brought back again and again. Or else the writer made readers believe that the novel was actually a form of familial or social history, as did Larry McMurty (*Lonesome Dove,* 1985, and *Texasville*), E.L. Doctorow (*World's Fair,* 1985, and *Billy Bathgate,* 1989), Don DeLillo (*Libra,* 1988, and *Underworld,* 1997), Charles Frazier (*Cold Mountain,* 1997), and Thomas Pynchon (*Mason and Dixon,* 1997).

The self-conscious satire of post-Modernist fiction was maintained by Barth (*Sabbatical,* 1982, and *Tidewater Tales,* 1987), T.C. Boyle (*Greasy Lake,* 1985, and *East Is East,* 1990), and Steven Milhauser (*In the Penny Arcade,* 1986). The most powerful post-Modernist novel of the era was William H. Gass's brilliant *The Tunnel* (1995), a tour de force that was destined to be one of the great, but largely unread, novels of the last half of the twentieth century. Other reactions against the minimalism of the 1980s can be seen in the on-the-road stories of Denis Johnson (*Jesus's Son,* 1993) and the spaced-out prose of Thom Jones (*Pugilist at Rest,* 1993, and *Cold Snap,* 1995).

The competition between the short story and the novel that dominated the marketplace in the early 1980s reached a truce of sorts in the late 1980s and early 1990s in two different ways. For one thing, several writers published short stories that they later stitched together into novels. Two of the best-known examples of this trend are Tim O'Brien's *The Things They Carried* (1990) and Louise Erdrich's *Tracks* (1988). The other way in which the two forms have merged is by a return to an interest in the novella, once so favored by Joseph Conrad and Henry James. Updike has, in his senior years, published longer, more leisurely narratives than the earlier *New Yorker* stories in his 1994 collection *The Afterlife,* and Andre Dubus, always a holdout against minimalism, has done the same in *Dancing after Hours* (1997). A number of writers who were part of the trend toward minimalism or hyperrealism during the 1980s have also turned to the novella. Ford's *Women with Men* (1997) is a collection of three novellas that unhurriedly explore character, and, in contrast to her earlier narratives, the novella title story of Beattie's *Park City* (1998) depends largely on novelistic techniques of expanded character exploration and realistic, nonmetaphoric detail.

It is often the case in American letters that poetry sets parameters for the other genres. Taking leads from the rebellions of the Beats or the increasing reliance on the autobiographical by such so-called confessional poets as Anne Sexton, Robert Lowell, John Berryman, and Sylvia Plath, fiction, memoir, and poetry have grown correspondingly autobiographical. In poems by Frank Bidart, Sharon Olds, Louise Gluck, Charles Wright, Carolyn Forche, Alan Shapiro, Lyn Lifshin, Jorie Graham, Rita Dove, Robert Hass, Robert Pinsky, and countless others, the personal appears to fuel the poetic voice. That the poem's experiences might not be factual is beside the point, for the sense of authentic and lived events appeals to today's readers. It is no coincidence that many contemporary poets are also essayists and memoirists, even writers of fiction, as in Shapiro's *Virgil* and Erdich's *The Blue Jay's Year.* There is also a tendency to combine forms within a single text, as Gloria Anzaldua has done in her essay and poem mélange *Borderlands* and as Sherman Alexie has done in the film *Smoke Signals,* based on his short fiction.

Readers conversant with the widely divergent strands of Modernism in American literature see a return to the insistence of such iconoclastic writers as Gertrude Stein and William Carlos Williams that writing be respected for itself and not hedged in by the confines of genre. One of the great qualities of American literature throughout history has been its drive to express the new, to create the genuine narrative or lyric, fostered in part by the excitement that true democratic principles create. To be free as people breaks into and through the formalist conventions of "good" literature and its sometimes oppressive traditions. The battle to achieve a literary form reflective of that ideal of freedom has pushed writers to create new forms—from the work of LANGUAGE poets like Clark Coolidge and Charles Bernstein to the emphatic feminist militancy of Marge Piercy, Judy Grahn, and Minnie Bruce Pratt, to Philip Levine's terse poems about class and, in fiction, from the deft post-Modernity of Ron Sukenik to the panoramic prose texts by DeLillo, Bartheleme, and David Foster Wallace, which are as various as their ostensible subjects.

The 1980s also saw an interesting return to an emphasis on verbal and linguistic pyrotechnics. Such playwrights as Mac Wellman, Eric Overmyer, and Len Jenkin reveled in the verbal detritus of pop culture deeded by advertising. In *On the Verge,* one of the most produced plays of the 1980s, Overmyer has three Victorian women traveling through a time warp into a world literally littered by 1950s cultural artifacts such as Cool Whip and "I Like Ike" buttons. Wellman's scripts are a vertiginous swirl of verbosity that characters spin into a dense, pun-filled poetical dialogue. But the most interesting aspect of contemporary dramatic writing resulted from another return, to that of the most minimalist of theatrical forms, storytelling. Labeled performance artists, many writers/performers simply created one-person shows knitted from the autobiographical musings of the performer (Spalding Gray, Karen Finley) or revuelike sketches of an odd assortment of character monologues (Whoopi Goldberg, Eric Bogosian, Lily Tomlin, Anna Deavere-Smith, and Danny Hoch, to name just a few of the most notable). Are they plays? If so, do they qualify as literature? The American theater during the past few decades has definitely stretched definitions.

Minimalism, post-Modernity, and other stylistic conventions, however, have increasingly yielded to the "maximizing" influence of multiculturalism on American literature, and the study of the literatures of the United States has broadened in scope to include an increasingly diverse group of writers. By the late twentieth century each of the country's many ethnic groups had produced writers who had already substantially affected the direction that American literature was taking into the next century. Among African Americans the leading male writers included Ernest Gaines, Ishmael Reed, John Edgar Wideman, Michael Harper, August Wilson, Charles Gordone, and Charles Johnson. Perhaps the most remarkable rise of a new author was that of the African American novelist Toni Morrison. Morrison published her first book, *The Bluest Eye,* in 1970. It was followed by *Sula, Tar Baby, Song of Solomon* (which won the National Book Critics Circle Award for 1977), *Beloved* (which won the 1988 Pulitzer Prize), and *Jazz* (1992). In 1993, two decades after she burst on the literary scene to critical and popular acclaim, Morrison received the Nobel Prize for literature. Besides Morrison, African American women authors of note included Maya Angelou, Gwendolyn Brooks, Nikki Giovanni, Ntozake Shange, Alice Walker, Toni Cade Bambara, Gloria Naylor, Rita Dove, Paule Marshall, and Terry McMillan. The increasing number of notable Asian American writers included, among others, Frank Chin, Jessica Hagedorn, Kimiko Hahn, Garrett Hongo, Richard Kim, John Okada, and Hisaye Yamamota.

In the closing decades of the twentieth century Native American writers began to incorporate in their novels themes other than the ritual quest. Erdrich (Ojibwa) focuses on family and community interrelationships in *Love Medicine* (1984), *Beet Queen* (1986), *Tracks* (1988), *The Bingo Palace* (1994), and *The Antelope Wife* (1998), all set in the writer's native North Dakota. Michael Dorris (Modoc), who was at one time married to Erdrich, will probably best be remembered for his touching memoir *The Broken Cord* (1990). Poetry has also been an important literary genre for Native Americans. Common themes include a sense of loss of tribal roots, closeness to nature and animals, the sense of displacement that urban Indians experience, and the traditional roles of tribal women. Among the most widely published Native American poets were Paula Gunn Allen (Laguna/Sioux), Joy Harjo (Creek), Simon J. Ortiz (Acoma), and Wendy Rose (Hopi-Miwok).

Hispanic writers, many of whom have Mexican and Mexican American roots, also received increasing recognition, especially during the 1980s and 1990s. The leading writers included Rudolfo Anaya, Gloria Anzaldua, Ana Castillo, Sandra Cisneros, Rolando Hinojosa, and Tomas Rivera. Oscar Hijuelos, a Cuban American novelist, and the Puerto Rican authors Tato Laviera and Nicholasa Mohr also made their marks.

As the twentieth century came to a close, others who had exerted influence included Richard Brautigan, Harry Crews, Joan Didion, James Donleavy, Thomas Flanagan, John Irving, Ken Kesey, Wright Morris, Joyce Carol Oates, Cynthia Ozick, Grace Paley, Susan Sontag, Wallace Stegner, Paul Theroux, and Barbara Kingsolver. Poets Galway Kinnell, William Stafford, John Ciardi, Donald Hall, and many others also participated in the dialogue that informed the literature. These writers and others too numerous to mention have made and continued to make distinctive contributions that shape American literature.

READING LIST

Bibliographies, Handbooks, etc.

American Literary Scholarship 1963— (annual review), 1965—.

Bailey, Leaonead, *Broadside Authors: A Biographical Directory,* 1971.

Bain, Robert, Joseph M. Flora, and Louis D. Rubin, Jr., editors, *Southern Writers: A Biographical Dictionary,* 1979.

Balderston, Daniel, *The Latin American Short Story: An Annotated Guide to Anthologies and Criticism,* 1992.

Barksdale, Richard and Keneth Kinnamon, editors, *Black Writers of America: A Comprehensive Anthology,* 1972.

Bean, Joseph, *In the Life: A Black Gay Anthology,* 1986.

Beidler, Peter G., *The American Indian in Short Fiction: An Annotated Bibliography,* 1979.

Bertens, Hans, and Theo D'haen, and Joris Duytschaever, and Richard Todd, editors, *Post-War Literatures in English: A Lexicon of Contemporary Authors,* 1988.

Blanck, Jacob, *Bibliography of American Literature,* 1997.

Bleznick, Donald William, *A Sourcebook for Hispanic Literature and Language: A Selected, Annotated Guide to Spanish, Spanish-American, and Chicano Bibliography, Literature, Linguistics, Journals and other Source Material,* 1983.

Bontemps, Arna and Langston Hughes, editors, *The Book of Negro Folklore,* 1958.

Brignano, Russell C., *Black Americans in Autobiography: An Annotated Bibliography of Bibliographies and Autobiographical Books Written since the Civil War,* revised edition, 1984.

Brooks, Cleanth, R.W.B. Lewis, and Robert Penn Warren, editors, *American Literature: The Makers and the Making,* 2 vols., 1973.

Brown-Guillory, Elizabeth, editor, *Their Place on the Stage: Black Women Playwrights in America,* 1988.

Bruccoli, Matthew J., and Judith S. Baughman, editors, *Bibliography of American Fiction, 1919-1988:* (Volume 1, *James Agee—John P. Marquand;* Volume 2, *Peter Matthiesen—Roger Zelazny*), 1991.

Buhle, Mari Jo, and Paul Buhle, and Dan Georgakas, editors, *Encyclopedia of the American Left,* 1990.

Butler, Deborah A., *American Women Writers on Vietnam: Unheard Voices, A Selected Annotated Bibliography,* 1990.

Castillo-Speed, Lillian, editor, *Chicana Studies Index,* 1992.

Catala, Rafael, James D. Anderson, and Sarah Park Anderson, *Index of American Periodical Verse* (annual), 1971—.

Chapman, Dorothy Hilton, *Index to Poetry by Black American Women,* 1986.

Cheung, King-Kok and Stan Yogi, *Asian American Literature: An Annotated Bibliography,* 1988.

Chielens, Edward E., *American Literary Magazines: The Twentieth Century,* 1992.

Clancy, James Thomas, *Native American References: A Cross-Indexed Bibliography of 17th Century American Imprints Pertaining to American Indians,* 1974.

Clark, Harry Hayden, *American Literature: Poe through Garland,* 1971.

Clements, William M., *Native American Folklore, 1879-1979,* 1984.

Cohen, Hennig, *Articles in American Studies 1954-1968,* 1972.

Contemporary Writers series *(Poets, Novelists, Dramatists, Literary Critics),* 1970— (each volume revised every 5 years).

Cook, Michael L., and Stephen T. Miller, *Mystery, Detective, and Espionage Fiction: A Checklist of Fiction in U.S. Pulp Magazines, 1915-1974, I & II,* 1988.

Dargan, Marion, *Guide to American Biography 1607-1933,* 2 vols., 1949-52.

Davis, Arthur P., *From the Dark Tower: Afro-American Writers 1900-1960,* 1982.

Davis, Gwenn, and Beverly A. Joyce, *Drama by Women to 1900,* 1992.

Davis, Gwenn, and Beverly A. Joyce, *Personal Writings by Women to 1900: A Bibliography of American and British Writers,* 1989.

Davis, Gwenn, and Beverly A. Joyce, editors, *Poetry by Women to 1900: A Bibliography of American and British Writers, Bibliographies of Writings by American and British Women to 1900,* 2 vols., 1991.

Davis, Richard Beale, *American Literature through Bryant 1585-1830,* 1969.

Deodene, Frank and William P. French, *Black American Fiction Since 1952: A Preliminary Checklist,* 1970.

Dictionary of American Biography, 17 vols., revised edition, 1981; supplement, 1988.

Dictionary of Literary Biography, 1978—.

Drew, Bernard A., *Action Series and Sequels: A Bibliography of Espionage, Vigilante, and Soldier of Fortune Novels,* 1988.

Eddleman, Floyd Eugene, *American Drama Criticism,* supplement II to second edition, 1989.

Eger, Ernestina N., *A Bibliography of Criticism of Contemporary Chicano Literature,* 1982.

Emanuel, James A. and Theodore L. Gross, editors, *Dark Symphony: Negro Literature in America,* 1968.

Erdman, David V., *The Romantic Movement: A Selective and Critical Bibliography for 1987,* 1988.

Fisher, Dexter, editor, *Minority Language and Literature: Retrospective and Prospective,* 1977.

Fleckner, John A., *Native American Archives: An Introduction,* 1984.

Fowler, Carolyn, *Black Arts and Black Aesthetics: A Bibliography,* 1981.

Frank, Frederick, S., *Gothic Fiction: A Master List of Twentieth Century Criticism and Research,* 1987.

Fried, Lewis, and Gene Brown, and Louis Harap, editors, *Handbook of American-Jewish Literature: An Analytical Guide to Topics, Themes, and Sources,* 1988.

Gilreath, James, and Elizabeth Carter Wills, *Federal Copyright Records, 1790-1800,* 1987.

Gohdes, Clarence, editor, *Bibliographical Guide to the Study of the Literature of the U.S.A.,* 1959; 5th edition, 1984.

Gould, Christopher, and Richard Parker Morgan, *South Carolina Imprints, 1731-1800: A Descriptive Bibliography,* 1985.

Grieb, Kenneth J., *Central America in the Nineteenth and Twentieth Centuries: An Annotated Bibliography,* 1988.

Harbert, Earl N., and Robert A. Rees, editors, *Fifteen American Authors before 1900: Bibliographical Essays on Research and Criticism,* 1984.

Hart, James D., *The Oxford Companion to American Literature*, 1941; 5th edition, 1983.

Havelice, Patricia, *Index to American Author Bibliographies*, 1971.

Hawes, Joseph M., and Ray N. Hiner, editors, *American Childhood: A Research Guide and Historical Handbook*, 1985.

Heard, J. Norman, *Handbook of the American Frontier: Four Centuries of Indian-White Relationships*, 1987.

Heisley, Michael, editor, *An Annotated Bibliography of Chicano Folklore from the Southwestern United States*, 1977.

Hill, Ruth Edmonds, editor, *Black Women's Oral History Collection at the Schlesinger Library, Radcliffe College*, 1989.

Hirschfelder, Arlene B., *The Native American Almanac: A Portrait of Native America Today*, 1993.

Holman, C. Hugh, *The American Novel through Henry James*, 1966; 2nd edition, 1979.

Howard, Sharon M., *African-American Women Fiction Writers, 1859-1986: An Annotated Bio-Bibliography*, 1994.

Hughes, Langston, and Arna Bontemps, editors, *The Poetry of the Negro, 1746-1970*, 1970.

Hughes, Langston, *The Best Short Stories by Negro Writers: An Anthology from 1899 to the Present*, 1967.

Humphreys, Nancy K., *American Women's Magazines: An Annotated Historical Guide*, 1989.

Inge, M. Thomas, editor, *Black American Writers*, 2 vols., 1978.

Inge, M. Thomas, editor, *Handbook of American Popular Culture*, 1988.

Jacobson, Angeline, *Contemporary Native American Literature: A Selected and Partially Annotated Bibliography*, 1977.

Jason, Philip K., *The Vietnam War in Literature: An Annotated Bibliography of Criticism*, 1992.

Jones, LeRoi, and Larry Neal, editors, *Black Fire: An Anthology of Afro-American Writing*, 1968.

Karkhanis, Sharad, *Jewish Heritage in America: An Annotated Bibliography*, 1988.

Kerri, James N., *American Indians: U.S. & Canada, A Bibliography of Contemporary Studies and Urban Research*, 1974.

Kim, Elaine H., "Asian American Writers: A Biographical Review," in *American Studies International*, 1984.

King, Woodie, and Ron Milner, editors, *Black Drama Anthology*, 1971.

Kolb, Harold H., Jr., *A Field Guide to the Study of American Literature*, 1976.

Kolin, Philip C., *American Playwrights since 1945: A Guide to Scholarship, Criticism, and Performance*, 1989.

Kunitz, Staniey J., and Howard Haycraft, *American Authors 1600-1900: A Biographical Dictionary of American Literature*, 1938.

Leary, Lewis, *American Literature: A Study and Research Guide*, 1976.

Leary, Lewis, *Articles on American Literature 1900-1950*, 1954; 1950-1967, 1970; 1968-1975, 1979.

Leonard, Angela M., editor, *Antislavery Materials at Bowdoin College: A Finding Guide*, 1992.

Ling, Amy, "Asian American Literature," in *Redefining American Literary History*, 1990.

Littlefield, Daniel F., *A Bibliography of Native American Writers, 1772-1924*, 1985.

Lomelí, Francisco A., and Donaldo W. Urioste, *Chicano Perspectives in Literature: A Critical and Annotated Bibliography*, 1976.

Lomelí, Francisco A., and Carl R. Shirley, *Dictionary of Literary Biography: Chicano Writers First Series*, 1989; *Second Series*, 1992.

Mainiero, Lina, editor, *American Women Writers*, 4 vols., 1979-82.

Malinowski, Sharon, editor, *Gay and Lesbian Literature*, 1994.

Martínez, Julio A., and Francisco A. Lomelí, editors, *Chicano Literature: A Reference Guide*, 1985.

Marting, Diane E., editor, *Spanish American Women Writers: A Bio-Bibliographical Source Book*, 1990.

Menendez, Albert J., *The Catholic Novel: An Annotated Bibliography*, 1988.

Mintz, Lawrence E., *Humor in America: A Research Guide to Genres and Topics*, 1988.

Mottram, Eric, and Malcolm Bradbury, editors, *U.S.A.*, in *The Penguin Companion to Literature 3*, 1971.

Myerson, Joel, editor, *The Transcendentalists: A Review of Research and Criticism*, 3 vols., 1984.

Nilon, Charles H., *Bibliography of Bibliographies of American Literature*, 1970.

Nilsen, Don L. F., *Humor in American Literature: A Selected Annotated Bibliography*, 1992.

Parker, Patricia L., *Early American Fiction: A Reference Guide*, 1984.

Peck, David R., *American Ethnic Literatures: Native American, African American, Chicano/Latino, and Asian American Writers and Their Backgrounds: An Annotated Bibliography*, 1992.

Prucha, Francis Paul, *Atlas of American Indian Affairs*, 1990.

Rebolledo, Tey Diana, and Eliana S. Rivero, editors, *Infinite Divisions: An Anthology of Chicana Writers*, 1993.

Rebolledo, Tey Diana, editor, *Las mujeres hablan: An Anthology of Nuevo Mexican Writers*, 1988.

Rees, Robert A., and Earl N. Harbert, editors, *Fifteen American Authors before 1900: Bibliographic Essays on Research and Criticism*, 1971; revised edition, 1984.

Robbins, J. Albert, editor, *American Literary Manuscripts*, 1960; revised edition, 1977.

Rock, Roger O., *The Native American in American Literature: A Selectively Annotated Bibliography*, 1985.

Rood, Karen L., editor, *American Literary Almanac: From 1608 to the Present; Orig. Compendium of Facts & Anecdotes about Lit. Life in United States of Amer.*, 1988.

Ruoff, A. LaVonne Brown, *American Indian Literature: An Introduction, Bibliographic Review, and Selected Bibliography*, 1990.

Ryan, Pat M., *American Drama Bibliography: A Checklist of Publications in English*, 1969.

Salzman, Jack, editor, *The Cambridge Handbook of American Literature*, 1986.

Schockley, Ann Allen, *Afro-American Women Writers, 1746-1933: An Anthology and Critical Guide*, 1988.

Scholnick, Robert J., *Bibliography: American Literature and Science through 1989*, in: Scholnick, Robert J., editor, *American Literature and Science*, 1992.

Shuman, R. Baird, *American Drama, 1918-1960: An Annotated Bibliography*, 1992.

Sklar, Morty and Robert Peters, editors, *Editor's Choice III: Fiction, Poetry & Art from the U.S. Small Presses; Selections from nominations made by the editors of independent, noncommercial literary presses and magazines, of works published by them from 1984 to 1990*, 1991.

Southern, Eileen, and Josephine Wright, *African American Traditions in Song, Sermon, Tale and Dance, 1600s-1920s: An Annotated Bibliography of Literature, Collections, and Artworks*, 1990.

Spiller, Robert E., and others, editors, *Literary History of the United States: Bibliography,* 1948; 4th edition, 1974.

Steiner, Michael, and Clarence Mondale, *Region and Regionalism in the United States: A Source Book for the Humanities and Social Sciences,* 1988.

Tanselle, G. Thomas, *Guide to the Study of United States Imprints,* 2 vols., 1971.

Taylor, Thomas J., *American Theater History: An Annotated Bibliography,* 1992.

Todd, Janet, editor, *A Dictionary of British and American Women Writers 1660-1800,* 1985.

Trujillo, Roberto G., and Andrés Rodríguez, compilers, *Literatura Chicana: Creative and Critical Writings through 1984,* 1985.

Twentieth-Century Writers series (*Children's Writers, Crime and Mystery Writers, Science-Fiction Writers, Romance and Gothic Writers, Western Writers*), 1978-- (each volume revised every 5 years).

Venzon, Anne Cipriano, *The Spanish-American War: An Annotated Bibliography,* 1990.

Verrall, Catherine, *Resource Reading List, 1990: An Annotated Bibliography of Resources by and about Native People,* 1990.

Weixlmann, Joe, *American Short-Fiction Criticism and Scholarship 1959-1977: A Checklist,* 1982.

West, Richard Samuel, *Bibliography of American Literature in Periodicals, 19th Century,* 1997.

White, Barbara A., *American Women's Fiction 1790-1870: A Reference Guide,* 1990.

Whiteman, Maxwell, *A Century of Fiction by American Negroes, 1853-1952: A Descriptive Bibliography,* 1955.

Winship, Michael, *Bibliography of American Literature: A Selective Index,* 1995.

Woll, Allen, *Dictionary of the Black Theatre: Broadway, Off-Broadway, and Selected Harlem Theatre,* 1983.

Woodress, James, editor, *American Fiction 1900-1950: A Guide to Information Sources,* 1975.

Wright, Lyle H., *American Fiction: A Contribution toward a Bibliography 1774-1850,* 1948, revised edition, 1966; *1851-1875,* 1965, revised edition, 1966; *1876-1900,* 1966.

Yancy, Preston M., *The Afro-American Short Story: A Comprehensive, Annotated Index with Selected Commentaries,* 1986.

Yanella, Donald, and John H. Roch, *Prose to 1820: A Guide to Information Sources,* 1979.

Yellin, Jean Fagan and Cynthia D. Bond, *The Pen Is Ours: A Listing of Writings by and about African American Women before 1910 with Secondary Bibliography to the Present,* 1991.

General Histories

Aaron, Daniel, *Writers on the Left: Episodes in American Literary Communism,* 1992.

Adamson, Joseph, and Hillary Clark, editors, *Scenes of Shame: Psychoanalysis, Shame, and Writing,* 1999.

Alpern, Sara, Joyce Antler, Elisabeth Israels Perry, and Ingrid Winther Scobie, editors, *The Challenge of Feminist Biography,* 1992.

Anderson, Douglas, *A House Undivided: Domesticity and Community in American Literature,* 1990.

Appiah, Kwame Anthony, *In My Father's House: Africa in the Philosophy of Culture,* 1992.

Arenal, Electa, and Stacey Schlau, *Untold Sisters: Hispanic Nuns in Their Own Works,* translated by Amanda Powell, 1989.

Attebery, Brian, *The Fantasy Tradition in American Literature from Irving to Le Guin,* 1980.

Baker, Houston A., Jr., *Long Black Song: Essays in Black American Literature and Culture,* 1990.

Barbour, James, and Tom Quirk, editors, *Writing the American Classics,* 1990.

Barbour, James, and Tom Quirk, editors, *Critical Essays in American Literature,* 1986.

Bartley, Numan V., editor, *The Evolution of Southern Culture,* 1988.

Battilana, Marilla, *The Colonial Roots of American Fiction: Notes toward a New Theory,* 1988.

Bauer, Dale M., *Feminist Dialogics: A Theory of Failed Community,* 1988.

Baym, Nina, *Feminism and American Literary History: Essays,* 1992.

Bell, Bernard, *The Afro-American Novel and Its Tradition,* 1987.

Bell, F. A., and D. K. Adams, editors, *American Literary Landscapes: The Fiction and the Fact,* 1988.

Bennett, Paula, *My Life a Loaded Gun: Female Creativity and Feminist Poetics,* 1986.

Benson, Thomas W., and Lewis Perry, editors, *American Rhetoric: Context and Criticism,* 1989.

Bercovitch, Sacvan, and Cyrus R.K. Patell, editors, *The Cambridge History of American Literature,* 1994.

Bercovitch, Sacvan, editor, *Reconstructing American Literary History,* 1986.

Binder, Wolfgang, editor, *Partial Autobiographies: Interviews with Twenty Chicano Poets,* 1985.

Blacksilver, Edith, editor, *The Ethnic American Woman: Problems, Protests, Lifestyle,* 1989.

Bloom, Clive, and Brian Docherty, editors, *American Poetry: The Modernist Ideal,* 1995.

Bogard, Travis, and others, *American Drama,* 1977.

Bone, Robert, *Down Home: A History of Afro-American Short Fiction from Its Beginning to the End of the Harlem Renaissance,* 1975.

Bridgman, Richard, *The Colloquial Style in America,* 1966.

Brooks, Van Wyck, *Makers and Finders: A History of the Writer in America 1800-1915,* 5 vols., 1936-52.

Brown, Julie, editor, *Ethnicity and the American Short Story* (Wellesley Studies in Critical Theory, Literary History and Culture, vol. 16), 1997.

Brown, Carolyn S., *The Tall Tale in American Folklore and Literature,* 1987.

Brown, Sterling, *Negro Poetry and Drama and The Negro in American Fiction,* 1972.

Bruce-Novoa, Juan, *Chicano Authors: Inquiry by Interview,* 1980.

Bruce-Novoa, Juan, *Chicano Poetry: A Critical Introduction,* 1986.

Brumble, H. David, *American Indian Autobiography,* 1988.

Budd, Louis J., Edwin H. Cady, and Carl L. Anderson, editors, *Toward a New American Literary History,* 1980.

Budd, Louis J., and Edwin H. Cady, editors, *On Humor: The Best from American Literature,* 1992.

Budick, Emily Miller, *Fiction and Historical Consciousness: The American Romance Tradition,* 1989.

Butters, Ronald R., John M. Clum, and Michael Moon, editors, *Displacing Homophobia: Gay Male Perspectives in Literature and Culture,* 1989.

Cain, William E., editor, *Reconceptualizing American Literary/Cultural Studies: Rhetoric, History, and Politics in the Humanities,* 1996.

Candelaria, Cordelia, *Chicano Poetry: A Critical Introduction,* 1986.

Carpenter, Lynette, and Wendy K. Kolmar, editors, *Haunting the House of Fiction: Feminist Perspectives on Ghost Stories by American Women,* 1991.

Chabot, C. Barry, *Writers for the Nation: American Literary Modernism,* 1997.

Chakovsky, Sergei, and M. Thomas Inge, editors, *Russian Eyes on American Literature,* 1992.

Cheung, King-Kok, *Articulate Silences: Hisaye Yamamoto, Maxine Hong Kingston, Joy Kogawa,* 1993.

Christian, Barbara, *Black Women Novelists: The Development of a Tradition, 1892-1976,* 1980.

Clark, Harry Hayden, editor, *Transitions in American Literary History,* 1953.

Clarke, Graham, editor, *The American City: Literary and Cultural Perspectives,* 1988.

Conkin, Paul K., *The Southern Agrarians,* 1988.

Covici, Pascal, *Humor and Revelation in American Literature: The Puritan Connection,* 1997.

Cowan, Bainard, and Joseph G. Kronick, editors, *Theorizing American Literature: Hegel, the Sign, and History,* 1991.

Cowie, Alexander, *The Rise of the American Novel,* 1948.

Culley, Margo, editor, *American Womens' Autobiography: Fea(s)ts of Memory,* 1992.

Cunliffe, Marcus, *The Literature of the United States,* 1954.

Cunliffe, Marcus, *The New Literature of the United States: American Literature to 1900,* 1987.

Davidson, Cathy N., editor, *Reading in America: Literature and Social History,* 1989.

Davidson, Cathy N., Patrick O'Donnell, Valerie Smith, and Christopher P. Wilson, editors, *The Columbia History of the American Novel,* 1991.

Davis, Robert Murray, *Playing Cowboys: Low Culture and High Art in the Western,* 1992.

Debo, Angie, *A History of the Indians of the United States,* 1970.

Dickason, Olive Patricia, *Canada's First Nations: A History of Founding Peoples from Earliest Times,* 1992.

Docherty, Brian, editor, *American Crime Fiction: Studies in the Genre,* 1988.

Docherty, Brian, editor, *American Horror Fiction: From Brockden Brown to Stephen King,* 1990.

Donaldson, Laura E., *Decolonizing Feminisms: Race, Gender, and Empire Building,* 1992.

Donoghue, Denis, *Reading America: Essays on American Literature,* 1988.

Eakin, Paul John, editor, *American Autobiography: Retrospect and Prospect,* 1991.

Elliott, Emory, general editor, *Columbia Literary History of the United States,* 1987.

Fabre, Genevieve, editor, *European Perspectives on Hispanic Literature of the United States,* 1988.

Fabre, Michael, *From Harlem to Paris: Black American Writers in France, 1840-1980,* 1991.

Fanning, Charles, *The Irish Voice in America: Irish-American Fiction from the 1760s to the 1980s,* 1990.

Farwell, Marilyn R., *Heterosexual Plots and Lesbian Narratives,* 1996.

Fender, Stephen, *Sea Changes: British Emigration & American Literature,* 1992.

Fenton, Jill Rubinson, Charles G. Waugh, Jane Russo, and Martin H. Greenberg, editors, *Women Writers from Page to Screen,* 1990.

Fichtelberg, Joseph, *The Complex Image: Faith and Method in American Autobiography,* 1989.

Fiedler, Leslie A., *Love and Death in the American Novel,* 1960.

Fiedler, Leslie A., *The Inadvertent Epic: From Uncle Tom's Cabin to Roots,* 1979.

Fisher, Marvin, *Continuities: Essays and Ideas in American Literature,* 1986.

Fishman, Sylvia Barack, editor, *Follow My Footprints: Changing Images of Women in American Jewish Fiction,* 1992.

Fowler, Lois J., and David H. Fowler, editors, *Revelations of Self: American Women in Autobiography,* 1990.

Franklin, Wayne, and Michael Steiner, editors, *Mapping American Culture,* 1992.

Gatta, John, *American Madonna: Images of the Divine Woman in Literary Culture,* 1997.

Gabler-Hover, Janet, *Truth in American Fiction: The Legacy of Rhetorical Idealism,* 1990.

Gelpi, Albert, *The Tenth Muse: The Psyche of the American Poet,* 1975.

Gibson, Arrell Morgan, *The American Indian: Prehistory to the Present,* 1980.

Gilbert, James, *Writers and Partisans: A History of Literary Radicalism in America,* 1992.

Giles, Paul, *American Catholic Arts and Fictions: Culture, Ideology, Aesthetics,* 1992.

Gish, Robert, *Beyond Bounds: Cross-Cultural Essays on Anglo, American Indian, & Chicano Literature,* 1996.

Goshgarian, G. M., *To Kiss the Chastening Rod: Domestic Fiction and Sexual Ideology in the American Renaissance,* 1992.

Grabher, Gundrun, M., and Maureen Devine, editors, *Women in Search of Literary Space,* 1992.

Guptka, R. K., *The Great Encounter: A Study of Indo-American Literary and Cultural Relations,* 1986.

Gutman, Huck, editor, *As Others Read Us: International Perspectives on American Literature,* 1991.

Gwin, Minrose C., *Black and White Women of the Old South: The Peculiar Sisterhood in American Literature,* 1985.

Habegger, Alfred, *Gender, Fantasy, and Realism in American Literature,* 1982.

Hamilton, Cynthia S., *Western and Hard Boiled Detective Fiction in America: From High Noon to Midnight,* 1987.

Handlin, Oscar, and others, *Harvard Guide to American History,* 1954 (and later editions).

Hanson, Elizabeth I., *The American Indian in American Literature: A Study in Metaphor,* 1988.

Hapke, Laura, *Tales of the Working Girl: Wage-Earning Women in American Literature, 1890-1925,* 1992.

Hardwick, Elizabeth, *Sight-Readings: American Fictions,* 1998.

Harrison, Elizabeth Jane, *Female Pastoral: Women Writers Re-Visioning the American South,* 1992.

Hart, James D., *The Popular Book: A History of America's Literary Taste,* 1950.

Herrera-Sobek, Maria, and Helena Maria Viramontes, editors, *Chicana Creativity and Criticism: Charting New Frontiers in American Literature,* 1988.

Herrera-Sobek, Maria, editor, *Reconstructing a Chicano/a Literary Heritage: Hispanic Colonial Literature of the Southwest,* 1993.

Huerta, Jorge A., *Chicano Theater: Themes and Forms,* 1982.

Hughes, Glenn, *A History of the American Theatre 1700-1950,* 1951.

Inness, Sherrie A., *The Lesbian Manace: Ideology, Identity, and the Representation of Lesbian Life,* 1997.

Jackson, Blyden, *A History of Afro-American Literature, Volume I: The Long Beginning, 1746-1895,* 1989.

Jason, Philip K., editor, *Fourteen Landing Zones: Approaches to Vietnam War Literature,* 1992.

Josephy, Alvin M., editor, *America in 1492: The World of the Indian Peoples before the Arrival of Columbus,* 1992.

Kamel, Rose Yalow, *Aggravating the Conscience: Jewish-American Literary Mothers in the Promised Land,* 1988.

Kanellos, Nicolás, *A History of Hispanic Theatre in the United States: Origins to 1940,* 1990.

Kazin, Alfred, *An American Procession: The Major Writers from 1830-1930,* 1984.

Kazin, Alfred, *God and the American Writer,* 1997.

Kazin, Alfred, *On Native Grounds: An Interpretation of Modern American Prose Literature,* 1942.

Kim, Elaine H., *Asian American Literature: An Introduction to the Writings and Their Social Contexts,* 1982.

Kronick, Joseph G., *American Poetics of History: From Emerson to the Moderns,* 1984.

Lee, A. Robert, editor, *First Person Singular: Studies in American Autobiography,* 1988.

Leisy, Ernest E., *The American Historical Novel,* 1950.

Levy, Andrew, *The Culture and Commerce of the American Short Story,* 1993.

Lewis, R.W.B., *Trials of the Word: Essays in American Literature and the Humanistic Tradition,* 1965.

Lim, Shirley Geok-lin, and Amy Ling, editors, *Reading the Literatures of Asian America,* 1992.

Limón, José Eduardo, *Mexican Ballads, Chicano Poems: History and Influence in Mexican-American Social Poetry,* 1992.

Lindberg, Gary, *The Confidence Man in American Literature,* 1982.

Ling, Amy, *Between Worlds: Women Writers of Chinese Ancestry,* 1990.

Liptzin, Solomon, *The Jew in American Literature,* 1966.

Luis, William, *Dance between Two Cultures: Latino Caribbean Literature Written in the United States,* 1997.

Machor, James L., *Pastoral Cities: Urban Ideals and the Symbolic Landscape of America,* 1987.

Maini, Darshan Singh, *The Spirit of American Literature,* 1988.

May, Charles, *The Short Story: The rEality of Artifice,* 1995.

Mayer, David R., *Door Stoops and Windowsills: Perspectives on the American Neighborhood Novel,* 1992.

McGregor, Gaile, *The Noble Savage in the New World Garden: Notes toward a Syntactics of Place,* 1988.

McIlwaine, Shields, *The Southern Poor-White from Lubberland to Tobacco Road,* 1939.

McNeil, Nellie, and Joyce Squibb, editors, *A Southern Appalachian Reader,* 1988.

McNickle, D'Arcy, *They Came Here First: The Epic of the American Indian,* 1975.

Meserve, Walter J., *An Outline History of American Drama,* 1965.

Mogen, David, Mark Busby, and Paul Bryant, editors, *The Frontier Experience and the American Dream: Essays on American Literature,* 1989.

Moreland, Kim Ileen, *The Medievalist Impulse in American Literature: Twain, Adams, Fitzgerald, and Hemingway,* 1996.

Morgan, Winifred, *An American Icon: Brother Jonathan and American Identity,* 1988.

Moses, Montrose J., and John Mason Brown, editors, *The American Theatre as Seen by Its Critics 1752-1934,* 1934.

Moss, Elizabeth, *Domestic Novelists in the South: Defenders of Southern Culture,* 1992.

Mott, Frank Luther, *American Journalism 1690-1960,* 1962.

Munk, Linda, *The Trivial Sublime: Theology and American Poetics,* 1992.

Murray, David, *Forked Tongues: Speech, Writing and Representation in North American Indian Texts,* 1991.

Nelson, Emmanuel S., editor, *AIDS: The Literary Response,* 1992.

Nelson, Emmanuel S., editor, *Connections: Essays on Black Literatures,* 1988.

Nye, Russel B., *The Unembarrassed Muse: The Popular Arts in America,* 1970.

Ousby, Ian, editor, *The Cambridge Guide to Literature in English,* 1988.

Owens, Louis, *Other Destinies: Understanding the American Indian Novel,* 1992.

Ozick, Cynthia, *Fame and Folly: Essays,* 1996.

Palmer, Jerry, *Potboilers: Methods, Concepts and Case Studies in Popular Fiction,* 1991.

Parrinder, Patrick, *Authors and Authority: English and American Criticism 1750-1990,* 1991.

Parrington, Vernon Louis, *Main Currents in American Thought: An Interpretation of American Literature from the Beginnings to 1920,* 3 vols., 1927-30.

Pearce, Roy Harvey, *The Continuity of American Poetry,* 1961; revised edition, 1987.

Pease, Donald E., *National Identities and Post-Americanist Narratives,* 1994.

Peden, William, *The American Short Story,* 1964; revised edition, 1975.

Poulsen, Richard C., *The Landscape of the Mind: Cultural Transformations of the American West,* 1992.

Quinn, Arthur Hobson, *A History of American Drama,* 3 vols., 1923-27; revised edition, 2 vols., 1936-43.

Quinn, Arthur Hobson, editor, *The Literature of the American People: An Historical and Critical Survey,* 1951.

Quirk, Tom, and Gary Scharnhorst, editors, *American Realism and the Canon,* 1995.

Rader, Barbara, and Howard G. Zettler, editors, *The Sleuth and the Scholar: Origins, Evolution, and Current Trends in Detective Fiction,* 1988.

Riler, Sam G., editor, *American Magazine Journalists, 1741-1850,* 1988.

Robinson, Cecil, *No Short Journeys: The Interplay of Cultures in the History and Literature of the Borderlands,* 1992.

Rotella, Carlo, *October Cities: The Redevelopment of Urban Literature,* 1998.

Roudane, Matthew C., editor, *American Dramatists,* 1989.

Rowe, Anne E., *The Idea of Florida in the American Literary Imagination,* 1992.

Rowe, Joyce A., *Equivocal Endings in Classic American Novels,* 1988.

Royot, Daniel, editor, *Interface: Essays on History, Myth and Art in American Literature,* 1985.

Rubin, Louis D., Jr., Blyden Jackson, S. Moore Rayburn, Lewis P. Simpson, and Thomas Daniel Young, editors, *The History of Southern Literature,* 1985.

Rubin, Louis D., Jr., editor, *The History of Southern Literature,* 1985.

Rubin, Louis D., Jr., *The Edge of the Swamp: A Study of the Literature and Society of the Old South,* 1989.

Ruoff, A. LaVonne Brown, and Jerry W. Ward, Jr., editors, *Redefining American Literary History*, 1990.

Sanders, Leslie Catherine, *The Development of Black Theater in America*, 1988.

Schnitzer, Deborah, *The Pictorial in Modernist Fiction from Stephen Crane to Hemingway*, 1988.

Scholnick, Robert J., editor, *American Literature and Science*, 1992.

Shirley, Carl R., and Paula W. Shirley, *Understanding Chicano Literature*, 1988.

Spiller, Robert E., and others, editors, *Literary History of the United States*, 3 vols., 1948; 4th edition, 2 vols., 1974.

Spiller, Robert E., *The Cycle of American Literature*, 1955; revised edition, 1967.

Spindler, Michael, *American Literature and Social Change: William Dean Howells to Arthur Miller*, 1983.

Stauffer, Donald Barlow, *A Short History of American Poetry*, 1974.

Stovall, Floyd, *The Development of American Literary Criticism*, 1955.

Tatum, Charles M., *Chicano Literature*, 1982.

Teague, David W., *The Southwest in American Literature and Art: The Rise of a Desert Aesthetic*, 1997.

Tebbel, John, *A History of Book Publishing in the United States*, 4 vols., 1972-81.

Terrell, John Upton, *American Indian Almanac*, 1971.

Thornton, Russell, *American Indian Holocaust and Survival: A Population History since 1492*, 1987.

Thorpe, James, *Principles of Textual Criticism*, 1990.

Tinker, George E., *Missionary Conquest: The Gospel and Native American Cultural Genocide*, 1993.

True, Michael, *An Energy Field More Intense Than War: The Nonviolent Tradition and American Literature*, 1995.

Turco, Lewis Putnam, *Visions and Revisions of American Poetry*, 1986.

Tuttleton, James W., *Vital Signs: Essays on American Literature and Criticism*, 1996.

Uffen, Ellen Serlen, *Strands of the Cable: The Place of the Past in Jewish Women's Writing*, 1992.

Utley, Robert Marshall, and Wilcomb E. Washburn, *The American Heritage History of the Indian Wars*, edited by Anne Moffat and Richard F. Snow, 1977.

Valis, Noel, and Carol Maier, editors, *In the Feminine Mode: Essays on Hispanic Women Writers*, 1990.

Vogel, Virgil J., *This Country Was Ours: A Documentary History of the American Indian*, 1972.

Voss, Arthur, *The American Short Story: A Critical Survey*, 1973.

Waggoner, Hyatt H., *American Poets from the Puritans to the Present*, 1968; revised edition, 1984.

Wagner, Peter, *A Short History of English and American Literature*, 1988.

Walcutt, Charles Child, *American Literary Naturalism: A Divided Stream*, 1956.

Walker, Nancy, *A Very Serious Thing: Women's Humor and American Culture*, 1988.

Walker, Nancy, and Zita Dresner, editors, *Redressing the Balance: American Women's Literary Humor from Colonial Times to the 1980s*, 1988.

Wardwell, Lelia, editor, *The Native American Experience*, 1991.

Washburn, Wilcomb E., *The American Indian and the United States: A Documentary History*, 1973.

Watts, Emily Stipes, *The Poetry of American Women from 1632 to 1945*, 1977.

Wear, Delese, and Lois LaCivita Nixon, *Literary Anatomies: Women's Bodies and Health in Literature*, 1994.

Weber, Ronald, *The Midwestern Ascendancy in American Writing*, 1992.

Weeks, Philip, editor, *The American Indian Experience: A Profile, 1524 to the Present*, 1988.

Weixlmann, Joe, and Houston A. Baker, Jr., editors, *Black Feminist Criticism and Critical Theory*, 1988.

Wesley, Marilyn C., *Secret Journeys: The Trope of Women's Travel in American Literature*, 1999.

West, James L. W., III, *American Authors and the Literary Marketplace since 1900*, 1988.

Westbrook, Max, and James H. Maguire, *A Literary History of the American West*, 1987.

Westbrook, Perry D., *A Literary History of New England*, 1988.

Williams, David R., *Wilderness Lost: The Religious Origins of the American Mind*, 1987.

Williams, John A., and Charles F. Harris, editors, *Amistad 1 & 2: Writings on Black History and Culture*, 1970 and 1971.

Wilson, Clyde N., editor, *American Historians, 1866-1912*, 1986.

Winchell, Mark Royden, *Cleanth Brooks and the Rise of Modern Criticism*, 1996.

Wong, Hertha Dawn, *Sending My Heart Back across the Years: Tradition and Innovation: Native American Autobiography*, 1992.

Wong, Sau-ling, *Reading Asian American Literature: From Necessity to Extravagance*, 1993.

American Literature to 1900: Critical Studies

Aaron, Daniel, *The Unwritten War: American Writers and the Civil War*, 1973.

American Renaissance Literary Report, I, 1987— (an annual).

Anderson, Quentin, *The Imperial Self: An Essay in American Literary and Cultural History*, 1971.

Andrews, William L., *To Tell a Free Story: The First Century of Afro-American Autobiography, 1760-1865*, 1988.

Armstrong, Nancy, and Leonard Tennenhouse, *The Imaginary Puritan: Literature, Intellectual Labor, and the Origins of Personal Life*, 1992.

Auchincloss, Louis, *Pioneers and Caretakers: A Study of Nine American Women Novelists*, 1965.

Auerbach, Jonathan, *The Romance of Failure: First-Person Fictions of Poe, Hawthorne, and James*, 1989.

Baker, Houston A., Jr., *The Journey Back: Issues in Black Literature and Criticism*, 1980.

Baker, Houston A., Jr., editor, *Three American Literatures: Essays in Chicano, Native American, and Asian-American Literature for Teachers of American Literature*, 1982.

Baym, Nina, *Novels, Readers, and Reviewers: Responses to Fiction in Antebellum America*, 1984.

Baym, Nina, *Women's Fiction: A Guide to Novels by and about Women in America 1820-1870*, 1978.

Bell, Michael Davitt, *The Development of American Romance: The Sacrifice of Relation*, 1983.

Bercovitch, Sacvan, *The American Jeremiad*, 1978.

Bercovitch, Sacvan, editor, *The American Puritan Imagination: Essays in Revaluation*, 1974.

Bercovitch, Sacvan, and Myra Jehien, editors, *Ideology and Classic American Literature*, 1986.

Bercovitch, Sacvan, *The Puritan Origins of the American Self*, 1975.

Bercovitch, Sacvan, editor, *Typology and Early American Literature*, 1972.

Berthoff, Warner, *The Ferment of Realism: American Literature 1884-1919*, 1965.

Bewley, Marius, *The Complex Fate: Hawthorne, Henry James, and Some Other American Writers*, 1952.

Bigelow, Gordon E., *Rhetoric and American Poetry of the Early National Period*, 1960.

Blair, Walter, *Native American Humor (1800-1900)*, 1937.

Bode, Carl, *The Anatomy of American Popular Culture 1840-1861*, 1959.

Boller, Paul F., Jr., *American Transcendentalism 1830-1860: An Intellectual Inquiry*, 1974.

Boswell, Jeanetta, *The American Renaissance and the Critics: The Best of a Century in Criticism*, 1990.

Bromell, Nicholas Knowles, *By the Sweat of the Brow: Literature and Labor in Antebellum America*, 1993.

Brown, Gillian, *Domestic Individualism: Imagining Self in Nineteenth-Century America*, 1990.

Brown, Herbert Ross, *The Sentimental Novel in America 1789-1860*, 1940.

Bruce-Novoa, Juan, *Retrospace: Collected Essays on Chicano Literature, Theory, and History*, 1990.

Cady, Edwin H., *The Light of Common Day: Realism in American Fiction*, 1951.

Calderón, Héctor, and José David Saldivar, editors, *Criticism in the Borderlands: Studies in Chicano Literature, Culture, and Ideology*, 1991.

Cameron, Kenneth Waiter, editor, *Concord Literary Renaissance: Ungathered Memorabilia of Emerson, Thoreau, Hawthorne, Sanborn, the Alcotts, Margaret Fuller & Their Connections*, 1988.

Carby, Hazel V., *Reconstructing Womanhood: The Emergence of the Afro-American Woman Novelist*, 1987.

Carter, Everett, *The American Idea: The Literary Response to American Optimism*, 1977.

Chai, Leon, *The Romantic Foundations of the American Renaissance*, 1987.

Charvat, William, *Literary Publishing in America 1790-1850*, 1959.

Charvat, William, *The Profession of Authorship in America 1800-1870*, edited by Matthew J. Brnccoli, 1968.

Current, Garcia Eugene, *The American Short Story before 1850*, 1985.

Daly, Robert, *God's Altar: The World and the Flesh in Puritan Poetry*, 1978.

Davis, Charles T., and Henry Louis Gates, Jr., editors, *The Slave's Narrative*, 1985.

Davis, Gwenn, and Beverly A. Joyce, *Drama by Women to 1900*, 1992.

Davis, Richard Beale, *Intellectual Life in the Colonial South 1585-1763*, 3 vols., 1978.

DeGrave, Kathleen R., *Swindler, Spy, Rebel: The Confidence Woman in Nineteenth-Century America*, 1989.

Dobson, Joanne, *Dickinson and the Strategies of Reticence: The Woman Writer in Nineteenth Century America*, 1989.

Donovan, Josephine, *New England Local Color Literature: A Women's Tradition*, 1983.

Dormon, James H., Jr., *Theater in the Ante-Bellum South 1815-1861*, 1967.

Douglas, Ann, *The Feminization of American Culture*, 1977.

Earnest, Ernest, *The American Eve in Fact and Fiction 1775-1914*, 1974.

Elder, Arlene, *The "Hindered Hand": Cultural Implications of Early African American Fiction*, 1978.

Elliott, Emory, *Revolutionary Writers: Literature and Authority in the New Republic 1725-1810*, 1982.

Emerson, Everett, editor, *American Literature 1764-1789: The Revolutionary Years*, 1977.

Emerson, Everett, editor, *Major Writers of Early American Literature*, 1972.

Emerson, Everett, *Puritanism in America 1620-1750*, 1977.

Fabre, Genevieve, editor, *European Perspectives on Hispanic Literature of the United States*, 1988.

Falk, Robert, *The Victorian Mode in American Fiction 1865-1885*, 1965.

Fiedler, Leslie A., *No! In Thunder: Essays on Myth and Literature*, 1960.

Forrer, Richard, editor, *Theodicies in Conflict: A Dilemma in Puritan Ethics and Nineteenth-Century American Literature*, 1986.

Franklin, Wayne, *Discoverers, Explorers, Settlers: The Diligent Writers of Early America*, 1989.

Fussell, Edwin, *Frontier: American Literature and the American West*, 1965.

Gaustad, E.S., *The Great Awakening in New England*, 1957.

Gilbert, Sandra M., and Susan Gubar, *The Madwoman in the Attic: The Woman Writer and the Nineteenth-Century Literary Imagination*, 1979.

Gilmore, Michael T., editor, *Early American Literature: A Collection of Critical Essays*, 1980.

Goddard, Harold Clarke, *Studies in New England Transcendentalism*, 1908.

González Berry, Erlinda, editor, *Pasó por aquí: Critical Essays on the Mexican Literary Tradition, 1542-1988*, 1989.

Gorsky, Susan Rubinow, *Feminity to Feminism: Women and Literature in the Nineteenth-Century*, 1992.

Granger, Bruce, *American Essay Serials from Franklin to Irving*, 1978.

Granger, Bruce, *Political Satire in the American Revolution 1763-1783*, 1960.

Greenfield, Bruce, *Narrating Discovery: The Romantic Explorer in American Literature, 1790-1855*, 1992.

Greenwald, Elissa, *Realism and the Romance: Nathaniel Hawthorne, Henry James, and American Fiction*, 1989.

Gura, Philip F., *The Wisdom of Words: Language, Theology, and Literature in the New England Renaissance*, 1981.

Hansen, Olaf, *Aesthetic Individualism and Practical Intellect: American Allegory in Emerson, Thoreau, Adams, and James*, 1990.

Harris, Susan K., *19th-Century American Women's Novels: Interpretative Strategies*, 1990.

Havens, Daniel F., *The Columbian Muse of Comedy: The Development of a Native Tradition in Early American Social Comedy, 1787-1845*, 1973.

Hernández, Guillermo E., *Chicano Satire: A Study in Literary Culture*, 1991.

Herrera-Sobek, María, *Beyond Stereotypes: The Critical Analysis of Chicana Literature*, 1985.

Heyne, Eric, editor, *Desert, Garden, Margin, Range: Literature on the American Frontier*, 1992.

Hoffman, Daniel, *Form and Fable in American Fiction*, 1961.

Holman, C. Hugh, *The Immoderate Past: The Southern Writer and History*, 1977.

Horno-Delgado, Asunción, and others, editors, *Breaking Boundaries: Latina Writings and Critical Readings*, 1989.

Howard, Leon, *The Connecticut Wits*, 1943.

Howe, Irving, *The American Newness: Culture and Politics in the Age of Emerson*, 1986.

Hubbell, Jay B., *The South in American Literature 1607-1900*, 1954.

Inge, M. Thomas, *The Frontier Humorists: Critical Views*, 1975.

Israel, Calvin, editor, *Discoveries and Considerations: Essays on Early American Literature and Aesthetics*, 1976.

Jiménez, Francisco, *The Identification and Analysis of Chicano Literature*, 1979.

Jones, Howard Mumford, *O Strange New World: American Culture: The Formative Years*, 1964.

Jones, Howard Mumford, *The Age of Energy: Varieties of American Experience 1865-1915*, 1971.

Jones, Howard Mumford, *Revolution and Romanticism*, 1974.

Kagle, Steven E., *American Diary Literature 1620-1799*, 1979.

Kagle, Steven E., *Early Nineteenth-Century American Diary Literature*, 1986.

Kagle, Steven E., *Late 19th Century American Diary Literature*, 1988.

Kammen, Michael, *A Season of Youth: The American Revolution and the Historical Imagination*, 1978.

Kanellos, Nicolás, editor, *Hispanic Theatre in the United States*, 1984.

Kanellos, Nicolás, *Mexican American Theater: Legacy and Reality*, 1987.

Keiser, Albert, *The Indian in American Literature*, 1933.

Kimbel, Bobby Ellen, and William E. Grant, editors, *American Short-Story Writers before 1880*, 1988.

Kolb, Harold H., Jr., *The Illusion of Life: American Realism as a Literary Form*, 1969.

Kolodny, Annette, *The Land before Her: Fantasy and Experience of the American Frontiers 1630-186O*, 1984.

Kolodny, Annette, *The Lay of the Land*, 1975.

Landy, Lino, *Las posibilidades de una literatura chicana/Possibilities of Chicano Literature*, 1973.

Lattin, Vernon E., editor, *Contemporary Chicano Fiction: A Critical Survey*, 1986.

Lawrence, D.H., *Studies in Classic American Literature*, 1923.

Leal, Luis, and others, editors, *A Decade of Chicano Literature (1970-1979): Critical Essays and Bibliography*, 1982.

Leal, Luis, *Aztlán y México: Perfiles literarios e históricos*, 1985.

Leary, Lewis, editor, *Soundings: Some Early American Writers*, 1975.

Lewis, R.W.B., *The American Adam: Innocence, Tragedy, and Tradition in the Nineteenth Century*, 1955.

Lichtenstein, Diane, *Writing Their Nations: The Tradition of Nineteenth-Century American Jewish Women Writers*, 1992.

Lockridge, Kenneth A., *On the Sources of Patriarchal Rage: The Commonplace Books of William Byrd and Thomas Jefferson and the Gendering of Power in the Eighteenth Century*, 1992.

López-González, Aralia, Amalia Malagamba, and Elena Urrutia, editors, *Mujer y literatura mexicana y chicana: Culturas en contacto*, 1988.

Love, Glen A., *New Americans: The Westerner and the Modern Experience in the American Novel*, 1982.

Lowance, Mason I., Jr., *The Language of Canaan: Metaphor and Symbol in New England from the Puritans to the Transcendentalists*, 1980.

Lund, Michael, *America's Continuing Story: An Introduction to Serial Fiction, 1850-1900*, 1992.

Martin, Jay, *Harvests of Change: American Literature 1865-1914*, 1967.

Martin, Ronald E., *American Literature and the Universe of Force*, 1981.

Martin, Terence, *The Instructed Vision: Scottish Common Sense Philosophy and the Origins of American Fiction*, 1961.

Marx, Leo, *The Machine in the Garden: Technology and the Pastoral Ideal in America*, 1964.

Matthiessen, F.O., *American Renaissance: Art and Expression in the Age of Emerson and Thoreau*, 1941.

McConachie, Bruce A., *Melodramatic Formations: American Theatre & Society, 1820-1870*, 1992.

McDowell, Deborah, and Arnold Rampersad, editors, *Slavery and the Literary Imagination*, 1989.

McKay, Janet Holmgrin, *Narration and Discourse in American Realistic Fiction*, 1982.

Miller, Perry, *Errand into the Wilderness*, 1956.

Miller, Perry, *The New England Mind*, 2 vols., 1939-53.

Miller, Perry, *The Raven and the Whale: The War of Words and Wits in the Era of Poe and Whitman*, 1956.

Miller, Ruth, editor, *Backgrounds to Blackamerican Literature*, 1971.

Morgan, Edmund S., *Visible Saints: The History of a Puritan Idea*, 1963.

Murdock, Kenneth B., *Literature and Theology in Colonial New England*, 1949.

Nye, Russel B., *American Literary History 1607-1830*, 1970.

Nye, Russel B., *The Cultural Life of the New Nation 1776-1830*, 1960.

Nye, Russel B., *Society and Culture in America 1830-1860*, 1974.

Parrington, Vernon Louis, *The Romantic Revolution in America, 1800-1860*, 1987.

Pattee, Fred Lewis, *The First Century of American Literature 1770-1870*, 1935.

Pease, Donald E., *Visionary Compacts: American Renaissance Writings in Cultural Context*, 1987.

Person, Leland S., Jr., *Aesthetic Headaches: Women and a Masculine Poetics in Poe, Melville, and Hawthorne*, 1988.

Petter, Henri, *The Early American Novel*, 1971.

Pizer, Donald G., *Realism and Naturalism in Nineteenth-Century American Literature*, 1961; revised edition, 1984.

Porte, Joel, *The Romance in America: Studies in Cooper, Poe, Hawthorne, Melville, and James*, 1969.

Rafia, Zafar, *We Wear the Mask: African Americans Write American Literature, 1760-1870*, 1997.

Redding, J. Saunders, *To Make a Poet Black*, 1988.

Reynolds, Larry J., *European Revolutions and the American Literary Renaissance*, 1988.

Richardson, Robert D., Jr., *Myth and Literature in the American Renaissance*, 1978.

Ringe, Donald A., *American Gothic: Imagination and Reason in Nineteenth-Century Fiction*, 1982.

Rodríguez del Pino, Salvador, *La novela chicana escrita en español: cinco autores comprometidos*, 1982.

Romo, Ricardo, and Raymund Paredes, editors, *New Directions in Chicano Scholarship*, 1978.

Rourke, Constance M., *American Humor: A Study of the National Character*, 1931.

Rowe, John Carlos, *At Emerson's Tomb: The Politics of Classical American Literature*, 1997.

Rowe, John Carlos, *Through the Custom-House: Nineteenth-Century American Fiction and Modern Theory*, 1982.

Rubin, Louis D., Jr., editor, *The Comic Imagination in American Literature*, 1973.

Rusk, Ralph Leslie, *The Literature of the Middle Western Frontier*, 2 vols., 1925.

Saldivar, Ramón, *Chicano Narrative: The Dialectics of Difference*, 1990.

Samuels, Shirley, editor, *The Culture of Sentiment: Race, Gender, and Sentimentality in Nineteenth-Century America*, 1992.

Sánchez, Marta Ester, *Contemporary Chicana Poetry: Critical Approaches to an Emerging Literature*, 1985.

Scheer, Steven C., *Pious Impostures and Unproven Words: The Romance of Deconstruction in Nineteenth-Century America*, 1990.

Schueller, Malini Johar, *U.S. Orientalisms: Race, Nation, and Gender in Literature, 1790-1890*, 1998.

Seelye, John D., *Prophetic Waters: The River in Early American Life and Literature*, 1977.

Sekora, John, and Darwin T. Turner, editors, *The Art of Slave Narrative*, 1982.

Shapiro, Ann R., *Unlikely Heroines: Nineteenth-Century American Women Writers and the Woman Question*, 1987.

Shea, Daniel B., Jr., *Spiritual Autobiography in Early America*, 1968.

Showalter, Elaine, *Sister's Choice: Tradition and Change in American Women's Writing; (Clarendon Lectures)*, 1989.

Shulman, Robert, *Social Criticism and Nineteenth-Century American Fictions*, 1987.

Simmen, Edward, editor, *The Chicano: From Caricature to Self-Portrait*, 1971.

Simpson, Lewis P., *The Man of Letters in New England and the South*, 1973.

Slotkin, Richard, *Regeneration through Violence: The Mythology of the American Frontier 1600-1860*, 1973.

Slotkin, Richard, *The Fatal Environment: The Myth of the Frontier in the Age of Industrialization 1800-1890*, 1985.

Smith, Henry Nash, *Democracy and the Novel: Popular Resistance to Classic American Writers*, 1978.

Sommers, Joseph, and Toman Ybarra-Frausto, editors, *Modern Chicano Writers: A Collection of Critical Essays*, 1979.

Somoza, Oscar U., *Narrative chicana contemporánea: Principios fundamentales*, 1983.

Spengemann, William C., *The Adventurous Muse: The Poetics of American Fiction 1789-1900*, 1977.

Stafford, John, *The Literary Criticism of "Young America": A Study of the Relationship of Politics and Literature 1837-1850*, 1952.

Stowell, Sheila, *A Stage of Their Own: Feminist Playwrights of the Suffrage Era*, 1992.

Sundquist, Asebrit, *Pocahontas & Co.: The Fictional American Indian Woman in Nineteenth-Century Literature: A Study of Method*, 1987.

Sundquist, Eric J., editor, *American Realism: New Essays*, 1982.

Taylor, Walter Fuller, *The Economic Novel in America*, 1942.

Tyler, Moses Coit, *A History of American Literature during the Colonial Period*, 2 vols., 1878; *The Literary History of the American Revolution*, 2 vols., 1897; abridged by Archie H. Jones, as *A History of American Literature 1607-1783*, 1967.

Villanueva, Tino, compiler, *Chicanos*, 1980.

Von Frank, Albert J., *The Sacred Game: Provincialism and Frontier Consciousness in American Literature 1630-1860*, 1985.

Walker, Cheryl, *Indian Nation: Native American Literature and Nineteenth-Century Nationalism*, 1997.

Walker, Cheryl, *The Nightingale's Burden: Women Poets and American Culture before 1900*, 1983.

Warner, Nicholas O., *Spirits of America: Intoxication in Nineteenth-Century American Literature*, 1997.

Wertheimer, Eric, *Imagined Empires: Incas, Aztecs, and the New World of American Literature, 1771-1876*, 1999.

Westbrook, Perry D., *Acres of Flint: Writers of New England 1870-1900*, 1951; revised edition, 1981.

White, Peter, editor, *Puritan Poets and Poetics: Seventeenth-Century American Poetry in Theory and Practice*, 1985.

Wilson, Edmund, *Axel's Castle: A Study in the Imaginative Literature of 1870-1930*, 1931.

Wilson, Edmund, *Patriotic Gore: Studies in the Literature of the American Civil War*, 1962.

Wilson, Edmund, editor, *The Shock of Recognition: The Development of Literature in the United States Recorded by the Men Who Made It*, 1943; enlarged edition, 1955.

Wright, Louis B., *The Cultural Life of the American Colonies 1607-1763*, 1957.

Yates, Norris W., *William T Porter and the Spirit of the Times: A Study of the Big Bear School of Humor*, 1957.

Ziff, Larzer, *The American 1890's: Life and Times of a Lost Generation*, 1966.

Ziff, Larzer, *Literary Democracy: The Declaration of Cultural Independence in America*, 1981.

American Literature since 1900: Critical Studies

Aaron, Daniel, *Writers on the Left: Episodes in American Literary Communism*, 1961.

Aiken, Conrad, *Scepticisms: Notes on Contemporary Poetry*, 1919.

Aldridge, John, *After the Lost Generation: A Critical Study of the Writers of Two Wars*, 1951.

Aldridge, John, *In Search of Heresy: American Literature in the Age of Conformity*, 1956.

Allen, Donald M., and Warren Tallman, *The Poetics of the New American Poetry*, 1974.

Atkinson, Brooks, *Broadway*, 1970.

Awkward, Michael, *Inspiriting Influences: Tradition, Revision, and Afro-American Women's Novels*, 1989.

Baker, Houston A., Jr., *Afro-American Poetics: Revisions of Harlem and the Black Aesthetic*, 1988.

Baker, Houston, Jr., and Patricia Redmond, editors, *Afro-American Literary Study in the 1990's*, 1990.

Barnstone, Aliki, Michael Tomasek Manson, and Carol J. Singley, editors, *The Calvinist Roots of the Modern Era*, 1997.

Baumbach, Jonathan, *The Landscape of Nightmare: Studies in the Contemporary American Novel*, 1965.

Beach, Joseph Warren, *American Fiction 1920-1940*, 1941.

Beach, Sylvia, *Shakespeare and Company*, 1959.

Beidler, Philip D., *American Literature and the Experience of Vietnam*, 1982.

Bentley, Eric, *The Dramatic Event: An American Chronicle*, 1954.

Berthoff, Warner, *A Literature without Qualities: American Writing since 1945*, 1979.

Berthoff, Warner, *Fictions and Events*, 1971.

Bigsby, C.W.E., *Confrontation and Commitment: A Study of Contemporary American Drama 1959-1966*, 1967.

Bigsby, C.W.E., editor, *A Critical Introduction to Twentieth-Century American Drama*, 3 vols., 1982-85.

Bigsby, C.W.E., editor, *The Black American Writer*, 2 vols., 1969.

Bigsby, C.W.E., editor, *The Second Black Renaissance*, 1980.

Blotner, Joseph, *The Modern American Political Novel 1900-1960*, 1966.

Bogan, Louise, *Achievement in American Poetry 1900-1950*, 1951.

Bornstein, George, *Representing Modernist Texts: Editing as Interpretation*, 1991.

Boyers, Robert, editor, *Contemporary Poetry in America*, 1974.

Bradbury, John M., *Renaissance in the South: A Critical History of the Literature 1920-1960*, 1963.

Bradbury, John M., *The Fugitives: A Critical Account*, 1958.

Bradbury, Malcolm, and David Palmer, editors, *The American Novel and the Nineteen Twenties*, 1971.

Bradbury, Malcolm, *The Modern American Novel*, 1983.

Brooks, Cleanth, *The Hidden God*, 1963.

Brooks, Cleanth, *Modern Poetry and the Tradition*, 1939.

Broussard, Louis, *American Drama: Contemporary Allegory from Eugene O'Neill to Tennessee Williams*, 1962.

Brown, John Mason, *Two on the Aisle: Ten Years of the American Theatre in Performance*, 1938.

Bruck, Peter, *The Afro-American Novel since 1960*, 1982.

Bryant, Jerry H., *The Open Decision: The Contemporary American Novel and Its Intellectual Background*, 1970.

Callahan, John F., *In the African-American Grain: The Pursuit of Voice in Twentieth-Century Black Fiction*, 1988.

Carruth, Hayden, *Suicides and Jazzers*, 1992.

Castro, Michael, *Interpreting the Indian: Twentieth Century Poets and the Native American*, 1983.

Charters, Samuel, *Some Poems/Poets: Studies in American Underground Poetry since 1945*, 1971.

Clurman, Harold, *The Fervent Years: The Story of the Group Theatre and the Thirties*, 1945.

Coffman, Stanley K., Jr., *Imagism: A Chapter for the History of Modern Poetry*, 1951.

Cohen, Sarah Blacher, *Comic Relief: Humor in Contemporary American Literature*, 1978.

Cohn, Ruby, *Dialogue in American Drama*, 1971.

Cooperman, Stanley, *World War I and the American Novel*, 1967.

Counts, Michael, L., *Coming Home: The Soldier's Return in Twentieth-Century American Drama*, 1988.

Cowan, Louise, *The Fugitive Group: A Literary History*, 1959.

Cowley, Malcolm, *A Second Flowering: Works and Days of the Lost Generation*, 1973.

Cowley, Malcolm, *--And I Worked at the Writer's Trade: Chapters of Literary History 1918-1978*, 1978.

Cowley, Malcolm, editor, *After the Genteel Tradition: American Writers since 1910*, 1937; revised edition, 1964.

Cowley, Malcolm, *Exile's Return: A Narrative of Ideas*, 1934; revised edition, as *Exile's Return: A Literary Odyssey of the 1920's*, 1951.

Davis, Arthur P., *From the Dark Tower: Afro-American Writers (1900 to 1960)*, 1974.

Dembo, L.S., *Conceptions of Reality in Modern American Poetry*, 1966.

Deutsch, Helen, and Stella Hanau, *The Provincetown: A Story of the Theatre*, 1951.

Dickey, James, *Babel to Byzantium: Poets and Poetry Now*, 1968.

Dodd, Elizabeth, *The Veiled Mirror and the Woman Poet: H.D., Louise Bogan, Elizabeth Bishop, and Louise Gluck*, 1992.

Donoghue, Denis, *Connoisseurs of Chaos: Ideas of Order in Modern American Poetry*, 1965.

Downer, Alan S., *Fifty Years of American Drama 1900-1950*, 1951.

Duberman, Martin, *Black Mountain: An Exploration in Community*, 1972.

Edel, Leon, *The Psychological Novel 1900-1950*, 1955; as *The Modern Psychological Novel*, 1959; revised edition, 1964.

Eisinger, Chester E., *Fiction of the Forties*, 1963.

Fabre, Genevieve, *Drumbeats, Masks, and Metaphors: Contemporary Afro-American Theatre*, translated by Melvin Dixon, 1983.

Fiedler, Leslie A., *Waiting for the End: The American Literary Scene from Hemingway to Baldwin*, 1964.

Fitch, Noel Riley, *Sylvia Beach and the Lost Generation: A History of Literary Paris in the Twenties and Thirties*, 1983.

Flanner, Janet, *Paris Was Yesterday 1925-1939*, edited by Irving Drutman, 1972.

Folsom, James K., editor, *The Western: A Collection of Critical Essays*, 1979.

Folsom, James K., *The American Western Novel*, 1966.

Fredman, Stephen, *Poet's Prose: The Crisis in American Verse*, 1984.

French, Warren, editor, *The Twenties [Thirties, Forties, Fifties]: Fiction, Poetry, Drama*, 4 vols., 1967-75.

French, Warren, *San Francisco Poetry Renaissance, 1955-1960*, 1991.

French, Warren, *The Social Novel at the End of an Era*, 1966.

Friebert, Stuart, and David Young, editors, *A Field Guide to Contemporary Poetry and Poetics*, 1980.

Frohock, Wilbur M., *The Novel of Violence in America*, revised edition, 1958.

Fullbrook, Kate, *Free Women: Ethics and Aesthetics in Twentieth-Century Women's Fiction*, 1990.

Fussell, Edwin, *Lucifer in Harness: American Meter, Metaphor, and Diction*, 1973.

Gaines, James R., *Wit's End: Days and Nights of the Algonquin Round Table*, 1977.

Galloway, David, *The Absurd Hero in American Fiction*, 1966; revised edition, 1970.

Gass, William H., *Fiction and the Figures of Life*, 1970.

Gassner, John, *Theatre at the Crossroads: Plays and Playwrights of the Mid-Century American Stage*, 1960.

Gates, Henry Louis, Jr., *The Signifying Monkey: A Theory of African-American Literary Criticism*, 1988.

Gayle, Addison, Jr., editor, *Black Expression: Essays by and about Black Americans in the Creative Arts*, 1969.

Gayle, Addison, Jr., editor, *The Black Aesthetic*, 1971.

Gayle, Addison, Jr., *The Way of the New World: The Black Novel in America*, 1975.

Geismar, Maxwell, *American Moderns: From Rebellion to Conformity*, 1958.

Geismar, Maxwell, *The Last of the Provincials: The American Novel 1915-1925*, 1947.

Geismar, Maxwell, *Rebels and Ancestors: The American Novel 1890-1915*, 1953.

Geismar, Maxwell, *Writers in Crisis: The American Novel Between Two Wars*, 1942.

Gelfant, Blanche Housman, *The American City Novel*, 1954.

Gibaldi, Joseph, *Introduction to Scholarship in Modern Languages and Literatures*, 1992.

Gibson, Donald B., *The Politics of Literary Expression: A Study of Major Black Witers,* 1981.

Gilbert, Sandra M., and Susan Gubar, *No Man's Land: The Place of the Woman Writer in the Twentieth Century, I: The War of the Words,* 1988; *II: Sexchanges,* 1989.

Glicksberg, Charles I., *The Sexual Revolution in Modern American Literature,* 1971.

Gloster, Hugh M., *Negro Voices in American Fiction,* 1948.

Gould, Jean, *American Women Poets: Pioneers of Modern Poetry,* 1980.

Gould, Jean, *Modern American Women Poets,* 1985.

Graff, Gerald, *Literature against Itself: Literary Ideas in Modern Society,* 1979.

Gregory, Horace, and Marya Zaturenska, *A History of American Poetry 1900-1940,* 1946.

Gunn, Giles, *Thinking across the American Grain: Ideology, Intellect, and the New Pragmatism,* 1992.

Guttmann, Allen, *The Jewish Writer in America: Assimilation and the Crisis of Identity,* 1971.

Guttmann, Allen, *The Wound in the Heart: America and the Spanish Civil War,* 1962.

Hall, Donald, *Remembering Poets,* 1978.

Handy, William, *Modern Fiction: A Formalist Approach,* 1971.

Hardwick, Elizabeth, *A View of My Own: Essays on Literature and Society,* 1962.

Harriman, Margaret Case, *The Vicious Circle: The Story of the Algonquin Round Table,* 1951.

Harris, Trudier, *Exorcising Blackness: Historical and Literary Lynching and Burning Rituals,* 1984.

Hassan, Ihab, *Contemporary American Literature 1945-1972,* 1973.

Hassan, Ihab, *Radical Innocence: Studies in the Contemporary American Novel,* 1961.

Hilfer, Anthony Channell, *The Revolt from the Village 1915-1930,* 1969.

Hill, Errol, editor, *The Theater of Black Americans: A Collection of Critical Essays,* 2 vols., 1980.

Hoffman, Daniel, editor, *Harvard Guide to Contemporary American Writing,* 1979.

Hoffman, Frederick J., *The Modern Novel in America 1900-1950,* 1951.

Hoffman, Frederick J., *The Twenties: American Writing in the Postwar Decade,* 1955; revised edition, 1962.

Hogue, W. Lawrence, *Race, Modernity, Postmodernity: A Look at the History and the Literatures of People of Color since the 1960s,* 1996.

Holman, C. Hugh, *Windows on the World: Essays on American Social Fiction,* 1979.

Honey, Maureen, editor, *Breaking the Ties that Bind: Popular Stories of New Woman, 1915-1930,* 1992.

Howard, Richard, *Alone with America: Essays on the Art of Poetry in the United States since 1950,* 1969; revised edition, 1980.

Huggins, Nathan, *Harlem Renaissance,* 1971.

Hymes, Dell, *"In Vain I Tried to Tell You": Essays in Native American Ethnopoetics,* 1981.

Jackson, Blyden, *The Waiting Years: Essays on American Negro Literature,* 1976.

Jarrell, Randall, *Poetry and the Age,* 1953.

Jones, Margaret C., *Prophets in Babylon: Five California Novelists in the 1930s,* 1992.

Jones, Peter G., *War and the Novelist: Appraising the American War Novel,* 1976.

Juhasz, Suzanne, *Naked and Fiery Forms: Modern American Poetry by Women,* 1976.

Kalstone, David, *Five Temperaments: Elizabeth Bishop, Robert Lowell, James Merrill, Adrienne Rich, John Ashbery,* 1977.

Karolides, Nicholas J., *The Pioneer in the American Novel 1900-1950,* 1967.

Kazin, Alfred, *Bright Book of Life: American Novelists and Storytellers from Hemingway to Mailer,* 1973.

Kazin, Alfred, *Contemporaries,* 1962.

Kenner, Hugh, *A Homemade World: The American Modernist Writers,* 1975.

Kenner, Hugh, *The Pound Era,* 1971.

Kerr, Walter, *Journey to the Center of the Theatre,* 1979.

Klein, Marcus, *After Alienation: American Novels in Mid-Century,* 1964.

Klein, Marcus, *Foreigners: The Making of American Literature 1900-1940,* 1981.

Klinkowitz, Jerome, *Literary Disruptions: The Making of a Post-Contemporary American Fiction,* 1975; revised edition, 1980.

Kostelanetz, Richard, *The End of Intelligent Writing: Literary Politics in America,* 1974.

Kramer, Dale, *Chicago Renaissance: The Literary Life in the Midwest 1900-1930,* 1966.

Krupat, Arnold, *The Voice in the Margin: Native American Literature and the Canon,* 1989.

Krutch, Joseph Wood, *The American Drama since 1918: An Informal History,* 1939; revised edition, 1957.

Labovitz, Esther Kleinbord, *The Myth of the Heroine: The Female Bildungsroman in the Twentieth Century,* 1986.

Lacey, Paul A., *The Inner War: Forms and Themes in Recent American Poetry,* 1972.

Langner, Lawrence, *The Magic Curtain,* 1951.

Lee, Robert Edson, *From West to East: Studies in the Literature of the American West,* 1966.

Lehan, Richard, *A Dangerous Crossing: French Literary Existentialism and the Modern American Novel,* 1973.

Levertov, Denise, *The Poet in the World,* 1973.

Lieberman, Laurence, *Unassigned Frequencies: American Poetry in Review 1964-77,* 1977.

Lincoln, Kenneth, *Native American Renaissance,* 1983.

Loeffelholz, Mary, *Experimental Lives: Women & Literature, 1900-1945,* 1992.

Lowell, Amy, *Tendencies in Modern American Poetry,* 1917.

Lynch, Michael F., *Creative Revolt: A Study of Wright, Ellison, and Dostoevsky,* 1990.

Madden, David, editor, *American Dreams, American Nightmares,* 1970.

Madden, David, editor, *Proletarian Writers of the Thirties,* 1968.

Madden, David, editor, *Tough Guy Writers of the Thirties,* 1968.

Malin, Irving, *Jews and Americans,* 1965.

Malin, Irving, *New American Gothic,* 1962.

Malkoff, Karl, *Escape from the Self: A Study in Contemporary American Poetry and Poetics,* 1977.

Margolies, Edward, *Native Sons: A Critical Study of Twentieth-Century Negro American Authors,* 1968.

Mariani, Paul, *A Usable Past: Essays in Modern and Contemporary Poetry,* 1984.

Martin, Gerald, *Journey through the Labyrinth: Latin American Fiction in the Twentieth Century,* 1989.

Mathews, Jane DeHart, *The Federal Theatre 1935-1939: Plays, Relief, and Politics,* 1967.

McCarthy, Mary, *Sights and Spectacles 1937-1956*, 1956; augmented edition, as *Theatre Chronicles 1937-1962*, 1963.

McRuer, Robert, *The Queer Renaissance: Contemporary American Literature and the Reinvention of Lesbian and Gay Identities*, 1997.

Melling, Philip, *American Literature and Vietnam*, 1990.

Middlebrook, Diane Wood, and Marilyn Yalom, editors, *Coming to Light: American Women Poets in the Twentieth Century*; (prepared under Auspices of Center for Research on Women, Stanford University), 1985.

Miller, J. Hillis, *Poets of Reality: Six Twentieth-Century Writers*, 1965.

Miller, James E., Jr., *The American Quest for a Supreme Fiction: Whitman's Legacy in the Personal Epic*, 1979.

Millgate, Michael, *American Social Fiction: James to Cozzens*, 1964.

Mills, Ralph J., Jr., *Contemporary American Poetry*, 1965.

Mordden, Ethan, *The American Theatre*, 1981.

Munt, Sally, editor, *New Lesbian Criticism: Literary and Cultural Readings*, 1992.

Murray, David, *Forked Tongues: Speech, Writing, and Representation in North American Indian Texts*, 1991.

Myers, Jack, and David Wojahn, *A Profile of Twentieth-Century Poetry*, 1991.

Neal, Larry, *Visions of a Liberated Future: Black Arts Movement Writings*, 1989.

Nemerov, Howard, *Figures of Thought: Speculations on the Meaning of Poetry and Other Essays*, 1978.

Nielsen, Aldon Lynn, *Reading Race: White American Poets and the Racial Discourse in the Twentieth Century*, 1988.

O'Hara, Daniel T., *Radical Parody: American Culture and Critical Agency after Foucault*, 1992.

Olderman, Raymond M., *Beyond the Waste Land: A Study of the American Novel in the Nineteen-Sixties*, 1972.

Owens, Louis, *Other Destinies: Understanding the American Indian Novel*, 1992.

Parkinson, Thomas, editor, *A Casebook on the Beat*, 1961.

Perkins, David, *A History of Modern Poetry: From the 1890's to the High Modernist Mode*, 1976.

Perloff, Marjorie, *Radical Artifice: Writing Poetry in the Age of Media*, 1992.

Phillips, Robert, *The Confessional Poets*, 1963.

Pinsker, Sanford, *The Schlemiel as Metaphor: Studies in the Yiddish and American-Jewish Novel*, 1971.

Pinsky, Robert, *The Situation of Poetry: Contemporary Poetry and Its Traditions*, 1976.

Pizer, Donald G., *Twentieth-Century American Literary Naturalism*, 1982.

Podhoretz, Norman, *Doings and Undoings: The Fifties and after in American Writing*, 1964.

Poirier, Richard, *The Performing Self: Compositions and Decompositions in the Language of Contemporary Life*, 1971.

Pryse, Majorie and Hortense J. Spillers, editors, *Conjuring: Black Women Fiction, and Literary Tradition*, 1985.

Quartermain, Peter, *Disjunctive Poetics: From Gertrude Stein and Louis Zukofsky to Susan Howe*, 1992.

Quinn, M. Bernetta, *The Metamorphic Tradition in Modern Poetry*, 1955.

Rabkin, Gerald, *Drama and Commitment: Politics in the American Theatre of the 1930's*, 1964.

Rahv, Philip, *Essays on Literature and Politics 1932-72*, edited by Arabel J. Porter and Andrew J. Dvorsin, 1978.

Ransom, John Crowe, *The New Criticism*, 1941.

Raper, Tulius Rowan, *Narcissus from Rubble: Competing Models of Character in Contemporary British and American Fiction*, 1992.

Rexroth, Kenneth, *American Poetry in the Twentieth Century*, 1971.

Rideout, Walter B., *The Radical Novel in the United States 1900-1954*, 1956.

Rosenblatt, Roger, *Black Fiction*, 1974.

Rosenthal, M.L., *The Modern Poets: A Critical Introduction*, 1960.

Sadler, Geoff, editor, *Twentieth-Century Western Writers*, 1991.

Sarris, Greg, *Keeping Slug Woman Alive: A Holistic Approach to American Indian Texts*, 1993.

Scholes, Robert, *The Fabulators*, 1967.

Shapiro, Karl, *The Poetry Wreck: Selected Essays 1950-1970*, 1975.

Sherzer, Joel, and Anthony C. Woodbury, *Native American Discourse: Poetics and Rhetoric*, 1987.

Simpson, Louis, *A Revolution in Taste: Studies of Dylan Thomas, Allen Ginsberg, Sylvia Plath, and Robert Lowell*, 1978.

Singal, Daniel J., *The War Within: From Victorian to Modernist Thought in the South 1919-1945*, 1982.

Solotaroff, Theodore, *The Red Hot Vacuum and Other Pieces on the Writing of the Sixties*, 1970.

Spears, Monroe K., *Dionysus and the City: Modernism in Twentieth-Century Poetry*, 1970.

Spiller, Robert E., editor, *A Time of Harvest: American Literature 1910-1960*, 1962.

Stanford, Donald E., *Revolution and Convention in Modern Poetry*, 1983.

Stewart, John L., *The Burden of Time: The Fugitives and Agrarians*, 1965.

Sutton, Walter, *American Free Verse: The Modern Revolution in Poetry*, 1973.

Swados, Harvey, *The American Writers and the Great Depression*, 1966.

Swann, Brian, and Arnold Krupat, *Recovering the Word: Essays on Native American Literature*, 1987.

Swann, Brian, editor, *Smoothing the Ground: Essays on Native American Oral Literature*, 1983.

Tanner, Tony, *City of Words: American Fiction 1950-1970*, 1971.

Taubman, Howard, *The Making of the American Theatre*, 1965; revised edition, 1967.

Taylor, Gordon O., *Chapters of Experience: Studies in Twentieth-Century American Autobiography*, 1983.

Thorp, Willard, *American Writing in the Twentieth Century*, 1960.

Thurber, James, *The Years with Ross* (on the *New Yorker* magazine), 1959.

Thurley, Geoffrey, *The American Moment: American Poetry in the Mid-Century*, 1977.

Tucker, Martin, general editor, *The Critical Temper, V: A Survey of Modern Criticism on English and American Literature from the Beginnings to the Twentieth Century*, 1989.

Tuttleton, James W., *The Novel of Manners in America*, 1972.

Tytell, John, *Naked Angels: The Lives and Literature of the Beat Generation*, 1976.

Valgemae, Mardi, *Accelerated Grimace: Expressionism in the American Drama of the 1920's*, 1972.

Vendler, Helen, *Part of Nature, Part of Us: Modern American Poets*, 1980.

Versluys, Kristiaan, editor, *Neo-Realism in Contemporary American Fiction*, 1992.

Vizenor, Gerald, editor, *Narrative Chance: Postmodern Discourse on Native American Indian Literatures*, 1993.

Watson, Steven, *The Birth of the Beat Generation: Visionaries, Rebels, and Hipsters, 1944-1960,* 1995.

Weales, Gerald, *American Drama since World War II,* 1962.

Weales, Gerald, *The Jumping-Off Place: American Drama in the 1960's,* 1969.

Weatherhead, A. Kingsley, *The Edge of the Image,* 1967.

Wellek, Rene, *American Criticism, 1900-1950,* 1986.

Werner, Craig Hansen, *Paradoxical Resolutions: American Fiction since James Joyce,* 1982.

West, Ray B., *The Short Story in America 1900-1950,* 1952.

Widmer, Kingsley, *The Literary Rebel,* 1965.

Wiger, Andrew, *Native American Literature,* 1985.

Williams, Ellen, *Harriet Monroe and the Poetry Renaissance: The First Ten Years of "Poetry" 1912-1922,* 1977.

Williamson, Alan, *Introspection and Contemporary Poetry,* 1984.

Wilson, Edmund, *The Bit Between My Teeth: A Literary Chronicle of 1950-1965,* 1965.

Wilson, Edmund, *Classics and Commercials: A Literary Chronicle of the Forties,* 1960.

Wilson, Edmund, *The Shores of Light: A Literary Chronicle of the Twenties and Thirties,* 1952.

Winters, Yvor, *On Modern Poets,* 1959.

Witham, W. Tasker, *The Adolescent in the American Novel 1920-1960,* 1964.

Writers at Work: The Paris Review Interviews, 1958—.

WRITERS

A

ADAMS, Henry (Brooks)

Born: Boston, Massachusetts, 16 February 1838; great grandson of John Adams, grandson of John Quincy Adams, and son of the writer Charles Francis Adams. **Education:** Harvard University, Cambridge, Massachusetts, 1854-58, A.B. 1858; studied law at the University of Berlin, 1858-59. **Family:** Married Marian Hooper in 1872 (died 1885). **Career:** Lived in Dresden, 1859-60; traveled in Italy writing for the Boston *Courier,* 1860; private secretary to his father when congressman from Massachusetts, in Washington, D.C., 1860-61, and when minister to the court of St. James, London, 1861-68; lived in Washington, D.C., and again in London, contributing to various American periodicals, 1869; editor, *North American Review,* Boston, and assistant professor of history, Harvard University, 1870-77; settled in Washington, D.C.; in later life spent six months in each year in France. President, American Historical Society, 1894. **Awards:** Loubat prize, for history, 1893; Pulitzer prize, for autobiography, 1919. LL.D.: Western Reserve University, Cleveland, 1892. **Member:** American Academy of Arts and Letters. **Died:** 27 March 1918.

PUBLICATIONS

Collections

Letters, edited by Worthington Chauncey Ford. 2 vols., 1930-38.
A Henry Adams Reader, edited by Elizabeth Stevenson. 1958.
The Education of Henry Adams and Other Selected Writings, edited by Edward N. Saveth. 1965.
Letters, edited by J.C. Levenson and others. 1983—.
Novels, Mont Saint Michel, The Education (Library of America), edited by Ernest and Jayne N. Samuels. 1983.
The Correspondence of Henry James and Henry Adams 1877-1914, edited by George Monteiro. 1992.
Henry Adams: Selected Letters, edited by Ernest Samuels. 1992.

Fiction

Democracy: An American Novel. 1880.
Esther. 1884.

Other

Chapters of Erie and Other Essays, with Charles Francis Adams, Jr. 1871.
Essays in Anglo-Saxon Law, with others. 1876.
The Life of Albert Gallatin. 1879.
John Randolph. 1882; revised edition, 1883.
History of the United States of America during the Administration of Jefferson and Madison. 9 vols., 1889-91; abridged version, edited by Herbert Agar, as *The Formative Years,* 2 vols., 1947; complete edition, edited by Earl Harbert (Library of America), 2 vols., 1986.
Historical Essays. 1891.
Memoirs of Marau, Last Queen of Tahiti. 1893; as *Memoirs of Arii,* 1901; edited by Robert E. Spiller, as *Tahiti: Memoirs of Arii Taimai,* 1947.

Recognition of Cuban Independence. 1896.
Mont-Saint-Michel and Chartres. 1904; revised edition, 1912.
The Education of Henry Adams: An Autobiography. 1907; edited by Ernest Samuels, 1974.
A Letter to American Teachers of History. 1910.
The Life of George Cabot Lodge. 1911.
The Degradation of the Democratic Dogma. 1919.
Letters to a Niece and Prayer to the Virgin of Chartres, edited by Mabel La Farge. 1920.
The Great Secession Winter of 1860-61 and Other Essays, edited by George Hochfield. 1958.

Editor, *Documents Relating to New England Federalism 1800-1815.* 1877.
Editor, *The Writings of Albert Gallatin.* 3 vols., 1879.
Editor, with Clara Louise Hay, *Letters of John Hay and Extracts from Diary.* 3 vols., 1908.

*

Bibliography: *Adams: A Reference Guide* by Earl Harbert, 1978.

Critical Studies: *The Young Adams, Adams: The Middle Years,* and *Adams: The Major Phase* all by Ernest Samuels, 3 vols., 1948-64; *Adams: Scientific Historian* by William H. Jordy, 1952; *Adams: A Biography* by Elizabeth Stevenson, 1955; *The Mind and Art of Adams* by J.C. Levenson, 1957; *Adams* by George Hochfield, 1962; *The Suspension of Adams: A Study of Manner and Matter* by Vern Wagner, 1970; *A Formula of His Own: Adams's Literary Experiment* by John Conder, 1970; *Symbol and Idea in Adams* by Melvin E. Lyon, 1970; *The Circle of Adams: Art and Artists* by Ernst Scheyer, 1970; *Adams* by Louis Auchincloss, 1971; *Adams* by James G. Murray, 1974; *The Force So Much Closer Home: Adams and the Adams Family* by Earl Harbert, 1977, and *Critical Essays on Adams* edited by Harbert, 1981; *Adams* by R.P. Blackmur, edited by Veronica A. Makowsky, 1980; *Adams: The Myth of Failure* by William Dusinberre, 1980; *Adams and the American Experiment* by David R. Contesta, 1980; *Power and Order: Adams and the Naturalist Tradition in American Fiction* by Harold Kaplan, 1981; *The Virgin of Chartres: An Intellectual and Psychological History of the Work of Adams* by Joseph F. Byrnes, 1981; *Both Sides of the Ocean: A Biography of Adams. His First Life 1838-1862* by Edward Chalfant, 1982; *The Ironies of Progress: Adams and the American Dream* by William Wasserstrom, 1984; "Autobiography in the American Renaissance" by Lawrence Buell in *American Autobiography: Retrospect and Prospect* edited by Paul John Eakin, 1991; *Better in Darkness: A Biography of Henry Adams: His Second Life, 1862-1891* by Edward Chalfant, 1994; *The Political Education of Henry Adams* by Brooks D. Simpson, 1995; *Male Authors, Female Subjects: The Women Within/Beyond the Borders of Henry Adams, Henry James and Others* by Duco van Oostrum, 1995; *The Medievalist Impulse in American Literature: Twain, Adams, Fitzgerald, and Hemingway* by Kim Ileen Moreland, 1996; *New Essays on the Education of Henry Adams* edited by John Carlos Rowe, 1996.

*   *   *

Standing in much the same relation to American culture in the latter half of the nineteenth century that Emerson did to the earlier period, Henry Adams might be said to have made a distinguished and melancholy career out of being the right sensibility for the wrong time and place. Dedicated to public service but shunted to the sidelines, genuinely committed to the orderly development of democratic processes but disillusioned by the post-Civil War expansionism that has been called "The Big Barbecue," Adams gradually contracted the sphere of his idealism, his sociality, and the generosity of his responses to a diminished center of bleak pessimism. Even so, this proved to be a sufficient base on which was built a noteworthy career as teacher (Harvard University), editor (*North American Review*), novelist (*Democracy* and *Esther*), and historian.

The two novels deal with pressing issues of the period, the growth of business in government and the strength of science in terms of religious dogma. The first of the two, *Democracy*, is a novel of considerable interest without being a great work of art. Taking place in Washington during the 1870s, it is a *roman á clef* in which contemporary readers were able to recognize several prominent political figures. The novel caused a sensation when it appeared in 1880, and tea tables and receptions buzzed with speculation about both the characters in the novel and the author; Adams had published the book anonymously and told only three of his closest friends that he had written it. There is far too much exposition and too little dramatic action in the story to make the novel first rate, and it becomes a little too melodramatic at the end. But after all these flaws are noted, the novel still has an appeal and is worth reading, primarily for Adams's depiction of Senator Silas P. Ratcliffe from Illinois, a character modeled after James G. Blaine, senator from Ohio, who was defeated for the Presidency by Grover Cleveland in 1884.

It is in Adams's twin meditations, *Mont-Saint-Michel and Chartres* and *The Education of Henry Adams,* that his erudition and mastery of the ironic mode fuse with a somber lyricism to produce a pair of eccentric masterpieces that combine autobiography, philosophy of history, and saturnine prophecy. Respectively subtitled "A Study of Thirteenth-Century Unity" and "A Study of Twentieth-Century Multiplicity," the books establish the figures of the virgin and the dynamo as the historically dominant symbols of forces that shape the values, the social organization, and the concepts of personality in both time-periods. The replacement of the former by the latter, in Adams's view, exemplifies what he believed to be the scientific principle of the acceleration of history. In these terms he attempts to understand and explain the loss of stable certitudes, the increased fragmentation of social groups, and the new burden of impotence and isolation on the individual psyche. Adams doubtless believed that his own shattered private life was an accurate reflection of this larger social and metaphysical explosion, and this personal despair lends a tone of mordant authority to his prose which almost precisely counters the accents of **Ralph Waldo Emerson**'s optimism. Brilliant, acerbic, and unsparing in its effort to conduct a grim cultural biopsy, Adams's work consummately articulates the outrage of the Genteel Tradition and stands as a major formulation of the ideology that would later be expressed by such alienated writers as **T.S. Eliot** and **Ezra Pound**.

—Earl Rovit and James Woodress

See the essay on *The Education of Henry Adams.*

ADE, George

Born: Kentland, Indiana, 9 February 1866. **Education:** Local schools, and Purdue University, Lafayette, Indiana, 1883-87 (editor, *Purdue*), B.S. 1887. **Career:** Reporter, Lafayette *Morning News,* 1888, and Lafayette *Call,* 1888-90; advertising writer, 1888; worked for Chicago *Morning News,* later *News-Record,* then the *Record,* 1890-1900: from 1893 collaborated with cartoonist John T. McCutcheon on a daily illustrated column about Chicago life ("Stories of the Street and of the Town"); settled on a farm near Brook, Indiana, 1904. Delegate, Republican National Convention, 1908; trustee, Purdue University, 1908-15, and promoted the Ross-Ade Stadium at Purdue, 1923-24; Grand Consul, Sigma Chi fraternity, 1909; publicity director, Indiana State Council of Defense, 1917-18; member, Indiana Commission for the Chicago World's Fair, 1933. L.H.D.: Purdue University, 1926. LL.D.: Indiana University, Bloomington, 1927. **Member:** American Academy, 1908. **Died:** 16 May 1944.

PUBLICATIONS

Collections

The Permanent Ade, edited by Fred C. Kelly. 1947.
The America of Ade: Fables, Short Stories, Essays, edited by Jean Shepherd. 1961.
Letters, edited by Terence Tobin. 1973.
The Best of Ade, edited by A.L. Lazarus. 1985.

Fiction

Stories of the Street and of the Town. 8 vols., 1894-1900; collected edition, 1941; as *Chicago Stories,* 1963.
What a Man Sees Who Goes Away from Home. 1896.
Circus Day. 1896.
Stories from History. 1896.
Artie. 1896.
Pink Marsh. 1897.
Doc' Horne. 1899.
Fables in Slang. 1900.
More Fables. 1900.
Forty Modern Fables. 1901.
Grouch at the Game. 1901.
The Girl Proposition. 1902.
People You Know. 1903.
Circus Day. 1903.
Handsome Cyril. 1903.
Clarence Allen. 1903.
In Babel. 1903.
Rollo Johnson. 1904.
Breaking into Society. 1904.
True Bills. 1904.
In Pastures New. 1906.
The Slim Princess. 1907.
I Knew Him When—. 1910.
Hoosier Hand Book. 1911.
Knocking the Neighbors. 1912.
Ades Fables. 1914.
Hand-Made Fables. 1920.

Single Blessedness and Other Observations. 1922.
Stay with Me Flagons. 1922.
Bang! Bang! 1928.

Plays

The Back-Stair Investigation (produced 1897).
The Night of the Fourth (produced 1901).
The Sultan of Sulu, music by Alfred G. Wathall (produced 1902). 1903.
The County Chairtan (produced 1903). 1924.
Peggy from Paris, music by William Loraine (produced 1903).
Bird Center: Cap Fry's Birthday Party (produced 1904).
The Sho-Gun, music by Gustav Luders (produced 1904).
The College Widow (produced 1904). 1924.
Just Out of College (produced 1905). 1924.
The Bad Samaritan (produced 1905).
Marse Covington (produced 1906). 1918.
Artie (produced 1907).
Father and the Boys (produced 1908). 1924.
Mrs. Peckham Carouse (produced 1908).
The Fair Co-ed, music by Gustav Luders (produced 1909).
The City Chap (produced 1910).
U.S. Minister Bedloe (produced 1910).
The Old Town (produced 1910).
The Mayor and the Manicure (produced 1912). 1923.
Nettie (produced 1914). 1923.
Speaking to Father. 1923.
The Persecuted Wife, in *Liberty,* 4 July 1925.
The Willing Performer, in *The Country Gentleman,* February 1928.
Aunt Fanny from Chautauqua. 1949.

Screenplays: many short films, and the following: *Our Leading Citizen,* with Waldemar Young, 1922; *Back Home and Broke,* with J. Clarkson Miller, 1922; *Woman-Proof,* with Tom Geraghty, 1923; *The Confidence Man,* with others, 1924; *Old Home Week,* with Tom Geraghty. 1925; *Freshman Love,* with Earl Felton and George Bricker, 1936.

Poetry

Verses and Jingles. 1911.

Other

The Old-Time Saloon (essays). 1931.
Revived Remarks on Mark Twain, edited by George Hiram Brownell. 1936.
One Afternoon with Mark Twain. 1939.

Editor, *An Invitation to You and Your Folks, from Jim and Some More of the Home Folks.* 1916.

*

Bibliography: *A Bibliography of Ade* by Dorothy R. Russo, 1947; "Supplements to the Standard Bibliographies of Ade, Bierce, Crane, Frederic, Fuller, Garland, Norris, and Twain" by James Stronks in *American Literary Realism 1870-1910,* Autumn 1983.

Critical Studies: *Ade, Warmhearted Satirist* by Fred C. Kelly, 1947; *Ade* by Lee Coyle, 1964; *"Ade: The City Uncle"* by Edmund Wilson, in *The Bit Between My Teeth,* 1965; *Small Town Chicago: The Comic Perspective of Finley Peter Dunne, Ade, and Ring Lardner* by James DeMuth, 1980; "George Ade: Forgotten Master of American Literature" by Harvey Pekar in *Gamut,* Fall 1981; "Hoosier Humorist, Three Letters" by Albert Asgforth in *American Scholar,* Autumn 1987; "Chicago's Tutors: The Humorous Columnists of the 1880's and 90's" by Janet St. Clair in *American Transcendental Quarterly,* September 1988; "George Ade at the 'Alfalfa European Hotel'" by Guy Szuberla, in *Midamerica: The Yearbook of the Society for the Study of Midwestern Literature,* 1995, pp. 10-24.

* * *

Born in a small Indiana town in 1866, George Ade grew up fascinated with the talk around Main Street shops and country stores. While attending Purdue College (later University) he became an avid theatergoer, rarely missing a minstrel show or musical comedy at the Lafayette Opera House. Not surprisingly, transcribing speech and writing plays became his lucrative livelihood. Following a stint as a hometown newspaper man, Ade went up to Chicago in 1890 to join his friend, the cartoonist John T. McCutcheon, on the Chicago *Morning News.*

In 1893 these two collaborated on a daily illustrated column, "All Roads Lead to the World's Fair," a potpourri of interviews and observations centered on the Columbian Exposition. After the Fair closed, their column continued as "Stories of the Streets and of the Town." Taking all Chicago as their province, Ade and McCutcheon described urban life and common speech in hundreds of vivid sketches. Stylistically, Ade experimented in the "Stories" with straight narrative, light verse, dramatic dialogue, and various ethnic dialects. The pieces were popular enough to be saved and sold in eight paperback collections between 1894 and 1900. Ade also extracted three recurring characters, stitched their scattered appearances into sustained narratives, and published the results as *Artie, Pink Marsh, and Doc' Horne.* The title characters were, respectively, a brash streetwise office worker, a black shoeshine boy in a basement barbershop, and a genial yarn-spinner living at the Alfalfa European Hotel. Not coherent enough to be considered novels, these books remain important as pioneering realistic transcriptions of urban vernacular voices—particularly Artie's colorful slang and Pink's northern Negro dialect.

Ade's best work is in his "Fables in Slang," the first of which appeared in the "Streets and Towns" column in 1897 after Ade had asked himself, "why not retain the archaic form and the stilted manner of composition (of the fable) and, for purposes of novelty, permit the language to be 'fly,' modern, undignified, quite up to the moment?" The fables became a regular Saturday feature, and were soon syndicated and collected into book form. Nine additional collections followed, the last in 1920. Most of Ade's fables were gently satiric examples of pretension and folly, set in Midwestern small towns or in Chicago, and capped by incongruous, undercutting moral tag lines. They follow his earlier work in reproducing familiar character types and common street talk. His master stroke was the use of capital letters for comic and ironic emphasis of the tendency of such talk toward platitudes and slang: "One morning a Modern Solomon, who had been chosen to preside as Judge in a divorce Mill, climbed to his Perch and unbuttoned his Vest for the Wearisome Grind." The fables brought to literary visibility a host of ordinary people: the bombastic preacher and the traveling salesman, college students, bohemian writers and fast-talking vaudevillians, and numbers of country folk lost in the city. They are valuable as a microcosm of Midwestern middle-class life at the turn of the century. More important, Ade's use of the vernacular instead of genteel-academic English provided a shot of vitality to the language, and helped make it more flexible for the next generation of American writers.

During his most productive decade, 1900-10, Ade also wrote over a dozen plays. Three were very successful on Broadway: *The Sultan of Sulu*, a musical-comedy satire on American assumption of the "white man's burden" in the South Pacific: *The County Chairman*, a comedy-drama about politics in the rural Midwest; and his best play, *The College Widow*, which introduced college life and football to the American stage.

—Charles Fanning

AGEE, James (Rufus)

Born: Knoxville, Tennessee, 27 November 1909. **Education:** St. Andrews School, Sewanee, Tennessee, 1919-24; Knoxville High School, 1924-25; Phillips Exeter Academy, Exeter, New Hampshire, 1925-28; Harvard University, Cambridge, Massachusetts (editor, *Harvard Advocate*), 1928-32, A.B. 1932. **Family:** Married 1) Olivia Saunders in 1933 (divorced 1937); 2) Alma Mailman, one son; 3) Mia Fritsch in 1946, one daughter. **Career:** Staff writer, *Fortune* and *Time* magazines, New York, 1932-48: film reviewer for *Time*, 1939-48; film critic, *Nation*, New York, 1942-48. Co-director of film *In the Street*, 1948. **Awards:** American Academy award, 1949; Pulitzer prize, 1958. **Died:** 16 May 1955.

PUBLICATIONS

Collections

Collected Poems and Collected Short Prose (includes excerpt of screenplay *Man's Fate*), edited by Robert Fitzgerald. 2 vols., 1968.
Agee: Selected Literary Documents, edited by Victor A. Kramer. 1996.

Fiction

The Morning Watch. 1951.
A Death in the Family. 1957.
Four Early Stories, edited by Elena Harap. 1964.

Plays

Agee on Film 2: Five Film Scripts (includes *The Blue Hotel, The African Queen, The Bride Comes to Yellow Sky, The Night of the Hunter*, and *Noa Noa*). 1960.

Screenplays: *The Quiet One* (documentary), 1949; *The African Queen*, with John Huston, 1951; *Genghis Khan* (English commentary), 1952; *The Bride Comes to Yellow Sky* (episode in *Face to Face*), 1953; *White Mane* (English commentary), 1953; *Green Magic* (English commentary), 1954; *The Night of the Hunter*, 1955.

Television Scripts: For *Omnibus* series, 1953.

Poetry

Permit Me Voyage. 1934.

Other

Let Us Now Praise Famous Men: Three Tenant Families, photographs by Walker Evans. 1941.
Agee on Film: Reviews and Comments. 1958.
Letters to Father Flye. 1962; revised edition, 1971.
A Way of Seeing: Photographs of New York, photographs by Helen Levitt. 1965.
Selected Journalism, edited by Paul Ashdown. 1985.

*

Bibliography: By Genevieve Fabre, in *Bulletin of Bibliography 24*, 1965; *John Hersey and Agee: A Reference Guide* by Nancy Lyman Huse, 1978; *Agee: An Annotated Bibliography of Published Primary and Secondary Sources 1925-1985* by Nancy Jane Richards, 1986; "Agee: A Bibliography of Secondary Sources" by Mary Moss, in *James Agee: Reconsiderations* edited by Michael A. Lofaro, 1992.

Critical Studies: *Agee* by Peter H. Ohlin, 1966; *Agee: Promise and Fulfillment* by Kenneth Seib, 1969; *Agee* by Erling Larsen, 1971; *A Way of Seeing: A Critical Study of Agee* by Alfred T. Barson, 1972; *Remembering Agee* edited by David Madden, 1974; *Irony in the Minds Life: Essays on Novels by Agee, Elizabeth Bowen, and George Eliot* by Robert Coles, 1974; *Agee* by Victor A. Kramer, 1975; *Agee: A Study of His Film Criticism* by John J. Snyder, 1977; *The Restless Journey of Agee* by Genevieve Moreau, 1977; *Tell Me Who I Am: Agee's Search for Selfhood* by Mark A. Doty, 1981; *Agee: A Life* by Laurence Bergreen, 1984; *Agee: His Life Remembered* edited by Ross Spears and Jude Cassidy, 1985; *American Silences: The Realism of Agee, Walker Evans, and Edward Hopper* by J.A. Ward, 1985; *Agee and Actuality: Artistic Vision in His Work* by Victor A. Kramer, 1991; *James Agee: Reconsiderations* edited by Michael A. Lofaro, 1992; *The Creative Process of James Agee* by James Lowe, 1994; *Documenting Lives: James Agee's and Walker Evans's Let Us Now Praise Famous Men* by Astrid Böger, 1994; *James Agee and the Legend of Himself: A Critical Study* by Alan Spiegel, 1998.

*   *   *

In 1941 James Agee and the photographer Walker Evans published *Let Us Now Praise Famous Men*. A long, journalistic piece that would become the central fixture of Agee's critical fame, the book was the result of eight months that he and Evans had spent in Alabama sympathetically chronicling in prose and photographs the daily lives of sharecropper families in the deep South.

Prior to the appearance of *Let Us Now Praise Famous Men*, Agee had published a book of poetry, *Permit Me Voyage*, as well as many magazine articles—most of them anonymously—as a member of the staff of *Fortune*. He had also begun writing film criticism for *Time*, an activity which he continued for the *Nation* and which signaled the beginnings of a deep involvement with cinema, not only as an outspoken critic of the medium but also as a writer of highly detailed screenplays.

Let Us Now Praise Famous Men and his film work aside, Agee is best remembered for his novels, *The Morning Watch* and *A Death in the Family,* the latter published two years after his death, earning him a posthumous Pulitzer Prize. Largely autobiographical, both novels reveal the influence in Agee's life and work of two elemental facts of his childhood: the death of his father when Agee was six years old, and the religious piety of his mother, a piety with which he would constantly struggle. *The Morning Watch,* for instance, is the story of a young student at a religious school who grows away from orthodoxy toward self-awareness and, eventually, alienation. And in *A Death in the Family* the young protagonist's father has been killed in an automobile accident—as Agee's own father had been killed—leaving the boy and his family to cope with his absence, even as had the Agee family.

Many critics have felt that Agee failed to reach the artistic achievement for which he seemed destined. Never one to settle on a particular genre, they point out, he chose instead to try it all: poetry, journalism, fiction, criticism, screenplays. And never one to care for his own health, he lived, as film director John Huston wrote, as though "body destruction was implicit in his make-up." Still, Agee achieved much in his 45 years, and his premature death meant, finally, that his greatest fame would have to come posthumously.

—Bruce A. Lohof

AIKEN, Conrad (Potter)

Born: Savannah, Georgia, 5 August 1889. **Education:** Middlesex School, Concord, Massachusetts; Harvard University, Cambridge, Massachusetts (president, *Harvard Advocate*), 1907-10, 1911-12, A.B. 1912. **Family:** Married 1) Jessie McDonald in 1912 (divorced 1929), one son and two daughters, the writers Jane Aiken Hodge and Joan Aiken; 2) Clarissa M. Lorenz in 1930 (divorced 1937); 3) Mary Hoover in 1937. **Career:** Contributing editor, *The Dial,* New York, 1916-19; American correspondent, *Athenaeum,* London, 1919-25, and London *Mercury,* 1921-22; lived in London, 1921-26 and 1930-39; instructor, Harvard University, 1927-28; London correspondent, *New Yorker,* 1934-36; lived in Brewster, Massachusetts, from 1940, and Savannah after 1962. Fellow, 1947, and consultant in poetry, 1950-52, Library of Congress, Washington, D.C. **Awards:** Pulitzer prize, 1930; Shelley Memorial award, 1930; Guggenheim fellowship, 1934; National Book award, 1954; Bollingen prize, 1956; Academy of American Poets fellowship, 1957; American Academy Gold Medal, 1958; Huntington Hartford Foundation award, 1960; Brandeis University Creative Arts award, 1967; National Medal for Literature, 1969. **Member:** American Academy, 1957. **Died:** 17 August 1973.

PUBLICATIONS

Short Stories

Bring! Bring! and Other Stories. 1925.
Costumes by Eros. 1928.
Among the Lost People. 1934.
The Short Stories. 1950.
The Collected Short Stories. 1960.

Novels

Blue Voyage. 1927.
Gehenna. 1930.
Great Circle. 1933.
King Coffin. 1935.
A Heart for the Gods of Mexico. 1939.
Conversation; or, Pilgrims' Progress. 1940; as *The Conversation,* 1948.
The Collected Novels. 1964.

Poetry

Earth Triumphant and Other Tales in Verse. 1914.
The Jig of Forslin: A Symphony. 1916.
Turns and Movies and Other Tales in Verse. 1916.
Nocturne of Remembered Spring and Other Poems. 1917.
The Charnel Rose, Senlin: A Biography, and Other Poems. 1918.
The House of Dust: A Symphony. 1920.
Punch: The Immortal Liar. 1921.
The Pilgrimage of Festus. 1923.
Priapus and the Pool and Other Poems. 1925.
[Selected Poems] edited by Louis Untermeyer. 1927.
Prelude. 1929.
Selected Poems. 1929.
John Deth: A Metaphysical Legend, and Other Poems. 1930.
Preludes for Memnon. 1931.
The Coming Forth by Day of Osiris Jones. 1931.
Landscape West of Eden. 1934.
Time in the Rock: Preludes to Definition. 1936.
And in the Human Heart. 1940.
Brownstone Eclogues and Other Poems. 1942.
The Soldier. 1944.
The Kid. 1947.
The Divine Pilgrim. 1949.
Skylight One: Fifteen Poems. 1949.
Collected Poems. 1953.
A Letter from Li Po and Other Poems. 1955.
The Flute Player. 1956.
Sheepfold Hill: Fifteen Poems. 1958.
Selected Poems. 1961.
The Morning Song of Lord Zero: Poems Old and New. 1963.
A Seizure of Limericks. 1964.
Preludes. 1966.
Thee. 1967.
The Clerk's Journal, Being the Diary of a Queer Man: An Undergraduate Poem, Together with a Brief Memoir of Dean LeBaron Russell Briggs, T.S. Eliot, and Harvard, in 1911. 1971.
Collected Poems 1916-1970. 1970.
A Little Who's Zoo of Mild Animals. 1977.

Play

Mr. Arcularis (produced 1949). 1957.

Other

Scepticisms: Notes on Contemporary Poetry. 1919.
Ushant: An Essay (autobiography). 1952.
A Reviewer's ABC: Collected Criticism from 1916 to the Present, edited by Rufus A. Blanshard. 1958; as *Collected Criticism,* 1968.

Cats and Bats and Things with Wings (for children). 1965.
Tom, Sue, and the Clock (for children). 1966.
Selected Letters, edited by Joseph Killorin. 1978.

Editor, *Modern American Poets.* 1922; revised edition, 1927; re-
    vised edition, as *Twentieth Century American Poetry,* 1945; re-
    vised edition, 1963.
Editor, *Selected Poems of Emily Dickinson.* 1924.
Editor, *American Poetry 1671-1928: A Comprehensive Anthology.*
    1929; revised edition, as *A Comprehensive Anthology of Ameri-
    can Poetry,* 1944.
Editor, with William Rose Benét, *An Anthology of Famous En-
    glish and American Poetry.* 1945.

*

Bibliography: *Aiken: A Bibliography (1902-1978)* by F.W. and
F.C. Bonnell, 1982; *Aiken: Critical Recognition 1914-1981: A Bibliographic Guide* by Catherine Kirk Harris, 1983.

Critical Studies: *Aiken: A Life of His Art* by Jay Martin, 1962;
Aiken by Frederick J. Hoffman, 1962; *Aiken* by Reuel Denney,
1964; *Lorelei Two: My Life with Aiken* by Clarissa M. Lorenz,
1983; *The Art of Knowing: The Poetry and Prose of Aiken* by
Harry Marten, 1988; *Aiken: Poet of White Horse Vale* by Edward
Butscher, 1988; *Aiken: A Priest of Consciousness* edited by Ted
R. Spirey and Arthur Waterman, 1989; *Time's Stop in Savannah:
Conrad Aiken's Inner Journey* by Ted Ray Spivey, 1997.

*   *   *

Characteristically, Conrad Aiken himself raises the essential critical problem in a note he wrote in 1917: "It is difficult to place Conrad
Aiken in the poetic firmament, so difficult that one sometimes wonders whether he deserves a place there at all" (*Collected Criticism*).
The problem is further complicated by the fact that Aiken was not
only a poet, but also a respected novelist and critic. The list of his
admirers is persuasive: R.P. Blackmur, **Allen Tate**, and Malcolm
Lowry all find in him one of the central voices of his age. Yet to the
contemporary reader such claims are likely to seem excessive.

About the scope of his ambition there can be no doubt. Five
long, complicated novels; many lengthy poetic sequences, or "symphonies," dealing with themes as varied, and as large, as the history of America (*The Kid*), the importance of his Puritan heritage
("Mayflower"), the problems of the self encountering the realities of love and death (*Preludes for Memnon* and *The Coming Forth
by Day of Osiris Jones*): all testify to the courageous attempt to
convey a rich, complex life in a wide-ranging, always technically
experimental art.

The center of this art lies in maintaining the difficult balance
between aesthetic purity and formal perfection on the one hand,
and the menacing chaos of terrifying experience on the other. It is
tempting to relate this to Aiken's very early experience as a child
when he discovered the bodies of his parents after a mutual suicide pact: this moment is placed at the center of his long autobiographical essay *Ushant.* This deeply buried memory may also have
encouraged Aiken's passionate interest in Freud. The five novels
show this interest everywhere: the hero of *Blue Voyage*, Demarest,
is on a voyage of self-discovery through journey, quest, and dream.
This novel, like *Great Circle*—which Freud himself admired—is
an elaborate metaphor for the author's psychic search, the explo-

ration of his own consciousness. At their best, the novels find a
language for disturbing, hidden states of the psyche: the combination of thriller form and psychoanalytic imagery in *King Coffin* is
uniquely memorable. But too often the novels slip into vagueness
and imprecision. As Frederick J. Hoffman has observed, their separate parts fail *quite* to cohere. The lack of adequate characterization, and the over-literariness of the enterprise, are at odds with
our valid expectations of prose fiction. It is significant, then, that
Aiken's "autobiography," *Ushant*, should seem to so many of his
critics his finest achievement in prose. Here, Aiken as writer, and
his literary friends, including **T.S. Eliot** and **Ezra Pound**, are at
the center of a "fictionalized" account of the author's life. Apart
from its other intrinsic interests, this quite extraordinary,
unclassifiable work is justified, almost alone, by the majestic sweep
and lyrical seductiveness of Aiken's rhetoric.

It is this majestic rhetoric that one also recognizes in the poetry: Malcolm Lowry referred to Aiken as "the truest and most
direct descendant of our own great Elizabethans." This quality is
immediately apparent in *Preludes for Memnon:*

> What dignity can death bestow on us,
> Who kiss beneath a street lamp, or hold hands
> Half hidden in a taxi, or replete
> With coffee, figs and Barsac make our way
> To a dark bedroom in a wormworn house?

The combination here of the common and quotidian—street
lamp, taxi, coffee—with noble, "Elizabethan" cadences, is the characteristic Aiken manner. It is a manner that frequently skirts parody
and pastiche, but equally often rises to a rich, solemn verbal music.
In poem after poem in his enormous output, Aiken sustains a long,
flowing musical line, celebrating, as in "Landscape West of Eden,"
the capacity of language to order the chaos of the unaccommodated
self. What one misses, however, in too much of this poetry, and what
contributes to a certain lack of *energy* in the verse, is any intense
verbal particularity, or, often, the sense of real feeling significantly
expressed. In *Time in the Rock,* one of his most ambitious pieces,
there is little sense of any real pressure or urgency behind the
words; they have a tendency, as it were, to slip off the edge of
the page as we read; nothing seems to make it all *cohere.*

His more objective, "dramatic" poems, like *The Kid* and "Mayflower," with their incorporation of historical and legendary material
and their evocations of New England landscape and geography are
perhaps more valuable, in the end, than his lyrical self-communings.
The contemporary reader is also likely to be more drawn to the lighter
side of Aiken: in a poem like "Blues for Ruby Matrix" the rhetoric
remains, but allied now to a delightful sexiness and tenderness.

Whatever the mode, however, there is always in Aiken, even if
only residually, that sense of horror, of terror, and of death—"The
somber note that gives the chord its power," as he puts it in "Palimpsest"—that gives the best poetry its capacity to hurt and
wound us. When, in *Preludes for Memnon,* he defines the role of
the poet, Aiken finds a definition that takes full note of this fundamental ground-bass of his own work: the poet is one

> who by imagination [apes]
> God, the supreme poet of despair . . .
> Knowing the rank intolerable taste of death,
> And walking dead on the living still earth.

—Neil Corcoran

AKINS, Zoë

Born: Humansville, Missouri, 30 October 1886. **Career:** Poet, novelist, screenwriter, and playwright. Contributor, *St. Louis Mirror*; screenwriter, Hollywood, late 1920s; under film contract to Paramount, 1930-31. **Awards:** Pulitzer prize for drama, for *The Old Maid*, 1935. **Died:** 29 October 1958.

PUBLICATIONS

Plays

The Magical City (produced 1915).
Papa (produced 1919). 1913.
Cake Upon the Waters. 1913.
Footloose (produced 1919).
Déclassée (produced 1919).
Daddy's Gone A-Hunting (produced 1921).
The Varying Shore (produced 1921).
The Texas Nightingale (produced 1922).
A Royal Fandango (produced 1923).
Déclassée, Daddy's Gone A-Hunting, and Greatness. 1923
The Moon-Flower (produced 1924).
Such a Charming Young Man: Comedy in One Act. 1924.
First Love (produced 1926).
The Crown Prince (produced 1927).
The Furies (produced 1928).
The Love Duel (produced 1929).
The Greeks Had a Word for It (produced 1930).
The Old Maid, adaptation of novella by Edith Wharton (produced 1935). 1935.
The Little Miracle. 1936.
O Evening Star! (produced 1936).
Mrs. January and Mr. Ex. 1948.

Screenplays: *Sarah and Son*, 1930; *Anybody's Woman*, with Doris Anderson, 1930; *The Right to Love*, 1930; *Women Love Once*, 1931; *Once a Lady*, with Samuel Hoffenstein, 1931; *Working Girls*, 1931; *Christopher Strong*, 1933; *Outcast Lady*, 1934; *Camille*, with Frances Marion and James Hilton, 1936; *Accused*, with George Barraud, 1936; *Lady of Secrets*, with Joseph Anthony, 1936; *The Toy Wife*, 1938; *Zaza*, 1938; *Desire Me*, with Marguerite Roberts, 1947.

Poetry

Interpretations: A Book of First Poems. 1912.
The Hills Grow Smaller. 1937.

Novel

Forever Young. 1941.

Other

In the Shadow of Parnassus: Zoë Akins's Essays on American Poetry, edited by Catherine N. Parke, 1994.

*

Critical Studies: *The Plays of Zoë Akins Rumbold* (dissertation) by Ronald Albert Mielech, 1974; "Edith Wharton's *The Old Maid*: Novella/Play/Film" by Margaret B. McDowell, in *College Literature*, fall 1987, pp. 246-62; "Zoë Akins and the Age of Excess: Broadway Melodrama in the 1920s" by Jennifer Bradley, in *Modern American Drama: The Female Canon*, 1990.

*   *   *

In the history of American dramatic literature Zoe Akins will be listed as the writer of a score of romantic dramas that held some appeal for American theatre audiences between the two world wars. Blending a certain sophistication with a preference for the sentimental, she was more charming than thought provoking in her plays, but that was certainly acceptable during times when amusement was either an end in itself or a necessary distraction from social upheavals. Consequently Akins became a popular playwright for a generation that watched the plays of Jessie Lynch Williams, Owen Davis, and Gilbert Emery while trying to adjust to the more penetrating theatrical experimentation of **Eugene O'Neill** and **Susan Glaspell.** When the new social realists appeared in the later 1920s—**Sidney Howard, Robert Sherwood,** and **Maxwell Anderson**—amidst a greater abundance of talented dramatists, Akins's plays were less distinctive. She nevertheless retained a little of her once popular reputation with the production of *The Old Maid* in 1935, an adaptation of **Edith Wharton**'s story.

In the history of the American theatre Akins will be remembered primarily as the author of *The Old Maid*, which was awarded a Pulitzer Prize. But this was not an entirely triumphant occasion in Zoe Akins's career. *The Old Maid* is the sentimental story of a woman who, having given up her illegitimate daughter at birth to be raised by a married cousin, endures her silent grief throughout her life and is rewarded by a glimmer of the daughter's love at the final curtain. *The Old Maid* was a box office success with a run of thirty-eight weeks. Unfortunately, with the competition particularly severe that year—**Lillian Hellman**'s *The Children's Hour*, **Clifford Odets'** *Awake and Sing!*, Sherwood's *The Petrified Forest*, and Anderson's *Valley Forge* were all considered stronger contenders for the Pulitzer—Akins's win resulted in a number of irate New York theatre critics. Stimulated by Helen Deutsch and others, including **George Jean Nathan,** the critics responded by establishing the Critics Circle Award at the end of the season. Their first award went to *Winterset* by Anderson. Sherwood received the Pulitzer Prize for *Idiot's Delight* in 1936. Presumably the Pulitzer Prize would be given to the most successful play on Broadway while the Critics Circle Award was for the most stimulating theatrical event.

Born in Missouri with her formative years spent in St. Louis, Akins developed her fascination for the theatre early in life. At seventeen she joined the Odeon Stock Company, and by 1908 she had helped establish the Juvenile Theatre of St. Louis. The following year she moved to New York to try her luck as an actress and playwright while continuing to write for magazines, including *McClure's*, where she found a friend in Willa Cather. Although her three-act "amorality play" *Papa* was published in 1913, it was not produced until 1916 when it was staged by an amateur company in Los Angeles. That same year the Washington Square Players in New York recognized her one-act verse drama *The Magical City* and gave her her first professional production. Her career really started, however, with *Declassee* (1919), which starred Ethel

Barrymore and showed off to advantage Akins's flair for getting the most from a dramatic situation. In the play a sophisticated woman must face divorce and the consequence of being *declassee*.

Other successes in the theatre quickly followed. *Daddy's Gone A-Hunting* (1921) builds upon the sentimental story of a mismatched husband and wife being kept together by a child. Like other dramatists of her time who tried to write thoughtful plays on social issues, Akins was unable to sustain a serious approach and maintain her popularity through her witty dialogue and characterization. *The Varying Shore* (1921) was an exciting romance of insignificant proportions. It was made interesting on stage through a variety of flashbacks revealing the story of a fallen woman in reverse—from the death of a rich old woman in Monte Carlo to her forced marriage at age seventeen. *Greatness*, produced in New York in 1922 under the title *The Texas Nightingale*, provides the best example of Akins's skillful dramatic dialogue and excellent characterization. Unfortunately the play failed in the theatre, according to contemporary critics, because it was terribly miscast. The story of an opera singer who had had four husbands, all blighted by their association with her, *Greatness* provided Akins with a fine opportunity for comedy as the temperamental diva reunites with her second husband and their son. Throughout the 1920s Akins turned out fanciful and sentimental romances such as *Pardon my Glove* (1926) and *The Greeks Had a Word for It* (1929), which played six months in London in 1934. She also adapted foreign plays such as *First Love* (1926) and *The Love Duel* (1929) for Ethel Barrymore; the latter featured a duel that ends in marriage. Like other dramatists of her time, Akins wrote quite a number of screenplays, including Edna Ferber's *Showboat* (1931), *Camille* for Greta Garbo (1936), and *Desire Me* (1947).

In 1923 when historian and theatre critic Oliver Sayler wrote in *Our American Theater* that "Zoe Akins is still the chief romancer of our stage," he may or may not have realized that he was identifying her for posterity. But it is not an unworthy epitaph, and it helps future students of the theatre understand both an audience and a theatre that could acknowledge and appreciate such an approach to life and to art.

—Walter J. Meserve

ALBEE, Edward

Born: Virginia, 12 March 1928. **Education:** Attended Trinity College, Hartford, Connecticut, 1946-47. **Career:** Has held a variety of jobs, including continuity writer for WNYC-Radio, office boy, record salesperson, and counterboy; messenger for Western Union, 1955-58; producer for New Playwrights Unit Workshop, 1963—; director of own plays, including *The Zoo Story, The Sandbox,* and *Listening*; codirector of Vivian Beaumont Theatre at Lincoln Center for the Performing Arts, New York City, since 1979. Founder of William Flanagan Center for Creative Persons, Montauk, New York, 1971. Lecturer at college campuses. U.S. State Department cultural exchange visitor to Union of Soviet Socialist Republics (now the Commonwealth of Independent States) and Latin American countries. Member of National Endowment grant-giving council; member of governing commission of New York State Council for the Arts. **Awards:** Berlin Festival award, 1959 and 1961; Rice Memorial award, 1960; Obie award, 1960; Argen-

tine Critics Circle award, 1961; best plays of the 1960-61 season honors from Foreign Press Association, 1961; Lola D'Annunzio award, 1961; selected as most promising playwright of 1962-63 season by the New York Drama Critics, 1963; New York Drama Critics Circle award, 1963; Foreign Press Association award, 1963; Antoinette Perry ("Tony") award, 1963; Outer Circle award, 1963; *Saturday Review* Drama Critics award, 1963; *Variety* Drama Critics' Poll award, 1963; *Evening Standard* award, 1964; Margo Jones award, with Richard Barr and Clinton Wilder, 1965; Pulitzer prize, 1967 and 1975; American Academy and Institute of Arts and Letters Gold Medal, 1980; inducted into Theater Hall of Fame, 1985; National Medal of Arts, 1996; Kennedy Center honoree, 1996. D. Litt. from Emerson College, 1967, and Trinity College, 1974. **Member:** National Institute of Arts and Letters. **Residence:** New York City.

PUBLICATIONS

Plays

The Zoo Story (produced Berlin, 1959; New York and London, 1960). Included in *The Zoo Story, The Death of Bessie Smith, The Sandbox: Three Plays,* 1960.

The Death of Bessie Smith (produced Berlin, 1960; New York and London, 1961). Included in *The Zoo Story, The Death of Bessie Smith, The Sandbox: Three Plays,* 1960.

The Sandbox (produced New York, 1960). Included in *The Zoo Story, The Death of Bessie Smith, The Sandbox: Three Plays,* 1960.

The Zoo Story, The Death of Bessie Smith, The Sandbox: Three Plays. 1960; as *The Zoo Story and Other Plays* (includes *The American Dream*), 1962.

Fam and Yam (produced Westport, Connecticut, 1960). 1961.

The American Dream (produced New York, 1961). 1961.

Who's Afraid of Virginia Woolf? (produced New York, 1962). 1962.

The American Dream, The Death of Bessie Smith, Fam and Yam. 1962.

The American Dream and The Zoo Story: Two Plays. 1963.

The Ballad of the Sad Cafe (adaptation of the novella by Carson McCullers; produced New York, 1963). Published as *The Ballad of the Sad Cafe, Carson McCullers's Novella Adapted to the Stage.* 1963.

Tiny Alice (produced New York, 1964). 1965.

Malcolm (adaptation of the novel by James Purdy; produced New York, 1966). Published as *Malcolm, Adapted by Edward Albee from the Novel by James Purdy.* 1966.

A Delicate Balance (produced New York, 1966). 1966.

Breakfast at Tiffany's (musical; adaptation of a story by Truman Capote; music by Bob Merrill; produced Philadelphia and New York, 1966).

Everything in the Garden (adaptation of play by Giles Cooper; produced New York, 1967). 1968.

Box [and] *Quotations from Chairman Mao Tse-Tung* (produced Buffalo, New York, and New York City, 1968). Published as *Box and Quotations from Chairman Mao Tse-Tung: Two Inter-Related Plays.* 1969.

All Over (produced New York, 1971). 1971.

Seascape (produced New York, 1975). 1975.

Counting the Ways (produced London, 1976; Hartford, Connecticut, 1977). Included in *Counting the Ways and Listening: Two Plays,* 1977.

Listening: A Chamber Play (produced as a radio play, BBC, 1976; produced Hartford, Connecticut, 1977). Included in *Counting the Ways and Listening: Two Plays,* 1977.
Counting the Ways and Listening: Two Plays. 1977.
The Lady from Dubuque (produced New York, 1980). 1980.
The Plays:
    Volume 1 (contains *The Zoo Story, The Death of Bessie Smith, The Sandbox,* and *The American Dream*). 1981.
    Volume 2 (contains *Tiny Alice, A Delicate Balance, Box,* and *Quotations from Chairman Mao Tse-Tung*). 1981.
    Volume 3 (contains *All Over, Seascape, Counting the Ways,* and *Listening*). 1982.
    Volume 4 (contains *Everything in the Garden, Malcolm,* and *The Ballad of the Sad Cafe*). 1983.
Lolita (adaptation of the novel by Vladimir Nabokov; produced Boston and New York, 1981). 1984.
The Man Who Had Three Arms (produced Miami, Florida, and Chicago, 1982). 1987.
The Marriage Play (produced Vienna, Austria, 1987; San Diego, California, 1989).
The Sandbox and The Death of Bessie Smith, with Fam and Yam. 1988.
Three Tall Women (produced 1991). 1995.
Fragments: A Sit Around (produced 1993). As *Edward Albee's Fragments: A Sit-Around,* 1995.
A Delicate Balance: A Play. 1997.

Screenplay: *A Delicate Balance,* 1976.

Radio Play: *Listening,* 1976.

Other

With James Hinton, Jr., *Bartleby* (opera; adaptation of a story by Herman Melville; produced New York, 1961).
Conversations with Edward Albee, edited by Philip C. Kolin. 1988.

*

Bibliography: *From Tension to Tonic: The Plays of Edward Albee* by Anne Paolucci, 1972; *Edward Albee at Home and Abroad* by Richard E. Amacher and Margaret Rule, 1973; *Edward Albee: An Annotated Bibliography 1968-1977* by Charles Lee Green, 1980; *Edward Albee: A Reference Guide* by Scott Giantvalley, 1987.

Critical Studies: *Seasons of Discontent* by Robert Brustein, 1965; *Edward Albee: Tradition and Renewal* by Gilbert Debusscher, 1967; *Edward Albee: Playwright in Protest* by Michael E. Rutenberg, 1969; *Edward Albee* by Ruby Cohn, 1969; *Edward Albee* by Richard E. Amacher, 1969, revised edition, 1982; *Albee* by C. W. E. Bigsby, 1969, and *Edward Albee: A Collection of Critical Essays* edited by Bigsby, 1975; *Who's Afraid of Edward Albee?* by Foster Hirsch, 1978; *Edward Albee: The Poet of Loss* by Anita Maria Stenz, 1978; *Culture Clash: The Making of Gay Sensibility* by Michael Bronski, 1984; *Critical Essays on Edward Albee* edited by Philip C. Kolin and J. Madison Davis, Hall, 1986; *We Can Always Call Them Bulgarians: The Emergence of Lesbians and Gay Men on the American Stage* by Kaier Curtin, 1987; *Understanding Edward Albee* by Matthew C. Roudane, 1987; *Conversations with Edward Albee* edited by Philip C. Kolin, 1988; *Edward Albee* edited by Harold Bloom, 1987; *Edward Albee* by

Gerry McCarthy, 1987; "American Variations on a British Theme: Giles Cooper and Edward Albee" by Peter Egri, in *Forked Tongues? Comparing Twentieth-Century British and American Literature,* edited by Ann Massa and Alistair Stead, 1994; in *The Playwright's Art: Conversations with Contemporary American Dramatists,* edited by Jackson R. Bryer, 1995; "Albee's Martha: Someone's Daughter, Someone's Wife, No One's Mother" by Bonnie Blumenthal Finkelstein, in *American Drama,* fall 1995, pp. 51-70; "Albee and Me" by Marian Seldes, in *American Theatre,* September 1996, pp. 24-26.

*   *   *

Critics are divided as to whether playwright Edward Albee is a realist or absurdist. Critics and public are divided as to the quality of his writing after *Who's Afraid of Virginia Woolf.* Actors and directors are divided as to whether he is wise to direct his own plays. Never one to soar above the battle, Albee wittily attacks his attackers.

The Zoo Story, completed in 1958 when he was thirty years old, played in New York City on the same bill as Samuel Beckett's *Krapp's Last Tape,* and Albee was immediately pigeonholed as an absurdist. Rather than dramatize a metaphysical impasse, however, Albee creates a protagonist, Jerry, who is a martyr to brotherly love. In arousing the smug Peter to enact a "zoo story," Jerry strikes hard at complacent conformity, and Albee strikes hard at conventional theater.

Albee's next few plays in the next few years are more traditionally satiric. *The Death of Bessie Smith* lacerates white racism; *The American Dream* and *The Sandbox* ridicule American materialism and mindlessness. In *Fam and Yam,* a slight piece, an old established playwright is confronted by a bright young novice.

For all the energetic idiom of *The Zoo Story* and the satiric verve of his other short plays, Albee remained a fringe playwright until *Who's Afraid of Virginia Woolf.* The play has been misunderstood as a marital problem play, a campus satire, or a portrait of veiled homosexuality, but even misunderstood, its verbal pyrotechnics attracted audiences. Slowly, its symbolic import has seeped through an apparently realistic surface. George and Martha, ostensibly a middle-aged American academic couple but related by name to the father (and mother) of the United States, have based their union on the fantasy of a child. On the eve of their imaginary child's twenty-first birthday, George and Martha return home from a campus party accompanied by a young academic and his wife. Drinking heavily, the older couple uses the younger one for "flagellation." As in O'Neill's *Long Day's Journey into Night,* alcohol proves confessional and penitential for all four characters. In the play's third act "exorcism," George kills their pretend son. The middle-aged couple, alone at daybreak, must learn to live with naked reality.

Albee continues the coruscating dialogue of *Virginia Woolf* into the first scene of *Tiny Alice* but then shifts to slower rhythms of mystery—both murder and metaphysics. As in *The Zoo Story* and *Virginia Woolf,* the protagonist of *Tiny Alice,* the lay brother Julian, seeks the reality beneath the surface. In this case, the surface glitters theatrically with such devices as a model castle, a cardinal of the Church who keeps caged cardinal birds, a beautiful woman disguised as an old crone, an operatic staircase, and visual reminders of the Pietà and Crucifixion. Brother Julian claims to be "dedicated to the reality of things, rather than the appearance." Abandoned on his wedding day by his bride Alice and her entourage, Julian finally lies in cruciform posture, clinging to illusion as he really dies.

A Delicate Balance returns to a more realistic surface; as in *Virginia Woolf,* the love relationship of one couple, Tobias and Agnes, is explored through their interaction with another couple. In act 1, set on a Friday, terrorized friends seek refuge with Tobias and Agnes; in Saturday's act 2, Tobias welcomes them, but his daughter Julia reacts hysterically. On Sunday, act 3, the friends know they are not welcome, and they know they would not have welcomed friends in a similar situation. They leave. The passion leads not to resurrection but to restitution of a delicate family balance.

After two related and exploratory plays called *Box-Mao-Box,* Albee returns in *All Over* to the upper-middle-class American milieu he stylizes so deftly. He brings to the center of this play a theme at the periphery of his other plays: the existential impact of death. In spite of the title, "all" is not quite "over," for a once powerful man is dying behind a stage screen. Waiting for his death are his wife, mistress, best friend, son, and daughter, whose mannered conversation traces the man's presence everywhere, or "all over." Death precariously joins this company, only to sunder them again, as each is suffused in his or her own unhappiness.

Between *A Delicate Balance* and *All Over,* both of them upper-middle-class plays in credible settings, Albee wrote the two "interrelated," experimental plays, *Box* and *Quotations from Chairman Mao Tse-tung. Box* is presented in two parts, which form "a parenthesis" around *Mao.* In *Box,* a brightly lit cube usurps the whole stage, while the audience hears the monologue of a middle-aged woman. Although apparently rambling, the speech is carefully structured: "When art hurts. That is what to remember." Quotations theatricalize the way that art can hurt. Within the cube, the deck of a steamship appears, with four characters on it—a silent minister, Chairman Mao speaking only in the titular quotations, a shabby old woman speaking only doggerel verse of Will Carleton, and a middle-class, middle-aged, long-winded lady whose discourse further develops the themes of art and suffering. Skillfully counterpointed, the three voices dramatize the frailty of art—how it is nourished by suffering and how it suffers.

After the jejune lapse of *Seascape* Albee created another two short experimental plays, *Listening* and *Counting the Ways. Listening,* a "chamber play" translated from radio, resembles a chamber quartet in its blend of four voices. Grouped about a fountain pool, the three visible characters engage in nonlinear dialogue on the theme of listening. The girl charges: "You don't listen.... Pay attention, rather, is what you don't do." Though the characters seem to speak in a limbo beyond life, the play is climaxed by a shocking suicide and a last reiteration of the girl's charge countered by the fifty-year-old woman: "I listen." Less resonant is the two-character *Counting the Ways,* "A Vaudeville" in twenty-one scenes depicting the varying moods of a love affair much as director Ingemar Bergman did that of a marriage in his film *Scenes from a Marriage.*

The Lady from Dubuque was first performed in New York in 1980, but rather than usher in a new theater decade, the play reflects earlier Albee hallmarks: witty repartee, preoccupation with death, skepticism about identity. Albee's eight characters (his largest cast) are centered on a woman in her thirties, who is dying of cancer. Neither she, her husband, Sam, nor the two couples they know can adequately deal with the fear and pain. Enter a mysterious black couple, Oscar and Elizabeth; the latter claims to be both the invalid's mother and the lady from Dubuque. Despite interference from the rest of the cast, the strange couple not only

ease the sick woman into death, they also confront the other characters with their deepest selves.

Although a decade separates Albee's *Three Tall Women* from *The Lady from Dubuque,* the former work also dramatizes dying. The three tall women are, in actuality, one, since they represent three different stages of one woman's life—at ages twenty-six, fifty-two, and ninety-two. Albee offers us nothing so simple as chronology, however. Act 1 presents us with "A," decrepit physically and mentally, yet spirited and even mischievous through her meandering memories. In act 2 the old woman is perfectly rational as she converses with her younger selves with whom she shares very little. "I used to be tall," she intones, "I've shrunk." And that is the resonant theme of Albee's play, for we all shrink towards death.

In contrast *The Play about the Baby* focuses on birth. As in *Virginia Woolf,* a younger and an older couple confront each other, and one couple nurtures the illusion of a child. But while the earlier work ended with a hesitant promise in the triumph over illusion, this play is tragicomically darker. Pointedly and with rhythmic skill, the older couple turn against the younger couple their own words about their imaginary infant. The lyrical phrases of act 1 metamorphose into the veiled threats of act 2. The renunciation of illusion leads only to questions.

The corpus of Albee's work shows stylistic variety and close attention to the nuances of language. Rarely facile, never clumsy, sometimes mannered, Albee has continued to dramatize deep themes in distinctive theatrical forms.

—Ruby Cohn

ALCOTT, Louisa May

Born: Germantown, Philadelphia, Pennsylvania, 29 November 1832; daughter of the philosopher Amos Bronson Alcott; grew up in Boston and later in Concord, Massachusetts. **Education:** At home by her father with instruction from Henry David Thoreau, Ralph Waldo Emerson, and Theodore Parker. **Career:** Began to write for publication, 1848; also worked as a teacher, seamstress, and domestic servant to support her family; army nurse at the Union Hospital, Georgetown, Washington, D.C., during the Civil War, 1862-63; visited Europe, 1865-66; editor of the children's magazine *Merry's Museum,* 1867; visited Europe, 1870-71, then settled in Boston. **Died:** 6 March 1888.

PUBLICATIONS

Collections

Glimpses of Louisa: A Centennial Sampling of the Best Short Stories, edited by Cornelia Meigs. 1968.
Works, edited by Claire Booss. 1982.
Short Stories. 1996.

Fiction

Flower Fables. 1855.
The Rose Family: A Fairy Tale. 1864.
On Picket Duty and Other Tales. 1864.

Moods. 1865; revised edition, 1882.
Morning-Glories and Other Stories. 1867; revised edition, 1868.
The Mysterious Key and What It Opened. 1867.
Proverb Stories. 1868; as *Three Proverb Stories,* n.d.
Kitty's Class Day. 1868.
Aunt Kipp. 1868.
Psyche's Art. 1868.
Little Women; or, Meg, Jo, Beth, and Amy. 2 vols., 1868-69; as *Little Women and Good Wives,* 1871; vol. 2 as *Little Women Wedded,* 1872, *Little Women Married,* 1873, and *Nice Wives,* 1875.
An Old-Fashioned Girl. 1870.
Will's Wonder Book. 1870.
VV; or, Plots and Counterplots. 1870.
Little Men: Life at Plumfield with Jo's Boys. 1871.
Aunt Jo's Scrap-Bag: My Boys, Shawl-Straps, Cupid and Chow-Chow, My Girls, Jimmy's Cruise in the Pinafore, An Old-Fashioned Thanksgiving. 6 vols., 1872-82.
Work: A Story of Experience. 1873.
Beginning Again, Being a Continuation of "Work." 1875.
Eight Cousins; or, The Aunt-Hill. 1875.
Silver Pitchers, and Independence: A Centennial Love Story. 1876; as *Silver Pitchers and Other Stories,* 1876.
Rose in Bloom: A Sequel to "Eight Cousins." 1876.
A Modern Mephistopheles. 1877.
Under the Lilacs. 1877.
Meadow Blossoms. 1879.
Water-Cresses. 1879.
Jack and Jill: A Village Story. 1880.
Proverb Stories. 1882.
Spinning-Wheel Stories. 1884.
Jo's Boys and How They Turned Out. 1886.
Lulu's Library: A Christmas Dream, The Frost King. Recollections. 3 vols., 1886-89; vol. 3 as *Recollections of My Childhood Days,* 1890.
A Garland for Girls. 1887.
A Modern Mephistopheles, and A Whisper in the Dark. 1889.
Louisa's Wonder Book: An Unknown Alcott Juvenile, edited by Madeleine B. Stern. 1975.
Behind a Mask: The Unknown Thrillers, edited by Madeleine B. Stern. 1975.
Plots and Counterplots: More Unknown Thrillers, edited by Madeleine B. Stern. 1976.
Fairy Tales and Fantasy Stories, edited by Daniel Shealy. 1992.
A Long Fatal Love Chase. 1995.
An Old-fashioned Thanksgiving and Other Stories. 1995.
Louisa May Alcott Unmasked: Collected Thrillers, edited by Madeline B. Stern. 1995.

Plays

Comic Tragedies Written by "Jo" and "Meg" and Acted by the "Little Women," edited by A.B. Pratt. 1893.

Other

Hospital Sketches. 1863; revised edition, as *Hospital Sketches and Camp and Fireside Stories,* 1869.
Nelly's Hospital. 1865.
Something to Do. 1873.
A Glorious Fourth. 1887.
What It Cost. 1887.

Jimmy's Lecture. 1887.
Alcott: Her Life, Letters, and Journals, edited by Ednah D. Cheney. 1889.
A Sprig of Andromeda: A Letter on the Death of Henry David Thoreau, edited by John L. Cooley. 1962.
Transcendental Wild Oats, and Excerpts from the Fruitlands Diary. 1981.
Louisa May Alcott's Little Instruction Book. 1995.
The Feminist Alcott: Stories of a Woman's Power. 1996.
Louisa May Alcott on Race, Sex, and Slavery, edited by Sarah Elbert. 1997.

*

Bibliography: In *Bibliography of American Literature* by Jacob Blanck, 1955; in *Louisa's Wonder Book* edited by Madeleine B. Stern, 1975; *Alcott: A Reference Guide* by Alma J. Payne, 1980.

Critical Studies: *Alcott* by Madeleine B. Stern, 1950, and *Critical Essays on Alcott* edited by Stern, 1984; *Miss Alcott of Concord* by Marjorie Worthington, 1958; *Alcott and the American Family Story* by Cornelia Meigs, 1970; *Louisa May: A Modern Biography of Alcott* by Martha Saxton, 1977; *The Alcotts: Biography of a Family* by Madelon Bedell, 1980; *Alcott* by Ruth MacDonald, 1983; *The Promise of Destiny: Children and Women in the Short Stories of Alcott* by Joy A. Marsella, 1983; *A Hunger for Home: Alcott and Little Women* by Sarah Elbert, 1984; *Victorian Domesticity: Families in the Life and Art of Alcott* by Charles Strickland, 1985; "The Limits of Sympathy: Louisa May Alcott and the Sentimental Novel" by Glenn Hendler in *American Literary History,* Winter 1991; *Sister's Choice: Tradition and Change in American Women's Writing: Clarendon Lectures, 1989* by Elaine Showalter, 1991; "Echoes of Literary Sisterhood: Louisa May Alcott and Kate Chopin" by Harbour Winn in *Studies in American Fiction,* Autumn 1992; *Louisa May Alcott: From Blood and Thunder to Hearth and Home* edited by Madeleine B. Stern, 1998.

*   *   *

Louisa May Alcott's reputation as one of America's best-loved writers is based upon *Little Women,* a domestic novel for girls that is also appealing to adults. *Little Women* reflects the Alcott family background of high-minded idealism while it glosses over the Alcott family problems. Its characters, the four March girls, were drawn from those of the author and her sisters, its scenes from the New England where she had grown up, and many of its episodes from those she and her family had experienced, although the literary influence of Bunyan, Dickens, Carlyle, **Hawthorne,** **Emerson,** Theodore Parker, and **Thoreau** may be traced.

In the creation of *Little Women,* Alcott was something of a pioneer, using her own life as the basis of a novel for children and achieving a realistic but wholesome picture of family life with which readers could readily identify. The Alcott poverty was sentimentalized, the eccentric Alcott father was an adumbrated shadow; yet the core of the domestic drama was apparent. Reported simply and directly in a style that applied her injunction, "Never use a long word, when a short one will do as well," the narrative embodied the simple facts and persons of a family, and so filled a gap in the literature of adolescence and domesticity.

There is no doubt that *Little Women* was the author's masterpiece. It had been preceded by a succession of literary efforts and experiments that gave Alcott a wide range of professional experience before she undertook her domestic novel. Her first published book, *Flower Fables,* consisted of "legends of faery land" and was dedicated to Emerson's daughter Ellen, for whom the tales were originally created. Her first novel, *Moods,* was a narrative of stormy violence, death, and intellectual love in which she attempted to apply Emerson's remark "Life is a train of moods like a string of beads." On and off she worked on an autobiographical, feminist novel, *Success,* subsequently retitled *Work: A Story of Experience.*

The Alcott bibliography encompasses nearly 300 books, articles, novels, short stories, and poems, many of which appeared in the periodicals of the day. They were written in a variety of literary genres: stories of sweetness and light; dramatic narratives of strong-minded women; realistic episodes of Civil War life based upon her experience as a nurse; pseudonymous blood-and-thunder thrillers of revenge and passion whose leading characters were usually manipulating and vindictive women. From the exigencies of serialization she developed the skills of cliff-hanger and page-turner. By 1868, when she began *Little Women,* Alcott had produced a broad spectrum of stories from tales of virtue rewarded to tales of vice unpunished.

Little Women was followed by a succession of wholesome domestic narratives, the so-called *Little Women Series,* in which the author continued to supply a persistent demand. More or less autobiographical in origin and perceptive in their characterizations of adolescents, all are in a sense sequels of *Little Women,* though none quite rises to its level. *An Old Fashioned Girl* is a domestic drama in reverse, exposing the fashionable absurdities of one home in contrast with the wholesome domesticity of another. *Eight Cousins* exalts the family hearth again, and *Jack and Jill* enlarges upon the theme of domesticity, describing the home life of a New England village rather than of a single family.

An exception to this preoccupation with domestic life was *A Modern Mephistopheles.* Here Alcott exploits a theme of Goethe in a novel that reverts to the sensationalism of her earlier thrillers. "Enjoyed doing it," she wrote in her journal, "being tired of providing moral pap for the young." Actually, this novel had first been written during the 1860s and rejected as "too sensational."

Alcott was a far more complex writer than has been recognized. Drawn to a variety of literary themes and techniques, she eschewed most of them in favor of the domestic novel she had perfected. Motivated by the "inspiration of necessity," she became a victim of her own success. She has inevitably achieved fame as the "Children's Friend" and the author of a single masterpiece. Thanks to its psychological perceptions, its realistic characterizations, and its honest domesticity, *Little Women* has become an embodiment of the American home at its best. As the Boston *Herald* commented after her death: "When the family history, out of which this remarkable authorship grew, shall be told to the public, it will be apparent that few New England homes have ever had closer converse with the great things of human destiny than that of the Alcotts." Imbedded in the domestic novel *Little Women* are "the great things of human destiny," for there the particular has been transmuted into the universal.

—Madeleine B. Stern

See the essay on *Little Women.*

ALGER, Horatio (Jr.)

Born: Chelsea, Massachusetts, 13 January 1832. **Education:** Chelsea Grammar School; Gates Academy, Marlborough, Massa-

chusetts, 1845-47; Harvard University, Cambridge, Massachusetts (Bowdoin prize, 1851), 1848-52, A.B. 1852 (Phi Beta Kappa); Harvard Divinity School, 1853, 1857-60, graduated 1860: ordained 1864. **Career:** Assistant editor, Boston *Daily Advertiser,* 1853-54; schoolteacher, East Greenwich, Rhode Island, 1854-55; principal, Deerfield Academy, Massachusetts, 1856; editorial writer, *True Flag,* and tutor, Boston, 1856-57; traveled in Europe, 1860-61; private tutor in Cambridge and Naliant, Massachusetts, 1861-64; minister, First Unitarian Church, Brewster, Massachusetts, 1864-66; lived in New York, 1866-96, and private tutor from 1869; lived in South Natick, Massachusetts, 1896-99. **Died:** 18 July 1899.

PUBLICATIONS

Collections

Alger Street: The Poetry, edited by Gilbert K. Westgard II. 1964.

Fiction

Bertha's Christmas Vision: An Autumn Sheaf (stories and verse). 1856.
Frank's Campaign; or, What Boys Can Do on the Farm for the Camp. 1864.
Paul Prescott's Charge. 1865; as *Paul Prescott the Runaway,* 1867.
Helen Ford. 1866.
Timothy Crump's Ward; or, The New Years Loan, and What Came of It. 1866; revised edition, as *Jack's Ward; or, The Boy Guardian,* 1875.
Charlie Codman's Cruise. 1866; as *Bill Sturdy; or, The Cruise of Kidnapped Charlie,* 1887.
Fame and Fortune; or, The Progress of Richard Hunter. 1868.
Ragged Dick; or, Street Life in New York with the Boot-Blacks. 1868.
Luck and Pluck; or, John Oakley's Inheritance. 1869.
The Match Boy; or, Richard Hunter's Ward. 1869.
Rough and Ready; or Life Among the New York Newsboys. 1869.
Ben, The Luggage Boy; or, Among the Wharves. 1870.
Rujus and Rose; or, The Fortunes of Rough and Ready. 1870.
Sink or Swim; or, Harry Raymond's Resolve. 1870; as *Paddle Your Own Canoe,* 1887.
Paul the Peddler; or, The Adventures of a Young Street Merchant. 1871; as *Plucky Paul,* 1888.
Strong and Steady; or, Paddle Your Own Canoe. 1871.
Tattered Tom; or, The Story of a Street Arab. 1871.
Phil, The Fiddler; or, The Story of a Young Street Musician. 1872.
Slow and Sure; or, From the Street to the Shop. 1872.
Strive and Succeed; or, The Progress of Walter Conrad. 1872.
Bound to Rise; or, Harry Walton's Motto. 1873.
Try and Trust; or, The Story of a Bound Boy. 1873; as *Trials and Adventures of Herbert Mason,* 1887.
Brave and Bold; or, The Fortunes of a Factory Boy. 1874.
Julius; or, The Street Boy Out West. 1874.
Risen from the Ranks; or, Harry Walton's Success. 1874.
Herbert Carter's Legacy; or The Inventor's Son. 1875; as *George Carter's Legacy,* 1887.
The Young Outlaw; or, Adrift in the Streets. 1875.
Sam's Chance, and How He Improved It. 1876.
Shifting for Himself, or, Gilbert Greyson's Fortunes. 1876; as *How His Ship Came Home,* 1887.

Wait and Hope; or, Ben Bradford's Motto. 1877.

The New Schoolma'am. 1877; as *A Fancy of Hers*, 1981.

The Western Boy; or, The Road to Success. 1878; as *Tom, The Bootblack*, 1880.

The Young Adventurer; or, Tom's Trip Across the Plains. 1878.

The Young Miner; or, Tom Nelson in California. 1879.

The Telegraph Boy. 1879; as *The District Telegraph Boy*, n.d.

The Young Explorer; or, Among the Sierras. 1880.

Tony, The Hero. 1880; as *Tony, The Tramp*, 1910(?).

Ben's Nugget; or, A Boy's Search for Fortune: A Story of the Pacific Coast. 1882.

The Train Boy. 1883.

The Young Circus Rider; or, The Mystery of Robert Rudd. 1883.

Dan, The Detective. 1884; as *Dan the Newsboy*, 1893; as *Dutiful Dan, The Brave Boy Detective*, 1895.

Do and Dare; or, A Brave Boy's Fight for Fortune. 1884.

Hector's Inheritance; or, The Boys of Smith Institute. 1885; as *Never Despair!*, 1887.

Helping Himself, or, Grant Thornton's Ambition. 1886.

Joe's Luck; or, A Boy's Adventure in California. 1887.

Frank Fowler, The Cash Boy. 1887.

Number 91; or, The Adventures of a New York Telegraph Boy. 1887.

The Store Boy; or, The Fortunes of Ben Barclay. 1887; as *The Fortunes of Ben Barclay*, 1896; as *Ben Barclay's Courage*, 1904.

Ben Stanton, The Explorer (includes *The Young Explorer* and *Ben's Nugget*). 1887.

Bob Burton. 1888; as *The Young Ranchman of the Missouri*, 1888.

The Errand Boy; or, How Phil Brent Won Success. 1888.

The Merchant's Crime. 1888; as *Ralph Raymond's Heir*, 1892.

Tom Temple's Career. 1888.

Tom Thatcher's Fortune. 1888.

Tom Tracy; or, The Trials of a New York Newsboy. 1888.

The Young Acrobat of the Great North American Circus. 1888; as *He Would Be a Mountebank*, 1888.

Luke Walton; or, The Chicago Newsboy. 1889.

Mark Stanton; or, Both Sides of the Continent. 1890.

Ned Newton; or, The Fortunes of a New York Bootblack. 1890.

A New York Boy. 1890.

The Odds Against Him; or, Carl Crawford's Experience. 1890; as *Driven from Home*, n.d.

Struggling Upward; or, Luke Larkin's Luck. 1890.

Dean Dunham. 1890; as *Wait Till the Clouds Roll By*, 1890.

The Erie Train Boy. 1890; as *The Straight Ahead*, 1891.

$500; or, Jacob Marlowe's Secret. 1890; as *Uncle Jacob's Secret*, 1890; as *The Five Hundred Dollar Check*, 1891.

Digging for Gold: A Story of California. 1892.

The Young Boatman of Pine Point. 1892.

Facing the World; or, The Haps and Mishaps of Harry Vane. 1893.

In a New World; or, Among the Gold-Fields of Australia. 1893; as *The Nugget Finders*, 1894; as *Val Vane's Victory; or, Well Won*, 1903(?).

Only an Irish Boy; or, Andy Burke's Fortunes and Misfortunes. 1894.

Victor Vane, The Young Secretary. 1894.

Adrift in the City; or, Oliver Conrad's Plucky Fight. 1895.

The Disagreeable Woman: A Social Mystery. 1895.

Frank Hunter's Peril. 1896.

The Young Salesman. 1896.

Walter Sherwood's Probation. 1897.

Frank and Fearless; or, The Fortunes of Jasper Kent. 1897.

The Young Bank Messenger. 1898.

A Boy's Fortune; or, The Strange Adventures of Ben Baker. 1898.

Rupert's Ambition. 1899.

Mark Mason's Victory: The Trials and Triumphs of a Telegraph Boy. 1899.

Jed, The Poorhouse Boy. 1900.

A Debt of Honor: The Story of Gerald Lane's Success in the Far West. 1900.

Out for Business; or, Robert Frost's Strange Career, completed by Edward Stratemeyer. 1900.

Falling in with Fortune; or, The Experiences of a Young Secretary, completed by Edward Stratemeyer. 1900.

Ben Bruce: Scenes in the Life of a Bowery Newsboy. 1901.

Lester's Luck. 1901.

Making His Mark. 1901.

Nelson the Newsboy; or, Afloat in New York, completed by Edward Stratemeyer. 1901.

Striving for Fortune; or, Walter Griffith's Trials and Successes. 1901; as *Walter Griffith*, 1901.

Tom Brace: Who He Was and How He Fared. 1901.

Young Captain Jack; or, The Son of a Soldier, completed by Edward Stratemeyer. 1901.

Andy Grant's Pluck. 1902.

A Rolling Stone; or, The Adventures of a Wanderer. 1902; as *Wren Winter's Triumph*, 1902.

Tom Turner's Legacy: The Story of How He Secured It. 1902.

The World Before Him. 1902.

Bernard Brook's Adventures: The Story of a Brave Boy's Trials. 1903.

Chester Rand; or, A New Path to Fortune. 1903.

Forging Ahead. 1903; as *Andy Gordon*, 1905.

Adrift in New York. 1903; revised edition, 1904.

Finding a Fortune. 1904; as *The Tin Box* 1905(?).

Jerry, The Backwoods Boy; or, The Parkhurst Treasure, completed by Edward Stratemeyer. 1904.

Lost at Sea; or, Robert Roscoe's Strange Cruise, completed by Edward Stratemeyer. 1904.

From Farm to Fortune; or, Nat Nason's Strange Experience, completed by Edward Stratemeyer. 1905.

Mark Manning's Mission; or, The Story of a Shoe Factory Boy. 1905.

The Young Book Agent; or, Frank Hardy's Road to Success, completed by Edward Stratemeyer. 1905.

Joe the Hotel Boy; or, Winning Out by Pluck, completed by Edward Stratemeyer. 1906.

Randy of the River; or, The Adventures of a Young Deckhand, completed by Edward Stratemeyer. 1906.

The Young Musician. 1906.

In Search of Treasure: The Story of Guy's Eventful Voyage. 1907.

Wait and Win: The Story of Jack Drummond's Pluck. 1908.

Ben Logan's Triumph; or, The Boys of Boxwood Academy, completed by Edward Stratemeyer. 1908.

Robert Coverdale's Struggle; or, On the Wave of Success. 1910.

Silas Snobden's Office Boy. 1973.

Cast upon the Breakers. 1974.

Hugo, The Deformed. 1978.

Madeline, The Temptress. 1981.

The Secret Drawer. 1981.

The Cooper's Ward. 1981.

Herbert Selden. 1981.

Manson, The Miser. 1981.

The Gipsy Nurse. 1981.
The Discarded Son. 1981.
The Mad Heiress. 1981.
Marie Bertrand. 1981.

Poetry

Nothing to Do: A Tilt at Our Best Society. 1857.
Grand'ther Baldwin's Thanksgiving with Other Ballads and Poems. 1875.

Other

From Canal Boy to President; or, The Boyhood and Manhood of James A. Garfield. 1881.
From Farm Boy to Senator, Being the History of the Boyhood and Manhood of Daniel Webster. 1882.
Abraham Lincoln, The Backwoods Boy. 1883.

*

Bibliography: *Alger: A Comprehensive Bibliography* by Bob Bennett, 1980; *Alger: An Annotated Bibliography of Comment and Criticism* by Gary Scharnhorst and Jack Bales, 1981; *Horatio Alger Books Published by M.A. Donohue & Co.* by Bradford S. Chase, 1994; *Enjoying Alger: An Anthology Listing of All Known Alger Works Designed for Readers and Collectors Together with Many Vintage Illustrations, Nostalgic Themes, and Forgotten Love* by Angelo Sylvester, 1995.

Critical Studies: *Alger: A Biography and Bibliography* by Frank Gruber, 1961; *Horatio's Boys: The Life and Works of Alger* by Edwin P. Hoyt, 1974; *Alger* by Gary Scharnhorst, 1980, and *The Lost Life of Alger* by Scharnhorst and Jack Bales, 1985; "Of Factories and Failures: Exploring the Invisible Factory Gates of Horatio Alger, Jr." by Carol Nackenoff in *Journal of Popular Culture* Spring 1992; *The Fictional Republic: Horatio Alger and American Political Discourse* by Carol Nackenoff, 1994.

*   *   *

In 1867 Horatio Alger, failed preacher and schoolmaster, entered upon a literary career that eventually produced more than a hundred so-called boys' novels, thereby becoming one of the most successful writers in history. Indeed, so successful was he that his name has entered the language to signify the rags-to-riches American hero who, though born in dire straits, follows a virtuous and diligent life to a position of respectability, and sometimes wealth and influence.

So prodigious an output necessarily dictated that Alger's characters were little more than caricatures, heroes with faces that "indicated a frank, sincere nature" (as in *The World Before Him*), and villains "with shifty black eyes and thin lips, shaded by a dark moustache" (*Adrift in New York*). His plots also inevitably located an impoverished but ingenuous lad, often an orphan, in a hostile environment, usually the city. There, possessed of those virtues that have become synonymous with the Alger myth—optimism, ambition, thrift, and self-reliance—the lad matured toward an adulthood of power, affluence, and respectability.

This conventional reading of the Alger stories and the myth to which they gave birth is, however, somewhat misleading. To the more careful reader Alger's novels carry a more ambiguous message. First, it is not simply individual virtue but virtue in the face of good fortune that brings success to Alger's boys. Thus, as the typical story unfolds, the hero chances to save the millionaire's grandson from drowning or to find and return the lost bag of bank notes. In a sense, then, the cultivation of virtue is really a ritual of purification that prepares Alger's hero for the providential moment when he will be tried and found not wanting. Luck, no less than pluck—not to mention virtue—figures deeply in the success of the Alger hero. Second, the Alger hero's virtues are often compromised by their countervailing vices. Thrift, for instance, routinely gives way to a profligate visit to the theater or a spendthrift ride on a ferry boat, and self-reliance is often submerged in the desire for security and dependence.

Alger's heroes, in short, are not of the unalloyed virtue that the myth would have one believe. And virtue itself, compromised as it is, is routinely abetted by dumb luck. Still, Alger's name lives in the language as a synonym for virtue rewarded. And Alger himself, a novelist of admittedly modest abilities, has been eclipsed by his own name in the minds of the millions who have never read his work.

—Bruce A. Lohof

ALGREN, Nelson

Born: Nelson Ahlgren Abraham in Detroit, Michigan, 28 March 1909. **Education:** Schools in Chicago; University of Illinois, Urbana, 1928-31, B.S. in journalism 1931. **Military Service:** Served in the U.S. Army Medical Corps, 1942-45: private. **Family:** Married 1) Amanda Kontowicz in 1936 (divorced 1939); 2) Betty Ann Jones in 1965 (divorced 1967). **Career:** Worked as salesman, migratory worker, carnival shill, and part owner of a gas station, 1931-35; editor, Illinois Writers Project, WPA (Works Progress Administration), 1936-40; editor, with Jack Conroy, *New Anvil,* Chicago, 1939-41; worked for the Venereal Disease Program of the Chicago Board of Health, 1941-42; teacher of creative writing, University of Iowa, Iowa City, 1967, and University of Florida, Gainesville, 1974; columnist, Chicago *Free Press,* 1970. **Awards:** American Academy grant, 1947, and Award of Merit Medal, 1974; Newberry Library fellowship, 1947; National Book award, 1950; National Endowment for the Arts grant, 1976. **Died:** 9 May 1981.

PUBLICATIONS

Collection

The Texas Stories of Nelson Algren, edited by Bettina Drew. 1995.

Short Stories

The Neon Wilderness. 1946.
The Last Carousel. 1973.

Novels

Somebody in Boots. 1935; as *The Jungle,* 1957.
Never Come Morning. 1942.

The Man with the Golden Arm. 1949.
A Walk on the Wild Side. 1956.
Calhoun (in German), edited by Carl Weissner. 1980; as *The Devil's Stocking,* 1983.

Other

Chicago: City on the Make. 1951.
Who Lost an American? Being a Guide to the Seamier Sides of New York City, Inner London, Paris, Dublin, Barcelona, Seville, Almería, Istanbul, Crete and Chicago, Illinois. 1963.
Conversations with Algren, with H.E.F. Donohue. 1964.
Notes from a Sea-Diary: Hemingway All the Way. 1965.
America Eats, edited by David E. Schoonover. 1992.
Nonconformity: Writing on Writing, edited by Daniel Simon. 1996.

Editor, *Algren's Own Book of Lonesome Monsters.* 1962; as *Algren's Book of Lonesome Monsters,* 1964.

*

Bibliography: *Algren: A Checklist* by Kenneth G. McCollum, 1973; *Algren: A Descriptive Bibliography* by Matthew J. Bruccoli and Judith Baughman, 1985.

Critical Studies: *Algren* by Martha Heasley Cox and Wayne Chatterton, 1975; *Confronting the Horror: The Novels of Algren* by James R. Giles, 1989; *Algren: A Life on the Wild Side* by Bettina Drew, 1989; "Interview with Nelson Algren" by Bob Perlongo, in *Arizona Quarterly,* Spring 1989; "The Hustler: Nelson Algren's Neon Wilderness" by Rick Hornung, in *Village Voice Literary Supplement,* December 1990; "A Jew from East Jesus: The Yiddishkeit of Nelson Algren" by James A. Lewin, in *Midamerica: The Yearbook of the Society for the Study of Midwestern Literature,* 1994, pp. 122-31.

*   *   *

Four novels, some fifty short stories, numerous sketches, essays, poems, travel books, book reviews, and other literary criticism produced over a period of more than forty years assure Nelson Algren a place in American literature. Chicago, where Algren lived for much of his life, is the setting for most of his work. Characters, themes, symbols, and imagery, as well as the Chicago settings, recur throughout his canon as he becomes the spokesman for the derelicts, professional tramps, prostitutes, addicts, convicts, prize-fighters, and baseball players who inhabit his city jungle, "The Neon Wilderness," as he titled one of his collections of short stories. While most of Algren's characters speak the dialogue of the gutter, his style varies from staccato reporting to the rich passages that have gained him the title "the poet of the Chicago slums." His books contain much offbeat information revealed with satire, irony, humor, and farce.

His first novel, *Somebody in Boots,* is a "Depression novel," a chronicle of poverty and failure dedicated to "those innumerable thousands: the homeless boys of America." His second, *Never Come Morning,* is a story of rape and murder with a doomed Chicago Polish boxer as its hero. His best known work, however, is his third novel, *The Man with the Golden Arm,* which won him the first National Book Award. In this book, written two decades before drug addiction became a national dilemma, Algren fictional-ized the world of the drug addict with as yet unsurpassed authority and impact.

His last novel, *A Walk on the Wild Side,* the result of an attempt to rework *Somebody in Boots,* was Algren's favorite work as well as that of most of his later critics. Though Algren once maintained that no one understood *A Walk on the Wild Side*—a book, he said, of a kind never before written, "an American fantasy—a poem written to an American beat as truly as *Huckleberry Finn*"—the novel is now acclaimed for its prophetic qualities and for its influence on later novels and films such as *Midnight Cowboy* and *Easy Rider.*

—Martha Heasley Cox

ALLEN, James Lane

Born: Near Lexington, Kentucky, 21 December 1849. **Education:** Transylvania Academy, Lexington, 1866-68; Kentucky University (now Transylvania University), Lexington, 1868-72, 1875-77, B.A. (honors) 1872, M.A. 1887. **Career:** Teacher at a district school in Fort Springs, Kentucky, 1872-73, and at a high school in Richmond, Missouri, 1872-74; teacher at his own school in Lexington, Missouri, 1875; principal, Transylvania Academy, 1878-80; professor of Latin, Bethany College, West Virginia, 1880-83; opened and taught at a private school in Lexington, Kentucky, 1883-85; thereafter full-time writer; moved to New York, 1893; lived in Europe, 1894, 1900, 1909. **Awards:** M.A.: Bethany College, 1880. LL.D.: Kentucky University, 1898. **Died:** 18 February 1925.

PUBLICATIONS

Collections

A Kentucky Cardinal, Aftermath, and Other Selected Works, edited by William K. Bottorff. 1967.

Fiction

Flute and Violin and Other Kentucky Tales and Romances. 1891.
John Gray: A Kentucky Tale of the Olden Time. 1893.
Kentucky Cardinal. 1895.
Aftermath. 1896.
Summer in Arcady: A Tale of Nature. 1896.
The Choir Invisible. 1897; revised edition, 1898.
The Reign of Law: A Tale of the Kentucky Hemp Fields. 1900; as *The Increasing Purpose,* 1900.
The Mettle of the Pasture. 1903.
The Bride of the Mistletoe. 1909.
The Doctor's Christmas Eve. 1910.
The Heroine in Bronze; or, A Portrait of a Girl: A Pastoral of the City. 1912.
The Last Christmas Tree: An Idyll of Immortality. 1914.
The Sword of Youth. 1915.
A Cathedral Singer. 1916.
The Kentucky Warbler. 1918.
The Emblems of Fidelity: A Comedy in Letters. 1919.
The Alabaster Box (stories). 1923.
The Landmark (stories). 1925.

Other

The Blue-Grass Region of Kentucky and Other Kentucky Articles. 1892.
Chimney Corner Graduates. 1900.

*

Bibliography: in *Bibliography of American Literature* by Jacob Blanck, 1955.

Critical Studies: *Allen* by John Wilson Townsend, 1927; *Allen and the Genteel Tradition* by Grant C. Knight, 1935; *Allen* by William K. Bottorff, 1964; "From Romance to Realism: James Lane Allen's Revisions of A Kentucky Cardinal" by Lee Harding, in *Mississippi Quarterly,* Winter 1985-86; *James Lane Allen and the Politics of Desire: A Study of Summer in Arcady* (dissertation) by Amy Johnson, 1995; "Reconstructing Southern Manhood: Race, Sentimentality, and Camp in the Plantation Myth" by Caroline Gebbard, in *Haunted Bodies: Gender and Southern Texts* edited by Anne Goodwyn Jones and Susan V. Donaldson, 1997.

*   *   *

James Lane Allen was ideally suited to purveying the kind of story and novel demanded by the popular reading audience of the 1890s. Because of his evangelical religious orthodoxy, his innate Southern chivalry, and his readings in **Nathaniel Hawthorne, T.S. Eliot,** Thackeray, and Dickens, he demonstrated the rigorous moral control so often admired by conservative readers of the *fin de siecle.*

Although Allen wrote during an era of fiction that is generally regarded as realistic, he himself is remembered as a romantic local colorist under the influence of Wordsworth, **Henry David Thoreau,** and Audubon, who tended to idealize nature by pointing out the "spiritual sustenance" nature offers (William K. Bottorff.) Allen's settings were often part of the central Kentucky landscape he knew so well.

There are essentially four groups of works in the Allen canon (see H.A. Toulmin, Jr., *Social Historians*). The first group sprang naturally from the disposition of a local colorist: a distinctive, sympathetic treatment of Kentucky life (*Flute and Violin and Other Kentucky Tales* and *The Blue-Grass Region of Kentucky*). The second group shows a certain philosophical growth in its treatment of nature (*A Kentucky Cardinal* and *Aftermath*). The third group champions the doctrines of evolution and the consequences of circumstance (*Summer in Arcady, The Reign of Law,* and *The Mettle of the Pasture*). The fourth vein of Allen's writings is the historical problem novel (*The Choir Invisible*).

It is to *Flute and Violin and Other Kentucky Tales* that the avid Allen reader returns. Three distinct weaknesses, however, become apparent in this early collection—sentimentality, an excessively adorned style, and a puritanical point of view that weaves, as Grant C. Knight says, "allegories and symbols into the pattern of the narratives." The title story has enjoyed considerable popularity owing to its sentimental portrayal of the Reverend James Moore who communes on his flute with the fatherless waif David, who plays the violin. The influence of Dickens is marked.

A Kentucky Cardinal is a love story set against the beauties of the rural Kentucky landscape just outside Lexington. The hero, Adam Moss, may well be Allen's finest and most Thoreau-like character. *The Choir Invisible,* a poorly unified work, sought to create a gentleman "in buckskins." The novel, set in Kentucky in

1795, brings to mind Eliot and Thackeray in its morality, humor, and pathos.

Allen's work began a marked decline early in the twentieth century. *The Mettle of the Pasture* had a mixed critical reception. *The Bride of the Mistletoe* and *The Doctor's Christmas Eve* met with indifference and disapproval, and his later works are all but forgotten.

Readers and critics of the late twentieth century will find it difficult to agree with Edmund Gosse's opinion that Allen's was "A pen possessed of every accomplishment." The contemporary literary historian will agree, however, that Allen's writings constitute some of the best moments of American local color. Allen may be regarded as the supreme southern Victorian in his medievalism, in his moral and didactic inclination, in his desire to experiment, and in his eclecticism. As Bottorff notes, from Hawthorne Allen drew his psychology, morality, and complexity, from Thoreau he learned his transcendentalism, and from **Henry James** the complexity of his psychological probings.

—George C. Longest

ALLEN, Paula Gunn

Born: Cubero, New Mexico, 24 October 1939. **Education:** University of Oregon, Eugene, B.A. 1966, M.F.A. 1968; University of New Mexico, Albuquerque, Ph.D. in American Studies 1975. **Family:** Divorced; three children. **Career:** Teacher at San Francisco State University, 1975-76, University of New Mexico, 1977-78, Fort Lewis College, Durango, Colorado, 1978-79, and University of California, Berkeley, 1982-86. Beginning 1990 professor of literature University of California at Los Angeles. **Awards:** Creative writing award and fellowship, both National Endowment for the Arts, both 1977-78; Pushcart Poetry prize nominations, 1979 and 1981; research fellowship, Institute of the Americas-American Indian Center for Research, 1981-82; citation for contributions to San Francisco Native American community, San Francisco Board of Supervisors, 1983; National Research Council Senior Post Doctoral fellow for Minority Scholars, 1984-85; American Book award, Before Columbus Foundation, for *Spider Woman's Granddaughters: Traditional Tales and Contemporary Writing by Native American Women,* 1990; Susan Koppelman award, Popular and American Culture Associations, and Native American prize for Literature, both 1990.

PUBLICATIONS

Collection

Life Is a Fatal Disease: Selected Poems, 1962-1995. 1996.

Poetry

Wyrds. 1967.
The Blind Lion. 1974.
Coyote's Daylight Trip. 1978.
A Cannon Between My Knees. 1981.
Shadow Country. 1982.
Skin and Bones. 1988.

Fiction

The Woman Who Owned the Shadows. 1986.

Other

The Sacred Hoop: Recovering the Feminine in American Indian Traditions. 1986.
Grandmother of the Light: A Medicine Woman's Sourcebook. 1991.
As Long as the Rivers Flow: The Stories of Nine Native Americans, with Patricia Clark Smith. 1996.
On the Reservation: Reflections on Boundary-Busting Border-Crossing Loose Canons. 1998.

Editor, *From the Center: A Folio of Native American Art and Poetry.* 1981.
Editor, *Studies In American Indian Literature: Critical Essays and Course Designs.* 1983.
Editor, *Spider Woman's Granddaughters: Traditional Tales and Contemporary Writing by Native American Women.* 1990.
Editor, *The Voice of the Turtle: Twentieth-Century American Indian Fiction.* 1994.
Editor, *Song of the Turtle: American Indian Fiction, 1974-1994.* 1995.

*

Critical Studies: "Paula Gunn Allen (Laguna-Sioux-Lebanese)" by John R. Milton in his *Four Indian Poets,* 1974; "A Laddered, Rain-bearing Rug: Paula Gunn Allen's Poetry" by Elaine Jahner in *Women and Western Literature,* edited by Helen Winter Stauffer and Susan Rosowski, 1982; "Paula Gunn Allen and Joy Harjo: Closing the Distance between Personal and Mythic Space" by James Ruppert in *American Indian Quarterly,* vol. 7, no. 1, 1983; interview with Franchot Ballinger and Brian Swann in *MELUS* vol. 10, no. 2, Summer 1983; "The Journey Back to Female Roots: A Laguna Pueblo Model" by Annette Van Dyke in *Lesbian Texts and Contexts: Radical Revisions* edited by Karla Jay and Joanne Glasgow, 1990; "Curing Ceremonies: The Novels of Leslie Marmon Silko and Paula Gunn Allen" by Annette Van Dyke in *The Search for a Woman-Centered Spirituality,* 1992; *Memory, Narrative, and Identity: New Essays in Ethnic American Literatures,* 1994; *Feminist Readings of Native American Literature: Coming to Voice* by Kathleen M. Donovan, 1998; *Feminist Rhetorical Theories* by Karen A. Foss, 1999.

*   *   *

In the burgeoning field of contemporary Native American literature, Paula Gunn Allen is a foremost literary critic, scholar, writer, and educator. Her 1975 germinal essay, "The Sacred Hoop: A Contemporary Perspective," now part of her collected essays, *The Sacred Hoop: Recovering the Feminine in American Indian Traditions* (1986), was one of the first to speak to the ritual function of Native American literature as opposed to Euro-American literature. The belief in the power of the oral tradition now embodied in poetry or prose to promote healing, rebirth, transformatory magic, survival, and continuance underlies all of Allen's work.

Although Allen writes from a Laguna Pueblo perspective, she often refers to herself as a "multicultural event," citing her Laguna Pueblo/Sioux/Lebanese/Scotch-American heritage. She believes that if she is able to communicate with others, then everyone should be able to communicate. Allen refers to Laguna Pueblo culture as female-centered in that descent was matrilineal, the ownership of houses was held by women, and the major deities were female. Delineating the world view of this culture is a major focus of Allen's work as well as confronting the difficulty of reconciling that world view in contemporary society.

A scholar of Native American literature, Allen edited an important collection on teaching Native American literature, containing an extensive bibliography and course designs, *Studies in American Indian Literature* (1983). The focus of her work, however, has moved steadily into addressing the loss, destruction, and attempted recovery of a separate Native American women's ritual tradition and of Native American women's experiences. Allen's novel, *The Woman Who Owned the Shadows* (1986), is a ritual journey of the protagonist to recover the women-centeredness of her culture and to recover her own spiritual way as a medicine woman or ceremonial lesbian. Her 1981 essay, "Lesbians in American Cultures," published in *Conditions* and reworked for *The Sacred Hoop,* articulates her ideas about the roles of Native American lesbians in traditional cultures.

Allen's 1984 essay, "Who Is Your Mother: Red Roots of White Feminism," published in *Sinister Wisdom* and then in *The Sacred Hoop,* was a startling and brilliant articulation of Native American contributions to democracy and feminism. Elaborating on the roles and power of Native American women, it counters the idea that there never were societies in which women's power was equal to men's. An edited collection, *Spider Woman's Granddaughters: Traditional Tales and Contemporary Writing by Native American Women* (1989), is an attempt to correct the literary invisibility of Native American women. In *Grandmother of the Light: A Medicine Woman's Sourcebook* (1991), Allen becomes the storyteller herself, thus extending her interest in the ritual experience of women as exhibited in traditional tales.

Also well-known as a poet, Allen often explores in her poetry the plight of contemporary and traditional Native American women who have lost both the cultural respect ordinarily accorded to them as well as the mythic dimensions of women's relationships to the sacred as expressed in poetry. Allen's verse is finely detailed, resonating with a sense of place—urban, reservation, or interior. She employs varying structures and rhythms which come from her multicultural background of Pueblo corn dances, Catholic masses, and Arabic chanting. She cites the non-linear writing of **Gertrude Stein** as a major influence.

A focus of Allen's poetry is to articulate the sense that everything is infused with spirit but not necessarily controllable by humans. She writes of layers of shadows and civilizations, attempting to bridge these as poet, as someone from a multicultural heritage, and to respond to the world with all its variations. Her multicultural Native American perspective continues to enrich American literature and feminism.

—Annette Van Dyke

ALLISON, Dorothy

Born: Greenville, South Carolina, 11 April 1949. **Education:** Florida Presbyterian College (now Eckerd College), B.A. 1971;

New School for Social Research, M.A. **Family:** One son. **Career:** Writer. **Awards:** Lambda Literary awards, for *Trash*, 1989; National Book award finalist, for *Bastard out of Carolina*, 1992.

PUBLICATIONS

Novels

Bastard out of Carolina. 1992.
Cavedweller. 1998.

Short Stories

Trash. 1988.

Poetry

The Women Who Hate Me. 1983.
The Women Who Hate Me: Poetry, 1980-1990. 1991.

Other

Skin. 1993; as *Skin: Talking About Sex, Class, and Literature,* 1994.
Two or Three Things I Know for Sure. 1995.

*

Critical Studies: "White Trash in Your Face: The Literary Descent of Dorothy Allison" by David Reynolds, in *Appalachian Journal: A Regional Studies Review*, summer 1993, pp. 356-66; "Cultural Borders: Working-Class Literature's Challenge to the Canon" by Renny Christopher, in *The Canon in the Classroom: The Pedagogical Implications of Canon Revision in American Literature*, 1995; "We're as American as You Can Get" by Michael Rowe, in *Harvard Gay and Lesbian Review*, winter 1995, pp. 5-10; "Novelist out of Carolina: Dorothy Allison: A Profile" by E.J. Graff, in *Poets and Writers Magazine*, January/February 1995; "Nonfelicitous Space and Survivor Discourse: Reading the Incest Story in Southern Women's Fiction" by Minrose Gwin, in *Haunted Bodies: Gender and Southern Texts*, edited by Anne Goodwyn Jones, 1997; "Telling Stories of 'Queer White Trash': Race, Class, and Sexuality in the Work of Dorothy Allison, in *White Trash: Race and Class in America*, edited by Matt Wray and Annalee Newitz, 1997; *The Accessibility and Relevance of Feminist Theory to Working Class Women: The Writing of Dorothy Allison* by Laura Buddendeck, 1998.

*   *   *

Dorothy Allison is known for her treatment of the difficult subjects of child abuse, incest, and domestic violence in her work. Allison makes these subjects palatable with her writing style, which can be described as toughly lyrical. In an essay from *Skin: Talking About Sex, Class and Literature*, Allison says, "I have wanted everything as a writer and a woman, but most of all a world changed utterly by my revelations. . . . When I sit down to make my stories I know very well that I want to take the reader by the throat, break her heart, and heal it again."

Growing up in extreme poverty in the South, Allison's poetry and fiction draw upon her experiences of being white, female, les-

bian, and working class. Her collected poems in *The Women Who Hate Me: Poetry, 1980-1990* (1991) fearlessly dissect a world that mainstream culture does not want to see. With surprising and sardonic language, the poems often draw upon images of food in a riveting union of physical and emotional need.

At the heart of her work is the exploration of relationships between women, sometimes sexual, but always with an eye to survival in an oppressive environment. One can trace the development of this theme from the poems, through the short stories in *Trash* (1998) and the novels *Bastard Out of Carolina* (1992) and *Cavedweller* (1998). After *Trash* the subject of lesbianism becomes less prominent, but always there is the question of how women both support and fail each other. A major theme in *Bastard* is the exploration of why women do not protect their children from sexual and physical abuse and the legacy of this violence. In *Cavedweller* the mother Delia returns to Georgia to recover her daughters, whom she left while fleeing the violence of her husband years before. To complicate matters, she brings with her the child of her union with a rock star. Allison chooses tough survivors—the girls Bone in *Bastard* and Cissy in *Cavedweller*—as her protagonists. *Bastard* ends with Bone reflecting on her legacy as a Boatwright woman—a kind of unforgiving acceptance of the situation of women. However, *Cavedweller* shows more hope. Delia's efforts are not entirely in vain, and her daughters have more choices in their lives.

Allison's early work was published by small feminist presses, but her novels have been published by mainstream presses and have received a good deal of attention from reviewers. *Bastard Out of Carolina* was made into a television film in 1996, bringing the subjects of child sexual and physical abuse to a wide audience. Allison has also been a well-known speaker on these difficult topics.

Her collection of essays, *Skin: Talking About Sex, Class & Literature*, explores Allison's experiences as a lesbian feminist activist and her journey to becoming a writer. The controversial essay "Public Silence, Private Terror" details activities which resulted in her being branded as a sexual rebel during the height of the feminist sexual debates for defending pornography and sadomasochism. Allison contends that "not addressing the basic issues of sexual fear, stereotyping, and stigmatization reinforces the rage and terror we all hide, while maintaining the status quo in a new guise."

Two or Three Things I Know for Sure (1995) is a memoir of her family and the complicated legacy of love, strong self-sacrificing women, violence, woman-hating, and poverty that produced her and her sisters. In it the reader can find Allison struggling with the same themes that run through all her work—survival in difficult times—but this time complete with family photographs. The memoir brings the reader hope for the future, embodied in the birth of Allison's son, Wolf. As in her other work, Allison laces the difficult themes of her life and fiction with the idea that "telling the story all the way through is an act of love."

—Annette Van Dyke

ALURISTA

Born: Alberto H. Urista, Mexico City, Mexico, 8 August 1947; immigrated to the U.S. in 1961. **Education:** San Diego State University, B.A. in psychology 1970, M.A. 1979; University of California, San Diego, Ph.D. in Latin American literature 1983. **Family:** Married 1) Irene Mercado in 1969 (divorced 1976), two children; 2) Xelina Rojas in 1977, two children. **Career:** Worked as a counselor at Friendly Center, Orange, California, 1963-67; psychiatric childcare worker, San Diego Children's Home, San Diego, California, 1967-68; co-founder of MECHA (Movimiento Estudiantil Chicano de Aztlan), 1967, of Chicano studies department in 1968, of Chicano Studies Center in 1969, and Centro Cultural de la Raza in 1971, all at San Diego State University, San Diego, where he also served as a lecturer in Chicano studies, 1968-74, 1976-83; coordinator and instructor in Volunteers in Service to America (VISTA), San Diego, summer, 1970; teacher corps instructor in 1971-72; organized Festival Floricanto, an annual literary event, 1973-78; instructor in psychology at Southwestern Junior College, 1973-74; lecturer in Chicano studies at University of Texas at Austin, 1974-76; founded *Maize,* a literary magazine and publishing house, 1976; distinguished visiting lecturer, University of Nebraska, 1979; assistant professor of Spanish at Colorado College, Colorado Springs, 1983-86; associate professor, foreign language department, California State Polytechnic, San Luis Obispo, 1986-1992. Beginning 1992 professor, Chicano Studies, University of California, Santa Barbara. **Awards:** Ford Foundation fellowship, 1976; California Art Council creative writing award, 1978; McArthur Chair of Spanish, McArthur Foundation, 1984. **Member:** Association of Mexican American Educators, International Academy of Poets, National Association of Chicano Studies, Association of Mexican-American Educators, Movimiento Estudiantil Chicano de Aztlán, Toltecas en Aztlán.

PUBLICATIONS

Poetry

Floricanto en Aztlan (Flower-and-Song in Aztlán). 1971.
Nationchild Plumaroja 1969-1972 (Nationchild Redfeather). 1972.
Timespace Huracan: Poems, 1972-1975. 1976.
A'nque (Even Though). 1979.
Spik in Glyph? 1981.
Return: Poems Collected and New. 1982.
Tremble Purple: Seven Poems. 1986.
Z Eros. 1995.
Et Tu...Raza? 1996.

Plays

Dawn, in *El Grito.* 1974.

Other

Coleccion Tula Y Tonan: Textos Generativos (for children), nine vols. 1973.

Editor, *El Ombligo en Aztlan: An Anthology of Chicano Student Poetry.* 1971.
Editor, *Space Flute and Barrio Paths,* by Alex Kiraca. 1972.
Editor, *And Her Children Lived,* by Gloriamalia Flores. 1974.
Editor, *Rebozos of Love,* by Juanfelipe Herrera. 1974.
Editor, *Happy Songs and Bleeding Hearts,* by Lin Romero. 1974.
Editor, *No Flights Out Tonight,* Ricardo Teall. 1975.

Editor, *Get Your Tortillas Together,* by Carmen Tafolla, Cecilio Garcia-Camarillo, and Reyes Cardenas. 1976.
Editor, *Festival Flor y Canto I and II: An Anthology of Chicano Literature.* 1979.
Editor, *Viendo Morir a Teresa y Otros Relatos,* by Herberto Espinoza. 1983.
Editor, with Xelina Rojas-Urista, *Tales of El Huitlacoche,* by Gary D. Keller. 1984.
Editor, with Xelina Rojas-Urista, *Ojo de la Cueva,* by Cordelia Candelaria. 1985.
Editor, with Xelina Rojas-Urista, *Para Todos los Panes no Estan Todos Presentes,* by Ricardo Cobian. 1985.
Editor, with Xelina Rojas-Urista, *Daily in All the Small,* by L. J. Griep-Ruiz. 1985.
Editor, with Xelina Rojas-Urista, *Southwest Tales: A Contemporary Collection.* 1986.

*

Critical Studies: *Poesia Chicana: Alurista, el Mero Chingon* by Jesus Maldonado, 1971; "Alurista: Three Attitudes Toward Love in His Poetry" by Daniel Testa in *Revista Chicano-Riquena,* winter 1976; "El concepto del barrio en tres poetas chicanos: Abelardo, Alurista y Ricardo Sánchez" by Francisco Lomeli and Donaldo Urioste in *De Colores,* volume 3, 1977; "Chicano Indigenismo: Alurista and Miguel Mendez M." by Gustavo Segade in *Xalman,* Spring 1977; "The Literary Strategies Available to the Bilingual Writer" by Gary D. Keller in *The Identification and Analysis of Chicano Literature,* 1979; "Alurista's Poetics: the Oral, the Bilingual, the Pre-Columbian" by Tomás Ybarra-Frausto in *Modern Chicano Writers,* 1979; interview with Juan Bruce-Novoa in *Chicano Writers: Inquiry by Interview,* 1980; "The Teachings of Alurista: A Chicano Way of Knowledge" by Juan Bruce-Novoa in *Chicano Poetry: A Response to Chaos,* 1982; "In Search of Aztlán" by Luis Leal in *Denver Quarterly,* 1981; *Chicano Poetry: A Critical Introduction* by Cordelia Candelaria, 1986; interview with Wolfgang Binder in *Partial Autobiographies: Interviews with Twenty Chicano Poets,* 1985; "Alurista's Flight to Aztlán: A Study of Poetic Effectiveness" in *Missions in Conflict,* 1986; "La Poesie chicano: Entre terre et poussierre" by Yves-Charles Grandjeat in *Revue Francaise d'Etudes Americaines,* 1991; "Alurista et les hieroglyphes du bilinguisme" in *Multilinguisme et multiculturalisme en Amerique du Nord,* 1988, "The Vicissitudes of Aztlán" in *Confluencia,* spring 1990, "The Evolution of Bilingualism in the Poetry of Alurista" by Elyette Audouard-Labarthe in *Confluencia,* Spring 1992.

*   *   *

Alberto H. Urista, best known by his pen name Alurista, was one of the most influential figures in Chicano cultural activities during the late 1960s and 1970s. Critics often repeat Juan Bruce-Novoa's statement from *Chicano Authors: Inquiry by Interview:* "He is the poet laureate of Aztlán." His first publications coincided with the student demonstrations related to the civil rights struggle by and for people of Mexican descent residing in the United States in 1969. Stylistically, Alurista—along with Jose Montoya and Ricardo Sánchez—popularized the interlingual text. Interlingualism is a term coined by Bruce-Novoa in the early 1970s to differentiate this practice from bilingualism. In interlingualism two or more languages enter into a state of tension which produces yet another code, an "inter" possibility of language. Bilingualism implies moving from one language code to another, while "interlingualism" implies the constant tension of the two at once. Thematically, however, Alurista was unique as the main exponent of the concept of Aztlán, the Mexican Amerindian ideology of an ancient homeland to which the descendants of the pre-Columbian people of Mexico must return. This concept, more than the formal experimentation, has had a lasting influence on Chicano thought, becoming a key symbol interpreted and utilized repeatedly by intellectuals and artists, as well as becoming fixture of popular culture. Alurista epitomized the 1960s socially committed writer, participating in university student activism, organizing community events, and insisting that literature have an ideological purpose. He was a co-founder of the student organization MECHA (Movimiento Estudiantil Chicano de Aztlan), the Chicano studies department at San Diego State University, the Floricanto literary festivals of the mid-1970s, and, with his wife Xelina, of the literary magazine and publishing house *Maize.* He is still spoken of as one of the most significant writers of what is now considered a closed period of Chicano writing, that of the Chicano Movement.

Alurista was born in Mexico City and immigrated to the United States as an adolescent, arriving in San Diego, California, in 1961 at the start of the cultural upheaval this decade would represent. Two years later he began to work in social service agencies with a therapeutic orientation. Later, when he turned to student activism and literature, this tendency to see himself as a social therapist continued. As the youth of the country was "turning on and dropping out" in search of alternative lifestyles, Alurista was following suit, albeit in an ethnic style. Like many counterculture youths, he was inspired by César Chávez's United Farm Workers' strikes in the mid 1960s, and by Carlos Castaneda's Amerindian philosophy and the Beatles' search for an Eastern transcendental solution to alienation as well. By the decade's end, he was focusing his efforts on organizing his own version of counterculture, the Chicano movement, on the campus of San Diego State University.

Alurista's familiarity with Far Eastern thought, western existentialism, and pre-Columbian Mexican philosophy often surprises readers. His eclectic cosmopolitanism should be read in the dual context of U.S. 1960s counterculture and the Mexican mid-century historical revisionism. The counterculture was dominated by the search for non-Western lifestyles, including Buddhism, Transcendental meditation, and popular nativist self-improvement programs like Carlos Castaneda's *The Teaching of Don Juan: A Yaqui Way of Knowledge.* There also was a focus on consciousness-raising and the constant questioning of the value of human action reminiscent of existentialism. In Mexico, the 1950s had seen the publication of Octavio Paz's *The Labyrinth of Solitude,* a reformulation of Mexican culture and history in terms of archetypes that represent the mestizo blend of forces eternally at work in the culture. Paz concluded that Mexico was the archetype of the modern human condition: a nation alienated from its origins and adrift in a world of ambiguous values. He proposed to help Mexico define its identity in order to be able to move into the future. Paz recommended a return to the sacred origins of all humankind, myth. In the same years, Miquel León Portilla published his monumental *Aztec Thought and Culture: A Study of the Ancient Nahuatl Mind.* Besides giving a general description of a philosophy of cosmic balance, Leon Portilla highlighted the tlamantini tradition of the poet/priest responsible for the moral, political, and physical well-

being of his people. In this context, he also related the story of Tlacaelel, the adviser to the Aztec emperors, who ordered the burning of the Indian codices—a century before the Spanish arrived—that contained the Aztec's humble origins. He then commanded the writing of new ones to create the glorious past of their pilgrimage to central Mexico from a homeland named Aztlán.

In his search for cultural alternatives to the "America Dream," Alurista combines these sources. As Paz recommended, he turned to archetypal myth, finding it outlined in León Portilla's work. In the latter he also found the mandate to serve the people as teacher, poet and healer, as well as the justification for playing fast and loose with history: Tlacaelel, the ancient figure of the recreator of national-origin myths for ideological and cultural ends. Applying this lesson to Tlacaelel's myth of Aztlán, Alurista relocated the homeland in the U.S. Southwest, thus creating something like a Chicano Israel.

Alurista's first collection of poetry, and still his best known and most influential book, *Floricanto en Aztlán* ("Flower-and-Song in Aztlán"), synthesizes these elements in a fairly balanced mixture of Spanish and English. He rejects modern alienation in favor of a return to a mythical ancestoral ideal of a utopian homeland of cosmic harmony. He couches the struggle in terms drawn straight from Carlos Castaneda, whom he cites in this book as well as his second. Chicanos are told to face and overcome fear through a series of rites of passage in which they discover their historical and mythical origins and prove themselves worthy of enlightenment. These rituals take the form of a pilgrimage back to the homeland, Aztlán. Since he locates Aztlán in the United States, the pilgrimage constitutes a revolution against cultural and political imperialism. His second book, *Nationchild Plumarojo, 1969-1972* (Nationchild Redfeather, 1969-1972), continued in the same line, but with more political content related to the contemporary Chicano movement.

In his third collection, *Timespace Huracan: Poems, 1972-1975,* Alurista shifted to Spanish as the dominant language of the poems. The title is yet another borrowing from the pre-Columbian practice of combining two nouns to form a concept not contained in either word alone. He explained the triple meaning of the term in an interview with Bruce-Novoa: the historical or "collective time-space, one that describes reality as accorded by a consensus of people," a personal one "individual, psychological," and a mythological one "that unifies the personal and historical time-space." He wants his work to achieve this triple fusion in order that it function as a therapeutic ritual for his people, providing a cultural point of reference from which they can derive the sense of their identity. The collection, however, lacks the tight thematic flow of his first book, and the political rhetoric starts to wear thin.

A'nque/Alurista features experimentation in punning and transformations through phonetic similarities. Spanish dominates almost exclusively, and at time the verses run on into paragraphs of rambling, prose-like discourse. Reading becomes impossible for the monolingual English-language reader, and extremely difficult for the average Chicano. While the poems in *Spik in Glyph* feature much more English, the content moves towards a mainstream social commentary and away from the Aztlán-based thematics with which Alurista's readers were familiar.

Return: Poems Collected and New, an attempt to go back to his more accessible use of language, was followed by a chapbook, *Tremble Purple: Seven Poems.* The former has the feel of a retrospective overview with a few newly written additions that fail to establish a strong sense of direction in which the poet is developing. None of these efforts match the balance between form and message of the early work, nor the matching of that message with the public's interest.

By the 1990s critics began to talk of Alurista in the past tense. Already in the 1980s most of the criticism on his work was coming from European scholars, the American critics having turned to more recent trends in Chicano poetry. Yet, he is still considered one of the most important founders of contemporary Chicano poetry. Some of Alurista's manuscripts are stored at the Nettie Lee Benson Collection, Latin American Collection, University of Texas, Austin.

—Juan Bruce-Novoa

AMMONS, A(rchie) R(andolph)

Born: Whiteville, North Carolina, 18 February 1926. **Education:** Wake Forest College, North Carolina, B.S. 1949; University of California, Berkeley, 1951-52. **Military Service:** Served in the U.S. Naval Reserve, 1944-46. **Family:** Married Phyllis Plumbo in 1949; one son. **Career:** Principal, Hatteras Elementary School, North Carolina, 1949-50; executive vice-president, Freidrich and Dimmock, Inc., glass manufacturers, Millville, New Jersey, 1952-61; poetry editor, *Nation,* New York City, 1963; assistant professor, 1964-68, associate professor, 1968-71, professor of English, since 1971, and Goldwin Smith Professor of English, since 1973, Cornell University, Ithaca, New York. Visiting professor, Wake Forest University, 1974-75; American Academy of Arts and Sciences fellow; member of the Institute of Arts and Letters and Fellowship of Southern Writers. **Awards:** Bread Loaf Writers Conference scholarship, 1961; Guggenheim fellowship, 1966; American Academy of Arts and Letters traveling fellowship, 1967, and award, 1977; *Poetry* magazine Levinson prize, 1970; National Book award, 1973; Bollingen prize, 1973-74; MacArthur fellowship, 1981; National Book Critics Circle award, 1982; Pulitzer prize, for *Garbage,* 1993; National Institute of Arts and Letters award; Rebekah Johnson Bobbit National prize for poetry, 1994; Ruth Lilly Poetry prize, 1995. D.Litt.: Wake Forest University, 1972; University of North Carolina, Chapel Hill, 1973. **Member:** Institute of Arts and Letters. **Residence:** Ithaca, New York.

PUBLICATIONS

Poetry

Ommateum, with Doxology. 1955.
Expressions of Sea Level. 1964.
Corsons Inlet. 1965.
Tape for the Turn of the Year. 1965.
Northfield Poems. 1966.
Selected Poems. 1968.
Uplands. 1970.
Briefings: Poems Small and Easy. 1971.
Collected Poems 1951-1971. 1972.
Sphere: The Form of a Motion. 1974.
Diversifications. 1975.
The Snow Poems. 1977.
The Selected Poems 1951-1977. 1977.

Highgate Road. 1977.
For Doyle Fosco. 1977.
Six-Piece Suite. 1979.
Selected Longer Poems. 1980.
A Coast of Trees. 1981.
Worldly Hopes. 1982.
Lake Effect Country. 1983.
The Selected Poems: Expanded Edition. 1986.
Sumerian Vistas. 1987.
The Really Short Poems of A. R. Ammons. 1990.
Garbage. 1993.
The North Carolina Poems. 1994.
Fear. 1995.
Brick Road. 1996.

Other

Set in Motion: Essays and Interviews. 1996.

Editor, with David Lehman, *Best American Poetry.* 1994.

*

Bibliography: *Ammons: A Bibliography 1954-1979* by Stuart Wright, 1980.

Critical Studies: "Ammons Issue" of *Diacritics,* 1974; *Ammons* by Alan Holder, 1978; *A. R. Ammons* edited by Harold Bloom, 1986; *A.R. Ammons and the Poetics of Widening* by Steven P. Schneider, 1994; *Critical Essays on A.R. Ammons,* edited by Robert Kirschten, 1997; *Approaching Prayer: Ritual and the Shape of Myth in A.R. Ammons and James Dickey* by Robert Kirschten, 1998; *Complexities of Motion: New Essays on A.R. Ammons's Long Poems,* edited by Steven P. Schneider, 1999.

*   *   *

A.R. Ammons is one of the most prolific poets of his generation, amassing to date more than twenty books of verse that have won him the National Book Award in 1973, for his *Collected Poems 1951-1971,* and several other important prizes. The earliest poems, searching boldly for a center of self from which to project his persona, achieve their best effect from his recklessly strewn imagery and the pressure of his imagination to find the edges and furthest barriers of experience. The excellent *Selected Poems* of 1968, a winnowing of all the early work, dramatizes this search with varied, often profoundly moving language.

Ammons's attention ranges from intricately detailed portraits of the landscape of upper New York state, to travels throughout the southwestern United States, and memories of his childhood growing up on a farm in North Carolina, where he is fresh and original. His reminiscence of the partly mute woman who raised him as a child, "Nelly Myers," is a minor classic of the modern elegy, with its lilting rhythms and its quiet, loving tribute to her wisdom and imperfections.

Much of Ammons's poetry depends upon a texture of rapid, rambling speech that precipitates a poem within often lush formations. The edge of his poem is not silence but the banter and commentary in which it lies embedded. This pointedly risky strategy of creating a lyric can, when it is not in control, produce tracts and harangues that run on tediously. When inspired, however, the language gives way to a charged form of words partly submerged in the verbal undergrowth. His poems are like statues half perceived lying in high grass.

His verbal felicity has, however, occasioned more dry commentary than inspired lyricism. In an experiment with writing on adding machine tape, which imposed a narrow frame on the poet, Ammons wrote a seemingly endless discourse on the minutiae of his life during the winter of 1964-65, published as *Tape for the Turn of the Year.* As a professor teaching at Cornell University and living in Ithaca, New York, the persona lacks adventure and change, and the poet's journal suffers from the uneventful pace of his days. In succeeding volumes, *Northfield Poems* and *Uplands,* the style is noticeably more clipped and abrupt, approaching Imagist concision. The poet is clearly inspired by natural phenomena, particularly in the latter volume where his attention to mountain scenery is keenly alert. In *Briefings* he continues to experiment with short, sudden articulations of feeling and momentary perceptions. But in *Sphere* the style changes again into a long sequential discourse patterned by sections of four triplets where language is only partly sculpted. *The Snow Poems* returns to the mode of shorter poems and is a large collection devoted to the poet's favorite landscape, the snow-laden terrain of the northeast.

Ammons's three collections, *A Coast of Trees, Worldly Hopes,* and *Lake Effect Country,* resolve all the earlier conflicts between form and language in poems that vigorously foreground a key figure and draw from it the inferences of an inner life beyond materiality. The language is now more reflexive and paradoxical, but it is Ammons's genius to preserve the natural speech of conversation in these richer, more demanding explorations of experience. Notable here is a quality of somber reflection upon mortality, and upon the elusive but omnipresent spirit in ordinary things. Ammons, like **Robert Frost** before him, has insisted upon modest subjects and situations for his poetry, but his claims upon them reach to metaphysical conclusions.

Alice Fulton argues, as she reviews *The Selected Poems: Expanded Edition* for *Poetry* (January 1988), that Ammons's "canon forms an ongoing, multifarious sequence." She proclaims that his distinctive vocabulary, punctuation, and "dazzling turns of abstraction" often recall **Emily Dickinson** and declares that "as with Dickinson, you have to read a lot of him in order to say you've read him at all." *Selected Poems* may, according to Fulton, provide the best introduction to Ammons's work, who she thinks may be "most famous as nature's scribe and prophet," whose verses "illuminate the marginal," though his work is formally experimental. As such, Fulton writes that the collection reflects "an inexhaustible intelligence keeping language on the stretch."

The title of the collection *Sumerian Vistas* harkens back to Sumeria, the site of the development of writing, and the volume is dedicated in part to exploring the evolution and nature of writing. In reviewing *Sumerian Vistas* in he same issue of *Poetry* Fulton likens Ammons to the god Janus looking "backward to antiquity and forward to mortality, seeking 'plateaus of staying and view.'" The long poem, "The Ridge Farm," comprises the first fifty pages of the book and examines, exalts, and explores the landscape, the divine, and the nature of holiness, while considering the "relationship of fluency and form, the paradoxical holding to 'the rigid line of the free and easy' within free verse." The last part of the book contains, for Fulton, "many superb poems." In these pages, he offers poems which Fulton claims console us into "celebrations,"

so that we feel, in Ammons's words, "that here the plainnest / majesty gave us what it could."

The Really Short Poems of A.R. Ammons is a volume delivering what it promises: the poems are rarely longer than ten lines. Fred Muratori, reviewing the collection for *Library Journal* (1 April 1991), remarks that it is "perfect for those who claim no time for poetry, [it] can be savored in bits or in batches." This remark, however, belies the delight of these really short poems, culled from forty years of Ammons work, about which Steven Cramer in *Poetry* (November 1991) writes they "flicker into focus, exchanging minor mystification for minor enlightenment. They dawn on you."

Like *Tape for the Turn of the Year* and *Sphere, Garbage* is a book-length poem. Garbage itself is a metaphor as Muratori explains his *Library Journal* (August 1993) review. In the poems of *Garbage,* according to the critic, we are "shown that what decomposes recomposes, what's refused re-fuses into new compounds of thought and experience," as Ammons defines "the line 'where passion and control waver / for the field.'"

—Paul Christensen, updated by Lisa C. Harper

ANAYA, Rudolfo A(lfonso)

Born: Pastura, New Mexico, 30 October 1937. **Education:** Browning Business School, 1956-58; University of New Mexico, B.A. in English 1963, M.A. in English 1968, M.A. in guidance and counseling 1972. **Family:** Married Patricia Lawless in 1966. **Career:** Teacher in Albuquerque, New Mexico, 1963-70; director of counseling, University of Albuquerque, Albuquerque, New Mexico, 1972-74. Beginning 1974, professor, University of New Mexico, and since 1993 professor emeritus. Teacher at New Mexico Writers Workshop, summers, 1977-79; lecturer at Universidad Anahuac, Mexico City, Mexico, summer, 1974, and at other universities, including Yale University, University of Michigan, Michigan State University, University of California at Los Angeles, University of Indiana, and University of Texas at Houston; vice president, Coordinating Council of Literary Magazines, 1974-80; founder and first President, Rio Grande Writers Association. **Awards:** Premio Quinto Sol literary award, 1971; University of New Mexico Mesa Chicana literary award, 1977; City of Los Angeles award, 1977; New Mexico Governor's Public Service award, 1978, 1980; National Chicano Council on Higher Education fellowships, 1979, 1980; Before Columbus Foundation American Book award, 1980; New Mexico Governor's award for Excellence and Achievement in Literature, 1980; literature award, Delta Kappa Gamma (New Mexico chapter), 1981; Hispanic Caucus of Teachers of English award for Achievement in Chicano Literature, 1983; Kellogg Foundation fellowship, 1983-85; Mexican Consulate of Albuquerque, New Mexico, Mexican Medal of Friendship, 1986; PEN-West Fiction award, 1993, for *Albuquerque*; Erna S. Fergusson award for exceptional accomplishment, University of New Mexico Alumni Association, 1994; Art Achievement award, Hispanic Heritage Celebration, 1995; El Fuego Nuevo award, 1995. **Honorary Doctorates:** University of Albuquerque, Marycrest College, University of New England, California Lutheran University, College of Santa Fe, University of New Mexico, and University of New Hampshire. **Residence:** Albuquerque, New Mexico.

PUBLICATIONS

Collection

The Anaya Reader. 1995.

Novels

Bless Me, Ultima. 1972.
Heart of Aztlán. 1976.
Tortuga. 1979.
The Legend of La Llorona. 1984.
Lord of the Dawn: The Legend of Quetzacoatl. 1987.
Zia Summer. 1995.
Jalamanta, a Message from the Desert. 1996.
Rio Grande Fall. 1996.

Plays

The Season of Llorona (produced 1979).
Who Killed Don José (produced 1987).
The Faralitos of Christmas (produced 1987).
Ay, Compadre (produced 1995).
Rosa Linda (unproduced). N.d.

Screenplay: *Bilingualism: Promise for Tomorrow,* 1976.

Short stories

The Silence of the Llano. 1982.

Poetry

The Adventures of Juan Chicaspatas. 1985.

Other

A Chicano in China. 1986.
Flow of the River. 1988.
Albuquerque. 1992.
Man on Fire: Luis Jimenez=EL hombre en llamas, with others. 1994.
Descansos: An Interrupted Journey, with Estevan Arellano and Denise Chávez. 1997.

Editor, with Jim Fisher, *Voices from the Rio Grande.* 1976.
Editor, with Antonio Márquez, *Cuentos Chicanos: A Short Story Anthology.* 1980.
Editor, with Simon J. Ortiz, *A Ceremony of Brotherhood, 1680-1980.* 1981.
Editor, *Voces: An Anthology of Nuevo Mexicano Writers.* 1987.
Editor, with Francisco Lomelí, *Aztlán: Essays on the Chicano Homeland.* 1989.
Editor, *Tierra: Contemporary Fiction of New Mexico.* 1989.

Translator, *Cuentos: Tales from the Hispanic Southwest,* edited by José Griego y Maestas. 1980.

*

Bibliography: *Chicano Perspectives in Literature: A Critical and Annotated Bibliography* by Francisco A. Lomelí and Donaldo W. Urioste, 1976.

Critical Studies: *Chicano Authors: Inquiry by Interview* by John David Bruce-Novoa, 1980; "Coming of Age in Novels by Rudolfo Anaya and Sandra Cisneros" by Dianne Klein, in *The English-Journal,* September 1992.

*   *   *

Rudolfo Anaya's literary career dates from the 1972 publication of his novel *Bless Me, Ultima.* More than twenty five years later, his artistic production has grown to include other novels, collections of short stories, poetry, essays, and drama. Anaya's readership is among the largest of all Mexican American authors, and his early fiction has now become an integral part of the canon of Chicano literature. Indeed, some critics have called him the "Godfather of Chicano Literature." Along with Tomás Rivera's *And the Earth Did Not Part* (*Y no se lo tragó la tierra*) and Rolando Hinojosa's *Sketches of the Valley and Other Works* (*Estampas del valle y otras obras*), Anaya's *Bless Me, Ultima* was instrumental in establishing a Chicano narrative tradition. All three were published in the early 1970s, and each won the prestigious Premio Quinto Sol literary award. Common themes and motifs of these and subsequent Chicano texts include an attachment to and celebration of place in fiction (in the works cited above, California, Texas, and New Mexico, respectively), and a conscious effort to transcend cultural and ethnic difference and articulate a common vision of Mexican American experience.

Another facet of Chicano literature particularly important in the works of Anaya is the cultural role of the story and the storyteller. Anaya has self-consciously identified himself with the *cuentero*, or traditional storyteller, who shapes and maintains cultural values and customs through stories. In his fiction Anaya the author writes from the perspective of one who is paradoxically immersed in, yet separate from, cultural traditions. In his fiction Anaya often includes *cuentero* figures, whose stories of shared communal values guide the protagonists in their moral and personal development. These figures are especially important in Anaya's most significant literary contribution, his first three novels, which constitute the so-called New Mexico trilogy. In each, Anaya creates an elderly *cuentero*-like character who guides the youthful protagonist on his journey to maturity and experience.

Anaya's best-known and most critically acclaimed work, *Bless Me, Ultima*, depicts seven-year-old Antonio Márez's passage from childhood innocence to maturity under the tutelage of the elderly sage Ultima. Though the story is told in the first person by Antonio, readers quickly recognize that the narrator is removed in time and, consequently, perspective from the events of the narrative. This structure enables Antonio to offer mature and introspective observations beyond the wisdom of a seven-year-old. The action begins with the arrival of Ultima, a *curandera,* or spiritual guide, to the home of the Márez family. A series of formative transitions and challenges, especially Antonio's entrance into public school, lay the foundation for his eventual emotional and moral development. Other notable rites of passage include Antonio's questioning of his Catholic faith and his witnessing of two violent killings and the drowning death of a friend. Amid these childhood traumas Antonio finds stability and meaning in traditional folkways through his apprenticeship with the *curandera* Ultima. *Bless Me, Ultima* was immediately hailed as a success by critics, and it has resulted in a large body of critical work.

The second work of Anaya's New Mexico trilogy, *Heart of Aztlán* (1976), traces the physical and emotional consequences of the Chávez family's move from the rural community of Guadalupe to an Albuquerque, New Mexico, barrio. While the novel explores how the Chávez family adjusts to urban life, the work highlights the spiritual and personal development of the father, Clemente. Removed from his sacred land, Clemente descends into a physical and moral stupor. He is led from this state by Crispín, a *cuentero* who, with his guitar and traditional songs, inspires Clemente to reassume his position as family and community leader. Like *Bless Me, Ultima*, Anaya's second work makes extensive use of symbolism to establish and resolve thematic oppositions. But unlike his first novel, *Heart of Aztlan* is overtly political in its critique of both capitalism and religion: members of the barrio community are exploited by the railroad and the Catholic Church. Many critics—and even Anaya himself—have faulted the novel for its failure to integrate its political and social critique with the plot and symbolism that characterize the trilogy. The third work of the trilogy, *Tortuga* (1980), tells the story of a sixteen-year-old boy encased in a body cast and known only by the nickname Tortuga, or Turtle. (Anaya himself sustained a serious spinal injury in 1954 and spent almost a year convalescing.) Like Antonio in *Bless Me, Ultima*, Tortuga journeys towards maturity and experience with the help of *curandero* figures.

The novels of the New Mexico trilogy share similar structural, thematic, and symbolic elements. All manifest a strong presence of magic, myth, dreams, spirituality, and religion. These elements have led some critics to comment on Anaya's mythic worldview. Moreover, all posit a communion between humankind and nature. Thematic elements include a pronounced attachment to place, the importance of the journey from youthful innocence to maturity, and a focus on the individual's place within society and family. Structurally, the novels share similar plots and characters. Together, these elements have resulted in a favorable reception of the New Mexico trilogy by readers of different backgrounds, including a Chicano audience that feels a commonality in outlook and experience and a broader cross-cultural reading public, which finds his fiction mysterious yet remarkably captivating.

More recently Anaya has explored a range of different subjects, including mystery (*Zia Summer*, 1995; *Rio Grande Fall*, 1996), New Mexico politics and place (*Alburquerque*, 1992), and spiritual life (*Jalamanta*, 1996). Though he continues to set his novels in New Mexico, Anaya has moved away from many of the themes and symbols that dominated his early fiction. His reputation as one of the founders of Chicano literature now rests almost exclusively on the critical and popular success of his first novel, *Bless Me Ultima*.

—Wade Williams and Joseph Deters

ANDERSON, Maxwell

Born: Atlantic, Pennsylvania, 15 December 1888; grew up in North Dakota. **Education:** Jamestown High School, North Dakota, graduated 1908; University of North Dakota, Grand Forks, 1908-11, B.A. 1911; Stanford University, California, 1913-14, M.A. in English 1914. **Family:** Married 1) Margaret C. Haskett in 1911 (died, 1931), three sons; 2) Gertrude Anthony in 1933 (died 1953), one daughter; 3) Gilda Oakleaf in 1954. **Career:** Principal and English teacher, Minnewaukan High School, North Dakota, 1911-13; English teacher, Polytechnic High School, San Francisco, 1914-

17; professor and head of the English department, Whittier College, California, 1917-18; staff member, *New Republic* magazine, New York, 1918-19, New York *Evening Globe,* 1919-21, and New York *World,* 1921-24; founding co-editor, *Measure* magazine, New York, 1921-26; founder, with Robert E. Sherwood, Elmer Rice, S.N. Behrman, Sidney Howard, and John F. Wharton, Playwrights Company, 1938. **Awards:** Pulitzer prize, 1933; New York Drama Critics Circle award, 1936, 1937; American Academy Gold Medal, 1954. Litt.D.: Columbia University, New York, 1946; University of North Dakota, 1958. **Member:** American Academy, 1955. **Died:** 28 February 1959.

PUBLICATIONS

Collection

Dramatist in America: Letters 1912-1958, edited by Laurence G. Avery. 1977.

Plays

White Desert (produced 1923).
What Price Glory? with Laurence Stallings (produced 1924). In *Three American Plays,* 1926.
First Flight, with Laurence Stallings (produced 1925). In *Three American Plays,* 1926.
The Buccaneer, with Laurence Stallings (produced 1925). In *Three American Plays.* 1926.
The Feud. 1925.
Outside Looking In, from the novel *Beggars of Life* by Jim Tully (produced 1925). With *Gods of the Lightning,* 1928.
Forfeits (produced 1926).
Saturday's Children (produced 1927). 1927.
Gods of the Lightning, with Harold Hickerson (produced 1928). With *Outside Looking In,* 1928.
Gypsy (produced 1929). Shortened version in *The Best Plays of 1928-29,* edited by Burns Mantle, 1929.
Elizabeth the Queen (produced 1930). 1930.
Night over Taos (produced 1932). 1932.
Sea-Wife (produced 1932).
Both Your Houses (produced 1933). 1933.
Mary of Scotland (produced 1933). 1933.
Valley Forge (produced 1934). 1934.
Winterset (produced 1935). 1935.
The Masque of Kings (produced 1937). 1936.
The Wingless Victory (produced 1936). 1936.
High Tor (produced 1937). 1937.
The Feast of Ortolans (broadcast 1937; produced 1938). 1938.
The Star-Wagon (produced 1937). 1937.
Knickerbocker Holiday, music by Kurt Weill (produced 1938). 1938.
Key Largo (produced 1939). 1939.
Eleven Verse Plays 1929-1939. 1940.
Second Overture (produced 1940). 1940.
Journey to Jerusalem (produced 1940). 1940.
The Miracle of the Danube (broadcast 1941). In *The Free Company Presents,* edited by James Boyd, 1941.
Candle in the Wind (produced 1941). 1941.
The Eve of St. Mark (produced 1942). 1942; revised edition, 1943.
Your Navy, in This Is War! 1942.

Letter to Jackie, in *The Best One-Act Plays of 1943,* edited by Margaret Mayorga. 1944.

Storm Operation (produced 1944). 1944.

Joan of Lorraine (produced 1946). 1946.

Truckline Cafe (produced 1946).

Anne of the Thousand Days (produced 1948). 1948.

Joan of Arc (screenplay), with Andrew Solt. 1948.

Lost in the Stars, music by Kurt Weill, from the novel *Cry, The Beloved Country* by Alan Paton (produced 1949). 1950.

Barefoot in Athens (produced 1951). 1951.

Bad Seed, from the novel *The Bad Seed* by William March (produced 1954). 1955.

A Christmas Carol, music by Bernard Heermann, from the story by Charles Dickens (televised 1954). 1955.

The Masque of Pedagogues, in *North Dakota Quarterly.* Spring 1957.

The Day the Money Stopped, from the novel by Brendan Gill (produced 1958).

The Golden Six (produced 1958). 1961.

Richard and Anne: A Play in Two Acts. 1995.

Screenplays: *All Quiet on the Western Front,* with others, 1930; *Rain,* 1932; *We Live Again,* with others, 1934; *Death Takes a Holiday,* with Gladys Lehman and Walter Ferris, 1934; *So Red the Rose,* with Laurence Stallings and Edwin Justus Mayer, 1935; *Joan of Arc,* with Andrew Solt, 1948; *The Wrong Man,* with Angus MacPhail, 1957.

Radio Plays: *The Feast of Ortolans,* 1937; *The Bastion Saint-Gervais,* 1938; *The Miracle of the Danube,* 1941; *The Greeks Remember Marathon,* 1944.

Television Play: *A Christmas Carol,* 1954.

Fiction

Morning, Winter, and Night. 1952.

Poetry

You Who Have Dreams. 1925.

Notes on a Dream, edited by Laurence G. Avery. 1971.

Other

The Essence of Tragedy and Other Footnotes and Papers. 1939.

The Bases of Artistic Creation: Essays, with Rhys Carpenter and Roy Harris. 1942.

Off Broadway: Essays about the Theatre. 1947.

*

Bibliography: *A Catalogue of the Anderson Collection at the University of Texas* by Laurence G. Avery, 1968; *Anderson and S.N. Behrman: A Reference Guide* by William Klink, 1977; *Maxwell Anderson: An Annotated Bibliography of Primary and Secondary Works,* 1985.

Critical Studies: *Anderson, The Man and His Plays* by Barrett H. Clark, 1933; *Anderson: The Playwright as Prophet* by Mabel Driscoll Bailey, 1957; *Life among the Playwrights* by John F. Wharton, 1974; *Anderson,* 1976, and *The Life of Anderson,* 1983, both by Alfred S. Shivers; *Maxwell Anderson and the New York Stage* edited by Nancy J. Doran Hazelton and Kenneth Krauss, 1991; *Maxwell Anderson on the European Stage 1929-1992: A Production History and Annotated Bibliography of Source Materials in Foreign Translation* by Ron Engle, 1996; *Maxwell Anderson: A Research and Production Sourcebook* by Barbara Lee Horn, 1996.

*   *   *

Maxwell Anderson became a playwright by accident, but once committed to a career in the theater, he set out to base his work on carefully wrought principles of composition. His dramatic theories were based on the practices of ancient Greece and the Elizabethan period, and he was fiercely dedicated to the ideal of the theater as the democratic cultural institution. He reintroduced the idea of poetic tragedy and attracted large audiences to his historical verse plays, though there are few striking passages of poetry in his work.

For Anderson the theater was both a spiritual experience and a commercial medium. While he agreed with Aristotle that the audience should be led by the playwright to experience strong emotions, he was sure that the proper mark of success was ticket sales. He accepted the maxim that no playwright deserves or will get posthumous adulation who has not attracted an enthusiastic audience during his lifetime. He attacked the New York critics for short-circuiting the gleaning process with their first-night reviews, but was personally willing to accept the audience's spontaneous judgment. He rejected the notion of government subsidization because he thought it would interfere with the natural selection process and resisted the lure of off-Broadway production on the grounds that only the more rigorous Broadway circuit was an ample test. Anderson successfully countered the commercial forces of Broadway for more than a quarter of a century and dominated American theater in the 1930s.

Anderson believed in a theater of ideas. In an essay called "Keeping the Faith" he enunciated as rule number one the necessity of having a central idea or conviction that cannot be excised without killing the play. His *Joan of Lorraine* dramatizes the process of making concessions to the realities of play production while trying to protect the central core of the play's integrity. Though his convictions changed markedly during his career, his use of the stage to express them did not. He attacked big government, defended democracy, preached pacifism, and urged commitment to war. As his ideas about war, for instance, changed from the cynicism of *What Price Glory?* (written with Laurence Stallings) to the patriotic fervor of *The Eve of St. Mark* and *Storm Operation,* he presented each new certainty with as much strength as the one before.

Anderson's overriding theme is the spiritual victory of humanity. In his essay "Off Broadway" he defined theater as "a religious institution devoted entirely to the exaltation of the spirit of man." He tried through the disillusionment of the 1920s, the depression of the 1930s, and the global war of the 1940s to present the triumphant human spirit. He has been accused of being a pessimist, but his view is essentially that of an optimistic humanist. He emphasized the importance of individual choice and the necessity of commitment. King McCloud of *Key Largo,* for instance having failed to make a stand in the last days of the Spanish Civil War, finds it hard to stop running. His spirit triumphs only when he finds something for which he is willing to die. Mio of *Winterset,* emotionally crippled by lust for revenge, becomes a complete person only when he accepts love.

In many plays Anderson used the lives of historical characters to illumine broad questions of power and choice. He wrote plays about Christ, Socrates, Elizabeth I, Mary Stuart, George Washington, and Peter Stuyvesant. A comparison of *Elizabeth the Queen* with *The Masque of Kings* illustrates the major problem in Anderson's method of historical tragedy. He is able to delineate Elizabeth's choice to have her lover Essex beheaded as a triumph of wise government over personal weakness, but Rudolph's suicide will not fit into such a neat pattern. As a result the third act of *The Masque of Kings* takes a different direction from the one we might reasonably expect after the recognition scene of Act II, and the ending is weak and inappropriate.

The high seriousness of his subject matter is often a mistake. It is unfortunate that he did not leaven his work with comedy more often. In *High Tor* and *Knickerbocker Holiday* (music by Kurt Weill) he demonstrated a rich gift for humor. *Both Your Houses,* a play about Congressional corruption, makes excellent use of satire and was highly praised by critics.

Anderson's deficiencies as a playwright seem to be related to conflicts between his intellectual approach to form and his spontaneous ideas for content. He wanted to emphasize the primacy of individual choice, for instance, but Aristotelian tragedy, which he chose to emulate, best communicates the powerful forces that neutralize free will. He wanted to write plays constructed around a second act recognition scene followed by spiritual triumph in physical defeat, but some of the historical characters he chose do not fit this pattern. He wanted to show the triumph of the human spirit, but one of his most successful plays, *Bad Seed,* demonstrates the victory of congenital evil. He wanted to treat universal themes, but in plays such as *Gods of the Lightning* and *The Wingless Victory* he got bogged down in heavy social commentary.

Anderson has been criticized for lack of innovation, and that is a fair criticism. His approach and subject matter are quite traditional. Echoes of *Medea* are clear in the plot of *The Wingless Victory,* and the parallels between *Winterset* and *Romeo and Juliet* are obvious. His concern is less with striking out into new territories than with re-vitalizing the old. The actors in *Elizabeth the Queen* actually use Shakespeare's lines, for instance, but the effect is to illuminate the Queen's character and judgment.

Anderson was a prolific writer whose work attracted audiences and made money; by his own criteria he was a success. In comparison with his fellow writers in the American theater he must also be rated a success; only O'Neill outshone him in his time. Anderson did not always overcome the problems posed by his own methods, but he did illuminate the mazes of power, freedom, and faith he set out to explore. For over a quarter of a century, especially with works such as *Elizabeth the Queen, High Tor,* and *Winterset,* he dramatized the human condition in some striking scenes and created some high moments in American theater.

—Barbara M. Perkins

ANDERSON, Robert (Woodruff)

Born: New York City, 28 April 1917. **Education:** Phillips Exeter Academy, Exeter, New Hampshire, 1931-35; Harvard University, Cambridge, Massachusetts, 1935-42, A.B. (magna cum laude) 1939, M.A. 1940. **Military Service:** Served in the U.S. Naval Reserve, 1942-46: lieutenant; Bronze Star. **Family:** Married 1) Phyllis Stohl in 1940 (died 1956); 2) the actress Teresa Wright in 1959 (divorced 1978). **Career:** Apprentice, South Shore Players, Cohasset, Massachusetts, summers 1937 and 1938; assistant in English, Harvard University, 1939-42; teacher, Erskine School, Boston, 1941; teacher of playwriting, American Theatre Wing, New York, 1946-51, and Actors Studio, New York, 1955-56; member of the faculty, Salzburg Seminar in American Studies, 1968; writer-in-residence, University of North Carolina, Chapel Hill, 1969, and University of Iowa Writers Workshop, Iowa City, 1976. Member of the Playwrights Producing Company, 1953-60; president, New Dramatists Committee, 1955-56, and Dramatists Guild, 1971-73; member of the Board of Governors, American Playwrights Theatre, 1963-79. Since 1965 member of the Council, and since 1980 vice president, Authors League of America. **Awards:** National Theatre Conference prize, 1945; Rockefeller fellowship, 1946; Writers Guild of America award, for screenplay, 1970; inducted into the Theater Hall of Fame, 1980; William Inge award for lifetime achievement in theater, 1985; ACE award, for television, 1991; Last Frontier award, Valdez, Alaska, 1997. **Member:** Theater Hall of Fame, 1980. **Residence:** Roxbury, Connecticut 06783.

PUBLICATIONS

Plays

Hour Town, book, music and lyrics by Anderson (produced 1938).
Come Marching Home (produced 1945).
The Eden Rose (produced 1949).
Sketches in *Dance Me a Song* (produced 1950).
Love Revisited (produced 1951).
All Summer Long, adaptation of the novel *A Wreath and a Curse* by Donald Wetzel (produced 1952). 1955.
Tea and Sympathy (produced 1953). 1953.
Silent Night, Lonely Night (produced 1959). 1960.
The Days Between (produced 1965). 1965.
You Know I Can't Hear You When the Water's Running (produced 1967). 1967.
I Never Sang for My Father (produced 1967). 1968; screenplay published, 1970.
Solitaire/Double Solitaire (produced 1971). 1972.
Free and Clear (produced 1983).
The Last Act Is a Solo (televised 1991). 1991.

Screenplays: *Tea and Sympathy,* 1956; *Until They Sail,* 1957; *The Nun's Story,* 1959; *The Sand Pebbles,* 1966; *I Never Sang for My Father,* 1970.

Radio Plays: *David Copperfield, Oliver Twist, Vanity Fair, The Glass Menagerie, Trilby, The Old Lady Shows Her Medals, The Petrified Forest, The Scarlet Pimpernel, A Farewell to Arms, Summer and Smoke, Arrowsmith,* and other adaptations, 1946-52.

Television Plays: *The Patricia Neal Story,* 1980; *The Last Act Is a Solo,* 1991; *Absolute Strangers,* 1991.

Novels

After. New York, Random House, and London, Barrie and Jenkins, 1973.
Getting Up and Going Home. New York, Simon and Schuster, 1978.

Other

Elements of Literature (textbook anthology). New York, Holt Rinehart, 6 vols., 1988.

*

Bibliography: *The Apprenticeship of Robert Anderson* by David Ayers, unpublished dissertation, Columbus, Ohio State University, 1969.

Manuscript Collection: Harvard University Theatre Collection, Cambridge, Massachusetts.

Critical Studies: *Life among the Playwrights* by John F. Wharton, New York, Quadrangle, 1974; *Playwrights Talk about Playwriting* edited by Lewis Funke, Chicago, Dramatic Publishing Company, 1975; *Robert Anderson* by Thomas Adler, Boston, Twayne, 1978; "A Dramatist's Inner Space," in *Dramatists Guild Quarterly* (New York), spring 1979; *The Strands Entwined* by Samuel Bernstein, Boston, Northeastern University Press, 1980; *Represented by Audrey Wood* by Audrey Wood and Max Wilk, New York, Doubleday, 1981; *The Playwright's Art* edited by Jackson Bryer, New Brunswick, New Jersey, Rutgers University Press, 1995.

*   *   *

Although Robert Anderson's play riting career extended for almost thirty years, from the mid-1940s to the early 1970s, he will always be associated with that group of psychological realists from the 1950s—among them principally **William Inge**—who peopled the American stage with characters, usually married, in the throes of romantic problems, emotional disorders, and sexual tribulations. Perhaps responding to the suspicion and paranoia rampant during the McCarthy era, the subtext in these dramatists' well-made problem plays was often the victimized individual's quest for freedom in an overtly patriarchal society. They frequently espoused the need to develop a moral or ethical relativism as an antidote to a restrictive social or religious authority. What secures for Anderson a position of more than passing interest is his recurrent focus on gender stereotyping and sexual roles; though he never pursues the issue of difference and the sexual other as insistently as Inge (or **Tennessee Williams**, arguably the major dramatist from the period), Anderson adopts for himself an original and prescient point of view about his middle-aged males who are disillusioned because life has not turned out as planned. These characters are fearful of expressing their feelings, they sublimate their fear of tenderness in a brooding sexuality that leaves their wives emotionally starved and themselves even lonelier, and they dread the passage of time as well as their own mortality.

Anderson was introduced to New York, though not Broadway, audiences with *Come Marching Home* (1946), an Ibsenite play in which a returning war hero enters a political fray and, in the face of a complacent electorate, must decide between retreating from the public arena altogether or adopting a sometimes irksome role as a messianic figure always marching one step ahead of the benighted majority. After two other plays seen in summer stock—*The Eden Rose* (1948) and *Love Revisited* (1951)—he reached a wider audience at Washington's Arena Stage in 1953 with *All Summer Long*, a philosophically dark Chekhovian mood play about a young boy's rite of passage into adolescence, adapted from a novel

by Donald Wetzel. Later that same year, he finally arrived on Broadway with what deservedly remains his best-known work, *Tea and Sympathy*. Set in a New England boarding school, the play tells of an artistic and not outwardly manly eighteen-year-old whose sexuality is questioned by his homophobic father and by a housemaster who himself may be a latent homosexual. Unable to perform sexually when he visits the town prostitute in order to prove his masculinity, the young man attempts suicide, only to be restored to belief in his own heterosexuality when the housemaster's wife tenderly takes him to bed. If Anderson admittedly had in mind **Henry David Thoreau**'s notion of marching to "a different drummer," neither was he unaware of how any deviation from perceived norms of behavior became fodder for persecution during the witch hunt unleashed by the House Un-American Activities Committee hearings, led by Senator Joseph McCarthy.

Anderson's last play of the 1950s, *Silent Night, Lonely Night* (1959), features two people, each married to someone else, coming together in a brief encounter, a sentimentally religious sexual union on a holy night that is sanctioned by a higher morality in rebellion against an inhibiting puritanical set of absolute norms. It was followed several years later by *The Days Between* (1965), seen widely in campus and regional theaters, whose technical novelty resides in its being told from the viewpoint of a woman who has totally submerged her own identity in that of her alcoholic and angst-ridden husband, a failed writer-teacher who is still plagued by an adolescent romanticization of marriage. Anderson returned to Broadway in 1967, scoring his biggest commercial hit (760 performances, forty-eight more than *Tea and Sympathy*'s 712) with *You Know I Can't Hear You When the Water's Running*, an evening of four one-act plays that explore some favorite Anderson topics: how the myth of masculinity that demands that men keep their emotions restrained promotes a macho aggressiveness; how differing sexual needs within marriage threaten lasting communion between the partners; and how the subjective truths of memory can help blunt the ravages of time.

Anderson's last two plays are technically somewhat more adventurous. In his autobiographical play *I Never Sang for My Father* (1968) Anderson's guilt-ridden narrator lacerates himself for having failed to love adequately an impossibly demanding father. *Solitaire, Double Solitaire* (1971) is another evening of long one-acts. The first features a dystopian technocracy in which the only relief from loss of identity comes through hiring Call Families in state-sanctioned houses of illusion; the second—more consequential and probably Anderson's finest achievement after *Tea and Sympathy*—uses the structure of the medieval morality play artfully blended with multimedia effects to tell of three generations of relationships founded on differing attitudes toward the importance of rituals and vows, with the men remaining romantics long after their wives have given up such illusions.

Although Anderson also wrote screenplays, most notably *The Nun's Story* (1959), and novels, including the autobiographical *After* (1973), his plays about married sexuality map out his most individual terrain. In them he reiterates certain central motifs: the need to set aside traditional moral codes that prevent people from responding openly to the emotional wounds of others; the idealization of sexuality that, while countering mortality and terror of the void, might only serve to objectify the loved one; the tendency of fathers to confuse manliness with strength and thus not foster sensitivity in their sons; women's propensity to sublimate their own identity and fulfillment in the needs of another.

Anderson's sympathy for lonely people seeking solace, and his compassion for those who are willing, if need be, to set aside longstanding moral codes in order to answer unselfishly the human cry for help, lend to his works their particularly magnanimous tonal quality and link his moral outlook closely to that of both Inge and Williams.

—Thomas P. Adler

ANDERSON, Sherwood (Berton)

Born: Camden, Ohio, 13 September 1876. **Education:** High school in Clyde, Ohio; Wittenberg Academy, Springfield, Ohio, 1899-1900. **Military Service:** Served in the U.S. Army in Cuba during the Spanish-American War, 1898-99. **Family:** Married 1) Cornelia Pratt Lane in 1904 (divorced 1916), two sons and one daughter; 2) Tennessee Claflin Mitchell in 1916 (divorced 1924); 3) Elizabeth Prall in 1924 (separated 1929; divorced 1932); 4) Eleanor Copenhaver in 1933. **Career:** Worked in a produce warehouse in Chicago, 1896-97; advertising copywriter, Long-Critchfield Company, Chicago, 1900-05; president, United Factories Company, Cleveland, 1906, and Anderson Manufacturing Company, paint manufacturers, Elyria, Ohio, 1907-12; freelance copywriter, then full-time writer, Chicago, 1913-20; visited France and England, 1921; lived in New Orleans, 1923-24; settled on a farm near Marion, Virginia, 1925: publisher, *Smyth Country News* and Marion *Democrat* from 1927; traveled extensively in the United States in mid-1930s reporting on Depression life. **Member:** American Academy, 1937. **Died:** 8 March 1941.

PUBLICATIONS

Collections

Anderson Reader, edited by Paul Rosenfeld. 1947.
The Portable Anderson, edited by Horace Gregory. 1949; revised edition, 1972.
Short Stories, edited by Maxwell Geismar. 1962.

Short Stories

Winesburg, Ohio: A Group of Tales of Ohio Small Town Life. 1919; edited by John H. Ferres, 1966.
The Triumph of the Egg: A Book of Impressions from American Life in Tales and Poems. 1921.
Horses and Men. 1923.
Alice, and The Lost Novel. 1929.
Death in the Woods and Other Stories. 1933.
Certain Things Last: The Selected Short Stories, edited by Charles E. Modlin. 1992.
The Egg and Other Stories, edited by Charles E. Modlin. 1992.

Novels

Windy McPherson's Son. 1916; revised edition, 1922.
Marching Men. 1917; edited by Ray Lewis White, 1972.
Poor White. 1920.
Many Marriages. 1923; edited by Douglas G. Rogers, 1978.

Dark Laughter. 1925.
Beyond Desire. 1932.
Kit Brandon: A Portrait. 1936.

Plays

Winesburg (produced 1934). In *Winesburg and Others*, 1937.
Mother (produced ?). In *Winesburg and Others*, 1937.
Winesburg and Others (includes *The Triumph of the Egg*, dramatized by Raymond O'Neil; *Mother, They Married Later*). 1937.
Above Suspicion (broadcast 1941). In *The Free Company Presents*, edited by James Boyd, 1941.
Textiles, in *Anderson: The Writer at His Craft*, edited by Jack Salzman and others. 1979.

Radio Play: *Above Suspicion*, 1941.

Other

Mid-American Chants. 1918.
A Story Teller's Story. 1924; edited by Ray Lewis White, 1968.
The Modern Writer. 1925.
Notebook. 1926.
Tar: A Midwest Childhood. 1926; edited by Ray Lewis White, 1969.
A New Testament. 1927.
Hello Towns! 1929.
Nearer the Grass Roots. 1929.
The American County Fair. 1930.
Perhaps Women. 1931.
No Swank. 1934.
Puzzled America. 1935.
A Writer's Conception of Realism. 1939.
Home Town. 1940.
Memoirs. 1942; edited by Ray Lewis White, 1969.
Letters, edited by Howard Mumford Jones and Walter B. Rideout. 1953.
Return to Winesburg: Selections from Four Years of Writing for a Country Newspaper, edited by Ray Lewis White. 1967.
The Buck Fever Papers, edited by Welford Dunaway Taylor. 1971.
Anderson/Gertrude Stein: Correspondence and Personal Essays, edited by Ray Lewis White. 1972.
The Writer's Book, edited by Martha Mulroy Curry. 1975.
France and Anderson: Paris Notebook 1921, edited by Michael Fanning. 1976.
Anderson: The Writer at His Craft, edited by Jack Salzman and others. 1979.
Selected Letters, edited by Charles E. Modlin. 1984.
Letters to Bab: Anderson to Marietta D. Finley 1916-1933, edited by William A. Sutton. 1985.
The Diaries, 1936-41, edited by Hilbert H. Campbell. 1987.
Early Writings, edited by Ray Lewis White. 1989.
Love Letters to Eleanor Copenhauer Anderson, edited by Charles E. Modlin. 1989.
Secret Love Letters; for Eleanor, a Letter a Day, edited by Ray Lewis White. 1991.

*

Bibliography: *Anderson: A Bibliography* by Eugene P. Sheehy and Kenneth A. Lohf, 1960; *Merrill Checklist of Anderson*, 1969, and *Anderson: A Reference Guide,* 1977, both by Ray Lewis White; *Anderson: A Selective, Annotated Bibliography* by Douglas G. Rogers, 1976.

Critical Studies: *Anderson: His Life and Work* by James Schevill, 1951; *Anderson* by Irving Howe, 1951; *Anderson* by Brom Weber, 1964; *Anderson* by Rex Burbank, 1964; *The Achievement of Anderson: Essays in Criticism* edited by Ray Lewis White, 1966; *Anderson: An Introduction and Interpretation* by David D. Anderson, 1967, and *Anderson: Dimensions of His Literary Art,* 1976, and *Critical Essays on Anderson,* 1981, both edited by David D. Anderson; *The Road to Winesburg: A Mosaic of the Imaginative Life of Anderson* by William A. Sutton, 1972; *Anderson: A Collection of Critical Essays* edited by Walter B. Rideout, 1974; *Anderson: Centennial Studies* edited by Hilbert H. Campbell and Charles E. Modlin, 1976; *Anderson* by Welford Dunaway Taylor, 1977; *Anderson: A Biography* by Kim Townsend, 1987; *A Storyteller and a City: Anderson's Chicago* by Kenny J. William, 1988; *New Essays on Winesburg, Ohio* edited by John W. Crowly, 1990; "Sherwood Anderson Special Issue" edited by David D. Anderson, in *Old Northwest,* Winter 1991-92; *Sherwood Anderson and the American Short Story* by P.A. Abraham, 1994; *A Comparative Study of Sherwood Anderson and Ryunoskue Akutagawa: Their Concepts of the Grotesquerie* by Hiromi Tsuchiya, 1996.

*   *   *

In an interview for the *Paris Review* (Spring 1956), **William Faulkner** stated that Sherwood Anderson was "the father of my generation of American writers and the tradition of American writing which our successors will carry on." Anderson's importance in literary history is accurately summed up in Faulkner's statement, for Anderson is a seminal figure whose prose style has had a significant impact on the direction of American literature in the twentieth century. As a boy from a small town in Ohio Anderson fell under the spell of **Mark Twain**'s *Huckleberry Finn* with its innocent narrator and non-literary, vernacular style. Later, as an aspiring writer in Chicago and New York, he became fascinated with **Gertrude Stein**'s attempt to use language as a plastic medium, the way an artist uses paints. These influences on Anderson resulted in the development of a simple, concrete style close to the rhythms of American speech, a style that left an indelible imprint on the prose of Hemingway and his followers.

Anderson also developed a number of characteristically American themes in his fiction. The celebration of youth and innocence is one of those distinguishing features of American writing, and Anderson, raised in the Midwest before the turn of the century, celebrates small-town life in the days of the horse and buggy. A boy's wonder and innocent joy in rural life, his love of horses and the open countryside, and his admiration for the craftsmen of the village are all part of a nostalgic vein running through Anderson's writing. But Anderson, raised in poverty, was intimate with another side of American life, one that he eventually termed "grotesque." As a young man he observed the people of his town caught in a struggle for material wealth and cowed by a repressive Puritan ethic, and consequently wrote with great feeling about people like his parents whose lives were made wretched by their society's values. Anderson is very sensitive in his fiction to movement, to the restlessness of the individual and to the movements of peoples within the ever-changing fabric of society. He documents America's transition from a rural to an industrial society,

and in several books he represents Americans, working in factories, as trapped in a form of living death. He saw the great masses of working Americans as alienated from creative work, and he pondered the artist's role in reawakening his countrymen to more meaningful forms of life.

Anderson's influence and reputation, however, outweigh his actual achievement as a writer. He published seven novels, but critics do not agree that any one of the novels is wholly successful. The first, *Windy McPherson's Son,* which at the outset effectively recreates something of Anderson's own youth, particularly his relation to his father, becomes a rambling, incoherent narrative about a man's quest for a family and meaningful work. *Marching Men* is an ideological novel with a cranky and finally incoherent vision of men marching for the betterment of humankind. *Poor White,* which dramatizes the industrialization of America, is usually considered the best of the novels, but the charges of diffuseness and unnecessary repetition are not without some justification. Critics generally feel Anderson's worst novel is *Many Marriages,* the story of a man on the verge of giving up his business and family in order to escape what has become for him a living death. Anderson himself walked out on his family and a successful career in order to become a writer, which explains perhaps his own fondness for *Many Marriages.* The other novels, *Dark Laughter, Beyond Desire,* and *Kit Brandon* all contain interesting variations on the theme of the individual's quest for a more vital existence, but none of these books succeeds completely in terms of characterization and especially plot. More valuable and interesting are Anderson's autobiographical writings, *A Story Tellers Story, Tar: A Midwest Childhood,* and the posthumous *Memoirs,* all of which fictionalize to a degree the actual events of Anderson's life and reveal the contrary and powerful impulses of the writer's imagination.

Anderson's success as a fiction writer, however, is undisputed in the short story form, and all of the collections he published contain at least one or two first rate pieces. Stories such as "I Want to Know Why," "I'm a Fool," and "The Man Who Became a Woman" in which he employs an innocent narrator and a simple, direct style, have a unified purpose and effect that is lacking in all of the longer fictions. These are initiation stories wherein a youth, usually an innocent boy from the country who loves horses, is awakened to fear, sexual guilt, and a knowledge of his own limitations. "Death in the Woods" is another short masterpiece; it describes a peasant woman's work-burdened existence with a simplicity and sureness of craft that has made critics compare it with the best of Turgenev's stories.

But the book for which Anderson will always be best known is *Winesburg, Ohio,* a cycle of stories about lonely people in a small Midwestern town. Anderson originally titled it *The Book of the Grotesque,* and in these stories he portrays, with both compassion and clinical accuracy, the secret lives of people who have been irreparably thwarted and frustrated in different ways. The narrator explains by means of a dream vision that the characters have become grotesque because they have chosen to believe in a single truth. Whether they believe in love, virginity, or godliness, the truth becomes a lie because such a narrow view distorts reality and tragically cuts people off from each other. The grotesques, caught up in their obsessive beliefs, are unable to communicate their ideas and feelings to each other. For example, a farmer consumed with the idea of being a biblical patriarch so confuses and terrifies his only grandson in a ritual of sacrifice that the boy runs away forever. A young man, obsessed with the idea that he is "queer," hopelessly different from other people, breaks into a frantic dance and physically strikes out at his one sympathetic listener. A shy woman, who has waited many years for the return of her lover, one night in desperation runs naked across her front lawn in the rain. Appearing in several stories is the young newspaper reporter, George Willard, to whom some of the grotesques tell their stories. George's mother, one of the aliens of the town, finds an ultimate release from her frustration and loneliness through death, but before she dies she prays that some day her son will "express something" for them both, that he will redeem their lives through art. The mother gives the book a tragic cast, for her prayer cannot be answered. The artists in Winesburg, Ohio, are ineffectual figures, often persons the least capable of expressing themselves. George Willard at the end of the book leaves Winesburg and we can assume he has written the stories we have read, but he has not been able to "save" his people because the underlying insight in his book is that each man lives by a truth and no one can fully understand or express that truth for someone else.

Anderson once described himself as "the minor author of a minor masterpiece," and one recognizes here an author's startlingly accurate self-assessment. But what Anderson's statement does not comprehend is the powerful influence he had on writers like **Ernest Hemingway** and Faulkner and on the course of American literature as a whole.

—David Stouck

See the essay on *Winesburg, Ohio.*

ANGELOU, Maya

Born: Marguerita Johnson in St. Louis, Missouri, 4 April 1928. **Education:** Attended public schools in Arkansas and California; studied dance with Martha Graham, Pearl Primus, and Ann Halprin; studied drama with Frank Silvera and Gene Frankel. **Family:** Married 1) Tosh Angelos (divorced); 2) Paul Du Feu in 1973 (divorced 1981); one son. **Career:** Dancer and actress, touring Europe and Africa in *Porgy and Bess,* 1954-55; appeared in Off-Broadway plays *Calypso Heatwave,* 1957, *The Blacks,* 1960, and *Cabaret for Freedom,* 1960; northern coordinator of Martin Luther King Jr.'s Southern Leadership Conference, 1959-60; associate editor, *Arab Observer,* Cairo, Egypt, 1962-63; assistant administrator, School of Music and Drama, University of Ghana, 1963-66; writer, *Ghanian Times,* Accra, 1963-65, and Ghanian Broadcasting Corporation, 1963-65; feature editor, *African Review,* Accra, 1965-66; returned to the United States and continued acting and writing careers, appearing in productions of *Medea,* 1966, *Look Away,* 1973, and in the television miniseries *Roots,* 1977; directed film *All Day Long,* 1974, and plays *And Still I Rise,* 1976, and *Moon on a Rainbow Shawl,* 1988; Reynolds Professor of American Studies, Wake Forest University, Winston- Salem, North Carolina, since 1981. Lecturer, University of California at Los Angeles, 1966; writer-in-residence, University of Kansas, 1970; visiting professor, Wake Forest University, Wichita State University, and California State University, all 1974; member, American Revolution Bicentennial Council, 1975-76, and National Commission on the Observance of International Women's Year. **Awards:** National Book Award nomination, 1970; Yale University fellowship, 1970; Pulitzer Prize nomination, 1972; Tony Award nomination, 1973; Rockefeller Foundation scholarship, 1975; Emmy Award nomination, 1977; named one of the top hundred most influential women by *Ladies Home Journal,* 1983; North Carolina Literature award, 1987; Woman of the Year, *Essence* magazine, 1992; Distinguished Women North Carolina, 1992; Horatio Alger award, 1992; Grammy award, best spoken word album, for *On the Pulse of the Morning,* 1994. Honorary degrees: Smith College, 1975; Mills College, 1975; Lawrence University, 1976. **Residence:** California.

PUBLICATIONS

Collection

The Complete Collected Poems of Maya Angelou. 1994.

Prose (autobiography)

I Know Why the Caged Bird Sings. 1970.
Gather Together in My Name. 1974.
Singin' and Swingin' and Gettin' Merry Like Christmas. 1976.
The Heart of a Woman. 1981.
All God's Children Need Traveling Shoes. 1986.
Even the Stars Look Lonesome. 1997.

Plays

Cabaret for Freedom, with Godfrey Cambridge (produced 1960).
The Least of These (produced 1966).
And Still I Rise (produced 1976).

Television Plays: *Blacks, Blues, Black,* 1968; *I Know Why the Caged Bird Sings,* 1979; *Sister, Sister,* 1982.

Screenplays: *Georgia, Georgia,* 1972; *All Day Long,* 1974.

Poetry

The True Believers, with Abbey Lincoln. N.d.
Just Give Me a Cool Drink of Water 'fore I Diiie. 1971.
Oh Pray My Wings Are Gonna Fit Me Well. 1975.
And Still I Rise. 1978.
Shaker, Why Don't You Sing. 1983.
Poems. 4 vols., 1986.
Now Sheba Sings the Song. 1987.
I Shall Not Be Moved. 1990.
Life Doesn't Frighten Me (for children). 1993.
On the Pulse of Morning. 1993.
Soul Looks Back in Wonder (for children). 1994.
Phenomenal Woman: Four Poems Celebrating Women. 1994.

Recordings: *The Poetry of Maya Angelou,* 1969; *On the Pulse of Morning.*

Other

All Day Long (short stories). N.d.
Mrs. Flowers: A Moment of Friendship (fiction). 1986.
Conversations with Maya Angelou. 1988.
Lessons in Living. 1993.
Wouldn't Take Nothin' for My Journey Now. 1994.

A Brave and Startling Truth. 1995.
Kofi and His Magic (for children). 1996.

*

Critical Studies: *Black Women Writers (1950-1980): A Critical Evaluation* edited by Mari Evans, 1984; *Afro-American Writers after 1955: Dramatists and Prose Writers* edited by Thadius M. Davis and Trudier Harris, 1985; *Studies in African and American Culture* edited by James L. Hill, 1990; *Southern Women Writers: The New Generation* edited by Tonette Bond Inge, 1990; *Heart of a Woman, Mind of a Writer, and Soul of a Poet: A Critical Analysis of the Writings of Maya Angelou* by Lyman B. Hagen, 1997; "Maya Angelou" in *Women Writers at Work: The Paris Review Interviews,* edited by George Plimpton, 1998; *Maya Angelou: A Critical Companion,* 1998; *Maya Angelou* by Terrasita A. Cuffie, 1999; *Maya Angelou* by Pamela Loos, 1999.

*   *   *

By the time she was in her early twenties, Maya Angelou had been a Creole cook, a streetcar conductor, a cocktail waitress, a dancer, a madam, and an unwed mother. The following decades saw her emerge as a successful singer, actress, and playwright, a lecturer and civil rights activist, and a popular author of four collections of poetry and five autobiographies. Lynn Z. Bloom in *Dictionary of Literary Biography* wrote that Angelou "is forever impelled by the restlessness for change and new realms to conquer that is the essence of the creative artist, and of exemplary American lives, white and black."

Angelou is hailed as one of the great voices of contemporary black literature and as a remarkable Renaissance woman. She began producing books after some notable friends, including author **James Baldwin**, heard Angelou's stories of her childhood spent shuttling between rural, segregated Stamps, Arkansas, where her devout grandmother ran a general store, and St. Louis, Missouri, where her worldly, glamorous mother lived. *I Know Why the Caged Bird Sings,* a chronicle of her life up to age sixteen (and ending with the birth of her son Guy) was published in 1970 with great critical and commercial success. Although many of the stories in the book are grim, as in the author's revelation that she was raped at age eight by her mother's boyfriend, the volume also recounts the self-awakening of the young Angelou. "Her genius as a writer is her ability to recapture the texture of the way of life in the texture of its idioms, its idiosyncratic vocabulary and especially in its process of image-making," reports Sidonie Ann Smith in *Southern Humanities Review.* "The imagery holds the reality, giving it immediacy. That [the author] chooses to recreate the past in its own sounds suggests to the reader that she accepts the past and recognizes its beauty and its ugliness, its assets and its liabilities, its strengths and its weaknesses. Here we witness a return to the final acceptance of the past in the return to and full acceptance of its language, the language a symbolic construct of a way of life. Ultimately Maya Angelou's style testifies to her reaffirmation of self-acceptance, [which] she achieves within the pattern of the autobiography."

Her next two volumes of autobiography, *Gather Together in My Name* and *Singin' and Swingin' and Gettin' Merry Like Christmas,* take Angelou from her late adolescence, when she flirted briefly with prostitution and drug addiction, to her early adulthood as she established a reputation as a performer among the avant-garde of the early 1950s. Not as commercially successful as *I Know Why the Caged Bird Sings,* the two books were guardedly praised by some critics. Lynn Sukenick, for example, remarks in *Village Voice* that *Gather Together in My Name* is "sculpted, concise, rich with flavor and surprises, exuding a natural confidence and command." Sukenick adds, however, that one fault lies "in the tone of the book . . . . [The author's] refusal to let her earlier self get off easy, and the self-mockery which is her means to honesty, finally becomes in itself a glossing over; although her laughter at herself is witty, intelligent, and a good preventative against maudlin confession, . . . it eventually becomes a tic and a substitute for a deeper look." Annie Gottlieb has another view of *Gather Together in My Name.* In her *New York Times Book Review* article, Gottlieb states that Angelou "writes like a song, and like the truth. The wisdom, rue and humor of her storytelling are borne on a lilting rhythm completely her own, the product of a born writer's senses nourished on black church singing and preaching, soft mother talk and salty street talk, and on literature."

The year 1981 brought the publication of *The Heart of a Woman,* a book that "covers one of the most exciting periods in recent African and Afro-American history," according to Adam David Miller in *Black Scholar.* Miller refers to the era of civil rights marches, the emergence of Martin Luther King, Jr., and Malcolm X, and the upheaval in Africa following the assassination of the Congolese statesman Patrice Lumumba. The 1960s see Angelou active in civil rights both in America and abroad; at the same time she enters into a romance with African activist Vusumzi Make, which dissolves when he cannot accept her independence or even promise fidelity. In a *Dictionary of Literary Biography* piece on Angelou, Lynn Z. Bloom considers *The Heart of a Woman* the author's best work since *I Know Why the Caged Bird Sings:* "Her enlarged focus and clear vision transcend the particulars and give this book a fascinating universality of perspective and psychological depth that almost matches the quality of [Angelou's first volume] . . . . Its motifs are commitment and betrayal."

Washington Post Book World critic David Levering Lewis also sees a universal message in *The Heart of a Woman.* "Angelou has rearranged, edited, and pointed up her coming of age and going abroad in the world with such just-rightness of timing and inner truthfulness that each of her books is a continuing autobiography of Afro-America. Her ability to shatter the opaque prisms of race and class between reader and subject is her special gift," he says. To Bloom, "it is clear from [this series of autobiographies] that Angelou is in the process of becoming a self-created Everywoman. In a literature and a culture where there are many fewer exemplary lives of women than of men, black or white, Angelou's autobiographical self, as it matures through successive volumes, is gradually assuming that exemplary stature."

In her fifth autobiographical work, *All God's Children Need Traveling Shoes,* Angelou describes her four-year stay in Ghana, "just as that African country had won its independence from European colonials," according to Barbara T. Christian in the *Chicago Tribune Book World.* Christian indicates that Angelou's "sojourn in Africa strengthens her bonds to her ancestral home even as she concretely experiences her distinctiveness as an Afro-American."

All God's Children Need Traveling Shoes has also received praise from reviewers. Wanda Coleman in the *Los Angeles Times Book Review* calls it "a thoroughly enjoyable segment from the life of a celebrity," while Christian describes it as "a thoughtful yet spirited account of one Afro-American woman's journey into the land of her ancestors." In Coleman's opinion, *All God's Children Need Traveling Shoes* is "an important document drawing more much needed attention to the hidden history of a people both African and American."

"As [Angelou] adds successive volumes to her life story," writes Bloom, "she is performing for contemporary black American women—and men, too—many of the same functions that escaped slave **Frederick Douglass** performed for his nineteenth-century peers through his autobiographical writings and lectures. Both became articulators of the nature and validity of a collective heritage as they interpret the particulars of a culture for a wide audience of whites as well as blacks . . . . As people who have lived varied and vigorous lives, they embody the quintessential experiences of their race and culture."

In addition to her autobiographical works, Angelou has also authored plays, screenplays, and fiction, and she continues to be a prolific poet. The 1990 volume *I Shall Not Be Moved* is Angelou's fifth collection of poetry, and the title for the book is drawn from the poem "Our Grandmothers," in which an elderly woman refuses to be moved from her "heartfelt stand," as Jacqueline Gropman writes in the *School Library Journal.* Angelou "is able to command our ear," declares Gloria T. Hull in *Belles Lettres.* "As I listen, what I hear in her open, colloquial poems is racial wit and earthy wisdom, honest black female pain and strength, humor, passion, and rhetorical force." Other themes include "loss of love and youth, human oneness in diversity, the strength of blacks in the face of racism and adversity," notes a reviewer in *Publishers Weekly. Library Journal* contributor Lenard D. Moore judges the poems to be "highly controlled and yet powerful," using language that is "precise and filled with imagery." Gropman concludes that the poems in *I Shall Not Be Moved* "possess the drama of the storyteller and the imagery and soul of the poet."

In 1993 Angelou published *On the Pulse of Morning,* the poem she delivered at the inauguration of U.S. President Bill Clinton. As with much of her other writing, *On the Pulse of Morning* continues Angelou's attempt to speak to diverse audience, here invoking the unity of a broad range of Americans. The breadth of such a topic illustrates Angelou's ability to consider a larger literary panorama, while her series of autobiographical works continue to express the particulars of African American experience through the details of her own compelling life.

—Denise Wiloch

ANZALDÚA, Gloria

Born: Jesus Maria of the Valley in South Texas, 26 September 1942. **Education:** Pan-American University, Edinburg, Texas, B.A. 1973; University of Texas at Austin, M.A. 1973; University of California at Santa Cruz. **Career:** Taught high school English and migrant, adult, and bilingual programs in Texas. Has taught creative writing, women's studies, Chicano studies at University of Texas at Austin, Vermont College of Norwich University, San Francisco State University, and University of California at Santa Cruz. Writer-in-residence at the Loft in Minneapolis, Minnesota; artist-in-residence at Pomona College, California. Contributing editor of *Sinister Wisdom.* Has given lectures, workshops, and appeared on panels throughout the United States, Canada, and Mexico. **Awards:** MacDowell Artist Colony fellowship, 1982; Before Columbus

Foundation American Book award, 1986; National Endowment of the Arts award for fiction, 1991; Astraea National Lesbian Action Foundation Lesbian Writers Fund Sappho award of Distinction, 1992. **Residence:** Santa Cruz, California.

PUBLICATIONS

Poetry

Borderlands—La Frontera: The New Mestiza (English and Spanish). 1987.

Other

Prietita Has a Friend—Prietita Tiene un Amigo (for children). 1991.
Lloronas, Women Who Howel: Autohistorias-Teorias and the Production of Writing, Knowledge and Identity. San Francisco, California Aunt Lute, c. 1994.
Prietita and the Ghost Woman (for children). 1995.

Editor, with Cherríe Moraga, *This Bridge Called My Back: Writings by Radical Women of Color.* 1981.
Editor, *Making Face, Making Soul—Hacienda Caras: Creative and Critical Perspectives by Feminists of Color.* 1990.

Recording: *This Bridge Called My Back: Writings by Women of Color,* 1983.

*

Critical Studies: "Reading Along the Dyke" by Valerie Mine in *Out/Look,* spring 1988; "Interview with Gloria Anzaldúa" by Eleanor J. Bader in *Matrix,* May 1988; "Borderlands: Transformation at the Crossroads" by Maya Valverde in *Woman of Power,* summer 1988; "Conversations at the Book Fair: Interview with Gloria Anzaldúa" by Suzanne de Lotbiniere-Harwood in *Trivia: A Journal of Ideas,* spring 1989; "On the Borderlands with Gloria Anzaldúa," in *Off Our Backs,* July 1991; "Gloria Anzaldúa" by Hector A. Torres in *Chicano Writers, Second Series,* edited by Carl R. Shirley and Francisco A. Lomeli, 1992; *American Women Writers,* Volume 5: *From Colonial Times to the Present; A Critical Reference Guide,* edited by Carol H. Green and Mary G. Mason, 1993; *Women Reading, Women Writing: Self-Invention in Paula Gunn Allen, Gloria Anzaldúa, and Audre Lorde* by AnaLouise Keating, 1996.

*   *   *

"Yo soy Patlache" ("I am Patlache") is how Gloria Anzaldúa introduced herself at a reading in Santa Cruz, California, in April 1993. Patlache is a *Nahuatl* (Native American) word for, as Anzaldúa said, "people like her"—lesbian. The word also connotes her identity as a mestiza, a woman of mixed European and Native American ancestry (in Anzaldúa's case, a mixture of Indian, Spanish, and Mexican). Anzaldúa has most commonly described herself as a Chicana-Tejana—that is, a Mexican living in Texas. These multiple identities permeate Anzaldúa's prose and poetry.

In her essay "La Prieta," Anzaldúa writes of her early life in Hargill, a Mexican community on the Rio Grande River in South

Texas. She was 15 years old when her father died and the family was reduced to poverty, wearing flour-sack clothing and working in the fields. Despite or perhaps because of her hard life, after learning English at age nine, Anzaldúa filled her life with stories. At night under the bed covers she read books voraciously and, because this was forbidden, told endless stories to her sister to keep her quiet. Consequently, Anzaldúa has done her best writing at night.

After her education, Anzaldúa moved from Texas (the first of her family in six generations to do so) and taught and wrote in Vermont and San Francisco. The move to San Francisco in the 1970s was pivotal for Anzaldúa. There she encountered other female writers of color, such as Cherríe Moraga, another Chicana looking at issues of identity in her writing. Feeling excluded by the white feminist writers' movement, Anzaldúa and Moraga spoke together of the need to expand the concept of feminism to encompass all women. In this vein, they coedited an anthology of writings by women of color entitled *This Bridge Called My Back: Writings by Radical Women of Color* (1981), first published by Persephone Press. *This Bridge Called My Back,* which included poetry, essays, and stories, has been immensely important to feminists and women of color. It sold widely, was translated into Spanish, won the 1986 Before Columbus Foundation American Book Award, and is used in university classrooms around the world. One section in *This Bridge Called My Back,* entitled "Between the Lines: On Culture, Class and Homophobia," contains prose and poetry by lesbians of color, many of whom were unknown to the reading public.

Continuing the ideas set out in *This Bridge Called My Back,* Anzaldua published a second anthology, *Making Face, Making Soul—Hacienda Caras: Creative and Critical Perspectives by Feminists of Color"* (1990). Works in *Making Face, Making Soul,* Anzaldua wrote, "confront the racism in the White Women's movement in a more thorough, personal, direct, empirical and theoretical way." *Making Face, Making Soul* gives voice to many writers unheard by the dominant white community.

Between the two anthologies, Anzaldúa published *Borderlands, La Frontera: The New Mestiza* (1987), which brought together many of her own writings for the first time. With essays on the nature of the mestiza, histories of Mexicans living on the U.S. border, stories and poems about her childhood, her family, and her lesbianism, and ancient myths and songs, *Borderlands* reaches out to all who live on the borders of race, class, sexuality, and culture. Playing with the idea of borders, Anzaldúa skillfully interweaves styles (essays, stories, poems) and languages (Spanish and English).

Since the publication of *Borderlands,* many scholars have commented upon and critiqued Anzaldúa's concept of the mestiza or mestizaje (mestiza-ness). AnaLouise Keating states that Anzaldúa "writes her own version of feminine mestizaje, inventing new metaphors (in Shamanism) that affirm the cultural specificities of her own heritage and open transcultural connections." Yvonne Yarbro-Bejarano describes the essays in *Borderlands* as a "serpentine movement through different kinds of mestizaje that produce a third thing that is neither this nor that but something else: the blending of Spanish, Indian, and African to produce the mestiza, of Spanish and English to produce Chicano language, of male and female to produce the queer, of mind and body to produce the animal soul, the writing that 'makes face.'"

In "Putting Coyolxauhqui Together: A Creative Process," her intriguing new essay on her "writing habits, rituals, and emotional upheavals," Anzaldúa uses the Nahuatl word *Nepantla* for "the space in between" where "you tap the inner stream of consciousness." *Nepantla* is the "symbol for the transitional process, both conscious and unconscious, that ... moves from rational to visionary states, from logistics to poetics, from focused to unfocused perception, from inner world to outer."

In the late 1990s Anzaldúa was working on a third anthology exploring the impact of *This Bridge Called My Back* both on individual readers and in feminist/queer/ethnic studies and theory. Anzaldúa has continued to use her writing to move herself along her autobiographical journey from Texas to California, from farmworker to academic/writer/theorist.

—Jacquelyn Marie

ARTHUR, Timothy Shay

Born: Near Newburgh, New York, 6 June 1809; moved with his family to Baltimore, 1817. **Education:** Public schools in Baltimore. **Family:** Married Eliza Alden in 1836; five sons and two daughters. **Career:** Apprentice, possibly for a tailor, then clerk in a counting room, Baltimore, 1830-33; western agent, Susquehanna Bridge and Banking Company, Baltimore, 1833; member of the editorial staff of various Baltimore journals, including *Athenaeum,* 1833-36, and *Saturday Visiter,* 1837-40; coeditor, Baltimore *Literary Monument,* 1836-39; editor, *Baltimore Merchant,* 1840; moved to Philadelphia, 1841, and became writer for *Saturday Courier, Graham's Magazine,* and *Godey's Lady's Book;* founder, *Arthur's Ladies' Magazine,* 1845; founder and publisher, *Arthur's Home Gazette Weekly* (*Arthur's Home Magazine* monthly, from 1853), 1850-85; publisher, *Children's Hour,* 1867-74, *Workingman,* 1869, and *Once a Month,* 1869-70. Wrote for children as Uncle Herbert. Member of the Executive Committee, Centennial Exhibition, Philadelphia, 1876. **Died:** 6 March 1885.

PUBLICATIONS

Fiction

Insubordination: An American Story of Real Life. 1841.
The Widow Morrison. 1841; as *Mary Ellis; or, The Runaway Match,* with Alice Mellville; or, *The Indiscretion,* 1850.
Tired of Housekeeping. 1842.
Six Nights with the Washingtonians (stories). 1842; revised edition, as *The Tavern-Keeper's Victims,* 1860.
The Ladies' Fair. 1843.
The Story Book. 1843.
Bell Martin; or, The Heiress. 1843; revised edition, 1849.
Fanny Dale; or, The First Year after Marriage. 1843.
The Tailor's Apprentice: A Story of Cruelty and Oppression. 1843.
The Little Pilgrims: A Sequel to The Tailor's Apprentice. 1843.
Madeline; or, A Daughter's Love, and Other Tales. 1843.
Making a Sensation and Other Tales. 1843.
The Ruined Family and Other Tales. 1843; as *Temperance Tales,* 1843.
Swearing Off and Other Tales. 1843.
The Seamstress. 1843.
The Stolen Wife. 1843.

Sweethearts and Wives; or, Before and after Marriage. 1843.
The Two Merchants. 1843.
The Village Doctors and Other Tales. 1843.
Cecilia Howard; or, The Young Lady Who Had Finished Her Education. 1844.
Pride or Principle—Which Makes the Lady? 1844.
Family Pride; or, The Palace and the Poor House. 1844.
Hints and Helps for the Home Circle; or, The Mother's Friend. 1844.
Hiram Elwood, The Banker; or, Like Father Like Son. 1844.
The Martyr Wife. 1844.
Prose Fictions Written for the Illustration of True Principles. 1844.
The Ruined Gamester; or, Two Eras in My Life. 1844.
The Two Sisters; or, Life's Changes. 1844.
Alice; or, The Victim of One Indiscretion. 1844.
The Maiden. 1845.
The Wife. 1845.
Anna Milnor, The Young Lady Who Was Not Punctual, and Other Tales. 1845.
The Heiress. 1845.
The Club Room and Other Temperance Tales. 1845.
Married and Single; or, Marriage and Celibacy Contrasted. 1845.
Lovers and Husbands. 1845.
Tales from Real Life. 1845.
The Two Husbands and Other Tales. 1845.
The Mother. 1846.
Random Recollections of an Old Doctor. 1846.
The Beautiful Widow. 1847.
Improving Stories for the Young. 1847.
Keeping Up Appearances. 1847.
Riches Have Wings. 1847.
The Young Lady at Home. 1847.
The Young Music Teacher and Other Tales. 1847.
Agnes; or, The Possessed: A Revelation of Mesmerism. 1848.
Debtor and Creditor. 1848.
The Lost Children. 1848.
Retiring from Business; or, The Rich Man's Error. 1848.
Love in a Cottage. 1848.
Rising in the World. 1848.
Stories for My Young Friends [Parents, Young Housekeepers]. 3 vols., 1848-51.
Temptations. 1848.
Lucy Sanford: A Story of the Heart. 1848.
Making Haste to Be Rich. 1848.
The Three Eras of a Woman's Life (includes The Maiden, The Wife, The Mother). 1848.
Love in High Life. 1849.
Mary Moreton; or, The Broken Promise. 1849.
Sketches of Life and Character. 1849.
Our Children: How Shall We Save Them? 1849.
All for the Best; or, The Old Peppermint Man. 1850.
The Debtor's Daughter. 1850.
The Divorced Wife. 1850.
Golden Grains from Life's Harvest Field. 1850.
Illustrated Temperance Tales. 1850; revised edition, as *The Lights and Shadows of Real Life,* 1851.
The Orphan Children. 1850.
Pride and Prudence; or, The Married Sisters. 1850.
Tales of Domestic Life. 1850.
True Riches and Other Tales. 1850.
The Two Brides. 1850.

The Young Artist; or, The Dream of Italy. 1850.
The Two Wives. 1851.
The Banker's Wife. 1851.
Lessons in Life for All Who Will Read Them. 1851.
Off-Hand Sketches. 1851.
Seed-Time and Harvest (stories). 1851.
The Way to Prosper; or, In Union There Is Strength and Other Tales. 1851.
Woman's Trials (stories). 1851.
Words for the Wise (stories). 1851.
Home Scenes and Home Influence. 1852.
The Tried and the Tempted. 1852.
Cedardale. 1852.
Pierre the Organ-Boy and Other Stories. 1852.
The Poor Wood-Cutter and Other Stories. 1852.
Jessie Hampton. 1852.
Uncle Ben's New-Year's Gift. 1852.
The Ways of Providence (stories). 1852.
Confessions of a Housekeeper. 1852; revised edition, as *Trials and Confessions of an American Housekeeper,* 1854; as *Ups and Downs,* 1857.
Who Are Happiest? and Other Stories. 1852.
Who Is Greatest? and Other Stories. 1852.
Haven't-Time and Don't-Be-in-a-Hurry and Other Stories. 1852.
The Last Penny and Other Stories. 1852.
Maggy's Baby and Other Stories. 1852.
The Wounded Boy and Other Stories. 1852.
Married Life: Its Shadows and Sunshine (stories). 1852.
The Lost Children and Other Stories. 1852.
Trials of a Needlewoman. 1853.
Before and After the Election; or, The Political Experiences of Mr. Patrick Murphy. 1853.
Finger Posts on the Way of Life. 1853.
The Fireside Angel. 1853.
Heart-Histories and Life-Pictures. 1853.
The Bar-Rooms at Brantley. 1877.
The Mill and the Tavern. 1878.
The Strike at Tivoh Mills and What Came of It. 1879.
Window Curtains. 1880.
Saved as by Fire. 1881.
Death-Dealing Gold. 1890.
The Little Savoyard and Other Stories. 1891.
Two Little Girls and What They Did. 1899.
Won by Waiting. n.d.

Other

The Young Wife's Book. 1836.
Hints and Helps for the Home Circle; or, The Mother's Friend. 1844.
A Christmas Box for the Sons and Daughters of Temperance. 1847.
Advice to Young Men [Ladies] on Their Duties and Conduct in Life. 2 vols., 1847.
Wreaths of Friendship: A Gift for the Young, with Francis Channing Woodworth. 1849.
A Wheat Sheaf Gathered from Our Own Field, with Francis Channing Woodworth. 1851.
Our Little Harry and Other Poems and Stories. 1852.
The History of Georgia, Kentucky, Virginia, New Jersey, New York, Ohio, Vermont, Connecticut, Pennsylvania, Tennessee, Illinois, with W.H. Carpenter. 11 vols., 1852-57.

The String of Pearls for Boys and Girls, with Francis Channing
    Woodworth. 1853.
Steps Towards Heaven (sermons). 1858.
Growler's Income Tax. 1864.
Talks with a Philosopher on the Ways of God and Man. 1871.
Strong Drink: The Curse and the Cure. 1877; as *Grappling with
    the Monster,* 1877.
Feet and Wings; or, Among the Beasts and Birds. 1880.
Adventures by Sea and Land. 1890.
Sow Well and Reap Well: A Book for the Young. n.d.
Story Sermons. n.d.
Talks with a Child on the Beatitudes. n.d.

Editor, with W.H. Carpenter, *The Baltimore Book.* 1838.
Editor, *The Sons of Temperance Offering.* 2 vols., 1849-50.
Editor, *The Brilliant: A Gift-Book.* 1850.
Editor, *The Crystal Fount for All Seasons.* 1850.
Editor, *The Temperance Gift.* 1854.
Editor, *The Temperance Offering.* 1854.
Editor, *Friends and Neighbors; or, Two Ways of Living in the
    World.* 1856.
Editor, *The Mother's Rule.* 1856.
Editor, *Our Homes.* 1856.
Editor, *The True Path and How to Walk Therein.* 1856.
Editor, *The Wedding Guest.* 1856.
Editor, *Words of Cheer for the Tempted, The Toiling, and the Sor-
    rowing.* 1856.
Editor, *Orange Blossoms.* 1857.
Editor, *Little Gems from the Children's Hour.* 1875.
Editor, *The Prattler.* 1876.
Editor, *The My Book.* 1877.
Editor, *The Budget.* 1877.
Editor, *My Pet Book.* 1877.
Editor, *My Primer.* 1877.
Editor, *The Playmate.* 1878.
Editor, *The Boys' and Girls' Treasury.* 1879.
Editor, *Pleasant Stories and Pictures.* 1880.
Editor, *Lucy Grey and Other Stories.* 1880.
Editor, *Sophy and Prince.* 1881.
Editor, *Uncle Herbert's Speaker.* 1886.
Editor, *Friendship's Token.* n.d.

*

Critical Studies: *T.S. Arthur: His Life and Works by One Who
Knows Him,* 1873; "Methods of T.S. Arthur" by D.L. Milliken
in *Writer,* October 1887; "Timothy Shay Arthur: Pioneer Business Novelist" by Warren French in *American Quarterly,* Spring
1958; "The Women's Press Goes for a Soldier: A Study in Propaganda, Patriotism and Public Image" by Kathleen L. Endres in *Civil
War History,* March 1984; *Marketplace Romances: Elusive Ambitions in the Fiction of T.S. Arthur, Edgar Allan Poe, and Nathaniel
Hawthorne* (dissertation) by Francis Timothy Ruppel, 1997.

*   *   *

Timothy Shay Arthur is likely to be recalled as the author of
Ten Nights in a Bar-Room, the popular melodrama about a small-
town miller turned saloon-keeper who brings misfortune upon his
family and community until the killing of his daughter by drunken
brawlers saves him and the town for temperance (which to Arthur

meant total prohibition). Actually he did not write the play, which
was one of the most often performed on the American stage during the late nineteenth century and which still survives, though
now it is usually burlesqued; the dramatization was prepared by
William W. Pratt from Arthur's novel. Nor did Arthur devote himself before the Civil War exclusively to the temperance cause, although he enjoyed his first success with *Six Nights with the Washingtonians,* tales about the work of this noble band that sought to
redeem drunkards through "moral suasion." After gaining experience as a contributor to literary magazines and then as co-editor
of several short-lived publications in Baltimore from 1834 to 1840,
he moved to Philadelphia, where, after several earlier experiments
in finding the profitable format for a journal devoted to "the good,
the true, and the beautiful," he founded in 1853 *Arthur's Home
Magazine,* which he edited until his death.

During these years he wrote about a hundred novels and un-
counted short stories, most of which appeared first either in his
magazines or in the many gift-books that he edited. Before the
Civil War, the majority of these tales were thinly fictionalized
guides to young people getting married and setting up a home and
business. *Three Eras of a Woman's Life* was only the most ambitious of about two dozen that advised maiden, wife, and mother
on the woman's proper "sphere" and duties. *Debtor and Creditor*
was one of many that warned against unsound business practices;
but Arthur was also one of the first American novelists, even before the age of the Robber Barons, to condemn unscrupulous business practices growing out of a greed for gain in an unexpectedly
bleak and cynical novel like *Nothing But Money.* Arthur was also
a member of the Church of the New Jerusalem, as the followers
of Emmanuel Swedenborg called themselves; he expounded the doctrines of the church in novels like *The Good Time Coming,* an
attempt to dissuade egotistical people from reckless courses. He
also, surprisingly, pioneered in fiction dealing with divorce—then
a scandalous subject. The *Hand But Not the Heart, After the Storm,*
and *Out in the World* castigate hasty marriage and easy divorce,
but grant that legal separation may be necessitated by a spouse's
philandering or intemperance.

After the Civil War left him disheartened about his fellow Americans, he devoted his fiction largely to the temperance crusade,
growing through *Three Years in a Man-Trap, Woman to the Rescue,* and *The Bar-Rooms at Brantley,* constantly more hysterical
in his denunciation of the evils of drink and shriller in his demands
for legal prohibition rather than a reliance upon self-reform. These
works in print or on the stage, however, failed to enjoy the success of his earlier writings.

—Warren French

ASHBERY, John (Lawrence)

Born: Rochester, New York, 28 July 1927. **Education:** Deerfield
Academy, Massachusetts; Harvard University, Cambridge, Mas-
sachusetts (member of the editorial board, *Harvard Advocate*),
A.B. in English 1949; Columbia University, New York, M.A. in
English 1951; New York University, 1957-58. **Career:** Copy-
writer, Oxford University Press, New York, 1951-54, and
McGraw-Hill Book Company, New York, 1954-55; co-editor, *One
Fourteen,* New York, 1952-53; art critic, European edition of New
York *Herald Tribune,* Paris, 1960-65, and *Art International,*

Lugano, Switzerland, 1961-64; editor, *Locus Solus* magazine, Lans-en-Vercors, France, 1960-62; editor, *Art and Literature,* Paris, 1963-66; Paris correspondent, 1964-65, and executive editor, 1965-72, *Art News,* New York City; professor of English, 1974-1980, and Distinguished Professor, 1980-1990, Brooklyn College; poetry editor, *Partisan Review,* New Brunswick, New Jersey, 1976-80; art critic, *New York* magazine, 1978-80, and *Newsweek,* New York, 1980-1985; Charles Eliot Norton Professor of Poetry, Harvard University, 1989-1990. Beginning 1990, Charles P. Stevenson Professor of Languages and Literature, Bard College. **Awards:** Fulbright fellowship to France, 1955, 1956; Yale Series of Younger Poets prize, 1956; Poets' Foundation grant, 1960, 1964; Ingram Merrill Foundation grant, 1962, 1972; *Poetry* magazine Harriet Monroe Poetry award, 1963, 1975; Union League Civic and Arts Foundation prize, 1966; Guggenheim fellowship, 1967, 1973; National Endowment for the Arts grant, 1968, 1969; American Academy award, 1969; Shelley Memorial award, 1973; Modern Poetry Association Frank O'Hara prize, 1974; National Book Critics Circle award, 1976; Pulitzer prize, 1976; National Book award, 1976; Rockefeller grant for playwriting, 1978; English Speaking Union prize, 1979; Mayor's award, New York City, 1983; Bard College Charles Flint Kellogg Award, 1983; Academy of American Poets fellowship, 1983; *American Poetry Review* Jerome J. Shestack Poetry award, 1984; Yale University Bollingen prize in poetry, 1984; *Nation* Lenore Marshall poetry prize, 1985; Wallace Stevens Fellow, Yale University, 1985; McArthur Foundation Fellow, 1985-1990; Modern Language Association Common Wealth award in literature, 1986; Brandeis University Creative Arts award, 1989; Ruth Lilly Poetry prize, *Poetry* magazine, 1992; awards from the Modern Poetry Association and American Council for Arts, 1992; Robert Frost medal, Poetry Society of America, 1995; Grand prize, Biennales International Poetry, Belgium, 1996. D.Litt.: Long Island University, Southampton, New York, 1979. **Member:** American Academy and Institute of Arts and Letters; American Academy of Arts and Sciences; chancellor of Academy of American Poets. **Residence:** New York City.

PUBLICATIONS

Collection

The Mooring of Starting Out: The First Five Books of Poetry (includes *Some Trees, The Tennis Court Oath, Rivers and Mountains, The Double Dream of Spring, Three Poems).* 1997.

Poetry

Turandot and Other Poems. 1953.
Some Trees. 1956.
The Poems. 1961(?).
The Tennis Court Oath. 1962.
Rivers and Mountains. 1966.
Selected Poems. 1967.
Three Madrigals. 1968.
Sunrise in Suburbia. 1968.
Fragment. 1969.
Evening in the Country. 1970.
The Double Dream of Spring. 1970.
The New Spirit. 1970. In *Three Poems.* 1989.
Penguin Modern Poets 19, with Lee Harwood and Tom Raworth. 1971.

Three Poems. 1972.
The Vermont Notebook. 1975.
The Serious Doll. 1975.
Self-Portrait in a Convex Mirror. 1975.
Houseboat Days. 1977. In *Three Poems.* 1993.
As We Know. 1979.
Shadow Train. 1981. In *Three Poems.* 1993.
A Wave. 1984. In *Three Poems.* 1993.
Selected Poems. 1985.
The Ice Storm. 1987.
April Galleons. 1987.
Three Poems ("The New Spirit," "The System," and "The Recital"). 1989.
Flow Chart. 1991.
Hotel Lautreamont. 1992.
Three Poems ("Houseboat Days," "Shadow Train," and "A Wave"). 1993.
And the Stars Were Shining. 1994.
Can You Hear, Bird: Poems. 1995.
Wakefulness: Poems. 1998.
Flow Chart. 1998.
Girls on the Run. 1999.

Plays

The Heroes (produced 1952). In *Three Plays,* 1978.
The Compromise (produced 1956). In *Three Plays,* 1978.
Three Plays. 1978.
The Philosopher (produced 1982). In *Three Plays.* 1978.

Fiction

A Nest of Ninnies, with James Schuyler. 1969.

Other

Ashbery and Kenneth Koch (A Conversation). 1965(?).
Reported Sightings: Art Chronicles, 1957-1987, edited by David Bergman. 1989.
Ellsworth Kelly: Plant Drawings. 1993.
Joan Mitchell Nineteen Ninety-Two, edited by John Cheim. 1993.

Editor, *Penguin Modern Poets 24.* 1973.
Editor, *Muck Arbour,* by Bruce Marcus. 1975.
Editor, *The Funny Place,* by Richard F. Snow. 1975.
Editor, *From Altar to Chimney-Piece,* by Mary Butts. 1992.

Translator, with Lawrence G. Blochman, *Murder in Montmartre,* by Noel Vexin. 1960.
Translator, *Melville,* by Jean-Jacques Mayoux. 1960.
Translator, with Lawrence G. Blochman, *The Deadlier Sex,* by Genevieve Manceron. 1961.
Translator, *Alberto Giacometti,* by Jacques Dupin. 1963(?).
Translator, *Fantomas,* by Marcel Allain and Pierre Souvestre. 1986.
Translator, *Every Question but One,* by Pierre Martory. 1990.
Translator, with others, *Selected Poems,* by Pierre Reverdy. 1991.
Translator, with others, *Things to Translate,* by Piotr Sommer. 1991.
Translator, *Hebdomeros and Other Writings,* by Giorgio De Chirico. 1992.

*

Bibliography: *John Ashbery: A Comprehensive Bibliography* by David K. Kermani, 1976.

Critical Studies: *Ashbery: An Introduction to the Poetry* by David Shapiro, 1979; *Beyond Amazement: New Essays on Ashbery* edited by David Lehman, 1980; *Poetry as Epitaph* by Karen Mills-Courts, 1990; *A Tradition of Subversion* by Margueritte Murphy, 1992; *On the Outside Looking Out: John Ashbery's Poetry* by John Shoptaw, 1994; *Politics and Form in Postmodern Poetry: O'Hara, Bishop, Ashbery, and Merrill* by Mutlu Konuk Blasing, 1995; *The Tribe of John: Ashbery and Contemporary Poetry,* edited by Susan M. Schultz, 1995; *Ashbery: The Modern Voice* by Cory Updyke, 1997; *An Open Possibility: John Ashbery and the Postmodern Prose Poem* by Robert Ring, 1998.

*   *   *

John Ashbery is considered by many to be the most important poet of the latter half of the twentieth-century. Certainly if one measures importance in terms of effect, then Ashbery's wide-ranging work, spanning four decades and a variety of formal positions, has dramatically affected the course of American poetry. Ashbery shares many affinities with **Wallace Stevens**, his favorite poet; both seek to articulate the mind's experience of experience rather than to depict experience per se. The difference between an art directed at embodying the physical world and an art that focuses on the mind's experience of the world is distinct and in the case of Ashbery frequently leads to rather elliptical poetry. Given the philosophical underpinnings both Stevens and Ashbery accept—primarily, the epistemological assertion that reality is either unknowable or incoherent—the poet must choose between writing poetry that pretends to know the unknowable (a sham) or make coherence out of chaos (an impossibility). Whereas Stevens settled for the construction of "supreme fictions" that allowed provisional "ideas of order" about the external world, Ashbery is much more postmodern in his skepticism toward such efforts. Flux, polyphony, formal experimentation are all methods that Ashbery uses to offer interstitial glimpses into the multitudinous and mysterious world. His poems are frequently humorous, ironic, and, occasionally, satirical. Whether or not Ashbery is the most important of late twentieth century poets, he is certainly a significant figure, and the undecidability of his poetry is certainly representative of an important intellectual current.

Ashbery's first full-length volume (excepting the small press *Turandot and Other Poems*) was the 1956 recipient of the Yale Younger Poets prize. *Some Trees* is indicative of certain elements that have become trademark in Ashbery's poetry; but before one asserts any notions as to signature qualities in Ashbery, a qualification is important. Ashbery is an exceptionally wide-ranging poet; various qualities that recur may manifest themselves in different ways at different points in his career. Thus, in his first book Ashbery established his playful yet compelling voice. His next book, *The Tennis Court Oath*, as the strange title might indicate, announced an abrupt change of direction; the wit of his first volume was replaced by a much more difficult sort of writing. Ashbery has described the creative process for the later work as being somewhat akin to automatic writing, and a short excerpt from "Our Youth" might reveal why:

> The Arabs took us. We knew
> The dead horses. We were discovering coffee,

> How it is to be drunk hot, with bare feet
> In Canada. And the immortal music of Chopin . . .

The poems are disjunctive yet engaging; the poems surprise, and this swerve away from his celebrated first volume marked an important point in the poet's career. Later works, including the powerful *Rivers and Mountains*, as well as *The Double Dream of Spring*, combine the more discursive style of Ashbery's early work with the imaginative free rein of the poems from the early sixties. This combination could be described as the signature Ashbery style. Whether part of a primarily lyrical poem such as "A Blessing in Disguise" or one of the lengthy prose poems of the early seventies or an extended meditation like "Self Portrait in a Convex Mirror," the quick imaginative leaps, the astonishing turns of phrase, and the vivid yet disconcerting imagery all make Ashbery's work engaging, even for the reader who might not be able to understand the pieces at first reading.

To look at Ashbery's work from another perspective, his poetry both violates and fulfills expectation; the casual, discursive voice prepares a reader for a poem in the romantic, meditative tradition. In Ashbery's poems, however, that voice is frequently undercut by the emergence of the banal, the unconnected, something mundane. Ashbery does this in order to make the reader think about how constructs—the romantic, meditative lyric of, say, Wordsworth, for instance—that presume to give form to reality are falsifying. Reality is far too large, too various, too bountiful for the poet's puny senses to somehow glean any meaning from it in a spontaneous overflow of powerful feeling. Hence, Ashbery tries to leave his poems open, able to sponsor multiple readings, multiple forms. Consequently, he employs multiple voices and multiple levels of diction, from the high lyrical to the cliché. For some readers, this variance on Ashbery's part is empowering, vitally connected to how art brings the world alive without suffocating it. For other readers, the gesture is seen as a failure, a kind of sophistry that allows automatic writing and laziness—albeit shaped by a sharp mind—to pass for high art. Although there seem to be more who celebrate Ashbery's work than who deride it, a reader should be aware that there are still many readers who are highly critical.

If awards are any indication of a poet's importance, then Ashbery has certainly exceeded any critical scrutiny. His most decorated book, *Self Portrait in a Convex Mirror,* won several important awards, including the Pulitzer Prize. He continues to publish prodigiously, writing nearly a book every year. *Flow Chart,* a 200-page-long poem, received a great deal of critical acclaim in the early nineties. He has published sixteen additional volumes since his first, and each of these has built on the success of that first book.

—Tod Marshall

ASIMOV, Isaac

Pseudonyms: Dr. A.; George E. Dale; Paul French; H.B. Ogden. **Born:** Petrovichi, U.S.S.R. (now Russia), 2 January 1920; immigrated to the United States in 1923; became U.S. citizen in 1928. **Education:** Boys High School of Brooklyn; Columbia University, B.S. in Chemistry 1939, M.A. 1941, Ph.D. 1948. **Military Service:** Employed at U.S. Navy Yard, Philadelphia, Pennsylvania,

1942-45; served in U.S. Army 1945-46. **Family:** Married 1) Gertrude Blugerman in 1942 (divorced 1973); 2) Janet Jeppson in 1973. **Career:** Appointed instructor in biochemistry, Boston University School of Medicine, 1949; became associate professor, 1958, professor beginning 1979; full-time writer, 1958-92; monthly columnist for *Magazine of Fantasy and Science Fiction,* 1958-92; editorial director of *Isaac Asimov's Science Fiction Magazine,* 1976-92. Published more than 100 science books for children, including the "ABCs of Science," "Ask Isaac Asimov," and the "Raintree Reader" series. **Awards:** Edison Foundation award, 1958; Blakeslee award of the American Heart Association, 1960; National Book award nomination, 1960; World Science Fiction Convention Hugo awards, 1963, 1966, 1973, 1977, 1983; Grady Medal for writing in the field of science, 1964; E.E. Smith Memorial award, 1967; American Association for the Advancement of Science-Westinghouse award for science writing, 1967; Science Fiction Writers of America (SFWA) Nebula award, 1973, 1977; SFWA Grand Master award, 1987. D.S.: Bridgewater State College, Bridgewater, Massachusetts, 1970; Rensselaer Polytechnic Institute, Troy, New York, 1971. Litt.D.: Alfred University, Alfred, New York, 1972; eleven other honorary degrees. **Died:** 6 April 1992.

PUBLICATIONS

Collections

The Collected Fiction of Isaac Asimov. 1979.
The Robot Collection: The Robot Novels. 1979.
The Complete Robot. 1982.
The Complete Stories. 2 vols., 1990-91.
Gold: The Final Science Fiction Collection. 1995.
Magic: The Final Fantasy Collection. 1996.

Novels

Pebble in the Sky. 1950.
Foundation. 1951.
The Stars, Like Dust—. 1951.
The Currents of Space. 1952.
David Starr: Space Ranger. 1952.
Foundation and Empire. 1952.
Lucky Starr and the Pirates of the Asteroids. 1953.
Second Foundation. 1953.
The Caves of Steel. 1954.
Lucky Starr and the Oceans of Venus. 1954.
The End of Eternity. 1955.
Lucky Starr and the Big Sun of Mercury. 1956.
Lucky Starr and the Moons of Jupiter. 1957.
The Naked Sun. 1957.
The Death Dealers. 1958; as *A Whiff of Death,* 1968.
Lucky Starr and the Rings of Saturn. 1958.
Fantastic Voyage. 1966.
The Gods Themselves. 1972.
Murder at the ABA. 1976.
Foundation's Edge. 1982.
Norby, the Mixed-up Robot, with Janet Asimov (for children). 1983.
The Robots of Dawn. 1983.
Norby's Other Secret, with Janet Asimov (for children). 1983.
Norby and the Invaders, with Janet Asimov (for children). 1984.
Norby and the Lost Princess, with Janet Asimov (for children). 1985.

Robots and Empire. 1985.
Foundation and Earth. 1986.
Norby and the Queen's Necklace, with Janet Asimov (for children). 1986.
Fantastic Voyage II: Destination Brain. 1987.
Norby Finds a Villain, with Janet Asimov (for children). 1987.
Norby: Robot for Hire, with Janet Asimov (for children). 1987.
The Norby Chronicles, with Janet Asimov (for children). 1988.
Norby Down to Earth, with Janet Asimov (for children). 1988.
Prelude to Foundation. 1988.
Nemesis. 1989.
Norby and Yobo's Great Adventure, with Janet Asimov (for children). 1989.
Nightfall, with Robert Silverberg. 1990.
Norby and the Oldest Dragon, with Janet Asimov (for children). 1990.
Norby and the Court Jester, with Janet Asimov. 1991.
The Ugly Little Boy, with Robert Silverberg. 1992.
Forward the Foundation. 1993.
The Positronic Man, with Robert Silverberg. 1993.

Short Stories

I, Robot. 1950.
The Martian Way and Other Stories. 1955.
Earth Is Room Enough. 1957.
Nine Tomorrows. 1959.
The Rest of the Robots. 1964.
Through a Glass, Clearly. 1967.
Asimov's Mysteries. 1968.
Nightfall and Other Stories. 1969.
The Best New Thing (for children). 1971.
The Early Asimov. 1972.
The Best of Isaac Asimov. 1973.
Have You Seen These? 1974.
Tales of the Black Widowers. 1974.
Buy Jupiter and Other Stories. 1975.
The Heavenly Host (for children). 1975.
The Bicentennial Man and Other Stories. 1976.
"The Dream," "Benjamin's Dream," "Benjamin's Bicentennial Blast." 1976.
Good Taste. 1976.
More Tales of the Black Widowers. 1976.
The Key Word and Other Mysteries (for children). 1977.
Casebook of the Black Widowers. 1980.
Three by Asimov: Three Science Fiction Tales. 1981.
The Union Club Mysteries. 1983.
The Winds of Change and Other Stories. 1983.
Banquets of the Black Widowers. 1984.
The Disappearing Man and Other Mysteries. 1985.
The Edge of Tomorrow. 1985.
It's Such a Beautiful Day (for children). 1985.
The Alternate Asimovs. 1986.
The Best Mysteries of Isaac Asimov. 1986.
The Best Science Fiction of Isaac Asimov. 1986.
Robot Dreams. 1986.
Science Fiction by Asimov. 1986.
Other Universes of Isaac Asimov. 1987.
Azazel. 1988.
All the Troubles of the World (for children). 1989.
Franchise (for children). 1989.
Robbie (for children). 1989.

Sally (for children). 1989.
Puzzles of the Black Widowers. 1990.

Poetry

Lecherous Limericks. 1975.
More Lecherous Limericks. 1976.
Asimov's Sherlockian Limericks. 1977.
Familiar Poems Annotated. 1977.
Still More Lecherous Limericks. 1977.
Limericks Too Gross, with John Ciardi. 1978.
A Grossery of Limericks, with John Ciardi. 1981.
Isaac Asimov's Limericks for Children. 1984.
Asimov Laughs Again. 1993.

Prose

Biochemistry and Human Metabolism, with William C. Boyd and Burnham S. Walker. 1952.
The Chemicals of Life: Enzymes, Vitamins, Hormones. 1954.
Races and People, with William C. Boyd. 1955.
Chemistry and Human Health, with Burnham S. Walker and Mary E. Nicholas. 1956.
Inside the Atom. 1956.
Only a Trillion. 1957; as *Marvels of Science,* 1963.
The World of Carbon. 1958.
The World of Nitrogen. 1958.
The Clock We Live On. 1959.
The Living River. 1959; as *The Bloodstream: River of Life,* 1961.
Realm of Numbers. 1959.
The Double Planet. 1960.
The Intelligent Man's Guide to Science. 2 vols., 1960; Vol. 1 as *The Intelligent Man's Guide to the Physical Sciences,* 1964; Vol. 2 as *The Intelligent Man's Guide to the Biological Sciences,* 1964; as *The New Intelligent Man's Guide to Science,* 1965; as *Asimov's Guide to Science,* 1972; as *Asimov's New Guide to Science,* 1984.
The Kingdom of the Sun. 1960.
The Wellsprings of Life. 1960.
Realm of Algebra. 1961.
Fact and Fancy. 1962.
Life and Energy. 1962.
The Search for the Elements. 1962.
The Genetic Code. 1963.
The Human Body: Its Structure and Operation. 1963; revised edition as *The Human Body: Its Structure and Operation,* 1992.
View from a Height. 1963.
Adding a Dimension: Seventeen Essays on the History of Science. 1964.
Asimov's Biographical Encyclopedia of Science and Technology. 1964; revised edition, 1982.
The Human Brain: Its Capabilities and Functions. 1964.
Planets for Man, with Stephen H. Dole. 1964.
Quick and Easy Math. 1964.
A Short History of Biology. 1964.
An Easy Introduction to the Slide Rule. 1965.
The Greeks: A Great Adventure. 1965.
Of Time and Space and Other Things. 1965.
A Short History of Chemistry. 1965.
From Earth to Heaven. 1966.
The Genetic Effects of Radiation, with Theodosius Dobzhansky. 1966.
The Neutrino: Ghost Particle of the Atom. 1966.

The Noble Gases. 1966.
The Roman Republic. 1966.
Understanding Physics. 1966.
The Universe: From Flat Earth to Quasar. 1966; as *The Universe: From Flat Earth to Black Holes—and Beyond,* 1980.
The Egyptians. 1967.
Environments Out There. 1967.
Is Anyone There? 1967.
The Roman Empire. 1967.
To the Ends of the Universe. 1967; revised edition, 1976.
The Dark Ages. 1968.
The Near East: Ten Thousand Years of History. 1968.
Science, Numbers and I. 1968.
Photosynthesis. 1969.
The Shaping of England. 1969.
Twentieth Century Discovery. 1969.
Constantinople: The Forgotten Empire. 1970.
The Solar System and Back. 1970.
The Land of Canaan. 1971.
The Stars in Their Courses. 1971.
Electricity and Man. 1972.
The Left Hand of the Electron. 1972.
The Shaping of France. 1972.
Worlds within Worlds: The Story of Nuclear Energy. 1972.
Jupiter, the Largest Planet. 1973.
Please Explain. 1973.
The Shaping of North America from Earliest Times to 1763. 1973.
Today and Tomorrow and. . . . 1973.
The Tragedy of the Moon. 1973.
Asimov on Astronomy. 1974; revised edition, 1979.
Asimov on Chemistry. 1974.
The Birth of the United States, 1763-1816. 1974.
Our World in Space. 1974.
The Ends of the Earth: The Polar Regions of the World. 1975.
Eyes on the Universe: A History of the Telescope. 1975.
Of Matters Great and Small. 1975.
Our Federal Union: The United States from 1816 to 1865. 1975.
Science Past, Science Future. 1975.
Alpha Centauri, the Nearest Star. 1976.
Asimov on Physics. 1976.
The Planet That Wasn't. 1976.
Asimov on Numbers. 1977.
The Beginning and the End. 1977.
The Collapsing Universe. 1977.
The Golden Door: The United States from 1865 to 1918. 1977.
Mars, the Red Planet. 1977.
Quasar, Quasar, Burning Bright. 1978.
A Choice of Catastrophes: The Disasters That Threaten Our World. 1979.
Extraterrestrial Civilizations. 1979.
In Memory Yet Green: The Autobiography of Isaac Asimov 1920-1954. 1979.
The Road to Infinity. 1979.
Saturn and Beyond. 1979.
In Joy Still Felt: The Autobiography of Isaac Asimov 1954-1978. 1980.
The Sun Shines Bright. 1980.
Venus, Near Neighbor of the Sun. 1980.
Visions of the Universe. 1981.
Exploring the Earth and the Cosmos: The Growth and Future of Human Knowledge. 1982.

Counting the Eons. 1983.
The Measure of the Universe. 1983.
The Roving Mind. 1983.
The History of Physics. 1984.
Living in the Future. 1984.
Science and Creationism. 1984.
X Stands for Unknown. 1984.
Asimov's Guide to Halley's Comet. 1985.
The Exploding Suns: The Secrets of the Supernovas. 1985.
Robots: Machines in Man's Image, with Karen Frenkel. 1985.
The Subatomic Monster. 1985.
The Dangers of Intelligence and Other Science Essays. 1986.
Future Days: A Nineteenth-Century Vision of the Year 2000. 1986.
Isaac Asimov's Wonderful Worldwide Science Bazaar. 1986.
Far as the Human Eye Could See. 1987.
How To Enjoy Writing: A Book of Aid and Comfort, with Janet Asimov. 1987.
Isaac Asimov Presents: From Harding to Hiroshima, with Barrington Boardman. 1988.
The Relativity of Wrong: Essays on the Solar System and Beyond. 1988.
Asimov on Science: A Thirty Year Retrospective. 1989.
Asimov's Chronology of Science and Technology. 1989.
The Secret of the Universe. 1989.
The Tyrannosaurus Prescription and One Hundred Other Essays. 1989.
Isaac Asimov's Library of the Universe. Index. 1990.
The March of the Millennia: A Key to Looking at History, with Frank White. 1990.
Out of the Everywhere. 1990.
Robot Visions. 1990.
Asimov's Chronology of the World. 1991.
Asimov's Guide to Earth and Space. 1991.
Atom: Journey Across the Subatomic Cosmos. 1991.
Frontiers: New Discoveries about Man and His Planet. 1991.
Our Angry Earth, with Frederik Pohl. 1991.
Frontiers II: More Recent Discoveries, with Janet Asimov. 1993.
I. Asimov: A Memoir. 1994.
Yours, Isaac Asimov: A Lifetime of Letters, edited by Stanley Asimov. 1995.

Other (editions and compilations)

Words of Science and the History Behind Them. 1959.
Words from the Myths. 1961.
Words in Genesis. 1962.
Words on the Map. 1962.
Words from the Exodus. 1963.
Asimov's Guide to the Bible. 2 vols., 1968-69.
Words from History. 1968.
Opus 100. 1969.
Asimov's Guide to Shakespeare. 1970.
Isaac Asimov's Treasury of Humor. 1971.
The Sensuous Dirty Old Man. 1971.
Asimov's Annotated "Don Juan." 1972.
More Words of Science. 1972.
The Story of Ruth. 1972.
Asimov's Annotated "Paradise Lost." 1974.
Isaac Asimov's Book of Facts. 1979.
Opus 200. 1979.
The Annotated "Gulliver's Travels." 1980.

Asimov on Science Fiction. 1981.
In the Beginning: Science Faces God in the Book of Genesis. 1981.
Would You Believe? 1981.
Isaac Asimov Presents Superquiz, with Ken Fisher. 1982.

Editor, *The Hugo Winners 1955-1961.* 1962.
Editor, *Tomorrow's Children: 18 Tales.* 1966.
Editor, *The Hugo Winners 1962-1970.* 1971.
Editor, *Where Do We Go From Here?* 1971.
Editor, *Nebula Award Stories Eight.* 1973.
Editor, *Before the Golden Age: A Science Fiction Anthology.* 1974.
Editor, *The Hugo Winners 1971-1975.* 1977.

*

Bibliography: *Asimov Science Fiction Bibliography* by Matthew B. Tepper, 1970; *Isaac Asimov: A Checklist of Works Published in the United States, March 1939-May 1972* by Marjorie M. Miller, 1972; *Isaac Asimov: An Annotated Bibliography of the Asimov Collection at Boston University* by Scott E. Green, 1995.

Critical Studies: *Asimov Analyzed* by Neil Goble, 1972; *The Science Fiction of Isaac Asimov* by Joseph Patrouch, 1974; *Isaac Asimov* edited by Martin H. Greenberg and Joseph D. Olander, 1977; *Isaac Asimov: The Foundations of Science Fiction* by James Gunn, 1982; *Isaac Asimov* by Jean Fiedler, 1982; *Isaac Asimov* by Donald Hassler, 1991; *Isaac Asimov* by William Touponce, 1991; *Asimov: The Unauthorized Life* by Michael White, 1994.

*   *   *

With nearly five hundred books to his credit, Isaac Asimov was probably the most prolific American writer of the twentieth century, and his range was as vast as his output. He was among other things a master at explaining science to the general public. In strictly literary terms, however, he is most noted for his science fiction. The conceptual contributions of his many novels and stories have profoundly influenced the genre since 1939, and in his nonfiction Asimov consistently championed science fiction as an important literary form.

Born in Russia in 1920 and brought to the United States at the age of three, Asimov grew up reading science fiction in his father's Brooklyn candy store. (He convinced his father that his reading was not trash by pointing to the word "science" on the various magazine covers.) Asimov's first published story, "Marooned Off Vesta," appeared in *Amazing Stories* in March 1939, but he had also been getting highly encouraging rejections from John W. Campbell, Jr., the pioneering editor of *Astounding Science Fiction.* Campbell soon bought Asimov's "Trends" and a fruitful editorial relationship began. Often Campbell would propose a story idea and Asimov would write it—such was the case with "Nightfall," a tale about the effects of darkness on a world where night comes only once every two thousand years: the effects are terror and madness. Asimov's "Nightfall" appeared in *Astounding* in 1941 and was later voted the best story in all of science fiction by the Science Fiction Writers of America.

Soon after breaking into *Astounding* Asimov began developing his landmark tales of robots and robotics (his coinage). Seeking to subvert the traditional image of robots as hostile to their creators, Asimov created the Three Laws of Robotics, which have since become the common property of science fiction writers:

1. A robot may not injure a human being, or, through in-action, allow a human being to come to harm.

2. A robot must obey the orders given it by human be-ings except where such orders would conflict with the First Law.

3. A robot must protect its own existence as long as such protection does not conflict with the First and Second Laws.

With these successively weaker laws, Asimov nullified at a stroke the imagined threat of robots and created the matrix of innumer-able story situations in which the three laws can create conflicts, dilemmas, and puzzles for both the robots and their human cre-ators.

A little later, in May 1942, Asimov began publishing in *As-tounding* the series of long short stories and novellas which when collected in volume form constitute the Foundation trilogy: *Foun-dation* (1951), *Foundation and Empire* (1952), and *Second Foun-dation* (1953). Two striking propositions underlie this epic work: the existence of a far-flung, far-future galactic empire subject to the changes inherent in all human enterprises, and the science of psychohistory, which enables its inventor, Hari Seldon, to pre-dict and guide the course of those changes. Asimov used the fate of the Roman and other empires as his models; Seldon's psychohistory is based on the idea that the behavior of human beings *en masse* is predictable, provided they do not know they are being studied. Like all empires, the First Galactic Empire will fall, but under Seldon's guidance (he reappears as a sort of holo-gram from time to time) its Dark Age can be shortened from ten to one thousand years. The "Foundation" of the title is a politi-cal, scientific, and cultural institution which undertakes to imple-ment Seldon's wisdom. Unknown to it a Second Foundation ex-ists, made up of mentalists and psychohistorians who believe that they are guiding the work of the first Foundation. Upon this grid of intrigue and veiled purposes are laid the stories of the many characters who inhabit Foundational space, including an unfore-seen genetic sport, the Mule, who upsets the forecasts of psychohistory.

This outline can suggest only some of the issues joined in the trilogy, which covers four hundred of the Seldon Plan's thousand years. Important among them is the conflict between the deter-minism which psychohistory implies and the free will which many of the characters seem to possess in abundance. There is also the question of power, which endlessly fascinates Asimov: who has it? who wants it? from whom to whom is it passing? Still, de-spite Campbell's encouragement, Asimov eventually wearied of the elaborate complications of the Foundation series; he did not return to it for almost thirty years. Asimov did not, of course, invent the saga of the galactic empire, but his Foundation novels present one of the most thoroughly rationalized and politically convincing pictures of future imperialism ever written. They won a special Hugo Award (science fiction's Oscar) in 1966.

Asimov's first published novel, *Pebble in the Sky* (1950), con-cerns neither robots nor foundations. It is set on a highly radioac-tive Earth at the height of the First Galactic Empire and it poses a question which Asimov pursued in later fictions: where amid the millions of inhabited worlds in the empire did humankind origi-nate? Can it have been upon this miserably insignificant planet, this pebble and pariah called Earth?

Asimov moves backward in time, takes the idea of Earth as out-cast or ghetto a step further, and elaborates the idea of robot cul-

ture in a pair of novels which merit the label detective science fiction: *The Caves of Steel* (1954) and *The Naked Sun* (1957). In these Asimov postulates the fifty Outer Worlds, highly advanced and highly dependent on robot technology, in conflict with a back-ward, agoraphobic Earth fearful of robots. The Outer Worlders main-tain a base on Earth and when one of them is murdered there, Detec-tive Elijah Baley is brought in (on the presumption that only Earth-dwellers are familiar with crime) and is provided, much to his initial dismay, with a partner, R. Daneel Olivaw, the R. standing for Robot. The interest of these novels is not just in the crimes committed but also in the interaction of the two major characters—the intuitive mind of Baley sparking against the logical brain of Olivaw—and in the im-plications of the laws of robotics, which, for example, oblige Olivaw to protect Baley even if that thwarts his investigations. Even so, some-thing strangely like affection develops between Baley and Olivaw.

The novels of the 1950s thus establish major points of interest in the Asimovian universe: earliest along the time line of Asimov's fictional future history are the robot/Outer World novels just men-tioned. Then come novels set during the growth and zenith of the First Galactic Empire; besides *Pebble in the Sky,* these include *The Stars, Like Dust—* (1951) and *The Currents of Space* (1952). Last come the Foundation stories, set during and after the Empire's collapse.

Asimov was also pursuing other interests during these years. Besides writing six novels about the adventures of Lucky Starr, Space Ranger (published under the pseudonym Paul French), he wrote a completely independent novel, *The End of Eternity* (1955), which acrobatically explores all of the possible paradoxes of time travel. Eternity is an extra-temporal organization whose agents at-tempt to manipulate human history to make it safer for us. All dangers and uncertainties are wiped out, which leads, in Asimov's basic paradox, to the human race itself being wiped out; to pre-vent this, Eternity must be destroyed.

In 1958 Asimov gave up his academic post at Boston Univer-sity and turned to writing full-time. During the 1960s he concen-trated on nonfiction but he came back to science fiction handsomely in 1972 with *The Gods Themselves,* which won the Hugo and Nebula Awards. The novel is something of a departure for Asimov: as an early disciple of John Campbell, who preached that humankind's manifest destiny was to spread to the empty stars, Asimov rarely wrote on such common science fiction subjects as alternate universes or alien encounters, but in this novel we have energy transfers between universes, and in the other universe en-tities as alien as one could wish.

Asimov returned to robots in 1976 with the short story "The Bicentennial Man," another Hugo winner. Then in the 1980s he began the most ambitious project in his fiction—an attempt to unify the story lines of the robot/Outer World novels and the Em-pire/Foundation novels, to push the latter backward in the Hugo-winning *Foundation's Edge* (1982) and *Foundation and Earth* (1986), and to move the former forward in *Robots of Dawn* (1983) and *Robots and Empire* (1985) until they meet, and to deal with the question of human origins which had first been mooted in *Pebble in the Sky* some thirty years before. Lastly, Asimov be-came interested in the figure of Hari Seldon himself and wrote of his career in *Prelude to Foundation* (1988) and the posthumously published *Forward the Foundation* (1993).

Asimov the man created a public persona, "the Good Doctor," a charming mix of intellect and ego leavened with humor and self-deprecation. Unlike many writers, he loved to write; he consis-tently worked eight hours a day, seven days a week, and he hated anything (holidays, vacations) which took him away from his desk. This devotion coupled with his famous refusal to fly limited the radius of his activities, yet he was in constant demand because he was a gifted and entertaining public speaker.

Asimov the writer is notable for a straightforward and unadorned style. The meaning of his fiction is very much on the surface and while important themes run throughout his stories (the question of the locus of power, for example), symbol-hunting generally goes unrewarded. He could create memorable characters (several of them robots) but like many science fiction writers of his generation he was at least as interested in idea as in character. His was an inventive mind and one can say of his ideas what E.M. Forster said of good characters: they surprise convincingly.

Asimov was a scientist and an apostle of rationalism and scientific discipline. He was literally a secular humanist, and his fiction, fully cognizant of human folly, celebrated human reason and human possibility.

—Michael Stanton

ATHERTON, Gertrude (Franklin)

Born: Gertrude Horn in San Francisco, California, 30 October 1857. **Education:** Private schools in California and Kentucky. **Family:** Married George H. Bowen Atherton in 1876 (died 1887). **Career:** Moved to New York, 1888, then traveled extensively and lived in Europe; lived in San Francisco after 1932. Trustee, San Francisco Public Library; member, San Francisco Art Commission; president, American National Academy of Literature, 1934; chairman of Letters, League of American Pen Women, 1939; president, Northern California Section of PEN. **Awards:** International Academy of Letters and Sciences of Italy Gold Medal; D.Litt.: Mills College, Oakland, California, 1935; LL.D.: University of California, Berkeley, 1937; chevalier, Legion of Honor (France), 1925. **Member:** American Academy, 1938. **Died:** 14 June 1948.

PUBLICATIONS

Fiction

What Dreams May Come. 1888.
Hermia Suydam. 1889; as *Hermia, An American Woman,* 1889.
Los Cerritos: A Romance of the Modern Time. 1890.
A Question of Time. 1891.
The Doomswoman. 1893.
Before the Gringo Came. 1894; revised edition, as *The Splendid Idle Forties: Stories of Old California,* 1902.
A Whirl Asunder. 1895.
His Fortunate Grace. 1897.
Patience Sparhawk and Her Times. 1897.
American Wives and English Husbands. 1898; revised edition, as *Transplanted,* 1919.
The Californians. 1898.
The Valiant Runaways. 1898.
A Daughter of the Vine. 1899.
Senator North. 1900.
The Aristocrats. 1901.

The Conqueror, Being the True and Romantic Story of Alexander Hamilton. 1902.
Heart of Hyacinth. 1903.
Mrs. Pendleton's Four-in-Hand. 1903.
Rulers of Kings. 1904.
The Bell in the Fog and Other Stories. 1905.
The Travelling Thirds. 1905.
Rezanov. 1906.
Ancestors. 1907.
The Gorgeous Isle: A Romance: Scene, Nevis, B.W.I., 1842. 1908.
Tower of Ivory. 1910.
Julia France and Her Times. 1912.
Perch of the Devil. 1914.
Mrs. Balfame. 1916.
The White Morning: A Novel of the Power of the German Women in Wartime. 1918.
The Avalanche: A Mystery Story. 1919.
The Sisters-in-Law: A Novel of Our Time. 1921.
Sleeping Fires. 1922; as *Dormant Fires,* 1922.
Black Oxen. 1923.
The Crystal Cup. 1925.
The Immortal Marriage. 1927.
The Jealous Gods: A Processional Novel of the Fifth Century B.C. (Concerning One Alcibiades). 1928; as *Vengeful Gods,* 1928.
Dido, Queen of Hearts. 1929.
The Sophisticates. 1931.
The Foghorn: Stories. 1934.
Golden Peacock. 1936.
Rezanov and Dona Concha. 1937.
The House of Lee. 1940.
The Horn of Life. 1942.

Screenplay: *Don't Neglect Your Wife,* with Louis Sherwin, 1921.

Other

California: An Intimate History. 1914; revised edition, 1927.
Life in the War Zone. 1916.
The Living Present (essays). 1917.
Adventures of a Novelist (autobiography). 1932.
Can Women Be Gentlemen? (essays). 1938.
Golden Gate Country. 1945.
My San Francisco: A Wayward Biography. 1946.

Editor, *A Few of Hamilton's Letters, Including His Description of the Great West Indian Hurricane of 1772.* 1903.

*

Bibliography: "A Checklist of the Writings of and about Atherton" by Charlotte S. McClure, in *American Literary Realism 1870-1910,* Spring 1976.

Critical Studies: *Atherton* by Joseph Henry Jackson, 1940; *Atherton,* 1976, and *Atherton,* 1979, both by Charlotte S. McClure; *California's Daughter: Gertrude Atherton and Her Times* by Emily Wortis Leider, 1991; "Through the Golden Gate: Madness and the Persephone Myth in Gertrude Atherton's *The Foghorn*" by Melissa McFarland Pennell, in *Images of Persephone: Feminist Readings in Western Literature* edited by Elizabeth T. Hayes, 1994; "Gertrude Atherton and Her San Francisco: A Wayward Writer in a Wayward Paradise" by Charlotte S. McClure, in *San Francisco in Fiction: Essays in a Regional Literature* edited by David Fine and Paul Skenazy, 1995.

* * *

Gertrude Atherton was a popular and prolific writer, publishing nearly forty novels, several volumes of short stories, three collections of essays, a history of California, two books about San Francisco, a selection of Alexander Hamilton's letters, and numerous uncollected articles. Although her novels lack great artistic merit, they are significant for the literary historian because they helped to free American literature from the shackles of Victorian prudery. From the beginning of her career Atherton rejected the Victorian myths about woman's moral superiority and sexual imbecility. Her heroines are sensual, egotistical, and intellectually ambitious. They seek an identity based on their own needs and talents rather than on the attributes ascribed to women by society. Her treatment of female sexuality in particular gained her considerable critical attention both in America and in England; liberal critics singled her out for her "fearless treatment of the problems of sex," while conservatives screamed that she exalted "the morals of the barn-yard into a social ideal" and accelerated "the corruption of private life and the destruction of the family relation."

Atherton's California fiction is of particular interest to the cultural historian, focusing, as it does, on the effects of the "gringo" coming to power at the expense of the Mexican aristocracy. Her best novel, *The Californians,* effectively analyzes the conflict between the heritages of Hispanic indolence and pride and Yankee shrewdness and pragmatism. In this novel Atherton's conception of her heroine is firmly rooted in her knowledge of the patriarchal, restrictive Spanish tradition as well as the shallow ambiance of San Francisco society. However, in many of her other California novels, Atherton romanticizes her subject matter. As Kevin Starr points out in *Americans and the California Dream,* Atherton speaks for the California elite which, on the one hand, mourned the loss of the Arcadian existence of other Hispanic settlers, but, on the other hand, repudiated that existence as inimical to the progress of the state.

In most of her fiction Atherton sensationalized her material. Thus, the heroine of *Patience Sparhawk and Her Times* is wrongly convicted of her husband's murder, the heroine of *Black Oxen* is a rejuvenated 58-year-old woman who falls in love with a man in his thirties, and the heroine of *The Immortal Marriage* is Aspasia, whom Atherton presents not as a prostitute, but as Pericles's beloved wife, supremely beautiful and intelligent enough to provoke admiration from men such as Sophocles and Socrates. Despite Atherton's artistic shortcomings, her lifelong concern with the contribution of women to civilization, as well as her fictional observation of fifty years of America's social history, suggest that her work deserves further examination by literary and cultural historians.

—Sybil B. Weir

AUCHINCLOSS, Louis (Stanton)

Born: Lawrence, New York, 27 September 1917. **Education:** Groton School, Massachusetts, graduated 1935; Yale University, New Haven, Connecticut, 1935-38; University of Virginia Law School, Charlottesville, LL.B. 1941; admitted to the New York bar, 1941. **Military Service;** Served in the U.S. Naval Reserve, 1941-45: lieutenant. **Family:** Married Adele Lawrence in 1957; three sons. **Career:** Associate lawyer, Sullivan and Cromwell, New York, 1941-51; associate, 1954-57, and since 1957 partner, Hawkins Delafield and Wood, New York. Chairman, Museum of the City of New York, beginning 1966; trustee, Josiah Macy Jr. Foundation, New York; former member of the executive committee, Association of the Bar of New York City. **Awards:** New York State Governor's award, 1985. D.Litt.: New York University, 1974; Pace College, New York, 1979. **Member:** (President)American Academy of Arts and Letters. **Residence:** New York, New York.

PUBLICATIONS

Collection

Collected Stories. 1994.

Fiction

The Indifferent Children. 1947.
The Injustice Collectors (stories). 1950.
Sybil. 1952.
A Law for the Lion. 1953.
The Romantic Egoists: A Reflection in Eight Minutes (stories). 1954.
The Great World and Timothy Colt. 1956.
Venus in Sparta. 1958.
Pursuit of the Prodigal. 1959.
The House of Five Talents. 1960.
Portrait in Brownstone. 1962.
Powers of Attorney (stories). 1963.
The Rector of Justin. 1964.
The Embezzler. 1966.
Tales of Manhattan. 1967.
A World of Profit. 1969.
Second Chance (stories). 1970.
I Come as a Thief. 1972.
The Partners. 1974.
The Winthrop Covenant. 1976.
The Dark Lady. 1977.
The Country Cousin. 1978.
The House of the Prophet. 1980; reprinted with new introduction by author, 1991.
The Cat and the King. 1981.
Watchfires. 1982.
Narcissa and Other Fables. 1983.
Exit Lady Masham. 1983.
The Book Class. 1984.
Honorable Men. 1986.
Diary of a Yuppie. 1987.
Skinny Island: More Tales of Manhattan. 1987.
The Golden Calves. 1989.
Fellow Passengers. 1989.
The Lady of Situations. 1990.
Fellow Passengers. 1991.
False Gods. 1992.

Three Lives. 1993.
Tales of Yesteryear. 1994.
The Education of Oscar Fairfax. 1995.
The Atonement. 1997.
The Anniversary. 1998.

Play

The Club Bedroom (produced 1967).

Other

Edith Wharton. 1961.
Reflections of a Jacobite. 1961.
Ellen Glasgow. 1964.
Motiveless Malignity (on Shakespeare). 1969.
Henry Adams. 1971.
Edith Wharton: A Woman in Her Time. 1971.
Richelieu. 1972.
A Writer's Capital (autobiography). 1974.
Reading Henry James. 1975.
Persons of Consequence: Queen Victoria and Her Circle. 1979.
Life, Law, and Letters: Essays and Sketches. 1979.
Three "Perfect Novels" and What They Have in Common. 1981.
Unseen Versailles. 1981.
False Dawn: Women in the Age of the Sun King. 1984.
Pioneers and Caretakers: A Study of 9 American Women Novelists. 1985.
The Vanderbilt Era: Profiles of a Gilded Age. 1989.
J.P. Morgan: The Financier as Collector. 1990.
Love Without Wings: Some Friendships in Literature and Politics. 1991.
The Style's a Man. 1994.
The Man Behind a Book. 1996.
La Gloire. 1996.

Editor, *An Edith Wharton Reader*. 1965.
Editor, *The Warden, and Barchester Towers*, by Anthony Trollope. 1966.
Editor, *Fables of Wit and Elegance*. 1975.
Editor, *Maverick in Mauve: The Diary of a Turn-of-the-Century Aristocrat*, by Florence Adele Sloane. 1983.
Editor, *The Hone and Strong Diaries of Old Manhattan*. 1989.

*

Bibliography: *Auchincloss and His Critics: A Bibliographical Record* by Jackson R. Bryer, 1977.

Critical Studies: *The Novel of Manners in America* by James W. Tuttleton, 1972; *Auchincloss* by Christopher C. Dahl, 1986; *Louis Auchincloss: The Growth of a Novelist* by Vincent Piket, 1991; *Louis Auchincloss: A Writer's Life* by Carol Gelderman, 1993.

*   *   *

Louis Auchincloss is a successor to **Edith Wharton** as a chronicler of the New York aristocracy. In this role he necessarily imbues his novels with an elegiac tone as he observes the passing beauties of the city and the fading power of the white Anglo-Saxon Protestants of old families and old money who can no longer sustain their position of dominance. His principal subjects are thus the manners and morals, the money and marriages, the families and houses, the schools and games, the language and arts of the New York aristocracy as he traces its rise, observes its present crisis, and meditates its possible fall and disappearance. The point of vantage from which he often observes the aristocracy is that of the lawyer who serves and frequently belongs to this class.

The idea of good family stands in an uneasy relation to money in Auchincloss's fiction. Auchincloss dramatizes the dilemma of the American aristocracy by showing that it is necessary to possess money to belong to this class but fatal to one's standing within the class to pursue money. People who have connections with those who are still in trade cannot themselves fully qualify as gentlemen, as the opportunistic Mr. Dale in *The Great World and Timothy Colt* shows. On the other hand, Auchincloss is clearly critical of those aristocrats like Bertie Millinder or Percy Prime who do nothing constructive and are engaged simply in the spending of money. Auchincloss recognizes that the family is the most important of aristocratic institutions and that its place in its class is guaranteed by the conservation of its resources. This task of preserving the family wealth falls to the lawyers, and his fiction is rich in the complexities, both moral and financial, of fiduciary responsibility; *Venus in Sparta* is a novel in point.

Auchincloss fully exploits the conflict between the marriage arranged for the good of the family, often by strong women, and romantic or sexual impulses that are destructive of purely social goals, as *Portrait in Brownstone* illustrates. Sex and love are enemies to the organicism of conservative societies, in which the will of the individual is vested in the whole. Auchincloss observes the workings of this organic notion in the structure of family and marriage as well as in institutions like the school and the club. Such institutions preserve a way of life and protect those who live by it from those on the outside who do not.

Auchincloss's fiction does more than present us with a mere record of the institutions that support the American aristocracy. The dramatic interest in his novels and whatever larger importance may be accorded them lies in his recognition that the entire class is in jeopardy and that individual aristocrats are often failures. Sometimes Auchincloss sees problems arising within the context of aristocracy itself, as when individual will or desire comes in conflict with the organicism; perhaps Reese Parmalee, in *Pursuit of the Prodigal*, makes the most significant rebellion of all Auchincloss's characters, but he is rejecting a decadent aristocracy and not aristocracy itself. But the real failures are those aristocrats who suffer, as so many of Auchincloss's male characters do, from a sense of inadequacy and insecurity that leads them to self-destructiveness. They are not strong and tough-fibred, as so many of the women are; they seem too fastidious and over-civilized, and they are failing the idea of society and their class. *A World of Profit* is the most explicit recognition of this failure.

Auchincloss has made his record of the New York aristocracy in a style that is clear and simple, occasionally elegant and brilliant, and sometimes self-consciously allusive. He has a gift for comedy of manners, which he has not sufficiently cultivated, and a fine model in Oscar Wilde. Yet among his faults as a novelist, especially evident because of the particular genre he has chosen, is a failure to give the reader a richness of detail. Furthermore, he sometimes loses control of his novels and permits action to overwhelm theme. The most serious criticism to be made of his work is that while he does indeed pose moral dilemmas for his characters, he too easily resolves their problems for them. He has given us, on balance, a full enough record of upper-class life in New York, but he has fallen short of the most penetrating and meaningful kinds of social insight that the best of the novelists of manners offer.

Of Auchincloss's later efforts, *The Golden Calves* is a novel of the high powered Manhattan art world, in which acquisition takes precedence over appreciation. In the *Times Literary Supplement,* Isabel Fonseca remarks that the buying and selling of art, "with its paranoia about circulation of fakes and its invocation of 'rights' in the service of privilege, is a nice metaphor for Society." As Fonseca points out, the collectors care more about whether their newest painting is authentic than whether it is truly great art. The reviewer found Auchincloss's tale is most convincing at this level, but also noted that his portrayal of love and affection, though integral to the plot, leaves much to be desired.

In *False Gods,* a collection of six novellas, which Kimberly G. Allen in *Library Journal* calls "finely crafted and eloquently written," Auchincloss continues to write about upper middle class Manhattanites. The stories use figures from Greek myths to inform contemporary narratives, a conceit that a *Publishers Weekly* reviewer believes "helps define the ancient yet contemporary ethical dilemmas" facing the characters. Likewise, *Three Lives* is also comprised of novellas about well-to-do New Yorkers. As with his other work, this volume finds Auchincloss continuing his ongoing chronicle of the American aristocracy and remaining faithful to his novel-of-manners style, a form he has carried forth from the early 1900s, even at the end of the twentieth century.

—Chester E. Eisinger, updated by Lisa C. Harper

B

BABCOCK, Winnifred Eaton. *See* EATON, Winnifred.

BACHMAN, Richard. *See* KING, Stephen (Edwin).

BALDWIN, James (Arthur)

Born: New York City, 2 August 1924. **Education:** Public School 139, Harlem, New York, and DeWitt Clinton High School, Bronx, New York, graduated 1942. **Career:** Worked as handyman, dishwasher, waiter, and office boy, New York, and in defense work, Belle Meade, New Jersey, in early 1940s; full-time writer from 1943; lived in Europe, mainly in Paris, 1948-56. Member, Actors Studio, New York; National Advisory Board of CORE (Congress on Racial Equality); and National Committee for a Sane Nuclear Policy. **Awards:** Saxton fellowship, 1945; Rosenwald fellowship, 1948; Guggenheim fellowship, 1954; American Academy award, 1956; Ford fellowship, 1958; National Conference of Christians and Jews Brotherhood award, 1962; George Polk award, 1963; Foreign Drama Critics award, 1964; Martin Luther King, Jr., award (City University of New York), 1978. D.Litt.: University of British Columbia, Vancouver, 1963. **Member:** American Academy, 1964. **Died:** 30 November 1987.

PUBLICATIONS

Collections

Collected Essays. 1998.
Early Novels and Stories. 1998.

Novels

Go Tell It on the Mountain. 1953.
Giovanni's Room. 1956.
Another Country. 1962.
Tell Me How Long the Train's Been Gone. 1968.
If Beale Street Could Talk. 1974.
Just above My Head. 1979.

Short Stories

Going to Meet the Man. 1965.

Plays

The Amen Corner (produced 1955). 1968.
Blues for Mister Charlie (produced 1964). 1964.
One Day, When I Was Lost: A Scenario Based on "The Autobiography of Malcolm X." 1972.
A Deed from the King of Spain (produced 1974).

Screenplay: *The Inheritance,* 1973.

Poetry

Jimmy's Blues: Selected Poems. 1983.

Other

Notes of a Native Son. 1955.
Nobody Knows My Name: More Notes of a Native Son. 1961.
The Fire Next Time. 1963.
Nothing Personal, photographs by Richard Avedon. 1964.
A Rap on Race, with Margaret Mead. 1971.
No Name in the Street. 1972.
A Dialogue: Baldwin and Nikki Giovanni. 1973.
Little Man, Little Man (for children). 1976.
The Devil Finds Work: An Essay. 1976.
The Price of a Ticket: Collected Nonfiction 1948-1985. 1985.
The Evidence of Things Not Seen. 1985.
Conversations, edited by Fred L. Standley and Louis H. Pratt. 1989.

*

Bibliography: "Baldwin: A Checklist 1947-1962" by Kathleen A. Kindt, and "Baldwin: A Bibliography 1947-1962" by Russell G. Fischer, both in *Bulletin of Bibliography,* January-April 1965; *Baldwin: A Reference Guide* by Fred L. and Nancy Standley, 1979.

Critical Studies: *The Furious Passage of Baldwin* by Fern Eckman, 1966; *Baldwin: A Critical Study* by Stanley Macebuh, 1973; *Baldwin: A Collection of Critical Essays* edited by Keneth Kinnamon, 1974; *Baldwin: A Critical Evaluation* edited by Therman B. O'Daniel, 1977; *Baldwin* by Louis H. Pratt, 1978; *Baldwin* by Carolyn W. Sylvander, 1980; *Baldwin: Three Interviews* by Kenneth B. Clark and Malcolm King, 1985; *Black Women in the Fiction of Baldwin* by Trudier Harris, 1985; *Stealing the Fire: The Art and Protest of Baldwin* by Horace Porter, 1988; *Baldwin: Artist on Fire* by W.J. Weatherby, 1989; *Baldwin: The Legacy* edited by Quincy Troupe, 1989; *Talking at the Gates: A Life of Baldwin* by James Campbell, 1991; *New Essays on Go Tell It on the Mountain,* 1996; *James Baldwin: Voice from Harlem* by Ted Gottfried, 1997; *The Critical Reception of James Baldwin in France* by Rosa Bobia, 1997.

*   *   *

James Baldwin's major theme has always been identity or its denial. He developed the complex personal and social dimensions of this theme in four main subjects: church, self, city, and race. The result is a substantial body of writing in fiction, drama, and the personal essay characterized by intense feeling, stylistic eloquence, and social urgency.

As Baldwin was making his first adolescent efforts to write, he was simultaneously preaching in store-front churches in Harlem. Of brief duration, his religious vocation both satisfied his need to prove his worth to his father and complicated his intellectual development. Seeming to simplify personal problems, his religious commitment actually generated tensions that were to make Baldwin an eloquent critic of Christianity, especially its pernicious social effects, as well as a witness of its emotional power and richness. The enduring fictional achievement of Baldwin's involvement with the church is his brilliant first novel, *Go Tell It on the Mountain.* By means of a carefully crafted tripartite structure, rich characterizations, and a distinctive stylistic voice, Baldwin tells the story not only of John Grimes, a Harlem youth undergoing a personal and religious crisis, but also of his stepfather, Gabriel; his stepfather's sister, Florence; and his mother, Elizabeth. With historical scope as well as personal immediacy, the author shows how gender, race, and religion affect the lives of these worshipers in the Temple of the Fire Baptized. Religious experience is conveyed to the reader with overwhelming emotional power, but he is also forced to recognize how it erodes social reality or even, in the case of Gabriel, becomes a means of oppression. The critique of the church is carried further in the play *The Amen Corner,* in which a fanatical woman preacher substitutes her small church for the love of her husband. Narrowly fulfilling, but in the final analysis life-denying, religion must be abandoned, Baldwin implies, if the self is to be realized.

Many of Baldwin's best early essays and stories—"Autobiographical Notes," "Notes of a Native Son," "Stranger in the Village," "The Discovery of What It Means to Be an American," "Previous Condition," "The Rockpile," "The Outing"—concern his search for self. His second novel, *Giovanni's Room,* explores the theme mainly as it relates to love and sexuality. David, an American expatriate in France, must choose between his mistress Hella and his lover Giovanni. By rejecting Giovanni, David denies his true homosexual self and his deepest feeling for another person in favor of socially sanctioned heterosexuality. As Baldwin develops it, the choice is also between America and Europe, conformity and freedom, safety and the risks necessary to realize love. In search of psychological security, David instead precipitates chaos and tragedy for himself, Hella, and Giovanni.

Both *Go Tell It on the Mountain* and *Giovanni's Room* express social concerns, but their emphasis is on psychological conflict. In his third novel, *Another Country,* Baldwin gives greater attention to the city itself as both the arena and the cause of personal problems. The New York setting of this novel, seething with hatred, corruption, and moral disarray, dooms the characters who inhabit its inhuman confines. The most obvious victim is Rufus Scott, a disconsolate black jazz musician who commits suicide at the end of the long first chapter, but the other seven major characters also suffer as they struggle to assuage their guilt and satisfy their craving for love in the unloving urban environment. Some of these concerns appear in the splendid earlier story, "Sonny's Blues" (1957), where, however, racial suffering in the northern city is controlled, expressed, and thus to some degree transcended through music. In *If Beale Street Could Talk,* Baldwin again tries to transcend the hostility of urban life, this time through a story of young love, but his effort is vitiated by sentimentality and problems of fictional technique.

With few exceptions, most of Baldwin's books have dealt in one way or another with race and racism. From youthful disengagement he has moved through commitment to interracial efforts to achieve civil rights to black nationalism to bitter prophecies of racial vengeance on the white West. *The Fire Next Time* is an eloquent statement of militant integrationism, but the play *Blues for Mister Charlie* expresses a deeper racial outrage and a diminished but not entirely abandoned hope for improvement. The social pathology revealed in this drama of race relations in the South derives from psychosexual origins much more than from political or economic causes. The shift from the nonviolent mode of resistance to racism to the advocacy of violence as the appropriate means of black self-defense begins in the play, and receives a stronger endorsement in the idealized portrait of Christopher, a fierce young black nationalist, in the novel *Tell Me How Long the Train's Been Gone.* The protagonist of this novel, a middle-aged actor named Leo Proudhammer, is an autobiographical character whose experience Baldwin sentimentalizes tiresomely, but in the autobiographical material of the tough-minded *No Name in the Street* the author avoids self-pity. Shifting back and forth between private experience and the public history of the violence-wracked 1960s, Baldwin offers in this work a sad and embittered testimony on race and racism. Quite different in its restrained tone and deliberately flat rhetoric from the hortatory *The Fire Next Time,* it is equally impressive.

By comparison Baldwin's later books are minor efforts that do not do justice to his stylistic resources, his capacity for feeling, and his thematic breadth. In any event, as a master of the personal essay, as racial commentator, and as a gifted if uneven novelist and short story writer, Baldwin has been one of the indispensable writers of the third quarter of the twentieth century.

—Kenneth Kinnamon

See the essay on *Go Tell It on the Mountain.*

BALDWIN, Joseph G(lover)

Born: Friendly Grove Factory, Virginia, 21 January 1815. **Education:** Schools in Staunton, Virginia, 1825-27; Staunton Academy, 1827-29; studied law, 1833-35; licensed 1835. **Family:** Married Sidney White in 1840; six children. **Career:** Deputy clerk, Old Chancery Court, Staunton, 1829-32; lawyer, DeKalb, Mississippi, 1836, and Gainesville, 1837-50, and Livingston, 1850-54, both Alabama; law partner of Philip Phillips, Mobile, Alabama, 1853; moved to San Francisco, 1854, and practiced law there; associate justice, California Supreme Court, 1858-62; returned to private practice. Whig member, Alabama House of Representatives, 1843; delegate, Whig Convention, Philadelphia, 1848; candidate for U.S. House of Representatives, 1848, and U.S. Senate, 1860. Copublisher, *Lexington Gazette* (later *Union*), 1835, and *Buchanan Advocate and Commercial Advertiser,* 1835-36, both Virginia. **Died:** 30 September 1864.

PUBLICATIONS

Fiction

The Flush Times of Alabama and Mississippi: A Series of Sketches. 1853; edited by William A. Owens, 1957.
The Flush Times of California, edited by Richard E. Amacher and George W. Polhemus. 1966.

Other

Party Leaders: Sketches of Jefferson, Hamilton, Jackson, Clay, Randolph of Roanoke. 1854.

*

Bibliography: in *Bibliography of American Literature* by Jacob Blanck, 1955.

Critical Studies: "Baldwin: Humorist or Moralist?" by Eugene Current-Garcia, in *The Frontier Humorists: Critical Essays* edited by M. Thomas Inge, 1975; "The Transfiguration of a Southwestern Humor Sketch: Joseph Glover Baldwin's 'Jo. Heyfron'" by Mark A. Keller, in *American Humor: An Interdisciplinary Newsletter,* Fall 1981; "Baldwin's Patrician Humor" by Mary Ann Wimsatt, in *Thalia: Studies in Literary Humor,* Fall-Winter 1983.

*　　*　　*

Although well known to American literary scholars for *The Flush Times of Alabama and Mississippi,* Joseph G. Baldwin has been little studied. As the title itself suggests, *Flush Times* constitutes an attempt to re-create in the *native* American tradition of the Old Southwest humorists a day and age with which Baldwin was well acquainted: an "age of litigation in a lawless country," as Eugene Current-Garcia says. A closer examination both of the author's life and the text of his work, however, suggests that Baldwin, in addition to being a frontier humorist, is a serious "moralist" who employs traditional conventions such as satire and irony in his exposure of the vices and weaknesses of humankind, thus bridging the gap between native Southwest humor and the older literary conventions of Europe.

Baldwin's purpose was doubtlessly moral, and his generic forte was essays and sketches rather than short stories. His literary models were, in all probability, Lamb and Dickens. His best character types remain self-important Virginians, inexperienced lawyers, and garrulous narrators. Two characters in particular are notable. Ovid Bolus, Esq., a truly artful liar, and Colonel Simon Suggs, Jr., to Current-Garcia the "symbol of his time, the epitome of a lawless, acquisitive society that had raised fraud and corruption to the level of 'super-Spartan roguery.'"

Nineteenth-century sensibilities extended, by contemporary standards, odd shadows. As a practicing attorney, Baldwin no doubt felt some sense of embarrassment over his authorship of *Flush Times,* a work that many American Victorians would have considered inconsequential. In order to demonstrate his talents for more serious writing, Baldwin published in 1854 *Party Leaders,* which is rarely read in the late twentieth century. Containing sketches of political leaders like **Thomas Jefferson**, Hamilton, Jackson, Clay, and Randolph, the book is motivated by the author's biographical and historical impulse and emphasizes moral instruction at the expense of humor.

Had Baldwin not died as suddenly as he did, he might well have become, as his wife believed, the Thucydides of the Civil War. In any event, his accomplishments as frontier humorist, moralist, and essayist continue to be admired by readers.

—George C. Longest

BAMBARA, Toni Cade

Also wrote as Toni Cade. **Born:** Toni Cade in New York City, 25 March 1939. **Education:** Queen's College, New York, 1955-59, B.A. in theater arts 1959; City College of New York, M.A. in literature 1963. **Family:** One daughter. **Career:** Worked as a so-cial worker, State Department of Social Welfare, New York, 1956-59; director of recreation, psychiatry department, Metropolitan Hospital, New York City, 1961-62; program director, Colony House Community Center, New York City, 1962-65; director and adviser, Theatre of the Black Experience, New York, 1965-69; English instructor, SEEK Program, City College of New York (now City College of the City University of New York), 1965-69; assistant professor, Livingstone College, Rutgers University, New Brunswick, New Jersey, 1969-74; founder and director, Pamoja Writers Collective, 1976-85; instructor, filmmaker, and videomaker, Scribe Video Center, Philadelphia, since 1986. Visiting professor, Duke University, Atlanta University, and Emory University, Atlanta, Georgia, 1975-79; artist-in-residence, Neighborhood Arts Center, Atlanta, 1975-79, Stephens College, Columbia, Missouri, 1976, and Spelman College, Atlanta, 1978-79. **Awards:** American Book Award, 1981; Langston Hughes Society Award, 1981, and Medallion, 1986. Honorary degree: SUNY-Albany, New York, 1990. **Residence:** Philadelphia. **Died:** 1995.

PUBLICATIONS

Short Stories

Gorilla, My Love. 1972.
The Seabirds Are Still Alive: Collected Stories. 1977.

Novels

The Salt Eaters. 1980.
If Blessing Comes. 1987.

Plays

Screenplays: *Zora,* 1971; *The Johnson Girls,* 1972; *Victory Gardens,* 1977; *Transactions,* 1979; *The Long Night,* 1981; *Epitaph for Willie,* 1982; *Tar Baby* (based on the novel by Toni Morrison), 1984; *Raymond's Run* (based on Bambara's story), 1985; *The Bombing of Osage,* 1986; *Celia B. Moore, Master Tactician of Direct Action,* 1987.

Other

Raymond's Run (for children). 1990.
Deep Sightings and Rescue Missions: Fiction, Essays, and Conversations, edited by Toni Morrison. 1996.

Editor (as Toni Cade), *The Black Woman: Anthology.* 1970.
Editor, *Tales and Stories for Black Folks* (for children). 1971.
Editor, with Leah Wise, *Southern Black Utterances Today.* 1975.

*

Bibliography: in *American Women Writing Fiction* edited by Mickey Pearlman, 1989.

Critical Studies: "Youth in Bambara's *Gorilla, My Love*" by Nancy D. Hargrove in *Women Writers of the Contemporary South,* edited by Peggy Whitman Prenshaw, 1984; "From Baptism to Resurrection: Bambara and the Incongruity of Language" by Ruth Elizabeth Burks in *Black Women Writers (1950-1980),* edited by

Mari Evans, 1984; "'What It Is I Think She's Doing Anyhow:' A Reading of Bambara's *The Salt Eaters*" by Gloria Hull in *Conjuring: Black Women, Fiction, and Literary Tradition,* edited by Marjorie Pryse and Hortense J. Spillers, 1985; "Problematizing the Individual: Bambara's Stories for the Revolution" in *Specifying: Black Women Writing the American Experience,* by Susan Willis, 1987; "The Dance of Characters and Community" by Martha M. Vertreace in *American Women Writing Fiction,* edited by Mickey Pearlman, 1989; "Go Eena Kumbla: A Comparison of Erna Brodber's *Jane and Louisa Will Soon Come Home* and Toni Cade Bambara's *The Salt Eaters*" by Daryl Cumber Dance in *Caribbean Women Writers: Essays from the First International Conference,* edited by Selwyn R. Cudjoe, 1990; "Women's Interracial Friendships and Visions of Community in *Meridian, The Salt Eaters, Civil Wars,* and *Dessa Rose*" by Nancy Porter in *Tradition and the Talents of Women,* edited by Florence Howe, 1991; "'Dialectics of Correctedness': Supernatural Elements in Novels by Bambara, Cisneros, Grahn, and Erdrich" by Wendy K. Kolmar in *Haunting the House of Fiction: Feminist Perspectives on Ghost Stories by American Women,* edited by Kolmar and Lynette Carpenter, 1991; "Time, Motion, Sound, and Fury in *The Sea Birds Are Still Alive*" by Lois F. Lyles in *College Language Association Journal,* 1992; "Toni Cade Bambara" by Nancy D. Hargrove, in *Contemporary Fiction Writers of the South: A Bio-Bibliographical Sourcebook,* edited by Joseph M. Flora and Robert Bain, 1993.

*   *   *

Widely respected for her collections of short stories (the most recent of which, *Deep Sightings and Rescue Missions,* was published posthumously in 1996), Toni Cade Bambara was a consummate wordsmith who blended her passionate social concerns with a deep appreciation for and understanding of African American and youth culture. A novelist, essayist, screenwriter, and short story writer, Bambara first gained national attention for her groundbreaking anthology *The Black Woman* (1970), which explored the intersection between race and gender in African American women's fiction. It was followed by the less ambitious *Tales and Stories of Black Folk* (1971), a collection of traditional African American folklore and short fiction. But Bambara's enduring literary reputation is the result of her particular narrative strength: her faithful renditions of the cadences and nuances of African American speech infuse her fiction with an arresting accuracy that powerfully captures the language and sensibility of African Americans.

Bambara is perhaps best known for her short fiction, which poignantly depicts adolescent life in a society rife with bigotry and injustice. Her first and most popular collection, *Gorilla, My Love* (1972), sensitively explores the struggles of young people—mostly females—growing up in a world that is alternately indifferent and hostile to them. The manner in which her pre-teen and teenage protagonists come to terms with the uncertain world where they live both reflects Bambara's understanding of the particular difficulties of youth and affirms her belief in the resilience of the human spirit.

In the short story "Happy Birthday," Ollie, a young orphan who lives with her grandfather, is forced to confront the loneliness that characterizes her young life. With her grandfather in a drunken stupor, Ollie spends her birthday in a doomed and desperate search for companionship and attention. Sadly, the only present Ollie receives is the tragic awareness that her birthday is no different from the other bleak, lonely days she has always known.

While childhood loneliness is the primary theme of "Happy Birthday," disillusionment is the focus of the title story, "Gorilla, My Love." Hazel, the narrator, believes her favorite uncle's promise to marry her when she grows up, and her discovery of her uncle's recent engagement leads her to the painful conclusion that no adult, not even a family member, can be trusted to keep his word. Angered by this betrayal, Hazel strikes out against the deceitful adult world, setting fire to the local movie theater's candy stand after the manager refuses to refund her money for a film that is not all that it was "advertised" to be. Whether or not Hazel's destructive tendencies continue depends ultimately on the questionable ability of the adults in her life to restore her faith in them.

"Raymond's Run," one of Bambara's most anthologized stories, explores the love that leads to true family unity. The life of the young narrator, Hazel Elizabeth Deborah Parker, centers on caring for her retarded brother Raymond and running. Threatened by the presence of another talented female runner in the neighborhood, Hazel is consumed by her desire to win the annual May Day race. But once the race begins, she discovers that it is Raymond, racing with her outside of the fence surrounding the track, who offers her the greatest challenge. Hazel realizes that by teaching Raymond to run she can make his life, and her own, far more meaningful. She wins the race, but her victory is less important than the joyous new awareness of her love for her brother.

More overtly political than her earlier works, Bambara's second collection of short stories, *The Sea Birds Are Still Alive* (1977), explores the personal impact of racial and gender inequality and stresses the need for an organized, community-wide response. In "A Girl's Story" Bambara uses a young girl's first menstruation to illustrate how female sexuality often is maligned in a male-dominated society. Rather than finding the support she needs to understand the important changes in her maturing body, the young protagonist Rae Ann is accused of having had a coat-hanger abortion by her brother and grandmother. Their cruel taunts perpetuate Rae Ann's sense of inferiority and feed her growing fear that she, unlike her brother, will be defined primarily by her bodily processes. In the title story, "The Sea Birds Are Still Alive," Bambara offers a thoughtful meditation on the enduring nature of the human spirit. Set on board an unidentified ship en route to an undisclosed destination, the story focuses on the conflicting thoughts and feelings of a group of people as they watch a mother and her daughter feed the birds that follow the vessel. The onlookers, either victims of or participants in a repressive social order, see the woman's actions as frivolous or ignorant according to their political beliefs. But none of the onlookers is aware of the irony of the situation: the mother, a former torture victim, allows her daughter to feed the birds with food given to her by one of her torturers. The sea birds that eat the presumably poisoned food survive, just as the woman has, symbolizing humanity's ability to endure even the bleakest of circumstances.

Bambara's novel *The Salt Eaters* (1981) continues her more explicit political themes. Winner of the American Book Society Award, the novel examines the connection between personal growth, spiritual healing, and social transformation in a small Southern community. Presented in a challenging nonlinear fashion, the novel traces the development of Velma Henry, a committed social activist, as she recovers from a suicide attempt and begins, with the help of her community, the difficult journey towards a place of peace and wholeness.

Underlying all of Bambara's works is the abiding belief that the best in all people, regardless of race or gender, needs to be recognized and constantly celebrated. Sometimes funny, often poignant, but always inspired, her fiction captures the ordinary lives of African Americans without sentimentality or condescension. Her unique vision offered valuable insight into what it has meant to be human in the twentieth century.

—Alisa A. Johnson

BANNISTER, Nathaniel (H.)

Born: 1813. **Family:** Married the widow of John Augustus Stone, 1835. **Career:** Playwright. Began career in New York and Philadelphia before moving to New Orleans, 1834. **Died:** 1847.

PUBLICATIONS

Plays

Gaulantus the Gaul. 1836.
The Destruction of Jerusalem. 1837.
The Gentleman of Lyons. 1838.
The Maine Question. 1839.
Putnam, the Iron Son of '76. 1844.

Other

Adapter, *Conaneheotah; or, the Indian's War Horse.* 1838.
Adapter, *Rookwood,* by William Harrison Ainsorth. 1844.

*   *   *

Unquestionably American in his outlook and professionally trained as actor and playwright to take advantage of the various and fickle fashions of American theater, Nathaniel H. Bannister made significant contributions to American dramatic literature during the second quarter of the nineteenth century. As he once wrote in an unpublished poem, "the stage but echoes back the Public Voice." During a brief career in which he wrote at least forty plays—mostly remembered by title only—he attempted, with moderate success, to follow the dictates of that voice. Five of this plays were published, one, *Gaulantas,* in a collection of four plays with J. R. Planche's *The Brigand,* Richard B. Sheridan's *Pizarro,* and **John Howard Payne**'s *Brutus.* His most popular play, *Putnam, the Iron Son of '76* (1844), had an initial run of seventy-eight nights at New York's Bowery Theatre and remained a favorite stage attraction for years.

In spite of Bannister's achievements as both actor and playwright, his reputation did not fare well with most twentieth-century theater historians. Montrose Moses and A. H. Quinn ignored both his spectacular melodramas, which the people had flocked to see, and his experimental plays, such as his fifteen-act version of *The Wandering Jew* and *The Destruction of Jerusalem,* in which his depictions of good and evil spirits so disturbed audiences that the theater manager, Francis Wemyss, withdrew it after six nights. Also, East Coast critics of his day, who in general disdained theatrical efforts in other parts of America, looked askance at this actor who in 1834 left New York and Philadelphia to join the acting company of the American Theatre in New Orleans.

In 1835 Bannister wrote five plays and married an actress, the widow of John Augustus Stone, author of *Metamora.* By the fall of 1837 Bannister had returned with his wife to Philadelphia and New York, where he began his association with the Bowery Theatre as both actor and playwright, an association that lasted for the rest of his life. The year before Bannister's death, a critic for the *Spirit of the Times* described his "peculiar powers for arranging terrific plots and for disposing spectacles to the best effect." In perspective, Bannister earned his excellent reputation as an actor and playwright in the American South and West and became a popular presence in New York.

Combining a patriotic theme and horses on stage—each of these having a rich history in theater around the world—Bannister created his most successful work, *Putnam, the Iron Son of '76,* a military drama in three acts that inspired a tradition in American theater. From the time the curtain opens upon a chorus singing, "Our tyrant shall tremble, we will be free," the patriotic theme rises and never falters. As for spectacle, audiences never tired of the famous run on horseback from the top of the theatre, 150 feet in height, down onto the stage. With romance, sentiment, crafty villains, and a plot in which a traitor is hanged and the British are duped as well as defeated, Bannister provided the exciting evening at the theater that the public of that time demanded. General Israel Putnam may have been the hero, but Black Vulture, the superbly trained horse, was the main attraction. Although imitations by other playwrights appeared immediately, *Putnam* was still being presented in New York thirty years later.

At a time when playwriting was hardly admired and certainly not lucrative, Bannister followed his dream—and died in poverty. For many of his plays he received nothing; his pay for *Putnam* was fifty dollars. Like most of his contemporaries, Bannister wrote for actors: at least one play for Edwin Forrest, several for Charles B. Parsons, most for himself. They were "powerful, vigorous and original" plays, according to Joseph Ireland, the nineteenth-century theater historian. With few exceptions Bannister's plays echoed the "Public Voice" that was America. In contrast to most contemporary actor-playwrights, however, he wrote mainly original plays, only occasionally adapting current fiction, such as William Harrison Ainsworth's *Rookwood* (1844) and *Conaneheotah; or, the Indian's War Horse* (1838) from a story in *Blackwood's Magazine.* For Yankee actors he wrote *The Yankee Duelist; or, Bunker's Hill Representative* (1838); emphasizing national issues, he wrote *The Maine Question* (1839) and *The Fall of San Antonio; or, Texas Victorious* (1836), among others. Responding to Americans' interest in Roman history, Bannister created a half dozen plays, including *Caius Silvius; or, the Slave of Carthage* (1835) and *Gaulantus the Gaul* (1836), a five-act tragedy in verse that boasts a moving spirit and exciting scenes remarkable for a twenty-three-year-old playwright. For *The Gentleman of Lyons; or, the Marriage Contract* (1838), Bannister undoubtedly took his title from Bulwer Lytton's *The Lady of Lyons,* which appeared in London that same year, but wove his own melodramatic plot while creating the effective scenes of comedy of manners that made this play one of the more skillfully crafted by an American to that date.

Clearly a hard-working professional in the theater, Bannister was an intelligent and well-read man, an imaginative writer who was always eager to please audiences and theater managers. Although he was an actor writing plays for his own talents—as were scores of other journeymen playwrights of this period in

America—the kind of plays he wrote suggests his hopes for the theater. Obviously creating plays for the moment (because the theater is always now), he was always mindful of that "Public Voice," which he tried to make heard with a distinctively American viewpoint. All of Bannister's extant plays include those dramatic scenes and stirring situations so necessary to Jacksonian era audiences. *Putnam, The Gentleman of Lyons,* and the last act of *Gaulantas* show Bannister as exemplary among his peers and one of whom still better things might have been expected had he lived longer.

—Walter J. Meserve

BARAKA, Amiri

Born: Everett LeRoi Jones in Newark, New Jersey, 7 October 1934; took name Amiri Baraka in 1968. **Education:** Central Avenue School and Barringer High School, Newark; Rutgers University, New Brunswick, New Jersey, 1951-52; Howard University, Washington, D.C., 1953-54, B.A. in English 1954; Columbia University, New York, M.A. in philosophy; New School for Social Research, New York, M.A. in German literature. **Military Service:** Served in the U.S. Air Force, 1954-57. **Family:** Married 1) Hettie Cohen in 1958 (divorced 1965), two daughters; 2) Sylvia Robinson (now Amini Baraka) in 1966, five children; also two step-daughters and one other daughter. **Career:** Teacher, New School for Social Research, New York, 1961-64, and summers, 1977-79, State University of New York, Buffalo, Summer 1964, and Columbia University, New York, 1964 and Spring 1980; visiting professor, San Francisco State College, 1966-67, Yale University, New Haven, Connecticut, 1977-78, George Washington University, Washington, D.C. 1978-79, and Rutgers University, 1988; since 1980 professor of African studies, State University of New York, Stony Brook. Founder, *Yugen* magazine and Totem Press, New York, 1958-62; editor, with Diane di Prima, *Floating Bear* magazine, New York, 1961-63; founding director, Black Arts Repertory Theatre, Harlem, New York, 1964-66; director of several of his own plays. Since 1966 founding director, Spirit House, Newark; involved in Newark politics: candidate, Newark community council, 1968, member of the United Brothers, 1967, and Committee for Unified Newark, 1969-75; Chairman, Congress of Afrikan People, 1972-75; member, All African Games, Pan African Federation, National Black Political Assembly (secretary general; co-governor), National Black United Front, Black Writers' Union, League of Revolutionary Struggle. **Awards:** Whitney fellowship, 1961; Obie award, for drama, 1964; Guggenheim fellowship, 1965; Yoruba Academy fellow, 1965; Dakar Festival prize, 1966; National Endowment for the Arts grant, 1966; Rockefeller grant, 1981; Poetry award, National Endowment for the Arts, 1981; New Jersey Council for the Arts award, 1982; Before Columbus Foundation award, 1984; American Book award, 1984; PEN-Faulkner award, 1989; Langston Hughes medal, for outstanding contribution to literature, 1989; Ferroni award, Italy, and Foreign Poet award, 1993; Playwright's award, Black Drama Festival, Winston-Salem North Carolina, 1997. D.H.L.: Malcolm X College, Chicago, 1972. **Member:** Black Academy of Arts and Letters. **Residence:** Newark, New Jersey.

PUBLICATIONS

Collections

Raise Race Rays Raze: Essays since 1965. 1971.
Selected Poetry of Amiri Baraka/LeRoi Jones. 1979.
Daggers and Javelins: Essays 1974-1979. 1984.
The LeRoi Jones/Amiri Baraka Reader. 1991.

Plays

A Good Girl Is Hard to Find (produced 1958).
Dante (produced 1961; as *The 8th Ditch,* produced 1964). In *The System of Dante's Hell,* 1965.
The Toilet (produced 1962). In *The Baptism, and The Toilet,* 1967.
Dutchman (produced 1964). In *Dutchman, and The Slave,* 1964.
The Slave (produced 1964). In *Dutchman, and The Slave,* 1964.
Dutchman, and The Slave. 1964.
The Baptism (produced 1964). In *The Baptism, and The Toilet,* 1967.
Jello (produced 1965). 1970.
Experimental Death Unit No. 1 (produced 1965). In *Four Black Revolutionary Plays.* 1969.
A Black Mass (produced 1966). In *Four Black Revolutionary Plays,* 1969.
The Baptism, and The Toilet. 1967.
Arm Yrself or Harm Yrself (produced 1967). 1967.
Slave Ship: A Historical Pageant (produced 1967). 1967.
Madheart (produced 1967). In *Four Black Revolutionary Plays,* 1969.
Great Goodness of Life (A Coon Show) (produced 1967). In *Four Black Revolutionary Plays,* 1969.
Home on the Range (produced 1968). In *Drama Review,* Summer 1968.
Police, in *Drama Review,* Summer 1968.
The Death of Malcolm X, in *New Plays from the Black Theatre,* edited by Ed Bullins. 1969.
Four Black Revolutionary Plays. 1969.
Insurrection (produced 1969).
Junkies are Full of (SHHH. . .) and *Bloodrites* (produced 1970). In *Black Drama Anthology,* edited by Woodie King and Ron Milner, 1971.
Black Dada Nihilismus (produced 1971).
BA-RA-KA, in *Spontaneous Combustion: Eight New American Plays,* edited by Rochelle Owens. 1972.
Columbia the Gem of the Ocean (produced 1973).
A Recent Killing (produced 1973).
The New Ark's a Moverin (produced 1974).
The Sidnee Poet Heroical (produced 1975). 1979.
S-1 (produced 1976). In *The Motion of History and Other Plays,* 1978.
America More of Less, with Frank Chin and Leslie Silko (produced 1973).
The Motion of History (produced 1977). In *The Motion of History and Other Plays,* 1978.
The Motion of History and Other Plays (includes *S-1* and *Slave Ship*). 1978.
What Was the Relationship of the Lone Ranger to the Means of Production? (produced 1979).
At the Dim'crackr Convention (produced 1980).
Boy and Tarzan Appear in a Clearing (produced 1981).

Weimar 2 (produced 1981).
Money:A Jazz Opera, with George Gruntz, music by Gruntz (produced 1982).
Song: A One Act Play about the Relationship of Art to Real Life (produced 1983).
Primitive World (produced 1984).
General Hag's Skeezag: A Play. In *Black Theater,* 1992.
The Election Machine Warehouse. 1997.

Screenplays: *Dutchman,* 1967; *Black Spring,* 1968; *Supercoon,* 1971; *A Fable,* 1971.

Fiction

The System of Dante's Hell. 1965.
Tales. 1967.

Poetry

Spring and So forth. 1960.
Preface to a Twenty Volume Suicide Note. 1961.
The Dead Lecturer. 1964.
Black Art. 1966.
A Poem for Black Hearts. 1967.
Black Magic: Poetry 1961-1967. 1969.
It's Nation Time. 1970.
In Our Terribleness: Some Elements and Meaning in Black Style, with Fundi (Billy Abernathy). 1970.
Spirit Reach. 1972.
Afrikan Revolution. 1973.
Hard Facts. 1976.
Selected Poetry. 1979.
AM/TRAK. 1979.
In the Tradition: For Black Arthur Blythe. 1980.
Reggae or Not! 1982.
Thoughts for You!. 1984.
LeRoi Jones-Amiri. 1991.
An Amiri Baraka/LeRoi Jones Poetry Sampler. 1991.
Transbluency: The Selected Poems of Amiri Baraka/LeRoi Jones (1961-1995). 1995.
Wise, Why's, Y's. 1995.
Funk Lore: New Poems, 1984-1995. 1996.

Other

Cuba Libre. 1961.
Blues People: Negro Music in White America. 1963.
Home: Social Essays. 1966.
Black Music. 1968.
A Black Value System. 1970.
Gary and Miami: Before and After. N.d.
Strategy and Tactics of a Pan African Nationalist Party. 1971.
Beginning of National Movement. 1972.
Kawaida Studies: The New Nationalism. 1972.
National Liberation and Politics. 1974.
Crisis in Boston! 1974.
Afrikan Free School. 1974.
Toward Ideological Clarity. 1974.
The Creation of the New Ark. 1975.
Selected Plays and Prose. 1979.
Spring Song. 1979.

The Autobiography of LeRoi Jones. 1984.
The Music: Reflections on Jazz and Blues. 1987.
Thornton Dial: Images of the Tiger. 1993.
Shy's Wise, Y's: The Griot's Tale. 1994.
Heathens and Revolutionary Art: Poems and Lecture. 1994.
Conversations with Amiri Baraka, edited by Charlie Reilly. 1994.
Eulogies. 1996.
Home: Social Essays. 1998.
Digging. 1999.

Editor, *January 1st 1959: Fidel Castro.* 1959.
Editor, *Four Young Lady Poets.* 1962.
Editor, *The Moderns: New Fiction in America.* 1963.
Editor and co-author, *In-formation.* 1965.
Editor, *Black and White,* by Gilbert Sorrentino. 1965.
Editor, *Hands Up!,* by Edward Dorn, 1965.
Editor and contributor, *Afro-American Festival of the Arts Magazine.* 1966; published as *Anthology of Our Black Selves,* 1969.
Editor, with Larry Neal, *Black Fire: An Anthology of Afro-American Writing.* 1968.
Editor, with Larry Neal and A.B. Spellman, *The Cricket: Black Music in Evolution.* 1968; published as *Trippin': A Need for Change,* 1969.
Editor, *African Congress: A Documentary of the First Modern Pan-African Congress.* 1972.
Editor, with Diane di Prima, *The Floating Bear: A Newsletter.* 1974.
Editor, with Amini Baraka, *Confirmation: An Anthology of African American Women.* 1983.

*

Bibliography: *Jones (Baraka): A Checklist of Works by and about Him* by Letitia Dace.

Critical Studies: *From Jones to Baraka: The Literary Works* by Theodore Hudson, 1973; *Baraka: The Renegade and the Mask* by Kimberly W. Benston, 1976, and *Baraka (Jones): A Collection of Critical Essays* edited by Benston, 1978; *Baraka/Jones: The Quest for a Populist Modernism* by Werner Sollors, 1978; *Baraka* by Lloyd W. Brown, 1980; *To Raise, Destroy, and Create: The Poetry, Drama, and Fiction of Baraka (Jones)* by Henry C. Lacey, 1981; *Theatre and Nationalism: Wole Soyinka and Jones* by Alain Ricard, 1983; *The Poetry and Poetics of Baraka: The Jazz Aesthetic* by William J. Harris, 1986. "From LeRoi Jones to Baraka and Back" by Johan Thielemans in *New Essays on American Drama,* 1989; "Amiri Baraka and the Politics of Pop Culture" by David Lionel Smith in *Politics and the Muse: Studies in the Politics of Recent American Culture,* 1989; "Ethnos and the Beat Poets" by Steve Harney in *Journal of American Studies* vol. 25, no. 3, 1991; "Jazz in the Poetry of Amiri Baraka and Roy Fisher" by Mary Ellison, in *Yearbook of English Studies,* 1994, pp. 117-45; "August Wilson and the Four B's: Influences" by Mark William Rocha in *August Wilson: A Casebook,* edited by Marilyn Elkins, 1994; "The Limits of African- American Political Realism: Baraka's *Dutchman* and Wilson's *Ma Rainey's Black Bottom*" by Eric Bergesen and William W. Demastes, in *Realism and the American Dramatic Tradition,* edited by William W. Demastes, 1996; "Looking into Black Skulls: Amiri Baraka's *Dutchman* and the Psychology of Race" by George Piggford, in *Modern Drama,* spring 1997, pp. 74-85; *A Nation Within a Nation: Amiri Baraka (LeRoi Jones) and Black Power Politics* by Komozi Woodard, 1999.

*   *   *

Amiri Baraka (born Everett LeRoi Jones) says he has "always tried to be a revolutionary." That is the consistent quality in a more than thirty-year career which has included writing in every literary genre and representing contradictory points of view.

The rebel in Baraka led him in his youth to prefer running with the ghetto gangs to remaining in his respectable middle-class home. At Howard University, which he found distastefully bourgeois, it led him to quit college after his junior year to join the Air Force. In New York in the late 1950s, it prompted him to become a Greenwich Village bohemian and a disciple of **Allen Ginsberg** and **Jack Kerouac**, to turn out lyric poetry and surreal fiction expressing the romantic angst and waggish frivolity which permitted publication under titles such as *The System of Dante's Hell* and *Preface to a Twenty Volume Suicide Note:* "My wife is left-handed. / which implies a fierce de- /termination. ITS WEIRD BABY. / The way some folks are always trying to be / different. A sin & a shame."

Jones in the late 1950s and early 1960s possessed a boundless energy and an extraordinarily diverse talent. He was still speaking to white people and writing for a racially mixed audience. He founded periodicals with two white women, the magazine *Yugen* with his wife Hettie Cohen and the newsletter *The Floating Bear*—its title derived from an A.A. Milne Winnie the Pooh story—with the poet Diane di Prima. His saturation in the western literary tradition (**William Carlos Williams**, **Walt Whitman**, **T.S. Eliot**, Yeats, **Ezra Pound**, and the Black Mountain poets) was clearly discernible in his poetry and novel. At that time Jones did not write specifically ethnic literature. Indeed, he alleged in 1959 that "Negro writing" can at best be folklore, for what is written out of racial consciousness cannot achieve literary status. In 1961 his poetry muses "Africa / is a foreign place. You are / as any other sad man here / american."

Yet even in the early work techniques analogous to black music—jazz and the blues—are evident, and Jones was also writing music criticism and essays expressing an increasingly inflammatory political consciousness. He was becoming politicized as early as 1960, when he visited Cuba and wrote the essay *Cuba Libre* in praise of Castro and that island's revolution. His verse became edgy, uneasy with his white life, and his essays and plays began to express an urgency which was turning, by 1964, to racial militancy.

Although a portion of his novel and the play *The Toilet* had been produced earlier, 1964 was the year that Baraka really won attention as a playwright. In March *The Eighth Ditch* (his Dante play) opened and was quickly closed by police on grounds of obscenity. Within a week *The Baptism,* an equally startling play, this one a religious satire which drew charges of both obscenity and blasphemy, jarred and amused its spectators. The very next day *Dutchman* opened, and later that year a double bill of *The Toilet* and *The Slave* further solidified Baraka's reputation. (A full-length play, *A Recent Killing,* which was written in this year but not produced until a decade later, dramatizes an interracial cooperation in which Jones was already losing faith.)

These plays are blistering in their dramatization of raw racial tensions on a realistic level, but they also function on an allegorical plane. *Dutchman,* in particular, is generally acknowledged to be his finest achievement. The Flying Dutchman constitutes one of the more obvious symbolic references in this play about a woman picking up a man on a New York City subway, but critical opinion has been divided over whether white Lula or black Clay embodies the legendary captain who is doomed to roam until his final peace can be purchased by a lover willing to die with

him. Perhaps it is white racism, as exemplified by the murderous Lula, that will not die, or possibly the swallowing of pride and suppression of rage, which the superficially assimilated Clay practices, represents what Jones had in mind. Whatever the parallel, a double death does not occur, so the spectre of racism is not exorcised.

Dutchman can also be interpreted as a modernization of the Adam and Eve story in which Lula—who keeps eating and offering apples—is a corrupter of the innocent, natural man of Africa and the cause of his expulsion from the paradise of the American dream. Other religious parables which have been discerned include that of Clay as Christ and Lula as Satan (with the young man at the end representing the resurrection) and the idea that Clay is being baptized in hellfire. *Dutchman* can therefore be viewed as a reference to disguise and the voluntary assumption of roles. Lula is an author creating a series of characters for herself. When Clay stops concealing his blackness behind white clothes, intellectual interests, and a courteous demeanor, Lula rewards his self-assertion with murder.

Equally playable and nearly equally subject to glosses (sometimes more arcane than illuminating), *The Toilet* and *The Slave* take somewhat different approaches to racial conflict. The earlier play, *The Toilet,* depicts interracial relations in a fashion which Baraka later came to regard as more sentimental than realistic, for the black gang leader really loves the white boy who is beaten up in the lavatory, and he returns to comfort Karolis when the bullies have left. A major factor in the play's appeal is Baraka's embodiment in his protagonist of a universal conflict between the gentle, nurturing, reflective aspect of the character (the "Ray" side of us) and the belligerent, aloof, authoritative aspect (the "Foots" side). The split in this particular temperament, of course, sets up a conflict between the assimilationist with aspirations to white goals (Ray, the good student who is attracted to Karolis) and the true black man (Foots, the natural leader).

Although *The Toilet* is milder than *Dutchman, The Slave* finds its protagonist has progressed beyond the birth of militance, which Clay barely reaches, to full leadership in a race war. Walker has left the insurgents just long enough to visit a white couple, his ex-wife and her new husband, the latter a college professor who represents the western culture to which Walker has bidden farewell. That he would pay such a call at all suggests that Walker is still something of a slave to the white liberal heritage, and the old slave whom Walker becomes in a long monologue reinforces that notion. Still, Walker is wiping out, literally, the old associations, and he, like Jones himself at this time of his life, sets a new, independent course.

Jones's drama had been by and large realistic and by and large addressed to a white or racially mixed audience. But the radical changes in his life—his departure in 1965 for Harlem and soon thereafter for the Newark ghetto, his divorce (subsequent to the prophetic *The Slave*) from the white wife (who now felt she was the enemy) and his marriage to a black woman, his conversion to the Kawaida sect of Muslim and his adoption of an African name, Amiri (prince) Baraka (blessedness), preceded for a time by the religious title Imamu (spiritual leader)—all reflect an ideological transformation which had a profound effect upon his writing. The essays grew violent, the poetry took on the dialect of black speech, and the plays increasingly spoke only to blacks and were presented in segregated theaters. Realism was generally rejected in favor of a technique sometimes expressionistic and sometimes a montage of brief episodes, cinematic juxtapositions.

The first plays of this black militant period, including *Experimental Death Unit No. 1, Jello, A Black Mass,* and *Madheart,* explicitly proclaim the superiority of black to white, of black revolutionist to assimilationist, and of male to female. *Jello* is also a quite funny parody of Jack Benny's radio show in which Rochester stops serving Benny and starts asserting his newfound black manhood, and *A Black Mass* is a lyrical evocation of a misguided black man's creation of the white race. While some later black nationalist plays by Baraka—*Arm Yrself or Harm Yrself,* for instance—are simple didactic dramas with lines which preach the point, others make considerable use of nonverbal techniques and are theatrical in ways Antonin Artaud would have appreciated. *Slave Ship,* for instance, forces its spectators to feel they themselves are manacled in the hold of that ship, and it employs Swahili and moans and groans quite as much as English dialogue. The play's spectacle of human suffering is marvelously powerful drama. Some other plays of the late 1960s are cinematic or surreal, and some experiment with language in ways outside the tradition of mainstream American drama.

A recent resurgence of the polemical in Baraka's dramaturgy has followed another political change. The creator of and foremost writer in the black arts movement by 1973 had become a Communist leader and had rejected his nationalist rage and rancor toward whites as racist. Therefore, *S-1* and *The Motion of History* employ agit-prop techniques, in the former to attack a proposed senate bill which opponents felt would have abridged freedom of speech and assembly, and in the latter to urge the solidarity of blacks and whites in a revolution to overthrow their oppressors. *The Motion of History* dramatizes instances from the past four centuries in which the ruling class has pitted poor blacks and whites against each other so as to obscure their common interests in ending exploitation. This play even ridicules the black militant, who is represented as a mindless robot chanting "the white man is the devil."

Although *The LeRoi Jones/Amiri Baraka Reader* includes representative works of the revolutionary author's long and loud career, it best clarifies the self-mythologized fourth period of Baraka's life, his "Third World Marxist Period (1974—)." This chapter of *The Reader* includes essays from *Daggers and Javelins* (including "The Revolutionary Tradition in Afro-American Literature"), two chapters from the 1984 *Autobiography of LeRoi Jones/Amiri Baraka,* and a section of Baraka's long essay on Jesse Jackson and the 1988 Democratic Convention. Other previously unpublished works include "Jimmy!" (a eulogy for **James Baldwin**), and more than a dozen sections of what may become an epic poem of African American history titled "Why's/Wise." Baraka's introductory note places "Why's/Wise" in the tradition of Williams' *Patterson* and **Charles Olson**'s *Maximus* poems in that "it tries to tell the history / life like an ongoing-off-coming Tale." Amiri Baraka's ongoing dramatic and poetic commentary on this "Tale," which integrates the dynamic energy of his "Beat Period" (1957-1962), his "Black Nationalist Period" (1965-1974), and his "Third World Marxist Period," continues to place Baraka as one of the leaders of African American radical intellectual thought.

—Tish Dace, updated by Andrew O. Jones

BARKER, James Nelson

Born: Philadelphia, Pennsylvania, 17 June 1784; son of General George Barker. **Education:** Schools in Philadelphia. **Military Ser-**

vice: Commissioned Captain in the 2nd U.S. Artillery, 1812; assistant adjutant-general, U.S. Army, rising to the rank of major, 1814-17. **Family:** Married Mary Rogers in 1811; one daughter. **Career:** Playwright, Philadelphia, 1804-08; studied government, Washington, D.C., 1809-10; returned to Philadelphia and resumed writing for the stage, 1812; contributed "The Drama" series to *Dramatic Pieces,* 1816-17; member, Board of Aldermen, Philadelphia, 1817-19, 1822-29: mayor, 1819-21; Collector of the Port of Philadelphia, 1829-38; controller, U.S. Department of the Treasury, Washington, D.C., 1838-41, and served various administrations as clerk in the office of the Chief Clerk of the Treasury. 1841-58. **Died:** 9 March 1858.

PUBLICATIONS

Plays

Tears and Smiles (produced 1807). 1808; edited by Paul H. Musser, in *Barker,* 1929.
The Embargo; or, What News? (produced 1808).
Travellers; or, Music's Fascination, from a work by Andrew Cherry (produced 1808).
The Indian Princess; or, La Belle Sauvage, music by John Bray (produced 1808). 1808; revised version, as *Pocahontas* (produced 1820).
Marmion; or, The Battle of Flodden Field, from the poem by Walter Scott (produced 1812). 1816.
The Armourer's Escape; or, Three Years at Nootka Sound (produced 1817).
How to Try a Lover (as *A Court of Love,* produced 1836). 1817.
Superstition; or, The Fanatic Father (produced 1824). 1826.

Other

Delaplaine's Repository of the Lives and Portraits of Distinguished American Characters, vol. 1, part 2. 1817.
Sketches of the Primitive Settlements on the River Delaware. 1827.

*

Critical Studies: *Barker* by Paul H. Musser, 1929 (includes bibliography); *The Romantic Indian: Sentimental Views from Nineteenth Century American Literature* by Charles M. Lombard, 1981; "James Nelson Barker's *Pocahontas*: The Theater and the Indian Question" by Eliana Crestani, in *Nineteenth Century Theatre,* Summer-Winter 1995, pp. 5-32; "Domesticating the Drama of Conquest: Barker's *Pocahontas* on the Popular Stage," in *American Transcendental Quarterly,* September 1996, pp. 231-43.

*   *   *

James Nelson Barker, Democratic mayor of Federalist Philadelphia and amateur historian, wrote for the Chestnut Street Theatre. His historical researches, political commitments, and talent for allegorical verse are all evident in his plays. His critical articles, such as "Tragedy of Character," examined the problems of adapting and performance and the social function of drama. Barker intended his earliest, unproduced "mask" (*America,* with "Liberty" singing) to conclude an unfinished dramatization of John Smith's 1624 history of Virginia. Instead, his popular but comically melodramatic opera *The Indian Princess* (John Bray's music) introduced the frequently repeated Pocahontas figure to the stage.

The stage for Barker addressed and shaped the partisan energies that preceded the War of 1812. *Tears and Smiles,* his clever sentimental comedy, marshaled early Yankee types, a patriotic sailor, fops, an Irishman, and mysterious European fugitives to question commercial aristocracy and praise domestic products in fashions, morals, and persons. *The Embargo,* written for a benefit performance, supported Jefferson's controversial ban on trade with Britain and France. After the war Barker's "melo-dramatic sketch" *The Armourer's Escape* let the Indian-captured sailor Jewitt play himself to capitalize on current (1817) interest in the Oregon boundary dispute.

How to Try a Lover, a singularly unpolitical gem in prose, was produced as *A Court of Love.* It celebrates blinding love, from insatiable lust to courtly and impractical idealism. Love's confusing possibilities are drawn, with literary parodies ("Almanzor" as hero-lover's pseudonym; conventional allegories of love/honor), through the neoclassically comic dance of a picaresque plot, while carefully described settings develop from dark Gothic vault toward brilliant court. Movements and situations belie the spoken words. Barker's balancing of his characters and their antithetical dialogue intensify the skeptical-romantic counterpoint in this play, the "only dream" that "satisfied" him as artist.

Barker's verse tragedies explored what politicians considered resolved. *Marmion* and *Superstition* are historical tragedies of personal and national character. "*The* American playwright" (New York review) and best adaptor of Scott's poem (London critic) reexamined Scott's sources, tightened the narrative, and alternated scenes for deeper psychological effect, with a view toward rallying sentiment for war against Britain—though in 1811-12 victory seemed unlikely. *Marmion* presents determining destiny against individual responsibility. In *Superstition* manifest destiny and liberty are threatened by public hysteria. The inspired leadership of the Puritan Unknown (a fugitive regicide) saves a New England community from Indian attack; but the perverting religious fervor of witch-hunts and narrow-mindedness, part of the colonial heritage, leave a Columbia-figure and the young lovers of a New World dead. The play also features spying courtiers who supply objectifying comedy. Behind the play's action loom the New England fathers and the war for independence from the mother country, as well as the current themes of Greek and South American struggles for independence, Philadelphia's epidemics and religious riots, and Barker's campaigning for Andrew Jackson (Hero of the People) against New England's Adams ("John the Second"). Though Barker the politician honored "The People," *Superstition* questions their readiness for genuine democracy and implies a vision of rational, tolerant, effective, and affective leadership, fatalistic action, and individual heroism. Allegory becomes symbolic and moving in these tragedies, the finest of early America.

—John G. Kuhn

BARLOW, Joel

Born: Redding, Connecticut, 24 March 1754. **Education:** Moor's School, Hanover, New Hampshire; Dartmouth College, Hanover, 1773-74; Yale University, New Haven, Connecticut, 1774-78.

B.A. 1778, M.A. 1781; admitted to the bar, 1786. **Military Service:** Served in the Massachusetts Brigade, 1780-83: chaplain. **Family:** Married Ruth Baldwin in 1781. **Career:** Lawyer after the Revolution; also schoolteacher and proprietor of a bookshop, Hartford, Connecticut; founding editor, with Elisha Babcock, *American Mercury,* 1784; lived in Europe, 1788-1805: European agent (to sell land in Ohio to Europeans), Scioto Associates, 1788-90; lived in London (friend of Thomas Paine), 1790-92, and in Paris after 1792: made honorary French citizen, became involved in French radical politics, and ran for National Assembly deputy (representing Savoy), 1793; shipping agent, Hamburg, 1794-95; U.S. Consul, Algiers, 1796; lived at his home Kalorama, near Washington, D.C., 1805-11; sent by President James Madison to negotiate with Napoleon, 1811-12. **Died:** 24 December 1812.

PUBLICATIONS

Collections

Works (facsimile edition), edited by William K. Bottorff and Arthur L. Ford. 2 vols., 1970.

Poetry

The Prospect of Peace. 1778.
A Poem, Spoken at the Public Commencement at Yale College. 1781.
An Elegy of the Late Titus Hosmer. 1782.
Doctor Watts's Imitation of the Psalms of David, Corrected and Enlarged. 1785; supplement, 1785.
The Vision of Columbus. 1787; revised edition, as *The Columbiad,* 1807.
The Conspiracy of Kings. 1792.
The Hasty-Pudding. 1796.
The Anarchiad: A New England Poem, with others, edited by Luther G. Riggs. 1861.

Other

Advice to the Privileged Orders in the Several States of Europe. 2 vols., 1792-93.
A Letter to the National Convention of France. 1793(?).
Lettre adessee aus habitans du Piemont. 1793; as *A Letter to the People of Piedmont,* 1795.
The History of England, 1765-95. 5 vols., 1795.
The Political Writings. 1796.
To His Fellow Citizens. 2 vols., 1799-1800.

Editor, *M'Fingal: A Modern Epic Poem,* by John Trumbull. 1792.

Translator, *New Travels in the United States of America in 1788,* by J.P. Brissot de Warville. 1792; revised edition, 1794.
Translator, *The Commerce of America with Europe,* by J.P. Brissot de Warville. 1794.
Translator, with Thomas Jefferson, *Volney's Ruins; or, Meditations on the Revolution of Empires.* 2 vols., 1802.

*

Critical Studies: *Life and Letters of Barlow* by Charles Burr Todd, 1886; *The Early Days of Barlow, A Connecticut Wit: His*

Life and Works from 1754 to 1787 by Theodore Albert Zunder, 1934 (includes bibliography); *The Connecticut Wits* by Leon Howard, 1943 (includes bibliography); *A Yankee's Odyssey: The Life of Barlow* by James Woodress, 1958; *Barlow* by Arthur L. Ford, 1971; *Poetry and Ideology in Revolutionary Connecticut* by William C. Dowling, 1990; "Joel Barlow, Edmund Burke, and Fears of Masonic Conspiracy in 1792" by Carla J. Mulford, in *Secret Texts: The Literature of Secret Societies* edited by Marie Mulvey Roberts and Lennon Hugh Ormsby, 1995; "Colonial Discourse and Early American Literary History: Ercilla, The Inca Garcilaso, and Joel Barlow's Conception of a New World Epic" by Ralph Bauer, in *Early American Literature,* 1995, pp. 230-32; *We Wear the Mask: African Americans Write American Literature, 1760-1870* by Rafia Zafar, 1997.

*   *   *

Although Joel Barlow had hoped to be remembered as an epic poet, only one mock-epic poem and a short, bitter piece of satiric verse give him what enduring interest he has as a poet. At the same time, however, he holds a secure place as a political pamphleteer in the early national period and as a minor figure in American history. He is a character of considerable interest, for his life touches many of the significant historical events between the Revolution and the War of 1812, and he stands as a representative figure of the American Enlightenment.

Going from a Connecticut farm to Yale on the eve of the Revolution, Barlow versified his way through college, and, after serving as a chaplain in Washington's army, he set about writing his epic, *The Vision of Columbus,* a poem in nine books of heroic couplets celebrating the history of America, past, present, and future. The poem was a considerable success in its day, but it seems unreadable in the twentieth century. Twenty years later Barlow brought out an expanded and revised version that he called *The Columbiad.* It appeared as a large quarto, leather bound and handsomely illustrated, the most beautiful book yet produced in America—but still unreadable.

The Hasty-Pudding, on the other hand, is a delightful piece of mock-heroic verse occasioned by Barlow's visit to Savoy in 1793 when he was running unsuccessfully for the French National Assembly. It was inspired by his being served a dish of corn meal mush (polenta, hasty pudding), which reminded him of his Connecticut boyhood. This poem has been reprinted many times and is often anthologized. The other notable piece of verse, "Advice to a Raven in Russia," was occasioned by Barlow's sharp reaction to Napoleon's campaign in Russia in 1812. It was written in the last month of Barlow's life when he had gone to Vilna in an effort to negotiate a treaty with Napoleon. To a Jeffersonian American the slaughter and carnage all about him evoked bitter criticism, and in a sense Barlow himself some days later was one of Napoleon's victims, for he caught pneumonia on the precipitous return to Paris from Lithuania after Napoleon's debacle.

During the years that Barlow was living in Europe (1788 to 1805), he plunged into political controversy. His tract *Advice to the Privileged Orders* was one of the important answers to Burke's *Reflections on the Revolution in France,* and it was proscribed in England, along with Paine's *The Rights of Man.* He also wrote political polemics in support of France and the Jeffersonians during the contentious days of Adams' administration, and as a result made himself unpopular with the conservative Federalists he had grown up with in Connecticut. Of all that group of writers known as the Connecticut Wits, who flourished in and about Hartford after the Revolution, Barlow was the only one who became a political liberal.

—James Woodress

BARNES, Djuna (Chappell)

Born: Near Cornwall-on-Hudson, New York, 12 June 1892. **Education:** Privately educated; studied art at Pratt Institute, Brooklyn, New York, 1911-12, and Art Students' League, New York, 1915. **Family:** Married Courtenay Lemon c. 1917 (divorced c. 1919). **Career:** Journalist and illustrator, 1913-31: with Brooklyn *Daily Eagle,* 1913, and *Press, World,* and *Morning Telegraph,* all New York, 1914; actress in New York, 1920-22; columnist, *Theatre Guild Magazine,* New York, 1929-31; lived in Paris, 1922-37 (with periods in New York, 1922-23, 1926-27, 1929-31), London, 1937-39, and New York, 1940-82. Also an artist: exhibition at Art of This Century Gallery, New York, 1946. Trustee, New York Committee of Dag Hammarskjold Foundation. **Member:** American Academy. **Died:** 18 June 1982.

PUBLICATIONS

Collection

Collected Stories. 1996.

Fiction

A Book (stories, verse, and plays). 1923; augmented edition, as *A Night among the Horses,* 1929; shortened version (stories only), as *Spillway,* 1962.
Ryder. 1928.
Nightwood. 1936; as *Nightwood: The Original Version and Related Drafts,* 1995.
Vagaries Malicieux: Two Stories. 1974.
Smoke and Other Early Stories, edited by Douglas Messerli. 1982.

Plays

Three from the Earth (produced 1919). In *A Book,* 1923.
Kurzy of the Sea (produced 1919).
An Irish Triangle (produced 1919). In *Playboy.* 1921.
To the Dogs, in *A Book.* 1923.
The Dove (produced 1926). In *A Book,* 1923.
She Tells Her Daughter, in *Smart Set,* 1923.
The Antiphon (produced 1961). 1958; revised version, in *Selected Works,* 1962.
At the Roots of the Stars: The Short Plays, edited by Douglas Messerli. 1995.

Poetry

The Book of Repulsive Women: Eight Rhythms and Five Drawings. 1915.
Creatures in an Alphabet. 1982.

Other

Ladies Almanack. 1928.
Selected Works. 1962.
Greenwich Village as It Is. 1978.
Interviews, edited by Alyce Barry. 1985.
I Could Never Be Lonely Without a Husband (interviews). 1987.
Poe's Mother: Selected Drawings of Djuna Barnes, edited by Douglas Messerli. 1995.

*

Bibliography: *Barnes: A Bibliography* by Douglas Messerli, 1976.

Critical Studies: *A Festschrift for Barnes on Her 80th Birthday* edited by Alex Gildzen, 1972; *Barnes* by James B. Scott, 1976; *The Art of Barnes: Duality and Damnation* by Louis F. Kannenstine, 1977; *Djuna: The Life and Times of Barnes* by Andrew Field, 1983, as *The Formidable Miss Barnes,* 1983; *Silence and Power: A Re-evaluation of Barnes* edited by Mary Lynn Broe, 1986; *All Contraries Confounded: The Lyrical Fiction of Virginia Woolf, Djuna Barnes, and Marguerite Duras* by Karen Kaivola, 1991; *(Sem)erotics: Theorizing Lesbian: Writing* by Elizabeth A. Meese, 1992; *Djuna: The Life and Work of Djuna Barnes* by Phillip F. Herring, 1995; *Following Djuna: Women Lovers and the Erotics of Loss* by Carolyn Allen, 1996; *Queer Poetics: Five Modernist Women Writers* by Mary E. Galvin, 1998.

*　　*　　*

Djuna Barnes was one of the original members of the Theater Guild and acted in New York in plays by Tolstoy and Paul Claudel in the early 1920s. By the late 1930s the publication of her novel *Nightwood,* with an enthusiastic introduction by **T.S. Eliot,** had led to her being considered the most important woman novelist living in Paris. In the fiction of **Anaïs Nin** she appears frequently as "Djuna," and David Gascoyne's poem "Noctambules" carries the dedication "Hommage a Djuna Barnes." When her play *The Antiphon* was published, Edwin Muir declared that it was "one of the greatest things written in our times." Yet, despite such high praise, her books were for many years available only in small editions.

Nightwood is about the obsession of two American women for each other in the 1920s. Their Paris is not the Paris of **F. Scott Fitzgerald** but that of Romaine Brooks, Natalie Clifford Barney, and the circle of "Amazonians" that surrounded them. Norah Flood, one of the protagonists of the novel, arranges publicity from time to time for the Denckman Circus, and she also runs a *salon.* Some thirty years before, Dr. Matthew O'Connor assisted at her birth; now living in Paris, he has given way to his homosexual-transvestite urges. He is called one night from a cafe to a nearby hotel to attend Robin Vote, a boyish young woman who has had a collapse. The doctor takes along with him his drinking companion, Baron Felix Volkbein, who falls in love with Robin and subsequently marries her. In due course Robin bears him a son, but she cannot stand the course of marriage and starts an affair with Norah. A passionate and tempestuous sequence of events follows and Robin's promiscuity nearly unhinges Norah's mind. Her old friend the doctor sits with her through the night, boozing and pouring forth great streams of disconnected thoughts on life, literature, and the vagaries of the human heart. Had the novel been adapted for radio, the role of the doctor was one that Dylan Thomas aspired to play.

The Antiphon, written in blank verse, recalls a Jacobean closet drama:

> You have such sons
> Would mate the pennies on a dead man's eyes
> To breed the sexton's fee.

But the setting is modern and takes place in England during World War II. Augusta Burley betrays her aristocratic lineage by marrying a coarse, uncultured Mormon from Salem, by whom she has three sons and a daughter. Now a widow, she arranges a reunion at Burley Hall for the whole family. Yet nothing is what it seems. For as two of the brothers and their sister await their third brother, he enjoys himself at their expense disguised as "a coachman." Recriminations and suppressed violence cause the two identified sons to plan a matricide, while their sister acts as inquisitor to her mother for marrying her father. Finally incensed by the desertion of her two sons, the mother turns on her daughter to kill her and brings about her own death at the same time. The original production of this powerful play—by the Royal Dramatic Theatre of Stockholm in 1961—was in a translation by Dag Hammarskjold.

Barnes also illustrated books and wrote poems, short stories, plays, journalism, and essays. Her *Ladies Almanack,* published anonymously in Paris, created a minor *succes de scandale* in the 1920s. In it a number of lesbians are gently mocked—among them Radclyffe Hall (Lady Buck-and-Balk), Natalie Clifford Barney (Evangeline Musset), and Lady Una Troubridge (Tilly-Tweed-in-Blood).

—Neville Braybrooke

BARRY, Philip

Born: Rochester, New York, 18 June 1896. **Education:** East High School, Rochester; Yale University, New Haven, Connecticut (editor, *Yale Review*), 1913-17, 1919, A.B. 1919; studied with George Pierce Baker at Harvard University, Cambridge, Massachusetts, 1919-21. Worked in the code department of the U.S. Embassy, London, 1918-19. **Family:** Married Ellen Semple in 1922; two sons and one daughter. **Career:** Worked in advertising, New York, 1921; full-time playwright from 1922; wrote for M.G.M., Hollywood, after 1934; lived in France, 1938-39. **Member:** American Academy. **Died:** 3 December 1949.

<small>PUBLICATIONS</small>

Collections

States of Grace: Eight Plays, edited by Brendan Gill. 1975.

Plays

Autonomy (produced 1919).
A Punch for Judy (produced 1921). 1922.
You and I (produced 1923; as *The Jilts,* produced 1923). 1923.
God Bless Our Home. 1924.
The Youngest (produced 1924). 1925.
In a Garden (produced 1925). 1926.
White Wings (produced 1926). 1927; revised version, music by Douglas Moore (produced 1935).

John (produced 1927). 1929.
Paris Bound (produced 1927). 1929.
Cock Robin, with Elmer Rice (produced 1928). 1929.
Holiday (produced 1928). 1929.
Hotel Universe (produced 1930). 1930.
Tomorrow and Tomorrow (produced 1931). 1931.
The Animal Kingdom (produced 1932). 1932.
The Joyous Season (produced 1934). 1934.
Bright Star (produced 1935).
Spring Dance, from a play by Eleanor Golden and Eloise Barrangon (produced 1936). 1936.
Here Come the Clowns (produced 1938). 1939.
The Philadelphia Story (produced 1939). 1939.
Liberty Jones (produced 1941). 1941.
Without Love (produced 1942). 1943.
Foolish Notion (produced 1945). Abridged version in *The Best Plays of 1944-45*, edited by Burns Mantle, 1945.
My Name Is Aquilon, from play by Jean Pierre Aumont (produced 1949).
Second Threshold, completed by Robert E. Sherwood (produced 1951). 1951.

Fiction

War in Heaven. 1938.

Other

The Dramatist and the Amateur Public. 1927.

*

Critical Studies: *The Drama of Barry* by Gerald Hamm, 1948; *Barry* by Joseph Patrick Roppolo, 1965.

*   *   *

American theater has never been particularly congenial to that honorable but somewhat amorphous genre *high comedy.* Philip Barry is one of the very few American playwrights who is a celebrated practitioner of the form. In plays like *Paris Bound, The Animal Kingdom, Without Love,* and—most famously—*Holiday* and *The Philadelphia Story,* he places articulate and well-to-do people in well-appointed homes and forces them to face domestic crises—usually a marriage in danger—with an equanimity that might be called courage and a wit that demands—but does not always get—audiences willing to listen for the precise meaning of lines that will direct them to the seriousness that lies at the heart of all the plays. That Barry is not simply an elegant entertainer can be seen in the variety of work in his canon—in which the successful comedies share space with a satirical extravaganza (*White Wings*), a biblical play more concerned with theology than anecdote (*John*), a mood play in which characters find spiritual regeneration through psychodrama (*Hotel Universe*), a parable of good and evil among vaudevillians (*Here Come the Clowns,* based on Barry's own novel *War in Heaven*), a symbolic political drama (*Liberty Jones*), and a mixture of the real and the imaginary (*Foolish Notion*).

The comedies tend to be more effective than the overtly earnest plays, in which art sometimes loses out to exposition. But the important thing about Barry as a serious playwright is that,

light or heavy, his work is informed by a major theme. Most of his plays, from *You and I* to *Second Threshold,* deal with man's need to be faithful to himself and his possibilities, personal and professional. The Barry protagonists have to escape the rigidities dictated by family (*The Youngest*), convention (*The Animal Kingdom*), society (*Holiday*). Sometimes, as with John and Herodias in *John,* the characters are trapped by their own preconceptions, and the luckier among them learn to live by discovering that, however benign their intentions, they too are manipulators (Nancy in *The Youngest,* Linda in *Holiday*) or by accepting their own imperfect, human condition (Tracy Lord in *The Philadelphia Story*). Barry's central concern is supported by recurrent minor themes—marriage as a bond of love, not a legal or religious ritual; work as a self-fulfilling activity. not a social imposition—and by the implicit religious assumptions that mark him even at his most secular. That *Holiday* and *The Philadelphia Story* are likely to remain Barry's most popular plays should not hide the fact that a number of the others—particularly the neglected *In a Garden*—deserve a place in the working American repertory.

—Gerald Weales

BARTH, John (Simmons)

Born: Cambridge, Maryland, 27 May 1930. **Education:** The Juilliard School of Music, New York; Johns Hopkins University, Baltimore, A.B. 1951, M.A. 1952. **Family:** Married 1) Anne Strickland in 1950 (divorced 1969), one daughter and two sons, 2) Shelly Rosenberg in 1970. **Career:** Junior instructor in English, Johns Hopkins University, 1951-53; instructor 1953-56, assistant professor, 1957-60, and associate professor of English, 1960-65, Pennsylvania State University, University Park; professor of English, 1965-71, and Butler Professor, 1971-73, State University of New York, Buffalo; Centennial Professor of English and creative writing, Johns Hopkins University, from 1973: became emeritus. **Awards:** Brandeis University Creative Arts award, 1965; Rockefeller grant, 1965; American Academy grant, 1966; National Book award, 1973; F. Scott Fitzgerald award for Outstanding Achievement in American fiction, 1997; Lannan Foundation Lifetime Achievement award, 1998; PEN/Malamud award for Excellence in the short story, 1998. Litt.D.: University of Maryland, College Park, 1969. **Member:** American Academy, 1974; American Academy of Arts and Sciences, 1974. **Residence:** Chestertown, Maryland.

PUBLICATIONS

Short Stories

Lost in the Funhouse: Fiction for Print, Tape, Live Voice. 1968.
Chimera. 1972.
Todd Andrews to the Author. 1979.
On With the Story. 1997.

Novels

The Floating Opera. 1956; revised edition, 1967.
The End of the Road. 1958; revised edition, 1967.

The Sot-Weed Factor. 1960; revised edition, 1967.
Giles Goat-Boy; or, the Revised New Syllabus. 1966.
Letters. 1979.
Sabbatical: A Romance. 1982.
The Tidewater Tales: A Novel. 1987.
The Last Voyage of Somebody the Sailor. 1991.
Once upon a Time. 1994.

Other

The Literature of Exhaustion, and The Literature of Replenishment
  (essays). 1982.
The Friday Book: Essays and Other Nonfiction. 1984.
Don't Count on It: A Note on the Number of the 1001 Nights. 1984.
Further Fridays. 1995.

*

Bibliography: *Barth: A Descriptive Primary and Annotated Secondary Bibliography* by Joseph Weixlmann, 1976; *Barth: An Annotated Bibliography* by Richard Allan Vine, 1977; *Barth, Jerzy Kosinski, and Thomas Pynchon: A Reference Guide* by Thomas P. Walsh and Cameron Northouse, 1977.

Critical Studies: *Barth* by Gerhard Joseph, 1970; *Barth: The Comic Sublimity of Paradox* by Jac Tharpe, 1974; *The Literature of Exhaustion: Borges, Nabokov, and Barth* by John O. Stark, 1974; *Barth: An Introduction* by David Morrell, 1976; *Critical Essays on Barth* edited by Joseph J. Waldmeir, 1980; *Passionate Virtuosity: The Fiction of Barth* by Charles B. Harris, 1983; *Barth* by Heide Ziegler, 1987; *Understanding Barth* by Stan Fogel and Gordon Slethaug, 1990; *A Reader's Guide to John Barth* by Zack R. Bowen, 1994; *Death in the Funhouse: John Barth and Poststructuralist Aesthetics* by Alan Lindsay, 1995.

*   *   *

Highly susceptible to the sport of metaphysical games and passionately attracted to the conundrums of self-consciousness, John Barth has moved steadily away from the objective and realistic toward myth and unashamed fable. His first two novels, *The Floating Opera* and *The End of the Road,* which he has claimed to be twin explorations of the comic and tragic aspects of philosophical nihilism, fall well within the conventions of realism. But his next novel, *The Sot- Weed Factor,* takes an entirely different direction. It is framed on a gigantic scale of multiple plots, disguises, coincidences, intrigues, and deceptions, and it is written in an exuberant and constantly inventive pastiche of seventeenth-century prose style. Mingling history, legend, fiction, and outrageous lie in a bawdy, funny, and learned parody of the initiation-and-quest novel, *The Sot-Weed Factor* purports to chronicle the life and career of **Ebenezer Cooke,** poet-laureate of Maryland. Partly a reinterpretation of the primal fall from innocence, and partly a reexamination of the rich ambiguities in the archetypal American experience, it is both a dazzling tour de force and a major contribution to the novel of fabulation.

Barth is even more ambitious in scope and substance in *Giles Goat-Boy.* In this gargantuan spoof, he attempts to fuse myth, allegory, satire, parody, and the conventions of science fiction to produce a comically revised New Testament that will expose the fictive sources of all myths while leaving a new one in their place.

Although the novel inevitably falls short of its excessive aims, its relative failure—it goes on too long and its plot becomes mechanical—is still a significant and startling achievement. In *Lost in the Funhouse and Chimera,* he has withdrawn into an increasingly abstract and cerebral style, deliberately focusing on the naked process of story-telling itself as a subject—if not a substitute—for telling stories. *Letters* features many of the characters in his previous fictions. The results are curiously mixed: over-clever, strained, whimsical, desperate, terrifying, boring, and funny. *Sabbatical: A Romance* (1982) takes place on the deck of a cruising sailboat and features two giddy literature lovers. It uses subplots, flashbacks, and every extraordinary occurrence from rape and incest to the C.I.A. and a sea monster. Likewise, *The Tidewater Tales* (1987) takes place on a sailboat, *Story,* where a husband and wife have gone to wait out a pregnancy and indulge their mutual love of storytelling. Through the counterpointing of anecdote and present-tense description of surroundings, the labyrinth of Chesapeake waterways become the topographical equivalent of the stories that emerge. A subtle thematic tension emerges between the cyclic and the linear, a tension that functions, like the metaphors of telling and sailing, to hold the collage of the novel together. *The Last Voyage of Somebody the Sailor* (1991) takes place in two worlds. Simon Behler is a twentieth-century American journalist who narrates his life and times to an audience in medieval Baghdad. Cast back in time, Simon is talking to Sinbad's family, staff, and potential business partners; his story is lifted with little modification from *The Arabian Knights.* Barth uses a potentially quite alien world, the medieval Orient, as a place to throw a 1950s-style American stag party. He exposes, among other things, the complex interplay of sex and domination that may suffuse both the art of pedagogy and the supposedly fallen realms of corporate and professional life. Whereas his earlier novels derided the systems—philosophical, literary, political, and social—by which people tried to stabilize experience, *The Last Voyage* indulges Barth's rancor and his prejudices, both racial and sexual. His most recent short story collection, *On with the Story* (1997), treats isolation and loss in scenes that are quickly drawn; the real interests of these stories are theories of time, the possibilities and limitations of fiction, and the problems of the reader's expectations. Many of the stories address the narrative conventions of beginning, middle, and end—and the delays within them. In the title story two characters discuss a story they are reading, and one of them questions the story's use of the "narrative pause button" to digress about relative motion and Zeno's paradox. The story proposes two endings for itself but chooses neither, closing with the question "On with the Story?" These stories, which weave Barth's wit into an interplay between realist fictional conventions and postmodern alternatives to these, are an example of the impressive range and ambition in Barth's work. There is little doubt that his literary intelligence and mastery of language place him in the forefront of his generation of writers.

—Earl Rovit, updated by Martha Sutro

BARTHELME, Donald

Born: Philadelphia, Pennsylvania, 7 April 1931; brother of the writer Frederick Barthelme. **Education:** University of Houston. **Military Service:** Served in the U.S. Army, 1953-55. **Family:**

Married 1) Birgit Barthelme; 2) Marion Knox in 1978; two daughters. **Career:** Reporter, Houston *Post,* 1951, 1955-56; worked on public relations and news service staff, and founding editor of the university literary magazine *Forum,* University of Houston, 1956-59; director, Contemporary Arts Museum, Houston, 1961-62; managing editor, *Location* magazine, New York, 1962-64; visiting professor, State University of New York, Buffalo, 1972, and Boston University, 1973; distinguished visiting professor, City College, New York, from 1974; visiting professor, University of Houston, from 1981. **Awards:** Guggenheim fellowship, 1966; National Book award, 1972; American Academy Morton Dauwen Zabel award, 1972. **Member:** American Academy. **Died:** 23 July 1989.

PUBLICATIONS

Short Stories

Come Back, Dr. Caligari. 1964.
Unspeakable Practices, Unnatural Acts. 1968.
City Life. 1970.
Sadness. 1972.
Guilty Pleasures. 1974.
Amateurs. 1976.
Great Days. 1979.
The Emerald. 1980.
Presents, collages by the author. 1980.
Sixty Stories. 1981.
Overnight to Many Distant Cities. 1983.
Forty Stories. 1987.
Sam's Bar. 1987.

Novels

Snow White. 1967.
The Dead Father. 1975.
Paradise. 1986.
The King. 1990.

Play

Great Days, from his own story (produced 1983).

Other

The Slightly Irregular Fire Engine; or, The Thithering Dithering Djinn (for children). 1971.
The Teachings; The Satires, Parodies, Fables, Illustrated Stories, and Plays, edited by Kim Herzinger. 1992.
Not-Knowing: The Essays and Interviews of Donald Barthelme. 1997.

*

Bibliography: *Barthelme: A Comprehensive Bibliography and Annotated Secondary Checklist* by Jerome Klinkowitz, Asa Pieratt, and Robert Murray Davis, 1977.

Critical Studies: "Barthelme Issue" of *Critique,* vol. 16, no. 3, 1975; *Barthelme* by Lois Gordon, 1981; *Barthelme* by Maurice

Courturier and Régis Durand, 1982; *The Metafictional Muse: The Works of Robert Coover, Barthelme, and William H. Gass* by Larry McCaffery, 1982; *Barthelme's Fiction: The Ironist Saved from Drowning* by Charles Molesworth, 1982; *The Shape of Art in the Short Stories of Barthelme* by Wayne B. Stengel, 1985; *Understanding Barthelme* by Alan Trachtenberg, 1990; *Barthelme: An Exhibition* by Jerome Klinkowitz, 1991; *Donald Barthelme and His Critics* (dissertation) by Alan Richard Asnen, 1994; *Postmodern Discourses of Love: Pynchon, Barth, Coover, Gass, and Barthelme* by Mira Sakrajda, 1997.

*   *   *

Since the American publication of two volumes of fictions by Argentinean Jorge Luis Borges in 1962, an interest in short, highly self-conscious, directly philosophical fiction has become apparent in the United States. Donald Barthelme is perhaps the best exemplar of this strain of fiction. His best work to date has been in the short story (for lack of a more expansive term), particularly in the substrain "metafiction," a term coined by **William H. Gass.** Like Borges, the Americans **John Barth,** Gass, and **Robert Coover,** and the Italian Italo Calvino, Barthelme has little interest in mimetic fiction that works from the bedrock of the "real" world. Instead of protracted social or psychological studies, he busied himself with very short, often truncated and discontinuous, literary pieces that depend on other literary works, philosophy, film, pop culture, and high art for their fictional matrices. There is throughout his work a suspicion of received morality or attitude, indeed of any unself-conscious and sustained human construct— including fiction. Thus his works are brief, constantly shifting in tone and style, evincing as much the juxtaposition and reverberation of image and language in modern poetry and the open randomness and "objectness" of the collage and much modern art as they do traditional fictional technique.

Barthelme's first work, *Come Back, Dr. Caligari,* was very well-reviewed, but one notes the bewilderment of critics who searched for "meaning" in his work. His best works have been collections of short fiction; of these, *City Life* and *Sadness* are most sustained in imagination and execution.

While Barthelme had little interest in miming reality, he did have a recurrent interest in modern consciousness, particularly as manifested in urban Americans. He issues elegant fictional reports on the state of consciousness in "The City," and, indeed, the daily sorrowful, maddening minutiae of city life—tattered marriages, the loss of innocence, the failure of love, the absurd hope of social or political "progress," the torrent of stimulation by the media—comprise the stuff of his reports. "The City" is dangerous and confusing, and is finally a configuration of human consciousness: "It heaves and palpitates. It is multi-dimensional and has a mayor. To describe it takes many hundreds of thousands of words. Our muck is only a part of a much greater muck—the nation state— which is itself the creation of that muck of mucks, human consciousness" (*City Life*).

Indeed, the human urban condition is Barthelme's major subject, and like his city, his vision can certainly appear bleak and pessimistic. Endlessly self-conscious (his narrators offer clues to the significance of their tales), satiric and parodic (Barthelme's liberated *Snow White* is hilarious), a mournful connoisseur of the many flavors of metaphysical malaise and angst of our time (a character "pickets" the human condition in an early story: "THE HUMAN CONDITION: WHY DOES IT HAVE TO BE THAT WAY?"), he can often seem depressing and negative. Yet his wit and humor are a delight, and his stylistic command is among the most deft of writers in English in our time.

Barthelme demands a creative reader, and he offered his own best apologia in writing on the work of Samuel Beckett: "His pessimism is the premise necessary to a marvelous pedantic high-wire performance, the wire itself supporting a comic turn of endless virtuosity. No one who writes as well as Beckett can be said to be doing anything but celebrating life."

—Jack Hicks

BAUM, L(yman) Frank

Born: Chittenango, New York, 15 May 1856. **Education:** Schools in Syracuse, New York, and Peekskill Military Academy, New York, 1868-69. **Family:** Married Maud Gage in 1882; four sons. **Career:** Reporter, New York *World,* 1873-75; founding editor, *New Era,* Bradford, Pennsylvania, 1876; actor (as Louis F. Baum and George Brooks), manager, Baum's Opera House, Richburg, New York, 1881-82, and producer, New York and on tour, 1881-83; poultry farmer and editor, *Poultry Record,* 1880s; salesman, Baum's Castorine axle grease, 1884-88; owner, Baum's Bazaar general store, Aberdeen, Dakota Territory, 1888-90; editor, *Saturday Pioneer,* Aberdeen, 1890-91; reporter, Chicago *Post,* buyer, Siegel Cooper and Company, Chicago, and salesman, Pitkin and Brooks, Chicago, 1891-97; founder, National Association of Window Trimmers, 1897, and founding editor and publisher, *Show Window* magazine, Chicago, 1897-1902; founding director, Oz Film Manufacturing Company, Los Angeles, 1914. **Died:** 6 May 1919.

PUBLICATIONS

Fiction

A New Wonderland. 1900; as *The Surprising Adventures of the Magical Monarch of Mo,* 1903.
The Wonderful Wizard of Oz. 1900; as *The New Wizard of Oz,* 1903; *The Annotated Wizard of Oz,* edited by Michael Patrick Hearn, 1973.
Dot and Tot of Merryland. 1901.
The Master Key: An Electrical Fairy Tale. 1901.
The Life and Adventures of Santa Claus. 1902.
The Enchanted Island of Yew. 1903.
The Marvelous Land of Oz. 1904.
Queen Zixi of Ix. 1905.
The Woggle-Bug Book. 1905.
The Fate of a Crown. 1905.
Daughters of Destiny. 1906.
John Dough and the Cherub. 1906.
Annabel. 1906.
Sam Steele's Adventures on Land and Sea. 1906; as *The Boy Fortune Hunters in Alaska,* 1908.
Aunt Jane's Nieces [Abroad, at Millville, at Work, in Society, and Uncle John, on Vacation, on the Ranch, Out West, in the Red Cross]. 10 vols., 1906-15.
Twinkle Tales. 6 vols., 1906; as *Twinkle and Chubbins,* 1911.
Tamawaca Folks. 1907.

Ozma of Oz. 1907; as *Princess Ozma of Oz,* 1942.
Sam Steele's Adventures in Panama. 1907; as *The Boy Fortune Hunters in Panama,* 1908.
Policeman Bluejay. 1907; as *Babes in Birdland,* 1911.
The Last Egyptian. 1908.
Dorothy and the Wizard in Oz. 1908.
The Boy Fortune Hunters in Egypt [China, Yucatan, the South Seas]. 4 vols., 1908-11.
The Road to Oz. 1909.
The Emerald City of Oz. 1910.
The Sea Fairies. 1911.
The Daring Twins. 1911.
The Flying Girl [and Her Chum]. 2 vols., 1911-12.
Sky Island. 1912.
Phoebe Daring. 1912.
The Patchwork Girl of Oz. 1913.
The Little Wizard Series. 6 vols., 1913; as *Little Wizard Stories of Oz,* 1914.
Tik-Tok of Oz. 1914.
The Scarecrow of Oz. 1915.
Rinkitink in Oz. 1916.
The Snuggle Tales. 6 vols., 1916-17; as *Oz-Man Tales,* 6 vols., 1920.
Mary Louise [in the Country, Solves a Mystery, and the Liberty Girls, Adopts a Soldier]. 5 vols., 1916-19.
The Lost Princess of Oz. 1917.
The Tin Woodman of Oz. 1918.
The Magic of Oz. 1919.
Glinda of Oz. 1920.
Jaglon and the Tiger Fairies. 1953.
A Kidnapped Santa Claus. 1961.
The Purple Dragon and Other Fantasies, edited by David L. Greene. 1976.
Baum's American Fairy Tales. 1997.

Plays

The Maid of Arran, music and lyrics by Baum, from the novel *A Princess of Thule* by William Black (produced 1882).
Matches (produced 1882).
Kilmourne; or, O'Connor's Dream (produced 1883).
The Wizard of Oz, music by Paul Tietjens, lyrics by Baum, from the story by Baum (produced 1902; revised version, as *There Is Something New under the Sun* produced 1903).
The Woggle-Bug, music by Frederic Chapin, from the story *The Marvelous Land of Oz* by Baum (produced 1905).
The Tik-Tok Man of Oz, music by Louis F. Gottschalk, from the story by Baum (produced 1913).
Stagecraft: The Adventures of a Strictly Moral Man, music by Louis F. Gottschalk (produced 1914).
The Uplift of Lucifer; or, Raising Hell, music by Louis F. Gottschalk (produced 1915). Edited by Manuel Weltman, 1963.
The Uplifters' Minstrels, music by Byron Gay (produced 1916).
The Orpheus Road Company, music by Louis F. Gottschalk (produced 1917).

Screenplays: *The Fairylogue and Radio-Plays,* 1908-09; *The Patchwork Girl of Oz,* 1914; *The Babes in the Wood,* 1914; *The Magic Cloak of Oz,* 1914; *The Last Egyptian,* 1914; *The New Wizard of Oz,* 1915.

Poetry

By the Candelabra's Glare. 1898.
Father Goose, His Book. 1899.
The Army Alphabet. 1900.
The Navy Alphabet. 1900.
The Songs of Father Goose, music by Alberta N. Hall. 1900.
Father Goose's Year Book: Quaint Quacks and Feathery Shafts for Mature Children. 1907.
The High-Jinks of Baum (songs for Uplifters). 1959.

Other

The Book of the Hamburgs: A Brief Treatise upon the Mating, Rearing, and Management of the Different Varieties of Hamburgs. 1886.
Mother Goose in Prose. 1897.
The Art of Decorating Dry Goods Windows and Interiors. 1900.
American Fairy Tales. 1901; augmented edition, 1908.
Baum's Juvenile Speaker (miscellany). 1910; as *Baum's Own Book for Children,* 1912.
Our Landlady (*Saturday Pioneer* columns). 1941.
Animal Fairy Tales. 1969.

*

Bibliography: in *The Annotated Wizard of Oz* edited by Michael Patrick Hearn, 1973.

Critical Studies: *The Wizard of Oz and Who He Was* edited by Russel Nye and Martin Gardner, 1957; *To Please a Child: A Biography of Baum* by Frank Joslyn Baum and Russell P. MacFall, 1961; *Wonderful Wizard, Marvelous Land* by Raylyn Moore, 1974; *Frank Baum: Royal Historian of Oz* by Angelica S. Carpenter and Jean L. Shirley, 1991; *Oz and Beyond: The Fantasy World of L. Frank Baum* by Michael O'Neal Riley, 1997.

*   *   *

L. Frank Baum's *The Wonderful Wizard of Oz,* illustrated by W.W. Denslow, is his masterpiece. It made him famous and, with its 13 sequels, has established him as a classic writer of children's stories.

The Wonderful Wizard of Oz was a novelty in children's books at the time it was published, lacking the didactic, moralizing, and stilted tone so common during the period. Its characters spoke the American vernacular; its plot was simple but intriguing and well structured. Moreover, Baum created five characters worthy to stand with Lewis Carroll's Alice and J.M. Barrie's Peter Pan. Dorothy and the Wizard, as well as the three nonhuman characters (the Tin Woodman, the Scarecrow, and the Cowardly Lion), are all archetypes yet sharply distinguished individuals. The quest of the Scarecrow for brains, the Woodman for a heart, and the Lion for courage, qualities they already possessed but did not know how to use, is the stuff of which classics are made.

The Wizard was also Baum's most successful, though not his best, example of what he called the American or modernized fairy tale. Responding to ideas expressed by **Hamlin Garland** and others, he intended to write fantasies that would be distinct from the European and New England tradition. They would recognize the existence and importance of the industry, technology, and social

concepts of the dawning twentieth century. He incorporated mechanical gadgets (particularly electricity, which fascinated him) into his works—*The Master Key: An Electrical Fairy Tale* is the best example—and dealt with such modern concepts as Populism. But in general his ambition to create a new genre was only partly successful. Though the visitors to Oz were American, the country itself was as foreign as **James Branch Cabell**'s Poictesme or Swift's Lilliput. Furthermore, he often used such traditional fairy tale paraphernalia as witches, gnomes, talking animals, and wishing caps. What many consider his best book, *Queen Ziri of Ix,* is entirely derived from European children's literature, though it contains many imaginative novelties.

Baum tired of his Oz series. But just as public demand kept Doyle writing his Sherlock Holmes stories when he would have preferred to concentrate on his more "serious" works, so it kept Baum at his Oz tales, though he did write many other children's books, few of them fantasies. Though written "to please a child" (Baum's phrase), the Oz books have also been popular with adults, who recognize subtleties that escaped them as children. *The Wonderful Wizard of Oz* is still popular, and now seems to have passed the judgment of time.

—Philip Jose Farmer

See the essay on *The Wonderful Wizard of Oz.*

BEATTIE, Ann

Born: Washington, D.C., 8 September 1947. **Education:** American University, Washington, D.C., B.A. 1969; University of Connecticut, Storrs, 1969-70, M.A. 1970. **Family:** Married 1) David Gates in 1973 (divorced); 2) Lincoln Perry. **Career:** Visiting lecturer, University of Virginia, Charlottesville, 1976-77 and 1980; Briggs Copeland Lecturer in English, Harvard University, Cambridge, Massachusetts, 1977-78. **Awards:** Guggenheim fellowship, 1977; American University Distinguished Alumnae award, 1980; American Academy and Institute of Arts and Letters award, 1980. L.H.D.: American University, 1983; Colby College, 1991. **Member:** American Academy of Arts and Letters, 1990. **Residence:** Maine and Florida.

PUBLICATIONS

Short Stories

Distortions. 1976.
Secrets and Surprises. 1978.
The Burning House. 1982.
Where You'll Find Me and Other Stories. 1986.
What Was Mine and Other Stories. 1991.
Park City: New and Selected Stories. 1998.

Novels

Chilly Scenes of Winter. 1976.
Falling in Place. 1980.
Love Always. 1985.
Picturing Will. 1990.

Another You. 1995.
My Life, Starring Dara Falcon. 1997.

Other

Spectacles (for children). 1985.
Alex Katz (monograph). 1987.

Editor, with Shannon Ravenel, *The Best American Short Stories 1987.* 1987.

*

Bibliography: "Ann Beattie (1947-): A Checklist" by Harry Opperman and Christina Murphy, in *Bulletin of Bibliography,* June 1987, pp. 111-118.

Critical Studies: "Beattie's Magic Slate or The End of the Sixties" by Blanche H. Gelfant, in *New England Review* 1, 1979; "Through "The Octascope': A View of Beattie" by John Gerlach, in *Studies in Short Fiction* 17, fall 1980; "Images of Void in Beattie's 'Shifting'" by Deborah DeZure, in *Studies in Short Fiction,* winter 1989; "Picturing Ann Beattie: A Dialogue" by Neila C. Seshchari, in *Weber Studies: An Interdisciplinary Humanities Journal,* spring 1990; "Ann Beattie: Emotional Loss and Strategies of Reparation" by Leo Schneiderman, in *The American Journal of Psychoanalysis,* December 1993, pp. 317-33; *The Critical Response to Ann Beattie* edited by Jaye Berman Montresor, 1993; "Philosophers Meet Feminism at 'The Burning House'" by Virginia A.K. Moran, in *Short Story,* fall 1995, pp. 47-53; "About Ann Beattie" by Don Lee, in *Ploughshares,* fall 1995, pp. 231-35; "Postmodernism and Its Children: The Case of Ann Beattie's 'A Windy Day at the Reservoir'" by Miriam Healy Clark, in *South Atlantic Review,* winter 1996, pp. 77-87.

*   *   *

Ann Beattie's short stories began to appear in small quarterlies in the early 1970s while she was a graduate student. When, after many rejections, the *New Yorker* accepted one of her stories in 1974, she began to devote herself to writing full time. Her first collection of stories, *Distortions,* and her first novel, *Chilly Scenes of Winter,* both appeared in 1976. Although critical opinion has always been split between those who admire her pinpoint portraits of the yuppie generation of the 1960s and 1970s and those who accuse her of psychological vacuity and sociological indifference, few can deny that, along with **Raymond Carver,** she was largely responsible for the renaissance of the American short story in the 1970s and 1980s. Seen as the spokesperson for the 1960s generation, Beattie has been alternately praised for her satiric view of that era's passivity and criticized for presenting slick, *New Yorker* magazine versions of superficial characters.

As with the fictional figures of the writers she claims as her literary progenitors, Samuel Beckett and **John Cheever,** Beattie's characters seldom know what makes them do what they do and have no real sense of purpose; thus, instead of engaging in deliberate action, they seem more often acted upon. They seldom experience the kind of epiphany of awareness associated with twentieth-century short fiction from James Joyce and **Sherwood Anderson** through **Eudora Welty** and **Bernard Malamud.** Moreover, since many of her stories are told in present tense, her char-

acters seldom engage in meditation or attempt to search for meaning; thus, there is little cause for her narrators to indulge in exposition or exploration.

Beattie's collection *Park City: New and Selected Stories* (1998) is a retrospective summation of her short-story career, containing such familiar stories from her previous five collections as "Dwarf House," "A Vintage Thunderbird," "Shifting," "The Lawn Party," "Jacklighting," "Greenwich Time," "The Burning House," "Weekend," "Janus," and "What Was Mine." In the twenty-odd years Beattie has been publishing short stories, mostly in the *New Yorker,* her milieu and her method have changed little; as a result, some critics charge that she harps too much on the same themes and has nothing new to say about the era she has evoked so sharply.

"Weekend," an early story, combines a typical Cheever-type male character with a female one typical of Beattie. A past-middle-age college professor tries to deny aging by sexually exploiting college girls who look up to him, while the thirty-four-year-old woman who lives with him passively accepts the "sick game" that he plays. Typical of Beattie's technique, the story ends with an image of a past moment in the life of the couple when things were somehow all right, but which is now lost forever. In "A Vintage Thunderbird," the central character is unable to commit himself to a relationship because of a fantasy desire for a woman who owns a vintage Thunderbird, a metaphor for some inaccessible goal. In "The Burning House," a young woman realizes she has fooled herself into thinking she knows the people around her just because she knows certain small personal things about them; however, like many Beattie characters, she discovers that she does not know them at all.

"Janus," a classic of Beattie's so-called minimalist phase, centers on a real-estate agent who uses an elegant bowl as a sort of trick to get buyers interested in a house. The bowl has a particular personal meaning for her, having been given to her by a man with whom she had an affair; it also has a mysterious symbolic significance: every house she puts it in becomes the home that she and her lover will never have because she is unwilling to leave her husband. In contrast to such compressed and metaphoric early stories, Beattie seemed to be moving more toward length and elaboration in her later short fiction, using such novelistic techniques as extended character development and realistic detail. "Windy Day at the Reservoir," the longest story in her collection *What Was Mine* (1991), focuses on a couple who, while house-sitting, make a number of unsettling discoveries both about the homeowners and about themselves. The point of view shifts from that of the house-sitting husband to that of his wife and then to that of the retarded son of the housekeeper, as he makes his way to the reservoir on a windy day to walk innocently into the water and drown. In the final section of this novella-length work, which focuses on the housekeeper after her son's death, the author provides a nonmetaphoric, novelistic resolution to the story of the two couples, who have since broken up.

In spite of the fact that Beattie has said she wishes to give up the short story and devote her time to the novel, her novels have not always been as well received as her stories. Her first novel, *Chilly Scenes of Winter,* did not fare as well with the critics as her first collection of stories, and her second novel, *Falling in Place* (1980), did not do much better. The reason seems to be a generic one, for Beattie's talent is for the small moment, a photographic snapshot of an almost frozen spatial reality. In such social comedies as *Love Always* (1985), Beattie is accused by critics of engaging in a kind of defensive irony in which she condescends to her characters, whereas in *Picturing Will* (1989), she is charged with seeming either unable or unwilling to develop her characters sufficiently to sustain the reader's interest or the narrative continuum. Her novel *My Life Starring Dara Falcon* (1997) has been scorned as her weakest yet; the *New York Times* called it an "ill-conceived experiment" that "must surely mark a low point" in her career.

Since Beattie began publishing short stories, her characters have remained much the same, and her technique has changed little. But her eye for detail is so piercing that it does not matter. In spite of the fact that she has published six less-than-brilliant novels, it is as a short-story writer that she has secured her reputation in American literature.

—Charles E. May

BEHRMAN, S(amuel) N(athaniel)

Born: Worcester, Massachusetts, 9 June 1893. **Education:** Providence Street School and Classical High School, both Worcester; Clark College (now Clark University), Worcester, 1912-14; Harvard University, Cambridge, Massachusetts, A.B. 1916 (Phi Beta Kappa); Columbia University, New York, M.A. 1918. **Family:** Married Elza Heifetz in 1936; one son and two step-children. **Career:** Advertising writer and book reviewer, *New York Times*, 1917-18; reviewer, *New Republic*, New York, and freelance publicist until early 1920s; columnist, *New Yorker*, from 1927. Founder, with Robert E. Sherwood, Elmer Rice, Maxwell Anderson, Sidney Howard, and John F. Wharton, Playwrights Company, 1938. Trustee, Clark University. **Awards:** American Academy grant, 1943; New York Drama Critics Circle award, 1944; Writers Guild of America West award, for screenplay, 1959; Brandeis University Creative Arts award, 1962. LL.D.: Clark University, 1949. **Member:** American Academy, 1943; American Academy of Arts and Sciences. **Died:** 9 September 1973.

PUBLICATIONS

Plays

Bedside Manners: A Comedy of Convalescence, with J. Kenyon Nicholson (produced 1923). 1924.
A Night's Work, with J. Kenyon Nicholson (produced 1924). 1926.
The Man Who Forgot, with Owen Davis (produced 1926).
The Second Man (produced 1927). 1927.
Love Is Like That, with J. Kenyon Nicholson (produced 1927).
Serena Blandish, from the novel by Enid Bagnold (produced 1929). In *Three Plays*, 1934.
Meteor (produced 1929). 1930.
Brief Moment (produced 1931). 1931.
Biography (produced 1932). 1933.
Love Story (produced 1933).
Three Plays: Serena Blandish, Meteor, The Second Man. 1934.
Rain from Heaven (produced 1934). 1935.
End of Summer (produced 1936). 1936.
Amphitryon 38, with Roger Gellert, from a play by Jean Giraudoux (produced 1937). 1938.
Wine of Choice (produced 1938). 1938.

No Time for Comedy (produced 1939). 1939.
The Talley Method (produced 1941). 1941.
The Pirate, from a play by Ludwig Fulda (produced 1942). 1943.
Jacobowsky and the Colonel, from a play by Franz Werfel (produced 1944). 1944.
Dunnigan's Daughter (produced 1945). 1946.
Jane, from a story by W. Somerset Maugham (produced 1946; as *The Foreign Language*, produced 1951). 1952.
I Know My Love, from a play by Marcel Achard (produced 1949). 1952.
Let Me Hear the Melody (produced 1951).
Fanny, with Joshua Logan, music by Harold Rome, from a trilogy by Marcel Pagnol (produced 1954). 1955.
Four Plays: The Second Man, Biography, Rain from Heaven, End of Summer. 1955.
The Cold Wind and the Warm (produced 1958). 1959.
The Beauty Part (produced 1962).
Lord Pengo: A Period Comedy, based on his book *Duveen* (produced 1962). 1963.
But for Whom Charlie (produced 1964). 1964.

Screenplays: *Liliom*, with Sonya Levien, 1930; *Lightnin'*, with Sonya Levien, 1930; *The Sea Wolf*, with Ralph Block, 1930; *The Brat*, with others, 1931; *Surrender*, with Sonya Levien, 1931; *Daddy Long Legs*, with Sonya Levien, 1931; *Delicious*, 1931; *Rebecca of Sunnybrook Farm*, with Sonya Levien, 1932; *Tess of the Storm Country*, with others, 1932; *Brief Moment*, 1933; *Queen Christina*, with Salka Viertel and H.M. Harwood, 1933; *Cavalcade*, 1933; *Hallelujah, I'm a Bum (Hallelujah, I'm a Tramp, Lazy Bones)*, with Ben Hecht, 1933; *My Lips Betray*, 1933; *As Husbands Go*, with Sonya Levien, 1934; *The Scarlet Pimpernel*, with others, 1934; *Anna Karenina*, with others, 1935; *A Tale of Two Cities*, with W.P. Lipscomb, 1935; *Conquest (Marie Walewska)*, with others, 1937; *Parnell*, with John van Druten, 1937; *The Cowboy and the Lady*, with Sonya Levien, 1938; *Waterloo Bridge*, with others, 1940; *Two Faced Woman*, with others, 1941; *Quo Vadis*, with others, 1951; *Me and the Colonel*, with George Froeschel, 1958; *Stowaway in the Sky* (English narration), 1962.

Fiction

The Burning-Glass. 1968.

Other

Duveen. 1952.
The Worcester Account (*New Yorker* sketches). 1954.
Portrait of Max: An Intimate Memoir of Sir Max Beerbohm. 1960; as *Conversation with Max*, 1960.
The Suspended Drawing Room. 1965.
People in a Diary: A Memoir. 1972; as *Tribulations and Laughter: A Memoir*, 1972.

*

Bibliography: *Maxwell Anderson and Behrman: A Reference Guide* by William Klink, 1977; updated in *Resources for American Literary Study*, vol. 12, 1982.

Critical Studies: *Life among the Playwrights* by John F. Wharton, 1974; *Behrman* by Kenneth T. Reed, 1975; *Behrman: The Major*

Plays by William Klink, 1978; in *The Man Behind the Book: Literary Profiles* by Louis Auchincloss, 1996.

*   *   *

It was 1927 when S.N. Behrman's *The Second Man* was produced by the Theatre Guild and made him famous. By the 1950s the material was old hat, and writers of comedies of manners (even better ones, such as **Philip Barry**) have become quite out of date. Behrman's work after the 1930s was fairly unimportant, largely adaptations. His sophisticated comedy belongs to an earlier generation. A revival of *The Second Man* looked very old-fashioned. It, of course, lacked the Lunts, who created roles in it (and Noël Coward and Raymond Massey, who played it in London), and it needed them.

In his time Behrman also had the assistance of stars like Greta Garbo, Ina Claire, Katherine Cornell, and Laurence Olivier. He, like the blase and aphoristic writer Clark Storey in *The Second Man,* said "(*Seriously*) Life is sad. I know it's sad. But I think it's gallant to pretend that it isn't." In the 1930s this approach made him an American Noël Coward and gave him "perhaps the most considerable reputation" among young playwrights (A.H. Quinn). But soon proletarian and "socially significant drama" was to render inoperable the approach of the heroine of *Biography,* which was to laugh at injustice because nothing could be done about it, and the hero of *No Time for Comedy,* who chose to write light comedy instead of propagandist melodrama. The depression and World War II wiped out Behrman's impassive, indifferent, intellectual sophisticates who gracefully soared above reality. In *Rain from Heaven,* even though it revolves around Fascists and German refugees, the sophisticates are still doing arabesques on the thin ice of political problems.

Behrman wrote a number of screenplays, including such movies as *Queen Christina* and *Anna Karenina* (both with Garbo), *Waterloo Bridge,* and *Quo Vadis.* For the *New Yorker* he wrote the sketches that became *Duveen* (about the art dealer who became Lord Millbank) and *The Worcester Account* (about his boyhood in Worcester, Massachusetts). These surpass his original comedies of manners, his adaptation of Giraudoux (*Amphitryon 38*) or Franz Werfel (*Jacobowsky and the Colonel*), his dramatization of stories by Enid Bagnold (*Serena Blandish*) and W. Somerset Maugham (*Jane*), all his theater work, and his cinema writing. It is unfortunate that he did not find time in his 80 years to write a work for the stage about the sort of people who enliven *The Worcester Account.* His cosmopolitan intellectuals may be well observed for a "brief moment" (as a 1931 play of his was called), but they are seen by a stranger, however clever. The people of Providence Street in Worcester, Behrman knew.

—Leonard R.N. Ashley

BELASCO, David

Born: San Francisco, California, 25 July 1853; moved with his family to Victoria, British Columbia, 1858. **Education:** A monastery in Victoria, 1858-62; in various schools in San Francisco, where his family returned in 1865; Lincoln Grammar School, San Francisco, graduated 1871. **Family:** Married Cecilia Loverich in 1873 (died 1925); two daughters. **Career:** Actor in repertory, tour-

ing California; acted at Piper's Opera House in Virginia City, Nevada, where he was employed briefly by Dion Boucicault as a secretary, 1873; stage manager, Maguire's Theatre, San Francisco, 1874; assistant to the manager, 1875-78, and stage manager, 1878-82, Lucky Baldwin's Academy of Music, San Francisco; began writing for the stage in the late 1870s; lighting manager, then stage manager, Madison Square Theatre, New York, 1882-86; manager, with David Frohman, Lyceum Theatre, New York, 1886-90; independent actor/manager, New York, 1890-1906; owner, Stuyvesant Theatre, later Belasco Theatre, New York, 1906-31. Produced more than 350 plays for Broadway and stock companies. **Awards:** Chevalier, Legion of Honor (France), 1924. **Died:** 14 May 1931.

PUBLICATIONS

Collections

The Plays of Henry C. DeMille and Belasco (includes *The Senator's Wife, Lord Chumley, The Charity Ball, Men and Women*), edited by Robert Hamilton Ball. 1941.
The Heart of Maryland and Other Plays (includes *The Stranglers of Paris, La Belle Russe, The Girl I Left Behind Me, Naughty Anthony*), edited by Glenn Hughes and George Savage. 1941.

Plays

Jim Black (produced 1865).
The Doll Master (produced 1874-75?).
Sylvia's Lovers (produced 1875?).
The Creole, from a play by Adolphe Belot (produced 1876-77?).
Olivia, from the novel *The Vicar of Wakefield* by Goldsmith (produced 1878).
Proof Positive (produced 1878).
Within an Inch of His Life, with James A. Herne, from a play by Emile Gaboriau (produced 1879). Edited by Arthur Hobson Quinn, in *The Early Plays of Herne,* 1940.
A Fast Family, from a play by Sardou (produced 1879).
The Millionaire's Daughter (produced 1879).
Marriage by Moonlight, with James A. Herne, from the play *Camilla's Husband* by Watts Phillips (produced 1879).
Drink, from a novel by Zola (produced 1879).
Hearts of Oak, with James A. Herne (as *Chums,* produced 1879; as *Hearts of Oak,* produced 1879). Edited by Mrs. James A. Herne, in *Shore Acres and Other Plays,* by Herne, 1928.
Paul Arniff; or, The Love of a Serf (produced 1880).
True to the Core, from the play by A. R. Slous (produced 1880).
La Belle Russe, from the plays *Forget-Me-Not* and *New Magdalen* (produced 1881). 1914; in *The Heart of Maryland and Other Plays,* 1941.
The Stranglers of Paris, from a novel by Adolphe Belot (produced 1881). In *The Heart of Maryland and Other Plays,* 1941.
The Curse of Cain, with Peter Robinson (produced 1882).
American Born, from the play *British Born* (produced 1882).
May Blossom (produced 1884). 1883.
Valerie, from a play by Sardou (produced 1886).
The Highest Bidder, from the play *Trade* by John Maddison Morton and Robert Reece (produced 1887).
Baron Rudolph, with Bronson Howard, revised version (produced 1887). Edited by Allen G. Halline, in *The Banker's Daughter and Other Plays,* by Howard, 1941.

Pawn Ticket 210, with Clay M. Greene (produced 1887).

The Senator's Wife, with Henry C. DeMille (as *The Wife,* produced 1887; as *The Senator's Wife,* produced 1892). In *The Plays of DeMille and Belasco,* 1941.

Lord Chumley, with Henry C. DeMille (produced 1888). In *The Plays of DeMille and Belasco,* 1941.

The Charity Ball, with Henry C. DeMille (produced 1889). In *The Plays of DeMille and Belasco,* 1941.

The Marquis, from a play by Sardou (produced 1889).

Men and Women, with Henry C. DeMille (produced 1890). *In The Plays of DeMille and Belasco,* 1941.

Miss Helyett, from a play by Maxime Boucheron (produced 1891).

The Girl I Left Behind Me; or The Country Ball, with Franklin Fyles (produced 1893). In *The Heart of Maryland and Other Plays,* 1941.

The Younger Son, from a play by O. Vischer (produced 1893).

The Heart of Maryland (produced 1895). In *The Heart of Maryland and Other Plays,* 1941.

Under the Polar Star, with Clay M. Greene (produced 1896).

Zaza, from a play by Pierre Berton and Charles Simon (produced 1898).

Naughty Anthony (produced 1899). In *The Heart of Maryland and Other Plays,* 1941.

Madame Butterfly, from the story by John Luther Long (produced 1900). In *Six Plays,* 1928.

Du Barry (produced 1901). In *Six Plays,* 1928.

The Darling of the Gods, with John Luther Long (produced 1902). In *Six Plays,* 1928.

Sweet Kitty Bellairs, from the novel *The Bath Comedy* by Agnes and Egerton Castle (produced 1903).

Adrea, with John Luther Long (produced 1904). In *Six Plays,* 1928.

The Girl of the Golden West (produced 1905). In *Six Plays,* 1928.

The Rose of the Rancho, from the play *Juanita* by Richard Walton Tally (produced 1906). 1936.

A Grand Army Man, with Pauline Phelps and Marion Short (produced 1907).

The Lily, from a play by Pierre Wolff and Gaston Leroux (produced 1909).

The Return of Peter Grimm (produced 1911). In *Six Plays,* 1928.

The Governor's Lady, with Alice Bradley (produced 1912).

The Secret, from a work by Henri Bernstein (produced 1913).

Van Der Decken: A Legendary Play of the Sea (produced 1915).

The Son-Daughter, with George Scarborough (produced 1919).

Timothy Shaft, with W. J. Hurlbut (produced 1921).

Kiki, from the play by Andre Picard (produced 1921).

The Merchant of Venice, from the play by Shakespeare (produced 1922). 1922.

The Comedian, from a play by Sacha Guitry (produced 1923).

Laugh, Clown, Laugh!, with Tom Cushing, from a play by Fausto Martini (produced 1923).

Salvage. 1925.

Fanny, with Willard Mack (produced 1926).

Mima, from a play by Molnar (produced 1928).

Six Plays (includes *Madame Butterfly, Du Barry, The Darling of the Gods, Adrea, The Girl of the Golden West, The Return of Peter Grimm*), edited by Montrose J. Moses. 1928.

Other

The Theatre through Its Stage Door, edited by Louis V. Defoe. 1919.

A Souvenir of Shakespeare's Merchant of Venice. 1923.

Editor, with Charles A. Byrne, *Fairy Tales Told by Seven Travellers at the Red Lion Inn.* 1906.

*

Bibliography: *Plays Produced under the Stage Direction of Belasco,* 1925.

Critical Studies: *The Life of Belasco* by William Winter, 2 vols., 1918; *The Bishop of Broadway: The Life and Work of Belasco* by Craig Timberlake, 1954; *Belasco: Naturalism in the American Theatre* by Lise-Lone Marker, 1975; *The First Born (1897): A Cultural, Historical, and Literary Study of Francis Powers and David Belasco's Unpublished Drama of Chinese Life in America* (dissertation) by Sheryl F. Nadler, 1994.

* * *

The parents of David Belasco came to San Francisco from England during the Gold Rush, and his early theatrical experience was gained entirely in the American and Canadian West. Humphrey Abraham Belasco was a harlequin turned shopkeeper, and his son at the age of eleven played the Duke of York to Charles Kean's Richard III. At twelve, he wrote and produced his first melodrama. He supered; prompted; played Hamlet, Uncle Tom, and Armand on tour; and in 1876 was secretary to Dion Boucicault, whose "sensation dramas" heavily influenced the would-be playwright.

While stage manager at Baldwin's Academy of Music, Belasco began to experiment with spectacle and stage lighting as well as adapting and collaborating on several plays, one of which, *La Belle Russe,* was a success in New York. Its derivative plot involves a woman's impersonation of her virtuous twin sister, even to the sister's titled husband. Here Belasco began treating "Strong," sometimes demonic, always sexual female characters and tense situations. The sketchy good twin also foreshadows Belasco's virtuous, suffering heroines such as Adrea and Cho-Cho-San.

In 1882 Belasco came east, where he was at times associated with the Frohmans, and in the late 1880s collaborated with Henry C. DeMille on four very popular but unmemorable plays. Belasco's real success as a playwright began with *The Heart of Maryland* in 1895, in which Mrs. Leslie Carter swung on the clapper of a bell to save her soldier-sweetheart, Belasco having been inspired by the Civil War and "Curfew Shall Not Ring Tonight!" Mrs. Carter, the star of a scandalous divorce trial, was taught to act by Belasco, who later wrote *Zaza, Du Barry,* and *Adrea* for her. Too high in voice and too low in stature to be effective on stage himself, he acted through the players he coached and in his own off-stage character as the silver-haired, clerical-collared "Bishop of Broadway."

In 1900 Belasco collaborated with John Luther Long on *Madame Butterfly,* from which Puccini derived his opera, and when the same composer set Belasco's *The Girl of the Golden West,* the playwright directed Caruso and the Metropolitan Opera cast for its 1910 premiere. Belasco's later work was largely as director and deviser of scenic effects, and the plays he dealt with were inconsequential except for his productions of Sacha Guitry's *Deburau, The Merchant of Venice* with David Warfield as Shylock, and Molnar's *Mima*—unsuccessful but stupendous.

It is doubtful that David Belasco did anything that could be called truly original, but he improved all he touched and he touched almost everything in the theater of his day. A master of the exciting plot, he developed from the physical sensationalism of Boucicault to the emotional sensationalism of Sardou. *In The Girl I Left Behind Me,* for example, he used elements of Boucicault's *Defense of Lucknow* for a situation that John Ford would adapt for his film *Stage Coach.* Belasco heroines such as Du Barry, Minnie, and Yo-San face Tosca's dilemma of proscribed lover and lascivious authority, while *Adrea* with its blind princess, wicked sister, exotic kingdom, disloyal lover, and tower of death recalls the extravagant costume dramas Sardou created for Sarah Bernhardt. Yet Belasco could also devise plays of quiet sentiment such as *The Return of Peter Grimm* with its affectionate ghost *ex machina* (and its only partly acknowledged debt to the young Cecil B. DeMille). As Belasco explained in *The Theatre Through Its Stage Door,* his plays appealed because he tried "to tug at the hearts of my audience: He also made those heart-strings zing with excitement, part of which arose from his extraordinary scenic effects.

Dion Boucicault had blown up steamboats on stage; Belasco created battlefields. Later, working in the tradition of realistic *mise en scene* introduced by Tom Robertson, Belasco used a real switchboard and telephone booths in his production of William C. DeMille's *The Woman* and re-created the interior of a Childs Restaurant on stage in *The Governor's Lady* by Alice Bradley. The theaters that he built (the Belasco and the Stuyvesant) contained the most sophisticated stage equipment of their day, and he experimented endlessly with electricity, first used by W. S. Gilbert at the Savoy Theatre.

Belasco believed that color and light could "communicate to audiences the underlying symbolism of a play." Cho-Cho-San's pathetic vigil was accompanied by fourteen minutes of mood lighting in which twilight darkened to night, stars appeared, lamps were lighted and flickered out one by one, and dawn broke. The River of Souls in *The Darling of the Gods* was composed of shadowy spirits "floating across and disappearing," an anticipation of back projection. For *The Girl of the Golden West,* Belasco spent three months designing a sunset, only to reject it—"It was a good sunset, but it was not Californian."

Although Belasco's meticulous realism is no longer fashionable, it is still significant in the *verismo* operas that Puccini based on his plays and productions. Moreover, like his predecessors Robertson and Gilbert, Belasco played a part in turning the stage from a star-dominated playhouse to a director's theater. Finally, the exciting motifs that he developed or adapted are still part of the vocabulary of American melodrama.

—Jane W. Stedman

BELLAMY, Edward

Born: Chicopee Falls, Massachusetts, 26 March 1850. **Education:** Local schools; at Union College, Schenectady, New York, 1867-68; traveled and studied in Germany, 1868-69; studied law in Springfield, Massachusetts: admitted to the Massachusetts bar, 1871, but never practiced. **Family:** Married Emma Sanderson in 1882; one son and one daughter. **Career:** Staff member, New York *Evening Post,* 1871-72; editorial writer and reviewer, Springfield *Union,* 1872-77; founder with his brother, Springfield *Daily News,* 1880; after 1885 writer and lecturer in support of the Nationalist movement (in favor of nationalization); founder, *New Nation,* Boston, 1891-96. **Died:** 22 May 1898.

PUBLICATIONS

Fiction

Six to One: A Nantucket Idyl. 1878.
Dr. Heidenhoff's Process. 1880.
Miss Ludington's Sister: A Romance of Immortality. 1884.
Looking Backward 2000-1887. 1888; edited by John L. Thomas, 1967.
Equality. 1897.
The Blindman's World and Other Stories. 1898.
The Duke of Stockbridge: A Romance of Shays' Rebellion, edited by Francis Bellamy. 1900; edited by Joseph Schiffman, 1962.

Other

Bellamy Speaks Again! Articles, Public Addresses, Letters. 1937.
Talks on Nationalism. 1938.
The Religion of Solidarity, edited by Arthur E. Morgan. 1940.
Selected Writings on Religion and Society, edited by Joseph Schiffman. 1955.

*

Bibliography: in *Bibliography of American Literature* by Jacob Blanck, 1955; *Edward Bellamy: An Annotated Bibliography of Secondary Criticism* by Richard Toby Widdicombe, 1988.

Critical Studies: *Bellamy,* 1944, and *The Philosophy of Bellamy,* 1945, both by Arthur E. Morgan; *The Year 2000: A Critical Biography of Bellamy* by Sylvia E. Bowman, 1958, and *Bellamy Abroad: An American Prophet's Influence* by Bowman and others, 1962; *Bellamy, Novelist and Reformer* by Daniel Aaron and Harry Levin, 1968; *Authoritarian Socialism in America: Bellamy and the Nationalist Movement* by Arthur Lipow, 1982; *Alternative America: Henry George, Bellamy, Henry Demarest Lloyd, and the Adversary Tradition* by John L. Thomas, 1983; *Looking Backward, 1988-1888: Essays on Edward Bellamy* edited by Daphne Patai, 1988; "Imagination and Inversion in Nineteenth-Century Utopian Writing" by Simon Dentith, in *Essays on Early Science Fiction and Its Precursors* edited by David Seed, 1995; *Edward Bellamy Writes Again* by Joseph R. Myers, 1997; "The Religious Ethics of Edward Bellamy and Jonathan Edwards" by Richard A. Spurgeon Hall, in *Utopian Studies,* 1997, pp. 13-31.

*   *   *

Edward Bellamy is known chiefly for his Utopian romance *Looking Backward 2000-1887,* which within a short time after its publication sold more than one million copies. The purpose of the book was to offer a blueprint of what Bellamy considered to be an ideal society. To make his presentation more palatable to the general reader, he encased it in a romantic plot: A young Bostonian after a hypnotic sleep of 113 years awakens in the year 2000 to discover a totally transformed social and economic order. Falling in love with a girl descended from his fiancee of 1887, he learns from her father, a physician, the details of the state socialism that has replaced the laissez-faire capitalism that was in effect before his long sleep. Under the new order all commerce, industry, and other economic and professional activities have been nationalized into one vast interlocking enterprise. All men and women between the ages of twenty-one and forty-five are required to engage in work suitable to their abilities and, when possible, to their tastes; and all, no matter what occupation they may be in, receive the same wages. Superior ability and productivity are rewarded by social recognition and by assignment to positions of leadership. After the age of forty-five all are retired and are free to do what they wish.

Looking Backward is one of a number of books expressing the dissatisfaction of many Americans with the conditions of labor, the rise of monopolies, and the political corruption that characterized the second half of the nineteenth century. But Bellamy's book enjoyed a greater popularity and exerted a stronger influence than any other, with the possible exception of Henry George's *Progress and Poverty* (1879). Bellamy called his program Nationalism, and in the 1890s many Nationalist Clubs were formed and began to wield a political influence, most notably on the newly formed and temporarily quite powerful Populist Party. As a sequel to *Looking Backward,* Bellamy wrote *Equality,* which he finished shortly before his death. But by this time the Nationalist movement was losing its momentum, though Bellamy's ideas continued to be an influence on later reform efforts. Bellamy's most lasting contribution, as one critic has put it, was in fostering "an attitude toward social change." For example, many of the innovations of the New Deal had been suggested and made familiar to the public by Bellamy's book.

Bellamy's literary career was not confined solely to reformist writing. He was an able newspaper and magazine editor and the author of nonpolitical fiction. Several of his novels, among them *Dr. Heidenhoff's Process* and *Miss Ludington's Sister* received favorable notice in their day; and his *The Duke of Stockbridge* (serialized 1879) has been called, perhaps extravagantly, "one of the greatest historical novels." Dealing with the revolt in 1786 and 1787 of Massachusetts farmers who were overburdened with debt and taxes and ruthlessly exploited by lawyers, merchants, and bankers, this book provides early evidence of Bellamy's concern with social and economic injustice—a concern that doubtless had its origin in his early awareness of the exploitation of workers in the Massachusetts mill town in which he grew up.

—Perry D. Westbrook

See the essay on *Looking Backward 2000-1887.*

BELLOW, Saul

Born: Lachine, Quebec, Canada, 10 June 1915; grew up in Montreal; moved with his family to Chicago, 1924. **Education:** Tuley High School, Chicago, graduated 1933; University of Chicago, 1933-35; Northwestern University, Evanston, Illinois, 1935-37, B.S. (honors) in sociology and anthropology 1937; did graduate work in anthropology at University of Wisconsin, Madison, 1937. **Military Service:** Served in the U.S. Merchant Marine, 1944-45. **Family:** Married 1) Anita Goshkin in 1937 (divorced), one son; 2) Alexandra Tschacbasov in 1956 (divorced), one son; 3) Susan Glassman in 1961 (divorced), one son; 4) Alexandra Ionescu Tulcea in 1975 (divorced 1986); 5) Janis Freedman in 1989. **Career:** Teacher, Pestalozzi-Froebel Teachers College, Chicago, 1938-42; member of the editorial department, "Great Books" Project, *Encyclopaedia Britannica,* Chicago, 1943-44; freelance editor and reviewer, New York, 1945-46; instructor, 1946, and assis-

tant professor of English, 1948-49, University of Minnesota, Minneapolis; visiting lecturer, New York University, 1950-52; creative writing fellow, Princeton University, New Jersey, 1952-53; member of the English faculty, Bard College, Annandale-on-Hudson, New York, 1953-54; associate professor of English, University of Minnesota, 1954-59; visiting professor of English, University of Puerto Rico, Rio Piedras, 1961; Romanes Lecturer, 1990; professor, and chairman, 1970-76, Committee on Social Thought, University of Chicago, from 1962; Gruiner Distinguished Services Professor. Beginning 1993 University Professor and professor of English, Boston University. Coeditor, *The Noble Savage,* New York, then Cleveland, 1960-62; coeditor, with Keith Botsford, *News from the Republic of Letters.* Fellow, Academy for Policy Study, 1966; Fellow, Branford College, Yale University, New Haven, Connecticut. **Awards:** Guggenheim fellowship, 1948, 1955; American Academy grant, 1952, and gold medal, 1977; National Book award, 1954, 1965, 1971; Ford grant, 1959, 1960; Friends of Literature award, 1960; James L. Dow award, 1964; International Literary prize, 1965; Jewish Heritage award, 1968; Formentor prize, 1970; Nobel prize for literature, 1976; Pulitzer prize, 1976; Neil Gunn International fellowship, 1977; Brandeis University Creative Arts award, 1978; Malaparte award (Italy), 1984; Scanno award (Italy), 1988; National Medal of Arts, 1988. D.Litt.: Northwestern University, 1962; Bard College, 1963. Litt.D.: New York University, 1970; Harvard University, Cambridge, Massachusetts, 1972; Yale University, 1972; McGill University, Montreal, 1973; Brandeis University, Waltham, Massachusetts, 1973; Hebrew Union College, Cincinnati, 1976; Trinity College, Dublin, 1976. Chevalier, Legion of Honor, 1983, and Commander, Order of Arts and Letters (France), 1985. **Member:** American Academy, 1970; Commander, Legion of Honor (France), 1983. **Residence:** Chicago, Illinois.

PUBLICATIONS

Short Stories

Seize the Day, with *Three Short Stories and a One-Act Play.* 1956.
Mosby's Memoirs and Other Stories. 1968.
Him with His Foot in His Mouth and Other Stories. 1984.
A Theft (novella). 1989.
The Bellarosa Connection. 1989.
Something To Remember Me By: Three Tales. 1992.

Novels

Dangling Man. 1944.
The Victim. 1947.
The Adventures of Augie March. 1953.
Henderson the Rain King. 1959.
Herzog. 1964.
Mr. Sammler's Planet. 1970.
Humboldt's Gift. 1975.
The Dean's December. 1982.
More Die of Heartbreak. 1987.
The Actual. 1997.

Plays

The Wrecker (televised 1964). Included in *Seize the Day,* 1956.
Scenes from Humanitas: A Farce, in Partisan Review. 1962.

The Last Analysis (produced 1964). 1965.

Under the Weather (includes "Out from Under," "A Wen," and "Orange Souffle") (produced 1966; as *The Bellow Plays*, produced 1966). "A Wen" published in *Esquire* (New York), January 1965; in *Traverse Plays*, edited by Jim Haynes, 1966; "Orange Souffle" published in *Traverse Plays*, 1966; in *Best Short Plays of the World Theatre 1968-1973*, edited by Stanley Richards. 1973.

Television Play: *The Wrecker*, 1964.

Other

Dessins, by Jesse Reichek; text by Bellow and Christian Zervos. 1960.

Recent American Fiction: A Lecture. 1963.

Like You're Nobody: The Letters of Louis Gallo to Saul Bellow, 1961-62. 1966.

Plus Oedipus-Schmoedipus, The Story That Started It All. 1966.

Technology and the Frontiers of Knowledge, with others. 1973.

The Portable Saul Bellow, edited by Gabriel Josipovici. 1974.

To Jerusalem and Back: A Personal Account. 1976.

Nobel Lecture. 1977.

Editor, *Great Jewish Short Stories*. 1963.

*

Bibliography: *Bellow: A Comprehensive Bibliography* by B.A. Sokoloff and Mark E. Posner, 1973; *Bellow, His Works and His Critics: An Annotated International Bibliography* by Marianne Nault, 1977; *Bellow: A Bibliography of Secondary Sources* by F. Lercangee, 1977; *Bellow: A Reference Guide* by Robert G. Noreen, 1978; *Bellow: An Annotated Bibliography* by Gloria L. Cronin, second edition, 1987.

Critical Studies: *Bellow* by Tony Tanner, 1965; *Bellow* by Earl Rovit, 1967, and *Bellow: A Collection of Critical Essays* edited by Rovit, 1975; *Bellow: A Critical Essay* by Robert Detweiler, 1967; *Bellow and the Critics* edited by Irving Malin, 1967, and *Bellow's Fiction* by Malin, 1969; *Bellow: In Defense of Man* by John Jacob Clayton, 1968, revised edition, 1979; *Bellow* by Robert R. Dutton, 1971, revised edition, 1982; *Bellow* by Brigitte Scheer-Schazler, 1973; *Bellow's Enigmatic Laughter* by Sarah Blacher Cohen, 1974; *Whence the Power? The Artistry and Humanity of Bellow* by M. Gilbert Porter, 1974; *Bellow: The Problem of Affirmation* by Chirantan Kulshrestha, 1978; *Critical Essays on Bellow* edited by Stanley Trachtenberg, 1979; *Quest for the Human: An Exploration of Bellow's Fiction* by Eusebio L. Rodrigues, 1981; *Bellow* by Malcolm Bradbury, 1983; *Bellow: Vision and Revision* by Daniel Fuchs, 1984; *Bellow and History* by Judie Newman, 1984; *A Sort of Columbus: The American Voyages of Bellow's Fiction* by Jeanne Braham, 1984; *On Bellow's Planet: Readings from the Dark Side* by Jonathan Wilson, 1984; *Bellow* by Robert F. Kiernan, 1988; *Bellow in the 1980's* edited by Gloria Cronin and L.H. Goldman, 1989; *Bellow and the Decline of Humanism* by Michael K. Glenday, 1990; *Bellow: Against the Grain* by Ellen Pifer, 1990; *Bellow: A Biography of the Imagination* by Ruth Miller, 1991; *Character and Narration in the Short Fiction of Saul Bellow* by Marianne M. Friedrich, 1995; *The Critical Response to Saul Bellow* edited by Gerhard Bach, 1995; *Character and Narration in the Short Fiction of Saul Bellow* by Marianne M. Friedrich, 1996; *Figures of Madness in Saul Bellow's Longer Fiction* by Walter Bigler, 1998.

*   *   *

Since receiving the Nobel Prize for literature, Saul Bellow has been assured an important position in American literature, but this position is not really a new one. For more than thirty years, at least since the publication of his popular *The Adventures of Augie March*, Bellow has been heralded as the major spokesman of realism in America, as an articulate voice for humanism, as the most sophisticated comedian of the modern predicament, and even as the one on whose shoulders has fallen the mantle of genius previously worn by **William Faulkner**. No matter how exaggerated these evaluations might seem, Bellow is surely one of the major postwar American novelists.

It is as a novelist that he assumes his important position. However, Bellow also writes essays, short stories, and plays. Most of his nonfiction is a clarification of his view of the duties of novelist and human being. For Bellow, fiction should be basically realistic; it should not obscure the human condition but should delve deeply into the psychological idiosyncrasies that explain an individual act. *To Jerusalem and Back* relates a visit to Israel less for the purpose of providing an answer to the Middle East question than for the fascinating personalized portraits of individuals. It is not sociology but psychology.

Most of Bellow's short pieces that appear in journals are sections of novels in progress, but some have remained short stories, the best of which have been collected in *Mosby's Memoirs*. Perhaps the best of these tales in relation to his major work is "The Old System," a short story that approaches one of Bellow's significant themes: the conflict between modern Jews and their ageless ties to a Jewish past. His plays, especially the one-act sketches, barely hint at the power of his novels; *The Last Analysis*, a full-length work, is his best attempt in this genre. The fragmentation, confusion, and discomfort of modern life color the play as much as they do the novels.

Bellow's first novel, *Dangling Man*, is a diary of a young man awaiting induction into the Army during World War II. Joseph quits his job, planning to relax and read before being subjected to the rigors of Army life. Instead, the period becomes one of inaction and meaninglessness. Joseph begins to question the value of his friendships, the meaning of his family, and finally even the goodness of life. After months of stultification, existence seems absurd; relief comes in the promise of the regimentation of military life. Joseph no longer awaits induction; he enlists.

The Victim is similar to *Dangling Man* in atmosphere and tone but dissimilar in form. Asa Leventhal is plagued by family responsibilities, human responsibilities, and anti-Semitism. He is the victim. But in his treatment, or rather his acceptance, of his major tormentor, Kirby Allbee, Asa victimizes both his tormentor and himself. The bleak picture of human irrationality, death, and sorrow is broken only by the end of an unbearably hot summer, the return of Asa's wife, and the philosophy of humanism that is spoken by the Yiddish Schlossberg. These reprieves assure Asa's escape.

The Adventures of Augie March was the novel that thrust Bellow before the American public. An exuberant picaresque tale of a Chicago boy born to a mentally retarded mother, Augie March asserts an American innocence and joy in existence that Bellow seemed shy of in his first novels. This joyousness is not, however, unadulterated. Augie is a Jewish bastard who must learn to fend for himself in the confused and constantly changing world of America in the 1940s: he encounters abortion, political manipulation, the black market, and sexual perversion. In the face of all of this, Augie can still laugh.

Seize the Day, a novella, tells how middle-aged Wilky Adler is forced to recognize the aimlessness of his life. Always a failure in his father's eyes, Wilky tries to establish an independent identity by attaining what his father most admires—wealth. Wilky is, of course, an abysmal failure, though he learns the valuelessness of money. His epiphany comes with the recognition of his shared humanity with all people. The beauty of humanity is not revealed in the predatory stalking for materialistic gain, but rather in the prayer over the corpse of a stranger.

Henderson the Rain King is a fantasy of a trip to Africa. Here on the continent that saw the first humans evolve, Eugene Henderson tries to return to fundamental living. Henderson leaves America as a man who feels his soul gnawed at by a demanding voice crying "I want! I want!" By the time he returns from Africa, after encountering the primitive power that is in a lion and in an African tribal king, he assumes the status of human being, with human grace and goodness. His desire to do good for others, his love for his family and wife, are directed now so that he can accept the joy of existence. Suffering is no longer his only means of definition.

In *Herzog* Bellow created a character who caught the consciousness of the American intellectual establishment of the 1960s. Moses Elkanah Herzog, on the brink of divorce (for the second time) and professional suicide, begins to develop his naturally reflective nature to the point of insanity. He writes letters—to his friends, to his family, to famous people both dead and alive, even notes to himself. These attempts to come to terms with his changing self-image center especially on his feelings about his Jewish past. During his adult life Moses has been a Jew totally assimilated into the Christian intellectual world; he has learned the history of the Christian West; he has accepted the precepts of the Christian philosophers and theologians; and he has taken a Christian wife. Suddenly, this life begins to disintegrate. Before Herzog can attain any equanimity he must learn how to balance his present individuality with his past tradition.

In *Mr. Sammler's Planet* the conflict between past and present is again a concern, but with many added ambiguities. Arthur Sammler, representative of the Old World and survivor of the Holocaust, is divorced from his Jewish past. He admires and studies the Christian ideals of the West. In America, his benefactor and nephew, Elya Bruner, a gynecologist who got rich by doing illegal abortions for the Mafia, is the representative of the Old World patterns. Despite his flaws, he follows the humanistic ideals that were the backbone of the East European *shtetl.* Only at the end of the novel can Sammler articulate the beauty that he sees in his nephew. Throughout most of the novel, Sammler endures life in New York, dodging nymphomaniacs, pickpockets, exhibitionists, violent madmen, and schizophrenics. In the face of such disruption of morals, his own delicacy is not the answer; Elya's goodness is the only philosophy that provides order.

Humboldt's Gift relates the growth of a dilettante writer, Charlie Citrine, who must learn the true value of his mad mentor, Von Humboldt Fleischer (a fictionalized portrait of the poet **Delmore Schwartz**). As a young man, Charlie worships the charismatic Humboldt. Moving east to follow his god, Charlie becomes a friend and colleague of the poet. Only after Charlie's success on Broadway do the two writers part—Humboldt accusing Charlie of stealing his personality for the hero of his play. This big, funny, and poignant novel centers on the young man's reflections on Humboldt and on his true value as an artist and mentor. Through flashbacks Charlie reveals the despair and paranoia that destroy his idol. The persistence of Humboldt's spiritual presence in Charlie's later life, long after the poet's death, bespeaks the importance of Humboldt to Charlie. The gift that the mentor leaves is really twofold. The most obvious gift is the absurdist play that will probably see great success as a film. But, more importantly, Humboldt serves as a model for Charlie's own life. The reflection of later years gradually reveals that Humboldt was indeed mad; he was a genius who was driven insane and finally killed by his own unwritten poems. He was one who misused his talents. After this realization Charlie is able to accept the memory of Humboldt. The reburial of the poet's body is a significant rite of passage for Charlie: no longer is he possessed by his mentor's personality.

The dean of *The Dean's December,* Albert Corde, is a character with some of the qualities of both Herzog and Sammler. In Chicago and Bucharest, the two worlds of the novel, his reputation is based on his charisma, especially with women, and his marriage to an eminent Russian-born astronomer, Minna. Corde's Chicago is a tough place, and from his protected position in the academy he researches this world, writes articles, and theorizes. The characters who serve to link Corde to a world to which he otherwise has no access, the friends of the poor, are Rufus Ridpath, a prison reformer, Toby Winthrop, who runs a detoxification center, and Sam Varennes, a public defender. They play roles in the several murders on which the novel touches. All act in Bellow's vision of the demoralized city. From the trial in Chicago of two blacks for the murder of a graduate student at Corde's university, to Bucharest, home of his wife's dying mother, Corde, who is at once both participant and observer, ruminates and writes about them. Both cities form the backdrop of his reporting on the articles he's written and, ultimately, for his dualistic study of old city and new city, and of the play on bravery and fearfulness that Albert Corde exemplifies.

In *More Die of Heartbreak,* Bellow presents a study of one of his primary concerns— family bonds. With characteristic irony and wit, the novel explores the affectionate bond between Benn Crader, a Midwestern botanist, and his nephew and the novel's narrator, Kenneth Trachtenberg, a young Russian literature scholar. Both characters present elaborate portraits of American intellectuals who need to talk about their worlds in order to exist within them. In their anti-dramatic world, all of the action occurs offstage. Benn has characteristic Bellowesque problems: as a gentlenatured intellectual, he is unmatched against the forces determined against him. His late marriage to the ambitious Matilda Layamon, whose family manipulates him, ultimately proves to be one of the situations that overwhelms him. The Layamon family wants him to threaten a lawsuit against his own uncle, a crooked machine boss, who had cheated Benn's family out of their share of the city's most valuable real estate. In the end, it is the strong kinship of the uncle and nephew that helps them both survive and, when they eventually depart on separate courses, each recognizes the futility of his overly cerebral escapism.

The Actual, published in 1997, is a novel of whimsy and trickery involving Sigismund Adletsky, a billionaire philanthropist, and Harry Trellman, an importer of damaged antiquities from China.

Siggy, in his nineties, is impressed by Harry's powers of observation and asks him to be a kind of intellectual companion for him. The relationship sets up Bellow's characteristic model of a father-son bond. Like many of Bellow's central characters, Siggy is sharp, canny, accustomed to power, and unfamiliar with compassion. Together with Harry he works out the problems of intellectual inheritance. Harry does not realize that Siggy has set up the opportunity for Harry to rejoin his lifelong love, Amy Wustrin. Ultimately, Siggy acknowledges that the love Harry and Amy choose is in part his creation and that, apart from the great cultivation of material wealth and intellectual legacy, the world of emotional completion and the chance to contribute to others in a loving way is the true gift of the mentor.

The variety and power of Bellow's novels are unquestioned. When Bellow resists the term "Jewish writer," it is because his art is not a chauvinistic and narrow one. But as readers we must not be misled by his resistance to this term: he is most assuredly a writer whose style, characters, form, and humor derive in large part from his Jewish past.

—R. Barbara Gitenstein, updated by Martha Sutro

BEMELMANS, Ludwig

Born: Meran, Austria (now Merano, Italy), 27 April 1898; moved to the United States in 1914; became citizen, 1918. **Education:** Schools in Regensburg and Rothenburg, Bavaria. **Military Service:** Served in the U.S. Army during World War I. **Family:** Married Madeline Freund in 1935; one daughter. **Career:** Worked in hotels and restaurants, 1914-17 and 1919-24; owner, Hapsburg House Restaurant, New York, 1925-35; writer for *New Yorker;* also an artist: exhibitions in galleries in the United States and abroad. **Awards:** American Library Association Caldecott Medal, for children's book, 1954. **Died:** 1 October 1962.

PUBLICATIONS

Collections

Tell Them It Was Wonderful: Selected Writings, edited by Madeline Bemelmans. 1985.

Fiction

I Love You, I Love You, I Love You (stories). 1942.
Now I Lay Me Down to Sleep. 1943.
The Blue Danube. 1945.
Dirty Eddie. 1947.
The Eye of God. 1947; as *The Snow Mountain,* 1950.
The Woman of My Life. 1957.
Are You Hungry, Are You Cold. 1960.
The Street Where the Heart Lies. 1963.

Other (for children)

Hansi. 1934.
The Golden Basket. 1936.
The Castle Number Nine. 1937.
Quito Express. 1938.

Madeline. 1939.
Fifi. 1940.
Rosebud. 1942.
A Tale of Two Glimps. 1947.
Sunshine. 1950.
The Happy Place. 1952.
Madeline's Rescue. 1953.
The High World. 1954.
Parsley. 1955.
Madeline and the Bad Hat. 1956.
Madeline and the Gypsies. 1959.
Welcome Home! 1960.
Madeline in London. 1961.
Marina. 1962.
Madeline's Christmas, completed by Madeline and Barbara Bemelmans. 1985.

Other

My War with the United States. 1937.
Life Class. 1938.
Small Beer. 1939.
At Your Service: The Way of Life in a Hotel. 1941.
Hotel Splendide. 1941.
The Donkey Inside. 1941.
Hotel Bemelmans. 1946.
The Best of Times: An Account of Europe Revisited. 1948.
How to Travel Incognito. 1952.
Father, Dear Father (autobiography). 1953.
To the One I Love the Best. 1955.
The World of Bemelmans. 1955.
My Life in Art. 1958.
How to Have Europe All to Yourself. 1960.
Italian Holiday. 1961.
On Board Noah's Ark. 1962.
La Bonne Table (writings and drawings), edited by Donald and Eleanor Friede. 1964.

Editor, *Holiday in France.* 1957.

*

Critical Studies: "Aesthetic Distancing in Ludwig Bemelmans' Madeline" by Jacqueline F. Eastman in *Children's Literature* vol. 19, 1991, and "Safety in the Structure of Art: Bemelmans' Madeline Books" by Eastman in *Cross-Culturalism in Children's Literature* edited by Susan R. Gannon and Ruth Anne Thompson, 1988; *A Study of the Madeline Books of Ludwig Bemelmans* (dissertation) by Jacqueline F. Eastman, 1990; "Aesthetic Distancing in Ludwig Bemelmans' *Madeline*" by Jacqueline F. Eastman in *Children's Literature: Annual of the Modern Language Association Division on Children's Literature,* 1991, pp. 75-89.

*   *   *

William McFee once wrote of Ludwig Bemelmans, the writer, stage designer, illustrator, and painter, that he was "one of those fortunate writers who have all the reviewers ranged on one side, rooting for him." Whether chronicling the adventures of Madeline, the irrepressible little French *gamine,* or reporting his own adventures as "El Senor Bnelemaas" in Ecuador (*The Donkey In-*

side) or as a waiter (in *Hotel Splendide*), he is delightful. He always wanted to be a painter (despite his family's belief that all artists are "hunger candidates") and only wrote because he had insomnia, but in his acerb and risible little essays, even more than in his drawings, every line is precisely right.

To him happen all the most fabulous things. He meets "Mr. Sigsag" of the Hotel Splendide and a host of other charming eccentrics. Just for him a war breaks out (*My War with the United States*) to galvanize a gallery of characters into action. He encounters a little girl who contrives to make her schoolmates livid with jealousy by having an appendix operation. For him tables and chairs have something droll about them. For him people do the most ludicrous things. The world ("I regard it as a curiosity") is funny and he has only to report it (*I Love You, I Love You, I Love You*). He claimed he had no imagination.

Bemelmans is always satirical but at his best when his unquenchable good humor is given free play, as in the novel *Now I Lay Me Down to Sleep* or the collection of *New Yorker* essays *Small Beer*. It is hard not to gush when mentioning his works, but his delightful humor disarms criticism.

—Leonard R.N. Ashley

BENCHLEY, Robert (Charles)

Born: Worcester, Massachusetts, 15 September 1889. **Education:** Worcester High School, 1904-07; Phillips Exeter Academy, New Hampshire, 1907-08; Harvard University, Cambridge, Massachusetts (president of the board of editors, *Harvard Lampoon*), 1908-12, A.B. 1913. **Family:** Married Gertrude Darling in 1914; two sons, including the writer Nathaniel Benchley. **Career:** Staff member, Boston Museum of Fine Art, 1912, and Curtis Publishing Company, 1912-14 (editor of the house journal *Obiter Dicta*); welfare worker in Boston and New York, 1914; worked in advertising, then as a reporter, New York *Tribune* and *Tribune* magazine, 1916-17; editor, *Tribune Graphic* Sunday supplement, 1918; drama critic, *Vanity Fair*, New York, and press agent for theatrical producers, 1917; news censor, Aircraft Board, Washington, D.C., 1918; promoter, Liberty Loan drive, 1919; managing editor, *Vanity Fair*, 1919-20; columnist, New York *World*, 1920-21; drama critic, 1920-24, and editor, 1924-29, *Life* magazine, New York; contributor, 1925-40, and drama critic, 1927-40, *New Yorker*; columnist, King Features Syndicate, 1933-36. Founder, with Dorothy Parker, Robert E. Sherwood, and others, Algonquin Hotel Round Table, 1920. Also an actor: stage debut, 1923; starred in numerous films (mainly shorts), 1928-45; radio broadcaster from 1938. **Awards:** Oscar, for acting in short film, 1935. **Died:** 21 November 1945.

PUBLICATIONS

Collection

The Best of Robert Benchley. 1995.

Essays and Sketches

Of All Things! 1921.
Love Conquers All. 1922.

Pluck and Luck. 1925.
The Early Worm. 1927.
The Bridges of Binding. 1928.
20,000 Leagues under the Sea; or, David Copperfield. 1928.
The Treasurer's Report and Other Aspects of Community Singing. 1930.
No Poems; or, Around the World Backwards and Sideways. 1932.
From Bed to Worse; or, Comforting Thoughts about the Bison. 1934.
Why Does Nobody Collect Me? 1935.
My Ten Years in a Quandary and How They Grew. 1936.
After 1903—What? 1938.
Inside Benchley (selection). 1942.
Benchley Beside Himself. 1943.
One Minute Please. 1945.
Benchley—or Else! 1947.
Chips Off the Old Benchley. 1949.
The "Reel" Benchley, edited by George Hornby. 1950.
The Bedside Manner; or, No More Nightmares. 1952.
The Benchley Roundup, edited by Nathaniel Benchley. 1954.
Benchley Lost and Found: 39 Prodigal Pieces. 1970.
Benchley at the Theatre (reviews). 1985.

Plays

Screenplays: *The Treasurer's Report*, 1928; *The Sex Life of the Polyp*, 1928; *The Spellbinder*, 1928; *Furnace Trouble*, 1929; *Lesson Number One*, 1929; *Stewed, Fried and Boiled*, 1929; *Sky Devils*, with others, 1932; *The Sport Parade*, 1932; *Your Technocracy and Mine*, 1933; *Murder on a Honeymoon*, with Seton I. Miller, 1935; *Foreign Correspondent*, with others, 1940; *No News Is Good News*, 1943; *Important Business*, 1944; *Why, Daddy?* 1944.

*

Bibliography: *Robert Benchley: An Annotated Bibliography*, 1995.

Critical Studies: *Benchley: A Biography* by Nathaniel Benchley, 1955; *Benchley* by Norris W. Yates, 1968; *Benchley: His Life and Good Times* by Babette Rosmond, 1970; *Starring Benchley: Those Magnificent Movie Shorts* by Robert Redding, 1973; *Benchley: A Biography* by Bill Altman, 1987; *Mr. B. or Comforting Thoughts about the Bison: A Critical Biography of Robert Benchley* by Wes D. Gehring, 1992.

*   *   *

After the customary false starts, forays into advertising and personnel work, Robert Benchley, like most of the American humorists of his generation, found his way to journalism. He began as a reporter for the New York *Tribune* in 1916 and within a few years became editor, columnist, or occasional contributor to *Collier's*, *Vanity Fair*, the New York *World*, *Life*, the *Bookman*, and the *New Yorker*. Aside from his comic writing, his most sustained work in the magazines was as a drama reviewer, primarily for *Life* and the *New Yorker*, and as a press critic, in which capacity he used a pseudonym, Guy Fawkes, and initiated "The Wayward Press" department in the *New Yorker*. His first book, *Of All Things!*, was published in 1921, and between that time and his death in 1945, some dozen more volumes appeared, all of them collections of pieces written for magazines or newspapers. Some of the later ones, like *Benchley Beside Himself,* cannibalize earlier collections.

In a letter to his mother written in 1922, **E.B. White** called *Of All Things!* "about as funny as anything there is on the market today," and, in a letter to Walter Blair in 1964, he admitted that he imitated Benchley in his early work. That writers like White and **James Thurber**, who so early found their own authentic voices, were influenced by Benchley is evidence not simply of the pervasiveness of his subject matter—the little indignities of daily life that have always beset humorists—but of the quality of his prose. Benchley could, like Frank Sullivan, rise to complete nonsense, but most of the time he wrote simple, deceptively rational sentences in which a judicious choice of adjective or a demanding parenthesis could turn the sentence, the whole piece, a conventional way of thinking inside out.

Benchley early developed a firm comic personality, and his persona became a Benchley after-image through the Gluyas Williams illustrations for his books and the bumbling character he played in movie shorts and in feature films. As he emerges in Benchley's writing, the character is more than the conventional little man so loved by humorists, cartoonists, and politicians. He is both vain and ponderous, using his own self-esteem as the banana peel on which to slip; he is easily embarrassed, but he will snarl—a bit tentatively—if he is cornered by too preposterous as assault from social usage. His ordinary antagonists are things like pigeons, road maps, ocean liners, and Christmas, but there are hints of darker enemies, as in "My Trouble," in which he asks, "Do all boys of 46 stop breathing when they go to bed?" This disquieting undertone emerges infrequently in Benchley's work; for the most part his confused and confusing other self is satisfied to worry a pomposity or a platitude to death and in the process leave the reader laughing.

—Gerald Weales

BENÉT, Stephen Vincent

Born: Bethlehem, Pennsylvania, 22 July 1898; brother of William Rose Benét. **Education:** Hitchcock Military Academy, Jacinto, California, 1910-11; Summerville Academy; Yale University, New Haven, Connecticut (chairman, *Yale Literary Magazine,* 1918), 1915-18, 1919-20, A.B. 1919, M.A. 1920; the Sorbonne, Paris, 1920-21. **Family:** Married Rosemary Carr in 1921; one son and two daughters. **Career:** Worked for the State Department, Washington, D.C., 1918, and for advertising agency, New York, 1919; lived in Paris, 1926-29; during 1930s and early 1940s was an active lecturer and radio propagandist for the liberal cause. Editor, Yale Younger Poets series. **Awards:** Poetry Society of America prize, 1921; Guggenheim fellowship, 1926; Pulitzer prize, 1929, 1944; O. Henry award, 1932, 1937, 1940; Shelley Memorial award, 1933; American Academy Gold Medal, 1943. **Member:** National Institute of Arts and Letters (vice-president), 1929. **Died:** 13 March 1943.

PUBLICATIONS

Collection

Selected Poetry and Prose, edited by Basil Davenport. 1960.

Short Stories

The Barefoot Saint. 1929.
The Litter of Rose Leaves. 1930.
Thirteen O'Clock: Stories of Several Worlds. 1937.
The Devil and Daniel Webster. 1937.
Johnny Pye and the Fool-Killer. 1938.
Tales Before Midnight. 1939.
Short Stories: A Selection. 1942.
O'Halloran's Luck and Other Short Stories. 1944.
The Last Circle: Stories and Poems. 1946.

Novels

The Beginning of Wisdom. 1921.
Young People's Pride. 1922.
Jean Huguenot. 1923.
Spanish Bayonet. 1926.
James Shore's Daughter. 1934.

Poetry

The Drug-Shop; or, Endymion in Edmonstoun. 1917.
Young Adventure. 1918.
Heavens and Earth. 1920.
The Ballad of William Sycamore 1790-1880. 1923.
King David. 1923.
Tiger Joy. 1925.
John Brown's Body. 1928.
Ballads and Poems 1915-1930. 1931.
A Book of Americans, with Rosemary Benét. 1933.
Burning City. 1936.
The Ballad of the Duke's Mercy. 1939.
Nightmare at Noon. 1940.
Listen to the People: Independence Day 1941. 1941.
Western Star. 1943.
Captain Kidd and Two Others. 1997.

Plays

Five Men and Pompey: A Series of Dramatic Portraits. 1915.
Nerves, with John Farrar (produced 1924).
That Awful Mrs. Eaton, with John Farrar (produced 1924).
The Headless Horseman, music by Douglas Moore (broadcast 1937). 1937.
The Devil and Daniel Webster, music by Douglas Moore, from the story by Benét (produced 1938). 1939.
Elementals (broadcast 1940-41). In *Best Broadcasts of 1940-41,* edited by Max Wylie, 1942.
Freedom's a Hard Bought Thing (broadcast 1941). In *The Free Company Presents,* edited by James Boyd, 1941.
Nightmare at Noon, in *The Treasury Star Parade,* edited by William A. Bacher. 1942.
A Child Is Born (broadcast 1942). 1942.
They Burned the Books (broadcast 1942). 1942.
All That Money Can Buy (screenplay), with Dan Totheroh, in *Twenty Best Film Plays,* edited by John Gassner and Dudley Nichols. 1943.
We Stand United and Other Radio Scripts (includes *A Child Is Born, The Undefended Border, Dear Adolf, Listen to the People, Thanksgiving Day—1941, They Burned the Books, A Time to Reap, Toward the Century of Modern Man, Your Army*). 1945.

Screenplays: *Abraham Lincoln,* with Gerrit Lloyd, 1930; *Cheers for Miss Bishop,* with Adelaide Heilbron and Sheridan Gibney, 1941; *All That Money Can Buy,* with Dan Totheroh, 1941.

Radio Plays: *The Headless Horseman,* 1937; *The Undefended Border,* 1940; *We Stand United,* 1940; *Elementals,* 1940-41; *Listen to the People,* 1941; *Thanksgiving Day—1941,* 1941; *Freedom's a Hard Bought Thing,* 1941; *Nightmare at Noon; A Child Is Born,* 1942; *Dear Adolf,* 1942; *They Burned the Books,* 1942; *A Time to Reap,* 1942; *Toward the Century of Modern Man,* 1942; *Your Army,* 1944.

Other

A Summons to the Free. 1941.
Selected Works. 2 vols., 1942.
America. 1944.
Selected Letters, edited by Charles A. Fenton. 1960.
Benét on Writing: A Great Writer's Letter of Advice to a Young Beginner, edited by George Abbe. 1964.

Editor, with others, *The Yale Book of Student Verse 1910-1919.* 1919.
Editor, with Monty Woolley, *Tamburlaine the Great,* by Christopher Marlowe. 1919.

*

Bibliography: by Gladys Louise Maddocks, in *Bulletin of Bibliography* 20, September 1951 and April 1952.

Critical Studies: *Benét* by William Rose Benét, 1943; *Benét: The Life and Times of an American Man of Letters* by Charles A. Fenton, 1958; *Benét* by Parry Stroud, 1962; "Benét's *The Devil and Daniel Webster*" by David Partenheimer, in *Explicator,* 1996, pp. 37-40.

*   *   *

Stephen Vincent Benét occupies a curiously equivocal position in American letters. One of America's best known and rewarded poets and storytellers, he has at the same time been virtually ignored in academic discussions of major twentieth-century writers and seldom anthologized. In light of the greater critical success enjoyed by his student friends at Yale—**Thornton Wilder, Archibald MacLeish,** and **Philip Barry,** themselves often unremarked among "major" writers—Benét's reputation seems thin indeed.

Benét's permanent place in the history of American fiction is nevertheless assured by the fact that among his many volumes of prose and verse there are several minor classics that are widely read and admired. His early light and ironic verse, such as "For City Spring" and "Evening and Morning," and such frolicking ballads as "Captain Kidd," "Thomas Jefferson," "The Mountain Whippoorwill," and "The Ballad of William Sycamore" are highly regarded. His long narrative poem about the Civil War, *John Brown's Body,* dramatized by Charles Laughton in 1953 and called by Henry Steele Commager "not only the best poem about the Civil War, and the best narrative, but also the best history," won Benét his first Pulitzer Prize. Benét's best known short story, "The Devil and Daniel Webster," which combines the author's flare

for fantasy and old folktale traditions, shares an equally prominent place in the tall-tale genre of American storytelling. Finally, *Western Star,* another long narrative poem about the heroic pioneering of America, begun in 1934 and incomplete at his death, won for Benét a second Pulitzer Prize in 1944.

Among the notes for the continuation of *Western Star* found after Benét's death, the following quatrain was saved:

> Now for my country that it still may live,
> All that I have, all that I am I'll give.
> It is not much beside the gift of the brave
> And yet accept it since tis all I have.

What Benét had—an unbounded, nineteenth-century faith in the promises of American democracy, and an expansive, Whitmanesque love for what seemed the nation's special attributes, diversity, amplitude, self-sufficiency, frankness, innocence—he poured into every poem, story, and novel he wrote. He praised New York as the communal achievement of the spirit of man, and America because there every man could most freely become what God meant him to be. "Out of your fever and your moving on," he said in the "Prelude" to *Western Star,* "Americans, Americans, Americans . . . I make my song."

Both in sentiment and in style, Benét's work attempts to embody the very democratic virtues it is about. Like **Carl Sandburg, Hart Crane,** and **Vachel Lindsay,** he uses the zesty tempos, conversational rhythms, and laconic vernacular to capture the spirit of greatness in the strength and simplicity of the nation's common people. In his book of 56 verses about famous American men and women, great and small, *A Book of Americans,* Benét says of the greatest and humblest of American native sons:

> Lincoln was a long man
> He liked out of doors.
> He liked the wind blowing
> And the talk in country stores.

Just as *John Brown's Body* projects Benét's sensitive feeling for half a dozen countrysides, racial strains, and political attitudes, so this book stands in praise of the nation's heroic ability to reconcile its opposites among that "varied lot" who "each by deed and speech / Adorned our history."

Despite the warmth, genuineness, and impish charm with which Benét celebrates the country's democratic potential, his failure to win wider critical respectability is clearly attributable to the fact that his breadth of sympathy and deep-rooted patriotism seem parochial and old-fashioned to modern audiences and that even his best work, viewed alongside the more realistic and richly inventive fiction of such contemporaries as Crane, Joyce, Proust, and **T.S. Eliot,** appears lacking in depth, subtlety, and originality. The pastoral rebellion of the earth against machines, against the "Age of Steam," which pervades so many of his poems, and his use of conventional verse forms and technical devices that have made him dear to school teachers, seem, in the words of one critic, "all too clear and all too facile." It is significant that Benét's writing has been praised more for its lively evocation of American history than for its aesthetic value.

—Lawrence R. Broer

See the essay on *John Brown's Body.*

BENÉT, William Rose

Born: Fort Hamilton, New York, 2 February 1886; brother of Stephen Vincent Benét. **Education:** Albany Academy, Albany, New York, graduated 1904; Yale University, New Haven, Connecticut (chairman, *Yale Courant;* editor, *Yale Record*), 1904-07, B.Phil. 1907. **Military Service:** Served in the U.S. Army Signal Corps, 1918: second lieutenant. **Family:** Married 1) Teresa Frances Thompson in 1912 (died 1919), one son and two daughters; 2) Elinor Wylie, in 1923 (died 1928); 3) Lora Baxter in 1932 (divorced 1937); 4) the writer Marjorie Flack in 1941. **Career:** Ship's clerk, 1908; lived in California, 1909-10; clerk and reader, 1911-14, and assistant editor, 1914-18, *Century* magazine, New York; advertising writer, 1918; assistant editor, *Nation's Business,* Washington, D.C., 1918-19; associate editor, *Literary Review,* supplement of New York *Evening Post,* 1920-24; founder, with Christopher Morley, 1924, associate editor, 1924-29, columnist ("The Phoenix Nest"), 1924-50, and contributing editor, 1929-50, *Saturday Review of Literature,* New York; editor, Brewer and Warren, publishers, New York, 1929-30. **Awards:** Pulitzer prize, 1942. **Member:** National Institute of Arts and Letters (secretary). **Died:** 4 May 1950.

PUBLICATIONS

Poetry

Merchants from Cathay. 1913.
The Falconer of God and Other Poems. 1914.
The Great White Wall. 1916.
The Burglar of the Zodiac and Other Poems. 1918.
Perpetual Light: A Memorial. 1919.
Moons of Grandeur. 1920.
Man Possessed: Selected Poems. 1927.
Sagacity. 1929.
Rip Tide: A Novel in Verse. 1932.
Starry Harness. 1933.
Golden Fleece. 1935.
Harlem and Other Poems. 1935.
A Baker's Dozen of Emblems. 1935.
With Wings as Eagles: Poems and Ballads of the Air. 1940.
The Dust Which Is God: A Novel in Verse. 1941.
Adolphus; or, The Adopted Dolphin and the Pirate's Daughter (for children), with Marjorie Hack. 1941.
Day of Deliverance. 1944.
The Stairway of Surprise. 1947.
Timothy's Angels (for children). 1947.
Poetry Package, with Christopher Morley. 1950.
The Spirit of the Scene. 1951.

Play

Day's End, in *The Best One-Act Plays of 1939,* edited by Margaret Mayorga. 1939.

Fiction

The First Person Singular. 1922.

Other

Saturday Papers (essays), with Henry Seidel Canby and Amy Loveman. 1921.
The Flying King of Kurio (for children). 1926.
Wild Goslings: A Selection of Fugitive Pieces. 1927.
The Prose and Poetry of Elinor Wylie. 1934.
Stephen Vincent Benét: My Brother Steve. 1943.

Editor, *Poems for Youth: An American Anthology.* 1925.
Editor, with John Drinkwater and Henry Seidel Canby, *Twentieth-Century Poetry.* 1929.
Editor, *Collected Poems, by Elinor Wylie.* 1932.
Editor, *Fifty Poets: An American Auto-Anthology.* 1933.
Editor, *Guide to Daily Reading.* 1934.
Editor, *The Pocket University.* 13 vols., 1934.
Editor, with others, *Adventures in English Literature.* 1936.
Editor, *Mother Goose: A Comprehensive Collection of the Rhymes.* 1936.
Editor, *From Robert to Elizabeth Barrett Browning* (letters). 1936.
Editor, with Norman Holmes Pearson, *The Oxford Anthology of American Literature.* 1938.
Editor, with Adolph Gillis, *Poems for Modern Youth.* 1938.
Editor, *Supplement to Great Poems of the English Language,* edited by Wallace Alvin Briggs. 1941.
Editor, with Conrad Aiken, *An Anthology of Famous English and American Poetry.* 1945.
Editor, with Norman Cousins, *The Poetry of Freedom.* 1945.
Editor, *The Reader's Encyclopedia.* 1948.

Translator, with Teresa Frances, *The East I Know,* by Paul Claudel. 1914.

*

Critical Study: in *Elinor Wylie, A Life Apart: A Biography* by Stanley Olson, 1979.

*   *   *

William Rose Benét has perhaps been more remarked upon in modern American literary history as the "older brother" of the writer **Stephen Vincent Benét** and as husband of **Elinor Wylie** than as an accomplished poet in his own right. Serious attention to his verse has also been diverted by his prominence as a reviewer, critic, and anthologist and by his numerous activities as a promoter of the arts. But despite this dispersion of energies, Benét managed to publish many volumes of verse whose value has not properly been acknowledged.

The obvious unevenness of Benét's creative output is hinted at by the fact that one critic rated him no better than a mere "journeyman of letters," while another claimed that he was a "builder [whose] strongest rhythms have the certitude of an arch . . . ." Certainly Benét's weakest poems are unapologetically romantic and lacking in intensity. When he announces his poetic intentions in his most celebrated work, *The Dust Which Is God,* as "I will be plain at least," he does more than alert us to what he hopes will be a poetic voice free of bombast and ornamentation; unwittingly, he indicts a good number of poems whose overstatedness results in an absence of color or emotional vitality. "Throw wide / The gates of the heart," he counsels in his poem "Study of Man," "Taking your part / In percipient life . . . Ever Extend / Your boundaries, and be / Inwardly free!"

Such direct statement issues from the poet's almost passionate reverence for the freedom and dignity of man, and for the ample spirit of God and nature, which he finds so abundantly manifest in his native America, as in "Men on Strike":

> The Country of the Free! Yes, a great land.
> Thank God that I have known it East to West
> And North to South, and still I love it best
> Of all the various world the seas command.

From the point of view of the wise primitivist, Benét celebrates the democratic virtues of common men, and envisions portents of disaster in the encroachments of the machine age. In "The Stricken Average," he writes:

> Little of brilliance did they write or say.
> They bore the battle of living, and were gay.
> Little of wealth or fame they left behind.
> They were merely honorable, brave, and kind.

He yearns for the "pristine creation / Unsullied by our civilization," ("Young Girl") whose elemental harmonies are forever threatened by factories, corporations, "towers of glass and steel" ("Shadow of the Mountain Man").

Such romantic attitudes were bound to lessen the appeal of Benét's work in an age whose best literary efforts were in direct opposition to such simple and sentimental verse. Yet there are indisputable qualities in Benét's best work, perhaps most forcibly realized in *The Dust Which Is God,* which in 1942 won him a Pulitzer Prize. An autobiographical verse narrative, it demonstrates a remarkable range of interests and intellect, and admirable versatility in the use of changing forms and rhythms to capture the diverse and sprawling nature of his subject—the birth and growth of the country, which he treats as synonymous with his own life. The poetry here reveals a lively and sophisticated grasp of cultural ideas, and often achieves a rich synthesis of opposites: classical and modern, noble and banal, holy and sensual, lyrical and prosaic. At their best, these "vignette illustrations" project for us a poetic talent of greater potential stature than that of the author's more celebrated brother—more original, more sensuous, and more varied and universal in scope.

—Lawrence R. Broer

BERKLEY, Helen. *See* **MOWATT, Anna Cora.**

BERRYMAN, John

Born: John Allyn Smith, in McAlester, Oklahoma, 25 October 1914; took step-father's surname, 1926. **Education:** Schools in Oklahoma, Florida, and New York City; South Kent School, Connecticut, 1928-32; Columbia University, New York (Rensselaer prize, 1935), 1932-36, A.B. 1936 (Phi Beta Kappa); Clare College, Cambridge (Kellett Fellow, 1936-37; Oldham Shakespeare Scholar, 1937), 1937-38, B.A. 1938. **Family:** Married 1) Eileen Patricia Mulligan in 1942 (divorced 1956); 2) Elizabeth Ann Levine

in 1956 (divorced 1959), one son; 3) Kathleen Donahue in 1961, two daughters. **Career:** Instructor in English, Wayne State University, Detroit, 1939-40, and Harvard University, Cambridge, Massachusetts, 1940-43; instructor in English, 1943, associate in creative writing, 1946-47, resident fellow, 1948-49, and Hodder Fellow, 1950-51, Princeton University, New Jersey; lecturer in English, University of Washington, Seattle, 1950; Elliston Professor of Poetry, University of Cincinnati, 1952; teacher of creative writing, University of Iowa, Iowa City, 1954; assistant professor, 1955-56, associate professor, 1957-62, professor, 1962-72, and Regents' Professor of Humanities, 1969-72, University of Minnesota, Minneapolis. U.S. Information Service lecturer, India, 1957. Visiting professor, University of California, Berkeley, 1960, and Brown University, Providence, Rhode Island, 1962-63. Poetry editor, *Nation,* New York, 1939. **Awards:** Rockefeller fellowship, 1944-46, 1956; Shelley Memorial award, 1949; Guggenheim fellowship. 1952, 1966; Harriet Monroe award, 1957; Brandeis University Creative Arts award, 1959; Ingram Merrill Foundation grant, 1964; Loines award, 1964; Pulitzer prize, 1965; Academy of American Poets fellowship, 1967; National Endowment for the Arts award, 1967, and senior fellowship, 1971; Bollingen prize, 1969; National Book award, 1969. D.Let.: Drake University, Des Moines, Iowa, 1971. **Member:** American Academy; American Academy of Arts and Sciences; Academy of American Poets. **Died:** 7 January 1972 (suicide).

PUBLICATIONS

Collections

Collected Poems 1934-1972, edited by Charles Thornbury. 1986.

Poetry

Five Young American Poets, with others. 1940.
Poems. 1942.
Two Poems. 1942.
The Dispossessed. 1948.
Homage to Mistress Bradstreet. 1956; as *Homage to Mistress Bradstreet and Other Poems,* 1959.
His Thought Made Pockets & the Plane Buckt. 1958.
77 Dream Songs. 1964.
Two Dream Songs. 1965.
Berryman's Sonnets. 1967.
Short Poems. 1967.
I Have Moved to Dublin . . . . 1967.
His Toy, His Dream, His Rest: 308 Dream Songs. 1968.
The Dream Songs. 1969.
Two Dream Songs. 1969.
Two Poems. 1970.
Love and Fame. 1970; revised edition, 1972.
Delusions, Etc. 1972.
Selected Poems 1938-1968. 1972.
Henry's Fate and Other Poems 1967-1972, edited by John Haffenden. 1977.
Shetland Poems. 1994.

Fiction

Recovery. 1973.

Other

Stephen Crane (biography). 1950.
The Freedom of the Poet (miscellany). 1976.
One Answer to a Question. 1981.
Stephen Crane: The Red Badge of Courage. 1981.

Editor, with Ralph Ross and Allen Tate, *The Arts of Reading* (anthology). 1960.
Editor, *The Unfortunate Traveller; or, The Life of Jack Wilton*, by Thomas Nashe. 1960.

*

Bibliography: *Berryman: A Checklist* by Richard J. Kelly, 1972; *Berryman: A Descriptive Bibliography* by Ernest C. Stefanik, Jr., 1974; *Berryman: A Reference Guide* by Gary Q. Arpin, 1976.

Critical Studies: *Berryman* by William J. Martz, 1969; *Berryman* by James M. Linebarger, 1974; *A Tumult for Berryman: A Homage* edited by Marguerite Harris, 1976; *The Poetry of Berryman* by Gary Q. Arpin, 1977; *Berryman: An Introduction to the Poetry* by Joel Conarroe, 1977; *Berryman: A Critical Commentary*, 1980, and *The Life of Berryman*, 1982, both by John Haffenden; *Poets in Their Youth* by Eileen Simpson, 1982; *The Stock of Available Reality: R. P. Blackmur and Berryman* by James D. Bloom, 1984; *The Soul under Stress: A Study of the Poetics of Berryman's Dream Songs* by Bo Gustavsson, 1984; *John Berryman and the Thirties* by E. M. Halliday, 1988; *Berryman's Understanding: Reflections on the Poetry of John Berryman* edited by Harry Thomas, 1988; *Dream Song: The Life of John Berryman* by Paul Mariani, 1990; "A Special Feature on John Berryman" edited by Peter Stitt, in *The Gettysburg Review* vol. 4, 1991; *Dream Song: The Life of John Berryman* by Paul L. Mariani, 1996; *John Berryman's Personal Library: A Catalogue* by Richard J. Kelly, 1998.

*　　*　　*

John Berryman spent his childhood on a farm in Oklahoma under the somber and difficult aegis of a father whose improvidence finally led to his suicide, an event that haunted and disturbed the poet for the rest of his life. From these dark beginnings, he leapt into the brighter world of his education, first at a private school in Connecticut, and then at Columbia University, where his immense energies and brilliance were manifested. A scholarship to Cambridge University led to his studies in Shakespeare and the English Renaissance, the stylistic exuberance of which was to influence his own discordant, richly embellished mode of verse. At Princeton University he began a frenzied pace of writing that led to his first full-length collection of short poems, *The Dispossessed*. He had also completed much of the cycle of poems later published as *Berryman's Sonnets*. In both volumes Berryman is a mature craftsman of traditional forms and meters, which he renewed with his energetic speech.

Berryman's major work begins with *Homage to Mistress Bradstreet*, which includes poems from *The Dispossessed*. The title poem, a sequence of fifty-seven eight-line stanzas, evokes the life and hardships of this American poet through an original strategy of merging the narrator's voice with his subject's, in which all the details of her sickness, frailty, and harsh family life are rendered with powerful immediacy. The poet's speech slips into the Colonial tongue and out again into a flinty modern colloquialism with masterful control. Berryman etches the character of Bradstreet and holds her up as an instance of the artist's eternal struggle against adversity:

> Headstones stagger under great draughts of time
> after heads pass out, and their world must reel
> speechless, blind in the end
> about its chilling star: thrift tuft,
> whin cushion—nothing. Already with the wounded flying
> dark air fills, I am a closet of secrets dying,
> races murder, foxholes hold men,
> reactor piles wage slow upon the wet brain rime.

Included in *Homage* is the series "The Nervous Songs," where he again inhabits other strained minds and articulates their emotions. They are important, however, chiefly for their form; each poem is cast in three six-line stanzas, the form employed throughout his greatest work, *The Dream Songs*.

The persona of the *Dream Songs* is variously referred to as Henry, Pussy-Cat, and Mr. Bones, and the poems evoke his daily inner life as he struggles through the routines of teaching, drying out from chronic alcoholism, and writing ambitious books of poems. His deepest dilemma is with his own identity, which fits him in the middle of every extreme of life: he is middle-aged, of the middle-class, and of middling talent. Against all these middlings he struggles to find an edge, by occasionally daubing burnt cork on his face, by heavy drinking, and by hard working, but each time falls back into the slough of his middleness depressed and exhausted:

> He lay in the middle of the world, and twicht.
> More Sparine for Pelides,
> human (half) & down here as he is,
> with probably insulting mail to open
> and certainly unworthy words to hear
> and his unforgivable memory.

Or again. "Henry felt baffled, in the middle of the thing," which is a refrain of his efforts and sufferings.

The desire to transcend his undefined existence wears down into defeat in later sections of this sequence, until "Henry hates the world. What the world to Henry did will not bear thought." The despair deepens into rejection: "This world is gradually becoming a place / where I do not care to be any more." He broods upon death in all its forms and nightmare possibilities, including the frequent lamentations for other poets who have died recently, and who seem to share his dark view of the world:

> I'm cross with God who has wrecked this generation.
> First he seized Ted [Roethke], then Richard [Blackmur],
> Randall [Jarrell], and now Delmore [Schwartz].
> In between he gorged on Sylvia Plath.
> That was a first rate haul. He left alive
> fools I could number like a kitchen knife
> but Lowell he did not touch.

In a later, grimmer juncture of the *Songs*, Henry remarks bitterly, "The world grows more disgusting dawn by dawn." The poems then take up a plot of sorts with a residence in Ireland, followed by a return to the United States and the long attempt to recover from alcoholism, a turn that also involves Henry in religious conversion.

The whole work, including the posthumous additions, *Henry's Fate,* amounts to a vast mosaic of pieces of Henry's life and character without transforming such pieces into a unified vision. The work is discordant throughout in its language and in its jagged progression of themes and motifs. It is essentially a long and despairing examination of a poet's alienation from the post-war world in which his brilliance and cultural inheritance appear to have no place or value. The grave, devoted artist founders and ultimately destroys himself, lamenting throughout the cursed and crooked fate of his fellow poets. This tragedy is lifted above self-pity and sentimentality by the essential good character of Henry, whose complications give us a Hamlet for this age.

Berryman's later works, *Love and Fame, Delusions, Etc.,* and the novel *Recovery,* turn away from the *Dream Songs* to treat more directly of the poet's life. *Love and Fame* is unabashed autobiography of the poet's education and rise to prominence, delivered in a flat, narrative style unlike his earlier verse. In *Delusions, Etc.* his religious turning is expressed in a section of liturgical poems where Berryman is again the effortless master of sonorous lyrics. *Recovery,* unfinished at the poet's death, exposes the torment of the alcoholic and eloquently pleads for understanding of this disease from which the poet suffered much of his life.

—Paul Christensen

See the essay on *The Dream Songs.*

BETTS, Doris Waugh

Born: Iredell County, North Carolina, 4 June 1932. **Education:** Statesville, North Carolina public schools; Woman's College of University of North Carolina; University of North Carolina Chapel Hill. **Family:** Married Lowry M. Betts. **Career:** Pianist, clerk, reporter, and typist, Statesville, North Carolina, 1945-52; office manager, secretary-treasurer, Simplified Farm Record Book Co., Chapel Hill, North Carolina, 1957-58; full-time feature writer, *Sanford Daily Herald,* 1958-60; editor, *Sanford News Leader,* 1960; lecturer, University of South Carolina, Chapel Hill, 1966-74; visiting lecturer, Duke University, 1971; lecturer, University of California, Davis, 1973. Associate professor, 1974-78, professor, 1978-80, and since 1980 Alumni Distinguished Professor of English, University of North Carolina, Chapel Hill. Member of staff of Indiana University summer writing conference, 1972-73, and Squaw Valley Writers Conference, 1974. Member of board, 1979-81 (chair, 1981) Associated writing programs, National Endowment for the Arts; member of North Carolina Tercentenary Commission, 1961-62; member of board of North Carolina Committee for Continuing Education in Humanities, 1972-75; consultant, North Carolina Department of Instruction, 1973-77; secretary, Lee County Arts Council, 1978; board member, Chatham Arts Council, 1997. **Awards:** Short-story prize, *Mademoiselle* College Fiction Contest, 1953; G.P. Putnam-University of North Carolina Fiction award, 1954; Sir Walter Raleigh awards for fiction, Historical Book Club of North Carolina, 1973; Tanner award for distinguished undergraduate teaching, 1974; Parker award for literary achievement, 1982-85; John Dos Passos award, 1983; Medal

of Merit, American Academy of Arts and Letters, 1989. Honorary degrees: Queens College; Erskine College; UNC-Greensboro; UNC-Pembroke; University of the South. **Member:** Fellowship of Southern Writers (chancellor 1997). **Residence:** Pittsboro, North Carolina.

PUBLICATIONS

Stories

The Gentle Insurrection. 1954.
The Astronomer and Other Stories. 1966.
Beasts of the Southern Wild. 1973.

Novels

Tall Houses in Winter. 1958.
The Scarlet Thread. 1965.
The River to Pickle Beach. 1972.
Heading West. 1981.
Souls Raised from the Dead. 1994.
The Sharp Teeth of Love. 1997.

Other

Creative Writing: The Short Story. n.d.

*

Manuscript Collection: Boston University Library, Betts Collection.

Critical Studies: in *Southern Literary Journal* edited by David Holman, 1982; in *Southern Quarterly,* 1983; *Doris Betts* by Elizabeth Evans, 1997.

*　　　*　　　*

Fiction writer and essayist Doris Betts made her initial reputation as a writer of short stories, building on the encouragement of her successful pursuit of the 1953 Mademoiselle College Fiction Contest. The following year, at age twenty-two, she won the Putnam-University of North Carolina prize for her first collection of short fiction, *The Gentle Insurrection and Other Stories.* These stories portray several "gentle insurrections," depicting the lives of ordinary persons whose humanity emerges as the reader comes to admire their quiet desperation.

Betts was determined, however, to be a novelist as well as a short story writer. The response to her first novel, *Tall Houses in Winter* (1957)—a study of an English professor with cancer of the larynx who returns to North Carolina to die but eventually chooses treatment earlier scorned—suggested that mastering this genre would be more difficult. A second novel, *The Scarlet Thread* (1964), a study of the rise of a North Carolina mill town at the turn of the century, did not fare much better. Betts was faulted for sensational gothicism and a literary structure that seemed too segmented, impressive more for parts than the whole—linked short stories, as it were.

In 1966 Harper & Row published *The Astronomer and Other Stories,* which provided further proof for those who judged short fiction Betts's forte. The title story, a novella, moved Betts closer to the success she sought in the longer form. "The Astronomer" depicts the life of a widowed and retired mill worker (his sons, too, are dead) who has focused his mind on space and his telescope and space but rediscovers that Earth is the right place for love after he rents a room to a young man who is soon joined by a woman who has walked away from her husband and children. The novella is followed by seven short stories that demonstrate Betts's continuing skill at finding meaning and humor in the lives of characters who come from the working-class world that shaped her, the daughter of a Statesville, North Carolina, mill worker.

The challenge of the novel still beckoned. Betts made great gains over her first two attempts with *The River at Pickle Beach* (1972), which follows a rural North Carolina couple whose lives are complicated by the appearance of the husband's old army buddy of the husband's, who is attracted to the wife. The novel touches numerous contemporary concerns of the 1970s—the generation gap, racial unease, pervasive violence. Betts received more praise for this novel than for her earlier efforts. The most satisfying accolade came from Jonathan Yardley in the *New York Times*, who called her "a tough, wise, and compassionate writer" still waiting to receive her due.

Betts's chances of getting her due were soon enhanced by the appearance of her third collection, *Beasts of the Southern Wild and Other Stories* (1973). In time, "The Ugliest Pilgrim," the lead story of the rich collection, would serve as the introduction to Betts for many readers and spread her fame outside the South. Frequently anthologized, the story recounts the journey of a young woman from Appalachia to see a faith healer in Tulsa, Oklahoma, for removal of a facial scar that has blighted her life. In 1981 "The Ugliest Pilgrim" was made into the film "Violet," which won an Oscar as best short feature. A musical stage version was produced in 1997.

With the publication of *Beasts,* Betts rested her case that she had mastered the short story. She set her mind more determinedly than ever on the challenge of the novel. Concluding that the short story is more useful to the young writer than to the older one, she looked to the novel to explore the themes and longer views that interested her. Longer in the making than any of her other novels, *Heading West* (1981) was her most ambitious. It explores territory far from her North Carolina base. The protagonist is a North Carolina librarian who is kidnapped by a psychopath and taken across the country, eventually arriving at the Grand Canyon. The descent into the canyon becomes her descent into herself and a new realization of the world and her place in it.

Although Betts still claims no complete satisfaction with any of her novels, she has earned a secure place among contemporary novelists. *Souls Raised from the Dead* (1994) and *The Sharp Teeth of Love* (1997) have added to her reputation as a novelist willing to take great risks—in technique as well as subject. *Souls* studies the death of a bright young girl and its effect on her family. *Teeth,* set mainly in and around contemporary Reno, Nevada, evokes the tragedy of the Donner Party of 1846 as it explores the various kinds of love that define human beings—loves that nurture and loves that devour.

No matter their social class, Betts's characters are always intelligent individuals who raise large questions. Although she rebelled against the conservative Presbyterianism of her youth, she has increasingly viewed life through the lens of faith. Like **Flannery O'Connor**, she has found it an advantage as a writer to have grown up in the Bible Belt. But unlike O'Connor, who said that

for the hard of hearing it is necessary to shout, Betts has preferred the whisper.

—Joseph M. Flora

BIERCE, Ambrose (Gwinnet)

Born: Horse Cave Creek, Meigs County, Ohio, 24 June 1842. **Education:** High school in Warsaw, Indiana; Kentucky Military Institute, Franklin Springs, 1859-60. **Military Service:** Served in the 9th Indiana Infantry of the Union Army during the Civil War, 1861-65: major. **Family:** Married Mollie Day in 1871 (separated 1888; divorced 1905); two sons and one daughter. **Career:** Printer's devil, *Northern Indianan* (anti-slavery paper), 1857-59; U.S. Treasury aide, Selma, Alabama, 1865; served on military mapping expedition, Omaha to San Francisco, 1866-67; night watchman and clerk, Sub-Treasury, San Francisco, 1867-78; editor and columnist ("Town Crier"), *News Letter,* San Francisco, 1868-71; lived in London, 1872-75: staff member, *Fun,* 1872-75, and editor, *Lantern,* 1875; worked in the assay office, U.S. Mint, San Francisco, after 1875; associate editor, *Argonaut,* 1877-79; agent, Black Hills Placer Mining Company, Rockervill, Dakota Territory, 1880-81; editor and columnist ("Prattle"), *Wasp,* San Francisco, 1881-86; columnist, San Francisco *Examiner,* 1887-1906, and New York *Journal,* 1896-1906; lived in Washington, D.C., 1900-13: Washington correspondent, New York *American,* 1900-06; columnist, *Cosmopolitan,* Washington, D.C., 1905-09; traveled in Mexico, 1913-14; served in Pancho Villa's forces and is presumed to have been killed at the Battle of Ojinaga. **Died:** 1914 (probably 11 January).

PUBLICATIONS

Collections

Collected Works, edited by Walter Neale. 12 vols., 1909-12.
Complete Short Stories, edited by Ernest Jerome Hopkins. 1970.
Stories and Fables, edited by Edward Wagenknecht. 1977.
The Devil's Advocate: A Reader, edited by Brian St. Pierre. 1987.

Short Stories

Nuggets and Dust Panned Out in California. 1873.
Cobwebs from an Empty Skull. 1874.
Tales of Soldiers and Civilians. 1891; as *In the Midst of Life,* 1892; revised edition, 1898.
Can Such Things Be? 1893.
Fantastic Fables. 1899.
Ambrose Bierce: Stories. 1994.
An Occurrence at Owl Creek Bridge and Other Stories. 1995.
The Moonlit Road and Other Ghost and Horror Stories. 1998.

Novels

The Fiend's Delight. 1873.
The Dance of Death, with Thomas A. Harcourt. 1877; revised edition, 1877.
The Monk and the Hangman's Daughter, from a translation by Gustav Adolph Danziger of a story by Richard Voss. 1892.

A Son of the Gods, and A Horseman in the Sky. 1907.
Battlefields and Ghosts. 1931.

Poetry

Black Beetles in Amber. 1892.
Shapes of Clay. 1903.
Poems of Ambrose Bierce. 1995.

Other

The Cynic's Word Book. 1906; as *The Devil's Dictionary,* 1911;
revised edition, by Ernest Jerome Hopkins, as *The Enlarged
Devil's Dictionary,* 1967.
The Shadow on the Dial and Other Essays, edited by S.O. Howes.
1909; revised edition, as *Antepenultimata* (in *Collected Works
11*), 1912.
Write It Right: A Little Black-List of Literary Faults. 1909.
Letters, edited by Bertha Clark Pope. 1921.
Twenty-One Letters, edited by Samuel Loveman. 1922.
Selections from Prattle, edited by Carroll D. Hall. 1936.
Satanic Reader: Selections from the Invective Journalism, edited
by Ernest Jerome Hopkins. 1968.
The Devil's Advocate: A Bierce Readers, edited by Brian St. Pierre.
1987.
Skepticism and Dissent: Selected Journalism, 1898-1901, edited
by Lawrence I. Berkove. 1986.
A Soul Survivor: Bits of Autobiography. 1998.

*

Bibliography: *Bierce: A Bibliography* by Vincent Starrett, 1929;
in *Bibliography of American Literature* by Jacob Blanck, 1955;
Bierce: Bibliographical and Biographical Data edited by Joseph
Gaer, 1968.

Critical Studies: *Bierce: A Biography* by Carey McWilliams,
1929; *Bierce, The Devil's Lexicographer,* 1951, and *Bierce and
the Black Hills,* 1956, both by Paul Fatout; *Bierce* by Robert A.
Wiggins, 1964; *The Short Stories of Bierce: A Study in Polarity* by
Stuart C. Woodruff, 1965; *Bierce: A Biography* by Richard
O'Connor, 1967; *Bierce* by M.E. Grenander, 1971; *Critical Es-
says on Bierce* edited by Cathy N. Davidson, 1982, and *The Ex-
perimental Fictions of Bierce: Structuring the Ineffable* by
Davidson, 1984; *Bierce: The Making of a Misanthrope* by Rich-
ard Saunders, 1985; "Ambrose Bierce's Civil War Stories and the
Critique of the Martial Spirit" by Giorgio Mariani, in *Studies in
American Fiction* vol. 19, 1991; *Ambrose Bierce: Alone in Bad
Company* by Ray Morris, 1995; *Questioning Truth: War and the
Art of Writing in Ambrose Bierce, Stephen Crane, Michael Herr,
and Tim O'Brien* (dissertation) by Dennis Keith Fudge, 1996; *Just
What War Is: The Civil War Writings of De Forest and Bierce* by
Michael W. Schaefer, 1997.

*　　*　　*

Though no longer widely read, Ambrose Bierce is a familiar
name in American letters. After several years of distinguished soldiering in the Civil War, the almost completely self-taught Bierce
turned to journalism and ended up being one of the most colorful
figures in late nineteenth- and early twentieth-century journalism

in the United States. In San Francisco, where he spent most of
his life, he was a newspaper editor and columnist and delighted in
exposing hypocrisy and stupidity in private and public life. Besides his witty and pungent journalistic writing, Bierce produced
a sizeable body of short stories and essays and also some verse,
chiefly occasional and satiric. His literary reputation, however,
must depend upon the stories collected in *Tales of Soldiers and
Civilians.* In "An Occurrence at Owl Creek Bridge" Bierce skillfully uses suspense not as a mere melodramatic device but as a
logical and calculating means of rendering believable the bizarre
plot, which concerns a young man about to be executed. In other
stories, like "One of the Missing," there is perhaps a heavier use
of coincidence than most readers will accept without protest.

If young Bierce dealt in the tall tale and broad western humor,
the older Bierce was a master of sardonic humor and mordant but
often sparkling wit. The best specimen of these qualities as well
as of Bierce's life-long cynicism is to be found, outside his journalism, in *The Devil's Dictionary,* a book quoted universally even
though many who quote from it may not be aware of the author's
identity. As a serious literary writer Bierce belongs to—and has
helped perpetuate (in a small measure)—the tradition of the absurd and grotesque in American writing. There is in his work a
marked interest in abnormal or intensified psychological states and
a persistent hostility to the realistic mode. One will look in vain
for a range of emotional experience in his writing and the depth of
serious feeling found in great literature. But for his picturesque
personality and his contribution as a committed and hard-hitting
journalist, and as a writer of some excellent stories, Bierce is an
enduring figure in the history of American literature.

—J.N. Sharma

See the essay on "One of the Missing."

BIRD, Robert Montgomery

Born: New Castle, Delaware, 5 February 1806. **Education:**
Germantown Academy, Philadelphia; University of Pennsylvania,
Philadelphia, 1824-27, M.D. 1827. **Family:** Married Mary Mayer
in 1837; one son. **Career:** Practiced as a physician in Philadelphia for one year, then gave up medicine to become a writer; wrote
plays for the actor-producer Edwin Forrest, 1831-34; wrote novels, 1835-40; suffered a breakdown and retired to a farm in Maryland, where he subsequently recovered, 1840; professor, Institutes
of Medicine and Materia Medica, Pennsylvania Medical College,
Philadelphia, 1841-43; literary editor and part owner, *North American,* Philadelphia, 1847-54. **Member:** Honorary member, English
Dramatic Authors Society. **Died:** 23 January 1854.

PUBLICATIONS

Collections

The Life and Dramatic Works (includes *Pelopidas, The Gladiator,
Oralloossa*), edited by Clement E. Foust. 1919.
The Cowled Lover and Other Plays (includes *Calidorf; or, The
Avenger; News of the Night; or, A Trip to Niagara; 'Twas All for
the Best; or 'Tis All a Notion*), edited by Edward O'Neill. 1941.

Plays

The Gladiator (produced 1831; also produced as *Spartacus*). In
  The Life and Dramatic Works, 1919.
Oralloossa (produced 1832). In *The Life and Dramatic Works*,
  1919.
The Broker of Bogota (produced 1834). Edited by Arthur Hobson
  Quinn, in *Representative American Plays*, 1917.
News of the Night; or, A Trip to Niagara (produced 1929). In *The
  Cowled Lover and Other Plays*, 1941.
The City Looking Glass: A Philadelphia Comedy, edited by Arthur
  Hobson Quinn (produced 1933). 1933.

Fiction

Calavar; or, The Knight of the Conquest. 1834; as *Abdalla the
  Moor and the Spanish Knight*, 1835.
The Infidel; or, The Fall of Mexico. 1835; as *Cortez*, 1835; as *The
  Infidel's Doom*, 1840.
The Hawks of Hawk-Hollow: A Tradition of Pennsylvania. 1835.
Sheppard Lee. 1836.
Nick of the Woods; or, The Jibbenainosay: A Tale of Kentucky.
  1837; edited by Cecil B. Williams, 1939.
Peter Pilgrim; or, A Rambler's Recollections. 1838.
The Adventures of Robin Day. 1839.

*

Bibliography: in *Bibliography of American Literature* by Jacob
Blanck, 1955.

Critical Studies: *Life of Bird* by Mary Mayer Bird, edited by
C. Seymour Thompson, 1945; *Bird* by Curtis Dahl, 1963; "Bird's
Bloody Romance: Nick of the Woods" by Robert P. Winston in
Southern Studies vol. 23, 1984; "Justified Bloodshed: Robert Mont-
gomery Bird's Nick of the Woods and the Origins of the Vigilante
Hero in American Literature and Culture" by Gary Hoppenstand,
in *Journal of American Culture* vol. 15, 1992.

*   *   *

One of the truly remarkable men of his time, Robert Montgomery Bird boasted sufficiently varied interests and equally responsive talents to lead his active mind through the fields of medicine, science, music, art, history, politics, pedagogy, and literature. Early in life he outlined a literary career in which he would
begin with poetry and drama, turn next to novels, and finally write
history. A scholarly man, widely read in the classics, he was also
very much a product of and a part of the Romantic tradition that
was being revealed in the idealism of **Emerson** and **Thoreau**, the
Gothic qualities in **Hawthorne** and **Poe**, and the concern for nature that distinguished the novels of **Cooper**, **John Pendleton
Kennedy** and **William Gilmore Simms**. Indeed, Bird was a significant force in bringing Romanticism to American literature, particularly the drama.

For his career as a dramatist, Bird projected at least fifty-five
plays, and in response to the play contests that Edwin Forrest
established in 1828, he began to write in earnest. Four of Forrest's
nine prize plays were written by Bird—*Pelopidas, The Gladiator, Oralloossa,* and *The Broker of Bogota*—but it did not prove
to be a completely happy arrangement. For his efforts Bird re-

ceived $1,000 for each play; Forrest, on the other hand, made hun-
dreds of thousands of dollars. When Bird realized that plays such
as *The Gladiator* and *The Broker of Bogota* would become permanent in Forrest's repertory, he complained, received no satisfaction, and stopped writing for the stage. "What a fool I was to
think of writing plays!" he confided in his *Secret Records.* In all
he completed only nine of his projected plays.

As a consequence of the events surrounding his relations with
Forrest, Bird turned to politics, journalism, and novels. Two of
his most popular novels are *The Hawks of Hawk-Hollow* and *Nick
of the Woods.* Bird's loss to American drama, however, must be
considered significant. An imaginative man, keenly aware of the
forces working upon his culture, he espoused theories of dramaturgy that not only reflected the Romanticism of his day but were
ideally suited to the style of acting then popular. The idealized
hero was the central force in his plays. All other dramatic elements—the plot, the dramatic incidents and spectacle, the poetic
speech, the passions of the characters, the theme of the play—
contributed to the creation of the hero and led to the climax of the
play. Bird obviously had the energy and the skill to write good
romantic melodrama. An early play, *The City Looking Glass* (written in 1828), also showed considerable potentiality for comedy.
Unfortunately, all of this talent was shelved when his indignation
was righteously ignited, and the help that copyright laws might
have provided was years in the future.

—Walter J. Meserve

BISHOP, Elizabeth

Born: Worcester, Massachusetts, 8 February 1911. **Education:**
Walnut Hill School, Natick, Massachusetts, 1927-30; Vassar College, Poughkeepsie, New York, 1930-34, A.B. 1934. **Career:**
Lived in Key West, Florida, in late 1930s and 1940s, and in Brazil, 1951-66. Consultant in poetry, Library of Congress, Washington, D.C., 1949-50; poet-in-residence, University of Washington, Seattle, 1966, 1973; lecturer in English, Harvard University, Cambridge, Massachusetts, 1970-79. **Awards:**
Guggenheim fellowship, 1947; American Academy grant, 1951;
Shelley Memorial award, 1953; Pulitzer prize, 1956; Amy
Lowell traveling fellowship, 1957; Chapelbrook fellowship,
1962; Academy of American Poets fellowship, 1964;
Rockefeller fellowship, 1967; Ingram Merrill Foundation grant,
1969; National Book award, 1970; Harriet Monroe Poetry
award, 1974; Neustadt prize, 1976; National Book Critics
Circle award, 1977. LL.D.: Smith College, Northampton, Massachusetts, 1968; Rutgers University, New Brunswick, New Jersey,
1972; Brown University, Providence, Rhode Island, 1972. Chancellor, Academy of American Poets, 1966. **Member:** Order of Rio
Branco (Brazil), 1971; American Academy, 1976. **Died:** 6 October 1979.

PUBLICATIONS

Collections

Complete Poems 1927-1979. 1983.
Collected Prose, edited by Robert Giroux. 1984.

Poetry

North and South. 1946.
Poems: North and South—A Cold Spring. 1955.
Poems. 1956.
Questions of Travel. 1965.
Selected Poems. 1967.
The Ballad of the Burglar of Babylon (for children). 1968.
The Complete Poems. 1969.
Geography III. 1977.

Other

Brazil, with the editors of *Life.* 1962.
One Art: Letters. 1994.
Conversations with Elizabeth Bishop. 1996.
Exchanging Hats: Paintings. 1996.

Editor, with Emanuel Brasil, and translator, *An Anthology of Twentieth-Century Brazilian Poetry.* 1972.

Translator, *The Diary of Helena Morley,* by Alice Brant. 1957.

*

Bibliography: *Bishop: A Bibliography 1927-1979* by Candace W. MacMahon, 1980; *Bishop and Howard Nemerov: A Reference Guide* by Diana E. Wyllie, 1983.

Critical Studies: *Bishop* by Anne Stevenson, 1966; *Bishop and Her Art* edited by Lloyd Schwartz and Sybil P. Estess, 1983; *The Unbeliever: The Poetry of Bishop* by Robert D. Parker, 1988; *Bishop: Her Artistic Development* by Thomas J. Travisano, 1988; *Bishop: The Biography of a Poet* by Lorrie Goldensohn, 1991; *Bishop: Questions of Mastery* by Bonnie Costello, 1991; *Reading and Writing Nature: The Poetry of Robert Frost, Wallace Stevens, Marianne Moore, and Elizabeth Bishop* by Guy Rotella, 1991; *The Veiled Mirror and the Woman Poet: H. D., Louise Bogan, Elizabeth Bishop, and Louise Gluck* by Elizabeth Dodd, 1992; *Remembering Elizabeth Bishop: An Oral Biography* by Gary Fountain, 1994; *Elizabeth Bishop: Her Poetics of Loss* by Susan McCabe, 1994; *Politics and Form in Postmodern Poetry: O'Hara, Bishop, Ashbery, and Merrill* by Mutlu Konuk Blasing, 1995; *Stein, Bishop, and Rich: Lyrics of Love, War, and Place* by Margaret Dickie, 1997; *Dazzling Dialectics: Elizabeth Bishop's Resonating Feminist Reality* by Sally Bishop Shigley, 1997; *Five Looks at Elizabeth Bishop* by Anne Stevenson, 1998.

*   *   *

Elizabeth Bishop's autobiographical "In the Village," a story that moves toward poetry and was originally included at the center of *Questions of Travel,* shows how the sounds and sights and textures of a Nova Scotia village enable a child to come to terms with the sound of the scream that signified her mother's madness and, ultimately, with human isolation, loss, mortality: the child's capacity for meticulous attention serves not merely as a method of escaping from intolerable pain but also as an opening from the prison of the self and its wounds to a rejoicing in both human creativity and the things and events of an ordinary day. The story, with its nod of homage to Chekhov, provides an accurate antici-

pation of the peculiar virtues of Bishop's poetry: her fantastic powers of observation, her impeccable ear, and her precise and often haunting sense of tone.

Her first volume, *North and South,* was a rigorous selection from earlier work. Although some of its poems are set in New York or Paris or New England or have no localized geographical setting, a number of the best ones are firmly placed in Nova Scotia or Florida. *A Cold Spring* continued the emphasis on place: a farm in Maryland, Nova Scotia again, Washington, D.C., Key West and New York, and, with "Arrival at Santos," Brazil, which was to be her home for a number of years. The poems in *Questions of Travel* are divided into two groups: "Brazil" and "Elsewhere." (Another result of her residence of Brazil was her beautiful translation of *The Diary of Helena Morley.*) The 1969 *Complete Poems* included new poems set in Brazil as well as translations from Carlos Drummond de Andrade and Joao Cabral de Melo Neto. The 1983 *Complete Poems* contained more translations from the Portuguese, Spanish, and French, and previously uncollected poems.

The title and some of the directions of *Geography III* were anticipated in the final line of "The Map," the first poem in her first volume: "More delicate than the historian's are the map-maker's colors." The map-maker (not the tourist) who comes truly to know differing peoples and their places for himself can see with fresh and multiple perspectives, and his discriminations may well be finer than the historian's if his powers of observation are intense, his sympathies wide, his moral judgments delicate, and his imagination that of a poet.

Bishop's geography is also of the imagination and the soul. Her poems treat their readers with unusual consideration. With the beginning of each poem we know that we are somewhere interesting (whether in a real or a surreal or a dream world), and we hear immediately a recognizable human voice: the poems make absorbing sense on a simple or naturalistic level. She is interested in, and asks our respectful attention for, everything that she puts into her poems; ultimate and "large" significances come only (and naturally) out of our experience of the whole.

The consideration is real, and one of its chief instruments is an unusual purity of diction. On a number of occasions one may be surprised to discover an image or detail or even a quoted phrase from the poetry of George Herbert. She found Herbert's example thoroughly congruent with one of the things she admired most about modernist poetry of the early twentieth century: the rejection of familiar public rhetoric and the consciously poetic for a language closer to that of a conversation between literate friends. Bishop consistently sustained her own high version of that standard: no inversions and no inflations, no Ciceronian periods, no elevated "poetic diction." Her indebtedness to **Marianne Moore**'s imaginative precision was handsomely acknowledged in "Invitation to Miss Marianne Moore" (the poem also owes something to Pablo Neruda). Her uses of other writers are markedly individual: her few epigrams are from Bunyan, Hopkins, and Sir Kenneth Clark; the poignant "Crusoe in England" owes as much to Charles Darwin as to Defoe.

Also like Herbert, Bishop seemed to seek a unique form for almost every poem. Her range extended from prose poems such as "Rainy Season; Sub-Tropics" and "12 O'Clock News" through relatively "free" and blank verse and unrhymed Horatian forms to strict quatrains and elaborately "counter-pointed" stanzas, a double sonnet ("The Prodigal," one of her best poems), sestinas and a villanelle, including along the way the lengthening triplets of "Roosters," derived from Crashaw's "Wishes to His (supposed)

Mistress," "Visits to St. Elizabeths," modeled on "The House that Jack Built," a true ballad, "The Burglar of Babylon," and the songs that she wrote for Billie Holiday. Whatever the forms, they provide opportunities rather than limitations, and their art is self-effacing: the lines of "Sestina" end with the words *house, grandmother, child, stove, almanac,* and *tears.* Her use of assonance and slant-rhymes and variable line lengths and rhyme patterns promised a useful freedom. Her example suggested to **Robert Lowell** the "way of breaking through the shell of my old manner" indicated by his "Skunk Hour."

Although Bishop's poetry is collected in a single volume of moderate size, Lowell remarked some years before her death, "When Elizabeth Bishop's letters are published (as they will be), she will be recognized as not only one of the best, but also one of the most prolific writers of our century." Most of her letters and papers have been collected by the Vassar College Library. David Kalstone's essay. "Prodigal Years: Elizabeth Bishop and Robert Lowell, 1947-49" (*Grand Street,* Summer 1985). provides a tantalizing promise of the riches still to come.

As a poet Bishop remained remarkably independent of schools or movements, religious, political, or literary. One modern practice that proved fruitful for her was that of the collage, in which the artist discovers subject and form in ordinary or unexpected materials and objects. ("Objects and Apparitions," Bishop's translation of "Octavio Paz's poems for Joseph Cornell, suggests the relation between collage and all art—as do her poems on the pictures of her great-uncle George.) Although the fictional speakers of her poems are often moving or witty (the Trollope of the Journals, a Brazilian friend in "Manuelzinho," Crusoe, a giant snail, a very small alien who reports on the writer's desk as a foreign landscape-all remarkable observers), in most of the poems the poet speaks in a voice recognizably her own. That the poems remain deeply personal rather than confessional may owe something to how firmly they are rooted in the "found": "Trouvée" in the flattened white hen on West 4th Street, "The Man Moth" in a newspaper misprint for *mammoth,* "The Burglar of Babylon" in the fact that on the hills of Rio the rich and poor live their melodramas and lives within sight and sound of each other, "The Moose" in the Nova Scotia bus ride, and "In the Waiting Room" in the events of late afternoon, "the fifth of February, 1918." Almost every poem by Bishop represents a human discovery both of the world and of an angle of vision. It is only superficially paradoxical that such creative novelty returns us, like "The Prodigal," to a familiar place and life: "But it took him a long time finally to make his mind up to go home."

—Joseph H. Summers

See the essay on "The Fish."

BISHOP, John Peale

Born: Charles Town (now Charleston), West Virginia, 21 May 1892. **Education:** Charles Town Academy; Washington County High School, Hagerstown, Maryland; Mercersburg Academy, Pennsylvania; Princeton University, New Jersey, 1913-17 (managing editor, *Nassau Literary Magazine*), Litt.B. 1917 (Phi Beta Kappa). **Military Service:** Served in the U.S. Army Infantry, 1917-19: first lieutenant; director of the Publications Program, 1941-42, and

special consultant, 1943, Office of the Coordinator of Inter-American Affairs, Washington, D.C. **Family:** Married Margaret Grosvenor Hutchins in 1922; three sons. **Career:** Managing editor, *Vanity Fair,* New York, 1920-22; freelance writer from 1922; lived in Paris and Sorrento, 1922-24, New York, 1924-26, France, 1926-33, Connecticut and Louisiana, 1933-37, and South Chatham, Massachusetts, 1937-44. **Died:** 4 April 1944.

PUBLICATIONS

Collections

Collected Poems, edited by Allen Tate. 1948; as *Selected Poems,* 1960.
Collected Essays, edited by Edmund Wilson. 1948.

Poetry

Green Fruit. 1917.
The Undertaker's Garland (poems and stories), with Edmund Wilson. 1922.
Now with His Love. 1933.
Minute Particulars. 1935.
Selected Poems. 1941.

Fiction

Many Thousands Gone (stories). 1931.
Act of Darkness. 1935.

Other

The Republic of Letters in America: The Correspondence of Bishop and Allen Tate, edited by Thomas Daniel Young and John J. Hindle. 1981.

Editor, with Allen Tate, *American Harvest: Twenty Years of Creative Writing in the United States.* 1942.

*

Bibliography: "Bishop: A Checklist" by J. Max Patrick and R.W. Stallman, in *Princeton University Library Chronicle,* vol. 7, 1946.

Critical Studies: *A Southern Vanguard: The Bishop Memorial Volume* edited by Allen Tate, 1947; "The Achievement of Bishop" by Joseph Frank, in *The Widening Gyre,* 1963; *Bishop* by Robert L. White, 1966; "Bishop and the Other Thirties" by Leslie Fiedler, in *Commentary* vol. 43, 1967; "Bishop" by Allen Tate, in *Essays of Four Decades,* 1968; *Bishop: A Biography* by Elizabeth Carroll Spindler, 1980; *The Republic of Letters in America: The Correspondence of John Peale Bishop & Allen Tate* edited by Thomas Daniel Young and John J. Hindle, 1981.

*   *   *

John Peale Bishop seems to owe his posthumous reputation to **Allen Tate** and **Edmund Wilson,** whose editing of the *Collected Poems* and *Collected Essays* in 1948 brought his most important work to the attention of a small audience. These books have long been out of print, but he continues to attract critics as different as Joseph Frank and **Leslie Fiedler,** and no account of American literary life between the two world wars is complete without his name. He was at Princeton with Wilson and **F. Scott Fitzgerald** and consequently has associations with the milieu popularized by Fitzgerald's early novels; indeed, he is the original for a character in *This Side of Paradise.* During the 1930s, especially after his return to the United States, he was thought of as a Southerner, partly because of his friendship with Tate. His two works of prose fiction are set in the "lost" part of West Virginia where he spent his boyhood and certainly have something in common with the Southern tradition of **Faulkner, Caroline Gordon,** and others.

Bishop, however, must be thought of mainly as a poet, and it is the verse of his last decade that is most impressive. His regional allegiances count for very little here, though his residence on Cape Cod after 1938 was surely responsible for such late poems as "A Subject of Sea Change" and the group called "The Statues." These meditations on the sea and the destiny of civilizations carry forward the strongly pictorial qualities of such earlier poems as "The Return." Eventually one should see Bishop as an American poet who is descended from a great tradition of European humanism, and his criticism of the American scene is conducted from this point of view. One of his finest poems, "The Burning Wheel," sets the American pioneers beside the figure of Aeneas:

> They, too, the stalwart conquerors of space,
> Each on his shoulders wore a wise delirium
> Of memory and age: ghostly embrace
> Of fathers slanted toward a western tomb.
>
> A hundred and a hundred years they stayed
> Aloft, until they were as light as autumn
> Shells of locusts. Where then were they laid?
> And in what wilderness oblivion?

This refined yet deeply felt humanism is perhaps not characteristic of American writers, and Bishop was a writer on a small scale, but his best work in poetry and criticism survives very well.

—Ashley Brown

BLOOM, Harold

Born: New York, New York, 11 July 1930. **Education:** Cornell University, B.A. 1951; Yale University, Ph.D. 1955. **Family:** Married Jeanne Gould in 1958; two sons. **Career:** Instructor, 1955-60; assistant professor, 1960-63, associate professor, 1963-65, professor of English, 1965-74, DeVane Professor of Humanities, 1974-77, processor of humanities, beginning1977, and since 1983 Sterling Professor of Humanities Yale University, New Haven, Connecticut. Visiting professor, Hebrew University, Jerusalem, 1959; Breadloaf Summer School, 1965-66; visiting professor, New School for Social Research, 1982-84; Charles Eliot Horton Professor of Poetry, Harvard University, 1987-88. **Awards:** Fulbright fellowship, 1955; John Addison Porter prize, Yale University, for *Shelley's Mythmaking,* 1956; Guggenheim fellowship, 1962-63; Newton Arvin award, 1967; Melville Cane award, Poetry Society of America, for *Yeats,* 1971; National Book awards juror, 1973;

Zabel prize, American Institute of Arts and Letters, 1982; MacArthur prize fellowship, 1985. D.H.L. Boston College, 1973; Yesgiva University, 1975. **Member:** American Academy of Arts and Sciences.

PUBLICATIONS

Prose

Shelley's Mythmaking. 1959.
The Visionary Company: A Reading of English Romantic Poetry. 1961.
Blake's Apocalypse. 1963.
The Poetry and Prose of William Blake. 1965; as *The Complete Prose and Poetry of William Blake,* 1982.
Yeats. 1970.
Romanticism and Consciousness: Essays in Criticism. 1970.
The Ringers in the Tower: Studies in Romantic Tradition. 1971.
The Anxiety of Influence: A Theory of Poetry. 1973.
A Map of Misreading. 1975.
Kabbalah and Criticism. 1976.
Poetry and Repression: Revisionism from Blake to Stevens. 1976.
Figures of Capable Imagination. 1976.
Wallace Stevens: The Poems of Our Climate. 1977.
The Flight to Lucifer: A Gnostic Fantasy. 1979.
Deconstruction and Criticism. 1979.
Agon: Toward a Theory of Revisionism. 1982.
The Breaking of the Vessels. 1982.
The Strong Light of the Canonical: Kafka, Freud, and Scholem as Revisionists of Jewish Culture and Thought. 1987.
Poetics of Influence. 1989.
Ruin the Sacred Truths: Poetry and Belief from the Bible to the Present. 1989.
The American Religion: The Emergence of the Post-Christian Nation. 1992.
The Western Canon: The Books and School of the Ages. 1994.
Omens of Millennium: The Gnosis of Angels, Dreams, and Resurrection. 1996.
Shakespeare: The Invention of the Human. 1998.

Other

Editor, *English Romantic Comedy, An Anthology.* 1961.
Editor, with John Hollander, *The Wind and the Rain.* 1961.
Editor, with Frederick W. Hilles, *From Sensibility to Romanticism: Essays Presented to Frederick A. Pottle.* 1965.
Editor, *The Literary Criticism of John Ruskin.* 1965.
Editor, *Selected Poetry,* by Percy Bysshe Shelley. 1966.
Editor, *Marius the Epicurean: His Sensations and Ideas,* by Walter Horatio Pater. 1970.
Editor, *Selected Poetry,* by Samuel Taylor Coleridge. 1972.
Editor, *The Romantic Tradition in American Literature* (33 Vols.). 1972.
Editor, with Lionel Trilling, *Romantic Prose and Poetry.* 1973.
Editor, with Lionel Trilling, *Victorian Prose and Poetry.* 1973.
Editor, with Frank Kermode, John Hollander, and others, *Oxford Anthology of English Literature* (2 Vols.). 1973.
Editor, *Selected Writings of Walter Pater.* 1974.
Editor, with Adrienne Munich, *Robert Browning: A Collection of Critical Essays.* 1979.

Editor, *Hamlet.* 1990.
Editor, *Caddy Compson.* 1990.
Editor, *Cleopatra.* 1990.
Editor, *French Poetry: The Renaissance through 1915.* 1990.
Editor, *Edwardian and Georgian Fiction, 1880 to 1914.* 1990.
Editor, *French Prose and Criticism, 1790 to World War II.* 1990.
Editor, *Holden Caulfield.* 1990.
Editor, *Huck Finn.* 1990.
Editor, *Clarissa Dalloway.* 1990.
Editor, *Modern Latin American Fiction.* 1990.
Editor, *Bigger Thomas.* 1990.
Editor, *Toni Morrison.* 1990.
Editor, *Sophocles.* 1990.
Editor, *Shylock.* 1991.
Editor, *Odysseus/Ulysses.* 1991.
Editor, *Ahab.* 1991.
Editor, *Antonia.* 1991.
Editor, *Brett Ashley.* 1991.
Editor, *Macbeth.* 1991.
Editor, *Willy Loman.* 1991.
Editor, *Gatsby.* 1991.
Editor, *Joan of Arc.* 1992.
Editor, *Falstaff.* 1992.
Editor, *David Copperfield.* 1992.
Editor, *Iago.* 1992.
Editor, *Caliban.* 1992.
Editor, *Marlow.* 1992.
Editor, *Isabel Archer.* 1992.
Editor, *King Lear.* 1992.
Editor, *Rosalind.* 1992.
Editor, *Heathcliff.* 1993.
Editor, *Lolita.* 1993.
Editor, *Classic Science Fiction Writers.* 1994.
Editor, *Classic Science Fiction Writers of the Golden Age.* 1994.
Editor, *Modern Fantasy Writers.* 1994.
Editor, *Modern Mystery Writers.* 1994.
Editor, *Classic Fantasy Writers.* 1994.
Editor, *Julius Caesar.* 1994.
Editor, *Black American Prose Writers of the Harlem Renaissance.* 1994.
Editor, *Black American Prose Writers: Before the Harlem Renaissance.* 1994.
Editor, *Black American Poets and Dramatists: Before the Harlem Renaissance.* 1994.
Editor, *Contemporary Horror Writers.* 1994.
Editor, *Major Modern Black American Writers.* 1994.
Editor, *Contemporary Black American Fiction Writers.* 1994.
Editor, *Classic Horror Writers.* 1994.
Editor, *Modern Horror Writers.* 1994.
Editor, *Modern Black American Poets and Dramatists.* 1994.
Editor, *Emma Bovary.* 1994.
Editor, *Contemporary Black American Poets and Dramatists.* 1994.
Editor, *Major Black American Writers through the Harlem Renaissance.* 1994.
Editor, *Black American Women Fiction Writers.* 1994.
Editor, *Modern Black American Fiction Writers.* 1995.
Editor, *Classic Mystery Writers.* 1995.
Editor, *Classic Crime and Suspense Writers.* 1995.
Editor, *Robinson Crusoe.* 1995.
Editor, *Modern Crime and Suspense Writers.* 1995.
Editor, *Beowulf.* 1996.

Editor, *Dante's Divine Comedy: The Inferno.* 1996.
Editor, *Wuthering Heights.* 1996.
Editor, *Great Expectations.* 1996.
Editor, *To Kill a Mockingbird.* 1996.
Editor, *Death of a Salesman.* 1996.
Editor, *The Adventures of Huckleberry Finn.* 1996.
Editor, *The Great Gatsby.* 1996.
Editor, *Heart of Darkness and The Secret Sharer.* 1996.
Editor, *Nineteen Eighty-Four.* 1996.
Editor, *The Odyssey.* 1996.
Editor, *Paradise Lost.* 1996.
Editor, *Sophocles' Oedipus Plays.* 1996.
Editor, *The Grapes of Wrath.* 1996.
Editor, *A Tale of Two Cities.* 1996.
Editor, *The Autobiography of Malcolm X.* 1996.
Editor, *The Scarlet Letter.* 1996.
Editor, *Uncle Tom's Cabin.* 1996.
Editor, *Othello.* 1996.
Editor, *Animal Farm.* 1996.
Editor, *A Midsummer Night's Dream.* 1996.
Editor, *Silas Marner.* 1996.
Editor, *Romeo and Juliet.* 1996.
Editor, *Jane Eyre.* 1996.
Editor, *Herman Melville's Billy Budd, Benito Cereno, and Bartleby the Scrivener.* 1996.
Editor, *I Know Why the Caged Bird Sings.* 1996.
Editor, *Black American women Poets and Dramatists.* 1996.
Editor, *Crime and Punishment.* 1996.
Editor, *Iliad.* 1996.
Editor, *The Sun Also Rises.* 1996.
Editor, *Invisible Man.* 1996.
Editor, *The Old Man and the Sea.* 1996.
Editor, *Native Son.* 1996.
Editor, *Tess of the D'Urbervilles.* 1996.
Editor, *Brave New World.* 1996.
Editor, *Frankenstein.* 1996.
Editor, *Pride and Prejudice.* 1996.
Editor, *Gulliver's Travels.* 1996.
Editor, *Aeneid.* 1996.
Editor, *Moby-Dick.* 1996.
Editor, *The Crucible.* 1996.
Editor, *The Red Badge of Courage.* 1996.
Editor, *Henry IV, Part 1.* 1996.
Editor, *A Farewell to Arms.* 1996.
Editor, *Lord of the Flies.* 1996.
Editor, *Of Mice and Men.* 1996.
Editor, *The Catcher in the Rye.* 1996.
Editor, *Caribbean Women Writers.* 1997.
Editor, *American Women Fiction Writers.* 1997.
Editor, *Asian American Women Writers.* 1997.
Editor, *British Women Fiction Writers, 1900-1960.* 1997.
Editor, *Lesbian and Bisexual Fiction Writers.* 1997.

*

Critical Studies: "Harold Bloom, The Western Canon: The Books and School of the Ages" by R.W. French, in *Walt Whitman Quarterly Review,* fall 1994.; "Harold Bloom: Joining the Fray" in *The Chronicle of Higher Education,* 1994.

*   *   *

Harold Bloom's extraordinary outpouring of literary criticism, even while rambunctious, stands second to none, and its impact has been incommensurable. His principal area of expertise is English literature—he has taught in the English Department at Yale University for decades, ever since he was hired in 1955 after earning his Ph.D. there. As a student he was notorious because, while drunk, he was able to recite **Hart Crane**'s "The Bridge" "frontwards, then backwards, quite like a tape recorder running wild." His favorite poets are William Blake, William Wordsworth, Samuel Taylor Coleridge, Lord Byron, Percy Bysshe Shelley, John Keats, and, of course, William Shakespeare, on whom he meditated profusely in his magisterial if chaotic study released in 1998 and subtitled *The Invention of the Human.* It is said that Bloom knows all of the Bard's plays by heart. He also claims that his only religion is "Bardolary," which he defines as "a secular worship of Shakespeare." In the American literary constellation, Bloom is akin to **Ralph Waldo Emerson** and **Wallace Stevens**.

He once explained the secret of his productivity—more than two dozen books and about 500 edited volumes for the Chelsea House Modern Critic Views series—quite simply: it is due to sleeplessness, he claimed, "and many, many enemies." (Aside from scores of feminists, this group also includes writer **John Updike** and poet **Howard Nemerov**, who have spoken, respectively, against Bloom's "torturous theories" and his "charlatanry"). The thesis for which he is popularly known was disseminated in *The Anxiety of Influence* (1973), a volume in which Bloom argues that poets do not compete against their contemporaries but against their precursors and that, deep at heart, every major poet shapes his oeuvre by misreading a chosen past master. Bloom's concepts of "anxiety" and "influence," strongly Freudian in tone, have entered the lexicon of global literary criticism. His education in an Orthodox Jewish family, where Yiddish was the language of home, prepared him for the rigors of intellectual analysis. The upbringing explains some of his adult interests: Franz Kafka, Sigmund Freud, and the doctrines of Cabala (a Jewish mystical tradition), to which he found access through the luminous work of the scholar Gershom Scholem, author of *Major Trends in Jewish Mysticism.* Bloom has reflected abundantly on Jewish topics, and his own personal quest seems to palpitate with biblical and rabbinic echoes. Perhaps his most notorious Jewish oeuvre is his introduction to David Rosenberg's translations of selected sections of the Pentateuch, released under the title *The Book of J* (1990). In it he discusses various textual interpretations of the Bible. He argues that its author might have been female and that she probably lived at the time of the kingdoms of David and Solomon. This scholarly path ultimately led him to Gnosticism—Bloom describes himself as "a Jewish Gnostic"—a lore indirectly influenced by Spinoza's philosophy and analyzed, along with other manifestation of religion in America, in the book *Omens of the Millennium (1995).*

Bloom's passion for poetry dates back to his teens, "when I became cathected," and, he says in his book *Agon,* "I have spent forty years trying to understand that initial cathexis." Since the publication of his doctoral dissertation, *Shelley's Mythmaking* (1959), he has explored the romantic literary procession, a prominent early field of study in his career, in one book after another. In *The Ringers in the Tower* (1971), he explores this tradition from its beginnings in the eighteenth century to its manifestations in late twentieth-century poets such as **A. R. Ammons** and **Allen Ginsberg**. Bloom's mind works centrifugally, expanding from the particular to the universal. From individual poets, he has moved to larger universal issues. This process reached its climax in 1994

with *The Western Canon,* wherein he discussed the various "schools of resentment" in the American academy, all of which, in unison, undermine the endurance of a literary "library of Platonic classics" that ideally should pertain and reach everyone everywhere. Bloom proceeded to prepare a list of classics and support each of his entries with a vigorous argument. The fact that the volume generated considerable controversy is no surprise, for it was published at a time when, with the ascent of multiculturalism, the humanities were undergoing a dramatic restructuring.

Bloom's stardom—he has gone from having his books released under the aegis of university presses like Oxford and Yale to mainstream New York houses like Riverhead, and a few of his titles have become best-sellers— coincided with the decline of the so-called New York intellectuals (a group including, among others, Irving Howe, Alfred Kazin, and Clement Greenberg). It symbolizes the transformation of academic critics from marginal entities, isolated in ivory towers, to major cultural figures. He is often compared—or better, contrasted—with another Jewish critic, albeit a French one, Jacques Derrida, who was born four days before him in 1930 and whose deconstructionism has exercised a noxious influence in American universities. While Derrida is much more obscure, the two share a disregard for social issues that makes them elitists, *i.e.,* not public intellectuals per se but snobbish scholars—this in spite of the fact that Bloom, at least, comes from a proletarian background. Bloom, a formidable teacher loved by his many pupils, once claimed:

> People cannot stand the saddest truth I know about the very nature of reading and writing imaginative literature, which is that poetry does not teach us how to talk to other people: it teaches us how to talk to ourselves. What I'm desperately trying to do is to get students to talk to themselves, and not someone else.

Indeed, one might say he lives his life in rhythmic, never-ending conversation with himself. In physical appearance he resembles Dr. Samuel Johnson, the British essayist and detective writer G. K. Chesterton, and his favorite Shakespearean character, Falstaff. Unfortunately, his lucid mind is not well served by his labyrinthine, ruminative prose. His sentences are convoluted, filled with abstract terminology. And yet, once the reader learns to travel through them, the rewards are at hand: sharpness, courage, and innovation. This is more than ought to be said about most critics.

—Ilan Stavans

BLY, Robert (Elwood)

Born: Madison, Minnesota, 23 December 1926. **Education:** St. Olaf College, Northfield, Minnesota, 1946-47; Harvard University, Cambridge, Massachusetts, A.B. (magna cum laude) 1950; University of Iowa, Iowa City, M.A. in creative writing, 1956. **Military Service:** Served in the U.S. Naval Reserve, 1944-46. **Family:** Married 1) Carolyn McLean in 1955 (divorced 1979), four children; 2) Ruth Counsell Ray in 1980. **Career:** Founding editor, beginning 1958, *The Fifties* magazine (later *The Sixties* and *The Seventies*), and the Fifties Press (later The Sixties and The Seventies Press), Madison, Minnesota. **Awards:** Fulbright fellowship, 1956; Amy Lowell traveling fellowship, 1964; Guggenheim fellowship, 1964, 1972; American Academy grant, 1965; Rockefeller fellowship, 1967; National Book award, 1968. **Residence:** Moose Lake and Minneapolis, Minnesota.

PUBLICATIONS

Poetry

The Lion's Tail and Eyes: Poems Written Out of Laziness and Silence, with James Wright and William Duffy. 1962.
Silence in the Snowy Fields. 1962.
The Light around the Body. 1967.
Chrysanthemums. 1967.
Ducks. 1968.
The Morning Glory: Another Thing That Will Never Be My Friend: Twelve Prose Poems. 1969; revised edition, 1970; complete version, 1975.
The Teeth Mother Naked at Last. 1970.
Poems for Tennessee, with William Stafford and William Matthews. 1971.
Water under the Earth. 1972.
Christmas Eve Service at Midnight at St. Michael's. 1972.
Jumping Out of Bed. 1973.
Sleepers Joining Hands (includes prose). 1973.
The Dead Seal near McClure's Beach. 1973.
The Hockey Poem. 1974.
Point Reyes Poems. 1974.
Grass from Two Years, Let's Leave. 1975.
Old Man Rubbing His Eyes. 1975.
The Loon. 1977.
This Body Is Made of Camphor and Gopherwood: Prose Poems. 1977.
This Tree Will Be Here for a Thousand Years. 1979; revised edition 1992.
Visiting Emily Dickinson's Grave and Other Poems. 1979.
The Man in the Black Coat Turns (includes prose). 1981.
Finding an Old Ant Mansion. 1981.
Four Ramages. 1983.
Out of the Rolling Ocean and Other Love Poems. 1984.
Loving a Woman in Two Worlds. 1985.
Selected Poems. 1986.
The Moon on a Fencepost. 1988.
A Little Book on the Human Shadow. 1988.
The Apple Found in the Plowing. 1989.
Angels of Pompeii. 1991.
What Have I Ever Lost by Dying?: Collected Prose Poems. 1992.
Gratitude to Old Teachers. 1993.
Meditations on the Insatiable Soul. 1994.
Morning Poems. 1997.
Holes the Crickets Have Eaten in Blankets. 1997.
Eating the Honey of Words: New and Selected Poems. 1999.

Other

A Broadsheet Against the New York Times Book Review. 1961.
Talking All Morning: Collected Conversations and Interviews. 1979.
The Eight Stages of Translation (includes poetry translations). 1983.
The Sibling Society. 1986.

The Pillow and the Key: Commentary on the Fairy Tale Iron John. 1987.
A Little Book on the Human Shadow, with William Booth. 1988.
American Poetry: Wildness and Domesticity (essays). 1990.
Iron John: A Book about Men. 1990.
Remembering James Wright. 1991.
The Maiden King: The Reunion of Masculine and Feminine, with Marion Woodman. 1999.

Editor, with David Ray, *A Poetry Reading Against the Vietnam War.* 1966.
Editor, *The Sea and the Honeycomb: A Book of Poems.* 1966.
Editor, *Forty Poems Touching on Recent American History.* 1970.
Editor, *Leaping Poetry: An Idea with Poems and Translations.* 1975.
Editor, *Selected Poems,* by David Ignatow. 1975.
Editor, *News of the Universe: Poems of Twofold Consciousness.* 1980.
Editor, *Ten Love Poems.* 1981.
Editor, *The Economy Spinning Faster and Faster,* by Goran Sonnevi. 1982.
Editor, *The Winged Life: The Poetic Voice of Henry David Thoreau.* 1986.
Editor, *The Rag and Bone Shop of the Heart: Poems for Men,* with others. 1992.
Editor, *The Darkness around Us Is Deep: Selected Poems of William Stafford.* 1993.
Editor, *The Soul Is Here for Its Own Joy: Sacred Poems from Many Cultures.* 1995.
Editor, *The Best American Poetry 1999.* 1999.

Translator, *The Illustrated Book about Reptiles and Amphibians of the World,* by Hans Hvass. 1960.
Translator, with James Wright, *Twenty Poems of Georg Trakl.* 1961.
Translator, *The Story of Gösta Berling,* by Selma Lagerlöf. 1962.
Translator, with James Wright and John Knoepfle, *Twenty Poems of César Vallejo.* 1962.
Translator, with Eric Sellin and Thomas Buckman, *Three Poems,* by Tomas Tranströmer. 1966.
Translator, *Hunger,* by Knut Hamsun. 1967.
Translator, with Christina Paulston, *I Do Best Alone at Night,* by Gunnar Ekelöf. 1967.
Translator, with Christina Paulston, *Late Arrival on Earth: Selected Poems of Gunnar Ekelöf.* 1967.
Translator, with others, *Selected Poems,* by Yvan Goll. 1968.
Translator, with James Wright, *Twenty Poems of Pablo Neruda.* 1968.
Translator, *Forty Poems of Juan Ramón Jiménez.* 1969.
Translator, *Ten Poems,* by Issa Kobayashi. 1969.
Translator, with James Wright and John Knoepfle, *Neruda and Vallejo: Selected Poems.* 1971; with a new preface, 1993.
Translator, *Twenty Poems of Tomas Tranströmer.* 1971.
Translator, *The Fish in the Sea Is Not Thirsty: Versions of Kabir.* 1971.
Translator, *Night Vision,* by Tomas Tranströmer. 1971.
Translator, *Ten Sonnets to Orpheus,* by Rainer Maria Rilke. 1972.
Translator, *Lorca and Jiménez: Selected Poems.* 1973.
Translator, *Elegy, Some October Notes,* by Tomas Tranströmer. 1973.

Translator, *Basho.* 1974.

Translator, *Friends, You Drank Some Darkness: Three Swedish Poets, Henry Martinson, Gunnar Ekelöf, Tomas Tranströmer.* 1975.

Translator, *Grass from Two Years,* by Kabir. 1975.

Translator, *Twenty-Eight Poems,* by Kabir. 1975.

Translator, *Try to Live to See This! Versions of Kabir.* 1976.

Translator, *The Kabir Book.* 1977.

Translator, *The Voices,* by Rainer Maria Rilke. 1977.

Translator, with Lewis Hyde, *Twenty Poems of Vicente Aleixandre.* 1977.

Translator, *Twenty Poems of Rolf Jacobson.* 1977.

Translator, *I Never Wanted Fame,* by Antonio Machado. 1979.

Translator, *Truth Barriers,* by Tomas Transtömer. 1980.

Translator, *Mirabai Versions.* 1980.

Translator, *I Am Too Alone in the World,* by Rainer Maria Rilke. 1980.

Translator, *Canciones,* by Antonio Machado. 1980.

Translator, *Truth Barriers,* by Tomas Transtömer. 1980.

Translator, *Selected Poems of Rainer Maria Rilke.* 1981.

Translator, with Coleman Barks, *Night and Sleep,* by Jelaluddin Rumi. 1981.

Translator, with Will Kirkland, *Selected Poems and Prose,* by Antonio Machado. 1983.

Translator, *Times Alone: Selected Poems of Antonio Machado.* 1983.

Translator, with others, *A Longing for the Light,* by Vicente Aleixandre. 1985.

Translator, *When Grapes Turn to Wine,* by Jelaluddin Rumi. 1986.

Translator, with others, *Tomas Transtömer: Selected Poems, 1954-1986.* 1987.

Translator, with others, *Light and Shadows,* by Juan Ramón Jiménez. 1987.

Translator, *Trusting Your Life to Water and Eternity: Twenty Poems of Olav H. Hauge.* 1987.

Translator, *Ten Poems of Francis Ponge* (with poems by Bly). 1990.

Translator, *The Lightening Should Have Fallen on Ghalib: Selected Poems of Ghalib,* with Sunil Dutta. 1999.

*

Bibliography: "Bly Checklist" by Sandy Dorbin, in *Schist 1,* fall 1973; *Robert Bly: A Primary and Secondary Bibliography* by William H. Roberson, 1986.

Critical Studies: *Alone with America* by Richard Howard, 1969, revised edition, 1980; *Four Poets and the Emotive Imagination* by Ronald Moran and George Lensing, 1976; *Moving Inward: A Study of Bly's Poetry* by Ingegerd Friberg, 1977; *Of Solitude and Silence: Writings on Bly* edited by Kate Daniels and Richard Jones, 1982; *Bly: An Introduction to the Poetry* by Howard Nelson, 1984; *Bly: When Sleepers Awake* edited by Joyce Peseroff, 1984; *Understanding Robert Bly* by William Davis, 1988; *The Incorporative Consciousness of Robert Bly* by Victoria Frenkel Harris, 1992; *Walking Swiftly: Writings on the Occasion of Robert Bly's 65th Birthday* edited by Thomas R. Smith, 1992; *Critical Essays on Robert Bly* edited by William V. Davis, 1992; *Robert Bly: The Poet and His Critics* edited by William V. Davis, 1994.

*   *   *

The spirited presence of Robert Bly is felt throughout the realms of modern poetry and literary criticism; he emerged from the early 1960s as one of the more stubbornly independent and critical poets of his generation, bold to state his positions against war and commercial monopoly, the spread of federal government, and crassness in literature wherever a forum was open to him. He was a dominating spokesman for the anti-war circles during the course of the Vietnam war, staging readings around the United States and compiling (with David Ray) the extraordinary poetic protests in the anthology *A Poetry Reading Against the Vietnam War.* Throughout his career, he has been a cranky but refreshing influence on American thought and culture for the very grandeur of his positions and the force he has given to his artistic individuality.

Although his output of poetry has been relatively small in an era of prolific poets, his books follow a distinctive course of deepening conviction and widening of conceptions. *Silence in the Snowy Fields,* his first book, is a slender collection of smooth, mildly surreal evocations of his life in Minnesota and of the landscape, with its harsh winters and huddled townships. Bly's brief poems animate natural settings with a secret, wilful life-force, as in this final stanza from "Snowfall in the Afternoon":

> The barn is full of corn, and moving toward us now,
> Like a hulk blown toward us in a storm at sea:
> All the sailors on deck have been blind for many years.

Silence in the Snowy Fields has an immediacy of the poet's personal life that reflects the inward shift of poetry during the late 1950s and early 1960s, a direction that Bly then actively retreated from, claiming poetry deserved a larger frame of experience than the poet's own circumstances and private dilemmas.

The Light around the Body moves into the political and social arena, with poems against corporate power and profiteering, presidential politics, and the Vietnam war. Here the poems are charged with greater flight of imagination and a more intensely surreal mode of discourse. The poems wildly juxtapose the familiar with the bizarre, in "A Dream of Suffocation"—"Accountants hover over the earth like helicopters, / Dropping bits of paper engraved with Hegel's name"—and "War and Silence"—

> Filaments of death grow out.
> The sheriff cuts off his black legs
> And nails them to a tree

To explain his poetic and to give it context, Bly edited a volume of poems entitled *Leaping Poetry* in which he argued that consciousness had now expanded to a new faculty of the brain where spiritual and supralogical awareness is stored. His commentary is wonderfully speculative and vivid, but bluffly assertive of its premise. Building on this provocative thesis, he commented in an essay, "I Came Out of the Mother Naked," part of his volume *Sleepers Joining Hands,* that society is now returning to a matriarchal order, where sensuousness of thought and synthetic reason are replacing the patriarchal emphasis on rationality and analytic thinking. *The Kabir Book,* Bly's translations of the fifteenth-century Indian poet, is an effort to present the work of a figure who both "leaps" in his poetry and illustrates the kind of thinking Bly has argued for recently.

In the preface to *This Tree Will Be Here for a Thousand Years,* Bly talks of "a consciousness out there among plants and animals," which is the "ground tone" of his new poems. Indeed, this duality is the theme of not only this book, but succeeding ones as well, especially his provocative and somber collection *Loving a Woman in Two Worlds* in which a figure moves freely between his own subjectivity and the brooding mind that surrounds him. The two worlds are like the realms of Martin Buber's I and Thou, an internal reality of the ego, and the lost sense of collective spirit belonging to the ancient world. Bly's poems are efforts to regain that lost sense of a vital universe in which selfhood is only an atom, though a necessary and participatory one. Bly's usual inventiveness is present throughout these poems, but his prose sketches in *The Man in the Black Coat Turns* are notable for their clarity, simplicity, and powerful evocation of this sense of doubleness.

Following the publication of *Iron John: A Book About Men,* Bly achieved national celebrity as the spiritual leader of a resurgent mythopoetic men's movement. In *Iron John,* Bly combined Jungian psychology, fairy tales, ancient religious myths, and his own problems in his relationship with his father to suggest that American men look to mythic archetypes to recapture their lost sense of worth. At the center of the book is the story of "Iron John," a wooly man who lives at the bottom of a lake and helps a young boy release his attachment to his mother and become a man. Bly's work was widely criticized by feminists, who accused Bly of encouraging masculine chest-thumping, but his message reached millions of men who participated in consciousness-raising seminars complete with tribal drum beating and spears. In 1992 Bly edited a book of poems dealing with men's experiences, titled *The Rag and Bone Shop of the Heart.*

—Paul Christensen, updated by Tom Pendergast

BODENHEIM, Maxwell

Born: Maxwell Bodenheimer in Hermanville, Mississippi, 26 May 1892. **Education:** Hyde Park High School, Chicago. **Military Service:** Served in the U.S. Army, c. 1908-11: jailed for desertion and discharged. **Family:** Married 1) Minna Schlein in 1918 (divorced 1938), one son; 2) Grace Finan in 1939 (died 1950); 3) Ruth Fagan in 1951(?). **Career:** Traveled in southwest U.S., 1911-12; lived in Chicago, 1912-15; settled in New York, 1916; writer for Chicago *Literary Times,* 1923-24; lived in Paris, 1929; worked for Federal Writers Project (Works Progress Administration), 1939-40 (fired for presumed association with Communist Party). **Died:** (murdered) 7 February 1954.

PUBLICATIONS

Fiction

Blackguard. 1923.
Crazy Man. 1924.
Cutie, A Warm Mamma, with Ben Hecht. 1924.
Replenishing Jessica. 1925.
Ninth Avenue. 1926.
Georgie May. 1928.
Sixty Seconds. 1929.
A Virtuous Girl. 1930.
Naked on Roller Skates. 1931.

Duke Herring. 1931.
6 A. M. 1932.
Run, Sheep, Run. 1932.
New York Madness. 1933.
Slow Vision. 1934.

Plays

Knot Holes (produced 1917).
The Gentle Furniture Shop (produced 1917). In *Drama 10,* 1920.

Poetry

Minna and Myself (includes play *The Master Poisoner* by Bodenheim and Ben Hecht). 1918.
Advice. 1920.
Introducing Irony: A Book of Poetic Short Stories and Poems. 1922.
Against This Age. 1923.
The Sardonic Arm. 1923.
Returning to Emotion. 1927.
The King of Spain. 1928.
Bringing Jazz! 1930.
Lights in the Valley. 1942.
Selected Poems 1914-1944. 1946.

Other

My Life and Loves in Greenwich Village (attributed to Bodenheim; ghostwritten by Sam Roth). 1954.

*

Critical Studies: *Bodenheim* by Jack B. Moore, 1970; "Maxwell Bodenheim's Harlem Slang" by Louis Phillips, in *Verbatim: The Language Quarterly,* autumn, 1988; "Maxwell Bodenheim: Catastrophe and Corrective" by Ben Yagoda, in *Boulevard,* spring 1995, pp. 199-209.

*   *   *

Maxwell Bodenheim's slow but steady and determined pursuit of self-destruction, as well as the frequently giddy capers he cut while parading (at first) and then lurching around New York's literary scene, have almost completely obscured his solid if inconsistent achievements as a writer. Easily forgotten, because buried under an avalanche of anecdotes, novels, and plays by other writers about his escapades during the Jazz Age and Depression years, is the undoubted evidence that he was sometimes a very powerful, often an innovative, and nearly always a fascinating poet-novelist of the world that ultimately passed him by.

Bodenheim's social and literary criticism are perhaps the least well known of his writings. **Ezra Pound** wanted to have published Bodenheim's "whole blooming book" on aesthetics although (or perhaps because) Pound claimed only he and a few other writers would understand it. In fact, only a few chapters of the book were ever printed, and these were published separately as essays. As a reviewer for many of the leading journals of the 1920s, he championed the work of such contemporaries as **Conrad Aiken, Wallace Stevens**, and **William Carlos Williams**; lambasted what he considered the sham pastoralism in modern fiction where "young men lie upon their backs in cornfields and feel oppressed by their bodies"; and tilted with the very popular and he felt often fake Freudianism of his times for trumpeting that "sex underlies all human motives and is the basis of all creations." He also sought out new writers. When he was one of the editors of the avant-garde little magazine *Others* he went out of his way to praise and secure publication for the very young **Hart Crane**.

From 1923 to 1934 he published some dozen novels, which, together with the poetry he wrote around the same period, refute the idea that he crippled himself as a writer simply through dissipating his resources in sordid adventures. He was by no means a major novelist, for his works lack artistic control. Too often he used the form as a way to settle personal scores, or, worse, did not attend strictly enough to technical details of his craft. He sometimes seemed more intent upon setting down striking phrases than on constructing a coherent and compelling story. But most of the novels display solid and significant attainments: the touching comic (and autobiographic) portrait of the young artist in *Blackguard;* the sad, sordid decline of the prostitute Georgie May; the urban nightmare of *Ninth Avenue;* and the parade of numbed derelicts that sleepwalk through *Slow Vision,* his Depression novel.

Bodenheim's artistic reputation rests most solidly upon his poetry, and his ultimate failure to become a first-rate poet is probably the saddest element of his professional career. Bodenheim was early considered one of the most promising writers taking part in the American literary renaissance of the second decade of the twentieth century: Harriet Monroe and Margaret Anderson, editors of the two most influential literary magazines of the day, both strove to be the first to announce the arrival of his genius. Conrad Aiken and William Carlos Williams were only two of the many writers who, though sometimes appalled by his antics, highly praised his poetry. Among his chief virtues as a poet were his ability to compose beautiful and exotic images and to weave them harmoniously into the texture of a unified poem, such as "Death." He could also write harshly and effectively about the ugliness of modern city life, as in "Summer Evening: New York Subway Station." His jazz poems, such as those in *Bringing Jazz!,* were interesting experiments in a form one critic said had been successfully employed only by one other poet—**T.S. Eliot.**

Bodenheim's artistic death, which long preceded his physical death, was lamentable, for he never came close to attaining the greatness his early promise and ability seemed to predict. Yet he accomplished far more than his relatively obscure reputation in the late twentieth century would suggest.

—Jack B. Moore

BOGAN, Louise

Born: Livermore Falls, Maine, 11 August 1897. **Education:** Mount St. Mary's Academy, Manchester, New Hampshire, 1907-09; Girls' Latin School, Boston, 1910-15; Boston University, 1915-16. **Family:** Married 1) Curt Alexander, 1916 (died 1920), one daughter; 2) Raymond Holden in 1925 (divorced 1935). **Career:** Freelance writer in New York, 1919-25; poetry editor, *New Yorker,* 1931-69. Fellow, 1944, and consultant in poetry, 1945, Library of Congress, Washington, D.C.; visiting professor, University of Washington, Seattle, 1948, University of Chicago, 1949, University of Arkansas, Fayetteville, 1952, Salzburg Seminar in

American Studies, 1958, and Brandeis University, Waltham, Massachusetts, 1964-65. **Awards:** Guggenheim grant, 1933, 1937; Harriet Monroe Poetry award, 1948; American Academy grant, 1951; Bollingen prize, 1955; Academy of American Poets fellowship, 1959; Brandeis University Creative Arts award, 1961; National Endowment for the Arts grant, 1967. L.H.D.: Western College for Women, Oxford, Ohio, 1956. Litt.D: Colby College, Waterville, Maine, 1960. **Member:** American Academy, 1951; Academy of American Poets, 1954. **Died:** 4 February 1970.

PUBLICATIONS

Collections

What the Woman Lived: Selected Letters 1920-1970, edited by Ruth Limmer. 1973.

Poetry

Body of This Death. 1923.
Dark Summer. 1929.
The Sleeping Fury. 1937.
Poems and New Poems. 1941.
Collected Poems 1923-1953. 1954.
The Blue Estuaries: Poems 1923-1968. 1968.

Other

Works in the Humanities Published in Great Britain 1939-1946: A Selected List. 1950.
Achievement in American Poetry 1920-1950. 1951.
Selected Criticism: Prose, Poetry. 1955.
Emily Dickinson: Three Views, with Archibald MacLeish and Richard Wilbur. 1960.
A Poet's Alphabet: Reflections on the Literary Art and Vocation, edited by Robert Phelps and Ruth Limmer. 1970.
Journey Around My Room: The Autobiography of Bogan: A Mosaic, edited by Ruth Limmer. 1980.

Editor and translator, with Elizabeth Roget, *Journal,* by Jules Renard. 1964.
Editor, with William Jay Smith, *The Golden Journey: Poems for Young People.* 1965.

Translator, with Elizabeth Mayer. *The Glass Bees,* by Ernst Juenger. 1961.
Translator, with Elizabeth Mayer, *Elective Affinities,* by Goethe. 1963.
Translator, with Elizabeth Mayer and (verse only) W.H. Auden, *The Sorrows of Young Werther* and *Novella,* by Goethe. 1971.

*

Bibliography: by Jane Couchman, in *Bulletin of Bibliography* vol. 33, 1976.

Critical Studies: *Bogan: A Woman's Words* by William Jay Smith, 1972; *Bogan: A Portrait* by Elizabeth Frank, 1985; *The Veiled Mirror and the Woman Poet: H. D., Louise Bogan, Elizabeth Bishop, and Louise Gluck* by Elizabeth Dodd, 1992; "Poets and Friends: The Correspondence of May Sarton and Louise Bogan" by Elizabeth Evans in *That Great Sanity: Critical Essays on May Sarton* edited by Susan Swartzlander, Marilyn R. Mumford, and Maureen Teresa McCarthy, 1992; "The Re-Making of a Poet: Louise Bogan" by Lee Upton in *The Centennial Review* fall, 1992; *Obsession and Release: Rereading the Poetry of Louise Bogan* by Lee Upton, 1996; *Our Thirty Year Friendship: Letters from Louise Bogan, Comments by Mildred Weston and Legacy: Poems from the Twenties to the Nineties* by Mildred Weston, 1997.

*   *   *

Louise Bogan's collected poems, *The Blue Estuaries,* make up a slender volume that brings together work published from 1923 to 1968. She rarely wrote poems longer than a page, and all her earlier published books are brief and cut to the bone. She was a relentless reviser of her work and a slow, cautious craftsman who refused publishers' urgings to increase her output.

Although she was keenly aware of the revolutions in poetic technique throughout her life, her poems adhered to rhyme and set meter and treated the themes of love, regret, death, memory, and landscape meditation in subtly alliterative language. Her style shows the influence of **Emily Dickinson** and perhaps the wit of Metaphysical poetry, but the essential charm of her best work is the quiet, feminine perception she expresses in her strict, tightly framed forms, as in "Second Song," an early poem:

I said out of sleeping:
Passion, farewell.
Take from my keeping
Bauble and shell.

Black salt, black provender.
Tender your store
To a new pensioner,
To me no more.

Although she relaxes into a certain lyric frankness of feeling in her later work, her style of spare restraint remains consistent throughout her work. In several of her poems a more strident feminine consciousness flares, as in "Women," with its sardonic portrayal of woman caught in her stereotype of the put-upon mate:

Their love is an eager meaninglessness
Too tense, or too lax.

They hear in every whisper that speaks to them
A shout and a cry.
As like as not, when they take life over their door-sills
They should let it go by.

Bogan regarded the poem as a deliberate and highly worked distillation of thought, and was perhaps too strict with her own imagination. The fire and wit of her mind are muted in most of her poetry but luxuriously displayed in her brilliant correspondence, collected in *What the Woman Lived,* where her sarcasm and acute critical nature are shared with a circle of notable literary figures of her time, including **Edmund Wilson**, Morton Dauwen Zabel, Rolfe Humphries, and **Theodore Roethke.**

Like her poetry, her critical writing eschewed partisanship and fashion in favor of a classical standard of moderation, balance, and form. As the poetry critic for the *New Yorker,* she was well known for her honest and abrasive judgments of the work of even her close friends, and her essays of these years, published in *A Poet's Alphabet,* endure in their accuracy and acumen. A brief treatise on modern poetry, *Achievement in American Poetry 1900-1950,* though merely a sketch of the main trends of these years, argues a provocative thesis that female poets of the late nineteenth century were chiefly responsible for revitalizing poetry with their sensuous, daring imaginations.

—Paul Christensen

BOKER, George Henry

Born: Philadelphia, Pennsylvania, 6 October 1823. **Education:** The College of New Jersey, now Princeton University (one of the founders of the *Nassau Monthly,* 1842), graduated 1842; also studied law. **Family:** Married Julia Mandeville Riggs in 1844; one son. **Career:** Writer from 1845; playwright from 1848; founding member, 1862, secretary, 1862-71, and president, 1879, Union Club, later Union League, Philadelphia; U.S. Ambassador to Turkey, 1871-75, and to Russia, 1875-78; president, Philadelphia Club, 1878; president, Fairmount Park Commission, Philadelphia, 1886-90. **Died:** 2 January 1890.

PUBLICATIONS

Collection

Glaucus and Other Plays (includes *The World a Mask, The Bankrupt*), edited by Sculley Bradley. 1940.

Plays

Calaynos (produced 1849). 1848.
Anne Boleyn (produced 1850). 1850.
The Betrothal (produced 1850). In *Plays and Poems,* 1856.
The World a Mask (produced 1851). 1856; in *Glaucus and Other Plays,* 1940.
The Widow's Marriage (produced 1852). In *Plays and Poems,* 1856.
Leonor de Guzman (produced 1853). In *Plays and Poems,* 1856.
Francesca da Rimini (produced 1855). In *Plays and Poems,* 1856.
The Bankrupt (produced 1855). In *Glaucus and Other Plays,* 1940.
Nydia, edited by Sculley Bradley. 1929; revised version, as *Glaucus,* in *Glaucus and Other Plays,* 1940.

Poetry

The Lesson of Life and Other Poems. 1848.
The Podesta's Daughter and Other Miscellaneous Poems. 1852.
Poems of the War. 1864.
Our Heroic Themes. 1865.
Konigsmark: The Legend of the Hounds and Other Poems. 1869.
The Book of the Dead: Poems. 1882.
Sonnets: A Sequence of Profane Love, edited by Sculley Bradley. 1929.

Other

Plays and Poems. 2 vols., 1856.

*

Bibliography: in *Bibliography of American Literature* by Jacob Blanck, 1955.

Critical Studies: *Boker, Poet and Patriot* by Sculley Bradley, 1927; *George Henry Boker* by Oliver H. Evans, 1984; *The Theatrical Life of George Henry Boker* by Thomas M. Kitts, 1994.

*   *   *

In keeping with his aspiration to live the life of the poet, George Henry Boker's first publication, *The Lesson of Life,* was a book of verse. The scion of a wealthy and aristocratic family who was classically educated at what would become Princeton University, Boker followed this first book with poems on public affairs, with patriotic verse, and with sonnets—a form with which he enjoyed particular felicity—on love and statesmanship. He subsequently collected many of these pieces into *Plays and Poems,* whose two volumes have been reprinted many times and are the most accessible source of Boker's verse. Despite his love for poetry, however, Boker is remembered primarily as a dramatist, having written nearly a dozen plays between his first, *Calaynos,* a tragedy in blank verse, and his last, *Nydia,* which he rewrote as *Glaucus* in 1886.

Surely the most famous of Boker's plays is *Francesca da Rimini,* completed in 1853 and first produced in New York two years later. Based on the tragic love story of thirteenth-century Italy that Dante celebrated in *The Inferno* and that had been reworked by so many other authors, Boker's *Francesca* consists of more than 3,500 lines of neo-Elizabethan verse, so befitting its author's poetic urges as well as the day's theatrical tastes. In these lines Boker chronicled once again the unhappy triangle of Francesca, a noblewoman of Ravenna, Paolo, a nobleman of Rimini to whom she had given her heart, and Lanciotto, Paolo's equally noble but sadly deformed brother to whom she had given her hand in marriage. A stirring success, *Francesca* ran on the New York and Philadelphia stage in 1855, and was reproduced for longer runs in 1882-83 and again in 1901-02.

As the corpus of his work reveals, Boker was a playwright whose sense of the literary matched his sense of the theatrical. Understandably, then, he is among the best remembered of American nineteenth-century dramatists.

—Brace A. Lohof

BOWLES, Paul (Frederick)

Born: New York City, 30 December 1910. **Education:** The School of Design and Liberal Arts, New York City, 1928; University of Virginia, Charlottesville, 1928-29; studied music with Aaron Copland in New York and Berlin, 1930-32, and with Virgil Thomson in Paris, 1933-34. **Family:** Married Jane Sydney Auer (i.e., the writer Jane Bowles) in 1938 (died 1973). **Career:** Music critic, New York *Herald-Tribune,* 1942-46; also composer; since 1947 has lived in Tangier, Morocco. **Awards:** Guggenheim fellowship, 1941; American Academy award, 1950; Rockefeller grant, 1959; Translation Center grant, 1975; National Endowment for the Arts grant, 1977. **Died:** 1986.

PUBLICATIONS

Collections

Collected Stories of Paul Bowles. 1992.
The Portable Paul and Jane Bowles. 1994.

Fiction

The Sheltering Sky. 1949.
The Delicate Prey and Other Stories. 1950.
A Little Stone: Stories. 1950.
Let It Come Down. 1952.
The Spider's House. 1955.
The Hours after Noon. 1959.
A Hundred Camels in the Courtyard (stories). 1962.
Up above the World. 1966.
The Time of Friendship (stories). 1967.
Pages from Cold Point and Other Stories. 1968.
Three Tales. 1975.
Things Gone and Things Still Here (stories). 1977.
Collected Stories 1939-1976. 1979.
Midnight Mass (stories). 1981.
Unwelcome Words: Seven Stories. 1987.
A Distant Episode: The Selected Stories. 1989.
A Thousand Days for Mokhtar, and Other Stories. 1989.

Plays

Senso, with Tennessee Williams, in *Two Screenplays,* by Luigi Visconti. 1970.

Screenplay: *Senso* (*The Wanton Countess,* English dialogue, with Tennessee Williams), 1949.

Poetry

Scenes. 1968.
The Thicket of Spring: Poems 1926-1969. 1972.
Next to Nothing. 1976.
Next to Nothing: Collected Poems 1926-1977. 1981.

Other

Yallah (travel). 1956.
Their Heads Are Green (travel). 1963; as *Their Heads Are Green and Their Hands Are Blue,* 1984.
Without Stopping: An Autobiography. 1972.
In the Red Room. 1981.
Points in Time (on Morocco). 1982.
Aperture. 1984.
Days, Tangier Journal: 1987-89. 1991.
Too Far From Home: The Selected Writings of Paul Bowles. 1993.
In Touch: The Letters of Paul Bowles, edited by Jeffrey Miller. 1993.

Morocco (travel). 1993.
Conversations with Paul Bowles, edited by Gena Dagel Caponi. 1993.
In Touch: The Letters of Paul Bowles. 1994.
Paul Bowles Photographs: "How Could I Send a Picture into the Desert?" 1994.

Translator, *No Exit,* by Jean-Paul Sartre. 1946.
Translator, *Lost Trail of the Sahara,* by Roger Firson-Roche. 1956.
Translator, *A Life Full of Holes,* by Driss ben Hamed Charhadi. 1964.
Translator, *Love with a Few Hairs,* by Mohammed Mrabet. 1967.
Translator, *The Lemon,* by Mohammed Mrabet. 1969.
Translator, *Mhashish,* by Mohammed Mrabet. 1969.
Translator, *The Boy Who Set the Fire and Other Stories,* by Mohammed Mrabet. 1974.
Translator, *For Bread Alone,* by Mohamed Choukri. 1974.
Translator, *Jean Genet in Tangier,* by Mohamed Choukri. 1974.
Translator, *The Oblivion Seekers,* by Isabelle Eberhardt. 1975.
Translator, *Hadidan Aharam,* by Mohammed Mrabet. 1975.
Translator, *Harmless Poisons, Blameless Sins,* by Mohammed Mrabet. 1976.
Translator, *Look and Move On,* by Mohammed Mrabet. 1976.
Translator, *The Big Mirror,* by Mohammed Mrabet. 1977.
Translator, *Five Eyes: Short Stories by Five Moroccans.* 1979.
Translator, *Tennessee Williams in Tangier,* by Mohamed Choukri. 1979.
Translator, *The Beach Café, and The Voice,* by Mohammed Mrabet. 1980.
Translator, *The Chest.* by Mohammed Mrabet. 1983.
Translator, *She Woke Me Up So I Killed Her.* 1985.
Translator, *The Beggar's Knife,* by Rodrigo Rey Rosa. 1985.
Translator, *Marriage with Papers,* by Mohammed Mrabet. 1986.
Translator, *Dust on Her Tongue,* by Rodrigo Rey Rosa. 1992.
Translator, *Chocolate Creams & Dollars,* by Mohammed Mrabet. 1993.

Published Music: *Tornado Blues* (chorus); *Music for a Farce* (chamber music); *Piano Sonatina; Huapango 1* and *2; Six Preludes for Piano; El Indio; El Bejuco; Sayula; La Cuelga; Sonata for Two Pianos; Night Waltz* (two pianos); *Songs: Heavenly Grass; Sugar in the Cane; Cabin; Lonesome Man; Letter to Freddy; The Years; Of All the Things I Love; A Little Closer, Please; David; In the Woods; Song of an Old Woman; Night without Sleep; Two Skies; Que te falta?; Ya Llego; Once a Lady Was Here; Bluebell Mountain; Three; On a Quiet Conscience; El Carbonero; Baby, Baby; Selected Songs,* Santa Fe, Soundings Press, 1984.

Operas: *Denmark Vesey,* 1937; *The Wind Remains,* 1941.

Ballets: *Yankee Clipper,* 1937; *Pastorella,* 1941; *Sentimental Colloquy,* 1944.

Incidental Music, for plays: *Horse Eats Hat,* 1936; *Dr Faustus,* 1937; *My Heart's in the Highlands,* 1939; *Love's Old Sweet Song,* 1940; *Twelfth Night,* 1940; *Liberty Jones,* 1941; *Watch on the Rhine,* 1941; *South Pacific,* 1943; *Jacobowsky and the Colonel,* 1944; *The Glass Menagerie,* 1945; *Twilight Bar,* 1946; *On Whitman Avenue,* 1946; *The Dancer,* 1946; *Cyrano de Bergerac,* 1946; *Land's End,* 1946; *Summer and Smoke,* 1948; *In the Summer House,* 1953; *Edwin Booth,* 1958; *Sweet Bird of Youth,* 1959; *The Milk Train Doesn't Stop Here Anymore,* 1963; for films: *Roots in the Soil,* 1940; *Congo,* 1944.

Recordings: *The Wind Remains; Cafe Sin Nombre; Sonata for Two Pianos; Night Waltz; Scenes d'Anabase; Music for a Farce; Song for My Sister; They Cannot Stop Death; Night without Sleep; Sailor's Song; Rain Rots the Wood; Sonata for Flute and Piano; Six Preludes; Huapango 1* and *2; A Picnic Cantata,* lyrics by James Schuyler, 1955; *El Bejuco and El Indio; Blue Mountain Ballads; Concerto for Two Pianos, Winds and Percussion; Once a Lady Was Here; Song of an Old Person; Six Latin American Pieces,* 1984; *Five Songs,* 1984.

*

Bibliography: *Bowles: A Descriptive Bibliography* by Jeffrey Miller, 1986.

Critical Studies: *Bowles: The Illumination of North Africa* by Lawrence D. Stewart, 1974; *Bowles: Staticity and Terror* by Eric Mottram, 1976; *The Fiction of Bowles: The Soul Is the Weariest Part of the Body* by Hans Bertens, 1979; "Bowles Issue" of *Review of Contemporary Fiction,* vol. 2, no. 3, 1982; *Bowles: The Inner Geography* by Wayne Pounds, 1985; "Paul Bowles Issue" of *Twentieth Century Literature: A Scholarly and Critical Journal,* fall-winter, 1986; *A World Outside: The Fiction of Paul Bowles* by Richard F. Patterson, 1987; *Paul Bowles: Romantic Savage* by Gena Dagel Caponi, 1994; *Paul Bowles* by Gena Dagel Caponi, 1998; *You Are Not I: A Portrait of Paul Bowles* by Millicent Dillon, 1998.

*   *   *

A prolific writer of music, Paul Bowles did not commit himself seriously to writing fiction until after World War II, when he was in his mid-thirties and living in New York after many years spent in North Africa. He has described the period as "the Atomic Age" in *The Sheltering Sky,* and his characters are appropriate to a period of fear and desolation—most are empty, deracinated, and hopeless, the hollow men of **T.S. Eliot,** as Chester E. Eisinger has described them in *Fiction of the Forties* (1963).

His first novel, *The Sheltering Sky,* may be taken as typical of most of his fiction. In it, three young Americans, a married couple and a male friend, have left fashionable New York for adventure in North Africa. There, they move steadily into the Sahara, leaving their morality, sense of purpose, and identities further behind them as they move from town to town. They become separated: Porter Moresby dies of typhoid after a horrifying vision of blood and excrement: his wife, Kit, a neurotic socialite, eventually loses her sanity after living with Arabs. Only their companion, Tunner, survives, left with the task of escorting the remnant of the woman he loves back to civilization. Some critics would agree with the reaction of Doubleday, the publishers who commissioned but then rejected the novel on the grounds that it lacked coherence and purpose. It is a charge that could be brought against several of his stories, which seem full of gratuitous violence and emptiness, as well as his second novel, *Let It Come Down,* which follows the steady degeneration of a single American, Dyar, in North Africa—he too moves steadily away from civilization and morality and toward murder and violence, ending with nothing but confirmation of his basic nature.

But what such a critical response ignores is the virility and vigor of the native life that is so central to Bowles's writing; his apathetic Europeans and Americans make a telling contrast to his vision of authenticity. Every native in his fiction is as much an individual as each European and American is not. His third novel, *The Spider's House,* is probably more successful than the first two because it gives considerable weight to such a native—Amar, the Moroccan youth who shares the story with a couple of Americans. Details and rituals of native life come into the foreground and the novel is given a liveliness and color that are rather lacking in the others. His fourth novel, *Up above the World,* although set in Central America, again charts disintegration into violence and death. More satisfying are Bowles's later translations of stories told by pre-literate Moroccan storytellers, in which the patterns of native life are once more dominant.

Though many of Bowles's works of fiction revolve around the theme of encounters between Western and Third World cultures, the vantage point from which the stories are told has gradually changed during the course of his career. That is, the perspective from which the stories are told has gradually moved from that of the Westerner to that of the Third World (often Moroccan) characters. In his earlier works of fiction, such as *The Sheltering Sky* and *Let It Come Down,* we encounter the narrative through the eyes and voices of the Westerners. In his later works we no longer view the Third World inhabitants through the eyes of the Westerners but, more and more, we view the Westerners through the eyes of the Third World characters. This pattern is discernable not only in Bowles's fiction but also in his non-fiction, such as his 1982 book *Points in Time*—a stylized history of Morocco including the legends of its past—and in the material he has translated, all of which assumes the Moroccan perspective as a vantage point. Beginning in the late 1940s and continuing over several decades, Bowles has translated a significant amount of Moroccan tales into English. This process completely eliminates the Western element of the story and causes the reader, as Bowles himself apparently has to some degree, to assume the perspective of the cultural other.

—Patrick Evans, updated by Craig Bryson

BOX, Edgar. *See* VIDAL, (Eugene Luther) Gore.

BOYD, James

Born: Harrisburg, Pennsylvania, 2 July 1888. **Education:** Hill School, Pottstown, Pennsylvania, 1901-06; Princeton University, New Jersey 1906-10, B.A. 1910; Trinity College, Cambridge, 1910-12. **Military Service:** Served in the New York Infantry, 1916, as a Red Cross volunteer, 1917, and in the U.S. Army Ambulance Service, in Italy and France, 1917-19: lieutenant. **Family:** Married Katharine Lamont in 1917; two sons and one daughter. **Career:** Staff writer and cartoonist, Harrisburg *Patriot,* 1910; teacher of English and French, Harrisburg Academy, 1912-14; member of the editorial staff, *Country Life in America,* New York, 1916; settled on a farm in Southern Pines, North Carolina, 1919: owner and editor, Southern Pines *Pilot,* 1941-44. Founder and first national chairman, Free Company of Players, 1941. **Award:** Honorary degree: University of North Carolina, Chapel Hill, 1938. **Member:** American Academy, 1937; Society of American Historians, 1939. **Died:** 25 February 1944.

PUBLICATIONS

Fiction

Drums. 1925.
Marching On. 1927.
Long Hunt. 1930.
Roll River. 1935.
Bitter Creek. 1939.
Old Pines and Other Stories. 1952.

Plays

One More Free Man (broadcast 1941). In *The Free Company Presents,* 1941.

Poetry

Eighteen Poems. 1944.

Other

Mr. Hugh David MacWhirr Looks after His $1.00 Investment in the Pilot Newspaper (sketches). 1943.

Editor, *The Free Company Presents: A Collection of Plays about the Meaning of America.* 1941.

*

Critical Studies: *James Boyd* by David E. Whisnant, 1972; *Books and Saddle: James Boyd, Author and Horseman,* 1994.

*   *   *

In the 1920s James Boyd was in the forefront of those who set about revitalizing and reconditioning the American historical novel, which had lapsed into romantic cliches and suspect authenticity. His deliberate apprenticeship in professional writing consisted of a series of experimental short stories testing his ability to master such techniques as dialogue, mood, and setting. Though his research for sketching in the Revolutionary milieu of *Drums* was facilitated by the availability of archival depositories then being developed and enlarged, he went a step further by uncovering period documents on his own and by visiting the scenes about which he would write. His authoritative historicity was never questioned. But Boyd's principal contribution to the historical novel was an emphasis on a "psychological realism" in addition to the romantic conventions and accuracy of detail. For example, in *Drums,* Boyd's most highly acclaimed work, the ambivalent loyalties of the backwoodsman Johnny Fraser during the dislocations of the American Revolution, as well as his slow development from an acceptance of British rule in the Colonies to his realization that change is inevitable, are never subsidiary to events, which instead are used to support the demands of characterization and motivation. From the hinterlands of North Carolina to the famed battle between the *Serapis* and John Paul Jones's *Bonhomme Richard,* the incidents of history are mere background to the novelist's multidimensional portrait of his hero.

In *Marching On* it is from the point of view of the Confederate infantryman James Fraser, descendant of Johnny Fraser, that the

Civil War is seen as "a rich man's war but a poor man's fight." In addition to such climactic chapters as that narrating James's participation in the Battle of Antietam, the novel provides social commentary in depicting and contrasting the lower segments of southern life, Fraser's middle class, and the landed aristocrats. Often criticized is Boyd's yielding to romantic practice in allowing his hero at war's end to marry the planter's daughter. *Long Hunt,* though it required as much research in gathering historical minutiae as did Boyd's first two books, is more properly defined as a frontier novel of the 1790s, when settlers moved from North Carolina across the mountains into Indian territory and on to the Mississippi River. *Roll River* represented a change in pace. In it Boyd wrote from personal observation of the shifting values among four generations of a proud, wealthy family in the city of Midian (the author's native Harrisburg, Pennsylvania). *Bitter Creek* is a cowboy western to which Boyd, as in the other books, applied his gift for psychological analysis.

His biographer wrote that Boyd saw man as "first of all a creature of history whose problems had to be understood in historical depth." His books, especially the two war novels that profited from his battlefield experience in World War I, were so highly regarded as exemplary of the "new" American historical novels that their other virtues have been for the most part overlooked by readers and critics alike.

—Richard Walser

BOYESEN, H(jalmar) H(jorth)

Born: Frederikvaern, Norway, 21 September 1848; immigrated to the United States in 1869. **Education:** The Latin School, Drammen; Christiania Gymnasium; Royal Fredriks University, postgraduate degree, 1868; University of Leipzig, 1873. **Family:** Married Elizabeth Keen in 1874. **Career:** Tutor in Latin and Greek, Urbana University, Ohio, 1869-70, 1871; editor, Norwegian weekly *Fremad* (Forward), Chicago, 1870; professor of German, Cornell University, Ithaca, New York, 1874-80; member of the German department, 1880-82, Gebhard Professor of German, 1882-90, and professor of Germanic languages and literatures, 1890-95, Columbia University, New York. **Died:** 2 October 1895.

PUBLICATIONS

Fiction

Gunnar: A Tale of Norse Life. 1874.
A Norseman's Pilgrimage. 1875.
Tales from Two Hemispheres. 1876.
Falconberg. 1879.
Ilka on the Hill-Top and Other Stories. 1881.
Queen Titania (stories). 1881.
A Daughter of the Philistines. 1883.
The Light of Her Countenance. 1889.
Vagabond Tales. 1889.
The Mammon of Unrighteousness. 1891.
The Golden Calf. 1892.
Social Strugglers. 1893.

Play

Alpine Roses, from his own story *Ilka on the Hill-Top* (produced 1884). 1884.

Poetry

Idylls of Norway and Other Poems. 1882.

Other

Goethe and Schiller: Their Lives and Works. 1879.
The Story of Norway. 1886.
The Modern Vikings: Stories of Life and Sport in the Norseland (for children). 1887.
Against Heavy Odds: A Tale of Norse Heroism (for children). 1890.
Essays on German Literature. 1892.
Boyhood in Norway: Stories of Boy-Life in the Land of the Midnight Sun (for children). 1892; as *The Battle of the Rafts and Other Stories,* 1893.
Norseland Tales (for children). 1894.
A Commentary on the Writings of Henrik Ibsen. 1894.
Literary and Social Silhouettes. 1894.
Essays on Scandinavian Literature. 1895.

*

Bibliography: in *Bibliography of American Literature* by Jacob Blanck, 1955.

Critical Studies: *Boyesen* by Clarence A. Glasrud, 1963; *Boyesen* by Robert S. Frederickson, 1980; *From Norwegian Romantic to American Realist: Studies in the Life and Writings of Hjalmar Hjorth Boyesen* by Per Seyersted, 1984.

*   *   *

H.H. Boyesen published his first novel, *Gunnar,* in 1874, five years after he came to the United States and mastered English. This romantic Norwegian idyll was influenced by Bjornstierne Bjornson's early fiction; Boyesen's success with this first effort was due in large part to his friendship with **William Dean Howells,** who helped polish the manuscript and serialized the story in the *Atlantic Monthly.* But though he was unquestionably a romantic by nature and early influence, Boyesen became a realist by conviction; with Howells he read and admired Turgenev and Tolstoy. Boyesen met Turgenev in Paris in 1873 with an introduction from a German critic; and Boyesen's second novel, *A Norseman's Pilgrimage,* was dedicated to Turgenev. Howells declined this romantically autobiographical story, warning the author that he was too hungry for publication; ten years elapsed before Turgenev approved one of the realistic stories Boyesen sent him ("A Dangerous Virtue").

Boyesen became one of America's best-known teachers and lecturers. His *Goethe and Schiller,* essentially an English reworking of German scholarship and criticism, went into ten editions. His three collections of essays on German and Scandinavian literature published in the 1890s are magazine pieces, usually reprinted without revision. Boyesen was a literary journalist and popularizer, not a scholar and critic. But he was an important European American liaison man who argued persuasively that Americans were so subservient to British literature that they ignored Goethe and Ibsen.

Boyesen's hundreds of articles, essays, and short stories reveal him as a magazinist who depended on the income from such writing, but they also reflect his changing experience and convictions. His articles and stories on Norwegian-Americans, including the novel *Falconberg,* are not convincing because he had little contact with his fellow immigrants. Boyesen lived in New York for fifteen years, on Fifth Avenue and at Southampton; and he was both fascinated and repelled by the social world of the newly rich.

He became sharply critical of American political and financial corruption, arguing that the American novelist was duty-bound to document and criticize American problems, and he tried to do this in such novels as *The Golden Calf* and *Social Strugglers.* For such efforts he was berated as an ungrateful foreigner and blamed for abandoning the idyllic vein of *Gunnar.* But Boyesen was consistent in his views, whether they were expressed in novels, essays, or speeches: when he died suddenly and unexpectedly in 1895, he was arguing vehemently for more realistic and responsible American fiction, citing the "high water mark" of realism established by the new Scandinavian writers.

In his long battle with the "purveyors of romance," Boyesen identified the American woman as the enemy of serious writing. She was "the Iron Madonna" who strangled the American novelist in her fond embrace because magazine editors and book publishers knew she was the reader and arbiter they must satisfy. The beautiful, vivacious, and independent women Boyesen found in the United States had fascinated him from his first arrival. He married one of them, and his subsequent efforts to augment a professor's salary by ceaseless writing and lecturing dissipated his talents and shortened his life. It seems significant that such women frustrate their Norwegian-born admirers in his earliest fiction, dominate their parents in later stories (*A Daughter of the Philistines*), and victimize their husbands, notably in his most ambitious work, *The Mammon of Unrighteousness.*

—Clarence A. Glasrud

BOYLE, Kay

Born: St. Paul, Minnesota, 19 February 1902. **Education:** The Cincinnati Conservatory of Music; Ohio Mechanics Institute, 1917-19. **Family:** Married 1) Richard Brault in 1922 (divorced); 2) Laurence Vail in 1931 (divorced), five daughters and one son; 3) Baron Joseph von Franckenstein in 1943 (died 1963). **Career:** Lived in Europe for 30 years. Foreign correspondent, *New Yorker,* 1946-53; lecturer, New School for Social Research, New York, 1962; fellow, Wesleyan University, Middletown, Connecticut, 1963; professor of English, San Francisco State University, 1963-80; professor emeritus, 1980-92; director, New York Writers Conference, Wagner College, New York, 1964; fellow, Radcliffe Institute for Independent Study, Cambridge, Massachusetts, 1964-65; writer-in-residence, University of Massachusetts, Amherst, 1967, Hollins College, Virginia, 1970-71, and Eastern Washington University, Cheney, 1982. **Awards:** Guggenheim fellowship, 1934, 1961; O. Henry award, 1935, 1941; San Francisco Art Commission award, 1978; National Endowment for the Arts grant, 1980; Before Columbus Foundation award, 1983; Celtic Foundation award, 1984; Los Angeles *Times* Kirsch award, 1986; Lannan Foundation award, 1989. D.Litt: Columbia College, Chicago, 1971; Southern Illinois University, Carbondale, 1982; D.H.L.: Skidmore College, Saratoga Springs, New York, 1977; L.H.D.: Bowling Green State University, Ohio, 1986; Ohio State University, Columbus, 1986. **Member:** American Academy, 1979. **Died:** 27 December 1992.

PUBLICATIONS

Short Stories

Short Stories. 1929.
Wedding Day and Other Stories. 1930.
The First Lover and Other Stories. 1933.
The White Horses of Vienna and Other Stories. 1936.
The Crazy Hunter: Three Short Novels. 1940; as *The Crazy Hunter and Other Stories,* 1940.
Thirty Stories. 1946.
The Smoking Mountain: Stories of Postwar Germany. 1951.
Three Short Novels. 1958.
Nothing Ever Breaks Except the Heart. 1966.
Fifty Stories. 1980.
Life Being the Best and Other Stories, edited by Sandra Whipple Spanier. 1988.

Novels

Plagued by the Nightingale. 1931.
Year before Last. 1932.
Gentlemen, I Address You Privately. 1933.
My Next Bride. 1934.
Death of a Man. 1936.
Monday Night. 1938.
Primer for Combat. 1942.
Avalanche. 1944.
A Frenchman Must Die. 1946.
1939. 1948.
His Human Majesty. 1949.
The Seagull on the Step. 1955.
Generation without Farewell. 1960.
The Underground Woman. 1975.

Poetry

A Statement. 1932.
A Glad Day. 1938.
American Citizen: Naturalized in Leadville, Colorado. 1944.
Collected Poems. 1962; augmented edition, 1991.
Testament for My Students and Other Poems. 1970.
This Is Not a Letter and Other Poems. 1985.

Other

The Youngest Camel (for children). 1939; revised edition, 1959.
Breaking the Silence: Why a Mother Tells Her Son about the Nazi Era. 1962.
Pinky, The Cat Who Liked to Sleep (for children). 1966.
Pinky in Persia (for children). 1968.
Being Geniuses Together 1920-1930, with Robert McAlmon. 1968.
The Long Walk at San Francisco State and Other Essays. 1970.
Four Visions of America, with others. 1977.

Words That Must Somehow Be Said: Selected Essays 1927-1984,
edited by Elizabeth S. Bell. 1985.

Ghostwriter, *Relations and Complications, Being the Recollections
of H. H. the Dayang Muda of Sarawak* by Gladys Palmer
Brooke, 1929.
Ghostwriter, *Yellow Dusk* by Bettina Bedwell, 1937.

Editor, with Laurence Vail and Nina Conarain, *365 Days.* 1936.
Editor, *The Autobiography of Emanuel Carnevali.* 1967.
Editor, with Justine Van Gundy, *Enough of Dying! An Anthology
of Peace Writings.* 1972.

Translator, *Don Juan,* by Joseph Delteil. 1931.
Translator, *Mr. Knife, Miss Fork,* by Rene Crevel. 1931.
Translator, *The Devil in the Flesh,* by Raymond Radiguet. 1932.
Translator, *Babylon,* by Rene Crevel. 1985.

*

Critical Studies: *Boyle, Artist and Activist* by Sandra Whipple
Spanier, 1986; *Boyle: A Study of the Short Fiction* by Elizabeth S.
Bell, 1992; *Kay Boyle: Author of Herself* by Joan Mellen, 1994; *Critical
Essays on Kay Boyle* edited by Marilyn Roberson Elkins, 1997.

*   *   *

Most memorable in Kay Boyle's fiction are specific scenes—
the sight of the sea tide building and crashing through the mouth
of a river; a young man, sick with tuberculosis, leaning over a ba-
sin to vomit blood; a bus-driver arguing recklessly with his passengers while the bus careens along a cliff road; a run-over dog
pulling itself forward, as its spilled-out entrails drag and turn white
in the dust; and Americans and Germans waiting over real fox holes
in a German forest, ready to club the young foxes as they come
out, and underground, moving through the tunnels, now near, now
distant, the sound of the yelping pack and pursuing dog.

Boyle's concern here is to heighten our responses to these
events. She asks us not only to respond to the vivid and extreme
sensations that they present, but to see them in sharp moral and
aesthetic terms, as beautiful or dangerous or agonizingly brutal.
She offers very little neutral ground on which we may look at
these scenes on our own. The youthful idealists, who play a major role in her novels, give us the right emotional cues for appreciating her work. Inexperienced in the ways of the world, their feelings are open and unmitigated; they do not quite believe in evil
and yet they are deeply troubled by pain and injustice. Bridget,
Victoria John, Mary Farrant, Milly Roberts—young Americans
whose destinies are connected with Europe—are such figures. If
the fictional situation would seem to echo **Henry James**, there
are major differences in its development, for Boyle's morality is
active rather than introspective.

Indeed, whether her heroes are young Americans in Europe or
former German soldiers, they express themselves in concrete acts.
What her heroes have in common is the courage to act—it is the
only thing people ever remember, one character says. But action
is, of course, no guarantee of success. Involved in every human
venture, it would seem, are elements that bring about its destruction. Those elements may be in nature—not malevolent but merely
indifferent—stupid accident, or man's incapacity to make a social
world that is supportive and helpful.

Thus, in *Plagued by the Nightingale,* the closely bound world
of a French family becomes so destructive that three daughters
and a son wait desperately for an escape. Only Charlotte, the
fourth daughter, loves her richly domestic life and her place within
the family; and only Charlotte is deprived of it by death. In *Year
before Last,* Martin, a young poet, dying of tuberculosis, and Eve,
his aunt, are bound together by their dedication to art. Yet the
emotion that shapes their lives is Eve's cruel jealousy of Hanah,
whom Martin loves and who would shield him from the agonies
of poverty and illness. In *My Next Bride,* the artist, Sorrel, uses
the common funds of the art colony to buy a magnificent and
expensive automobile. In this shallow attempt to escape poverty
and ugliness, he betrays the destitute craftsmen who work for him,
as well as the artistic creed by which he has professed to live.

The qualities of Boyle's strongest characters—courage to act
as a counter to failure, energy rather than hopeless despair—admit the possibility of tragedy. Very often these qualities seem
wasted, for although Boyle insists upon courageous action, the
possible choices she sees in such action are limited. Also, perhaps equally harmful, these choices do not necessarily grow out
of the fictional situation; they are fixed from the beginning. It is
for this reason, perhaps, that her characters adopt unreal positions—in *Avalanche,* the mountain men are total in their dedication to a good cause, the German agent, total in his dedication to a
bad one; in *The Seagull on the Step,* the doctor commits melodramatic villainies, the teacher-reformer, heroic deeds; in *Generation
without Farewell,* the American colonel is brutal and gross, his
wife and daughter are gentle and sensitive. Such extreme divisions
in realistic novels fail to convince.

But what gives her work strength is her understanding that our
human connections lie finally in our limitations, most of all in our
common mortality. This understanding is sometimes expressed
with startling clarity. In *Plagued by the Nightingale* Charlotte's
family is hastily called to her bedside. Those who have waited
through the day—Charlotte's young children, her sisters—make
their way through the dark, wet autumn night, to Charlotte's house,
up the great stairs and to her room. There they wait in silence
until the door is opened, and the children walk "calmly into the
roar of Charlotte's death." In *Generation without Farewell* a power
shovel in downtown Frankfurt accidentally unearths an underground air raid shelter and releases a single survivor, entombed
there since the war. As the mad, tattered figure runs wildly across
the upturned ground, bewildered by his resurrection, any ideals
we may hold about nationality, military success, and moral justification diminish into nothingness. Only a sense of our common
inhumanity persists.

—Jacqueline Hoefer

BRACKENRIDGE, Hugh Henry

Born: Kintyre, near Campbeltown, Argyll, Scotland, in 1748; immigrated with his family to a farm in York County, Pennsylvania,
1753. **Education:** Slate Ridge School and Fagg's Manor; College
of New Jersey (now Princeton University), 1768-71, B.A. 1771,
M.A. 1774; studied law under Samuel Chase in Annapolis, Maryland, 1780: admitted to Philadelphia bar 1780. **Military Service:**
Served in George Washington's army during the Revolutionary
War, 1777-78: chaplain. **Family:** Married 1) Miss Montgomery

in 1785 (died 1788), one son; 2) Sabina Wolfe in 1790, two sons and one daughter. **Career:** Teacher in a public school, Gunpowder Falls, Maryland, 1763-67, and at Somerset Academy, Back Creek, Maryland, 1772-76; founding editor, *United States Magazine,* Philadelphia, 1779; founder, *Tree of Liberty* newspaper, 1780; moved to Pittsburgh, and practiced law there, 1781-99: founder, Pittsburgh *Gazette,* 1786; Pennsylvania state assemblyman, 1786-88; established Pittsburgh Academy, 1786, and the first bookshop in Pittsburgh, 1789; Justice of the Pennsylvania Supreme Court, 1799-1816. **Died:** 25 June 1816.

PUBLICATIONS

Collections

A Brackenridge Reader, edited by Daniel Marder. 1970.

Fiction

Modern Chivalry. 6 vols., 1792-1805; revised edition, 1815, 1819; edited by Claude Milton Newlin, 1937.
Father Bombo's Pilgrimage to Mecca 1770, with Philip Freneau, edited by Michael Davitt Bell. 1975.

Plays

The Battle of Bunkers-Hill. 1776.
The Death of General Montgomery at the Siege of Quebec. 1777.

Poetry

A Poem on the Rising Glory of America, with Philip Freneau. 1772.
A Poem on Divine Revelation. 1774.
An Epistle to Walter Scott. 1811(?).

Other

Six Political Discourses Founded on the Scriptures. 1778.
An Eulogium of the Brave Men Who Have Fallen in the Contest with Great Britain. 1779.
Incidents of the Insurrection in the Western Parts of Pennsylvania in 1794. 1795; edited by Daniel Marder, 1972.
The Standard of Liberty. 1802.
Gazette Publications (miscellany). 1806.
Law Miscellanies. 1814.

Editor, *Narratives of a Late Expedition Against the Indians.* 1783.

*

Bibliography: in *Bibliography of American Literature* by Jacob Blanck, 1955; *A Bibliography of the Writings of Brackenridge* by Charles F. Heartman, 1968.

Critical Studies: *The Life and Writings of Brackenridge* by Claude Milton Newlin, 1932; *Brackenridge* by Daniel Marder, 1967; "Representation in Brackenridge's *Modern Chivalry*" by Mark R. Patterson, in *Texas Studies in Literature and Language,* summer, 1986; "Brackenridge, *Modern Chivalry,* and American Humor" by John Engell, in *Early American Literature,* spring, 1987;

"Brackenridge's *Modern Chivalry*: A Reassessment" by Darlene Harbour Unrue, in *History and Humanities: Essays in Honor of Wilbur S. Shepperson* edited by Francis X. Hartigan, 1989; "Dress and Undress in Brackenridge's *Modern Chivalry*" by Caryn Chaden, in *Early American Literature,* vol. 26, 1991.

*   *   *

Although Hugh Henry Brackenridge wrote in a number of different genres—poetry, drama, and nonfictional prose—his one real claim to our attention in the late twentieth century is for the first part of *Modern Chivalry,* an extended piece of satiric fiction published in four volumes between 1792 and 1797. It can hardly be called a novel. The narrative line is thin, merely holding together a series of episodes involving a modern American Quixote, Captain John Farrago, and his Irish servant, Teague O'Regan, as they travel together on the western frontier and later visit the city of Philadelphia. It moves toward no climax in either plot or meaning but merely illustrates through their adventures various failings of American democracy.

But if *Modern Chivalry* is weak in both narrative and thematic development, it is strong in its realistic pictures of frontier life and manners—exaggerated though they may be for satiric purposes—and in the simple, straightforward style through which both the incidents and the authorial discussions of them are presented. Various kinds of dialect—Irish, Scotch, and African American—are well reproduced in its pages, and, though the characters may not be fully developed, they are sharply and skillfully sketched through their language and actions. Thus, the book has often been justly praised as an early piece of American realism.

It is also important for what it has to say about the theory and practice of American democracy. Most of the satire is directed against the Teague O'Regans, ignorant and ambitious men who are eager to accept honors and positions for which they are not qualified, and against an electorate that will put such men in office. But the book is not antidemocratic. It attacks as well those men of wealth or inherited position who are no more suited to rule and members of organizations who admit unqualified persons to their ranks. What the book affirms is the basic principle of democracy: that positions of leadership should be given only to men of ability and integrity, qualities that may appear at any level of society but that must be developed through education.

Only this first part is wholly successful. Brackenridge published the second in 1804-05 and extended the work yet again in the edition of 1815. His satiric touch was gone, however, and with it much of the charm of the book. The second part even lacks the narrative line of the first and becomes, in effect, an endlessly redundant lecture. It more than doubles the size of *Modern Chivalry,* but it does not add appreciably to what Brackenridge had accomplished in the 1790s.

—Donald A. Ringe

See the essay on *Modern Chivalry.*

BRADBURY, Ray (Douglas)

Born: Waukegan, Illinois, 22 August 1920. **Education:** Los Angeles High School, graduated 1938. **Family:** Married Marguerite

Susan McClure in 1947; four daughters. **Career:** Full-time writer, from 1943. President, Science-Fantasy Writers of America, 1951-53. Member of the board of directors, Screen Writers Guild of America, 1957-61. **Awards:** O. Henry prize, 1947, 1948; Benjamin Franklin award, 1954; American Academy award, 1954; Boys' Clubs of America Junior Book award, 1956; Golden Eagle award, for screenplay, 1957; Ann Radcliffe award, 1965, 1971; Writers Guild award, 1974; World Fantasy award for lifetime achievement, 1977; Aviation and Space Writers award, for television documentary, 1979; Balrog award, best poet, 1979; Gandalf award, 1980; PEN Body of Work award, 1985. D.Litt.: Whittier College, California, 1979. **Residence:** Los Angeles, California.

Publications

Short Stories

Dark Carnival. 1947; abridged edition, 1948; abridged edition, as *The Small Assassin,* 1962.
The Martian Chronicles. 1950; as *The Silver Locusts,* 1951.
The Illustrated Man. 1951.
The Golden Apples of the Sun. 1953.
The October Country. 1955.
Sun and Shadow. 1957.
A Medicine for Melancholy. 1959; as *The Day It Rained Forever,* 1959.
The Pedestrian. 1962.
The Machineries of Joy. 1964.
The Vintage Bradbury. 1965.
The Autumn People. 1965.
Tomorrow Midnight. 1966.
Twice Twenty Two (selection). 1966.
I Sing the Body Electric! 1969.
Bloch and Bradbury, with Robert Bloch. 1969; as *Fever Dreams and Other Fantasies,* 1970.
(Selected Stories), edited by Anthony Adams. 1975.
Long after Midnight. 1976.
The Best of Bradbury. 5 vols., 1976.
To Sing Strange Songs. 1979.
The Aqueduct. 1979.
The Stories of Bradbury. 1980.
The Last Circus, and The Electrocution. 1980.
The Love Affair (includes verse). 1982.
Dinosaur Tales. 1983.
A Memory of Murder. 1984.
Fever Dream. 1987.
The Other Foot. 1987.
The Veldt. 1987.
The Fog Horn. 1987.
The April Witch. 1987.
The Dragon. 1988.
The Toynbee Convector. 1988.
There Will Come Soft Rains. 1989.
The Smile. 1991.
Driving Blind: Stories. 1997.

Novels

Fahrenheit 451. 1953.
Dandelion Wine. 1957.

Something Wicked This Way Comes. 1962.
Death Is a Lonely Business. 1985.
A Graveyard for Lunatics: Another Tale of Two Cities. 1990.
Green Shadows, White Whale. 1992.

Plays

The Meadow, in *Best One-Act Plays of 1947-48,* edited by Margaret Mayorga. 1948.
The Anthem Sprinters and Other Antics (produced 1968). 1963.
The World of Bradbury (produced 1964).
The Wonderful Ice-Cream Suit (produced 1965; musical version, music by Jose Feliciano, produced 1990). Included in *The Wonderful Ice-Cream Suit and Other Plays,* 1972.
The Day It Rained Forever, music by Bill Whitefield (produced 1988). 1966.
Christus Apollo, music by Jerry Goldsmith (produced 1969).
The Wonderful Ice-Cream Suit and Other Plays (includes *The Veldt* and *To the Chicago Abyss*). 1972.
Leviathan 99 (produced 1972).
Pillar of Fire and Other Plays for Today, Tomorrow, and Beyond Tomorrow (includes *Kaleidoscope* and *The Foghorn*). 1975.
The Foghorn (produced 1977). Included in *Pillar of Fire and Other Plays,* 1975.
That Ghost, That Bride of Time: Excerpts from a Play-in-Progress. 1976.
Forever and the Earth (radio play). 1984.
Flying Machine. 1986.
A Device Out of Time. 1986.
The Martian Chronicles, adaptation of his own stories (produced 1977). 1986.
Fahrenheit 451, adaptation of his own novel (produced 1979). 1986.
Dandelion Wine, adaptation of his own story (produced 1977). 1988.
Falling Upward (produced 1988). 1988.
Bradbury on Stage. 1991.

Screenplays: *It Came from Outer Space,* with David Schwartz, 1952; *Moby-Dick,* with John Huston, 1956; *Icarus Montgolfier Wright,* with George C. Johnston, 1961; *Picasso Summer* (as Douglas Spaulding), with Edwin Booth, 1972; *Something Wicked this Way Comes,* 1983.

Television Plays: *Shopping for Death,* 1956, *Design for Loving,* 1958, *Special Delivery,* 1959, *The Faith of Aaron Menefee,* 1962, and *The Life Work of Juan Diaz,* 1963 (all *Alfred Hitchcock Presents* series); *The Marked Bullet* (*Jane Wyman's Fireside Theater* series), 1956; *The Gift* (*Steve Canyon* series), 1958; *Tunnel to Yesterday* (*Trouble Shooters* series), 1960; *I Sing the Body Electric!,* 1962, and *The Elevator,* 1986 (both *Twilight Zone* series); *The Jail* (*Alcoa Premier* series), 1962; *The Groom* (*Curiosity Shop* series), 1971; *Marionettes, Inc.,* 1985, *The Playground,* 1985, *The Crowd,* 1985, *Banshee,* 1986, *The Screaming Woman,* 1986, and *The Town Where No One Got Off,* 1986 (all *Bradbury Theatre* series); *Walking on Air,* 1987; *The Coffin,* 1988 (U.K.); *The Fruit at the Bottom of the Bowl,* 1988; *Skeleton,* 1988; *The Emissary,* 1988; *Gotcha!,* 1988; *The Man Upstairs,* 1988; *The Small Assassin,* 1988; *Punishment without Crime,* 1988; *On the Orient, North,* 1988; *Tyrannosaurous Rex,* 1988; *There Was an Old Woman,* 1988; *And So Died Raibouchinska,* 1988; *The Dwarf,* 1989; *A Miracle of Rare Device,* 1989; *The Lake,* 1989; *The Wind,* 1989; *The Pedestrian,*

1989; *A Sound of Thunder*, 1989; *The Wonderful Death of Dudley Stone*, 1989; *The Haunting of the New*, 1989; *To the Chicago Abyss*, 1989; *Hail and Farewell*, 1989; *The Veldt*, 1989; *Boys! Raise Giant Mushrooms in Your Cellar!*, 1989; *Mars Is Heaven*, 1990; *The Murderer*, 1990; *Touched with Fire*, 1990; *The Black Ferris*, 1990; *Usher II*, 1990; *Exorcism*, 1990; *The Day It Rained Forever*, 1990; *A Touch of Petulance*, 1990; — *And the Moon Be Still as Bright*, 1990; *The Toynbee Convector*, 1990; *The Long Years*, 1990; *Here There Be Tygers*, 1990; *The Earth Men*, 1992; *Zero Hour*, 1992; *The Jar*, 1992; *Colonel Stonesteel and the "Desperate Empties"*, 1992; *The Concrete Mixer*, 1992; *The Utterly Perfect Murder*, 1992; *Let's Play Poison*, 1992; *The Martian*, 1992; *The Lonely One*, 1992; *The Happiness Machine*, 1992; *The Long Rain*, 1992; *Down Wind from Gettysbury*, 1992; *Some Live like Lazarus*, 1992; *Fee Fi Fo Fum*, 1992; *Dora and the Great Wide World*, 1992.

Poetry

Old Ahab's Friend, and Friend to Noah, Speaks His Piece: A Celebration. 1971.
When Elephants Last in the Dooryard Bloomed: Celebrations for Almost Any Day in the Year. 1973.
That Son of Richard III: A Birth Announcement. Privately printed, 1974.
Where Robot Mice and Robot Men Run Round in Robot Towns: New Poems, Both Light and Dark. 1977.
Twin Hieroglyphs That Swim the River Dust. 1978.
The Attic Where the Meadow Greens. 1980.
The Haunted Computer and the Android Pope. 1981.
The Complete Poems of Bradbury. 1982.
October. 1983.
Long after Ecclesiastes. 1985.
Death Has Lost Its Charm for Me. 1987.
The Climate of Palettes. 1989.

Other

Switch on the Night (for children). 1955.
R Is for Rocket (for children). 1962.
S Is for Space (for children). 1966.
Teacher's Guide: Science Fiction, with Lewy Olfson. 1971.
The Halloween Tree (for children). 1972.
Zen and the Art of Writing, and The Joy of Writing. 1973.
The Mummies of Guanajuato, photographs by Archie Lieberman. 1978.
Beyond 1984: Remembrance of Things Future. 1979.
The Ghosts of Forever, illustrated by Aldo Sessa. 1981.
The Art of Playboy (text by Bradbury). 1985.
Zen in the Art of Writing (essays). 1990.
Yestermorrow: Obvious Answers to Impossible Futures (essays). 1991.

Editor, *Timeless Stories for Today and Tomorrow.* 1952.
Editor, *The Circus of Dr. Lao and Other Improbable Stories.* 1956.

*

Bibliography: in *The Bradbury Companion* by William F. Nolan, 1975; *Bradbury* edited by Joseph D. Olander and Martin H. Greenberg, 1980.

Critical Studies: introduction by Gilbert Highet to *The Vintage Bradbury*, 1965; "The Revival of Fantasy" by Russell Kirk, in *Triumph* (Washington, D.C.), May 1968; *The Bradbury Companion* (includes bibliography) by William F. Nolan, 1975; *The Bradbury Chronicles* by George Edgar Slusser, 1977; *Bradbury* (includes bibliography) edited by Joseph D. Olander and Martin H. Greenberg, 1980; *Bradbury* by Wayne L. Johnson, 1980; *Bradbury and the Poetics of Reverie: Fantasy, Science Fiction, and the Reader* by William F. Toupence, 1984; *Bradbury* by David Mogen, 1986; *Ray Bradbury and the Poetics of Reverie: Gaston Bachelard, Wolfgang Iser, and the Reader's Response to Fantastic Literature* by William F. Touponce, 1998.

*   *   *

Ray Douglas Bradbury is probably the first American writer of science fiction to become widely known outside the field. Although his reputation rests in considerable part on two early novels, *The Martian Chronicles* (1950) and *Fahrenheit 451* (1953), many of his short stories are perennial anthology favorites. His fiction is noted for its poetic and lyrical qualities, but he has also written a number of dramatic works.

Bradbury was born in Waukegan, Illinois, in 1920; after some nomadic years his family settled in Los Angeles in 1934 and Bradbury has lived there ever since. His long residence on the West Coast notwithstanding, the Midwest of his boyhood is a persistent image in his work: a small-town American utopia of the past with green lawns, shady streets, and friendly neighbors. The image pervades his quasi-autobiographical novel *Dandelion Wine* (1957), and in *The Martian Chronicles* the Martians cruelly use it to enchant and destroy spacemen from Earth.

In the 1940s Bradbury made his way into large circulation magazines like *Collier's* and the *Saturday Evening Post.* The poetic quality of his work seemed to burst the confines of the genre, which made purists uncomfortable. Bradbury was in fact one of the few science fiction writers of note then who was neither a disciple of John W. Campbell, Jr., the innovative editor of *Astounding Science Fiction,* nor possessed of a technical or scientific education. His prize-winning short stories of the late 1940s led to his first novel, *The Martian Chronicles,* in 1950.

In form *The Martian Chronicles* is more a sequence of episodes (some had been previously published) than a novel. They stretch from 1999 to 2026, as the native Martians are destroyed by an Earth-borne plague (chicken pox), and Earth itself is made uninhabitable by nuclear holocaust. A few survivors flee to Mars: in the last chapter a man promises to show his children the true Martians and points to their own reflections in a pool of water.

Free water on Mars suggests that Bradbury's red planet is a poetic image, not a scientific fact. Strict definers of science fiction have had difficulty with Bradbury's inattention to scientific probability, and with attitudes in his fiction which seem downright anti-scientific. Yet Bradbury's concern is not with science in the abstract but with the human use or abuse of it. Science and technology, as represented in his fiction, are often the occasion for displays of human pride and folly, which is only to say that much of Bradbury's work is satire, a posture characteristic of science fiction. One of Bradbury's best-known short stories, "The Veldt," illustrates the point: the Hadleys have put a technologically advanced playroom in place of their own care for their children. Their indifference finally kills them as the simulated African landscape becomes all too real.

That was futuristic enough for 1950, but generally the face of Bradbury's fiction is turned firmly toward the past, as in the idyllic

portrayals of mid-America in perhaps the 1920s. In another noted short story, "The Sound of Thunder," a time traveler is actually shot for altering the past, so precious it seems. In one sense, his fiction warns us about what we can lose.

The future world of *Fahrenheit 451,* for example, is one in which firemen set fires; they burn books. In the totalitarian regime postulated, effective thought control means destroying the heritage of the past, the knowledge that can make human beings wise and free. But this picture of a repressive dystopia ends with praise for the irrepressible human spirit: some people refuse to abandon their past. They memorize great literary and philosophical works; they carry within themselves and in a way become Swift or **Thoreau** or Thomas Love Peacock.

Since the 1960s Bradbury has turned from science fiction and fantasy to poetry (his *Collected Poems* appeared in 1982), drama, including productions of his own plays, and mystery fiction: his *Death is a Lonely Business* came out in 1986. Clearly Bradbury is a versatile writer, but the science fiction which established his name remains a poetic blend of the pastoral and the scientific, of the nostalgic and the satiric.

—Michael N. Stanton

BRADFORD, Roark

Born: Lauderdale County, Tennessee, 21 August 1896. **Education:** Local schools. **Military Service:** Served in the Artillery Reserve of the U.S. Army, 1917-20: lieutenant; U.S. Naval Reserve, assigned to the Bureau of Aeronautics Training Literature Division, Navy Department, Washington, D.C., 1942-45. **Family:** Married Mary Rose Himler; one son. **Career:** Reporter, Atlanta *Georgian,* 1920-22, Macon *Telegraph,* Georgia, 1923, and Lafayette *Daily Advertiser,* Louisiana, 1923; night city editor, later Sunday editor, New Orleans *Times Picayune,* 1924-26; full time writer from 1929. **Awards:** O. Henry Award, 1927. **Member:** American Academy. **Died:** 13 November 1948.

PUBLICATIONS

Fiction

Ol' Man Adam an' His Chillun. 1928.
This Side of Jordan. 1929.
Ol' King David and the Philistine Boys. 1930.
John Henry. 1931.
Kingdom Coming. 1933.
Let the Band Play Dixie and Other Stories. 1934.
The Three-Headed Angel. 1937.

Plays

How Come Christmas: A Modern Morality. 1930.
John Henry, music by Jacques Wolfe, from the story by Bradford. 1939.

Other

The Green Roller (miscellany). 1949.

* * *

To read the stories and novels of Roark Bradford is to enter into a world separated from us by time, space, and especially temperament. In his depiction of the life on Southern plantations, the white man's world fades into the background, becoming neither more nor less important than the plowing of fields or the picking of cotton. Bradford wrote of Southern blacks out of a deep respect and love, which, coupled with his uncanny gift for imitating dialectical speech, makes his writing altogether unique in a white man.

Bradford turned to writing full time in 1929, concerning himself not with philosophical or moral evaluations of the Southern black's life but rather with the reality of his situation and the problems of coping with it. His prose, like his characters, is simple and direct, even childlike, but never sentimental. Death can come quickly and unromantically to them, and when it does, they face it with the deep faith that was a part of the author himself until his death in 1948.

Above all, Bradford was a storyteller. His work vibrates with the strong, simple rhythms of speech, whether in his realistic novels or in his modern myths like *John Henry*: "The night John Henry was born the moon was copper-colored and the sky was black. . . . Forked lightning cleaved the air and the earth trembled like a leaf. The panthers squalled in the brake like a baby and the Mississippi ran upstream a thousand miles."

Bradford won the O. Henry Award in 1927 with his second published short story, "Child of God." His retelling of biblical stories, *Ol' Man Adam an' His Chillun,* was adapted for the stage by **Marc Connelly** and became the highly successful play *The Green Pastures.*

—Walter Bode

BRADFORD, William

Born: Austerfield, Yorkshire, England; baptized 19 March 1590. **Family:** Married 1) Dorothy May in 1613 (died 1620), one son; 2) Alice Carpenter Southworth in 1623, one daughter, two sons and two stepsons. **Career:** Joined a non-conformist congregation at age 12 and a church in Scrooby, Nottinghamshire (which met at the house of William Brewster), 1606; moved with this congregation to Holland, 1608; silk worker, Amsterdam, 1608-09; fustian worker, Leyden, 1609-20; sailed from Delftshaven and Plymouth on ship *Speedwell* (later transferred to the *Mayflower*), signed Mayflower Compact, and was member of Miles Standish's initial exploring expeditions that decided to settle at Plymouth, 1620; governor, Plymouth Colony, 1621, and re-elected 30 times, 1622-56 (served as assistant governor, 5 years); principal judge and treasurer until 1637; with other Plymouth leaders bought out the London colonial investors, 1627. **Died:** 9 May 1657.

PUBLICATIONS

Collections

Collected Verse, edited by Michael G. Runyan. 1974.

Prose

A Relation or Journal of the Beginning and Proceedings of the English Plantation Settled at Plymouth (Mourt's Relation), with Edward Winslow. 1622; edited by Dwight B. Heath, 1963.

Of Plymouth Plantation (facsimile edition), edited by John A. Doyle. 1896; as *History of Plymouth Plantation,* edited by Worthington Chauncey Ford, 2 vols., 1912; edited by Samuel Eliot Morison, 1952.

*

Critical Studies: *Saints and Strangers, Being the Lives of the Pilgrim Fathers and Their Families* by George F. Willison, 1945; *Bradford of Plymouth* by Bradford Smith, 1952; *Bradford* by Perry D. Westbrook, 1978; *Style as Structure and Meaning: Bradford's Of Plymouth Plantation* by Floyd Ogburn, Jr., 1981; "Ideology and the American Frontier" by Norman S. Grabo, in *Early American Literature* vol. 22, 1987; "William Bradford's American Sublime" by David Laurence, in *PMLA: Publications of the Modern Language Association of America* January, 1987; *Sodometries: Renaissance Texts, Modern Sexualities* by Jonathan Goldberg, 1992; *William Bradford: Artist at the Water's Edge* by Albert F. Benac, 1996; *William Bradford of the Mayflower and His Descendants for Four Generations* by Robert S. Wakefield, 1997.

*   *   *

William Bradford was a man of enormous energy and diverse talents. He was governor of Plymouth Plantation during most of his life after 1620, and his leadership, business acumen, and general good sense contributed vitally to the survival of the colony. He was also the historian of the colony—the author of a work that became known as *History of Plymouth Plantation* (titled *Of Plimmoth Plantation, 1620-1657* by him). Bradford had a flair for writing, and his pages are seldom dull. He was self-educated, acquiring over the years some mastery of Latin, Greek, and Hebrew. In England and Holland, as well as in the United States, he had access to the rather extensive library of his good friend and mentor, William Brewster, who had attended Cambridge University. Both by inclination and by his studies, Bradford was prepared for authorship.

But behind Bradford's writing there is another compelling motive—a sense of duty. The early colonists in New England, whether Puritan or Separatist, were Calvinists. As such, they believed that their venture in the wilderness was under the close guidance and scrutiny of God. Indeed, they thought of themselves as a chosen people, fleeing from the Egyptian darkness of Europe and entrusted with the founding of a New Jerusalem where God's will for His people could finally be fulfilled. The leaders of such an undertaking would obviously feel obligated to record the events in the struggle to accomplish what God had mandated. Thus, historians abounded in New England. They called themselves "God's rememberancers," chroniclers for future generations of the what **Cotton Mather** called *Magnalia Christi Americana*—the great works of Christ in America.

Bradford was the first "God's rememberancer" in New England, but during his lifetime only one of his writings was published. This was a section of a book titled *A Relation or Journal of the Beginning and Proceedings of the English Plantation Settled at Plymouth* (commonly known as *Mourt's Relation,* after its supposed editor, G. Mourt), published in London in 1622. Bradford's contribution to the book, it is generally agreed, was a lengthy account of the settlers' landing at Cape Cod, their exploration of the area, and their first winter at Plymouth. The narrative is swift-paced and concrete and pleasantly colloquial in language. Since the purpose of the book was to interest others in coming to New En-

gland, the authors either omitted or toned down many of the difficulties and hardships endured by the colonists during their first year.

In Mourt's Relation the religious motif is less pervasive than in Bradford's major work, *History of Plymouth Plantation.* In the latter Bradford recounts many "special providences," events that demonstrate God's hand in the progress of the colony. Thus the Indian Squanto, who taught the newcomers how to plant maize, was put on the scene by God. Similarly, God intervened when, during the Atlantic voyage, He afflicted with a fatal disease a young man who planned to throw half of the Mayflower passengers overboard. On the other hand, unfavorable events were taken as signs of divine displeasure. Bradford, indeed, regarded the Plymouth venture as nothing less than a crucial episode in the rise of Protestantism, crucial to its eventual triumph over the Church of Rome; and in the first part of the *History* he develops this idea by relating the adventures of his group of Separatists during the years before 1620. The second and by far the larger part of the *History* is in the form of annals, recording in graphic, at times amusing detail the daily life of the colonists as well as the political and military events that shaped their destiny. It gives character sketches of various persons, both saintly and disreputable, who visited or lived in the colony. Bradford himself announced that his writing would be in the "plain style" favored by the Puritans over the ornate style that they associated with orthodox Anglican authors, but his style is not plain to the point of dullness. Its almost chatty tone and diction and its imagery drawn from everyday life and the fast pace of the narrative sections make the book very readable. Most appealing to modern readers would be Samuel Eliot Morison's edition (1952), in which spelling and punctuation have been modernized.

The manuscript of the *History* was mined for material by New England historians throughout the colonial period. After being lost for seventy-five years following the American Revolution, the manuscript turned up in the Fulham Palace Library in London. It was then first published in its entirety by the Massachusetts Historical Society (1856). A small body of additional writing by Bradford—some undistinguished verse and two religious dialogues—have been published. The reader who ignores them will miss nothing. Bradford's very considerable and well deserved literary reputation rests on his *History.*

—Perry D. Westbrook

BRADSTREET, Anne

Born: Anne Dudley, probably in Northampton, England, in 1612 or 1613. **Education:** Privately educated. **Family:** Married Simon Bradstreet, later Governor of Massachusetts, in 1628(?) (died 1697); four sons and four daughters. **Career:** Immigrated to Massachusetts with the Winthrops, 1630; lived in Salem and near Boston, 1630-35, Ipswich, 1635-45, and North Andover, 1645-72. **Died:** 16 September 1672.

PUBLICATIONS

Collections

Works, edited by Jeannine Hensley. 1967.
Poems, edited by Robert Hutchinson. 1969.

Complete Works, edited by Joseph R. McElrath, Jr., and Allan P. Robb. 1981.
A Woman's Inner World: Selected Poetry and Prose, edited by Adelaide P. Amore. 1982.

Poetry

The Tenth Muse Lately Sprung Up in America. 1650; revised edition, as *Several Poems Compiled with Great Variety of Wit and Learning,* 1678.

*

Bibliography: "A List of Editions of the Poems of Bradstreet" by Oscar Wegelin, in *American Book Collector 4,* 1933; "Bradstreet: An Annotated Checklist" by Ann Stanford, in *Bulletin of Bibliography 27,* 1970.

Critical Studies: *Bradstreet and Her Time* by Helen S. Campbell, 1891; *Bradstreet* by Josephine K. Piercy, 1965; *Bradstreet: The Tenth Muse* by Elizabeth Wade White, 1971; *Bradstreet, The Worldly Puritan* by Ann Stanford, 1974, and *Critical Essays on Bradstreet* edited by Stanford and Pattie Cowell, 1983; *An American Triptych: Bradstreet, Emily Dickinson, Adrienne Rich* by Wendy Martin, 1984; *Anne Bradstreet: A Reference Guide* by Raymond F. Dolle, 1990; *Gender Roles, Literary Authority, and Three American Women Writers: Anne Dudley Bradstreet, Mercy Otis Warren, Margaret Fuller Ossoli* by Theresa Freda Nicolay, 1995; *Anne Bradstreet: The Sacred and the Profane* (dissertation) by Sandra Gamble, 1998; *The Flesh and the Spirit: The Female Subject and the Body in the Spiritual Autobiographies of Anne Hutchinson, Anne Bradstreet and Mary Rolandson* (dissertation) by Mary Clare Carruth, 1998.

*   *   *

Anne Bradstreet has long been recognized as the first genuine poet to develop in the English-speaking New World. A biographer, Elizabeth Wade White, maintains further that she "was also the first significant woman poet of England." The one volume that appeared during her lifetime as *The Tenth Muse Lately Sprung Up in America*—published in England without her knowledge and with a title she did not supply—was the first collection of poetry to come out of the New England colonies, to which Bradstreet had immigrated as a young wife in 1630.

Paradoxically, Bradstreet continues to attract an appreciative audience not for the poetry in *The Tenth Muse* but for a considerable number of poems that were first published in 1678, six years after her death. Of the thirteen poems in *The Tenth Muse,* only one, the 48-line "Prologue," appeals to the modern reader; the others are lengthy and tedious exercises in imitation of various poets—chiefly Guillaume du Bartas (as rendered into English by Joshua Sylvester), Spenser, and Sidney. Their works, together with Raleigh's *The History of the World,* she first read as a precocious child in the library of her indulgent father, Thomas Dudley, for many years steward to the Earl of Lincoln. Bradstreet's obvious indebtedness to these authors suggests that she carried her favorite books aboard the *Arbella* and into the New England wilderness in 1630.

Life in that wilderness, however—rather than her father's books—prompted the poetry that has won for her a modest but permanent place in English-American literature. Her *Several Poems* contained—in addition to the pieces in *The Tenth Muse*—almost a score of poems that show her abandoning her old models and striking out with nuances, texture, and techniques that are her own. One of these is "The Author to Her Book," a well-controlled sustained metaphor that dramatizes her chagrin on first seeing the poorly printed *The Tenth Muse.* "Contemplations," often regarded as her best poem, anticipates the romantic view of nature and hints at her discomfort lest her physical reactions be at odds with her spiritual convictions. A number of love poems written for her devoted husband, Simon Bradstreet, a busy colonial official often away from home, reveal a healthy sensuality and suggest that, although she was a Puritan, she was not puritanical. In other poems to and about her children and about the fortunes and misfortunes of her family, she avoids sentimentality and brings to her work the same quiet strength that helped her to survive for forty-two years in remote Massachusetts.

—Thomas F. O'Donnell

See the essay on *The Tenth Muse.*

BRAUTIGAN, Richard (Gary)

Born: Tacoma, Washington, 30 January 1935. **Family:** Married 1) Virginia Dionne Adler in Reno, Nevada, 8 June 1957 (divorced), one daughter; 2) Akiko, 1978 (divorced 1980). **Career:** Poet in residence at California Institute of Technology, 1967; instructor at Montana State University, Bozeman, 1982. Coeditor, *Change* (single-issue magazine), 1963. **Awards:** National Endowment for the Arts grant, 1968. **Died:** (possibly suicide) September 1984.

PUBLICATIONS

Collections

Trout Fishing in America, The Pill Versus the Springhill Mine Disaster, and In Watermelon Sugar. 1968.
Revenge of the Lawn; The Abortion; So the Wind Won't Blow It Away. 1995.
I Watched the World Glide Effortlessly Bye: And Other Pieces. 1996.

Short Stories

Revenge of the Lawn: Stories 1962-1970. 1971.

Novels

A Confederate General from Big Sur. 1965.
Trout Fishing in America. 1967.
In Watermelon Sugar. 1968.
The Abortion: An Historical Romance, 1966. 1971.
The Hawkline Monster: A Gothic Western. 1974.
Willard and His Bowling Trophies: A Perverse Mystery. 1975.
Sombrero Fallout: A Japanese Novel. 1976
Dreaming of Babylon: A Private Eye Novel 1942. 1977.
The Tokyo-Montana Express. 1980.
So the Wind Won't Blow It All Away. 1982.

Poetry

The Return of the Rivers. 1957.
The Galilee Hitch-Hiker. 1958.
Lay the Marble Tea: Twenty-four Poems. 1959.
The Octopus Frontier. 1960.
All Watched Over by Machines of Loving Grace. 1967.
The Pill Versus the Springhill Mine Disaster. 1968.
Please Plant This Book. 1968.
The San Francisco Weather Report. 1969.
Rommel Drives on Deep into Egypt. 1970.
Loading Mercury with a Pitchfork. 1976.
June 30th, June 30th. 1978.

Other

Would You Like to Saddle Up a Couple of Goldfish and Swim to Alaska? 1995.

Recording: *Listening to Richard Brautigan.* N.d.

*

Bibliography: *Richard Brautigan: An Annotated Bibliography* by John F. Barber, 1990.

Critical Studies: *Richard Brautigan: Writer for the Seventies* by Terence Malley, 1972; "Richard Brautigan: The Politics of Woodstock" by John Clayton, in *New American Review* vol. 11, 1971; "Some Observations on A Confederate General from Big Sur" by Gerald Locklin and Charles Stetler, in *Critique* vol. 13, no. 3, 1971; "Trout Fishing in America: Brautigan's Funky Fishing Yarn" by Kenneth Seib, in *Critique* vol. 13, no. 3, 1971; "The Man on the Quaker Oats Box: Characteristics of Recent Experimental Fiction" by John Ditsky, in *Georgia Review,* fall 1972; "The Poetry of Richard Brautigan" by Robert Novak, in *The Windless Orchard,* vol. 14, 1973; "Richard Brautigan and the Modern Pastoral" by Neil Schmitz, in *Modern Fiction Studies* vol. 19, spring 1973; "Escape Through Imagination in Trout Fishing in America" by Thomas Hearron, in *Critique* vol. 16, no. 1, 1974; "Author's Intent: In Watermelon Sugar" by Patricia Hernlund, in *Critique,* vol. 16, no. 1, 1974; "Trout Fishing in America and the American Tradition" by David L. Vanderwerken, in *Critique* vol. 16, no. 1, 1974; "Fishing the Ambivalence, or, A Reading of Trout Fishing in America" by Kent Bales, in *Western Humanities Review* vol. 29, winter 1975; "Williams, Brautigan, and the Poetics of Primitivism" by Robert Kern, in *Chicago Review* vol. 27, no. 1, summer 1975; "The Life and Death of Richard Brautigan" by Lawrence Wright, in *Rolling Stone,* April 11, 1985; *Reading Richard Brautigan's Trout Fishing in America* by Joseph Mills, 1998.

*   *   *

Richard Brautigan once stated that he had written poetry for seven years to learn how to write a sentence because he wanted to write novels and thought that he could not write a novel until he could write a sentence: "I used poetry as a lover but I never made her my old lady."

The popularity of his books spread from California in the 1960s to a larger American audience in the wake of the movement often called "The Greening of America." In 1969 Kurt Vonnegut reported to Delacorte Press the West Coast popularity of Brautigan's paperbacks published by a small San Francisco press, Four Seasons Foundation. Delacorte successfully bargained for two novels, *Trout Fishing in America* and *In Watermelon Sugar,* and a book of poetry, *The Pill Versus the Springhill Mine Disaster,* and they appeared in 1969. Three hundred thousand copies of this trilogy sold that first year, and 1,390,000 had been sold as of 1977. Soon the Japanese discovered him, and he began living there on and off, using Japan for settings and finally marrying a Japanese woman. His minimalist poetry had always had a haiku quality, and one might argue that his surrealist prose has a Japanese feel for nature.

A controversial writer because he seems to encourage the self-adoring anti-intellectualism of the young, Brautigan is commonly seen as the bridge between the Beat movement of the 1950s and the youth revolution of the late 1960s. In a full-length study of his work, Terence Malley identifies the common theme of Brautigan's first four novels as "the shy loner trying to find a 'good world' in the inhospitable America of the 1960s." Josephine Hendin has noted that Brautigan's characters are marked by their lack of a passionate attachment to anyone and to any place; they never permit themselves to feel. Perhaps an even better case can be made that Brautigan's major theme is borrowed from the Romantic poets—that of the transforming power of the imagination, that both the comedy and beauty of art lie in the power of the artist's imagination.

Trout Fishing in America (written in 1961 but not published until 1968) seems like a collage. Terence Malley, however, has explained its thematic structure and, like John Clayton, calls it an "unnovel." It has a traditional theme of American novels: the influence of the American frontier and wilderness on America's imagination, its lifestyle, its economics, its ethics, its therapies, its religion, its politics. The narrator as a child and later as a husband and a father searches for the mythical Eden of the perfect trout stream that America has promised. He finds that the spirit of such a vision of America has become perverted into a legless man in a chrome-plated wheel chair, a Hollywood hero called Trout Fishing in America Shorty, and that the Cleveland Wrecking Yard has used trout streams stacked and for sale at $6.50 per foot. *Trout Fishing in America* is Brautigan's **Hemingway** book, a kind of "Big Two-Hearted River" as seen through the disillusioned eyes of a flower child. Its pervading tone of melancholy arises from the sense that the American child, indoctrinated by our literature, movies, and commerce to believe in the American myth of the Edenic wilderness, has been betrayed. The melancholy is saved from sentimentality by unconventional plots, exaggerated figures of speech that have become Brautigan's trademark, and a style uncomplicated by difficult syntax of logical relationships. Speaking of one trout creek, the narrator says its canyon was sometimes so narrow that the creek poured out "like water from a faucet. You had to be a plumber to fish that trout creek." And the Missouri River at Great Falls, Montana, "looks like a Deanna Durbin movie, like a chorus girl who wanted to go to college." The real heroes in the book are probably the sixth-graders who terrorize first-graders by chalking "Trout Fishing in America" on their backs. John Clayton praised the book's imagination but complained of its political stance of disengagement a la Woodstock. Others noted the "latency of violence and death" in the book, along with its "humor and zaniness," its pessimism about the search for the pastoral myth, and the ambivalence in Brautigan's relation to the American myth and symbols.

Based on the proposition that one can combine stories about hippies at Big Sur and San Francisco in the 1960s and a putative General in the Battle of the Wilderness of the Civil War, Brautigan's first published novel, *A Confederate General from Big Sur* (1965), humorously portrays the lifestyles of Jessie, the narrator; Lee Mellon, the man who thinks he is a Confederate general; and their hippie women. It is Brautigan's **Stephen Crane** Civil War book. In it, Brautigan's playful vision of America satirizes the hippie lifestyle.

The twenty-nine-year-old narrator "without a regular name" of *In Watermelon Sugar* (1968) is an ex-sculptor who has recently taken up writing. He describes three days in his commune at a small town oddly called ideath [sic], population 375. A flashback describes how the town's hoodlum gang committed mass ritual suicide to restore the town. There is also an accompanying story of how the narrator grows bored with his mistress, who he feels has gone bad by consorting with the hoodlum gang, and how she commits suicide because she is displaced by a new mistress. This tragic love triangle is underplayed, and the death seems merely a sad annoyance to everybody. The real hero is the environment and the multipurpose watermelon sugar. The sun is a different color for each day of the week, there are streams everywhere, even in the living room, and houses, lighting oil, and clothes are made from watermelon sugar.

To Malley, this commune is a group of traumatized survivors of a holocaust trying to cope; they are ritualized and deprogrammed from their egoism and previous ideology. He noted, however, that some people read the book as "an acid allegory of altered consciousness" and "watermelon sugar as an euphemism for LSD or some other hallucinogen." He recognized the "curious lack of emotion" in the town and the condemnation of whiskey drinking, which is treated favorably in other Brautigan books. Such detail has led Patricia Hernlund to argue that Brautigan sees the utopian commune as an unsuccessful counterculture without pity and joy.

Revenge of the Lawn: Stories 1962-1970 (1971) contains sixty-two vignettes and short stories that are unified by the theme of the stoicism necessary for healthy survival after one loses the easy life of the child. Many of the sketches seem to detail Brautigan's own childhood in the 1940s and 1950s in the Pacific Northwest as a lonely poor boy addicted to fishing, an enthusiasm for World War II, and writing. The humor of the title story, arising from the story's digressive structure and deadpan tone, is reminiscent of **Mark Twain.** Hemingway's influence on these stories is also clear in Brautigan's feeling for nature, his subdued tone, and the frequent use of the point of view of an adolescent. Those stories set in California are ambivalent about its kinky inhabitants (the man who rebuilt his house with poetry, the woman who buried her dog in an expensive Chinese rug, the Christians having outdoor services in Yosemite). The title story humorously tells about the narrator's bootlegging grandmother, her handyman who hated the lawn, and his comic troubles with drunken geese and bees who feed on rotting pears.

Perhaps the prototypal image occurs at the end of this story: the narrator's earliest memory is of a man cutting down a pear tree, soaking it with gasoline, and setting fire to it while the pears are still green on its branches. It combines both the Brautigan surrealistic image (burning the green pears) and the uneasy relationships the Brautigan characters have with nature. Again, Brautigan's theme of the imagination's ability to reshape reality comes out of these stories in the figures of speech and the imaginative incidents, such as the geese with hangovers, the witch's bedroom filled with flowers, the child who wants to become a deer, and the customer whom the narrator sees in City Lights Bookstore debating with himself whether to buy a Brautigan book.

So the Wind Won't Blow It All Away (1982), Brautigan's last novel and also his best, commemorates a series of people whom the protagonist, who may be autobiographical, knew from the age of five to thirteen "before television crippled the imagination of America." The title, a refrain throughout the book, refers to the writer's attempt to remember these vivid, often eccentric characters: a middle-aged couple who brought their couch, cookstove, and other furniture to set up an outdoor house where they fished; a fifteen-year-old athlete and popular friend whom the narrator accidentally shot to death; two old men who befriended the boy; and one who ran a gas station that sold mostly fishworms and the other who lived in isolation in a one-room shack built of crates. The Northwest seen from a bright, poverty-stricken boy's point of view through the war years and aftermath produces people he does not wish to forget. This book, having sufficient provocative human details, uses few of the usual Brautigan surrealistic figures of speech. It moves the heart instead of the head.

The Pill Versus the Springhill Mine Disaster (1968), ninety-eight poems including the nine parts of "The Galilee Hitch-Hiker," gets its title from its four-line poem about the birth-control pill. Eighteen people read its "Love Poem" on the *Listening to Richard Brautigan* record, and because of this wonderful performance the poem becomes the book's most memorable piece. The feel of the book is The Greening of America, Consciousness III, which passes no moral judgment ("Winos on Potrero Hill"), celebrates psychedelic or surreal visions ("pomegranates go by in their metallic costumes"), and alludes to such popular music groups as The Grateful Dead and The Mamas and the Papas. The most successful poem is the high school grade card poem "Gee, You're So Beautiful That It's Starting to Rain." The poem "1942" will later be elaborated into the whole book *June 30th, June 30th* and is Brautigan's finest mastery of tone.

Brautigan's novels are best appreciated by the principles of the New Fiction ("Post-Modern"), spelled out in an article in *TriQuarterly* by Philip Stevick, and are marked by their deliberately chosen, limited audience and the joy the observer finds in the mere texture of the data of the fiction. Thomas Hearron explains how Brautigan's imagination works in his metaphors. Brautigan's theme is usually the power of the imagination to give zest, poetry, and humanness to life as well as to literature. The youth audience was reading him expecting either affirmation (unfulfilled) of the 1960s counterculture or titillation from his style and a literary equivalent of the drug experience. Professionals read him expecting enlightenment on the youth culture. He was aware of several currents of American tradition, especially that of the new American Eden as created by **Thoreau** in *Walden,* by Twain in Huckleberry Finn's escape to the Mississippi River, and by the Californian myth since the Gold Rush days, and Brautigan tends to condemn the new America because it has betrayed the promises of the new American Eden.

—Robert Novak

BRENT, Linda. *See* **JACOBS, Harriet Ann.**

BROMFIELD, Louis

Born: Mansfield, Ohio, 27 December 1896. **Education:** Cornell University Agricultural College, Ithaca, New York, 1914-15; School of Journalism, Columbia University, New York, 1916, honorary war degree 1920. **Military Service:** Served in the American Ambulance Corps, with the 34th and 168th divisions of the French Army, 1917-19: Croix de Guerre. **Family:** Married Mary Appleton Wood in 1921 (died 1952); three daughters. **Career:** Reporter, City News Service and Associated Press, New York, 1920-22; editor and/or critic, *Musical America, The Bookman,* and *Time,* also worked as an assistant to a theatrical producer and as advertising manager of Putnam's, publishers, all New York, 1922-25; lived in Senlis, France, 1925-38; lived on a farm in Richland County, Ohio, 1939-56. President, Emergency Committee for the American Wounded in Spain, 1938. Director, U.S. Chamber of Commerce. **Awards:** Pulitzer prize, 1927; Chevalier, Legion of Honor (France), 1939. LL.D: Marshall College, Huntington, West Virginia; Parsons College, Fairfield, Iowa. Litt.D.: Ohio Northern University. **Member:** American Academy. **Died:** 18 March 1956.

PUBLICATIONS

Collection

Return to Pleasant Valley: Louis Bromfield's Best from Malabar Farm and His Country Classics: Including Special Selections. 1996.

Fiction

The Green Bay Tree. 1924.
Possession. 1925; as *Lilli Barr,* 1926.
Early Autumn. 1926.
A Good Woman. 1927.
The Strange Case of Miss Annie Spragg. 1928.
Awake and Rehearse (stories). 1929.
Tabloid News (stories). 1930.
Twenty-Four Hours. 1930.
Modern Hero. 1932.
The Farm. 1933.
Here Today and Gone Tomorrow: Four Short Novels. 1934.
The Man Who Had Everything. 1935.
It Had to Happen. 1936.
The Rains Came: A Novel of Modern India. 1937.
It Takes All Kinds (omnibus). 1939; selection, as *You Get What You Give,* 1951.
Night in Bombay. 1940.
Wild Is the River. 1941.
Until the Day Break. 1942.
Mrs. Parkington. 1943.
Bitter Lotus. 1944.
What Became of Anna Bolton. 1944.
The World We Live In: Stories. 1944.
Colorado. 1947.
Kenny. 1947.
McLeod's Folly. 1948.
The Wild Country. 1948.
Mr. Smith. 1951.

Plays

The House of Women, from his novel *The Green Bay Tree* (produced 1927).
DeLuxe, with John Gearnon (produced 1934).
Times Have Changed (produced 1935).

Screenplays: *One Heavenly Night,* with Sidney Howard, 1930; *Brigham Young—Frontiersman,* with Lamar Trotti, 1940.

Other

The Work of Robert Nathan. 1927.
England, A Dying Oligarchy. 1939.
Pleasant Valley. 1945.
A Few Brass Tacks. 1946.
Malabar Farm. 1948.
Out of the Earth. 1950.
The Wealth of the Soil. 1952.
A New Pattern for a Tired World. 1954.
From My Experience: The Pleasures and Miseries of Life on a Farm. 1955.
Animals and Other People. 1955.
Walt Disney's Vanishing Prairie. 1956(?).

*

Critical Studies: *Bromfield and His Books* by Morrison Brown, 1956; *The Heritage: A Daughters Memories of Bromfield* by Ellen Geld, 1962; *Bromfield* by David D. Anderson, 1964; "The Village Grown Up: Sherwood Anderson and Louis Bromfield" by Roger J. Bresnahan, in *Midamerica: The Yearbook of the Society for the Study of Midwestern Literature* vol. 12, 1985; "Literary Gardeners: Louis Bromfield and Jean de Boschere" by Victor Llona, in *Laurels,* fall, 1988; *Louis Bromfield and the Malabar Farm Experience* by John T. Carter, 1995; *Louis Bromfield, Novelist and Agrarian Reformer: The Forgotten Author* by Ivan Scott, 1998.

*   *   *

One of the most promising young American novelists of the 1920s, Louis Bromfield fell into critical disfavor in the early 1930s, a condition that prevailed until his death in 1956 in spite of a continued prodigious production of novels and short stories and a remarkable popular success. To assess his contributions to American literature is not difficult; the many literary shortcomings that prevented the fulfillment of his early literary promise are sufficient to keep him out of the first rank of American novelists. But at the same time he deserves a better literary fate than he has received: his effective style, his character portrayal, and his narrative technique are consistently strong, and his interpretations of American life are effective and intelligent.

The themes with which he dealt are significant: the decline of American individualism and agrarian democracy and the growth of industrialism; the unique role of the strong woman in American life; the egalitarian philosophy that permits a young person to rise above his origins. In his use of them in his work he came close to the essence of American life as thoughtful Americans know it. That he did not go on to chronicle the rise of an industrial democracy, as the Marxist critics of the 1930s demanded, but attempted instead to return to the past contributed to the demise of his reputation, but it resulted in some of his best works, those in which he develops his major themes effectively as he reiterates the values upon which the country was built and emphasizes the need to return to those values in an increasingly materialistic age.

Among his substantial literary contributions must be included his four panel novels, *The Green Bay Tree, Possession, Early Autumn,* and *A Good Woman,* which document in human terms the impact of sweeping social changes and perverted values in the early years of the twentieth century. These novels also illustrate his literary talents: a forthright, literate style; characters who are human and intense; and strong narratives. To these novels must be added *The Farm,* his best single work, *Twenty Four Hours,* a remarkably controlled work in spite of its lapses, and *The Rains Came,* the most dramatic and philosophically unified of his books. Of his later work, *Mrs. Parkington* is an intensely human portrait of a magnificent American woman, and *The Wild Country* comes close to a definitive expression of the American Midwestern experience in transition from frontier to civilization.

Also worth noting are Bromfield's contributions to the literature of nature, folklore, and agriculture. Most of the best of his folklore and nature writing is included in *Animals and Other People,* while *Pleasant Valley* and *Malabar Farm* indicate what technical writing may achieve when it is lively, imaginative, and literate.

Unfortunately, Bromfield still suffers from the fact that he has received little objective criticism. The unfair criticisms of the early 1930s have discouraged later critics from looking at his work clearly and coherently. He wrote too well too easily, and his early critical and commercial successes ultimately worked to his disadvantage. But in almost all of his work he wrote well, and he constructed memorable characters and situations—uncommon abilities in any age.

—David D. Anderson

BROOKS, Gwendolyn

Born: Topeka, Kansas, 7 June 1917. **Education:** Wilson Junior College, Chicago, graduated 1936. **Family:** Married Henry L. Blakely in 1939 (divorced); one son and one daughter. **Career:** Publicity director, NAACP Youth Council, Chicago, 1937-38. Taught at Northeastern Illinois State College, Chicago; Columbia College, Chicago, Illinois; Elmhurst College, Illinois; and University of Wisconsin, Madison; Distinguished Professor of the Arts, City College, City University of New York, 1971; editor, *Black Position* magazine; Consultant in Poetry, Library of Congress, Washington, D.C., 1986. **Awards:** Named woman of the year, *Mademoiselle* magazine, 1945; National Institute of Arts and Letters grant, 1946; Guggenheim fellowships, 1946, 1947; American Academy grant, 1946; Eunice Tietjens Memorial prize, *Poetry* magazine, 1949; Pulitzer prize, 1950; Anisfield-Wolf award, 1968; Poet Laureate of Illinois, 1968; Black Academy of Arts and Letters award, 1971; Shelley Memorial award, 1976; inducted into National Women's Hall of Fame, 1988; Lifetime Achievement Award from the National Endowment for the Arts, 1989; Society for Literature award, University of Thessaloniki, Athens, Greece, 1990; Aiken-Taylor award, 1992; Jefferson lecturer award, 1994; National Book Foundation medal for lifetime achievement, 1994; National medal of Arts, 1995. Received honorary degrees from: Columbia College, 1964. D.Litt.: Lake Forest College, Chicago, 1965; Brown University, Providence, Rhode Island, 1974. **Residence:** Chicago.

Poetry

A Street in Bronzeville. 1945.
Annie Allen. 1949.
Bronzeville Boys and Girls (for children). 1956.
The Bean Eaters. 1960.
Selected Poems. 1963.
In the Time of Detachment, In the Time of Cold. 1965.
In the Mecca. 1968.
For Illinois 1968: A Sesquicentennial Poem. 1968.
Riot. 1970.
The Wall. N.d.
Family Pictures. 1970.
World of Gwendolyn Brooks. 1971.
Aloneness. 1971.
Aurora. 1972.
Beckonings. 1975.
To Disembark. 1981.
Black Love. 1982.
Selected Poems. 1982.
Gottschalk and the Grand Tarantelle. 1988.
Mayor Harold Washington and *Chicago, The I Will City.* 1983.
The Near Johannesburg Boy. 1986.
Blacks. 1991.
Children Coming Home. 1991.
Primer for Blacks. 1991.

Fiction

Maud Martha. 1953.
The Tiger Who Wore White Gloves; or, What You Are You Are (for children). 1974.

Other

A Portion of That Field, with others. 1967.
The World of Brooks (miscellany). 1971.
Report from Part One: An Autobiography. 1972.
A Capsule Course in Black Poetry Writing, with Haki R. Madhubuti, Keorapetse Kgositsilc, and Dudley Randall. 1975.
Young Poets' Primer. 1981.
Very Young Poets. 1983.
Winnie (about Winnie Mandela). 1991.

Editor, *A Broadside Treasury.* 1971.
Editor, *Jump Bad: A New Chicago Anthology.* 1971.

*

Bibliography: *Langston Hughes and Brooks: A Reference Guide* by R. Baxter Miller, 1978. "Bibliographical Scholarship on Three Black Writers" by Vincent Prestianni in *Obsidian-II:-Black- Literature-in-Review* vol. 5, no. 1, Spring 1990.

Critical Studies: Essays on Brooks in *Black American Literature and Humanism* edited by Baxter R. Miller, 1981; Essays on Brooks in *Black Women Writers (1950-1980): A Critical Evaluation* edited by Mari Evans, 1984; Essays on Brooks in *Black American Poets between Worlds, 1940-1960* edited by Baxter R. Miller,

1986; *Brooks: Poetry and the Heroic Voice* by D.H. Melhem, 1987; *A Life Distilled: Brooks, Her Poetry and Fiction* edited by Maria K. Mootry and Gary Smith, 1987; *A Life of Gwendolyn Brooks* by George E. Kent, 1990; *Race, Gender, and Class Perspectives in the Works of Maya Angelou, Gwendolyn Brooks, Rita Dove, Nikki Giovanni, and Audre Lorde,* by Ekaterini Georgoudaki, 1991; *On Gwendolyn Brooks: Reliant Contemplation,* 1996.

*   *   *

The recipient of a Pulitzer Prize in 1950 for her volume of poetry *Annie Allen,* Gwendolyn Brooks stands as one of the premier American poets of the twentieth century. Brooks writes both powerfully and universally out of the black American milieu, exploring the nature of racism, sexism, and classism in the United States in a distinctive poetic style. In her poetry, Brooks experiments with a wide range of narrative and poetic strategies, exploring the spectrum of American social, economic, and cultural problems. Throughout her diverse work, Brooks's most consistent achievement is her marriage of poetry and politics. Her poems may sometimes be bitter, angry, or threatening, but they always maintain an aesthetic and resist being read merely as propaganda.

By often focusing on characters who live in urban ghettos or who are members of disempowered communities, Brooks depicts the struggles as well as the triumphs of the American underclass. Brooks not only explores the nature of racial relations and racial justice in her poetry, she addresses the plight of women in America as well as the vital quest for personal and national peace. Houston A. Baker Jr. has noted in *A Life Distilled: Gwendolyn Brooks, Her Poetry and Fiction* that Brook's characters and the subjects of her poetry "transcend the ghetto life of many black Americans. They reflect the joy of childhood, the burdens and contentment of motherhood, the distortions of the war-torn psyche, the horror of blood-guiltiness, and the pains of an antihero confronted with a heroic ideal." Baker continues, explaining that "Brook's protagonists, personae, and speakers, in short, capture all of life's complexities, particularly the complexity of an industrialized age characterized by swift change, depersonalization, and war."

In her earliest book of poetry, *A Street in Bronzeville* (1945), Brooks celebrates black culture in Chicago, creating vivid characters who pulse with life. In "The Sundays of Satin-Legs Smith," for example, Brooks chronicles the Sunday morning ritual of a lively man who dresses in "Wonder-suits in yellow and in wine, / Sarcastic green and zebra-striped cobalt. / With shoulder padding that is wide / And cocky and determined as his pride." After rising from a raucous Saturday night's revelry: "He dances down the hotel steps that keep / Remnants of last night's high life and distress."

Brooks's descriptions invest her characters with a vivacity and a lust for life that virtually enables them to leap off the printed page and to dance wildly across the room.

In *Annie Allen* (1949) and *The Bean Eaters* (1960), Brooks continues to create vivid characters who are ripe with the ecstasy and the tragedy of day-to-day life in lower class black America. In her poem "The Anniead," Brooks elevates a young black woman's experiences to epic proportions, modeling the title as well as the structure of her poem after Vergil's *Aeneid.* But the love scenes of "The Anniead" do not take place in ancient Carthage, as they do in Vergil's epic, but rather in a Chicago tenement:

Think of almost thoroughly
Derelict and dim and done.
Stroking swallows from the sweat.
Fingering faint violet.
Hugging old and Sunday sun.
Kissing in her kitchenette
The minuets of memory.

The title characters of "The Bean Eaters" also live a mythic life in their creaking tenement, pursuing daily routines and remembering life "as they lean over the beans in their rented back room that is full of beads and receipts and dolls and cloths, tobacco crumbs, vases and fringes." Brooks's representation of such larger-than-life characters in her poetry is supplemented by the invocation of street language and colloquial speech, making her poetry truly a celebration of proletarian existence.

Brooks's lyrical voice turns sharply towards black solidarity and black pride in her poetry from the 1960s, reflecting her increasing awareness of the political potential of poetry. *In the Mecca,* published in 1968, and especially the poems published since, reflect Brooks's conversion from deep racial pride to the harsher militancy that she experienced under the tutelage of a group of young blacks at a meeting at Fisk University in 1967. Thus she speaks in "Young Africans" (from *Family Pictures*) of "our black revival, our black vinegar, / our hands and our hot blood," and warns in 1970 in the acerbic *Riot,* "Cabot! John! You are a desperate man / and the desperate die expensively today." But nearly always Brooks finds the tight poetic structure, the form in which to embody the idea, so that the reader comes away with a sense of surprise and delight at the insight.

Brooks's only substantial work of fiction, *Maud Martha,* published in 1953, has been largely overlooked, but it is notable for being one of the first representations of a black woman in fiction who is not a walking stereotype but is instead a complex, multidimensional human being. *Maud Martha* is an African-American bildungsroman which focuses upon the spiritual and inner development of a young black girl in Chicago in the 1930s and 1940s.

Brooks has devoted much of her time since the late 1960s to helping young black Americans, and especially writers. Throughout her writing, Brooks consistently strives to reveal the presence and the passion of black life in America in a poetic style which is complex, subtle, and challenging. Her use of idiomatic language, black English, and colloquial speech skillfully combine in a style which is uniquely alive and throbbing with the dual pulse of poetry and politics. Perhaps more so than any other contemporary poet, Gwendolyn Brooks speaks out of the American consciousness and to the American conscience, combining poetry and politics into a rare, precious, and seamless whole.

—Alan R. Shucard, updated by Allison Hersh

BROUGHAM, John

Born: Dublin, Ireland, 9 May 1810; became U.S. citizen. **Education:** Trinity College and Peter Street Hospital. **Career:** Had to give up education to help his family with financial difficulties. Actor, Queen's Theatre Company, 1830, and with Madame Vestris's Company, 1831; began American career as actor with the play *His Last Legs,* New York, 1842; actor and playwright,

William Burton's Company; visited England, 1860-65; became impoverished and lived on an annual annuity raised by friends. **Died:** 7 January 1880.

PUBLICATIONS

Collection

Life Stories and Poems of John Broughman, edited by William Winter. 1881.

Plays

Love's Livery. 1840(?).
Life in the Clouds; or, Olympus in an Uproar. 1840.
Night and Morning. 1846.
A Grandioso, Amoroso, Serioso, Verisoso, Polyglotte-Anglo-Italio-Americano Opera: Being the Account of an Unfortunate Druidical Delinquent Who Had Neither Pa, Nor-Ma! 1847.
Dombey and Son, adaptation of Charles Dickens. 1849(?).
A Basket of Chips. 1855.
Po-ca-hon-tas. 1855.
The Game of Love. 1855.
All's Fair in Love: An Original Dramatic Story. 1856.
Dred; or The Dismal Swamp, adaptation of Harriet Beecher Stowe. 1856.
Irish Yankee; or, The Birth-day of Freedom. 1856.
Life in New York; or, Tom and Jerry on a Visit. 1856.
Temptation; or, The Irish Emigrant. 1856.
The Red Mask; or, The Wolf of Lithuania. 1856.
Franklin; A New and Original Historical Drama. 1856.
Columbus el Filibustero!! 1857.
Metamora; or, The Last of the Pollywogs. 1857(?).
Much Ado about a Merchant of Venice. 1858.
The Great Tragic Revival. 1858.
The Miller of New Jersey; or, The Prison Hulk. 1858.
The Musard Ball; or, Love at the Academy. 1858.
Neptune's Defeat; or, The Seizure of the Seas. 1858.
Humorous Stories. 1858.
Art and Artifice; or, Woman's Love. 1859.
Flies in the Web. 1860.
Playing with Fire. 1860.
The Duke's Motto. 1870.
Bel Demonio. 1870.
La Belle Sauvage. 1870.
Lotos Leaves, edited by Brougham and John Elderkin. 1875.

Critical Studies: "The Hibernian Experience: John Brougham's Irish-American Plays" by Pat M. Ryan, in *MELUS: The Journal of the Society for the Study of the Multi-Ethnic Literature of the United States,* summer 1983; in *When Conscience Trod the Stage: American Plays of Social Awareness* edited by Mollie Ann and Walter J. Meserve, 1998; in *Romanticism and Colonialism: Writing and Empire, 1780-1830* edited by Tim Fulford and Peter Kitson, 1998.

*   *   *

Born in Dublin, John Brougham garnered experience as an actor with Mme. Vestris in England before coming to America in 1842.

Critics in New York City immediately singled him out as a lively actor with a rich brogue and a "truly Irish countenance." As a playwright he quickly struck the pace that a large part of America enjoyed with the farcical *Jupiter Jealous; or, Life in the Clouds,* which played at William Mitchell's popular Olympic Theatre. During the next eight years Brougham wrote at least twenty plays, not counting his claim that he was a substantial coauthor with Dion Boucicault of *London Assurance.* By 1850 his name as an actor and a playwright was recognized in the major theaters across America. Introducing *Brougham's Dramatic Works,* published by Samuel French in 1856, Dr. Sheldon MacKinzie, the theater critic and writer to whom a substantial number of American playwrights appealed for advice, described Brougham as "one of the most successful of living dramatists." During his long career Brougham wrote 126 dramatic works; his prodigious output inspired Laurence Hutton, writing about "The American Burlesque" for *Harper's New Monthly* (1890), to dub Brougham the "Aristophanes" of American drama.

It is that tag, celebrating Brougham's farces and burlesques, that has followed him through theater history. During the 1840s the only theatre to make money in New York was the Olympic, which catered to patriotic, rowdy, fun-loving Jacksonian individualists. With that audience in mind, Brougham wrote *Life in New York* and *Declaration of Independence,* both in 1844. With *Met-a-mora; or, the Last of the Polywogs* (1847), however, he discovered what he did best: parody events and popular works by other dramatists. In this instance he burlesqued both the subject matter of John Augustus Stone's *Metamora; or, the Last of the Wampanoags* and the acting techniques of Edwin Forrest, for whom Stone's play was written—a combination that had adorned American stages for a generation. In Brougham's hands, Stone's Metamora became "the ultimate Polywog"; a majestic dying panther became a frightened pig; and Forrest's dramatic delivery of "Hah!" became a ridiculous "Ugh!" Brougham's reputation was established. It was an evening of broad farcical entertainment enlivened with vaudevillian one-liners and minstrel-show humor.

Like the best of dramatists, Brougham provided the public with amusing diversions while pointing out conditions worthy of serious attention. *The Ruling Passion* (1859) focused on love and money. *The Game of Life* (1853) showed a game of scoundrels, gossip, and scandal. *The Game of Love* (1855) revealed a social affair in which characters generally got what they deserved. *The Irish Emigrant; or Temptation* (1856) focused on two social problems of the day. Like all actor-playwrights, Brougham also followed the popular trend of adapting novels for the stage. He was particularly partial to the works of Charles Dickens and dramatized *Dombey and Son* (1848) and *Bleak House* (1853). In his version of *David Copperfield* (1851) Brougham played Wilkins Micawber, who controlled the action of the play, foiled the villain, and had the final curtain speech in the play. Brougham also did his share of adapting sentimental popular fiction, producing *Orion, the Gold Beater* and *Karmel the Scout; or, the Rebel of the Jerseys,* both in 1857.

Although Brougham wrote several burlesques, only one rivals *Met-a-mora.* In *Po-ca-hon-tas; or, the Gentle Savage* (1855) he took considerable liberties with the familiar story while creating on stage a hilariously funny Pow-ha-tan I, "King of the Tuscaroras, a crotchety monarch, in fact, a Semi-Brave." With such Indians as the medicine man Kod-liv-royal and Po-ca-hon-tas's friends Dahlin-duk and Lum-pa-shuga, Brougham employed puns, songs, dances, slapstick comedy, and topical satire to amuse his audiences. His other burlesques before the Civil War never quite caught the public fancy. In *Columbus el Filibustero* (1857) Brougham showed a more thoughtful wit. *The Great Tragic Revival* (1858) included such characters as Marcus Brutus Richelieu Smith and probably much improbable stage business.

Brougham was associated with several major American theaters. After first appearing at the Park Theatre in 1842, he went on tour, only to lose all of his money in a Mississippi riverboat poker game. By 1848 he was stage manager at the Burton's Chambers Street Theatre. Twice he attempted to manage theaters—Brougham's Broadway Lyceum (1850-52) and the Old Bowery (1856-57)—neither successfully. For several years he was employed at Wallack's Theatre as actor-playwright, a position he later held—after spending the Civil War years in London—at the Winter Garden and at Daly's Fifth Avenue Theatre.

In an essay in *Wags of the Stage* (1902), Joseph Whitton claimed that Brougham "excelled all other burlesque writers in the flash of his humour and in the apt and prolific use of the *jeu-d'esprit*. But his forte was speechmaking." During the post-Civil War years the social elite of Manhattan basked in the personal charm, grace, and humor of "Genial John" Brougham. Seemingly a happy-go-lucky man, yet one who experienced depths of despair that contrasted sharply with the soaring good nature most people saw in him, Brougham enjoyed the American theater scene; he took chances as he found them and had his share of success and failure. He was a charitable man whose thoughts and conversations often dwelt upon the disparity of conditions in society and the struggles of the poor. A fine actor, he was a bungling theater manager. Both vocations, however, forced him to write plays—the first to provide vehicles for his acting talents, generally in Irish roles; the second to keep his theaters open. On both accounts he left some memorable farces and burlesques for the ephemeral popular entertainment, farces that reveal an inexhaustible supply of good humor and a sharp tongue to match the fancy of his imagination.

—Walter J. Meserve

BROWN, Charles Brockden

Born: Philadelphia, Pennsylvania, 17 January 1771. **Education:** The Friends' Latin School, Philadelphia, 1781-86; studied law in the office of Alexander Wilcocks, Philadelphia, 1787-92, but never practiced. **Family:** Married Elizabeth Linn in 1804; three sons and one daughter. **Career:** Lived in New York and was associated with the Friendly Society there, 1798-1801: editor of the society's *Monthly Magazine and American Review,* 1799-1800; returned to Philadelphia and worked in his brother's importing business, 1800-06, and as an independent trader, 1807-10. Editor, *Literary Magazine,* 1803-07, and *American Register,* 1807-10. **Died:** 21 February 1810.

PUBLICATIONS

Collections

Novels. 7 vols., 1827.
Novels and Related Works, edited by Sydney J. Krause. 1977—.

Fiction

Wieland; or, The Transformation: An American Tale. 1798.
Ormond; or The Secret Witness. 1799.
Arthur Mervyn; or, Memoirs of the Year 1793. 2 vols., 1799-1800.
Edgar Huntly; or, Memoirs of a Sleep-Walker. 1799; edited by David Lee Clark, 1928.
Clara Howard. 1801; as *Philip Stanley; or, The Enthusiasm of Love,* 1807.
Jane Talbot. 1801.
Carwin the Biloquist and Other American Tales and Pieces. 1822.
Memoirs of Stephen Calvert, edited by Hans Borchers. 1978.
Three Gothic Novels. 1998.

Other

Alcuin: A Dialogue. 1798; edited by Lee R. Edwards, 1971.
An Address to the Government on the Cession of Louisiana to the French. 1803; revised edition, 1803.
Monroe's Embassy. 1803.
An Address on the Utility and Justice of Restrictions upon Foreign Commerce. 1809.
The Rhapsodist and Other Uncollected Writings, edited by Harry R. Warfel. 1943.

Translator, *A View of the Soil and Climate of the United States of America,* by C.F. Volney. 1804.

*

Bibliography: in *Bibliography of American Literature* by Jacob Blanck, 1955; "A Census of the Works of Brown" by Sydney J. Krause and Jane Nieset, in *Serif 3,* 1966; *Brown: A Reference Guide* by Patricia Parker, 1980.

Critical Studies: *The Life of Brown* by William Dunlap, 2 vols., 1815, as *Memoirs of Brown,* 1822; *Brown, American Gothic Novelist* by Harry R. Warfel, 1949; *Brown, Pioneer Voice of America* by David Lee Clark, 1952; *Brown* by Donald A. Ringe, 1966; *Rational Fictions: A Study of Brown* by Arthur G. Kimball, 1968; *Critical Essays on Brown* edited by Bernard Rosenthal, 1981; *The Coincidental Art of Brown* by Norman S. Grabo, 1981; *Brown: An American Tale* by Alan Axelrod, 1983; *A Right View of the Subject: Feminism in the Works of Brown and John Neal* by Fritz Fleischmann, 1983; *Conspiracy and Romance: Studies in Brockden Brown, Cooper, Hawthorne and Melville* by Robert Levine, 1989; *The Godwinian Novel: The Rational Fictions of Godwin, Brockden Brown, Mary Shelley* by Pamela Clemit, 1993; *The Apparition in the Glass: Charles Brockden Brown's American Gothic* by Bill Christophersen, 1994; *The Ideological Polyphony in the Fictional World of Charles Brockden Brown* (dissertation) by Dingquan Zhang, 1995; *The Novel Historicism of Charles Brockden Brown* (dissertation) by Mark L. Kamrath, 1996; *Private Property: Charles Brockden Brown's Gendered Economics of Virtue* by Elizabeth Jane Wall Hinds, 1997.

*   *   *

When Charles Brockden Brown began to write fiction in the latter half of the 1790s, he turned for his models to the popular novels of his time: the Gothic romances of England and Germany, the sentimental tale of seduction, and the novel of purpose. All of these types of fiction had a strong influence on the young American, and each of his six novels can be classified under one or more of these headings. But however much he may have learned from his wide reading, Brown was no mere imitator. He shaped his models to his own artistic ends and turned even such unpromising forms as the Gothic and sentimental romance into vehicles for the development of important themes. He left his indelible mark on everything he wrote.

A major characteristic of Brown's fiction is its intense intellectuality. Though *Wieland* and *Ormond* may both be viewed as tales of seduction, and *Wieland* and *Edgar Huntly* as tales of terror, all three carry a weight of thematic meaning not commonly found in the sentimental or Gothic romance. Sensationalist psychology, theories of education, and the sources of mania are major concerns in *Wieland;* utopian theories, the proper training for women, and the place of religion in education in *Ormond;* and benevolist principles in *Edgar Huntly.* Other of Brown's books are equally intellectual. Benevolist theory also appears in *Arthur Mervyn,* a book modeled on William Godwin's *Caleb Williams,* and Godwinian rationalism clashes with religion in *Jane Talbot,* a sentimental romance.

This is not to say that Brown is a propagandist. He used his fiction, as one critic has observed, not for the exposition, but for the discovery of ideas, which he puts to the test through the actions of his characters. The mistakes that the mad Theodore Wieland, the distraught Clara Wieland, and the rationalistic Henry Pleyel make in attempting to act on the basis of misinterpreted sensations, and the disaster that Edgar Huntly causes by acting on benevolist principles well illustrate Brown's technique. He forces the reader to examine the ideas in the context of the action, but he draws no conclusion himself. Indeed, since all of his books are first-person narrations, told through the voices of one or more characters or through a series of letters, the reader must often penetrate the psychology of the narrator before he can discover the thematic meaning embodied in the action.

In *Ormond* the point of view causes relatively little trouble, for the story is told in a straightforward manner by a rational character who, throughout most of the book, plays no major role in the action. In other novels, however, where the protagonists tell their own stories, the problem can be difficult. Blessed with an innocent face and a glib tongue, Arthur Mervyn always presents himself in a favorable light, but he exists in a world where appearances are often deceiving, and his actions seem to belie the purity of motive that he consistently attributes to himself. He is, therefore, extremely difficult to penetrate, and critics are divided over the meaning of his experience. The protagonists in *Wieland* and *Edgar Huntly* present a different problem, for both are mentally disturbed. Clara Wieland lapses into madness in the course of her narrative, and Edgar Huntly is driven by strange compulsions from the very first pages of the book. Both narrators are, presumably, brought back to sanity by the close of their stories, but neither is easy for the reader to plumb.

In both of these Gothic tales, however, Brown found effective means for revealing the mental state of his disturbed narrators. Through the use of enclosures in *Wieland*—the temple, the summer house, and Clara's room and closet—he suggests the isolation and introspection of all the Wielands, including Clara; through the labyrinthine paths and deep cave in *Edgar Huntly*, he projects his protagonist's mental journey and withdrawal into himself. Other devices, too—Clara's dream, Edgar Huntly's somnambulism, and the appearance of his double, Clithero Edny—help the reader to understand their psychology. All of these were excellent inventions that function well in their respective books. Through them, Brown helped to establish the kind of psychological Gothic that became so popular throughout the nineteenth century in the works of Poe, Hawthorne, and even James.

Brown's position at the head of that tradition accounts for part of the interest he generates among modern readers, but his historical importance is not his only claim to attention. Though he never wrote a wholly satisfactory novel—even his best books are marred by structural flaws and a defective style—he achieved so great an intellectual and imaginative intensity in such works as *Wieland, Edgar Huntly,* and *Arthur Mervyn* that one can forgive the weaknesses for the strengths. All are told by protagonists whose psychological state fascinates, and the tales they recount appeal to both the intellect and the emotions of the reader. The ideas Brown explores are always interesting, and the means he found to reveal the psychology of the narrators and to advance the action are absorbing. Though a hasty and careless writer—he hurried all six of his novels through the press in about three years—Brown instilled in the best of his books a vitality yet apparent almost two centuries after they were written.

—Donald A. Ringe

BROWN, Rita Mae

Born: Hanover, Pennsylvania, 28 November 1944 and adopted in infancy by Ralph and Julia Brown. **Education:** University of Florida, 1962-64; Broward Junior College, A.A. 1965; New York University, B.A. in English and Classics 1968; School of the Visual Arts, Cinematography Degree 1968; Institute for Policy Studies, Ph.D. in English and Political Science 1976. **Family:** Companion of Martina Navratilova 1979-81; companion of Judy Nelson 1992. **Career:** Photography editor, Sterling Publishing Company, New York City, 1969-70; lecturer in sociology, Federal City College, Washington, D.C., 1971; research fellow, Institute for Policy Studies, Washington, D.C., 1971-73; visiting instructor, Goddard College, Plainfield, Vermont, 1973; member of board and teacher, Sagaris (an experimental feminist school in Vermont), 1973-75; writer-in-residence, Cazenovia College, Cazenovia, New York, 1977-78; moved to Charlottesville, Virginia, 1981; founder and president of American Artists, Inc., 1981 (to option novels for television and film); visiting instructor at University of Virginia, 1992. Organizing member, Furies Collective, Washington, D.C., 1971-72; founding editor, *Quest,* 1971; book reviewer for major newspapers since 1978. **Awards:** fiction grant, Massachusetts Council on Arts and Humanities, 1977; fiction grant, National Endowment for the Arts, 1978; shared in Writers Guild of America award and Emmy award nomination, both 1982, both for television special "I Love Liberty"; Emmy Award nomination, 1985, for *The Long Hot Summer;* Literary Lion award, New York Public Library, 1986. **Residence:** Charlottesville, Virginia.

PUBLICATIONS

Novels

Rubyfruit Jungle. 1973.
In Her Day. 1976.
Six Of One. 1978.

Southern Discomfort. 1982.
Sudden Death. 1983.
High Hearts. 1986.
Bingo. 1988.
Wish You Were Here. 1990.
Rest in Pieces. 1992.
Venus Envy. 1993.
Dolley: A Novel of Dolley Madison in Love and War. 1994.
Murder at Monticello, or Old Sins. 1994.
Pay Dirt, or Adventures at Ash Lawn. 1996.
Murder, She Meowed. 1996.
Riding Shotgun. 1997.
Murder on the Prowl. 1998.
Loose Lips. 1999.
Cat on the Scent. 1999.

Poetry

The Hand That Cradles the Rock. 1971.
Songs to a Handsome Woman. 1973.
Poems. 1987.

Prose

A Plain Brown Rapper. 1976.
Starting From Scratch: A Different Kind of Writers' Manual. 1988.
Rita Will: Memoir of a Literary Rabble-Rouser. 1997.

Other

Screenplays: *Sleepless Nights* (produced as *Slumber Party Massacre*), 1982, and *Rubyfruit Jungle.* Television screenplays: *I Love Liberty,* with others, 1982; *The Long Hot Summer,* with others, 1985; *My Two Loves,* with others, 1986.

Translator, *Hrotsvitra: Six Medieval Latin Plays.* 1971.

*

Critical Studies: "Rita Mae Brown: 'The Issue for the Future is Power'" by Delores Alexander in *Ms.,* September 1974; "The Fugitive Hero in New Southern Fiction" by Gary Davenport in *Sewanee Review,* Summer 1983; "Rita Mae Brown: Feminist Theorist and Southern Novelist" by Martha Chew in *Women Writers of the Contemporary South* edited by Peggy Prenshaw, 1984; "Rubyfruit Jungle: Lesbianism, Feminism, and Narcissism" by Leslie Fishbein in *International Journal of Women's Studies,* March/April 1984; "Questions of Genre and Gender: Contemporary American Versions of the Feminine Picaresque" by James Mandrell in *Novel,* Winter 1987; "The Dominant and the Deviant" by Jonathan Dollimore in *Homosexual Themes in Literary Studies* edited by Wayne R. Dynes and Stephen Donaldson, 1992; *Rita Mae Brown* by Carol M. Ward, 1993; in *Ladies Laughing: Wit as Control in Contemporary American Women Writers* by Barbara Levy, 1997; in *The Bluelight Corner: Black Women Writing on Passion, Sex, and Romantic Love,* edited by Rosemarie Robotham, 1999.

*   *   *

"I'm a writer and I'm a woman and I'm from the South," proclaimed Rita Mae Brown in a 1978 *Publisher's Weekly* interview,

in an attempt to refocus critical attention from the openly lesbian-feminist aspect of her fiction to the eternal human verities explored in her controversial literary works. Indeed, her novels have won the admiration of increasingly mainstream audiences because of their broad slapstick humor, their biting social satire of small-town hypocrisy, and their outlandish characters and situations. Her humor and celebration of lesbian themes have endeared her to gay audiences, earning her a respected niche in gay/lesbian literature, while her interest in history, family, and community, particularly in relationship to her rural Southern roots, has broadened her appeal to the general reading public. Although her books have received little serious critical attention from literary scholars, Brown has experimented with narrative structure as she relates her unique vision of society and of the individual's struggles to find her place within it. In Brown's fictional universe, characters are evaluated on their ability to rediscover their "root selves," their basic human natures before society instilled prejudices, labels, definitions, and limits on individual free will. She envisions a world where tolerance and diversity prevail, where basic human goodness emerges, and love is "the wildcard of existence."

Brown's philosophy evolved out of her life experiences; she was able to create in fiction what she could not always have in the real world. Born on November 28, 1944 in Pennsylvania, Brown was adopted in infancy by Ralph and Julia Brown. Despite the loving family ties she developed with the Brown family, the social stigma of illegitimacy and the feeling of not belonging haunted Brown, becoming a major component of her work. The search for a home and the need to strike a balance between individuality and community (a community based on kindred spirit if not on blood) determine the trajectory of her fictional quests for selfhood. Another formative feature of her early autobiography was her emerging sexuality, which also classified her as an outsider, different from the other children. Admittedly "pansexual," Brown experienced rejection by her family and peers in Fort Lauderdale, Florida, where the family had moved in 1955, when her affections for another young woman were discovered by the girl's father. A similar revelation later in college (along with her involvement in the civil rights movement) would lead to the loss of her scholarship and her eventual journey to New York City in search of an education and an accepting environment. These adventures and her eventual reunion with her mother are chronicled in her first novel, *Rubyfruit Jungle* (1973). An immediate cult favorite, *Rubyfruit Jungle* borrows from **Mark Twain** and the picaresque tradition to create a modern feminist Huck Finn in the outspoken heroine Molly Bolt. Bolt shares with Brown a burning desire to transcend without denying her working class background, to employ her wits and education as a weapon against hypocrisy, to be accepted on her own terms without compromise of her ideals and principles.

In New York City, Brown's political consciousness was shaped not only by her own battles against sexism and homophobia but also by the tumultuous social climate of the 1960s. She became an activist for women's rights and for gay rights in such organizations as the Student Homophile League at New York University, the Redstockings (a radical feminist group), the newly formed National Organization for Women (NOW), the Radicalesbians (for which she co-authored the influential lesbian manifesto "Woman Identified Woman"), and later the Furies Collective in Washington, D.C. Her political thought and experience found vivid expression in the many essays she wrote for feminist journals (collected and published in 1976 as *A Plain Brown Rapper*), in her volumes of poetry (*The Hand That Cradles the Rock* in 1971 and *Songs to a Handsome Woman* in 1973), and in a disappointing second novel, *In Her Day* (1976). Relying heavily on her life in the Furies Collective for characters and situations, in this second novel Brown portrays the relationship between a fiery young radical lesbian and a sophisticated college professor who discover that they both have their own contributions to make to the women's movement. The professor decides that she can still contribute to the cause if she moves away from New York to return to her roots in the South, a move that Brown herself made in 1978 when she took up residence in Charlottesville, Virginia.

After the overt politicizing of *In Her Day,* Brown tones down her rhetoric in *Six Of One* (1978), which also deals with the theme of returning home to the South, but does so with restraint, complexity, and power. In what is probably her most artistically successful novel, Brown experiments with a flashback narrative structure as she contemplates the effect of history and the Southern landscape on a community of interrelated women characters, past and present. In it Brown's alter ego Nichole (Nickel) returns to the old family homestead. In the process of her reintegration into society, she observes the antics of her aging mother and aunt and learns the history of a group of extraordinary women (including beautiful and wealthy lesbians, speakeasy proprietors, and socialists), who lived very open and free lives during the tumultuous era from 1909 through World War II. In a central event in the novel, Nickel recalls the legend of her own adoption, a story that directly parallels Brown's own experience. Brown later revisits the mythical town of Runnymede in a loosely related sequel to *Six of One* entitled *Bingo* (1988), which concentrates more straightforwardly on the contemporary set of characters. A jaded and weary Nickel again returns home, this time to recuperate from an unsuccessful lesbian relationship and to run the local newspaper. After an affair with her best friend's husband, Nickel brings the community together with the birth of twins and marriage to the local gay hairdresser, Mr. Pierre.

Southern history continues to fascinate Brown in her next several novels. Set in early twentieth century Montgomery, Alabama, *Southern Discomfort* (1982) contrasts the manners and mores of hypocritical politicians, whorehouse prostitutes, a movie star couple, aspiring middle class blacks, and the upper crust of southern white society. Brown's characters break gender, racial, and social barriers in order to free their spirits from deadly conformity and forge fresh identities. In *High Hearts* (1986), Brown sees the Civil War as a similar time when the normal rules and traditions of society could be bent and broken with liberating effect. Her heroine dons a Confederate uniform, charges off to battle, and discovers her true self in the process.

Brown's romantic relationship with tennis champion Martina Navratilova from 1979 to 1981 is reflected in *Sudden Death* (1983), which Brown claims that she wrote as a promise to a dying friend. An avid tennis player herself, Brown captures the fast-paced world of the professional tennis circuit in thinly veiled portraits of contemporary players, while revealing the sexism and homophobia of the sport. After her separation from Navratilova (and partly because of the financial strain of "divorce"), Brown became more involved in writing for television and movies. Although she has written and sold many scripts, only a few have been produced, with varying results. Her script *Sleepless Nights* was transformed into an exploitative horror film entitled *Slumber Party Massacre* (1982), while her scripts for television, *I Love Liberty* (1982) and *The Long Hot Summer* (1985) were nominated for Emmy Awards.

Her teleplay *My Two Loves* (1986), co-written with Reginald Rose for ABC, was one of the first television movies to deal with lesbianism.

Brown's experiences as a writing instructor at various colleges as well as her belief in the necessity of storytelling led her to encourage future writers with her witty and entertaining writers' manual, *Starting From Scratch* (1988). In it she claims that all writers must be bisexual in order to understand the complexity and diversity of human nature. In other recent writings, in a startling change from the often depressing tones of the heroine of *Bingo,* Brown indulges in the fantasy of a Kitty Crime series of books co-written with her cat Sneaky Pie Brown. Despite the frivolity of such a premise, *Wish You Were Here* (1990) and *Rest in Pieces* (1992) contain Brown's usual astute observations of small-town life and her unique views of human as well as animal behavior. These books, which focus on the heroine's attempt to rebuild her life after her divorce, are the first not to have lesbian characters. Although Brown has expanded her audience with this venture into the mystery genre, she has not left behind her gay readership; *Venus Envy* (1993) confronts the results of a successful woman's coming out to her family and friends in Charlottesville, Virginia. A classical scholar, Brown displays her knowledge in a fanciful sequence where the heroine romps with the ancient gods to achieve a cosmic affirmation of her life. As in her other treatments of the coming out theme, Brown dwells less on the psychological subtleties of homosexuality than on the reaction of others and how the heroine will overcome their prejudice and attempts at social ostracism.

In Brown's universe, the heroine's sexual preference never brings her feelings of guilt, shame, or fear as in much of earlier lesbian literature. Brown's characters believe fiercely in themselves and fight to attain the respect that they deserve. To them, an individual's character is far more important than empty rituals, unquestioned social strictures, and the blind following of tradition. Brown's early political idealism, coupled with her Southern love of the land, has led her to describe a sort of grass roots battle for individual freedom. Social change for women, blacks, and gays is inevitable but it is not easy; as she writes in the introduction to her essay collection, "Change, it becomes apparent, is not a convulsion of history but the slow, steady push of people over decades." People must fight their battles where they are, not just in New York and San Francisco, but in Runnymede and Charlottesville. In addition to this note of optimism, Brown's fiction provides much-needed levity and common sense to lesbian literature, which often reflects more of the negative aspects of homosexuality than the positive. Through the use of humor as a subversive literary device, Brown is able to make people see the possibility for change; her characters not only survive, they triumph.

—Carol M. Ward

BROWN, Sterling A(llen)

Born: Washington, D.C., 1 May 1901. **Education:** Dunbar High School, Washington, D.C.; Williams College, Williamstown, Massachusetts, 1918-22, A.B 1922 (Phi Beta Kappa); Harvard University, Cambridge, Massachusetts, M.A. 1923. **Family:** Married Daisy Turnbull in 1927; one son. **Career:** Teacher at Virginia Seminary and College, Lynchburg, 1923-26, Lincoln University, Jefferson

City, Missouri, 1926-28, and Fisk University, Nashville, Tennessee, 1929; professor of English, Howard University, Washington, D.C. 1929-69, emeritus professor, 1969-89; visiting professor, New York University, New School for Social Research, New York, Vassar College, Poughkeepsie, New York, and University of Minnesota, Minneapolis. Literary editor, *Opportunity* magazine, Washington, D.C., 1930s; editor of *Negro Affairs* for the Federal Writers' Project, 1936-39; staff member, *American Dilemma*. **Awards:** Guggenheim fellowship, 1937; Lenore Marshall prize, 1981; Poet Laureate of the District of Columbia, 1984. Honorary degrees: Atlanta University; Boston University; Brown University, Providence, Rhode Island; Harvard University; Howard University; Lewis and Clark College, Portland, Oregon; Lincoln University, Pennsylvania; University of Maryland, College Park; University of Massachusetts, Amherst; Northwestern University, Evanston, Illinois; University of Pennsylvania, Philadelphia; Williams College; Yale University. **Died:** 13 January 1989.

PUBLICATIONS

Collections

The Collected Poems of Sterling A. Brown, edited by Michael S. Harper. 1980.

Poetry

Southern Road. 1932.
The Last Ride of Wild Bill and Eleven Narrative Poems. 1975.

Other

Outline for the Study of the Poetry of American Negroes (study guide for James Weldon Johnson's *The Book of American Negro Poetry*). 1931.
The Negro in American Fiction. 1937.
Negro Poetry and Drama. 1937.
James Weldon Johnson, with A.B. Spingarn and Carl Van Vechten. c. 1941.
The Negro in Washington, with *The Negro Newcomers in Detroit,* by George Edmund Haynes. 1969.
A Son's Return: Selected Essays of Sterling A. Brown, edited by Mark A. Sanders. 1996.

Editor, *The Negro in Virginia.* 1940.
Editor, with Arthur P. Davis and Ulysses Lee, *The Negro Caravan: Writings by American Negroes.* 2 vols., 1941.

Recording: *A Celebration of Sterling A. Brown, American Poet and Cultural Worker,* 1998.

*

Bibliography: *An Annotated Bibliography of the Works of Sterling A. Brown* by Robert G. O'Meally, in *The Collected Poems* edited by Michael S. Harper, 1980.

Critical Studies: "Brown Issue" in *Callaloo,* February-March 1982; "Sterling Brown, Poet, His Place in Afro-American Literary History" by Charles Nichols, in *The Harlem Renaissance: Re-*

valuations edited by Amritjit Singh, William Shiver, and Stanley Brodwin, 1989; "Sterling A. Brown: Outsider in the Harlem Renaissance" by Robert B. Stepto, in *The Harlem Renaissance: Revaluations* edited by Amritjit Singh, William Shiver, and Stanley Brodwin, 1989; "Sterling Brown's Folk Odyssey" by John S. Wright, in *American Literature, Culture, and Ideology: Essays in Memory of Henry Nash Smith* edited by Beverly R. Voloshin, 1990; "The Ballad, the Hero, and the Ride: A Reading of Sterling A. Brown's *The Ride of Wild Bill*" by Mark A. Sanders, in *College Language Association Journal,* December 1994, pp. 162-82; "Irony without Condescension: Sterling A. Brown's Nod to Robert Frost" by Mark Jeffreys, in *Literary Influence and African-American Writers* edited by Tracy Mishkin, 1996; "The Role of Music in the Self-Reflexive Poetry of the Harlem Renaissance" by Hartmut Grandel, in *Poetics in the Poem: Critical Essays on American Self-Reflexive Poetry* edited by Dorothy Z. Baker, 1997.

*   *   *

Essentially a traditional song maker and storyteller, Sterling A. Brown witnessed crosscurrents of American literature and chose in his poetry to depict blacks and the clash of their roles with those of whites in the variegated society of the American South, particularly in the time caught between two world wars. Analyzing Brown's "tragic universe" in his book *Black Poets of the United States,* Jean Wagner notices that the "dominant note in Brown's poetry is provided by his acute understanding of the tragic destiny that had been the black people's on the American soil." Brown's poetry depicts and orchestrates the dramatic notes of that particular atmosphere, the cosmic and universally tragic time and space in which "the characters" of his poems are forced to live their lives. The tragedy of the black people becomes a universal tragedy, and their destinies are perceived as a collective saga of sorrow. "No one else had depicted the black man as so alone and powerless, confronting a universe all of whose elements are in league against him," says Wagner.

The 1920s, when Brown graduated, were the years of the Harlem Renaissance, the era of the New Negro, effervescent times of change, when black artists tried to create a universe of their own, a new and strong culture deeply rooted in the African tradition. His poetry was collected in anthologies as early as **James Weldon Johnson**'s *The Book of American Negro Poetry* (1922), and, like Johnson himself and **Langston Hughes**, he set about disrupting the patently false and banal image of the docile American Negro with his charming *patois,* artificially stylized and mimicked by the whites in the minstrel shows still popular in the 1920s and 1930s. Johnson says in his preface on Hughes and Brown that they "*do* use a dialect, but it is not the dialect of the comic minstrel tradition or the sentimental plantation tradition; it is the common, racy, 'living, authentic speech of the Negro in certain phases of real life."

Brown uses original Afro-American ballads such as "Casey Jones," "John Henry," and "Staggolee" as counterpoint for his modern ones, but the portent of his ironic wit should not be underestimated, for it is actually a tool to shape an ironic, infernal vision of American life as Hades: "The Place was Dixie I took for Hell," says Slim in "Slim in Hell." The American Negro is heralded not as Black Orpheus but as modern tragic hero Mose, a leader of *all* people while futilely attempting to save his own: "A soft song, filled with a misery/Older than Mose will be." In "Sharecropper" he is broken as Christ was broken; his landlord "shot him in the side" to put him out of his misery; he is lost and wild as Odysseus in "Odyssey of a Big Boy"; and found again:

Man wanta live
Man want find himself
Man gotta learn
How to go it alone.

Though small in quantity, Brown's poetry is epic in conception; his ballad, blues, and jazz forms are the vehicles for creative insight into themes of American life.

—Carol Lee Saffioti, updated by Dayana Stetco

BROWN, William Wells

Born: In 1813 on a plantation near Lexington, Kentucky; son of a slave owner and one of his slaves. **Family:** Married Elizabeth Schooner in 1834; three daughters. **Career:** Taken to St. Louis as a boy and hired out on a steamboat; worked in the print shop of the editor of the St. Louis *Times;* then again hired out on a steamboat; escaped from slavery to Cincinnati, 1834 (assumed the name of a man who befriended him); moved to Cleveland, then to Monroe, Michigan, where he ran a barbershop and set up a bank; steamboat steward on Lake Erie and helped fugitive slaves escape to Canada; moved to Buffalo, 1836, and became active in abolitionist activities: lecturer for abolitionist movement, New York and Massachusetts, 1843-49, and England, 1849-54; also associated with other reform movements: represented the American Peace Society at the Peace Congress, Paris, 1849; studied medicine and had medical practice in Boston for many years. **Died:** 6 November 1884.

PUBLICATIONS

Fiction

Clotel; or, The President's Daughter: A Narrative of Slave Life in the United States. 1853; other versions published as *Clotelle: A Tale of the Southern States,* 1864, and *Clotelle; or, The Colored Heroine,* 1867; edited by William Edward Farrison, with *Narrative of Brown,* 1969.

Play

The Escape; or, A Leap for Freedom. 1858.

Other

Narrative of Brown, A Fugitive Slave. 1847; revised edition, 1848, 1849; edited by William Edward Farrison, with *Clotel,* 1969.
Three Years in Europe; or, Places I Have Seen and People I Have Met. 1852; revised edition, as *The American Fugitive in Europe,* 1855.
The Black Man: His Antecedents, His Genius, and His Achievements. 1863; revised edition, 1863.
The Negro in the American Rebellion: His Heroism and His Fidelity. 1867.

The Rising Son; or, The Antecedents and Advancement of the Colored Race. 1874.
My Southern Home; or, The South and Its People. 1880.

Editor, *The Anti-Slavery Harp: A Collection of Songs for Anti-Slavery Meetings.* 1848.

*

Bibliography: *Brown and Martin R. Delany: A Reference Guide* by Curtis W. Ellison and E.W. Metcalf, 1978.

Critical Studies: *Brown, Author and Reformer* (includes bibliography) by William Edward Farrison, 1969; *Brown and Clotelle: A Portrait of the Artist in the First Negro Novel* by J. Noel Heermance, 1969; *My Chains Fell Off: Brown, Fugitive Abolitionist* by L.H. Whelchel, Jr., 1985; "Mark Twain, William Wells Brown, and the Problem of Authority in New South Writing" by William H. Andrews, in *Southern Literature and Literary Theory* edited by Jefferson Humphries, 1990; "Her Side of His Story: A Feminist Analysis of Two Nineteenth-Century Antebellum Novels—William Wells Browns' *Clotel* and Harriet E. Wilson's *Our Nig*" by Angelyn Mitchell, in *American Literary Realism, 1870-1910* spring, 1992; *To Steal Away Home: Tracing Race, Slavery, and Difference in Selected Writings of Thomas Jefferson, David Walker, William Wells Brown, Ralph Waldo Emerson, and Pauline Elizabeth Hopkins* (dissertation) by Verner D. Mitchell, 1995; "Representing Slavery in Nineteenth-Century Britain: The Anxiety of Non/Fictional Authorship in Charles Dickens' *American Notes* and William Brown's *Clotel*" by M. Giulia Fabi, in *Images of America: Through the European Looking-Glass* edited by William L. Chew, 1997; "Whiseky, Blacking and All: Temperance and Race in William Wells Brown's *Clotel*" by Robert S. Levine, in *The Serpent in the Cup: Temperance in American Literature* edited by David S. Reynolds and Debra J. Rosenthal, 1997.

*   *   *

Born a slave in Kentucky, William Wells Brown was schooled by the "peculiar institution" for life-long work as a reformer. Within two years of his own escape from bondage in 1834, he was conducting others to freedom on the underground railroad, and by the 1850s he was among the most famous abolitionists in Europe as well as America.

Crusaders then as now employed every medium available to their talents to advance their cause. In this company, Brown was remarkable, for besides oration and documentary reports he also produced a novel, a European travel book, plays, several historical studies, and reflective memoirs. The novel, *Clotel,* the travel book, *Three Years in Europe,* and the five-act drama, *The Escape,* are first examples of their type written by a black American. Together with the range of his other writings they assure Brown a place in American literary history.

Brown's narrative of life in slavery was a bestseller. His novel found a broad audience by virtue of its appearance in several versions, and his histories and recollections went through multiple editions. Their contemporary appeal seems to have been due largely to their reaffirmation of standard arguments in their use of familiar literary conventions.

Yet it is the evident redundancy in his work that accounts for Brown's present significance. In his autobiography, Brown's first published book, he describes his master as stealing him as soon as he was born. His mother, he explains, bore seven children by seven different men, including a white relative of the master, who fathered William. Each infant was claimed by the master as his property without regard to lineage or paternal affection. William and his mother tried to escape slavery but were caught, and his mother sold into the deep South "to die on a . . . plantation!" Later, when he made his way alone to freedom in Ohio, he joined the name his mother had given him with that of Wells Brown, his first white friend and surrogate father. These autobiographical facts reveal the terms in which Brown saw destiny. Thus, his fiction centers upon mulatto characters whose very existence images violation and relates incidents where neither blood, race, nor intimacy prevent subjugation. Carried into nonfiction, where he argued the case for equality on the basis of achievement and service, Brown adapts his motifs into a plea for reconciliation within the human family.

It is repeated examination of fate in an America where essential humanity is divided by brutal practice that gives Brown continued importance. For this first black man of letters established in literature the prevalent Afro-American concern with identity.

—John M. Reilly

BRYANT, William Cullen

Born: Cummington, Massachusetts, 3 November 1794. **Education:** Privately educated and at Williams College, Williamstown, Massachusetts, 1810-11; studied law under Elias Howe, Worthington, Massachusetts, 1811-14, and in the office of William Baylies, Bridgewater, Massachusetts, 1814-15: admitted to the Massachusetts bar, 1815. **Family:** Married Frances Fairchild in 1821 (died 1866); two daughters. **Career:** Lawyer, Plainfield, 1816, and Great Barrington, 1817-25, both Massachusetts; editor, with Henry J. Anderson, *New York Review and Athenaeum Magazine,* 1825-26; assistant editor, *United States Review,* 1826-27; assistant editor, 1826-29, and editor and part owner, 1829-78, New York *Evening Post.* President, American Free Trade League, 1865-69. **Died:** 12 June 1878.

PUBLICATIONS

Collections

Poetical Works, Prose Writings, edited by Parke Godwin. 4 vols., 1883-84.
Poetical Works, edited by Henry C. Sturges and Richard Henry Stoddard. 1903.
Selections, edited by Samuel Sillen. 1945.
Letters, edited by William Cullen Bryant II and Thomas G. Voss. 6 vols., 1975-92.

Poetry

The Embargo; or, Sketches of the Times: A Satire. 1808.
The Embargo and Other Poems. 1809.
Poems. 1821.
Poems. 1832; London edition, edited by Washington Irving, 1832; revised edition, 1834, 1836, 1850.
The Fountain and Other Poems. 1842.

The White-Footed Deer and Other Poems. 1844.
Poems. 2 vols., 1855.
Thirty Poems. 1864.
Hymns. 1864; revised edition, 1869.
Poems. 1871.
Poems. 3 vols., 1875.
Poems. 1876.

Other

Letters of a Traveller; or, Notes of Things Seen in Europe and America. 1850; as *The Picturesque Souvenir,* 1851.
Reminiscences of The Evening Post. 1851.
Letters of a Traveller, Second Series. 1859.
A Discourse on the Life, Character, and Genius of Washington Irving. 1860.
Letters from the East. 1869.
Some Notices of the Life and Writings of Fitz-Greene Halleck. 1869.
Orations and Addresses. 1873.

Editor, *Tales of Glauber-Spa.* 2 vols., 1832.
Editor, *Selections from the American Poets.* 1840.
Editor, *The Berkshire Jubilee.* 1845.
Editor, *A Library of Poetry and Song.* 1871; revised edition, as *A New Library,* 1876(?).
Editor, with Oliver B. Bunce, *Picturesque America; or, The Land We Live In.* 2 vols., 1872-74.
Editor, *A Popular History of the United States,* vols. 1-2, by Sydney Howard Gay. 1876-78.
Editor, with Evert A. Duyckinck, *Complete Works of Shakespeare.* 25 vols., 1888.

Translator, *The Iliad and The Odyssey of Homer.* 4 vols., 1870-72.

*

Bibliography: in *Bibliography of American Literature* by Jacob Blanck, 1955; *A Bibliography of Bryant and His Critics, 1808-1972* by Judith T. Phair, 1975.

Critical Studies: *A Biography of Bryant* (includes letters) by Parke Godwin, 2 vols., 1883; *Gotham Yankee: A Biography of Bryant* by Harry Houston Peckham, 1950; *Politics and a Belly Full: The Journalistic Career of Bryant* by Curtiss S. Johnson, 1962; *Bryant* by Albert F. McLean, Jr., 1964, revised edition, 1989; *Bryant* by Charles H. Brown, 1971; *Bryant and His America* edited by Stanley Brodwin and Michael D'Innocenzo, 1983; "The Poet As Planter: William Cullen Bryant, Landscaper and Horticulturalist" by Cathy E. Sabol, in *Plants and People* edited by Peter Benes and Jane Montague Benes, 1995; "The Unsurveyed Interior: William Cullen Bryant and the Prairie State" by Jack Vespa, in *American Transcendental Quarterly,* December 1997, pp. 285-308; "William Cullen Bryant to Josiah Whitney Barstow: Three Letters" by George Monteiro, in *ANQ: A Quarterly Journal of Short Articles, Notes, and Reviews,* spring 1998, pp. 32-34.

*   *   *

When in his poem "The Poet" William Cullen Bryant urges a writer to eschew the "empty gust / Of passion" but to express "feelings of calm power and mighty sweep, / Like currents journeying through the windless deep," he is making an apt comment on his own best work. For though in "A Fable for Critics" **James Russell Lowell** goes too far in joking at Bryant for his coldness, his lack of enthusiasm, his "supreme *ice*olation," Bryant's strong points are indeed not passion, not delicacy, not soaring imagination, but dignity and power. Even though his lighter poems sound a strong didactic note that reminds one that his literary forebears were New England Puritans, his work also has overtones of the sober eighteenth-century neoclassicism of Gray and Collins. He is at his best when with stately force he depicts the grand sweeping cycle of life that carries all away with its resistless current.

Thus, his first major poem, "Thanatopsis," written in the tradition of the British Graveyard Poets in sober, resounding lines, pictures man, even new American man, living on the tombs of countless races. When we too join the caravan to the inevitable tomb, Bryant says, may we face our fate with stoic dignity. "The Journey of Life," "The Ages," "The Past," and "The Flood of Years," though with a more specifically Christian hope of immortality, similarly emphasize with stately resonance and images the cyclical patterns of human existence. The same theme is effectively voiced in such poems as "The Prairies," "Monument Mountain," and "An Indian at the Burial Place of His Fathers," which delineate the successive destruction of America's aboriginal races and remind the white man that he too may disappear. Because of such epic grandeur in his own themes it is not surprising that Bryant was a highly successful translator of Homer.

But the classic dignity of much of Bryant's best work is nicely balanced by his Romantic sense of the soothing power and divinity of nature. Bryant was America's first major Romantic poet. Poems like "A Forest Hymn," "Green River," and "Inscription for the Entrance to a Wood" earnestly inculcate the creed that nature can give solace to the weary heart. Some of these poems verge on pantheism and foreshadow **Ralph Waldo Emerson**'s doctrine that the divine creation has never ceased. Throughout even the simple nature poems, such as "The Yellow Violet" and "To a Fringed Gentian," Bryant preaches sometimes somberly, sometimes wittily; his favorite lyric form is a series of descriptive stanzas followed by one or two of moral. Though he is playful in "A Meditation on Rhode Island Coal" and "Robert of Lincoln," he rarely writes for fun. Yet in such a poem as "To a Waterfowl" he can so superbly blend his moralism with telling imagery and restrained emotion that it becomes an integral part of a powerful work of art, indeed one of America's finest lyrics.

Though Bryant was intensely concerned with mutability and nature, he was also acutely awake to American life around him. His first published volume, *The Embargo,* was a satire against the Jeffersonians. Not only was he the writer of powerful liberal editorials in the New York *Evening Post,* of which for many years he was editor, but he also wrote many effective and graceful occasional poems such as his elegy on Lincoln. Like the Hudson River School painters with whom he was closely associated (see "To Cole, The Painter, Departing for Europe"), he patriotically celebrated American landscape, American nature, and American history and legend. He even edited a collection of essays and engravings entitled *Picturesque America.* He wrote on popular causes such as slavery ("The African Chief") and Greek independence ("The Massacre at Scio"). Sometimes, as in "The Death of the Flowers," he verged toward the mawkish sentimentalism that was the bane of America's "Feminine Fifties," but his lack of pretentiousness, quiet integrity, and basic good sense, seen also in his anthologies of American poetry and especially in his first-rate critical essays on poets and poetry, generally saved him from banality. Like so many American authors of his time he also wrote hymns.

With some justice Bryant's poetry has been derogated as bloodless, undramatic, too orotund, too much concerned with death and mutability, out of touch with vivid life, even morbid. To read his verse, Marius Bewley says, is "a little like listening to a harmonium with the pedal stuck," and his poetry gives the impression of "a best parlor filled with marmoreal statuary." But such comment is unfair. Bryant is a significant pioneer in American literature. His best work is also still worthy to be read for what Lowell calls "the grace, strength, and dignity" of his art and for the quiet depth and earnestness of his vision of the ever-flowing stream of nature and human life. His was surely the most powerful poetic voice in America between **Edward Taylor** and **Edgar Allan Poe.**

—Curtis Dahl

See the essay on "Thanatopsis."

BUCK, Pearl S(ydenstricker)

Born: Hillsboro, West Virginia, 26 June 1892; daughter of Presbyterian missionaries in China. **Education:** Boarding school in Shanghai, 1907-09; Randolph-Macon Woman's College, Lynchburg, Virginia, B.A. 1914 (Phi Beta Kappa); Cornell University, Ithaca, New York, M.A. 1926. **Family:** Married 1) John Lossing Buck in 1917 (divorced 1935), one daughter; 2) Richard J. Walsh in 1935 (died 1960); eight adopted children. **Career:** Psychology teacher, Randolph-Macon Woman's College, 1914; English teacher, University of Nanking, 1921-31, Southeastern University, Nanking, 1925-27, and Chung Yang University, Nanking, 1928-31; returned to the United States, 1935; coeditor, *Asia* magazine, New York, 1941-46; founder and director, *East and West* Association, 1941-51; founder, Welcome House, an adoption agency, 1949, and Pearl S. Buck Foundation, 1964; member of the board of directors, Weather Engineering Corporation of America, Manchester, New Hampshire, 1966. **Awards:** Pulitzer prize, 1932; American Academy Howells Medal, 1935; Nobel prize for Literature, 1938; National Conference of Christians and Jews Brotherhood award, 1955; President's Commission on Employment of the Physically Handicapped citation, 1958; Women's National Book Association Skinner award, 1960; ELA award, 1969. M.A.: Yale University, New Haven, Connecticut, 1933. D.Litt.: University of West Virginia, Morgantown, 1940; St. Lawrence University, Canton, New York, 1942; Delaware Valley College, Doylestown, Pennsylvania, 1965. LL.D.: Howard University, Washington, D.C.. 1942; Muhlenberg College, Allentown, Pennsylvania, 1966. L.H.D.: Lincoln University, Pennsylvania, 1953; Woman's Medical College of Philadelphia, 1954; University of Pittsburgh, 1960; Bethany College, West Virginia, 1963; Hahnemann Medical College, Philadelphia, 1966; Rutgers University, New Brunswick, New Jersey. 1969. D.Mus.: Combs College of Music, Philadelphia, 1962. D.H.: West Virginia State College, Institute, 1963. **Member:** American Academy. **Died:** 6 March 1973.

PUBLICATIONS

Fiction

East Wind: West Wind. 1930.
The Good Earth. 1931.
Sons. 1932.
The First Wife and Other Stories. 1933.
The Mother. 1934.
A House Divided. 1935.
House of Earth. 1935.
This Proud Heart. 1938.
The Patriot. 1939.
Other Gods: An American Legend. 1940.
Today and Forever: Stories of China. 1941.
China Sly. 1942.
Dragon Seed. 1942.
The Promise. 1943.
China Flight. 1945.
The Townsman. 1945.
Portrait of a Marriage. 1945.
Pavilion of Women. 1946.
The Angry Wife. 1947.
Far and Near: Stories of Japan, China, and America. 1948.
Peony. 1948; as *The Bondmaid,* 1949.
Kinfolk. 1949.
The Long Love. 1949.
God's Men. 1950.
The Hidden Flower. 1952.
Satan Never Sleeps. 1952.
Bright Procession. 1952.
Come, My Beloved. 1953.
Voices in the House. 1953.
Imperial Woman. 1956.
Letter from Peking. 1957.
Command the Morning. 1959.
Fourteen Stories. 1961; as *With a Delicate Air and Other Stories,* 1962.
Hearts Come Home and Other Stories. 1962.
The Living Reed. 1963.
Stories of China. 1964.
Death in the Castle. 1965.
The Time Is Noon. 1967.
The New Year. 1968.
The Good Deed and Other Stories of Asia, Past and Present. 1969.
The Three Daughters of Madame Liang. 1969.
Mandala. 1970.
The Goddess Abides. 1972.
All under Heaven. 1973.
The Rainbow. 1974.
Book of Christmas (stories). 1974.
East and West (stories). 1975.
Secrets of the Heart (stories). 1976.
The Lovers and Other Stories. 1977.
The Woman Who Was Changed and Other Stories. 1979.

Plays

Flight into China (produced 1939).
Sun Yat Sen: A Play, Preceded by a Lecture by Dr. Hu-Shih. 1944(?).

China to America (radio play), in *Free World Theatre,* edited by Arch Oboler and Stephen Longstreet. 1944.
Will This Earth Hold? (radio play), in *Radio Drama in Action,* edited by Erik Barnouw. 1945.
The First Wife (produced 1945).
A Desert Incident (produced 1959).
Christine, with Charles K. Peck, Jr., music by Sammy Fain, from the book *My Indian Family* by Hilda Wernher (produced 1960).
The Guide, from the novel by R.K. Narayan (produced 1965).

Screenplays: *The Big Wave,* with Ted Danielewski, 1962; *The Guide,* with Danielewski, 1965.

Poetry

Words of Love. 1974.

Other (for children)

The Young Revolutionist. 1932.
Stories for Little Children. 1940.
When Fun Begins. 1941.
The Chinese Children Next Door. 1942.
The Water Buffalo Children. 1943.
The Dragon Fish. 1944.
Yu Lan: Flying Boy of China. 1945.
The Big Wave. 1948.
One Bright Day. 1950; as *One Bright Day and Other Stories for Children,* 1952.
The Man Who Changed China: The Story of Sun Yat Sen. 1953.
The Beech Tree. 1954.
Johnny Jack and His Beginnings. 1954.
Christmas Miniature. 1957; as *The Christmas Mouse,* 1958.
The Christmas Ghost. 1960.
Welcome Child. 1964.
The Big Fight. 1965.
The Little Fox in the Middle. 1966.
Matthew, Mark, Luke, and John. 1967.
The Chinese Storyteller. 1971.
A Gift for the Children. 1973.
Mrs. Starling's Problem. 1973.

Other

Is There a Case for Foreign Missions? 1932.
East and West and the Novel: Sources of the Early Chinese Novel. 1932.
The Exile (biography). 1936.
Fighting Angel: Portrait of a Soul (biography). 1936.
The Chinese Novel. 1939.
Of Men and Women. 1941.
American Unity and Asia. 1942; as *Asia and Democracy,* 1943.
What America Means to Me. 1943.
Talk about Russia, with Masha Scott. 1945.
Tell the People: Talks with James Yen about the Mass Education Movement. 1945.
How It Happens: Talk about the German People. 1914-1933, with Erna von Pustau. 1947.
American Argument, with Eslanda Goode Robeson. 1949.
The Child Who Never Grew. 1950.
My Several Worlds (autobiography). 1954.

Friend to Friend, with Carlos P. Romulo. 1958.
The Delights of Learning. 1960.
A Bridge for Passing (autobiography). 1962.
The Joy of Children. 1964.
The Gifts They Bring: Our Debts to the Mentally Retarded, with Gweneth T. Zarfoss. 1965.
Children for Adoption. 1965.
The People of Japan. 1966.
For Spacious Skies: Journey in Dialogue, with Theodore F. Harris. 1966.
My Mothers House, with others. 1966.
To My Daughters, With Love. 1967.
The People of China. 1968.
The Kennedy Women: A Personal Appraisal. 1970.
China as I See It, edited by Theodore F. Harris. 1970.
The Story Bible. 1971.
China Past and Present. 1972.
A Community Success Story: The Founding of the Pearl Buck Center. 1972.
Oriental Cookbook. 1972.

Editor, *China in Black and White: An Album of Woodcuts by Contemporary Chinese Artists.* 1945.
Editor, *Fairy Tales of the Orient.* 1965.

Translator, *All Men Are Brothers,* by Shui Hu Chan. 2 vols., 1933.

*

Bibliography: by Lucille S. Zinn, in *Bulletin of Bibliography 36,* 1979.

Critical Studies: *Buck* by Paul A. Doyle, 1965, revised edition, 1980; *Buck: A Biography* by Theodore F. Harris, 2 vols., 1969-71; *Buck: A Woman in Conflict* by Nora Stirling, 1983; *Pearl S. Buck: A Cultural Biography* by Peter J. Conn, 1996.

*   *   *

The amount and variety of Pearl S. Buck's writing and the strong correlation between her writing and her life make critical analysis complex. She admired the work of such naturalists as Zola and **Dreiser** and often emphasized the power of nature and culture, but she was never sordid nor pessimistic, and her realistic details of places, events, and people are organized around such romantic tenets as individuality, the nobility of common people, the corrupting influence of wealth and cities, and the universal interest in "love." Her years in China, her missionary connections, her exposure to many forms of domestic life, and her humanitarian projects furnished both the material and the themes of her stories. And while her masterpiece, *The Good Earth,* and the biographies of her parents, *The Exile* and *Fighting Angel,* are widely regarded as classics, much of the rest of her work is of uneven artistic merit.

The Good Earth achieves a perfect blending of appropriate diction, informative detail, epic structure, and universal themes. Such semi-biblical lines as "I am with child," and such "Chinese" lines as "There is this woman of mine," are held together with such thematic lines as: "He had no articulate thought of anything; there was only this perfect sympathy of movement, of turning this earth of theirs over and over to the sun, this earth which formed their

home and fed their bodies and made their gods." Occasionally there are poetic lines as delicate as a Chinese painting: "A small soft wind blew gently from the east, a wind mild and murmurous and full of rain." While she used a similar style in her other Chinese books, she both modernized and Americanized the language when appropriate.

The Good Earth is the "epic" of a "rags-to-riches" farmer-hero of Old China, practicing his native customs but experiencing the universal drama of birth and death, prosperity and famine, work and sex, tradition and change. The plot is structured by Wang's relationship to three wives—and to his land. The "good" wives sympathize with his love of the land; the "bad" wife hates the land. Like nearly all of Buck's male characters, Wang is inept in human relations, controlled by forces he never understands, yet capable of resisting social pressure and remaining loyal to personal qualities of honesty and kindness. In contrast, nearly all of her female characters are wiser, or craftier, than the men they are destined to serve—an "autobiographical" point of view especially apparent in *This Proud Heart, Pavilion of Women, Peony,* and *Letter from Peking.*

Throughout her writing Buck portrays religion, slavery, economic tyranny, war, and government as capable of being manipulated by individuals. And although she occasionally generalizes about settings or classes, her character development is consistent, the variety of her "solutions" credible. Certainly her informative depiction of cultural conflicts served her overriding aims—freedom and reconciliation.

—Esther Marian Greenwell Smith

BULLINS, Ed

Born: Philadelphia, Pennsylvania, 2 July 1935. **Education:** Philadelphia public schools; at William Penn Business Institute, Philadelphia; Los Angeles City College; San Francisco State College. **Military Service:** Served in the U.S. Navy, 1952-55. **Career:** Playwright-in-residence and associate director, New Lafayette Theatre, Harlem, New York, 1967-73; Mellon Lecturer, Amherst College, Massachusetts, 1977; since 1995 professor of theater, Northeastern University, Boston, Massachusetts. Editor, *Black Theatre* magazine, New York, 1969-74. New York Shakespeare Festival, writers unit coordinator/press assistant, 1975-82; New York University, School of Continuing Education, instructor of dramatic writing, 1981; Berkeley Black Repertory, public relations director, 1982; City College of San Francisco, CA, instructor in drama, 1984-88; Antioch University, CA, student instructor of playwriting and assistant in public information and recruitment, 1986-87; The Bullins Memorial Theatre, Emeryville, CA, producer/playwright, 1988; lecturer at Sonoma University, CA, and University of California, Berkeley. **Awards:** Rockefeller grant, 1968, 1970, 1973; Vernon Rice award, 1968; American Place grant, 1968; Obie award, 1971, 1975; Guggenheim grant, 1971, and fellowship 1976; Creative Artists Public Service grant, 1973; National Endowment for the Arts grant, 1974; AUDELCO award, Harlem Theatre; New York Drama Critics Circle award, 1975, 1977. D.L.: Columbia College, Chicago, 1976; Gwendolyn Brooks Center for Black Literature and Creative Writing award, Chicago State University, 1993; National Black Theatre Festival "Living Legend" award, 1997. **Residence:** Roxbury, Massachusetts.

Collections

New/Lost Plays by Ed Bullins: Six Plays, edited by Ethel Pitts-Walker. 1994.

Plays

How Do You Do? (produced 1965). 1965.
Clara's Ole Man (produced 1965). In *Five Plays*, 1969.
Dialect Determinism; or, The Rally (produced 1965). In *The Theme Is Blackness*, 1973.
The Theme Is Blackness (produced 1966). In *The Theme Is Blackness*, 1973.
It Has No Choice (produced 1966). In *The Theme Is Blackness*, 1973.
A Minor Scene (produced 1966). In *The Theme is Blackness*, 1973.
The Game of Adam and Eve, with Shirley Tarbell (produced 1966).
In New England Winter (produced 1967). In *New Plays from the Black Theatre*, edited by Bullins, 1969.
In the Wine Time (produced 1968). In *Five Plays*, 1969.
A Son, Come Home (produced New York, 1968). In *Five Plays*, 1969.
The Electronic Nigger (produced 1968). In *Five Plays*, 1969.
Goin' a Buffalo: A Tragifantasy (produced 1968). In *Five Plays*, 1969.
The Gentleman Caller (produced 1969). In *Illuminations 5*, 1968; in *The Black Quartet*.
The Corner (produced 1968).
Five Plays. 1969; as *The Electronic Nigger and Other Plays*, 1970.
We Righteous Bombers, from a work by Camus (produced 1969).
The Man Who Dug Fish (produced 1969). In *The Theme Is Blackness*, 1973.
Street Sounds (produced 1970). In *The Theme Is Blackness*, 1973.
The Helper (produced 1970). In *The Theme Is Blackness*, 1973.
A Ritual To Raise the Dead and Foretell the Future (produced 1970). In *The Theme Is Blackness*, 1973.
The Fabulous Miss Marie (produced 1970). In *The New Lafayette Theatre Presents*, edited by Bullins, 1974.
Four Dynamite Plays: It Bees Dat Way, Death List, The Pig Pen, Night of the Beast (produced 1970). 1971.
The Duplex: A Black Love Fable in Four Movements (produced 1970). 1971.
The Devil Catchers (produced 1971).
The Psychic Pretenders (produced 1972).
You Gonna Let Me Take You Out Tonight, Baby (produced 1972).
Next Time, in *City Stops* (produced 1972).
House Party, music by Pat Patrick, lyrics by Bullins (produced 1973).
The Theme Is Blackness: The Corner and Other Plays (includes *Dialect Determinism, or The Rally; It Has No Choice; The Helper; A Minor Scene; The Theme Is Blackness; The Man Who Dug Fish; Street Sounds;* and the scenarios and short plays *Black Commercial No. 2, The American Flag Ritual, State Office Bldg. Curse, One-Minute Commercial, A Street Play, A Short Play for a Small Theatre,* and *The Play of the Play*). 1973.
The Taking of Miss Janie (produced 1975). In *Famous American Plays of the1970s*.
The Mystery of Phyllis Wheatley (produced 1976).
I Am Lucy Terry (produced 1976). In *New/Lost Plays of Ed Bullins*, 1994.

Jo Anne!!! (produced 1976). In *New/Lost Plays of Ed Bullins*, 1994.
Home Boy, music by Aaron Bell, lyrics by Bullins (produced 1976).
Daddy (produced 1977).
Sepia Star, music and lyrics by Mildred Kayden (produced 1977).
Storyville, music and lyrics by Mildred Kayden (produced 1977; revised version, produced 1979).
Michael (produced 1978).
C'mon Back to Heavenly House (produced 1978).
Leavings (produced 1980).
Steve and Velma (produced 1980).

Screenplays: *Night of the Beast*, 1971; *The Ritual Masters*, 1972.

Fiction

The Hungered One: Early Writings. 1971.
The Reluctant Rapist. 1973.

Poetry

To Raise the Dead and Foretell the Future. 1971.

Other

Editor, *New Plays from the Black Theatre*. 1969.
Editor, *The New Lafayette Theatre Presents: Plays with Aesthetic Comments by 6 Black Playwrights*. 1974.

*

Bibliography: in *Black Image on the American Stage* by James V. Hatch, 1970.

Critical Studies: "The Polished Protest: Aesthetics and the Black Writer" in *Contact Magazine*, 1962; "The Theatre of Reality" in *Black World*, 1966; "Up from Politics" in *Performance*, 1972; "Bullins: The Quest and Failure of an Ethnic Community Theatre" by Peter Bruck, in *Essays on Contemporary American Drama* edited by Hedwig Bock and Albert Wertheim, 1981; "'Dialect Determinism': Bullins' Critique of the Rhetoric of the Black Power Movement" by Leslie Sanders, in *Belief vs Theory in Black American Literary Criticism* edited by Joe Weixlmann and Chester Fontenot, 1986; "Bullins: Black Theatre as Ritual" by Arlene Elder, in *Connections: Essays on Black Literatures* edited by Emmanuel Nelson, 1988; *Ed Bullins: A Literary Biography* by Samuel A. Hay, 1997.

*   *   *

Ed Bullins is the most original and prolific playwright of the American Black Theatre movement. To quote him: "To make an open secret more public: in the area of playwriting, Ed Bullins, at this moment in time, is almost without peer in America—black, white or imported." Written in 1973, the statement exaggerates little. It appears in *The Theme Is Blackness*, a title that polemically reduces Bullins's actual thematic range; he dramatizes many relationships of black people—family, friendship, business, the business of crime. From urban black ghettos Bullins draws characters who speak with humor, obscenity, and sophistication. Whereas **Langston Hughes** had to strain to capture underworld idiom in Harlem, Bullins modulates a language that ignores the black as well as the white middle class.

As ambitious as **Eugene O'Neill,** Bullins has embarked on a Twentieth Century Cycle of twenty plays, to depict the lives of certain Afro-Americans between 1900 and 1999. The first five plays very loosely trace the experiences of the Dawsons—it would be inaccurate to call them a family, since the men find households, abandon them, disappear, reappear. Even incomplete, the cycle stresses the necessarily fragmentary nature of relationships of black urban males in twentieth-century America. Each of the plays focuses on a complete action, free in dramatic form, often embellished with song and dance, rich in rhythmic speech and terse imagery that Bullins crafts so beautifully. Indefatigable, Bullins has also written agit-prop Dynamite Plays, in which his anti-white rage is indistinguishable from that of **Amiri Baraka.** Other extra-cycle plays resemble Chekhov in their evocation of a dying class, e.g., *Clara's Ole Man* and *Goin' a Buffalo.* Like Chekhov, Bullins dramatizes the foibles of his people, endearing them to us through a poignant humor. Bullins, however, questioned the idea of theatre as mere entertainment. As long as the public continued to regard theatre as a Fun House, no change could be expected in "the vacuum" existing in the modern American theatre, as William Couch, Jr., puts it in his "Introduction" to New Black Playwrights.

The unrecorded troubled history of the African Americans deserves wonderful moments of spontaneity and creativity contained by the plays of the modern Black writers. Bullins's dramatic work suggests that however "revolutionary" these spontaneous moments may be, they bring forth the claims of a younger generation of playwrights, a revival of the theatre tradition itself, and, for what it is worth, an attempt to educate the public in appreciating something that is beyond stereotypical behavior and entertainment.

—Ruby Cohn, updated by Dayana Stetco

BULOSAN, Carlos

Born: Binalonan, Pangasinan, Philippines, 24 November 1914; immigrated to the United States in 1931. **Education:** Public school in Binalonan and high school in Lingayen; quit school to go to work; mainly self-educated during two-year hospitalization for tuberculosis in the United States. **Career:** Worked as field laborer and market helper in the Philippines; migrant laborer on farms and in canneries from Southern California to Alaska in United States; union activist, 1935-41. **Died:** 11 September 1956.

PUBLICATIONS

Collections

The Power of the People, edited by Epifanio San Juan, Jr. 1977.
If You Want to Know What We Are: A Carlos Bulosan Reader, edited by Epifanio San Juan, Jr. 1983.
On Becoming Fillipino: Selected Writings of Carlos Bulosan. 1995.

Short Stories

The Philippines Is in the Heart: A Collection of Short Stories, edited by Epifanio San Juan, Jr. 1979.

Poetry

Letter from America. 1942.
The Voice of Bataan. 1943.

Other

The Laughter of My Father. 1944.
The Dark People. 1944.
America Is in the Heart (autobiography). 1946; reprinted 1973.
Sound of Falling Light: Letters in Exile, edited by Dolores Feria. 1960.
The Cry and the Dedication. 1995.

Editor, *Chorus for America: Six Filipino Poets.* 1942.

*

Bibliography: "Writings of Bulosan" by Epifanio San Juan, Jr., in *Amerasia Journal,* May 1979; *Bulosan: An Introduction with Selections* edited by Epifanio San Juan, Jr., 1983; *Remembering Bulosan: His Heart Affair with America* by P.C. Morantte, 1984; *Bulosan and His Poetry: A Biography and Anthology* edited by Susan Evangelista, 1985.

Critical Studies: "Bulosan: The Politics of Literature" by Petronilo Bn. Daroy, in *Saint Louis Quarterly* vol. 6, 1968; *Bulosan and the Imagination of the Class Struggle,* 1972, and *Writing and National Liberation: Essays in Critical Practice,* 1991, both by Epifanio San Juan, Jr.; "Two Letters from America: Bulosan and the Act of Writing" by Oscar V. Campomanes and Todd S. Gernes, in *MELUS* vol. 15, no. 3, fall 1988; "The Female Principle and Woman Reading in Bulosan Story" by Lina B. Diaz de Rivera, in *Diliman Review* vol. 37, no. 3, 1989; *Subversion or Affirmation: The Text and Subtext of America Is in the Heart* by Marilyn Alquizola, 1991; "Carlos Bulosan: A Quagmire for Critics" by L. M. Grow, in *Pilipinas,* spring 1992; *Carlos Bulosan: Conceptual Progenitor of Multicultural Education* (dissertation) by Greg S. Castilla, 1995; *The Americas of Asian American Literature: Nationalism, Gender, and Sexuality in Bulosan's America Is in the Heart, Jen's Typical American, and Hagedorn's Dogeaters* (dissertation) by Rachel C. Lee, 1995.

*   *   *

"There is a beautiful lady/surrounded with swords," Ronald Takaki recites from a Tagalog riddle in *Strangers from a Different Shore* (1989). This riddle exemplifies how *manongs*—first-generation Filipinos—warned newcomers to America. It metaphorically splits America into two halves and engenders each: one half as the beautiful lady (presumably the Statue of Liberty), for whom male immigrants yearn, and the other as the masculine phallic symbols that forbid any communion or wedding with the "essence" of America—its femininity. A somewhat crude division, this metaphor in fact describes well the postcolonial complex manifested in the sexual tensions found in Bulosan's writings. Bulosan's fascination for the feminine America shapes itself into the form of "colonial romance," which is complicated by his social activism against the masculine America. The alleged two faces of the New World complement each other in the postcolonial subject's subconsciousness. The harsher the American men, who are owners of factories and farms or are members of police forces along the West Coast, persecute colonial subjects, the more desperately the victims embrace the escapist icon of Caucasian women.

Bulosan grew up in an impoverished peasant family in the Philippines. Following in the footsteps of many Filipino young men, he came to the United States in search of a better life, and as with so many other immigrants, he found himself in the hostile and racist environment of the Depression. His presence was hated, despite or because of the cheap labor he was able to provide. Bulosan recorded his wretched life in his short stories and poetry. His *magnum opus, America Is in the Heart,* is an autobiographical fiction that relates his individual experiences as well as the collective Pinoy (Filipino) experience as immigrants from the island-nation to the United States.

Part I of *America* is a series of bittersweet memories of the narrator's childhood in the Philippines. Farmers there lead a life plagued by absentee landlords, corrupt authority, illiteracy, and other problems, resulting in extreme deprivation. In addition to family support that offers temporary psychological relief, the only way out seems to be to travel to the promised land, a dream perpetuated by colonialism and the subsequent cultural imperialism. The scramble for an English education even at the expense of selling the last piece of family land most vividly evidences the dream in the story. Bulosan's dispossessed background sets the stage for his later conversion to union activist. Because of his own origin, he relates easily to the plight of workers in a capitalist country. But even at this early stage of the book, the pattern of entanglement of social commitment to the oppressed and of sexual fantasy for Caucasian women has presented itself. In the midst of the protagonist's misery, Mary Strandon from Spencer, Iowa, appears like a guardian angel to deliver him. The deification and idolization of white women are strengthened by Strandon's story of Abraham Lincoln who liberated the slaves. Her presence supposedly foretells the narrator's own emancipation.

Part II of *America* meticulously reconstructs a Pinoy's life along the West Coast in the 1930s and 1940s. The Pinoys are brutalized in the underworld immigrants are forced to inhabit and by the indifferent or even malicious American society. To add to their affliction, the Pinoys no longer enjoy family support. The narrator's two brothers who came to the United States earlier had turned hardened and ruthless themselves. As the narrator begins to degenerate, the socialist awakening and Caucasian female saviors proliferate. The two strands eventually become inseparable, since women are portrayed as, among other roles, mentors introducing him to various readings to raise his consciousness. Parts III and IV continue this model of labor activities intermingled deeply with colonial romance; socialism intertwined with the fetishism of white women.

This ambiguous blending of public commitment and personal fantasy by Bulosan has been separately investigated by critics. Elaine Kim pointed out in *Asian American Literature* (1982) that white women offer some kind of saving grace in the hostile land of *America Is in the Heart.* On the other hand, Epifanio San Juan, Jr., has exhaustively studied socialist leanings within Bulosan's works. But the most fascinating dimension of Bulosan's career is the rather incongruous fusion of the two forces; for the unrelenting maltreatment he experienced comes to consolidate a postcolonial subject's faith in the fantasized, feminized America. Caucasian women, physically and symbolically, serve as an escape clause to "light out of" the demeaning territory and to hold together a Pinoy's decomposing dream. These women rarely dis-

illusion immigrants because they have merged with the land, so immense and transcendental that they enjoy some sort of impunity. A case in point is the object of admiration in "Five Poems for Josephine," whose body coalesces with America:

> Now I contemplate this our land, flowing
> With her full breasts into hamlets and villages,
> Full of life and strength, with her arteries . . .
>
> And my new country! And my new paradise!
> O Josephine! O Josephine! O Josephine!

Indeed, even during the darkest moments inflicted by American males, the conviction in this feminized America holds up: "And this land . . . is not yet denuded by the rapacity of *men.* Rolling like a beautiful woman with an overflowing abundance of fecundity and murmurous with her eternal mystery, there she lies before us like a great mother" ("Be American"; emphasis added).

In addition to these personal reveries, Bulosan leaves behind much discourse on the public realm, such as his works on the war effort against Japan and about his beloved countries—his native Philippines and adopted America. Bulosan's episodic and fragmentary style has prompted critics such as L.M. Grow to complain that "[m]ore effort has already been spent on Bulosan than his literary status warrants" and Petronilo Bn. Daroy to assert that "[Bulosan] did not bother with form. He wrote as he had lived." Despite these obvious flaws, Bulosan has received a great deal of attention because of his unique status as a Filipino American writer at a time when very few of such voices could be heard. More significantly, his third-world, working-class background is rarely found among those ethnic writers who did confront social injustice, a dimension of Bulosan that endears him to a great many critics and readers.

—Sheng-mei Ma

BURKE, Kenneth (Duva)

Born: Pittsburgh, Pennsylvania, 5 May 1897. **Education:** Peabody High School, Pittsburgh; Ohio State University, Columbus, 1916-17; Columbia University, New York, 1917-18. **Family:** Married 1) Lillian Mary Batterham in 1919 (divorced), three daughters; 2) Elizabeth Batterham in 1933, two sons. Lived in New York City, 1918-21, and Andover New Jersey, since 1921; **Career:** Co-editor, *Secession,* 1923; research worker, Laura Spelman Rockefeller Memorial, New York City, 1926-27; music critic, *Dial,* New York City, 1927-29, and *The Nation,* New York City, 1934-36; editor, Bureau of Social Hygiene, New York City, 1928-29; lecturer, New School for Social Research, New York City, 1937; University of Chicago, 1938, 1949-50; Bennington College, Vermont, 1943-61; Princeton University, New Jersey, 1949, 1975; Kenyon College, Gambier, Ohio, 1950; Indiana University, Bloomington, 1953, 1958; Drew University, Madison, New Jersey, 1962, 1964; Pennsylvania State University, University Park, 1963; Regents' Professor, University of California, Santa Barbara, 1964-65; professor, Central Washington State University, Ellensburg, 1966; Harvard University, Cambridge, Massachusetts, 1967-68; Washington University, St. Louis, 1970-71; Wesleyan University, Middletown, Connecticut, 1972; University of Pittsburgh, 1972;

University of Nevada, Reno, 1976. Andrew W. Mellon Visiting Professor of English, University of Pittsburgh, 1974; Walker-Ames Visiting Professor of English, Washington University, 1976. **Awards:** Guggenheim fellowship, 1935; American Academy grant, 1946, and Gold Medal, 1975; Princeton Institute for Advanced Studies fellowship, 1949; Stanford University Center for Advanced Study in Behavioral Sciences fellowship, 1957; Rockefeller grant, 1966; Brandeis University Creative Arts Award, 1967; National Endowment for the Arts award, 1968; New School for Social Research Horace Gregory Award, 1970; Ingram Merrill Foundation award, 1970; American Academy of Arts and Sciences award, 1977; National Medal for Literature, 1981; Bobst Award, 1983. D.Litt: Bennington College, 1966; Rutgers University, New Brunswick, New Jersey, 1968; Dartmouth College, Hanover, New Hampshire, 1969; Fairfield University, Connecticut, 1970; Northwestern University, Evanston, Illinois, 1972; University of Rochester, New York, 1972; Indiana State University, Terre Haute, 1976; Kenyon College, 1979. **Member:** American Academy of Arts and Letters and American Academy of Arts and Sciences; honorary fellow, Modern Language Association. **Died:** 1993.

PUBLICATIONS

Collections

Collected Poems 1915-1967. 1968.
The Complete White Oxen: Collected Short Fiction. 1968.

Poetry

Book of Moments: Poems 1915-1954. 1955.

Fiction

The White Oxen and Other Stories. 1924.
Toward a Better Life: Being a Series of Epistles or Declamations. 1932; revised edition, 1966.

Other

Counter-Statement. 1931; revised edition, 1968.
Permanence and Change: An Anatomy of Purpose. 1935; revised edition, 1954; with a new afterword, 1984.
Attitudes toward History. 2 vols., 1937; revised edition, 1959; with a new afterword, 1984.
The Philosophy of Literary Form: Studies in Symbolic Action. 1941; revised edition, 1957.
A Grammar of Motives. 1945.
A Rhetoric of Motives. 1950.
The Rhetoric of Religion: Studies in Logology. 1961.
Perspectives by Incongruity (includes *Terms for Order*), edited by Stanley Edgar Hyman. 1964.
Language as Symbolic Action: Essays on Life, Literature and Method. 1966.
Dramatism and Development. 1972.
Ideas for Environment, with Julie Kranhold. 10 vols., 1973-74.
William Carlos Williams (lectures), with Emily H. Wallace. 1974.
The Selected Correspondence of Kenneth Burke and Malcolm Cowley, edited by Paul Jay. 1988.

On Symbols and Society, edited by Joseph R. Gusfield. 1989.
A New Approach to Shakespeare's Early Comedies: Theoretical Foundations. 1998.

Translator, *Death in Venice,* by Thomas Mann. 1925; revised edition, 1970.
Translator, *Genius and Character,* by Emil Ludwig. 1927.
Translator, *Saint Paul,* by Emile Baumann. 1929.

*

Critical Studies: *Critical Moments: Burke's Categories and Critiques* by George Knox, 1957; *Burke and the Drama of Human Relations* by William H. Rueckert, 1963, revised edition, 1982, and *Critical Responses to Burke 1924-1966* edited by Rueckert, 1969 (includes checklist by Armin and Mechtchild Frank); *Burke* by Armin Frank, 1969; *Burke* by Merle E. Brown, 1969; *Representing Kenneth Burke* edited by Hayden White and Margaret Brose, 1982; *Kenneth Burke: Literature and Language as Symbolic Action* by Greig E. Henderson, 1988; *The Legacy of Kenneth Burke* edited by Herbert W. Simons and Trevor Melia, 1989; "Theory and Equipment for (Postmodern) Living," by Thomas McLaughlin in *Practicing Theory in Introductory College Literature Courses* edited by James M. Cahalan and David B. Downing, 1991; "The Ethics of Argument: Kenneth Burke's Influence on the Teaching of Writing," by Ann Dobyns in *Rhetoric and Ethics: Historical and Theoretical Perspectives* edited by Victoria Aarons and Willis A. Salomon, 1991; *Critical Moments in the Rhetoric of Kenneth Burke: Implications for Composition* by Martin Behr, 1996; *Kenneth Burke and the 21st Century,* 1999; *Kenneth Burke and the Conversation After Philosophy* by Timothy W. Crusius, 1999.

*   *   *

In his poem "The Momentary, Migratory Symptom" found in *Book of Moments* Kenneth Burke as narrator makes a curious remark that happens to contain the formula for his broadly based literary criticism, which encompasses rhetorical and verbal analysis, psychology, politics, economics, philosophy, logic, theology, history, and music—to say nothing of literature itself. It also contains the formula for his general attitude toward life, now and in the hereafter. Burke confesses that he went to see a doctor about a recurrent shooting pain: "I wanted him to help me track it down/ With every verb and adjective and noun." Here then are the formulaic elements in his thinking: the belief that the right words, strategically used, can solve all or most problems; the revelation of motives by means of rhetoric; the representation of symbolic action through the strategic use of words; the (potential) "dramatistic" schematization of a situation, for the purpose of clarification, whereby one of five essential elements (act, scene, agent, agency, purpose) is shown to predominate, and whose importance in relation to the other elements can be studied. Burke's skill in rhetoric analysis, his remarkably wide reading in the ancients and moderns, and his powers of association have astounded many literary scholars. Still, there is a dismaying deeply-rooted tendency in Burke to float impractical, frivolous sounding ideas and to indulge in nonsensical and occasionally tasteless wordplay.

A few examples of Burke's over-reliance on abstractions, cloud-castle theorizing, and negligible associations of meaning may be given. "War is a disease of cooperation which should be curable by means of 'creative and peaceful verbal acts' " (to paraphrase William H. Rueckert in his essay "Some of the Many Kenneth Burkes" in *Representing Kenneth Burke*). Burke, in the essay "Literature as Equipment for Living" (*The Philosophy of Literary Form*), instead of discussing the vital, down-to- earth application of literature to human problems and needs, "throws away his line" and lapses into woolly generalizations and constructs. Using a series of proverbs and their extension into literary works, he suggests the formation of a "sociological criticism" for codifying and classifying the strategies that artists have formulated for "the naming of situations." And in *Attitudes toward History,* Burke traces James Joyce's punning to his guilt for having rejected Catholicism and his thereby being caught in an incongruous situation. This leads Burke to the American "Knock, knock, who's where?" game of pun-making in the 1930s (whose popularity Burke sees as a reflection of national uncertainty about authority-symbols in business). Next Burke leaps to Thomas De Quincey's discussion of the guilt-symbol of the knocking at the gate in *Macbeth;* he goes from there to the Negro spiritual "Somebody's Knocking at Your Door," and finally to **Edgar Allan Poe**'s "The Raven," with its tapping and rapping at the chamber door.

On the other hand, though Burke has not been closely identified with any one group of critics—despite his Marxist leanings in the 1930s and 1940s—his ongoing intense concern with the complexities of language and meaning in the text has linked him with the newer and more fashionable schools of criticism. According to Hayden White, in his Preface to *Representing Kenneth Burke,* Burke had already by 1977 begun working on deconstructive criticism (wherein meaning in a text is no longer an absolute, no longer subject to a rank-order of importance), and it was obvious at that time that he had anticipated both the structuralist and post-structuralist movements before they had come into existence. This restlessly inquiring, penetrating approach (fueled by Burke's close familiarity with the history of Western philosophy, and with Greek and Latin rhetorical modes) makes for very exciting reading, *when* he sticks to literature. Two examples of how well "he illuminates texts" (I am borrowing **Howard Nemerov**'s apt expression) are the article on Mark Antony— "Antony in Behalf of the Play," and his discussion of Coleridge and "The Rime of the Ancient Mariner" (both in *The Philosophy of Literary Form*). Important as rhetorical analysis and dialectical exposition are to Burke, his intense concern with naming, renaming, and classifying critical concepts and categories must also be included among his accomplishments—although this particular concern can be quite wearying. A good, concise overview of this situation is given by Rueckert in "Some of the Many Kenneth Burkes": one instance of Burke's seemingly gratuitous word-coinages is his shifting from "dialectics" to "logologic" and then to a more encompassing term, "logology."

Burke's poems and his overly academic and philosophical attempts at fiction (*The White Oxen* and *Towards a Better Life*) will not be dealt with here. His first non-fiction book, *Counter-Statement,* written during the 1920s, reflects Burke's interest in political forces and deals with the status of art in society—and the various ways in which art has been regarded. A long "set-piece," "Lexicon Rhetoricae," shows Burke already embarked on a naming and classifying project. His aim, in exemplifying thirty-nine terms ("Patterns of experience," "The Symbol," " 'Priority' of forms," "Ideology," etc.), is to explain the foundations of literature's appeal, the way that writers produce their effects. *Per-*

manence and Change, written at the beginning of the Depression, when it seemed to Burke that there might be more than a major change to come in the "traditional ways"—in fact "a permanent collapse"—seeks an alleviation of the fear and anxiety felt by Burke and people like him. Though the book contains an intriguing section on Burke's fruitful concept of "perspective by incongruity," it unmistakably reads as though Burke were living in a private universe and spinning out happy, idealistic theories to keep his spirits up. Communication problems in society, viewed through Burke's tinted lenses, constitute the subject matter of *Permanence and Change;* Burke even posits an "Ideal New Order," following his examination of old, modified, and outworn meanings and signs.

Attitudes Toward History is another therapeutic attempt to deal with the "troubled thirties"—this time by examining the way people have felt about "life in political communities." Burke first examines the positions of "Acceptance and Rejection"; next he creates a five-act drama, "The Curve of History," which moves from the emergence of Evangelical Christianity to Collectivism; then he deals with rituals and routines; finally he generates a "Dictionary of Pivotal Terms"—"attitudinal" expressions such as "Discounting," "Efficiency," "Problem of Evil," "Rituals of Rebirth"— used to confront dilemmas at various periods in history. *The Philosophy of Literary Form,* subtitled "Studies in Symbolic Action," consists of writings also produced during the 1930s, fascinatingly written attempts to relate somehow "political programs and cultural concerns in general." Any verbal act, according to Burke, may be taken as a "symbolic action"—the *act* being "the *dancing of an attitude"* (a concept Burke adapts from I. A. Richards's original idea), in such a way as to involve the entire body, and to evoke the tenets of behavioristic psychology.

A Grammar of Motives deals at length with Burke's system of "dramatism," and is considered one of his most important contributions to literary criticism. The book also includes an extensive section on the dialectic process, as well as an appendix consisting of four articles. One of these, "Four Master Tropes," shows Burke once more renaming and classifying: metaphor, metonymy, synecdoche, and irony become, respectively, perspective, reduction, representation, and dialectic (in the narrow sense). A sequel, *A Rhetoric of Motives,* continues to reflect Burke's social concerns. By discovering rhetorical motives in unsuspected places and by developing a "philosophy of rhetoric" while emphasizing the key terms "identification" and "persuasion," he seeks to promote tolerance and contemplation, thereby (as he so fondly hopes) reducing the ill-will so widespread at the time—the end of the 1940s.

In his article "Theory as Equipment for (Postmodern) Living" Thomas McLaughlin discusses Burke's original approach to literature. Paraphrasing the title of one of Burke's most anthologized essays, "Literature as Equipment for Living," McLaughlin points out the author's fascination with words. In Burke's metaphorical vision of the world, literature does powerful social and political work, functioning as a means of survival and communication, as a huge dictionary of potential meanings. "Each work of art," says Burke, "is the addition of a word to an informal dictionary." Thus, literature becomes a game which manipulates meanings and feelings, a dream whose analysis is made possible by reading. In this context theory becomes "a strategy" of reading, a necessary equipment for (postmodern) life, a means of decoding the complex process of naming, in other words, of attaching meanings to different combination of sounds. Naming means mastering, grasping the hidden meaning behind symbols. Burke's *Rhetoric of Motives* produced a resurgence of interest in the study of rhetoric as a part of humanities.

Analyzing Burke's influence on modern theories of rhetoric in her essay appearing in *Rhetoric and Ethics*, Ann Dobyns proves that Burke's rhetoric indicates a shift in emphasis from persuasion to identification. Indebted to Aristotle, Burke asks the modern speaker to identify the "ideas" (Aristotle's "places") in persuasive images; however, this happens only if the images are persuasive to the hearer also. This requires an ethical dimension of rhetoric, a better communication between the speaker and the hearer, in other words, acknowledges persuasion as a necessary condition of being human. Applied in a classroom, Burke's theory teaches the students the importance of the argument. Rhetoric thus becomes a dialectic art depending on persuasion and argument, not on an absolute objective criterion. This new pedagogical approach "compels students to take positions which follow logically from an analysis of complex ideas, it involves, in other words, critical thinkings," says Dobyns. *The Rhetoric of Religion* pursues the matter of rhetoric-as-persuasion into the field of religion, just far enough to deal with nomenclature: specifically, the individual's "relationship to the word 'God.' "For this reason, Burke explains, he has subtitled the book "Studies in Logology"; the subject matter is "words-about-words."

Despite Burke's many accomplishments the reader is tempted to raise a few questions. They have to do with matters dearest to Burke's heart: rhetoric, dialectic, symbolic action, motives. It never occurred to him, in all the decades he has been writing, that he has continued to describe individuals in the abstract *only as males,* as if females who are not designated by legal names do not exist. He has never been aware that his voluminous body of esoteric, highly specialized writings, reflecting his ongoing desire to move society "towards a better life" (to borrow the title of his anti-novel), could not possibly have the intended effect—on grounds both of practicality and probability. Few could digest his abstruse arguments, fewer still could act on them in any meaningful way. Ergo: have not his lifelong efforts at literary-political writing really been motivated by the desire to take the easy way out, while at the same time assuaging a chronically-nagging social conscience? Despite these objections, Burke's theories of literature and rhetoric continue to influence modern pedagogy and philosophy. His patterns of interpretation add a new dimension to language in general, and to communication in particular, compelling the speaker/teacher/writer to assume the entire responsibility of his words in his attempt to persuade his public and make a valid argument.

—Samuel Irving Bellman, updated by Dayana Stetco

BURNETT, Frances (Eliza) Hodgson

Born: Cheetham Hill, Manchester, England, 24 November 1849; immigrated with her mother to New Market, Tennessee, 1865; became citizen, 1905. **Education:** Schools in Manchester. **Family:** Married 1) Dr. Swan Moses Burnett in 1873 (divorced 1898), two sons; 2) Stephen Townesend in 1900 (separated 1901; died 1914). **Career:** Lived in Knoxville, 1869-74, Europe, 1875-76, and Washington, D.C., 1877-87; after 1887 traveled frequently between the United States and Europe. **Died:** 29 October 1924.

PUBLICATIONS

Fiction

Surly Tim and Other Stories. 1877.
Theo: A Love Story. 1877.
Pretty Polly Pemberton: A Love Story. 1877.
That Lass o' Lowrie's. 1877.
Dolly: A Love Story. 1877; as *Vagabondia,* 1883.
Kathleen: A Love Story. 1878.
Miss Crespigny: A Love Story. 1878.
Earlier Stories. 1878; second series, 1878.
A Quiet Life, and The Tide on the Moaning Bar. 1878.
Our Neighbour Opposite. 1878.
Jarl's Daughter and Other Stories. 1879.
Natalie and Other Stories. 1879.
Haworth's. 1879.
Louisiana. 1880.
A Fair Barbarian. 1881.
Through One Administration. 1883.
Little Lord Fauntleroy. 1886.
A Woman's Will; or, Miss Defarge. 1887.
Sara Crewe; or, What Happened at Miss Minchin's. 1887.
Editha's Burglar. 1888.
The Fortunes of Philippa Fairfax. 1888.
The Pretty Sister of Jose. 1889.
Little Saint Elizabeth and Other Stories. 1890.
Children I Have Known. 1892; as *Giovanni and the Other: Children Who Have Made Stories,* 1892.
Piccino and Other Child Stories. 1894; as *The Captain's Youngest, Piccino and Other Child Stories,* 1894.
Two Little Pilgrims' Progress: A Story of the City Beautiful. 1895.
A Lady of Quality. 1896.
His Grace of Osmonde. 1897.
In Connection with the De Willoughby Claim. 1899.
The Making of a Marchioness. 1901; revised edition, 1901.
The Methods of Lady Walderhurst. 1901.
In the Closed Room. 1904.
A Little Princess, Being the Whole Story of Sara Crewe Now Told for the First Time. 1905.
Racketty-Packetty House. 1906.
The Dawn of a To-morrow. 1906.
Queen Silver-Bell. 1906; as *The Troubles of Queen Silver Bell,* 1907.
The Cozy Lion, as Told by Queen Crosspatch. 1907.
The Shuttle. 1907.
The Spring Cleaning, as Told by Queen Crosspatch. 1908.
The Good Wolf 1908.
Barty Crusoe and His Man Saturday. 1909.
The Land of the Blue Flower. 1909.
The Secret Garden. 1911.
My Robin. 1912.
T. Tembarom. 1913.
The Lost Prince. 1915.
The Way to the House of Santa Claus: A Christmas Story. 1916.
Little Hunchback Zia. 1916.
The White People. 1917.
The Head of the House of Coombe. 1922.
Robin. 1922.

Plays

That Lass o' Lowrie's, with Julian Magnus, from the novel by
  Burnett (produced 1878). *Esmeralda,* with William Gillette (pro-
  duced 1881; as *Young Folks' Ways,* produced 1883). 1881.
The Real Little Lord Fauntleroy, from her own novel (produced
  1888). *Phyllis,* from her novel *The Fortunes of Philippa Fairfax*
  (produced 1889).
Editha's Burglar, with Stephen Townesend, from the novel by
  Burnett (produced 1890; as *Nixie,* produced 1890). *The
  Showman's Daughter,* with Stephen Townesend (produced
  1891).
The First Gentleman of Europe, with Constance Fletcher (pro-
  duced 1897).
A Lady of Quality, with Stephen Townesend, from the novel by
  Burnett (produced 1897).
A Little Princess, from her own novel *Sara Crewe* (as *A Little
  Unfairy Princess,* produced 1902; as *A Little Princess,* produced
  1903). In *Treasury of Plays for Children,* edited by Montrose
  J. Moses, 1921.
The Pretty Sister of Jose, from her own novel (produced 1903).
That Man and I, from her novel *In Connection with the De
  Willoughby Claim* (produced 1903).
Dawn of a Tomorrow, from her own novel (produced 1909).
Racketty-Packetty House, from her own novel (produced 1912).

Other

The Drury Lane Boys' Club. 1892.
The One I Knew Best of All: A Memory of the Mind of a Child
  (autobiography). 1893.
In the Garden. 1925.

*

Critical Studies: *Mrs. Ewing, Mrs. Molesworth, and Mrs. Burnett*
by Marghanita Laski, 1950; *Happily Ever After: A Portrait of
Burnett* by Constance Buel Burnett, 1969; *Waiting for the Party:
The Life of Burnett* by Ann Thwaite, 1974; *Burnett* by Phyllis
Bixler, 1984; *What Katy Read: Feminist Re-readings of "Classic"
Stories for Girls* by Shirley Foster, 1995; in *New Essays on the
Maternal Voice in the Nineteenth Century* edited by Barbara Thaden,
1995; *The Secret Garden: Nature's Magic* by Phyllis Bixler, 1996.

*   *   *

When Frances Hodgson Burnett died in 1924, the *Times*'s obituary writer praised her work in helping to bring about the 1911
Copyright Act but decided that it was almost solely by her "idyll
of child life" *Little Lord Fauntleroy* that Burnett would be remembered. *Times* readers rushed to deny that her claims to permanence were so limited. Some of her adult novels and, of course,
The Secret Garden were mentioned. In fact, since her death her
three major children's books, *Fauntleroy, A Little Princess,* and
The Secret Garden, have never been out of print. *Fauntleroy* made
an immediate impact on its first publication. Along with *King
Solomon's Mines* and *War and Peace,* it was one of the best-selling novels of 1886 in the United States, read by old and young
alike. The descriptions of the "handsome, blooming, curly-headed
little fellow" may be nauseating to modern taste, but it remains an
excellent story.

Its wild success changed Burnett's career. Up until this time,
she had been gradually establishing herself as a serious and important novelist. In 1877 her American publisher, Scribner, wrote
to her English publisher, Warne, "She is considered by good judges
as the 'Coming Woman' in literature." The Boston *Transcript* wrote
of her first full-length novel, *That Loss o' Lowrie's:* "We know of
no more powerful work from a woman's hand in the English language, not even excepting the best of George Eliot." Both this novel
and *Haworth's* were set in industrial Lancashire with a liberal use
of the dialect that had fascinated her even as a young child in
Manchester.

Through One Administration, her last adult novel before
Fauntleroy, is a considerable achievement, proving that Burnett
was indeed much more than the romantic middle-brow novelist
her later books suggest. It was not the love between Bertha Amory
and Tredennis that interested her; it was the lack of love between
Bertha and Richard Amory. And the novel's picture of Washington lobbying, of machinations and intrigues, is vivid and convincing. It was at this time (in an article in the July 1883 issue of the
Century) that Burnett was named as one of the five writers in
America "who hold the front rank today in general estimation."
Then came *Fauntleroy,* a great deal of money and a pattern of
writing that had to keep pace with her new way of life—large
houses, numerous crossings of the Atlantic, and a constant demand for her talents.

The most interesting of her later adult books are *A Woman's
Will,* her autobiography, *The One I Knew the Best of All, The
Shuttle,* and *The Making of a Marchioness.* In Marghanita Laski's
words, the last is a "fairy story diluted with unromantic realism,"
and it is that realistic treatment of its period that gives it its special appeal in the late twentieth century.

Much of the appeal of her children's story *A Little Princess* is
its period charm. But its incredible coincidences do not conceal
Burnett's understanding of children. Sara is real in an unreal story.
The Secret Garden has real children in a real story. Two unhappy
children are convincingly transformed, not by outside intervention but by their own determination. It is a book that made no
great impact on publication, but it has steadily established itself
as one of the few real classics of children's literature.

—Ann Thwaite

BURNS, Tex. *See* **L'AMOUR, Louis (Dearborn).**

BURROUGHS, Edgar Rice

Born: Chicago, Illinois, 1 September 1875. **Education:** The
Harvard School, Chicago, 1888-91; Phillips Academy, Andover,
Massachusetts, 1891-92; Michigan Military Academy, Orchard
Lake, 1892-95. **Military Service:** Served in the U.S. 7th Cav-
alry, 1896-97; Illinois Reserve Militia, 1918-19. **Family:** Mar-
ried 1) Emma Centennia Hulbert in 1900 (divorced 1934), two
sons and one daughter; 2) Florence Dearholt in 1935 (divorced
1942). **Career:** Instructor and Assistant Commandant, Michigan
Military Academy, 1895-96; owner of a stationery store, Pocatello,
Idaho, 1898; worked in his father's American Battery Company,
Chicago, 1899-1903; joined his brother's Sweetser-Burroughs Mining Company, Idaho, 1903-04; railroad policeman, Oregon Short

Line Railroad Company, Salt Lake City, 1904; manager of the Stenographic Department, Sears Roebuck and Company, Chicago, 1906-08; partner, Burroughs and Dentzer, advertising contractors, Chicago, 1908-09; office manager, Physicians Co-Operative Association, Chicago, 1909; partner, State Burroughs Company, salesmanship firm, Chicago, 1909; worked for Champlain Yardley Company, stationers, Chicago, 1910-11; manager, System Service Bureau, Chicago, 1912-13; free-lance writer after 1913; formed Edgar Rice Burroughs, Inc., publishers, 1913, Burroughs-Tarzan Enterprises, 1934-39, and Burroughs-Tarzan Pictures, 1934-37; lived in California after 1919; mayor of Malibu Beach, 1933; also United Press correspondent in the Pacific during World War II, and columnist ("Laugh It Off"), Honolulu *Advertiser*, 1941-42, 1945. **Died:** 19 March 1950.

PUBLICATIONS

Fiction

Tarzan of the Apes. 1914.
The Return of Tarzan. 1915.
The Beasts of Tarzan. 1916.
The Son of Tarzan. 1917.
A Princess of Mars. 1917.
Tarzan and the Jewels of Opar. 1918.
The Gods of Mars. 1918.
Jungle Tales of Tarzan. 1919.
The Warlord of Mars. 1919.
Tarzan the Untamed (stories). 1920.
Thuvia, Maid of Mars. 1920.
Tarzan the Terrible. 1921.
The Mucker (stories). 1921; as *The Mucker* and *The Man without a Soul*, 2 vols., 1921-22.
The Chessmen of Mars. 1922.
At the Earth's Core. 1922.
Tarzan and the Golden Lion. 1923.
The Girl from Hollywood. 1923.
Pellucidar. 1923.
Tarzan and the Ant Men. 1924.
The Land That Time Forgot (stories). 1924; selections, as *The Land That Time Forgot, The People That Time Forgot,* and *Out of Time's Abyss*, 3 vols., 1963.
The Bandit of Hell's Bend. 1925.
The Eternal Lover (stories). 1925; as *The Eternal Savage*, 1963.
The Cave Girl (stories). 1925.
The Mad King (stories). 1926.
The Moon Maid (stories). 1926; selection, as *The Moon Men*, 1962.
The Tarzan Twins (for children). 1927.
The Outlaw of Torn. 1927.
The War Chief. 1927.
Tarzan, Lord of the Jungle. 1928.
The Master Mind of Mars. 1928.
Tarzan and the Lost Empire. 1929.
The Monster Men. 1929.
Tarzan at the Earth's Core. 1930.
Tanar of Pellucidar. 1930.
Tarzan the Invincible. 1931.
A Fighting Man of Mars. 1931.
Tarzan Triumphant. 1932.
Jungle Girl. 1932; as *The Land of Hidden Men*, 1963.

Tarzan and the City of Gold. 1933.
Apache Devil. 1933.
Tarzan and the Lion-Man. 1934.
Pirates of Venus. 1934.
Tarzan and the Leopard Men. 1935.
Lost on Venus. 1935.
Tarzan and the Tarzan Twins, with Jad-Bal-Ja, The Golden Lion (for children). 1936.
Tarzan's Quest. 1936.
Swords of Mars. 1936.
The Oakdale Affair; The Rider. 1937.
Back to the Stone Age. 1937.
Tarzan and the Forbidden City. 1938.
The Lad and the Lion. 1938.
Tarzan the Magnificent (stories). 1939.
Carson of Venus. 1939.
The Deputy Sheriff of Comanche County. 1940.
Synthetic Men of Mars. 1940.
Land of Terror. 1944.
Escape on Venus. 1946.
Tarzan and the Foreign Legion. 1947.
Llana of Gathol (stories). 1948.
Beyond Thirty. 1955; as *The Lost Continent*, 1963.
The Man-Eater (story). 1955.
Savage Pellucidar (stories). 1963.
Tales of Three Planets. 1964.
John Carter of Mars (stories). 1964.
Beyond the Farthest Star. 1964.
Tarzan and the Castaways (stories). 1964.
Tarzan and the Madman. 1964.
The Girl from Farris's. 1965.
The Efficiency Expert. 1966.
I Am a Barbarian. 1967.
Pirate Blood. 1970.
The Wizard of Venus. 1970.

Other

Official Guide of the Tarzan Clans of America. 1939.

*

Critical Studies: *Edgar Rice Burroughs, Master of Adventure,* 1965, revised edition, 1968, and *Barsoom: Burroughs and the Martian Vision,* 1976, both by Richard A. Lupoff; *Tarzan Alive: A Definitive Biography of Lord Greystoke* by Philip Jose Farmer, 1972; *Burroughs' Science Fiction* by Robert R. Kudlay and Joan Leiby, 1973; *Burroughs, The Man Who Created Tarzan* (includes bibliography) by Irwin Forges, 1975; *Guide to Barsoom* by John Flint Roy, 1976; *The Burroughs Bestiary: An Encyclopedia of Monsters and Imaginary Beings Created by Burroughs* by David Day, 1978; *Tarzan and Tradition: Classical Myth in Popular Literature* by Erling B. Holtsmark, 1981; *Science Fiction Writers: Critical Studies of the Major Authors from the Early Nineteenth Century to the Present Day* edited by Franklin Everett Bleiler, 1982; "The Time and Place of Edgar Rice Burroughs's Early Martian Trilogy" by Benjamin S. Lawson, in *Extrapolation: A Journal of Science Fiction and Fantasy,* fall 1986; *Investigating the Unliterary: Six Readings of Edgar Rice Burroughs' Tarzan of the Apes* edited by Richard J. Utz, 1995; *The Burroughs Encyclopedia: Characters, Places, Fauna, Flora, Technologies, Languages, and*

Terminologies Found in the Works of Edgar Rice Burroughs by Clark A. Brady, 1996; "The World According to Normal Bean: Edgar Rice Burroughs' Popular Culture" by Harry Stecopoulos, in *Race and the Subject of Masculinities* edited by Harry Stecopoulos, 1997.

*   *   *

When he was almost thirty-six years old, with a wife and three children, disappointed in his military and various business careers, Edgar Rice Burroughs decided to try writing fiction. His first sale, later printed in hardcover as *A Princess of Mars,* was serialized in *All-Story Magazine* in 1912. The first of a series still immensely popular, the novel illustrates most of the strengths and weaknesses of Burroughs's works. Fast-paced, colorful, and strikingly imaginative, it stimulates the sense of wonder, especially of children and adolescents. But the characters are one-dimensional, either evil or good, and coincidences abound. Though Burroughs presents the "Barsoomian" cultures vividly, he does not develop them in depth. The historical novel *The Outlaw of Torn* and his "realistic" stories, notably those of crime and corruption in Chicago and Hollywood, illustrated his failure to be convincing at anything other than fantasy. He dealt much more effectively with the never-never lands of Mars, darkest Africa, the earth's center-worlds that neither he nor his readers knew much about.

Burroughs is best known as the creator of Tarzan, son of an English peer, Lord Greystoke, raised from the age of one in the African jungle by language-using great apes. Critics have maintained that Burroughs wrote *Tarzan of the Apes* to demonstrate his belief in the superiority of heredity over environment, and especially of the superior heredity of the British upper classes. In one sense they are correct. Tarzan's human genes gave him an intelligence superior to the apes'; they gave him an innate curiosity and drive that would have taken him out of any lowly station into which he had been born. But in the end it is the environment that molds Tarzan's character. Raised as a feral child, he is a classic example of the outsider, one who has an objective view of human society because he has not imbibed its irrationalities along with his mother's milk. Through Tarzan's eyes Burroughs satirizes Homo sapiens, as he did through some of his other heroes, notably Carson Napier of the "Venus" series.

However, Burroughs's ape-man is neither a Voltairean observer nor a noble savage. He regards pre-literates as superior in their way of life to civilized peoples, and he himself is never quite human. He is, when in the jungle, free of the mundane, drab, wearing, and often tragic restrictions of civilized, social life. Tarzan's being a law unto himself and his closeness to nature are part of his appeal. But Burroughs, though unconsciously, also gave him most of the attributes of the pre-literate and classical hero of fairy tale, legend, and mythology, including the Trickster. Tarzan is the last of the Golden Age heroes, a literary character who reflects the archetypal images and feelings of the unconscious mind noted by Carl Jung and Joseph Campbell.

Like Arthur Conan Doyle, Burroughs had the gift of writing adventure stories with an indefinable quality that made them endure while thousands of similar works dropped into oblivion. Like Doyle he created a classical fictional character of whom he wearied. The later Tarzan novels, in fact all of his works written in the latter part of his career, show a flagging invention, repetitiveness of plot and incident, excess of coincidences and improbabilities, and failure to develop promising themes.

Burroughs never thought of himself as anything but a commercial writer of romances. His works betray the bias, conservatism, and timidity of his social class and time, and his style is old-fashioned. With the exception of Tarzan and a few others, his characters are cardboard. His genius was in the creation of an archetypal feral man and the writing of many pseudoscientific romances that have enthralled generations of young—and not so young—readers.

—Philip Jose Farmer

BURROUGHS, William S(eward)

Pseudonyms: William Lee and Willy Lee. **Born:** St. Louis, Missouri, 5 February 1914. **Education:** Harvard University, A.B. 1936, graduate study, 1938; University of Vienna, 1937; Mexico City College, 1949-50. **Military Service:** Served in the U.S. Army, 1942. **Family:** Married 1) Ilse Herzfeld Klapper, 1937 (divorced 1946); 2) Joan Vollmer, 1946 (died 1951, of an accidental gunshot wound); one son, the writer William S. Burroughs, Jr. (died 1981). **Career:** Advertising copywriter in New York in early 1940s; has also worked as bartender, exterminator, and private detective. Actor in motion picture *Drugstore Cowboy,* 1989; has appeared in numerous music videos. Lived in Lawrence, Kansas. **Awards:** National Institute of Arts and Letters and American Academy award in literature, 1975, named member, 1983. The Nova Convention, a four-day arts festival held in New York in 1978, and the Final Academy, held in London in 1982, were organized as tributes to Burroughs. **Died:** 2 August 1997.

PUBLICATIONS

Collections

A William Burroughs Reader, edited by John Calder. 1982.
The Burroughs File (includes *The White Subway, Cobble Stone Gardens,* and *The Retreat Diaries*). 1984.
Word Virus: The William S. Burroughs Reader. 1998.

Novels

Junkie: Confessions of an Unredeemed Drug Addict (as William Lee; bound with *Narcotic Agent* by Maurice Helbrant). 1953; reissued, 1957; published separately under name William S. Burroughs, 1964; unexpurgated edition published as *Junky,* 1977.
The Naked Lunch. 1959; reissued, 1964; as *Naked Lunch,* 1962.
The Soft Machine. 1961; enlarged edition, 1966; enlarged edition, 1968.
The Ticket That Exploded. 1962; revised edition, 1967; reissued, 1968.
Dead Fingers Talk (contains excerpts from *Naked Lunch, The Soft Machine,* and *The Ticket That Exploded*). 1963.
Nova Express. 1964; reissued, 1966.
The Wild Boys: A Book of the Dead. 1971; reissued, 1972; revised edition, 1979.
Short Novels. 1978.
Port of Saints. 1979; reissued, 1983.
Blade Runner: A Movie. 1979.
The Soft Machine, Nova Express, The Wild Boys. 1980.

Cities of the Red Night: A Boy's Book. 1981.
The Place of Dead Roads. 1983; reissued, 1984.
Queer. 1985; reissued, 1986.
The Western Lands. 1987.
Routine. 1987.
Tornado Alley. 1989.

Short Stories

Exterminator! 1973; reissued, 1975.
Early Routines. 1981.
The Streets of Chance. 1981.

Plays

The Last Words of Dutch Schultz: A Fiction in the Form of a Film Script. 1970; reissued, 1975.

Librettist, *The Black Rider,* music by Tom Waits, directed by Robert Wilson. 1992.

Screenplays: With Brion Gysin, *Towers Open Fire,* 1963; with Antony Balch, *Bill and Tony,* 1966; *The Cut-Ups.*

Other

The Exterminator, with Brion Gysin. 1960.
Minutes to Go (poems), with Brion Gysin, Sinclair Beiles, and Gregory Corso. 1960; reissued, 1968.
The Yage Letters, with Allen Ginsberg. 1963.
Takis (exhibition catalog). 1963.
Roosevelt after Inauguration (as Willy Lee). 1964; as *Roosevelt after Inauguration, and Other Atrocities.* 1979.
Valentine's Day Reading. 1965.
The White Subway, edited by James Pennington. 1965.
Health Bulletin: APO:33: A Metabolic Regulator. 1965; revised edition as *APO:33: A Report on the Synthesis of the Apomorphine Formula,* 1966.
Darayt, with Lee Harwood. 1965.
So Who Owns Death TV?, with Claude Pelieu and Carl Weissner. 1967.
They Do Not Always Remember. 1968.
Ali's Smile. 1969.
The Dead Star. 1969.
Entretiens avec William Burroughs, with Daniel Odier. 1969; revised, enlarged, and translated as *The Job: Interviews with William S. Burroughs* (includes *Electronic Revolution*), 1970; with additional material as *The Job: Topical Writings and Interviews,* 1984.
The Braille Film, with Carl Weissner. 1970.
Jack Kerouac (in French), with Claude Pelieu. 1971.
Electronic Revolution. 1971.
Brion Gysin Let the Mice In, with Brion Gysin and Ian Somerville, edited by Jan Herman. 1973.
Mayfair Academy Series More or Less. 1973.
The Book of Breeething. 1974; reissued, 1975.
Snack: Two Tape Transcripts, with Eric Mottram. 1975.
Sidetripping, with Charles Gatewood. 1975.
Cobble Stone Gardens. 1976.
The Retreat Diaries (bound with *The Dream of Tibet* by Allen Ginsberg). 1976.
Naked Scientology. 1978.

The Third Mind, with Brion Gysin. 1978; reissued, 1979.
Doctor Benway: A Variant Passage from "The Naked Lunch." 1979.
Ah Pook Is Here, and Other Texts (includes *The Book of Breeething, Electronic Revolution*). 1979; reissued, 1982.
Letters to Allen Ginsberg, 1953-1957. 1981.
The Four Horsemen of the Apocalypse. 1984.
The Adding Machine: Collected Essays. 1985; reissued, 1986.
Interzone. 1989.
Uncommon Quotes (poetry). 1989.
Ghost of a Chance (essays). 1991.
The Letters of William S. Burroughs, 1945-1959. 1994.
My Education: A Book of Dreams. 1995.
Concrete and Buckshot: William S. Burroughs Paintings, 1987-1996. 1996.
Collected Interviews of William S. Burroughs. 1997.

Composer, *Old Lady Sloan,* recorded by Mortal Micronotz. 1982.

Recordings: *Call Me Burroughs,* 1965; *William S. Burroughs/John Giorno,* 1975; *You're the Man I Want to Share My Money With,* 1981; *Nothing Here Now but the Recordings,* 1981; *Revolutions per Minute (The Art Record),* 1982; *Dead City Radio,* 1988; with Gus Van Sant, *Elvis of Letters;* with Kurt Cobain, *The Priest They Called Him,* 1993; *Spare Ass Annie,* 1993.

*

Bibliography: *William S. Burroughs: An Annotated Bibliography of His Works and Criticism* by Michael Barry Goodman, 1975; *William S. Burroughs: A Bibliography 1953-73* by Joe Maynard and Barry Miles, 1978; *William S. Burroughs: A Reference Guide* by Michael B. Goodman and Lemuel B. Coley, 1990; *William S. Burroughs and Allen Ginsberg: A Select Bibliography of Works in the UCLA University Library,* 1998.

Critical Studies: *William Burroughs: The Algebra of Need* by Eric Mottram, 1971, second edition, 1977; *Naked Angels: The Lives and Literature of the Beat Generation* by John Tytell, 1976; *Contemporary Literary Censorship: The Case History of Burroughs's Naked Lunch* by Michael B. Goodman, 1981; *With William Burroughs: A Report from the Bunker* edited by Victor Bokris, 1981; *William Burroughs* by Jennie Skerl, 1985; *Literary Outlaw: The Life and Times of William S. Burroughs* by Ted Morgan, 1988; *Contemporary Gay American Novelists* edited by Emmanuel S. Nelson, 1993; *William Burroughs: El Hombre Invisible* by Barry Miles, Hyperion, 1993; *Ports of Entry: William S. Burroughs and the Arts* by Robert A. Sobieszek, 1996; *Gentleman Junkie: The Life and Legacy of William S. Burroughs* by Graham Caveney, 1998; *William Burroughs: The Priest They Called Him* by Graham Caveney, 1999.

*   *   *

There are two fields of experience central to the life and work of William S. Burroughs. They mark points at which criticism of his work must begin, and around which controversy has swirled. Scion of the Burroughs Adding Machine family, he traveled for much of adult life, during which time he became addicted to heroin in 1944, remaining so across three continents and fourteen years. His addiction and cure (the last and presumably final in 1957) have provided the controlling metaphor for an *oeuvre* of cosmic dimensions.

The second area of concern is, like Burroughs's opiate addiction, an extended series of drug experiences. In 1953 he journeyed to the Peruvian Amazon expressly for the purpose of taking *yage*, a mescaline-like natural hallucinogen used sacramentally by the Indians of the region. These and subsequent psychedelic experiences provided not only primary materials for *Naked Lunch, The Soft Machine,* and *The Ticket That Exploded,* but served to expand and intensify his vision beyond the relative solipsism of "junk."

For Burroughs's most fervent admirers he has become a cult figure: an international underworld traveler, a gifted teacher, a universal personage reborn, at least partially, from innumerable deaths, returned to speak and write of his experiences. For this group, his life is an example and his writing is a report, a formal statement of an entire lifestyle. He is a beatific figure, the madman-saint, like de Sade, Artaud, Céline and his contemporary Genet. His life is a message, as Alan Ansen writes unabashedly: "In the case of Burroughs, the writing is only a by-product, however brilliant, of a force. What I am writing is not only a paean to a writer; it is also a variant of hagiography." His detractors are equally enthusiastic: George Garrett speaks for Jolin Wain, George Steiner, **Anaïs Nin,** and others when he complains: "Do we have to become connoisseurs of vomit? Is the world doing so badly a job at tearing itself apart that it needs the aid of gifted writers to finish it off?"

The indelible image of the heroin addict is presented in Burroughs's first work, *Junkie*—the addict slumped nodding in his chair or out on the street, waiting, making his ruins public. The rhetoric of this small book has the economy and force of needle and spoon, and its initial sociological value is as reportage, in the lucid pictures of the addict world. But more, in the linking of the heroin addict with the metaphysical condition of the "enslaved" condition of modern man, it establishes the single radical image from which Burroughs's "new mythology for the space age" develops.

Naked Lunch is Burroughs's most famous work. Admitted for publication to the United States after several famous obscenity trials, "composed" with aid from his friends **Allen Ginsberg** and **Jack Kerouac,** the novel is a series of fantastic episodes arranged in collage form, the whole being held together by a manic and comic narrative voice that turns matters inevitably to the theme of human control. *Naked Lunch* becomes increasingly disjointed and surrealistic in technique, and it displays the misogynist-homosexual concerns and the satiric comic vision that have become Burroughs's signatures.

Subsequent longer works, especially *The Soft Machine* and *The Ticket That Exploded,* have ranged from anthropological pre-history to the uncertain future of dystopian science fiction but share a predilection for radical linguistic and textual experiment: the "cut-up," the "fold in," and similar dislocations. As revealed in *The Job* (interviews with Daniel Odier), Burroughs's recent interests have been less in fiction than in the possibilities for human growth—evidenced especially in his fascination with out-of-body experience and psychobiology. *Exterminator!* and *The Wild Boys* are more accessible than much of his previous work, but no less unsettling. John Tytell, for one, suggests that *The Wild Boys* is Burroughs's best work since *Naked Lunch.*

The piercing of flesh by the needle, the body by the phallus, the rending of language and—finally—the physical cosmos itself, these are transformations. William Burroughs's endless, cranky linguistic experiments—with cut-ups, fold-ins, the shattering of images, sentences and words, with nightclub routines and carnival "drums" and surreal war and sex fantasies—flawed and confusing as they can be, I see as an attempt to use The Word itself to negate its own power, to lay bare the multiple prisons of corporeal existence, the passage of time, the deceits of language, the illusions of individual consciousness, the endless charades of mass social and political existence.

—Jack Hicks

BYRD, William, II

Born: Westover, Virginia, 28 March 1674. **Education:** Felsted Grammar School, Essex, England; trained in business, London, 1690-91; studied at Middle Temple, London, 1692-95; called to the bar, 1695. **Family:** Married Lucy Parke in 1706 (died 1716), two daughters and two sons; 2) Maria Taylor in 1724, three daughters and one son. **Career:** Returned to Virginia, 1696; elected to House of Burgesses, Williamsburg, for Henrico County, 1696; represented Virginia Assembly in London, 1697, and colonial agent, 1698-1705; returned to Virginia and appointed Receiver-General, 1705; member, Virginia Council, 1709-44: represented Council against Lieutenant-Governor Spotswood in London, 1715-19, and as agent, 1721-26; President of Council, 1743. Commissioner in boundary dispute between Virginia and North Carolina, 1728, and crown representative in survey of Northern Neck of Virginia, 1735-36; rebuilt his estate at Westover, 1730-31. **Member:** Royal Society (London), 1696. **Died:** 26 August 1744.

PUBLICATIONS

Collections

Prose Works, edited by Louis B. Wright. 1966.
The Correspondence of the Three William Byrds of Westover, Virginia 1684-1776, edited by Marion Tialing. 2 vols., 1977.

Prose

A Discourse Concerning the Plague, With Some Preservations Against It (possibly not by Byrd). 1721.
Description of the Dismal Swamp and a Proposal to Drain the Swamp, edited by Earl Gregg Swem. 1922.
A Journey to the Land of Eden and Other Papers, edited by Mark Van Doren. 1928.
Histories of the Dividing Line Betwixt Virginia and North Carolina, edited by William K. Boyd. 1929.
Natural History of Virginia; or, The Newly Discovered Eden (probably not by Byrd), edited and translated (from 1737 German version) by Richmond Croom Beatty and William J. Mulloy. 1940.
The Secret Diary 1709-1712, edited by Louis B. Wright and Marion Tialing. 1941; selection, as *The Great American Gentleman: Byrd of Westover in Virginia,* 1963.
Another Secret Diary 1739-1741, edited by Maude H. Woodfin and Marion Tialing. 1942.
The London Diary 1717-1721, and Other Writings, edited by Louis B. Wright and Marion Tinling. 1958.

*

Bibliography: *John and William Bartram, William Byrd II and St. John de Crévecour: A Reference Guide* by Rose Marie Cutting, 1976.

Critical Studies: *Byrd of Westover* by Richmond Croom Beatty, 1932; *The Byrds of Virginia* by Alden Hatch, 1969; *Byrd of Westover 1674-1744* by Pierre Marambaud, 1971; *The Diary, and Life, of William Byrd II of Virginia, 1674-1744*, 1987, and *On the Sources of Patriarchal Rage: The Commonplace Books of William Byrd and Thomas Jefferson and the Gendering of Power in the Eighteenth Century*, 1992, both by Kenneth A. Lockridge.

*   *   *

The reputation of William Byrd II of Westover has grown steadily in importance among scholars and historians of American culture during the last decades of the twentieth century. Critics have labeled him a belated Restoration cavalier and satirist, a Queen Anne wit, a pamphleteer, a promoter, an American Pepys, a travel writer, a naturalist, and a historian. He was all of these things, but he was also a model for what would become the Southern gentleman planter and a founder of the Southern school of letters.

Some have questioned Byrd's position as a writer because he published so little. It is true that his only published works during his lifetime were a scientific paper in the *Philosophical Transactions* of the Royal Society in 1698, the anonymous pamphlet *A Discourse Concerning the Plague* in 1721, and a few poems attributed to him, but he was writing constantly. He produced almost without fail daily entries in his diary and wrote four complete travel narratives, love poetry and occasional verse, character sketches, satiric essays, translations, literary exercises, and a large body of correspondence-business, family, and love letters. Writing was an integral part of his life, and he expressed himself with all the rhetorical skills of the published writer.

Byrd clearly had some theories of composition and understood the importance of style and audience. Many of his ideas might have been absorbed from his contemporaries and colleagues in England—William Congreve, Nicholas Rowe, John Oldmixon, and William Wycherley were among his friends—and he frequently attended the theater at Drury Lane and Lincoln's Inn when in residence. We know that Byrd prepared a second version of his *History of the Dividing Line* specifically for publication, although he never submitted it to the printer. A comparison of both versions shows that he was aware of audience—the first was witty and satirical of things Virginians would understand, and the second is more serious and directed to a British audience with a distinct promotional slant. The manuscripts of his narratives *A Progress to the Mines in the Year 1732* and *A Journey to the Land of Eden Anno 1773* were copied out apparently with publication in mind, and there exist fair-hand copies of other pieces that seem to have been intended for the printer. Most of his writings, however, were known only to the friends among whom they circulated.

The diaries, the least literary of Byrd's manuscripts, were not written with the assumption that anyone would read them, thus his use of a cryptic shorthand. We need not exclude the possibility, however, that he entertained the notion of writing an autobiography some day for which the entries would provide an outline. There is, in any case, little of the refined wit and bawdy humor one finds in Byrd's public writings, but once the reader adjusts to the routine of the daily formula for entries, little nuggets of insight and activity appear that flesh out Byrd's life and personality. We observe the skills necessary for the management of a large estate; the political duties of a prominent Virginia aristocrat; Byrd's pursuit of learning and literature as a scholar and author; his reading habits; his private dreams and superstitions; his religious beliefs; his interest in other women besides his wife; his drinking, gambling, horse-play, and lewd language; his bowel movements and practice of masturbation; and the quality of his domestic life, including his wife's moods, their marital arguments, and even where they had sex ("In the afternoon my wife and I had a little quarrel which I reconciled with a flourish. Then she read a sermon in Dr. Tillotson to me. It is to be observed that the flourish was performed on the billiard table."—30 July 1710). In short, Byrd emerges from these pages a broad-minded, engaging, and warmly human individual.

Throughout Byrd's writings, both public and private, satire and irony remained central to his perspective and style. "Satire is much the easier work of the understanding," he once noted, "because Nature is always at hand to assist us, when we attempt to sink the character of our neighbor below our own. . . ." This implies his theory of humor—that comedy depends on viewing others as inferior to one's self. His comic sense is nowhere more evident than in the *History of the Dividing Line,* where he chronicles the habits and peculiarities of the inhabitants of North Carolina, which he calls condescendingly "Lubberland." In such passages lies the genesis of a mainstream of Southern humor populated by a series of opportunists and disreputable poor white trash, such as Sut Lovingood, Simon Suggs, Flem Snopes, and Snuffy Smith.

Much of the myth and idea of the American South originated with Byrd in the colonial period. Long before the Revolution and the formal organization of several of the states into a Southern political bloc, as a writer and a man Byrd anticipated many of the characteristics of what would become known as Southern culture. Because of the wide range of his work in style, sophistication, and subject matter, Byrd may also be entitled to recognition as the South's first man of letters.

—M. Thomas Inge

C

CABELL, James Branch

Born: Richmond, Virginia, 14 April 1879. **Education:** The College of William and Mary, Williamsburg, Virginia, 1894-98, A.B. 1898. **Family:** Married 1) Priscilla Bradley Shepherd in 1913 (died 1949), one son; 2) Margaret Waller Freedman in 1950. **Career:** Instructor in Greek and French at the College of William and Mary while an undergraduate, 1896-97; staff member, Richmond *Times,* 1898, New York *Herald,* 1899-1901, and Richmond *News,* 1901; engaged in genealogical research in America and Europe, 1901-11; office worker at coal mine in West Virginia, 1911-13; genealogist, Virginia Society of Colonial Wars, 1916-28, and Virginia Sons of the American Revolution, 1917-24; editor, Virginia War History Commission, 1919-26; silent editor, *Reviewer,* Richmond, 1921; editor, *American Spectator,* 1932-35. President, Virginia Writers Association, 1918-21. **Member:** American Academy. **Died:** 5 May 1958.

PUBLICATIONS

Collections

The Letters, edited by Edward Wagenknecht. 1975.

Fiction

The Eagle's Shadow. 1904; revised edition, 1923.
The Line of Love (stories). 1905; revised edition, 1921.
Gallantry (stories). 1907; revised edition, 1922.
Chivalry (stories). 1909; revised edition, 1921.
The Cords of Vanity. 1909; revised edition, 1920.
The Soul of Melicent. 1913; revised edition, as *Domnei,* 1920.
The Rivet in Grandfather's Neck. 1915.
The Certain Hour (stories). 1916.
The Cream of the Jest. 1917; revised edition, 1923.
Beyond Life. 1919.
Jurgen. 1919.
Figures of Earth. 1921.
The High Place. 1923.
The Silver Stallion. 1926.
The Music from Behind the Moon (stories). 1926.
Something about Eve. 1927.
The Works (Storisende Edition; includes "The Biography of the Life of Manuel": revised editions of earlier works, plus new material). 18 vols., 1927-30.
The White Robe (stories). 1928.
The Way of Ecben. 1929.
Smirt: An Urbane Nightmare. 1934.
Smith: A Sylvan Interlude. 1935.
Smire: An Acceptance in the Third Person. 1937.
The King Was in His Counting House. 1938.
Hamlet Had an Uncle. 1940.
The First Gentleman of America. 1942; as *The First American Gentleman,* 1942.
There Were Two Pirates. 1946.

The Witch-Woman (includes revised editions of *The Music from Behind the Moon, The Way of Ecben, The White Robe*). 1948.
The Devil's Own Dear Son. 1949.

Play

The Jewel Merchants. 1921.

Poetry

From the Hidden Way. 1916; revised edition, 1924.
Ballades from the Hidden Way. 1928.
Sonnets from Antan. 1929.

Other

Branchiana (genealogy). 1907.
Branch of Abingden. 1911.
The Majors and Their Marriages. 1915.
The Judging of Jurgen. 1920.
Jurgen and the Censor. 1920.
Taboo: A Legend Retold from the Dirghic of Saevius Nicanor. 1921.
Joseph Hergesheimer. 1921.
The Lineage of Lichfield: An Essay in Eugenics. 1922.
Straws and Prayer-Books. 1924.
Some of Us: An Essay in Epitaphs. 1930.
Townsend of Lichfield. 1930.
Between Dawn and Sunrise: Selections, edited by John Macy. 1930.
These Restless Heads: A Trilogy of Romantics. 1932.
Special Delivery: A Packet of Replies. 1933.
Ladies and Gentlemen: A Parcel of Reconsiderations. 1934.
Preface to the Past. 1936.
The Nightmare Has Triplets: An Author's Note on Smire. 1937.
On Ellen Glasgow. 1938.
The St. Johns: A Parade of Diversities, H. L. with A.J. Hanna. 1943.
Let Me Lie. 1947.
Quiet, Please. 1952.
As I Remember It: Some Epilogues in Recollection. 1955.
Between Friends: Letters of Cabell and Others, edited by Padraic Colum and Margaret Freeman Cabell. 1962.

*

Bibliography: *Cabell: A Complete Bibliography* by James N. Hall, 1974; *Cabell: A Reference Guide* by Maurice Duke, 1979.

Critical Studies: *No Place on Earth: Ellen Glasgow, Cabell, and Richmond-in-Virginia* by Louis D. Rubin, Jr., 1959; *Cabell* by Joe Lee Davis, 1962; *Jesting Moses: A Study in Cabellian Comedy* by Arvin R. Wells, 1962; *Cabell: The Dream and the Reality* by Desmond Tarrant, 1967; *Cabell: Three Essays* by Carl Van Doren, H.L. Mencken, and Hugh Walpole, 1967; *Cabell under Fire: Four Essays* by Geoffrey Morley-Mower, 1975; *Cabell: The Richmond Iconoclast* by Dorothy B. Schlegel, 1975; *In Quest of Cabell: Five Exploratory Essays* by William Leigh Godshalk, 1976; *Cabell: Centennial Essays* edited by M. Thomas Inge and Edgar E.

MacDonald, 1983; *From Satire to Subversion: The Fantasies of James Branch Cabell* by James D. Riemer, 1989.

*   *   *

Regarded as belonging in the top echelon of American writers throughout the 1920s, James Branch Cabell has never regained the prestige he then knew. But even during the decade of his greatest fame, Cabell was outside the mainstream. While his contemporaries found increasing fascination with life in their period and used the standard of critical realism to treat the immediate, Cabell's preference was for romance and myth. He defined his preference brilliantly in *Beyond Life* and reiterated it in essays and romances throughout his long career. He avowed "The auctorial virtues of distinction and clarity, of beauty and symmetry, of tenderness and truth and urbanity."

Cabell's tastes, like his ancestry, were aristocratic and mannered. The elegant prose style he perfected was appropriate to his Virginia roots and his subject matter. It is ironic that so cultivated a writer with a specialized appeal became so popular. One important reason was that Cabell was almost the only sign of hope **H.L. Mencken** could find that the culture of the post-Civil War South was not to be damned totally, and Mencken made very loud noises about Cabell's work. More important was *Jurgen,* the tale of a medieval pawnbroker in Cabell's mythical kingdom of Poictesme. Jurgen was ever willing to do the gentlemanly thing, and word got around that Cabell's book was lascivious. It was suppressed in 1920, but Cabell's cause rallied the foes of censorship, ensuring booming sales. The novel, which certainly has it Rabelaisian touches, was exonerated in court in 1922.

Jurgen is a part of Cabell's most ambitious and most important work, the eighteen-volume "Biography of the Life of Manuel." Dom Manuel is the founder of Poictesme, and his followers and offspring (legitimate and otherwise) inherit his legend and face the same tensions between the dream (the dynamic illusion) and the frustrating reality of everyday life. The most brilliant of the Romances besides *Jurgen* are *Figures of Earth, The Silver Stallion, The High Place,* and *Something about Eve.* Cabell revised his earlier Romances of Virginia as later volumes of the Biography because they, too, were illustrative of the attitudes of Chivalry, Gallantry, and Poetry treated in the more famous books. Virginia and Poictesme have much in common.

After the completion of the Biography, Cabell published for a time under the name Branch Cabell, to symbolize the completion of his grand design and perhaps in recognition of the end of the era of his greatest fame. During the years of the Depression and World War II, Cabell tenaciously followed his own ideals and eschewed the contemporary. A trilogy of high satire (Smirt, Smith, Smire) treated the dream life of the writer, mirroring the dream experience more fully than anything Cabell had written previously. Another trilogy dealt with murder, conquest, and intrigue in Hamlet's Denmark, the family circle of Cosimo dei Medici, and the Virginia of Nemattanon, an Indian prince during the time of the Spanish conquests. A final trilogy explored Florida's legendary past.

Cabell then focused attention on his own life with several volumes of reminiscences and assessments of his career and those of many of his contemporaries. He viewed his progress with humor and detachment. His professed goal was to write beautifully of beautiful happenings. Although he can certainly sting his readers with a sense of reality, it seems clear that writing gave him great joy. He wrote mainly for himself, he tells us, but he did so with such humor and insight that he insures himself a loyal group of enthusiasts.

—Joseph M. Flora

CABLE, George Washington

Born: New Orleans, Louisiana, 12 October 1844. **Education:** New Orleans public schools until 1859. **Military Service:** Served in the 4th Mississippi Cavalry during the Civil War, 1863-65. **Family:** Married 1) Louisa Stewart Bartlett in 1869 (died 1904), six children; 2) Eva C. Stevenson in 1906 (died 1923); 3) Hanna Cowing in 1923. **Career:** State surveyor in Louisiana, 1865-66; incapacitated by malaria, 1866-68; reporter and columnist ("Drop Shot") New Orleans *Picayune,* 1870; accountant and correspondence clerk, A.C. Black and Company, cotton factors, New Orleans, 1869-79; accountant with cotton exchange, 1879-81; full-time writer from 1881; after 1884 made yearly tours of the U.S. reading his own works; lived in Northampton, Massachusetts, from 1885; organized the Home-Culture Club, Northampton, 1886 (renamed Northampton People's Institute, 1909); published the journals *Letter,* 1892-96, and *Symposium,* 1896. **Awards:** A.M.: Yale University, New Haven, Connecticut, 1883. D.Litt.: Washington and Lee University, Lexington, Virginia, 1882; Yale University, 1901; Bowdoin College, Brunswick, Maine, 1904. **Member:** American Academy. **Died:** 31 January 1925.

PUBLICATIONS

Collections

Creoles and Cajuns: Stories of Old Louisiana, edited by Arlin Turner. 1959.

Fiction

Old Creole Days (stories). 1879.
The Grandissimes: A Story of Creole Life. 1880.
Madame Delphine. 1881.
Dr. Sevier. 1884.
Madame Delphine, Carancro, Grande Pointe. 1887.
Bonaventure: A Prose Pastoral of Acadian Louisiana. 1888.
Strange True Stories of Louisiana. 1889.
John March, Southerner. 1894.
Strong Hearts. 1899.
The Cavalier. 1901.
Pete Raphael. 1901.
Bylow Hill. 1902.
Kincaid's Battery. 1908.
"Posson Jone' " and Pére Raphaël. 1909.
Gideon's Band: A Tale of the Mississippi. 1914.
The Amateur Garden. 1914.
The Flower of the Chapdelaines. 1918.
Lovers of Louisiana (Today). 1918.

Other

The Creoles of Louisiana. 1884.
The Silent South. 1885; revised edition, 1889.

The Negro Question. 1890.
A Busy Man's Bible. 1891.
A Memory of Roswell Smith. 1892.
A Southerner Looks at Negro Discrimination: Selected Writings, edited by Isabel Cable Manes. 1946.
Twins of Genius: Letters of Mark Twain, Cable, and Others, edited by Guy A. Cardwell. 1953.
The Negro Question: A Selection of Writings on Civil Rights in the South, edited by Arlin Turner. 1958.
Mark Twain and Cable: The Record of a Literary Friendship, edited by Arlin Turner. 1960.

*

Bibliography: *Cable: An Annotated Bibliography* by William H. Roberson, 1982.

Critical Studies: *Cable: His Life and Letters* by Lucy Leffingwell Cable Bikle, 1928; *Cable: A Study of His Early Life and Work* by Kjell Ekstrom, 1950; *Cable: A Biography* by Arlin Turner, 1956, and *Critical Essays on Cable* edited by Turner, 1980; *Cable: The Northampton Years,* 1959, and *Cable,* 1962, both by Philip Butcher; *Cable: The Life and Times of a Southern Heretic* by Louis D. Rubin, Jr., 1969; *The Grandissimes: Centennial Essays* edited by Thomas J. Richardson, 1981; "'An Atmosphere of Hints and Allusions': Bras-Coupe and the Context of Black Insurrection in The Grandissimes" by Barbara Ladd in *The Southern Quarterly: A Journal of the Arts in the South,* spring 1991; "Native Outsider: George Washington Cable" by Alice Hall Petry, in *Literary New Orleans: Essays and Meditations,* edited by Richard S. Kennedy, 1992; "George Washington Cable's 'My Politics': Context and Revision of a Southern Memoir" by James Robert Payne in *Multicultural Autobiography: American Lives* edited and introduction by James Robert Payne, 1992; *Nationalism and the Color Line in George Washington Cable, Mark Twain, and William Faulkner* by Barbara Ladd, 1996; *George Washington Cable Revisited* by John Cleman, 1996.

*   *   *

George Washington Cable was one of the first progressive writers of the "New South." His father's German background and his mother's New England Protestantism contributed to his own sense of isolation in a community whose leaders were primarily French and Catholic. Cable's position as an outsider may have stimulated his interest in sociological problems and made him more sensitive to the needs of minorities, especially southern blacks. His father's untimely death and the Civil War prevented him from completing his formal education, but he was always an avid reader and enjoyed writing. In his late twenties he took a part-time job on the New Orleans *Picayune,* where his "Drop Shot" column, though occasionally controversial, was well-received. At this time Cable began writing a series of short stories and was discovered by Scribner's Edward King, who was touring Louisiana in search of materials for his "Great South" series. Although Scribner's rejected "Bibi," Cable's story of a tormented slave-prince, on the grounds of its unpleasant subject matter, they published his character sketch of an old Creole, " 'Sieur George," in 1873. Richard Watson Gilder, editor of *Scribner's Monthly* and the *Century,* considered Cable one of his leading local colorists, who would contribute to Gilder's plan for reconciling the North and South through litera-

ture. **H.H. Boyesen** also took an interest in Cable's writing and initiated a correspondence helpful to the latter's career.

In 1879 Cable's *Old Creole Days,* a collection of short stories, was published, and the first installments of *The Grandissimes,* which incorporated the "Bibi" materials, appeared in *Scribner's Monthly.* In 1880 *The Grandissimes* was published in book form, as was *Madame Delphine,* a novella. These two books represent Cable's highest achievement, anticipating the complex drama of Faulkner's works. Each deals with racial injustice, the continuing problems caused by exploitation of the black community, and the Creoles' resistance to social change. He described the lush, exotic world of the deep South unknown to most Americans. Topics considered off limits to the genteel authors of the Tidewater region or the wholesome humorists of the Piedmont are insightfully probed: miscegenation, the cruelties of the *Code Noire,* and the arrogance and indolence of the aristocracy.

By 1882 Cable began a full-time career as a writer, completing *Dr. Sevier,* a serious novel dealing with prison reform, which was followed by a *Century* exposé, "The Convict Lease System in the Southern States," and a history, *The Creoles of Louisiana.* These three works, openly polemical, offended Gilder and caused tremendous resentment throughout the South. A reading tour with **Mark Twain** brought Cable some additional income and popularity, but his increasingly fervent publications on the Negro's dilemma, especially "A Freedman's Case in Equity" and *The Silent South,* made him notorious in New Orleans, and he eventually settled in Northampton, Massachusetts.

There Cable organized the Home-Culture clubs, racially integrated reading groups designed to raise the educational level of average citizens. The success of the movement was due in part to the national atmosphere of self-improvement and upward mobility in the last quarter of the 19th century.

When Cable was fifty he published *John March, Southerner,* an ambiguous portrait of a Southern aristocrat during the reconstruction era. As in his earlier fiction he examined outmoded conceptions of chivalry and honor, racial injustice, and anachronistic social and political attitudes. This was his last attempt at social satire. He continued to be an outspoken essayist, but his fiction became unashamedly romantic. The public taste of the period and his editors reinforced his tendency toward sentimentalism. *The Cavalier* was Cable's greatest popular success. He even overcame his Calvinistic distrust of the stage and authorized a dramatic version of the novel, starring Julia Marlowe. Energetic until the end, he wrote three novels in his seventies and shaped an optimistic vision of technological progress in the New South and the eventual integration of the races.

Perhaps because he remained too dependent on the family magazine audience and the taste of his editors, Cable did not live up to his early potential as a major southern writer. Nevertheless, in his best fiction he transcended the limitations of the local color genre and revealed a daring and prophetic intelligence.

—Kimball King

CADE, Toni. *See* **BAMBARA, Toni Cade.**

CAHAN, Abraham

Born: Podberezy, near Vilna, Lithuania, 7 July 1860; immigrated to the United States in 1882; later became citizen. **Education:**

The Vilna Teachers Institute, 1877-81; later attended law school in New York. **Family:** Married Anna Bronstein in 1887. **Career:** Settled in New York: worked in a cigar factory, and as tutor and free-lance writer, from 1882; coeditor, *Neie Tseit* (New Era) Yiddish socialist paper, 1886; editor, *Arbeiter Zeitung,* 1891-94, and *Die Zukunft,* 1893-94; reporter, *Commercial Advertiser,* New York, 1897-1901; helped found, 1897, and editor, 1902 and 1903-51, *Vorwärts* (Jewish Daily Forward) Yiddish newspaper, New York. **Died:** 31 August 1951.

PUBLICATIONS

Fiction

Yekl: A Tale of New York Ghetto. 1896.
The Imported Bridegroom and Other Stories of the New York Ghetto. 1898.
The White Terror and the Red: A Novel of Revolutionary Russia. 1905.
Rafael Naarizokh (story). 1907.
Neshoma Yesorah; Fanny's Khasonim (Fanny's Suitors; novellas). 1913(?).
The Rise of David Levinsky. 1917.
Yekl and the Imported Bridegroom and Other Stories of the New York Ghetto. 1970.

Other

Social Remedies. 1889.
Historia fun di Fareingte Shtaaten (History of the United States). 2 vols., 1910-12.
Bleter fun Mein Leben. 5 vols., 1926-31; vols. 1 and 2 as *The Education of Cahan,* 2 vols., 1969.
Palestina. 1934.
Rashel: A Biografia. 1938.
Grandma Never Lived in America: The New Journalism of Cahan, edited by Moses Rischin. 1986.

Editor, *Hear the Other Side: A Symposium of Democratic Socialist Opinion.* 1934.

*

Bibliography: *Cahan: A Bibliography* by Ephim H. Joshurin, 1941; by Sanford E. Marovitz and Lewis Fried, in *American Literary Realism 1870-1910,* no. 3, 1970.

Critical Studies: *From the Ghetto: The Fiction of Cahan* by Jules Chametzky, 1977; "The Secular Trinity of a Lonely Millionaire: Language, Sex and Power in The Rise of David Levinsky" by Sanford E. Marovitz, in *Studies in American Jewish Literature* vol. 2, 1982; "Cahan's David Levinsky: An Inner Profile" by Bernard Weinstein, in *MELUS: The Journal of the Society for the Study of the Multi Ethnic Literature of the United States,* fall 1983; "The Objectivity of Abraham Cahan" by Albert Waldinger, in *Proteus: A Journal of Ideas,* spring 1990; *Abraham Cahan* by Sanford E. Marovitz, 1996; *Jewish Socialists in the United States: The Cahan Debate, 1925-1926* edited by Jacob Goldstein and Abraham Cahan, 1998.

*   *   *

Abraham Cahan is perhaps more notable for his leadership in the Yiddish-speaking community of the Lower East Side than he is for any of his English prose. For more than forty years he was the editor of the popular Yiddish newspaper the *Jewish Daily Forward.* As such he guided the immigrant Jewish populace in their Americanization. His editorials, his Yiddish fiction, and his work as a union organizer all bespoke his socialist goals and didactic prejudices.

It was not until 1895 that he published his first short story in English. At least as early as the 1880s, however, he was contributing nonfiction prose to the New York *World* and the New York *Sun and Press.* In these pieces Cahan introduced the East Side ghetto to non-Jewish America. In the career of Cahan, however, these articles are not as important as the writing he did in the offices of the *Commercial Advertiser* (1897-1901). The relationship between Cahan and his colleagues on the English newspaper was mutually beneficial: Hutchins Hapgood and Lincoln Steffens learned of the intellectual turmoil and excitement of the Lower East Side; Cahan learned more sophisticated techniques of journalism.

Before his tenure on the *Commercial Advertiser,* Cahan had published only two short stories and a novella in English. These three pieces are local color treatments of immigrant life, reflecting Cahan's strong moralizing temperament and his socialist criticism of the dehumanization of capitalism.

Cahan never abandoned this socialist didacticism, but his later fiction is more successful in keeping it under aesthetic control. Cahan grew more interested in presenting the dilemma of his old world immigrants in modern America, whose struggles result from the conflict between the teachings and expectations of the past and the realities and threats of the present. In short story form, Cahan's most successful treatment of this conflict is "The Imported Bridegroom," a tale of the repercussions of the modern world vision on Jews in different stages of alienation from their Jewish past.

It is, however, the novel *The Rise of David Levinsky* that assures Cahan his significance in American literature. Past ideals and present desires plague the rise of this Jewish Silas Lapham. The title clearly alludes to the famous novel of **William Dean Howells,** Cahan's favorite American writer and his staunch supporter in the American literary establishment. The story of David is different from that of Silas: unlike the Protestant version of the rags to riches hero, Cahan's hero never effects a moral rise, never learns to balance his present reality with his past expectations.

Cahan's novel is one of the most powerful about immigrant life in America and one of the most telling portraits of the joylessness of the moneyed life without spiritual fulfillment. After this great success, Cahan seemed to have finished his discourse with English-speaking America. The rest of his career was centered on the *Jewish Daily Forward* and his autobiography in Yiddish.

—R. Barbara Gitenstein

CAIN, James M(allahan)

Born: Annapolis, Maryland, 1 July 1892. **Education:** Washington College, Chesterton, Maryland, B.A. 1910, M.A. 1917. **Military Service:** Served in the U.S. Army during World War I (editor-in-chief of *Lorraine Cross,* 79th Division newspaper). **Family:** Married 1) Mary Rebecca Clough in 1920 (divorced 1923); 2) Elina Sjösted Tyszecha in 1927 (divorced 1942); 3) Aileen Pringle in 1944 (divorced 1945); 4) Florence Macbeth Whitwell in 1947 (died 1966). **Career:** Reporter, Baltimore *American,* 1917-18; Baltimore *Sun,* 1919-23; professor of journalism, St. John's College, Annapolis, 1923-24; editorial writer, *New York World,* 1924-31; screenwriter, 1932-48. **Award:** Mystery Writers of America Grand Master award, 1970. **Died:** 27 October 1977.

PUBLICATIONS

Collection

Three Complete Novels. 1994.

Fiction

The Postman Always Rings Twice. 1934.
Serenade. 1937.
Mildred Pierce. 1941; edited by Albert J. LaValley, 1980.
Love's Lovely Counterfeit. 1942.
Career in C Major and Other Stories. 1943.
Three of a Kind: Career in C Major, The Embezzler, Double Indemnity. 1944; *Career in C Major* and *The Embezzler* published as *Everybody Does It,* 1949.
Past All Dishonor. 1946.
The Butterfly. 1947.
Sinful Woman. 1947.
The Moth. 1948.
Three of Hearts (omnibus). 1949.
Jealous Woman. 1950.
The Root of His Evil. 1952; as *Shameless,* 1958.
Galatea. 1953.
Mignon. 1962.
The Magician's Wife. 1965.
Rainbow's End. 1975.
The Institute. 1976.
The Baby in the Icebox and Other Short Fiction, edited by Roy Hoopes. 1981.
Cloud Nine. 1984.
The Enchanted Isle. 1985.
Career in C Major and Other Fiction, edited by Roy Hoopes. 1986.

Plays

Hero; Hemp; Red, White, and Blue; Trial by Jury; Theological Interlude; Citizenship; Will of the People (short plays), in *American Mercury 6* to *29,* 1926-29.
The Postman Always Rings Twice, from his own novel (produced 1936).
Algiers (screenplay), with John Howard Lawson, in *Foremost Films of 1938,* edited by Frank Vreeland. 1939.

Screenplays: *Algiers,* with John Howard Lawson, 1938; *Stand Up and Fight,* with others, 1939; *When Tomorrow Comes,* with Dwight Taylor, 1939; *Gypsy Wildcat,* with others, 1944; *Everybody Does It,* with Nunnally Johnson, 1949.

Other

Our Government. 1930.
Sixty Years of Journalism. edited by Roy Hoopes. 1986.

Editor, *79th Division Headquarters Troop: A Record,* with Malcolm Gilbert. 1919.
Editor, *For Men Only: A Collection of Short Stories.* 1944.

*

Critical Studies: "Man under Sentence of Death: The Novels of Cain" by Joyce Carol Oates, in *Tough Guy Writers of the Thirties* edited by David Madden, 1968, and *Cain,* 1970, and *Cain's Craft,* 1985, both by Madden; *Cain: The Biography* by Roy Hoopes, 1982; "Sexuality, Guilt and Detection: Tension between History and Suspense" by Richard Bradbury, in *American Crime Fiction: Studies in the Genre* edited by Brian Docherty, 1988; *James M. Cain* by Paul Skenazy, 1989; *The American Roman Noir: Hammett, Cain, and Chandler* by William Marling, 1995.

*   *   *

James M. Cain is the twenty-minute egg of the hard-boiled school. The tough-guy novel made a lasting impact on "serious" American and European fiction; for instance, Albert Camus admitted that *The Postman Always Rings Twice* was a model for *The Stranger.* Cain said he had only one story to tell: a love story. "I write of the wish that comes true, for some reason a terrifying concept . . . I think my stories have some quality of the opening of a forbidden box." The act of forcing the wish to come true isolates Cain's obsessed lovers from society and places them on what he calls a "love-rack."

If Cain's "heels and harpies" are to consummate and prolong their sexual passion, they must commit a crime. Frank Chambers and Cora in *The Postman* must murder Cora's husband; in *Serenade* Juana must slaughter Winston Hawes, a homosexual symphony conductor, to ensure the sexual salvation of her lover, Howard Sharp, an opera singer; sex and money are the motives in Walter's and Phyllis's murder of her husband in *Double Indemnity;* in *The Butterfly,* when his apparently incestuous lust for his daughter Kady is threatened, Jess Tyler, a West Virginia farmer, shoots Moke Blue.

In his novels dealing with criminal love, even in his romances *Career in C Major* and *Galatea* and his historical novels *Past All Dishonor* and *Mignon,* Cain effectively dramatizes profound insights into the American character and scene and into the way American dreams degenerate into nightmares. In his novels of character, *Mildred Pierce* and *The Moth,* set in the depression years, his scrutiny is most direct. Physically and often intellectually aggressive, Cain's audacious American male is an inside-dopester equipped with great know-how in many areas (even food, music, and the art of biography); but self-dramatizing inclinations, a suppressed sentimentality, and a misconceived American romanticism and optimism often defeat him. The female is realistic, ruthless, materialistic, and sensitive to minor social taboos even while violating major laws. A deadly pair, they are more often destroyed by their own sexual and materialistic overreaching than by the police. In their total commitment to each other, severing all ties to other people, Cain's lovers experience a blazing, self-consuming flash of self-deceptive purity and hideous innocence.

Without style and technique, Cain's rich and fascinating subject matter, energized by imagination and controlled by formula, would lack sustaining power. A few characters and a simple plot with a first-person narrator—that is the magic combination of a Cain "natural," producing a style like the "metal of an automatic," a pace like "a motorcycle," and a sense of immediacy that hypnotizes the reader. The first person narration enables Cain to use basic technical devices with special skill and appropriateness. His distinctive dialog is especially powerful when it is all of a piece with the cold objectivity and immediacy of the arrogant, commanding first-person voice. Cain, whose conscious intention was to "cast a spell on the beholder," stated that he developed "the habit of needling a story at the least hint of a breakdown," striving for a "rising coefficient of intensity."

Cain would never have used the term "existential," but as a consequence of his primary intention to tell a story superbly well, he created an objective, disinterested, often pessimistic view of life that is simultaneously terrifying and starkly beautiful.

—David Madden

CALDWELL, Erskine (Preston)

Born: Moreland, Georgia, 17 December 1903. **Education:** Erskine College, Due West, South Carolina, 1920-21; University of Virginia, Charlottesville, 1922, 1925-26; University of Pennsylvania, Philadelphia, 1924. **Family:** Married 1) Helen Lannigan in 1925 (divorced 1938), two sons and one daughter; 2) the photographer Margaret Bourke-White in 1939 (divorced 1942); 3) June Johnson in 1942 (divorced 1955), one son; 4) Virginia Moffett Fletcher in 1957. **Career:** Played professional football, Wilkes-Barre, Pennsylvania, 1920s; reporter, Atlanta *Journal,* 1925-26; freelance writer from 1926; ran a bookstore in Portland, Maine, 1928; screenwriter, Hollywood, 1930-34, 1942-43; foreign correspondent in Mexico, Spain, Czechoslovakia, Russia, and China, 1938-41; editor, American Folkways series (25 vols.), 1941-55. **Awards:** Order of Cultural Merit (Poland), 1981. **Member:** National Institute of Arts and Letters, 1942; American Academy, 1984; Commander, Order of Arts and Letters (France), 1984. **Died:** 11 April 1987.

PUBLICATIONS

Short Stories

American Earth. 1931; as *A Swell-Looking Girl,* 1951.
Mama's Little Girl (story). 1932.
A Message for Genevieve (story). 1933.
We Are the Living: Brief Stories. 1933.
Kneel to the Rising Sun and Other Stories. 1935.
The Sacrilege of Alan Kent (story). 1936.
Southways: Stories. 1938.
Jackpot: The Short Stories. 1940; abridged edition, as *Midsummer Passion,* 1948.
Georgia Boy. 1943.
A Day's Wooing and Other Stories. 1944.
Stories by Caldwell: 24 Representative Stories, edited by Henry Seidel Canby. 1944; as *The Pocket Book of Caldwell Stories,* 1947.

The Caldwell Caravan: Novels and Stories. 1946.
Where the Girls Were Different and Other Stories, edited by Donald A. Wollheim. 1948.
A Woman in the House. 1949.
The Humorous Side of Caldwell, edited by Robert Cantwell. 1951; as *Where the Girls Were Different and Other Stories,* 1962.
The Courting of Susie Brown. 1952.
The Complete Stories. 1953.
Gulf Coast Stories. 1956.
Certain Women. 1957.
When You Think of Me. 1959.
Men and Women: 22 Stories. 1961.
Stories. 1980.
Stories of Life: North and South. 1983.
The Black and White Stories of Caldwell. 1984.
Midsummer Passion and Other Tales of Maine Cussedness, edited by Charles G. Waugh and Martin H. Greenberg. 1990.

Novels

The Bastard. 1930.
Poor Fool. 1930.
Tobacco Road. 1932.
God's Little Acre. 1933.
Journeyman. 1935; revised edition, 1938.
Trouble in July. 1940.
All Night Long: A Novel of Guerrilla Warfare in Russia. 1942.
Tragic Ground. 1944.
A House in the Uplands. 1946.
The Sure Hand of God. 1947.
This Very Earth. 1948.
Place Called Estherville. 1949.
Episode in Palmetto. 1950.
A Lamp for Nightfall. 1952.
Love and Money. 1954.
Gretta. 1955.
Claudelle Inglish. 1959; as *Claudell,* 1959.
Jenny by Nature. 1961.
Close to Home. 1962.
The Last Night of Summer. 1963.
Miss Mama Aimee. 1967.
Summertime Island. 1968.
The Weather Shelter. 1969.
The Earnshaw Neighborhood. 1971.
Annette. 1973.

Plays

Screenplays: *A Nation Dances* (documentary), 1943; *Volcano,* 1953.

Other

In Defense of Myself. 1930.
Tenant Farmer. 1935.
Some American People. 1935.
You Have Seen Their Faces, photographs by Margaret Bourke-White. 1937.
North of the Danube, photographs by Margaret Bourke-White. 1939.
Say! Is This the U.S.A.?, photographs by Margaret Bourke-White. 1941.

All-Out on the Road to Smolensk. 1942; as *Moscow Under Fire:*
  A Wartime Diary 1941, 1942.
Russia at War, photographs by Margaret Bourke-White. 1942.
Call It Experience: The Years of Learning How to Write. 1951.
Molly Cottontail (for children). 1958.
Around About America. 1964.
In Search of Bisco. 1965.
The Deer at Our House (for children). 1966.
In the Shadow of the Steeple. 1967.
Writing in America. 1967.
Deep South: Memory and Observation (includes *In the Shadow of*
  the Steeple). 1968.
Afternoons in Mid-America: Observations and Impressions. 1976.
With All My Might: An Autobiography. 1987.
Conversations with Caldwell, edited by Edwin T. Arnold. 1988.

Editor, *Smokey Mountain Country,* by North Callahan. 1988.

*

Critical Studies: *The Southern Poor-White from Lubberland to
Tobacco Road* by Shields McIlwaine, 1939; *Caldwell* by James
Korges, 1969; *Black Like It Is/Was: Caldwell's Treatment of Ra-
cial Themes* by William A. Sutton, 1974; *Critical Essays on
Caldwell* edited by Scott MacDonald, 1981; *Caldwell* by James
E. Devlin, 1984; *Caldwell Reconsidered* edited by Edwin T. Arnold,
1990; *Erskine Caldwell and the Fiction of Poverty: The Flesh and
the Spirit* by Sylvia Jenkins Cook, 1991; *Erskine Caldwell: His
Early Life and Works* (dissertation) by Erik Bledsoe, 1995; *The
People's War: Erskine Caldwell and the South* by Wayne Mixon,
1995; *The Critical Response to Erskine Caldwell* edited by Robert L. McDonald, 1997.

*   *   *

The degenerate side of life that Erskine Caldwell exploited so
successfully in 1932 in *Tobacco Road* extends back some 200 years
in Southern life, suggesting some kinship between his work and
that of the frontier humorists. A hallmark of Caldwell's exploitation of Southern folk and folkways is his use of what Shields
McIlwaine calls "idiotic gravity," emanating from characters who
are in dead earnest in their sometimes misguided, if not perverted,
commitment.

Caldwell's humorous approach to the seaminess and poverty
of Southern life, whether in *Tobacco Road, God's Little Acre,* or
Georgia Boy, accounts for his avoidance of the melodramatic and
banal. As Robert Cantwell suggested, Caldwell's comic treatment
of materials makes the poverty of his characters "unforgettable."

In terms of literary tradition, it is Caldwell's Chaucerian treatment of sex that places his novels in the mainstream of the *fabliau,*
McIlwaine noting that the author's poor whites like Ty Ty Walden
(*God's Little Acre*) and Jeeter Lester (*Tobacco Road*) enjoy the
"game of sex without self consciousness." Cantwell, moreover,
points out that Caldwell's sexual scenes normally have witnesses—
visitors, Negroes peering over fences, etc.—thus suggesting an initiation process. Caldwell's frank treatment of sex marks in the
1930s a major shift in popular literature. After the success of *Tobacco Road*—especially in resisting suppression—similar works by
later writers became a staple of commercial fiction. But, with the exception of *Trouble in July* (1940), few of Caldwell's own novels after
God's Little Acre add to his stature as a creative artist.

In an equally important sense the Caldwell canon owes much
to the tradition of naturalism in American writing. Thus Caldwell's
characters—oppressed by barren land, mill life, heredity, or other
circumstances beyond their control—fail to perceive any solution
in flight. The author, moreover, creates with some consistency
character after character who is a victim of his heredity and/or
environment. Jeeter Lester (*Tobacco Road*), for example, is but
the inevitable outcome of 100 years of family degeneration and
disintegration, whereas Ty Ty Walden's degeneracy (*God's Little
Acre*) is owed to a "perverted idealism" (McIlwaine).

Current criticism of Caldwell's work, however, places it in the
American Gothic vein. The author's use of deformed and sometimes mentally deficient and perverted characters defines his purpose. In *Tobacco Road* one is confronted by a grandmother consumed by pellagra, in *God's Little Acre* by Pluto's obesity, and in
Tragic Ground by Bubber's permanent grin. Whereas eighteenth-
and nineteenth-century Gothicists exploited setting and the supernatural as vehicles, both Caldwell and **William Faulkner** turned
Southern sociology and misshapen personalities into effective Gothic
pronouncements concerning the quality of modern life.

The Complete Stories reveals the author's true métier: Southern
settings, disenfranchised blacks and poor whites, a depression
background. "Candy-Man Beechum," his most frequently anthologized story, presents the artist at his best: passionate in his commitment to social values, primitive in his rhythmic articulation,
and genuine in the sense of uncontrolled fate that he evokes.

—George C. Longest

CALISHER, Hortense

Born: New York City, 20 December 1911. **Education:** Hunter
College High School, New York; Barnard College, New York, A.B.
in philosophy 1932. **Family:** Married 1) H. B. Heffelfinger in
1935, one daughter and one son; 2) Curtis Harnack in 1959. **Career:** Worked for Department of Public Welfare, New York, 1933-
34; adjunct professor of English, Barnard College, 1956-57; visiting professor, University of Iowa, Iowa City, 1957, 1959-60,
Stanford University, California, 1958, Sarah Lawrence College,
Bronxville, New York, 1962, 1967 and Brandeis University,
Waltham, Massachusetts, 1963-64; writer in residence, 1965, and
visiting lecturer, 1968, University of Pennsylvania, Philadelphia;
adjunct professor of English, Columbia University, New York,
1968-70 and 1972-73; Clark Lecturer, Scripps College, Claremont,
California, 1969; visiting professor, City College of the City Uni-
versity of New York, New York, 1970-71 and State University of
New York, Purchase, 1971-72; Regents' Professor, University of
California, Irvine, Spring 1976; visiting writer, Bennington Col-
lege, Vermont, 1978 and in West Germany, Yugoslavia, Romania,
and Hungary, 1978; Hurst Professor, Washington University, St.
Louis, 1979; National Endowment for the Arts lecturer, Cooper
Union, New York, 1983; visiting professor, Brown University,
Providence, Rhode Island, 1986. **Awards:** Guggenheim fellowship,
1952, 1955; Department of State American Specialists grant, 1958;
American Academy award, 1967; National Endowment for the
Arts grant, 1967; Hurst fellowship, Washington University, St.
Louis, Missouri, 1979; National Book award nominations, 1962,
1973, 1976; National Endowment for the Arts award for Lifetime
Achievement, 1988; four O'Henry prize story awards. Litt.D.:

Skidmore College, Saratoga Springs, New York, 1980, Grinnell College, Iowa, 1986. **Member:** American Academy and Institute of Arts and Letters, (president 1987-90.) **Residence:** New York City.

Publications

Collections

The Collected Stories. 1975.
The Collected Stories of Hortense Calisher. 1984.
The Novellas of Hortense Calisher. 1998.

Fiction

In the Absence of Angels: Stories. 1951.
False Entry. 1961.
Tale for the Mirror: A Novella and Other Stories. 1962.
Textures of Life. 1963.
Extreme Magic: A Novella and Other Stories. 1964.
Journal from Ellipsia. 1965.
The Railway Police and The Last Trolley Ride (two novellas). 1966.
The New Yorkers. 1966.
Queenie. 1971.
Standard Dreaming. 1972.
Eagle Eye. 1973.
On Keeping Women. 1977.
Mysteries of Motion. 1983.
Saratoga, Hot (stories). 1985.
The Bobby-Soxer. 1986.
Age. 1987.
In the Palace of the Movie King. 1993.
In the Slammer, with Carol Smith. 1997.

Other

What Novels Are (lecture). 1969.
Herself (memoir). 1972.
Kissing Cousins (memoir). 1988.

Editor, with Shannon Ravenel, *The Best American Short Stories.* 1981.

*

Bibliography: "Calisher: A Bibliography, 1948-1986" by Kathleen Snodgrass in *Bulletin of Bibliography,* March 1988.

Critical Studies: article by Cynthia Ozick in *Midstream,* 1969; interview in *Paris Review,* Winter 1987; "A Conversation with Calisher" in *Southwest Review,* Spring 1986; "The Writer's Role: Responses to Calisher" by Richard Wilbur and others in *New Criterion,* February 1983; article by Christina Stead in *Yale Review,* Winter 1987; *The Fiction of Hortense Calisher* by Kathleen Snodgrass, 1993; in *Jewish Women Fiction Writers,* edited by Harold Bloom, 1998.

*   *   *

Hortense Calisher's fiction may be too demanding to find a wide audience, despite her remarkable perceptions and formidable talent. She marks a dense, elliptical narrative with subtle, verbal hu-

mor and penetrating examinations of the heart. The patient reader is always richly rewarded by her wit and her lush writing style. Calisher has been compared to both **Edith Wharton** and **Henry James** for her novelistic focus upon upper-class bourgeois experience and the artifice and manners that typify that lifestyle. Like Wharton and James, Calisher uncovers meaning beneath the layers of social decorum, unveiling the complexities of the mind and heart through her evocative writing style. Calisher describes her own prose style as poetic. As she explains in a 1987 interview in the *Paris Review,* "Prose can have its own strong, profound rhythms. And its own lyric. Both as powerful as poetry."

Her shorter fiction is, generally speaking, more successful than her full-length novels. The mandarin precision in the telling is better sustained in "an apocalypse, served in a very small cup," in Calisher's own definition of a story. Her range is astonishing: as serious as children confronting death by way of professional mourners; as levitous as a dinner party at which the women suddenly decide to remove their blouses. In *Extreme Magic* two people suffering from the intensity of emotional scars find solace in each other's pain and memory, singled out for the implication in the title of this novella. In another, *The Railway Police*—which is, perhaps, Calisher's most powerful work—a woman abandons the artificial identity represented by her collection of elaborate wigs in order to face the world, bravely and fearlessly, with a bald skull.

Textures of Life, an early novel, represents Calisher at her most accessible: a conventional, even romantic plot salvaged from the ordinary by a vast intelligence and compassion. *False Entry* and *The New Yorkers,* loosely connected novels of rich complexity in both plot and narrative, contain brilliant set pieces—the Ku Klux Klan section in the former, the childhood story of a Hungarian immigrant in the latter. *Journal from Ellipsia,* which "only the uninitiate still call science fiction," has an interplanetary Gulliver as heroine and sometime narrator; it anticipates *Mysteries of Motion* a decade later, Calisher's interplanetary epic that weaves the lives of several contemporary types together for a first civilian flight into space. *On Keeping Women* and *The Bobby-Soxer* are modern novels of marital and non-marital relationships, spun out in her customary elegance; and *Saratoga, Hot,* a collection of "little novels," as she has termed them, contains some of her best stories to date, notably "Gargantua," as painful as any she has written, and "The Passenger," one of her autobiographical pieces, its cruel self-assessment cut with her deadpan humor and rich compassion. *Queenie* is perhaps the best example of her delicious wit, a verbal tour de force in the disguise of a sexual fable in answer to Portnoy, by way of Colette, and a 1970s bawdy tale of immaculate taste.

Calisher's autobiography, *Herself,* discloses less about the author than about her view of art, including, in "Pushing Around the Pantheon," an entertaining and enlightening discussion of sexuality in literature in relation to the masculine and feminine roles tradition has imposed on writers. *Herself,* originally titled *The Autobiography of a Writer,* began as a collection of Calisher's non-fictional writings and ended up as an unconventional autobiography in that it focuses, almost exclusively, on Calisher's life as a writer, eschewing extraneous personal detail. The opening lines of *Herself* are representative of Calisher's poetic prose style:

> Put your ear to an old faucet, do you hear the lifeblood of art drip-dripping, leaking like tapwater?—it's only the old ivory-tower blues; she hears it every day. A faucet has realms of being for everybody; that is hers.
>
> Meanwhile, ordinary life-under-death waits at the

mousehole. She tosses it theater like everybody, learns like them to build honeycomb houses for whoever shall be there with her: the flesh of her body and other guests.

For Calisher, it seems, art exists everywhere, even within the pipes of an old faucet, and it is the task of the writer to turn the knob and to collect the precious waters.

In her more recent novels like *Age* and *In The Palace of the Movie King,* Calisher continues to explore class relations and to investigate the complexity of human emotions beneath the deceptively still surface of language and gestures. Calisher's fiction continues to captivate with its style and its substance. "The magic is in her writing," Marya Mannes has written, "the marvel is in her range."

—Bruce Kellner, updated by Allison Hersh

CALLAHAN, S(ophia) Alice

Born: Sulphur Springs, Texas, 1 January 1868. **Education:** Attended Wesleyan Female Institute in Staunton, Virginia; took an examination for a teacher's certificate in the subjects of grammar, arithmetic, geography, history, and physics in 1892. **Career:** Teacher, Creek Nation Wealaka Mission School in Indian Territory, later Oklahoma, 1892-93; Harrell Institute (a high school) in Muskogee, 1893. Served as Correspondence Secretary, Conference Officers of Parsonages and Home Mission Society of the Methodist Church, 1893. **Died:** 7 January 1894.

PUBLICATIONS

Novels

Wynema, A Child of the Forest. 1891.

*

Critical Studies: "S. Alice Callahan: Author of *Wynema, A Child of the Forest*" by Carolyn Thomas Foreman, in *Chronicles of Oklahoma,* vol. 33, autumn 1955; "Justice for Indians and Women: The Protest Fiction of Alice Callahan and Pauline Johnson" by A. LaVonne Brown Ruoff, in *World Literature Today,* vol. 66, no. 2, spring 1992; "An Introduction to *Wynema, A Child of the Forest* by Sophia Alice Callahan" by Annette Van Dyke, in *Studies in American Indian Literatures,* vol. 4, nos. 2-3, summer/fall 1992; "Two Ideas above an Oyster: Gender Roles in S. Alice Callahan's *Wynema*" by LaVonne Ruoff, in *Native American Women in Literature and Culture* edited by Susan Castillo and Victor M. P. Da Rosa, 1997.

*   *   *

Wynema, A Child of the Forest is believed to be the first novel written by a Native American and the first to be written in Oklahoma, then Indian Territory. The book enjoyed some success after its publication in 1891 but then disappeared from circulation until 1955, when a historian rediscovered the only known copy in the Library of Congress. Until later in the twentieth century, this copy was misplaced, and therefore it has received very little attention from scholars of Native American literature.

Of mostly historical significance, *Wynema* is a romantic novel protesting the treatment of Native Americans. The dedication reads:

> TO THE INDIAN TRIBES OF NORTH AMERICA: Who have felt the wrongs and oppressions of their pale-faced brothers, I lovingly dedicate this work, praying that it may serve to open the eyes and heart of the world to our afflictions, and thus speedily issue into existence an era of good feeling and just dealing toward us and our more oppressed brothers.

Wynema traces the education of a young Creek girl, Wynema, to her becoming a teacher and to her marriage to the brother of her Methodist woman teacher. The story is seldom told from the Native American characters' perspectives, and the chapters that focus on the very real problems facing the Native Americans of the time, such as the 1890 Massacre at Wounded Knee, seem disruptive of the romantic plot. Despite her awkward format, Callahan does manage to record Creek culture, including blue dumplings (a favorite food), the busk or green corn ceremony, and the death chant. Her characters also discuss allotment (the Dawes Act of 1887), temperance, and suffrage for women.

Callahan was the daughter of Captain Samuel Benton Callahan, a prominent cattle rancher and member of the Creek Nation. The newspaper accounts of the day referred to them as part of the "Creek aristocracy." The family had been forced from Alabama to Indian Territory in 1833 along with others of the Creek Nation as part of the mass eviction known as the Trail of Tears. Although Callahan was well-educated and promotes the value of Christian education and the Protestant work ethic in her novel, her real point is not to convert the non-Christian Native Americans, but to stop their slaughter and unfair treatment. Evincing a maternal ethic common to other novels of the nineteenth century such as **Harriet Beecher Stowe**'s *Uncle Tom's Cabin,* she visualizes Native Americans and Euro-Americans living side by side in peace. Her untimely death at age twenty-six of acute pleurisy cut short her writing and teaching career and left only this first novel.

—Annette Van Dyke

CAPOTE, Truman

Born: Truman Streckfus Persons in New Orleans, Louisiana, 30 September 1924; took step-father's surname. **Education:** Trinity School and St. John's Academy, New York; Greenwich High School, Connecticut. **Career:** Worked in the art department and wrote for "Talk of the Town," *New Yorker,* early 1940s; then full-time writer. **Awards:** O. Henry award, 1946, 1948, 1951; American Academy grant, 1959; Mystery Writers of America Edgar Allen Poe award, 1966; Emmy award, for television adaptation, 1967. **Member:** American Academy. **Died:** 25 August 1984.

PUBLICATIONS

Collections

A Capote Reader. 1987.

Short Stories

Other Voices, Other Rooms. 1948.
A Tree of Night and Other Stories. 1949.
Breakfast at Tiffany's: A Short Novel and Three Stories. 1958.
A Christmas Memory (story). 1966.

Novels

The Grass Harp. 1951.
Answered Prayers (unfinished). 1986.

Plays

The Grass Harp, from his own novel (produced 1952). 1952.
House of Flowers, music by Harold Arlen, lyrics by Capote and
    Arlen (produced 1954; revised version, produced 1968). 1968.
The Thanksgiving Visitor, from his own story (televised 1968).
    1968.
Trilogy (screenplay, with Eleanor Perry), in *Trilogy.* 1969.

Screenplays: *Beat the Devil,* with John Huston, 1953; *Indiscre-
tion of an American Wife,* with others, 1954; *The Innocents,* with
William Archibald and John Mortimer, 1961; *Trilogy,* with
Eleanor Perry, 1969.

Television Plays and Films (includes documentaries): *A
Christmas Memory,* with Eleanor Perry, from the story by
Capote, 1966; *Among the Paths to Eden,* with Eleanor Perry,
from the story by Capote, 1967; *Laura,* from the play by Vera
Caspary, 1968; *The Thanksgiving Visitor,* from his own story,
1968; *Behind Prison Walls,* 1972; *The Glass House,* with Tracy
Keenan Wynn and Wyatt Cooper, 1972; *Crimewatch,* 1973.

Other

Local Color. 1950.
*The Muses Are Heard: An Account of the Porgy and Bess Tour to
    Leningrad.* 1956.
Observations, photographs by Richard Avedon. 1959.
Selected Writings, edited by Mark Schorer. 1963.
*In Cold Blood: A True Account of a Multiple Murder and Its Con-
    sequences.* 1966.
Trilogy: An Experiment in Multimedia, with Frank and Eleanor
    Perry. 1969.
The Dogs Bark: Public People and Private Places. 1973.
*Then It All Came Down: Criminal Justice Today Discussed by Po-
    lice, Criminals, and Correction Officers with Comments by
    Capote.* 1976.
Music for Chameleons. 1980.
One Christmas (memoir). 1983.
Conversations with Capote, with Lawrence Grobel. 1985.
Capote: Conversations, edited by M. Thomas Inge. 1987.

*

Bibliography: *Capote: A Primary and Secondary Bibliography*
by Robert J. Stanton, 1980.

Critical Studies: *The Worlds of Capote* by William L. Nance,
1970; *Capote* by Helen S. Garson, 1980; *Capote* by Kenneth Reid,

1981; *Capote* by Marie Rudisill and James C. Simmons, 1983;
Footnote to a Friendship: A Memoir of Capote and Others by
Donald Windham, 1983; *Capote: Dear Heart, Old Buddy* by John
Malcolm Brinnin, 1986, as *Capote, A Memoir,* 1987; *Capote: A
Biography* by Gerald Clarke, 1988; "Literature, Criticism, and Fac-
tual Reporting" by Alan Collett, in *Philosophy and Literature,* Oc-
tober 1989; *Truman Capote: A Study of the Short Fiction* by Helen
S. Garson, 1992; *Literary Reflections: Michener on Michener,
Hemingway, Capote, and Others* by James A. Michener, 1993;
*Truman Capote: In Which Various Friends, Enemies, Acquaintan-
ces, and Detractors Recall His Turbulent Career* by George
Plimpton, 1997.

*   *   *

Few contemporary writers have projected a public image as
compelling or as enduring as that of Truman Capote. John W.
Aldridge in *After the Lost Generation,* for example, compared the
popular image of Capote to that of **Hemingway** and Byron, noting that the author's publishers exploited him in order to reinforce
the reader's "impression of fragile aestheticism" evident in his
works. Certainly Capote's personal idiosyncrasies and the superficial effects of the style and atmosphere of his work did much to
enhance his popular following.

Although the art of Capote speaks directly to his own day and
age, the best of it is rooted in nineteenth-century American literary traditions reflected in **Hawthorne** and **James.** Like Hawthorne,
for example, his work focuses upon the dichotomy of good and
evil, light and dark. Capote's craft, moreover, is that of the romance as defined by James. Dream symbolism adds to the Gothic
impact of the author's resonance.

Critics in the late twentieth century have tended to divide Capote's works into two fictional modes, the nocturnal and the daylight, or the dark and the light. The light
Capote fiction tends to take place in a public world (*The
Grass Harp*) and reveals an often aggressive social order. The
daylight fiction, moreover, is marked by a realistic, colloquial,
often funny, first-person narrative (*Breakfast at Tiffany's*). The
nocturnal, by contrast, is manifest in the dreamlike, detached,
inverted, third-person narrative focusing on an inner complex
world, often approaching the surreal as in *Other Voices, Other
Rooms.*

Because of the romance tradition implicit in his work, Capote's
characters are rooted in Gothic narcissism. As an instance of that
narcissism, a major Capote theme is the discovery of one's *real*
identity. In a supernatural context a character often confronts his
alter ego, as in *Other Voices, Other Rooms.* The tree house in *The
Grass Harp* becomes a place for wish fulfillment, a refuge for
fighting off the hypocrisy of the social order. Even Holly
Golightly's rebellion in *Breakfast at Tiffany's* suggests a degree of
self-love. *In Cold Blood* emphasizes the nocturnal motif, the use
of the modern Gothic, and the skillful manipulation of narcissus.
This experiment with what has been called the nonfiction novel,
is an excellent example of Capote's skillful penetration of the nightmarish enigma of evil, suggesting again his kinship to Hawthorne,
Melville, and James.

—George C. Longest

CARTER, Nick. *See* **SMITH, Martin Cruz.**

CARVER, Raymond (Clevie, Jr.)

Born: Clatskanie, Oregon, 25 May 1938. **Education:** Yakima High School, Yakima, Washington, 1953-56; Chico State College, Chico, California (editor, first issue of *Selection,* 1960), 1958-60; Humbolt State College, Arcata, California (editor, *Toyon,* spring 1963), A.B. in English 1963; University of Iowa, Iowa Writers' Workshop, Iowa City, Iowa (fellowship), 1963-64; Sacramento State College, Sacramento, California, 1966. **Family:** Married 1) Maryann Burke in 1957 (divorced 1982), one daughter and one son; 2) poet Tess Gallagher in 1988. **Career:** Worked miscellaneous blue-collar jobs as a mill hand, trucker, gas-station attendant, and hospital custodian in Washington and northern California to support his family and attend college, 1958-66; textbook editor, Science Research Associates (SRA), Palo Alto, California, 1967-68; accompanied wife to Israel when she received a one-year scholarship from Tel Aviv University, 1968-69; rehired as advertising director for SRA, 1969-70; visiting lecturer in creative writing, University of California, Santa Cruz (founding advisory editor, *Quarry,* 1971), 1971-72; visiting lecturer in fiction writing, University of California, Berkeley, 1972; visiting lecturer, Iowa Writers' Workshop, Iowa City, 1973-74; visiting lecturer, University of California, Santa Barbara (advisory editor, *Spectrum,* 1974), 1974; drinking and domestic problems while living in Cupertino, California, 1974-77; hospitalized for alcohol dependency and stopped drinking on 2 June 1977; distinguished writer-in-residence, University of Texas El Paso, 1978-79; professor of English, Syracuse University, Syracuse, New York, 1980-83; resigned from teaching to write full time in Port Angeles, Washington, 1983-88; reading tour of Argentina and Brazil for U. S. Information Service, 1984; traveled through Europe from April to July, 1987; treated for lung cancer, Seattle, Washington, 1988. **Awards:** The Best American Short Stories awards, 1964, 1967, 1982, 1988; National Endowment for the Arts Discovery award, 1970; San Francisco Foundation Joseph Henry Jackson award for fiction (honorable mention), 1971; Stanford University Wallace E. Stegner Creative Writing fellowship, 1972; O. Henry award, 1973, 1983, 1988; Pushcart prize, 1976, 1981, 1983, 1984; National Book award nomination, 1977; John Simon Guggenheim fellowship, 1978; National Endowment for the Arts fellowship for fiction, 1980; *Columbia* magazine Carlos Fuentes Fiction award, 1981; American Academy and Institute of Arts and Letters Mildred and Harold Strauss Livings award, 1983-88; National Book Critics Circle award nomination for fiction, 1983, 1989; Pulitzer prize nomination for fiction, 1984, 1989; *Poetry* magazine Levinson prize, 1985; *Los Angeles Times* book prize, 1986; Brandeis University Creative Arts award Citation for Fiction, 1988; Seattle Foundation Maxine Cushing Gray Fellowship (posthumously), 1989; English-Speaking Union Ambassador Book award (posthumously), 1989. D.Litt.: University of Hartford, Hartford, Connecticut, 1988. **Member:** Corporation of Yaddo, 1982; International PEN; Authors Guild. **Died:** 2 August 1988.

PUBLICATIONS

Collections

Fires: Essays, Poems, Stories. 1984.
The Stories of Raymond Carver. 1985.
Where I'm Calling From: New and Selected Stories. 1988.

Short Cuts: Selected Stories. 1993.
All Of Us: Raymond Carver, the Collected Poems. 1996.

Short Stories

Put Yourself in My Shoes. 1974.
Will You Please Be Quiet, Please? 1976.
Furious Seasons and Other Stories. 1977.
What We Talk About When We Talk About Love. 1981.
The Pheasant. 1982.
Cathedral. 1983.
If It Please You. 1984.
Elephant and Other Stories. 1988.

Recordings: *Raymond Carver Reads Three Stories* ("Nobody Said Anything," "A Serious Talk," and "Fat"), 1983.

Poetry

Near Klamath. 1968.
Winter Insomnia. 1970.
At Night the Salmon Move. 1976.
Two Poems ("The Baker" and "Louise"). 1982.
Where Water Comes Together with Other Water. 1985.
Ultramarine. 1986.
Two Poems ("Reaching" and "Soda Crackers"). 1986.
In a Marine Light. 1987.
A New Path to the Waterfall. 1989.
All of Us: The Collected Poems. 1998.

Plays

Carnations: A One-Act Play (produced 1962). 1992.

Screenplays: *Dostoevsky: A Screenplay,* with Tess Gallagher, 1985.

Other

Those Days: Early Writings by Raymond Carver: Eleven Poems and a Story, edited by William L. Stull. 1987.
No Heroics Please: Uncollected Writings, edited by William L. Stull. 1992.

Editor, with Shannon Ravenel, *The Best American Short Stories 1986.* 1986.
Editor, with Tom Jenks, *American Short Story Masterpieces.* 1987.

*

Bibliography: "Raymond Carver: A Bibliographical Checklist" by William L. Stull, in *American Book Collector* vol. 8, no. 1, 1987.

Critical Studies: "Raymond Carver" by William L. Stull, in *DLB Yearbook 1984;* "Raymond Carver" by William L. Stull, in *DLB Yearbook 1988; Understanding Raymond Carver* by Arthur Saltzman, 1988; *Conversations with Raymond Carver* edited by Marshall Bruce Gentry and William L. Stull, 1990; *Raymond Carver: A Study of the Short Fiction* by Ewing Campbell, 1992; *Reading Raymond Carver* by Randolph Paul Runyan, 1992; *Raymond Carver* by Adam Meyer, 1994; *Raymond Carver: An*

Oral Biography by Sam Halpert, 1995; *Raymond Carver's Where I'm Calling From: A Reflection of His Life and Art* by John Magee, 1997.

*   *   *

Raymond Carver earned popular and critical acclaim for reviving the short story during the 1970s and 1980s. Within a twelve-year span, he published four major-press collections, which garnered for him the most prestigious endowments, nominations, and awards in American literature and the arts. Carver's indebtedness to Anton Chekhov and **Ernest Hemingway** is evident in his brusque characterizations and his concise style. In fact, his early stories were hailed as minimalist masterpieces, though he regretted their being thus labeled. As his career evolved, he sought "more generous" results and tried to make his writing "open up," as he mentioned in an interview for *The London Review of Books* (15 September 1987). On occasion, he would return to a previously published story, completely rework it, and include the expanded "new" version in a later collection, giving readers an opportunity to witness first hand what he felt to be life-affirming changes. A corecipient in 1983 of the first American Academy of Arts and Letters Mildred and Harold Strauss Livings Award, he drew unqualified praise during the next five years for his achievements. Carver's reputation endures, and among critics he is acknowledged as the most gifted short-story writer of his generation.

Carver felt privileged to be a writer. Born into a working-class family, he experienced the paralyzing economic hardships that typified growing up in the logging districts of the Pacific Northwest. His father filed saws, and his mother either waited tables or clerked in retail stores to bring in needed money. Though his father had a knack for telling family anecdotes and stories, he also enjoyed drinking with his friends. When he failed to come home after work, Carver recalled that a feeling of despair lingered over the dinner table. After graduating from Yakima High, for six despondent months he followed his father into the local saw mill before deciding he wanted a different type of life. After leaving, he never forgot or made light of the futility that he associated with the lives of those whom he had met. From them he found his most defining topics, including the strife in relationships between men and women and the way people struggle to survive in situations that threaten to overpower them.

A husband and father by the age of nineteen, Carver pointed to responsibility as his primary antagonist. He worked every job that came his way in order to pay rent and cover college tuition costs. Finding the time and reserving the energy to write were never easy for him, but by the late 1960s he was publishing stories about the domestic "dis-ease" afflicting his own marriage. His success led to a number of temporary teaching positions at universities interested in promoting their creative writing programs. Privately, however, alcoholism was destroying his family and his career. While separated from his wife, he sought treatment on four occasions and finally stopped drinking on 2 June 1977. Thankful for this "second-life," this "post-drinking life," Carver referred to his subsequent optimistic poems and stories as "gifts" that he would have been denied had he stayed on his self-destructive course.

In a conversation for *The Paris Review* (summer 1983), Carver stressed that many people " . . . don't succeed at what they try to do, at the things they most want to do, the large or small things

that support the life." In his first major collection, *Will You Please Be Quiet, Please?* (1976), Carver investigates the vast distance between what his characters had once envisioned for themselves and what they have become. Pulling together stories written over a thirteen-year span, he focuses on people who have been inattentive to their responsibilities to themselves as well as to others. Without their knowing quite when or how, their expectations have been vandalized, and they seemingly lack the resources to do anything about it. Feeling estranged, they have difficulty recognizing themselves in the lives they are living.

Drawn from his blue-collar background, Carver's people either are out of work or are handcuffed to menial, low-paying jobs that offer no benefits. Debts accrue; creditors knock at their doors. Meanwhile, they drink cheap liquor, smoke marijuana, sell off their belongings, and betray their spouses. Since intimacy escapes or confuses them, they are enticed by grimy indecencies like spying on the couple next door as they get ready for bed. Other people's enjoyments simply are more interesting than their own. However, like Bill and Arlene Miller in "Neighbors," somewhere along the line they absent-mindedly lock themselves out of life's more promising ventures and slink back into the routines that have brought them to the doorstep of frustration. In doing so, they are apprehensive that tomorrow will be exactly the same as today.

Carver's second major collection generated as much controversy for its style as it did for its subject matter. A majority of the stories in *What We Talk About When We Talk About Love* (1981) once again involve marital or family unrest, but their impending cruelty is tightened up a notch. For Claire in "So Much Water So Close to Home" and the mother, Ann Weiss, in "The Bath," comfort and security dissolve in the grievous fragment of an hour or a day. Life is tenuous in Carver's stories, and his characters experience shame and remorse when it occurs to them that they do not really know the people with whom they live. Isolated within their relationships, they never find the right words for articulating their feelings. And once the talking stops, silence becomes haunting.

To underscore these impoverished attempts at communication, Carver refined a lean prose style based on Hemingway's theory of omission. From his mentor **John Gardner** and his editor Gordon Lisch, he was encouraged to leave out everything that hindered a story from driving tenaciously toward its end. He told *The Bloomsbury Review* (January/February 1988) that "Pare, pare, and pare some more" became his obsessive tenet for nearly two years as he cut "to the marrow, not just to the bone." A thirty-five page draft might be subjected to twenty revisions until the finished ten-page story offered only the barest details about setting, character, and plot. Carver wanted his stories to "work invisibly." As he declares in his essay "On Writing" (1983): "What creates tension in a piece of fiction is partly the way concrete words are linked together to make up the visible action of the story. But it's also the things that are left out, that are implied, the landscape just under the smooth (but sometimes broken and unsettled) surface of things." Although his style became the literary sensation of the 1980s, he was troubled by the "minimalist" tag reviewers attached to his fiction. In his mind, the term made his people seem pathetic and superficial, just as it devalued the self-conscious precision he exerted while completing the book.

The accolades for *What We Talk About* conferred celebrity status upon Carver as the most resonant voice of his day, yet he told Mona Simpson (*The Paris Review*, summer 1983): "Any farther in that direction and I'd be at a dead end—writing stuff and publishing stuff I wouldn't want to read myself." After a six month drought, he experienced a dramatic breakthrough while writing "Cathedral," which would become the title of his third and most heralded collection. His technique and vision suddenly expanded as a result of the positive changes occurring in his personal life. His conquering alcohol, his Guggenheim fellowship, his faculty appointment at Syracuse, his confidence in the value of his work, and his love for Tess Gallagher coalesced into a feeling of renewed hope, which extends through his best writing in *Cathedral* (1983) and in the seven new stories collected in *Where I'm Calling From* (1988). His characters share many of the same adversities and disappointments as their precursors, but Carver allows for ordinary human kindness to point the way toward healing. Whether prompted by a good luck kiss or by the touch of a blind stranger, his protagonists look into their lives for the meaningful small surprises that inspire understanding amid the detritus of addiction, divorce, bankruptcy, and death. They share, they console, and they forgive. As elliptical omissions are replaced by conventionally developed passages and scenes, Carver deals optimistically with the "dis-eases" that compelled him to become a writer. Generosity distinguishes the final stories he composed, reinforcing that the courage to change is one of life's most sustaining principles.

From an unlikely beginning, Carver's reputation continued to advance throughout his twenty-five-year career. Though he never anticipated fame to come his way, he told *Publishers Weekly* just six months before he died of cancer: "I can't think of anything else I'd rather be called than a writer, unless it's a poet." Because his fastidiously crafted prose delivers authentic news about America's underclass, Carver ranks among the most insightful and influential short-story writers of the twentieth century.

—Joe Nordgren

See the essay on "The Cathedral."

CATHER, Willa (Sibert)

Born: Back Creek Valley, near Winchester, Virginia, 7 December 1873; moved with her family to a farm near Red Cloud, Nebraska, 1883. **Education:** Red Cloud High School, graduated 1890; Latin School, Lincoln, Nebraska, 1890-91; University of Nebraska, Lincoln, 1891-95, A.B. 1895. **Career:** Columnist, Lincoln *State Journal,* 1893-95; lived briefly in Red Cloud, 1896; editor, *Home Monthly,* Pittsburgh, 1896-97; telegraph editor and drama critic, Pittsburgh *Daily Leader,* 1896-1900; contributor, the *Library,* Pittsburgh, 1900; Latin and English teacher, Central High School, Pittsburgh, 1901-03; English teacher, Allegheny High School, Pittsburgh, 1903-06; staff writer, later managing editor, *McClure's* magazine, New York, 1906-11; full-time writer from 1912. **Awards:** Pulitzer prize, 1923; American Academy Howells Medal, 1930, and Gold Medal, 1944; Prix Fémina Américaine, 1932. Litt.D.: University of Nebraska, 1917; University of Michigan, Ann Arbor, 1922; Columbia University, New York, 1928; Yale University, New Haven, Connecticut, 1929; Princeton University, New Jersey, 1931. D.L.: Creighton University, Omaha, Nebraska, 1928. LL.D.: University of California, Berkeley, 1931. L.H.D.: Smith College, Northampton, Massachusetts, 1933. **Member:** American Academy. **Died:** 24 April 1947.

PUBLICATIONS

Collections

Early Novels and Stories (Library of America), edited by Sharon O'Brien. 1987.
The Short Stories, edited by Hermoine Lee. 1989.
Great Short Works of Cather, edited by Robert K. Miller. 1989.
Later Novels (Library of America), edited by Sharon O'Brien. 1990.
Stories, Poems, and Other Writings (Library of America), edited by Sharon O'Brien. 1992.
Willa Cather: Stories. 1994.

Short Stories

The Troll Garden. 1905; variorum edition, edited by James Woodress, 1983.
Youth and the Bright Medusa. 1920.
The Fear That Walks by Noonday. 1931.
Obscure Destinies. 1932.
Novels and Stories. 13 vols., 1937-41.
The Old Beauty and Others. 1948.
Early Stories, edited by Mildred R. Bennett. 1957.
Collected Short Fiction 1892-1912, edited by Virginia Faulkner. 1965.
Uncle Valentine and Other Stories: Uncollected Fiction 1915-1929, edited by Bernice Slote. 1973.
Paul's Case and Other Stories. 1996.

Novels

Alexander's Bridge. 1912; as *Alexander's Bridges,* 1912.
O Pioneers! 1913.
The Song of the Lark. 1915.
My Ántonia. 1918.
One of Ours. 1922.
A Lost Lady. 1923.
The Professor's House. 1925.
My Mortal Enemy. 1926.
Death Comes for the Archbishop. 1927.
Shadows on the Rock. 1931.
Lucy Gayheart. 1935.
Sapphira and the Slave Girl. 1940.

Poetry

April Twilights. 1903.
April Twilights and Other Poems. 1923; revised edition, 1933; edited by Bernice Slote, 1962; revised edition, 1968.

Other

The Life of Mary Baker G. Eddy, and the History of Christian Science, by Georgine Milmine (ghostwritten by Cather). 1909.
My Autobiography, by S. S. McClure (ghostwritten by Cather). 1914.
Not Under Forty. 1936.
On Writing: Critical Studies on Writing as an Art. 1949.
Writings from Cather's Campus Years, edited by James R. Shively. 1950.

Cather in Europe: Her Own Story of the First Journey, edited by George N. Kates. 1956.
The Kingdom of Art: Cather's First Principles and Critical Principles 1893-1896, edited by Bernice Slote. 1967.
The World and the Parish: Cather's Articles and Reviews 1893-1902, edited by William M. Curtin. 2 vols., 1970.

Editor, *The Best Stories of Sarah Orne Jewett.* 2 vols., 1925.

*

Bibliography: *Cather: A Bibliography* by Joan Crane, 1982.

Critical Studies: *Cather: A Critical Introduction* by David Daiches, 1951; *Cather: A Critical Biography* by E. K. Brown, completed by Leon Edel, 1953; *The Landscape and the Looking Glass: Cather's Search for Value* by John H. Randall III, 1960; *The World of Cather* by Mildred R. Bennett, 1961; *Cather's Gift of Sympathy* by Edward and Lillian Bloom, 1962; *Cather* by Dorothy Van Ghent, 1964; *Cather and Her Critics* edited by James Schroeter, 1967; *Cather: Her Life and Art,* 1970, and *Cather: A Literary Life,* 1987, both by James Woodress; *Cather* by Dorothy McFarland Tuck, 1972; *Cather: A Pictorial Memoir* by Bernice Slote, 1973, and *The Art of Cather* edited by Slote and Virginia Faulkner, 1974; *Five Essays on Cather,* 1974, and *Critical Essays on Cather,* 1984, both edited by John J. Murphy; *Cather's Imagination* by David Stouck, 1975; *Cather* by Philip L. Gerber, 1975; *Chrysalis: Cather in Pittsburgh 1896-1906* by Kathleen D. Byrne and Richard C. Snyder, 1982; *Willa: The Life of Cather* by Phyllis C. Robinson, 1983; *Cather's Short Fiction,* 1984, and *Cather: A Reference Guide,* 1986, both by Marilyn Arnold; *The Voyage Perilous: Cather's Romanticism* by Susan Rosowski, 1986; *Cather: The Emerging Voice* by Sharon O'Brien, 1986; *Cather in Person: Interviews, Speeches and Letters* edited by L. Brent Bohlke, 1987; *Cather: Life as Art* by Jamie Ambrose, 1987; *Cather in France: In Search of the Last Language* by Robert J. Nelson, 1988; *Cather: A Life Saved Up* by Hermoine Lee, 1989, as *Cather: Double Lives,* 1990; *Cather* by Susie Thomas, 1989; *Cather: A Study of the Short Fiction* by Loretta Wasserman, 1991; *Willa Cather: A Memoir* by Elizabeth Shepley Sergeant, 1992; *Willa Cather and John Milton: The Search for Paradise* (dissertation) by Paula F. Fessler, 1995; *Becoming Modern: Willa Cather's Journalism* (dissertation) by Cathy Downs, 1996; *Sigrid Undset and Willa Cather: Literary Correspondences* (dissertation) by Sherill M. Harbison, 1996; "Willa Cather's *Sapphira and the Slave Girl*: Extending the Boundaries of the Body" by Angela M. Salas, in *College Literature,* June 1997, pp. 97-108.

*   *   *

Willa Cather, who can be ranked among the most important American writers of the first half of the twentieth century, is best known for her novels and stories depicting the early years of Nebraska. Her range is considerably broader, however, and also includes notable work set in the American Southwest, Quebec, and Virginia. Her reputation is based on an extraordinary ability to capture the sense of place and a meticulous craftsmanship that combines a very clear prose style with effective use of myth and symbol. In an age when authors were increasingly able to exploit their literary talents in the marketplace, Cather displayed an awesome dedication to her art. She wrote slowly and carefully, consistently refused to allow her works to be anthologized, dramatized, or sold in paperback editions. When she died she had produced twelve novels and at least fifty-five stories of consistently high quality.

Cather served a long literary apprenticeship before she was able to cut loose from journalism and devote her time exclusively to writing. Her ideas and values, however, were formed early, as the volumes of her early newspaper writings show. During her early years of journalism and teaching she wrote mostly short fiction, producing forty-five stories before 1912, when she resigned from her editorship of *McClure's.* These stories, which show a slowly maturing talent, explore themes and subjects that she later employed in her novels. Her first book, however, was *April Twilights,* a volume of verse published while she was teaching high school in Pittsburgh. Her first fiction was a collection of stories, *The Troll Garden.* These stories deal in various ways with the artist and society and show a strong Jamesian influence. They also make use of Western material, particularly "A Sculptor's Funeral" and "A Wagner Matinee," but the tone of these last is more akin to the revolt-from-the-village strain in early twentieth-century American literature than Cather's later work celebrating the land in novels like *O Pioneers!* and *My Ántonia.*

In 1911 Cather took a leave from *McClure's* and wrote "The Bohemian Girl," a long story that uses for the first time in a nostalgic and affirmative manner the memories of her early years on a Nebraska farm and in the prairie village of Red Cloud. She blends a realistic use of detail with a romantic sensibility in a very successful story that encouraged her to plunge into full-length novels of the same genre. Even before writing "The Bohemian Girl," however, she had published her first novel, *Alexander's Bridge,* but, despite the fact that it is a well-written work of considerable interest, she later deprecated the book and regarded it as a false start. The novel is very Jamesian, takes place in Boston and London, and concerns a bridge-builder whose bridge, like his character, contains a fatal flaw. The story ends with the collapse of the bridge and the death of the protagonist.

O Pioneers!, The Song of the Lark, My Ántonia, One of Ours, and *A Lost Lady* are set entirely or in part in Nebraska, and form the basis for Cather's identification with that part of the United States. It is important to note that she began using this material nearly two decades after she had left Nebraska to live in the east. By then the youthful experience was ripe and ready for artistic employment. In a 1925 introduction to the stories of **Sarah Orne Jewett,** who had been her friend and a literary influence, she quoted from a letter from Jewett: "The thing that teases the mind over and over for years, and at last gets itself put down rightly on paper—whether little or great, it belongs to literature." This was a literary principle in which Cather thoroughly believed, and it places Cather closer to Wordsworth with his view of poetry as "emotion recollected in tranquility" than it does to the realists or naturalists of the late nineteenth and early twentieth centuries like **Howells, Garland,** or **Dreiser,** who "worked up" their materials.

O Pioneers! is the story of Alexandra Bergson, a Swedish immigrant who tames the wild land in the pioneer days of Nebraska. Alexandra's life is a success story told with a loving affirmation of the beauty of the land and the value of the pioneer struggle. The novel is not all light, however, as two of Alexandra's brothers turn out to be mean-spirited materialists and her beloved younger brother dies at the hand of a Czech farmer whose wife he has fallen in love with. *The Song of the Lark* combines Cather's memories of her young life in Red Cloud with her great interest in music and in particular the Wagnerian soprano Olive Fremstad, who had grown up in an immigrant family in Minnesota. Thus the youth of the singer is Cather's own youth and the career of the artist is a fictionalized biography of Olive Fremstad. *My Ántonia,* regarded by many readers as Cather's best novel, creates a memorable character in a Bohemian immigrant heroine who had her prototype in a childhood friend. This story is told retrospectively by a male narrator whose experience growing up on a farm and in the town of Black Hawk (Red Cloud) parallels Cather's own life. Again the same sense of place is evoked memorably, and the land and its pioneer settlers are presented with a haunting nostalgia. The book is episodic in character, which is typical of Cather, and contains stories within stories. The novel is carefully constructed, however, and given an organic form that suits the material.

One of Ours is less successful, though the early parts of the novel set in Nebraska create a vivid picture of life on a Nebraska farm and in a college town like Lincoln where Cather attended the university. The story was suggested by the life of her cousin who was killed in France during the First World War. Ironically, this novel won a Pulitzer Prize and brought Cather handsome royalties for the first time. She returned to an all-Nebraska setting in *A Lost Lady,* and again evoked childhood memories in the creation of Captain and Mrs. Forrester, the chief characters. The setting is again a fictionalized Red Cloud, and the story of the lost lady, lost only to the point-of-view character, is told from the perspective of a boy growing up in the small town. This novel demonstrates the literary technique that Cather explains in her essay "The Novel Démeublé." It is a work of about 50,000 words in which all the excess detail is stripped away. "The higher processes of art are all processes of simplification" she wrote. She also was fond of quoting Dumas *pére,* who once had said that to make a drama all "a man needed [was] one passion, and four walls."

The Professor's House is a different sort of novel from the Nebraska stories, the tale of a middle-aged professor of history who loses the will to live and barely escapes death. Although he had won an important literary prize and apparently had everything to live for, he is profoundly depressed by the materialism of his family and his culture. There is a good deal of autobiography in this novel, for Cather, too, felt that for her "the world broke in two in 1922 or thereabouts." There is a long tale inserted in the middle of this novel, "Tom Outland's Story," that evokes the ancient civilization of the Mesa Verde Indians in sharp contrast to the 1920s and also reflects Cather's growing interest in the Southwest.

Her most significant use of the Southwest came two years later in *Death Comes for the Archbishop,* the novel that she thought her best. It creates in episodic form the life of Jean Latour, the first bishop of New Mexico. She long had been fascinated by the story of the Catholic church in the Southwest, and had begun visiting the area as early as 1912. When she ran across a letter collection that gave her a clear account of the real Bishop Lamy's career in New Mexico in the nineteenth century, she found her story and produced a distinguished historical novel. Much of the detail is fiction and it is romanticized, but the material does not do violence to history or to the historical characters it recreates. The work represents Cather at the peak of her creative powers.

Two more historical novels, *Shadows on the Rock* and *Sapphira and the Slave Girl,* followed, and Cather after 1927 seemed to take refuge in writing about the past. *Shadows,* a novel that is dramatically thin but pictorially rich, is a story of Quebec at the end of the seventeenth century. *Sapphira,* the only novel Cather ever wrote about her native Virginia, takes place in the Shenandoah Valley before the Civil War and deals with an incident of family history, her grandmother's successful efforts to help a slave escape to Canada. *Lucy Gayheart,* one of Cather's lesser novels, returns to the use of Red Cloud and a musician's life in Chicago.

—James Woodress

See the essay on *My Ántonia.*

CHANDLER, Raymond (Thornton)

Born: Chicago, Illinois, 23 July 1888; moved to England with his mother: became British citizen, 1907; again became American citizen, 1956. **Education:** A local school in Upper Norwood, London; Dulwich College, London, 1900-05; studied in France and Germany, 1905-07. **Military Service:** Served in the Gordon Highlanders, Canadian Army, 1917-18, and in the Royal Air Force, 1918-19. **Family:** Married Pearl Cecily Hurlburt in 1924 (died 1954). **Career:** Worked in supply and accounting departments of the Almiralty, London, 1907; reporter, London *Daily Express* and Bristol *Western Gazette,* 1908-12; returned to the United States, 1912; worked in St. Louis, then on a ranch and in a sporting goods firm in California; accountant and bookkeeper, Los Angeles Creamery, 1912-17; worked in a bank in San Francisco, 1919; staff member, Los Angeles *Daily Express,* 1919; bookkeeper, then auditor, Dabney Oil Syndicate, Los Angeles, 1922-32; full-time writer from 1933. **Member:** Mystery Writers of America, president, 1959. **Awards:** Mystery Writers of America Edgar Allan Poe award, for screenplay, 1946, for novel, 1954. **Died:** 26 March 1959.

PUBLICATIONS

Collections

Selected Letters, edited by Frank MacShane. 1981.
Stories and Early Novels. 1995.
Later Novels and Other Writings. 1995.

Fiction

The Big Sleep. 1939.
Farewell, My Lovely. 1940.
The High Window. 1942.
The Lady in the Lake. 1943.
Five Murderers (stories). 1944.
Five Sinister Characters (stories). 1945.
Finger Man and Other Stories. 1946.
Red Wind (stories). 1946.
Spanish Blood (stories). 1946.
The Little Sister. 1949; as *Marlowe,* 1969.
The Simple Art of Murder (stories). 1950; as *Trouble Is My Business, Pick-Up on Noon Street,* and *The Simple Art of Murder,* 3 vols., 1951-53.
The Long Goodbye. 1953.
Smart Aleck Kill (stories). 1953.
Pearls Are a Nuisance (stories). 1953.

Playback. 1958.
Poodle Springs (unfinished novel), in *Chandler Speaking.* 1962.
Killer in the Rain (stories), edited by Philip Durham. 1964.
The Smell of Fear. 1965.
The Midnight Chandler (omnibus), edited by Joan Kalin. 1971.

Plays

Double Indemnity, with Billy Wilder, in *Best Film Plays 1945,* edited by John Gassner and Dudley Nichols. 1946.
The Blue Dahlia (screenplay), edited by Matthew J. Bruccoli. 1976.
Chandler's Unknown Thriller: The Screenplay of Playback. 1985.

Screenplays: *And Now Tomorrow,* with Frank Partos, 1944; *Double Indemnity,* with Billy Wilder, 1944; *The Unseen,* with Hagar Wilde and Ken Englund, 1945; *The Blue Dahlia,* 1946; *Strangers on a Train,* with Czenzi Ormonde and Whitfield Cook, 1951.

Other

Chandler Speaking, edited by Dorothy Gardiner and Kathrine Sorley Walker. 1962.
Chandler Before Marlowe: Chandler's Early Prose and Poetry 1908-1912, edited by Matthew J. Bruccoli. 1973.
The Notebooks of Chandler, and English Summer: A Gothic Romance, edited by Frank MacShane. 1976.
Chandler and James M. Fox: Letters. 1979.

*

Bibliography: *Chandler: A Descriptive Bibliography* by Matthew J. Bruccoli, 1979; *Dashiell Hammett and Raymond Chandler: A Checklist and Bibliography of Their Paperback Appearances* by Gary Lovisi, 1994.

Critical Studies: *Down These Mean Streets a Man Must Go: Chandler's Knight* by Philip Durham, 1963; *The Life of Chandler* by Frank MacShane, 1976; *The World of Chandler* edited by Miriam Gross, 1977; *Chandler* by Jerry Spier, 1981; *Chandlertown: The Los Angeles of Philip Marlowe* by Edward Thorpe, 1983; *Something More Than Night: The Case of Chandler* by Peter Wolfe, 1985; *Raymond Chandler's Pearl* by J.O. Tate, in *Clues: A Journal of Detection,* fall-winter 1992; *The Australian Love Letters of Raymond Chandler* by Alan Close, 1995; *Quickness of Fancy: Raymond Chandler's Philip Marlowe* (dissertation) by Charles Mason Smith, 1997; *Raymond Chandler: A Biography* by Tom Hiney, 1997; *Wholeness Restored: Love of Symmetry as a Shaping Force in the Writings of Henry James, Kurt Vonnegut, Samuel Butler, and Raymond Chandler* by Ralf Norrman, 1998; *Modernity and Identity in the Detective Novels of Raymond Chandler* by Christopher Routledge, 1998.

*   *   *

Raymond Chandler first attempted a literary career in London in his early twenties, when he unsuccessfully tried to establish himself as a poet and critic. Twenty years later, after losing his important job with an oil company because of his drinking, he tried again, writing stories for pulp magazines, notably *Black Mask.* This time he was immediately successful, and, along with **Dashiell**

Hammett, became the principal champion of the "hard-boiled" school of detective fiction.

Chandler was scornful of the English school of detective fiction that, as he said in a famous remark, was an "affair of the upper classes, the weekend house party and the vicar's rose garden." He believed that crime fiction should deal with real criminals and should employ the language actually used by murderers and policemen. Chandler used what he called the "objective method," which assures authenticity. At the same time, his work has a strong emotional center that is capable of illuminating "an utterly unexpected range of sensitivity."

In 1939 he published *The Big Sleep,* his first novel. In quick succession he published *Farewell, My Lovely, The High Window,* and *The Lady in the Lake,* reworking material from his earlier stories. Chandler's novels are narrated by the central character, Philip Marlowe, an idealistic and romantic detective who is also tough and cynical. The books are dramatic and funny: Chandler's prose is formal but his vocabulary is full of the slang of his characters. The prose is a mirror of the political and financial corruption that lies under the bland surface of California life. Chandler was the first to give Los Angeles a literary identity.

During the 1940s and early 1950s Chandler wrote movie scripts in Hollywood, notably *Double Indemnity* (with Billy Wilder), *The Blue Dahlia,* and *Strangers on a Train.* Chandler disliked Hollywood, but earned enough money to retire with his wife, Cissy, to La Jolla, where he returned to fiction, writing *The Little Sister* and his most ambitious novel, *The Long Goodbye.* This book is a conscious effort to stretch the conventions of the detective novel so as to convert it into a general work of fiction. It brings crime fiction to the highest level it has attained in modern times. Chandler also wrote an essay, "The Simple Art of Murder," which places his work in the context of other crime novelists. It attempts to justify his blend of idealism and realism and may be considered his literary testament. He also wrote incisively about Hollywood.

Following the death of his wife, Chandler spent much time in England, where he became a celebrity, acknowledged as a master of contemporary fiction. Nevertheless, he was lonely and withdrawn and succeeded in writing only one further novel, *Playback.* Since his death his stature has continued to grow, and he is generally considered to be among the most important American novelists of his time.

—Frank MacShane

See the essay on *The Big Sleep.*

CHANNING, William Ellery

Born: Boston, Massachusetts, 29 November 1817; nephew of the writer William Ellery Channing. **Education:** Round Hill School, Northampton, Massachusetts; Boston Latin School; Harvard University, Cambridge, Massachusetts, 1834. **Family:** Married Ellen Fuller in 1842 (died 1856); five children. **Career:** Farmer, Woodstock, Illinois, 1839-40; tutor and journalist, Cincinnati, 1840-41; settled in Concord, Massachusetts, to be near Emerson, 1842: associated with other members of the Concord community, especially Thoreau; lived in New York, writing for the *Tribune,* 1844; visited France and Italy, 1846; editor, New Bedford *Mercury,* Massachusetts, 1855-58. **Died:** 23 December 1901.

PUBLICATIONS

Collections

Poems of Sixty-Five Years, edited by F.B. Sanborn. 1902.
Collected Poems (facsimile edition), edited by Walter Harding. 1967.

Poetry

Poems. 1843; second series, 1847.
Conversations in Rome: Between an Artist, A Catholic, and a Critic. 1847.
The Woodman and Other Poems. 1849.
Near Home. 1858.
The Wanderer: A Colloquial Poem. 1871.
The Burial of John Brown. 1878.
Eliot. 1885.
John Brown and the Heroes of Harper's Ferry. 1886.

Other

Thoreau, The Poet-Naturalist. 1873; revised edition, 1902.

Editor, with Sophia Thoreau, *The Maine Woods,* by Henry David Thoreau. 1864.
Editor, with Sophia Thoreau, *Cape Cod,* by Henry David Thoreau. 1865.
Editor, with Sophia Thoreau, *A Yankee in Canada, with Anti-Slavery and Reform Papers,* by Henry David Thoreau. 1866.

*

Bibliography: in *Bibliography of American Literature* by Jacob Blanck, 1957.

Critical Studies: *Channing of Concord: A Life* by Frederick T. McGill, 1967; *Channing* by Robert N. Hudspeth, 1973; "'That Sainted Spirit': William Ellery Channing and the Unitarian Milton" by Kevin P. Van Anglen, in *Studies in the American Renaissance,* 1983; "William Ellery Channing II" by Francis B. Dedmond, in *The Transcendentalists: A Review of Research and Criticism* edited by Joel Myerson, vol. 19, 1984; "The Wisdom of William Ellery Channing" by Hyatt H. Waggoner, in *Modern Age: A Quarterly Review,* summer-fall 1986; "The Selected Letters of William Ellery Channing the Younger (Part One)," 1989, "The Selected Letters of William Ellery Channing the Younger (Part 2)," 1990, "The Selected Letters of William Ellery Channing the Younger (Part Three)," 1991, "The Selected Letters of William Ellery Channing the Younger (Part Four)," 1992, all by Francis B. Dedmond, in *Studies in the American Renaissance*; *Channing: Paradigm Transition Figure* by Jeffrey James Ake, 1995; *Providence and Love: Studies in Wordsworth, Channing, Myers, George Eliot, and Ruskin* by John B. Beer, 1998.

*   *   *

When **Ralph Waldo Emerson** helped found *The Dial* in 1840, it was just such a poet as William Ellery Channing for whom he intended the new magazine. Channing was a young man with a talent but with no readily available place for his verses. Under Emerson's sponsorship, Channing went on to publish not only poems in *The Dial* but two books of lyrics and four book-length poems later in his life. These early lyrics are in many ways most characteristic of him. His themes were beauty, self-reliance, and nature. He was hostile to the development of urban America, and in such poems as "Reverence" and "Walden Spring" he gave voice to his fears and to his longings for a pastoral life that was quickly vanishing in the 1840s. What he wanted was the union of nature and self such as he imaged in "Wachusett":

> It went within my inmost heart,
> The overhanging Arch to see,
> The liquid stream, became a part
> Of my internal Harmony.

Typical of his time and place, he insisted on a union of art and life. To write well was to live well; to be a poet was itself a creation of supreme importance.

His increasing awareness of his own loneliness and his isolation was most apparent in two of his book-length poems, *Near Home* and *The Wanderer.* The first of these is a charming hymn to New England as a place of healing power.

> Perpetual newness and the health in things.
> This, is the startling theme, the lovely birth
> Each morn of a new day, so wholly new,
> So absolutely penetrated by itself,
> The fresh, the fair, the ever-living grace.

In *The Wanderer,* Channing completed his journey from the simplicity of his lyrics to a more complex recognition of the tensions between man's love of nature and the forces working against the fulfillment of his pastoral idealism. The poem counterpoises a reverence for the land with a stark awareness of the destructive forces of death and technology. A poetic career beginning in enthusiasm ends in a mature perception of frustration.

Beyond the achievement of his poetry, Channing's career included the first biography of **Henry David Thoreau**, who had been Channing's close friend from 1841. *Thoreau, The Poet-Naturalist* is a narrative built on extensive quotations from Thoreau's journal, which was then unpublished. The book had the virtue of thus putting before the public quite a bit of Thoreau's little known writing, and it also offered a cogent commentary by Channing who rightly emphasized the ethical strictness and the aesthetic craftsmanship in Thoreau's writing. Appearing at a time when Thoreau was all but unknown, the biography had the virtue of keeping his name alive and making his work more readily accessible.

Finally, it is as a friend that Channing may be best remembered. He was the only close friend of Thoreau; he was a constant companion of Emerson for forty years; he was a frequent visitor in the homes of **Louisa May Alcott** and **Nathaniel Hawthorne**; and he was Margaret Fuller's brother-in-law. Channing was a brilliant talker, full of wit and spontaneity. The universal report from his contemporaries was that be spoke better than he wrote. Emerson was convinced that "In walking with Ellery you shall always see what was never before shown to the eye of man." For his part, Hawthorne wrote in *Mosses from an Old Manse,* "Could he have drawn out that virgin gold [of his conversation] and stamped it with the mint mark that alone gives currency, the world might have had the profit, and he the fame." In a narrow society such as New England was, the vitality of Channing's conversation was not to be ignored. He showed his gifted friends how they might see better; he was a receptive audience, a sympathetic and shrewd critic, one who made it possible for men such as Emerson and Thoreau to act on their talent.

—Robert N. Hudspeth

CHÁVEZ, Fray Angélico

Born: Manuel Ezequiel Chávez in Wagon Mound, New Mexico, 10 April 1910; took the name Fray Angélico in 1929 when he became a Franciscan. **Education:** St. Francis Seminary, Cincinnati, Ohio, 1924-29; Duns Scotus College, Detroit, Michigan, 1930-34, B.A. 1934; Franciscan House of Studies, Oldenburg, Indiana, 1934-37. **Career:** Entered the Franciscan Order in 1929; ordained Roman Catholic priest, Santa Fe, 1937; missionary priest throughout New Mexico, 1937-72; served as chaplain in the U.S. Army, 1943-46 in South Pacific and 1950-52 in Texas and Germany; retired from priestly duties, 1972. Southwest book review editor, *New Mexico Magazine,* 1970-78; lecturer, University of Albuquerque, 1972-74; archivist, Catholic Archdiocese of Santa Fe, beginning 1975. Associate member, Academy of American Franciscan History (beginning 1967); vice president, Catholic Poetry Society of America (1946-48); regent, Museum of New Mexico, 1946-57; state chaplain, American Legion, 1948. **Awards:** Catholic Poetry Society of America award, 1948; Cardinal Newman Key award, 1949; National Conference of Christians and Jews lyric poetry award, 1963; New Mexico Governor's literary award, 1976. D.H.L.: University of New Mexico, Albuquerque, 1974. D.Litt.: University of Albuquerque, 1963. LL.D: New Mexico State University, Las Cruces, 1975. **Died:** 18 March 1996.

PUBLICATIONS

Collections

Selected Poems, With an Apologia. 1969.
The Short Stories of Fray Angélico Chávez, edited by Genaro Padilla. 1987.

Novels

The Lady from Toledo, illustrated by Fray Angélico Chávez. 1960; abridged edition, 1993.

Short Stories

New Mexico Triptych. 1940.
From an Altar Screen/ El retablo: Tales from New Mexico. 1957; as *When the Santos Talked: A Retablo of New Mexico Tales,* 1977.

Poetry

Clothed with the Sun. 1939.
Eleven Lady-Lyrics and Other Poems. 1945.
The Single Rose: the Rose Unica and Commentary of Fray Manuel de Santa Clara. 1948.
The Virgin of Port Lligat. 1959.

Other

Seraphic Days. 1940.
Our Lady of the Conquest. 1948.
La Conquistadora: The Autobiography of an Ancient Statue. 1954.
Origins of New Mexico Families in the Spanish Colonial Period. 1954; revised as *Origins of New Mexico Families: A Genealogy of the Spanish Colonial Period.* 1993.
Coronado's Friars. 1968.
The Song of Francis. 1973.
My Penitente Land: Reflections on Spanish New Mexico. 1974.
But Time and Chance: The Story of Padre Martínez of Taos, 1793-1867. 1981.
Tres Macho—He Said. 1985.
Chávez: A Distinctive American Clan of New Mexico. 1989.

Editor and translator with Eleanor B. Adams, *Missions of New Mexico, 1776, A Description by Fray Atanasio Domínguez.* 1956.
Editor, *Archives of the Archdiocese of Santa Fe, 1678-1900.* 1957.
Editor and translator, *The Oroz Codex,* by Fray Pedro Oroz. 1972.

Translator, *The Domínguez-Escalante Journal.* 1976.

*

Bibliography: *Fray Angélico Chávez: A Bibliography of His Published Writings (1925-1978)* by Phyllis S. Morales, 1980.

Critical Studies: "Fray Angélico Chávez and His Lady Lyrics" by Robert Hunt, in *Southwest Review* vol. 31, Summer 1946; "Fray Angélico Chavez: 20th-Century Renaissance Man" by Robert Huber, in *New Mexico Magazine,* March-April 1970; review of *My Penitente Land* by Kenneth R. Weber, in *Journal of Ethnic Studies* vol. 3, no. 2, 1975; review of *My Penitente Land* by Francisco A. Lomelí, in *New Scholar* vol. 8, nos. 1-2, 1982; "The Social Allegories of Fray Angélico Chávez" by Genaro Padilla, in *Pasó por Aquí: Critical Essays on the New Mexico Literary Tradition,* 1989.

*   *   *

Fray Angélico Chávez, poet, author and one of New Mexico's first native-born Franciscan priests, devoted his long and productive literary career to the study of New Mexico's Hispanic heritage, finding Biblical roots in its social, religious and historical traditions. For his ability to capture in poetry and prose the essence of this Hispanic tradition, he has been honored as one of the Southwest's most remarkable writers and recognized with numerous awards and degrees.

Even as a youth Chávez enjoyed reading histories of New Mexico and was first attracted to the Franciscan Order because of its importance for the history of his beloved homeland. He completed his undergraduate and seminary education in the Midwest, entering the Franciscan Order in 1929. An avid painter at the time, he took the name Fray Angélico after the renowned Italian Renaissance artist Fra Angélico, whose work he admired. All but the author's earliest writings have been published under that name.

At age 27 he returned to New Mexico to be ordained a Roman Catholic priest in the cathedral in Santa Fe. From that date until his retirement in 1972, he followed a dual career as both author and parish priest to several towns and pueblos in New Mexico, including Peña Blanca, Cochití, Santa Domingo, Jémez, San Felipe, and Cerrillos. During World War II and the Korean War he served as chaplain in the U.S. Army, spending time in the Pacific and later in Texas and Germany. In 1975 he was appointed archivist to the Archdiocese of Santa Fe, having retired from his priestly duties but not from his membership in the Franciscan Order.

Chávez's interest in writing began at an early age. He was already publishing poems for the school paper while still a seminary student in Cincinnati. Some of these early poems are in fact included in his first published book of poems, *Clothed With the Sun* (1939). In this volume, whose title is taken from the Apocalypse, his aim, drawing from personal experience, is to capture the emotional impact of a religious life. Some of the settings are New Mexican, and the sun here is a metaphor for the Southwest, but, more importantly, also a reference to the rebirth of the Christian soul in God. According to Chávez in his "Apologia" to *Selected Poems* (1969), he was engaged in a "quest for that rare poem which, without any seeming effort, fixes a few simple Anglo-Saxon words into a thing of beauty that brings on rapture." He found his spiritual progenitors in English lyric poetry, particularly poets William Blake and John Donne.

With time his poetry became increasingly complex and ambitious, while retaining an essentially religious world view. *The Single Rose* (1948) recalls the biblical Song of Songs in its evocation of human and divine love, particularly the love that binds the poet to the homeland and the Creator to the chosen people. The allegory of the rose, on which this poem is based, is from a late-medieval literary tradition that Chávez revived in his own mystical and emotional vision.

It was a painting by Salvador Dali that inspired the poet to write *The Virgin of Port Lligat* (1959), a poem that **T.S. Eliot** praised as a "very considerable achievement." The narrator's perspective is essentially a positive one as he addresses the significance of human life and the condition of Western man in the atomic age. It was selected as one of the forty best books of 1959 for adults by the Catholic Library Association.

In 1948 the Catholic Poetry Society of America honored him with its annual poetry award and poet Jessica Powers in *The Commonweal* called him "one of the great hopes of Catholic poetry." However, by the mid-sixties, Chávez had become disillusioned with the writing of poetry. His lyric style, he wrote in the "Apologia," had become "outmoded . . . in an age opposed to regular rhythm and rhyme." *Selected Poems With an Apologia,* published in 1969, marks the end of his career as an active poet.

A longtime interest in folk art and folk tales led him to the writing of original historical fiction about Hispanic New Mexico. Occasionally, as in the *New Mexico Triptych* (1940) and *The Lady From Toledo* (1960), these stories were accompanied by his own illustrations. The stories capture the mood of an earlier age and bring to life the faith in miracles and naive beauty that are exemplified in the painted altar screens of eighteenth-century rural New Mexican churches, with their colorful portrayals of saints and sacred mysteries. *La Conquistadora* (1954) is an imaginative tale of adventure told from the perspective of a famous statue of the Virgin in the cathedral in Santa Fe. She is the unofficial patroness of colonial New Mexico and was brought to that Spanish kingdom by Diego de Vargas in his reconquest of the area following the 1680 Pueblo Indian revolt. *The Lady From Toledo* (1960) also employs a setting in colonial New Mexico to recount events leading up to that revolt. While the story is based on historical documents of the period, the fictional characters—an invalid girl miraculously

cured, a sinister rebel, a native religious convert caught between conflicting loyalties, a martyred missionary—are stylized constructs who act out their parts as in a medieval mystery play. The "Lady" referred to in the title is herself an icon, a small statue of the Virgin Mary said to have prophesied the impending rebellion. In the fiction of Fray Angélico, art, life and the miraculous are inextricably fused.

Chávez's writings reflect his life-long interest in the history of Hispanic New Mexico - his intent being to present the story of his people, told from their own perspective, which is sometimes at odds with non-Hispanic accounts. He has studied, and written extensively about Spanish culture in the Southwest and possesses an extraordinary knowledge of documentary sources. The several important Spanish-language sources that he has translated and published include *Missions of New Mexico 1776; Archives of the Archdiocese of Santa Fe, 1678-1900; The Domínguez-Escalante Journal;* and *The Oroz Codex, 1584-1586.* Based on early and previously untranslated documents such as these, Chávez's groundbreaking studies have contributed much to advancing our understanding of Southwest history. *Coronado's Friars* (1968), for example, resolved four centuries of confusion about the role of Franciscans who participated in that historic expedition; *But Time and Chance* (1981) was written in defense of Padre Antonio José Martínez, one of New Mexico's most maligned ecclesiastics. Chávez's goal of reaching a popular audience with the history of the achievements of New Mexico's Hispanics was furthered when he completed the biography of José Manuel Gallegos of Albuquerque, New Mexico's first U.S. Congressman, *Tres Macho—He Said* (1985). Access to original documents also facilitated his interest in tracing family genealogies, as in *Origins of New Mexico Families in the Spanish Colonial Period* (1954) and in an account of his own ancestors, *Chávez: A Distinctive American Clan of New Mexico* (1989).

The most personal of all Chávez's prose writings is *My Penitente Land* (1974), a panegyric in praise of New Mexico's landscape and Hispanic history told from an intensely personal perspective. In his words, "It is a long story of blood in connection with landscape—a shepherd blood and its *hesed* upon upland landscapes of severe bright colors, crystal skies, and sparse rains." Drawing upon his talents as poet, historian, theologian and storyteller, Chávez weaves together biblical episodes, historical anecdotes and personal memories to create a lyric vision of a difficult land of divine promise. He sees a powerful connection between terrain, racial ancestry, and Hispanic character, a conjunction that finds expression in the people's religious beliefs, especially the Penitente Brotherhood.

Chávez's multi-faceted talents, which in their breadth and energy evoke the analytic enthusiasm of the Renaissance, have reinforced each other to articulate with uncommon clarity the world view of Hispanic New Mexicans—the visionary faith that for centuries has guided them, their sense of an organic and nourishing connection to Spanish civilization, and their growth out of a land both hard and beautiful.

—Clark Colahan

CHAYEFSKY, Paddy

Born: Sidney Chayefsky in the Bronx, New York, 29 January 1923. **Education:** DeWitt Clinton High School, Bronx, graduated

1939; City College, New York, B.S. in social science 1943. **Military Service:** Served in the U.S. Army, 1943-45: private; Purple Heart. **Family:** Married Susan Sackler in 1949; one son. **Career:** Worked for a printer, New York, 1946; writer in Hollywood, late 1940s; gag writer for Robert Q. Lewis, New York, 1950. President, Sudan Productions, 1956, Carnegie Productions, 1957, S.P.D. Productions after 1959, Sidney Productions after 1967, and Simcha Productions after 1971, all New York. Council member, Dramatists Guild, from 1962. **Awards:** Screen Writers Guild award, 1954, 1971; Oscar, for screenplay, 1955, 1971, 1976; New York Film Critics award, 1956, 1971, 1976; British Academy award, 1976. **Died:** 1 August 1981.

PUBLICATIONS

Collection

The Collected Works of Paddy Chayefsky. 1994.

Plays

No T.O. for Love, music by Jimmy Livingston (produced 1945).
Printer's Measure (televised 1953). In *Television Plays,* 1955.
Middle of the Night (televised 1954; revised version, produced 1956). 1957.
Television Plays (includes *The Bachelor Party, The Big Deal, Holiday Song, Marty, The Mother,* and *Printer's Measure*). 1955.
The Bachelor Party (screenplay). 1957.
The Goddess (screenplay; stage version produced 1971). 1958.
The Tenth Man (produced 1959). 1960.
Gideon (produced 1961). 1962.
The Passion of Josef D. (produced 1964). 1964.
The Latent Heterosexual (produced 1968). 1967.

Screenplays: *The True Glory* (uncredited), with Garson Kanin, 1945; *As Young as You Feel,* with Lamar Trotti, 1951; *Marty,* 1955; *The Bachelor Party,* 1957; *The Goddess,* 1958; *Middle of the Night,* 1959; *The Americanization of Emily,* 1964; *Paint Your Wagon,* with Alan Jay Lerner, 1969; *The Hospital,* 1971; *Network,* 1975; *Altered States,* 1979.

Radio Plays: *The Meanest Man in the World, Tommy,* and *Over 21* (all in *Theater Guild of the Air* series), 1951-52; scripts for *Cavalcade of America.*

Television Plays: scripts for *Danger* and *Manhunt* series; *Holiday Song,* 1952; *The Reluctant Citizen,* 1952; *Printer's Measure,* 1953; *Marty,* 1953; *The Big Deal,* 1953; *The Bachelor Party,* 1953; *The Sixth Year,* 1953; *Catch My Boy on Sunday,* 1953; *The Mother,* 1954; *Middle of the Night,* 1954; *The Catered Affair,* 1955; *The Great American Hoax,* 1957.

Fiction

Altered States. 1978.

*

Critical Studies: *Chayefsky* by John M. Clum, 1976; "Paddy Chayefsky's Jews and Jewish Dialogues" by Leslie Field, in *From*

Hester Street to Hollywood: The Jewish-American Stage and Screen edited by Sarah Blacher Cohen, 1983; *Mad As Hell: The Life and Work of Paddy Chayefsky* by Shaun Considine, 1994.

*   *   *

"I write out of social necessity," Paddy Chayefsky once explained, but he might have said with equal candor, "I write out of personal conviction." A determined idealist who believed the message of his plays, Chayefsky wrote about men—*The Man Who Made the Mountains Shake* (an earlier title of the unproduced *Fifth from Garibaldi*), *The Tenth Man, The Latent Heterosexual, Marty, Gideon and Josef D.*—and about the agony man suffers in the *Middle of the Night* and the doom he senses when lost in *The Hospital* or inhumanly controlled within the *Network.* "I write a call to disaster," Chayefsky also once said, and the echoes of that "call," early and late, presented in stage plays, screenplays, and plays for television, detail Chayefsky's progress from a writer with a wholesome faith in man and his power to love to a man who found in his despair that love was not enough.

Chayefsky's early work clearly illustrates his positive approach to the world, the world of the common man whose urgent search for values in his real and spiritual existence absorbed the playwright. Chayefsky's overwhelming sympathy for poor, trapped, and self-defeated people drove him to explore post-war urban society in America and, with his own abundant faith, to boost their self-esteem. Mario Fortunato, the ditch digger in the Boston Navy Yard who once "made the mountains shake" must recognize his own worth, not through wealth or his son's activities but as a man loved by his sons. How does one find meaning in life? That was Chayefsky's question, and in the personal dramas he created for television during the 1950s he contrived the simple and sentimental answers that first made him popular. His secret was a combination of distinctive craftsmanship, a belief in his art and a medium (television) that he found most suitable for his talents in creating a sense of reality among everyday crises. With a natural ear for human speech that earned him the reputation of the best writer of realistic dialogue in America, Chayefsky created a memorably poignant sense of frail humanity within the television framework of 53 minutes. In the early years his work was an affirmation of faith, revealed in such teleplays as *Holiday Song* and *The Reluctant Citizen.* Marty was just an ordinary, fat, ugly man with certain values and many conflicts who at the end of 53 minutes began a new and purposeful life.

The three best and most successful plays of Chayefsky's career epitomize the playwright of faith whose balanced approach to the frailties of man was buttressed by an empyreal sense of humor. In *Middle of the Night,* a 53-year-old widowed manufacturer and a 24-year-old girl, both beset by greedy and insensitive people, decide that "even a few years of happiness you don't throw away. We'll get married." They are gentle and likeable people who flaunt social conventions with a nervous laugh and a calculated gamble. Arthur Landau in *The Tenth Man* has a terrifyingly perceptive view of modern life that underscores his assertion that he believes in nothing. This is his dybbuk. When he is commandeered to help fulfill the requirement for Jewish worship and discovers his fondness for a girl whose more conventional dybbuk arouses the Jews and their Cabalist to perform an exorcism, Arthur finds himself purged. It is a tender tale, realistically told, and the urban hero, feeling the power of love—or God, if you will—asserts himself and takes the girl away. According to Chayefsky,

Gideon tests the God he knows, once again illustrating the playwright's very human view of man's relationship to his Old Testament God whose patience is indeed tried by this "vain ass" whose power to contemplate God evokes only his ingenuous but reasonable request that he be allowed to believe in himself. And God agrees—he loves Gideon—but with a cosmic sense of mocking humor; let man try to be God if he can.

Although Chayefsky's thoughtful concern for man remained prominent in his work, his convictions changed. His faith in the power of love to free a trapped mankind was replaced by fears for humanity. In *The Passion of Josef D.* belief in God becomes no longer possible. "Nothing is real," says Lenin; the gods that men create for themselves are illusions. Although *The Latent Heterosexual* is undeniably a serious play showing the wretched horror of the times, it is also frequently crude and brutal with a hero whose ego denies him real emotions, serious thoughts, or any recognizable values. After these plays, Chayefsky wrote only screenplays. *The Hospital* shows "the whole wounded madhouse of our times," a sick society in which the hero, struggling to regain his sense of purpose, finally recognizes a need "to be responsible." *Network* also pictures a grotesque and dehumanized world where there is no hope for man. The craftsmanship that was a hallmark of Chayefsky's work remained, but he now dramatized a total disillusionment where sentimental faith had become a fearful bitterness and hope had changed to horror in the world around him.

—Walter J. Meserve

CHEEVER, John (William)

Born: Quincy, Massachusetts, 27 May 1912. **Education:** Thayer Academy, South Braintree, Massachusetts. **Military Service:** Served in the U.S. Army Signal Corps, 1943-45: sergeant. **Family:** Married Mary M. Winternitz in 1941; one daughter and two sons. **Career:** Full-time writer in New York City, 1930-51, Scarborough, New York, 1951-60, and Ossining, New York, after 1961; teacher at Barnard College, New York, 1956-57, Ossining Correctional Facility (Sing Sing prison), 1971-72, and University of Iowa Writers Workshop, Iowa City, 1973; visiting professor of creative writing, Boston University, 1974-75. **Awards:** Guggenheim fellowship, 1951, and second fellowship; Benjamin Franklin award, 1955; O. Henry award, 1956, 1964; American Academy grant, 1956, and Howells Medal, 1965; National Book award, 1958; National Book Critics Circle award, 1979; Pulitzer prize, 1979; MacDowell Medal, 1979; American Book award, for paperback, 1981; National Medal for literature, 1982. Litt.D.: Harvard University, Cambridge, Massachusetts, 1978. **Member:** American Academy, 1958. **Died:** 18 June 1982.

Publications

Short Stories

The Way Some People Live: A Book of Stories. 1943.
The Enormous Radio and Other Stories. 1953.
Stories, with others. 1956; as *A Book of Stories*, 1957.
The Housebreaker of Shady Hill and Other Stories. 1958.
Some People, Places, and Things That Will Not Appear in My Next Novel. 1961.

The Brigadier and the Golf Widow. 1964.
The World of Apples. 1973.
The Stories. 1978.
The Day the Pig Fell into the Well (story). 1978.
The Leaves, The Lion-Fish and the Bear (story). 1980.
The Uncollected Stories. 1988.
Thirteen Uncollected Stories. 1994.

Novels

The Wapshot Chronicle. 1957.
The Wapshot Scandal. 1964.
Bullet Park. 1969.
Falconer. 1977.
Oh, What a Paradise It Seems. 1982.

Plays

Television Plays: scripts for *Life with Father* series; *The Shady Hill Kidnapping*, 1982.

Other

Conversations with Cheever, edited by Scott Donaldson. 1987.
The Letters, edited by Benjamin Cheever. 1988.
The Journals. 1991.
Glad Tidings: A Friendship in Letters: The Correspondence of John Cheever and John D. Weaver, 1945-1982. 1993.

*

Bibliography: *Cheever: A Reference Guide* by Francis J. Bosha, 1981.

Critical Studies: *Cheever* by Samuel Coale, 1977; *Cheever* by Lynne Waldeland, 1979; *Critical Essays on Cheever* edited by R.G. Collins, 1982; *Cheever: The Hobgoblin Company of Love* by George W. Hunt, 1983; *Home before Dark: A Biographical Memoir of Cheever* by Susan Cheever, 1984; *Cheever: A Study of the Short Fiction* by James Eugene O'Hara, 1989; "Writing the Cheever" by Scott Donaldson, in *Sewanee Review*, summer 1990; "Shutting the Door on Someone" by Helen Barolini, in *Southwest Review*, autumn 1990; "John Cheever's Contingent Imagination" by Daniel T. O'Hara, in *South Atlantic Quarterly*, summer 1992; *Dragons and Martinis: The Skewed Realism of John Cheever* by Michael D. Byrne, 1993; *John Cheever Revisited* by Patrick Meanor, 1995.

*   *   *

John Cheever made his mark as a chronicler of a modern American sensibility that is well educated, disoriented, and generally bitter toward the situations, sexual and cultural, in which it finds itself. That sensibility is usually represented as able to look back on an earlier generation in which moral codes were fixed and confident; that fixity and confidence almost constitute a romantic backdrop against which the frustrations of current life play out their inconclusive courses. These courses are often presented in short stories that combine the irony of sheer event with Cheever's own comments on what is happening—happening to persons who endure the events rather than understand them. For example, one story, "The Swimmer" (in *The Brigadier and the Golf Widow*), illustrates the texture and scope of many a Cheever tale. A man decides, for reasons that he does not clearly understand, to reach his home by swimming through all the private pools that extend toward his own home and pool. In the course of his feat, no more sensible than climbing the Himalayas, the swimmer has contact, ironic for Cheever and his readers, with several aspects of the swimmer's society. At the end, the swimmer arrives at his own pool, only to find his house empty; there is no explanation of this shocking conclusion. The man's dismay is but an intensification of the pressures that set him on his way.

Novels allowed Cheever to explore at greater length destinies no more controlled and intelligible than the afternoon efforts of the swimmer. Two closely related novels, *The Wapshot Chronicle* and *The Wapshot Scandal,* represent the decline of a "good family" in a small New England community; the modest certainties of an older generation unravel in the adventures of two sons as they wander from job to job and from one sexual relation to another. Stories loosely connected with the fates of the two young men ornament the novels and illustrate the impact of conspicuous wealth. American go-getting, scientific research, and the soft life that lies in wait for most Cheever characters. *Bullet Park* presents these themes with more rigor as they apply to two men, Hammer and Nailles. In Nailles appears a man who is fairly content with the disintegrating Zion where he finds himself. In Hammer, Cheever offers a man whose wealth and success create in him only a nameless bitterness. It is a bitterness that leads Hammer to an envy of the complacent Nailles, whose unconsidered contentment he tries to destroy; Hammer attempts to crucify Nailles' son.

Is this the end of the road? *Falconer* seems to say "Not necessarily." Farragut, the hero of this novel, has one of the bitterest experiences that Cheever ever contrived. The man is a drug addict who has been sent to prison for the murder of his brother. In a highly unified narrative, Farragut experiences the heartless pressures of the prison system, goes through the routine inhumanity, homosexuality, and sheer boredom of prison life—and has enough energy left to contrive his escape into a world whose qualities are not necessarily superior to the concentrated hell of the prison. Farragut's will to persist, to continue in a life made up of the absurdities that society and fate and Cheever contrive, sums up the counsel that Cheever offers.

Counsel less definite appears in Cheever's last book, *Oh, What a Paradise It Seems.* In this brief tale, a suitable coda to Cheever's work, several persons are briefly stirred to action by a commercial threat to a local pond. But the encounter of the persons at the village meeting is brief, and it is clear that all the participants will go their separate ways. And such dispersion is enough, at least for Cheever. For the mark of a superior intelligence is to be able to look down on the minds and deeds of others.

So once more advice is offered with a skill that is ingenious and deft. It is advice that comes from an authorial consciousness that is condescending rather than sympathetic.

—Harold H. Watts

See the essay on "The Swimmer."

CHESNUTT, Charles Waddell

Born: Cleveland, Ohio, 20 June 1858; moved with his family to Fayetteville, North Carolina, 1866. **Education:** Privately educated, and at local schools. **Family:** Married Susan U. Perry in 1878; four children. **Career:** Teacher, North Carolina public schools, 1873-77; assistant principal, 1877-79, and principal, 1880-83, Howard Normal School, Fayetteville; reporter, New York *Mail and Express,* 1883; clerk for railway company, Cleveland, 1883, then stenographer for the company's lawyer and studied law (admitted to Ohio bar, 1887); owned a stenographic business, mid-1880s-1899 and after 1902. **Awards:** NAACP Spingarn Medal, 1928. **Died:** 15 November 1932.

PUBLICATIONS

Collections

The Short Fiction, edited by Sylvia Lyons Render. 1974.
Charles W. Chesnutt: Stories. 1994.

Short Stories

The Conjure Woman. 1899.
The Wife of His Youth and Other Stories of the Color Line. 1899.

Novels

The House Behind the Cedars. 1900.
The Marrow of Tradition. 1901.
The Colonel's Dream. 1905.
Mandy Oxendine: A Novel. 1997.
Paul Merchand, F.M.C. 1998.

Other

Frederick Douglass. 1899.
To Be an Author: Letters of Charles W. Chesnutt, 1889-1905. 1997.

*

Bibliography: "The Works of Chesnutt: A Checklist" by William L. Andrews, in *Bulletin of Bibliography,* January 1976; *Chesnutt: A Reference Guide* by Curtis W. Ellison and E.W. Metcalf, Jr., 1977.

Critical Studies: *Chesnutt, Pioneer of the Color Line* by Helen M. Chesnutt, 1952; *Chesnutt: America's First Great Black Novelist* by J. Noel Heermance, 1974; *An American Crusade: The Life of Chesnutt* by Frances Richardson Keller, 1978; *The Literary Career of Chesnutt* by William L. Andrews, 1980; *Chesnutt* by Sylvia Lyons Render, 1980; "The Framing of Charles W. Chesnutt: Practical Deconstruction in the Afro-American Tradition" by Craig Werner, in *Southern Literature and Literary Theory* edited by Jefferson Humphries, vol. 18, 1990; "Who 'Goophered' Whom: The Afro-American Fabulist and His Tale in Charles Chesnutt's The Conjure Woman" by Joyce Hope Scott, in *Bestia: Yearbook of the Beast Fable Society,* May 1990; *Chesnutt* by Cliff Thompson, 1992; *Charles W. Chesnutt and the Progressive Movement* by Ernestine Williams Pickens, 1994; *The Absent Man: The Narrative Craft of Charles W. Chesnutt* by Charles Duncan, 1998; *Charles W. Chesnutt: A Study of the Short Fiction* by Henry B. Wonham, 1998.

*   *   *

Charles Waddell Chesnutt, a "voluntary Negro," reflects in his writings major inter- and intraracial tensions of the nineteenth-century United States. Beginning and ending his life in Cleveland, Ohio, and from age seven to twenty-five living in North Carolina, he found the major motivations and materials of his works in his own life and that of contemporaries or immediate forebears on both sides of the Mason-Dixon line. Chesnutt's preoccupations with the problems of powerless blacks and poor whites is doubtless a reflection not only of the trauma that marked his own poverty-stricken youth but also of the resultant resolve to improve the quality of life for all those denied access to the fullness of American life because of color and/or class.

Chesnutt's fiction ranges in form from simple tale to highly plotted novel, in mood from comic to tragic. The subject matter reflects the major contemporary concerns of black Americans. However, the general reading public, primarily white, rejected Chesnutt's increasingly explicit advocacy of equal rights for blacks and other under-privileged citizens. Consequently, after *The Colonel's Dream* in 1905, Chesnutt terminated his writing career.

By that time, however, Chesnutt had won a permanent place in American literary history, especially for his short fiction. His serious consideration as a conscious, accomplished author by critics such as **William Dean Howells** and **George Washington Cable** was unprecedented for a black American prose writer. His works, usually presented from a black perspective, are historically and sociologically accurate as well as aesthetically satisfying and ethically admirable. Chesnutt is recognized as "the first real Negro novelist," "the pioneer of the color line," and the first American writer not only to use the folk tale for social protest but also extensively to characterize black Americans.

After he stopped writing Chesnutt used in other ways his increasing influence to improve the status of his fellow blacks. In recognition of his achievements, the National Association for the Advancement of Colored People awarded him its annual Spingarn Medal in 1928. Upon Chesnutt's death in 1932, a friend summed up accurately: "His great contribution in letters is a monument to our race and . . . to our national life."

—Sylvia Lyons Render

CHILD, Lydia Maria

Pseudonyms: L. Maria Child; Mrs. Child. **Born:** Lydia Francis in Medford, Massachusetts, 11 February 1802. **Education:** Schools in Medford, Massachusetts, and Norridgewock, Maine. **Family:** Married David Lee Child in 1828. **Career:** Taught at a girls' school in Gardiner, Maine, 1820-21; began literary career with publication of historical novel, *Hobomok,* in 1824; taught school in Watertown, Massachusetts, 1826-27, and in Dorchester Heights, Massachusetts, 1830; founded and edited *The Juvenile Miscellany,* 1826-34; publication of *An Appeal in Favor of That Class of Americans Called Africans* in 1833 marked beginning of active public commitment to antislavery cause; edited *The National Anti-Slavery Standard* in New York, 1841-43; remained in New York, estranged from her husband, during the 1840s and published fiction in *The Columbian Lady's and Gentleman's Magazine* and *The Union Magazine,* 1845-49; reunited with David Child and returned to the Boston area in 1850; edited Harriet Jacobs's

Incidents in the Life of a Slave Girl in 1861; after the Civil War, continued to write and edit books, including a text for freed slaves, *The Freedmen's Book* (1865); a novel, *A Romance of the Republic* (1867); and *An Appeal for the Indians* (1868). **Died:** 20 October 1880.

PUBLICATIONS

Collections

Letters of Lydia Maria Child with a Biographical Introduction by John G. Whittier and an Appendix by Wendell Phillips. 1882.
The Collected Correspondence of Lydia Maria Child, 1817-1880, edited by Patricia G. Holland, Milton Meltzer, and Francine Krasno, 1980.
Lydia Maria Child: Selected Letters, 1817-1880, edited by Patricia G. Holland, Milton Meltzer, and Francine Krasno, 1982.
Hobomok & Other Writings on Indians, edited by Carolyn L. Karcher. 1986.
A Lydia Maria Child Reader, edited by Carolyn L. Karcher, 1997.

Novels

Hobomok, A Tale of Early Times. 1824.
The Rebels, or Boston before the Revolution. 1825; revised edition, 1850.
Philothea. A Romance. 1836; published as *Philothea: A Grecian Romance.* 1845.
A Romance of the Republic. 1867; published as *Rose and Flora,* 2 volumes, 1867.

Short Stories

The Coronal. A Collection of Miscellaneous Pieces, Written at Various Times. 1832; enlarged edition published as *The Mother's Story Book; or, Western Coronal. A Collection of Miscellaneous Pieces. By Mrs. Child . . . To which are added, a few tales, by Mary Howitt, and Caroline Fry.* 1833.
The Happy Grandmother. By Mrs. Child. To Which Is Added, The White Palfrey. c. 1835.
Fact and Fiction: A Collection of Stories. 1846; published as *The Children of Mt. Ida, and Other Stories.* 1871.
Sketches from Real Life. I. The Power of Kindness. II. Home and Politics. 1850; published as *The Power of Kindness; and Other Stories.* 1853.
Autumnal Leaves: Tales and Sketches in Prose and Rhyme. 1857.

Prose

The Frugal Housewife. 1829; revised edition, 1830; published as *The American Frugal Housewife,* beginning with the eighth edition, 1832.
The Mother's Book. 1831; revised edition, 1844.
The Biographies of Madame de Stael, and Madame Roland. 1832; published in part as *The Biography of Madame de Stael.* 1836; published as *Memoirs of Madame de Stael, and of Madame Roland.* 1847.
The Biographies of Lady Russell, and Madame Guyon. 1832; published in part as *The Biography of Lady Russell.* 1836.

Good Wives. 1833; published as *Biographies of Good Wives.* 1846; published as *Celebrated Women; Or, Biographies of Good Wives.* 1861; published as *Married Women: Biographies of Good Wives.* 1871.

An Appeal in Favor of That Class of Americans Called Africans. 1833.

The History of the Condition of Women, in Various Ages and Nations, 2 volumes. 1835; revised edition published as *Brief History of the Condition of Women, in Various Ages and Nations,* 2 volumes. 1845.

No. 1. Authentic Anecdotes of American Slavery . . . Aged Slaves (published anonymously). 1835.

No. 2. Authentic Anecdotes of American Slavery (published anonymously). 1835.

Anti-Slavery Catechism. 1836.

The Evils of Slavery, and The Cure of Slavery. The First Proved by the Opinions of Southerners Themselves, The Last Shown by Historical Evidence. 1836.

The Family Nurse; or Companion of The Frugal Housewife. 1837.

No. 3. Authentic Anecdotes of American Slavery (published anonymously). 1837.

Letters from New-York, [First Series], 1843; extended edition, 1844.

Letters from New York. Second Series. 1845.

Isaac T. Hopper: A True Life. 1853.

The Progress of Religious Ideas, through Successive Ages, 3 volumes. 1855.

Correspondence between Lydia Maria Child and Gov. Wise and Mrs. Mason, of Virginia. 1860.

The Right Way the Safe Way, Proved by Emancipation in the British West Indies, and Elsewhere. 1860; enlarged edition, 1862.

The Duty of Disobedience to the Fugitive Slave Act: An Appeal to the Legislators of Massachusetts. 1860.

An Appeal for the Indians. 1868.

Other (for children)

Evenings in New England. Intended for Juvenile Amusement and Instruction. 1824.

Emily Parker, or Impulse, Not Principle. Intended for Young Persons. 1827.

Biographical Sketches of Great and Good Men. Designed for the Amusement and Instruction of Young Persons. 1828.

The First Settlers of New-England: or, Conquests of the Pequods, Narragansets and Pokanokets: As Related by a Mother to Her Children, and Designed for the Instruction of Youth. 1829.

The Little Girl's Own Book. 1831; enlarged edition, 1834.

Flowers for Children, 3 volumes, 1844, 1845, 1847; volume 1 published as *The Christ-Child, and Other Stories.* 1869; volume 2 published as *Good Little Mitty, and Other Stories.* 1869; volume 3 published as *Making Something, and Other Stories.* 1869.

The Childrens' [sic] *Gems. The Brother and Sister: And Other Stories* (published anonymously). 1852.

A New Flower for Children. 1856.

Other

Compiler, *The Patriarchal Institution, As Described by Members of Its Own Family.* 1860.

Editor and contributor, *The Juvenile Souvenir.* 1827.
Editor and contributor, *The Oasis.* 1834.

Editor, *Memoir of Benjamin Lay: Compiled from Various Sources.* 1842.

Editor, *American Anti-Slavery Almanac [for 1843].* 1843.

Editor, *Linda Brent (Harriet A. Jacobs), Incidents in the Life of a Slave Girl.* 1861; published as *The Deeper Wrong; or Incidents in the Life of a Slave Girl.* 1862.

Editor and contributor, *Looking Toward Sunset. From Sources Old and New, Original and Selected.* 1865.

Editor and contributor, *The Freedmen's Book.* 1865.

Editor, *Aspirations of the World. A Chain of Opals.* 1878.

*

Critical Studies: *The Heart Is Like Heaven: The Life of Lydia Maria Child* by Helene G. Baer, 1964; *Tongue of Flame: The Life of Lydia Maria Child* by Milton Meltzer, 1965; *Lydia Maria Child* by William S. Osborne, 1980; *Women & Sisters: The Antislavery Feminists in American Culture* by Jean Fagan Yellin, 1989; *Crusader for Freedom: A Life of Lydia Maria Child* by Deborah Pickman Clifford, 1992; *The First Woman in the Republic: A Cultural Biography of Lydia Maria Child* by Carolyn L. Karcher, 1994; *Cultural Reformists: Lydia Maria Child and the Literature of Reform* by Bruce Mills, 1994.

*   *   *

In the July 1833 issue of the prestigious *North American Review,* Grenville Mellen championed Lydia Maria Child as perhaps the foremost woman writer in the United States. "Few female writers, if any," he asserted, "have done more or better things for our literature, in its lighter and graver departments." Indeed, Child had contributed much to the entertainment and elevation of American readers: a controversial but acclaimed historical novel, *Hobomok* (1824); one of the first successful children's magazines, *The Juvenile Miscellany* (1826-34); a domestic manual that would see more than thirty editions, *The Frugal Housewife* (1829); and a biography series of famous women that would culminate in two volumes used extensively by Margaret Fuller, Elizabeth Cady Stanton, and Susan B. Anthony, *The History of the Condition of Women, in Various Ages and Nations* (1835). With the publication of her abolitionist text *An Appeal in Favor of That Class of Americans Called Africans* in the same year as Mellen's review, however, she dramatically entered the antislavery cause and thus changed the way she would be received by the American public. Before a public struggling to interpret its democratic mission, Child contributed fiction and nonfiction that played influential roles in American literary and social circles.

Born in 1802 in Medford, Massachusetts, Child was the youngest of seven children. Her parents, Susannah Rand and Convers Francis, a prosperous baker and strict Calvinist, had been raised in families who had endured the hardships of the Revolutionary War. The Rands had been forced from their homes during the Battle of Bunker Hill, and Convers Francis's father had fought with the Minutemen at Concord and Lexington in 1775. Tempered in the fire of such events and baptized with the harsh faith of their forbearers, Child's parents formed a household that strongly asserted the values of frugality, industry, and duty to God. Reflecting upon her youth in 1863, Lydia Maria Child characterized her parents as "hard-working people, who had had small opportunity for culture." Thus, though she would reflect an assimilation of her family's republican values in *The Frugal Housewife* and *An Ap-*

peal, Child repeatedly lamented that these early years were uncongenial to a literary life.

Upon the death of her mother in 1814, Child joined her newly-wed sister, Mary Preston, in the "frontier" town of Norridgewock, Maine. While evidently designed to educate her in the domestic realm that her father wished to consign her, Child benefited from being freed from the more oppressive qualities of a Calvinist home. The stay with her sister proved as important to her literary imagination as to her domestic skills. In Maine, she imbibed the power of the landscape and visited the Penobscot Indians still residing along the Kennebec River. Area legend would later have it that Child was one of the first women to scale Mount Katahdin, an apparently erroneous rumor that confirms her reputation as one who broke barriers common to women of the nineteenth century.

During her time in Maine, Child continued a rich exchange with her brother Convers Francis, the sibling closest in age and temperament to Lydia. Child herself would later write that she owed her "literary tendencies" to her brother's early influence. Having been given the opportunity of a trade or an education, Convers had chosen the latter, entered Harvard, and eventually became a Unitarian minister. After teaching a year at a girls' school in Gardiner, Maine, she joined her brother and his wife at his Watertown, Massachusetts, home in the summer of 1821. Joining Convers initiated a significant transition in Child's life. In fact, as if to celebrate this new beginning, she renamed herself Lydia Maria, preferring from this point to be called Maria.

The Francis home proved to be the setting that Child longed for when she was younger. During her stay, she met such notables as **Ralph Waldo Emerson**, Theodore Parker, **John Greenleaf Whittier**, and Margaret Fuller. It was during this time as well that, while reading the April 1821 issue of the *North American Review,* Child ran across a review of James Wallis Eastburn and Robert Sands's narrative poem *Yamoyden.* Written by her brother's college friend John Gorham Palfrey, the article called upon American writers to make fictional use of those features that distinguished the nation: the vast landscape, Puritan history, and the exotic qualities of Indian culture. Just twenty-two years old, Child responded to Palfrey's summons by writing the historical novel *Hobomok* in six weeks. However, though the book answered the call for a national literature, it offended readers by portraying the miscegenation of a Puritan woman and a Native American man. According to the *North American Review* (July 1824), this union was "not only unnatural, but revolting . . . to every feeling of delicacy in man or woman." Still, through the influence of powerful Bostonians like Harvard professor George Ticknor, the book earned favorable reviews and thus won for the aspiring writer entrance into elite literary and social circles.

In depicting a union that violated cultural taboos, Child distinguished herself as a writer who tested literary and cultural boundaries regarding race and gender. While uneasy with her fictional portrayal of an interracial marriage, however, literary and social arbiters still saw in Child an author who scripted acceptable democratic principles. She most clearly articulated these principles in the magazines and books she published between 1824 and 1830. In her works for children, such as *Evenings in New England* (1825) and the *Juvenile Miscellany,* she included tales of Revolutionary War heroes such as George Washington and **Benjamin Franklin,** urging many of the values that Franklin himself delineated in his autobiography: frugality, industry, temperance, and moderation. Designed for those "who are not ashamed of economy," *The Frugal Housewife* also encouraged similar values. And, though her stories within the *Miscellany* would begin to reflect antislavery sentiment in the early 1830s, in the 1820s they still promoted the views of prominent Bostonians who held that patience not emancipation was the answer to the slavery question.

Attention to these virtues belied the undercurrent of radical reform that would pour forth from Child in the next decade. After her marriage to David Lee Child in 1828, Child grew increasingly concerned with such national ills as the policy toward the Cherokee Indians and slavery. Through David, a lawyer known for championing unpopular causes, Maria first met William Lloyd Garrison, the fiery abolitionist whose publication of *The Liberator* in 1831 marked the beginning of a more strident call for immediate emancipation. Converted to the antislavery cause, she penned one of the central abolitionist texts of the period, *An Appeal in Favor of That Class of Americans Called Africans.* "I am fully aware of the unpopularity of the task I have undertaken," Child wrote in the preface, "but though I expect ridicule and censure, it is not in my nature to fear them."

In calling for immediate and unconditional emancipation of slaves, Child indeed drew the censure she expected. The Boston Athenaeum, an extensive private library whose members included the elite of the city, withdrew Child's membership in the spring of 1835. (In 1832, she had become the first woman since Hannah Adams to be given access to the prestigious library.) Moreover, the public response to her abolitionist views led Child to give up editorship of the lucrative *Juvenile Miscellany.* Given these setbacks and the burdensome debt that David had incurred from lawsuits, the Childs departed for Northampton, Massachusetts, in 1838 and began what proved to be an unsuccessful venture in raising sugar beets. Both had hoped their efforts would decrease dependence upon slave-produced sugar. In 1841, Child moved to New York and accepted the editorship of the *National Anti-Slavery Standard,* a position she held until 1843.

Child's dedication to reform did not mean that she entirely abandoned the career for which she first gained national attention. Along with her reform activities in Boston during the 1830s, she also engaged in literary functions, attending **Ralph Waldo Emerson**'s lectures and Fuller's conversation group. In addition, she remained in contact with her brother who, along with Emerson, **Bronson Alcott**, and others, formed the Transcendentalist Club. Her intimate ties to both the literary and social reforms of the time led to the publication of *Philothea* (1836), a novel that develops antislavery and transcendental themes in portraying the philosophical Philothea and her slave friend Eudora. Child's personal and literary interest in transcendentalism later evolved into *Letters from New York* (1843), a collection of journalistic essays first published in the *National Anti-Slavery Standard.* These essays on topics ranging from mesmerism, prison reform, and women's rights reestablished Child's literary reputation. In part because of the repeated criticism from more strident abolitionists for her editorial style at the *Standard* and the persistent financial crises precipitated by David Child, Child became estranged from both the antislavery cause and her marriage.

During the 1840s, Child rededicated herself to her literary career, publishing more than twenty-four sketches and short stories in *The Columbian Lady's and Gentleman's Magazine* and *The Union Magazine* (known also as *Sartain's Union Magazine*). During this time she also renewed her friendship with Margaret Fuller, then working as a journalist for Horace Greeley's *New York Tribune.* In all, the decade of the 1840s saw the publication of some of Child's best work, including *Letters from New York, Second*

Series (1845) and some of her collected magazine fiction in *Fact and Fiction* (1846).

Her sabbatical from a central role in the antislavery cause during the 1840s did not signal her abandonment of reform principles. In fact, though Child distanced herself for a time from the abolitionist ranks, she continued to lace her stories with messages consistent with antislavery principles. Her reunion with David Child and her return to the Boston area in 1850, however, presaged a renewed commitment to the cause. Sparked by the events of the Kansas-Missouri conflict over the slavery issue, Child wrote "The Kansas Emigrants" (1855), a story that depicted peaceful New England settlers' efforts to defend their homestead from the proslavery "Border Ruffians" who sought to turn Kansas into a slave state. Within less than five years, she published antislavery pamphlets that further galvanized public sentiment against slavery. Having initially sought to nurse John Brown after his capture at Harper's Ferry in October of 1859, she produced a powerful defense of Brown in *Correspondence between Lydia Maria Child and Gov. Wise and Mrs. Mason, of Virginia* (1860), a work that eventually sold 300,000 copies. Within a year, she published two more pamphlets and edited **Harriet Jacobs**'s *Incidents in the Life of Slave Girl* (1861).

After the Civil War, Child continued to write and edit numerous books against racial prejudice. In *The Freedmen's Book* (1865), a text designed for emancipated slaves, she included stories by or about famous men and women of African descent, including Frances E.W. Harper, **Frederick Douglass**, and **Phillis Wheatley**. Described by Child as a novel designed to undermine prejudice, *A Romance of the Republic* (1867) imagines interracial marriage as an emblem for reconstruction. And, in *An Appeal for the Indians* (1868), she argued for just policies regarding Plains Indians. Even in these later works, then, Child continued her legacy of literary reform. "Besides playing a key role in the most important reform movements of her epoch," Carolyn L. Karcher writes in the *Dictionary of Literary Biography*, "she had pioneered almost every genre of nineteenth-century American letters, from the historical novel and the science fiction tale to children's fiction and the domestic advice book . . . . Clearly, as one who consistently encouraged readers to imagine alternative resolutions to national conflicts, Child endures as a central figure in antebellum literature and culture."

—Bruce Mills

CHILDRESS, Alice

Born: Charleston, South Carolina, 12 October 1920. **Education:** New York City public schools. **Family:** Married Nathan Woodard in 1957 (second marriage); one child (first marriage). **Career:** Actress, director, and playwright with American Negro Theatre, New York, eleven years; actress in *On Strivers Row,* 1940, *Natural Man,* 1941, *Anna Lucasta,* 1944, *Florence,* 1949, *The World of Sholom Aleichem,* and *The Cool World;* performer on Broadway and television; visiting scholar, 1966-68, Radcliff Institute for Independent Study (now Mary Ingraham Bunting Institute), Cambridge, Massachusetts; lecturer at universities and schools. Member of Frances Delafield Hospital governing board. **Awards:** Obie award for best original off-Broadway play, 1956; John Golden Fund for Playwrights grant, 1957; Rockefeller grant, 1967; *New York Times*

Book Review outstanding books of the year citation, 1973; Jane Addams Children's Book Honor award, 1974; named honorary citizen of Atlanta, Georgia, 1975; Sojourner Truth award; National Association of Negro Business and Professional Women's Clubs, 1975; Lewis Carroll Shelf award, 1975, University of Wisconsin; Virgin Islands film festival award for best screen play, 1977; first Paul Robeson award for outstanding contributions to the performing arts; Black Filmmakers Hall of Fame, 1977; "Alice Childress Week" observed in Charleston and Columbia, South Carolina, 1977; *New York Times* outstanding books of the year citation, 1982. **Died:** 1994.

PUBLICATIONS

Plays

Florence (produced 1949).
Just a Little Simple, based on Langston Hughes' short story collection *Simple Speaks His Mind* (produced 1950).
Gold through the Trees (produced 1955). Revised edition in *Black Theatre: A Twentieth Century Collection of the Work of Its Best Playwrights,* edited by Lindsay Patterson. 1971.
Trouble in Mind. 1955.
Like One of the Family (produced 1956).
Wedding Band: A Love/Hate Story in Black and White (produced 1966).
The Freedom Drum (produced 1969; produced as *Young Man Martin Luther King,* 1969).
A Man Bearing a Pitcher. 1969.
Martin Luther King at Montgomery, Alabama. 1969.
String, based on Guy de Maupassant's *A Piece of String* (produced 1969).
Mojo: A Black Love Story (produced 1970).
The African Garden. 1971.
Mojo [and] *String.* 1971.
When the Rattlesnake Sounds: A Play (for children). 1975.
Let's Hear It for the Queen: A Play (for children). 1976.
Sea Island Song (produced 1977; produced as *Gullah,* 1984).
Moms: A Praise Play for a Black Comedienne (produced 1986).
Wine in the Wilderness (screenplay). In *Black Theatre USA,* 1996.

Screenplays: *Wine in the Wilderness: A Comedy-Drama,* 1969; *Wedding Band,* 1973; *A Hero Ain't Nothin' but a Sandwich,* 1978; *String,* 1979.

Novels

A Hero Ain't Nothin' but a Sandwich. 1973.
A Short Walk. 1979.
Rainbow Jordan. 1981.

Other

Like One of the Family: Conversations from a Domestic's Life. 1956.
Many Closets. 1987.
Those Other People. 1989.

Editor, *Black Scenes.* 1971.

*

Critical Studies: *Black Women Writers (1950-1980): A Critical Evaluation,* 1984; "Alice Childress: Black Woman Playwright as Feminist Critic" by Gayle Austin in *The Southern Quarterly: A Journal of the Arts in the South,* Spring 1987; "Alice Childress: A Pioneering Spirit" by Elizabeth Brown-Guillory in *Sage: A Scholarly Journal on Black Women,* Spring 1987; *Modern American Drama: The Female Canon,* 1990; *Alice Childress* by La Vinia Delois Jennings, 1995; in *The Playwright's Art: Conversations with Contemporary American Dramatists,* edited by Jackson R. Bryer, 1995; *Modern Black American Poets and Dramatists,* edited by Harold Bloom, 1995; *Shackles on a Writer's Pen: Dialogism in Plays by Alice Childress, Lorraine Hansbery, Adrienne Kennedy, and Ntozake Shange* (dissertation) by Elizabeth Barnsley Brown, 1996.

*   *   *

Although Alice Childress is best known for her participation in theater arts, the impact Childress has had upon the theater far exceeds the recognition she has received. Childress began her career as an actress and director with the American Negro Theater in New York. Her first performance was in *On Strivers Row* (1940), but within nine years Childress had written and directed her own play *Florence* (1949). In 1952, Childress became the first black woman to write a play and have it professionally produced on the New York stage. *Florence* went on to be performed on Broadway. Along with several of her other works, including *Wine in the Wilderness: A Comedy-Drama* (1969), *Wedding Band: A Love/Hate Story in Black and White* (1973), *A Hero Ain't Nothin' but a Sandwich* (1978), and *String* (1979), for which Childress wrote screenplays, *Florence* was produced for television.

At a time when the country found itself embroiled in many racial conflicts, Childress chose to explore racial concerns through her art. Due to her frank representations of racial issues, however, her work often received unfair treatment. *Wine in the Wilderness,* for example, was banned by the state of Alabama and *A Hero Ain't Nothin' but a Sandwich* was barred from the school library system of Savannah, Georgia. And some affiliate television stations refused to air her plays. Childress has been characterized as a forerunner of her time because her choice of subject matter challenged audiences to establish new ways of understanding race in America. By refusing to accept race and gender concerns as binary oppositions she positioned herself as more than an artist, playwright, or novelist by laying the groundwork for valuable social critiques.

Childress' writings dismiss much of the negative imagery so common in representations of the black community and replace stereotypical characters with vibrant themes that celebrate black experiences. Unlike the psychological characterizations prevalent in contemporary theater, in the plays of **Eugene O'Neill, Tennessee Williams,** and **Arthur Miller** for instance, Childress emphasizes theme rather than character. In her essay, "A Candle in a Gale Wind," Childress explains: "My writing attempts to interpret the 'ordinary' because they are not ordinary. Each human is uniquely different. Like snowflakes, the human pattern is never cast twice. We are uncommonly and marvelously intricate in thought and action, our problems are most complex and, too often, silently borne." In her exploration of the particularities of individuals and their specific situations, Childress finds the content of her work.

Childress' writings depict the heroic nature of the struggle to do more than simply survive the racist institutions which circum-

scribe the lives of her characters. Whether through the use of fiction, television, or the stage, Childress' work seeks to be a vehicle of transformation for social concerns. In her novel *A Hero Ain't Nothin' but a Sandwich,* as well as the television production by the same name, to give one example, she explores the potential of human relationships to impact the life of a teenaged heroine addict either positively or negatively. The novel ends without a resolution but Childress invests a tremendous amount of hope in man's ability to reach out to his stepson. It is the "human" part which most interests Childress in her work because it is the part that is most unwilling to be defeated and the most likely to overcome.

—Valerie Sweeney Prince

CHIN, Frank (Chew, Jr.)

Born: Berkeley, California, 25 February 1940. **Education:** University of California at Berkeley, 1958-61; State University of Iowa, 1961-63; University of California at Santa Barbara, B.A. 1965. **Family:** Married Dana Lynn Spradling (third marriage); two children. **Career:** Worked as a clerk with the Western Pacific Railroad Company, Oakland, California, 1962-65; brakeman, Southern Pacific Railroad, Oakland, California, 1966; production writer, story editor and writer, KING-TV, Seattle, Washington, 1966-69; freelance consultant and lecturer on Chinese-America and racism, 1969-70; part-time lecturer in Asian American Studies, University of California at Davis, and San Francisco State College (now San Francisco State University), 1969-70; lecturer in creative writing, University of California at Berkeley, 1972; film consultant, Western Washington State College (now Western Washington University); artistic director, Asian American Theater workshop, San Francisco, since 1976; lecturer in Department of Sociology and Asian American Studies, University of California at Santa Barbara, 1980; lecturer in Department of English, University of Oklahoma, Norman, 1988. **Awards:** Joseph Henry Jackson award, 1965; James T. Phelan award, 1966; East-West Players Playwriting award, 1971; Jack J. Flaks Memorial Grant, 1972; San Francisco Foundation Playwrights fellowship, 1974; Rockefeller Playwright's grant, 1974; National Endowment for the Arts grant, 1974, 1980; Before Columbus-American Book award, 1981, 1989; Rockefeller American Generations Grant-University of California, Los Angeles, 1991-92; Lannan Foundation Literary Fellowship, 1992. **Residence:** Los Angeles.

Publications

Plays

The Chickencoop Chinaman (produced 1972). 1981.
The Year of the Dragon (produced 1974). 1981.
Gee, Pop! (produced 1974).
America More or Less, with Amiri Baraka and Leslie Marmon Silko, music by Tony Greco, lyrics by Arnold Weinstein (produced 1976).
Lullaby, with Leslie Marmon Silko, from her story (produced 1976).
America Peek-a-Boo Kabuki, World War II and Me (produced 1985).
Flood of Blood. 1988.

Television documentaries: *TSRT: Act Two,* 1966; *The Bel Canto Carols,* 1966; *A Man and His Music,* 1967; *Seafair Preview,* 1967; *The Year of the Ram,* 1967; *"And Still Champion . . . !" The Story of Archie Moore,* 1967; *Mary,* 1967; *"Chinaman's Chance . . ." A Portrait of Changing Chinese America,* 1971.

Television plays: *Rainlight, Rainvision,* 1969.

Short Stories

The Chinaman Pacific & Frisco R. R. Co. 1988.

Novels

Donald Duk. 1991.
Gunga Din Highway. 1994.

Other

Rescue at Wild Boar Forest (for children). 1988.
Lin Chong's Revenge (for children). 1989.
Bulletproof Buddhists and Other Essays. 1998.

Coeditor, *Aiiieeeee!: An Anthology of Asian American Writers.* 1974.
Coeditor, *Yardbird Reader.* Volume 3, 1974.
Coeditor, *The Big Aiiieeeee!* 1991.

*

Critical Studies: "Introduction" by Dorothy Ritsuko McDonald to Frank Chin's *The Chickencoop Chinaman [and] The Year of the Dragon,* 1981; "Chinatown Cowboys and Warrior Women: Searching for a New Self-Image" in *Asian American Literature: An Introduction to the Writings and Their Social Context,* 1982 and "'Such Opposite Creatures': Men and Women in Asian American Literature" in *Michigan Quarterly Review* vol. 39, no. 1, 1990, both by Elaine H. Kim; "An Introduction to Chinese-American and Japanese-American Literature" by Walter J. Ong in *Three American Literatures: Essays in Chicano, Native American, and Asian-American Literature for Teachers of American Literature* edited by Ong and Houston B. Baker, Jr., 1982; "The Woman Warrior versus the Chinaman Pacific: Must the Chinese American Critic Choose between Feminism and Heroism?" by King-kok Cheung in *Conflicts in Feminism* edited by Marianne Hirsch and Evelyn Fox Keller, 1990; "The Formation of Frank Chin and Formations of Chinese American Literature" in *Asian Americans: Comparative and Global Perspectives* edited by Shirley Hune, Hyung-chan Kim, Stephen S. Fugita, and Amy Ling, 1991 and "The Production of Chinese American Tradition: Displacing American Orientalist Discourse" in *Reading the Literatures of Asian America* edited by Shirley Geok-lin Lim and Amy Ling, 1992, both by David Leiwei Ling; "Frank Chin: Iconoclastic Icon" by Robert Murray Davis in *Redneck Review of Literature* no. 23, 1992; "Dublin to Chinatown: James Joyce to Frank Chin" by Robert Murray Davis, in *Hungarian Journal of English and American Studies,* 1996, pp. 117-22; "Tripmaster Monkey, Frank Chin, and the Chinese Heroic Tradition" by Patricia P. Chu, in *Arizona Quarterly: A Journal of American Literature, Culture, and Theory,* Autumn 1997, pp. 117-39.

*   *   *

Since the 1960s, Frank Chin has played a significant role in the development of Asian American literature. Chin's writing over the years, filled with wit and vitriol, sardonic humor and unrelenting pathos, placed a signature emphasis on correcting the demeaning and debilitating stereotypes assigned to Asian Americans by mainstream American society. Chin's work began to appear at a time of heightened social awareness of racial problems in the United States and in the context of various third world liberation movements of the 1960s and 1970s. Consequently, his work has often been seen as a militant call to Asian Americans to resist the imposition of stereotypes which mark them as inveterately humble, industrious, self-effacing, and law-abiding—in short, a "model minority" to be held up as a disciplinary example for other, presumably less model, minorities. For Chin, these stereotypes stood in the way of more accurate representations of Asian Americans as well as a more realistic understanding of the dynamics of race in American life. Chin's vociferous debunking of long-cherished misrepresentations of Asian Americans helped open the way for a new generation of Asian American writers whose aesthetic and political sensibilities had been shaped by the social tumult of the 1960s and 1970s.

Chin grew up in the Chinatowns of Oakland and San Francisco. He attended the University of California at Berkeley, gained a fellowship to the Writer's Workshop at the University of Iowa, and received a bachelor's degree in English from the University of California at Santa Barbara in 1965. Before returning to school to complete his degree, Chin worked in various clerk jobs with the Western Pacific Railroad in Oakland, California, and upon graduation hired on as the first Chinese American brakeman for the Southern Pacific Railroad. After leaving the railroad in the summer of 1966, Chin began working with KING-TV, a television station in Seattle. While in Seattle, he wrote and produced documentaries on topics including the Chinese New Year's celebration and Chinese American history in Seattle, and on the Light Heavyweight Champion, Archie Moore. He also contributed scripts for *Sesame Street.*

Early recognition of his work came in the wake of the American Place Theatre's productions of his plays *The Chickencoop Chinaman* (1972) and *The Year of the Dragon* (1974). The first Chinese American plays to be produced on the New York stage, they garnered praise from critics who welcomed the dismantling of long-cherished stereotypes of Asian Americans, and drew criticism from those who were puzzled by the seemingly uncharacteristic representations of Asian Americans and offended by the rawness of the language. In 1973 Chin started the Asian American Theatre Workshop in San Francisco, and remained its director until 1977. Over the years, Chin has taught courses on Asian American subjects at San Francisco State College (now San Francisco State University), the University of California at Berkeley, Davis and Santa Barbara, and the University of Oklahoma in Norman. Throughout the 1980s and the early 1990s, Chin's work has gained recognition in the form of numerous awards and grants, including the Lannan Foundation Literary Fellowship in 1992.

Driving Chin's work are two related concerns: the search for a usable past with which to make sense of the present, and the struggle between assimilation and nativism. His first play, *The Chickencoop Chinaman,* deals with the search for cultural and linguistic roots. In this, and in some of his other writings, the son's quest to find and to know the father functions also as a metaphor for the search by Chinese Americans for a Chinese-American history that will enable them to claim a stake in American life. The play also raises the issue of how language constitutes not only a mode of expression but also a mode of being. The main character in the play, who "talk[s] the talk of orphans," being "born to none of [his] own" is forever scouring the range of American dialects available to him as the child of a low-income neighborhood in Oakland, California (a range which includes holy roller, hipster, gangster, and standard English) for one in which to ground his identity.

In *The Year of the Dragon,* an immigrant Chinese American father's experiences of a racially hostile society outside of Chinatown leave him profoundly skeptical of his son's chances for survival and success in the larger society. The son, whose aspirations to become a writer have largely been crushed by familial obligations that require him to abandon his writing in order to return to Chinatown to take over the family business, tries to balance the tenuous hope that he might yet write with his immediate obligations to his family. The dilemma posed by the father-son relationship is, for Chin, simultaneously the dilemma confronting the Chinese American forced to choose between individual fulfillment (assimilation) and familial obligation (retention of native culture). In this play, it is the daughter, however, who makes that choice by leaving Chinatown, but who leaves at the cost of estranging herself from her family and the Chinatown community. Her assimilation into American life via marriage to a white husband in Boston and via financial success as the author of bestselling Chinese cookbooks is contrasted with the son's reluctance to relinquish what he perceives to be the only identity allowed him—a Chinese American identity bound up with Chinatown. The daughter's actions bespeak betrayal of family and culture, and the son's actions, while upholding family and culture, ultimately bespeak debilitating self-contempt. Decay, futility, self-loathing, and death are the thematic touchstones here. The father eventually dies, the daughter is banished from Chinatown by her older brother, the reluctant heir to the Chinatown mantle, and the play ends with the image of Chinatown awash in a sea of self-contemptuous drool.

Chin's fictional world of ne'er-do-wells, has-beens, cripples, traitors, well-intentioned liberals, and general misfits is also inhabited by the figure of the trickster-outlaw which offers transformative possibilities. This trickster-outlaw, at once fast-talking, wisecracking, witty, and licentious, is Chin's antidote to the bumbling, tongue-twisted if not tongue-tied Charlie Chans of American popular culture. But even the trickster's verbal virtuosity can be throttled by the dying clutch of Chinatown. At the end of *The Year of the Dragon,* the oldest son, who works as a Chinatown tour guide in the family travel agency, finds himself, as the stage directions tell us, dressed in the image of a "shrunken Charlie Chan, an image of death." Shortly after he begins his tour guide spiel, he finds himself at "the end of language" itself. The trickster's speech has been reduced to "some kind of awful pissed off wounded animal language," hardly the language of transformative possibility.

In the eight stories collected in *The Chinaman Pacific & Frisco R. R. Co.,* the themes of decay, crippling, and death are revisited. But at the same time, there is a greater urgency here about recovering the heroism of the Chinese American past. As the title of the collection suggests, Chinese American history for Chin is intimately bound up with the construction of the transcontinental railroad. The choice of the railroad as the actual and symbolic site of Chinese American heroism is more fully developed in Chin's first novel, *Donald Duk.* The novel tells the story of a Chinese American boy's coming of age in San Francisco's Chinatown. The Chinatown of *Donald Duk* is, however, no longer inhabited by the dead and the dying. Instead, it is a newly revitalized cultural

and commercial enclave which ultimately comes to claim the boy's respect and allegiance rather than his contempt. This difference between the two representations of San Francisco's Chinatown can be traced in part to demographic changes. The earlier depictions, conceived in the late 1960s, reflected a common assumption of the times that Chinatowns and their inhabitants were dying out because of restrictive immigration laws dating back to the Chinese Exclusion Act of 1882 that drastically limited the numbers of Chinese allowed to enter the country. With a disproportionately high number of Chinese men in relation to Chinese women, Chinatowns and their largely aging bachelor populations seemed unlikely to reproduce themselves. With the liberalization of the immigration laws in 1965, the ratio of men to women began to balance out and the numbers of Chinese Americans grew significantly. By 1990, San Francisco's Chinatown was filled with not only new immigrants from Hong Kong, the People's Republic of China and Taiwan, but also ethnic Chinese from other Southeast Asian countries. The Chinatown that the character Donald Duk inhabits is a far cry from the one experienced by the characters in *The Year of the Dragon.*

In *Donald Duk,* the revitalization of Chinatown is tied to the recovery of a heroic Chinese and Chinese American past. Martial arts heroes from the fourteenth-century Chinese classic *Water Margin* surface in the novel to mingle with equally heroic nineteenth-century Chinese railroad workers in the Sierra Nevadas. The eponymous hero is himself transported back in time—by way of nightly dreams—to 1869 and the completion of the transcontinental railroad at Promontory Point, Utah. In witnessing the valiant struggles of the Chinese railroad workers in the face of racist employers and the unforgiving elements, Donald Duk gains an understanding of the actualities of Chinese American history that has hitherto been obscured for him by the prevailing stereotypes of Chinese Americans. He subsequently becomes proud of his heritage, and becomes indignant over the harsh treatment of the Chinese in the past and the continuing omission from American history texts of the Chinese railroad workers' contribution to the making of America.

Most critics would point to Chin's recovery of a viable Chinese American identity as his single most important contribution to the development of Asian American literature and culture. Others, while acknowledging the importance of this contribution, would recognize some of its problematic consequences, one of which stems from what critics have noted as Chin's male-centered vision of Chinese American identity. In *Aiiieeeee!: An Anthology of Asian-American Writers* (1974), an influential collection of writings that Chin co-edited with Jeffery Paul Chan, Lawson Fusao Inada and Shawn Wong, the editors called for the recognition of a distinct Asian American voice cast in the "style of Asian American manhood." The conflation of Asian American manhood with Asian American identity was to prove troubling for many readers. The editors wanted a style that valorized daring, physicality, adventurousness, and verbal aggressiveness, which are qualities more often associated with notions of the masculine than the feminine. Along with this narrowly prescriptive definition of Chinese American identity, some readers have also objected to what they perceived to be negative portrayals of women throughout Chin's work.

However controversial Chin's work has been and continues to be, it remains indisputably of signal importance to the history of Asian American literature. His work (in particular, the early plays and polemical essays) offered not only a corrective for mainstream audiences more attuned to popular culture stereotypes of Asians, but also enabled Asian Americans themselves to rethink, through the interplay of symbolic fictions, their individual or group situation as Asian Americans. Coming as it did in a period of American history marked by racial discontent and social upheaval, Frank Chin's work contributed not only to the growth of Asian American literature but also to the opening up of the American literary landscape to the efflorescence of a multitude of culturally diverse voices.

—Shelley Sunn Wong

CHIVERS, Thomas Holley

Born: Near Washington, Georgia, 18 October 1809. **Education:** A preparatory school in Georgia; Transylvania University, Lexington, Kentucky, M.D. (honors) 1830. **Family:** Married 1) his cousin Frances Elizabeth Chivers in 1827, one daughter; 2) Harriette Hunt in 1837, two sons and two daughters. **Career:** Practiced medicine briefly, then full-time writer; contributed to numerous periodicals throughout his life; corresponded with Edgar Allan Poe from 1840, met him in 1845, and was later involved in a controversy about plagiarism of Poe's work. **Died:** 18 December 1858.

PUBLICATIONS

Collections

Chivers: A Selection, edited by Lewis Chase. 1929.
Correspondence 1838-1858, edited by Emma Lester Chase and Lois Ferry Parks. 1957.

Poetry

The Path of Sorrow; or, The Lament of Youth. 1832.
Nacoochee; or, The Beautiful Star, with Other Poems. 1837.
The Lost Pleiad and Other Poems. 1845.
Eonchs of Ruby: A Gift of Love. 1851; revised edition, as *Memoralia; or, Phials of Amber Full of the Tears of Love,* 1853.
Virginalia; or, Songs of My Summer Nights: A Gift of Love for the Beautiful. 1853.
Atlanta; or, The True Blessed Island of Poesy: A Paul Epic in Three Lustra. 1853.
Birth-Day Song of Liberty: A Paean of Glory for the Heroes of Freedom. 1856.

Plays

Conrad and Eudora; or, The Death of Alonzo. 1834.
The Sons of Usna: A Tragi-Apotheosis. 1858.
The Unpublished Plays (includes *Count Julian, Osceola, Charles Stuart, Leoni*), edited by Charles M. Lombard. 1980.

Other

Search after Truth; or, A New Revelation of the Psycho-Physiological Nature of Man. 1848.
Life of Poe, edited by Richard Beale Davis. 1952.

*

Bibliography: in *Bibliography of American Literature* by Jacob Blanck, 1957; by John O. Eidson, in *A Bibliographical Guide to the Study of Southern Literature* edited by Louis D. Rubin, Jr., 1969.

Critical Studies: *Chivers, Friend of Poe* (with selections) by S. Foster Damon, 1930; *Chivers: His Literary Career and His Poetry* by Charles H. Watts, 1956; *Chivers* by Charles M. Lombard, 1979; *The Unpublished Plays of Thomas Holley Chivers* edited by Charles M. Lombard, 1980.

*   *   *

Unlike many of his American and Southern contemporaries, Thomas Holley Chivers was free to devote himself to poetry since he had independent means, and, though he could hardly be called a professional man of letters, he took literature seriously and developed a theory of poetry and an aesthetic. Over a period of twenty-five years he published, usually at his own expense, a great deal of verse and a smattering of prose in periodicals in Washington and Decatur, Georgia, as well as occasionally in the *Knickerbocker* and *Graham's,* and in book form in Macon, Georgia, and Franklin, Tennessee, as well as in New York and Philadelphia.

Chivers's theory of poetry as expressed in his prefaces to his collections of poems, especially *Nacoochee, Memoralia,* and *Atlanta,* and in his unpublished and incomplete articles and lectures is, according to Edd Winfield Parks, that true poetry is "divinely inspired" and the poet is "at once the mediator and the revelator of God." "Poets," Chivers says in "The Beauties of Poetry," "are the apostles of divine thought, who are clothed with an authority from the Most High, to work miracles in the minds of men." The poet sees all things with "*internal,* or spiritual eyes," though, admittedly, celestial beauty can only be partially glimpsed on earth. Still, the inspired writer can recognize transcendental truth and can "convey the idea of a heavenly truth by an earthly one."

In his own practice Chivers tried the usual forms—drama, ode, sonnet, narrative—but he gradually became fascinated with rhythm, diction, sound, and with the lore and melodies of the Indian, the Negro, and the folk tradition of Georgia. His experimentation with ballad-like forms, refrains, and language led him to a special vocabulary and declamatory style that manifest themselves in, among others, "Lily Adair," "Avalon," "Apollo," and "Rosalie Lee."

The first and last of these poems, to be sure, suggest the work of Poe, as do such earlier pieces as "Isadore" and "To Allegra Florence." Still, despite a certain amount of critical attention in the last decades of the twentieth century, Chivers's work is largely of interest because of its relationship to Poe's. The thorny problems of precedence and influence have not yet been fully resolved, despite efforts by scholars interested in each poet. Even if it is established that Chivers provided Poe with hints concerning rhythm, meter, and refrain, the disinterested critic can only conclude with Jay B. Hubbell in *The South in American Literature* that Poe's supposed "borrowings" are "all assimilated and transformed into something original and Poesque." This, of course, is to say nothing of Chivers's borrowings from Poe, nor to mention that nothing was said of plagiarism until Poe was dead.

Whatever one may say, however, of the Poe-Chivers matter, one must also conclude that Chivers's work, erratic and uneven as it may be, is fascinating in its own right and deserves more critical consideration than it has hitherto received.

—Rayburn S. Moore

CHOPIN, Kate

Born: Katherine O'Flaherty in St. Louis, Missouri, 8 February 1851. **Education:** Academy of the Sacred Heart, St. Louis, graduated 1868. **Family:** Married Oscar Chopin in 1870 (died 1883); five sons and one daughter. **Career:** Lived in New Orleans, 1870-79, on her husband's plantation in Cloutierville, Louisiana, 1880-82, and in St. Louis after 1884. **Died:** 22 August 1904.

PUBLICATIONS

Collections

Complete Works, edited by Per Seyersted. 2 vols., 1969.

Short Stories

Bayou Folk. 1894.
A Night in Acadie. 1897.
The Awakening and Other Stories, edited by Lewis Leary. 1970.
Portraits: Short Stories, edited by Helen Taylor. 1979.
The Awakening and Selected Stories, edited by Sandra M. Gilbert. 1984.
Beyond the Bayou. 1996.

Novels

At Fault. 1890.
The Awakening. 1899; edited by Margaret Culley, 1976.

Other

A Chopin Miscellany, edited by Per Seyersted and Emily Toth. 1979.
Kate Chopin's Private Papers. 1998.

*

Bibliography: in *Bibliography of American Literature* by Jacob Blanck, 1957; *Edith Wharton and Chopin: A Reference Guide* by Marlene Springer, 1976; *Kate Chopin: An Annotated Bibliography of Critical Works* by Suzanne Disheroon Green, 1999.

Critical Studies: *Chopin and Her Creole Stories* by Daniel S. Rankin, 1932; *The American 1890's: Life and Times of a Lost Generation* by Larzer Ziff, 1966; *Chopin: A Critical Biography* by Per Seyersted, 1969; *Chopin* by Peggy Skaggs, 1985; *Chopin* by Barbara C. Ewell, 1986; *Forbidden Fruit: On the Relationship between Women and Knowledge in Doris Lessing, Slema Lagerlöf, Chopin, and Margaret Atwood* by Bonnie St. Andrews, 1986; *New Essays on The Awakening* edited by Wendy Martin, 1988; *Chopin* by Emily Toth, 1988; *Gender, Race, and Religion in the Writings of Grace King, Ruth McEnery Stuart, and Chopin* by Helen Taylor, 1989; *Verging on the Abyss: The Social Fiction of Chopin and Edith Wharton* by Mary E. Papke, 1990; *Kate Chopin Reconsidered: Beyond the Bayou* edited by Lynda S. Boren and Sara deSaussure Davis, 1992; *Perspectives on Kate Chopin: Proceedings from the Kate Chopin International Conference, April 6, 7, 8, 1989* edited by Grady Ballenger, Karen Cole, Katherine Kearnes, and Tom Samet, 1992; *Kate Chopin: A Study of the Short Fiction*

by Bernard Koloski, 1996; *Critical Essays on Kate Chopin* edited by Alice Hall Petry, 1996; *Kate Chopin, Edith Wharton and Charlotte Perkins Gilman: Studies in Short Fiction* by Janet Beer, 1997; *Unveiling Kate Chopin* by Emily Toth, 1999.

*   *   *

In 1894, when Kate Chopin published *Bayou Folk,* a collection of Louisiana stories, she was greeted as an outstanding local color writer. In 1899, when she brought out *The Awakening,* a novel that in certain respects is an American *Madame Bovary,* she so shocked the public that some libraries banned the book. As a result, her creative spirit was stifled, and, when she died in 1904, she was forgotten. But in 1969, when *The Complete Works of Kate Chopin* appeared, the time was ripe for a reassessment and revival of this writer. She became recognized both as a literary artist of the American realist movement and as a particularly significant commentator on the female experience.

Chopin grew up in the French atmosphere of her mother's family in St. Louis, and she married a Creole, and lived in New Orleans and on a Louisiana plantation for thirteen years. Her *oeuvre* consists of two novels and about 100 stories. Nearly all she wrote is set in Louisiana, and she makes the atmosphere of this picturesque state vivid, with the enchanting physical setting and the charming peculiarities of the Creoles, Cajuns, and blacks of the region.

But she used local color discreetly, never as an end in itself; rather, her interest was general human nature. As a child she had been taught to face life without fear and embarrassment and to observe people without judging them. She did not believe in idealism, and she disliked moral reformers. In her first novel, *At Fault,* she lets a woman (who has forced a man to remarry his divorced drunkard wife in order to redeem her) come to the conclusion that no one has the right to submit others to the "exacting and ignorant rule of . . . moral conventionalities."

From an early age Chopin was an avid reader, with a particular interest in books dealing with women's position. She was especially influenced by Maupassant, probably because she felt he spoke secretly to her with his frank treatments of the hidden life of women. This fitted in with her own ambition, which was to portray especially the lives of women, as truthfully and openly as America would permit. Her first extant story deals with a "feminine" or traditional heroine who submissively leaves it to the man to decide her fate, and the second with an "emancipated" woman who insists on deciding for herself about her own life. Most of her later heroines are variations on these two types. She often wrote about them in pairs, thus keeping up a kind of balanced dialogue between traditional and emancipated women.

As Chopin gained in self-confidence, she became more daring in her descriptions of unconventional women. When she had just been nationally praised for *Bayou Folk* she wrote "The Story of an Hour," a tale about a woman who, when told that her husband has suddenly died, whispers "free, free, free!" A few weeks later the author in a sense answered this extreme example of the self-assertive woman with an entry in her diary, where she wrote that could she get her husband back, she would have been willing to give up "the past ten years of my growth—my real growth."

Chopin's ultimate examples of the feminine and the emancipated woman are found in *The Awakening.* Adele Ratignolle strikingly illustrates the patriarchal ideal of the self-forgetting woman. A Creole and a Catholic, she is likened to a "Faultless Madonna" and described as a "mother-woman," that is, one who lives for and through her family and who considers it "a holy privilege to efface themselves as individuals." She is a perfect foil for Edna Pontellier, an American married to a New Orleans Creole and the mother of two, who says: "I would give up the unessential; I would . . . give my life for my children; but I wouldn't give myself." What she means by this becomes clear as she gradually awakens to a self-assertion both in the physical and spiritual field. Like Emma Bovary, she becomes estranged from her husband, neglects her children, has lovers, and finally takes her life. But while Emma acts out roles inherited from romantic literature and gains little self-knowledge, Edna outgrows her romantic notions and learns "to look with her own eyes [and] to apprehend the deeper under-currents of life."

She realizes that the physical side of love can live apart from the spiritual one, and that sex is a basic force that—in the guise of romantic emotions—drives us blindly on toward procreation. She understands that, for her, a return to the submission and self-delusion of the past is impossible. She refuses to let the children "drag her into the soul's slavery for the rest of her days," but she finally accepts a responsibility not to give them a bad name and takes her life. While defeated by her environment, she is also victorious: finally understanding her own nature and her situation as a woman, she exerts her inner freedom by assuming sole responsibility for her life.

The critics had to concede that, artistically, *The Awakening* is a small masterpiece. But just as with Dreiser's *Sister Carrie* a year later, they could not accept an author who in no way condemns such a heroine. Larzer Ziff has said of Chopin's silence after this setback that it was "a loss to American letters of the order of the untimely deaths of **Crane** and **Norris**." At the end of the twentieth century *The Awakening* was available in numerous editions, and with this novel and her best stories Kate Chopin seems assured a permanent place in American literature.

—Per Seyersted

See the essay on *The Awakening*.

CHURCHILL, Winston

Born: St. Louis, Missouri, 10 November 1871. **Education:** Smith Academy, St. Louis, 1879-88; U.S. Naval Academy, Annapolis, Maryland, 1890-94; naval cadet on the cruiser *San Francisco*, New York Navy Yard, 1894. **Family:** Married Mabel Harlakenden Hall in 1895 (died 1945); one daughter and two sons. **Career:** Editor, *Army and Navy Journal*, New York, 1894; managing editor, *Cosmopolitan*, New York, 1895; full-time writer from 1895; Republican member for Cornish, New Hampshire Legislature, 1903-05; delegate for New Hampshire, Republican National Convention, Chicago, 1904; Progressive Party candidate for the New Hampshire governorship, 1912; toured European battle fronts, and wrote for *Scribner's*, New York, 1917-18. President, Authors League of America, 1913. **Died:** 12 March 1947.

PUBLICATIONS

Fiction

The Celebrity: An Episode. 1898.
Richard Carvel. 1899.

The Crisis. 1901.
Mr. Keegan's Elopement (stories). 1903.
The Crossing. 1904.
Coniston. 1906.
Mr Crewe's Career. 1908.
A Modern Chronicle. 1910.
The Inside of the Cup. 1913.
A Far Country. 1915.
The Dwelling-Place of Light. 1917.
The Faith of Frances Craniford (story). 1917.

Plays

The Title-Mart (produced 1905). 1905.
Dr Jonathan. 1919.

Other

A Traveller in War-Time, with an Essay on the American Contribution and the Democratic Idea. 1918.
The Green Bay Tree. 1920.
The Uncharted Way: The Psychology of the Gospel Doctrine. 1940.

*

Bibliography: *Churchill: A Reference Guide* by Eric Steinbaugh, 1985.

Critical Studies: *The Romantic Compromise in the Novels of Churchill* by Charles C. Walcutt, 1951; *Churchill* by Warren I. Titus, 1963; *Novelist to a Generation: The Life and Thought of Churchill* by Robert W. Schneider, 1976.

*   *   *

Winston Churchill (no relation to the British statesman) was a gifted storyteller who became very popular with well-researched but episodic romances concerning the American Revolution in *Richard Carvel*, the Civil War in *The Crisis*, and the settlement of Tennessee and Kentucky in *The Crossing*. Drawing upon his personal experience as a legislator and candidate for gubernatorial nomination in New Hampshire, Churchill then became a more serious social critic in *Coniston*, a novel about political bossism. The boss, Jethro Bass (based on a real political figure, Ruel Durkee), is a complex mixture of good and evil who in part manipulates the system and is in part a product of it. He is probably Churchill's best developed and most human character. *Mr. Crewe's Career* does not so much concern the bumbling political efforts of the amateur politician Humphrey Crewe (said by Churchill to be a self-satire) as it concerns the corrupting influence of the railroad and other industries on the state legislature and the courts. Churchill mars these two novels by resolving the conflicts with a marriage between a daughter and a son of the opposing major figures. Although this device was supposed to show how the dynamism of industry could be combined with the idealism of politics, it actually leaves the essential differences of the two views unsettled, and reflects Churchill's mild "Progressive" approach in these novels (he was a friend and admirer of Theodore Roosevelt).

Churchill first evidenced in his fiction a concern for religion in *The Inside of the Cup*, a novel that concerns a clergyman of an unspecified persuasion (Churchill was an active Episcopal layman) who comes to see the necessity for preaching a social gospel rather than a purely "spiritual" one. Although he meets resistance from a slum landlord in his congregation, the minister makes many converts to his position and remains in the good graces of his church. The novel is therefore less hard hitting than, say, Charles Monroe Sheldon's *In His Steps*. *A Far Country* deals even more forcefully with the conflict Churchill saw between Christianity and capitalism and with society's ill-treatment of unwed mothers. Churchill lent his pen to the propaganda effort during World War I, but immediately afterward returned in *Dr. Jonathan* to call for more social justice and a more equitable distribution of wealth.

Churchill's popularity declined gradually after he forsook the historical romance, but in 1920 he found himself almost without an audience. He then devoted twenty years to research in psychology and theology before publishing a nonfiction reinterpretation of the world and of the Bible, *The Uncharted Way*. Churchill did not think his analysis of history as the conflict between the "moral" self and the "technical" self, the generous and selfish side of each man, would be immediately understood but looked to future generations for vindication.

—William Higgins

CIARDI, John (Anthony)

Born: Boston, Massachusetts, 24 June 1916. **Education:** Medford High School, Massachusetts, 1929-33; Bates College, Lewiston, Maine, 1934-36; Tufts College, Medford, Massachusetts, B.A. (magna cum laude) 1938; University of Michigan, Ann Arbor, M.A. 1939. **Military Service:** Served in the U.S. Army Air Corps as a B-29 gunner on Saipan, 1942-45; technical sergeant; received Air Medal with Oak Leaf Cluster. **Family:** Married Judith Hostetter in 1946; two sons and a daughter. **Career:** Instructor in English, University of Kansas City, Missouri, 1940-42 and 1946; Briggs-Copeland Instructor, 1946-48, and assistant professor of English, 1948-53, Harvard University, Cambridge, Massachusetts; founder and editor of the Twayne Library of Modern Poetry, 1949-51, and executive editor, 1951 to c. 1957, Twayne Publishers; poetry lecturer at Salzburg Seminar in American Culture, Austria, 1951; instructor, 1953-54, associate professor, 1954-56, and professor, 1956-61, Rutgers University, New Brunswick, New Jersey; director, Bread Loaf Writers' Conference of Middlebury College, Vermont, 1955-72; poetry editor, *Saturday Review,* 1956-72; lecturer, 1961-86; host of CBS TV's *Accent* program, 1961-62; author of "Manner of Speaking" column, *Saturday Review,* 1961-72; contributing editor, *World* magazine (later merged with new *Saturday Review),* 1973-80; resident etymologist for National Public Radio weekly *A Word in Your Ear* program, 1978-86. National spokesman and fund raiser for Henry Wallace's Progressive Party bid for the presidency, 1946-48. **Awards:** Avery Hopwood award for Poetry, 1939; from *Poetry:* Oscar Blumenthal prize, 1943, the Eunice Tietjens award, 1945, the Levinson prize, 1946, and the Harriet Monroe Memorial prize, 1955; New England Poetry Club Golden Rose Trophy, 1948; fellow, American Academy of Arts and Sciences, 1953; American Academy of Arts and Letters Prix de Rome, 1956-57; National Council of Teachers of English award for poetry for children, 1982. D.Litt.: Tufts University, 1960; Wayne State University, Detroit,

Michigan, 1963; Ursinus College, Collegeville, Pennsylvania, 1964; Kalamazoo College, Michigan, 1964; Bates College, 1970; Washington University, St. Louis, Missouri, 1971; Kean College, Union, New Jersey, 1977. **Member:** National College English Association, director, 1955-57, president, 1958-59; National Institute of Arts and Letters. **Died:** 30 March 1986.

PUBLICATIONS

Collections

Dialogue with an Audience (*Saturday Review* essays). 1963.
The Achievement of John Ciardi. 1969.
Manner of Speaking (*Saturday Review* essays). 1972.

Poetry

Homeward to America. 1940.
Other Skies. 1947.
Live Another Day. 1949.
Live Time to Time. 1951.
As If. 1955.
I Marry You. 1958.
39 Poems. 1959.
In the Stoneworks. 1961.
In Fact. 1962.
Person to Person. 1965.
This Strangest Everything. 1966.
A Genesis. 1967.
Lives of X. 1971.
The Little That Is All. 1974.
Limericks Too Gross, with Isaac Asimov. 1978.
For Instance. 1979.
A Grossery of Limericks, with Isaac Asimov. 1981.
Selected Poems. 1984.
The Birds of Pompeii. 1985.
Poems of Love and Marriage. 1988.
Echoes. 1989.
Stations of the Air. 1993.

Recordings: *As If,* 1956; *John Ciardi and W.D. Snodgrass,* 1961; *This Strangest Everything,* 1966; *John Ciardi,* 1972; *What Is a Poem?,* 1974.

Verse (for children)

The Reason for the Pelican. 1959.
Scrappy the Pup. 1960.
The Man Who Sang the Sillies. 1961.
I Met a Man. 1961.
The Wish Tree. 1962.
You Read to Me, I'll Read to You. 1962.
John J. Plenty and Fiddler Dan. 1962.
You Know Who. 1964.
The King Who Saved Himself from Being Saved. 1965.
The Monster Den. 1966.
Someone Could Win a Polar Bear. 1970.
Fast and Slow. 1975.
Doodle Soup. 1985.
Blabberhead, Bobbie-Bud & Spade. 1988.

The Hopeful Trout. 1989.
Mummy Took Cooking Lessons. 1990.

Recordings: *You Read to Me, I'll Read to You,* 1962; *You Know Who,* 1966; *The King Who Saved Himself,* 1971; *Someone Could Win a Polar Bear,* 1974; *About Eskimos and Other Poems,* 1974; *What Do You Know about Poetry,* 1974; *Why Noah Praised the Whale,* 1974.

Prose

Saipan: The War Diary of John Ciardi. 1988.
Selected Letters of John Ciardi, edited by Edward M. Cifelli. 1991.

Other

How Does a Poem Mean? (textbook). 1960; 2nd edition, with Miller Williams, 1975.
Poetry: A Closer Look, with James M. Reid and Laurence Perrine (textbook). 1963.
A Browser's Dictionary and Native's Guide to the Unknown American Language. 1980.
A Second Browser's Dictionary and Native's Guide to the Unknown American Language. 1983.
Good Words to You. 1987.

Editor, *Mid-Century American Poets.* 1950.

Translator, *Dante's Inferno.* 1954.
Translator, *Dante's Purgatorio.* 1961.
Translator, *Dante's Paradiso.* 1970.
Translator, *The Divine Comedy,* by Dante. 1977.

Recording: *The Inferno,* 1954.

*

Bibliography: *John Ciardi: A Bibliography* by William White, 1959.

Critical Studies: Interview with Roy Newquist in *Counter Point,* 1964; "Nothing Is Really Hard But to Be Real" by Miller Williams, in *The Achievement of John Ciardi,* 1969; "The Size of John Ciardi's Song" by Edward M. Cifelli, in *CEA Critic,* November 1973, reprinted in the introduction to Ciardi's *Saipan,* 1988; *John Ciardi* by Edward Krickel, 1980; "An Archetypal World: Images of Italy in the Poetry of John Ciardi" by Fedora Giordano, in *Rivista di Studi Anglo-Americani,* 1984-85; "Ciardi's Art" by Judson Jerome, in *Writer's Digest,* October 1985; "John Ciardi, 1916-1986" by Richard Wilbur, in *Proceedings of the American Academy,* 1986; "John Ciardi: The Many Lives of Poetry" by John Frederick Nims, in *Poetry,* August 1986; *John Ciardi: Measure of the Man* edited by Vince Clemente, 1987; "John Ciardi," in *The Writer's Mind: Interviews with American Authors Vol. 1* edited by Irv Broughton, 1989; *Whose Woods These Are: A History of the Bread Loaf Writers' Conference* by David Haward Bain, 1993; "Lancelot in Hell: John Ciardi's Medievalism" by Klaus P. Jankofsky, in *SiM,* 1994, pp. 163-73.

*   *   *

John Ciardi was one of the most prolific and talented men of letters in mid-century America. His poetry is often brilliant in language and inventive in form, but his independence as an artist kept him working apart from the group movements of his time such as the Beats or the Confessional Poets, whom he occasionally offended with disparaging remarks in his literary criticism. Moreover, by standing apart, Ciardi became something of a puzzle to literary historians, who found it difficult to place him among the other poets of his time. Evaluating Ciardi's contribution to mid-century American letters is made even more difficult for historians and literary critics by the diversity of his genius, for he was not only an excellent poet but an award-winning writer of children's verse, one of the finest translators of Dante in the twentieth century, a daunting poetry editor at the *Saturday Review* for some twenty years, the controversial director of the Bread Loaf Writers' Conference between 1955 and 1972, an expert word historian, and a popular international lecturer.

Ciardi was born in 1916 in Boston. His father died in a freak automobile accident in 1919, after which his mother moved her family, three daughters and a young son, to nearby Medford. In 1934, after graduating from high school, Ciardi enrolled at Bates College, where he remained for a year and a half before returning home and to Medford's own Tufts College. At Tufts, Ciardi studied poetry under one of the finest poet-teachers of his time, John Holmes, who sent his young protégé to the University of Michigan. At Michigan, Ciardi won the $1200 Avery Hopwood Award for Poetry and published his award-winning manuscript the next year as *Homeward to America.* With the help of Holmes and the poet Louis Untermeyer, Ciardi secured his first teaching position in 1940 at the University of Kansas City.

Ciardi entered the United States Army Air Corps in 1942 and initially trained to be a navigator, but was later sent to gunnery school where he became a turret gunner on B-29 aircraft, serving on Saipan and flying bombing missions over Japan. After the war, Ciardi taught one semester at the University of Kansas City, married Judith Hostetter, and then took a post as Briggs-Copeland instructor of English at Harvard, where he remained for the next seven years. He published *Other Skies,* an important book of war poems, in 1947. At this time, Ciardi became a national spokesman and fund-raiser for the Progressive Party, which nominated Henry Wallace for president. Ciardi then became poetry editor for the newly-incorporated Twayne Publishers and guided into existence its first-book contest and Library of Modern Poets. In 1950, he edited one of the most important anthologies of its time, *Mid-Century American Poets,* which boldly identified the premier poets of the 1940s and predicted greater things for them all in the new decade: **Robert Lowell, Richard Wilbur, Theodore Roethke, Elizabeth Bishop, Karl Shapiro, Delmore Schwartz,** and others, including Ciardi himself.

Ciardi began the decade of the fifties on leave from Harvard, lecturing on poetry at the Salzburg Seminar on American Studies and then moving to Rome, where he worked on his translation of Dante's *Inferno.* This translation was published in 1954 to enthusiastic reviews and has since been adopted widely for classroom use. Ciardi left his position at Harvard to direct a writing program at Rutgers University. Two years later, he reluctantly took over the directorship of the Bread Loaf Writer's Conference in Vermont. Although he loved the conference, he felt he was too busy to add such a large responsibility to his annual workload. Nonetheless, he continued there as director until 1972, when he left amid controversy and criticism, as a younger generation became irritated by Ciardi's old-fashioned insistence upon poetic craftsmanship and his unwillingness to allow undisciplined writing to pass as free verse.

Ciardi was invited by Norman Cousins to become poetry editor at *Saturday Review* in 1956, a post he held for some twenty years; he subsequently began contributing a regular column, "Manner of Speaking," to the magazine. One of his early reviews, a scathing indictment of badly-written poetry occasioned by the work of Anne Morrow Lindbergh, caused an unprecedented reaction and established Ciardi in the national consciousness as both confrontational and controversial. Whether he had intended it or not, he had established himself as a spokesman for modern poetry, helping readers cope with it and insisting that poets be precise in their execution of it. Though wary of free verse and fads like the Beat movement, Ciardi championed poetry from his various platforms and helped frame new attitudes that lasted for the rest of the century. Nor did any of his wide-ranging side interests keep Ciardi from his real work: four books of his new poems appeared in the 1950s. He published his first book of children's verse in 1959, *The Reason for the Pelican,* and translated Dante's *Purgatorio* for publication two years later.

In order to pursue the financial opportunities that accompanied his celebrity status, Ciardi resigned his professorship at Rutgers in 1961 and branched out into television, hosting a program called "Accent" on the CBS television network. He had always been popular on the lecture circuit, an income possibility that he exploited during the summers from the late 1940s on, but once freed from teaching responsibilities, Ciardi began undertaking two lecture sweeps per year, earning more than enough money to allow him to write for the rest of the year. He dabbled in real estate, invested wisely, and by the middle of the decade had accumulated a million dollars in assets. And he continued to produce: ten books in ten years. He published his translations of both *Purgatorio* and *Paradiso* during this period; a widely influential textbook, *How Does a Poem Mean?;* a book of essays, *Dialogue with an Audience;* four books of new poems; two books of children's verses; and a collection of his poems, edited by Miller Williams, *The Achievement of John Ciardi.*

Ciardi's influence on the American poetry written in the second half of the twentieth century began to decline after he resigned under pressure as director of the Bread Loaf Writers' Conference. For seventeen years he had reigned as one of the senior statesmen in the world of modern poetry, for Bread Loaf had provided him with a bully pulpit. It was the granddaddy of all the writers' conferences to follow, not only because it was the oldest, going back to the 1920s, but also because it had the presence and sanction of **Robert Frost** to legitimize it. Ciardi took the loss of his position very badly, and for the rest of his life he bitterly viewed the palace revolt that had unseated him as an act of the blackest betrayal. Another factor in the decline of Ciardi's influence was the demise of *Saturday Review.* The magazine had undergone many changes in the early 1970s: it was sold, changed format, went bankrupt, was rescued by Norman Cousins and folded into his new magazine *World,* and then launched again on its own. Through most of the changes, Ciardi remained as a columnist, but his role as poetry editor gradually declined as the magazine stopped printing poetry. Despite his fading influence, the decade of the 1970s saw several important Ciardi books come into print, including a sequence of self-examinations called *Lives of X,* which combines long narrative techniques and masterfully controlled verse into a major contribution to the genre of autobiographical litera-

ture, and a hardcover edition of Ciardi's complete translation of *The Divine Comedy.*

During the late 1970s Ciardi became passionately and happily obsessed with word histories, what he called "felonious footnotery," and began a weekly program on the subject that was distributed to more than 200 stations on the National Public Radio network. In 1980, he published the first of three books on the subject, *A Browser's Dictionary and Native's Guide to the Unknown American Language.* The second volume appeared in 1983 and the third in 1987 after his death. Ciardi broke away from his attic dictionary room, where he had collected hundreds of etymological reference books, long enough to prepare his *Selected Poems* and to see two more books of poetry into print, *The Birds of Pompeii* for adults and *Doodle Soup* for children. He died of a heart attack on Easter Sunday in 1986, but three more books of his poetry have been published posthumously, along with his war diary and *Selected Letters.*

—Edward M. Cifelli

CISNEROS, Sandra

Born: Chicago, Illinois, 20 December 1954. **Education:** Loyola University, Chicago, B. A. in English, 1976; University of Iowa, M.F.A. in creative writing, 1978. **Career:** Instructor, Latino Youth Alternative High School, Chicago, Illinois, 1978-80; taught poetry workshops for the Illinois Arts Council, 1979-82; artist in residence, Fondation Michael Karolyi, Vence, France, Spring, 1983; guest lecturer at Texas Lutheran College, Seguin, Texas, 1985, and California State University in Chico, 1988, and at Guadalupe Cultural Arts Center, San Antonio, Texas, and University of California—Irvine. **Awards:** National Endowment for the Arts writing fellowship, 1981-82; Illinois Arts Council grant, 1984; American Book award, 1985; Dobie-Paisano fellowship, Texas, 1985-86; National Endowment for the Arts fellowship in fiction, 1987; Lannan Foundation Literary award, 1991; MacArthur fellow, 1995. **Residence:** Chicago, Illinois.

PUBLICATIONS

Fiction

The House on Mango Street. 1983.
Woman Hollering Creek and Other Stories. 1991.
Hairs: Pelitos. 1994.

Poetry

Bad Boys. 1980.
The Rodrigo Poems. 1985.
My Wicked, Wicked Ways. 1987.
Loose Woman. 1994.

*

Critical Studies: "The Book on Mango Street: Escritura y liberación en la obra de Sandra Cisneros" in *Mujer y literatura mexicana y chicana: culturas en contacto,* 1990; "On the Solitary of Being Mexican, Female, Wicked and Thirty-Three: An Interview with Writer Sandra Cisneros" by Pilar E. Rodríguez-Aranda in *Americas Review: A Review of Hispanic Literature & Art of the USA,* Spring 1990; "Latina Narrative and Politics of Signification: Articulation, Antagonism, and Populist Rupture" by Ellen McCracken in *Crítica: A Journal of Critical Essays,* 1990; "Fables of the Fallen Guy" by Renato Rosaldo in *Criticism in the Borderlands: Studies in Chicano Literature* edited by Calderón and Saldívar, 1991; "Coming of Age in Novels by Rudolfo Anaya and Sandra Cisneros" by Dianne Klein in *The English Journal,* September 1992; "In Search of Identity in Cisneros' *The House on Mango Street*" by María Elena de Valdés in *Canadian Review of American Studies,* Fall 1992; *Mirrors Beneath the Earth: Short Fiction by Chicano Writers,* edited by Ray González, 1992; *Creating Safe Space: Violence and Women's Writing,* edited by Tomoko Kuribayashi and Julie Ann Tharp, 1998.

* * *

Sandra Cisneros's father migrated from Mexico, leaving a family of some privilege and means; her mother's family, also of Mexican stock, albeit humbler and working class, had been in the United States for several generations. The married couple and their seven children traveled constantly between Chicago and Mexico, having to find new living quarters after each trip. Cisneros's childhood was spent in a variety of run-down Hispanic neighborhoods that offered experiences that have found their way into her writing. Constant moves and changes of schools made Cisneros an introspective child who retreated to books and the writing of poetry. In 1966, her parents purchased their first home, a small two-story bungalow, painted red, in a Puerto Rican neighborhood on the north side of Chicago. Experiences there served as inspiration for many of the tales in *The House on Mango Street.* The poet admits she had no awareness of being different from classmates, or even of being Chicana, until her graduation from Loyola University. At most she felt Mexican, maybe even part Puerto Rican, because of the neighborhood she had grown up in. All of her education had been in mainstream English, as had her reading and writing.

Cisneros admits that at the beginning of her graduate studies in Iowa she was very young, immature, and insecure as a person and as a writer. She floundered, while imitating a variety of writing styles: her teachers', established authors', even her classmates' in the writing program. None of these approaches worked. Cisneros then realized that she was very different from her elite and privileged classmates, many of whom were educated in private schools and groomed for the arts. The styles, structures, and themes that the workshop encouraged just did not fit her; she felt like a weed amidst a collection of cultivated hot-house blooms. By probing into her past inner-city life and those experiences she had always been embarrassed about, she found within herself the child-voice that emerged in the short tales from *Mango Street.* That side of her life inspired many poems, as well.

Bad Boys is a short collection of poems that demonstrates the early stage of Cisneros's writing. The poem "South Sangamon," talks about a wife-beating scene in the inner city, overheard by a neighboring child and recounted in that child's voice. "Blue Dress" tells of the awkward encounter of a young man with the girl he made pregnant; the visual images are vivid, the lines brief and clipped.

The Rodrigo Poems is a collection that reflects a more mature writer; many of the texts inspired during Cisneros's travels in Europe. Gone are the child's voice and humorous observations. Instead, one reads about amorous encounters with roguish European men, all of whom can be identified by the name "Rodrigo." In this collection, Cisneros uses much of the style, imagery, and technique that characterizes her most recent work. She uses words as a painter would use brief strokes of a brush; each word, its sound, its shape, and its placement on the paper, serves to produce a sensation for the reader. Her style could be called minimalist for its compactness, whether the text takes the shape of a poem or of prose; in the balance, Cisneros is essentially a poet. The poem "No Mercy" presents a theme common to Cisneros, that of the unfaithful man who hurts women who, in turn, must somehow vindicate themselves. In this text two previous wives have abandoned a pitiful man, plucking from the kitchen sink their long hair, their rings, and their domestic comb. "You must've said something cruel/ you must've done something mean/ for women to gather/ all of their things."

The Rodrigo poems were included in a later collection of poems titled *My Wicked, Wicked Ways.* In addition to the group of Rodrigo-type poems, there are others, similar in content, based on European travels. Only a few of these texts are voiced by the small child who observes people and events in her neighborhood.

By the time Cisneros published *The House on Mango Street,* she had developed her very own style of poetic prose. The short tales recounted by Esperanza, a fictional adolescent girl, reflect the incisive musings of this young person as she observes other women around her and then matches their existential situation with what may possibly await Esperanza herself in the future. While humorous in many ways, each story offers a brief portrait of a young woman in Esperanza's immediate neighborhood, most of whom have less than ideal lives. Thus, the *persona* observes adolescent girls who are rushing into adult experiences, others who already face the dilemmas of a domineering husband or father, the raising of children, being trapped in a life situation that offers little hope for improvement or growth. In essence, the tongue in cheek humor of each story also reveals a tragic side. This book earned Cisneros a national award as well as important recognition as an author. Her next work received the important recognition of being published by a major U.S. publisher—quite a triumph for a writer who is a member of a minority group, many of whom must struggle to get published.

Woman Hollering Creek and Other Stories is a very rich album of female portraits. The dedication reads: "for my mama . . . y para mi papá . . . . " signaling both the bicultural and bilingual nature of this work. Although written totally in Cisneros's polished inimitable style of English, there appear enough Spanish references or words to root the stories in a long tradition of Mexican-American culture. The tales show a progression in narrative voice and in the fictional world depicted. They begin with the voice of the adolescent narrator, found in early poems, and in *Mango.* "Mericans" is a representative story recounting the dilemma faced by Chicano authors in their life and their art. The protagonists are children born and raised in the United States, who travel to visit grandmother in Mexico. While one of them recounts her observations of religious rituals and superstitious beliefs practiced by the older generation, they are addressed in broken Spanish by an American tourist who offers them chewing gum in exchange for taking a snapshot of lovely "native" children. The tourist is perplexed when she hears the children speak amongst themselves in perfect English; of course, they admit they are "mericans," a curious neologism signifying a mixture of Mexican and American.

Only the first seven of the twenty-two stories deal with childhood scenes, akin to those in *Mango*. The remaining stories progress through a variety of Hispanic women's experiences coming from all social and educational classes, as well as from many regions of the United States. "The Eyes of Zapata" offers the portrait of the Mexican revolutionary hero's wife; she is the only character in the book who is totally Mexican, untouched by contact with U.S. cultural values and customs. This narrative is extremely rich in descriptive detail, and while it purports to talk about the man Zapata, it tells even more about the woman narrator, her character strengths, and the power she unobtrusively holds in a culture that is traditionally patriarchal and sexist.

The outstanding fact about all of the stories is that they focus on the conditions of women, are narrated from a woman's vantage point, and describe how women adjust, submit, rebel, or perhaps work through the dynamics of the interrelationship of the sexes. The lead story, which gives the book its title, tells of a young Mexican woman who marries a Mexican-American. Her life goes from poor to wretched, yet toward the end it is a female network that saves her and shows her there are other ways to exit from her life situation. The beauty and richness in this book is that Cisneros has intricately woven together a myriad of cultural details, popular sayings, folk traditions, and legends in a way not seen before.

—Eduardo F. Elías

CLARK, Walter Van Tilburg

Born: East Orland, Maine, 3 August 1909. **Education:** Reno High School, Nevada, graduated 1926; University of Nevada, Reno, 1926-31, B.A. 1931, M.A. 1932; University of Vermont, Burlington, M.A. 1934. **Family:** Married Barbara Frances Morse in 1933 (died); one daughter and one son. **Career:** English teacher and basketball coach, Cazenovia Central School, Cazenovia, New York, 1933-45; and a school in Rye, New York, 1945-46; lecturer, 1950-53, and writer-in-residence, 1962-71, University of Nevada; Rockefeller Lecturer, 1953; associate professor of English, University of Montana, Missoula, 1953-56; professor of English and creative writing, San Francisco State College, 1956-62; fellow in fiction, Center for Advanced Studies, Wesleyan University, Middletown, Connecticut, 1960-61. **Awards:** O. Henry award, 1945. Litt.D.: Colgate University, Hamilton, New York, 1958; University of Nevada, 1969. **Died:** 10 November 1971.

PUBLICATIONS

Fiction

The Ox-Bow Incident. 1940.
The City of Trembling Leaves. 1945; as *Tim Hazard,* 1951.
The Track of the Cat. 1949.
The Watchful Gods and Other Stories. 1950.

Poetry

Christmas Comes to Hjalsen, Reno. 1930.
Ten Women in Gale's House and Shorter Poems. 1932.

Other

Editor, *The Journals of Alfred Doten 1849-1903.* 3 vols., 1973.

*

Bibliography: "Clark: A Bibliography" by Richard W. Etulain, in *South Dakota Review,* autumn 1965.

Critical Studies: *Clark* by Max Westbrook, 1969; *Clark* by L.L. Lee, 1973; *Clark: Critiques* edited by Charlton Laird, 1983; "Conversation with Clark" by John R. Milton, in *South Dakota Review,* winter 1988; "Three Influential Novels of the American West" by Robert Roripaugh, in *South Dakota Review,* autumn 1991; "Law and Morality in Billy Budd and The Ox-Bow Incident" by John M. Budd, in *College Language Association Journal,* December 1991; "Walter Van Tilburg Clark's *Ox Bow Incident*: Prototype for the Antiheroic Western" by A.H. Walle, in *Platte Valley Review,* winter 1995, pp. 50-67; "Clark's *The Wind and the Snow of Winter* and Celtic Oisin" by Franklin E. Court, in *Studies in Short Fiction,* spring 1996, pp. 219-28.

*   *   *

The place of Walter Van Tilburg Clark in literary history rests on two of his three novels, *The Ox-Bow Incident* and *The Track of the Cat.* If that perch is narrow, it is also firm, not merely because both were made into memorable films but, more importantly, because both are sensitive psychological studies of great impact.

Taken as a parable of fascism at the time of its writing, *The Ox-Bow Incident,* set in the American west, is a powerful examination of leadership and mob violence. Against a drytinder backdrop of lassitude reminiscent of the setting of **William Faulkner**'s "dry September," the men of Bridger's Wells need only an act of violence and the imposition of a strong will to be ignited into a flaming mob. The point is that violence triumphs by default; that a single-minded person can take charge and use the vast energy latent in boredom and resentment for evil as long as no one will take steps sufficient to stop him.

Four years after his jejune second novel, *The City of Trembling Leaves,* Clark published his second successful novel, *The Track of the Cat.* Much more self-consciously artistic than *The Ox-Bow Incident,* the novel uses as its focus a mountain lion that becomes, literally and symbolically, the *bete noire* of the men who are tracking it. In the death of the two men, there is penetrating insight into human character: one, the overbearing realist, cannot cope with the mythic dimensions of the cat and falls from a cliff in fear of it; the other, the arch romantic, forgets the cat's deadly reality and is struck down.

Clark's problem as a novelist resides in his inability to proportion characters appropriately to plot. He invests no one in *The Track of the Cat,* for example, with stature commensurate with the great task of hunting the real and mythic beast. His characters are sometimes sententious. But in his two fine western novels, he largely overcomes the problem by sheer narrative force and by showing his audience some revealing habits of the human animal.

—Alan R. Shucard

CLEMENS, Samuel Langhorne. *See* **TWAIN, Mark.**

COFER, Judith Ortiz

Born: Hormigueros, Puerto Rico, 24 February 1952; immigrated to U.S. in 1954. **Education:** Schools in Paterson, New Jersey, and Augusta, Georgia; Augusta College, B.A. in English 1974 (Dean's list student); Florida International University, M.A. in English 1977; Oxford University (Scholar of English Speaking Union), 1977. **Family:** Married John Cofer in 1971; one daughter. **Career:** Worked as bilingual teacher at public schools in Palm Beach County, Florida, 1974-75; adjunct instructor in English, 1978-80, and instructor in Spanish, 1979, Broward Community College, Fort Lauderdale, Florida; adjunct instructor in English, Palm Beach Junior College, 1978-80; lecturer in English, University of Miami, Coral Gables, 1980-84; administrative staff, Bread Loaf Writers' Conference, 1983-85; instructor in English, University of Georgia, Athens, 1984-87; instructor in English, Georgia Center for Continuing Education, University of Georgia, 1987-88; instructor in English, Macon College, 1988-89. Beginning 1990 Atlanta Elderhostel Coordinator, Mercer University College, Forsyth, Georgia, 1990. Visiting King/Chavez/Parks Professor, American Cultural Department, University of Michigan, 1991; associate teaching staff of Bread Loaf Writers' Conference since 1991; assistant professor of English and creative writing, University of Georgia since 1992. **Awards:** Janet Rice Memorial fellowship, Florida Atlantic University, 1975; Poetry fellowship, Florida Fine Arts Council, 1980; Working scholarship, Bread Loaf Writers' conference, 1981; John Atherton scholarship in poetry, Bread Loaf Writers' conference, 1982; Virginia Center for the Creative Arts fellowship, 1985; first prize, Riverstone International Chapbook competition, 1986; Artist Initiated grant, Georgia Council for the Arts, 1987; Witter Bynner Foundation for Poetry grant, 1988; U.S. National Endowment for the Arts fellowship in poetry, 1989; Pulitzer prize nomination, 1989; Pushcart prize for Nonfiction, 1990. **Member:** Academy of American Poets. **Residence:** Louisville, Georgia.

PUBLICATIONS

Collection

The Year of Our Revolution: New and Selected Stories and Poems. 1998.

Novels

The Line of the Sun. 1989.

Plays

Latin Women Pray (produced 1984).

Poetry

Latin Women Pray. 1980.
The Native Dancer. 1981.
Among the Ancestors. 1981.
Peregrina. 1986.
Reaching for the Mainland in *Triple Crown: Chicano, Puerto Rican and Cuban American Poetry.* 1987.

Terms of Survival. 1987.
Reaching for the Mainland and Selected New Poems. 1995.

Other

Silent Dancing: A Partial Remembrance of a Puerto Rican Childhood. 1990.
The Latin Deli: Prose & Poetry. 1993.
An Island Like You: Stories of the Barrio (for children). 1995.

*

Bibliography: "Judith Ortiz Cofer" by Nicolás Kanellos, in *Bibliographical Dictionary of Hispanic Literature in the United States: The Literature of Puerto Ricans, Cuban Americans, and Other Hispanic Writers,* 1989; "Judith Ortiz Cofer" in *Hispanic Writers* edited by Bryan Ryan, 1991; "Judith Ortiz Cofer" by Marian C. Gonsior in *Notable Hispanic American Women,* 1993.

Critical Studies: "Judith Ortiz Cofer's Rituals of Movement" by Juan Bruce-Novoa in *The Americas Review* vol. 19, no. 3-4, 1991; "His and Her Panics" by José Piedra in *Dispositio* vol. 16, no. 41, 1991; "Puerto Rican Literature in Georgia? Interview with Judith Ortiz Cofer" by Rafael Ocasio in *The Kenyon Review* vol. XIV, no. 4, 1992; "Speaking in Puerto Rican: An Interview with Judith Ortiz Cofer" in *Bilingual Review/Revista Bilingüe* vol. XVII, no. 2, 1992; *Puerto Rican Voices in English: Interviews with Writers* by Carmen Dolores Hernandez, 1997.

*   *   *

Judith Ortiz Cofer offers in her poetry and prose a new direction to Puerto Rican literature written in the United States. Two distinctive features mark her literary style: her use of conventional American English in her discourse on Puerto Rican identity, and her independence from the Puerto Rican literary group based in the City of New York, a strong center of Puerto Rican culture. Public recognition for her work included a poetry fellowship from the Florida Fine Arts Council; a Bread Loaf Writers' Conference poetry scholarship; and a grant from the Witter Bynner Foundation for Poetry. Her first novel, *The Line of the Sun,* the first novel published by the University of Georgia Press, received a nomination for the Pulitzer Prize.

Born in Hormigueros, Puerto Rico, Cofer resettled at the age of two with her family in Paterson, New Jersey, where her father had enlisted in the U.S. Navy for economic reasons. She often repeated the process of adapting to a new culture and a new language, since she traveled to Puerto Rico with her mother and her younger brother for long periods every time her father left for duty abroad. These trips allowed Cofer to retain her use of the Spanish language, encouraged her ties to Puerto Rican culture, and, especially, gave her an opportunity to know and to become a part of the intimate association among Puerto Rican women. These periods of her life in the Hispanic barrio of New Jersey and in Puerto Rico were pivotal but relatively brief. She was fourteen when her family moved to Augusta, Georgia, because of the Paterson riots and because of her father's retirement from the Navy in 1968.

After earning an M.A. in English in 1977—her thesis examines the works of **Lillian Hellman**—Cofer began her literary career as a poet. Her first works, *Latin Women Pray* and *The Native Dancer,* give concrete expression of Puerto Rican culture in the

United States beyond the life in the barrio of New York City. Published in chapbook format, the two works use typical autobiographical elements of key moments in the formation of a psyche that is clearly feminine and Latina. Cofer presents personal experiences in standard English, a departure from the linguistic experimentations of Spanish-English compound forms traditionally associated with depictions of characters in the barrio.

Cofer's academic and literary formation, rooted in classic U.S. models, led her to a critical selectivity of content and style, introducing new polish into the genre called "minority literature." For example, her first poetry collection, *Peregrina,* was highly praised by critics and won a first-place award in the Riverstone International Chapbook competition in 1986. With new emphasis on refinement of literary expression, she used this collection to explore the function of the political voice in ethnic literature. As its Spanish title suggests, *Peregrina* ("The Female Wanderer") proposes a metaphorical representation of the Puerto Rican search for identity in the U.S. Here, as in most of her poetry, the continual existential search takes place within non-Latino social structures of the U.S.

Certainly, Cofer helps to promote exploration of the complex systems of U.S. ethnicity. In *Reaching for the Mainland* and *Terms of Survival,* her first two collections of poems in book form, there is powerful emphasis on reconstructing "Puerto Rican-ness" by means of autobiographical memory, which in turn scrutinizes her own process of intellectual maturation. Cofer draws away from the intent to make a photographic copy of life in the barrio evident in the work of so many Puerto Rican and Latino contemporary poets. She prefers to focus on key moments of her own adaptation to American life, finding in her dual identity material suitable for her poetic expression. This approach results in a feminist activism conspicuous in her creation of numerous female characters who reject their social position as members of a minority.

In *Silent Dancing: A Partial Remembrance of a Puerto Rican Childhood,* Cofer experiments with a combination of poetry and personal essays to articulate the Puerto Rican personality in the U.S. From her childhood spent partly in Puerto Rico and partly in New Jersey, as indicated in the subtitle, autobiographical memory reproduces the linguistic dilemma of the Puerto Rican immigrant: Spanish in family life and English outside the community. This constant suspension between opposing social and cultural institutions causes the Puerto Rican (and, by extension, a member of any other Latino group) to live simultaneously vital experiences that are clearly separated into English and Spanish, each representing its respective society. Living in these linguistically opposed worlds is precisely the motif of the essay "One More Lesson." It captures the exact moment when each of the two spheres of language (and, therefore, of culture) demands supremacy. The author brings back into reality a confrontation with a U.S. teacher who had brutally punished her as a child for her inability to communicate in English. The writer recalls that even as a little girl she had realized the secret for survival: "I instinctively understood then that language is the only weapon a child has against the absolute power of adults."

After this crisis with languages has been suffered and overcome, the literary personality—Puerto Rican and American—accepts cultural duality and gives it specific form in the novel *The Line of the Sun.* Like members of other ethnic groups (and especially among women writers within those groups), Cofer recognizes that choice of language and use of language determines the essence of a literary work. The axis of *The Line of the Sun* is the adaptation of

semantic codes in Spanish that, incorporated into the English text, manifest the mind of the Puerto Rican in the United States. Specifically, Cofer explores in depth the concept of Puerto Ricanness in the U.S., projecting a painting of that ethnic group against the background of U.S. society.

The novel's action is placed inside a building in the Latino section of Paterson. There, a Puerto Rican family representing two generations lives together in an extremely limited space. The mother uses Spanish and the father prefers English. The children, as first-generation Americans, must absorb both cultures. The clash between these two worlds is severely painful for the adolescent daughter Marisol, or the "little American" as she is known in the neighborhood. Her nickname shows her movement away from the central character of the Puerto Rican community. It is notable that she is the narrator of the family saga and that it is from this position as "historian" that she interprets her existence within two Puerto Rican cultures: that of the island and that of New Jersey.

Typical of the new Puerto Rican brought up between the two cultures, Marisol represents a living bridge between the two worlds. In a flash of insight as she witnesses a spiritist ceremony, she experiences the Puerto Rican-ness produced by conciliation of ancestral Hispanic and African cultures on the island in earlier times in processes similar to her own adaptation to American culture. As the metaphysical concepts of this religious expression are revealed to her, Marisol recognizes and accepts her duality and the forces that produced it: "I learned something during those days: though I would always carry my Island heritage on my back like a snail, I belonged in the world of phones, offices, concrete buildings, and the English language."

The Latin Deli, a collection of essays, short stories and poems, continues Cofer's experimentation with the interconnection of genres in her search for the "perfect" literary medium for expressing the complex history of the Puerto Rican exile in the United States. Again, as in *Silent Dancing,* ethnic depiction of the Puerto Rican is for Cofer only one point of departure in her examination of the urban American psyche. The Puerto Rican community and their popular, social, and economic culture, produce symbols illustrative of a community articulated by social elements. In Cofer the social symbolism—the Latin deli, for example—attains official character as literary material, not as a sociological device.

Cofer incorporates Puerto Rican exile into the history of immigrant experiences in the United States. Her work promotes the analysis of linguistic symbols present in the much discussed concept of American "ethnicity." Her interpretation of Puerto Ricanness and her exploration of the Puerto Rican way of life in the United States are fertile literary material. For Cofer, the existence of a Puerto Rican personality in the United States is one more example of the multiracial, multicultural society of the United States, which is in continual renewal and reinvention.

—Rafael Ocasio

COHAN, George M(ichael)

Born: Providence, Rhode Island, 3 July 1878; son of the vaudevillians Jerry and Helen Cohan. **Education:** Briefly attended two elementary schools in Providence; received no formal education after age 8. **Family:** Married 1) Ethelia Fowler (the actress Ethel Levey) in 1899, one daughter; 2) Agnes Nolan in 1907, two daughters and one son. **Career:** Traveled with his parents as a child and made his stage debut with them in 1887; thereafter regularly appeared with his parents and sister as The Four Cohans; appeared as an actor in *Peck's Bad Boy,* in New York, 1890; toured the United States with The Four Cohans throughout the 1890s, and was appearing with them in leading vaudeville houses in New York and Chicago by 1900; produced first musical for the New York stage, starring The Four Cohans and his wife, in 1901; formed producing partnership with Sam Harris, 1904, and wrote, presented, and starred in a number of musical hits on Broadway; presented plays with Harris at the New Gaiety Theater, New York, 1908-10, and at the George M. Cohan Theater, New York, 1910-20; lived in semi-retirement after 1920, occasionally appearing on the New York stage. Produced 150 plays and wrote more than 500 songs. **Awards:** U.S. Congress gold medal, 1940. **Died:** 5 November 1942.

PUBLICATIONS

Plays

The Governor's Son (produced 1901). Songs published c.1901.
Running for Office (produced 1903); revised version, as *The Honeymooners* (produced 1907).
Little Johnny Jones (produced 1904).
Popularity (produced 1906).
Forty-Five Minutes from Broadway (produced 1906).
George Washington, Jr. (produced 1906).
Fifty Miles from Boston (produced 1907).
The Talk of New York (produced 1907).
The American Idea (produced 1908). 1909.
The Yankee Prince (produced 1908).
The Man Who Owns Broadway (produced 1909). Songs published c.1909.
Get-Rich-Quick Wallingford, from a story by George Randolph Chester (produced 1910).
The Little Millionaire (produced 1911). 1911.
Broadway Jones (produced 1912). 1923; revised version, music by the author, as *The Two of Us* (as *Billie,* produced 1928), 1928.
Seven Keys to Baldpate, from the novel by Earl Derr Biggers (produced 1913). 1914.
The Miracle Man, from a story by Frank L. Packard (produced 1914).
Hello, Broadway!, music by the author (produced 1914).
What Advertising Brings, with L. Grant (produced 1915).
Hit-the-Trail Holliday (produced 1915). 1916.
The Cohan Revue 1916 (produced 1916).
Honest John O'Brien (produced 1916).
The Cohan Revue 1918 (produced 1918).
The Voice of McConnell (produced 1918).
The Fireman's Picnic. 1918.
A Prince There Was, from the novel *Enchanted Hearts* by Darragh Aldrich (produced 1918). 1927.
The Royal Vagabond, with Stephen Ivor-Szinny and William Cary Duncan, music by Anselm Goetzl (produced 1919). 1919.
The Farrell Case: A One Act Mystery (produced 1919).
Madeleine and the Movies (produced 1922).
Little Nelly Kelly (produced 1922).
The Song and Dance Man (produced 1923).

The Rise of Rosie O'Reilly (produced 1923). Songs published c.1923.
American Born (produced 1925).
The Home-Towners (produced 1926).
The Baby Cyclone (produced 1927). 1929.
The Merry Malones (produced 1927).
Whispering Friends (produced 1928).
Gambling (produced 1929).
Friendship (produced 1931).
Confidential Service. 1932.
Pigeons and People (produced 1933). 1941.
Dear Old Darling (produced 1935).
Fulton of Oak Falls, from a story by Parker Fennelly (produced 1936).
The Return of the Vagabond (produced 1940). 1940.

Poetry

Songs of Yesteryear. 1924.

Other

Twenty Years on Broadway, and the Years It Took to Get There. 1925.

*

Critical Studies: *Cohan, The Man Who Owned Broadway* by John McCabe, 1980; "The Missing Will and George M. Cohan's 'Money to Burn'" by Stephen M. Vallillo, in *Performing Arts Resources* 16, 1991.

*   *   *

Cohan the dramatist? Surely not. Cohan the Yankee Doodle Dandy, the song and dance man, the song writer (not only "Yankee Doodle Dandy" but also "Mary's a Grand Old Name" and "Give My Regards to Broadway"). But Cohan the playwright is as unknown in the late twentieth century as Cohan the vaudevillian and Cohan the movie star. The only play of his that is still remembered is probably *Seven Keys to Baldpate,* a comedy thriller filmed five times.

In his own time, however, Cohan was significant not only as an actor but as a playwright. As Alan S. Downer puts it (in *Fifty Years of American Drama,* 1951), "Out of the variety houses and into the legitimate theater came George M. Cohan, the apostle of rampant Americanism. With a sharp ear for the colloquial speech of New York . . ., with his single-minded devotion to the color combination in Old Glory, he created a wise-cracking, quick-footed, dashing young hero who could instantaneously declare and prove his superiority to all lesser mortals, 'reubens' or 'limeys' or both." From his success derive plays such as those of Winchell Smith and **George Kelly,** the tough talk of the 1930s films, the snappy wisecracks of Kaufman and **Dorothy Parker.**

The best of the plays are probably *Little Johnny Jones, Forty-Five Minutes from Broadway, Get-Rich-Quick Wallingford, Seven Keys to Baldpate, The Miracle Man,* and *Gambling.* Cohan learned his craft in the 1880s and 1890s and seldom went beyond what he learned. He used theatrical tricks in many of the plays, shocked the audience by putting Billy Sunday on the stage in *Hit-the-Trail Holliday,* kept the title character offstage in *The Miracle Man,* had no intermission in *Pigeons and People*, revealed the identity of the robber in the first act of *Confidential Service*, always with an eye on theatrical effect. His one rule was to "wow them."

—Leonard R.N. Ashley

CONNELLY, Marc(us Cook)

Born: McKeesport, Pennsylvania, 13 December 1890. **Education:** Trinity Hall, Washington, Pennsylvania, 1902-07. **Family:** Married Madeline Hurlock in 1930 (divorced 1935). **Career:** Reporter and drama critic, Pittsburgh *Press* and *Gazette-Times*, 1908-15; moved to New York, 1915; free-lance writer and actor, 1915-33; reporter, New York *Morning Telegraph*, 1918-21; helped found the *New Yorker*, 1925; wrote screenplays and directed in Hollywood, 1933-44; professor of playwriting, Yale University Drama School, New Haven, Connecticut, 1947-52. U.S. Commissioner to United Nations Educational, Scientific, and Cultural Organization (UNESCO), 1951; adviser, Equity Theatre Library, 1960. Council member of Dramatists Guild, from 1920; member of the Executive Committee, U.S. National Committee for UNESCO. **Awards:** Pulitzer Prize, 1930; O. Henry award, for short story, 1930. Litt.D.: Bowdoin College, Brunswick, Maine, 1952; Baldwin Wallace College, Berea, Ohio, 1962. **Member:** President, Authors League of America; President, National Institute of Arts and Letters, 1953-56. **Died:** 21 December 1980.

PUBLICATIONS

Plays

$2.50 (produced 1913).
The Lady of Luzon (lyrics only), book by Alfred Ward Birdsall, music by Zoel Parenteau (produced 1914).
Follow the Girl (lyrics only, uncredited; produced 1915).
The Amber Empress, music by Zoel Parenteau (produced 1916; as *The Amber Princess*, produced 1917).
Dulcy, with George S. Kaufman (produced 1921). 1921.
Erminie, revised version of a play by Henry Paulton (produced 1921).
To the Ladies!, with George S. Kaufman (produced 1922). 1923.
No, Sirree!, with George S. Kaufman (produced 1922).
The 49ers, with George S. Kaufman (produced 1922).
West of Pittsburgh, with George S. Kaufman (produced 1922; revised version, as *The Deep Tangled Wildwood*, produced 1923).
Merton of the Movies, with George S. Kaufman, from the story by Harry Leon Wilson (produced 1922). 1925.
A Christmas Carol, with George S. Kaufman, from the story by Dickens, in *Bookman*, December 1922.
Helen of Troy, New York, with George S. Kaufman, music and lyrics by Harry Ruby and Bert Kalmar (produced 1923).
Beggar on Horseback, with George S. Kaufman, music by Deems Taylor, from a play by Paul Apel (produced 1924). 1925.
Be Yourself, with George S. Kaufman, music and lyrics by Lewis Genzler and Milton Schwarzwald, additional lyrics by Ira Gershwin (produced 1924).
The Wisdom Tooth: A Fantastic Comedy (produced 1926). 1927.
The Wild Man of Borneo, with Herman J. Mankiewicz (produced 1927).

How's the King? (produced 1927).
The Green Pastures: A Fable Suggested by Roark Bradford's Southern Sketches "Ol' Man Adam an' His Chillun" (produced 1930). 1929.
The Survey (skit), in the *New Yorker*, 1934.
The Farmer Takes a Wife, with Frank B. Elser, from the novel *Rome Haul* by Walter D. Edmonds (produced 1934). Abridgement in *Best Plays of 1934-1935*, edited by Burns Mantle, 1935.
Little David: An Unproduced Scene from "The Green Pastures." 1937.
Everywhere I Roam, with Arnold Sundgaard (produced 1938).
The Traveler. 1939.
The Mole on Lincoln's Cheek (broadcast 1941). In *The Free Company Presents*, edited by James Boyd, 1941.
The Flowers of Virtue (produced 1942).
The Good Earth, with others, in *Twenty Best Film Plays*, edited by John Gassner and Dudley Nichols. 1943.
A Story for Strangers (produced 1948).
Hunter's Moon (produced 1958).
The Portable Yenberry (produced 1962).
The Green Pastures (screenplay), edited by Thomas Cripps. 1979.
The Stitch in Time (produced 1981).

Screenplays: *Whispers*, 1920; *Exit Smiling*, with others, 1926; *The Bridegroom, The Burglar, The Suitor*, and *The Uncle* (film shorts), 1929; *The Unemployed Ghost* (film short), 1931; *The Cradle Song*, 1933; *The Little Duchess* (film short), 1934; *The Green Pastures*, 1936; *The Farmer Takes a Wife*, 1937; *Captains Courageous*, with John Lee Mahin and Dale Van Emery, 1937; *The Good Earth*, with others, 1937; *I Married a Witch*, with Robert Pirosh, 1942; *Reunion* (*Reunion in France*), with others, 1942; *The Imposter* (additional dialogue), 1944; *Fabiola* (English dialogue), 1951; *Crowded Paradise* (additional scenes), 1956.

Radio Play: *The Mole on Lincoln's Cheek*, 1941.

Fiction

A Souvenir from Qam. 1965.

Other

Voices Off-Stage: A Book of Memoirs. 1968.

*

Critical Studies: *Connelly* by Paul T. Nolan, 1969; "George S. Kaufman's Exploitation of Women (Characters): Dramaturgy and Feminism" by David K. Sauer, in *American Drama*, spring 1995, pp. 55-80.

*   *   *

Born to parents who had both had stage careers, Marc Connelly early became dedicated to the theater. As a young child, he says in his memoirs, he got the "feeling that going to the theater is like going to an unusual church, where the spirit is nourished in mystical ways, and pure magic may occur at any moment." Connelly spent his life as a man of the theater seeking to produce that pure magic—as actor, director, and playwright.

Convinced that there was much to be enjoyed in life, Connelly as a young man fell in naturally with the famed "Round Table" of the 1920s at New York's Algonquin Hotel. His first New York stage venture had been the lyrics for the musical *The Amber Empress* (1916), but success did not come until the collaborations with George S. Kaufman. In 1921 their *Dulcy*, a mixture of gentle satire and fun, helped to set the standard for the Broadway comedy of the 1920s. They collaborated on six other plays. Their *Merton of the Movies*, based on the story by Harry Leon Wilson, inaugurated an era of Broadway satires on Hollywood. The play's success was marked by Hollywood's reproduction.

The most important play of the Kaufman-Connelly collaboration was *Beggar on Horseback*, a masterpiece of American expressionism and a fitting symbol of the *joie de vivre* the collaborators consistently sought to bring to the stage. The play is based on Paul Apel's *Hans Sonnestossers Hollenfahrt*, but it is no slavish copy of the German play—the expressionism has been completely Americanized in technique and in its satiric ends. Framed by scenes of comic realism, the visual and audial effects of the expressionism, helped by cinematic techniques, are more varied than those of **Elmer Rice**'s *The Adding Machine* (1923).

After the success of *Beggar on Horseback*, the collaborators decided to pursue their careers apart. Connelly wrote musicals and plays (most successfully *The Wisdom Tooth*) and wrote short stories for the *New Yorker* (he was on the editorial board of the struggling new magazine), but it was not until he read **Roark Bradford**'s *Ol' Man Adam an' His Chillun* that he wrote the play that insured his unique position in twentieth-century drama. In Bradford's rendering of Old Testament stories from the viewpoint of uneducated Louisiana Negroes, Connelly immediately perceived the basis of a drama where pure magic might nourish the human spirit. The result was *The Green Pastures*, a work that, while it contained much of the fun of Bradford, gave it a greater dignity and a greater vision. Connelly's Lawd is a growing protagonist; his play's action concerns man's search for God and God's search for man. Connelly enhanced his episodically structured play through the use of Negro spirituals, suggesting other aspects of the folk longings. By framing the play with a children's Sunday School, Connelly conveyed the value of his material: unless one becomes as a little child, the play's vision would be beyond him. Broadway had long been without a religious play, and an all-Negro cast was also unusual. Connelly had difficulty getting backing for the play, but the production (directed by himself) proved the skeptics wrong. The play ran for five years, totaling 1642 performances.

Connelly was in Hollywood often in the 1930s, writing screenplays (some of the best of the period) and directing (he would later act in *Our Town* and in other plays). Although Connelly wrote some scripts and other plays, none matched his earlier successes. *A Souvenir from Qam*, his only novel, satirizes spy stories. He reminisced about his many years on the stage and in the movies in *Voices Off-Stage*, which gives brief glimpses of famous contemporaries but is most valuable for its account of *The Green Pastures*.

—Joseph M. Flora

COOKE, Ebenezer

Surname also spelled Cook. **Born:** London, England, c. 1667. **Career:** First came to Maryland c. 1694; returned to London c. 1700

and again before 1708; in Maryland after 1712, when he inherited a family estate in Dorchester County. Deputy Receiver-General, Cecil County, after 1720; also land agent; admitted to Prince George's County bar, 1728. **Died:** c. 1732.

PUBLICATIONS

Poetry

The Sot-Weed Factor; or, A Voyage to Maryland. 1708; edited by Brantz Mayer, 1865.
Sotweed Redivivus; or, The Planter's Looking-Glass. 1730.
The Maryland Muse (includes *The Sot-Weed Factor* and *The History of Colonel Nathaniel Bacon's Rebellion in Virginia*). 1731.

*

Critical Studies: *Men of Letters in Colonial Maryland* by J.A. Leo Lemay, 1972; *Cooke: The Sot-Weed Canon* by Edward H. Cohen, 1975; "Cooke: Satire in the Colonial South" by Robert D. Arner, in *Southern Literary Journal* vol. 8, 1975; "The Case against Ebenezer Cooke's Sot-Weed Factor" by Robert Micklus, in *American Literature: A Journal of Literary History, Criticism, and Bibliography*, May 1984; "The Poem as Con Game: Dual Satire and the Three Levels of Narrative in Ebenezer Cooke's 'The Sot-Weed Factor'" by Gregory A. Carey, in *Southern Literary Journal*, fall 1990; "The Process of Americanization as Portrayed in Ebenezer Cooke's *The Sot-Weed Factor*" by Charles League, in *Southern Literary Journal*, fall 1996, pp. 18-25.

*   *   *

Known as the self-proclaimed "Poet Laureate" of colonial Maryland, Ebenezer Cooke was among the first American poets to write satire about the colonies from the point of view of a disgruntled colonist. He is also recognized as the most popular and successful of America's early Southern poets and a precursor of the frontier humorists of the nineteenth century.

While little is known for certain about Cooke's early life, he is thought to have been born in England, to have spent a brief period of time in Maryland in 1694, and to have migrated there sometime after 1712. His first visit to the "Western Shoars" is thought to have inspired his most famous work, *The Sot-Weed Factor*, published in London in 1708 but believed to have been written much earlier. About the experiences of a British tobacco merchant who comes to America to trade with the colonists and who is cheated and insulted during the course of his visit, *The Sot-Weed Factor* is biting satire on the manners and mores of the people who lived in the colony of Maryland at the beginning of the eighteenth century. Written in Hudibrastic couplets, the poem burlesques the escapades of drunken lawyers, inept physicians, illiterate and often dishonest planters, crude and debased women, and degenerate Indians, all of whom are said to typify New World culture, or the lack thereof. Omitted in the American edition of 1731, the final lines of the poem are a "Curse," delivered by the narrator as he departs from America for England, on the "Inhospitable Shoar" that he has just visited, "Where no Man's Faithful, nor a Woman Chast."

A sequel to *The Sot-Weed Factor*, once attributed to an imitator but later correctly attributed to Cooke, was published in Maryland in 1730 by William Parks under the title *Sotweed Redivivus*. By the time of the poem's publication, Cooke had permanently established himself in Maryland, where he had become a respected member of the community. As a result, *Sotweed Redivivus* is less a satire of colonial manners than an attempt to write serious didactic poetry on the necessity of remedying the economic woes of Maryland through legislative reform. According to Cooke, the standard of living in Maryland would be greatly improved if its people would endorse legislation to control inflation, limit the production of tobacco for which there was no market, curtail the slave trade, and halt the indiscriminate waste of natural resources, particularly the wanton destruction of forests.

Other poems in the Cooke canon that merit critical analysis are "The History of Colonel Nathaniel Bacon's Rebellion in Virginia," published along with *The Sot-Weed Factor* in *The Maryland Muse*, and a series of elegies on the deaths of public figures with whom Cooke associated. A mock-heroic epic of the type then popular in England, "The History of Colonel Nathaniel Bacon's Rebellion" reflects Cooke's conservative thinking on the subject of revolution and colonial self-government. Far from praising Nathaniel Bacon, the popular American hero who in 1676 had led the people of frontier Virginia to revolt against the tyrannical administration of Governor William Berkeley, Cooke's stated aim in writing a history of the rebellion was to "Cooke *this* Bacon" whose "dire . . . Wars" he considered a threat to civilization and an act of extreme folly. Although they lack the clever wit and polished charm of his other poems, Cooke's elegies are numbered among the finest surviving examples of colonial American elegiac verse. Particularly noteworthy is "An Elegy on the Death of the Honourable William Lock" (1732), in which Cooke uses the death of a local dignitary as the occasion for poetic commentary on the universality of death.

After 1732 Cooke stopped writing poetry, and because nothing is known about his subsequent activities, scholars have assumed that he died at this time. Cooke attracted the attention of **John Barth**, whose novel *The Sot-Weed Factor* (1960) alone earned Cooke a lasting reputation in the annals of American literary history.

—James A. Levernier

COOKE, John Esten

Born: Winchester, Virginia, 3 November 1830. **Education:** Schools in Charleston and Richmond, Virginia; studied law with his father: admitted to Virginia bar, 1851. **Military Service:** Served in the Confederate army during the Civil War, 1861-65: captain. **Family:** Married Mary Frances Page in 1867 (died 1878); three children. **Career:** Lawyer in Richmond, 1851-52 and intermittently, 1853-54; temporary editor, *Southern Literary Messenger*, Richmond, 1851 and 1854, and Richmond *Express*, 1854; full-time writer from 1854; moved to an estate near Millwood, Virginia, 1868; thereafter writer and farmer. **Died:** 27 September 1886.

PUBLICATIONS

Fiction

Leather Stocking and Silk; or, Hunter John Myers and His Times: A Story of the Valley of Virginia. 1854; as *Leather and Silk*, 1892.

The Virginia Comedians; or, Old Days in the Old Dominion. 1854; as *Beatrice Hallam and Captain Ralph*, 2 vols., 1892.
Ellie; or, The Human Comedy. 1855.
The Last of the Foresters; or, Humors on the Border: A Story of the Old Virginia Frontier. 1856.
Henry St. John, Gentleman, of "Flower of Hundreds" in the County of Prince George, Virginia: A Tale of 1774-'75. 1859; as *Bonnybel Vane*, 1883; as *Miss Bonnybel*, 1892.
Surry of Eagle's-Nest; or, The Memoirs of a Staff-Officer Serving in Virginia. 1866.
Fairfax; or, The Master of Greenway Court: A Chronicle of the Valley of the Shenandoah. 1868; as *Lord Fairfax*, 1888.
Mohun; or, The Last Days of Lee and His Paladins: Final Memories of a Staff Officer Serving in Virginia. 1869.
Hilt to Hilt; or, Days and Nights on the Banks of the Shenandoah in the Autumn of 1864. 1869.
The Heir of Gaymount. 1870.
Hammer and Rapier. 1870.
Out of the Foam. 1871; as *Westbrooke Hall*, 1891.
Doctor Vandyke. 1872.
Her Majesty the Queen. 1873.
Pretty Mrs. Gaston and Other Stories. 1874.
Justin Harley: A Romance of Old Virginia. 1875.
Canolles: The Fortunes of a Partisan of '81. 1877.
Professor Pressensee, Materialist and Inventor. 1878.
Stories of the Old Dominion from the Settlement to the End of the Revolution. 1879.
Mr. Grantley's Idea. 1879.
The Virginia Bohemians. 1880.
Fanchette, by One of Her Admirers. 1883.
My Lady Pokahontas: A True Relation of Virginia. 1885.
The Maurice Mystery. 1885; as *Col. Ross of Piedmont*, 1893.

Other

The Youth of Jefferson; or, A Chronicle of College Scrapes at Williamsburg, in Virginia. A.D. 1764. 1854.
The Life of Stonewall Jackson. 1863; revised edition, as *Stonewall Jackson: A Military Biography*, 1866.
Wearing of the Gray. Being Personal Portraits, Scenes, and Adventures of the War. 1867; edited by Philip Van Doren Stern, 1960.
A Life of Gen. Robert E. Lee. 1871.
Virginia: A History of the People. 1883.
Poe as a Literary Critic, edited by N. Bryllion Fagin. 1946.
Stonewall Jackson and the Old Stonewall Brigade, edited by Richard Barksdale Harwell. 1954.
Outlines from the Outpost, edited by Richard Barksdale Harwell. 1961.
Autobiographical Memo, edited by John R. Welsh. 1969.

*

Bibliography: *A Bibliography of the Separate Writings of Cooke* by Oscar Wegelin, 1925, revised edition, 1941; in *Bibliography of American Literature* by Jacob Blanck, 1957; by Theodore L. Gross, in *A Bibliographical Guide to the Study of Southern Literature* edited by Louis D. Rubin, Jr., 1969.

Critical Studies: *Cooke, Virginian* by John O. Beaty, 1922; "John Esten Cooke and His 'Confederate Lies'" by Mary Jo Bratton, in

Southern Literary Journal, Spring 1981; "John Esten Cooke's My Lady Pokahontas: The Popular Novel on History" by Thomas S. Gladsky in *Southern Studies: An Interdisciplinary Journal of the South,* Fall 1984; "The Novelist as Soldier: Cooke and DeForest" by Eric Solomon, in *American Literary Realism, 1870-1910,* Spring 1987; "Responding to the 'Airplant' Tradition: Cooke's My Lady Pokahontas" by A. Carl Bredahl, in *Southern Literary Journal,* Fall 1988.

*   *   *

Although John Esten Cooke, the younger brother of Philip Pendleton Cooke (1816-1850) and cousin of **John Pendleton Kennedy** (1795-1870), was best known in his own time and afterwards as a writer of long fiction, he was also something of a poet, one of whose fugitive pieces—"The Band in the Pines"—is still occasionally anthologized; a biographer, whose lives of Lee and Stonewall Jackson are worthy of attention but more as accounts of battles than as biography; and a historian, whose Virginia, though hardly scholarly according to modern standards, is a pleasant narrative of the early days of the Commonwealth.

Along with stories, sketches, essays, verse, and other contributions to periodicals, Cooke produced at least five novels before the Civil War, four of which are actually historical romances—*Leather Stocking and Silk, The Virginia Comedians, Henry St. John, Gentleman,* and *Fairfax* (serialized in 1859). The second of these is, according to the author, "intended to be a picture of our curiously graded Virginia society just before the Revolution" and included portraits of Patrick Henry and Lewis Hallam's actors in the Williamsburg area. It remains his best work of historical fiction, despite the fact that many of his numerous books on the war are based on his own first-hand experience.

Surry of Eagle's-Nest, the most notable of the war novels and his most popular long fiction, and its sequel, *Mohun,* cover many of the great battles of Lee's army, military actions in which Cooke participated, from the first engagement at Bull Run to Appomattox—priceless material for a novelist. Cooke found it difficult, nevertheless, to fuse fact and fiction in these novels and to refrain, any more than had his predecessors Scott, **Cooper, Irving,** and **Simms,** from introducing extraneous materials into his structure, in these particular instances Gothic characters, melodrama, and sub-plots in works that are essentially historical or even realistic. But when, for example, the narrative focuses on Surry and military adventure, it moves swiftly and with eyewitness authority. Though much of Cooke's long fiction seems romantic and dated in the late twentieth century, some of it anticipates Mary Johnston (*Canolles*) and **Ellen Glasgow** (*The Heir of Gaymount*), and his style remains charming and graceful; his appreciation of the past manifests itself in the antebellum work, and his military experience lends authenticity to the best of the Civil War romances.

—Rayburn S. Moore

COOLIDGE, Clark

Born: Providence, Rhode Island, 26 February 1939. **Education:** Brown University, Providence, 1956-58. **Family:** Married Susan Hopkins, one daughter. **Career:** Editor, *Joglars* magazine, Provi-

dence, 1964-66. **Awards:** National Endowment for the Arts grant, 1966; New York Poets Foundation award, 1968.

PUBLICATIONS

Poetry

Flag Flutter and U.S. Electric. 1966.
(Poems). 1967.
Ing. 1969.
Space. 1970.
The So. 1971.
Moroccan Variations. 1971.
Suite V. 1973.
The Maintains. 1974.
Polaroid. 1975.
Quartz Hearts. 1978.
Own Face. 1978.
Smithsonian Depositions, and Subject to a Film. 1980.
American Ones. 1981.
A Geology. 1981.
Research. 1982.
Mine: the One that Enters the Stories. 1982.
Solution Passage: Poems, 1978-1981. 1986.
The Crystal Text. 1986.
Mesh. 1988.
At Egypt. 1988.
A Geology. 1988.
Sound As Thought: Poems 1982-1984. 1990.
The Book of During. 1991.
Odes to Roba. 1991.
Baffling Means. 1991.
On the Slates. 1992.
Lowell Connector: Lines & Shots from Kerouac's Town. 1993.
Registers: (People in All). 1994.
The ROVA Improvisations. 1994.
Keys to the Caverns. 1995.
For Kurt Cobain. 1995.
The Crystal Text. 1995.
The Names. 1997.
Book of Stirs. 1998.

Play

To Obtain the Value of the Cake Measure from Zero, with Tom Veitch. 1970.

*

Critical Studies: "Clark Coolidge Issue" of *Big Sky 3,* 1972; interview in *This 4,* Spring 1973; in *The End of Intelligent Writing* by Richard Kostelanetz, 1974; "A Symposium on Clark Coolidge" in *Stations 5,* Winter 1978; in *Postmodern Poetry: The Talisman Interviews* by Edward Halsey Foster, 1994.

*   *   *

Clark Coolidge's poetry and prose has consistently extended the artistic usage of language beyond the conventions of grammar, syntax, and narrative. From his earliest explorations of "cut-up" techniques borrowed from the novelist **William Burroughs** to his latest book-length poems and texts, Coolidge demonstrates a powerful attraction to the material side of language: its spatial dispensation on the page, its sounds and rhythms, its syllabic textures and weights. Accordingly, he has also been fascinated with the problematic relation of words to material objects—rocks and other geological entities are of special importance to him—and with the objectlike resistance to meaning words may take on once they are displaced from their usual contexts into unusual, artificial ones chosen by the poet.

Coolidge's early book *Space* includes a number of very spare arrangements of words that are meant to be autonomous of any identifiable speaker, statement, narrative, or overarching symbolic meaning. While they are not, strictly speaking, "concrete poems," which tend to use written language to compose pictorial or sculptural icons to support the meaning of the words, Coolidge's poems do insist on their literal, space-occupying presence on the page:

of   about

since   dot

This poem forms a clearly demarcated square, its center empty and its corners occupied by its four sole words; however, nothing in particular is symbolized by either the figure or the words. Nevertheless, it need not be seen as a "meaningless" exercise, for it does invite serious questions and possible interpretations of the text. For example, we can take "of," "about," and "dot" in a spatial sense, to designate three kinds of spatial relations: inclusion, surrounding, and punctual position. Taken as tools for exploring this space, these would allow us to identify an inside and an outside, as well as specific points within both domains. And if with these terms we have the three dimensions of the space of this little cosmos, with "since" we gain the fourth dimension: time. The terms also point to linguistic meanings. In their linguistic functions, "of" and "about" can be taken to be roughly similar: in the phrases "the history of World War I" and "this book about World War I," the terms are synonymous; but in "a story of my father" and "a story about my father," they define the poles of subject and object, the teller and that which is told. "Dot" indicates the bounds of the sentence, the basic unit within which meaning and reference take place. Generating the dimensions of time, space, meaning, reference, causality, objectivity, and subjectivity, all out of four word-units, Coolidge's arrangement thus works as a kind of minimal machine for generating a significant "world."

His later writing explores a variety of poetic means. His 1974 book *The Maintains,* for example, explores arrangements of words that defy sentence structure or often even the syntax of phrases:

he in of tree dial a pod
age code time or ball with another
cod to a proper close
lands of cake egg strut
snail rung at no two
to bay
the verb to toupee

These lines focus the reader's attention on the complicated relations of the sonorous, orthographic, and significant aspects of language. For example, in the lines just quoted, the *tü* sound appears in the words "two," "to," and "toupee." In the absence of a definite syntactical environment or sense, one cannot know whether "to bay" is a spatial designation (the sound of ringing traveling to the bay) or a verb (to bay like a dog). The unit "the verb," however, could pertain to either "to bay" or "to toupee" (a neologism meaning "to cover with a toupee"); or it could be the object of "to bay," perhaps as if the dog's barking was the sound of the verb itself ("bay! bay!"). Nothing here is certain, but the lines force us to look for possible coherences that stretch the functions of words beyond their normal uses.

Most recently Coolidge has incorporated this close attention to word, grammar, and syntax into a number of longer poems, in which the ambiguities are projected onto larger-scale structure. For example, in his book-length poem "Research," he uses self-contained phrases or sentences to shift frames continually. From line to line there is a semblance of sense, but the concatenation of lines leads to the impression of an elusive, open-ended narrative constantly surfacing and being erased:

Behind the scene there was a large ape of yellow metal
He thought his mind had gone backwards from the age
      of seventeen
Threats, apparel, vitamins, a treadmill, the wall receding
I had to hand you
My name is Jan, as in January, as in Jan & Dean, as in
      Jansen, as in Emil Jannings,
The moon was already full but grew brighter behind the
      slogan MARRY ME FIRST
There were pipes all over the place, those and empty
      hoardings
The exact turnpike was described in my this year's
      calendar

At his most ambitious, as in his 1994 book *The Rova Improvisations,* Coolidge elaborates such obliquities over the structure of a 200-page collection. This book, as Coolidge notes, originated with the task of writing liner notes for an album by the Rova Saxophone Quartet, an avant-garde jazz ensemble. The first section of the book was composed while listening to all the recorded music of Rova in the order of its recording; the second, complementary section was written while reading through the first sequence. Coolidge's structure raises a whole set of issues about the relation of sound and sense, poetry and music, originality and secondariness. Both sections, he suggests, are something like the negative imprints of experiences (listening, reading) that register only in the traces of their absence. "One [section was] written in the hollows of the music," he remarks. "The other in the silence of the words."

—Tyrus Miller

COOPER, James Fenimore

Born: Burlington, New Jersey, 15 September 1789; moved with his family to Cooperstown, New York, 1790. **Education:** Village school at Cooperstown; in the household of the rector of St.

Peter's, Albany, New York, 1800-02; Yale University, New Haven, Connecticut, 1803-05: dismissed for misconduct; thereafter prepared for a naval career: served on the *Sterling*, 1806-07; commissioned midshipman in the U.S. Navy, 1808; served on the *Vesuvius*, 1808; for a brief time in command on Lake Champlain, also served on the *Wasp* in the Atlantic, 1809; resigned commission, 1811. **Family:** Married Susan Augusta DeLancey in 1811; five daughters and two sons. **Career:** Lived in Mamaroneck, New York, 1811-14, Cooperstown, 1814-17, and Scarsdale, 1817-21; began to write in 1820; lived in New York, 1821-26, and Europe, 1826-33; returned to New York, 1833, and lived in Cooperstown, 1834-51. **Awards:** M.A.: Columbia University, 1824. **Died:** 14 September 1851.

PUBLICATIONS

Collections

Works. 33 vols., 1895-1900.
Representative Selections, edited by Robert E. Spiller. 1936.
Letters and Journals, edited by James Franklin Beard. 6 vols., 1960-68.
Writings, edited by James Franklin Beard. 1980—

Fiction

Precaution. 1820.
The Spy: A Tale of the Neutral Ground. 1821.
The Leatherstocking Tales (Library of America), edited by Blake Nevius. 2 vols., 1985.
    The Pioneers; or, The Sources of the Susquehanna: A Descriptive Tale. 1823.
    The Last of the Mohicans: A Narrative of 1757. 1826.
    The Prairie: A Tale. 1827.
    The Pathfinder; or, The Inland Sea. 1840.
    The Deerslayer; or, The First War-Path: A Tale. 1841.
Tales for Fifteen; or, Imagination and Heart. 1823.
The Pilot: A Tale of the Sea. 1823.
Lionel Lincoln; or, The Leaguer of Boston. 1825.
The Red Rover: A Tale. 1827; edited by Warren S. Walker, 1963; edited by Thomas Phillbrick and Marianne Phillbrick, 1991.
The Borderers: A Tale. 1829; as *The Wept of Wish Ton-Tish,* 1829; as *The Heathcotes,* 1854.
The Water Witch; or, The Skimmer of the Seas: A Tale. 1830.
The Bravo: A Venetian Story. 1831.
The Heidenmauer; or, The Benedictines. 1832.
The Headsman; or, The Abbaye des Vignerons: A Tale. 1833.
The Monikins: A Tale. 1835.
Homeward Bound; or, The Chase: A Tale of the Sea. 1838.
Home as Found. 1838; as *Eve Effingham; or, Home,* 1838.
Mercedes of Castile; or, The Voyage to Cathay. 1840.
The Two Admirals: A Tale of the Sea. 1842.
The Jack O'Lantern (Le Feu-Follet); or, The Privateer. 1842; as *The Wing-and-Wing; or, Le Feu-Follet,* 1842.
Le Mouchoir: An Autobiographical Romance. 1843; as *The French Governess; or, The Embroidered Handkerchief,* 1843; edited by George F. Horner and Raymond Adams, as *Autobiography of a Pocket Handkerchief,* 1949.
Wyandotte; or, The Hutted Knoll. 1843.
Afloat and Ashore; or, The Adventures of Miles Wailingford. 1844.

Lucy Harding: A Second Series of Afloat and Ashore. 1844; as *Afloat and Ashore,* vols. 3-4, 1844.
Satanstoe; or, The Family of Littlepage: A Tale of the Colony. 1845; as *Satanstoe; or, The Littlepage Manuscripts,* 1845; edited by Robert E. Spiller and Joseph D. Coppock, 1937.
The Chainbearer; or, The Littlepage Manuscripts. 1845.
Ravensnest; or, The Redskins. 1846; as *The Redskins; or Indian and Injin, Being the Conclusion of the Littlepage Manuscripts,* 1846.
Mark's Reef; or, The Crater: A Tale of the Pacific. 1847; as *The Crater; or, Vulcan's Peak,* 1847; edited by Thomas Philbrick, 1962.
Captain Spike; or, The Islets of the Gulf. 1848; as *Jack Tier; or, The Florida Reef,* 1848.
The Bee-Hunter; or, The Oak Openings. 1848; as *The Oak Openings,* 1848.
The Sea Lions; or, The Lost Sealers. 1849; edited by Warren S. Walker, 1965.
The Ways of the Hour: A Tale. 1850.
The Lake Gun, edited by Robert E. Spiller. 1932.

Other

Notions of the Americans, Picked Up by a Travelling Bachelor. 2 vols., 1828; as *America and the Americans,* 1836.
Letter to Gen. Lafayette. 1831.
A Letter to His Countrymen. 1834.
Sketches of Switzerland. 2 vols., 1836; as *Excursions in Switzerland,* 1836.
A Residence in France with a Second Visit to Switzerland. 2 vols., 1836; as *Sketches of Switzerland, Part Second,* 1836.
Recollections of Europe. 2 vols., 1837; as *Gleanings in Europe,* 1837.
England, with Sketches of Society in the Metropolis. 2 vols., 1837; as *Gleanings in Europe: England,* 1837.
Excursions in Italy. 2 vols., 1838; as *Gleanings in Europe: Italy,* 1838.
The American Democrat. 1838; edited by George Dekker and Larry Johnston, 1969.
The Chronicles of Cooperstown. 1838.
The History of the Navy of the United States of America. 2 vols., 1839.
The Battle of Lake Erie. 1843.
Ned Myers; or, A Life Before the Mast. 1843.
Lives of Distinguished American Naval Officers. 2 vols., 1846.
The Works, revised by the author. 12 vols., 1849-51.
New York, edited by Dixon Ryan Fox. 1930.
Early Critical Essays 1820-1822, edited by James Franklin Beard. 1955.

Editor, *Elinor Wyllys,* by Susan A. Fenimore Cooper. 1845.

*

Bibliography: *A Descriptive Bibliography of the Writings of Cooper* by Robert E. Spiller and Philip C. Blackburn, 1934; in *Bibliography of American Literature* by Jacob Blanck, 1957.

Critical Studies: *Cooper, Critic of His Times,* 1931, and *Cooper,* 1965, both by Robert E. Spiller; *Cooper* by James Grossman, 1949; *Cooper and the Development of American Sea Fiction* by Thomas Philbrick, 1961; *Cooper* by Donald A. Ringe, 1962; *Coo-*

per: An Introduction and Interpretation, 1962, and *Plots and Characters in the Fiction of Cooper,* 1979, both by Warren S. Walker; *Cooper's Americans* by Kay House, 1966; *Cooper the Novelist* by George Dekker, 1967, as *Cooper, The American Scott,* 1967, and *Cooper: The Critical Heritage* edited by Dekker and J.P. McWilliams, 1973; *Cooper: The Last of the Mohicans* (study guide) by Jack B. Moore, 1971; *Cooper's Landscapes: An Essay on the Picturesque Vision* by Blake Nevius, 1976; *A World by Itself: The Pastoral Moment in Cooper's Fiction* by H. Daniel Peck, 1977; *Cooper: A Study of His Life and Imagination* by Stephen Railton, 1978; *Cooper: A Collection of Critical Essays* edited by Wayne Fields, 1979; *The New World of Cooper* by Wayne Franklin, 1982; *Plotting America's Past: Cooper and the Leatherstocking Tales* by William P. Kelly, 1983; *Early Cooper and His Audience* by James D. Wallace, 1986; *Cooper: New Critical Essays* edited by Robert Clark, 1986; *Cooper* by Robert Emmet Long, 1990; *Cooper: His Country and His Art; Papers from the Bicentennial Conf., 1989* edited by George A. Test, 1991; *Cooper's Leather-Stocking Novels: A Secular Reading* by Geoffrey Rans, 1991; *The Lasting of the Mohicans: History of an American Myth* by Martin Barker, 1995; *James Fenimore Cooper: The Critical Heritage,* 1997; *The Search for a Fatherland: James Fenimore Cooper in Germany* (dissertation) by Barton Carl Beebe, 1998.

*   *   *

James Fenimore Cooper will always be remembered first for his Leatherstocking tales: *The Pioneers, The Last of the Mohicans, The Prairie, The Pathfinder,* and *The Deerslayer.* These five books recount the experiences of an American frontiersman, variously named Deerslayer, Hawkeye, Pathfinder, Leatherstocking, and the trapper, between the early 1740s, when British America was a line of settlements along the Atlantic coast, and 1805 to 1806, when the Lewis and Clark expedition crossed the continent. Though the books were not written in the order of the events they portray, they form, nonetheless, a kind of American epic concerned not only with the opening of the West but also with the costs involved in the process: the cutting of the forests, the killing of the game, and the displacement of the Indian. Leatherstocking, a man of the woods, wants to preserve the natural environment and use it only as needed, but by acting as hunter and scout, he opens the wilderness to the very settlers whose wasteful ways he abhors. Cooper details both the social and moral consequences of the process, and though he laments the fate of the Indian and warns his countrymen against the destruction of their resources, he does not place his values in Leatherstocking alone. He consistently affirms, rather, the Christian civilization that must supplant the wilderness. The problem America faces, these books seem to say, is to insure that the new society will be a just and democratic one ruled by the most talented and virtuous men who will not needlessly destroy the bounties of nature. To develop the social aspects of his theme, Cooper includes a wide range of characters, both white and Indian, who illustrate the various attitudes that men have toward God, nature, and society, and he uses his physical setting—both dense woods and desolate prairie—to reveal the moral state of his characters and their relation to a transcendent system of value revealed in the landscape—one that Leatherstocking always recognizes, but that too many of his fellow countrymen fail to perceive.

The neutral ground in *The Spy,* where contending irregulars fight during the American Revolution, typifies well a moral world where motives and identities are masked and loyalties are uncertain. The isolated frontier settlements in *The Wept of Wish Ton-Tish* and *Wyandotte* clearly represent the islands of peace and order that the colonists try to establish in a moral chaos. Even the sea in the maritime novels functions in a similar fashion. In the two series of *Afloat and Ashore,* it serves a dual purpose as a testing ground for men. Here the right to rule, by virtue of character, training, and knowledge, may be established in the handling of a ship, but here too the weakness of even the most capable men before the power of God may be starkly revealed. Indeed, in *The Crater,* Cooper uses both the sea and the isolated settlement, some islands in the Pacific, to establish the relation between the moral basis of a society and its ability to survive.

Much of Cooper's success as an artist derives from his ability to project his meaning through setting, whether it be a frontier fort in America, a ship at sea, or a part of the European scene: the city of Venice in *The Bravo,* an isolated valley in Germany in *The Heidenmauer,* or the breathtaking landscape of Switzerland in *The Headsman.* That meaning, moreover, is always both moral and social. At times, of course, one or the other aspect may dominate, and, especially in the social criticism, the moral basis may be muted or unexpressed, but it is never completely absent. His attacks on aristocracy in his three European novels and on the excesses of American democracy in the books that followed derive from his consistent belief that the evils of society are caused by the fallen nature of men, who must humble themselves before God and act, not from economic, but from moral motives if society is ever to escape the wrongs and injustices that have plagued it in the past.

Cooper detested aristocracy wherever he found it and wrote the European novels not merely to attack it in the abstract, but also to make clear the evils of such societies wherever they might appear. Though Cooper was thinking of contemporary England and of the France of Louis Philippe when he wrote these books, he also wished to warn his countrymen that a similar oligarchy, based on commerce, could develop in the United States and subvert its political principles. When he viewed American democracy, on the other hand, he saw a quite different problem. The leveling democrat is impelled by an economic motive no less strong than that of the aristocrat; he wishes to remove all distinctions among men and rule, not through a governing class, but through the manipulation of the electoral process. In place of the aristocrat, there appears the demagogue.

Cooper never found a completely suitable means for presenting his criticism of American democracy, and most of his novels attacking the failings of contemporary America do not succeed as fiction. Yet all of them are interesting. In *The Monikins,* he satirized English, American, and French society through a race of monkeys who live in Antarctica, and in *Homeward Bound* and *Home as Found,* he attempted to depict a cross section of American life through the experience of the Effingham family, descendants of the founder of Templeton in *The Pioneers,* who are returning home after a sojourn in Europe. The device gave him the opportunity to attack the leveling democrats and the social climbers, the Anglophiles and the super-patriots of America, while affirming through the Effinghams what true Americans should be. His major characters are rather wooden, however, and though each book has its interest—the adventure parts of the former are very well done— both are rather weak novels.

Cooper did better in some of his later works: the Littlepage series and his final book, *The Ways of the Hour.* Critics have sometimes set the Littlepage series against the Leatherstocking tales to illustrate a bifurcation in Cooper's fiction, but the two series actually complement each other. The Leatherstocking tales, after all, have much to say about American society, and the first two Littlepage books, *Satanstoe* and *The Chainbearer,* contain major frontier episodes. They portray the rise of the Littlepage family during the eighteenth century and their successful struggle to maintain their possessions against both French and Indian invaders and New England squatters. The third book, *The Redskins,* shows them defending their property against insurgent radical democrats in contemporary New York, but the book is too polemical to work as fiction. *The Ways of the Hour,* focused upon a jury trial for murder, is a far more effective treatment of the failings of American democracy.

Not all of Cooper's novels fit into the two main categories for which he is best known: frontier romance and social criticism. A third major type is one he created, the tale of the sea. Cooper's maritime novels cover a wide range, from delightful romantic fictions, like *The Red Rover* and *The Water Witch,* to serious explorations of moral problems, like *The Two Admirals* and *The Wing-and-Wing.* They include the patriotic *The Pilot,* the grim *Jack Tier,* in which all value seems to have been lost, and the deeply religious *The Sea Lions,* which, like *The Oak Openings,* a late tale of the wilderness, makes a strong affirmation of Christian faith. These tales of the sea may appear diverse in theme and tone, but, seen in the broad pattern of Cooper's thirty-year career as a novelist, their relation to his other work is clear. His successful sailors are men who, like Leatherstocking, submit to the God they perceive in the natural setting. Those who fail to do so cause the many evils and injustices that, Cooper believed, always result when men act from selfish motives in this fallen world.

Cooper also wrote a significant amount of good nonfiction. *Notions of the Americans* and *The American Democrat* are sound statements of American beliefs and principles; his five travel volumes (1836-38) not only describe his sojourn abroad, but also make sharp observations on European society; and *The History of the Navy of the United States of America* and *Lives of Distinguished American Naval Officers* are sound historical works. Though Cooper's claim to our attention must always rest on his fiction, these miscellaneous works made a real contribution to nineteenth-century American thought and are still of interest to serious readers of the late twentieth century.

—Donald A. Ringe

See the essay on *The Last of the Mohicans.*

COOVER, Robert (Lowell)

Born: Charles City, Iowa, 4 February 1932. **Education:** Southern Illinois University, Carbondale, 1949-51; Indiana University, Bloomington, B.A. 1953; University of Chicago, 1958-61, M.A. 1965. **Military Service:** Served in the U.S. Navy, 1953-57: lieutenant. **Family:** Married Maria del SansMallafré in 1959; two daughters and one son. **Career:** Taught at Bard College, Annandale-on-Hudson, New York, 1966-67, University of Iowa, Iowa City, 1967-69, Columbia University, New York, 1972, Princeton University, New Jersey, 1972-73, Virginia Military Institute, Lexington, 1976, and Brandeis University, Waltham, Massachusetts, 1981; writer-in-residence, Brown University, Providence, Rhode Island,

beginning 1981. Fiction editor, *Iowa Review,* Iowa City, 1974-77. **Awards:** Faulkner award, 1966; Brandeis University Creative Arts award, 1969; Rockefeller fellowship, 1969; Guggenheim fellowship, 1971, 1974; American Academy award, 1976; National Endowment for the Arts grant, 1985; Rea award, for short story, 1987.

PUBLICATIONS

Short Stories

Pricksongs and Descants. 1969.
Hair o' the Chine. 1979.
After Lazarus: A Filmscript. 1980.
Charlie in the House of Rue. 1980.
A Political Fable (novella). 1980.
The Convention. 1982.
In Bed One Night and Other Brief Encounters. 1983.
Aesop's Forest, with *The Plot of the Mice and Other Stories,* by Brian Swann. 1986.
A Night at the Movies; or, You Must Remember This. 1987.

Novels

The Origin of the Brunists. 1966.
The Universal Baseball Association, Inc., J. Henry Waugh, Prop. 1968.
The Public Burning. 1977.
Spanking the Maid. 1982.
Gerald's Party. 1986.
Whatever Happened to Gloomy Gus of the Chicago Bears? 1987.
Pinocchio in Venice. 1991.
John's Wife. 1996.
Briar Rose. 1997.
Ghost Town. 1998.

Plays

The Kid (produced 1972). Included in *A Theological Position,* 1972.
A Theological Position (includes *A Theological Position, The Kid, Love Scene, Rip Awake*). 1972.
Love Scene (as *Scène d'amour,* produced 1973; as *Love Scene,* produced 1974). Included in *A Theological Position,* 1972.
Rip Awake (produced 1975). Included in *A Theological Position,* 1972.
A Theological Position (produced 1977). Included in *A Theological Position,* 1972.
Bridge Hand (produced 1981).
Spanking the Maid (produced 1987).
A Pedestrian Accident (produced 1998).
Charlie in the House of Rue (produced 1999).

Other

Editor, with Kent Dixon, *The Stone Wall Book of Short Fiction.* 1973.
Editor, with Elliott Anderson, *Minute Stories.* 1976.

Theatrical Activities: Director: **Film**—*On a Confrontation in Iowa City,* 1969.

*

Critical Studies: *Fiction and the Figures of Life* by William H. Gass, 1970; *Black Humor Fiction of the Sixties* by Max Schulz, 1973; "Coover and the Hazards of Metafiction" by Neil Schmitz, in *Novel 7,* 1974; "Humor and Balance in Coover's *The Universal Baseball Association, Inc.*" by Frank W. Shelton, in *Critique 17,* 1975; "Coover, Metafictions, and Freedom" by Margaret Heckard, in *Twentieth Century Literature 22,* 1976; "The Dice of God: Einstein, Heisenberg, and Coover" by Arlen J. Hansen, in *Novel 10,* 1976; "Structure as Revelation: Coover's *Pricksongs and Descants*" by Jessie Gunn, in *Linguistics in Literature,* vol. 2 no. 1, 1977; *The Metafictional Muse: The Works of Coover, Donald Barthelme, and William H. Gass* by Larry McCaffery, 1982; *Coover: The Universal Fictionmaking Process* by Lois Gordon, 1983; *Coover's Fictions* by Jackson I. Cope, 1986; *Dissident Postmodernists: Barthelme, Coover, Pynchon* by Paul Maltby, 1991; *Robert Coover: A Study of the Short Fiction* by Thomas E. Kennedy, 1992; *Comic Sense: Reading Coover, Stanley Elkin, Philip Roth* by Thomas Pughe, 1994.

*   *   *

Emerging from the 1960s as one of the most thematically interesting and technically successful novelists within the era's great outpouring of innovative fiction, Robert Coover has developed as a writer ever on the cutting edge of his literary culture. The nature of his work—brainy, quirkily comic, and subversive of established beliefs—has denied him a great popular readership. Yet among academics and fanciers of intellectually serious fiction, he remains accessible, thanks to his basis in vernacular language and the iconology of mass society.

Coover's debut novel, *The Origin of the Brunists,* anticipated the characteristics that would both define its author's career and limit the scope of his achievements. Set in the coal-mining region of the lower Middle West where, after his birth in Iowa, Coover was raised, this novel dramatizes a newspaper writer's reaction to the birth of a small-time religious movement. A mining explosion has killed ninety-seven men, but one has miraculously survived, and around his survival grows an apocalyptic religious movement. As a storyteller, Coover focuses more on the response to these events than on the movement itself. Along the way peoples' attitudes toward religion are examined, but the author's interests (and the liveliness of his writing) are given broader scope for expression when they fix upon the peculiarities of reactive behavior. Appropriately *The Origin of the Brunists* was hailed for its artistic rather than commercial success, receiving the 1966 William Faulkner Prize established for new and under-recognized young writers.

With *The Universal Baseball Association, Inc., J. Henry Waugh, Prop.,* Coover first employed the metafictive devices that, in the hands of **John Barth**, Ronald Sukenick, and others, were defining the innovative style of his generation. Set alternately in the apartment of the player of a tabletop baseball game and on the projected baseball field of that game itself, this novel's true story is of the metafictive impulse in action. As fiction that explores the conditions of its own making, metafiction withholds the suspension of disbelief in favor of showing how a tale is created. That is exactly what J. Henry Waugh does in the narrative, coming home each night from a colorless job to breathe drama and excitement into the card-turning, dice-throwing game he has devised to simulate not just a baseball contest but an entire world of players, teams, and leagues. A Walter Mitty type, Waugh at times gets caught up in the putative reality of his creation; but readers are privileged to see the manipulations taking place above, no matter how convincing the tabletop narrative.

Yet it is the charm of baseball Americana that makes *The Universal Baseball Association* so agreeable, and it is an especially artful mix of similarly popular images of American history and recent politics that generates appeal in Coover's major work, *The Public Burning.* In structure this novel pursues another strategy of innovative fiction, that of the mega-novel, where everything, from size and scope to nature of expression, is taken to deliberate excess. As in **Thomas Pynchon**'s *Gravity's Rainbow,* the impulse is to create a book big enough to contain an entire world, though with Coover there is the added intention of bowling readers over with the onrush of overwritten language. Coover's talent consists partly in finding the right occasion for such work; here it is the execution of accused atom-bomb spies Julius and Ethel Rosenberg amid the excesses of 1950s American popular culture. That talent extends to mixing media in a broadly comic, even slapstick manner, combining ridiculously overstated impossibilities with rare, true historical details to the extent that the reader is unable to decipher which is actual and which is farce. Did Richard Nixon, a character in the novel, really do and say such things? Coover's manner in *The Public Burning* is to make it hard to tell.

The Public Burning, a closely typeset, 534-page monster of a book, was originally drafted and published (in *TriQuarterly* No. 26, Winter 1973) as part of a planned novella, *The Public Burning of Julius and Ethel Rosenberg.* Throughout his career Coover has experimented with the novella form, making a collage of children's books and politics for *The Cat in the Hat for President,* exploring the Sadean qualities of self-generating narrative in *Spanking the Maid,* and toying with the ephemera and narrative style of professional sports in *Whatever Happened to Gloomy Gus of the Chicago Bears?* In their playfulness with literary devices, these works reflect the more closely technical interests of Coover's short stories, collected in *Pricksongs and Descants, In Bed One Night,* and *A Night at the Movies.* It is their fascination with the excesses of narrative choice that allies them with the author's subsequent, self-consciously bizarre novels.

Written and published in an age of literary deconstruction, where conventional assumptions are systematically dismantled to reveal the true nature of a work beneath, *Gerald's Party* grants a narrator the privilege of taking apart the premises of an average, everyday cocktail party—albeit one that results in the almost total destruction of the host's home. That Coover wishes to spoof certain literary conventions is obvious from the first sentence, where in murder-mystery fashion, a body is discovered with no explanation as to the cause of death. From here the narrator backtracks to describe the scene and detail the action, all of which has developed slowly and with great subtlety at Gerald's party. The art of it is that for a long time, nothing much happens. The occasion is arranged, guests arrive, the first drinks are poured, and mingling begins. But with the first spill of something on the rug, a tenor of disorder begins, paced by the arrival of more guests and a steady increase in the group's level of inebriation. More accidents and eventually absurdities and random acts of violence follow, all predicated against the inexplicable presence of the dead body and the constantly reasserted gestures towards normality (such as guests ducking away from the crime scene for a moment to check the basketball scores on TV). Coover's method for such madness—and madness it surely is by novel's end—is to see how much chaos can be generated from a minimal introduction of disorder.

As a canonically accepted author, Coover glories in the exercise of writerly privilege. This once revolutionary tactic now conforms to readerly acceptance; it is, indeed, what is expected in advancing old age from one who was once a Young Turk. Yet in key respects Coover is still breaking new ground. The massive novel *John's Wife* uses the now familiar device of a party gone wild to explore the history of an entire community, from real estate deals and civic scandals to small-time philandering and poorly disguised lusts. Heavily detailed but minimally punctuated paragraphs give each community member a voice, and to the extent that action exists, it is in a swirl of language expressing each person's point of view in an ever-shimmering collage. *Briar Rose,* just eighty-six pages in length, looks back to medieval times for the retelling of a fairy tale in strikingly postmodern terms—by itself nothing new for Coover (nor, especially, for his contemporary **Donald Barthelme**, famous for doing the same in *Snow White*), but significant here for its ongoing alternation between the voices of the prince, the sleeping beauty herself (named Rose), and the evil fairy who has bewitched her (but who can control the narrative only at times). *Ghost Town* succeeds best as a tour de force example of Coover's method, a virtuoso display in which the resulting work is almost pure performance. Familiarity of subject (the Wild West of history, myth, and popular culture) allows blatant unfamiliarity of writing technique, a condition ideally suited to narrative styles that might elsewhere collapse into surrealistic nightmare; here, what would otherwise escape sharp focus remains almost painfully in full view.

Throughout his career Coover has welcomed occasions to deliberately overwrite. These occasions include chances to make the historical figure of Richard Nixon seem preposterous beyond belief (in *The Public Burning*) and to make a postmodern professor suffer deconstructions otherwise feasible only for a wooden puppet (*Pinocchio in Venice*). Some critics feel his aim corresponds with the art-for-art's-sake side of innovative fiction, granting himself occasions for mere virtuoso performance, but Coover's reputation rests more securely in a notion the innovators have developed in league with postmodern literary theory: that what is accepted as reality itself is a construct liable to manipulation, exploitation, and ultimately insightful enjoyment by those whose can make its tricks their own.

—Jerome Klinkowitz

COWLEY, Malcolm

Born: Belsano, Pennsylvania, 24 August 1898. **Education:** Harvard University, B.A. 1920 (cum laude); Universite de Montpellier, diplome 1922. **Military Service:** American Filed Service, 1917; served in France, U.S. Army, artillery officers' training school, 1918. **Family:** Married 1) Marguerite Frances Baird in 1919 (divorced 1932); 2) Muriel Maurer in 1932; one son. **Career:** Writer, editor, and lecturer. Employee, Sweet's Architectural Service, New York City; freelance writer and translator, 1925-29; literary editor, *New Republic*, 1929-40; member of staff, Office of Facts and Figures, Washington, DC; literary advisor, Viking Press, New York City, 1948-85. Visiting professor, University of Washington, 1950-51, Stanford University, 1956-57, 1959-61, and 1965, University of Michigan, 1957-58, University of California, 1962-63, Cornell University, 1964-65, Hollins College,

1968-69, 1970-71, University of Minnesota, 1971-72, and University of Warwick, 1973. Contributor, *Gargoyle*, 1922, *Horizon* and *Sewanee Review*; associated editor, *Broom*, 1928, and *Secession*; associate editor and book critic, *New Republic*, 1929-44. Organized first American Writers Congress, 1935. Cofounder, resultant League of American Writers; director, Corporation of Yaddo; chairman of zoning board, Sherman, Connecticut, 1945-68. **Awards:** Levinson prize, 1928, and Harriet Monroe Memorial prize, 1939, both for verse published in *Poetry*; National Institute of Arts and Letters grant in literature, 1946; National Endowment for the Arts grant, 1967; Signet Society Medal, 1976; Hubbell Medal for service to the study of American letters, 1979; National Institute Gold Medal, 1981; Who's Who in America Achievement award, 1984; Elmer Holmes Bobst award for Arts and Letters, New York University, for literary criticism, 1985. Litt.D.: Franklin and Marshall College, 1961; Colby College, 1962; University of Warwick, 1975; University of New Haven, 1976; Monmouth College, 1978; Indiana University of Pennsylvania, 1985. **Member:** American Academy of Arts and Letters (chancellor, 1967-76). **Died:** 27 March 1989.

PUBLICATIONS

Collection

The Portable Malcolm Cowley, edited by Donald W. Faulkner. 1990.

Prose

Racine. 1923.
Exile's Return: A Narrative of Ideas. 1934; revised edition *Exile's Return: A Literary Odyssey of the 1920s,* 1951.
The Literary Situation. 1954.
Black Cargoes: A History of the Atlantic Slave Trade, 1518-1865, with Daniel Pratt Mannix. 1962.
Van Wyck Brooks, with R.D. Oakes. 1963.
Think Back on Us: A Contemporary Chronicle of the 1930s, edited by Henry Dan Piper. 1969.
A Many-Windowed House: Collected Essays on American Writers and American Writing, edited by Henry Dan Piper. 1970.
The Lesson of the Masters, with Howard Hugo. 1971.
A Second Flowering: Works and Days of the Lost Generation. 1973.
The View from Eighty. 1980.
The Flower and the Leaf: A Contemporary Record of American Writing Since 1941, edited by Donald W. Faulkner. 1985.
Unshaken Friend: Profile of Maxwell Perkins. 1986.
New England Writers and Writing, edited by Donald W. Faulkner. 1996.

Poetry

Blue Juniata. 1929; revised as *Blue Juniata: Collected Poems,* 1968.
The Dry Season. 1941.
Blue Juniata: A Life: Collected and New Poems. 1985.
The Urn. 1986.

Recordings: *Malcolm Cowley Reading His Poems in the Recording Laboratory,* 1954; *Malcolm Cowley and Theodore Russell Weiss Reading and Discussing Their Poems in the Coolidge Auditorium,* 1969; *Malcolm Cowley Talks About the "Lost Gen-*

eration," 1980; *Malcolm Cowley Talks About His Life in Criticism and the Process of Aging,* 1982.

Other

The Faulkner-Cowley File: Letters and Memoirs, 1944-62. 1966.
—And I Work at the Writer's Trade (memoirs). 1978.
The Dream of the Golden Mountains: Remembering the 1930s (memoirs). 1980.
Conversations with Malcolm Cowley. 1986.
The Selected Correspondence of Kenneth Burke and Malcolm Cowley, 1915-1981. 1988.

Editor, *Adventures of an African Slaver; Being a True Account of the Life of Captain Theodore Canot, Trader in Gold, Ivory and Slaves on the Coast of Guinea: His Own Story as Told in the Year 1854 to Brantz Mayer* by Mayer Brantz.
Editor, *After the Genteel Tradition: American Writers Since 1910.* 1937; revised edition, 1964.
Editor, with Bernard Smith, *Books That Changed Our Minds.* 1940.
Editor, *The Viking Portable Hemingway.* 1944.
Editor, with Hannah Josephson, *Aragon, Poet of the French Resistance.* 1945; as *Aragon, Poet of Resurgent France,* 1946.
Editor, *The Portable Faulkner.* 1946; as *The Essential Faulkner,* 1967.
Editor, *The Portable Hawthorne.* 1948; as *Nathaniel Hawthorne: The Selected Works,* 1971.
Editor, *The Complete Poetry and Prose of Walt Whitman.* 1948; as *The Works of Walt Whitman,* 1968.
Editor, *The Stories of F. Scott Fitzgerald: A Selection of Twenty-Eight Stories.* 1951.
Editor, *Tender Is the Night: A Romance* by F. Scott Fitzgerald. 1951.
Editor, *Three Novels of F. Scott Fitzgerald: The Great Gatsby; Tender Is the Night (with the Author's Final Revisions); The Last Tycoon.* 1953.
Editor, *Great Tales of the Deep South.* 1955.
Editor, *Writers at Work: The "Paris Review" Interviews.* 1958.
Editor, *Leaves of Grass: The First Edition* by Walt Whitman. 1959.
Editor, *Winesburg, Ohio* by Sherwood Anderson. 1960.
Editor, *Three Novels of Ernest Hemingway.* 1962.
Editor, *The Bodley Head F. Scott Fitzgerald...Short Stories.* 1963.
Editor, with Robert Cowley, *Fitzgerald and the Jazz Age.* 1966.

Translator, *On Board the Morning Star* by Pierre MacOrlan. 1924.
Translator, *Joan of Arc* by Joseph Delteil. 1926.
Translator, *Catherine-Paris* by Marthe Lucie Bibesco. 1928.
Translator, *The Green Parrot* by M.L. Bibesco. 1929.
Translator, *The Sacred Hill* by Maurice Barres. 1929.
Translator, *The Count's Ball* by Raymond Radiguet. 1929.
Translator, *Imaginary Interviews* by André Gide. 1944.
Translator, with James R. Lawler, *Leonardo, Poe, Mallarme* by P. Valery. 1972.

*

Manuscript Collection: Newberry Library, Chicago.

Critical Studies: *Malcolm Cowley's Path to William Faulkner* by Lawrence H. Schwartz, 1982; *The Early Career of Malcolm*

Cowley: A Humanist Among the Moderns by James Michael Kempf, 1985; *Malcolm Cowley: The Formative Years* by Hans Bak, 1993.

*   *   *

A strong case can be made that Malcolm Cowley and Edmund Wilson are the most important literary critics of the twentieth century. Cowley's books read like good novels or the best biographies, which in a way, of course, they are. His *Exile's Return,* for example, about the expatriate, post-World War One generation of American writers in Paris, did perhaps more than any other work of criticism to place rebel authors like Ernest Hemingway, Ford Madox Ford, and many others firmly in the literary canon. While making the case for these writers' first books, Cowley also succeeded in presenting their exciting lives in one of the most romantic, dynamic settings in the world.

In *The Literary Situation,* Cowley stretched the traditional boundaries of literary criticism. In addition to the expected summary and interpretation of important novels, Cowley included his version of how writers get started and how they make a living; one piece examines the domestic habits of writers, while another concentrates on the writer as public figure (or, in our time, as celebrity).

In the famous chronological sequels to *Exile's Return, A Second Flowering* and *The Dream of the Golden Mountains,* Cowley's talent as social critic and chronicler rivals his brilliant abilities in literature. "American society, and business society over the world, and the trade of writing had all been stumbling downhill since the Wall Street Crash . . .," he writes. "But there was hope as well, the apocalyptic hope that a City of Man would rise on the other side of disaster. By surrendering their middle-class identities, by joining the workers in an idealized army, writers might help to overthrow 'the system' and might go marching with comrades, shoulder to shoulder, out of injustice and illogic into the golden mountains." In the thirties and forties, especially, Cowley served as a kind of first witness to the high points and disasters as that dream played out in coal strikes and the New Deal, Communist parades and hunger marches, and the flowering of writers such as Clifford Odets, F. Scott Fitzgerald, Hart Crane, and others who lived lives of social activism that seem odd and antique among today's more cynical and narcissistic mainstream writers.

No discussion of Malcolm Cowley would be complete without mentioning his work as an editor and his poetry. It is reasonable to assume that so acute an observer as Cowley would also make a superior editor. Such was the case, particularly at *The New Republic,* where he guided new writers into print and promoted the work of the generation he knew best for fifteen years. Cowley is also generally acknowledged as the man who revived William Faulkner's career by editing a selection of his work for Viking.

Cowley's poems are perhaps unfairly overshadowed by his reputation as a critic and editor. His definitive statement in verse was collected late in his life in *Blue Juniata: Collected Poems.* The poetry leans toward traditional meters, relaxed rhymes, and free verse that seems, at times, to nod to the poetry of T. S. Eliot. His subjects vary from country life to campus life to the writing life—the latter always his favorite obsession. Perhaps his strongest poem is "The Flower and the Leaf," a poignant elegy for the generation of writers he observed so closely.

Since Malcolm Cowley's death, no American critic has even remotely approached his breadth of vision, his generosity, and—

most remarkable in a critic—his fairness. Cowley's sensibility and style bring even to unfavorable criticism a sense of compassionate sweetness. One who knows Cowley's work firsthand thinks of him today as many baseball fans must think of the late Joe DiMaggio: with excitement, with awe, and with sadness that the great man's time among us has ended. One need only consider the current crop of leading critics to miss Malcolm Cowley, to feel the terrible sadness of his, and serious literary criticism's, passing.

—Robert McDowell

COZZENS, James Gould

Born: Chicago, Illinois, 19 August 1903. **Education:** Kent School, Connecticut, 1916-22, graduated 1922; Harvard University, Cambridge, Massachusetts, 1922-24. **Military Service:** Served in the U.S. Army Air Force, 1942-45: major. **Family:** Married Sylvia Bernice Baumgarten in 1927. **Career:** Tutor, Santa Clara, Cuba, 1925, and in Europe, 1926-27; librarian, New York Athletic Club, 1927; guest editor, *Fortune* magazine, New York, 1938. **Awards:** O. Henry award, 1936; Pulitzer prize, 1949; American Academy Howells Medal, 1960. Litt.D.: Harvard University, 1952. **Member:** American Academy, 1943. **Died:** 9 August 1978.

PUBLICATIONS

Collections

Just Representations: A Cozzens Reader, edited by Matthew J. Bruccoli. 1978.

Fiction

Confusion. 1924.
Michael Scarlett: A History. 1925.
Cock Pit. 1928.
The Son of Perdition. 1929.
S.S. San Pedro: A Tale of the Sea. 1931.
The Last Adam. 1933; as *A Cure of Flesh,* 1933.
Castaway. 1934.
Men and Brethren. 1936.
Ask Me Tomorrow; or, The Pleasant Comedy of Young Fortunatus. 1940.
The Just and the Unjust. 1942.
Guard of Honor. 1948.
By Love Possessed. 1957.
Children and Others (stories). 1964.
Morning Noon and Night. 1968.
A Flower in Her Hair (stories). 1974.

Other

A Rope for Dr. Webster (essay). 1976.
Some Putative Facts of Hard Record. 1978.
A Time of War: Air Force Diaries and Pentagon Memos 1943-45, edited by Matthew J. Bruccoli. 1984.
Selected Notebooks 1960-1967, edited by Matthew J. Bruccoli. 1984.

*

Bibliography: *Cozzens: A Descriptive Bibliography* by Matthew J. Bruccoli, 1981.

Critical Studies: *The Novels of Cozzens* by Frederick Bracher, 1959; *Cozzens: Novelist of Intellect* by Harry John Mooney, Jr., 1963; *Cozzens* by D.E.S. Maxwell, 1964; *Cozzens* by Granville Hicks, 1966; *Cozzens* by Pierre Michel, 1974; *Cozzens: A New Acquist of True Experience,* 1979, and *Cozzens: A Life Apart,* 1983, both by Matthew J. Bruccoli; "The Manuscripts of James Gould Cozzens's *By Love Possessed*" by Anne Clough Little, in *Resources for American Literary Study,* 1995, pp. 189-205; "A Just Representation of Life and People: The Artistic Technique of James Gould Cozzens" by Gordon Van Ness, in *The Professions of Authorship: Essays in Honor of Matthew J. Bruccoli* edited by Richard Layman and Joel Myerson, 1996.

*   *   *

James Gould Cozzens was a writer whose work offers, with a quiet persistence, an account of American life that is not really duplicated elsewhere. After tentative starts in novels that were modish when they were published, Cozzens found a stride that carried him off in a more personal direction. The early novel *Confusion* played off the refinement of Europe against the crudity of America, as many novelists of the time were doing. The somewhat later novel, *The Last Adam,* stridently celebrated the lusty and primitive energy of the hero as if he were cousin to the gamekeeper in *Lady Chatterley's Lover.*

But these novels—and *The Last Adam* is excellent in its own right—were apprentice exercises: a cutting-away of underbrush that kept Cozzens from reaching his own territory. This territory is kept strictly to in novels like *The Just and the Unjust* and *By Love Possessed.* It is only apparently departed from in *Men and Brethren,* Cozzens's "clerical" novel with a big-city setting, and *Guard of Honor,* a "war" novel with an army base for its background. Cozzens's domination of his territory has not been difficult; few other American writers have wanted to enter it. Of those who seem to, it is **Louis Auchincloss** who comes closest to Cozzens; both Auchincloss and Cozzens depict the lives of a privileged minority. But Auchincloss's characters are both more wealthy and more powerful than Cozzens's, "big city" and mobile. In contrast, Cozzens's "right people" are provincial and fixed in their habitations and their careers.

The typical Cozzens heroes, most fully displayed in *The Just and the Unjust* and *By Love Possessed* but represented elsewhere, are the latest members of families that have enjoyed privilege, education, and position for several generations in American towns of medium size. The heroes are at the center of the web of custom and law that continues to hold together the communities they serve, often as lawyers and always as thoughtful and responsible citizens. Both men have fathers who speak of the order they supported in their days; the fathers encourage their sons to continue the quiet battle of preserving a way of life that is already old, shadowed by elms and dominated by court-house domes and the law-courts beneath those domes. It is a way of life best enjoyed by people of substance and privilege—a way both misunderstood and resented by those who are "outside the law": Poles, Irish Catholics, and blacks. For these persons, whose drunkenness and violence often take them into the lawyers' offices, the lawyers (and Cozzens the novelist) offer sympathy and comprehension but hardly acceptance; the clients' disorder is part of a more general confusion that is always threatening not just the privileged but the entire community.

This confusion—as most of Cozzens's narratives suggest—can be held back by law and custom; it will not cease. So, in face of the disorder in "alien" behavior and the outbreaks of lust and malice in their own beings, the Cozzens heroes fight and learn while they fight. Their battles are related by Cozzens in such a way that all events, all human deliberations, are bathed in a rationality that is calm and unmilitant; absent from the novels is the self-righteousness of many a novelist whose orientation is liberal. Cozzens has faith in what he says, but the faith is not excessive. Absent also are the transcendental hopes of novelists who have heard a gospel. Cozzens and his heroes are committed to a kind of dubiety, a dubiety both provincial and shrewd. It is a world in which expectations of happiness are both clear and quite modest.

Cozzens's analysis of human motive is sharp. Cozzens and his most perceptive characters—he is not easily to be separated from them—are armed with generations of common sense and desultory talk rather than with the Freudian or Jungian strategies that are useful to many of Cozzens's contemporaries. Cozzens was—differences being allowed for—the Anthony Trollope of the recent American day, judging the life he knew with sharp intelligence rather than dismissing it with contempt or violence.

—Harold H. Watts

CRADDOCK, Charles Egbert. *See* **MURFREE, Mary Noailles.**

CRANE, (Harold) Hart

Born: Garrettsville, Ohio, 21 July 1899. **Education:** East High School, Cleveland, 1914-15. **Career:** Lived in New York, 1916-17; worked in munitions plant, Cleveland, 1918; reporter, Cleveland *Plain Dealer,* 1918-19; advertising manager, *Little Review,* and clerk, Rheinthal and Newman, both New York, 1919; worked for his father in Akron and Cleveland, 1920-21; advertising copywriter, Cleveland, 1922-23; worked at office jobs in advertising and sales, New York, 1923-25; given money by financier Otto Kahn, 1925 and 1927; traveled in Europe, 1928-29, and Mexico, 1931-32. **Awards:** Guggenheim fellowship, 1931. **Died:** (suicide) 27 April 1932.

PUBLICATIONS

Collections

Letters 1916-1932, edited by Brom Weber. 1952.
Complete Poems and Selected Letters and Prose, edited by Brom Weber. 1966; revised edition, 1984.
Poems, edited by Marc Simon. 1986.

Poetry

White Buildings. 1926.
The Bridge. 1930.
Seven Lyrics. 1966.
Ten Unpublished Poems. 1972.

Other

Twenty-One Letters to George Bryan, edited by Joseph Katz and others. 1968.
Robber Rocks: Letters and Memories of Crane 1923-1932 edited by Susan Jenkins Brown. 1969.
Letters of Crane and His Family, edited by Thomas S.W. Lewis. 1974.
Crane and Yvor Winters: Their Literary Correspondence, edited by Thomas Parkinson. 1978.
O My Land, My Friends: The Selected Letters of Hart Crane. 1997.
The Correspondence between Hart Crane and Waldo Frank. 1998.

*

Bibliography: *Crane: A Descriptive Bibliography* by Joseph Schwartz and Robert C. Schweik, 1972; *Crane: A Reference Guide* by Joseph Schwartz, 1983.

Critical Studies: *Crane: A Biographical and Critical Study* by Brom Weber, 1948; *Crane: An Introduction and Interpretation* by Samuel Hazo, 1963, revised edition, as *Smithereened Apart: A Critique of Crane,* 1978; *Crane* by Vincent Quinn, 1963; *Crane* by Monroe K. Spears, 1965; *The Poetry of Crane* by R.W.B. Lewis, 1967; *The Crane Voyages* by Hunce Voelcker, 1967; *Crane: An Introduction to the Poetry* by Herbert A. Leibowitz, 1968; *Voyager: A Life of Crane* by John Unterecker, 1969 (*Notes,* 1970); *The Broken Arc: A Study of Crane* by R.W. Butterfield, 1969; *Hart's Bridge* by Sherman Paul, 1972; *Crane: The Patterns of His Poetry* by Margaret Dickie Uroff, 1974; *Crane's Bridge: A Description of Its Life* by Richard P. Sugg, 1977; *Vision of the Voyage: Crane and the Psychology of Romanticism* by Robert Combs, 1978; *Crane's Divided Vision: An Analysis of The Bridge* by Helge Nilsen, 1980; *Crane's Holy Vision: White Buildings* by Alfred Hanley, 1981; *Crane: A Collection of Critical Essays* edited by Alan Trachtenberg, 1982; *Critical Essays on Crane* edited by David R. Clark, 1982; *Splendid Failure: Crane and the Making of The Bridge* by Edward Brunner, 1984; *Crane: The Contexts of The Bridge* by Paul Giles, 1986; *'The Imaged Word': The Infrastructure of Crane's White Buildings* by Ernest Smith, 1990; *Brooklyn Parable: A Study of Allegory in Two Poems by Vladimir Mayakovsky and Hart Crane* by Christopher Caes, 1997.

* * *

It is difficult to give a final and objective estimate of Hart Crane's place as a poet. He is important, on more than one count, for what he set out to do, but critics have differed widely as to his actual achievement. Furthermore, there is the legend, as we may call it, of his life. We are presented with the picture of a man driven by compulsive and self-destructive urges, both alcoholic and homosexual, culminating in a spectacular suicide. Crane himself identified with such doomed and outcast figures as Christopher Marlowe and Arthur Rimbaud, and it is easy to make him into the romantic scapegoat of American civilization. On the other hand, a critic like **Yvor Winters** can too readily move from a moral disapproval of the undisciplined life to a total dismissal of the work.

The Bridge is Crane's longest and clearly his most important poem. In form it is modeled on **T.S. Eliot**'s *The Waste Land,* and it is generally agreed that Crane intended his own poem as a kind of riposte, giving a positive rather than a negative view of the modern metropolitan city. In *The Waste Land,* and in James Joyce's *Ulysses,* the protagonist moves about the city—London or Dublin—which becomes a symbolic landscape, crowded with mythical and heroic archetypes. Past splendors contrast with modern squalor. *The Bridge* follows the same plan. The setting is New York. The protagonist wakes in the morning, passes over Brooklyn Bridge, wanders about the city and returns in the evening by the subway under the Hudson River. Crane tries to create a mythology for America out of scraps of literature, history, and tradition. Columbus, Rip Van Winkle, and the Wright brothers appear, as well as **Walt Whitman**, **Edgar Allan Poe**, **Emily Dickinson**, and Isadora Duncan. In the section entitled "Powhatan's Daughter" Pocahontas represents the American earth itself and its Indian past: "Lie to us. Dance us back our tribal dawn." In "The Tunnel," through the suffocating atmosphere of a rush hour subway, Crane encounters the ghost of Poe:

And why do I often meet your visage here,
Your eyes like agate lanterns—on and on
Below the toothpaste and the dandruff ads?

And did their riding eyes right through your side,

And did their eyes like unwashed platters ride?
And Death, aloft,—gigantically down
Probing through you—toward me, O evermore!

In this remarkable passage, Crane shows that he is aware that the American dream of materialistic, technological progress has its reverse side of neurotic nightmare, and that Poe represents this nightmare. But it is Brooklyn Bridge itself that is the unifying symbol of the poem. The bridge unites the two halves of the city, and by the railroad that it carries unites the city with the country and thus its present with its past. As a feat of engineering it denotes human achievement, and in its clean functional beauty, the union of aesthetics and technics.

We may thus consider Crane, as does **Harold Bloom**, as standing in the succession of Romantic, myth making, and visionary poets. He is one of the explorers of what Charles Williams called "the Image of the City." But as an urban poet he differs sharply from his American and British successors of the 1930s in that his poetry is almost devoid of social and political comment. He has indeed been reproached by left-wing critics for his unreflecting celebration of the American capitalist system. Indeed, the sudden collapse of that system in the Depression was one of the factors contributing to his despair and his suicide.

Crane may also be considered, at least in part, as the most notable representative in the English-speaking world of the Futurist movement founded in 1909 and extending through the 1920s. The term "Futurism" was coined by the Italian Marinetti, a figure more notable for self-publicity than literary genius. But his claim that art should celebrate the achievements and imitate the rhythms of a machine civilization influenced poets better than himself. These included Apollinaire in France and Mayakovsky in Russia. The latter, like Crane, found his new faith inadequate to sustain him and ended in suicide. But Crane, as we have seen, did not regard the traditions of the past as irrelevant. He suffered, however, from a certain paucity in his own cultural background: it really does seem that he thought the phrase "Panis angelicus" that he quotes in the "Cape Hatteras" section of *The Bridge* meant "angelic Pan" and could be applied to Walt Whitman. And some may feel that

the only religious tradition he seems to have been acquainted with, his mother's Christian Science, lacked a richness compared with the theological currents that fertilized the work of Eliot and Joyce.

Although Whitman's populist rhetoric represents one of Crane's stances, his free verse is not in the least Whitmanesque. Like that of Eliot, it is based on an extension of principles already found in the blank verse of Shakespeare's contemporaries. But while Eliot's is founded upon that of Webster and his generation, that of Crane is to be related to the practice of Marlowe, with its strongly stressed iambic rhythm and its terminal pause. As in Marlowe there is an element of bombast in Crane, and a certain degree of rhythmical monotony. At his best he sweeps us along by the sheer energy of his writing, in spite of the frequent difficulty of grasping the exact sense of what he is saying. Crane is undeniably often very obscure. But his much quoted letter to Harriet Monroe, defending his poem, "At Melville's Tomb," shows that he was very much intellectually in control. The poem consists in fact of a series of compressed conceits, rather different from the extended metaphysical conceits of Donne and his school. At times it is difficult to translate these into completely logical terms. These lines (from "Voyages") are typical—"In all the argosy of your bright hair, I dreamed / Nothing so flagless as this piracy"—yet their haunting quality is manifest. As a visual poet Crane is remote from Pound and the Imagists; instead of a clear pictorial impression of a scene or object we get a kind of kaleidoscope of sense impressions. His style might best be described as manneristic, and in this respect his affinities are less with his contemporaries and immediate predecessors than with certain poets who came into prominence a decade later, such as George Barker and Dylan Thomas. Crane has indeed been claimed as an influence on the latter poet, but this is difficult to determine.

When Crane moved from the early short poems of *White Buildings* to the elaborately planned *The Bridge* he was attempting to encompass something in the nature of an epic style. What he in fact achieved might more properly be described as quasi-Pindaric or dithyrambic lyric. This dithyrambic quality is even more marked in "For the Marriage of Faustus and Helen." This sequence of three poems continues some of the themes of *The Bridge.* Faustus's evocation of the shade of Helen is, of course, one of the most memorable moments in Marlowe's *Doctor Faustus;* and Marlowe, as we have seen, was one of Crane's heroes. The marriage of Faust and Helena, in the second part of Goethe's *Faust,* was a symbol of the union of the modern with the antique spirit. Crane may have taken his cue from this, since the theme of these three poems is the union of American technological civilization with the traditional idea of beauty. Crane here forces language almost to the breaking point as he strives to evoke Helen first from a vision of the metropolitan city, second (it would seem) from a scene of jazz revelry at the summit of a skyscraper, and third from the airman's conquest of distance:

Capped arbiter of beauty in this street
That narrows darkly into motor dawn,—
You, here beside me, delicate ambassador
Of intricate slain numbers that arise
In whispers, naked of steel;
religious gunman!
Who faithfully, yourself, will fall too soon,
And in other ways than as the wind settles
On the sixteen thrifty bridges of the city:
Let us unbind our throats of fear and pity.

In contrast to this, the series of poems entitled "Voyages" represents Crane's return to a purer and more personal lyricism. These may in the end constitute his most enduring, though not his most ambitious achievement. In these poems Crane thinks of himself united with one of his lovers, a merchant seaman, as he voyages through imaginary seascapes. The verse of these poems has a new kind of music, and they are less rhetorically accentuated. Crane now uses enjambment with effect, especially a characteristic trick of ending a line with a grammatically unimportant word as in the second line of the following quotation:

> O minstrel galleons of Carib fire,
> Bequeath us to no earthly shore until
> Is answered in the vortex of our grave
> The seal's wide spindrift gaze toward paradise.

Crane's final days were spent in Mexico. He had gone there on a grant from the Guggenheim Foundation, with a project to compose a long poem on the Spanish Conquest of Mexico. This historical theme, almost too highly charged with imaginative potential, has more than once proved a trap for poets. What Crane might have made of it we can only conjecture. In fact his Mexican days were a disaster, and, before he committed suicide by drowning on his return voyage, he knew that he had no work on the project to show and in the light of the changed economic situation it was unlikely his grant would be renewed. Nevertheless, some of the last poems, such as "The Idiot" and "Bacardi Spreads the Eagle's Wings," give a compassionate view of the poor and outcast that hints at a grasp of reality previously somewhat wanting in Crane's poetry.

—John Heath-Stubbs

See the essay on *The Bridge.*

CRANE, Stephen

Born: Newark, New Jersey, 1 November 1871. **Education:** Schools in Port Jervis, New York, 1878-83, and Asbury Park, New Jersey, 1883-84; Pennington Seminary, 1885-87; Claverack College, and Hudson River Institute, Claverack, New York, 1888-90; Lafayette College, Easton, Pennsylvania, 1890; Syracuse University, New York, 1891. **Family:** Lived with Cora Taylor from 1897. **Career:** News agency reporter, New York *Tribune,* 1891-92; wrote sketches of New York life for New York *Press,* 1894; traveled in the western U.S. and Mexico, writing for the Bacheller and Johnson Syndicate, 1895; sent by Bacheller to report on the insurrection in Cuba, 1896: shipwrecked on the voyage, 1897; went to Greece to report the Greco-Turkish War for New York *Journal* and *Westminster Gazette,* London, 1897; lived in England after 1897; reported the Spanish-American War in Cuba for the New York *World,* later for the New York *Journal,* 1898. **Died:** 5 June 1900.

PUBLICATIONS

Collections

The Complete Short Stories and Sketches, edited by Thomas A. Gullason. 1963.

The Portable Crane, edited by Joseph Katz. 1969.
Works, edited by Fredson Bowers. 10 vols., 1969-76.
Prose and Poetry (Library of America), edited by J.C. Levenson. 1984.
Stories and Collected Poems. 1997.

Short Stories

The Little Regiment and Other Episodes of the American Civil War. 1896.
The Open Boat and Other Tales of Adventure. 1898.
The Monster and Other Stories. 1899; augmented edition, 1901.
Whilomville Stories. 1900.
Wounds in the Rain: War Stories. 1900.
The Sullivan County Sketches, edited by Melvin Schoberlin. 1949; revised edition, edited by R.W. Stallman, as *Sullivan County Tales and Sketches,* 1968.
The Man Without a Country and Other Tales. 1995.

Novels

Maggie, a Girl of the Streets (A Story of New York). 1893; revised edition, 1896.
The Red Badge of Courage: An Episode of the American Civil War. 1895.
George's Mother. 1896.
The Third Violet. 1897.
Active Service. 1899.
Last Words. 1902.
The O'Ruddy: A Romance, with Robert Barr. 1903.

Play

The Blood of the Martyr. 1940.

Poetry

The Black Riders and Other Lines. 1895.
A Souvenir and a Medley: Seven Poems and a Sketch. 1896.
War Is Kind. 1899.

Other

Great Battles of the War. 1901.
Et Cetera: A Collector's Scrap-Book. 1924.
A Battle in Greece. 1936.
Letters, edited by R.W. Stallman and Lillian Gilkes. 1960.
Uncollected Writings, edited by Olov W. Fryckstedt. 1963.
The War Despatches, edited by R.W. Stallman and E.R. Hagemann. 1964.
The New York City Sketches and Related Pieces, edited by R.W. Stallman and E.R. Hagemann. 1966.
Notebook, edited by Donald J. and Ellen B. Greiner. 1969.
Crane in the West and Mexico, edited by Joseph Katz. 1970.
The Western Writings, edited by Frank Bergon. 1979.
The Correspondence, edited by Stanley Wertheim and Paul Sorrentino. 2 vols., 1988.

*

Bibliography: *Crane: A Critical Bibliography* by R.W. Stallman, 1972; *Crane: An Annotated Bibliography* by John C. Sherwood,

1983; *Crane: An Annotated Bibliography of Secondary Scholarship* by Patrick K. Dooley, 1992; *A Stephen Crane Encyclopedia* by Stanley Wertheim, 1997.

Critical Studies: *Crane: A Study in American Letters* by Thomas Beer, 1923; *Crane,* 1950, and *Crane: The Red Badge of Courage,* 1981, both by John Berryman; "Naturalistic Fiction: 'The Open Boat'" by Richard P. Adams, in *Tulane Studies in English* 4, 1954; *The Poetry of Crane* by Daniel Hoffman, 1957; "Realistic Devices in Crane's 'The Open Boat'" by Charles R. Metzger, in *Midwest Quarterly* 4, 1962; *Crane* by Edwin H. Cady, 1962, revised edition, 1980; *Crane in England,* 1964, and *Crane: From Parody to Realism,* 1966, both by Eric Solomon; "Crane's 'The Bride Comes to Yellow Sky'" by A.M. Tibbets, in *English Journal* 54, 1965; "Interpretation through Language: A Study of the Metaphors in Crane's 'The Open Boat'" by Leedice Kissane, in *Rendezvous* 1, 1966; *Crane: A Biography* by R.W. Stallman, 1968; *The Fiction of Crane,* 1968, and *The Red Badge of Courage: Redefining the Hero,* 1988, both by Donald B. Gibson; *A Reading of Crane* by Marston LaFrance, 1971; *Cylinder of Vision: The Fiction and Journalistic Writing of Crane* by Milne Holton, 1972; *Crane: The Critical Heritage* edited by Richard Weatherford, 1973; *Crane's Artistry* by Frank Bergon, 1975; *Crane and Literary Impressionism* by James Nagel, 1980; *The Anger of Crane: Fiction and the Epic Tradition* by Chester L. Wolford, 1983; *Crane* by James B. Colvert, 1984; "Crane's Vaudeville Marriage: 'The Bride Comes to Yellow Sky'" by Samuel I. Bellman, in *Selected Essays: International Conference on Wit and Humor* edited by Dorothy M. Joiner, 1986; *New Essays on The Red Badge of Courage* edited by Lee Clerk Mitchell, 1986; *Crane* by Bettina L. Knapp, 1987; *Crane* edited by Harold Bloom, 1987; *Crane: A Pioneer in Technique* by H.S.S. Bais, 1988; *The Red Badge of Courage: Redefining the Hero* by Donald B. Gibson, 1988; *The Color of the Sky: A Study of Crane* by David Haliburton, 1989; *Crane: A Study of the Short Fiction* by Chester L. Wolford, 1989; *Critical Essays on Crane* edited by Donald Pizer, 1990; *The Double Life of Crane* by Christopher E.G. Benfey, 1992; *The Virtues of the Vicious Jacob Riis, Stephen Crane, and the Spectacle of the Slum* by Keith Gandal, 1997; *Stephen Crane, Journalism, and the Making of Modern American Literature* by Michael Robertson, 1997; *Badge of Courage: The Life of Stephen Crane* by Linda H. Davis, 1998; *Readings on Stephen Crane* edited by Bonnie Szumski, 1998.

*   *   *

Stephen Crane was a descendant of Methodist ministers and of Revolutionary soldiers. One ancestor was a founder of the city of Newark, New Jersey; a grandfather was a bishop and founder of Syracuse University. His father was a parson, his mother a journalist for religious newspapers. This ancestry of military and civic virtue and literate religious vocation influenced Stephen's responses to experience.

Crane's life was brief; he was dead of tuberculosis before his thirtieth birthday. His career as an author lasted only from 1892 to 1900. Yet he wrote the first naturalistic novel of city life in the United States (*Maggie, a Girl of the Streets*); the greatest novel of the American Civil War, perhaps the best fictional study in English of fear (*The Red Badge of Courage*); and poems that in their avoidance of debilitated Victorian verse conventions seem heralds of the modernist movement (*The Black Riders, War Is Kind*). He wrote incomparable short stories—of shipwreck and survival

("The Open Boat"), of violence in the American west ("The Bride Comes to Yellow Sky," "The Blue Hotel"); a volume of unsentimental local-color stories of a village childhood (*Whilomville Stories*); and a novella ("The Monster") comparable to Ibsen's *An Enemy of the People* in its treatment of alienation and the callousness of society. In addition to these works, he was a prolific journalist whose sketches—of war in the Caribbean and the Balkans, of the underside of New York City life, of travels in the American west and Mexico—are stylistically distinguished and raise journalistic occasions to an imaginative intensity close to that in his fiction. Crane was the doomed boy wonder of American literature.

As varied as his subjects were his fictional modes. Critics still debate whether Crane was an impressionist, a realist, or a naturalist. With little formal education—he dropped out of college after two semesters, during which he played on the baseball team, smoked cigarettes, and wrote the draft of *Maggie*—he was a natural writer who absorbed from the literature around him the then dominant methods of writing and transformed these with imaginative energy into the instrument of his own purposes. At the time he wrote *Maggie,* his only literary acquaintance was the midwestern realist Hamlin Garland. On its appearance, **William Dean Howells** recognized and encouraged the genius of this youth whose work differed so greatly from his own. *The Red Badge of Courage* made Crane famous overnight; he was sent by a newspaper syndicate to cover the Cuban insurrection and the Spanish-American War; later, he reported the war between Greece and Turkey. He went, he said, to test his knowledge in *The Red Badge of Courage.* This novel about a conflict that had ended seven years before Crane's birth had been grounded on his experience on the football field, where "the opposing team is the enemy tribe." After seeing war up close, "*The Red Badge,*" Crane concluded, "is all right." In fact there were other models beside football: Crane had read Zola's *The Downfall* (*La Debacle*) and Tolstoy's *Sebastopol;* he had studied the reminiscences and memoirs in the *Century* series "Battles and Leaders of the Civil War"; he had absorbed and internalized the creed of aesthetic realism held by the war correspondent in Kipling's *The Light That Failed.*

These influences were welded together by a sensibility that found in war the externalization of its obsessive psychological conflicts. There is war everywhere in Crane's work. *Maggie* shows family life in perpetual conflict, the social environment as hostile there as Nature is to the men adrift in "The Open Boat." In "The Blue Hotel," the immigrant Swede, stranded by a blizzard, brings to a frontier outpost the mental image of the violence he expects to find in the west. Crane encapsulated the theme in a brief poem:

A man feared that he might find an assassin;
Another that he might find a victim.
One was more wise than the other.

One of his ironic war tales is titled "The Mystery of Heroism." Crane was possessed by that mystery; he called *The Red Badge of Courage* "a study of fear." His life was such a study, and a conquest of its subject.

He brought to all of his writings a style at once metaphoric, animistic, striated with color, dense with implication. "An artist," he once wrote, "is nothing but a powerful memory that can move itself at will through certain experiences sideways and every artist must be in some things powerless as a dead snake," thus granting his vocation at once freedom from and subjection to necessity.

His influence on later American writers is considerable. His theme of grace under pressure in a masculine world of conflict provided **Ernest Hemingway** with a model, while Crane's metaphoric, ironic style anticipates **Flannery O'Connor**.

As a poet Crane's work was too fragmentary and his career too brief to affect the glib versifiers of the American 1890s, but after 1912, when the imagist movement had begun and the conventions Crane avoided were being defied by the new modernists, he was revived and remembered as a forerunner. His theme is the alienation of man in an uncaring universe. He rebels against the pieties of conventional Christianity, overthrows the rule of its vengeful God, proposes a kinder deity. Certain of his poems, such as "War Is Kind" and "A Man Adrift on a Slim Spar," crystallize the themes of his fiction. This one typifies his parabolic brevity:

> A man said to the universe:
> "Sir, I exist!"
> "However," replied the universe,
> "The fact has not created in me
> A sense of obligation."

Crane's personal life in the decade of his authorship was as vivid as any of his fictions. As a reporter he frequented the Bowery in New York City, seeking subjects for his sketches. He befriended a woman whom he saw being entrapped by police on a charge of soliciting; after testifying in her defense he was run out of town by the police department. On his way to Cuba to sail aboard the gun-running tug whose shipwreck led him to write "The Open Boat," he met in Jacksonville, Florida, the undivorced wife of a son of the British Governor General of India. Cora Taylor was then the madame of a pleasure parlor. She and Crane lived together as man and wife until his death. Cora went with Stephen to the Balkans as the first woman war correspondent. While in England, as tenants of Morton Frewen's manor house, Brede Place, in Surrey, they entertained **Henry James**, Joseph Conrad, H.G. Wells, and other notable writers. The preacher's son Stephen Crane lived in notoriety and scandal. He and Cora were spendthrift, always in need of money. His last two years, while sick and dying, were spent desperately in hack work.

Crane remains the most interesting American writer of the 1890s. His work is of lasting value. What is local and dated in it (his struggle against the dour God of his fire-eating, Evangelistic background) is subsumed in what anticipates the spiritual negation of the war-torn twentieth century: his sense of the world as a juggernaut of impersonal force against which the precious values of the individual life must be precariously maintained by heroic struggle.

—Daniel Hoffman

See the essay on *The Red Badge of Courage.*

CRAWFORD, F(rancis) Marion

Born: Bagni di Lucca, Tuscany, Italy, 2 August 1854; son of the sculptor Thomas Crawford. **Education:** Privately educated in Rome, 1860-66; at St. Paul's School, Concord, New Hampshire, 1866-69; privately in Hatfield Broad Oak, Essex, England, 1870-73; Trinity College, Cambridge, 1873; Technische Hochschule, Karlsruhe, Germany, 1874-76; University of Heidelberg, 1876; University of Rome, 1878. **Family:** Married Elizabeth Berdan in 1884; two daughters and two sons. **Career:** Correspondent, London *Daily Telegraph,* late 1870s; editor, *Indian Herald,* Allahabad, 1879-80; converted to Roman Catholicism, 1880; full-time writer from 1881; lived in Boston, 1881-83, Rome, 1883-84, and Sorrento, Italy, after 1885. **Died:** 9 April 1909.

PUBLICATIONS

Collections

Novels. 30 vols., 1919.

Fiction

Mr. Isaacs: A Tale of Modern India. 1882.
Doctor Claudius: A True Story. 1883.
To Leeward. 1883.
A Roman Singer. 1884.
An American Politician. 1884.
Zoroaster. 1885.
A Tale of a Lonely Parish. 1886.
Saracinesca. 1887.
Marzio's Crucifix. 1887.
Paul Patoff. 1887.
With the Immortals. 1888.
Greifenstein. 1889.
Sant' Ilario. 1889.
A Cigarette-Maker's Romance. 1890.
Khaled: A Tale of Arabia. 1891.
The Witch of Prague. 1891.
The Three Fates. 1892.
Don Orsino. 1892.
The Children of the King. 1893.
Pietro Ghisleri. 1893.
Marion Darche. 1893.
Katharine Lauderdale. 1894.
The Upper Berth (stories). 1894.
Love in Idleness. 1894.
The Ralstons. 1895.
Casa Braccio. 1895.
Taquisara. 1896.
Adam Johnstone's Son. 1896.
A Rose of Yesterday. 1897.
Corleone. 1897.
Via Crucis: A Romance of the Second Crusade. 1899.
In the Palace of the King: A Love Story of Old Madrid. 1900.
Marietta, a Maid of Venice. 1901.
Cecilia: A Story of Modern Rome. 1902.
Man Overboard! 1903.
The Heart of Rome: A Tale of the "Lost Water". 1903.
Whosoever Shall Offend. 1904.
Soprano: A Portrait. 1905; as *Fair Margaret,* 1905.
A Lady of Rome. 1906.
Arethusa. 1907.
The Little City of Hope: A Christmas Story. 1907.
The Primadonna: A Sequel to Soprano. 1908.
The Diva's Ruby: A Sequel to Soprano and Primadonna. 1908.
The White Sister. 1909.

Stradella: An Old Italian Love Tale. 1909.
The Undesirable Governess. 1910.
Uncanny Tales. 1911; as *Wandering Ghosts*, 1911.
For the Blood Is the Life: And Other Stories. 1996.

Plays

Doctor Claudius, with Harry St. Maur, from the novel by Crawford (produced 1897).
Francesca Da Rimini (produced 1902). 1980.
The Ideal Wife, from a work by M. Prage (produced 1912).
The White Sister, with Walter Hackett, from the novel by Crawford. 1937.

Other

Our Silver. 1881.
The Novel: What It Is. 1893.
Constantinople. 1895.
Bar Harbor. 1896.
Ave, Roma Immortalis: Studies from the Chronicles of Rome. 2 vols., 1898; revised edition, 1902.
The Rulers of the South, Sicily, Calabria, Malta. 2 vols., 1900; as *Southern Italy and Sicily,* and *The Rulers of the South,* 1905.
Salve Venetia: Gleanings from Venetian History. 2 vols., 1905; as *Venice, The Place and the People,* 1909.

*

Critical Studies: *My Cousin Crawford* by Maud Howe Elliott, 1934; *Crawford* by John Pilkington, Jr., 1964; *The American 1890s: Life and Times of a Lost Generation* by Lorzer Ziff, 1966; *A Crawford Companion* by John C. Moran, 1981; "The Wandering Ghosts of F. Marion Crawford" by Douglas Robillard, in *American Supernatural Fiction: From Edith Wharton to the Weird Tales Writers,* edited by Douglas Robillard, 1996.

*   *   *

F. Marion Crawford was America's most successful novelist at the end of the nineteenth century. He sometimes published three novels a year, simultaneously in New York and London, and Macmillan paid him $10,000 in advance for each of them in the 1890s. All of his forty-two novels are marred by haste and a kind of contempt for the esthetics of fiction. In *The Novel: What It Is* Crawford argued that the novel is "an intellectual artistic luxury" that had one essential ingredient, "a story or romance," and one purpose—to entertain. Crawford knew exotic and lowly places in many lands. He could tell a story easily and naturally, and his fast-moving romances are not impeded by subtleties or significance. He held to traditional values and opposed social, political, and economic change; he upheld the genteel, moral, and ideal in literature and the chivalric code of honor of Christian gentlemen.

The glamor of "the magnificent Marion Crawford," the "Prince of Sorrento," was a factor in his success. He was born in Rome, son of a New England heiress (the sister of Julia Ward Howe) and the Irish-American expatriate sculptor Thomas Crawford, whose circle Hawthorne pictured in *The Marble Faun* (1860). His mother gave her son an international education, designed for an aristocratic genius: private tutors in Rome, St. Paul's School in New Hampshire (which he hated), and additional schooling in England

and Germany in preparation for brief periods at Cambridge and Heidelberg. He considered himself both a Roman and an American. He was a linguistic genius and reputedly knew 16 languages. His wide travels gave him a "special and accurate knowledge that created a perfect illusion" (Van Wyck Brooks) of such places as Constantinople (where he was married), St. Petersburg, Munich (where he wrote *A Cigarette-Maker's Romance* and *The Witch of Prague* in 1890), of Iceland and India—as well as Paris, London, and Rome. To a wide audience, many of them attaining great wealth and seeking easy sophistication, Crawford seemed the most cosmopolitan of writers: in a letter to **William Dean Howells**, **Henry James** petulantly called Crawford "a six-penny humbug"—and begged Howells not to betray his jealous outburst!

His first novel, *Mr. Isaacs,* is the fictional portrait of an enormously wealthy and powerful Persian diamond merchant Crawford had met two years before when he edited a newspaper in Allahabad. With this novel, which anticipated Rudyard Kipling in its vivid pictures of Indian life, Crawford made himself world famous; Gladstone called it a "literary marvel." Within the same year Crawford published a second semi-biographical novel, *Doctor Claudius:* a Swedish-born Heidelberg Ph.D. inherits an American fortune and marries a Russian countess after saving her inheritance. *A Roman Singer* is based on Crawford's own attempts to become an opera singer. His weakest efforts are the American novels: *An American Politician, Katharine Lauderdale,* and *The Ralstons.* His best are *Saracinesca* and its three sequels, which deal with the Roman social world of his childhood; the others are *Sant' Ilario, Don Orsino,* and *Corleone.* Literary historians exempt these novels from their general condemnation of nineteenth-century melodramatic costume romances and note some other Crawford successes: the English countryside in *A Tale of a Lonely Parish* and the evocation of Phillip II of Spain in *In the Palace of the King.*

—Clarence A. Glasrud

CREELEY, Robert (White)

Born: Arlington, Massachusetts, 21 May 1926. **Education:** Holderness School, Plymouth, New Hampshire; Harvard University, Cambridge, Massachusetts, 1943-44, 1945-47; Black Mountain College, North Carolina, B.A. 1956; University of New Mexico, Albuquerque, M.A. 1960. **Military Service:** Served in the American Field Service in India and Burma, 1944-45. **Family:** Married 1) Ann MacKinnon in 1946 (divorced 1955), two sons and one daughter; 2) Bobbie Louise Hall in 1957 (divorced 1976), three daughters; 3) Penelope Highton in 1977, one son and one daughter. **Career:** Farmer near Littleton, New Hampshire, 1948-51; lived in France, 1951-52, and Mallorca, 1952-53; instructor, Black Mountain College, 1954-55; teacher in a boys' school, Albuquerque, 1956-59, and on a *finca* in Guatemala, 1959-61; visiting lecturer, 1961-62, and visiting professor, 1963-66, 1968-69, 1978-80, University of New Mexico; lecturer, University of British Columbia, Vancouver, 1962-63; visiting professor, 1966-67, professor, 1967-78, Gray Professor of Poetry and Letters, 1978-89; director of poetics program, 1990-91, and beginning 1989 Capen Professor of Poetry and Humanities, and, State University of New York, Buffalo. Visiting professor, San Francisco State College, 1970-71; Bicentennial Chair of American Studies, 1988-89,

Helsinki University; operated the Divers Press, Palma de Mallorca, 1953-55; editor, *Black Mountain Review*, North Carolina, 1954-57; associated with *Wake, Golden Goose, Origin, Fragmente, Vou, Contact, CIV/n,* and *Merlin* magazines in early 1950s, and other magazines subsequently. **Awards:** D.H. Lawrence fellowship, 1960; Levinson prize, 1960, and Blumenthal-Leviton award, 1965, *Poetry* magazine; Guggenheim fellowship, 1964, 1971; Rockefeller grant, 1965; Union League Civic and Arts Foundation prize, *Poetry* magazine, 1967; Shelley Memorial award, 1981; National Endowment for the Arts grant, 1982; DAAD fellowship, 1983, 1987; Leone D'Oro Premio Speciale, 1985; Frost Medal, Poetry Society of America, 1987; State Poet of New York, 1989-91; Distinguished Professor, State University of New York, 1989; Horst Bienek Lyrikpreis, Bavarian Academy of Fine Arts, Munich, 1993; America award in poetry, 1995; Fulbright, University of Auckland, New Zealand, 1995; Lila Wallace/Reader's Digest award, 1996. Honorary degree: University of New Mexico, 1993. **Member:** American Academy; National Institute of Arts and Letters. **Residence:** Waldoboro, Maine.

PUBLICATIONS

Poetry

LeFou. 1952.
The Kind of Act Of. 1953.
The Immoral Proposition. 1953.
A Snarling Garland of Xmas Verses. 1954.
All That Is Lovely in Men. 1955.
Ferrini and Others, with others. 1955.
If You. 1956.
The Whip. 1957.
A Form of Woman. 1959.
For Love: Poems 1950-1960. 1962.
Distance. 1964.
Two Poems. 1964.
Hi There! 1965.
Words. 1965.
About Women. 1966.
Poems 1950-1965. 1966.
For Joel. 1966.
A Sight. 1967.
Words. 1967.
Creeley Reads (with recording). 1967.
The Finger. 1968.
5 Numbers. 1968.
The Charm: Early and Uncollected Poems. 1968.
The Boy. 1968.
Numbers. 1968.
Divisions and Other Early Poems. 1968.
Pieces. 1968.
Hero. 1969.
A Wall. 1969.
Mazatlan: Sea. 1969.
Mary's Fancy. 1970.
In London. 1970.
The Finger: Poems 1966-1969. 1970.
For Betsy and Tom. 1970.
For Benny and Sabina. 1970.
As Now It Would Be Snow. 1970.

America. 1970.
Christmas: May 10, 1970. 1970.
St. Martin's. 1971.
Sea. 1971.
1.2.3.4.5.6.7.8.9.0. 1971.
For the Graduation. 1971.
Change. 1972.
One Day after Another. 1972.
A Day Book (includes prose). 1972.
For My Mother. 1973.
Kitchen. 1973.
His Idea. 1973.
Sitting Here. 1974.
Thirty Things. 1974.
Backwards. 1975.
Away. 1976.
Selected Poems. 1976.
Myself. 1977.
Thanks. 1977.
The Children. 1978.
Hello: A Journal, February 23—May 3, 1976. 1978.
Later. 1978.
Desultory Days. 1978.
Later: New Poems. 1979.
Corn Close. 1980.
The Collected Poems 1945-1975. 1982.
Echoes. 1982.
A Calendar. 1983.
Mirrors. 1983.
Memories. 1984.
A Calendar: Twelve Poems. 1984.
Memory Gardens. 1986.
The Company. 1988.
7 & 6, with Robert Therrien and Michel Butor (photography and poetry). 1988.
It, with Francesco Clemente (pastels and poetry). 1989.
Have a Heart. 1990.
Places. 1990.
Windows. 1990.
Selected Poems. 1991.
A Poetry Anthology. 1992.
Selected Poems. 1993.
Life and Death. 1998.
So There, Poems 1976-1983. 1998.

Play

Listen (produced 1972). 1972.

Fiction

The Gold Diggers. 1954.
The Island. 1963.
Mister Blue. 1964.
The Gold Diggers and Other Stories. 1965.

Other

An American Sense (essay). 1965(?).
Contexts of Poetry. 1968.
A Quick Graph: Collected Notes and Essays. 1970.

A Day Book. 1970.

Notebook. 1972.

A Sense of Measure (essays). 1972.

The Creative. 1973.

Contexts of Poetry: Interviews 1961-1971, edited by Donald Allen. 1973.

Inside Out: Notes on the Autobiographical Mode. 1973.

Presences: A Text for Marisol. 1976.

Mabel: A Story, and Other Prose. 1976.

Was That a Real Poem or Did You Just Make It Up Yourself. 1976.

Was That a Real Poem and Other Essays, edited by Donald Allen. 1979.

The Collected Prose. 1984.

The Collected Essays of Robert Creeley. 1989.

Autobiograpy. 1990.

Charles Olson and Robert Creeley: The Complete Correspondence, edited by George F. Butterick. 5 vols., 1980-83. 1990.

Irving Layton and Robert Creeley: The Complete Correspondence, edited by Ekbert Faas. 1990.

Robert Creeley and the Genius of the American Commonplace: Together with the Poet's Own Autobiography, with Tom Clark. 1993.

Tales Out of School, Selected Interviews. 1993.

Editor, *Mayan Letters,* by Charles Olson. 1953.

Editor, with Donald Allen, *New American Story.* 1965.

Editor, *Selected Writings,* by Charles Olson. 1966.

Editor, with Donald Allen, *The New Writing in the U.S.A.* 1967.

Editor, *Whitman.* 1973.

Editor, *Going On: Selected Poems, 1958-80,* by Joanne Kyger. 1983.

Editor, *Essential Burns.* 1989.

Editor, *Tim Prythero.* 1990.

Editor, *Charles Olson, Selected Poems.* 1993.

*

Bibliography: *Creeley: An Inventory 1945-1970* by Mary Novik, 1973; *A Year by Year Bibliography of Robert Creeley* by Timothy Murray and Stephen Boardway, 1984; *Robert Creeley, Edward Dorn, and Robert Duncan: A Reference Guide* by Willard Fox, III, 1988.

Critical Studies: *Three Essays on Creeley* by Warren Tallman, 1973; *Measures: Creeley's Poetry* by Ann Mandel, 1974; "Creeley Issue" of *Boundary 2,* spring-fall 1978; *Creeley's Poetry: A Critical Introduction* by Cynthia Edelberg, 1978; *Creeley* by Arthur L. Ford, 1978; *The Lost America of Love: Rereading Creeley, Edward Dorn, and Robert Duncan* by Sherman Paul, 1981; *Robert Creeley: The Poet's Workshop* edited by Carroll F. Terrell, 1984; *Robert Creeley's Life and Work: A Sense of Increment* edited by John Wilson, 1986; *Pieces of a Mirror: Robert Creeley's Later Poetry* by Fred Moramarco, 1987; *The Lyric and Modern Poetry: Olsen, Creeley, Bunting* by Brian Conniff, 1988; *Robert Creeley and the Genius of the American Common Place* by Tom Clark, 1993; *Understanding the Black Mountain Poets* by Edward Halsey Foster, 1994.

*   *   *

In his 1967 Berlin lecture, "I'm Given to Write Poems," Robert Creeley acknowledged his indebtedness to **William Carlos Williams** for teaching him the use of an American speech in poetry and for the emotional perception he has achieved, as well as his debt to **Charles Olson** for "the *freedom* I have as a poet." This freedom lies not in the lyric itself, which is tightly restrained from committing verbal excess, but in the flow of the thought, which ranges freely over a complex psychological interior. Creeley's best poems contain remarkable articulation of shades and hues of mood, often achieved by the subtle word play of the discourse. The poems, brief seizures of attention, are a chronicle of his two marriages, in which the self undergoes remorseless scrutiny and analysis. The larger canon of these miniature self-portraits reveals a life of emotional isolation as a man attempts both to possess and submit to women who are repelled by his profound vulnerability.

The early poems, collected in *For Love: Poems 1950-1960,* are intensely formal in their compactness and closure. Many tend toward epigram in their brevity and pithy advice. A typical instance is "The Warning":

> For Love—I would
> split open your head and put
> a candle in
> behind the eyes.
>
> Love is dead in us
> if we forget
> the virtue of an amulet
> and quick surprise.

But the best of the short poems define the self from an oblique but penetrating angle of insight, as in the three couplets of "The End":

> When I know what people think of me
> I am plunged into my loneliness. The grey
>
> hat bought earlier sickens.
> I have no purpose no longer distinguishable.
>
> A feeling like being choked
> enters my throat.

Creeley's marital theme is expressed in the majority of poems in *For Love,* but "The Whip," "A Form of Women," "The Way," "A Marriage," and "Ballad of the Despairing Husband" capture its dilemmas with deep poignancy. Other poems in this large collection depict the female not only as a sexual partner, but as a force or element to sustain male consciousness. "The Door," among the longest and most ambitious of these poems, explores the female in her divine and archetypal aspect.

More recently Creeley has dissolved the formalism of his verse in order to create verse fields in book-length serial compositions, in the manner of Charles Olson and **Robert Duncan.** He has abandoned the structural neatness of his earlier verse, but the more fluid compositions of *Words, Pieces,* and *A Day Book* tend to be lax and to include much trivial detail of his daily life.

In *Later,* as the title suggests, Creeley has made reassessments of his outlook; the style may not have changed, but the attitude is now one of reconciliation with life, with ordinary events, with the nature of experience. His tone here is one of serene resignation to the will of his surroundings, which he surmises with appreciation. More importantly, this and later books make stark contrast between the exaggerations of a mercantile society that sells everything with excessive flair, and these quietly accurate, penetrating descriptions of life simply as it is. As he remarks in "Prayer to Hermes" near the end of *Later*, "Imagination / is the wonder / of the real . . . . " It is his defense against the "cheapshit world of / fake commerce, *buy and sell*," a point made in *Mirrors*, which features some of his most expansive lyrics. *Mirrors*, with its suggestion of a new reflectiveness, comes after his massive *The Collected Poems 1945-1975*, which sums up a corpus of rigorously taciturn poetry.

His prose work follows the themes of his verse. The novel *The Island* deals with his first marriage. Creeley's prose is unique in modern fiction: his use of detail is extraordinarily delicate and precise, producing an uncanny perceptiveness in his narrators. Self-absorption in *The Island* is all the more compelling as the narrator dismantles his own thinking process to inspect the deterioration jealousy causes in him. Although Creeley is a highly provocative writer of prose, his poetry has had a more pervasive influence.

In his criticism *A Quick Graph*, in interviews, collected in *Contexts of Poetry*, and in *Was That a Real Poem and Other Essays*, Creeley has proved an astute chronicler of modern poetry, particularly on the work and influence of Charles Olson, with whom he launched the movement that became known as Black Mountain poetry.

From 1989 to 1991, Creeley was poet laureate of the state of New York. In *Windows*, which was published during this period, Creeley "continues to prod the boundaries of language and expression," according to *Publishers Weekly*. In his signature spare style, the poems function something like "frames" through which Creeley examines his subjects. Ultimately, the *Publishers Weekly* reviewer remarks, the volume reflects Creeley's "concern with the relationship between speech and silence," time and human experience.

Selected Poems was published at the end of Creeley's tenure as poet laureate and offers selections from both his traditional and more experimental verse. The reviewer for *Publishers Weekly* describes the volume as one whose poems "cope with the rush of memories, the chaos of dreams, the sudden flare of feelings," and Creeley himself as a poet "who delights in words and remains true to self." Reviewing the same volume for *Poetry*, William Logan calls Creeley's "terse minimalism . . . unusual in American poetry because his austerity is not religious." For Logan, the volume reveals a personage who is not so much unsympathetic as lacking in sympathy. Consequently, Logan believes that the poems are most convincing as "send-up[s] of his own [thin-lipped] manner." Logan notes that Creeley's often anthologized "I Know a Man" is so successful because of the highly suggestive style that imparts meaning to poem beyond the content of its lines and the "ironic regard [which] exposes the limitations of character." Creeley's poems, Logan writes, "seem dreams of dreams of depression rather than an accommodation with suffering slowly arrived at."

—Paul Christensen, updated by Lisa C. Harper

CREWS, Harry (Eugene)

Born: Alma, Georgia, 6 June 1935. **Education:** University of Florida, B.A. 1960, M.S. Ed. 1962. **Military Service:** Served in the U.S. Marine Corps, 1953-1956; sergeant. **Family:** Married Sally Thornton Ellis, 1960 (divorced), two sons (one deceased). **Career:** Taught English, Broward Junior College, Ft. Lauderdale,

Florida, 1962-1968. Associate professor, 1968-1974, and since 1974 professor of English, University of Florida, Gainesville. **Awards:** American Academy of Arts and Sciences Award, 1972; National Endowment for the Arts grant, 1974. **Residence:** Gainesville, Florida.

PUBLICATIONS

Collections

Florida Frenzy. 1982.
Classic Crews: A Harry Crews Reader. 1993.

Short Stories

The Enthusiast. 1981.
Two. 1984.

Novels

The Gospel Singer. 1968.
Naked in Garden Hills. 1969.
This Thing Don't Lead to Heaven. 1970.
Karate Is a Thing of the Spirit. 1971.
Car. 1972.
The Hawk Is Dying. 1973.
The Gypsy's Curse. 1974.
A Feast of Snakes. 1976.
All We Need of Hell. 1987.
The Knockout Artist. 1988.
Body. 1990.
Scar Lover. 1992.
The Mulching of America. 1995.
Celebration: A Novel. 1998.

Other

A Childhood: The Biography of a Place. 1978.
Blood and Grits. 1979.
Where Does One Go When There's No Place Left to Go? 1998.

*

Bibliography: *Harry Crews: A First Bibliography* by Michael Hargraves, 1981.

Critical Studies: "Matters of Life and Death: The Novels of Harry Crews" by Allen Shepherd in *Critique* vol. 20, no. 1, 1978; *Dictionary of Literary Biography*, vol. VI: *American Novelists Since World War II, Second Series*, 1980; *A Grit's Triumph: Essays on the Works of Harry Crews* edited by David K. Jeffrey, 1983; *Writing in the Southern Tradition: Interviews with Five Contemporary Authors* edited by A.S. Crowder, 1990; "Harry Crews After *A Childhood*" by Frank Shelton in *The Southern Literary Journal* vol. 24, no. 2, 1992; "The Violent Bear It As Best They Can: Social Conflicts in the Novels of Harry Crews" by William M. Teem IV, in *Cultural Conflict in Contemporary Southern Fiction*, edited by Victor A. Kramer, 1994.

*   *   *

Between 1968 and 1998 Harry Crews published twenty-one books, of which fourteen novels and an autobiography are the most noteworthy. His short fiction and essays are interesting principally as they illuminate his other work. He remains one of the most original, prolific, uneven, and compelling of the post-**Styron** generation of Southern writers. In whatever form it is manifest, his vision is powerful and idiosyncratic and does not cater to any conventional moral message, social insight, or economic imperative. Although bemused reviewers, after an exclamatory plot summary, continue to compare him to such diverse notables as Barry Hannah, **Jim Harrison**, **Flannery O'Connor**, and **William Faulkner**, Crews is very much his own man.

The essence of Crews's art is experiential and aesthetic risk-taking: excess is his norm. His fiction is fast, derisive, extraordinarily violent, and often horrifyingly funny—altogether an unsettling combination. Most of his books bear rereading, but the intensity of his characters' resistance to the brutal stringencies of their lives makes an engaged reading of Crews's fiction painful work.

In Crews's fictional world, things relentlessly go wrong, yet self-discipline and craftsmanship do not altogether fail; people suffer and die but struggle to make their lives mean something. The body, however powerful, finally gives out; the spirit, bereft of wholeness, hungers. Religion seldom yields meaning. *The Gospel Singer,* for example, reaches its climax with the title character's lynching. Typically, physical ritual or performance is at last unsatisfying. Thus *Karate Is a Thing of the Spirit* ends with its battered young hero driving an old Volkswagen off to a revived domesticity.

In the widely admired *A Feast of Snakes* Crews delivers an agonizing company of ex-high school football All-Americans, a rattlesnake-handling preacher, and a pack of pit bull dogs mercilessly trained and eagerly waiting to kill each other. The novel's hero finally, mercifully, and perhaps inevitably, goes berserk, killing four people before disappearing into the snake-collecting pit. Only in such violence does he achieve what he has never had: the power to decide, a sense of being at last, however briefly, in control.

After an eleven-year absence from fiction (from 1976 to 1987), Crews returned to it more irascible and less likely than before to worry his way through a complex sentence or thought. *All We Need of Hell* is among his least inspired work; it offers a plot extemporaneously haphazard and characters who rarely aspire above cliché, set down in a notably erratic style. *The Knockout Artist,* however, represents an equally noteworthy recovery. The tale of a glass-jawed hero who knocks himself out for delighted patrons is suited to the dramatization of virtually all of Crews's major thematic concerns.

The protagonist of *Body,* Shereel Dupont (born Dorothy Turnipseed), tries and ultimately fails to pump her way out of an embarrassing, dirt-poor past through body building and supremely willed re-creation. *Scar Lover* offers equal helpings of grim humor and deeply felt charity as it exemplifies the primal Crewsian truth that pain lets you know who you are. Pete Butcher, embroiled in his own dark past and trying desperately to be left alone by the world, finds himself so enmeshed in Sarah Leamer's tragedies that he ultimately has to face his own greatest scar from the past.

Characters from the rural South, shaped by sweat, cruelty, and hardship, continue to be the staples of Crews's recent novels. In *The Mulching of America,* celebrated as one of his best, Hickum Looney, a door-to-door salesman, is the traveler through the grotesque and tragic worlds of a boss, a lover, a bodybuilder, and a chauffeur. At the same time that the vision of the novel comically and incisively opens up the lives of these characters, it also ex-

poses just as sharply the emptiness and depravity of the New South. *Celebration* is another satire in which Too Much, a voluptuous young woman who shares the bed of a one-armed trailer park owner, Stump, attempts to bring redemption, "life where there had only been death," to the worlds of the old folks passively waiting to go to the morgue.

Crews's heroes and heroines have mastered a remarkable variety of athletic activities, including karate, gymnastics, rattlesnake hunting, dog fighting, hawk taming, football (all levels), weight lifting, marathon running, rock climbing, white water canoeing, body building, rodeo performing, bicycle racing, handball, and boxing. The prominence of athletic figures in Crews's novels probably reflects the fact that it is they, more than any other characters drawn from our culture, who epitomize the duality of mind and body at the heart of the human condition.

Crews came from a family of Georgia tenant farmers; their lives, as he describes them in his autobiography, *A Childhood: The Biography of a Place,* were often hard, even nightmarish. The restrictive realities of his early years figure prominently in his fiction; indeed, Crews could almost be a character in one of his novels. As a child, he recalls, he fell into a vat of boiling water, had infantile paralysis, moved practically every year, and believed his uncle was his father. Crews left his birthplace of Alma, Georgia, in 1953 for the U.S. Marine Corps, was discharged as a sergeant in 1956, received B.A. and M.S. Ed. degrees from the University of Florida, and, largely by accident, he says, began teaching English, first at a junior college in Fort Lauderdale in 1962 and more recently at the University of Florida, Gainesville. He has found his largest audience as an *Esquire* columnist and *Playboy* contributor; his periodical essays are collected in *Blood and Grits* and *Florida Frenzy.*

In terms of fictional techniques, Crews is a traditional storyteller, raised in a society of storytelling people. Unlikely as it seems, Crews learned how to fashion a story, discovered what would work on the page, by sedulous analytical study of Graham Greene's fiction. Crews most often writes about present-day, small-town, blue-collar Georgians and Floridians, some of whom have escaped their godforsaken homes, more of whom die trying. In Crews's work, the rural life has few charms. Personal history is what counts, and the afflicted—dwarfs, mutes, giants, the immensely fat, people missing limbs—are numerous. Crews, who himself as a child felt like a freak, creates characters with limited options for self-concealment, men and women who are true by and to nature.

Crews's work is strikingly uneven. The only discernible pattern is radical inconsistency. *A Feast of Snakes* may well be his best novel. Certainly its immediate successor, *A Childhood,* is a highly praised book—fresh, beautifully crafted, and very touching. It is not advisable to read too much of Crews at a single sitting, but his obsessive depth of penetration amply compensates for his characteristic breadth and variety, and probably no other present-day novelist is better suited to make sense of the aberrant, the deviant, the murderous, and the desperate among us.

—Allen Shepherd, updated by Martha Sutro

CROTHERS, Rachel

Born: Bloomington, Illinois, 12 December 1878. **Education:** Illinois State University Normal High School, Bloomington, graduated 1891; New England School of Dramatic Instruction, certificate 1892; Stanhope-Wheatcroft School of Acting, New York, 1897. **Career:** Elocution teacher, Bloomington, 1892-96; teacher, Stanhope-Wheatcroft School, 1897-1901; directed and staged her own plays. Founder, Stage Women's War Relief Fund, 1917; President, Stage Relief Fund, 1932-51; founder and first President, American Theatre Wing, and organized American Theatre Wing for War Relief, 1940. **Awards:** Megrue prize, 1933; Chi Omega award, 1939. **Died:** 5 July 1958.

PUBLICATIONS

Plays

Elizabeth (produced 1899).
Criss-Cross (produced 1899). 1904.
Mrs. John Hobbs (produced 1899).
The Rector (produced 1902). 1905.
Nora (produced 1903).
The Point of View (produced 1904).
The Three of Us (produced 1906). 1916.
The Coming of Mrs. Patrick (produced 1907).
Myself, Bettina (produced 1908).
Kiddie. 1909.
A Man's World (produced 1910). 1915.
He and She (as *The Herfords,* produced 1912; as *He and She,* produced 1920). 1932.
Ourselves (produced 1913).
Young Wisdom (produced 1914). 1913.
The Heart of Paddy Whack (produced 1914). 1925.
Old Lady 31, from the novel by Louise Forsslund (produced 1916). In *Mary the Third . . .*, 1923.
Mother Carey's Chickens, with Kate Douglas Wiggin, from the novel by Wiggin (produced 1917). 1925.
A Little Journey (produced 1918). In *Mary the Third . . .*, 1923.
Once upon a Time (produced 1918). 1925.
39 East (produced 1919). In *Expressing Willie . . .*, 1924.
Everyday (produced 1921). 1930.
Nice People (produced 1921). In *Expressing Willie . . .*, 1924.
Mary the Third (produced 1923). In *Mary the Third . . .*, 1923.
Mary the Third, Old Lady 31, A Little Journey: Three Plays. 1923.
Expressing Willie (produced 1924). In *Expressing Willie . . .*, 1924.
Expressing Willie, Nice People, 39 East: Three Plays. 1924.
Six One-Act Plays (includes *The Importance of Being Clothed, The Importance of Being Nice, The Importance of Being Married, The Importance of Being a Woman, What They Think, Peggy*). 1925.
A Lady's Virtue (produced 1925). 1925.
Venus (produced 1927). 1927.
Let Us Be Gay (produced 1929). 1929.
As Husbands Go (produced 1931). 1931.
Caught Wet (produced 1931). 1932.
When Ladies Meet (produced 1932). 1932.
The Valiant One. 1937.
Susan and God (produced 1937). 1938.

Screenplay: *Splendor,* 1935.

*

Critical Studies: *Crothers* by Lois C. Gottlieb, 1979; *Rachel Crothers: A Research and Production Sourcebook* by Colette Lindroth, 1995.

*   *   *

Rachel Crothers was that rarity, a total woman of the theater. Seldom had such complex personal supervision over an entire theatrical production been seen: she exercised complete control over her plays, which were generally directed, and occasionally even acted in, by her. Most extraordinary was the fact that she was a woman who had such a multileveled theatrical success and over so long a period of time. Altogether, the career of Rachel Crothers was unparalleled.

As a writer, she was a playwright and a playwright only, and the singlemindedness of her literary style also became the singlemindedness of her essential theme, that of woman emerging from the oppressions of society. Her "problem comedies"—which were notable for their witty and natural dialogue—dealt with such themes as career versus marriage (*He and She*), the "liberated" girl of the 1920s (*Nice People*), the generation gap (*Mary the Third*), divorce (*Let Us Be Gay*), adultery (*When Ladies Meet*), and emotional-cum-spiritual restlessness (*Susan and God*).

Crothers was critically and popularly acclaimed as America's foremost woman playwright for more than thirty years. Always concerned with human dignity, Crothers organized war relief committees in both world wars. This patriotism carried into her work, for, in addition to her depiction of her theme of the feminine view of life in many variations, she was a very endemically American playwright. Speaking of her play on love firmly rooted in Yankee soil (*Old Lady 31*), a *New York Times* article compared her to **Booth Tarkington,** saying "Rachel Crothers must be admitted to the small and select group of those who tend to reveal America to the Americans."

In her time she was enormously successful, and perhaps the wholesomeness of her approach and the sound common sense and decency of spirit underlying all her plays (which stand up theatrically because of their timely situations and excellent dialogue) are the essential reasons behind this resounding success. Her interest in the "balanced or everyday life" was epitomized in her work: it is her plea for "sanity in all art," as she herself termed it, that her plays so ably exemplify.

—Zoe Coralnik Kaplan

CULLEN, Countée

Born: Countée Leroy Porter in Louisville, Kentucky, 30 May 1903; adopted by Frederick Asbury Cullen, 1918. **Education:** De Witt Clinton High School, New York, graduated 1922; New York University, 1922-25, B.A. 1925 (Phi Beta Kappa); Harvard University, Cambridge, Massachusetts, A.M. in English 1926. **Family:** Married 1) Yolande Du Bois (daughter of W.E.B. Du Bois) in 1928 (divorced 1930); 2) Ida Mae Roberson in 1940. **Career:** Assistant editor and columnist ("From the Dark Tower"), *Opportunity,* magazine of the National Urban League, 1927; lived in France, 1928-30; French teacher, Frederick Douglass Junior High School, New York, 1934-46. **Awards:** Guggenheim fellowship, 1928. **Died:** 9 January 1946.

PUBLICATIONS

Collections

On These I Stand: An Anthology of the Best Poems of Cullen. 1947.

Poetry

Color. 1925.
Copper Sun. 1927.
The Ballad of the Brown Girl: An Old Ballad Retold. 1927.
The Black Christ and Other Poems. 1929.
The Medea and Some Poems. 1935.
The Lost Zoo (A Rhyme for the Young, but Not Too Young). 1940.

Plays

St. Louis Woman, with Arna Bontemps, from novel *God Sends Sunday* by Bontemps (produced 1946). In *Black Theater,* edited by Lindsay Patterson, 1971.
The Third Fourth of July, with Owen Dodson, in *Theatre Arts,* August 1946.

Fiction

One Way to Heaven. 1932.
My Lives and How I Lost Them (for children). 1942.

Other

Editor, *Caroling Dusk: An Anthology of Verse by Negro Poets.* 1927.

*

Bibliography: *A Bio-Bibliography of Cullen* by Margaret Perry, 1971.

Critical Studies: *Roots of Negro Racial Consciousness: Three Harlem Renaissance Authors* by Stephen H. Bronz, 1964; *Cullen and the Negro Renaissance* by Blanche E. Ferguson, 1966; *In a Minor Chord* (on Cullen, Hurston, and Toomer) by Darwin T. Turner, 1971; *A Many-Colored Coat of Dreams: The Poetry of Cullen* by Houston A. Baker, Jr., 1974; *Cullen* by Alan R. Shucard, 1984; "The Bible and Countee Cullen: Portraying the Outcast and Resolving the Conflict" by Lonnell E. Johnson, in *Mount Olive Review,* spring 1991; "Dual Reality: Echoes of Blake's Tiger in Cullen's *Heritage*" by Ronald E. Sheasby, in *College Language Association Journal,* December 1995, pp. 219-27; "Missing the Boat: Countee Cullen's *The Lost Zoo*" by Gillian Adams, in *Lion and the Unicorn: A Critical Journal of Children's Literature,* January 1997, pp. 40-58; "Countee Cullen: How Teaching Rewrites the Genre of Writer" by Hans Ostrum, in *Genre and Writing: Issues, Arguments, Alternatives* edited by Wendy Bishop and Hans Ostrum, 1997; "Cullen's *Yet Do I Marvel*" by Fred M. Fetrow, in *Explicator,* winter 1998, pp. 103-05.

*   *   *

Countée Cullen, a black American, was a lyricist who found his inspiration among the nineteenth-century romantic poets, es-

pecially Keats. As Cullen himself said in 1928, "good poetry is a lofty thought beautifully expressed" (*St. Louis Argus,* 3 February 1928). Even though Cullen wrote poetry that was racially inspired, he was, first of all, a poet consciously in search of beauty.

Cullen was described frequently as being the least race-conscious among the early modern black poets who achieved fame in the 1920s during the period labeled the Harlem Renaissance. Cullen suffered in his efforts to pay homage to Beauty and his race, and critics were divided about the effect of this conflict of universal vs. black experience (few then, including Cullen, speculated on aesthetic value from a strictly black point of view). When Cullen's first book, *Color,* appeared, one reviewer wrote, "Countee Cullen is a supreme master of Beauty." What a reader of Cullen's poetry must understand, however, is that Cullen was trying to place all of his poetry on the same level of achievement, rather than have his "racial" poetry (e.g., "Heritage," "Shroud of Color") judged by one set of standards and his "non-racial" poetry (e.g., "Wisdom Cometh with the Years," "To John Keats, Poet. At Spring Time") judged upon another, more universal, academic set.

As a black man, Cullen was not insensitive to the genre of music and sound indigenous to black Africa. The influence on Cullen's poetry, in most cases, is extremely subtle. Indeed, there is an interesting combination of black sensuousness and Romantic language in such lines as "Her walk is like the replica / Of some barbaric dance / Wherein the soul of Africa / Is winged with arrogance" ("A Song of Praise"). In his poetry Cullen was consistently absorbed by the themes of love (both its joy and sorrow), beauty, and the evanescence of life as well as racial sorrow and racial problems; and he also revealed a romantic evocation of the African heritage he shared with his fellow poets in Harlem.

In his one novel, *One Way to Heaven,* Cullen displayed deftness at characterization and symbolism. His novel was, in Cullen's words, a "two-toned picture" of the upper and lower classes of blacks in Harlem during the 1920s.

Cullen never achieved the heights many felt he was destined to reach when the reading public was exposed to his famous poem "Heritage" in March 1925. But he may have been restrained by the poignant last lines of this particular poem—"Yet do I marvel at this curious thing / To make a poet black and bid him sing!"

—Margaret Perry

CUMMINGS, E(dward) E(stlin)

Born: Cambridge, Massachusetts, 14 October 1894. **Education:** A private school in Cambridge; Cambridge High and Latin School; Harvard University, Cambridge, 1911-16 (cofounder, Harvard Poetry Society, 1915), A.B. (magna cum laude) in Greek 1915, A.M. 1916. **Military Service:** Served in the Norton-Harjes Ambulance Group, 1917; interned in France, 1917-18; served in the U.S. Army, 1918-19. **Family:** Married 1) Elaine Orr Thayer in 1924 (divorced 1924), one daughter; 2) Anne Barton in 1929 (divorced 1932); 3) Marion Morehouse c. 1934. **Career:** Worked at P.F. Collier and Company, mail order books, New York, 1917; lived in Paris 1921-23; writer, *Vanity Fair,* New York, 1925-27. Artist: paintings included several times in group shows at the Society of Independent Artists, Paris; individual shows include Painters and Sculptors Gallery, New York, 1932; American British Art Center, New York, 1944, 1949; Rochester Memorial Art Gallery, New York,

1945, 1950, 1954, 1957. Charles Eliot Norton Professor of Poetry, Harvard University, 1952-53. **Awards:** Guggenheim fellowship, 1933; Shelley Memorial award, 1945; Academy of American Poets fellowship, 1950; Harriet Monroe Poetry award, 1950; National Book award, 1955; Bollingen prize, 1958; Ford Foundation grant, 1959. **Died:** 3 September 1962.

PUBLICATIONS

Collections

Three Plays and a Ballet, edited by George James Firmage. 1967.
Poems 1905-1962, edited by George James Firmage. 1973.
Complete Poems 1910-1962, edited by George James Firmage. 2 vols., 1981.

Poetry

Tulips and Chimneys. 1923; complete edition, 1937; edited by George James Firmage, 1976.
Puella Mea. 1923.
XLI Poems. 1925.
&. 1925.
Is 5. 1926.
Christmas Tree. 1928.
(No Title). 1930.
VV (Viva: Seventy New Poems). 1931; edited by George James Firmage, 1979.
No Thanks. 1935; edited by George James Firmage, 1978.
1/20 (One Over Twenty). 1936.
Collected Poems. 1938.
50 Poems. 1940.
1 x 1. 1944.
Xaipe. 1950; edited by George James Firmage, 1979.
Poems 1923-1954. 1954.
95 Poems. 1958.
100 Selected Poems. 1959.
Selected Poems 1923-1958. 1960.
73 Poems. 1963.
Etcetera: The Unpublished Poems, edited by George James Firmage and Richard S. Kennedy. 1983.
Hist Whist and Other Poems for Children, edited by George James Firmage. 1983.

Plays

Him (produced 1928). 1927.
Tom: A Ballet. 1935.
Anthropos; or, The Future of Art. 1945.
Santa Claus: A Morality. 1946.

Fiction

The Enormous Room. 1922; edited by George James Firmage, 1978.

Other

CIOPW (drawings and paintings). 1931.
Eimi (travel). 1933.

i: Six Nonlectures. 1953.
A Miscellany, edited by George James Firmage. 1958; revised edition, 1965.
Adventures in Verse, photographs by Marion Morehouse. 1962.
Fairy Tales (for children). 1965.
Selected Letters, edited by F.W. Dupee and George Stade. 1969.
Pound/Cummings: The Correspondence of Ezra Pound and E.E. Cummings, edited by Barry Ahearn. 1996.

Translator, *The Red Front,* by Louis Aragon. 1933.

*

Bibliography: *Cummings: A Bibliography* by George James Firmage, 1960; *Cummings: A Reference Guide* by Guy L. Rotella, 1979.

Critical Studies: *The Magic-Maker: Cummings* by Charles Norman, 1958, revised edition, 1964, 1972; *Cummings: The Art of His Poetry,* 1960, and *Cummings: The Growth of a Writer,* 1964, both by Norman Friedman, and *Cummings: A Collection of Critical Essays* edited by Friedman, 1972; *Cummings and the Critics* edited by S.V. Baum, 1962; *Cummings* by Barry Marks, 1964; *The Poetry and Prose of Cummings* by Robert E. Wegner, 1965; *Cummings* by Eve Triem, 1969; *Cummings: A Remembrance of Miracles* by Bethany K. Dumas, 1974; *Cummings and Ungrammar: A Study of Syntactic Deviance in His Poems* by Irene R. Fairley, 1975; *I Am: A Study of Cummings' Poems* by Gary Lane, 1976; *Cummings: An Introduction to the Poetry* by Rushworth M. Kidder, 1979; *Dreams in the Mirror: A Biography of Cummings* by Richard S. Kennedy, 1980; *Poet and Painter: The Aesthetics of Cummings's Early Work* by Milton A. Cohen, 1987; *E.E. Cummings Revisited* by Richard S. Kennedy, 1994.

*   *   *

Edward Estlin Cummings, better known in lower case as e.e. cummings, is a major poet of the modern period who grew up in a comfortable, liberal household in Cambridge, Massachusetts, where ingenuity was energetically cultivated. The neighborhood of the Irving Street home was populated by Harvard faculty; his father had taught at Harvard before becoming a Unitarian minister of considerable renown in Boston. Cummings's parents had been introduced to each other by the distinguished psychologist and writer **William James**, also a neighbor. Summers were spent on the family farm in New Hampshire, where the young Cummings spent his hours musing in a study his father had built him; another was situated in a tree behind their Cambridge house. Both father and mother encouraged the gifted youth to paint and write and, by their excessive indulgence, perhaps nurtured his diffident character. At Harvard Cummings distinguished himself and graduated with honors in Greek and English studies and delivered a commencement address entitled "The New Art," his survey of Cubism, new music, and the writings of **Gertrude Stein** and **Amy Lowell**, all of which he defended with insight and daring before his proper Bostonian audience. It was an early declaration of Cummings's bold taste and artistic direction.

At Harvard Cummings wrote and published poems in the undergraduate reviews, but most of them were conventional and uninspired, except for a brief collection of poems issued in a privately printed anthology, *Eight Harvard Poets* (1917). After a brief stint of work in a mail-order publishing house, the first and only regular employment in his career, Cummings quit and volunteered for service in the Norton-Harjes Ambulance Group in France. Soon after he and a friend, William Slater Brown, were interrogated by security police regarding Brown's correspondence with a German professor at Columbia University, and both were incarcerated in a French concentration camp. Cummings was freed after three months but only after his father had written to President Wilson requesting special attention to his son's internment. From that experience, Cummings wrote *The Enormous Room,* a World War I classic, at the insistence of his father, who viewed the incident as a sinister act of an ally. The long autobiographical account sparkles with reportorial details, insight, and comic invention and asserts a theme of anti-authoritarianism throughout.

Cummings submitted his first book of poems to Boni, the publisher of *The Enormous Room,* but was refused there and at other houses. The large manuscript, entitled *Tulips and Chimneys,* contained 152 poems ranging from a long, rambling epithalamion and other derivative exercises to short, pithy works of explosive energy and significant innovation. As a last resort Cummings's old classmate John Dos Passos found a publisher for a shortened version of sixty poems in 1923. Two years later forty-one more poems were issued as *XLI,* and Cummings printed the remaining poems with some additions in *&.* In 1937 the original manuscript was issued in its entirety under its first title and came to stand as one of the great classics of Modernist poetry.

For lyric energy, imagination, and verve, few books of poems compare with it. Even Cummings's later books do not have the vigor of this first work. Among the poems in the collection are "All in green went my love riding," "In Just," "O sweet spontaneous," and "Buffalo Bill's / defunct." The work is astounding for its variety of voice, tone, technique, and theme, and the content ranges widely from outrageous satire to jazzy lyrics, from naive rhymes to sexually explicit portraits. Cummings caught the irreverent, slapdash tonality of the jazz age in his sprawling, sensuous lyrics. The old decorums were exploded and replaced by a humor Cummings had absorbed from vaudeville shows, burlesque houses, and music halls of the day.

But there is more to these experiments than we might suspect. The young Cummings was fascinated with the asyntactic language of Stein, the grotesque, paralogical imagery of Amy Lowell, and the dismantled shapes of Cubist paintings, all of which seemed to liberate the artist from traditional logic. The new art made spontaneous perception the basis of expression. This was equally the force of jazz itself: the soloist departed from the melodic pattern to perform his own spontaneous variations according to his mood. Cummings attacked the conventional lyric with the lesson of these other arts. He took the formal lyric apart and redistributed each of its components: punctuation becomes a series of arbitrary signals he sometimes uses even as words. The function of nouns, pronouns, adverbs, and adjectives could all be interchanged in verbal flights. The barrel shape of the standard lyric could simply be blown open, as though the staves had all been unhooped. Language drips, spills, dribbles, runs over the frame in one of

Cummings's Cubist-style poems. The genius in the experiment is that Cummings evolved a series of innovations that seemed to Americanize the European-born lyric poem: in his irreverent care the poem had become a display of verbal energy and exuberance, a vehicle of melting-pot humor and extravagance, a youthfully arrogant jazz variation of an old standard form. The modern lyric has continued to sprawl whimsically down the page ever since Cummings first scattered it in *Tulips and Chimneys.*

Cummings's innovations in other forms and media are less sure and significant, but he is nonetheless a refreshing influence. In the play form he was drawn to over-subtle psychological comedy, as in *Him,* but he was far ahead of his time in his absurdist dialogue and surreal sets and costumes. Cummings was also a prolific graphic artist who worked in most media. Some of this work was published in *CIOPW.* Cummings strained the immediacy of prose with his massive account of a visit to Russia entitled *Eimi,* in which he assails the Marxist state and the regimented condition of Soviet citizens. The book offended the American left at home, which dominated the publishing field during the first years of the depression, and for several years Cummings published little work. A volume entitled *No Thanks,* the title directed at publishers who had rejected the manuscript, appeared in 1935, followed three years later by his first *Collected Poems.*

The many books of poems that succeeded *Tulips and Chimneys* sustained the nervous energy of his first experiments, but Cummings did not advance in new techniques so much as refine and consolidate his discoveries from the first book. As Norman Friedman points out, Cummings experimented with different aspects of his style in the years after 1923. In the 1930s, in *VV* and *No Thanks,* Cummings sought the limits of typographical experiment, extending to the curious strategy known as *tmesis,* or the breaking up and mingling of words to achieve intense immediacy. The dismantled language of his poems focused attention on the individual word and its component letters, and often gave expressiveness to the word through its spatial arrangement. A famous poem of his later years, "l(a," is an arrangement of letters that plummet abruptly down the page, emblematic of a falling leaf and of autumn.

Over the span of his career, Cummings moved slowly away from the simple delight in love, in the seasons, in nature and simplicity, to more urgent and didactic poems that finally came to preach the virtues of naive existence, as in *Xaipe* and *95 Poems.* His argument against science, which he sometimes equated with "death," may have turned him too much against the modern world and toward pastoral themes. As a result, he is a poet of a large canon of work that is marked by much repetition of theme and perspective, but his status as a major poet is secure; one has only to "look" at an anthology of new poems to see his pervasive influence.

—Paul Christensen

See the essay on "Somewhere i have never travelled, gladly beyond."

D

DAHLBERG, Edward

Born: Boston, Massachusetts, 22 July 1900. **Education:** Schools in Kansas City; Jewish Orphan Asylum, Cleveland, 1912-17; University of California, Berkeley, 1922-23; Columbia University, New York, 1923-25, B.S. in philosophy 1925. **Military Service:** Served in the U.S. Army, 1918: private. **Family:** Married 1) Fanya Fass in 1926 (divorced); 2) Winifred Sheehan Moore in 1942, two sons; 3) Rlene LaFleur Howell in 1950; 4) Julia Lawlor in 1967. **Career:** Messenger, Western Union, Cleveland, 1917-18; stockyard drover, Kansas City, 1918; traveled and worked at odd jobs in western United States, 1919-20; lived in Europe, 1926-28; teacher, Boston University, 1947; lecturer, School of General Education, New York University, 1961-62; Cockefair Professor, 1964-65, and Professor of Language and Literature, 1966, University of Missouri, Kansas City; teacher, Columbia University, 1968. **Awards:** Longview Foundation award, 1961; American Academy award, 1961; Rockefeller grant, 1965; Ariadne Foundation award, 1970; Cultural Council Foundation award, 1971. **Member:** American Academy, 1968. **Died:** 27 February 1977.

PUBLICATIONS

Fiction

Bottom Dogs. 1929.
From Flushing to Calvary. 1932.
Kentucky Blue Grass Henry Smith (story). 1932.
Those Who Perish. 1934.
Because I Was Flesh. 1964.
The Olive of Minerva; or, The Comedy of a Cuckold. 1976.
Bottom Dogs, From Flushing to Calvary, Those Who Perish, and Hitherto Unpublished and Uncollected Works. 1976.

Poetry

Cipango's Hinder Door. 1965.

Other

Do These Bones Live. 1941; as *Sing, O Barren,* 1947; revised edition, as *Can These Bones Live,* 1960.
The Flea of Sodom. 1950.
The Sorrows of Priapus. 1957.
Truth Is More Sacred: A Critical Exchange on Modern Literature, with Herbert Read. 1961.
Alms for Oblivion: Essays. 1964.
Reasons of the Heart: Maxims. 1965.
The Dahlberg Reader, edited by Paul Carroll. 1967.
Epitaphs of Our Times: The Letters of Dahlberg. 1967.
The Leafless American, edited by Harold Billings. 1967.
The Carnal Myth: A Search into Classical Sensuality. 1968.
The Confessions of Dahlberg. 1971.

Editor, *The Gold of Ophir: Travels, Myths and Legends in the New World.* 1972.

*

Bibliography: *A Bibliography of Dahlberg* by Harold Billings, 1971.

Critical Studies: *Dahlberg: American Ishmael of Letters* edited by Harold Billings, 1968; *Dahlberg: A Tribute* edited by Jonathan Williams, 1970; *Dahlberg* by Fred Moramarco, 1972; *The Wages of Expectation: A Biography of Dahlberg* by Charles DeFanti, 1978; "Dahlberg's View of Women in Can These Bones Live" by Kyoko Kondo, in *Sophia-English-Studies* 4, 1979; "Because I Was Flesh: Dahlberg and the Rhetoric of American Identity" by Carol Schloss, in *Massachusetts Review: A Quarterly of Literature, the Arts and Public Affairs,* autumn 1981; *Charles Olson and Dahlberg: A Portrait of a Friendship* by John Cech, 1982; "Dahlberg's Kansas City: Two Views" by Robert L. Kindrick, in *Midamerica: The Yearbook of the Society for the Study of Midwestern Literature* 10, 1983; "Dahlberg and Kansas City" by Conger Beasley, Jr., in *New-Letters,* winter 1984-85; "Politics and Rhetoric in the Novel in the 1930s" by William Solomon, in *American Literature: A Journal of Literary History, Criticism, and Bibliography,* December 1996, pp. 799-818.

* * *

Edward Dahlberg was the illegitimate son of a lady barber whose hardships and endurance were to be a central subject in his work. His first book, *Bottom Dogs,* was published with a preface by D.H. Lawrence. Based on his own experience of poverty, it shows the influence of his left-wing politics. His next two novels, *From Flushing to Calvary* and *Those Who Perish,* were reportorial pieces of social realism, the first affected by the hardships of the depression, the second by anti-Nazi sentiments, the result of a trip to Germany. For a while, Dahlberg was associated with the Communist Party, but he abandoned politics for aesthetic reasons. He then entered a long period of silence broken only by occasional works of literary criticism such as *Do These Bones Live* and *Sing, O Barren* that examine the heritage of **Poe**, **Thoreau**, **Melville**, and other writers, as well as the sexlessness of American literature. Dahlberg's years of study and rumination bore fruit in *Because I Was Flesh,* an autobiography in fictional form. The book is a rewriting of *Bottom Dogs,* but the events and characters are related to literary and mythical antecedents. The prose is aphoristic and affects classical and biblical overtones. *Because I Was Flesh* is Dahlberg's most universal book and is already considered a masterpiece of contemporary prose.

In 1965 Dahlberg returned to America after living abroad for many years, mainly in Spain and Ireland. In the last decade of his life he made up for his long silence by publishing an average of a book a year—poems, a collection of aphorisms, essays, fiction, a selection of letters and a literary autobiography entitled *The Confessions of Edward Dahlberg.* Writing in a style reminiscent of Sir Thomas Browne, Dahlberg was a literary Jeremiah, attacking materialism and lamenting the loneliness of human existence. He was also a steadfast foe of modernism, opposed to the work of **William Faulkner**, **Ernest Hemingway**, **Ezra Pound**, **T.S. Eliot**, and Joyce. He felt kinship with **Sherwood Anderson**, **Theodore Dreiser**, and **William Carlos Williams**.

Dahlberg's writing is extremely individualistic, purposefully unfashionable. He thought our age desiccated; he wanted flesh and blood in life as well as literature. He influenced many of his contemporaries but remained an isolated naysayer.

—Frank MacShane

DALE, George E. *See* **ASIMOV, Isaac.**

DALY, Augustin

Born: Plymouth, North Carolina, 20 July 1838; grew up in New York City. **Education:** Local schools. **Family:** Married Mary Dolores Duff in 1869, two sons. **Career:** Worked for house furnishers in mid-1850s; writer, New York *Sunday Courier*, 1859-67; drama critic, New York *Express*, 1864-67, *Sun*, 1866-67, *Citizen*, 1867, and *Times*, 1867-69; professional playwright from 1862; manager for Batemans, Philadelphia, 1863; manager of the Fifth Avenue Theatre, New York, where he established his own company of actors, 1869, until the theatre burned down in 1873; took over the New York Theatre and reopened it as Daly's Broadway Theatre, 1873; also formed the first professional organization of theatrical managers in New York, 1873; managed the Grand Opera House, New York, 1873, and the New Fifth Avenue Theatre, 1873-77; visited Italy and England, 1878-79; returned to New York and converted Wood's Museum into Daly's Theatre, where he assembled a new company of actors and subsequently became internationally known for his productions of Shakespeare: managed the theatre and company, 1879-99; toured London, 1884, 1886, also Germany and Ireland, 1888, 1890, 1891, 1896, 1897, and Paris, 1888, 1891; ran Daly's Theatre, London, 1893-95. **Died:** 7 June 1899.

PUBLICATIONS

Collections

Man and Wife and Other Plays (includes *Divorce, The Big Bonanza, Pique, Needles and Pins*), edited by Catherine Sturtevant. 1942.
Plays (includes *A Flash of Lightning, Horizon, Love on Crutches*), edited by Don B. Wilmeth and Rosemary Cullen. 1984.

Plays

Leah the Forsaken, from a play by S.H. von Mosenthal (produced 1862). 1863.
Taming a Butterfly, with Frank Wood, from a play by Sardou (produced 1864). 1867; revised version as *Delmonico's; or, Lurks up the Hudson* (produced 1871).
Lorlie's Wedding, from a play by C. Birchpfeiffer (produced 1864).
Judith, the Daughter of Merari, with Paul Nicholson (produced 1864).

The Sorceress (produced 1864).
Griffith Gaunt; or, Jealousy, from the novel by Charles Reade (produced 1866). 1867(?).
Hazardous Ground, from a play by Sardou (produced 1867). 1868.
Under the Gaslight; or, Life and Death in These Times (produced 1867). 1867; revised version (produced 1881); in *Hiss the Villain: Six English and American Melodramas*, edited by Michael Booth, 1964.
A Legend of "Norwood"; or, Village Life in New England, with Joseph W. Howard, from the novel *Norwood* by Henry Ward Beecher (produced 1867). 1867.
The Pickwick Papers, from the novel by Dickens (produced 1868).
A Flash of Lightning (produced 1868). 1885; in *Plays*, 1984.
The Red Scarf; or, Scenes in Aroostock (produced 1868).
Fernanda, with Hart Jackson, from a play by Sardou (produced 1870).
The Red Ribbon (produced 1870).
Frou-Frou, from a play by Henri Meilhac and Ludovic Halevy (produced 1870). 1870(?).
Man and Wife, from the novel by Wilkie Collins (produced 1870). 1885; in *Man and Wife and Other Plays*, 1942.
Come Here; or, The Debutante's Test, from a play by F. von Elsholtz (produced 1870).
Divorce, from the novel *He Knew He Was Right* by Trollope (produced 1871). 1884; in *Man and Wife and Other Plays*, 1942.
Horizon (produced 1871). 1885; in *Plays*, 1984.
No Name, from the novel by Wilkie Collins (produced 1871).
Article 47, from a play by Adolphe Belot (produced 1872).
King Carrot, from a play by Sardou, music by Offenbach (produced 1872).
Round the Clock; or, New York by Dark (produced 1872).
Alixe, from a play by Théodore Barrière and A. Règnauld de Prebois (produced 1873).
Roughing It! (produced 1873).
Uncle Sam; or, The Flirtation, from a play by Sardou (produced 1873).
Madelaine Morel, from a play by S.H. von Mosenthal (produced 1873). 1884.
The Parricide, from a play by Adolphe Belot (produced 1873).
Folline, from a play by Sardou (produced 1874).
Monsieur Alphonse, from a play by Dumas fils (produced 1874). 1886.
What Should She Do? or, Jealousy, from a novel by E. About (produced 1874).
The Two Widows, from a play by F. Mallefille (produced 1874).
The Critic, from the play by Sheridan (produced 1874); as *Rehearsing the Tragedy*, (produced 1888). 1889.
Yorick, from a play by M. Tamayo y Baus (produced 1874).
The School for Scandal, from the play by Sheridan (produced 1874). 1891.
The Big Bonanza; or, Riches and Matches, from a play by Gustav von Moser (produced 1875). 1884; in *Man and Wife and Other Plays*, 1942.
Pique (produced 1875; as *Only a Woman*, produced 1882; as *Her Own Enemy*, produced 1884). 1884; in *Man and Wife and Other Plays*, 1942.
Life (produced 1876).
The American, from a play by Dumas fils (produced 1876).
Lemons; or, Wedlock for Seven, from a play by Julius Rosen (produced 1877). 1877.
Blue Grass, from a play by J.B. von Schweitzer (produced 1877).

The Princess Royal, from a play by J. Adenis and J. Rostaing (produced 1877).

Vesta, from a play by D.A. Parodi (produced 1877).

The Dark City! and Its Bright Side, from a play by T. Cogniard and L.F. Nicolaie (produced 1877).

The Assommoir, from a novel by Zola (produced 1879).

Love's Young Dream, from a French play (produced 1879). In *Three Preludes to the Play*, n.d.

An Arabian Night in the Nineteenth Century, from a play by Gustav von Moser (produced 1879). 1884.

Needles and Pins, from a play by Julius Rosen (produced 1880). 1884; in *Man and Wife and Other Plays*, 1942.

The Royal Middy, with Frederick Williams, from an opera by F. Zell, music by R. Genée (produced 1880).

The Way We Live, from a play by A. L'Arronge (produced 1880).

Tiote; or, A Young Girl's Heart, from a translation by Frederick Williams of a play by M. Drach (produced 1880).

Zanina; or, The Rover of Cambaye, from an opera by A. West and F. Zell, music by R. Genée (produced 1880).

Quits; or, A Game of Tit for Tat (produced 1881).

Royal Youth, from a play by Dumas père and fils (produced 1881).

The Passing Regiment, from a play by Gustav von Moser and Franz von Schönthan (produced 1881). 1884.

Odette, from a play by Sardou (produced 1882).

Mankind, from the play by P. Merritt and G. Conquest (produced 1882).

Our English Friend, from a play by Gustav von Moser (produced 1882). 1884.

She Would and She Would Not, from the play by Colley Cibber (produced 1883). 1884.

Serge Panine, from a play by G. Ohnet (produced 1883).

7-20-8; or, Casting the Boomerang, from a play by Franz von Schönthan (produced 1883). 1886.

Dollars and Sense; or, The Heedless Ones, from a play by A. L'Arronge (produced 1883). 1885.

The Country Girl, from Garrick's adaptation of the play *The Country Wife* by Wycherley (produced 1884). 1898.

Red Letter Nights; or, Catching a Croesus, from a play by E. Jacobson (produced 1884).

A Woman Won't, from a play by M. Röttinger (produced 1884).

A Wooden Spoon; or, Perdita's Penates, from a play by Franz von Schönthan (produced 1884).

Love on Crutches, from a play by H. Stobitzer (produced 1884). 1885; in *Plays*, 1984.

A Night Off or, A Page from Balzac, from a play by Franz and P. von Schönthan (produced 1885). 1885.

The Recruiting Officer, from the play by Farquhar (produced 1885). 1885.

Denise, from a play by Dumas fils (produced 1885).

Living for Show, from a German play (produced 1885).

Nancy and Company, from a play by Julius Rosen (produced 1886). 1884.

The Merry Wives of Windsor, from the play by Shakespeare (produced 1886). 1886.

A Wet Blanket, from a play by P. Bilhaud and J. Lévy (produced 1886). In *Three Preludes to the Play*, n.d.

A Sudden Shower, from a play by F. Beissier (produced 1886). In *Three Preludes to the Play*, n.d.

After Business Hours, from a play by Oscar Blumenthal (produced 1886). 1886.

Love in Harness; or, Hints to Hymen, from a play by Albin Valabrègue (produced 1886). 1887.

The Taming of the Shrew, from the play by Shakespeare (produced 1887). 1887.

The Railroad of Love, from a play by Franz von Schönthan and G. Kadelburg (produced 1887). 1887(?).

A Midsummer Night's Dream, from the play by Shakespeare (produced 1888). 1888.

The Lottery of Love, from a play by A. Bisson and A. Mars (produced 1888). 1889.

The Undercurrent (produced 1888).

The Inconstant; or, The Way to Win Him, from the play by Farquhar (produced 1889). 1889.

An International Match, from a play by Franz von Schönthan (produced 1889). 1890.

Samson and Delilah, from a play by A. Bisson and J. Moineaux (produced 1889).

The Golden Widow, from a play by Sardou (produced 1889).

Roger la Honte; or, A Man's Shadow, from the play by R. Buchanan (produced 1889).

The Great Unknown, from a play by Franz von Schönthan and G. Kadelburg (produced 1889). 1890.

As You Like It, from the play by Shakespeare (produced 1889). 1890.

Miss Hoyden's Husband, from the play *A Trip to Scarborough* by Sheridan (produced 1890).

The Last Word, from a play by Franz von Schönthan (produced 1890). 1891.

The Prodigal Son, from a play by M. Carré fils, music by A. Wormser (produced 1891).

Love's Labour's Lost, from a play by Shakespeare (produced 1891). 1891.

A Sister's Sacrfice, in *Werner's Readings and Recitations 4*, edited by Elsie M. Wilbor. 1891.

Love in Tandem, from a play by H. Bocage and C. de Courcy (produced 1892). 1892.

Little Miss Million, from a play by Oscar Blumenthal (produced 1892). 1893.

A Test Case; or, Grass Versus Granite, from a play by Oscar Blumenthal and G. Kadelburg (produced 1892). 1893.

The Hunchback, from the play by Sheridan Knowles (produced 1892). 1893.

The Belle's Stratagem, from the play by Hannah Cowley (produced 1892). 1893.

The Foresters, from the play by Tennyson, music by Arthur Sullivan (produced 1892).

Twelfth Night, from the play by Shakespeare (produced 1893). 1893.

The Wonder. 1893.

The Orient Express, from a play by Oscar Blumenthal and G. Kadelburg (produced 1895).

Two Gentlemen of Verona, from the play by Shakespeare (produced 1895). 1895.

A Bundle of Lies, from a play by K. Laufs and W. Jacoby (produced 1895).

The Transit of Leo, from a play by B. Köhler and Oscar Blumenthal (produced 1895).

The Countess Gucki, from a play by Franz von Schönthan and F. Koppel-Ellfeld (produced 1896). 1895.

Much Ado about Nothing, from the play by Shakespeare (produced 1896). 1897.

The Wonder! A Woman Keeps a Secret, from the play by Susanna Centlivre (produced 1897). In *Two Old Comedies,* 1897.

The Tempest, from the play by Shakespeare (produced 1897). 1897.

Number Nine; or, The Lady of Ostend, with F.C. Burnand, from a play by Oscar Blumenthal and G. Kadelburg (produced 1897).

Cyrano de Bergerac, from a translation by G. Thomas and M.F. Guillemard of a play by Rostand (produced 1898).

The Merchant of Venice, from the play by Shakespeare (produced 1898). 1898.

Other

Woffington: A Tribute to the Actress and the Woman. 1888.

*

Critical Studies: *Memories of Daly's Theatres* by E.A. Dithmar, 1896; *The Life of Daly* by Joseph F. Daly, 1917; *Daly's: The Biography of a Theatre* by D. F. Winslow, 1944; *The Theatre of Daly* by Marvin Felheim, 1956; "Literary Stepchildren: Nineteenth-Century Dramatists" by Brenda Murphy, in *Blacksburg Review* 8, 1986; "Two Vulgar Geniuses: Augustin Daly and David Belasco" by Stanley Kaufman, in *The Yale Review,* summer 1987; "The Face of Fear" by Jeffrey D. Mason, in *Melodrama* edited by James Redmond, 1992; "Shaw's Reviews of Daly's Shakespeare: The Wooing of Ada Rehan" by Russell Jackson, in *Theatre Research International,* autumn 1994, pp. 203-13.

*   *   *

The career of Augustin Daly is particularly difficult to summarize. A man of tremendous energies and almost total dedication to the theatre, he became the most powerful man in American theatre during his lifetime. A drama critic, theatre manager, playwright, and adapter of foreign plays, he was also the manager of a company of actors that successfully performed Shakespearean drama in England and Europe. In the modern sense of the term he was the first stage director in America, and the strict control he exercised over all aspects of a theatrical production, even the lives of his actors, suggests both his tyranny and his devotion.

Theories of modern theatre might strongly object against such training, which gives the actor little room for his own interpretation. The fact that Daly cast actors in roles for which their personalities and appearance suited them is again questionable. Playing the same type of roles, actors lose the ability to transform themselves, to "adopt" a different personality, to improvise.

The two most important trends in late nineteenth-century American drama were an interest in social comedy and realism. Daly contributed to both, while illustrating in his plays that he was living in the age of spectacular melodrama as well as the rise of realism. Both *Divorce* and *Pique* suggest the slowly developing social comedy. *Under the Gaslight* was his first successful melodrama and boasted such realistic scenes as the Blue Room at Delmonico's, the New York pier, and the famous railroad scene in which the heroine switches the train and saves the life of the hero, who is tied to the tracks. His other spectacular melodramas include *A Flash of Lightning,* with its water and fire thrills, and *The Red Scarf,* in which the hero was tied to a log and sent to the saw mill.

After twenty years of activity, in 1880 his theatre became "the polite and refined" theatre that he had always dreamed of, and his comedies had, as reviewers of the time put it, "a polished look." In large measure Daly succeeded because of his strong stock system, and because, flawless or amendable, his was the only "school" of acting at the time.

Daly had the amazing quality to be praised and blamed for the same things: he was an extremely efficient and practical manager but a despotic director, and his vision of theater was not very flexible or open to suggestions. A strong-minded impresario, Daly was primarily interested in giving audiences what they wanted. Because he relied heavily on structure and action, his theatrical productions were "natural" in dialogue and presented that "perfect illusion of reality" that the public seemed to enjoy so much, but they lacked the charm of novelty or the courage of the experiment. Daly's writing, mostly adaptation of novels, was "new" in its attempt to Americanize French and German works. The performance of his original plays pleased, but never surprised audiences. His comedies were tame but successful, and his influence in the realm of theatrical realism was overwhelming.

Although he tried to encourage playwriting, even tried to work with **Mark Twain** and **William Dean Howells**, he was not an innovator. Realism was spectacle to him, not a theory of living and writing. Plays by George Bernard Shaw and Henrik Ibsen were never produced on his stage, and his encouragement to playwrights was always governed by the limitations that he felt the public dictated. As for his own plays, either original or adaptations, there is still some mystery concerning the part that his brother Joseph Daly contributed to their writing. Because he understood the requirements of the theatre he was able to inject the right ingredients into his plays and meet the demands of commercial theatre. But for this same reason he did not contribute markedly to the development of American drama and, in some ways, considering the force of his standing in theatrical circles, was a negative influence. Mainly he was a contriver of effects, a bold and ingenious creator of theatrical magic from his position as a *régisseur.* But in his best commercial successes, in both the manner of production and the material dramatized, he suggested certain truths about society that melodrama may reflect.

—Walter J. Meserve, updated by Dayana Stetco

DANA, Richard Henry, Jr.

Born: Cambridge, Massachusetts, 1 August 1815; son of the writer Richard Henry Dana, Sr. **Education:** Harvard University, Cambridge, Massachusetts, 1831, 1832; sailor on the brig *Pilgrim,* and on the *Alert,* 1834-36; returned to Harvard, 1836, graduated 1837; attended Harvard Law School, 1837-40, and taught elocution at Harvard, 1839-40; admitted to Massachusetts bar, 1840. **Family:** Married Sarah Watson in 1841, six children. **Career:** Lawyer, specializing in maritime cases, Boston, 1840-78; a founder, Free Soil Party, 1848; member of the convention for the revision of the Constitution of Massachusetts, 1853; visited England, 1856 and 1866; U.S. District Attorney for Massachusetts, 1861-66; lecturer, Harvard Law School, 1866-68; member, Massachusetts House of Representatives, and counsel for the United States in the proceedings against Jefferson Davis, 1867-68; candidate for U.S. House of Representatives, 1868; nominated ambassador to England by President Grant, 1876 (appointment not confirmed by the Senate); senior counsel for the United States before the Fisheries Commission at Halifax, 1877; lived in Europe, studying and writing on international law, 1878-82. Overseer, Harvard University, 1865-77. LL.D.: Harvard University, 1866. **Died:** 6 January 1882.

PUBLICATIONS

Prose

Two Years before the Mast: A Personal Narrative of Life at Sea.
    1840; revised edition, 1869; edited by Thomas Philbrick, 1981.
The Seaman's Friend. 1841; as *The Seaman's Manual,* 1841.
To Cuba and Back: A Vacation Voyage. 1859; edited by C. Harvey
    Gardiner, 1966.
Speeches in Stirring Times, and Letters to a Son, edited by Rich-
    ard Henry Dana, 3rd. 1910.
An Autobiographical Sketch (1815-1842), edited by Robert F.
    Metzdorf. 1953.
Journal, edited by Robert F. Lucid. 1968.

Editor, *Lectures on Art and Poems,* by Washington Allston. 2
    vols., 1850.
Editor, *Elements of International Law,* 8th edition, by Henry
    Wheaton. 1866.

*

Bibliography: in *Bibliography of American Literature* by Jacob
Blanck, 1957; *The Parkman Dexter Howe Library: A Descriptive
Catalogue of the Richard Henry Dana, Jr., Collection* by Kevin
B. MacDonnell, 1986.

Critical Studies: *The Seaman's Friend* by R. H. Madison, 1851;
Dana by Samuel Shapiro, 1961; *Dana* by Robert L. Gale, 1969;
"Richard Henry Dana and 'The Only Romantic Spot on the
Coast'" by Karl Keller, in *Seacoast,* January 1981; "Redburn's
Seamanship and Dana's Guide-Book" by R. D. Madison, in
Melville Society Extracts, February 1984; "Richard Henry Dana's
Two Years before the Mast: Autobiography Completing Life" by
James M. Cox, in *The Dialectic of Discovery: Essays on the Teach-
ing and Interpretation of Literature Presented to Lawrence E.
Harvey* edited by John D. Lyons and Nancy J. Vickers, 1984;
"Richard Henry Dana, Jr. and *Two Years before the Mast:* Strate-
gies for Objectifying the Subjective Self" by Bryce Conrad, in *Criti-
cism: A Quarterly for Literature and the Arts,* summer 1987; "'One
of them': The Voyage of Style in Dana's *Two Years before the
Mast*" by Hugh Egan in *American Transcendental Quarterly,* September 1988; "Two Boston Fugitives: Dana and Parkman" by
Daniel Aaron, in *American Literature, Culture, and Ideology: Essays in Memory of Henry Nash Smith* edited by Beverly R.
Voloshin, 1990; *Limited Engagements: The Traveler as Subject and
Social Critic in Nineteenth Century American Literature* (dissertation) by David Henry Elderbrock, 1995.

*   *   *

Richard Henry Dana, Jr., was the author of the best known of
three outstanding nineteenth-century travel books dealing with
what were then largely unexplored sections of the American continent. *Two Years before the Mast* has won a reputation as an adventure story for boys, while the other books, **Francis Parkman**'s
The Oregon Trail and Lewis Hector Garrard's *Wah-to-yah and*

the Taos Trail, survive principally because of their historical, as
well as literary, value. Dana would surely have preferred a similar
fate for his book; its popularity among boys was a reputation he
neither sought nor welcomed.

This popularity is curious, for the book's complex, if precise,
prose might make it seem less accessible than, in particular, *Wah-
to-yah,* characterized as it is by a rather colloquial and flowing
style. Undoubtedly the major reason for the popularity of Dana's
book is its series of high adventures, vividly and objectively described. Parkman and Garrard lived with Indians—but Dana did
that and much more. His realistic narrative deals effectively with
a wide range of adventures that include not only life on shipboard
but also life in what became the American southwest, then a seemingly exotic region known to most Americans only through rumor. *Two Years before the Mast* still makes Dana's adventures seem
exciting and unique, long after the type of customs and way of
life he experienced have vanished.

After the publication of *Two Years before the Mast,* Dana became
a lawyer and was never able to duplicate its success. He published a
travel book based on a trip to Canada and wrote a popular handbook
for sailors, *The Seaman's Friend,* but neither book has literary interest for readers of the late twentieth century.

—Edward Halsey Foster

DANNAY, Frederic. *See* **QUEEN, Ellery.**

DAVIDSON, Donald (Grady)

Born: Campbellsville, Tennessee, 18 August 1893. **Education:**
Branham and Hughes School, Spring Hill, Tennessee, 1905-09;
Vanderbilt University, Nashville, Tennessee, 1910-11, 1914-17,
A.B. 1917, M.A. 1922. **Military Service:** Served in the 324th
Infantry, 81st Division of the U.S. Army, in France, 1917-19: first
lieutenant. **Family:** Married Theresa Sherrer in 1918; one daugh-
ter. **Career:** Teacher at schools in Cedar Hill and Mooresville,
1910-14, and Pulaski, 1916-17, all Tennessee; head of the English
Department, Kentucky Wesleyan College, Owensboro, 1919-20;
instructor, 1920-24, assistant professor, 1924-27, associate professor, 1927-36, professor of English, 1937-64, and Professor
Emeritus from 1964, Vanderbilt University. Teacher, Bread Loaf
School of English, Middlebury College, Vermont, summers 1931-
68. Staff member, 1920, and columnist ("Spyglass") and book page
editor, Nashville *Tennessean,* 1924-30 member of the Fugitive group
of poets: cofounder, *The Fugitive,* Nashville, 1922; advisory board
member, *Modern Age and Intercollegiate Review.* Chairman, Tennessee Federation for Constitutional Government, 1955-59.
Awards: Litt.D.: Cumberland College, 1946; Washington and Lee
University, Lexington, Virginia, 1948. L.H.D.: Middlebury College, 1965. **Died:** 25 April 1968.

PUBLICATIONS

Poetry

Avalon, with *Armageddon* by John Crowe Ransom, and *A Fragment* by William Alexander Percy. 1923.
An Outland Piper. 1924.

The Tall Men. 1927; revised version in *Lee in the Mountains,* 1938.
Lee in the Mountains and Other Poems. 1938.
The Long Street. 1961.
Poems 1922-1961. 1966.

Novel

The Big Ballad Jamboree: A Novel. 1996.

Play

Singin' Billy, music by Charles Faulkner Bryan (produced 1952).

Other

I'll Take My Stand: The South and the Agrarian Tradition, with
    others. 1930.
Who Owns America? A New Declaration of Independence, with
    others, edited by Herbert Agar and Allen Tate. 1936.
*The Attack on Leviathan: Regionalism and Nationalism in the
    United States.* 1938.
American Composition and Rhetoric. 1939; revised edition, with
    Ivar Lou Myhr, 1947, 1953.
The Tennessee. 2 vols., 1946-48.
Twenty Lessons in Reading and Writing Prose. 1955.
Still Rebels, Still Yankees, and Other Essays. 1957.
Southern Writers in the Modern World. 1958.
The Spyglass: Views and Reviews 1924-1930, edited by John Tyree
    Fain. 1963.
Concise American Composition and Rhetoric. 1964.
*It Happened to Them: Character Studies of New Testament Men
    and Women.* 1965.
The Literary Correspondence of Davidson and Allen Tate, edited
    by John Tyree Fain and Thomas Daniel Young. 1974.

Editor, *British Poetry of the Eighteen-Nineties.* 1937.
Editor, with Sidney Erwin Glenn, *Readings for Composition, From
    Prose Models.* 1942; revised edition, 1957.
Editor, *Selected Essays and Other Writings of John Donald Wade.*
    1966.
Editor, with Mary C. Simms Oliphant, *Voltmeier; or, The Moun-
    tain Men,* by William Gilmore Simms. 1969.

*

Critical Studies: *The Fugitive Group,* 1959, and *The Southern
Critics,* 1971, both by Louise Cowan; *The Fugitive Poets* edited
by William Pratt, 1965; *Davidson: An Essay and a Bibliography,*
1965, and *Davidson,* 1971, both by Thomas Daniel Young and
M. Thomas Inge; *The Method of Truth in Metaphysics* by Donald
Davidson, edited by Peter A. French, Theodore E. Uehling, Jr.,
and Howard K. Wettstein, 1977; *Donald Davidson and Allen Tate*
by Thomas Daniel Young, 1984; *Essays on Davidson: Actions and
Events* edited by Bruce Vermazen and Merrill B. Hintikka, 1985;
"Communication and Convention" by Donald Davidson, in *Dia-
logue: An Interdisciplinary Approach* edited by Marcelo Dascal
and Hubert Cuyckens, 1985; "The Fugitives: Ransom, Davidson,
Tate" by Thomas Daniel Young, in *The History of Southern Literature* edited by Louis D. Rubin, Jr., Blyden Jackson, S. Moore
Rayburn, Lewis P. Simpson, and Thomas Daniel Young, 1985;
"Metaphor According to Davidson and de Man" by Samuel C.

Wheeler III, in *Redrawing the Lines: Analytic Philosophy,
Deconstruction, and Literary Theory* edited by Reed W.
Dasenbrock, 1989; *The Unregenerate South: The Agrarian
Thought of John Crowe Ransom, Allen Tate, and Donald Davidson*
by Mark G. Malvasi, 1997.

*   *   *

An original member of the group of poets who published *The Fugitive,* Donald Davidson published some of his first poems in that
journal. From 1924 to 1930 he was literary editor of the Nashville
Tennessean and produced what one critic has called the "best literary
page ever published in the South." He contributed to both agrarian symposia, *I'll Take My Stand* and *Who Owns America?,* and was widely
known and respected as a poet, essayist, editor, historian, and critic.

Davidson's reputation as a poet must stand on *The Tall Men,*
"Lee in the Mountains" (1934), and a half dozen poems from *The
Long Street. The Tall Men,* a book-length narrative, is organized
around a young man's search for a meaningful tradition, a heritage
of heroism and humanism. The exploration of Davidson's protagonist, a modern southern American, is not a vague, nostalgic
meandering into a far distant past. Instead, his excruciating self-
analysis is an attempt "to name and set apart from time / One
sudden face" and to understand his present situation by discovering how he is related to the history and history makers of his
own section of the country. He finally becomes aware not only of
his traditional heritage but of the forces that would destroy it.
"Lee in the Mountains," Davidson's most widely anthologized
poem, presents his art at its best. In its epic dignity, its purity of
form, its dramatic presentation of theme, it demonstrates as no
other poem of his does the totality of his vision and the range of
his imagination. The force and clarity of his presentation in this
and many other of his poems give him a place almost unique among
the poets of his generation. For Davidson, however, prose was
the dominant means of expression throughout his career. As literary critic and social and political philosopher he offered cogent
and convincing arguments in a prose that was lucid, smooth, and
supple. As a prose stylist Davidson has few peers in contemporary American literature.

—Thomas Daniel Young

DAVIS, Rebecca (Blaine) Harding

Born: Washington, Pennsylvania, 24 June 1831; moved with her fam-
ily to Alabama, then to Wheeling, West Virginia. **Family:** Married L.
Clarke Davis in 1863 (died 1904); two sons (including Richard Harding
Davis) and one daughter. **Career:** Professional writer from 1861; lived
in Philadelphia, 1863-1910; member of the editorial staff, New York
Tribune from 1869. **Died:** 29 September 1910.

Publications

Collections

*A Rebecca Harding Davis Reader: Life in the Iron Mills, Selected
    Fictions, and Essays,* edited by Jean Pfaelzer, 1995.
Rebecca Harding Davis: Stories. 1996.

Fiction

Margret Howth: A Story of Today. 1862.
Dallas Galbraith. 1868.
Waiting for the Verdict. 1868.
Kitty's Choice (stories). 1874(?).
John Andross. 1874.
A Law unto Herself. 1878.
Natasqua. 1886.
Kent Hampden (for children). 1892.
Silhouettes of American Life. 1892.
Dr. Warrick's Daughters. 1896.
Frances Waldeaux. 1897.
Life in the Iron Mills; or, The Korl Woman. 1972.

Other

Pro Aris et Focis: A Plea for Our Altars and Hearths. 1870.
Bits of Gossip. 1904.

*

Critical Studies: *The Richard Harding Davis Years: A Biography of a Mother and Son* by Gerald Langford, 1961; afterword by Tillie Olsen to *Life in the Iron Mills,* 1972; "Reading 'Life in the Iron-Mills' Contextually: A Key to Rebecca Harding Davis's Fiction" by Jane Atteridge Rose, in *Conversations: Contemporary Critical Theory and the Teaching of Literature* edited by Charles Moran and Elizabeth F. Penfield, 1990; *Rebecca Harding Davis and American Realism* by Sharon M. Harris, 1991; "The Artist Manque in the Fiction of Rebecca Harding Davis" by Jane Atteridge Rose, in *Writing the Woman Artist: Essays on Poetics, Politics, and Portraiture,* 1991; *Led By a Woman's Hand: Rebecca Harding Davis's Gendered Economics As a Countervoice to Philosophies of Culture and Art* (dissertation) by Michele L. Mock, 1996; *Parlor Radical: Rebecca Harding Davis and the Origins of American Social Realism* by Jean Pfaelzer, 1996.

*   *   *

When Rebecca Harding Davis died in 1910, she was remembered in the New York *Times* obituary primarily as the mother of Richard Harding Davis and secondarily as a novelist who had, in 1861, written a story about the "grinding life of the working people" that was so stern in its realism that "many thought the author must be a man." Nearly eighty years after her death, aside from an occasional mention of that story, "Life in the Iron Mills," in literary histories, her work is almost entirely unknown, although later in the twentieth century feminist critics such as Tillie Olson have sought to reclaim her from obscurity. Davis was not a prolific writer—some dozen works, novels, short stories, and improving essays during a writing career of forty years—and not a particularly good one. Her plots are slipshod, her prose awkward. Her chief gift lies in the creation of character. But having acknowledged her limitations, a critic must recognize her achievement. She lived for her first thirty-two years the proper life of a middle-class spinster in the frontier industrial town of Wheeling, West Virginia, out of touch with literary circles, restricted in her social contacts. Yet she wrought out of this limited life a coherent theory of literary realism that preceded by a quarter of a century the admonition of **William Dean Howells** that fiction ought to be true to the life of actual men and women.

In her first, and most important, novel, *Margret Howth: A Story of Today,* she attacks her readers' preference for "idylls delicately tinted." She wants them instead to "dig into this commonplace, this vulgar American life and see what is in it." She finds "a new and awful significance" in the grim underlife of the industrial city where workers live thwarted lives amidst the "white leprosy of poverty." Her heroine, Margret, has been deserted by her fiancé and has gone to work as a bookkeeper in a woolen mill to support her ill and aging parents. The novel is a romance, and ultimately her fiancé is restored to his senses and her arms, but in the course of the narrative, as in "Life in the Iron Mills," Davis provides a fully realized image of the oppressive noise, stench, and grime of industrial work. In addition, she creates in Margret a new kind of heroine—plain, blunt, occasionally pettish about the sacrifices she is required to make. Margret is the first of a series of Davis heroines who are, as one is described in a later novel, "built for use and not for show."

Davis always wrote about contemporary issues—the Civil War, the problem of the free black, and, in *John Andross* (probably her strongest work), political corruption. Contemporary critics were not kind to her. They found her subjects disagreeable, her prose mawkish, her attitude overly didactic. But one critic, writing in the *Nation* in 1878, acknowledged that despite these flaws she contrived in her "grim and powerful etchings" to evoke the American atmosphere, "its vague excitement, its strife of effort, its varying possibilities." That is a more apt summary of her contribution to American letters than the *Times* obituary.

—Louise Duus

See the essay on *Margret Howth.*

DAVIS, Richard Harding

Born: Philadelphia, Pennsylvania, 18 April 1864; son of Rebecca Harding Davis. **Education:** The Episcopal Academy, Swarthmore, Pennsylvania; Ulrich's Preparatory School, Bethlehem, Pennsylvania; Lehigh University, Bethlehem, 1882-85; Johns Hopkins University, Baltimore, 1885-86. **Family:** Married 1) Cecil Clark in 1899 (divorced 1910); 2) Elizabeth Genevieve McEvoy in 1912, one daughter. **Career:** Journalist from 1886: reporter, Philadelphia *Record,* 1886, *Press,* 1886-89, and New York *Sun,* 1889-90; managing editor, *Harper's Weekly,* New York, 1890-95; correspondent for various newspapers and journals, including *Harper's Monthly, Collier's Weekly,* New York *Sun, Journal,* and *Herald,* London *Times,* and *Daily Mail* from 1890; covered Queen Victoria's Jubilee in London, Spanish War in Cuba, the Greco-Turkish War, Spanish-American War, Boer War, and World War I; most widely known reporter of his generation. **Member:** Fellow, Royal Geographical Society (UK). **Died:** 11 April 1916.

Publications

Collections

From "Gallegher" to "The Deserter": The Best Stories, edited by Roger Burlinghame. 1927.
Richard Harding Davis: Stories. 1994.

Fiction

Gallegher and Other Stories. 1891.
Stories for Boys. 1891.
Van Bibber and Others (stories). 1892.
The Exiles and Other Stories. 1894.
Cinderella and Other Stories. 1896.
Soldiers of Fortune. 1897.
The King's Jackal. 1898.
Episodes in Van Bibber's Life. 1899.
The Lion and the Unicorn. 1899.
In the Fog. 1901.
Ranson's Folly. 1902.
Captain Macklin, His Memoirs. 1902.
The Bar Sinister. 1903.
Real Soldiers of Fortune. 1906.
The Scarlet Car. 1907.
Vera the Medium. 1908.
The White Mice. 1909.
Once upon a Time. 1910.
The Man Who Could Not Lose (stories). 1911.
The Red Cross Girl (stories). 1912.
The Lost Road (stories). 1913.
The Boy Scout (stories). 1914.
Somewhere in France (stories). 1915.
Novels and Stories. 12 vols., 1916.

Plays

The Other Woman (produced 1893).
The Disreputable Mr. Reagan (produced 1895).
The Princess Aline. 1895.
Soldiers of Fortune (produced 1902).
The Taming of Helen (produced 1903).
Ranson's Folly (produced 1904).
The Dictator (produced 1904). In *Farces,* 1906.
The Galloper (produced 1905). In *Farces,* 1906.
Miss Civilization, from a story by James Harvey Smith (produced 1906). 1905.
Farces: The Dictator, The Galloper, Miss Civilization. 1906.
A Yankee Tourist, music by Alfred G. Robyn, lyrics by Wallace Irwin (produced 1907). Music published 1907.
Vera, the Medium (produced 1908).
The Seventh Daughter (produced 1910).
The Consul. 1911.
Blackmail (produced 1913).
Who's Who (produced 1913).
The Trap, with Jules Eckert Goodman (produced 1914).
The Zone Police (produced 1916). 1914.
Peace Manoeuvres (produced 1917). 1914.

Other

The Adventures of My Freshman. 1884.
The West from a Car-Window. 1892.
The Rulers of the Mediterranean. 1894.
Our English Cousins. 1894.
About Paris. 1895.
Three Gringos in Venezuela and Central America. 1896.
Dr. Jameson's Raiders vs. the Johannesburg Reformers. 1897.
Cuba in War Time. 1897.

A Year from a Reporter's Note-Book. 1897; as *A Year from a Correspondent's Note-Book,* 1897.
The Cuban and Porto Rican Campaigns. 1898.
With Both Armies in South Africa. 1900.
The Congo and Coasts of Africa. 1907.
Notes of a War Correspondent. 1910.
With the Allies. 1914.
The New Sing Sing. 1915.
With the French in France and Salonika. 1916.
The Adventures and Letters, edited by Charles Belmont Davis. 1917.

*

Bibliography: *Davis: A Bibliography* by Henry Cole Quinby, 1924; in *Bibliography of American Literature* by Jacob Blanck, 1957; "Davis: A Checklist of Secondary Comment" by Clayton L. Eichelberger and Ann McDonald, in *American Literary Realism 4,* 1971; "Richard Harding Davis's Gallegher: A Bibliographical Note" by Jim Riser, in *American Literary Realism, 1870-1910,* spring 1981.

Critical Studies: *Davis: His Day* by Fairfax D. Downey, 1933; *The Davis Years: A Biography of a Mother and Son* by Gerald Langford, 1961; *Davis* by Scott C. Osborn and Robert L. Phillips, Jr., 1978; "Une Oeuvre fictive de Richard Harding Davis: 'How I Did Not Become a War Correspondent'" by Jean Bernard, in *Annales du Centre de Recherches sur l'Amerique Anglophone* vol. 5 edited by Jean Beranger, Jean Cazemajou, and Pierre Spriet, 1980; "Richard Harding Davis's The Boys in the Adirondacks" by Joseph R. McElrath, Jr., in *American Literary Realism, 1870-1910,* autumn 1981; "Norris's 'Van Bubbles' Story': Bursting the Bubble of the Davis Mystique" by Douglas K. Burgess, in *Frank Norris Studies,* spring 1993, pp. 10-13.

*   *   *

Although the close connection between journalistic and fictional writing in the late nineteenth century in America has never been adequately analyzed, critics have often claimed that Richard Harding Davis failed as a writer of fiction because he excelled as a journalist. Such a judgment may be less than accurate, for Davis incorporated in his fiction the best qualities of his journalism—his quick recognition of the picturesque, his unerring selection of interest-arousing features, his keen eye for external detail, his easy phrasing of remarkably lively impressionistic passages, his youthful appreciation of adventure and movement. These qualities explain his immense contemporary popularity.

But beneath the pace and vivid detail and youthful verve of Davis's fiction, a certain emptiness bothered the serious critics. Journalistic superficiality and haste were blamed. "Smart and shallow," Ludwig Lewisohn briefly intoned in *Expression in America* (1932); and others had said much the same thing. Davis wrote too much too rapidly. He never probed beneath the surfaces. Although clever, he was unconvincing; although satisfying, never profound. At his best he exhibited impressive dramatic power, but too often the drama drifted into theatricality. His stories always charmed, but they were rarely memorable. Those who waited for Davis's exceptional promise to be fulfilled, waited in vain. "Like many handsome and idolized American college men," wrote Francis Hackett in the *New Republic* (2 March 1918), Davis "never quite graduated." Although his fiction excited, it did not confront or deal meaningfully with those issues of humanity that contribute timelessness to a literary work.

Despite the reluctant acknowledgment of serious literary critics, however, and despite their occasional condescending tributes to Davis as the best of the journalistic novelists, his work was not without value in his own time, nor is it in ours. He was the very symbol of achievement for the mass of Americans at the turn of the century, and so serves as an index to a cultural state. Not only was he the visible embodiment of the exuberant life style of the Strenuous Age, but he was also a vocal exponent of ideals that for many readers pointed direction in their dreams. Further, in both his journalistic and his fictional work, he, perhaps better than any other writer, preserved "for all ages," as Thomas Beer noted in *Liberty* (October 1924), "the adventurous, expansionist spirit of the decades that ushered in the twentieth century, the world war, and our own times."

—Clayton L. Eichelberger

De FOREST, John William

Born: Humphreysville (now Seymour), Connecticut, 31 March 1826. **Education:** Local schools. **Family:** Married Harriet Silliman Shepard in 1856 (died 1878); one son. **Career:** Lived in Syria, 1846-48, and in Florence and Paris, 1850-55; writer from 1856; active soldier during the Civil War: recruited and became Captain of Company I, 12th Connecticut Volunteers, 1862-64; Inspector-General, 1st Division, XIX Corps of the U.S. Army; commissioned Major, United States Volunteers, 1865; also wrote descriptions of battle scenes for *Harper's Monthly* during the war; Commanding Captain, Veterans Reserve Corps of Company I, 14th Regiment, Washington, D.C., 1865; commander of a district of the Freedman's Bureau, Greenville, South Carolina, 1866-68; full-time writer, mainly for magazines, New York and New Haven, Connecticut, 1868-81; inactive as writer after 1880s; invalid, in hospital, from 1903. **Award:** A.M. (honorary): Amherst College, Massachusetts, 1859. **Died:** 17 July 1906.

PUBLICATIONS

Fiction

Seacliff; or, The Mystery of the Westervelts. 1859.
Miss Ravenel's Conversion from Secession to Loyalty. 1867; revised edition, 1939.
Overland. 1871.
Kate Beaumont. 1872.
The Wetherel Affair. 1873.
Honest John Vane. 1875.
Playing the Mischief. 1875.
Justine's Lovers. 1878.
Irene the Missionary. 1879.
The Bloody Chasm. 1881; as *The Oddest of Courtships*, 1882.
A Lover's Revolt. 1898.
Witching Times, edited by Alfred Appel, Jr. 1967.

Poetry

The Downing Legends: Stories in Rhyme. 1901.
Poems: Medley and Palestina. 1902.

Other

History of the Indians of Connecticut from the Earliest Known Period to 1850. 1851.
Oriental Acquaintance; or, Letters from Syria. 1856.
European Acquaintance. 1858.
The De Forests of Avesnes (and of New Netherland): A Huguenot Thread in American Colonial History 1494 to the Present Time. 1900.
"The First Time under Fire" of the 12th Regiment, Connecticut Volunteers. 1907.
A Volunteer's Adventures: A Union Captain's Record of the Civil War, edited by James H. Croushore. 1946.
A Union Officer in the Reconstruction, edited by James H. Croushore and David Morris Potter. 1948.

*

Bibliography: in *Bibliography of American Literature* by Jacob Blanck, 1957; "De Forest: A Critical Bibliography of Secondary Comment" by James F. Light, in *American Literary Realism 4*, 1968.

Critical Studies: *Patriotic Gore: Studies in the Literature of the American Civil War* by Edmund Wilson, 1962; *De Forest* by James F. Light, 1965; *The Worthy Gentleman of Democracy: John William De Forest and the American Dream* by Frank Bergmann, 1971; *Critical Essays on De Forest* edited by James W. Gargano, 1981; "The Novelist as Bureaucrat: The Structure of De Forest's *A Union Officer in the Reconstruction*" by William J. McGilel, in *Critical Essays on John William De Forest* edited by James W. Gargano, 1981; "*Miss Ravenel's Conversion*: A Neglected American Novel" by Robert William Antoni, in *The Southern Quarterly: A Journal of the Arts in the South,* spring 1986; "The Novelist as Soldier: Cooke and DeForest" by Eric Solomon, in *American Literary Realism, 1870-1910,* spring 1987; "Genre Wars and the Rhetoric of Manhood in Miss Ravenel's Conversion from Secession to Loyalty" by Thomas H. Fick, in *Nineteenth Century Literature,* March 1992; *Just What War Is: The Civil War Writings of De Forest and Bierce* by Michael W. Schaefer, 1997.

*   *   *

John William De Forest was in his own day a prolific but little-read author. Despite the praise of **William Dean Howells**, nineteenth-century readers, with their love for melodrama and romance, could not accept De Forest's realism. Yet unquestionably De Forest deserves the credit as an innovator that literary critics such as Edmund Wilson and Van Wyck Brooks have accorded him. Three of his novels, *Miss Ravenel's Conversion from Secession to Loyalty, Kate Beaumont,* and *Playing the Mischief,* are particularly fine examples of realistic fiction.

In his first published work, *History of the Indians of Connecticut from the Earliest Known Period to 1850,* he demonstrated the objectivity and the penchant for debunking romantic myths that characterize his fictional style. By the time the Civil War began he had written two novels. *Witching Times* is set during the hysteria of the Salem witch trials. *Seacliff,* a country-house novel with a mystery theme, presents Mrs. Westervelt, the first of his wealthy, bored, neurotic middle-aged women. The story is told from a limited first-person point of view, a technique later perfected by **Henry James**. De Forest also published two travel books, *Oriental Acquaintance* and *European Acquaintance,* during this pre-war period.

The author and his family left Charleston, South Carolina, just before Fort Sumter was fired on. In 1862 the thirty-six-year-old De Forest, a successful author and a family man, became captain of a company of Connecticut volunteers. This Civil War service became the raw material for a series of magazine articles collected and published posthumously under the title *A Volunteer's Adventures,* and for his most famous novel, *Miss Ravenel's Conversion.* His post-war stint in the Freedmen's Bureau gave him local settings for *Kate Beaumont* and *The Bloody Chasm* and the materials for essays in *A Union Officer in the Reconstruction.*

De Forest's descriptions of war are unemotional, graphic and vivid. Perhaps his maturity at the time he had his wartime experience accounts in part for his dispassionate style, but the same objectivity and ironic detachment characterize all his best fiction. Though the fever pitch of the early war years had been lessened by the tragedy of Bull Run, the war was for most Northern readers still the great crusade; the notion that promotions were ruled by political patronage or that generals caused needless deaths through incompetence were unwelcome dashes of cold water. Descriptions of grim field hospitals with amputated limbs and co-agulating blood under the operating table or the dead blackening and bloating in the hot Louisiana sun were too strong for the mass audience.

Howells blamed De Forest's lack of success on the female reader. Certainly it is true that De Forest does not romanticize many female figures in his work. Mrs. La Rue of *Miss Ravenel's Conversion* and Mrs. Chester of *Kate Beaumont* are fading flirts still trying to attract young men. Though Mrs. Chester ultimately goes mad, Mrs. La Rue succeeds in captivating Miss Ravenel's first husband and, after his death, finding another influential lover who helps her to recoup her fortunes lost in the war. Josie Murray of *Playing the Mischief* and Olympia Smiles Vane of *Honest John Vane* manipulate men for material gain with complete success; there may be storm clouds in their futures, but they are secure as the novels end. Even the chaste ingenues like Lily Ravenel and Clara Van Dieman of *Overland* respond passionately to the sexual aspects of the men they marry. The Howells theory has, no doubt, an element of truth in it, but other factors enter in as well.

De Forest suffered as Melville, Hawthorne and others did from the unfavorable conditions of American publishing in their day. With no international copyright protection from European rivals and the high volume of sales needed to turn a profit, one after another of De Forest's publishers went bankrupt. De Forest approached his work with the detachment of a scientist; even when exposing the scandal and malfeasance of the war and the Grant era, his tone is clinical and detached. His post-war work eschews sermonizing and he either lets the scene speak for itself or comments with ironic indirection. This lack of passion and subtlety of point of view may have been too demanding for his readers. Moreover, the author's cynicism may have disturbed some readers. There are no gods in his pantheon. Democracy is failing in his Washington novels; the women's suffrage movement produces humor but no greatness; romantic love is a delusion better buried, as in *A Lover's Revolt,* in more compelling public issues.

Although occasionally De Forest could not resist the lure of popular taste—*Overland* and *The Bloody Chasm* have highly contrived melodramatic plots—at his best he carefully deflates romantic situations. Josie Murray entraps two Congressional lov-

ers, but the man she really admires escapes one romantic embrace after another, coolly appraising the dangers of commitment to an enticing but amoral woman. Nelly Armitage, Kate Beaumont's sister, lured by passion into marriage with a handsome drunkard, is praised for her fortitude in staying with him. She replies, "It is mere hardened callousness and want of feeling. I ceased some time ago to be a woman. I am a species of brute." Captain Colburne, the hero of *Miss Ravenel's Conversion,* is bored during the bombardment of Port Hudson and finds his freed servant is not saintly Uncle Tom, but a pilferer who must be constantly watched. De Forest's last novel, *A Lover's Revolt,* demonstrates the conflict between the romantic plot elements he knew the mass audience wanted and the realistic passages he wrote so successfully. The book contains the required love story, but the author's prime concern is the military situation in Boston of 1775-76; the love triangle is mechanically and scantily disposed of.

De Forest wrote many fine stories and novels in the years immediately following the war, and he explored new ground with almost every effort, but his books did not sell. He hoped to leave a standard edition of his work as a "little monument," but no publisher would agree to the venture. Finally this accomplished writer gave up in discouragement; he wrote little during the last two decades of his life.

—Barbara M. Perkins

DELAND, Margaret

Born: Margaretta Wade Campbell, near Allegheny, Pennsylvania, 23 February 1857; orphaned: raised by her aunt and uncle in Manchester, Pennsylvania. **Education:** Local schools, and at Pelham Priory, New Rochelle, New York, 1873-75; studied art and design at Cooper Union, New York, 1875-76. **Family:** Married Lorin F. Deland in 1880 (died 1917). **Career:** Assistant instructor of Drawing and Design, Normal College of the City of New York (later Hunter College), 1876-80; lived in Boston from 1880; with her husband created a hostel, in their home, for unmarried mothers, 1880-84; full-time writer from 1886. **Awards:** Honorary degrees: Rutgers University, New Brunswick, New Jersey, 1917; Tufts College, Medford, Massachusetts, 1920; Bates College, Lewiston, Maine, 1920; Bowdoin College, Brunswick, Maine, 1931. **Member:** American Academy, 1926. **Died:** 13 January 1945.

PUBLICATIONS

Fiction

John Ward, Preacher. 1888.
A Summer Day. 1889.
Sidney. 1890.
The Story of a Child. 1892.
Mr. Tommy Dove and Other Stories. 1893.
Philip and His Wife. 1894.
The Wisdom of Fools. 1897.
Old Chester Tales. 1898.
Good for the Soul. 1899.
Dr. Lavendar's People. 1903.

The Awakening of Helena Richie. 1906.
An Encore. 1907.
R.J.'s Mother and Some Other People. 1908.
The Way to Peace. 1910.
The Iron Woman. 1911.
The Voice. 1912.
Partners. 1913.
The Hands of Esau. 1914.
Around Old Chester. 1915.
The Rising Tide. 1916.
The Promises of Alice. 1919.
An Old Chester Secret. 1920.
The Vehement Flame. 1922.
New Friends in Old Chester. 1924.
The Kays. 1926.
Captain Archer's Daughter. 1932.
Old Chester Days. 1937.

Play

Screenplay: *Smouldering Fires,* with others, 1925.

Poetry

The Old Garden and Other Verses. 1886.

Other

Florida Days. 1889.
The Common Way. 1904.
Small Things. 1919.
If This Be I, As I Suppose It Be (autobiography). 1935.
Golden Yesterdays (autobiography). 1941.

*

Critical Studies: "Breaking the Silent Partnership: Business-women in Popular Fiction" by Susan Albertine, in *American Literature: A Journal of Literary History, Criticism, and Bibliography,* June 1990; in *Ripples of Dissent: Women's Stories of Marriage in the 1890s* edited by Bridget Bennett, 1996.

*   *   *

In 1888 Margaret Deland, who had previously written only one book of poetry, *The Old Garden and Other Verses,* published a novel, *John Ward, Preacher.* A complex, thesis-ridden saga of Puritan zealotry gone rigid and perverse, the book became an infamous best-seller and made its author a celebrity. John Ward, an unreconstructed Calvinist, is married to an Episcopalian woman who, as Percy H. Boynton has written (in *America in Contemporary Fiction*), "is so devoted to her husband that she can ignore his bigotry if only he will permit her to. He believes, however, that the salvation of her soul is more imperative than the survival of his home, sends her away, breaks down under the strain, and dies."

In the years that followed the publication of *John Ward,* Deland moved from the infamous and realistic to the conventional and placid. Her Old Chester pieces—many of which were collected in *Old Chester Tales* and *Dr. Lavendar's People*—for which she is best remembered, told of life in the turn-of-the-century village.

Old Chester, a fictionalized Manchester, the small Pennsylvania town in which Deland had spent a part of her childhood, was not drawn with the cynicism of **Sinclair Lewis**'s Gopher Prairie or the grotesquery of **Sherwood Anderson**'s Winesburg or even with the zeal of Deland's own *John Ward.* Hers, rather, was an image of small-town Americana both peaceful and homiletic.

Reminiscences of her earlier realism were signaled now and again in Old Chester, however. In *The Awakening of Helena Richie,* for instance, the protagonist comes to the village to escape the drunkenness of her husband and her own adulterous past, only to be revealed by Dr. Lavendar and subsequently shown the path of penitence. And in a sequel, *The Iron Woman,* the awakened Helena leads the next generation away from the realistically portrayed pitfalls of adultery and divorce.

Born before the Civil War, Deland was a sometimes outspoken defender of marriage, family, and community. But by the time of her death in 1945, one could scarcely imagine that so benign a spokesperson had ever been thought provocative. Indeed, the very virtues that she had stood for seemed to be in disarray.

—Bruce A. Lohof

DELANY, Martin Robinson

Born: Charles Town, Virginia (now Charleston, West Virginia), 6 May 1812. **Family:** Married Kate A. Richards in 1843. **Career:** Editor of *Mystery,* a black newspaper in Pittsburgh, 1847; coedited the *North Star* newspaper with Frederick Douglass, 1847-48; studied medicine with local physicians in Pittsburgh, 1848-49; entered Harvard medical school in 1850, but was not allowed to continue enrollment due to student protest; established medical practice in Pittsburgh, 1851; originated and presided over a National Emigration Convention, 1854; moved with his family to Chatham, Canada West (now Ontario), along with a large population of African Americans, after the passage of the Fugitive Slave Act, 1856; led expedition to the Niger Valley in Africa to explore the possibility of African American emigration, 1859-61; recruiter for the Union Army's black military units, 1863-65; commissioned as major in the U.S. Army (the first African American to gain this rank), 1865; assigned to the army's Freedman's Bureau in South Carolina; served as a member of the State Executive Committee of South Carolina and as a lt. colonel in the South Carolina State Militia, 1868-73; appointed customs inspector of Charleston, South Carolina, 1873; appointed trial judge for the third ward of Charleston, 1874; ran unsuccessfully for Lt. Governor of South Carolina, 1874; tried on charge of breach of trust, pardoned and re-appointed as judge, but subsequently lost office, 1876; became treasurer of the Liberian Exodus Joint Stock Steamship Company, 1878-84, to explore emigration plans; campaigner for Republican candidate John Desendorf. **Died:** 24 January 1885.

PUBLICATIONS

Novels

Blake; or the Huts of America (serialized in *Anglo-African* and *Weekly Anglo-African,* 1859-1862). 1970.

Prose

*The Condition, Elevation, Emigration, and Destiny of the Colored
    People of the United States, Politically Considered.* 1852.
The Origins and Objects of Ancient Freemasonry. 1853.
"Political Destiny of the Colored Race on the American Conti-
    nent," in *Proceedings of the National Emigration Convention of
    Colored People Held at Cleveland, Ohio the 24th, 25th, and 26th
    of August, 1854.* 1854.
Official Report of the Niger Valley Exploring Party. 1861.
University Pamphlets: A Series of Four Tracts on National Polity.
    1870.
Principia of Ethnology. 1879.

*

Bibliography: *William Wells Brown and Martin R. Delany: A Reference Guide* by Curtis W. Ellison and E.W. Metcalf, Jr., 1978.

Critical Studies: *Life and Public Services of Martin R. Delany*
by Frank A. Rollin (Frances A. Rollin Whipper), 1868, reprinted
in *Two Biographies by African-American Women* edited by William L. Andrews, 1991; *Martin R. Delany: The Beginnings of Black
Nationalism* by Victor Ulman, 1971; *Violence in the Black Imagination* by Ronald Takaki, 1973; *The African Dream: Martin R.
Delany and the Emergence of Pan-African Thought* by Cyril W.
Griffith, 1975; *To Wake the Nations: Race in the Making of American Literature* by Eric J. Sundquist, 1993.

*   *   *

Acknowledged as the founder of African American nationalism
in the United States, Martin Robinson Delany led a varied career
as a reporter and editor for black newspapers, a medical doctor, a
novelist, a judge, a politician, and the first black major in the U.S.
Army. Although at one time best known as coeditor of the *North
Star* with American abolitionist **Frederick Douglass**, Delany is
an important historical figure in his own right who developed strong
ideological viewpoints in all of his writings. He is also the author
of *Blake; or The Huts of America,* an early African American novel,
which, although it never appeared in book form in Delany's lifetime, has been of lasting interest to scholars and readers.

Martin Delany was born in Charles Town, Virginia, to Pati
Delany, a free woman, and Samuel Delany, a slave. Delany learned
to read from a white man, in violation of a 1819 law that forbade
black children from being educated; in 1822, as a result, Pati Davis
had to flee with her children to Chambersburg, Pennsylvania, to
avoid imprisonment. Samuel Delany was able to purchase his freedom and join his family a year later.

As a young man, Martin Delany moved to Pittsburgh to continue his education and begin studying medicine under a local doctor. During his years in Pittsburgh, Delany became politically active, eventually becoming editor of the *Mystery,* an early black
newspaper. When supporting this newspaper proved to be a financial hardship, he closed it and became coeditor of the *North
Star* with Frederick Douglass. The newspaper was published in
Rochester, New York, but Delany remained stationed in Pittsburgh
as a correspondent and agent. The partnership did not last long,
however; Delany's more radical stances clashed with Douglass's
views, leading Douglass to announce in 1849 that Delany was no
longer associated with the paper.

In 1852, after briefly attending medical school at Harvard but
having been denied readmittance due to protests by white students, Delany wrote *The Condition, Elevation, Emigration, and
Destiny of the Colored People of the United States, Politically Considered.* In this polemical work, Delany took a position in stark
contrast to Douglass's integrationist views. Delany claimed that
"the colored people are not yet known, even to their most professed friends among the white Americans; for the reason that politicians, religionists, colonializationists, and abolitionists, have each
and all, at different times, presumed to think for, dictate to, and
know better what suited colored people, than they knew for themselves." He doubted that white America would ever sufficiently
recognize black America, or that black Americans, lacking the numbers, organization, and wealth of white Americans, could ever force
their acceptance as equals. He advocated, therefore, the establishment of an African American state in Central America that would
use economic means to undermine American slavery. *Condition*
was widely reviewed by the abolitionist press, but was not warmly
accepted. William Lloyd Garrison's *Liberator* and *Frederick
Douglass's Paper,* for instance, both found virtues in the book but
disagreed with its conclusions. Nonetheless, the work is frequently
cited as the beginning of the black emigrationist movement that
Marcus Garvey was to advance in the early twentieth century.

Delany's second work, however, was largely ignored at the time
of its publication, and has not received much attention since. In
this history of black freemasonry called *The Origins and Objects
of Ancient Freemasonry: Its Introduction into the United States
and Legitimacy among Colored Men* (1853), Delany tried to prove
that freemasonry began in ancient Egypt and Ethiopia as a means
of improving government. To exclude blacks from freemasonry,
Delany argued, was to deny blacks their rightful African heritage,
one that could help elevate blacks from the downtrodden and enslaved conditions under which many lived.

In August of 1854, Delany led a National Emigration Conven-
tion in Cleveland, where he delivered an important nationalist
speech, "Political Destiny of the Colored Race on the American
Continent." In this paper, he attacked the efforts of the American
Colonization Society to colonize Liberia with freedmen from the
U.S. Instead, he urged emigration to Central America, with the
purpose of establishing an independent, self-governing, pan-
Africanist nation.

Although the exact dates of composition are not entirely clear,
Delany began working on his only novel, *Blake; or the Huts of
America,* sometime in 1852 or 1853—probably in reaction to
Harriet Beecher Stowe's *Uncle Tom's Cabin*—and continued
working on it at least until 1859, when it began to be serialized in
the *Anglo-African* magazine. Only part of it was to appear that
year, however. The entire novel was not printed until serialized
again in 1861 and 1862 in the *Weekly Anglo-African* magazine, and
was not printed in book form until 1970. *Blake,* which was written to dramatize Delany's political positions, focuses on organized
resistance to slavery by blacks. However, as Floyd Miller notes
in his introduction to the modern reprint of the novel, *Blake* can
be viewed as both the accumulation and culmination of Delany's
pre-Civil War thinking about slavery, since the meandering plot
touches on a variety of his perspectives on the topic.

The main character of *Blake* is Henricus Blacus, usually called
Henry Blake, a West Indian black who is kidnaped into slavery,
after which he marries Maggie, a slave woman who is the daughter of her owner, Colonel Stephen Franks. When Maggie is sold
to a Northern judge who takes her down to Cuba, Blake vows to

get her back. He escapes from slavery, and travels throughout the South, observing slavery and trying to plant the seeds for an eventual slave revolt. After returning to the Franks plantation, Blake escapes again with a number of other slaves to Canada.

Part II of the novel traces Blake's rise to a position of leadership in a black rebel army in Cuba. Blake sails down to Cuba as a servant and helps Maggie buy her freedom. Afterwards, he ships out with a slave-trading vessel (appropriately named the *Vulture*) to Africa, planning to organize the enslaved Africans on the return trip and seize the ship. Although the plot is eventually attempted, it fizzles out for reasons that are never made clear. Nonetheless, Blake is able to spread the story that these slaves attempted a revolt. As a result, there are few bidders when they are brought to auction, and most of the slaves are sold to agents of abolitionists who plan to set them free. Blake's role in this episode helps get him appointed general to an army that is forming to fight for Cuban independence and freedom for black slaves. As the novel ends, the troops are still gathering to plan strategy, and the outcome of the rebellion is never detailed.

It becomes obvious in *Blake* that Delany is committed to the prospect of violence in attaining black freedom. Nonetheless, the book remains notably circumspect about portraying blacks committing violence. The revolution that Blake hopes to incite through his travels in the South never occurs; the on-ship rebellion begun by enslaved Africans on board the *Vulture* ends vaguely; and the revolution headed by Blake is still in the planning stage when the novel ends, although the novel strongly implies that battle is inevitable. It is quite possible that Blake wanted to raise the prospect of a slave revolt as a warning to the South, but transposed the conflict to Cuba, where the smaller scale and the nationalist sentiment for Cuban independence from Spain facilitated the fictional depiction of a slave uprising. It is also likely that while Delany intended to present the possibility of a violent black insurrection, he wanted to avoid some of the criticism that might have resulted from a direct depiction of such an event. Nonetheless, Delany's *Blake* is a thorough statement of a radical, anti-slavery militancy that was rare for its time.

From 1859 to 1861, Delany traveled with Robert Campbell to the Niger Valley in Africa to explore the possibility of establishing a settlement of black Americans there. When he returned, he published his *Official Report of the Niger Valley Exploring Party* in 1861, an account of his journey and intentions, to publicize the emigration project. Although the *Report* brought Delany a great deal of exposure, his plans for an emigration project were interrupted by the Civil War. By 1863 he had become a recruiter for black soldiers to fight in the Union Army, and in 1865, he was commissioned as a Major in the U.S. Army and assigned to the Freedman's Bureau in Beaufort, South Carolina, a Union stronghold in the South. After the war, he continued to be active in politics, serving posts within the Republican party, running unsuccessfully for lieutenant governor of South Carolina, and serving twice as a trial judge in Charleston, South Carolina.

Delany's last literary effort, *The Principia of Ethnology: The Origin of Races and Color with an Archeological Compendium of Ethiopian and Egyptian Civilization,* was published in 1879. Appearing at a time when the theory of African origins of ancient civilization had fallen into disfavor among Euro-American scholars, Delany's work was meant as a correction. Not only did Delany point out that Ancient Egyptian and Ethiopian civilizations were far more advanced than their European counterparts, he also asserted the superiority of pure-blooded Africans over those descended from mixed races. Regardless of the scientific merit of Delany's biological arguments, there can be no denying the value of his attempt to counter the widespread contemporary pseudo-scientific theories on the inferiority of blacks.

Although Delany's first major polemical text, *The Condition, Elevation, Emigration, and Destiny of the Colored People of the United States, Politically Considered,* was for many years considered his most important work, scholarship on black nationalist themes in literature led to a revival of interest in *Blake* in the late 1960s. An extended discussion of *Blake* by Eric Sundquist in his 1993 work *To Wake the Nations* has also drawn attention to this early African American novel. Because all of his works were clearly polemical, Delany is seldom considered primarily as a literary artist. Instead, he is recognized as an early and powerful voice for the African American nationalist and pan-Africanist movements.

—Thomas Cassidy

DELANY, Samuel R(ay Jr.)

Pseudonym: K. Leslie Steiner. **Born:** New York City, 1 April 1942. **Education:** Dalton Elementary, a private school in Manhattan, 1947-1956; Bronx High School of Science, 1956-1960; City College (now the City University of New York), 1960, 1962-63. **Family:** Married the poet Marilyn Hacker in 1961 (separated 1975; divorced 1980); one daughter. **Career:** Earned living as folk singer and guitarist in Greenwich Village coffee houses and nightclubs in the 1960s; worked as an actor, teacher, reviewer, freelance writer, 1960-64; hitchhiked from New York to Texas Gulf Coast to work on shrimp boats, June 1965; visited Europe, Greece, Turkey, and England and worked as troubadour, July 1965-summer 1966; returned to New York, lived in Heavenly Breakfast commune, played with Heavenly Breakfast rock band, 1967; moved to San Francisco, 1969-70; returned to New York City, 1970; filmmaker and editor for the short films *Tiresias,* 1970, and *The Orchard,* 1971; wrote two comic book scripts for *Wonder Woman,* 1972; Visiting Butler Professor of English, State University of New York at Buffalo, 1975; senior fellow at the Center for Twentieth Century Studies, University of Wisconsin-Milwaukee, 1977; senior fellow at the Society for the Humanities, Cornell University, 1987; professor of comparative literature, University of Massachusetts—Amherst, 1988—; fellow, Institute for Humanities, University of Michigan, spring 1993. Coeditor, with Marilyn Hacker, *Quark,* 1970-71; served on editorial board, *The Little Magazine,* 1981-86. **Awards:** Breadloaf Writers Conference Fellowship, 1960; Science Fiction Writers of America, Nebula awards for best novel, 1966 and 1967, for best short story, 1967, and for best novelette, 1969; Hugo award, best short story, 1970; American Book Award nomination, 1980; Science Fiction Research Association Pilgrim award for Excellence in Science Fiction Criticism, 1985; James Whitehead Memorial award for Lifetime of Excellence for Gay and Lesbian Literature, 1993. **Residence:** New York City.

PUBLICATIONS

Collections

The Ballad of Beta-2 [and] Empire Star. 1975.

Short Fiction

Driftglass: Ten Tales of Speculative Fiction. 1971.
Distant Stars. 1981.

Novels

The Jewels of Aptor, abridged edition bound with *Second Ending* by James White. 1962; hardcover edition, 1968.
Captives of the Flame, bound with *Psionic Menace* by Keith Woodcott. 1963; revised edition published under original title *Out of the Dead City,* 1968.
The Towers of Toron, bound with *The Lunar Eye* by Robert Moore Williams. 1964; 1968.
City of a Thousand Suns. 1965.
The Ballad of Beta-2, bound with *Alpha Yes, Terra No!* by Emil Petaja. 1965.
Empire Star, bound with *The Tree Lord of Imeten* by Tom Purdom. 1966.
Babel-17. 1966.
The Einstein Intersection (slightly abridged edition). 1967; complete edition, 1972.
Nova. 1968.
The Fall of the Towers (trilogy). 1970.
The Tides of Lust. 1973.
Dhalgren. 1975.
Triton. 1976.
Empire: A Visual Novel, illustrations by Howard V. Chaykin. 1978.
"Return to Neveryon" series:
   Tales of Neveryon. 1979.
   Neveryona; or The Tale of Signs and Cities. 1983.
   Flight from Neveryon. 1985.
   The Bridge of Lost Desire. 1987; as *Return to Neveryon,* 1994..
Stars in My Pocket Like Grains of Sand. 1984.
The Star Pit, bound with *Tango Charlie* and *Foxtrot Romeo* by John Varley. 1989.
They Fly at Ciron. 1993.
Equinox. 1994.
The Mad Man. 1994.
Atlantis: Three Tales. 1995.
Trouble on Triton: An Ambiguous Heterotopia. 1996.
Hogg. 1996.

Plays

Radio Play: *The Star Pit* (adapted from Delany's short story), 1972.

Other

The Jewel-Hinged Jaw: Notes on the Language of Science Fiction (criticism). 1977.
The American Shore: Meditations on a Tale of Science Fiction by Thomas M. Disch— "Angouleme." 1978.
Heavenly Breakfast: An Essay on the Winter of Love. 1979.
Starboard Wine: More Notes on the Language of Science Fiction (essays). 1984.
Wagner/Artaud (critical monograph). 1988.
The Motion of Light on Water: Sex and Science Fiction Writing in the East Village, 1957-1965. 1988.
The Straits of Messina (essays; originally published in magazines under pseudonym, K. Leslie Steiner). 1989.

Silent Interviews: On Languages, Sex, Science Fiction, and Some Comics. 1994.
Longer Views: Extended Essays. 1996.
Bread and Wine: An Erotic Tale of New York City: An Autobiographical Account. 1998.
Times Square Red, Times Square Blue. 1999.

Editor, *Nebula Awards Thirteen.* 1980.

*

Bibliography: *Samuel R. Delany: A Primary and Secondary Bibliography, 1962-1979* by Michale W. Peplow and Robert S. Bravard, 1980; "Through a Glass Darkly: Bibliographing Samuel R. Delany" and "Samuel R. Delany: A Selective Primary and Secondary Bibliography, 1979-1983" both by Robert S. Brevard and Michale W. Peplow in *Black American Literature Forum,* summer 1984.

Critical Studies: *Samuel R. Delany* by Jane Weedman, 1982; *Conscientious Sorcerers: The Black Postmodernist Ficton of LeRoi Jones/Amiri Baraka, Ishmael Reed, and Samuel R. Delany* by Robert Elliot Fox, 1987; *Ash of Stars: On the Writing of Samuel R. Delany,* edited by James Sallis, 1996.

*   *   *

Born in Harlem to Samuel R. Delany Sr. and Margaret Carey Boyd Delany, writer, editor, critic, and teacher Samuel R. "Chip" Delany Jr. survived a privileged yet problematic childhood to become one of the most widely celebrated and highly acclaimed authors of science fiction and fantasy literature. In addition, Delany was also the first successful African-American to write in this genre. A brilliant, if rebellious and precocious youngster, Delany was the product of a financially-stable black middle-class upbringing. His father, a North Carolina migrant to New York, owned Levy and Delany, a Seventh Avenue Harlem funeral home. His mother, a native of the Bronx, worked as a library clerk and was a licensed funeral director. A large extended family gathered yearly for family picnics at Hopewell Junction, New York, and for several years, Delany attended Camp Woodland, a private summer camp.

Educated outside of Harlem at private, prestigious, and progressive Dalton Elementary, the young Delany was the product of both an African American community and the upper-class white world of New York's Manhattan. In a letter to Peplow and Bravard excerpted in the introduction to their bibliography, Delany described his life between ages five through thirteen as a "ballistic trip through a socio-psychological barrier." At Dalton, he was well accepted by his classmates and peers, and Delany's teachers found him intelligent, talented, imaginative, and independent, if undisciplined; verbally creative, if unable to spell or read at grade level. As advanced as Dalton was, teachers at the school did not recognize Delany's dyslexia and recommended he take remedial work and obtain counseling to help him learn discipline. This same rebelliousness contributed to a tension at home between Delany and his father. At twelve, the racial, social, and cultural boundaries that Delany constantly negotiated, coupled to an advanced sexual precociousness, led him to record in a notebook erotic sexual fantasies that went unattended by the psychiatrist his mother took him to for therapy. These were, he reported in the extended memoir, *The Motion of Light and Water,* "rather grandiose, homoerotic, full of kings and warriors, leather armor, slaves, swords, and brocade, mixing the inflated language and the power fantasies of Robert E. Howard (*Conan the Conqueror*) and **Frank Yerby** (*The Saracen Blade*)."

Sometimes called a child prodigy, other times a "wunderkind," at an early age Delany had demonstrated a commitment to both music and literature. He learned to play the violin and the guitar and became very interested in folk music; his interest in literature was fed from a variety of different cultural sources including selections from Greek and Roman mythology and the tales about King Arthur's Round Table as well as the stories and novels of black American authors such as **Paul Laurence Dunbar, Langston Hughes, Chester Himes,** and **Amiri Baraka,** and those of science fiction authors Arthur C. Clark, Theodore Sturgeon, and **Robert Heinlein.** He began to write fiction, and to be published, while enrolled in summer camp in 1955. His first science fiction story, a tale based on a dream, was published the next summer. In 1956, following his graduation from Dalton, and through the intervention of his uncle, Judge Hubert Delany, and his father, Delany was allowed to enroll in Bronx High School for Science. It was here he met Marilyn Hacker, herself a child prodigy and a poet. Despite differences in ethnic backgrounds—she was Jewish, he was black—they married in 1961. The Bronx high school provided a very stimulating environment for the young Delany. He did well in his majors, math and physics; he began another journal; and he wrote several stories that earned both recognition and awards. His personal life, however, had become more difficult. Arguments with his father caused Delany to run away from home; he also began missing classes. Then, in 1959, his father contracted lung cancer; he died the following year. But 1960 was also the year Delany graduated from high school, had an essay accepted by a national journal, and won a fellowship to the Breadloaf Writer's Conference in Vermont.

Delany emerged as a science fiction writer of extraordinary ability and imagination with the publication of *The Jewels of Aptor* in 1962; he was nineteen at the time. He worked hard and lived fast; the strain produced acute anxiety which made Delany believe that the subway would kill him or that he should commit suicide. He was hospitalized and treated. Throughout the 1960s Delany cut the exotic bohemian artist figure. A folk singer and musician in Greenwich Village, he hitchhiked to Texas to work on shrimp boats in June of 1965; the next month, he flew to Europe with a friend and stayed, visited Greece and Turkey, wrote fiction, and earned some money as a wandering troubadour for a little more than a year. On the way back to the United States, he stopped in England and with several English science fiction authors, including Michael Moorcock, editor of *New World,* who encouraged Delany to revise *The Fall of the Towers* for British publication. Between 1963 through 1967 Delany penned seven science fiction novels and published four short stories. Of the novels, *Babel-17* and *Einstein Intersection* won Nebula awards in 1967 and 1968 respectively. *Einstein* was also nominated for a Hugo. Delany's shorter fiction in this period, "The Star Pit," "Aye, and Gomorrah...," "Driftglass," and "Corona," also brought him critical success and awards.

In Delany's fiction from the mid-sixties through 1973, his characters, the themes, and sometimes the setting of his novels or stories were extrapolated from stories told by friends he and Marilyn Hacker met or they reflected his dreams; the stories also sprang from his own diverse experiences as itinerant musician and artist observing, working, and living among a constantly shifting mosaic of people and being exposed to some of the more earthy experiences of urban life. Typically, his heroes are poet or artist figures, outcasts, or criminals; authentic sexual relations are embedded in his texts; his female characters are as heroic and as fully drawn as his male protagonists; his protagonists are frequently black or nonwhite; often they may be physically scarred or psychologically wounded. Delany interwove many of the conventions typically connected to the genre with more aesthetic issues. Thus, standard science fiction elements—starships, aliens, life on other worlds, intergalactic war, epic struggles to save planets, technology abused or gone awry, and adaptive changes to human beings—are merged with a study of power relationships, slavery and freedom, racism and oppression, language and language systems, frank reconfigurations and dramatizations of sexuality, and new mythologies sprung from the ruins of decayed civilizations.

Nova (1968), nominated for both the Hugo and Nebula awards, is a stirring science fiction adventure saga which features a race to obtain a rare element from an exploding star, but it would prove to be the last of Delany's conventional science fiction. For an interview in *Callaloo* (spring 1991), Delany noted that during the 1960s when "New Wave" science fiction was emerging, he had remained a thematically "conservative SF writer," maintaining an interest in "space opera and hardware" while writers identified with the New Wave were spurning such an emphasis.

In 1973 Delany published *The Tides of Lust,* a pornographic novel; in 1975 came *Dhalgren,* and in 1976, *Triton. Dhalgren,* nominated for a Nebula in 1975, is a huge dystopian novel examining a chaotic, violent, oppressive "near future" earth. It has a sprawling plot, all manner of sexual relationships, and a wandering poet, called Kid, as the hero who records and helps to right the problems of the community. *Triton,* nominated for a Nebula in 1976, features an almost totally unsympathetic, insensitive figure for a protagonist and explores very fluid, very explicit, racial and sexual relationships.

Delany was one of a very few science fiction writers to explore diversity in human sexuality through his fiction. Lust, desire, love, sex as commodity, and varying forms of sexual orientation or sexual drives are all present, as is his concern for language or variations on narrative form. By taking his science fiction and fantasy in this direction Delany noted in the *Callaloo* interview that "what I am doing in almost all my books is the genre equivalent of 'gender bending.' That's how all genres expand, progress, survive. It's a paradox that when the results look most revolutionary, that's when the writer is attending most to the tradition." His "Neveryon" series of the 1980s is, as Michael Morrison declared in a review in *Washington Post Book World* (January 31, 1988), a sword-and-sorcery fantasy that "constructs self-conscious metafictions about social and sexual behavior, the play of language and power, and ... the possibilities and limitations of narrative." Morrison considered the last book in the series, *The Bridge of Lost Desire* (1987), "eminently readable and gorgeously entertaining." Delany viewed the function of the series as a way "to articulate for adults the hidden and subterranean currents that are forever at play in the largely infantile genre of sword and sorcery; to make explicit ... the sadomasochistic and homoerotic elements without which Conan the Conqueror would never have survived."

Distant Stars (1981) is an illustrated collection of several Delany novellas and short stories. *Stars in My Pocket Like Grains of Sand* (1984), set in the far future, was to have been the first in a diptych of novels; the concluding novel remains in progress. *They Fly at Ciron* (1993) developed from a short story Delany wrote in 1962, being substantially revised and expanded for the novel form.

In 1980, Delany and Marilyn Hacker were divorced. They had maintained the most open and flexible of marriages and remained friendly, sharing child care responsibilities after the divorce was final. Feeling a need to provide a more stable environment for child rearing, Delany accepted a position as the Visiting Butler Chair of English at the State University of New York at Buffalo. His pace as a novelist and short story writer slackened, and he began to devote more time to nonfiction and critical texts. In 1978-79 he published *The Jewel Hinged Jaw, Starboard Wine, The American Shore,* and *Heavenly Breakfast,* a slim memoir of his youth while living in a commune in Greenwich Village. His *The Motion of Light in Water: Sex and Science Fiction Writing in the East Village, 1957-1965* further expanded the boundaries of autobiographical revelation. In 1988, after completing the "Neveryon" series, Delany became professor of comparative literature at the University of Massachusetts—Amherst and has devoted most of his energy to teaching.

—Sandra Y. Govan

DeLILLO, Don

Born: New York City, 20 November 1936. **Education:** Cardinal Hayes High School, 1954; Fordham University, 1958. **Family:** Married Barbara Bennett, 1975. **Career:** Ad writer for Ogilvy & Mather ad agency, 1959-64; supported himself as a hack writer while working on his early novels, 1964-79; lived in Greece on Guggenheim grant while researching and writing *The Names,* 1979-82. **Awards:** Guggenheim fellowship, 1979; American Academy and Institute of Arts and Letters award in Literature, 1984; American Book award and nomination for National Book Critics Circle award, both for *White Noise,* 1986; *Irish Times*-Aer Lingus International Fiction prize and nominations for the American Book award and the National Book Critics Circle award, all for *Libra,* 1989; PEN/Faulkner award for *Mao II,* 1992.

PUBLICATIONS

Novels

Americana. 1971.
End Zone. 1972.
Great Jones Street. 1973.
Ratner's Star. 1976.
Players. 1977.
Running Dog. 1978.
Amazons. 1980.
The Names. 1982.
White Noise. 1985.
Libra. 1988.
Mao II. 1991.
Underworld. 1997.

Plays

The Engineer of Moonlight. 1979.
The Day Room (produced 1986). 1987.
The Rapture of the Athlete Assumed into Heaven (produced 1990).
Valparaiso (produced 1999). 1999.

*

Bibliography: by James Dean Young, in *Critique,* 1978; by Paula Bryant, in *Bulletin of Bibliography,* September 1988.

Critical Studies: *In the Loop: Don DeLillo and the Systems Novel* by Tom LeClair, 1987; *South Atlantic Quarterly* special issue on Don DeLillo, 1990; *Introducing Don DeLillo* edited by Frank Lentricchia, 1991, and *New Essays on White Noise* edited by Lentricchia; *Don DeLillo* by Douglas Keesey, 1993; *Nobody's Home: Speech, Self, and Place in American Fiction from Hawthorne to DeLillo* by Arnold Weinstein, 1993; *American Literary Naturalism and Its Twentieth-Century Transformations: Frank Norris, Ernest Hemingway, Don DeLillo* by Paul Civello, 1994; *Conspiracy and Paranoia in Contemporary American Fiction: The Works of Don DeLillo and Joseph McElroy* by Steffen Hantke, 1994; *Static Beauty: The Retreats of Don DeLillo* by Andrew Roe, 1996; *Postmodern Culture at Risk: Late Capitalism in the Works of Cherrie Moraga, Don DeLillo, and Manuel Puig,* 1999.

*   *   *

Don DeLillo has written ten novels that have put him in the front rank of contemporary American writers, a status recognized in the several awards he received in the 1980s. Although his first seven novels were generally well reviewed, DeLillo did not have a big novel, one that would establish him on college reading lists and in the paperback market, until *White Noise* (1985), which earned him an American Book Award. This success was followed by *Libra* (1989), a fictionalized account of U.S. President John F. Kennedy's assassination, which won him more award nominations. DeLillo's solid place in American letters was acknowledged in a special issue of *South Atlantic Quarterly* in 1990 that subjected his work to analysis by highbrow cultural critics.

The title of DeLillo's first novel, *Americana* (1971), describes well the themes and preoccupations of his fiction as a whole. *Americana* launched DeLillo's career in a reliable format for the beginning writer: a first-person spiritual odyssey, a sort of survey of the landscape in which areas are outlined that will be colored in later. The protagonist, David Bell, makes his pilgrimage west from Maine in a car, since "cars are religious now and this is a religious trip." With Bell are several companions given implausible but resonant names and best described as comic fantastics: a hitchhiker named Kyrie Eleison and a fat young man, Leonard Zajac, known as the Young Man Carbuncular. These comic-book creations, absurd but always wildly funny, recur in various reincarnations throughout the next seven novels and often take up the slack left by thin plots.

DeLillo's second novel, *End Zone* (1972), focused on two of America's most intense obsessions: college football and scenarios for nuclear war. The protagonist is a talented halfback, Gary Harkness, who has come to tiny Logos College in West Texas after botched starts at Syracuse and Penn State. Gary hangs out with some entertaining eccentrics while not on the field, but his real interest is his long dialogues about nuclear apocalypse with Major Staley of ROTC. Despite the emotional succor he gets from Myna Corbett, a classmate in Mexican geography who keeps her weight at 165 pounds to avoid "the responsibility of being beautiful," Gary's control over his world wastes away until the story ends with his being fed through tubes while confined to an infirmary bed.

The first two novels are distinguished by their sparkling language (DeLillo has himself described language as "a subject as well as an instrument") and characters who, although freakish and scruffy, are bright and ingratiating. In *Great Jones Street* (1973), the language keeps pace but the characters—a rock star named Bucky Wunderlick and an assortment of drug dealers and urban refuse—fail to engage the reader; what happens to them cannot matter much.

DeLillo's fourth novel, *Ratner's Star* (1976), is a long, fantastic excursion often in the spirit of Book Three of Swift's *Gulliver's Travels*. The fourteen-year-old genius Billy Twillig, winner of the first Nobel Prize in Mathematics, is summoned to the Center for the Refinement of Ideational Structures, a Connecticut think tank, to decode the message in a mysterious radio signal coming from a planet orbiting Ratner's star. The loony characters exceed even DeLillo's best previous efforts: an obstetrician named Hoy Hing Toy, who once concluded a delivery by polishing off the placenta in "five huge gulps"; a mad Honduran financier; a gnome; and finally, a young woman named Thorkild, who will not allow Billy to see her naked because she has no lap. The two parts of *Ratner's Star* recall Lewis Carroll's *Alice's Adventures in Wonderland* (1865) and *Through the Looking-Glass* (1871). This fantastic romp displays DeLillo's grasp of mathematical logic in a way that would have pleased Carroll (pseudonym of the English mathematician Charles Lutwidge Dodgson), and the verbal intricacy and high jinks are some of DeLillo's best. Perhaps most significant is the further development of the basic DeLillo protagonist: the young man who goes to ground to escape menace from a dangerous world. That is what Billy Twillig does in the final pages—runs for a foxhole when his reading of events convinces him the end is near.

In *Players* (1977) there is hardly a likable character to be found. The major "players," Lyle and Pammy, are mere puppets who get caught in a terrorist plot and a failed marriage. Only the reliable DeLillo language carries *Players* through to the end. *Running Dog* (1978) parades DeLillo's most repellent characters so far, but the intricate plot elements—the search for a home movie shot in Hitler's bunker during his last hours; hanky panky between a CIA rogue, Glenn Selvy, and a crusading senator; the goings-on among pornography dealers—are woven together complexly. Along with the terrorists of *Players,* the shady characters in *Running Dog* elicit the same kind of fascination as creatures found under a rotting log. And in both novels the protagonist goes to ground: Lyle in his role as go-between for the terrorists and the FBI, and Selvy in his retreat to a remote Texas training ground for covert agents, where he seeks to escape from a porn dealer's hit men.

In many ways DeLillo's most intellectually challenging novel is *The Names* (1982). Set during the Iran hostage crisis in 1980, the story is narrated by James Axton, an American working in Athens, who seeks to puzzle out the mystery of a strange alphabet cult. The cult's mission is the murder of people whose initials match those of the village in which they live. The cult murders demonstrate "how far men will go to satisfy a pattern, or find a pattern, or fit together the elements of a pattern." *The Names* is rich in other forms of word play: brief etymological lectures, nicely shaped narrative ornaments formed from proper names, a decorative mishmash of notes on epigraphy, and much more.

White Noise (1985) was the big success that DeLillo needed to establish his reputation. Cultural critics fastened on the toxic cloud that menaces the college town in which events take place, as well as on the cornucopia represented by the supermarket, to draw grim morals about life under capitalism. The familiar comic creations return, especially in the character of Murray Jay Siskind, who reads *American Transvestite* and confesses an urge to hire a

prostitute on whom to perform the Heimlich maneuver. Jack Gladney is the history professor hero, whose wife, Babette, has been secretly taking an experimental drug, Dylar, to calm her fear of death. Noise is everywhere—in the supermarket, in the background hum of technology, and especially in that little murmur in the back of our minds that keeps reminding us we are going to die.

In *Libra* (1989) many of the elements of the earlier works come together in an imaginative recreation of President Kennedy's assassination—the paranoid right wing, the American obsession with guns and violence, the conspiracy theories, and that archetypal figure of both American life and DeLillo's novels, the alienated loner who broods too much and often buckles under stress. *Libra* (the title comes from Lee Harvey Oswald's astrological sign) is a brilliantly conceived but dark vision of America.

The title of DeLillo's tenth novel, *Mao II,* derives from the pop artist Andy Warhol's *Mao* series of the early 1970s. The novel returns to terrorism for its theme, as a reclusive novelist, Bill Gray, is lured to Beirut in a futile attempt to effect the release of a political hostage. *Mao II* pleases in its opening set piece, a Moonie mass wedding of 6,500 couples in Yankee Stadium, but struggles to maintain a plot. A disquisition on the parallels between terrorists and novelists picks up a little speed, especially in the terrorist philosopher's insistence on the need for authority, for the absolutist who will help societies struggling to rehabilitate themselves.

After the high accomplishment of *White Noise* and *Libra, Mao II* mostly disappointed, but DeLillo regained a lot of ground with *Underworld,* which in its 827 pages made the traditional "loose, baggy monster" novel look close knit. But no matter—nobody reads DeLillo for Aristotelian beginnings, middles, and ends, and *Underworld* offers rich rewards in terms of language, atmosphere, and nostalgia. The story opens with Jackie Gleason vomiting on Frank Sinatra's shoes as they sit with Toots Shor and J. Edgar Hoover watching the historic 1951 baseball game in which Bobby Thompson hit a dramatic three-run homer, crushing the Dodgers and sending the Giants to the World Series. A black youth named Cotter Martin has sneaked into the stadium, and the home run ball that he recovers becomes one of the symbols that appear and reappear throughout this long survey of Americana that goes back in spirit to DeLillo's first novel. Some old DeLillo topics return: the insider chatter about nuclear weapons and the war scenarios that rounded out the football story in *End Zone* and a lost film from 1932 by Sergei Eisenstein titled *Unterwelt* (*Underworld*), which recalls perhaps the movie from Hitler's bunker in *Running Dog.* The many characters walk on and off the stage, unannounced, from 1951 through the middle nineties, always talking in that distinctive DeLillo voice that makes turning the pages a compulsion when he hits the right pitch. One of DeLillo's mini-essays in *Underworld* praises *Sprachgefühl* ("a feeling for speech")—a good choice of subject for DeLillo, who has this quality in abundance and whose works would shrink and dry up without it.

—Frank Day

DELL, Floyd

Born: Barry, Illinois, 28 June 1887. **Education:** Schools in Barry and Quincy, Illinois, and Davenport High School, Iowa. **Military**

Service: Served in the U.S. Army, 1918. **Family:** Married 1) Margery Curry in 1909 (separated 1913; divorced 1916); 2) Berta Marie Gage in 1919, two sons. **Career:** Reporter, Davenport *Times,* 1905; editor, *Tri-City Workers' Magazine,* Davenport, 1906; reporter, Davenport *Democrat,* 1906; reporter, Chicago *Evening Post,* 1909, and assistant editor, 1909-10, associate editor, 1910-11, and editor, 1911-13, *Evening Post Friday Literary Review;* moved to New York, 1913: managing editor, *The Masses,* 1914-17, and associate editor of its successor, *The Liberator,* 1918-20; tried for sedition for his pacifist writings, 1917; full-time writer from 1921; editor for the WPA (Works Progress Administration), Washington, D.C., 1935-47. **Died:** 23 July 1969.

PUBLICATIONS

Fiction

Moon-Calf. 1920.
The Briary-Bush. 1921.
Janet March. 1923; revised edition, 1927.
This Mad Ideal. 1925.
Runaway. 1925.
Love in Greenwich Village (stories and poems). 1926.
An Old Man's Folly. 1926.
An Unmarried Father. 1927; as *Little Accident,* 1930.
Souvenir. 1929.
Love without Money. 1931.
Diana Stair. 1932.
The Golden Spike. 1934.

Plays

Human Nature (as *A Five Minute Problem Play,* produced 1913). In *King Arthur's Socks. . .,* 1922.
The Chaste Adventures of Joseph (produced 1914). In *King Arthur's Socks . . .,* 1922.
Ibsen Revisited (produced 1914). In *King Arthur's Socks. . .,* 1922.
Enigma (produced 1915). In *King Arthur's Socks. . .,* 1922.
Legend (as *My Lady's Mirror,* produced 1915). In *King Arthur's Socks. . .,* 1922.
The Rim of the World (produced 1915). In *King Arthur's Socks. . .,* 1922.
King Arthur's Socks (produced 1916). In *King Arthur's Socks. . .,* 1922.
The Angel Intrudes (produced 1917). 1918.
A Long Time Ago (produced 1917). In *King Arthur's Socks. . .,* 1922.
Sweet and Twenty (produced 1918). 1921.
Poor Harold! (produced 1920). In *King Arthur's Socks. . .,* 1922.
King Arthur's Socks and Other Village Plays. 1922.
Little Accident, with Thomas Mitchell, from the novel *An Unmarried Father* by Dell (produced 1928).
Cloudy with Showers, with Thomas Mitchell (produced 1931).

Other

Women as World Builders: Studies in Modern Feminism. 1913.
Were You Ever a Child? 1919.
Looking at Life. 1924.
Intellectual Vagabondage: An Apology for the Intelligentsia. 1926.

The Outline of Marriage. 1926.
Upton Sinclair: A Study in Social Protest. 1927.
Love in the Machine Age: A Psychological Study of the Transition from Patriarchal Society. 1930.
Homecoming: An Autobiography. 1933.
Children and the Machine Age. 1934.
Floyd Dell: Essays from the Friday Literary Review, 1909-1913. 1995.

Editor, *Poems,* by Wilfrid Scawen Blunt. 1923.
Editor, *Poems of Robert Herrick.* 1924.
Editor, *Poems and Prose of William Blake.* 1925.
Editor, with Paul Jordan-Smith, *The Anatomy of Melancholy,* by Robert Burton. 1927.
Editor, *Daughter of the Revolution and Other Stories,* by John Reed. 1927.

*

Bibliography: *Dell: An Annotated Bibliography of Secondary Sources 1910-1981* by Judith Nierman, 1984.

Critical Studies: *Dell* by John E. Hart, 1971; "Floyd Dell, Literary Radical: The Apple Pie Evolution" by Thomas N. Walters, in *Pembroke Magazine* vol. 11, 1979; "Floyd Dell in the Western Illinois Region" by Clarence A. Andrews, in *Western Illinois Regional Studies,* fall 1985; "Remembering Floyd Dell" by Craig R. Sautter, in *Midwestern Miscellany* vol. 13, 1985; "Floyd Dell in Iowa" by William H. Roba, in *Books at Iowa* vol. 44, 1986; *Freud und die amerikanische Literatur (1920-1940): Studien zur Rezeption der Psychoanalyse in den literarischen Zeitschriften und den Werken von Conrad Aiken, Ludwig Lewisohn und Floyd Dell* by Hans Borchert, 1987; *Floyd Dell: The Life and Times of an American Rebel* by Douglas Clayton, 1994; "Willa Cather and Floyd Dell" by William Holtz, in *Willa Cather Pioneer Memorial Newsletter,* summer 1994, pp. 34-36.

*   *   *

In a writing career running from 1908 to 1935, Floyd Dell published more than twenty books and roughly one thousand periodical pieces. They, like his life, fall into several distinct periods and reflect his connection with many of the important literary movements and intellectual concerns in the United States during the first quarter of the twentieth century.

In his Chicago period (1908-13), his output consisted chiefly of book reviews and essays for the *Friday Literary Review* of the Chicago *Evening Post,* which during his editorship found itself at the heart of what has come to be known as the Chicago Renaissance. His brisk and often highly personal discussions for the *Review* championed the "new" literature, introduced the work of many continental novelists, and surveyed current books on socialism and sex; one of his series of articles, "Modern Women," taking up the views of ten feminists, became his first book, *Women as World Builders.*

His Greenwich Village years (1913-20, chronicled nostalgically in prose sketches, short stories, and poetry in *Love in Greenwich Village*), coincided with a period of intense creative and intellectual activity there, and he became one of the leading figures both through his participation in the little theater movement—several of his short plays gently satirizing the intellectual concerns of the

Villagers were collected as *King Arthur's Socks and Other Village Plays*—and his writings as an editor of the socialistic journals *The Masses* and its successor, *The Liberator.* The books that resulted from this writing reflect the dualism both of Dell and of these magazines, which were concerned with art as well as politics and were often as conservative in the former as they were radical in the latter. *Looking at Life* draws together forty short pieces, largely unconnected with socialism; they display an acute intelligence playing lightly and entertainingly, but seldom profoundly, over a wide range of subjects. *Were You Ever a Child?,* based on a series in *The Liberator,* is a plea for educational reform, popularizing the ideas of **John Dewey** and other educational theorists and presenting them with humor and playfulness (and often in dialogue form). *Intellectual Vagabondage,* based on another series written for *The Liberator* (but after Dell left the Village), is the most important of the three, and is Dell's most ambitious effort at interpreting literature from a social and economic standpoint; with characteristic lightness of touch he traces the historical role of the intelligentsia and then, more significantly, sets forth the "spiritual autobiography" of his own generation, depicting, among other things, the idealistic revolt of youth against the restraints of a commercial world.

This perennial theme of Dell's runs through the novels that he produced during what may be regarded as his third period, the years when he lived at Croton-on-the-Hudson, New York (1920-35). His first—and most famous and best—novel, *Moon-Calf,* draws heavily on his own pre-Chicago years and describes with great sensitivity the intellectual development of a young dreamer and poet; with it he made the analysis of moon-calves, and their adjustment to reality, his own special province. In ten succeeding novels he continued to explore the predicaments of youthful idealists, who in the end find happiness by accepting conventions; like his other writings, these novels are facile and exhibit a keen sense of irony and humor, but they do not fulfill the promise suggested by *Moon-Calf.* The interest in psychological and social problems manifested in the novels reaches its climax in Dell's substantial study of adolescent adjustment, *Love in the Machine Age,* a well-written exposition of the thesis that the neuroses of the modern world are the result of outmoded but still operative patriarchal conventions.

For psychological insight, however, readers are likely to prefer his autobiography, *Homecoming,* especially the first half dealing with the years covered fictionally in *Moon-Calf.* As the title implies, the movement of the book and of his life is toward the stability finally found in marriage and a home, but he never lost the ability to write perceptively of youthful rebellion, and the book contains some of his best work. The dust jacket calls it "not Floyd Dell's autobiography but your own," a remark that points to Dell's importance as a representative figure. He will be best remembered as an intelligent and articulate commentator on the characteristic concerns of a sizable segment of his literary generation.

—G. Thomas Tanselle

DEWEY, John

Born: Burlington, Vermont, 20 October 1859. **Education:** Schools in Burlington; University of Vermont, Burlington, 1875-79, B.A. 1879; Johns Hopkins University, Baltimore, 1882-84, Ph.D. 1884.

Family: Married 1) Alice Chipman in 1886 (died 1927), three sons, three daughters, and one adopted son; 2) Roberta L. Grant in 1946, one son and one daughter, both adopted. **Career:** High school teacher, Oil City, Pennsylvania, 1879-81; assistant professor, 1886-88, and professor of philosophy, 1889-94, University of Michigan, Ann Arbor; visiting professor of philosophy, University of Minnesota, Minneapolis, 1888-89; professor of philosophy and chairman of the department of philosophy, psychology and pedagogy, University of Chicago, 1894-1904 (founder, Laboratory School, 1896; director, School of Education, 1902-04); professor of philosophy, 1904-30, Professor Emeritus in Residence, 1930-39, and Professor Emeritus, 1939-52, Columbia University, New York. Lecturer, Imperial University of Tokyo, 1919, and National Universities of Peking and Nanking, 1919-21; Clifford Lecturer, University of Edinburgh, 1929; William James Lecturer, Harvard University, Cambridge, Massachusetts, 1930; Dwight Harrington Terry Lecturer, Yale University, New Haven, Connecticut, 1934. Conducted surveys of education in Turkey, 1924, Mexico, 1926, and the Soviet Union, 1928; chairman, Commission of Inquiry into the charges made against Leon Trotsky in the Moscow Trials, 1937. President, American Psychological Association, 1899, and Eastern Division of American Philosophical Association, 1905-06; a founder and first president, American Association of University Professors, 1915. **Awards:** Honorary degrees: University of Wisconsin, Madison, 1904; University of Vermont, 1910; University of Michigan, 1913; Johns Hopkins University, 1915; University of Peking, 1920; University of St. Andrews, Scotland, 1929; Columbia University, 1929; University of Paris, 1930; Harvard University, 1932; University of Pennsylvania, Philadelphia, 1946; University of Oslo, 1946; Yale University, 1951. **Member:** National Academy of Sciences, 1910. **Died:** 1 June 1952.

PUBLICATIONS

Collections

The Early Works 1882-1898, edited by Jo Ann Boydston. 5 vols., 1967-72.
The Middle Works 1899-1924, edited by Jo Ann Boydston. 15 vols., 1976-83.
The Poems, edited by Jo Ann Boydston. 1977.
The Later Works 1925-1953, edited by Jo Ann Boydston. 1981—.
The Essential Dewey. 1998.

Prose

Psychology. 1887; revised edition, 1889, 1891.
Leibniz's New Essays Concerning the Human Understanding: A Critical Exposition. 1888.
The Ethics of Democracy. 1888.
Applied Psychology: An Introduction to the Principles and Practices of Education, with J.A. McLellan. 1889.
Outlines of a Critical Theory of Ethics. 1891.
The Study of Ethics: A Syllabus. 1894.
The Psychology of Number and Its Applications to Methods of Teaching Arithmetic, with J.A. McLellan. 1895.
My Pedagogic Creed, with *The Demands of Sociology upon Pedagogy,* by Albion W. Small. 1897.
The Significance of the Problem of Knowledge. 1897.

Psychology and Philosophic Method. 1899.

The School and Society. 1899; revised edition, 1915; edited by Jo Ann Boydston, 1980.

Psychology and Social Practice. 1901.

The Child and the Curriculum. 1902.

The Educational Situation. 1902.

Studies in Logical Theory, with others. 1903.

Logical Conditions of a Scientific Treatment of Morality. 1903.

The School and the Child, Being Selections from the Educational Essays of Dewey, edited by J.J. Findlay. 1907.

Ethics (lecture). 1908.

Ethics, with James H. Tufts. 1908; revised edition, 1932; selection, as *Theory of the Moral Life,* 1960.

Moral Principles in Education. 1909.

How We Think. 1910; revised edition, 1933.

The Influence of Darwin on Philosophy and Other Essays in Contemporary Thought. 1910.

Educational Essays, edited by J.J. Findlay. 1910.

Interest and Effort in Education. 1913.

Some Dangers in the Present Movement for Industrial Education. 1913.

German Philosophy and Politics. 1915.

Schools of To-morrow, with Evelyn Dewey. 1915.

Democracy and Education: An Introduction to the Philosophy of Education. 1916.

Essays in Experimental Logic. 1916.

Creative Intelligence: Essays in the Pragmatic Attitude, with others. 1917.

Enlistment for the Farm. 1917.

Vocational Education in the Light of the World War. 1918.

Letters from China and Japan, with Alice Chipman Dewey, edited by Evelyn Dewey. 1920.

Reconstruction in Philosophy. 1920; revised edition, 1948.

China, Japan and the U.S.A.: Present-Day Conditions in the Far East and Their Bearing on the Washington Conference. 1921.

Human Nature and Conduct: An Introduction to Social Psychology. 1922.

Experience and Nature. 1925; revised edition, 1929.

The Public and Its Problems. 1927.

The Philosophy of Dewey, edited by Joseph Ratner. 1928.

Progressive Education and the Science of Education. 1928.

Impressions of Soviet Russia and the Revolutionary World: Mexico, China, Turkey. 1929.

Characters and Events: Popular Essays in Social and Political Philosophy, edited by Joseph Ratner. 2 vols., 1929.

Art and Education, with others. 1929.

The Quest for Certainty: A Study of the Relation of Knowledge and Action. 1929.

The Sources of a Science of Education. 1929.

Individualism, Old and New. 1930.

Construction and Criticism. 1930.

Context and Thought. 1931.

Philosophy and Civilization. 1931.

The Way Out of Educational Confusion. 1931.

American Education Past and Future. 1931.

The Place of Minor Parties in the American Scene. 1932.

The Educational Frontier, with others. 1933.

Steps to Economic Recovery. 1933(?).

Education and the Social Order. 1934.

The Meaning of Marx: A Symposium, with others. 1934.

Art as Experience. 1934.

A Common Faith. 1934.

Liberalism and Social Action. 1935.

The Teacher and Society, with others. 1937.

The Case of Leon Trotsky: Report of the Hearings of the Charges Made against Him in the Moscow Trials, with others. 1937.

Not Guilty: Report of the Commission of Inquiry into the Charges Made against Leon Trotsky in the Moscow Trials, with others. 1938.

Logic: The Theory of Inquiry. 1938.

Experience and Education. 1938.

Democracy and Education in the World of Today. 1938.

Intelligence in the Modern World: Dewey's Philosophy, edited by Joseph Ratner. 1939.

Freedom and Culture. 1939.

Theory of Valuation. 1939.

What Is Democracy? with others. 1939.

Education Today, edited by Joseph Ratner. 1940.

Problems of Men. 1946.

Knowing and the Known, with Arthur F. Bentley. 1949.

The Wit and Wisdom of Dewey, edited by A.H. Johnson. 1949.

David Dubinsky: A Pictorial Biography. 1951.

Dewey: His Contribution to the American Tradition, edited by Irwin Edman. 1955.

Dewey on Education, edited by Martin S. Dworkin. 1959.

Dictionary of Education, edited by Ralph B. Winn. 1959.

On Experience, Nature, and Freedom: Representative Selections, edited by Richard J. Bernstein. 1960.

Philosophy, Psychology, and Social Practice: Essays, edited by Joseph Ratner. 1963.

Dewey and Arthur F. Bentley: A Philosophical Correspondence 1932-1951, edited by Sidney Ratner and Jules Altman. 1964.

Dewey on Education, edited by Reginald D. Archambault. 1966.

Lectures in the Philosophy of Education 1899, edited by Reginald D. Archambault. 1966.

Selected Educational Writings, edited by F.W. Garforth. 1966.

(Selections), edited by Malcolm Skilbeck. 1970.

The Philosophy of Dewey: The Structure of Experience and *The Lived Experience,* edited by John J. McDermott. 2 vols., 1973.

Lectures in China 1919-1920, edited and translated by Robert W. Clopton and Tsuin-chen Ou. 1973.

Lectures on Psychological and Political Ethics 1898, edited by Donald F. Koch. 1976.

The Moral Writings, edited by James Gouinlock. 1976.

The Essential Writings, edited by David Sidorsky. 1977.

Principals of Instrumental Logic: John Dewey's Lectures in Ethics and Political Ethics, 1895-1896. 1998.

Editor, *New York and the Seabury Investigation.* 1933.

Editor, *The Living Thoughts of Thomas Jefferson.* 1940.

Editor, with Horace M. Kallen, *The Bertrand Russell Case.* 1941.

*

Bibliography: *Dewey: A Centennial Bibliography* by Milton Halsey Thomas, 1962; *Checklist of Writings about Dewey 1887-1977* by Jo Ann Boydston and Kathleen Poulos, 1978.

Critical Studies: *Dewey: An Intellectual Portrait* by Sidney Hook, 1939, and *Dewey, Philosopher of Science and Freedom: A Symposium* edited by Hook, 1967; *The Philosophy of Dewey* edited by Paul Arthur Schilpp, 1939; *The Logic of Pragmatism: An Exami-

nation of Dewey's Logic by H.S. Thayer, 1952; *The Nihilism of Dewey* by Paul K. Crosser, 1955; *Dewey in Perspective* by George R. Geiger, 1958; *Dewey: His Thought and Influence* edited by John Blewett, 1960; *Dewey as Educator: His Design for Work in Education 1894-1904* by Arthur G. Wirth, 1966; *Guide to the Works of Dewey* edited by Jo Ann Boydston, 1970; *Dewey* by Harry M. Campbell, 1971; *Dewey's Philosophy of Value* by James Gouinlock, 1972; *The Life and Mind of Dewey* by George Dykhuizen, 1973; *Dewey and His Influence* by Robert C. Whittemore, 1973; *Young Dewey: An Essay in American Intellectual History* by Neil Coughlan, 1975; *Dewey's Aesthetic Philosophy* by Philip M. Zeltner, 1975; *Dewey Reconsidered* edited by R.S. Peters, 1977; *New Studies in the Philosophy of Dewey* edited by Steven M. Cahn, 1977; *John Dewey: The Later Works, 1925-1953,* 5 volumes, 1981-84; *Dewey: Recollections* edited by Robert Bruce Williams, 1982; *The Politics of Dewey* edited by Gary Bullert, 1984; "Dewey's Message to China" by Jane Cauvel, in *Hypatia: Essays in Classics, Comparative Literature, and Philosophy Presented to Hazel E. Barnes on Her Seventieth Birthday* edited by William M. Calder, Ulrich K. Goldsmith, and Phyllis B. Kevevan, 1985; "Scientific Rhetoric in the Nineteenth and Early Twentieth Centuries: Herbert Spencer, Thomas H. Huxley, and John Dewey" by James P. Zappan, in *Textual Dynamics of the Professions: Historical and Contemporary Studies of Writing in Professional Communities* edited by Charles Bazerman and James Paradis, 1991; *John Dewey's Ethical Thought* by Jennifer Welchman, 1995; *William James and John Dewey* by Gordon Haddon Clark, 1995; *John Dewey's Argument for Social Control: Its Relevance to Contemporary American Problems* by Tanya S. Francis, 1996; *Reflection in Teacher Education: A Study of John Dewey's Theory and the Practice of Katherine Taylor and Lucy Sprague Mitchell* by Carol Richardson Rodgers, 1996; *Dewey and Eros: Wisdom and Desire in the Art of Teaching* by James W. Garrison, 1997; *John Dewey and the High Tide of American Liberalism* by Alan Ryan, 1997; *John Dewey and Karl Jaspers: Main Philosophic Concepts and Educational Implications* by Fernando M. Soares Silva, 1998; *Thought and Action: John Dewey at the University of Michigan* by Brian A. Williams, 1998; *The Political Philosophy of John Dewey: Towards a Constructive Renewal* by Terry Hoy, 1998; *Naturalizing Philosophy of Education: John Dewey in the Postanalytic Period* by Jerome A. Popp, 1998; *Reading Dewey: Interpretations for a Postmodern Generation* edited by Larry Hickman, 1998; *John Dewey and the Lessons of Art* by Philip W. Jackson, 1998.

*   *   *

John Dewey's writings are a notable exception to the frequently expressed despair that philosophy affords no answers to problems of living. Dewey's greatness as a philosopher derives from his recognition that this despair articulates a need to transcend the Western philosophical tradition, to advance a view that "re-understands" the human condition, a view that in Dewey's words (in *Reconstruction in Philosophy*) "would have an active share in the work of construction of a moral human science which serves as a needful precursor of reconstruction of the actual state of human life toward order and toward other conditions of a fuller life than man has yet enjoyed." So, what conceptual disease explains the impotence of traditional philosophy in the face of life's perils? What therapy is there? What philosophical outlook can ground this "moral human science?"

Dewey's therapy resembles that prescribed by such thinkers as Wittgenstein and Heidegger. Dewey recommends reflection upon the natural and socio-cultural history of those dualisms that have preoccupied the Western tradition: Mind-Matter, Subject-Object, Certainty/Knowledge-Belief/Doing, Experience-Nature, Contemplation-Action—a "naturalistic Hegelianism," as it were. Dewey contends that these dualisms are rooted in certain primitive evaluations of remote antiquity, according an inherently "higher" value to "religious" over "technological" attempts at securing human existence.

"Philosophy inherited the realm with which religion had been concerned" and rationally justified the value-distinction between its inherited realm and the realm of technics. Technics comprised "bodies of information that corresponded to the everyday arts, the store of matter-of-fact knowledge, . . . things men knew because of what they did" (*The Quest for Certainty*). Philosophy, however, sought genuine knowledge of a realm "higher" than the earthly realm of technics. It aspired accurately to represent an immutable, eternal Reality.

These conceptions—of Philosophy as genuine knowledge, of genuine knowledge as representation of Reality, of Reality as eternal and thus independent of human existence—engendered a picture of Mind's relation to Reality that is pivotal in the Western tradition, what Dewey calls the "spectator theory of knowledge." It portrays Mind as metaphysically removed from Reality, as beholding Reality through a conceptual veil.

The theory motivates the concern over whether we shall ever know if Thought truthfully represents Reality. We cannot "hold up" our moral and scientific theories in comparison with Reality—we cannot wedge Thought between Mind and Reality. Indeed, our scientific theories demonstrate that various qualities ascribed to Reality—colors, sounds, etc.—are effects on sensory receptors, merely subjective experiential representations of Reality; and as a measure of the Real, such theories cast moral and aesthetic values as ontologically aberrant. Seeking comfort in a Kantian bastion of transcendental deduction is illusory: assimilating the empirically real to the transcendentally ideal.

According to Dewey, we must reject the spectatorial separation of Mind from Reality. We must recognize Mind as part of Reality: Thinking and Knowing are activities, things we do. Their fruits are simply further ways of dealing with life's perils. We must recognize "Doing" as the heart of "Knowing," "regard knowings and reasonings and mathematical and scientific adventurings even up to their highest abstraction, as activities . . ." (*The Quest for Certainty*).

Philosophy must attempt to integrate "our cognitive beliefs, our beliefs resting upon the most dependable methods of inquiry, with the practical beliefs about the values, the ends and purposes, that should control human action in the things of large and liberal human import" (*Experience and Nature*). The integration is to be conducted methodologically: our "most dependable methods" being the experimental methods characteristic of physical science, Philosophy must advance a framework for introducing these methods into the "human sciences."

Initially such a framework seems incoherent. Physical science cannot be unified with human science. The latter countenances mental, moral, and aesthetic entities; these are not entities physical science can countenance. However, Dewey asserts we should not construe physical science as the measure of Reality. Following the pragmatic instrumentalism of Charles Sanders Peirce and **William James**, he maintains that physical science should not be construed as true by virtue of successful reference to an objective Reality whose nature is antecedent to observation and inquiry. Physical science is an "instrument" that helps explain regularities governing phenomena observable in everyday life; its "truth" is gauged by its consequences in life.

The project introduces tensions. Dewey urges that we abandon traditional metaphysics. However, he aspires toward an account "of the generic traits manifested by existence of all kinds without regard to their differentiation into physical and mental . . ." (*Experience and Nature*). Why do we need such an account? Does it resolve the above tension? However, a thoroughgoing instrumentalism does that. But can such an instrumentalism be coherently maintained? It is a problem in the theory of meaning whether one can distinguish "theoretical" from "observational" as instrumentalism requires. Finally, it is questionable whether Dewey's diagnosis of the tradition is adequate; in this he stands trial with Wittgenstein and Heidegger.

These difficulties aside, Dewey's philosophical view at least outlines a framework in which all fields of human endeavor can buttress each other towards creating "conditions of a fuller life than man has yet enjoyed."

—James M. Drayton

DICKEY, James (Lafayette)

Born: Atlanta, Georgia, 2 February 1923. **Education:** Clemson College, South Carolina, 1942; Vanderbilt University, Nashville, Tennessee, B.A. (magna cum laude) 1949, M.A. 1950. **Military Service:** Served as a pilot in the U.S. Army Air Force during World War II and as a training officer in the Air Force during the Korean War. **Family:** Married 1) Maxine Syerson in 1948 (died 1976), two sons; 2) Deborah Dodson in 1976, one daughter. **Career:** Teacher at Rice University, Houston, 1950, 1952-54, and University of Florida, Gainesville, 1955-56; poet-in-residence, Reed College, Portland, Oregon, 1962-64, San Fernando Valley State College, Northridge, California, 1964-66, and University of Wisconsin, Madison, 1966; consultant in poetry, Library of Congress, Washington, D.C., 1966-68; professor of English and writer-in-residence, University of South Carolina, Columbia, 1969-97. Yale Younger Poets contest, judge, 1989-94. **Awards:** Vachel Lindsay prize, 1959; Longview Foundation award, 1960; Guggenheim fellowship, 1961; Melville Cane award, 1966; National Book award, 1966; American Academy grant, 1966; Medicis prize, for novel, 1971; Levinson prize, 1981. **Member:** American Academy. **Died:** 19 January 1997.

PUBLICATIONS

Poetry

Into the Stone and Other Poems. 1960.
Drowning with Others. 1962; selection, as *The Owl King,* 1977.
Helmets. 1964.
Two Poems of the Air. 1964.
Buckdancer's Choice. 1965.
Poems 1957-1967. 1967.
The Achievement of Dickey: A Comprehensive Selection of His Poems, edited by Laurence Lieberman. 1968.

The Eye-Beaters, Blood, Victory, Madness, Buckhead and Mercy. 1970.
The Zodiac. 1976; revised edition, 1976.
The Strength of Fields. 1977; revised edition, 1979.
Veteran Birth: The Gadfly Poems 1947-1949. 1978.
Head-Deep in Strange Sounds: Free-Flight Improvisations from the UnEnglish. 1979.
Falling, May Day Sermon, and Other Poems. 1981.
The Early Motion. 1981.
Puella. 1982.
The Central Motion: Poems, 1968-1979. 1983.
False Youth—Four Seasons. 1983.
Night Hurdling. 1983.
Intervisions: Poems and Photographs, photographs by Sharon Anglin Kuhne. 1983.
Bronwen, the Traw, and the Shape-Shifter. 1986.
Of Prisons and Ideas. 1987.
Summons. 1988.
The Eagle's Mile. 1990.
The Whole Motion: Collected Poems, 1945-1992. 1992.
James Dickey: The Selected Poems. 1998.

Fiction

Deliverance. 1970.
Alnilam. 1987.
To the White Sea. 1993.

Plays

Deliverance: A Screenplay, edited by Matthew J. Bruccoli. 1981.

Screenplay: *Deliverance,* 1972.

Television Play: *The Call of the Wild,* from the novel by Jack London, 1976.

Other

The Suspect in Poetry. 1964.
A Private Brinksmanship (address). 1965.
Spinning the Crystal Ball: Some Guesses at the Future of American Poetry. 1967.
Metaphor as Pure Adventure (lecture). 1968.
Babel to Byzantium: Poets and Poetry Now. 1968.
Self-Interviews, edited by Barbara and James Reiss. 1970.
Sorties (essays). 1971.
Exchanges . . . . : Being in the Form of a Dialogue with Joseph Trumbull Stickney. 1971.
Jericho: The South Beheld, paintings by Hubert Shuptrine. 1974.
God's Images: The Bible: A New Vision, illustrated by Marvin Hayes. 1977.
Tucky the Hunter (for children). 1978.
The Enemy from Eden. 1978.
In Pursuit of the Grey Soul (on fishing). 1979.
The Water-Bug's Mittens: Ezra Pound, What We Can Use (lecture). 1980.
Scion. 1980.
The Starry Place between the Antlers: Why I Live in South Carolina. 1981.
The Eagle's Mile. 1981.

The Poet Turns on Himself. 1982.
How to Enjoy Poetry. 1982.
For a Time and Place. 1983.
Night Hurdling: Poems, Essays, Conversations, Commencements, and Afterwords. 1983.
Wayfarer: A Voice from the Southern Mountains, with William A. Bake. 1988.
The Voiced Connections of James Dickey: Interview and Conversations, edited by Ronald Baughman. 1989.
Southern Light, photographs by James Valentine. 1991.
Striking In: The Early Notebooks of James Dickey. 1996.

Editor, *From the Green Horseshoe.* 1987.

Translator, *Stolen Apples,* by Yevgeny Yevtushenko. 1971.

*

Bibliography: *Dickey: A Bibliography 1947-1974* by Jim Elledge, 1979; *Dickey: A Bibliography* by Stuart Wright, 1982; *James Dickey: A Descriptive Bibliography* by Matthew J. Bruccoli, 1990.

Critical Studies: *Dickey: The Expansive Imagination: A Collection of Critical Essays* edited by Richard J. Calhoun, 1973, and *Dickey* by Calhoun and Robert W. Hill, 1983; "Dickey Issue" of *South Carolina Review,* April 1978; *Dickey: Splintered Sunlight* edited by Patricia De La Fuente, 1979; *The Imagination as Glory: Essays on the Poetry of Dickey* edited by Bruce Weigl and T.R. Hummer, 1984; *Understanding Dickey* by Ronald Baughman, 1985; *Dickey: The Poet as Pitchman* by Neal Bowers, 1985; *James Dickey* edited by Harold Bloom, 1987; *Outbelieving Existence: The Measured Motion of Dickey* by Gordon Van Ness, 1992; *Critical Essays on James Dickey* edited by Robert Kirschten, 1994; *Approaching Prayer: Ritual and the Shape of Myth in A.R. Ammons and James Dickey* by Robert Kirschten, 1998.

*   *   *

James Dickey emerged as an important American poet and as a still underrated literary critic through an astonishing period of creative productivity from 1957 to 1967. He was regarded so much as a poet without imitators and without specific social or political concerns that his important contributions to postmodernism both as a poet and critic were not adequately recognized. But Dickey should be seen as a postmodernist romantic—because of his desire to make imaginative contact with natural forces that have been lost to modern man, because of his romantic faith in the power of his imagination, and because of the expansive affirmative character of most of his poems.

Dickey has always violated the modernist practice of impersonality in his poetry, for there has always been a close correspondence between the chronology of his poems and his life. In his earliest poems he drew from such autobiographical data as the death (before Dickey was born) of his brother Eugene and his experiences as a fighter pilot in two destructive wars, as well as from his love for hunting, archery, and the Southern landscape. Many of these poems feature encounters leading to vividly imagined exchanges of identity between the living and the dead, between men and "unthinking" nature, for the purpose of understanding through the imagination what reason alone cannot comprehend.

Dickey early declared himself an affirmative poet, with an acknowledged affinity for the poetry of his friend and mentor **Theodore Roethke**; but his affirmations are from the knowing perspective of a grateful survivor of two wars. His poems have always portrayed those who were *not* survivors and affirmed the risk inherent in an exchange of identity. In later poems, especially in *The Eye-Beaters,* Dickey has exhibited a fascination with fantasy, with what he has called his "country surrealism," blurring distinctions between reality and dreams, even suggesting hallucinations. His intention has been to produce a poetry that releases the unconscious and the irrational, with results that are both life affirmative and life threatening.

Two poems that might serve as transitions from earlier to later themes are "Power and Light" and "Falling," both from *Poems 1957-1967.* There is a shift of emphasis from a celebration of "more life" through the imaginative comprehension of nature to the necessity of confronting destructive forces and of finding spiritual resources for that confrontation. Dickey's formal interests likewise shifted from regular towards more irregular forms, from the directness of "the simple declarative sentence" to the intimations of open and "big forms," and to such devices as split space punctuation within lines—effective in a tour de force like "Falling," but less effective in some later poems.

In the 1970s Dickey's production of poetry lessened with a developing interest in the novel, television and film scripts, and in a form of literary criticism, the self-interview. His successful novel *Deliverance* shares with his poetry a concern with the cycle of entry into "unthinking nature," followed by a return to the world, perhaps having become while in nature "another thing." The return to the human realm is just as important as the entry into the natural. *New York Times Book Review* contributor Robert Towers called *Deliverance* "a macho adventure story moving with an arrow's precision from the soft banalities of middle-class life into a Gothic nightmare of rape, death and almost unbearable tension."

Dickey also became engaged in writing coffee-table sized prose-poem celebrations of the Southern landscape (*Jericho*) and of the King James version of the Bible (*God's Images*). He produced one book of poetic "imitations" to mixed reviews from his critics, *The Zodiac,* his versions of the poems of a drunken Dutch sailor-poet of the 1940s. This book seemingly exhausted the wildness and madness in Dickey's poetry. *The Strength of Fields* marked a change in tone towards acceptance and kindness. He offered additional translations, or, more properly, imitations. There are new war poems, but these are not poems about death and Dickey as survivor but more positive poems of acceptance of war and death. *Puella* displays an even more radical experiment in poetic voice. As the title suggests, Dickey adopts not his usual very masculine voice but the perspective of a girl, "male imagined." He traces the development of the girl Deborah from girlhood to womanhood and shows her relationship to the four traditional elements, fire, air, water, earth.

Dickey is by birth and residence a Southern poet, with academic credentials from the stronghold of agrarianism, Vanderbilt University. Yet he has always made it clear that he is no "latter-day Agrarian." Still, like **John Crowe Ransom**, who feared the loss of "the world's body," and **Allen Tate**, who feared the loss of "complete knowledge" of man and his universe in an era dominated by science and technology, Dickey has his own version of agrarian fears of technology and urbanization. He has always been "much more interested in man's relationship to the God-made world, or the universe made than to the man made." He has made his best poetic subject clear in *Self-Interviews:* "The relationship of the human being to the great natural cycles of birth, the seasons, the growing up of seasons out of dead leaves, the generations of animals and of men, all on the heraldic wheel of existence is very beautiful to me."

In 1987, seventeen years after the publication of *Deliverance,* Dickey returned to the novel form to pen *Alnilam,* the story of a blinded man who travels to a U.S. Army Air Corps training base to investigate the disappearance of a son he has never met. The father, Frank Cahill, slowly unravels the mystery of his son's apparent death in an airplane crash, discovering that the 19-year-old was the leader of a semi-fascist cult known as Alnilam. Along the way Dickey takes Cahill and the reader on a series of wild and dizzying airplane rides, including descriptions of aerial combat that must have been lifted from the author's own experiences. "I've tried to do for the air what Melville did for water," Dickey told *Time.* Towers called *Alnilam* an "extended hymn to air, light, wind and the ecstasies of flight." Dickey's next novel, *To the White Sea,* begins with a violent plane crash at the end of World War II. Tailgunner Muldrow survives the crash but must tap all of his considerable knowledge as a woodsman and a killer to escape from behind enemy lines. Dickey manages to make Muldrow both likeable and monstrous at the same time. A *Newsweek* reviewer wrote: "Dickey means to give you the creeps, and he succeeds mightily in a great novel."

—Richard J. Calhoun, updated by Tom Pendergast

DICKINSON, Emily (Elizabeth)

Born: Amherst, Massachusetts, 10 December 1830. **Education:** Amherst Academy; Mount Holyoke Female Seminary, South Hadley, Massachusetts, 1847. **Career:** Lived a secluded life in Amherst except for brief visits to Washington, D.C., Philadelphia, and Boston; semi-invalid, 1884-86. **Died:** 15 May 1886.

PUBLICATIONS

Collections

The Poems, edited by Thomas H. Johnson. 3 vols., 1955.
Letters, edited by Thomas H. Johnson and Theodora Ward. 3 vols., 1958; *Selected Letters,* 1971.
Complete Poems (single version of all poems), edited by Thomas H. Johnson. 1960; *Final Harvest* (selections), 1961.
The Manuscript Books, edited by R.W. Franklin. 2 vols., 1981.
The Essential Dickinson, edited by Joyce Carol Oates. 1996.

Poetry

Poems, edited by Mabel Loomis Todd and T.W. Higginson. 1890; *Second Series,* 1891; *Third Series,* edited by Todd, 1896.
The Single Hound: Poems of a Lifetime, edited by Martha Dickinson Bianchi. 1914.
The Complete Poems, edited by Martha Dickinson Bianchi. 1924.
Further Poems, edited by Martha Dickinson Bianchi and Alfred Leete Hampson. 1929.

Unpublished Poems, edited by Martha Dickinson Bianchi and Alfred Leete Hampson. 1935.
Bolts of Melody: New Poems, edited by Mabel Loomis Todd and Millicent Todd Bingham. 1945.
A Light Exists in Spring, and Other Poems. 1996.
A Murmur in the Trees. 1998.

Other

Letters (includes some poems), edited by Mabel Loomis Todd. 2 vols., 1894.
Emily Dickinson's Open Folios: Scenes of Reading, Surfaces of Writing. 1995.
Open Me Carefully: Emily Dickinson's Intimate Letters to Susan Huntington Dickinson. 1998.

*

Bibliography: *Dickinson: An Annotated Bibliography: Writings, Scholarship, Criticism, and Ana 1850-1968* by Willis J. Buckingham, 1970; *The Poems of Dickinson: An Annotated Guide to Commentary Published in English 1890-1977* by Joseph Duchac, 1979; *A Reference Guide to the Bible in Emily Dickinson's Poetry* by Fordyce R. Bennett, 1997.

Critical Studies: *The Life and Letters of Dickinson* by Martha Dickinson Bianchi, 1924; *Dickinson* by Richard Chase, 1951; *Dickinson: An Interpretive Biography* by Thomas H. Johnson, 1955; *The Years and Hours of Dickinson* edited by Jay Leyda, 2 vols., 1960; *Dickinson's Poetry: Stairway of Surprise* by Charles R. Anderson, 1960; *Dickinson: A Collection of Critical Essays* edited by Richard B. Sewall, 1963, and *The Life of Dickinson* by Sewall, 2 vols., 1974; *The Recognition of Dickinson: Selected Criticism since 1890* edited by Caesar R. Blake and Carlton F. Wells, 1964; *The Long Shadow: Dickinson's Tragic Poetry* by Clark Griffith, 1964; *Dickinson: The Mind of the Poet* by Albert J. Gelpi, 1965; *The Editing of Dickinson: A Reconsideration* by R.W. Franklin, 1967; *Dickinson: An Introduction and Interpretation* by John B. Pickard, 1967; *The Poetry of Dickinson* by Ruth Miller, 1968; *The Voice of the Poet: Aspects of Style in the Poetry of Dickinson* by Brita Lindberg-Seyersted, 1968; *Circumference and Circumstance: Stages in the Mind and Art of Dickinson* by William R. Sherwood, 1968; *Dickinson* by Denis Donoghue, 1969; *After Great Pain: The Inner Life of Dickinson* by John J. Cody, 1971; *Dickinson's Poetry* by Robert Weisbuch, 1975; *Dickinson and the Image of Home* by Jean McClure Mudge, 1975; *Dickinson* by Paul J. Ferlazzo, 1976, and *Critical Essays on Dickinson* edited by Ferlazzo, 1984; *The Only Kangaroo among the Beauty: Dickinson and America* by Karl Keller, 1979; *Dickinson's Imagery* by Rebecca Patterson, edited by Margaret H. Freeman, 1979; *Lyric Time: Dickinson and the Limits of Genre* by Sharon Cameron, 1979; *Dickinson: The Modern Idiom* by David Porter, 1981; *Dickinson and the Romantic Imagination* by Joanne Feit Diehi, 1982; *Dickinson: When a Writer is a Daughter* by Barbara A.C. Mossberg, 1983; *The Marriage of Dickinson: A Study of the Fascicles* by William Shurr, 1983; *Feminist Critics Read Dickinson* edited by Suzanne Juhasz, 1983, and *The Undiscovered Continent: Dickinson and the Space of the Mind* by Juhasz, 1984; *Dickinson: The Anxiety of Gender* by Vivian R. Pollak, 1984; *Dickinson: A Voice of War* by Shira Wolosky, 1984; *Dickinson and Her Culture: The Soul's Society* by Barton Levi St. Armand,

1985; *Dickinson: Strategies of Limitation* by Jane Donahue Eberwein, 1985; *Dickinson* by Helen McNeil, 1986; *Dickinson and the Life of Language: A Study in Symbolic Poetics* by E. Miller Budick, 1986; *Dickinson: The Lives of a Poet* edited by Christopher Benfey, 1986; *Dickinson* by John Robinson, 1986; *Dickinson: A Biography* by Cynthia Griffin Wolff, 1986; *On Dickinson: The Best from American Literature* edited by Edwin H. Cady and Louis J. Budd, 1990; "'The Orient Is in the West': Emily Dickinson's Reading of Anthony and Cleopatra" by Paula Bennett, in *Women's Re-Visions of Shakespeare: On the Responses of Dickinson, Woolf, Rich, H.D., George Eliot, and Others* edited by Marianne Novy and Carol Thomas Neely, 1990; "Homelessness at Home: Placing Emily Dickinson in (Women's) History" by Thomas Foster, in *Engendering Men: The Question of Male Feminist Criticism* edited by Joseph A. Boone and Michael Cadden, 1990; *Emily Dickinson: Woman Poet* by Paula Bennett, 1990; *Emily Dickinson's Readings of Men and Books: Sacred Soundings* by Benjamin Lease, 1990; "Dickinson's Paradoxical Losses" by Alfred Corn, in *Conversant Essays: Contemporary Poets on Poetry* edited by James McCorkle, 1990; *Positive as Sound: Emily Dickinson's Rhyme* by Judy Jo Small, 1990; "The Pea That Duty Locks: Lesbian and Feminist-Heterosexual Readings of Emily Dickinson's Poetry" by Paula Bennett, in *Lesbian Texts and Contexts: Radical Revisions* edited by Carla Jay and Joanne Glasgow, 1990; *Lyric Contingencies: Emily Dickinson and Wallace Stevens* by Margaret Dickie, 1991; *The Passion of Emily Dickinson* by Judith Farr, 1992; *Rowing in Eden: Rereading Emily Dickinson* by Martha Nell Smith, 1992; *Skies in Blossom: The Nature Poetry of Emily Dickinson* edited by Jonathan Cott and Mary Frank, 1995; *The Seductions of Emily Dickinson* by Robert McClure Smith, 1996; *The Death-Motif in the Poetry of Emily Dickinson and Christina Rossetti* by Claudia Ottlinger, 1996; *A Critical Study of Emily Dickinson's Letters: The Prose of a Poet* by Robert Graham Lambert, 1996; *Emily Dickinson's Gothic: Goblin with a Gauge* by Daneen Wardrop, 1996; *Emily Dickinson: Daughter of Prophecy* by Beth Maclay Doriani, 1996; *Emily Dickinson's Use of Anglo-American Legal Concepts and Vocabulary in Her Poetry: Muse at the Bar* by Robert Graham Lambert, 1997; *Inflections of the Pen: Dash and Voice in Emily Dickinson* by Paul Crumbley, 1997; *Readings on Emily Dickinson* edited by Tamara Johnson, 1997; *Emily Dickinson's Secret Love: Mystery "Master" Behind Poems* by Bill Arnold, 1998; *Emily Dickinson and the Art of Belief* by Roger Lundin, 1998; *Emily Dickinson's Vision: Illness and Identity in Her Poetry* by James R. Guthrie, 1998; *Emily Dickinson: Singular Poet* by Carol Dommermuth-Costa, 1998; *An Emily Dickinson Encyclopedia* edited by Jane Donahue Eberwein, 1998.

*   *   *

Emily Dickinson's importance as a poet is not in any doubt. Her cause may have been damaged by injudicious partisanship during the 1930s, but a longer retrospect sets her firmly among the major poets who have written in English. She never prepared her poems for publication, and had she done so she in all probability would have rejected many of those that are now in print. It follows from this that the general reader is likely to read no more than a selection of her work; yet nothing that she wrote is without interest, and even the "failures" take their place in an *oeuvre* that is marked by a distinctive union of style and sensibility. In this respect, then, she satisfies **T.S. Eliot**'s criterion (see his "What Is Minor Poetry?," *On Poetry and Poets*) by which all

the work of a major poet should be read. Nor can we deny that her work possesses "significant unity," another of Eliot's desiderata; if we accept his third point, that a poet's majority does not depend on his having written lengthy works, then Dickinson's status cannot be in doubt.

Even the most enthusiastic appreciations of her work have tended, however, to contain a note of reservation. She has been reproached for faults of technique, and her idiosyncratic sensibility has been criticized on account of the alleged whimsicality of its perceptions. The technical objections fall, insofar as they are not merely general, into three categories. First there is the question of her "bad grammar" (**Yvor Winters** wrote, in his *Maule's Curse*, of her "habitual carelessness"). The chief issue here is that of her very frequent use of a sort of subjunctive mood, of which the following lines provide an instance:

> Time is a test of trouble
> But not a remedy.
> If such it prove, it prove too
> There was no malady.

The usage here is surely justified, at least in the case of the first "prove," insofar as the subjunctive mood expresses an awareness that the statement is provisional: time may or may not "prove" a remedy. And the second "prove" contains a similar elliptical suggestion: "may prove" or "will prove" are implied. At all events, this feature of Dickinson's poetry occurs far too often to be ascribed to "carelessness," and is better seen as a (largely successful) attempt to express linguistically the poet's tentative and scrupulous searching for the truth, which she could never see as straightforward or self-evident. Nor should we forget that there are, especially during the period of Dickinson's greatest creative power in the early 1860s, many poems of confident assertion, strongly indicative in mood, like "Because I could not stop for Death."

Other critics speak of failings in meter and in rhyme. It is certainly difficult to find any consistent explanation for the irregularities of Dickinson's verse, any principle on which they can be said deliberately to occur. This does not, however, oblige us to consider such irregularities as weaknesses. Dickinson composed by instinct (which is not to say automatically), adapting the basic rhythms of the hymns she had heard from childhood; and her instinct told her that mechanical regularity would make for monotony. Her poems are a great deal more varied than their appearance on the page might suggest. Generalization is inappropriate in this connection, for her rhythms, considered as personal variations on a rigid pattern, are to be acclaimed or found wanting according to the shapes and sounds of particular poems. To my ear, at least, her rhythmic sense is seldom absolutely deficient, and often inspired.

In the matter of rhyme, it is probably equally misconceived to search for a uniform pattern, although some have tried to show that her use of assonance in place of full rhyme is always deliberate artistry. It would be truer to say that full rhyme usually, though not invariably, accompanies moods of confidence, while assonance implies uncertainty. But there are significant exceptions to this rule. All we can safely assert is that she felt no compulsion to find exact rhymes, and that the use of assonance also helped her to get away from the mechanical jingle of hymn-forms.

Those who object to the quality of Dickinson's sensibility cannot, of course, be answered "in good set terms." This is inevitably a subjective matter; moreover, the idiosyncratic vision of which we are speaking is not evident only intermittently, in this image or that turn of phrase, but informs every line, so that despite their differences Dickinson's poems are always unmistakably hers. One can do no more here than offer a brief sketch of her sensibility, hoping to counter the charge of whimsicality or childishness—as opposed to what might be called child*like*ness that certainly is present in her work, and helps to account for the immediacy as well as the strangeness of such an image as "Great streets of silence led away / To neighborhoods of pause." Immediacy of perception; a predominantly spatial (rather than temporal) apprehension; a direct and yet uncanny confrontation with natural phenomena—these qualities, epitomized in poems such as "A narrow fellow in the grass" or "I started early, took my dog" go to make up the distinctive atmosphere of her work. But, although these qualities might in themselves be called childlike or naif, those epithets would quite fail to characterize Dickinson's poetry as a whole. In the following, for instance, we find indeed a physical image, but this is no more than the beginning of the poem, the vivid introduction to the metaphor whose meaning the lines develop:

> It dropped so low in my regard
> I heard it hit the ground
> And go to pieces on the stones
> At bottom of my mind;
>
> Yet blamed the fate that fractured less
> Than I reviled myself
> For entertaining plated wares
> Upon my silver shelf.

This is scarcely the observation of a child. The poem, moreover, is typical in this respect of its author's work. The clarity of physical image serves above all to enforce what we must call the poem's abstract meaning, which in this case is moral and psychological. Similarly, the poem "Presentiment is that long shadow on the lawn" does not describe any particular lawn at dusk so much as it invokes, with wonderful economy, the essential nature of all presentiment and all nightfalls. The same, finally, is true of many of those poems whose theme is death. If we think of the graphic spareness of "There's been a death in the opposite house," of the more exuberant images of "As far from pity as complaint," or of the triumphantly bold conceit that ends "Ample make this bed" ("Let no sunrise' yellow noise / Interrupt this ground"), we recognize that the poet has not only made alive for us an unfamiliar world of the senses, but in doing so has created a new awareness of the experience underlying the phenomena that she has described.

The underlying common quality that especially characterizes Dickinson's poetry is best denoted by her own term "awe." Awe is fear divested of its physical attributes and raised to the status of a mental attitude. It is the spiritual form of fear, or the corporeal form of reverence, and defines the nature of the childlike sensibility's response to the wonder and ecstasy of simple existence. This sense of awe is clearly present in a poem like "I know some lonely houses off the road," but it is also a general presence, found to some degree even in so brief and seemingly impersonal a poem as this:

> How still the bells in steeples stand
> Till swollen with the sky,
> They leap upon their silver feet
> In frantic melody.

The sensibility that perceived bells in this way was not, it goes without saying, "normal"—any more than were the sensibilities of John Clare or Vincent van Gogh. But the intensity of the vision defies the charge of eccentricity, and the perception, although so wholly personal, is at the same time universal. The analogy with van Gogh can be pursued, for in the case of the poet as of the painter an initial sense of strangeness gives way to a recognition that we too have known just such experiences as are being depicted, but could never acknowledge them as ours until they were articulated for us by another's art.

In order further to apprehend, if not to understand, the success of this articulation, we have to consider Dickinson's language. To examine her use of words in constructing the world in which she lived out her poems is a long and rewarding study that cannot be undertaken here. One might usefully begin with a consideration of her undoubted sensitivity to the quality that makes English unique among European languages as a poetic medium, its contrasting and complementary Saxon and Romance elements. Not all poets have recognized the exceptional resources of this vocabulary, but the greatest, of whom Chaucer and Shakespeare are the pre-eminent examples, have undoubtedly done so. Dickinson, as a close reading of her poems will confirm, is to be counted among their number.

—James Reeves

See the essay on "Because I could not stop for Death."

DIDION, Joan

Born: Sacramento, California, 5 December 1934. **Education:** California Junior High and C.K. McClatchy Senior High, 1948-1952; University of California, Berkeley, B.A., 1956. **Family:** Married writer John Gregory Dunne in 1964; one daughter. **Career:** Promotional copywriter, then associate feature editor for *Vogue,* New York, 1956-63, resigned editorship but continued writing as film critic, 1963; moved to Los Angeles in 1964; columnist for the *Saturday Evening Post,* 1967-69; columnist for *Life,* 1969-70; columnist for *Esquire,* 1976-77; contributor of articles, short stories, and reviews to numerous magazines in the 1960s and 1970s, including *Harper's Bazaar, Holiday, New Yorker, New York Review of Books,* the *New York Times Book Review,* and the *National Review;* moved to a beach house in Trancas, on the Pacific Coast north of Los Angeles, 1971; visiting regents lecturer in English, University of California, Berkeley, 1975; moved to Brentwood Park, Los Angeles, 1978. **Awards:** First prize, *Vogue*'s Prix de Paris, 1956; Bread Loaf fellowship in fiction, 1963; Morton Dauwen Zabel Award, National Institute of Arts and Letters, 1978; Edward MacDowell medal, 1996. **Residence:** New York City.

PUBLICATIONS

Novels

Run River. 1963.
Play It As It Lays. 1970.
A Book of Common Prayer. 1977.

Democracy. 1984.
The Last Thing He Wanted. 1996.

Essays

Slouching towards Bethlehem. 1968.
The White Album. 1979.
Salvador. 1983.
Miami. 1987.
After Henry. 1992.

Screenplays: *Panic In Needle Park,* with John Gregory Dunne, 1971; *Play It As It Lays,* with John Gregory Dunne, 1972; *A Star Is Born,* with John Gregory Dunne, 1976; *True Confessions,* with John Gregory Dunne, 1981; *Up Close and Personal,* with John Gregory Dunne, 1996.

Other

Telling Stories. 1978.

*

Bibliography: *A Bibliography of Writings about Joan Didion* by Katherine Usher Henderson, 1989; "Joan Didion: A Checklist, 1955-1980" by Donna Olendorf, in *Bulletin of Bibliography,* January-March 1981.

Critical Studies: *Bright Book of Life: American Novelists and Storytellers from Hemingway to Mailer* by Alfred Kazin, 1973; *Joan Didion* by Mark Royden Winchell, 1980; *The Art of Fact: Contemporary Artists of Nonfiction* by Barbara Lounsberry, 1990; *Strategies of Reticence: Silence and Meaning in the Works of Jane Austen, Willa Cather, Katherine Ann Porter, and Joan Didion* by Janis P. Stout, 1990; *Writing War: Fiction, Gender, and Memory* by Lynne Hanley, 1991; "A Hard Story to Tell: The Vietnam War in Joan Didion's *Democracy*" by Stuart Ching, in *Fourteen Landing Zones: Approaches to Vietnam War Literature,* 1992; "Joan Didion and the Problem of Journalistic Travel Writing" by Mark Z. Muggli, in *Temperamental Journeys: Essays on the Modern Literature of Travel* edited by Michael Kowalewski, 1992; *The Critical Response to Joan Didion* edited by Sharon Felton, 1994; *Through the Window, Out the Door: Women's Narratives of Departure, from Austin and Cather to Tyler, Morrison, and Didion* by Janis P. Stout, 1998; *Women Writers at Work: The Paris Review Interviews* edited by George Plimpton, 1998.

*   *   *

"We tell ourselves stories in order to live," writes Joan Didion in the opening lines of *The White Album.* "The naked woman on the ledge outside the window on the sixteenth floor is a victim of accidie, or the naked woman is an exhibitionist . . . . We look for the sermon in the suicide, for the social or moral lesson in the murder of five. We interpret what we see, select the most workable of multiple choices." Journalist, essayist, and novelist, Didion is most known for her precise and unsentimental view of contemporary California life. She admits that she is not an intellectual writer (intellectuals deal with abstractions, she says), and is more concerned with facts and details than with ideas and theories. Her training as a journalist and film critic have contributed much to

her atypical literary voice. One of the most common themes of her work is the deterioration of society in the twentieth century, a theme captured in the quotation from William Butler Yeats that she uses as an epigraph to her essay collection *Slouching towards Bethlehem:* "Things fall apart; the center cannot hold;/Mere anarchy is loosed upon the world." According to Michiko Kakutani in *Essays and Conversations,* Didion creates in her books "one of the most devastating and distinctive portraits of modern America to be found in fiction or non-fiction." How people survive in this landscape of spiritual poverty is the subject of most of Didion's work.

Didion's pioneer ancestry is evident in her writings. Her family came to the Sacramento Valley in the 1800s, and her great-great grandmother, Nancy Hardin Cornwall, was an original member of the 1846 Donner party. (By the time the party was trapped in a mountain pass in a storm and had to resort to cannibalism to stay alive, Nancy Hardin Cornwall had already separated with a group from the party and had headed north through Oregon). This heritage noticeably enriches Didion's writing, for she writes about individualists, extremes, and frontiers. To her, a "frontier" may be psychological, political, or geographical.

In her first novel, *Run River,* she depicts the frontier of the postwar California Sacramento Valley. The heroine, Lily Knight McClellan, sees some of the values she has grown up with challenged in her adult life and obliterated by social and economic change. The author dramatizes the impact of World War II and the ensuing industrial and housing expansion that followed it by contrasting it against the image of the rich Sacramento River and the fertile valley that it supplies. In the background of the story lies one of Didion's favorite subjects, the history of the westward migration in America and the toppling of the romantic idea that California's first settlers were heroes poised for a new Eden, where freedom and riches awaited. Both Lily and Everett's families have lived in the valley since the 1850s and neither one of them wakes fully from the illusion that the Sacramento Valley is a paradise unto itself where no one hurts anyone and nothing from the outside can penetrate. But the novel ultimately concerns Lily's failed marriage and her attempt to gain control of a life in shambles; by the time the book ends, there are two suicides, an abortion, and a murder.

Didion attests that she had a happy childhood in the Sacramento Valley but that she was jittery and lived with a constant dread of something: bombs, drowning in the Sacramento river, crossing bridges. Her mother suggested that she write to distract her from these fears. Her first story, about a woman who dreams she is freezing to death in the Arctic, who awakens to find she is actually burning in the desert sun. Didion was only five.

During World War II, while Didion was still young, the family followed her father around the country from one Air Corps base to another, settling for brief periods in Washington, North Carolina, and Colorado. When the war ended, the family returned to Sacramento, but it was a long time before Didion felt settled. The theme of the stories she wrote at this time seems to reflect her despair and detachment. Her central characters commit suicide by jumping off a bridge or by walking into the ocean. It was in her early teens, however, that Didion began writing in earnest. Not only did she spend hours alone writing her own stories, but she also practiced typing whole chapters from the fiction of **Ernest Hemingway,** Joseph Conrad, and **Henry James.**

Didion majored in English at the University of California at Berkeley, publishing her first short story in the campus magazine *Oc-*

cident. In 1955, her senior year at Berkeley, she won first prize in *Vogue's* Prix de Paris with an article on William Wilson Wurster, the founder of the San Francisco style of architecture. *Vogue* offered her a choice of prizes: a cash prize and a job at their New York office or a trip to France. Didion took the job and the cash prize and moved to New York, where she began as a promotional copywriter. During her eight-year stay with the magazine, she was promoted to associate feature editor and met John Gregory Dunne, a staff writer at *Time,* whom she married in 1964.

In her highly praised collection of essays, *Slouching towards Bethlehem,* Didion presents herself as one well acquainted with the edge. To garner more material for her essays, she lived among the hippies of Haight-Ashbury in San Francisco. The collection includes twenty essays from the years 1963 to 1968 divided into three sections: section one is comprised of eight journalistic feature articles; section two consists of five personal essays; section three's seven essays are written in a style that mixes journalistic and personal techniques. Drug-dazed children, convicted murderers, and narcissistic rock bands haunt the essays. Didion writes of cases of "bad nerves," of taking "gin and hot water to blunt the pain and [taking] Dexedrine to blunt the gin." And, of course, social and philosophical questions riddle *Slouching towards Bethlehem.* Didion tackles issues on the level of the community and the nation at first and then looks for continuity with her own personal history in light of contemporary events. Questions such as "What makes us American?" "How do we choose our heroes?" "How much responsibility does one have for one's own actions?" unite the sketches. These themes give framework to a drama that is otherwise fragmented, much like the lives of its real-life characters.

With the publication of *Play It As It Lays* in 1970, Didion was established as a major talent among American novelists. To the author's surprise, the book immediately became a national best seller and was nominated for a National Book Award. Like *Run River, Play It As It Lays* details the impact of industrialization on a generation taught to respect religion, marriage, and democracy. Again mining her native California for evidence of the general social deterioration, Didion creates a protagonist who struggles to make sense of a meaningless life. The heroine, Maria Wyeth, faces a world that has no moral center, a world of barrenness and lovelessness. She harbors a dream of familial harmony while living and working in Beverly Hills and Hollywood, places whose citizens value physical beauty, power, and success. Maria's father explains that life is like a craps game: it must be played as it lies. The novel becomes a record of Maria's emotional breakdown. The action takes place in Maria's tortured mind, which has weathered a "successful" modeling career in New York, an unstable marriage, a friend's suicide, and a therapeutic abortion. Maria cannot survive with the Hollywood jet set, yet she never stops trying to make sense of her world. Like a writer who attempts to make sense of the things she sees happening in the world, Maria is trying to make meaning out of the "plot" of her life, but all she sees are "images with no meaning." Carol Anshaw of the *Village Voice* is correct when she links the author to her heroines. Like the women in her books, says Anshaw, Didion "stands observant in the shadows, numbed and jaded from too much acquaintance with celebrity and money and power, drawn to their observances and rituals even as she dismisses them."

A discernable heroine appears in most of Didion's works of both fiction and nonfiction: a wanderer, outsider, a survivor who manages to continue playing the game despite the odds. Although her heroines have been disappointed by promises, have lost their lovers to divorce, cancer, or suicide, and have been separated from their children, they survive.

Didion's third novel, *A Book of Common Prayer,* is another testimonial to chaos and violence. Every character in the novel is touched by some measure of political violence. Grace Strasser-Mendana, the narrator, is the mother of a rebel in Central America; Charlotte Douglass, the main character, is the mother of a student outlaw in the United States; Charlotte's husband Leonard is a lawyer who arranges the purchase of artillery for international revolutionaries. Investigating the consequences of societal breakdown on parents and children, Didion shows us that parents' failure to explain the world to their children is a consequence of their own failure to understand it. Didion registers familiar feelings of her generation: as Hendrick Hertzberg notes in a review of Didion for the *New York Times Book Review,* "she is an expert geographer of the landscape of American public culture, and she knows that the lines on the maps most of us use seldom correspond to the real boundaries."

The White Album, Didion's second volume of essays, is a continuation of her nonfictional account of the decade of the sixties in the United States. Kakutani relates that Didion found the Beatles' *White Album* "ominous and disturbing, an album inextricably connected to the Manson murders and the dissonance of the 60's." Like a photo album, *The White Album* contains images, fragments of the era: the Beatles' album of the same title (suggested by the plain white cover of the book), conversations with musicians the Doors and Janis Joplin, the media accounts of the Manson murders, student protests, barricades and bombings, political assassinations, the Vietnam War. *The White Album* was nationally acclaimed for its insight into the sixties in the United States as well as for its precision and economy of style. The essays cover a wide range of subjects. This "album" also includes a sketch of a Mexican gardener who raises orchids in Malibu, California; an essay on Hollywood as the "last extant stable society"; a tribute to the artist Georgia O'Keeffe and to the poet Doris Lessing. At the beginning of the book Didion copies verbatim a psychiatric report of her depression based on tests that she took as an outpatient in a Santa Monica clinic in 1968. As narrator of the collage of images that make up the *White Album,* Didion presents herself as one alienated from the mainstream culture: "You are getting a woman who somewhere along the line misplaced whatever slight faith she ever had in the social contract . . . in the whole grand pattern of human endeavor." This "voice from the fringe" best characterizes the author of *The White Album.* As Carol Anshaw puts it in the *Village Voice:* "Everything Didion writes has a land's-end edginess to it—a hyperattentive eye on the dramas found on the outskirts of the human condition."

After Henry, Didion's third collection of essays, is dedicated to her editor and mentor, Henry Robbins, who died in 1979. Three broad subjects carry the book: Washington, D.C., California, and New York City. Underlying the "Washington" section with the theory that presidential campaigns are a collaborative effort of journalists and candidates, she shrewdly examines the Reagan presidency and 1988 presidential campaign. In the seven essays that comprise the "California" section, Didion explores the psychological and political implications of everything from the state's fires and earthquakes to Hollywood screenwriting to Los Angeles zoning laws for a new international airport. "New York" centers around the social and political implications of the famous "Central Park Jogger Crime" of 1989. She proceeds, in journalistic fashion, to delineate the clash between those who "seized upon the attack on the jogger as an exact representation of what was wrong with the city" and those who believed almost the opposite, that the rapist was also a victim of a ruined environment. Didion relates the manner in which the media reports collaborate with the stories New Yorkers told themselves about the attack to offer "a sentimental reading of class differences and human suffering, a reading that promises both resolution and retribution," but that in fact serves "as a built-in source of natural morphine working to blur the edges of real and to a great extent insoluble problems."

In addition to writing novels and essays, Didion occasionally writes screenplays with her husband, John Gregory Dunne. The two collaborated on a screenplay of *Play It As It Lays, Panic in Needle Park* (based on a James Mills book of the same title), *A Star Is Born,* and *True Confessions* (based on Dunne's novel of the same title). The two have edited each other's work since their marriage.

Whether Didion is writing as an essayist, journalist, short story writer, or novelist, she always adheres to her self-proclaimed mission as a writer: "to witness well." Like George Orwell, who from his early teen-age years developed the habit of observing the smallest concrete detail, Didion conveys abstract truths through the description of concretely rendered scenes. As Kakutani puts it, Didion is "a gifted reporter with an eye for the telling detail . . . she is also a prescient witness, finding in her own experiences parallels of the times."

—Susan A. Bunn

DILLARD, Annie

Born: Pittsburgh, Pennsylvania, 30 April 1945. **Education:** The Ellis School, Pittsburgh, Pennsylvania, 1955-63; Hollins College, Roanoke, Virginia, 1963-68, B.A. 1967, M.A. 1968. **Family:** Married 1) Richard Dillard in 1965 (divorced 1975); 2) Gary Clevidence in 1979 (divorced 1988), one daughter; 3) Robert Richardson in 1989. **Career:** Writer. Scholar-in-residence, Western Washington University, 1975-79; visiting professor, 1979-1981, adjunct professor, beginning 1983, and beginning 1987 writer-in-residence Wesleyan University. Contributing editor, *Harper's* magazine, 1974-81, 1983-85. **Awards:** Pulitzer prize, for general nonfiction, 1975; New York Press Club award for Excellence, 1975; Washington's Governor's award for Literature, 1977; Connecticut's Governor's Arts award, 1993; Best foreign book, 1990; Western Pennsylvania Historical Society History Makers award, 1993; National Endowment for the Arts/Literature grant, 1982-83; Phi Beta Kappa Orator, Harvard Commencement Exercises, 1983; New York Public Library Literary Lion, 1984; John Guggenheim Foundation grant, 1986; Appalachian Gold Medallion, 1989; St. Botolph's club foundation award in the arts, Boston, 1989; Ambassador Book award in letters, English Speaking Union, 1989; Boston Globe "Best Books of the Decade"; Milton prize, 1994; The Campion award, 1994; Connecticut Women's Hall of Fame, 1997; fellow, Calhoun College, Yale, beginning 1997; award in literature, American Academy of Arts and Letters, 1998 Honorary degrees: Boston College; University of Hartford; Connecticut College. **Residence:** Connecticut.

PUBLICATIONS

Collection

The Annie Dillard Reader. 1994.

Nonfiction

Pilgrim at Tinker Creek. 1974.
Holy the Firm. 1977.
Living By Fiction. 1982.
Teaching a Stone to Talk. 1982.
Encounters with Chinese Writers. 1984.
An American Childhood. 1987.
The Writing Life. 1989.
The Living. 1992.
For the Time Being. 1999.

Poetry

Tickets for a Prayer Wheel. 1974.

Other

Editor, *Inventing the Truth: The Art and Craft of Memoir.* 1987.
Best Essays of 1998, with Robert Atwan. 1998.

*

Manuscript Collection: Beinecke Library, Yale University.

Critical Studies: "The Spirit of Quest in Two Works by Annie Dillard" by Richard Messer, in *Journal of Evolutionary Psychology,* 1988; "Fellow Rebels: Annie Dillard and Maxine Hong Kingston" by Joan Bischoff, in *The English Journal,* December 1989, pp. 62-67; *Annie Dillard's Aesthetic* (dissertation) by Cam Balzer, 1991; *Annie Dillard* by Linda L. Smith, 1991; *Seeking Awareness in American Nature Writing* by Scott Slovic, 1992; "Following the Paths of Thoreau and Dillard" by Karen Werkenthin, in *English Journal,* October 1992; *The Space Between* by Sandra Humble Johnson, 1992; *The Environmental Imagination* by Lawrence Buell, 1995; *Lee Smith, Annie Dillard* by Nancy Parrish, 1998.

*   *   *

Annie Dillard's 1999 induction into the prestigious American Academy of Arts and Letters attests to her contribution to postmodern literature. Winning approval from most critics, Dillard has been described as a writer who explores mankind's relationship to God and asks vital questions about the meaning of life and death. A meditative and inspirational tone unites her work, which includes autobiography, nature studies, literary criticism, fiction, and poetry. She takes her readers on journeys of spiritual discovery, and although the means of exploration vary from book to book, they invariably seek to reach the destinations of self-awareness and recognition of divinity. She explores relationships between the individual and the infinite as a modern metaphysician, seeking abstract wisdom by examining concrete realities, teaching her readers how to see the intricacies of the commonplace. In her essays, memoirs, poems, and novel, Dillard explores life, evil, and the significance of belief in God.

Beginning with her first publication *Tickets for a Prayer Wheel,* a book of contemplative poems, she expresses the need to discover God's presence, a theme that pervades her works. Her nonfiction *Pilgrim at Tinker's Creek,* for which she was awarded the Pulitzer Prize, examines the divinity of nature in a series of observations organized, like **Henry David Thoreau**'s *Walden,* around a calendar year from January to December. The experiences and meditations recorded in the book take place at a remote cabin and creek in the Roanoke Valley of Virginia. Here Dillard examines the bilateral conditions of the natural world, the existence of pain and peace, the phenomenon of life and death, and uses them as metaphors for the complexities of human life. In these essays containing abundant scientific facts, detailed descriptions of nature, and intense personal reactions, she reaches beyond the material reality to grasp the spiritual essence of life.

In a similar vein Dillard also combines nature writing and personal memoir in *Teaching a Stone to Talk: Expeditions and Encounters.* She reflects upon life's meaning as gleaned from her observations of local and exotic places, reacting with as much awe to an eclipse in central Washington state as to a tarantula in an Ecuadorean jungle. The fourteen essays in this book continue in the style of *Pilgrim at Tinker Creek*— contemplative, personal observations presented with the poetic grace that established her critical reputation. As in *Teaching a Stone to Talk,* Dillard's work often develops from her journeys. For example, she describes a visit to China in 1982 in *Encounters with Chinese Writers,* and in doing so, she explores the Chinese and American cultures.

Dillard followed *Pilgrim at Tinker Creek* with *Holy the Firm,* in which she questions the intentions of a God who allows the innocent to suffer. Presented in the form of a journal of autumn days on Washington's Puget Sound, Dillard's thoughts arise from her need to examine her own religious beliefs after hearing that a neighbor's child has been hurt in a plane crash. In her analyses of natural violence and random human suffering, she concludes that one cannot understand divine intent. She voices these musings again in *For the Time Being.* This book contains a "quilted" pattern of Dillard's considerations about the Baal Shem Tov, the charismatic leader of the Hasidim, and the Jesuit paleontologist and theologian Teilhard de Chardin, interspersed with descriptions of visits to China and Israel, and contemplation about birth defects, clouds, mass executions, and sand. The accumulation of despairing images prompts her to suggest that when God prays He might say, "May it be my will that my mercy overcome my anger." She concludes these often-disturbing thoughts with an anecdote that implies the forward progression of mankind. Her main point here as well as throughout her work is that hope lies within the individual. Her purpose, it seems, is to present the intricacies of existence so that, somewhere in the collage, the reader may see his own reflection, enabling him to propel himself along a path of divinity rather than evil.

For the Time Being is an example of a kind of literary structure that Dillard applauds. In an earlier book, *Living by Fiction,* she discusses structural forms of modern literature as a way to understand the twentieth century. Using her own term "contemporary modernists" to classify writers such as Italo Calvino, Manuel Puig, Alain Robbe-Grillet, Carlos Fuentes, Jorge Luis Borges, Samuel Beckett, **John Barth**, **Donald Barthelme**, and **Thomas Pynchon**, Dillard examines how they interpret the modern world. Part of their appeal to her lies in their ability to create "narrative collages" that capture the fragmented reality of contemporary life. These writers, according to Dillard, offer an intellectual depth rather than the emotional depth of traditional fiction. The annular structure that Dillard admires appears in her own works, notably *An American Childhood, The Living,* and *For the Time Being,* and has been the cause of both critical praise and disapproval. She has also used a method that resembles collage in the construction of a book of poetry, *Mornings Like This: Found Poems,* which consists of fragments of pre-existing texts from such disparate sources as a junior high school English book and a nineteenth-century medical tract. Here and throughout her work, Dillard's use of the collage method may appear random and her writing full of apparently trivial facts, but in the end, the segments add up to a complex, unified whole.

Most of Dillard's nonfiction uses personal memoir as a minor, but integral part of a collage that actually has a larger focus. *An American Childhood,* though, makes its main focus Dillard's own life, offering an account of her inquisitiveness, imagination, and developing intellectual proclivity during her early years growing up in an elite Presbyterian community of Pittsburgh. In a break from traditional autobiography, she has written an autobiography of the mind rather than a narrative of the events in her life. It contains the same kind of meditative, mystical observations that exist in her other works, only here they are recorded as memories of childhood experiences. Some critics fault the book for its lack of narrative structure and well-developed character, but Dillard's intention is to show the degree to which incidents of observation and intellectual pursuits shaped her life even from childhood. Dillard also focuses on herself, although somewhat peripherally, in *The Writing Life,* in which she shares her experiences as an author, her worldview, and her reactions to literature as sources for her own work. She informs the reader of the struggles that she and well-known authors of the past have endured in the creation of literature.

A diverse talent, Dillard has also produced a novel, *The Living,* set between 1855 and 1897 in the state of Washington. In epic style it tells of the Chinese, European, and Yankee settlers drawn to the northwest by the promise of opportunity and of the Native Americans displaced by them. *The Living* contains much intricate detail, bears witness to Dillard's intense interest in nature, and is written in a cyclical, collagelike form—all chacteristics that continually recur in her nonfiction work.

— Sharon Brown

DOCTOROW, E(dgar) L(aurence)

Born: New York City, 6 January 1931. **Education:** Kenyon College, Gambier, Ohio, A.B. (with honors), 1952; Columbia University, New York, NY, graduate study, 1952-53. **Military Service:** Served in the U.S. Army Signal Corps, 1953-55. **Family:** Married Helen Esther Setzer in 1954, one son and two daughters. **Career:** Worked as script reader, Columbia Pictures Industries, Inc., New York City; senior editor, New American Library, New York City, 1959-64; editor-in-chief, Dial Press, New York City, 1964-69; vice-president, publisher, Dial Press, New York City, 1968-69; writer-in-residence, University of California, Irvine, 1969-70; faculty member, Sarah Lawrence College, Bronxville, NY, 1971-78; Glucksman Professor of English and American Letters, New York University, New York City, 1982—; creative writing fellow, Yale School of Drama, New Haven, Connecticut, 1974-75; visiting professor, University of Utah, Salt Lake City, 1975; visiting senior fellow, Princeton University, Princeton, New Jersey, 1980-81. **Awards:** National Book award nomination, 1972; Guggenheim Fellowship, 1973; Creative Artists Service Fellow, 1973-74; National Book Critics Circle award and Arts and Letters award, 1976; National Book award Nomination, 1980; National Book award, 1986; Edith Wharton citation of merit for fiction and New York State author, 1989-91; PEN/Faulkner award for Fiction, National Book Critics Circle award, and William Dean Howells Medal, 1990. **Member:** American Academy and Institute of Arts and Letters. **Residence:** New York City.

PUBLICATIONS

Collections

Jack London, Hemingway, & the Constitution: Selected Writings, 1977-1992. 1993.
Three Complete Novels. 1994.

Short Fiction

Lives of the Poets: Six Stories and a Novella. 1984.

Novels

Welcome to Hard Times. 1960; as *Bad Man From Bodie.* 1961.
Big As Life. 1966.
The Book of Daniel. 1971.
Ragtime. 1975.
Loon Lake. 1980.
World's Fair. 1985.
Billy Bathgate. 1989.
The Waterworks. 1994.

Plays

Drinks before Dinner (produced 1978). 1979.

Screenplay: *Daniel* (based on *The Book of Daniel*). 1983.

Other

Conversations with E.L. Doctorow. 1999.

*

Critical Studies: *E. L. Doctorow: Essays and Conversations* edited by Richard Trenner, 1983; *Models of Misrepresentation: On the Fiction of E. L. Doctorow* by Christopher D. Morris, 1991; *E. L. Doctorow* by John G. Parks, 1991; "The Politics of Polyphony: The Fiction of E.L. Doctorow" by John G. Parks in *Twentieth-Century Literature* Winter 1991; interview with Christopher D. Morris in *Michigan Quarterly Review* vol. 30, no. 3, Summer 1991; "The Musical World of Doctorow's *Ragtime*" by Berndt Ostendorf in *American Quarterly* vol. 43, no. 4, December 1991; *Understanding E. L. Doctorow* by Douglas Fowler, 1992; "Cultural Hegemony Goes to the Fair: The Case of E. L. Doctorow's World's Fair" by Michael Robertson in *American Studies* vol. 33, no. 1, Spring 1992; "Genealogy/Narrative/Power: Questions of

Postmodernity in Doctorow's *The Book of Daniel* by T. V. Reed in *American Literary History* vol. 4, no. 2, Summer 1992; *Fiction As False Document: The Reception of E.L. Doctorow in the Postmodern Age* by John Williams, 1996; *The Political Fiction of E.L. Doctorow: Skeptical Comment* by Michelle M. Tokarczyk, 1999.

*   *   *

Edgar Laurence Doctorow has enjoyed considerable popular and critical success since his first book, *Welcome to Hard Times,* was published, later winning numerous awards and honors. He is best known, however, for *Ragtime,* one of his three novels that have been adapted for the movies, the other two being *Welcome to Hard Times* and *Billy Bathgate.* Still, a number of well-informed readers have hedged or withheld their approval of certain of his works on technical grounds, objecting to the liberties he has taken with traditional modes of novel and play construction. His critics also point out that Doctorow has failed to exert significant literary influence on younger writers.

Born in New York City in 1931—his father a music store proprietor, his mother a pianist—Doctorow early on was steeped in the topography and atmosphere of the huge metropolitan area he would later write about in such close detail. In addition he received an excellent education from precisely the kinds of academic institutions that would help to prepare him to deal as a writer with large subjects relating to the American experience. Doctorow received a B.A. degree (with honors) in 1952 from Kenyon College, the rural Ohio institution renowned for its academic critics and creative writers and for its literary studies, and attended graduate school at Columbia University. After military service and a job as script reader for Columbia Pictures, he enjoyed a highly successful career in the New York publishing business. He left publishing in 1969 to further his career as a writer.

Doctorow's flouting of literary conventions and his not having inspired literary followers (quite unlike such literary trailblazers as **Sherwood Anderson, Ernest Hemingway,** and **William Faulkner)** are closely related matters. As for the former, Doctorow has been criticized for deliberately obscuring his narrative point of view, making it unclear who is telling the story or even what the storyline is all about. He has also been faulted for taking liberties with American history and historical figures (in *Ragtime*), and for eliminating the concept of character in his stage-piece *Drinks before Dinner.*

While it is true that Doctorow's creative work has occasionally been experimental, challenging the very basis of literary communication between writer and reader, so has a notable portion of American (and foreign) literature posed such a challenge, steadily since the 1950s. Setting aside the early landmark in the overthrow of literary convention—Laurence Sterne's *Tristram Shandy* (1759-67), which did not alter the developmental course of the novel—a major literary revolution began taking place in the early 1950s. From this time on, numerous writers—among them Beckett, **Ionesco, Barth, Barthelme, Burroughs, Coover, Gass, Pynchon, Albee,** Cortazar, Robbe-Grillet, and Pinter—have been refashioning literature for a new age. (A few, such as Borges and Landolfi, began even earlier.)

Thus Doctorow's occasional departures from conventional literary norms should be considered as part of this long tradition, despite the unwillingness of many readers, and some critics as well, to accept them. Moreover, in the latter half of the twentieth century it has been difficult for a writer to be innovative enough to really break new ground—which was not the case when Anderson, Hemingway and Faulkner were developing their stylistic techniques. Hence Doctorow, for all his somewhat qualified popular and critical success, can hardly be expected to have become a strong literary influence on other writers. Distinctive as his writing is, in terms of his large aims and his depictions of the multifarious struggles of the weak against the strong, Doctorow is, finally, one more representative of a broad literary trend too powerful for many serious contemporaneous writers to resist. Notwithstanding all this, Doctorow is worthy of serious consideration in his own right, if only for the particular subject he chooses for each individual work and for how he deals with that subject.

Immediately evident upon consideration of Doctorow's varied works is one of the most interesting features of his literary career: his rich diversity of subject matter and personal interests. Critics and reviewers have spoken of his historical treatment of the American experience from his own social and political perspectives. They have also noted his ability to adapt familiar genres to his own ends, in accordance with his private vision. A brief look at the Doctorow canon should help clarify his contribution to contemporary American literature.

Welcome to Hard Times is a Western in which a psychopathic destroyer terrorizes a frontier town in the Dakota Territory. The sensitive, grieving mayor (20 years a widower), narrator of the horrific events, kills the evil man but agonizes over what has happened. *Big As Life* is a science-fiction fantasy about two monstrously huge nude human figures, suggesting a supernatural, supercolossal Adam and Eve, who make a sudden appearance in New York harbor. The result is chaos and controversy over what to do with the two enormous intruders. *The Book of Daniel* is a political polemical novel, a fictional recreation of—and a departure from—the story of the orphaned children of Julius and Ethel Rosenberg, who were convicted of espionage and executed in 1953.

Ragtime, Doctorow's most popular novel and one of the easiest of his works to read and enjoy, is a fictionalized social history of the earliest years of the twentieth century. Suggesting **John Dos Passos**'s *USA* trilogy, the novel offers a number of fascinating elements. Among these are: immigrants making their way in America, disadvantaged blacks in their relations with both good and bad whites, and an array of historical figures (Henry Ford, J.P. Morgan, **Emma Goldman**, and others) doing things that have never been recorded.

Doctorow's play *Drinks before Dinner* is concerned more with language and its intended effect on the reader than with anything else and in consequence it has been criticized for its shortcomings as a play. The action features slightly more than half a dozen "talking heads" at a New York City dinner party. The character Edgar (here as in *World's Fair,* Doctorow has bestowed his own first name on his protagonist; additional autobiographical hints are found in the play) complains at length about modern civilization. He subsequently brandishes an unloaded gun and behaves outrageously to an eminent guest, leaving all those inside and outside the play (except possibly Doctorow himself) puzzled about his purpose and meaning.

Loon Lake, perhaps Doctorow's most difficult book, is another fictionalized social history of, roughly, the first half of the twentieth century, with emphasis on the period of the Great Depression. It too suggests Dos Passos's *USA,* but it is the antithesis of *Ragtime* in mood and in narrative effectiveness. The story is largely about the effect of an industrial and business tycoon, F.W. Bennett, owner of Loon Lake and its adjunctive estate in the New York

Adirondacks, on the people around him. These include his aviatrix wife, the gangsters he entertains at Loon Lake, innumerable people dependent on him for a livelihood, and two curious outsiders who find a home of sorts on his property.

Edgar in *Drinks before Dinner* seems to bear a slight resemblance to Jonathan, the narrator in the novella "Lives of the Poets," included in the story collection of that name. Having walked out on his wife and children, Jonathan, a successful writer, ruminates over the broken domestic relationships and the crumbling society he sees all around him.

World's Fair, winner of the American Book Award for Fiction, is a veiled (*i.e.,* fictionalized) autobiography covering Doctorow's first decade or so of life in the Bronx. The shabby-genteel childhood of the protagonist, Edgar Altschuler, is described not only in terms of his growing awareness of things, but also contextually—through an elaborate mapping of locations and occasional references to popular-culture trivia and current events. At the close of the story, Edgar wins honorable mention in a World's Fair essay contest and gets to take his whole family to the fair. Finally, he makes his own time capsule of memorabilia in response to the World's Fair Time Capsule with its historic cultural artifacts. The novel has been compared with James Joyce's *A Portrait of the Artist as a Young Man,* but it lacks the depth and intensity of that book.

A significant reference in *World's Fair* to the mobster Dutch Schultz is a harbinger of Doctorow's gangster novel *Billy Bathgate,* a book praised for its vibrant, colorful style. It has been interpreted politically as an indictment of the gangsterism that underlies the capitalist system, sociologically as a realization of the American Dream, and literarily as the saga of a Depression-period Huck Finn and as a rags-to-riches fable. Billy Bathgate, a fatherless street urchin doing juggling tricks, is noticed by Schultz and earns a position of trust in the mob. At the end of his account of his life in crime, the conscienceless Billy gives thanks to God for all the terror he has known. Despite the gusto with which Doctorow depicts his rogues' gallery, these figures nevertheless seem flat and contrived.

Arguably his best and most important work to date is Doctorow's gothic detective-novel *Waterworks* (1994). Revealing an array of provocative themes and concerns, *Waterworks* is a rough guide to the politics, topography, and sociology of New York in 1871—in Doctorow's imagination. Always keen on rewriting American history when doing so might provide him with a good tale to tell (example, *Ragtime*), Doctorow utilizes the notorious Tweed Ring (the elaborate political network run by William M. "Boss" Tweed) as the background in dealing with a shady medical genius, Dr. Sartorius, whose medical experiments involve waifs plucked from the mean streets of New York. Clearly, *Waterworks* is no mere horror novel. Storyline aside, it is filled with philosophical speculations and commentary about science and morality, the profession and ethics of journalism, and the philosophy of painting. Beyond all this, it poses a challenge no other single work by Doctorow seems to throw at the reader. What is it about this book that makes the whole so much greater than the sum of its parts, so much grander than the dynamic interplay of themes, characters, symbols, and social and philosophical issues?

A many-sided writer, Doctorow seems to be fascinated by the very weak and the very strong, while always attempting to find a suitable voice (understandable or not to the reader) for his currently developing fantasy. In years to come he may be remembered less as a brilliant novelist or playwright than as an experimental stylist working seriously not with the sound of silence but with the sound of the inexpressible.

—Samuel Bellman

DOMINI, Rey. *See* **LORDE, Audre (Geraldine).**

DONLEAVY, J(ames) P(atrick)

Born: Brooklyn, New York, 23 April 1926. **Education:** Trinity College, Dublin. Became Irish citizen in 1967. **Military Service:** Served in the U.S. Navy during World War II. **Family:** Married 1) Valerie Heron (divorced), one daughter and one son; 2) Mary Wilson Price, one daughter and one son. **Career:** Cofounder, with son Philip and producer Robert Mitchell, of the De Alfonce Tennis Association for the Promotion of the Superlative Game of Eccentric Champions. **Awards:** Most Promising Playwright award, *Evening Standard,* 1960; Brandeis University Creative Arts award, 1961-62; citation from the National Institute and American Academy of Arts and Letters, 1975; Gold award, Worldfest, Houston, Texas, 1993; Cine Golden Eagle, for television, 1993. **Residence:** Westmeath County, Ireland.

PUBLICATIONS

Collection

An Author and His Image: The Collected Shorter Pieces. 1997.

Novels

The Ginger Man. 1955; introduction by Arland Ussher, 1956; complete and unexpurgated edition, 1965.
A Singular Man. 1963.
The Saddest Summer of Samuel S. 1966.
The Beastly Beatitudes of Balthazar B. 1968.
The Onion Eaters. 1971.
A Fairy Tale of New York. 1973.
The Destinies of Darcy Dancer, Gentleman. 1977.
Schultz. 1979.
Leila: Further in the Destinies of Darcy Dancer, Gentleman. 1983.
Are You Listening Rabbi Löw? 1987.
A Singular Country. 1990.
That Darcy, That Dancer, That Gentleman. 1990.
The Lady Who Liked Clean Rest Rooms. 1997.
Wrong Information Is Being Given Out at Princeton. 1998.

Short Stories

Meet My Maker the Mad Molecule. 1964.

Plays

The Ginger Man (adaptation of Donleavy's novel of the same title; produced 1959). 1959.
Fairy Tales of New York (adaptation of Donleavy's novel of the same title; produced 1961). 1961.

A Singular Man (adaptation of Donleavy's novel of the same title; produced 1964). 1964.
The Plays of J.P. Donleavy; with a Preface by the Author. 1973.
The Beastly Beatitudes of Balthazar B (adaptation of Donleavy's novel of the same title; produced 1981). 1981.

Radio Play: *Helen,* 1956.

Television: *J.P. Donleavy's Ireland in All Her Sins and Graces,* 1993.

Other

The Unexpurgated Code: A Complete Manual of Survival and Manners, illustrated by the author. 1975.
De Alfonce Tennis: The Superlative Game of Eccentric Champions, Its History, Accoutrements, Rules, Conduct, and Regimen. 1984.
J.P. Donleavy's Ireland: In All Her Sins and in Some of Her Graces. 1986; as *Ireland: In All Her Sins and in Some of Her Graces,* 1986.

*

Critical Studies: "No Face and No Exit: The Fiction of James Purdy and Donleavy" by Gerald Weales, in *Contemporary American Novelists* edited by Harry T. Moore, 1964; "A Case of Death: The Fiction of Donleavy" by Tom LeClair, in *Contemporary Literature* vol. 12, summer 1970; *Donleavy: The Style of His Sadness* by Charles G. Masinton, 1975.

* * *

J.P. Donleavy's first novel, *The Ginger Man,* introduced a most peculiar character by the name of Sebastian Dangerfield. He was the first in a series of characters whose names have become more and more easy to recognize as Donleavy's creations (which include Balthazar B, Sebastian S, Darcy Dancer, Cornelius Christian). Dangerfield was the first, however, to represent the perfect exile, the eternal stranger, the uncompromising loser. Although presented in a Kafkaesque vision against the absurdist background of a society that constantly requires compromises in order to accept him, Dangerfield is clearly Donleavy's alter ego. Like young Donleavy, Dangerfield aspires to success and recognition. He wishes to become "Sebastian Bullion Dangerfield, Chairman of Quids, Inc., largest banking firm in the world," but will never agree to become a puppet in the social game. No matter how greedy or envious, Dangerfield will never sacrifice his spirit in order to attain material success; however, he is not a liberated spirit. As William E. Grant states in an essay for the *Dictionary of Literary Biography,* "Sebastian reads law but creates chaos. Rabelaisian in his carnal appetites, Dangerfield exemplifies in his relentless search for alcohol and women all the excesses and failures of character society normally condemns: he lies, cheats, steals, and sponges without conscience."

After a series of rejections, *The Ginger Man* was published by Olympia Press in Paris and quickly established itself as a bestseller. Almost in spite of his own will, Sebastian Dangerfield became the antihero of a whole generation of college students. Nonconformist, theatrical, immoral, and persuasive, he is obsessed with death and incapable of love; he is, in other words, the dream of all restless, angry young men.

American literary criticism, as well as the Irish literary market find labeling Donleavy's work a difficult task. Like Dangerfield, author Donleavy refuses compromise. Disappointed by his American experience that, especially after the war, turned out to be sad and bitter, in 1946 Donleavy became a student of Trinity College in Dublin. Throughout the years he continued to return to America in search of the promised land that he never found, but the journeys brought neither peace nor happiness. In his essay "An Expatriate Looks at America" Donleavy confesses: "As far away as you may go, or as foreign as your life can ever become, there is something American that always stays stained American in you."

Donleavy's characters in his subsequent books seem somewhat related to Sebastian Dangerfield in the successful work *The Ginger Man.* They have in common their quixotic quest for a land that they could call home, and where they could finally learn how to live. Something is always in the way of their hopes, though; something that they mistakenly try to identify outside themselves, in the lives of the others.

George Smith, the hero of *A Singular Man,* is, as the title of the book presents him, a unique character obsessed by the idea of building a monumental mausoleum in the Renown Cemetery. If Dangerfield fights death, Smith is fascinated by it; he would even consider living in the mausoleum if that were not against the regulations of the cemetery. If Dangerfield and Smith, almost paranoid in their resentment of society, can still experience short and chaotic love stories, Samuel S (*The Saddest Summer of Samuel S*) finds himself trapped in a dead-end situation. He desperately wants to have a relationship, a family and children, but his efforts are dissipated by years of unsuccessful psychoanalytical treatment. At the end of his summers, Samuel S is lonely and defeated, a stranger in his own isolated world.

What saves Donleavy's novels from being perfect melodramas is his bitter sense of humor. His characters perceive the world and the society in which they live as a huge joke. History, or geography, for that matter, are of no importance: Donleavy's heroes inhabit nightmarish landscapes and live in hostile times. For some reason, the world does not work out for them. There comes a time, then, when like Kafka's K. or Melville's Bartleby, his heroes "prefer not to" live anymore their lives of quiet desperation and become, like their creator, silent and empty of feeling.

—Dayana Stetco

DONNELLY, Ignatius

Born: Philadelphia, Pennsylvania, 3 November 1831. **Education:** Central High School, Philadelphia, graduated 1849; read law in the office of Benjamin Harris Brewster, Philadelphia, 1850-52: admitted to Pennsylvania bar, 1852. **Family:** Married 1) Katharine McCaffrey in 1855 (died 1894), three children; 2) Marian Hanson in 1898. **Career:** Practiced law and active in Democratic politics, Philadelphia, 1852-56; moved to Minnesota, 1856; involved in unsuccessful attempt to develop Nininger City, Minnesota, 1857; left Democratic Party over slavery issue, 1857, and joined Republican Party; Lieutenant Governor of Minnesota, 1859-63; member (Republican, Minnesota), U.S. House of Representatives, Washington, D.C., 1863-69; lobbyist for railroad interests and correspondent for St. Paul *Dispatch,* Washington, D.C., 1869-70; President, National Anti-Monopoly Convention, 1872, and edi-

tor, *Anti-Monopolist* newspaper, 1874-79; member of the Minnesota Senate, 1874-78; Greenback-Democrat candidate for House of Representatives, 1878 (also candidate in 1884 and 1889); farmer and writer after 1878; Farmers Alliance member, Minnesota State Legislature, 1887; President, State Farmers Alliance of Minnesota, 1890, and helped turn Alliance into Populist Party, 1891-92 (wrote preamble to Populist Party's "Omaha Platform," 1892); Populist candidate for Governor of Minnesota, 1892, and nominee for U.S. Vice-President, 1898; founding editor, St. Paul *Representative,* from 1895. After 1878 developed theory that Francis Bacon wrote Shakespeare's plays. **Died:** 1 January 1901.

PUBLICATIONS

Fiction

Caesar's Column: A Story of the Twentieth Century. 1890; edited by Walter B. Rideout, 1960.
Doctor Huguet. 1891.
The Golden Bottle; or, The Story of Ephraim Benezet of Kansas. 1892.

Poetry

The Mourner's Vision. 1850.

Other

Nininger City. 1856.
The Sonnets of Shakespeare: An Essay. 1859.
Atlantis: The Antediluvian World. 1882; edited by Egerton Sykes, 1949.
Ragnarok: The Age of Fire and Gravel. 1883.
The Great Cryptogram: Francis Bacon's Cipher in the So-Called Shakespeare Plays. 1888.
In Memoriam Mrs. Katharine Donnelly. 1895.
The American People's Money. 1895; revised edition, as *The Bryan Campaign for the American People's Money,* 1896.
The Cipher in the Plays and on the Tombstone. 1899.

*

Bibliography: in *Bibliography of American Literature* by Jacob Blanck, 1957.

Critical Studies: *North Star Sage: The Story of Donnelly* by Oscar M. Sullivan, 1953; *Donnelly: Portrait of a Politician* by Martin Ridge, 1962; *Donnelly* by David D. Anderson, 1980; "Caesar no Kinechu Saiko" by Koji Oi, in *Yamakawa Kozo Kyoju Taikan Kinen Ronbunshu,* 1981; "Ignatius Donnelly: Caesar's Column: A Story of the Twentieth Century (1890)" by Hans Joachim Lang, in *Die Utopie in der angloamerikanischen Literatur: Interpretationen* edited by Hartmut Heuermann and Bernd Peter Lange, 1984; "Ignatius Donnelly Meets the Swedes" by Helen M. White, in *Minnesota History,* spring 1996.

*   *   *

Ignatius Donnelly's works are imaginative, eccentric, and occasionally startling in their perceptions. *Atlantis: The Antediluvian*

World is an attempt to demonstrate and expand upon Plato's myth of a great civilization that once supposedly existed near the mouth of the Mediterranean long before any similarly high culture, an island society suddenly destroyed by the gods because of its decadence. In his stupifyingly data-crammed book, Donnelly argued not only that Atlantis actually existed but that it was "the region where man first rose from a state of barbarism to civilization." Furthermore, Atlantis was the source of most of the world's gods, legends, inventions, languages, architectural styles, plants, and animals.

The book was extremely popular, running through over twenty editions, and it inspired countless imitators and followers to publish their corroborative findings. Since, as Martin Gardner says in *Fads and Fallacies,* there is "not a shred of reliable evidence, geological or archeological, to support" the myth, this popularity seems a testament to Donnelly's ability to immerse his readers in an impressively assembled mass of highly interesting but nearly totally misleading information. Donnelly's argument is dense and the farrago of seemingly expert testimony he scraped together from a wide variety of library nooks and crannies is mountainous: his own literary style is far from ornate, however, and though assertive seems simply the straight-from-the-shoulder truth of a no-nonsense scholar. The work is fun to read, filled with arcane stories and ingenious, wild yoking of disparate cultural phenomena. He advances all his evidence quite seriously, including parallel lists showing the similarities between the Sioux and Danish languages, and hilarious drawings of skulls from Central America and Egypt artificially deformed in the same fashion. In *Ragnarok: The Age of Fire and Gravel* he theorized that long ago the Earth passed through the tail of a giant comet, producing world-wide catastrophe, "rearings, howlings, . . . hissings," and great heat. When the fires from this heat subsided, an Age of Darkness began, followed by the Ice Age. In *The Great Cryptogram* he produced a thousand pages of cipher analyses and lists of parallel quotations to prove that Francis Bacon wrote Shakespeare's plays. One critic used Donnelly's de-coding formula to demonstrate that a passage from Hamlet really read "Dou-nill-he, the author, politician, and mountebanke, will work out the secret of this play. The sage is a daysie."

But it would be a mistake to dismiss Donnelly as a crank. He was, according to David W. Noble in *The Progressive Mind 1890-1917,* "one of the most important critics who represented and expressed the . . . fears which ultimately found political expression in the Populist Party of the 1890's." He is frequently fascinating and his forays into scientific theory or literary criticism display impressive if ill-digested and misguided learning, and sensitivity to literary values. Both *Ragnarok* and *Atlantis,* in some ways freakish books, also contain attacks upon the harsher aspects of social Darwinism, and *Atlantis* argues for the simpler virtues and systems of the early Jeffersonian Republic. Furthermore, in his fiction he seriously addressed social problems such as agricultural decay and the political weakness of the poor in *The Golden Bottle,* and racial intolerance in *Doctor Huguet,* a novel tracing complications following exchanges in racial identity. *Caesar's Column* is a minor anti-Utopian classic predicting class warfare between the economic oppressors and oppressed, forces equally matched in their brutality. Marred only by two silly love stories, the novel accurately depicts many technological horrors of the future—such as air raids—and, more importantly, discusses specific social reforms such as an eight-hour work day and socialized medicine. The book's central image is a grotesque symbol of modern civilization: Caesar's column is a gigantic pillar of dead bodies from both sides killed in the slaughter of war.

—Jack B. Moore

DOOLITTLE, Hilda

Writes as H.D. **Born:** Bethlehem, Pennsylvania, 10 September 1886. **Education:** Gordon School, and Friends' Central School, 1902-04, both Philadelphia; Bryn Mawr College, Pennsylvania, 1905-06. **Family:** Married the writer Richard Aldington in 1913 (separated 1918; divorced 1938); one daughter by Cecil Gray. **Career:** Lived in Europe after 1911; closely associated with the Imagist movement after 1912; editor, *Egoist* magazine, London, 1916-17 (took over editorship from Aldington); began long relationship with the writer Bryher (Annie Winifred Ellerman) in 1919; joint founder, *Close Up* film journal, Territet, Switzerland, 1927-33. **Awards:** Brandeis University Creative Arts award, 1959; American Academy award of Merit Medal, 1960. **Died:** 27 September 1961.

PUBLICATIONS

Collections

Collected Poems 1912-1944, edited by Louis L. Martz. 1983.

Poetry

Sea Garden. 1916.
Choruses from the Iphigenia in Aulis by Euripides. 1916.
The Tribute, and Circe: Two Poems. 1917.
Choruses from the Iphigenia in Aulis and the Hippolytus by Euripides. 1919.
Hymen. 1921.
Heliodora and Other Poems. 1924.
Collected Poems. 1925.
(Poems), edited by Hughes Mearns. 1926.
Red Roses for Bronze. 1931.
The Usual Star. 1934.
What Do I Love. 1943(?).
Trilogy. 1973.
   The Walls Do Not Fall. 1944.
   Tribute to the Angels. 1945.
   The Flowering of the Rod. 1946.
By Avon River. 1949; revised edition, 1986.
Selected Poems. 1957.
Helen in Egypt. 1961.
Two Poems. 1971.
Hermetic Definition. 1972.
The Poet and the Dancer. 1975.
Priest, and A Dead Priestess Speaks. 1983.

Plays

Hippolytus Temporizes. 1927; revised version, 1985.
Ion, from the play by Euripides. 1937; revised version, 1985.

Fiction

Palimpsest. 1926; revised edition, 1968.
Hedylus. 1928; revised edition, 1980.
Kora and Ka. 1934.
Nights. 1935.
The Hedgehog (for children). 1936.
Bid Me to Live: A Madrigal. 1960; revised edition, 1983.
HERmione. 1981; as *Her,* 1984.

Other

Borderline. 1930.
Tribute to Freud, with Unpublished Letters by Freud to the Author. 1956; revised edition, 1974.
Temple of the Sun. 1972.
End to Torment: A Memoir of Ezra Pound (includes poems by Pound), edited by Norman Holmes Pearson and Michael King. 1979.
The Gift (memoir). 1982; as *The Gift: The Complete Text,* 1998.
Notes on Thought and Vision, and The Wise Sappho. 1982.
Between History and Poetry: The Letters of H.D. and Norman Holmes Pearson. 1997.

*

Bibliography: "H.D.: A Preliminary Checklist" by Jackson R. Bryer and Pamela Roblyer, in *Contemporary Literature 10* ("H.D. Issue"), 1969.

Critical Studies: *The Heart of Artemis: A Writer's Memoirs* by Bryher, 1962; *The Classical World of H.D.* by Thomas Burnett Swann, 1962; *Doolittle/H.D.* by Vincent Quinn, 1967; *Psyche Reborn: The Emergence of H.D.* by Susan Stanford Friedman, 1981; *H.D.: The Life and Work of an American Poet* by Janice S. Robinson, 1982; *Herself Defined: The Poet H.D. and Her World* by Barbara Guest, 1984; *H.D.: Woman and Poet* edited by Michael King, 1986; *H.D.: The Career of That Struggle* by Rachel Blau DuPlessis, 1986; "H.D. and A.C. Swinburne: Decadence and Sapphic Modernism" by Cassandra Laity, in *Lesbian Texts and Contexts: Radical Revisions* edited by Karla Jay, Joanna Glasgow, and Catharine R. Stimpson, 1990; *H.D.: The Poetics of Childbirth* by Donna Krolik Hollenberg, 1991; "H.D.'s The Gift: 'Hide-and-Seek' with the 'Skeleton-Hand of Death'" by Miriam Fuchs, in *Redefining Autobiography in Twentieth-Century Women's Fiction: An Essay Collection* edited by Janice Morgan, Colette T. Hall, and Carol L. Snyder, 1991; "'O Careless, Unspeakable Mother': Irigaray, H.D. and Maternal Origin" by Claire Buck, in *Feminist Criticism: Theory and Practice* edited by Susan Sellers, Linda Hutcheon, and Paul Perron, 1991; "Science and the Mythopoeic Mind: The Case of H.D." by Adalaide Morris, in *Chaos and Order: Complex Dynamics in Literature and Science* edited by N. Katherine Hayles, 1991; "Canon, Gender, and Text: The Case of H.D." by Lawrence S. Rainey, in *Representing Modernist Texts: Editing as Interpretation* edited by George Bornstein, 1991; *Richard Aldington & H.D.: The Early Years in Letters* edited by Caroline Zilboorg, 1992; *The Veiled Mirror and the Woman Poet: H.D., Louise Bogan, Elizabeth Bishop, and Louise Gluck* by Elizabeth Dodd, 1992; *Out of Line: History, Psychoanalysis, and Montage in H.D.'s Long Poems* by Susan Edmunds, 1994; *H.D. and the Victorian Fin de Siècle: Gender, Modernism, and Decadence* by Cassandra Laity, 1996; *H.D. and Hellenism: Classic Lines* by Eileen Gregory, 1997.

*   *   *

H.D., the pen name for Hilda Doolittle, was a poet of considerable significance. Her work itself is precise, careful, sharp, and compressed; it gives one the sense that the poet is excluding much more than she expresses. Natural objects (e.g., "Oread," "Pear Tree") are presented in lines that are free of conventional poetic rhythms and that are yet as carefully shaped as a piece of Greek statuary. So the immediate pleasure of much of H.D.'s work is a response to an object that is created by a few carefully chosen phrases: phrases that exist in the presence of easy and facile language that has been excluded. As painters say, the "negative space"—the area around a represented object—is as important as the object itself.

H.D.'s work has an air of being isolated, of being simply her considered and purified record of what has stirred her senses and her emotions: the natural world with, for human context, the ancient Greek world as H.D. remembers it. Birds fly through air that is radiantly Greek, love intensifies its expression in the presence of Helen and Lais, and the mysteries of life and death bring into view satyrs and not Christian saints.

But H.D.'s work did not actually proceed in isolation; she was closely associated with the Imagist movement from 1913 onwards. **Ezra Pound**, **John Gould Fletcher**, **Amy Lowell**, and others thought of their poetic effort as a realization of **Walt Whitman**'s demand for new words that would bring poetry closer to the object it was "rendering" and free poetic expression from the abstractions and the overt moral purposes that had made much nineteenth-century poetry vague and imprecise. Poetry—and this was a main drive of Imagist theory—was a medium in which could appear the poet's direct apprehension of physical entities and the poet's immediate reaction to those entities. In pursuit of object and emotion, the poet should be free to discard both conventional rhythms and shop-worn poetic diction. Much of H.D.'s poetry achieves these aims. Thus, the emotion in many a poem is coerced, to be recreated in the mind of the reader, by the carefully selected physical details—details that pass before the reader following a syntax that is simple and uninvolved and expressed in words that are familiar and unmysterious. But the poems, in the long run, are not free of general impressions or even abstractions although they state very few. The impressions and abstractions must vary from reader to reader, but they concern the beneficence that reaches the human mind through the senses; it is a beneficence unsullied by ancient dogma and more recent social purpose. Poets like Shelley and Tennyson did not hesitate to offer "gospels." If there is some sort of message in much of H.D.'s work, it is very neatly fused with the external world she duplicates.

A modification of these effects appears in a later work like *The Walls Do Not Fall.* Using the techniques of the writer's previous verse, H.D. moves beyond the innocent and "natural" invocations of Greek health—health that is also of the physical world. But the destruction of World War II make the Greek health an insufficient corrective to modern chaos. *The Walls Do Not Fall* becomes quite specific about the sources of human health. Those sources find expression not only in halcyon flight and the play of light on the Aegean Sea. They can be traced in the essence of all great religions, and it is particularly the work of Egyptian gods that allows us to see the physical world achieving completion in myths and rituals. In such a body of faith as the Egyptian are myth and

"Vision" coming into a focus of great human relevance. H.D. sees the Egyptian Amen and the later "Christos" as identical. They and other August entities are the symbols, if not the ultimate elan, of the eternal cycles of excellence and health that modern insanity—in its pursuit of power and inferior sorts of knowledge—has ignored.

This concluding attitude in the work of H.D. may strike some readers as going beyond the confines of the early Imagism. The attitude can also be regarded as an effort to defend and exploit the initial stance of Imagist simplicity and directness. These are opposing judgments. At any rate, in her later work, H.D.'s implications intensify and complicate themselves. But the modes of expression do not change. Perhaps their persistence indicates an essential continuity in the entire body of her poetry.

—Harold H. Watts

DORRIS, Michael Anthony

Born: Dayton, Washington, 30 January 1945. **Education:** Georgetown University, Washington, D.C. (honors), B.A. 1967; Yale University, New Haven, Connecticut, M. Phil. 1970. **Family:** Married the writer Louise Erdrich in 1981; six children. **Career:** Graduate assistant, Yale University, 1969-70; assistant professor of anthropology, Johnston College, University of Redlands, Redlands, California, 1970-71; assistant professor, Franconia College, Franconia, New Hampshire, 1971-72; professor, Dartmouth College, Hanover, New Hampshire, 1972-97; founder, chairman of Department of Native American Studies, Dartmouth College, 1972-85. Editor of *Viewpoint,* 1967-68, *A Sourcebook for Native American Studies,* 1977; member of editorial board for *American Indian Culture Center Journal,* University of California, Los Angeles, beginning 1974; board of directors Save the Children, 1991-92. **Awards:** Danford graduate fellow, 1967; Woodrow Wilson graduate fellow, 1967; National Institute of Mental Health fellow, 1970, grantee, 1971; Spaulding-Potter Program grant, 1973; Guggenheim fellow, 1978; Woodrow Wilson faculty fellow, 1980; Rockefeller fellow, 1985-86; Indian achievement award, 1985; PEN Syndicated Fiction award, 1988; National Endowment for Arts creative writing fellow, 1989; Christopher award, 1990; Heartland Prize, 1990; National Book Critics award, 1990; Sara Josepha Hale award, 1991; Scott O'Dell award for Best Historical Fiction for Young Readers, 1992; *Boston Review* Best Short Story of 1992 award; International pathfinder award, World Conference on the Family, 1992; Award for Excellence, Center for Anthropology and Journalism, 1992; Minnesota Book award for best young adult fiction, 1996, for *Sees Behind Trees.* **Member:** Smithsonian Council, American Anthropological Association, Council on Anthropology and Education, American Folklore Society, National Congress of American Indians, Native American Rights Fund, National Indian Education Association, National Indian Youth Council, United Indian Planners Association. **Died:** (suicide) 11 April 1997.

PUBLICATIONS

Novels

A Yellow Raft in Blue Water. 1987.
The Crown of Columbus, with Louise Erdrich. 1991.

Morning Child (for children). 1992.
Guests (for children). 1994.
Sees Behind Trees. 1996.
Cloud Chamber. 1997.
The Window (for children). 1997.

Short Stories

Working Men. 1993.

Plays

Groom Service, adaptation of his own story (produced 1993).

Other

Native Americans: Five Hundred Years After, photographs by Joseph Farber. 1975.
A Guide to Research on North American Indians, with Arlene Hirschfelder and Mary Lou Byler. 1984.
The Broken Cord: A Family's Ongoing Struggle with Fetal Alcohol Syndrome (nonfiction). 1989.
Route Two (nonfiction), with Louise Erdrich. 1990.
Rooms in the House of Stone (nonfiction). 1993.
Paper Trail (essays). 1994.

Editor, *The Most Wonderful Books: Writers on Discovering the Pleasures of Reading.* 1997.

*

Critical Studies: "Acts of Recovery: The American Indian Novel in the '80s" by Louis Owens, in *Western American Literature,* vol. 22, no. 1, 1987, and "Erdrich and Dorris's Mixedbloods and Multiple Narratives" by Owens, in *Other Destinies: Understanding the American Indian Novel,* 1992; "An Interview with Louise Erdrich and Dorris" by Hertha D. Wong, in *North Dakota Quarterly* vol. 55, no. 1, 1987; "An Interview with Louise Erdrich and Dorris" by Kay Bonetti, in *Missouri Review,* vol. 11, no. 2, 1988; "Exploring the Meaning of Discovery in *The Crown of Columbus*" by Thomas Matchie, in *North Dakota Quarterly,* vol. 59, no. 4, 1991; "Shifting Identity in the Work of Louise Erdrich and Dorris" by Ann Rayson, in *Studies in American Indian Literatures,* vol. 3, no. 4, 1991; *Conversations with Louise Erdrich and Michael Dorris* by Louise Erdrich, 1994; "Storytelling As Deconstruction and Seduction: The Columbus Novels of Stephen Marlowe and Michael Dorris/Louise Erdrich" by Helmbrecht Breinig, in *Historiographic Metafiction in Modern American and Canadian Literature* edited by Bernd Engler and Kurt Muller, 1994; "The Rhythm of Three Strands: Cultural Braiding in Dorris's *A Yellow Raft in Blue Water*" by David Cowart, in *Studies in American Indian Literatures: The Journal of the Association for the Study of American,* spring 1996, pp. 1-12; "Louise Erdrich and Michael Dorris" by Kay Bonetti, in *Conversations with American Novelists: The Best Interviews from The Missouri Review and the American Audio Prose Library,* 1997.

*　　*　　*

Part Modoc on his father's side, Michael Dorris helped promote the study of Native American culture by publishing *A Guide to Research on North American Indians* (with Arlene Hirschfelder and Mary Lou Byler) and by founding, in 1972, the Native American Studies Department at Dartmouth College. As a writer of nonfiction, he has helped to educate the public about the dangers of drinking alcohol during pregnancy. Particularly on reservations, where the rate of alcohol abuse is much higher than the national average, Fetal Alcohol Syndrome (FAS) is a tragic problem. Dorris knew firsthand about the severe mental impairment and physical disabilities that are symptomatic of the syndrome. His heartrending book, *The Broken Cord,* recounts his struggle to raise his adopted son, Adam, a Sioux child born with FAS. The book won the National Book Critics Circle Award, the Heartland Prize, and the Christopher Award. As a writer of fiction, Dorris made the theme of family his trademark, and he has demonstrated the curious ability for a male author of creating vivid and utterly believable female characters. While the main characters in his acclaimed first novel, *A Yellow Raft in Blue Water,* are reservation-affiliated Native Americans, this story of a family in conflict is concerned with universal issues of love, responsibility, and loyalty. Yet, if Dorris, in his fiction, seems less concerned than other Native American novelists with exploring problems peculiar to Indians in contemporary society, it would be a mistake to underestimate his awareness of the crisis over identity that many Native Americans face in the late twentieth century.

Set in the states of Montana and Washington, *A Yellow Raft in Blue Water* is divided into three sections, each narrated by one of its female protagonists: Rayona (daughter), Christine (mother), and Ida (grandmother). In the closing scene of the novel, Ida begins to braid her hair ("the rhythm of three strands"), a neat metaphor for the book itself. Each of the narrators represents a strand in a braid—though a braid fraught with frustrating knots and tangles. Quite simply, these three women have a hard time getting along, and they are all prone to blaming each other for their unhappiness. The fact remains, however, that their lives, like the strands in the braid, are undeniably and inextricably entwined. Rayona, a teenager, cannot forgive her mother for abandoning her at "Aunt" Ida's house on the reservation. Rayona's feelings of rejection and alienation are compounded by the fact that she, the daughter of a Native American woman and an African American man, is twice an outcast in American society. Thus, race is a central issue in this novel, especially for fragile Rayona. Christine, too, feels unloved by her mother, and for good reason. Even when Ida speaks for herself in the last section of the novel, she is as stern and acerbic as her daughter and granddaughter have portrayed her to be. "I'm a woman who's lived for fifty-seven years," says Ida, "and worn resentment like a medicine charm for forty." Ida, who has never lived anywhere but on the reservation, once experienced strong feelings for a man with a disfigured face. In the present time of the novel, however, she finds all the companionship she desires by regularly tuning in to her favorite television soap operas and game shows.

The message that one encounters in such seminal works of Native American fiction as **N. Scott Momaday**'s *House Made of Dawn* and **Leslie Marmon Silko**'s *Ceremony* is that the key to achieving self-fulfillment for the protagonist lay in reclaiming his tribal identity. This message is not to be found in *A Yellow Raft in Blue Water.* By its absence, Dorris seems to be making the sad point that a once vital culture has been irretrievably lost. That Rayona, Christine, and Ida belong to a nameless tribe, living on a nameless reservation, underscores the lack of a basic identity that, collectively, these women can call their own. The traditional language, which Ida speaks fluently, though primarily for the purpose of being secretive in front of others, also lacks a specific name; Rayona and Christine refer to it generically as "Indian." The emptiness left by the disappearance of traditional customs, ceremonies, and religion has been inadequately filled by the popular movies, television programs, and songs of mass culture to which the characters are constantly alluding as a way of explaining their situations and defining their roles. In addition to being a serious, tightly woven story about three generations of embattled women, *A Yellow Raft in Blue Water* is often a very humorous book, particularly in its satire of popular culture.

It is interesting to note, considering the skill with which Dorris depicts strong, realistic female characters, that the author originally conceived the character of Rayona as a boy named Raymond. The anthology *The New Native American Novel: Works in Progress* (1986) contains an early draft of a chapter from *A Yellow Raft in Blue Water,* narrated by Raymond. Regarding other aspects of his creative process, Dorris gave much credit for the success of his work to his wife, Louise Erdrich, the highly regarded author of *Love Medicine* and other novels. In interviews, Dorris and Erdrich called all of their work a collaboration; and in *The Broken Cord,* Dorris states: "Louise and I had become involved more and more with each other's writing, from the conception of fictional characters to the final copyediting of a manuscript. . . . By the time any submission left our house,. . . we had achieved—after many a heated literary argument—consensus on every word." Be that as it may, *The Crown of Columbus* is the only novel that bears both Dorris's and Erdrich's names. For these two widely praised authors, it also represents their only critical failure.

Published to coincide with the fanfare surrounding the five-hundredth anniversary of Columbus's discovery of the New World, *The Crown of Columbus* is a contrived piece of fiction narrated alternately by Vivian Twostar and Roger Williams, two Dartmouth professors doing research on Columbus. Pompous, competitive, and Eurocentric, Roger seems the very stereotype of the white, male academician. Vivian's character is more original, and her struggle to preserve her career as well as her relationships with her troubled teenaged son and her live-in Navajo grandmother makes hers the more sympathetic character, too. Before the novel begins, she and Roger have had an affair, conceived a child, and broken up. Eventually they will reach a reconciliation, but not before Dorris and Erdrich's busy plot takes them on a farcical trip to the Bahamas as guests of Henry Cobb, who covets the pages from Columbus' diary that Vivian has uncovered in the Dartmouth library. While *The Crown of Columbus* has its defenders, they are outnumbered by those critics who expressed disappointment over this much publicized collaboration. In an opinion that speaks for the majority, Robert Houston notes in the *New York Times Book Review* (28 April 1991): "In the end, 'The Crown of Columbus' never really finds itself."

A collection of short stories, *Working Men,* returned Dorris to good standing with the critics. All of the distinctive characteristics of Dorris the fiction writer are on display in these stories: the use of first-person narrators, the seriocomic tone, and the focus on family and romantic relationships. Despite the emphasis on masculinity in the title, not all of these stories are about men. Even those that are feature women in prominent roles, proving, once again, that Dorris can write sensitively and convincingly about women. Furthermore, when the narrator of the story "Layaway" (chosen as the Best Short Story of 1992 by the *Boston Review*) reveals the supposedly telling detail that his family "ate out at McDonald's slightly more often than at Burger King," Dorris is making one of his favorite points about how we allow consumer culture to define who we are.

Stories about Native Americans account for just two of the fourteen works included in this rich collection, yet they are among the best. "Groom Service" concerns a young Native American man who endures a prolonged, ritualized, and humiliating courtship before finally gaining permission to marry the young woman he loves. The attention to social codes in this story reminds the reader that Dorris is a trained anthropologist. This connection is even more obvious in "Shining Agate," where the protagonist, a white man, is performing anthropological field work among Native Americans in Alaska. His acceptance by the native community comes only after he has stood up to a ghost.

Despite the paucity of Native American characters in *Working Men,* Dorris will continue, no doubt, to be thought of as a Native American author. He was clearly a versatile writer, however, capable of depicting a wide range of characters and of working in more than one genre. Successful at whatever form of creative writing he has attempted, Dorris was awarded the 1992 Scott O'Dell Award for Best Historical Fiction for Young Readers for his children's novel *Morning Child,* a book with Native American characters and themes.

—Paul Hadella

DOS PASSOS, John (Roderigo)

Born: Chicago, Illinois, 14 January 1896. **Education:** Choate School, Wallingford, Connecticut, 1907-11; Harvard University, Cambridge, Massachusetts (editor, *Harvard Monthly*), 1912-16, A.B. (cum laude) 1916; studied in Castile, 1916-17. **Military Service:** Served in the Norton-Harjes Ambulance Group in France, 1917, and the American Red Cross Ambulance Corps in Italy, 1918; served in the U.S. Medical Corps, 1918-19. **Family:** Married 1) Katharine F. Smith in 1929 (died 1947); 2) Elizabeth Hamlin Holdridge in 1949, one daughter. **Career:** Lived in Spain and Portugal, 1919; traveled in the Near East with the Near East Relief Organization, 1921; lived in New York, 1922; traveled in Spain, 1923; cofounder, *New Masses,* New York, 1926, and contributor until early 1930s; director, New Playwrights Theatre, New York, 1927-29; visited the U.S.S.R., 1928; contributor, *Common Sense,* 1932; screenwriter in Hollywood, 1934; war correspondent in the Pacific, and at Nuremberg, 1945, and in South America, 1948, for *Life* magazine, New York. Treasurer, National Committee for the Defense of Political Prisoners, 1931; chairman, National Committee to Aid Striking Miners, 1931; treasurer, Campaign for Political Refugees, 1940; U.S. delegate, International PEN Club Congress, England, 1941. Artist: individual show of sketches, New York, 1937. **Awards:** Guggenheim fellowship, 1939, 1940, 1942; American Academy Gold Medal, 1957; Feltrinelli prize (Italy), 1967. **Member:** American Academy, 1947. **Died:** 28 September 1970.

PUBLICATIONS

Fiction

One Man's Initiation—1917. 1920; as *First Encounter,* 1945; complete edition, 1969.

Three Soldiers. 1921.
Streets of Night. 1923.
Manhattan Transfer. 1925.
U.S.A. 1938.
    The 42nd Parallel. 1930.
    1919. 1932.
    The Big Money. 1936.
Chosen Country. 1951.
District of Columbia. 1952.
    Adventures of a Young Man. 1939.
    Number One. 1943.
    The Grand Design. 1949.
Most Likely to Succeed. 1954.
The Great Days. 1958.
Midcentury: A Contemporary Chronicle. 1961.
Century's Ebb: The Thirteenth Chronicle. 1975.

Plays

The Garbage Man: A Parade with Shouting (as *The Moon Is a Gong,* produced 1925; as *The Garbage Man,* produced 1926). 1926.
Airways, Inc. (produced 1927). 1928.
Fortune Heights (produced 1933). In *Three Plays,* 1934.
Three Plays. 1934.
USA: A Dramatic Review, with Paul Shyre. 1963.

Screenplay: *The Devil Is a Woman,* with S.K. Winston, 1935.

Poetry

A Pushcart at the Curb. 1922.

Other

Rosinante to the Road Again. 1922.
Orient Express. 1927.
Facing the Chair: The Story of the Americanization of Two Foreignborn Workmen (on Sacco and Vanzetti). 1927.
In All Countries. 1934.
The Villages Are the Heart of Spain. 1937.
Journeys between Wars. 1938.
The Ground We Stand On: Some Examples from the History of a Political Creed. 1941.
State of the Nation. 1944.
Tour of Duty. 1946.
The Prospect Before Us. 1950.
Life's Picture History of World War II. 1950.
The Head and Heart of Thomas Jefferson. 1954.
The Theme Is Freedom. 1956.
The Men Who Made the Nation. 1957.
Prospects of a Golden Age. 1959.
Mr. Wilson's War. 1962.
Brazil on the Move. 1963.
Thomas Jefferson: The Making of a President (for children). 1964.
Occasions and Protests: Essays 1936-1964. 1964.
The Shackles of Power 1801-1826: Three Jeffersonian Decades. 1966.
The Best Times: An Informal Memoir. 1966.
The Portugal Story: Three Centuries of Exploration and Discovery. 1969.

Easter Island: Island of Enigmas. 1971.
The Fourteenth Chronicle: Letters and Diaries, edited by
Townsend Ludington. 1973.

Editor, *The Living Thoughts of Tom Paine.* 1940.

Translator, *Metropolis,* by Manuel Maples Arce. 1929.
Translator, *Panama: or, The Adventures of My Seven Uncles,* by
Blaise Cendrars. 1931.

*

Bibliography: *A Bibliography of Dos Passos* by Jack Potter,
1950; *Dos Passos: A Reference Guide* by John Rohrkemper, 1980;
Dos Passos: A Comprehensive Bibliography by David Sanders,
1986.

Critical Studies: *Dos Passos* by John H. Wrenn, 1961; *Dos
Passos* by Robert Gorham Davis, 1962; *The Fiction of Dos Passos*
by John D. Brantley, 1968; *Dos Passos, The Critics, and the
Writer's Intention* edited by Allen Belkind, 1971; *Dos Passos' Path
to U.S.A.: A Political Biography 1912-1936* by Melvin Landsberg,
1972; *Dos Passos: A Collection of Critical Essays* edited by Andrew Hook, 1974; *Dos Passos* by George J. Becker, 1974; *Dos
Passos and the Fiction of Despair* by Iain Colley, 1978; *Dos
Passos: Artist as American* by Linda W. Wagner, 1979; *Dos
Passos: A Twentieth-Century Odyssey* by Townsend Ludington,
1980; *Dos Passos: Politics and the Writer* by Robert C. Rosen,
1981; *John Dos Passos* by Hidekazu Hirose, 1981; *Twentieth-Cen-
tury American Literary Naturalism: An Interpretation* by Donald
Pizer, 1982; *Dos Passos: A Life* by Virginia Spencer Carr, 1984;
Naturalism in American Fiction: The Classic Phase by John J.
Conder, 1984; "A 'sublime and atrocious' Spectacle: New York
and Iconography of Manhattan Island" by Graham Clarke, in *The
American City: Literary and Cultural Perspectives* edited by
Clarke, 1988; *John Dos Passos: The Major Nonfictional Prose* by
Donald Pizer, 1988; *Dos Passos' U.S.A.: A Critical Study* by
Donald Pizer, 1988; "The Collapse of Faith and the Failure of
Language: John Dos Passos and the Spanish Civil War" by John
Rohrkemper, in *Rewriting the Good Fight: Critical Essays on the
Literature of the Spanish Civil War* edited by Frieda S. Brown,
Malcolm Alan Compitello, Victor M. Howard, and Robert A. Mar-
tin, 1989; "Hart Crane and John Dos Passos" by Joseph W. Slade,
in *American Literature and Science* edited by Robert J. Scholnick,
1992; *My Father, John Dos Passos* by Lucy Dos Passos Coggin,
1996; *John Dos Passos Revisited* by Lisa Nanney, 1998; *Dos
Passos and the Ideology of the Feminine* by Janet Galligani Casey,
1998.

*   *   *

John Dos Passos was involved in many of the episodes that
have played an important part in twentieth-century literary history; not surprisingly, these had an important effect on his writing. After a lonely childhood living in Europe and then being a
bookish student among advocates of the strenuous life at the
Choate School in Wallingford, Connecticut, he went through
Harvard University with a number of the writers who became part
of the artistic renaissance that started during the period just before World War I. **T.S. Eliot** was still at Harvard while Dos Passos
was there; **e.e. cummings**, Robert Hillyer, and Stewart Mitchell

were among his close friends. He drove an ambulance during World
War I, then roamed the Continent afterward and passed frequently
through the Paris expatriate scene, though he was never truly a
part of it. He was a friend of writers such as **F. Scott Fitzgerald,
Upton Sinclair,** Van Wyck Brooks and a close friend of **Archibald
MacLeish, Edmund Wilson,** and—for a while—**Ernest
Hemingway,** among others. He became deeply involved in political radicalism during the 1920s but was never the activist that his
writings made him seem; he interviewed and wrote about the Italian anarchists Sacco and Vanzetti, who had been found guilty of
murder on dubious evidence; he worked as a director of a left-
wing, experimental drama group, the New Playwrights, in the late
1920s; he traveled to Russia in 1928; he visited the Harlan County,
Kentucky, coal mines with **Theodore Dreiser** in 1931; he experienced the "big money" briefly as a screenwriter in Hollywood
in 1934; and he went to Spain many times, returning in 1937 with
Hemingway to report on the Civil War. During World War II he
wrote about the domestic scene, visited the Pacific, and reported
on Europe and the war-crimes trials in Germany after the war. In
the 1940s and subsequently he took an interest in capitalism—
this time viewing it favorably—in Jeffersonian liberalism, and in
the development of Latin America.

Although his reputation is not what it was in 1938 when Jean-
Paul Sartre declared, "I regard Dos Passos as the greatest writer
of our time," his works of fiction, which he came to call chronicles,
and his non-fiction continue to be read widely. He is one of the
two or three most important political novelists the United States
has produced, and certain of his books—in particular *Three Soldiers, Manhattan Transfer,* and the three volumes of *U.S.A.*—are
landmarks in the nation's literary history. *Three Soldiers* was the
first of the significant novels to come from an American writer's
experiences during World War I. *Manhattan Transfer* represents
Dos Passos's innovative application to literature of the artistic
theories and techniques that emerged during the decades before
and after the turn of the century, when a veritable revolution in
the arts occurred in Europe and then in the United States. This
chronicle of the city incorporates impressionism, expressionism,
montage, simultaneity, reportage, and other techniques of "the new"
in the arts and is important also for its themes of alienation and
loss, as well as for its satiric treatment of the urban scene.

The three volumes of *U.S.A.* are Dos Passos's attempt to employ his techniques of art to chronicle American civilization from
1900 to the beginning of the Great Depression in 1929. While he
was writing *U.S.A.* from 1927 to 1936, he was far to the left politically, although he began turning toward the center by 1934. The
trilogy, a panorama of the nation's life from his political perspective, is deeply satiric about business and the materialistic society
it had created. The period he was chronicling, he wrote the critic
Malcolm Cowley, was a time when the country moved from "competitive" to "monopoly" capitalism.

From being a political leftist, Dos Passos moved toward the
right after believing himself personally betrayed by the Communists, a feeling culminating with the execution—he claimed at the
hands of the Communists—of his close friend Jose Robles in Spain
in 1937. Betrayal by the Communists became the fate of the hero
in his next novel, the distinctly anti-left *Adventures of a Young
Man.* Dos Passos's own adventure with the left was over by then;
his subsequent chronicles, which extended through the 1960s, were
increasingly strident satires, most of them about the modern liberalism and government bureaucracy that he saw to be the heritage of Franklin Roosevelt's New Deal administration. A single

exception is *Chosen Country* where, through the adventures of an autobiographical hero, Jay Pignatelli, Dos Passos told of his gradual allegiance to the United States and his romance with his first wife, Katharine Smith.

But Dos Passos was not only a novelist. He wrote numerous books of reportage describing his world travels and analyzing the life and politics of his own and other nations. After 1937, he began also to write histories, repeatedly considering the origins of the United States in books such as *The Ground We Stand On, The Men Who Made the Nation, Prospects of a Golden Age,* and *The Shackles of Power: Three Jeffersonian Decades.* He became fascinated by **Thomas Jefferson**, who was, in fact, a sort of hero for him; he wrote a biography—*The Head and Heart of Thomas Jefferson*—as well as several studies of the man and his era. In addition to all of these works he wrote a volume of poetry, several plays, and many articles about politics, drama, and art, among other subjects.

In the early 1950s, he sympathized with Senator Joseph McCarthy's efforts to ferret Communists out of the government but did not support McCarthy's methods. In 1964 he supported Senator Barry Goldwater for the Presidency; yet Dos Passos's conservatism was never the simplistic matter his critics took it to be. Always critical rather than doctrinaire, Dos Passos wanted to remain independent, something of the anarchist, in his works supporting individual freedoms against bureaucracies and monoliths wherever he saw them, while portraying the swirl of life in his chosen country. Granting Dos Passos his political perspectives, the reader can get from his works a remarkably broad chronicle of the twentieth-century United States.

—Townsend Ludington

See the essay on *U.S.A.*

DOUGLASS, Frederick

Born: Frederick Augustus Washington Bailey in Tuckahoe, Talbot County, Maryland, 1818; took name Douglass upon escape from slavery. On plantation until 1825; house servant, Baltimore, 1825-33 (learned to read and write); inherited by new owner and worked as field hand, St. Michael's, Maryland, 1833-36: unsuccessfully conspired to escape, 1836; sent to Baltimore and trained as ship's caulker (allowed to do some free-lance work), 1837-38; escaped to New York, 1838. **Family:** Married 1) Anna Murray in 1838, one daughter and three sons; 2) Helen Pitts in 1884. **Career:** Shipyard laborer, New Bedford, 1838-41, and Lynn, 1842, both Massachusetts; agent, Massachusetts Anti-Slavery Society from 1841, and central figure in the New England anti-slavery campaigns, and, after 1848, in the women's rights movement; lectured in Britain and Ireland, 1845-47; British friends bought his freedom, 1847; founder, *North Star* abolitionist paper (became *Frederick Douglass' Paper,* 1851), Rochester, New York, 1847-60, and *Frederick Douglass' Monthly,* 1858-63; escaped to Canada, 1859, and lived in Britain, 1859-60, when named as accomplice to John Brown in Harper's Ferry raid; recruited black regiments (Massachusetts 54th and 55th), 1863, and worked for civil rights during Reconstruction; owner, *New National Era* newspaper, Washington, D.C., 1870-74; assistant secretary, Santo Domingo annexation commission, 1871; president, Freedman's Sav-

ings and Trust Company, 1873-74; U.S. marshal, 1877-81, and recorder of deeds after 1881, Washington, D.C.; U.S. minister to Haiti, 1889-91. **Died:** 20 February 1895.

PUBLICATIONS

Collections

Life and Writings, edited by Philip S. Foner. 4 vols., 1950-55.
Papers, edited by John W. Blassingame. 1979—.
The Narrative and Selected Writings, edited by Michael Meyer. 1984.

Prose

Narrative of the Life of Douglass, An American Slave. 1845, edited by Houston A. Baker, Jr., 1982; revised edition, as *My Bondage and My Freedom,* 1855; as *Life and Times of Douglass,* 1881, revised edition, 1892.
Douglass on Women's Rights, edited by Philip S. Foner. 1976.
A Black Diplomat in Haiti: The Diplomatic Correspondence of U.S. Minister Douglass from Haiti 1889-1891, edited by Norma Brown. 2 vols., 1977.

*

Critical Studies: *Douglass* by Charles Waddell Chesnutt, 1899; *Douglass* by Booker T. Washington, 1907; *Douglass* by Benjamin Quarles, 1948, and *Douglass* edited by Quarles, 1968; *Douglass: A Biography* by Philip S. Foner, 1964; *Free at Last: The Life of Douglass* by Arna Bontemps, 1971; *Young Douglass: The Maryland Years* by Dickson J. Preston, 1980; *Slave and Citizen: The Life of Douglass* by Nathan Irvin Huggins, edited by Oscar Handlin, 1980; *The Mind of Douglass* by Waldo E. Martin, Jr., 1986; *Frederick Douglass's Narrative of the Life of Frederick Douglass* edited by Harold Bloom, 1988; "Between Politics and Poetics: Frederick Douglass and Postmodernity" by John Carlos Rowe, in *Reconstructing American Literary and Historical Studies* edited by Gunter H. Lenz, Hartmut Keil, and Sabine Brock-Sallah, 1990; *Frederick Douglass: New Literary and Historical Essays* edited by Eric J. Sundquist, 1991; *Frederick Douglass on Slave Art and Work* by Sterling Stuckey, 1998; *On Racial Frontiers: The New Culture of Frederick Douglass, Ralph Ellison, and Bob Marley* by Gregory Stephens, 1999.

* * *

Born a slave on a plantation in Maryland, Frederick Douglass escaped to freedom in the North at the age of twenty-one and eventually rose to international prominence as a lecturer, journalist, editor, autobiographer, and political activist. Although he was almost totally a self-educated man, his brilliant rhetorical powers as well as tireless efforts on behalf of the oppressed made Douglass a forceful leader in the abolitionist movement of the late 1840s and 1850s, earning him the title in the twentieth century of "Father of the Civil Rights Movement."

As a writer Douglass is primarily remembered for the *Narrative of the Life of Frederick Douglass.* An autobiographical account of Douglass's life as a slave, this work has been called a "landmark in the literary crusade against slavery" and "one of the most influential pieces of reform propaganda in American literature." Unlike many other works in the sub-genre of American writing known as the "slave narrative," the Douglass *Narrative* has never ceased to attract an audience. Within just a few months of its publication in 1845, some 5,000 copies had been sold. More than thirty thousand copies are estimated to have been printed during the ten years that followed; revised and enlarged editions were published in 1855 under the title *My Bondage and My Freedom* and in 1881 under the title *Life and Times of Frederick Douglass.* During the twentieth century, Douglass's autobiography has been almost continually in print.

Several factors have been noted as contributing to the *Narrative*'s appeal as a lasting work of literature. Unlike many of the other works of its kind, the Douglass *Narrative,* as its introductions by William Lloyd Garrison and Wendell Phillips attest, was written by Douglass himself, without the assistance of an editor or ghostwriter. As such, the *Narrative* possesses the genuine force of eyewitness conviction that was often lost in similar accounts whose editors and transcribers could not resist the impulse to sentimentalize or fictionalize for the sake of stylization and emotional effect. Throughout the *Narrative,* Douglass remains true to the facts of his experience, and those facts themselves provide a relentless condemnation of slavery and its supporters. Clear and direct, the style of Douglass's writing is one that the average individual can easily assimilate, and its clarity and directness only tend to underscore the barbarities and inhumanities described in the book: the separation of families, a total disregard on the part of slave owners and overseers for the human rights of their slaves, and brutal beatings meant to dehumanize the slaves and rob them of their personal identities and dignity. Moreover, as late-twentieth-century scholarship has shown, carefully developed patterns of animal and maritime imagery reinforce tensions and themes present in the *Narrative* as a whole, making it, in the words of one commentator, "the first native American autobiography to create a black identity in style and form adequate to the pressures of historic black experience."

As editor of and contributor to the *North Star, Douglass' Monthly,* and the *New National Era,* Douglass further distinguished himself in literary and political circles. For his work on the *North Star,* Douglass has been called a "champion of literary taste." Although the major editorial philosophy behind Douglass's weekly was the furtherance of the cause of emancipation and civil rights, he nonetheless published works of literature on a variety of topics and by a variety of authors, including Emerson, Coleridge, Tennyson, and Dickens. As a result, his paper has been praised as one of the most "respected guides to cultural and literary taste in the nineteenth century" and "a source of lasting pride" for both back and white Americans.

—James A. Levernier

DOVE, Rita (Frances)

Born: Akron, Ohio, 28 August 1952. **Education:** Miami University, Oxford, Ohio, B.A., 1973 (summa cum laude); attended Universitaet Tuebingen, West Germany, 1974-75; University of Iowa, M.F.A., 1977. **Family:** Married the writer Fred Viebahn; one daughter. **Career:** Assistant professor, 1981-84, associate professor, 1984-87, and professor of English, 1987-89, Arizona State

University, Tempe; Tuskegee Institute, writer in residence, Tuskegee Institute, Alabama, 1982; University of Virginia, Charlottesville, commonwealth professor of English, beginning 1989; Poet Laureate of the United States, 1993-95. Member of literature panel, National Endowment for the Arts, 1984-86, chair of poetry grants panel, 1985; member of board of directors, Associated Writing Programs, 1985-88, president, 1986-87; associate editor of *Callaloo,* beginning 1986. **Awards:** Fullbright fellowship, 1974-75; grants from National Endowment for the Arts, 1978, and Ohio Arts Council, 1979; International Working Period for Authors fellowship for West Germany, 1980; Portia Pittman fellowship at Tuskegee Institute from National Endowment for the Humanities, 1982; John Simon Guggenheim fellowship, 1983; Peter I.B. Lavan Younger Poets award, Academy of American Poets, 1986; Pulitzer prize in poetry, 1987; General Electric Foundation award for Younger Writers, 1987; Bellagio (Italy) Residency, Rockefeller Foundation, 1988; Ohio Governor's award, 1988; Andrew W. Mellon fellowship, National Humanities Center, North Carolina, 1988-89; named Poet Laureate of the United States, 1993; Renaissance Forum award for leadership in the literary arts, Folger Shakespeare Library, 1994; Golden Plate award, American Academy of Achievement, 1994; Carl Sandburg award, 1994; fund for new American plays, Kennedy Center, 1995; The Heinz award in the Arts and Humanities, 1996; The Charles Frankel prize/National medal in the Humanities, 1996; Levinson prize, 1998. Honorary degrees: Dartmouth College; Miami University, 1988; University of Pennsylvania; University of Notre Dame; Tuskegee University; Washington University; Spelman College; Knox College; Northeastern University; University of Akron; University of North Carolina Chapel Hill; Boston College; University of Miami; Arizona State University; Case Western Reserve University; Columbia University. **Member:** Academy of American Poets; American Philosophical Society, 1996. **Residence:** Charlottesville, Virginia.

PUBLICATIONS

Collections

Selected Poems. 1993.

Poetry

Ten Poems. 1977.
The Only Dark Spot in the Sky. 1980.
The Yellow House on the Corner. 1980.
Mandolin. 1982.
Museum. 1983.
Thomas and Beulah. 1986.
The Other Side of the House, photography by Tamarra Kaida. 1988.
Grace Notes. 1989.
Mother Love. 1996.
On the Bus with Rosa Parks. 1999.

Recording: *Selected Poems.* 1993.

Fiction

Fifth Sunday (short stories). 1985.
Through the Ivory Gate: A Novel. 1992.

Plays

The Siberian Village. In *Callaloo,* Vol. 14, No. 2, 1991.
The Darker Face of the Earth (produced 1996). 1994.

*

Critical Studies: "Coming Home: An Interview with Rita Dove" by Steven Schneider, in *The Iowa Review* vol. 19, no. 3, 1989; "The Assembling Vision of Rita Dove" by Robert McDowell, in *Conversant Essays: Contemporary Poets on Poetry* edited by James McCorkle, 1990; "An Interview with Maryse Conde and Rita Dove" by Mohamed B. Taleb-Khyar, in *Callaloo* vol. 12, no. 2, spring 1991; "Scars and Wings: Rita Dove's *Grace Notes*" by Bonnie Costello, in *Callaloo* vol. 14, no. 2, spring 1991; *Race, Gender, and Class Perspectives in the Works of Maya Angelou, Gwendolyn Brooks, Rita Dove, Nikki Giovanni, and Audre Lourde* by Ekaterini Georgoudaki, 1991; "Folk Idiom in the Literary Expression of Two African American Authors: Rita Dove and Yusef Komunyakaa" by Kirkland C. Jones, in *Language and Literature in the African American Imagination* edited by Carol Aisha Belay-Blackshire, 1992; in *The Given and the Made: Strategies of Poetic Redefinition* by Helen Hennessy Vendler, 1995.

*   *   *

Rita Dove, the youngest person ever appointed Poet Laureate of the United States, declared in the November-December 1993 issue of *Ms.,* "Writing poetry is the most intimate of arts. . . . Poetry is one person talking, whispering to another. Connection is one of the most incredible experiences that a human being can have. Connect with your own innermost feelings, render them through language in a poem, then give that to someone else." In her own poetry, fiction, and drama, as well as her teaching and public speaking, Dove has been making those connections—as an African American artist from a Midwestern working-class family, and as a talented and well-traveled writer and musician. Though much of her writing captures the richness of her African American culture, her larger subject is humanity, as she declared in the *Washington Post*: "Obviously, as a black woman, I am concerned with race. . . . But certainly not every poem of mine mentions the fact of being black. They are poems about humanity, and sometimes humanity happens to be black. I cannot run from, I won't run from any kind of truth." What Rita Dove achieves in her ten books of poetry, two books of fiction, and her verse play is the fundamental connection of her life with the world.

The author's career has won her many grants, awards, and fellowships, including National Endowment for the Arts and Guggenheim fellowships, a Pulitzer Prize for her *Thomas and Beulah* family history in poetry (making her the second black woman, after Gwendolyn Brooks, to receive a Pulitzer), and her appointment as Poet Laureate of the United States in 1993—all by the age of forty-one. In her 1993 *Selected Poems* collection (culled from three of her books, *The Yellow House, Museum,* and *Thomas and Beulah*), and in the publication of her first novel, *Through the Ivory Gate,* we begin to assess her writing career and her importance as a female African American writer.

In the poems in *The Yellow House on the Corner* (1980) Dove portrays old neighborhood scenes and her own emerging sense of self growing up in Akron, Ohio. It also establishes her fine sense of detail. As Donna M. Williams has noted in *Ms.,* "The power of Dove's poetry lies in her ability to wrest beauty from the most ordinary of life's moments: leafing through *Jet* magazine, eating figs, unpacking a bottle of Heinz ketchup. Her poems are obsessively crafted; it may take twenty to forty drafts for the poem to 'breathe on its own.'" This art of making the ordinary into the extraordinary by perceiving its music and expressing it with lyric intensity is what gives Dove's writing its striking form. Life is taken in and reflected back with lyric form and resonance through the poet's perception. Her own musical training as a cellist and her early love of writing and art heighten the lyricism of her art. As Williams put it, Dove's "writing throbs with melody and rhythm. Music is not just a metaphor; it is life. Indeed, she asserts that a poem that doesn't have its own music isn't really a poem." Dove celebrates the music of life particularly well in poems such as "David Walker (1785-1830)."

The poems in Dove's collection *Museum* are almost too diverse and diffuse. It is not until part three of that book, "My Father's Telescope," that she finds her subject in the love and humor of her father's life. Through her intensely felt family portraits she is able to achieve a larger sense of the human family. Nowhere is that felt more strongly than in her book *Thomas and Beulah.* Based on the lives of her maternal grandparents, it captures the texture of their lives—the meeting, marriage, work, family, and death. Williams described the book in *Ms.*: "In microcosm it is the story of the great migration of southern blacks northward to find work in the factories and a modicum of peace in the post-slavery U.S." The book won her immediate critical praise and the Pulitzer Prize in 1987 for best book of poetry. It is her most "connected" book, even as she writes of a distant past kept alive through family stories. Dove's ability to project the narrative of these two lives is remarkable here. The book presents quiet themes of struggle and pain that are met by a simple courage and a sustaining love and humor. In some poems the characters of Thomas and Beulah reflect their own tales, as in "Roast Possum" and "Courtship, Diligence." "The Satisfaction Coal Company" is a vivid portrait of a man's love and sacrifice for family. These poems achieve their own music of loving and lusting, of laboring and mothering, and finally of dying and mourning.

Dove has maintained these roots while extending her own experience in her 1989 collection, *Grace Notes,* which the *Christian Science Monitor* praised: "What a chorus of voices—bold, sly, anguished, determined—and each one is spotlighted briefly on the darkened stage of story or poem. [Her] poems are . . . intimate, but still resonate with the voices of friends and family, still captivate us with her startling sense of the particular." Her ability to handle characterization, storytelling, and a realistic, though suggestive, imagery were acclaimed by the *Chicago Tribune*: "What makes Rita Dove's work appealing is her ability to draw real characters holding jobs, raising families, drinking beer, playing music, and eating catfish dripping with hot sauce." This has been followed by two books: *Mother Love* (1995), a sonnet sequence using the Greek myth of Demeter and Persephone to examine the deep bond of mother and daughter, and *On the Bus with Rosa Parks* (1999), which engages the author more fully in the historical social struggle of races and people. Using the figure of civil right demonstrator Rosa Parks, Dove reveals our human capacity for heroism in the face of need.

For an intimate, though fictionalized, sense of Dove's own life, one need only read her 1992 novel *Through the Ivory Gate.* Using an overlaid and cinematic style, the author jumps through time periods to capture the many layers of her heroine's young life. Virginia King, in her mid-twenties, returns as an artist-in-residence to her native Akron, Ohio, to work as a puppeteer in the schools. She brings with her memories of her working-class childhood in Akron and of her family's unexplained move to Arizona while she was in junior high school. There are also layers of college life with its theater classes, training on the cello, and working with the theater group "Puppets and People" in Wisconsin; friendships, love affairs, and frustrations echo back. In Akron she is ambushed by her own past: an urban landscape that etched itself into her consciousness, a wise though cranky grandmother, a wounded aunt, the challenge of a new job of teaching, and a confused longing for human connection.

The *Christian Science Monitor* described *Through the Ivory Gate*'s scope and intention: "Whether she is evoking the look of a landscape or depicting the nuances of a family quarrel, Dove sees with the keen eye of an artist and writes with the finely honed diction of a poet. . . . She demonstrates a strong grasp of the complexities of human character and interpersonal relationships." Virginia represents a young African American woman struggling to make peace with the past and the present as we watch her evolve through her life, work, and loves. There are vivid panoramic views of the working-class life as well as personal portraits of strong characters. Though the work is complex, almost dizzying at times in its shifts, a consistent theme is expressed through Virginia's grandmother: "Love is such a little thing. . . . That's why we're all the time running around looking for it. And it's delicate. But pain . . . pain is strong; pain goes on a long time. And it's selfish, it needs itself to feed on." Kelly Cherry described the book's motive and charm for the *Los Angeles Times Book Review*: "Virginia's progress is from a history of hurt to a new hopefulness. Sweet purity suffuses the story, runs through it like a melodic line. . . . Such writing is felt by the reader as a kind of caress."

In 1997 Dove enlarged her range and content with the opening of her verse play *The Darker Face of the Earth* at the Kennedy Center in Washington, D.C. Les Gutman of *Curtain Up* described the drama: "The themes are intricate, the main characters full-bodied, and the language—Oh, the language—nothing short of stunning." It is a retelling of the Oedipus tragedy set on a South Carolina slave plantation and has as its theme the single rootedness of all peoples and cultures. Rita Dove has emerged as a major voice in literature, but also as a woman, African American, and compassionate writer of human union.

—Larry Smith

DRAKE, Joseph Rodman

Born: New York City, 7 August 1795. **Education:** Studied medicine at a school on Barclay Street, New York, and qualified 1816. **Family:** Married Sarah Eckford in 1816. **Career:** Toured Europe, 1816-19; partner, with William Langstaff, in a drugstore in New York, 1819-20. **Died:** 21 September 1820.

PUBLICATIONS

Collection

Life and Works: A Memoir and Complete Text of His Poems and Prose, by Frank Lester Pleadwell. 1935.

Poetry

Poems, with Fitz-Greene Halleck, 1819; revised edition, as *The Croakers,* 1860.
The Culprit Fay and Other Poems. 1835.

*

Bibliography: in *Bibliography of American Literature* by Jacob Blanck, 1957.

*   *   *

Joseph Rodman Drake is an American member of the brotherhood of poets whose small measure of lasting fame depends on one or two popular successes. His fanciful 639-line poem "The Culprit Fay"—written in 1816 but not published until long after his death—continues to please many readers. "The American Flag," written and published pseudonymously in 1819, was widely admired in the United States and set to music by numerous composers (including Dvorak). His memory also survives because of the monody "On the Death of Joseph Rodman Drake," written by his friend **Fitz-Greene Halleck**, that opens with the well known quatrain:

Green be the turf above thee,
Friend of my better days!
None knew thee but to love thee,
Nor named thee but to praise.

Otherwise, Drake is remembered only by some historical critics who—following the example set by **Edgar Allan Poe** in the 1830s—are still outraged by the vogue that Drake's work enjoyed in America after his death.

Except for one excursion abroad, Drake lived out his short life in New York City. Trained as a physician, he never aspired to literary fame; he published little during his lifetime, and he reportedly requested on his deathbed that his poetry manuscripts be burned as "valueless." The request was ignored, however, and when his verse appeared in 1835 he was revealed as one of the authors (the other was his friend Halleck) of the "Croaker" poems that had titillated readers of New York newspapers during the summer of 1819. This revelation, together with the appearance of Drake's only long poem, "The Culprit Fay," prompted extravagant praise that Poe deplored (*Southern Literary Messenger,* April 1836), as did later critics. Later, a biographer of Poe (Vincent Buranelli, *Edgar Allan Poe,* 1961) labeled Drake "a third-rate versifier."

Despite such judgments, Drake's poetry reflects a promising if aborted talent. A number of his "Croaker" poems—"To Ennui," "The National Painting," "To John Minshull, Esquire," to name only a few—poke healthy fun at an America that was already beginning to take itself too seriously. In "The Culprit Fay"—reportedly written in three days—Drake anticipated both **Washington Irving** and **James Kirke Paulding** in experimenting with fantasy; the poem tells the story of a Hudson River fairy who, for having fallen in love with "an earthly maid," is sentenced by his "lily-king" to perform herculean tasks in miniature. Derivative as it is, "The Culprit Fay" reflects not only Drake's perceptive reading of great masters—ranging from Shakespeare and Michael Drayton to his own contemporaries Coleridge and Keats—but an exciting young imagination that was too soon stilled by death.

—Thomas F. O'Donnell

DREISER, Theodore (Herman Albert)

Born: Terre Haute, Indiana, 27 August 1871. **Education:** Public schools in Warsaw, Terre Haute, Sullivan, and Evansville, all Indiana; Indiana University, Bloomington, 1889-90. **Family:** Married 1) Sara Osborne White in 1898 (separated 1914; died 1942); 2) Helen Patges Richardson in 1944. **Career:** Worked in a restaurant and for a hardware company, in Chicago, 1887-89; real estate clerk and collection agent, Chicago, 1890-92; reporter, Chicago *Globe,* 1892; dramatic editor, St. Louis *Globe-Democrat,* 1892-93; reporter, St. Louis *Republic,* 1893; columnist, Pittsburgh *Dispatch,* 1894; moved to New York, 1894; editor, *Ev'ry Month,* New York, 1895-97; free-lance magazine writer, 1897-99; had no settled job or home, 1900-03; editor, *Smith's Magazine,* 1905-06, and *Broadway Magazine,* 1906-07, both New York; managing editor, Butterick Publications, New York, and editor of Butterick's *Delineator,* 1907-10; editor, *Bohemian* magazine, 1909-10; full-time writer from 1911; lived in Los Angeles, 1919-23 and after 1938; coeditor, *American Spectator,* 1932-34; applied for membership of the Communist Party, 1945. Chairman, National Committee for the Defense of Political Prisoners, 1931. **Awards:** American Academy Award of Merit Medal, 1944. **Died:** 28 December 1945.

Publications

Collections

Letters: A Selection, edited by Robert H. Elias. 3 vols., 1959.
A Dreiser Reader, edited by James T. Farrell. 1962.
Selected Poems, edited by Robert P. Saalback. 1969.
Works (Pennsylvania Edition), edited by Neda Westlake and James L.W. West III. 1981–
Theodore Dreiser: Stories. 1996.

Fiction

Sister Carrie. 1900.
Jennie Gerhardt. 1911.
The Financier. 1912; revised edition, 1927.
The Titan. 1914.
The "Genius." 1915.
Free and Other Stories. 1918.
Twelve Men. 1919.
An American Tragedy. 1925.
Chains: Lesser Novels and Stories. 1927.
A Gallery of Women. 1929.
Fine Furniture (stories). 1930.
The Bulwark. 1946.
The Stoic. 1947.

Plays

Laughing Gas (produced 1916). In *Plays,* 1916.

Plays of the Natural and the Supernatural (includes *The Girl in the Coffin, The Blue Sphere, Laughing Gas, In the Dark, The Spring Recital, The Light in the Window, The Old Ragpicker*). 1916; augmented editions, 1926 (includes *Phantasmagoria* and *The Count of Progress*) and 1927 (includes *The Dream*); as *Plays, Natural and Supernatural* (includes *The Anaesthetic Revelation*), 1930.
The Girl in the Coffin (produced 1917). In *Plays,* 1916.
The Old Ragpicker (produced 1918). In *Plays,* 1916.
The Hand of the Potter (produced 1921). 1919; revised version, 1927.

Poetry

Moods, Cadenced and Declaimed. 1926; revised edition, 1928; as *Moods Philosophic and Emotional, Cadenced and Declaimed,* 1935.
The Aspirant. 1929.
Epitaph. 1930.

Other

A Traveler at Forty. 1913.
A Hoosier Holiday. 1916.
Life, Art, and America. 1917.
Hey Rub-a-Dub-Dub: A Book of the Mystery and Wonder and Terror of Life. 1920.
A Book about Myself. 1922; as *Newspaper Days,* 1931.
The Color of a Great City (on New York City). 1923.
Dreiser Looks at Russia. 1928; shortened version, as *Dreiser's Russia,* 1928.
My City. 1929.
The Carnegie Works at Pittsburgh. 1929(?).
Dawn: A History of Myself. 1931.
Tragic America. 1931.
Tom Mooney. 1933.
America Is Worth Saving. 1941
Letters to Louise, edited by Louise Campbell. 1959.
Autobiography. 2 vols., 1965.
Notes on Life, edited by Marguerite Tjader and John J. McAleer. 1974.
A Selection of Uncollected Prose, edited by Donald Pizer. 1977.
Selected Magazine Articles of Dreiser: Life and Art in the American 1890's, edited by Yoshinobu Hakutani. 1986.
Theodore Dreiser Journalism: Newspaper Writings, 1892-1895, vol. 1, edited by T.D. Nostwich, 1988.
Dreiser's Russian Diary. 1996.

Editor, *The Living Thoughts of Thoreau.* 1939.

*

Bibliography: *Dreiser: A Primary and Secondary Bibliography* by Donald Pizer and others, 1975, and *Dreiser: A Primary Bibliography and Reference Guide* by Pizer, 1991; *Dreiser and the Critics, 1911-1982: A Bibliography with Selective Annotations* by Jeanetta Boswell, 1986.

Critical Studies: *Dreiser, Apostle of Nature* by Robert H. Elias, 1949, revised edition, 1970; *Dreiser* by F.O. Matthiessen, 1951, revised edition, 1973; *The Stature of Dreiser* edited by Alfred Kazin and Charles Shapiro, 1955, and *Dreiser: Our Bitter Patriot* by Shapiro, 1962; *Dreiser,* 1964, *Plots and Characters in the Fiction of Dreiser,* 1977, and *Dreiser Revisited,* 1992, all by Philip L. Gerber; *Dreiser* by W.A. Swanberg, 1965; *Dreiser: A New Dimension* by Marguerite Tjader, 1965; *Dreiser: An Introduction and Interpretation* by John J. McAleer, 1968; *Two Dreiser* by Ellen Moers, 1969; *Dreiser: His World and His Novels* by Richard Lehan, 1969; *Dreiser: A Collection of Critical Essays* edited by John Lydenberg, 1971; *Homage to Dreiser* by Robert Penn Warren, 1971; *Dreiser* by W.H. Frohock, 1972; *Dreiser: The Critical Reception* edited by Jack Salzman, 1972; *Dreiser: American Editor and Novelist* by Alan L. Paley, 1973; *Dreiser* by James Lundquist, 1974; *The Novels of Dreiser: A Critical Study* by Donald Pizer, 1976, and *Critical Essays on Dreiser* edited by Pizer, 1981; *Young Dreiser: A Critical Study* by Yoshinobu Hakutani, 1980; *Dreiser and His Fiction: A Twentieth-Century Quest* by Lawrence E. Hussman, 1983; *The Small Canvas: An Introduction to Dreiser's Short Stories* by Joseph Griffin, 1985; *Dreiser: At the Gates of the City 1871-1907* (vol. 1 of biography), 1986, and *Dreiser: An American Journey, 1908-1945* (vol. 2 of biography), 1990, both by Richard Lingeman; *Mechanism and Mysticism: The Influence of Science on the Thought and Work of Theodore Dreiser* by Louis J. Zanine, 1993; *Sexualizing Power in Naturalism: Theodore Dreiser and Frederick Philip Grove* by Irene Gammel, 1994; *Theodore Dreiser: Beyond Naturalism* edited by Miriam Gogol, 1995; *Dreiser and Veblen, Saboteurs of the Status Quo* by Clare Virginia Eby, 1998.

*   *   *

The first major writer to emerge from America's "melting pot" population (his father was a German-Catholic weaver), Theodore Dreiser almost single-handedly created and made respectable a socially oriented fiction that surprisingly complements the romance tradition of **Hawthorne** and **Melville** while expanding the narrowly focused realism of **Howells** and **James**. His achievement is vast, paradoxical, and, considering the conditions of his birth and the poverty of his youth, highly unlikely. Personally ungainly, erratically educated, and possessing an unusually shoddy conception of aesthetics, he succeeds through a combination of passionate integrity and a brutal determination to exhaust his material completely. For the first time in American fiction, he introduced on an epic scale a literary effort in which the social environment was given a detailed attention equal to, if not greater than, that which was focused on the individual protagonist. His heroes are neither orphans set adrift in a bewildering chaotic world nor archetypal symbols occupying spaces in a moral or allegorical diagram. Instead, they are begotten out of concrete family relationships within particular socioeconomic situations. And although Dreiser's characters are never the mere pawns of their social and biological circumstances, still they can only be understood in terms of those circumstances. Sex and money have ever been the twin thematic strands out of which novels are built, but Dreiser is the first American novelist to scrutinize these concerns with a consistently unashamed and unaverted gaze. His reluctance to apply moralistic judgments and the spacious compassion with which he views the behavior of his characters infuse his fiction with a vitality and a sense of wonder that transcend by far the mechanical operations of the naturalistic formulas that are sometimes invoked to explain—or explain away—his work.

Partly influenced by Herbert Spencer's interpretation of evolution and excited by the honesty he found in the novels of Balzac, Tolstoy, Zola, and Hardy, Dreiser is, of course, far less intellectual than his intellectual influences. Nearer to the bone, he drew upon the checkered adventures of his own large family and his personal experiences as an ill-favored ambitious young man struggling to make good in the big blustering city. With the successes and failures of his brothers and sisters in mind, he had no need of philosophical theory to perceive the sharp disparity between the sanctimonious cant of the pulpit and the popular press and the actual practices of life in the booming economy of the last years of the nineteenth century. And, perhaps most important, his capacity to project himself autobiographically into such different personalities as Carrie Meeber, Hurstwood, Drouet, Jennie Gerhardt, Frank Cowperwood, and Clyde Griffiths makes his novels both impersonal and personal—widescale renderings of American life as viewed from a detached, brooding perspective and intimately felt transcriptions of the loneliness, frustration, and burning desire to succeed that torment the sensibilities of the American temperament.

His first novel, *Sister Carrie,* already shows Dreiser in full possession of his powers. The pilgrimage of the eighteen-year-old country girl to Chicago and then later to stardom on the New York stage follows the hackneyed scenario of the sentimental fiction (the **Horatio Alger**-Cinderella fairy tale) that Dreiser knew well as an editor for Butterick publications. But Dreiser does more than simply refuse to disapprove of his amoral heroine; he transforms these stock melodramatic materials into a dispassionate dissection of the factors that conjoin for success and failure in a society where "making" and "being" good are sometimes in radical disalignment. Carrie's rise, Drouet's complacent survival, and Hurstwood's fall are complementary elements in the turbulence of a collective life-force surging and ebbing in accord with its own laws of movement. Man may attempt to resist or try to ride along with the current, but, in terms of his most profoundly cherished ideals, he is alien to the purposes of life and doomed to recurrent and ultimate dissatisfaction.

Sister Carrie introduces the themes that were to preoccupy Dreiser throughout his career and also displays his novelistic techniques in full maturity. Although he has been frequently condemned by critics as a wretched stylist, it might be more accurate to suggest that he simply had no personal style at all. Instead, he absorbed the highly detailed, prolix, occasionally ornate but usually lucid magazine-style of the Mauve Decade and employed it as an impersonal instrument in the fashioning of his fiction. In Dreiser's case, his personal style may be more fruitfully sought in his characteristic use of structure. He built his novels in large narrative blocks, each of them composed of simple sequences of action; these he relates unhurriedly, setting minutely observed detail upon detail like a workman laying bricks. These narrative sequences succeed one another in ponderous waves of relentless motion suggesting a sense of the irrevocable passage of time, a cumulative weight of authenticity, and a rhythm of inevitability. With the writing of *Sister Carrie,* Dreiser's development as a novelist was complete. In his subsequent novels he might intensify, broaden, or polish aspects of his ideas and craftsmanship, but his work would remain within the same methodology and frame of bemused compassion that constitute his signature in *Sister Carrie.*

After *Jennie Gerhardt*—a curiously neglected novel that turns *Sister Carrie* inside-out, as it were, and presents in its title character the nearest approach to a saint that Dreiser ever made—he produced his study of an American "robber baron" in *The Financier* and *The Titan.* Modeling his protagonist, Frank Cowperwood, on the millionaire Charles T. Yerkes, Dreiser's intention is to show the obverse side of the Darwinian coin—the ruthless Superman, coolly aware of the amoral rules of the game, who stakes his formidable energies in a single-minded drive for power. Utterly persuasive in its grasp of the political and financial minutiae of stock transfers and bond issues, Dreiser's treatment of Cowperwood's career is easily the authoritative—if caricatured—portrait of the American businessman, relentless in his pursuit of wealth and power, but destined to the same frustration as the weak and victimized people whom he manipulates.

The last of Dreiser's major novels and perhaps his single most impressive work is *An American Tragedy*. Here Dreiser is at the very peak of his ability, identifying closely with his protagonist, Clyde Griffiths, even as he broods with Olympian resignation over the wretched banality of Clyde's life. Dreiser reveals that life with magisterial authority, piece by painstaking piece, from Clyde's beginnings as a small embarrassed boy walking the city streets with his missionary parents to his final state execution for murder. More like a massive monument that turns in slow-motion before the reader than a literary portrait, *An American Tragedy* patiently and inexorably amasses evidence to show how a weak, malleable personality can be so thoroughly molded by his circumstances and by the shallow values of his culture as to become virtually negligible as a generative force in himself. By the end of the novel, the reader so fully understands the elements that have created Clyde that the character himself almost recedes into the landscape of the novel as merely one more passive factor. And although—or because—every relevant fact in his life has been clearly illumined, the reader can no more determine to what extent Clyde is a murderer and to what extent a victim than can Clyde himself.

Dreiser not only wrote long novels, but he was prolific in many genres. Of the poetry, short stories, plays, and nonfiction as well as other novels, we might cite as of special interest *A Book About Myself* and *Dawn*, two volumes of memoirs, *Hey Rub-a-Dub-Dub*, a characteristic volume of essays, and *The "Genius,"* his least successful but most nakedly autobiographical novel. Dreiser's stature in American letters is huge, stubborn, and undeniable. As the nineteenth-century Russian novelists are supposed to have climbed out from under Gogol's overcoat, so one might suggest that Dreiser must bear a similar paternal responsibility for the fiction of the 1920s (**Anderson, Faulkner, Fitzgerald, Hemingway, Lewis, Wolfe**), the 1930s (**Farrell, Steinbeck, Wright**), and even the 1940s (**Bellow, Mailer**). There is a sense in which his achievement may seem crude, I suppose, but it required something stronger than gentility to clear a continent in which his successors could pursue their visions of truth unimpeded by the barriers of hypocrisy, reticence, and prudential caution. The momentum of history was in this direction, of course, but yet some of the richness and power of the modern American novel is due to Dreiser's sweeping redefinition of the novelist's task.

—Earl Rovit

See the essay on *Sister Carrie*.

Du BOIS, W(illiam) E(dward) B(urghardt)

Born: Great Barrington, Massachusetts, 23 February 1868; immigrated to Ghana, 1961; became citizen, 1963. **Education:** Public schools in Great Barrington; Fisk University, Nashville, Tennessee (editor, *Fisk Herald*), 1885-88, A.B. 1888; Harvard University, Cambridge, Massachusetts, 1888-90, A.M. 1891, Ph.D. 1895; University of Berlin, 1892-94. **Family:** Married 1) Nina Gomer in 1896 (died 1950), one son and one daughter; 2) Shirley Graham in 1951. **Career:** Professor of Greek and Latin, Wilberforce University, Ohio, 1894-96; assistant instructor in sociology, University of Pennsylvania, Philadelphia, 1896-97; professor of economics and history, Atlanta University, 1897-1910; editor, *Moon Illustrated Weekly,* Memphis, Tennessee, 1906, and *Horizon,* Washington, D.C., 1907-10; a founder of the National Association for the Advancement of Colored People, 1910, and director of publicity and research for the NAACP and editor of the NAACP's magazine *Crisis,* New York, 1910-34; editor, with A.G. Dill, *Brownies' Book,* 1920-22; columnist ("A Forum of Fact and Opinion"), Pittsburgh *Courier,* 1936-38 and ("As the Crow Flies"), *Amsterdam News,* New York, 1939-44; editor, *Phylon,* Atlanta, 1940-44; director of the Department of Special Research, NAACP, New York, 1944-48; columnist ("The Winds of Time"), Chicago *Defender,* 1945-48, and *People's Voice,* 1947-48. Founder, Pan-African Congress, 1900, and Niagara Movement, 1904; vice-chairman, Council on African Affairs, 1949-54; candidate for U.S. Senate, from New York, 1950. **Awards:** Spingarn Medal, 1920; International Peace prize, 1952. Knight Commander, Liberian Order of African Redemption; fellow, American Association for the Advancement of Science. **Member:** American Academy. **Died:** 27 August 1963.

PUBLICATIONS

Collections

The Seventh Son: The Thought and Writings of Du Bois, edited by Julius Lester. 2 vols., 1971.
Correspondence, edited by Herbert Aptheker. 3 vols., 1973-78.
Writings (Library of America), edited by Nathan Huggins. 1986.
The Oxford W.E.B. Du Bois Reader, edited by Eric Sundquist. 1996.

Fiction

The Quest of the Silver Fleece. 1911.
Dark Princess: A Romance. 1928.
The Black Flame
　The Ordeal of Mansart. 1957.
　Mansart Builds a School. 1959.
　Worlds of Color. 1961.

Plays

The Star of Ethiopia (pageant, produced ?). 1913.
Haiti, in *Federal Theatre Plays,* edited by Pierre de Rohan. 1938.

Poetry

Selected Poems. 1965.

Other

The Suppression of African Slave-Trade to the United States of America 1638-1870. 1896.

The Conservation of Races. 1897.

The Philadelphia Negro: A Social Study, with *A Report on Domestic Service* by Isabel Eaton. 1899.

Possibilities of the Negro: The Advance Guard of Race. 1903.

Souls of Black Folk: Essays and Sketches. 1903; revised edition, 1953.

Of the Wings of Atlanta. 1904.

The Black Vote of Philadelphia. 1905.

The Negro South and North. 1905.

The Negro in the South: His Economic Progress in Relation to His Moral and Religious Development, with Booker T. Washington. 1907; as *The American Negro* (Southern States), 1909.

John Brown (biography). 1909.

The Social Evolution of the Black South. 1911.

Disfranchisement. 1912.

The Negro. 1915.

Darkwater: Voices from within the Veil. 1920.

The Gift of Black Folk: Negroes in the Making of America. 1924.

Africa: Its Geography, People, and Products. 1930.

Africa: Its Place in Modern History. 1930.

Black Reconstruction in America: An Essay. 1935.

A Pageant in Seven Decades 1868-1938. 1938.

Black Folk Then and Now: An Essay in the History and Sociology of the Negro Race. 1939.

The Revelation of Saint Orgne, The Damned. 1939.

Dusk of Dawn: An Essay Toward an Autobiography of a Race Concept. 1940.

Encyclopedia of the Negro: Preparatory Volume. 1945; revised edition, 1946.

Color and Democracy: Colonies and Peace. 1945.

The World and Africa. 1947; revised edition, 1965.

In Battle for Peace: The Story of My 83rd Birthday. 1952.

The Story of Benjamin Franklin. 1956.

Africa in Battle against Colonialism, Racialism, Imperialism. 1960.

An ABC of Color. 1963.

Autobiography. 1968.

The Black North in 1901: A Social Study. 1969.

Du Bois Speaks: Speeches and Addresses 1890-1963, edited by Philip Foner. 2 vols., 1970.

Du Bois: A Reader, edited by Meyer Weinberg. 1970.

A Du Bois Reader, edited by Andrew D. Paschal. 1971.

The Crisis Writings, edited by Daniel Walden. 1972.

The Emerging Thought of Du Bois: Essays and Editorials from The Crisis, edited by Henry Lee Moon. 1972.

The Education of Black People: Ten Critiques 1906-1960, edited by Herbert Aptheker. 1973.

Book Reviews, edited by Herbert Aptheker. 1977.

Du Bois on Sociology and the Black Community, edited by Dan S. Green and Edwin D. Driver. 1978.

Prayers for Dark People, edited by Herbert Aptheker. 1980.

Selections from The Crisis, edited by Herbert Aptheker. 1983.

Against Racism: Unpublished Essays, Papers, Addresses 1887-1961, edited by Herbert Aptheker. 1985.

The Selected Speeches of W.E.B. Du Bois. 1996.

Editor, *An Appeal to the World.* 1947.

Editor, *Atlanta University Publications* (pamphlets published in 1898-1913). 2 vols., 1968-69.

*

Bibliography: *Annotated Bibliography of the Published Writings of Du Bois* by Herbert Aptheker, 1973; *Du Bois: A Bibliography of His Published Writings* by Paul G. Partington, 1979, supplement, 1984; *W.E.B. Du Bois: An Annotated Bibliography* by Jennifer Wagner, 1994.

Critical Studies: *Du Bois* by Elliott M. Rudwick, 1960; *His Day Is Marching On: A Memoir of Du Bois,* 1971, and *Du Bois: A Pictorial Biography,* 1978, both by Shirley Graham; *Du Bois: A Profile* by Rayford W. Logan, 1971; *The Art and Imagination of Du Bois,* 1976, and *Slavery and the Literary Imagination: Du Bois's "The Souls of Black Folk;" Selected Papers,* 1989, both by Arnold Rampersad; *Du Bois* by Jack B. Moore, 1981; *The Social Thought of Du Bois* by Joseph P. DeMarco, 1983; *Critical Essays on Du Bois* edited by William L. Andrews, 1985; *Dubois and Expansionism: A Black Man's View of Empire* by Helene Christol, 1991; *W.E.B. Du Bois: Of Racial and Cultural Identity* edited by Robert Gooding-Williams, 1994; *W.E.B. Du Bois* by David L. Lewis, 1994; *Dark Voices: W.E.B. Du Bois and American Thought, 1888-1903* by Shamoon Zamir, 1995; *W.E.B. Du Bois and American Political Thought: Fabianism and the Color Line* by Adolph L. Reed, 1997.

*   *   *

At the age of thirty-five, in 1903, W.E.B. Du Bois took intellectual leadership of those within the Afro-American world who preferred liberal idealism to compensatory realism. Du Bois was prepared for his role by rigorous training in the traditional liberal arts as well as the newer empirical social sciences. But it was confidence in the moral absolute of truth and a poetic imagination that were to prove the sources of his effectiveness.

Souls of Black Folk, the book in which Du Bois publicly announced his differences with Booker T. Washington, is constructed from first-hand observation, historical research, and reasoned analysis. Its power, however, derives from the images of divided consciousness (souls), a culturally united black nation (folk), and the veil behind which black remained nearly invisible. In a time when Jim Crow shaped perception as much as policy, Du Bois's metaphors represented intellectual liberation, giving blacks a profoundly dignified way of conceiving their own lives and history. The cultural nationalism of *Souls of Black Folk* had been implicit in the earlier study *The Philadelphia Negro,* in which Du Bois documented class structure and shared institutions. It reappeared as motivation for the utopian vision of agricultural cooperatives in *The Quest of the Silver Fleece* and the romantic narrative of worldwide organization for colored people in *Dark Princess.*

Du Bois's well-known commitment to the idea of leadership by a talented tenth has its counterpart in the learned rhetoric of his essays and the grandiose design of his novels. It is no wonder that writing as a critic in *Crisis* he was unsympathetic to the experimentation and modern realism of the younger generation in the Negro Renaissance. Still, he made his own characteristic contribution to the "new Negro." His book *The Negro,* anticipating anti-colonial conferences organized after World War I, corrected popular impressions that American blacks were without roots by celebrating the African past. Then *Black Reconstruction in America,* written out of Du Bois's new enthusiasm for Marxism in the 1930s, recovered the significance of black people in the history of the south. Despite limitations of style, these historical reevaluations initiated a scholarly revisionism comparable to the redirection of thought in the book *Souls of Black Folk.*

Nearing the end of his life, Du Bois published his most comprehensive treatment of America, *The Black Flame*, a trilogy binding into one narrative a historical account of the years corresponding roughly to his own life and a fictional account of Manuel Mansart. That the plots are meant to inter-relate goes without saying. More to the point is the observation that Du Bois's career, capped by the trilogy, was his most important dialectical demonstration. Seeking to write as truthfully as possible, he became not only a scribe of history but its maker.

—John M. Reilly

See the essay on *Souls of Black Folk.*

DUBUS, André

Born: Lake Charles, Louisiana, 11 August 1936. **Education:** McNeese State College, B.A. in 1958; University of Iowa, M.F.A. in 1966. **Family:** Married 1) Patricia Lowe in 1958 (divorced 1970), two daughters and two sons; 2) Tommie Gail Cotter in 1975 (divorced 1977); 3) Peggy Rambach in 1979, two daughters. **Career:** U.S. Marine Corps, 1958-64 (left service as captain); teacher of modern fiction and creative writing, Bradford College, Bradford, Massachusetts, 1966-84. Visiting teacher at colleges and universities, including University of Alabama and Boston University. **Died:** March 1999.

PUBLICATIONS

Short Stories

Separate Flights. 1975.
Adultery and Other Choices. 1977.
Finding a Girl in America. 1980.
The Times Are Never So Bad. 1983.
We Don't Live Here Anymore. 1984.
Land Where My Father Died. 1984.
The Last Worthless Evening. 1986.
Selected Stories. 1988.
The Cage Keeper and Other Stories. 1989.
Dancing after Hours: Stories. 1996.

Novel and Novella

The Lieutenant (novel). 1967.
Voices from the Moon (novella). 1984.
We Don't Live Here Anymore: The Novellas of Andre Dubus. 1984.

Other

Blessings. 1987.
Broken Vessels. 1991.
Bluesman. 1993.

*

Critical Studies: "André Dubus" by John B. Breslin, in *Commonweal,* 1999, pp. 10.

*   *   *

The conflict between flesh and spirit is at the center of the short stories and essays of André Dubus. A lifelong Catholic, Dubus brings a deep religious sensibility to his treatment of sexuality, betrayal, loss, guilt, joy, and the presence of grace in even the most flawed and insignificant of lives. Though these thematic concerns have prompted comparisons with the work of **Flannery O'Connor**, Dubus eschews her grotesque humor and exaggeration; the influence of **Ernest Hemingway**, **William Faulkner**, and Anton Chekhov is more evident in his somber, plainly written, and empathic stories.

Though he grew up in the South, Dubus lived most of his adult life near the decaying mill towns north of Boston in which much of his work is set. His characters are undistinguished types: bartenders, construction workers, cops, and waitresses who sense the fallen nature of their lives but lack the ability to change much. They betray or are betrayed, and often these betrayals lead to violent actions—yet their pain comes less from anger than from their sorrowful recognition of their inevitable weaknesses. In some ways, these concerns resemble those of Dubus's contemporary, **Raymond Carver**, who also wrote brilliantly about marginalized lives. But while Carver's approach is understated, minimalist, and ironic, Dubus's approach is fully developed and emotional, often achieving an intimate sympathy of feeling but sometimes tending toward the oversentimentalized and didactic.

Many of Dubus's typical concerns can be found in "If They Knew Yvonne," the first-person account of a young Catholic boy's discovery of sex and love. The story begins with the boy's struggles to control his sexual urges, as the Christian Brothers at his school have taught him. The result, however, is confusion and guilt. A few years later, however, the boy meets Yvonne and discovers that sex can be good. He describes the course of their relationship, from what he thinks is love and its consummation to what he slowly realizes is just physical attraction. The priest to whom he finally confesses this more mature awareness is sensitive and understanding; the young man is absolved but is left with the knowledge of his betrayed ideal. Sexuality betrayed is also central to "Killings," in which a grieving father avenges the murder of his adult son. Though the acts of violence dominate the plot, they are set in motion by an earlier act of adultery—itself prompted by the more elusive betrayal of a sexual love turned base. This pattern emerges again in "The Pretty Girl," about a young woman who realizes too late that she has married a brute; when she leaves him for another man, he rapes her, and she eventually kills him.

Betrayed innocence also underlies "Rose," the third-person story of a woman who believes that she has done only one good thing in her life—saved her children from their abusive father. The story's apparently autobiographical narrator, an ex-marine, writer, and teacher, reimagines Rose's life as the story of idealized love gone bad: "On the car seat of courtship she had dreamed of this, and in the first year of marriage she lived the dream: joined him in the shower and made love with him, still damp, before they went to the dinner kept warm on the stove, then back to the bed's tossed sheets to lie in the dark, smoking, talking, touching, and they made love again; and later, again, until they could only lie side by side waiting for their breathing to slow, before they slept. Now at the tired ends of days they took release from each other, and she anxiously slept, waiting for a baby to cry." For Dubus, the deterioration of a marriage is a tragedy and a sin, for it is the betrayal of a sacrament; an unloving marriage can only result in pain or violence—in Rose's case, both. Yet the story also stresses the superhuman strength of which seemingly weak human beings can be capable and the grace that can be achieved when flawed people choose to act against evil.

"Rose" also reveals, however, the excessive romanticizing and didacticism that are Dubus's weaknesses. The narrator does not merely tell Rose's story; he preaches and judges: "But if the outlaw rapes, tortures, gratuitously kills, or if he makes children suffer, we hate him with a purity we seldom feel: our hatred has no roots in prejudice, or self-righteousness, but in horror. . . . So I hate Jim Cormier, and cannot understand him; cannot with my imagination cross the distance between myself and him, enter his soul and know how it felt to live even five minutes of his life. And I forgive Rose, but as I write I resist that compassion, or perhaps merely empathy, and force myself to think instead of the three children, and Rose living there, knowing what she knew. She was young." In order to forgive, the narrator must first assign blame—an unusual, and perhaps morally arrogant, perspective for a character not directly involved in the story's events.

Rose is both weak and flawed, but she is also morally aware, and her story show's Dubus's ability to portray his female characters as fully complex beings instead of mere props in stories about men.

Dubus writes convincingly as well about physical life, describing his awareness of the body's beauty and of the intimate pleasures of running, sweating, walking, and lifting weights. Dubus's perspective on such physical joys was suddenly challenged, however, when in 1986 he was struck by an automobile after stopping to assist a stranded motorist; he lost one leg and the use of the other and lived the rest of his life in a wheelchair. Dubus probed his feelings about this loss in several personal essays. Like his fiction, these are distinguished by their unguarded emotion and their awareness of spiritual mystery; several deal directly with religious content. While some of these pieces are considered overdone or stale, the best of them offer such wisdom as that which concludes "A Country Road Song," in which Dubus describes the transcendence he found in running, and then writes, "I mourn this, and I sing in gratitude for loving this, and in gratitude for all the roads I ran on and walked on, for the hills I climbed and descended, for trees and grass and sky, and for being spared losing running and walking sooner than I did: ten years sooner, or eight seasons, or three; or one day."

—Elizabeth Shostak

DUMAS, Henry L.

Born: Sweet Home, Arkansas, 20 July 1934. **Education:** City College (now the City University of New York) and Rutgers University, 1958-61; studied in residence with the musician and philosopher Sun Ra. **Military Service:** Served in the U.S. Air Force, 1953-57, stationed at Lackland Air Force Base in Texas, and later in the Arabian Peninsula. **Family:** Married Loretta Ponton in 1955; two sons. **Career:** Printing machine operator for IBM, 1963-64; social worker for the state of New York, 1965-66; assistant director of Upward Bound at Hiram College in Hiram, Ohio, 1967; teacher-counselor and director of language workshops for Southern Illinois University's Experiment in Higher Education,

1967-68; published "Rain God" in *Negro Digest* and "Mosaic Harlem," "Knock on Wood," and "Cuttin Down to Size" in *Black Fire: An Anthology of Afro-American Writing,* edited by LeRoi Jones and Larry Neal, 1968. **Died:** 23 May 1968.

PUBLICATIONS

Novels

Jonoah and the Green Stone. 1976.

Short Fiction

Ark of Bones and Other Stories. 1970.
Rope of Wind and Other Stories. 1979.
Goodbye Sweetwater. 1988.

Poetry

Poetry for My People. 1970; as *Play Ebony, Play Ivory,* 1974.
Knees of A Natural Man: The Selected Poetry of Henry Dumas. 1989.

*

Critical Studies: "The Poet's Work" by Clyde Taylor, in *Black World,* September 1975; "Combining Traditions of the Black Experience" by Barbara Smith, in *Freedomways* vol. 15, no. 1, 1975; special Henry Dumas issue of *Black American Literature Forum,* summer 1988; "Locating a Text: Implications of Afrocentric Theory" by Molefi Kete Asante, in *Language and Literature in the African American Imagination* edited by Carol Aisha Blackshire-Belay, 1992; *The Liberating Imagination: Politics of Vision in the Art of Edward Kamau Brathwaite and Henry Dumas* (dissertation) by Paul Anderson Griffith, 1995.

*   *   *

Henry Dumas's life was cut tragically short in 1968—at the age of thirty-four—when he was shot by a policeman during a subway incident that was eventually determined to have been a case of mistaken identity. Nevertheless, he still managed to produce a small body of literature that is of a high and lasting quality. Dumas has been hailed by such authors as **Toni Morrison** and Molefi Asante as a writer who focused on African American values of community and whose writing embodies an Afrocentric viewpoint.

Because most of his work was published only posthumously, Dumas's reputation grew slowly but surely in the years after his death. His first short story collection, *Ark of Bones,* was the most crucial work in establishing Dumas's permanent place in the world of African American letters, and the title story of that collection is frequently noted as one of his strongest efforts. As is typical of Dumas's fiction, the main characters are known only by their nicknames, Headeye and Fish-Hound. Headeye takes the younger Fish-Hound down to the edge of the Mississippi River, where a small boat takes them to a fantastic ark in the middle of the river. As is typical of Dumas's stories that have an element of the fantastic, no explanation is given for the appearance of the ark. Its purpose, however, is to dredge the bones of African Americans from the Mississippi River and record each one, so the dead will not be forgotten. As the priest in charge of this sacred duty says to Fish-Hound, "Every African who lives in America has a part of his soul in this ark." Headeye has come to be initiated into the ranks of those who record the bones; Fish-Hound has been called to be a witness. When the two return to the shore, they discover that a lynching has taken place while they were gone. Headeye disappears for a few days after that, then returns to the ark for good, while Fish-Hound remains to spread the word—not about the ark (which he does not think anyone would believe)—but about "Ezekiel in the valley of dry bones." His experience with the ark of bones has made him a deep believer in the power and the spirit of African American people; he has become a prophet of that spirit.

Equally impressive is Dumas's short story "Rope of Wind," collected in the short story collection of the same name. It tells of Johnny B's attempt to thwart a deputy sheriff bent on lynching the Reverend Westland. Johnny spots the deputy and tries to warn Westland ahead of time, but Westland calmly accepts his fate, well knowing that he is helpless before it. As the men drive Westland away, Johnny races after them on foot, hoping to intervene in some way. Summoning incredible powers of endurance and intuition—and inspired by the memory of another man he'd seen murdered—Johnny is able to keep the car in sight, but he is unable to overtake it; when it finally stops, he is still helpless to intervene and save Westland. He is, however, able to cut Westland's dead body free from the sack they have stuffed it in, and then race back to the town to say where the reverend's body lies. At the end of this supreme effort Johnny B dies. Although unsuccessful in his attempt to save Westland, he has prevented any further desecration of the man's body and he has brought news to Westland's son about his father's fate.

The same spiritual vision that can be seen in Dumas's fiction is also displayed in his poetry. First published in 1970 as *Poetry for My People,* this volume is equally well-known under the 1974 title of *Play Ebony, Play Ivory.* The title poem, "Play Ebony, Play Ivory," re-imagines the piano as an African percussion instrument, capable of making notes and chords reminiscent of African drums. This poem also expresses Dumas's deep feelings about the spiritual nature of music, as he urges the piano player to "play ebony play ivory. / play my people / all my people who breathe / the breath of earth." The piano player seems to merge with the piano, as the poet urges, "now touch / and hear and see / let your lungs scream." There is no clear distinction between the music, the performer, the instrument, and the audience of "all my people who are keys and chords."

Dumas's poem "Son of Msippi" in many ways recalls Langston Hughes's poem, "The Negro Speaks of Rivers," as the voice in this poem recalls that "Up / from Msippi I grew." But the Mississippi River is in this poem, "the river of death," much as it is in the short story, "Ark of Bones." As in "Ark of Bones," the Mississippi River is "the bone-filled Mississippi," and is associated with spirituality and music, as the speaker "grew, / wailing a song with every strain."

Dumas's sole novel, *Jonoah and the Green Stone,* is about another son of the Mississippi, Jonoah, born John, but renamed after both Noah and Jonah when he is found by a black family—the Mastersons—floating on a boat on the Mississippi in the middle of a flood. The novel's most complete section is set during the great 1937 flood of the Mississippi and tells of Jonoah's separation from his parents, who are lost and presumably drowned in the flood. When Old Man Hearth, who was to pilot the feverish Jonoah to safety, is also lost to the waters, the boat drifts aimlessly until Jonoah is saved by Jubal, a precociously worldly six year old. Jubal and his entire family (including his sister, parents, and aunt, and many of their animals) crowd onto Jonoah's boat and they immediately become his family. When they stop to help Dog Whitlock, a white man who has lost everything in the flood, Whitlock then tries to take control of the boat. He torments the entire family to assert himself over them and eventually knocks the parents—Mamada and Papa Lem—both into the water before losing interest and wading to the shore, since the weather has cleared and the boat has come to higher ground.

The rest of the novel traces Jonoah's migration up north, during which time his moral sense of direction begins to drift. He eventually returns down south to offer his support to the ongoing civil rights movement and to find an ambiguous Green Stone that serves as an emblem of identity, although the meaning is never fully clarified. Because *Jonoah and the Green Stone* was never completed, this section of the novel is the most sketchy. Yet, as Herman Cromwell Gilbert has pointed out, Dumas's visions comes through in these sections with a special haunting power by "teasing the reader with the wonder of things just beyond the reach of knowing."

Although Dumas's vision was spiritual and musical, he could still infuse his vision with wit without undermining the power of his spiritual message. This is apparent in some of the poetry in the "Blues Songs" section of *Poetry for My People,* and nowhere more strongly than in "Machines Can Do It Too / (IBM Blues)," which ends, "If I find a machine in bed with me, / that's the time I'm through." Equally witty, if also more serious, is a story from *Ark of Bones* called "Will the Circle Be Unbroken?," which focuses on a jazz musician, Probe, and his new music, played on an afro-horn (which produces vibrations said to be too intense for those not of African origins). When three white jazz enthusiasts gain entrance by swearing to be black, they are overcome by the music of Probe's afro-horn and die immediately. Dumas's point in this brief story seems to be that black art has a distinct role to play within the black community and that black artists need to create art for this unbroken circle that radiates from Africa.

While waiting on a train platform in Harlem on the 23 May 1968, Dumas was approached by a Transit Authority policeman, who later said that Dumas had been singing and acting erratically. The exact details of Dumas's death are somewhat unclear; when Dumas put his hands in his pockets, the officer apparently thought Dumas was reaching for a gun and fired. The incident was later ruled as one of mistaken identity. Naturally, much of the writing on Dumas has commented on the tragedy of a writer's life being so senselessly cut short as his art was still maturing. Nonetheless, Dumas produced a body of literature that, although small in size, is high in quality and as rich and full of spirit as the Mississippi he used so well in some of his finest work.

—Thomas Cassidy

DUNBAR, Paul Laurence

Born: Dayton, Ohio, 27 June 1872; son of a former slave. **Education:** Dayton High School, graduated 1891. **Family:** Married Alice Ruth Moore in 1898. **Career:** Elevator operator, Dayton,

1891-93; worked at the Haiti Building, World's Columbian Exposition, Chicago, 1894; encouraged in his writing by prominent Dayton men and by William Dean Howells, at whose instigation he joined the Pond Lecture Bureau, 1896; attained great popularity throughout the United States as a reader of his own works, and visited England, 1897; assistant in the Library of Congress, Washington, D.C., 1897-98. Suffered from tuberculosis. **Died:** 9 February 1906.

PUBLICATIONS

Collections

Complete Poems. 1913.
The Dunbar Reader, edited by Jay Martin and Gossie H. Hudson. 1975.

Poetry

Oak and Ivy. 1893.
Majors and Minors. 1895.
Lyrics of Lowly Life. 1896.
Lyrics of the Hearthside. 1899.
Poems of Cabin and Field. 1899.
Candle-Lightin' Time. 1901.
Lyrics of Love and Laughter. 1903.
When Malindy Sings. 1903.
Li'l' Gal. 1904.
Chris'mus Is A-Comin' and Other Poems. 1905.
Howdy, Honey, Howdy. 1905.
Lyrics of Sunshine and Shadow. 1905.
Joggin' Erlong. 1906.
Speakin' o' Christmas and Other Christmas and Special Poems. 1914.
I Greet the Dawn, edited by Ashley Bryan. 1978.

Plays

The Gambler's Wife, in *Dayton Tattler,* Ohio, 13, 20, and 27 December 1890.
African Romances, music by Samuel Coleridge Taylor. 1897.
Clorindy; or, The Origin of the Cakewalk, music by Will Marion Cook. 1898.
Dream Lovers, music by Samuel Coleridge Taylor. 1898.
Jes Lak White Fo'ks (lyrics only, with others), music by Will Marion Cook. 1900.
Uncle Eph's Christmas, music by Will Marion Cook. 1900.
Plantation Melodies, Old and New (lyrics only, with others), music by H.T. Burleigh. 1901.
In Dahomey (lyrics only, with others), music by Will Marion Cook. 1903.
My Lady (lyrics only, with others), music by Will Marion Cook. 1914.

Fiction

The Uncalled. 1898.
Folks from Dixie (stories). 1898.
The Love of Landry. 1900.
The Strength of Gideon and Other Stories. 1900.

The Fanatics. 1901.
The Sport of the Gods. 1902; as *The Jest of Fate,* 1902.
In Old Plantation Days (stories). 1903.
The Heart of Happy Hollow (stories). 1904.

*

Bibliography: *Dunbar: A Bibliography* by E.W. Metcalf, Jr., 1975.

Critical Studies: *The Life and Works of Dunbar,* biography by Lida Keck Wiggins, 1907; *Dunbar and His Song* by Virginia Cunningham, 1947; *Oak and Ivy: A Biography of Dunbar* by Addison Gayle, Jr., 1971; *A Singer in the Dawn: Reinterpretations of Dunbar* edited by Jay Martin, 1975; "The 'Limitless' Freedom of Myth: Paul Lawrence Dunbar's *The Sport of the Gods* and the Criticism of Afro-American Literature" by Houston A. Baker, Jr., in *The American Self* edited by Sam B. Girgus, 1981; "Dunbar: Straightening the Record" by Emeka Okeke Ezigbo, June 1981, and "Dunbar: Master Player in a Fixed Game" by Ralph Story, September 1983, both in *College Language Association Journal.*

*   *   *

There were, in truth, two Paul Laurence Dunbars. One was the writer supported by the interest of white Americans because some of his work was sufficiently faithful to black stereotypical images designed and demanded by white Americans. The other, in a sense the more "real" Dunbar, was the writer of genuine literary talent and dramatic sensibility, whose true literary worth could not be widely assessed until a wide range of his work was gathered and published as late as 1975 in *The Dunbar Reader.*

In his first manifestation, that of dialect poet, Dunbar was not so much pandering to the demands of white editors and a white reading public as indulging his own natural affinity for the rhythms of common speech and often for comedy; dialect in literature was, after all, very much *à la mode* with the interest in local color in late nineteenth-century America. That he had a gift as a dialect poet is undeniable, but it is rather too bad that his white audience could not accept him as anything more.

Much more he was, as **William Dean Howells** recognized early. As a writer of fiction and essays, he used the stuff of black lore to greater effect than any previous black writer, and at least as well as such whites as **Joel Chandler Harris** had done. Particularly noteworthy in his work is the reflection of religion in black American life and of the implications of the black migration to American cities. As a poet, Dunbar often superbly starched his ready lyricism with a keen sense of drama. It is a truism to say that while his material was mainly black, his insights were universal.

Dunbar did not choose to be the exemplar of the white view of black America in his time—but he was, and he made a sturdy pivot. He managed to entertain and enlighten whites while helping to imbue fellow blacks with a sense of history and importance, making him a close spiritual ancestor of **Countée Cullen, Langston Hughes, James Baldwin,** and the other powerful twentieth-century black American voices.

—Alan R. Shucard

DUNCAN, Robert

Pseudonym: Robert Edward Symmes (until 1942). **Born:** Edward Howard Duncan in Oakland, California, 7 January 1919; adopted in 1920 and given name Robert Edward Symmes; took original surname, 1941. **Education:** University of California, Berkeley, 1936-38 and 1948-50. **Military Service:** Served in the U.S. Army, 1941. **Family:** Companion of Jess Collins. **Career:** Editor, *Experimental Review*, 1938-40, *Phoenix*, and *Berkeley Miscellany*, 1948-49, Berkeley, California; teacher at Black Mountain College, Black Mountain, North Carolina, 1956; assistant director of Poetry Center, 1956-57, and lecturer in poetry workshop, 1965, San Francisco State College, California; lecturer in creative writing workshop, University of British Columbia, Vancouver, 1963; organizer of and participant in poetry readings and workshops, San Francisco. **Awards:** Ford grant, 1956-57; *Poetry* Union League Civic and Arts Foundation prize, 1957; *Poetry* Harriet Monroe prize, 1961; Guggenheim fellowship, 1963-64; *Poetry* Levinson prize, 1964; Miles Poetry prize, 1964; National Endowment for the Arts grants, 1965 and 1966-67; *Poetry* Eunice Tietjens Memorial prize, 1967; National Book Critics Circle Award nomination, 1984; Shelley Memorial award, 1984; National Poetry award, 1985; Before Columbus Foundation American Book award, 1986; Bay Area Book Reviewers Association Fred Cody award for Lifetime Literary Excellence, 1986. **Died:** 7 January 1988.

PUBLICATIONS

Collection

Selected Poems. 1997.

Poetry

Heavenly City, Earthly City. 1947.
Poems 1948-49. 1949.
Medieval Scenes. 1950; with preface by the author, 1978.
The Song of the Border-Guard. 1952.
Fragments of a Disordered Devotion. 1952.
Caesar's Gate: Poems 1949-1950 with Collages by Jess Collins. 1955; published as *Caesar's Gate: Poems 1949-50 with Paste-Ups by Jess,* with preface by the author, 1972.
Letters: Poems MCMLIII-MCMLVI, and illustrator. 1958.
Selected Poems. 1959.
The Opening of the Field. 1960; revised, 1973.
Roots and Branches. 1964.
Writing, Writing: A Composition Book of Madison 1953, Stein Imitations (poems and essays). 1964.
Wine. 1964.
Uprising. 1965.
A Book of Resemblances: Poems 1950-1953. 1966.
Of the War: Passages 22-27. 1966.
The Years as Catches: First Poems (1939-1946). 1966.
Boob. 1966.
Epilogos. 1967.
The Cat and the Blackbird (for children), illustrations by Jess Collins. 1967.
Christmas Present, Christmas Presence! 1967.
Bending the Bow. 1968.

My Mother Would Be a Falconess. 1968.
Names of People. 1968.
The First Decade: Selected Poems 1940-1950. 1968.
Derivations: Selected Poems 1950-1956. 1968.
Play Time, Pseudo Stein [and] *1942, a Story* [and] *A Fairy Play: From the Laboratory Records Notebook of 1953, a Tribute to Mother Carey's Chickens.* 1969; with preface by the author, 1969.
Achilles' Song. 1969.
Poetic Disturbances. 1970.
Bring It Up from the Dark. 1970.
Tribunals: Passages 31-35. 1970.
Structure of Rime XXVIII: In Memoriam Wallace Stevens. 1972.
Poems from the Margins of Thom Gunn's Moly. 1972.
A Seventeenth Century Suite in Homage to the Metaphysical Genius in English Poetry (1590-1690): Being Imitations, Derivations, and Variations upon Certain Conceits and Findings Made among Strong Lines, c. November 5, 1971-December 16, 1971. 1973.
An Ode and Arcadia, with Jack Spicer. 1974.
Dante. 1974.
The Venice Poem. 1978.
Veil, Turbine, Cord, and Bird. 1979.
The Five Songs. 1981.
Ground Work: Before the War. 1984.
The Regulators. 1985.
Ground Work II: In the Dark. 1987.
Selected Poems, edited by Robert J. Bertholf. 1993.

Plays

Faust Foutu (produced San Francisco, 1955). Published as *Faust Foutu: Act One of Four Acts: A Comic Mask, 1952-54,* decorations by the author, 1958; published as *Faust Foutu: An Entertainment in Four Parts,* 1959.
Medea at Kolchis: The Maiden Head (produced Black Mountain, North Carolina, 1956). 1965.

Essays

As Testimony: The Poem and the Scene. 1964.
The Truth and Life of Myth: An Essay in Essential Autobiography. 1968.
Fictive Certainties: Five Essays in Essential Autobiography. 1979.

Other

The Artist's View. 1952.
The Sweetness and Greatness of Dante's "Divine Comedy," 1263-1965 (lecture presented at Dominican College of San Raphael, 1965). 1965.
Six Prose Pieces. 1966.
Adam's Way: A Play on Theosophical Themes. 1966.
Audit/Robert Duncan (first published as special issue of *Audit/Poetry,* Vol. 4, No. 3). 1967.
A Selection of Sixty-five Drawings from One Drawing Book, 1952-1956. 1970.
Notes on Grossinger's "Solar Journal: Oecological Sections." 1970.
A Prospectus for the Prepublication of Ground Work to Certain Friends of the Poet. 1971.

An Epithalamium. 1980.
Quand le Grand Foyer. 1981.
In Blood's Domain. 1982.
Towards an Open Universe. Published in *Poets on Poetry,* edited by Howard Nemerov, 1966; 1982.
In Passage. 1983.

*

Bibliography: *A Bibliography of the White Rabbit Press* by Johnston Alastair, 1985; *Robert Creeley, Edward Dorn, and Robert Duncan: A Reference Guide* by Willard Fox, 1989.

Critical Studies: *Godawful Streets of Man* by Warren Tallman, 1976; *Robert Duncan: Scales of the Marvelous* edited by Robert J. Bertholf and Ian Reid, 1979; *The Lost America of Love: Rereading Robert Creeley, Edward Dorn, and Duncan* by Sherman Paul, 1981; *Young Duncan: Portrait of the Poet As Homosexual in Society* by Ekbert Faas, 1983; *Duncan: A Descriptive Biography* by Robert J. Bertholf with preface by Robert Creeley, 1986; *Duncan* by Mark Andrew Johnson, 1988; *Hear the Voice of the Bard! Who Present, Past, and Future Sees: Three Cores of Bardic Attention—The Early Bards, William Blake, and Robert Duncan* by David Annwn, 1995; *Robert Duncan in San Francisco* by Michael Rumaker, 1996.

*   *   *

The poet, Robert Duncan has said, is akin to the paranoiac: everything seems to belong to the plot. Raised in a Theosophist environment, Duncan in much of his work seeks, like the paranoiac but without his fear, for something that does *not* belong to the coherent cosmic plot. Duncan, therefore (as he expounds it most clearly in the sections of the incomplete "The H. D. Book"), lives in a world in which "things strive to speak," where the poet seems to read "the language of things" and where "the poet must attend not to what he means to say but to what what he says means" (*Caterpillar* 7). The poet is, then, subject not to "inspiration" so much as he is to "possession," where he may be had by an idea, and poetry is—in Duncan's language—"an Office": the text the poet writes is part of a larger text, "the Poem," and the office of poet is subsumed in the larger Office, of Poet.

It is thus perhaps to be expected that Duncan, of all poets associated with Black Mountain College and with post-modernism, should be the American writer most closely associated with the great tradition of English poetry and of mystical poetry, while at the same time he is the one who seems most consistently and perversely to be at odds with the traditions and conventions of English poetry. Such apparent perversity arises in part from Duncan's insistence, drawn from Heraclitus, that "an unapparent connexion is stronger than an apparent": it derives also, in part, from "the strongest drive of my life, that things have not come to the conclusions I saw around me, and this involved the conclusions that I saw shaping in my own thought and actions" (*Caterpillar* 8/9). Thus, "A Poem Beginning with a Line by Pindar" (1958) is a combination of traditional devices, forms, and sources with the unexpected and unconventional. The synecdoche of "the light foot *hears*," quoted from Pindar's First Pythian Ode, involves the breaking of things "normal" in the language; this in turn suggests a range of possible meanings for "*light* foot." The poem, an extended meditation and discovery on—among other things—the notion of Adulthood, proposes a world in which the Real is found, not in a landscape, but "in an obscurity"—hidden, that is to say, from normal, familiar, conventional (or mortal) sight. In two essays central to his work, "Ideas of the Meaning of Form" (*Kulchur* 4) and "Man's Fulfillment in Order and Strife" (*Caterpillar* 8/9), Duncan insists that "to the conventional mind" form is "what can be imposed," and, in all of his writing, conventional syntax and language are a part of conventional form, and man is a creature of language. In section two of the "Pindar" poem the language, individual words and syllables, breaks down, loses its articulation, becomes almost nonsense. The breakdown is triggered by the word "stroke," which—initially of a brush, painting, or of a pen writing—becomes a medical stroke (Eisenhower's?), and the poem, which at that point seems to be struggling to a halt, moves into a firm political rhetoric that reveals adulthood as a condition of nations as well as of individuals, and the condition itself as a process. Reading the poem, we witness the testimony of the poet discovering the world as it reveals itself to him through language. Meaning, in such poems as this, is to be found in the play of possible meanings, rather than in the conventionally ordered exposition of rational or reasonable thought. Duncan's insistence "not to reach a conclusion but to keep our exposure to what we do not know" has led to "Passages," a series of rhetorical poems that, resting on the Julian motto "The even is bounded, but the uneven is without bounds," explores all possible voices as its testimony to What Is.

—Peter Quartermain

DUNLAP, William

Born: Perth Amboy, New Jersey, 19 February 1766. **Education:** Local schools until his family moved to New York City in 1777; then studied painting with a New York artist. **Family:** Married Elizabeth Woolsey in 1789; one son and one daughter. **Career:** Clerk in his father's store, then portrait painter, New York, 1782-84; studied art with Benjamin West in London, 1784-87; returned to New York and abandoned painting to write for the stage; manager and part owner, Old American Company, at the John Street Theatre, later at the Park Theatre, New York, presenting his own plays as well as current French and German plays in translation, 1796 until he went bankrupt, 1805; itinerant painter of miniatures, 1805-06; general assistant to the new manager of the Park Theatre, 1806-11; freelance writer and editor, 1811-15; founder, *Monthly Record,* New York, 1813; Assistant Paymaster-General, New York Militia, 1814-16; painter of miniatures, portraits, and religious commissions, 1816-mid-1830s. Founder member, 1826, and vice-president, 1831-38, National Academy of Design. **Died:** 28 September 1839.

PUBLICATIONS

Collections

Four Plays (1789-1812) (includes *The Father of an Only Child, Leicester, The Italian Father, Yankee Chronology*), edited by Julian Mates. 1976.

Musical Works (includes *Darby's Return, The Archers, The Wild-Goose Chase, The Glory of Columbia*), edited by Julian Mates. 1980.

More Plays of William Dunlap. 1995.

Plays

The Father; or, American Shandy-ism (produced 1789). 1789; revised version, as *The Father of an Only Child*, in *Dramatic Works*, 1806; in *Four Plays*, 1976.

Darby's Return (produced 1789). 1789; edited by Walter J. Meserve and William R. Reardon, in *Satiric Comedies*, 1969; in *Musical Works*, 1980.

The Miser's Wedding (produced 1793).

Leicester (as *The Fatal Deception; or, The Progress of Guilt*, produced 1794). In *Dramatic Works*, 1806; in *Four Plays*, 1976.

Shelty's Travels (produced 1794).

Fountainville Abbey (produced 1795). In *Dramatic Works*, 1806.

The Archers; or, Mountaineers of Switzerland, music by Benjamin Carr (produced 1796). 1796; in *Musical Works*, 1980.

Ribbemont; or, The Feudal Baron (as *The Mysterious Monk*, produced 1796). 1803.

The Knight's Adventure (produced 1797). 1807.

The Man of Fortitude, with John Hodgkinson (produced 1797). 1807.

Tell Truth and Shame the Devil, from a play by A. L. B. Robineau (produced 1797). 1797.

The Stranger, from a play by Kotzebue (produced 1798). 1798.

André (produced 1798). 1798.

False Shame; or, The American Orphan in Germany, from a play by Kotzebue (produced 1798). Edited by Oral Sumner Coad, with *Thirty Years*, 1940.

The Natural Daughter (produced 1799).

The Temple of Independence (produced 1799).

Don Carlos, from the play by Schiller (produced 1799).

Indians in England, from a play by Kotzebue (produced 1799).

The School for Soldiers, from a play by L.S. Mercier (produced 1799).

The Robbery, from a play by Boutet de Monval (produced 1799).

The Italian Father, from the play *The Honest Whore* by Dekker (produced 1799). 1810; in *Four Plays*, 1976.

Graf Benyowsky, from a play by Kotzebue (produced 1799).

Sterne's Maria; or, The Vintage (produced 1799).

Lovers' Vows, from a play by Kotzebue (produced 1799). 1814.

The Force of Calumny, from a play by Kotzebue (produced 1800).

The Stranger's Birthday, from a play by Kotzebue (produced 1800).

The Knight of Guadalquiver (produced 1800).

The Wild-Goose Chase, music by J. Hewitt, from a play by Kotzebue (produced 1800). 1800; in *Musical Works*, 1980.

The Virgin of the Sun, from a play by Kotzebue (produced 1800). 1800.

Pizarro in Peru; or, The Death of Rolla, from a play by Kotzebue and the version by Sheridan (produced 1800). 1800.

Fraternal Discord, from a play by Kotzebue (produced 1800). 1809.

The Soldier of '76 (produced 1801).

Abée de l'Epée, from a play by Jean Bouilly (produced 1801).

Where Is He?, from a German play (produced 1801).

Abaellino, The Great Bandit, from a play by J. H. D. Zschokke (produced 1801). 1802.

The Merry Gardener, from a French play (produced 1802).

The Retrospect; or, The American Revolution (produced 1802).

Peter the Great; or, The Russian Mother, from a play by J. M. Babo (produced 1802). 1814.

The Good Neighbor: An Interlude, from a work by A. W. Iffland (produced 1803). 1814.

Blue Beard: A Dramatic Romance, from the play by George Colman the Younger. 1803.

The Voice of Nature, from a play by L. C. Caigniez (produced 1803). 1803.

The Blind Boy, from a play by Kotzebue (produced 1803).

Bonaparte in England (produced 1803).

The Proverb; or, Conceit Can Cure, Conceit Can Kill (produced 1804).

Lewis of Monte Blanco; or, The Transplanted Irishman (produced 1804).

Nina, from a play by Joseph Marsollier (produced 1804).

Chains of the Heart; or, The Slave of Choice, from a play by Prince Hoare (produced?). 1804.

The Wife of Two Husbands, from a play by Pixérécourt (produced 1804). 1804.

The Shipwreck, from a play by Samuel James Arnold (produced ?). 1805.

Dramatic Works. 3 vols., 1806-16.

Alberto Albertini; or, The Robber King (produced 1811).

Yankee Chronology; or, Huzza for the Constitution! (produced 1812). 1812; in *Four Plays*, 1976.

The Glory of Columbia: Her Yeomanry! (produced 1813). 1817; in *Musical Works*, 1980.

The Flying Dutchman (produced 1827).

A Trip to Niagara; or Travellers in America (produced 1828). 1830.

Thirty Years; or, The Gambler's Fate, from a play by Prosper Goubaux and Victor Ducange (produced 1828). Edited by Oral Sumner Coad, with *False Shame*, 1940.

Other

Memoirs of the Life of George Frederick Cooke. 2 vols., 1813; revised edition, as *The Life of Cooke*, 1815.

A Record, Literary and Political, of Five Months in the Year 1813, with others. 1813.

The Life of the Most Noble Arthur, Marquis and Earl of Wellington, with Francis L. Clarke. 1814.

A Narrative of the Events Which Followed Bonaparte's Campaign in Russia. 1814.

The Life of Charles Brockden Brown, with Selections. 2 vols., 1815; as *Memoirs of Charles Brockden Brown*, 1822.

A History of the American Theatre. 1832.

History of the Rise and Progress of the Arts of Design in the United States. 2 vols., 1834; revised edition, edited by Alexander Wyckoff, 1965.

Thirty Years Ago; or, The Memoirs of a Water Drinker. 2 vols., 1836.

A History of New York, for Schools. 2 vols., 1837.

History of the New Netherlands, Province of New York, and the State of New York. 2 vols., 1839-40.

Diary: The Memoirs of a Dramatist, Theatrical Manager, Painter, Critic, Novelist, and Historian, edited by Dorothy C. Barck. 3 vols., 1930.

*

Bibliography: in *False Shame, and Thirty Years* edited by Oral Sumner Coad, 1940; in *Bibliography of American Literature* by Jacob Blanck, 1957.

Critical Studies: *Dunlap: A Study of His Life and Works and of His Place in Contemporary Culture* by Oral Sumner Coad, 1917; *Arts of the Young Republic: The Age of Dunlap* by Harold E. Dickson, 1968; *Dunlap* by Robert H. Canary, 1970; *Four Plays (1789-1812),* 1976, and *The Musical Works of William Dunlap,* 1980, both by Julian Mates; *Virtuosity and Theatricality: A Study of William Dunlap and Charles Brockden Brown* (dissertation) by Colin Jeffrey Morris, 1994.

*   *   *

"The American Vasari" and "Father of American Theatre" are phrases that honor William Dunlap as the first historian of American arts. But his *Rise and Progress of the Arts,* though richly anecdotal, is a moralistic, opinionated source of biographical sketches. His *American Theatre* concentrates on 1787 to 1811, when Dunlap, as a playwright and manager, knew everyone in the business and contributed to its growth from a British "provincial" company to a theatre bragging of native-born stars and playwrights. Dunlap proposed federal subsidies, questioned the star system, and despised the new Scribean play-factories—despite having translated the lurid *Thirty Years.*

This democratic abolitionist and artist saw himself as an antipartisan reconciler. Because the best European models required an indefinable purification of "old world vices," Dunlap was left without dependable aesthetic grounds for resisting commercial standardization. He became the compromiser who packaged the acceptable best. More than half of his plays introduced fashionable continental dramatists into the American repertory. After successfully adapting *The Stranger,* Dunlap depended particularly upon the popularity of Kotzebue's plays (twelve translations) with their affecting sentimentality coupled with, admittedly, "false philosophy and unsound morals." *False Shame* typically puts all major characters through set-piece confessions of "false shame" before redeeming them by inter-marriage or new-found family relationships. It conforms in kind to Dunlap's own sentimental comedies.

Dunlap's first produced play, *The Father,* uses the stock comic doctor and country maidservant to give some savor to its purposeful actions: an American patriot's reunion with his son, an English officer; the redemption of a mildly rakish husband; a pallid literary borrowing from Sterne. Art, politics, and business "now in Virtue's cause engage/And rear that glorious thing, a *Moral Stage.*" For benefit performances or historical occasions Dunlap framed narrative songs. In *Yankee Chronology* a sailor returns to tell and sing of the 1812 victory of the (parable-pun) U.S.S. Constitution. Contradicting the travel writers, *A Trip to Niagara* frames a moving diorama with interesting American (and British) types to persuade an English snob of some American virtues.

Only an unsophisticated audience could tolerate the ghastliness, disguises, and mistaken identities of the Gothic *The Mysterious Monk* and the romantic *The Fatal Deception*—harmlessly abstract figures justified by much talk in verse about honor. But idea and theme, finally, make *André* a substantial and significant tragedy. General Washington and Major André are its heroic figures, while young Bland tries to be Otway's Pierre. Captain Bland and the other American officers play out their neoclassic alternatives of

mind or heart, and the poetic drama gathers relevant force in their debate of the modes, moralities, and reconciliations necessary for an independent country in 1780, or in 1798 (the year of production).

Dunlap fashioned his controversial, unpopular, but finest play into a popular celebration. Incoherent and delightful, *The Glory of Columbia: Her Yeomanry!* wraps pieces of *André* with a despicable Benedict Arnold, some honest Yankee soldiers who capture André, a singing sister Sal in uniform, and a canny Irishman. He changes sides for a final victory pageant at Yorktown and a chorale to "Columbia's Son, Immortal Washington!"

—John G. Kuhn

DUNNE, Finley Peter

Born: Peter Dunne in Chicago, Illinois, 10 July 1867. **Education:** West Division High School, Chicago, graduated 1884. **Family:** Married Margaret Abbott in 1902; three sons and one daughter. **Career:** Journalist from 1885; city editor, *Times,* 1888-89, editor, *Tribune* Sunday edition, 1890-91, editorial page editor, *Evening Post,* 1892-97, and managing editor, *Journal,* 1897-1900, all Chicago; editor, New York *Morning Telegraph,* 1902-04; writer, *Collier's,* 1902, and editor, *Collier's Weekly,* 1917-19, both New York; editor, with Ida Tarbell and Lincoln Steffens, 1906, and contributor, 1906-15, *American Magazine,* New York. **Member:** American Academy. **Died:** 24 April 1936.

PUBLICATIONS

Collections

Mr. Dooley and the Chicago Irish, edited by Charles Fanning. 1976.

Prose

Mr. Dooley in Peace and in War. 1898.
Mr. Dooley in the Hearts of His Countrymen. 1899.
What Dooley Says. 1899.
Mr. Dooley's Philosophy. 1900.
Mr. Dooley's Opinions. 1901.
Observations by Mr. Dooley. 1902.
Dissertations by Mr. Dooley. 1906.
Mr. Dooley Says. 1910.
New Dooley Book. 1911.
Mr. Dooley on Making a Will and Other Necessary Evils. 1919.
Mr. Dooley at His Best, edited by Elmer Ellis. 1938.
The World of Mr. Dooley, edited by Louis Filler. 1962.
Mr. Dooley Remembers: The Informal Memoirs of Dunne, edited by Philip Dunne. 1963.

*

Critical Studies: *Mr. Dooley's America: The Life of Dunne* by Elmer Ellis, 1941; *Mr. Dooley's Chicago* by Barbara C. Schaaf, 1977; *Dunne and Mr. Dooley: The Chicago Years* by Charles Fanning, 1978; *Small Town Chicago: The Comic Perspective of Dunne, George Ade, and Ring Lardner* by James DeMuth, 1980; *Dunne* by Grace Eckley, 1981; *Mr. Dooley and Mr. Dunne: The Literary Life of a Chicago Catholic* by Edward J. Bander, 1981.

*　　*　　*

Finley Peter Dunne is best known for having created Mr. Martin Dooley, an aging Irish saloon keeper from Chicago, who began appearing in a weekly column in the Chicago *Evening Post* in October 1893. Dunne's own parents had been Irish immigrants to Chicago, and he began his journalistic career there in 1884 at age seventeen. After working on several different newspapers, he settled as precocious editorial chairman at the *Post* in 1892. The last in a series of dialect experiments for his creator, Mr. Dooley succeeded Colonel Malachi McNeery, a downtown Chicago barkeep modeled on a friend of Dunne's, who had become a popular *Post* feature during the World's Fair of 1893. Unlike McNeery, Mr. Dooley was placed on Chicago's South Side, in the Irish working-class neighborhood of Bridgeport. Between 1893 and 1898, 215 Dooley pieces appeared in the *Post*. Taken together, they form a coherent body of work, in which a vivid, detailed world comes into existence—that of Bridgeport, a self-contained immigrant culture, with its own customs and ceremonies and a social structure rooted in family, geography, and occupation. Included are memories of Ireland and emigration, descriptions of the daily round of Bridgeport life, and inside narratives of rough-and-tumble politics in a city ward. In addition, other pieces contain wholly serious treatments of suffering and starvation among the poor, the divisive scramble for middle-class respectability, and conflict between immigrant parents and their American children. In these Bridgeport pieces, Dunne contributed to the development of literary realism in America. In depicting this immigrant community and its working-class inhabitants through the medium of Irish vernacular dialect, he gave Chicagoans a weekly example of the realist's faith in the potentiality for serious fiction to use common speech and to show everyday life.

Dunne's career took a sharp turn in 1898, when Mr. Dooley's satirical coverage of the Spanish-American War brought him to the attention of readers outside Chicago. Beginning with his scoop of "Cousin George" Dewey's victory at Manila, Mr. Dooley's reports of military and political bungling during the "splendid little war" were widely reprinted, and national syndication soon followed. By the time Dunne moved to New York in 1900, Mr. Dooley was the most popular figure in American journalism. From this point until World War I, Dunne's gadfly mind ranged over the spectrum of newsworthy events and characters, both national and international: from Teddy Roosevelt's health fads to Andrew Carnegie's passion for libraries; from the invariable silliness of politics to society doings at Newport; from the Boer and Boxer Rebellions to the Negro, Indian, and immigration "problems." Mr. Dooley's perspective was consistently skeptical and critical. The salutary effect of most pieces was the exposure of affectation and hypocrisy through undercutting humor and common sense. The most frequently quoted Dooleyisms indicate this thrust: Teddy Roosevelt's egocentric account of the Rough Riders is retitled, "Alone in Cubia"; Henry Cabot Lodge's imperialist rationale becomes "Take up th' white man's burden an' hand it to th' coons"; a fanatic is defined as "a man that does what he thinks th' Lord wud do if He knew th' facts iv th' case." Although he joined Ida Tarbell and Lincoln Steffens in taking over the *American Magazine* in 1906, Dunne was not himself a progressive reformer. He viewed the world as irrevocably fallen and unimproveable, and

many Dooley pieces reflect their author's tendency toward cynicism, pessimism, and fatalism. More pronounced in the early Chicago work than in the lighter national commentary, Dunne's darker side may be explained by his Irish background and his journalist's education into the realities of nineteenth-century urban life.

Mr. Dooley was the first Irish voice in American literature to transcend the confines of "stage Irish" ethnic humor. Dunne's accomplishment divides (at 1898) into two parts: the Chicago pieces, which contain pioneering realistic sketches of an urban immigrant community, and the pieces written for a national audience, which contain some of the best social and political satire ever penned in America.

—Charles Fanning

DWIGHT, Timothy

Born: Northampton, Massachusetts, 14 May 1752. **Education:** Yale University, New Haven, Connecticut, 1766-69, 1771-72, B.A. 1769, M.A. 1772. **Military Service:** Served in General Parson's Connecticut Brigade during the Revolutionary War, 1777-79: chaplain. **Family:** Married Mary Woolsey in 1777; eight sons. **Career:** Headmaster, Hopkins Grammar School, New Haven, Connecticut, 1769-71; tutor, Yale University, 1771-77; licensed to preach, 1777; member, Massachusetts Legislature, 1781-82; ordained to the ministry of the Congregational Church, 1783; pastor, Greenfield Hill Congregational Church, Connecticut, 1783-95 (also schoolmaster in Greenfield); professor of divinity, and president, Yale University, 1795-1817 (founder of the medical department). Helped establish the Andover Theological Seminary and Missionary Society of Connecticut; member, American Board of Commissioners for Foreign Missions. **Awards:** LL.D.: Harvard University, Cambridge, Massachusetts, 1810. **Died:** 11 January 1817.

PUBLICATIONS

Poetry

America; or, A Poem on the Settlement of the British Colonies. 1780(?).
The Conquest of Canaan. 1785.
The Triumph of Infidelity. 1788.
Greenfield Hill. 1794.
The Psalms of David, by Watts, altered by Dwight. 1801.

Other

The Nature, and Danger, of Infidel Philosophy. 1798.
Remarks on the Review of Inchiquin's Letters. 1815.
Theology Explained and Defended in a Series of Sermons. 5 vols., 1818-19; abridged edition, as *Beauties of Dwight,* 4 vols., 1823.
Travels in New-England and New-York. 4 vols., 1821-22; edited by Barbara Miller Solomon, 4 vols., 1969.
An Essay on the Stage. 1824.
Sermons. 2 vols., 1828.

*

Bibliography: in *Bibliography of American Literature* by Jacob Blanck, 1957.

Critical Studies: *A Sketch of the Life and Character of Dwight* by Benjamin Silliman, 1817; *Dwight: A Biography* by Charles E. Cunningham, 1942; *Dwight* by Kenneth Silverman, 1969; *Calvinism versus Democracy: Dwight and the Origins of American Evangelical Orthodoxy* by Stephen E. Berk, 1974; *Poetry and Ideology in Revolutionary Connecticut* by William C. Dowling, 1990; *President Timothy Dwight at Yale: On Earth As It Is In Heaven* by Pamela J. Jason, 1994; *Timothy Dwight's Greenfield Hill* by John Willson, 1995; *New England's Moral Legislator: A Life of Timothy Dwight, 1752-1817* by John R. Fitzmier, 1998.

*   *   *

In his own time Timothy Dwight was a figure of towering significance. President of Yale University, he was an educator, theologian, and foremost among the Hartford Wits. In the late twentieth century, however, he is mainly remembered as a staunch advocate of Federalist and Calvinist orthodoxies in a world of change and as a poet who made modest if seminal contributions to the growth of an indigenous American literature.

Dwight's reputation for obstinacy originates mostly in his crabbed and dogmatic prose works. In 1798, for instance, with Deism and **Thomas Jefferson** on the rise, he announced in his sermon "The Duty of Americans, at the Present Crisis" that a return to Calvin and to Federalism was mandatory. In *The Nature, and Danger, of Infidel Philosophy,* published that same year, he castigated the liberal politics of John Locke, David Hume, and **Thomas Paine**. As for his own hero he would go on record two years later with a laudatory "Discourse on the Character of George Washington." And his *Theology Explained and Defended,* a five-volume collection of sermons that he had delivered to his students at Yale, was an apologia for the theocracy that he sought to maintain.

Dwight's orthodoxy also informed some of his verse. For example, *The Conquest of Canaan,* an epic in eleven books reminiscent of Milton, was a veiled allegory of the American War for Independence, with Joshua in the role of Washington. And his most venomous verse, *The Triumph of Infidelity,* recounted in heroic couplets the sins of Voltaire, Hume, and other expositors of liberalism. Still other of his poems, however, revealed another, softer, side of Dwight. In his most famous poem, *Greenfield Hill,* for instance, he spoke in seven different sections—now as narrator, now as rural mother or clergyman or farmer—of the virtues of pastoral life in the new nation in ways that are actually Jeffersonian in intonation.

It was also in *Greenfield Hill,* and to a lesser degree in *The Conquest of Canaan,* that Dwight made an important contribution to the growth of an indigenous literature by employing landscapes and personalities of an indubitably American nature. Unfortunately, the more reactionary of Dwight's writings, together with the prevailing view that the setting of poetry should be other than American, conspired to hide Dwight's attempts at a native literature. In another generation, however, the authors of the American Renaissance would build a successfully native literature upon the earlier efforts of poets such as Dwight.

—Bruce A. Lohof

E

EATON, Winnifred

Pseudonym: Onoto Watanna. Also wrote as Winnifred Eaton Babcock and Winnifred Eaton Reeve. **Born:** Lillie Winnifred Eaton in Montreal, Canada, 21 August 1875; sister of author Sui Sin Far (Edith Maud Eaton). **Family:** Married 1) Bertrand W. Babcock in 1901 (divorced 1916), four children; 2) Francis Fournier Reeve in 1917. **Career:** Reporter in Jamaica; typist for stockyards in Chicago; writer in New York, 1900-17, and in Calgary, Alberta, Canada, 1917-24; scenarist, Universal Studios, New York, 1924; screenwriter for Universal Pictures and Metro-Goldwyn-Mayer, Hollywood, 1925-31. **Died:** 8 April 1954.

PUBLICATIONS

Novels

Miss Numè of Japan; a Japanese-American Romance. 1899.
A Japanese Nightingale. 1901.
The Wooing of Wistaria. 1902.
The Heart of Hyacinth. 1903.
Daughters of Nijo, a Romance of Japan. 1904.
The Love of Azalea. 1904.
A Japanese Blossom. 1906.
The Diary of Delia; Being a Veracious Chronicle of the Kitchen, with Some Side-Lights on the Parlour. 1907.
Tama. 1910.
The Honorable Miss Moonlight. 1912.
Sunny-San. 1922.
Cattle. 1923.
His Royal Nibs. 1925.

Plays

Screenplays: *False Kisses,* 1921; *The Mississippi Gambler,* with H.H. Van Loan, 1929; *Shanghai Lady,* with Houston Branch, 1929; *East Is West,* 1930; *Undertow,* with Edward T. Lowe, Jr, 1930; *Young Desire,* 1930.

Other

Chinese-Japanese Cook Book, with Sara Bosse. 1914.
Me, a Book of Remembrance. 1915.
Marion; the Story of an Artist's Model, by Herself and the Author of "Me." 1916.

*

Critical Studies: "Winnifred Eaton: Ethnic Chameleon and Popular Success" by Amy Ling, in *MELUS: The Journal of the Society for the Study of the Multi-Ethnic Literature of the United States,* vol. 11, no. 3, 1984; *Between Worlds: Women Writers of Chinese Ancestry* by Ling, 1990, and "Creating Themselves: The Eaton Sisters" by Ling, in *Reading the Literatures of Asian America* edited by Shirley Geok-Lin Lim and Ling, 1992; "Cross-Dressing and Cross-Naming: Decoding Onoto Watanna" by Yuko Matsukawa, in *Tricksterism in Turn-of-the-Century U.S. Literature* edited by Elizabeth Ammons and Annette White-Parks, 1994.

*   *   *

Unlike her sister, the writer Edith Maud Eaton, who celebrated her Chinese heritage by writing under the Chinese pseudonym Sui Sin Far, turn-of-the-century writer Winnifred Eaton adopted the Japanese-sounding "Onoto Watanna" as her pseudonym to write numerous essays and short stories as well as sixteen novels, many of them with Japanese themes, during her long career. That she was a successful writer illustrates her audience's enthusiasm for things "oriental" in the late-nineteenth and early-twentieth centuries; that she chose to write under a Japanese-sounding pen name and to cultivate a distinctly Japanese(-American) writing persona suggests that Eaton not only catered to the popular reading audience's desire for orientalist romances but also used this literary masquerade as a strategy to combat the anti-Chinese sentiment that led to the anti-Chinese immigration policies of the United States and Canada in the late 1800s.

In order to maintain this authorial identity, Eaton shrouded the details of her real life in mystery. The fiction that she was the daughter of a Japanese noblewoman from Nagasaki, Japan, and an English diplomat who had been stationed there was widely accepted during her lifetime. Furthermore, her fictionalized autobiography *Me, a Book of Remembrance* (1915), in which she calls herself Nora Ascough, as well as the novel based on her sister Sara Bosse's experiences, entitled *Marion; the Story of an Artist's Model* (1916), contributed to the confusion about the details of her life. In fact, Winnifred Eaton was born in Montreal, Canada, in 1875 to Grace Trepesis (1847-1922), a Chinese woman who had been reared by an English missionary couple, and Edward Eaton (1838-1915), an English traveler and artist. Theirs was a large family without an adequate income (Winnifred was the eighth of sixteen children, fourteen of whom lived to be adults). So by her late teens, Eaton was ready to leave home and support herself. She first obtained work in Jamaica as a reporter but soon came back up north to work as a typist and stenographer in Chicago. It was during her stay in Chicago that she wrote her first book, *Miss Numè of Japan* (1899), published by Rand, McNally & Company, which launched her career and her writing persona as Onoto Watanna.

"Two years ago the name of Onoto Watanna was entirely unknown, except to a coterie in Chicago; to-day it is known everywhere," declared *Harper's Weekly* in the supplement to its December 5, 1903 issue. This proclamation provides us with a sense of Eaton's swift rise to popularity during the first few decades of the twentieth century as a writer who specialized in romances set in Japan. Eaton made the leap from local to national stardom by moving to New York in 1900 and writing prolifically, producing almost a book a year between 1901 and 1916. It was there that she met and married her first husband (who later became her literary agent), Bertrand W. Babcock, who was a reporter for the *Brooklyn Eagle.* Her second novel, *A Japanese Nightingale* (1901) was a tremendous hit: it was translated into many languages, adapted for the stage by Sir William Young in 1903 and then made into a motion picture in 1918. *A Japanese Nightingale* was quickly followed by titles such as *The Wooing of Wistaria* (1902), *The Heart of Hyacinth* (1903), and *The Love of Azalea* (1904), all of which capitalized on the reading public's fascination for exotic fiction.

Eaton's publishers—Harper & Brothers, Macmillan, and Dodd, Mead, among others—cooperated in the marketing of Onoto Watanna and her "oriental" tales by making the books themselves exotic and ornamented. Many of the volumes had decorative covers and gilt edges with specially commissioned illustrations drawn by Japanese artists. The texts were often printed upon sheets of paper embellished with orientalized drawings in the wide margins. In her publicity photos, Eaton reinforced her image as a Eurasian writer by donning kimonos and holding fans. Hence both the books and Onoto Watanna were consciously produced for popular consumption.

Eaton's knowledge of Japan and of the Japanese language was shaky at best but this did not faze her, nor did it seem to disturb her audience. Her novels are formulaic, fanciful romances, most of which either are set in Japan or contain Japanese characters. The plots are mostly love stories and many feature interracial romances, more often than not between a Japanese woman and a Caucasian man (*Miss Numè of Japan, The Love of Azalea*) or a Eurasian woman and a Caucasian man (*A Japanese Nightingale, Tama, Sunny-San*). By setting these romances against the backdrop of an imaginary Japan, Eaton diffuses the potentially disruptive subject of interracial romance and miscegenation in order to safely explore the intersections of culture and gender relations. We may surmise that these plots draw from Eaton's parents' relationship as well as from her own identity as a Eurasian woman; though the nationalities are different, these family romances are rewritten and reworked repeatedly.

Eaton divorced Babcock in 1916 and the following year married Francis Fournier Reeve, a cattle rancher who later made his fortune in oil. Eaton and her husband then moved to Calgary, Alberta, where she supported the arts and continued her writing. During her Calgary years she wrote her last Japanese novel, *Sunny-San* (1922) and two novels set in the Canadian West, *Cattle* (1923) and *His Royal Nibs* (1925). In the 1920s, Eaton embarked upon a new career: she worked on movie scripts, first in New York City and then in Hollywood, writing for both Universal Pictures and MGM. Since the film industry then was making the transition from silent to sound films, the role of the script writer was also undergoing changes to accommodate the new technology. Because of the flux in the function of the writer, none of Eaton's credits appear as the writer of a screenplay (a term that came into use as soon as the production of sound films stabilized) but rather, she is listed as adapter, dialog writer, and/or scenarist. The ease with which she assumed these roles and the orientalist themes of some of the films—for instance, *Shanghai Lady* (1929) and *East Is West* (1930)—suggest that even in Hollywood, Eaton was drawing on her expertise as a writer of exotic romances to satisfy the demands of this newly developing narrative medium.

Once her writing contracts with Hollywood expired, Eaton returned to Calgary to be with her family. She actively participated in and supported regional and Canadian literary organizations and theater groups. Her papers are preserved in the archives of the University of Calgary where there is a theater named after Winnifred and her husband Francis, who donated the funds for the construction of the building. Winnifred Eaton passed away on 8 April 1954, in Butte, Montana, on her way home from a vacation in Phoenix, Arizona.

Despite the fact that her novels are out of print and that major bibliographical, biographical, and critical work needs to be done in order to excavate and examine her life and writings, Winnifred Eaton merits our attention because she makes visible, through her self-representation and texts, not only the choices that women writers of color had to make in order to make themselves heard at the turn of the century but also the constructed nature of literary identity. And as one of the earliest Asian American writers, she also offers us, along with her sister, Edith Eaton, a point of departure from which we may chart the trajectory of Asian American writing.

—Yuko Matsukawa

EBERHART, Richard (Ghormley)

Born: Austin, Minnesota, 5 April 1904. **Education:** The University of Minnesota, Minneapolis, 1922-23; Dartmouth College, Hanover, New Hampshire, B.A. 1926; St. John's College, Cambridge, B.A. 1929, M.A. 1933; Harvard University, Cambridge, Massachusetts, 1932-33. **Military Service:** Served in the U.S. Naval Reserve, 1942-6: lieutenant commander. **Family:** Married Helen Butcher in 1941; two children. **Career:** Tutor to the son of King Prajadhipok of Siam, 1930-31; English teacher, St. Mark's School, Southboro, Massachusetts, 1933-41, and Cambridge School, Kendal Green, Massachusetts, 1941-42; assistant manager to Vice-President, Butcher Polish Company, Boston, Massachusetts, 1946-52, now honorary vice-president and member of board of directors; visiting professor, University of Washington, Seattle, 1952-53, 1967, 1972; professor of English, University of Connecticut, Storrs, 1953-54; visiting professor, Wheaton College, Norton, Massachusetts, 1954-55; resident fellow and Gauss Lecturer, Princeton University, New Jersey, 1955-56; Dartmouth College, professor of English and poet-in-residence, 1956-68, Class of 1925 Professor, 1968-70, Professor Emeritus, 1970—; Elliston Lecturer, University of Cincinnati, 1961; visiting professor, University of Florida, Gainesville, winter term, 1974-82, Columbia University, New York, 1975, and University of California, Davis, 1975; Wallace Stevens Fellow, Timothy Dwight College, Yale University, New Haven, Connecticut, 1976. Founder, 1950, and first president, Poets' Theatre, Cambridge, Massachusetts; Phi Beta Kappa Poet at Tufts University, 1941, Brown University, Providence, Rhode Island, 1957, Swarthmore College, 1963, Trinity College, 1963, College of William and Mary, 1963, University of New Hampshire, 1964, and Harvard University, 1967; member, 1955, and since 1964, director, Yaddo Corporation; member, since 1959, advisory committee on the arts, John F. Kennedy Memorial Theatre; consultant in poetry, plays, 1959-61, and Honorary Consultant in American Letters, 1963-69, Library of Congress, Washington, D.C. **Awards:** New England Poetry Club Golden Rose, 1950; Shelley Memorial award, 1952; Harriet Monroe Poetry award, 1955; National Institute of Arts and Letters, 1955; Bollingen prize, 1962; Pulitzer prize, 1966; Academy of American Poets fellowship, 1969; National Book award, 1977; President's Medallion, University of Florida, 1977; Poet Laureate of New Hampshire, 1979; Rhode Island Governor proclaimed a "Richard Eberhart Day" in 1982; Sarah Josepha Hale award, 1982; Robert Frost Medal, Poetry Society of America, 1986. D.Litt: Dartmouth College, 1954; Skidmore College, Saratoga, New York,

1966; College of Wooster, Ohio, 1969; Colgate University, Hamilton, New York, 1974. D.H.L.: Franklin Pierce College, Rindge, New Hampshire, 1978. **Member:** Poetry Society of America, honorary president, 1972—; Academy of American Poets fellow; American Academy and Institute of Arts and Letters; American Academy of Arts and Sciences. **Residence:** Hanover, New Hampshire.

PUBLICATIONS

Poetry

A Bravery of Earth. 1930.
Reading the Spirit. 1936.
Song and Idea. 1940.
A World-View. 1941.
Poems, New and Selected. 1944.
Rumination. 1947.
Burr Oaks. 1947.
Brotherhood of Men. 1949.
An Herb Basket. 1950.
Selected Poems. 1951.
Undercliff: Poems 1946-1953. 1953.
Great Praises. 1957.
The Oak: A Poem. 1957.
Collected Poems 1930-1960, Including 51 New Poems. 1960.
The Quarry: New Poems. 1964.
The Vastness and Indifference of the World. 1965.
Fishing for Snakes. 1965.
Selected Poems 1930-1965. 1965.
Thirty One Sonnets. 1967.
Shifts of Being. 1968.
The Achievement of Eberhart: A Comprehensive Selection of His Poems, edited by Bernard F. Engel. 1968.
Three Poems. 1968.
Fields of Grace. 1972.
Two Poems. 1975.
Collected Poems 1930-1976, Including 43 New Poems. 1976.
Poems to Poets. 1976.
Hour, Gnats. 1977.
Survivors. 1979.
Ways of Light: Poems 1972-1980. 1980.
New Hampshire: Nine Poems. 1980.
Four Poems. 1980.
Florida Poems. 1981.
In the Fourth World. 1983.
The Long Reach: New and Uncollected Poems 1948-1983. 1984.
Snowy Owl. 1984.
Throwing Yourself Away. 1984.
Collected Poems, 1930-1986. 1988.
Maine Poems. 1988.
New and Selected Poems, 1930-1990. 1990.

Plays

The Apparition (produced 1951). *In Collected Verse Plays,* 1962.
The Visionary Farms (produced 1951). *In Collected Verse Plays,* 1962.
Triptych (produced 1955). *In Collected Verse Plays,* 1962.
Devils and Angels (produced 1956). *In Collected Verse Plays,* 1962.

The Mad Musician (produced 1962). *In Collected Verse Plays,* 1962.
Collected Verse Plays (includes *Triptych, The Visionary Farms, The Apparition, The Mad Musician, Devils and Angels, Preamble I and II*). 1962.
The Bride from Mantua, from a play by Lope de Vega (produced 1964).
Chocurua. 1981.

Other

Poetry as a Creative Principle (lecture). 1952.
Of Poetry and Poets. 1979.

Editor, with others, *Free Gunner's Handbook,* revised edition, 1944.
Editor, with Selden Rodman, *War and the Poet: An Anthology of Poetry Expressing Man's Attitude to War from Ancient Times to the Present.* 1945.
Editor, *Dartmouth Poems.* 12 vols., 1958-59, 1962-71.

*

Critical Studies: *Eberhart* by Ralph J. Mills, Jr., 1966; *Eberhart: The Progress of an American Poet* by Joel Roache, 1971; *Eberhart* by Bernard F. Engel, 1972; *Eberhart: A Celebration* edited by Sydney Lea and Jay Pafrini, 1980.

*   *   *

Poetry is a recognition
of man's estate
and of his fate, and
ultimately, poetry is
praise.

Even Richard Eberhart's most ardent admirers admit the striking unevenness of his work—stirring and exquisite poems published alongside lines marred by sentimentality, pedantic diction, and banal abstractions. That his work is so uneven derives from Eberhart's personal definition of poetry, as well as his method of composition: "Poetry is dynamic, Protean," he writes. "In the rigors of composition . . . the poet's mind is a filament, informed with the irrational vitality of energy as it was discovered in our time in quantum mechanics. The quanta may shoot off any way." Eberhart rewrites little. His is an inspirational verse; through it he discovers life's significances: "You breathe in maybe God;" and at those moments, "the poet writes with a whole clarity."

Unlike many of his contemporaries during the 1930s, Eberhart never worked for the hard, spare line; he rejected the ironic mode and created no personae. He wrote a personal poetry, much in the vein of the Romantics, especially Blake, Wordsworth, and **Whitman**—a poetry concerned with understanding and transcending concrete experience. Regardless of the inevitable problems such an aesthetic might invite, there remains a large body of inspired and original verse wherein Eberhart has been able to "aggravate" perception into life. His best work results from his success in transforming keenly felt sense perceptions, through the language of the experience itself, into meaning—moral, metaphysical, mystical, even religious. His most impressive work retains the urgency and radiance of the felt experience, as it simultaneously transforms it into the significant; Eberhart is epiphanic, much like Gerard Manley Hopkins. "The poet," he states, "makes the world anew; something grows out of the old, which he locks in words."

In Eberhart's first volume, *A Bravery of Earth,* he writes about the three types of "awareness" one must gain in the progress toward maturity—of mortality, mentality, and men's actions. These goals have been reflected throughout his career. Particular subjects have also persisted, such as the poet's sheer wonder in nature and the fierce exhilaration inspired by "lyric" and "lovely" nature within which "God" "incarnate" resides. Intimate involvement with physical nature involves the poet in its cycles of growth and decay, and Eberhart, always aware of his own mortality, searches for intimations of immortality.

Eberhart's compassion extends toward all living things which share a common fate. "The Groundhog," one of his best known poems, evokes a wild, extravagant transcendence in the face of physical decay. The poet now experiences an exhilaration not through an awareness of nature's eternal, recurrent cycles but rather through his creative articulation of the fact of decay. Returning year after year to the dead groundhog, he wishes for its absorption within nature's processes but instead witnesses its transformation from simple decay—"I saw a groundhog lying dead. / Dead lay he"—to something aesthetically moving, its few bones "bleaching in the sunlight / Beautiful as architecture." Eberhart moves from a sense of "naked frailty" to "strange love," "a fever," "a passion of the blood." Elsewhere, Eberhart has said: "Poetry is a spell against death," and he concludes "The Groundhog" with:

> I stood there in the whirling summer,
> My hand capped a withered heart,
> And thought of China and of Greece,
> Of Alexander in his tent;
> Of Montaigne and his tower,
> Of Saint Theresa in her wild lament.

Eberhart comes to identify with the mighty figures of the past who transcended the ravages of time through the very energy of their creative living and through the legacy of historical memory and art. The poet has transcended through the creation of his poem.

He writes about the variety of experiences associated with death. In "Imagining How It Would Be to Be Dead" and "When Golden Flies upon My Caracass Come," he tries to apprehend his own death. It may be the moment of revelation and transcendence, of "worldless Ecstasy / Of mystery." But death may also be "merely death"—"This is a very ordinary experience. / A name may be glorious but death is death" ("I Walked over the Grave of Henry James"). In "The Cancer Cells," he expresses an aesthetic glee in the artistic design of malignant cells: "They looked like art itself. . . / I think Leonardo would have in his disinterest / enjoyed them precisely with a sharp pencil."

Poems like "If I Could Only Live at the Pitch That Is Near Madness" represent another theme in Eberhart's poetry—his desire to retain the intensity of childhood, "the incomparable light," "when everything is as it was in my childhood / Violent, vivid, and of infinite possibility." But Eberhart accepts, indeed embraces, the "moral answer," the awareness that one cannot leave the world of men and maturity, and, as he returns "into a realm of complexity," there is a sense of new wonder

and exaltation, as of joyful paternity, in his acceptance of the responsibilities of adulthood. One must not just feel experience; one must understand and articulate it.

Also recurrent are the variety of images of man's fallen state, his cruelty to his fellow man, the varieties of human suffering that grow out of social, political, and family strife. One is under obligation, implies Eberhart in his famous "Am I My Neighbor's Keeper," to care for his fellow man. Perhaps best known among this group is "The Fury of Aerial Bombardment," one of his many poems concerned with the inhumanity of war, where the poet ultimately wonders what sort of God would permit the barbarism of war: "You would feel that after so many centuries / God would give man to relent."

Familiar themes recur in *Ways of Light,* poems written between 1972 and 1980: man's relation to nature, his fate, and the larger themes of life, such as "love and the challenge of time." The poet listens, once more, to the owl cry ("Who") and returns to the rowboat of his youth to contemplate the seals and the "loon's cry far beyond the human." These shake his "sense to worldlessness" and make a "mystical matter of his involvement." Although he would seem to repeat that the ways of light remain through love, he admits that neither age and love nor honor and fame have brought him wisdom or certitude. Wonder and mystery remain in a world forever rich and unfathomable. *The Long Reach* intensifies Eberhart's sense of the fragility of life and immutability of death. Once again, confronting experience in his typically non-ironic, direct, and occasionally naive terms, he accepts the variegated conditions of life and the oblivion of death.

The immensity of Eberhart's lifetime output will most likely overwhelm the reader who opens Eberhart's *Collected Poems, 1930-1986.* His more recent, and more manageable, selections of his work bring to light what critic Jay Parini calls Eberhart's "buried beauties," those often-anthologized and sometimes newly-discovered works that remind us why Eberhart continues to be an important—if somewhat anachronistic—force in American poetry. Eberhart's *Maine Poems,* for instance, exemplify the author's favorite themes of the permanence of nature and a childlike wonder with characters and settings that could have been lifted from **Sarah Orne Jewett**'s *The Country of the Pointed Firs.* Readers exhausted from a trip through Eberhart's *Collected Poems* will appreciate the consistent excellence and manageability of *Maine Poems.*

Throughout his more than sixty years of writing, Eberhart has emphasized the need for a transcending credo—a personal belief structure created through both personal and concrete experience. As intensely aware of man's existential condition as many of his contemporaries, Eberhart has always focused on life and its creative possibilities. (In his speech accepting the 1977 National Book Award he lamented the suicides of some of his contemporaries and said: "Poets should not die for poetry but live for it.") For him, words lead to "joy" and "ecstasy": "The only triumph is some elegance of style."

But each person is a poet, in a sense, for everyone is, in everyday life, the creator of any meaning that life can have. Everyone must "make [his] own myth," because nature remains benignly indifferent. As one of his reviewers put it, the owl's cry tells man nothing unless one goes "somewhere beyond realism" and learns to "listen to the tune of the spiritual. Nature does not love or heed us. We are the lovers of nature."

—Lois Gordon, updated by Andrew O. Jones

EDWARDS, Jonathan

Born: East Windsor, Connecticut, 5 October 1703. **Education:** Home, and at Yale University, Wethersfield, later New Haven, Connecticut, 1716-20, B.A. 1720; studied theology, 1720-22. **Family:** Married Sarah Pierpont in 1727; 11 children. **Career:** Presbyterian minister, New York, 1722-23; tutor, Yale University, 1724-25; assistant minister, later minister, Congregational church, Northampton, Massachusetts, 1726-50 (dismissed by congregation); missionary to Mohican Indians and minister, Stockbridge, Massachusetts, after 1751; president, College of New Jersey (now Princeton University), 1757-58. **Died:** 22 March 1758.

PUBLICATIONS

Collections

Works (Leeds Edition), edited by Edward Williams and Edward Parsons. 8 vols., 1806-11; revised edition, 10 vols., 1847.
Representative Selections, edited by Clarence H. Faust and Thomas H. Johnson. 1935; revised edition, 1962.
Works, edited by Perry Miller. 1957—.
Basic Writings, edited by Ola Elizabeth Winslow. 1966.
A Jonathan Edwards Reader. 1995.

Prose

God Glorified in the Work of Redemption. 1731.
A Divine and Supernatural Light. 1734.
A Faithful Narrative of the Surprising Work of God in the Conversion of Many Hundred Souls in Northampton. 1737.
A Letter to the Author of the Pamphlet Called An Answer to the Hampshire Narrative. 1737.
Discourses on Various Important Subjects. 1738.
The Distinguishing Marks of a Work of the Spirit of God. 1741.
The Resort and Remedy of Those That Are Bereaved by the Death of an Eminent Minister. 1741.
Sinners in the Hands of an Angry God. 1741.
Some Thoughts Concerning the Present Revival of Religion in New England. 1742.
The Great Concern of a Watchman for Souls. 1743.
The True Excellency of a Minister of the Gospel. 1744.
Copies of the Two Letters Cited by Rev. Mr. Clap. 1745.
An Expostulatory Letter. 1745.
The Church's Marriage to Her Sons and to Her God. 1746.
A Treatise Concerning Religious Affections. 1746; in *Works* 2, 1959.
True Saints, When Absent from the Body, Are Present with the Lord. 1747.
An Humble Attempt to Promote Explicit Agreement and Visible Union of God's People in Extraordinary Prayer. 1747.
A Strong Rod Broken and Withered. 1748.
An Account of the Life of the Late Reverend Mr. David Brainerd. 1749; in *Works* 7, 1984.
An Humble Inquiry into the Rules of the Word of God Concerning . . . Communion. 1749.
Christ the Great Example of Gospel Ministers. 1750.
A Farewell Sermon Preached at the First Precinct in Northampton. 1751.
Misrepresentations Corrected and Truth Vindicated. 1752.
True Grace Distinguished from the Experience of Devils. 1753.
A Careful and Strict Enquiry into . . . Freedom of Will. . . . 1754; in *Works* 1, 1957; as *Freedom of the Will,* edited by Arnold S. Kaufman and William K. Frankena, 1969.
The Great Christian Doctrine of Original Sin Defended. 1758.
Two Dissertations: Concerning the End of Which God Created the World; The Nature of True Virtue. 1765.
The Life and Character of Edwards, with a Number of His Sermons, edited by Samuel Hopkins. 1765.
A History of the Work of Redemption. 1774.
Sermons, edited by Jonathan Edwards the Younger. 1780.
Practical Sermons, edited by Jonathan Edwards the Younger. 1788.
Miscellaneous Observations. 1793.
Remarks on Important Theological Controversies. 1796.
Charity and Its Fruits, edited by Tryon Edwards. 1852.
Selections from the Unpublished Writings, edited by Alexander B. Grosart. 1865.
Observations Concerning the Scripture Economy of the Trinity and Covenant of Redemption, edited by Egbert C. Smyth. 1880.
An Unpublished Essay on the Trinity, edited by George P. Fisher. 1903.
Selected Sermons, edited by H. Norman Gardiner. 1904.
Images; or, Shadows of Divine Things, edited by Perry Miller. 1948.
Puritan Sage: Collected Writings, edited by Vergilius Ferm. 1953.
The Philosophy of Edwards from His Private Notebooks, edited by Harvey G. Townsend. 1955.
Sermon Outlines, edited by Sheldon B. Quincer. 1958.
The Mind: A Reconstructed Text, edited by Leon Howard. 1963.
Treatise on Grace and Other Posthumously Published Writings, edited by Paul Helm. 1971.
Ecclesiastical Writings. 1994.
Altogether Lovely: Jonathan Edwards on the Glory and Excellency of Jesus Christ. 1997.
Instrumental Music in the Public Worship of the Church. 1997.
Pressing into the Kingdom: On Seeking Salvation. 1998.
The Work of the Holy Spirit in the Human Heart: Being Two Tracts on That Subject. 1998.

Other

Letters and Personal Writings. 1998.

*

Bibliography: *The Printed Writings of Edwards: A Bibliography* by Thomas H. Johnson, 1940; *Edwards: A Reference Guide* by Milton X. Lesser, 1981; *Edwards: Bibliographical Synopses* by Nancy Manspeaker, 1981; *Jonathan Edwards: An Annotated Bibliography, 1979-1993* by M.X. Lesser, 1994.

Critical Studies: *Edwards* by Arthur Cushman McGiffert, Jr., 1932; *Edwards: A Biography* by Ola Elizabeth Winslow, 1940; *Edwards* by Perry Miller, 1949; *Edwards* by Alfred Owen Aldridge, 1964; *Edwards: The Narrative of a Puritan Mind* by Edward H. Davidson, 1966; *Edwards and the Visibility of God* by James Carse, 1967; *Beauty and Sensibility in the Thought of Edwards* by Roland Andre Delattre, 1968; *Edwards: A Profile* edited by David Levin, 1969; *Edwards* by Edward Griffin, 1971; *Edwards: His Life and Influence* edited by Charles Angoff, 1975; *The Writings of Edwards: Theme, Motif, and Style* by William J.

Scheik, 1975, and *Critical Essays on Edwards* edited by Scheik, 1980; *Edwards, Pastor: Religion and Society in Eighteenth-Century Northampton* by Patricia Tracy, 1980; *Edwards: Art and the Sense of the Heart* by Terrence Erdt, 1980; *Edwards's Moral Thought and Its British Context* by Norman Fiering, 1981; *The Philosophy of Jonathan Edwards: A Study of Divine Semiotics* by Stephen H. Daniel, 1994; *Jonathan Edwards: Evangelist* by John H. Gerstner, 1995; *Jonathan Edwards, Religious Tradition, and American Culture* by Joseph A. Conforti, 1995; *Jonathan Edwards and the Catholic Version of Salvation* by Anri Morimoto, 1995; *Jonathan Edwards's Writings: Text, Context, Interpretation* edited by Stephen J. Stein, 1996; *Making the American Self: Jonathan Edwards to Abraham Lincoln* by Daniel Walker Howe, 1997; *Jonathan Edwards and the Limits of Enlightenment Philosophy* by Leon Chai, 1998; *Encounters with God: An Approach to the Theology of Jonathan Edwards* by Michael James McClymond, 1998.

*   *   *

Jonathan Edwards is legendary in American history and letters not just as a Calvinist minister of fire and brimstone but, more importantly, as a revolutionary thinker who incorporated contemporary psychological and scientific ideas into his discourses on the human mind, natural science, and religion. A man who epitomized the mystical and practical (the evangelical and Puritan) tendencies of his time, Edwards was instrumental in the mid-eighteenth-century revival of American Calvinism known as the Great Awakening. Edwards strove to destroy the increasingly popular Arminianist propositions that rejected the doctrines of predestination and the enslavement of the will. Arminianism asserted a doctrine of universal redemption based on the *election,* rather than the *predetermination,* of salvation. Edwards was unyielding in his strict adherence to the absolute primacy of deity and the utter subordination of man, to the Calvinist concept of the depravity of man and grace of the Gospel—to a belief system focusing on God as an inscrutable power that, while constituting humanity and nature, lacked complete identification with either. Throughout his life, despite the growing religious liberalism, Edwards repudiated all modern claims to man's natural rights and free will: "The unconverted are guilty and deserve the punishment awaiting them; this punishment is given by an infinite God in His justice; and the only hope of escape is by the gift of salvation which cannot be won by man's effort."

According to Perry Miller, Edwards's reading of John Locke's *An Essay Concerning Human Understanding* was the major event in his intellectual life. From it, Edwards refined his idea that whatever the mind knows as idea depends upon sensation, rather than reason or speculation. As such, through a series of light images in *A Divine and Supernatural Light,* he discusses religious certainty in empirical terms: one intuits or feels grace (the loveliness of God's holiness) through supernatural illumination. One "does not merely rationally believe that God is glorious but he has a sense of the gloriousness of God in his heart." Religious conversion is an overwhelming intuition.

"Justification of Faith Alone" (1734) amplifies Edwards's thesis that the covenant between God and man is one of grace, not works; but "faith actualizes grace." Again, consonant with the science of his day, Edwards incorporates Newton's causation theory, that effect exists, regardless of cause (atoms adhere not because of their inherent physical properties but because of an undefined

Cause). To Edwards, as gravity adheres in matter, so God inheres in gravity and gives being and oneness to all. Man is therefore not justified just through faith. He has faith because he is first justified through God's grace. Man's state is not prior but posterior to God's grace.

"Personal Narrative" details his conversion twenty years earlier. Grace is a "Divine and Supernatural Light" that gives the regenerate a "new apprehension and disposition to love divine decrees." He traces his regeneration out of the "swamp" into the "meadow" of experience, how he saw divine beauty in everything and experienced "vehement longings of soul after God and Christ and after more holiness." The mention of a single word in the Bible caused his heart to burn with the "ardency of soul" and a "flood of tears and weeping aloud." Edwards yearned to "be nothing before God . . . that God might be all." For the saved, there is a mystical-aesthetic intuition of divine beauty through supernatural illumination.

Despite growing resentment toward his frightening portraits of the unredeemed, Edwards delivered the famous sermon *Sinners in the Hands of an Angry God* in Enfield, 8 July 1741. In a formidable examination of the blackness of death and the emptiness of non-being, he amplified how man is subject to spiritual disintegration. Expounding upon Deuteronomy 32:35 ("their foot shall slide in due time"), the sermon speaks of damnation, "The wrath of God is like great waves . . . [that] increase more and more, and rise higher and higher." By convincing the sinner that only divine mercy will protect him, Edwards hoped to convey a "new sense of the heart." "On Virtue" had already stated that all creation continuously depends on God's action, in which all goodness is constituted.

Edwards's many essays on the psychology of religion include *The Distinguishing Marks of a Work of the Spirit of God,* which separates "true signs" and "false signs," and *A Treatise Concerning Religious Affections,* which distinguishes understanding and will. The first is related to reason, judgment, and perception; the latter to feeling, the heart, and the more essential experience of religion. One of his most virulent adversaries, Charles Chauncey, continued to argue that God's presence could not be proved by experience, that Christianity is rational, and that emotionalism should be equated less with holiness than Satan. Nevertheless, *An Humble Inquiry* reiterated Edwards's insistence that church membership could only be open to those with visible evidence of grace.

Because of this kind of single-mindedness, Edwards was dismissed, in 1750, from his prestigious Northampton, Massachusetts, pulpit. From the frontier settlement at Stockbridge, he wrote the great *Freedom of the Will* and posited that will is not separate from mind but indissolubly connected to intellect: man *chooses* what he understands to be the greatest good. One will do only the "greatest good," and God is man's most apparent good. Furthermore, if the will and intellect are inseparable, then the true inner man (and "morality") will be manifest in man's actions. Edwards also argued that although man is free to gratify his will, he is not free to determine what he chooses. Prior to will is divine determination. *A History of the Work of Redemption* is his apocalyptic view of divine and human history from the creation to the final judgment; *The Great Christian Doctrine of Original Sin Defended* posits that we are all corrupted offspring of Adam, damned to utter alienation. The more positive *The Nature of True Virtue* argues that virtue is a kind of moral beauty that is love—benevolence toward Being, one's neighbor, and God. It also exemplifies Edwards's typical tripartite sermon structure: text (thesis, with biblical passage and commentary); doctrine (thematic implications, the heart of the essay); sermon or application (the bulk of the essay).

—Lois Gordon

See the essay on "Personal Narrative."

EGGLESTON, Edward

Born: Vevay, Indiana, 10 December 1837. **Education:** Indiana country schools, and at Amelia Academy, Virginia, 1854-55. **Family:** Married 1) Lizzie Snider in 1858 (died 1890), three daughters; 2) Frances E. Goode in 1891. **Career:** Teacher, Madison, Indiana, 1855; entered the Methodist ministry, 1857: circuit rider in southeast Indiana, 1856-57; preacher, Traverse and St. Peter, 1857-58, St. Paul, 1858-60, Stillwater, 1860-61, St. Paul, 1862-63, and Winona, 1864-66, all Minnesota; associate editor, *Little Corporal* magazine, and columnist, Chicago *Evening Journal,* 1866-67; editor, *National Sunday School Teacher,* Chicago, 1867-69; literary editor, 1870, and superintending editor, 1871, New York *Independent;* editor, *Hearth and Home,* New York, 1871-72; left the Methodist ministry, 1874; founder and pastor of the non-sectarian Church of the Christian Endeavor, Brooklyn, New York, 1874-79. Cofounder, Authors' Club, 1882; president, American Historical Association, 1900. **Awards:** D.D.: University of Indiana, Bloomington, 1870. D.H.L.: Allegheny College, Meadville, Pennsylvania, 1893. **Died:** 2 September 1902.

PUBLICATIONS

Fiction

Mr. Blake's Walking-Stick: A Christmas Story for Boys and Girls. 1870.
The Book of Queer Stories, and Stories Told on a Cellar Door. 1871.
The Hoosier School-Master. 1871; revised edition, 1892.
The End of the World: A Love Story. 1872.
The Mystery of Metropolisville. 1873.
The Circuit Rider: A Tale of the Heroic Age. 1874.
The Schoolmaster's Stories for Boys and Girls. 1874.
Roxy. 1878.
The Hoosier School-Boy. 1882.
Queer Stories for Boys and Girls. 1884.
The Graysons: A Story of Illinois. 1888.
The Faith Doctor: A Story of New York. 1891.
Duffels (collected stories). 1893.

Other

Sunday School Conventions and Institutes. 1867; revised edition, 1870.
The Manual: A Practical Guide to the Sunday-School Work. 1869.
Improved Sunday School Record. 1869.
Tracts for Sunday School Teachers. 1872(?).
Tecumseh and the Shawnee Prophet, with Lillie Eggleston Seelye. 1878; as *The Shawnee Prophet,* 1880.

Pocahontas, with Lillie Eggleston Seelye. 1879; as *The Indian Princess,* 1881.
Brant and Red Jacket, with Lillie Eggleston Seelye. 1879; as *The Rival Warriors, Chiefs of the Five Nations,* 1881.
Montezuma and the Conquest of Mexico, with Lillie Eggleston Seelye. 1880; as *The Mexican Prince,* 1881.
A History of the United States and Its People, for the Use of Schools. 1888.
A First Book in American History. 1889.
Stories of Great Americans for Little Americans: Second Reader Grade. 1895.
Stories of American Life and Adventures: Third Reader Grade. 1895.
The Beginners of a Nation. 1896.
The Transit of Civilization from England to America in the Seventeenth Century. 1901.
The New Century History of the United States, edited by G.C. Eggleston. 1904.

Editor, *Christ in Literature.* 1875.
Editor, *Christ in Art.* 1875.
Editor, with Elizabeth Eggleston Seelye, *The Story of Columbus.* 1892.
Editor, with Elizabeth Eggleston Seelye, *The Story of Washington.* 1893.

*

Bibliography: in *Bibliography of American Literature* by Jacob Blanck, 1959; "Eggleston" by William Peirce Randel, in *American Literary Realism* 1, 1967.

Critical Studies: *Eggleston, Author of "The Hoosier School-Master,"* 1946, and *Eggleston,* 1963, both by William Peirce Randel; *From Here to Modernity: Nation Building, the Writing of Place, and the Provincial Ideal in Hugh Miller and Edward Eggleston* (dissertation) by Bruce Evan Levy, 1993.

*   *   *

In 1871 Edward Eggleston, a former Methodist clergyman from Indiana who had become a successful editor of popular magazines for children and adults, published *The Hoosier School-Master,* thereby launching the first of two literary careers that made him an important—if decidedly minor—figure. In the adventures of a fictional frontier Indiana schoolteacher, Eggleston the novelist created a pioneering piece of western dialect fiction, and also contributed seminally to the growth of a Midwestern realism, a genre that would subsequently be developed by **Hamlin Garland**.

Written initially for serialization in Eggleston's magazine *Hearth and Home,* with the early installments in print well before the later portions were in outline, *The Hoosier School-Master* has rightly been criticized for its many structural flaws. But Eggleston soon followed with a series of finer though curiously less famous novels in the same realistic vein: *The End of the World,* based upon the Millerite delusion of the 1840s; *The Mystery of Metropolisville,* a poorly constructed but equally realistic saga of boom and bust on the Midwestern frontier; *The Circuit Rider,* a novel of remembrance, as the erstwhile preacher Eggleston wrote in its dedication, for his "Comrades of Other Years . . . with whom I had the honor to be associate in a frontier ministry"; and *Roxy,* the story of a small-town Ohio girl, thought by some to be Eggleston's best fictional work. Throughout his novels Eggleston sought to portray the commonplace in nineteenth-century American life. As he stated in *The Mystery of Metropolisville,* a novel "needs to be true to human nature in its permanent and essential qualities, and it should truthfully represent . . . some form of society."

Given the realistic character of his fiction, it was a short step for Eggleston to his next and final career, that of historian. In 1888 he published *A History of the United States and Its People.* And in 1896 appeared *The Beginners of a Nation,* the first of a projected multi-volume "History of Life in the United States." True to his proclivities as a realist, Eggleston had planned, as he said in 1880, for his history to be "a history of . . . the life of the people, the sources of their ideas and habits, the course of their development from beginnings." And had he been able to complete his series he surely would have joined Moses Coit Tyler and John Bach McMaster as one of the great founders of American social history. Unfortunately he came to history too late in life and with too expansive a plan; after publishing the second volume in the series, *The Transit of Civilization,* he died in 1902.

—Bruce A. Lohof

ELIOT, T(homas) S(tearns)

Born: St. Louis, Missouri, 26 September 1888; became British citizen, 1927. **Education:** Mrs. Lockwood's school, St. Louis; Smith Academy, St. Louis, 1898-1905; Milton Academy, Massachusetts, 1905-06; Harvard University, Cambridge, Massachusetts (board member, *Harvard Advocate,* 1909-10; Sheldon Traveling Fellowship, 1914), 1906-10, 1911-14, A.B. 1909, A.M. in English 1910; the Sorbonne, Paris, 1910-11; Merton College, Oxford, 1914-15. **Family:** Married 1) Vivien (born Vivienne) Haigh-Wood in 1915 (separated, 1933; died, 1947); 2) Esme Valerie Fletcher in 1957. **Career:** Teacher, High Wycombe Grammar School, Buckinghamshire, 1915-16, and Highgate Junior School, London, 1916; tutor, University of London Extension Board, Southall, 1916-19; clerk in the Colonial and Foreign Department, then in charge of the Foreign Office Information Bureau, Lloyd's Bank, London, 1917-25; editor, later director, Faber and Gwyer, 1925-28, and Faber and Faber, publishers, London, 1929-65. Assistant editor, *The Egoist,* London, 1917-19; regular contributor, *Times Literary Supplement,* London, from 1919; founding editor, *The Criterion,* London, 1922-39; member of the editorial board, *New English Weekly,* London, 1934-44, and *Christian News Letter,* Oxford, 1939-46. Clark Lecturer, Trinity College, Cambridge, 1926; Charles Eliot Norton Professor of Poetry, 1932-33, and Theodore Spencer Memorial Lecturer, 1950, Harvard University; Page-Barbour Lecturer, University of Virginia, Charlottesville, 1933; visiting fellow, Institute for Advanced Studies, Princeton University, New Jersey, 1948. Joined Church of England, 1927. **Awards:** Nobel prize for Literature, 1948; New York Drama Critics Circle award, 1950; Hanseatic-Goethe prize (Hamburg), 1954; Dante Gold Medal (Florence), 1959; Order of Merit (Bonn), 1959; Emerson-Thoreau Medal, 1960; U.S. Medal of Freedom, 1964. Litt.D.: Columbia University, New York, 1933; Cambridge University, 1938; University of Bristol, 1938; University of Leeds, 1939; Harvard University, 1947; Princeton University, 1947; Yale University, New Haven, Connecticut, 1947; Washington University, St. Louis, 1953; University of Rome, 1958; University of Sheffield, 1959; University of Bologna, 1967. LL.D.: University of Edinburgh, 1937; St. Andrews University, Fife, Scotland, 1953. D.Litt.: Oxford University, 1948. D.Lit.: University of London, 1950. D. es L.: University of Paris, 1951; University of Aix-Marseille, 1959; University of Rennes, 1959. D.Phil.: University of Munich, 1959. Honorary Fellow, Magdalene College, Cambridge, 1948, and Merton College, Oxford, 1949. O.M. (Order of Merit), 1948; Officer, Legion of Honor, and Commander, Order of Arts and Letters (France), 1950. **Member:** American Academy (honorary); foreign member, Accademia dei Lincei (Rome) and Akademie der Schonen Kunste. **Died:** 4 January 1965.

Publications

Collections

Selected Prose, edited by Frank Kermode. 1975.

Poetry

Prufrock and Other Observations. 1917.
Poems. 1919.
Ara Vos Prec. 1920; as *Poems,* 1920.
The Waste Land. 1922; *A Facsimile and Transcripts of the Original Drafts Including the Annotations of Ezra Pound,* edited by Valerie Eliot, 1971.
Poems 1909-1925. 1925.
Journey of the Magi. 1927.
A Song for Simeon. 1928.
Animula. 1929.
Ash-Wednesday. 1930.
Marina. 1930.
Triumphal March. 1931.
Words for Music. 1935.
Two Poems. 1935.
Collected Poems 1909-1935. 1936.
Old Possum's Book of Practical Cats. 1939.
The Waste Land and Other Poems. 1940.
East Coker. 1940.
Later Poems 1925-35. 1941.
The Dry Salvages. 1941.
Little Gidding. 1942.
Four Quartets (includes *Burnt Norton, East Coker, The Dry Salvages, Little Gidding*). 1943.
A Practical Possum. 1947.
Selected Poems. 1948.
The Undergraduate Poems. 1949.
Poems Written in Early Youth, edited by John Hayward. 1950.
The Cultivation of Christmas Trees. 1954.
Collected Poems 1909-1962. 1963.

Plays

Sweeney Agonistes: Fragments of an Aristophanic Melodrama (produced 1933). 1932.
The Rock: A Pageant Play (produced 1934). 1934.
Murder in the Cathedral (produced 1935). 1935; revised version, in *The Film of Murder in the Cathedral,* with George Hoellering, 1952.

The Family Reunion (produced 1939). 1939.
The Cocktail Party (produced 1949). 1950; revised edition, 1950.
The Confidential Clerk (produced 1953). 1954.
The Elder Statesman (produced 1958). 1959.
Collected Plays: Murder in the Cathedral, The Family Reunion, The Cocktail Party, The Confidential Clerk, The Elder Statesman. 1962; as *The Complete Plays,* 1969.

Other

Ezra Pound: His Metric and Poetry. 1918.
The Sacred Wood: Essays on Poetry and Criticism. 1920.
Homage to John Dryden: Three Essays on Poetry in the Seventeenth Century. 1924.
Shakespeare and the Stoicism of Seneca. 1927.
For Lancelot Andrewes: Essays on Style and Order. 1928.
Dante. 1929.
Charles Whibley: A Memoir. 1931.
Thoughts after Lambeth. 1931.
Selected Essays 1917-1932. 1932; revised edition, 1950.
John Dryden: The Poet, The Dramatist, The Critic. 1932.
The Use of Poetry and the Use of Criticism: Studies in the Relation of Criticism to Poetry in England. 1933.
After Strange Gods: A Primer of Modern Heresy. 1934.
Elizabethan Essays. 1934; as *Elizabethan Dramatists,* 1963; selection, as *Essays on Elizabethan Drama,* 1956.
Essays Ancient and Modern. 1936.
The Idea of a Christian Society. 1939.
Points of View, edited by John Hayward. 1941.
The Classics and the Man of Letters. 1942.
The Music of Poetry. 1942.
Reunion by Destruction: Reflections on a Scheme for Church Unity in South India Addressed to the Laity. 1943.
What Is a Classic? 1945.
Die Einheit der Europaischen Kultur. 1946.
On Poetry. 1947.
Milton. 1947.
From Poe to Valery. 1948.
A Sermon Preached in Magdalene College Chapel. 1948.
Notes Towards the Definition of Culture. 1948.
The Aims of Poetic Drama. 1949.
Poetry and Drama. 1951.
The Value and Use of Cathedrals in England Today. 1952.
An Address to the Members of the London Library. 1952.
The Complete Poems and Plays. 1952.
Selected Prose, edited by John Hayward. 1953.
American Literature and the American Language. 1953.
The Three Voices of Poetry. 1953.
Religious Drama, Medieval and Modern. 1954.
The Literature of Politics. 1955.
The Frontiers of Criticism. 1956.
On Poetry and Poets. 1957.
Geoffrey Faber 1889-1961. 1961.
George Herbert. 1962.
Knowledge and Experience in the Philosophy of F. H. Bradley (doctoral dissertation). 1964.
To Criticize the Critic and Other Writings. 1965.

Editor, *Selected Poems,* by Ezra Pound. 1928; revised edition, 1949.
Editor, *A Choice of Kipling's Verse.* 1941.

Editor, *Introducing James Joyce.* 1942.
Editor, *Literary Essays of Ezra Pound.* 1954.
Editor, *The Criterion 1922-1939.* 18 vols., 1967.

Translator, *Anabasis: A Poem,* by Saint-John Perse. 1930; revised editions, 1938, 1949, 1959.

*

Bibliography: *Eliot: A Bibliography* by Donald Gallup, 1952, revised edition, 1969; *The Merrill Checklist of Eliot* by B. Gunter, 1970; *Eliot: A Bibliography of Secondary Works* by Beatrice Ricks, 1980; *Eliot: Man and Poet, II: An Annotated Bibliography of a Decade of Eliot Criticism, 1977-1986* by Sebastian Knowles and Scott A. Leonard, 1992; *A Concordance to the Complete Poems and Plays of T.S. Eliot* by J.L. Dawson, 1995.

Critical Studies: *The Achievement of Eliot: An Essay on the Nature of Poetry* by F.O. Matthiessen, 1935, revised edition, 1949, with additional material by C.L. Barber, 1958; *Four Quartets Rehearsed* by R. Preston, 1946; *Eliot: A Symposium* edited by Richard March and Tambimuttu, 1948; *Eliot: The Design of His Poetry* by Elizabeth Drew, 1949; *The Art of Eliot,* 1949, *Eliot and the English Poetic Tradition,* 1965, and *The Composition of Four Quartets,* 1978, all by Helen Gardner; *The Poetry of Eliot* by D.E.S. Maxwell, 1952; *A Reader's Guide to Eliot* by George Williamson, 1953, revised edition, 1966; *Eliot's Poetry and Plays: A Study in Sources and Meaning,* 1956, revised edition, 1975, and *The Waste Land,* 1983, both by Grover Smith; *Eliot: A Symposium for His Seventieth Birthday* edited by Neville Braybrooke, 1958; *The Invisible Poet: Eliot* by Hugh Kenner, 1959, and *Eliot: A Collection of Critical Essays* edited by Kenner, 1962; *Eliot's Dramatic Theory and Practice* by Carol H. Smith, 1963; *Eliot* by Northrop Frye, 1963, revised edition, 1968; *Notes on Some Figures Behind Eliot* by Herbert Howarth, 1964; *Eliot* by Philip Headings, 1964, revised edition, 1982; *Eliot: The Dialectical Structure of His Theory of Poetry* by Fei-pai Lu, 1965; *Eliot: The Man and His Work* edited by Allen Tate, 1966; *Eliot: Movements and Patterns* by Leonard Unger, 1966; *A Student's Guide to the Selected Poems of Eliot* by B.C. Southam, 1968, revised edition, 1981; *Twentieth-Century Interpretations of The Waste Land* edited by Jay Martin, 1968; *The Waste Land: A Casebook* edited by C.B. Cox and Arnold P. Hinchliffe, 1968; *Eliot's Four Quartets: A Casebook* edited by Bernard Bergonzi, 1969, and *Eliot* by Bergonzi, 1972, revised edition, 1978; *The Making of Eliot's Plays* by E. Martin Browne, 1969; *Eliot: Poems in the Making* by Gertrude Patterson, 1971; *Eliot's Intellectual Development 1922-1939* by John D. Margolis, 1972; *Eliot: Poet and Dramatist* by Joseph Chiari, 1972, revised edition, 1979; *Critics on Eliot* edited by Sheila Sullivan, 1973; *Eliot in His Time: Essays on the Occasion of the Fiftieth Anniversary of The Waste Land* edited by A. Walton Litz, 1973; *Eliot's Impersonal Theory of Poetry* by Mowbray Allan, 1974; *Eliot: A Collection of Criticism* edited by Linda W. Wagner, 1974; *Eliot* by Stephen Spender, 1975; *Eliot: The Pattern in the Carpet* by Elisabeth W. Schneider, 1975; *Eliot: The Longer Poems* by Derek A. Traversi, 1976; *Eliot's Personal Waste Land: Exorcism of the Demons* by James E. Miller, Jr., 1977; *Eliot's Early Years* by Lyndall Gordon, 1977; *The Literary Criticism of Eliot: New Essays* edited by David Newton-De Molina, 1977; *Eliot: Poet* by A.D. Moody, 1979; *Eliot and the Romantic Critical Tradition* by Edward Lobb, 1981; *Eliot: The Poet and His Critics* by Robert H. Canary, 1982; *Eliot* by

Burton Raffel, 1982; *Eliot: The Critical Heritage* edited by Michael Grant, 2 vols., 1982; *Eliot: A Chronology of His Life and Works* by Caroline Behr, 1983; *Eliot and the Poetics of Literary History* by Gregory S. Jay, 1983; *Eliot: A Study in Character and Style* by Ronald Bush, 1984; *Eliot: A Life* by Peter Ackroyd, 1984; *Critical Essays on Eliot: The Sweeney Motif* edited by Kinley Roby, 1985; *An Eliot Companion: Life and Works* edited by F.B. Pinion, 1986; *The Serious Poet in a Secularized Society: Reflections on Eliot and Twentieth-Century Culture* by Cleanth Brooks, 1991; *Trans-Culturality and Inter-Culturality in French and German Translations of Eliot's The Waste Land* by Armin Paul Frank and Birgit Bodeker, 1991; *The Poetry of Eliot: A Study in Religious Sensibility* by Narsingh Srivastava, 1991; *The English Eliot: Design, Language and Landscape in Four Quarters* by Steve Ellis, 1991; *The Russian Man at Russell Square: Reflections on the Critical Conception of Eliot* by Dmitry Urnov, 1992; *Falling Towers: The Trojan Imagination in the Waste Land, The Dunciad, and Speke, Parrot* by J.A. Richardson, 1992; *T.S. Eliot's The Waste Land* by Gareth Reeves, 1994; *Where the Words Are Valid: T.S. Eliot's Communities of Drama* by Randy Malamud, 1994; *Mastery and Escape: T.S. Eliot and the Dialectic of Modernism* by Jewel Spears Brooker, 1994; *Puritan Sensibility in T.S. Eliot's Poetry* by Dal-Yong Kim, 1994; *Construction of "the Jew" in English Literature and Society: Racial Representations, 1875-1945* by Bryan Cheyette, 1995; *Religious Quest in the Poetry of T.S. Eliot* by Caroline Phillips, 1995; *T.S. Eliot and Ideology* by Kenneth George Asher, 1995; *A Deconstruction of T.S. Eliot: The Fire and the Rose* by William James Austin, 1996; *Tracing T.S. Eliot's Spirit: Essays on His Poetry and Thought* by Anthony David Moody, 1996; *The Poetics of Fascism: Ezra Pound, T.S. Eliot, Paul de Man* by Paul Morrison, 1996; *T.S. Eliot: Mystic, Son, and Lover* by Donald J. Childs, 1997; *T.S. Eliot's Use of Popular Sources* by Manju Jaidka, 1997; *The Golden Lotus: Buddhist Influence in T.S. Eliot's Four Quartets* by Paul Foster, 1998; *T.S. Eliot and American Poetry* by Lee Oser, 1998; *Deviant Modernism: Sexual Errancy in T.S. Eliot, James Joyce, and Marcel Proust* by Colleen Lamos, 1998; *Aethereal Rumors: T.S. Eliot's Physics and Poetics* by Benjamin G. Lockerd, 1998.

*　　*　　*

T.S. Eliot's influence was predominant in English poetry in the period between the two world wars. His first small volume of poems, *Prufrock and Other Observations,* appeared in 1917. The title is significant. Eliot's earliest verse is composed of *observations,* detached, ironic, and alternately disillusioned and nostalgic in tone. The prevailing influence is that of French poetry and in particular of Jules Laforgue; the mood is one of reaction against the comfortable certainties of "Georgian" poetry, the projection of a world that presented itself to the poet and his generation as disconcerting, uncertain, and very possibly heading for destruction.

The longest poem in the volume, "The Love Song of J. Alfred Prufrock," shows these qualities but goes beyond them. The speaker is a kind of modern Hamlet, a man who after a life passed in devotion to the trivial has awakened to a sense of his own futility and to that of the world around him. He feels that some decisive act of commitment is needed to break the meaningless flow of events that his life offers. The question, however, is whether he really dares to reverse the entire course of his existence by a decision the nature of which eludes him:

And indeed there will be time
To wonder, "Do I dare?" and, "Do I dare?"
Time to turn back and descend the stair,
With a bald spot in the middle of my hair . . .
Do I dare
Disturb the universe?

The answer, for Prufrock, is negative. Dominated by his fear of life, misunderstood when he tries to express his sense of a possible revelation, Prufrock concludes "No! I am not Prince Hamlet, nor was meant to be," refuses to accept the role that life for a moment seemed to have thrust upon him, and returns to the stagnation that his vision of reality imposes.

Eliot's earliest poems are American in theme and inspiration, and reflect his experiences there, especially while studying philosophy at Harvard. The outbreak of war in 1914 found him in England, where he eventually made his home and where his conception of his art underwent a considerable change. After a second small volume, published in 1919, which shows, especially in its most impressive poem, "Gerontion," a notable deepening into tragedy, came the publication in 1922 of *The Waste Land.* Written in part in Switzerland, while Eliot was recovering from a period of deep depression, the poem underwent considerable changes at the suggestion of **Ezra Pound**, before bursting upon its readers with the effect of a literary revolution. Many of its first readers found it arid and incomprehensible, though it was in fact neither. The poet tells us that he is working through "a heap of broken images." He does this because it is a world of dissociated fragments that he is describing; but his aim, like that of any artist, is not merely an evocation of chaos. The poem is built on the interweaving of two great themes: the broken pieces of the present, as it presents itself to a disillusioned contemporary understanding, and the significant continuity of tradition. These two strains begin apart, like two separate themes in a musical composition, but the poem is animated by the hope, the *method,* that at the end they will converge into some kind of unity. Some critics, reading it in the light of Eliot's later development, have tried to find in the poem a specifically "religious" content which is not there. At best, there is a suggestion at the close that such a content, were it available, might provide a way out of the "waste land" situation, that the life-giving rain may be on the point of relieving the intolerable drought; but the poet cannot honestly propose such a resolution and the step that might have affirmed it is never rendered actual.

For some years after 1922, Eliot wrote little poetry and the greater part of his effort went into critical prose, much of it published in *The Criterion,* the literary quarterly that he edited until 1939. Eliot's criticism, which profoundly affected the literary taste of his generation, contributed to the revaluation of certain writers—the lesser Elizabethan dramatists, Donne, Marvell, Dryden—and, more controversially, to the depreciation of others, such as Milton (concerning whom, however, Eliot later modified his views) and some of the Romantic poets. It was the work of a poet whose interest in other writers was largely conditioned by the search for solutions to the problems raised by his own art; and, as such, it was marked by the idiosyncrasies that constitute at once its strength and its limitation.

In 1928, in his preface to the collection of essays *For Lancelot Andrewes,* Eliot declared himself Anglo-Catholic in religion, royalist in politics, classicist in literature: a typically enigmatic statement that indicated the direction he was to give to the work of his later years. *Ash-Wednesday,* published in 1930, was his first considerable poem of explicitly Christian inspiration: a work at once religious in content and modern in inspiration, personal yet without concession to sentiment. The main theme is an acceptance of conversion as a necessary and irretrievable act. The answer to the question posed by Prufrock—"Do I dare / Disturb the universe?"— is seen, in the translation of the first line of the Italian poet Guido Cavalcanti's ballad, "Because I do not hope to turn again," as an embarkation, dangerous but decisive, upon the adventure of faith.

The consequences of this development were explored in the last and in some respects the most ambitious of Eliot's poetic efforts: the sequence of poems initiated in 1935 and finally published, in 1943, under the title of *Four Quartets.* The series opens, in *Burnt Norton,* with an exploration of the *possible* significance of certain moments that seem to penetrate, briefly and elusively, a reality beyond that of normal temporal experience. "To be conscious," the poem suggests, "is not to be in time": only to balance that possibility with the counter-assertion that "Only through time time is conquered." The first step towards an understanding of the problems raised in the *Quartets* is a recognition that time, though inseparable from our human experience, is not the whole of it. If we consider time as an ultimate reality, our spiritual intuitions are turned into an illusion: whereas if we seek to deny the reality of time, our experience becomes impossible. The two elements—the temporal and the timeless—need to be woven together in an embracing pattern of experience that is, in fact, the end to which the entire sequence points.

The later "quartets" build upon this provisional foundation in the light of the poet's experience as artist and human being. The impulse to create in words reflects another, still more fundamental impulse that prompts men to seek *form,* coherence, and meaning in the broken intuitions that their experience offers them. The nature of the search is such that it can never be complete in time. The true value of our actions only begins to emerge when we abstract ourselves from the temporal sequence—"time before and time after"—in which they were realized; and the final sense of our experience only reveals itself when the pattern is completed, at the moment of death. This moment, indeed, is not properly speaking a single final point, but a reality that covers the whole course of our existence.

These reflections lead the poet, in the last two poems of the series, *The Dry Salvages* and *Little Gidding,* to acceptance and even to a certain optimism. The end of the journey becomes the key to its beginning, and this in turn an invitation to confidence: "Not fare well, / But fare forward, voyagers." The doctrine of detachment explored in the second poem, *East Coker,* becomes an "expanding" one of "love beyond desire." The conclusion stresses the continuity between the "birth" and "death" that are simultaneously present in each moment, in each individual life, and in the history of the human race. It is true, as the closing section of *Little Gidding* puts it, that "we die with the dying"; but it is equally true that "we are born with the dead." We die, in other words, as part of the tragedy that the fact of our humanity implies, but we are born again when, having understood the temporal process in its true light, we are ready to accept our present position within a still-living and continually unfolding tradition.

Eliot's poetic output was relatively small and intensely concentrated: a fact that at once confirms its value and constitutes, in some sense, a limiting factor. It should be mentioned that in his later years he devoted himself to the writing of verse plays, in an attempt to create a contemporary mode of poetic drama. The ear-

lier plays, *Murder in the Cathedral* and *The Family Reunion,* which are also the best, take up the themes that were being explored at the same time in his poetry and develop them in ways that are often interesting and dramatically effective. *The Cocktail Party,* though still a skillful work, shows some decline in conception and execution, and the later plays—*The Confidential Clerk* and *The Elder Statesman*—while they seem to show that he was arriving towards the end of his life at a more accepting view of the world, can safely be said to add little to Eliot's achievement.

—Derek A. Traversi

See the essays on "The Love Song of J. Alfred Prufrock," *Murder in the Cathedral,* and *The Waste Land.*

ELKIN, Stanley L(awrence)

Born: New York City, 11 May 1930. **Education:** University of Illinois (A.B., 1952; M.A., 1953; Ph.D., 1961). **Military Service:** Served in the U.S. Army, 1955-57. **Family:** Married Joan Marion Jacobson in 1953, two sons and one daughter. **Career:** Washington University, St. Louis, Missouri, instructor, 1960-62, assistant professor, 1962-66, associate professor, 1966-69, beginning 1969 professor of English, and beginning 1983 Merle Kling Professor of Modern Letters; visiting professor at Smith College, 1964-65, University of California, Santa Barbara, 1967, University of Wisconsin—Milwaukee, 1969, University of Iowa, 1974, Yale University, 1975, and Boston University, 1976. **Awards:** Longview Foundation award, 1962; Paris Review humor prize, 1965; Guggenheim fellowship, 1966-67; Rockefeller Foundation grant, 1968-69; National Endowment for the Arts and Humanities grant, 1972; American Academy of Arts and Letters award, 1974; Richard and Hinda Rosenthal award, 1980; Sewanee Review prize, 1981; National Book Critics Circle award, 1982; Creative Arts award, Brandeis University, 1986; Elmer Holmes Bobst award, New York University, 1991. **Member:** American Academy. **Died:** 31 May 1995.

PUBLICATIONS

Collections

Stanley Elkin's Greatest Hits, foreword by Robert Coover. 1980.
Early Elkin. 1985.

Novels

Boswell: A Modern Comedy. 1964; reprinted, 1980.
A Bad Man. 1967; reprinted, 1980.
The Dick Gibson Show. 1971.
The Franchiser. 1976.
The First George Mills. 1981.
George Mills. 1982.
Stanley Elkin's Magic Kingdom. 1985.
The Rabbi of Lud. 1987.
The MacGuffin. 1991.
Mrs. Ted Bliss. 1995.

Short Stories and Novellas

Criers and Kibitzers, Kibitzers and Criers (stories). 1966; reprinted, 1980.
The Making of Ashenden (novella). 1972.
Searches and Seizures. 1973; in England as *Eligible Men: Three Short Novels,* 1974; as *Alex and the Gypsy,* 1977.
The Living End. 1979.
The Coffee Room. 1988.
Van Gogh's Room at Arles: Three Novellas. 1993.

Other

Pieces of Soap: Essays by Stanley Elkin. 1992.

Editor, *Stories from the Sixties.* 1971.
Editor, with Shannon Ravenal, *The Best American Short Stories of 1980* (and introduction). 1980.

*

Bibliography: by Marc Chenetier, in *Delta,* February 1985; by Larry McCaffrey, in *Bulletin of Bibliography* vol. 34, 1977; by William M. Robbins, in *Critique* vol. 26, 1985.

Critical Studies: "The Obsessional Fiction of Stanley Elkin" by Thomas LeClair, in *Contemporary Literature* vol. 16, 1974; "The Power of the Guest: Stanley Elkin's Fiction" by Francine O. Hardaway, in *Rocky Mountain Review of Language and Literature* vol. 32, 1977; "Stanley Elkin's Recovery of the Ordinary" by Larry McCaffrey, in *Critique* vol. 21, 1978; "The American Salesman as Pitchman and Poet in the Fiction of Stanley Elkin" by Robert Edward Colbert, in *Critique* vol. 21, 1978; *The Fiction of Stanley Elkin,* 1980, and "The Orphan Adopted: Stanley Elkin's *The Franchiser*" in *Studies in American Jewish Literature* vol. 2, 1982, both by Doris Bargen; "Death as Grotesque: The Fiction of Stanley Elkin" in *Hollins Critic,* June 1982; "M.S. as Metaphor" in *Delta,* February 1985, and *Reading Stanley Elkin,* 1985, both by Peter Joseph Bailey; "Elkin's *George Mills,* or How to Make an Ectoplasm Schmooze" by Maurice Couturier, in *Delta,* February 1985; "Stanley Elkin and 'Everything': The Problem of Surfaces and Fullness in the Novels" by Charles Molesworth, in *Delta,* February 1985; "Stanley Elkin and Jewish Black Humor" by Maurice Charney, in *Jewish Wry* edited by Sarah Blacher Cohen, 1987; "Ego and Appetite in Stanley Elkin's Fiction" by Arthur M. Saltzman, in *Literary Review* vol. 32, 1988; interview with David C. Dougherty, in *Literary Review,* winter 1991; *Stanley Elkin* by David C. Dougherty, 1991; "Stanley Elkin and the Revival of the Familiar Essay" in *The Old Northwest,* fall 1992; *Comic Sense: Reading Robert Coover, Stanley Elkin, Philip Roth* by Thomas Pughe, 1994; *Love as the Cause of Death, Death as the Cause of Love: The Fiction of Stanley Elkin* by Jeffrey Michael Popovich, 1997.

*   *   *

Stanley Elkin's fiction can be discussed within a variety of contexts: Jewish-American literature, black humor, metafiction. His protagonists tend to be gathered from the rootless and disenchanted, from those who quest after elusive, often wacky goals in an effort to overcompensate for absent families or feelings of powerlessness. But it is Elkin's dazzling style, rather than his plots, that both creates his characters and moves them beyond comic complications to versions of individuality and psychic health. His style is to language what a sideshow contortionist is to the human body. Thus, he can stretch a normal sentence structure until the knees find themselves draped around the neck, elbows are twisted almost beyond recognition, and the trunk—magically, impossibly—disappears. His paragraphs often take on the shape of pretzels or, perhaps, pachyderms. Indeed, everything he writes seems analogous to an overnight bag packed for a two-week vacation, which is to say that his characteristic style strikes readers as comically, delightfully overstuffed.

After eleven novels and four collections of short fiction, readers know, or at least think they know, what to expect when they encounter a new book by Elkin. It will be darkly comic and wildly irreverent, inventive and masterful, simultaneously gruff and tender-hearted—all the predictable labels reviewers pasted on his fictions for at least two decades. What professional Elkin-watchers cannot so easily account for, however, is the way style and shtick (comic bits) become virtually indistinguishable or how it is that even Elkin aficionados continue to find themselves surprised by the surprises of his language. No doubt his wizardry is connected to his playful brand of curiosity, as well as to the sheer delight he takes in crafting sentences with a requisite shape and feel; and no doubt fellow writers would put all this more simply: Elkin, they would insist, is blessed with a great ear.

Here, for example, is how an essay entitled "Pieces of Soap" describes his penchant for soap-stealing. What makes his peccadillo, and his resulting mock confessional about it, so peculiar is that this solidly upright citizen, this Dr. Jekyll who "would never think of swiping a towel or making off with so much as a wire coat hanger," turns into a sticky-fingered Mr. Hyde whenever he spots the chance to pilfer yet another slender bar of complimentary soap. He becomes, as Elkin himself puts it,

> this conscienceless soap yegg and soap poacher, this footpad of handsoap, something exponential in the blood that made me this, well, brigand of the bath, this simple soapsy-sud fetishist, this collector-plunderer/hunter-gatherer of special soap booty, grabbing up my pieces of soap like pieces of eight, handfuls of discrete, magic, anal greed, filling my pockets, *shtupping* all my clothing like a contestant let loose in a supermarket.

In less skillful hands such snowballing analogies would fall over from their accumulated weight, but Elkin long ago mastered the tricky art of inventing memorable characters by letting them, as it were, rip. "The Bailbondsman," one of the novellas collected in *Searches and Seizures* (1973), is a case in point. In this ostensible account of a single day in the high-energy life of Alexander Main, an aging bail bondsman, the protagonists's voice matters in ways the "plot" never quite does: "I go surety . . . . My conditions classic and my terms terminal. Listen, I haven't much law—though what I have is on my side, binding as clay, advantage to the house—but am as at home in replevin, debenture, and gage as someone on his own toilet seat with the door closed and the house empty."

Elkin brings a similar spirit to novels such as *The Living End,* in which jumbo-sized paragraphs detail, in an exquisite specificity the likes of which we have not seen since the days of Rabelais or S. J. Perelman, just how comically shameful the cliches of our popular culture actually are. Since *The Franchiser,* however, a novel in which the protagonist finds himself stricken with multiple sclerosis, disease and the body's wreck have increasingly become Elkin's congenial subject.

That his personal essays should talk about the heart attack he experienced at the relatively young age of thirty-seven, which led him, as he wrote (in "Pieces of Soap") "toward revenge—a writer's revenge, anyway, the revenge . . . of style," is hardly surprising. But in a novel such as *The Magic Kingdom,* where a melange of exotic diseases provides the building blocks of its dark, complicated art, and in two of the novellas collected in *Van Gogh's Room at Arles,* illness has taken a center position on the fictional stage. Elkin may describe himself as "not a particularly brave man and, most certainly, not in the least a reticent one. I publicly whine, I mean. I don't keep myself to myself, which is where, in all probability, I probably belong," but the collection as a whole suggests otherwise. Indeed, the word that best describes his deliciously wicked account of Hollywood's Big Night ("At the Academy Awards") or his graduate school memories of an extravagantly expensive yellow shirt he wore to a 1953 reading by T. S. Eliot is not "whine" but, rather, brio. For Elkin has an eye for the wacky and vibrant, the idiosyncratic and the downright zany that is at least the equal of his ear for language bent into surprising configurations.

Sometimes, as in *The Living End,* the cliches we live and die by provide Elkin all the comic material he needs; in other cases, such as *The Rabbi of Lud* or *The MacGuffin,* elaborately embroidered humor unrolls from relatively simple premises. From at least *The Magic Kingdom* onward, however, one begins to feel not only the damp hand of melancholy or evidence of disease, but also the increasing toll of bodies contorted by physical suffering. *Van Gogh's Room at Arles* is, among other things, a study in protagonists' literally falling apart.

Elkin's final novel, *Mrs. Ted Bliss,* is not about disintegration, however, but rather survival. At first glance Dorothy Bliss seems an unlikely heroine for any novelist, much less one like Elkin, who prefers to give middle-aged—usually male—failures the comic treatment they deserve. Mrs. Bliss, by contrast, can be numbered among the ever-growing tribe of moderately well-heeled Jewish widows who carve new lives out of the theme nights, bingo games, and squeaky-clean accoutrements of their Miami Beach condos. At the same time, however, Elkin gives his protagonist enough definition (she had "passed over into a new state of being, existed on a plane different from grief out of reach of cumulate time's ministering comforts and platitudes") and enough diversion (in her early eighties, she suddenly finds herself swept up in a series of comic misadventures—with South American drug dealers, quack therapists, and con men) to make her one of contemporary American literature's more interesting characters.

Elkin's orphans, bachelors, and widows, his sufferers and comic whiners, pursue ideas of order at their peril. In the process, however, Elkin demonstrates as much elegance as grotesquerie, and he makes us see the human condition as simultaneously comic and precious.

—Sanford Pinsker

ELLISON, Ralph (Waldo)

Born: Oklahoma City, Oklahoma, 1 March 1914. **Education:** A high school in Oklahoma City, and at Tuskegee Institute, Alabama,

1933-36. **Military Service:** Served in the United States Merchant Marine, 1943-45. **Family:** Married Fanny McConnell in 1946. **Career:** Writer from 1936; lecturer, Salzburg Seminar in American Studies, 1954; instructor in Russian and American Literature, Bard College, Annandale-on-Hudson, New York, 1958-61; Alexander White Visiting Professor, University of Chicago, 1961; visiting professor of writing, Rutgers University, New Brunswick, New Jersey, 1962-64; Whittall Lecturer, Library of Congress, Washington, D.C., 1964; Ewing Lecturer, University of California, Los Angeles, 1964; visiting fellow in American studies, Yale University, New Haven, Connecticut, 1966; Albert Schweitzer Professor in the Humanities, New York University, 1970-79; now emeritus. Chairman, Literary Grants Committee, American Academy, 1964-67; member, National Council on the Arts, 1965-67; member, Carnegie Commission on Educational Television, 1966-67; member of the editorial board, *American Scholar,* Washington, D.C., 1966-69; honorary consultant in American Letters, Library of Congress, Washington, D.C., 1966-72. Trustee, John F. Kennedy Center of the Performing Arts, Washington, D.C., New School for Social Research, New York, Bennington College, Vermont, Educational Broadcasting Corporation, and Colonial Williamsburg Foundation. **Awards:** Rosenwald fellowship, 1945; National Book award, 1953; National Newspaper Publishers Association Russwarm award, 1953; American Academy Rome prize, 1955, 1956; United States Medal of Freedom, 1969; National Medal of Arts, 1985; Coordinating Council of Literary Magazines-General Electric Foundation award, 1988. Ph.D. in Humane Letters: Tuskegee Institute, 1963. Litt.D.: Rutgers University, 1966; University of Michigan, Ann Arbor, 1967; Williams College, Williamstown, Massachusetts, 1970; Long Island University, New York, 1971; College of William and Mary, Williamsburg, Virginia, 1972; Wake Forest College, Winston-Salem, North Carolina, 1974; Harvard University, Cambridge, Massachusetts, 1974. L.H.D.: Grinnell College, Iowa, 1967; Adelphi University, Garden City, New York, 1971; University of Maryland, College Park, 1974. Commandant, Order of Arts and Letters (France), 1970. **Member:** American Academy, 1975. **Died:** 16 April 1994.

PUBLICATIONS

Novels

Invisible Man. 1952.
Juneteenth. 1999.

Other

The Writer's Experience, with Karl Shapiro. 1964.
Shadow and Act (essays). 1964.
The City in Crisis, with Whitney M. Young and Herbert Gnas. 1968.
Going to the Territory (essays). 1986.

*

Bibliography: "A Bibliography of Ellison's Published Writings" by Bernard Benoit and Michel Fabre, in *Studies in Black Literature* (Fredericksburg, Virginia), autumn 1971; *The Blinking Eye: Ellison and His American, French, German and Italian Critics 1952-1971* by Jacqueline Covo, 1974.

Critical Studies: *The Negro Novel in America,* revised edition, by Robert A. Bone, 1958; "The Blues as a Literary Theme" by Gene Bluestein, in *Massachusetts Review* (Amherst), autumn 1967; *Five Black Writers: Essays* by Donald B. Gibson, 1970; *Twentieth-Century Interpretations of Invisible Man* edited by John M. Reilly, 1970; "Ellison Issue" of *CLA Journal* (Baltimore), March 1970; interview in *Atlantic* (Boston), December 1970; *The Merrill Studies in Invisible Man* edited by Ronald Gottesman, 1971; *Ellison: A Collection of Critical Essays* edited by John Hersey, 1973; article by Leonard J. Deutsch, in *American Novelists since World War II* edited by Jeffrey Heltermann and Richard Layman, 1978; *Folklore and Myth in Ellison's Early Works* by Dorothea Fischer-Hornung, 1979; *The Craft of Ellison,* 1980, and "The Rules of Magic: Hemingway as Ellison's 'Ancestor,'" in *Southern Review* (Baton Rouge, Louisiana), summer 1985, both by Robert G. O'Meally, and *New Essays on Invisible Man* edited by O'Meally, 1988; *Ellison: The Genesis of an Artist* by Rudolf F. Dietze, 1982; introduction by the author to 30th anniversary edition of *Invisible Man,* 1982; "Ellison and Dostoevsky" by Joseph Frank, in *New Criterion* (New York), September 1983; *Speaking for You: The Vision of Ellison* edited by Kimberly W. Benston, 1987; *Invisible Criticism: Ellison and the American Canon* by Alan Nadel, 1988; *Creative Revolt: A Study of Wright, Ellison, and Dostoevsky* by Michael F. Lynch, 1990; *Visible Ellison: A Study of Ralph Ellison's Fiction* by Edith Schor, 1993; *Deprogramming through Cultural Nationalism: Achebe and Ellison* by Prema Kumari Dheram, 1994; *Commitment as a Theme in African American Literature: A Study of James Baldwin and Ralph Ellison* by R. Jothiprakash, 1994; "On Burke and the Vernacular: Ralph Ellison's Boomerang of History" by Robert G. O'Meally, in *History and Memory in African-American Culture,* edited by Genevieve Fabre and Robert O'Meally, 1994; " The Politics of Carnival and Heteroglossia in Toni Morrison's *Song of Solomon* and Ralph Ellison's *Invisible Man*" by Elliott Butler-Evans, in *The Ethnic Canon: Histories, Institutions, and Interventions,* edited by David Palumbo Liu, 1995; *Conversations with Ralph Ellison,* edited by Maryemma Graham, 1995; *On Racial Frontiers: The New Culture of Frederick Douglas, Ralph Ellison, and Bob Marley* by Gregory Stephens, 1999.

*   *   *

A bookish as well as a musical child, Ralph Ellison began to read some of the classics of modern literature, including *The Waste Land,* while a student at Tuskegee. His literary education was accelerated after he met **Richard Wright** in 1937. In addition to providing an example of commitment to social and racial justice, Wright helped to persuade Ellison to direct his creative energies to writing, encouraging him to turn to "those works in which writing was discussed as a craft . . . to **Henry James**' prefaces, to Conrad, to Joseph Warren Beach and to the letters of Dostoievsky" (*Shadow and Act*). Despite some later disavowals, Ellison was deeply influenced by Wright's own fiction as well as by his literary tutelage. Such early short stories as "Slick Gonna Learn" and "Mister Toussan," for example, reveal how carefully Ellison had read Wright's *Uncle Tom's Children.*

When one looks at *Invisible Man,* however, one sees that Ellison's creative consciousness encompasses a vast range of the world's literature. Such modern giants as **Eliot,** Joyce, Malraux, **Hemingway, Pound, Stein,** and **Faulkner** are clearly part of his literary inheritance, but so are the writers of the Harlem Renaissance; the Continental (especially Dostoevsky), British, and American (especially **Melville** and **Twain**) masters of 19th-century fiction; and his namesake **Emerson** and other Transcendentalists. Some critics have argued for *The Odyssey* or *The Aeneid* as major influences on Ellison's novel. However allusive, Ellison is also profoundly original, putting his sophisticated technique and literary education to the service of his vision of the racial and human condition in America.

Invisible Man concerns the quest of an unnamed young black man for personal identity and racial community as he travels from South to North, from innocence to experience, from self-deception to knowledge, from a spurious visibility to an existential invisibility. These journeys take place in the immediate context of the late Depression, but, as they unfold, their implications extend backward in time to the Reconstruction, slavery, and the founding of the Republic, and outward from the protagonist's self to the social situation of black America and to the very nature of the democratic experiment.

Framed by a prologue and an epilogue set in an underground chamber to which the protagonist has retreated from the chaos of life above ground, the narrative proper begins in the deep South with his initiation rite into the social order of white supremacy as he graduates from high school and prepares to matriculate at a black college closely resembling Tuskegee Institute, where he hopes to learn to become a black leader. There the idyllic setting and his personal ambition are disrupted by his naivety, by a northern white capitalist's ambiguous "philanthropy," and by the ruthless self-aggrandizement of Dr. Bledsoe, the black president of the institution. Expelled from college and from the South, the protagonist travels to New York to seek employment in a white-collar position. Unsuccessful in that effort, he undergoes a still more disastrous experience as an industrial worker in the Liberty Paint plant. After these repeated failures in his personal pursuit of success, the protagonist becomes involved with the Brotherhood, a radical political organization paralleling the Communist Party. Here, he hopes, he can achieve self-realization while contributing to social amelioration. But political radicalism fails him—and his race—just as completely as southern segregation and northern employment, and for similar reasons of personal and racial exploitation. When his very physical existence is threatened in a Harlem race riot, he goes underground for sanctuary and reassessment. Ending in the epilogue where it began in the prologue, the narrative completes its circular ("boomerang") structure. Whatever one thinks of the rather forced optimism concerning a possible resurrection and return to the world above ground, the success of which may be viewed as problematical given his repeated rebuffs, the protagonist has at last and at least achieved for himself and for the reader the kind of self-actualization that knowledge of self and society can bring. To that extent he is no longer an invisible man.

Shadow and Act is a prose miscellany deriving some unity from its tripartite arrangement: "The Seer and the Seen"—topics in literature (especially his own career) and folklore; "Sound and the Mainstream"—topics in music, especially the blues and jazz; and "The Shadow and the Act"—black American social and cultural conditions in the context of national patterns. This organization emphasizes the lifelong interests of the author: books, music, and race.

Ellison's long second novel on religion and politics, published excerpts from which indicate high quality, has been in progress for three decades. It is clear that Ellison's reputation as a novelist will rest not on an ample *oeuvre* but on the brilliance, verbal dexterity, and mythic and social dimensions of one or two books.

—Keneth Kinnamon

EMERSON, Ralph Waldo

Born: Boston, Massachusetts, 25 May 1803. **Education:** Boston Latin School; Harvard University, Cambridge, Massachusetts (class poet), A.B. 1821; Harvard Divinity School. **Family:** Married 1) Ellen Louisa Tucker in 1829 (died 1831); 2) Lydian Jackson in 1835, two sons and two daughters. **Career:** Schoolmaster in 1820s; assistant pastor, then pastor, Old Second Church (Unitarian), Boston, 1829-32 (resigned); visited Europe, 1832-33; lyceum lecturer after 1833; moved to Concord, Massachusetts, 1834; a leader of the Transcendental Club from 1836, and contributor to the club's periodical *The Dial*, 1840-44 (editor, 1842-44); lectured in England, 1847-48; active abolitionist in 1850s. **Award:** LL.D.: Harvard University, 1866. **Died:** 27 April 1882.

Publications

Collections

Complete Works. 12 vols., 1883-93; edited by Edward Waldo Emerson, 12 vols., 1903-04.
Letters, edited by Ralph L. Rusk. 6 vols., 1939.
Collected Works, edited by Alfred R. Ferguson. 1971—.
Essays and Lectures (Library of America), edited by Joel Porte. 1983.
The Complete Sermons of Ralph Waldo Emerson, edited by Ronald A. Bosco. 3 vols., 1991.
Collected Poems and Translations, edited by Harold Bloom and Paul Kane. 1994.

Poetry

Poems. 1847.
Selected Poems. 1876.
The Concord Hymn and Other Poems. 1996.

Other

Nature. 1836.
Essays. 1841; revised edition, as *Essays: First Series,* 1847; Second Series, 1844; revised edition, 1850.
The Young American. 1844.
Nature: An Essay, and Lectures of the Times. 1844.
Orations, Lectures, and Addresses. 1844.
Nature: Addresses and Lectures. 1849.
Representative Men: Seven Lectures. 1850.
English Traits. 1856.
The Conduct of Life. 1860.
Complete Works. 2 vols., 1866.
May-Day and Other Pieces. 1867.
Prose Works. 3 vols., 1868-78(?).
Society and Solitude. 1870.
Letters and Social Aims. 1876.

The Preacher. 1880.
The Correspondence of Carlyle and Emerson 1834-1872, edited by Charles Eliot Norton. 2 vols., 1883; supplement, 1886; edited by Joseph Slater, 1964.
The Senses and the Soul, and Moral Sentiment in Religion: Two Essays. 1884.
Two Unpublished Essays: The Character of Socrates, The Present State of Ethical Philosophy. 1896.
Journals 1820-76, edited by Edward Waldo Emerson and Waldo Emerson Forbes. 10 vols., 1909-14.
Uncollected Writings, edited by Charles C. Bigelow. 1912.
Uncollected Lectures, edited by Clarence Gohdes. 1932.
Young Emerson Speaks: Unpublished Discourses on Many Subjects, edited by Arthur Cushman McGiffert, Jr. 1938.
The Portable Emerson, edited by Mark Van Doren. 1946; revised edition, edited by Carl Bode and Malcolm Cowley, 1981.
Selections, edited by Stephen E. Whicher. 1957.
Early Lectures, edited by Stephen E. Whicher, Robert E. Spiller, and Wallace E. Williams. 3 vols., 1959-72.
Journals and Miscellaneous Notebooks, edited by William H. Gilman and Ralph H. Orth. 16 vols., 1960-83; selection, as *Emerson in His Journals,* edited by Joel Porte, 1982.
Literary Criticism, edited by Eric W. Carlson. 1979.
Selected Essays, edited by Larzer Ziff. 1982.
Poetry Notebooks, edited by Ralph H. Orth and others. 1985.
The Selected Letters of Ralph Waldo Emerson, 1803-1882. 1997.

Editor, *Essays and Poems,* by Jones Very. 1839.
Editor, with James Freeman Clarke and W.H. Channing, *Memoirs of Margaret Fuller Ossoli.* 2 vols., 1852.
Editor, *Excursions,* by Henry David Thoreau. 1863.
Editor, *Letters to Various Persons,* by Henry David Thoreau. 1865.
Editor, *Parnassus* (poetry anthology). 1875.

Translator, *Vita Nuova,* by Dante, edited by J. Chesley Mathews. 1960.

*

Bibliography: *Emerson and the Critics: A Checklist of Criticism 1900-1977* by Jeanetta Boswell, 1979; *Emerson: A Descriptive Bibliography* by Joel Myerson, 1982, and *Emerson: An Annotated Secondary Bibliography* by Myerson and Robert E. Burkholder, 1985; *Ralph Waldo Emerson: An Annotated Bibliography of Criticism, 1980-1991* by Robert E. Burkholder, 1994.

Critical Studies: *The Life of Emerson* by Ralph L. Rusk, 1949; *Spires of Form: A Study of Emerson's Aesthetic Theory* by Vivian C. Hopkins, 1951; *Emerson's Angle of Vision: Man and Nature in American Experience* by Sherman Paul, 1952; *Emerson Handbook* by Frederic I. Carpenter, 1953; *Freedom and Fate: An Inner Life of Emerson* by Stephen E. Whicher, 1953, *Emerson: A Collection of Critical Essays* edited by Whicher and Milton R. Konvitz, 1962, and *The Recognition of Emerson: Selected Criticism since 1837* edited by Konvitz, 1972; *Emerson and Thoreau: Transcendentalists in Conflict,* 1966, and *Representative Man: Emerson in His Time,* 1979, both by Joel Porte, and *Emerson: Prospect and Retrospect* edited by Porte, 1982; *Emerson among His Contemporaries* edited by Kenneth Walter Cameron, 1967; *Emerson: A Portrait* edited by Carl Bode, 1968; *Emerson's Nature: Origin, Growth, Meaning* edited by Merton M. Sealts, Jr., and Alfred R. Ferguson,

1969, revised edition, edited by Sealts, 1979; *Emerson: Portrait of a Balanced Soul* by Edward Wagenknecht, 1974; *Emerson as Poet* by Hyatt H. Waggoner, 1974; *Emerson: Prophecy, Metamorphosis, and Influence* edited by David Levin, 1975; *The Slender Human Word: Emerson's Artistry in Prose* by William J. Scheik, 1978; *Emerson and Literary Change* by David Porter, 1978; *Emerson and the Orphic Poet in America* by R.A. Yoder, 1978; *Emerson: An Interpretive Essay* by Lewis Leary, 1980; *The Trans-Parent: Sexual Politics in the Language of Emerson* by Eric Cheyfitz, 1981; *Emerson: A Biography* by Gay Wilson Allen, 1981; *Emerson's Fall: A New Interpretation of the Major Essays* by B.L. Packer, 1982; *Emerson, Whitman, and the American Muse* by Jerome Loving, 1982; *Emerson* by Donald Yannella, 1982; *Apostle of Culture: Emerson as Preacher and Lecturer* by David Robinson, 1982; *Emerson Centenary Essays* edited by Joel Myerson, 1982, *Critical Essays on Emerson* edited by Myerson and Robert E. Burkholder, 1983, and *Emerson and Thoreau: The Contemporary Reviews* edited by Myerson, 1992; *Emerson's Romantic Style* by Julie Ellison, 1984; *Emerson: Days of Encounter* by John J. McAleer, 1984; *Transcendentalist Hermeneutics: Institutional Authority and the Higher Criticism of the Bible* by Richard A. Grusin, 1991; *Philosophical Passages: Wittgenstein, Emerson, Austin, Derrida* by Stanley Cavell, 1995; *Emerson in His Sermons: A Man-Made Self* by Susan L. Roberson, 1995; *Sublime Thoughts/Penny Wisdom: Situating Emerson and Thoreau in the American Market* by Richard E. Teichgraeber, 1995; *Emerson: The Mind on Fire: A Biography* by Robert D. Richardson, 1995; *Ralph Waldo Emerson: Preacher and Lecturer* by Earl Lloyd Rohler, 1995; *Emerson among the Eccentrics: A Group Portrait* by Carlos Baker, 1996; *The Emerson Effect: Individualism and Submission in America* by Christopher Newfield, 1996; *Emerson and Power: Creative Antagonism in the Nineteenth Century* by Michael Lopez, 1996; *The Romance of Desire: Emerson's Commitment to Incompletion* by Susan L. Field, 1997; *Emerson's Sublime Science* by Eric Wilson, 1998; *Masters of Repetition: Poetry, Culture and Work in Thomson, Wordsworth, Shelley, and Emerson* by Lisa M. Steinman, 1998.

*   *   *

Ralph Waldo Emerson was the most distinguished of the New England Transcendentalists and one of the most brilliant American poets and thinkers of the nineteenth century. Although Transcendentalism as a mode of Romantic thought has been largely discredited by modern scientific theory, Emerson's essays and poems remain remarkably provocative—and much more tough-minded than they have frequently been given credit for being.

Emerson was not a highly systematic philosopher. His thought was an amalgam from a wide variety of sources: 1) New England religious thought and related English writings of the seventeenth and eighteenth centuries; 2) Scottish realism, which he absorbed principally while at Harvard; 3) French and English skepticism, the lasting effects of which should not be underestimated; 4) Neo-Platonism, the dominant element in his thought, especially as it was interpreted by the English Romantic poets and the German and French Idealists; 5) Oriental mystical writings, even though he never accepted their fatalism or their concept of transmigration; 6) Yankee pragmatism, which was latent in almost all of his work and which muted his Romantic Idealism, especially in his essays on political and economic affairs. In Coleridge's explanation of Platonic dualism Emerson found the ordering principle for these disparate strands of thought. The discovery of Coleridge's distinction between the Reason and the Understanding brought such a surge of confidence in him that it is hardly an exaggeration to say that it transformed Emerson's life. Certainly it transformed his thinking.

Within one great Unity, he came to believe, there are two levels of reality, the supernatural and the natural. The supernatural is essence, spirit, or Oversoul as Emerson most frequently called it. It is an impersonal force that is eternal, moral, harmonious, and beneficent in tendency. The individual soul is a part of the Oversoul, and man has access to it through his intuition (which like Coleridge Emerson called the Reason, thereby confusing his readers then and now). One of the tendencies of the Oversoul is to express itself in form, hence the world of nature as an emanation of the world of spirit. The individual has access to this secondary level of reality through the senses and the understanding (the rational faculty). To explain the relation between the spiritual and physical levels of being, Emerson used such oppositions as One and Many, cause and effect, unity and diversity, object and symbol, reality and appearance, truth and hypothesis, being and becoming. Since laws of correspondence relate the two levels of being, the study of physical laws can generate intuitions of spiritual truths. What especially delighted Emerson about this dualism was that it allowed him to entertain both faith and doubt: to accept the promptings of the intuition without question and yet to view the hypotheses of the understanding as only tentative and hence constantly open to question.

In his earlier essays, Emerson particularly stressed the unlimited potential of the individual. The most notable of these, *Nature,* argues that, although nature serves as commodity, beauty, language, and discipline, its most important function is to excite the intuition so that the individual, through a mystical experience, becomes aware of the power of the Oversoul residing within him. "Nature always speaks of Spirit. It suggests the absolute." "The American Scholar" (1837) warns that books and scholarship can divert one from seeking the spiritual power within, and the "Divinity School Address" (1838) suggests that historical Christianity can do the same. "Self Reliance" (1844), in metaphor after metaphor, challenges the reader to seek the truths of the Reason: "Trust thyself; every heart vibrates to that iron string." In many respects "Self Reliance" is the capstone of American Romanticism. Later essays are more guarded in announcing the individual's limitless potential. In "Experience" (1844), for example, Emerson admits that such this-world elements as health, temperament, and illusion can prevent one from exploiting all of the vast possibilities asserted in *Nature.* The enormous confidence of his earlier essays dwindles to "Patience and Patience, we shall win at last."

On subjects of public interest, Emerson's philosophical liberalism had to contend with his pragmatism. At most he was a cautious liberal. The Democrats, he thought, had the better causes, the Whigs the better men. Following Adam Smith, he believed that "affairs themselves show the best way they should be handled." So he was for *laissez-faire* and free trade, though he was more of an agrarian than Smith. Of the followers of Smith he rejected the utilitarians and the pessimists, and approved of only the optimists, particularly such members of the American school as Daniel Raymond, A.H. Everett, and Henry C. Carey. Emerson had nothing against wealth *per se,* but was against rule by the wealthy because the wealthy were too likely to be nothing more than materialists, persons without intuitive insight. Rule by an upper class, however, was agreeable to him so long as the upper class consisted of persons wise, temperate, and cultivated; persons with the insight and courage necessary to protect the poor and weak against the predatory. Clearly his thinking did not drift far in the direction of Marxism. Nor was he willing to admit that the socialistic experiments of Owen and Fourier, though he admired their objectives, had the magic key to Utopia. Even the Transcendental experiments at Fruitlands and Brook Farm he believed impractical. Bereft of their romance, he said, they were projects that well might make their participants less intuitive and self-reliant rather than more so. Of the other major reforms of his day, Emerson lectured only in favor of child labor legislation, a public land policy, and the abolition of slavery. The passage of the Fugitive Slave Bill in 1850 made him as angry as he probably ever became on a public issue. More practical than most abolitionists, however, he argued that slavery was basically an economic matter, and that if the Northern church people really wanted to emancipate the slaves they should sell their church silver, buy up the slaves, and themselves set them free. He saw the Civil War not only as necessary for liberating the slave but "a hope for the liberation of American culture."

Emerson's aesthetic theory, to the extent that he had one, is a direct outgrowth of his Idealistic philosophy. As he conceived of it, the great work of art is not an imitation of nature but a symbolization of Truth realized intuitively. It is the result of resigning oneself to the "divine *aura* which breathes through forms." In his most quoted statement on the subject he put it this way: "It is not metres, but a metre-making argument that makes a poem—a thought so passionate and alive that like the spirit of a plant or animal it has an architecture of its own, and adorns nature with a new thing." Thus the poet (or any great artist) must first of all be the Seer, intuitively experiencing the absolutes of the Oversoul, and secondly the Sayer, communicating those absolutes so compellingly that readers are stimulated to have intuitions of their own. Emerson was realistic enough to realize that such a process is not easy. Intuitions fade quickly. And words, being but symbols of symbols, are inadequate even at best to convey them. The most that a writer can do is to suggest his intuitions by a series of half-truths. The greatest writing, therefore, must be provocative, not descriptive or explanatory. Such a conviction lies behind Emerson's epigrammatic prose style and the liberties he takes with poetic conventions.

There is a good reason for considering Emerson as primarily a poet, even though one must go to his journals and essays to realize the fullness of his thought. His concentration on the concrete image, the simplicity of his symbols and words, and his willingness, within limits, to let form follow function were practices that profoundly influenced such widely divergent followers as **Whitman** and **Dickinson**, and through them much of modern poetry. Many of Emerson's best-known poems, such as "Concord Hymn" and "The Snow Storm," celebrate local events. But his more notable ones give expression to elements of his philosophy. Through the voice of the cosmic force, "Brahma" suggests the enclosure of all diversity in the one great Unity; so does "Each and All" in which the beauty and meaning of "each" is seen to be dependent upon its context, or the "all." "The Problem" contrasts the unlimited freedom of the poet's imagination with the stultifying routine of the "cowed churchman." Perhaps Emerson's most poignant poem is "Threnody," written in two periods after the death of his young son Waldo. The first part, composed immediately after Waldo's death, describes the poet's disillusionment with nature, indeed with the cosmic scheme, which he had spent so many years celebrating. The second part, written several years

later, asserts his resurgent confidence. **Nathaniel Hawthorne** probably spoke for some modern readers when he said that he "admired Emerson as a poet of deep beauty and austere tenderness, but sought nothing from him as a philosopher." Yet his philosophy cannot be dismissed so summarily. It resulted in a freedom of spirit, a respect for the individual human being, a sense of awe and wonder before the inexplicable that many modern readers still find stirring and reassuring.

—John C. Gerber

See the essay on *Nature.*

ERDRICH, (Karen) Louise

Pseudonyms: Heidi Louise (with her sister Heidi) and Milou North (with husband, Michael Dorris). **Born:** Little Falls, Montana, 7 June 1954 (one source cites 6 July 1954). **Education:** Various schools in Wahpeton, North Dakota, 1960-72; Dartmouth College, New Hampshire, 1972-76, B.A. in English, 1976; Johns Hopkins University, 1978-79, M.A. in English, 1979. **Family:** Married writer and professor Michael Anthony Dorris, *q.v.,* in 1981 (committed suicide 1997); seven children. **Career:** Worked as waitress, psychiatric aide, lifeguard, and writing contest judge; North Dakota State Arts Council, visiting poet and teacher, 1977-78; Johns Hopkins University, Baltimore, Maryland, writing instructor, 1978-79; Boston Indian Council, Boston, Massachusetts, communications director and editor of *Circle,* 1979-80; Charles Merrill Co., textbook writer, 1980; writer of poetry, prose, and fiction. **Awards:** Fellowships from Johns Hopkins University in 1979, MacDowell Colony in 1980, Yaddo Colony in 1981, and Dartmouth College in 1981; first prize in *Chicago* magazine's Nelson Algren fiction competition, 1982; Pushcart prize, 1983; National Magazine Fiction awards, 1983, 1987; National Book Critics Circle award for best work of fiction, 1984; Virginia McCormick Scully prize for best book of the year, 1984; *Los Angeles Times* award for best novel; best first fiction award from the American Academy and Institute of Arts and Letters, 1985; Sue Kaufman prize, 1985; *New York Times Book Review* "best eleven books of 1985" citation; Guggenheim fellowship, 1985-86; *Publishers Weekly*'s best books citation, 1986; O. Henry award first prize, 1987. **Member:** Enrolled as a member of the Turtle Mountain Band of Ojibwa in Belcourt, North Dakota; International Writers. **Residence:** Hanover, New Hampshire.

PUBLICATIONS

Novels

Love Medicine. 1984; expanded edition, 1993.
The Beet Queen. 1986.
Tracks. 1988.
The Crown of Columbus, with Michael Dorris. 1991.
The Bingo Palace. 1994.
The Blue Jay's Dance: A Birth Year. 1995.
Tales of Burning Love. 1996.
Grandmother's Pigeon. 1996.
The Antelope Wife. 1998.

Poetry

Jacklight. 1984.
Baptism of Desire. 1989.

Other

Imagination (textbook). 1980.
Conversations with Louise Erdrich and Michael Dorris. 1994.
The Birchbark House (for children). 1999.

Editor, *The Best American Short Stories., 1993.* 1993.

*

Bibliography: *American Indian Literatures: An Introduction, Bibliographic Review, and Selected Bibliography* by A. LaVonne Brown Ruoff, 1990.

Critical Studies: "Reading between Worlds: Narrativity in the Fiction of Louise Erdrich" by Catherine Rainwater in *American Literature* vol. 62, no. 3, 1990; "Transformation and Continuance: Native American Tradition in the Novels of Louise Erdrich" by Debra C. Holt in *Entering the 90s: The North American Experience,* 1991; "Toward a Native American 'Realism': The Amphibious Fiction of Louise Erdrich" by Hans Bak in *Neo-Realism in Contemporary American Fiction,* 1992; *Conversations with Louise Erdrich and Michael Dorris* edited by Allan Chavkin and Nancy Feyl Chavkin, 1994; "Erdrich's *Love Medicine*" by Jeanne-Marie Zeck, in *The Explicator,* fall 1995, pp. 58-60; "Storytelling: Tradition and Preservation in Louise Erdrich's *Tracks*" by Jennifer Sergi, in *World Literature Today,* spring 1995, pp. 279-82; *Louise Erdrich: A Critical Companion* by Lorena Laura Stookey, 1999; *A Reader's Guide to the Novels of Louise Erdrich* by Peter G. Beidler, 1999.

*   *   *

One of the most prolific and widely respected Native American writers, Louise Erdrich shows her Chippewa and German-American heritage in her poetry, prose, and fiction. Her first novel, *Love Medicine*, published when she was only twenty-nine, won both the National Book Critics Circle Award and the Virginia McCormick Scully Prize as the best book of 1984. It also won the award for best first fiction from the American Academy of Arts and Letters and the Sue Kaufman Prize and was listed as one of the best books of the year by the *New York Times Book Review*. *Love Medicine* was the first in what was to become a series of novels set in and around an imaginary North Dakota town and Indian reservation. Although the critical reception of Erdrich's subsequent fiction has not been quite so enthusiastic, it has nevertheless been highly favorable. *The Beet Queen* was named one of the best books of 1986 by *Publishers Weekly,* won first prize in the O. Henry Awards for 1987, and was nominated for a National Book Critics Circle Award. Her 1988 novel *Tracks* quickly became the subject of intense and warm critical scrutiny. Her two books of poetry, *Jacklight* and *Baptism of Desire*, have also earned praise but have drawn less critical attention. *The Crown of Columbus,* Erdrich's 1991 collaboration with her husband, Michael Dorris, is a story about Christopher Columbus's discovery of America as it pertained to Native Americans; the book received significant critical and popular attention.

Erdrich began her writing at an early age. Her father, a teacher for the Bureau of Indian Affairs schools, paid her a nickel for each story she wrote as a child, and her half-Chippewa mother wove covers for them—not a bad form of royalty and publication for one so young. The events in her life served to shape and influence her writing. She worked at a number of jobs—waitress, flagperson for a construction team, weeder in a beet farm, psychiatric aide in a hospital in Vermont, teacher of poetry in prisons, lifeguard, judge of writing contests—all of which gave depth, confidence, and compassion to her writing. At Dartmouth she took a course taught by Dorris, a part-Native American writer and anthropologist who had recently been hired to head the school's new Native American studies program. He encouraged her to get in touch with her Native American roots and helped her with her writing. They later married and became a supportive and productive husband-and-wife writing team. Their alliance continued until they separated in the late 1990s; Dorris subsequently committed suicide.

Love Medicine is the flagship of a series of novels about white and Indian families who live on and around an Indian reservation in the fictional town of Argus, North Dakota. The novel introduces characters and themes that continue to inform Erdrich's writing the way that the similarly fictional Winesburg, Ohio, did for **Sherwood Anderson** and Yoknapatawpha County, Mississippi, for **William Faulkner**. The characters in this little corner of the world cannot quite be said to make a microcosm of the larger world, but they do resonate with readers from all over the globe (*Love Medicine* has been translated into at least ten other languages). There is some question whether *Love Medicine* is less a novel than a collection of short stories unified by slender threads of character, setting, and theme, but how it is classified has little effect on the book's impact. Certainly one of its most impressive chapters is its first, "The World's Greatest Fishermen," an impressive achievement in its own right. Published separately before the larger *Love Medicine* was conceived, it won first prize in *Chicago* magazine's 1982 Nelson Algren fiction competition. It tells the haunting tale of a young woman who freezes to death. The woman's story forms one of many strong threads that serve to unify *Love Medicine*.

The Beet Queen, Erdrich's second novel, explores the white community of Argus. Beginning in 1932 the novel takes the reader to a time before most of the events in *Love Medicine*. Its central characters are white—Mary Adare, her brother Karl, and their cousin Sita—but their part-Chippewa friend Celestine is also important. The narrative ends some forty years later after Mary and Karl achieve whatever healing they are likely to achieve given their father's early death and their mother's dramatic flight. That flight is pure Erdrich. No one who reads the novel can ever forget the scene in which the widowed Adelaide impulsively boards the plane of the Great Omar, an airplane stunt artist, and flies away with him, leaving on the field behind her newborn daughter and older siblings Mary and Karl. A neighbor takes the baby, leaving the fourteen-year-old Karl and his eleven-year-old sister, Mary, to fend for themselves. They do so by jumping a boxcar for their own flight, and the novel opens when Karl and Mary show up in Argus to live with their Aunt Fritzi.

Tracks, published two years after *The Beet Queen*, goes back even further in time—to the period from 1912 to 1932—to the reservation and to the origins of some of the characters and many of the difficulties that surface in *Love Medicine*. Like the earlier two novels, *Tracks* also begins with cold and with the death or abandonment of a young woman. The young woman in this case is Fleur Pillager, the feverish, near-frozen seventeen-year-old survivor of an outbreak of tuberculosis that has killed the rest of her family. She is rescued by one of the novel's narrators, a Native American tribal leader named Nanapush, who nurses the young woman back to health. Fleur is eventually raped by three white poker players in Argus and later gives birth to a daughter named Lulu. The chapters are narrated alternately by Nanapush, who knows and believes in the old ways, and by Pauline, a half-breed woman who is torn between reservation life and the change that white civilization offers. In the novel Pauline also gives birth to a daughter, named Marie. Lulu and Marie both figure prominently in the events of *Love Medicine*. *Tracks* is a brilliant book—funny, serious, political, human, spare, moving.

Erdrich's poetry and the collaborative novel *The Crown of Columbus* are also brilliant in their own ways. The appeal of the verse is limited, but it is attractive to those appreciative of good poetry. *The Crown of Columbus*, which was designed to find a large audience and to capitalize on the interest in the quincentennial of Columbus's "discovery" of America and the Native American role in that event, seems, finally, temporary and topical. It has the earnestness of Erdrich's other fiction but not the haunted quality that keeps many readers coming back.

Erdrich's fourth novel set in Argus, *The Bingo Palace*, was published in 1994. It returns to the reservation and to some of the characters made familiar in *Love Medicine*. Her fifth novel, *Tales of Burning Love*, set mostly in Fargo, North Dakota, involves a part-Ojibwa contractor named Jack Mauser and his five wives, two of whom, June and Dot, are known to readers from their earlier appearance in *Love Medicine* and other novels. Her sixth novel, *The Antelope Wife*, takes the reader east to Minneapolis. It has no overlap with characters in earlier novels. This complex work treats the lives of a half-dozen generations of the descendants of a U.S. cavalry soldier and the surviving victims of his attack on an Indian village shortly after the Civil War. The main action of the novel, however, takes place in the 1980s and 1990s in contemporary Minneapolis. This action the reader sees through the recording consciousness of Cally Roy, who is related to most of the important characters in the novel. In addition to her work in fiction, Erdrich also contributed prefaces to her husband's award-winning nonfiction book *The Broken Cord* and author Desmond Hogan's *A Link with the River*.

Erdrich is likely to be an enduring voice in American fiction. She has the writing skills that enable her to capture in words the vividness of life. She speaks of common people in common language. She knows, apparently by instinct, when to describe details and when to leave them out. She has done what all writers dream but few accomplish: created a world of her own in which enough of the characters breathe that it does not matter others remain lifeless. She brings to American literature a timely and honest authenticity about the multiple cultures in the United States, moves easily in both the dominant and a minority culture, and knows how to write with both grace and force about what it is to be a woman in contemporary America.

—Peter G. Beidler

F

FARRELL, James T(homas)

Born: Chicago, Illinois, 27 February 1904. **Education:** St. Anselm Grammar School and St. Cyril High School, both Chicago; DePaul University, Chicago, 1924-25; University of Chicago, 1926-29; New York University, 1941. **Family:** Married 1) Dorothy Butler in 1931 (divorced); 2) Hortense Alden (divorced 1955), one son; 3) remarried Dorothy Butler in 1955 (separated 1958). **Career:** Clerk for an express company, Chicago, 1922-24; writer from 1930; lived in Paris, 1931-32; adjunct professor, St. Peter's College, Jersey City, New Jersey, 1964-65; writer-in-residence, Richmond College, Virginia, 1969-70, and Glassboro State College, New Jersey, 1973. Chairman, National Board, Workers Defense League. **Awards:** Guggenheim fellowship, 1936; Emerson-Thoreau Medal, 1979. D.Litt.: Miami University, Oxford, Ohio, 1968; Columbia College, Chicago, 1974. **Member:** American Academy, 1941. **Died:** 22 August 1979.

PUBLICATIONS

Collection

Chicago Stories, edited by Charles Fanning. 1998.

Fiction

Studs Lonigan (trilogy). 1935.
    Young Lonigan: A Boyhood in Chicago Streets. 1932.
    The Young Manhood of Studs Lonigan. 1934.
    Judgment Day. 1935.
Gas-House McGinty. 1933.
Calico Shoes and Other Stories. 1934; as *Seventeen and Other Stories,* 1959.
Guillotine Party and Other Stories. 1935.
Danny O'Neill pentalogy
    A World I Never Made. 1936.
    No Star Is Lost. 1938.
    Father and Son. 1940; as *A Father and His Son,* 1943.
    My Days of Anger. 1943.
    The Face of Time. 1953.
Can All This Grandeur Perish? and Other Stories. 1937.
The Short Stories. 1937; as *Fellow Countrymen: Collected Stories,* 1937.
Tommy Gallagher's Crusade. 1939.
Ellen Rogers. 1941.
$1000 a Week and Other Stories. 1942.
Fifteen Selected Stories. 1943.
To Whom It May Concern and Other Stories. 1944.
When Boyhood Dreams Come True. 1946.
More Fellow Countrymen. 1946.
Bernard Carr trilogy:
    Bernard Clare. 1946; as *Bernard Clayre,* 1948; as *Bernard Carr,* 1952.

    The Road Between. 1949.
    Yet Other Waters. 1952.
The Life Adventurous and Other Stories. 1947.
Yesterday's Love and Eleven Other Stories, edited by Donald A. Wollheim. 1948.
A Misunderstanding (story). 1949.
A Hell of a Good Time and Other Stories, edited by Donald A. Wollheim. 1950.
An American Dream Girl (stories). 1950.
This Man and This Woman. 1951.
French Girls Are Vicious and Other Stories. 1955.
An Omnibus of Short Stories. 1956.
A Dangerous Woman and Other Stories. 1957.
Saturday Night and Other Stories. 1958.
The Girls at the Sphinx (stories). 1959.
Looking 'em Over (stories). 1960.
Side Street and Other Stories. 1961.
Boarding House Blues. 1961.
Sound of a City. 1962.
A Universe of Time series:
    The Silence of History. 1963.
    What Time Collects. 1964.
    When Time Was Born. 1966.
    Lonely for the Future. 1966.
    A Brand New Life. 1968.
    Judith. 1969.
    Invisible Swords. 1971.
    Judith and Other Stories. 1973.
    The Dunne Family. 1976.
    The Death of Nora Ryan. 1978.
    Olive and Mary Anne (stories). 1978.
New Year's Eve/1929. 1967.
Childhood Is Not Forever and Other Stories. 1969.
Sam Holman. 1983.

Poetry

The Collected Poems. 1965.

Other

A Note on Literary Criticism. 1936.
The League of Frightened Philistines and Other Papers. 1945.
The Fate of Writing in America. 1946.
Literature and Morality. 1947.
The Name Is Fogarty: Private Papers on Public Matters. 1950.
Poet of the People: An Evaluation of James Whitcomb Riley, with Horace Gregory and Jeannette Covert Nolan. 1951.
Reflections at Fifty and Other Essays. 1954.
My Baseball Diary: A Famed Author Recalls the Wonderful World of Baseball, Yesterday and Today. 1957.
It Has Come to Pass (on Israel). 1958.
Dialogue with John Dewey, with others. 1959.
Selected Essays, edited by Luna Wolf. 1964.
Literary Essays 1954-1974, edited by Jack Alan Robbins. 1976.
On Irish Themes, edited by Dennis Flynn. 1982.
Hearing Out Farrell (lectures), edited by Donald Phelps. 1985.

Editor, *Prejudices: A Selection,* by H.L. Mencken. 1958.
Editor, *A Dreiser Reader.* 1962.

*

Bibliography: *A Bibliography of Farrell's Writings 1921-1957* by Edgar M. Branch, 1959, supplements in *American Book Collector 11,* 1961, *17,* 1967, and *26,* 1976.

Critical Studies: *Farrell* by Edgar M. Branch, 1971; *Farrell: The Revolutionary Socialist Years* by Alan M. Wald, 1978; *Death and Revery in Farrell's O'Neill-O'Flaherty Novels* by Charles Fanning, 1988; *A Paris Year: Dorothy and James T. Farrell, 1931-1932* by Edgar Marquess Branch, 1998.

*   *   *

The son and grandson of Irish Catholic working-class laborers, James T. Farrell was raised in a southside Chicago neighborhood that became the source for much of his remarkable body of work, which constitutes the greatest sustained production in twentieth-century America of uncompromisingly realistic fiction. Filling some fifty volumes, this corpus includes four large fictional cycles, three of which are further connected as progressive explorations of their main characters' varying responses to an urban ethnic environment similar to Farrell's. Published between 1932 and 1953, these three related groups are the Studs Lonigan trilogy, the O'Neill-O'Flaherty pentalogy, and the Bernard Carr trilogy.

Begun with Farrell's first novel, *Young Lonigan,* the first group traces the downward drift to death at twenty-nine of its weak-willed, misguided protagonist. A normally inquisitive boy, Studs shows signs of intelligence, even imagination, in early scenes. And yet he assumes the facile and corrupting "tough guy" values of the Chicago street-corner society to which he is drawn after graduation from eighth grade. As a partial explanation of the boy's failure of judgment, the trilogy chronicles the breakdown in the twentieth-century city of the previously directing institutions of family, school, and church, and Studs's origin in a well-fixed, middle-class family makes the indictment of urban "spiritual poverty" (Farrell's phrase) all the more severe. The result is a powerful narrative, terrifying in its seemingly inexorable progress to *Judgment Day,* an American tragedy in the Dreiserian mold.

In the O'Neill-O'Flaherty novels, Farrell uses his own family history much more directly. The main figure is Danny O'Neill, a slightly younger contemporary of Studs Lonigan who takes an opposite road—out of Chicago and toward understanding and control of his own life. More intelligent than Studs, Danny is driven by a persistent dream of accomplishment that crystallizes into the desire to be a writer. On the other hand, he also sometimes slips into aimless idling and drinking, and his economic and family situations are potentially dangerous to his normal development. The O'Neills are so poor that some of the children, including Danny, have had to be raised by his mother's parents, the O'Flahertys. This arrangement alienates Danny but provides the pentalogy with a large number of major characters, including his grandfather, Tom O'Flaherty, an aging immigrant teamster, fully evoked in *The Face of Time,* and his grandmother, an archetypal Irish-American matriarch, strong-willed and fiercely maternal, who dominates the early novels of the series. Danny's father, Jim O'Neill, works his way from teamster to shipping clerk, only to be dealt a cruel, decisive blow by a series of paralyzing strokes.

His hysterical, hyper-religious wife, Lizz, is no help to him, and in *Father and Son* Jim faces inutility, boredom, and approaching death—but with lonely courage and dignity that make him one of the most memorable characters in Farrell's fiction. Painful attempts at closeness between "father and son," Danny's high school graduation, and Jim's death bring the novel to its climax. In *My Days of Anger,* Danny begins to find his way, through attendance at the University of Chicago, great gulps of reading, and a final decision in 1927 to leave Chicago for New York and a writing career.

Instead of the tight, fatalistic narrative drive of the Lonigan trilogy, the five O'Neill-O'Flaherty novels are diffused and episodic; and in this looser structure is embodied a broader, more open and optimistic, but still unsentimentalized view of urban society. Moreover, in his complex creation of the interrelated lives of the O'Neills and O'Flahertys, Farrell has provided the most thoroughly realized immigrant-ethnic community in American literature.

The Bernard Carr trilogy, published between 1946 and 1952, continues the action of the O'Neill novels in dealing with the young manhood of a working-class Chicago Irishman with literary ambitions who has fled to New York in search of experience and perspective. His ambition is akin to that of Joyce's Stephen Dedalus, with whom Farrell's O'Neill/Carr figure has much in common. In these novels of education, Bernard Carr learns to reject the Catholic Church, his own naive appropriation of Nietzsche, and the Communist Party, all of which he comes to find as threatening to his artistic integrity. His emergence as a successful writer rounds out the Lonigan-O'Neill-Carr connected cycles. The Carr trilogy lacks the rootedness in place and community of the previous Chicago-based novels, but it compensates by providing a vivid rendering of the lives of New York left-wing intellectuals in the 1930s, with particular attention given to their passionate engagement with the question of the relationship between the artist and society.

In addition to his large cycles and a few isolated novels, Farrell published about 250 short stories and novelettes, in which his presentation of twentieth-century life became even more inclusive. Many stories concern the protagonists of his novels (there are fifty about Danny O'Neill alone); others place new characters in familiar Chicago or New York settings, and still others are set in Europe, especially Paris. True to Farrell's realistic aesthetic, the stories are strong on character revelation and spurn machinations of plot.

Farrell's critical writings also fill several volumes; these contain useful explanations of the relationship between his life and his work, appreciations of writers who have been important to him, including **Theodore Dreiser**, James Joyce, and **Sherwood Anderson**, and declarations of his position as a realist who writes "as part of an attempt to explore the nature of experience."

In 1963 Farrell published *The Silence of History,* his sixteenth novel, and the first of *A Universe of Time,* his fourth fictional cycle, which, in his heroic projection, would have run to thirty volumes. Integrated by the central recurrent character of Eddie Ryan, another Chicago writer, born, like his creator, in 1904, the *Universe* cycle embodies a reassessment of Farrell's life-long concern with the experience of the artist in the modern world, as well as a continuation of the "lifework" that he defined, in an introduction to the new cycle's sixth unit, *Judith,* as "a panoramic story of our days and years, a story which would continue through as many books as I would be able to write."

Farrell was first and foremost an American realist: fiercely and scrupulously honest, immune to sentimentality, and, in the earlier novels especially, pioneering in his commitment to giving serious literary consideration to the common life in an urban-immigrant-ethnic community. In his later fiction he often went beyond Chicago and the Irish to explore more widely his most important themes—the possibilities in modern life for self-knowledge, growth, and creativity. Farrell died in 1979, leaving much fiction in manuscript. His first posthumously published work, *Sam Holman,* is a novel of New York intellectual life in the 1930s.

Farrell's great strengths as a novelist are his development of convincing characters, the firm placement of these characters in a detailed, realistic urban setting, and the ability to conceive and carry through monumental fictional cycles. In addition, he perfected an urban American plain style, an appropriate mode for registering the self-consciousness of ordinary people living relatively uneventful lives. In his best work, a hard-won, minimal eloquence emerges from the convincingly registered thoughts of such characters as Jim O'Neill and Old Tom O'Flaherty. Farrell achieved what he declared to be "my constant and major aim as a writer—to write so that life may speak for itself." In this vein, his fullest and most compassionate creation remains Chicago's Irish Catholic South Side, which emerges in his fiction as a realized world, as whole and coherent as **William Faulkner**'s Mississippi.

—Charles Fanning

FAULKNER, William

Born: William Cuthbert Falkner in New Albany, Mississippi, 25 September 1897; moved with his family to Oxford, Mississippi, 1902. **Education:** Local schools in Oxford; University of Mississippi, Oxford, 1919-20. **Military Service:** Served in the Royal Canadian Air Force, 1918. **Family:** Married Estelle Oldham Franklin in 1929; two daughters. **Career:** Bookkeeper in bank, 1916-18; worked in Doubleday Bookshop, New York, 1921; postmaster, University of Mississippi Post Office, 1921-24; lived in New Orleans and contributed to New Orleans *Times-Picayune,* 1925; traveled in Europe, 1925-26; returned to Oxford, 1927; thereafter a full-time writer; screenwriter for Metro-Goldwyn-Mayer, 1932-33, Twentieth Century-Fox, 1935-37, and Warner Brothers, 1942-45. Writer-in-residence, University of Virginia, Charlottesville, 1957, and part of each year, 1958-62. **Awards:** O. Henry award, 1939, 1949; Nobel prize for literature, 1950; American Academy Howells Medal, 1950; National Book award, 1951, 1955; Pulitzer prize, 1955, 1963; American Academy of Arts and Letters Gold Medal, 1962. **Member:** Nation Letters, 1939; American Academy, 1948. **Died:** 6 July 1962.

PUBLICATIONS

Collections

The Portable Faulkner, edited by Malcolm Cowley. 1946; revised edition, 1967.
The Faulkner Reader, edited by Saxe Commins. 1954.
Novels 1930-1935 (Library of America), edited by Joseph Blotner and Noel Polk. 1985.
Novels 1936-1940 (Library of America), edited by Joseph Blotner. 1990.

Collected Stories. 1995.
Novels 1957-1962 (Library of America). 1999.

Short Stories

These 13: Stories. 1931.
Doctor Martino and Other Stories. 1934.
Go Down, Moses, and Other Stories. 1942.
Knight's Gambit. 1949.
Collected Stories. 1950.
Big Woods. 1955.
Jealousy and Episode: Two Stories. 1955.
Uncle Willy and Other Stories. 1958.
Selected Short Stories. 1961.
Barn Burning and Other Stories. 1977.
Uncollected Stories, edited by Joseph Blotner. 1979.

Novels

Soldiers' Pay. 1926.
Mosquitoes. 1927.
Sartoris. 1929; original version, as *Flags in the Dust,* edited by Douglas Day, 1973.
The Sound and the Fury. 1929.
As I Lay Dying. 1930.
Sanctuary. 1931.
Idyll in the Desert. 1931.
Light in August. 1932.
Miss Zilphia Gant. 1932.
Pylon. 1935.
Absalom, Absalom! 1936.
The Unvanquished. 1938.
The Wild Palms (includes *Old Man*). 1939.
The Hamlet. 1940; excerpt, as *The Long Hot Summer,* 1958.
Intruder in the Dust. 1948.
Notes on a Horsethief. 1950.
Requiem for a Nun. 1951.
A Fable. 1954.
Faulkner County. 1955.
The Town. 1957.
The Mansion. 1959.
The Reivers: A Reminiscence. 1962.
Father Abraham, edited by James B. Meriwether. 1984.

Plays

The Marionettes (produced 1920). 1975; edited by Noel Polk, 1977.
Requiem for a Nun (produced 1957). 1951.
The Big Sleep, with Leigh Brackett and Jules Furthman, in *Film Scripts One,* edited by George P. Garrett, O.B. Harrison, Jr., and Jane Gelfmann. 1971.
To Have and Have Not (screenplay), with Jules Furthman. 1980.
The Road to Glory (screenplay), with Joel Sayre. 1981.
Faulkner's MGM Screenplays, edited by Bruce F. Kawin. 1983.
The DeGaulle Story (unproduced screenplay), edited by Louis Daniel Brodsky and Robert W. Hamblin. 1984.
Battle Cry (unproduced screenplay), edited by Louis Daniel Brodsky and Robert W. Hamblin. 1985.
Stallion Road: A Screenplay, edited by Louis Daniel Brodsky and Robert W. Hamblin. 1989.

Screenplays: *Today We Live,* with Edith Fitzgerald and Dwight Taylor, 1933; *The Road to Glory,* with Joel Sayre, 1936; *Slave Ship,* with others, 1937; *Air Force* (uncredited), with Dudley Nichols, 1943; *To Have and Have Not,* with Jules Furthman, 1945; *The Big Sleep,* with Leigh Brackett and Jules Furthman, 1946; *Land of the Pharaohs,* with Harry Kurnitz and Harold Jack Bloom, 1955.

Television Play: *The Graduation Dress,* with Joan Williams, 1960.

Poetry

The Marble Faun. 1924.
Salmagundi (includes prose), edited by Paul Romaine. 1932.
This Earth. 1932.
A Green Bough. 1933.
Mississippi Poems. 1979.
Helen: A Courtship, and *Mississippi Poems.* 1981.
Vision in Spring. 1984.

Other

Mirrors of Chartres Street. 1953.
New Orleans Sketches, edited by Ichiro Nishizaki, 1955; revised edition, edited by Carvel Collins, 1958.
On Truth and Freedom. 1955(?).
Faulkner at Nagano (interview), edited by Robert A. Jelliffe. 1956.
Faulkner in the University (interviews), edited by Frederick L. Gwynn and Joseph Blotner. 1959.
University Pieces, edited by Carvel Collins. 1962.
Early Prose and Poetry, edited by Carvel Collins. 1962.
Faulkner at West Point (interviews), edited by Joseph L. Fant and Robert Ashley. 1964.
The Faulkner-Cowley File: Letters and Memories 1944-1962, with Malcolm Cowley. 1966.
Essays, Speeches, and Public Letters, edited by James B. Meriwether. 1966.
The Wishing Tree (for children). 1967.
Lion in the Garden: Interviews with Faulkner 1926-1962, edited by James B. Meriwether and Michael Millgate. 1968.
Selected Letters, edited by Joseph Blotner. 1977.
Mayday. 1978.
Letters, edited by Louis Daniel Brodsky and Robert W. Hamblin. 1984.
Sherwood Anderson and Other Famous Creoles. 1986.
Thinking of Home (letters), edited by James G. Watson. 1992.
Conversations with William Faulkner. 1999.

*

Bibliography: *The Literary Career of Faulkner: A Bibliographical Study* by James B. Meriwether, 1961; *Faulkner: A Reference Guide* by Thomas L. McHaney, 1976; *Faulkner: A Bibliography of Secondary Works* by Beatrice Ricks, 1981; *Faulkner: The Bio-Bibliography* by Louis Daniel Brodsky and Robert W. Hamblin, 1982; *Faulkner: An Annotated Checklist of Recent Criticism* by John Earl Bassett, 1983; *Faulkner's Poetry: A Bibliographical Guide to Texts and Criticisms* by Judith L. Sensibar and Nancy L. Stegall, 1988; *A William Faulkner Encyclopedia* by Robert W. Hamblin and Charles A. Peek, 1999.

Critical Studies: *Faulkner: A Critical Study* by Irving Howe, 1952, revised edition, 1962, 1975; *Faulkner* by Hyatt H. Waggoner, 1959; *The Novels of Faulkner* by Olga W. Vickery, 1959, revised edition, 1964; *Faulkner* by Frederick J. Hoffman, 1961, revised edition, 1966; *Bear, Man, and God* edited by Francis L. Utley, Lynn Z. Bloom, and Arthur F. Kinney, 1963, revised edition, 1971; *Faulkner: The Yoknapatawpha Country,* 1963, *Faulkner: Toward Yoknapatawpha and Beyond,* 1978, and *Faulkner: First Encounters,* 1983, all by Cleanth Brooks; *Faulkner's People* by Robert W. Kirk and Marvin Klotz, 1963; *A Reader's Guide to Faulkner* by Edmond L. Volpe, 1964; *Faulkner: A Collection of Critical Essays* edited by Robert Penn Warren, 1966; *The Achievement of Faulkner* by Michael Millgate, 1966; *Faulkner: Myth and Motion* by Richard P. Adams, 1968; *Faulkner of Yoknapatawpha County* by Lewis Leary, 1973; *Faulkner's Narrative* by Joseph W. Reed, Jr., 1973; *Faulkner: Four Decades of Criticism* edited by Linda W. Wagner, 1973, and *Hemingway and Faulkner: Inventors/Masters* by Wagner, 1975; *Faulkner: A Collection of Criticism* edited by Dean M. Schmitter, 1973; *Faulkner: The Abstract and the Actual* by Panthea Reid Broughton, 1974; *Faulkner: A Biography* by Joseph Blotner, 2 vols., 1974, revised and condensed edition, 1 vol., 1984; *A Faulkner Miscellany* edited by James B. Meriwether, 1974; *Doubling and the Incest/Repetition and Revenge: A Speculative Reading of Faulkner* by John T. Irwin, 1975; *Faulkner: The Critical Heritage* edited by John Earl Bassett, 1975; *A Glossary of Faulkner's South* by Calvin S. Brown, 1976; *The Most Splendid Failure: Faulkner's The Sound and the Fury* by André Bleikasten, 1976, and *Faulkner's The Sound and the Fury: A Critical Casebook* edited by Bleikasten, 1982; *Faulkner's Heroic Design: The Yoknapatawpha Novels* by Lynn Levins, 1976; *Faulkner's Craft of Revision* by Joanne V. Creighton, 1977; *Faulkner's Women: The Myth and the Muse* by David L. Williams, 1977; *Faulkner's Narrative Poetics* by Arthur F. Kinney, 1978, and *Critical Essays on Faulkner: The Compson Family,* 1982, and *The Sartoris Family,* 1985, both edited by Kinney; *The Fragile Thread: The Meaning of Form in Faulkner's Novels* by Donald M. Kartiganer, 1979; *Faulkner's Career: An Internal Literary History* by Gary Lee Stonum, 1979; *Faulkner: The Transfiguration of Biography* by Judith Wittenberg, 1979; *Faulkner's Yoknapatawpha Comedy* by Lyall H. Powers, 1980; *Faulkner: His Life and Work* by David Minter, 1980; *The Heart of Yoknapatawpha* by John Pilkington, 1981; *Faulkner's Characters: An Index to the Published and Unpublished Fiction* by Thomas E. Dasher, 1981; *Faulkner: The Short Story Career—An Outline of Faulkner's Short Story Writing from 1919 to 1962,* 1981, and *Faulkner: The Novelist as Short Story Writer,* 1985, both by Hans H. Skei; *A Faulkner Overview: Six Perspectives* by Victor Strandberg, 1981; *Faulkner: Biographical and Reference Guide and Critical Collection* edited by Leland H. Cox, 2 vols., 1982; *The Play of Faulkner's Language* by John T. Matthews, 1982; *The Art of Faulkner* by John Pikoulis, 1982; *Faulkner's "Negro": Art and the Southern Context* by Thadious M. Davis, 1983; *Faulkner: The House Divided* by Eric J. Sundquist, 1983; *Faulkner's Yoknapatawpha* by Elizabeth M. Kerr, 1983; *Faulkner: New Perspectives* edited by Richard Brodhead, 1983; *The Origins of Faulkner's Art* by Judith Sensibar, 1984; *Uses of the Past in the Novels of Faulkner* by Carl E. Rollyson, Jr., 1984; *Faulkner's Absalom, Absalom! A Critical Casebook* edited by Elizabeth Muhlenfeld, 1984; *A Faulkner Chronology* by Michel Gresset, 1985; *Faulkner's Short Stories* by James B. Carothers, 1985; *Faulkner* by Alan Warren Friedman, 1985; *Genius of Place:*

Faulkner's Triumphant Beginnings by Max Putzel, 1985; *Faulkner's Humor,* 1986, *Faulkner and Women,* 1986, *Faulkner and Race,* 1988, *Faulkner and the Craft of Fiction,* 1989, *Faulkner and Popular Culture,* 1990, and *Faulkner and Religion,* 1991, all edited by Doreen Fowler and Ann J. Abadie; *Figures of Division: Faulkner's Major Novels* by James A. Snead, 1986; *Heart in Conflict: Faulkner's Struggles with Vocation* by Michael Grimwood, 1986; *Faulkner: The Man and the Artist* by Stephen B. Oates, 1987; *Faulkner: The Art of Stylization* by Lothar Hönnighausen, 1987; *Faulkner* by David Dowling, 1988; *Fiction, Film, and Faulkner: The Art of Adaptation* by Gene D. Phillips, 1988; *Faulkner, American Writer* by Frederick Karl, 1989; *Faulkner's Country Matters: Folklore and Fable in Yoknapatawpha* by Daniel Hoffman, 1989; *Faulkner's Marginal Couple* by John N. Duvall, 1990; *Faulkner: The Yoknapatawpha Fiction* edited by A. Robert Lee, 1990; *Faulkner's Fables of Creativity: The Non-Yoknapatawpha Novels* by Gary Harrington, 1990; *Faulkner: Life Glimpses* by Louis Daniel Brodsky, 1990; *Faulkner's Short Fiction* by James Ferguson, 1991; *Faulkner and Thoroughly Modern Novel* by Virginia V. James Hlavsa, 1991; *American Designs: The Late Novels of James and Faulkner* by Jeanne Campbell Reesman, 1991; *Novel Frames: Literature as Guide to Race, Sex, and History in American Culture,* 1991, and *Faulkner's Apocrypha: A Fable, Snopes, and the Spirit of Human Rebellion,* 1991, both by Joseph R. Urgo; *Ordered by Words: Language and Narration in the Novels of Faulkner* by Judith Lockyer, 1991; *Reading for the Plot: Design and Intention in Narrative* by Peter Brooks, 1992; *The Novels of William Faulkner: A Critical Interpretation* by Olga Vickery, 1995; *The Life of William Faulkner: A Critical Biography* by Richard Gray, 1996; *Faulkner: The Return of the Repressed* by Doreen Fowler, 1997; *Faulkner's Place* by Michael Millgate, 1997; *Fictions of Labor: William Faulkner and the South's Long Revolution* by Richard Godden, 1997; *Natural Aristocracy: History, Ideology, and the Production of William Faulkner* by Kevin Railey, 1999; *William Faulkner's Postcolonial South* by Charles Baker, 1999; *Producing American Races: Henry James, William Faulkner, Toni Morrison* by Patricia McKee, 1999.

*   *   *

William Faulkner often said that he regarded poetry as the most difficult genre and himself as a "failed poet." Although he wrote prose quite early, he devoted most of his energy as a beginning writer to verse, imitating Housman and Swinburne, translating French Symbolist poets, and coming under the spell of **Ezra Pound** and **T.S. Eliot**. *The Marble Faun,* however, was a cycle of pastoral poems, and one of the keys to both the complexity and power of his mature prose is the carryover of poetic techniques and pastoral imagery into his realistic fiction. In his Waste Land novel, *Soldiers' Pay,* he struck the contemporary note of postwar disillusionment, but in his third, *Sartoris,* he set his scene in Mississippi and began to mine the resources of his native region. Conventional in technique, this novel drew upon his own family, especially Colonel William C. Faulkner, in the creation of Colonel John Sartoris and his troubled descendants. Placed in opposition to them were the Snopeses, a family of landless whites. In their craft, rapacity, and savagery, they represented the negative aspects of the rise of the new man in the New South but also perennial facets of human nature castigated by literature's classic moralists and satirists.

By the time Faulkner began his next novel he had not only read Joyce and imitated Eliot, he had also composed highly experimental drama and prose tales. All of this exploration and maturation, together with the frustration he felt at repeated rejections of the manuscript of *Sartoris,* combined to produce in his new work a novel of extraordinary power and poetic sensibility. In *The Sound and the Fury* he told the story of the tragic Compson family from four different points of view, employing complex patterns of image and symbol and exploiting the stream of consciousness technique quite as much as Joyce had done. This novel, showing him suddenly at the height of his powers, would later be studied and explicated almost as much as Joyce's *Ulysses.*

In his next two works he employed the Chickasaw name he had chosen for his apocryphal county: Yoknapatawpha. One of these, *Sanctuary,* seemed *grand guignol* to some readers, updated Greek tragedy to others. Its violence and atrocities in a gangland setting, combined with ribald humor and poetic sensibility, constituted a virtuoso performance that gained Faulkner the mass attention that had eluded him. But books such as *As I Lay Dying* repelled many readers, not only because their poor Southern whites seemed strange and often violent, but also because of the technical complexity with which Faulkner presented them, employing fifty-nine separate interior monologues to tell the story of the Bundrens and their disaster-plagued journey undertaken to bury their mother in her family plot.

In novels such as *Light in August* Faulkner continued his exploration of the range of human possibility, not only "the human heart in conflict with itself," but also man in conflict with society, as in the case of Joe Christmas, who does not know whether he is white or black and cannot come to terms with life in either of these worlds. Here Faulkner continued his probing into the psychologies of his characters, their lives deeply determined by their past. Increasingly he employed flashbacks, shifts in chronology, and poetic renderings of perception combined with vivid factual narration and scrupulous use of dialects both black and white.

Now clearly a master of prose fiction, Faulkner published his second and last book of verse, *A Green Bough,* comprising poems written over a decade or more. Embodying several different styles, they showed his versatility but justified his earlier judgment that he was primarily a fiction writer and not a poet. One critic, however, would aptly call him an epic poet in prose.

When *Absalom, Absalom!* appeared (the novel that would challenge *The Sound and the Fury* for pre-eminence), it revealed not only the further exploration of Yoknapatawpha County and its people but also Faulkner's use of the mystery story genre in his attempts to understand history. In part a narrative of the Civil War, it went beyond the regional and the particular to constants in human experience. Like *The Sound and the Fury,* it left some questions unanswered in a kind of aesthetic expression of a principle of indeterminacy in human life. Continuing his work in shorter fiction, Faulkner depicted his county in the days before the white man came in a sequence of Indian stories that showed his imaginative grasp of another people's culture. Other short stories were later reworked, deepened, and augmented to form novels: *The Unvanquished,* a further tale of the Sartoris family and the South; *The Hamlet,* an account of country people and particularly the Snopeses, whose rise would be further chronicled in *The Town* and *The Mansion;* and *Go Down, Moses,* a narrative of the relations between black and white in Yoknapatawpha County.

A striking quality in his fiction was the interrelationships from book to book, as though the whole panorama of his creation was there in his mind at once, with people, places, and events to be summoned up at will, at times even seeming to obsess him, demanding his creative efforts whether he willed it or not. Nearly twenty years after *Sanctuary* he brought back the ill-starred Temple Drake in a work that explored her partial atonement and that of her husband for their sins in *Sanctuary*. Begun as a play, *Requiem for a Nun* refused to coalesce for Faulkner, and so he turned to narrative prose, introducing each act with a long prologue that set this new drama of passion and murder against the history of Yoknapatawpha County, beginning in the dawn of time and coming up to the present.

Faulkner did not, however, limit himself to settings in Yoknapatawpha, as *A Fable,* set in France during the Great War, testified. More than ten years in the writing, this book was the only one, Faulkner would say, that he had ever written from an idea: what would happen if Christ were to return, giving man his last chance not only for salvation but for survival? His retelling of the story of Christ's Passion and Death during the false armistice on the Western Front was in its way his most explicit statement of his own humanistic faith, using conventional Christian lore as a metaphor. The novel was an ambitious if not wholly successful attempt at a kind of summary statement.

But it was in the Yoknapatawpha novels that his genius found its fullest expression. *The Town* and *The Mansion* completed his chronicle of the rise of the Snopeses and the decline of the Sartoris class, reflecting social changes in the South over the better part of a century yet at the same time remaining faithful to such patterns in other times and other societies. Though these novels had in them something of the same quality of family chronicle as had the earlier *Sartoris,* he continued his technical experimentation, passing the narration from one major character to another and intervening in an omniscient narrative voice when his strategy demanded it. In this latter part of his career, a volume of detective stories and a volume of hunting stories testified to his continuing vigor and versatility. One book, *Intruder in the Dust,* had begun as a detective story turned into a novel, and evolved as well into a study of racial prejudice and conflict in the South and the process by which a young white boy came to see the humanity of the innocent Negro whom he helped to save from lynching. Faulkner's last book, a kind of valedictory, was a retrospective and often mellow novel, a story of a boy's initiation that was amusing and touching by turns. *The Reivers* showed him once more as master of this domain he had created and exploited as no one had done since Balzac.

Thus it is that he can be called the greatest of modern American novelists. To his strongest admirers he is the greatest of American novelists, a claim that rests upon his prodigious creativity and productivity, his extraordinary mastery of literary techniques, and a breadth of characterization and insight into the human condition that made Yoknapatawpha County a paradigm for the larger world beyond its forests and rivers.

—Joseph Blotner

See the essays on *Absalom, Absalom!* and *The Sound and the Fury.*

FEARING, Kenneth (Flexner)

Born: Oak Park, Illinois, 28 July 1902. **Education:** Public schools in Oak Park; University of Wisconsin, Madison, B.A. 1924. **Family:** Married 1) Rachel Meltzer in 1933, one son; 2) Nan Lurie in 1945 (divorced 1958). **Career:** Reporter in Chicago; freelance writer in New York City from 1925: contributor to poetry magazines, and staff writer, *Time* magazine. **Awards:** Guggenheim fellowship, 1936, 1939; American Academy award, 1945. **Died:** 26 June 1961.

PUBLICATIONS

Collection

Kenneth Fearing: Complete Poems. 1994.

Poetry

Angel Arms. 1929.
Poems. 1935.
Dead Reckoning. 1938.
Collected Poems. 1940.
Afternoon of a Pawnbroker and Other Poems. 1943.
Stranger at Coney Island and Other Poems. 1948.
New and Selected Poems. 1956.

Fiction

The Hospital. 1939.
Dagger of the Mind. 1941; as *Cry Killer!,* 1958.
Clark Gifford's Body. 1942.
The Big Clock. 1946.
John Barry, with Donald Friede and Henry Bedford-Jones. 1947.
Loneliest Girl in the World. 1951; as *The Sound of Murder,* 1952.
The Generous Heart. 1954.
The Crozart Story. 1960.

*

Critical Studies: "The Meaning of Fearing's Poetry" by M.L. Rosenthal, in *Poetry,* July 1944; "The Life of Kenneth Flexner Fearing (1902-1961)" by Patricia B. Santora, in *College Language Association Journal,* 1989; *Fear Ruled Them All: Kenneth Fearing's Literature of Corporate Conspiracy* by Andrew R. Anderson, 1996.

*   *   *

Poet, novelist, and editor Kenneth Fearing is associated with the literature of disillusionment written in America during the 1930s and 1940s, when technological achievements and social institutions appeared incapable of remedying the profound evils of economic depression. Severely affected by the senseless suffering he perceived in his environment, Fearing became disillusioned with capitalistic systems of government and industry, espousing instead a Marxist belief in the inherent goodness of common men, whom he hoped would unite and lead the world into a new era of utopian humanism.

Into this crusade for social justice, Fearing enlisted his talents as a writer. His poetry earned him the admiration of his contemporaries and a lasting position of respect in modern literature. The deft ironic tone that characterizes much of Fearing's poetry, and that undercuts the optimism of the Whitmanesque lines in which he wrote, is admirably suited to capturing his anger and bitterness at the disregard of institutions for the liberties of the individual, and his sympathy and pity for those people who were trapped by social circumstance in sterile urban environments where they were forced by industrial and political taskmasters to lead mechanical lives of quiet desperation.

But if the economic and social conditions of the 1930s provided Fearing with the subject matter for his poetry, they also limited the scope of his poetic growth. In many respects, Fearing's hatreds and fears shackle his imagination to themes and obsessions that do not sustain repeated or extended treatment. As a result, the reader who indulges in more than one volume of Fearing's poems receives the impression that while the setting and characters of his poems may vary from volume to volume the ideas that they embody remain the same. In his best poems, however, Fearing captures the anxieties, hopes, and frustrations of his generation with sensitivity and depth. At least two of Fearing's books of poetry, *Dead Reckoning* and *Afternoon of a Pawnbroker*, repay close reading.

As a novelist Fearing specialized in pulp thrillers into which he interjected social commentary. His first novel, *The Hospital*, is replete with scandals and intrigues that expose the machinations behind the workings of the medical profession. Equally shocking and equally involved are *Clark Gifford's Body*, a murder mystery that explores the possibility of revolution in America, and *The Generous Heart*, a novel that depicts the graft and greed involved in the misappropriation of funds by a charitable organization. Another novel, *The Big Clock*, proved so popular that it became the subject of a film. Ostensibly about a murder, *The Big Clock* also analyzes the ruthlessness of journalistic rivalry and muckraking. Fearing excelled in the use of multiple, first-person narrators, and while this technique sometimes detracted from the movement of his plots, it allowed him the opportunity to develop in his many detective and mystery novels considerably more psychological complexity than most of his predecessors in these genres had been able to accomplish.

—James A. Levernier

FERBER, Edna

Born: Kalamazoo, Michigan, 15 August 1885. **Education:** Ryan High School, Appleton, Wisconsin, graduated 1902. **Career:** Reporter, Appleton *Daily Crescent*, 1902-04, Milwaukee *Journal*, 1905-08, and Chicago *Tribune;* full-time writer from 1910; lived in New York City after 1912; served with the Writers War Board and as a war correspondent with the U.S. Army Air Force during World War II. **Awards:** Pulitzer prize, 1924. Litt.D.: Columbia University, New York; Adelphi College, Garden City, New York. **Member:** American Academy. **Died:** 16 April 1968.

PUBLICATIONS

Fiction

Dawn O'Hara, The Girl Who Laughed. 1911.
Buttered Side Down (stories). 1912.
Roast Beef Medium: The Business Adventures of Emma McChesney and Her Son, Jock. 1913.

Personality Plus: Some Experiences of Emma McChesney and Her Son, Jock. 1914.
Emma McChesney & Co. 1915.
Fanny Herself. 1917.
Cheerful, By Request (stories). 1918.
Half Portions (stories). 1920.
The Girls. 1921.
Gigolo (stories). 1922; as *Among Those Present*, 1923.
So Big. 1924.
Show Boat. 1926.
Mother Knows Best. 1927.
Cimarron. 1930.
American Beauty. 1931.
They Brought Their Women (stories). 1933.
Come and Get It. 1935.
Nobody's in Town (includes *Trees Die at the Top*). 1938.
No Room at the Inn (stories). 1941.
Saratoga Trunk. 1941.
Great Son. 1945.
One Basket: Thirty-One Stories. 1947.
Giant. 1952.
Ice Palace. 1958.
Edna Ferber: Stories. 1996.

Plays

Our Mrs. McChesney, with George V. Hobart (produced 1915).
$1200 a Year, with Newman Levy. 1920.
Minick, with George S. Kaufman, from the story "Old Man Minick" by Ferber (produced 1924). In *Old Man Minick: A Short Story. . . Minick: A Play,* 1924.
The Eldest: A Drama of American Life. 1925.
The Royal Family, with George S. Kaufman (produced 1927). 1928; as *Theatre Royal* (produced 1935), 1936.
Dinner at Eight with George S. Kaufman (produced 1932). 1932.
Stage Door, with George S. Kaufman (produced 1936). 1936.
The Land Is Bright, with George S. Kaufman (produced 1941). 1941.
Bravo!, with George S. Kaufman (produced 1948). 1949.

Screenplay: *A Gay Old Dog,* 1919.

Other (autobiographies)

A Peculiar Treasure. 1939.
A Kind of Magic. 1963.

*

Critical Studies: *Women and Success in American Society in the Works of Ferber* by Mary Rose Shaughnessy, 1977; *Ferber: A Biography* by Julie Goldsmith Gilbert, 1978; "The Americanization of Edna: A Study of Ms. Ferber's Jewish American Identity" by Steven P. Horowitz and Miriam J. Landsman, in *Studies in American Jewish Literature*, 1982; "The Inherited and the Disinherited: The Polish Farmer in New England Literature" by Stanislaus A. Blejwas, in *Connecticut Review*, 1992; "Show Boat: The Revival, the Racism" by Robin Breon, in *TDR*, summer 1995, pp. 86-105; "Pax Americana: The Case of Show Boat" by Lauren Berlant, in *Cultural Institutions of the Novel* edited by Deidre Lynch and William B. Warner, 1996.

*   *   *

Although many of Edna Ferber's novels were best-sellers, she acquired among some critics the reputation of being more than an entertainer. Grant Overton, for instance, called her a social critic, but it is primarily as a social historian that she made her critical reputation. William Allen White said of her books that there is "no better picture of America in the first three decades of this century." And it is this aspect of her work—appearing to tell the unvarnished truth about American life—that has most appealed to her serious readers.

Whatever the final judgment about Ferber's work, there is no doubt that her finger was always on the pulse of what many American readers felt or wanted to feel about American life. She had the journalist's gift of "working up" her subject with a minimum of research and often no first-hand experience, though doubtless her earliest books about shrewd, hard-driving working girls came out of her own early career. Books like *Dawn O'Hara, Roast Beef, Medium,* and *Emma McChesney & Co.* helped establish her reputation as a writer who knew the facts about American life. She won the Pulitzer Prize in 1924 for *So Big,* a novel dealing with farm life, a subject, she confessed, about which she knew nothing first-hand. Later books were written after quick trips to the locale to get the feel of the territory and gather a few facts.

Cimarron purported to deal with the opening of the Oklahoma Territory and the discovery of oil, *Saratoga Trunk* with the career of a nineteenth-century self-made millionaire (whose exciting life story newspaper reporters refused to believe). *Giant* dealt with the fabulous excesses of the Texas new-rich. These books, as well as Ferber's two dozen or so others, are movie-like romances about the lure of money and big-time success, presented with a clever blend of voyeuristic fascination and a satirical undercutting that permits the reader to luxuriate in the fantasy but at the same time feel superior to it.

In addition to romances about working girls, farmers, Oklahoma roustabouts, Indians, and self-made millionaires, Ferber also published several collections of short stories, two autobiographical volumes, and several plays (most written in collaboration with George S. Kaufman). A number of her novels have also been turned into successful stage musicals and motion pictures, *Show Boat* and *Saratoga Trunk* being perhaps the best known. Ferber's popularity and the critical attention she has received suggest that when the definitive study of popular taste in America is written, her novels, plays, and short stories will have to be reckoned with.

—W.J. Stuckey

FERLINGHETTI, Lawrence

Born: Lawrence Ferling in Yonkers, New York, 24 March 1919. **Education:** Mount Hermon School, University of North Carolina, A.B. 1941; Columbia University, M.A. 1948; Sorbonne University of Paris, Doctorat de l'Universite (with honors) 1951. **Military Service:** United States Navy, 1941-45; lieutenant commander. **Family:** Married Seldon Kirby-Smith in 1951 (divorced 1976); two children. **Career:** Editor and publisher, City Lights Books, San Francisco, California; poet, playwright, painter, poetry-and-jazz performer; owner and manager, City Lights Bookshop, San Francisco. **Awards:** Commonwealth Club of California Silver Medal for poetry, 1986; recipient of poetry prize, City of Rome, 1993; San Francisco street named in his honor, 1994.

PUBLICATIONS

Novels

Her. 1960.
Love in the Days of Rage. 1988.

Plays

Unfair Arguments with Existence: Seven Plays for a New Theatre. 1963.
Routines. 1964.
3 by Ferlinghetti. 1970.

Screenplay: *Have You Sold Your Dozen Roses?,* 1957.

Poetry

Pictures of a Gone World. 1955.
A Coney Island of the Mind. 1958.
Starting from San Francisco. 1961; revised edition, 1967.
One Thousand Fearful Words for Fidel Castro. 1961.
An Eye on the World: Selected Poems. 1967.
The Secret Meaning of Things. 1969.
Tyrannus Rex. 1969; revised edition, 1973.
The Mexican Night. 1970.
Back Roads to Far Places. 1971.
Open Eye, Open Heart. 1973.
Who Are We Now? 1976.
Northwest Ecolog. 1978.
Landscapes of Living and Dying. 1979.
A Trip to Italy and France. 1980.
Endless Life: Selected Poems. 1981.
The Populist Manifestos. 1983.
Over All the Obscene Boundaries: European Poems and Translations. 1984.
Inside the Trojan Horse. 1987.
Wild Drams of a New Beginning. 1988.
When I Look at Pictures. 1990.
These Are My Rivers: New & Selected Poems, 1955-1993. 1993.
A Far Rockaway of the Heart. 1997.
The Street's Kiss. 1998.

Other

The Mexican Night Travel Journal. 1970.
Literary San Francisco: A Pictorial History, with Nancy Joyce Peters. 1980.
Leaves of Life: Fifty Drawings from the Model. 1985.
Lawrence Ferlinghetti: In Search of Eros. 1995.
Leaves of Life: Thirty Drawings from the Model. 1995.
From Work-in-Progress. 1996.

Editor, *Beatitude Anthology.* 1960.
Editor, *Hunk of Skin,* by Pablo Picasso. 1969.
Editor, *Panic Grass,* by Charles Upton. 1969.
Editor, *City Lights Anthology.* 1974.
Coeditor, *City Lights Review. No. 1.* 1987.
Coeditor, *City Lights Review, No. 2.* 1988.

Translator, *Selections from Paroles,* by Jacques Prevert. 1958.

Recordings: *Poetry Reading in "The Cellar,"* with Kenneth Rexroth, 1958; *Tentative Description of a Dinner Given to Promote the Impeachment of President Eisenhower & Other Poems,* 1959; *Tyrannus Rex? & Assassination Raga,* 1971; *Contemporary Poets Read Their Works: Lawrence Ferlinghetti,* 1972; *Into the Deeper Pools . . . ,* 1984.

*

Bibliography: *Six Poets of the San Francisco Renaissance* by David Kherdian, 1967; *Lawrence Ferlinghetti: A Descriptive Bibliography* by Bill Morgan, 1981.

Critical Studies: *Howl of the Censor* by J.W. Ehrlich, 1961; *Some Poems/Poets: Studies in American Underground Poetry Since 1945* by Samuel Charters, 1971; "Lawrence Ferlinghetti," an interview with David Meltzer in *The San Francisco Poets,* 1971 (revised as *Golden Gate,* 1976); *Archetype West: The Pacific Coast as a Literary Region* by William Everson, 1976; *Naked Angels: The Lives & Literature of the Beat Generation* by John Tytell, 1976; *Ferlinghetti: A Biography* by Neeli Cherkovski, 1979; *Lawrence Ferlinghetti: Poet-At-Large* by Larry Smith, 1983; *Ferlinghetti, The Artist in His Time* by Barry Silesky, 1990.

*   *   *

Lawrence Ferlinghetti is the author of one of America's most popular poetry books of all time, *A Coney Island of the Mind* (1958), as well as experimental novels and plays; he is also founder and publisher of one of the country's vital alternative presses, City Lights Books. He remains a literary force more than forty years after helping to launch the Beat movement in America in 1957. Having moved to San Francisco from New York in 1951, the young Ferlinghetti had already lived part of his childhood and college years in France. Significantly, he can best be understood in the international tradition of the artist as one who is socially and politically engaged. His own influences included such European writers as William Blake, Arthur Rimbaud, Blaise Cendrars, Jacques Prévert, Jean-Paul Sartre, Albert Camus, and the French surrealists, as well as the Americans **Walt Whitman, Henry David Thoreau, E.E. Cummings, Ezra Pound, William Carlos Williams,** and **Thomas Wolfe.** As part of a 1950s group of American writers of dissent, including **Kenneth Rexroth, Henry Miller, Kenneth Patchen,** and **Charles Olson,** Ferlinghetti helped to foster the Beat movement and soon became an artistic peer of and publisher for such writers as **Allen Ginsberg, Jack Kerouac, Gary Snyder,** Philip Whalen, and Gregory Corso.

When the Beat writers Ginsberg and Kerouac arrived in San Francisco's North Beach area from New York City in 1955, Ferlinghetti was already there, established among the bohemian artists, jazz musicians, and aging Italian anarchists. As cofounder with Peter Martin of America's first all-paperback bookstore, City Lights Bookshop (named after the film by rebel artist Charlie Chaplin), Ferlinghetti had become active in the arts scene by writing reviews for the *San Francisco Chronicle* and creating his own tragicomic verse. He launched the City Lights Books publishing house in 1955 with his own *Pictures of a Gone World,* followed immediately by books by Williams, Rexroth, and Patchen in the celebrated Pocket Poets Series. The fifth volume in that series represented the merger of the San Francisco poetry renaissance with the East Coast Beat movement; the work was Ginsberg's *Howl and Other Poems* (1957), a book whose innovative form and pro-

vocative content helped create a movement. In the censorship trial that followed its release and censure by the U.S. Customs Office during the politically repressive McCarthy period, Ferlinghetti and his press stood as a voice for freedom of artistic expression. At the age of 38, the shy poet emerged as a public figure and spokesperson for the rights and obligations of the artist, a position he maintained and continued to use to promote issues of human rights and social justice. At times this active protest led to arrest and imprisonment, as in the 1967 Oakland, California, demonstration against the Vietnam War, which resulted Ferlinghetti's serving a nineteen-day jail term.

The poet's relentless demand for a writing of engagement eventually led to his 1959 quarrel with the Beat movement, in which he decried the East Coast "hipster" attitude of Beat aloofness or "disengagement." He publicly asserted his own position on the cover notes to his recording of his political poem "Tentative Description of a Dinner Given to Promote the Impeachment of President Eisenhower," writing:

> Jean-Paul Sartre cares and has always hollered that the writer especially should be committed. Engagement is one of his favorite dirty words. He would give the horse laugh to the idea of Disengagement. . . . Only the dead are disengaged.

This stance, along with his support of unpopular causes (among them, the leadership of Fidel Castro), often placed Ferlinghetti and his work under critical and political attack.

Because of his instrumental role in fostering the Beat movement, Ferlinghetti often was labeled as a "Beat writer," even though his career and innovations have extended the vision of that movement and outlived it by 30 years. A close look at Ferlinghetti's artistic works reveals a surprising diversity of form, as well as the achievement of a remarkable and authentic art. An early innovation tied to his painting was his development of a visual poetry akin to that of Cummings and the French avante-garde poet Guillaume Apollinaire. In these works the sight and sound "happen" upon the page in a verbal abstract expressionism, as in many of the lyric visual poems of his *Pictures of a Gone World.* He also developed a cinematic poetic form for rendering contemporary slices of life, exemplified in his poem "The Old Italians Dying," and a polemic form used to confront issues, evident in the three "Populist Manifesto" poems. The latter are important statements and challenges to poets to create a dynamic and accessible art.

Another of Ferlinghetti's innovations was his development of an oral poetry form, one that was both rhetorically functional and socially vital. Using colloquial bluntness, mocking alliteration, internal and multiple rhymes, puns, incongruent diction, and comic allusions, he creates a vehicle for both satire and real sentiment. Strong examples of this style from his early work include "Junkman's Obbligato," "Autobiography," and the Beatest of Beat poems, "Dog." Examples from the middle to later period include "Bickford's Buddha," "Assassination Raga," "Moscow in the Wilderness/Segovia in the Snow," "The Old Italians Dying," and the three "Populist Manifesto" poems. In all of these there is a sense of the poet as activist abroad in the world. [AU: your meaning preserved in this condensed version?] As he exclaims in his "First Populist Manifesto":

> Poets, come out of your closets,
> Open your windows, open your doors,

You have been holed-up too long
in your closed worlds.

In many of his poems Ferlinghetti performs the role of the poet observer or poet journalist; in others, he is the recorder of his own life. It was not until Neeli Cherkovski published *Ferlinghetti: A Biography* (1979), however, that readers began to understand the strong autobiographical basis of much of this work, including such poems as "The Pennycandystore Beyond the El," "Director of Alienation," "True Confessional," "Endless Life," and even Ferlinghetti's two semisurrealistic novels *Her* and *Love in the Days of Rage*. He was born the last of five sons to Italian-American Charles Ferlinghetti and Portuguese-Jewish Clemence Mendes-Monsanto; his birth followed his father's sudden death, and not long afterward his mother was institutionalized. The young Ferlinghetti was then whisked off by his mother's sister to Paris, where he spent his early childhood. "Open eye open heart where / do I wander / I cried and ran off / into the heart of the world," he recounts in "True Confessional." Back in New York at age six, he was abandoned by his aunt and adopted by the wealthy and older Bisland family of Bronxville. Suddenly all his physical needs were met but not his longing for affection: "I was a wind-up toy / someone had dropped wound-up / into a world / already running down." In many ways he turned to the books in the Bisland's library as a kind of foster parents.

There followed a friendship with the Zilla Larned Wilson family, including a more typical yet turbulent adolescence. "I still can hear the paper thump / on lost porches . . . / I got caught stealing pencils / from the Five and Ten Cent Store / the same month I made Eagle Scout," he wrote in "Autobiography." Following high school at Mount Mermon came college at the University of North Carolina at Chapel Hill, a freight train trip to Mexico, then a stint in the U.S. Navy during World War II. Back home in 1945, he lived in New York City's Greenwich Village neighborhood while earning a graduate degree (1948) from Columbia University. This led to study at the Sorbonne in Paris, where in addition to completing a doctoral thesis on "The City as Symbol in Modern Poetry," he also wrote his early "Palimpsest" poems and much of the Thomas Wolfean novel *The Way of the Dispossessed* and started his surrealistic novel *Her*. Returning to the United States in 1950, he married Seldon Kirby-Smith ("Kirby") and settled in San Francisco, that most cosmopolitan of American cities, where he has maintained an interest in ecology, Zen Buddhism, and world politics and art.

Today Ferlinghetti finds himself the good gray poet, declared the first poet laureate of San Francisco in 1998 at age 79. His City Lights Bookshop at 261 Columbus Avenue has become a fixture of the literary landscape. He is seen by biographer Cherkovski as "a living symbol of the bohemian life-style that had attracted him." Ferlinghetti has never abandoned his romantic ideals, as is apparent in his tribute to an "Endless Life":

> Endless the splendid life of the world
> Endless its lovely living and breathing
> its lovely sentient beings
> seeing and hearing feeling and thinking
> laughing and dancing singing and crying
> through endless afternoons endless nights.

Cherkovski commends Ferlinghetti for thinking "on a universal scale—but always with a human perspective. He has never lost

an innate ability to capture the mood and tenor of 'everyman,' . . . more of a see-er than a seer. He writes with his eyes first, above all else, then with his ear for language, and then with his intellect."

In his third decade as a writer, his works appear more often in collected and selected works, as in the volume *These Are My Rivers: New and Selected Poems* (1993). But in 1997 he surprised even himself with what he termed "a poetry seizure," which resulted in *A Far Rockaway of the Heart*. Calling the new work a sequel to *A Coney Island of the Mind, Booklist* commented that it "reveals how he has weighted the scales this time more to heart-side than mind, offering a far more personalized narrative of familial, poetical, and social history." Bonding old forms and new vision, Ferlinghetti has created poems that "burn through modern America's absurdities and unrepentant historical revision in a glorious rant against mediocrity, greed, capitalism and boring poetry, with copious riffs on painting and love" (*Publishers Weekly*). Maintaining his engaged stance as poet, painter, playwright, publisher, and provocateur, Ferlinghetti has molded a powerful and popular art for creating change.

—Larry Smith

FIEDLER, Leslie A.

Born: Newark, New Jersey, 8 March 1917. **Education:** Public schools in Newark; New York University, B.A. 1938; University of Wisconsin, M.A. 1939, Ph.D. 1941; postdoctoral work at Harvard, Cambridge, Massachusetts and at Japanese Language school, 1943-44. **Military Service:** United States Navy, 1943-45. **Family:** Married 1) Margaret Shipley (divorced 1973); 2) Sally Andersen; three daughters, three sons, and two stepsons. **Career:** Teacher, University of Montana, Missoula, Montana, 1941-63. Beginning 1964, professor of English, State University of New York at Buffalo. Junior fellow, Indiana School of Letters, 1954-73; associate fellow, Calhoun College, Yale University. Visiting professor in Bologna, Rome, Paris, Venice, Athens, Sussex, and Princeton University. **Awards:** Rockefeller fellowship, 1946-47; Fulbright fellowship, 1951-53, 1961-62; Kenyon Review fellowship in criticism, 1956; Guggenheim fellowship, 1970-71; Furioso Poetry prize; Alumni award of New York University, 1985; Distinguished professor, State University of New York, 1987; Chancellor Charles P. Norton medal, 1989; Hubbell Medal for Lifetime contribution to the Study of American Literature, Modern Language Association, 1994; Ivan Sandorf award for lifetime contribution of American Arts and Letters, National Book Critics Circle, New York, 1998. **Member:** American Academy and Institute of Letters, 1988. **Residence:** Buffalo, New York.

PUBLICATIONS

Collection

A Fiedler Reader. 1977.

Literary Criticism

An End to Innocence: Essays on Culture and Politics. 1955.
The Art of the Essay. 1958; revised 1969.

No! In Thunder: Essays on Myth and Literature. 1960.
Waiting for the End. 1964.
The Continuing Debate, with Jacob Vinocur. 1966.
Love and Death in the American Novel. 1966.
The Return of the Vanishing America. 1968.
Being Busted. 1970.
The Collected Essays of Leslie Fiedler. 1972.
The Stranger in Shakespeare. 1972.
The Messengers Will Come No More. 1974.
Freaks: Myths and Images in the Secret Self. 1978.
The Inadvertent Epic. 1979.
What Was Literature? 1982.
Olaf Stapledon. 1982.
Fiedler on the Roof: Essays on Literature and Jewish Identity. 1991.
Tyranny of the Normal. 1996.
Back to Innocence. n.d.

Fiction

Pull Down Vanity and Other Stories. 1962.
The Second Stone: A Love Story. 1963.
Back to China. 1965.
The Last Jew in America. 1966.
Nude Croquet and Other Stories. 1969.

Other

Editor, *In Dreams Awake: Anthology of Science Fiction.* 1976.

*

Critical Studies: *Leslie Fiedler and American Culture,* edited by Steven G. Kellman, 1999.

* * *

Few critics of American literature have aroused as much controversy as Leslie Fiedler. Though his views on the workings of myth and gender in classic American fiction initially prompted disdain from the critical establishment, many of Fiedler's arguments have since been acknowledged as brilliant expositions of archetypal patterns at the core of American identity. By the 1970s, Fiedler's psychoanalytic and Marxist approach had been eclipsed by the deconstructionist movement, but his exploration of the psychic ambivalence within American fiction continues to be of lasting importance.

Fiedler, who did his Ph.D. work on John Donne and has written poetry and fiction in addition to criticism, was an unknown professor of English at the University of Montana when he published his sensational essay "Come Back to the Raft Ag'in, Huck Honey!" in 1948 in the *Partisan Review.* The essay, reprinted in Fiedler's first collection, *An End to Innocence* (1955), stemmed from his fascination with America's " . . . implacable nostalgia for the infantile." Fiedler argued in the essay that the fundamental archetype underlying American fiction is a homoerotic bond between the white man and a "Dark Other." This bond—as seen between Natty Bumppo and Chingachgook in the novels of James Fenimore Cooper, Ishmael and Queequeg in *Moby Dick,* and Huck and Jim in *The Adventures of Huckleberry Finn*—is essentially adolescent, predicated on the desire to escape from mature sexual relationships with women (*i.e.,* civilization) and to find instead an idealized isolation in undefiled nature (the inevitable setting of "the Sacred Marriage of males").

Mainstream literary critics found this argument scandalous. Some misread it as an attempt to prove that Huck and Jim were homosexuals; others considered the essay a joke. Partly in order to set the record straight, Fiedler expanded and developed his thesis in his masterwork *Love and Death in the American Novel* (1960). An erudite and rigorously argued work based on a thorough understanding of English models, particularly Henry Fielding's novel *Clarissa, Love and Death* shows that American literary myths and forms derived from the erosion of Puritan values. The strict Calvinist belief in the innate depravity of humankind, on which Puritanism had been founded, had proved emotionally too demanding to be sustained and had eroded into an essentially sentimental view that polarized good and evil rather than recognizing their coexistence within each person. In effect, the decay of Puritanism led to a psychological "splitting" in American literature, through which conflicting elements (reason and emotion, innocence and corruption, spiritual and physical) were associated with symbolic opposites: the innocent, nonsexual, white-skinned blonde woman, for example, contrasted with the corrupting, sexual, dark-skinned woman. Though in psychoanalytic terms these types represent two sides of one divided self, they remain split in a literary tradition that displaces negative qualities onto a symbolic other.

The American experience, Fiedler argued, was particularly suited to this symbolic view of conflicted reality. While the new country had been founded on romantic ideals that consciously rejected the corrupt political structures of Europe, America had not lived up to its ideal. The twin evils of slavery and genocide remained as stark reminders of human imperfection and evil. The ambivalence and guilt arising from this profound discrepancy, Fiedler showed, have uniquely shaped American identity and created a literature that is typically gothic or sentimental, extreme, and heavily symbolic.

Within this context, the archetypal American character became a symbol of alienation, embodied in a young male who can achieve a satisfactory union with neither the pure maiden nor the dangerous dark temptress and therefore rejects both. "It is maturity above all things that the American writer fears," Fiedler commented, "and marriage seems to him its essential sign. For marriage stands traditionally . . . for a reconciliation with the divided self . . . [and] also a compromise with society . . . ." The American hero seeks instead an idealized existence in undefiled nature, where he finds a chaste homoerotic bond with a dark-skinned male (who symbolizes both the untamed wilderness and the hero's own darker self). Such a relationship "symbolically joins the white man to nature and his own unconscious . . . . This is the pure marriage of males—sexless and holy, a kind of counter-matrimony, in which the white refugee from society and the dark-skinned primitive are joined till death do them part."

Fiedler's recognition of this primal myth in *Uncle Tom's Cabin,* a critically scorned yet immensely popular book, led him in subsequent works to explore the mythic dynamic in romance, science fiction, Westerns, television and movies, comic books, and pornography. Although the thesis of *Love and Death* had become increasingly accepted, the attack he leveled at the literary canon in *What Was Literature?* (1982) again outraged the academic world. Writing as a self-described "barbarian within the gates," who, as a Jew, was sensitive to being marginalized within WASP culture, Fiedler vigorously challenged notions of "high" and "low" literature, arguing that American fiction is essentially hostile "to the modes and canons of High Art." Criticizing professors of English for acting as "gatekeepers," he argued that popular works often present "not mythology once removed [as in *Ulysses* or *The Waste Land*] but primary myth." Conservative critics rejected Fiedler's view as subversive, but more liberal elements embraced his anti-elitist argument. This acceptance helped to fuel movements that challenged the canon of "dead white males" and paved the way for such new academic disciplines as cultural studies.

Literary and social criticism converged in both *Freaks* (1978), Fiedler's only best-seller, and *The Tyranny of the Normal* (1996), both of which considered a broader range of topics than the merely literary. The former book, the culmination of Fiedler's career-long fascination with symbolic duality, explored the ways in which "the Freak, the Monster, the congenital malformation" is seen as "a more ultimate Other." Similar bioethical concerns emerged in *The Tyranny of the Normal*, a collection of essays on topics ranging from revisionist religious movements to child abuse to images of the disabled in literature. Though Fiedler's viewpoints here were basically rearticulations of his previous work, the book made fascinating and provocative connections between his literary criticism and contemporary social problems and issues.

Despite increasing skepticism about Freudian theory and archetypal criticism, Fiedler's influence as a literary critic has endured. His enthusiasm for popular forms helped to shape new attitudes toward "high" and "low" art. And *Love and Death in the American Novel* remains a seminal critical text that, despite some outdated elements, identifies what is essentially American in our literature and culture.

—Elizabeth Shostak

FIELD, Eugene

Born: St. Louis, Missouri, 2 (or 3) September 1850. **Education:** A school in Monson, Massachusetts; Williams College, Williamstown, Massachusetts, 1868-69; Knox College, Galesburg, Illinois, 1869-70; University of Missouri, Columbia, 1870-71. **Family:** Married Julia Sutherland Comstock in 1873; eight children. **Career:** Traveled in Europe, 1872-73; reporter and city editor, St. Louis *Evening Journal,* 1873-75; city editor, St. Joseph *Gazette,* Missouri, 1875-76; editorial writer, St. Louis *Times-Journal,* 1876-80; managing editor, Kansas City *Times,* 1880-81, and Denver *Tribune,* 1881-83; columnist ("Sharps and Flats"), Chicago *Morning News* (later called Chicago *Record*), 1883-95. **Died:** 4 November 1895.

PUBLICATIONS

Collections

Writings in Prose and Verse. 10 vols., 1896.
Hoosier Lyrics, edited by Charles Walter Brown. 1905.
Poems, Complete Edition. 1910.
Eugene Field: An Anthology in Memoriam, 1850-1895. 1995.

Poetry

A Little Book of Western Verse. 1889; revised edition, 1890.
Echoes from the Sabine Farm, Being Certain Horatian Lyrics, with Roswell M. Field. 1891; revised edition, 1893.

Second Book of Verse. 1892.
Love-Songs of Childhood. 1894.
Songs and Other Verse. 1896.
A Little Book of Tribune Verse: A Number of Hitherto Uncollected Poems, Grave and Gay, edited by Joseph G. Brown. 1901.
A Little Book of Nonsense, edited by Edward B. Morgan. 1901.
John Smith U.S.A., edited by Charles Walter Brown. 1905.
The Gingham Dog and the Calico Cat: A Poem. 1994.
Wynken, Blynken, and Nod: A Poem. 1998.

Fiction

A Little Book of Profitable Tales. 1889.
The Holy-Cross and Other Tales. 1893.
The House: An Episode in the Lives of Reuben Baker, Astronomer, and of His Wife Alice. 1896.
Second Book of Tales. 1896.
How One Friar Met the Devil and Two Pursued Him. 1900; as *The Temptation of Friar Goncol,* 1900.
The Stars: A Slumber Story, edited by Will M. Clemens. 1901.
The Coquettish Doll. 1995.

Other

Tribune Primer. 1881.
The Model Primer. 1882.
Culture's Garland, Being Memoranda of the Gradual Rise of Literature, Art, Music, and Society in Chicago and Other Western Ganglia. 1887.
With Trumpet and Drum. 1892.
The Love Affairs of a Bibliomaniac. 1896.
Field to Francis Wilson: Some Attentions. 1896.
Florence Bardsley's Story: The Life and Death of a Remarkable Woman. 1897.
The Field Book: Verses, Stories, and Letters, edited by Mary E. Burt and Mary B. Cable. 1898.
Sharps and Flats, edited by Slason Thompson. 2 vols., 1900.
Clippings from Denver Tribune 1881-1883, edited by Willard S. Morse. 1909.
Verse and Prose from the George H. Yenowine Collection, edited by Henry H. Harper. 1917.
Some Love Letters. 1927.

*

Bibliography: in *Bibliography of American Literature* by Jacob Blanck, 1959.

Critical Studies: *Field: A Study in Heredity and Contradictions,* 2 vols., 1901, and *Life of Field, The Poet of Childhood,* 1927, both by Slason Thompson; *Field's Creative Years* by Charles H. Dennis, 1924; *The Gay Poet: The Story of Field* by Jeannette Covert Nolan, 1940; *Field Days: The Life, Times, and Reputation of Field* by Robert Conrow, 1974; "There Ought to Be Clowns: American Humor and Literary Naturalism" by Hamlin Hill, in *Journal of American Cultural Studies,* 1980; "Chicago's Tutors: The Humorous Columnists of the 1880's and 90's" by Janet St. Clair, in *American Transcendental,* 1988.

*   *   *

Eugene Field's was a motley genius, for he was a modern jester, the man and his works being a puzzling combination of perverse contrasts. Field is generally remembered as a children's writer of charming if dated bits of verse like "Little Boy Blue" and "Wynken, Blynken, and Nod," yet he still enjoys a sub rosa reputation for off-color lines, his "Little Willie" perhaps the best known of these naughty verses. Field openly professed a dislike for children— other than his own—and his *Tribune Primer,* written in sardonic imitation of grade-school readers, encourages young folks to culti- vate the acquaintanceship of wasps and gluepots. While capable of turning out in apparent sincerity the most pious of verses like "The Divine Lullaby," Field was the libidinous originator of por- nographic exercises that, like "Bangin' on the Rhine," enjoyed a long underground life even before seeing formal (if surreptitious) print.

Commencing his career as a newspaper columnist of the hu- morous one-liner breed, Field, despite his New England birth and education, was fond of identifying himself with the west, hence with the vital western tradition of journalism that produced **Mark Twain**, **Ambrose Bierce**, and (closer in generation and region to Field) **James Whitcomb Riley**. It is a tradition that accommo- dates Field's many sides, his love of hoaxes, his use of public print to roast friends and enemies alike, his fierce (in all senses) loyalties, his displays of saccharine sentimentality, and his airing of public dislikes and private passions. Most of what he wrote did not outlive him, and he died relatively young, at the height of his career and powers. Though he was a skillful and witty occa- sional poet, that alone doomed his work to ephemerality. The best of his writing is the early dialect verse that in its masculine vital- ity and mining-camp settings anticipates Robert Service and par- allels in chronology and spirit Kipling's barrack-room voice.

Field possessed a genuinely comic sense, which from his invet- erate love of practical jokes to his humorous verse and prose, was thoroughly of his times and did not transcend them. He was a classic instance of Victorian madness, in which dilettantism took on a thoroughly middle-class, cigar-smoking, feet-on-desk pose, and self-conscious archaism gained a popular audience. Born in 1850, he was absolutely in synchronization with his half-century, and died, most timely, five years before it ran out.

—Catherine Seelye

FISHER, Vardis (Alvero)

Born: Annis, Idaho, 31 March 1895. **Education:** Rigby High School, Idaho, graduated 1915; University of Utah, Salt Lake City, B.A. 1920; University of Chicago, A.M. 1922, Ph.D. (magna cum laude) 1925. **Military Service:** Served in the U.S. Army Artil- lery Corps, 1918: corporal. **Family:** Married 1) Leona McMurtrey in 1917 (died 1924), two sons; 2) Margaret Trusler in 1928 (di- vorced 1939), one son; 3) Opal Laurel Holmes in 1940. **Career:** Assistant professor of English, University of Utah, 1925-28, and New York University, 1928-31; full-time writer from 1931; teacher at Montana State University, Bozeman, summers 1932-33; direc- tor, Idaho Writers' Project and Historical Records Project (Works Progress Administration), 1935-39; syndicated columnist ("Vardis Fisher Says") in Idaho newspapers, 1941-68. **Awards:** Western Writers of America Spur award, for novel, 1966, for nonfiction, 1969. **Died:** 9 July 1968.

Fiction

Toilers of the Hills. 1928.
Dark Bridwell. 1931; as *The Wild Ones,* 1952.
Vridar Hunter tetralogy
    In Tragic Life. 1932; as *I See No Sin,* 1934.
    Passions Spin the Plot. 1934.
    We Are Betrayed. 1935.
    No Villain Need Be. 1936.
April: A Fable of Love. 1937.
Odyssey of a Hero. 1937.
Forgive Us Our Virtues: A Comedy of Evasions. 1938.
Children of God. 1939.
City of Illusion. 1941.
The Mothers. 1943.
Darkness and the Deep. 1943.
The Golden Rooms. 1944.
Intimations of Eve. 1946.
Adam and the Serpent. 1947.
The Divine Passion. 1948.
The Valley of Vision. 1951.
The Island of the Innocent. 1952.
Jesus Came Again: A Parable. 1956.
A Goat for Azazel. 1956.
Pemmican: A Novel of the Hudson's Bay Company. 1956.
Peace Like a River. 1957; as *The Passion Within,* 1960.
My Holy Satan: A Novel of Christian Twilight. 1958.
Tale of Valor: A Novel of the Lewis and Clark Expedition. 1958.
Love and Death: The Complete Stories. 1959.
Orphans in Gethsemane. 1960; as *For Passion, For Heaven* and
    The Great Confession, 2 vols., 1962.
Mountain Man. 1965.

Poetry

Sonnets to an Imaginary Madonna. 1927.

Other

The Neurotic Nightingale. 1935.
The Caxton Printers in Idaho: A Short History. 1944.
God or Caesar? The Writing of Fiction for Beginners. 1953.
*Suicide or Murder? The Strange Death of Governor Meriwether
    Lewis.* 1962.
Thomas Wolfe as I Knew Him and Other Essays. 1963.
Gold Rushes and Mining Camps of the Early American West, with
    Opal Laurel Holmes. 1968.
*Three West: Conversations with Fisher, Max Evans, Michael
    Straight,* by John R. Milton. 1970.

Editor, *Idaho: A Guide in Word and Picture.* 1937.
Editor, *The Idaho Encyclopedia.* 1938.
Editor, *Idaho Lore.* 1939.

*

Bibliography: "Fisher: A Bibliography" by George Kellogg, in *Western American Literature,* spring 1970.

Critical Studies: "Fisher Issue" of *American Book Collector,* September 1963; *Fisher* by Joseph M. Flora, 1965; *Fisher: The Frontier and Regional Works* by Wayne Chatterton, 1972; *Fisher: The Novelist as Poet* and *A Solitary Voice: Fisher* both by Dorys C. Grover, 1973; *The Epic of Evolution: Its Ideology and Art: A Study of Fisher's Testament of Man* by Alfred K. Thomas, 1973; *The Past in the Present: Two Essays on History and Myth in Fisher's Testament of Man* by Lester Strong, 1979; *Fisher* by Louie W. Attebery, 1987; "Wagons West: Vardis Fisher's and John Ford's Vision of the Mormon Movement West" by Larry W. Ranney, in *The Image of the Frontier in Literature, the Media, and Society* edited by Will Wright and Steven Kaplan, 1997.

*   *   *

Vardis Fisher is usually placed with the naturalists in American literature and among the strident voices of protest in the 1930s. Although his greatest fame came in the Depression years—reaching its height in 1939 with *Children of God*—he was a prolific writer whose work spanned four decades. He wore no labels easily and relished defying definition. Not interested in literary trends, he stuck doggedly to the goals he set himself. He survived numerous battles with publishers and lived to see a modest but genuine revival of interest in his work.

Fisher's youth in an isolated area along the Snake River in Idaho was lonely and terrifying. Alfred Kazin called him America's last authentic novelist of the frontier. More important, Fisher was the first to write significant novels of the Rocky Mountain west. His passionate, sometimes violent and ambiguous response to his mountain country produced his best work. His first published novel, *Toilers of the Hills,* gave a poignant rendering of pioneer efforts to farm the difficult Antelope Hills bordering the South Fork of the Snake. The sense of place and people was even stronger in his second novel, *Dark Bridwell*—his most satisfying work of fiction. Fisher seemed on the way to founding a western counterpart to Faulkner's Yoknapatawpha County, for he was also writing short stories and poems about the people of the Antelope Hills. Vridar Hunter, the protagonist of *In Tragic Life,* had already appeared as a minor character in *Dark Bridwell;* and Dock Hunter, the farmer of *Toilers of the Hills,* is Vridar's uncle.

But Vridar was not simply a character who had played a part in the earlier novel. As his name indicates, he was also an autobiographical figure. *In Tragic Life* renders Fisher's first eighteen, largely agonized, years forcefully. The book became the first volume of an autobiographical tetralogy—and as the other volumes appeared Antelope became less significant. It became clear that Fisher was intent on exploring his own agonies more than a region. His first wife had committed suicide while he was a graduate student, and there were major psychological problems he had to work out. The confessional aspect of his work is large. Vridar made an unusual hero, for Fisher was often castigating him. Hence, the tetralogy becomes increasingly intellectual and loaded with indictments of a world Vridar never made—the final volume being decidedly a novel of ideas.

Not overly concerned with critical objections to his tetralogy, Fisher felt that his autobiographical searches had not led him to understand Vridar as he would have liked. Even as he finished the tetralogy, Fisher made plans for his *Testament of Man* novels—a series to be based on extended research into man's evolutionary development, particularly his ideas about divinity. Beginning with *Darkness and the Deep,* when man is little more than an ape and

possessed only the simplest speech, Fisher traces man's "progress" until he eventually retells Vridar's story as the final volume in the series of twelve. The most successful books are the first two and the final one. The later volumes become increasingly discursive and the presentation of research as experience less successfully integrated.

Still, Fisher has an important place among the American writers of historical novels. The impetus behind his famous *Children of God* was a search into his most immediate religious heritage—Mormonism. He focuses directly on the lives of Joseph Smith and Brigham Young for the major part of his long novel. His intention was to be as accurate as possible. The success of *Children of God* led Fisher to pursue other aspects of the western American past, with the goal of accurate rendering a prime consideration. He also wrote nonfictional works about the west as well as about writing.

Fisher's final novel, *Mountain Man,* is vastly different from his other historical novels of the west. Although based on an actual mountain man, "Liver-eating" Johnson, the novel is markedly unlike such factual novels as *Children of God* or *The Mothers.* It is patterned on music and highlights the romantic spirit more carefully hidden in his other work.

—Joseph M. Flora

FITCH, (William) Clyde

Born: Elmira, New York, 2 May 1865. **Education:** Hartford Public High School, Connecticut; Holderness School, New Hampshire; Amherst College, Massachusetts (editor, *Student*), 1882-86, B.A. 1886, M.A. 1902. **Career:** Freelance writer and tutor, New York, 1886: wrote for *Life* and *Puck;* visited Paris and London, and met writers in the aesthetic movement, 1888; returned to New York, and wrote children's stories for *Churchman, Independent,* and other magazines; full-time playwright and producer/director of his own plays from 1898. **Died:** 4 September 1909.

PUBLICATIONS

Collections

Plays (includes *Beau Brummell, Lovers' Lane, Nathan Hale, Barbara Frietchie, Captain Jinks of the Horse Marines, The Climbers, The Stubbornness of Geraldine, The Girl with the Green Eyes, Her Own Way, The Woman in the Case, The Truth, The City*), edited by Montrose J. Moses and Virginia Gerson. 4 vols., 1915.

Plays

Beau Brummell (produced 1890). 1908; in *Plays,* 1915.
Frederick Lemaitre (produced 1890). Edited by Oscar Cargill, in *The Social Revolt,* 1933.
Betty's Finish (produced 1890).
Pamela's Prodigy (produced 1891). 1893.
A Modern Match (produced 1892; as *Marriage,* produced 1892).
The Masked Ball, from a play by Alexandre Bisson and Albert Carre (produced 1892).

The Moth and the Flame (as *The Harvest*, produced 1893; revised version, as *The Moth and the Flame*, produced 1898). 1908; edited by Montrose J. Moses, in *Representative Plays*, 1921.
April Weather (produced 1893).
A Shattered Idol, from a novel by Balzac (produced 1893).
The Social Swim, from a play by Sardou (produced 1893).
An American Duchess, from a play by Henri Lavedan (produced 1893).
Mrs. Grundy, Jr., from a French play (produced 1893).
His Grace de Grammont (produced 1894).
Gossip, with Leo Ditrichstein, from a play by Jules Claretie (produced 1895).
Mistress Betty (produced 1895; revised version, as *The Toast of the Town*, produced 1905).
Bohemia, from a play by Theodore Barriere and Henri Murger (produced 1896).
The Liar, from a play by Alexandre Bisson (produced 1896).
A Superfluous Husband, with Leo Ditrichstein, from a play by Ludwig Fulda (produced 1897).
The Head of the Family, with Leo Ditrichstein, from a play by Adolph L'Arronge (produced 1898).
Nathan Hale (produced 1898). 1899; in *Plays*, 1915.
The Merry-Go-Round, with F. Kinsey Peile (produced 1898).
The Cowboy and the Lady (produced 1899). 1908.
Barbara Frietchie, The Frederick Girl (produced 1899). 1900; in *Plays*, 1915.
Sappho, from the play by Daudet and Belot, based on the story by Daudet (produced 1899).
Captain Jinks of the Horse Marines (produced 1901). 1902; in *Plays*, 1915.
The Climbers (produced 1901). 1906; in *Plays*, 1915.
Lovers' Lane (produced 1901). In *Plays*, 1915.
The Marriage Game, from a play by Emile Augier (produced 1901).
The Last of the Dandies (produced 1901).
The Way of the World (produced 1901).
The Girl and the Judge (produced 1901).
The Stubbornness of Geraldine (produced 1902). 1906; in *Plays*, 1915.
The Girl with the Green Eyes (produced 1902). 1905; in *Plays*, 1915.
The Bird in the Cage, from a play by Ernst von Wildenbruch (produced 1903).
The Frisky Mrs. Johnson, from a play by Paul Gavault and Georges Beer (produced 1903). 1908.
Her Own Way (produced 1903). 1907; in *Plays*, 1915.
Algy (produced 1903).
Major Andre (produced 1903).
Glad of It (produced 1903).
The Coronet of the Duchess (produced 1904).
Granny, from a play by Georges Michell (produced 1904).
Cousin Billy, from a play by Labiche and Martin (produced 1905).
The Woman in the Case (produced 1905). In *Plays*, 1915.
Her Great Match (produced 1905). Edited by Arthur Hobson Quinn, in *Representative American Plays*, 1917.
Wolfville, with Willis Steell, from a novel by Alfred Henry Lewis (produced 1905).
Toddles, from a play by Godferneaux and Bernard (produced 1906).
The House of Mirth, with Edith Wharton, from the novel by Wharton (produced 1906). Edited by Glenn Loney, 1981.

The Girl Who Has Everything (produced 1906).
The Straight Road (produced 1907).
The Truth (produced 1907). 1907; in *Plays*, 1915.
Miss McCobb, Manicurist (produced 1907).
Her Sister, with Cosmo Gordon-Lennox (produced 1907).
The Honor of the Family, from a play by Emile Fabre based on a novel by Balzac (produced 1908).
Girls, from a play by Alexander Engel and Julius Horst (produced 1908).
The Blue Mouse, from a play by Alexander Engel and Julius Horst (produced 1908).
A Happy Marriage (produced 1909).
The Bachelor (produced 1909).
The City: A Modern Play of American Life (produced 1909). In *Plays*, 1915.

Fiction

The Knighting of the Twins and Ten Other Tales (for children). 1891.
A Wave of Life. 1909.

Other

Some Correspondence and Six Conversations. 1896.
The Smart Set: Correspondence and Conversations. 1897.
Fitch and His Letters, edited by Montrose J. Moses and Virginia Gerson. 1924.

*

Critical Study: *The Fitch I Knew* by Archie Bell, 1909.

*   *   *

No playwright in the history of American drama has been able to match the commercial success of Clyde Fitch and at the same time achieve the international reputation that his work brought him. Many have written better plays; probably some have made more money; but none has equaled his cumulative success. Clearly aided by the copyright law of 1891 and his membership in the "Syndicate School," Fitch produced a considerable body of work (more than fifty plays, including many adaptations of foreign works), became the first millionaire dramatist in America, and showed himself to be not just an extremely colorful man of the theater but a dramatist of some sensitivity whose plays were produced in several countries.

His theory of playwriting reflected the prevailing nineteenth-century attitudes toward literature and art. "Try to be truthful," Fitch explained: true to the details of life and environment that he saw, true to every emotion, every motive, every occupation, every class. Fitch himself was most successful in portraying the upper levels of society that in a few plays occasionally reflected the realistic and truthful detail of noteworthy drama. In most instances, however, his concern for truth lacked the necessary perspective, and he simply imitated the popular melodramatic caricature of life with an excess of what became recognized as "Fitchian detail."

As a flamboyant man-about-town Fitch enjoyed the places frequented by New York society. The problems of married life, the peculiarities of individuals, the faults and foibles of a rapidly changing society—these were the aspects of life that appealed to Fitch and that he tried to picture truthfully in his plays. His first full-length social drama was *A Modern Match,* concerned with a selfish woman who refused to assume the responsibilities of marriage. *The Climbers* is one of his better social melodramas, ridiculing the hypocrisy and materialism of New York society. *The Stubbornness of Geraldine* and *Her Great Match* reflect the international social scene. In *The Truth,* concerned with a pathological liar, and *The Girl with the Green Eyes,* which dramatized what he termed an "inherited" jealousy, Fitch was at his melodramatic best, using the particular personal insight that distinguished the plays. In his final play, *The City,* he attempted to present a serious view of city life disintegrating under a weight of moral, economic, and political problems, but the lighter and satiric view of high society was his proper metier.

As one who prepared the way for an established social comedy in America Fitch deserves attention. He was above all a man of that society, and a craftsman of the commercial theater whose interest in truthfulness in drama helped him create some believable characters and memorable social scenes against a background of melodrama.

—Walter J. Meserve

FITZGERALD, F(rancis) Scott (Key)

Born: St. Paul, Minnesota, 24 September 1896. **Education:** St. Paul Academy, 1908-11; Newman School, Hackensack, New Jersey, 1911-13; Princeton University, New Jersey, 1913-17. **Military Service:** Served in the U.S. Army, 1917-19: 2nd lieutenant. **Family:** Married Zelda Sayre in 1920; one daughter. **Career:** Advertising copywriter, Barron Collier Agency, New York, 1919-20; full-time writer from 1920; lived in Europe, 1924-26, 1929-31; screenwriter for Metro-Goldwyn-Mayer, Hollywood, 1937-38. **Died:** 21 December 1940.

PUBLICATIONS

Collections

The Bodley Head Fitzgerald, edited by Malcolm Cowley and J.B. Priestley. 6 vols., 1958-63.
The Fitzgerald Reader, edited by Arthur Mizener. 1963.
The Short Stories, edited by Matthew J. Bruccoli. 1989.
The Selected Works of F. Scott Fitzgerald. 1996.

Short Stories

Flappers and Philosophers. 1920.
Tales of the Jazz Age. 1922.
All the Sad Young Men. 1926.
Taps at Reveille. 1935.
The Stories, edited by Malcolm Cowley. 1951.
The Mystery of the Raymond Mortgage (story). 1960.
The Pat Hobby Stories, edited by Arnold Gingrich. 1962.
The Apprentice Fiction of Fitzgerald 1909-1917, edited by John Kuehl. 1965.
Bits of Paradise: 21 Uncollected Stories, with Zelda Fitzgerald, edited by Matthew J. Bruccoli and Scottie Fitzgerald Smith. 1973.

The Basil and Josephine Stories, edited by Jackson R. Bryer and John Kuehl. 1973.
The Price Was High: The Last Uncollected Stories of Fitzgerald, edited by Matthew J. Bruccoli. 1979.
Babylon Revisited and Other Stories. 1996.
Bernice Bobs Her Hair and Other Stories. 1996.
The Diamond As Big As the Ritz and Other Stories. 1997.
The Rich Boy and Other Stories. 1998.
The Ice Palace and Other Stories. 1998.

Novels

This Side of Paradise. 1920.
The Beautiful and Damned. 1922.
John Jackson's Arcady, edited by Lilian Holmes Stack. 1924.
The Great Gatsby. 1925; *A Facsimile of the Manuscript* edited by Matthew J. Bruccoli, 1973; *Apparatus* edited by Bruccoli, 1974.
Tender Is the Night: A Romance. 1934; revised edition, edited by Malcolm Cowley, 1951.
The Last Tycoon: An Unfinished Novel, Together with The Great Gatsby and Selected Writings, edited by Edmund Wilson. 1941.
Dearly Beloved. 1969.

Plays

Fie! Fie! Fi-Fi! (plot and lyrics only), book by Walker M. Ellis, music by D.D. Griffin, A.L. Booth, and P.B. Dickey (produced 1914). 1914.
The Evil Eye (lyrics only), book by Edmund Wilson, music by P.B. Dickey and F. Warburton Guilbert (produced 1915). 1915.
Safety First (lyrics only), book by J.F. Bohmfalk and J. Biggs, Jr., music by P.B. Dickey, F. Warburton Guilbert, and E. Harris (produced 1916). 1916.
The Vegetable; or, From President to Postman (produced 1923). 1923.
Screenplay for Three Comrades, edited by Matthew J. Bruccoli. 1978.

Screenplays: *A Yank at Oxford* (uncredited), with others, 1937; *Three Comrades,* with Edward E. Paramore, 1938.

Radio Play: *Let's Go Out and Play,* 1935.

Poetry

Poems 1911-1940, edited by Matthew J. Bruccoli. 1981.

Other

The Crack-Up, with Other Uncollected Pieces, Note-Books, and Unpublished Letters, edited by Edmund Wilson. 1945.
Afternoon of an Author: A Selection of Uncollected Stories and Essays, edited by Arthur Mizener. 1957.
The Letters of Fitzgerald, edited by Arthur Turnbull. 1963.
Thoughtbook, edited by John Kuehl. 1965.
Fitzgerald in His Own Time: A Miscellany, edited by Matthew J. Bruccoli and Jackson R. Bryer. 1971.
Dear Scott/Dear Max: The Fitzgerald-Perkins Correspondence, edited by John Kuehl and Jackson R. Bryer. 1971.
As Ever, Scott Fitz—: Letters Between Fitzgerald and His Literary Agent Harold Ober 1919-1940, edited by Matthew J. Bruccoli and Jennifer Atkinson. 1972.
Ledger, edited by Matthew J. Bruccoli. 1973.

The Cruise of the Rolling Junk (travel). 1976.
The Notebooks, edited by Matthew J. Bruccoli. 1978.
Correspondence, edited by Matthew J. Bruccoli and Margaret M. Duggan. 1980.
Fitzgerald on Writing, edited by Larry W. Phillips. 1985.
A Life in Letters. 1994.
F. Scott Fitzgerald and Authorship. 1996.

*

Bibliography: *The Critical Reception of Fitzgerald: A Bibliographical Study* by Jackson R. Bryer, 1967, supplement 1984; *Fitzgerald: A Descriptive Bibliography* by Matthew J. Bruccoli, 1972, supplement 1980, revised edition, 1987; *The Foreign Critical Reception of Fitzgerald: An Analysis and Annotated Bibliography* by Linda C. Stanley, 1980; *F. Scott Fitzgerald A to Z: The Essential Reference to His Life and Work* by Mary Jo Tate, 1998; *An F. Scott Fitzgerald Encyclopedia* by Robert L. Gale, 1998.

Critical Studies: *The Far Side of Paradise: A Biography of Fitzgerald* by Arthur Mizener, 1951, revised edition, 1965, and *Fitzgerald: A Collection of Critical Essays* edited by Mizener, 1963; *The Fictional Technique of Fitzgerald* by James E. Miller, Jr., 1957, revised edition, as *Fitzgerald: His Art and His Technique,* 1964; *Beloved Infidel: The Education of a Woman* (with Gerold Frank), 1958, and *The Real Fitzgerald: Thirty-Five Years Later,* 1976, both by Sheilah Graham; *Fitzgerald* by Andrew Turnbull, 1962; *The Composition of Tender Is the Night,* 1963, *Scott and Ernest: The Authority of Failure and the Authority of Success,* 1978, and *Some Sort of Epic Grandeur: The Life of Fitzgerald,* 1981, all by Matthew J. Bruccoli, and *New Essays on The Great Gatsby* edited by Bruccoli, 1985; *Fitzgerald* by Kenneth Eble, 1963, revised edition, 1977, and *Fitzgerald: A Collection of Criticism* edited by Eble, 1973; *Fitzgerald and His Contemporaries* by William F. Goldhurst, 1963; *Fitzgerald: A Critical Portrait* by Henry Dan Piper, 1965; *The Art of Fitzgerald* by Sergio Perosa, 1965; *Fitzgerald and the Craft of Fiction* by Richard D. Lehan, 1966; *Fitzgerald: The Last Laocoön* by Robert Sklar, 1967; *Fitzgerald: An Introduction and Interpretation* by Milton Hindus, 1968; *Zelda: A Biography* by Nancy Milford, 1970, as *Zelda Fitzgerald,* 1970; *The Illusions of a Nation: Myth and History in the Novels of Fitzgerald* by John F. Callahan, 1972; *Fitzgerald: The Critical Reception,* 1978, and *The Short Stories of Fitzgerald: New Approaches in Criticism,* 1982, both edited by Jackson R. Bryer; *Candles and Carnival Lights: The Catholic Sensibility of Fitzgerald* by Joan M. Allen, 1978; *Fitzgerald* by Rose Adrienne Gallo, 1978; *Fitzgerald: Crisis in an American Identity* by Thomas J. Stavola, 1979; *The Achieving of The Great Gatsby: Fitzgerald 1920-1925* by Robert Emmet Long, 1979; *Fitzgerald and the Art of Social Fiction* by Brian Way, 1980; *Fitzgerald: A Biography* by André Le Vot, 1983; *Fool for Love: Fitzgerald* by Scott Donaldson, 1983, and *Critical Essays on Fitzgerald's The Great Gatsby* edited by Donaldson, 1984; *Invented Lives: The Marriage of F. Scott and Zelda Fitzgerald* by James R. Mellow, 1984; *The Novels of Fitzgerald* by John B. Chambers, 1989; *Fitzgerald's Craft of Short Fiction: The Collected Stories 1920-1935* by Alice Hall Petry, 1989; *Gatsby* edited by Harold Bloom, 1991; *A Fortune Yet: Money in the Art of Fitzgerald's Short Stories* by Bryant Mangum, 1991; *Gatsby's Party* by Patti White, 1992; *Fitzgerald and Hemingway: A Dangerous Friendship* by Matthew Joseph Bruccoli, 1994; *The Winding Road to West Egg: The Artistic Development of F. Scott Fitzgerald* by Robert Roulston, 1994; *Tender Is the Night: The Broken Universe* by Milton R. Stern, 1994; *American Dream Visions: Chaucer's Surprising Influence on F. Scott Fitzgerald* by Deborah Davis Schlacks, 1994; *The Great Gatsby and Modern Times* by Ronald Berman, 1994; *The Politics of Exile: Ideology in Henry James, F. Scott Fitzgerald, and James Baldwin* by Bryan R. Washington, 1995; *Enchanted Places: The Use of Setting in F. Scott Fitzgerald's Fiction* by Aiping Zhang, 1997; *Understanding the Great Gatsby: A Student Casebook to Issues, Sources, and Historical Document* by Dalton Gross, 1998.

*   *   *

Like so many modern American writers, F. Scott Fitzgerald created a public image of himself as a representative figure of his times, which may have been a part of the promotional campaign to sell his fiction. It worked for a while, with such success that any effort to evoke the Jazz Age or the Roaring Twenties is inevitably accompanied by a reference to or a photograph of Fitzgerald. But the public memory is fickle, and after he and Zelda had left the big stage and the gossip columnists no longer had their reckless antics to report, people forgot that he was once considered a writer of great promise and talent, and few realized that he had produced a body of work that bids well to bring him status as a writer for all times.

When Fitzgerald appeared on the literary scene in 1920 with *This Side of Paradise,* a semi-autobiographical guide to life at Princeton and the story of a sensitive young man who is trying to find his place in society, the critics were taken with its sophisticated style, its use of the social milieu, its honest treatment of emotional experience, and its somewhat bold portrayal of the younger generation. His readers, then, looked for even better writing in the following five years, but few would agree that he fulfilled his promise. Neither the two collections of intriguing, skillful, but often uneven short stories, *Flappers and Philosophers* and *Tales of the Jazz Age,* nor the weak play *The Vegetable* seemed to satisfy their expectations. His second novel, *The Beautiful and Damned,* was looked to more eagerly and was more widely reviewed than any other work by the author. The hero, Fitzgerald said in a letter to his publisher, was intended as "one of those many with the tastes and weaknesses of an artist but with no actual creative inspiration," and the novel related how he and his beautiful young wife were "wrecked on the shoals of dissipation." The use of autobiographical details again occasioned some speculation and caused the book to sell well, but many critics found it an unsuccessful effort at a somber tragedy of a typical American sensibility and thought that it lacked organization or focus. Some later critics, however, have felt it to be a better novel than contemporary readers realized.

Whatever faults one may find in Fitzgerald's early work, with the publication of *The Great Gatsby* he fulfilled his highest promise and gave to American literature one of its masterworks. On the surface, of course, *The Great Gatsby* is much a part of its age as a brilliant dramatization of the social and economic corruptions of the jazz age, marked by Prohibition, gangsterism, blasé flappers, and uprootedness. American morality was marked by questionable business ethics, commercial criteria for success, and ultraconservatism in social and political thinking. Historians like Charles Beard were insisting that materialistic and economic factors rather than idealistic motives had determined the course of American history. Through character and theme, Fitzgerald dealt in one way or another with all of these historic factors with such a sensitivity that one can even intuit in the text slight prophetic reverberations of the stock market crash of 1929 and the Great Depression in the offing.

Beyond these surface concerns, the novel deals symbolically with the failure of the American dream of success, which in Fitzgerald's time was still best known through the **Horatio Alger** novels. Like **Benjamin Franklin** before him, Horatio Alger expounded, by way of his dime novels, the possibility of rising from rags to riches through industry, ambition, self-reliance, honesty, and temperance. In this myth, and the frontier tradition of self-reliance, lies the genesis of what impels Gatsby. Behind his simple and touching study and work schedule in the copy of *Hopalong Cassidy* cherished by his father lies the childhood dreams of a Franklin or a Thomas Edison, the lectures on self-improvement of a Russell Conwell or a Dale Carnegie, the lessons on bodily development of a Charles Atlas, and the tradition that every American boy could make a million dollars or become President. But what an ironic reversal! By imitating the great American moralists, Gatsby rises to be a rich and powerful criminal.

A second significant thematic concern of the novel relates to its symbolic use of the Midwest as a contrast with the east. In his nostalgic reverie on the midwest near the end of the novel, Nick Carraway concludes, "I see now that this has been a story of the West, after all—Tom and Gatsby, Daisy, Jordan, and I, were all Westerners, and perhaps we possessed some deficiency in common which made us subtly unadaptable to Eastern life." This last line is ironic, because Nick left his Minnesota home originally because it "seemed like the ragged edge of the universe," but by the end of the novel it is the place to which he returns to regain a sense of balance and moral equilibrium. Fitzgerald is playing with the traditional American dichotomy between the east as a model of European sophistication and corruption and the west as a repository of the fundamental decencies and virtues derived from contact with the American soil, the new Garden of Eden.

A figure who lurks in the background of the novel is Dan Cody, whose name suggests the mythic traditions surrounding Daniel Boone and Buffalo Bill Cody. Cody had helped settle the nation and made a fortune besides, and therefore he represents the energies that sparked the western frontier movement. But as Frederick Jackson Turner had reminded everyone in 1893, the frontier had been closed and no longer carried the significance it once had as the source of sudden wealth and the place of refuge for those seeking a second chance. By the time Gatsby met him, Dan Cody had degenerated into a senile old man subject to the advances of opportunists and gold-diggers. Gatsby takes him as his ideal, nevertheless, and, like the romantic that he is, he refuses to let historic circumstance stand in his way. Rather than wrest his fortune from the raw earth, he pioneers eastward and conquers the urban wilderness through adapting its devious means to the romantic end of recapturing the past. But history cannot be repeated, and the historic promise that Gatsby learned from Cody was, Nick notes, "already behind him, somewhere back in that vast obscurity beyond the city, where the dark fields of the republic rolled on under the night."

Jay Gatsby, then, is the ultimate American arch-romantic. Because he lacked the wealth and timing, he missed the girl on whom he had focused what Nick calls his "heightened sensitivity to the promises of life." After obtaining the wealth through corrupt means, he returns five years later to fulfill his "incorruptible dream" by attempting to repeat the one golden moment of his life when he possessed that "elusive rhythm," that "fragment of lost words" that we all seek to recall in this mundane existence from a former life, time or world. Not since Don Quixote's pursuit of Dulcinea has literature seen such a noble, heartbreaking, and impossible quest.

Adopting a modified first-person narrative form from Conrad, Fitzgerald unfolds Gatsby's tragedy for us through the eyes of the narrator, Nick Carraway. What we learn through Nick is that pure willpower divorced from rationality and decency leads to destruction, and that a merely selfish dream or notion is insufficient to justify the enormous amount of energy and life expended by Gatsby. It is a lesson that this nation would not learn for almost another fifty years, and a suggestion that Fitzgerald's prophetic vision saw farther into the future than the Depression years. When Gatsby is viewed against the moral decadence and cowardly conduct of the Buchanans—"You're worth the whole damn bunch put together," Nick tells him—his unassailable romanticism makes him appear heroic. As an individual, then, who dreams higher than he can achieve, whose reach exceeds his grasp, Gatsby is at the heart of the tragic condition and thus shares certain characteristics with Oedipus, Hamlet, and other tragic heroes of Western literature. Unlike **Arthur Miller**'s modern tragic figure, Willy Loman, Gatsby doesn't evoke mere pity and disgust at the end, as he faithfully waits for a phone call that will never come.

Aside from its concern with social and moral questions of continuing consequence, *The Great Gatsby* is one of the most carefully constructed and precisely written novels in American literature. The subtle complexity of the language; the calculated use of colors, references, and connotations; the striking configurations of verbal patterns and repetitions—all lead the reader to read and reread sentences time and time again to catch the multi-level nuances of meaning. The style is poetic and repays the application of the techniques of studied explication.

Because of the disarray of his personal life, his dwindling financial resources, and his increasing self-doubts as a writer, Fitzgerald was unable to bring his artistry to such a perfect pitch again. His numerous short stories written primarily for pay (some of which were collected in *All the Sad Young Men* and *Taps at Reveille*) and his indifferent work for Hollywood only occasionally encouraged his best talents. His next novel, *Tender Is the Night,* which came nine years after *Gatsby,* used European locales and his experiences with his wife's mental illness, another foray into autobiographical materials. What some critics felt was an unresolved problem in structure and a failure to provide clear character motivation caused many to overlook its impressive sweep of characters and its admirable effort to deal with significant psychological and social themes.

The doomed anti-hero of *Tender Is the Night,* Dick Diver, a psychiatrist turned husband/keeper of the beautiful, spoiled, wealthy Nicole, is, in part, a dark version of Fitzgerald's fears for his own crackup into alcoholism and decadence. The sprawling canvas of the novel—set in the south of France, full of echoes of America and equally filled with brilliant cameos of lost American expatriates—catches the tone of the Depression United States both in the personal despair of the Divers and in the social clarity that highlights the waste of spirit and money that leads to a society's collapse. In his attempt to write a "big" novel, Fitzgerald tries to control his variety of themes, characters, and settings by techniques that are almost, but not quite, triumphant: the use of an innocent eye as narrative viewpoint in the book's opening, through Rosemary, a young, tough but unspoiled Hollywood actress who over-identifies with the glamorous Divers' surface; then a long flashback section to World War I and

Dick's psychiatric career as well as Nicole's illness, told from an omniscient viewpoint that concentrates on Dick's thoughts; finally a scattered, staccato ending of drunkenness and violence shown through both Dick's and Nicole's minds.

After his death, the fragments of a novel, *The Last Tycoon,* were found, many pages of which suggest that Fitzgerald was regaining control of his creative skills at the last. Despite his lapses and occasional self-indulgence, the high quality of his best work, and most certainly the striking achievement in *The Great Gatsby,* has brought his work the esteem that eluded Fitzgerald himself during his own lifetime.

—M. Thomas Inge and Eric Solomon

See the essay on *The Great Gatsby.*

FLETCHER, John Gould

Born: Little Rock, Arkansas, 3 January 1886. **Education:** Little Rock High School, 1899-1902; Phillips Academy, Andover, Massachusetts, 1902-03; Harvard University, Cambridge, Massachusetts, 1903-07. **Family:** Married 1) Florence Emily Arbuthnot in 1916 (divorced 1936); 2) Charlie May Hogue Simon in 1936. **Career:** Lived in Italy, 1907-08, and England, 1909-14 and 1916-33: associated with the Imagist movement; returned to the United States and settled in Arkansas, 1933; founder, Arkansas Folk Lore Society, 1935. **Awards:** Pulitzer prize, 1939. LL.D.: University of Arkansas, Fayetteville, 1933. **Member:** American Academy. **Died:** (suicide) 10 May 1950.

PUBLICATIONS

Poetry

The Book of Nature 1910-1912. 1913.
The Dominant City (1911-1912). 1913.
Fire and Wine. 1913.
Fool's Gold. 1913.
Visions of the Evening. 1913.
Irradiations: Sand and Spray. 1915.
Goblins and Pagodas. 1916.
Japanese Prints. 1918.
The Tree of Life. 1918.
Breakers and Granite. 1921.
Preludes and Symphonies. 1922.
Parables. 1925.
Branches of Adam. 1926.
The Black Rock. 1928.
XXIV Elegies. 1935.
The Epic of Arkansas. 1936.
Selected Poems. 1938.
South Star. 1941.
The Burning Mountain. 1946.

Other

La Poesie d'Andre Fontainas. 1919.
Some Contemporary American Poets. 1920.

Paul Gauguin: His Life and Art. 1921.
John Smith—Also Pocahontas. 1928.
The Crisis of the Film. 1929.
The Two Frontiers: A Study in Historical Psychology (on Russia and America). 1930; as *Europe's Two Frontiers,* 1930.
I'll Take My Stand: The South and the Agrarian Tradition, with others. 1930.
Life Is My Song (autobiography). 1937.
Arkansas. 1947.

Editor, *Edgar Allan Poe.* 1926.

Translator, *The Dance over Fire and Water,* by Elie Faure. 1926.
Translator, *The Reveries of a Solitary,* by Rousseau. 1927.
Translator, with others, *Jean sans terre/Landless John,* by Yvan Goll. 1944.

*

Bibliography: *Fletcher: A Bibliography* by Bruce Morton, 1979.

Critical Studies: *Fletcher* by Edna B. Stephens, 1967; *Fletcher and Imagism* by Edmund S. de Chasca, 1978; *John Gould Fletcher and Southern Modernism* by Lucas Carpenter, 1990; *Fierce Solitude: A Life of John Gould Fletcher* by Ben F. Johnson, 1994.

*   *   *

Although most often linked with the Imagist movement because of his early association with **Amy Lowell**, John Gould Fletcher belongs to no one "school" of poetry; his work covers a wide range of styles and themes. But in all of his work an emphasis upon the visual is a reflection not only of his interest in art but of his early experience with Imagist philosophy. In 1907, at the age of twenty-two, Fletcher left America for Europe and spent the next twenty-five years moving between the two continents. In 1913, having published, at his own expense, five volumes of poetry, he went to Paris where he came under the influence of Impressionist art, new music, and **Ezra Pound**. But it was with Amy Lowell that he aligned himself, joining her Imagist circle in 1914; Lowell included some of Fletcher's poems in her anthologies, he dedicated some of his work to her, and together they formulated a poetic style of "polyphonic prose."

Of Fletcher's many works, the most famous are his "symphonies"; these are expressions of mood symbolized by a distinct color, one for each symphony. They are all divided into movements (the poems of *Irradiations: Sand and Spray* are even given tempo markings), each reflecting another aspect of the color stressed in the imagery of the poem. The result is an effective synaesthetic blend of verbal, visual, and musical elements. In "White Symphony," for instance, mood is reflected in white peonies "like rockets in the twilight," the "white snow-water of my dreams," and a "white-laden" snowy landscape. Fletcher retains the idea of symphonic form in later poems as well. Orientalism, so influential upon the Imagists, also had a profound effect upon Fletcher; Chinese philosophy and Japanese poetry (especially *haiku*) were important to the writing of the symphonies, and Fletcher's viewing of Oriental art exhibited in America in 1914 and 1915 is reflected in *Goblins and Pagodas* and *Japanese Prints.* The subjects of the latter volume are not necessarily Japanese, as Fletcher notes in his preface, "but all illustrate something of the charm I have found in Japanese poetry and art." Here he seeks "to universalize our emotions," to show "that the universe is just as much in the shape of a hand as it is in armies, politicians, astronomy, or the exhortations of gospel-mongers; that style and technique rest on the thing conveyed and not the means of conveyance." This emphasis upon the concrete remains constant throughout all of Fletcher's poetry, which, in general, is fairly traditional in form.

In the 1920s, traveling through the American south, Fletcher met the writers of the agrarian "Fugitive" movement, in whom he had been interested for several years. Although he did not embrace the Fugitives' belief in purely intellectual poetry, he did share their concept of southern agrarian culture as a bastion against modern industrialism. His contribution to the 1929 Fugitive symposium was a discussion of "Education, Past and Present" (published in 1930 in *I'll Take My Stand*), in which he stressed the importance of encouraging folk education to help the south maintain its distinct culture. In 1933, Fletcher returned to his native Little Rock, and from that point he can be considered a southern regional writer.

—Jane S. Gabin

FORCHÉ, Carolyn

Born: Carolyn Sidlosky in Detroit, Michigan, 28 April 1950. **Education:** Michigan State University, East Lansing, B.A. in international relations and creative writing; Bowling Green State University, M.F.A. 1975. **Family:** Married Harry E. Mattison in 1984; one son. **Career:** Visiting lecturer, Michigan State University, 1974; visiting lecturer, 1975, and assistant professor, 1976-78, San Diego State University; visiting lecturer, University of Virginia, Charlottesville, 1979, 1982-83; assistant professor, 1980, and associate professor, 1981, University of Arkansas, Fayetteville; visiting lecturer, New York University, 1983, 1985, and Vassar College, Poughkeepsie, New York, 1984; adjunct professor, Columbia University, 1984-85; writer-in-residence, State University of New York, Albany, 1985; visiting associate professor, University of Minnesota, Minneapolis, summer 1985. Poetry editor, *Tendril,* Green Harbor, Massachusetts. Journalist for Amnesty International in El Salvador, 1978-80, and Beirut correspondent, "All Things Considered" radio program, 1983. **Awards:** Yale Series of younger Poets award, 1975; *Chicago Review* award, 1975; Devine Memorial prize, 1975; Bread Loaf Writer's Conference Tennessee Williams fellowship, 1977, 1984; Guggenheim fellowship, 1978; Emily Clark Balch prize, 1979; Lamont Poetry Selection award, 1981; Edita and Ira Morris Award for Peace and Culture, 1998. H.D.L.: Russell Sage College, Troy, New York, 1985.

PUBLICATIONS

Poetry

Gathering the Tribes. 1976.
The Country Between Us. 1981.
The Angel of History. 1994.

Other

Women in American Labor History, 1825-1935: An Annotated Bibliography, with Martha Jane Soltow. 1972.

El Salvador: The Work of Thirty Photographers. 1983.
Colors Come from God-Just Like Me, illustrated by Charles Cox. 1995.
Lani Maestro: Essays, with Rina Carvajal and Stephen Horne. 1996.

Editor, *Women and War in El Salvador.* 1980.
Editor, *Against Forgetting: Twentieth-Century Poetry of Witness.* 1993.

Translator, *Flowers from the Volcano,* by Claribel Algeria. 1982.
Translator, *Sorrow,* by Claribel Alegria. 1999.

*

Critical Studies: By Terrence Diggory, in *Salmagundi,* Spring 1984.

* * *

Leaving her home in Detroit, Michigan, to attend college in East Lansing, Carolyn Sidlosky carried with her a strong sense of family—a richly varied family, memorialized in the persona of Anna, her Slovak immigrant grandmother. She studied for a B.A. degree at Michigan State University, where she majored in creative writing and English—and won most of the campus poetry contests. While there, she also married. Finding her way to Breadloaf as an undergraduate, she created a reputation for herself even before going to Bowling Green (Ohio) State University's master of fine arts program, where she taught writing courses, worked with Frederick Eckman, and spent several years traveling in the deserts of Utah and living with the Pueblo Indians near Taos, New Mexico. Many of the poems from her study there appeared in her first book, *Gathering the Tribes,* which won the Yale Younger Poets Award in 1975.

During the next few years Forché won a National Endowment for the Arts grant and a Guggenheim fellowship. She lived first in Spain and then in El Salvador, where she documented human rights violations for Amnesty International. Between 1978 and 1980, she worked closely with Monsignor Oscar Romero—until he was assassinated by a right-wing death squad. Many of the poems in Forché's second book, *The Country Between Us,* which won the Lamont Poetry Award in 1982, speak of the desperate plight of human beings in El Salvador and elsewhere. In 1982 she also published *Flowers from the Volcano,* poems by Claribel Alegria, and an edited book, *El Salvador: The Work of Thirty Photographers.* Forché continued to work for Amnesty International in Israel, Lebanon, and South Africa. She taught at many universities, finally becoming a professor of English at George Mason University in Fairfax, Virginia; she makes her home in Virginia with her husband, a documentary photographer, and son.

In 1991 she published—and was partial translator from the French for—*The Selected Poems of Robert Desnos,* as well as another edited book, *Shooting Back: Photography by and about the Homeless.* Concurrently, she worked years developing her 1993 poetry anthology, *Against Forgetting: Twentieth-Century Poetry of Witness,* and in 1994 published the book that places her among the century's leading poets, *The Angel of History.* Drawing from Walter Benjamin's concept of human responsibility, her third book records an almost unvoiced lament, a Kadish for humankind. Quite different from either of her first books, this collection takes Forché from the category of lyric poet, though never so spare or so apparently artless as Williams or Frost, to a class closer to that of prophetic poet. In her art, she has moved from a cogent and precise mastery of language, sound, and form to an appropriate, groping hesitancy. Because of the intensity of the poet's response to her subject matter, her style has changed to allow a glimpse into wider worlds: lines break away to float, gossamer-like, ready to attach themselves to some different, separate mass; lines have not only lives of their own but multiple lives.

The Angel of History is a book of fragmented images, of characters—named and unnamed—and of their largely silenced stories. Regardless of who a person is, his or her placement in this narrative signals participation in one of another of this century's horrors. From the personal familial tragedy to the Holocaust, from the debacle of war to the even more threatening debacle of genocidal murder, Forché's characters live their pain. We believe the poet when she writes, "There is no other way to say this."

Rather than the stark, inevitable image, Forché here creates an enigmatic landscape, although an intentionally placeless one, of partial objects. These graphic, concrete images, which spark immediate recognition, stop short of "meaning." The white dress hanging behind the door remains evocative—we surround the image with our contextualizations of woman's dress, whiteness, specialness, vestigial memory. The dress hovers in the reader's mind, finally named as a wedding dress but still not providing an answer to the riddle of the poem entire.

From these decades of mourning, Forché creates a figure, part religious, part mythic, and part human. Her angel observes, attempts to record, and tries to find language, speech. Never an intrusive consciousness, Forché's angel most often chooses the personae of bereaved women as its points of consciousness or avenues of expression. This is far from a didactic poem. It is also far from a domestic one. The life events described here are the monumental human events of the twentieth century—the wars, the genocide, the bomb—but they are reflected through the prism of a woman's experiences. And often, a lone woman.

Part of the textual fabric consists, in fact, of small, single voices, flutelike, piercing the shadows. Sometimes unintelligible, rarely complete, these reedy syllables mark—nothing. They sound but without any tangible narrative. They lament but are absent a specific reference. Strangest of all, when they do speak, they try to remember the positive: "We went on. When my son was born I became mortal. My husband was a soldier against the Nazis. He even returned to me."

Woven from such splinters of voice, Forché's poem pulls as well from remarkable long lines of some authorial memory. *The Angel of History* is a poem about both the personal and the historical, the voiced and the voiceless, the shards of memory that comprise what we know—or ever will know—of time past: ". . . a little residue of nothing . . . . And the world is worse now than it was then."

—Linda Wagner-Martin

FORD, Richard

Born: Jackson, Mississippi, 16 February 1944. **Education:** Public schools in Jackson, 1950-62; Michigan State University, East Lansing, 1962-66, B.A. 1966; Washington University Law School,

St. Louis, 1966-67; University of California, Irvine, 1968-70, M.F.A. 1970. **Family:** Married Kristina Hensley in 1968. **Career:** Assistant professor, University of Michigan, 1975-76; assistant professor of English, Williams College, Williamstown, Massachusetts, 1978-79; lecturer and George Perkins fellow in the Humanities, Princeton University, New Jersey, 1980-81; lecturer, Harvard University, 1994; visiting professor, Northwestern University, 1997-98. **Awards:** Fellow, Society of Fellows, University of Michigan, 1971-74; Great Lakes College Association Best First Novel award, 1976; Guggenheim fellowship, 1977; National Endowment for the Arts fellowship, 1979, 1986; Pushcart prize story, 1986; Best American Short Stories prize story, 1986; Mississippi Academy of Arts and Letters Award for Literature, 1987; PEN-Faulkner Award for Fiction (citation), 1987; Northwest Booksellers Award for Fiction, 1988; New York Public Library Literary Lion award, 1989; American Academy award, 1989; Echoing Green Foundation award, 1991; Avery Hopwood Memorial Lecturer, University of Michigan, 1992; Governor's Award for Artistic Achievement (Mississippi), 1993; Fulbright fellowship (Sweden), 1993; The Lyndhurst prize, 1993; The Rea Award for the Short Story, 1995; Officier, L'Ordre Des Arts Des Lettres, Republic of France, 1996; Pulitzer prize for Fiction, 1996; Finalist, National Book Critics Circle award, 1996; PEN-Faulkner award for Fiction, 1996; Humanist of the Year, Louisiana Endowment for the Humanities, 1997; Award for Merit in the Novel, American Academy of Arts and Letters, 1997. Honorary degrees: University of Rennes, France, 1995; Loyola University, 1996; University of Michigan, 1998. **Member:** American Academy of Arts and Letters, 1998. **Residence:** New Orleans, Louisiana.

PUBLICATIONS

Novels

A Piece of My Heart. 1976.
The Ultimate Good Luck. 1981.
The Sportswriter. 1986.
Wildlife. 1990.
Independence Day. 1995.

Short Stories

Rock Springs. 1987.
Women with Men. 1997.

Plays

American Tropical. 1983.

Screenplays: *Bright Angel,* 1991.

Other

Editor, with Shannon Ravenel, *The Best American Short Stories 1990.* 1990.
Editor, *The Granta Book of the American Short Story.* 1992.
Editor, *Ploughshares.* Fall, 1996.
Editor, with Constance Sullivan, *The Fights.* 1996.
Editor, with Michael Kreyling, *Eudora Welty: Collected Writings.* n.d.

*

Manuscript Collection: Michigan State University, East Lansing.

Critical Studies: "Richard Ford" by Frank W. Shelton, in *Contemporary Fiction Writers of the South: A Bio-Bibliographical Sourcebook* edited by Joseph Flora, 1993; "Frank Bascombe Awakes to Lessons of Independence" by Merle Rubin, in *The Christian Science Monitor,* July 1995, pp.19; "The Poetry of Real Estate" by Raymond A. Schroth, in *Commonweal,* October 1995, pp. 27-8; "Richard Ford: Important Acts" in *Passion and Craft: Conversations with Notable Writers* edited by Bonnie Lyons and Bill Oliver, 1998.

*   *   *

Richard Ford is often linked with his friends **Raymond Carver** and **Tobias Wolff** as representative of the so-called dirty realism of the late 1980s. Like them, he tries to accomplish what he says rock singer Bruce Springsteen does with his music: dignify "small feelings with the gravity of real emotion" and give "a voice of consequence to the unlistened to."

Born and raised in Jackson, Mississippi, Ford made his one attempt to capture the history-haunted South in his first novel, *A Piece of My Heart* (1976). This "hello and farewell" to a southern literary tradition focuses on two men who return to the South to find out who they are but fail to discover anything except that it is futile to search for meaning either in the past or in a place. The book received some good reviews but sold few copies, which may have led Ford to try a more popular genre in his second book, *The Ultimate Good Luck* (1981), an intrigue about a Vietnam veteran who tries to free the brother of a former girlfriend from a Mexican prison. More interesting than the film noir conspiracies in this Graham Greene-like "entertainment," however, is Ford's creation of a rootless and detached male protagonist who, even though he wants involvement, avoids commitment.

In his third novel, Ford further develops this protagonist, making him softer and more philosophical. Frank Bascombe, the thirty-eight-year-old hero of *The Sportswriter*, is a sort of American everyman who means well but tries to avoid repeating the pains of the past by remaining on the surface of reality. Bascombe cannot get over his failure to fulfill his early promise as a fiction writer, the death of his nine-year old son, and the breakup of his marriage. As a writer for a New York sports magazine, he contrasts his own introspection and dissatisfaction with the comfortable, unexamined self-image of the athletes about whom he writes.

Bascombe is primarily characterized by his inability to get close to anyone or to face the truth about himself and get on with his life. In one encounter, a disabled ex-pro-football player challenges Bascombe to face his own crippled state, but he refuses. In a more significant encounter, a friend comes to Bascombe for understanding and sympathy after his wife has run off with another man, but Bascombe once again turns away from sympathetic identification. When the friend commits suicide, Bascombe seems on the verge of some rebirth but insists that he has no responsibility to anyone but himself.

The Sportswriter received the PEN/Faulkner award for fiction and got almost universally good reviews, establishing Ford's reputation, which was solidified the following year with his highly praised collection of short stories, *Rock Springs*. One of the most frequently anthologized stories in the collection is the title story, in which the protagonist, Earl, heads off to Tampa in a stolen car, accompanied by his daughter, Cheryl, and his girlfriend, Edna, full of high hopes—that is, until his luck runs out when they break

down in Rock Springs, Wyoming. Things completely fall apart when they retreat to a Ramada Inn so that Earl can steal another car and Edna leaves him. In a poignant conclusion, Earl wanders the motel parking lot, wondering how someone observing his actions would react: "Would you think he was trying to get his head cleared? . . . Would you think he was anybody like you?"

Wildlife, Ford's fourth novel, a coming-of-age spin-off of the short story "Great Falls," focuses on Joe Brinson, the first-person narrator who recalls his adolescence during the fall of 1960, which was also marked a fall from innocence. Set historically on the cusp of a turbulent decade, metaphorically framed by a wildfire that threatens the town of Great Falls, Montana, the story deals with a family's loss of security and a boy's determination to hold on to some meaningful center.

Independence Day, Ford's successful sequel to *The Sportswriter*, begins six years later, when Frank Bascombe has given up writing to become a real estate agent, an occupation that allows Ford to explore the narrative metaphor of the American search for a dream home and gives him the opportunity to confront Bascombe with a wide range of modern American types, not the least of which is the impossible-to-satisfy couple to whom he shows forty-five different homes. As in *The Sportswriter*, however, Bascombe is not focused outward on the world but inward on his memories. Still haunted by the sense of "dreaminess" created by the death of his son, he longs for family security, even going so far as to buy his former wife's house to create a sense of the familiar past.

Just as the Easter holiday suggested the metaphoric need for rebirth in *The Sportswriter*, *Independence Day* revolves around the Fourth of July weekend and Bascombe's own desire for independence. He takes his "emotionally underdeveloped" but intellectually gifted fifteen-year-old son, Paul, to the Baseball Hall of Fame to try to reconnect with him, only to see the boy dangerously beaned by a pitching machine. Although Frank does not get what he wants, the novel concludes with a sense that there is "much that's left till later." *Independence Day* was the first book to simultaneously win the Pulitzer Prize and the PEN/Faulkner Award for Fiction.

In his seventh book, *Women with Men* (1997), a collection of short novels, Ford was still concerned with the initiation of adolescent males and the dilemma of drifting middle-aged men. In two stories that focus on Americans in Paris—"The Womanizer" and "Occidentals"—the central characters drift passively through relationships, affecting others only negatively. "Jealous" is more successful, not only because it is set in Montana, a place with which Ford is more engaged, but also because it is told from the point of view of the 17-year-old boy rather than by the lazily ruminative voice of "Womanizer" and "Occidentals."

In the late 1990s Ford was reportedly thinking about bringing Frank Bascombe back. He told an interviewer that to have written one book without even thinking about a second and then to have written it, "you would have to be naive to think that you couldn't contemplate a third."

—Charles E. May

FORNÉS, María Irene

Born: Havana, Cuba, 14 May 1930; immigrated to the United States, 1945; became citizen, 1951. **Education:** Educated in Havana public schools. **Career:** Lived in Europe, 1954-57; painter and textile designer; costume designer, Judson Poets Theatre and New Dramatists Committee productions, 1965-70; teacher at the Teachers and Writers Collaborative, New York, privately, and at numerous drama festivals and workshops, from 1965. President, New York Theatre Strategy, 1973-80. **Awards:** Whitney fellowship, 1961; Centro Mexicano de Escritores fellowship, 1962; Office for Advanced Drama Research grant, 1965; Obie award, 1965, 1977, 1979, 1982, 1984, 1985, 1988; Cintas Foundation fellowship, 1967; Yale University fellowship, 1967, 1968; Rockefeller fellowship, 1971, 1985; Guggenheim fellowship, 1972; Creative Artists Public Service grant, 1972, 1975; National Endowment for the Arts grant, 1974; American Academy award, 1985; Home Box Office award, 1986. **Residence:** New York City.

PUBLICATIONS

Plays

The Widow (produced 1961). Published, as *La Viuda*, in *Teatro Cubano*, 1961.

Tango Palace (as *There! You Died*, produced 1963; as *Tango Palace*, produced 1964; revised version produced 1965). Included in *Promenade and Other Plays*, 1971.

The Successful Life of Three: A Skit for Vaudeville (produced 1965). Included in *Promenade and Other Plays*, 1971.

Promenade, music by Al Carmines (produced 1965; revised version produced New York, 1969). Included in *Promenade and Other Plays*, 1971.

The Office (produced 1966).

A Vietnamese Wedding (produced 1967). Included in *Promenade and Other Plays*, 1971.

The Annunciation (also director: produced 1967).

Dr. Kheal (produced 1968). Included in *Promenade and Other Plays*, 1971.

The Red Burning Light; or, Mission XQ3 (produced 1968). Included in *Promenade and Other Plays*, 1971.

Molly's Dream, music by Cosmos Savage (produced 1968). Included in *Promenade and Other Plays*, 1971.

Promenade and Other Plays. 1971; revised edition, 1987.

The Curse of the Langston House, in *Baboon!!!* (produced 1972).

Dance, with Remy Charlip (also co-director: produced 1972).

Aurora, music by John FitzGibbon (also director: produced 1974).

Cap-a-Pie, music by José Raúl Bernardo (also director: produced 1975).

Lines of Vision (lyrics only), book by Richard Foreman, music by George Quincy (produced 1976).

Washing (produced 1976).

Fefu and Her Friends (also director: produced 1977). Published in *Wordplays 1*, 1980.

Lolita in the Garden, music by Richard Weinstock (also director: produced 1977).

In Service (also director: produced 1978).

Eyes on the Harem (produced 1979).

Blood Wedding, adaptation of a play by García Lorca (produced 1980).

Evelyn Brown: A Diary (also director: produced 1980).

Life Is Dream, adaptation of a play by Calderón, music by George Quincy (also director: produced 1981).

A Visit, music by George Quincy (also director: produced 1981).

The Danube (also director: produced 1982). Included in *Plays*, 1986.

Mud (also director: produced 1983; revised version, also director: produced 1985). Included in *Plays*, 1986.

Sarita, music by Leon Odenz (also director: produced 1984). Included in *Plays*, 1986.

Abingdon Square (produced 1984).

The Conduct of Life (also director: produced 1985). Included in *Plays*, 1986.

Cold Air, adaptation of a play by Virgilio Piñera (also director: produced 1985). 1985.

Drowning, adaptation of a story by Chekhov, in *Orchards* (produced 1985). 1986.

The Trial of Joan of Arc on a Matter of Faith (also director: produced 1986).

Lovers and Keepers, music by Tito Puente and Ferrando Rivas, lyrics by Fornés (also director: produced 1986). 1987.

Art, in *Box Plays* (produced 1986).

The Mothers (also director: produced 1986).

Plays. 1986.

A Matter of Faith (produced 1986).

Uncle Vanya, adaptation of the play by Anton Chekhov (also director: produced 1987).

Hunger (also director: produced 1988).

And What of the Night? (also director: produced 1989).

Oscar and Bertha (produced 1991).

*

Manuscript Collection: Lincoln Center Library of the Performing Arts, New York.

Critical Studies: interviews with Rob Creese in *Drama Review*, December 1977, with Gayle Austin in *Theatre Times*, March 1984, with Allen Frame in *Bomb*, Fall 1984, and with Scott Cummings in *Theater*, Winter 1985; "The Real Life of María Irene Fornés," in *Theatre Writings* by Bonnie Marranca, 1984; "Creative Danger" by Fornés, in *American Theatre*, September 1985; preface by Susan Sontag to *Plays*, 1986; "The Search for Identity in the Theater of Three Cuban American Female Dramatists" by Maida Watson, in *The Bilingual Review*, May-December 1991, pp. 188-96; "Fornés's Odd Couple: Oscar and Bertha at the Magic Theatre" by Scott T. Cummings, in *Journal of Dramatic Theory and Criticism*, Spring 1994, pp. 147-56; *How Shall I Live?: Community and Moral Vision in Selected Plays by María Irene Fornés* (dissertation) by Diane Rao, 1995; *María Irene Fornés and Her Critics* by Assunta Bartolomucci Kent, 1996; *Fornés: Theater in Present Tense* by Diane Lynn Moroff, 1996: *Invasion of the Temple: Women Speaking on the Ground of the Abject in the Plays of María Irene Fornés* (dissertation) by Julia Jeanette Norstrand, 1996; "Wordscapes on the Body: Performative Language as Gestus in María Irene Fornés's Plays" by Deborah R. Geis and "Drama and the Dialogic Imagination: *The Heidi Chronicles* and *Fefu and Her Friends*" by Helene Keyssar, both in *Feminist Theatre and Theory* edited by Helene Keyssar, 1996; "Feminism, Metatheatricality, and Mise-en-scene in María Irene Fornés's *Fefu and Her Friends*" by Penny Farfan, in *Modern Drama*, Winter 1997, pp. 442-53; "Pity and Terror As Public Acts: Reading Feminist Politics in the Plays of María Irene Fornés" by Tracy C. Davis, in *Staging Resistance: Essays on Political Theater* edited by Jeanne M. Colleran and Jenny S. Spencer, 1998; *The Theater of María Irene Fornés* edited by Marc Robinson, 1999.

Theatrical Activities:
Director: **Plays**—several of her own plays; *Exiles* by Ana Maria Simo, New York, 1982; *Uncle Vanya* by Anton Chekhov, New York, 1987; *Going to New England* by Ana Maria Simo, New York, 1990.

*   *   *

Maria Irene Fornes is one of the American theater's great cultural treasures, although her work has largely escaped notice by the general public. Still, she is the only playwright to have an off-Broadway theater named after one of her works—*Promenade*—and she has won more Obie awards than any other living playwright except for **Sam Shepard**. During the 1999-2000 season, New York's Signature Theatre devoted its year to her work after having previously focused only on men, including **Edward Albee**, Shepard, and **Arthur Miller**. She deserves such company.

Over the past four decades Fornes has written dozens of plays in a wide range of styles and set in various countries, cultures, and periods. She has translated and adapted the works of Rilke, Chekhov, Ibsen, Calderon, and Virgilio Pinera. One reason sometimes cited for her lack of productions is that she often insists on directing her own plays. In addition, much of her time is spent teaching, and, in fact, her reputation as an educator and playwriting teacher may eventually approach her notable accomplishments as a writer.

Given Fornes's lack of formal schooling (her mother taught English in Cuba, and Irene attended school through the sixth grade before they emigrated when she was 15), it is not surprising that many of her plays feature characters farcically trying to teach some subject (*Dr. Kheal*) or characters in search of education (*Fefu and Her Friends, The Danube,* and *Mud*). Fornes's work is completely idiosyncratic, and she is adamant about not being pigeonholed into any "school." In her introduction to one play collection, former roommate **Susan Sontag** calls her an "autodidact."

Fornes studied visual arts early on, and she has claimed that before she became a dramatist the only play she read was *Hedda Gabler* and the only play she saw performed was the original production in Paris of *Waiting for Godot*. Fittingly enough, Fornes's work can be divided by these influences. Her early work tends toward the farcical slapstick absurdism of plays like *Tango Palace, Promenade,* and *Dr. Kheal*; her later work has a grittier, earthbound realism—not naturalism—as in *Mud, Conduct of Life,* and *The Danube*. Lanford Wilson, another playwright born from the 1960s off-Broadway movement, once said of his colleague, "Her work has no precedents, it isn't derived from anything." Fornes continued writing through the 1990s, but her late plays have yielded the least critical enthusiasm. Her Christopher Columbus project *Terra Incognita* never totally set sail, and *Oscar and Bertha* had only limited runs in regional theaters.

The dividing line between her early and later styles can roughly be marked by one of Fornes's most enduring creations, *Fefu and Her Friends* (1977). The play concerns a group of women in the 1930s who have retired to a country home, ostensibly to discuss educational issues. The strange tension-filled relationships are revealed in the second act, in which the audience is divided into four parts and moves to a quartet of locations around the "house" to witness four different scenes that occur simultaneously. The hostess—a Hedda Gabler-like figure—fires a rifle at her husband in a strange personal game as characters speak in typical Fornes dialogue peppered with non sequiturs. Of course, as in all good melodrama, the gun goes off at the end with tragic consequences, but with totally different ones than anyone would expect in a work of pure naturalism.

Fornes's singular talent, in fact, is for surprise. Part of this is due to her process, for she works serendipity into her scripts. For *Promenade* she wrote character ideas on index cards, made two stacks, shuffled them, and drew cards from each pile to create scenes. *Mud* is a series of blackout sketches in which the trio of actors freezes after every scene because Fornes initially staged the play outdoors and needed to indicate scene endings. Yet their frozen attitudes at the end of each of the 17 scenes also theatrically represent how these three poor, uneducated people are mired in "still lives." Mae, the woman in the triangle, attends school (at one point we reads aloud from a textbook on starfidh), but the most important knowledge she gains—that she should leave the two men—has tragic consequences. Likewise, *The Danube*, a haunting romance set during an unnamed war, was occasioned by an old 78-rpm recording of a Hungarian language lesson Fornes found at a used record store. In an interview Fornes described how the "tenderness" of the simple English and Hungarian phrases spurred her on. The result is one of her most moving and theatrically adventurous scripts (at one point puppets play the characters), in which a young couple's growing love is juxtaposed with a deteriorating world that literally ends with an explosion and blackout. *Fefu*'s half-dozen characters were written for six dresses the playwright found at a thrift store. The second, "promenade," act occurred because the original theater had spaces that Fornes wanted to use.

A little known fact of Fornes's career is that early on, in the 1960s, she worked on a Broadway musical, *The Office*, with Jerome Robbins. For reasons unknown, the play closed in previews. But the idea that one of America's most singular theater voices might have had a completely different career is the kind of chance quirk of fate that enlivens and infuses so much of Fornes's life and work.

—John Istel

FOSTER, Hannah (Webster)

Born: Salisbury, Massachusetts, 10 September 1758. **Education:** A boarding school after 1762. **Family:** Married the Reverend John Foster in 1785; six children. **Career:** Lived in her husband's parish of Brighton, Massachusetts until his death, then settled with her daughters in Montreal. **Died:** 17 April 1840.

PUBLICATIONS

Fiction

The Coquette; or, The History of Eliza Wharton. 1797.
The Boarding School; or, Lessons of a Preceptress to Her Pupils. 1798.

*

Bibliography: in *Bibliography of American Literature* by Jacob Blanck, 1959.

Critical Studies: "Flirting with Destiny: Ambivalence and Form in the Early American Sentimental Novel" by Cathy N. Davidson, in *Studies in American Fiction,* spring 1982; "'Fallen under My Observation': Vision and Virtue in *The Coquette*" by David Waldstreicher, in *Early American Literature* vol. 27, no. 3, 1992; "Sisterhood in a Separate Sphere: Female Friendship in Hannah Webster Foster's *The Coquette* and *The Boarding School*" by Claire C. Pettengill, in *Early American Literature* vol. 27, no. 3, 1992; "Hannah Webster Foster" by Claire C. Pettengill, in *Legacy: A Journal of American Women Writers,* 1995, pp. 133-41; "Detested Be the Epithet!: Definition, Maxim, and the Language of Social Dicta in Hannah Webster Foster's *The Coquette*" by Dorothy Z. Baker, in *Essays in Literature,* spring 1996, pp. 58-68; "Consent, Coquetry, and Consequences" by Gillian Brown, in *American Literary History,* winter 1997, pp. 625-52; "The Politics of Seduction: Theater, Sexuality, and National Virtue in the Novels of Hannah Foster" by Jeffrey H. Richards, in *Exceptional Spaces: Essays in Performance and History* edited by Della Pollock, 1998.

*   *   *

Two of the earliest essays into American fiction were designed to "expose the dangerous consequences of seduction." William Hill Brown's *The Power of Sympathy* and Hannah Foster's *The Coquette* are cut from the same Richardsonian pattern. Of the two the more convincing and more durable is the Foster book. Better constructed and more single-minded in its purpose, it can still appeal to readers in the late twentieth century.

Moreover, *The Coquette* is based on fact and thus achieves a kind of realism more becoming to American than English taste. Eliza Wharton, the heroine, was in reality Elizabeth Whitman and her lover was Pierpont Edwards, both of good Massachusetts families. The newspaper accounts tell of her elopement with him and of her death in the Bell Tavern in Danvers, Massachusetts. A secret marriage is hinted at, but that part of the story remains a mystery. These events took place ten years before the appearance of the novel; but even more compelling is the fact that Foster's husband was the cousin of the wife of Deacon John Whitman of Stow, himself a cousin of Elizabeth Whitman's father. It seems probable that Foster, through these family connections, was in possession of the facts.

The Coquette is an imitation of Richardson's *Clarissa,* but it is one of the most successful in a long series of seduction novels written in its period. The characters of Major Peter Sanford, the seducer, and Eliza Wharton are convincing and straightforward. The other characters are skillfully used to build the plot and comment on the unfortunate lovers, so that the reader's attention never moves away from the unfolding tragedy. The motivation is real and the moments of tortured self-revelation raise the novel above the sensationalism and sentimentality of many novels of this genre. Moreover, Foster does not fall into the obvious excesses of the epistolary form; she does not tax the credulity of the reader, nor does she intrude with tedious editorializing.

—Dominic J. Bisignano

FOSTER, Stephen Collins

Born: Pittsburgh, Pennsylvania, 4 July 1826. **Education:** Privately educated, Allegheny, and at Towanda Academy, Athens Academy, Tioga Point, 1840-41, and Jefferson College, Canonsburg, 1841, all in Pennsylvania. **Family:** Married Jane McDowell in 1850; one daughter. **Career:** Bookkeeper for his brother, Cincinnati, 1847; then songwriter: contracted to Firth Pond and Company from 1849. **Died:** 13 January 1864.

PUBLICATIONS

Collections

The Melodies. 1909.
Foster's Forgotten Songs, edited by Hamilton A. Gordon. 1941.
A Treasury of Foster. 1946.

*

Bibliography: *A Pictorial Bibliography of the First Editions of Foster* by James J. Fuld, 1957.

Critical Studies: *Foster, America's Troubadour,* 1935, and *The Literature of Foster,* 1944, both by John T. Howard; *Foster, Boy Minstrel* by Helen B. Higgins, 1944; *The Songs of Foster* by William W. Austin, 1975; "T.S. Eliot and Stephen Foster" by George Monteiro, in *Explicator,* spring 1987; *Doo-dah!: Stephen Foster and the Rise of American Popular Culture* by Ken Emerson, 1997.

*   *   *

While Stephen Collins Foster's literary output is inextricably linked to the music to which he set it, he must nevertheless be considered as a poet and more influential in his writing of words than of music. The abstract art of his music surrounds and complements his lyrics in an inimitable Bellinian "simplicity of genius," but his carefully crafted words ultimately reflect and refine the mores of American society in the pre-Civil War period: optimistic, sentimental, patriotic, and proudly unsophisticated.

Foster has been criticized as too sentimental, as having embodied the patronizing racism of his time, and of having been not a poet at all but a musician who wrote some of his own lyrics. About a third of Foster's 180-odd songs were, it is true, written to the texts of others, but only two or three of these have survived among the forty and more Foster songs with which most Americans are familiar. As a musician, he responded best to himself as poet.

Of Foster's own lyrics, most, and the most important, form two groups: the sentimental ballad and the Negro dialect song. His few political, patriotic, and non-dialect comic lyrics are neither greatly distinguished in themselves nor sources of memorable musical accompaniments. The sentimental ballads, such as "Beautiful Dreamer," "Come Where My Love Lies Dreaming," and "Jeannie with the Light Brown Hair" are comparable in intensity of emotion to, and less pretentious stylistically than, the sentimental poetry of such contemporaries as **Edgar Allan Poe** and **Sidney Lanier.** At the same time, his lyrics are more metrically and verbally sophisticated than those of his contemporaries who wrote not as poets but only as lyricists.

The Negro-dialect lyrics, or "Etheopian Songs" as they were popularly known, demonstrate Foster's keen ear for the rhythms and patterns of black speech. In his earliest efforts, such as "Oh Susanna" and "Old Folks at Home," some crudities and a tendency to see the black, slave or free, as a happy buffoon, can be traced. But the poet's close observation of blacks for both poetic and musical veracity resulted in a gradual and progressive move away from stereotype to the image of the black person as dignified, sensitive, and empathetic rather than simple and ridiculous. He jettisoned objectionable words commonly descriptive of blacks, leading to later lyrics such as "Old Black Joe" in which dialect disappears entirely, though by then his grasp of it, in "Nelly Bly," "My Old Kentucky Home," and "Massa's in de Cold Ground" demonstrate a command equal to Lanier's of the contemporary white southerner.

The Civil War, which abolished black servitude and replaced sentimentality with expansionism and urbanism, cut off the possibility of Foster's being an influence on the poetry that followed his death, and froze him into the posture of a spokesman for a vanished age. The strong American sense of nostalgia has thus deified him, and the mythic figure thus created has so far repelled any serious study of his considerable talents as a poet.

—William J. Collins

FRANK, Waldo (David)

Born: Long Branch, New Jersey, 25 August 1889. **Education:** De Witt Clinton High School, New York, 1902-06; Les Chamettes Pensionnat, Lausanne, Switzerland, 1906-07; Yale University, New Haven, Connecticut, B.A. and M.A. 1911. **Family:** Married 1) Margaret Naumberg in 1916 (divorced 1926), one son; 2) Alma Magoon in 1927 (divorced 1943), two daughters; 3) Jean Klempner in 1943, two sons. **Career:** Theater critic, New Haven *Courier-Journal,* 1910-11; reporter, New York *Evening Post,* 1911-12, and New York *Times,* 1912; lived abroad, 1913-14; associate editor, *Seven Arts,* New York, 1916; conscientious objector during World War I; staff member, *Ellsworth County Leader,* Kansas, 1919; contributing editor, *New Republic,* New York, 1925-40, and *New Masses,* New York, 1926; lecturer, New School for Social Research, New York, 1927; honorary professor, Central University of Ecuador, 1949. Chairperson, Independent Miners' Relief Committee, 1932; first chairperson, League of American Writers, 1935. **Awards:** Litt.D.: Universidad Nacional de San Marcos, Lima, Peru, 1929. **Member:** American Academy, 1952. **Died:** 9 January 1967.

PUBLICATIONS

Fiction

The Unwelcome Man. 1917.
The Dark Mother. 1920.
Rahab. 1922.
City Block. 1922.
Holiday. 1923.
Chalk Face. 1924.
The Death and Birth of David Markand: An American Story. 1934.
The Bridegroom Cometh. 1938.
Summer Never Ends. 1941.
Island in the Atlantic. 1946.
The Invaders. 1948.
Not Heaven. 1953.

Play

New Year's Eve. 1929.

Other

The Art of the Vieux Colombier: A Contribution of France to the Contemporary Stage. 1918.
Our America. 1919; as *The New America,* 1922.
Salvos: An Informal Book about Books and Plays. 1924.
Time Exposures, By Search-Light. 1926.
Virgin Spain: Scenes from the Spiritual Drama of a Great People. 1926; revised edition, 1942.
Five Arts, with others. 1929.
The Re-Discovery of America: An Introduction to a Philosophy of American Life. 1929.
America Hispana: A Portrait and a Prospect. 1931.
Dawn in Russia: The Record of a Journey. 1932.
In the American Jungle 1925-1936. 1937.
Chart for Rough Water: Our Role in a New World. 1940.
South American Journey. 1943.
The Jew in Our Day. 1944.
Birth of a World: Bolivar in Terms of His Peoples. 1951.
Bridgehead: The Drama of Israel. 1957.
The Rediscovery of Man: A Memoir and a Methodology of Modern Life. 1958.
Cuba, Prophetic Island. 1961.
Memoirs, edited by Alan Trachtenberg. 1973.

Editor, *Tales from the Argentine,* translated by Anita Brenner. 1930.
Editor, *The Collected Poems of Hart Crane.* 1933; revised edition, as *The Complete Poems,* 1958.
Editor, with others, *America and Alfred Stieglitz: A Collective Portrait.* 1934.

Translator, *Lucienne,* by Jules Romains. 1925.

*

Critical Studies: *The Novels of Frank* by William Bittner, 1958; *The Shared Vision of Frank and Hart Crane* by Robert L. Perry, 1966; *Frank* by Paul J. Carter, 1967; "Sherwood Anderson and Waldo Frank" by Charles E. Modlin, in *The Old Northwest: A Journal of Regional Life and Letters,* winter 1991-92; *Waldo Frank: Prophet of Hispanic Regeneration* by Michael A. Orgorzaly, 1994.

*   *   *

Although Waldo Frank produced a large and varied body of work in prose—history, fiction, essays—he considered himself a poet. In his memoirs, he refers to himself as a poet, describes his novels as lyrical, and says that *Virgin Spain* represents a subjective, lyrical expression of the author. The memoirs provide a useful introduction to the man and to the genesis and the attitudes informing some of his important books.

Surprisingly, his important books are history, not fiction or essays. Frank's essays were written for periodicals, and consist principally of commentary on literature, the theater, the current American scene, and the position of the Jew in the modern world. Occasionally they are listed as criticism, but Frank lacked the tools of criticism. He also lacked wit and humor, as is painfully evident in a collection of brief "Profiles," first published in the *New Yorker.* Like his history and fiction, his essays offer a poet's vision and use of language. In the best, in the introduction to **Hart Crane**'s poems, for example, this vision enlarges the reader's understanding. It tends to vitiate much of his other writing, especially his fiction.

At the heart of Frank's work is his vision of a social and personal Whole—variously termed Cosmos or Being or The Great Tradition—achieved in western Europe in the middle ages by the church, through the teaching of Jesus. In succeeding ages, according to Frank, this very teaching—that the Kingdom of God is within man—gave rise to an ego that, particularly in America, replaced the Ptolemaic universe with a secular, mechanistic multiverse. The chaos of the multiverse is but a stage, however, in man's history, which must culminate in the Whole once more, the knowledge that God, the universal, is within man, whose life therefore has purpose and direction.

The timeless, spaceless nature of this vision of the Whole precludes the development of character and situation in Frank's fiction, as he himself asserts. Consequently, his short stories are made up essentially of moments of epiphany, and his novels contain inert ideological and symbolic material. Like a poet, he attempts to re-create language, using nouns as verbs and adjectives as nouns. These usages and his poetic descriptions unhappily abound to the point of embarrassment in his writing.

On account of his vision, his histories of North and South America, Russia, and Spain must be accepted on his terms, as works of art. His considerable research gives substance to some that otherwise would amount to little more than poetic travel books. As history, *Birth of a World* is his best, undoubtedly in part because it was commissioned by the Venezuelan government and because Bolivar, not Frank, is at the center of the narrative. Most important for the reader's comprehension and intelligent assessment of Frank's work is *The Re-Discovery of America.* For it presents his vision, interpreting religion and history from a poet's perspectives, with a poet's insights.

—Robert F. Richards

FRANKLIN, Benjamin

Born: Boston, Massachusetts, 17 January 1706. **Education:** Boston Grammar School, 1714; George Brownell's School, Boston. **Family:** Married Deborah Read in 1730 (died 1774); one son and one daughter; also an illegitimate son (William Franklin, loyalist governor of New Jersey) and daughter. **Career:** Worked in his father's tallow chandler business, Boston, from age ten; apprenticed as printer to his half-brother James, 1718; worked on James's *New-England Courant:* contributed "Silence Dogood" articles, 1721-23, and published paper during James's imprisonment, 1722; moved to Philadelphia, 1723; worked for printer Samuel Keimer, 1723-24; sent to London to buy printing equipment and worked for printers Palmer, then Watt, 1724-25; clerk for Denham, a merchant, Philadelphia, 1726-27, and Keimer, 1728; established own printing business, Philadelphia, 1729: publisher, 1729-48, and copublisher, 1748-66, *Pennsylvania Gazette;* publisher, *Philadelphische Zeitung,* 1732; editor, *General Magazine,* Philadelphia, 1741; retired and turned over running of business to partner, 1748. Clerk, 1736-51, member for Philadelphia, 1751-64, and

Speaker, 1764, Pennsylvania Assembly: London agent for the Assembly, chiefly on taxation matters, 1757-62 and 1764-75 (involved in passage and repeal of the Stamp Act); also colonial agent for Georgia, 1768, New Jersey, 1769, and Massachusetts, 1770; deputy postmaster, Philadelphia, 1737-53, and joint deputy postmaster of the colonies, 1753-74 (dismissed by British; elected postmaster general of the colonies by Continental Congress, 1775); delegate, Albany Congress (to unite colonies in French and Indian War), 1754. Returned to America from London and delegate to Second Continental Congress, 1775-76; member of the drafting committee and signatory, Declaration of Independence, 1776; sent by Congress as one of three commissioners to negotiate with the French, 1776, and became sole commissioner, 1778 (treaty of commerce and defensive alliance signed, 1778); lived at Passy, near Paris, and established a press there, 1776-85; member, with John Jay and John Adams, of commission to negotiate peace with Britain, from 1781 (treaty signed, 1783); returned to Philadelphia, 1785; president, Pennsylvania Executive Council, 1785-87; delegate, Constitutional Convention, Philadelphia, 1787 (helped arrange the compromise on representation incorporated into the Constitution); president, Pennsylvania Society for the Abolition of Slavery, 1787. Involved in Philadelphia community affairs: worked on projects to establish police force and street paving and cleaning schemes; helped found Library Company of Philadelphia (first circulating library in America), 1731, Union Fire Company, 1736, American Philosophical Society, 1743, Academy for the Education of Youth (later University of Pennsylvania), 1751, and Philadelphia City Hospital, 1751. Invented "Franklin Stove" or "Pennsylvania Fireplace," 1739; studied electricity after 1746: performed kite experiment to test identity of lightning and electricity, and invented lightning rod, 1752. **Awards:** Royal Society Copley Medal, 1753. M.A.: Harvard University, Cambridge, Massachusetts, 1753; Yale University, New Haven, Connecticut, 1753; College of William and Mary, Williamsburg, Virginia, 1756. LL.D.: University of St. Andrews, Fife, Scotland, 1759. D.C.L.: Oxford University, 1762. Fellow, Royal Society (London), 1756. **Member:** French Academy of Sciences, 1772. **Died:** 17 April 1790.

PUBLICATIONS

Collections

Writings, edited by Albert Henry Smyth. 10 vols., 1905-07.
Representative Selections, edited by Frank Luther Mott and Chester E. Jorgenson. 1936; revised edition, 1962.
Papers, edited by Leonard W. Labaree and William B. Willcox. 1959.
Collected Works (Library of America), edited by J.A. Leo Lemay. 1987.

Prose

A Dissertation on Liberty and Necessity, Pleasure and Pain. 1725.
A Modest Enquiry into the Nature and Necessity of a Paper-Currency. 1729.
Poor Richard: An Almanack 1733 [through *1747*]. 1732-46; as *Poor Richard Improved 1748* [through *1763*], 1747-64; *The Complete Poor Richard Almanacks,* edited by Whitfield Bell, Jr., 2 vols., 1970.
A Defense of the Rev. Mr. Hemphill's Observations. 1735.

A Letter to a Friend in the Country. 1735.

Some Observations on the Proceedings against the Rev. Mr. Hemphill. 1735; as *Some Sermons,* 1735.

A Proposal for Promoting Useful Knowledge among the British Plantations in America. 1743.

An Account of the New Invented Pennsylvania Fire-Places. 1744.

Reflections on Courtship and Marriage. 1746.

Plain Truth. 1747.

Proposals Relating to the Education of Youth in Pennsylvania. 1749.

Experiments and Observations on Electricity. 1751; *Supplemental Experiments,* 1753; *New Experiments and Observations,* 1754; revised edition, 1769, 1774.

Idea of the English School. 1751.

Some Account of the Pennsylvania Hospital. 1754.

Some Account of the Success of Inoculation for the Small-Pox. 1759.

A Parable against Persecution. 1759 (?).

Father Abraham's Speech. 1760; as *The Way to Wealth,* 1774.

The Interest of Great Britain Considered, with Regard to Her Colonies. 1760.

Cool Thoughts on the Present Situation of Our Public Affairs. 1764.

A Narrative of Late Massacres, in Lancaster County, of a Number of Indians, Friends of This Province, by Persons Unknown. 1764.

Remarks on a Late Protest against the Appointment of Mr. Franklin an Agent for This Province. 1764.

The Examination of Doctor Franklin, Relative to the Repeal of the American Stamp Act. 1766.

Physical and Meteorological Observations and Suppositions. 1766.

Oeuvres (in French), edited by Jacques Dubourg. 2 vols., 1773.

Political, Miscellaneous, and Philosophical Pieces, edited by Benjamin Vaughan. 1779.

Remarks Concerning the Savages of North America. 1784.

Information to Those Who Would Remove to America. 1784(?).

Philosophical and Miscellaneous Papers, edited by Edward Bancroft. 1787.

Observations on the Causes and Cure of Smoky Chimneys. 1787.

Rules for Reducing a Great Empire to a Small One. 1793.

The Art of Swimming. 1816(?).

The Private Correspondence, edited by William Temple Franklin. 2 vols., 1817.

A Collection of the Familiar Letters and Miscellaneous Papers, edited by Jared Sparks. 1833.

Autobiography, edited by John Bigelow. 1868; edited by Leonard W. Labaree and others, 1964; *The Autobiography: A Genetic Text,* edited by J.A. Leo Lemay and P.M. Zall, 1981.

An Address to the Good People of Ireland, on Behalf of America . . . 1778, edited by Paul Leicester Ford. 1891.

Franklin's Contribution to Medicine, edited by Theodore Diller. 1912.

Letters to Madame Helvetius and Madame La Frete, edited by Luther S. Livingston. 1924.

My Dear Girl: The Correspondence of Franklin with Polly Stevenson, Georgiana and Catherine Shipley, edited by James Madison Stifler. 1927.

Account Books, edited by George Simpson Eddy. 2 vols., 1928-29.

Advice to a Young Man on Choosing a Mistress, edited by Harold D. Carew. 1930.

The Ingenious Dr. Franklin: Selected Scientific Letters, edited by Nathan G. Goodman. 1931.

Satires and Bagatelles, edited by Paul McPharlin. 1937.

The General Magazine and Historical Chronicle for All the British Plantations in America (issued 1741), edited by Lyon N. Richardson. 1938.

Autobiographical Writings, edited by Carl Van Doren. 1945.

A Franklin Reader, edited by Nathan G. Goodman. 1945; as *The Franklin Sampler,* 1956.

Letters and Papers of Franklin and Richard Jackson 1753-1785, edited by Carl Van Doren. 1947.

Memoirs: Parallel Text Edition, edited by Max Farrand. 1949.

The Will of Franklin 1757, edited by Carl Van Doren. 1949.

Franklin and Catharine Ray Greene: Their Correspondence 1775-1790, edited by William Greene Roelker. 1949.

Letters of Franklin and Jane Mecom, edited by Carl Van Doren. 1950.

Letters to the Press 1758-1775, edited by Verner W. Crane. 1950.

Franklin's Wit and Folly: The Bagatelles, edited by Richard E. Amacher. 1953.

Mr. Franklin: A Selection from His Personal Letters, edited by Leonard W. Labaree and Whitfield J. Bell, Jr. 1956.

Franklin on Education, edited by John Hardin Best. 1962.

The Political Thought of Franklin, edited by Ralph L. Ketcham. 1965.

The Bagatelles from Passy, edited by Claude-Anne Lopez and Willard F. Trask. 1967.

Franklin Laughing: Anecdotes from Original Sources by and about Franklin, edited by P.M. Zall. 1980.

Selected Writings of Benjamin Franklin. 1996.

*

Bibliography: *Franklin Bibliography* by Paul Leicester Ford, 1889; *Franklin's Philadelphia Printing 1728-1766: A Descriptive Bibliography* by C. William Miller, 1974; *Franklin 1721-1906: A Reference Guide* by Melvin H. Buxbaum, 1983.

Critical Studies: *Franklin* by Carl Van Doren, 1938, and *Meet Dr. Franklin* edited by Van Doren, 1943; *Franklin: His Contribution to the American Tradition* by I. Bernard Cohen, 1953; *Franklin* by Richard E. Amacher, 1962; *Franklin: An American Man of Letters* by Bruce Ingham Granger, 1964; *Franklin, Philosopher and Man,* 1965, and *Franklin and Nature's God,* 1967, both by Alfred Owen Aldridge; *Franklin* by Ralph L. Ketcham, 1965; *The Private Franklin: The Man and His Family* by Claude-Anne Lopez and Eugenia W. Herbert, 1975; *Franklin* by David Freeman Hawke, 1976; *The Oldest Revolutionary: Essays on Franklin* edited by J.A. Leo Lemay, 1976, *The Canon of Franklin: New Attributions and Reconsiderations* by Lemay, 1986, and *Benjamin Franklin: Optimist or Pessimist?* by Lemay, 1991; *Franklin: A Collection of Critical Essays* edited by Brian M. Barbour, 1979; *Franklin: A Biography* by Ronald W. Clark, 1983; *Cotton Mather and Franklin: The Price of Representative Personality* by Mitchell Robert Breitwieser, 1984; *Franklin of Philadelphia* by Esmond Wright, 1986, and *Franklin: His Life as He Wrote It* edited by Wright, 1990; *Benjamin Franklin in American Thought and Culture, 1790-1990* by Nian-Sheng Huang, 1994; *The Devious Dr. Franklin, Colonial Agent: Benjamin Franklin's Years in London* by David T. Morgan, 1996; *The Radical Enlightenments of Benjamin Franklin* by Douglas Anderson, 1997.

*   *   *

Benjamin Franklin is an American idol. One of the founders of the American political tradition and a distinguished scientist, diplomat, and humanitarian, Franklin was also, to quote David Hume, the "first great man of letters" for whom Europe was beholden to America.

In his every accomplishment, Franklin epitomized the American Enlightenment. Possessed of an infinitely curious mind fixed on understanding and improving the world around him, he sought a better life for people of all classes and situations. A Deist, he tried to reconcile rationalism and science with the belief in God, urging faith and good will and always advocating the application of faith based on intelligence; he never spared humor in meeting the contingencies of the human condition.

He brought to his writing this broad humanism and selflessness, and a grace and wit that made him one of America's greatest writers. He gave an American flavor to the epistolary and essay forms, mastered the use of persona in creating the first memorable American comic character, and left for succeeding generations to emulate a crackerbarrel and homey humor. Always, Franklin's work appeals to human reason and retains as its purpose social and moral betterment. "No Piece can properly be called good . . . which is void of any tendency to benefit the [Reader's] . . . Virtue or his Knowledge."

His essays include the "Do-Good Papers," "Busy-Body Papers," and *Bagatelles.* The first—fourteen essays that appeared in his half-brother's *New-England Courant* and written under the name of Silence Dogood—is the essential Franklin. His persona, a parson's widow writing of both the serious and ridiculous—provides the author distance for irony and satire. Her subjects include "Pride and Hoop Petticoats," women as the cause of men's sins, and the more serious problems of excessive religious zeal, alcoholism, and the plight of widows (this was written shortly after the smallpox epidemic and Indian wars of 1722); "The Temple of Learning" is a hearty satire of Harvard University; there are also essays of literary criticism, one on Arminianism, and many on other topical matters. The essays represent early social criticism in American journalism. The "Busy-Body Papers" comprises thirty-two letters addressed to a competing newspaper, the *American Weekly Mercury.* On subjects like religion, morality, and various social issues, Franklin accomplishes his retaliation against the publisher Samuel Keimer, who shortly thereafter went bankrupt. The fifteen *Bagatelles,* short and urbane essays written in his seventies, cover a broad range of subjects and include "The Ephemera," "Parable against Persecution," and "The Whistle." Some are in the vein of Swift's *A Modest Proposal.* "Rules by Which a Great Empire May Be Reduced to a Small One," for example, contains twenty rules by which the British empire may be reduced, like a cake. "I would propose that all the Capitals of the several Provinces should be burnt to the Ground, and that they cut the throats of all the inhabitants: Men, Women, and Children, and scalp them, to serve as an Example." Franklin also wrote a prodigious number of letters.

Poor Richard's Almanack, the early work that brought him great success in the colonies and then abroad, epitomizes Franklin's passion for improving himself and others: "I write Almanacks with no other View than that of the publick Good." Like the popular almanacs of the time, Franklin's includes weather predictions, short sayings, a history of European kings and dates of courts, tides, fairs, recipes, maxims, movements of planets and eclipses, a calendar of meetings, and the distance between towns. Unique is Franklin's fictional character, his persona Richard Saunders who,

married to the proud and talkative Bridget, is shamed into writing because she can't stand his obsessive gazing at the stars. Franklin dramatizes a very funny battle between the sexes and once again utilizes the persona device to distinguish his work from the tired, moralizing pieces popular at the time. The self-denying Richard frequently illustrates the dangers of frugality.

The book is filled with maxims that Franklin gathered from a vast number of sources, many of which he adapts to the circumstances of his impoverished Richard. Franklin gives a homespun flavor to the gospel of American folk wisdom. He alters, for example, "Fresh fish and poor friends become soon ill sav'd [savored]" to "Fresh fish and visitors stink in three days." Other sayings include:

> Early to bed, early to rise, makes a man healthy, wealthy, and wise.
> It is hard for an empty sack to stand upright.
> Neither a fortress nor a maidenhead will hold out long after they begin to parley.
> Men and Melons are hard to know.

The first *Almanack* sold so well that "as poor Richard says" became a household phrase on thrift. *The Way to Wealth,* Father Abraham's speech on the nature of the times, contains ninety maxims on "industry, frugality, and prudence," many of which are from *Poor Richard's Almanack.*

The very popular *Autobiography* was dedicated to Franklin's son, on how "from the poverty and obscurity in which I was born . . . I have raised myself to a state of affluence and some degree of celebrity in the world." Although unfinished, these "Memoirs," in four sections, portray both the didactic and witty Franklin. They expound the thirteen virtues of his self-improvement course: Temperance, Silence, Order, Resolution, Frugality, Industry, Sincerity, Justice, Moderation, Cleanliness, Tranquility, Chastity, and Humility. The book is appealing not only as a guide to morality but as an early **Horatio Alger** tale, a story about the American dream and Franklin's particular application of common sense in the brave new world of opportunity.

Franklin wrote more than 20,000 works; his stylistic goals were clarity, precision, and propriety. He was extraordinarily well-read: his major literary influences were Addison, Locke, Swift, Bunyan, and Defoe. In his many political tracts, letters, satires, essays, fables, pamphlets, and even hoaxes, he made clear his belief in God and man's capabilities and responsibilities: "I believe in one God, Creator of the Universe. That He governs it by his Providence. That the most acceptable service we render to Him is doing good to His other children. That the soul of man is immortal and will be treated with justice in another life respecting its conduct in this."

—Lois Gordon

FREDERIC, Harold

Born: Utica, New York, 19 August 1856. **Education:** The Advanced School, Utica, graduated 1871. **Family:** Married Grace Williams in 1877, two daughters and two sons; also had two daughters and one son by Kate Lyon. **Career:** Photographer's assistant and retoucher, Utica, 1871-73, and Boston, 1873-74; proofreader, Utica *Morning Herald,* 1875; reporter, 1875-80, and editor, 1880-82, Utica *Observer;* editor-in-chief, Albany *Evening Journal,* 1882-84; London correspondent, *New York Times,* 1884-98. **Died:** 19 October 1898.

PUBLICATIONS

Collections

Stories of York State, edited by Thomas F. O'Donnell. 1966.
(Works), edited by Stanton Garner. 1977—.

Fiction

Seth's Brother's Wife: A Study of Life in the Greater New York.
   1887.
The Lawton Girl. 1890.
In the Valley. 1890.
The Return of the O'Mahony. 1892.
The Copperhead. 1893.
The Copperhead and Other Stories of the North During the American War. 1894.
Marsena and Other Stories of the Wartime. 1894.
The Damnation of Theron Ware. 1896; as *Illumination,* 1896; edited by Everett Carter, 1960.
Mrs. Albert Grundy: Observations in Philistia. 1896.
March Hares. 1896.
In the Sixties (stories). 1897.
Gloria Mundi. 1898; abridged version, as *Pomps and Vanities,*
   1913.
The Deserter and Other Stories: A Book of Two Wars. 1898.
The Market-Place. 1899.

Other

The Young Emperor William II of Germany: A Study in Character Development on a Throne. 1891.
The New Exodus: A Study of Israel in Russia. 1892.

*

Bibliography: *A Bibliography of Writings by and about Frederic* by Thomas F. O'Donnell, Stanton Garner, and Robert H. Woodward, 1975; *The Literary Manuscripts of Frederic: A Catalogue* by Noel Polk, 1979.

Critical Studies: *Frederic* by Thomas F. O'Donnell and Hoyt C. Franchere, 1961; *The Novels of Frederic* by Austin Briggs, Jr., 1969; *Frederic* by Stanton Garner, 1969; "'With Their Tongues Doom Men to Death': Christian Science and the Case of Harold Frederic" by Susan Albertine, in *American Literary Realism, 1870-1910,* spring 1989; "Resurrecting Man: Desire and *The Damnation of Theron Ware*" by Lisa Watt MacFarlane, in *Studies in American Fiction,* autumn 1992; *Reluctant Expatriate: The Life of Harold Frederic* by Robert M. Myers, 1995; *The Damnation of Harold Frederic: His Lives and Works* by Bridget Bennett, 1997; *An Examination of Political Pessimism in the Works of Harold Frederic* by Jean S. Filetti, 1998.

*   *   *

Two distinct strains, realistic and romantic, mix in Harold Frederic's fiction. He regarded Erckmann-Chatrian and **Nathaniel Hawthorne** as the principal influences on his own work. His reading of popular romance, together with qualities inherent in his temperament and the pattern of his career, manifests itself in certain romantic effects. He lapses into melodrama and sentimentality and recurrently draws central figures who are young, hopeful, naive, and embark on fairy-tale adventures of personal fulfillment. Frederic's romanticism matures in the brief course of his writing career, however, from an initial schoolboy emulation of Erckmann-Chatrian in the earliest stories towards a Hawthorne-like probing of the ambiguities manifest in human character, and of the inner and outer pressures that determine behavior. Frederic's reputation and his distinctive character as a writer depend primarily on his talents as a realist who exploited materials pertaining to the Mohawk Valley region of New York. In the autobiographical derivation of his fiction, in his faithful representation of everyday language, behavior, and scene, and in his dramatic method (i.e., his letting the tale tell itself rather than interpreting it for the reader) Frederic has been compared to **William Dean Howells,** whom he greatly admired. His essentially comic vision also associates him with Howells and with an underlying American optimism ultimately deriving from **Ralph Waldo Emerson.**

Frederic's first novel, *Seth's Brother's Wife,* his masterwork *The Damnation of Theron Ware,* and his best stories are all realistic. They draw upon his childhood experiences in a working-class, Methodist home during the Civil War era and upon his subsequent observations as a photographer's apprentice and a journalist in upstate New York. Seth is a young journalist variously involved with his job, politics, and his brother's wife, his story enacted against the dreary background of a poor upstate farming district. Theron Ware is a small-town Methodist minister whose intellectual, aesthetic, and sexual initiations under the influence of town sophisticates paradoxically result in both *eclaircissement* and moral degeneration. Here as elsewhere Frederic's overt treatment of sexuality and his preoccupation with the type of the modern woman are manifest. The Civil War stories are highly original, dealing with ambivalent attitudes toward the war and with its effects upon civilians at home rather than celebrating military heroics. Written in 1892-93 these have been collected in a modern edition as *Stories of York State. The Lawton Girl,* a moderately successful sequel to *Seth,* and *In the Valley,* a historical romance of the Revolutionary War, are also set in the Mohawk Valley.

Frederic was a highly successful foreign correspondent, and his fiction writing represented a second career in part motivated by financial objectives. All his fiction except the early stories was written in England, and he initially attempted to assimilate European materials in *The Return of the O'Mahony.* This far-fetched, comical, trivial romance is Frederic's deepest plunge into Irish folk materials, although folklore, legend, and genealogy interested him throughout his career, and his interest in the New York Irish predated his journalistic immersion in Irish politics. *March Hares,* set in London, is believed to be a fictional celebration of Frederic's liaison with Kate Lyon. Its deft, urbane, and comic tone, characteristic of Frederic's mature voice, is reminiscent of that of his bachelor narrator in *Mrs. Albert Grundy,* a series of fictionalized satirical sketches originally published in the *National Observer* in 1892 as "Observations in Philistia."

In his last two novels, *Gloria Mundi* and *The Market-Place,* Frederic makes his most serious attempts to discover European materials of sufficient richness to replace the New York regionalist material that he had substantially worked through. Of these *Gloria Mundi*, a Cinderella tale of a young man's coming into a dukedom and an inheritance, is the less successful. Frederic was ill-advised to attempt the depiction of a social milieu inaccessible to him, and the novel lacks the authenticity that characterizes his scene-painting of rural New York. In *The Market-Place*, however, a romance of commercial enterprise dealing with life in the City and with the interaction of political and philanthropic motives, Frederic opens up a vein of material that he might easily have exploited thereafter. Taken together, the central figures of *Theron Ware*, *Gloria Mundi*, and *The Market-Place* manifest a deepening psychological insight and an ever-increasing subtlety and ambiguity in rendering the relationships between character and environment. The peculiar strength of *Theron Ware*, which is generally regarded as a minor classic, may in fact derive from its bringing together the New York regionalist material at which Frederic was a sure hand, with his increasingly subtle probing into the forces that shape and thwart human development.

Frederic's novels reveal curious mixtures of disparate treatment, material, and attitudes within individual works. A sort of intellectual omnivorousness characterizes him, though some of the inconsistencies may result from lack of time for revision. In any case, the diversity of his talents, attitudes, and experiments is in itself remarkable. His novels characteristically reveal multiple perspectives, a tendency to view experience from more than one point of view. The problem of distinguishing between mere inconsistencies and calculated ironies is a crux in assessing individual works fairly and in forming a conclusive judgment of his achievement as a novelist.

—Jean Frantz Blackall

See the essay on *The Damnation of Theron Ware*.

FREEMAN, Mary E(leanor) Wilkins

Born: Randolph, Massachusetts, 31 October 1852; brought up in Randolph, then in Brattleboro, Vermont; returned to Randolph, 1883. **Education:** Brattleboro High School; Holyoke Female Seminary, South Hadley, Massachusetts, 1870-71; Glenwood Seminary, West Brattleboro, 1871. **Family:** Married Charles M. Freeman in 1902 (died 1923). **Career:** Lived in Metuchen, New Jersey, after 1902. **Awards:** American Academy Howells Medal, 1925. **Member:** American Academy, 1926. **Died:** 13 March 1930.

PUBLICATIONS

Collections

Selected Stories, edited by Marjorie Pryse. 1983.
The Infant Sphinx: Collected Letters, edited by Brent L. Kendrick. 1985.

Fiction

A Humble Romance and Other Stories. 1887; as *A Far-Away Melody and Other Stories*, 1890.
A New England Nun and Other Stories. 1891.

Jane Field. 1892.
Pembroke. 1894; edited by Perry D. Westbrook, 1971.
Madelon. 1896.
Jerome, A Poor Many. 1897.
Silence and Other Stories. 1898.
The People of Our Neighborhood. 1898; as *Some of Our Neighbours*, 1898.
The Jamesons. 1899.
In Colonial Times. 1899.
The Heart's Highway: A Romance of Virginia in the Seventeenth Century. 1900.
The Love of Parson Lord and Other Stories. 1900.
Understudies (stories). 1901.
The Portion of Labor. 1901.
Six Trees (stories). 1903.
The Wind in the Rose-Bush and Other Stories of the Supernatural. 1903.
The Givers (stories). 1904.
The Debtor. 1905.
"Doc" Gordon. 1906.
By the Light of the Soul. 1907.
The Fair Lavinia and Others. 1907.
The Shoulders of Atlas. 1908.
The Winning Lady and Others. 1909.
The Butterfly House. 1912.
The Yates Pride. 1912.
The Copy-Cat and Other Stories. 1914.
An Alabaster Box, with Florence Morse Kingsley. 1917.
Edgewater People (stories). 1918.
The Best Stories, edited by Henry Wysham Lanier. 1927.

Play

Giles Corey, Yeoman. 1893.

Other (for children)

Goody Two-Shoes and Other Famous Nursery Tales, with Clara Doty Bates. 1883.
Decorative Plaques (verse), designs by George F. Barnes. 1883.
The Cow with Golden Horns and Other Stories. 1884(?).
The Adventures of Ann: Stories of Colonial Times. 1886.
The Pot of Gold and Other Stories. 1892.
Young Lucretia and Other Stories. 1892.
Comfort Pease and Her Gold Ring. 1895.
Once Upon a Time and Other Child-Verses. 1897.
The Green Door. 1910.

*

Bibliography: in *Bibliography of American Literature* by Jacob Blanck, 1959.

Critical Studies: *Freeman* by Edward Foster, 1956; *Freeman* by Perry D. Westbrook, 1967, revised edition, 1988; *The Infant Sphinx: Collected Letters of Freeman* edited by Brent L. Kendrick, 1985.

*   *   *

Mary E. Wilkins Freeman, who wrote almost exclusively about rural and village life in New England, ranks among the foremost

American local colorists or regionalists. Brought up in a family of modest means and station in the small towns of Randolph, Massachusetts, and Brattleboro, Vermont, she drew the material for her fiction from her own experience; and when she started, in her early twenties, to write stories with New England settings she was hailed as an expert in the dialect, customs, and character traits of the people of her region. Thus she won a place among the early realists in American literature, receiving praise from **William Dean Howells**, a leader in the realist movement.

Freeman's keenest personal interest and her greatest strength were in the psychological analysis of characters representative of the final phase of Puritanism. In her day the old religion and culture lingered in the back country, but in an advanced state of decay. This was a period in the rural areas that one literary historian felicitously described as "the terminal moraine of New England Puritanism." Among the people the old Puritan strengths had degenerated into eccentricity, neurosis, and worse; and these warpings of personality are portrayed unforgettably in Freeman's works. Especially fascinating to her was the transformation of the Puritan will—once considered to be under God's direction—into pathological compulsions and obsessions: a man who will not enter his church but sits on its porch for ten years during Sabbath services because of a minor doctrinal difference with the minister ("A Conflict Ended"); a village seamstress who faints from hunger rather than receive payment for two patchwork quilts because she keeps misplacing one rag and forces herself to redo her work twice ("An Honest Soul"); a woman who waits fifteen years for her lover to return from Australia, finds on his return that he is in love with another girl, and lives out the rest of her life in self-imposed solitude ("A New England Nun"); a young farmer who breaks his engagement with his fiancee because of an insignificant political disagreement with her father and postpones reconciliation for ten years (Pembroke).

Freeman's best writing is in the form of short fiction, which from the beginning of her career found ready acceptance in periodicals like *Harper's New Monthly*. The best known among the many volumes of her tales were the first two to be published—*A Humble Romance and Other Stories* and *A New England Nun and Other Stories*. Freeman also wrote a number of novels, the most notable of which are *Jane Field* and *Pembroke*, both dealing with New England village life. The latter is a powerful novel, which received high praise from Arthur Machen and Arthur Conan Doyle. In all her writing Freeman's style is simple and direct, though at times she proves herself adept at using symbols (the chained dog and caged canary in "A New England Nun"). In the late twentieth century, because of her sympathetic and realistic fictional treatment of women, she has aroused considerable interest among feminist critics in America.

—Perry D. Westbrook

FRENCH, Paul. *See* **ASIMOV, Isaac.**

FRENEAU, Philip (Morin)

Born: New York City, 2 January 1752. **Education:** Privately educated; College of New Jersey (now Princeton University), 1768-71, B.A. 1771. **Military Service:** Enlisted in New Jersey militia and served as crew member on blockade runners, 1778-80: captured by the British, 1780. **Family:** Married Eleanor Forman in 1790. **Career:** Teacher on Long Island, New York, 1772, and at Somerset Academy, Back Creek, Maryland, 1773-74; lived in New York, 1775; planter's secretary and sailor, Santa Cruz, West Indies, 1776-78; editorial staff member, *Freeman's Journal,* Philadelphia, 1781-84; post office clerk, Philadelphia, 1782-84; master of a brig bound for Jamaica, 1784, and officer on ships in the Caribbean and Atlantic coast trade, 1785-89; editor, New York *Daily Advertiser,* 1790-91; translating clerk, U.S. Department of State, and editor, *National Gazette,* Philadelphia, 1791-93; bookseller and farmer, 1795, and editor, *Jersey Chronicle,* 1795-96, Mount Pleasant, New Jersey; editor, *Time-Piece,* New York, 1796-98; managed his New Jersey farm, 1799-1801 and after 1808; sailor, 1802-07. **Died:** 18 or 19 December 1832.

PUBLICATIONS

Collections

Poems, edited by Fred Lewis Pattee. 3 vols., 1902-07.
Poems, edited by Harry Hayden Clark. 1929.
Prose, edited by Philip M. Marsh. 1955.
A Freneau Sampler, edited by Philip M. Marsh. 1963.

Poetry

A Poem on the Rising Glory of America, with Hugh Henry Brackenridge. 1772.
The American Village. 1772.
American Liberty. 1775.
A Voyage to Boston. 1775.
General Gage's Soliloquy. 1775.
General Gage's Confession. 1775.
The British Prison-Ship. 1781.
The Poems. 1786; as *Poems on Various Occasions,* 1861.
A Journey from Philadelphia to New-York. 1787; as *A Laughable Poem,* 1809.
The Village Merchant. 1794.
Poems Written between the Years 1768 and 1794. 1795.
Poems, Written and Published during the American Revolutionary War. 2 vols., 1809.
A Collection of Poems on American Affairs. 2 vols., 1815.
Some Account of the Capture of the Ship Aurora, edited by Jay Miller. 1899.
Last Poems, edited by Lewis Leary. 1946.
The Final Poems of Philip Freneau (1827-1828), edited by Judith R. Hiltner. 1979.

Fiction

Father Bombo's Pilgrimage to Mecca 1770, with Hugh Henry Brackenridge, edited by Michael Davitt Bell. 1975.

Other

Miscellaneous Works. 1788.
Letters on Various Interesting and Important Subjects. 1799.
Unpublished Freneauana, edited by Charles F. Heartman. 1918.
The Writings of Hezekiah Salem, edited by Lewis Leary. 1975.

Editor, *An Historical Sketch of the Life of Silas Talbot.* 1803.

Translator, *New Travels through North America,* by Abbe Claude Robin. 1783.

*

Bibliography: *A Bibliography of the Separate and Collected Works of Freneau* by Victor Hugo Paltsits, 1903; in *Bibliography of American Literature* by Jacob Blanck, 1959; *Freneau's Published Prose: A Bibliography* by Philip M. Marsh, 1970.

Critical Studies: *That Rascal Freneau: A Study in Literary Failure* by Lewis Leary, 1941; *Freneau and the Cosmic Enigma* by Nelson F. Adkins, 1949; *The Prose of Freneau,* 1955, *Freneau, Poet and Journalist,* 1967, and *The Works of Freneau: A Critical Study,* 1968, all by Philip M. Marsh; *Freneau: Champion of Democracy* by Jacob Axelrad, 1967; *Freneau* by Mary Weatherspoon Bowden, 1976; *Land and Sea: The Lyric Poetry of Freneau* by Richard C. Vitzthum, 1978; "Philip Freneau: First American Poet to Write about the Caribbean" by Samuel B. Bandara, in *Revista Interamericana de Bibliografia Inter-American Review of Bibliography* vol. 36, 1986; "Early American Literature Worth Teaching: Philip Freneau's 'Indian' Poems" by John Baker in *Virginia English Bulletin,* winter 1986.

*   *   *

Philip Freneau's poetry and prose reflect his life and times: he gloried in matching the image of the Enlightened gentleman-scholar, one who could be as content administering his estate as intriguing in the latest political uproar, as happy translating the classics as being the master of a ship safely brought into port. Current politics, the latest scientific discovery, the newest philosophy, the recent misfortune of a neighbor, the chance observation of a terrapin: Freneau thought all fit subjects for his pen.

Many of his poems were propaganda, either for a political party or for the United States during the two wars against Great Britain. In his poems of the Revolution, he moved from personal attacks on the British ("Cain, Nimrod, Nero—fiends in human guise, / Herod, Domitian—these in judgment rise, / And, envious of his deeds, I hear them say / None but a George could be more vile than they") to calls for greater exertion by the patriots ("Rouse from your sleep, and crush the thievish band, / Defeat, destroy, and sweep them from the land"). But his War of 1812 verse is more urbane: both sides are pictured with wit and humor. Freneau was also involved in other causes: for the Revolution in France, against the American lack of support for poetry ("An age employed in edging steel / Can no poetic raptures feel"), against the dislocation of the Indians, against debtors' prisons. Much of this occasional verse, written in the heat of the moment, deserves to be forgotten, but sometimes, as in "Stanzas to an Alien" or "Stanzas on the Decease of Thomas Paine," he achieves lasting feeling.

Freneau's best known prose is that in his several series of essays. In the early series, the major characters, "The Pilgrim" and "The Philosopher of the Forest," tend to be preachy and fuzzily drawn. The Indian "Tomo-Cheeki" of another series voices the expected noble-savage statements in elegant prose: he is but a device for social criticism through the contrast of cultures. Used somewhat similarly is "Hezekiah Salem," the chief character of a light series that appeared in New York. As a New Englander, Salem is

an early progenitor of American humor based on regional differences. But Freneau's greatest prose creation was Robert Slender, spokesman of an electioneering series. Robert Slender is the common man: he peaks as one, he feels as one, his fears are those of one. He views government from the point of view of everyday life, as here where he talks to himself on the way to a tavern:

> Had I, said I, (talking to myself all the while) the disposal of but half the income of the United States, I could at least so order matters, that a man might walk to his next neighbour's without splashing his stockings, or being in danger of breaking his legs in ruts, holes, gutts, and gullies. I do not know, says I to myself, as I moralized on my splash'd stocking, but money might with more profit be laid out in repairing the roads, than in marine establishments, supporting a standing army, useless embassies, exorbitant salaries, given to many flashy fellows that are no honour to us, or to themselves, and chartering whole ships to carry a single man to another nation.

Freneau's best prose pieces are those in which he speaks in this colloquial, common style.

But the works of Freneau that are read in the late twentieth century are not the occasional verse that made him famous, nor his prose, but poems that capture the melancholy so admired by the pre-Romantics. Best known of this type is "The Wild Honeysuckle," which presents the inevitable decay of the flower's beauty: "Smit with those charms, that must decay, / I grieve to see your future doom." The emotion is restrained, is never permitted to become more than a pleasing melancholy:

> From morning suns and evening dews
> At first thy little being came
> If nothing once, you nothing lose,
> For when you die you are the same;
> The space between, is but an hour,
> The frail duration of a flower.

As Freneau revised the last couplet several times, so he revised his best poems frequently, polishing them as a craftsman. One of his best is "Ode to Fancy," a late revision of his very early "The Power of Fancy." The poem begins with Fancy's origin and nature: "Wakeful, vagrant, restless thing, / Ever wandering on the wing, / Who thy wondrous source can find, / Fancy, regent of the mind." The poet then presents the analogy between the creations of man's fancy and the elements of the universe, "Ideas of the Almighty mind!" After a description of Fancy's power, the poem ends with this plea: "Come, O come-perceiv'd by none, / You and I will walk alone." The whole is a unified, satisfying poem. As, later in life, Freneau became a better poet, he also became a more philosophical one, often presenting in verse his views on nature and the universe, still clinging to that most cherished virtue of the Enlightenment-moderation. In one of his last poems, "Winter," he again emphasizes this virtue:

> Happy with wine we may indulge an hour;
> The noblest beverage of the mildest power.
> Happy, with Love, to solace every care,
> Happy with sense and wit an hour to share;
> These to the mind a thousand pleasures bring
> And give to winter's frosts the smiles of spring.

These virtues appear also in Freneau's works: they show wit and sense, and feeling.

—Mary Weatherspoon Bowden

FROST, Robert (Lee)

Born: San Francisco, California, 26 March 1874. **Education:** Lawrence High School, Massachusetts, graduated 1892; Dartmouth College, Hanover, New Hampshire, 1892; Harvard University, Cambridge, Massachusetts, 1897-99. **Family:** Married Elinor Miriam White in 1895; one son and three daughters. **Career:** Mill worker and teacher, Lawrence, 1892-97; farmer, Derry, New Hampshire, 1900-12; English teacher, Pinkerton Academy, Derry, 1905-11; conducted course in psychology, State Normal School, Plymouth, New Hampshire, 1911-12; sold his farm, and lived in England, 1912-15; returned to America and settled on a farm near Franconia, New Hampshire, 1915; poet in residence, Amherst College, Massachusetts, 1916-20; subsequently visiting lecturer at Wesleyan University, Middletown, Connecticut; University of Michigan, Ann Arbor, 1921-23, 1925-26; Dartmouth College; Yale University, New Haven, Connecticut; and Harvard University. A founder, Bread Loaf School, Middlebury College, Vermont, 1920. Poetry Consultant, Library of Congress, Washington, D.C., 1958. **Awards:** Pulitzer prize, 1924, 1931, 1937, 1943; New England Poetry Club Golden Rose, 1928; Loines award, 1931; American Academy Gold Medal, 1939; Academy of American Poets fellowship, 1953; Sarah Josepha Hale award, 1956; Emerson-Thoreau Medal, 1959; U.S. Senate Citation of Honor, 1960; Poetry Society of America Gold Medal, 1962; MacDowell Medal, 1962; Bollingen prize, 1963. Litt.D.: Cambridge University, 1957. D.Litt.: Oxford University, 1957. **Member:** American Academy. **Died:** 29 January 1963.

PUBLICATIONS

Collections

Selected Letters, edited by Lawrance Thompson. 1964.
Selected Prose, edited by Hyde Cox and Edward Connery Lathem. 1966.
The Poetry, edited by Edward Connery Lathem. 1969.
Collected Poems, Prose, and Plays. 1995.
Early Poems. 1998.

Poetry

Twilight. 1894.
A Boy's Will. 1913.
North of Boston. 1914.
Mountain Interval. 1916.
Selected Poems. 1923.
New Hampshire: A Poem with Notes and Grace Notes. 1923.
West-Running Brook. 1928.
The Lovely Shall Be Choosers. 1929.
Collected Poems. 1930; revised edition, 1939.
The Lone Striker. 1933.
Three Poems. 1935.
The Gold Hesperides. 1935.
From Snow to Snow. 1936.
Further Range. 1936.
Selected Poems. 1936.
A Considerable Speck. 1939.
A Witness Tree. 1942.
Come In and Other Poems, edited by Louis Untermeyer. 1943; revised edition, as *The Road Not Taken,* 1951.
A Masque of Reason. 1945.
The Courage to Be New. 1946.
Poems. 1946.
Steeple Bush. 1947.
A Masque of Mercy. 1947.
Complete Poems. 1949.
Hard Not to Be King. 1951.
Aforesaid. 1954.
Selected Poems. 1955.
Dedication: The Gift Outright. 1961.
In the Clearing. 1962.
One Favored Acorn. 1969.
Three Books (includes *A Boy's Will, North of Boston, Mountain Interval*). 1997.

Recording: *Robert Frost: Poetry Reading,* 1953.

Plays

A Way Out (produced 1919?). 1929.
The Cow's in the Corn. 1929.

Other

Two Letters. 1931.
Frost and John Bartlett: The Record of a Friendship, edited by Margaret Bartlett Anderson. 1963.
Letters to Louis Untermeyer. 1963.
Frost: Farm-Poultryman, edited by Edward Connery Lathem and Lawrance Thompson. 1963.
Frost: Life and Talks—Walking, edited by Louis Mertins. 1965.
Frost and the Lawrence, Massachusetts "High School Bulletin": The Beginning of a Literary Career, edited by Edward Connery Lathem and Lawrance Thompson. 1966.
Interviews with Frost, edited by Edward Connery Lathem. 1967.
Family Letters of Robert and Elinor Frost, edited by Arnold Grade. 1972.
Frost on Writing, edited by Elaine Barry. 1973.
A Time to Talk, edited by Robert Francis. 1973.
Frost and Sidney Cox: Forty Years of Friendship, edited by William R. Evans. 1981.
Stories for Lesley (for children), edited by Roger D. Sell. 1984.

*

Bibliography: *A Descriptive Catalogue of Books and Manuscripts in the Clifton Waller Barrett Library, University of Virginia* by Joan St. C. Crane, 1974; *The Critical Reception of Frost: An Annotated Bibliography of Secondary Comment* by Peter VanEgmond, 1974; *Frost: A Bibliography 1913-1974* by Frank and Melissa C. Lentricchia, 1976; *Robert Frost's Reading: An Annotated Bibliography* by David W. Tutein, 1997.

Critical Studies: *Human Values in the Poetry of Frost: A Study of a Poet's Convictions* by George W. Nitchie, 1960; *The Pastoral Art of Frost* by John F. Lynen, 1960; *Frost: A Collection of Critical Essays* edited by James M. Cox, 1962; *An Introduction to Frost* by Elizabeth Isaacs, 1962; *The Major Themes of Frost* by Radcliffe Squires, 1963; *The Poetry of Frost: Constellations of Intention* by Reuben Brower, 1963; *Frost* by Elizabeth Jennings, 1964; *Frost* by James Doyle, 1965; *Frost* by Philip L. Gerber, 1966, revised edition, 1982, and *Critical Essays on Frost* edited by Gerber, 1982; *Frost: The Early Years,* 1966, *The Years of Triumph,* 1970, and *The Later Years,* 1977, by Lawrance Thompson and R. H. Winnick (one vol. edition, edited by Edward Connery Lathem, 1982); *Frost* by Elaine Barry, 1973; *Frost* by Reginald Cook, 1974; *Frost: The Poet and His Critics* by Donald J. Greiner, 1974; *Frost: Centennial Essays 1-3* edited by Jac Tharpe, 3 vols., 1974-78; *Frost: Modern Poetics and the Landscapes of Self* by Frank Lentricchia, 1975; *Frost's Imagery and the Poetic Consciousness* by Dennis Vail, 1976; *Frost: The Critical Reception* edited by Linda W. Wagner, 1977; *Frost: The Work of Knowing* by Richard Poirier, 1977; *Frost and New England: The Poet as Regionalist* by John C. Kemp, 1979; *Frost: Studies of the Poetry* by Kathryn Gibbs Harris, 1979; *Frost Handbook* by James L. Potter, 1980; *Frost: Contours of Belief* by Dorothy Judd Hall, 1984; *Frost: A Literary Life Reconsidered* by William H. Pritchard, 1984; *Frost and the Opposing Lights of the Hour* by Richard Wakefield, 1984; *Frost Himself* by Stanley Burnshaw, 1986; *Frost and the New England Renaissance* by George Monteiro, 1988; *Toward Frost: The Reader and the Poet* by Judith Oster, 1991; *Reading and Writing Nature: The Poetry of Robert Frost, Wallace Stevens, Marianne Moore, and Elizabeth Bishop* by Guy Rotella, 1991; *Robert Frost and a Poetics of Appetite* by Katherine Kearns, 1994; *Robert Frost and the Challenge of Darwin* by Robert Faggen, 1997; *The Ordeal of Robert Frost: The Poet and His Poetics* by Mark Richardson, 1997; *On the Sonnets of Robert Frost: A Critical Examination of the 37 Poems* by H.A. Maxson, 1997; *Robert Frost and Feminine Literary Tradition* by Karen L. Kilcup, 1998.

*   *   *

In 1959, at a dinner celebrating Robert Frost's eighty-fifth birthday, **Lionel Trilling** gave an after-dinner address that was later incorporated in "A Speech on Robert Frost: A Cultural Episode." Trilling announced his antipathy for those poems by Frost that expressed a "distaste for the life of the city" and for "the demand that is made upon intellect to deal with whatever are the causes of complexity, uncertainty, anxiety." Then Trilling specified poems he did admire, poems that led him to define Frost as a "terrifying poet" who depicted a "terrifying universe." The speech confused Frost (who was not sure whether he had been attacked or praised), outraged many of his friends, and caused quite a furor.

It would seem ludicrous that as late as Frost's eighty-fifth birthday there could be so much confusion concerning what constituted his basic point of view. Yet several factors make this situation plausible. For one thing, although such critics as **John Crowe Ransom** and **Randall Jarrell** praised Frost's poetry, his work gained comparatively little critical attention in the decades when the practitioners of the New Criticism reigned supreme. Further complications were caused by many of the critics who did laud his work. These admirers touted precisely the glib, sentimental, shallow poems by Frost that Trilling disliked. The main source of the confusion, however, was Frost himself. Because Frost hun-

gered so insatiably for popularity and esteem, he meticulously created a "folksy" public image of himself that his audiences would be entranced by. He never read any of his somber poems in public. He saw to it that his unattractive traits—his obsessive need to win at everything, his violent temper, his delight in back-biting, his race prejudices—remained totally unknown to the public. With equal skill, he hid his family misfortunes—his sister's insanity, his severe marital problems, his son's suicide, a daughter's insanity.

It is no wonder, then, that although Frost began writing in the late nineteenth century, we are still only beginning to formulate an intelligent evaluation of his poetry. Yet, despite all the obfuscations, such an evaluation is well worth pursuing, for Frost's best poems—and there are many of them—are of a very high quality. Frost was a consummate craftsman. He mastered a variety of forms; he wrote excellent sonnets, heroic couplets, and blank verse poems. His rhyme patterns are deftly wrought. He was even more adroit in matters of meter and rhythm. He proved repeatedly that there is no reason to believe that traditional rhythmical patterns inevitably lead to monotony.

What ultimately makes Frost's best poems valuable, however, is their dynamic view of our daily life. Frost believed that we live in a God-directed universe, but despite all his religious meditations Frost found God's ways absolutely inscrutable. At his most grim, as represented in "Design," Frost not only acknowledges the presence of the appalling in physical reality, but wonders if there is any cosmic design at all. It is certain in any case, as "Nothing Gold Can Stay" states, that no purity can abide in physical reality. What is pure is almost immediately contaminated. Nature is lovely at times, yet its very loveliness can prove fatally alluring, as the speaker in "Stopping by Woods on a Snowy Evening" testifies. Nor can we imitate the animal world and rely on our instincts; "The White-Tailed Hornet" reports that nature's creatures, acting on pure instinct, often blunder ridiculously.

Man experiences no clarifying visions. "The Fear" insists that we live surrounded by a literal and metaphorical darkness that harbors the hostile and the terrifying ambiguous. Weariness and loneliness define the archetypal human being who narrates "Acquainted with the Night." Isolation and poverty can crush a person physically, mentally, and spiritually, as they do characters in "A Servant to Servants" and "The Hill Wife." Moreover, man is badgered by his suppressed desires—the point of "The Sound of the Trees." Yet "The Flood" states that man cannot always control his destructive urges.

Frost also makes it clear that people cannot easily offer each other solace. The difficulty of understanding another human being is sometimes insurmountable. In "Home Burial," a husband and wife attempt to cope with the death of their child in two different ways. Neither can understand the other's attitude or behavior; neither can in any way help the other.

In his essay "'The Death of the Hired Man': Modernism and Transcendence," Warren French pinpoints why Frost's poetry is especially valuable in the late twentieth century. French remarks that, aware of modern man's grim situation, Frost—unlike the premodernists—did not proclaim the need for every individual to retreat at all costs to the safety of society; nor did Frost adopt or advocate the lifestyle lauded by modernist writers—the deliberate withdrawal on the part of the individual from society. Instead, Frost concentrated on what marks him—in French's term—as a "post-modernist." He struggled to discover what positive course is possible for a man who wants to maintain his individuality without exiling himself from society.

The affirmative albeit starkly limited goal Frost strove for and suggested to others is best indicated by his statement that his poems offer "a momentary stay against confusion." A series of momentary stays, created by the individual, is all man can hope for. As Lawrance Thompson wrote in his introduction to Frost's *Selected Letters,* Frost "bluntly rejected all the conventional stays which dogmatists call permanent"; they are too inflexible to contend successfully with physical reality's evershifting conditions. Frost was equally uninterested in trying to transcend the physical—material—world. He thought that the label "materialist" was used too quickly as a pejorative term. He said that it was "wrong to call anybody a materialist simply because he tried to say spirit in terms of matter, as if that were a sin." Nor did Frost fall back on the Romantic belief that man is basically good. He spurned the view that because man and nature are God's creations, they can do no wrong.

According to Frost, in order to achieve a momentary stay against confusion the first thing man needs is courage. A character in *A Masque of Mercy* says, "The saddest thing in life / Is that the best thing in it should be courage." Man must also try to maintain his equilibrium. Again and again, as in "The Vantage Point," "Goodbye and Keep Cold," and "To Earthward," Frost underscores the need to have the right perspective on all things, including oneself. Men should focus on the facts—and not daydream. In "Mowing," he declares that "The fact is the sweetest dream that labor knows." "Labor" is another key word. In "Two Tramps in Mud Time," he states that we should work and that our work should be motivated simultaneously by "love" and "need."

In some ways, nature can be supportive. "The Onset" and "The Need of Being Versed in Country Things" remind us that many things on earth are cyclical; this means that although evil comes to us, it will not last. So, too, nature is a revitalizing force, and sometimes awesomely beautiful, as described in "Iris by Night." It can also startle us out of a black mood created by too much self-centeredness—the development recorded in "Dust of Snow." It should also be remembered, as "Our Hold on the Planet" points out, that nature is at least "one fraction of one per cent" in "favor of man"—otherwise we would never have been able to thrive on earth.

Finally, Frost specifically advises us to preserve our individual integrity, but to link ourselves to society. Frost's emphasis on the value of society (often symbolized by the home) is coupled with his emphasis on the value of love. Love can be tenderly lyrical, as described in "Meeting and Passing." "Putting in the Seed" proclaims that love can be dynamically fertile. Love can alter reality—the point in "Never Again Would Birds' Song Be the Same." Love, breeding forgiveness and acceptance, provides a home against adversity. This is what Mary, in "The Death of the Hired Man," knows to be so, and what her husband, Warren, comes to realize. They decide to nurse Silas, their old hired man, but also to allow him his self-respect. Perhaps the finest example of Frost's stress on the importance of a viable balance between the individual and society is "The Silken Tent." Here, the woman described is a vibrant individual, yet held—willingly—by "countless ties of love and thought / To everything on earth."

—Robert K. Johnson

See the essay on "The Death of the Hired Man."

FRYE, (Herman) Northrop

Born: Sherbrooke, Quebec, Canada, 14 July 1912. **Education:** Victorian College, Toronto, B.A. 1933; Emmanuel College, ordained 1936; Merton College, Oxford, M.A. 1940. **Family:** Married Helen Kemp 1937. **Career:** Lecturer in English, 1939-41, assistant professor, 1942-46, associate professor, 1947, professor of English, 1948, chairman of department, 1952, University Professor, beginning 1967, Victoria College, University of Toronto. Visiting professor, Harvard University, Princeton University, Columbia University, Indiana University, University of Washington, and University of British Columbia. **Awards:** Guggenheim fellow, 1950-51; Lorne Pierce Medal of the Royal Society of Canada, 1958. Honorary degrees: Carleton University; Queen's University; Mount Allison University; University of New Brunswick; University of Manitoba; St. Lawrence University; University of British Columbia. **Member:** Modern Language Association (executive council member, 1958-62). **Died:** 23 January 1991.

PUBLICATIONS

Criticism

Fearful Symmetry: A Study of William Blake. 1947.
Anatomy of Criticism: Four Essays. 1957.
The English and Romantic Poets and Essayists: A Review of Research and Criticism. 1957.
Culture and the National Will. 1957.
Three Lectures. 1958.
By Liberal Things. 1959.
Myth and Symbol: Critical Approaches and Applications. 1963.
The Developing Imagination. 1963.
The Well-tempered Critic. 1963.
T.S. Eliot. 1963.
Fables of Identity: Studies in Poetic Mythology. 1963.
The Educated Imagination. 1964.
A Natural Perspective: The Development of Shakespearean Comedy and Romance. 1965.
The Return of Eden: Five Essays on Milton's Epics. 1965.
Fools in Time: Studies in Shakespearean Tragedy. 1967.
The Modern Century. 1967.

Editor, *Shakespeare The Tempest.* 1959.
Editor, *Design for Learning.* 1962.
Editor, *Blake: A Collection of Critical Essays.* 1966.

*   *   *

Northrop Frye, arguably the most influential literary critic of the twentieth century, belongs in the philosophical tradition of Immanuel Kant and the mythic tradition of Giovanni Battista Vico. Along with other neo-Kantians, such as Ernst Cassirer, Frye insists that the mythic symbol is constitutive of reality and not merely a mimetic mirror held up to a pre-existing world. What Frye means by the archetypal context for literature is not Jungian images but rather the context of literature itself.

For Frye myth criticism is the isolation of that aspect of the work that is conventional—that is, held in common with other works of the same genre or category. Literary form or shape, says Frye, does not come from life but only from literary tradition and thus, ultimately, from myth. The most recent heir to this approach, which received further impetus from the structuralist and poststructuralist critics of the 1970s and 1980s, is intertextualism, an approach that has revived interest in genre study—a field Frye said in his famous 1957 *Anatomy of Criticism* was stuck precisely where Aristotle had left it.

Frye's first book *Fearful Symmetry* (1947) was an analysis of the mythological framework of the poetry of William Blake. This work not only rescued that romantic mystic from relegation to the role of ecstatic madman by revealing the extraordinary systematic nature of his total body of work, but more important, it introduced Frye as a theoretical critic of the first magnitude who was as interested in developing the basic principles of literary study as he was in uncovering the highly developed genius of Blake.

Frye's ground-breaking work, however, after which literary criticism would never again be the same, was *Anatomy of Criticism* (1957). In what many critics have claimed is the single most influential work of criticism in the twentieth century, Frye argues that the shortest answer to the question of why criticism exists is that it can talk, while all the arts are dumb. He calls for criticism to leap to a new ground, discovering the organizing or containing forms of literature's conceptual framework. The most obvious example of a containing form, says Frye, is genre, but criticism, he points out, has no coherent conception of genre: "The very word sticks out in an English sentence as the unpronounceable and alien thing it is." Frye argued criticism had up to that time failed to organize literature, which appeared only as a huge aggregate or miscellaneous pile of creative efforts. The only organizing principle yet discovered, according to Frye, is chronology; however, literature does not exist only in time, "but spread out in conceptual space from some kind of center that criticism can locate."

The critical response to the literary work, Frye insists, begins when the temporal, participatory response to "what happens next" ends, when we can see the entire work as a total design. For Frye, theme is equivalent to Aristotle's dianoia—that is, the details of the plot in relation to a spatial unity rather than to a linear progression. A good introduction to Frye's intertextuality can be found in the opening chapter of his 1971 book *The Critical Path*. Criticism, says Frye, must develop its own historical overview on the basis of what is inside literature rather than what is outside—that is, conventions, genres, and recurring image-groups, or archetypes. Frye argues that the critic must avoid both the centrifugal fallacy, which asserts that literature lacks a social reference unless we associate its content with something nonliterary, as well as the centripetal fallacy, in which we fail to separate criticism from the direct experience of literature. "I wanted a historical approach to literature," he wrote, but an approach that would be a genuine history of literature, a history of its conventions, genres, and archetypal image clusters and "not simply the assimilating of literature to some other kind of history."

In one of his last books, *The Secular Scripture* (1976), Frye suggests that the romance form is the structural core of all fiction, bringing us closest to fiction as an epic of the human vision of life as a quest. The only way "reality" can be presented in literature is within conventions of literary structure, although, he complains, very few writers or critics recognize this limitation. One of the most important models for his basic assumption, says Frye, is Oscar Wilde's "The Decay of Lying," which pointed out that since life has no shape and literature does, literature throws away its one distinctive feature when it tries to imitate life. In Frye's view, Wilde anticipated a new age in literature, which it has taken critics a hundred years to accept. Thus, imagination is always a form of "lying," a creation in which coherence rather than correspondence to reality is the benchmark for truth. For the critic, "life" should be only "the seed-plot of literature," Frye says, "a vast mass of potential literary forms."

Throughout his long career, Frye continued to contribute to the understanding of Milton and Shakespeare. He also furthered the study of the relationship between criticism and society, the role of literature in culture and education, Canadian literary culture, and education in the humanities. One of Frye's last major projects, *The Grand Code: The Bible and Literature*, was not so much a scholarly work as what Frye called the result of his "own personal encounter" with the Bible; rather than an examination of the Bible as a series of separate literary works, it is, in typical Frye fashion, a study of the grand design—the Bible as an overarching embodiment of the mythological framework of Western literature.

Not since Matthew Arnold has a critic had such a profound influence on how we understand literature. Although such superstars as Jacques Derrida and Roland Barthes have superseded Frye in the last quarter of the twentieth century, he was the first to claim a significant role for literary criticism among the modern human sciences.

—Charles E. May

FULLER, Henry Blake

Born: Chicago, Illinois, 9 January 1857. **Education:** South Division High School, Chicago, 1872, 1875-76; Allison Classical Academy, Oconomowoc, Wisconsin, 1873-74. **Career:** Worked at Ovington's Crockery, 1875-76, and Home National Bank, 1877-78, Chicago; toured Europe, 1879-80; freelance writer in Chicago, 1880-82 and after 1885, Rome, 1883, and Boston, 1884-85; wrote for *Chicago Tribune,* 1884, and book review section of *Chicago Evening Post,* 1901-02; editorial writer, *Chicago Record-Herald,* 1911-13. Member of the advisory committee, *Poetry,* Chicago, 1912-29. **Died:** 28 July 1929.

PUBLICATIONS

Fiction

The Chevalier of Pensieri-Vani (stories). 1890; revised edition, 1892.
The Chatelaine of La Trinite. 1892.
The Cliff-Dwellers. 1893.
With the Procession. 1895.
From the Other Side: Stories of Transatlantic Travel. 1898.
The New Flag: Satires. 1899.
The Last Refuge: A Sicilian Romance. 1900.
Under the Skylights (stories). 1901.
Waldo Trench and Others: Stories of Americans in Italy. 1908.
Lines Long and Short: Biographical Sketches in Various Rhythms (stories). 1917.
On the Stairs. 1918.
Bertram Cope's Year. 1919.

Gardens of This World. 1929.
Not on the Screen. 1930.

Plays

O, That Way Madness Lies: A Play for Marionettes, in *Chap-book 4,* December 1895.
The Puppet-Booth: Twelve Plays. 1896.
The Coffee-House, and *The Fan,* from plays by Goldoni. 2 vols., 1925-26.
The Red Carpet, in *Fuller: A Critical Biography* by Constance Griffin. 1939.

Other

Editor, *The So-Called Human Race,* by Bert Leston Taylor. 1922.

*

Bibliography: *Fuller and Hamlin Garland: A Reference Guide* by Charles L.P. Silet, 1977; "Supplements to the Standard Bibliographies of Ade, Bierce, Crane, Frederic, Fuller, Garland, Norris, and Twain" by James Stronks, in *American Literary Realism, 1870-1910,* autumn 1983.

Critical Studies: *Fuller: A Critical Biography* by Constance Griffin, 1939; *Fuller* by John Pilkington, 1970; *Fuller of Chicago: The Ordeal of a Genteel Realist in Ungenteel America* by Bernard R. Bowron, Jr., 1974; *A Varied Harvest: The Life and Works of Fuller* by Kenneth Scambray, 1987; "The Chevalier of Pensieri-Vani: Henry Fuller's Not-So-Elusive Anatomy" by William D. Burns, in *Rocky Mountain Review of Language and Literature,* 1996, pp. 147-63.

*   *   *

A writer whose work suggests **Henry James** or **William Dean Howells,** but without the former's strength and without the latter's variety, Henry Blake Fuller strikes his admirers as subtle and his detractors as dull. In his best novels the style is elegant and spare, distinguished by a dry wit; in verse and drama, and in his last two novels, however, the performance is uncertain and even embarrassing. An "unconquerable reticence," in Harriet Monroe's phrase, and the "deliberate flatness" that **Edmund Wilson** observed do not encourage many readers to pursue this decorous writer. Three novels and several stories, however, do not deserve their present neglect.

Fuller's fictions pass in Italy or in Chicago. In the first group, somewhat vulgar Americans encounter sophisticated Europeans in a series of books beginning with *The Chevalier of Pensieri-Vani.* An elderly American woman, for example, longs to escape her crass new country for the older, presumably better one; an Italian nobleman is persuaded to alter his family's villa to suit the whims of tasteless Americans; on a train, an American encounters a traveling theatrical troupe and mistakes it for royalty. These ironic miniatures are finely honed and atmospheric, but they are less persuasive than the best of the Chicago novels.

With the Procession traces a middle-class family's pathetic attempts to social climb. An older generation has made the modest family fortune that a younger one wastes. The son is a posturing dilettante, the daughter a fatuous spinster, each aspiring to join Chicago's social "procession." *On the Stairs* follows the equally mediocre lives of two boys, the rise of one and the fall of the other, through two generations that blur the social distinctions that separated them in youth and separate them through economic ones.

Fuller's preoccupation with failures—despite his wry humor—may account, in part, for the indifference with which his best novel was greeted. *Bertram Cope's Year* attempts to overcome Fuller's "unconquerable reticence" in dealing with homosexuals, but in a manner sufficiently elliptical to obscure its intentions. Cope, an androgynous young man of surpassing good looks, attracts everyone despite his seeming diffidence and lack of marked intellect, but the attraction is only superficial. Cope is the *beau ideal* with little to offer, and his catastrophic effect on a variety of people is emotional rather than physical, spun in Fuller's most indirect manner. Critics seem to have misunderstood the novel, and Fuller's friends were embarrassed by it. A decade later he wrote two other novels, but at the time of the failure of *Bertram Cope's Year* he said, "No further novels likely: too much effort and too little return—often none." It deserves attention.

—Bruce Kellner

GADDIS, William

Born: New York City in 1922. **Education:** Harvard University, Cambridge, Massachusetts. **Family:** One son and one daughter. **Career:** Staff member, *New Yorker,* 1946-47; lived in Latin America, Europe, and North Africa, 1947-55; freelance speech and filmscript writer, from 1956 to the 1970s. **Awards:** American Academy grant, 1963; National Endowment for the Arts grant, 1966, 1974; National Book award, 1976, 1994; Guggenheim fellowship, 1981; MacArthur prize, 1982; National Book Critics' Circle award, for *A Frolic of His Own,* 1995. **Member:** American Academy, 1984; Institute of Arts and Letters. **Died:** 16 December 1998.

PUBLICATIONS

Fiction

The Recognitions. 1955.
JR. 1975.
Carpenter's Gothic. 1985.
A Frolic of His Own. 1993.

*

Critical Studies: *City of Words* by Tony Tanner, 1971; *A Reader's Guide to Gaddis's The Recognitions* by Steven Moore, 1982, and *In Recognition of Gaddis* edited by Moore and John Kuehl, 1984; "Gaddis Issue" of *Review of Contemporary Fiction,* vol. 2, no. 2, 1982; *American Fictions 1940-1980* by Frederick Karl, 1983; *The Contemporary American Comic Epic: The Novels of Barth, Pynchon, Gaddis, and Kesey* by Elaine B. Safer, 1988; "His Master's Voice: On William Gaddis's *JR*" by Patrick J. O'Donnell, in *Postmodern Culture: An Electronic Journal of Interdisciplinary Criticism,* vol. 1, no. 2, 1991; *Fire the Bastards* by Jack Green, 1992.

*   *   *

William Gaddis's novels are, without exception, long and complex, and all are marked by technical departures from ordinary conventions of narrative. The esteem for these works may testify to a widespread impatience with old fashions of narrative and a thirst for other ways of presenting experience. Among these "other ways"—ways that can also be observed in **John Barth, Thomas Pynchon, Richard Brautigan,** and others—are the modes of transmuting reality, perhaps getting at its essence by stringent rearrangement, which the reader meets in *The Recognitions* and *JR.*

JR is, as a story, an account of the fraudulent manipulation of stocks by a sixth-grader in a Long Island school for delinquents. The boy (JR) uses adults as agents and exploits for his own benefit the fatuities and self-deceptions of the great American world of trade and "development." An amusing anecdote. But Gaddis opens it out to deal with all that takes place in the universe that

is composed of stock flotation, management of industry, manipulation of bequests, and even in the arts, which are not independent of the commercial textures that surround them. In these tossing seas, the little craft of the boy JR often vanishes from view to reappear a hundred pages later.

All this is presented in a way that leaves a realistic copying of the world to one side. Interminable conversations, by telephone or face-to-face, blend with other conversations, and one learns by osmosis rather than by explicit statement that characters are speaking on a certain page. Moreover, many characters are endowed with knowledge they would not have in "real life"; obscure Christian heresies or references to **T.S. Eliot**'s *The Waste Land* occasionally sum up what a fumbling speaker is trying to say. To some readers, the result of all this is just confusion; others will find *JR* an often comic and revealing view of a world in which conventional pieties, familial and sexual, conform to the laws of trade. From this point of view, the novel is a confident innovation that refines a reader's awareness and encourages his detachment from what the bulk of mankind regards as important.

The earlier novel, *The Recognitions,* also views a great variety of persons and settings, but under the sign of religion rather than money. Persons try to see the sum of human meaning expressed by the various religions of the world and express some of these meanings in works of art and, even, in personal involvements. If Gaddis himself has an attitude toward the motley adventures and aspirations he reports, it is perhaps indicated by several references to Frazer's *Golden Bough,* where the effort of a scholar's mind to free itself from delusion is displayed. But such a firm center to *The Recognitions* becomes dim as endless inconsequence and violence mingle, undoing the "noble" hope of this character or that one. Scenes of great comic power alternate with interminable discussion.

Carpenter's Gothic, which took Gaddis ten years to write, has a plot. But, as is usual with Gaddis, the course of events comes to us filtered through a thick-meshed screen. The screen, in this novel, is the way in which the characters usually speak. Now and then a man called McCandless is allowed to express himself rather clearly on fundamentalism and other evils. But otherwise each utterance is a blend of what the particular character is saying and what that character might well be thinking. This is particularly true of the utterances of the scatter-brained heroine, Liz. Each new topic that enters her mind is obscured by the ferment of the topics that are already present. And Liz's habit of thought is, for the most part, the mode of expression with which Gaddis endows all the other characters.

Gaddis's presentation in *Carpenter's Gothic* is once more unconventional and difficult. But the plot, unlike that of *JR* and *The Recognitions,* is as full of conventional surprises as a thriller. McCandless is no tower of sense, but is actually insane. Liz's best friend Edie not only discovers Liz's body but drives off with Liz's husband, both well content. However, it is not in these events that the interest of *Carpenter's Gothic* lies but in the dense texture of spoken discourse, of conversations where minds, as often as not, do not meet.

In 1993 Gaddis released a fourth novel, *A Frolic of His Own.* In the same manner that *The Recognitions* examines religion and *JR* confronts trade, *A Frolic of His Own* is concerned with the ramifications of legal proceedings. The book's protagonist, Oscar Crease, is a middle-aged history professor who becomes consumed by two lawsuits. After he is run over by a Japanese-built car, Crease sues the manufacturer. He adds to his legal woes by bringing suit against a filmmaker, alleging that a play he had written was stolen and used as the basis for a movie. As in *Carpenter's Gothic,* Gaddis relates this straightforward plot with a tangle of voices, forgoing description and traditional narrative conceits. The result is a fast-paced and often humorous review of the contemporary American mania for pursuing litigation. It also indicates that Gaddis remained committed to his unique and experimental style of fiction.

—Harold H. Watts, updated by Craig Bryson

GAINES, Ernest J(ames)

Born: Oscar, Louisiana, 15 October 1933. **Education:** Educated at a high school in Vallejo, California; Vallejo Junior College; San Francisco State College, B.A. 1957; Stanford University, 1958-59. **Military Service:** Served in the United States Army, 1953-55. **Family:** Married Dianne Saulney in 1993. **Career:** Writer-in- residence, Denison University, Granville, Ohio, 1971; writer-in- residence, Stanford University, Stanford, California, 1981. Beginning 1983 professor of English and writer-in-residence, University of Southwestern Louisiana, Lafayette, Louisiana. Visiting professor, 1983, and writer-in-residence, 1986, Whittier College, Whittier, California. **Awards:** Wallace Stegner fellowship, Stanford University, 1957; San Francisco Foundation Joseph Henry Jackson award, 1959; National Endowment for the Arts grant, 1967; Rockefeller grant, 1970; Guggenheim fellowship, 1971; Black Academy of Arts and Letters award, 1972; Commonwealth Club of California fiction gold medal, 1972, for *The Autobiography of Miss Jane Pittman,* and 1984, for *A Gathering of Old Men;* American Academy and Institute of Arts and Letters literary award, 1987; Louisiana Endowment for the Humanities Humanist of the Year, 1989; MacArthur Foundation award, 1993; National Book Critics Circle award, 1994; Pulitzer prize, for *A Lesson Before Dying,* 1994. D. Litt.: Denison University, 1980; Brown University, 1985; Bard College, 1985; Louisiana State University, 1987. D.H.L.: Whittier College, 1986. **Residence:** Lafayette, Louisiana, and San Francisco, California.

PUBLICATIONS

Novels

Catherine Carmier. 1964.
Of Love and Dust. 1967.
The Autobiography of Miss Jane Pittman. 1971.
In My Father's House. 1978.
A Gathering of Old Men. 1983.
A Lesson before Dying. 1993.

Short Stories

Bloodline. 1968.
A Long Day in November (originally published in *Bloodline*). 1971.
The Sky Is Gray (originally published in *Bloodline*). 1993.

Other

Porch Talk with Ernest Gaines. 1990.
Conversations with Ernest Gaines. 1995.

*

Bibliography: "Ernest Gaines: An Annotated Bibliography, 1956-1988" by Mary Ellen Doyle, in *Black American Literature Forum,* vol. 24, no. 1.

Critical Studies: *Porch Talk with Ernest Gaines: Conversations on the Writer's Craft* by Marcia Gaudet and Carl Wooton, 1990; *Ernest Gaines* by Valerie Melissa Babb, 1991; *Critical Reflections on the Fiction of Ernest J. Gaines* edited by David Estes, 1994; *Wrestling Angles into Song: The Fictions of Ernest J. Gaines and James Alan McPherson* by Herman Beavers, 1995; *Ernest J. Gaines: A Critical Companion* by Karen Carmean, 1998.

*   *   *

Ernest J. Gaines came to the attention of the American public with the broadcast of a made-for-television movie based on his 1971 novel *The Autobiography of Miss Jane Pittman.* The story of a 108-year-old woman who lived from the time of slavery through the civil rights movement struck a chord with a nation seeking a deeper understanding of its past. The movie was popular in part because it drew from the novel what Gaines has successfully created in all his fiction: a sense of history lived by ordinary people rather than larger-than-life heroes. In all of his novels and short stories, he portrays men and women struggling for dignity in the racially and culturally complex world of rural Louisiana.

Gaines is able to depict this world so precisely because he grew up in it. His parents, Manuel and Adrienne Colar Gaines, were sharecroppers on the River Lake Plantation near Oscar, Louisiana. Gaines has commented several times on his experience of digging potatoes in the fields at the age of five. Also significant in his development was his Aunt Augusteen, a woman who, though unable to walk, managed to care for Ernest and his younger brothers while their parents worked. She became for him the symbol of the devout and determined black woman who refused to be overwhelmed by circumstances; such women appear in virtually all of his works. At the age of fifteen, he moved to California to join his mother and stepfather. It was here that he began a habit of voracious reading that gave him formal models for the kind of storytelling he wanted to do. What he did not discover in the great Russian writers or in American realists was any sense of the world he came from, and it was this he wanted to re-create.

His early novels reflect the restraints and frustrations in a rural Louisiana populated by African Americans, Cajuns, and black and white Creoles. Both *Catherine Carmier* (1964) and *Of Love and Dust* (1967) focus on pain and violence caused by generations of racial and cultural domination and misunderstanding. All of the characters, regardless of background, are trapped by their history; the best that can be hoped for is pride in surviving under such difficult circumstances. With the short story collection *Bloodline* (1968), Gaines began to assert a more positive role for folk culture and the individuals who live according to its values. For example, in "Just Like a Tree," a family and community gather around Aunt Fe, who is dying, though some members of the family want to deny this. She is the strong matriarch who represents tradition and endurance. Visiting her becomes the occasion for telling stories and for passing communal wisdom to a younger generation. But she also recognizes the value of change; she offers a blessing to Emmanuel, who has become a civil rights activist in opposition to the wishes of his conservative and fearful relatives. Similarly, "The Sky Is Gray" tells the story of a young boy's relationship to his mother, who is trying to raise her children alone in extreme poverty. She is typical of many of Gaines's heroic figures in being almost Hemingwayesque in her silent endurance of difficult circumstances. She teaches her son the meaning of manhood as she prepares him to be a responsible member of the family.

These literary qualities come together in Gaines's best-known work, *The Autobiography of Miss Jane Pittman* (1971). Jane tells her own story of over a century of African American life in rural Louisiana. Her voice is one of her author's great achievements; she offers folk wisdom, humor, and a personal version of an extended period of American history. She tells of tragedies, she talks to trees, she describes her religious experiences, and she discusses the importance of Joe Louis and Jackie Robinson to ordinary blacks. Through it all runs a theme of human dignity in spite of the pain and frustration of racial oppression. She recounts the lives of the various local heroes who sacrificed themselves for the improvement of black life. It is in fact her telling that brings them into history. Through her, Gaines allows readers to see Southern and African-American history and culture as a concrete human experience rather than an abstraction. In letting her tell the story, he proclaims the value of the lives of the black masses.

In his later work, Gaines focuses primarily on the experiences of black men, though women often play important roles. *In My Father's House* (1978) examines the life of a minister and leader of the local civil rights movement as he comes to terms with a past that he believed had disappeared. He discovers the need to embrace even the most disreputable aspects of history in order to fully live in the present. This work is disappointing in part because the lessons learned about the value of traditional black life do not seem to apply here. The characters all seem lost and uncertain, without any resources to draw upon. *A Gathering of Old Men* (1983) is more successful, in part perhaps because Gaines seems more comfortable with a rural setting. Like *Jane Pittman,* this work was made into a successful television production. It tells the story of the killing of a Cajun bully who has abused blacks for years. Soon after his body is discovered, all of the older black men show up with their guns having been recently fired. The sheriff tries to sort out the facts by interviewing each of them. In the process, they each tell of experiences of cruelty and humiliation that have shaped their lives. Every one of them has reason to kill some white person, but virtually all of them have suffered in silence for years. This death becomes the opportunity for a communal catharsis through which they can reclaim their manhood. As in *Jane Pittman,* it is the voices of the folk and the history they speak rather than the plot of the murder mystery that is important. *A Lesson before Dying* (1993) continues the theme of manhood in its narrative of a young man who is condemned to die and the schoolteacher who is asked to talk with him. The issue for Gaines is not so much the fairness of the legal system as it is the means by which self-worth can be achieved and maintained under adverse conditions. He is interested, in other words, in what Hemingway called "grace under pressure." This has special resonance for Gaines's work since to the personal struggle must be added the reality of racial oppression. Grant's task in the novel is not to save Jefferson but rather to convince him that he is not the "hog" he was described as being by his own lawyer in the trial.

The focus of Gaines on black humanity and dignity has won him considerable recognition over his career. He has received National Endowment for the Arts, Guggenheim, and Rockefeller grants, in addition to a number of local and state awards. In 1993, he was awarded a MacArthur Foundation "genius" grant. This recognition comes as a result of his success at doing what many great writers have done: making a small world a microcosm of universal human experience. Like one of his models, **William Faulkner,** Gaines has taken a "postage stamp" of the South and turned it into the world.

—Keith E. Byerman

GALE, Zona

Born: Portage, Wisconsin, 26 August 1874. **Education:** Portage public schools and at the University of Wisconsin, Madison, 1891-95, B.L. 1895, M.L. 1899. **Family:** Married William L. Breese in 1928; one adopted daughter. **Career:** Reporter, Milwaukee *Evening Wisconsin,* 1895-96, Milwaukee *Journal,* 1896-1901, and New York *Evening World,* 1901-03; returned to Portage, 1904; thereafter a full-time writer. Member, Wisconsin Library Commission, 1920-32; member, Board of Regents, 1923-29, and Board of Visitors, 1936-38, University of Wisconsin; Wisconsin delegate, International Congress of Women, Chicago, 1933. **Awards:** Butterick prize, 1911; Pulitzer prize, for drama, 1921. D.Litt.: Ripon College, Wisconsin, 1922; University of Wisconsin, 1929; Rollins College, Winter Park, Florida, 1930. **Died:** 27 December 1938.

PUBLICATIONS

Fiction

Romance Island. 1906.
The Loves of Pelleas and Etarre (stories). 1907.
Friendship Village (stories). 1908.
Friendship Village Love Stories. 1909.
Mothers to Men. 1911.
Christmas: A Story. 1912.
Neighborhood Stories. 1914.
Heart's Kindred. 1915.
A Daughter of the Morning. 1917.
Birth. 1918.
Peace in Friendship Village (stories). 1919.
Miss Lulu Bett. 1920.
Faint Perfume. 1923.
Preface to a Life. 1926.
Yellow Gentians and Blue (stories). 1927.
Borgia. 1929.
Bridal Pond (stories). 1930.
Papa La Fleur. 1933.
Old-Fashioned Tales. 1933.
Light Woman. 1937.
Magna. 1939.

Plays

The Neighbours (produced 1912). 1926.
Miss Lulu Bett, from her own novel (produced 1920). 1921.
Uncle Jimmy. 1922.
Mister Pitt (produced 1925). 1925.
Evening Clothes. 1932.
Faint Perfume, from her own novel. 1934.
The Clouds. 1936.

Radio Play: *Neighbors,* with Marian de Forest, from stories in *Friendship Village* by Gale, 1933.

Poetry

The Secret Way. 1921.

Other

Civic Improvement in Little Towns. 1913.
When I Was Little Girl. 1913.
What Women Won in Wisconsin. 1922.
Portage, Wisconsin, and Other Essays. 1928.
Frank Miller of Mission Inn. 1938.

*

Bibliography: "Gale" by Harold P. Simonson, in *American Literary Realism 3,* 1968.

Critical Studies: *Still Small Voice: The Biography of Gale* by August Derleth, 1940; *Gale* by Harold P. Simonson, 1962; "Miss Lulu Bett Revived" by Katherine A. White, in *Turn of the Century Women,* winter 1984; "Zona Gale" by William Maxwell, in *The Yale Review,* winter 1987.

*   *   *

"There is no contemporary author," wrote Joseph Wood Krutch in 1929, "whose evolution is more interesting than that of Zona Gale." Although she lived most of her life in the village of her birth—Portage, Wisconsin—and wrote largely in the village vein that attracted the talents of so many other writers of her generation, she was nevertheless a child of her age who responded to the astonishing variety of its pressures.

After four years in New York, during which she wrote *Romance Island* and *The Loves of Pelleas and Etarre,* two works of saccharine sentimentality, Gale returned to Portage to write a series of novels and tales, including *Friendship Village, Friendship Village Love Stories, Neighborhood Stories,* and *Peace in Friendship Village.* Unlike the meanness of **Sinclair Lewis**'s Gopher Prairie, the grotesquery of **Sherwood Anderson**'s Winesburg, or the enervation of **Hamlin Garland**'s Middle Border, Gale's Friendship Village, though not so sentimentally drawn as her earlier Romance Island, was an idyllic and hospitable town dedicated to children, family, and community.

However, her pastoral rendering of Friendship Village obscured her growing concerns with the issues and movements of her day—pacifism, women's rights, prohibition, civil liberties, progressivism, and others—even as it did her labors in their behalf: writing pamphlets and delivering speeches, campaigning for the progressive La Follettes of her native Wisconsin, joining the ill-fated pro-

test against the execution of Sacco and Vanzetti. In truth, Gale's increasingly realistic image of the world found its way even into the Friendship Village tales, which by the decade's end had begun to compromise the idyll with an occasional suggestion of reform. More important, her growing politicization was signaled in three novels of social relevance, all written during the Friendship Village period. *Heart's Kindred,* a pacifist piece; *A Daughter of the Morning,* a portrait of the working woman's plight; and what is perhaps her best work, *Birth.* In the last of these three, readers found a vision of small-town Americana whose acerbity approaches that of the better-known realist writers of her time. Indeed, *Birth,* along with *Miss Lulu Bett,* an equally acerbic novel of village life for which, after dramatization, Gale was awarded the Pulitzer Prize, nearly established their author as an authentic if minor realist writer.

Gale soon moved on, however. Prompted on a personal level by the death of her doting mother and more generally by the rise of a variety of New Thought movements in which she took an interest, Gale moved from realism to spiritualism and the occult, a vantage point from which she wrote a number of short stories and also *Preface to a Life,* a novel whose major character, though living on some higher astral plane, is understood by his fellow villagers to be insane.

Her talent having been a modest one, Gale has fallen into the obscurity that most critics agree she deserves. Still, she was in tune with many of the social currents of her day. And had her powers of imagination been greater, had her artistic control been stronger, her contribution to American letters might well have been of a high rank.

—Bruce A. Lohof

GALINDO, P. *See* **HINOJOSA, Rolando.**

GARDNER, Erle Stanley

Pseudonym: A.A. Fair. **Born:** Malden, Massachusetts, 17 July 1889. **Education:** Palo Alto High School, California, graduated 1909; Valparaiso University, Indiana, 1909; studied in law offices and admitted to the California bar, 1911. **Family:** Married 1) Natalie Talbert in 1912 (separated 1935; died 1968), one daughter; 2) Agnes Jean Bethell in 1968. **Career:** Lawyer, Oxnard, California, 1911-18; salesman, Consolidated Sales Company, 1918-21; lawyer, Ventura, California, 1921-33; contributed hundreds of stories, often under pseudonyms, to magazines, 1923-32; self-employed writer after 1933. Founding member, Court of Last Resort (now the Case Review Committee), 1948-60; frequent reporter on criminal trials; founder, Paisano Productions, 1957. **Awards:** Mystery Writers of America Edgar Allan Poe award, 1952, and Grand Master award, 1961. Honorary alumnus: Kansas City University, 1955. D.L.: McGeorge College of Law, Sacramento, California, 1956. **Member:** American Polygraph Association, honorary life member. **Died:** 11 March 1970.

PUBLICATIONS

Fiction

The Case of the Velvet Claws. 1933.
The Case of the Sulky Girl. 1933.

The Case of the Howling Dog. 1934.
The Case of the Curious Bride. 1934.
The Case of the Lucky Legs. 1934.
The Case of the Counterfeit Eye. 1935.
The Case of the Caretaker's Cat. 1935.
The Clew of the Forgotten Murder. 1935.
This Is Murder. 1935.
The Case of the Sleepwalker's Niece. 1936.
The Case of the Stuttering Bishop. 1936.
The Case of the Dangerous Dowager. 1937.
The Case of the Lame Canary. 1937.
The D.A. Calls It Murder. 1937.
Murder up My Sleeve. 1937.
The Case of the Shoplifter's Shoe. 1938.
The Case of the Substitute Face. 1938.
The D.A. Holds a Candle. 1938.
The Case of the Perjured Parrot. 1939.
The Case of the Rolling Bones. 1939.
The D.A. Draws a Circle. 1939.
The Bigger They Come. 1939; as *Lam to the Slaughter,* 1939.
The Case of the Baited Hook. 1940.
Gold Comes in Bricks. 1940.
Turn on the Heat. 1940.
The Case of the Silent Partner. 1940.
The D.A. Goes to Trial. 1940.
The Case of the Haunted Husband. 1941.
The Case of the Turning Tide. 1941.
The Case of the Empty Pin. 1941.
Double or Quits. 1941.
Spill the Jackpot! 1941.
Bats Fly at Dusk. 1942.
Owls Don't Blink. 1942.
The Case of the Careless Kitten. 1942.
The Case of the Drowning Duck. 1942.
The D.A. Cooks a Goose. 1942.
The Case of the Buried Clock. 1943.
Case of the Drowsy Mosquito. 1943.
Case of the Smoking Chimney. 1943.
Cats Prowl at Night. 1943.
Give 'em the Ax. 1944; as *An Axe to Grind,* 1951.
D.A. Calls a Turn. 1944.
The Case of the Crooked Candle. 1944.
Case of the Black-Eyed Blonde. 1944.
Case of the Half-Wakened Wife. 1945.
Over the Hump. 1945.
Case of the Golddigger's Purse. 1945.
The Case of the Borrowed Brunette. 1946.
The Case of the Backward Mule. 1946.
The D.A. Breaks the Seal. 1946.
Crows Can't Count. 1946.
Fools Die on Friday. 1947.
The Case of the Fan-Dancer's Horse. 1947.
The Case of the Lazy Lover. 1947.
Two Clues: The Clue of the Runaway Blonde, The Clue of the Hungry Horse. 1947.
The D.A. Takes a Chance. 1948.
The Case of the Vagabond Virgin. 1948.
The Case of the Lonely Heiress. 1948.
The Case of the Dubious Bridegroom. 1949.
The D.A. Breaks an Egg. 1949.
Bedrooms Have Windows. 1949.

The Case of the Cautious Coquette. 1949.
The Case of the Musical Cow. 1950.
The Case of the Negligent Nymph. 1950.
The Case of the One-Eyed Witness. 1950.
The Case of the Angry Mourner. 1951.
The Case of the Fiery Fingers. 1951.
The Case of the Moth-Eaten Mink. 1952.
The Case of the Grinning Gorilla. 1952.
Top of the Heap. 1952.
Some Women Won't Wait. 1953.
The Case of the Green-Eyed Sister. 1953.
The Case of the Hesitant Hostess. 1953.
The Case of the Runaway Corpse. 1954.
The Case of the Fugitive Nurse. 1954.
The Case of the Restless Redhead. 1954.
The Case of the Glamorous Ghost. 1955.
The Case of the Sun Bathers Diary. 1955.
The Case of the Nervous Accomplice. 1955.
The Case of the Terrified Typist. 1956.
The Case of the Gilded Lily. 1956.
The Case of the Demure Defendant. 1956.
Beware the Curves. 1956.
Some Slips Don't Show. 1957.
You Can Die Laughing. 1957.
The Case of the Daring Decoy. 1957.
The Case of the Lucky Loser. 1957.
The Case of the Screaming Woman. 1957.
The Case of the Long-Legged Models. 1958.
The Case of the Foot-Loose Doll. 1958.
The Case of the Calendar Girl. 1958.
The Count of Nine. 1958.
Pass the Gravy. 1959.
The Case of the Singing Skirt. 1959.
The Case of the Mythical Monkeys. 1959.
The Case of the Deadly Toy. 1959.
The Case of the Waylaid Wolf. 1960.
The Case of the Shapely Shadow. 1960.
The Case of the Duplicate Daughter. 1960.
Kept Women Can't Quit. 1960.
Bachelors Get Lonely. 1961.
Shills Can't Cash Chips. 1961; as *Stop at the Red Light.* 1962.
The Case of the Bigamous Spouse. 1961.
The Case of the Spurious Spinster. 1961.
The Case of the Reluctant Model. 1962.
The Case of the Blonde Bonanza. 1962.
The Case of the Ice-Cold Hands. 1962.
Try Anything Once. 1962.
Fish or Cut Bait. 1963.
The Case of the Amorous Aunt. 1963.
The Case of the Mischievous Doll. 1963.
The Case of the Stepdaughter's Secret. 1963.
The Case of the Phantom Fortune. 1964.
Up for Grabs. 1964
The Case of the Horrified Heirs. 1964.
The Case of the Daring Divorcee. 1964.
The Case of the Beautiful Beggar. 1965.
Cut Thin to Win. 1965.
The Case of the Troubled Trustee. 1965.
Widows Wear Weeds. 1966.
The Case of the Worried Waitress. 1966.
The Case of the Queenly Contestant. 1967.

Traps Need New Bait. 1967.

The Case of the Careless Cupid. 1968.

The Case of the Murderers Bride and Other Stories, edited by Ellery Queen. 1969.

The Case of the Fabulous Fake. 1969.

All Grass Isn't Green. 1970.

The Case of the Crimson Kiss (stories). 1971.

The Case of the Crying Swallow (stories). 1971.

The Case of the Fenced-In Woman. 1972.

The Case of the Irate Witness (stories). 1972.

The Case of the Postponed Murder. 1973.

The Amazing Adventures of Lester Leith (stories), edited by Ellery Queen. 1981.

The Human Zero: The Science Fiction Stories, edited by Martin H. Greenberg and Charles G. Waugh. 1981.

Whispering Sands: Stories of Gold Fever and the Western Desert, edited by Charles G. Waugh and Martin H. Greenberg. 1981.

Pay Dirt and Other Whispering Sands Stories, edited by Charles G. Waugh and Martin H. Greenberg. 1983.

Other

The Land of Shorter Shadows. 1948.

The Court of Last Resort. 1952.

Neighborhood Frontiers. 1954.

The Case of the Boy Who Wrote "The Case of the Missing Clue" with Perry Mason. 1959.

Hunting the Desert Whale. 1960.

Hovering over Baja. 1961.

The Hidden Heart of Baja. 1962.

The Desert Is Yours. 1963.

The World of Water. 1965.

Hunting Lost Mines by Helicopter. 1965.

Off the Beaten Track in Baja. 1967.

Gypsy Days on the Delta. 1967.

Mexico's Magic Square. 1968.

Drifting Down the Delta. 1969.

Host with the Big Hat (on Mexico) 1970.

Cops on Campus and Crime in the Street. 1970.

*

Critical Studies: *The Case of Gardner* by Alva Johnston, 1947; *Gardner: The Case of the Real Perry Mason* by Dorothy B. Hughes, 1978 (includes bibliography by Ruth Moore); *Murder in the Millions: Gardner, Mickey Spillane, Ian Fleming* by J. Kenneth Van Dover, 1984; *Erle Stanley Gardner's Ventura: The Birthplace of Perry Mason* by Richard L. Senate, 1996.

*   *   *

Erle Stanley Gardner spent much of his childhood traveling with his mining-engineer father through the remote regions of California, Oregon, and the Klondike. In his teens he not only boxed for money but promoted a number of unlicensed matches. Soon after entering college he was, by his own account, expelled for slugging a professor. But in the practice of law he found the form of combat he seemed born to master. He was admitted to the California bar in 1911 and opened an office in Oxnard, where he represented the Chinese community and gained a reputation for flamboyant trial tactics. In one case, for instance, he had dozens of Chinese

merchants exchange identities so that he could discredit a policeman's identification of a client. In the early 1920s he began to write Western and mystery stories for magazines, and eventually he was turning out and selling the equivalent of a short novel every three nights while still lawyering during the business day. With the sale of his first novel in 1933 he gave up the practice of law and devoted himself to full-time writing, or more precisely to dictating. Thanks to the popularity of his series characters—lawyer-detective Perry Mason, his loyal secretary Della Street, his private detective Paul Drake, and the foxy trio of Sergeant Holcomb, Lieutenant Tragg and District Attorney Hamilton Burger—Gardner became one of the wealthiest mystery writers of all time.

The 82 Mason adventures from *The Case of the Velvet Claws* (1933) to the posthumously published *The Case of the Postponed Murder* (1973) contain few of the literary graces. Characterization and description are perfunctory and often reduced to a few lines that are repeated in similar situations book after book. Indeed virtually every word not within quotation marks could be deleted and little would be lost. For what vivifies these novels is the sheer readability, the breakneck pacing, the involuted plots, the fireworks displays of courtroom tactics (many based on gimmicks Gardner used in his own law practice), and the dialogue, where each line is a jab in a complex form of oral combat.

The first nine Masons are steeped in the hard-boiled tradition of *Black Mask* magazine, their taut understated realism leavened with raw wit, sentimentality, and a positive zest for the dog-eat-dog milieu of the free enterprise system during its worst depression. The Mason of these novels is a tiger in the social-Darwinian jungle, totally self-reliant, asking no favors, despising the weaklings who want society to care for them, willing to take any risk for a client no matter how unfairly the client plays the game with him. Asked what he does for a living, he replies: "I fight!" or "I am a paid gladiator." He will bribe policemen for information, loosen a hostile witness' tongue by pretending to frame him for a murder, twist the evidence to get a guilty client acquitted and manipulate estate funds to prevent a guilty non-client from obtaining money for his defense. Besides *Velvet Claws,* perhaps the best early Mason novels are *The Case of the Howling Dog* and *The Case of the Curious Bride* (both 1934).

From the late 1930s to the late 1950s the main influence on Gardner was not *Black Mask* but the *Saturday Evening Post,* which serialized most of the Mason novels before book publication. In these novels the tough-guy notes are muted, "love interest" plays a stronger role, and Mason is less willing to play fast and loose with the law. Still the oral combat remains breathlessly exciting, the pace never slackens and the plots are as labyrinthine as before, most of them centering on various sharp-witted and greedy people battling over control of capital. Mason, of course, is Gardner's alter ego throughout the series, but in several novels of the second period another author-surrogate arrives on the scene in the person of a philosophical old desert rat or prospector who delights in living alone in the wilderness, discrediting by his example the greed of the urban wealth- and power-hunters. Among the best cases of this period are *Lazy Lover; Hesitant Hostess,* which deals with Mason's breaking down a single prosecution witness; and *Lucky Loser* and *Foot-Loose Doll* with their spectacularly complex plots.

Gardner worked without credit as script supervisor for the long-running *Perry Mason* television series (1957-66), starring Raymond Burr, and within a few years television's restrictive influence had infiltrated the new Mason novels. The lawyer evolved into a ponderous bureaucrat mindful of the law's niceties, just as Burr played him, and the plots became chaotic and the courtroom sequences mediocre, as happened all too often in the TV scripts. But by the mid-1960s the libertarian decisions of the Supreme Court under Chief Justice Earl Warren had already undermined a basic premise of the Mason novels, namely that defendants menaced by the sneaky tactics of police and prosecutors needed a pyrotechnician like Mason in their corner. Once the Court ruled that such tactics required reversal of convictions gained thereby, Mason had lost his *raison d'etre*.

Several other detective series sprang from Gardner's dictating machine during his peak years. The 29 novels he wrote under the by-line of A.A. Fair about diminutive private eye Donald Lam and his huge irascible partner Bertha Cool are often preferred over the Masons because of their fusion of corkscrew plots with fresh writing, characterizations, and humor. The high spots of the series are *The Bigger They Come* and *Beware the Curves*. And in his nine books about small-town district attorney Doug Selby, Gardner reversed the polarities of the Mason series, making the prosecutor his hero and the defense lawyer the oft-confounded trickster. But most of Gardner's reputation stems from Perry Mason, and his best novels in both this and his other series offer abundant evidence of his natural storytelling talent, which is likely to retain its appeal as long as people read at all.

—Francis M. Nevins, Jr.

GARDNER, John (Champlin, Jr.)

Born: Batavia, New York, 21 July 1933. **Education:** DePauw University, Greencastle, Indiana, 1951-53; Washington University, St. Louis, A.B. 1955; University of Iowa (Woodrow Wilson Fellow, 1955-56), M.A. 1956, Ph.D. 1958. **Family:** Married 1) Joan Louise Patterson in 1953, one son and one daughter; 2) Liz Rosenberg in 1980. **Career:** Teacher at Oberlin College, Ohio, 1958-59; California State University, Chico, 1959-62, and San Francisco, 1962-65; Southern Illinois University, Carbondale, 1965-74; Bennington College, Vermont, 1974-76; Williams College, Williamstown, Massachusetts, and Skidmore College, Saratoga Springs, New York, 1976-77; George Mason University, Fairfax, Virginia, 1977-78; member of the English department, State University of New York, Binghamton, 1978-82. Visiting professor, University of Detroit, 1970-71, and Northwestern University, Evanston, Illinois, 1973. Editor, *MSS* and Southern Illinois University Press Literary Structures series. **Awards:** Danforth fellowship, 1970; National Endowment for the Arts grant, 1972; American Academy award, 1975; National Book Critics Circle award, 1976. **Died:** 14 September 1982.

PUBLICATIONS

Fiction

The Resurrection. 1966.
The Wreckage of Agathon. 1970.
Grendel. 1971.
The Sunlight Dialogues. 1972.

Jason and Medeia (novel in verse). 1973.
Nickel Mountain: A Pastoral Novel. 1973.
The King's Indian: Stories and Tales. 1974.
October Light. 1976.
In the Suicide Mountains. 1977.
Vlemk, The Box-Painter. 1979.
Freddy's Book. 1980.
The Art of Living and Other Stories. 1981.
Mickelsson's Ghosts. 1982.
Stillness, and Shadows, edited by Nicholas Delbanco. 1986.

Plays

William Wilson (libretto). 1978.
Three Libretti (includes *William Wilson, Frankenstein, Rumpelstiltskin*). 1979.

Poetry

Poems. 1978.

Other

The Gawain-Poet. 1967.
Le Morte D'Arthur. 1967.
The Construction of the Wakefield Cycle. 1974.
Dragon, Dragon and Other Timeless Tales (for children). 1975.
The Construction of Christian Poetry in Old English. 1975.
Gudgekin the Thistle Girl and Other Tales (for children). 1976.
A Child's Bestiary (for children). 1977.
The Poetry of Chaucer. 1977.
The Life and Times of Chaucer. 1977.
The King of the Hummingbirds and Other Tales (for children). 1977.
On Moral Fiction. 1978.
On Becoming a Novelist. 1983.
The Art of Fiction: Notes on Craft for Young Writers. 1984.

Editor, with Lennis Dunlap, *The Forms of Fiction.* 1962.
Editor, *The Complete Works of the Gawain-Poet in a Modern English Version with a Critical Introduction.* 1965.
Editor, with Nicholas Joost, *Papers on the Art and Age of Geoffrey Chaucer.* 1967.
Editor, *The Alliterative Morte Arthure, The Owl and the Nightingale, and Five Other Middle English Poems, in a Modernized Version, with Comments on the Poems, and Notes.* 1971.
Editor, with Shannon Ravenel, *The Best American Short Stories 1982.* 1982.

Translator, with Nobuko Tsukni, *Tengu Child,* by Kikuo Itaya. 1983.
Translator, with John Maier, *Gilgamesh.* 1984.

*

Bibliography: *Gardner: A Bibliographical Profile* by John M. Howell, 1980; *Gardner: An Annotated Secondary Bibliography* by Robert A. Morace, 1984.

Critical Studies: *Gardner: Critical Perspectives* edited by Robert A. Morace and Kathryn VanSpanckeren, 1982; *Arches and*

Light: The Fiction of Gardner by David Cowart, 1983; *A World of Order and Light: The Fiction of Gardner* by Gregory L. Morris, 1984; *Thor's Hammer: Essays on Gardner* edited by Jeff Henderson and Robert E. Lowrey, 1985; *The Novels of John Gardner: Making Life Art as a Moral Process* by Leonard Butts, 1988; *Conversations with John Gardner* edited by Allan Chavkin, 1990; *The Art of John Gardner: Instruction and Exploration* by Per Winther, 1992; *Understanding John Gardner* by John M. Howell, 1993.

* * *

In his treatise *On Moral Fiction* John Gardner is quite specific: a good book is "one that, for its time, is wise, sane, and magical, one that clarifies life and tends to improve it." His best works give testimony to this belief. Gardner was not only a fine novelist, but also a critic, historian, and respected medieval and classical scholar. The canon renders these pursuits inseparable. This integrity is unsurprising in view of his general thesis that "We recognize true art by its careful, thoroughly honest search for and analysis of values." Art, it is said, seeks that which is "good," and such a search entails a wholeness of vision; an account taken of all the possibilities. It is this honest search for, and examination of values that characterizes Gardner's fiction. It promotes the dualisms so often remarked upon as typical and provides his recurring theme. Against an existential world, Gardner posits the transcending power of love and imagination.

The theme becomes apparent in *Grendel* in which Gardner, turned modern fabulator, re-creates the story of Beowulf from the monster's point of view. When Grendel begins his story he has already been at war with the Hrothgars for twelve years and, in a retrospective first-person narrative, must already be bleeding to death. His story is a tragi-comic lament to brute existence, inspired by the nihilism he has acquired from the Dragon. The Dragon, borrowing from Sartre and others, has told Grendel everything that an existentialist would. You are the "brute existent—the blunt facts of their mortality." Grendel, pointless ridiculous monster that he is, becomes an archetypal absurd hero. His monstrous set of values threaten civilization and form an ironic commentary on Hrothgar's attempts to live the Anglo-Saxon heroic ideal. Opposing the brute existence with a belief in the holy and miraculous, is the high priest Ork. Gardner, it seems, believed neither. At the end of the book, he tells us, is another Dragon whose opinions oppose those of the first. This "dragon" is Beowulf, whispering to Grendel that "Time is mind, the hand that makes (fingers on harpstrings, heroswords, the acts, the eyes of queens). By that I kill you." Civilization is redeemed by an act of imagination.

The constant search for value lends a quality of literary evolution to the canon. The last "dragon" in *Grendel,* says Gardner, expresses the views of William Blake. *Nickel Mountain,* rightly subtitled *A Pastoral Novel,* finds Henry Soames coming to a "mariner"-like awareness of the holiness of all things, so that, at the end of the novel, he sees life "less as a yarn told after dinner," and more as "a kind of church service—communion, say, or a wedding." In *The King's Indian* one hears the voice of Melville and others, and *October Light* is colored by the gentle wisdom of Matthew Arnold. Style, likewise, matches content.

In *Mickelsson's Ghosts,* Gardner's last and most demanding novel, the lyricism found in *Grendel* and the naturalism of *October Light* give way to a hard-edged contemporary prose. This, with the modern setting and the novel's sheer complexity, sug-

gests some attempt to culminate ideas in what is, necessarily, an open-ended form. The novel follows Gardner's recurrent pattern. A philosopher of ethics, Mickelsson is brought to the brink of insanity and despair by a multiplicity of sorrows. He must, in common with other Gardner characters, travel an anguished road toward self-regeneration. The book is, in essence, a modern morality play. Ghosts, merely evocative in previous novels, visibly haunt the protagonist of this one. Mickelsson faces the living ghosts of family and friends whom he feels he has failed, and the ghosts of dead philosophers whom he blames for the modern world's insanity. A modern "everyman," Mickelsson must wrestle with their ideas. Heidegger, Luther, Nietzsche, Wittgenstein, and others are evoked to create the dualisms that negate the obvious, and force Mickelsson to a recognition of his common humanity. The resolution, when it comes, takes place on the very brink of possibility. Surrounded by all of life, Mickelsson makes love: "oblivious to the tumbling, roaring bones and blood . . . pitiful emptyheaded nothings complaining to be born."

Gardner does not expect his contemporary heroes to slay monsters. A clumsy affirmation of love, or some small gesture towards responsible action may be all that denies what, in *October Light,* is called "gravity." Even language, low speech, it is understood, suffers gravity. "Everything decent supported the struggle upward." Such affirmation is unusual in the twentieth century, but since his death, Gardner's stature as a major American writer has been confirmed. His influence is likely to be lasting.

—Jan Pilditch

GARDONS, S.S. *See* **SNODGRASS, W.D.**

GARLAND, (Hannibal) Hamlin

Born: Near West Salem, Wisconsin, 14 September 1860. **Education:** Cedar Valley Seminary, Osage, Iowa, 1876-81. **Family:** Married Zulime Taft in 1899; two daughters. **Career:** Taught at a country school, Grundy County, Ohio, 1882-83; homesteader in McPherson County, Dakota Territory, 1883-84; student, then teacher, Boston School of Oratory, 1884-91; full-time writer from 1891: lived in Chicago, 1893-1916, New York, 1916-30, and Los Angeles, 1930-40. Founding president, Cliff Dwellers, Chicago. 1907. **Awards:** Pulitzer prize, for biography, 1922; Roosevelt Memorial Association Gold Medal, 1931. D.Litt: University of Wisconsin, Madison, 1926; Northwestern University, Evanston, Illinois, 1933; University of Southern California, Los Angeles, 1937. **Member:** American Academy, 1918, director, 1920. **Died:** 5 March 1940.

PUBLICATIONS

Fiction

Main-Travelled Roads: Six Mississippi Valley Stories. 1891; revised edition, 1899, 1922, 1930; edited by Thomas A. Bledsoe, 1954.
A Member of the Third House. 1892.

Jason Edwards: An Average Man. 1892.
A Little Norsk; or, Ol' Pap's Flaxen. 1892.
A Spoil of Office. 1892.
Prairie Folks (stories). 1893; revised edition, 1899.
Rose of Dutcher's Coolly. 1895; revised edition, 1899; edited by
  Donald Pizer, 1969.
Wayside Courtships (stories). 1897.
The Spirit of Sweetwater. 1898; revised edition, as *Witch's Gold,* 1906.
The Eagle's Heart. 1900.
Her Mountain Lover. 1901.
The Captain of the Gray-Horse Troop. 1902.
Hesper. 1903.
The Light of the Star. 1904.
The Tyranny of the Dark. 1905.
Money Magic. 1907; as *Mart Haney's Mate,* 1922.
The Moccasin Ranch. 1909.
Cavanagh, Forest Ranger. 1910.
Other Main-Travelled Roads (includes *Prairie Folks* and *Wayside
  Courtships*). 1910.
Victor Ollnee's Discipline. 1911.
The Forester's Daughter. 1914.
They of the High Trails (stories). 1916.
Hamlin Garland: Stories. 1994.

Play

Under the Wheel. 1890.

Poetry

Prairie Songs. 1893.
Iowa, O Iowa! 1935.

Other

Crumbling Idols: Twelve Essays on Art. 1894; edited by Jane
  Johnson, 1960.
Ulysses S. Grant: His Life and Character. 1898.
*The Trail of the Goldseekers: A Record of Travel in Prose and
  Verse.* 1899.
Boy Life on the Prairie. 1899; revised edition, 1908.
The Long Trail (for children). 1907.
The Shadow World. 1908.
A Son of the Middle Border. 1917; edited by Henry M. Christman,
  1962.
A Daughter of the Middle Border. 1921.
A Pioneer Mother. 1922.
Commemorative Tribute to James Whitcomb Riley. 1922.
The Book of the American Indian. 1923.
Trail-Makers of the Middle Border. 1926.
The Westward March of American Settlement. 1927.
Back-Trailers from the Middle Border. 1928.
Prairie Song and Western Story (miscellany). 1928.
Roadside Meetings. 1930.
Companions on the Trail: A Literary Chronicle. 1931.
My Friendly Contemporaries: A Literary Log. 1932.
Afternoon Neighbors: Further Excerpts from a Literary Log. 1934.
Joys of the Trail. 1935.
Forty Years of Psychic Research: A Plain Narrative of Fact. 1936.
*The Mystery of the Buried Crosses: A Narrative of Psychic Explo-
  ration.* 1939.

Diaries, edited by Donald Pizer. 1968.
Observations on the American Indian 1895-1905, edited by Lonnie
  E. Underhill and Daniel F. Littlefield, Jr. 1976.
Selected Letters of Hamlin Garland. 1998.

*

Bibliography: *Garland and the Critics: An Annotated Bibliogra-
phy* by Jackson R. Bryer and Eugene Harding, 1973; *Henry Blake
Fuller and Garland: A Reference Guide* by Charles L.P. Silet, 1977;
*Hamlin Garland: A Bibliography, with a Checklist of Unpublished
Letters* by Keith Newlin, 1998.

Critical Studies: *Garland: A Biography* by Jean Holloway, 1960;
Garland's Early Work and Career by Donald Pizer, 1960; *Garland: L'Homme et l'oeuvre* by Robert Mane, 1968; *Garland: The
Far West* by Robert Gish, 1976; *Garland* by Joseph B.
McCullough, 1978; *Critical Essays on Garland* edited by James
Nagel, 1982; *The Critical Reception of Garland 1891-1978* edited
by Charles L.P. Silet and Robert E. Welch, 1985; "The Uncollected Letters of Hamlin Garland to Walt Whitman" by Kenneth
M. Price and Robert C. Leitz III, in *Walt Whitman Quarterly Review,* winter 1988; "Representing Regionalism" by David Jordan,
in *Canadian Review of American Studies,* winter 1993.

*　　*　　*

Hamlin Garland played an important role in the development
of realism in America, but the work of enduring significance that
he bequeathed to the last half of the twentieth century is modest.
One volume of stories, one novel, and his autobiography are
all that a contemporary reader need bother about. Garland is
one of the most uneven of American writers, for the gulf is
wide between the stories in *Main-Travelled Roads* and the popular fiction he later turned out for the *Saturday Evening Post.*
His fall from realism into sentimental romance is simply embarrassing.

After Garland left the Midwest and went to Boston to become
a writer, he was encouraged by Joseph Kirkland, a realist writer,
to make use of his farm background. No authentic farmer yet had
appeared in American literature, and the subject was virgin. This
advice came in 1887 as Garland was returning from a visit to see
his mother, who had had a stroke, and he was burning with indignation over the privations and injustices of farm life. In addition,
the 1880s were a period of farm depression, for too much new
land had been opened up too fast and the invention of farm ma-
chinery had over-stimulated production. Out of this context came
the six stories that made up the original edition of *Main-Travelled
Roads.* They are "A Branch-Road," "Up the Coule," "Among the
Corn Rows," "The Return of a Private," "Under the Lion's Paw,"
and "Mrs. Ripley's Trip." Some take place in Wisconsin where
Garland was born, some in Iowa where the Garlands homesteaded
after the Civil War, and one makes use of the Dakotas where Garland homesteaded himself before leaving for Boston to become a
writer. The general theme is the hard lot of the farmer, and especially the farm wife, but the stories are not all somber. "Mrs.
Ripley's Trip" is bucolic comedy and "Among the Corn Rows"
ends with an elopement and high hopes. All of the stories, however, are filled with closely observed detail that make them good
examples of literary realism. There are some naturalistic elements
in the victimization of the characters by forces beyond their con-

trol, but Garland is not really a naturalist. It is above all the intensity of his feeling that carries these stories.

That Garland's compulsion to write these stories lay mostly in his anger of the moment and not in deeply held convictions is shown by subsequent developments. After he settled his mother in Wisconsin and began to prosper, he lost his zeal for social criticism. He was not dishonest, but he saw the world in terms of himself and later lapsed into a terrible respectability. He continued to write stories, however, and the six stories in *Main-Travelled Roads* eventually grew to twelve, but the later tales are inferior and lapse into sentimentality. He also produced another volume of somber tales, *Prairie Folks,* before his indignation abated, and he wrote four novels worth mentioning. The first, *A Little Norsk,* has something of the hard Dakota farm life in it, but it is marred by sentimentality. His best novel, and one that still can be recommended, is *Rose of Dutcher's Coolly,* the story of a farm girl who goes to the state university and then to Chicago to pursue a career. The detail is good, especially the childhood and adolescence of Rose on the farm, and it deals with feminist problems of the 1890s. *Jason Edwards* is single-tax propaganda written after Garland had met Henry George and become a supporter of the single-tax panacea for economic ills. *A Spoil of Office* is a populist novel attacking political corruption and reminding modern readers who stumble on it that 1892 was the year that James Weaver led the United States' most successful third party movement.

Garland made a literary comeback in 1917 when he wrote his autobiography, *A Son of the Middle Border.* This is a first-rate work that ranks with the best that Garland accomplished in the 1890s. He followed this with three other volumes of family history: *A Daughter of the Middle Border, Trail-Makers of the Middle Border* (this one fictionalized), and *Back-Trailers from the Middle Border,* but these are less interesting than the first. Because Garland lived a long time and made a point of meeting writers and public figures, students of literary history will find considerable interest in his literary reminiscences: *Roadside Meetings, Companions on the Trail, My Friendly Contemporaries,* and *Afternoon Neighbors.* Also noteworthy is Garland's one venture into literary criticism, *Crumbling Idols,* in which he makes a strong defense of realism.

—James Woodress

See the essay on *Main-Travelled Roads.*

GASS, William H(oward)

Born: Fargo, North Dakota, 30 July 1924. **Education:** Kenyon College, A.B. 1947; Cornell University, Ph.D. 1954. **Military Service:** U.S. Navy 1943-46. **Family:** Married 1) Mary Patricia O'Kelly in 1952; one son and one daughter; 2) Mary Alice Henderson in 1969; two daughters. **Career:** Instructor in philosophy, College of Wooster, Wooster, Ohio, 1950-54; assistant professor, 1954-60, associate professor, 1960-66, and professor of philosophy, 1966-69, Purdue University, Lafayette, Indiana; professor of philosophy, 1969-79, and beginning 1979 the David May Distinguished University Professor in the Humanities, Washington University, St. Louis, Missouri. **Awards:** Longview Foundation award in fiction, 1959; Rockefeller grant for fiction, 1965-66; Standard Oil Teaching award, Purdue University, 1967; Sigma Delta Chi Best Teacher award, Purdue University, 1967 and 1968; Guggenheim fellowship, 1969-70; National Medal of Merit for fiction, 1979; National Book Critics Circle award for criticism, for *The Habitants of the World: Essays,* 1986; PEN/Faulkner award for fiction, 1996; National Book Critics Circle award, for *Finding a Form,* 1997; Lifetime Achievement award, The Lannan Foundation Literary awards, 1997. D.Litt: Kenyon College, 1974; George Washington University, 1982; Purdue University, 1985.

PUBLICATIONS

Novels

Omensetter's Luck. 1966.
The Tunnel. 1994.

Short Stories

In the Heart of the Heart of the Country. 1968.
The First Winter of My married Life. 1979.
Culp. 1985.

Novellas

Willie Masters' Lonesome Wife. 1968.

Other

Fiction and Figures of Life. 1970.
On Being Blue. 1975.
The World Within the World. 1978.
The House VI Book. 1980.
The Habitations of the World: Essays. 1984.
Words About the Nature of Things. 1985.
A Temple of Texts. 1990.
Fifty Literary Pillars: A Temple of Texts: An Exhibition to Inaugurate the International Writers Center. 1991.
Finding a Form: Essays. 1996.
Art and Science: Investigating Matter. 1996.
Writing in Politics. 1996.
with Johanna Drucker, *The Dead Muse: The Writer as Artist, the Artist as Writer.* 1997.
Reading Rilke: Reflections on the Problems of Translation. 1999.

Editor, with Lorin Cuoco, *The Writer in Politics.* 1996.

*

Critical Studies: *Into the Tunnel: Readings of Gass's Novel* by Steven G. Kellman, 1998.

*   *   *

William H. Gass is America's most important philosophical novelist, not in the discursive sense by which we identify other novelists with a freight of ideology to illustrate, but rather as a philosopher of language who is also a powerful fiction-maker with the courage of his convictions. Gass has been the most articulate and forceful contemporary proponent of the importance of aesthetic beauty and artistic structure, even as critics and writers around him have caved in to the social message of cultural correctness.

In his fourth collection of essays, *Finding a Form* (1996), Gass remains one of the last unashamed advocates for the great Greek ideal of form, exploring with the precision usually reserved for poetry the relationship between language and mind and the tension between nature and culture. His every sentence carefully carved, Gass is the best example of his own belief that there is music in prose and that language must be carefully crafted so that it can be heard. Throughout the book Gass returns untiringly to his central conviction—that the artist's fundamental loyalty is to form and not to ideology or content. "Every other diddly desire can find expression; every crackpot idea or local obsession, every bias and graciousness and mark of malice, may have an hour," says Gass, "but it must never be allowed to carry the day."

Gass has been singing this tune since his first collection of essays, *Fiction and the Figures of Life* (1970), in which he established his primary premise about fiction: "stories and the places and people in them are merely made of words as chairs are made of smoothed sticks and sometimes of cloth and metal tubes." His formalist conviction that a novel or short story is ideally a self-contained meaning system is his most controversial principle, one that he explores with equal fervor in his other two collections of essays, *The World Within the Word* (1978) and *Habitations of the Word* (1985).

Gass's first novel, *Omensetter's Luck* (1966), was met with almost overwhelming critical success. Reviewers praised its lyrical beauty and its intellectual depth, calling it an important contribution to the literature of its time, even the most important work of fiction by an American writer of its generation. The plot of the novel is simple, for Gass has never been interested in mere plot. It deals with an old man who tries to tell about Omensetter, a craftsman who settled in a town in Ohio in the late nineteenth century. However, this voice is less important than the voice of the Reverend Jethro Furber, Omensetter's antagonist. A parody of folk legend, the novel is about how to represent the world in words, the theme of all of Gass's fiction. A verbal duel between the two main characters, the book explores basic philosophical conflicts between mind and body, human and object, reason and feeling.

Two years later Gass published his second work of fiction, *In the Heart of the Heart of the Country*, which included a novella, *The Pedersen Kid*, a hallucinatory detective story and quest romance about coming of age in the midst of madness and death, and four short stories. Gass has said that the best of these latter pieces is "Order of Insects," a story about a woman who limits her vision so obsessively that she transforms insects into metaphoric, mythic creatures. Her fascination with insects centers on their order and wholeness in death, for, unlike those of humans, their skeletons are on the outside; thus they retain their form. Never seeming to decay, they are perfect geometric shapes of pure order.

The best-known story in the collection is the title story, a lyrical meditation in thirty-two sections, which, in between its Yeatsean beginning—"I have sailed the seas and come . . . to B . . . a small . . . town fastened to a field in Indiana"—and its transcendent conclusion of "Joy to the World," explores the narrator's efforts to pull himself together poetically after a failed affair that makes him feel he has "love left over" that he would like to lose. The story has become a classic anthology piece, a representative of experimental short fiction of the 1960s, often placed alongside

the stories of **Donald Barthelme**, **John Barth**, and **Robert Coover** to illustrate the self-reflexivity of postmodernism.

Gass's most thoroughly experimental, self-reflexive fiction, however, is his novella *Willie Master's Lonesome Wife* (1968). This is a work that seeks to create the illusion that the book the reader holds in his hands is indeed the lonesome wife herself and that the reading process is a sexual encounter—a metaphor to which Gass calls the reader's attention by using different paper textures, photographs, and a variety of typographical devices to suggest that words are sensuous objects that must be encountered concretely and not merely a transparent lens through which we perceive "reality."

The Tunnel, Gass's masterwork on which he labored for twenty-five years, creates the voice of William Frederick Kohler, a history professor who, while trying to write a simple, self-congratulatory preface to his own magnum opus, *Guilt and Innocence in Hitler's Germany*, becomes blocked and writes about his own life instead. Filled with bitterness, hatred, lies, self-pity, and self-indulgence, Kohler resents his hard-fisted father and his self-pitying mother, loathes his fat, slothful wife, and has nothing but contempt for his nondescript adolescent sons, his pedantic colleagues, and his superficial lovers. In spite of the protagonist's abhorrent personality, however, and because the voice of Kohler is expressed in Gass's highly polished prose, wonderfully sustained for over six hundred pages, the novel is not a self-indulgent diatribe but a complex philosophic exploration of the relationship between historical fascism and domestic solipsism.

Gass's most recent collection of stories, *The Cartesian Sonata* (1998), ranges from the somewhat conventional "Bed and Breakfast," in which an ineffectual traveling businessman loses himself in the textual world of books, to the self-reflexive, poetic reverie "Emma Enters a Sentence of Elizabeth Bishop's" and the Kafkaesque "The Master of Secret Revenges." In these stories Gass continues to fly in the face of late-twentieth-century realism by creating fictional figures caught in the web of language and thought.

—Charles E. May

GATES, Henry Louis, Jr.

Born: Keyser, West Virginia, 16 September 1950. **Education:** Yale University, B.A 1973; Clare College, Cambridge, Massachusetts, M.A. 1974, Ph.D. 1979. **Family:** Married Sharon Lynn Adams in 1979; two daughters. **Career:** General anesthetist, Anglican Mission Hospital, Kilimatinde, Tanzania, 1970-71; director of student affairs, John D. Rockefeller gubernatorial campaign, Charleston, West Virginia, 1971 and director of research, 1972; staff correspondent, *Time,* London Bureau, London, 1973-75; lecturer, 1976-79, and assistant professor, 1979-84, associate professor of English and Afro-American Studies, 1979-84, and director of undergraduate Afro-American studies, Yale University, New Haven, Connecticut; professor of English, comparative literature and African Studies, Cornell University, Ithica, New York, 1985-88, and W.E.B. DuBois Professor of Literature, 1988-90. Beginning 1990 John Spencer Bassett Professor of English and Literature, Duke University, Durham, North Carolina. W.E.B. DuBois Professor of the Humanities, professor of English, and chair of Afro-American Studies, Harvard University, Cambridge, Massachusetts, beginning 1990. **Awards:** Carnegie Foundation Fellowship for Africa, 1970-71; Phelps Fellowship, Yale University, 1970-71; Mellon fellowships, Cambridge University, 1973-75, and National Humanities Center, 1989-90; grants from Ford Foundation, 1976-77 and 1984-85, and National Endowment for the Humanities, 1980-86; A. Whitney Griswold Fellowship, 1980; Rockefeller Foundation fellowships, 1981 and 1990; MacArthur prize fellowship, MacArthur Foundation, 1981-86; Yale Afro-American teaching prize, 1983; award from Whitney Humanities Center, 1983-85; Princeton University Council of the Humanities lectureship, 1985; Award for Creative Scholarship, Zora Neale Hurston Society, 1986; associate fellowship from W.E.B. DuBois Institute, Harvard University, 1987-88 and 1988-89; John Hope Franklin prize honorable mention, American Studies Association, 1988; Woodrow Wilson National Fellow, 1988-89 and 1989-90; Candle award, Morehouse College, 1989; American Book award and Anisfield-Wolf Book award for Race Relations, both 1989, both for *The Signifying Monkey: Towards a Theory of Afro-American Literary Criticism*; Potomac State College Alumni award, 1991; Bellagio Conference Center Fellowship, 1992; Clarendon Lecturer, Oxford University, 1992; Best New Journal of the Year award, Association of American Publishers, 1992; Golden Plate Achievement award, 1993; African American Students Faculty award, 1993; George Polk award for Social Commentary, 1993; Heartland prize for nonfiction, for *Colored People: A Memoir,* 1994; Lillian Smith Book award, 1994; West Virginian of the Year, 1995; Humanities award, West Virginia Humanities Council, 1995; Ethics award, *Tikun* magazine, 1996; Distinguished Editorial Achievement, 1996. Honorary degrees: Dartmouth College, 1989; University of West Virginia, 1990; University of Rochester, 1990; Pratt Institute, 1990; University of Bridgeport, 1991 (declined); University of New Hampshire, 1991; Bryant College, 1992; Manhattan Community College, 1992; George Washington University, 1993; University of Massachusetts at Amherst, 1993; Williams College, 1993; Emory University, 1995; Colby College, 1995; Bard College, 1995, and Bates College, 1995. **Member:** American Academy of Arts and Sciences, 1993.

PUBLICATIONS

Prose

Figures in Black: Words, Signs, and the 'Radical Self'. 1987.
The Signifying Monkey: Towards a Theory of Afro-American Literary Criticism. 1988.
Loose Canons: Notes on the Culture Wars. 1992.
Colored People: A Memoir. 1994.
Speaking of Race: Hate Speech, Civil Rights, and Civil Liberties. 1995.
The Future of the Race, with Cornel West. 1996.
Thirteen Ways of Looking at a Black Man. 1997.
Wonders of the African World. 1999.

Other

Editor, *Black Is the Color of the Cosmos: Charles T. Davis's Essays on Afro-American Literature and Culture, 1942-1981.* 1982.
Editor, *Our Nig; or, sketches from the Life of a Free Black,* by Harriet E. Wilson. 1983.
Editor, *Black Literature and Literary Theory.* 1984.

Editor, *The Slave's Narrative: Texts and Contexts.* 1986.
Editor, *Race, Writing, and Difference.* 1986.
Editor, *The Classic Slave Narratives.* 1987.
Editor, *In the House of Oshugbo: A Collection of Essays on Wole Soyinka.* 1988.
Editor, *The Oxford-Schomburg Library of Nineteenth-Century Black Women Writers* (30 Vols.). 1988-.
Editor, *The Souls of Black Folk,* by W.E.B. DuBois. 1989; as *The Souls of Black Folk: Authoritative Text, Contexts, Criticism,* 1999.
Editor, *The Autobiography of an Ex-Colored Man,* by James Weldon Johnson. 1989.
Editor, *Three Classic African-American Novels.* 1990.
Editor, *Their Eyes Were Watching God,* by Zora Neale Hurston. 1990.
Editor, *Jonah's Gourd Vine,* by Zora Neale Hurston. 1990.
Editor, *Tell My Horse,* by Zora Neale Hurston. 1990.
Editor, *Mules and Men,* by Zora Neale Hurston. 1990.
Editor, *Reading Black, Reading Feminist: A Critical Anthology.* 1990.
Editor, *Voodoo Gods of Haiti.* 1991.
Editor, *The Schomburg Library of Nineteenth-Century Black women Writers.* 1991.
Editor, with Randall K. Burkett and Nancy Hall Burkett, *Black Biography 1790-1950: A Cumulative Index.* 1991.
Editor, with George Bass, *Mulebone: A Comedy of Negro Life,* by Langton Hughes and Zora Neale Hurston. 1991.
Editor, *Bearing Witness: Selections from African American Autobiography in the Twentieth Century.* 1991.
Editor, with Anthony Appiah, *Gloria Naylor: Critical Perspectives Past and Present.* 1993.
Editor, with Anthony Appiah, *Alice Walker: Critical Perspectives Past and Present.* 1993.
Editor, with Anthony Appiah, *Langton Hughes: Critical Perspectives Past and Present.* 1993.
Editor, with Anthony Appiah, *Richard Wright: Critical Perspectives Past and Present.* 1993.
Editor, with Anthony Appiah, *Toni Morrison: Critical Perspectives Past and Present.* 1993.
Editor, with Anthony Appiah, *Zora Neale Hurston: Critical Perspectives Past and Present.* 1993.
Editor, *The Amistad Chronology of African American History form 1445-1990.* 1993.
Editor, *Frederick Douglass: Autobiographies.* 1994.
Editor, with Anthony Appiah, *The Dictionary of Global Culture.* 1995.
Editor, *The Complete Stories of Zora Neale Hurston.* 1995.
Editor, with Anthony Appiah, *Identities.* 1996.
Editor, *Ann Petry: Critical Perspectives Past and Present.* 1997.
Editor, *Chinua Achebe: Critical Perspectives Past and Present.* 1997.
Editor, *Harriet A. Jacobs: Critical Perspectives Past and Present.* 1997.
Editor, *Ralph Ellison: Critical Perspectives Past and Present.* 1997.
Editor, *Wole Soyinka: Critical Perspectives Past and Present.* 1997.
Editor, *Frederick Douglass: Critical Perspectives Past and Present.* 1997.
Editor, with William L. Andrews, *Pioneers of the Black Atlantic: Five Slave Narratives from the Enlightenment, 1772-1815.* 1998.
Editor, *The Essential Soyinka: A Reader.* 1998.
Editor, *Critical Essays on Zora Neale Hurston.* 1998.
Editor, *Black Imagination and the Middle Passage.* 1999.

*

Critical Studies: "The Crisis in Black American Literary Criticism and the Postmodern Cures of Houston A. Baker, Jr. and Henry Louis Gates, Jr." in *Double-Consciousness/Double Bind: Theoretical Issues in Twentieth-Century Black Literature* by Sandra Adell, 1994.

*   *   *

Although Henry Louis Gates, Jr., has both devotees and detractors, he is undoubtedly one of the most influential critics and social commentators of our time. Gates has said of his work, "My task is to explicate black texts," and it seems that he has set about this task with gusto, casting a wide net over the publishing community, both past and present. He has been involved in such diverse projects as the *Norton Anthology of African American Literature,* which he coedited, to the revival of what is considered the first African American novel, Harriet E. Wilson's *Our Nig; or Sketches from the Life of a Free Black,* to regular contributions to the *New Yorker* magazine that range from the moderately serious to the puff profile piece.

One of the things that put Gates in the literary spotlight was the Black Periodical Fiction Project, established to find and revive black fiction that had been published in nineteenth-century periodicals. It was the 1983 republication of *Our Nig,* edited and with an introduction by Gates, that first established him as an important African American literary scholar. He soon followed with the publication of the essay "On 'The Blackness of Blackness': A Critique of the Sign and the Signifying Monkey" in *Critical Inquiry,* which began his project of reexamining and recontextualizing African American literature.

It now seems that Gates began his career rather shrewdly, working somewhat outside the black arts movement and calling for an examination of black literature that would remove it from the realm of art as a literal transliteration of life and place it firmly in the context of the literature that has preceded it. Gates attempts to tether the history of African American literature together so that a tug at one end may cause a text at the other end to jump, shake, or slide. The individual text does not stand alone, cashing in on the author's experiences or attitudes, but rather gives a reinterpretation similar to the way a jazz musician riffs on a theme or performs a song differently from one session to the next, thus reflecting on the text that has come before, whether it be spoken, written, or sung. Gates's metaphor for the inclusion of a work in this extended literary history is, as he spells it, "signifyin(g)." He announces, outlines, and details at length the signifying of African American literature in his books *Figures in Black: Words, Signs and the Racial Self* and *The Signifying Monkey: Towards a Theory of Afro-American Literary Criticism.* Gates retraces the transmission of ritual and mythology from the Yoruba to the Caribbean and the United States. As a member of the modern form of this community of writers and artists, he participates in the tradition of signifying, describing and reflecting on the black heritage in his criticism, memoirs, and essays.

There is something very attractive about the idea of a contemporary author participating in the work of the significant artists of the past, perhaps recalling the concept of the living word or the muse and mentor. It seems to add a mystical, cross-media element to the literary efforts of contemporary writers. It may seem less like hard scholarship, although hard scholarship it is, but perhaps, as with the case of Gates's criticism, with more popular appeal. Gates has said, however, that he does not have the time to do an original work of scholarship. "I worry," he has said, "that I haven't published a scholarly work since 1988."

The combination of Gates's critical stance, or the lack thereof since 1988, and of what has been perceived as his almost tireless self-promotion has created a nesting place for a number of detractors. In many ways his popularity seems to have watered down his message. In an attempt to link the past with the present, Gates tends to be rather extrainclusive, so that many works that may have historical value are elevated despite an evident lack of literary merit. Still, historical significance is a form of significance and is probably worth promoting. But that is primarily what Gates seems to do anymore—promote. When approaching the work of a black author, Gates's stance often seems to be one of pulling punches, if indeed there are any punches to be pulled, so as to include the individual whose work may be inferior. He may quote someone else's criticism of a work, but he rarely is critical himself.

One notable exception to this rule is his profile of Anatole Broyard in *Thirteen Ways of Looking at a Black Man,* in which Gates allows himself to imply a kind of subtle disapproval of Broyard's behavior, though not of his work. Throughout his career as a book critic for the *New York Times,* Broyard allowed the general public to think that he was white. Gates, it seems, would rather the world know that this well-respected critic for the *Times* was, indeed, black. In this essay Gates is at his best as a prose stylist, writing with lively elegance. The argument may be made that, when he allows himself to be honest in this way, he is at his most absorbing as an essayist and critic. After all, conflict is interesting, even invigorating, and so why not allow it? Although if there is one thing that can certainly be said about the writing of Gates, it is that he can be a terribly absorbing writer, even when his politics may be confounding.

Perhaps it is not as important as it may seem that Gates is not a perfect critic, essayist, or anything else. Perhaps what is more important is the influence he has had on African American literature through his criticism and promotion of other writers, through his editorial work, and through his essays. That influence is, in the long run, both positive and immeasurable.

—Terry Bain

GIBBONS, Kaye

Born: Nash County, North Carolina, 1960. **Education:** Attended North Carolina State University and the University of North Carolina at Chapel Hill. **Family:** 1) Married and divorced; 2) partner of Frank Ward; three daughters. **Career:** Writer. **Awards:** Sue Kaufman prize for first fiction; National Endowment for the Arts fellowship, for *A Virtuous Woman*; Nelson Algren Heartland award for fiction, *Chicago Tribune,* for *A Cure for Dreams,* 1991.

PUBLICATIONS

Novels

Ellen Foster. 1987.
A Virtuous Woman. 1989.
A Cure for Dreams. 1991.

Charms for the Easy Life. 1993.
Sights Unseen. 1995.
On the Occasion of My Last Afternoon. 1998.

Other

Frost and Flower: My Life with Manic Depression So Far (limited edition). 1995.

*

Critical Studies: "The Only Hard Part Was the Food: Recipes for Self-Nurture in Kaye Gibbons's Novels" by Veronica Makowsky, in *The Southern Quarterly: A Journal of the Arts in the South,* winter-spring, 1992, pp. 103-12; "Women and the Gift for Gab: Revisionary Strategies in *A Cure for Dreams*" by Tonita Branan, in *Southern Literary Journal,* spring 1994, pp. 91-101; "Kaye Gibbons: Her Full-Time Women" by Nancy Lewis, in *Southern Writers at Century's End,* edited by Jeffrey Folks and James A. Perkins, 1997; "Simply Talking: Women and Language in Kaye Gibbon's *A Cure for Dreams*" by Kathryn McKee, in *Southern Quarterly,* summer 1997, pp. 97-106.

*　　*　　*

Kaye Gibbons, whose meteoric rise to prominence began in 1987 with her first novel, *Ellen Foster,* is truly a product of North Carolina. She was born in 1960 in Nash County and educated at the University of North Carolina at Chapel Hill and at North Carolina State University at Raleigh, where she later went to teach. Her first novels were published by Algonquin Press of Carrboro, the house founded and run by Louis Rubin, Jr., a professor of English at the University of North Carolina, and much of the impetus for the early years of her career came from the phenomenon of the Southern renaissance, particularly interest in the work of women writers.

More importantly, the subject matter of *Ellen Foster* is recognizably Southern. Delving into the lives of poor white and black families in rural North Carolina, the prizewinning novel tells the story of a culture so steeped in prejudices of class and gender as well as race that little social or human justice is possible. After the suicide of her mother, eleven-year-old Ellen is first abandoned to the careless life and eventual abuse of her alcoholic father. She is then sent from home to home of equally careless relatives, members of her mother's better-placed family, who are memorable for their cruelty to the child of a marriage they thought was beneath their daughter and sister. The voice of the child, who is the book's narrator, captured readers' imaginations, and *Ellen Foster* not only won the Sue Kaufman Prize for First Fiction, given by the American Academy and Institute of Arts and Letters, but also was a runner-up for the Ernest Hemingway Prize. Marked by what readers saw as "Southern humor" and with consistent irony—in that Ellen chooses to name herself for the foster family she also chooses to live with—the book is a remarkable and rewriting of **Mark Twain**'s *Huckleberry Finn.*

Ellen Foster marked the beginning of a career that has come to encompass six novels, all varied, all well received, all structured to show the versatility of an extremely talented writer. With the aid of a fellowship from the National Endowment for the Arts, Gibbons completed *A Virtuous Woman,* the alternating stories of Ruby Stokes's death from cancer, which she tells in flashback,

and the congruent memories of her bereaved husband. A narrative tour de force, the novel, which was published in 1989, was followed by Gibbons's 1991 multigenerational novel, *A Cure for Dreams.* This book won both the Nelson Algren Heartland Award for Fiction, given by the *Chicago Tribune,* and a PEN/Revson Foundation fellowship. In 1993, with *Charms for the Easy Life,* Gibbons moved to Putnam as her publisher, and although she was already widely known outside the South, the change of venue meant greater marketing scope and finesse.

Each of the novels after *Ellen Foster* was successful. Each told women's stories, and each presented some aspect of Southern experience. *Charms for the Easy Life,* for example, focused on World War II and its effect on the lives of modest Southern women. The strong depiction of ignorance about race had softened, so that it was clear that Gibbons was more interested in gender issues than in the plight of African Americans in North Carolina. The readership that had found Gibbons with *Ellen Foster* continued to follow her enthusiastically, but with her fifth and sixth novels she again showed her versatility in taking on new kinds of themes and in using different modes to present them.

Sights Unseen, published in 1995, reverted to a seemingly more comic mode as Gibbons tried to evoke the way an adolescent daughter feels about her manic-depressive mother. Although many of the episodes are humorous, the underlying tone is somber. Gibbons used the work as a vehicle to illustrate cultural blindness about mental illness, much as she had used Ellen Foster's reaction to Starletta and her family to illustrate racial prejudice. To readers the novel seemed different—much less Southern, for one thing—and reviewers were somewhat perplexed.

With *On the Occasion of My Last Afternoon,* Gibbons abandoned humor almost entirely. In this 1998 novel Gibbons showed that she could write in a beautifully modulated Victorian woman's voice, that of a Raleigh doctor's wife who had survived the Civil War, taking into her home hospital the wounded of both North and South. Fleeing her prejudiced family to marry a young liberal doctor who had come to the South, Gibbons's protagonist—like Ellen Foster—was herself the victim of gender, class, and ideological prejudice. The actual narration, which takes place, one presumes, during her last afternoon, is a performance much like **William Faulkner**'s in *The Reivers,* using a single telling, a single voice. Like the rest of Gibbons's oeuvre, *On the Occasion of My Last Afternoon* is a moving, impressive, and thoroughly controlled work by a writer of the highest order.

—Linda Wagner-Martin

GILBERT, Sandra M. and Susan GUBAR

GILBERT, Sandra M.: Born: New York, New York, 27 December 1936. **Education:** Cornell University, B.A. 1957; New York University, M.A. 1961; Columbia University, Ph.D. 1968. **Family:** Married Elliot Lewis Gilbert in 1957; one son and two daughters. **Career:** Lecturer in English, Queens College of the City University of New York, 1963-64; lecturer in English, Sacramento State College, 1967-68; assistant professor of English, California State College, Hayward, 1968-71; lecturer in English, St. Mary's College, Moraga, California, 1972; professor, University of California, Davis, 1975-85; professor of English, Princeton University, 1985-89. Beginning 1989 professor of English, University of California, Davis. **Awards:** National Endowment for the Humanities fellowship, 1980-81; Rockefeller Foundation fellowship, 1982; Guggenheim fellowship, 1983; Woman of the Year award, *Ms.* Magazine, 1986; University of California-Davis Humanities Institute fellowship, 1987-88; Charity Randall award, International Poetry Foundation, 1990; University of California President's fellowship, 1991-92. D. Litt: Weslyan University, 1988. **GUBAR, Susan: Born:** 1944. **Career:** Professor of English, Indiana University, Bloomington. **Awards:** National Book Critics Circle Award nomination, for outstanding book of criticism, for *The Madwoman in the Attic: The Woman Writer and the Nineteenth-Century Literary Imagination,* 1979; *Ms.* Magazine woman of the year citation, 1986.

PUBLICATIONS

Prose

Shakespeare's Twelfth Night (by Gilbert only). 1964.

Two Novels by E.M. Forster (by Gilbert only). 1965.

D.H. Lawrence's Sons and Lovers (by Gilbert only). 1965.

The Poetry of W.B. Yeats (by Gilbert only). 1965.

Two Novels by Virginia Woolf (by Gilbert only). 1966.

Acts of Attention: The Poems of D.H. Lawrence (by Gilbert only). 1973.

In the Fourth World: Poems (by Gilbert only). 1978.

The Madwoman in the Attic: A Study of Women and the Nineteenth-Century Literary Imagination. 1979.

The Summer Kitchen: Poems (by Gilbert only). 1983.

Emily's Bread: Poems (by Gilbert only). 1984.

Blood Pressure: Poems (by Gilbert only). 1988.

No Man's Land: the Place of the Women Writer in the Twentieth Century (3 Vols). 1988-1994.

Masterpiece Theatre: An Academic Melodrama. 1995.

Ghost Volcano: Poems (by Gilbert only). 1995.

Wrongful Death: A Medical Tragedy (by Gilbert only). 1995.

with Diana O'Hehir, *Mothersongs: Poems For, By, and about Mothers.* 1995.

Teaching with the Norton Anthology of Literature by Women: Second Edition: A Guide for Instructors. 1996.

Race Changes: White Skin, Black Face in American Culture (by Gubar only). 1997.

Other

Editor, *Shakespeare's Sisters: Feminist Essays on Women Poets.* 1979.

Editor, *The Norton Anthology of Literature by Women: The Tradition in English.* 1985.

Editor, with Joan Hoff *For Adult Users Only: The Dilemma of Violent Pornography* (by Gubar only). 1989.

Editor, with Jonathan Kamholtz *English Inside and Out: The Places of Literary Criticism* (by Gubar only). 1992.

*   *   *

Their numerous pioneering and highly suggestive contributions to the study of women's writing have placed Sandra Gilbert and Susan Gubar at the forefront of the movement to develop a more woman-centered approach to literary criticism. Moving away from critical approaches that studied female characters primarily on the basis of their authenticity and value as role models, Gilbert and Gubar spearheaded the search for distinctively female literary imagination in the works of nineteenth- and twentieth-century women writers. Gilbert and Gubar were among the first to argue for a historical continuity in women's literature and to assert the significance of studying works written by women in their own— i.e., female—context. While both have published widely as individuals, they are best known for their groundbreaking collaborative efforts. Gilbert and Gubar co-edited the influential *Norton Anthology of Literature by Women* (1985), a pioneering anthology that greatly extended the exposure of women writers across the ages. But it was the publication of their landmark works *The Madwoman in the Attic* (1979) and the subsequent three-volume series *No Man's Land* (1988-1994) that established Gilbert and Gubar as two of the most innovative thinkers in the field of literary studies.

In their groundbreaking work *The Madwoman in the Attic: The Woman Writer and the Nineteenth-Century Literary Imagination* (1979) Gilbert and Gubar analyze the methods nineteenth-century women writers employed to cope with the restrictions imposed by a male-dominated society. Constricted by a culture that viewed writing strictly as a male profession and hampered by their own artistic insecurities (which were constantly fed by a disapproving public), women writers such as Jane Austen, Mary Shelley, and the Brontë sisters (Charlotte, Emily, and Anne) developed a clandestine literary style designed to disguise the deeper, often subversive, meanings of their works beneath a socially acceptable veneer. This clandestine style often included the construction of a wrathful alter ego that expressed the dark emotions that neither the author nor her female characters could reveal safely. Using the character of Bertha Mason Rochester, the imprisoned madwoman in Charlotte Brontë's *Jane Eyre*, to symbolize the repressed emotions and experiences of women writers, Gilbert and Gubar probe the manner in which these writers created works that simultaneously conformed to and worked against established traditional literary standards. In providing an explanation for some of the more puzzling aspects of nineteenth-century women's literature, the authors argue for a continuous tradition in women's literature that has been heretofore unacknowledged.

Their succeeding three-volume study, *No Man's Land: The Place of the Woman Writer in the Twentieth Century*, uses social and cultural theory, literary criticism, and textual analysis to explore the impact of changing gender roles on the literary imaginations of male and female writers. In volume one, *The War of the Words* (1988), Gilbert and Gubar concentrate on the ways in which the development of literary modernism was directly affected by the shifting position of women in society. Using World War I as both a backdrop and a metaphor, the authors examine the ways the sexual conflict between men and women, generated by the death of traditional notions about femininity and the rise in feminism, was expressed in the literature then produced. Gilbert and Gubar theorize that the bold experimentation male modernist writers engaged in was a direct response to the anxiety they felt about the rise in feminism and the movement towards the liberation of women.

Volume two, *Sex-Changes* (1989), continues the focus on the social and literary impact of the war between the sexes in the twentieth century. In this volume, Gilbert and Gubar argue that growing male hostility towards increasing female sovereignty led to a cultural confusion about and destabilization of gender definition. Women writers, including Edith Wharton, Gertrude Stein, and Virginia Woolf, expressed this conclusion in their works by blurring the boundaries of gender and experimenting with sexual roles. Seeking to construct an authentic female identity, women writers experimented with existing concepts of gender, often impersonating or performing traditional feminine roles in order to locate a genuine female identity.

Letters from the Front (1994), the final volume of the trilogy, moves the "front lines" of society's war of the sexes from the battlefield to the home front. Asserting that the frustration both males and females felt about their proscribed roles in World War II only increased the alienation between the sexes, Gilbert and Gubar trace the beginnings of postmodern sensibilities back to the efforts of disconcerted male and female writers to locate new sources of gender identity. Broadly surveying the literature produced between the two World Wars, including works by poets Edna St. Vincent Millay and H.D. and Harlem Renaissance writers Jessie Fauset and Zora Neale Hurston, the authors investigate the ways in which women writers, caught in transition between old and new modes of thought, revised and reinterpreted history in their search for genuine modes of self-expression.

The collaboration of Sandra Gilbert and Susan Gubar has produced some of the most original and suggestive interpretations of women's literature of the past three decades. Their ability to interweave social and cultural criticism, history, and philosophy with close textual analysis in order to lay bare the intricacies and contradictions within the works they explore is the defining characteristic of their work together. Gilbert and Gubar's extraordinary efforts to chart the essential role women have played in shaping British and American literature has provided one of the most significant and enduring bridges between the works of women writers—past, present, and future.

—Alisa Johnson

GILCHRIST, Ellen

Born: Vicksburg, Mississippi, 20 February 1935. **Education:** Vanderbilt University, Nashville, Tennessee; Millsaps College, Jackson, Mississippi, B.A. 1967; University of Arkansas, Fayetteville, 1976. **Family:** Married several times; divorced; three sons. **Career:** Freelance writer, journalist; commentator for *Morning Edition,* National Public Radio, Washington, DC, 1984-85. **Awards:** Mississippi Arts Festival poetry award, 1968; University of Arkansas poetry award, 1976; *New York Quarterly* craft in poetry award, 1978; National Endowment for the Arts grant in fiction, 1979; Pushcart Prize, Pushcart Press, 1979-80, 1983; Prairie Schooner fiction award, 1981; Louisiana Library Association Honor Book, 1981; Mississippi Academy of Arts and Sciences fiction award, 1982, 1985; Saxifrage Award, 1983; American Book Award, 1984; University of Arkansas J. William Fulbright Prize, 1985; Mississippi Institute of Arts and Letters literature award, 1985, 1990, 1991; Pushcart prizes, 1995; O. Henry short story award, 1995. Litt.D., Millsaps College, 1987. **Residence:** Fayetteville, Arkansas.

PUBLICATIONS

Short Stories

In the Land of Dreamy Dreams. 1981.
Victory over Japan. 1984.
Drunk with Love. 1986.
Two Stories: "Some Blue Hills at Sundown" and "The Man Who Kicked Cancer's Ass." 1988.
Light Can Be Both Wave and Particle. 1989.
I Cannot Get You Close Enough: Three Novellas. 1990.
The Blue-Eyed Buddhist and Other Stories. 1990.
The Age of Miracles: Stories. 1995.
Rhoda: A Life in Stories. 1995.
The Courts of Love: A Novella and Stories. 1996.
Flights of Angels: Stories. 1998.

Novels

The Annunciation. 1983.
The Anna Papers. 1988.
I Cannot Get You Close Enough (three novellas). 1990.
Net of Jewels. 1992.
Anabasis: A Journey to the Interior. 1994.
Starcarbon: A Meditation on Love. 1994.
Sarah Conley: A Novel. 1997.

Poetry

The Land Surveyor's Daughter. 1979.
Riding Out the Tropical Depression. 1986.

Other

Falling through Space: The Journals of Ellen Gilchrist. 1987.

*

Bibliography: in *Contemporary Literary Criticism,* 1988; in *Louisiana Women Writers: New Essays and a Comprehensive Bibliography* edited by Dorothy Brown and Barbara Ewell, 1992.

Critical Studies: "The Miracle of Realism: The Bid for Self-Knowledge in the Fiction of Ellen Gilchrist" by Jeanie Thompson and Anita Miller, in *Southern Quarterly,* vol. 22, no. 1, 1983; *In the Vernacular: Interviews at Yale with Sculptors of Culture* edited by Melissa E. Biggs, 1987; "Ellen Gilchrist's Characters and the Southern Women's Experience" by Margaret Jones Bolsterli, in *New Orleans Review,* vol. 15, no. 1, 1988; "The Evolution of Caddy: An Intertextual Reading of The Sound and the Fury and Ellen Gilchrist's The Annunciation" by Margaret D. Bauer, in *Southern Literary Journal,* vol. 25, no. 1, 1992, and "Water and Women: Ellen Gilchrist Explores Two Life Sources" by Margaret D. Bauer, in *Louisiana Literature,* Fall 1992; "Ellen Gilchrist" by Robert Bain, in *Contemporary Fiction Writers of the South: A Bio-Bibliographical Sourcebook* edited by Joseph M. Flora and Robert Bain, 1993; *Ellen Gilchrist* by Mary A. McCay, 1997.

*   *   *

Ellen Gilchrist, a native of Mississippi and a lifetime resident of the American South, has achieved prominence among a generation of contemporary Southern women fiction writers. Gilchrist's work centers on the deep South after World War II and is often compared with the work of **Carson McCullers, Flannery O'Connor, Eudora Welty** (with whom she studied for a year at Millsaps College in 1966), and **William Faulkner**. But the social geography of her work complements its regional focus: most of her stories focus on the decline of the Southern upper class and the adjustments her protagonists (mostly women) must make to their changing class status. Gilchrist's writings alternate between the mundane and the shocking, between clichés and surprise endings, reflecting the disorientation of her characters in a changing world. Her fiction chronicles the "imaginative strategies by which [Southern women] fend off boredom, inertia, heat, and the aimlessness of their lives," according to Brian Morton in the *Times Literary Supplement.*

Gilchrist's own career reflects the dramatic turns of her characters' lives: after four marriages and three children, she began writing and editing poetry for the *Vieux Carré Courier* in Mississippi in 1975. Her work came to the attention of poet and novelist Jim Whitehead, who encouraged her to study writing at the University of Arkansas. She began writing professionally in 1976 at the age of forty and moved to Fayetteville after the publication of her first volume of poetry, *The Land Surveyor's Daughter.* Her focus shifted to fiction writing with her first collection of short stories, *In the Land of Dreamy Dreams,* which received positive reviews when it was published in 1981. Since then, she has written four more books of short stories, four novels, a second volume of poetry, and a television screenplay based on stories by Eudora Welty.

Most critics agree that Gilchrist is at her finest in her short fiction. Her stories' protagonists are outsiders, often children and adolescents, alienated by their social environments and disintegrating relationships. Gilchrist's most vivid characters are women; the men in her stories are often ineffectual or absent, in contrast to the strength and power of the women. For example, Amanda McCamey, in Gilchrist's first novel, *The Annunciation,* attempts to flee the destructive social forces of upper-class New Orleans by turning to alcohol and illicit relationships. She ultimately seeks refuge in a writer's commune and takes work as a translator for what Jeanie Thompson and Anita Garner in the *Southern Quarterly* call her "bid for freedom through self-knowledge."

One of the distinguishing features of Gilchrist's short fiction is her recurring characters, who are portrayed at various stages of life in different stories. The effect of interweaving personalities and themes among her stories is a cumulative one, giving her stories the feel of a loosely constructed novel in which characters emerge and grow. One such recurring character is Rhoda Manning. Jim Crace, in the *Times Literary Supplement,* observes that Gilchrist's primary subject is the coming-of-age struggle of her young female characters, and Rhoda Manning's development is no exception. Gilchrist extends her portrait of Rhoda into a novel, *Net of Jewels,* which chronicles Rhoda's late adolescence and college years, filling in the gaps between her previous appearances. Gilchrist gets to know her recurring characters in the process of writing them; in a 1987 interview with Melissa Biggs of *Yale Vernacular,* she characterizes her relationship with Rhoda as "a friendship . . . you pick up the conversation where you left off."

Another such character is Anna Hand, who first appears in "Anna, Part I" in *Drunk with Love.* The 1988 novel *The Anna*

Papers builds on this story and draws on the narrative structure of **Henry James**'s *The Aspern Papers,* opening with Anna's suicide after she has been diagnosed with cancer. Anna and her extended family are further developed in the three novellas that make up *I Cannot Get You Close Enough.* Gilchrist notes in a *Publishers Weekly* interview with Wendy Smith that the wider scope of the novel form allows for more characters and more sustained development of "the vision I currently have of reality. . . . What I'm trying to do now is make a study of existence. . . . I want it to be as true to what I know about human beings as it can be." In keeping with this string of assertive, independent heroines is Auria, the protagonist of *Anabasis: A Journey to the Interior.* As a runaway slave girl during the Peloponnesian War, Auria reflects Gilchrist's childhood fascination with Greek myths, and Gilchrist says she started creating the character when she was a child.

The 1995 collection *The Age of Miracles* features Rhoda in middle-age, still unconventional, strong-willed, and impetuous, and enticing enough to Gilchrist to be employed as the narrator of many of these stories. Gilchrist uses the stories as a forum to speak out about abortion rights, the effects of AIDS, and even the insurance industry, but it is what she calls the "massive tentacles of . . . family" that continue to haunt her characters. Diane Cold, in the *New York Times Book Review,* concluded that Gilchrist "possesses a distinct voice, and at her best she blends a sense of poignancy with an often outrageously gothic humor."

Also published the same year, *Rhoda: A Life in Stories,* features an excerpt from the *Net of Jewels* and all twenty-one of the Rhoda stories. In the introduction to the collection Gilchrist reveals that some of the stories are "made up" and some are "blatantly autobiographical." Critics generally agree that the exploits of Rhoda in her youth are better than the portraits of her in midlife or later.

In a departure from Rhoda, *The Courts of Love: A Novella and Other Stories* showed another popular character, Nora Jane Whittington, in a more thoughtful and complex series of studies on the interactions of memory and desire and the question of how much satisfaction an individual can expect of life. The stories in the second half of the book are told from divergent viewpoints: a nostalgic, middle-aged wife; an aspiring poet; a teenager; an AIDS patient; even a bear cub. Many critics found Gilchrist to be unusually contemplative in this collection.

The novel *Sarah Conley,* Gilchrist's fifteenth book, portrays a middle-aged editor at *Time* who, critics agree, seems to work out everything in surface melodrama. Sarah, the protagonist and the archetypal Gilchrist female, seems to have all the dilemmas and complexities of the high-powered writer; ultimately she faces the classic choice between the man she loves and the career opportunity of a lifetime.

Gilchrist is perhaps at her best when writing about the dilemmas of being young and female, and in her 1998 book *Flights of Angels* she returns to the issues of the artistic, emotional Southern women of her earlier work. *Booklist* noted that Gilchrist's "dual senses of comedy and poignancy continue in close partnership" in this collection.

The entries in Gilchrist's published journal, *Falling through Space,* express in nonfictional form many of the themes she develops in her fiction. The journal includes many of Gilchrist's editorial essays and witty radio commentaries for the National Public Radio news show *Morning Edition,* which reached a wide audience during her stint as a commentator in 1984 and 1985. The journal also includes meditations on her writing process: Gilchrist writes that "a piece of writing is the product of a series of explosions in the mind." The heroines and their rebellions in Gilchrist's fiction reflect these creative explosions. Much like their creator, these women reshape their experience of declining Southern society to fit their independent spirits.

Gilchrist's fiction has received mixed critical reactions; critics generally praise her early work, and her short fiction in particular, while pointing out the inconsistencies and clichés of her novels and later work in general. But there is no doubt that Gilchrist's subtle eye for detail, vivid characters, and confident and stylish prose have earned her widespread recognition as one of the foremost contemporary writers of the American South.

—Linda P. Bachman, updated by Martha Sutro

GILLETTE, William (Hooker)

Born: Hartford, Connecticut, 24 July 1853. **Education:** Hartford High School, graduated 1873; Monroe School of Oratory, Boston University, 1875-76. **Family:** Married Helen Nickles in 1882 (died 1888). **Career:** Debuted as actor, St. Louis and New Orleans, 1873-74; acted in New York and Boston, 1875; appeared with Boston Museum Company, 1876, and Bernard Macauley's company, Cincinnati and Louisville, 1876-78; returned to New York and from 1881 was one of the most prominent actors on the New York and London stage; appeared in most of his own plays: especially noted for his portrayal of Sherlock Holmes; retired in 1919 to an estate in Connecticut, but later came out of retirement to reprise his early roles in New York and on U.S. tours; retired again in 1936. **Awards:** American Academy Gold Medal, 1931. M.A.: Yale University, New Haven, Connecticut, 1930; Trinity College, Hartford, Connecticut, 1930. LL.D.: Dartmouth College, Hanover, New Hampshire, 1930; Columbia University, New York, 1930. **Member:** National Institute of Arts and Letters, 1898; American Academy, 1915. **Died:** 29 April 1937.

PUBLICATIONS

Collection

Plays (includes *All the Comforts of Home, Secret Service, Sherlock Holmes*), edited by Rosemary Cullen and Don B. Wilmeth. 1983.

Plays

Ballywingle the Beloved (produced 1873).
The Professor (produced 1881; as *The Professor's Wooing*, produced 1881).
Esmeralda, with Frances Hodgson Burnett (produced 1881; as *Young Folks' Ways*, produced 1883). 1881.
Digby's Secretary, from play by Gottfried von Moser (produced 1884; revised version, as *The Private Secretary*, produced 1884).
Held by the Enemy (produced 1886; revised version, produced 1886). 1898.
She, from the novel by Rider Haggard (produced 1887). *A Legal Wreck* (produced 1888). 1900.

Robert Elsmere, from the novel by Mrs. Humphry Ward (produced 1889).
All the Comforts of Home, with H.C. Duckworth, from a play by Carl Lauf (produced 1890). 1897; in *Plays*, 1983.
Mr Wilkinson's Widows, from a play by Alexandre Bisson (produced 1891).
Settled Out of Court, from a play by Alexandre Bisson (produced 1892).
Ninety Days (produced 1893).
Too Much Johnson, from a play by Maurice Ordonneau (produced 1894). 1912.
Secret Service (produced 1895). 1898; revised version, in *Representative American Plays*, edited by Arthur Hobson Quinn, 1917; in *Plays*, 1983.
Because She Loved Him So, from a play by Alexandre Bisson and Adolphe Leclerq (produced 1898).
Sherlock Holmes, with Arthur Conan Doyle, from works by Doyle (produced 1899). 1922; revised version, 1935; in *Plays*, 1983.
The Painful Predicament of Sherlock Holmes (produced 1905). 1955.
Clarice (produced 1905; revised version, produced 1905).
That Little Affair at Boyd's (produced 1908; as *Ticey*, produced 1908).
The Red Owl (as *The Robber*, produced 1909). 1924.
Among Thieves (produced 1909). In *One-Act Plays for Stage and Study 2*, 1925.
Electricity (produced 1910). 1913.
Diplomacy, from translation of play by Sardou (produced 1914).
The Dream Maker, from story by Howard E. Morton (produced 1921).
Winnie and the Wolves, from stories by Bertram Akey (produced 1923).
How Well George Does It! 1936.

Fiction

A Legal Wreck. 1888.
The Astounding Crime on Torrington Road. 1927.

Other

The Illusion of the First Time in Acting. 1915.

Editor, *How to Write a Play: Letters from Augier, Banville, Dennery, Dumas, Gondinet, Labiche, Legouve, Pailleron, Sardou, and Zola*, translated by Dudley Miles. 1916.

*

Critical Studies: *Sherlock Holmes and Much More; or Some Facts about Gillette* by Doris Cook, 1970; "William Gillette and Sherlock Holmes" by Georg W. Schuttler, in *Journal of Popular Culture*, spring 1982, and "William Gillette: Marathon Actor and Playwright" by Schuttler, in *Journal of Popular Culture*, winter 1983; *William Hooker Gillette, Director* (dissertation) by Marcia Lee Merrill Nash, 1996.

*   *   *

William Gillette was one of the first to profess that an actor should build his characterization on the dominant qualities of his own personality; his first major performance, with an assist from **Mark Twain**, was in *Faint Heart Ne'er Won Fair Lady* in 1875. He appeared in several stock companies before opening his own play, *The Professor*, at Madison Square Garden in 1881. Thereafter, except for roles in *Samson, Diplomacy, The Admirable Crichton, A Successful Calamity,* and *Dear Brutus,* he appeared in his own plays, in which he did his best work. He was at his best portraying the "cool man of action," whether it was the title role in *Sherlock Holmes* (he played the part for 30 years), Brant in *Held by the Enemy* (a melodrama, but the first successful play about the Civil War), or *Secret Service* (his most popular Civil War play). Notable among his other plays are *A Legal Wreck,* set in a coastal New England town, and *The Painful Predicament of Sherlock Holmes,* an hysterically funny miniplay sequel to *Sherlock Holmes* featuring a bumbling, loquacious, accident-prone escapee from a mental hospital who, while appealing for help to the always silent Holmes, accidentally destroys his violin, violin bow, lamp, cocaine pot, crime notes, and photographs before Holmes's servant can summon sanatorium assistance.

Gillette's best claim to fame lies in *Sherlock Holmes* (written with Arthur Conan Doyle), revived gloriously by the Royal Shakespeare Company in 1974 at the Aldwych and transferred in triumph to New York. The play skillfully blends dialogue and the most dramatic moments directly from Doyle's "A Scandal in Bohemia" and "The Final Problem," though the melodramatic tension is Gillette's own. He not only demonstrates Holmes's great skill against Moriarty, the Napoleon of Crime, but also shows Holmes falling in love with the heroine, Alice Faulkner, though one sometimes wonders whether he will shoot Moriarty or cocaine. A good script editor can easily keep the play's many dramatic turns from becoming too intricate, and its melodramatic turns from becoming maudlin, since Holmes, besottedly in love, could have provided a deadly melodramatic element, especially when coupled with Alice's innocence and naivety. Romance spurs interest in the triumph of good, however. Holmes quickly solves the mystery, foils the thugs, recovers the blackmail papers (50 percent honestly), jails Moriarty, and, to the audience's delight, has Alice fall ecstatically into his arms at the final curtain.

—Louis Charles Stagg

GILMAN, Charlotte (Anna) Perkins (Stetson)

Born: Hartford, Connecticut, 3 July 1860. **Education:** Studied art, Rhode Island School of Design, Providence, 1878-79. **Family:** Married 1) (Charles) Walter Stetson in 1884 (divorced 1894), one daughter (died 1979); 2) George Houghton Gilman in 1900 (died 1943). **Career:** Treated for hysteria by Dr. S. Weir Mitchell, 1886; moved to Pasadena, California, 1888; playwright with Grace Channing, 1888-91; ran a boarding house, 1890s; coeditor, *The Impress* journal, San Francisco, 1894; full-time writer, activist in women's suffrage movement, public speaker, and lecturer, from mid-1890s; moved to New York City, 1900; lectured in Europe, 1905; editor and writer, *The Forerunner* magazine, 1909-16; moved to Pasadena, 1934. **Died:** (suicide) 17 August 1935.

PUBLICATIONS

Collections

Herland and Selected Writings, edited by Denise D. Knight. 1999.
The Charlotte Perkins Gilman Reader, edited by Ann J. Lane. 1999.
Charlotte Perkins Gilman's Utopian Novels. 1999.

Short Stories

The Yellow Wallpaper (novella). 1899; edited by Elaine Hedge, 1973.
The Yellow Wallpaper and Other Stories. 1995.

Novels

The Crux. 1911.
Moving the Mountain. 1911.
What Diantha Did. 1912.
Herland: A Lost Feminist Utopia, edited by Ann J. Lane. 1979.
Benigna Machiavelli. 1994.
With Her in Ourland: A Sequel to Herland. 1997.
Unpunished: A Mystery. 1997.

Poetry

In This Our World. 1893.
Suffrage Songs and Verses. 1911.
The Later Poetry of Charlotte Perkins Gilman. 1996.

Other

A Clarion Call to Redeem the Race! 1890.
Women and Economics. 1898.
Concerning Children. 1900.
The Home, Its Work and Influence. 1903.
Human Work. 1904.
The Punishment that Educates. 1907.
The Man-Made World; or, Our Androcentric Culture. 1911.
His Religion and Hers: A Study of the Faith of Our Fathers and the Work of Our Mothers. 1923.
The Living of Gilman (autobiography). 1935.
The Gilman Reader: "The Yellow Wallpaper" and Other Fiction, edited by Ann J. Lane. 1980.
Gilman: A Non-Fiction Reader, edited by Larry Ceplair. 1991.
The Diaries of Charlotte Perkins Gilman. 1994; as *The Abridged Diaries of Charlotte Perkins Gilman,* edited by Denise D. Knight, 1998.
A Journey from Within: The Love Letters of Charlotte Perkins Gilman, 1897-1900. 1995.

*

Bibliography: *Gilman: A Bibliography* by Gary Scharnhorst, 1985.

Critical Studies: "Gilman on the Theory and Practice of Feminism" by Carl N. Degler, in *American Quarterly,* spring 1956; *Gilman: The Making of a Radical Feminist* by Mary A. Hill, 1980; *Building Domestic Liberty: Gilman's Architectural Feminism* by Polly Wynn Allen, 1988; *Gilman: The Woman and Her Work* edited by Sheryl L. Meyering, 1989; *To Herland and Beyond: The Life and Work of Gilman* by Ann J. Lane, 1990; *The Captive Imagination: A Casebook on The Yellow Wallpaper* edited by Catherine Golden, 1992; *Critical Essays on Gilman* edited by Joanne B. Karpinski, 1992; *Charlotte Perkins Gilman: A Study of the Short Fiction* by Denise D. Knight, 1997; *Kate Chopin, Edith Wharton, and Charlotte Perkins Gilman: Studies in Short Fiction* by Janet Beer, 1997; *A Very Different Story: Studies on the Fiction of Charlotte Perkins Gilman* edited by Val Gough and Jill Rudd, 1998.

*   *   *

"In this republican country," wrote **Nathaniel Hawthorne** in *The House of Seven Gables,* "amid the fluctuating waves of our social life, somebody is always at the drowning point." The force of his statement is nowhere better illustrated than in a consideration of the life, writings, and reputation of Charlotte Perkins Gilman. Whereas Hawthorne's ironies and ambiguity detach both reader and author from the victim, Gilman and her readers measure the efficacy of her life and works by their effect on saving the victim—or perhaps more accurately in showing how one does not have to be a victim. This overriding ethical impulse pervades her life and work as it continues for her readers in the late twentieth century as the measure of her value.

As a grandniece of **Harriet Beecher Stowe**, Gilman may be said to have come by the ethical imperative almost genetically. Yet her early life was marked less by the doing of good than by genteel poverty and her parents' separation shortly after her birth. These limited opportunities for Gilman in an age in which young women (of a certain background and respectability) already faced what we would consider significant restrictions on their life choices. If, on the one hand, she was heir to a great American family, on the other, she was on the verge of receiving so little education and possessing so little opportunity that she herself might have slipped below the surface. The young Charlotte was, if nothing else, strong-willed, an aspect best seen in her insistence that she attend the Rhode Island School of Design over and against her mother's objections. Her courtship with her first husband, the painter Charles Walter Stetson, also manifests this determination—the young woman fell in love and decided to marry without seeking permission from her mother or father.

Her marriage, ironically enough, came at the expense of an earlier resolution not to marry so that she could, like so many of her female peers, do some good in the world. Walter's insistence—and her own genuine feeling—overcame this desire, but at the expense of a depression that grew, especially after the birth of her daughter. Having agreed more or less amicably to separate, the then Charlotte Stetson left her husband in Providence to stay with the family of her best friend, Grace Ellery Channing, in Pasadena.

It was in Pasadena in 1891 that she wrote *The Yellow Wallpaper,* the story for which she is probably best known to late-twentieth-century readers. The story is the first person narration of a young wife whose husband, a physician, has diagnosed in her a "temporary nervous depression—a slight hysterical tendency" and prescribed a domestic version of the rest cure. The narrator comes to believe that a woman is imprisoned behind the pattern of the wallpaper of her bedroom and the story culminates in her ripping off the paper, telling her shocked husband "I've got out at last." Gilman clearly drew on her own experiences, both of the depression itself and of a somewhat truncated course of treatment with **S. Weir Mitchell**, for the story.

As the most famous of her works, *The Yellow Wallpaper* is illuminating and yet misleading. In its concern for the plight of a woman and implicit objection to the idea that women were and should be dependent on others, the story announces a, perhaps the, major theme of Gilman's work. Yet the story, written as a series of increasingly fragmented diary entries and ending somewhat ambiguously (is she finally sane or insane?) is formally very different from the other stories and novels Gilman was to write with similar themes. Most often written in the third person, those texts (see, for example, "Three Thanksgivings," "Martha's Mother" and "Making a Change") focus on women who reject such dependence and succeed both economically and psychologically. Unlike "The Yellow Wallpaper," these stories are clear and unambiguous in their narrative form and point of view. They end in the successful triumph of their female protagonists, whose own actions establish their autonomy.

Until the later part of the twentieth century, *The Yellow Wallpaper* was most often read as a horror story in the tradition of **Edgar Allan Poe**—and as such a story was regarded highly. It was reprinted in 1899, again by **William Dean Howells** in his *Great American Short Stories* and at least twice more. Its reinterpretation as a feminist narrative stems from the late 1960s when Gilman's *Women and Economics* was reprinted. That book was the source of Gilman's fame in her lifetime, going through seven American editions and ultimately being translated into seven other languages. Although Gilman was known as a lecturer before its appearance, the success of *Women and Economics* made her internationally famous. The book brings together the three great themes of Gilman's public life—her socialism, her feminism, and her adaptation of evolutionary arguments. Exhibiting faith in the goodness and inevitability of progress, Gilman drew upon examples from the natural world to argue that the extremity of sexual difference insisted upon in her society had penalized women and retarded the advance of humanity. Most important, as the title indicates, she critiqued the nuclear family of her time because it was an economic unit rather than an affectionate one. The economic independence of woman, possible for Gilman in a (non-Marxian) socialist world, would lead to equality for women and true marriage.

Gilman, then, may be said to be a conservative in her ideas of marriage and domesticity and a radical insofar as she called for radical changes in self and society to achieve the former. Between 1898 and the First World War, she repeated and developed the themes of *Women and Economics* in lectures and a series of books: *Concerning Children, The Home: Its Work and Influence, Human Work* and *The Man-Made World; or Our Androcentric Culture.* Indeed, she was so committed to the home as purely a center of affection that she advocated communal kitchens and laundries. Her happy marriage to her cousin, George Houghton Gilman in 1900, might be seen to illustrate her ideas about combining marriage and independence.

Despite the apparent evidence of *The Yellow Wallpaper,* Gilman valued the work of art insofar as it led to changes in the world outside the self. Gilman continued writing fiction and poetry, especially for her magazine *The Forerunner.* She not only wrote every word but also accepted advertisements only for those products that she could personally endorse. The most famous and influential fiction written for *The Forerunner* is *Herland,* a utopian novel. Especially since Gilman's public career as a thinker and lecturer had begun with her adoption of the ideas of **Edward Bellamy**'s *Looking Backward,* it seems fitting that she should have adopted this form for her own work.

Herland is the story of three male explorers, Terry, Jeff, and Van (the narrator), who seek and find a land rumored to be inhabited only by women. The novel begins with their assumption that the story cannot be true. Thus, when they first fly over Herland, Van speaks for them: "Why, this is a *civilized* country! . . . There must be men." Eventually, they are compelled to admit the truth that an all-female society has created a truly civilized society as they learn the culture and customs during an enforced stay.

Herland is not only a society of women; it is also a world in which all women are literally as well as figuratively sisters. Its history begins with a natural disaster that kills almost all the men; the rest die in a slave revolt that in turn leads to a revolution of the women against their new masters. With all the men dead and facing extinction, a miracle occurs: via parthenogenesis, a woman becomes pregnant. She eventually gives birth to five girls, who themselves each have five female children. From this original mother, all the women are descended. Over the 2,000 years of their history, the women of Herland have transformed their natural environment into a park-like setting and the social order into a communal and harmonious society. The idea of individual possession, whether of property or of children, has vanished. As well, because Herland has been without men for so long, the idea of romantic love has disappeared. Thus, although each of the men falls in love with and marries an inhabitant, they are stymied by the inability of their wives to respond positively to domesticity and sexuality.

The three male characters cannot deny the evidence of their senses, but of them, only Van is able to change his preconceived ideas about weakness and dependence of women. Jeff is happy to remain in Herland, but never gives up idealizing women as angelic figures. Terry, who from the start has articulated the values of masculine predatoriness and possessiveness, eventually attempts to rape his wife and is made to leave having given his promise not to tell about the country. Only Van makes significant progress in accepting the ideal of equality and with it a marriage more companionate than passionate. The difficulties that these characters have suggest that Gilman did not, unlike Bellamy, imagine that utopia was right around the corner.

Herland does illustrate Gilman's faith in the power of humans to direct evolutionary progress and her belief that almost all our problems result from the misorganization of society. In the utopian tradition of *Looking Backward,* Gilman's novel suggests that criminality and insanity stem from culture, not nature. What cannot be overstressed is the crucial addition of her work to the utopian tradition: the argument that sexual difference has gained an importance out of proportion to its real significance and that to reform the world, we must fundamentally alter our ideas about masculinity and femininity.

Gilman's career dwindled after the First World War. Already at odds with some of her former allies because of her support for the war, she also reacted negatively to the influence of Sigmund Freud, arguing that his work vastly overemphasized sexuality. Furthermore, with suffrage for women achieved in the 19th Amendment, the organized feminist movement lost much of its energy. This latter point is ironic, for Gilman had never defined her political objectives so narrowly. She continued to seek lecturing opportunities throughout the 1920s, but her influence diminished. Her final work, *The Living of Charlotte Perkins Gilman: An Autobiography,* is a fascinating but detached record of the events of her life. While the account of her early years records some of her feelings and conflicts, especially those with her mother, most of

the book adopts a journalistic prose to describe what she was thinking, doing and saying at any particular time.

—Ross J. Pudaloff

GINSBERG, Allen

Born: Newark, New Jersey, 3 June 1926. Son of Louis and Naomi (Levy) Ginsberg. **Education:** Paterson High School, New Jersey; Columbia University, New York, 1943-45, 1946-48, A.B. 1948. Served in the Military Sea Transport Service. **Career:** Book reviewer, *Newsweek,* New York, 1950; market researcher, New York, 1951-53, and San Francisco, 1954; University of British Columbia, Vancouver, instructor, 1963; freelance writer: participant in many poetry readings and demonstrations; organizer of Gathering of the Tribes for a Human Be-In, San Francisco, 1967; read poetry and gave lectures at universities, coffee houses, and art galleries around the world; beginning 1971 director, Committee on Poetry Foundation, New York; co-founder, 1974, and director, Kerouac School of Poetics, Naropa Institute, Boulder, Colorado. **Awards:** Woodbury Poetry prize; Guggenheim fellowship, 1963; National Endowment for the Arts grant, 1966; National Institute of Arts and Letters award, 1969; American Academy grant, 1969; National Book award for Poetry for *The Fall of America,* 1974; National Arts Club Gold Medal, 1979; Los Angeles *Times* award, 1982; National Endowment for the Arts fellowship, 1986; Golden Wreath prize, 1986; Poetry Society of America gold medal, 1986; Mayor Dinkins (of New York City) award for Arts Excellence, 1989; Lifetime Achievement award, 1990; Harriet Monroe Poetry award, University of Chicago, 1991; Chevalier de l'Ordre des Artes et des Lettres, 1992; fellow, American Academy of Arts and Sciences, 1992. **Member:** American Academy; American Institute of Arts and Letters; PEN (vice-president of American Chapter 1987-88); New York Eternal Committee for Conservation of Freedom in the Arts. **Died:** 5 April 1997.

PUBLICATIONS

Collections

Collected Poems, 1947-1985. 1995.
Selected Poems, 1947-1995. 1996.

Poetry

Howl and Other Poems. 1956; revised edition, 1971.
Siesta in Xbalba and Return to the States. 1956.
Empty Mirror: Early Poems. 1961.
Kaddish and Other Poems 1958-60. 1961.
A Strange New Cottage in Berkeley. 1963.
Reality Sandwiches 1953-60. 1963.
Penguin Modern Poets 5, with Lawrence Ferlinghetti and Gregory Corso. 1963.
The Change. 1963.
Kral Majales. 1965.
Prose Contribution to Cuban Revolution. 1966.
Wichita Vortex Sutra. 1966.
T.V. Baby Poems. 1967.

Wales—A Visitation, July 29, 1967. 1968.
Scrap Leaves, Hasty Scribbles. 1968.
Message II. 1968.
Planet News 1961-1967. 1968.
Airplane Dreams: Compositions from Journals. 1968.
Ankor Wat. 1968.
The Moments Return. 1970.
Notes after an Evening with William Carlos Williams. 1970.
Iron Horse. 1972.
The Fall of America: Poems of These States 1965-1971. 1972.
The Gates of Wrath: Rhymed Poems 1948-1952. 1972.
Open Head, with *Open Eye,* by Lawrence Ferlinghetti. 1972.
New Year Blues. 1972.
Bixby Canyon Ocean Path Word Breeze. 1972.
Sad Dust Glories. 1975.
First Blues: Rags, Ballads, and Harmonium Songs 1971-1974. 1975.
Mind Breaths: Poems 1972-1977. 1978.
Poems All Over the Place: Mostly Seventies. 1978.
Mostly Sitting Haiku. 1978; revised edition, 1979.
Careless Love: Two Rhymes. 1978.
Straight Hearts' Delight: Love Poems and Selected Letters 1947-1980, with Peter Orlovsky, edited by Winston Leyland. 1980.
Plutonian Ode: Poems 1977-1980. 1982.
Collected Poems 1947-1980. 1984.
White Shroud: Poems 1980-1985. 1986.
Cosmopolitan Greetings: Poems, 1986-1992. 1994.
Making It Up: Poetry Composed at St. Marks Church on May 9, 1979. 1994.
Allen Ginsberg: Shared Dreams, Some Roots and Later Leaves, Some Sources and Descendants, edited by David Cope. 1994.
Luminous Dreams. 1997.

Recordings: *Holy Soul Jelly Roll Poems and Songs 1949-1993,* 1994; *The Ballad of the Skeletons,* with Philip Glass and Paul McCartney, 1996; *The Lion for Real,* with Mark Bingham, 1997; *Howl and Other Poems,* 1998.

Plays

Don't Go Away Mad, in *Pardon Me, Sir, But Is My Eye Hurting Your Elbow?,* edited by Bob Booker and George Foster. 1968.
Kaddish (produced 1972).

Other

The Yage Letters, with William S. Burroughs. 1963.
Notes on an Interview with Ginsberg, by Edward Lucie-Smith. 1965.
Indian Journals: March 1962—May 1963: Notebooks, Diary, Blank Pages, Writings. 1970.
Improvised Poetics, edited by Mark Robison. 1971.
Declaration of Independence for Dr. Timothy Leary. 1971.
Gay Sunshine Interview, with Allen Young. 1974.
Allen Verbatim: Lectures on Poetry, Politics, Consciousness, edited by Gordon Ball. 1974.
The Visions of the Great Rememberer (on Jack Kerouac). 1974.
Chicago Trial Testimony. 1975.
To Eberhart from Ginsberg. 1976.
The Dream of Tibet, with *The Retreat Diaries,* by William S. Burroughs. 1976.

As Ever: The Collected Correspondence of Allen Ginsberg and Neal Cassady, edited by Barry Gifford. 1977.
Journals: Early Fifties—Early Sixties, edited by Gordon Ball. 1977.
Composed on the Tongue: Literary Conversations 1967-1977, edited by Donald Allen. 1980.
Beat Legacy: Connections, Influence: Allen Ginsberg. 1994.
Poem, Interview, Photographs. 1994.
Mind Writing Slogans. 1994.
Journals: Mid-Fifties, 1954-1958, edited by Gordon Ball. 1995.

*

Bibliography: *A Bibliography of Works of Ginsberg October 1943-July 1, 1967* by George Dowden, 1970; *Ginsberg: An Annotated Bibliography 1969-1977* by Michelle P. Kraus, 1980; *The Response to Allen Ginsberg, 1926-1994: A Bibliography of Secondary Sources* by Bill Morgan, 1996.

Critical Studies: *Ginsberg in America* by Jane Kramer, 1968, as *Paterfamilias,* 1970; *Ginsberg* by Thomas F. Merrill, 1969; *Scenes along the Road* edited by Ann Charters, 1971; *Ginsberg in the '60s* by Eric Mottram, 1972; *The Visionary Poetics of Ginsberg* by Paul Portuges, 1978; *Cometh with Clouds (Memory: Ginsberg)* by Dick McBride, 1983; *Great Poet's Howl: A Study of Ginsberg's Poetry 1943-1955* by Glen Burns, 1983; *On the Poetry of Ginsberg* edited by Lewis Hyde, 1984; "An Interview with Ginsberg," in *American Writing Today* edited by Richard Kostelanetz, 1991; *Dharma Lion: A Critical Biography of Allen Ginsberg* by Michael Schumacher, 1994; "*Howl* Revisited: The Poet as Jew" by Alicia Ostriker, in *American Poetry Review,* July-August 1997, pp. 28-31; "Allen Ginsberg" by Regina Weinrich, in *Five Points,* fall 1997, pp. 30-46; "Madness, Speech, and Prophecy in Allen Ginsberg's *Howl*" by Frank D. Casale, in *Spectacle,* spring 1998, pp. 101-12.

*   *   *

Like **Walt Whitman,** his forebear, Allen Ginsberg was a prolific poet who wrote too much: some of his work is, like Whitman's, unfocused, emotionally scattered, and prone to large abstractions unrelated to any concrete particularity. And, like Whitman, Ginsberg insisted that any subject is a fit one for poetry. And so, like Whitman, he has been attacked for his vulgarity, for his failure to be "proper" or dignified; yet at the same time, like both Whitman and Blake (from whom he has learned much), he appeals to the young and to those who do not think that poetry and the business of daily life are essentially grave matters whose languages have to be separated from one another. Ginsberg was a World-Poet, like Neruda and Yevtushenko and like Gibran, Tagore, Whitman, and Blake in previous times. And, like each of these, he wrote a quantity of slight but interesting occasional verse, of which "Portland Coliseum" (in *Planet News*), about a Beatles concert, is representative.

In *Improvised Poetics* Ginsberg talks about writing this poem. "I changed things," he said, "like Hands waving LIKE myriad snakes of thought to Hands waving myriad / snakes of thought. Ah . . . The million children OF the thousand worlds, so I just changed The million children, / the thousand worlds." These apparently minor revisions are significant: Ginsberg talks about his "paragraphal" mode of composition and explains, "when I'd get three or four [phrases] that made an apposition I'd start a new paragraph." In taking out "a lot of syntactical fat" and thus "putting two short lines together that had just images in them," Ginsberg prunes the lines of prepositions that express relationship and embraces the technique of juxtaposition, learned from Pound. The danger of such technique is that the poem can degenerate into a mere list (although, as Emerson remarked in *The Poet,* "bare lists of words are found suggestive to an imaginative and excited mind"). The value of such appositional language is that it can imply cause-and-effect relationships, but it does not state them: cause and effect are not to be assumed in or about the world of event; it is a world of immediacy. That is to say, the reader is moved into a world of event, a place *where things happen,* for (to quote Emerson again) "the quality of the imagination is to flow, and not to freeze." Ginsberg's reader can, therefore, often be overwhelmed by a rush of sensory, social, political and/ or intellectual data to very good effect, as in poems like *Howl* or *Kaddish.*

The concern of the poet is for registering the precise nature of the occurrence (his thought, his feeling, the particularities from which they arise) in the here and now. So Ginsberg, like other modernists, finds crucial the accuracy of the poem as notation of the spoken voice or as notation of the process of thought. The notation is exact: in *Airplane Dreams* the lines of the long poem "New York to San Fran" are, in Ginsberg's words, "hung out on the page a little to the right . . . A little bit like diagramming a sentence, you know, the old syntactical diagrammatic method of making a little platform and you put the subject and object on it and hang adjectives and adverbial clauses down" (*Improvised Poetics*). Here is a short sequence from "Portland Coloseum":

> The million children
> the thousand worlds
> bounce in their seats, bash
> each other's sides, press
> legs together nervous
> Scream again & clap hand

Like Olson's, Ginsberg's line-breaks serve an emphatic, syntactic purpose, in which the slight hesitancy at the end of the line provides for unexpected semantic conjunctions and emphases, while at the same time they direct the reader's voice into the (in this case slightly nervous) rhythm and rhetorical inflection of the verse.

Such a line, the unit of thought or the unit of speech, reinforces the air of spontaneous improvisation characteristic of much of Ginsberg's work. The publication of *Howl* in 1956 brought Ginsberg to prominence and gave wide currency to the notion that poetry might be a spontaneous art, requiring little or no skill or revision. Deceptively simple in appearance, *Howl* rests on an extensive apprenticeship in rhymed verse (some of which has been published in *The Gates of Wrath*) and in conscious craftsmanship. As Ginsberg wrote to Richard Eberhart, the "general ground plan" of the poem, "quite symmetrical, surprisingly," structures the three sections of the poem round three main devices: the fixed base of "who" and a long line; the repetition and variation of the fixed base "Moloch"; and the "fixed base / reply / fixed base / longer reply" of the final section. Such writing is not always done, of course, in a single extended burst of composition (the result of a fairly extended gestation): Ginsberg's compositions are often leisurely and deliberative, and very often, in revising a poem, Ginsberg in effect composes a completely new one. "Sunflower

Sutra," for example, is a revised version of "In Back of the Real." It is fundamentally a different poem that came about as the result of "re-seeing" the same event. With its long lines, its introduction of a second person into the poem, and its focus on the perceiver of the flower, "Sunflower Sutra" is both less general and more immediate in its effect. At the same time it is, as is much of Ginsberg's work, more a celebration and affirmation of the individual, of the personal, and of nature than a denunciation of the world of man. Ginsberg's great strengths as a poet are to be found in such visionary poems as this, with its long and carefully controlled lines juxtaposed against shorter lines, leading the poem to a crescendo that is not rhetorical only but quite literally *physical:* Ginsberg's long interest in yoga and in the breath as a measure in verse led him to speculate on the correlations in Sanskrit poetry between prosody and human physiology, and led him to attempt similar correlations in his own work. At the same time, the unabashed frankness of his words and the declarative nature of much of his writing have made the work accessible to the casual reader, and have thus given Ginsberg a wide following.

—Peter Quartermain

See the essay on *Howl.*

GIOVANNI, Nikki (Yolande Cornelia, Jr.)

Born: Knoxville, Tennessee, 7 June 1943. **Education:** Fisk University, Nashville, Tennessee, 1960-67, A.B. 1967; University of Pennsylvania School of Social Work, Philadelphia; Columbia University School of Fine Arts, New York, 1967. **Family:** One son. **Career:** National Foundation of the Arts, assistant professor of black studies, Queens College, City University of New York, Flushing, 1968; associate professor of English, 1969-70, Rutgers University, New Brunswick, New Jersey; visiting professor of English, 1984, Ohio State University, Columbus; professor of creative writing, 1985-87, College of Mount St. Joseph on the Ohio; professor of English, 1987, Virginia Polytechnic Institute and State University, Blacksburg; Honors Week visiting professor of humanities, Texas Christian University, Fort Worth, 1991. Founded publishing firm, Niktom, Ltd., 1970; participated in the International Poetry Festival, Ultrecht, Holland, 1991; has traveled throughout the United States giving lectures and poetry readings, as well as to Europe, Africa, the Caribbean, Haiti, and Barbados. Co-chair of Literary Arts Festival for the State of Tennessee Homecoming, 1986; appointed to Ohio Humanities Council, 1987; director of Warm Hearth Writer's Workshop, 1988; elected to board of directors, Virginia Foundation for the Humanities and Public Policy, 1990-93. **Awards:** Ford Foundation grant, 1967; National Endowment for the Arts award, 1968; Harlem Cultural Council award, 1969; *Mademoiselle* Woman of the Year award, 1971; Omega Psi Phi Fraternity award, 1971; Cook County Jail meritorious plaque for service, 1971; Prince Matchabelli Sun Shower award, 1971; National Council of Negro Women, life member and scroll, 1972; National Association of Radio and Television Announcers award for best spoken word album, 1972; *Ladies Home Journal,* Woman of the Year Youth Leadership award, 1972; National Book award nomination for *Gemini: An Extended Autobiographical Statement of My First Twenty-five Years of Being a Black Poet,* 1973; American Library Association best books for young adults citation, 1973;

Cincinnati Chapter YWCA Woman of the Year citation, 1983; elected to Ohio Women's Hall of Fame, 1985; Detroit City Council distinguished recognition award, 1986; Ohioana Book Award for *Sacred Cows . . . and Other Edibles,* 1988; Lynchburg Virginia Chapter, National Association for the Advancement of Colored People, Woman of the Year citation, 1989; The Jeanine Rae award for the Advancement of Women's Culture, 1995. Doctorate of humanities: Wilberforce University and Fisk University, both 1972. Doctorate of literature: University of Maryland at Princess Anne and Ripon University, both 1974; Smith College, 1975; College of Mount St. Joseph, 1983. Doctorate of Humane Letters: Mount St. Mary College.

PUBLICATIONS

Poetry

Black Feeling, Black Talk. 1968; 3rd edition, 1970.
Black Judgement. 1968.
Black Feeling, Black Talk and Black Judgement. 1970.
Re: Creation. 1970.
Poem of Angela Yvonne Davis. 1970.
Spin a Soft Black Song: Poems for Children. 1971; revised edition, 1987.
My House. 1972.
Ego-Tripping and Other Poems for Young People. 1973.
The Women and the Men. 1975.
Cotton Candy on a Rainy Day. 1978.
Vacation Time: Poems for Children. 1980.
Those Who Ride the Night Winds. 1983.
Knoxville, Tennessee (for children). 1994.
Grand Mothers. 1994.
The Selected Poems of Nikki Giovanni. 1996.
The Genie in the Jar, illustrated by Chris Raschka (for children). 1996.
The Sun Is So Quiet, illustrated by Ashley Bryan (for children). 1996.
Love Poems. 1997.
Blues: For All the Changes. 1999.

Prose

Gemini: An Extended Autobiographical Statement of My First Twenty-five Years of Being a Black Poet. 1971.
A Dialogue: James Baldwin and Nikki Giovanni, with James Baldwin. 1973.
A Poetic Equation: Conversations between Nikki Giovanni and Margaret Walker, with Margaret Walker. 1974.
Appalachian Elders: A Warm Hearth Sampler, with Cathee Dennison. 1991.
Conversations with Nikki Giovanni, edited by Virginia C. Fowler. 1992.

Other

Sacred Cows . . . And Other Edibles. 1988.

Editor, *Night Comes Softly: An Anthology of Black Female Voices.* 1970.
Editor, with Jessie Carney Smith, *Images of Blacks in American Culture: A Reference Guide to Information Sources.* 1988.

Editor, *Grand Fathers: Reminiscences, Poems, Recipes and Photos of the Keepers of Our Traditions.* 1999.

Recordings: *Truth Is on Its Way,* 1971; *Like a Ripple on a Pond,* 1973; *The Way I Feel,* 1974; *Legacies: The Poetry of Nikki Giovanni,* 1976; *The Reason I Like Chocolate,* 1976; *Cotton Candy on a Rainy Day,* 1978; *Nikki Giovanni in Philadelphia; Jackie Stealing Home: For Jackie Robinson.*

*

Bibliography: *Nikki Giovanni: An Introduction to Her Life and Works* edited by Virginia C. Fowler, 1992.

Critical Studies: *Dynamite Voices I: Black Poets of the 1960's* by Don L. Lee, 1971; *Modern Black Poets: A Collection of Critical Essays* edited by Donald B. Givson, 1973; *Understanding the New Black Poetry: Black Speech and Black Music as Poetic References* by Stephen Henderson, 1973; *Black Women Writers at Work* by Claudia Tate, 1983; *Black Women Writers, 1950-1980: A Critical Evaluation* edited by Mari Evans, 1984; *Imagining the Body in Contemporary Women's Poetry: Helga Novak, Ursula Krechel, Carolyn Forché, Nikki Giovanni* by Amy Stawser, 1999.

*   *   *

Nikki Giovanni is an important literary figure and academician whose poetry, speeches, and lectures are appealing to all ages, especially young people. Outspoken and assertive, she emerged from the black revolutionary movement of the 1960s as an artistic voice for change. Enthusiasm, creativity, intellectual brilliance, exuberance, humor, and incisiveness are characteristics of both her prose and verse. Over a thirty-year period she has developed from social critic and activist to literary genius with penetrating insight and artistic charm. She has published several volumes of poetry and nonfiction works, including her autobiographical statement, *Gemini.* Her poetry readings, recorded with musical accompaniment, also have wide appeal. She is in great demand as a lecturer and professor of English and creative writing, and has won many awards and citations for her works. She has taught at Queens College (New York), Rutgers University (New Jersey), Ohio State University (Columbus), Virginia Polytechnic Institute and State University (Blacksburg), and other places. Perhaps her most noted awards have been her honorary doctorate degrees and her selection as a featured poet in the International Poetry Festival of Ultrecht, Holland, in 1991.

Giovanni developed artistically and professionally during an exciting time in American history. She was in the thick of the action of the Civil Rights/black liberation movement of the 1960s and 1970s. Since that time she has continued to grow and expand and deepen, while sharpening her skills. While a student at Fisk University she participated in the Fisk Writers Workshop under the direction of the accomplished author John O. Killens. After graduation in 1967, she planned and directed the first Cincinnati Black Arts Festival, one of a number of efforts in the black communities throughout the country designed to awaken cultural awareness. As a part of this new black renaissance, the Cincinnati project developed into a theater movement known as the New Theater. Active involvement in one cultural or educational project after another enabled the poet to exercise and sharpen her intellectual and creative skills.

After attendance at the University of Pennsylvania School of Social Work under a Ford Foundation grant, and the School of Fine Arts at Columbia University in 1968, she was involved in the SEEK Program at Queens College. Out of active community participation such as this Giovanni wrote talkative, ritually recitative lyrics that reflect personal reactions to the social and spiritual encounters and interactions of the time. Her first two volumes of poetry, *Black Feeling, Black Talk* (1967), and *Black Judgement* (1968) represent immersion in the black cultural awakening that was characteristic of that era. The poems are insightful and critical of people, places, incidents, attitudes, and social and political situations, such as the assassinations of political and social figures like Martin Luther King, Jr., and Robert Kennedy.

Among other projects Giovanni engaged in was her publishing cooperative known as Niktom, Ltd., through which she published works of other poets such as **Gwendolyn Brooks**, Mari Evans, and **Margaret Walker**. This began in 1970, the year her third volume of poetry came out, titled *Re: Creation,* another collection of revolutionary verse. In the meantime travels to the Caribbean and other places tended to broaden her perspective and stimulate her intellect. This is reflected in the self-examination process we see her undergoing in *Gemini: An Extended Autobiographical Statement on My First Twenty-five Years of Being a Black Poet* (1971). In the same year we see a result of this self-search in the new book of poems, *Spin a Soft Black Song: Poems for Children.* The movement of the poet has been from the revolutionary to the introspective. This book was dedicated to her son. Her recording of the album *Truth Is on Its Way* in 1971, in which she reads some of her poetry against the background of gospel music, brought Giovanni national prominence. Churches and social organizations, such as the National Council of Negro Women were attracted to her, and Giovanni came to be in popular demand as a lecturer, especially on college campuses. She began receiving awards and was featured in magazines such as *Ebony, Jet,* and *Harper's Bazaar.*

After travels to Africa and Europe in July of 1971, Giovanni published another volume of poetry titled *My House* (1972), which shows a significant transformation in her thinking. She has broadened to a more inclusive social perspective, and her poetry here is softer, more lyrical, rhythmical and eloquent. Thoughts are more of home and family, love, and her two-year old son Thomas. In 1973 she published *Ego-Tripping and Other Poems for Young People,* a special edition of her poetry that she collected and edited especially for youth. Within this period Giovanni further enriched her intellectual and artistic perspective by engaging in published dialogues with two other prominent African American authors, **James Baldwin** and Margaret Walker. The former is taken from a taped conversation with Baldwin for the television program "South" in London, England, in 1971. It represents the interaction of two brilliant thinkers on subjects like black men and women, black people and American society, and literary criticism. A year later Giovanni appeared on the **Paul Lawrence Dunbar** centennial program at the University of Dayton with other writers, including Margaret Walker. From her encounter with Walker on this program grew a request for the two to do a "Conversation Book" together. In 1974 there appeared *A Poetic Equation: Conversations between Nikki Giovanni and Margaret Walker.* These two women of high intelligence but of different generations and backgrounds exchange rather revealing and pungent views, sometimes agreeing and other times arguing and debating with each other, on subjects such as the black liberation movement, black women, war, and American society.

All of Giovanni's later publications of poetry, *The Women and the Men* (1975), *Cotton Candy on a Rainy Day* (1978), *Vacation Time: Poems for Children* (1980), and *Those Who Ride the Night Winds* (1983), reflect an evolving, changing, growing poet and intellect who draws much from life and experience. In the process, her creativity and artistic skills become better and better. As a result, Giovanni has evolved into one of the finest lyrical poets on the American scene. In her works one finds a mastery of words in the expression of all the ranges of human feelings—joy, loneliness, love, emptiness, delight, sorrow, hope, pain. One also finds an ever changing style reflecting the changes in content and emphasis in her writing.

—Mozella G. Mitchell

GLASGOW, Ellen (Anderson)

Born: Richmond, Virginia, 22 April 1873. **Education:** Tutored at home and educated in private schools in Richmond; began to lose her hearing at age 16 and eventually went deaf. **Career:** Writer from 1896; lived in New York, 1911-16. President, Richmond Society for the Prevention of Cruelty to Animals, 1924-25. **Awards:** American Academy Howells Medal, 1941; Pulitzer prize, 1942. Litt.D.: University of North Carolina, Chapel Hill, 1930. LL.D.: University of Richmond, 1938; Duke University, Durham, North Carolina, 1938; College of William and Mary, Williamsburg, Virginia, 1939. **Member:** American Academy, 1938. **Died:** 21 November 1945.

PUBLICATIONS

Collections

Letters, edited by Blair Rouse. 1958.
Collected Stories, edited by Richard K. Meeker. 1963.

Fiction

The Descendant. 1897.
Phases of an Inferior Planet. 1898.
The Voice of the People. 1900; edited by William L. Godshalk, 1972.
The Battle-Ground. 1902.
The Deliverance. 1904.
The Wheel of Life. 1906.
The Ancient Law. 1908.
The Romance of Plain Man. 1909.
The Miller of Old Church. 1911.
Virginia. 1913.
Life and Gabriella. 1916.
The Builders. 1919.
One Man in His Time. 1922.
The Shadowy Third and Other Stories. 1923; as *Dare's Gift and Other Stories,* 1924.
Barren Ground. 1925.
The Romantic Comedians. 1926.
They Stooped to Folly: A Comedy of Morals. 1929.
The Sheltered Life. 1932.

Vein of Iron. 1935.
In This Our Life. 1941.
Beyond Defeat: An Epilogue to an Era, edited by Luther Y. Gore. 1966.

Poetry

The Freeman and Other Poems. 1902.

Other

Works (Old Dominion Edition). 8 vols., 1929-33.
Works (Virginia Edition). 12 vols., 1938.
A Certain Measure: An Interpretation of Prose Fiction (prefaces to Virginia Edition). 1943.
The Woman Within (autobiography). 1954.

*

Bibliography: *Glasgow: A Bibliography* by William W. Kelly, edited by Oliver L. Steele, 1964.

Critical Studies: *On Glasgow* by James Branch Cabell, 1938; *No Place on Earth: Glasgow, James Branch Cabell, and Richmond-in-Virginia* by Louis D. Rubin, Jr., 1959; *Glasgow and the Ironic Art of Fiction* by Frederick P. W. McDowell, 1960; *Glasgow* by Blair Rouse, 1962; *Glasgow* by Louis Auchincloss, 1964; *Glasgow's American Dream* by Joan Foster Santas, 1966; *Three Modes of Modern Southern Fiction: Glasgow, Faulkner, and Wolfe* by C. Hugh Holman, 1966; *Without Shelter: The Early Career of Glasgow* by J.R. Raper, 1971, and *From the Sunken Garden: The Fiction of Glasgow 1916-1945* by Raper, 1980; *Glasgow's Development as a Novelist* by Marion K. Richards, 1971; *Glasgow and the Woman Within* by E. Stanly Godbold, Jr., 1972; *Glasgow: Centennial Essays* edited by M. Thomas Inge, 1976; *The Social Situation of Women in the Novels of Glasgow* by Elizabeth Gallup Myer, 1978; *The End of a Legend: Glasgow's History of Southern Women* by Barbro Ekman, 1979; *Glasgow* by Marcelle Thiebaux, 1982; *Glasgow: Beyond Convention* by Linda W. Wagner, 1982; *The Southern Belle in the American Novel* by Kathryn Lee Seidel, 1985; *Writing the Margins: Edith Wharton, Ellen Glasgow, and the Literary Tradition of the Ruined Woman* by Catherine E. Saunders, 1987; *Ellen Glasgow and a Woman's Traditions* by Pamela R. Matthews, 1994; *Ellen Glasgow: New Perspectives* edited by Dorothy McInnis Scura, 1995; *Ellen Glasgow: A Biography* by Susan Goodman, 1998.

*   *   *

Ellen Glasgow was the first clear voice in the movement that became known as the Southern Literary Renaissance. She was the first writer to apply the principles of critical realism and a detached and ironic point of view to the people, the region, and the problems of the American South. Beginning with her first novel, *The Descendant,* in 1897 and ending with *Beyond Defeat,* posthumously published in 1966, she produced twenty novels in which with varying degrees of success she brought to Virginia and the South what she felt it most needed, "blood and irony." In addition to these novels, she published a volume of critical introductions to a collected edition of her novels, *A Certain Measure;* a

volume of undistinguished verse, *The Freeman and Other Poems;* and a collection of mediocre short stories, *The Shadowy Third.*

Her first two novels, both set in New York, point to her later work only in attempting a clear-eyed realism and in having southern characters. But beginning in 1900, with *The Voice of the People,* and continuing through *The Battle-Ground, The Deliverance, The Romance of a Plain Man, The Miller of Old Church, Virginia,* and *Life and Gabriella,* Glasgow constructed a fictional social history of the Commonwealth of Virginia from the Civil War to World War I, placing a particular emphasis upon the transition from a ruling aristocracy to the rise of the middle class to political and economic power. In this series of novels, she traced the petrifaction of the aristocratic ideals of pre-war Virginia and recorded through the lives of fictional characters the major social revolution that the rise of the middle class produced. These novels are historical only in the sense that all historical novels deal with issues of manners, politics, and economic forces in an earlier age; they do not deal with historical personages or actual events. She treated social history with detachment, irony, and a self-consciously witty style. In 1925 she published *Barren Ground,* a novel of a lower-middle-class country woman, Dorinda Oakley, in her struggle with self, circumstance, and the soil. In this novel Glasgow reached the highest expression of her historical view, although there are no historical events as such in the novel. *Barren Ground* is a grim story, reminiscent of the works of Thomas Hardy, whom she greatly admired. It recounts, she declared, events that could happen "wherever the spirit of fortitude has triumphed over the sense of futility." She also said that it demonstrated that "one may learn to live, one may even learn to live gallantly without delight." Though she was acquainted with modern scientific, social, and anthropological views of man and society, her fundamental view of life remained shaped, as this statement suggests, by a firm but nontheological Calvinistic determinism.

Barren Ground not only summed up the first period in her active career—a period that had seen, in addition to the works named, the publication of four minor novels and her short stories and poetry—it also launched the most productive and artistically successful period in her career. In 1926 she published *The Romantic Comedians,* an almost perfectly constructed novel of manners, laid in Queenborough, her name for her native city of Richmond. The novel, centered in the marriage of an old man to a young girl, is a witty and amusing attack upon the social customs of the surviving Virginia aristocracy. She followed *The Romantic Comedians* with *They Stooped to Folly,* another comedy of manners laid in Queenborough, which plays amusing variations on the idea of the ruined woman through three generations of a Virginia family. *The Sheltered Life,* a tragi-comedy that concludes the Queenborough trilogy, ranks with *Barren Ground* as one of her two best works. *The Sheltered Life* is particularly noteworthy for its treatment of time and memory. "The Deep Past," a section of the novel consisting of the recollections of a very old man, is her finest single piece of work. The last two novels published during her lifetime portray the growing darkness of her view of life. *Vein of Iron* is a grim picture of life in the Virginia mountains, a story that she called "a drama of mortal conflict with fate." In *This Our Life,* a Pulitzer Prize-winner, is a despairing view of modern life in Queenborough, a book that, she said, shows "that character is an end in itself." *Beyond Defeat,* written as a sequel to it, strongly supports this view.

Glasgow was a committed realist with a tragic view of human potentialities. Her world view was strongly shaped by a sense of imperfection and failure in all human efforts. Supremely the novelist and fictional historian of her native Virginia, she maintained toward the places in which she lived and the people whom she loved an ironic detachment largely the result of her witty and polished and consciously fashioned style. A half-dozen of her novels, including *Virginia, Barren Ground,* the Queenborough trilogy, and *Vein of Iron* are works of considerable distinction. In her own time, she enjoyed both popular and critical respect. Since her death she has received little attention, but she deserves to be better known and more widely read.

—C. Hugh Holman

GLASPELL, Susan (Keating)

Born: Davenport, Iowa, 1 July 1882 (possibly 1876). **Education:** Davenport schools; Drake University, Des Moines, Iowa, Ph.D. 1899; University of Chicago, 1902. **Family:** Married 1) the writer George Cram Cook in 1913 (died 1924); 2) the writer Norman Matson in 1925 (divorced 1932). **Career:** Reporter, Des Moines *Daily News* and *Capital,* 1899-1901; freelance writer in Davenport, 1901-11; founder, with George Cram Cook, Provincetown Players, 1915, and wrote for the company in Provincetown, Massachusetts, and New York, 1915-22; lived in Greece, 1922-24; director, Midwest Play Bureau of the Federal Theater Project, Chicago, 1936-38. **Awards:** Pulitzer prize, 1931. **Died:** 27 July 1948.

PUBLICATIONS

Plays

Suppressed Desires, with George Cram Cook (produced 1915). In *Plays,* 1920.
Trifles (produced 1916). In *Plays,* 1920.
The People (produced 1917). 1918.
Close the Book (produced 1917). With *The People,* 1918.
The Outside (produced 1917). In *Plays,* 1920.
Woman's Honor (produced 1918). In *Plays.* 1920.
Tickless Time, with George Cram Cook (produced 1918). In *Plays,* 1920.
Bernice (produced 1919). In *Plays,* 1920.
Plays. 1920; as *Trifles and Other Short Plays,* 1926.
Inheritors (produced 1921). 1921.
The Verge (produced 1921). 1922.
Chains of Dew (produced 1922).
The Comic Artist, with Norman Matson (produced 1928; revised version, produced 1933). 1927.
Alison's House (produced 1930). 1930.

Fiction

The Glory of the Conquered. 1909.
The Visioning. 1911.
Lifted Masks: Stories. 1912.
Fidelity. 1915.
A Jury of Her Peers (stories). 1927.
Brook Evans. 1928; as *The Right to Love,* 1930.

Fugitive's Return. 1929.
Ambrose Holt and Family. 1931.
The Morning Is near Us. 1940.
Cherished and Shared of Old. 1940.
Norma Ashe. 1942.
Judd Rankin's Daughter. 1945; as *Prodigal Giver,* 1946.

Other

The Road to the Temple (on George Cram Cook). 1926.

Editor, *Greek Coins* (verse), by George Cram Cook. 1925.

*

Critical Studies: *Glaspell* by Arthur E. Waterman, 1966; "On the Edge: The Plays of Susan Glaspell" by Christine Dymkowski, in *Modern Drama,* March 1988; "Susan Glaspell's Contributions to Contemporary Women Playwrights" by Linda Ben-Zvi, in *Feminine Focus: The New Women Playwrights* edited by Enoch Brater, 1989, and "'Murder, She Wrote': The Genesis of Susan Glaspell's *Trifles*" by Ben-Zvi, in *Theatre Journal,* May 1992; "Rebellion and Rejection: The Plays of Susan Glaspell" by Barbara Oziebolo, in *Modern American Drama: The Female Canon* edited by June Schlueter, 1990; *Susan Glaspell: Essays on Her Theater and Fiction* edited by Linda Ben-Zvi, 1995; *Making Room for Creative Women: Female Artists in the Works of Susan Glaspell* (dissertation) by Karen Hollingsworth Gardiner, 1996.

* * *

When the Provincetown Players opened a subscription theater in Greenwich Village in 1916, their two major playwrights were **Eugene O'Neill** and Susan Glaspell. With her husband, George Cram "Jig" Cook, Glaspell was a founder of the Provincetown Players and, before his dissatisfaction with the direction the theater was taking and their departure for Greece in 1922, she was a substantial contributor to the success of the group. Although she lacked O'Neill's theatricality at this time, she was much closer to O'Neill in his concern for intense, meaningful drama than any of their contemporaries.

An intelligent and perceptive person, confident in her art and the values she found meaningful, she was most impressive in her thoughtful and theatrically effective one-act plays. *Suppressed Desires* (written with Cook) is a clever satire on the idea of complete freedom in self-expression. *Trifles* combines mystery with a penetrating understanding of a woman's character in a single tense scene. Other one-act plays performed by the Provincetown Players were *The People, The Outside,* and *Woman's Honor.*

Her full-length plays, all of which reveal a liberal woman's approach with force and dignity, never quite reached the quality she seemed capable of producing. *Bernice,* although too conversational and contrived, shows the power and thoughtful ingenuity of a loving wife to effect a dramatic and sustaining change upon her husband after her death. One of her most popular plays from this period is *Inheritors,* which dramatizes the problems of a Midwestern college in carrying on the liberal ideas of its founder over the conservatism of its present board of trustees. It is in *The Verge* that Glaspell came closest to portraying the emotional struggles that were central to O'Neill's plays. Searching for an understanding of herself, the heroine is on the "verge" both of insanity and that answer that eludes her. In language and idea the play suggests a power that was never completely dramatized.

After her husband's death in Greece, Glaspell wrote *The Road to the Temple*, a moving and interesting biography-autobiography of their work together in theater and of his last years. She also produced a number of short stories and novels that did little for her reputation as a writer. Her single outstanding work of this later period was the Pulitzer Prize-winning *Alison's House*, a thought-provoking and beautifully expressed play based on **Emily Dickinson**'s life. Her major contribution to American drama and theater, however, rests almost entirely on those years of the Provincetown Players, an extremely important time in the growth of American drama.

—Walter J. Meserve

GLÜCK, Louise (Elizabeth)

Born: New York City, 22 April 1943. **Education:** Sarah Lawrence College, Bronxville, New York, 1962; Columbia University School of General Studies, 1963-66; Columbia University, School of Arts, 1967-68. **Family:** Married 1) Charles Hertz, Jr., in 1967 (divorced 1968); 2) John Darrow in 1977 (divorced 1993), one son. **Career:** Taught at Goddard College, Plainfield, Vermont, 1971-72, 1973-74, 1976-80, University of Virginia, Charlottesville, 1973, University of North Carolina, Greensboro, 1973, University of Iowa, Iowa City, University of Cincinnati, 1978, Columbia University, 1979, Warren Wilson College, Swannanoa, North Carolina, 1978-80, University of Califronia at Berkeley, 1982, at Davis, 1983, at Irvine, 1984. Senior lecturer in English, 1984-98 and beginning 1998 Preston S. Parish '41 Third Century Lecturer in English, Williams College, Williamstown, Massachusetts. Regents professor, University of California, Los Angeles, 1985-87; visiting professor, Harvard University, Cambridge, Massachusetts, January-May 1995; Hurst Professor, Brandeis University, Waltham, Massachusetts, January-May, 1996. **Awards:** Rockefeller grant in poetry, 1968-69; National Endowment for the arts fellowship, 1969-70, 1979-80, 1988-89; Eunice Tietjens prize, 1971; Guggenheim fellowship, 1975-76, in poetry, 1987-88; Vermont Council for the Arts grant, 1978-79; American Academy and Institute of Arts and Letters, award in literature, 1981; Melville Cane award, 1985; National Book Critics Circle award, 1985; Sara Teasdale memorial prize, 1986; Boston Globe poetry prize, 1987; Bobbitt National poetry prize, 1992; Jerome J. Shestack prize, 1992; William Carols Williams award, 1993; Pulitzer prize, 1993; American Academy of Arts and Sciences, fellow, 1993; Vermont State poet, 1994; P.E.N. Martha Albrand award, first nonfiction, 1995. Honorary degrees: Williams College, 1993; Skidmore College, 1995; Middlebury College, 1996. **Member:** American Academy of Arts and Letters, 1996. **Residence:** Cambridge, Massachusetts.

PUBLICATIONS

Poetry

Firstborn. 1968.
The House on Marshland. 1975.
The Garden. 1976.
Descending Figure. 1980.
The Triumph of Achilles. 1985.
Ararat. 1990.
The Wild Iris. 1992.
The First Four Books of Poems. 1995.
Meadowlands. 1996.
Vita Nova. 1999.

Other

Proofs and Theories. 1994.

Editor, with David Lehman, *The Best American Poetry 1993*. 1993.

*

Critical Studies: "The Poetry of Louise Glück" by Burton Raffel, in *The Literary Review: An International Journal of Contemporary Writing*, Spring 1988; "'Free/of Blossom and Subterfuge': Louise Glück and the Language of Renunciation" by Lynn Keller, in *World, Self, Poems: Essays on Contemporary Poetry form the "Jubilation of Poets,"* edited by Leonard M. Trawick, 1990; "The Harsher Figure of Descending Figure: Louise Glück's 'Dive into the Wreck'" by Laurie E. George, in *Women's Studies*, 1990; *The Veiled Mirror and the Woman Poet: H.D., Louise Bogan, Elizabeth Bishop, and Louise Glück* by Elizabeth Caroline Dodd, 1992; "Without Relation: Family and Freedom in the Poetry of Louise Glück" by Suzanne Matson, in *Mid-America Review*, 1994; *The Muse of Abandonment: Origin, Identity, Mastery, in Five American Poets* by Lee Upton, 1998.

*   *   *

Pulitzer Prize-winning poet Louise Glück is a member of the American Academy of Arts and Letters and was elected to the board of chancellors of the Academy of American Poets in 1999. *The First Four Books of Poetry* (1995) is a collection that includes *Firstborn* (1968), *The House on Marshland* (1975), *Descending Figure* (1980), and the *Triumph of Achilles* (1985). Other books of poetry include *Ararat* (1990), *Meadowlands* (1996), and *The Wild Iris,* for which she won the Pulitzer Prize in 1993. Glück has received the National Book Critics Circle Award for Poetry, the Boston Globe Literary Press Award, the Poetry Society of American Melville Kane Award, and the William Carlos Williams Award. In addition, Glück wrote a collection of essays, *Proofs and Theories*, which garnered the PEN/Martha Albrand Award for Nonfiction.

In *Firstborn*, "The Chicago Train," a powerfully evocative poem, expresses ugly images of death, poison, and lice as the narrator observes a couple with their child on a train. "The Egg" depicts a woman addressing her lover and describing her emotions of loss stemming from a traumatic abortion. Birth and death are juxtaposed in this poem. *The House on Marshland*, another collection, deals with the pains of love. In "Pomegranate" the narrator says, "First he gave me / his heart. It was red fruit containing / many seeds . . . I preferred / to starve." In "Here Are My Black Clothes," a woman gives her lover her black clothes because she will not mourn him in her new life. The poet addresses her lover's mother in "Love Poem," where she comments that the mother knits scarves while marrying "over and over."

Descending Figure opens with a poignant, sad poem called "The Drowned Children." The theme of the difficulty of love resounds in "Palais des Arts," where the narrator notes that a woman cannot touch her man's arm in innocence anymore, without the obligation of what Glück calls the "thrust and ache." "Epithalamium" recalls the disillusion with marriage, which continues in "The Mirror." Here the woman is critical of her lover as he shaves and cuts himself. In "Tango" the female voice complains that "envy / is a dance, too; the need to hurt / binds you to your partner." This poem and "For My Sister" includes a reminiscence about Glück's dead sister, whom she cannot forget. Besides her mother and sister, the speaker recalls her grandmother's marriage in "Grandmother," and she comments about her grandfather's silencing of his wife—"his hand over her mouth." Another theme of the collection is hunger ("Dedication to Hunger"), including the hunger of anorexia ("The Deviation") as a means of controlling the self and achieving perfection: "It is the same need to perfect, / of which death is the mere byproduct."

In *The Triumph of Achilles*, classical references are interspersed with modern ones. From the earlier, more structured rhymes of "The Chicago Train" in *Firstborn*, Glück moved toward easier rhymes in "Here Are My Black Clothes" in *The House on Marshland*, and into even looser rhymes in "The Triumph of Achilles." The title poem relates the loss of Petroclus and Achilles' grief. On an optimistic note, the poet has the power to bring lovers together in poetry in "The Tribute." But "The End of the World" expresses pessimism about death and the inability of a god to save even one person. Combining the classical and the modern, "The Mountain" tells of a teacher who compares her artistic endeavors to those of Sisyphus laboring to push a boulder up a hill. Taking up the subject of family again, the narrator recalls her grandfather from Hungary in "Legend." She admires his principles, especially his belief in speaking the truth, which gives "the illusion of freedom." The collection ends with "Horse," where the speaker complains that her husband is closer to his horse than to her, and: "Then I know what lies behind your silence / scorn, hatred of me, marriage."

In *Meadowlands* Glück made use of Homer's *The Odyssey*, juxtaposed with modern events, to highlight the dissolution of a marriage. Penelope, Odysseus, Telemachus, and Circe appear in these poems, as well as a contemporary couple who engage in conversation related to everyday concerns. "Penelope's Song" tells of her struggle to hold on to the memory of Odysseus and to entice him to return to her. She calls out to him with her "dark song." The tedium of daily life rankles the modern wife who complains in "Ceremony" about her husband's refusal to have guests and about his routines: "Living with you is like living / at boarding school: / chicken Monday, fish Tuesday." Penelope's and Odysseus's son Telemachus looks at his parents' lives in several poems, displaying wisdom beyond his years. In "Telemachus' Guilt" he complains that because his mother did not know he existed, he smiled when she wept. The goddess Circe comments upon her prowess: "Some people are pigs; I make them / look like pigs." The power of this book derives from conversational language, the posing of questions, and acute observations. The combination of classical and contemporary allows the reader to understand the timelessness of love and its loss.

Glück's work remains in the forefront of American poetry because she is able to articulate themes such as the painfulness of love, adversarial gender relationships, poignant memories of family, and perceptions of nature and environment. Following in the

tradition of confessional poets like Anne Sexton and Sylvia Plath, Glück embodies a post-confessional perspective with the poet's persona aligned with the mythic and classical. The female voice expresses both the noise and the silence of the difficulties of family life and engages in the dialectic between helplessness and assertiveness. While affording a source of subject matter and imagery, domestic life can be hurtful. Thus, Glück emerges as a post-feminist poet who explores the psychological, familial dimensions of women's experience.

—Shirley J. Paolini

GOLDMAN, Emma

Born: Kovno, Russia, 27 June 1869. Immigrated to Rochester, New York, 1886. **Family:** Married 1) Jacob Kreshner in 1886 (divorced 1887); 2) James Colton in 1925. **Career:** Worked in garment and corset factories in Rochester, New York, and New York City, beginning c. 1886; became active in anarchist movement, c. 1887; met companion Alexander Berkman, 1892; attempted, with Berkman, to kill Henry Clay Frick, 1892; sentenced to one year for inciting a riot, 1895; began publishing *Mother Earth,* 1906; sentenced to 15 days for lecturing on birth control, 1915; sentenced along with Berkman to two years for anti-conscription activity, 1917; deported to Russia with Berkman in 1919; met Vladimir Lenin, 1920; deported from Russia with Berkman, 1921, and traveled to Berlin and London; in exile in Saint-Tropez, France, began writing autobiography *Living My Life,* 1928; published *Living My Life,* 1931. **Died:** 14 May 1940.

PUBLICATIONS

Collections

Red Emma Speaks: An Emma Goldman Reader, compiled and edited by Alix Kates Shulman. 1972.
Anarchist Notebook: A Compilation of the Writings of Emma Goldman. 1996.

Other

Anarchism and Other Essays. 1910.
The Social Significance of Modern Drama. 1914.
My Disillusionment in Russia. 1925.
Living My Life. 1931.
The Traffic in Women and Other Essays on Feminism, with bibliography by Alix Kates Shulman. 1970.

*

Critical Studies: *Emma Goldman: An Intimate Life* by Alix Kates Shulman, 1984; "Living Our Life" by Shulman, in *Between Women: Biographers, Novelists, Critics, Teachers, and Artists Write about Their Work on Women,* 1984; "Epistolary Politics: The Correspondence of Emma Goldman and Alexander Berkman" by Wendy Deutelbaum, in *Prose Studies: History, Theory, Criticism* vol. 9, no. 1, 1986; *Emma Goldman* by Martha Solomon, 1987; "Speaking Her Own Piece: Emma Goldman and the Discursive Skeins of

Autobiography" by Blanche H. Gelfant, in *Reconstructing the 'Self' in America: Patterns in Immigrant Women's Autobiographies* by Betty-Ann Bergland, 1991; *Emma Goldman and the American Left* by Marian J. Morton, 1992; *Emma Goldman and the Anxiety of Biography* by Alice Wexler, 1992; *Red Emma, Queen of the Anarchists* by Carol Bolt, 1994; "Charlotte Perkins Gilman and Emma Goldman Reformer and Radical" by Margaret Jackson Smith, in *The Arkansas Review: A Journal of Criticism,* spring 1994, pp. 152-67; *Emma Goldman: A Guide to Her Life and Documentary Sources,* 1995; "Neither Tired nor Poor nor Huddled: Emma Goldman and the Limits of the American Dream" by Una M. Cadegan, in *University of Dayton Review,* winter 1995-96, pp. 47-53.

*   *   *

Known for her fiery oratory as well as her revolutionary views of marriage, sex, and politics, Emma Goldman commanded the attention of many in early-twentieth-century America. An anarchist by her own definition and a radical feminist according to many others, Goldman sought notoriety and an audience as a means of communicating her ideas to revolutionize the American political and social structures. Because Goldman's fame came as a result of her ability to rally a crowd to fever pitch, much of the understanding of her legendary status died with her. Goldman did, however, publish a small newspaper/newsletter called *Mother Earth* for twelve years that contained many of the speeches she and other anarchists gave around the United States. Most often accompanied by her lifelong lover/companion, Alexander Berkman, Goldman endured three stays in prison, two deportations, and finally the wrath of what was once her constituency. Perhaps the most complete and compelling account of Goldman's beliefs and activities is her autobiography, *Living My Life,* which she wrote at the end of her life while in exile.

Goldman stayed in her birthplace in a czarist Russian ghetto named Kovno only until 1886. At 17 she fled to Rochester, New York, where her sister Lena lived. The roots of what was to become Goldman's feminism began in her early years in Russia. Goldman's father discouraged her from pursuing an education. Marriage, he told his daughter, was women's only alternative, and one that a woman did not need an education for. Goldman's father tried to force Emma to marry, thus precipitating her flight to the United States. Ironically, upon arriving in Rochester, Goldman married Jacob Kreshner. As Goldman reasons in her autobiography, her job in a garment factory was not enough to support her; thus, Kreshner's additional income proved helpful. This marriage quickly dissolved, however. Goldman's increased awareness and involvement in the anarchist movement in New York City drew her away from Kreshner and toward the city, to which she moved two years after her 1887 divorce.

Goldman marks the hanging of four anarchists as a result of the Chicago Haymarket trials of 1887 as her "birth." While working in a corset factory in New York City, Goldman devoted all of her leisure time to the anarchist movement, attending lectures and adopting Johann Most, a prominent anarchist speaker, as her mentor. At the encouragement of Most, Goldman gave her first public speech in 1891. Years later, after Goldman had gained her own devout following, and after she distinguished herself as decidedly different from Most, Goldman poignantly demonstrated her distaste for Most and his beliefs by publicly horsewhipping Most during one of her speeches that he heckled. In 1892 Goldman met and began her lifelong relationship with Alexander Berkman, a fellow anarchist.

In her speeches Goldman denigrated the institution of marriage as inherently unequal and ridiculously prudish. Goldman advocated both in her speeches and her actions a free love in which partners could unite and part as they wished. Goldman's ability to arouse wild enthusiasm and violent disdain by lecturing on such topics earned her the reputation of a diabolically dangerous woman. Eventually this reputation led to Goldman's frequent censorship and difficulty in finding a landlord willing to rent her an apartment.

In 1892 Goldman and Berkman hoped to make an effective and lasting step toward anarchism. Their "Attentat" or action toward anarchism was to kill Henry Clay Frick, the owner of Carnegie Steel. To Goldman and Berkman, Frick symbolized gross consumption and unconscionable exploitation. Berkman succeeded only in wounding Frick, however. While Goldman was not charged in the attempted murder, Berkman was sentenced to 22 years at Blackwell, a prison notorious for its horrible conditions.

Although Goldman continued and even picked up her lecture pace, frequently using Berkman as an example of the proper devotion the anarchist movement needed, Goldman felt guilt for having come out of the Frick affair unharmed. This evasion of the penal system was not to last, however. Goldman's first sentencing came in 1895 as a result of one of her lectures on anarchism. Sentenced to one year for inciting a riot, Goldman's stay in prison did nothing to calm her fervor. Indeed, it was as a result of this sentence and Goldman's bolstered defiance that her celebrity status as the most dangerous woman in America was launched. The 1901 assassination of President McKinley immediately brought Goldman under suspicion as a conspirator in the murder. Although unknown to Goldman, the young Czolgosz who shot McKinley named Goldman as his inspiration.

Goldman increased her audience with the publication of *Mother Earth* in 1906. Frequently threatened by lack of finances and by raids on its offices by the police, *Mother Earth* remained in publication, often only through Goldman's efforts, until 1918, when it was successfully censored by the American government. Within its pages Goldman espoused the tenets of anarchism through her own as well as other anarchists' words. Goldman's lecture schedule and published speeches frequently appeared in the publication. The collection *Anarchism and Other Essays,* 1910, contains a number of essays and speeches that also appeared in *Mother Earth.*

In 1915, Goldman was jailed for a second time as a result of her lecture on birth control at Carnegie Hall. At the height of her lecturing career, Goldman was giving more than 120 lectures a year in 37 cities in 25 states to some 25,000 paying and non-paying attendants. While she traveled, Goldman continued to publish *Mother Earth* as well as a series on Russian and American drama that still receives praise for its insights. A collection of her essays on drama appears in *The Social Significance of Modern Drama,* 1914. However, Goldman's past and present reputation as a radical and frequently outrageous anarchist overshadows these other accomplishments.

In 1917, Goldman and Berkman were both sentenced to a two-year sentence and deportation for their anti-conscription activity. They served their sentences while awaiting the U. S. Supreme Court's ruling on their deportation hearings. Goldman and Berkman were released from jail two years later and immediately deported to Russia. Goldman's legendary status followed her to Russia, where in 1921 both she and Berkman were put into solitary confinement in order for the Russian government to examine the nature of their political beliefs. As Goldman had long looked forward to joining the Bolshevik Revolution, which she saw as confirming the practicability of anarchist principles, her disappointment with the revolution devastated her belief not only in the Russians' struggle, but in the merits of anarchism as well. She would write of her experiences in Russia in *My Disillusionment in Russia,* published in 1925.

Despite Goldman's notoriety and popularity among radicals and intellectuals in the United States and Russia, during the late 1910s and early 1920s her popularity became tainted with disillusionment. More and more of her followers and comrades began to look to Berkman for leadership; Goldman, they argued, no longer seemed the fearless and fierce woman she once was. What had been the only consistent relationship in her life, her relationship with Berkman, also began to collapse. After their deportation from Russia to Berlin in 1921, Goldman and Berkman grew increasingly apart. Goldman eventually left, alone, for London, where she continued to lecture, although unsuccessfully. She married a Welsh miner, James Colton, in 1925, supposedly as a favor to him so he could gain British citizenship, which she herself had recently acquired. Goldman began writing her autobiography, *Living My Life,* in 1928 in Saint-Tropez, France, and published it in 1931. Berkman committed suicide in 1936, and Goldman, while living in yet another country, Canada, died in 1940.

—Kathleen Grimm Garrett

GOODMAN, Paul

Born: New York City, 9 September 1911. **Education:** City College, New York, B.A. 1931; University of Chicago, Ph.D. 1940 (received 1954). **Family:** Married twice; two daughters and one son. **Career:** Reader, Metro-Goldwyn-Mayer, 1931; instructor, University of Chicago, 1939-40; teacher of Latin, physics, history and mathematics, Manumit School of Progressive Education, Pawling, New York, 1942; also teacher at New York University, 1948, Black Mountain College, North Carolina, 1950, and Sarah Lawrence College, Bronxville, New York, 1961; Knapp Professor, University of Wisconsin, Madison, 1964; teacher at Experimental College of San Francisco State College, 1966, and University of Hawaii, Honolulu, 1969, 1971. Editor, *Complex* magazine, New York; film editor, *Partisan Review,* New Brunswick, New Jersey; television critic, *New Republic,* Washington, D.C.; editor *Liberation* magazine, New York, 1962-70. **Awards:** American Council of Learned Societies fellowship, 1940; American Academy grant, 1953. **Died:** 3 August 1972.

PUBLICATIONS

Collections

Collected Poems, edited by Taylor Stoehr. 1974.
Collected Stories, edited by Taylor Stoehr. 4 vols., 1978-80.

Fiction

The Grand Piano; or, The Almanac of Alienation. 1942.
The Facts of Life (stories). 1945.

The State of Nature. 1946.
The Break-Up of Our Camp and Other Stories. 1949.
The Dead of Spring. 1950.
Parents Day. 1951.
The Empire City. 1959.
Our Visit to Niagara (stories). 1960.
Making Do. 1963.
Adam and His Works: Collected Stories. 1968.
Don Juan; or, The Continuum of the Libido, edited by Taylor Stoehr. 1979.

Plays

Childish Jokes: Crying Backstage. 1938.
The Tower of Babel, in *New Directions in Prose and Poetry 5.* 1940.
2 Noh Plays (produced 1950). In *Stop-Light,* 1941.
Stop-Light: 5 Dance Poems (Noh plays: *Dusk: A Noh Play, The Birthday, The Three Disciples, The Cyclist, The Stop Light*). 1941.
Faustina (produced 1949). In *Three Plays,* 1965.
Theory of Tragedy, in *Quarterly Review of Literature,* winter 1950.
Jonah (produced 1950; revised version, produced 1966). In *Three Plays,* 1965.
Abraham (cycle of Abraham plays; produced 1953). *Abraham and Isaac* in *Cambridge Review,* November 1955.
The Young Disciple (produced 1955). In *Three Plays,* 1965.
Little Hero (produced 1957). In *Tragedy and Comedy: Four Cubist Plays,* 1970.
The Cave at Machpelah, music by Ned Rorem (produced 1959). In *Commentary,* June 1958.
Three Plays. 1965.
Tragedy and Comedy: Four Cubist Plays (includes *Structure of Tragedy, After Aeschylus; Structure of Tragedy, After Sophocles; Structure of Pathos, After Euripides; Little Hero, After Moliere*). 1970.

Poetry

Ten Lyric Poems. 1934.
12 Ethical Sonnets. 1935.
15 Poems with Time Expressions. 1936.
Homecoming and Departure. 1937.
A Warning at My Leisure. 1939.
Five Young American Poets, with others. 1942.
Pieces of Three, with Meyer Liben and Edouard Roditi. 1942.
The Copernican Revolution. 1946; revised edition, 1947.
Day and Other Poems. 1954(?).
Red Jacket. 1955.
Berg Goodman Mezey, with Stephen Berg and Robert Mezey. 1957.
The Well of Bethlehem. 1957.
Ten Poems. 1961.
The Lordly Hudson: Collected Poems. 1962.
Hawkweed. 1967.
North Percy. 1968.
Homespun of Oatmeal Gray. 1970.
Two Sentences. 1970.

Other

Art and Social Nature (essays). 1946.
Kafka's Prayer. 1947.
Communitas: Means of Livelihood and Ways of Life, with Percival Goodman. 1947; revised edition, 1960.

Gestalt Therapy: Excitement and Growth in the Human Personality, with Frederick S. Perls and Ralph F. Hefferline. 1951.
The Structure of Literature. 1954.
Censorship and Pornography on the Stage, and Are Writers Shirking Their Political Duty? 1959(?).
Growing Up Absurd: Problems of Youth in the Organized System. 1960.
Drawing the Line. 1962.
The Community of Scholars. 1962.
Utopian Essays and Practical Proposals. 1962.
The Society I Live in Is Mine. 1963.
Compulsory Mis-Education. 1964; revised edition, 1971.
People or Personnel: Decentralizing and the Mixed System. 1965.
Mass Education in Science. 1966.
Five Years: Thoughts During a Useless Time. 1966.
The Moral Ambiguity of America. 1966; revised edition, as *Like a Conquered Province: The Moral Ambiguity of America,* 1967.
The Open Look. 1969.
New Reformation: Notes of a Neolithic Conservative. 1970.
Speaking and Language: Defence of Poetry. 1972.
Little Prayers and Finite Experience. 1972.
Drawing the Line: The Political Essays, edited by Taylor Stoehr. 1977.
Nature Heals: The Psychological Essays, edited by Taylor Stoehr. 1977.
Creator Spirit, Come! The Literary Essays, edited by Taylor Stoehr. 1977.
The Black Flag of Anarchism. 1978.
Crazy Hope and Finite Experience: Final Essays of Paul Goodman, edited by Taylor Stoehr. 1994.
Format and Anxiety: Paul Goodman Critiques the Media. 1995.

Editor, *Seeds of Liberation.* 1964.

*

Bibliography: *Adam and His Work: A Bibliography of Sources by and about Goodman* by Tom Nicely, 1979.

Critical Studies: *The Literary Rebel,* 1965, and *Goodman,* 1980, both by Kingsley Widmer; *Toward an Effective Critique of American Education* by James E. MacLellan, 1968; *The Party of Eros: Radical Socialist Thought and the Realm of Freedom* by Richard King, 1972; *Goodman et le reconquete du present* by Bernard Vincent, 1976; *Artist of the Actual: Essays on Paul Goodman* edited by Peter Parisi, 1986; "An Investigation of Paul Goodman and Black Mountain" by Stephen P. Horowitz, in *American Poetry,* fall 1989; "Paul Goodman, the Living Theater, and the Great Despair" by Taylor Stoehr, in *Theater,* winter-spring 1989-1990; *Decentralizing Power: Paul Goodman's Social Criticism* edited by Taylor Stoehr, 1994; *Here Now Next: Paul Goodman and the Origins of Gestalt Therapy* by Taylor Stoehr, 1994.

*   *   *

Toward the end of his life Paul Goodman became a cult figure among young, disaffected Americans. His writings were in favor of sexual liberation (he was avowedly bisexual) and freedom from planners' control, and they passionately protested against the American involvement in Vietnam—these were all causes that could be and were embraced by a large number of students and their sympathizers. Goodman became suddenly famous, his books went into paperback, he led marches, he received many offers to speak on and off campus, and in a sense he wore himself out trying to make the armies of the night into an efficient fighting force against corporation America.

Cult figures rise and fall. But Goodman is a far more substantial figure than his brief celebrity status might make him appear. Probably comparatively few of those who began buying his books in the 1960s managed to work their way through them. And this is not because the books are poor, or badly written, but because Goodman was a tough-minded thinker, a man of real intellectual distinction, who refused to be caught out in simplistic postures, and who never pandered to popular demands that he should become a generation's guru. In short, Goodman is in no way to be blamed for the odd, upward turn of his reputation during those last hopeful, bewildering, and finally sad years of his life. (The sadness was caused by a series of heart attacks and more grievously by the death of his beloved son, Matty, about which he writes in a series of moving poems in *Homespun of Oatmeal Gray.*)

Perhaps the single work that did most to endear him to the young was *Growing Up Absurd,* which he subtitled "Problems of youth in the organized system." Yet this is not a glib tract for the times: on the contrary, it clearly grew out of Goodman's lifelong dedication to his own particular brand of intellectual anarchism, his deeply held and passionately argued belief that the life of the individual was being more and more threatened by the state. Goodman is really a descendant of John Stuart Mill and **Walt Whitman**: he longs to invite his soul to loaf, but he fears that the time for loafing may well be past. The themes of *Growing Up Absurd* are also presented in fictional form in many of his stories, in *The Empire City,* and, particularly, in *Making Do.*

Behind *Growing Up Absurd* is a quite magnificent study of the American city as it is and as it might be, *Communitas,* written with his brother Percival. Wonderfully well-written, rigorous in method, argument, and detailed application, *Communitas* is a deeply sane and wise book. And the same may be said for most of the essays in *Utopian Essays and Practical Proposals.* Goodman is indeed an extraordinarily good essayist, better, I would say, than Orwell; he is also a minor poet of some distinction (his posthumous *Little Prayers and Finite Experience* is an interesting experiment in intercutting small lyrical prayers-in-verse with longer prose meditations); and also, though not so successfully, a writer of fiction. Reviewing *Growing Up Absurd,* Webster Schott pointed out that Goodman is "a rational Utopian who has most of the analytical apparatus and theoretical formulations of modern sociology, psychology. historiography and aesthetics at his finger tips." This almost terrifying breadth and depth—along with his warm and loving heart—help give Goodman his distinction.

—John Lucas

GORDON, Caroline

Born: Todd County, Kentucky, 6 October 1895. **Education:** Bethany College, West Virginia, A.B. in Greek 1916. **Family:** Married Allen Tate in 1924 (divorced and remarried 1946; separated 1955; divorced 1959); one daughter. **Career:** High school teacher, 1917-19; reporter, Chattanooga *News,* Tennessee, 1920-24; secretary to the writer Ford Madox Ford, New York, 1926-28; lived in Europe, 1928-29 and 1932-33; writer-in-residence,

University of North Carolina Woman's College, Greensboro, 1938-39; lecturer in creative writing, School of General Studies, Columbia University, New York, from 1946; visiting professor of English, University of Washington, Seattle, 1953; writer-in-residence, University of Kansas, Lawrence, 1956, University of California, Davis, 1962-63, and Purdue University, Lafayette, Indiana, 1963; teacher of creative writing, University of Dallas, after 1973. Joined Catholic Church, 1947. **Awards:** Guggenheim fellowship, 1932; O. Henry award, 1934; American Academy grant, 1950; National Endowment for the Arts grant, 1966. D.Litt.: Bethany College, 1946; St. Mary's College, Notre Dame, Indiana, 1964. **Died:** 11 April 1981.

PUBLICATIONS

Collection

Collected Stories. 1981.

Fiction

Penhally. 1931.
Aleck Maury, Sportsman. 1934; as *The Pastimes of Aleck Maury: The Life of a True Sportsman,* 1935.
None Shall Look Back. 1937.
The Garden of Adonis. 1937.
Green Centuries. 1941.
The Women on the Porch. 1944.
The Forest of the South (stories). 1945.
The Strange Children. 1951.
The Malefactors. 1956.
Old Red and Other Stories. 1963.
The Glory of Hera. 1972.

Other

How to Read a Novel. 1957.
A Good Soldier: A Key to the Novels of Ford Madox Ford. 1963.
Exiles and Fugitives: The Letters of Jacques and Raissa Maritain, Allen Tate, and Caroline Gordon, with Jacques and Raissa Maritain and Allen Tate, edited by John M. Dunaway. 1992.

Editor, with Allen Tate, *The House of Fiction: An Anthology of the Short Story.* 1950; revised edition, 1960.

*

Bibliography: *Flannery O'Connor and Gordon: A Reference Guide* by Robert E. Golden and Mary C. Sullivan, 1977.

Critical Studies: *Gordon* by Frederick P.W. McDowell, 1966; *Gordon* by W.J. Stuckey, 1972; *The Short Fiction of Gordon: A Critical Symposium* edited by Thomas H. Landess, 1972; *Gordon as Novelist and Woman of Letters* by Rose Ann C. Fraistat, 1984; *Close Connections: Caroline Gordon and the Southern Renaissance* by Ann Waldron, 1989; *Caroline Gordon: A Biography* by Veronica A. Makowsky, 1989; *The Underground Stream: The Life and Art of Caroline Gordon* by Nancylee Novell Jonza, 1995.

*   *   *

Caroline Gordon is rightly grouped with writers of the so-called Southern Literary Renaissance but is sometimes inappropriately called a regionalist. Most of her novels and short stories are set in her native Kentucky and in other nearby regions of the south, but her fiction strives toward the kind of universality achieved by the writers she most admired: Flaubert, **Henry James**, and James Joyce. She was an artist of the "dramatic" school—that is, she attempted to efface herself as author and allow her fiction to speak for itself. In addition to her nine novels and two short story collections, *The Forest of the South* and *Old Red and Other Stories,* Gordon wrote a critical book, *How to Read a Novel,* in which she set down the theoretical basis for her own fiction. With **Allen Tate** she edited *The House of Fiction,* an anthology of the short story with critical commentary on the craft and teaching of the short story form.

Gordon was a novelist, however, not a critic. Her life-long theme was the quest for heroic paradigms, a search that led her back to pioneer Kentucky (*Green Centuries*), to the pre-Civil War south (*Penhally*), to the war itself (*None Shall Look Back*) and, in modern times, to a southern plantation in the 1930s (*The Garden of Adonis*) ruined by drought and the Depression. Gordon's heroes are men or women who, on principle or out of commitment to a cause, stand up for what they believe to be right. This quest, as her fictions moved toward the twentieth century, necessarily involved her with the widespread modern preference for the anti-hero and its attendant cultural implications, particularly with the view that meaningful action is impossible to an intellectually aware individual. In *The Women on the Porch,* set in New York and Kentucky, she took as her hero a deracinated intellectual-poet and "saved" him from emotional detachment through a final reconciliation with his estranged wife, a resolution that points toward the next stage in Gordon's development. In *The Strange Children,* narrated by a young girl, the hero—also an intellectual—comes to the realization that what is missing from his life is religious faith. *The Malefactors* carries this resolution a step further: the hero, Thomas Claiborne, cures his emotional paralysis by entering the Catholic Church. In *The Glory of Hera,* Gordon returned once more to the past, finding her hero and her heroic paradigm in Hercules; she set forth his story with all the sharpness of detail and dramatic enactment that characterized her earlier work.

The fiction of Gordon has much in common with the major fiction of the modern period, particularly with Hemingway's tightly controlled, dramatic, impersonal symbolic novels and stories, and reflects the same attachment to the natural world and traditional values to be found in southern writers generally and **William Faulkner** in particular. The chief difference, perhaps, between the work of Gordon and that of her contemporaries is in her lack of moral ambiguity. Her fiction is less a discovery of acceptable shades of meaning than a bodying forth in enigmatic form of timeless moral truths.

—W.J. Stuckey

GOTTSCHALK, Laura Riding. *See* **RIDING, Laura.**

GREEN, Paul (Eliot)

Born: Near Lillington, North Carolina, 17 March 1894. **Education:** Buies Creek Academy (now Campbell College), North Carolina, graduated 1914; University of North Carolina, Chapel Hill,

1916-17 and 1919-21, A.B. 1921 (Phi Beta Kappa), graduate study, 1921-22; Cornell University, Ithaca, New York, 1922-23. **Military Service:** Served in the U.S. Army Engineers, 1917-19: lieutenant. **Family:** Married Elizabeth Atkinson Lay in 1922; one son and three daughters. **Career:** School principal, Olive Branch, North Carolina, 1914-17; lecturer, then associate professor of philosophy, 1923-39, professor of dramatic art, 1939-44, and professor of radio, television and motion pictures, 1962-63, University of North Carolina. Editor, *Reviewer* magazine, Chapel Hill, 1925. President, National Folk Festival, 1934-45, National Theatre Conference, 1940-42, and North Carolina State Literary and Historical Association, 1942-43; member, U.S. Executive Committee and National Commission, United Nations Educational, Scientific, and Cultural Organization (UNESCO), 1950-52; Rockefeller Foundation lecturer in Asia, 1951; director, American National Theatre Company, 1959-61; delegate, International Conference on the Performing Arts, Athens, 1962. **Awards:** Pulitzer prize, 1927; Guggenheim fellowship, 1928, 1929; Claire M. Senie Drama Study award, 1937; Freedoms Foundation George Washington Medal, 1951, 1956, 1967; Yale School of Drama award, 1964; Susanne M. Davis award, 1966; National Theatre Conference citation, 1974; American Theatre Association award, 1978. Litt. D.: Western Reserve University, Cleveland, 1941; Davidson College, North Carolina, 1948; University of North Carolina, 1956; Berea College, Kentucky, 1957; University of Louisville, Kentucky, 1957; Campbell College, Buies Creek, North Carolina, 1969; Duke University, Durham, North Carolina, 1980. D.F.A.: North Carolina School of the Arts, Winston-Salem, 1976. L.H.D.: Moravian College, Bethlehem, Pennsylvania, 1976. **Member:** American Academy, 1941. **Died:** 4 May 1981.

PUBLICATIONS

Collection

A Paul Green Reader. 1998.

Plays

Surrender to the Enemy (produced 1917).
Souvenir (produced 1919).
The Last of the Lowries (produced 1920). In *The Lord's Will and Other Carolina Plays*, 1925.
The Long Night, in *Carolina Magazine*, 1920.
Granny Boling, in *Drama*, August-September 1921.
Old Wash Lucas (The Miser) (produced 1921). In *The Lord's Will and Other Carolina Plays*, 1925.
The Old Man of Edenton (produced 1921). In *The Lord's Will and Other Carolina Plays*, 1925.
The Lord's Will (produced 1922). In *The Lord's Will and Other Carolina Plays*, 1925.
Blackbeard, with Elizabeth Lay Green (produced 1922). In *The Lord's Will and Other Carolina Plays*, 1925.
White Dresses (produced 1923). In *Lonesome Road*, 1926.
Wrack P'int (produced 1923).
Sam Tucker, in *Poet Lore*, summer 1923; revised version, as *Your Fiery Furnace*, in *Lonesome Road*, 1926.
Fixin's, with Erma Green (produced 1924). 1934.
The No 'Count Boy (produced 1925). In *The Lord's Will and Other Carolina Plays*. 1925; revised (white) version, 1953.
In Aunt Mahaly's Cabin: A Negro Melodrama (produced, 1925). 1925.

The Lord's Will and Other Carolina Plays (includes *Blackbeard, Old Wash Lucas (The Miser), The No 'Count Boy, The Old Man of Edenton, The Last of the Lowries*). 1925.
Quare Medicine (produced 1925). In *In the Valley and Other Carolina Plays*, 1928.
The Man Who Died at Twelve O'Clock (produced 1925). 1927.
In Abraham's Bosom (produced 1926). In *The Field God, and In Abraham's Bosom*, 1927.
Lonesome Road: Six Plays for the Negro Theatre (includes *In Abraham's Bosom*, one-act version; *White Dresses*; *The Hot Iron*; *The Prayer Meeting*; *The End of the Row*; *Your Fiery Furnace*). 1926.
The Hot Iron, in *Lonesome Road*, 1926; revised version as *Lay This Body Down* (produced 1972), in *Wings for to Fly*, 1959.
The Field God (produced 1927). In *The Field God, and In Abraham's Bosom*, 1927.
The Field God, and In Abraham's Bosom. 1927.
Bread and Butter Come to Supper. 1928; as *Chair Endowed* (produced in *Salvation on a String*, 1954).
In the Valley and Other Carolina Plays (includes *Quare Medicine, Supper for the Dead, Saturday Night, The Man Who Died at Twelve O'Clock, In Aunt Mahaly's Cabin, The No 'Count Boy, The Man on the House, The Picnic, Unto Such Glory, The Goodbye*). 1928.
Supper for the Dead (produced in *Salvation on a String*, 1954). Included in *In the Valley and Other Carolina Plays*, 1928.
Unto Such Glory (produced 1936). In *In the Valley and Other Carolina Plays*, 1928.
The Goodbye (produced 1954). In *In the Valley and Other Carolina Plays*, 1928.
Blue Thunder; or, *The Man Who Married a Snake*, in *One Act Plays for Stage and Study*. 1928.
Old Christmas, in *Wide Fields*. 1928.
The House of Connelly (produced 1931). In *The House of Connelly and Other Plays*, 1931; revised version (produced 1959), in *Five Plays of the South*, 1963.
The House of Connelly and Other Plays (includes *Potter's Field* and *Tread the Green Grass*). 1931.
Potter's Field (produced 1934). In *The House of Connelly and Other Plays*, 1931; revised version, as *Roll Sweet Chariot: A Symphonic Play of the Negro People*, music by Dolphe Martin (produced 1934), 1935.
Tread the Green Grass, music by Lamar Stringfield (produced 1932). In *The House of Connelly and Other Plays*, 1931.
Shroud My Body Down (produced 1934), 1935; revised version, as *The Honeycomb*, 1972.
The Enchanted Maze: The Story of a Modern Student in Dramatic Form (produced 1935). 1939.
Hymn to the Rising Sun (produced 1936). 1939.
Johnny Johnson: The Biography of a Common Man, music by Kurt Weill (produced 1936). 1937; revised version, 1972.
The Southern Cross (produced 1936). 1938.
The Lost Colony (produced 1937). 1937; revised version, 1939, 1946, 1954, 1980.
Alma Mater, in *The Best One-Act Plays of 1938*, edited by Margaret Mayorga. 1938.
Out of the South: The Life of a People in Dramatic Form (includes *The House of Connelly*; *The Field God*; *In Abraham's Bosom*; *Potter's Field*; *Johnny Johnson*; *The Lost Colony*; *The No 'Count Boy*; *Saturday Night*; *Quare Medicine*; *The Hot Iron*; *Unto Such Glory*; *Supper for the Dead*; *The Man Who Died at Twelve O'Clock*; *White Dresses*; *Hymn to the Rising Sun*). 1939.

The Critical Year: A One-Act Sketch of American History and the Beginning of the Constitution. 1939.
Franklin and the King. 1939.
The Highland Call: A Symphonic Play of American History (produced 1939). 1941; revised version, 1975.
Native Son (The Biography of a Young American), with Richard Wright, from the novel by Wright (produced 1941). 1941; revised version, 1980.
A Start in Life (broadcast 1941). In *The Free Company Presents,* edited by James Boyd, 1941; as *Fine Wagon,* in *Wings for to Fly,* 1959.
The Common Glory: A Symphonic Drama of American History (produced 1947). 1948; revised version, 1975.
Faith of Our Fathers (produced 1950).
Peer Gynt, from the play by Ibsen (produced 1951). 1951.
The Seventeenth Star (produced 1953).
Serenata, with Josefina Niggli (produced 1953).
Carmen, from the libretto by H. Meilhac and L. Halevy, music by Bizet (produced 1954).
This Declaration. 1954.
Salvation on a String (includes *Chair Endowed, The No 'Count Boy, Supper for the Dead*) (produced 1954).
Wilderness Road: A Symphonic Outdoor Drama (produced 1955; revised version, produced 1972). 1956.
The Founders: A Symphonic Outdoor Drama (produced 1957). 1957.
The Confederacy: A Symphonic Outdoor Drama Based on the Life of General Robert E. Lee (produced 1958). 1959.
The Stephen Foster Story: A Symphonic Drama Based on the Life and Music of the Composer (produced 1959). 1960.
Wings for to Fly: Three Plays of Negro Life, Mostly for the Ear but Also for the Eye (includes *The Thirsting Heart, Lay This Body Down, Fine Wagon*). 1959.
The Thirsting Heart (produced 1971). In *Wings for to Fly,* 1959.
Five Plays of the South (includes revised versions of *The House of Connelly, In Abraham's Bosom, Johnny Johnson, Hymn to the Rising Sun, White Dresses*). 1963.
Cross and Sword: A Symphonic Drama of the Spanish Settlement of Florida (produced 1965). 1966.
The Sheltering Plaid. 1965.
Texas: A Symphonic Outdoor Drama of American Life (produced 1966). 1967.
Sing All a Green Willow (produced 1969).
Trumpet in the Land (produced 1970). 1972.
Drumbeats in Georgia: A Symphonic Drama of the Founding of Georgia by James Edward Oglethorpe (produced 1973).
Louisiana Cavalier: A Symphonic Drama of the 18th Century French and Spanish Struggle for the Settling of Louisiana (produced 1976).
We the People: A Symphonic Drama of George Washington and the Establishment of the United States Government (produced 1976).
The Lone Star: A Symphonic Drama of Sam Houston and the Winning of Texas Independence from Mexico (produced 1977).
Palo Duro: A Sound and Light Drama (produced 1979).

Screenplays: *Cabin in the Cotton,* 1932; *State Fair,* with Sonya Levien, 1933; *Dr. Bull,* 1933; *Voltaire,* with Maude T. Howell, 1933; *The Rosary,* 1933; *Carolina,* 1934; *David Harum,* 1934; *Time Out of Mind,* 1947; *Roseanna McCoy,* 1949; *Red Shoes Run Faster,* 1949.

Radio Play: *A Start in Life,* 1941.

Fiction

Wide Fields (stories). 1928.
The Laughing Pioneer: A Sketch of Country Life. 1932.
This Body the Earth. 1935.
Salvation on a String and Other Tales of the South. 1946.
Dog on the Sun: A Volume of Stories. 1949.
Words and Ways: Stories and Incidents from My Cape Fear Valley Folklore Collection. 1968.
Home to My Valley (stories). 1970.
Land of Nod and Other Stories: A Volume of Black Stories. 1976.

Poetry

Trifles of Thought. 1917.
The Lost Colony Song-Book. 1938.
The Highland Call Song-Book. 1941.
Song in the Wilderness, music by Charles Vardell. 1947.
The Common Glory Song-Book. 1951.
Texas Song-Book. 1967.
Texas Forever. 1967.

Other

Contemporary American Literature: A Study of Fourteen Outstanding American Writers, with Elizabeth Lay Green. 1925; revised edition, 1927.
The Hawthorn Tree: Some Papers and Letters on Life and the Theatre. 1943.
Forever Growing: Some Notes on a Credo for Teachers. 1945.
Dramatic Heritage (essays). 1953.
Challenge to Citizenship (address). 1956.
Drama and the Weather: Some Notes and Papers on Life and the Theatre. 1958.
The University in a Nuclear Age (address). 1963.
Plough and Furrow: Some Essays and Papers on Life and the Theatre. 1963.
A Southern Life: Letters of Paul Green, 1916-1981. 1994.

*

Critical Studies: *Green* by Barrett H. Clark, 1928; *Green of Chapel Hill* by Agatha Boyd Adams, 1951; *Green* by Walter S. Lazenby, 1970; *Green* by Vincent S. Kenny, 1971; *The Green I Know* by Elizabeth Lay Green, 1978; "*White Dresses, Sweet Chariots, In Abraham's Bosom, The No 'Count Boy* and *A Hymn*: Paul Green's Vehicles for the Black Actor" by Glenda E. Gill, in *Southern Literary Journal,* spring 1990; "On Meeting Paul Green" by Ed Devany, in *North Carolina Literary Review,* spring 1994, p. 53; *Paul Green's Celebration of Man, with a Bibliography* edited by Sue Laslie Kimball and Lynn Veach Sadler, 1994.

*   *   *

Paul Green's career as a playwright can be divided conveniently into four overlapping periods. In the first he used the history, dialect, superstitions, customs, and beliefs of both white and black inhabitants of his native region in eastern North Carolina and began by writing short realistic folkplays, comedies, and tragedies.

Noticeable from the outset was a compassion for society's expendibles, those cast-offs who, though victims of social injustice, held within them the dreams and hopes common to all mankind. The full-length *In Abraham's Bosom,* its protagonist a luckless black schoolteacher, was an extended treatment of a one-act play. It was followed on Broadway by *The Field God,* dealing with the oppressive religious orthodoxy among back-country whites.

Tread the Green Grass, a deliberate experiment, turned from realism toward a mythic non-realistic folk drama, but retained the kind of rustic characters who were now his special province. Green's stylized blend of pantomime, dance, ritual, dream sequences, puppetlike movements, fantasy and legend, with music an integral part of the play as with the Greeks, expanded, he believed, the accepted concepts of time and space on the stage. For those of his plays synthesizing the theatrical arts—plays like *Roll Sweet Chariot* (earlier title, *Potter's Field*), *Shroud My Body Down,* and *Sing All a Green Willow*—Green coined the term "symphonic drama," intending apparently to devise an American *Gesamtkunstwerk.*

Meanwhile he did not abandon the commercial theater. *The House of Connelly,* a dramatization of the fluctuating conditions among aristocrats and "poor whites" in the post-Civil War south, conformed to Broadway standards of what a well-made play should be. The anti-war musical *Johnny Johnson* was a collaborative effort with Kurt Weill, and *Native Son* an adaptation of **Richard Wright**'s tragic story of a black misfit in Chicago. For the New York stage he provided an English version of *Peer Gynt,* and for an opera theater in Colorado, a translation of *Carmen.*

The fourth phase began in 1937 with *The Lost Colony,* an "outdoor symphonic drama" produced on the very spot where Sir Walter Raleigh's colonists landed in 1587. Applying the elements of his experimental plays, and superimposing upon an event in history a tightly drawn plot, Green was finally permitted, on the huge open-air stage, the freedom of sweeping folk dances, large choruses, and broad movements of men, women, and children. The throngs of unsophisticated ticket-buyers who attended *The Lost Colony* inspired him to establish away from Broadway a "theater of the people." In 1947 came *The Common Glory* for Virginia, then *Faith of Our Fathers* (Washington, D.C.), and other plays like *Wilderness Road* (Kentucky), *Cross and Sword* (Florida), *Texas,* and *Trumpet in the Land* (Ohio). Green and his followers used his "formula" for more than sixty similar works, spread out from the Atlantic coastline to California and Alaska. Never satisfied with his last versions, Green constantly revised the annual summertime repetitions of his outdoor plays.

—Richard Walser

GREGORY, Horace (Victor)

Born: Milwaukee, Wisconsin, 10 April 1898. **Education:** The Milwaukee School of Fine Arts, summers 1913-16; German-English Academy, Milwaukee, 1914-19; University of Wisconsin, Madison, 1919-23, B.A. 1923. **Family:** Married the poet Marya Zaturenska in 1925 (died 1982); one daughter and one son. **Career:** Free-lance writer, New York, 1923-33; member of the English department, 1934-60, and professor emeritus, 1960-82, Sarah Lawrence College, Bronxville, New York. Lecturer, New School

for Social Research, New York, 1955-56. Associate editor, *Tiger's Eye* magazine, New York. **Awards:** Russell Loines award, 1942; Guggenheim fellowship, 1951; Academy of American Poets fellowship, 1961; Bollingen prize, 1965; Horace Gregory Foundation award, 1969. D.Litt.: University of Wisconsin, Milwaukee, 1977. **Member:** American Academy, 1964. **Died:** 11 March 1982.

PUBLICATIONS

Poetry

Chelsea Rooming House. 1930; as *Rooming House,* 1932.
No Retreat. 1933.
A Wreath for Margery. 1933.
Chorus for Survival. 1935.
Poems 1930-1940. 1941.
Selected Poems. 1951.
Medusa in Gramercy Park. 1961.
Alphabet for Joanna (for children). 1963.
Collected Poems. 1964.
Another Look. 1976.

Other

Pilgrim of the Apocalypse: A Critical Study of D. H. Lawrence. 1933; revised edition, 1957.
The Shield of Achilles: Essays on Beliefs in Poetry. 1944.
A History of American Poetry 1900-1940, with Marya Zaturenska. 1946.
Poet of the People: An Evaluation of James Whitcomb Riley, with James T. Farrell and Jeannette Covert Nolan. 1951.
Amy Lowell: Portrait of the Poet in Her Time. 1958.
The World of James McNeill Whistler. 1959.
The Dying Gladiators and Other Essays. 1961.
Dorothy Richardson: An Adventure in Self-Discovery. 1967.
The House on Jefferson Street: A Cycle of Memories. 1971.
Spirit of Time and Place: Collected Essays. 1973.

Editor, with Eleanor Clark, *New Letters in America.* 1937.
Editor, *Critical Remarks on the Metaphysical Poets,* by Samuel Johnson. 1943.
Editor, *The Triumph of Life: Poems of Consolation for the English-Speaking World.* 1943.
Editor, *The Portable Sherwood Anderson.* 1949; revised edition, 1972.
Editor, *The Snake Lady and Other Stories,* by Vernon Lee. 1954.
Editor, *Selected Poetry,* by Robert Browning. 1956.
Editor, with Marya Zaturenska, *The Mentor Book of Religious Verse.* 1957.
Editor, with Marya Zaturenska, *The Crystal Cabinet: An Invitation to Poetry.* 1962.
Editor, with others, *Riverside Poetry 4: An Anthology of Student Verse.* 1962.
Editor, *Evangeline and Selected Tales and Poems of Longfellow.* 1964.
Editor, *Selected Poems,* by e. e. cummings. 1965.
Editor, with Marya Zaturenska, *The Silver Swan: Poems of Romance and Mystery.* 1966.
Editor, *Selected Poems of Lord Byron.* 1969.

Translator, *The Poems of Catullus.* 1931.
Translator, *Poems,* by Catullus. 1956.
Translator, *The Metamorphoses,* by Ovid. 1958.
Translator, *Love Poems of Ovid.* 1964.

*

Critical Studies: "Gregory Issue" of *Modern Poetry Studies,* May 1973; "Visiting the Gregorys" by Robert Phillips, in *The New Criterion,* September 1990.

*   *   *

Horace Gregory was perhaps best known as the translator of Catullus and Ovid. But he was a poet in his own right and also wrote studies of **Amy Lowell,** D.H. Lawrence, James McNeill Whistler, and others. Collaborating with his wife, the poet Marya Zaturenska, he produced the study *A History of American Poetry 1900-1940.*

In regard to his poetry, Elizabeth Drew wrote that Gregory's "emotional range is perhaps the most comprehensive among modern poets," and Louis Untermeyer wrote that Gregory "does not share Eliot's disillusions or Crane's disorganization," a statement that is unfair to all three poets. However, poems like "Valediction to My Contemporaries" compare interestingly with Hart Crane's *The Bridge* in language, idealism, and purposes; and many of Gregory's efforts to recapture in monologues the pathos and cacophony of life in the modern city remind one of Eliot. In the final analysis, however, authenticity and integrity may not be enough; subtleties of syntax, powers of condensation, and originality of imagery distinguish Eliot and Crane from those, such as Gregory, who wrote with comparable verve.

Gregory is academic, ordered, descriptive, even-paced; he might be quite properly compared with MacLeish for his intellectual ambition, rhetorical power, and sense of American history. Most of his poems are based on classical subjects in one way or another, though he often juxtaposes classical imagery with modernistic impressions; he also has many poems about paintings, European scenes, and—like MacLeish—his country's cultural history. His well-known poem on Emerson recapitulates Emerson's life in an investigation of the intellectual's role ("To know too well, to think too long") in a land where action and immortality are even more akin than rhetoric and relevance. Gregory, like MacLeish, bears a heavy weight of idealism at all times, perhaps more than his country's history can support. Because the idealism is more muted in his Chelsea rooming house poems, they are perhaps more appealing than his verse that had more epic ambitions. In poems like "McAlpin Garfinkel, Poet" and "Time and Isidore Lefkowitz," Gregory seems to have absorbed the influence of **Edwin Arlington Robinson** and to have looked forward to the work of poets like **Kenneth Fearing:**

Look at Isidore Lefkowitz,
biting his nails, telling how
he seduces Beautiful French Canadian
Five and Ten Cent Store Girls,
beautiful, by God, and how they cry
and moan, wrapping their arms
and legs around him
when he leaves them . . . .

In an age when we have come to think of poems as the swiftly captured sound of madness, Gregory's work stands as a celebration of order, with the glimpsed backstreet life crying out to have a part of that order and the consideration due to it.

How can I unlearn
the arts of love within a single hour:
How can I close my eyes before a mirror,
believe I am not wanted, that hands, lips, breast
are merely deeper shadows behind the door
where all is dark?

—David Ray

GREGORY, J. Dennis. *See* **WILLIAMS, John A(lfred).**

GREY, Zane

Born: Pearl Zane Gray in Zanesville, Ohio, 31 January 1872. **Education:** Moore High School, Zanesville; University of Pennsylvania, Philadelphia, D.D.S. 1896. **Family:** Married Lina Elise Roth in 1905; two sons and one daughter. **Career:** Dentist in New York, 1896-1904; thereafter a full-time writer; traveled in the western United States, 1907-18; settled in California, 1918. **Died:** 23 October 1939.

PUBLICATIONS

Fiction

Betty Zane. 1903.
The Spirit of the Border. 1906.
The Last of the Plainsmen. 1908.
The Lost Trail. 1909.
The Heritage of the Desert. 1910.
Riders of the Purple Sage. 1912.
Desert Gold. 1913.
The Light of Western Stars. 1914.
The Rustlers of Pecos County. 1914.
The Lone Star Ranger. 1915.
The Rainbow Trail. 1915.
The Border Legion. 1916.
Wildfire. 1917.
The U.P. Trail. 1918; as *The Roaring U.P. Trail,* 1918.
The Desert of Wheat. 1919.
The Man of the Forest. 1920.
The Mysterious Rider. 1921.
To the Lost Man. 1922.
The Day of the Beast. 1922.
Wanderer of the Wasteland. 1923.
The Call of the Canyon. 1924.
Roping Lions in the Grand Canyon. 1924.
The Thundering Herd. 1925.
The Vanishing American. 1925; as *The Vanishing Indian,* 1926.
Under the Tonto Rim. 1926.
Forlorn River. 1927.
Nevada. 1928.

Wild Horse Mesa. 1928.
Fighting Caravans. 1929.
The Shepherd of Guadaloupe. 1930.
Sunset Pass. 1931.
Arizona Ames. 1932.
Robbers' Roost. 1932; abridged edition, as *Thieves' Canyon,* 1965.
The Drift Fence. 1933.
The Hash Knife Oust. 1933.
Code of the West. 1934.
Thunder Mountain. 1935.
The Trail Driver. 1936.
The Lost Wagon Train. 1936.
West of the Pecos. 1937.
Tex Thorne Comes Out of the West. 1937.
Majesty's Rancho. 1938.
Raiders of the Spanish Peaks. 1938.
Western Union. 1939.
Knights of the Range. 1939.
30,000 on the Hoof. 1940.
Twin Sombreros. 1941.
Stairs of Sand. 1943.
Wilderness Trek. 1944.
Shadow of the Trail. 1946.
Valley of Wild Horses. 1947.
Rogue River Feud. 1948.
The Deer Stalker. 1949.
The Maverick Queen. 1950.
The Dude Ranger. 1951.
Captives of the Desert. 1952.
Wyoming. 1953.
Lost Pueblo. 1954.
Black Mesa. 1955.
Stranger from the Tonto. 1956.
The Fugitive Trail. 1957.
The Arizona Clan. 1958.
Horse Heaven Hill. 1959.
Boulder Dam. 1963.
Grey, Outdoorsman: Best Hunting and Fishing Tales, edited by George Reiger. 1972.
Greatest Western [Indian, Animal] Stories, edited by Loren Grey. 3 vols., 1975.
The Big Land, edited by Loren Grey. 1976.
Yaqui and Other Great Indian Stories, edited by Loren Grey. 1976.
Shark! Tales of Man-Eating Sharks, edited by Loren Grey. 1976.
The Reef Girl, edited by Loren Grey. 1977.
The Buffalo Hunter, edited by Loren Grey. 1977.
The Westerner, edited by Loren Grey. 1977.
Savage Kingdom. 1979.
The Undiscovered Fishing Stories, edited by George Reiger. 1983.

Plays

Screenplays: *The Vanishing Pioneer,* with others, 1928; *Rangle River,* with Charles and Elsa Chauvel, 1936.

Other (for children)

The Short-Stop. 1909.
The Young Forester. 1910.
The Young Pitcher. 1911.

The Young Lion Hunter. 1911.
Ken Ward in the Jungle. 1912.
The Red-Headed Outfield and Other Baseball Stories. 1920.
Tappan's Burro and Other Stories. 1923.
Don: The Story of a Lion Dog. 1928.
The Wolf Tracker. 1930.
Book of Camps and Trails. 1931.
King of the Royal Mounted [and the Northern Treasure, in the Far North, Gets His Man, Policing the Far North, and the Great Jewel Mystery, and the Ghost Guns of Roaring River]. 7 vols., 1936-46.
The Ranger and Other Stories. 1960.
Blue Feather and Other Stories. 1961.

Other

Nassau, Cuba, Yucatan, Mexico: A Personal Note of Appreciation of These Nearby Foreign Lands. 1909.
Tales of Fishes [Lonely Trails, Southern Rivers, Fishing Virgin Seas, The Angler's Eldorado—New Zealand, Swordfish and Tuna, Fresh-Water Fishing, Tahitian Waters]. 8 vols., 1919-31; augmented edition of *Tales of the Angler's El Dorado,* as *Angler's El Dorado: Grey in New Zealand,* 1982.
An American Angler in Australia. 1936.
Adventures in Fishing, edited by Ed Zern. 1952.
Tales from a Fisherman's Log. 1978.
Grey: A Photographic Odyssey (Zane Grey's photographs), text by Loren Grey. 1985.

*

Bibliography: *Grey, Born to the West: A Reference Guide* by Kenneth W. Scott, 1979; *Grey, A Documented Portrait: The Man, the Bibliography, the Filmography* by G.M. Farley, 1985.

Critical Studies: *Grey: A Biography* by Frank Gruber, 1970; *Grey* by Carlton Jackson, 1973; *Grey* by Ann Ronald, 1975; *Grey, Story Teller* by Carol Gay, 1979; *Grey's Arizona* by Candace C. Kant, 1984; "Zane Grey's Western Eroticism" by William Bloodworth, in *South Dakota Review,* autumn 1985; "Silent Walls: 'Nature' in Grey's *The Vanishing American*" by Arthur Kimball, in *South Dakota Review,* spring 1988; "Zane Grey and the American, Hypervisual Tradition" by William E.H. Meyer, Jr., in *Journal of American Culture,* winter 1989; *Zane Grey and the Images of the American West* by Kevin S. Blake, 1995; *Zane Grey: Romancing the West* by Stephen May, 1997.

*   *   *

Zane Grey's literary career typifies the American **Horatio Alger** success story, and Grey helped to perpetuate the Alger myth, using striking settings in the American West. At the beginning of his career Grey struggled for several years in New York City and near Lackawaxen, Pennsylvania, writing essays on fishing and a trilogy based on the Zane family history in the settlement of the Ohio Valley. But he received little encouragement, save from his wife, and gathered rejection slips until he found his subject in the American West as a result of a visit to Arizona at the request of C.J. "Buffalo" Jones, a business entrepreneur.

Grey's own taste in literature was for the romantic, and he realized that the West was still close enough to frontier conditions for him to use it as a splendid testing ground of a man's worth. **Owen Wister** had discovered the cowboy as romantic hero with *The Virginian* (1902), and Grey was quick to capitalize on Wister's discovery. He paid his debt to Wister by using the subtitle of Wister's famous novel as the title for his first book about the West, *The Last of the Plainsmen.*

That book was largely a narrative of travel and was followed by his first proper novel of the West, *The Heritage of the Desert.* The success in sales was moderate, but in the story of the rise to manhood of an eastern misfit, John Hare, Grey had found those elements of adventure, suspense, and history that were to make him the most popular writer of his time. *Riders of the Purple Sage,* his next Western, was to insure that Grey's struggles to establish himself as a writer were at an end. From then on he easily outdistanced other American writers in sales and popular, although not critical, appreciation.

Grey was bothered by the reaction of critics to his work. There is, however, much of the formula in his work. He is often melodramatic and sentimental, and his style is stilted or awkward. But his fiction has emphasized the importance of the West to the American psyche, and embodied values in American life that those given critical acclaim frequently scoffed at or ignored. Grey was concerned about changing mores in American society. His *The Call of the Canyon,* for example, is contemporary in its concern for the plight of the returned soldier and in its objection to the "new woman." Grey's views, obviously, reflected a large segment of popular opinion in the 1920s, when he was frequently at or near the top of the best-seller lists.

Although Grey also wrote many books for boys and books about the outdoors, he will continue to be known for his Western fiction. His energies were so great that new Grey titles were published for years after his death. His work is perennially popular.

—Joseph M. Flora

GUARE, John (Edward)

Born: New York City, 5 February 1938. **Education:** Joan of Arc Elementary School, and St. John's Preparatory School, New York; Georgetown University, Washington, D.C., 1956-60, A.B. 1960; Yale University School of Drama, 1960-63, M.F.A. 1963. **Military Service:** Served in the U.S. Air Force Reserve, 1963. **Family:** Married Adele Chatfield-Taylor in 1981. **Career:** Assistant to the manager, National Theatre, Washington, D.C., 1960; member, Barr/Wilder/Albee Playwrights Unit, New York, 1964; founding member, Eugene O'Neill Playwrights Conference, Waterford, Connecticut, 1965; playwright-in-residence, New York Shakespeare Festival, 1976-77; adjunct professor of playwriting, Yale University, 1978. Visiting artist, Harvard University, 1990-91; fellow, Julliard School, 1993-94; lecturer, New York University and City College of New York. Council member, Dramatists Guild, 1971; vice-president, Theatre Communications Group, 1986. **Awards:** ABC-Yale University fellowship, 1966; Obie award, 1968, 1971; *Variety* award, 1969; Cannes Film Festival award, for screenplay, 1971; New York Drama Critics Circle award, 1971, 1972; Tony award, 1972, 1986; Joseph Jefferson award, 1977; Venice Film Festival Golden Lion, National Society of Film Critics award, New York Film Critics Circle award, and Los Angeles Film Critics award,

all for screenplay, 1980; American Academy Award of Merit Medal, 1981; named Literary Lion, New York Public Library, 1986; New York Institute for the Humanities fellowship, 1987. **Residence:** New York City.

PUBLICATIONS

Plays

Theatre Girl (produced 1959).
The Toadstool Boy (produced 1960).
The Golden Cherub (produced 1962(?)).
Did You Write My Name in the Snow? (produced 1963).
To Wally Pantoni, We Leave a Credenza (produced 1965).
The Loveliest Afternoon of the Year, and Something I'll Tell You Tuesday (produced 1966; *The Loveliest Afternoon of the Year* produced 1972). 1968.
Muzeeka (produced 1967). Included in *Off-Broadway Plays*, 1970; in *Cop-Out, Muzeeka, Home Fires*, 1971.
Cop-Out (produced 1968). Included in *Off-Broadway Plays*, 1970; in *Cop-Out, Muzeeka, Home Fires*, 1971.
Home Fires (produced 1969). Included in *Cop-Out, Muzeeka, Home Fires*, 1971.
Kissing Sweet (televised 1969). With *A Day for Surprises*, 1971.
A Day for Surprises (produced 1970). With *Kissing Sweet*, 1971.
The House of Blue Leaves (produced 1971). 1972.
Two Gentlemen of Verona, with Mel Shapiro, music by Galt MacDermot, lyrics by Guare, adaptation of the play by Shakespeare (produced 1971).1973.
Cop-Out, Muzeeka, Home Fires. 1971.
Taking Off (screenplay), with others. 1971.
Optimism; or, The Misadventures of Candide, with Harold Stone, based on a novel by Voltaire (produced 1973).
Rich and Famous (produced 1974). 1977.
Marco Polo Sings a Solo (produced 1976; revised version produced 1977). 1977.
Landscape of the Body (produced 1977). 1978.
Take a Dream (produced 1978).
Bosoms and Neglect (produced 1979). 1980.
In Fireworks Lie Secret Codes (produced in *Holidays*, 1979; also director: produced separately, 1981). 1981.
Nantucket series:
  Lydie Breeze (produced 1982). 1982.
  Gardenia (produced 1982). 1982.
  Women and Water (produced 1984; revised version produced 1985). 1990.
Three Exposures (includes *The House of Blue Leaves, Landscape of the Body, Bosoms and Neglect*). 1982.
Hey, Stay a While, music by Galt MacDermot, lyrics by Guare (produced 1984).
Gluttony, in *Faustus in Hell* (produced 1985).
The Talking Dog, adaptation of a story by Chekhov, in *Orchards* (produced 1985). 1986.
The House of Blue Leaves and Two Other Plays (includes *Landscape of the Body* and *Bosoms and Neglect*). 1987.
Moon over Miami (produced 1989).
Six Degrees of Separation (produced 1990). 1990.
Four Baboons Adoring the Sun (produced 1992). Published in *Antaeus*, 1992.
The War against the Kitchen Sink. 1996.

Screenplays: *Taking Off*, with others, 1971; *Atlantic City*, 1980.

Television Play: *Kissing Sweet* (*Foul!* series), 1969.

Film Adaptation: *Six Degrees of Separation*.

*

Manuscript Collection: Beinecke Library, Yale University, New Haven, Connecticut.

Critical Studies: article and checklist by John Harrop, in *New Theatre Quarterly 10*, May 1987; "John Guare" by John DiGaetani, in *A Search for a Postmodern Theater: Interviews with Contemporary Playwrights* edited by John DiGaetani, 1991; "Fierce Love and Fierce Response: Intervening in the Cultural Politics of Race, Sexuality, and AIDS" by David Roman, in *Critical Essays: Gay and Lesbian Writers of Color* edited by Emmanuel S. Nelson, 1993; "Life Is a Silken Net: Mourning the Beloved Monstrous in Lydie Breeze" by Robert F. Gross, in *Journal of Dramatic Theory and Criticism*, Fall 1994, pp. 21-43.

Theatrical Activities:
Director: **Play**—*In Fireworks Lie Secret Codes*, 1981.

*   *   *

John Guare's work is marked by an unsparing theatricality that is blended with a deeply personal narrative style. Guare has often voiced his distrust and aversion to naturalism and realism. In Guare's words, "Naturalism kills; it's deadly to the theater." Indeed, a collection of John Guare's theatrical works is entitled *The War against the Kitchen Sink*.

According to Guare, "reality doesn't always supply us with the payoff. Reality just gives us the agony." Guare's work, like that of Samuel Beckett, whose drama he champions, explores the agony of existence. But even if Guare's work is not truly realistic, unlike that of Beckett, it is contained within the storm cloud of everyday life. Guare's drama, his settings, and his characters are all structured from a realistic base from which leaps are made into a fantasy world of improbability and exhilaration. This ability to vault into a world of near magical realism was perhaps acquired from those playwrights of Guare's youth by whom he was inspired: **Eugene O'Neill, Sidney Kingsley,** and especially **Thornton Wilder.** The link to Wilder is most clearly seen in *Marco Polo Sings a Solo* (1973), Guare's excursion into absurdist theater, incorporating such settings as icebergs and outer space.

But unlike O'Neill, **Arthur Miller, Tennessee Williams,** and other such totemic modern American playwrights, Guare's stage is never completely populated with lost souls. Instead, there seems to be an air of cautious optimism that infuses Guare's theatrical world. Guare says that "In every one of my plays there is that feeling of, 'If I could only show you who I really am, you would love me totally.'" In Guare's drama there always seems to be a sense of joy at the almost comical indomitability of the human condition, and awestruck wonder at the lengths to which humanity will go to relieve the emptiness, loneliness, and horror of twentieth-century life.

Guare maintains that in his fourth decade of play writing he is still perplexed by those same questions of existence that haunted

him as a young writer: "What's real and what isn't? How do we tell what's real in our lives? How do we see things as they really are? What is my role in life?" It is Guare's search for the answers to these questions that creates the autobiographical basis for his drama as he continues to examine and chronicle mankind's dogged determination to matter in this universe. Continually, Guare's theater work is a consideration of "what time does and what time doesn't change—the demons we never outgrow." This is a particularly apt recapitulation of *Bosoms and Neglect* (1979), Guare's broadly humorous psychoanalytic satire distilled through an enigmatic mother-son relationship.

Noted for his skillful use of language, Guare considers language to be both the writer's "formal mask" and his "weapon." Guare believes it is the playwright's obligation "to write about that which you don't want to write about. Whatever it is that wakes you up at four o'clock in the morning, that's what you have to write about. You have to write about the nightmares."

Guare's two most successful works, *The House of Blue Leaves* (1970) and *Six Degrees of Separation* (1990), conveniently bookend his play writing career. This does not diminish the quality of the rest of Guare's oeuvre, but emphasizes the impact that these two works have had upon contemporary American theater. *The House of Blue Leaves* features the household of Artie Shaughnessy, a largely unsuccessful songwriter, and his touching and fragile wife Bananas as they prepare to celebrate the Pope's 1965 visit to New York City. *Six Degrees of Separation* is a comedy with tragic implications, involving a wealthy art dealer caught in a scam perpetrated by a young African American man claiming to be the son of actor Sidney Poitier. Yet, despite the two plays' disparate characters, Guare acknowledges the connections they have to one another: "What is *Six Degrees of Separation* but *The House of Blue Leaves* with money?" Each of these plays, like the entire body of Guare's work, seems to revel in the obsessive drive of humans to both engage in and disengage from civilization. Throughout his work, Guare has remained focused upon this paradoxical attempt to simultaneously escape and make sense of the sordid decay of daily life.

—Arthur Horowitz

GUINEY, Louise Imogen

Born: Roxbury, Boston, Massachusetts, 7 January 1861. **Education:** Convent of the Sacred Heart, Elmhurst, Rhode Island. **Career:** Worked for a time as a journalist; postmistress, Auburndale, Massachusetts; worked in the cataloging department, Boston Public Library; editor, with Alice Brown, *Pilgrim Scrip*; moved to England, 1895. **Died:** 2 November 1920.

PUBLICATIONS

Poetry

Songs at the Start. 1884.
The White Sail and Other Poems. 1887.
A Roadside Harp. 1893.
Nine Sonnets Written at Oxford. 1895.
England and Yesterday: A Book of Short Poems. 1898.

The Martyrs' Idyl and Shorter Poems. 1899.
Happy Ending: Collected Lyrics. 1909; revised edition, 1927.

Fiction

Lovers', Saint Ruth's, and Three Other Tales. 1895.

Other

Goose-Quill Papers. 1885.
Brownies and Bogles (for children). 1888.
Monsieur Henri: A Foot-Note to French History. 1892.
A Little English Gallery. 1894.
Three Heroines in New England Romance: Their True Stories, with
 Harriet Prescott Spoffard and Alice Brown. 1894.
*Patrins, To Which Is Added an Inquirendo into the Wit and Other
 Good Parts of His Late Majesty King Charles the Second.* 1897.
Robert Emmet: A Survey of His Rebellion and of His Romance.
 1904.
Blessed Edmund Campion. 1908.
Letters, edited by Grace Guiney. 2 vols., 1926.
*Colonel Guiney and the Ninth Massachusetts: A Filial Apprecia-
 tion.* 1932.

Editor, *James Clarence Mangan: His Selected Poems.* 1897.
Editor, *Sohrab and Rustum and Other Poems,* by Matthew Arnold.
 1899.
Editor, *The Mount of Olives and Primitive Holiness,* by Henry
 Vaughan. 1902.
Editor, *Selected Poems,* by Katherine Philips. 2 vols., 1904-05.
Editor, *Hurrell Froude: Memoranda and Comments.* 1904.
Editor, *Thomas Stanley: His Original Lyrics, Complete.* 1907.
Editor, *Some Poems of Lionel Johnson.* 1912.
Editor, *Arthur Laurie Thomas: A Memoir,* by F.E. Thomas. 1920.
Editor, with Geoffrey Bliss, *Recusant Poets.* 1938.

Translator, *The Sermon to the Birds and the Wolf of Gubbio.* 1898.
Translator, *The Secret of Fougereuse: A Romance of the Fifteenth
 Century,* by Louise Morvan. 1898.

*

Bibliography: in *Bibliography of American Literature* by Jacob
Blanck, 1959.

Critical Studies: *Guiney* by Alice Brown, 1921; *Guiney: Her
Life and Works* by E.M. Tenison, 1923; *Guiney: Laureate of the
Lost* by Henry G. Fairbanks, 1972; "Heroic Failures and the Lit-
erary Career of Louise Imogen Guiney" by Sheila A. Tully, in
American Transcendental Quarterly, summer-fall 1980; *Regional-
ism and Nationalism in Victorian American Writing: Stoddard,
Guiney, Tabb, and Shea* by Paul Gerard Robichaud, 1994; "Fred
Holland Day, Louise Imogen Guiney, and the Text of Stephen
Crane's *The Black Riders*" by James B. Colvert, in *American Lit-
erary Realism,* winter 1996, pp. 18-24.

*   *   *

Although she published nearly thirty books and a hundred articles, Louise Imogen Guiney is relatively forgotten in the late twentieth century. Her best volume of verse, *A Roadside Harp,* brings

to maturity the themes and attitudes that she introduced in two
previous collections, *Songs at the Start* and *The White Sail and
Other Poems,* and that were to preoccupy her throughout her career: an attachment to the past, a fondness for nature, and a love
for religion and learning. Technically, Guiney's poetry is conservative and genteel. Its carefully measured rhythms and conventional forms earned her the admiration of **Oliver Wendell
Holmes**, who called her his "little golden guinea," and the disapproval of the editor and critic Horace Scudder, who found her work
excessively "oblique and allusive."

For her models, Guiney looked toward the classics, in which
she was extraordinarily well instructed, and the Renaissance, in
which she was an acknowledged expert. Guiney was particularly
fond of sonnets and elegies. *Nine Sonnets Written at Oxford* was
considered by many to be one of the finest collections of sonnets
published during the nineteenth century. So precise was her attention to form and so classical were her tastes that several of
Guiney's poems were mistaken for translations of Greek originals. Guiney's longer narrative poetry, which she herself disparaged for its lack of unity, was less successful. At its best Guiney's
poetry sparkles with wit and allusion; at its worst it is imitative
and artificial.

Later in life, Guiney found it increasingly more difficult to write
poetry, and she turned instead toward scholarship. A poorly written collection of stories, *Lovers', St. Ruth's, and Three Other Tales,*
early convinced her that the essay, not fiction, was the form of
prose most suited to her talents. Her most famous book of essays, *Patrins,* avoids the stylistic pitfalls of an earlier collection,
Goose-Quill Papers, which bordered on the precious and even, at
times, the euphuistic. In *Patrins* she summarizes her critical theory,
articulated previously in her preface to a translation of Merimee's
Carmen and in the introduction to her edition of the poetry of
James Clarence Mangan, that literature should be emphatically humanistic and that it should express "joy" rather than what she
termed "willful sadness." But Guiney's critical theories, while pronounced, were by no means intolerant. Although she disapproved
of realism and naturalism, she was not beyond appreciating the
artistry and talent of someone like **Harold Frederic**, whom she
called a "country boy of genius."

Guiney's many biographical works, which include *A Little English Gallery, Robert Emmet,* and *Blessed Edmund Campion,* display the painstaking exactitude and genuine devotion to learning
that characterize nearly everything she wrote. A knowledgeable
editor, Guiney published selections from the works of Henry
Vaughan, Matthew Arnold, Hurrell Froude, Thomas Stanley, and
Lionel Johnson, among others. Many of her essays express her
lifelong commitment to Roman Catholicism, and at the time of
her death, she was working on a collection, with copious biographical and bibliographical notes, of poetry written by Catholics in England from 1535 to 1735, posthumously published as
Recusant Poets.

—James A. Levernier

GUTHRIE, Ramon

Born: New York City, 14 January 1896. **Education:** Mt. Hermon,
1912-14; University of Toulouse, Docteur en Droit, 1922; the
Sorbonne, Paris, 1919, 1922-23. **Military Service:** Served in the

American Field Service, 1916-17; U.S. Army Air Corps, 1917-19; Office of Strategic Services, 1943-45: Silver Star. **Family:** Married Marguerite Maurey in 1922. **Career:** Assistant professor of romance languages, University of Arizona, Tucson, 1924-26; professor of French, 1930-63, and professor emeritus, 1963-73, Dartmouth College, Hanover, New Hampshire. **Awards:** National Endowment for the Arts, grant, 1969, 1971; Marjorie Peabody Waite award, 1970. M.A., 1939, and D.Litt., 1971, Dartmouth College. **Died:** 22 November 1973.

PUBLICATIONS

Collections

Maximum Security Ward and Other Poems, edited by Sally M. Gall. 1984.

Poetry

Trobar Clus. 1923.
A World Too Old. 1927.
The Legend of Ermengarde. 1929.
Scherzo, From a Poem to be Entitled "The Proud City." 1933.
Graffiti. 1959.
Asbestos Phoenix. 1968.
Maximum Security Ward 1964-1970. 1970.

Fiction

Marcabrun. 1926.
Parachute. 1928.

Other

Editor, with George E. Diller, *French Literature and Thought since the Revolution.* 1942.
Editor, with George E. Diller, *Prose and Poetry of Modern France.* 1964.

Translator, *The Revolutionary Spirit in France and America,* by Bernard Fay. 1927.
Translator, *The Other Kingdom,* by David Rousset. 1947.
Translator, *The Republic of Silence,* edited by A.J. Liebling. 1947.

*

Critical Studies: *Guthrie Kaleidoscope,* 1963 (includes bibliography by Alan Cooke); *Guthrie's Maximum Security Ward* by Sally M. Gall, 1984.

*   *   *

Ramon Guthrie's last and most important work, *Maximum Security Ward,* appeared when he was 74. Indeed, although he was a contemporary of **E.E. Cummings** and **Hart Crane,** most of his significant work belongs to the late 1950s and 1960s and is collected in *Graffiti, Asbestos Phoenix,* and *Maximum Security Ward.* All three books contain striking poems, but the cumulative force of the last, which derives from its dramatic center, is by far Guthrie's most sustained success. The speaker, a critically ill and suffering old man, uses all the resources of his imagination, memory, intellect, and humor to overcome his bewildering isolation and disappointment in himself and his fellow human beings. The book is a particularly valuable addition to the genre of the modern lyric sequence.

The best introduction to the poet and his style comes in the first of the forty-nine poems of *Maximum Security Ward:*

> So name her Vivian. I, scarecrow Merlin—
> our Broceliande this frantic bramble of
> glass and plastic tubes and stainless steel—
> could count off such illusions as I have
> on a quarter of my thumbs.

Here are all the hallmarks of Guthrie's mature verse: the passionate immediacy of the speaking voice; the subtle internal rhymes and skillful assonance, alliteration, and colliteration (the use of related consonants); the unpretentious, humorous, colloquial tone combined with a scholarly range of reference and romantic wistfulness; and the recurrent reference to French art and literature, particularly medieval romance, as a psychological touchstone.

Guthrie was bilingual and a Francophile, and his intimate knowledge of France is reflected in his poetry. He lived, studied, and wrote in France during most of the 1920s and sporadically thereafter and knew the expatriate community of artists well. He served in France in two wars, married a French woman, and taught French literature throughout his academic career. His earliest important literary influences were French, and Proust was his philosophical mentor. But he was an eminently American poet, writing out of the traditions of American verse and at times satirizing his country's hypocrisies and cruelties—particularly its role in Vietnam—for the good of the body politic. Of course, his great subject in Maximum Security Ward is supranational: the meaning of the whole human enterprise—what it is to be fully human psychologically, socially, politically—and the role of any artist, whether writer, painter, musician, or sculptor, in uncovering what is essentially a sacred meaning.

A good amateur painter, Guthrie had a visual imagination that matched and reinforced his great love for the texture of language and that enhanced the exquisitely tactile sensuousness of some of his most evocative passages:

> this smooth knoll of your shoulder,
> this cwm of flank, this moss-delineated quite
> un-Platonic cave. . . .

> Everywhere about is landscape as far as foot can feel
> lamps exude their light on flagstones
> there are quaint quiet trains in
> corridors of pure perspective

Guthrie's poems are filled with concrete, memorable phrases and imagery; he moves skillfully from tone to tone, from the most jarring to the most lyrical; wit, intelligence, and a deep sympathy and humanity inform his work. It is a pity it is not better known.

—Sally M. Gall

H

HAGEDORN, Jessica Tarahata

Also writes as Jessica Hagedorn. **Born:** Manila, Philippines, 22 May 1949. Immigrated to the United States, 1963. **Education:** Manila and San Francisco. **Career:** Poet, fiction writer, musician, screenwriter, multi-media theater and performance artist since early 1970s. Joined American Conservatory Theater's training program in San Francisco, 1972; revisited Philippines, from 1975; organized and performed in West Coast Gangster Choir, 1975-78; moved to New York City, 1978; performed in Gangster Choir, 1978-85, and Thought Music, 1988-92; returned to Philippines to cover national elections, 1992; commentator for *Crossroads,* syndicated weekly newsmagazine on public radio, beginning 1990. **Awards:** American Book award, 1983, 1990; nominee for National Book award, 1990. **Residence:** New York City.

PUBLICATIONS

Collections

Danger and Beauty. 1993.

Poetry

Four Young Women: Poems by Jessica Tarahata Hagedorn, Alice Karle, Barbara Szerlip, and Carol Tinker, edited by Kenneth Rexroth. 1973.

Novels

Dogeaters. 1990.
The Gangster of Love. 1996.

Plays

Mango Tango (produced 1978). 1978.
Where the Mississippi Meets the Amazon, with Ntozake Shange and Thulani Davis (produced 1978).
Tenement Lover: no palm trees/in new york city (performance piece; produced 1981).
Teenytown, with Laurie Carlos and Robbie McCauley (produced 1988).
Airport Music, with Han Ong (produced 1994).
Dogeaters, adapted from her novel (produced 1998).

Television Plays: *Chiquita Banana,* 1972, in *Third World Women,* 1972; *Tenement Lover,* 1981, in *Between Worlds: Contemporary Asian-American Plays,* 1990; *A Nun's Story,* 1988.

Radio Play: *Holy Food,* 1989.

Screenplays: *Kiss Kiss Kill Kill,* 1992; *Fresh Kill,* 1992.

Other

Dangerous Music (verse and fiction). 1975.

Pet Food & Tropical Apparitions (verse and fiction). 1981.

Editor, *Charlie Chan Is Dead: An Anthology of Contemporary Asian American Fiction.* 1993.

*

Critical Studies: "Jessica Hagedorn: Pinay Poet" by Susan Evangelista, in *Philippine Studies,* vol. 35, no. 4, 1987; "Bangungot and the Philippine Dream in Hagedorn" by Leonard Casper, in *Solidarity,* July-September 1990; "Jessica Hagedorn's *Dogeaters:* A Feminist Reading" by Maria Teresa De Manuel, in *Likha,* vol. 12, no. 2, 1990-91; "Notes of a Native Daughter" by Margaret Talbot, in *San Francisco Examiner Image Magazine,* 13 January 1991; "Jessica Hagedorn" (interview), in *Listen to Their Voices: Twenty Interviews with Women Who Write* edited by Mickey Pearlman, 1993.

*   *   *

A prominent figure in contemporary Asian American literature, Jessica Hagedorn has gained acclaim in a variety of artistic modes, including fiction, poetry, music, video, multimedia, theater, and performance art. Despite the protean quality of her achievement, a spirit of ethnic consciousness and an undercurrent of social protest serve to unify much of her work. Having witnessed the pernicious effects of racism and economic exploitation during her early life in the Philippines and as a teenager in San Francisco, she frequently explores themes of colonialism, violence, and psychological debilitation. Additionally, she offers an insider's appreciation of the cultural vitality and ethos of contemporary urban communities.

Although politically engaged, Hagedorn remains too skeptical to confuse artistic gesture with social result and too playful and satiric to be bound to a dominant ideology. At times she implies that art should possess a social utility—but never at the expense of its obligation to continually reinvent itself. Hence, her writings are often marked by leaps across artistic genres, by collage-like effects, and by other maneuvers that run the risk of confusing or alienating her audiences. Her work resists simple categorization into popular or high culture but instead, borrowing from both, explores the tensions between them.

Hagedorn's multiple interests in theater, cinema, music, and poetry have had a valuable cross-pollinating effect upon her work. An early interest in music, especially in urban-based rock, jazz, and rhythm and blues, led in 1975 to the formation of the West Coast Gangster Choir, a band rechristened in 1978 in New York as the Gangster Choir. From her early experiments with dramatic sketches performed during the pauses between her songs, Hagedorn has steadily explored the possibilities of performance art. A number of her theatrical works and teleplays have been produced, including at New York's Public Theater. One of her early performance pieces, the one-act teleplay *Chiquita Banana* (1972), satirically protests the exploitation of women of color and features take-offs on a variety of Hollywood figures. The work effectively evokes anger and militance while experimenting with fragments of song, poetry, and dance. The 1981 performance piece *Tenement*

Lover: no palm trees/in new york city uses multiple devices—tableaux, slides, songs, and letters—to open a space for rethinking the way theatrical arts may intersect with such themes as colonialism, revolution, urban anomie, and the yearning for home. Her performance/theater trio, Thought Music (1988-92), was similarly a product of Hagedorn's desire to work across traditional genres.

Her earliest published poems appear in *Four Young Women: Poems*, a 1973 anthology edited by Kenneth Rexroth. Marked by bursts of street vernacular, edgy rhythms, and a sense of incipient violence, they provide an introduction to her nontraditional poetics. Variously hip or mocking, brassy or belligerent, the voices in these poems depict an American youth culture that simultaneously rebels from and complies with the social vectors of capitalist mass culture.

Inspired by her continuing experiments with music and by a return to the Philippines after a prolonged absence, Hagedorn explores in more depth both the performative possibilities of literature and her own cultural identity in *Dangerous Music*, her 1975 collection of poetry and prose. While the first section conveys her bittersweet memories of her homeland, pays tribute to family members, and acknowledges the transformative powers of art, the long third section experiments with blending music and dance rhythms into the text. More jittery than reflective, and dense with private allusions, the words themselves seem to dart across the page as if intent on escaping analytical confinement; these poems are paeans to the spontaneous, lunatic, carnivalesque part of ourselves that daily life seeks to repress. Between these two sections appears "The Blossoming of Bongbong," a story evoking, then undermining, Euro-American conventions of the quest and the bildungsroman. While the immigrant Bongbong appears to pursue an American Dream of success and to engage in a process of growth, in the end the dream comes to nothing, and the youth's sanity disintegrates. Obedience to such conventions, the story implies, constitutes surrender to a literary colonialism that commonly regulates and compromises the complex narratives of immigration.

Pet Food and Tropical Apparitions (1981) is marked by a deeper awakening of the range of her poetic gifts and by a harder look at inner-city street life. Sexually charged, the poems include a depiction of a transvestite with a blue wig, an earthy hymn to the reggae singer Bob Marley, a sado-masochistic declaration of female liberation and a reclamation of Asian masculinity. But Hagedorn conveys ambivalence regarding street culture, recognizing both its contributions to the vitality of the city and its inherently self-destructive capacity for excess. The comic novella *Pet Food* offers a condensation of this idea. With a cast of street denizens, artists, pornographers, and drug abusers, the narrative taps into the jarring unpredictability and spontaneity of the counter-cultural life while exploring an assortment of related topics, including race relations and imperialism. But the narrative also makes clear that this surrealistic vitality is tied to various forms of violent self-destruction, and it finally turns longingly to such traditional values as commitment and personal growth.

Hagedorn's range of social and political interests and her sardonic wit reach a high point in her darkly comic novel *Dogeaters* (1990), which masterfully coordinates a panoply of characters and intersecting themes. Nominated for the National Book Award and a recipient of the American Book Award, *Dogeaters* (derogatory slang for Filipinos) inflates the trope of the exploited inner-city into that of the exploited nation, while bringing to fruition Hagedorn's earlier experiments in prose narrative. Situated entirely in the Philippines and set primarily in the 1950s under a repressive and corrupt regime, the novel offers an acerbic look at class divisions, foiled ambitions, rampant commercialism, unimpeded violence, and the varieties of corruption in a country deeply afflicted by centuries of Western colonialism and internecine conflict. The first half of the novel introduces an array of characters—the vile plutocrat Severo Alacran; the street savvy hustler and disc jockey Joey; a former Miss Philippines who joins a band of rebel guerrillas; an assortment of aspiring, current, and fading movie stars; a working-class sales girl caught in a meager, deluded life; middle-class families with a range of obsessions; and various government officials who actively repress or simply ignore human rights. The second half of the novel centers on a political assassination and its spiraling effects on this multitude of characters. Amidst the mayhem, the sometime-narrator Rio emerges as a voice of sanity, perseverance, and unspoiled hope. A tour-de-force in its orchestration of character and theme, *Dogeaters* is also notable for its stylistic daring. By interspersing fabricated and actual news items, a public address by William McKinley, poetry, a gossip column, dramatic dialogue, and book and letter excerpts, the novel forces the reader to acknowledge that an authentic depiction of the Philippines can only be pieced together from unreliable literary and verbal representations. Thus, Hagedorn both documents her native country and culture and eschews any claim to have told its true story.

In 1993 Hagedorn edited *Charlie Chan Is Dead: An Anthology of Contemporary Asian American Fiction*, the first anthology of Asian American fiction to be produced and distributed by a commercial publisher in America. The book boasts figures steeped in the early traditions of Asian American fiction, including **Carlos Bulosan**, **Hisaye Yamamoto** (DeSoto), and **Toshio Mori**, as well as others who have achieved substantial recognition in recent years, such as Gish Jen, Cynthia Kadohata, **Maxine Hong Kingston**, David Wong Louie, **Bharati Mukherjee**, and **Amy Tan**. But with nearly half the total of forty-eight writers enjoying publication in a major collection for the first time, the book goes farther than any other in both celebrating and extending the existing canon of Asian American fiction. While Hagedorn seeks to combat the stereotype of the humorless, non-assertive, exotic Asian perpetuated in popular media and incarnated in the image of the inscrutable Oriental detective Charlie Chan, she does so, as in her own art, with a keen respect for the multitudinous facets of Asian America.

In 1996 Hagedorn published her second novel, *The Gangster of Love*, a chronicle of a young woman from the Philippines, Raquel Rivera, who (as her nickname "Rocky" implies) struggles in America amidst personal and family turmoil to establish her musical and artistic career, as well as, in time, to raise a daughter. *Gangster* experiments with shifting narrators and dream-like accounts as a way of simultaneously expanding the narrative surface and enlarging the non-mimetic dimensions of understanding. While the novel boasts an oddball supporting cast—the talented, self-absorbed Keiko; the alluring, magisterial mother, Milagros; the wired, doomed Sly; the smoldering lover Elvis Chang—with the exception of Milagros its strength lies not so much in the originality of these characters as in the simultaneous attractions and disattractions that their associations produce. The most compelling figure remains Rocky herself—gifted, temperamental, self-examining, imaginative, and tortuously honest—as she finds the life about her changing and herself drawn inexorably into middle age. Although on the whole the issues at stake are smaller and more private than the ones in *Dogeaters*, Hagedorn's second novel attests to her continuing and undiminished powers as a writer.

—George Uba

HALL, Donald

Born: New Haven, Connecticut, 20 September 1928. **Education:** Phillips Exeter Academy, New Hampshire; Harvard University, Cambridge, Massachusetts (Garrison and Sergeant prizes, 1951), B.A. 1951; Oxford University (Newdigate prize, 1952), B. Litt. 1953; Stanford University, California (creative writing fellow), 1953-54. **Family:** Married in 1952 (divorced 1969), one son and one daughter; 2) Jane Kenyon, *q.v.*, in 1972 (died 1995). **Career:** Junior fellow, Society of Fellows, Harvard University, 1954-57; Assistant Professor, 1957-61, Associate Professor, 1961-66, and Professor of English, 1966-75, University of Michigan, Ann Arbor. Poetry editor, *Paris Review,* Paris and New York, 1953-62; member of the editorial board for poetry, Weslyan University Press, 1958-64. Consultant, Harper and Row publishers, 1964-81. Lived in England, 1959-60, 1963-64. Deacon, South Danbury Church, New Hampshire. **Awards:** Lamont Poetry Selection award, 1955; Edna St. Vincent Millay memorial prize, 1956; Longview Foundation award, 1960; Guggenheim fellowship, 1963, 1972; Sarah Joseph Hale award, 1983; Lenore Marshall award, 1987; N.B.C.C. award, 1989; for *The One Day;* Robert Frost Silver medal, Poetry Society of America, 1991; Lifetime Achievement award, New Hampshire Writers and Publishers Project, 1992; New England Book award for nonfiction, 1993; Lily prize for poetry, 1994. Honorary degrees: Presbyterian College; Colby-Sawyer College; Daniel Webster College; New England college; State University of New York; Bates College; University of New Hampshire; University of Michigan; Plymouth State College. Poet Laureate of New Hampshire, 1984-89. **Member:** American Academy of Arts and Letters, 1989.

PUBLICATIONS

Poetry

(Poems). 1952.
Exile. 1952.
To the Loud Wind and Other Poems. 1955.
Exiles and Marriages. 1955.
The Dark Houses. 1958.
A Roof of Tiger Lilies. 1964.
The Alligator Bride. 1968.
The Alligator Bride: Poems New and Selected. 1969.
The Yellow Room: Love Poems. 1971.
A Blue Wing Tilts at the Edge of the Sea: Selected Poems 1964-1974. 1975.
The Town of Hill. 1975.
Kicking the Leaves. 1978.
The Toy Bone. 1979.
The Twelve Seasons. 1983.
Brief Lives. 1983.
Great Day in the Cows' House. 1984.
The Happy Man. 1986.

The One Day: A Poem in Three Parts. 1988.
Old and New Poems. 1990.
The One Day and Poems (1947-1990). 1991.
The Museum of Clear Ideas. 1993.
The Old Life. 1996.
Without. 1998.

Recordings: *Today's Poets 1,* with others, 1967; *Donald Hall Prose and Poetry,* 1967; *Names of Horses,* 1985.

Plays

An Evening's Frost (produced 1965).
Bread and Roses (produced 1975).
Ragged Mountain Elegies (produced 1983).
The Bone Ring (produced 1986). 1987.

Short Stories

The Ideal Bakery. 1987.

Other

Andrew the Lion Farmer (for children). 1959.
String Too Short to Be Saved. 1961.
Henry Moore: The Life and Work of a Great Sculptor. 1966.
Marianne Moore: The Cage and the Animal. 1970.
As the Eye Moves: A Sculpture by Henry Moore. 1970.
The Gentleman's Alphabet Book. 1972.
Writing Well. 1973.
Playing Around: The Million-Dollar Infield Goes to Florida, with others. 1974.
Dock Ellis in the Country of Baseball, with Dock Ellis. 1976.
Riddle Rat (for children). 1977.
Remembering Poets: Reminiscences and Opinions–Dylan Thomas, Robert Frost, T.S. Eliot, Ezra Pound. 1978.
Goatfoot Milktongue Twinbird: Interviews, Essays, and Notes on Poetry 1970-6. 1978.
Ox-Cart Man (for children). 1979.
To Keep Moving, Essays 1959-1969. 1980.
To Read Literature: Fiction, Poetry, Drama. 1981.
The Weather for Poetry: Essays, Reviews, and Notes on Poetry 1977-81. 1982.
The Man Who Lived Alone. 1984.
Fathers Playing Catch with Sons: Essays on Sport (Mostly Baseball). 1985.
Seasons at Eagle Pond. 1987.
Poetry and Ambition: Essays 1982-1988. 1988.
Anecdotes of Modern Art, with pat Corrigan Wykes. 1990.
Here at Eagle Pond. 1990.
Their Ancient Glittering Eyes. 1992.
Life Work. 1993.
Death to Death of Poetry. 1994.
Farm Summer 1942 (for children). 1994.
I Am the Dog, I am the Cat (for children). 1994.
Lucy's Christmas (for children). 1994.
Death to the Death of Poetry: Essays, Reviews, Notes, Interviews. 1994.
Old Home Day. 1994.
Farm Summer, 1942. 1994.
Lucy's Summer (for children). 1995.

Principal Products of Portugal. 1995.
The Milkman's Boy (for children). 1997.

Editor, *The Harvard Advocate Anthology.* 1950.
Editor, with Robert Pack and Louis Simpson, *New Poets of England and America.* 1957.
Editor, *Whittier.* 1961.
Editor, *Contemporary American Poetry.* 1962.
Editor, *A Poetry Sampler.* 1962.
Editor, with Stephen Spender, *The Concise Encyclopedia of English and American Poets and Poetry.* 1963.
Editor, with Warren Taylor, *Poetry in English.* 1963.
Editor, *The Faber Book of Modern Verse.* 1965.
Editor, *A Choice of Whitman's Verse.* 1968.
Editor, *The Modern Stylists: Writers on the Art of Writing.* 1968.
Editor, *Man and Boy: An Anthology.* 1968.
Editor, *American Poetry: An Introductory Anthology.* 1969.
Editor, *The Pleasures of Poetry.* 1971.
Editor, with D.L. Emblen, *A Writer's Reader.* 1976.
Editor, *To Read Literature.* 1980.
Editor, *To Read Poetry.* 1981.
Editor, *The Oxford Book of American Literary Anecdotes.* 1981.
Editor, *Claims for Poetry.* 1982.
Editor, *The Contemporary Essay.* 1984.
Editor, *The Oxford Book of Children's Verse in America.* 1985.
Editor, *To Read Fiction.* 1987.
Editor, with David Lehman, *The Best American Poetry.* 1989.
Editor, *The Essential Andrew Marvell.* 1991.
Editor, *The Essential E.A. Robinson.* 1993.

*

Critical Studies: *The Day I Was Older: Collected Writings on the Poetry of Donald Hall,* edited by Liam Rector, 1989.

*　　*　　*

Donald Hall's prolific career in poetry contains an impressive travelogue of styles and a consistent mature vision of life in service to work, God, the past, art, community, and loved ones. Hall's early poems, through the volume *The Dark Houses* (1958), are traditionally formal, inventive, and complex. In *A Roof of Tiger Lilies* (1964) Hall embarks on a wild early-middle period during which he forsakes formal for free verse, echoes some of the work of the Beats, and opens his ear to poetic influences from translation, particularly the Far East.

With his move from Michigan to his ancestral farm in New Hampshire, Hall's poetry, beginning with the breakthrough volume *Kicking the Leaves,* reclaims many of its traditionally formal strengths while honing to razor sharpness its most compelling point of view. Through six additional, ambitious volumes, writing out of the shadows of precursors such as **T. S. Eliot**, Horace, and **Robert Frost**, among others, Hall composed some of the best American poems about life lived harmoniously on the land, at times rivaling his talented contemporary Wendell Berry for the title of America's "Parson of Poetry." Of particular note in this vein are his poems "Names of Horses," "Great Day in the Cows' House," and "Ox Cart Man."

Another strong suit in Hall's verse is the use of the dramatic monologue and the development of compelling characters (for example, in "Merle Bascom's .22," and "Carlotta's Confes-

sion"). This interest in creating in poetry a cast of memorable people who, together, make up a convincing community in a recognizable place made Hall a sympathetic, if stern, commentator and model for the younger poets who sparked the resurgence of narrative poetry in the 1980s and '90s. His poem "Wolf Knife" and the book-length poem, *The One Day* (1988), are superior representatives of this aspect of his work. In the latter Hall deftly lays out his philosophy as man, mate, and artist:

> He walks delicately, impeccably, trembling in outrage,
> among criminals in New York, like a sick fox
> seeking the hay floor. When my sister drowns
> my lungs fill also: We are one cell perpetually
> dying and being born, led by a single day that presides
> over our passage through the thirty thousand days
> from highchair past work and love to suffering death.

> We plant; we store the seedcorn. Our sons and daughters
> topdress old trees. Two chimneys require:
> Work, love, build a house, and die. But build a house.

Work, love, build a house, be it of masonry or of words. These, Hall says, are the things on which our survival depends.

One other channel of Hall's poetry bears attention. During his own serious illness and after the fatal illness of his wife, the poet **Jane Kenyon**, Hall wrote an extraordinary series of poems (collected in *Without,* 1998) on sickness, care-giving, and grieving. They are painful and uplifting to read as they chart, with startling clarity, the daily struggles of the dying and those who attend them. Bitter, raging, funny, and terribly sad, in the end the poems break through to the wisdom of endurance, to the conviction that birth and death are but two doors on opposite sides of a room of indeterminate size and complexity. Seldom has contemporary poetry been so brutally honest about humankind's greatest fears and challenges. Over the course of a remarkable journey that is still in progress, Donald Hall has been an honest, independent, innovative force in American verse.

—Robert McDowell

HALLECK, Fitz-Greene

Born: Guilford, Connecticut, 8 July 1790. **Education:** Public schools in Guilford. **Career:** Worked in a store in Guilford, 1806-11; clerk in the banking house of Jacob Barker, New York, 1812-30; toured Europe, 1822; confidential clerk in the banking house of John Jacob Astor, 1832-49; retired to Guilford on an annuity left him by Astor, 1849. Leading member of the Knickerbocker Group, New York; vice-president, Authors Club, New York, 1837. **Died:** 19 November 1867.

PUBLICATIONS

Collections

Poetical Writings, edited by James Grant Wilson. 1868.

Poetry

Poems, with Joseph Rodman Drake. 1819; revised edition, as *The Croakers,* 1860.
Fanny. 1819; revised edition, 1821.
Alnwick Castle with Other Poems. 1827.
The Recorder with Other Poems. 1833.
Fanny with Other Poems. 1839.
Poetical Works. 1847.
Young America. 1865.

Other

A Letter Written to Joel Lewis Griffing in 1814. 1921.

Editor, *The Works of Lord Byron in Verse and Prose.* 1833.
Editor, *Selections from the British Poets.* 2 vols., 1840.

*

Bibliography: in *Bibliography of American Literature* by Jacob Blanck, 1959.

Critical Studies: *Life and Letters of Halleck* by James Grant Wilson, 1869; *Some Notices of the Life and Writings of Halleck* by William Cullen Bryant, 1869; *Halleck: An Early Knickerbocker Wit and Poet* by Nelson Frederick Adkins, 1930.

* * *

With the exception of **William Cullen Bryant**, Fitz-Greene Halleck was, among his contemporaries, the most popular of the Knickerbocker poets, and although such once-famous Knickerbockers as Samuel Woodworth, Robert Sands, and George Pope Morris have long been forgotten by virtually everyone except literary historians, Halleck is still remembered as a minor poet and satirist of New York society in the early nineteenth century.

Poetry was for Halleck, as for other Knickerbockers, an avocation, a pleasant diversion for gentlemen. His poetry is also exceedingly derivative. Campbell, Scott, and Moore are among those who most influenced him, but no poet's influence was greater then Byron's—an influence that Halleck freely acknowledged. (Indeed Halleck repaid the debt in his memoir and collected edition of Byron's works, the first such edition to be published on either side of the Atlantic.)

Although Halleck published little poetry of consequence, its range was large, including the heroic ("Marco Bozzaris"), the pastoral ("Wyoming"), the sentimental ("Alnwick Castle"), the elegiac ("On the Death of Joseph Rodman Drake"), and the satiric (*Fanny*). His reputation was established in 1819 with the publication of "The Croaker Papers," written jointly with **Joseph Rodman Drake**. These poems, widely read and praised in their day, satirize prominent figures in the financial, political, and social life of New York. *Fanny,* Halleck's most sustained literary effort and his best, is a pointed but delicate satire of fashionable New York society, a world that Halleck knew well. During the last four decades of his life, Halleck, who died in 1867, published little of interest.

Despite his satires of fashionable New York, it was in that New York that Halleck was most at home. As personal secretary to John Jacob Astor, he was assured of access to the social realm he most admired. Here literature was a pastime, a diversion. Astor's world was the ideal setting for the accomplished but amateur poet that Halleck indisputably was.

—Edward Halsey Foster

HAMMETT, (Samuel) Dashiell

Born: St. Mary's County, Maryland, 27 May 1894. **Education:** Baltimore Polytechnic Institute to age 13. **Military Service:** Served in the Motor Ambulance Corps of the U.S. Army, 1918-19: sergeant; also served in the U.S. Army Signal Corps in the Aleutian Islands, 1942-45. **Family:** Married Josephine Annas Dolan in 1920 (divorced 1937); two daughters. **Career:** Worked as a clerk, stevedore, and advertising manager; private detective, Pinkerton Agency, 1908-22; full-time writer from 1922: book reviewer, *Saturday Review of Literature,* New York, 1927-29, and *New York Evening Post,* 1930; lived in Hollywood, 1930-42; began long relationship with Lillian Hellman in 1930; teacher of creative writing, Jefferson School of Social Science, New York, 1946-56. Convicted of contempt of Congress and sentenced to six months in prison, 1951. Member of Civil Rights Congress of New York, 1946-47; member of the advisory board, *Soviet Russia Today.* **Member:** League of American Writers, president, 1942. **Died:** 10 January 1961.

PUBLICATIONS

Collection

The Big Knockover: Selected Stories and Short Novels, edited by Lillian Hellman. 1966; as *The Hammett Story Omnibus,* 1966; as *The Big Knockover* and *The Continental Op,* 2 vols., 1967.

Fiction

Red Harvest. 1929.
The Dain Curse. 1929.
The Maltese Falcon. 1930.
The Glass Key. 1931.
The Thin Man. 1934.
$106,000 Blood Money. 1943; as *Blood Money,* 1943; as *The Big Knockover,* 1948.
The Adventures of Sam Spade and Other Stories, edited by Ellery Queen. 1944; as *They Can Only Hang You Once,* 1949; selection, as *A Man Called Spade,* 1945.
The Continental Op, edited by Ellery Queen. 1945.
The Return of the Continental Op, edited by Ellery Queen. 1945.
Hammett Homicides, edited by Ellery Queen. 1946.
Dead Yellow Women, edited by Ellery Queen. 1947.
Nightmare Town, edited by Ellery Queen. 1948.
The Creeping Siamese, edited by Ellery Queen. 1950.
Woman in the Dark, edited by Ellery Queen. 1951.
A Man Named Thin and Other Stories, edited by Ellery Queen. 1962.
The Continental Op, edited by Steven Marcus. 1974.

Plays

Watch on the Rhine (screenplay), with Lillian Hellman, in *Best Film Plays of 1943-44,* edited by John Gassner and Dudley Nichols. 1945.

Screenplays: *City Streets,* with Oliver H.P. Garrett and Max Marcin, 1931; *Woman in the Dark,* with others, 1934; *After the Thin Man,* with Frances Goodrich and Albert Hackett, 1936; *Another Thin Man,* with Frances Goodrich and Albert Hackett, 1939; *Watch on the Rhine,* with Lillian Hellman, 1943.

Other

Secret Agent X-9 (cartoon strip), with Alex Raymond. 2 vols., 1934.
The Battle of the Aleutians, with Robert Colodny. 1944.
Hellman and Hammett: The Legendary Passion of Lillian Hellman and Dashiell Hammett. 1996.

Editor, *Creeps by Night.* 1931; as *Modern Tales of Horror,* 1932; as *The Red Brain,* 1961; as *Breakdown,* 1968.

*

Bibliography: *Hammett: A Descriptive Bibliography* by Richard Layman, 1979; *Dashiell Hammett and Raymond Chandler: A Checklist and Bibliography of Their Paperback Appearances* by Gary Lovisi, 1994.

Critical Studies: "The Black Mask School" by Philip Durham and "The Poetics of the Private-Eye: The Novels of Hammett" by Robert I. Edenbaum, both in *Tough Guy Writers of the Thirties* edited by David Madden, 1968; *Hammett: A Casebook,* 1969, and *Hammett: A Life at the Edge,* 1983, both by William F. Nolan; *An Unfinished Woman,* 1969, *Pentimento,* 1973, and *Scoundrel Time,* 1976, all by Lillian Hellman; *Beams Falling: The Art of Hammett* by Peter Wolfe, 1980; *Shadow Man: The Life of Hammett* by Richard Layman, 1981; *Zur Rolle der Syntax im Erzahlkunstwerk* by Wolfgand G. Muller, 1981; *The New Wild West: The Urban Mysteries of Dashiell Hammett and Raymond Chandler* by Paul Skenazy, 1982; "The Case for the Private Eye" by Thomas Chastain, in *The Murder Mystique: Crime Writers on Their Art* edited by Lucy Freeman, 1982; *Hammett* by Dennis Dooley, 1983; *Hammett: A Life* by Diane Johnson, 1983, as *The Life of Hammett,* 1984; *Hammett* by William Marling, 1983; "Dashiell Hammett and Raymond Chandler: An Anatomy of the Rich" by Bernard Benstock, in *All Men Are Created Equal: Ideologies* edited by Jean Pierre Martin, 1983; *California Writers: Jack London, John Steinbeck, the Tough Guys* by Stoddard Martin, 1983; "Imparare semiotica dal Falcone Maltese" by Massimo Bonfantini, in *Letteratura: Percorsi possibili* edited by Franca Mariani, 1983; "Dashiell Hammett and the Poetics of Hard-Boiled Detection" by James Naremore, in *Art in Crime Writing: Essays on Detective Fiction* edited by Bernard Benstock, 1983; *Dashiell Hammett* by William Marling, 1983; *Dashiell Hammett* by Dennis Dooley, 1984; *Private Investigations: The Novels of Hammett* by Sinda Gregory, 1984; *The Hard-Boiled Explicator: A Guide to the Study of Dashiell Hammett, Raymond Chandler, and Ross Macdonald* by Robert E. Skinner, 1985; *Hammett* by Julian Symons, 1985; "Laughing with the Corpses: Hard-Boiled Humor" by Frederick

Isaac, in *Comic Crime* edited by Earl F. Bargainnier, 1987; "Investigating the Investigator: Hammett's Continental Op" by Gary Day, "Radical Anger: Dashiell Hammett's *Red Harvest*" by Christopher Bentley, and "Camera Eye/Private Eye" by Peter Humm, all in *American Crime Fiction: Studies in the Genre* edited by Brian Docherty, 1988; *Jameson, Genre, and Gumshoes: The Maltese Falcon As Inverted Romance* by Jasmine Yong Hall, 1990; *The American Roman Noir: Hammett, Cain, and Chandler* by William Marling, 1995.

*   *   *

In the same year (1923) that he began publishing his stories of the Continental Op in *Black Mask,* the monthly pulp magazine founded by **H.L. Mencken** and **George Jean Nathan**, Dashiell Hammett contributed to their more sophisticated *Smart Set* a collection of terse observations about his career as a Pinkerton agent under a title echoing the writings of his former employer: "From the Memoirs of a Private Detective." In form these "memoirs" play against familiar conventions of detective literature. A wry remark such as "I know a forger who left his wife because she had learned to smoke cigarettes while he was serving a term in prison" diminishes the categorical morality of crime literature, and other comments on the inadequacy of fingerprints as clues or the number of unsolved cases in a detective's files disparage all accounts of infallible detective procedures. Since the stories of the Continental Op, Ned Beaumont, Sam Spade, and Nick Charles similarly transgress familiar conventions, it is not hard to see why readers, like **Raymond Chandler** in his famous essay "The Simple Art of Murder," consider Hammett to have added realism to a form grown effete by its emphasis on the myths of ratiocinative detection.

Hammett is notable for the verisimilitude in his use of criminal argot and the description of underworld life, but that cannot be confused with imitation of *the real world.* And his use of American vernacular speech in the first-person narrations of the Continental Op or Nick Charles and the density of action and dialogue in the futile quest for the Maltese falcon or the political crimes of *The Glass Key* should be seen as the requirement of the contract between author and reader of fiction that there be a specific world within the fiction. The extraordinarily complicated, and unlikely, plotting even in the novelettes about the Op, are as incongruent with the reader's known world as the private detectives are unlike their real-life counterparts who occupy themselves with tawdry divorce cases or employee theft.

What, then, is Hammett's achievement, if it is not in mimetic narrative? The answer seems to be that he supplants the mystery puzzle and idealized heroes of earlier detective fiction with themes that codify a modern sense of urban disorder. He achieves this, first of all, by creation of a milieu of pervasive corruption. In his novels—all but *The Thin Man* originally serialized in *Black Mask*—and short stories, the socially reputable are as criminal as the gangsters with whom they often collaborate. The action of plot necessarily follows. Everyone becomes involved in crime, while the force of violence is the common expression of will for those who recognize no law but their own domination, and for the detective because his reason is insufficient alone. When the systems of our social and political myths cannot account for the feel of confusion and menace in urban life, the caricature of a naturalistic world in Hammett's fiction becomes a plausible image.

Similarly, Hammett's stylized representation of hard-boiled detectives offers an appropriate common-sense theme of behavior.

Sam Spade repressing sentiment, Ned Beaumont acting on motives that are unclear even to himself, the Continental Op just doing his job, and Nick Charles affecting sophistication are all masked figures. Behind the tough and cool face they maintain before their world, as though there were no such thing as subjective psychology, we sense a vulnerability that becomes justification for wariness and a disposition to violence. We are intrigued by the thought that Hammett's detectives are what Huck Finn would have become when he found that the Territory in which he hoped to escape civilization was dotted with cities, and in adulthood converted his sense of complicity in events beyond his control into a principle of behavior.

—John M. Reilly

HANSBERRY, Lorraine (Vivian)

Born: Chicago, Illinois, 19 May 1930. **Education:** The Art Institute, Chicago; University of Wisconsin, Madison, 1948-50. **Family:** Married Robert Nemiroff in 1953 (divorced 1964). **Career:** Journalist, 1950-51, and associate editor after 1952, *Freedom,* New York. **Awards:** New York Drama Critics Circle award, 1959. **Died:** 12 January 1965.

PUBLICATIONS

Collections

Les Blancs: The Collected Last Plays (includes *Les Blancs, The Drinking Gourd, What Use Are Flowers?*), edited by Robert Nemiroff. 1972.

Plays

A Raisin in the Sun (produced 1959). 1959.
The Sign in Sidney Brustein's Window (produced 1964). 1965.
To Be Young, Gifted, and Black: A Portrait of Hansberry in Her Own Words, adapted by Robert Nemiroff (produced 1969). 1971.
Les Blancs, edited by Robert Nemiroff (produced 1970). In *Les Blancs* (collection), 1972.

Screenplay: *A Raisin in the Sun,* 1961.

Other

The Movement: Documentary of a Struggle for Equality. 1964; as *A Matter of Colour,* 1965.
To Be Young, Gifted, and Black: A Portrait of Hansberry in Her Own Words, edited by Robert Nemiroff. 1969.

*

Critical Studies: "Hansberry Issue" of *Freedomways 19,* 1979; *Hansberry* by Anne Cheney, 1984; "A Raisin in the Sun Revisited" by J. Charles Washington, in *Black American Literature Forum,* spring 1988; "Colonialism and Culture in Lorraine Hansberry's *Les Blancs*" by Steven R. Carter, in *The Journal of the Society for the Study of the Multi-Ethnic Literature of the United States,* spring 1988, and "Lorraine Hansberry's Toussaint" by Carter, in *Black American Literature Forum,* spring 1989; "Inter-Ethnic Issues in Lorraine Hansberry's *The Sign in Sidney Brustein's Window*" by Steven R. Carter and Helen MacLam, in *Explorations in Ethnic Studies,* July 1988; "Rites and Responsibilities: The Drama of Black American Women" by Helene Keyssar, in *Feminine Focus: The New Women Playwrights* edited by Enoch Brater, 1989; "Lorraine Hansberry and the Great Black Way" by Leonard R. Ashley, in *Modern American Drama: The Female Canon* edited by June Schlueter, 1990; "Excavating Our History: The Importance of Biographies of Women of Color" by Margaret B. Wilkerson, in *Black American Literature Forum,* spring 1990; "Living the Answer: The Emergence of African American Feminist Drama" by Thelma J. Shinn, in *Studies in the Humanities,* December 1990; "From Lorraine Hansberry to August Wilson: An Interview with Lloyd Richards" by Sandra G. Shannon, in *Callaloo,* winter 1991; "Hymns of Sedition: Portraits of the Artist in Contemporary African American Drama" by James C. McKelly, in *Arizona Quarterly,* spring 1992; "Lies That Kill: Lorraine Hansberry's Answer to *Heart of Darkness* in *Les Blancs*" by John Gruesser, in *American Drama,* spring 1992; "A Raisin in the Sun: A Study in Afro-American Culture" by Sandra Seaton, in *Midwestern Miscellany,* vol. 20, 1992; *The Work of Democracy: Ralph Bunche, Kenneth B. Clark, Lorraine Hansberry, and the Cultural Politics of Race* by Ben Keppel, 1995; *A Raisin in the Sun, Lorraine Hansberry* by Joyce Stewart, 1996; *Lorraine Hansberry: A Research and Production Sourcebook* by Richard M. Leeson, 1997; *Black Women's Writing: Quest for Identity in the Plays of Lorraine Hansberry and Ntozake Shange* by Y.S. Sharadha, 1998.

* * *

The importance of Lorraine Hansberry as an American dramatist rests with two plays, *A Raisin in the Sun* and *The Sign in Sidney Brustein's Window,* both produced during her tragically short life of 34 years. The first, by all measurements, was a major success. The second was a commercial failure, meeting only limited critical support. There were two posthumous productions, the effective but somewhat pasted-up collection presented as *To Be Young, Gifted, and Black* and *Les Blancs,* more or less complete but obviously still unfinished.

Hansberry is an important, though minor, figure in American drama if for no more than the fact that she wrote an outstanding play of substantial popular and critical success as a black writer contributing to an essentially white-oriented commercial theater during a period when the black identity in American letters was at a very delicate stage. It was a period when a strong pull existed between those blacks who preferred to stand on their achievements as artists, irrespective of race, and those who preferred to take a stand, artistic as well as social or political, because of the very fact of their blackness. This dichotomy is clear in the opinions of critics who evaluate Hansberry as a black writer. While she herself was completely uncontroversial and avoided the pointedly racial-political involvements associated with black writers of her era, there is some controversy as to whether or not her two major plays were merely outstanding, relatively conventional, dramatic works of a fine young American playwright of promising talent who happened to be black, or were the works of a dedicated black playwright treating subjects directly involved in the causes espoused by the writers overtly conscious of their race.

A Raisin in the Sun at first glance would suggest that Hansberry is allied to those black writers who choose to place onstage the social issue of the ghetto-trapped family. The specifications are there, from the exasperated young black male, fumbling and frustrated in The Man's world, to the matriarch holding the fatherless family together. But Hansberry actually composed a solid, almost conventional "well-made" play, centering upon a theme that could have at one time as easily been Irish, Jewish, or Oriental, but that happens, given the time it was written and the knowledge of its creator, to be black. True, the plight of the Youngers, a serious and prevalent American theme, exists almost entirely *because* they are black, but the confrontations, save for that with the rather pitiful Linder, who brings the outside forces briefly into the Youngers' living room, remain offstage or are postponed until after the curtain falls. Audience interest in the Youngers is in their human, not their racial, qualities.

The Sign in Sidney Brustein's Window is a sensitive comedy far removed in subject and intent from *Raisin*. The world of a white Jewish flat in Greenwich Village, visited by attractive, if not always "normal" characters and centered upon a strictly local political campaign, is not the usual subject associated with a black writer intent on attacks against the social injustices of a racist society. Hansberry attacks petty individual prejudices, those against black or sexual deviant, as well as personal selfishness that can be fatal to those one ought to love.

It is impossible to know where Hansberry might have gone. Perhaps she would have become "radicalized" or perhaps she was already more radicalized than we recognize. It hardly matters. Judgment of her two important plays shows that she was a writer of singular promise, a very important voice in an uncertain historical and social period.

—Jordan Y. Miller

See the essay on *A Raisin in the Sun.*

HARJO, Joy

Born: Tulsa, Oklahoma, 9 May 1951. Enrolled member of the Muscogee (Creek) tribe, Oklahoma. **Education:** The Institute of American Indian Arts, 1968; University of New Mexico, B.A., 1976; University of Iowa, M.F.A., 1978; non-degree study in filmmaking, Anthropology Film Center, 1982. **Family:** One son and one daughter. **Career:** Toured as a dancer with an all-Indian troupe, 1968; writer-in-residence, New Mexico Poetry in the Schools Program, 1974-76 and 1980; writer-in-residence, Navajo Community College, 1978; instructor, Institute of American Indian Arts, Santa Fe, 1978-79 and 1983-85; State Arts Council of Oklahoma, 1980-81; part-time instructor in creative writing and poetry, Arizona State University, Tempe, 1980-81; Richard Hugo Chair, University of Montana, spring 1985; assistant professor, University of Colorado, Boulder, 1985-88; writer-in-residence, State University of New York at Stony Brook, October 1987; associate professor, University of Arizona, Tucson, 1988-90; full professor, University of New Mexico, Albuquerque, 1991-1997. Has given poetry readings and musical performances on the saxophone throughout the United States, Alaska, Canada, Central America, and Europe; poetry editor, *High Plains Literary Review;* contributing editor, *Tyuonyi* and *Contact II.* **Awards:** Academy of

American Poetry first place award, 1976; University of Colorado Writers Forum first place in poetry, 1977; NEA fellowship in creative writing, 1978; Santa Fe Festival for the Arts first place in poetry, 1980; Pushcart Prize for poetry, 1987-88; Arizona Commission on the Arts Creative Writing fellow, 1989; American Indian Distinguished Achievement in the Arts award, 1990; PEN Oakland Josephine Miles Poetry award, 1991; William Carlos Williams award for best book of poetry, 1991; Before Columbus Foundation American Book award, 1991; New York University Delmore Schwartz Memorial Award, 1991; Wittner Bynner Poetry fellowship, 1994; Lifetime Achievement award, Native Writers' Circle of America, 1995; Oklahoma Book Arts award, for *The Woman Who Fell from the Sky,* 1995; Plains Booksellers' award, for *In Mad Love and War,* 1995. **Member:** International PEN; Board of Directors, Native American Public Broadcasting Consortium, 1980-83; National Indian Youth Council, 1980-83; Policy Panel, National Endowment for the Arts, 1980-83; American Film Institute; National Third World Writers Association, 1980-81; Steering Committee, En'owkin Centre International School of Writing; Advisory Panel, New Mexico Arts Commission; Writers Union. **Residence:** Albuquerque, New Mexico.

PUBLICATIONS

Poetry

The Last Song. 1975.
What Moon Drove Me to This? 1980.
She Had Some Horses. 1983.
In Mad Love and War. 1990.
The Woman Who Fell from the Sky. 1996.

Prose

Secrets from the Center of the World, photographs by Stephen Strom. 1989.

Screenplays: *The Gaan Story,* with Henry Greenberg (produced 1979-84); *The Beginning,* with Henry Greenberg (1983-84); *We Are One, Umonho* (produced 1984); *Maiden of Deception Pass* (1984-85); *Origin of Apache Crown Dance* (1985); *I Am Different from My Brother* (1986); *The Runaway* (1986); *Indians and AIDS* (1988); *When We Used to Be Humans* (1990).

Recordings: *Furious Light,* 1985; PBS *Power of the Word* Series (video), 1989; Lamman Foundation (video), 1989; *A Moveable Feast,* 1991; *New Letters on the Air,* 1991; *Joy Harjo Reading,* 1994.

Other

The Spiral of Memory: Interviews. 1996.

Editor, with Gloria Bird, *Reinventing the Enemy's Language: North American Native Women's Writing.* 1997.

*

Critical Studies: "Paula Gunn Allen and Joy Harjo: Closing the Distance Between Personal and Mythic Space" by Jim

Ruppert in *American Indian Quarterly*, vol. 7, no. 1, 1983; interview in *Survival This Way: Interviews with American Indian Poets* by Joseph Bruchac, 1987; "Joy Harjo: A Mystical Sense of Beauty," by John Nizalowski in *Pasatiempo*, August 26, 1989; "Spinning Dreams Into Words" (interview) in *Tucson Weekly*, December 27, 1989; "Joy Harjo" (interview) in *This Is about Vision: Interviews with Southwestern Writers*, 1990; "Ode to Joy" by Dan Bellm in *Village Voice Literary Supplement*, April 2, 1991; *Through Landscape toward Story/Through Story toward Landscape: A Study of Four Native American Women Poets* by Nancy Helene Lang, 1991; "Representing Real Worlds: The Evolving Poetry of Joy Harjo" by John Scarry in *World Literature Today*, Spring 1992; "The Spectrum of Other Languages: An Interview with Joy Harjo" in *Tamaqua*, Spring 1992; "Joy Harjo" (interview) in *Poets & Writers*, July-August 1993; "Joy Harjo" in *Listen to Their Voices: Twenty Interviews with Women Who Write* by Mickey Pearlman, 1993; *Tribal Selves: Subversive Identity in Asian American and Native American Literature* (dissertation) by Sharon S. Suzuki-Martinez, 1996; *Joy Harjo* by Rhonda S. Pettit, 1998.

*   *   *

Joy Harjo has worked as a painter, a dancer, a musician, a screenwriter, and a teacher, but it is as a poet that she has reached her widest audience and has made the deepest impression beyond her immediate Native American culture. Of the many Native American poets who have come to prominence in the past two decades, few have produced such imaginative and provocative work as Harjo. More than one critic has commented on Harjo's deep feeling for the myths and world view of her people, a feeling she has translated into works that have found an increasingly appreciative audience. As Dan Bellm has noted in the *Village Voice Literary Supplement*, Harjo is "now writing a visionary poetry that is among the very best we have." It is this strong sense of ancient Native American values coupled with untraditional visions of our larger society that enables Harjo's poetry to transcend a particular culture or a single period of time.

Harjo uses poetry to travel to her own internal landscapes and then return to the visible world. The poet not only employs visual images to report on these journeys, she also uses the connected sounds she has heard in her mind since childhood. "Often when I write poems," she told the *Tucson Weekly* in 1989, "I start not even with an image but a sound." This use of sound as a starting point for her poetry is an important part of her artistic thinking, as important to her as her early experience with painting. In an interview in *Pasatiempo* in 1989, Harjo is quoted as saying that her approach to writing is similar to a painter's technique, as "images overlap until they become one piece." Other influences on Harjo's work are even more specific. For example, there was her experience at an Indian boarding school in 1967, when a creative Native American atmosphere immediately stimulated her artistic ambitions. In addition, one of the first poetry readings she attended was given by **Galway Kinnell**, an event that helped turn her mind in the direction of literature. In a 1993 *Poets and Writers* interview, Harjo indicated some of the other poets she admires, among them Pablo Neruda, Okot p'Bitek (a writer from Uganda), **Audre Lorde**, and **Gwendolyn Brooks**. Harjo cites **Leslie Marmon Silko** and **N. Scott Momaday** among the writers of prose she most esteems; it is noteworthy that Harjo has often paid tribute to Silko as the writer to whom she is most deeply indebted. Underscoring her ability to draw upon prose writers for

poetic inspiration, Harjo, in the *Poets and Writers* interview, characterized another important work, Momaday's *House Made of Dawn*, as "a novel that was pretty much a poem."

Many of the poems in Harjo's first collection, a 1975 chapbook entitled *The Last Song*, are directly rooted in the writer's own Southwest: such titles as "For a Hopi Silversmith" and "Watching Crows, Looking South Towards the Manzano Mountains" give a local flavor to much of this earliest work. Her second collection appeared five years later as *What Moon Drove Me to This?* and contains all of the material published in *The Last Song* in addition to forty-eight new poems. This second book gives a clear indication of the writer's desire to encompass wider themes and to work in the atmosphere of the larger society: the book contains such new poems as "Chicago and Albuquerque," "Crossing the Border into Canada," and, in "Blackbirds," a consideration of the destruction that can take place when the military comes in contact with creatures from the wild. Despite the promise contained in this second volume, Harjo does not have positive feelings about the book. "It should stay out of print," she told *Poets and Writers* magazine in 1993, "It was a very young book. . . . You could see the beginnings of something, but it wasn't quite cooked."

One section of *What Moon Drove Me to This?* contains "Four Horse Songs" and represents an early use of that animal as a symbol in her work. The motif of the horse finds its fullest expression in her 1983 volume *She Had Some Horses*. Harjo has pointed out more than once that this is the one poem she is most often asked about and the one she least wants to discuss. Certainly the horse is one of the most recognizable Native American images, but in Harjo's poetry the animal achieves what has been called "psychic dualism," a view of our human nature that allows us to see ourselves as a part of, and at the same time apart from, the rest of nature. In the view of Dan Bellm, "The title poem is a long litany of the 'horses' inside a woman who is trying to become whole." The book contains several other poems in which the horse is used, in varying degrees, as a symbol for the poet's meanings; these poems include "Call It Fear," "Night Out," "The Black Room," and "Kansas City," among others. At least one other poem in this volume looks forward to a later autobiographical essay: "For Alva Benson, And for Those Who Have Learned to Speak" directly prefigures the prose piece "Three Generations of Native American Women's Birth Experience" that Harjo published in the July-August 1991 issue of *Ms.* magazine. Other poems in *She Had Some Horses* take us to earlier and later expressions of ideas that are strongly connected to each other. For example, "Nandia" and "Anchorage" are reminiscent of what we find in many parts of *Secrets from the Center of the World*, while "Rain" is a seminal expression of at least two poems in *In Mad Love and War*, "A Hard Rain" and "The Real Revolution Is Love." It is also instructive to read "Your Phone Call at 8 AM" in connection with "Are You Still There," a poem that appeared in her first collection, *The Last Song*.

In her first book-length collaboration Harjo expanded on several of her major ideas and concerns. *Secrets from the Center of the World* (1989) combines poetic texts by Harjo with photographs by Stephen Strom; the images are designed to expand the meanings of the printed words. The book not only provides an unusual view of the American landscape, it also illustrates many of Harjo's Native American mythic beliefs and poetic visions. In her preface to the book, the poet observes that Strom's photographs show that the world "is not static but inside a field that vibrates. The whole earth vibrates." This echoes one of Harjo's long-held beliefs, that "in the real world all is in motion, in a state of change." In this book, as in so much of her work, the poet uses language to represent what she sees as a constant flow of landscape, history, and myth.

Harjo's 1990 book of poetry, *In Mad Love and War,* marks a very different direction for the writer. Although the setting and symbols of the book's opening poem, "Deer Dancer," are clearly drawn from Native American mythology, much of the book shows a wide variety of other concerns, ranging from the strictly autobiographical ("Rainy Dawn" is about her daughter), to American music ("Bird" and "We Encounter Nat King Cole as We Invent the Future"), to an intense concern with the power of love, often seen in a social and political context ("City of Fire" and "The Real Revolution is Love").

In her fourth book, *The Woman Who Fell from the Sky* (1994), Harjo sets twenty-five prayer-like prose poems in a mysterious land of myth, depicting an ongoing moral "war" between forces of creation and forces of destruction. In a celebration of her tribal affiliation, Harjo seeks to find a place for the "unknowable" Native American spirit in contemporary American life. In the title poem, based on the Iroquoian myth of the falling creatrix, the goddess becomes a "strange beauty in heels" who falls through a plate glass grocery window and is aided and redeemed by a lost Indian named Saint Coincidence, whom she in turn redeems. In all of the poems, Harjo melds the present with the mythic past.

The quality of Harjo's poetry has placed her in the first rank of Native American writers. Her work conveys her very personal vision of reality with images from her own culture illuminating the wider American landscape. In 1992 Harjo told interviewers from *Tamaqua* magazine that her writing technique "is a fusion, much the way jazz is a fusion." Harjo is a mystical poet who works from dreams, but many of her poems are firmly rooted in the landscapes of politics and social justice, and her work freely indulges in sensual images as an integral part of her meaning. Her further ability to deal fluidly with the themes of past and present—in historic and even prehistoric terms—gives increased depth to her work. Dan Bellm has written this succinct appreciation of the writer's output: "Harjo's work draws from the river of Native tradition, but it also swims freely in the currents of Anglo-American verse—feminist poetry of personal/political resistance, deep-image poetry of the unconscious, 'new-narrative' explorations of story and rhythm in prose-poem form."

Harjo also invites comparison with poets of a wider tradition. Brian Swann, in his introduction to *Harper's Anthology of 20th Century Native American Poetry,* quotes **Richard Hugo**'s 1975 comment to the effect that Native American poets are similar to such writers as **T. S. Eliot** and William Butler Yeats. As in the case of the Anglo-Irish Yeats, Harjo is able to thrive in the larger culture while still breathing deeply of her own native air. Her poetry is permeated with the spirit and symbols of the Native American experience, but it also reverberates with every dimension of the human experience.

—John Scarry, updated by Martha Sutro

HARPER, Frances Ellen Watkins

Born: Baltimore, Maryland, 24 September 1825. **Education:** The Watkins Academy, Baltimore, Maryland, until the age of 13. **Fam-**ily: Married Fenton Harper, 22 November 1860; one daughter. **Career:** Worked as instructor, Union Seminary, near Columbus, Ohio, 1851-52; taught in Little York, Pennsylvania, 1852-53; became lecturer for the Maine Anti-Slavery Society, 1854; traveled Great Lakes region and Canada and lectured for the Pennsylvania Anti-Slavery Society, 1857-1858; toured southern states, 1867-1871; worked as a spokesperson and lecturer for women's rights with the American Women's Suffrage Association, Women's Christian Temperance Union, and the National Council of Women; elected vice president, National Council of Negro Women. **Died:** 22 February 1911.

PUBLICATIONS

Collections

Complete Poems of Frances E.W. Harper, edited by Maryemma Graham. 1988.
A Brighter Coming Day: A Frances Ellen Watkins Harper Reader, edited by Frances Smith Foster. 1990.
Three Rediscovered Novels: Minnie's Sacrifice, Sowing and Reaping, Trial and Triumph. 1994.

Poetry

Forest Leaves, also known as *Autumn Leaves.* c. 1845.
Poems on Miscellaneous Subjects. 1854.
Poems on Miscellaneous Subjects. 1855; second enlarged edition, 1857; 20th enlarged edition, 1871.
Poems. 1857.
Moses: A Story of the Nile. Second edition, 1869; enlarged edition, 1889.
Sketches of Southern Life. 1872; enlarged edition, 1886; as *Idylls of the Bible,* 1901.
The Sparrow's Fall and Other Poems. 1894.
Atlanta Offering: Poems. 1895.
Martyr of Alabama and Other Poems. 1895.
Poems. 1895.

Novels

Iola Leroy; Or, Shadows Uplifted. 1892.

*

Critical Studies: *The Underground Rail Road* by William Still, 1872, reprinted 1970; *Black Women in Nineteenth-Century American Life* by Bert Lowenberg and Ruth Bogin, 1976; *Black Women Novelists* by Barbara Christian, 1980; "'Let Me Make the Songs for the People'" by Patricia Liggins Hill, in *Black American Literature Forum,* summer 1981, and "Frances Watkins Harper's *Moses: A Study of the Nile*" by Hill, in *The AME Zion Quarterly Review* vol. 95, 1984; *When and Where I Enter* by Paula Giddings, 1984; "Frances Ellen Watkins Harper" by Elizabeth Ammons, in *Legacy* vol. 2, 1985; *Prologue: The Novels of Black American Women* by Carole Watson, 1985; *Reconstructing Womanhood* by Hazel Carby, 1987; "'One Great Bundle of Humanity': Frances Ellen Watkins Harper" by Margaret Hope Bacon, in *The Pennsylvania Magazine of History and Biography* vol. 113 no. 1, January 1989; *Discarded Legacy: Politics and Poetics in the Life of Frances*

E.W. Harper, 1825-1911 by Melba Joyce Boyd, 1994; *Beyond the Pale: Unsettling Race and Womanhood in the Novels of Harper, Hopkins, Fauset and Larsen* (dissertation) by Teresa Christine Zackodnik, 1996.

*   *   *

Although Frances Ellen Watkins Harper published more than ten volumes of poetry, a novel, and numerous essays and was one of the most popular writers of the nineteenth century, many modern critics of American literature disregarded her or judged her literary efforts as substandard. Until the late twentieth century, Harper's works were considered overly sentimental and didactic, lacking in style. But, as Frances Smith Foster acknowledges, to judge Harper by contemporary standards and conventions is to do her a grave disservice. Indeed, doing so attempts to invalidate all that Harper accomplished as a poet, novelist, essayist, women's rights activist, and social reformer. In a letter to William Still, written circa 1859, Harper wrote, "Oh, life is fading away, and we have but an hour of time! Should we not, therefore, endeavor to let its history gladden the earth? The nearer we ally ourselves to the wants and woes of humanity in the spirit of Christ, the closer we get to the great heart of God; the nearer we stand by the beating of the pulse of universal love." Thus, Harper succinctly captured her religious, racial, and personal philosophies: to serve God through the redemption and uplift of all peoples.

Harper was born in 1825 in Baltimore, Maryland, to free black parents. Her status as a free-born black did not, however, safeguard her from the difficulties encountered by blacks who were slaves. Orphaned by the time she was three years old, Watkins lived with an uncle, William Watkins, and his family. Watkins was a prominent minister, abolitionist and educator. He educated Frances and his own three children at the Watkins Academy, a school for free black children he established. Frances' education ended when she was about thirteen, at which time she began working as a domestic for a white family who allowed her use of the bookshop they owned once her literary talents were made obvious.

Her first collection of prose and poetry, *Forest Leaves* was published by the time she was twenty-one. No copies of this work have survived. Some six years later, in 1851, Harper left Baltimore for Ohio. There, she became the first female teacher at Union Seminary. After teaching for a brief time, Harper moved to Little York, Pennsylvania, in 1852, where she was also employed as a teacher. Still noted the twofold dilemma Harper faced in Pennsylvania: "Here she not only had to encounter the trouble of dealing with unruly children, she was sorely oppressed with the thought of the condition of her people in Maryland." As a result, Harper decided to leave the teaching profession. Two factors aided Harper in making this decision. First, the number of runaway slaves seeking refuge in the North and Canada intensified greatly as a result of the 1850 Fugitive Slave Act. Second, Watkins' home state, Maryland, passed its own law that denied free blacks who lived in the North the right to enter Maryland. Doing so would result in their being sold into slavery. Harper and other free blacks who lived and worked in the North became immediate exiles. One free black man who decided to return to Maryland was captured and sold South into slavery. After attempting to escape on a paddleboat traveling down the Mississippi, he was recaptured and later died of exposure. After learning of this incident, Harper's decision to serve her people as an abolitionist (instead of as a teacher) was

firmly fixed. Writing to a friend, Harper proclaimed, "Upon that grave I pledged myself to the Anti-Slavery cause."

Harper's work for the anti-slavery cause initially consisted of public lectures and addresses and later included published volumes of poetry. She also traveled extensively, often refusing to accept fees for speaking. In 1854 Harper's second volume of poetry, *Poems on Miscellaneous Subjects,* was published in Boston and Philadelphia. The work featured an introduction by noted abolitionist William Lloyd Garrison, and contained such poems as "A Mother's Heroism," "The Slave Mother," and "Eliza Harris," which Harper wrote in response to **Harriet Beecher Stowe**'s *Uncle Tom's Cabin.* The poems in this collection established early in Harper's literary career the themes of heroic womanhood, religious fortitude, and racial injustices that are reflected in later volumes. Also included in this work were three prose selections, "The Bible," "Christianity," and "The Colored People of America." The success of the book—it was reprinted five times—established Harper as a literary success.

While many of the poems in this volume were written as antislavery anthems, others, such as "The Burial of Moses," render Biblical accounts in detailed narrative form. Perhaps the poem most familiar in this collection is "The Slave Mother." Addressing the cruelty imposed on slaves, especially slave women, who are forcefully separated from those they love, "The Slave Mother" provides a moving narrative that builds towards its conclusion: the suffering mother's shriek echoes through the poem as she and her child are parted. As Foster notes, "though she wrote to change minds and actions, hers was not the poetry of confrontation, but of gentle persuasion. Harper played her audience, used her poetry to strike chords of sentiment, to improvise upon familiar themes, and thereby to create songs more in harmony with what she knew as the dictates of Christianity and democracy." As a result, Harper's works were widely read; by its 1857 Philadelphia printing, there were over ten thousand copies of *Poems on Miscellaneous Subjects* in print.

Harper's career as an antislavery lecturer was equally successful. After moving from Philadelphia (where she lived at an Underground Railroad station) to Boston and later to New Bedford, Massachusetts, Harper was asked to lecture at a public meeting of blacks and whites. As a result of her "maiden lecture," "The Elevation and Education of Our People," Harper was hired by the Maine Anti-Slavery Society. Harper was rarely overlooked or ignored when she spoke. Frances Smith Foster writes in *A Brighter Coming Day,* " As a writer and lecturer, [Harper] was a complex and confounding figure. Her language was 'chaste,' her literature was 'moral,' and contemporary reporters rarely failed to note her 'slender and graceful' form and her 'soft, musical voice.' . . . [Harper's] brand of abolitionism, firmly grounded in the philosophy of Christian morality, was of the same radical persuasion as that of Still, John Brown, and Henry Highland Garner." In 1857 Harper left Massachusetts to begin lecturing with the Pennsylvania Anti-Slavery Society in eastern Pennsylvania and New Jersey. The following year she ended her speaking engagements for the Pennsylvania Anti-Slavery Society and began lecturing in the Midwest. While in Ohio Harper attended the Ohio State Convention of Negroes, helping to draw up the constitution for the Ohio State Anti-Slavery Society, which was formed during the convention.

Simultaneously, Harper's literary career continued to flourish. *The Anglo-African* magazine published Harper's poetry, and in 1859 proclaimed her one of the best-known blacks in the United

States. During the same year, Harper published "The Two Offers," generally considered the first published short story by a black woman writer. "The Two Offers" tells the story of Laura, who has received two marriage proposals. Unable to decide which offer to accept, she confides in her cousin Janet, who advises her not to accept either offer if Laura cannot decide which of the two men she loves best. Janet has also been in love but has never married. Instead, she is a completely self-reliant woman who supports herself through her own talents and efforts. Laura ignores Janet's council and marries an attractive wastrel. She later dies of an illness compounded by the misery of a seldom present husband and the heartache of an unhappy marriage.

While traveling in Ohio, Harper met and married Fenton Harper, a widower with three children. As a result of worsening health (the results of strenuous traveling and speaking engagements) and her marriage to Harper, Frances Harper accepted fewer invitations to lecture, although she did continue to travel and speak on a more limited basis. The Harpers' only child, Mary, was born a few years after the 1860 marriage. Some four years later Fenton Harper died, leaving his wife in debt. The farmhouse, which she had helped purchase, was seized and the furniture sold. Addressing the Eleventh Woman's Rights Convention in 1866, Harper noted, "Had I died instead of my husband, how different might have been the result! By this time he would have another wife, it is likely; and no administrator would have gone into his home, sold his bed, and taken away his means of support." Harper did not remarry; instead, she returned to the lecture circuit, speaking at the National Convention of Colored Men barely five months after her husband's death. During the three-year period following Fenton Harper's death, Harper divided her time between her writing—publishing several new poems and a serialized novel—and a difficult and demanding travel schedule. Immediately after the Civil War, Harper visited the Reconstruction states, lecturing the newly freed slaves and others on Christian morality, temperance, and the need for education. As she traveled through each of the southern states (her tour included all except Arkansas and Texas), Harper became more concerned with the needs of black women and often lectured privately to small groups of women on their rights. Harper concluded her southern travels in February 1871, returning to Philadelphia where she and daughter Mary settled in a house Harper had purchased in 1870. *Sketches of Southern Life* appeared in 1872. Harper's writings in this volume, which contained nine poems, were based solely on her travels and experiences in the South., Considered her best work, *Sketches,* writes Maryemma Graham "is both a culmination of the formal structure Harper had used in her earliest poetry and an incorporation of a vernacular mode." *Sketches* also introduced Aunt Chloe, who narrates several of the poems. A former slave, Aunt Chloe's voice of maturity and wisdom reflected Harper's major themes: the cruelties of slavery, the strength and endurance of black women who suffered mightily during slavery, and the former slaves' desire for education. As a result, Harper's Aunt Chloe later influenced the writings of poets such as Dunbar, Campbell, and Davis.

After her return to Philadelphia, Harper continued the work she had begun before her travels south. As one of the few black women affiliated with women's suffrage, Harper argued for the rights of all women. She also spoke out most vehemently for the need of black enfranchisement and the passage of the Fifteenth Amendment while also noting the particular needs of black women. In 1866 Harper had joined the American Equal Rights Association (ERA); when this organization split, Harper allied herself with the more moderate branch, the American Woman's Suffrage Association (AWSA), which supported the Fifteenth Amendment. In addition to women's suffrage, Harper worked tirelessly with the Women's Christian Temperance Union, becoming the Pennsylvania State Superintendent of Work among the Colored People and the first Superintendent of the Negro Section. During this time Harper's literary works included the novel for which she is best known, *Iola Leroy, Or, Shadows Uplifted.* Harper was sixty-seven years old when *Iola Leroy* was published in 1892. The novel, dedicated to Harper's daughter, Mary, addresses several themes of Harper's writings: temperance, self-reliance, education, women's rights, and religious values. Iola, the novel's heroine, grows up believing herself to be white. After her white father dies, Iola is confronted with her black heritage. She steadfastly refuses to pass for white, even though doing so would significantly better her life. Instead, Iola works to help her people, becoming a nurse, teacher, and social activist. After Iola reunites her family, she marries a black physician who is equally dedicated to the service and uplift of black people. The novel and its depiction of the antebellum South was immediately successful. While reflecting in some ways the era's popular theme of the tragic mulatta, *Iola Leroy* goes far beyond this trope and provides the literary background for the black women writers who followed Harper. Iola's strength and determination and her desire to be of service are characteristics present in feminist and womanist texts of the twentieth century.

Between 1894 and 1900, Harper published three volumes of poetry. After 1901 there are few public records of Harper's life and events, though she continued to be an active spokesperson for blacks. She died of heart failure in 1911. Despite the elements of sentimentality, didacticism, and reliance on content over style, Harper's writings are once again being recognized as a ground breaking body of American literature that has served as a major influence for writers during the last half twentieth century.

—Lillie Jones

HARPER, Michael S(teven)

Born: Brooklyn, New York, 18 March 1938; moved to Los Angeles in 1951. **Education:** Susan Miller Dorsey High School, Los Angeles, 1955; attended Los Angeles City College, A.A. 1959, Los Angeles State College of Applied Arts and Sciences (now California State University at Los Angeles), B.A. 1961 and M.A. 1963; University of Iowa, M.A. 1963; pursued postgraduate studies at the Center for Advanced Studies at the University of Illinois, 1970-71. **Family:** Married Shirley Ann Buffington in 1965; five children (two deceased during infancy). **Career:** Instructor, Contra Costa College, 1964-68; visiting professor, Reed College and Lewis and Clark College, 1968-69; associate professor, California State College (now University) at Hayward, 1969-70; associate professor, 1971-73, full professor, 1973—, and beginning 1983 Director of Writing Program, Brown University; visiting professor at Harvard, 1974-77, Yale, 1976, Carleton College, 1979, University of Cincinnati, 1979, University of Delaware, 1988, and Macalester College, 1989. Bicentennial Poet, Bicentennary Exchange: Britain/USA, 1976; American Specialist, International Congress of Africanists (ICA) State Department tour of Africa, 1977; lecturer, German University ICA tour of nine universities, 1978; judge, National Book Awards in Poetry, 1978; Council Member,

Massachusetts Council on the Arts and Humanities, 1977-80; founding member, African Continuum, St. Louis; board member, Yaddo Artists Colony, Sarasota Springs; editorial board member, *TriQuarterly, Georgia Review,* and *Obsidian.* **Awards:** National Book award nomination, 1971, 1978; Black Academy of Arts and Letters poetry award, 1972; National Institute of Arts and Letters award, 1972; Guggenheim Fellowship for poetry, 1976; NEA Creative Writing award, 1977; Melville-Cane award, 1978; National Humanities Distinguished Professor, Colgate University, 1985; Honorary Doctorate of Letters, Trinity College, 1987; first Poet Laureate of Rhode Island, 1988; Robert Hayden Memorial Poetry award, 1990; Honorary Doctorate of Humane Letter, Coe College, 1990; Phi Beta Kappa visiting scholar, 1991. **Member:** American Academy of Arts and Letters.

PUBLICATIONS

Poetry

Dear John, Dear Coltrane. 1970.
History Is Your Own Heartbeat. 1971.
Photographs: Negatives: History as Apple Tree. 1972.
Song: I Want a Witness. 1972.
Debridement. 1973.
Nightmare Begins Responsibility. 1974.
Images of Kin: New and Selected Poems. 1977.
Rhode Island: Eight Poems. 1981.
Healing Song for the Inner Ear: Poems. 1985.
Honorable Amendments. 1995.

Recording: *Hearing Where Coltrane Is,* 1971; *Michael S. Harper and Quincy Troupe Reading Their Poems,* 1994.

Other

Editor, *Leaving Eden: Poems by Ralph Dickey.* 1974.
Editor, *Heartblow: Black Veils* (anthology). 1974.
Editor, with Robert B. Stepto, *Chant of Saints: A Gathering of Afro-American Literature, Art, and Scholarship.* 1979.
Editor, *The Collected Poems of Sterling A. Brown by Sterling A. Brown.* 1980.
Editor, with John Wright, *The Carleton Miscellany: A Ralph Ellison Festival.* 1980.
Editor, with Anthony Walton, *Every Shut Eye Ain't Asleep: An Anthology of Poetry by African Americans since 1945.* 1994.

*

Critical Studies: "Michael Harper" in *Interviews with Black Writers* edited by John O'Brien, 1973; "An Interview with Michael S. Harper" by Abraham Chapman in *Arts in Society,* Fall 1974/Winter 1975; "Double-Conscious Poet in the Veil (for Michael S. Harper)" by Edwin Fussell in *Parnassus: Poetry in Review,* Fall/Winter 1975; "The Poetics of Michael S. Harper" by Arnold Rampersad in *Poetry Miscellany,* vol. 6, 1976; "Michael S. Harper, Poet as Kinsman: The Family Sequences" by Robert B. Stepto in *Massachusetts Review,* Autumn 1976; "The Testifying Voice in Michael Harper's Image of Kin" by John F. Callahan in *Black American Literature Forum,* Fall 1979; "An Interview with Michael S. Harper" by James Randall in *Ploughshares,* vol. 7,

no.1, 1981; "Magic: Power: Activation: Transformation" by Richard Jackson in *Acts of Mind: Conversations with Contemporary Poets,* 1983; "Black Poetry and Black Music: History and Tradition: Michael Harper and John Coltrane" by Gunter H. Lenze in *History and Tradition in Afro-American Culture* edited by Lenze, 1984; "Michael S. Harper" by Norris B. Clark in *Afro-American Poets Since 1955,* 1985; "Their Long Scars Touch Ours: A Reflection on the Poetry of Michael Harper" by Joseph A. Brown in *Callaloo,* Winter, 1986; "Interview with Michael S. Harper" by David Lloyd in *TriQuarterly,* Winter 1986; "Michael S. Harper: American Poet" by John F. Callahan et al in *Callaloo,* Fall, 1990; "'Down Don't Worry Me': An Interview with Michael S. Harper" by Charles H. Rowell in *Callaloo,* Fall 1990; "Jazz Modalities" by Galy Jones in *Liberating Voices: Oral Tradition in African American Literature* by Jones, 1991.

*   *   *

Michael S. Harper, Poet Laureate of Rhode Island and Israel K. Kapstein Professor of English at Brown University, has had a distinguished career both as a poet and as an educator. The books of poems he has published over a period of more than two decades have brought him critical acclaim, including two nominations for the National Book Award for poetry as well as other honors and prizes. Among his former students are accomplished writers such as Shirley Anne Williams, Melvin Dixon, and **Gayl Jones.** Writing as a black American who seeks to reconnect the severed links between the majority and the minority, individual and society, and past and present, Harper persistently probes into the historical roots of the painful realities of America, and in the process offers a holistic vision of healing.

Harper's first collection, *Dear John, Dear Coltrane,* is an apotheosis of the jazz musician, John Coltrane, a saxophone virtuoso known for his avant-garde experimentations. Coltrane, whom Harper regards as his own Orpheus, demonstrates "a love supreme" that can only be "played through pain," i.e., achieved through the artist's passionate and energetic devotion to art; for Harper, he epitomizes the celebration of Life as Song in spite of the tragedies, losses, griefs, and pains in one's personal, familial, and communal experiences. Besides Coltrane, Harper also pays tribute to other musicians by way of exploring the relationship between his poetry and black musical forms, thus situating his work within the African American cultural tradition. A poetics based on black music arises from such a connection. According to this musical poetics, jazz, which Harper regards with biblical reverence, exemplifies what **Ralph Ellison** calls "antagonistic cooperation," a process by which the soloist, while improvising, cooperates with the band through exchanges of call and response. The improvisor and the band, thus engaging one another in mutual stimulation and support, epitomize the relationship between the poet and his community not only in Harper's first book but also throughout his career. As is evident from the volume, blues music has inspired Harper as well. Again the influence is not only stylistic but also philosophical. The most important lesson blues have taught Harper is to "always say *yes* to life" and "meet life's terms but never accept them." Both aesthetically and thematically, Harper's poetry is largely informed by these two forms of music, which share in common a melding together of the private and the historical.

With the publication of the second collection, *History Is Your Own Heartbeat,* it becomes clear that the celebration of Life as Song is concomitant with Harper's insistence to reckon with the violence, oppression, and suffering in history, especially with regard to the experience of African Americans and Native Americans. According to Harper, who concurs with **William Carlos Williams**'s view that "History for us begins with murder and enslavement, not with discovery" (*In the American Grain,* 1925), the "amnesia level" of Americans with regard to history and moral ideas is high. Hence, as a poet Harper is particularly interested in the reconstruction of history in order to connect the individual experience with the historical experience, with a view to clearing a ground for recovery. To this end, Harper treats history largely in pathological and clinical terms. His use of medical metaphors in connection with history (e.g., history as gallstone; history as bandage) thus looms large in this volume, which derives its title from the last line of the opening poem, "Blue Ruth: America." The poem portrays Ruth (Ruth McLaughlin Buffington, mother of Harper's wife and the subject of Part One subtitled *Ruth's Blues*) as a patient with grievous health problems. From the sequence it can be gathered that Ruth, after living in Minnesota in isolation, joins her estranged kin in Oregon in order to undergo surgery and convalescence; in this personal epic quest for health she rediscovers her family and is rediscovered by them. While portraying her and meditating on her malady, Harper probes into the historical and cultural significance of Ruth's predicament and asserts that "*history is your own heartbeat*" by demonstrating how Ruth can be regarded as the personification of America itself. America is seriously ill because, for historical reasons, family ties have been denied and severed as a result of racial discord, but recovery is possible once America's and the individual's heartbeats are seen as one and the same.

Harper's musical idiom and clinical imagery are joined by the language of photography in *Photographs: Negatives: History as Apple Tree,* a series of poems first published in a limited edition and then incorporated in *Song: I Want a Witness.* In the poem titled "History as Apple Tree," Harper recounts the legend of Roger Williams, who established the Providence Plantation in 1636 upon his banishment by Massachusetts Puritans for his outspoken views. Crucial to Williams's founding of Rhode Island are the various Indian tribes residing there; without their consent to give him a tract of land his whole venture would not have been possible. As a fugitive, he was not unlike the black men who escaped into Canonicus chief sachem's tribe. Hence, when Harper describes himself as a black man visiting Williams' grave (from which grows a giant apple tree) to meditate on the skeleton buried underneath, he is in effect revising the history of America in multiracial terms: America is a joint effort to which the apple tree bears the fruit of witness. The myth of the American Dream is also revised when the poet acknowledges the skeleton-appletree as his own myth and wills himself to become a "black human photograph: apple tree." Condensed in the overlapping metaphor of the skeleton-appletree-photograph is a rhetoric of testimony, which Harper further develops into a testament in *Song: I Want a Witness* (the book, originally, was to be titled *The Appletree*). The title poem offers glimpses of the racial violence of the Civil Rights era, with blacks who have been subjected to "an army of white dust" and "black smoke" calling upon the nation to testify and to redeem.

Harper's testamental temper finds its fullest and most unified expression in *Debridement.* The book is dedicated to his five children (three surviving and two deceased) and consists of three parts, with each focusing on a particular period in African American history. "History as Cap'n Brown" (Part I), which is inspired by abolitionist John Brown, deals with a range of issues and events related to slavery, slave uprisings, the abolition movement, the underground railway, the Civil War, and African American leaders such as **Frederick Douglass** and **W.E.B. DuBois**. As variations on the theme that "the price of repression is greater than the cost of liberty," the poems reconfigure the contours of American history. In "Heartblow" (Part II), as a counterpoint to John Brown, Harper evokes (sympathetically but also critically) **Richard Wright**, author of *Black Boy* and *Native Son,* and uses Bigger Thomas's predicament as a metaphor for the reality of African Americans in the first half of the 20th century. The section titled "Debridement" (Part III) deals with the generation of the Vietnam War, a generation in which a disproportionately large number of blacks served in the American military. The medical term "debridement," which refers to "the cutting away of dead or contaminated tissue from a wound to prevent infection" (debridement is also performed to heal or clean up infection), serves as a governing metaphor. Clinical images abound in this section, which consists of a sequence of poems narrating the experience of John Henry Louis, a semi-fictional black Vietnam veteran who has been recognized as a member of the Congressional Medal of Honor Society. The fact that he meets his death in the United States rather than Vietnam as a result of racism is ironic, but through his tragedy he also rises to a mythical height.

The title of Harper's next volume, *Nightmare Begins Responsibility,* recalls **Delmore Schwartz**'s book of poems titled In *Dreams Begin Responsibility* (1938), which in turn is derived from a line from W.B. Yeats's *Responsibilities* (1913). The Nightmare vs. Dream formulation also reminds us of Malcolm X's interpretation of the American Dream as the American Nightmare. The phrase "Nightmare begins responsibility" has already surfaced as a concept in some of Harper's earlier volumes, and here it appears in association with the deaths of his two sons; it suggests that taking responsibility, especially in the face of hardship, violence, suffering, and grief, is an integral part of his poetics. The pervasive presence of kin (in the broad sense of the term) also ties the book to the next volume, *Images of Kin,* which consists of selections from all previous volumes as well as two new groups of poems. The first group, "Healing Songs," addresses issues of literary art and serves as the wellspring for *Healing Song for the Inner Ear.* The second group, "Uplift from a Dark Tower," explores the ideas of the three preeminent leaders of African Americans—Frederick Douglass, Booker T. Washington, and W.E.B. Dubois—and looks at their historical circumstances in connection with the white racism that has engendered the history of America. As a retrospective and prospective volume, *Images of Kin* consolidates the best of Harper's work and showcases the complexity as well as breadth and depth of his thought. Appropriately for such a summation, the book received the Melville-Cane award and was nominated for the National Book award in 1978.

As a poet, Harper believes that he is both black *and* American, not "either/or." To be recognized as such, in his poetry he has to dismantle the fundamental myth—understood as a lie—that the American Dream can conveniently encompass the experience of all Americans including minorities. Harper attempts to accomplish this difficult task by various means, but essentially his efforts concentrate on the reconstruction of history through personal and familial realities, the revision of the American experience in terms of minority perspectives, and the reconnection of the mainstream and the minority. By referring generously to kinsfolk, friends, and fellow artists throughout his poetry, he is writing in the "honoring of kin" tradition in African American culture. Understood as a rally cry that exhorts all Americans to take the responsibility of waking up after the nightmare, the honoring of kin also paves the way for healing historical wounds. As is evident from his more recent works, Harper has formulated a holistic vision, a philosophy of inclusion and diversity, that is determined to overcome the "dualistic schizophrenia" and "historical amnesia" of American society.

—Balance Chow

HARRIGAN, Edward

Born: New York City, 26 October 1844. **Education:** Received little schooling. **Family:** Married Annie T. Braham in 1876; seven children. **Career:** Left home for San Francisco and appeared in vaudeville in the west, 1867-70; returned to New York and appeared on stage with Sam Rickey as a vaudeville comic team, 1870; first appeared with Anthony J. Cannon (stage name: Tony Hart), as Harrigan and Hart, 1871, and with him managed and appeared at the Theatre Comique, New York, 1871 until the theater was torn down, 1881: during this period wrote more than 80 sketches, music by David Braham, which developed into the complete plays of his later career in which he always acted the leading part; with Hart, opened the New Theatre Comique, 1881, and managed it until it was destroyed by fire, 1884; partnership with Hart ended, 1885; leased Harrigan's Park Theatre, 1884-88; built Harrigan's, later the Garrick, Theatre, 1891-95; retired, 1908. **Died:** 6 June 1911.

PUBLICATIONS

Collections

The Famous Songs of Harrigan and Hart, edited by Edward B. Marks. 1938.

Plays and Sketches

The Mulcahey Twins (produced 1870). Songs published 1872.
The Little Fraud (produced 1871). Songs published 1870.
The Big and Little of It (produced 1871).
The Day We Went West (produced 1871).
The German Emigrants (produced 1871).
The Irish Emigrant (produced 1871).
You 'spute Me (produced 1871).
Ireland vs. Italy (also called *Who Owns the Line?*) (produced 1872).
Shamus O'Brien at Home (produced 1872).
Sing Sing (produced 1872).
The Mulligan Guard (produced 1873). Songs published 1873.
St. Patrick's Day Parade (also called *The Day We Celebrate*) (produced 1873; revised 1874 and thereafter). Songs published 1884.
The Absent-Minded Couple (produced 1873).
An Editor's Troubles (produced 1873). 1875.
The Mixed Couple (produced 1873).
Eureka, with John Woodard (produced 1874).
Muldoon, The Solid Man (produced 1874).
The Raffle for Mrs. Hennessey's Clock (produced 1874).
The Regular Army, O! (produced 1874).

A Terrible Example (produced 1874).
Who Stole the Monkey? (produced 1874).
The Skidmores (produced 1874).
The Invalid Corps (produced 1874).
Going Home Again (produced 1874).
The Night Clerk's Troubles; or, The Fifth Avenue Hotel (also called *The Porter's Troubles*) (produced 1875). 1875.
The Blue and the Gray (produced 1875). 1875.
Fee-Gee (produced 1875).
The Doyle Brothers, with John Woodard (produced 1875).
April Fool (produced 1875).
Innocence at Home (produced 1875).
No Irish Wanted Here (produced 1875).
The Donovans (produced 1875).
King Calico's Body Guard (produced 1875).
The Two Awfuls (produced 1875).
Behind the Scenes (produced 1875).
Slavery Days (produced 1875). Songs published 1875.
Down Broadway; or, From Central Park to the Battery (produced 1875). Songs published 1878.
The Bradys (produced 1876).
The Italian Ballet Master (produced 1876).
Malone's Night (produced 1876).
The Bold Hibernian Boys (produced 1876).
S.O.T (Sons of Temperance) (produced 1876). Songs published 1876.
Iascaire (produced 1876).
Walkin' for Dat Cake (produced 1876). Songs published 1877.
Bar Ber Ous (produced 1876).
Down in Dixie (produced 1876).
Matrimonial Ads (produced 1877).
The Rising Star (produced 1877).
The Telephone (produced 1877).
Christmas Joys and Sorrows (produced 1877). 1877.
The Grand Duke's Opera House (produced 1877).
Old Lavender (also called *Old Lavender Water* and *Around the Docks*) (produced 1877; revised version, 1878, 1885). 1877.
My Wife's Mother (produced 1878). 1877.
Callahan the Detective (produced 1877).
The Crushed Actors (produced 1877).
The Pillsbury Muddle (produced 1877).
Sullivan's Christmas (produced 1877).
Our Irish Cousins (produced 1877).
The Two Young Fellows and Her Majesty's Marines (produced 1877).
Love vs. Insurance (produced 1878).
A Celebrated Hard Case (produced 1878). 1878.
The Lorgaire (produced 1878; revised 1888). 1878.
The Mulligan Guard Picnic (produced 1878). 1880.
Coloured Baby Show (produced 1878).
The Italian Junkman (produced 1878).
The Lady of Lions (produced 1878).
Our Low Makers (produced 1878).
O'Brien, Counselor-at-Low (produced 1879).
The Great In-Toe-Natural Walking Match (produced 1879).
The Mulligan Guard Ball (produced 1879). 1879.
The Mulligan Guard Chowder (produced 1879). 1879.
The Mulligan Guards' Christmas (produced 1879). 1879.
The Mulligan Guard Nominee (produced 1880). 1880.
The Mulligan Guards' Surprise (produced 1880). 1880.
The Major (produced 1881). 1881.

The Mulligans' Silver Wedding (produced 1881). 1881.

Squatter Sovereignty (produced 1882). 1881.

Our Cranks, with G.L. Stout (produced 1881).

Mordecai Lyons (produced 1882). 1882.

McSorley's Inflation (produced 1882). 1882.

The Muddy Day (also called *Bunch o' Berries*) (produced 1883). Songs published 1883.

Cordelia's Aspirations (produced 1883).

Dan's Tribulations (also called *Tribulations*) (produced 1884). Songs published 1893.

Investigation (produced 1884). Songs published 1884.

McAllister's Legacy (produced 1885).

Are You Insured? (produced 1885).

The Grip (produced 1885).

The O'Reagans (produced 1886).

The Leather Patch (produced 1886). Songs published 1886.

McNooney's Visit (produced 1887).

Pete (produced 1887).

Waddy Googan (produced 1888). Songs published 1893.

Reilly and the Four Hundred (produced 1890). Songs published 1890.

The Last of the Hogans (produced 1891; shortened version, as *Sergeant Hickey,* produced 1897). Songs published 1891.

The Woollen Stocking (produced 1893). Songs published 1893.

Notoriety (produced 1894). Songs published 1894.

The Blue Ribbon (produced 1894).

My Son Dan (produced 1896).

Marty Malone (produced 1896).

Low Life (produced 1897).

An Old New Yorker (produced 1899).

Under Cover (produced 1903).

The Simple Life (produced 1905).

In the North Woods (produced 1907).

The Lord Mayor of Dublin (produced 1908).

Fiction

The Mulligans. 1901.

Poetry

Songs for the Banjo. 1888.

Songs. 1893.

Other

Comique Joker, with Tony Hart. 1870(?).

Pictorial History of the Mulligan Guard Ball. 1879.

*

Bibliography: "An Edward Harrigan Bibliography" by Alicia Kae Koger, in *Nineteenth Century Theatre,* summer 1991.

Critical Studies: *The Merry Partners: The Age of Harrigan and Hart* by E.J. Kahn, Jr., 1955; *Harrigan: From Corlear's Hook to Herald Square* by Richard Moody, 1980; "Ethnic Cultures of the Mind: The Harrigan-Hart Mosaic" by James H. Dormon, in *American Studies,* fall 1992.

*   *   *

The enthusiastic comparisons that critics applied to Edward Harrigan's plays would seem to have assured him an international reputation. **William Dean Howells** (in *Harper's,* July 1886) described him as the American Goldoni and a playwright who created "the spring of a true American Comedy." Others compared him to Hogarth, Balzac, Zola, and Dickens. At a time when American literature and art were firmly caught up in the rise of realism Harrigan deserved this critical attention through his successful depiction of Lower East Side New York life. As a comedian and a playwright he believed in "Holding the Mirror Up to Nature," as he explained it in an essay in *Pearson's Magazine* (November 1903), and providing a series of photographs of "life today in the Empire City" (*Harper's Weekly,* 2 February 1889). By using authentic scenes, character types, speech, dress, and gestures he provided realistic farce-comedy in which he infused his own belief in the kindness and good nature of the majority of people. As riotous fun, his plays and performances were both a reflection of the serious artistic and social movements of his generation and an antidote to the grimness that they frequently unveiled.

Harrigan, after several years in vaudeville, formed a comedy team with Anthony J. Cannon, who soon changed his name to Hart. As "Harriganandhart" they performed for fourteen years, and Harrigan began writing the sketches, with music by David Braham, that often developed into full-length plays. Many of the most memorable take place in Mulligan's Alley in New York's Sixth Ward. It was a part of New York that Harrigan researched and knew very well—a jumbled population of Germans, Italians, Chinese, blacks, and Irish who took their ward politics seriously as well as their social activities that seemed always haunted by the "battle of the sexes." There was the Wee Drop Saloon run by Walfingham McSweeny, an Italian junk shop, a Chinese laundry-lodging combination, Lochmuller's butcher shop, and a black social club called the Full Moon Union. It was an international community that Harrigan brought to life with elaborate stage-business, meticulous attention to realistic detail, and a comedian's enthusiasm for the "general melee" that characterized his plays.

Harrigan's most famous plays involved the Mulligans—*The Mulligan Guard, The Mulligan Guard Ball, The Mulligan Guard Nominee,* and so on—through which he satirized contemporary military organization, social life on the Lower East Side, and politics. *Cordelia's Aspirations* and *Dan's Tribulations* also involve Dan Mulligan and his wife. His other important plays include *Old Lavender, Waddy Googan,* and *Reilly and the Four Hundred.* The people and their ideas were real if slight, and the spectators came to see something of themselves on stage. Trying always to be "truthful to the laws that govern society," Harrigan also confessed to being provincial and optimistic. Although he did not fulfill the potentiality that some critics saw or stimulate followers for his theory of American comedy, he was a major favorite for a generation or more of New York theater-goers.

—Walter J. Meserve

HARRIS, George Washington

Born: Allegheny City, Pennsylvania, 20 March 1814; grew up in Knoxville, Tennessee. **Education:** Local schools; apprenticed to a metalworker, Knoxville, 1826-33. **Family:** Married 1) Mary Emeline Nance in 1835 (died 1867), six children; 2) Jane E. Pride in 1869. **Career:** Captain of the *Knoxville,* a Tennessee River boat, 1833-38; farmer, Tucaleeche Cove, Tennessee, 1839-43; opened a metalworking shop in Knoxville, 1843; superintendent, Holston Glass Works, 1849; captain of the steamboat *Alida,* Tennessee River, 1854; copper mine surveyor, Ducktown, Tennessee, 1854; alderman, Fourth Ward of Knoxville, 1856; postmaster, Knoxville, 1857-58; conductor, 1859, and freight agent, 1860-61, Nashville and Chattanooga Railroad; lived in Nashville, 1862, and in various parts of the South during the Civil War, 1862-65; worked for the Wills Valley Railroad, Chattanooga, Tennessee, 1866-69. Delegate to the secessionist Southern Commercial Convention, Savannah, Georgia, 1856; member of Democratic State Central Committee, Tennessee, 1859. **Died:** 11 December 1869.

PUBLICATIONS

Collection

Sut Lovingood's Yarns, and *High Times and Hard Times,* edited by M. Thomas Inge. 2 vols., 1966-67.

Prose

Sut Lovingood: Yarns Spun by a "Nat'ral Born Durn'd Fool: Warped and Wove for Public Wear." 1867.
Sut Lovingood: Travels with Old Abe Lincoln. 1937.

*

Bibliography: in *Bibliography of American Literature* by Jacob Blanck, 1959.

Critical Studies: *The Lovingood Papers* edited by Ben Harris McClary, 4 vols., 1962-65; *Harris* by Milton Rickels, 1966; *The Frontier Humorists: Critical Views* edited by M. Thomas Inge, 1975; "George Washington Harris's Newspaper Grotesques" by Milton Rickels, in *University of Mississippi Studies in English,* vol. 2, 1981; "The Identity of George Washington Harris's 'Man in the Swamp'" by William E. Lenz, in *Notes on Mississippi Writers,* vol. 13, 1981; "George Washington Harris and Supernaturalism" by Benjamin Franklin Fisher, in *Publications of the Mississippi Philological Association,* summer 1982; "That George Washington Harris 'Christmas Story': A Reconsideration of Authorship" by Mark A. Keller, in *American Literature,* May 1982; "A Nat'ral Born Durn'd Fool" by Thomas Daniel Young, in *Thalia,* fall/winter 1983; "Sut Lovingood: Backwoods Existentialist" by Elaine Gardiner, in *Southern Studies,* summer 1983; "The Grotesque Body of Southwestern Humor" by Milton Rickels, in *Critical Essays on American Humor* edited by W. Craig Turner, 1984; "Sut Lovingood: A Nat'ral Born Durn'd Yarnspinner" by Carolyn S. Brown, in *Southern Literary Journal,* fall 1985, and *The Tall Tale in American Folklore and Literature* by Brown, 1987; "George Washington Harris's 'Special Vision': His Yarns as Historical Sourcebook" by Ben Harris McClary, in *No Fairer Land: Studies in Southern Literature before 1900* edited by J. Lasley Dameron and James W. Mathews, introduction by James H. Justus, 1986; "Newly Discovered Reprintings of G.W. Harris's Tales and Letters" by Janet Galligani Casey, in *Studies in American Humor,* spring 1986; "Sut Lovingood's Yarns and the Politics of Performance" by John Wenke, in *Studies in American Fiction,* autumn 1987; "Sut Lovingood at the Camp Meeting: A Practical Joker among the Back-

woods Believers" by David C. Estes, in *Southern Quarterly,* winter 1987; "A Nat'ral Born Durn'd Fool: L'Irresistible decheance de Sut Lovingood" by Daniel Royot, in *Caliban,* vol. 26, 1989; *Sut Lovingood's Nat'ral Born Yarnspinner: Essays on George Washington Harris* edited by James Edward Caron and M. Thomas Inge, 1996.

*   *   *

George Washington Harris was neither a writer by trade nor a southerner by birth. Yet he contributed to American literature one of its most distinctively southern comic figures in Sut Lovingood and brought the American literary vernacular to its highest level of achievement before **Mark Twain**.

Harris had been brought as a child to Knoxville, Tennessee, by his half-brother from the place of his birth in Allegheny City, Pennsylvania, and he adapted to the attitudes and mores of the antebellum South with spirited enthusiasm. With little education in the formal sense, he had learned from a wide range of occupations, including metal working, captaining a steamboat, farming, running a glass works and a sawmill, surveying, running for political office, serving as a postmaster, and working for the railroad. Such diverse experience gave Harris a large reservoir of material from which to draw in his writing.

Writing was a leisure time activity for Harris, who began as an author of political sketches for local newspapers and sporting epistles for the New York *Spirit of the Times.* He quickly developed a facility for local color and dialect and a skill for bringing backwoods scenes and events to life on the printed page. When he contributed the first Sut Lovingood sketch to the *Spirit* (4 November 1854), he outdistanced all the other humorists of the Old Southwest by allowing one central character to tell his own stories in his own vernacular and by granting him (without authorial comment) a lease on life according to the integrity and consistency of that character's independence in thought and action. Mark Twain would learn this lesson well from Harris, whose one collection of stories, *Sut Lovingood: Yarns,* he reviewed, and put it to effective use in *Adventures of Huckleberry Finn.*

While authors and critics such as **William Dean Howells** and **Edmund Wilson** have found Sut Lovingood repugnant, others such as Mark Twain, **William Faulkner**, and F.O. Matthiessen have paid tribute to Harris's genius. What makes Sut distinctive is the combination in his character of such human failings as bigotry, vulgarity, cowardice, brutality, and offensive behavior, along with a steadfast opposition to hypocrisy, dishonesty, and all limitations set on personal and social freedom. Many readers find it difficult to like Sut, but few find it possible to resist his appeal, especially evident when he reveals hypocritic sins and recounts the brutal punishment of those who take advantage of innocence. Sut is a minister of justice in coarse southern homespun whose wildly funny pranks and incorrigible attitudes make him one of the most intriguing characters in American literary history.

—M. Thomas Inge

HARRISON, Jim

Born: Grayling, Michigan, 11 December 1937. **Education:** Michigan State University, B.A. 1960, M.A. 1964. **Family:** Married Linda King in 1960; two daughters. **Career:** Writer. Assistant professor of English, State University of New York at Stony Brook, 1965-66. Screenwriter for Warner Bothers and other film companies. **Awards:** National Endowment for the Arts grant, 1967-69; Guggenheim fellowship, 1969-70; two awards from National Literary Anthology.

PUBLICATIONS

Novels

Wolf: A False Memoir. 1971.
A Good Day to Die. 1973.
Farmer. 1975.
Legends of the Fall. 1979.
Warlock. 1981.
Sundog: The Story of an American Foreman, Robert Corvus Strang. 1984.
Dalva. 1988.
The Woman Lit by Fireflies. 1990.
Country Stores. 1993.
Julip. 1994.

Poetry

Plain Song. 1965.
Locations. 1968.
Walking. 1969.
Outlyer and Ghazals. 1971.
Letters to Yesinin. 1973.
Returning to Earth. 1977.
Selected Poems. 1982.
The Theory and Practice of Rivers and New Poems. 1989.
After Ikkyu and Other Poems. 1996.

Recording: *Poetry Reading with Jim Harrison,* 1996.

Other

Pathways to a Southern Coast, with Jerry Blackwelder. 1986.
The Passing: Perspectives of Rural America. 1988.
Just Before Dark: Collected Nonfiction. 1991.

Screenplays: *Wolf,* with Wesley Strick, 1994.

*

Critical Studies: *Jim Harrison* by Edward C. Reilly, 1996.

*   *   *

Jim Harrison has produced strong work in several genres, including the novel, novella, short story, poem, screenplay, and essay. Less recognized in terms of awards and prizes than some of his generational peers, Harrison has produced a body of work that is unified by thematic considerations, as well as by a commitment to exploring the formal shapes of narrative technique. Harrison's work continues the lineage of **Ernest Hemingway**, while still offering its own signatory imprint; if his work is stark, stylistically taut, and in some ways focused upon "masculine" narratives of quest and conquest, there are still enough deviations from this tem-

plate in his oeuvre to suggest a far more ambitious palette than one would find in a more derivative writer. The use of a female narrator in two of the three sections of the novel *Dalva,* for instance, is certainly indicative of his willingness to break the mold. Nevertheless, the recurrence of violence, of a brutal and indifferent natural world, of protagonists searching for existential rather than transcendent meaning—these elements certainly tie Harrison to Hemingway.

Harrison's protagonists frequently confront death, whether their own or that of a friend, loved one, or even a stranger. These encounters usually force the characters into a reexamination of the life lived; that is, when faced with nothingness, they come to understand the compulsion to give meaning to their brief life spans. This meaning is not connected to religiosity or ideological convictions, though Harrison is a writer well acquainted with Kierkegaard, Kant, and other important thinkers. The other significant theme in Harrison's work concerns the individual's attempts to understand, survive in, and come to terms with contemporary society; Harrison recognizes a panoply of forces—economic, political, and social—that alienate the individual, and this alienation contributes to the existential journeys of his characters.

Harrison's first novel *Wolf,* in which several critics have noted autobiographical elements, is an account of a camping trip in Michigan's Upper Peninsula. The protagonist is thirty-three-year-old Carol Swanson, and the events revolve around Swanson's desire to see a wolf—a creature with which he, as a loner, identifies, and through which he can somehow envision a connection to the world. In reminiscences and ruminations, Swanson philosophizes on a variety of topics concerning contemporary life. His quest ends in failure, though, as he reverts to disconnectedness fueled by drink and self-pity. Simply, he has proved incapable of finding meaning in the world to answer the emptiness he feels inside.

The rather despairing conclusion of *Wolf* is echoed by *A Good Day to Die,* Harrison's next novel. A trio of self-identified "ecoterrorists" sets out from Florida to blow up dams in the western United States. Their drug use, abuse of others (the narrator has abandoned his wife and child), and extremist reason for their mission all contribute to the desperate conclusion of the novel, in which their one attempt to bomb a dam leads to the death of one of the trio. In spite of this grisly end, the narrator reveals that physical pleasures such as "Sylvia [one of the trio], and the food that even now Rosie was slinging on the table. And in whiskey and fishing." This emphasis on the physical is one of the ways in which Harrison's protagonists find meaning in the world; the absence of any transcendence, coupled with the vacuousness of contemporary culture, leaves the characters with their own empirical experience as the only "true sentence" (to borrow Hemingway's phrase) in which they can find meaning. The danger, of course, with such a dynamic is that the characters may succumb to mere hedonism, abandoning altogether the quest for meaning; Harrison explores this dynamic in both *Farmer* and *Warlock,* emphasizing the need for both a realist's experience of the world and a romanticist's hope for something more.

Dalva is both a strong psychological portrait and a vivid indictment of the ill effects of what Harrison understands as our legacy of mistreatment of the Native American people. In a 1988 *Paris Review* interview, Harrison said, "To me, the Indians are our curse on the house of Atreus. They're our doom. They way we killed them is also what's killing us now." Utilizing sections written in the form of a diary, some of which work better than others (why, for example, does Dalva write of her sister's sexual exploits in a diary account intended for her son?), the novel addresses Dalva's search for this son, whom she gave up when she was sixteen. The novel also presents a graphic picture of the disintegration of the Lakota nation at the hands of corrupt treaties and profit-seeking whites. Never sliding into mere didacticism, the book manages to have both a strong plot and a compelling discursive side.

Two other aspects of Harrison's work are worth mentioning. Although his writing style is frequently subdued, many critics have noted the poetic quality of the prose. As a practicing poet, Harrison is certainly attentive to the rhythmic quality of the language he uses; his poetry is also strong. *The Theory and Practice of Rivers* is a fine collection that reveals both the author's ability to render a strong sense of place (northern Michigan) and his facility with the difficult Arabic lyric form called the ghazel. His *Selected and New Poems*, however, which includes earlier work, should not be ignored; it contains the same lyrical and narrative strength of the later poems, utilizing a shorter, tauter line, yet also showing a facility for a variety of fixed forms.

In the previously mentioned interview, Harrison said, "If there's anything more gruesome than Republican politics, it's literary politics." Whether this attitude has anything to do with the failure of the literary community to fully celebrate Harrison's work is debatable. Regardless, he is an important writer of the same generation as Alice Munro, **Tim O'Brien**, **Joyce Carol Oates**, and Margaret Atwood, and he deserves to be read with the same reverence.

—Tod Marshall

HART, Moss

Born: New York City, 24 October 1904. **Education:** New York public schools to 7th grade. **Family:** Married the actress Kitty Carlisle in 1946; one son and one daughter. **Career:** Delivery boy, clerk, and furrier in New York, late 1910s and early 1920s; worked for theatrical agent Augustus Pitou, 1923; actor and director on little theater circuit, and resort camp social director, later 1920s; full-time playwright from 1930, often in collaboration with George S. Kaufman; also produced and directed for the Broadway stage. **Awards:** Megrue prize, 1930; Pulitzer prize, 1937; New York Drama Critics Circle award, for directing, 1955; Tony award, for directing, 1957. **Member:** Dramatists Guild, president, 1947-55; Authors League, president, 1955-61. **Died:** 21 December 1961.

PUBLICATIONS

Plays

The Hold-Up Man (produced 1923).
Jonica, with Dorothy Heyward, music by Joseph Meyer, lyrics by William Moll (produced 1930).
No Retreat (produced 1930).
Once in a Lifetime, with George S. Kaufman (produced 1930). 1930.
Face the Music, music by Irving Berlin (produced 1932).
As Thousands Cheer, with Irving Berlin, music and lyrics by Edward Heyman and Richard Myers (produced 1933).
The Great Waltz, from a play by Ernst Marischka and others, music by Johann Strauss (produced 1934).
Merrily We Roll Along, with George S. Kaufman (produced 1934). 1934.

The Paperhanger, with George S. Kaufman. 1935(?).
Jubilee, music by Cole Porter (produced 1935).
The Show Is On (revue), with others (produced 1936).
You Can't Take It with You, with George S. Kaufman (produced 1936). 1937.
I'd Rather Be Right, with George S. Kaufman, music by Richard Rodgers, lyrics by Lorenz Hart (produced 1937). 1937.
The Fabulous Invalid, with George S. Kaufman (produced 1938). 1938.
The American Way, with George S. Kaufman, music by Oscar Levant (produced 1939). 1939.
The Man Who Came to Dinner, with George S. Kaufman (produced 1939). 1939.
George Washington Slept Here, with George S. Kaufman (produced 1940). 1940.
Lady in the Dark, music by Kurt Weill, lyrics by Ira Gershwin (produced 1941). 1941.
Winged Victory (produced 1943). 1943.
Christopher Blake (produced 1946). 1947.
Light Up the Sky (produced 1948). 1949.
The Climate of Eden, from the novel *Shadows Move among Them* by Edgar Mittelholzer (produced 1952). 1953.

Screenplays: *Flesh*, with Edmund Goulding, 1932; *Broadway Melody of 1936*, with Jack McGowan and Sid Silvers, 1935; *Frankie and Johnny*, with Jack Kirkland, 1936; *Winged Victory*, 1944; *Gentleman's Agreement*, 1947; *Hans Christian Andersen*, with Myles Connolly, 1952; *A Star Is Born*, 1954; *Prince of Players*, 1954.

Other

Act One: An Autobiography. 1959.

*

Critical Studies: *American Dreams: Analyzing Moss Hart, Ira Gershwin, and Kurt Weill's Lady in the Dark* (dissertation) by Bruce D. McClung, 1997; "The Screenwriting Life: A Memory of Moss Hart" by Mann Rubin, in *Creative Screenwriting*, fall 1997, pp. 76-78.

*   *   *

Moss Hart's first play, *The Hold-Up Man*, written when he was nineteen, folded in Chicago. But his *Once in a Lifetime* caught Sam Harris's eye, he was given **George S. Kaufman** as a collaborator (a story wittily told in Hart's autobiography, *Act One*), and the rest is history. Their play *Once in a Lifetime* was a success and the team continued with *Merrily We Roll Along*, the classic *You Can't Take It with You*, *The Man Who Came to Dinner*, and *George Washington Slept Here*.

Then Hart, never secure alone, sought other collaborators and produced more important work. Having written *Face the Music* and *As Thousands Cheer* with Irving Berlin, *Jubilee* with Cole Porter, and *I'd Rather Be Right* with Kaufman and Rodgers and Lorenz Hart, he carried on his musical success in 1941 with Kurt Weill and Ira Gershwin: *Lady in the Dark*. This was probably the highlight of his own musical work though he directed such hits by others as Irving Berlin's *Miss Liberty* (1949) and the Lerner and Loewe blockbusters *My Fair Lady* (1956) and *Camelot* (1960). In

1943 he created a "spectacle in two acts and seventeen scenes" for the U.S. Air Force called *Winged Victory,* starring 300 servicemen, including Red Buttons and Lee J. Cobb. "The Army Emergency Relief Fund needs the money," was Lewis Nichols's review in the New York Times, but he patriotically if not critically added that it was "a wonderful show." After World War II Hart gave us *Christopher Blake*—which can be forgotten. *Light Up the Sky,* however, is a fine play about theater folk—slick, sentimental, simplistic, and very funny. It is a delightful expansion of real life. In *The Climate of Eden,* "Eden" turns out to be the British Guiana mission of Gregory Hawke's uncle, and there our hero, feeling guilty for his wife's death, is obsessed with various problems. More interesting are Hart's films such as *Gentleman's Agreement* and *A Star Is Born.*

Hart was always the innovative sort of theater man who could call for four revolving stages where no one had ever used more than two before—and the dependent sort of theater man that leaned on collaborators but also got four times as much out of them, and himself, as had ever been obtained before. He was also the sort who could submit *Once in a Lifetime* to six managers (all of whom accepted it) and then sell it to Sam Harris with the understanding that Kaufman would collaborate.

That collaboration produced one of the best comedies of the American theater, *The Man Who Came to Dinner.* Of course, "real life" made them a gift of the inimitable Alexander Woollcott, but they knew what to do with him. It also takes a crack at Noël Coward, one of the Marx Brothers, the Lizzie Borden story (which is rather ineptly worked in), and the Midwest, would-be writers, fussy nurses, "the most chic actress on the New York or London stage," etc. The plot (largely Hart's?) is carpentry, but the wisecracks (mostly Kaufman's) are pure gold.

—Leonard R.N. Ashley

HARTE, (Francis) Bret(t)

Born: Albany, New York, 25 August 1836; lived with his family in various cities in the northeast, then in New York City after 1845. **Education:** Local schools to age 13. **Family:** Married Anna Griswold in 1862; four children. **Career:** Worked in a lawyer's office, then a merchant's counting room, New York; moved to Oakland, California, 1854; teacher, LaGrange, apothecary's clerk, Oakland, and express-man in various California towns, 1854-55; private tutor, 1856; guard on Wells Fargo stagecoach, 1857; printer and reporter, Arcata *Northern Californian,* 1858-60; moved to San Francisco: typesetter, *Golden Era,* 1860-61; clerk, Surveyor General's office, 1861-63; secretary, U.S. branch mint, 1863-69; contributor and occasional acting editor, *Californian,* 1864-66; first editor, *Overland Monthly,* 1868-71; lived in New Jersey and New York, 1871-78; went on lecture tours, 1872-74; tried unsuccessfully to establish *Capitol* magazine, 1878; U.S. commercial agent, Krefeld, Germany, 1878-80; U.S. Consul, Glasgow, 1880-85; lived in London, 1885-1902. **Died:** 5 May 1902.

PUBLICATIONS

Collections

Writings. 20 vols., 1896-1914.
Representative Selections, edited by Joseph B. Harrison. 1941.

The Best Short Stories, edited by Robert N. Linscott. 1967.
Bret Harte: Stories. 1994.
Selected Stories and Sketches, edited by David Wyatt. 1995.
Bret Harte's Gold Rush: "Outcasts of Poker Flat," "The Luck of Roaring Camp," "Tennessee's Partner," and Other Favorites. 1997.

Short Stories

The Lost Galleon and Other Tales. 1867.
The Luck of Roaring Camp and Other Sketches. 1870; revised edition, 1871.
Stories of the Sierras and Other Sketches. 1872.
Mrs. Skaggs's Husbands and Other Sketches. 1873.
An Episode of Fiddletown and Other Sketches. 1873.
Tales of the Argonauts and Other Sketches. 1875.
Wan Lee, The Pagan and Other Sketches. 1876.
My Friend, The Tramp. 1877.
The Man on the Beach. 1878.
Jinny. 1878.
Drift from Two Shores. 1878; as *The Hoodlum Bard and Other Stories,* 1878.
An Heiress of Red Dog and Other Sketches. 1879.
The Twins of Table Mountain. 1879.
Jeff Briggs's Love Story and Other Sketches. 1880.
Flip and Other Stories. 1882.
On the Frontier. 1884.
California Stories. 1884.
The Heritage of Dedlow Marsh and Other Tales. 1889.
A Sappho of Green Springs and Other Tales. 1891.
Sally Dows, Etc. 1893.
A Protegee of Jack Hamlin's and Other Stories. 1894.
The Bell-Ringer of Angel's and Other Stories. 1894.
Barker's Luck and Other Stories. 1896.
The Ancestors of Peter Atherly and Other Tales. 1897.
Tales of Trail and Town. 1898.
Stories in Light and Shadow. 1898.
Mr. Jack Hamlin's Mediation and Other Stories. 1899.
Trent's Trust and Other Stories. 1903.

Novels

Condensed Novels and Other Papers. 1867; revised edition, 1871.
The Little Drummer; or, The Christmas Gift That Came to Rupert: A Story for Children. 1872.
Idyls of the Foothills. 1874.
Gabriel Conroy. 1876.
Thankful Blossom: A Romance of the Jerseys 1779. 1877.
Thankful Blossom and Other Tales. 1877.
The Story of a Mine. 1877.
In the Carquinez Woods. 1883.
By Shore and Sedge. 1885.
Maruja. 1885.
Snow-Bound at Eagle's. 1886.
The Queen of the Pirate Isle. 1886.
A Millionaire of Rough-and-Ready, and Devil's Ford. 1887.
The Crusade of the Excelsior. 1887.
A Phyllis of the Sierras, and A Drift from Redwood Camp. 1888.
The Argonauts of North Liberty. 1888.
Cressy. 1889.
Captain Jim's Friend, and The Argonauts of North Liberty. 1889.

A Waif of the Plains. 1890.
A Ward of the Golden Gate. 1890.
A First Family of Tasajara. 1891.
Colonel Starbottle's Client and Some Other People. 1892.
Susy: A Story of the Plains. 1893.
Clarence. 1895.
In a Hollow of the Hills. 1895.
Three Partners; or, The Big Strike on Heavy Tree Hill. 1897.
From Sand Hill to Pine. 1900.
Under the Redwoods. 1901.
Openings in the Old Trail. 1902; as *On the Old Trail,* 1902.
Condensed Novels: Second Series: New Burlesques. 1902.

Plays

Two Men of Sandy Bar, from his story "Mr. Thompson's Prodigal." 1876.
Ah Sin, with Mark Twain (produced 1877). Edited by Frederick Anderson, 1961.
Sue, with T. Edgar Pemberton, from the story "The Judgment of Bolinas Plain" by Harte (produced 1896). 1902; as *Held Up* (produced 1903).

Poetry

The Heathen Chinee. 1870.
Poems. 1871.
That Heathen Chinee and Other Poems, Mostly Humorous. 1871.
East and West Poems. 1871.
Poetical Works. 1872; revised edition, 1896, 1902.
Echoes of the Foot-Hills. 1874.
Some Later Verses. 1898.
Unpublished Limericks and Cartoons. 1933.

Other

Complete Works. 1872.
Prose and Poetry. 2 vols., 1872.
Lectures, edited by Charles Meeker Kozlay. 1909.
Stories and Poems and Other Uncollected Writings, edited by Charles Meeker Kozlay. 1914.
Sketches of the Sixties by Harte and Mark Twain from "The Californian" 1864-67. 1926; revised edition, 1927.
Letters, edited by Geoffrey Bret Harte. 1926.
San Francisco in 1866, Being Letters to the Springfield Republican, edited by George R. Stewart and Edwin S. Fussell. 1951.
Selected Letters of Bret Harte. 1997.

Editor, *Outcroppings, Being Selections of California Verse.* 1865.
Editor, *Poems,* by Charles Warren Stoddard. 1867.

*

Bibliography: in *Bibliography of American Literature* by Jacob Blanck, 1959; *Harte: A Reference Guide* by Linda D. Barnett, 1980.

Critical Studies: *Harte, Argonaut and Exile* by George R. Stewart, 1931; *Mark Twain and Harte* by Margaret Duckett, 1964; *Harte: A Biography* by Richard O'Connor, 1966; *Harte* by Patrick Morrow, 1972, *Harte, Literary Critic* by Morrow, 1979, and "Bret Harte, Mark Twain, and the San Francisco Circle" by Morrow, in

A Literary History of the American West, 1987; "Francis Bret Harte: Ironie und Konvention" by Klaus P. Hansen, in *Arbeiten aus Anglistik und Amerikanistik,* vol. 9, 1984; "John Hay and the Western School of Literature" by George Monteiro, in *Western Illinois Regional Studies,* spring 1984; "The End of a Friendship: Two Unpublished Letters from Twain to Howells about Bret Harte" by Francis Murphy, in *New England Quarterly,* March 1985; "Bret Hart to Robert Roosevelt on Two Men of Sandy Bar: A Newly Discovered Letter" by G.A. Cevasco and Richard Harmond, in *American Literary Realism, 1870-1910,* fall 1988; *Bret Harte's California: Letters to the Springfield Republican and Christian Register, 1866-67* edited by Gary Scharnhorst, 1990, and *Bret Harte* by Scharnhorst, 1992; "McTeague as Metafiction? Frank Norris' Parodies of Bret Harte and the Dime Novel" by William J. Hug, in *Western American Literature,* November 1991; "Rewriting the Gold Rush: Twain, Harte, and Homosociality" by Peter Stonely, in *Journal of American Studies,* August 1996, pp. 189-209; "Bierstadt's Settings, Harte's Plots" by Lee Mitchell, in *Reading the West: New Essays on the Literature of the American West* edited by Michael Kowalewski, 1996; "She War a Woman: Family Roles, Gender, and Sexuality in Bret Harte's Western Fiction" by J. David Stevens, in *American Literature,* September 1997, pp. 571-93; "Lord of Romance: Bret Harte's Later Career Reconsidered" by Axel Nissen, in *American Literary Realism,* spring 1997, pp. 64-81.

*   *   *

Because of the nature of his fiction and the timing of his publication of "The Luck of Roaring Camp" (1868), Bret Harte is often remembered as the earliest of American local colorists. Insofar as his craftsmanship is concerned, however, Harte may be considered the logical extension of earlier southern humorists like **Augustus Baldwin Longstreet,** William Tappan Thompson, **Johnson Jones Hooper,** and **Joseph Baldwin,** all of whom were realists writing with broad humor of the more primitive moments of southern frontier life.

Critics have consistently pointed out the influence of Dickens on Harte's work. Joseph B. Harrison in his introduction to *Bret Harte: Representative Selections,* has pinpointed several Dickens influences, e.g., the mixture of humor and sentiment, the exploitation of unique characters in unique situations and environment, the simplification of character to the point of caricature, extravagant dialect and names (Hash, Starbottle, Rats), the love of stupid but good people, opposition to the hypocritical, and satire on injustice.

Harte's literary career lends itself to easy if not simplistic geographic division, i.e., stories composed while the author was living in California, in New York, and in Europe. Scholars consistently point out the gradual deterioration of the artist as he moved further and further from California. In any event, the scholarly consensus is that Harte's literary reputation rests largely on his work completed before the end of 1871, when he returned to the East to write for magazines. Work completed after 1878, when Harte sailed to Europe to be a consul in Prussia, is generally considered hack work and has been all but ignored.

The use of contrast is perhaps the most genuine hallmark of Harte's fiction. Arthur Hobson Quinn, for example, noted Harte's use of "moral contrast," and John Erskine attributed Harte's successful humor to his perception of contrast in American life itself. "The Outcasts of Poker Flat," which vies with "The Luck of

Roaring Camp" for the honor of Harte's best work, centers on use of contrasts: four degenerates are juxtaposed with two innocents, a harlot starves herself to death in order to save a virgin, the gambler Oakhurst gives up his chance for safety to the Innocent and then commits suicide. Erskine notes that Harte perceives the good qualities in the life of the lowly as in "Tennessee's Partner" and that his use of parody in *Condensed Novels,* which satirizes popular sentimental and idealistic novels, is comparable to that of Swinburne.

Local color stories, because of their nature, depend to a large extent upon their fidelity to detail. Harte's stories like "The Outcasts of Poker Flat" or "Miggles," are, therefore, frequently praised for their meaningful use of detail. Some of the best short stories Harte ever wrote were written for the *Overland:* "The Outcasts of Poker Flat," "Miggles," "Tennessee's Partner," "The Idyl of Red Gulch," and "Brown of Calaveras." Scholars generally agree that Harte never again equaled their freshness, spontaneity, compression, and unity.

"Tennessee's Partner" is the third most frequently anthologized Harte story. Here, Harte makes chance, fate, and accident the normal, the customary. The sentimentality in the story satisfied the taste of the reading audience of the late nineteenth century.

Of the more than 200 poems in the standard edition of Harte, more than one half are narrative and one third humorous or satirical. Some are entirely or partially dialect. Although the great strength of Harte's poetry is brevity, he fails to unite this brevity with symbolism and emotional implication, a unity necessary to successful poetry. Harte's best poetry is always his satirical and humorous verse; the two best—and most frequently reprinted—poems are "Plain Language from Truthful James" and "The Society upon the Stanislaus." As a novelist, Harte has generally been judged superficial, for his characters, like many of Dickens's poorer characters, are wooden and puppet-like. The characters, for example, in *Gabriel Conroy, A Waif of the Plains,* and *In the Carquinez Woods* have neither ideas nor passions to be sustained or complicated.

Harte's real achievement, then, is to be found in his local color stories written, for the most part, before 1871, stories that bear his hallmarks of brevity, dramatic action reporting, the new morality of the far west, humor, contrast, and uncluttered style. G.K. Chesterton observed that Harte's fiction serves, realistically, to remind us that "while it is very rare indeed in the world to find a thoroughly good man, it is rarer still, rare to the point of monstrosity, to find a man who does not either desire to be one or imagine that he is one already."

—George C. Longest

See the essay on "The Luck of Roaring Camp."

HASS, Robert

Born: San Francisco, California, 1 March 1941. **Education:** St. Mary's College, Moraga, California, B.A. 1963; Stanford University, California (Woodrow Wilson Fellow; Danforth Fellow), 1964-67, M.A. 1965, Ph.D. 1976. **Family:** Married Earlene Leif in 1962; three children. **Career:** Teacher, State University of New York, Buffalo, 1967-71, St. Mary's College, Moraga, California, 1971-74, 1975-89, and University of Virginia, Charlottesville, 1974. Beginning 1989 professor of English, University of California, Ber-

keley. Poet-in-residence, The Frost Place, Franconia, New Hampshire, 1978. U.S. Poet/Laureate/Consultant in Poetry, Library of Congress, 1995-97. **Awards:** Yale series of Younger Poets award, 1972; US-UK Bicentennial Exchange fellowship, 1976; William Carlos Williams award, 1979; Guggenheim fellowship, 1980; American Academy award, 1984; MacArthur Foundation fellowship, 1984-89; NBCC award, for criticism, 1985; P.E.N./ B.A.B.R.A. award for translation, 1986. Poet Laureate/Consultant in Poetry, Library of Congress, 1995-97.

PUBLICATIONS

Poetry

Field Guide. 1973.
Winter Morning in Charlottesville. 1977.
Praise. 1981.
Five American Poets, with Others. 1979.
Spring Drawing. 1988.
Human Wishes. 1989.
Sun under Wood: New Poems. 1996.

Recording: *A Story about the Body,* 1988.

Other

Twentieth Century Pleasures: Prose on Poetry. 1984.
Poet's Choice: Poems for Everyday Life. 1998.
An Unnamed Flowing. 1999.

Editor, *Rock and Hawk: A Selection of Shorter Poems,* by Robinson Jeffers. 1987.
Editor, *Selected Poems 1954-1986,* by Tomas Tranströmer. 1987.
Editor, with Stephen Mitchell, *Into the Garden: A Wedding Anthology: Poetry and Prose on Love and Marriage.* 1993.
Editor, *The Essential Haiku: Versions of Basho, Buson, and Issa.* 1994.

Translator, with Robert Pinskey, *The Separate Notebooks,* by Czeslaw Milosz. 1984.
Translator, with Czeslaw Milosz, *Unattainable Earth,* by Milosz. 1986.
Translator, with others, *Collected Poems,* by Czeslaw Milosz. 1988.
Translator, with Czeslaw Milosz, *Provinces* by Milosz. 1993.

*

Critical Studies: In *Regions of Unlikeness: Explaining Contemporary Poetry* by Thomas Gardner, 1999.

*   *   *

Robert Hass is one of the most important contemporary American poets. His work embraces and distills a variety of traditions, including a sharp imagistic eye for detail and a broad-ranging philosophical sensibility. Hass asserts that two of the most profound influences on his work are William Wordsworth and **Ezra Pound.** In the case of his earlier work, the recognition of such a debt is accurate—if one adds the importance of **Wallace Stevens, Robert Lowell,** and **Theodore Roethke.** Additional influences, evident in his later work, include Hass's involvement with the works of the Polish Nobel laureate Czeslaw Milosz; the San Francisco Language poets such as Michael Palmer; and Hass's intense interest in haiku, particularly the work of Basho, Issa, and Buson.

Hass's first book, *Field Guide*, was the recipient of the Yale Younger Poet's Award. Like many first books, this one reveals the poet engaging a range of material with a range of formal techniques. Some of the most successful poems reveal his allegiance to Pound. At the end of "Song," for example, where Hass writes, "Slices of green pepper / on a bone white dish," one hears the cadences of Pound's famous "In a Station of the Metro." Other poems reveal the romantic sensibility more vividly, showing an individual attempting to make sense of the world through his relationship to nature. One should add, though, that Hass's depiction of "things in the world" shows little faith in the ability of the poet to reveal any sort of "natural piety." Instead, nature is beautiful and distant, something with which one may strive to connect—although often without success. At the end of "On the Coast Near Sausalito," for instance, the speaker holds up a cabezone fish; unable to see any thing but otherness in the creature, he and the fish "stare down the centuries."

Hass's second book, *Praise*, represents a formative moment in American poetry of the closing decades of the twentieth century. One of the most celebrated poems in the book, "Meditation at Lagunitas," has become representative of the meditative lyric, a poem of introspection and philosophical inquiry that is, of course, in some ways indebted to romantic meditative lyrics such as Wordsworth's "Tintern Abbey." The philosophical discourse of "Meditation," though, is much more evident in Hass's poetry, as is the self-reflexivity, the awareness of and interrogation of the poem's construction. In this poem and others in this collection, Hass combines the romantic's attentiveness to the sublime in the natural world with a very contemporary skepticism about the ability of such attention to perceive sublimity and the adequacy of language to embody it. Other poems, including "Heroic Simile," "The Yellow Bicycle," and "Against Botticelli," explore similar issues, respectively—the "limits to the imagination," the relationship between eros and desire, and the juxtaposition of Renaissance depictions of bodiliness and stark human need. The book ends with a long meditation on family, death, aesthetics, and childhood in "Songs to Survive the Summer." The poem certainly owes a debt to Stevens's "Credences of Summer," but Hass uses a shorter line and his epistemological and metaphysical inquiry is always tempered by a keen sense of the vivid presence of things.

Human Wishes, Hass's third collection, is more formally experimental than his earlier work. Some of the poems rely on filmic "cuts" to stitch together images, memories, allusions, and quotations. This accretive style is certainly connected to the Hass's interest in the ideogrammatic method of Pound, a technique that arranges sometimes connected, sometimes disparate materials in order to gain energy from the arrangement. However, Hass's method also seems connected to the work of Michael Palmer, particularly Palmer's collection *Notes from Echo Lake*, a book Hass has said he was reading when he started writing the poems in the first section of his book. The conditional mood is characteristic of many of these poems; they shift focus rapidly and accrete meaning through these shifts. There are also prose poems and poems that focus on the domestic. Some of the last poems in the book, including "On Squaw Peak," offer poignant moments of self-examination, plumbing the depths of relationships and responses to regret and loss.

Sun Under Wood was published during Hass's service as poet laureate of the United States. The book continues to, as Hass has put it, unravel the threads of his childhood. "My Mother's Nipples" is a particularly brilliant poem in this regard; formally innovative, the poem uses prose, rhymed sections, and free verse in a wide polyphonic investigation of a mother-son relationship. Other poems consider the efficacy of language, the history of the English language, and the movement from post-divorce pain to a new romantic life. The poems are also imbued—more so than those in any of his previous collections—with humor; "Shame: An Aria," for instance, has many comic sections. Perhaps this use of humor is connected to Hass's desire as poet laureate to explore ways in which poetry can appeal to a larger audience.

Hass's poetry places him as one of the most significant writers of the late twentieth century. He has also written a remarkable prose volume, however, *Twentieth Century Pleasures,* for which he received the National Book Critics Circle award; this collection, gracefully written and brilliantly argued, offers several exceptional essays on a variety of subjects connected to twentieth-century poetry. For instance, there are essays on free verse, the image, Rilke, and an informative introduction to the works of Czeslaw Milosz. Hass collaborated with Milosz for many years to translate his works into English, and these translations represent an important body of work in their own right. Finally, Hass also translated three of the most important haiku artists, Basho, Buson, and Issa, and the collection, *The Essential Haiku*, is a substantial literary contribution. Hass is widely recognized as one of the most important poets of his time; his work is original and strong, resplendent with a variety of different lineages in American and international literature.

—Tod Marshall

HAWKES, John (Clendennin Burne, Jr.)

Born: Stamford, Connecticut, 17 August 1925. **Education:** Trinity School, 1940-41; Pawling High School, 1941-43; Harvard University, Cambridge, Massachusetts, 1943-49, A.B. 1949. **Military Service:** Served as an ambulance driver in the American Field Service in Italy and Germany, 1944-45. **Family:** Married Sophie Goode Tazewell in 1947; three sons and one daughter. **Career:** Assistant to the production manager, Harvard University Press, 1949-55; visiting lecturer, 1955-56, and instructor in English, 1956-58, Harvard University; assistant professor, 1958-62, associate professor, 1962-67, professor of English, 1967-73, T.B. Stowell University Professor, 1973-88, since 1988 professor emeritus, Brown University, Providence, Rhode Island. Visiting assistant professor, Massachusetts Institute of Technology, 1959; special guest, Aspen Institute for Humanistic Studies, Colorado, 1962; staff member, Utah Writers Conference, summer 1962, and Bread Loaf Writers Conference, Middlebury College, Vermont, summer 1963; visiting professor of creative writing, Stanford University, California, 1966-67; visiting distinguished professor of creative writing, City College, New York, 1971-72. Member, Panel on Educational Innovation, Washington, D.C., 1966-67. **Awards:** American Academy grant, 1962; Guggenheim fellowship, 1962; Ford fellowship, 1964; Rockefeller fellowship, 1968; Foreign Book prize (France), 1974. A.M.: Brown University, 1962. **Member:** American Academy of Arts and Sciences, 1973; American Academy, 1980. **Died:** 1998.

PUBLICATIONS

Fiction

The Cannibal. 1949.
The Beetle Leg. 1951.
The Goose on the Grave, and The Owl: Two Short Novels. 1954;
   The Owl published separately, 1977.
The Lime Twig. 1961.
Second Skin. 1964.
Lunar Landscapes: Stories and Short Novels 1949-1963. 1969.
The Blood Oranges. 1971.
Death, Sleep, and the Traveler. 1974.
Travesty. 1976.
The Universal Fears (story). 1978.
The Passion Artist. 1979.
Virginie: Her Two Lives. 1982.
Innocence in Extremis (story). 1985.
Adventures in the Alaskan Skin Trade. 1985.
Island Fire. 1988.
Whistlejacket. 1988.
Sweet William: A Memoir of Old Horse. 1993.
The Frog. 1996.
The Lime Twig, Second Skin, Travesty. 1996.
An Irish Eye. 1997.

Plays

The Wax Museum (produced 1966). In *The Innocent Party,* 1966;
   1999.
The Questions (produced 1966). In *The Innocent Party,* 1966.
The Innocent Party: Four Short Plays. 1966.
The Undertaker (produced 1967). In *The Innocent Party,* 1966.
The Innocent Party (produced 1968).

Poetry

Fiasco Hall. 1943.

Other

Humors of Blood and Skin: A John Hawkes Reader. 1984.
Hawkes Scrapbook: A New Taste in Literature. 1991.

Editor, with others, *The Personal Voice: A Contemporary Prose
   Reader.* 1964.
Editor, with others, *The American Literary Anthology 1: The 1st
   Annual Collection of the Best from the Literary Magazines.* 1968.

*

Bibliography: *Three Contemporary Novelists: An Annotated Bibliography* by Robert M. Scotto, 1977; *Hawkes: An Annotated Bibliography* by Carol A. Hryciw, 1977, revised edition, as *Hawkes:
A Research Guide,* 1986.

Critical Studies: *Hawkes: A Guide to His Fictions* by Frederick
Busch, 1973; *Comic Terror: The Novels of Hawkes,* 1973, revised
edition, 1978, and *Understanding Hawkes,* 1985, both by Donald

J. Greiner; *Hawkes and the Craft of Conflict* by John Kuehl, 1975;
A Hawkes Symposium edited by Anthony C. Santore and Michael
N. Pocalyko, 1977; *A Poetry of Force and Darkness: The Fiction
of Hawkes* by Eliot Berry, 1979; *John Fowles, Hawkes, Claude
Simon: Problems of Self and Form in the Post-Modernist Novel*
by Robert Burden, 1980; *Hawkes* by Patrick O'Donnell, 1982;
"Hawkes Issue" of *Review of Contemporary Fiction,* vol. 3, no. 3,
1983; *God the Artist* by Jan Gorak, 1987; "John Hawkes, Skin
Trader" in *Nobody's Home: Speech, Self, and Place in American
Fiction from Hawthorne to DeLillo* by Arnold L. Weinstein, 1993;
Innocence, Power, and the Novels of John Hawkes by Rita Ferrari,
1996; *Crystals Out of Chaos: John Hawkes and the Shapes of
Apocalypse* by Lesley Marx, 1997; *Navigating the Minefield:
Hawkes' Narratives of Perversion* by Michaele Whelan, 1998.

*   *   *

American letters has not, on the whole, been particularly receptive to the cultivation of truly esoteric talents, probably because some appeal to a general audience is almost morally as well
as commercially compulsory in American culture. John Hawkes,
however, comes close to being a writer whose intransigent dedication to a special conception of art provides the exception to this
rule. But if he has colonized for himself a separate place in contemporary fiction, he has done so not through the promulgation
of an exotic or cultist philosophy, nor through the projection of a
public personality that cuts against the grain of conventional mores, but preeminently as a prose stylist. In his first novel, *The
Cannibal,* he staked out the literary area which he would make
uniquely his own: the creation of an uncompromising verbal artifice that aims at rendering sensuously and in the modern idiom
the melodramatic atmosphere of traditional gothic materials in a
manner designed to implicate the reader in ambivalent sado-masochistic responses. That is, Hawkes has deliberately conceived of
his fiction as a premeditated assault against a victimized reader.
The establishment of a powerful tension between the outrageously
unacceptable behavior of the plot and characters and the equally
undeniable visceral reactions of the individual reader results in that
impasse of aesthetic distortion that is usually assumed to be within
the provenance of "the grotesque." And in Hawkes's work the
largest part of the burden in achieving this goal is entrusted to his
style—a lean, elusive, visual-kinetic succession of images that alternately beguiles, frustrates, and shocks the reader's expectations.

Set in a fantastic post-World War II Occupied Germany, *The
Cannibal* ignores conventional time- sequences, character development, and cause-effect probabilities to describe the triumphant
uprising of the defeated nation in the persons of a crippled handful of mutated life-forms tortuously emerging from the debris of
their own corruption. Belying its own stoic bitterness, the novel
moves casually back and forth through time, dispassionately issuing a series of vividly etched vignettes of murder, betrayal, cannibalism, and destructive perversions of love. And although the
work occasionally suggests the experimentalism of Dada and Surrealism, its rigorous stylistic attachment to the matter-of-fact conventions of realism forces it on the reader with the imperative of
a personal nightmare.

After *The Cannibal,* Hawkes experimented with a bleak parody
of the Western (*The Beetle Leg*) and a grim excursion in archaism
(*The Goose on the Grave*) before producing the masterful *The
Lime Twig.* Partly indebted to Brighton Rock and the post-war
British movies, and partly a sardonic parody of the detective novel,
The Lime Twig depicts brilliantly the ironic confluence of banal

bourgeois fantasies (Hencher, Margaret and Michael Banks) and a ruthless underworld gang that brings those fantasies to terrible realization as it endeavors to make a fortune on a horse-race. Hawkes's uncanny evocation of the seedy atmosphere of the British demi-monde and his persuasive characterization of the twisted loneliness of Hencher and the semi-voluntary brutalization of the Bankses give this novel a quality of sadistic and yet poetic grotesquerie remarkable in its integrity to its own cruel aesthetic purposes.

With *Second Skin* Hawkes inaugurates a new direction in narrative focus, restricting himself to the consciousness of the first-person point of view (the Skipper's), throwing some doubt on the reliability of that point of view, and adding an element of playfulness to the chronicle of the horrible events (rape, sodomy, suicide) that mark the Skipper's journey toward ambiguous self-understanding. And in the trilogy of novels that followed (*The Blood Oranges; Death, Sleep, and the Traveler;* and *Travesty*), this use of an increasingly unreliable narrator and a playfulness that sometimes borders on the frivolous have become even more marked. But if these novels show a falling off from the concentrated purity of Hawkes's earlier excursions in seductive horror, his prose style has remained as sensuous, supple, and shocking as it was in the beginning.

Hawkes continued to refine and extend his range through the 1980s. *The Passion Artist* returns to the bleak fictional world of *The Cannibal. Virginie* is a Nabokovian tour de force that started as a novel based on the life of the Marquis de Sade, but the erotic bliss it presents exists in the realm of poetic artifice. *Adventures in the Alaskan Skin Trade* is the longest of Hawkes's fictions, and the most realistic in method; it employs such surprising (for Hawkes) material as the tall tale. In *Whistlejacket,* Hawkes returns to the fascination with horses that provided a center for the violence and sexuality, respectively, of *The Lime Twig* and *The Passion Artist.* In this book, the characters are obsessed with horses and with the paintings of horses created by eighteenth-century artist George Stubbs, who literally skinned the animals to understand their structure. When the stud horse owned by the wealthy Van Fleet family tramples the patriarch to death, an outsider steps in to play stud to both his wife and daughter. "While *Whistlejacket* involves several deaths and a good deal of erotica," wrote Patrick McGrath in the *New York Times Book Review,* "it is as a brilliantly sustained reflection on surface and depth, illusion and exposure, and the construction of meaning that it must finally be seen."

Hawkes remains well outside the mainstream of contemporary fiction, but he has settled a small, solid island of stylistic rigor which stands as a kind of navigational guide for his contemporaries and for those who voyage after him. McGrath called Hawkes "the most consistently interesting writer, in terms of formal inventiveness, intelligence and the sheer grace of the prose, at work in the United States today."

—Earl Rovit, updated by Tom Pendergast

HAWTHORNE, Nathaniel

Born: Nathaniel Hathorne in Salem, Massachusetts, 4 July 1804. **Education:** Samuel Archer's School, Salem, 1819; Bowdoin College, Brunswick, Maine, 1821-25. **Family:** Married Sophia Peabody in 1842; two daughters and one son. **Career:** Lived with his mother in Salem, writing and contributing to periodicals, 1825-36; editor, *American Magazine of Useful and Entertaining Knowledge,* Boston, 1836; weigher and gager, Boston Customs House, 1839-41; invested in the Brook Farm commune, West Roxbury, Massachusetts, and lived there, 1841-42; lived in Concord, Massachusetts, 1842-45, 1852, and 1860-64; surveyor, Salem Customs House, 1846-49; lived in Lenox, 1850-51, and West Newton, 1851, both Massachusetts; U.S. consul, Liverpool, England, 1853-57; lived in Italy, 1858-59, and London, 1859-60. **Died:** 19 May 1864.

PUBLICATIONS

Collections

Complete Writings. 22 vols., 1900.
Complete Novels and Selected Tales, edited by Norman Holmes Pearson. 1937.
The Portable Hawthorne, edited by Malcolm Cowley. 1948; revised edition, 1969; as *Hawthorne: Selected Works,* 1971.
Works (Centenary Edition), edited by William Charvat and others. 1963—.
Poems, edited by Richard E. Peck. 1967.
Tales and Sketches (Library of America), edited by Roy Harvey Pearce. 1982.
Novels (Library of America), edited by Millicent Bell. 1983.
Nathaniel Hawthorne: Three Complete Novels. 1993.
Miscellaneous Prose and Verse. 1994.
Haunting Tales. 1998.

Fiction

Fanshawe: A Tale. 1828.
Twice-Told Tales. 1837; revised edition, 1842.
The Celestial Rail-Road. 1843.
Mosses from an Old Manse. 1846.
The Scarlet Letter: A Romance. 1850.
The House of the Seven Gables: A Romance. 1851.
The Snow-Image and Other Twice-Told Tales. 1851.
The Blithedale Romance. 1852.
Transformation; or, The Romance of Monte Beni. 1860; as *The Marble Faun,* 1860.
Pansie: A Fragment. 1864.
Septimius: A Romance, edited by Una Hawthorne and Robert Browning. 1872; as *Septimius Felton; or, The Elixir of Life,* 1872.
The Dolliver Romance and Other Pieces, edited by Sophia Hawthorne. 1876.
Fanshawe and Other Pieces. 1876.
Dr. Grimshaw's Secret: A Romance, edited by Julian Hawthorne. 1883; edited by Edward H. Davidson, 1954.
The Ghost of Dr. Harris. 1900.
The Great Stone Face. 1997.

Other

Grandfather's Chair: A History for Youth. 1841, revised edition, 1842.
Famous Old People, Being the Second Epoch of Grandfather's Chair, 1841.

Liberty Tree, with the Last Words of Grandfather's Chair, 1841.

Biographical Stories for Children. 1842.

True Stories from History and Biography. 1851.

A Wonder-Book for Girls and Boys. 1851.

Life of Franklin Pierce (campaign biography). 1852.

Tanglewood Tales for Girls and Boys, Being a Second Wonder Book. 1853.

Our Old Home: A Series of English Sketches. 1863; in *Works,* 1970.

Passages from the American Note-Books, edited by Sophia Hawthorne. 2 vols., 1868.

Passages from the English Note-Books, edited by Sophia Hawthorne. 2 vols., 1870.

Passages from the French and Italian Note-Books, edited by Una Hawthorne. 2 vols., 1871.

Twenty Days with Julian and Little Bunny: A Diary. 1904.

Love Letters. 2 vols., 1907.

Letters to William D. Ticknor. 2 vols., 1910.

The Heart of Hawthorne's Journal, edited by Newton Arvin. 1929.

The American Notebooks, edited by Randall Stewart. 1932; in *Works,* 1972.

The English Notebooks, edited by Randall Stewart. 1941.

Hawthorne as Editor: Selections from His Writings in the American Magazine of Useful and Entertaining Knowledge, edited by Arlin Turner. 1941.

Hawthorne's Lost Notebook 1835-1841, edited by Barbara S. Mouffe. 1978.

Editor, with Elizabeth Hawthorne, *Peter Parley's Universal History.* 2 vols., 1837; as *Peter Parley's Common School History,* 1838.

Editor, *Journal of an African Cruiser,* by Horatio Bridge. 1845.

Editor, *The Yarn of a Yankee Privateer,* by Benjamin Frederick Browne(?). 1926.

*

Bibliography: *Hawthorne: A Descriptive Bibliography* by C.E. Frazer Clark, Jr., 1978; *Hawthorne and the Critics: A Checklist of Criticism 1900-1978* by Jeanetta Boswell, 1982.

Critical Studies: *Hawthorne* by Henry James, 1879; *Hawthorne: A Biography* by Randall Stewart, 1948; *Hawthorne* by Mark Van Doren, 1949; *Hawthorne's Fiction: The Light and the Dark,* 1952, revised edition, 1964, and *Hawthorne's Imagery,* 1969, both by Richard Harter Fogle; *Hawthorne: A Critical Study,* 1955, revised edition, 1963, and *The Presence of Hawthorne,* 1979, both by Hyatt H. Waggoner; *Hawthorne's Tragic Vision* by Roy R. Male, 1957; *Hawthorne, Man and Writer* by Edward Wagenknecht, 1961; *Hawthorne: An Introduction and Interpretation,* 1961, and *Hawthorne: A Biography,* 1980, both by Arlin Turner; *Hawthorne Centenary Essays* edited by Roy Harvey Pearce, 1964; *Hawthorne* by Terence Martin, 1965, revised edition, 1983; *The Sins of the Fathers: Hawthorne's Psychological Themes* by Frederick Crews, 1966; *Hawthorne: A Collection of Critical Essays* edited by A.N. Kaul, 1966; *Twentieth-Century Interpretations of The Scarlet Letter* edited by John C. Gerber, 1968; *Plots and Characters in the Fiction and Sketches of Hawthorne* by Robert L. Gale, 1968; *Hawthorne, Transcendental Symbolist* by Marjorie Elder, 1969; *The Recognition of Hawthorne: Selected Criticism since 1828* edited by B. Bernard Cohen, 1969; *Hawthorne as Myth-Maker: A Study in Imagination* by Hugo McPherson, 1969; *Hawthorne: The*

Critical Heritage, 1970, and *Hawthorne: A Collection of Criticism,* 1975, both edited by J. Donald Crowley; *The Pursuit of Form: A Study of Hawthorne and the Romance* by John Caldwell Stubbs, 1970; *Hawthorne's Early Tales: A Critical Study* by Neal F. Doubleday, 1972; *Hawthorne's Career* by Nina Baym, 1976; *Hawthorne: The Poetics of Enchantment* by Edgar A. Dryden, 1977; *Rediscovering Hawthorne* by Kenneth Dauber, 1977; *Hawthorne and the Truth of Dreams* by Rita K. Gollin, 1979; *A Reader's Guide to the Short Stories of Hawthorne* by Lea B.V. Newman, 1979; *Hawthorne: The English Experience 1853-1864* by Raymona E. Hull, 1980; *Hawthorne in His Times* by James R. Mellow, 1980; *The Productive Tension of Hawthorne's Art* by Claudia D. Johnson, 1981; *Hawthorne: New Critical Essays* edited by A. Robert Lee, 1982; *Family Themes in Hawthorne's Fiction* by Gloria C. Erlich, 1984; *The Province of Piety: Moral History in Hawthorne's Early Tales* by Michael J. Colacurcio, 1984, and *New Essays on The Scarlet Letter* edited by Colacurcio, 1985; *Hawthorne's Secret: An Un-told Tale* by Philip Young, 1984; "Romance and the Prose of the World: Hegelian Reflections on Hawthorne" by Joseph G. Kronick, in *Theorizing American Literature: Hegel, the Sign, and History* edited by Bainard Cowan and Kronick, 1991; *Critical Essays on Hawthorne's Short Stories* edited by Albert J. von Frank, 1991; *Fiktion und Wirklichkeit: Zur narrativen Vermittlung erkenntnisskeptischer Positionen bei Hawthorne und Melville* by Bernd Engler, 1991; *Salem Is My Dwelling Place: A Life of Nathaniel Hawthorne* by Edwin Haviland Miller, 1991; *Contexts for Hawthorne: The Marble Faun and the Politics of Openness and Closure in American Literature* by Milton R. Stern, 1991; *The Office of the Scarlet Letter* by Sacvan Bercovitch, 1991; *Using Lacan, Reading Fiction* by James M. Mellard, 1991; *The Production of Personal Life: Class, Gender, and the Psychological in Hawthorne's Fiction* by Joel Pfister, 1991; "Soul Murder and Other Crimes of the Heart: Familial Abuse in Nathaniel Hawthorne's Fictional Psychodramas" by Maryhelen C. Harmon, in *The Aching Hearth: Family Violence in Life and Literature,* edited by Sara Munson Deats and Lagretta Tallent Lenker, 1991; *The Critical Response to Nathaniel Hawthorne's The Scarlet Letter* edited and introduced by Gary Scharnhorst, 1992; "The Romantic Poetics of Hawthorne" by Maya Koreneva, in *Russian Eyes on American Literature* edited by Sergei Chakovsky and M. Thomas Inge, 1992; *Hawthorne's Literature for Children* by Laura Laffrado, 1992; "Hawthorne, Emerson and the Forms of the Frontier" by James Barszcz, in *Desert, Garden, Margin, Range: Literature on the American Frontier* edited by Eric Heyne, 1992; *Nathaniel Hawthorne: A Study of the Short Fiction* by Nancy Bunge, 1993; *A Thick and Darksome Veil: The Rhetoric of Hawthorne's Sketches, Prefaces, and Essays* by Thomas R. Moore, 1994; *Nathaniel Hawthorne: The Contemporary Reviews,* 1994; *Engendering Romance: Women Writers and the Hawthorne Tradition* by E. Miller Budick, 1994; *The Province of Piety: Moral History in Hawthorne's Early Tales* by Michael J. Colacurcio, 1995; *Hawthorne's Narrative Strategies* by Michael Dunne, 1995; *The Making of the Hawthorne Subject* by Alison Easton, 1996; *Liquid Fire: Transcendental Mysticism in the Romances of Nathaniel Hawthorne* by Harvey L. Gable, 1997; *Mesmerism and Hawthorne: Mediums of American Romance* by Samuel Coale, 1998; *The Salem World of Nathaniel Hawthorne* by Margaret B. Moore, 1998; *Rhetorical Deception in the Short Fiction of Hawthorne, Poe, and Melville* by Terry J. Martin, 1998; *Citizens of Somewhere Else: Nathaniel Hawthorne and Henry James* by Dan McCall, 1999; *Hawthorne and Women: Engendering and Ex-*

panding the Hawthorne Tradition edited by John L. Idol and Melinda M. Ponder, 1999.

*   *   *

Nathaniel Hawthorne's fiction is unique in two important respects. He was the first major novelist in English to combine high moral seriousness with transcendent dedication to art. He was also the first major novelist in English to insist upon the basic unreality of his works. An imaginative genius gifted with considerable linguistic skill, he opened a path in literature that few have followed with comparable success. Like all great writers he was original in that fundamental sense in which the work resists duplication because it remains identified with the creative individuality of the author. George Eliot followed Hawthorne in the attempt to wed morality to art, but he attempted the fusion within a framework of realistic verisimilitude. Most writers since Hawthorne who have worked outside of the framework of realism have been less concerned than he with the moral seriousness of their works.

Isolation stands at the heart of his development as an artist. For twelve years after his graduation from Bowdoin College he lived in his mother's house in Salem, publishing *Fanshawe* at his own expense and numerous tales and sketches in magazines and gift annuals at rates so low that the income from the 27 tales he published in the *Token* amounted to less than $350. Since all of this early material was published either anonymously or under pseudonyms, he achieved no reputation and acquired no literary friends. In terms of financial success, indeed, it probably would not have mattered much if he had acquired friends and a reputation early. Like other American writers of his time he suffered even during the years of his greatest popularity from the lack of an international copyright law; he could neither compete at home with cheap editions of famous English authors nor reap much income from his sales in England. Although *The Scarlet Letter* made him a name, it earned him a pitifully small income (probably not more than $1,500 from the American sales during his lifetime). Under the circumstances, it is not surprising that he developed a literary aesthetic in which mass appeal had no place. He wrote to please himself and also that occasional isolated reader who would share with him his aesthetic and moral sensibilities.

He early formed the habit of working from the inside outward. Unlike his friend **Melville** he possessed no well of exotic experience from which to draw his subject matter. His material came from his thoughts, his reading, his brooding upon New England and its history. Coming to believe that all the truth that matters is inner ("the truth," as he expressed it, "of the human heart"), he considered externalities to be inherently deceptive. Consequently he considered verisimilitude, in the sense of faithfulness to the world of actuality, to be a highly questionable merit in fiction. Much more important to him was the construction of a fictive world that remained faithful to the artist's inmost vision. Hence his insistence that his works were to be judged as romances rather than novels. Hence, too, the considerable drive toward symbol and allegory.

He is a romantic writer, but not because his material is distant in time and place. Among his longer fictions, *The House of the Seven Gables, The Blithedale Romance,* and *The Marble Faun* are contemporary with his own time. *The Scarlet Letter* and many of the tales are set in that Puritan New England that he knew so intimately. He is romantic in the more important sense of considering verifiable fact to be a less important commodity in the world than the unverifiable discoveries of imagination and intuition. He

is also romantic in the particularly American sense of possessing a visionary idea of a society in which perfect freedom, equality, and justice might one day prevail, though no such society has yet appeared on earth. It is against such a vision that *The Scarlet Letter* especially must be read; it is the vision that places Hawthorne, for all his idiosyncrasy, in the direct line of American novelists from **Cooper** through Melville, **Twain**, and **James**.

His most frequent themes revolve around the sanctity of the individual, the necessity for warm human relationships, the nature of sin, a distrust of science and the intellect, and a belief in the fundamental ambiguity of earthly phenomena. All are closely related in his work, with an exploration of the nature of sin the tie that binds the others together. Thus the characters of Rappaccini ("Rappaccini's Daughter"), Ethan Brand ("Ethan Brand"), and Roger Chillingworth (*The Scarlet Letter*) mix their sin from the same ingredients: all are coldly intellectual, scientifically detached individuals who possess no effectively warm human relationships, are willing and even eager to intrude upon the privacy of others, and are convinced of the possibility of ultimate triumph over the mysteries of the phenomenal world. The sin of adultery that Hester Prynne of *The Scarlet Letter* has committed is much less sweeping than this. The result of a natural need for human warmth, it is clothed in ambiguity. There are sins and sins. In a more perfect society Hester's act would be no sin. If there exists, however, the unpardonable sin that Ethan Brand seeks it is very close to that attributed to Roger Chillingworth by Arthur Dimmesdale in *The Scarlet Letter*: "He has violated, in cold blood, the sanctity of a human heart."

The terrific "power of blackness" that Melville saw in Hawthorne begins in the isolation of the artist and ends in the ambiguity of his work. As artist he must break through the isolation or remain self-incased and unread. His artistry drives him inward, away from the human contact that is necessary for survival both as a writer and as a man. In his works he must remain true to his deepest vision, including for Hawthorne an abiding sense of the world's unshakeable ambiguities, but he must also make this vision accessible to others. In "The Minister's Black Veil" and "Young Goodman Brown" the touchstones of isolation and ambiguity are given splendid emphasis, but they remain important to the effect of large numbers of other works as well, from deceptively simple sketches such as "Wakefield" or "The Ambitious Guest" through the relative lightness of *The House of the Seven Gables* to the dark complexities of *The Marble Faun.*

In the end, the peculiar conditions of his creative life served him well. Steeped in the New England that he depicted so effectively in the majority of his works, he created masterly short fiction because the form came naturally to him. He probed beneath the surfaces of his subjects because he saw so little in the outward appearances that was of lasting interest. Without the financial support of the British three-decker tradition, he wrote much shorter novels than Dickens or Eliot, but his works gain in impact through compression. Few novelists in English have accomplished so much in so few words as is accomplished in *The Scarlet Letter.* Few have displayed better than Hawthorne does in his best works the power of romance, or, by inference, the limitations of superficial realism. Seldom have the modes of symbol and allegory been so effectively rendered in prose.

—George Perkins

See the essays on "Ethan Brand" and *The Scarlet Letter.*

HAYDEN, Robert (Earl)

Born: Detroit, Michigan, 4 August 1913. **Education:** Detroit public schools; Detroit City College (now Wayne State University), 1932-36, B.A. 1942; University of Michigan, Ann Arbor (Hopwood award, 1938, 1942) part-time 1938-40, full-time 1941-44, M.A. in English 1944. **Family:** Married Erma Inez Morris in 1940; one daughter. **Career:** Writer and researcher, Federal Writers Project (Works Progress Administration), Detroit, 1936-40; teaching assistant in English, University of Michigan, 1944-46; assistant professor, 1946-53, associate professor, 1954-66, and professor of English, 1967-69, Fisk University, Nashville, Tennessee; visiting professor, 1968, and professor of English, 1969-80, University of Michigan. Poet-in-residence, Indiana State University, Terre Haute, summer 1967; Bingham Professor, University of Louisville, Kentucky, spring 1969; poet-in-residence, University of Washington, Seattle, summer 1969, Denison University, Granville, Ohio, 1971, and Connecticut College, New London, 1974; staff member, Bread Loaf Writers Conference, Middlebury College, Vermont, 1972. Joined Baha'i Faith, 1942; poetry editor of Baha'i magazine *World Order* from 1967. Consultant, Scott Foresman, publishers, Glenview, Illinois, from 1970; consultant in poetry, Library of Congress, Washington, D.C., 1976-78. **Awards:** Rosenwald fellowship, 1947; Ford Foundation grant, 1954; World Festival of Negro Arts (Dakar, Senegal) poetry prize, 1966; American Academy Loines award, 1970; Academy of American Poets fellowship, 1975. D.Litt.: Grand Valley State College, Allendale, Michigan, 1975. D.H.L.: Brown University, Providence, Rhode Island, 1976; Benedict College, Columbia, South Carolina, 1977; Wayne State University, 1977. **Member:** American Academy, 1979. **Died:** 25 February 1980.

PUBLICATIONS

Collections

Collected Prose, edited by Frederick Glaysher. 1984.

Poetry

Heart-Shape in the Dust. 1940.
The Lion and the Archer, with Myron O'Higgins. 1948.
Figure of Time. 1955.
A Ballad of Remembrance. 1962.
Selected Poems. 1966.
Words in the Mourning Time. 1970.
The Night-Blooming Cereus. 1972.
Angle of Ascent: New and Selected Poems. 1975.
American Journal. 1978; revised edition, 1982.

Other

How I Write 1, with Judson Philips and Lawson Carter. 1972.
Nine Black American Doctors (for children), with Jacqueline Harris. 1976.

Editor, *Kaleidoscope: Poems by American Negro Poets.* 1967.
Editor, with David J. Burrows and Frederick R. Lapides, *Afro American Literature: An Introduction.* 1971.

Editor, with James E. Miller, Jr., and Robert O'Neal, *The United States in Literature.* 1973.

*

Bibliography: "Robert Hayden" by Xavier Nicholas, in *Bulletin of Bibliography,* September 1985.

Critical Studies: "Reconsiderations and Reviews: A Remembrance for Robert Hayden, 1913-1980" by Vilma Raskin Potter, in *Journal of the Society for the Study of the Multi-ethnic Literature of the United States,* spring 1981; "Remembering Robert Hayden" by Michael S. Harper, in *Michigan Quarterly Review,* winter 1982; "Homage to a Mystery Boy" by John S. Wright, in *Georgia Review,* winter 1982; *From the Auroral Darkness: The Life and Poetry of Hayden* by John Hatcher, 1984; "Robert Hayden's Meditation on Art: The Final Sequence of Words in the Mourning Time" by Fritz Oehlschlaeger, in *Black American Literature Forum,* fall 1985; "Robert Hayden in the 1940's" by Reginald Gibbons, in *TriQuarterly,* winter 1985; "Robert Hayden and Michael S. Harper: A Literary Friendship" by Xavier Nicholas, in *Callaloo: A Journal of African American and African Arts and Letters,* fall 1994, pp. 975-1016; "Freud and Hayden: A Speculative Note on Striking Parallel" by Robert J. Kloss, in *Journal of Evolutionary Psychology,* August 1997, pp. 160-63.

*   *   *

Much in the manner of **Countée Cullen,** the Harlem Renaissance poet, though more comfortable experimenting with free forms of verse, Robert Hayden steadfastly claimed his refusal to write racial poetry but was quite consistently at his poetic best precisely when he used the material of the black American experience. He warned in *Kaleidoscope* against placing the black writer in "a kind of literary ghetto," where he would be "not considered a writer but a species of race-relations man, the leader of a cause, the voice of protest." It must be said that even when Hayden employs racial material and themes, he usually molds them into interesting and often exquisite universal shapes that make him far more than a mere "race-relations man." If there is a criticism to be leveled at him, it would be that he is occasionally too academic (indeed, he has spent much of his life in academe), occasionally lapsing into preciousness (e.g., in "Veracruz": "Thus reality / bedizened in the warring colors /or a dream . . . ").

Mostly, however, Hayden composes with notable power and beauty. For example, his evocation, in "The Ballad of Nat Turner," of the nineteenth-century leader of a slave uprising is perhaps the most succinct and spiritually true in all of imaginative literature. Such poems as "The Diver" capture the essence of the moment or act (in this case the descent of a sea diver "through easeful azure" to the time when "somehow began the measured rise") with the felicitous marriage of sound and sense that is quintessential poetry.

—Alan R. Shucard

HAY, John (Milton)

Born: Salem, Indiana, 8 October 1838. **Education:** A private school in Pittsfield and a college in Springfield, both Illinois; Brown

University, Providence, Rhode Island, 1855-58, graduated, 1858; studied law in the office of Milton Hay, Springfield; admitted to Illinois bar, 1861. **Military Service:** Served with the Union forces during the Civil War: colonel. **Family:** Married Clara Louise Stone in 1874. **Career:** Secretary to President Abraham Lincoln, Washington, D.C., 1861-64; in the U.S. Diplomatic Service: first secretary of the legation in Paris, 1865-67; charge d'affaires, Vienna, 1867-68; first secretary of the legation in Madrid, 1868-70; first assistant secretary of state, Washington, D.C., 1879-81; ambassador to Great Britain, 1897-98; secretary of state, to President McKinley, 1898-1901, and to President Theodore Roosevelt, 1901-05. Worked in business, Cleveland, 1875-79. Staff member, 1870-75, and editor, 1881, New York *Tribune*. **Awards:** LL.D.: Western Reserve University, Cleveland; Princeton University, New Jersey; Dartmouth College, Hanover, New Hampshire; Yale University, New Haven, Connecticut; Harvard University, Cambridge, Massachusetts. **Member:** American Academy, 1904. **Died:** 1 July 1905.

Publications

Collections

Complete Poetical Works, edited by Clarence L. Hay. 1916.
Hay's Pike County, edited by George Monteiro. 1984.

Poetry

Jim Bludso of the Prairie Belle, and Little Breeches. 1871.
Pike County Ballads and Other Pieces. 1871; as *Little Breeches and Other Pieces,* 1871.
Poems. 1890.

Fiction

The Bread-Winners: A Social Study. 1884.
The Blood Seedling and Other Tales: The Uncollected Fiction of Hay, edited by George Monteiro. 1972.

Other

Castilian Days. 1871; revised edition, 1890; revised abridgement, 1903.
Abraham Lincoln: A History, with John G. Nicolay. 10 vols., 1890.
Addresses. 1906.
Letters and Extracts from Diary, edited by Henry Adams and Clara Louise Hay. 3 vols., 1908.
A Poet in Exile: Early Letters, edited by Caroline Ticknor. 1910.
A College Friendship: A Series of Letters to Hannah Angell. 1938.
Lincoln and the Civil War in the Diaries and Letters of Hay, edited by Tyler Dennett. 1939.
Henry James and Hay: The Record of a Friendship, edited by George Monteiro. 1965.
The Hay-Howells Letters: The Correspondence of Hay and William Dean Howells 1861-1905, edited by George Monteiro and Brenda Murphy. 1980.
Inside Lincoln's White House: The Complete Civil War Diary of John Hay. 1997.
Lincoln's Journalist: John Hay's Anonymous Writings for the Press, 1860-1864. 1998.

Editor, with John G. Nicolay, *Complete Works,* by Abraham Lincoln. 2 vols., 1894.

*

Bibliography: in *Bibliography of American Literature* by Jacob Blanck, 1963.

Critical Studies: *Life and Letters of Hay* by William Roscoe Thayer, 2 vols., 1915; *Hay: From Poetry to Politics* by Tyler Dennett, 1933; *Hay as a Man of Letters* by Kelly Thurman, 1974; *Hay: The Gentleman as Diplomat* by Kenton J. Clymer, 1975; *Hay: The Union of Poetry* by Howard I. Kushner and Anne Hummel Sherrill, 1977; *Hay* by Robert L. Gale, 1978; "Henry James on the Death of Del Hay: A New Letter" by George Monteiro, in *American Literary Realism, 1870-1910,* spring 1987, and "Henry James and the Secretary of State: A New Letter" by Monteiro, in *American Literary Realism, 1870-1910,* fall, 1989.

*   *   *

In 1904 John Hay was numbered among the first seven individuals elected to the American Academy of Arts and Letters. He was given this honor as the famous author of *Castilian Days,* essays on Spain; *Pike County Ballads and Other Pieces; Poems,* a collected edition; and *Abraham Lincoln: A History,* ten volumes written in collaboration with John G. Nicolay. Forgotten were the essays and stories he had published in the 1860s and 1870s in *Putnam's, Harper's,* and the *Atlantic.* It had not yet been established, moreover, that Hay was also the author of *The Bread-Winners,* an anti-labor novel that so closely reflected Hay's alarm over the growing threats to society posed by the violent strikes of 1877 and their aftermath, and one that so obviously drew upon his own sense of himself as a beleaguered member of the establishment, that the prudent author chose to publish his novel anonymously. Its authorship, a closely guarded secret for decades, was acknowledged only after his death. *The Bread-Winners* lives on, less for its reactionary argument, than for its sharp portrait of Maud Matchin, a self-made girl. In this pert and impertinent high-school graduate Hay created a portrait of American girlhood to stand beside those of **James**'s Daisy Miller and **Howells**'s Lydia Blood.

Hay's short fiction antedates *The Bread-Winners,* some of it by more than twenty years. Even though the stories constitute early work, they continue to warrant serious attention, both for their intrinsic merit and for their surprisingly skillful anticipation of many of the major technical and thematic interests of the American realists. The principal concerns of his fiction can be described as the dangers awaiting innocent and not-so-innocent Americans trying to make their way in Paris ("Shelby Cabell" and "Kane and Abel"), the duties of those who would be faithful to the Union ("Red, White and Blue"), the wages of love and miscegenation ("The Foster-Brothers") and the murderous proclivities in the heart of the midwestern farmer ("The Blood Seedling").

The last of these stories presents the Golyers, a family that figures as well in the Pike County ballads, the first three of which, "Banty Tim," "Jim Bludso, of the Prairie Belle," and "Little Breeches," catapulted Hay to immediate fame. Contemporary arguments over whether Hay or his friend **Bret Harte** had been the first to exploit the dialects of the American West served both to promote their fame and to delay the assessment of Hay's achievement. If there was no doubt that his poems captured the rhythmic speech of the Pike County Man, the notion that such speech did not provide fit substance for poetry would long plague Hay. It was not immediately recognized that the poems were not primarily attacks on common poetic speech, but rather sly barbs aimed at the conventional morality of his day. In Jim Bludso he presents a hard-talking bigamist who is nevertheless capable of Christian self-sacrifice. This rude practitioner of a religion of humanity, according to the poet, could hardly suffer retribution from a true Christian God. If this poetically unconventional statement did not receive unanimous approval, it did tap a vein of largely unexpressed feelings. With tears in her eyes, George Eliot frequently recited by heart "Jim Bludso," and in *Ulysses* Joyce has Leopold Bloom, on his way to the brothel, ruminate: "I did alla white man could . . . Jim Bludso. Hold her nozzle again the bank."

At other times Hay wrote more conventional poems that continue to appeal, among them the political "A Triumph of Order," the skillfully devised "Una," and the witty, self-ironic "A Dream of Bric-a-Brac." But when poets are again permitted to tell stories in verse, Hay's spirited ballads will recover something of the favor they enjoyed in 1897 when, on the occasion of Hay's appointment as ambassador to the Court of St. James's, English publishers, passing up *Castilian Days* and *Abraham Lincoln,* brought out an edition of Hay's poems, ignoring his properly understated title in 1890 for his collected *Poems* in favor of *Pike County Ballads and Other Poems,* one harking back to his first collection.

—George Monteiro

HAYNE, Paul Hamilton

Born: Charleston, South Carolina, 1 January 1830. **Education:** Cotes's School, Charleston; College of Charleston, graduated 1850; studied law but abandoned practice for a literary career, 1852. **Military Service:** Served on Governor Pickens's staff, 1861-62. **Family:** Married Mary Middleton Michel in 1852; one son. **Career:** Associate editor, 1852, 1854-55, and editor, 1852-54, *Southern Literary Gazette,* Charleston; founding editor, *Russell's Magazine,* Charleston, 1857-60; made homeless and bankrupt by Civil War: moved to Grovetown, near Augusta, Georgia; news editor, Augusta *Constitutionalist,* 1865; farmer and freelance writer from 1866. **Awards:** LL.D.: Washington and Lee College, Lexington, Virginia, 1882. **Died:** 6 July 1886.

PUBLICATIONS

Collections

The Southern Poets, with Sidney Lanier and Henry Timrod, edited by J.W. Abernethy. 1904.

Poetry

Poems. 1854.
Sonnets and Other Poems. 1857.
Avolio: A Legend of the Island of Cos, with Poems Lyrical, Miscellaneous, and Dramatic. 1859.
Legends and Lyrics. 1872.

The Mountain of the Lovers, with Poems of Nature and Tradition. 1875.
Poems, Complete Edition. 1882.
The Broken Battalions. 1885.

Other

Lives of Robert Young Hayne and Hugh Swinton Legare. 1878.
A Collection of Hayne Letters, edited by Daniel Morley McKeithan. 1944.
The Correspondence of Bayard Taylor and Hayne, edited by Charles Duffy. 1945.
A Man of Letters in the Nineteenth-Century South: Selected Letters of Hayne, edited by Rayburn S. Moore. 1982.

Editor, *The Poems of Henry Timrod.* 1873.

*

Bibliography: in *Bibliography of American Literature* by Jacob Blanck, 1963; by Rayburn S. Moore, in *A Bibliographical Guide to Southern Literature* edited by Louis D. Rubin, Jr., 1969; *Sidney Lanier, Henry Timrod, and Hayne: A Reference Guide* by Jack De Bellis, 1978.

Critical Studies: *Hayne* by Rayburn S. Moore, 1972; *A Man of Letters in the Nineteenth-Century South: Selected Letters of Paul Hamilton Hayne* edited by Moore, 1982, "'A Great Poet and Original Genius': Hayne Champions Poe" by Moore, in *Southern Literary Journal,* fall 1983, and "Paul Hamilton Hayne and William Gilmore Simms: Friends, Colleagues, and Members of the Guild; Essays in Honor of Thomas Cary Duncan Eaves" by Moore, in *Long Years of Neglect: The Work and Reputation of William Gilmore Simms* edited by John Caldwell, 1988; "Paul Hamilton Hayne's Defense of Francis Orray Ticknor" by Doris Lanier, in *American Notes and Queries,* September/October 1981; "Letter from O.B. Mayer to Paul Hamilton Hayne: Some Notes on Literary Relationships" by Ed Piacentino, in *Mississippi Quarterly: The Journal of Southern Culture,* winter 1996-97, pp. 117-23.

* * *

Paul Hamilton Hayne began publishing poems at the age of fifteen, and by 1861 his poetry had appeared in *Graham's Magazine,* the *Atlantic Monthly,* and the *Southern Literary Messenger* and he had collected three volumes of romantic verse based chiefly on the examples of Keats, Hunt, **Poe,** Tennyson, and **Longfellow.** His work attracted the critical attention of **Lowell** and Whipple, but the Civil War temporarily interrupted his development.

After the war Hayne's muse continued to develop in the mainstream of the Anglo-American tradition. He became a versatile versifier and employed a wide range of forms, metrical schemes, and techniques. His short poems—sonnets and nature lyrics in particular—demonstrate his work at its best. In fact, as his career progressed, Hayne became a leading American sonneteer, and such pieces as "Aspects of the Pines," "The Voice in the Pines," "To a Bee," "The First Mocking-Bird in Spring," "Hints of Spring," and "Midsummer (on the Farm)" reflect his achievement as a lyricist on nature.

At the same time Hayne could also write successful long poems, narratives like "The Wife of Brittany," an interpretation of

Chaucer's "Franklin's Tale" and Hayne's most ambitious and fully realized long poem; "Cambyses and the Macrobian Bow," succinct, with a minimum of sentimentality, and, according to **Sidney Lanier**, a "fearful tale beautifully told" in blank verse; and irregular odes like "Muscadines," a sensuous piece whose verbal melody derives from Keats and the "liquid magic" of the southern grape, and "Unveiled," an ode whose tone and view of nature suggest a philosophical kinship with Wordsworth's "Tintern Abbey." Even late in his career Hayne continued to write long poems, frequently celebrating occasions or commemorating events such as the centennials of the battles of King's Mountain and Yorktown in 1881 or the sesquicentennial of the founding of Georgia in 1883, among others. The ode on Georgia, it should be noted, and the production of his last four years, including three additional long poems, a fine sonnet on Robert E. Lee, and a handful of lyrics that are among the best he ever wrote on his own locale, were never collected.

After **William Gilmore Simms**'s death in 1870, Hayne became the "representative" poet and literary spokesperson for the South. Indeed, in the scope, versatility, and bulk of his production, he remains a substantial minor American poet of the period, even though a sizable proportion of his output is ephemeral magazine verse. Admittedly, few of his poems come near the perfection of, say, Poe's "To Helen," for he lacked Poe's sense of art and critical acumen. Moreover, he accepted without challenge the conventions of the nineteenth-century Anglo-American poetic tradition, and many of his poems embody certain aspects of its weakest features—ornate and artificial language, empty abstractions, unalloyed bookishness, and monotonous metrical regularity. But these standards of time and taste cannot change the fact that Hayne's canon reflects the full scope of a striving for expression in a spectrum of poetic types and structures, nor should they in any way detract from the devotion he rendered his muse despite discouraging and distressing conditions of poverty and ill health during the last part of his life. His accomplishment was modest, but his dedication to literature was exemplary.

—Rayburn S. Moore

H.D. *See* **DOOLITTLE, Hilda.**

HEARN, (Patricio) Lafcadio (Tessima Carlos)

Born: On the island of Santa Maura, Greece, 27 June 1850; brought up in Dublin; became Japanese citizen, 1891. **Education:** St. Cuthbert's College, Ushaw, County Durham, England, 1863-66; Petits Precepteurs, Yvetot, near Rouen, France, 1867. **Family:** Married Setsuko Koizumi in 1891; three sons. **Career:** Lived in Paris, 1869, and New York, 1869-71; worked at various jobs in Cincinnati, 1872; proofreader, Robert Clarke Company, then staff member, *Trade List* weekly, and reporter, Cincinnati *Enquirer,* 1873-76, and Cincinnati *Commercial,* 1876-77; cofounder, *Ye Giglampz* satirical journal, Cincinnati, 1874; assistant editor, New Orleans *Item,* 1877-81; staff member, New Orleans *Times-Democrat,* 1881-87; lived in Martinique and wrote for *Harper's,* 1887-89; moved to Japan, 1890; teacher, Ordinary Middle School,

Matsue, 1890-91, and Government College, Kumamoto, 1891-94; worked for Kobe *Chronicle,* 1894-95; professor of English literature, Imperial University, Tokyo, 1896-1903; English teacher, Waseda University, 1904. **Died:** 26 September 1904.

PUBLICATIONS

Collections

Writings. 16 vols., 1922.
Selected Writings, edited by Henry Goodman. 1949.
Manuscripts and Letters, edited by Hojin Yano and others. 1974—.

Fiction

Chita: A Memory of Last Island. 1889.
Youma: The Story of a West-Indian Slave. 1890.
Barbarous Barbers and Other Stories, edited by Ichiro Nishizaki. 1939.

Other

Stray Leaves from Strange Literature. 1884.
Some Chinese Ghosts. 1887.
Two Years in the French West Indies. 1890.
Glimpses of Unfamiliar Japan. 2 vols., 1894.
Out of the East: Reveries and Studies in New Japan. 1895.
Kokoro: Hints and Echoes of Japanese Inner Life. 1896.
Gleanings in Buddha-Fields: Studies of Hand and Soul in the Far East. 1897.
Exotics and Retrospectives. 1898.
In Ghostly Japan. 1899.
Shadowings. 1900.
A Japanese Miscellany. 1901.
Kotto, Being Japanese Curios, with Sundry Cobwebs. 1902.
Kwaidan: Stories and Studies of Strange Things. 1904.
Japan: An Attempt at Interpretation. 1904.
The Romance of the Milky Way and Other Studies and Stories. 1905.
Letters from the Raven, Being the Correspondence of Hearn with Henry Watkin, edited by Milton Bronner. 1907.
The Japanese Letters, edited by Elizabeth Bisland. 1910.
Leaves from the Diary of an Impressionist: Early Writings, edited by Ferris Greenslet. 1911.
Editorials from the Kobe Chronicle, edited by Merle Johnson. 1913; edited by Makoto Sangu, 1960.
Fantastics and Other Fancies, edited by Charles Woodward Hutson. 1914.
Karma, edited by Albert Mordell. 1918.
Essays in European and Oriental Literature, edited by Albert Mordell. 1923.
Creole Sketches, edited by Charles Woodward Hutson. 1924.
An American Miscellany: Articles and Stories Now First Collected, edited by Albert Mordell. 2 vols., 1924; as *Miscellanies,* 1924.
Occidental Gleanings: Sketches and Essays Now First Collected, edited by Albert Mordell. 2 vols., 1925.
Some New Letters and Writings, edited by Sanki Ichikawa. 1925.
Editorials, edited by Charles Woodward Hutson. 1926.
Facts and Fancies, edited by R. Tanabe. 1929.

Essays on American Literature, edited by Sanki Ichikawa. 1929.

Gibbeted: Execution of a Youthful Murderer, edited by P.D. Perkins. 1933.

Spirit Photography, edited by P.D. Perkins. 1933.

Letters to a Pagan, edited by R.B. Powers. 1933.

Letters from Shimane and Kyushu. 1935.

American Articles, edited by Ichiro Nishizaki. 4 vols., 1939.

Buying Christmas Toys and Other Essays, edited by Ichiro Nishizaki. 1939.

Literary Essays, edited by Ichiro Nishizaki. 1939.

The New Radiance and Other Scientific Sketches, edited by Ichiro Nishizaki. 1939.

Oriental Articles, edited by Ichiro Nishizaki. 1939.

An Orange Christmas. 1941.

Children of the Levee, edited by O.W. Frost. 1957.

Japan's Religions: Shinto and Buddhism, edited by Kazumitsu Kato. 1966.

The Buddhist Writings, edited by Kenneth Rexroth. 1977.

Writings from Japan, edited by Francis King. 1984.

A Day in the Life of Old Japan. 1995.

Lafcadio Hearn's Japan: An Anthology of His Writings on the Country and Its People. 1997.

Editor, *La Cuisine Creole: A Collection of Recipes*. 1885.

Translator, *One of Cleopatra's Nights*, by Gautier. 1882.

Translator, *Gombo Zhebes: Little Dictionary of Creole Proverbs*. 1885.

Translator, *The Crime of Sylvestre Bonnard*, by Anatole France. 1890.

Translator, *Japanese Fairy Tale* series. 5 vols., 1898-1922.

Translator, *The Temptation of St. Anthony*, by Gustave Flaubert. 1910.

Translator, *Japanese Lyrics*. 1915.

Translator, *Saint Anthony and Other Stories*, by Guy de Maupassant, edited by Albert Mordell. 1924.

Translator, *The Adventures of Walter Schnaffs and Other Stories*, by Guy de Maupassant, edited by Albert Mordell. 1931.

Translator, *Stories*, by Pierre Loti, edited by Albert Mordell. 1933.

Translator, *Stories*, by Émile Zola, edited by Albert Mordell. 1935.

Translator, *Sketches and Tales from the French*, edited by Albert Mordell. 1935.

Lecture notes of Hearn's Japanese students published: *Interpretations of Literature*, 2 vols., 1915, *Appreciations of Poetry*, 1916, *Life and Literature*, 1917, and *Pre-Raphaelite and Other Poets*, 1922, all edited by John Erskine; *A History of English Literature*, 2 vols., 1927, supplement, 1927, revised edition, 1941, *Complete Lectures on Art, Literature, and Philosophy*, 1932, *On Poetry*, 1934, and *On Poets*, 1934, all edited by R. Tanabe; *Lectures on Shakespeare*, edited by Sanki Ichikawa, 1928; *Lectures on Prosody*, 1929; *Victorian Philosophy*, 1930; *Lectures on Tennyson*, edited by Shigetsugu Kishi, 1941.

*

Bibliography: *Hearn: A Bibliography of His Writings* by F.R. and Ione Perkins, 1934; in *Bibliography of American Literature* by Jacob Blanck, 1963.

Critical Studies: *Life and Letters* by Elizabeth Bisland, 2 vols., 1906; *Hearn* by Marcel Robert, 2 vols., 1950-51; *Young Hearn* by O.W. Frost, 1958; *Hearn* by Elizabeth Stevenson, 1961; *An Ape of Gods: The Art and Thought of Hearn* by Beongcheon Yu, 1964; *Discoveries: Essays on Hearn* by Albert Mordell, 1964; *Hearn* by Arthur E. Kunst. 1969; "Ye Giglampz and the Apprenticeship of Lafcadio Hearn" by Jon Christopher Hughes, in *American Literary Realism, 1870-1910*, autumn 1982; "After the War: Romance and the Reconstruction of Southern Literature" by Michael Kreyling, in *Southern Literature in Transition: Heritage and Promise* edited by Philip Castille and William Osborne, 1983; *Lafcadio Hearn and His German Critics: An Examination of His Appeal* by Kathleen M. Webb, 1984; "Lafcadio Hearn's Chita and Kate Chopin's The Awakening: Two Naturalistic Tales of the Gulf Islands" by Joyce Coyne Dyer, in *Southern Studies*, winter 1984; "Lafcadio Hearn et la mer" by Bernadette Lemoine, in *Cahiers Victoriens et Edouardiens*, April 1986, and "Aspects de l'exotisme de Lafcadio Hearn" by Lemoine, in *Le Voyage romantique et ses reecritures* edited by Christian La Cassagnere, 1987; "Was She Really Reconciled? Ghost Wife Stories in Chinese, Korean, Japanese and American Literatures" by Sukehiro Hirakawa, in *Tamkang Review*, autumn 1988; "Lafcadio Hearn, W.B. Yeats and Japan" by Barbara Hayley, in *Literature and the Art of Creation* edited by Robert Welch and Suheil Badi Bushrui, 1988; "Lafcadio Hearn's Translations and the Origins of Imagist Aesthetics" by Daniel Stempel, in *Comparative Literature East and West: Traditions and Trends* edited by Cornelia Moore and Raymond A. Moody, 1989; "East Meets West in Lafcadio Hearn" by Margaret Hodges, in *The Image of the Childe* edited by Sylvia Patterson Iskander, 1991; "Valery et l'Extreme-Orient" by Tsunejiro Tanji, in *Bulletin des Etudes Valeryennes*, June 1991; "Lafcadio Hearn in Japan" by Amy Vladeck Heinrich, in *Columbia Library Columns*, May, 1991; "Cultural Translator: Lafcadio Hearn" by Hephzibah Roskelly, in *Literary New Orleans: Essays and Meditations* edited by Richard S. Kennedy, 1992; "Light in New Orleans: Change in the Writings of Mark Twain, Lafcadio Hearn, William Faulkner, and Walker Percy" by Thomas Bonner, Jr., in *University of Mississippi Studies in English*, vol. 10, 1992; *Lafcadio Hearn (Koizumi Yakumo): His Life, Work, and Irish Background* by Sean G. Ronan, 1996; *Rediscovering Lafcadio Hearn: Japanese Legends, Life, and Culture* edited by Sukehiro Hirakawa, 1997; *A Fantastic Journey: The Life and Literature of Lafcadio Hearn* by Paul Murray, 1997.

*   *   *

Parental desertion and a rootless, restless childhood left Lafcadio Hearn with a heart "like a bird fluttering impatiently for the migrating season," spurning the "egotistical individualism," "constitutional morality," and scientific positivism of an Anglo-Saxon world from which he "considered (him)self ostracized, tabooed, outlawed." Initially he sought in creole New Orleans ("the paradise of the South") and the tropical Caribbean that "sensuous life . . . , the life desire" that would favor "the development of a morbid nervous sensibility to material impressions, . . . absolute loss of thinking, . . . numbing and clouding of memory." But it was the less languid, more ascetic culture of the Orient that finally offered him the refuge of "feelings, so strangely far away from all the nineteenth century part of me, that the faint blind stirrings of them make one afraid— deliciously afraid."

At his best, Hearn evokes both in form and content an ethos "as gentle as the light of dreams," "the all-temperate world," "soft serenity" and "passionless tenderness" and "the vague but immeasurable emotion of Shinto" of his adoptive home-land. "Depth does not exist in the Japanese soulstream," he observed, and the evocative, picturesque surfaces of his essays seem to gain from his own ocular deficiency: "a landscape necessarily suggests less to the keen-sighted man than to the myope. The keener the view the less depth in the impression produced." His penchant, derived from a journalistic training, was for the quick sketch and fleeting apercu; *Two Years in the French West Indies* he described as "simple note-making," "impressions of the moment," a method disclosed by the very titles of his later work: *Glimpses of Unfamiliar Japan, Gleanings in Buddha-Fields, Stray Leaves from Strange Literature,* the latter being "reconstructions of what impressed me as most fantastically beautiful in the most exotic literature." *Some Chinese Ghosts, Shadowings,* and *In Ghostly Japan* likewise retell a society through its most impalpable manifestations. Herbert Spencer's evolutionary vitalism taught him "a new reverence for all kinds of faith," which Hearn transferred to the cult of ancestor-worship. Seeking to reconcile his western sense of fragmentary but unique identity with oriental quietism and self-abnegation, he came to believe that "We are, each and all, infinite compounds of anterior lives" (*Gleanings*), and that "the thoughts and acts of each being, projected beyond the individual existence, shape other lives unborn" (*Out of the East*). He saw the past as subliminal echoes investing the present, and in the Japanese Festival of the Dead found a ceremonious symbolism of the human condition: "Are we not ourselves as lanterns launched upon a deeper and a dimmer sea, and ever separating further and further one from another as we drift to the inevitable dissolution?" (*In Ghostly Japan*).

Hearn's style, like that he admired in **Poe** and Gautier, is an "engraved gem-work of words," rich with "voluptuous delicacy"—exquisite, precious, given to elaborate catalogues of isolated details and a self-conscious, sesquipedalian cadence that can overwhelm the sense ("mesmeric lentor," "the stridulous telegraphy of crickets," "a limpid magnificence of light indescribable"). In his sympathy for the intangible and evanescent he can also rise to poignancy and at times a sharp, racy vigor.

—Stan Smith

HECHT, Ben

Born: New York City, 28 February 1894; moved with his family to Chicago then to Racine, Wisconsin. **Education:** Racine High School, graduated 1910. **Family:** Married 1) Marie Armstrong in 1915 (divorced 1925), one daughter; 2) Rose Caylor in 1925, one daughter. **Career:** Reporter, Chicago *Journal,* 1910-14; reporter, 1914-18, correspondent in Berlin, 1918-19, and columnist, 1919-23, Chicago *News;* founding editor and publisher, *Chicago Literary Times,* 1923-24; thereafter a full-time writer for the stage and for films, from 1933; formed a production company with Charles MacArthur, 1934-36; columnist ("1001 Afternoons in Manhattan"), *PM* newspaper, Long Island, New York, 1940-41. Active Zionist from 1946: cochair, American League for a Free Palestine. **Awards:** Academy award, 1928, 1936. **Died:** 18 April 1964.

Publications

Plays

The Wonder Hat: A Harlequinade, with Kenneth Sawyer Goodman (produced 1916). 1920.
The Hero of Santa Maria, with Kenneth Sawyer Goodman (produced 1917). 1920.
The Master Poisoner, with Maxwell Bodenheim, in *Minna and Myself,* by Bodenheim. 1918.
The Hand of Siva, with Kenneth Sawyer Goodman. 1920.
The Egoist (produced 1922).
The Wonder Hat and Other One-Act Plays (includes *The Two Lamps, An Idyll of the Shops, The Hand of Siva,* and *The Hero of Santa Maria*), with Kenneth Sawyer Goodman. 1925.
The Stork, from a play by Laszlo Fodor (produced 1925).
Man Eating Tiger (produced 1927).
Christmas Eve: A Morality Play (produced 1939). 1928.
The Front Page, with Charles MacArthur (produced 1928). 1928.
Twentieth Century, with Charles MacArthur (produced 1932). 1932.
The Great Magoo, with Gene Fowler (produced 1932). 1933.
Jumbo, with Charles MacArthur, music by Richard Rodgers, lyrics by Lorenz Hart (produced 1935). 1935.
To Quito and Back (produced 1937). 1937.
Ladies and Gentlemen, with Charles MacArthur, from a play by Ladislas Bus-Fekete (produced 1939). 1941.
Fun to Be Free: Patriotic Pageant, with Charles MacArthur (produced 1941). 1941.
Lily of the Valley (produced 1942).
We Will Never Die (produced 1943). 1943.
Wuthering Heights (screenplay), with Charles MacArthur, in *Twenty Best Film Plays,* edited by John Gassner and Dudley Nichols. 1943.
A Tribute to Gallantry, in *The Best One-Act Plays of 1943,* edited by Margaret Mayorga. 1943.
Miracle on the Pullman (broadcast 1944). In *The Best One Act Plays of 1944,* edited by Margaret Mayorga, 1945.
The Common Man (produced 1944).
Swan Song, with Charles MacArthur, from a story by Ramon Romero and Harriett Hinsdale (produced 1946). In *Stage Works of MacArthur,* 1974.
A Flag Is Born, music by Kurt Weill (produced 1946). 1946.
Spellbound (screenplay), with Angus MacPhail, in *Best Film Plays 1945,* edited by John Gassner and Dudley Nichols. 1946.
Hazel Flagg, music by Jule Styne, lyrics by Bob Hilliard, from a story by James Street and the screenplay *Nothing Sacred* (produced 1953). 1953.
Winkelberg (produced 1958). 1958.
Simon, from play by Bertolt Brecht and Lion Feuchtwanger (produced 1962).

Screenplays: *Underworld (Paying the Penalty),* with others, 1927; *The Big Noise,* with George Marion, Jr., and Tom Geraghty, 1928; *The Unholy Night,* with others, 1929 (also French version, *Le Spectre vert,* 1930); *The Great Gabbo,* with Hugh Herbert, 1929; *Roadhouse Nights (The River Inn),* with Garrett Fort, 1930; *The Unholy Garden,* with Charles MacArthur, 1931; *Scarface, The Shame of the Nation,* with others, 1932; *Turn Back the Clock,* with Edgar Selwyn, 1933; *Design for Living,* 1933; *Hallelujah, I'm a Bum (Hallelujah, I'm a Tramp, Lazy Bones),* with S.N. Behrman, 1933; *Viva Villa!,* with Howard Hawks, 1934; *Twentieth Century,* with Charles MacArthur, 1934; *Crime without Passion,* with Charles MacArthur, 1934; *Upperworld,* with others, 1934; *The Scoundrel,* with Charles MacArthur, 1935; *Barbary Coast,* with Charles MacArthur, 1935; *Once in a Blue Moon,* with Charles MacArthur, 1935; *Soak the Rich,* with Charles MacArthur, 1936; *Nothing Sacred,* 1937; *The Goldwyn Follies,* with others, 1938; *Gunga Din,* with others, 1939; *Lady of the Tropics,* 1939; *Wuthering Heights,* with Charles MacArthur, 1939; *It's a Wonderful World,* with Herman J. Mankiewicz, 1939; *Let Freedom Ring (Song of the West),* 1939; *Angels over Broadway,* 1940; *Comrade X,* with Charles Lederer and Walter Reisch, 1940; *Lydia,* with others, 1941; *Tales of Manhattan,* with others, 1942; *The Black Swan,* with Seton I. Miller, 1942; *China Girl,* with Melville Crossman, 1942; *Spellbound,* with Angus MacPhail, 1945; *Watchtower over Tomorrow* (short), 1945; *Specter of the Rose,* 1946; *Notorious,* 1946; *Her Husband's Affairs,* with Charles Lederer, 1947; *Kiss of Death,* with Charles Lederer and Eleazar Lipsky, 1947; *Ride the Pink Horse,* with Charles Lederer, 1947; *The Miracle of the Bells,* with Quentin Reynolds, 1948; *Whirlpool,* with Andrew Solt, 1950; *Where the Sidewalk Ends,* with others, 1950; *Actors and Sin,* 1951; *Monkey Business,* with Charles Lederer and I.A.L. Diamond, 1952; *The Indian Fighter,* with Frank Davis and Ben Kadish, 1955; *Ulisse (Ulysses),* with others, 1955; *Miracle in the Rain,* 1956; *The Iron Petticoat,* 1956; *Legend of the Lost,* with Robert Presnell, Jr., 1957; *A Farewell to Arms,* 1957; *Queen of Outer Space,* with Charles Beaumont, 1958; *Circus World (The Magnificent Showman),* 1964; uncredited collaborations (selection)—*The Front Page,* 1931; *Back Street,* 1932; *Topaze,* 1933; *The President Vanishes (The Strange Conspiracy), 1934; The Hurricane,* 1937; *His Girl Friday,* 1939; *The Shop around the Corner,* 1940; *Roxie Hart,* 1942; *Gilda,* 1946; *Dishonored Lady,* 1947; *Rope,* 1948; *Love Happy,* 1949; *The Thing (The Thing from Another World),* 1951; *The Secret of Convict Lake,* 1951; *Roman Holiday,* 1953; *John Paul Jones,* 1959; *Mutiny on the Bounty,* 1962; *Casino Royale,* 1967.

Radio Plays: *Miracle on the Pullman,* 1944; *Miracle of a Bum,* 1945.

Television Plays: *Light's Diamond Jubilee,* 1954; *Hello Charlie,* from his book *Charlie,* 1959; *The Third Commandment,* 1959.

Fiction

Erik Dorn. 1921.
Fantazius Mallare: A Mysterious Oath. 1922.
A Thousand and One Afternoons in Chicago (stories). 1922.
Gargoyles. 1922.
The Florentine Dagger. 1923.
Humpty Dumpty. 1924.
The Kingdom of Evil: A Continuation of the Journal of Fantazius Mallare. 1924.
Cutie, A Warm Mamma, with Maxwell Bodenheim. 1924.
Broken Necks and Other Stories. 1924.
Tales of Chicago Streets. 1924.
Broken Necks, Containing More 1001 Afternoons (stories). 1926.
Count Bruga. 1926.
Infatuation and Other Stories of Love's Misfits. 1927.
Jazz and Other Stories of Young Love. 1927.

The Unlovely Sin and Other Stories of Desire's Pawns. 1927.
The Policewoman's Love-Hungry Daughter and Other Stories of Chicago Life. 1927.
The Sinister Sex and Other Stories of Marriage. 1927.
A Jew in Love. 1931.
The Champion from Far Away (stories). 1931.
Actor's Blood (stories). 1936.
A Book of Miracles (stories). 1939.
1001 Afternoons in New York. 1941.
Miracle in the Rain. 1943.
I Hate Actors! 1944; as *Hollywood Mystery!,* 1946.
The Collected Stories. 1945.
Concerning a Woman of Sin and Other Stories. 1947.
The Cat That Jumped out of the Story (for children). 1947.
The Sensualists. 1959.
In the Midst of Death. 1964.

Other

A Guide for the Bedevilled. 1944.
A Child of the Century (autobiography). 1954.
Charlie: The Improbable Life and Times of Charles MacArthur. 1957.
A Treasury of Hecht. 1959.
Perfidy. 1961.
Gaily, Gaily (autobiography). 1963.
Letters from Bohemia. 1964.

Film director: *Crime without Passion,* 1934, *The Scoundrel,* 1935, *Once in a Blue Moon,* 1935, and *Soak the Rich,* 1936, all with Charles MacArthur; *Angels over Broadway,* 1940, *Specter of the Rose,* 1946, and *Actors and Sin,* 1951, all with Lee Garmes.

*

Critical Studies: *The Five Lives of Hecht* by Doug Fetherling, 1977; "Sherwood Anderson and Ben Hecht: Fancy and Fact" by Walter Gobel, in *Winesburg Eagle,* November 1982; "The Chicago Literary Times: A Description and a Book Review Index" by Ray Lewis White, in *Midamerica,* vol. 9, 1982; "His Girl Friday in the Cell: A Case Study of Theatre-to-Film Adaptation" by Jeffrey A. Smith, in *Literature Film Quarterly,* vol. 13, 1985; *Hecht, Hollywood Screenwriter* by Jeffrey Brown Martin, 1985; *Rediscovering Ben Hecht* by Florice Whyte Kovan, 1997.

*   *   *

Ben Hecht began his writing career before the evolution of "play lovers" into "play decipherers," the "audience renaissance" that he analyzed in a 1963 *Theatre Arts* article. By this evolution the status of the theatre as "our most ancient bridgehead of lucidity" was undermined. Hecht's earliest literary values, influenced by his career in journalism, taught him that "whatever confusions possessed the other arts, the art of the theatre remained basically that of a Western Union telegram—terse and informative." These principles were to govern most of his dramatic output, and partially explain why such a disciplined, intelligent, and prolific writer has only intermittently attracted critical attention.

The journalist's attention to incident and detail the "katatonic armor" that shields him in daily contact with life's severities, and the craft of shaping these into a "story" are all prominent factors in his plays. Hecht's most famous collaboration with **Charles MacArthur**, *The Front Page,* has often been dismissed as a romantic melodrama about journalism; however, it also generates a poignant dilemma between public and private values, articulated with a vigorous realism that was all but unique on Broadway in 1928. *To Quito and Back,* considered by many to be the best play that Hecht wrote alone, also introduces a journalist as a secondary character to sift out a situation in Ecuador not unlike that of the Spanish Civil War. However, the diversity of content and style in Hecht's drama is almost as great as in his screenplays. His early one-act plays (written between 1914 and 1918) show experimentation with various types of stylization then fashionable in "art theatres," a tendency that declines after the death of his first collaborator, the more experienced playwright Kenneth Sawyer Goodman, in 1918. Working with MacArthur, Hecht produced the Hollywood satire *Twentieth Century,* the musical extravaganza *Jumbo,* and the murder melodrama *Swan Song;* with Gene Fowler, he wrote the "dramatic cartoon" *The Great Magoo;* with Kurt Weill, he collaborated in the pageant of Jewish history *A Flag Is Born,* which gave a starring part to the young Marlon Brando, and netted nearly one million dollars for the Zionist cause in 1946. Several of Hecht's later plays are also graveyard dramas: *Lily of the Valley* is a purgatorial allegory, and *Winkelberg* is a work of expressionistic nostalgia. The stylistic eclecticism of Hecht's drama is reflected in the range of collaborators with whom he proved compatible, but his claim to a place in American dramatic history must rest on his tough, anecdotal realism.

Antedating Hecht's "audience renaissance" was the "Chicago Renaissance" to which he was a central contributor, and which provided the context of Winkelberg. Assessments of Hecht's novels have been increasingly unfavorable since the 1950s, and criticism of the "clever saccharinity" of the Chicago school is substantiated by a reading of his earliest prose fiction, from *Erik Dorn* to *Gargoyles.* Hecht's role as founding editor of the Chicago *Literary Times* (which he also printed, published, managed, proofed, and helped distribute) was a watershed in his career, and it was a much less pretentious Hecht who emerged to write *The Front Page;* his original purpose in that play was to reflect his "intellectual disdain of and superiority to the Newspaper" but a much more honest, frontal attitude to his writing developed, resulting in his finest novel, *A Jew in Love,* as well as the best of his short stones.

Ironically, it was only late in his career that Hecht found a commitment that would have given cohesive solidity to his central output. Jews and journalists abound in his early novels and plays, but it is only in his later autobiographical writings that he deliberately anatomizes his own identity as an American Jew.

—Howard McNaughton

HEINLEIN, Robert Anson

Pseudonyms: Anson MacDonald; Lyle Monroe; John Riverside; Caleb Saunders; Simon York. **Born:** Butler, Missouri, 7 July 1907. **Education:** The Kansas City school system; graduated from Central High School, 1924; University of Missouri, 1924-25; U.S. Naval Academy, graduate (twentieth in a class of 243), 1929; University of California, Los Angeles, graduate study, 1934-35. **Military Service:** Served in the U.S. Navy, 1929-34. **Family:** Married 1) Leslyn McDonald (divorced 1947); 2) Virginia Gerstenfeld

in 1948. **Career:** Worked as silver miner in Colorado; real estate salesperson; politician in California; writer from 1939; civilian engineer (with fellow science fiction writers Isaac Asimov and L. Sprague de Camp), Naval Air Experimental Station, Philadelphia, Pennsylvania, 1942-45; lived in California, in Colorado from 1950-66, and again in California for the remainder of his life; Columbia Broadcasting System, guest commentator during Apollo lunar landing, 1969; James V. Forrestal Lecturer, U.S. Naval Academy, 1973. **Awards:** World Science Fiction Conventions Guest of Honor, 1941, 1961, and 1976; World Science Fiction Convention Hugo awards, 1956, 1960, 1962, and 1976; Boys' Clubs of America Book award, 1959; Oklahoma Library Association Sequoyah Children's Book award of Oklahoma, 1961; *LOCUS* magazine readers' polls best all-time author, 1973 and 1975; National Rare Blood Club Humanitarian award, 1974; Science Fiction Writers of America Nebula Grand Master award, 1975; Council of Community Blood Centers award, 1977; American Association of Blood Banks award, 1977; Inkpot award, 1977; NASA Distinguished Public Service Medal, 1988. L.H.D.: Eastern Michigan University, 1977. **Member:** American Institute of Astronautics and Aeronautics; Authors' League of America; Navy League; Air Force Association; Air Power Council; Association of the Army of the United States; United States Naval Academy Alumni Association; American Association for the Advancement of Science. **Died:** 8 May 1988.

PUBLICATIONS

Collections

The Man Who Sold the Moon. 1950.
The Green Hills of Earth. 1951.
Universe. 1951; as *Orphans of the Sky,* 1964.
Assignment in Eternity. 1953.
The Menace from Earth. 1959.
The Unpleasant Profession of Jonathan Hoag. 1959.
Three by Heinlein. 1965; as *A Heinlein Triad,* 1966.
The Worlds of Robert A. Heinlein. 1966.
The Past Through Tomorrow. 1967.
The Best of Robert Heinlein, 1939-1959. 1973.
Destination Moon. 1979.
Expanded Universe. 1980.
Requiem. 1992.

Novels

Rocket Ship Galileo. 1947.
Beyond This Horizon. 1948.
Space Cadet. 1948.
Red Planet. 1949.
Sixth Column. 1949; as *The Day after Tomorrow,* 1951.
Farmer in the Sky. 1950.
Waldo and Magic, Inc. 1950; as *Waldo: Genius in Orbit,* 1958.
Between Planets. 1951.
The Puppet Masters. 1951.
The Rolling Stones. 1952; as *Space Family Stone,* 1969.
Revolt in 2100. 1953.
Starman Jones. 1953.
Star Beast. 1954.
Tunnel in the Sky. 1955.
Double Star. 1956.

Time for the Stars. 1956.
Citizen of the Galaxy. 1957.
The Door into Summer. 1957.
Have Space Suit, Will Travel. 1958.
Methuselah's Children. 1958.
Starship Troopers. 1959.
Stranger in a Strange Land. 1961, unabridged edition as *Stranger in a Strange Land: The Uncut Version,* 1991.
Glory Road. 1963.
Podkayne of Mars. 1963.
Farnham's Freehold. 1964.
The Moon Is a Harsh Mistress. 1966.
I Will Fear No Evil. 1971.
Time Enough for Love. 1973.
The Notebooks of Lazarus Long. 1978.
The Number of the Beast. 1980.
Friday. 1982.
Job: A Comedy of Justice. 1984.
The Cat Who Walks through Walls. 1985.
To Sail Beyond the Sunset. 1987.
Ordeal in Space. 1990.

Plays

Screenplays: *Destination Moon,* 1950; *Project Moonbase,* 1953.

Other

Famous Science Fiction Stories, with others. 1957.
The Science Fiction Novel, with others. 1959
Grumbles from the Grave (letters). 1990.
Tramp Royale (travels). 1992.
How to Take Back Your Government (nonfiction). 1993.

Editor, *Tomorrow, the Stars.* 1952.

*

Bibliography: *Robert A. Heinlein: A Bibliography* by Mark Owings, 1973; "Bibliography," in *Grumbles from the Grave* edited by Virginia Heinlein, 1990.

Critical Studies: *Heinlein in Dimension* by Alexei Panshin, 1968; *Robert A. Heinlein: Stranger in His Own Land* by George Edgar Slusser, 1976, and *The Classic Years of Robert A. Heinlein* by Slusser, 1977; *Robert A. Heinlein* edited by Joseph D. Olander and Martin Harry Greenberg, 1978; *Robert A. Heinlein: America as Science Fiction* by H. Bruce Franklin, 1980; *Robert A. Heinlein* by Peter Nicholls, 1982; *Robert A. Heinlein* by Leon Stover, 1987; *Robert A. Heinlein* by Thomas D. Clareson, 1988; *A Guide through the Worlds of Robert A. Heinlein* by J. Lincoln Thorner, 1989; *Robert Anson Heinlein* by Gordon Beason, Jr., 1990; *Self-begetting, Self-devouring: Jungian Archetypes in the Fiction of Robert A. Heinlein* by Robin Usher, 1996.

*　　*　　*

If literary history continues to be of interest in years to come, then science fiction may well come to be seen as one of the most important literary movements of the twentieth century. In that case three of its most important figures will surely be Robert A.

Heinlein, **Isaac Asimov**, and John W. Campbell, Jr., Heinlein and Asimov for what they wrote, Campbell for the editorial standards that he set and for the writers (including Heinlein and Asimov) that he nurtured.

Heinlein did not set out to become a writer. He wanted to be an admiral. Following an older brother's example, he attended the U.S. Naval Academy at Annapolis and went to sea in ships. His chosen career was barely under way when he developed tuberculosis and had to accept early retirement. In 1934, at the age of twenty-seven, he was unexpectedly a man without a goal, rudderless on a strange new sea. A married man with financial responsibilities, he tried a variety of ways to earn a living, but none of them gave him what he was looking for: a long-term, life-guiding occupation. Then he chanced upon an ad in a science fiction magazine for a short story contest, the winner of which would earn $50. He wrote a story, liked it enough to send it to Campbell at *Astounding,* and "won" $70. When "Life-Line" was published in August 1939, Heinlein had found his new career.

Over the next three years Heinlein published nearly thirty stories of various lengths, mostly in Campbell's *Astounding.* Campbell wanted stories written as if they were intended for magazines contemporaneous with the events in the stories; that is, stories that took their backgrounds for granted. Just as stories in today's magazines don't take up their readers' time with explanations of automobiles, television sets, and jetliners, so the stories Campbell wanted should not bog down in explanations of the devices of the future. Heinlein became an acknowledged master at exposition, and the writers of science fiction's "Golden Age" (1939-57) all admitted to following his examples. This is what made the initial three years of Heinlein's career so important in the history of science fiction. In this period Heinlein combined his skill in exposition with a clear and colloquial writing style, a rapidly developing sense of story structure, and an often strong emotional content to produce some of the most memorable stories to appear in science fiction, stories like "Requiem," "The Roads Must Roll," "Universe," and *Beyond This Horizon.*

Then came the Second World War. Writing entertaining stories for Campbell was suddenly not that important. His request for a return to active duty denied because of continuing poor health (a life-long problem), Heinlein made his contribution to the war effort as a civilian engineer at the Philadelphia Navy Yard. Five years later, at the end of the war, he returned to his writing.

And what a return it was! His apprenticeship under Campbell over, he began to open up new, higher-paying markets for himself and by extension for all science fiction writers. He sold to slick magazines like the *Saturday Evening Post, Argosy,* and *Bluebook,* and he reworked many of his pre-war stories for publication in hardback, this at a time when there was little or no market for science fiction in hardback. Most importantly, he began a series of "juveniles" for Scribners, a series some readers feel will turn out to be his most significant and enduring work. This series consists of twelve short novels beginning with *Rocket Ship Galileo* in 1947 and ending with *Have Spacesuit, Will Travel* in 1958. While the books in this series do not feature continuing characters (as is the case with the Hardy Boys or Nancy Drew), they do all have young protagonists (both male and female) learning to function responsibly in an adult world; in fact, the youngsters often behave more responsibly than many of the adults, who often turn out to be the antagonists. The series also turns out to be a sort of Future History combined with a Tour of the Solar System: each novel takes its characters farther away from the earth, from the moon in the first novel all the way out to the Lesser Magellanic Cloud in the last. In addition to these "juveniles" (all of which can be recommended, although of course different readers will have different favorites), Heinlein was also producing several novels for adults, novels like *The Puppet Masters* (1953) and *Double Star* (1956). When one adds in his work on the very successful film *Destination Moon* (script 1948), it is easy to see that in the decade after the Second World War Heinlein was at the top of his game.

But a major change was coming in his writing. In 1957 he turned fifty years old, the biggest fish in the little-respected science fiction pond. Also, in the spring of that year, he participated in a series of lectures at the University of Chicago, along with fellow science fiction writers C. M. Kornbluth, Alfred Bester, and Robert Bloch. Heinlein's talk was a defense of science fiction, while Bloch attacked science fiction's conservatism, drawing his examples from the works of science fiction's most respected practitioner, Robert A. Heinlein. Surely Heinlein knew Bloch's lecture—all four were eventually published in a single volume, *The Science Fiction Novel: Imagination and Social Criticism,* edited by Basil Davenport (1959). Among many other things, Bloch pointed out that the standard science fiction hero fights "to restore the 'normal' culture and value-standards of the mass-minds of the Twentieth Century. You won't find him fighting in defense of incest, homosexuality, free love, [or] nihilism." The first novel Heinlein wrote after the Chicago lectures was *Starship Troopers* (1959), which he intended as the thirteenth in his series of juveniles for Scribners. But its overt militarism and extreme violence led the editors at Scribners to reject it unanimously, thus ending the series. *Starship Troopers* instantly became—and remains—one of Heinlein's most successful books.

More important was Heinlein's next novel, *Stranger in a Strange Land* (1961). The basic story idea—a human infant being raised by aliens on their own planet—had been suggested to Heinlein by his wife Virginia in 1949. He had started work on the novel in the early 1950s, but had been unable to finish it. Now, in late 1959, after his fiftieth birthday, after the Chicago lectures, after the collapse of his juvenile series for Scribners, after establishing himself financially with a substantial body of work, Heinlein decided to turn to an adult book for an adult audience with adult themes. In a letter dated October 21, 1960, he writes that the two themes he emphasized most were religion and sex, monotheism and monogamy. For example, of the first he writes, "My book says: a personal God is unprovable, most unlikely, and *all* contemporary theology is superstitious twaddle insulting to a mature mind," and of the second, "monogamy is merely a social pattern useful to certain structures of society . . . and a myriad of other patterns are possible." Whether it was written directly in response to Bloch's criticism or not, *Stranger in a Strange Land* deliberately challenges "the value-standards of the mass-minds of the Twentieth Century." It is meant to make its readers think by raising questions about our fundamental assumptions about religion and society, as are the rest of Heinlein's novels from 1961 until his death in 1988.

Unfortunately, in switching from writing for what he perceived as a juvenile audience to an adult one, he eventually abandoned many of the techniques that had won him his widespread readership and prestige in the first place. When he wrote in the "old" way—as in, say, *Farnham's Freehold* (1964) or what many consider to be his best novel, *The Moon is a Harsh Mistress* (1966)—his success was unquestioned. But evidently he came to feel that

adult readers are more interested in issues directly discussed by the author or by "talking heads," and so he lost his science fiction audience with two novels it considered bloated and badly in need of editing: *I Will Fear No Evil* (1970) and *The Number of the Beast* (1980). As a result, his last four novels have not been given the critical attention they need and, considering their author, surely deserve.

The keynote of Heinlein's work has always been an intense curiosity about how things work, and especially about how people and societies work today, have worked in the past, and could work in the future. Heinlein made his readers aware that things—social institutions like government and marriage and the military—don't have to continue to be the way they are today. If we can improve our airplanes and television sets, why can't we also improve the ways in which people relate to one another? His novels are constant inquiries into—and, at their best, demonstrations of—possible ways in which we can change, improve, our lives in the future. Heinlein is constantly setting before us tentative responses to the eternal question, what is the nature of the good life?

—Joseph Patrouch

HEJINIAN, Lyn

Born: Alameda, California, 17 May 1941. **Education:** Harvard University, 1959-63, B.A. 1963. **Family:** Married John P. Hejinian in 1961 (divorced 1972), one daughter and one son; 2) Lawrence M. Ochs in 1972. **Career:** Teacher, Humanities Department, California of Arts and Crafts, 1978; visiting lecturer, University of California, San Diego, 1992; faculty, summer writing program, Naropa Institute, 1992, 1995, 1998; Robert Holloway Lecturer in the Practice of Poetry, University of California, Berkeley, 1993; adjunct faculty, University of California at Berkeley, 1994-95; Coal Royalty Chair in Creative Writing, University of Alabama, 1996; guest lecturer, University of Iowa, 1998. Beginning fall 1990 member of core faculty, Poetics Program, New College of California. Editor and publisher, Tuumba Press, 1976-84; co-producer and co-host (with Kit Robinson), "In the American Tree: New Writing by Poets," June 1978; coeditor and publisher, *Poetics Journal,* beginning 1981; corresponding editor, *Logos,* 1989-91; coeditor, *Atelos,* beginning 1995. Literature panel, National Endowment for the Arts, 1979-81, 1990, 1991, 1992, 1993; literature panel, California arts council, 1982-84; member, board of directors, LINES, Detroit Art Institute, 1985-90; member, board of directors, Small Press Distribution, beginning 1987; member, steering committee, Oakland Strategic Plan for Cultural Development, 1993-94; consultant, University of California press, 1994-96. **Awards:** James D. Phelan award in literature, 1974; Editor's grant, National Endowment for the Arts, 1978, 1979, 1986; Editor's Grants, California Arts Council, 1983, 1985, 1988; Pushcart prize, 1981, 1987; Poetry Center Book award, 1988; National Endowment for the Arts Translators fellowship grant, 1988; California Arts council Individual Artist's grant, 1989; E- Independent Literary award, 1989; travel grant, Fund for U.S. Artists at International Festivals and Exhibitions, sponsored by the NEA, Rockefeller Foundation, Pew charitable Trust, and USIA, August 1989; Fund for Poetry grant, 1990. **Residence:** Berkeley, California.

PUBLICATIONS

Poetry

A Thought in the Bride of What Thinking. 1976.
A Mask of Motion. 1977.
Gesualdo. 1978.
Writing Is an Aid to Memory. 1978.
My Life. 1980.
The Guard. 1984.
Redo. 1984.
My Life (second version). 1987.
Individuals, with Kit Robinson. 1988.
Leningrad, with Michael Davidson, Ron Silliman, Barrett Watten. 1991.
The Hunt. 1991.
Oxota: A Short Russian Novel. 1991.
The Cell. 1992.
Jour de Chasse. 1992.
The Cold of Poetry. 1994.
Two Stein Talks. 1996.
Wicker, with Jack Collom. 1996.
The Little Book of a Thousand Eyes. 1996.
Guide, Grammar, Watch, and The Thirty Nights. 1996.
The Traveler and the Hill and the Hill, a collaboration with Elimlie Clark. 1998.
Sight, with Leslie Scalapino. 1999.
The Language of Inquiry. 1999.
A Border Comedy. 1999.

Other

Translator, *Description,* poems by Arkadii Dragomoshchenko. 1990.
Translator, *Xenia,* poems by Arkadii Dragomoshchenko. 1994.

*

Manuscript Collection: University of California, San Diego.

Critical Studies: "The World As Such: L=A=N=G=U=A=G=E Poetry in the Eighties" by Marjorie Perloff, in *American Poetry Review,* May-June 1984; "The World in the Work: Toward a Psychology of Form" by Barrett Watten, in *Total Syntax,* 1985, pp. 146-49; "What Then Is a Window" by Marnie Parsons, in *Touch Monkeys: Nonsense Strategies for Reading Twentieth-Century Poetry,* 1994; "Some Problems about Agency in the Theories of Radical Poetics" by Charles Altieri, in *Contemporary Literature,* vol 37, no 2, summer 1996; "Eight Justifications for Canonizing Lyn Hejinian's *My Life*" by Lisa Samuels, in *Modern Language Studies,* spring 1997.

*   *   *

Lyn Hejinian's poetry and poetic prose have consistently explored the complex, interlocking relations between personal identity, memory, narrative, and writing. In her work the forms of writing give shape and contour to the restless movements of perception and thought, while in turn, her thinking opens poetic forms to unexpected breaks and turns, straining against the framework of the formal structure. Hejinian's first major book of poetry, *Writ-*

ing Is An Aid To Memory, illustrates clearly how the formal design of her poem also expresses an aspect of subjective thought, the temporal dynamics of remembrance and forgetting. Hejinian's text is a disjunctive montage of minutely registered moments of an on-going process, a flux of time and space, in which the perceiving subject, the perceived object, and bits of speech mingle in fragmentary complexes:

> many comedies emerge and in particular a group
>   of girls
>   how can it be
>   composed when brilliantly objective and cast a little
>   further
> and with such care disintegrates
>   rub tinged
>   fall what
>   heck car

Some pieces of this passage seem to connect into relatively coherent, meaningful phrases across line breaks, such as the unit "a group / of girls"; in others, words or phrases appear to have been lost or erased. "What [the] / heck [were you doing on that] car [?]" might, for example, be a plausible—though never definitively establishable—reconstruction of the last two lines, perhaps asked about someone who, goofing around on a car, accidentally fell off. By entertaining this hypothetical interpretation, we can imagine these lines as an episode in a vaguely implied narrative: this ridiculous fall off of a car being perhaps one of the "many comedies" involving the "group of girls" mentioned earlier.

It is not only the submerged grammatical and narrative elements of such passages that serve to structure Hejinian's highly fragmentary poem but also the jagged, apparently chaotic typography. Its seeming visual disorder conceals a highly rigorous system of constraint chosen by the poet and applied consistently throughout the book-length sequence: the opening letter of the first word in each line determines the number of spaces from the left margin the line will begin. Thus, the first line quoted above, beginning with the letter "m," the thirteenth letter of the alphabet, is indented thirteen spaces, while the fourth line, beginning with "c," is indented only three spaces. The alphabet, out of which all the words in the book are of course generated, is thus given a kind of metaphorical presence in the appearance of the page. This typographical device also dramatizes the fundamental antitheses that are the main themes of the poem: freedom and necessity, memory and forgetting, simultaneous presence and the irreversible passage of time. The visual chaos of the page—resembling a cubist design of overlapping planes—plays against the stringently determined placement of the lines, although these deterministic features in turn follow from the poet's subjective decisions about which word will begin a given line. Similarly, if the alphabet is linked to memory—because it is the foundation of writing, memory's "aid"—it also gives rise here to the white space of the indentation, a kind of visual metaphor for oblivion and loss.

Hejinian's most celebrated work has been her long verse and prose sequences that treat autobiographical experience in light of her thinking about literary forms and her philosophical concerns with time and personal identity. Key among these works are her two versions of *My Life.* The first version was written in 1978, when Hejinian was thirty-seven. Taking her age as a formal device for structuring the text, she created thirty-seven sections consisting of thirty-seven sentences each. Although the reader can discern a chronological movement from section to section, passing from childhood experiences through adulthood and into the present, there is also a sophisticated ensemble of echoes, anticipations, and other sorts of eddies in time that break up the linear "plot" of the life story. As in *Writing Is An Aid To Memory,* Hejinian is interested not so much in registering the experiences of an essentially continuous and unchanging self as in conveying how a single, stable self comes to take shape despite constant change, through countless acts of attention, memory, and projection of future possibilities. When Hejinian republished *My Life* eight years later, she remained faithful to her original design: she added eight sentences to each section and eight new sections to the work, effectively bringing it into the present while augmenting the earlier sections with new depths of memory. The reader of Hejinian's *My Life* is thus faced with a paradox: a text that is far from a conventional autobiography but that nevertheless applies a basic concept of autobiography—the expressive relation between the life as lived and the life as written—with exceptional rigor. Other works that further develop this autobiographical tendency include Hejinian's book-length verse sequence, *Oxota: A Short Russian Novel,* and the long sequences from the late 1980s and 1990s such as *The Person* and *The Cell.*

—Tyrus Miller

HELLER, Joseph

Born: Brooklyn, New York, 1 May 1923. **Education:** Abraham Lincoln High School, New York, graduated 1941; University of Southern California, Los Angeles, 1945-46; New York University, 1946-48, B.A. in English 1948 (Phi Beta Kappa); Columbia University, New York, M.A. 1949; Oxford University (Fulbright Scholar), 1949-50. **Military Service:** Served in the U.S. Army Air Force, 1942-45: lieutenant. **Family:** Married Shirley Held in 1945; one son and one daughter. **Career:** Instructor in English, Pennsylvania State University, University Park, 1950-52; advertising writer, *Time* magazine, New York, 1952-56, and *Look* magazine, New York, 1956-58; promotion manager, *McCalls* magazine, New York, 1958-61. **Awards:** American Academy grant, 1963; Medicis prize (France), 1985; Interallie prize (France), 1985. **Member:** American Academy, 1977. **Residence:** Long Island, New York.

PUBLICATIONS

Fiction

Catch-22. 1961.
Something Happened. 1974.
Good as Gold. 1979.
God Knows. 1984.
Picture This. 1988.
Closing Time. 1994.

Plays

We Bombed in New Haven (produced 1967). 1968.
Catch-22, from his own novel (produced 1971). 1973.

Clevinger's Trial, from chapter 8 of his novel *Catch-22* (produced 1974). 1973.

Screenplays: *Sex and the Single Girl,* with David R. Schwartz, 1964; *Casino Royale* (uncredited), 1967; *Dirty Dingus Magee,* with Tom and Frank Waldman, 1970.

Other

No Laughing Matter (autobiographical), with Speed Vogel. 1986.
Joseph Heller: An Interview. 1988.
Conversations with Joseph Heller, edited by Adam J. Sorkin. 1993.
Now and Then: From Coney Island to Here. 1998.

*

Bibliography: *Three Contemporary Novelists: An Annotated Bibliography* by Robert M. Scotto, 1977; *Heller: A Reference Guide* by Brenda M. Keegan, 1978.

Critical Studies: *A Catch-22 Casebook* edited by Frederick T. Kiley and Walter McDonald, 1973; *Critical Essays on Catch-22,* 1974, and *Critical Essays on Heller,* 1984, both edited by James Nagel; *From Here to Absurdity: The Moral Battlefields of Heller* by Stephen W. Potts, 1982; *Joseph Heller* by Robert Merrill, 1987; *The Fiction of Joseph Heller: Against the Grain* by David Seed, 1989; *Understanding Joseph Heller* by Sanford Pinsker, 1991; *From Here to Absurdity: The Moral Battlefields of Joseph Heller* by Stephen Potts, 1995.

*   *   *

Joseph Heller is not only regarded as a major contemporary novelist, but also as one who has achieved the rare distinction of balancing academic plaudits with widespread popular success. Even more impressive, the title of his first novel, *Catch-22,* has become a household phrase, one defined by *Webster's New World Dictionary of the American Language* as "a paradox in law, regulation, or practice that makes one a victim of its provisions no matter what one does." In Heller's novel it is the deadly "catch" that specified "that a concern for one's safety in the face of dangers that were real and immediate was the process of a rational mind." Fliers designated as "crazy" are relieved of combat duty; to fly missions designed to produce "tight bombing patterns" and little else is *crazy.* But therein lies *Catch-22*'s deadly rub: fliers who recognize the absurdity of their situation are, by definition, sane—and, of course, they must continue to fly missions.

Catch-22 is nominally a World War II novel, but with important differences. Set in Italy at the tag- end of the war, it focuses on a group of American fliers who discover that the bureaucratic double-shuffle can be as deadly as enemy gunfire. In this sense, it begins where World War I novels like **Hemingway**'s *A Farewell to Arms* or Erich Maria Remarque's *All Quiet on the Western Front* end. Gallows humor replaces innocence, and staying alive counts for more than saving the world for democracy.

In short, the novel addressed itself to a generation coming of age in the 1960s. It had exactly the right mix of black humor and satiric bite to speak for those bent on kicking the System in its slats. Yossarian, Heller's protagonist, is the classical Outsider, the man who cannot quite shake the image of a fellow flier (significantly enough, named Snowden) freezing to death as his insides seep through a flak jacket. For all of *Catch-22's* hijinks, its brilliantly comic asides, and its fractured chronology, the narrative always arcs back to the image of the dying Snowden.

Heller's next novel, *Something Happened,* transported the nervous energy and the abiding paranoia of *Catch-22* to corporate America and the "willies" Bob Slocum gets when he sees a closed door: " . . . something horrible is happening behind it, something that is going to affect me adversely . . . . Something must have happened to me sometime." Slocum—surely a neurotic among contemporary American literature's vast array of neurotics—picks away at the scab that has become his life, trying to figure out where things went wrong. Slocum is a middling man caught in the world of middle management. But, unlike Yossarian, he prefers wringing his hands to tilting at windmills.

Something Happened is, among other things, an extended study in moral bankruptcy. Slocum's first- person narration makes for a draining read. One looks at Slocum with nearly equal doses of fascination and dread. If, as some critics have suggested, he is our Everyman, the portrait Heller holds up to the nature of corporate life is a chilling one indeed. Nonetheless, there are good reasons for supposing that *Something Happened* is the tortoise that will one day overtake *Catch-22*'s hare.

By contrast, Heller's most recent novels—*Good as Gold, God Knows* and *Picture This*—are not likely candidates to survive the cold eye of subsequent readings. *Good as Gold* is, in effect, three books masquerading as one: a Jewish family comedy in the mode of **Philip Roth**, a satire of academic life, and a piece of political invective. Unfortunately, the parts are not equal, and, more to the point, they do not mesh. The family dinner scenes, for example, are wonderfully funny, but the lop-sided harangues directed against Henry Kissinger are sophomoric and, even now, terribly dated.

God Knows is yet another extended (i.e., undisciplined) exercise—this time a Borscht Belt version of the King David story with Heller, rather than George Burns, playing God. Heller mixes biblical text and contemporary detail with what he hopes will be wild abandon, but the sad truth is that writers have been mining this particular vein of humor for some time. Juxtapositions of this sort—Yiddish inflections stuffed into the mouths of biblical giants—can work in a short story (one thinks, for example, of Isaac Rosenfeld's "King Solomon"), but the thread is too slender by far to sustain a novel.

Picture This compares the societies of ancient Greece, seventeenth-century Holland, and modern America, focusing on subjects such as art, war, injustice, and democracy. It is part history, part novel, and part political tract.

Given the slippery nature of literary success in America, it is unlikely that Heller will write a novel that could join *Catch-22* in that select circle reserved for "contemporary classics." On the other hand, Heller clearly has too much talent for us to imagine that he will continue to turn out "disappointments." He is, after all, a major contemporary writer, and not only because he happens to be the author of *Catch-22*.

—Sanford Pinsker, updated by Denise Wiloch

HELLMAN, Lillian (Florence)

Born: New Orleans, Louisiana, 20 June 1905 (some sources give 1906). **Education:** New York University, 1924-25; Columbia University, New York, 1925. **Family:** Married the writer Arthur Kober in 1925 (divorced 1932). **Career:** Reader, Horace Liveright, publishers, New York, 1924-25; reviewer, New York *Herald-Tribune,* 1925-28; theatrical play reader, 1927-30; reader, Metro-Goldwyn Mayer, 1930-32; began long relationship with Dashiell Hammett, in 1930; teacher at Yale University, New Haven, Connecticut, 1966, and at Harvard University, Cambridge, Massachusetts, Massachusetts Institute of Technology, Cambridge, and University of California, Berkeley. **Awards:** New York Drama Critics Circle award, 1941, 1960; Brandeis University Creative Arts award, 1960; American Academy Gold Medal, 1964; National Book award, for nonfiction, 1970; Paul Robeson award, 1976; MacDowell Medal, 1976. M.A.: Tufts College, Medford, Massachusetts, 1940. Litt.D.: Wheaton College, Norton, Massachusetts, 1961; Rutgers University, New Brunswick, New Jersey, 1963; Brandeis University, Waltham, Massachusetts, 1965; Yale University, New Haven, Connecticut, 1974; Smith College, Northampton, Massachusetts, 1974; New York University, 1974; Franklin and Marshall College, Lancaster, Pennsylvania, 1975; Columbia University, 1976. **Member:** American Academy of Arts and Sciences, 1960; vice president, National Institute of Arts and Letters, 1962; American Academy, 1963. **Died:** 30 June 1984.

PUBLICATIONS

Plays

The Children's Hour (produced 1934). 1934.
Days to Come (produced 1936). 1936.
The Little Foxes (produced 1939). 1939.
Watch on the Rhine (produced 1941). 1941.
Four Plays (includes *The Children Hour, Days to Come, The Little Foxes, Watch on the Rhine*). 1942.
The North Star: A Motion Picture about Some Russian People. 1943.
The Searching Wind (produced 1944). 1944.
Watch on the Rhine (screenplay), with Dashiell Hammett, in *Best Film Plays of 1943-44,* edited by John Gassner and Dudley Nichols. 1945.
Another Part of the Forest (produced 1946). 1947.
Montserrat, from a play by Emmanuel Robles (produced 1949). 1950.
Regina, music by Marc Blitzstein (produced 1949).
The Autumn Garden (produced 1951). 1951.
The Lark, from a play by Jean Anouilh (produced 1955). 1956.
Candide, music by Leonard Bernstein, lyrics by Richard Wilbur, John LaTouche, and Dorothy Parker, from the novel by Voltaire (produced 1956). 1957.
Toys in the Attic (produced 1960). 1960.
Six Plays. 1960.
My Mother, My Father, and Me, from the novel *How Much?* by Burt Blechman (produced 1963). 1963.
The Collected Plays (includes *The Children's Hour, Days to Come, The Little Foxes, Watch on the Rhine, The Searching Wind, Another Part of the Forest, Montserrat, The Autumn Garden, The Lark, Candide, Toys in the Attic,* and *My Mother, My Father, and Me*). 1972.

Screenplays: *The Dark Angel,* with Mordaunt Shairp, 1935; *These Three,* 1936; *Dead End,* 1937; *The Little Foxes,* with others, 1941; *Watch on the Rhine*, with Dashiell Hammett, 1943; *The North Star*, 1943; *The Searching Wind*, 1946; *The Children's Hour (The Loudest Whisper)*, with John Michael Hayes, 1961; *The Chase*, 1966.

Other

Three. 1979.
    An Unfinished Woman: A Memoir. 1969.
    Pentimento: A Book of Portraits. 1973.
    Scoundrel Time. 1976.
Maybe: A Story. 1980.
Eating Together: Recollections and Recipes, with Peter Feibleman. 1984.
Conversations with Hellman (interviews), edited by Jackson R. Bryer. 1986.

Editor, *Selected Letters*, by Anton Chekhov, translated by Sidonie K. Lederer. 1955.
Editor, *The Big Knockover: Selected Stories and Short Novels*, by Dashiell Hammett. 1966; as *The Hammett Story Omnibus*, 1966; as *The Big Knockover* and *The Continental Op*, 2 vols., 1967.

*

Bibliography: *Hellman: An Annotated Bibliography* by Steven H. Bills, 1979; *Hellman: Plays, Films, Memoirs: A Reference Guide* by Mark W. Estrin, 1980; *Hellman: A Bibliography 1926-1978* by Mary Marguerite Riordan, 1980.

Critical Studies: *Hellman* by Jacob Adler, 1969; *Hellman, Playwright* by Richard Moody, 1972; *Hellman* by Doris V. Falk, 1978; *Hellman* by Katherine Lederer, 1979; *Hellman in Hollywood* by Bernard F. Dick, 1982; "Lillian Hellman: 'The First Jewish Nun on Prytania Street'" by Bonnie Lyons, in *From Hester Street to Hollywood: The Jewish-American Stage and Screen*, 1983; "Manners, Morals and Success in Modern American Drama" by Wolfgang Binder, in *From Rags to Riches: Le Mythe du self-made man*, 1984; "Modern Southern Drama" by Jacob H. Adler, in *The History of Southern Literature* edited by Louis D. Rubin, Jr., Blyden Jackson, S. Moore Rayburn, Lewis P. Simpson, and Thomas Daniel Young, 1985; *Hellman: A Life* by William Wright, 1986; "Reference and the Representative in American Autobiography: Mary McCarthy and Lillian Hellman" by Paul John Eakin, in *Identita e scrittura: Studi sull'autobiografia nord-americana* edited by Anna Lucia Accardo, Maria Ornella Marotti, and Igina Tattoni, 1988; "The Exchange of Women and Male Homosocial Desire in Arthur Miller's *Death of a Salesman* and Lillian Hellman's *Another Part of the Forest*" by Gayle Austin, in *Feminist Rereadings of Modern American Drama* edited by June Schlueter, 1989; "Women in Lillian Hellman's Plays, 1930-1950" by Ekaterini Georgoudaki, in *Women and War: The Changing Status of American Women from the 1930s to the 1950s* edited by Maria Diedrich and Dorothea Fischer-Hornung, 1990; "The Fox's Cubs: Lillian Hellman, Arthur Miller, and Tennessee Williams" by Charlotte Goodman, in *Modern American Drama: The Female Canon* edited by June Schlueter, 1990; *Telling Lies in Modern American Autobiography* by Timothy Dow Adams, 1990; "The Foxes in Hellman's Family Forest" by Lagretta Tallent Lenker, in *The Aching Hearth: Family Violence in Life and Literature* edited by Sara Munson Deats and Lenker, 1991; *Feminine Sense in South-*

ern Memoir: Smith, Glasgow, Welty, Hellman, Porter, and Hurston by Will Brantley, 1995; *Lillian Hellman, Rebel Playwright* by Ruth Turk, 1995; *Hellman and Hammett: The Legendary Passion of Lillian Hellman and Dashiell Hammett* by Joan Mellen, 1996; *The Stolen Legacy of Anne Frank: Meyer Levin, Lillian Hellman, and the Staging of the Diary* by Ralph Melnick, 1997; *Lillian Hellman: A Research and Production Sourcebook* by Barbara Lee Horn, 1998; *Understanding Lillian Hellman* by Alice Griffin, 1998.

*   *   *

Lillian Hellman ranks as one of America's major dramatists. She entered a male-dominated field when she was nearly thirty years old and wrote some dozen plays in three decades. Her early model was Ibsen, and she shared his love of tightly knit plots and emphasis on sociological and psychological forces. Her best plays, like Ibsen's, are those in which a powerful character cuts loose and transcends the limitations of the play's rigid symmetry and plot contrivance. Along with **Clifford Odets**, the other significant writing talent of the 1930s, Hellman showed a keen interest in Marxist theory and explored the relationship between the nuclear family and capitalism. Hellman, more than Odets, held ambiguous views of man and society. Her antagonists are not wholly the products of environment but seem at times innately malicious. The quest for power fascinated the author and her characters became famous for their ruthlessness and cunning. Most of her plays verge on melodrama but are admired for their energetic protagonists and swift-moving plots.

In her first play, *The Children's Hour*, Hellman showed how the capricious wielding of power could ruin innocent people. Two young women at a girl's school are falsely accused of having a lesbian relationship by a disturbed child. They are brought to trial by outraged parents and eventually lose their case—and their school. One of the teachers commits suicide and, too late, the child's treachery is discovered. The homosexual motif, though discreetly handled, accounted for the play's notoriety in 1934; but the abuse of power by an arrogant elite is its enduring theme.

Usurping power is also the motivating force in Hellman's best-known play, *The Little Foxes*, at once a political statement and a complex study of family dynamics. The rapacious Hubbard family represents a new brand of southern capitalist who subordinates all traditions and human values to the goal of acquiring wealth and property. The strength of the play lies in Hellman's implicit comparison of the Hubbard siblings' rivalries with the competitiveness of Americans in the free enterprise system. The role of Regina Hubbard, who withholds her dying husband's heart medicine and who outwits her equally greedy brothers in a major business coup, has become a favorite vehicle for American actresses.

At the beginning of World War II Hellman wrote *Watch on the Rhine* and *The Searching Wind*, which both dealt with the fascist menace. The former play contains some witty repartee and suspenseful moments; but its solutions to the international crisis are simplistic, and it is better described as an adventure story than a thesis play.

When the war ended, Hellman returned to the easy-to-hate Hubbard family in *Another Part of the Forest*. Unfortunately the exaggerated spitefulness and hysteria of the characters and the unrelieved high-tension atmosphere of this play become nearly ludicrous. The concept of personal manipulation had become an obsession with the author, and a correlation seemed to have developed between her studies of social and societal exploitation and

her own excessive control over plot characterization and stage effects. Perhaps the playwright realized this, because in her last plays
she turned from Ibsen to Chekhov for inspiration. Both *The Autumn Garden* and *Toys in the Attic* recall the mood and ambiguous
moral judgments of Chekhov. Neither of these plays has a truly
pernicious villain, and most of the characters seem to be suffering
from a Chekhovian paralysis of will. The atmosphere is deterministic and the plots are truer to life. What has changed is that
all bids for personal power prove self-defeating—the predatory
are caught in traps of their own making and hardly struggle before
acknowledging defeat. Nevertheless these plays also include sharp,
amusing verbal exchanges and the famous blackmail scenes associated with Hellman. Blackmail, present in all of her plays, is
Hellman's favorite metaphor for personal manipulation; but in the
later works she uses blackmail and other devices with greater
subtlety, and presents a somewhat blurred but more convincing
vision of stumbling modern man and his society.

Hellman's dramatic mode, based on her adherence to continental models, is bound to an earlier era. Most of her experiments
with screenwriting proved frustrating. Her best later works were
autobiographical sketches: in *An Unfinished Woman, Pentimento,*
and *Scoundrel Time* she reveals her penetrating intelligence but tacitly acknowledges that her insights and talents are better suited to
the historical memoir.

—Kimball King

See the essay on *The Little Foxes.*

HEMINGWAY, Ernest (Miller)

Born: Oak Park, Illinois, 21 July 1899. **Education:** Oak Park High
School, graduated 1917. **Military Service:** Served as a Red Cross
ambulance driver in Italy, 1918; also served on the western front
with the Italian Arditi; wounded in action: Medaglia d'Argento al
Valore Militare; Croce de Guerra; involved in anti-submarine patrol duty off the coast of Cuba, 1942-44. **Family:** Married 1)
Hadley Richardson in 1921 (divorced 1927), one son; 2) Pauline
Pfeiffer in 1927 (divorced 1940), two sons; 3) the writer Martha
Gellhorn in 1940 (divorced 1946); 4) Mary Welsh in 1946. **Career:** Reporter, Kansas *City Star,* 1917; reporter, then foreign correspondent, Toronto *Star* and *Star Weekly,* 1920-23: covered the
Greco-Turkish War, 1922; moved to Paris, 1921, and became associated with the expatriate community, including Gertrude Stein
and Ezra Pound; correspondent in Paris for Hearst newspapers,
1924-27; settled in Key West, Florida, 1928; moved to Cuba, 1940,
and to Idaho, 1958; war correspondent for North American Newspaper Alliance, in Spain, 1937-38, and for *Collier's* in Europe,
1944-45: Bronze Star. **Awards:** Bancarella prize (Italy), 1953;
Pulitzer prize, 1953; Nobel prize for Literature, 1954; American Academy award of Merit Medal, 1954. **Died:** (suicide) 2 July 1961.

PUBLICATIONS

Collections

A Hemingway Selection, edited by Dennis Pepper. 1972.
The Enduring Hemingway, edited by Charles Scribner, Jr. 1974.

88 Poems, edited by Nicholas Gerogiannis. 1979; as *Complete Po-
ems,* 1983.
Selected Letters 1917-1961, edited by Carlos Baker. 1981.
The Complete Short Stories, edited by Finta Vigia. 1987.
The Collected Stories. 1995.
The Short Stories. 1995.

Fiction

Three Stories and Ten Poems. 1923.
In Our Time (sketches). 1924.
In Our Time: Stories. 1925; revised edition, 1930.
*The Torrents of Spring: A Romantic Novel in Honor of the Pass-
ing of a Great Race.* 1926.
The Sun Also Rises. 1926; as *Fiesta,* 1927.
Men without Women (stories). 1927.
A Farewell to Arms. 1929.
God Rest You Merry Gentlemen (stories). 1933.
Winner Take Nothing (stories). 1933.
To Have and Have Not. 1937.
The Fifth Column and the First Forty-Nine Stories (includes play).
1938.
For Whom the Bell Tolls. 1940.
The Portable Hemingway, edited by Malcolm Cowley. 1944.
The Essential Hemingway. 1947.
Across the River and into the Trees. 1950.
The Old Man and the Sea. 1952.
Hemingway in Michigan (stories), edited by Constance Cappel
Montgomery. 1966.
The Fifth Column and Four Stories of the Spanish Civil War. 1969.
Islands in the Stream. 1970.
The Nick Adams Stories, edited by Philip Young. 1972.
A Divine Gesture: A Fable. 1974.
The Garden of Eden. 1986.
The Good Lion. 1998.
True at First Light: A Fictional Memoir. 1999.

Plays

Today Is Friday. 1926.
The Spanish Earth (screenplay). 1938.
The Fifth Column (produced 1940). In *The Fifth Column . . . ,*
1938.

Screenplays (documentaries): *Spain in Flames,* with others,
1937; *The Spanish Earth,* 1937.

Poetry

Collected Poems. 1960.

Other

Death in the Afternoon. 1932.
Green Hills of Africa. 1935
The Hemingway Reader, edited by Charles Poore. 1953
Hemingway: The Wild Years (newspaper articles), edited by Gene
Z. Hanrahan. 1962.
A Moveable Feast (autobiography). 1964.
*By-Line: Hemingway. Selected Articles and Dispatches of Four
Decades,* edited by William White. 1967.

Hemingway: Cub Reporter; "Kansas City Star" Stories, edited by Matthew J. Bruccoli. 1970.
The Faithful Bull (for children). 1980.
Hemingway on Writing, edited by Larry W. Phillips. 1984.
The Dangerous Summer. 1985.
Dateline: Toronto: The Complete Toronto Star Dispatches, 1920 to 1924, edited by William White. 1985.
Conversations with Hemingway (interviews), edited by Bruccoli. 1986.
The Only Thing That Counts: The Ernest Hemingway/Maxwell Perkins Correspondence, 1925-1947. 1996.

Editor, *Men at War: The Best War Stories of All Time.* 1942.

*

Bibliography: *Hemingway: A Comprehensive Bibliography* by Audre Hanneman, 1967, supplement, 1975; *Hemingway: A Reference Guide* by Linda W. Wagner, 1977.

Critical Studies: *Hemingway: The Writer As Artist,* 1952, revised edition 1972, and *Hemingway: A Life Story,* 1969, both by Carlos Baker, and *Hemingway and His Critics: An International Anthology* edited by Baker, 1961; *Hemingway* by Philip Young, 1952, revised edition, as *Hemingway: A Reconsideration,* 1966; *Hemingway* by Stewart F. Sanderson, 1961; *Hemingway: A Collection of Critical Essays* edited by Robert P. Weeks, 1962; *Hemingway* by Earl Rovit, 1963; *Hemingway: An Introduction and Interpretation* by Sheridan Baker, 1967; *Hemingway and the Pursuit of Heroism* by Leo Gurko, 1968; *Hemingway's Nonfiction: The Public Voice* by Robert O. Stephens. 1968, and *Hemingway: The Critical Reception* edited by Stephens, 1977; *Hemingway: The Inward Terrain* by Richard B. Hovey, 1968; *Hemingway's Heroes* by Delbert E. Wylder, 1969; *Hemingway: The Writer's Art of Self-Defense* by Jackson R. Benson, 1969, and *The Short Stories of Hemingway: Critical Essays* edited by Benson, 1975; *A Reader's Guide to Hemingway* by Arthur Waldhorn, 1972; *Hemingway's Craft* by Sheldon Norman Grebstein, 1973; *Hemingway: Five Decades of Criticism* edited by Linda W. Wagner, 1974, and *Hemingway and Faulkner: Inventors / Masters* by Wagner, 1975; *By Force of Will: The Life and Art of Hemingway* by Scott Donaldson, 1977; *Scott and Ernest: The Authority of Failure and the Authority of Success* by Matthew J. Bruccoli, 1978, and *Conversations with Hemingway* (interviews) edited by Bruccoli, 1986; *Hemingway and His World* by Anthony Burgess, 1978; *The Tragic Art of Hemingway* by Wirt Williams, 1981; *Hemingway: The Critical Heritage* edited by Jeffrey Meyers, 1982, and *Hemingway: A Biography* by Meyers, 1985; *Hemingway's Nick Adams* by Joseph M. Flora, 1982; *Hemingway* by Samuel Shaw, 1982; *Hemingway: New Critical Essays* edited by A. Robert Lee, 1983; *The Hemingway Women* by Bernice Kert, 1983; *Hemingway and The Sun Also Rises: The Crafting of a Style* by Frederic J. Svoboda, 1983; *Hemingway: The Writer in Context* edited by James Nagel, 1984; *Concealments in Hemingway's Work* by Gerry Brenner, 1984; *Hemingway: Life and Works* (chronology) by Gerald B. Nelson and Glory Jones, 1984; *Cassandra's Daughters: Women in Hemingway* by Roger Whitlow, 1984; *The Young Hemingway* by Michael Reynolds, 1986; "Brett's Problem" by Wolfgang E.H. Rudat, in *Brett Ashley* edited by Harold Bloom, 1991, and *Alchemy in the Sun Also Rises: Hidden Gold in Hemingway's Narrative* by Rudat, 1992; *Hemingway: Essays of Reassessment* edited by Frank Scafella, 1991; "Modernist Eruptions" by Margot Norris, in *The* *Columbia History of the American Novel* edited by Cathy N. Davidson, Patrick O'Donnell, Valerie Smith, and Christopher P. Wilson, 1991; "Ernest Hemingway: The Road to Literary Craft" by Natalia Yakimenko, in *Russian Eyes on American Literature* edited by Sergei Chakovsky and M. Thomas Inge, 1992; *Ernest Hemingway* by Peter Messent, 1992; "Comrades-in-Arms: Models for Fiction. Hemingway and the Exiles from Nazi Germany" by Guy Stern, in *German and International Perspectives on the Spanish Civil War: The Aesthetics of Partisanship* edited by Luis Costa, Richard Critchfield, Richard Glosan, and Wulf Koepke, 1992; *Blowing the Bridge: Essays on Hemingway and "For Whom the Bell Tolls"* edited by Rena Sanderson, 1992; *Hemingway's "In Our Time": Lyrical Dimensions* by Wendolyn E. Tetlow, 1992; *Hemingway's Genders: Rereading the Hemingway Text* by Nancy R. Comley, 1994; *The Novels of Huxley and Hemingway: A Study in Two Planes of Reality* by Sanjukta Dasgupta, 1996; *New Essays on Hemingway's Short Fiction* edited by Paul Smith, 1998; *Ernest Hemingway: Seven Decades of Criticism* edited by Linda Wagner-Martin, 1998; *Hemingway: The Final Years* by Michael S. Reynolds, 1999; *Ernest Hemingway, A to Z: The Essential Reference to His Life and Work* by Charles M. Oliver, 1999; *Hemingway's Fetishism: Psychoanalysis and the Mirror of Manhood* by Carl P. Eby, 1999.

*   *   *

When Ernest Hemingway was awarded the Nobel Prize for Literature, the Swedish Academy commented on the central themes of his work. Courage and compassion in a world of violence and death were seen as the distinguishing marks of "one of the great writers of our time . . . who, honestly and undauntedly, reproduces the genuine features of the hard countenance of the age." These comments sum up perceptively the characteristic preoccupations of Hemingway's fiction and of the heroic code of behavior that it explores. But they do less than justice to another aspect of his writing. Hemingway was also a deliberate and careful artist, for whom every book was, in his own words, "a new beginning" in which the writer "should always try for something that has never been done."

Hemingway started his working life as a newspaper reporter, an excellent training in writing graphic declaratory prose. Covering crime stories was one introduction to a violent world, service with a Red Cross ambulance unit in Italy another. Severely wounded just before his nineteenth birthday, he received further emotional wounds when rejected by an American nurse with whom he fell in love. These experiences epitomize themes he was to explore in his short stories and novels, in prose that he deliberately stripped bare of adjectival coloring and rhetorical flourishes.

His first books, *Three Stories and Ten Poems* and *In Our Time,* were slim volumes that attracted coterie attention. The second of them consisted of twelve stark vignettes—scenes of war, bull-fighting, murder—which in a later edition were interleaved between lengthier short stories in which the Hemingway hero, and the heroic code of grace under pressure, first appear. Seven of the stories are episodes in the experience of a young man whose sensitivity has been violated in various ways, physically, emotionally, and spiritually. One day, he knows, his traumata will be healed, but this will take time, courage, and an effort of will. In the meantime he holds on stoically.

The Torrents of Spring, an uncharacteristic burlesque, is unimportant except as an indication of Hemingway's considerable skill as a comic satirist: it foreshadows the very funny ironical humor in, for instance, passages of *Death in the Afternoon* and *A Moveable Feast. In Our Time,* however, is the matrix from which the rest of his fiction is cast, both the later volumes of short stories and the succession of brilliantly finished, though occasionally flawed, novels. *The Sun Also Rises* established Hemingway beyond question as a significant new novelist. Narrated in the first person, it deals with the predicament of the hero, emasculated by an unlucky war wound, in his frustrated love for an Englishwoman whom time and misfortune have driven into alcoholism, promiscuity, and self-destructive irresponsibility. Charting the mores of Paris cafe society playboys and would-be artists, Hemingway for some readers obscured the moral seriousness of his novel through the brilliance of his writing, especially in the scenes at the fiesta in Pamplona. But the message is there. The hero has learnt to accept his plight with honesty and courage; and even the heroine, though morally ruined, is honest with herself and in her own fashion also honorable. The hero's own moral strength allows him to treat her with compassion.

In his next novel Hemingway settled for third-person narration. A romantic tragedy of love and war, *A Farewell to Arms* shows considerable technical development. Formally constructed in five acts, it is closely knit by complex sub-structure. Symbols of weather and topography unobtrusively counterpoint the action, while contrasts of profane and sacred love are made both overtly and covertly in the evolving relationship between the hero and the novel's innocent tragic heroine. In this novel, too, Hemingway tried to communicate directly his own experience of being wounded by trench mortar fire, in a cardinal passage that supports his occasionally expressed view that writing is a kind of self-therapy.

Hemingway's views on fiction, which incidentally show how closely he had studied the English, French, and Russian novelists, are for the most part woven into his classic study of bullfighting, *Death in the Afternoon.* In brief, his aim was to write simply and directly about directly received experience. The more precisely a writer can express the essential impact of experience, the more precisely he will impress that experience on his readers. His task is to set down "the sequence of motion and fact which made the emotion," which "with luck and if you stated it purely enough" should remain valid always. By concentrating on describing his characters in action a writer should be able to communicate unwritten emotional reverberations, whereas to write as an omniscient commentator is to spoil his fiction by adding what is structurally unnecessary and undesirable. In a famous comparison, Hemingway likens the artist's work to the tip of an iceberg, whose dignity of movement is due to only one-eighth of it being above water. It is an austere approach to the writer's craft, but one whose discipline gives Hemingway's work unmistakable authority and strength.

While many writers in the early 1930s were as much concerned with political as with literary preoccupations, Hemingway fed his experience and his literary production by big-game hunting, fishing, and shooting. This is the period of some of his best short stories, including "The Snows of Kilimanjaro," technically superb in its accumulated moves from reality to illusory vision. His novel *To Have and Have Not* is less satisfying. An attempt to portray characters under economic stress in the depression, it was cobbled together from two earlier short stories and was written hastily between visits to Spain during the Civil War. This also is the period of *The Fifth Column,* an undistinguished venture into the theater.

The Spanish Civil War, however, provided Hemingway with the theme of another outstanding novel, *For Whom the Bell Tolls,* in which again he extended his techniques. The story is built around twin themes, the dynamiting of a bridge by a guerrilla group and the love affair of an American partisan and a girl in the group. The action is restricted to some seventy hours, the location to a single valley, the personae to a handful; but by dipping into the stream of the hero's thoughts about his former life and by having various characters recount their memories, Hemingway works beyond these confines to create an ample but tightly organized novel of epic dimensions. There is an optimistic shift, too, in the heroic code, in that the hero is now in command of himself and meets death alone but fearless. Contemporary judgments of this novel were often politically colored, ranging from allegations that Hemingway had "largely sloughed off his Stalinism" to accusations of Fascist sympathies: these variant views reflect clearly the success of Hemingway's sympathetic treatment of the complexity of political and human predicaments. Of the novel's literary quality there has never been any doubt.

His next two novels, *Across the River and into the Trees* and *The Old Man and the Sea,* take the heroic code further. The latter's message that a man can be destroyed but not defeated carries a suggestion of Christian salvation. Though *Across the River and into the Trees* contains some of Hemingway's most intense writing (e.g., the description of the duck-shoot with which the novel opens), it is flawed by occasional obtrusions of the author's own personality and by his as yet incomplete mastery of new modes of symbolism operating at multiple levels. These are under perfect control in *The Old Man and the Sea,* a work of flawless craftsmanship that can be read literally, or as an allegory of human life, or of the Crucifixion, or of the artist's struggle to dominate his material.

The posthumous publication of the long, uneven *Islands in the Stream* and *The Garden of Eden,* unrevised by his skilled hand, neither adds to nor detracts from the reputation of a dedicated and sensitive artist, one of the greatest and most influential prose writers of the twentieth century.

—Stewart F. Sanderson

See the essays on "Big Two-Hearted River" and *The Sun Also Rises.*

HENRY, O.

A pseudonym for William Sydney (or Sidney) Porter. **Born:** Greensboro, North Carolina, 11 September 1862. **Education:** His aunt's private school in Greensboro to age 7; apprentice pharmacist in Greensboro, 1878-81; licensed by the North Carolina Pharmaceutical Association, 1881. **Family:** Married 1) Athol Estes Roach in 1887 (died 1897), one son and one daughter; 2) Sara Lindsay Coleman in 1907. **Career:** Moved to Texas, 1882, and worked on a ranch in LaSalle County, 1882-84; bookkeeper in Austin, 1884-86; contributed to Detroit *Free Press,* 1887; draftsman, Texas Land office, Austin, 1887-91; teller, First National Bank, Austin, 1891-94; founding editor, *Iconoclast,* later *Rolling Stone* magazine, Houston, 1894-95; columnist ("Tales of the Town," later "Some Postscripts"), Houston *Post,* 1895-96; accused of embezzling funds from his previous employers, First National

Bank, Austin, 1895; fled to Honduras to avoid trial, 1896-97; returned to Austin because of wife's illness, 1897; jailed for embezzling in the federal penitentiary, Columbus, Ohio, 1898-1901 (5-year sentence reduced to 3): while in prison began publishing stories as O. Henry; moved to Pittsburgh, 1901, and New York, 1902; thereafter a full-time writer; regular contributor, New York *Sunday World*, 1903-05. O. Henry Memorial Award established by the Society of Arts and Sciences, 1918. **Died:** 5 June 1910.

PUBLICATIONS

Collections

Complete Works. 1926.
Stories, edited by Harry Hansen. 1965.
Tales of O. Henry. 1993.
Collected Stories. 1994.
New Yorkers' Short Stories. 1995.
100 Selected Stories. 1995.
O. Henry's New York. 1996.

Fiction (stories)

Cabbages and Kings. 1904.
The Four Million. 1906.
The Trimmed Lamp and Other Stories of the Four Million. 1907.
Heart of the West. 1907.
The Voice of the City: Further Stories of the Four Million. 1908.
The Gentle Grafter. 1908.
Roads of Destiny. 1909.
Options. 1909.
Strictly Business: More Stories of the Four Million. 1910.
Whirligigs. 1910.
Let Me Feel Your Pulse. 1910.
The Two Women. 1910.
Sixes and Sevens. 1911.
Rolling Stones. 1912.
Waifs and Strays. 1917.
Selected Stories, edited by C. Alphonse Smith. 1922.
The Best of O. Henry. 1929.
More O. Henry. 1933.
The Best Short Stories of O. Henry, edited by Bennett Cerf and Van H. Cartmell. 1945.
The Pocket Book of O. Henry, edited by Harry Hansen. 1948.
Cops and Robbers, edited by Ellery Queen. 1948.
O. Henry Westerns, edited by Patrick Thornhill. 1961.

Play

Lo, with Franklin P. Adams, music by A. Baldwin Sloane (produced 1909).

Other

Complete Writings, 14 vols., 1918.
O. Henryana: Seven Odds and Ends: Poetry and Short Stories. 1920.
Letters to Lithopolis from O. Henry to Mabel Wagnalls. 1922.
Postscripts (from Houston *Post*), edited by Florence Stratton. 1923.

O. Henry Encore: Stories and Illustrations (from Houston *Post*), edited by *Mary Sunlocks Harrell*. 1939.

*

Bibliography: *A Bibliography of Porter (O. Henry)* by Paul S. Clarkson, 1938; *Porter (O. Henry): A Reference Guide* by Richard C. Harris, 1980; in *Bibliography of American Literature* by Jacob Blanck, edited by Virginia L. Smyers and Michael Winship, 1983.

Critical Studies: *O. Henry Biography* by C. Alphonse Smith, 1916; *The Caliph of Bagdad* by Robert H. Davis and Arthur B. Maurice, 1931; *O. Henry: The Man and His Work*, 1949, and *O. Henry: American Regionalist*, 1969, both by Eugene Hudson Long; *The Heart of O. Henry* by Dale Kramer, 1954; *Alias O. Henry: A Biography* by Gerald Langford, 1957; *O. Henry from Polecat Creek* by Ethel Stephens Arnett, 1962; *O. Henry (Porter)* by Eugene Current Garcia, 1965; *O. Henry: The Legendary Life of Porter* by Richard O'Connor, 1970; *From Alamo Plaza to Jack Harris's Saloon: O. Henry and the Southwest He Knew* by Joseph Gallegly, 1970; *O. Henry: A Biography* by David Stuart, 1986; *Cheap Rooms and Restless Hearts: A Study in Formula in the Urban Tales of William Sydney Porter* by Karen Charmaine Blansfield, 1988; *O. Henry: A Study of the Short Fiction* by Eugene Current Garcia, 1993.

*   *   *

William Sydney Porter's first story to appear in a national magazine was published in September 1898 while he was in prison, and it was in prison that he began writing in earnest. Following his release, Porter moved to New York where he wrote prodigiously; during 1904 and 1905 he is said to have produced a story a week for the New York *World*. Fame and notoriety, which he shunned, came to him quickly, as did money, which he spent lavishly and usually unwisely. *Cabbages and Kings*, his first collection of stories, established him as an author to be taken seriously. By 1908, with the publication of *The Voice of the City*, he was hailed as having "breathed new life into the short story; the stigma of the genre is wearing off, and for its rehabilitation . . . (Porter) is responsible"; and in 1914, in a symposium conducted by the New York *Times*, "A Municipal Report" was voted "the greatest American short story ever written."

By 1920, ten years after his death, five million volumes of Porter's stories had been sold, but the current of critical opinion had turned against them and their author: not uncharacteristic is **H.L. Mencken**'s pronouncement that "in the whole canon of O. Henry's work you will not find a single recognizable human character." A just estimate of Porter's fiction lies somewhere between such extremes. O. Henry brought verve, excitement, and humor to the genre. Enormously interested in people, he is capable of swift and compassionate insights into the average person, and his sympathy for the underdog, the little man or woman dwarfed in the maze of contemporary life, to a degree accounted for his enormous popularity. He was a good reporter with a keen eye for the significant detail, and he had a feeling for setting unmatched by most of his contemporaries. His brisk openings and the engrossing narrative pace of even his least successful stories are perhaps the major reasons for his instant appeal. Perhaps most important of all, he influenced an entire generation of writers and helped provide an enthusiastic audience for their work.

Porter's faults are as conspicuous as his assets—contrivance, sentimentality, repetition, and melodrama; his trick endings, particularly, seemed patently dated in the context of the new realism of the 1920s. He wrote rapidly— "once I begin a yarn I must finish it without stopping or it kinda goes dead on me"—and revised seldom. Haunted by memories of the past, increasingly engulfed in alcohol, Porter had no illusions about his literary shortcomings. "I'm a failure," he wrote to a friend. "My stories? No, they don't satisfy me. It depresses me to have people point me out as 'a celebrated author.' It seems such a big label for such picayune goods."

Porter's work, as one of his contemporaries commented, never did justice to his talents. Perhaps the soundest estimate of his contribution has been made by one of the most important modern English writers of fiction, H.E. Bates. However one belittles O. Henry, Bates wrote in *The Modern Short Story,* "he still emerges, by his huge achievement and the immense popularity of his particular method, as an astonishingly persistent influence on the short story of almost every decade since his day."

—William Peden

See the essay on "Gifts of the Magi."

HERGESHEIMER, Joseph

Born: Philadelphia, Pennsylvania, 15 February 1880. **Education:** A Quaker school in Germantown, Philadelphia; studied painting at Pennsylvania Academy of Fine Arts, Philadelphia. **Family:** Married Dorothy Hemphill in 1907. **Career:** Settled in Virginia, 1900; regular contributor to *Saturday Evening Post,* 1915-38; lived in West Chester, Pennsylvania, and Stone Harbor, New Jersey, after 1945. **Member:** American Academy, 1921. **Died:** 25 April 1954.

PUBLICATIONS

Fiction

The Lay Anthony. 1914; revised edition, 1919.
Mountain Blood. 1915; revised edition, 1930.
The Three Black Pennys. 1917.
Gold and Iron. 1918.
The Happy End (stories). 1919.
Linda Condon. 1919.
Java Head. 1919.
Cytherea. 1922.
The Bright Shawl. 1922.
Tol'able David (stories). 1923.
Balisand. 1924.
Merry Dale. 1924.
Tampico. 1926.
Quiet Cities (stories). 1928.
Triall by Armes (stories). 1929.
The Party Dress. 1930.
The Limestone Tree. 1931.
Love in the United States, and The Big Shot. 1932.

Tropical Winter (stories). 1933.
The Foolscap Rose. 1934.

Play

Screenplay: *Flower of Night,* with Willis Goldbeck, 1925.

Other

Hugh Walpole: An Appreciation. 1919.
San Cristobal de la Habana. 1920.
The Presbyterian Child (autobiography). 1923.
From an Old House (autobiography). 1925.
Swords and Roses. 1929.
Sheridan: A Military Narrative. 1931.
Berlin. 1932.

*

Bibliography: "Hergesheimer: A Selected Bibliography 1913-1945" by James J. Napier, in *Bulletin of Bibliography 24,* 1963-64.

Critical Studies: *Hergesheimer: The Man and His Books* by Llewellyn Jones, 1920; *Hergesheimer* by James Branch Cabell, 1921; *The Fiction of Hergesheimer* by Ronald E. Martin, 1965; *Ingenue among the Lions: Letters of Emily Clark to Hergesheimer* edited by Gerald Langford, 1965; *Hergesheimer* by Victor E. Gimmestad, 1984.

*   *   *

James Branch Cabell called Joseph Hergesheimer "the most insistently superficial of writers" and meant it as a compliment; many decades later the remark speaks unintentionally for his detractors. Writing from "aspiration hopelessly in advance of accomplishment," as Hergesheimer described his endeavors, he was reputed one of America's foremost novelists; in the late twentieth century he is almost forgotten, and many readers would think deservedly so. After several quasi-historical novels, Hergesheimer turned to his immediate milieu—the American 1920s—and made the subject glossily his own. Later, his attempts at *belles lettres*—travel books and descriptions of old houses in fancy prose—blurred into his fiction, and flesh and blood disappeared into the architecture.

Of his early books, *Java Head* is an excellent adventure story of clipper ships and miscegenation in eighteenth-century Salem, with a Manchu princess as catalyst. *The Three Black Pennys* is an underrated novel about a Pennsylvania coal mining family, tracing an emotional decline from the eldest, sober and hard-working, to the youngest, a dilettante; finely written, even moving, it is undeserving of its present neglect.

The later novels "flash and glitter like so many fricaseed rainbows," according to George Jean Nathan. *Linda Condon* and *Cytherea* trace the hedonism of the 1920s—prohibition, permanent waves, "extraordinary quantities of superlative jewels and superfine textures"—with ironic detachment. In *The Party Dress,* however, written at the end of the decade, Hergesheimer detailed the mystique of golf—not only the shots in a game but the look of the greens and the quality of the clubs—in deadly earnest, and he lavished as much attention on his characters' houses, clothing, table manners, including the silver and crystal, as he did on their love affairs. Later historical novels, *Balisand* and *The Limestone Tree*, for example, had not even the glamour of the 1920s to enliven them.

Alfred Kazin spotted the quintessential Hergesheimer passage in *Cytherea*: "'I want to be outraged!' Her low ringing cry seemed suppressed, deadened as though the damasked and florid gilt and rosewood, now inexpressibly shocked, had combined to muffle the expression, the agony, of her body." Kazin called Hergesheimer's passion "vulgar"; Wilson Follett called it an "aristocratic distinction" although "a distinctly un-American trait."

Readers in an audio-visual age may grow impatient with Hergesheimer's tales of beautiful women and wise men stifled by sybaritic description; but many of the novels accurately reflect their own time, however meretricious that time was. Hergesheimer still has much to say, by the fact of his reputation during the 1920s, to a later period preoccupied with pop culture.

—Bruce Kellner

HERNE, James A.

Born: James Ahern in Cohoes, New York, 1 February 1839. **Education:** Local schools to age 13. **Family:** Married 1) Helen Western in 1866 (divorced); 2) the actress Katherine Corcoran in 1878, three daughters. **Career:** Debut as an actor, in repertory, Troy, New York, 1859; appeared with John Ford's company in Baltimore and Washington, D.C., during the Civil War; leading man in the Lucille Western Company, touring the United States, 1865-67; thereafter managed the Grand Opera House, New York; stage director, Lucky Baldwin's Academy of Music, San Francisco, 1875-80; began writing for the stage by collaborating with his associate David Belasco in 1879; starred in *Hearts of Oak* for the next seven years, a success that allowed him to retire to Dorchester, Massachusetts, and become a full-time writer; lost his fortune on his next play: forced to move back to New York and work as stage manager for Klaw and Erlanger, 1891; appeared in *Shore Acres*, 1892-98, the success of which restored his fortunes; retired to Southampton, Long Island. **Died:** 2 June 1901.

PUBLICATIONS

Collections

Shore Acres and Other Plays (includes *Sag Harbor, Hearts of Oak*), edited by Mrs. James A. Herne. 1928.
The Early Plays (includes *The Minute Men of 1774-1775, Drifting Apart, The Reverend Griffith Davenport, Within an Inch of His Life*), edited by Arthur Hobson Quinn. 1940.

Plays

Within an Inch of His Life, with David Belasco, from a play by Emile Gaboriau (produced 1879). In *The Early Plays, 1940.*
Marriage by Moonlight, with David Belasco, from the play *Camilla's Husband* by Watts Phillips (produced 1879).
Hearts of Oak, with David Belasco (as *Chums*, produced 1879; as *Hearts of Oak*, produced 1879). In *Shore Acres and Other Plays*, 1928; revised version by Herne, as *Sag Harbor* (produced 1900), in *Shore Acres and Other Plays*, 1928.

The Minute Men of 1774-1775 (produced 1886). In *The Early Plays*, 1940.
Drifting Apart (produced 1888). In *The Early Plays*, 1940.
Margaret Fleming (produced 1890). Edited by Myron Matlaw, in *The Black Crook and Other 19th-Century American Plays*, 1967.
My Colleen (produced 1892).
Shore Acres (produced 1893). In *Shore Acres and Other Plays*, 1928.
The Reverend Griffith Davenport, from the novel *An Unofficial Patriot* by Helen H. Gardener (produced 1899). In *The Early Plays*, 1940; Act III edited by Arthur Hobson Quinn, in *American Literature 24*, 1952.

*

Bibliography: "Selected Bibliography of Herne" by John Perry, in *Bulletin of Bibliography 31*, 1974; "James A. Herne: A Bibliography" by Barbara C. Gannon, in *American Literary Realism: 1870-1910*, spring 1983.

Critical Studies: *Herne: The Rise of Realism in the American Drama* by Herbert J. Edwards and Julie A. Herne, 1964; *Herne, The American Ibsen* by John Perry, 1978; "The Legacy of James A. Herne: American Realities and Realisms" by Patricia D. Denison, in *Realism and the American Dramatic Tradition* edited by William Demastes, 1996.

*   *   *

Most of the plays by the accomplished actor James A. Herne remain in the limbo of strictly minor American drama. *The Minute Men of 1774-1775, Drifting Apart, My Colleen,* or *The Reverend Griffith Davenport,* and even those written in collaboration with **David Belasco**, including *Within an Inch of His Life, Marriage by Moonlight,* or *Hearts of Oak,* redone by Herne as *Sag Harbor,* have become so obscure as to be virtually unobtainable save in limited library collections. But with *Margaret Fleming* and *Shore Acres* Herne has survived as the most important pivotal American playwright of the late nineteenth century. In these two plays, particularly the former, Herne took the most significant steps of any American dramatist of his time away from the well-made artificialities of nineteenth-century romance and melodrama toward the development of effective dramatic realism.

Margaret Fleming abounds in nineteenth-century conventions and artifices: the wronged young girl who must bear her child in shame and die; the threatened vengeance of the shamed girl's sister, a servant in the home of the seducer; the angelic wife struck blind as she learns of her husband's faithlessness. But the play goes well beyond the surface cliches. The seducer is no caddish rogue, but a successful manufacturer, Philip Fleming, obviously well-respected within the community, and deeply in love with his wife. He is no villain, but neither is he a hero. He is in truth a "fallen man," and it is his suffering and redemption that motivate a good part of the action, not the fate of the fallen woman who, in life and death, remains offstage, merely a point of reference. The problem of Philip Fleming's infidelity is strictly a domestic matter to be recognized and discussed by husband, wife, and family physician. Margaret Fleming, stunned by her husband's inadequately explained deed, refuses to be martyred and she survives through firmness and conviction evolving out of common sense and rational behavior. Her own behavior as an offended human being, not merely a stereotyped wronged woman, renders her far superior to her husband, whom she permits to return to her but only on her conditions. Reconciliation remains solely a dim hope in the indefinite future.

Thus Herne's skill in giving his central characters the strengths, weaknesses, and motivations of recognizable human individuals well developed within a recognizable contemporary society keeps *Margaret Fleming* from collapsing into sentimental bathos. The last act, which survives today through Herne's daughter's reconstruction, refuses to tie up the threads in conventionally neat fashion. There will be a life together for Philip and Margaret Fleming, but the ending, rather than "happy," is believable and eminently satisfactory. The wall remains between husband and wife, but, as Herne acknowledges in this ending (he apparently experimented with several) so shocking to nineteenth-century audiences, men and women, do, in reality, survive such traumas. They continue their lives; the world does not end; the drama does not conclude with the descent of the final curtain. The "ever after," as in life, is uncertain, possibly dangerous, and even terrifying.

Shore Acres, a lesser play, has too many outdated melodramatics. Still, Herne permits no heroes, no heroines, and no villains. There are logic and sound reason behind the businessman who would foreclose and subdivide the homestead. The love affair and its complications, if we ignore the dark and stormy night syndrome, are understandable. Uncle Nat, the prime mover, talks and acts with reasonable believability. The minor characters, relatively well-developed, enter and depart with clear motivation. For all the frequent transparent arbitrariness, there is a realistic aura in setting, action, and language.

Neither play is a great work of dramatic art. Both, however, are significant. To criticize the creaks and groans of structure is to miss the point of their artistic advances. Though *Margaret Fleming* may have been quite literally driven from the stage by adverse reaction to its daring theme and shocking ending, the courage of the playwright in creating it is recognized for the exceptional deed that it was. The significance of the play, together in a lesser degree with *Shore Acres,* in providing the substantial push behind the American drama's movement toward full-fledged artistic participation in twentieth-century world theater is abundantly apparent.

—Jordan Y. Miller

See the essay on *Margaret Fleming.*

HERRICK, Robert (Welch)

Born: Cambridge, Massachusetts, 26 April 1868. **Education:** Cambridge High School, 1881-85; Harvard University, Cambridge (editor, *Harvard Monthly,* 1888), 1885-90, graduated 1890. **Family:** Married Harriet Emery in 1894 (divorced 1916), two daughters and one son. **Career:** Instructor in rhetoric, Massachusetts Institute of Technology, Cambridge, 1890-93; member of the faculty from 1893, and professor of English, 1905-23, University of Chicago; teacher, Rollins College, Winter Park, Florida, 1931; secretary to the Governor of the Virgin Islands, 1935-38. **Died:** 23 December 1938.

PUBLICATIONS

Fiction

Literary Love-Letters and Other Stories. 1897.
The Man Who Wins. 1897.
The Gospel of Freedom. 1898.
Love's Dilemmas (stories). 1898.
The Web of Life. 1900.
The Real World. 1901; as *Jock o' Dreams,* 1908.
Their Child (stories). 1903.
The Common Lot. 1904.
The Memoirs of an American Citizen. 1905; edited by Daniel Aaron, 1963.
The Master of the Inn (stories). 1908.
Together. 1908.
A Life for a Life. 1910.
The Healer. 1911.
His Great Adventure. 1913.
One Woman's Life. 1913.
Clark's Field. 1914.
The Conscript Mother (stories). 1916.
Homely Lilla. 1923.
Waste. 1924.
Wanderings (stories). 1925.
Chimes. 1926.
The End of Desire. 1932.
Sometime. 1933.

Other

Composition and Rhetoric for Schools, with Lindsay Todd Damon. 1899; revised edition, 1902, 1911, 1922.
Teaching English, with May Estelle Cook and Lindsay Todd Damon. 1899.
The World Decision. 1916.
Little Black Dog. 1931.

*

Critical Studies: *Herrick: The Development of a Novelist* by Blake Nevius, 1962; *Herrick* by Louis J. Budd, 1971; in *The Man Behind the Book: Literary Profiles* by Louis Auchincloss, 1996.

*   *   *

In his first novelette, *The Man Who Wins,* Robert Herrick dealt with the question that was to be central to his entire work: what is success? A dedicated medical researcher is diverted into a lucrative practice, but late in life he sees his mistake and encourages young men not to seek material gain. Similarly, in *The Web of Life* a doctor samples and rejects the luxurious life of a society physician and refuses to marry the daughter of a capitalist until she renounces her wealth. *The Master of the Inn* presents a doctor who heals with simple methods in a rural hospital although he commands a knowledge of modern medicine. *The Healer* deals with a Canadian doctor who is traduced by his wife into leaving his spiritually rewarding life in the wild for a financially rewarding practice in Chicago. Disgusted by the avarice of city doctors, the doctor recommends that the professions all become "great monastic orders," and returns to his home.

Other novels contrast the proper use of technical knowledge to help mankind with the use of knowledge for selfish gain. An architect in *The Common Lot* exploits his profession until his shady practices cause several people to be killed in a fire. Business executives climb to the top in their fields before realizing the hollowness of their triumphs in *The Real World, A Life for a Life*, and *Waste*. All the executives atone by working for small, struggling businesses and crusading against trusts. Only the central character of *The Memoirs of an American Citizen*, a meat-packer named Van Harrington who claws his way to a fortune and a seat in the Senate, seems to have few regrets. Herrick was more proud of this characterization than any other, and it is doubtless his best. Herrick enlivened these novels with interesting details from the worlds of business and the professions, freighting them with symbolic weight that skillfully clarified the conflict between the central figures. However, it is not always clear why small businesses in the West are more moral and rewarding than large ones in the East.

In all these novels Herrick buttressed the main plot with a subplot contrasting the sordid family relationships of the rich and the more loving and simple ones of the working classes. In *Together, One Woman's Life, Homely Lilla*, and *The End of Desire*, he placed his main emphasis on the problem of women's rights, sexual liberation, and modern marriage. Advanced for his day in these matters, Herrick recommended that women share men's work and that men relieve women from the drudgery of housework and child-rearing. As with business, Herrick finds greed the enemy of good marriages.

Clark's Field shows why private property should not be allowed to restrict urban growth; *Chimes* deals with academic life. Herrick's views on many subjects are summarized in his Utopian novel of the future, *Sometime*.

Even if his novels are occasionally resolved by flimsy devices such as earthquakes or fires, Herrick deserves serious attention for his incisive criticism of his culture and his accurate picture of it.

—William Higgins

HIJUELOS, Oscar

Born: New York City, 24 August 1951. **Education:** The City College of the City University of New York, B.A. 1975, M.A. in English/Writing 1976. **Career:** Worked as an advertising media traffic manager for Transportation Display, Winston Network, New York City, 1977-84; writer since 1984; lived in Italy and traveled through Europe, Turkey, and Africa, 1984-89. Beginning 1989 educator at Hofstra University. **Awards:** Oscar Cintas fiction writing grant, 1978; Bread Loaf Writers Conference scholarship, 1980; Creative Artists Program Service grant, 1982; Ingram Merrill award, 1983; National Endowment for the Arts Fellowship for Creative Writers, 1985; Rome Fellowship in Literature of the American Academy and Institute of Arts and Letter, 1985; National Book Award and National Book Critics Circle award nominations, 1989; Guggenheim fellowship, 1990; Pulitzer prize for fiction, 1990. **Member:** International PEN. **Residence:** Manhattan.

PUBLICATIONS

Novels

Our House in the Last World. 1983.

The Mambo Kings Play Songs of Love. 1989.
The Fourteen Sisters of Emilio Montez O'Brien. 1993.
Mr. Ives' Christmas. 1995.
Empress of the Splendid Season. 1999.

*

Critical Studies: "Rum, Rump, and Rumba: Cuban Contexts for *The Mambo Kings Play Songs of Love*" by Gustavo Pérez Firmat in *Dispositio*, vol. 16, no. 41, 1991; "Oscar Hijuelos, novelista" by Ilan Stavans in *Revista Iberoamericana*, vol. 57, no. 155-56, 1991; *Imagining the Present of the Americas: Three Readings of The Mambo Kings Play Songs of Love and The Kiss of the Spider Woman* (dissertation) by Adrián Pérez Melgosa, 1995.

*   *   *

The bittersweet experiences of immigrant life are compellingly portrayed in the critically-acclaimed novels of Oscar Hijuelos. Through well-paced, accessible prose, Hijuelos explores the tangle of contradictory hopes and expectations within the immigrant psyche, the struggle to assert an ethnic American identity, and the relationships—between genders, generations, and the individual and ethnic community—that shape the immigrant's self-image. Vivid and provocative, the narratives never lose sight of the ambiguity that is central to the ethnic minority experience. The musings of his characters reveal the unstable interplay of memory and nostalgia, culture and language, assimilation and identity; this uncertainty grants a dimension of poignant complexity to Hijuelos's immigrants and their descendants.

Our House in the Last World is an account of the strife and tribulations of the Santinio family. The novel begins in the Cuba of the 1930s with the courtship and early years of marriage of the "small town dandy" Alejo Santinio and the shy, déclassée Mercedes Sorrea. Lured by the American Dream, the young couple relocates to Spanish Harlem in 1943; the dream is soon replaced by brutal reality as the unfortunate immigrants and their sons Horacio and Hector pass their days in squalor, barely surviving on Alejo's earnings as a hotel cook. Watching their friends and relatives thrive in the land of opportunity, Mercedes becomes increasingly bitter and high-strung while her husband turns to drink. Their oldest son Horacio, rebellious and angry, comes of age on the mean streets of New York. In contrast, the overprotected, sickly Hector grows into a withdrawn individual who exudes an aura of frailty. The story of their turbulent lives ends in the 1970s, shortly after the death of Alejo.

The individual voices of these characters affirm the author's concern with questions of perspective and diversity of experience. Challenging the notion of a "typical" or "representative" immigrant narrative, Hijuelos compassionately depicts how each of the unequal participants in the American Dream is transformed by the process of assimilation. The autobiographical references and elements of Cuban culture are presented in a manner that is ever mindful of readers of different cultural backgrounds; however, Hijuelos does not permit the explanations and alternative discourses necessitated by such a readership to compromise the artistic integrity of his writing.

The prestigious Pulitzer Prize for fiction was awarded to Hijuelos for his second novel, *The Mambo Kings Play Songs of*

Love. This vivid portrayal of the musical world of the 1950s uses two circumscribed flash-backs to recount the lives of Cuban immigrants César and Nestor Castillo, brothers who achieve a degree of fame during the heyday of the mambo. The untimely death of the thoughtful, sensitive Nestor (whose composition "Beautiful María of My Soul" is their only hit song) cuts short their careers. César never recovers from the loss; wrecked by the wear and tear of life and fate, the aged Mambo King becomes increasingly preoccupied with the re-examination of his past: his decisions, squandered hopes, and the unfulfilled promise of greatness augured by the two brothers' guest appearance on the "I Love Lucy" television show.

Viewed individually, elements of the novel seem awkwardly exaggerated: the boldly-drawn central characters are over-assertive in their masculinity or intemperately melancholic, the narration revels in the strong language of the street and daily talk, and the bawdy sex scenes are envisioned with an unwavering male gaze. But Hijuelos, ever the conscious and deliberate artist, concentrates each detail to secure unity of tone. The repeated portrayals of emotional and physical excess imbue the narrative with an energy, a vibrancy that seeks but never finds climax nor resolution. This intense potentiality, along with the presence of overwhelming nostalgia, are key ingredients of this successful study in disillusionment. A master stroke in this depiction of lost opportunities is the use of television as a transgenerational bridge: the reruns of "I Love Lucy" painfully remind César of his misplaced dreams, while causing Eugenio (Nestor's son) to long for the father that he barely remembers.

Ambitious and triumphant, *The Fourteen Sisters of Emilio Montez O'Brien* weaves a marvelous tapestry from the individual stories of the immigrants Nelson O'Brien and Mariela Montez and their fifteen children. The head of the rambunctious Montez O'Brien family is an Irish immigrant who meets his wife while a photographer in Cuba during the Spanish-American War. The couple and their oldest daughter—Margarita, born at sea—settle in a small town in Pennsylvania shortly after the turn of the century. Nelson maintains his family, ultimately composed of fourteen daughters and a son, through his photography trade and by running the local Jewel Box Movie Theater.

Although the novel eloquently grants a voice to all of the individual characters, the most developed subplots are those that deal with Nelson, Mariela, Margarita, and Emilio. Through Nelson and Mariela, Hijuelos explores two diverse immigrant experiences. For the young Nelson, enterprising and motivated, relocating to the U.S. is an escape from an abusive father, a chance for adventure, and the opportunity to achieve a modicum of success. On the other hand, the aristocratic, poetic Mariela finds herself isolated—from her English-speaking children as well as the American community—and is never able to overcome her feelings of dislocation. Margarita, who has a long and full life, recounts through reminiscences much about the complex interfamily relationships that exist among the members of the Montez O'Brien family. She studies Spanish as an adult in an attempt to assert an ethnic minority identity, only to discover that being "half Cuban by blood" does not make her privy to the immigrant psyche or the emotional turmoil of the exiled islanders. Emilio's uneasiness with the feminine world of his family provokes an ambiguous relationship with his sisters and mother, and a life of restlessness. Nonetheless, *The*

Fourteen Sisters of Emilio Montez O'Brien is a celebration, even in its darkest moments, of the strength of love and family.

—Bridget M. Morgan

HILLERMAN, Tony

Born: Sacred Heart, Oklahoma, 27 May 1925. **Education:** Oklahoma State University, 1942- 43; University of Oklahoma, B.A. 1948; University of New Mexico, M.A. in English 1965. **Military Service:** Served in the U.S. Army, 1943-45; received Bronze Star, Silver Star, Purple Heart. **Family:** Married Mary Unzner in 1948; three daughters and three sons. **Career:** Police reporter, *Borger News Herald,* Borger, Texas, 1948; reporter, then city editor, *Morning Press-Constitution,* Lawton, Oklahoma, 1948-50; United Press International, political reporter, Oklahoma City, Oklahoma, 1950-52, bureau manager in Santa Fe, New Mexico, 1952-54; reporter, then executive editor, *New Mexican,* Santa Fe, New Mexico, 1954-63; member of journalism department, University of New Mexico, Albuquerque, 1965-85, chairman of the department, 1966-73, assistant to the president, 1975-80, and beginning 1985 Professor Emeritus. **Awards:** Mystery Writers of America Edgar Allan Poe award, 1974, Grand Master award, 1991; Anthony award, 1987; Western Writers of America Golden Spur award, 1987; Navajo Tribal Council Special Friend of Dineh award, 1987; Department of the Interior award, 1990; American Anthropological Association media award, 1990; Center for the Indian ambassador award, 1992; Grand Prix de Litterature Policiére (France). D.Litt.: University of New Mexico, 1990; Arizona State University, 1991. **Member:** Mystery Writers of America, president, 1988. **Residence:** Albuquerque, New Mexico.

PUBLICATIONS

Collections

The Joe Leaphorn Mysteries. 1989.
Leaphorn and Chee: Three Classic Mysteries Featuring Lt. Joe Leaphorn and Officer Jim Chee. 1992.
The Jim Chee Mysteries. 1993.

Novels

The Blessing Way. 1970.
The Fly on the Wall. 1971.
The Boy Who Made Dragonfly: A Zuni Myth (for children). 1972.
Dance Hall of the Dead. 1973.
Listening Woman. 1977.
The People of Darkness. 1978.
The Dark Wind. 1981.
Ghostway. 1984.
A Thief of Time. 1985.
Skinwalkers. 1986.
Talking God. 1989.
Coyote Waits. 1990.
Mudhead Kiva. 1992.
Sacred Clowns. 1993.
Finding Moon. 1995.
The Fallen Man. 1997.
The First Eagle. 1999.

Other

The Great Taos Bank Robbery and Other Indian Country Affairs (essays). 1980.
Indian Country: America's Sacred Land (pictorial). 1987.
Words, Weather, and Wolfmen: Conversations with Tony Hillerman, with Ernie Bulow. 1989; revised as *Talking Mysteries: A Conversation with Tony Hillerman.* 1991.
Hillerman Country: A Journey through the Southwest with Tony Hillerman (pictorial). 1991.
New Mexico, Rio Grande, and Other Essays. 1992.

Editor, *The Spell of New Mexico.* 1984.
Editor, *Best of the West: An Anthology of Classic Writing from the American West.* 1991.

*

Bibliography: *Tony Hillerman: From "The Blessing Way" to "Talking God": A Bibliography* by Louis Hieb, 1990.

Critical Studies: "Mystery Literature and Ethnography: Fictional Detectives as Anthropologists" by James C. Pierson in *Literature and Anthropology,* edited by Philip Dennis, n.d.; *Tony Hillerman* by Fred Erisman, 1989; "Weaving Mysteries that Tell of Life among the Navajos" by Michael Parfit in *Smithsonian,* vol. 21, no. 9, 1990; *This Is about Vision: Interviews with Southwestern Writers* edited by William Balassi and John F. Crawford, 1990; "Tony Hillerman's Jim Chee and the Shaman's Dilemma" by Fred Erisman in *Lamar Journal of the Humanities,* vol. 17, no. 1, 1992; "Landscape and Place in Tony Hillerman's Mysteries" by Leonard Engel in *Western American Literature,* vol. 28, no. 2, 1993; *The Tony Hillerman Companion: A Comprehensive Guide to His Life and Work,* edited by Martin Harry Greenberg, 1994; *Tony Hillerman: A Public Life* by John Sobol, 1994; *Tony Hillerman: A Critical Companion* by John M. Reilly, 1996; *Slaying the Monsters: Native American Spirituality in the Works of Tony Hillerman* (dissertation) by Beverly G. Six, 1998.

*   *   *

Tony Hillerman is primarily known for his mystery novels set in the Navajo country of the American Southwest. From *The Blessing Way* to *Sacred Clowns,* a generation of readers has enjoyed getting to know Jim Chee and Joe Leaphorn, the protagonists of most of Hillerman's thirteen detective novels and stories. Hillerman's fiction draws upon his background in journalism for its realism and topicality, and he cites such diverse literary influences as Eric Ambler, **Raymond Chandler, Joan Didion,** Graham Greene, **E.B. White,** and **Ernest Hemingway.** He has won numerous awards for his mysteries, several of which, including *Talking God* and *Coyote Waits,* have become best-sellers. Through his extensive attention to landscape and culture in his fiction and essays, and his editing of such collections as *The Best of the West: An Anthology of Classic Writing from the American West,* he has achieved wide recognition as a literary ambassador for the Southwest.

Hillerman, a native of Oklahoma, began his career with a degree in journalism from the University of Oklahoma and gained extensive writing and editing experience at a variety of newspapers in Oklahoma, Texas, and New Mexico. In the mid-1960s, he returned to the University of New Mexico to earn his master's degree in English and became a professor of journalism and the assistant to the president before retiring from academic work in 1985. Hillerman's journalistic background informs all of his writing; critics have widely noted how Hillerman's detective plots resonate with contemporary events and issues. In an interview with Ernie Bulow published in *Words, Weather, and Wolfmen,* Hillerman comments: "It's very important to me that the stories seem realistic. They seem [to be] about people who could really *be* people and things that could really happen. I'm writing about the reality, and frequently the headlines happen after the book is started, or long finished."

The reality to which Hillerman addresses himself is often the Native American cultures of the Southwest. From his plots, which often center on Native American traditions, legends, and rituals, to his characterizations of Navajo detectives Jim Chee and Joe Leaphorn, who struggle to reconcile their Navajo heritage with their Anglo education and U.S. government jobs, Hillerman's fiction is valuable for its portrayal of cross-cultural perspectives. Although not of Native American heritage himself, Hillerman told Patricia Holt in a *Publishers Weekly* interview: "For me, studying [Native American cultures] has been absolutely fascinating, and I think it's important to show how aspects of ancient Indian ways are still very much alive and are highly germane even to our ways." Indeed, many critics have compared Hillerman's mysteries to ethnographies, as they provide a fictional window into the cultural and political issues of contemporary Navajo life.

Critics and reviewers also praise Hillerman's infusion of Southwestern landscapes into his fiction and nonfiction writing. Essays such as *New Mexico, Rio Grande,* and the pictorial essay *Indian Country: America's Sacred Land* incorporate a sense of place and regional identity directly, but Hillerman's detective fiction also depends on a deep knowledge of Southwestern landscape. "For some reason when I'm writing it's essential for me to have in my mind a memory of the landscape, the place where that chapter's action is to take place," he told Bulow. *Listening Woman,* for instance, opens with a vivid description of the wind that "howled across the emptiness of the Moenkopi plateau, and made a thousand strange sounds in windows of the old Hopi villages at Shongopovi and Second Mesa . . . . It sandblasted the stone sculptures of Monument Valley Navajo Tribal Park and whistled eastward across the maze of canyons," finally bringing the narrative to the dust-covered brush arbor sheltering the three main characters.

Like the Southwest wind, Hillerman's fiction sweeps across the vastness, rich textures and colors, and desolate beauty of the Southwest landscape, giving his stories and characters a rich sense of place and history linked with the region. It is no wonder that Hillerman has won awards for best Western as well as best mystery: readers emerge from his tales with a deep sense of the character of the Southwest and of the convergence of landscape, history, and cultures that shape the detective plots, characters, and themes of his mysteries.

—Linda P. Bachman

HIMES, Chester

Born: Jefferson City, Missouri, 29 July 1909. **Education:** Attended Ohio State University, 1926-27. **Family:** Married 1) Jean

Lucinda Johnson in 1937 (divorced); 2) remarried, wife's name, Lesley. **Career:** Convicted of armed robbery at the age of nineteen and sentenced to twenty-to-twenty-five years in Ohio State Penitentiary; began writing short stories while in prison, which were published first in black newspapers and magazines and later by *Esquire;* released from prison in 1936; worked for Federal Writer's Project, completing an unpublished history of Cleveland; wrote for the *Cleveland Daily News;* worked in shipyards and aircraft factories in Los Angeles and in San Francisco during World War II; moved to Europe in 1953; suffered a stroke in 1965 and become temporarily inactive; spent the last fifteen years of his life in Spain. **Awards:** Julius Rosenwald fellowship in Creative Writing 1944-45; Yaddo fellowship, 1948; Grand Prix Policier, 1958. **Died:** 12 November 1984.

PUBLICATIONS

Collections

The Collected Stories of Chester Himes. 1991.
The Harlem Cycle. 1996.

Novels

If He Hollers, Let Him Go. 1945.
Lonely Crusade. 1947.
Cast the First Stone. 1952.
The Third Generation. 1954.
The Primitive. 1955; revised edition published as *The End of a Primitive*, 1997.
For Love of Imabelle. 1957; revised edition published as *A Page in Harlem*, 1965.
Il pleut des coups durs, translation by C. Wourgaft. 1958; as *The Real Cool Killers.* 1959.
The Crazy Kill. Originally published in French, 1958; English edition, 1959.
Couche dans le pain, translation by J. Herisson and H. Robillot. 1959.
Tout pour plaire, translation by Yves Marlartic. 1959; as *The Big Gold Dream*, 1960.
Dare-dare, translation by Pierre Verrier. 1959; as *Run Man, Run*, 1966.
Imbroglio Negro, translation by J. Fillon. 1960; as *All Shot Up.* 1960.
The Heat's On. Originally published in French, 1960; English edition, 1966; as *Come Back Charleston Blue*, 1967.
Pinktoes. 1961.
Ne nous enervons pas! (title means "Be Calm"), translation by J. Fillon. 1961.
Mamie Mason; ou, Un Exercise de la bonne volonte, translation by Andre Mathieu. 1963.
Une Affaire de viol, translation by Mathieu. 1963; published in English as *A Case of Rape*, 1984.
Retour en Afrigue, translation by Pierre Sergent. 1964; as *Cotton Comes to Harlem*, 1965.
Blind Man with a Pistol. 1969; as *Hot Day Hot Night*, 1970.
Plan B. Originally published in French, 1983; English edition, 1993.

Other

The Autobiography of Chester Himes, Volume 1: *The Quality of Hurt.* 1972.

Black on Black: Baby Sister and Selected Writings (stories). 1973.
The Autobiography of Chester Himes, Volume 2: *My Life of Absurdity.* 1977.
Conversations with Chester Himes. 1995.

*

Bibliography: *Chester Himes: An Annotated Primary and Secondary Bibliography* by M. Fabre, 1992.

Critical Studies: *Native Sons: A Critical Study of Twentieth-Century Negro American Authors,* 1968, and *Which Way Did He Go?: The Private Eye in Dashiell Hammett, Raymond Chandler, Chester Himes, and Ross MacDonald,* 1982, both by Edward Margolies; *Chester Himes: A Critical Appraisal* by Stephen Milliken, 1976; *Two Guys from Harlem: The Detective Fiction of Chester Himes* by Robert E. Skinner, 1989; *Airing Dirty Laundry* by Ishmael Reed, 1993; *The Several Lives of Chester Himes* by Edward Margolies, 1997.

*   *   *

Robert E. Skinner begins his discussion of Chester Himes by saying: "It is one of the greatest ironies of Chester Himes' life that it did not begin in the gutter." The son of middle class parents, Himes did not begin in the gutter, but from his earliest childhood until the time he entered the Ohio State Penitentiary, his life was filled with fear, rage, hate, guilt, and uncertainty.

There was always internal friction between Himes's parents, and because Estelle Bomar Himes believed that her background (Himes once wrote that she "was a octoroon or perhaps white") made her superior to her husband, she often dominated and humiliated him. Despite family conflicts, Himes graduated from Cleveland's East High School in 1926 and matriculated at Ohio State University in the fall of that year. He stayed at the university for two quarters but his drinking and carousing, along with his poor grades, caused him to drop out.

After leaving the university, Himes returned to Cleveland and entered the underworld of crime. He committed petty crimes until 1928, when he was convicted of grand larceny and sentenced to twenty-to-twenty-five years in Ohio State Prison. Himes's captivity forced him to turn inward; in prison he began to write short fiction about his experiences there. His first short stories were published in black weekly newspapers such as *The Atlanta Word, The Pittsburgh Courier,* and *The Afro-American.* Later his works appeared in *Esquire.*

One may divide Himes's literary career into two broad areas: the early period of protest literature and the expatriate period in which he wrote popular fiction including the Harlem Domestic Novels. Himes wrote five novels that are considered his "serious writing": *If He Hollers, Let Him Go, Lonely Crusade, Cast the First Stone, The Primitive,* and *The Third Generation.* The first two novels, *If He Hollers* and *Lonely Crusade,* are set in California during World War II and explore the racial tensions, the prejudice, and the alienation that blacks experienced in the war industry. *If He Hollers* is centered in the experiences of Robert Jones, a conflicted man who supervises a group of black mechanics at a Los Angeles shipyard. Robert is insulted by a white female, Madge Perkins, and follows her home to attack her for humiliating him. However, when he discovers that Madge really wants him to seduce her, he becomes afraid and runs. Later Madge finds Robert in a secluded area of a ship, locks them in and proceeds to seduce him, but when she realizes that she could be caught in a comprising situation with a black male, she cries rape. Robert is arrested and drafted into the Army.

Lonely Crusade is also set in Los Angeles during the war years. The protagonist, Lee Gordon, a college graduate, copes with long unemployment because he refuses to work as a menial laborer. Eventually Lee finds employment as a union organizer attempting to organize the black employees of Comstock Aircraft Cooperation. He is also experiencing marital problems with his wife Ruth because of his chronic unemployment, and is kicked out by his white girlfriend, Jacke Folks. Finding himself unemployed and on skid row, Lee marches to his death as the standard bearer for the union. In *Lonely Crusade,* as in *If He Hollers,* Himes dramatizes the effects of prejudice and racism on blacks in general and the black male in particular. The novelist suggests that racism is a deterministic force that limits the hopes and destroys the dreams of blacks. Discussing the novel's unpopularity, Himes once said, "The left hated it, the right hated it, Jews hated it, blacks hated it." Himes became so depressed over the reception of this novel that he did not approach his writing seriously for another five years.

Himes's third published novel was the first he had written. The original title was *Black Sheep,* reflecting, perhaps, Himes's concept of his position in his family. The novel was published as *Cast the First Stone,* and although the experiences the protagonist Jimmy Monroe relates are parallel to the ones Himes experienced while incarcerated at Ohio State Penitentiary, Jimmy is white. Himes, through Jimmy, forces the reader to see prison for what it is, an institution where gambling, homosexuality, and violence are rampant. Despite the novel's negativity, James Lundquist, author of *Chester Himes,* maintains: "Though it deals, exhaustively, with aberrations in the behavior of caged men, *Cast the First Stone,* at times a very funny book, is always a very hopeful one."

While all of Himes's novels represent chapters of his life, the last two protest novels, which were published in America after he went to Europe, are truly autobiographical. *The Third Generation* explores the novelist's formative years, and differs from Himes's autobiography, *The Quality of Hurt,* in that the human encounters in the novel are much more intensified, and much of what is barely suggested in the autobiography is graphically explained in the novel. Stephen Milliken sums up *The Third Generation* by noting that Himes "reduced the complexity of class struggle to the confrontation between one plebeian male and one aristocratic female, father and mother, and their struggle for control of their own sons, a struggle finally centered on one son the most sensitive and the most loved."

The Primitive, like *The Third Generation,* represents a slice of Himes's private life, for he confesses: "my book *The Primitive* was about [an] affair." Set in New York, the novel takes as its focus seven days in the lives of a white woman, Kriss Cummings, and her black lover, Jesse Robinson. The affair ends tragically when Jesse, in a drunken stupor, kills Kriss. Structurally and stylistically, this novel is Himes's most effective work. Using a point-counter-point construct, the plot shifts smoothly from one character to the other, allowing the reader to see each character's daily activities. Using flashbacks, Himes allows the reader to observe the mental and emotional state of each character; then he brings the two characters together for the final combat. The dramatic effects of the final chapters of this novel are disquieting, for Himes clearly demonstrates the pernicious effects of racism and how it destroys meaningful relationships.

After completing *The Primitive,* Himes turned to popular fiction. Finding himself destitute in Paris, he turned to detective fiction when he was approached by French publisher Marcel Duhamel. Nine of these novels are set in Harlem and are known as the Harlem Domestic Series. Eight of the novels have as their central characters two detectives known as Coffin Ed Johnson and Grave Digger Jones.

The Harlem Domestic Series deals with the seamy side of life of New York's inner city, presenting the pimps, the prostitutes, the hustlers, the gays, the drunks, the numbers runners, and the crooked ministers and politicians. In Himes's world, there are two kinds of people: the villains who are always on the "take" and the gullible squares who are always "taken." Unlike most detective novels, in Himes's series there is very little plot and no concern for ratiocination. Instead, Himes relies on his uncanny ability to describe the quirky, the grotesque, the comical. Robert E. Skinner, who has written most comprehensively on the crime series, says of these novels: "Though many critics have derided the work of Chester Himes for over forty years as ugly and hateful or cheap and gaudy, it is a inescapable fact that in these eight short novels he has done something significant . . . he told the story of a race of people who lived in the mean streets of Black America at mid-century."

During his late expatriate period Himes wrote the last two of the Harlem novels, *Blind Man with a Pistol* and *Plan B.* While the detective novels are basically entertaining, these last two novels are more serious. In the earlier novels the violence is gratuitous, but in these two novels the violence is planned; it is for a purpose. *Blind Man,* for example, is just as disjointed as the earlier novels. It seems to be divided into three distinct sections, but the major concept throughout the novel is that Harlem is about to explode in an all-consuming race riot and that there is very little anyone can do to prevent this inevitable explosion. Robert Skinner says that as a crime story *Blind Man* is "a confusing work," but he maintains that the piece "is a effective protest novel which depicts in a harsh light the destructive forces that American race relations threaten to unleash in the big city."

Whereas *Blind Man with a Pistol,* one of the last of Himes's Harlem novels, suggests that violence in Harlem is imminent, *Plan B,* Himes's final work, depicts violence on a grand scale. In a interview with **John A. Williams**, Himes discussed *Plan B* as being his bloodiest book. He says: "I don't know what the American publishers will do about this book, but one thing I do know, Johnny, they will hesitate, and it will cause them a great deal of revulsion, because the scenes I have described will be revolting scenes." The novel describes the activities of Tomsson Black, a former 1960s radical who has become a successful businessman and who has been accepted by the white community. Black uses his wealth and his social position to purchase and to distribute arms to all black males across America in an attempt to overthrow the government.

One of Himes's work to be published in the late twentieth century is a volume titled *The Collected Short Stories of Chester Himes.* This collection includes pieces that Himes wrote in prison as well as later works. According to Ishmael Reed, who reviewed the collection for the *Los Angeles Times Book Review,* "Chester Himes is highly successful when he uses 'comic aggression,'" but "the 'serious' and 'earnest' writing in the Collection often falls flat. . . ." The short stories, however, are extremely important for students and scholars who are interested in Himes's writings, for it is through the short stories that one sees how Himes develops his character and his style. The naturalistic style Himes introduced in his prison stories is fully developed in his novels, and some of the characters that first appear in the short stories are later developed in the novels.

With the re-emergence of Himes as a writer of the detective novel, a new interest was begun in his career. James Lundquist, Stephen Ben, Gilbert Muller, Robert Skinner, and Matthew Lawrence have added their literary voices in books honoring Himes's talent. Later critics such as Ishmael Reed, Luc Sante, and Michel Fabre have continued the appraisal. Many years after his death and many more years since he became an expatriate, Himes is finding his niche in the American literary canon.

—Ralph Reckley

HINOJOSA, Rolando

Pseudonyms: Rolando Hinojosa-S., Rolando R. Hinojosa-S., Rolando Hinojosa-Smith; and P. Galindo. **Born:** Mercedes, Texas, 21 January 1929. **Education:** Educated at University of Texas, B.A. in Spanish 1953; New Mexico Highlands University, M.A. 1963; University of Illinois, Ph.D. 1969. **Military Service:** Army and Reserves, 1956-63, 2nd lieutenant. **Family:** Married Patricia Sorensen in 1963 (divorced, 1989); two daughters and one son. **Career:** High school teacher, Brownsville, Texas, 1954-56; assistant professor in modern languages, Trinity University, San Antonio, 1968-70; associate professor, 1970-74, dean of College of Arts and Sciences, 1974-76, vice president for academic affairs, 1976-77, Texas A&I University, Kingsville; chair of Chicano studies, 1977-80, professor of Chicano studies, 1980-81, University of Minnesota—Minneapolis; professor of English, 1981-85, E.C. Garwood Professor, beginning 1985, Mari Subusawa Michener chair in English, 1989, University of Texas at Austin; director of Texas Center for Writers 1989-94. Consultant to Minneapolis Education Association 1978-80; U.S. Information Agency, 1980, 1989; Texas Commission for the Humanities 1981-82. **Awards:** Premio Quinto Sol (Best Novel), 1972; Casa de Las Americas Premio Mejor Novela (Cuba), 1976; Ford Foundation fellow, 1979; Southwest Conference on Latin American Studies, Best Writing in Humanities, 1981; University of Illinois College of Liberal Arts Distinguished Alumnus, 1988. **Member:** Modern Language Association, PEN-America, Academia Real Norteamericana de la Lengua Española, Texas Institute of Letters, fellow of Society of Spanish and Spanish American Studies; University of Illinois Alumni Achievement award, 1998. **Residence:** Austin, Texas.

PUBLICATIONS

Collections

The Rolando Hinojosa Reader, edited by Jose David Saldivar. 1985.

Novels

"Klail City Death Trip" series
  Estampas del valle y otras obras. 1972; bilingual edition published as *Sketches of the Valley and Other Works,* translated by Gustavo Valadez and Jose Reyna, 1980; as *Estampas del Valle,* 1993.

  Klail City y sus alrededores, bilingual edition translated by Rosaura Sanchez. 1976; published under name Rolando R. Hinojosa-S. as *Generaciones y semblanzas* (title means "Generations and Lineages"), 1977; as *Klail City,* translation by Hinojosa, 1987.

  Korean Love Songs from Klail City Death Trip (novel in verse form). 1978; German-English version as *Korean Love Songs/ Korea Liebes Lieder,* 1993.

  Claros varones de Belken. 1981; bilingual edition published as *Fair Gentlemen of Belken County,* translated by Julia Cruz, 1987.

  Mi querido Rafa. 1981; as *Dear Rafe,* translation by Hinojosa, 1985.

  Rites and Witnesses. 1982.

  Generaciones, notas, y brechas/Generations, Notes, and Trails. 1978.

  Partners in Crime. 1985.

  Becky and Her Friends. 1990; translated edition published as *Los amigos de Becky,* 1991.

  The Useless Servants. 1993.

  El Condado de Belken-Klail City. 1993.

  Ask a Policeman. 1998.

Other

Criticism in the Borderlands: Studies in Chicano Literature, Culture, and Ideology, with Hector Calderon, Jose David Saldivar. 1991.

Coeditor, *Tomas Rivera 1935-1984: The Man and His Work.* 1988.

*

Bibliography: "Rolando Hinojosa-S." in *Chicano Perspectives in Literature: A Critical and Annotated Bibliography* edited by Francisco Lomeli and Donaldo W. Urioste, n.d.; "Rolando Hinojosa-Smith" in *Chicano Literature: A Reference Guide* edited by Julio Martinez and Francisco A. Lomeli, 1985.

Critical Studies: "Rolando Hinojosa" in *Chicano Authors: Inquiry by Interview* by Juan Bruce-Novoa, 1980; "Faulkernerian Elements in Rolando Hinojosa's *The Valley*" by Mark Busby, in *MELUS,* vol. 11, 1984; "From Heterogeneity to Contradiction: Hinojosa's Novel" by Rosaura Sanchez, in *Revista Chicano-Riqueña,* vol. 12, 1984; "Discourse and Plot in Rolando Hinojosa's *The Valley:* Narrativity and the Recovery of Chicano Heritage" by Hector Torres, in *Confluencia: Revista Hispanica de Cultura y Literatura,* vol. 2, 1986; "Who's Killing Whom in Belken County: Rolando Hinojosa's Narrative Production" by Juan Bruce-Novoa, in *Monographic Review/ Revista Monografica,* vol. 3, 1987; "An Interview with Rolando Hinojosa" by Reed Dasenbrock, in *Translation Review,* vol. 27, 1988; *Rolando Hinojosa and the American Dream* by Joyce Glover Lee, 1997.

*   *   *

Rolando Hinojosa is one of the foremost Chicano authors of the twentieth century. A recipient of the Premio Casa de las Americas for his *Klail City y sus alrededores* in 1976, translated as *Klail City* (1987), Hinojosa has populated his fictional world of Belken County with more than one thousand characters. His six-novel "Klail City Death Trip" series, and his other works of fiction, piece together the life of this county through a unique blend of narratives, dialogues, monologues, newspaper accounts, testimonials, and interviews with residents. His work has been critically acclaimed and has strongly influenced a new generation of Chicano authors. Hinojosa might well be described as the Chicano **Faulkner**, both in importance and in his creation of a world unto itself.

Raised in the Lower Rio Grande valley along the border with Mexico, speaking only Spanish until he entered junior high, Hinojosa comes from the rich borderlands heritage of Mexican Americans. After a stint in the Army, he, like many of his family members, became a teacher, and later, taking advanced degrees in New Mexico and Illinois, a professor of Spanish and English literature and language. He has held prominent administrative and faculty positions in Texas and Minnesota. Returning to Texas in 1985 to teach at the University of Texas, he was appointed the Mari Subusawa Michener Chair and the directorship of the Texas Center for Writing. In addition to his fiction, which he prefers to write in Spanish, he has authored numerous critical works, and has translated the writing of others into English.

The "Klail City Death Trip" series captures the flavor of the Valley and its people though a multitude of characters and a bricolage of narrative strategies. The effect of the multiple layering of individual voices, the collective history of Belken County, mirroring the Chicano experience in general, is to create an internal and regional history of Chicano culture, rather than a history imposed from outside the region, from the dominant culture. Weaving his most prominent narrators, Jehú Malacara and Rafe Buenrostro, into all the disparate voices of Valley residents, Hinojosa de-stabilizes the typically American omniscient epic voice, and retains a uniquely Mexican American tone to tell their stories.

The dual publication of Hinojosa's novels in Spanish and English also reflects an important moment in American literature. The mixture of both English and Spanish and the fluid boundaries between original publication and translation, frequently including a simultaneous publication, demonstrate both the popularity of Hinojosa's writing as well as the importance of both languages to Chicano readers.

Not to be outdone by his recurrent characters, Hinojosa has published "The Mexican American Devil's Dictionary" under the pseudonym P. Galindo, a character who appears also as the interviewer in *Claros varones de Belken*. Hinojosa has also tried his hand at the formula detective novel, *Partners in Crime,* which, because of its Belken County setting, rises above the conventions of the genre and adds color and mystery to the life of Klail City. Hinojosa continues to fascinate general readers, scholars and reviewers with his work, showing no signs of letting up. His work has drawn scholarly attention from Latin America and Europe, and many of these critical studies have been published in Spanish, German, and French publications. Hinojosa's appeal lies in his ability to unite the voices of his Valley childhood into the multivalent, humorous, and colorful lives of his fictional world. A major figure in Chicano letters, Hinojosa represents America to much of the literary world as well, and has garnered the highest respect of that community.

—Jay Ann Cox

HOFFMAN, Charles Fenno

Born: New York City, 7 February 1806. **Education:** Schools in New York and New Jersey; Columbia University, New York,
1821-23; studied law with Harmanus Bleecker, Albany, New York; admitted to New York bar, 1827. **Career:** Lawyer in New York City, 1827-30; editor with Charles King, New York *American,* 1829-33; editor, *Knickerbocker* magazine, New York, 1833; toured the Midwest, 1833-34; editor, *American Monthly,* New York, 1835-37, and New York *Mirror,* 1837; full-time writer, 1838-39; associate editor with Horace Greeley, *New Yorker,* 1840; third chief clerk, 1841-43, and deputy surveyor, 1843-44, Office of the Surveyor of Customs of the Port of New York; full-time writer, 1844-47; editor, *Literary World,* New York, 1847-49; became insane and confined to the State Hospital, Harrisburg, Pennsylvania, 1849-84. **Award:** A.M.: Columbia University, 1837. **Died:** 7 June 1884.

PUBLICATIONS

Poetry

The Vigil of Faith and Other Poems. 1842; revised edition, as *Songs and Other Poems,* 1846.
The Echo; or, Borrowed Notes for Home Circulation. 1844.
Love's Calendar, Lays of the Hudson, and Other Poems. 1847.
Poems, edited by Edward F. Hoffman. 1873.

Fiction

Wild Scenes in the Forest and Prairie. 1839.
Greyslaer: A Romance of the Mohawk. 1840.

Other

A Winter in the West. 2 vols., 1835.
The Pioneers of New-York. 1848.

Editor, *The New-York Book of Poetry.* 1837; as *The Gems of American Poetry,* 1840.

*

Bibliography: in *Bibliography of American Literature* by Jacob Blanck, 1963.

Critical Studies: *Hoffman* by Homer F. Barnes, 1930; "Dark Lady Triumphant: Innovations in American Romance in Charles Fenno Hoffman's *Greyslaer: A Romance of the Mohawk*" by Melissa McFarland Pennell, in *Mid-Hudson Language Studies,* 1988; "The New Revenge Tragedy: Comparative Treatments of the Beauchamp Case" by William Goldhurst, in *Southern Literary Journal,* fall 1989.

*   *   *

During the 1830s and 1840s Charles Fenno Hoffman was among the more influential of a group of "literati," as **Edgar Allan Poe** referred to them, who called themselves the "Knickerbockers," a term made famous by **Washington Irving**'s *A History of New York* (written as Diedrich Knickerbocker) and by the *Knickerbocker* magazine (1833-65), which Hoffman helped to found. This group, which included **James Fenimore Cooper, William Cullen Bryant,** and Irving, among others, tried to shape the literary tastes of the nation and to make New York the literary center of the day. It especially encouraged the writing of literature on American themes, and it was dedicated to improving the quality and variety of American literature as it then existed.

Hoffman's works reflect the concerns and preoccupations of the Knickerbocker group. His best poems are those that romanticize the splendor and potentiality of the American landscape. Of these, the most memorable include "To the Hudson River," "The Morning Hymn," "Forest Musings," and "Moonlight on the Hudson." Skilled in the art of prosody, Hoffman injected a lyrical quality into his verse that made many of his poems extremely popular, especially those that were set to music. "Monterey," for example, was for many years one of the most popular ballads written in America, and it continues to be sung.

Hoffman's prose, like his verse, was strongly nationalistic in its intentions and themes. His best known novel, *Greyslaer: A Romance of the Mohawk,* was a fictional adaptation of the infamous Beauchamp-Sharp murder case. Critics appreciated *Greyslaer;* it went into two editions, and for a time competed successfully with the frontier romances of Cooper and **William Gilmore Simms**. The result of an excursion on horseback through Ohio, Illinois, Michigan, Iowa, and Pennsylvania, *A Winter in the West* provided many Americans with their first detailed account of life on the western frontier as it existed in the early 1830s. A skilled observer, Hoffman mastered the genre of travel literature. His discrimination and learning allowed him to select and describe incidents and characters that transcend regional particularities and that, even in the late twentieth century, provide insight into whatever part of America he visited.

As a critic and editor for some of the most influential literary magazines of his day, Hoffman encouraged the writing and publication of books and literature on American subjects. He believed that it was the critic's function to encourage excellence rather than to denigrate needlessly. He especially encouraged young writers who he felt might profit from some degree of public recognition, even if undeserved. About *Typee,* **Herman Melville**'s first novel, Hoffman wrote: "One of the most delightful and well written narratives that ever came from an American pen." He was also instrumental in helping such then unknown writers as **Francis Parkman**, whose classic account of overland adventure, *The California and Oregon Trail,* was recommended by Hoffman for publication.

Regrettably, Hoffman's literary career was cut short by illness and financial worries. Unable to support himself by writing, he was forced to take a position in a New York customs office. For several years he had been working on an historical novel to be called *Red Spur of the Ramapo,* which he hoped would be his greatest literary success but which was accidentally destroyed by his maid, who used it as kindling. This unfortunate mishap proved too much for Hoffman. With nerves already weakened from excessive toil and worry, he began treatment for a mental disorder that eventuated in his incarceration at the state hospital in Harrisburg, Pennsylvania, where he spent the remaining 35 years of his life, contented but hopelessly insane.

—James A. Levernier

HOLMES, Oliver Wendell

Born: Cambridge, Massachusetts, 29 August 1809. **Education:** Phillips Academy, Andover, Massachusetts; Harvard University,

Cambridge, Massachusetts, graduated 1829; studied law for one year; studied medicine in Paris, 1834-35, and at Harvard Medical School, M.D. 1836. **Family:** Married Amelia Lee Jackson in 1840; two sons (including the jurist Oliver Wendell Holmes, Jr.) and one daughter. **Career:** Practiced medicine in Boston; professor of anatomy and physiology, Dartmouth College, Hanover, New Hampshire, 1839-40; discovered that puerperal fever is contagious, 1843; Parkman Professor of Anatomy, Harvard Medical School, 1847-82. **Awards:** Boylston prize, for medical essays, 1836, 1837. Honorary degrees: Edinburgh University, 1886; Oxford University, 1887; Cambridge University, 1887. **Died:** 7 October 1894.

PUBLICATIONS

Collections

Complete Poetical Works, edited by Horace E. Scudder. 1895.
Representative Selections, edited by S.I. Hayakawa and Howard Mumford Jones. 1939.
Poetical Works, edited by Eleanor M. Tilton. 1975.

Poetry

The Harbinger: A May-Gift. 1833.
Poems. 1836; revised editions, 1846, 1848, 1849.
Urania: A Rhymed Lesson. 1846.
Astraea: The Balance of Illusions. 1850.
Poetical Works. 1852.
Songs and Poems of the Class of 1829, second edition. 1859; revised edition, 1868.
Songs of Many Seasons. 1861.
Poems. 1862.
Humorous Poems. 1865.
Songs of Many Seasons 1862-1874. 1874.
Poetical Works. 1877.
The Iron Gate and Other Poems. 1880.
Poetical Works. 2 vols., 1881.
Illustrated Poems. 1885.
Before the Curfew and Other Poems, Chiefly Occasional. 1888.
At Dartmouth: The Phi Beta Kappa Poem 1839. 1940.
Grandmother's Story of Bunker Hill Battle: As She Saw It from the Belfry. 1995.

Fiction

Elsie Venner: A Romance of Destiny. 1861.
The Guardian Angel. 1867.
A Mortal Antipathy: First Opening of the New Portfolio. 1885.

Other

Boylston Prize Dissertations for 1836 and 1837. 1838.
Homoeopathy and Its Kindred Delusions (lectures). 1842.
The Autocrat of the Breakfast-Table. 1858.
The Professor at the Breakfast-Table, with the Story of Iris. 1860.
Currents and Counter-Currents in Medical Science, with Other Addresses and Essays. 1861.
Soundings from the Atlantic. 1863.
Mechanism in Thought and Morals. 1871.

The Poet at the Breakfast-Table: His Talks with His Fellow-Boarders and the Reader. 1872.
John Lothrop Motley: A Memoir. 1878.
The School-Boy. 1879
Poems and Prose Passages, edited by Josephine E. Hodgdon. 1881.
Medical Essays 1842-1882. 1883.
Pages from an Old Volume of Life: A Collection of Essays 1857-1881. 1883.
Ralph Waldo Emerson. 1884.
Our Hundred Days in Europe. 1887.
Over the Teacups. 1890.
Writings. 14 vols., 1891-92.
A Dissertation on Acute Pericarditis. 1937.
The Autocrat's Miscellanies, edited by Albert Mordell. 1959.

Editor, with Jacob Bigelow, *Principles of the Theory and Practice of Medicine,* by Marshall Hall. 1839.
Editor, with Donald Grant Mitchell, *The Atlantic Almanac 1868.* 1867.

*

Bibliography: *Bibliography of Holmes* by Thomas Franklin Currier and Eleanor M. Tilton, 1953; in *Bibliography of American Literature* by Jacob Blanck, 1963.

Critical Studies: *Life and Letters of Holmes* by John T. Morse, Jr., 2 vols., 1896; *Holmes of the Breakfast-Table* by M. A. De Wolfe Howe, 1936; *Amiable Autocrat: A Biography of Holmes* by Eleanor M. Tilton, 1947; *Holmes* by Miriam R. Small, 1963; *The Improper Bostonian* by Edwin P. Hoyt, 1979; "Oliver Wendell Holmes" by Barry Menikoff, in *Fifteen American Authors before 1900: Bibliographical Essays on Research and Criticism* edited by Earl N. Harbert and Robert A. Rees, 1984; "Holmes's Emerson and the Conservative Critique of Realism" by Len Gougeon, in *South Atlantic Review,* January 1994, pp. 107-25; "Disfigurement and Reconstruction in Oliver Wendell Holmes's *The Human Wheel, Its Spokes and Felloes*" by David D. Yuan, in *The Body and Physical Difference: Discourses of Disability* edited by David T. Mitchell and Sharon L. Snyder, 1997.

*   *   *

The great popular reputation of Oliver Wendell Holmes in the nineteenth century receded with the eclipse of New England preeminence. Except for the rural **Whittier**, Holmes was the most provincial of the New England writers, and unlike the others he did not espouse causes. The Boston of his occasional verse and genial essays was not (according to the editors of *Representative Selections*) "the rebellious Boston, out of which came the antislavery societies, transcendentalism, and the feminist movement." In the opening chapter of his first novel (*Elsie Venner*) Holmes describes and provides a lasting label for cultured, mercantile Bostonians with Bulfinch houses, Beacon Street addresses, and ancestral portraits. He became the spokesperson for this "Brahmin Caste of New England" when his *The Autocrat of the Breakfast-Table* began to appear in the *Atlantic Monthly* in 1857. Although his public had read his occasional poems even since he was a Harvard undergraduate, his new image as "the Autocrat" established Holmes's reputation as a major American writer.

There had been little time for writing prose between 1830 and 1857, for Holmes had become a physician and held professorships of anatomy at Dartmouth and Harvard. But Holmes was a brilliant and incessant talker, and when he hit upon the scheme of jotting down his own talks, he had the matter for his essay series. Literary historians agree that his personality imposed itself on and gave unity to his writing—poetry, essays, and fiction alike. There is a consistent mental set in his writing also: he was a clear-headed rationalist who disliked even the "bullying" of science and abhorred the dogmatism of theology. His attacks on Calvinism were his closest approximation to taking up a cause, but it later seemed strange that Boston thought of him as an American Voltaire. However, Holmes liked to point out the parallels between his own life and Dr. Johnson's. Johnson was born in 1709, Holmes in 1809; both were urban beings, and Holmes's devotion to Boston matched Johnson's love of London. Both were great talkers and were devoted to common sense; and, though his wit has not survived as well as Johnson's, one, at least, of Holmes's remarks is remembered: "Boston State-House is the hub of the solar system. You couldn't pry that out of a Boston man if you had the tire of all creation straightened out for a crowbar."

The *Atlantic Monthly* version of *The Autocrat of the Breakfast-Table* begins, "I was just going to say, when I was interrupted." After the twelve *Atlantic* installments had become a book in 1858, the author explains that the interruption had lasted a quarter of a century, since two articles entitled "The Autocrat of the Breakfast Table" had appeared in the *New England Magazine* in 1831 and 1832. He had matured and gained confidence in the 25-year interval: along with his medical practice and professorships, he had published important medical essays and a volume of poems. His Harvard lectures were as celebrated for their wit as for their intellect, and from 1841 to 1857 he was a sought-after lyceum lecturer on literary as well as medical subjects. But Dr. Holmes was becoming even better known in Boston and Cambridge as a genial humorist and master of conversation.

His fellow-Brahmin, **James Russell Lowell**, accepted the editorship of the *Atlantic Monthly* on the condition that Holmes become a regular contributor. Holmes had suggested the name for the new magazine and there were Holmes's poems, essays, articles, and reviews or installments of novels in the magazine every year until 1893. The *Atlantic* published sixty-five Holmes poems, each of his three novels, three series of *Autocrat* sequels—*The Professor at the Breakfast-Table, The Poet at the Breakfast-Table,* and *Over the Teacups*—and *Our Hundred Days in Europe.*

It is difficult to evaluate Holmes's writing on medical subjects, or determine how his role as a doctor and professor of anatomy related to his literary career. Scientific medicine was just beginning a phenomenal advance in Holmes's day, but it is generally agreed that his own chief claim to medical distinction was his excellence as a teacher. Most interest in the late twentieth century has focused on his three "medicated novels" (Holmes accepted the term of a "dear old lady" who refused to read them): *Elsie Venner, The Guardian Angel,* and *A Moral Antipathy* have been judged "so absurd that it hardly bears repetition." Psychologists and psychiatrists have found validity and importance in the neuroses pictured in these novels, some of them profoundly shocking to Holmes's readers a hundred years ago.

To the twentieth century, Oliver Wendell Holmes was a writer of verse, not poetry—which even his contemporaries might have conceded. Significantly, both "The Deacon's Masterpiece" (or "One Hoss Shay"—sometimes interpreted as an allegory of New

England Calvinism) and "The Chambered Nautilus," his acknowledged masterpiece, were both "recited" by the Autocrat of the Breakfast Table.

To the generations growing up in the first half of the twentieth century, the name Oliver Wendell Holmes meant the distinguished jurist whom Franklin Roosevelt had hailed in 1933 as "the greatest living American." This son and namesake, the only member of his family to outlive Dr. Holmes, had his father's clear-headed rationalistic turn of mind—but none of his other traits. Fifty years after the son's death, the elder Holmes again emerged as a distinct figure: the conservative but clear-sighted, talkative Brahmin, who liked mill-owners better than abolitionists and transcendentalists, and who lived long enough to write graceful poetic tributes to nearly all of the nineteenth-century New England worthies.

—Clarence A. Glasrud

HONGO, Garrett Kaoru

Born: Volcano, Hawaii, 30 May 1951. **Education:** Gardena (California) High School; Pomona College, B.A. 1973; University of Michigan, 1974-75; University of California, Irvine, M.F.A. 1980. **Family:** Married Cynthia Thiessen, 1982; two children. **Career:** Traveled to Japan, 1973-74; founder and artistic director, Asian Exclusion Act (theater group), Seattle, 1975-77; executive director, Asian Multi Media Center, Seattle, 1976-77; poet-in-residence, Seattle Arts Commission, 1977-78; teaching assistant, 1980-82, and visiting poet, 1983-84, University of California, Irvine; visiting assistant professor, University of Southern California, 1982-83; assistant professor, University of Missouri, Columbia, 1984-89; poetry editor, *Missouri Review,* 1984-89; visiting associate professor, University of Houston, 1988; professor of English and director of creative writing, University of Oregon, Eugene, 1990—. Regular visits to Volcano, Hawaii, 1985-1991. Member of Associated Writing Programs. **Awards:** Thomas J. Watson fellowship, 1973-74; Hopwood Poetry prize, 1975; Discovery/*The Nation* award, 1981; NEA fellowships, 1982, 1988; Pushcart selection, 1986; Lamont Poetry selection, 1987; Pulitzer prize finalist, 1989; *Los Angeles Times* Book award finalist, 1989; Guggenheim fellowship, 1990-91; Rockefeller Residency fellowship at Bellagio Study Center, Italy, 1992. **Residence:** Eugene, Oregon.

PUBLICATIONS

Poetry

The Buddha Bandits Down Highway 99, with Alan Chong Lau and Lawson Fusao Inada. 1978.
Yellow Light. 1982.
The River of Heaven. 1988.

Plays

Nisei Bar and Grill. 1976.

Other

Volcano Journal (memoir). 1995.

Editor, *Greenfield Review* (special literary anthology of Asian American writers). 1977.
Editor, *The Open Boat* (poetry anthology). 1993.
Editor, *Songs My Mother Taught Me: Stories, Plays, Memoir* by Wakako Yamauchi. 1994.

Recordings: *The Power of the Word,* 1989.

*

Critical Studies: "The 'Doctor of Magic'" by Susan Yim in *Honolulu Star Bulletin* December 27, 1982; "Middle Class Poetry" by Diane Wakoski in *American Book Review* vol. 6, no. 2, 1984; "Yellow Light" by George Uba in *The Journal of Ethnic Studies* vol. 12, no. 4, 1985; "Hongo Offers a Poet's View of Japanese American Experience" by J. K. Yamamoto in *Pacific Citizen* February 20, 1987; "Writers On Writing: Voices of Democracy" by Phoebe Pettingell in *The New Leader* June 13, 1988; "Passionate Virtuosity" by Robert Schultz in *Hudson Review* vol. 17, no. 1, 1989; "A Vicious Kind of Tenderness: An Interview with Garrett Hongo" by Alice Evans in *Poets and Writers Magazine* September-October, 1992; *Garrett Hongo* by Laurie Filipelli, 1997.

*   *   *

Garrett Kaoru Hongo came to national prominence in the 1980s as a poet of urgent, lyrical narratives. His poetic impulse has been to recover the histories of the oppressed and dispossessed, locating previously untold stories that confer coherence and beauty upon ordinary experience and that speak directly to issues of ethnic identity. For Hongo, poetic account inevitably crosses into social history and cultural critique but simultaneously declares faith in the transfigurative powers of language itself. At its best, his poetry achieves a formal elegance that borrows from the rhythms of religious ceremonies. These rhythms lend spiritual density to his character portraits and elevate his preoccupation with the past above the level of nostalgia. While he remains a poet of painful memory and private yearning, it is memory transformed by luminescent moments of unity and yearning exalted by social desire.

Hongo made his earliest mark among a principally Asian American audience. He wrote, produced, and directed the 1976 play *Nisei Bar and Grill,* which depicts the interactions of a group of Japanese American veterans of the Korean War and explores issues related to biculturalism and sexuality. In 1978 he coauthored with Alan Chong Lau and Lawson Fusao Inada a small-press book entitled *The Buddha Bandits Down Highway 99.* Hongo's contribution, the nine-part "Cruising 99," is a singularly daring pastiche that incorporates a variety of poetic styles and a range of voices from urban funk to Whitmanian lyricism. At times noticeably improvisational, the poem nevertheless constitutes a distinctly ceremonial quest for "Paradise," whose earthly incarnation is a ghostly hermit mystically transformed into the highway itself. Later included as the longest poem in his first solo volume of poetry, "Cruising 99" demonstrates Hongo's attention to the particularities of ethnic experience and the spiritual searching he believes should regulate our lives.

Hongo gained further recognition when he was selected one of four winners in the annual Discovery/The Nation poetry contest in 1980. His work having already begun appearing in such venerable literary outlets as the *New Yorker,* the *Nation,* and *Antaeus,* his book of poetry, *Yellow Light*, was published in 1982 by Wesleyan University Press. The book offers taut, lyrical expressions of personal experiences, with moving tributes to family members and others whose lives are distinguished not by material accomplishment but by fullness of heart. At the book's ideological core, however, lies the search for ethnic and cultural roots. This search leads Hongo back in time to the rich, often troubling heritage of Japanese Americans both in Hawaii and the continental United States. Isolation, grinding toil, racial discrimination, internment camps, the oppression of field workers in Hawaii—all form essential parts of this historical record. But so too do endurance, imagination, and artistic achievement. The poet also conducts a spatial odyssey to Japan, where he seeks to discover cultural connections even as this ancestral land races through its astonishing postwar transformation.

Hongo's next book, *The River of Heaven* (1988), won the Lamont Poetry Award, given annually to a distinguished second book of poetry. This award was followed by a 1989 nomination for the Pulitzer Prize in Poetry. Divided into two parts, the book initially traces the poet's attempt to recover family connections and ancestral history relating to Hawaii, Hongo's place of birth. Beginning with a lush, inchoate catalogue of recalled things, the poet proceeds to piece together coherent versions of past lives from the story fragments he overhears. The book's second half offers a more random excursion into the past. Situated primarily in various urban enclaves of Southern California, the poems offer a series of anecdotes about lives that are variously ordinary, vagrant, or privileged, and about the disturbing intersections among them. The intense concentration on class divisions is augmented by a keen attention to racial differences. Occasionally, the poet celebrates a fragile moment of racial harmony; more frequently he coldly notes a pervading distrust or disrespect. Complicating these tensions, although at the same time enriching his conception of Asian America, is his depiction of more recent immigrants and refugees in several of the poems. Their full stories, it is implied, await further telling.

In general, Hongo's poetry is distinguished by its breadth, power, and ambition. With their sweeping, grandiose lines, his poems insist on the splendor of human experience and the inseparability of beauty and pain. The spirit craves respite from suffering and deprivation but can only appreciate relief by having prior knowledge of pain and can only achieve it through the formal eloquence of art. Socially self-conscious, such poetry is equal parts anger and love. Stylistically, it is memorable for its subtle variations of voice; its rich, voluptuous images that boldly insist on the lyrical capacities of narrative; and its ability to use ceremonial rhythms that lend formal dignity to even the humblest activity or event. For both philosophical and literary reasons, *Yellow Light* and *The River of Heaven* are among the important books of poetry to be produced by an Asian American.

In 1993 Hongo edited the poetry anthology *The Open Boat*. Continuing the work of recent anthologists, though potentially reaching out to another audience, the book seeks to reconfigure Asian American poetry as something richer and more diverse than the traditional categories of Chinese American, Japanese American, and Filipino American allow by including Indian and other South Asian, as well as biracial, writers. But beyond the issue of inclusion, Hongo believes that a narrow and repressive literary authority has been exerted over Asian American poets and writers in the form of a counter-cultural poetics attuned to various forms of social activism and dissent but intolerant of alternative

practices, ignorant of the history of poetry, and blind to poetic nuance. *The Open Boat*, which includes many writers boasting "conventional" literary credentials, seeks to reopen the question of the Asian American poetic canon and the aesthetic criteria that govern it by taking a position that has left its editor vulnerable, according to his detractors, to charges of accommodation, elitism, and exaggeration.

Hongo's first extended prose work was the evocative *Volcano: A Memoir of Hawai'i* (1995). Hongo left his birthplace as an infant, so the book is scarcely a reminiscence. Like other memoirs, *Volcano* is a work both of recovery and discovery, but additionally, it is an incantation and a conjuration of a place and a past that serve as the author's spiritual center. The geological and botanical descriptions are exceedingly lavish, at times reading like the field manual of a latter-day **Thoreau** and reminding us of the poet's passion for verbal abundance. Some readers are apt to turn with relief to a section like "Self Portrait," where the author revealingly examines his relationships with former teachers and mentors. But key to understanding the work and its descriptive luxuriance is to recognize it as a "book of origins"—origins related to a particular locale, to an evolving natural history, and to a family not exactly shrouded in mystery but somehow (like so many Nisei before the redress movement) detaching itself from its own beginnings. The book marks the author's brave effort to stave off alienation, to resist brooding, and to modulate defiance by finding "a way to belong and a place to belong to."

—George Uba

HOOPER, Johnson Jones

Born: Wilmington, North Carolina, 9 June 1815. **Education:** Local schools. **Family:** Married Mary Mildred Brantley in 1842; two sons and one daughter. **Career:** Printer's devil on newspapers, Charleston, South Carolina, 1826-32; read law with his brother in La Fayette, Alabama, 1835-37: admitted to Alabama bar, 1838; census taker for Tallapoosa County, Dadeville, Alabama, 1840; lawyer from 1841 (in practice with his brother from 1842); editor, La Fayette *East Alabamian*, 1843-45, and Wetumpka *Whig,* Alabama, 1845-46; member of the editorial staff, *Alabama Journal,* Montgomery, 1846-49; editor and part owner, Chambers *County Tribune,* La Fayette, 1850-53; solicitor, 9th Alabama Judicial Circuit, 1849-53; editor, Montgomery *Mail,* 1854-61; secretary, Allegheny Mining Company, 1859; secretary, Provisional Congress of the Southern States, Richmond, 1861-62. **Died:** 7 June 1862.

PUBLICATIONS

Fiction and Sketches

Some Adventures of Captain Simon Suggs, Late of the Tallapoosa Volunteers, Together with Taking the Census and Other Alabama Sketches. 1845; augmented edition, 1848.

A Ride with Old Kit Kuncker and Other Sketches and Scenes of Alabama. 1849.

The Widow Rugby's Husband, A Night at the Ugly Man's, and Other Tales of Alabama. 1851.

Dog and Gun: A Few Loose Chapters on Shooting. 1856.

Other

Editor, *Reminiscences of the Creek, or Muscogee Indians,* by Thomas S. Woodward. 1859.

*

Critical Studies: *The Southern Poor-White from Lubberland to Tobacco Road* by Shields McIlwaine, 1939; *Alias Simon Suggs: The Life and Times of Hooper* by W. Stanley Hoole, 1952; *Hooper: A Critical Study* by Howard Winston Smith, 1963; introduction by Manly Wade Wellman to *Adventures of Captain Simon Suggs,* 1969; *Johnson J. Hooper* by Paul Somers, Jr., 1984; "Writing with a Forked Pen: Racial Dynamics and Johnson Jones Hooper's Twin Tale of Swindling Indians" by Sheila Ruzycki O'Brien, in *American Studies,* fall 1994, pp. 95-113.

*   *   *

The achievement of Johnson Jones Hooper is rooted in his contributions to nineteenth-century Southwest humor, a broadly realistic, often satiric, sometimes cold-blooded, oral-vernacular tale-telling revealing a near absence of civilized standards of conduct. Some establishment critics of the early twentieth century tended virtually to dismiss Hooper's art as "discomfiture"—an "ancient, primitive, anti-social kind of merry-making." Despite such narrow judgment, Hooper's work was well received in its own day, appearing in such popular American humor anthologies as *The Big Bear of Arkansas* and *Polly Peablossom's Wedding and Other Tales.* Moreover, within an eighteen-year period twenty-one editions of Hooper's books appeared, eleven editions of his masterpiece, *Some Adventures of Captain Simon Suggs,* appearing between 1845 and 1856.

In form, the work has long been viewed as campaign biography, and hence tied to the political machinations of frontier folk. The work, however, can be taken as a burlesque of campaign biography, with specific events based on Andrew Jackson's military career.

Suggs himself is perhaps the "bad boy" of American literature, a man proficient in the art of drinking, joking, and staying just a step ahead of his creditors. Hooper's biographer, W. Stanley Hoole, cites Bird Young of Tallapoosa County as the historical model for Suggs. As fictional creation, Suggs, however, is the epitome of the poor-white. Shields McIlwaine notes that the adventurer has a "long nose hung above a mouth stained by the filthy weed . . . ," his family living in "woolhat poverty." As a cultural-sociological phenomenon, Suggs originates perhaps in the Lubberland of **William Byrd II**.

More than any other character from frontier humor, however, Suggs is indebted to the European tradition of the picaresque. As Howard Winston Smith has noted in his helpful critical study, both Suggs and Don Quixote undergo imitation promotions (Suggs to captaincy and Quixote to knighthood), and both works are episodic in nature. The general picaresque trait of the "picaro and the priest," moreover, originating in *Lazarillo de Tormes,* accounts in large part for Hooper's greatest moment in his most frequently anthologized chapter, "The Captain Attends a Camp Meeting." That particular chapter ultimately became the source for chapter twenty of *Huckleberry Finn.* Hooper ties together the many episodes by having each end in the triumph of frontier rascality over both innocence and sophistication.

None of Hooper's later writings has been judged equal to his first book. Both *The Widow Rugby's Husband, A Night at the Ugly Man's, and Other Tales of Alabama* and *Dog and Gun* attest to the author's love of the life he knew, but neither work reveals the real Hooper that Thackeray judged the "most promising writer of his day."

—George C. Longest

HOPKINSON, Francis

Born: Philadelphia, Pennsylvania, 2 October 1737. **Education:** The Academy of Philadelphia (now University of Pennsylvania), 1751-57, A.B. 1757, A.M. 1760; studied law with Benjamin Chew, 1757-61: admitted to Pennsylvania bar, 1761, and New Jersey bar, 1775. **Family:** Married Ann Borden in 1768; one son. **Career:** Began study of harpsichord, 1754; gave first public performance, 1757, and later set poems and psalms to music: first American-born composer of secular songs, 1759; developed improved method of quilling harpsichords; collector of customs, Port of Salem, New Jersey, 1763, and New Castle, Delaware, 1772; lawyer in Philadelphia and Bordentown, New Jersey, in 1760s and 1770s; also ran a store in Philadelphia; member, New Jersey Governor's Council, 1774, and New Jersey Provincial Congress, 1774-76; delegate from New Jersey, Second Continental Congress, 1775-76; signed the Declaration of Independence; subsequently served the new U.S. Government as chairman of the Continental Navy Board, 1776-78, and treasurer of the Continental Loan Office, 1778-81; Judge of Admiralty for Pennsylvania, 1779-89; member, Pennsylvania convention to ratify the Constitution, 1787; judge, U.S. District Court for Pennsylvania, 1789-91. Founding member, American Philosophical Society; a designer of the Great Seal of New Jersey, 1776; credited with the design of the American flag, 1777; secretary of the convention that organized the Protestant Episcopal Church, 1789. **Died:** 9 May 1791.

Publications

Collections

The First American Composer, edited by Harold V. Milligan. 1919.
Comical Spirit of Seventy-Six: The Humor of Hopkinson, edited by P.M. Zall. 1976.

Poetry

An Exercise. 1761.
Science. 1762.
A Collection of Psalm Tunes. 1762.
A Psalm of Thanksgiving. 1766.
The Psalms of David in Metre. 1767.
The Battle of the Kegs. 1779.
An Ode. 1788.
A Set of Eight Songs. 1788.
Ode from Ossian's Poems. 1794.

Play

The Temple of Minerva (oratorio), music by Hopkinson (produced 1781).

Fiction

A Pretty Story, Written in the Year of Our Lord 2774. 1774; as *The Old Farm and the New Farm: A Political Allegory,* 1857.

Other

Errata; or, The Art of Printing Incorrectly. 1763.
Account of the Grand Federal Procession. 1788.
Judgments in the Admiralty of Pennsylvania. 1789.
Miscellaneous Essays and Occasional Writings. 3 vols., 1792.

*

Critical Studies: *The Life and Works of Hopkinson* by George E. Hastings, 1926 (includes bibliography); "Hopkinson and Franklin" by Dixon Wecter, in *American Literature 12,* 1940; *Forrest's Curious Old Play: Or Hopkinson's Disappointment* by Mary D. Shepherd, 1994.

* * *

Poet, politician, musician, judge, scientist, and artist Francis Hopkinson excelled in so many activities that his contributions to American culture defy easy classification. A college friend of the Philadelphia writers Nathaniel Evans, Thomas Godfrey, and Jacob Duche, Hopkinson early showed an interest in a literary career. More than any other event, however, the Revolutionary War shaped Hopkinson's interests, and it is with the war that he eventually became associated. As a member of the Second Continental Congress, Hopkinson signed the Declaration of Independence, an action that alone was enough to guarantee him a place in history.

Not the least of his accomplishments were the many poems and essays he wrote in support of his country's decision to separate from Great Britain. His verses, most of which satirized the British and praised the Americans, were light, humorous, and deft. While not the stuff of great poetry, they accomplished what they were intended to do. Easily set to music, they lifted the spirits of American soldiers who sang them at the front, and they helped to demoralize the British by good naturedly ridiculing their cause. Hopkinson's most famous poem, "The Battle of the Kegs," recounts in ballad form how the British, unfamiliar with explosives, battled relentlessly with a flotilla of mines that American patriots had ingeniously floated in kegs down the Delaware River toward their camp. Other famous poems written by Hopkinson during the Revolutionary War include "A Camp Ballad," "The Toast," and "Tory Medley." Together these poems made Hopkinson one of the most popular American poets of his day—"penman of the Revolution."

Equally popular were the prose essays and tracts that Hopkinson directed against the British. From Arbuthnot, Swift, Addison, and Steele, Hopkinson developed a fondness for satire, particularly when it was couched in the form of allegory or a fabricated letter. Like his verse, Hopkinson's prose was extremely effective anti-British propaganda. Written in the form of a humorous allegory, and inspired by Arbuthnot's *History of John Bull, A Pretty Story* depicts the events that led the Colonies to declare their independence. In "A Prophecy," also an allegory, Hopkinson uses the persona of a biblical prophet who predicts the establishment of a new and prosperous government in North America.

Although Hopkinson frequently contributed poems and essays to such periodicals as the *American Magazine,* the *Columbian Magazine,* and the *Pennsylvania Packet,* his writing before and after the war lacked the vigor that the conflict itself inspired in him. With the possible exception of "My Days Have Been So Wondrous Free" (1759), a work thought to be the oldest American song known, his early and late poetry, for the most part dull and uninteresting, is rarely read in the late twentieth century. His letters are more profitable because he corresponded with the most important statesmen of his day, including George Washington, **Benjamin Franklin,** and **Thomas Jefferson.** *Miscellaneous Essays and Occasional Writings,* collected by Hopkinson himself, contains only a small portion of his total literary output. Many of his writings, particularly those written for periodicals, have yet to be collected.

—James A. Levernier

HOVEY, Richard

Born: Normal, Illinois, 4 May 1864. **Education:** Dartmouth College, Hanover, New Hampshire (editor, *Aegis*), 1881-85, B.A. (cum laude) 1885; Episcopal Seminary, New York, 1886. **Family:** Married Henrietta Russell in 1894; one son. **Career:** Teacher, Thomas Davidson's Summer School of Philosophy, 1888; actor, 1890; lived in England, 1894, and France, 1895-96; teacher, Barnard College, New York, 1899-1900. **Died:** 24 February 1900.

PUBLICATIONS

Poetry

Poems. 1880.
The Laurel: An Ode to Mary Day Lanier. 1889.
Harmonics. 1890.
Seaward: An Elegy on the Death of Thomas William Parsons. 1893.
Vagabondia books
    Songs from Vagabondia, with Bliss Carman. 1894.
    More Songs, 1896.
    Last Songs, 1900.
Along the Trail: A Book of Lyrics. 1898.
To the End of the Trail, edited by Mrs. Richard Hovey. 1908.
Dartmouth Lyrics, edited by Edwin Osgood Grover. 1924.
A Poem and Three Letters. 1935.

Plays

Launcelot and Guenevere: A Poem in Dramas (includes *The Quest of Merlin* and *The Marriage of Guenevere*). 1891; revised versions of *The Marriage of Guenevere,* 1895, and of *The Quest of Merlin,* 1898.
The Birth of Galahad. 1898.
Taliesin: A Masque. 1899.
The Holy Grail and Other Fragments, Being the Uncompleted Parts of the Arthurian Dramas, edited by Mrs. Richard Hovey. 1907.

Other

Hanover by Gaslight; or, Ways That Are Dark, Being an Expose of the Sophomoric Career of '85. 1883(?).

Translator, *The Plays of Maurice Maeterlinck: Princess Maleine, The Intruder, The Blind, The Seven Princesses.* 1894; second series (includes *Alladine and Palomides, Pelleas and Melisande, Home, The Death of Tintagiles*), 1896.

*

Bibliography: in *Bibliography of American Literature* by Jacob Blanck, 1963.

Critical Studies: *Hovey, Man and Craftsman* by Allan Houston Macdonald, 1957 (includes bibliography by Edward Connery Lathem); *Hovey* by William R. Linneman, 1976.

*   *   *

Like his contemporary **Stephen Crane**, Richard Hovey died tragically young, before he could fulfill the artistic promise he demonstrated, before he could make himself felt as a major force in modern poetry. But unlike Crane, Hovey did not seek to confront the turbulence and brutality of his age; yet he rebelled against it in *fin de siecle* aestheticism, in the spirit of bohemianism, of carefree youth, cheerful pleasures, and hearty fellowship. This spirit ruled his life and his poetry.

After graduating in 1885 from Dartmouth College, where he was active in campus literary life (Hovey celebrates the college in many poems, including "Men of Dartmouth," "Hanover Winter Song," and "Our Liege Lady, Dartmouth"), he studied to become an Episcopal priest, but left the seminary after one year. In 1887, he met the artist Tom Meteyard and the Canadian poet Bliss Carman, with both of whom he collaborated on the *Vagabondia* books. The dominant theme in these little volumes is that of the bold and energetic young man, "Wandering with the wandering wind, / Vagabond and unconfined!" ("The Wander-Lovers"); these short lyrics describe Hovey's world, one of adventurous, genteel Bohemianism, dedicated to comradeship and a love of Art. Hovey and Carman each wrote about half the number of poems in the books, which were popular, especially among college students, around the turn of the century.

Hovey was also a serious dramatic poet, planning (but never finishing) a series of verse plays on the Arthurian legends (a world popular with much escapist art and literature of the late nineteenth century).

A major influence acknowledged by Hovey is that of the American poet **Sidney Lanier**. Hovey's ode *The Laurel* (dedicated to Mrs. Lanier) and his serious lyric poetry, notably the elegy *Seaward*, reflect Lanier's rhythms and images. Hovey was also influenced by the French *symbolistes*, and translated Mallarmé and Maeterlinck. But he did not have enough time in which to develop his own lyrical talent into a unique or influential poetic voice.

—Jane S. Gabin

HOWARD, Bronson (Crocker)

Born: Detroit, Michigan, 7 October 1842. **Education:** Schools in Detroit and at Russell's Institute, New Haven, Connecticut. **Family:** Married Alice Wyndham in 1880. **Career:** Staff member, *Detroit Free Press;* began writing for the stage, 1864; moved to New York, 1865, and worked as a reporter for *Evening Mail, Tribune,* and *Evening Post,* until his first dramatic success, 1870; thereafter a full-time playwright. **Member:** Founder, 1891, and first president, American Dramatists Club (later the Society of American Dramatists and Composers). **Died:** 4 August 1908.

PUBLICATIONS

Collection

The Banker's Daughter and Other Plays (includes *Old Love Letters, One of Our Girls, Hurricanes, Knave and Queen, Baron Rudolph*), edited by Allan G. Halline. 1941.

Plays

Fantine (produced 1864).
Saratoga; or, Pistols for Seven (produced 1870). 1870.
Ingomar the Idiotic; or, The Miser, the Maid, and the Mangle, with Oswald Allen (produced 1871).
Diamonds (produced 1872).
The Banker's Daughter (as *Lilian's Lost Love,* produced 1873; revised version as *The Banker's Daughter,* produced 1878; as *The Old Love and the New,* produced 1879). 1878; in *The Banker's Daughter and Other Plays,* 1941.
Moorcroft; or, The Double Wedding (produced 1874).
Knave and Queen, with Charles L. Young (as *Ivers Dean,* produced 1877). In *The Banker's Daughter and Other Plays,* 1941.
Old Love Letters (produced 1878). 1897; in *The Banker's Daughter and Other Plays,* 1941.
Hurricanes (produced 1878; as *Truth,* produced 1878). In *The Banker's Daughter and Other Plays,* 1941.
Wives, from a play by Moliere (produced 1879).
The Amateur Benefit. 1881.
Baron Rudolph (produced 1881; revised version, with David Belasco, produced 1887). In *The Banker's Daughter and Other Plays,* 1941.
Fun in a Green Room (produced 1882).
Young Mrs. Winthrop (produced 1882). 1899.
One of Our Girls (produced 1885; as *Cousin Kate,* produced 1889). 1897; in *The Banker's Daughter and Other Plays,* 1941.
Camping Out (produced 1886).
Met by Chance (produced 1887).
The Henrietta (produced 1887). 1901; edited by Allan G. Halline, in *American Plays,* 1935.
Shenandoah (produced 1888). 1897; edited by Arthur Hobson Quinn, in *Representative American Plays,* 1917.
Aristocracy (produced 1892). 1898.
Peter Stuyvesant, with Brander Matthews (produced 1899).

Fiction

Kate. 1906.

Other

The Autobiography of a Play (on *The Banker's Daughter*). 1914.

*

Critical Studies: *In Memoriam Bronson Howard* (addresses), 1910; "Bronson Howard: Dean of American Drama, 1842-1908" by Barbara C. Gannon, in *American Literary Realism, 1870-1910,* spring 1982 (includes bibliography).

*   *   *

The contribution to American drama that inspired some critics to describe Bronson Howard as the "Dean of American Drama" derives largely from his ability to support himself as a dramatist, the first American to achieve this distinction. As a professional dramatist he founded the American Dramatists Club in 1891, lectured at Harvard on what he termed "The Laws of Dramatic Composition," established himself firmly as the major playwright to deal with the American businessman, and brought to American drama the international social scene that was then being exploited in fiction with considerable success by **Henry James** and **William Dean Howells**.

The fact that Howard could make a career as a playwright suggests something about his abilities. A good craftsman of the stage, he understood and accepted the commercially oriented conventions and limiting requirements of the late nineteenth-century American theater. Although he was markedly more farsighted than his contemporaries in terms of his chosen themes and materials, he carefully adhered to his own outline of a well-constructed play that must be "satisfactory" to an audience and reach a properly moral and happy conclusion. Toward the end of his career he weakened his position as a man of independent thought by joining the stable of playwrights of the Theatrical Syndicate. He was always a man of the theater, sometimes belligerently so, and it was never his intention to pull together the established rift in America between theater and drama. Indeed, his expressed antagonism toward dramatic literature and literary people probably further delayed a developing American drama.

A major characteristic of his playwriting was the carefully crafted and commercially successful work that suggested a direction for future dramatists whose careers among theater managers would be more secure after Howard's efforts. His first success was a play called *Saratoga,* for which he embroidered the usual farce action with better than average farce dialogue and used a favorite American resort as his scene. The fact that the play was transferred successfully to English circumstances by Frank Marshall as *Brighton* (1874) suggests something of his style. More significant are his business plays. *Young Mrs. Winthrop* showed the difficulties that the demands of the business world may bring to married life. *The Henrietta* satirized life on the New York Stock Exchange. *Aristocracy* combined Howard's interest in the American businessman and the socially intriguing international scene by revealing that the obvious route by which new wealth of the American West might unite with New York traditional society was through London aristocracy. In an earlier play, *One of Our Girls,* Howard contrasted American and French social conventions. His single play— a very successful one—which remains outside his usual society-oriented work is *Shenandoah,* a romantic tale of the Civil War.

Basically a transitional dramatist in American theater, Howard helped to diminish the popularity of foreign plays on the American stage and give the American dramatist greater importance in the theater. This is his real contribution. Otherwise, he was a generally skillful dramatist for his time who could write entertaining and sentimental social melodrama.

—Walter J. Meserve

HOWARD, Sidney (Coe)

Born: Oakland, California, 26 June 1891. **Education:** The University of California, Berkeley (editor, *Occident*), 1911-15, B.A. 1915; studied with George Pierce Baker at Harvard University, Cambridge, Massachusetts, 1915-16, A.M. 1916. **Military Service:** Served in the American Ambulance Corps, and later in the U.S. Army Air Corps, during World War I: captain; Silver Star. **Family:** Married 1) the actress Clare Jenness Eames in 1922 (divorced 1930), one daughter; 2) Leopoldine Blaine Damrosch in 1931, one daughter and one son. **Career:** Member of the editorial staff, 1919-22, and literary editor, 1922, *Life* magazine, New York; special investigator and feature writer, *New Republic* and *Hearst's International Magazine,* New York, 1923; full-time playwright from 1923; founder, with Robert E. Sherwood, Elmer Rice, Maxwell Anderson, S. N. Behrman, and John F. Wharton, Playwrights Company, 1938. Member, Board of Directors, American Civil Liberties Union; President, Dramatists Guild, 1935-37. **Awards:** Pulitzer prize, 1925; Academy award, for screenplay, 1940. Litt.D.: Washington and Jefferson College, Washington, Pennsylvania, 1935. **Member:** American Academy. **Died:** 23 August 1939.

PUBLICATIONS

Plays

The Sons of Spain (produced 1914).
Swords (produced 1921). 1921.
S.S. Tenacity, from work by Charles Vildrac (produced 1922).
Sancho Panza, from play by Melchior Lengyel (produced 1923).
Casanova, from a play by Lorenzo de Azertis (produced 1923). 1924.
They Knew What They Wanted (produced 1924). 1925.
Bewitched, with Edward Sheldon (produced 1924).
Lexington (produced 1925). 1924(?).
Michel Auclair (produced 1925). In *Plays for College Theater,* edited by Garrett H. Leverton, 1932.
The Last Night of Don Juan, from a play by Edmond Rostand (produced 1925).
Morals, from a play by Ludwig Thoma (produced 1925).
Lucky Sam McCarver (produced 1925). 1926.
Ned McCobb's Daughter (produced 1926). 1926.
The Silver Cord (produced 1926). 1927.
Salvation with Charles MacArthur (produced 1928). In *Stage Works of MacArthur,* 1974.
Olympia, from a play by Ferenc Molnar (produced 1928). 1928.
Half Gods (produced 1929). 1930.
Lute Song, with Will Irwin (as *Pi-Pa-Ki,* produced 1930); revised version, as *Lute Song,* music by Raymond Scott, lyrics by Bernard Hanighen (produced 1946). 1955.
President, from a play by Ferenc Molnar (as *One, Two, Three* produced 1930). In *Romantic Comedies,* by Molnar, 1952.
Marseilles, from a work by Marcel Pagnol (produced 1930).
The Late Christopher Bean, from a play by Rene Fauchois (produced 1932). 1933.
Alien Corn (produced 1933). 1933.
Gather Ye Rosebuds, with Robert Littell (produced 1934).
Ode to Liberty, from a play by Michel Duran (produced 1934).
Dodsworth, from the novel by Sinclair Lewis (produced 1934). 1934.

Yellow Jack, with Paul de Kruif, from a work by de Kruif (produced 1934). 1934.
Paths of Glory, from the novel by Humphrey Cobb (produced 1935). 1935.
The Ghost of Yankee Doodle (produced 1937). 1938.
Madam, Will You Walk? (produced 1953). 1955.
GWTW [Gone with the Wind]: *The Screenplay,* edited by Richard Harwell. 1980.

Screenplays: *Bulldog Drummond,* with Wallace Smith, 1929; *Condemned,* 1929; *A Lady to Love,* 1930; *Raffles,* 1930; *One Heavenly Night,* with Louis Bromfield, 1930; *Arrowsmith,* 1931; *The Greeks Had a Word for Them,* 1932; *Dodsworth,* 1936; *Gone with the Wind,* 1939; *Raffles,* with John van Druten, 1940.

Fiction

Three Flights Up (stories). 1924.

Other

The Labor Spy: A Survey of Industrial Espionage, with Robert Dunn. 1921; revised edition, 1924.
Professional Patriots, with John Hearley, edited by Norman Hapgood. 1927.

*

Critical Study: *Howard* by Sidney H. White, 1977.

*   *   *

The first major writer of social drama after American drama approached the age of maturity following World War I, Sidney Howard mixed melodrama and comedy with the established mode of realism in literature to reflect a dominant social idea of the 1920s—*They Knew What They Wanted.* As the title of one of his best plays, it presented the positive individualism of his generation, which other playwrights (**Philip Barry, S. N. Behrman, Maxwell Anderson, Paul Green**) soon emphasized. In contrast to some of his outstanding contemporaries, Howard was not an innovator in dramatic form nor a particularly profound writer. He readily admitted such shortcomings, if indeed they were that. Instead, he was a substantial playwright of considerable theatrical skill and imagination who stepped into the ongoing stream of social drama in America and produced at least two major plays in that genre.

They Knew What They Wanted is a modern version of the Paolo-Francesca love story but with a modern twist that none of those who told the story from Dante to Wagner would have accepted. But Howard's intelligently expedient people, battling the exigencies of the modern world, know what they want, and his hero, Tony, can become, as Frank Loesser's musical adaptation made him, "The Most Happy Fella." In *The Silver Cord* Howard took advantage of ideas propounded by Strindberg and Freud. With a diabolic cunning worthy of Strindberg's Laura, Howard's protagonist fights for the control of her sons in an emotion-packed drama that remains one of America's best thesis plays. Emotion and spectacle are always major aspects of a Howard play. He wrote about people, frequently with a strong sense of irony, and all of his plays held at least one spectacular scene that he

handled with a craftsmanship critics have admired. The best include *Lucky Sam McCarver, Ned McCobb's Daughter,* and *The Late Christopher Bean;* he also adapted Sinclair Lewis's *Dodsworth* for the stage.

During a life cut short by a farm accident in 1939 Howard wrote some twenty plays, most of them either adaptations or collaborations. But his reputation in American drama rests solidly upon the plays he wrote by himself, the best of which appeared during the 1920s. He seemed unable to relate successfully to the social atmosphere of the Depression years that followed.

—Walter J. Meserve

HOWE, E(dgar) W(atson)

Born: Near Treaty, Wabash County, Indiana, 3 May 1853. **Education:** Local schools in Missouri. **Family:** Married Clara L. Frank in 1873 (divorced 1901); five children. **Career:** Apprentice printer on his father's newspaper, *Union of States,* Bethany, Missouri, 1864-65; printer in Missouri, Iowa, Illinois, Nebraska, Wyoming, and Utah, 1866-72; publisher, *Globe,* Golden, Colorado, 1873-75; founder with his brother James, and editor, 1877-1910, Atchison *Globe,* Kansas; editor and publisher, *E.W. Howe's Monthly,* Atchison, 1911-33. **Awards:** Litt.D.: Rollins College, Winter Park, Florida, 1926; Washburn College, Topeka, Kansas, 1927. **Died:** 3 October 1937.

Pᴜʙʟɪᴄᴀᴛɪᴏɴs

Fiction

The Story of a Country Town. 1883; edited by Brom Weber, 1964.
The Mystery of The Locks. 1885.
A Moonlight Boy. 1886.
A Man Story. 1889.
An Ante-Mortem Statement. 1891.
The Confession of John Whitlock, Late Preacher of the Gospel. 1891.
Dying Like a Gentleman and Other Stories. 1926.
The Covered Wagon and the West (stories). 1928.
Her Fifth Marriage and Other Stories. 1928.
When a Woman Enjoys Herself and Other Tales of a Small Town. 1928.

Other

Mark Antony De Wolfe Howe 1808-1895: A Brief Record of a Long Life. 1897.
Daily Notes of a Trip Around the World. 2 vols., 1907.
The Trip to the West Indies. 1910.
Country Town Sayings: A Collection of Paragraphs from the Atchison Globe. 1911.
Travel Letters from New Zealand, Australia, and Africa. 1913.
Success Easier Than Failure. 1917.
The Blessing of Business. 1918.
Ventures in Common Sense, edited by H.L. Mencken. 1919; as *Adventures in Common Sense,* 1922.
The Anthology of Another Town. 1920.

Notes for My Biographer: Terse Paragraphs on Life and Letters.
1926.
Preaching from the Audience: Candid Comments on Life. 1926.
Sinner Sermons: A Selection of the Best Paragraphs of Howe. 1926.
Plain People (autobiography). 1929.
The Indignations of Howe. 1933.

*

Critical Studies: *Howe, Country Town Philosopher* by Calder
M. Pickett, 1968; *Howe* by S.J. Sackett, 1972; *Howe* by Martin
Bucco, 1977.

*   *   *

"I come of a long line of plain people," E.W. Howe writes at
the beginning of his autobiography *Plain People,* but as a famous
editor in the days of personal journalism and as a minor novelist
of the late nineteenth century, Howe achieved a measure of distinction in his own day and a small niche in the history of American life and culture. He is the author of one novel that continues
to be reprinted and read, and his autobiography, long out of print,
deserves to be better known. Howe is an authentic bit of Americana woven into the fabric of national experience—a figure to be
compared in this respect with **Benjamin Franklin**, **Horatio
Alger**, **H.L. Mencken**, and Will Rogers.

After establishing himself as a newspaper editor, Howe turned
toward literature. For months in the early 1880s he worked over
the manuscript of *The Story of a Country Town* at the kitchen
table after finishing a long day in the newspaper office. When commercial publishers turned down his book, he published it himself.
The novel was an immediate success and encouraged him to write
several more, all of which were failures and never have been reprinted. Eventually he resigned himself to filling his newspaper
columns with aphoristic paragraphs that attracted national attention. He continued to write books for the rest of his life, but they
are mostly forgotten travel letters, tracts on business, and collections of his newspaper and magazine paragraphs. One other, however, is worth reading: *The Anthology of Another Town,* a prose
version of and answer to **Edgar Lee Masters**'s *Spoon River Anthology.*

The Story of a Country Town draws on the life of Howe's father and Howe's own experience growing up in northwest Missouri where the novel takes place. It is basically a melodramatic
tragedy of a backwoods Othello who becomes insanely jealous
when he discovers that his wife was once in love with another
man. As a work of art, it is full of crudities, but the story is told
with such a passionate intensity by Howe's persona, young Ned
Westlake, who observes the action, that readers are swept along
by it.

Both **Howells** and **Twain**, who received copies from the author, wrote flattering letters about the novel. Howells thought it a
"very remarkable piece of realism" and praised the fidelity of the
country town setting although he objected to the sentimentality
of the tragic romance. The novel generally has been classed with
early examples of realism, but it is only partly realistic, and Howe's
later novels demonstrated that he was really a sentimental romancer
at heart. *The Story of a Country Town* can be seen, with its bitter
memories of the narrator's youth, as a forerunner of the revolt-
from-the-village literature of **Sinclair Lewis**, **Sherwood Anderson**, and Masters, but Howe during his later years filled his news-

paper columns with the most blatant Chamber-of-Commerce puff-
ery and really believed that all virtue resided in the small town
and in rural life.

—James Woodress

HOWE, Susan

Born: 1937. **Education:** Museum of Fine Arts, Boston, B.F.A.
in painting 1961. **Family:** Married 1) Harvey Quaytam in 1960
(divorced 1965), one daughter; 2) David von Schlegell in 1965 (died
1992), one son. **Career:** Butler fellow, SUNY Buffalo, New York,
1988; visiting professor, SUNY Buffalo, New York, 1989; visiting professor, Temple University, Philadelphia, Pennsylvania, 1990
and 1991. Beginning 1992 full professor with tenure, department
of English, SUNY Buffalo. Leo Block Chair for Visiting Artist-
Scholar, University of Denver, 1993-94; visiting professor,
Stanford University, spring 1998. Visiting poet, Kootenay School
of Writing, 1987, Naropa Institute, Boulder, Colorado, summer
1991, Bard College, 1993, George Mason University, 1994, University of Wisconsin at Madison, 1994, University of Arizona,
Tempe, April 1994, Oberlin College, November 1995, and St.
Joseph's College, Hartford, Connecticut, June 1996. Also an artist: exhibitions in Paley and Lowe Gallery, New York, 1972;
Albright Knox Museum, Buffalo, 1973; and Philadelphia Institute of Contemporary Art, 1976. **Awards:** Before Columbus Foundation American Book award, for *Secret History of the Dividing
Line,* 1980, and for *My Emily Dickinson,* 1986; Fund for Poetry
award, 1987, 1989; New York State council of the Arts Grant to
be Poet-in-Residence at George Arts Project, 1987; Roy Harvey
Pearce award for Work by a Poet and Critic, for *The Birth-mark:
Unsettling the Wilderness in American Literary History,* 1996; John
Simon Guggenheim Memorial fellowship, 1996; distinguished fellow,
Stanford Humanities Center, 1998. **Member:** Connecticut Academy
of Arts and Sciences. **Residence:** Guilford, Connecticut.

PUBLICATIONS

Poetry

Hinge Picture. 1974.
The Western Borders. 1976.
Cabbage Gardens. 1979.
Secret History of the Dividing Line. 1979.
The Liberties. 1980.
Pythagorean Silence. 1982.
Defenestration of Prague. 1983.
Articulation of Sound Forms in Time. 1987.
A Bibliography of the King's Book or, Eikon Basilike. 1989.
The Europe of Trusts: Selected Poems. 1989.
Singularities. 1990.
The Nonconformist's Memorial: Poems by Susan Howe. 1993.
Frame Structures: Early Poems, 1974-1978. 1996.
Pierce-Arrow. 1999.

Other

My Emily Dickinson. 1985.

Incloser. 1992.

The Birth-mark: Unsettling the Wilderness in American Literary History. 1993.

Translator, *Marginalia de Melville.* 1997.
Translator, *Deux et.* 1998.

*

Critical Studies: "Howe: Open Letter" by Tina Darragh, in *Language 4,* Winter 1982; "*The Defenestration of Prague*" by Lori Chamberlin, in *Sulfur, 9, 1984;* "our law/ vocables/ of shape or sound: The Work of Susan Howe" by Rachel Blau du Plessis, in *Howe(ever),* May 1984; "Recharging the Canon: Some Reflections on Feminist Poetics and the Avant-garde" by Marjorie Perloff, in *The American Poetry Review,* July-August 1986; "Susan Howe's *My Emily Dickinson*" by John Taggart, in *Conjunctions,* 1986; "The Mysterious Vision of Susan Howe" by George Butterick, in *North Dakota Quarterly,* Fall 1987; "'Collision or Collusion with History': The Narrative Lyric of Susan Howe" by Marjorie Perloff, in *Contemporary Literature,* Winter 1989; "And the Without: An Interpretive Essay on Susan Howe" by Peter Quartermain, in *The Difficulties, Susan Howe Issue,* 1989; "A Tangent on Lines by Susan Howe" by Rosemarie Waldrop, in *Talisman,* Spring 1990; *Radical Affair: Writing Poetry in the Age of Media* by Marjorie Perloff, 1991; "On Ice: Julia Kristeva, Susan Howe, and Avant Garde Poetics" by Peter Middleton, in *Contemporary Poetry Meets Modern Theory* edited by Anthony Easthope and John Thompson, 1991; "Reading Susan Howe: Notes Toward a Review" by Merle-Lyn Bachman, in *Talisman,* Spring 1994; "An End of Abstraction: An Essay on Susan Howe's Historicism" by John Palattella, in *Denver Quarterly,* Winter 1995; "Into/The Very of Silence': Reading Susan Howe" by Thomas Vogler, in *Hambone,* Fall 1995; "Waging Political Babble: Susan Howe's Visual Prosody and the Politics of Noise" by Craig Douglas Dworkin, in *Word and Image,* October-December 1996.

*   *   *

Over the course of ten books of poetry and two critical studies of classic American literature, Susan Howe has developed a unique poetic mode. In it she mingles the historical archivist techniques pioneered by **Ezra Pound** and **Charles Olson** in *The Cantos* and *The Maximus Poems* with the heterodox prophetic stance of William Blake, **Emily Dickinson**, **Henry David Thoreau**, and **Herman Melville**. A self-proclaimed "library cormorant" like two of her heroes, Samuel Taylor Coleridge and Melville, she combs through obscure texts of the past for traces of a forgotten history—unfamiliar vocabularies, quirky narratives, obsolete spellings, irregular printings—that reveal the presence of a material "wilderness" surrounding the confines of normative modern culture.

Howe's poems similarly often explore crossings between culture and wilderness through her choice of source texts and themes. For example, her poetic sequence *Hope Atherton's Wanderings* is based on a seventeenth-century narrative of an Indian captivity. To be precise, in fact, it is the story of Hope Atherton's failure to be taken captive and his wandering in a no-man's land between the settler's society and that of the native inhabitants. Howe conveys this background information to her reader through further layers of historical documentation and testimony, in a letter from 1781, written over a century after the events, which she cites as

the preface to her sequence. The author of that letter recounts being told by Atherton's son that the Indians had told him about the inconsequential, almost silly episode of Atherton's noncaptivity: "the Indians told him that after the fall fight, a little man with a black coat and without any hat, came toward them, but they were afraid and ran from him, thinking it was the Englishman's God." The poetic sequence itself represents the experience of Hope Atherton's errancy in the forest from within, from inside his scattered consciousness and in the form of his anachronistic vocabulary and spellings:

> Two blew bird eggs plat
> Habitants before dark
> Little way went mistook awake
> abt again Clay Gully
> espied bounds to leop over

Later in the sequence, Howe's own prophetic commentary begins to enter, suggesting the ambiguity of the figure of Atherton, oscillating between the bounded laws of colonial settlement and the anarchy of the forest, in which all fixed categories are dissolved. In this light, Atherton becomes Howe's archetypal modern American, also compounded of such contradictory qualities:

> Impulsion of a myth of beginning
> The figure of a far-off Wanderer
>
> Grail face of bronze and brass
> Grass and weeds cover the face
>
> Colonades of rigorous Americanism
> Portents of lonely destructivism
>
> Knowledge narrowly fixed knowledge
> Whose bounds in theories slay

Howe has further noted that "Hope" is generally thought of as a woman's name, so that not only does he embody the potential to wander between native and settler identities and between American wilderness and European civilization, but also between masculinity and femininity.

Another poetic sequence *thorow* explores analogous themes in a nineteenth-century setting, while further radicalizing the techniques developed in the earlier piece. The title itself indicates one of the main strategies of the work, a complex use of nonstandard spellings and irregular typography to bring to the fore the material properties of words as composed of printed letters; the title "thorow" can be taken to point simultaneously to the words "through," "throw," and "thorough," as well as to the name "Thoreau." The reader must read the letters of the misspelled words as if "scouting" along the littered floor of the forest, as if interpreting animal tracks, indices of weather, patterns of leaves, and other natural signs to discover the proper way through the thicket. Howe presents this task as a kind of exposure of the self to the radical "otherness" of the natural world, an experience both frighteningly disorienting and potentially enlightening, because it may reveal the lineaments of another order concealed, as Thoreau discovered at Walden, by the bustle and noise of everyday life:

> The expanse of unconcealment
> so different from all maps

Spiritual typography of elegy

Nature in us as a Nature
the actual one the ideal Self

tent tree sere leaf spectre
Unconscious demarkations range

I pick my compass to pieces

Howe's most complicated pages are not even reproducible, as they employ upside-down or diagonal printings of words and over-printing of lines. They are intended as analogues of a unique eco-logical configuration, glimpsed as a patterned whole at a moment in time. The most striking instance of this technique comes in two facing pages in the third part of *thorow*. In these two poems Howe repeats the same elements word-for-word, but arranges them dif-ferently, scattering the phrases across the page as if they were fallen leaves on the surface of a pond, agitated by a breeze. The reader must literally rotate the book to read the poems, and they are explicitly meant to be slowly taken in and compared for their similarities and differences, their local elements, and their overall shape. As poems, they waver between visual artworks and texts, ultimately serving less to convey a particular verbal meaning than to offer a kind of hieroglyphic image of a unique moment, regis-tering its brief presence in the enduring medium of the printed word.

—Tyrus Miller

HOWELLS, William Dean

Born: Martinsville (later Martins Ferry), Ohio, 1 March 1837. **Education:** Schools in Hamilton and Dayton, Ohio. **Family:** Married Elinor Gertrude Mead in 1862 (died 1910); two daugh-ters and one son. **Career:** Compositor, *Ohio State Journal,* Co-lumbus, 1851-60; contributor to his father's newspaper, *Jefferson Sentinel,* Ohio, from 1852; columnist ("Letter from Columbus," 1857-58, and "Letter from New York," 1866), Cin-cinnati *Gazette;* columnist, Cleveland *Herald,* 1858; reader, Follett and Foster, publishers, Columbus, 1860; U.S. Consul, Venice, 1861-65; columnist ("Letter from Venice"), Boston *Daily Advertiser,* 1862-64; columnist ("Minor Topics"), *The Nation,* New York, 1865-66; assistant editor, 1866-71, and editor-in-chief, 1871-81, *Atlantic Monthly,* Boston; University Lecturer in Modern Literature, Harvard University, Cambridge, Massa-chusetts, 1869-71; Lowell Lecturer, Boston, 1870; freelance writer, 1881-85; columnist ("Editor's Study," 1886-92, and "Editor's Easy Chair," from 1900), *Harper's* monthly, New York ("Life and Letters"), *Harper's Weekly,* New York, 1895-98, and ("American Letter"), *Literature,* 1898-99; lived in New York after 1891; coeditor, *Cosmopolitan,* New York, 1892. **Awards:** American Academy Gold Medal, 1915. M.A.: Harvard University, 1867. Litt.D.: Yale University, New Haven, Con-necticut, 1901; Oxford University, 1904; Columbia University, New York, 1905. L.H.D.: Princeton University, New Jersey, 1912. Honorary Fellow, Royal Society of Literature, 1901; president, American Academy, 1908-20. **Died:** 11 May 1920.

PUBLICATIONS

Collections

Representative Selections, edited by Clara Marburg Kirk and Rudolf Kirk. 1950.
Selected Writings, edited by Henry Steele Commager. 1950.
Complete Plays, edited by Walter J. Meserve. 1960.
Selected Edition, edited by Ronald Gottesman and others. 1968-.
Novels 1875-1886 (Library of America), edited by Edwin H. Cady. 1982.
Selected Short Stories of William Dean Howells. 1997.

Fiction

Their Wedding Journey. 1872; edited by John K. Reeves, in *Se-lected Edition,* 1968.
A Chance Acquaintance. 1873; edited by Ronald Gottesman, David J. Nordloh, and Jonathan Thomas, in *Selected Edition,* 1971.
A Foregone Conclusion. 1874.
The Lady of the Aroostook. 1879.
The Undiscovered Country. 1880.
A Fearful Responsibility and Other Stories. 1881; as *A Fearful Re-sponsibility and Tonnelli's Marriage,* 1882.
Doctor Breen's Practice. 1881.
A Modern Instance. 1882; edited by David J. Nordloh and David Kleinman, in *Selected Edition,* 1977.
A Woman's Reason. 1883.
The Rise of Silas Lapham. 1885; edited by Don L. Cook, 1982.
Indian Summer. 1886; edited by Scott Bennett and David J. Nordloh, in *Selected Edition,* 1971.
The Minister's Charge; or, The Apprenticeship of Lemuel Barker. 1886; edited by David J. Nordloh and David Kleinman, in *Se-lected Edition,* 1978.
April Hopes. 1887.
Annie Kilburn. 1888.
A Hazard of New Fortunes. 1889; edited by David J. Nordloh, in *Selected Edition,* 1976.
The Shadow of a Dream. 1890; with *An Imperative Duty,* edited by Martha Banta, Ronald Gottesman, and David J. Nordloh, in *Selected Edition,* 1970.
An Imperative Duty. 1891; with *The Shadow of a Dream,* edited by Martha Banta, Ronald Gottesman, and David J. Nordloh, in *Selected Edition,* 1970.
Mercy. 1892; as *The Quality of Mercy,* 1892; edited by James P. Elliott, in *Selected Edition,* 1979.
The World of Chance. 1893.
The Coast of Bohemia. 1893.
A Traveler from Altruria. 1894; complete edition, edited by Clara Marburg Kirk and Rudolf Kirk, as *Letters of an Altrurian Trav-eller (1893-1894),* 1961; with *Between the Dark and the Day-light,* in *Selected Edition,* 1968.
The Day of Their Wedding. 1896.
A Parting and a Meeting. 1896; with *The Day of Their Wedding,* as *Idyls in Drab,* 1896.
The Landlord at Lion's Head. 1897.
An Open-Eyed Conspiracy: An Idyl of Saratoga. 1897.
The Story of a Play. 1898.
Ragged Lady. 1899.
Their Silver Wedding Journey. 1899; abridged edition, as *Hither and Thither in Germany,* 1920.

A Pair of Patient Lovers (stories). 1901.
The Kentons. 1902; in *Selected Edition,* 1971.
The Flight of Pony Baker: A Boy's Town Story. 1902.
Questionable Shapes. 1903.
Letters Home. 1903.
The Son of Royal Langbrith. 1904; edited by David Burrows, Ronald Gottesman, and David J. Nordloh, in *Selected Edition,* 1969.
Miss Bellard's Inspiration. 1905.
Through the Eye of the Needle. 1907.
Between the Dark and the Daylight: Romances. 1907; with *A Traveler from Altruria,* in *Selected Edition,* 1968.
Fennel and Rue. 1908.
New Leaf Mills: A Chronicle. 1913.
The Leatherwood God. 1916; in *Selected Edition,* 1976.
The Vacation of the Kelwyns: An Idyl of the Middle Eighteen-Seventies. 1920.
Mrs. Farrell. 1921.

Plays

Samson, from the play by Ippolito D'Aste (produced 1874). 1889.
The Parlor Car. 1876.
Out of the Question. 1877.
A Counterfeit Presentment (produced 1877; revised version, produced 1877). 1877.
Yorick's Love, from a play by Manuel Tamayo y Baus (as *A New Play,* produced 1878; as *Yorick's Love,* produced 1880). In *Complete Plays,* 1960.
The Sleeping-Car (produced 1887). 1883.
The Register. 1884.
The Elevator (produced 1885). 1885.
The Garroters (produced 1886). 1886.
A Foregone Conclusion, with William Poel, from the novel by Howells (produced 1886). In *Complete Plays,* 1960.
Colonel Sellers as a Scientist, with Mark Twain, from the novel *The Gilded Age* by Twain and Charles Dudley Warner (produced 1887). In *Complete Plays,* 1960.
The Mouse-Trap (produced 1887-88?). In *The Mouse-Trap and Other Farces,* 1889.
A Sea-Change; or, Love's Stowaway: A Lyricated Farce, music by George Henschel. 1888.
The Mouse-Trap and Other Farces (includes *A Likely Story, Five O'Clock Tea, The Garroters*). 1889.
The Sleeping-Car and Other Farces (includes *The Parlor Car, The Register, The Elevator*). 1889.
The Albany Depot. 1891.
A Letter of Introduction. 1892.
The Unexpected Guests. 1893.
Evening Dress (produced 1894). 1893.
Bride Roses (produced 1894). 1900.
A Dangerous Ruffian (produced 1895).
A Previous Engagement. 1897.
Room Forty-Five. 1900.
An Indian Giver. 1900.
The Smoking Car. 1900.
Minor Dramas. 2 vols., 1907.
The Mother and the Father. 1909.
Parting Friends. 1911.
The Night Before Christmas, and Self-Sacrifice, in *The Daughter of the Storage and Other Things in Prose and Verse,* 1916.

Poetry

Poems of Two Friends, with John J. Piatt. 1860.
No Love Lost: A Romance of Travel. 1869.
Poems. 1873; revised edition, 1886.
Stops of Various Quills. 1895.
The Mulberries in Pay's Garden. 1907.

Other

Lives and Speeches of Abraham Lincoln and Hannibal Hamlin, with J. L. Hayes. 1860.
Venetian Life. 1866; revised edition, 1867, 1872; 2 vols., 1907.
Italian Journeys. 1867; revised edition, 1872, 1901.
Suburban Sketches. 1871; revised edition, 1872; abridged edition, as *A Day's Pleasure,* 1876.
Sketch of the Life and Character of Rutherford B. Hayes. 1876.
A Little Girl among the Old Masters. 1884.
Three Villages. 1884.
Tuscan Cities. 1885.
Modern Italian Poets: Essays and Versions. 1887.
A Boy's Town (for children). 1890.
Criticism and Fiction. 1891.
A Little Swiss Sojourn. 1892.
Christmas Every Day and Other Stories Told for Children. 1892.
My Year in a Log Cabin. 1893.
My Literary Passions. 1895.
Impressions and Experiences. 1896.
Stories of Ohio. 1897.
Doorstep Acquaintance and Other Sketches. 1900.
Literary Friends and Acquaintance: A Personal Retrospect of American Authorship. 1900; edited by David F. Hiatt and Edwin H. Cady, in *Selected Edition,* 1968.
Heroines of Fiction. 2 vols., 1901.
Literature and Life: Studies. 1902.
London Films. 1905.
Certain Delightful English Towns. 1906.
Roman Holidays and Others. 1908.
Seven English Cities. 1909.
My Mark Twain: Reminiscences and Criticisms. 1910; edited by Marilyn Austin Baldwin, 1967.
Imaginary Interviews. 1910.
Familiar Spanish Travels. 1913.
The Seen and Unseen at Stratford-on-Avon: A Fantasy. 1914.
The Daughter of the Storage and Other Things in Prose and Verse. 1916.
Years of My Youth (autobiography). 1916; in *Selected Edition,* 1975.
Life in Letters of Howells, edited by Mildred Howells. 2 vols., 1928.
Prefaces to Contemporaries (1882-1920), edited by George Arms, William M. Gibson, and Frederic C. Marston, Jr. 1957.
Criticism and Fiction and Other Essays, edited by Clara Marburg Kirk and Rudolf Kirk. 1959.
Mark Twain-Howells Letters: The Correspondence of Samuel L. Clemens and Howells 1872-1910, edited by Henry Nash Smith and William M. Gibson. 2 vols., 1960; abridged edition, as *Selected Mark Twain-Howells Letters,* 1967.
Discovery of a Genius: Howells and Henry James, edited by Albert Mordell. 1961.
Howells as Critic, edited by Edwin H. Cady. 1973.
Interviews with Howells, edited by Ulrich Halfmann. 1973.

The John Hay-Howells Letters: The Correspondence of John Milton Hay and Howells 1861-1905, edited by George Monteiro and Brenda Murphy. 1980.

The Editor's Study: A Comprehensive Edition of Howells's Column, edited by James W. Simpson. 1983.

A Realist in the American Theatre: Selected Drama Criticism of William Dean Howells, edited by Brenda Murphy. 1992.

Staging Howells: Plays and Correspondence with Lawrence Barrett. 1994.

Editor, *Three Years in Chili,* by Mrs. C. B. Merwin. 1861; as *Chili through American Spectacles,* n.d.

Editor, *Choice Autobiographies.* 8 vols., 1877-78.

Editor, with Thomas Sergeant Perry, *Library of Universal Adventure by Sea and Land.* 1888.

Editor, *Mark Twain's Library of Humor.* 1888.

Editor, *Poems of George Pellew.* 1892.

Editor, *Recollections of Life in Ohio from 1813 to 1840,* by William Cooper Howells. 1895.

Editor, with Russell Sturgis. *Florence in Art and Literature.* 1901.

Editor, with Henry Mills Alden, *Harper's Novelettes.* 8 vols., 1906-08.

Editor, *The Great Modern American Short Stories: An Anthology.* 1920.

Editor, *Don Quixote,* by Cervantes, translated by Charles Jarvis. 1923.

Translator, *Venice, Her Art-Treasures and Historical Associations: A Guide,* by Adalbert Müller. 1864.

*

Bibliography: *A Bibliography of Howells* by William M. Gibson and George Arms, 1948; in *Bibliography of American Literature* by Jacob Blanck, 1963; *Howells: A Bibliography* by Vito J. Brenni, 1973; *Published Comment on Howells through 1920: A Research Bibliography* by Clayton L. Eichelberger, 1976.

Critical Studies: *Howells and Italy* by James Woodress, 1952; *The Road to Realism: The Early Years, 1837-1885, of Howells* and *The Realist at War: The Mature Years, 1885-1920, of Howells* by Edwin H. Cady, 2 vols., 1956-58, and *Critical Essays on Howells 1866-1920* edited by Edwin H. and Norma W. Cady, 1983; *Howells: The Development of a Novelist,* 1959, and *The Realism of Howells 1889-1920,* 1973, both by George N. Bennett; *Howells: His Life and World* by Van Wyck Brooks, 1959; *Howells: A Century of Criticism* edited by Kenneth E. Eble, 1962, and *Howells* by Eble, 1982; *Howells, Traveler from Altruria 1889-1894,* 1962, and *Howells and Art in His Time,* 1965, both by Clara Marburg Kirk, and *Howells* by Clara Marburg Kirk and Rudolf Kirk, 1962; *The Immense Complex Drama: The World and Art of the Howells Novel* by George C. Carrington, Jr., 1966, and *Plots and Characters in the Fiction of Howells,* by George C. Carrington, Jr., and Ildiko Carrington, 1976; *The Literary Realism of Howells* by William McMurray, 1967; *Howells* by William M. Gibson, 1967; *The Achievement of Howells: A Reinterpretation* by Kermit Vanderbilt, 1968; *Howells: The Friendly Eye* by Edward Wagenknecht, 1969; *Howells: An American Life* by Kenneth S. Lynn, 1971; *Critics on Howells* edited by Paul A. Escholz, 1975; *The Circle of Eros: Sexuality in the Work of Howells* by Elizabeth Stevens Prioleau, 1983; *The Black Heart's Truth: The Early Career of Howells* by

John W. Crowley, 1985; *'A Heart of Ideality in My Realism' and Other Essays on Howells and Twain* by John E. Bassett, 1991; *New Essays on 'The Rise of Silas Lapham'* edited by Donald E. Pease, 1991; *The Riddle of the Painful Earth: Suffering and Society in W.D. Howell's Major Writings of the Early 1890s* by Robert Mielke, 1994; *Language and Gender in American Fiction: Howells, James, Wharton, and Cather* by Elsa Nettels, 1997; *The Social Self: Hawthorne, Howells, William James, and Nineteenth-Century Psychology* by Joseph Alkana, 1997.

*   *   *

William Dean Howells's literary career was remarkable not only for its length and variousness but for its continuous and conscientious productivity. For more than fifty years, extending from the nineteenth well into the twentieth century, Howells appeared in print as a journalist, a poet, a sensitively observant but unsentimental traveler, a novelist, a playwright, a critic and a polemicist in the cause of realism (these last two functions merging in *Criticism and Fiction*), a publicist and explicator of foreign writers for an ill-informed American public, and the educator of that same public to the greatness of its own writers like James and Twain.

The experience behind this writing was also rich and varied, directly furnishing much of the material for the immense productivity. Moreover, it was an experience that had its public occasions, most notably Howells's outspoken opposition to the treatment of the Chicago anarchists in the Haymarket affair. Beneath the surface of a life that moved from Midwestern print-shops and newspapers through the consulship at Venice and the editorship of the *Atlantic Monthly* to the new center of literary activity in New York, and brought varied relationships with the literary giants of New England and deep literary and personal friendships with the new giants of American literature, James and Twain, there was profound personal experience: the challenge of Darwinian science to religious faith, and an increasing awareness of cultural dislocations, political corruptions, and economic inequities. Thus, Howells's writing became a permanently valuable record of a broad spectrum of the American literary, social, economic, religious, and moral experience. Even more importantly, in an impressive number of his fiction writings Howells achieved the transmutation of actual and vicarious experience into realistic art, and met his own criterion of "dispersing the conventional acceptations by which men live on easy terms with themselves" without falling into the error of claiming thereby to have solved "the riddle of the painful earth."

Howells's relatively late decision to become a novelist kept him close to his own experience and led to the unsophisticated literary devices in the early novels. The tentatively novelistic *Their Wedding Journey* stated his intention to deal with "poor Real life." But the pronouncement stemmed more from his distrust of his ability to manage a sustained narrative and his desire to employ the methods of the travel book than from a theory of realism. *A Chance Acquaintance* also employed the narrative structure of the journey, but it also developed a situation in which the moral spontaneity of an unsophisticated American girl (a portrait highly praised by James) served to reveal the stultifying snobbishness of a proper Bostonian, and, to the dissatisfaction of many, chose the "realistic" mode of an "unhappy" ending in which the girl rejected the ungentlemanly gentleman. Throughout this apprenticeship period, Howells continued to exploit the kind of confrontation labeled by Edwin H. Cady the "conventional-unconventional formula." He also put to use his own experience in summer boardinghouses in *Mrs. Farrell* (serialized as *Private Theatricals*) and in pre-Jamesian versions of the international novel in *A Foregone Conclusion* and *The Lady of the Aroostook*. The former is often cited as a benchmark in the terrain of Howells's early novels because of its skillful dramatic development (a lesson learned from Turgenev) of a "tragic" involvement of an Italian priest and another of Howells's radically innocent American girls.

Beginning in 1880 with *The Undiscovered Country,* Howells's fiction began to take account of issues not easily confined within the limits of the novel of manners (the terminology most frequently applied to his pre- and post-"economic" fiction). That novel has begun to receive deserved attention as an original transformation of Hawthornian themes into a probing study of the problem of religious faith and as Howells's first major attempt to achieve a reconciliation of the American present with its past through a pastoral vision. It was followed by *A Modern Instance,* in any accounting, including Howells's own, one of his most penetrating studies of American life. In spite of general contemporary misunderstanding, it was a contemporary reviewer who noted that the novel was not an anti-divorce tract but "a demonstration of a state of society of which divorce was the index." As the novel expands from a brilliant study of the disintegration of a marriage through a failure of moral discipline, that state of society is depicted as one marked by the decay of vital religious faith, of family solidarity as the nexus of social stability, of the social ethic that is being displaced by purely commercial principles. *The Rise of Silas Lapham* also involves a questioning of American commercial society as Lapham's moral rise is achieved by the sacrifice of the materialistic success for which he very nearly sold his soul. Moreover, it was so far from being a mere comedy of manners—as many readers have termed it because of Lapham's attempts to gain entrance into Boston society and because of the apparent submergence of the moral issue to the romantic sub-plot (the relationship of the plots is a point of extensive critical debate)—that Howells suffered some kind of psychic breakdown in being confronted with the issues it raised: the degree and nature of his commitment to a democracy that included the Irish and Jews; his own relationship with proper Bostonians and New England literati, most of whom had little appreciation for the realistic art to which he had committed himself. The increasing doubts about the America with which he had once been thoroughly optimistic but which he came to feel, as he told James, was "coming out all wrong in the end," made him ripe for the reading of Tolstoy (begun in 1885) and for the expression of a newly open radicalism in the novels of the 1890s that Everett Carter distinguished as works of "critical realism."

The most important of these was *A Hazard of New Fortunes.* It was preceded by *Annie Kilburn,* a demonstration of the Tolstoyan lesson of the necessity for "justice not *alms*" as the corrective for the economic and social ills of the polity. It was followed by *The Quality of Mercy,* an accusation of a system of which embezzlers were merely symptomatic, and *The World of Chance,* an examination of the malfunctioning or absence of causality in not only the business world but in all human involvements. Howells then abandoned the realistic novel as the vehicle of his socialistic ideas and turned to an openly dialectical form in two Altrurian (Utopian) romances.

The recovery of a "usable" Howells after a period in which he was the largely unread touchstone of timid gentility and Victorian morality for writers and critics like **Sinclair Lewis** and **H.L. Mencken** was directly due to the rediscovery of these two Utopias, with their socio-economic criticisms of American life. Critical debate continues in the late twentieth century concerning their artistic quality and their significance to the totality of Howells's career: they have often been seen, even in approaches modified from the doctrinaire criticism of the 1930s, as marking the limit of Howells's artistic growth, and as evidencing a "tragic vision" absent from his other work (and shaped not only by Tolstoy but by a number of profound personal experiences, including the hazard of his career in defense of the Haymarket anarchists and the protracted illness and agonizing death of his daughter). Consequently, his career has been seen as a growth through the comedy of manners to social realism to a unique critical realism and then a falling away. That falling away has been variously explained as simply an exhaustion of the creative impulse; as a failure of nerve in questioning the values and value of American society; as a recognition of his inability to provide solutions to the problems he examined; as a deliberate return to the intellectually and financially safe fiction of his earlier career. The complications of Howells's reputation can be seen in the various interpretations of *A Hazard of New Fortunes,* a key novel. It has been seen variously as a comedy of manners, a symbolic myth of Christian atonement, a realistic tragedy, a treatise on aesthetics, and a combined "psychological" and "economic" novel.

After 1893, Howells still had 27 years of productive life during which he published a dozen or so novels. Of these, almost half— *The Landlord at Lion's Head, The Kentons, The Son of Royal Langbrith, The Leatherwood God,* and the posthumous *The Vacation of the Kelwyns*—have, from various critical perspectives, been judged worthy to be included in the permanent Howells canon. If that canon is initiated by *A Modern Instance*—indeed, a case may be made for the earlier *A Foregone Conclusion* or *The Undiscovered Country*—the continuous excellence of Howells's realistic fiction throughout his career assures him an important place in the history of the development of American fiction. And, if there is added to that assessment his also continuous and influential role in his associations with the *Atlantic, Harper's,* and other journals, his importance as a force in American literature is difficult to overstate.

—George N. Bennett

See the essay on *The Rise of Silas Lapham.*

HOYT, Charles

Born: 1860. **Career:** Professional playwright. Committed to the Retreat for the Insane, Hartford, 1900. **Died:** 1900.

PUBLICATIONS

Plays

Rag Baby. 1884.
A Bunch of Keys. 1882.
The Brass Monkey. 1888.
A Texas Steer. 1890.
A Temperence Town. 1893.

A Milk White Flag. 1893.
A Runaway Colt. 1895.
A Trip to Chinatown. 1891.

*   *   *

Theater was a commercial endeavor for Charles Hoyt, one that he mastered through long hours of meticulous attention to audience reactions and constant rewriting to perfect gags and stage business. Farce was his métier, and his success appeared in the gales of merriment that theater patrons could expect; yet there was also a concern for social issues that filtered through his sometimes loosely constructed plots. In most years he would earn $100,000, and in so doing he created a milestone in the development of America's most impressive contribution to dramatic literature—the satiric farce. But his career was to be unfortunately brief.

Born in Concord, New Hampshire, Hoyt moved to Charlestown, New Hampshire, when he was eight years old and forever afterward considered this village his home. He was twenty-one when he wrote his first successful play, a melodrama called *Gifford's Luck* (1881), at the urging of William Harris, who controlled the old Howard Athenaeum in Boston. But he came into playwriting through a variety of unrelated occupational doorways. After a haphazard youthful education, including some time at the Boston Latin School, he studied law in the office of a Boston firm, became a journalist in St. Albans, Vermont, and worked on a cattle ranch in Colorado.

Writing appealed to Hoyt, and by the time he was nineteen he was on the permanent staff of the *Boston Post*, where he wrote a daily semi-humorous front-page column called "All Sorts," which combined local news events with witty comments. Later, those columns would reveal the beginnings of characters and ideas that appeared in his plays. At the *Boston Post* Hoyt was also the music, sports, and drama critic. Known throughout his career as a generous and sentimental man who would host banquet dinners after his plays, he was a conservative critic. An upstanding playwright whose works were family fare, he believed that offending good taste was bad business and was quick to condemn vulgarity in his drama reviews.

In 1882 Hoyt wrote *Cazalia*, which quickly failed in Boston. Then he found his proper dramatic form with *A Bunch of Keys* (1883), based on his father's experience as a hotel keeper. After trial and error and revision, the play became a great success in New York. By this time Hoyt had formed a partnership with Charles W. Thomas, a colleague from the *Boston Post*. Quitting their jobs, they worked very successfully together—Thomas handing the business details—for ten years. The two eventually leased the Madison Square Theater in 1892 (later renamed the Hoyt Theater), and the partnership made Hoyt a very rich man. His plays appeared regularly: *A Rag Baby* (1884), *A Parlor Match* (1884), *A Tin Soldier* (1885), and fourteen more plays before the turn of the century. Only one was a dismal failure: *The Maid and the Moonshine* (1886). Never again did Hoyt begin a play title with "The."

As many American journeyman playwrights of the past had done, Hoyt concentrated on contemporary events, on the movements and fascinations of the day. Unlike other playwrights, he did not stop with simply mentioning a public fad but wrote an entire play on the subject. *A Texas Steer* (1890) makes fun of Congress, elections, and Texas businessmen; *A Temperance Town* (1893) comments on local option and prohibition; *A Milk White Flag* (1894) pokes fun at home guard companies; *A Runaway Colt* (1895) features a famous baseball player, "Pop" Anson of the Chicago Cubs, to deal with bribery in the game; and *A Contented Woman* (1897) satirizes the women's suffrage movement by featuring a wife who enters a mayoral contest against her husband because she has incorrectly sewn a button on his shirt. Within all of these plays, however, there was the "hilarious confusion" for which Hoyt was famous.

Hoyt's early playwriting technique might appear casual because plot structure is submerged as each play achieves its effect through fast action and slapstick comedy. Later, by the 1890s, Hoyt was emphasizing a tighter construction and more carefully drawn characters. His habit was to make notes on scraps of paper, jot down witty remarks he had heard, and remember strange names and peculiar people. After creating a play script and putting it into rehearsal, he would constantly work with it. Touring with the theater company, he would sit in the audience night after night gauging reactions until he had just the right movement, the exact word, the best business. Using ordinary American people at whom he poked genial fun, his satire was pleasant and kind in tone at a time when social sensitivity was not politicized and people were allowed to laugh at themselves.

Among Hoyt's many successes was the record-setting run of *A Trip to Chinatown* (1891)—657 consecutive performances in New York. In 1892 his home state of New Hampshire elected him to its state assembly, where he served two terms. He was married twice: Flora Walsh Hoyt died while rehearsing her role in *A Temperance Town* in 1892; Caroline Miskel Hoyt, also an actress, died in 1898. Following her death, Hoyt's health began to decline rapidly. In July 1900 he was declared an incurable paretic and committed to an asylum in Hartford, Connecticut. Released to the care of his home town of Charlestown in August, he died on November 20, 1900.

—Walter J. Meserve

HUGHES, (James) Langston

Born: Joplin, Missouri, 1 February 1902. **Education:** Central High School, Cleveland, 1916-20; Columbia University, New York, 1921-22; Lincoln University, Pennsylvania (Witter Bynner award, 1926), 1926-29, B.A. 1929. **Career:** During World War II, member of the Music and Writers war boards. English teacher in Mexico, 1920-21; seaman, 1923-24; busboy, Wardman Park Hotel, Washington, D.C., 1925; Madrid correspondent, Baltimore *Afro-American,* 1937; columnist ("Simple"), Chicago *Defender,* 1943-67, and New York *Post,* 1962-67; lived in Harlem, New York, after 1947. Founder Harlem Suitcase Theater, New York, 1938, New Negro Theater, Los Angeles, 1939, and Skyloft Players, Chicago, 1941. Visiting professor of creative writing, Atlanta University, 1947; poet-in-residence, University of Chicago Laboratory School, 1949. **Awards:** Harmon Gold Medal, 1931; Rosenwald fellowship, 1931, 1940; Guggenheim fellowship, 1935; American Academy grant, 1946; Anisfield-Wolf Award, 1953; Spingarn Medal, 1960. D.Litt: Lincoln University, 1943; Howard University, Washington, D.C., 1963; Western Reserve University, Cleveland, 1964. **Member:** American Academy, 1961; American Academy of Arts and Sciences. **Died:** 22 May 1967.

PUBLICATIONS

Collections

Short Stories of Langston Hughes. 1996.
The Collected Poems of Langston Hughes. 1996.

Poetry

The Weary Blues. 1926.
Fine Clothes to the Jew. 1927.
Dear Lovely Death. 1931.
The Negro Mother and Other Dramatic Recitations. 1931.
The Dream-Keeper and Other Poems. 1932.
Scottsboro Limited: Four Poems and a Play in Verse. 1932.
A New Song. 1938.
Shakespeare in Harlem. 1942.
Jim Crow's Last Stand. 1943.
Lament for Dark Peoples and Other Poems, edited by H. Driessen. 1944.
Fields of Wonder. 1947.
One- Way Ticket. 1949.
Montage of a Dream Deferred. 1951.
Selected Poems. 1959.
Ask Your Mama: 12 Moods for Jazz. 1961.
The Panther and the Lash: Poems of Our Times. 1967.
Don't You Turn Back (for children), edited by Lee Bennett Hopkins. 1969.
The Block (for children). 1995.
Carol of the Brown King: Nativity Poems. 1998.

Recording: *The Voice of Langston Hughes, Selected Poetry and Prose Read by the Author* (Smithsonian Folkways), 1995.

Plays

The Gold Piece, in *Brownies' Book,* July 1921.
Mulatto (produced 1935; original version produced 1939). In *Five Plays,* 1963.
Little Ham (produced 1935). In *Five Plays,* 1963.
Troubled Island (produced 1935; revised version, music by William Grant Still, produced 1949). 1949.
When the Jack Hollers, with Arna Bontemps (produced 1936).
Joy to My Soul (produced 1937).
Soul Gone Home (produced 1937?). In *Five Plays,* 1963.
Don't You Want to Be Free?, music by Carroll Tate (produced 1937). In *One Act Play Magazine,* October 1938.
Front Porch (produced 1938).
The Organizer, music by James P. Johnson (produced 1939).
The Sun Do Move (produced 1942).
Freedom's Plow (broadcast 1943). 1943.
Pvt. Jim Crow (radio script), in *Negro Story,* May-June 1945.
Booker T. Washington at Atlanta (broadcast 1945). In *Radio Drama in Action,* edited by Eric Barnouw, 1945.
Street Scene (lyrics only), book by Elmer Rice, music by Kurt Weill (produced 1947). 1948.
The Barrier, music by Jan Meyerowitz (produced 1950).
Just Around the Corner (lyrics only), book by Abby Mann and Bernard Drew, music by Joe Sherman (produced 1951).
Simply Heavenly, music by David Martin (produced 1957). 1959.
Esther, music by Jan Meyerowitz (produced 1957).

Shakespeare in Harlem, with James Weldon Johnson (produced 1959).
Port Town, music by Jan Meyerowitz (produced 1960).
The Ballad of the Brown King, music by Margaret Bonds (produced 1960).
Black Nativity (produced 1961).
Gospel Glow (produced 1962).
Let Us Remember Him, music by David Amram (produced 1963).
Tambourines to Glory, music by Jobe Huntley, from the novel by Hughes (produced 1963). In *Five Plays,* 1963.
Five Plays (includes *Mulatto, Soul Gone Home, Little Ham, Simply Heavenly, Tambourines to Glory*), edited by Webster Smalley. 1963.
Jerico-Jim Crow (produced 1963).
The Prodigal Son (produced 1965).

Screenplay: *Way Down South,* with Clarence Muse, 1939.

Radio Scripts: *Jubilee,* with Arna Bontemps, 1941; *Brothers,* 1942; *Freedom's Plow,* 1943; *John Henry Hammers It Out,* with Peter Lyons, 1943; *In the Service of My Country,* 1944; *The Man Who Went to War,* 1944 (UK); *Booker T. Washington at Atlanta,* 1945; *Swing Time at the Savoy,* with Noble Sissle, 1949.

Television Scripts: *The Big Sea,* 1965; *It's a Mighty World,* 1965; *Strollin' Twenties,* 1966.

Fiction

Not Without Laughter. 1930.
The Ways of White Folks (stories). 1934.
Simple Speaks His Mind. 1950.
Laughing to Keep from Crying (stories). 1952.
Simple Takes a Wife. 1953.
Simple Stakes a Claim. 1957.
Tambourines to Glory. 1958.
The Best of Simple. 1961.
Something in Common and Other Stories. 1963.
Simple's Uncle Sam. 1965.
The Return of Simple. 1994.

Other (for children)

Popo and Fifina: Children of Haiti, with Arna Bontemps. 1932.
The First Book of Negroes. 1952.
The First Book of Rhythms. 1954.
Famous American Negroes. 1954.
Famous Negro Music-Makers. 1955.
The First Book of Jazz. 1955; revised edition, 1962.
The First Book of the West Indies. 1956; as *The First Book of the Caribbean,* 1965.
The Hughes Reader. 1958.
Famous Negro Heroes of America. 1958.
The First Book of Africa. 1960; revised edition, 1964.
The Sweet and Sour Animal Book. 1994.

Other

The Big Sea: An Autobiography. 1940.
The Sweet Flypaper of Life (on Harlem), with Roy De Carava. 1955.

A Pictorial History of the Negro in America, with Milton Meltzer. 1956; revised edition, 1963, 1968.
I Wonder as I Wander: An Autobiographical Journey. 1956.
The Hughes Reader. 1958.
Fight for Freedom: The Story of the NAACP. 1962.
Black Magic: A Pictorial History of the Negro in American Entertainment, with Milton Meltzer. 1967.
Black Misery. 1969.
Good Morning, Revolution: Uncollected Social Protest Writings, edited by Faith Berry. 1973.
Hughes in the Hispanic World and Haiti, edited by Edward J. Mullen. 1977.
Arna Bontemps-Hughes: Letters 1925-1967, edited by Charles H. Nichols. 1980.
Langston Hughes and the Chicago Defender: Essays on Race, Politics, and Culture, 1942-1962. 1995.

Editor, *Four Lincoln University Poets.* 1930.
Editor, with Arna Bontemps, *The Poetry of the Negro 1746 1949: An Anthology.* 1949; revised edition, 1970.
Editor, with Waring Guney and Bruce M. Wright, *Lincoln University Poets.* 1954.
Editor, with Arna Bontemps, *The Book of Negro Folklore.* 1958.
Editor, *An Africa Treasury: Articles, Essays, Stories, Poems by Black Africans.* 1960.
Editor, *Poems from Black Africa.* 1963.
Editor, *New Negro Poets: USA.* 1964.
Editor, *The Book of Negro Humor.* 1966.
Editor, *La Poesie Negro-Americaine* (bilingual edition). 1966.
Editor, *Anthologie Africaine et Malgache.* 1966.
Editor, *The Best Short Stories by Negro Writers.* 1967.

Translator, with Mercer Cook, *Masters of the Dew,* by Jacques Roumain. 1947.
Translator, with Ben Frederic Carruthers, *Cuba Libre,* by Nicolas Guillen. 1948.
Translator, *Gypsy Ballads,* by Federico Garcia Lorca. 1951.
Translator, *Selected Poems of Gabriela Mistral.* 1957.

*

Bibliography: *A Bio-Bibliography of Hughes 1902-1967* by Donald C. Dickinson, 1967, revised edition, 1972; *Hughes and Gwendolyn Brooks: A Reference Guide* by R. Baxter Miller, 1978; *Hughes: A Bio-bibliography* by Thomas A. Mikolyzk, 1990.

Critical Studies: *Hughes* by James A. Emanuel, 1967; *Hughes: A Biography* by Milton Meltzer, 1968; *Hughes, Black Genius: A Critical Evaluation* edited by Therman B. O'Daniel, 1971 (includes bibliography); *Hughes: An Introduction to the Poetry* by Onwuchekwa Jemie, 1976; *Hughes: The Poet and His Critics* by Richard K. Barksdale, 1977; *Hughes: Before and Beyond Harlem* by Faith Berry, 1983; *I, Too, Sing America* (vol.1 of *The Life of Hughes*) by Arnold Rampersad, 1986; "Langston Hughes: Black America's Poet Laureate" by Larry Neal, in *American Writing Today* edited by Richard Kostelanetz, 1991; *Langston Hughes: A Study of the Short Fiction* by Hans Ostrom, 1993; *Langston Hughes, Folk Dramatist in the Protest Tradition, 1921-1943* by Joseph McLaren, 1997; *Langston Hughes: The Contemporary Reviews,* 1997.

*   *   *

As impressive as Langston Hughes is for his versatility and productivity, his claim to enduring literary importance rests chiefly on his poetry and his Simple sketches. In his poetry his sure lyric touch, his poignant insight into the urban black folk soul rendered with remarkable fidelity to a variety of black idioms, his negative capability of subordinating his own personality so as to convey a vivid impression of scene or incident or mood or character, and his willingness to experiment are his richest endowments, though one also often finds in his verse the comic sense (often ironic or bittersweet), the broad democratic faith, and the total understanding of character that so irradiate the Simple tales.

Although Hughes wrote some verse without specific racial reference, the three major categories of his poetry comprise poems related to black music, poems of racial protest, and poems of racial affirmation. These categories naturally overlap, but it is convenient to discuss them separately.

For the entire course of his literary career, Hughes was fascinated by black music: blues, jazz in its several varieties, and gospel. The classic blues stanzaic form, consisting of a statement of a problem or situation in the first line repeated in the second (often with a slight variation) followed by a third line resolving, interpreting, or commenting on the first two, appears frequently in Hughes, as in the following from "Red Sun Blues":

> Gray skies, gray skies, won't you let the sun shine through?
> Gray skies, gray skies, won't you let that sun shine through?
> My baby's left me, I don't know what to do.

Elsewhere, as in the title poem of *The Weary Blues,* Hughes uses the blues and bluesmen as subject in a poem that may incorporate blues stanzas but has its own larger structure. His poems deriving from jazz are more complicated in their experimentation. Taken together, they provide a kind of poetic graph of developments in jazz from the Harlem cabaret life of the exuberant 1920s, through the boogie-woogie of the 1930s and the bebop of the 1940s, to the progressive jazz of the 1950s. From such early examples as "Jazzonia" and "The Cat and the Saxophone" to the ambitious later works *Montage of a Dream Deferred* and *Ask Your Mama,* Hughes used the varieties of jazz as both subject and style, designing the last-named work for musical accompaniment and often reading his poetry on tour to a jazz background. Though less prominently than blues and jazz, spirituals and gospel music figure in Hughes's poetry (for example, the "Feet of Jesus" section in *Selected Poems*), as well as in his numerous song-plays.

As a poet of racial protest Hughes was less strident than some other well-known black writers, but not necessarily less trenchant or effective. Such poems as "I, Too" and "Let America Be America Again" express a wistful longing for racial equality. Others, such as "Brass Spittoons" and "Ballad of the Landlord" develop miniature dramas of the hardships and injustices of black life in a racist society. Some of the later poems included in the "Words on Fire" section of *The Panther and the Lash* sound notes of rising militancy. Surely among Hughes's best poems in this category are "American Heartbreak," whose laconic understatement achieves a sense of bitter finality, and "Song for a Dark Girl," a starkly tragic and strangely beautiful lyric about a girl's response to the lynching of her lover. Whether wistful, dramatic, angry, or tragic in mood,

Hughes was always alive throughout his career to the oppression of his people.

He was equally sensitive to the dignity with which they endured or resisted that oppression. "Mother to Son" and "The Negro Mother" are among his many poems celebrating the black quest for freedom and social justice. Hughes was one of the first writers to use "soul" in a special racial sense, as in his very early poem "The Negro Speaks of Rivers." Color itself delights the poet in the carefully crafted "Dream Variation" and the delicious "Harlem Sweeties." And his comic vision to be developed in such loving detail in the Simple sketches is prefigured in "Sylvester's Dying Bed" and the Madam Alberta K. Johnson poems. Lowlife and working-class blacks, shunned by bourgeois spokesmen of the Harlem Renaissance, often receive special tribute in Hughes's poems of racial affirmation.

Hughes's interest in fiction developed later than his instinct for poetry. The novels *Not Without Laughter* and *Tambourines to Glory* are highly readable if somewhat weak in structure. The best of his sixty-six published short stories are proficient in technique and perceptive in their treatment of a variety of human situations. The most striking achievement in fiction is the creation of Jesse B. Simple. As Richard K. Barksdale has noted, Simple "had just the right blend of qualities to be Black America's new spokesman— just enough urban humor, cynicism, and sardonic levity and just enough down-home simplicity, mother-wit, innocence, and naivete" (*Black Writers of America,* edited by Richard K. Barksdale and Keneth Kinnamon). The marvelous talk elicited from this fully realized black working man by the middle-class, intellectual narrator of the sketches constitutes one of the most valuable treasures of American literary humor.

In drama Hughes is perhaps more important for the extent of his activity and the stimulus he gave to black theater than for the intrinsic artistic merit of his own plays. As translator, anthologist, historian, and biographer he played a major role in popularizing Afro-American, Afro-Caribbean, and African subjects. As devoted friend and sponsor of generations of aspiring writers he was at the center of black literary activity for more than four decades. Together with his own accomplishments as poet and humorist, these efforts constitute a total contribution to literature matched by that of few writers in the twentieth century.

—Keneth Kinnamon

See the essay on *The Weary Blues.*

HUGO, Richard (Franklin)

Born: Seattle, Washington, 21 December 1923. **Education:** University of Washington, Seattle, B.A. 1948, M.A. 1952. **Military Service:** Served in the U.S. Army Air Corps during World War II: bombardier. **Family:** Married and divorced. **Career:** Worked for Boeing Company, Seattle, 1951-63; member of the English department, then professor of English, University of Montana, Missoula. Editor, Yale Younger Poets series, from 1977. **Awards:** Northwest Writers award, 1966; Rockefeller fellowship, 1967; Guggenheim fellowship, 1977; Academy of American Poets fellowship, 1981. **Died:** 22 October 1982.

PUBLICATIONS

Collections

Making Certain It Goes On: The Collected Poems. 1983.

Poetry

A Run of Jacks. 1961.
Five Poets of the Pacific, with others, edited by Robin Skelton. 1964.
Death of the Kapowsin Tavern. 1965.
Good Luck in Cracked Italian. 1969.
The Lady in Kicking Horse Reservoir. 1973.
What Thou Lovest Well, Remains American. 1975.
Rain Five Days and I Love It. 1975.
Duwamish Head. 1976.
31 Letters and 13 Dreams. 1977.
Selected Poems. 1979.
White Center. 1980.
The Right Madness on Skye. 1980.

Other

The Triggering Town: Lectures and Essays on Poetry and Writing. 1979.
The Real West Marginal Way: A Poet's Autobiography, edited by Ripley S. Hugo and others. 1986.

*

Critical Studies: *We Are Called Human: The Poetry of Hugo* by Michael S. Allen, 1982; *A Trout in the Milk: A Composite Portrait of Hugo* edited by Jack Myers, 1982; *Hugo* by Donna Gerstenberger, 1983; *The Writer's Mind: Interviews with American Authors (Volume II)* edited by Irv Broughton, 1990; "West Marginal Way: Richard Hugo's Poetry as Self-Psychoanalysis" by Jonathan Holden, in *Mid-America Review,* 1995, pp. 26-32.

*   *   *

The last poem in *Making Certain It Goes On,* Richard Hugo's collected poems, ends with a speculation that the community, which has emerged as the subject of the poem, will be "going strong another hundred years." The simple, almost naive, affirmation strikes the reader with conviction and inspires confidence in its probability. That reaction is all the more notable because the poem begins with a drunk fisherman at an unpromising trout stream, steadfastly refusing to engage any of the positive opportunities that surround him. Hugo's concerns in his poetry move between these contraries of the isolated, often alienated individual and the communities of people whose bonds and relationships lie beyond the understanding of the casual observer or the curious newcomer. In the late poems, especially *White Center* and *The Right Madness on Skye,* Hugo characteristically poses as a traveler or refugee happening into a new place or situation that at first seems only vaguely interesting, but that finally reveals a sense of connection with other places and other people. The speaker, always very conscious of being an outsider, thrills to the new knowledge and often invites or challenges the reader to join in the delights and the responsibilities that the insight offers. The concern and

focus of many of the later poems revolve around this simultaneous presence of individuality and self-awareness and access to
the deep and mysterious cohesion of communities. "Distances,"
one of Hugo's last poems, opens with "Driving a Prairie," thus
establishing the fluid, tentative relationship between the speaker
and his setting and the low definition of the landscape that almost
taunts an observer to try to make a point. When the speaker can
manage the confidence needed to observe that "Whole symphonies
live between / here and a distant whatever-we-look-at," Hugo has won
the struggle to celebrate self, community, and place in his poetry.

The early poems in *A Run of Jacks* and *Death of the Kapowsin
Tavern* usually focused on places. Indeed, Hugo is often identified with the American Northwest because he so often uses specific places as occasions for his poems. Perhaps this sense of identification with place is more understandable in the early poems
because Hugo's speakers often elaborate on an experience in a
place and in the process of elaboration reveal a significant aspect
of the experience. A poem such as "G.I. Graves in Tuscany" begins with the speaker, although also a traveler, involved in his reaction to the graves and in the course of elaborating that experience finding a sense of his own meaning in the scene. These early
poems are regional only in the sense that Hugo, like most poets,
draws on personal experiences. The early poems show a modernist cast in their preference for leaving much of the revelation unstated or only suggested. While the speaker clearly has a change
during the course of the experience, the reader must fill in the gaps
to develop a sense of meaning.

In the burst of work Hugo published between 1973 and 1977,
the stance of the poet and his speakers shifts to a greater concern:
that the communication initiated by the speaker work on the reader.
In *The Lady in Kicking Horse Reservoir* and *What Thou Lovest
Well, Remains American* Hugo regularly brings the speaker's concerns around to issues recognizable as important to larger groups
of fellow citizens. He wants the poems to identify a connection
between the collective personal experiences and discoveries of
groups of people. This process of increasing concern for community culminates in the 1977 volume, *31 Letters and 13 Dreams,*
which established Hugo as a master of the very difficult form of
the letter poem. These letter poems play off the tension and challenges of the dependable, accessible format of the letter against
the lyric and ritualized forms of poetry. The musical and stylized
language that calls attention to itself in so much of Hugo's poetry
always lurks behind the comfortable, casual prose forms of the
letter. At a moment, the very pleasant letter enfolds into a tightly
organized and powerful poetic utterance. The flow back and forth
between the two forms justifies the focus on common and ordinary
subjects and points out the origins and historical functions of poems.

Hugo's search for and interest in simple concerns such as innocence, sincerity, and beauty at first glance seem naive and sentimental. But his care in establishing appropriate postures and his
mastery of language create the justification for his concerns and
the conditions under which his search succeeds.

—Richard C. Turner

HUNEKER, James (Gibbons)

Born: Philadelphia, Pennsylvania, 31 January 1857. **Education:**
Roth's Military Academy, Philadelphia; subsequently studied law;

studied piano in Paris with Georges Mathias and in New York
with Rafael Joseffy. **Career:** Music critic and editor, *Musical Courier,* 1887-1902; teacher of piano, National Conservatory, 1888-
98; music critic, 1900-02, drama critic, 1902-04, and art critic,
1906-12, New York *Sun;* foreign correspondent on the arts, 1912-
13, and music critic, 1918-19, New York *Times;* music critic, New
York *World,* 1919-21. **Died:** 9 February 1921.

PUBLICATIONS

Collections

Letters and Intimate Letters, edited by Josephine Huneker. 1922-24.
Essays, edited by H.L. Mencken. 1929.
Americans in the Arts 1890-1920: Critiques by Huneker, edited
by Arnold T. Schwab. 1985.

Fiction

Melomaniacs (stories). 1902.
Visionaries (stories). 1905.
Painted Veils. 1920.

Other

Mezzotints in Modern Music. 1899.
Chopin: The Man and His Music. 1900.
Overtones: A Book of Temperaments. 1904.
Iconoclasts: A Book of Dramatists. 1905.
Egoists: A Book of Supermen. 1909.
Promenades of an Impressionist. 1910.
Franz Liszt. 1911.
The Pathos of Distance: A Book of a Thousand and One Moments. 1913.
Old Fogy: His Musical Opinions and Grotesques. 1913.
New Cosmopolis: A Book of Images. 1915.
Ivory, Apes, and Peacocks. 1915.
Unicorns. 1917.
*The Philharmonic Society of New York and Its Seventy-Fifth Anni-
versary: A Retrospect.* 1917(?).
The Steinway Collection of Paintings by American Artists. 1919.
Bedouins (essays and stories). 1920.
Steeplejack (autobiography). 2 vols., 1920.
Variations. 1921.

Music editions: *Forty Piano Compositions* by Chopin, 1902; *Forty
Songs* by Brahms, 1903; *The Greater Chopin,* 1908; *Forty Songs*
by Strauss, 1910; *Forty Songs* by Tchaikovsky, 1912; *Romantic Preludes and Studies for Piano,* 1919.

*

Bibliography: in *Bibliography of American Literature* by Jacob
Blanck, 1963.

Critical Studies: *Huneker* by Benjamin DeCasseres, 1925;
Huneker, Critic of the Seven Arts by Arnold T. Schwab, 1963;
"Huneker and Other Lost Arts" by Arno Karlen, in *Antioch Re-
view,* fall 1981; "James Huneker & America's Musical Coming of
Age" by Samuel Lipman, in *New Criterion,* June 1987.

*   *   *

James Huneker is probably America's most versatile critic. Beginning in the late 1880s as a music critic, he acquired an international reputation in the next fifteen years, especially for his writings on Chopin, Liszt, and Richard Strauss. The musical associations of Baudelaire, Gautier, Huysmans, George Moore, and others led him to their non-musical books and thus into literary criticism, of which his best book was *Egoists*. His deep interest in the new psychology quickly attuned him to the work of Ibsen, Strindberg, Shaw, Maeterlinck, Hauptmann, and Sudermann, and his *Iconoclasts* was the most brilliant study of these playwrights to appear in America.

Best known for popularizing contemporary or near-contemporary Continental writers, Huneker also singled out the best American novelists of his day—**James**, **Howells**, **Wharton**, **Norris**, **Dreiser**—and called attention to **Whitman**, **Poe**, **Dickinson**, and **Robinson** at a time when these poets were either vilified or ignored by many other critics. But his talent in detecting the most enduring of early-twentieth-century American artists (thoroughly revealed only later in his *Americans in the Arts*) was most notably reflected, perhaps, in his praise of painters such as Bellows, Davies, Henri, Luks, Marin, Maurer, Prendergast, Shinn, and Sloan.

As a critic, Huneker was probably most comfortable, technically, in music (he had studied and taught piano) and least secure, despite his perspicacity, in art. Fond of anecdotes, puns, and parodies, he produced essays admired for their wit, humor, urbanity, and range. His tendency to dart from topic to topic, idea to idea, name to name, paying little attention to connecting links and logical development, sometimes made him seem superficial or irritating to those who valued clear sustained reasoning above the picturesque phrase and the evocative association. But the staccato manner and the incessant allusions sprang from a mind richly loaded with gleanings from life and literature and quick with intuitive perception and sympathy. Not hesitating to pass judgment, in an undogmatic way, on artists of his own day, he was usually right: few of his swans turned out to be geese.

In his short stories—collected in *Melomaniacs*, *Visionaries*, and *Bedouins*—and in his one novel, *Painted Veils*, Huneker displayed the wide-reading, powerful curiosity about the artist as a human being, the fascination with sexual or sensory abnormality, and the colorful, epigrammatic style reflected in his criticism. If the stories smack a bit too much of the grotesqueries of Hoffmann and Poe, they achieve some originality in Huneker's attempt to penetrate and portray the emotional life of the musician. In coming to grips with sexual themes, he was clearly ahead of his time in his fiction as well as his criticism. His plots reveal his flair for the humorously bizarre, and touches of comic description accompany his lively imagination. If his skill in execution—especially in characterization and dialogue—had matched his inventive facility, Huneker might have become the outstanding writer of fiction he always wanted to be.

—Arnold T. Schwab

HURSTON, Zora Neale

Born: Eatonville, Florida, 7 January 1901(?). **Education:** Robert Hungerford School, Eatonville, and a school in Jacksonville, Florida; Morgan Academy, Baltimore, 1917-18; Howard Preparatory School, 1918-19, and Howard University, part-time 1920-

24, Washington, D.C.; Barnard College, New York, 1925-28, B.A. 1928. **Family:** Married 1) Herbert Sheen in 1927 (divorced 1931); 2) Albert Price III in 1939 (divorced 1943). **Career:** Maid with traveling repertory company, 1915-16; waitress while at Howard Preparatory School and University, 1918-24; folklore researcher in Alabama, Florida, and Louisiana, 1927-32, and in Haiti and the British West Indies, 1936-38; drama instructor, Bethune Cookman College, Daytona, Florida, 1933-34; editor, Federal Writers Project, Florida, 1938-39; member of the Drama Department, North Carolina College for Negroes, Durham, 1939-40; story consultant, Paramount, Hollywood, 1941-42; part-time teacher, Florida Normal College, St. Augustine, 1942; maid in Florida, 1949-50; reporter, Pittsburgh *Courier*, 1952; librarian, Patrick Air Force Base, Florida, 1956-57; reporter, Fort Pierce *Chronicle*, Florida, 1957-59; substitute teacher, Lincoln Park Academy, Fort Pierce, 1958-59. **Awards:** Rosenwald fellowship, 1934; Guggenheim fellowship, 1936, 1937; Anisfield Wolf Award, 1942; Howard University award, 1943. Litt.D.: Morgan State College, Baltimore, 1939. **Died:** 28 January 1960.

PUBLICATIONS

Collection

I Love Myself When I am Laughing . . . and Then Again When I Am Looking Mean and Impressive: A Hurston Reader, edited by Alice Walker. 1979.

Fiction

Jonah's Gourd Vine. 1934.
Their Eyes Were Watching God. 1937.
Moses, Man of the Mountain. 1939.
Seraph on the Suwanee. 1948.
The Sanctified Church. 1981.
Sweat. 1997.

Plays

Color Struck, in *Fire!!*, November 1926.
The First One, in *Ebony and Topaz*, edited by Charles S. Johnson. 1927.
The Great Day (produced 1932).
Singing Steel (produced 1934).

Other

Mules and Men. 1935.
Tell My Horse. 1938; as *Voodoo Gods: An Inquiry into Native Myths and Magic in Jamaica and Haiti*, 1939.
Dust Tracks on a Road: An Autobiography. 1942.

Editor, *Caribbean Melodies*. 1947.

*

Critical Studies: *In A Minor Chord* (on Hurston, Cullen, and Toomer) by Darwin T. Turner, 1971; *Hurston: A Literary Biography* by Robert E. Hemenway, 1977; *Hurston* by Lillie P. Howard, 1980; *Zora in Florida* edited by Steve Glassman and Kathryn Lee Seidel, 1991; *Jump at the Sun: Zora Neale Hurston's Cosmic Comedy* by John Lowe, 1994; *Making Her Way with Thun-*

der: A Reappraisal of Zora Neale Hurston's Narrative Art by Janet Carter-Sigglow, 1994; *Social Rituals and the Verbal Art of Zora Neale Hurston* by Lynda Marion Hill, 1996; *Zora Neale Hurston: Southern Storyteller* by Della A. Yannuzzi, 1996.

*   *   *

The leading fact about Zora Neale Hurston is her identification with black folklore. She spent her childhood in the black town of Eatonville, Florida. As a student in anthropology, she recorded the oral literature of the black South and Caribbean, and her best writing employs the intangible artifacts of traditional culture. Yet her preoccupation with folk life had ambivalence. As Robert E. Hemenway has shown, she experienced conflict between her role as a scientific observer of culture and the need to express her feelings as an intuitive participant. She never denied the value of science, but eventually art alone claimed her talents.

Art, however, had its own ambivalence. For, while the substance of Hurston's work derived from spontaneous folk life, she was, of course, a deliberate literary writer. *Mules and Men* represents an early effort to resolve the consequent aesthetic problem. In it Hurston adapts folklore to the requirements of written literature by creating a persona and framing folktales in the context of a return home. This structure provides readers with a sense of entry into the community. One feels a privileged listener, but it must be remembered that one actually heard Hurston's selectively condensed version of the tales. Several years later, in *Moses, Man of the Mountain,* Hurston's confidence in her ability to reshape folk matter permitted her to assume the role openly. Taking as her premise the traditional parallel between the children of Israel and enslaved Africans she synthesizes legends and images to establish Moses as a humanized African-American.

Still more literary ways of using folk life appear in *Jonah's Gourd Vine* and *Their Eyes Were Watching God.* The first book presents as its central figure a preacher endowed with magnificent command of poetic language who thereby typifies the creativity of folk culture. At the same time he is morally flawed by a sexual drive that continually brings him low. Possibly through this flaw Hurston meant to create a tragic figure, but there can be no doubt that with the preacher's wife she touched the theme of her most distinguished book. *Their Eyes Were Watching God,* a novel about Janie Crawford's disappointing marriages and exhilarating love affair with the ebullient Tea Cake, fully merges author and folk subject. The theme of a woman struggling to realize herself was inevitable for a female artist as independent as Hurston. That Janie becomes free within the culture of the black South, however, represents both a social and an aesthetic resolution. The social resolution appears as preference for black cultural values despite shortcomings, the aesthetic resolution as the assimilation of folk to the consciousness of a modern artist.

—John M. Reilly

See the essay on *Their Eyes Were Watching God.*

HWANG, David Henry

Born: Los Angeles, California, 11 August 1957. **Education:** Harvard Boys School in the Hollywood Hills; Stanford Univer-

sity, Stanford, California, B.A. 1979 (Phi Beta Kappa); Yale University School of Drama, New Haven, 1980-81. **Family:** Married 1) Ophelia Y.M. Chong in 1985 (divorced 1989); 2) Kathryn A. Layng in 1993, one son. **Career:** Moved to New York and developed play for Joseph Papp's New York Shakespeare Festival Public Theatre, 1979-80; taught English and writing, Menlo-Atherton High School, Menlo Park, California, 1980; withdrew from Yale and moved back to New York, 1981; directed plays, 1980-90; cofounder, Stanford Asian American Theatre Project; traveled in Europe, Asia, and Canada, 1984-85; moved back to Los Angeles, 1985; wrote television projects, 1985; dramaturg, Asian-American Theatre Center, San Francisco, California, beginning 1987; wrote screenplays, 1993; moved back to New York, 1994; artist-in-residence, Trinity Repertory Company, beginning 1996. Member of the boards of directors of Theatre Communications Group beginning 1987, Dramatists Guild beginning 1988, China Institute, beginning 1994; member of the President's Committee on the Arts and Humanities, beginning 1994; New York Council on the Humanities, beginning 1998; Center for Arts and Culture, beginning 1998. **Awards:** Drama-Logue award, 1980, 1986; Obie award for best play, 1981, and for playwriting, 1997; CINE Golden Eagle, 1982; Rockefeller Foundation playwright-in-residence award, 1983; National Endowment for the Arts artistic associate fellowship, 1983-84; Guggenheim fellowship, 1984; New York State Council on the Arts fellowship, 1985; National Endowment for the Arts fellowship, 1987; Antoinette Perry ("Tony") award, 1988; Drama Desk award, 1988; Outer Critics Circle award, 1988; John Gassner award, 1988; Pulitzer prize nomination, 1989; Los Angeles Drama Critics Award, 1991; Obie award, 1997; the Organization of Chinese Americans' "Outstanding Citizens award," 1997; Antoinette Perry ("Tony") and Outer Critics Circle award nominations, 1998. Honorary degree: Columbia College, 1998. **Residence:** New York.

PUBLICATIONS

Collections

Broken Promises: Four Plays. 1983.
FOB and Other Plays, 1990.

Plays

FOB (produced 1979). With *The House of Sleeping Beauties,* 1983.
The Dance and the Railroad (produced 1981). With *Family Devotions,* 1983.
Family Devotions (produced 1981). With *The Dance and the Railroad,* 1983.
Sound and Beauty, omnibus title for two one-acts, *The House of Sleeping Beauties* and *The Sound of a Voice* (produced 1983).
The House of Sleeping Beauties (produced 1983). With *FOB,* 1983.
Broken Promises: Four Plays (and author of introduction). 1983.
The Sound of a Voice (produced 1983). 1984.
Rich Relations (produced 1986). In *FOB and Other Plays* (and author of introduction), 1990.
As the Crow Flies (produced 1986).
Broken Promises, omnibus title for two one-acts, *The Dance and the Railroad* and *The House of Sleeping Beauties* (produced 1987).
M. Butterfly (and author of author's notes; produced 1988). 1988.
1000 Airplanes on the Roof, music by Philip Glass, projections by Jerome Sirlin (produced 1988). 1989.

Dances in Exile, with Ruby Shang (produced 1991).
Bondage (produced 1992). In *The Best American Short Plays 1992-93,* 1993.
The Voyage, music by Philip Glass (produced 1992).
Face Value (produced 1993).
Trying to Find Chinatown (produced 1996).
Golden Child (produced 1996). 1998.
The Silver River, music by Bright Sheng (produced 1997).
Peer Gynt, adaptation of Ibsen, with Stephen Müller (produced 1998).
After Eros, with Maureen Fleming (produced 1998).

Screenplays: *M. Butterfly,* 1993; *Golden Gate,* 1993.

Television Plays: *Blind Alleys,* with Frederic Kimball, 1985; *My American Son,* 1987.

*

Critical Studies: *David Henry Hwang* by Douglas Street, 1989; interview with John Louis DiGaetani, in *TDR,* March 1989; "Breaking the Butterfly: The Politics of David Henry Hwang" by Robert Skloot, in *Modern Drama,* March 1990; "David Henry Hwang's *M. Butterfly* and Philip Kan Gotanda's *Yankee Dawg You Die:* Repositioning Chinese American Marginality on the American Stage," in *Theatre Journal,* March 1990; "Intimacy or Cruel Love: Displacing the Other by Self Assertion" by Kent Neely, in *Journal of Dramatic Theory and Criticism,* Spring 1991; *Intrinsic Intertextuality: A Methodology for Analyzing the Seamless Intertext* by Karen Sue Mitchell, 1991; "David Henry Hwang's *M. Butterfly:* The Eye on the Wing" by Janet Haedicke, in *Journal of Dramatic Theory and Criticism,* Fall 1992; "'Who's to Say?' or Making Space for Gender and Ethnicity in *M. Butterfly*" by Karen Shimakawa, in *Theatre Journal,* Fall 1993; "In the Shadows of a Diva: Committing Homosexuality in David Henry Hwang's *M. Butterfly*" by David L. Eng, in *Amerasia Journal,* 1994, pp. 93-116; "The Theatre of Punishment: David Henry Hwang's *M. Butterfly* and Michel Foucault's *Discipline and Punish*" by Kathryn Remen, in *Modern Drama,* Fall 1994; "David Henry Hwang" by Devorah Frockt, in *The Playwright's Art: Conversations with Contemporary American Dramatists* edited by Jackson R. Bryer, 1995; "New Theatrical Statements: Asian Western Mergers in the Plays of David Henry Hwang" by Robert Cooperman, in *Staging Difference: Cultural Pluralism in American Theatre and Drama* edited by *Marc Maufort,* 1995; "Ethnic Fiction and Survival Ethics: Toni Morrison, Louise Erdrich, David H. Hwang" by Alfred Hornung, in *Ethics and Aesthetics: The Moral Turn of Postmodernism* edited by Gerhard Hoffman and Alfred Hornung, 1996.

*   *   *

Catapulted into the theatrical limelight at age twenty-two by his Obie Award-winning first play, David Henry Hwang, by age thirty-one, had garnered a Tony Award and a Pulitzer Prize nomination for *M. Butterfly.* Hwang is widely lauded as the pre-eminent Asian American playwright, yet this designation understates his importance in and potential impact on American drama. Though most of his plays concern East-West cultural confrontations, Hwang's real subject is an America where multiculturalism is not fad but fact. Urging a new cultural model not only reflected but

foreshadowed by America's artists, Hwang proclaims in the "Introduction" to his first published plays that "American theater is beginning to discover Americans." Actually, Hwang views all American theater as "ethnic" since mainstream "universality" emerges from dramatizing a particular group, such as **Tennessee Williams**'s white Southerners. Hwang has consciously evolved his focus from ethnic marginalization to any form of subordination for the purpose of bolstering a dominant cultural identity.

Born to successful Chinese immigrant parents, Hwang grew up in an Evangelical Christian, English-speaking home, his parents withdrawing their children from Chinese language classes for fear of adverse affects on their English. His family's assimilation and the multi-ethnic character of his Los Angeles suburb led Hwang to consider his ethnicity a trait no more significant than hair or eye color. Accomplished in both debate and violin, which he was taught by his musician mother, Hwang entered an exclusive boys' school, where he formulated vague ambitions to study law. Only at Stanford did Hwang develop an interest in theater as well as an ethnic consciousness. An English major, Hwang became enthralled with playwright **Sam Shepard**'s dramatization of American myth and was convinced that Chinese American history constitutes a part of that myth. Thus, in the "Playwright's Note" to his first play, Hwang describes the roots of *FOB,* his original sketch about a limousine trip having been "invaded" by two characters from American literature, as "thoroughly American." From **Frank Chin**'s play *Gee, Pop!* came the Chinese warrior-god Gwan Gung, whom *FOB*'s Steve claims to be; from **Maxine Hong Kingston**'s *The Woman Warrior* came Fa Mu Lan, a father-surrogate warrior whom another character, Grace, conjures in her fantasies. A first-generation Chinese-American college student, Grace finds herself torn between Steve, the FOB (Fresh off the Boat) Chinese student, and Dale, her second-generation, belligerently assimilated cousin, who despises "clumsy, ugly, greasy" FOBs. Grace's Fa Mu Lan-Gwan Gung ritual battle and final exit with Steve signal a resurrection of ethnic heritage that will allow for a true Chinese American identity. Backed by the Stanford Asian American Theatre Project, which Hwang co-founded, and performed at Okada House dormitory in 1979, *FOB* was selected for development at the O'Neill National Playwrights' Conference after which it was picked up by Joseph Papp's Public Theatre and awarded the 1981 Obie.

At Yale in late 1980, Hwang wrote *The Dance and the Railroad,* another examination of immigrant identity. Set in 1867 during a transcontinental railroad strike, the play features two "coolie" laborers: Lone, a two-year veteran, and Ma, a newly arrived optimist. Themes from *FOB* recur as the naive Ma confronts the cynical Lone on the mountaintop where he withdraws to practice for the Peking Opera, in which he had become qualified to play Gwan Gung. Becoming Lone's apprentice, Ma aspires to play the warrior-god for the laborers below, but, disillusioned by the outcome of the strike, he gets "the fear" from Lone. Inspired by John Lone, who received his training in the Chinese opera circuit and who acted in and directed *The Dance and the Railroad,* the play was successfully staged by the Public Theatre in 1981, as was Hwang's third play four months later. *Family Devotions* was developed after Hwang had withdrawn from Yale and moved to New York. Dedicated to Sam Shepard, the play evidences a more Western theatrical form, farcically but tragically depicting three generations of an Asian American family in conflict over assimilation. The autobiographical drama is set in the luxurious California home of an Evangelical Christian family who perform daily devotions. Supported by the aggressively capitalist father but dominated by two elderly women, the household awaits the arrival of the brother who personifies heritage. The atheist brother, however, explodes their ethnic, religious, and familial mythologizing, killing them in the process and exiting with the third-generation violinist nephew. The play emphasizes that exalting a fabricated Chinese past or a stereotypical American present forecloses all possibilities of identity.

Intentionally, Hwang turned from Chinese America to Japan in developing two one-act plays as playwright-in-residence for the Public Theatre. Produced in 1983 as *Sound and Beauty, The House of Sleeping Beauties* and *The Sound of a Voice* again portray the entry of an outsider into a mythic domain. Here the domain is female: the house of the first play is a Tokyo brothel; the house of the second is a forest hermitage. A fantasy springing from a novelette by and subsequent suicide of Japanese novelist Kawabata, *Hwang's House* depicts the writer's succumbing to the seduction of drug-induced sleep next to a drugged "sleeping beauty" and the elderly madam who assists his suicide. *Sound* depicts an aging Samurai warrior who changes his mind about killing his hermit-hostess only to cause her suicide. Though off-putting to critics, these stylized plays nonetheless earned an extended run. In 1986 Hwang wrote another one-act companion for *The Sound of a Voice* at the request of the Los Angeles Theatre Center. *As the Crow Flies* portrays a black domestic servant of an elderly Chinese woman in a play that again conveys mythic dimensions. Also produced in 1986 and also reflecting an attempt to defy ethnic literary segregation, *Rich Relations,* containing no Asian characters, became the playwright's first failure. Hwang admits that the play emerged as an autobiographical narrative with white characters as substitutes. Echoing *Family Devotions, Rich Relations* calls for spiritual resurrection from materialist hell, but it is a call deflected by dramatic flaws.

Asserting that failure was cathartic, Hwang shortly thereafter heard of the incident that would spawn his first Broadway production. Finding a May 1986 *New York Times* report of an espionage trial confirmed his idea for *M. Butterfly,* which proved an astounding success in 1988. A French diplomat, M. Bouriscot, and his lover, M. Shi, a Chinese Opera singer, were sentenced to prison for six years after Bouriscot confessed to passing information to Shi, whom for twenty years he mistook for a woman. Fascinated by the "fantasy stereotype" of the modest Asian woman, Hwang, in the "Author's Notes," describes his fictionalized version of Bouriscot's story as "a deconstructivist *Madama Butterfly.*" Puccini's 1904 opera, wherein a Japanese woman commits suicide when spurned by the American Pinkerton, embodied for Hwang racial and gender stereotypes; thus *M. Butterfly* subverts Puccini's plot as the Westerner, Gallimard, plays out his Pinkerton-power fantasies with the Chinese diva only to learn, when "she" exposes herself as man and spy, that it is he who is the love-ruined Butterfly. Dressed in her discarded costume, Gallimard re-enacts the opera's finale with his own ritual suicide. Hwang's hope was that this reversal would prompt the audience to examine their own attraction to stereotypes. Though some critics branded the play as misogynist or racist itself, Hwang insists that *M. Butterfly* is not a sexist, anti-American diatribe but a plea to both women and men, East and West, to discard mythic misperceptions. Reaping the Tony, the Outer Critics Circle, the John Gassner, and the Drama Desk awards for best play as well as a Pulitzer Prize nomination, the play has been produced in over thirty countries.

Still determined to stretch perceptual boundaries, Hwang wrote the text for another 1988 production, a science-fiction musical drama called *1000 Airplanes on the Roof.* With music by Philip Glass and projection by Jerome Sirkin, this collaboration features a character whose monologue exudes distress over his possible kidnapping by aliens. Another collaboration with Glass was *The Voyage,* produced by the Metropolitan Opera for the Columbus quincentennial. Also in 1992, Hwang's one-act play *Bondage* was produced at the Humana Theatre Festival. Reflecting Hwang's avowed goal of a multicultural theater, *Bondage,* set in a "fantasy bondage parlor," examines racial and sexual power structures as the masked dominatrix and her client assume various ethnic identities before revealing themselves as a white woman and an Asian man. Race and gender issues also emerge in *Face Values,* a farce prompted by the controversy over the casting of a Caucasian to play an Asian character in a production of the musical *Miss Saigon* in Boston in 1993.

Regretting his own "bunker mentality" during this controversy, Hwang, in an *American Theatre* article, repeats the call for art that transcends racial boundaries and allows for a cross-cultural dialogue. Such a dialogue arises between the two characters of *Trying to Find Chinatown,* produced at the Humana Theatre Festival in 1996, as a Caucasian man adopted at birth by Asian Americans seeks direction to Chinatown from an Asian American street violinist who sees his heritage as musical rather than racial. Conflicts of heritage also constitute the subject of *Golden Child,* produced by the Public Theatre in 1996 and on Broadway in 1998. Based on Hwang's transcription as a ten-year-old of his dying grandmother's memories of life as the favored child, the play depicts a fearful prospective father visited by the ghost of his grandmother. Her dramatized flashback to the power struggle among the three wives of her father, who decreed a household conversion to Christianity, represents the collision of cultures in the China of eighty years ago and in the lives of descendants in America today.

Regarding this latest production as "a much more forgiving look at the same issues" than were his earlier plays, Hwang's beliefs have evolved from the disparagement of assimilation his works evidenced in the 1970s. He now advocates a "Dynamic Assimilation," with equal influence among ethnic groups, in the belief that genuine multiculturalism can effect "interculturalism"—a redefined America now evident in the theater in large part because of Hwang.

—Janet V. Haedicke

I

INGE, William (Motter)

Born: Independence, Kansas, 3 May 1913. **Education:** Montgomery County High School, Independence, graduated 1930; University of Kansas, Lawrence, 1930-35, A.B. 1935; Peabody Teachers College, Nashville, Tennessee, 1935-36, M.A. 1938; Yale University, New Haven, Connecticut, 1940. **Career:** Announcer, KFH Radio, Wichita, Kansas, 1936-37; teacher at Columbus High School, Kansas, 1937-38, Stephens College, Columbia, Missouri, 1938-43, and Washington University, St. Louis, 1946-49; arts critic, St. Louis *Star-Times*, 1943-46; story consultant, *Bus Stop* television series, 1961-62; lecturer, University of North Carolina, Chapel Hill, 1969, and University of California, Irvine, 1970. **Awards:** George Jean Nathan award, 1951; Pulitzer prize, 1953; New York Drama Critics Circle award, 1953; Donaldson award, 1953; Oscar, for screenplay, 1962. **Died:** (suicide) 10 June 1973.

PUBLICATIONS

Plays

The Dark at the Top of the Stairs (as *Farther Off from Heaven*, produced 1947; revised version, as *The Dark at the Top of the Stairs,* produced 1957). 1958.
Come Back, Little Sheba (produced 1949). 1950.
Picnic: A Summer Romance (produced New York, 1953). 1953; revised version, as *Summer Brave* (produced 1962), In *Summer Brave and Eleven Short Plays*, 1962.
Bus Stop (produced 1955). 1955.
Four Plays (includes *Come Back, Little Sheba; Picnic; Bus Stop; The Dark at the Top of the Stairs*). 1958.
Glory in the Flower (produced 1959). In *24 Favorite One-Act Plays*, edited by Bennett Cerf and Van H. Cartmell, 1958.
The Tiny Closet (produced 1959). In *Summer Brave and Eleven Short Plays*, 1962.
A Loss of Roses (produced 1959). 1960.
Splendor in the Grass: A Screenplay. 1961.
Natural Affection (produced 1962). 1963.
Summer Brave and Eleven Short Plays (includes *To Bobolink, For Her Spirit; A Social Event; The Boy in the Basement; The Tiny Closet; Memory of Summer; The Rainy Afternoon; The Mall; An Incident at the Standish Arms; People in the Wind; Bus Riley's Back in Town; The Strains of Triumph*). 1962.
Where's Daddy? (as *Family Things, Etc.*, produced 1965; as *Where's Daddy?,* produced 1966). 1966.
The Disposal (as *Don't Go Gentle*, produced 1968; as *The Last Pad,* produced 1972). In *Best Short Plays of the World Theatre, 1958-1967*, edited by Stanley Richards, 1968; revised version, as *The Disposal*, music by Anthony Caldarella, lyrics by Judith Gero (produced 1973).
Two Short Plays: The Call, and A Murder. 1968.
Midwestern Manic, in *Best Short Plays 1969*, edited by Stanley Richards. 1969.
Overnight (produced 1969).
Caesarian Operations (produced 1972).

Love Death Plays: Dialogue for Two Men, Midwestern Music, The Love Death, Venus and Adonis, The Wake, The Star (produced 1975).

Screenplays: *Splendor in the Grass,* 1961; *All Fall Down,* 1962; *Bus Riley's Back in Town,* 1965.

Television Play: *Out on the Outskirts of Town,* 1964.

Fiction

Good Luck, Miss Wyckoff. 1971.
My Son Is a Splendid Driver. 1972.

*

Bibliography: *Inge: A Bibliography* by Arthur F. McClure, 1982.

Critical Studies: *Inge* by R. Baird Shuman, 1966, as *William Inge,* 1989; "Social and Cultural Prophecy in the Works of William Inge" by Jane Courant, in *Studies in American Drama 1945-Present,* 1991; *William Inge: A Research and Production Sourcebook* by Richard M. Leeson, 1994.

*   *   *

William Inge remains an interesting phenomenon in American drama. His impact upon critic and public alike demands that he be included in any serious consideration of the postwar theater, but in subject matter and in style he was so counter to the patterns of his contemporaries as to seem to belong to quite another generation. Leaving behind a minimal impression upon the development of late-twentieth-century American drama, his name rapidly fading, he was nonetheless a major figure for almost a decade and wrote some of the most appealing dramatic pieces of the late 1940s and 1950s.

Inge's significance in American drama is limited to four plays: *Come Back, Little Sheba, Picnic, Bus Stop,* and *The Dark at the Top of the Stairs.* His first, *Farther Off from Heaven,* produced by Margo Jones in Dallas, got to New York only in a much-revised version. *A Loss of Roses* failed completely, as did *Natural Affection* and *Family Things, Etc.* His screenplays, though they were made into notable films, brought no added fame, and his prose fiction is limited in appeal.

While **Tennessee Williams**, **Arthur Miller**, and **Eugene O'Neill** dwelt upon the tragic nature of their often inauspicious characters, Inge chose to emphasize his characters' fundamentally pathetic and frequently comic nature. The tragic fates are nowhere in evidence. Inge's appeal lies in a compassionate understanding of and a great sensitivity toward his petty little people, as he conveys successfully to his audiences the universally amusing and simultaneously agonizing quality of ordinary human nature under very ordinary circumstances. Furthermore, at a time when his major contemporaries favored impressionistic stagings, stylized settings, politico-historical themes, and regional emphases, Inge remained consistently a writer of straightforward, single-set plays of Ibsenesque realism. His characters, straight from the unprepossessing streets and towns of the vast mid-section of contemporary America, moved within settings, both geographical and theatrical, remarkable for their unobtrusive, innocuous nature. Inge is one of the most regional of dramatists, but he is emphatically not a "regionalist"; that is, his chosen locale is so lacking in specific regional association and importance, and hence influence upon his characters, as to be virtually neutral. The importance of the surroundings into which Inge places his characters lies precisely in their lack of any importance at all.

Nor does Inge permit the many individual problems of his characters to become the central "problem" of the plays as a whole. His first success, *Come Back, Little Sheba,* is a fine case in point. For instance, we learn a great deal about A.A. and alcoholism, but it is not a play *about* alcoholism. Sexual restraints, taboos, and frustrations, past and present, cause serious personal problems for Doc and Lola, but the play is in no way *about* sex. The air of pessimistic hopelessness surrounding the Delaneys may be the strongest theme, but the play refuses to dwell upon the subject and, in fact, displays a considerable awareness of the positive aspect of human resilience *and* ultimate hope. *Come Back, Little Sheba,* is, then, a play that sends out strong shock waves from all of these problems, permitting none of them to dominate the action. The audience finds itself attracted to these wholly undistinguished people in this undistinguished small town by bonds of mutual sympathy and understanding, together with an appreciation of Inge's outstanding ability to demonstrate what human love, patience, and endurance really mean to virtually all of us. Much has been lost by Doc and Lola in the course of the action, but much has been gained in return. Everybody, at the final curtain, is back at the beginning, more or less, and that, in the end, is far more the way of the world than otherwise. Inge's characters, here and elsewhere, will move no mountains in their lifetimes, but they are, as one critic has said, the salt of the earth, their importance lying almost entirely in the fact of their being human.

Picnic, as one opening night critic observed, is still "basic Inge." The sensation of the season, the play won a Pulitzer Prize and remains probably Inge's most famous play. Adding a few characters and moving them from kitchen to back yard, Inge proved that his formula for the dramatic impact of *Sheba* had been no fluke. "Affectionate, understanding, interesting, engagingly funny, emotionally touching, with fascinating characters" were the critical terms that greeted the play's portrayal of what happens on a Labor Day weekend in a Kansas backyard among a group of almost embarrassingly stock stage figures from clucking-hen mother to sexually frustrated old-maid schoolteacher. Highly emotional things happen in *Picnic,* as they do in *Sheba,* caused mainly by the intrusion of the handsome semi-clad drifter who causes a general loosening of assorted libidos, culminating in fornication, drunkenness, and elopement. But none of these things in themselves, any more than in *Sheba,* is the point. What matters is Inge's highly skilled and absolutely convincing portrayal of the driving human forces of underlying desires, frustrations, fears, and joys of these routinely bland people in an equally bland environment.

In *Bus Stop* Inge falls back on a device that worked for Shakespeare on Prospero's island, for **Melville** aboard the *Pequod,* and for **James Jones** in his pre-Pearl Harbor army. Into Grace's microcosmic lunchroom, driven by the unalterable force of a prairie blizzard, the playwright sends a group of individuals as stereotyped and undistinguished as anything he or many another artist has attempted. What emerges, for all that, is a wholly delightful

human comedy with an underlying drama of deep human pathos. The pursuit and capture of the pitifully floozy "chantoosie" by the frantically infatuated, rambunctious but innocent cowboy is superbly comic, beautifully controlled. Simultaneously, the parallel affair of the decadent professor and the naive waitress, while ever on the edge of the pit of gratuitous sensation, carries the more serious theme with touching effectiveness. Before he is through with us, Inge has made us care a great deal about Bo, Cherie, Lyman, Elma, and Virgil. Normally we, as well as the rest of the world, would take little note of them, but Inge has shown us that they are highly important people to themselves and in many ways to each other. Cherie, hopelessly tarnished, artistically a fiasco, has stood her ground with dignity while vigorously defending her womanly honor against the onrushing Bo. He in turn, literally forced to bow before her, has learned, to his wondering astonishment, that women are not calves to be bulldogged, hogtied, and subdued. Elma has come dangerously close to the total destruction of her innocence, but that very innocence has given the aging sensualist pause enough to permit both of them, for the time, to escape. By the time Inge returns all on stage to equilibrium and sends his bus on its journey, we have encountered a touching human experience of lasting impressiveness.

In his final and least noteworthy "success," *The Dark at the Top of the Stairs,* Inge unfortunately surrenders to artificialities of plot, less than subtle symbolism, gratuitous violence, and remarkably unconvincing characters. There is much of the "basic Inge" to be seen and, upon occasion, praised, but the strong human appeal of the first three plays is lost amid generally unsatisfactory handling of marital problems, racial prejudices, and parent-child relationships. We may still understand some of the reasons for Rubin Flood's infidelity and Sonny's mamma's boy behavior, as well as little Sammy's suicide, but, on the whole, there is too much of the trite and unimaginative to be as convincing as we would like.

The ultimate appeal of Inge seems to lie in his ability to transform the lives and behavior of drab people in drab surroundings into a significant drama of human experience. Taking us inside and outside the houses most of us pass every day down the block and around the corner, he reveals some rather profound human truths, and he grips us in fascination as he does so.

—Jordan Y. Miller

See the essay on *Picnic.*

INGRAHAM, Joseph Holt

Born: Portland, Maine, 26 January 1809. **Education:** Hallowell Academy, Maine; Yale University, New Haven, Connecticut, 1828-29. **Family:** Married Mary Brookes in 1849; three daughters and one son. **Career:** Teacher, Jefferson College, Washington, Mississippi, after 1830; writer of romances from 1835; established a girls school in Nashville, Tennessee, 1849; began theological studies: ordained deacon, 1851, and priest, 1852, in the Protestant Episcopal Church, and thereafter wrote books with religious themes; missionary in Aberdeen, Mississippi, 1852-53; rector, St. John's Church, Mobile, Alabama, 1853-57, a church in Riverside, Tennessee, 1857-58, and Christ Church, Holly Springs, Mississippi, 1858-60. **Died:** 18 December 1860.

The Brigantine; or, Guitierro and the Castilian: A Tale Both of Boston and Cuba (includes *The Old Bean*). 1847.

Edward Manning; or, The Bride and the Maiden. 1847.

Beatrice, The Goldsmith's Daughter: A Story of the Reign of the Last Charles. 1847.

Ringold Griffitt; or, The Raftsman of the Susquehannah: A Tale of Pennsylvania. 1847.

The Free-Trader; or, the Cruiser of Narragansett Bay. 1847.

The Texan Ranger; or, The Maid of Matamoras (includes *Alice Brandon*). 1847.

Wildash; or, The Cruiser of the Capes. 1847.

Jennette Alison; or, The Young Strawberry Girl. 1848.

Nobody's Son; or, The Life and Adventures of Percival Mayberry. 1851.

The Arrow of Gold; or, The Shell Gatherer. 1854(?).

The Prince of the House of David; or, Three Years in the Holy City. 1855.

Rivingstone; or, The Young Ranger Hussar: A Romance of the Revolution. 1855.

The Pillar of Fire; or, Israel in Bondage. 1859.

The Throne of David: From the Consecration of the Shepherd of Bethlehem to the Rebellion of Prince Absalom. 1860.

The Sunny South; or, The Southerner at Home. 1860; as *Not "A Fool's Errand,"* 1880; as *Kate's Experiences,* 1880.

Mortimer; or, The Bankrupt's Heiress. 1865.

Wildbird; or, The Three Chances. 1869.

The Avenging Brother; or, The Two Maidens. 1869.

The Pirate Chief; or, The Cutter of the Ocean. n.d.

Other

The South-West. 2 vols., 1835.

Pamphlets for the People, in Illustration of the Claims of the Church and Methodism. 1854.

*

Bibliography: in *Bibliography of American Literature* by Jacob Blanck, 1963.

Critical Study: *Ingraham* by Robert W. Weathersby II, 1980.

*   *   *

Joseph Holt Ingraham was one of the first Americans to try to make a living by writing fiction, and his career provides a paradigm of the forms to which early would-be professionals turned in their efforts to meet the destructive competition from imported works in the days before international copyright.

After achieving success with his non-fiction account of his travels in Louisiana and Mississippi (*The South-West*), he turned to the then favorite two-volume historical novel after the manner of Scott and Cooper. His first, *Lafitte, The Pirate of the Gulf,* a conventional romance about a patriotic Louisiana pirate who turns out to have been highborn, was his most successful and remained in print well into the twentieth century. *Burton* (which is about the Canadian campaign of Aaron Burr during the American Revolution) and *Captain Kyd* (another fantasy about a famous pirate) were less successful; despite the appeal of the subjects, the stories were too preposterous and chaotically constructed even for readers accustomed to Gothic fiction. A fourth double-decker, *The*

Quadroone, another tale of baby-switching during the Spanish occupation of New Orleans in the eighteenth century, was coldly received; and a projected fifth, *The Dancing Feather,* an unlikely tale of contemporary piracy in New York harbor, had to be ended abruptly after the tenth chapter of a planned fifty and published as a cheap paperback.

During the next five years, Ingraham led in productivity a pack of hungry writers churning out the hundred-page pamphlets that new high-speed printing presses made it possible to sell for 25 cents. Ingraham wrote at least sixty; most were stories of pirates and other nautical adventurers, though some were early tales of the shady side of big city life. Typical and most interesting are *The Beautiful Cigar Vendor* and its sequel *Herman de Ruyter,* in which Ingraham provides his own solution to the mystery of the disappearance of Mary Cecilia Rogers, a New York girl who inspired also Poe's "The Mystery of Marie Roget."

When Ingraham entered the work of the Protestant Episcopal church in 1847, what the *Knickerbocker* magazine called his "cheap and nasty," "immoral" stories ceased to flow from his pen, although in 1851 he produced a final short work, *Nobody's Son,* protesting the mistreatment of orphans in the manner of Dickens's popular fictions.

Ingraham's greatest success and major contribution to literature came late in his life, however, when, as he was engaged in the ministry, he began to write a life of Christ in the form of a series of letters from an impressionable young Egyptian girl visiting the Holy Land in Christ's time. These developed into *The Prince of the House of David,* the first religious bestseller, and the prototype of a vein that has flourished through the works of **Lew Wallace,** Lloyd Douglas, and others to the present day. Further attempts, however, to tell the story of Moses (*The Pillar of Fire*) and the founding of the Hebrew kingdom (*The Throne of David*) were less successful because the novels became too long-winded and were clumsily constructed. He failed to find a publisher for a projected fourth novel, *St. Paul, The Roman Citizen,* before his sudden and still mysterious death.

—Warren French

IRVING, John (Winslow)

Born: Exeter, New Hampshire, 2 March 1942. **Education:** Phillips Exeter Academy in New Hampshire; University of Pittsburgh, 1961-62; Institute of European Studies, University of Vienna, 1963-64; University of New Hampshire, B.A. (cum laude) 1965; University of Iowa, M.F.A. 1967. **Family:** Married 1) Shyla Leary in 1964 (divorced 1981), two sons; 2) Janet Turnbull in 1987, one son. **Career:** Assistant wrestling coach, Phillips Exeter Academy, 1964-65; assistant professor of English, Windham College, 1967-69, 1970-72; Mount Holyoke College, 1975-78; writer-in-residence, University of Iowa, 1972-75; Bread Loaf Writer's Conference, 1976; Brandeis University, 1978-79; assistant wrestling coach, Northfield Mt. Hermon School, 1981-83; Fessenden School, 1984-86; head wrestling coach, Vermont Academy, 1987-89. **Awards:** Rockefeller Foundation grant, 1971-72; National Endowment for the Arts fellowship, 1974-75; Guggenheim award, 1976-77; National Book award nomination, 1979; American Book award, 1980; honored in 1988 by the National Women's Political Caucus. **Residence:** Dorset, Vermont.

PUBLICATIONS

Collections

3 by Irving. 1980.
Trying to Save Piggy Sneed. 1996.

Novels

Setting Free the Bears. 1969.
The Water-Method Man. 1972.
The 158-Pound Marriage. 1974.
The World According to Garp. 1978.
The Hotel New Hampshire. 1981.
The Cider House Rules. 1985.
A Prayer for Owen Meany. 1989.
A Son of the Circus. 1994.
A Widow for One Year. 1998.

*

Bibliography: "A John Irving Bibliography" by Edward C. Reilly, in *Bulletin of Bibliography,* 1985.

Critical Studies: *John Irving* by Gabriel Miller, 1982; *John Irving* by Carol C. Harter and James R. Thompson, 1986; *Understanding John Irving* by Edward C. Reilly, 1991; "The Postmodern Novel: The Example of John Irving's *The World According to Garp* by Raymond Wilson, in *Critique,* Fall 1992; "Double Discourse in John Irving's *The World According to Garp*" by Kim McKay, in *Twentieth-Century Literature,* Winter 1992.

*   *   *

Novelist John Irving is a gifted storyteller with a remarkably fertile imagination and a penchant for meshing the comic and tragic. Irving is perhaps best known for his critically acclaimed bestseller *The World According to Garp.* The book's publication came at just the right time for Irving. Although the author's earlier works *Setting Free the Bears* and *The Water-Method Man* sold over six thousand copies each, *The 158-Pound Marriage* sold only 2,500. When Irving switched from Random House to E. P. Dutton, the move proved beneficial for both Dutton and Irving. Amid a Garpomania advertising blitz, *The World According to Garp* initially sold 120,000 hardbound copies and eventually more than three million hardbound and paperback copies. The work gained Irving an avid reading public, and he became a significant voice in contemporary American fiction. In recommending Garp for publication, Dutton editor Henry Robbins acclaimed that it was a "major novel" and "sure to be the 'breakthrough' book by an immensely talented novelist in his mid-30s." R. Z. Sheppard emphasized in an article in *Time* (August 31, 1981) *Garp*'s and Irving's importance: "In the 1950s **J. D. Salinger** produced *Catcher in the Rye,* the Huckleberry Finn for the Silent Generation. Readers in the 1960s and early 1970s rallied around **Kurt Vonnegut**'s *Cat's Cradle* with its 'karass,' and the casually philosophical 'so it goes' from *Slaughter-House Five.* The end of the decade belong[s] to Irving and Garpomania."

Although Irving says his life has been average, happy, and basically uninteresting, he stresses that he uses his experiences but translates them through his imagination into the art of fiction. His prep school days became, accordingly, backgrounds for Steering School (*Garp*) and Gravesend Academy (*Owen Meany*), and his college years became the grist for settings in *The Water-Method Man, The 158-Pound Marriage,* and *Owen Meany.* Irving's wrestling experiences provide the symbols and metaphors in *Setting Free the Bears, The 158-Pound Marriage,* and *Garp,* as well as the sports metaphors in *The Hotel New Hampshire* (weight lifting) and *Owen Meany* (slam-dunking basketballs). Irving's sojourn in Vienna, Austria, is the basis not only for his literary world vision, but also for his protagonists' rites of passage in the first five novels. Because Irving never knew his biological father, a World War II airman who was shot down but survived the war, Irving's young characters may either be true orphans like Homer Wells (*The Cider House Rules*) or may have lost one parent like T. S. Garp, Siegfried Javotnik (*Bears*), the Berry children (*Hotel New Hampshire*), or John Wheelwright (*Owen Meany*). In imitating the nineteenth-century novelists whom he admired, especially Charles Dickens, Irving produces expansive, action-filled novels with a great deal of interest in character and plot. "I do mean to move characters through time," he told Joyce Renwick in *Fiction International* (1982), "so we can see how they've changed—in their lives and by their lives. I think the novel that interests me right now is a novel that shows us how people end up. . . . I feel I am programmed to write big novels, or at least long ones."

In developing his plots, Irving blesses and then curses his characters, an idea he underscored when he told Larry McCaffery in *Contemporary Literature* (1982), "I always try to place my characters under the most and least favorable circumstances to see how they will react, to test them. . . . I visit all the worst kinds of extreme things on these people to see how they would deal with extremes of adversity, just as earlier they had to cope with success." This technique of emotional extremes, moreover, meshes with his characters' rites-of-passage, with the plots' juxtaposition of tragedy and comedy, with those contemporary issues Irving writes about, and with the sudden violence and death at the core of Irving's fictional universe. Yet despite the tragedy and violence in his characters' lives, the novels end affirmatively, or, as he wryly remarked about *Garp* to Joyce Renwick, "I've written a life-affirming novel in which everyone dies." Accordingly, his novels' epilogues—also a nineteenth-century tradition—underscore Irving's affirmative visions, and in *Publisher's Weekly* (24 April 1978) he told Barbara Bannon, "I wanted to write about the passing of time and the softening of pain. An epilogue inevitably has nostalgia in it—it's a way of saying, 'It's not so bad what happened to that little child.' No one has a 'happy ending.' 'Ending' is by definition not a happy occurrence."

Although *Setting Free the Bears* is Irving's only novel with European settings and characters, and although *The Water-Method Man* is his only truly comic novel, all of his novels share Irvingesque trademarks. They are all about eccentric characters, most of whom experience a rite of passage in an essentially violent world. His plots also rely on symbols, a technique he stressed when talking with Laura de Coppet in *Interview* (1981): "There's not much point in symbols if people don't understand them. If you're going to be symbolic, you'd better let people know you are." In addition, Irving uses "refrains" that he described to de Coppet as "little litanies . . . that serve to mark how far you've come, and also forewarn you about where you're going." In each of his novels, either World War II or the Vietnam War (the latter in *Owen Meany*), as well as the wars' aftermaths, spawn the violence at the core of twentieth-century life and Irving's literary world vision. This violence is assuaged, however, in each novel's affirmative epilogue, which always highlights life's positive values—for example, responsibility, family solidarity, and, above all, compassion and love. In the main, the symbols, refrains, and themes complement settings, characterizations, and conflicts. More importantly, they underscore Irving's intricately woven plotting techniques, especially in his two most admired novels, *Garp* and *Hotel New Hampshire.*

In the McCaffery interview, Irving emphasized that *The World According to Garp* is "the best of the four published books . . . . *Garp* seemed to bring together a lot of things I'd only been getting started in my other books. It summarized the other books for me, finished the cycle I had started."

Reviewers, critics, and scholars also acclaim the novel's merits. In the main, the plot traces T. S. Garp's rite of passage from childhood to adulthood and his assassination in the Steering School wrestling room. In its richly layered plot, however, it is also about Garp's mother, Jenny Fields; Helen Holm, Garp's wife; his children, Duncan, Walt, and Jenny; Ernie Holm, Garp's father-in-law; Garp's friends, Roberta Muldoon, Ellen James, Alice and Harrison Fletcher; and about Vienna, Steering School, and the omnipresent Under Toad. It is also about women's liberation, transvestism, radical extremism, self-mutilation, rape, death, and ultimately about family solidarity and the pleasures gracing life. The work's strengths are evident in Irving's already established techniques and themes. "The Pension Grillparzer," "Vigilance," and "The World According to Bensenhaver" are narratives within the main narrative that illuminate incidents and themes. The third-person point of view is technically sound because, as Irving remarked to Laura de Coppet, "The practical reason for . . . the third person is that they are all terminal cases; they are all going to die. . . . In other words, the last chapter is an obituary, and there's no one to tell the story if the story isn't in the third person." In addition, the rite of passage motif applies to Garp's, Helen's, and his children's lives since they all move through experience to knowledge about life. Complementing settings, characterizations, and themes are the novel's symbols, especially wrestling, the wrestling room, and the Under Toad. Finally, despite the mayhem and death plaguing the characters' lives, the epilogue is technically sounder and even more ebullient than those of the preceding novels in that all of the characters transcend the violence and death and live happy lives.

The Hotel New Hampshire focuses on the eccentric Berry family: Winslow Berry (Father), Mary Bates (Mother), and the five children—Franny, Frank, John (protagonist/narrator), Lilly, and Egg; the family circle also includes Iowa Bob Bates, the grandfather; Sorrow, the Labrador retriever; and State O'Maine (Earl), a performing bear. The novel is also about Freud, Susie the Bear, Junior Jones, Chipper Dove, and about rape, incest, terrorism, suicide, family solidarity, and hotels. Win Berry invests in three hotels during the course of the narrative and moves his family from hotel to hotel, one being the second Hotel New Hampshire in Vienna and part of the characters' obligatory trip as well as their rite of passage. In typical Irvingesque plot twists, violence and tragedy stalk the Berrys—Franny is gang-raped on the night Sorrow is put to sleep; Iowa Bob dies of a heart attack when the stuffed Sorrow glides out of John's closet; Mother and Egg die in a plane crash at sea; and Lilly commits suicide. In thwarting the young German radicals' plot to blow up the Vienna State Opera House, Win Berry is blinded in the blast, and John literally squeezes Argbeiter to death in a bear hug. Despite the violence and death, the novel ends with a life-affirming epilogue: Franny is

a successful movie starlet, Frank is a successful businessman, Win is content with the third hotel, and John marries Susie.

Regarding *Hotel New Hampshire,* Irving told Richard West in *New York Magazine* (1981), "There is no question in my mind it's better than *The World According to Garp.* It certainly is every bit as big a book, and it means much more. It's a more ambitious novel symbolically but with a different point of view, deliberately narrower than *Garp.*" The first-person narration is chronological and thus easier to read than the convoluted plot shiftings and points of view in his first two novels. The narrative plot line is also not interrupted by stories within the main narrative, a disconcerting technique for some readers of *Garp. The Hotel New Hampshire* is indeed a "more ambitious book symbolically" in its number of symbols, which include State O'Maine and Susie the Bear, the man in the white dinner jacket, weight lifting, Sorrow, Vienna, the three different hotels, and even Freud and his experiences in the concentration camps and with the young neo-Nazi terrorists.

Irving's eighth novel, *A Son of the Circus* (1994) was considered a disappointment after the critical success of *Owen Meany.* The story of a physician caught up in the search for a serial killer of prostitutes in Bombay, *Circus* contains the expected assortment of Irving misfits as well as his trademark labyrinthine plotting and obsession with the grotesque: sideshow freaks; a transsexual cult; a giant dildo used for drug smuggling. What could have been a rich exploration of social alienation, however, was instead a book that many critics found unengaging, limp, and merely titillating. Irving returned to form, though, with *A Widow for One Year* (1998), in many ways his most *Garp*-like book since *Garp.* About family, love, betrayal, and loss, *Widow* recycles many of *Garp*'s trademark elements, including the death of children in a car accident and a parent's lasting grief. The story concerns a family of writers. Ted Cole is an author and illustrator of children's books whose womanizing has alienated his wife. The summer that Ted and Marion separate, Ted hires teenager Eddie O'Hare to work as his assistant. Eddie and Marion embark on a lusty affair, after which Ted sues for custody of four-year-old Ruth. Marion disappears—only to turn up years later as a pseudonymous writer—and Ruth becomes a best-selling novelist. Various traumas await the adult Ruth, including her witnessing of a prostitute's murder in Amsterdam, but after having been widowed for one year, she finally finds happiness. Throughout the novel, the characters' experiences show up in amusing ways in their books—a clever device that allows Irving to explore the ways in which art imitates life and life imitates art. Though reviewers were not blind to the novel's faults, among them some flatness of characterization and a tendency to over-narrate trivial plot details, many hailed the book as evidence that Irving's comic sensibility and inventive plotting were still robust.

Some critics believe that Irving is a trendy or popular writer because he focuses on contemporary problems and issues ranging from homosexuality, lesbianism, transvestism, and women's rights to radical extremism, rape, incest, abortion, suicide, and assassination; other critics believe that he is a serious writer because of his insights into and analyses of these problems and issues and their effects on the modern world. On the other hand, Irving believes that the writer's aesthetic responsibility is to tell a good story, and in the McCaffery interview he said: "The writer's responsibility is to take hard stuff and make it as accessible as the stuff can be made. Art and entertainment aren't contradictions. It's only been in the last decade, or last twenty years, that there has somehow developed this rubric under which art is expected to be difficult. . . . By creating a taste for literature that needs interpretation, we, of course, create jobs for reviewers, for critics, for the academy. I like books that can be read without those middlemen." In other words, like Charles Dickens, one of his avowed favorites, Irving examines contemporary issues, and in so doing, he tries to tell a good comic story.

—Edward C. Reilly, updated by Elizabeth Shostak

IRVING, Washington

Born: New York City, 3 April 1783. **Education:** Local schools; studied law in the offices of Henry Masterton, 1799, Brockholst Livingstone, 1801, and Josiah Ogden Hoffman, 1802; admitted to New York bar, 1806, but practiced only intermittently. **Career:** Served as military aide to New York Governor Tompkins in the U.S. Army during the War of 1812. Traveled in Europe, 1804-06; became partner, with his brothers, in family hardware business, New York and Liverpool, England, 1810; representative of the business in England, 1815 until the firm collapsed, 1818; editor, *Analectic* magazine, Philadelphia and New York, 1812-14; lived in Dresden, Germany, 1822-23, London, England, 1824, Paris, France, 1825, and Madrid, Spain, as member of the U.S. Legation, 1826-29; secretary, U.S. Legation, London, 1829-32; returned to New York, then toured the southern and western United States, 1832; lived at the manor house "Sunny-side," Tarrytown-on-Hudson, New York, 1836-42; U.S. Ambassador to Spain, in Barcelona and Madrid, 1842-45; then returned to Tarrytown. President, Astor Library (later New York Public Library), 1848-59. **Awards:** Royal Society of Literature medal, 1830. LL.D.: Oxford University, 1831. Honorary degree: Columbia University, New York; Harvard University, Cambridge, Massachusetts. **Member:** Royal Academy of History (Spain), corresponding member, 1829. **Died:** 28 November 1859.

PUBLICATIONS

Collections

Works (Author's Revised Edition). 15 vols., 1848-51.
Representative Selections, edited by Henry A. Pochmann. 1934.
Complete Works, edited by Richard Dilworth Rust and others. 1969—.
Complete Tales, edited by Charles Neider. 1975.
History, Tales and Sketches (Library of America), edited by James W. Tuttleton. 1983.
Washington Irving: Stories. 1994.

Fiction and Sketches

Salmagundi; or, The Whim-Whams and Opinions of Launcelot Langstaff, Esq., and Others, with James Kirke Paulding and William Irving. 2 vols., 1807-08; revised (by Washington Irving only), 1824.
The Sketch Book of Geoffrey Crayon, Gent. 7 vols., 1819-20; revised edition, 2 vols., 1820.
Bracebridge Hall; or, The Humourists: A Medley. 1822; edited by J.D. Colclough, 1898.

Letters of Jonathan Oldstyle, Gent. 1824.
Tales of a Traveller. 1824.
The Alhambra: A Series of Tales and Sketches of the Moors and Spaniards. 1832.
Essays and Sketches. 1837.
Chronicles of Wolfert's Roost and Other Papers. 1855.

Plays

Charles the Second; or, The Merry Monarch, with John Howard Payne, from a play by Alexandre Duval (produced 1824). 1824; edited by Arthur Hobson Quinn, in *Representative American Plays,* 1917.
Richelieu: A Domestic Tragedy, with John Howard Payne, from a play by Alexandre Duval (produced 1826; as *The French Libertine,* produced 1826). 1826.
Abu Hassan. 1924.
The Wild Huntsman, from a play by Friedrich Kind. 1924.
An Unwritten Play of Lord Byron. 1925.

Poetry

The Poems, edited by William R. Langfeld. 1931.

Other

A History of New-York from the Beginning of the World to the End of the Dutch Dynasty. 2 vols., 1809; revised edition, 1812, 1848.
A History of the Life and Voyages of Christopher Columbus. 4 vols., 1828; edited by Winifred Hulbert, as *The Voyages of Columbus,* 1931.
A Chronicle of the Conquest of Granada. 2 vols., 1829.
Voyages and Discoveries of the Companions of Columbus. 1831.
Miscellanies (A Tour on the Prairies, Abbotsford and Newstead Abbey, Legends of the Conquest of Spain). 3 vols., 1835; *A Tour on the Prairies* edited by John Francis McDermott, 1956.
Astoria; or, Anecdotes of an Enterprise Beyond the Rocky Mountains. 2 vols., 1836; edited by Edgeley W. Todd, 1964.
Adventures of Captain Bonneville; or, Scenes Beyond the Rocky Mountains of the Far West, based on journals of B.L.E. Bonneville. 3 vols., 1837; as *The Rocky Mountains,* 1837.
The Life of Oliver Goldsmith, with Selections from His Writings. 2 vols., 1840; revised edition, as Oliver Goldsmith: A Biography, in *Works II,* 1849; edited by G.S. Blakely. 1916.
Biography and Poetical Remains of the Late Margaret Miller Davidson. 1841.
A Book of the Hudson. 1849.
Mahomet and His Successors, in *Works.* 2 vols., 1850.
Life of George Washington. 5 vols., 1855-59; abridged and edited by Charles Neider, 1976.
Spanish Papers and Other Miscellanies, edited by Pierre M. Irving. 2 vols., 1866.
Letters to Mrs. William Renwick and to Her Son James Renwick. 1915.
Letters to Henry Brevoort, edited by George S. Hellman. 2 vols., 1915.
The Journals (Hitherto Unpublished), edited by William P. Trent and George S. Hellman. 3 vols., 1919.
Notes and Journal of Travel in Europe 1804-1805. 3 vols., 1921.
Diary: Spain 1828-1829, edited by Clara Louisa Penney. 1926.
Notes While Preparing Sketch Book 1817, edited by Stanley T. Williams. 1927.

Tour in Scotland 1817, and Other Manuscript Notes, edited by Stanley T. Williams. 1927.

Letters from Sunnyside and Spain, edited by Stanley T. Williams. 1928.

Journal (1823-1824), edited by Stanley T. Williams. 1931.

Irving and the Storrows: Letters from England and the Continent 1821-1828, edited by Stanley T. Williams. 1933.

Journal 1803, edited by Stanley T. Williams. 1934.

Journal 1828, and Miscellaneous Notes on Moorish Legend and History, edited by Stanley T. Williams. 1937.

The Western Journals, edited by John Francis McDermott. 1944.

Contributions to the Corrector, edited by Martin Roth. 1968.

Irving and the House of Murray (letters), edited by Ben Harris McClary. 1969.

Editor, *The Miscellaneous Works of Goldsmith.* 4 vols., 1825.

Editor, *Poems* (London edition), by William Cullen Bryant. 1832.

Editor, *Harvey's Scenes of the Primitive Forest of America.* 1841.

Translator, with Peter Irving and Georges Caines, *A Voyage to the Eastern Part of Terra Firma; or, The Spanish Main,* by F. Depons. 3 vols., 1806.

*

Bibliography: *A Bibliography of the Writings of Irving* by Stanley T. Williams and Mary Allen Edge, 1936; in *Bibliography of American Literature* by Jacob Blanck, 1969; *Irving: A Reference Guide* by Haskell Springer, 1976; *Washington Irving Papers: 1759-1898: Guide to the Scholarly Resources Microfilm Edition,* 1996.

Critical Studies: *Life and Letters of Irving* by Pierre M. Irving, 4 vols., 1862-64; *The Life of Irving* by Stanley T. Williams, 2 vols., 1935; *The World of Irving* by Van Wyck Brooks, 1944; *Irving and Germany* by Walter A. Reichart, 1957; *Irving: Moderation Displayed* by Edward Wagenknecht, 1962; *Irving* by Lewis Leary, 1963; *Irving: An American Study 1802-1835* by William L. Hedges, 1965; *Irving Reconsidered: A Symposium* edited by Ralph Aderman, 1969; *The Worlds of Irving,* 1974, and *A Century of Commentary on the Works of Irving,* 1976, both edited by Andrew B. Myers; *Comedy and America: The Lost World of Irving* by Martin Roth, 1976; *Pierre M. Irving and Washington Irving: A Collaboration in Life and Letters* by Wayne R. Kime, 1977; *Irving* by Mary Weatherspoon Bowden, 1981; *Tales of Adventurous Enterprise: Washington Irving and the Poetics of Western Expansion* by Peter Antelyes, 1990; *Critical Essays on Washington Irving* edited by Ralph M. Aderman, 1990; "Irving's *The Legend of Sleepy Hollow*" by Raymond Benoit, in *Explicator,* fall 1996; *Debatable Ground: Westward Expansion, Sentimental Aesthetics, and the Literary Personas of Washington Irving* (dissertation) by Richard Vogtel McLamore, 1997; "Days of the Patriarchs: Washington Irving's *A History of New York*" by Phillip Lopate, in *Boulevard,* winter 1997; "Origins of American Literary Regionalism: Gender in Irving, Stowe, Longstreet" by Marjorie Pryse, in *Breaking Boundaries: New Perspectives on Women's Regional Writing* edited by Sherrie A. Inness and Diana Royer, 1997.

*   *   *

Born in 1783, the year in which the American Revolution ended, Washington Irving, son of a prosperous New York hardware mer-

chant, became the first author of the new country to be acclaimed in England. Although he never wrote a novel—indeed, his chief achievement resides in perhaps a dozen sketches and short stories—he must be acknowledged as the first man of letters in the United States. He lived until 1859, much admired by **Edgar Allan Poe** and **Nathaniel Hawthorne,** whose grapplings with the darker side of human nature were as foreign to Irving's own sanguine temperament as were their respective interests in ideas and in the extended development of plot and character. Yet Irving had managed to win not only their admiration but also that of Walter Scott, Samuel Coleridge, and Lord Byron. By the time he published *The Sketch Book of Geoffrey Crayon, Gent* in 1819-20, his best work had been done. In the succeeding forty years he, like his contemporary **William Cullen Bryant,** became enshrined as a living figurehead of literary culture in America, though the conditions of American life rapidly outstripped Irving's preparation or inclination to treat them in his writing.

In the event, however, Irving did bring to his vocation a belletristic sensibility, and a style that combined grace and poise with an inimitable pictorial quality. This style seems a fusion of Augustan balance with the sentiments of early Romanticism; it is among the first purely literary artifacts in the culture of the new republic. Irving's stylistic influence is visible in Hawthorne, in the tales of **Bret Harte** set in Spanish California, and even in **Henry James** (e.g., the description of Gardencourt in *The Portrait of a Lady*). But a decade before achieving the grade and strength of this style in *The Sketch Book,* Irving had scored a literary triumph of a different stripe with *A History of New-York* (as the pseudonymous Diedrich Knickerbocker). This burlesque, Hudibrastic in its energy, is a satiric debunking of the Colonial history of Dutch New York, published in 1809; its author's and its country's twenty-sixth year. Although Irving was not to be so boldly satirical again, this youthful extravagance also exhibits another aspect of his sensibility that stayed with him to the end: his fascination with the past.

Not one to stay tied to the family hardware business, Irving served in the War of 1812 as a staff colonel, and in 1815 returned to Europe (he had taken a grand tour in 1804)—little knowing that he would not see New York again for seventeen years. Arriving in England, he sought out Scott, who had admired his *History.* Irving quickly became Scott's disciple, and, as is seen in *The Sketch Book,* he turned, in his most memorable stories, to the local settings and legends of the same Dutch ancestors whose political figures he had, as Diedrich Knickerbocker, lampooned a decade earlier. But Irving, although he anticipates by half a century the local color movement in fiction, was not merely a local colorist. He used the color of his native locale the Hudson Valley, to impart the tinge of native realism to fables he deftly appropriated from European literature. "Rip Van Winkle," the tale that would bring Irving world-wide fame, is in part a nearly literal rendering from Otmar's *Volkssagen.* "The Legend of Sleepy Hollow," Irving's other masterpiece, is similarly based on Burger's *Der Wilde Jager* and one of the Rubezahl tales. Yet Irving did more than give these Germanic folk motifs a local habitation and a name. He infused them with subliminal universal significance, and at the same time, by an authorial alchemy no doubt unconscious on his part, expressed in them the very spirit of his nation and of his time.

In "Rip Van Winkle" the localization of the ancient German tale is perfect. Rip, a shrew-bedeviled husband, is a stock comic figure seeking regressive freedom in his bottle and in the wilderness of the mountaintop. There, encountering the ghosts of Hendrik

Hudson's crew, he drinks their magical draught—and awakens as an old man, his fowling gun rusted beside him. In the meantime, however, life had gone on in the village below: that life included the American Revolution. So Rip's return from the blessed otherworld of the irretrievable past is to a new, busy, bustling nation he can neither understand nor enter. Irving's pervasive theme of nostalgia for the unrecoverable past is here at once mythologized and made unforgettable.

In "The Legend of Sleepy Hollow" Irving again appropriates a comic stereotype in Ichabod Crane. The Yankee schoolmaster is akin to satirical versions of the Puritan character—calculating, narrow-gauged, lacking in spontaneity—found in the popular culture of the time. With intuitive prescience Irving puts Ichabod in opposition to Brom Bones, a brawny, forthright Dutchman whose character resembles that of such frontier folk heroes yet to come as Mike Fink or Davy Crockett. Thus, at the beginning of American literature, Irving anticipates the regional conflict between East and West, between the Puritan, urban, prudential character and the freedom of the natural man. He further imbeds this story in the expressive energies of popular culture by making the plot hinge on a tall tale that is also the frontiersman's hoax. Ichabod, known to be superstitious, is run out of town by the headless horseman. Brom Bones, in the saddle with the pumpkin head in his lap, stays in Kinderhook to marry the girl. Thus Irving bestows his favor on an American of the coming century. In his own life, however, Irving was not as lucky as Brom Bones. His fiancee, Matilda Hoffman, daughter of a judge, died, and it may be that this early loss colored Irving's Romantic nostalgia.

Elsewhere in *The Sketch Book* Irving wrote at lower levels of intensity, exploring the folk customs of English Christmas, describing "A Country Church," "A Sunday in London," and the like. These at best are gentle impressionistic evocations of nostalgic moods. In *Bracebridge Hall* and *Tales of a Traveller* he reiterated similar subjects: *Chronicles of Wolfert's Roost* draws on Irving's travels in Germany and Spain, but the best tales are "Kidd the Pirate" and "The Devil and Tom Walker," the one an American legend, the other a native adaptation of the Faustian theme. Little in these books has lived, though in their time they doubtless enriched American literature with an antiquarian's love of the vanished or vanishing folkways of Europe.

Irving spent the winter of 1825 in Dresden, the next three years in Madrid, and then served from 1829 until his return in 1832 as Secretary of the American legation in London. His Spanish sojourn led to his writing the tales in *The Alhambra* and to his lengthy biographies of Mahomet and Columbus. These, as Stanley Williams has observed, are really romances rather than factual accounts of their subjects. After returning to America, Irving, aware of the public's desire for fictional treatments of the west, took a tour of the wilds and provided them with *A Tour on the Prairies, Astoria* (an account of John Jacob Astor's success in the fur trade), and *Adventures of Captain Bonneville.* Thus the famous writer tried to obviate suspicion of his long exile, but these writings bring to the west only the pictorialist's eye trained in London and Madrid. Irving could not romanticize such subjects.

It was characteristic of this genial author's temperament that he chose as his private vehicle the sketch during the decades when the short story was supplanting it in popularity. In fact his own tales served as models for Poe, Hawthorne, and other authors whose fictions hurried the genre of the sketch into oblivion. If Irving's works of lasting value are but few and those few brief, his career is nonetheless significant; not only did he write some

incomparable tales, and prove that authorship was a possible profession in a new country, but at the very moment when American literary consciousness was first developing he enriched his nation's culture with his cosmopolitan reflection of the themes and modes of British and continental Romanticism.

—Daniel Hoffman

See the essay on "The Legend of Sleepy Hollow."

ISHERWOOD, Christopher (William Bradshaw)

Born: High Lane, Cheshire, England, 26 August 1904; immigrated to the United States, 1939; naturalized citizen, 1946. **Education:** Repton School, 1919-22; Corpus Christi College, Cambridge, 1924-25; medical student at King's College, London, 1928-29. **Family:** Companion of artist Don Bachardy. **Career:** Secretary to French violinist Andre Mangeot and his Music Society String Quartet, London, 1926-27; private tutor, London, 1926-27; English teacher, Berlin, Germany, 1930-33; film script work, Gaumont Films, England; dialogue writer, Metro-Goldwyn-Mayer, Hollywood, California, 1940; worked in hostel for Central European refugees, American Friends Service Committee, Haverford, Pennsylvania, 1941-42; coeditor, with Swami Prabhavananda, *Vedanta and the West,* Vedanta Society of Southern California, 1943-45. Guest professor: Los Angeles State College (now California State University, Los Angeles) and University of California, Santa Barbara, 1959-62; regents professor, University of California, Los Angeles, 1965, and University of California, Riverside, 1966. **Awards:** Brandeis University Creative Arts award, 1974-75; PEN award for body of work, 1983; Common Wealth Award for distinguished service in literature, 1984. **Died:** 4 January 1986.

PUBLICATIONS

Collection

The Mortmere Stories. 1994.

Novels

All the Conspirators. 1928.
The Memorial: Portrait of a Family. 1932.
The Last of Mr. Norris. 1935; as *Mr. Norris Changes Trains,* 1935; in *The Berlin Stories,* 1946.
Sally Bowles. 1937; in *The Berlin Stories,* 1946.
Goodbye to Berlin. 1939; in *The Berlin Stories,* 1946.
Prater Violet. New York, 1945.
The Berlin Stories (contains *Mr. Norris Changes Trains, Sally Bowles,* and *Goodbye to Berlin*). 1946; as *The Berlin of Sally Bowles,* 1975.
The World in the Evening. 1954.
Down There on a Visit. 1964.
A Single Man. 1964.
A Meeting by the River. 1967.

Plays

The Dog Beneath the Skin; or, Where Is Francis?, with W.H. Auden (produced London, 1936; revised and produced London, 1937). 1935.

The Ascent of F6, with W.H. Auden (produced London, 1937; New York, 1939). 1937.

A Melodrama in Three Acts: On the Frontier, with W.H. Auden (produced Cambridge, England, 1938). 1938; as *On the Frontier: A Melodrama in Three Acts,* 1939.

The Adventures of the Black Girl in Her Search for God (based on a novella by George Bernard Shaw; produced Los Angeles, 1969).

A Meeting by the River, with Don Bachardy (based on Isherwood's novel; produced Los Angeles, 1972; on Broadway, 1979).

Plays and Other Dramatic Writings: W.H. Auden and Christopher Isherwood, 1928-1938, with W.H. Auden, edited by Edward Mendelson. 1988.

Screenplays: *Little Friend,* with others, 1934; *A Woman's Face,* with others, 1941; *Rage in Heaven,* with Robert Thoeren (based on novel by James Hilton), 1941; *Forever and a Day,* with others, 1943; *The Great Sinner,* with Ladislas Fodor, 1949; *Diane,* 1955; *The Loved One,* with Terry Southern (based on novel by Evelyn Waugh), 1965; *The Sailor from Gibraltar,* with Don Magner and Tony Richardson (based on novel by Marguerite Duras), 1967; *Frankenstein: The True Story,* with Don Bachardy (based on novel by Mary Shelley), produced 1972, published 1973.

Television play: *The Legend of Silent Night* (adapted from a story by Paul Gallico), 1969.

Other

Lions and Shadows (autobiography). 1938.
Journey to War, with W.H. Auden. 1939.
The Condor and the Cows: A South American Travel Diary. 1949.
An Approach to Vedanta. 1963.
Ramakrishna and His Disciples (biography). 1965.
Exhumations: Stories, Articles, Verses. 1966.
Essentials of Vedanta. 1969.
Kathleen and Frank (autobiography). 1971.
My Guru and His Disciple. 1980.
Christopher and His Kind (autobiography). 1980.
People One Ought to Know, with Sylvain Mangeot (poems). 1982.
October (autobiography). 1983.
The Wishing Tree: Christopher Isherwood on Mystical Religion, edited by Robert Adjemian. 1987.
Diaries. 1996.
The Repton Letters. 1997.

Editor, *Vedanta for the Western World.* 1945; as *Vedanta and the West,* 1951.
Editor, *Vedanta for Modern Man.* 1951.
Editor, *Great English Short Stories.* 1957.

Translator, *Penny for the Poor* by Bertolt Brecht. 1937; as *Threepenny Novel,* 1956.
Translator with Swami Prabhavananda, *Bhagavad-Gita: The Song of God.* 1944; as *The Song of God: Bhagavad-Gita,* 1951.
Translator and editor, with Swami Prabhavananda, *Crest-Jewel of Discrimination* by Swami Shankara. 1947.
Translator, *Intimate Journals* by Charles Baudelaire. 1947.
Translator and editor, with Swami Prabhavananda, *How to Know God: The Yoga Aphorisms of Patanjali.* 1953.

*

Bibliography: *Christopher Isherwood: A Bibliography 1923-1967* by Selmer Westby and Clayton M. Brown, 1968; "Christopher Isherwood: A Checklist, 1968-1975" by Stathis Orphanis, in *Twentieth-Century Literature,* October 1976; *Christopher Isherwood: A Reference Guide* by Robert W. Funk, 1979; *Christopher Isherwood: A Bibliography of His Personal Papers* edited by James White and William H. White, 1987.

Critical Studies: *The Modern Novel in Britain and the United States* by Walter Allen, 1964; *Christopher Isherwood* by Carolyn C. Heilbrun ("Columbia Essays on Modern Literature" series), 1970; *Christopher Isherwood* by Carolyn G. Heilbrun, 1970; *Christopher Isherwood* by Alan Wilde ("Twayne's United States Authors Series" series), 1971; *The Auden Generation: Literature and Politics in England in the 1930s* by Samuel L. Hynes, 1976; *Christopher Isherwood* by Francis King ("Writers and Their Work" series), 1976; *Isherwood: A Biography of Christopher Isherwood* by Jonathan Fryer, 1977; *Christopher Isherwood: Myth and Anti-Myth* by Paul Piazza, 1978; *Christopher Isherwood: A Critical Biography* by Brian Finney, 1979; *Christopher Isherwood* by Claude J. Summers, 1980; *Christopher Isherwood: A Personal Memoir* by John Lehmann, 1988; *Isherwood's Fiction: The Self and Technique* by Lisa M. Schwerdt, 1989; *Gay Fictions: Wilde to Stonewall* by Claude J. Summers, 1990; *Christopher Isherwood: A World in Evening* by Kay Ferres, 1994; *Auden and Isherwood: The Berlin Years* by Page Norman, 1998.

*   *   *

When Christopher Isherwood died on 4 January 1986, he was widely mourned as a deeply revered icon of contemporary Anglo-American gay culture, a courageous teacher who had wrestled with themes that haunt the twentieth-century psyche—alienation and isolation, sexuality and spirituality—and one who had voiced the fears and aspirations of gay men in difficult and dangerous times. His fascinating life's journey from an angry young man of the 1920s and 1930s to the ironic moralist and gay liberation activist of the 1970s and 1980s was itself the source of his art. Isherwood found in his mirror the personal reflection of universal predicaments, yet his work was never self-indulgent. Indeed, his greatest contribution to gay literature was to depict the homosexual as a faithful mirror of the human condition.

He was born Christopher William Bradshaw Isherwood on 26 August 1904 into an old and distinguished family, the principal landowners in Cheshire, England. In May of 1915, while a student at St. Edmund's preparatory school in Surrey, he learned of the death of his father in World War I, a loss that would haunt his early writings. He was educated at Repton School and Corpus Christi College, Cambridge, but was sent down from the university without a degree in 1925 for answering examination questions facetiously. Shortly thereafter he renewed his friendship with W.H. Auden, his former classmate at St. Edmund's, with whom he was to share a sporadic and unromantic sexual relationship for more than ten years. Auden, who quickly emerged as his generation's greatest poet, cast Isherwood in the role of literary mentor and soon introduced him to a fellow Oxford undergraduate, Stephen Spender. The trio formed the nucleus of the "Auden Gang," the young poets and novelists who dominated the English literary scene of the 1930s.

From 1930 to 1933, Isherwood lived in Berlin, where the city's political excitement and sexual freedom became the stuff of his art. He immersed himself in the world of male prostitutes, living almost anonymously in shabbily genteel and working class areas of the city and translating his experience of the demimonde into what would eventually become the definitive portrait of pre-Hitler Germany, *The Berlin Stories*. During his stay in Berlin, Isherwood fell in love with a working-class youth, Heinz, with whom he was to wander restlessly from one European country to another in search of a place where the two could settle together. The odyssey finally ended when Heinz had to return to Germany, where he was arrested, sentenced to prison for homosexual activities, and then to service in the German army. Isherwood's knowledge of Heinz's conscription in the German army contributed to his pacifism on the eve of the outbreak of World War II.

Having collaborated with Auden on three avant-garde plays and having supported various leftist causes, Isherwood gained a reputation for ideological commitment in the 1930s. But partly because of his growing self-consciousness as a homosexual, he deeply distrusted communism and became increasingly uncomfortable with the vacuity of political rhetoric of all stripes. In 1939, Isherwood and Auden immigrated to the United States, settling at first in New York City. But where Auden found the city exhilarating, Isherwood was soon deeply depressed. He decided to settle in Los Angeles, where he soon found a job in the motion picture industry. In 1940, under the influence of a Hindu monk and surrogate father, he converted to vedantism, a philosophy that would influence all his later work.

Isherwood was a conscientious objector during World War II and became a U.S. citizen in 1946. In 1953, he fell in love with an eighteen-year-old college student, Don Bachardy, who was to achieve independent success as a portrait artist. The relationship was to last the rest of Isherwood's life. At the conclusion of his 1976 autobiography, *Christopher and His Kind,* he described Bachardy as "the ideal companion to whom you can reveal yourself totally and yet be loved for what you are, not what you pretend to be." During the 1970s and 1980s Isherwood and Bachardy were active participants in the burgeoning American gay liberation movement, a movement that Isherwood's work of the 1950s and 1960s had anticipated and inspired.

The impact of Isherwood's homosexuality on his writing is pervasive and incalculable, felt both directly and indirectly. His interest in certain psychological predicaments and in recurring character types and themes, as well as his fascination with the antiheroic hero, his rebellion against bourgeois respectability, his empathy with "The Lost" (his code name for the alienated and the excluded), and his ironic perspective, are all related to his awareness of himself as a homosexual. Even when suppressed or disguised for legal or artistic reasons, homosexuality is a felt presence in Isherwood's novels. It is a crucial component of the myth of the outsider that he developed so painstakingly, and a symbol not merely of alienation and isolation, but also of individuality and of the variousness of fully human possibilities.

In his early works, Isherwood presents homosexuality unapologetically and naturally. He domesticates aspects of gay life that lesser writers sensationalized, and he reveals considerable insight into the dynamics of gay relationships. His first novel, *All the Conspirators,* published in 1928, indicts the repression of homosexual feelings, a motif that will recur throughout his canon; his second novel, 1932's *The Memorial,* brilliantly portrays a homosexual's grief at the loss of his best friend in World War I. *The Berlin Stories* (consisting of *The Last of Mr. Norris,* 1935, and *Goodbye to Berlin,* 1939), which brought him international fame, depicts a wide range of homosexual characters, from Baron Kuno von Pregnitz, whose secret fantasies revolve around English schoolboy adventure stories, to Peter Wilkinson and Otto Nowak, who share a spoiled homosexual idyll on Reugen Island. In *The Berlin Stories,* the unhappiness that plagues the gay characters is attributed not to their homosexuality but to their infection with the soul sickness that denies life and distorts reality, an infection that they share with everyone else in the doomed city. In the early works, the gay characters are juxtaposed with the heterosexual ones to reveal, beneath their apparent polarities, a shared reality of the deadened spirit.

Isherwood's American novels, beginning with *The World in the Evening,* published in 1954, focus more directly on the social plight of the homosexual in a homophobic society. In these novels, Isherwood anticipates the concerns of the nascent gay liberation movement, as he presents homosexuals as a legitimate minority among the sea of minorities that constitute Western democracies. By conceiving of homosexuals as an aggrieved minority, Isherwood both softens the stigma linked to homosexuality and encourages solidarity among gay people, while also implying the possibility of a political redress to injustice by forming alliances with other disadvantaged minorities. The dilemma faced by the gay characters of Isherwood's later novels is crystallized in their apparently irreconcilable needs to assert their individuality and to feel a sense of community.

In Bob Wood, the Quaker artist of *The World in the Evening,* Isherwood offers one of the earliest sympathetic portraits of a gay activist in Anglo-American literature. Wood bitterly criticizes the heterosexual majority for its failure to accept the gay minority. Sick of futile discussions of the etiology of homosexuality, he would like to "march down the street with a banner saying, 'We're queer because we're queer because we're queer.'" But even this protest, wildly unlikely in the 1940s, when the action of the novel takes place, is impossible: his lover, Charles, a Jew who has changed his name, "is sick of belonging to these whining, militant minorities." After much soul searching, Wood finally enlists in the Navy, despite the ban against homosexuals in the U.S. military. His motives are defiant rather than patriotic: "what they're claiming is that us queers are unfit for their beautiful pure Army and Navy—when they ought to be glad to have us." Wood's militancy and his solidarity with other homosexuals are extremely rare in the literature of the 1950s.

Isherwood's sensitivity to the injustices felt by homosexuals is also apparent in 1962's *Down There on a Visit.* Ambrose, an expatriate Englishman who has created an anarchic community on a Greek island, fantasizes a homosexual kingdom in which heterosexuality is illegal: "meanwhile it'll be winked at, of course, as long as it's practiced in decent privacy. I think we shall even allow a few bars to be opened for people with those unfortunate tendencies, in certain quarters of the larger cities." This comic riff parodies the unjust reality in which homosexuals are excluded from the larger community, even as it betrays Ambrose's secret desire for involvement in the world.

In Isherwood's 1962 masterpiece, *A Single Man,* the need for community is also an issue. Focusing on George, a late-middle-aged and lonely expatriate Briton grieving at the death of his lover of many years, the novel more fully develops the context of gay oppression than do the earlier works and places it within a still larger context of spiritual transcendence. *A Single Man* regards the assertions of individual uniqueness and minority consciousness as necessary worldly and political goals, but it finally subsumes them in the vedantic idea of the universal consciousness. In making concrete this resolution, the novel presents a moving portrait of male homosexual love; and George emerges as an Everyman figure whose homosexuality is a simple given. Presaging the gay liberation movement, *A Single Man* presents homosexuality as a human variation that should be accorded respect and depicts homosexuals as a minority whose grievances need to be addressed.

Isherwood's final novel, *A Meeting by the River,* pivots on the unsuccessful attempt of a bisexual movie producer to dissuade his younger brother from taking final vows as a Hindu monk. The producer, Patrick, finally retreats to a cowardly conformity, but his Whitmanesque vision of a homosexual union "in which two men learn to trust each other so completely that there's no fear left and they experience and share everything together in the flesh and in the spirit" complements his brother's search for spiritual brotherhood in a monastery. This vedantic novel discovers in the concept of brotherhood a means of escaping the imprisoning ego.

Described by **Gore Vidal** as "the best prose writer in English," Isherwood was a masterful stylist, a subtle ironist, a witty and compassionate moralist, and an insightful observer of the human condition. He was, in fact, one of the best writers of his generation. Central to his achievement was his depiction of homosexuality in casual, occasionally elevated, and always human terms. Incorporating gay liberation perspectives into his novels, especially the need for solidarity among homosexuals and the recognition of homosexuals as a legitimate minority, Isherwood created characters whose homosexuality is an integral part of their personality and an emblem of their common humanity.

—Claude J. Summers

J

JACKSON, Helen (Maria) Hunt

Born: Born Helen (Maria) Hunt Fiske, Amherst, Massachusetts, 15 October 1830. **Education:** Ipswich Female Seminary, Massachusetts, and Spingler Institute, New York. **Family:** Married 1) Edward Bissell Hunt in 1852 (died 1863), two sons; 2) William Sharpless Jackson in 1875. **Career:** Neighbor and schoolmate of Emily Dickinson, who remained her life-long friend; after her first marriage, traveled throughout the United States with her husband, an officer in the Army Corps of Engineers; lived in Newport, Rhode Island, 1866-74; traveled in Europe, 1868-70; lived in Colorado Springs, 1875-85; commissioner, Bureau of Indian Affairs, to investigate conditions of the Mission Indians of California, 1882-83. **Died:** 12 August 1885.

PUBLICATIONS

Fiction

Saxe Holm's Stories. 2 vols., 1874-78.
The Story of Boon. 1874.
Mercy Philbrick's Choice. 1876.
Hetty's Strange History. 1877.
Nelly's Silver Mine: A Story of Colorado Life. 1878.
The Hunter Cats of Connorloa. 1884.
Ramona. 1884.
Zeph: A Posthumous Story. 1885.
Pansy Billings and Popsy: Two Stories of Girl Life. 1898.

Poetry

Verses. 1870; revised edition, 1871, 1874.
Easter Bells. 1884.
Pansies and Orchids, edited by Susie B. Skelding. 1884.
Sonnets and Lyrics. 1886.

Other

Bits of Travel. 1872.
Bits of Talk about Home Matters. 1873.
Bits of Talk, in Verse and Prose, for Young Folks. 1876.
Bits of Travel at Home. 1878.
A Century of Dishonor: A Sketch of the United States Government's Dealings with Some of the Indian Tribes. 1881; edited by Andrew F. Rolle, 1965.
Mammy Tittleback and Family: A True Story of Seventeen Cats. (for children). 1881.
The Training of Children. 1882.
Report on the Condition and Needs of the Mission Indians of California, with Abbot Kinney. 1883; *Father Junipero and His Work* edited by Richard B. Yale, 1966.
Glimpses of Three Coasts. 1886.
Between Whiles. 1887.
Westward to a High Mountain: The Colorado Writings of Helen Hunt Jackson. 1994.

The Indian Reform Letters of Helen Hunt Jackson, 1879-1885. 1998.

Editor, *Letters from a Cat,* by Deborah Fiske. 1879.

Translator, *Bathmendi,* by J.P.C. de Florian. 1867.

*

Bibliography: in *Bibliography of American Literature* by Jacob Blanck, 1963.

Critical Studies: *Jackson* by Ruth Odell, 1939; "Jackson, Sentimentalist vs. Realist" by Allan Nevins, in *American Scholar,* summer 1941; *Jackson* by Evelyn I. Banning, 1973; *Helen Hunt Jackson* by Rosemary Whitaker, 1987; *Helen Hunt Jackson: Writer with a Cause* by Pat Edwards, 1998.

*   *   *

When Helen Hunt Jackson died in 1885, **Emily Dickinson** promised her immortality: "Helen of Troy will die, but Helen of Colorado, never." At the time of her death her reputation was at its height as the result of two works, *A Century of Dishonor* and *Ramona,* both produced partly in consequence of Jackson's move to Colorado and the west after her second marriage in 1875. Thomas Wentworth Higginson compared her to George Eliot; another critic thought her verse in some respects superior to that of Elizabeth Barrett Browning. *A Century of Dishonor* went out of print in 1885 and remained so until 1965, but *Ramona* went through more than 300 printings in the intervening years and was transferred to both stage and screen.

Paradoxically, these two works alone do not give much understanding of either the writer's background or of her cultural and literary drives. In essence, she was a New Englander whose closest friends and influences included not only Dickinson and Higginson but **Nathaniel Hawthorne**, Horace Greeley, and the sculptors Horace Greenough and William Wetmore Story. Much of her verse and prose was filled by preoccupations with sin and morality, with the evil in man and the need for moral struggle. Allan Nevins argued in *American Scholar* (1941) that *A Century of Dishonor* is too sentimental, and he is correct in that its purpose was polemical rather than literary or historical. But there is far less sentimentality in the main body of Jackson's work. Though her descriptions are often too cozy, her sympathies are defined by a rationalism and an individualism that make her characters, in the end, fully responsible for their fates, and she does not bring excess emotion to the telling of their destinies. Her characters survive and struggle on after what other novelists of the day would have seen as the final and crippling climax, as can be seen in both *Hetty's Strange History* and *Mercy Philbrick's Choice.*

Such a modern sounding quality is linked to what some of her contemporary critics felt needed apology: a devaluing of narrative in some of her work. At times the results are anti-climactic, for it is difficult to sustain the dramatic tension once the central focus of the plot has been passed. The difference in the characters' lives before and after this point is often too extremely presented, but the great advantage is escape from denouement. It is possible that Jackson's emphasis on the continuity of life was one aspect of an outlook partly formed by a vigorous and intelligent sense of humor, though this quality is to be found more in her ephemeral writings like *Bits of Travel at Home* than in the more formal works.

Modern readers would be attracted not only by her sympathy for the Native American but also by her strong feminism. Her heroines are the prime movers of her plots; the men revolve about them. Her women tend to be socially committed, fulfilling themselves through the exercise of their talents in the world, and, if introspective, they are so only in a way that strengthens them when in contact with others. The women she describes would not have been at home among the New England millworkers; their freedom of action depended on their freedom from poverty. Her lack of interest in this connection prevented her being swamped by naturalism and has deprived her of readers in a century that demands it.

In life Jackson was vivacious, articulate, intelligent, and active. Her work deserves respect as that of a modern woman in the thirty years after the Civil War.

—R.A. Burchell

JACKSON, Laura Riding. *See* **RIDING, Laura.**

JACKSON, Mrs. Schuyler B. *See* **RIDING, Laura.**

JACKSON, Shirley (Hardie)

Born: San Francisco, California, 14 December 1916. **Education:** Burlingame High School, California; Brighton High School, Rochester, New York; University of Rochester, 1934-36; Syracuse University, New York, 1937-40, B.A. 1940. **Family:** Married the writer Stanley Edgar Hyman in 1940; two sons and two daughters. **Career:** Lived in North Bennington, Vermont, after 1945. **Awards:** Mystery Writers of America Edgar Allan Poe award, 1961. **Died:** 8 August 1965.

PUBLICATIONS

Collections

The Magic of Jackson, edited by Stanley Edgar Hyman. 1966.
Just an Ordinary Day. 1996.
The Masterpieces of Shirley Jackson. 1996.
The Road through the Wall; Hangsaman; The Bird's Nest. 1998.

Short Stories

The Lottery; or, The Adventures of James Harris (stories). 1949.

Novels

The Road Through the Wall. 1948; as *The Other Side of the Street,* 1956.
Hangsaman. 1951.

The Bird's Nest. 1954; as *Lizzie,* 1957.
The Sundial. 1958.
The Haunting of Hill House. 1959.
We Have Always Lived in the Castle. 1962.

Plays

The Lottery, from her own story, in *Best Television Plays 1950-1951,* edited by William I. Kauffman. 1952.
The Bad Children: A Play in One Act for Bad Children. 1959.

Other

Life among the Savages. 1953.
The Witchcraft of Salem Village (for children). 1956.
Raising Demons. 1957.
Special Delivery: A Useful Book for Brand-New Mothers. 1960; as *And Baby Makes Three,* 1960.
9 Magic Wishes (for children). 1963.
Famous Sally (for children). 1966.
Come Along with Me: Part of a Novel, Sixteen Stories, and Three Lectures, edited by Stanley Edgar Hyman. 1968.

*

Critical Studies: *Jackson* by Lenemaja Friedman, 1975; *Private Demons: The Life of Jackson* by Judy Oppenheiner, 1988; *Jackson: A Study of the Short Fiction* by Joan Wylie Hall, 1993.

*   *   *

Throughout her work Shirley Jackson focuses on incongruities in an everyday setting, whether for comic or sinister effect. This is as true of her "disrespectful memoir" of her children, *Life among the Savages,* and its equally hilarious sequel, *Raising Demons,* as of the dark psychological explorations of her novels and short stories. In her later fiction she wrote about extraordinary characters and situations, but these were always located in an ordinary setting, the juxtaposition providing her staple ingredient of incongruity.

Much of Jackson's work is concerned with an attempt to gain, or regain, an identity. *The Bird's Nest* concerns a mentally disturbed girl who has four different voices and identities. It is triumphantly structured, but, like the earlier *Hangsaman,* the positive note on which it ends fails to remove our doubts about the future of the main character. In *The Sundial* Jackson focuses on an eccentric group of characters in the Halloran family house, where, directed by a dead relative, they await the end of the world in the belief that they alone will be saved. Allegorical relationships emerge between the characters, and the narrative, characteristically both comic and macabre, develops baroque motifs of sundial and maze.

Like *The Sundial* and her famous spine-chiller *The Haunting of Hill House* (with its "clashing disharmonies"), *We Have Always Lived in the Castle* centers on a house. Even more than *The Sundial* the reader is induced to identify with its inhabitants—eccentric or criminal though they may be—against "them" in the world outside. Eighteen-year-old "Merricat" describes her life with her sister Constance after the latter's acquittal from a charge of poisoning the rest of the family—a charge of which the local police believe her to be guilty. The destructive invasion of the world outside parallels the set-piece of the peaceable invasion of the locals invited to the final barbecue in *The Sundial*. The portrayal of the sisters' loving relationship, albeit in macabre circumstances, makes *We Have Always Lived in the Castle* the most remarkable of Jackson's books.

A few of Jackson's short stories delight in the incongruous for its own sake; however, most of her stories, including the title story of *The Lottery* (which caused a sensation on its publication in the *New Yorker* in 1948), are informed by a genuine sense of evil. The stories generally center on an isolated female, often the inadequate victim of a demon lover (such as James Harris in *The Lottery*). These characters are lost in the concrete jungle of the Kafkaesque city or are on long-distance journeys "to the end of the night." This theme is habitually announced by laughter, lines from songs and poems, or nursery rhymes, transmuted to sinister leitmotifs.

To portray the fragmented personality Jackson resorted to a kind of zany verbal logic and semantic irony. Yet, though there are passages in her work reminiscent of Borges, she kept any experimental tendency in her writing subordinated to the demands of storytelling, her prime consideration, as the lectures in *Come Along with Me* make clear.

—Val Warner

JACOBS, Harriet Ann

Pseudonym: Linda Brent. **Born:** Edenton, North Carolina, 1813. **Family:** One daughter and one son by U.S. Congressman Samuel Tredwell Sawyer. **Career:** Ran away from master, Dr. James Norcom, 1835; hid in grandmother's garret for seven years and escaped to New York, 1842; fled Norcom and slave catchers by moving to Boston, 1843; traveled to England, 1845; moved to New York, 1846, and to Rochester, 1849; worked in anti-slavery reading room, Rochester, 1849-50; nursemaid, 1850; with passage of the Fugitive Slave Law she fled again to Massachusetts to elude her master, 1852; legally defined as a slave until her purchase from southern owners by Northern friends for the sum of 300 dollars, 1852; her autobiography published as *Incidents in the Life of a Slave Girl*, 1868; traveled to London, England to raise funds for orphanage in Savannah, 1868; worked in Alexandria, Edenton, and Savannah as a nurse and reformer to improve the economic, health, and social conditions among recently freed slaves, both during and after the Civil War; took part in foundational meetings of the National Association of Colored Women, Washington, D.C., 1896. **Died:** 7 March 1897.

PUBLICATIONS

Autobiography (slave narratives)

"Letter from a Fugitive Slave" in *New York Tribune*. 1855.
Incidents in the Life of a Slave Girl, edited by Lydia Maria Child. 1861; in England, as *The Deeper Wrong,* 1862; edited and with an introduction by Jean Fagan Yellin, 1987.

*

Critical Studies: "Written by Herself: Jacobs' Slave Narrative" in *American Literature*, vol. 53, no. 3, 1981, "Texts and Con-

texts of Jacobs' *Incidents in the Life of A Slave Girl: Written by Herself*," in *The Slave's Narrative* edited by Charles T. Davis and Henry Louis Gates, 1985, and *Women & Sisters: Anti-Slavery Feminists in American Culture*, 1989, all by Jean Fagan Yellin; "Jacobs' *Incidents in the Life of a Slave Girl*: The Re-definition of the Slave Narrative Genre" by Joanne Braxton in *Massachusetts Review*, vol. 27, no. 2, 1986; *Reconstructing Womanhood: The Emergence of the Afro-American Woman Novelist* by Hazel Carby, 1987; "The Spoken and the Silenced in *Incidents in the Life of a Slave Girl* and *Our Nig*" by Gabrielle Foreman, in *Callaloo*, vol. 13, no. 2, 1990; *Stowe, Jacobs, Wilson: White Plots and Black Counterplots* by Phyllis Cole, 1990; *The Girls Who Became the Women: Childhood Memories in the Autobiographies of Jacobs, Mary Church Terrell, and Anne Moody* by Nellie McKay, 1991; "Black Womanhood in Nineteenth-Century America: Subversion and Self-Construction in Two Women's Autobiographies" by Beth Doriani, in *American Quarterly,* vol. 43, no. 2, 1991; *The Changing Moral Discourse of Nineteenth-Century African American Women's Autobiography: Jacobs and Elizabeth Keckley* by William Andrews, 1992; *Touching Liberty: Abolition, Feminism, and the Politics of the Body* by Karen Sanchez-Eppler, 1993; "The Queen of America Goes to Washington City: Jacobs, Frances Harper, and Anita Hill" by Lauren Berlant, in *American Literature,* vol. 65, no. 3, 1993; *Jacobs: Critical Perspectives Past & Present*, 1994; *Harriet Jacobs and Incidents in the Life of a Slave Girl: New Critical Essays*, 1996; *The Voices of African American Women: The Use of Narrative and Authorial Voice in the Works of Harriet Jacobs, Zora Neale Hurston, and Alice Walker* by Yvonne Johnson, 1996; "Irruptions of the Grotesque in Harriet Jacobs' *Incidents in the Life of a Slave Girl*" by Elaine Marshall, in *JAISA*, spring 1997.

*   *   *

"I was born a slave" begins Harriet Jacobs in *Incidents in the Life of a Slave Girl*, an autobiography and slave narrative that strives to claim selfhood for a self that suffered the double negation of woman and slave in antebellum America. But, despite this assertion of identity, the danger of recapture at the hands of slave catchers dictates that she cloak her name and family with the pseudonym of Linda Brent. And although she asserts the veracity of her narrative, readers and critics saw *Incidents* as the fictional offspring of white abolitionist and feminist Lydia Maria Child. It is the ability of Jacobs to negotiate these borders between chattel and person, truth and fiction, and freedom and slavery that has made *Incidents,* since expansion of the literary canon by feminist scholars in the 1970s, a seminal text in any survey of American literature in general or African American literature in particular.

Before *Incidents* appeared in 1861, there were few other publications that had permitted African American women, in their own voice, to express their peculiar sexual plight and outraged motherhood. Certainly **Frederick Douglass** and other fugitive slave men had gained much for the antislavery cause with their narratives, but their accounts only briefly touch upon the gender inequities involved in slavery. **Harriet Beecher Stowe** in *Uncle Tom's Cabin* drew more attention to the condition of women under slavery, but Jacobs no doubt found this novelistic treatment inadequate, and she wrote Amy Post on October 9, 1853, that "I refused to have my history in her key [*Key to Uncle Tom's Cabin*]. To inform Northerners about her two million sisters held in bondage, and without surrendering control of her story to a white editor, Jacobs resolved to author her own narrative. Her heroic decision, however, entailed a series of complications; most serious was the fact that autobiography in her case was an immodest act, not simply because she was a woman speaking publicly, but also because her story meant the disclosure of her history of sexual harassment, seduction, and unwed motherhood.

Jacobs' narrator, Linda Brent, recounts her trials as a fifteen-year-old slave girl struggling to resist the increasingly violent sexual advances of her master. Having scant options, she finds the only way to evade her master's insistent demands is to begin a sexual relationship with a white lover, Mr. Sands. Explaining herself to her Northern audience, Brent writes, "There is something akin to freedom in having a lover who has no control over you, except that which he gains by kindness and attachment." In an era in which the so-called "cult of true womanhood" demanded that the "fairer sex" conform to Victorian models of delicacy, honesty, and purity, Brent twice violated feminine norms, once by having unmarried, interracial sex and then once again by publishing that fact. Yet her confession contains an incisive questioning of these standards: how is it possible, she asks, to judge the slave girl for not complying with these expectations when the system of slavery carries with it the constant threat of rape and seduction? In pointed asides throughout her narrative, Brent reminds white women readers of their relative security and autonomy in comparison to the South's female chattel. In contrast to a work such as *Louisa Picquet: The Octoroon* (1861) in which a white minister pries into a slave woman's sexual history, Brent discloses her seduction to interrogate social standards and those who would appeal to such standards to condemn her.

This focus upon seduction and women's embattled domesticity has prompted numerous critics, most notably Jean Fagan Yellin, Valerie Smith, and **Henry Louis Gates** in their introductions to *Incidents,* to compare Jacobs' work to the sensation novel, popular especially among women in nineteenth-century culture. Even as such chapters as "The Hairbreadth Escape" and "A Perilous Passage in the Slave Girl's Life" display her indebtedness to contemporary melodramatic fiction, Jacobs adapts popular forms as a vehicle to express her own agenda that examines an oppression that is at once racial and gendered. Given that the slave narrative genre had been primarily used by men, *Incidents* is singular and distinctive in its use of feminine literary models to depict the specific sufferings of women under the South's "peculiar institution."

Two children resulted from her liaison with Mr. Sands, causing Brent to seek freedom, not for herself, but for her children. This resolve that privileges familial freedom over personal freedom underscores a further distinction between *Incidents* and many men's slave narratives. Whereas critics have often remarked upon the individual and masculine character of freedom in a text such as Douglass's *Narrative of the Life of Frederick Douglass,* Jacobs' autobiography suggests a different image of freedom understood along shared, maternal lines. To achieve her goal for her children, Brent escapes from her master's plantation, but she also refuses to flee to the North. Instead, she remains in her neighborhood where she can be close to and watch over her children until they are brought across the Mason-Dixon line. She hides in neighbors' storerooms, beneath kitchen floorboards, and finally, for seven years, she lies in her grandmother's attic garret, a "little dismal hole, almost deprived of light and air, and with no space to move my limbs." Brent thus locates her struggle for freedom within domestic spaces as a collective enterprise. As author, Jacobs seconds this communal sensibility in her construction of a narrative that includes sketches of the surrounding plantations, the oppression of other slave mothers, and the effect of Nat Turner's slave insurrection on the slave community. When a rare opportunity for escape on a northbound vessel is found, Brent "passes" herself off as a white woman. Later when she thinks about her reunion with her children, she expresses her happiness even as she again signals her difference from the white woman reading her story: "O reader, can you imagine my joy? No, you cannot, unless you have been a slave mother."

Although most antebellum slave narratives end with a successful escape from bondage, *Incidents* continues long after her arrival in the North to comment upon how racial prejudice mars a supposed freedom. The Fugitive Slave Law, persistent worries that her former master's family will kidnap her back into slavery, and pervasive racism all cause Brent to view the United States with sarcasm and disdain. Freedom for her is attained only amidst the keenest irony. When friends buy Brent and present her with the bill of sale, she thinks, "So I was *sold* at last!" commenting upon the fact that even at the moment of her emancipation she remains an article of merchandise. A bitter echo of the African American spiritual, "Free at Last," her words stand as an accusation of the continual deferral of freedom within nineteenth-century American racial politics.

In addition to her tremendous impact upon literary critics and historians, Harriet Jacobs is a foundational figure in African American literary tradition. For example, in her 1987 introduction to *Incidents,* Yellin suggests that Jacobs' autobiography influenced other black women writers including **Frances Ellen Watkins Harper** and **Zora Neale Hurston**. The always postponed status of freedom at the end of *Incidents,* combined with the final yet unsettling image of "a dark and troubled sea" perhaps accounts for her narrative's lasting significance.

—Russ Castronovo

JAMES, Henry

Born: New York City, 15 April 1843; brother of the philosopher William James; became British citizen, 1915. **Education:** The Richard Pulling Jenks School, New York; traveled with his family in Europe from an early age: studied with tutors in Geneva, London, Paris, and Boulogne, 1855-58, Geneva, 1859, and Bonn, 1860; lived with his family in Newport, Rhode Island, 1860-62; attended Harvard Law School, Cambridge, Massachusetts, 1862-63. **Career:** Lived with his family in Cambridge and wrote for *Nation* and *Atlantic Monthly,* 1866-69; toured Europe, 1869-70; returned to Cambridge, 1870-72; art critic, *Atlantic Monthly,* 1871-72; lived in Europe, 1872-74, Cambridge, 1875, and Paris, 1875-76; writer for New York *Tribune,* Paris, 1875-76; moved to London, 1876, and lived in England for the rest of his life; settled in Rye, Sussex, 1896; traveled throughout the United States, 1904-05. **Awards:** L.H.D.: Harvard University, 1911; Oxford University, 1912. Order of Merit, 1916. **Died:** 28 February 1916.

Collections

Novels and Stories, edited by Percy Lubbock. 35 vols., 1921-24.
Complete Plays, edited by Leon Edel. 1949.
Complete Tales, edited by Leon Edel. 12 vols., 1962-64.
Representative Selections, revised edition, edited by Lyon N. Richardson. 1966.
Tales, edited by Maqbool Aziz. 1973—.
Novels 1871-1880 and 1881-1886 (Library of America), edited by William T. Stafford. 2 vols., 1983-85.
Literary Criticism (Library of America), edited by Leon Edel. 2 vols., 1984.
Tales, edited by Christof Wegelin. 1984.
Novels 1886-1890 (Library of America), edited by Daniel M. Fogel. 1987.

Short Stories

A Passionate Pilgrim and Other Tales. 1875.
Daisy Miller: A Study. 1878.
The Madonna of the Future and Other Tales. 1879.
A Bundle of Letters. 1880.
The Diary of a Man of Fifty, and A Bundle of Letters. 1880.
Novels and Tales. 14 vols., 1883.
The Siege of London, The Pension Beaurepas, and The Point of View. 1883; revised edition, 1884.
Tales of Three Cities. 1884.
The Author of Beltraffio, Pandora, Georgina's Reasons, The Path of Duty, Four Meetings. 1885.
Stories Revived. 1885.
The Aspern Papers, Louisa Pallant, The Modern Warning. 1888.
A London Life, The Patagonia, The Liar, Mrs. Temperly. 1889.
The Lesson of the Master, The Marriages, The Pupil, Brooksmith, The Solution, Sir Edmund Orme. 1892.
The Real Thing and Other Tales. 1893.
The Private Life, The Wheel of Time, Lord Beaupré, The Visits, Collaboration, Owen Wingrave. 1893.
Terminations: The Death of the Lion, The Coxon Fund, The Middle Years, The Altar of the Dead. 1895.
Embarrassments: The Figure in the Carpet, Glasses, The Next Time, The Way It Came. 1896.
The Two Magics: The Turn of the Screw, Covering End. 1898; *The Turn of the Screw,* edited by Robert Kimbrough, 1966.
The Soft Side. 1900.
The Better Sort. 1903.
Novels and Tales (New York Edition), revised by James. 26 vols., 1907-17.
Travelling Companions, edited by Albert Mordell. 1919.
A Landscape Painter, edited by Albert Mordell. 1919.
Master Eustace. 1920.
Eight Uncollected Tales, edited by Edna Kenton. 1950.

Novels

Roderick Hudson. 1875; revised edition, 1879.
The American. 1877.
Watch and Ward. 1878.
The Europeans: A Sketch. 1878.
An International Episode. 1879.

Confidence. 1879.
Washington Square. 1881.
The Portrait of a Lady. 1881.
The Bostonians. 1886.
The Princess Casamassima. 1886.
The Reverberator. 1888.
The Tragic Muse. 1890.
The Other House. 1896.
The Spoils of Poynton. 1897; edited by Bernard Richards, 1982.
What Maisie Knew. 1897; edited by Douglas Jefferson, 1966.
In the Cage. 1898; edited by Morton Dauwen Zabel, 1958.
The Awkward Age. 1899; edited by Vivien Jones, 1984.
The Sacred Fount. 1901; edited by Leon Edel, 1953.
The Wings of the Dove. 1902; edited by Peter Brooks, 1984.
The Ambassadors. 1903; edited by Christopher Butler, 1985.
The Golden Bowl. 1904; edited by Virginia Llewellyn Smith, 1983.
Julia Bride. 1909.
The Finer Grain. 1910.
The Outcry. 1911.
The Ivory Tower, edited by Percy Lubbock. 1917.
The Sense of the Past, edited by Percy Lubbock. 1917.
Gabrielle de Bergerac, edited by Albert Mordell. 1918.

Plays

Daisy Miller, from his own story. 1883.
The American, from his own novel (produced 1891). 1891.
Guy Domville (produced 1895). 1894.
Theatricals (includes *Tenants, Disengaged*) (produced 1909). 1894.
Theatricals: Second Series (includes *The Album, The Reprobate*) (produced 1919). 1894.
The High Bid (produced 1908). In *Complete Plays,* 1949.
The Saloon (produced 1911). In *Complete Plays,* 1949.
The Outcry (produced 1917). In *Complete Plays,* 1949.

Other

Transatlantic Sketches. 1875; revised edition, as *Foreign Parts,* 1883.
French Poets and Novelists. 1878; revised edition, 1883; edited by Leon Edel, 1964.
Hawthorne. 1879; edited by William M. Sale, Jr., 1956.
Portraits of Places. 1883.
Notes on a Collection of Drawings by George du Maurier. 1884.
A Little Tour in France. 1884; revised edition, 1900.
The Art of Fiction, with Walter Besant. 1885 (?); edited by Leon Edel, in *The House of Fiction,* 1957.
Partial Portraits. 1888.
Picture and Text. 1893.
Essays in London and Elsewhere. 1893.
William Wetmore Story and His Friends. 2 vols., 1903.
The Question of Our Speech, The Lesson of Balzac: Two Lectures. 1905.
English Hours. 1905; edited by Alma Louise Lowe, 1960.
The American Scene. 1907; edited by Leon Edel, 1968.
View and Reviews. 1908.
Italian Hours. 1909.
The Henry James Year Book, edited by Evelyn Garnaut Smalley. 1911.
A Small Boy and Others. 1913.
Notes of a Son and Brother. 1914.

The Middle Years, edited by Percy Lubbock. 1917.
Notes on Novelists and Some Other Notes. 1914.
Letters to an Editor. 1916.
Within the Rim and Other Essays 1914-1915. 1919.
Letters, edited by Percy Lubbock. 2 vols., 1920.
Notes and Reviews. 1921.
A Most Unholy Trade, Being Letters on the Drama. 1923.
Three Letters to Joseph Conrad, edited by Gerard Jean-Aubry. 1926.
Letters to Walter Berry. 1928.
Letters to A. C. Benson and Auguste Monod, edited by E. F. Benson. 1930.
Theatre and Friendship: Some James Letters, edited by Elizabeth Robins. 1932.
The Art of the Novel: Critical Prefaces, edited by R. P. Blackmur. 1934.
Notebooks, edited by F. O. Matthiessen and Kenneth B. Murdock. 1947.
The Art of Fiction and Other Essays, edited by Morris Roberts. 1948.
James and Robert Louis Stevenson: A Record of Friendship and Criticism, edited by Janet Adam Smith. 1948.
The Scenic Art: Notes on Acting and the Drama 1872-1901, edited by Allan Wade. 1948.
Daumier, Caricaturist. 1954.
The American Essays, edited by Leon Edel. 1956.
Autobiography, edited by F.W. Dupee. 1956.
The Future of the Novel: Essays on the Art of the Novel, edited by Leon Edel. 1956; as *The House of Fiction,* 1957.
The Painter's Eye: Notes and Essays on the Pictorial Arts, edited by John L. Sweeney. 1956.
Parisian Sketches: Letters to the New York Tribune 1875-1876, edited by Leon Edel and Ilse Dusoir Lind. 1957.
Literary Reviews and Essays on American, English, and French Literature, edited by Albert Mordell. 1957.
James and H.G. Wells: A Record of Their Friendship, Their Debate on the Art of Fiction, and Their Quarrel, edited by Leon Edel and Gordon N. Ray. 1958.
The Art of Travel: Scenes and Journeys in America, England, France, and Italy, edited by Morton Dauwen Zabel. 1958.
French Writers and American Women: Essays, edited by Peter Buitenhuis. 1960.
Selected Literary Criticism, edited by Morris Shapira. 1963.
James and John Hay: The Record of a Friendship, edited by George Monteiro. 1965.
Switzerland in the Life and Work of James: The Clare Benedict Collection of Letters from James, edited by Jörg Hasler. 1966.
The Art of Criticism: James on the Theory and Practice of Fiction, edited by William Veeder and Susan M. Griffin. 1986.
The Complete Notebooks, edited by Leon Edel and Lyall H. Powers. 1986.
Letters, edited by Leon Edel. 4 vols., 1974-84; *Selected Letters,* 1987.
The Critical Muse: Selected Literary Criticism, edited by Roger Gard. 1987.
Selected Letters to Edmund Gosse 1882-1915: A Literary Friendship, edited by Rayburn S. Moore. 1988.
Letters 1900-1915, with Edith Wharton, edited by Lyall H. Powers. 1990.
Pardon My Delay: Letters from Henry James to Bruce Richmond. 1994.

Henry James: Essays on Art and Drama. 1996.
Letters, Fictions, Lives: Henry James and William Dean Howells. 1997.
William and Henry James: Selected Letters. 1997.

Translator, *Port Tarascon,* by Alphonse Daudet. 1891.

*

Bibliography: *A Bibliography of James* by Leon Edel and Dan H. Laurence, 1957, revised edition, 1961, 1982; *James: A Bibliography of Secondary Works* by Beatrice Ricks, 1975; *James 1917-1959: A Reference Guide* by Kristin Pruitt McColgan, 1979; *James 1960-1974: A Reference Guide* by Dorothy M. Scura, 1979; *James 1866-1916: A Reference Guide* by Linda J. Taylor, 1982; *James: A Bibliography of Criticism 1975-1981* by John Budd, 1983; *An Annotated Critical Bibliography of James* by Nicola Bradbury, 1987; *James 1975-1987: A Reference Guide* by Judith E. Funston, 1991.

Critical Studies: *James* by Rebecca West, 1916; *James: The Major Phase,* 1944, and *The James Family,* 1947, both by F.O. Matthiessen; *The Great Tradition: George Eliot, James, Joseph Conrad* by F.R. Leavis, 1948; *James* (biography) by Leon Edel, 5 vols., 1953-72, revised edition, 2 vols., 1978; *The American James* by Quentin Anderson, 1957; *The Comic Sense of James: A Study of the Early Novels* by Richard Poirier, 1960; *The Novels of James* by Oscar Cargill, 1961; *The Imagination of Disaster: Evil in the Fiction of James,* 1961, and *Search for Form: Studies in the Structure of James's Fiction,* 1967, both by J.A. Ward; *The Ordeal of Consciousness in James* by Dorothea Krook, 1962; *James and the Jacobites* by Maxwell Geismar, 1963, as *James and His Cult,* 1964; *The Expense of Vision: Essays on the Craft of James* by Laurence B. Holland, 1964; *The Caught Image: Figurative Language in the Fiction of James,* 1964, *Plots and Characters in the Fiction of James,* 1965, and *A James Encyclopedia,* 1989, all by Robert L. Gale; *Technique in the Tales of James* by K.B. Vaid, 1964; *The Imagination of Loving: James's Legacy to the Novel* by Naomi Lebowitz, 1965; *The Ironic Dimension in the Fiction of James* by John A. Clair, 1965; *An Anatomy of The Turn of the Screw* by Thomas Mabry Cranfill and Robert Lanier Clark, Jr., 1965; *James* by Bruce McElderry, 1965; *James: A Reader's Guide,* 1966, as *A Reader's Guide to James,* 1966, and *A Preface to James,* 1986, both by S. Gorley Putt; *James and the Children: A Consideration of James's The Turn of the Screw* by Eli Siegel, edited by Martha Baird, 1968; *James: The Critical Heritage* edited by Roger Gard, 1968; *James,* 1968, and *James: The Writer and His Work,* 1985, both by Tony Tanner; *The Negative Imagination: Form and Perspective in the Novels of James* by Sallie Sears, 1969; *The Early Tales of James* by James Kraft, 1969; *The Fictional Characters of James* by Muriel G. Shine, 1969; *James and the Visual Arts* by Viola Hopkins Winner, 1970; *The Grasping Imagination: The American Writings of James* by Peter Buitenhuis, 1970; *James and the Naturalist Movement* by Lyall H. Powers, 1971; *The Ambiguity of James* by Charles Thomas Samuels, 1971; *James and the Occult* by Martha Banta, 1972, and *New Essays on The American* edited by Banta, 1987; *James and the French Novel* by Philip Grover, 1973; *Reading James* by Louis Auchincloss, 1975; *James: The Drama of Fulfilment: An Approach to the Novels* by Kenneth Graham, 1975; *James and the Comic Form* by Ronald Wallace, 1975; *James, The Lessons of the Master: Popular Fiction and Per-*

sonal Style in the Nineteenth Century by William Veeder, 1975; Communities of Honor and Love in James by Manfred Mackenzie, 1976; Language and Knowledge in the Late Novels of James by Ruth Bernard Yeazell, 1976; Who's Who in James by Glenda Leeming, 1976; Person, Place and Thing in James's Novels by Charles R. Anderson, 1977; The Crystal Cage: Adventures of the Imagination in the Fiction of James by Daniel J. Schneider, 1978; A Rhetoric of Literary Character: Some Women of James by Mary Doyle Springer, 1978; Eve and James: Portraits of Women and Girls in His Fiction, 1978, The Novels of James, 1983, and The Tales of James, 1984, all by Edward Wagenknecht; James and the Experimental Novel by Sergio Perosa, 1978; The Novels of James: A Study of Culture and Consciousness by Brian Lee, 1978; James: The Later Novels by Nicola Bradbury, 1979; Love and the Quest for Identity in the Fiction of James by Philip Sicker, 1980; Writing and Reading in James by Susanne Kappeler, 1980; Culture and Conduct in the Novels of James by Alwyn Berland, 1981; The Literary Criticism of James by Sarah B. Daugherty, 1981; James and the Structure of the Romantic Imagination by Daniel M. Fogel, 1981; James and Impressionism by James J. Kirschke, 1981; The Insecure World of James's Fiction: Intensity and Ambiguity by Ralf Norrman, 1982; The Drama of Discrimination in James by Susan Reibel Moore, 1982; The Expense of Vision: Essays on the Craft of James edited by Laurence B. Holland, 1982; James: The Early Novels by Robert Emmet Long, 1983; James and the Mass Market by Marcia Ann Jacobson, 1983; Studies in James by R.P. Blackmur, edited by Veronica A. Makowsky, 1983; The Phenomenology of James by Paul Armstrong, 1983; James: Interviews and Recollections edited by Norman Page, 1984; Imagination and Desire in the Novels of James by Carren Kaston, 1984; James the Critic by Vivien Jones, 1984; James and the Art of Power by Mark Seltzer, 1984; A Woman's Place in the Novels of James by Elizabeth Allen, 1984; The Ambassadors, 1984, and James, 1988, both by Alan W. Bellringer; James: Fiction as History, 1984, and James and the Past, 1990, both edited by Ian F.A. Bell; Women of Grace: James's Plays and the Comedy of Manners by Susan Carlson, 1985; The Theoretical Dimensions of James by John Carlos Rowe, 1985; James and the Darkest Abyss of Romance by William R. Goetz, 1986; The Museum World of James, 1986, and The Book World of James, 1987, both by Adeline R. Tintner; Friction with the Market: James and the Profession of Authorship by Michael Anesko, 1986; Desire and Repression: The Dialectic of Self and Other in the Late Works of James by Donna Przybylowicz, 1986; Critical Essays on James edited by James W. Gargano, 2 vols., 1987; James and the Evolution of Consciousness: A Study of The Ambassadors by Courtney Johnson, Jr., 1987; Order and Design: James's Titled Story Sequences by Richard P. Gage, 1988; A Ring of Conspirators: James and His Literary Circle 1895-1915 by Miranda Seymour, 1988; Desire and Love in James: A Study of the Late Novels by David McWhirter, 1989; Thinking in James by Sharon Cameron, 1989; James and the "Woman Business" by Alfred Habegger, 1989; James's Portrait of the Writer as Hero by Sara S. Chapman, 1990; New Essays on The Portrait of a Lady edited by Joel Porte, 1990; Professions of Taste: James, British Aestheticism, and Commodity Culture by Jonathan Freedman, 1990; The French Side of James by Edwin Fussell, 1990; James: A Study of the Short Fiction by Richard A. Hocks, 1991; James: The Imagination of Genius (biography) by Fred Kaplan, 1992; Henry James and Masculinity: The Man at the Margins by Kelly Cannon, 1994; Henry James and the Ghostly by T.J. Lustig, 1994; Suicide in Henry James's Fiction by Mary J. Joseph, 1994; Male Authors, Female

Subjects: The Women within/beyond the Borders of Henry Adams, Henry James, and Others by Duco van Oostrum, 1995; Reading Henry James in French Cultural Contexts by Pierre A. Walker, 1995; Henry James and the Art of Nonfiction by Tony Tanner, 1995; Henry James, Gertrude Stein, and the Biographical Act by Charles Caramello, 1996; Henry James's The Ambassadors: A Critical Study by Dorothea Krook-Gilead, 1996; Henry James in the Periodicals by Arthur Sherbo, 1997; Enacting History in Henry James: Narrative, Power, and Ethics, 1997; Henry James and the Culture of Publicity by Richard Salmon, 1997; Henry James's Last Romance: Making Sense of the Past and the American Scene by Beverly Haviland, 1997; Henry James and Homo-erotic Desire edited by John R. Bradley, 1998; Henry James's Legacy: The Afterlife of His Figure and Fiction by Adeline R. Tintner, 1998; Henry James and Sexuality by Hugh Stevens, 1998; The Cambridge Companion to Henry James, 1998; The Turn of the Mind: Constituting Consciousness in Henry James by Adré Marshall, 1998.

* * *

Few who accord the novels and short stories of Henry James the attention they deserve come away from the experience unmoved by the subject matter and unenlightened by the artistry, yet it is probably true that James would be little read in the late twentieth century if it were not for the continuing enthusiasm of individuals who discover him first as a reading assignment in a college or university course. More than almost any other great novelist, James is a writer whose best works require a sympathetic power of attention that the casual reader is not disposed to give. For most people James is an acquired taste. Unless they approach him in the right spirit they never acquire the taste at all. Yet he is certainly one of the great writers in English, one of those artists of another era who nevertheless seems perennially modern.

His dedication to literature for fifty years, from the Civil War until his death in 1916, produced a body of work of monumental scope. He never married, never carried on anything resembling a conventional courtship. His friendships were virtually all rooted in shared literary or artistic enthusiasms. He travelled—often, it seems, merely to reinvigorate himself for a new assault upon his artistic problems. With less talent and similar dedication he might have produced novels and tales that consisted mainly of the same stories retold, the same techniques exploited again and again in order to recapture prior successes. Something of this tendency resides in his work as it does in the work of all masters, but there is also an extraordinary continual development that reaches its peak in three late masterpieces: The Wings of the Dove, The Ambassadors, and The Golden Bowl. The late work of some poets can best be read largely in the light of the education gained by studying their earlier efforts: James is one of a relatively few novelists whose work cries out to be approached in a similar manner.

"It's a complex fate being an American," James once wrote, "and one of the responsibilities it entails is fighting against a superstitious valuation of Europe." Herein is expressed the essence of the "international theme" that runs through much of his work. In a time when more than a few novelists were making capital out of the social complications that arise when individuals from one side of the Atlantic confront the natives of the other side upon their home ground, James made this subject peculiarly his own by returning to it in work after work. So doing, he lifted it outside the confines of drawing room comedy and placed it squarely at the crossroads of the two great traditions of the nineteenth-century novel in English. Among the best of James's international novels and tales are *The American, The Europeans, Daisy Miller, The Portrait of a Lady, The Wings of the Dove, The Ambassadors,* and *The Golden Bowl.* In these works, the central concerns of previous novelists in English come together in a confrontation almost mythic in its implications. Simply expressed, the central concern of English novelists from Austen through Scott, Dickens, and Eliot was the accommodation of individual aspirations within the sheltering embrace of the social framework; both their social view and their art were shaped by a realistic vision of compromise. Just as simply expressed, the central concern of American novelists from **James Fenimore Cooper** through **Nathaniel Hawthorne, Herman Melville,** and **Mark Twain,** was with those individual aspirations that are incapable of accommodation within any social framework except the as-yet-unrealized American dream of perfect freedom, equality, and justice; their social view and their art were shaped by a vision that looked toward a world considerably more ideal than the world they lived in. James brought these visions together in an amalgamation inherently tragic. His best works express in metaphor how much the condition of modern man hangs continually in the balance between the European dream of social accommodation and the American dream of perfect freedom.

Closely related to the international theme is James's continual emphasis upon partial perspectives. Human knowledge, he insists, and consequently human action, is sharply limited by inescapable conditions of time and place. From Christopher Newman to Lambert Strether, his Americans achieve their destiny because the perspectives forced upon them by birth and education allow them no choices except the ones they inevitably make. From Madame de Cintre to Madame de Vionnet his Europeans are similarly limited. This at least is the theory: the novel is realistic, as James most often intended it should be, when the fates of the characters follow inevitably from the conditions that surround them; it is romantic, as James sometimes allowed, when the fates evolve from conditions imposed by the author that are quite distinct from the facts of observable reality. The realistic effect that he intended for most of his novels derives from the success with which he developed techniques for objectifying the partial perspectives from which humans direct their lives.

An important part of his work is also the theme of awareness that comes too late. His people are concerned above all with the question of how to live, but most of them have not any clear idea of how to begin. Sometimes they are wealthy, like Christopher Newman in *The American,* Millie Theale in *The Wings of the Dove,* and Maggie Verver in *The Golden Bowl.* Sometimes they become wealthy, like Isabel Archer in *The Portrait of a Lady.* Sometimes they live in expectation of wealth, like Kate Croy in *The Wings of the Dove.* In most instances they have at least, like Lambert Strether in *The Ambassadors,* enough to enable them to live comfortably, though it is often true of the less attractive figures that they suppose themselves in need of more than they possess. In any event, they are mostly free of the more mundane cares of life and have nearly total leisure in which to pursue happiness through courtship, marriage, liaisons, social activity, travel, the search for culture: whatever, in short, seems most attractive to them. To live most fully, James makes clear in a number of places, is to be most fully aware of one's possibilities so that one may make the best of them. Since, however, the most interesting possibilities come from human relationships that are inherently a tissue of subtle complexities, to be most fully aware is to possess a depth of sympathetic insight that comes to few people until it is too late to take advantage of it. Total freedom for James's characters involves the freedom to make social commitments different from those that all too often they make, wrongly, in bondage to some mistaken understanding, or do not make at all because, sadly, they fail to perceive the opportunity that lies before them.

A great critic, James is also a great technical experimenter. The best of his criticism is preserved in individual essays such as "The Art of Fiction" and in his *Notebooks* and the prefaces that he wrote for the New York edition of his works. All are read most profitably in conjunction with the example of his fiction. His technical experiments are most readily approached through those many fictions in which he enforces the theme of partial perspectives by contriving severely limited perspectives from which to narrate. Some of the easier works in which this theme and this method are important are the early *Daisy Miller* and the later "The Beast in the Jungle." Because Daisy is never seen except from the partial view that Winterbourne enjoys, the reader remains in danger of sharing Winterbourne's misunderstanding of her character. Because May Bartram, in "The Beast in the Jungle," is never seen except in a view accessible to Marcher, the same potential exists. Fundamentally simple in these works, both theme and technique become more complex in "The Aspern Papers," *The Turn of the Screw,* and *The Sacred Fount.* In all three the careful reader is aware that there may be some aspect of the truth that remains dark to the central vision of the narrator; in *The Turn of the Screw* there are good reasons to suppose both that the ghosts do and do not exist; in *The Sacred Fount* the puzzle that begins the novel becomes not less but more of a puzzle as it ends. In *The Portrait of a Lady, The Wings of the Dove, The Ambassadors,* and *The Golden Bowl,* the theme of partial perspectives (which involves often the theme of too late awareness) merges with the international theme to provide the substance of James's most lasting achievement.

Many of James's fictions conclude upon a sense of loss. In his deepest vision, human life is fundamentally tragic because of the eternal tension between the individual's sense of his vast human opportunities and his frequently inadequate awareness of his personal limitations. Like Isabel Archer or Lambert Strether, twentieth-century readers, too, are possessed by dreams of boundless freedom. Like both, they make in the end the choices that they can make—which are often not all the choices that they would make if they lived in a world in which a just and equal perfect freedom came less insistently into conflict with the requirements of social accommodation.

—George Perkins

See the essays on *The Ambassadors, The Portrait of a Lady,* and *The Turn of the Screw.*

JAMES, William

Born: New York City, 11 January 1842; brother of Henry James. **Education:** Europe, 1857-60; studied art with William Morris Hunt, Newport, Rhode Island, 1860-61; attended Lawrence Scientific School, 1861-63, and Harvard Medical School, M.D. 1869, both Cambridge, Massachusetts. **Family:** Married Alice Howe Gibbens in 1878; four sons and one daughter. **Career:** Member of the Thayer Expedition to Brazil (led by Louis Agassiz), 1865-66; traveled and studied in Germany, 1867-68; instructor in anatomy and physiology, 1873-76, assistant professor of physiology, 1876-80, assistant professor of psychology, 1880-85, and professor of physiology, 1885-1907, Harvard University. Gifford Lecturer, University of Edinburgh, 1901-02; Lowell Institute Lecturer, Boston, 1906; Hibbert Lecturer, Manchester College, Oxford, 1908. **Awards:** LL.D., Harvard University. **Died:** 26 August 1910.

PUBLICATIONS

Collections

Letters, edited by Henry James (William's son). 2 vols., 1920.
Selected Letters, edited by Elizabeth Hardwick. 1961.
Works, edited by Frederick H. Burkhardt, Fredson Bowers, and Ignas K. Skrupskelis. 1975—.
Writings, edited by John J. McDermott. 1977.
Selected Writings, edited by Robert Coles. 1997.

Prose

The Principles of Psychology. 2 vols., 1890; chapter *Habit* published separately, 1914.
Psychology (Briefer Course). 1892; as *Text-Book of Psychology,* 1892.
Is Life Worth Living? 1896.
The Will to Believe, and Other Essays in Popular Philosophy. 1897.
Human Immortality: Two Supposed Objections to the Doctrine. 1898.
Talks to Teachers on Psychology, and to Students on Some of Life's Ideals. 1899; selection, as *On Some of Life's Ideals,* 1912.
The Varieties of Religious Experience: A Study in Human Nature. 1902.
Pragmatism: A New Name for Some Old Ways of Thinking. 1907.
The Energies of Men. 1908.
The Meaning of Truth: A Sequel to "Pragmatism." 1909.
A Pluralistic Universe: Hibbert Lectures at Manchester College on the Present Situation in Philosophy. 1909.
Some Problems of Philosophy: A Beginning of an Introduction to Philosophy, edited by Henry James (William's son). 1911.
Memories and Studies, edited by Henry James (William's son). 1911.
Essays in Radical Empiricism, edited by Ralph Barton Perry. 1912.
Selected Papers on Philosophy, edited by C.M. Bakewell. 1917.
Collected Essays and Reviews, edited by Ralph Barton Perry. 1920.
The Philosophy of James. 1925.
As James Said: Extracts from the Published Writings, edited by Elizabeth Perkins Aldrich. 1942.
Essays on Faith and Morals, edited by Ralph Barton Perry. 1943.
James on Psychical Research, edited by Gardner Murphy. 1960.
Letters of James and Theodore Flournoy, edited by Robert C. LeClair. 1966.
The Moral Equivalent of War and Other Essays, and Selections from Some Problems of Philosophy, edited by John K. Roth. 1971.
The Moral Philosophy of James, edited by John K. Roth. 1971.
The Essential Writings, edited by Bruce W. Wilshire. 1971.

A James Reader, edited by Gay Wilson Allen. 1972.
Selected Unpublished Correspondence 1885-1910, edited by Frederick J. D. Scott. 1986.
The Correspondence of William James. 1998.

Editor, *The Literary Remains of the Late Henry James* (William's father). 1885.
Editor, *The Foundation of Ethics,* by John Edward Maude. 1887.

*

Bibliography: in *Writings* edited by John J. McDermott, 1977; *James: A Reference Guide* by Ignas K. Skrupskelis, 1977.

Critical Studies: *The Thought and Character of James* by Ralph Barton Perry, 2 vols., 1935; *The James Family* by F.O. Matthiessen, 1947; *The Thirteen Pragmatisms and Other Essays* by Arthur O. Lovejoy, 1963; *James* by Edward Carter Moore, 1965; *Introduction to James* by Andrew J. Reck, 1967; *James: A Biography,* 1967, and *James,* 1970, both by Gay Wilson Allen; *James* by Bernard P. Brennan, 1968; *Freedom and the Moral Life: The Ethics of James* by John K. Roth, 1969; *The Radical Empiricism of James* by John Wild, 1969; *Henry James and Pragmatistic Thought: A Study in the Relationship between the Philosophy of William James and the Literary Art of Henry James* by Richard A. Hocks, 1974; *Purpose and Thought: The Meaning of Pragmatism* by John E. Smith, 1978; *Chaos and Context: A Study in James* by Charlene H. Seigfried, 1978; *A Stroll with James* by Jacques Barzun, 1983; *Becoming James* by Howard M. Feinstein, 1984; *James: His Life and Thought* by Gerald E. Meyers, 1986; *The Trial of Curiosity: Henry James, William James, and the Challenge of Modernity* by Ross Posnock, 1991; *American Designs: The Late Novels of James and Faulkner* by Jeanne-Campbell Reesman, 1991; *Poetry and Pragmatism* by Richard Poirier, 1992; *Thinking across the American Grain: Ideology, Intellect, and the New Pragmatism* by Giles Gunn, 1992; *William James and the Affirmation of God* by George P. Graham, 1992; *William James and John Dewey* by Gordon Haddon Clark, 1995; *Manhood at Harvard: William James and Others* by Kim Townsend, 1996; *Democratic Temperament: The Legacy of William James* by Joshua Miller, 1997; *Genuine Reality: A Life of William James* by Linda Simon, 1998; *William James and the Metaphysics of Experience* by David C. Lamberth, 1999; *The Divided Self of William James* by Richard M. Gale, 1999.

*   *   *

It was once said that William James was not really a philosopher: his excursions into philosophy were more "in the nature of raids." This is something of an exaggeration. Nevertheless, those viewing James only from the vantage points of his pragmatism and radical empiricism, or who consider him meaningful only because he anticipated various philosophic courses, underestimate his contribution. James wrote mainly for the public mind and his skill in the presentation of ideas was consummate. His journals and letters are a charming insight into the life of a famous nineteenth-century family, and his witty, eloquent and heavily metaphorical style has much appeal even in the late twentieth century. His qualities and cast of mind are dateless. With James, the philosophic enterprise begins again. He attempted to provide a method of inquiry that would mediate between the evolutive procession of nature and the realization of uniquely human concerns. This attempt can best be seen in the contexts of nineteenth-century evolutionary theory, James's belief in an intelligible, continuous, but unfinished universe, and his personal confrontation with nihilism.

In 1869 and 1870 James underwent a personal crisis of despair that culminated in a rejection of suicide in favor of a possibly creative life unsupported by certitude. Reading Renouvier's second *Essais,* he saw no reason why that definition of free will, "the sustaining of a thought because I choose to when I might have other thoughts" need be the definition of an illusion. He writes in his diary of 30 April 1870: "My first act of free will shall be to believe in free will." This Promethean quality pervades his work. The dramatic and active role of belief is asserted in *The Will to Believe.* In the physical world a belief that a certain task is possible can contribute to its being achieved. In the spiritual or moral realm belief in potential goodness may help a person achieve it. To refuse belief until viewing all the evidence is irrational. Decisions, even in science, are the product of human selectivity, so, James suggests, we have a right to belief, when it accords with our "passional nature." This is particularly true of religious and moral beliefs as their worth lies not in their source, but in the effects they are capable of promoting.

James, however, was not a subjectivist. He did not deny humanity's inextricable bond with nature, but, in view of evolutionary theory, neither could he imbue nature with meaning, as did Emerson. In *Pragmatism,* which insists that the truth of an assertion be estimated solely by its bearing on practical human interests, he pronounces: "Woe to him whose beliefs play fast and loose with the order which realities follow in his experience; they will lead him nowhere . . . . " Belief was not to be perpetrated beyond its ability to generate supporting evidence, but was, rather, to provide a liberating dimension in life, while acknowledging that facts are both stubborn and irreducible. James was profoundly aware of the need to affirm a view of the world that would allow for such a doctrine. Throughout life he argued that the universe was open and pluralistic. It was neither a monastic whole, nor a number of independent parts. "There can be no difference anywhere," says James, "that doesn't make a difference elsewhere." The universe then is open to initiative from the human mind.

The Principles of Psychology was published in 1890 to great acclaim, and the chapter "Habit" remains a classic statement on that aspect of human life. "Habit is the enormous fly-wheel of society, its most precious conservative agent," James says with typical exuberance. He had rejected the idea of becoming a painter early in life, but his painter's sensitivity and eye for vivid portrayal remained with him. The work is a storehouse of human experience, and is James's endeavor to explain mind in terms of evolution. He took psychology out of metaphysics, and into science, creating a work that explored possibilities and indicated directions. **John Dewey** remarks that it forms a junction between the traditional methods of psychology: behaviorism and introspection. Behaviorism was foreshadowed by the James-Lange theory, which suggested that emotion was nothing but the subjective feelings engendered by body changes or action. We do not cry because we feel sorry, rather " . . . we feel sorry because we cry." On the other hand, consciousness could be known only through introspection. James discovered that no one "ever had a simple sensation by itself." His notion of a stream of consciousness continues to inspire new literary techniques. Further, consciousness behaved like an organism with interests. It would favor some interests over others. "The knower is an actor," James says.

The insights of James refuse to be localized. He provided initiatives for existentialism, phenomenism, and the operational philosophy of science. For the ordinary reader he provides a way of thinking that is creative and honest. His *Pragmatism* has become a part of popular consciousness. Philosophy, he once said, is the habit of always seeing an alternative. "My belief, to be sure, can't be optimistic—but I will posit life (the real, the good) in the self-governing resistance of the ego to the world. Life shall be built in doing and suffering and creating."

—Jan Pilditch

JARRELL, Randall

Born: Nashville, Tennessee, 6 May 1914. **Education:** Vanderbilt University, Nashville (editor, *Masquerader*), B.S. in psychology 1936 (Phi Beta Kappa), M.A. in English 1939. **Military Service:** Served as a celestial navigation tower operator in the U.S. Army Air Corps, 1942-46. **Family:** Married 1) Mackie Langham in 1940; 2) Mary Eloise von Schrader in 1952. **Career:** Instructor in English, Kenyon College, Gambier, Ohio, 1937-39, University of Texas, Austin, 1939-42, and Sarah Lawrence College, Bronxville, New York, 1946-47; associate professor, 1947-58, and professor of English, 1958-65, Woman's College of the University of North Carolina (later University of North Carolina at Greensboro). Lecturer, Salzburg Seminar in American Civilization, 1948; Visiting Fellow in Creative Writing, Princeton University, New Jersey, 1951-52; fellow, Indiana School of Letters, Bloomington, summer 1952; visiting professor of English, University of Illinois, Urbana, 1953; Elliston lecturer, University of Cincinnati, Ohio, 1958. Acting literary editor, *The Nation,* New York, 1946-47; poetry critic, *Partisan Review,* New Brunswick, New Jersey, 1949-53, and *Yale Review,* New Haven, Connecticut, 1955-57; member of the Editorial Board, *American Scholar,* Washington, D.C., 1957-65. Consultant in Poetry, Library of Congress, Washington, D.C., 1956-58. **Awards:** Guggenheim fellowship, 1946; American Academy grant, 1951; National Book award, 1961; University of North Carolina Gardner award, 1962; American Association of University Women award, 1964; Ingram Merrill award, 1965. D.H.L.: Bard College, Annandale-on-Hudson, New York, 1962. **Member:** American Academy. 1961; chancellor, Academy of American Poets, 1965. **Died:** 14 October 1965.

PUBLICATIONS

Collections

The Complete Poems. 1969.
The Achievement of Jarrell: A Comprehensive Selection of His Poems, edited by Frederick J. Hoffman. 1970.
Jarrell's Letters: An Autobiographical and Literary Selection, edited by Mary Jarrell. 1985.

Poetry

Five Young American Poets, with others. 1940.
Blood for a Stranger. 1942.
Little Friend, Little Friend. 1945.

Losses. 1948.
The Seven-League Crutches. 1951.
Selected Poems. 1955.
Uncollected Poems. 1958.
The Woman at the Washington Zoo: Poems and Translations.
  1960.
Selected Poems. 1964.
The Lost World: New Poems. 1965.
Jerome: The Biography of a Poem. 1971.

Play

The Three Sisters, adaptation of a play by Chekhov (produced
  1964). 1969.

Fiction

Pictures from an Institution: A Comedy. 1954.

Other (for children)

The Rabbit Catcher and Other Fairy Tales of Ludwig Bechstein.
  1962.
The Golden Bird and Other Fairy Tales by the Brothers Grimm.
  1962.
The Gingerbread Rabbit. 1964.
The Bat-Poet. 1964.
The Animal Family. 1965.
Snow-White and Other Fairy Tales from the Brothers Grimm. 1972.
The Juniper Tree and Other Tales from Grimm, with Lore Segal.
  1973.
Fly by Night. 1976.
A Bat is Born. 1978.
The Fisherman and His Wife. 1980.

Other

Poetry and the Age. 1953.
Poets, Critics, and Readers (address). 1959.
A Sad Heart at the Supermarket: Essays and Fables. 1962.
The Third Book of Criticism. 1969.
Kipling. Auden & Co.: Essays and Reviews 1935-1964. 1980.
No Other Book: Selected Essays. 1995.

Editor, *The Anchor Book of Stories.* 1958.
Editor, *The Best Short Stories of Rudyard Kipling.* 1961; as *In the
  Vernacular: The English in India and The English in England,*
  2 vols., 1963.
Editor, *Six Russian Short Novels.* 1963.

Translator, with Moses Hadas, *The Ghetto and the Jews of Rome,*
  by Ferdinand Gregorovius. 1948.
Translator, *Goethe's Faust, Part One.* 1976.

*

Bibliography: "Jarrell: A Bibliographical Checklist" by Robert
A. Wilson, in *American Book Collector,* May-June 1982; "Jarrell:
A Bibliography of Criticism 1941-1981" by Jeffrey Meyers, in
Bulletin of Bibliography, December 1982; *Jarrell: A Descriptive
Bibliography 1929-1983* by Stuart Wright, 1986.

Critical Studies: *Jarrell 1914-1965* edited by Robert Lowell,
Peter Taylor, and Robert Penn Warren, 1967; *Jarrell* by Karl
Shapiro, 1967; *Jarrell* by Suzanne Ferguson, 1971, and *Critical
Essays on Jarrell* edited by Ferguson, 1983; *Jarrell* by M.L.
Rosenthal, 1972; *Jarrell* by Bernetta Quinn, 1981; *Worlds and
Lives: The Poetry of Jarrell* by Charlotte H. Beck, 1983; *Jarrell's
Children's Books* by Jerry Griswold, 1984; *Randall Jarrell and
Lost World of Childhood* by Richard Flynn, 1990; *A Different
Poem: Rainer Maria Rilke's American Translators Randall Jarrell,
Robert Lowell, and Robert Bly* by Hartmut Heep, 1996.

*   *   *

Shortly after his death the elegant, brilliant, and quixotic Randall
Jarrell was eulogized by **Karl Shapiro** as the greatest poet-critic
since **T.S. Eliot.** At a memorial service at Yale, such men as **Robert Lowell, Robert Penn Warren,** and **Richard Eberhart** came
to honor their dead friend as a master among men of their craft.
Lowell called him "the most heartbreaking English poet of his generation." Celebrated as well was Jarrell's literary criticism, for in
work like *Poetry and the Age,* he had altered dominant critical trends
and tastes. He had brought **Walt Whitman** into prominence, and
he had brought into focus **Robert Frost, Wallace Stevens, William Carlos Williams,** and **Marianne Moore,** among others; he
had attacked the New Critics, and he had affirmed the relevance
of art to life. Not unlike **Ezra Pound,** Jarrell was one of those
truly committed critics who, although a poet himself, had helped
the writers around him to define twentieth-century art.

As Walter Rideout in his essay in *Poets in Progress* (edited by
Edward Hungerford, 1962) noted, when Jarrell published his *Selected Poems* in 1955, he grouped them in such a way as to obscure the rather marked delineations in central subject matter that
had distinguished volume after volume. The style of his first book
Blood for a Stranger, however, is noticeably derivative, and shows
the influence of **Allen Tate, John Crowe Ransom,** and particularly **W. H. Auden** in its experiments with villanelles, sestinas,
and unusual rhyming patterns, as well as in its intellectual brilliance and metaphysical questionings. The volume cries out against
a world politically heaving itself toward catastrophe. Jarrell's tone
is one of existential loneliness and despair.

Little Friend, Little Friend and *Losses* are less formal; Jarrell
establishes a more direct and characteristic tone; the poet seems,
in fact, personally more attracted to death. Jarrell's ambiguous view
of humanity, man as murderer and victim, innocent and guilty, ultimately like the child facing the "capricious infinite" parental
power, found its perfect expression in these war poems. But
Jarrell's war poems treat the human condition, their central image,
man as soldier/prisoner. Jarrell dramatizes man's guilt and suffering upon a stage of worldwide struggle. *Losses* treats all sorts of
prisoners—children, black Americans, displaced persons at Haifa,
Jews in concentration camps—and focuses upon how each is a victim within "the necessities that governed every act." Even the enemy
contains the child, who, when called upon to commit a terrible act of
violence, is himself an innocent. Using the perspective of the child,
Jarrell makes the outcome of war the product of innocence:

> The other murderers troop in yawning;
> Three of them play Pitch, one sleeps, and one
> Lies counting missions, lies there sweating
> Till even his heart beats: One; One; One.
> O *murderers!* . . . Still, this is how it's done.

Reality is defined as nightmare, "experience" before and after life as the dream. In "The Death of the Ball Turret Gunner," he writes: "From my mother's sleep I fell into the State/. . . I woke to black flak and the nightmare fighters." Jarrell supports no conventional political position, no "program for chance." Instead, the man-child is "a ticket / Someone bought and lost on, a stray animal/. . . Bewildered . . . /What have you understood, to die?" His compassion extends even to the enemy; the powerful also suffer: "Who will teach the Makers how to die?" he writes.

Jarrell's great and fertile period concluded with *The Seven League Crutches.* The early works focused upon lost childhood and innocence, the terrible shock of awareness of adult hypocrisy and social disintegration. Jarrell now moved away from more public concerns to private life; his poems are more relaxed. Although the theme of illness remains in the poems about children, his work is more psychological, more dream-filled. One senses now, in addition, "a way out," in the face of "Necessity": "Man you must learn to live / though you want nothing but to die." Stoical, compassionate, and even at times capable of a bittersweet humor, some of Jarrell's most mature work now appeared. Man may perhaps even transcend Necessity through the imaginative life, the creation and perception of art.

After this, Jarrell turned to the fairy tale, becoming preoccupied with children's stories and German Romanticism. The fairy tale offered him the innocent's victory over the potent and evil forces of the universe. In "The Marchen" (Grimm's Tales), he wrote, for example:

> We felled our islands there, at last, with iron.
> The sunlight fell to them, according to our wish,
> And we believed, till nightfall, in that wish;
> And we believed, till nightfall, in our lives.

The title poem of *The Woman at the Washington Zoo,* a return to Jarrell's more formal style of the 1940s, crystallizes the poet's concern with aging and loneliness. The woman cries out for relief, for transformation again, from her empty life: "the world goes by my cage and never sees me." She cries: "You know what I was, / You see what I am: change me, change me!"

In *The Lost World,* published after a nervous breakdown, many of his recurrent themes appear: loneliness, lovelessness, age, lost youth, the world's hypocrisy, and, as Lowell put it, childhood, "above all childhood!" *The Lost World* fails to exhibit the brilliance, power, elegance, and diversity that characterize his earlier work. More importantly, there is about it too much of a confessional quality; the poems are awkward and read like revelations on the analyst's couch. The speaker appears filled with a sense of guilt and helplessness. He tries to forgive, especially, his parents, but he is unsuccessful. In "The Piano Player," for example, he confesses: "I go over, hold my hands out, play I play— / If only, somehow, I had learned to live!" His childhood football hero, Daddy Lipscomb, admits: "I've been scared / Most of my life. You wouldn't think so to look at me./ It gets so bad I cry myself to sleep." Many of these poems contain a female persona, a woman sometimes unfaithful to her lover, often cruel to people and animals to the point of murder, but, most frequently, unmitigatingly unkind to her child. Although one senses Jarrell's attempt to understand and forgive these people, the poet remains in despair: "I identify myself, as always / With something that there's something wrong with."

One feels a debt toward Jarrell for his enormous encouragement and advice to the poets of his time. But one must also regard him as an important poet with a brilliant intelligence, elegance, and humor. Jarrell's uniqueness remains in his special combination of sophistication with undiminished yearnings for childhood; that bittersweet faith that through art, or dreams, or fairy tales, one could regain childhood innocence and joy and negate the inevitable processes of aging, isolation, and death.

—Lois Gordon

JEFFERS, (John) Robinson

Born: Pittsburgh, Pennsylvania, 10 January 1887. **Education:** Tutored by his father; private schools in Switzerland and Germany; University of Western Pennsylvania (now University of Pittsburgh), 1902-03; Occidental College, Los Angeles (editor, *Aurora*), 1903-05, B.A. 1905; University of Southern California, Los Angeles, 1905-06, 1907-10, M.A.; University of Zurich, 1906-07; studied forestry at University of Washington, Seattle, 1910-11. **Family:** Married Una Call Kuster in 1913 (died 1950); one daughter and twin sons. **Career:** Lived near Carmel, California, from 1914. **Awards:** Academy of American Poets fellowship, 1958; Shelley Memorial award, 1961. D.H.L.: Occidental College, 1937; University of Southern California, 1939. **Member:** American Academy; chancellor, Academy of American Poets, 1945-56. **Died:** 20 January 1962.

PUBLICATIONS

Collections

Selected Poems. 1965.
Selected Letters 1897-1962, edited by Ann N. Ridgeway. 1968.

Poetry

Flagons and Apples. 1912.
Californians. 1916.
Tamar and Other Poems. 1924.
Roan Stallion, Tamar, and Other Poems. 1925.
The Women at Point Sur. 1927.
Poems. 1928.
An Artist. 1928.
Cawdor and Other Poems. 1928.
Dear Judas and Other Poems. 1929.
Stars. 1930.
Apology for Bad Dreams. 1930.
Descent to the Dead: Poems Written in Ireland and Great Britain. 1931.
Thurso's Landing and Other Poems. 1932.
Give Your Heart to the Hawks and Other Poems. 1933.
Return. 1934.
Solstice and Other Poems. 1935.
The Beaks of Eagles. 1936.
Such Counsels You Gave to Me and Other Poems. 1937.
The Selected Poetry. 1938.
Two Consolations. 1940.

Be Angry at the Sun. 1941.
The Double Axe and Other Poems. 1948.
Hungerfield and Other Poems. 1954.
The Loving Shepherdess. 1956.
The Beginning and the End and Other Poems. 1963.
The Alpine Christ and Other Poems, edited by William Everson. 1973.
Brides of the South Wind: Poems 1917-1922, edited by William Everson. 1974.
Granite and Cypress, edited by William Everson. 1975.
The Women at Point Sur and Other Poems. 1977.
The Double Axe and Other Poems, edited by William Everson. 1977.
What Odd Expedients and Other Poems, edited by Robert Ian Scott. 1981.

Plays

Medea, from a play by Euripides (produced 1947). 1946.
The Cretan Women, from a play by Euripides (produced 1954?). In *From the Modern Repertoire 3,* edited by Eric Bentley, 1956.

Other

Poetry, Gongorism, and a Thousand Years. 1949.
Themes in My Poems. 1956.
Tragedy Has Obligations. 1973.
Meditation on Saviors. 1994.
RJ on RJ: Robinson Jeffers and The Subtle Passion. 1996.

*

Bibliography: *A Bibliography of the Works of Jeffers* by S.S. Alberts, 1933; *The Critical Reception of Jeffers: A Bibliographical Study* by Alex A. Vardamis, 1972.

Critical Studies: *Jeffers: The Man and His Works* by Lawrence Clark Powell, 1940; *The Loyalties of Jeffers* by Radcliffe Squires, 1956; *Jeffers* by Frederic I. Carpenter, 1962; *The Stone Mason of Tor House: The Life and Work of Jeffers* by Melba B. Bennett, 1966; *Jeffers: Fragments of an Older Fury* by Brother Antoninus (William Everson), 1968; *Jeffers, Poet of Inhumanism* by Arthur B. Coffin, 1971; *Jeffers: Myth, Ritual, and Symbol in His Narrative Poems,* 1973, revised edition, 1976, and *Jeffers,* 1975, both by Robert J. Brophy; *In This Wild Water: The Suppressed Poems of Jeffers* by James Shebl, 1976; *Shining Clarity: God and Man in the Works of Jeffers* by Marlan Beilke, 1977; *Rock and Hawk: Jeffers and the Romantic Agony* by William H. Nolte, 1978; *The Cliffs of Solitude: A Reading of Jeffers* by Robert Zaller, 1983; *Critical Essays on Robinson Jeffers* edited by James Karman, 1990; *Centennial Essays for Robinson Jeffers* edited by Robert Zaller, 1991; *The Collected Poetry of Robinson Jeffers, 1939-1962: Volume III* edited by Tim Hunt, 1991; *Robinson Jeffers, Dimensions of a Poet* edited by Robert J. Brophy, 1995; *Robinson Jeffers and the Sources of His Muse* by Jean O'Brien, 1996; *Jeffers Country Revisited: Beauty without Price* by Richard Kohlman Hughey, 1996.

* * *

In 1925 *Roan Stallion, Tamar, and Other Poems* established Robinson Jeffers as one of the major poets of his generation. But beginning in 1927 with *The Women at Point Sur* his repeated use of forbidden themes alienated many readers, and in 1941 his opposition to American participation in World War II all but destroyed his reputation. Since his death in 1962 a better perspective has been achieved, and he became recognized as one of the most powerful—if also most controversial—of the modern poets.

Most of his volumes include one or more long narrative poems, together with many shorter lyrics. And these longer poems all deal, either implicitly or explicitly, with the materials of myth. His *Medea,* for instance, is a free adaptation of the play of Euripides, but *Solstice* attempts to domesticate the violent Greek myth in a realistic California setting. His most successful narrative poems, such as "Roan Stallion"—that describes a woman's passionate adoration of a horse—use mythical materials most unobtrusively. But the aura of myth and the forbidden passions that the old myths described, such as incest, parricide, and the love of man for beast, all trouble the narrative poetry of Jeffers.

Besides these myths, his poetry gives vivid expression to an extraordinary sense of place. The wild coast of the country south of Carmel, where he lived all his creative life, provides both actual setting and the conviction of immediate reality for all his poems, both narrative and lyric. But most significant of all is the symbolic nature of this actual country. Here is "Continent's End," both in fact and in idea, "the long migrations' end," where human civilization now faces "the final Pacific" and looks westward toward its first beginnings in "mother Asia."

In his poetry, this realistic sense of place combines with a consciousness of the symbolic significance of this place and a remembrance of the prehistoric origins of civilization suggested by the ancient myths. At its best this poetry realizes a vision of human history unique in its temporal scope and its imaginative power. It is small wonder if it sometimes fails to unify these disparate elements and to realize this all-inclusive vision.

The volume that first established Jeffers's reputation probably remains his best, and the three narrative poems that it includes illustrate the various combinations of narrative realism with mythical symbolism that his later poetry developed. "Roan Stallion" is the most completely realistic, and perhaps for this reason has remained the favorite of traditional minded readers. "Tamar" is most extreme, both in plot and in technique, although the strange story of incest plays itself out in a California setting. "The Tower Beyond Tragedy" retells the story of the Oresteia in its original Greek setting, but with modern characterization.

The heroine of "Roan Stallion" is named "California," and both name and plot recall the Greek myth of Europa. But the god-like stallion remains simply an animal, and the woman's adoration for him remains psychological. Meanwhile the mythical dimensions of the naturalistic story are emphasized by poetic suggestion:

> The fire threw up figures
> And symbols meanwhile, racial myths formed and
> dissolved in it, the phantom rulers of humanity
> That without being are yet more real than what
> they are born of, and without shape, shape that
> which makes them.

"Tamar" is a very different poem, perhaps unique in literature. Its incestuous heroine rejects all the inhibitions of civilization, but her seemingly realistic actions are motivated by passages of dream, vision, and racial memory until the modern story seems to reenact the earliest creation myths of the incestuous union of Coelus and Terra, of gods and men. The heroine's absolute rejection of morality is paralleled only by that of the later *The Women at Point Sur*. But here the repeated use of dream and vision transforms the realistic story into the realm of timeless myth.

"The Tower Beyond Tragedy" narrates the plot of the Oresteia in realistic terms, but focuses on the character of Cassandra and her predictions of doom. Midway through the poem these enlarge into an all-embracing prophecy of the ultimate destruction of future empires, ending with "a mightier to be cursed and a higher for malediction," America. The poem concludes with the refusal of Orestes to inherit Mycenae, or imperial power, and an eloquent poetic statement of his philosophy of total detachment in a "tower beyond tragedy."

This denunciation of imperial power and this celebration of human detachment is also the theme of many of Jeffers's best shorter poems, such as "Shine, Perishing Republic" and "Continent's End." Other lyrics celebrate simply the beauty of nature, such as "Night" and "Boats in a Fog." Perhaps the best of his short poems is "To the Stone Cutters," which treats the ancient theme of mutability.

After the *Roan Stallion* volume, *The Women at Point Sur* narrated a story of the total rejection of traditional morality by a renegade Christian minister. But this longest of Jeffers's poems was also most realistic, so that the mythical and instinctual incest of "Tamar" became calculated and explicit. Actually, the poem recalls the story of Euripides's *Bacchae*, which Jeffers also used in his short poem "The Humanist's Tragedy," but the longer poem abandoned all reference to myth and symbol. Although most contemporary readers rejected it, Jeffers's chief modern disciple, William Everson (Brother Antoninus), has praised it highly in *Jeffers: Fragments of an Older Fury*.

In *Dear Judas* Jeffers retold the gospel story with new characterization, as he had retold the Oresteia in "The Tower Beyond Tragedy." The striking originality of his conception and the soaring poetry with which he clothed it make the poem memorable. But his rejection of Christian orthodoxy seemed blasphemous to many readers. "The Loving Shepherdess", a companion narrative poem, created a character of such beauty that her story seems unique among Jeffers's dark tragedies.

In the 1930s Jeffers turned to a series of more realistic long poems with contemporary California settings and without mythical overtones. "Cawdor," "Thurso's Landing," and "Give Your Heart to the Hawks" all take place in "Jeffers Country" south of Carmel, and all develop their tragic stories effectively. Only some names and passages of poetic commentary suggest larger themes. Near the end of "Thurso's Landing" the poet comments:

> The platform is like a rough plank theatre-stage
> Built on the brow of the promontory: as if our blood had
> labored all around the earth from Asia
> To play its mystery before strict judges at last, the final
> ocean and sky, to prove our nature
> More shining than that of the other animals. It is rather
> ignoble in its quiet times, mean in its pleasures,
> Slavish in the mass; but at stricken moments it can shine
> terribly against the dark magnificence of things.

After 1935 Jeffers published new volumes every few years, but only a few of the narrative poems achieved excellence. "At the Birth of an Age" develops incidents from the Niblung Saga, but the poetry overshadows the story, and the mythical and philo-

sophic elements that it illustrates find powerful expression. The second narrative poem in *The Double Axe*, "The Inhumanist," creates a hermit-hero who gives expression to Jeffers's philosophy both in speech and in action. Finally, "Hungerfield" creates a brief modern myth recalling that of Herakles.

Many readers prefer Jeffers's shorter poems to his long narratives. His "Apology for Bad Dreams" offers both illustration and explanation of the violent imagery and pessimistic philosophy that characterize all his poetry. A later poem, "The Bloody Sire," gives perfect expression to this philosophy of violence, ending: "Who would remember Helen's face/ Lacking the terrible halo of spears?"

Much of the difficulty of his poetry stems from his insistence upon the philosophy of "Inhumanism," which he attempted to define in his later writing. His opposition both to human self-importance and to the classical tradition of humanism emphasized instead the modern search for objective truth. In contrast to T. S. Eliot's traditional classicism, Jeffers celebrated the values of science and discovery.

—Frederic I. Carpenter

JEFFERSON, Thomas

Born: Shadwell, Goochland (now Albemarle) County, Virginia, 13 April 1743. **Education:** Educated by tutors at his uncle's estate, Tuckahoe, 1748-51; at William Douglas's Latin School, 1752-57; James Maury's School, 1758-59; College of William and Mary, Williamsburg, Virginia, 1760-62, graduated 1762; studied law with George Wythe, 1762-67: admitted to bar, 1767, and practiced law until 1774. **Military Service:** Served as commander of the Albemarle militia, 1775. **Family:** Married Martha Wayles Skelton in 1772 (died 1782); five daughters and one son. **Career:** Member, Virginia House of Burgesses, 1769-75: held strongly anti-British views; lieutenant, 1770, and surveyor, 1773, Albemarle County; delegate, Second Continental Congress, 1775-76; member of the drafting committee, principal author, and signatory, Declaration of Independence, 1776; member, Virginia House of Delegates, 1776-79, 1782: wrote preamble to Virginia's Constitution and drew up a statute establishing religious freedom (which became model for the First Amendment of the U.S. Constitution); governor of Virginia, 1779-81, re-elected 1781, but resigned when British forces captured Richmond and raided his home, Monticello, near Charlottesville; appointed to peace commission to Europe, 1782 (commission withdrawn); delegate, 1783, and chairman, 1784, Continental Congress; foreign minister to negotiate commercial treaties, 1784-87 (successful treaty with Prussia, 1785; unsuccessful negotiations with Britain, 1786, and Morocco, 1787); minister to France, 1785-89: negotiated consular convention, 1788; first U.S. secretary of state in administration of George Washington, New York, 1790, and Philadelphia, 1791-93: considerable policy differences with Secretary of the Treasury Alexander Hamilton led to formation of Republican (Jefferson) and Federalist (Hamilton) parties; lived at Monticello, 1794-96; U.S. vice president in Federalist administration of John Adams, Philadelphia, 1797-1800: main duty was to preside over Senate; U.S. president, Washington, D.C., 1801-09 (initially tied in election with Aaron Burr, who became his first administration vice president; reelected 1805, with George Clinton as vice president); during presidency: Louisiana Purchase, 1803, Lewis and Clark expedition, 1804-05, treaty with

Tripoli and Morocco over Barbary pirates, 1805, trial of Aaron Burr, 1807, embargo against Britain, 1807-09; lived at Monticello, 1809-26 (began work on the estate, 1768). Trustee, Albemarle Academy, from 1814; member of the Board of Visitors, Central College, Charlottesville, 1817 (chartered as University of Virginia, 1819; opened, 1825); rector, University of Virginia, 1819-26: designed and supervised construction of many campus buildings. President, American Philosophical Society, 1797-1815; associate, Institute of France, 1801. **Died:** 4 July 1826.

PUBLICATIONS

Collections

Writings, edited by Paul Leicester Ford. 10 vols., 1892-99.
Papers, edited by Julian P. Boyd. 1950—The Portable Jefferson, edited by Merrill D. Peterson. 1975.
Writings (Library of America), edited by Merrill D. Peterson. 1984.
The Essential Thomas Jefferson. 1994.

Prose

A Summary View of the Rights of British America. 1774.
The Declaration of Independence, with others. 1776.
Notes on the State of Virginia. 1785.
An Act for Establishing Religious Freedom. 1786.
An Appendix to the Notes on Virginia Relative to the Murder of Logan's Family. 1800.
A Manual of Parliamentary Practice for Use in the Senate of the United States. 1801.
Early History of the University of Virginia, as Contained in the Letters of Jefferson and Joseph C. Cabell, edited by Nathaniel Francis Cabell. 1856.
The Life and Morals of Jesus of Nazareth (The Jefferson Bible). 1902; complete edition, 1904; edited by Henry Wilder Foote, 1951.
The Complete Anas, edited by Franklin B. Sawvel. 1903.
Germantown Letters, edited by Charles Francis Jenkins. 1906.
The Confidential Letters to William Wirt. 1912.
Autobiography, edited by Paul Leicester Ford. 1914.
Correspondence, Printed from the Originals in the Collections of William K. Bixby, edited by Worthington Chauncey Ford. 1916.
The Best Letters, edited by Joseph G. de Roulhac Hamilton. 1926.
The Commonplace Book of Jefferson: A Repertory of His Ideas on Government, edited by Gilbert Chinard. 1928.
The Literary Bible of Jefferson: His Commonplace Book of Philosophers and Poets, edited by Gilbert Chinard. 1928.
Jeffersonian Principles, edited by James Truslow Adams. 1928.
The Letters of Lafayette and Jefferson, edited by Gilbert Chinard. 1929.
Jefferson and Education in a Republic, edited by Charles Flinn Arrowood. 1930.
Correspondence Between Jefferson and Pierre Samuel du Pont de Nemours 1798-1817, edited by Dumas Malone. 1930.
The *Correspondence of Jefferson and du Pont de Nemours,* edited by Gilbert Chinard. 1931; revised edition, 1970.
Alexander Hamilton and Jefferson: Representative Selections, edited by Frederick C. Prescott. 1934.

Democracy, edited by Saul K. Padover. 1939; as *Jefferson on Democracy,* 1954.
The Living Thoughts of Jefferson, edited by John Dewey. 1940.
The Wisdom of Jefferson, edited by Edward Boykin. 1941.
Jefferson Himself: The Personal Narrative, edited by Bernard Mayo. 1942.
Jefferson and His Unknown Brother Randolph: Twenty-Eight Letters 1807 to 1815, edited by Bernard Mayo. 1942.
The Complete Jefferson, edited by Saul K. Padover. 1943.
Jefferson's Garden Book 1766-1824, with Relevant Extracts from *His Other Writings,* edited by Edwin Morris Betts. 1944.
The Life and Selected Writings of Jefferson, edited by Adrienne Koch and William Peden. 1944.
Basic Writings, edited by Philip S. Foner. 1944.
Correspondence of Jefferson and Francis Walker Gilmer 1814-1826, edited by Richard Beale Davis. 1946.
Jefferson's Ideas on a University Library: Letters from the Founder of the University of Virginia to a Boston Bookseller, edited by Elizabeth Cometti. 1950.
Farm Book, edited by Edwin Morris Betts. 1953.
The Political Writings: Representative Selections, edited by Edward Dumbauld. 1955.
A Jefferson Profile as Revealed in His Letters, edited by Saul K. Padover. 1956.
The Adams-Jefferson Letters: The Complete Correspondence Between Jefferson and Abigail and John Adams, edited by Lester J. Cappon. 2 vols., 1959.
The Jefferson-Dunglison Letters, edited by John M. Dorsey. 1960.
Architectural Drawings, edited by Frederick Doveton Nichols. 1960; revised edition, 1961.
Crusade Against Ignorance: Jefferson on Education, edited by Gordon C. Lee. 1961.
The Essential Jefferson, edited by Albert Fried. 1963.
To the Girls and Boys (letters), edited by Edward Boykin. 1964.
Jefferson and the Foundations of American Freedom, edited by Saul K. Padover. 1965.
The Family Letters, edited by Edwin Morris Betts and James Adam Bear, Jr. 1966.
Citizen Jefferson: The Wit and Wisdom of an American Sage. 1994.
The Republic of Letters: The Correspondence between Thomas Jefferson and James Madison, 1776-1826. 1995.
The Papers of Thomas Jefferson, edited by John Catanzariti. 1997.
Jefferson's Memorandum Books: Accounts, with Legal Records and Miscellany, 1767-1826. 2 vols., 1997.
Jefferson in Love: Love Letters between Thomas Jefferson and Maria Cosway. 1998.

Translator, with Joel Barlow, *Volney's Ruins; or, Meditations on the Revolution of Empires.* 2 vols., 1802.

*

Bibliography: *Jefferson: A Reference Guide* by Eugene L. Huddleston, 1982; *Jefferson: A Comprehensive, Annotated Bibliography of Writings About Him (1926-1980)* by Frank Shuffleton, 1983.

Critical Studies: *The Jefferson Cyclopedia* by John P. Foley, 1900; *The Philosophy of Jefferson* by Adrienne Koch, 1943; *The Declaration of Independence: The Evolution of the Text* by Julian P. Boyd, 1945; *Jefferson among the Arts: An Essay in Early Ameri-*

can Esthetics by Eleanor Davidson Berman, 1947; Jefferson and His Time by Dumas Malone, 6 vols., 1948-81; The Head and Heart of Jefferson by John Dos Passos, 1954; The Jefferson Image in the American Mind, 1960, and Jefferson and the New Nation, 1970, both by Merrill D. Peterson, and Jefferson: A Profile edited by Peterson, 1967; A Casebook on the Declaration of Independence edited by Robert Ginsberg, 1967; Jefferson: An Intimate History by Fawn M. Brodie, 1974; Inventing America: Jefferson's Declaration of Independence by Garry Wills, 1978; Jefferson by William K. Bottorff, 1979; Jefferson's Monticello by W. Howard Adams, 1983; Describing Early America: Bartram, Jefferson, Crevecoeur, and the Rhetoric of Natural History by Pamela Regis, 1992; Liberalism and Republicanism in the Historical Imagination by Joyce Appleby, 1992; On the Sources of Patriarchal Rage: The Commonplace Books of William Byrd and Thomas Jefferson and the Gendering of Power in the Eighteenth Century by Kenneth A. Lockridge, 1992; The Inner Jefferson: Portrait of a Grieving Optimist by Andrew Burstein, 1995; American Sphinx: The Character of Thomas Jefferson by Joseph J. Ellis, 1996; The Long Affair: Thomas Jefferson and the French Revolution, 1785-1800 by Conor Cruise O'Brien, 1996; Thomas Jefferson and Sally Hemings: An American Controversy by Annette Gordon-Reed, 1997; From Radical to Respectable: The Declining Influence of Jefferson's Political Thought on Twentieth Century American Liberalism by Jeffrey L. Taylor, 1997; Money and Modernity: Pound, Williams, and the Spirit of Jefferson by Alec Marsh, 1998; Jefferson's Declaration of Independence: Origins, Philosophy, and Theology by Allen Jayne, 1998.

*   *   *

Thomas Jefferson is one of the great writers of the Revolutionary and Early National eras, and among American presidents who wrote with distinction, his only rivals are Abraham Lincoln and Woodrow Wilson. The ideas of the founding fathers of the American republic are nowhere better articulated than in the writings of Jefferson, in his public papers, in his one book, and in his letters. He was extremely conscious of the great events taking place in America in the last quarter of the eighteenth century, and his writings are wise and lucid, felicitously phrased, and continuously important for anyone wishing to understand the foundations of the republic, its ideological underpinning, and its development during its first half century.

Jefferson was born the son of a self-made, little educated man, Peter Jefferson, who became a prosperous landowner and member of the Virginia House of Burgesses, and Jane Randolph, who came from one of the most prominent families of the colony. As a member of a distinguished and affluent family, Jefferson was given the best education available. His years of study culminated in his graduation from the College of William and Mary and post-graduate work reading law with the celebrated George Wythe. The classical education that he received, which is reflected in his writings, was a shaping influence on his life. He wrote Joseph Priestley in 1800 that to read the Latin and Greek authors in their original text is a sublime luxury: "I thank Him who directed my early education, for having put into my possession this rich source of delight; and I would not exchange it for anything which I could then have acquired."

Jefferson was a member of the Virginia Assembly when events were moving inexorably towards the Revolution, and his first important writing was A Summary View of the Rights of British America, a strong plea for natural rights for the British colonies and a stern indictment of British tyranny. It was read at the Virginia convention in Williamsburg in August 1774 but it was considered too revolutionary and was not adopted. The resolutions it contained, however, were widely circulated, and Jefferson acquired a reputation as an eloquent spokesman for the developing American point of view. This document led to his appointment to the committee, containing John Adams and **Benjamin Franklin**, charged by Congress to write the Declaration of Independence. The Declaration, though edited somewhat by Adams, Franklin, and Congress, is almost entirely the work of Jefferson and states brilliantly the social contract theory of government then gaining currency during the Enlightenment.

When the Revolution was in its final days, Jefferson retired as governor of Virginia and returned to his home at Monticello. There he wrote the one book published during his lifetime: Notes on the State of Virginia, still a remarkably interesting volume after 200 years. It was cast in the form of answers to queries posed by the secretary of the French legation in Philadelphia, and it covers every aspect of the state, its history, government, ethnology, religion, geology, flora, and fauna. It shows Jefferson as an eighteenth-century polymath, a man intensely interested in ideas, curious about all sides of human nature and science, and widely read in authors ancient and modern.

During the years that Jefferson was actively engaged in government on the national level; as Washington's secretary of state; vice president under John Adams; and then as president for two terms, he wrote many state papers that are notable for their cogency and clarity. After his years in Europe as American minister to France, he returned with a knowledge of world affairs and statecraft far beyond most Americans, who on the whole were provincial in outlook. His state papers reflect this broad experience and vision. His first inaugural address, one of his most memorable statements, was delivered after the turmoil of the Adams years and the intense partisan struggle that ended in his election as president. It is an eloquent call for unity and harmony: "We are all republicans—we are all Federalists. If there be any among us who would wish to dissolve the Union or to change its republican form, let them stand undisturbed as monuments of the safety with which error of opinion may be tolerated where reason is left to combat it."

After Jefferson retired from the presidency, he continued his intellectual interests and carried on a distinguished correspondence with important scientists, philosophers, and statesmen in America and Europe. The hundreds of letters he wrote went, to name a few; to Lafayette, Kosciusko, Priestley, and Thomas Cooper in Europe; to Madison and Monroe, his successors in the presidency; and to Benjamin Rush and Benjamin Waterhouse in the United States. The list is legion, and the subjects discussed are innumerable; but perhaps the most interesting is the extensive correspondence with his old political rival Adams. These letters constitute an important exchange of ideas between two of the founding fathers as they reflect back on their careers from the perspective of old age. Jefferson, also in his last years, wrote a partial autobiography that is an important record of his career down to 1790.

In his declining years, Jefferson devoted much of his attention to education, and the opening of the University of Virginia the year before he died was the culmination of years of planning. He believed passionately that education was an end in itself, the way to happiness, and the foundation on which self-government rested. He planned the university, chose the books for the library, selected the faculty, drew up the curriculum, designed the buildings, and oversaw their construction. He even wrote "An Essay on the Anglo-Saxon Language," one of his many interests, for his new university. When he died fifty years to the day following the signing of the Declaration of Independence, he directed that his tombstone record the three accomplishments of which he was most proud: author of the Statute of Virginia for Religious Freedom, the Declaration of Independence, and the founder of the University of Virginia.

—James Woodress

JEWETT, (Theodora) Sarah Orne

Born: South Berwick, Maine, 3 September 1849. **Education:** Educated as Miss Raynes's School, 1855, and Berwick Academy, 1861-66, graduated 1866. **Career:** Full-time writer in Berwick from 1866: contributed to *Atlantic Monthly* from 1869. **Award:** Litt.D.: Bowdoin College, Brunswick, Maine, 1901. **Died:** 24 June 1909.

PUBLICATIONS

Collections

Stories and Tales. 7 vols., 1910.
The Best Stories, edited by Willa Cather. 2 vols., 1925.
Letters, edited by Richard Cary. 1956; revised edition, 1967.
The Country of the Pointed Firs and Other Stories, edited by Mary Ellen Chase. 1968.
Best Stories, edited by Josephine Donovan, Martin Greenberg, and Charles Waugh. 1988.
Novels and Stories. 1994.
The Irish Stories of Sarah Orne Jewett. 1996.

Short Stories

Deephaven. 1877; edited by Richard Cary, with other stories, 1966.
Old Friends and New (stories). 1879.
Country By-Ways. 1881.
The Mate of the Daylight, and Friends Ashore (stories). 1883.
A White Heron and Other Stories. 1886.
The King of Folly Island and Other People. 1888.
Tales of New England. 1890.
A Native of Winby and Other Tales. 1893.
The Life of Nancy (stories). 1895.
The Country of the Pointed Firs. 1896.
The Queen's Twin and Other Stories. 1899.
Uncollected Short Stories, edited by Richard Cary. 1971.

Novels

A Country Doctor. 1884.
A Marsh Island. 1885.
Strangers and Wayfarers. 1890.
The Tory Lover. 1901.
An Empty Purse: A Christmas Story. 1905.

Poetry

Verses, edited by M. A. De Wolfe Howe. 1916.

Other

Play Days: A Book of Stories for Children. 1878.
The Story of the Normans (for children). 1887.
Betty Leicester: A Story for Girls. 1890.
Betty Leicester's English Xmas (for children). 1894; as *Betty Leicester's Christmas,* 1899.
Letters, edited by Annie Fields. 1911.
Letters Now in Colby College Library, edited by Carl J. Weber. 1947.

Editor, *Stories and Poems for Children,* by Celia Thaxter. 1895.
Editor, *The Poems of Celia Thaxter.* 1896.
Editor, *Letters of Sarah Wyman Whitman.* 1907.

*

Bibliography: *A Bibliography of the Published Writings of Jewett* by Clara Carter Weber and Carl J. Weber, 1949; in *Bibliography of American Literature* by Jacob Blanck, 1969; *Jewett: A Reference Guide* by Gwen L. Nagel and James Nagel, 1978.

Critical Studies: *Jewett* by F.O. Mattheissen, 1929; *Acres of Flint: Writers of New England 1870-1900* by Perry D. Westbrook, 1951, revised edition, as *Acres of Flint: Jewett and Her Contemporaries,* 1981; *Jewett* by John Eldridge Frost, 1960; *Jewett* by Richard Cary, 1962, and *Appreciation of Jewett: 29 Interpretive Essays* edited by Cary, 1973; *Jewett* by Margaret Farrand Thorp, 1966; "The Child in Jewett" by Eugene Hillhouse Pool, in *Colby Library Quarterly* 7, 1967; "Women and Nature in Modern Fiction" by Annis Pratt, in *Contemporary Literature* 13, 1972; "The Double Consciousness of the Narrator in Jewett's Fiction" by Catherine Barnes Stevenson, in *Colby Library Quarterly* 11, 1975; "The World of Dreams: Sexual Symbolism in 'A White Heron'" by James Ellis, in *Nassau Review* 3, 1977; "'Once Upon a Time': Jewett's 'A White Heron' as Fairy Tale" by Theodore Hovet, in *Studies in Short Fiction* 15, 1978; "Free Heron or Dead Sparrow: Sylvia's Choice in Jewett's 'A White Heron'" by Richard Brenzo, in *Colby Library Quarterly* 14, 1978; *Jewett* by Josephine Donovan, 1980; "The Necessary Extravagance of Jewett: Voices of Authority in 'A White Heron'" by Michael Atkinson, in *Studies in Short Fiction* 19, 1982; "The Language of Transcendence in Jewett's 'A White Heron'" by Gwen Nagel, in *Colby Library Quarterly* 19, 1983; *"A White Heron" and the Question of Minor Literature* by Louis A. Renza, 1984; *Critical Essays on Jewett* edited by Gwen L. Nagel, 1984; "The Shape of Violence in Jewett's 'A White Heron'" by Elizabeth Ammons, in *Colby Library Quarterly* 22, 1986; *Jewett, An American Persephone* by Sarah Way Sherman, 1989; *Folk Roots and Mythic Wings in Sarah Orne Jewett and Toni Morrison: The Cultural Function of Narrative* by Marilyn-Sanders Mobley, 1991; *Jewett: Reconstructing Gender* by Margaret Roman, 1992; *The Home Plot: Women, Writing & Domestic Ritual* by Ann Romines, 1992; *New Essays on The Country of the Pointed Firs,* 1994; "Domesticity, Cultivation, and Vocation in Jane Addams and Sarah Orne Jewett" by Francesca Sawaya, in *Nineteenth-Century Literature,* March 1994, pp. 507-28; "Visions of Time in *The Country of the Pointed Firs*" by Margaret Baker Graham, in *Studies in Short Fiction,* winter 1995, pp. 29-37; "Narrative Meditation in Sarah Orne Jewett's *The Country of the Pointed Firs*" by Allison T. Hild, in *Colby Quarterly,* June 1995, pp. 114-22; "Unraveling Regions, Unsettling Periods: Sarah Orne Jewett and American Literary History" by June Howard, in *American Literature: A Journal of Literary History, Criticism, and Bibliography,* June 1996, pp. 365-84.

*   *   *

Willa Cather ranked Sarah Orne Jewett's *The Country of the Pointed Firs,* with **Nathaniel Hawthorne's** *The Scarlet Letter* and **Mark Twain's** *Huckleberry Finn,* as one of the three American prose literary works most likely to endure. The estimate is probably overenthusiastic; yet *The Country of the Pointed Firs,* a loosely constructed episodic novel set on the Maine coast, is at least a minor classic and will continue to be read for many years to come. Jewett was an eminently successful literary regionalist—a depicter of setting and character in the area where she had been born and brought up in a patrician family whose sympathies had been Loyalist during the Revolutionary War. Yet her somewhat aristocratic viewpoint—she was inordinately proud of her Anglo-Norman ancestry—in no way affected her understanding and admiration of the fishing and farming people she wrote about in her best work.

Her first book, *Deephaven,* fashioned from sketches that had previously appeared in the *Atlantic Monthly,* deals with life among all classes in a typical Maine seaport, with emphasis upon social and economic decay as commerce and shipping became more and more concentrated in the larger ports like Boston and New York. Jewett's tone in this volume, as in much of her writing, is one of nostalgia for a time when her region had figured vitally in the maritime life of the nation and had nurtured a population of hardy seafarers who sailed their vessels to all the great ports of the world. These days, regrettably, were past, but Jewett still found much to praise among the Maine folk of her time. *The Country of the Pointed Firs* is her major tribute to these quiet, resourceful, hardworking people, the significance of whose lives, now that the adventurous seafaring days were gone, Jewett found to be in the success with which they had adjusted to a harsh environment. The women especially (and most of Jewett's strong characters are women) had learned to live in harmony with their native region—a rocky, island-studded coast with steep pastures and forested mountains rising close back from the water. The most notable of these women, the widow Almira Todd, subsisted as a herbalist, thus personifying the Maine folks' ability to draw life-giving strength from a seemingly sterile land.

Jewett, in her Preface to *Deephaven,* stated that she considered one of her functions as a regional writer was to make the rest of the nation acquainted with the lives and characteristics of a little-known segment of the population. But more important, taking her cue from a statement by George Sand regarding the French peasantry, Jewett believed that the scrutiny to which she, as a writer, subjected her Maine neighbors would reveal a human worth and gentle heroism rarely found elsewhere. Jewett, indeed, saw a physical resemblance between the Maine Coast and the coast and isles of Greece, and she saw classical qualities in her Maine characters. Thus Mrs. Todd, standing on an Atlantic headland and mourning her husband drowned in shipwreck, reminds Jewett of Antigone "alone on the Theban plain." Elsewhere Mrs. Todd, as an herbalist, reminds Jewett of the enchantress Medea. Such allu-

sions, inserted in passing, underline Jewett's point in this and other books: that the simplest persons can attain a dignity, even a tragic grandeur, essentially the same as that found in the great classical works. She did not always find these qualities only among maritime people. The persons in her fiction include upcountry farmers, elderly ladies in elm-shaded inland towns, and Irish maid-servants, and almost invariably she presents them as possessing, and exhibiting, a potential for the full range of human experience from tragedy to ecstasy.

Jewett's prose is notable for its purity and variety. Her descriptions of the land and sea are lyrically evocative. Her narrative style is direct and flowing. In her dialogue she succeeds better than any other New England writer in reproducing the accents and, especially, the rhythms of speech native to her region. Unlike many local-colorists, she does not strive for phonetic renderings of dialect—efforts that usually result in grotesque and nearly unintelligible manglings of spelling. Jewett emphasizes regional diction, idiom, and cadence with only minor alterations in spelling. The result is not only readable but authentic.

Jewett in her lifetime was an admired and popular writer, publishing a sizable number of novels and collections of tales and sketches. Among the novels, *A Country Doctor,* which draws from her experiences in accompanying her physician father on his rounds, deserves mention, as does *A Marsh Island,* an idyllic celebration of life on a coastal farm. Among her volumes of short fiction and sketches, three of the richest are *Country By-Ways, A White Heron and Other Stories* (the title piece being her most famous story), and *The King of Folly Island and Other People,* containing the superb story "Miss Tempy's Watchers."

Though born and brought up in a small Maine town and always fiercely loyal to the place of her birth, Jewett was very much in touch with, and an influence in, the literary life of her times. A close friend of Mrs. James Fields, wife of the prominent Boston publisher, she was active in Boston literary circles and met many of the nation's and world's great writers as they visited the publisher's home. Eventually she became recognized as the author who carried local color, or regionalism, to the highest artistic level it has attained in America. Her writing has served as a model for other American authors, not all of them local-colorists, especially women of her and later generations. For example, Cather, following Jewett's example and personal advice, redirected her early efforts from rather mediocre fiction in the manner of **Henry James** to the writing of highly successful novels based on life in the Midwestern farm-lands where she had been brought up. Jewett always held that an author's chief source of materials should be his or her own locale and personal experience. To this conviction she remained faithful throughout her writing career.

—Perry D. Westbrook

See the essay on *The Country of the Pointed Firs.*

JOHNSON, Charles (Richard)

Born: Evanston, Illinois, 23 April 1948. **Education:** Southern Illinois University, Carbondale, B.A. in journalism 1971, M.A. in philosophy 1973; State University of New York, Stony Brook, 1973-76. **Family:** Married Joan New in 1970; two children. **Career:** Reporter and cartoonist, Chicago *Tribune,* 1969-70; member of art staff, St. Louis *Proud,* Missouri, 1971-72; fiction editor, Seattle *Review,* 1978—; assistant professor of English, 1976-79, associate professor of English, 1979- 82, and professor of English, 1982—, University of Washington, Seattle; director, 1979-81, and member of board of directors, 1983—, Associated Writing Programs Award Series in Short Fiction; writer and cartoonist. **Awards:** Southern Illinois University journalism alumnus of the year, 1981; State of Washington Governor's award for Literature, 1983; *Callaloo* Creative Writing award, 1983; Writer's Guild award, 1986; PEN American Center PEN/Faulkner award nomination, 1987; National Book award, 1990. **Residence:** Seattle, Washington.

PUBLICATIONS

Collection

I Call Myself an Artist: Writings By and About Charles Johnson. 1999.

Novels

Faith and the Good Thing. 1974.
Oxherding Tale. 1982.
Middle Passage. 1990.
Dreamer. 1998.

Short Stories

The Sorcerer's Apprentice: Tales and Conjuration. 1988.

Play

Olly Olly Oxen Free. 1988.

Television Plays: *Charlie's Pad,* 1971; *Charlie Smith and the Fritter Tree,* 1978; *For Me Myself,* 1982; *A Place for Myself,* 1982; *Booker,* with John Allmann, 1984.

Other

Black Humor (cartoons). 1970.
Half-Past Nation Time (cartoons). 1972.
Being and Race: Black Writing Since 1970. 1988.
All This and Moonlight. 1990.
In Search of a Voice, with Ron Chernow (juvenile). 1991.

*

Critical Studies: "Writers Should Be Able to Write Everything: Ken McCullough Talks to Johnson" in *Coda: Poets and Writers Newsletter* September/October 1978; "Reflections on Fiction, Philosophy, and Film: An Interview with Johnson" in *Callaloo* October 1978; "Novels of the New Black Renaissance (1960-1977): A Thematic Survey" by Arthur Davis in *CLA Journal* June 1978; "American Literature, 1974-1976: The People Fell to Earth" by Raymond Olderman in *Contemporary Literature* June 1978; "The Heirs of Ralph Ellison" by Elizabeth Shultz in *CLA Journal* December 1978; "Johnson, Free at Last" by Stanley Crouch in *Village Voice* July 1983; "Johnson's Revolutionary *Oxherding Tale*" by Jonathan Little in *Studies in American Fiction* vol. 19, no. 2,

1991; "The Phenomenology of the Allmuseri: Johnson and the Subject of the Narrative of Slavery" by Ashraf Rushdy in *African American Review* vol. 26, no. 3, 1992; *African Culture as Tradition: A Reading of Tales of the Congaree, Middle Passage, Benito Cereno, and Black Thunder* (dissertation) by Sandra M. Grayson, 1994; *Towards a Unified Articulation of the Self: Aesthetic Theory and Practice in Charles Johnson's Fiction* (dissertation) by William Richardson Nash, 1994; *Charles Johnson's Spiritual Imagination* by Jonathan Little, 1997.

*   *   *

In modern phenomenological study, the definition of reality is subject to controversy. Novelist **Henry James**, for instance, believes that "the measure of reality is very difficult to fix. . . . Humanity is immense, and reality has a myriad forms." Other modern phenomenalists such as Paul Armstrong also posit that truth, instead of being a fixed, determinate object, is "the ever-shifting goal of the infinitely variable activity of creating and construing meaning." African American novelist Charles Johnson's writing is strongly influenced by the phenomenological approach in literary criticism and theory. In his three masterpieces, *Faith and the Good Thing* (1974), *Oxherding Tale* (1982), and *Middle Passage* (1990), he invites readers to participate in reconstructing history, an activity that Johnson believes can be as subjective as it is objective.

Johnson developed an interest in both philosophy and creative writing while he was a student at Southern Illinois University in Carbondale, Illinois; his mentor there was **John Gardner**, his creative writing instructor. Johnson once showed Gardner manuscripts of six completed novels for critique. Gardner's encouragement was what helped Johnson to stay focused in creative writing. The seventh manuscript that Johnson finished was eventually published as the novel *Faith and the Good Thing.*

Johnson's novels are characterized by a strong interest in philosophy and history. Since, like other phenomenalists, Johnson strongly believes that reality can be defined as a sum of many perceptions, he subjects the reconstruction of African American history and the recreation of the world of African American experience to many different perspectives and possibilities. Indeed, while many writers are content with what is available in traditional literary conventions, Johnson is more interested in enriching contemporary American literature by searching for appropriate approaches and forms that can help reclaim African Americans' sense of history and identity. As is suggested by Maryemma Graham, Johnson's three critically acclaimed novels help to both establish and define the "new fiction," which began in the middle of the 1970s.

Johnson's novels are as philosophical as they are historical. But each novel has a different focus. In *Faith and the Good Thing,* for example, Johnson creates a character whose search for an ideal forces her to visit not only the past, but also the metaphysical world. Faith's metaphysical world is home to a werewitch (Swamp Woman) and a mad professor, while present in her physical world are Faith's male clients, a sanctimonious husband, and an ex-lover. Faith is the only character in the book who can cross the border that separates the two worlds, but she is also the only one who has to learn how to balance her relationship with both.

Johnson worked for the Public Broadcasting System, writing television scripts and programs, for eight years before he published his second novel, *Oxherding Tale.* Several critics have correctly pointed out that *Oxherding Tale* is a modern slave narrative. By using a controversial form that is as old as the slavery system, Johnson challenges the reader to reconstruct a piece of history from a modern phenomenological point of view. In *Oxherding Tale* Johnson, nevertheless, modifies his metaphysical accentuation to represent a time during which accidents and chances appeared to play as much a determinate role as destiny.

Middle Passage is, without doubt, Johnson's best work. The book won the 1990 National Book award and has received favorable critical reviews. *Middle Passage* follows the same tradition as **Herman Melville**'s *Moby-Dick,* but its epic scope and humorous tone set the book apart from nineteenth-century American sea-faring literature. In *Middle Passage,* the main character, Rutherford Calhoun, is a newly freed slave. Working his passage on an illegal slave clipper bound for Africa, Calhoun has to fight off Captain Ebenezer Falcon's "courtship" whose words are just as seductive as the nightmare of the god of Allmuseri is tormenting.

After Calhoun's observation leads him to the conclusion that all forty crew members aboard the *Republic* are loners in search of a new frontier, "refugees from responsibility and, like social misfits ever pushing westward to escape citified life, took to the sea as the last frontier that welcomed miscreants, dreamers, and fools," he comes to believe that, despite Captain Falcon's ominous talk about a person's "nonself," he is not searching for his self, but creating one. Calhoun's strengthened faith in self-centered individualism makes it possible for him to play a game with both the captain and the other crew members, as well as with himself. But after he betrays the Allmuseri captives by informing the captain of the god of the Allmuseri, Calhoun is tormented by a sense of guilt. After spending three days feeding the Allmuseri god and meeting his long-lost father and himself, Calhoun believes he has reached a new level of self-awareness.

In *Middle Passage,* Johnson follows the trickster tradition in African American literature. Calhoun reminds the reader of **Ralph Ellison**'s Rinehart in *Invisible Man,* a character who has many personalities: Calhoun is at the same time a learned African American former slave, a pragmatic liar, a survival specialist, a wooer, and the one who is being wooed. He thus becomes the ultimate symbol of history, of life, and of America. If Faith in *Faith and the Good Thing* has to learn how to balance the metaphysical world and the physical one to walk the tightrope that connects life and death, in *Middle Passage,* Calhoun has to learn how to balance the influence of both Western culture (epitomized in the book by Captain Falcon's propensity to philosophize life) and the indigenous African culture (represented by the presence of the Allmuseri god) to protect his emotional integrity and individuality.

Critics have compared *Middle Passage* to Melville's *Moby Dick* (1851) and "Benito Cereno" (1855), **Edgar Allan Poe**'s *The Narrative of Arthur Gordon Pym* (1838), Ralph Ellison's *Invisible Man* (1952), and Gardner's novella *The King's Indian* (1974). But Calhoun's professed candor and the book's philosophical accentuation also remind the reader of Voltaire's "contes philosophiques," which are as hilariously humorous as they are deadly serious. Johnson's use of historical allusions, twisted cliches, and nonsensical coincidences works cohesively with his attempt to destroy his readers' traditional logical sense and to invite them to participate in the reconstruction of history. Indeed, by intermingling philosophy and history, the past and the present, and the metaphysical world and the physical world, Johnson is able to turn the unexpected into the expected, to bridge the parallel worlds of the visible and the invisible, and to make comprehensible what would otherwise remain incongruous.

As is demonstrated throughout his works, Johnson's interest in phenomenology is as strong as his interest in sociology and history. In 1997 Johnson, together with John McCluskey, Jr., published a book on the political, social, and cultural status of African American men. *Black Men Speaking* calls readers' attention to not only the intercultural but also the intracultural conflict within the African American community. In 1998, Johnson worked with Patricia Smith to write and produce a television series for WGBH in Boston, Massachusetts. The series, later published by Harcourt Brace, is a study and portrayal of African Americans' struggle through slavery. Johnson's 1998 novel, *Dreamer,* is a biographical fiction of Martin Luther King, Jr. In the novel, the author again experiments with the style and form to destroy the boundaries that purport to separate reality from imagination and history from fiction.

—Qun Wang

JOHNSON, James Weldon

Born: Jacksonville, Florida, 17 June 1871. **Education:** Atlanta University, A.B. 1894, A.M. 1904; also studied at Columbia University, New York, for three years. **Family:** Married Grace Nail in 1910. **Career:** Principal, Stanton Central Grammar School for Negroes, Jacksonville; helped found Jacksonville *Daily American;* admitted to Florida bar, and practiced in Jacksonville, 1897-1901; moved to New York, to collaborate with his brother, the composer J. Rosamond Johnson, in writing popular songs and light opera, 1901-06; U.S. consul, Puerto Cabello, Venezuela, 1906-09, and Corinto, Nicaragua, 1909-12; executive secretary, National Association for the Advancement of Colored People, 1916-30; Spence professor of creative literature, Fisk University, Nashville, Tennessee, 1930-38; visiting professor of creative literature, New York University, 1934. Columnist, *New York Age.* Director, American Fund for Public Service; trustee, Atlanta University. **Awards:** Spingarn Medal, 1925; Du Bois prize for Negro Literature, 1933. Litt.D.: Talladega College, Alabama, 1917; Howard University, Washington, D.C., 1923. **Member:** Academy of Political Science. **Died:** 26 June 1938.

PUBLICATIONS

Collection

The Selected Writings of James Weldon Johnson. 1995.

Poetry

Fifty Years and Other Poems. 1917.
God's Trombones: Seven Negro Sermons in Verse. 1927.
Saint Peter Relates an Incident of the Resurrection Day. 1930.
Saint Peter Relates an Incident: Selected Poems. 1935.

Plays

Goyescas; or, The Rival Lovers, from a play by Fernando Periquet, music by Enrique Granados (produced 1915). 1915.
Shakespeare in Harlem, with Langston Hughes (produced 1959).

Fiction

The Autobiography of an Ex-Colored Man. 1912.

Other

The Changing Status of Negro Labor. 1918.
Africa in the World Democracy, with Horace M. Kallen. 1919.
Self-Determining Hayti. N.d.
Lynching: America's National Disgrace. 1924.
The Race Problem and Peace. 1924.
Fundamentalism Versus Spiritualism: A Layman's Viewpoint. 1925.
Native African Races and Culture. 1927.
Legal Aspects of the Negro Problem. N.d.
Black Manhattan. 1930.
The Shining Life. 1932.
Along This Way (autobiography). 1933.
Negro Americans, What Now? 1934.
Lift Every Voice and Sing. 1993.

Editor, *The Book of American Negro Poetry.* 1922; revised edition, 1931.
Editor, *The Book of American Negro Spirituals.* 1925; *Second Book,* 1926.

*

Bibliography: *Johnson and Arna Wendell Bontemps: A Reference Guide* by Robert E. Fleming, 1978.

Critical Studies: *Johnson* by Sterling A. Brown, Carl Van Vechten, and A.B. Spingarn, 1941(?); *Roots of Negro Racial Consciousness: Three Harlem Renaissance Authors* by Stephen H. Bronz, 1964; *Johnson, Black Leader Black Voice* by Eugene D. Levy, 1973 (includes bibliography); *Black Poets of the United States* by Jean Wagner, 1973; *James Weldon Johnson* by Robert E. Fleming, 1987; *Politics in the African-American Novel: James Weldon Johnson, W.E.B. Du Bois, Richard Wright, and Ralph Ellison* by Richard Kostelanetz, 1991; *Critical Essays on James Weldon Johnson,* 1997.

*   *   *

James Weldon Johnson's literary output was slight, but it is a solid achievement and one that proves crucial when viewed as that of a black American aspiring to a literary career in the early twentieth century. In *God's Trombones: Seven Negro Sermons in Verse,* Johnson achieved considerable success in melding African American folk and European-American sophisticated modes of expression to gain the kind of artistic synthesis he hoped would assist in confirming the right to full citizenship for peoples of African descent in the United States, by virtue of a demonstrated capacity (which their detractors would argue they did not possess) to contribute significantly to the formation of a new national culture. This task of recuperation became a theme in Johnson's influential picaresque novel, later regarded as a classic, *The Autobiography of an Ex-Colored Man,* first published anonymously in 1912. The novel's "tragic mulatto" protagonist is a trained musician who earns his way as an inspired ragtime pianist. He professes, however ironically (and it is to Johnson's skillful manipulation of irony that the novel owes the greater part of its suc-

cess), to bring "glory and honour to the Negro race." This he intends to achieve through compositions in the European classical tradition incorporating elements of African American folk music, the projected field research for which, however, never gets done. Further insight into Johnson's aims is available in the important prefaces to two editions of his equally influential and classic anthology, *The Book of American Negro Poetry.* In these, he compares the African American poet's need to achieve a distinct mode of expression rooted in and supportive of African American life ("a form that will express the racial spirit by symbols from within" rather than from without) to that recognized by the Irish poet-playwright J.M. Synge that led to the assimilation of indigenous folk material into his works.

Johnson's accidental death cut short his efforts, but his poems in *God's Trombones* mark a significant step in the direction of his goal. This work has continued to serve as an inspiration and a model for African American writers. Stylistically inspired by the folk preaching Johnson observed in African American churches, the poems assume the form and essential rhythm of the sermons and prayers he heard. As such, they are a marked stylistic departure from the prevailing Anglo-American poetic tradition of the day. Also, they constitute a corrective to the artificial and, as Johnson saw it, denigrating folk speech of the stereotype-fostering dialect mode that had been grafted onto that tradition, including its use in Johnson's own early dialect poetry. On the Euro-American side, the poems in *God's Trombones* are biblical-Whitmanesque, gaining an appeal at once sophisticated and folk-oriented. Similarly, *The Autobiography of an Ex-Colored Man* delineates the artistic defusing of various stereotypes that African American writers were coming to recognize as an obligatory function of their works. Toward that end, Johnson imbues his protagonist with the superficialities of the "tragic mulatto" stereotype, but portrays him with a psychological verisimilitude and with irony, thus enabling the stereotypical aspect to achieve a virtual self-destruction. He thus carried forward a tradition of corrective aesthetics pioneered by his predecessors, Charles W. Chesnutt and, to a lesser degree, **Paul Laurence Dunbar.**

—Alvin Aubert

JONES, Everett LeRoi. *See* **BARAKA, Amiri.**

JONES, Gayl

Born: 1949. **Education:** In segregated schools, Lexington, Kentucky; Connecticut College; Brown University. **Career:** Professional novelist, poet, and dramatist.

PUBLICATIONS

Fiction

Corregidora. 1975.
White Rat and Other Short Stories. 1977.
Song for Anninho. 1981.
The Hermit Woman. 1983.

Poetry

Xargue and Other Poems. 1985.

*   *   *

The African American writer Gayl Jones has published a volume of narrative poetry, *Song for Anninho* (1981), but her reputation is founded on her fiction; her early work celebrated the harsh lives of her characters in equally harsh prose. Her short stories, written from 1971 on, and collected in *White Rat* (1977) are, with one exception, first-person narratives, and in them repetitive snatches of dialogue and a conspicuous lack of emotional commentary convey the despair of people whose lives are crippled by poverty, racism, and mental illness. "White Rat," the lead story, is narrated by a black man nicknamed White Rat because he looks Caucasian, a fact that hatefully defines him and that psychologically paralyzes him. Characteristic of Gayl Jones in this story are a bitter humor and a strong sense of the speaking voice—for example, when White Rat describes his wedding: "We went down to the courthouse and fore I even said a word, the man behind the glass cage look up at us and say, 'Round here nigger don't marry white.' I don't say nothing just standing up there looking at him and he looking like a white toad, and I'm wondering if they call him 'white toad' more likely 'white turd.' But I just keep looking at him."

The novel *Corregidora* (1975) is a devastating account of Brazilian slavery (a topic that Jones studied at college) and its destructive effects on Ursa, a beautiful blues singer living in Kentucky, struggling against its legacy of hatred and sexual perversion. Ursa must undergo a hysterectomy after she is attacked by her jealous husband, and poignantly regrets that she cannot "make generations." It is the tragedy of the novel that she has been repeatedly exhorted by her mother and grandmother to "make generations," or have children, for the purpose of immortalizing the memory of the vile slave owner Corregidora. Although the novel ends on a note of cautious optimism as Ursa meets her estranged husband years later, it is the story of a horrific and malignant obsession.

The most striking aspect of *Corregidora* is the eloquence of its absences: the absence of any description of Ursa's haunting beauty, which is always implied, and the absence of any description of her singing, the only way Ursa can give articulate expression to her pain. Ursa's narrative itself is deliberately flat, crude, and violent, implying rather than expressing the depths of her pain. Jones uses the same technique in her second novel, *Eva's Man* (1976), narrated by Eva, a somber, pathetic woman who is constantly, through the references to her hair, compared with Medusa. Eva has been imprisoned for murdering her lover, and she is regarded with an intrusive and morbid fascination by all the other characters because she had bitten off his penis. As Elvira, one of her fellow inmates, puts it laconically, "I guess what you done excites people." *Eva's Man* functions as a kind of detective story as we retrace her steps to this act of violence, and it is also an extended meditation on the cruelties of imprisonment.

The Healing (1998) is the narrative of an itinerant faith healer in the South, told colloquially but in a more sophisticated way than her first two novels. The healer, Harlan, establishes early on that she is herself by nature skeptical: "In the evening we'll go to the basement of the Freewill Baptist Church and then I'll show 'em my miracles and wonders. Of course they's always three kinds of people there: them that believes without questioning, those that believe only when it's themselves being healed, and those who could suck a cactus dry—they ain't got cactus in this region, but the region I just come from, little town name Cuba, New Mexico—and 'ud still tell you it ain't got no juice in it. I'll tell y'all the truth. If I wasn't the one doing the healing, I'd be among the tough nuts." This skepticism amusingly infiltrates the story, which Harlan tells backwards, so that we not only track, in reverse, her previous lives as the wife of a medical missionary traveling in Africa, as a beautician, and as the personal manager of a rock star, but at the same time gradually unravel her development as a spiritual phenomenon. Harlan tells her story with the ruthless candor and the vivid imagery of one of **Toni Cade Bambara**'s protagonists, and as she moves through Africa and the South she displays the anthropological enthusiasms of **Alice Walker**'s later heroines.

As her ground-breaking critical work, *Liberating Voices: Oral Tradition in African American Literature* (1991), has demonstrated, Jones has a consuming interest in the reproduction of the speaking voice as a literary device and in its status as part of a long and distinguished tradition in African American culture. Jones's work is especially brilliant in its depiction of the interaction between the artist and her audience, whether that artist is a purveyor of deadly gossip, a blues singer, or a shaman.

—Mary Condé

JONES, James

Born: Robinson, Illinois, 6 November 1921. **Education:** University of Hawaii, Honolulu, 1942; New York University, 1945. **Military Service:** Served in the U.S. Army, 1939-44: Bronze Star; Purple Heart. **Family:** Married Gloria Mosolino in 1957; one son and one daughter. **Career:** Lived in Paris, 1958-74; writer-in-residence, Florida International University, Miami, 1974-77. **Awards:** National Book award, 1952. **Died:** 9 May 1977.

PUBLICATIONS

Fiction

From Here to Eternity. 1951.
Some Came Running. 1957.
The Pistol. 1959.
The Thin Red Line. 1962.
Go to the Widow-Maker. 1967.
The Ice-Cream Headache and Other Stories. 1968.
The Merry Month of May. 1971.
A Touch of Danger. 1973.
Whistle: A Work-in-Progress. 1974; complete version, as *Whistle*, 1978.

Play

Screenplay: *The Longest Day,* with others, 1962.

Other

Viet Journal. 1974.
WWII, with Art Weithas. 1975.

*

Bibliography: *Jones: A Checklist* by John R. Hopkins, 1974.

Critical Studies: *Jones: A Friendship* by Willie Morris, 1978; *Jones* by James R. Giles, 1981; *Jones* by George Garrett, 1984; *Into Eternity: Jones—The Life of an American Writer* by Frank MacShane, 1985; "Jones's *From Here to Eternity*" by Laurie Champion, in *Explicator,* summer 1996, pp. 342-44; "Not Following in the Groove: Lowney Handy, James Jones, and the Handy Colony for Writers" by Thomas J. Wood, in *Illinois Historical Journal,* summer 1997, pp. 82-96; "Thoughts for the Times on War and Death: Militarism and Its Discontents" by Christopher Lane, in *Literature and Psychology,* 1995, pp. 1-12.

*   *   *

Generally regarded as the most successful "war-novelist" to emerge from World War II, James Jones, at his best, writes the way a good combat infantryman serves out a campaign. His prose is direct, muscular, prepared to take advantage of tactical opportunities, efficient, cynical without being pessimistic, and cannily aware of the ambiguous areas where fear mingles with bravery, and self-interest and self-sacrifice shade together. One of the few modern writers to depict the character of man-as-warrior sympathetically and without romantic illusions, Jones will probably be remembered for *From Here to Eternity, The Thin Red Line,* and his acute nonfictional study, *WWII: A Chronicle of Soldiering.*

In *From Here to Eternity,* Jones found a story perfectly adequate to his thematic interests: the heroic struggle of the warrior-individual trying to maintain his sense of self against the pressures of the very system that provides him with his cherished identity. Prewitt, the doomed protagonist, becomes an indelible figure in the gallery of American fictional soldiers that runs from Crane's Henry Fleming through Hemingway's Frederic Henry to Joseph Heller's Yossarian. Unlike the others, however, Prewitt is a soldier by choice and devotion; he is neither a rebel against, nor a victim of, the institution in which he finds his fullest realization. Jones's non-military fiction—including *Some Came Running, Go to the Widow-Maker,* and *The Merry Month of May*—tends to lack the controlled narrative focus of his war novels; characteristically, the prose is much looser, the action moves toward the melodramatic and sensational, and the novels suffer from a combination of verbosity and sentimentality.

—Earl Rovit

K

KAUFMAN, George S.

Born: Pittsburgh, Pennsylvania, 16 November 1889. **Education:** Liberty School, New Castle School, and Central High School, Pittsburgh, graduated 1907; Western University of Pennsylvania Law School (now University of Pittsburgh), 1907. **Family:** Married 1) Beatrice Bakrow in 1917 (died 1945), one adopted daughter; 2) the actress Leueen MacGrath in 1949 (divorced 1957). **Career:** Worked as a surveyor, clerk in the Allegheny County Tax Office, and stenographer for the Pittsburgh Coal Company; traveling salesman, Columbia Ribbon Company, Paterson, New Jersey, 1909-12; columnist, Washington *Times,* 1912-13; drama critic, New York *Tribune,* 1914-15; columnist, New York *Evening Mail,* 1915; drama critic, later drama editor, New York *Times,* 1917-30. Writer for the stage from 1918, often in collaboration; stage director from 1928; panelist, *This Is Show Business* radio and TV program, 1948-52. Chairman of the Board, Dramatists Guild 1927. **Awards:** Megrue prize, 1931; Pulitzer prize, 1932, 1937; Tony award, for directing, 1951. **Died:** 2 June 1961.

PUBLICATIONS

Collections

By George: A Kaufman Collection, edited by Donald Oliver. 1979.

Plays

Among Those Present, with Larry Evans and Walter C. Percival (produced 1918; as *Someone in the House,* produced 1918).
Jacques Duval, from play by Hans Miller (produced 1919).
Dulcy, with Marc Connelly (produced 1921). 1921.
To the ladies!, with Marc Connelly (produced 1922). 1923.
No, Sirree!, with Marc Connelly (produced 1922).
The 49ers, with Marc Connelly (produced 1922).
West of Pittsburgh, with Marc Connelly (produced 1922; revised version, as *The Deep Tangled Wildwood,* produced 1923).
Merton of the Movies, with Marc Connelly, from the story by Harry Leon Wilson (produced 1922). 1925.
A Christmas Carol, with Marc Connelly, from the story by Dickens, in Bookman, December 1922.
Helen of Troy, New York, with Marc Connelly, music and lyrics by Harry Ruby and Bert Kalmar (produced 1923).
Beggar on Horseback, with Marc Connelly. music by Deems Taylor, from a play by Paul Apel (produced 1924). 1925.
Sketches, in *'Round the Town* (produced 1924).
Be Yourself, with Marc Connelly, music and lyrics by Lewis Genzler and Milton Schwarzwald, additional lyrics by Ira Gershwin (produced 1924).
Minick, with Edna Ferber, from the story "Old Man Minick" by Ferber (produced 1924). In *Old Man Minick: A Short Story ... Minick: A Play,* 1924.
The Butter and Egg Man (produced 1925). 1926.
The Cocoanuts, music by Irving Berlin (produced 1925). 1925.
Business Is Business, with Dorothy Parker (produced 1925).

If Men Played Cards Like Women Do. 1926.
The Good Fellow, with Herman J. Mankiewicz (produced 1926). 1931.
The Royal Family, with Edna Ferber (produced 1927). 1928; as *Theatre Royal* (produced 1935), 1936.
Animal Crackers, with Morrie Ryskind, music and lyrics by Harry Ruby and Bert Kalmar (produced 1928).
The Still Alarm (sketch), in *The Little Show* (produced 1929). 1930.
June Moon, with Ring Lardner, from the story "Some Like Them Cold" by Lardner (produced 1929). 1930.
The Channel Road, with Alexander Woollcott (produced 1929).
Strike Up the Band, book by Morrie Ryskind from a libretto by Kaufman, music by George Gershwin, lyrics by Ira Gershwin (produced 1930).
Once in a Lifetime, with Moss Hart (produced 1930). 1930.
The Band Wagon, with Howard Dietz, music by Arthur Schwartz (produced 1931).
Eldorado, with Laurence Stallings (produced 1931).
Of Thee I Sing, with Morrie Ryskind, music by George Gershwin, lyrics by Ira Gershwin (produced 1931). 1932.
Dinner at Eight, with Edna Ferber (produced 1932). 1932.
Let 'em Eat Cake, with Morrie Ryskind, music by George Gershwin, lyrics by Ira Gershwin (produced 1933). 1933.
The Dark Tower, with Alexander Woollcott (produced 1933). 1934.
Merrily We Roll Along, with Moss Hart (produced 1934). 1934.
Bring on the Girls, with Morrie Ryskind (produced 1934). Prom Night. 1934.
Cheating the Kidnappers. 1935.
The Paperhanger, with Moss Hart. 1935(?).
First Lady, with Katharine Dayton (produced 1935). 1935.
Stage Door, with Edna Ferber (produced 1936). 1936.
You Can't Take It with You, with Moss Hart (produced 1936). 1937.
I'd Rather Be Right, with Moss Hart, music by Richard Rodgers, lyrics by Lorenz Hart (produced 1937). 1937.
The Fabulous Invalid, with Moss Hart (produced 1938). 1938.
The American Way, with Moss Hart, music by Oscar Levant (produced 1939). 1939.
The Man Who Came to Dinner, with Moss Hart (produced 1939). 1939.
George Washington Slept Here, with Moss Hart (produced 1940). 1940.
The Land Is Bright, with Edna Ferber (produced 1941). 1941.
Six Plays, with Moss Hart. 1942.
The Late George Apley, with John P. Marquand, from the novel by Marquand (produced 1944). 1946.
Local Boy Makes Good, in The Seven Lively Arts (produced 1944).
Hollywood Pinafore (produced 1945).
Park Avenue, with Nunnally Johnson, music by Arthur Schwartz, lyrics by Ira Gershwin (produced 1946).
Bravo!, with Edna Ferber (produced 1948). 1949.
The Small Hours, with Leueen MacGrath (produced 1951). 1951.
Fancy Meeting You Again, with Leueen MacGrath (produced 1952). 1952.
The Solid Gold Cadillac, with Howard Teichmann (produced 1953). 1954.

Silk Stockings, with Leueen MacGrath and Abe Burrows, music by Cole Porter, suggested by Melchior Lengyel (produced 1955). 1955.

Amicable Parting, with Leueen MacGrath (produced 1957). 1957.

Screenplays: *Roman Scandals,* with others, 1933; *A Night at the Opera,* with Morrie Ryskind and James Kevin McGuinness, 1935; *Star Spangled Rhythm,* with others, 1942.

Film director: *The Senator Was Indiscreet (Mr. Ashton Was Indiscreet),* 1947.

*

Critical Studies: *Act One* by Moss Hart, 1959; *Kaufman: An Intimate Portrait* by Howard Teichmann, 1972; *Kaufman and His Friends* by Scott Meredith, 1974, abridged version, as *Kaufman and the Algonquin Round Table,* 1977; *Kaufman: His Life, His Theater* by Malcolm Goldstein, 1979; "The Fool and the Clown: The Ironic Vision of George S. Kaufman" by Jeffery D. Mason, in *Farce* edited by James Redmond, 1988; in *American Playwrights, 1880-1945: A Research and Production Sourcebook* edited by William W. Demastes, 1995.

*   *   *

George S. Kaufman was a devastating wit and a serious satirist who worked— almost always in collaboration—on successful plays, musicals, and films. He was especially effective with **Moss Hart,** and their partnership was a productive blend of talents much studied and admired: "Their most distinguished works, *You Can't Take It with You* and *The Man Who Came to Dinner,* reveal Kaufman and Hart," says Milton Levin (in *The Reader's Encyclopedia of World Drama*), "as the best satirists in American drama."

Kaufman's first play was with the team of Larry Evans and Walter C. Percival. Then he and Marc Connelly (another newspaperman from Pennsylvania active in New York) worked on a series of collaborations: *Dulcy, To the ladies!, Merton of the Movies, The Deep Tangled Wildwood,* and *Beggar on Horseback.* Of these, only *The Deep Tangled Wildwood* (a satire "upon the Winchell-Smith type of play") was a failure. *Merton of the Movies,* the story of a movie-struck clerk who achieves success because he, unconsciously, burlesques serious roles, was a delight. The dream sequence of *Beggar on Horseback* (a penniless composer, Neil McRae is given a sedative and has nightmares about having to work in a "widget" factory and then a Consolidated Art Factory, where he has to write music for songs like: "You've broken my heart like you broke my heart/So why should you break it again?") was considered "a fine expression of the resentment of the artist" for those who are "contemptuous of those who show originality" (A.H. Quinn). *Beggar on Horseback* is considered a milestone in American expressionism. The team broke up and Kaufman wrote his one unaided work, *The Butter and Egg Man* (1925), and Connelly tried an original also, *The Wisdom Tooth* (1926). Neither was much good, for Kaufman's farce and Connelly's fantasy did not seem to work separately.

"I have always been smart enough to attach myself to the most promising lad that came along in the theater," said Kaufman, and he joined forces with a number of burgeoning, bright talents. With **Edna Ferber** he wrote *Minick, The Royal Family, Dinner at Eight,*

Stage Door, and *The Land is Bright.* With Herman J. Mankiewicz, another journalist and wit, he wrote *The Good Fellow,* which flopped (Mankiewicz went on to success as a screenwriter, probably writing most of Citizen Kane though that is still argued), but Kaufman had a hit with **Ring Lardner,** that "wonderful man" with such a great ear for American speech, in an hilarious take-off of Tin-Pan Alley, *June Moon.* About the same time, Kaufman began to work with one of the madcap writers behind the Marx Brothers, the too little-acknowledged zany genius, Morrie Ryskind. With Ryskind, Kaufman entered the world of Broadway musicals, starting with *Animal Crackers.* Their collaboration was later to produce *Of Thee I Sing* (with the Gershwins; Pulitzer Prize 1932) and *Let 'em Eat Cake* (with the Gershwins), satires of politics and revolutionaries. With Alexander Woollcott, Kaufman wrote *The Channel Road* and, not much better, *The Dark Tower.* With Katharine Dayton he did a comedy of Washington politics and social life, *First Lady.* In the 1930s he was at his best with Moss Hart. *Once in a Lifetime* was a facile but funny satire on Hollywood. *Merrily We Roll Along* cleverly told its story backwards, taking the middle-aged failure back to the promise of his youth. *I'd Rather Be Right* took its title from a Henry Clay speech of 1850 ("I would rather be right than be President"), but attacked the administration of Franklin Delano Roosevelt. *You Can't Take It with You* well deserved its Pulitzer Prize, for the crazy Sycamore family creates one of the fastest, most furious, funniest farces ever and manages to effect a sweet, sentimental ending as well. The musicals *Strike Up the Band* and *The Band Wagon* (with Howard Dietz) were fun—but *The Man Who Came to Dinner,* with Hart, was fabulous. At the center of the chaos stands (or sits, in a wheelchair) Sheridan Whiteside, described by Monty Woolley in the film biography of Cole Porter as "an intolerable ass." As Woolley played him on stage and screen, this caricature of Alexander Woollcott was irresistible and, though the play is cluttered with other matters (such as cartoons of Noel Coward, one of the Marx Brothers, and a Lizzie Borden character), he delightfully dominates the action as he dominates the poor family who were unlucky enough to have him break a hip on their premises. The play contains some of the best single lines in American comedy.

The Man Who Came to Dinner may be the high point of Kaufman's career. *George Washington Slept Here* was accurately reviewed as "George Kaufman slipped here" and later work such as *The Late George Apley* (with novelist John P. Marquand) and *The Solid Gold Cadillac* (with Howard Teichmann) were a part of Kaufman's long career as a play doctor, though much of their success was no doubt due to his expertise. He also worked with other play doctors (such as Abe Burrows) and with Nunnally Johnson, Leueen MacGrath and others.

Kaufman gained various strengths from various collaborators— farce, fantasy, satire, structure—but, to put it briefly, he can best be understood if one thinks of him as a Jewish comedian. He was a leader among the "Broadway intellectuals" (with Hart, Dorothy Parker, **S.N. Behrman,** George Jean Nathan) and a master of the wisecrack. His is the *echt* Jewish humor that plays with language (as in Goodman Ace); often sees the world as *ash und porukh* (ashes and dust) but will hang on to see what happens ("You might as well live"—Dorothy Parker); deals in insult; sometimes takes off into nonsense, intoxicated by words (**S.J. Perelman**), and sometimes into sentimentality (Sam Levine), attracted to nostalgia for better times; is repelled by pretension and more than a little attracted to cynicism (though not at Kaufman's time going as far as Lenny Bruce) and always loves to tinker with logic until it explodes. In *World of Our Fathers* (1977), Irving Howe dissects this Jewish humor that chooses laughter as the alternative to tears and often uses satire as both a defensive and an offensive weapon. Howe quotes Gilbert Seldes, who claimed that the Jewish entertainers' "daemonic" approach was traceable to "their fine carelessness about our superstitions of politeness and gentility . . . contempt for artificial notions of propriety."

Kaufman was businessman enough to know that an all-out assault on the Establishment would not pay off. His pose was that of the hero of *The Butter and Egg Man,* the naif in the big city. His targets were the obvious, safe ones that are best suited to musical comedy and farce. When he tried something "positive" like *The American Way* (a patriotic panorama), he was at his weakest. A wisecrack has to be a *zinger,* not a compliment. He never let himself get bitter; that was the kind of satire, as he said, which "closes on Sunday night." He wasn't a *kvetch* or a nag or a moralist, just a very funny wisecracking wit, one of the best.

—Leonard R.N. Ashley

KELLY, George (Edward)

Born: Schuykill Falls, Pennsylvania, 16 January 1887. **Education:** Privately educated. **Military Service:** Served in the U.S. Army, 1917. **Career:** Debut as actor, 1908; subsequently acted in touring companies and vaudeville. **Awards:** Pulitzer prize, 1926; Brandeis University Creative Arts award, 1959. A.F.D.: LaSalle College, Philadelphia, 1962. **Died:** 18 June 1974.

PUBLICATIONS

Plays

One of Those Things (produced 1913). In *One-Act Plays for Stage and Study,* 3rd series, 1927.
Finders-Keepers (produced 1916). 1923.
Mrs. Ritter Appears (produced 1917; revised version, as *The Torchbearers: A Satirical Comedy* produced 1922). 1923; revised version of Act III, as *Mrs. Ritter Appears,* 1964.
The Flattering Word (produced 1919). In *The Flattering Word and Other One-Act Plays,* 1925.
The Weak Spot (produced 1922). In *The Flattering Word and Other One-Act Plays,* 1925.
Poor Aubrey (produced 1922). In *The Flattering Word and Other One-Act Plays,* 1925; revised version, as *The Show-Off: A Transcript of Life* (produced 1924), 1924.
Mrs. Wellington's Surprise (produced 1922).
Smarty's Party (produced 1923). In *The Flattering Word and Other One-Act Plays,* 1925.
The Flattering Word and Other One-Act Plays. 1925.
Craig's Wife (produced 1925). 1926.
Daisy Mayme (produced 1926). 1927.
Behold the Bridegroom (produced 1927). 1928.
A La Carte (sketches and lyrics only; produced 1927).
Maggie the Magnificent (produced 1929).
Philip Goes Forth (produced 1931). 1931.
Reflected Glory (produced 1936). 1937.

The Deep Mrs. Sykes (produced 1945). 1946.
The Fatal Weakness (produced 1946). 1947.

Screenplay: *Old Hutch,* 1936.

*

Bibliography: *"Kelly: An Eclectic Bibliography"* by Paul A. Doyle, in *Bulletin of Bibliography,* September-December 1965.

Critical Studies: in *Theatre Chronicles* 1937-1962 by Mary McCarthy, 1963; *Kelly* by Foster Hirsch, 1975.

*   *   *

George Kelly had a lot of brothers and sisters and he followed his older brother Walter ("The Virginia Judge" of vaudeville) into the theater. In those days it was not quite so unusual a place to find a moralist, even an anti-romantic, deeply puritanical one.

Kelly played juveniles on the Keith and Orpheum circuits and began to write sketches such as *One of Those Things, Finders-Keepers, The Flattering Word,* and *Poor Aubrey.* They were light little satires on character flaws such as vanity and bragging. People who overstepped the accepted moral code were given their come-uppance, like the adventuress who outsmarts herself in *Smarty's Party.* They were popular enough: really trenchant satire (as **George S. Kaufman** remarked) "closes on Saturday night," but audiences like to see obvious targets hit skillfully and wittily.

But then Kelly expanded *Poor Aubrey* into the full-length play of *The Show-Off,* in which vanity Aubrey Piper's bragging and bluffing are exposed and his lies and pretensions exploded. It was Kelly's first success, for *The Torchbearers,* a rather gentle send-up of the pretensions of Little Theatres with even littler talent in them, did not catch on at first, though it later was to achieve some recognition.

Kelly achieved the height of his career (and the Pulitzer Prize) with *Craig's Wife.* The vanity of *The Flattering Word* and the manipulator defeated of *Smarty's Party* combine in the well-constructed but rather grimly determined story of a woman whose concern with appearances and control of her sterile environment give "Good Housekeeping" a bad name. But character study is confused with the problem play and Kelly is no Ibsen. Mrs. Craig was unforgettable but essentially just revealed, not developed. A revival of the play in the 1970s made the theatrical success of a half century before look too theatrical and the character of Mrs. Craig too static and that of her long-suffering husband too trivial.

After *Craig's Wife,* Kelly was on the slide. He had four failures in a row: *Daisy Mayme* was talky; *Behold the Bridegroom* was worse, preachy; *Maggie the Magnificent* and *Philip Goes Forth* convinced the dramatist to give up Broadway, though he returned with *Reflected Glory,* and *The Deep Mrs. Sykes.* After the poor reception of *The Fatal Weakness* in 1946, Kelly seemed to recognize his own fatal weaknesses as a playwright—getting in the way of the characters, imposing himself and his views on the situation and using the stage as a soapbox without the brilliance of Shaw or the cleverness of Brecht—and retired. In the late twentieth century he is known as the author of *Craig's Wife* and *The Torchbearers.*

—Leonard R.N. Ashley

KENNEDY, John Pendleton

Born: Baltimore, Maryland, 25 October 1795. **Education:** The Sinclair Academy, Baltimore, and Baltimore College; graduated 1812; studied law: admitted to Maryland bar, 1816. **Military Service:** Served in the U.S. Army during the War of 1812. **Family:** Married 1) Mary Tennant in 1824 (died 1824); 2) Elizabeth Gray in 1829. **Career:** Lawyer in Baltimore from 1816; Maryland House of Delegates, 1820-23; inherited large income from an uncle c. 1830 and increasingly gave up the law for literature and politics; member from Maryland, U.S. House of Representatives, 1838, 1840-44; chairman of the Congressional Committee on Commerce; member of the Maryland House of Delegates and speaker of the house, 1846-48; secretary of the Navy, under President Millard Fillmore, 1852-53; organized Commodore Perry's expedition to Japan, 1852. Provost, University of Maryland; president, Board of Trustees, Peabody Institute, Baltimore. **Member:** American Philosophical Society. **Died:** 18 August 1870.

PUBLICATIONS

Collections

Collected Works. 10 vols., 1871-72.

Fiction

Swallow Barn; or, A Sojourn in the Old Dominion. 1832; edited by Jay B. Hubbell, 1929.
Horse-Shoe Robinson: A Tale of the Tory Ascendency. 1835; edited by Ernest E. Leisy, 1937.
Rob of the Bowl: A Legend of St. Inigoe's. 1838; edited by William S. Osborne, 1965.
Quodlibet, Containing Some Annals Thereof. 1840.

Other

The Red Book, with Peter Hoffman Cruse. 2 vols., 1820-21.
Defence of the Whigs. 1844.
Memoirs of the Life of William Wirt, Attorney General of the United States. 2 vols., 1849; revised edition, 1850.
The Border States. 1860.
Mr. Ambrose's Letters on the Rebellion. 1865.

Editor, with Alexander Bliss, *Autograph Leaves of Our Country's Authors.* 1864.

*

Bibliography: in *Bibliography of American Literature* by Jacob Blanck, 1969.

Critical Studies: *The Life of Kennedy* by Henry T. Tuckerman, in *Collected Works,* 1871; *Kennedy, Gentleman from Baltimore* by Charles H. Bohner, 1961; *Kennedy* by J.V. Ridgely, 1966; "Time and Timelessness in Images of the Old South: Pastoral in John Pendleton Kennedy's *Swallow Barn* and *Horse-Shoe Robinson*" by Jan Bakker, in *Tennessee Studies in Literature,* 1981; "Frontier Yeoman versus Cavalier: The Dilemma of Antebellum Southern Fiction" by Richie D. Watson, in *The Frontier Experience and the*

American Dream: Essays on American Literature edited by David Mogen, Mark Busby, and Paul Bryant, 1989; *What Happened to Horseshoe Robinson? A Study of John P. Kennedy's 1835 Novel, Horseshoe Robinson* by Thomas Weldon Christopher, 1995.

* * *

Only two of John Pendleton Kennedy's four works of fiction can really be called novels. Much like **Washington Irving**'s *Bracebridge Hall,* which it both resembles and satirizes, *Swallow Barn* is hardly more than a series of sketches loosely held together by common characters and a pair of shadowy plot lines, and *Quodlibet* is a satire on Jacksonian politics and policies of the 1830s projected through a history of the imaginary borough of Quodlibet. *Horse-Shoe Robinson* and *Rob of the Bowl* are thus his only true novels. Both are historical romances of the kind made popular by Scott and Cooper.

Swallow Barn is in many ways his most attractive book. Hardly the realistic work it has sometimes been called, it makes good-natured fun of a group of Virginia planters in the early nineteenth century, burlesques their chivalric ideals and pretensions, yet also treats with respect many of the gentlemanly values they attempt to preserve. *Quodlibet,* by contrast, attacks the leveling democrats through one of their number. Solomon Secondthoughts recounts the history of Quodlibet in such a way as to damn the very policies and practices he thinks he is upholding. The work is a clever, if dated, piece of satire.

Horse-Shoe Robinson and *Rob of the Bowl,* on the other hand, develop their themes through the use of history. Kennedy sought to maintain historical accuracy in both, but like other historical romances, the books are concerned not so much with demonstrable fact as with the meaning to be found in the events of the past. Thus, *Horse-Shoe Robinson* portrays the American Revolution as a desperate struggle by young patrician leaders and their yeoman supporters to establish a free society, and *Rob of the Bowl* depicts the successful defense of seventeenth-century Maryland against both Puritan rebels and lawless buccaneers as the maintenance of established order against the threat of disruption.

Kennedy's four books would thus seem to work at cross purposes: *Horse-Shoe Robinson* affirming the need for progressive social change, and *Rob of the Bowl* upholding the value of social stability; *Swallow Barn* satirizing Virginia aristocrats, and *Quodlibet* attacking leveling democrats. Yet the books are not so diverse in meaning as they may seem. The issues they present are those that troubled American thinking during the 1830s, and Kennedy seems to suggest that some kind of balance among the conflicting ideas should be maintained: though American society must progress, it should not change so radically as to destroy the personal and social values that had come to it from the past. Taken together, then, his four works of fiction indicate the skill with which Kennedy, who did not think of himself as a professional man of letters, was able to develop a complex social theme.

—Donald A. Ringe

KENYON, Jane

Born: Ann Arbor, Michigan, 23 May 1947. **Education:** University of Michigan, B.A. 1970, M.A. 1972. **Family:** Married Donald

Hall, *q.v.,* in 1972. **Career:** Visiting writer, State Department cultural exchange in China and Japan, 1986, and India, 1991 and 1993. Cofounder and coeditor, *Green House.* Regular guest editorial writer, *Concord Monitor,* New Hampshire. **Awards:** Avery and Jule Hopwood award, University of Michigan, 1969; National Endowment for the Arts fellowship, 1981; New Hampshire State Council on the Arts fellowship, 1984; Granite State award, Plymouth State College, New Hampshire, 1989; Sara Teasdale award, Wellesley College, 1991; St. Botolph Club award, Boston, 1991; Guggenheim fellowship, 1992; PEN Voelcker award, 1994. **Died:** 22 April 1995.

PUBLICATIONS

Collection

Otherwise: New and Selected Poems. 1996.

Poetry

From Room to Room. 1978.
The Boat of Quiet Hours. 1986.
Let Evening Come. 1990.
Constance. 1993.

Other

A Hundred White Daffodils, 1999.

Translator, *Twenty Poems of Anna Akhmatova.* 1985.

*   *   *

Jane Kenyon's tragic, untimely death in 1995 at age forty-seven cut short one of America's most promising poetry lives. After just four individual volumes, *From Room to Room, The Boat of Quiet Hours, Let Evening Come,* and *Constance,* and in *Otherwise: New and Selected Poems,* which she and her poet-husband, **Donald Hall,** put together in the last months of her life, Kenyon could claim an unusually large and diverse audience.

Others have speculated that she reached so many readers, both inside and out of the academy, because she wrote so openly and well about clinical depression (see her "Having It Out with Melancholy"), perhaps better than anyone else in her time. But this explains only part of her poetry's appeal. In addition to her ability to write concisely about the darkest, non-verbal moments of life, Kenyon also wrote with inspiring compression and clarity, as, for example, in "Otherwise":

> I got out of bed
> on two strong legs.
> It might have been
> otherwise. I ate
> cereal, sweet
> milk, ripe, flawless
> peach. It might
> have been otherwise.
> I took the dog uphill
> to the birch wood.
> All morning I did

> the work I love.
> At noon I lay down
> with my mate. It might
> have been otherwise.
> We ate dinner together
> at a table with silver
> candlesticks. It might
> have been otherwise.
> I slept in a bed
> in a room with paintings
> on the walls, and
> planned another day
> just like this day.
> But one day, I know,
> it will be otherwise.

Wedding the ominous to a sense of the divine links Kenyon, in both spiritual outlook and in style of poems, to Anna Akhmatova, whom she translated. It also invests her work with a greater sense of hope and almost heroic resignation than that of prematurely doomed American precursors like **Sylvia Plath,** Thomas James, and **Anne Sexton.** A further distinction between Kenyon, Plath, and Sexton is that Kenyon can also be read as a religious poet, a nature poet, and a poet of happy domesticity. She is a poet of whom one can say that the spirit of her location in the natural world entered and enriched the poetry itself.

In Kenyon's case, as in her husband Hall's, that landscape consisted mainly of the New Hampshire farm where the two lived and wrote together for nearly 20 years. There she recorded in poems their routines—walking the dog, gardening, attending service at the village church, taking part in community events, writing, cooking, making love. But in poetry the routines took on unusual qualities, became almost ceremonial in their bright, ephemeral humility and sweetness. If this is the greatest challenge faced by the poet of daily affairs, then Kenyon must be included in their front rank. Consider the heartbreaking yet heroic tenor of "Let Evening Come":

> Let the light of late afternoon
> shine through chinks in the barn, moving
> up the bales as the sun moves down.

> Let the cricket take up chafing
> as a woman takes up her needles
> and her yarn. Let evening come.

> Let dew collect on the hoe abandoned
> in long grass. Let the stars appear
> and the moon disclose her silver horn.

> Let the fox go back to its sandy den.
> Let the wind die down. Let the shed
> go black inside. Let evening come.

> To the bottle in the ditch, to the scoop
> in the oats, to air in the lung
> let evening come.

> Let it come, as it will, and don't
> be afraid. God does not leave us
> comfortless, so let evening come.

Few poems of this period so successfully capture the fragile nobility of our time together on this earth.

—Robert McDowell

KEROUAC, Jack

Born: Jean Louis Lebris de Kerouac in Lowell, Massachusetts, 12 March 1922. **Education:** Lowell High School; Horace Mann School, New York, 1939-40; Columbia University, New York, 1940-41, 1942. **Military Service:** Served in the U.S. Merchant Marine, 1942, 1943, and U.S. Navy, 1943. **Family:** Married 1) Edie Parker in 1944 (annulled 1945); 2) Joan Haverty in 1950 (divorced), one daughter; 3) Stella Sampas in 1966. **Career:** Sports reporter, Lowell *Sun,* 1942; worked at various jobs from 1944; brakeman, Southern Pacific Railroad, San Francisco, 1952-53; traveled throughout the United States and Mexico, 1953-56; fire lookout for U.S. Agricultural Service in Washington State, 1956; full-time writer from 1957. **Died:** 21 October 1969.

PUBLICATIONS

Fiction

The Town and the City. 1950.
On the Road. 1957; edited by Scott Donaldson, 1978.
The Subterraneans. 1958.
The Dharma Bums. 1958.
Doctor Sax: Faust Part Three. 1959.
Maggie Cassidy. 1959.
Excerpts from Visions of Cody. 1959.
Tristessa. 1960.
Book of Dreams. 1960.
Big Sur. 1962.
Visions of Gerard. 1963.
Desolation Angels. 1965.
Satori in Paris. 1966.
Vanity of Duluoz: An Adventurous Education 1935-46. 1968.
Pic. 1971.
Visions of Cody. 1973.
Two Early Stories. 1973.

Plays

Screenplay: *Pull My Daisy,* 1959.

Poetry

Mexico City Blues. 1959.
Hymn—God Pray for Me. 1959.
Rimbaud. 1960.
The Scripture of the Golden Eternity. 1960.
Poem. 1962.
A Pun for Al Gelpi. 1966.
Hugo Weber. 1967.
Someday You'll Be Lying. 1968.
A Last Haiku. 1969.

Scattered Poems. 1971.
Trip Trap: Haiku along the Road from San Francisco to New York 1959, with Albert Saijo and Lew Welch. 1973.
Heaven and Other Poems, edited by Donald Allen. 1977.

Other

Lonesome Traveler, drawings by Larry Rivers. 1960.
Old Angel Midnight. N.d.
Dear Carolyn (letters to Carolyn Cassady), edited by Arthur and Kit Knight. 1983.

*

Bibliography: *A Bibliography of Works by Kerouac 1939-1967* by Ann Charters, 1967, revised edition, 1975; *Kerouac: An Annotated Bibliography of Secondary Sources 1944-1979* by Robert J. Milewski, 1981.

Critical Studies: *No Pie in the Sky: The Hobo as American Cultural Hero in the Works of Jack London, John Dos Passos, and Kerouac* by Frederick Feied, 1964; *Kerouac: A Biography* by Ann Charters, 1973; *Kerouac's Town* by Barry Gifford, 1973, revised edition, 1977, and *Jack's Book: An Oral Biography* by Gifford and Lawrence Lee, 1978; *Visions of Kerouac* by Charles E. Jarvis, 1974; *The Visions of the Great Rememberer* by Allen Ginsberg, 1974; *Heart Beat: My Life with Jack and Neal* by Carolyn Cassady, 1976; *Kerouac, Prophet of the New Romanticism: A Critical Study* by Robert A. Hipkiss, 1976; *Kerouac: The New Picaroon* by Luc Gaffie, 1977; *Kerouac* by Harry Russell Huebel, 1979; *Desolate Angel: Kerouac, The Beats, and America* by Dennis McNally, 1979; *Kerouac's Crooked Road: The Development of a Fiction* by Tim Hunt, 1981; *The Kerouac We Knew: Unposed Portraits, Action Shots* edited by John Montgomery, 1982; *Memory Babe: A Critical Biography of Kerouac* by Gerald Nicosia, 1983; "Kerouac Issue" of *Review of Contemporary Fiction,* vol. 3, no. 2, 1983; *Kerouac* by Tom Clark, 1984; *Quest for Kerouac* by Chris Challis, 1984; *Kerouac* by Warren French, 1986; *A Map of Mexico City Blues: Jack Kerouac as Poet* by James T. Jones, 1992; *Soul in the City: A Guide to Jack Kerouac's Lowell* by Paul A. Maher, 1998; *The Long Slow Death of Jack Kerouac* by Jim Christy, 1998; *Jack Kerouac, King of the Beats: A Portrait* by Barry Miles, 1998; *Subterranean Kerouac: The Hidden Life of Jack Kerouac* by Ellis Amburn, 1998.

*   *   *

Along with **Gary Snyder, Allen Ginsberg, William Burroughs,** Neal Cassady, and their compatriots, Jack Kerouac was an unlikely cultural hero. Each, in his own very different way, was a thread in the vast social fabric of the United States. Kerouac was rooted more than most in a traditional American mythos. Raised in a working-class Catholic family in Lowell, Massachusetts, and given to normal boyhood fantasies of early greatness as a football star (he very nearly recognized them in his brief stay at Columbia University), he later became the leading prose writer of the Beat movement. His group and its substantial youthful following sparked a cultural renaissance in mid-twentieth-century America—in literature, music, painting, and the larger realms of society and politics—that will not soon be forgotten.

Kerouac's favorite early nickname was "memory babe," suggestive of his own prodigious memory and the accompanying later desire to preserve, in a weakly fictionalized pickle, the experiences of childhood and youth in Lowell, his days on the road in the heart of America, and particularly his friends and exploits along the way. From his first and most conventional work, *The Town and the City,* he sought to preserve in their essences: himself (as Peter Martin, Sal Paradise, and Jack Duluoz), Snyder (as Japhy Ryder), Ginsberg (as Carlo Marx and Irwin Garden), Burroughs (as Old Bull Lee and Bull Hubbard), and Neal Cassady (as Dean Moriarity and Cody Pomeray). He had hoped, in later life, to collect his works—uniformly bound as multi-volumes of a single gigantic work, with real names and places restored.

Kerouac, the man and the writer, represented a revitalization of the romantic spirit in America. He idealized a return to a more essential and authentic life and intense existence in the present, be it in the streets of his fictional Lowell (*The Town and the City, Doctor Sax*), along the streams and fire trails of his fictional Oregon (*The Dharma Bums*), in the barrios of his fictional California and Mexico (*On the Road, Big Sur, Mexico City Blues*), or in subterranean clubs of New York, Denver, San Francisco, and points along the way. His biographers, particularly Ann Charters and Charles Marcus, document his own fierce and often troubled individualism, recurrent optimism, and reverence for sentient life, and the tragedy of his later years—virtually alone in Florida and finally Lowell.

Kerouac's work depicted both the ideals of the "hot" beats—those like Neal Cassady, who burned their lives as filaments in a quest for "IT!," and "Kicks," pure ecstatic existence in what **Norman Mailer** calls "the enormous present"—and the "cool" beats—Gary Snyder and kindred spirits who sought a return to essence in the more Eastern detached, ascetic realms of Zen and allied philosophies. A keynote of his fiction and poetry is the notion that the act of creating literature is in itself a performance, an authentic act testifying to intensely felt experience. (We should recall the great popularity of poetry as a declaimed form, a song as well as a text, often combined with jazz, during the Beat years.) Thus Kerouac's work rarely responds well to the techniques of close textual reading. He claimed to have written *On the Road* "at white heat" in several weeks on an unbroken roll of teletype paper; his later work was rarely revised, very loose in form, episodic and lyrical at best, improvised like the jazz the Beats so admired, given to humor and nostalgia and the crests and valleys of romantic fiction.

Like many of his fellow Beats (a predominantly masculine group), Kerouac was widely lauded and damned—in his own day and in the present. Like Burroughs and Cassady and Ginsberg, Kerouac lived his life as a kind of work of art, an action painting, a jazz riff. Their experiments in sexuality, with drugs, with the many and often frightening potentialities of psychic and social order and disorder, their bold and often naive desires to re-awaken dormant chords in American life and writing—these have rarely been met with balanced opinions. And Kerouac, as the central figure of the most well-defined literary movement in twentieth-century America, like most truly revolutionary figures, found no final peace in his life and will not soon rest easily in mass thought or literary history.

—Jack Hicks

See the essay on *On the Road.*

KESEY, Ken (Elton)

Born: La Junta, Colorado, 17 September 1935. **Education:** The University of Oregon, B.A. 1957; Stanford University, graduate study in creative writing, 1958-61, 1963. **Family:** Married Faye Haxby in 1956; two sons and two daughters. **Career:** Worked as a multi-media artist and farmer, and a night attendant in psychiatric Veterans Administration Hospital, 1956-61; writer since 1962; president, Intrepid Trips, Inc. (film company), 1964. Beginning 1974 lived with his wife on his farm in Oregon raising prime beef cattle, teaching occasional courses in fiction writing at a nearby university, and working on novels, children's books, and articles. **Awards:** Woodrow Wilson fellowship; Saxton Fund fellowship, 1959; Distinguished Service award, State of Oregon, 1978. **Residence:** Oregon.

PUBLICATIONS

Collections

Kesey's Garage Sale. 1973.
Demon Box. 1986.

Novels

One Flew Over the Cuckoo's Nest. 1962; new edition with criticism, edited by John C. Pratt, 1973.
Sometimes a Great Notion. 1964.
Little Tricker the Squirrel Meets Big Double the Bear (for children). 1988.
Caverns, with others. 1989.
The Sea Lion (for children). 1991.
Sailor Song. 1992.
Last Go Round. 1994.

Screenplay: *The Further Inquiry.* 1990.

Other

Co-editor, *The Last Supplement to the Whole Earth Catalog.* 1971.

*

Critical Studies: *Ken Kesey's One Flew over the Cuckoo's Nest: Text and Criticism* edited by John Clark Pratt, 1963; *A Casebook on Ken Kesey's "One Flew over the Cuckoo's Nest"* edited by George J. Searles, 1970; *Ken Kesey* by Barry H. Leeds, 1981; *The Art of Grit: Ken Kesey's Fiction* by M. Gilbert Porter, 1982; *Ken Kesey* by Stephen L. Tanner, 1983; *The Contemporary American Comic Epic: The Novels of Barth, Pynchon, Gaddis and Kesey* by Elaine B. Safer, 1988; *On the Bus: The Complete Guide to the Legendary Trip of Ken Kesey and the Merry Pranksters and the Birth of the Counterculture* by Paul Perry, 1990.

* * *

Ken Kesey, best known as the author of the novel *One Flew over the Cuckoo's Nest,* which was made into an Academy-Award winning film starring Jack Nicholson, is one of the few remaining cultural heroes of the 1960s. Like the poet and activist **Allen Ginsberg**, Kesey is a superb performer of his own work whose public appearances testify to his tireless resistance to repressive social attitudes and his unflagging quest for heightened personal consciousness. In addition to his literary production, Kesey achieved renown in the 1960s as the organizer of The Merry Pranksters, a group of friends advocating the use of LSD who traveled the American highways coast-to-coast in a bus painted in flowing psychedelic designs. The bus was driven by the legendary Neal Cassady, who had been celebrated as the central character "Dean Moriarty" in **Jack Kerouac**'s "true-life" novel *On the Road* (1957). Influenced by earlier Beat Generation authors like Kerouac, Kesey has been characterized as "the Beat Paul Bunyan" by the poet **Lawrence Ferlinghetti** in reference to the characteristic elements of folkloric humor and tall-tale narrative in Kesey's writing.

Ken Kesey's upbringing in the Pacific Northwest developed interests that he has retained all his life—a fascination with magic and illusions, a commitment to risk-taking in feats of physical endurance like wrestling, and a love of the rural countryside near his home in Eugene, Oregon. After his marriage to his high school sweetheart, Faye Haxby, he and his wife moved from Oregon to California, where he enrolled in the creative writing program at Stanford University. He has remained close friends with his fellow students there who also went on to become well-known writers: Wendell Berry, **Larry McMurtry**, and Robert Stone.

In 1962 Kesey catapulted to literary fame with the publication of his first novel *One Flew over the Cuckoo's Nest,* written while he was a graduate student in the Stanford writing program. Kesey's instructor at Stanford and editor for that book was **Malcolm Cowley**, who had been Kerouac's editor five years earlier for *On the Road.* Both novels celebrate the resilience of the human spirit in a conformist postwar American society shaped by materialistic consumer values.

In Kesey's novel, his hero Randle Patrick McMurphy, who himself committed to a mental hospital to avoid work in a prison farm, challenges the repressive authority of Nurse Ratched, the woman who runs the ward. After McMurphy inspires the dehumanized patients to rebel, Nurse Ratched has him lobotomized. As a 1960s book, Kesey's portrayal of Nurse Ratched provoked considerable negative comment from feminist critics twenty years later. Kesey has explained that in his view, the nurse "just happens to be a woman. She represents the values of the Combine, that is white, western society, and she'll go on winning just like the Combine because she has all the power of the Combine behind her."

All of Kesey's novels and children's stories convey his sense of himself as a "privileged American. I don't know what's right, but I do know what's fair." A self-proclaimed romantic, his prose is always shaped toward communication and persuasion. His prophecy is not the nihilistic message of coming doom in the next millennium but the optimistic belief in available grace, and his writing is a vital testimony to the endurance of hope and humor in this country's literature.

—Ann Charters

KHANSHENDEL, Chiron. *See* **ROSE, Wendy (Bronwen Elizabeth Edwards).**

KIM, Richard E(unkook)

Born: Hamheung, Korea, 13 March 1932. **Education:** Primary and secondary schools in North and South Korea; Middlebury College, 1955-59; Johns Hopkins University, M.A. 1960; University of Iowa, M.F.A. 1962; Harvard University, M.A. 1963. **Military Service:** Served in the Republic of Korea Marines and Army, 1950-54; honorably discharged as first lieutenant, Infantry, December 1954. **Family:** Married Penelope Ann Groll in 1960; one daughter and one son. **Career:** Instructor in English, California State University, Long Beach, 1963-64; assistant professor of English, University of Massachusetts, Amherst, 1964-67, associate professor of English, 1968-69, adjunct associate professor of English, 1969-70. Director, University of Massachusetts Imaginative Writers' Workshop, Nantucket, summers 1967-69; visiting writer, Mediterranean Institute, Mallorca, 1969; visiting professor of English, Syracuse University, 1970-71; visiting professor of English, California State University, San Diego, 1975-77; Fulbright professor of English, Seoul National University, Korea, 1981-83; reporter, narrator, and interviewer for television documentaries, including *200 Years of Christianity in Korea, The Korean War, Reflections on the Wartime Massacres/The Korean War, In Search of Lost Koreans in the Soviet Union,* and *The Great Trans-Siberian Railway;* columnist, *Chosun Ilbo* (*Korea Daily*), and *Korea Herald,* Seoul, Korea, 1981-84; president of Trans-Lit Agency, Shutesbury, Massachusetts, beginning 1985. **Awards:** Johns Hopkins University graduate fellowship, 1959; University of Iowa Writers Workshop fellowship, 1960; Mary Roberts Rinehart Foundation literary fellowship, 1962; Ford Foundation Foreign Area fellowship, 1962; Guggenheim fellowship, 1966; first award, Modern Korean Literature Translation awards, 1974; National Endowment for the Arts literary fellowship, 1978; Fulbright Scholar, 1981-83. **Residence:** Shutesbury, Massachusetts.

PUBLICATIONS

Novels

The Martyred. 1964.
The Innocent. 1968.

Short Stories

Lost Names: Scenes from a Korean Boyhood. 1970.

Other

A Blue Bird (children's story). 1983.
In Search of Lost Years (essays). 1985.
In Search of "Lost" Koreans in China and Russia (photo-essays). 1989.

Translator, *Arrow to the Sun,* by Gerald McDermott. 1982.
Translator, *Picture World 100* (20 volumes of Korean children's stories). 1983.
Translator, *Touch the Earth,* by T.C. McLuhan. 1983.
Co-translator, *The Ascent of Man,* by J. Bronowski. 1985.
Translator, *Three Little Chipmunks and the Sly Old Fox,* by Richard E. Walker. 1986.

Translator, *The Garden of Eden,* by Ernest Hemingway. 1986.
Co-translator, *More Die of Heartbreak,* by Saul Bellow. 1987.

*

Critical Studies: "The Love Stance: Kim's *The Martyred*" by David D. Galloway, in *Critique,* winter 1964-65; "Faith and Despair: A Comparative Study of a Narrative Theme" by Mario J. Valdes, in *Hispania,* September 1966; "The Humanism of Kim" by Robert J. Goar, in *Midwest Quarterly,* summer 1980.

*   *   *

Richard E. Kim's literary reputation is primarily based on his first novel, *The Martyred,* which was a critically acclaimed best-seller in the United States. *The Martyred* was subsequently made into a play and an opera, and in Korea it formed the basis for a film. Critics have praised Kim's writing for its evocation of complex moral themes and grand passions through a modest and economical prose style. Kim's fiction characteristically takes the form of an unobtrusive, chronological, first-person narrative. The emotional tension beneath this narrative is compounded by the carefully restrained and understated manner of the narration.

Kim's style is appropriate to his main theme that is the endurance of the human spirit in the face of the senseless violence of social and political conflict. His writings are informed by existentialist and Korean Christian humanist thought.

All of Kim's fiction explores the human response to the violence of war, revolution, and imperial occupation. Kim's fiction is situated in the context of modern Korean history, whether that context is the Japanese occupation of Korea (*Lost Names*), the Korean War (*The Martyred*), or the volatile national politics of postwar South Korea (*The Innocent*). While these periods correspond roughly with the author's own experiences of growing up in North and South Korea and of serving in the Republic of Korea military, his stories are not, strictly speaking, autobiographical. Kim always maintains his first-person and autobiographical narratives as fiction. The influence of European existentialist thought is apparent throughout his work, most notably in *The Martyred,* which is dedicated to Albert Camus. Kim's writing focuses on the crisis in personal morality that occurs in times of political conflict. To the extent that Kim always sets his work within Korean struggles for national liberation, Kim's existentialism takes the form of passionate political commitment similar to Camus' active commitment to the French Resistance and the movement for Algerian independence.

The Martyred takes place in the early phase of the Korean War from June of 1950 to May of 1951. The narrator, Captain Lee, is assigned by Colonel Chang, the Chief of Army Political Intelligence, to investigate the deaths of twelve Christian ministers in Pyongyang who were executed while in detention by North Korean forces. Colonel Chang hopes to use this incident as political propaganda in the war effort against North Korea. Captain Lee, a former university instructor, is interested in the academic, and later personal, "truth" behind the facts of the execution. Lee's investigation leads him to the two ministers who survived the detention, Mr. Hahn and Mr. Shin. Mr. Hahn has become insane as a result of the ordeal, and Mr. Shin is uncooperative and reticent about the experience. As Captain Lee's investigation continues, a complex moral drama unfolds that draws half a dozen characters into

separate, individual reconciliations with the agony and human frailty exposed by Mr. Shin's varying testimonies. Critics have compared Mr. Shin—as a cleric tormented by doubt, guilt, and despair—with the cleric in Miguel de Unamuno's *San Manuel Bueno, martir* written in Spain in 1931. The theme, setting, and subject of *The Martyred* combined with its spare, austere narration has also led critics to compare *The Martyred* with Camus' *The Stranger* and *The Plague.*

Kim's second novel, *The Innocent,* was not as successful as *The Martyred* but is nevertheless a competently written, briskly paced novel of political intrigue. In *The Innocent* Captain Lee returns as a major; this time he is a conspirator in a military coup against a corrupt South Korean government. The plot is complicated by the profusion of minor characters, especially on the revolutionary council, whose roles and identities are not always clear. While this confusion of characters may reflect the atmosphere of an actual coup, the early part of the novel is sometimes distracted by stiff, cumbersome dialogue between these characters. The central relationship in the novel between Major Lee and the coup leader, Colonel Min, is also flawed by Major Lee's unremittingly naive hopes for a bloodless coup. Major Lee's character has not developed from his experiences as Captain Lee in *The Martyred.* The moral climax of the novel is sustained by Colonel Min who, as the pragmatic leader, tries to balance inevitable bloodshed with the ideals of the revolution. The wider international plot involving the presence of the Chinese, the uneasy collaboration with the American advisor, and scenes from an earlier history of Russian involvement, add informative dimensions to the central plot of the internal South Korean military coup.

Lost Names is a collection of six short stories set in Korea from 1932 to 1945, the last thirteen years of the Japanese occupation. The title refers to the Japanese practice of forcing Koreans to give up their Korean names for Japanese ones. The stories are told from the perspective of a young boy who comes of age as the Japanese imperial occupation is coming to an end. The stories exude warmth and humor through intimate details of family life in rural Korea. However, the stories do not sentimentalize the brutality of foreign domination. In each story there are conscientious acts of endurance and resistance in the face of the Japanese oppressor. Nevertheless, the enduring emotion of each tale is not that of rigid resentment or hate. Rather, the stories are arranged as scenes in the process of the boy's maturation as a historical agent of a new Korean society. In the collection's final story, "In the Making of History—Together," the narrator explain to his father: "We will be all right, Father. We are going to be different from your generation, stronger and more confident." This optimism for Korea's future, in spite of the turmoil of modern Korean history, is the consistent theme of Kim's writings. While Kim lives and writes primarily in the United States, the matter of Korea occupies his central concerns and is the chief social ground over which he unravels his existentialist and Christian humanist themes.

Since 1981 Kim has worked mainly in television and translation. He has also written and translated literature for children. Kim's work of this period often returns to the subjects and interests of the main period of his literary output from 1964 to 1970: displaced Koreans, the Korean endurance of political oppression, and the experience of childhood.

—Tomo Hattori

KING, Stephen (Edwin)

Pseudonyms: Richard Bachman and John Swithen. **Born:** Portland, Maine, 21 September 1947. **Education:** Lisbon Falls, Maine, high school, 1962-66; University of Maine, Orono, B.A. in English, 1970. **Family:** Married Tabitha Spruce in 1971; three children. **Career:** Worked as laborer in industrial laundry, 1970; English teacher, Hampden Academy, Hampden, Maine, 1971-73; wrote several unpublished novels and short stories prior to publication of first book *Carrie,* 1974; lived in Boulder, Colorado, 1974; writer in residence, University of Maine, 1978-79; taught classes in creative writing and gothic fiction; judge, World Fantasy Awards, 1978. Owner, Philtrum Press and WZON-AM, a radio station, Bangor, Maine. Has appeared in several films, making cameo appearances: *Knightriders,* 1981, *Creepshow,* 1982, *Maximum Overdrive,* 1986, and *Pet Sematary,* 1989. **Awards:** Balrog Awards second place in best novel category, and second place in best collection category, 1979; named to American Library Association's list of best books for young adults, 1979, 1981; World Fantasy award for contributions to the field, 1980, and for story, 1982; University of Maine at Orono Career Alumni award, 1981; Science Fiction Writers of America Nebula award nomination, 1981; Hugo award and British Fantasy award, 1982; *Us* magazine Best Fiction Writer of the Year, 1982; Locus award, 1986; selected by *People* magazine as one of twenty individuals who have defined the decade of the eighties; Bram Stoker award for best horror collection, 1990; World Fantasy award for short story, for *The Man in the Black Suit,* 1995. **Residence:** Maine.

PUBLICATIONS

Collections

Stephen King (novel compilation). 1981.
The Bachman Books: Four Early Novels by Stephen King. 1985.

Novels

Carrie. 1974.
'Salem's Lot. 1975.
Rage. 1977.
The Shining. 1977.
The Stand. 1978; revised edition, 1990.
The Dead Zone. 1979.
The Long Walk. 1979.
Firestarter. 1980.
Cujo. 1981.
Roadwork. 1981.
Different Seasons (novellas). 1982.
"The Dark Tower" series:
  The Dark Tower: The Gunslinger, illustrations by Michael Whelan. 1982.
  The Dark Tower II: Drawing of the Three, illustrations by Phil Hale. 1987.
  The Dark Tower III: The Waste Lands, illustrated by Ned Dameron. 1991.
  The Dark Tower Trilogy: The Gunslinger; Drawing of the Three; The Waste Lands. 1993.
The Running Man. 1982.

Christine. 1983.
Pet Sematary. 1983.
Cycle of the Werewolf (novella), illustrations by Berni Wrightson. 1983.
The Eyes of the Dragon. 1984.
The Talisman, with Peter Straub. 1984.
Thinner. 1984.
It. 1986.
Misery. 1987.
The Tommyknockers. 1987.
The Dark Half. 1989.
Needful Things. 1991.
Dolores Claiborne. 1992.
Gerald's Game. 1992.
Four Past Midnight (novellas). 1990.
Insomnia. 1994.
Rose Madder. 1994.
The Green Mile. 1996.
Desperation. 1996.
The Two Dead Girls. 1996.
The Regulators. 1996.
Wizard and Glass. 1997.
Bag of Bones. 1998.
The Girl Who Loved Tom Gordon. 1999.

Recordings: *Rita Hayworth and Shawshank Redemption: Different Seasons I, The Body: Different Seasons II, Apt Pupil: Different Seasons III,* and *The Breathing Method: Different Seasons IV,* 1984; *The Gunslinger* and *Drawing of the Three,* 1988; *One Past Midnight, Two Past Midnight, Three Past Midnight,* and *Four Past Midnight,* 1990.

Short Stories

Night Shift (short stories). 1978.
Skeleton Crew (short stories), illustrations by J. K. Potter. 1985.
My Pretty Pony, illustrations by Barbara Kruger. 1989.
Nightmares and Dreamscapes (short stories). 1993.

Plays

The Shawshank Redemption: The Shooting Script (screenplay). 1996.

Screenplays: *Stephen King's Creep Show,* 1982; *Cat's Eye,* 1984; *Silver Bullet,* 1985; *Maximum Overdrive,* 1986; *Pet Sematary,* 1989; *Sleepwalkers,* 1992; *The Shawshank Redemption,* 1996.

Television Plays: *Golden Years* (limited series), 1991; *The Stand,* 1994.

Poetry

Another Quarter Mile: Poetry. 1979.

Other

Danse Macabre (nonfiction) 1981.
The Plant (serial comic horror novel). 1982. 1983. 1985.
Black Magic and Music: A Novelists Perspective of Bangor (nonfiction). 1983.
Nightmares in the Sky: Gargoyles and Grotesques, photographs by f-stop Fitzgerald. 1988.

*

Bibliography: *The Work of Stephen King: An Annotated Bibliography and Guide* by Michael R. Collings, 1996.

Critical Studies: *Fear Itself: The Horror Fiction of Stephen King* 1982, *Kingdom of Fear: The World of Stephen King* 1986, *Bare Bones: Conversations on Terror with Stephen King* (interviews) 1988, *Feast of Fear: Conversations with Stephen King* (interviews) 1989, all edited by Tim Underwood and Chuck Miller; *Stephen King: The Art of Darkness* by Douglas Winter, 1984, and interview with Winter in *The Faces of Fear: Encounters with the Creators of Modern Horror* 1985; *Stephen King As Richard Bachman* 1985, and *The Many Facets of Stephen King* 1985, both by Michael R. Collings; *Stephen King: The First Decade* by Joseph Reino, 1988; *Reign of Fear: Fiction and Film of Stephen King* edited by Don Herron, 1988; *Landscape of Fear: Stephen King's American Gothic* 1988, *Stephen King: The Second Decade* 1992, both by Tony Magistrale, and *The Dark Descent: Essays Defining Stephen King's Horrorscape* edited by Magistrale, 1992; *The Stephen King Companion* edited by George Beahm, 1989; *American Horror Fiction: From Brockden Brown to Stephen King* edited by Brian Docherty, 1990; *The Shape under the Sheet: The Complete Stephen King Encyclopedia* edited by Stephen J. Spignesi, 1991; *Family Survival: Domestic Ideology and Destructive Paternity in the Horror Fictions of Stephen King* (dissertation) by Joe M. Abbott, 1994; *Stephen King's America* by Jonathan P. Davis, 1994; *Observations from the Terminator: Thoughts on Stephen King and Other Modern Masters of Horror Fiction* by Tyson Blue, 1996; *Stephen King: A Critical Companion* by Sharon A. Russell, 1996; *Forbidden Texts: The Ambivalence of Knowledge and Writing in Horror Fiction from Mary Shelley to Stephen King* (dissertation) by Steven R. Glickman, 1997; *Discovering Stephen King's The Shining: Essays on the Bestselling Novel by America's Premier Horror Writer,* edited by Tony Magistrale, 1998; *Stephen King from A to Z: An Encyclopedia of His Life and Work* by George W. Beahm, 1998; *Stephen King* by John F. Wukovits, 1999.

*   *   *

In the past two decades, Stephen King has emerged as arguably the most popular writer in America. In 1989, Viking unleashed 1.5 million hardcover copies of *The Dark Half,* the largest first- edition printing in publishing history. He was, in addition, the first writer to have had five titles appear simultaneously on the *New York Times*'s bestseller list. But attendant to such enormous popularity come questions regarding the quality of King's substantial fictional canon. Despite an emerging corpus of film and literary criticism in the past few years that has treated King's work quite seriously, his long-standing artistic reputation is still considered in doubt. Is he merely an enduring fad in the popular imagination, a writer who panders to America's love affair with poorly crafted action novels emphasizing violence and the supernatural? Or does Stephen King offer something more substantial, continuing an American literary tradition that certainly dates back to **Edgar Allan Poe** and **Nathaniel Hawthorne** in the nineteenth century, and even further if we wish to view King as an heir to British and German gothicism?

Critics and English teachers have debated these issues since King's emergence; but perhaps what is most significant is the fact that these questions, both embodying essential truths about King's literary contribution, have even been asked—and continue to be asked—at all. The careful reader of Stephen King senses that he is up to something important in his work, in the same way that **William Faulkner** and **Shirley Jackson**, two of King's favorite novelists, are doing something important in theirs—and in a way that Danielle Steele or Tom Clancy, for instance, are not. But exactly what is Stephen King doing that makes him interesting both to readers who dislike literature and seldom read any writer other than King and those who are scholars of American literature?

Writing about the demographics and personalities represented in King's diverse audience in "Stephen King and His Readers: A Dirty, Compelling Romance," Brian Kent acknowledges King's attraction to, and utilization of, high and low culture: "King can write to please university professors if he chooses, and he often chooses, but his special gift is his ability to use the tools of sophisticated literary construction in such a way that . . . the bulk of his readership [is] not put off or intimidated and still gets the point." Kent's commentary is often echoed by King himself, as when he insisted in an interview that the "story must be paramount, because it defines the entire work of fiction. All other considerations are secondary—theme, mood, even characterizations and language."

Even as King would appear to relegate the craft of storytelling to the story itself, it is clear that he has created a highly complex body of work that reflects—in terms of its narrative experimentation, character development, and the essential conflict which often occurs between the individual and his or her environment—a deep awareness of America's rich literary tradition. King's descriptions of his native Maine in a novel such as *Pet Sematary,* the close scrutiny of character, tradition, and the clash between civilized values and the wilderness, find their closest points of comparison in the writing of Hawthorne. From Poe, King learned how to visualize the confinement of an interior atmosphere. *The Shining* would not produce the same levels of terror and claustrophobic anxiety were it not for King's awareness of "The Fall of the House of Usher" and "Masque of the Red Death." In addition, King has been strongly influenced by the naturalistic fiction of writers such as **Theodore Dreiser, Frank Norris,** and **Ernest Hemingway.** *Cujo* and particularly the novels published under the Richard Bachman pseudonym speak directly to naturalistic concerns: the sense of the individual alone and at odds with an environment that is actively opposed to human survival. Lastly, but by no means exhausting his ability to bridge the immediate and familiar landscape of contemporary America with the tradition of nineteenth-and twentieth-century American literature, Stephen King is the novelist who perhaps best approximates William Faulkner's bifurcated vision of the regional merging into the transcendent. Faulkner's contributions to the development of the modern novel, for example, were important influences on the narrative structure of King's 1986 novel *It.* Both writers represented, through their use of experimental narrative structures, the insistence that survival and identity, for individuals as well as for social communities, were possible only when the past was acknowledged and viewed in direct relationship to the present. Just as Faulkner frequently dispenses with the typical characteristics found in conventional narratives in order to provide the reader with a deeper and multifaceted understanding of history, King likewise employs a narrative—incorporating time dislocations and convergences, and multiple and subjective perspectives on a shared past—that is drawn from a variety of historical consciousnesses.

In addition to experimenting with various narratological points of view and stylistic inclusions which reflect these purposes,

Faulkner composed a unique vision of the South in his Yoknapatawpha cycle. King presents us with a similar attempt to create a unified myth of place in his portrait of Castle Rock and its surrounding Maine communities. The rural social environments in novels such as *'Salem's Lot, The Tommyknockers, The Body, It, Thinner,* and *Needful Things* represent large portions of each book. King sets up an opposition between a vampire-like megacharacter, the Maine town upon which it "feeds," and several central characters who resist the megacharacter's intrusion. In each of these novels the town as a community revolves around some locus of decay: in *It,* it is the Derry sewer system; in *Lot,* the Marston House; in *Tommyknockers,* the ship in the woods; and in *Needful Things,* the stranger, Leland Gaunt, preys upon the baser instincts of Castle Rock's citizenry. While King is highly critical of his small-town societies and their attendant institutions, individual Maine men and women often find themselves in positions where they must rise above their unassuming and oppressive origins to engage in heroic action. Against the collective antagonistic energy of the town itself, King places several protagonists who represent the life force in their stubborn refusal to capitulate to evil's corrosive momentum; they are always alone in their estrangement from the collective negative psyche that engulfs their respective communities.

King's work has been shaped by high and low culture alike; his art may be seen as the very embodiment of a postmodernist aesthetic. At the same time as the influences of Poe and Faulkner must be acknowledged, scholars need also to account for less mainstream writers such as Ira Levin (*Rosemary's Baby*) and Charles Beaumont (teleplays for the "Twilight Zone" series) who shaped King's ability to exploit what he calls "phobic pressure points," the potential for terror inherent in everyday occurrences. King labors deliberately to create an easily identifiable world littered with touchstones of reality: corporate brand names, products, recent political and historical figures and events. Moreover, his typical protagonists are ordinary middle-class men and women who suddenly find themselves in extraordinary circumstances. King establishes these believable contexts in order to place the reader in a position where he or she is forced to establish a bond with the protagonist under siege. This strategy makes the terror more real. As he argues throughout *Danse Macabre,* "If horror has redeeming social merit, it is because of that ability to form liaisons between the real and unreal." Consequently, King's greatest terrors have little to do with the supernatural per se. He is far more interested in reminding us about what is terrifying in real life: our technological hazards; familial tensions, particularly in the form of unresponsive and openly antagonistic parents; the destructive potential of alcohol and drugs on a permissive society that often glorifies their use; the general inability of social institutions to maintain their viability in the shape of changing values and needs; the tragic consequences of patriarchal privilege and abuse.

King's stories often speak to us of unresolved tensions that are both endemic to our time and particular to an individual's identity formation. A novel such as *The Shining,* for example, is disturbing not only because of its obvious gothic trappings—animated hedge animals, ghosts moving in the night—but also because the novel forces the reader into recognizing childhood phobias about parental discord, devouring mother and father figures, separation and abandonment anxieties, and child abuse itself. Similarly, *Gerald's Game* suggests that only by confronting the darkest memories of childhood is it possible for the adult to attain true liberation.

In novels as diverse as *Misery, It, The Shining, The Stand, Cujo, Pet Sematary* and *Gerald's Game,* King is interested in probing what the past represents to both the individual characters who must confront it directly, and to the larger American culture that has shaped its meaning. In his work, the past is both a curse and a means for survival. Individual characters are menaced by the sins of the past and its influence upon the present, as in the evil representations of *It,* the Micmac burial ground, or the Overlook Hotel. Conversely, King's fictional survivors frequently thwart evil's design by relying upon the power of memory: the shared childhood loyalties and friendships in *It,* the willingness to face the terrors of one's personal history in *Gerald's Game* and *Dolores Claiborne* and in doing so uncover a means for establishing a stronger identity in the present.

What is perhaps more impressive than the number of book titles King has published in two decades of writing is the range of literary genres and traditions he has incorporated into his art. His canon belies the reductive characteristics often ascribed to popular fiction and horror in particular. In *The Shining* and *Pet Sematary* critics have noted classical tragic paradigms; science fiction themes and hardware are found in *The Tommyknockers, The Running Man,* and several of his short stories; epic and mythic archetypes dominate *The Stand, It,* and *The Talisman;* the genres of the fairy tale and the American western are modelled in *Eyes of the Dragon* and *The Dark Tower,* respectively; the political-historical novel is treated in *Apt Pupil* and *The Dead Zone;* and in his most recent fiction, *Gerald's Game* and *Dolores Claiborne,* King has created narratives from strong feminist perspectives. Although his work has often been dismissed by critics who argue that King does not produce "serious" fiction, it is clear that those who would posit such an assessment have either failed to read this writer carefully, or have not bothered to read him at all.

—Tony Magistrale

KINGSLEY, Sidney

Born: Sidney Kirshner in New York City, 22 October 1906. **Education:** Townsend Harris Hall, New York, 1920-24; Cornell University, Ithaca (state scholarship), 1924-28, B.A. 1928. **Military Service:** Served in the U.S. Army, 1941-43: lieutenant. **Family:** Married the actress Madge Evans in 1939 (died). **Career:** Actor in the Tremont Stock Company, Bronx, 1928-29; thereafter playreader and scenario writer for Columbia Pictures; full-time writer and stage director from 1934; president, Dramatists Guild, 1961-69. **Awards:** Pulitzer prize, 1934; New York Theatre Club medal, 1934, 1936, 1943; New York Drama Critics Circle award, 1943, 1951; New York Newspaper Guild Front Page award, 1943, and Page One Citation, 1949; Mystery Writers of America Edgar Allan Poe award, 1950; Donaldson award, 1951; American Academy Award of Merit Medal, 1951, Gold Medal, 1986; Yeshiva University award, 1965; named to Theatre Hall of Fame, 1983. D.Litt.: Monmouth College, West Long Branch, New Jersey, 1978; Ramapo College, Mahwah, New Jersey, 1978. **Died:** 1995.

PUBLICATIONS

Plays

Men in White (produced 1933). 1933.
Dead End (produced 1935). 1936.

Ten Million Ghosts (produced 1936).
The World We Make, from the novel *The Outward Room* by
    Millen Brand (produced 1939). 1939.
The Patriots (produced 1943). 1943.
Detective Story (produced 1949). 1949.
Darkness at Noon, from the novel by Arthur Koestler (produced
    1951). 1951.
Lunatics and Lovers (produced 1954). Condensed version in *Theater 1955,* 1955.
Night Life (produced 1962). 1966.
The Art Scene. 1969.
Sidney Kingsley: Five Prizewinning Plays (includes *Men in White;*
    Dead End; The Patriots; Detective Story; Darkness at Noon).
    1995.

Screenplay: *Homecoming,* with Paul Osborn and Jan Lustig, 1948.

*

Critical Study: "Sidney Kingsley's Men in White" by Evangeline
Morphos in *The Drama Review* winter 1984.

*   *   *

Sidney Kingsley was one of "the young radicals our colleges
are said to be full of nowadays," as **S. N. Behrman** put it in *End
of Summer.* His agit-prop approach to theatre was a bit less strident than that of some other proletarian dramatists, but sufficient
to endear him to the famous Group Theater, whose financial life
he saved early in its career with the success of his first play, *Men
in White.*

The story of *Men in White* is accurately told by John Mason
Brown in *Two on the Aisle:* it "is a piffling script, mildewed in its
hokum, childishly sketchy in its characterization, and so commonplace in its every written word that it in no way justifies its own
unpleasantness." Moreover, "the finished result . . . is *only remarkable because it is not real.*" Kingsley's approach has since
been copied, in its dab-hand dramaturgy and somewhat fuzzy concern with ethical standards, in **Paddy Chayefsky**'s *The Hospital*
and *Network* and in many television soap operas and feature films.

Also seminal was *Dead End,* establishing for the cinema many
of the cliches of slum-life sociology. Brooks Atkinson called it "a
raucous tone-poem of the modern city," a shaky melodrama set
down in a handsome set with a pier-head jutting right into the
orchestra pit. The contrived plot brings the Dead End kids and
other poor folk into contact with some rich East Siders in New
York: the facade of the wealthy apartment house is under repair,
which brings the rich people round to the back and right on stage.
Unfortunately for Kingsley, he does not seem to remember poverty without sentimentality and, at least before the considerable
success of *Dead End,* seems never to have met anyone rich. His
sociology is superficial and his dramaturgy profoundly pedestrian.
Ten Million Ghosts is a confused discussion of munitions mag-
nates. Kingsley was well out of his intellectual depth. *The World
We Make* was not much better, although for once in the 1930s the
emphasis is upon character rather than upon "The System" and
environment. *The Patriots* is about a decade in the life of **Thomas
Jefferson.** In none of these plays did Kingsley have the advantages he had in *Dead End.* He desperately needed stars and set
designers and a whole team to "make something" of his scripts.
He once half perceived this when he said: "When two people have

a baby, the baby is a bit of a surprise. In the theater we have a
marriage of many people. I can't really tell how the baby will
come out."

Kingsley became known to wider audiences through such films
as *Men in White, Dead End,* and *Detective Story.* He was at his
best whenever he had help: the committed cast of *Men in White,*
the street arabs and street scene of *Dead End,* Millen Brand's novel
The Outward Room as a basis for *The World We Make,* Madge
Evans to help with *The Patriots,* Arthur Koestler's novel behind
Darkness at Noon. Crowell's Handbook of Contemporary Drama
gives as fair an estimate as any: "In most of his work Kingsley
relies on a sense of atmosphere generated by realistic re-creation
of a particular world—hospitals, slums, police stations, prisons—
a vivid milieu that supplies much of the vivid impact of the play
and also constitutes its limitation. The plays are frequently melodramatic in plot and sketchy in characterization; timely issues
have made them at first appear more substantial than they later
are seen to be."

Kingsley's theatre is not made to be read as "a text." The "atmosphere" that he heavily relies on has to be created on stage
with the proper commitment of the actors, with a set of which
the importance needs to be exaggerated, and with an unusual lighting design. Otherwise his plays, which are extremely easy to follow, pose no questions, arouse no interest. To the sophisticated
imagination of the modern theatre goer, the actions are dull and
lack moments of fascination. To the non-initiated spectator, always concerned with "what happens next," his plays seem to be
dragging. Ordinary people busy themselves with ordinary actions,
and still, surprisingly enough, they seem to re-create a particular
world, a shadow-image of our trivial lives, a duplicate of an already known original.

—Leonard R.N. Ashley, updated by Dayana Stetco

KINGSOLVER, Barbara

Born: Annapolis, Maryland, 8 April 1955. **Education:** DePauw
University, B.A. (Magna cum laude) 1977; University of Arizona,
M.S. 1981. **Family:** Married Joseph Hoffman in 1985 (divorced),
one daughter. **Career:** Research assistant in department of physiology, 1977-79; technical writer in office of arid land studies, 1981-
85; freelance journalist, 1985-87. Since 1987 full-time writer. Book
reviewer, *New York Times,* beginning 1988. **Awards:** Feature-writ-
ing award, Arizona Press club, 1986; American Library Association awards for *The Bean Trees,* 1988, and for *Homeland,* 1990;
citation of accomplishment from United Nations National Council of Women, 1989; PEN fiction prize and Edward Abbey
Ecofiction award, for *Animal Dreams,* 1991; Woodrow Wilson/
Lila Wallace fellow, 1992-93. D.Litt.: De Pauw University, 1994.

PUBLICATIONS

Novels

The Bean Trees. 1988.
Animal Dreams. 1990.
Pigs in Heaven. 1993.
The Poisonwood Bible. 1998.

Short Stories

Homeland and Other Stories. 1989.

Poetry

Another America/Otra America. 1993.

Other

Holding the Line: Women in the Great Arizona Mine Strike of 1983. 1989.
High Tide in Tucson: Essays from Now or Never. 1995.

*

Critical Studies: *A Reader's Guide to the Fiction of Barbara Kingsolver: The Bean Trees, Homeland and Other Stories, Animal Dreams, Pigs in Heaven* by Jennifer Fleischner, 1994; *Kentucky Literature* by George Brosi, 1994; "Barbara Kingsolver" by Robin Epstein, in *The Progressive,* February 1996, pp. 33; *Barbara Kingsolver: A Critical Companion* by Mary Jean DeMarr, 1999.

*   *   *

Barbara Kingsolver is an original and engaging writer who has already created a diverse body of work. In 1988 Kingsolver came upon the American fiction scene with an award-winning novel, *The Bean Trees,* which traces a young woman's travels from rural Kentucky to the deserts of Arizona. Along her journey, Taylor Greer meets a host of unusual characters, including Turtle, a Native American girl that she adopts as her daughter. This popular novel examines the costs of uprooting and the values of creating new communities, as Taylor learns to connect with other women and to empower herself. Kingsolver has described the loose design of this first novel by comparing it to dumping out an old purse of ideas and characters: ". . . there lies this pile of junk. You start picking through it, and assembling it into what you hope will be a statement of your life's great themes." She also admits that this book, conceived while she was pregnant with her first daughter, was written during many nights of insomnia. In an early review in the *New York Times Book Review,* Jack Butler praised the book's "stark fine poetry," and concluded, "Barbara Kingsolver can write. On any page of this accomplished first novel, you can find a striking image and fine dialogue or a telling bit of drama. . . . It is one thing to create a vivid and realistic scene, and it quite another to handle the harmonics of many such scenes, to cause all the images and implications to work together."

Kingsolver's next book was a historical chronicle titled *Holding the Line: Women in the Great Mine Strike of 1983* (1989), comprised of oral narration and social criticism. It won early praise as a politically and socially engaged work. A critic in the *Industrial and Labor Relations Review* called the book "a stirring, densely documented narrative that works as drama and as social history." Like the renowned 1956 film *Salt of the Earth,* this nonfiction book lays out a socially engaged stance through rich human portraits, which celebrate women and a communal sense of empowerment. Kingsolver declared, "I believe the creation of empathy is a political act. The ability to understand and really feel for people who are different from ourselves—that's a world-changing event.

It's the antidote to bigotry and spiritual meanness, and all the terrible things those deficiencies lead us into. That is why I feel lucky to get to do what I do: I get a little shot at changing the world."

Though one might predict from this early manifesto a canon of work that assumes a political platform, in fact, what has emerged from Kingsolver is a series of delightful fictions that are as human and humorous as **Mark Twain**'s *Adventures of Huckleberry Finn.* She moves the reader from within, with her vision and empathy for human diversity.

Kingsolver's writing career actually began ignominiously as a science writer for the University of Arizona in Tucson, where she earned a master's degree in biology. She also had been writing freelance journalism and short fiction in the early 1980s. In the 1970s she went to DePaw University in Indiana to study music but earned a degree in biology and ecology; there she also became an activist against the war in Vietnam and for social and environmental responsibility. All of these concerns she has extended into her fiction and essays. Kingsolver became socially aware as a child growing up in rural Nicholas County, Kentucky, where her father was a country doctor and where, she confides, "You can't help seeing the difference between the haves and have-nots. . . . The options were limited—grow up to be a farmer or a farmer's wife." The family's life took a surprising turn when Kingsolver was eight years old; they moved to Africa, where her father ran a medical clinic, and the family became a racial minority—a situation she used in her 1998 opus *The Poisonwood Bible.* Though Kingsolver declares that the characters in her writings are not based on "real people" that she knows personally, the settings are always vividly real and close to home.

A pivot now in the direction of her work after these early premiers reveals that her two veins, personal essays of commitment and deeply human fictions, are actually integral. Her 1989 *Homeland and Other Stories* further revealed the diversity of her fictional world, the unity of her sense of character and place, her vibrant language and wit, and her deeply felt themes. This collection of twelve tales received an important review from fellow writer Russell Banks in the *New York Times Book Review,* where he noted her originality yet placed her with other engaged writers of the working-class, including **Grace Paley, Raymond Carver,** and, by implication, himself. "There is a moral toughness in her characters . . . Like Paley and Raymond Carver, Ms. Kingsolver mixes argot with aphorism, sexual frankness with delicate high-mindedness, the purely personal with class-consciousness. There is an interesting ingratiating style, miles from the high cool of minimalism, but just as carefully wrought, and it seems especially suited to, and respectful of, the lives she wishes to dramatize." Though the stories are a bit uneven in quality, the title story "Homeland" is recognized as a small classic of character and place. Kingsolver emerged as a major American fiction writer here.

While not strictly a "feminist" writer, Kingsolver clearly and repeatedly delineates the struggles of women and reveals women's ways of experiencing and surviving. This is evident in her next two novels, *Animal Dreams* (1990) and *Pigs in Heaven* (1993). The former concerns two estranged sisters, Codi and Hallie Noline; Codi is returning from a life of drifting to Arizona where she will care for her father, suffering from Alzheimers disease. Hallie is a political activist in Nicaragua, yet maintains her connections to her home and sister with her letters home. The book is carefully structured and weaves themes of social responsibility with personal integration. *Pigs in Heaven* picks up the Greer family from *The Bean Trees* as Taylor and her daughter struggle together with personal needs and Native American cultural laws, ultimately integrating the values of the individual and the communities, recurring themes for Kingsolver. Novelist Hilma Wolitzer found the book's strength in its fairness, "It is the author's particular achievement that both sides of the issue are wholly sympathetic, and that in the midst of this compelling story we're given an undidactic, historical overview of the oppression and deconstruction of the Native American family" (*Chicago Tribune*, July 11, 1993).

Following these novels, Kingsolver published a collection of personal essays that used generous wit and political and cultural insight to deal with contemporary American life. In *High Tide in Tucson: Essays from Now and Never* (1995) issues of family, community, environmental concerns, motherhood, and social responsibility are treated through Kingsolver's light style yet committed approach. A review in the *New York Times* suggested the book's special charm: "Kingsolver's essays should be savored like quiet afternoons with a friend . . . [She] speaks in a language rich with music and replete with good sense"

In 1998 Kingsolver found herself in a new marriage with ornithologist Steven Hopp, with a new daughter, and with her most ambitious book to date, *The Poisonwood Bible*. For her setting the author went back to the Africa of her youth, only this time her characters were a family lead by Baptist minister Nathan Price. The story is told in a series of narratives by each of the women of that family: mother Orleanna Price, self-absorbed teenager Rachel, twins Leah and Adah, and five-year-old Ruth May. Suspense and tragedy compel this drama of the Western assault on African culture. The Reverend Price has neither understanding of nor appreciation for tribal culture and so creates havoc for them and his family. Kingsolver has admitted in interviews that she had to wait thirty years for the maturity to write this epic, but its acclaim seems worth the wait. Critics have cited the moral perception of the book and its fully realized narrative achievement. Novelist Jane Smiley stated in *Washington Post Book World*, "There are few ambitious, successful, and beautiful novels. Lucky for us, we have one now, in Barbara Kingsolver's *The Poisonwood Bible*. This awed reviewer hardly knows where to begin."

Ultimately, Kingsolver's empathetic writing has worked to change the consciousness and thus the conscience. It has created a wide path for a deeply human literature. She declares, "I have a commitment to accessibility. I believe in plot. I want an English professor to understand the symbolism while at the same time I want the people I grew up with . . . to read my books." With such commitment and craft Kingsolver builds bridges with each book.

—Larry Smith

KINGSTON, Maxine (Ting Ting) Hong

Born: Stockton, California, 27 October 1940. **Education:** University of California, Berkeley, A.B. in English, 1962. Earned teaching certificate, 1965. **Family:** Married Earll Kingston, 1962; one son. **Career:** English and mathematics teacher, Sunset High School, Hayward, California, 1965-1967; teacher, Kahuku High School, Hawaii, 1967-68; teacher, Drop-In School, Kahaluu, Hawaii, 1968-69; teacher, Kailua High School, Hawaii, 1969; English teacher,

Honolulu Business College, Honolulu, Hawaii, 1969-70; teacher, Mid-Pacific Institute, 1970-76; visiting associate professor of English, University of Hawaii, Honolulu, 1976-77; visiting professor at Eastern Michigan University, 1986-87. Beginning 1990 English and creative writing instructor, University of California at Berkeley. **Awards:** National Book Critics Circle award, 1976; *Mademoiselle* magazine award, 1977; Anisfield-Wolf Race Relations award, 1978; *Time* magazine's Top Ten Nonfiction Works of the Decade list, 1979; National Endowment for the Arts writing fellow, 1980; named Living Treasure of Hawaii, 1980; American Book award for general nonfiction, 1981; Woman of the year, Asian Pacific Women's Network, 1981; Stockton, California, Arts Commission Award, 1981; Hawaii Writers award, 1983; PEN award in fiction, 1987; Lila Wallace Reader's Digest Writing award, 1992; Cyril Magnin award for Outstanding Achievement in the Arts, 1996; Fred Cody Lifetime Achievement award, 1998; John Dos Passos prize for Literature, 1998. **Member:** American Academy of Arts and Science. **Residence:** Oakland, California.

PUBLICATIONS

Novels

The Woman Warrior: Memoirs of a Girlhood among Ghosts. 1975.
China Men. 1977.
Tripmaster Monkey: His Fake Book. 1987.

Poetry

The Open Boat, edited by Garrett Hongo. 1992.

Other

Hawai'i One Summer. 1987.

*

Critical Studies: *A Poetics of Women's Autobiography: Marginality and the Fictions of Self-Representation* edited by Sidonie Smith, 1987; *Approaches to Teaching Kingston's The Woman Warrior* edited by Shirley Geok-lin Lim, 1991; "The High Note of the Barbarian Reed Pipe: Maxine Hong Kingston" by Gloria Chun, *Journal of Ethnic Studies* vol. 19, no. 3, 1991; *Haunting the House of Fiction: Feminist Perspectives on Ghost Stories by American Women* edited by Wendy Kolmar, 1991; *Critical Essays on Maxine Hong Kingston* edited by Laura E. Skandera-Trombley, 1998; *Conversations with Maxine Hong Kingston* edited by Paul Skenazy, 1998; *The Female Bildungsroman by Toni Morrison and Maxine Hong Kingston: A Postmodern Reading* by Pin-chia Feng, 1998; *Maxine Hong Kingston* by Diane Simmons, 1999; *Maxine Hong Kingston's The Woman Warrior: A Casebook* edited by Sau-ling Cynthia Wong, 1999.

*   *   *

The publication of *The Woman Warrior* in 1976 and its immediate critical success and embracement by feminists propelled Maxine Hong Kingston to fame and recognition. *The Woman Warrior*'s companion text, *China Men,* and her later novel

Tripmaster Monkey: His Fake Book have met with similarly warm critical receptions, although not nearly the same commercial success as her first novel.

Since its publication, *The Woman Warrior: Memories of a Girlhood among Ghosts* has become, according to Gloria Chun, "the most widely taught book by a living writer in U.S. colleges and universities." It appears in courses under such diverse departments such as Literature, Asian American Studies, Ethnic Studies, Women's Studies, Sociology, History, Anthropology, and Political Science. *Washington Post Book World* reviewer William McPherson wrote that *The Woman Warrior* is "a strange, sometimes savagely terrifying and, in the literal sense, wonderful story of growing up caught between two highly sophisticated and utterly alien cultures, both vivid, often menacing and equally mysterious." Frederick Wakeman, Jr., in a review of *China Men* for the *New York Review of Books,* notes that "as Kingston herself has admitted, many of the myths she describes are largely her own reconstructions . . . precisely because the myths are usually so consciously contrived, her pieces of distant China lore often seem jejune and even inauthentic—especially to readers who know a little bit about the original high culture which Kingston claims as her birthright."

These two reviews characterize a debate over the generic literary status (whether autobiography, fiction, or both) of *The Woman Warrior* and *China Men* that has consumed Asian American scholars and literary critics since their publication. This debate over generic classification has been particularly intense on the topic of how accurately Kingston should represent Chinese American experiences in her writing. These texts are marketed as autobiography and are viewed as factual in most of the classes that use them. Since Kingston incorporates loosely interpreted and even revised Chinese and Western myths, utilizes a non-linear chronological structure and tells multiple versions of single events in these texts, distinguishing fact from fiction as well as actual Chinese culture from American distortions are daunting, if not impossible. Given the extremely wide popularity of *The Woman Warrior* and its inclusion on many high school and college course syllabi, this debate over authenticity has wide-ranging implications.

According to Kingston: "*The Woman Warrior* and *China Men* were supposed to be one book. I had conceived of one huge book. However, part of the reason for two books is history. The women had their own time and place and their lives were coherent; there was a women's way of thinking. My men's stories seemed to interfere. They were weakening the feminist point of view. So I took all the men's stories out, and then I had *The Woman Warrior.*" The structure of *China Men* exhibits this comparative incoherence. Unlike *The Woman Warrior,* which is a largely first-person narrative focussing primarily on the relationship between the second generation Chinese American female protagonist and her mother, *China Men* incorporates stories of four generations of Chinese American men in the protagonist's family. Great-grandfather, Bak Goong, worked in the cane sugar plantations in Hawaii, while the grandfather, Ah Goong, labored on the first transcontinental railroad. The father alternately owns and operates a laundry and gambling house, and the brother is a pacifist who teaches high school writing and is reluctantly drafted into the Vietnam War. In *China Men,* the narrator attempts to come to terms with her father's culturally-based misogynist attitudes: "What I want from you is for you to tell me that those curses are only common Chinese sayings. That you did not mean to make me sicken at being female. 'Those were only sayings,' I want you to say to me. 'I

didn't mean you or your mother. I didn't mean your sister or grandmothers or women in general.'"

The narrator also must cope with her father's mysterious silences and contradictorily multiple versions of his past, especially regarding the details of his immigration to the United States and his fifteen years there before he sends for his wife, Brave Orchid. Thus, Kingston fabricates narratives of her father's youth and training to be a scholar and village teacher in China, his ocean voyage to the United States, and his bachelor lifestyle in New York before his wife joins him. Kingston emphasizes the imagined nature of her narrative when she tells two versions of her father's passage to the United States. The first story is that he is a stowaway in a crate on a ship that lands in Florida, while the second is that he enters the country legally as a passenger on a ship but is detained and ruthlessly interrogated at Angel Island, the immigration detention center off the coast near San Francisco. In both versions of the story, her father endures great hardship and anxiety in his decision to leave China and in the actual voyage to the United States.

However, Kingston's narrative in *China Men* extends beyond personal memoir or autobiography. This is evident in the first chapter, "On Discovery." In this quasi-myth, Tang Ao discovers a land of women who subject him to humiliating and torturous physical deformations such as footbinding, hair tweezing, and ear piercing in order to transform him for display before their queen; in short, they strip him of his masculinity. The final sentence, which notes that this country is rumored to have been in North America, is a lightly veiled allusion to the similarly humiliating emasculation of the Chinese immigrants who were lured by the Gold Rush and promise of wealth, only to find low-paying domestic employment such as laundry, cooking, and houseserving. In constructing the narratives of her own forefather's and brother's stories, Kingston also aims to humanize and masculinize the historical experiences of the "Chinamen" who were major contributors to such historically significant American phenomenon as the first transcontinental railroad and the Hawaiian cane sugar plantations. It was primarily Chinamen laborers who did the dangerous work of dynamiting and laying down railroad track on the most difficult terrain through the Sierra Nevadas, as well as the backbreaking work of harvesting cane. Also, in telling stories about rare Chinamen such as "Alaska China Men," she reclaims an obscure Chinese American history and disputes biased mainstream newspaper reporting that distorts the Chinamen into sub-human beings such as the "Wild Man of the Green Swamp." In addition, the chapter "The Laws," which is simply a listing of all the actual laws that discriminated against and victimized Chinese Americans, is a sobering implication of the extreme obstacles they faced. With the final story on the Brother in Vietnam, Kingston's narrative of an idealist and pacifist brother who is vehemently opposed to the war and yet serves his duty when he is drafted, reveals a sensitive and ethical man, one who submits to the military training, but who nevertheless "had not gotten killed" and who "had not killed anyone."

In Kingston's novel *Tripmaster Monkey: His Fake Book,* she again focuses on a singular protagonist, who is also a Chinese American man and idealist, but her method of writing undergoes a dramatic change. *Tripmaster Monkey* has been called an epic novel as well as a postmodern text. While *The Woman Warrior* and *China Men* incorporate much first person narration, *Tripmaster Monkey* is told from a third person narrative, and extends her use of diverse forms of writing to include not only myths and Chinese traditions and culture, but also exhaustive references to famous poets (**Walt Whitman**, who is Wittman's namesake, Rilke, and **Allen Ginsberg**), literature, and American popular culture of the 1960s. Protagonist Wittman Ah Sing is a self-assured, frenetic playwright who takes his artist persona very seriously. The book begins with Wittman's dramatic thoughts of suicide by jumping off the Golden Gate Bridge, and ends with his successful staging of a three-day-long epic play based on the Chinese classical myth, "The Romance of Three Kingdoms," with an immense cast that represents nearly the entire community in the book. In the course of the several months in his life that comprise the book, his daily activities are followed very closely, as well as his witty and impassioned stream-of-consciousness type of thoughts. Since its publication, the character of Wittman has been rumored to be heavily based upon the personality of Kingston's real-life literary foe, the irrepressible playwright and novelist **Frank Chin**, who has criticized Kingston for making her books cater to white Euro-sensibilities.

This is an interesting speculation, since Kingston seems to use Wittman's aggressively honest and indignant voice to protest racial inequality as well as awaken Chinese and Asian American passivity to speak out against racism and stereotypes of Asian Americans. Wittman's own actions bespeak a temperament that many mainstream readers would feel uncomfortable with. He sports a long-haired hippie look, is always precariously employed, and in fact gets fired from his job as a clerk in a department store, partakes of the 60s drug culture at parties, marries a white woman several days after he meets her in an unconventional, unofficial wedding ceremony, and talks nonstop throughout the book, even to strangers on a bus. However, his eccentric personality and background (his mother is a former Floradora nightclub dancer and his father a former nightclub emcee) attest to the diversity of the Chinese American experience. In the novel, the densely packed references to Chinese and Western-misinterpretations-of-Chinese cultural phenomenon that often run unprefaced into one another leads to the observation that "representation and reality, the socially constructed stereotypical, and the experiential are inseparably mixed in Wittman's perceptions of ethnic difference." Though Wittman resists being pigeonholed into a simplistic Asian stereotype, he also rails against being subsumed into a "melting pot" ideology that denies very real gender, class, and race boundaries in America. Instead, in his final "community play," he calls for a celebration of radical ethnic differences and an assertion of ethnic pride that is strategically political: "It's our fault they call us gook and chinky chinaman. We've been here all this time, before Columbus, and haven't named ourselves. Look at the Blacks beautifully defining themselves." Even in identifying with the Chinese mythical Monkey King, a mischievous figure who tricks the gods and is irreverent toward authority, Wittman articulates an identity that seems disruptive, but upon closer inspection, is "firmly anchored to the culture, but subject to change."

—Karen Chow

KINNELL, Galway

Born: Providence, Rhode Island, 1 February 1927. **Education:** Public schools in Pawtucket, Rhode Island; Wilbraham Academy (private school), Massachusetts, 1944; Black Mountain School,

North Carolina, summer 1947; Princeton University, A.B. (summa cum laude) 1948; University of Rochester, M.A. in English 1949. **Military Service:** Served in the United States Navy, 1944-46. **Family:** Married Ines Delgado de Torres in 1965 (divorced 1985); one daughter and one son. **Career:** Poet and translator, 1949—. Instructor in English, Alfred University, Alfred, New York, 1949-51; director of liberal arts program, University of Chicago, Illinois, 1951-55; American lecturer, University of Grenoble, Grenoble, France, 1956-57; lecturer in summer session, 1957, and Fulbright lecturer, 1978, University of Nice, France; adjunct assistant professor, New York University, New York City, 1957-59; Fulbright lecturer, University of Iran, Teheran, 1959-60; field worker, Congress of Racial Equality (CORE), Hammond, Louisiana, 1963; poet-in-residence at Juniata College, 1964, Reed College, 1966-67, Colorado State University, 1968, University of Washington, 1968, University of California, Irvine, 1968-69, University of Iowa, 1970; resident writer, Deya University, Mallorca, Spain, 1969-70; visiting professor, Queens College of the City University of New York, and Pittsburgh Poetry Forum, 1971; adjunct associate professor, 1972, and adjunct professor, 1974, 1976, Columbia University, New York City; visiting poet, Sarah Lawrence College, 1972-78; visiting professor, Brandeis University, 1974, and Skidmore College, 1975; visiting poet, Princeton University, 1976; poet-in-residence, Holy Cross College, 1977; visiting poet, University of Hawaii, 1977; visiting professor, University of Delaware, 1978; visiting writer, MacQuarrie University, Sydney, Australia, 1979; Citizen's professor, University of Hawaii at Manoa, Honolulu, 1979-81; director of writing program, New York University, New York City, 1981-84; Mellon professor, University of Pittsburgh, Pennsylvania, 1983; professor, State University of New York, Binghamton, 1984-85. Beginning 1985 Samuel F. B. Morse professor of Arts and Sciences, New York University; Erich Maria Remarque professor, 1990. Participated in public readings against war in Vietnam; organized anti-nuclear reading, New York City, 1982. Member of board of directors, 1979-84, and poetry consultant, 1985—, Squaw Valley Community of Writers; president of American PEN, 1983-84; board member of PEN, 1983-89; board member of Poetry Society of America, 1985-87; board member of Poets House, 1986; board member of Poets and Writers, 1986—; member of board of trustees, Princeton University, 1988—. **Awards:** Ford Grant, 1955; Fulbright scholarship to Paris, 1955-56; Guggenheim fellowships, 1961-62, 1974-75; National Institute of Arts and Letters grant, 1961; Longview Foundation award, 1962; Rockefeller Foundation grants, 1962-63, 1968; *Poetry* magazine Bess Hokin prize, 1965; *Poetry* magazine Eunice Tietjens prize, 1966; Ohio University Press Cecil Hemley Poetry prize for translation of Yves Bonnefoy's work, 1968; National Book award for poetry special mention, 1969; Ingram Merrill Foundation award, 1969; Amy Lowell traveling fellowship, 1969-70; National Endowment for the Arts grant, 1969-70; Brandeis University Creative Arts award, 1969; Poetry Society of America Shelley prize, 1974; National Institute of Arts and Letters Medal of Merit, 1975; Landan Translation prize, 1979; co-recipient of American Book Award for poetry, 1983, Pulitzer Prize, 1983, and National Book Award for Poetry, 1984, all for *Selected Poems;* MacArthur Fellowship, 1984-89; appointed Vermont State Poet, 1989-93; University of Chicago Harriet Monroe prize, 1990. Honorary degrees from Kalamazoo College, 1986, Hofstra University, 1988, and Southern Vermont College, 1990. **Member:** National Academy and Institute of Arts and Letters, 1980—. **Residence:** Vermont.

PUBLICATIONS

Poetry

What a Kingdom It Was. 1960.
Flower Herding on Mount Monadnock. 1964.
Body Rags. 1967.
Poems of Night. 1968.
The Hen Flower. 1969.
First Poems: 1946-1954. 1971.
The Shoes of Wandering. 1971.
The Book of Nightmares. 1971.
The Avenue Bearing the Initial of Christ into the New World: Poems 1946-1964. 1974.
Mortal Acts, Mortal Words. 1980.
Selected Poems. 1982.
The Past. 1985.
When One Has Lived a Long Time Alone. 1990.
Three Books. 1993.
Imperfect Thirst. 1994.

Fiction

Black Light. 1966.

Other

The Poetics of the Physical World (lecture). 1969
Walking Down the Stairs: Selections from Interviews. 1977.
How the Alligator Missed Breakfast (juvenile). 1982.
Thoughts Occasioned by the Most Insignificant of all Human Events (essay). 1982.
Remarks on Accepting the American Book Award. 1984.

Editor, *The Essential Whitman.* 1987.

Translator, *Pre-Columbian Ceramics,* by Henri Lehman. 1962.
Translator, *The Poems of Francois Villon.* 1965.
Translator, *Bitter Victory,* by Rene Hardy. 1965.
Translator, *On the Motion and Immobility of Douve,* by Yves Bonnefoy. 1966.
Translator, *Lackawanna,* by Yvan Goll. 1970.
Translator, *Early Poems, 1947-1959,* by Yves Bonnefoy. 1993.

*

Critical Studies: *Recent American Poetry* by Glauco Cambon, 1961; *Babel to Byzantium: Poets and Poetry Now* by James Dickey, 1968; *Alone with America: Essays on the Art of Poetry in America since 1950* by Richard Howard, 1969; *Cry of the Human* by Ralph J. Mills, 1975; *The Fierce Embrace* by Charles Molesworth, 1979; *Self and Sensibility in Contemporary American Poetry* by Charles Altieri, 1984; *Our Last First Poets: Vision and History in Contemporary American Poetry* by Cary Nelson, 1984; *Introspection and Contemporary Poetry* by Alan Williamson, 1984; *On the Poetry of Galway Kinnell* edited by Howard Nelson, 1987; *Intricate and Simple Things: The Poetry of Galway Kinnell* by Lee Zimmerman, 1987; "Being with Reality: An Interview with Galway Kinnell" in *Columbia: A Magazine of Poetry & Prose,* 1989; *Galway Kinnell* by Richard J. Calhoun, 1991; "Theodore Roethke and Galway Kinnell: Voices in Contemporary American Romanticism," in *Northwest Review* vol. 29, no. 2, 1991; "The Language of Sexuality: Walt Whitman and Galway Kinnell" by Nancy Tuten, in *Walt Whitman Quarterly Review* vol. 9, no. 3, 1992; "'The Seekonk Woods': Kinnell's Frostian 'Directive' to the Wilderness" by Nancy Tuten, in *Robert Frost Review* fall 1992; *Critical Essays on Galway Kinnell,* edited by nancy Lewis Tuten, 1996.

*   *   *

Galway Kinnell is now acknowledged as a major American poet, even though he may lack the popular name recognition of **John Ashbery**, **James Merrill**, his former Princeton classmate **W.S. Merwin**, or **James Dickey**, to whom he often has been compared. This is not to say that Kinnell does not have his devoted readers and appreciators, especially among those who have fallen under the spell of his compelling public readings of his poetry. Richly deserved critical acclaim has become more common since the early 1980s, when Kinnell won both the National Book Award and the Pulitzer Prize for poetry.

Kinnell has been appropriately regarded as an important neo-Romantic postmodernist in the great Romantic tradition of Blake, Rilke, the early Yeats, and Walt Whitman. As a fellow poet and a dedicated Whitman scholar, he has acknowledged the poetic energy that came out of the special relationship between Whitman and the physical things of his world, and has attempted, with an additional debt to **William Carlos Williams**, his own version of a poetics of the physical world. Death is a crucial issue to both poets. Whitman takes the position of a positive Romantic with ultimate faith in a life force so powerful that he can assert in "Song of Myself" that "the smallest sprout shows there is really no death." Kinnell's version is more existential; the ultimate reality for all living things is the pain of death.

In two recent literary histories, David Perkins's *History of Modern Poetry* and Emory Elliott's *Columbia Literary History of the United States,* Kinnell's postmodernism has been categorized with the surrealism of deep image poetry, a poetic faction comprised of W. S. Merwin, **Louis Simpson**, **James Wright**, and **Robert Bly**, all variously engaged in a search for an alternative to modernism through recovering "deep image" material from the subconscious. Kinnell's contribution has been a preoccupation with the self and its relation to the forces of wildness and violence, mutability and mortality. To Kinnell and the "deep image" poets, as well as to James Dickey with his self-styled "country surrealism," only a thin framework of civilization conceals the primitive underpinnings of existence. Kinnell's poetry manifests the serious concern in modern poetry with the relationship of the self to a primitive underside of surface life. To Kinnell, bona fide meaning can be approached only through a willful acceptance of the terminal common mortality of all living things. No contemporary poet has asserted more severely the inevitability of mortality and the ambivalences associated with the reality of death. Death involves loss of identity, the terror of extinction; but Kinnell believes also in the possibility of a death leading to a rebirth more alive and more related to natural life.

James Dickey gave early testimony to Kinnell's promise as a poet as originating from a necessary involvement of poems with the author's life. Kinnell's poetry does come out of his own experience, sometimes directly, but more frequently obliquely, in some degree analogous to **Emily Dickinson**. He has indeed written autobiographical and family poems about brother, wife, children, and several substantial poems come out of his political commitments; but he has never resorted to trendy confessional poetry or fashioned life chronicles.

Kinnell began writing poetry during the heyday of impersonal modernism in poetry and new critical formalism in criticism; but since, as Charles Molesworth has made apparent, he has intended a poetry of immersion into experience; he has always needed the personal encounters in nature characteristic of the Romantics and neo-Romantic postmodernists. Kinnell's version of Whitman-esque empathy from these encounters is an acceptance of animal nature and of death that leads to affinity with all living mortal things. He has written two of the most intense contemporary animal poems, "The Bear" and "The Porcupine." In his most acclaimed works, *The Book of Nightmares* and *Mortal Acts, Mortal Words,* he has reverted to archetypal imagery, notably fire imagery, in existential ultimate concern with death and immortality. Richard Howard has identified the crucial action of Kinnell's poetry as an ordeal by fire, affirming that the hope for regeneration is through consumption by fire.

Kinnell's poems are demonstrably from his own times. He is not an academic poet, though he is every so often a *New Yorker* poet; but his poems engage urgent philosophical concerns of his generation. The two philosophical movements most influential during his formative years as a poet were existentialism and phenomenology. If Kinnell is a product of what **Robert Lowell** called the existential fifties, he also is one of the most phenomenological poets of his generation in his concern, as recurrently a poet of landscapes, with things observed on a journey, the infrastructure of many of his long meditative poems. In the existential fifties, ultimate concern was accorded the absurdity of death. In the face of death, the appropriate choice was to create meaning through discoveries about and in choices defining one's own existence.

Kinnell's poems of the 1950s express some of the existential concerns of that decade; the kingdom of *What a Kingdom It Was* is one in which humankind must realize that the only escape from loneliness and separation is through conscious acceptance of kinship and identity in experiences shared with all living things. The poems of the 1960s and the 1970s add an articulation of the social and political concerns over civil rights, the war in Vietnam, and the dehumanizing effects of technology: "The Avenue Bearing the Initial of Christ into the New World" is Kinnell's wasteland view of modern life; "Vapor Trail Reflected in the Frog Pond" parodies Whitman's "I Hear America Singing" by detailing the violent crimes against humanity modern technology has abetted in Vietnam and in the desegregating South; "The Last River" mythologizes his personal journey to jail in segregated Louisiana into a journey into Hades. The poems of the 1980s, in *Mortal Acts, Mortal Words* and in *The Past,* and of the 1990s have turned more to the phenomenology of everyday events and to personal friendships and family values and incertitudes, adding a warmer touch of humanity to Kinnell's poetry. His first book of the 1990s, *When One Has Lived a Long Time Alone,* goes further, specifying the need for love, or at least for the presence of another creature, any creature, to negate loneliness. More than lonely immersion of self into nature is now required; lovers, friends, some kind of companionship, as well as the order and form that song and poems bring into life, are all now integral.

—Richard J. Calhoun

KIRKLAND, Joseph

Born: Geneva, New York, 7 January 1830; grew up in Michigan and Illinois. **Education:** Received little formal education; studied law, 1873-80: admitted to Illinois bar, 1880. **Military Service:** Served in the Civil War, in the Illinois 12th Regiment, 1861, as aide-de-camp. Adjutant-General's Department, Washington, D.C., 1861, and on the staff of Generals Fitz-John Porter and George McClellan, 1862-63: major. **Family:** Married Theodosia Burr Wilkinson in 1863; four children. **Career:** Sailor on packet ship to Europe, 1847; clerk, New York City, 1848-52; clerk and reader, *Putnam's Monthly,* New York, 1852-55; auditor, Illinois Central Railroad, Chicago, 1855-58; supervisor, Carbon Coal Company, Tilton, Illinois, 1858-61 and 1863-64; cofounder, *Prairie Chicken* literary journal, Tilton, 1864-65; established coal mining business in Tilton, 1865, and a retail coal business in Chicago, 1868 (business destroyed in Chicago fire, 1871); worked for U.S. Revenue Service 1873-80; lawyer, in partnership with Mark Bangs, Chicago, 1880-90; special correspondent and literary editor, Chicago *Tribune,* 1889-93. **Member:** Committee on the World's Columbian Exposition in Chicago, 1893. **Died:** 28 April 1894.

PUBLICATIONS

Fiction

Zury, The Meanest Man in Spring County: A Novel of Western Life. 1887; revised edition, 1888.
The McVeys (An Episode). 1888.
The Captain of Company K. 1891.

Plays

Sidonie, The Married Flirt, with James B. Runnion, from a novel by Alphonse Daudet (produced 1877).

Other

The Story of Chicago, completed by Caroline Kirkland. 2 vols., 1892-94; revised edition of vol. 1, 1892.
The Chicago Massacre of 1812. 1893.

Editor, *Lily Pearl and the Mistress of Rosedale,* by Ida Glen-wood. 1892.
Editor, with John Moses, *The History of Chicago.* 2 vols., 1895.

*

Bibliography: in *Bibliography of American Literature* by Jacob Blanck, 1969.

Critical Study: *Kirkland* by Clyde E. Henson, 1962.

*   *   *

Joseph Kirkland's claim to fame rests entirely on one book, *Zury,* and a superficial reading of it is likely to be misleading. Literary historians have been too quick to classify Kirkland with other "agrarian realists" and "protest novelists." It is true that *Zury* contains many details conveying the narrowness, brutality, and deprivation of Midwestern farm life in the middle of the nineteenth century. *Zury* (the name is short for Usury) has a beloved sister who dies as a result of the primitive conditions on the farm, and the family has no coins with which to weight her eyelids. Since she dies in mid-winter, the family has no choice but to let the body freeze and wait for the spring thaw to bury her.

The novel also forcefully describes the cruelty and niggardliness Zury must possess to accumulate his modest fortune. Having been made selfish by his environment, he seeks to avoid his responsibility for making pregnant Anne Sparrow, the young and innocent schoolteacher from the east. He arranges to marry her to a local idler, John McVey.

However, to emphasize these details is to neglect the end of *Zury* and the entirety of the sequel, *The McVeys.* The second volume followed soon after the first, and in it Zury sees his error and takes an interest in his and Anne's twin children (McVey has conveniently died). Although she at first rejects him, Zury and Anne eventually marry and symbolically combine the vitality and toughness of Zury's West with the culture and refinement of Anne's East; the last scene of *The McVeys* finds them cozy and happy in a prosperous farmhouse. One might suggest that Kirkland was ultimately more "realistic" than some of his more bitter contemporaries, and certainly more entertaining.

After writing *The Captain of Company K,* an episodic but vivid story of the Civil War, Kirkland showed little interest in artistic creation, and devoted himself to editorial and historical work.

—William Higgins

KNIGHT, Etheridge

Born: Corinth, Mississippi, 19 April 1931. **Education:** Attended high school for two years, then self-taught and educated during prison sentence. **Military Service:** U.S. Army, Guam, Hawaii, and Korea, 1947-51. **Family:** Married 1) Sonia Sanchez (divorced); 2) Mary Ann McAnally in 1973 (divorced), one daughter and one son; 3) Charlene Blackburn, one son, three step-children. **Career:** Poet. Inmate, Indiana State Prison, 1960-68; writer-in-residence, University of Pittsburgh, Pittsburgh, Pennsylvania, 1968-69, University of Hartford, Hartford, Connecticut, 1969-70, and Lincoln University, Jefferson City, Missouri, 1972. **Awards:** Pulitzer prize and National Book award nominee. **Died:** 10 March 1991.

PUBLICATIONS

Collection

The Essential Etheridge Knight. 1986.

Poetry

Poems from Prison. 1968.
A Poem for Brother/Man (After His Recovery from an O.D.). 1972.
Belly Song and Other Poems. 1973.

Born of a Woman: New and Selected Poems. 1980.
Freedom and Fame (limited edition). 1990.

Recording: *Etheridge Knight Reads Poems from Prison,* 1969.

*

Critical Studies: *The New Black Aesthetic As a Counterpoetics: The Poetry of Etheridge Knight* (dissertation) by Patricia Alveda Liggins Hill, 1977; *Belly Songs: The Poetry of Etheridge Knight* by Howard Nelson, 1981; "The Poet, the Poem, the People: Etheridge Knight's Aesthetic" by Craig Werner, in *Obsidian,* summer-winter 1981, pp. 7-17; "Voice As Lifesaver: Defining the Function of Orality in Etheridge Knight's Poetry" by Ugo Rubeo, in *The Black Columbiad: Defining Moments in African American Literature and Culture* edited by Werner Sollors and Maria Diedrich, 1994; "An Interview with Etheridge Knight" by Charles H. Rowell, in *Callaloo,* fall 1996; "Etheridge Knight: Poet and Prisoner: An Introduction" by Jean Anaporte Easton, in *Callaloo,* fall 1996, pp. 941-46.

*   *   *

Etheridge Knight was one of the pivotal African American voices to emerge in American poetry in the 1960s. With fellow poets **Sterling A. Brown**, Dudley Randall, **Amiri Baraka**, Don Lee, and Al Young, Knight must always be seen as a multicultural pioneer. Yet, even more than his peers (with the possible exception of Baraka), Knight brought into the canon experiences from a world of hurt and anguish that mainstream America was seldom aware of.

When his *Poems from Prison* appeared in 1968, the year of the Martin Luther King and Robert F. Kennedy assassinations, America's long bandaged, racial wounds were naked and bleeding. Knight's raw, explosive, often horrifying free verse written out of confinement helped, in their way, to convey some of the more unsavory aspects that inspired the civil rights struggle. In this way his poems were meaningful to the white, literate middle-class and white academics whose activism often lacked a solid understanding of the worldwide problem—racism—under attack.

As for his African American audience, Knight understood early on that he had a responsibility to ingest and speak for them and for their communities, dreams, triumphs, and failures. He lived up to this responsibility more diligently than any African American poet of his time.

It was not an easy thing to do. Autobiographical notes appended to his aforementioned first book chillingly suggest the emotional gulf that Knight had to cross: "I died in Korea from a shrapnel wound and narcotics resurrected me. I died in 1960 from a prison sentence and poetry brought me back to life."

The poetry that brought him back to life during his imprisonment was more than the pouring out of his own experience. From the beginning Knight had the gift of looking outside himself to the characters and situations all around him. In torrid free verse, in accomplished Haiku sequences, and in wrenching narrative elegies, Knight told the stories of unforgettable but often overlooked characters like Hard Rock, a legendary prison tough guy finally controlled by brain surgery, or the black stoker who successfully escapes the Titanic, or the "beautiful fascist" fresh out of the Hole, who challenges the poet-prisoner, asking "why ain't you / *doing something?*" The poet's answer is to stay up all night writing five thousand words, but in the end he is not convinced that he is making the contribution he thinks he should be making.

This social conscience politicizes Knight's poetry and sets him apart from so many contemporary poets who confine their verses to commentaries on their personal lives. As a result, the emotional range in Knight's poems is impressive. This poet was not afraid to rage at his readers. In "A Poem for 3rd World Brothers," he warns those he addresses about the consequences of accepting U.S. overtures: "By the time white thighs wrap round your head / white / america will send the thrill of the pill / to kill you." In "On Watching Politicians Perform at Martin Luther King's Funeral," he is no more forgiving: "Hypocrits shed tears / like shiny snake skins."

One could not make the claim for emotional range in Knight's poetry, however, were he not capable of unexpected but utterly believable tenderness, as, for example, in "For Mary Ellen McAnally" from *Belly Song and Other Poems*:

Who is
a perfect poem
and a song
pulse of love
world of wonders
and the warm black earth
falling
thru my fingers.

Longer than the seventeen syllables of the Haiku, this poem is still driven and shaped by the ancient form. In "One Day We Shall All Go Back," the poet expands his vision of love to the lost home:

One day we shall all go back—
we shall all go back (down home
where the blood of our fathers
has fed the black earth (down home
where the slow/flowing rivers, dark and silent,
sing to the bones of our brothers (down home. . .

This poignant look back on hard racial history, the open parentheses and repetition represent endurance, survival, and promise yet unfulfilled. A resurrection in poetry aims this high. It keeps the promise in sight and sometimes brings it home. Knight knew this. He breathed it, lived it, wrote it.

Such content is guileless, tender, sweet. This last is a word that one would not immediately associate with the poetry of Knight. But the superior poet will surprise even the most knowledgeable reader. Such surprises come often, rewarding the reader who embraces the entire oeuvre.

—Robert McDowell

KNOWLES, John

Born: Fairmont, West Virginia, 16 September 1926. **Education:** Phillips Exeter Academy, Exeter, New Hampshire, 1942-44; Yale University, New Haven, Connecticut (editorial board, *Yale Daily News*), 1946-49, B.A. 1949. **Military Service:** Served in the U.S. Army Air Force, 1945. **Career:** Assistant editor, *Yale Alumni* magazine, 1949; reporter and drama critic, *Hartford Courant*, Connecti-

cut, 1950-52; free-lance writer in Italy, France, and New York, 1952-56; associate editor, *Holiday* magazine, Philadelphia, 1957-60; full-time writer, 1960—; traveled in Europe and Middle East, 1960-62; lived in New York City, 1962-70. Writer-in-residence, University of North Carolina, Chapel Hill, 1963-64, and Princeton University, New Jersey, 1968-69. **Awards:** National Institute of Arts and Letters Richard and Hinda Rosenthal Foundation award, 1960; William Faulkner Foundation award, 1960; National Association of Independent Schools award, 1961. **Residence:** Southampton, Long Island.

PUBLICATIONS

Novels

A Separate Peace. 1959.
Morning in Antibes. 1962.
Indian Summer. 1966.
The Paragon. 1971.
Spreading Fires. 1974.
A Vein of Riches. 1978.
Peace Breaks Out. 1981.
A Stolen Past. 1983.
The Private Life of Axie Reed. 1986.

Short Stories

Phineas: Six Stories. 1968.

Other

Double Vision: American Thoughts Abroad. 1964.

*

Critical Studies: "John Knowles's Short Novels" by Jay L. Halio in *Studies in Short Fiction* vol. 1, no. 2, 1964; "A Separate Peace: The Fall from Innocence" by James Ellis in *English Journal* vol. 53, no. 5, 1964; "Narrative Method in *A Separate Peace*" by Ronald Weber in *Studies in Short Fiction* vol. 3, no. 1, 1965; "*A Separate Peace*: A Study in Structural Ambiguity" by Paul Witherington in *English Journal* vol. 54, no. 9, 1965; "The Novels of John Knowles" by James L. McDonald in *Arizona Quarterly* vol. 23, no. 4, 1967; "The Impact of Knowles's *A Separate Peace*" by Peter Wolfe in *University Review* vol. 36, no. 3, 1970; *A Separate Peace: The War Within* by Hallman Bell Bryant, 1990; *Readings on A Separate Peace,* edited by Jill Karson, 1999.

*   *   *

First-novel success is both a blessing and a curse. It assures the young writer of an eager publisher and public for subsequent books, but also guarantees an uphill struggle with the critics. New novels will always be measured by the yardstick of the first, and often found to be lacking. Such is the case with the American novelist, John Knowles. His first novel, *A Separate Peace,* was an instant critical success, winning both the prestigious Rosenthal Award as well as the William Faulkner Award, and it established Knowles overnight as one of the bright young men of American letters. In the eight novels since, Knowles has fought to make people forget *A Separate Peace* and judge each succeeding book on its own merits. The fact of repeating themes in the subsequent novels has not made this task any easier. Knowles is an explorer of the borderland between rational and instinctual man; of the internal battle between a life lived by formula and one invented by experience. And in all his novels, Knowles—who is resonant of **F. Scott Fitzgerald** in this respect— surveys the terrain of the rich and affluent and describes their battle to feel, to burst out of the emotional bonds of the upper middle class.

It is a terrain Knowles understands quite well. Born the third of four children in 1926 to Mary Beatrice Shea Knowles and James Myron Knowles, he was brought up comfortably in Fairmont, West Virginia. His father was the vice president of Consolidation Coal Company; his was a childhood that wanted for little. At fifteen, Knowles became a student at Phillips Exeter Academy in New Hampshire, a location which served as the inspiration for the private school in *A Separate Peace.* After a short stint in the U.S. Army Air Force, he attended Yale, both swimming for the university and editing the *Yale Daily News.* During his college years he began writing short stories and was mentored by the novelist **Thornton Wilder.** After graduation and a couple of years spent on a Connecticut paper, Knowles travelled in Europe, writing an unpublished first novel, *Descent into Proselito,* and taking up skindiving on the Riviera. The year abroad was a valuable one: Knowles now had his major themes in hand as well as the two locations to which he returns over and over in his novels, New England and Europe.

By 1957 Knowles had moved to Philadelphia where he became the associate editor for *Holiday.* Having developed an acute ability to describe local color, he set to work on the novel that would make his fame. Two of his short stories, "A Turn in the Sun" and "Phineas," had been published in the mid-1950s, and of these, "Phineas" is the more important for what would come next because that story, which explored the relationship between two adolescents, was the germ of *A Separate Peace.* Gene Forrester and his friend Finney (Phineas)—students at a private school during World War II—are a study in contrasts: Gene, introverted and conscientious, and Finney, outgoing and athletic. They share a bond of friendship that becomes strained through the competition that Gene begins to feel toward his friend. Initially attracted to the freewheeling Finney and to the free-spirited element in himself, Gene comes to reject that aspect of his own personality, opting for the "cautious Protestant," as Knowles has termed it. When Gene tricks Finney into injuring himself by jumping out of a tree, Finney is hurt badly enough that he will in all likelihood be kept out of the war—creating a separate peace for him. The friends are later reconciled only to have Finney die from a fall down the school stairs, but Gene becomes transformed by the experience. The book is a study, Knowles has said, "of how adolescent personality develops, identifying with an admired person, then repudiating that person." Gene's separate peace results from his ultimate withdrawal from the outside influences of his peers to mold his own character. Critics on both sides of the Atlantic were quick to praise the book. In England, *The Times Literary Supplement* called it "a novel of altogether exceptional power and distinction," while in the U.S., *Time* concurred, terming *A Separate Peace* an "excellent first novel." The book has been grist for the literary magazine mills ever since, spawning dozens of critical articles and placing it in the same coming-of-age canon as *Catcher in the Rye.*

The critical and financial success of his first novel allowed Knowles to quit his job at *Holiday* and devote himself full time to writing. He travelled in the Middle East and Greece for the next two years and in 1962 published *Morning in Antibes.* Set on the French Riviera, Knowles's second novel deals with the struggles of a young American to save his marriage. Reminiscent of the lost generation of the twenties and thirties, the book was panned by some critics for its underdeveloped characterizations, though most agreed that its evocation of scene is powerful. Knowles followed this with a travel book, *Double Vision,* an account of the author's travels in the Middle East and Greece which allowed him an insight into his own country, hence the double vision of the title.

Returning to the U.S., Knowles also returned to an earlier theme with his third novel, *Indian Summer,* a Literary Guild Selection dedicated to Thornton Wilder. In the book we have a Finney-like character, Cleet Kinsolving, part Native American and the embodiment of the free spirit. Seduced for a time by the privileged life of Neil Reardon, his old friend, Cleet ultimately opts for his former free life. Again Knowles is posing the savage element against the "cautious Protestant" in the American vein, yet most reviewers felt the symbolic content outweighed the story line.

Invited to be writer-in-residence at Princeton University for the 1968-69 school year, Knowles published a volume of short stories, *Phineas: Six Stories,* in 1968. He then took up residence in Southampton on Long Island in 1970 and became the neighbor of such literary luminaries as **Truman Capote** and Irwin Shaw. With his fourth novel, *The Paragon,* set at Yale in 1953, Knowles recaptured some of the literary respect earned with *A Separate Peace.* Reminiscent of Fitzgerald's *The Great Gatsby,* Knowles's novel tells the story of a university sophomore, full of confused idealism, who is in love with an older actress. It was called "a beautiful, funny, moving novel about a young man in trouble," by Webster Schott in the *New York Times Book Review.* Other critics, however, did not agree. Writing in the *Antioch Review* James Aronson found that "the dialogue is faked and stagy, the characters are stereotyped, the parallels between 1950 and 1970 are tritely obvious, and the shape of the novel is curiously disjointed."

In 1972 the movie version of *A Separate Peace* was released, further assuring Knowles's economic security, and two years later he published his fifth novel, *Spreading Fires,* set in the south of France and detailing the decadence of the upper classes through the struggle between open sexuality and repression. Writing in the *New York Times,* Christopher Lehmann-Haupt found the book an "abortive thriller." With his 1978 novel, *A Vein of Riches,* Knowles mined new territory. This time his story was set in his native West Virginia in the early boom years of the twentieth century. The central conflict in the novel is money—as represented by the wealthy and powerful Catherwood family—versus land and the laboring classes. In the course of the novel, Knowles lays bare the ugliness of capitalism gone mad, implying that the real vein of riches lies in the emotions and intellect. Despite the deeply felt local atmosphere and its pretensions to a more epic form, *A Vein of Riches* is generally thought to be Knowles's least powerful work.

With *Peace Breaks Out* in 1981, Knowles returned to Devon Academy, the setting for *A Separate Peace.* The plot is very similar to the earlier novel, but this time the story is told through the point of view of a war-weary instructor, and the action takes place several years later than in *A Separate Peace.* Again the central incident is the death of a student at the academy, although the vision is bleaker in *Peace Breaks Out:* there is no redemption, no realization as a result of the incident. The war has wrought terrible changes not only in the shape of the outer world, but also in the inner world of conscience. Some reviewers, such as Peter S. Prescott in *Newsweek,* felt similarities between the two books were too great. He wrote, "Going back to your old school is a risky business: the old pranks you used to play will never work again." But others favorably compared it with *A Separate Peace.* "[*Peace Breaks Out*] will take its place alongside the earlier book as a fine novel," Dick Abrahamson noted in the *English Journal.*

Two more novels followed in the 1980s: *A Stolen Past,* again set at Yale and which *Publishers Weekly* called a "gripping, thoroughly absorbing tale" about the career of three writers; and *The Private Life of Axie Reed,* the remembrances of an actress, which was generally considered to be of lesser importance. Reviewing that book in the *New York Times,* Michiko Kakutani argued that Knowles has "demonstrated a seemingly durable, if slender talent for delineating the emotional geometry connecting certain members of certain rarified worlds (prep school, Yale University, the Riviera) in deft, coolly-refined prose." It is a judgement that might stand for Knowles's entire body of work, as well.

—J. Sydney Jones

KOMUNYAKAA, Yusef

Born: Bogalusa, Louisiana, 29 April 1947. **Education:** University of Colorado, B.A. (magna cum Laude) in English/Sociology 1975; Colorado State University, M.A. in Creative Writing 1978; University of California, Irvine, M.F.A. in Creative Writing 1980. **Military Service:** Served in Vietnam as a correspondent and editor of *The Southern Cross*: bronze star. **Family:** Married Mandy Sayer. **Career:** Associate instructor, Colorado State University, 1976-78; teaching assistant in poetry, University of California Irvine, 1980; instructor of English composition and American Literature, University of New Orleans, 1982-84; poet-in-the-schools, New Orleans, 1984-85. Visiting assistant professor of English, 1985-86, associate professor of English and African-American Studies, 1986-93, and beginning 1993 professor of English and African American Studies, Indiana University, Bloomington. Visiting associate professor of English, fall 1991, Holloway Lecturer, spring 1992; University of California, Berkeley. Production editor, *The Southern Cross* (newspaper), American Division in Chu Lai, South Vietnam, 1970; editor, *UCCA News and Riverrun,* University of Colorado, 1973-75; co-editor and publisher, *Gumbo: A Magazine for the Arts,* 1976-79; administrative consultant, *Indiana Review*; advisor, *Callaloo,* Johns Hopkins University. **Awards:** First Place poetry award, Rocky Mountain Writers Forum, 1974, 1977; Fine Arts Work Center Writing fellowship, Provincetown, 1980-81; National Endowment for the Arts Creative Writing fellowship, 1981-82, 1987-88; Louisiana Arts fellowship, 1985; San Francisco Poetry award, 1986, for *I Apologize for the Eyes in My Head*; the Dark Room Poetry prize, 1989, for *Dien Cai Dau*; Best Books for Young Adults selection, American Literary Association, for *Dien Cai Dau*; Thomas Forcade award, University of Massachusetts, Boston, 1990; *Kenyon Review* award for literary excellence, 1991; *The Village Voice* twenty-five best books selection, 1992; Kingsley Tufts Poetry award, 1994; Pulitzer prize for poetry, 1994.

PUBLICATIONS

Poetry

Dedications and Other Dark Horses. 1977.
Lost in the Bonewheel Factory. 1979.
Copacetic. 1984.
Toys in a Field. 1986.
I Apologize for the Eyes in My Head. 1986.
Dien Cai Dau. 1988.
February in Sydney. 1989.
Magic City. 1992.
Neon Vernacular (New and Selected Poems 1977-1989). 1994.
Thieves of Paradise. 1998.

Other

Editor, with J.A. Sascha Feinstein, *The Jazz Poetry Anthology.* 1991.

Translator, with Martha Collins, *The Insomnia of Fire* by Nguyen Quang Thieu. 1995.

*   *   *

Yusef Komunyakaa has emerged as one of the most celebrated poets of his generation. His work insistently ties itself to direct experience, whether the sensual flights of jazz, the trials and traumas of combat in Vietnam, or life in the humid delta of Louisiana. Each of these—and any material with which Komunyakaa might be working—finds vivid presence in his poetry. To put it another way, although memory and perception are important threads in his work, Komunyakaa's poetry seldom launches into epistemological, metaphysical, or ontological inquiry; unlike that of many other contemporary poets steeped in literary theory and postmodern skepticism. For Komunyakaa, the world simply exists, and the poet's attention to that given—a given rife with beauty and cruelty, joy and pain, light and darkness—is what makes strong poetry, powerful imagery, emotional resonance. Like Bruce Weigl and John Balaban, he is one of the most important poets of the Vietnam generation.

Dedications & Other Darkhorses announced Komunyakaa's talents. Published during a period when many American poets were turning toward a more meditative vein, propelled by the epistemological and aesthetic inquiry of **John Ashbery** and the personal, romantic meditations of **Robert Hass**, Komunyakaa's poetry offers readers a very different experience. The sonic texture is Hopkinsesque, punchy, stress-ridden, sometimes cacophonous; the subject matter is sensual and sensory driven; formally, the poems usually rely upon a fairly short free verse line, a shape to which Komunyakaa has frequently returned. Consider these opening lines from "The Tongue Is":

> xeroxed on brainmatter.
> Grid-squares of words spread
> like dirty oil over a lake.
> The tongue even lies to itself,
> gathering wildfire for songs of gibe.
> Malcontented clamor, swish of reeds.
> Slow, erratic, memory's loose
> grain goes deep as water
> in the savage green of oleander.

Komunyakaa's work is sometimes sassy, frequently acerbic, and occasionally elegiac. His tonal control is tight, especially in the poems where he considers his experience in the Vietnam conflict.

In the transitional collection *Lost in the Bonewheel Factory*, Komunyakaa wrote of his familial past in Bogalusa, Louisiana, and many of the dark shadows of childhood—sexuality, racism, the possibilities of violence and love. Perhaps this consideration of the past allowed Komunyakaa the compelling authority of the four volumes that were to follow. Whatever the case may be, the poems of *Lost in the Bonewheel Factory* are sometimes nostalgic, sometimes angry, and closer in many ways to the historical-auto-biographical work of many poets of the period than the starkly powerful *Copacetic* and *I Apologize for the Eyes in My Head*, Komunyakaa's next volumes. The two books in which he reaches a full command of his tonal, formal, and thematic range, *Toys in a Field* and *Dien Cai Dau*, are also the books in which his work most poignantly deals with the Vietnam War. Consider this short poem from *Dien Cai Dau*, "We Never Know":

> He danced with tall grass
> for a moment, like he was swaying
> with a woman. Our gun barrels
> glowed white hot.
> When I got to him,
> a blue halo
> of flies had already claimed him.
> I pulled the crumbled photograph
> from his fingers.
> There's no other way
> to say this: I fell in love.
> The morning cleared again,
> except for distant mortar
> & somewhere choppers taking off.
> I slid the wallet into his pocket
> & turned him over, so he wouldn't be
> kissing the ground.

This poem articulates one of Komunyakaa's primary concerns: how to somehow give dignity, even grace, to brutality, whether the brutality is that of the household or the battlefield. The sensuality of the soldier's last dance, the "blue halo" over his body, the inability of language to capture the full emotional impact of the experience, coupled to the necessity to make the attempt—these are characteristic gestures in Komunyakaa's work. He is one of the most important poets of the Vietnam generation, and his attempts to describe the physical and emotional landscapes of this experience are an important part of American literature of the closing decades of the twentieth century.

Another important aspect of Komunyakaa's work is his attraction to jazz. Frequently attempting to emulate the fluid movement of jazz music, Komunyakaa recognizes how the energetic qualities of this music can translate into poetry, especially in his most recent writing. These lines from "Blue Light Lounge Sutra for the Performance Poets at Harold Park Hotel" are representative:

> the need gotta be
> so deep words can't
> answer simple questions
> all night long notes
> stumble off the tongue

> & color the air indigo
> so deep fragments of gut
> & flesh cling to the song

The poem ends:

> the need gotta be basic
> animal need to see
> & know the terror
> we are made of honey
> cause if you wanna dance
> this boogie be ready
> to let the devil use your head
> for a drum

Dexter Gordon, Charlie Parker, Miles Davis, and other important jazz figures find their way into many of these poems, poems which are sometimes elegiac, sometimes celebratory.

Although the linking of jazz and poetry has been a project of many writers since the Beats, Komunyakaa's work offers a new thread, one that relies on a percussive stress and fluid vowels in order to mimic the strains of the music. His ability to emulate these rhythms is indicative of his formal control, an element that is important to his success as a writer; lesser talents who might have experienced the trials of the battlefield would rely simply on the "subject matter" available. Unwilling to be reduced to the label of "Vietnam" writer, Komunyakaa has continued throughout his career to refine and redirect his poetry.

—Tod Marshall

KOPIT, Arthur (Lee)

Born: New York City, 10 May 1937. **Education:** Lawrence High School, New York, graduated 1955; Harvard University, Cambridge, Massachusetts, A.B. (cum laude) 1959 (Phi Beta Kappa). **Family:** Married to Leslie Ann Garis; two sons and one daughter. **Career:** Playwright-in-residence, Wesleyan University, Middletown, Connecticut, 1975-76; CBS fellow, 1976-77, and adjunct professor of playwriting, 1977-80, Yale University, New Haven, Connecticut. Beginning 1982 taught playwriting workshop at City College, New York. Council member, Dramatists Guild, from 1982. **Awards:** Vernon Rice award, 1962; Outer Circle award, 1962; Guggenheim fellowship, 1967; Rockefeller grant, 1968; American Academy award, 1971; National Endowment for the Arts grant, 1974; Wesleyan University Center for the Humanities fellowship, 1974; Italia prize, for radio play, 1979. **Residence:** Connecticut.

PUBLICATIONS

Plays

The Questioning of Nick (produced 1957). In *The Day the Whores Came Out to Play Tennis and Other Plays*, 1965.
Gemini (produced 1957).
Don Juan in Texas, with Wally Lawrence (produced 1957).
On the Runway of Life, You Never Know What's Coming Off Next (produced 1958).

Across the River and into the Jungle (produced 1958).

To Dwell in a Place of Strangers, Act I published in *Harvard Advocate,* May 1958.

Aubade (produced 1959).

Sing to Me through Open Windows (produced 1959; revised version produced 1965). In *The Day the Whores Came Out to Play Tennis and Other Plays,* 1965.

Oh Dad, Poor Dad, Mamma's Hung You in the Closet and I'm Feelin' So Sad: A Pseudoclassical Tragifarce in a Bastard French Tradition (produced 1960). 1960.

Mhil'daim (produced 1963).

Asylum; or, What the Gentlemen Are Up To, and As for the Ladies (produced 1963; *And As for the Ladies* produced as *Chamber Music,* 1971). *Chamber Music* in *The Day the Whores Came Out to Play Tennis and Other Plays,* 1965.

The Conquest of Everest (produced 1964). In *The Day the Whores Came Out to Play Tennis and Other Plays,* 1965.

The Hero (produced 1964). In *The Day the Whores Came Out to Play Tennis and Other Plays,* 1965.

The Day the Whores Came Out to Play Tennis (produced 1965). In *The Day the Whores Came Out to Play Tennis and Other Plays,* 1965.

The Day the Whores Came Out to Play Tennis and Other Plays. 1965; as *Chamber Music and Other Plays,* 1969.

Indians (produced 1968). 1969.

An Incident in the Park, in *Pardon Me, Sir, but Is My Eye Hurting Your Elbow?* edited by Bob Booker and George Foster. 1968.

What's Happened to the Thorne's House? (produced 1972).

Louisiana Territory; or, Lewis and Clark—Lost and Found (produced 1975).

Secrets of the Rich (produced 1976). 1978.

Wings (produced 1978). 1978.

Nine (libretto), music and lyrics by Maury Yeston, from an adaptation by Mario Fratti of the screenplay *8 1/2* by Federico Fellini (produced 1981). 1983.

Good Help Is Hard to Find (produced 1981). 1982.

Ghosts, from a play by Henrik Ibsen (produced 1982).

End of the World (With a Symposium to Follow) (produced 1984; as *The Assignment,* produced 1985). In *Best American Plays,* 1993; published separately 1994.

Road to Nirvana (as *Bone-the-Fish,* produced 1989). 1991.

Peace Plays Two. 1990.

Phantom, music and lyrics by Maury Yeston; from the novel *The Phantom of the Opera* by Gaston Leroux. 1992.

Roswell (screenplay). 1993.

Three Plays (includes *Oh Dad, Poor Dad, Mamma's Hung You in the Closet and I'm Feelin' So Sad; Indians; Wings*). 1997.

Television Plays: *The Conquest of Television,* 1966; *Promontory Point Revisited,* 1969; *Phantom,* 1992.

*

Critical Study: *Sam Shepard, Kopit, and the Off-Broadway Theater* by Doris Auerbach, 1982.

*   *   *

"Do I exaggerate?" asks Michael Trent in his first speech in *End of the World.* "Of course. That is my method. I am a playwright." The line is a comic one which becomes ironic in the face of a theme—the prospect of global annihilation—which turns even the grandest theatrical exaggeration into austere understatement. Out of context, the words provide a suitable description of the way Arthur Kopit works.

At 23, fresh out of Harvard, Kopit escaped—or appeared to escape—the cocoon of university production when *Oh Dad, Poor Dad, Mamma Hung You in the Closet and I'm Feelin' So Sad* was published by a house that specializes in serious drama and went on to production in London and New York. A fashionable success, it established Kopit as a dramatist, but it also saddled him with the label "undergraduate playwright" which stayed with him long after the playfulness of *Oh Dad* had given way to the mixed-genre method that marks his best and most complex plays. One reason the epithet stuck is that the work that immediately followed *Oh Dad* lacked the flash of that play and offered little substance in consolation. *The Day the Whores Came Out to Play Tennis and Other Plays,* which contained some of his student work along with his post-*Oh Dad* efforts, seemed to confirm the critics who saw him simply as a clever young man noodling around.

Such a judgment is far too dismissive. Although some of *Oh Dad*'s games—the parody references to **Tennessee Williams**, for instance—seem too cute in retrospect, it is an early indication of the dramatic virtues that have become increasingly apparent in Kopit's work: a facility with language, an ear for the cliches of art and life, an eye for the effective stage image (the waltz scene in which Madame Rosepettle breaks Commodore Roseabove, for instance), a strategic use of caricature, the talent for being funny about a subject that is not at all comic. All of these are in evidence in *Oh Dad* and all of them are in the service of a serious theme (or one that seemed serious in 1960)—the emasculation of the American male by the too protective mother, the iron-maiden temptress and the little girl as seducer.

In an interview in *Mademoiselle* (August 1962), Kopit said, "Comedy is a very powerful tool . . . . You take the most serious thing you can think of and treat it as comically as you can." Although he invoked Shaw, *Oh Dad* is the immediate reference. Since then, he has thought of more serious things—war, death, nuclear destruction—and has treated them seriously. And comically, as *Indians* and *End of the World* indicate. The Bantam edition of *Indians* (1971) prints a long interview with John Lahr in which Kopit identifies his play as a response to "the madness of our involvement in Vietnam," but he chose to approach the subject obliquely, going back to the eviction of the American Indian from his land. The play shows the distance between official words and deeds, the power of platitude and the way in which myths are made and used. The central figure is Buffalo Bill, who begins as a friend of the Indians and ends—a star of his own show—as an apologist for slaughter. The play moves back and forth between comic and serious scenes, from the broad farce of the play within the play and the cartoon Ol' Time President to the powerful accusatory ending in which the Wild West Show is invaded by the dead Indians. For some, the funny scenes fit uncomfortably with the solemn subject matter, but they are not simply entertaining decoration. The comedy is thematic. The disastrous production of the Ned Buntline melodrama at the White House is both an instance of the creation of myth and a critique of it.

End of the World is a similar fusion of genres. It concerns a playwright who is commissioned to write a play about the dangers of nuclear proliferation—as Kopit was, in fact—and finds that he can only do so by writing a play about a playwright who is commissioned to write a play about nuclear proliferation. The parody, private-eye frame of the play (the playwright as detective), the agents' lunch at the Russian Tea Room, and the three interviews in which the rationale of nuclear stockpiling and scenarios of destruction are presented as comic turns are all central to the play's assumption that there are personal, artistic, and official ways of not facing up to the impending horror. Michael Trent learns in the play that all the nuclear strategists know the situation is hopeless but do not believe what they know, and that he was chosen to write the play because, like the men he interviews, he has an attraction to evil and destruction. A painful and funny play, it provides no solution, only an insistence on the probability of catastrophe and, unlike the conventional post-bomb melodrama, no promise of rebirth.

If *Indians* and *End of the World* share dramatic method, *Wings* is an indication of Kopit's unpredictability. There are funny lines in the play, but it is primarily a lyric exploration of death, perhaps prompted by the recent death of his father. It is about a woman who suffers a stroke, struggles to make her fragmented speech fit her still coherent thoughts and, after a second stroke, becomes eloquent as she sees herself flying into the unknown. A wing-walker in her youth, her profession/art provides the main metaphor for her final sense of exhilarating discovery. The play evokes both the concerned narrowness of medicine's perception of the woman and the imagination that continues to carry her above her stammering exasperation with herself and those around her. It is an indication—along with *Indians* and *End of the World*—that Kopit is wing-walking far above the bravura fight of *Oh Dad*.

Kopit returned to the ground with *Road to Nirvana,* which was originally produced as *Bone-the-Fish.* In fact, a *New York* magazine reviewer accused Kopit of scraping "rock bottom in taste, wit, and substance." The play mocks **David Mamet**'s successful play *Speed-the-Plow* in its exploration of the absurdly nightmarish world of Hollywood glitz, and takes satirical jabs at the pop-singer Madonna, the model for the main character. A *New Republic* reviewer called the play "one of the most relentlessly scatological satires of our time . . . . Dazzling in its capacity for insult, and animated by unsuppressed ferocity, *Bone-the-Fish* is destined to create a scandal wherever it is performed." More suited to mainstream audiences was Kopit's adaptation of Gaston Leroux's novel *The Phantom of the Opera.* The lavish musical, called simply *Phantom,* proved immensely popular and toured for a number of years after its introduction.

—Gerald Weales, updated by Tom Pendergast

KOSINSKI, Jerzy (Nikodem)

Pseudonym: Joseph Novack. **Born:** Lodz, Poland, 14 June 1933; immigrated to the United States in 1957; became citizen, 1965. **Education:** The University of Lodz, 1950-55, M.A. in political science 1953, M.A. in history 1955; Columbia University, New York (Ford Foundation Fellow), 1958-64; New School for Social Research, New York, 1962-65. **Family:** Married 1) Mary Hayward Weir in 1962 (divorced 1966); 2) Katherina von Fraunhofer in 1987. **Career:** Ski instructor, Zakopane, Poland, winters 1950-56; aspirant (graduate assistant), Polish Academy of Science, Warsaw, 1955-57; visiting researcher, Lomosov University, Moscow, 1957; laborer, truck driver, chauffeur, and projectionist on arriv-

ing in United States; fellow, Center for Advanced Studies, Wesleyan University, Middletown, Connecticut, 1968-69; senior fellow, Council for the Humanities, and visiting lecturer, Princeton University, New Jersey, 1969-70; professor of English prose and criticism, School of Drama, and resident fellow, Davenport College, Yale University, New Haven, Connecticut, 1970-73. Photographer: individual show—Crooked Circle Gallery, Warsaw, 1957. President, PEN American Center, 1973-75. Member of the Executive Board, National Writers Club; director, International League for Human Rights, 1973-79. **Awards:** Polish Academy of Science grant, 1955; Foreign Book prize (France), 1966; Guggenheim fellowship, 1967; National Book award, 1969; American Academy award, 1970; Yale University John Golden Fellowship in Playwriting, 1970; Brith Sholom Humanitarian Freedom award, 1974; American Civil Liberties Union First Amendment award, 1978; Writers Guild of America award, for screenplay, 1979; Polonia Media award, 1980; BAFTA award, for screenplay, 1981; Spertus College Humanitarian award, 1982. Doctor of Hebrew Letters: Spertus College, Chicago, 1982. **Died:** (suicide) 3 May 1991.

PUBLICATIONS

Fiction

The Painted Bird. 1965; revised edition, 1970.
Steps. 1968.
Being There. 1971.
The Devil Tree. 1973; revised edition, 1981.
Cockpit. 1975.
Blind Date. 1977.
Passion Play. 1979.
Pinball. 1982.
The Hermit of 69th Street. 1986.

Plays

Being There. 1973; revised edition, 1980.
Passion Play. 1982.

Screenplay: *Being There,* 1980.

Other

Dokumenty walki o czlowieka (Documents of the Struggle for Man). 1955.
Program rewolucji ludowej Jakoba Jaworskiego (Jakob Jaworski's Program of People's Revolution). 1955.
The Future Is Ours, Comrade: Conversations with Russians. 1960.
No Third Path. 1962.
Notes of the Author on The Painted Bird 1965. 1965.
The Art of the Self. Essays a propos Steps. 1968.
Passing By: Selected Essays. 1992.
Conversations with Jerzy Kosinski, edited by Tom Teicholz. 1993.

Editor, *Socjologia Amerykanska* (American Sociology). 1962.

*

Bibliography: *John Barth, Kosinski, and Thomas Pynchon: A Reference Guide* by Thomas P. Walsh and Cameron Northouse, 1977.

Critical Studies: *Kosinski: Literary Alarm Clock* by Byron L. Sherwin, 1981; *Kosinski* by Norman Lavers, 1982; *Words in Search of Victims: The Achievement of Kosinski* by Paul R. Lilly, Jr., 1988; *Plays of Passion, Games of Chance: Kosinski and His Fiction* by Barbara Lupack, 1988; *Jerzy Kosinski: A Biography* by James Park Sloan, 1996; *Critical Essays on Jerzy Kosinski,* 1998.

*   *   *

In Jerzy Kosinski's first novel, *The Painted Bird,* there is an incident that not only sums up the thrust of the novel in which it appears, but points to the core of the great variety of experiences that appear in Kosinski's later novels. A peasant catches a raven, paints it with brilliant colors, and releases it to return to its fellows. But the other birds will not accept it and tear it to pieces. This image is a metaphor that expresses the experience of the narrator in the novel, a child of dark aspect ("gypsy" or "Jewish" by turns) who wanders through Poland, deprived of his parents and depending on the ungentle mercies of the peasants he encounters; the peasants, blond and stupid, regard the child as full of evil magic. And the "painted" child learns to survive by duplicity; he endures a solitude that he has not chosen; the only morality he knows is that of survival.

It is a morality that, with appropriate alterations, the central figures of the other novels sense; just so do they define and experience their existences. Such a morality is tested—admired from several angles—in *Steps,* a collection of narrative fragments and mostly unlocalized amorous dialogues. Much of this material is linked with the education and migration to a foreign country of a young man who is, like the child in *The Painted Bird,* on the run, exploited and exploiting wherever he goes. To him every new acquaintance is both an affront and an opportunity.

Kosinski's traumatic childhood informs most of his novels. Born to Jewish parents, he became separated from them during the Nazi invasion of Poland in World War II. He escaped the Holocaust by wandering the countryside disguised as a peasant. From this vantage point, he witnessed the horrors and desolation of war. These experiences color his fiction.

For a change of pace, the hero of *Being There* is no person displaced by war; rather, he is an orphan without identity, unable to read, skillful only as a gardener. But when he leaves the Eden where he has learned his only skills, his oddity and peculiar vulnerability arouse wonder and respect, rather than antipathy as in *The Painted Bird.* His trivial remarks about gardening are taken as profound and enigmatic insights by those he encounters; businessmen, TV reporters, and others surround him with an aura of ultimate authority. In *The Devil Tree,* a young man named Jonathan James Whalen wanders through another landscape of solitude, this one created by his great inherited wealth. There is practically nothing that he cannot purchase and manipulate, and the absolute control he can exercise separates him from other persons as fully as does, for example, the "gypsy" aspect of the child in *The Painted Bird.* Whatever can be purchased can also be thrown away; this is the core of Whalen's experience.

The wanderings presented in *Cockpit* are those of a secret agent named Tarden. Born in a Communist country, he soon learns what his precious endowment is: intelligence and guile that surpass the intelligence and guile of all other persons. Every person he meets is a predestined victim whom Tarden can mislead and abuse, all with the intent of showing that Tarden is one "painted bird" whom his hostile peers cannot destroy.

Blind Date unites, within the confines of one novel, intense realizations of themes dispersed elsewhere. There is the solitude of a man, George Levanter, who has left his native Russia, has succeeded as an investment broker, and can afford the luxury of satisfying all his whims. He travels, he has many sexual encounters, and (a little odd in this context) he is an occasional enforcer of justice in an unjust world. In short, Levanter is both a knight errant and, more often, just an exile errant, all in a luxurious world that only superlatives can describe.

Two other novels—*Pinball* and *Passion Play*—are also variations on basic themes, ornamented with special attention to materials not treated elsewhere. Both novels present human beings incommunicado. In *Pinball* a girl seeks to find a rock star, and in *Passion Play* a polo player wants to discover competitors who are his equals. Each novel has its individual note: rock versus traditional music in *Pinball* and horsemanship in *Passion Play.*

Each of Kosinski's novels is a demonstration of one variety of solipsism. Community of any kind is a figment that misleads inferior imaginations. Each of Kosinski's novels dissolves such illusions. Innocence, wealth, and guile are alternate strategies, but they have a common goal. All confirm that each human being is alone, and those who have a degree of wisdom recognize their solitude and enforce it.

—Harold H. Watts, updated by Denise Wiloch

KUNITZ, Stanley (Jasspon)

Born: Worcester, Massachusetts, 29 July 1905. **Education:** Classical High School, Worcester, graduated 1922; Harvard University, Cambridge, Massachusetts (Garrison Medal, 1926), A.B. (summa cum laude) 1926 (Phi Beta Kappa), A.M. 1927. **Military Service:** Served in the U.S. Army Air Transport Command, 1943-45; sergeant. **Family:** Married 1) Helen Pearce in 1930 (divorced 1937); 2) Eleanor Evans in 1939 (divorced 1958), one daughter; 3) Elise Asher in 1958. **Career:** Editor, Wilson Library Bulletin, New York, 1928-43; member of the faculty, Bennington College, Vermont, 1946-49; professor of English, Potsdam State Teachers College (now State University of New York), 1949-50, and summers, 1949-53; lecturer, New School for Social Research, New York, 1950-57; visiting professor, University of Washington, Seattle, 1955-56, Queens College, Flushing, New York, 1956-57, Brandeis University, Waltham, Massachusetts, 1958-59, Yale University, New Haven, Connecticut, 1970-72, Rutgers University, Camden, New Jersey, 1974, Princeton University, New Jersey, 1978, and Vassar College, Poughkeepsie, New York, 1981. Director, YM-YWHA Poetry Workshop, New York, 1958-62; Danforth Visiting Lecturer, 1961-63; lecturer, 1963-67, and adjunct professor of writing, 1967-85, Columbia University, New York; associated with the Fine Arts Work Center, Provincetown, Massachusetts, 1968—; chancellor, Academy of American Poets, 1970; Senior Fellow in Humanities, Princeton University, 1978; editor, Yale Younger Poets series, Yale University Press, New Haven, Connecticut, 1969-77; consultant in poetry, 1974-76, honorary consultant in American letters, 1976-83, Library of Congress, Washington, D.C.; president, Poets House, New York City, 1985—; secretary, American Academy; cultural exchange lecturer, U.S.S.R., Poland, Senegal, Ghana, Israel, and Egypt. **Awards:** Oscar Blumenthal prize, 1941, Guggenheim fellowship, 1945; Amy

Lowell traveling fellowship, 1953; Levinson prize, *Poetry* magazine, 1956; Harriet Monroe award, 1958; Pulitzer prize, 1959; Ford grant, 1959; American Academy grant, 1959; Brandeis University Creative Arts award, 1964; Academy of American Poets fellowship, 1968; Fellow, Yale University, 1969; New England Poetry Club Golden Rose trophy, 1970; Notable book citation, American Library Association, 1979; Lenore Marshall award, 1980; National Endowment for the Arts senior fellowship, 1984; Bollingen prize, 1987; Walt Whitman award citation of merit, with designation as State Poet of New York, 1987; named Walt Whitman Birthplace Poet, 1989. Litt.D.: Clark University, Worcester, Massachusetts, 1961; Anna Maria College, Paxton, Massachusetts, 1977; L.H.D.: Worcester State College, Massachusetts, 1980. **Residence:** New York City.

PUBLICATIONS

Poetry

Intellectual Things. 1930.
Passport to the War: A Selection of Poems. 1944.
Selected Poems 1928-1958. 1958.
The Testing-Tree. 1971.
The Terrible Threshold: Selected Poems 1940-1970. 1974.
The Coat without a Seam: Sixty Poems 1930-1972. 1974.
The Lincoln Relics. 1978.
The Poems of Stanley Kunitz 1928-1978. 1979.
The Wellfleet Whale and Companion Poems. 1983.
Next-to-Last Things (includes essays). 1985.
Interviews and Encounters with Stanley Kunitz. 1993.
Passing Through: The Later Poems, New and Selected. 1995.

Other

Robert Lowell, Poet of Terribilita (lecture). 1974.
A Kind of Order, A Kind of Folly: Essays and Conversations. 1975.
From Feathers to Iron (lecture). 1976.
Interviews and Encounters with Stanley Kunitz. 1993.

Editor, *Living Authors: A Book of Biographies*. 1931.
Editor, with Howard Haycraft and Wilbur C. Hadden, *Authors Today and Yesterday: A Companion Volume to Living Authors*. 1933.
Editor, with others, *The Junior Book of Authors*. 1934; revised edition, 1961.
Editor, with Howard Haycraft, *British Authors of the Nineteenth Century*. 1936.
Editor, with Howard Haycraft, *American Authors 1600-1900: A Biographical Dictionary of American Literature*. 1938.
Editor, with Howard Haycraft, *Twentieth Century Authors: A Biographical Dictionary of Modern Literature*. 1942; first supplement, with Vineta Colby, 1955.
Editor, with Howard Haycraft, *British Authors before 1800: A Biographical Dictionary*. 1952.
Editor, *Poems of John Keats*. 1964.
Editor, with Vineta Colby, *European Authors 1000-1900: A Biographical Dictionary of European Literature*. 1967.
Editor and translator, with Max Hayward, *Poems of Akhmatova*. 1973.
Editor and co-translator, *Orchard Lamps*, by Ivan Drach. 1978.

Editor, with John Wakeman, *World Authors, 1970-1975: A Biographical Dictionary*. 1980.
Editor, *The Essential Blake*. 1987.

Translator, with others, *Stolen Apples*, by Yevgeny Yevtushenko. 1972.
Translator, with others, *Story under Full Sail*, by Andrei Voznesensky. 1974.
Translator, with others, *Window on the Black Sea: Bulgarian Poetry in Translation*. 1992.

*

Critical Studies: *Kunitz* by Marie Henault, 1980; *Kunitz: An Introduction to the Poetry* by Gregory Orr, 1985; *A Celebration for Kunitz on His Eightieth Birthday,* 1986; "An Interview with Stanley Kunitz" in the *Gettysburg Review,* Spring, 1992.

*   *   *

Stanley Kunitz's *Selected Poems 1928-1958* offers us a good standard of the classic forms and modes of poetry that largely governed American poets of these three decades. Kunitz has more often fought the form imposed on his sometimes extravagant lyrical language than given in to it, and where this creative conflict between a restless content and a rigid, enveloping form is sustained the result has unusual vigor and freshness. The effect is of loosely woven statements held under intense pressure of symmetry and repeated rhythm, as in this nervous, jaggedly expressed love lyric, "Green Ways":

> Let me not say it, let me not reveal
> How like a god my heart begins to climb
> The trellis of the crystal
> In the rose-green moon;
> Let me not say it, let me leave untold
> This legend, while the nights snow emerald.
> Let me not say it, let me not confess
> How in the leaflight of my green-celled world
> In self's pre-history
> The blind moulds kiss;
> Let me not say it, let me but endure
> This ritual like feather and like star.
> Let me proclaim it—human be my lot!—
> How from my pit of green horse-bones
> I turn, in a wilderness of sweat,
> To the moon-breasted sibylline,
> And lift this garland, Danger, from her throat
> To blaze it in the foundries of the night.

But "Green Ways" is the balance that Kunitz has not always been able to strike in his poetry; here passion and form give way to each other, but in some of his work the feeling has been too thoroughly subdued by order and conscious craft, creating a lyric that is too dry and rehearsed in its utterance. But even in the severest of his poems, the reader is aware of the intensity of the poet's mind, the irrepressible energy of his imagination.

Often called the poet's poet, a term he has tended to dismiss more vigorously in later years, Kunitz has himself defended the unruly side of the poetic medium. As editor of the Yale Younger Poets series, Kunitz has been enthusiastic in his advocacy of poetry of process and impulsive strategies. In his occasional and critical prose, he has also tended to favor the ungoverned muse: in his essay "A Kind of Order" he says: "With young writers I make a nuisance of myself talking about order, for the good reason that order is teachable; but in my bones I know that only the troubled spirits among them, those who recognize the disorder without and within, have a chance to become poets."

In the strictest balance, however, Kunitz's *Selected Poems* conveys, even in its most rigid formulations of lyric, a stubbornly individual mind that has known all the extremes of feeling and mood. "Night-Piece," "The Man Upstairs" with its Eliotic strain of irony and wit, the poems gathered under the section "The Terrible Threshold," and much else in this collection are provocative and vital.

In the most recent edition of his selected poems (*The Poems 1928-1978*), which covers fifty years of poetry, Kunitz follows the bent of his disorderly side, not only in breaking up the thematic order of the older edition, but in putting first his new poems, and then arranging the rest in chronological order. The new poems are livelier, fresher, and freer in tone and method. Kunitz is fortunately one of those in whom age is an access to one's youth, as he reports in his opening poem, "The Knot," with its image of the "obstinate bud, / sticky with life." *Next-to-Last Things* contains new poems and essays, which bears as part of its epigraph a line that reads, "that he might risk his soul in the streets." Though few, these are some of his most charming poems; the prose section following is a reckoning with age and his changed views: "A poem is at once the most primitive and most sophisticated use of language, but my emphasis is on the former," he writes in "The Wisdom of the Body." In recent years, the wisdom, the guidance, and the dozens of book introductions that Kunitz has shared with grateful authors have been repaid by the many poets he has helped during his long lifetime. *A Celebration for Kunitz on His Eightieth Birthday* compiles many poems written for or about the elder statesman of poetry, while *Interviews and Encounters with Stanley Kunitz*, edited by Stanley Moss, reminds us why this poet's words have been such a help to aspiring writers for more than sixty years.

—Paul Christensen, updated by Andrew O. Jones

KUSHNER, Tony

Born: New York City, 16 July 1956. Grew up in Lake Charles, Louisiana. **Education:** Columbia University, New York, B.A. 1978; New York University, M.F.A. in directing 1984. **Career:** Beginning 1989 guest artist, New York University Graduate Theatre Program, Yale University, New Haven, Connecticut, and Princeton University, New Jersey. Director, Literary Services, Theatre Communications Group, New York, 1990-91; playwright-in-residence, Juilliard School of Drama, New York, 1990-92. **Awards:** National Endowment for the Arts directing fellowship, 1985; Princess Grace award, 1986; New York State Council on the Arts playwrighting fellowship, 1986; New York Foundation for the Arts playwrighting fellowship, 1987; John Whiting award, 1990; Kennedy Center/American Express Fund for New American Plays award, 1990, 1992; National Arts Club Kesselring award, 1991; Will Glickman playwrighting prize, 1992; *Evening Standard* award, 1992; Pulitzer prize for drama, Tony award for best play, and New York Drama

Critics Circle award for best new play, all 1993, all for *Millennium Approaches,* part 1 of *Angels in America*; American Academy of Arts and Letters award, 1994; Tony award for *Perestroika,* part two of *Angels in America,* 1994; Lambda Literary award, Lesbian and Gay drama, for *Thinking about the Longstanding Problems of Virtue and Happiness,* 1996. **Residence:** Brooklyn, New York.

PUBLICATIONS

Plays

Yes, Yes, No, No (for children; produced 1985). Published in *Plays in Process,* vol. 7, no. 11, 1987.
Stella, adaptation of the play by Goethe (produced 1987).
A Bright Room Called Day (produced 1987). 1991.
Hydriotaphia (produced 1987).
The Illusion, adaptation of a play by Pierre Corneille (produced 1988; revised version produced 1990). 1991.
Widows, with Ariel Dorfman, adaptation of the novel by Dorfman (produced 1991).
Angels in America, Part One: Millennium Approaches (produced 1991). 1992; with *Angels in America, Part Two: Perestroika,* 1993.
Angels in America, Part Two: Perestroika (produced 1992). With *Angels in America, Part One: Millennium Approaches,* 1993; revised version, 1996.

Other

Thinking about the Longstanding Problems of Virtue and Happiness. 1995.
A Prayer (excerpt from *Slavs!: Thinking about the Longstanding Problems of Virtue and Happiness*). 1995.
Tony Kushner in Conversation, edited by Robert Vorlicky. 1998.

Translator, *A Dybbuk.* 1998.

*

Critical Studies: "Tony Kushner Considers the Longstanding Problems of Virtue and Happiness" by David Savran, in *American Theatre,* 1994, pp. 20-27, 100-04; *Essays on Kushner's Angels* edited by Per K. Brask, 1995; "The Angels of Fructification: Tennessee Williams, Tony Kushner, and Images of Homosexuality on the American Stage" by James Fisher, in *Mississippi Quarterly: The Journal of Southern Culture,* Winter 1995-96, pp. 13-32; "*Angels in America:* Tony Kushner's Theses on the Philosophy of History" by Charles McNully, in *Modern Drama,* Spring 1996; "Authors in America: Tony Kushner, Arthur Miller, and Anna Deveare Smith" by Iris Smith, in *the Centennial Review,* Winter 1996, pp. 125-42; *Approaching the Millennium: Essays on Angels in America* edited by Deborah R. Geis and Steven F. Kruger, 1997.

Theatrical Activities:

Director: **Plays**–*Yes Yes Yes No No: The Solace-of-Solstice, Apogee/Perigee, Bestial/Celestial Holiday Show,* 1985; *In Great Eliza's Golden Time,* 1986; *Golden Boy,* 1986.

Actor: **Play**–*Letter from New York to Sarajevo*, 1995. **Television**–*The 47ᵗʰ Annual Tony Awards*, 1993; *In Search of Angels*, 1994.

*　　*　　*

"I read the histories of Germany. I read the Book of Revelations. I read the *Times*. I sense parallels," says Zillah in Tony Kushner's early play *A Bright Room Called Day*. The contemporary American Jewish character with "Anarcho-Punk tendencies" could just as well be describing her creator's modus operandi. For Kushner's plays interweave a vivid historical consciousness, a deep religious and spiritual fascination, and a journalistic ability to sense a culture's zeitgeist. His plays, even the ponderous and uneven ones like *A Bright Room . . . ,* are so rich, intelligent, and dramatically challenging that his early promise marked him as one of the finest writers for the American theater in the second half of the twentieth century.

Almost all of Kushner's work for the theater focuses on the actions of characters caught in brutish, bellicose societies under siege: Reagan-era America (*Angels in America*); Germany in the 1930s (*Bright Room*); post-*Perestroika* Russia (*Slavs!*). How humans react in and amidst these social situations is Kushner's territory. What defines heroic behavior? What are the morally acceptable courses of action? How does one keep one's faith when the world is crumbling? And, most important, what faith should one keep? The faded Marxist-Leninism bandied about in *Slavs!* by party apparatchiks? Joe's conservative Republicanism or Louis's "radical democracy" in *Angels in America*? These outsized questions make his plays potent and important. History does not stand still in Kushner's plays; it is an object lesson as stationary and staid as an oncoming locomotive.

Because history is a narrative continually being written, as Kushner's plays suggest, humankind may as well try to break any destructive repeating cycles. That is why the contemporary American Zillah is so important to a play whose other characters all inhabit the increasingly corrupt society of Germany during the raise of Nazism. Comparing the United States of the 1980s to pre-Nazi Germany may seem a bit hysterical—unless the writer creates a character who admits to being paranoid enough to consider the parallel.

Most of Kushner's reputation has been occasioned by the wild success—both critical and popular—of his two-part epic *Angels in America*, produced on Broadway, across the United States, and around the world. The play's subtitle—"A Gay Fantasia on National Themes"—directly refers to George Bernard Shaw's subtitle for *Heartbreak House*. And although Kushner owes some debt to Shaw in his tendency to mix social consciousness and political philosophy with a light comedic touch, his influences cannot be confined to a single individual. He is enthralled equally it seems with cabala, Karl Marx, and the politics of homosexuality. And his theatrical techniques—the use of projected scene titles, direct address, taped voices, and other nonnaturalistic elements—are more Brechtian than Shavian.

Thanks to graduate theater training in directing, Kushner developed the ability to theatricalize his heady ideals in a flamboyant fashion: angels burst through the ceiling onto the stage; a Communist party leader leaps around the stage and then falls over dead. As the character Roy Cohn in *Angels* (based on the McCarthy-era lawyer and Nixon supporter) says of the musical version of *La Cage aux Folles*, it's "fabulous." That tradition, largely gay, of a "theater of the fabulous" is one that Kushner also claims. The closing benediction of the dying character Prior in *Angels* suggests this when he says, "Bye now. You are fabulous creatures, each and every one." Kushner makes plays that could be called—borrowing from a popular Latin American literary genre—"magic theaterism." Small wonder then that he has adapted classics of world drama that exhibit similar sensibilities, most notably *The Illusion* by Pierre Corneille and Ansky's *The Dybbuk*.

It remains to be seen if *Angels of America* will be regarded ultimately as a great universal drama for the ages or as an almost baroque period piece about the United States in the 1990s. A case can be made that the play's theatrical strokes—reincarnated characters from earlier centuries, hallucinations, angels—will keep audiences engaged, as will the epic's love triangle. What is sure to endure, however, is the critical assessment of Kushner's ability to combine intellectual ferocity with an informed worldview to make explosive, engaging theatrical works.

—John Istel

See the essay on *Angels in America.*

L

LA FARGE, Oliver (Hazard Perry)

Born: New York City, 19 December 1901. **Education:** The Groton Academy, Lowell, Massachusetts, graduated 1920; Harvard University, Cambridge, Massachusetts (editor, *Harvard Lampoon;* president, *Advocate;* class poet), 1920-24, B.A. 1924, then did graduate work in anthropology (Hemenway Fellow), M.A. 1929. **Military Service:** Served in the U.S. Army, 1942-46: lieutenant-colonel; Legion of Merit, 1946. **Family:** Married 1) Wanden E. Mathews in 1929 (divorced 1937), one son and one daughter; 2) Consuelo Otille C. de Baca in 1939, one son. **Career:** Anthropologist: involved in expeditions for the Peabody Museum, Harvard, in Arizona, 1921, 1922, 1924; Assistant in Ethnology, Department of Middle American Research, Tulane University, New Orleans, 1925-26; involved in research expeditions to Mexico and Guatemala, 1926-28; Research Associate in Ethnology, Columbia University, New York, 1931; director of the Columbia University expedition to Guatemala, 1932; thereafter a full-time writer and historian; columnist, Santa Fe *New Mexican,* 1950-63. president, Association on American Indian Affairs, 1932-41, 1948. **Awards:** Pulitzer prize, 1930; O. Henry award, 1931; Guggenheim fellowship, 1941; A.M., Brown University, Providence, Rhode Island, 1932; fellow, American Association for the Advancement of Science, 1938, American Anthropological Association, 1947, and American Academy of Arts and Sciences, 1953. **Member:** American Academy, 1957. **Died:** 2 August 1963.

PUBLICATIONS

Fiction

Laughing Boy. 1929.
Sparks Fly Upward. 1931.
Long Pennant. 1933.
All the Young Men (stories). 1935.
The Enemy Gods. 1937.
The Copper Pot. 1942.
A Pause in the Desert (stories). 1957.
The Door in the Wall (stories). 1965.

Plays

Screenplay: *Behold My Wife,* with William R. Lipman, 1934.

Other

Tribes and Temples: A Record of the Expedition to Middle America Conducted by the Tulane University of Louisiana in 1925, with Frans Blom. 2 vols., 1926-27.
The Year Bearers People, with Douglas Byers. 1931.
An Alphabet for Writing the Navajo Language, with J. P. Harrington. 1936.
As Long as the Grass Shall Grow, photographs by Helen M. Post. 1940.

War below Zero: The Battle for Greenland, with Bernt Balchen and Corey Ford. 1944.
Raw Material (autobiography). 1945.
Santa Eulalia: The Religion of a Cuchumatan Indian Town. 1947.
The Eagle in the Egg. 1949.
Cochise of Arizona: The Pipe of Peace Is Broken (for children). 1953.
The Mother Ditch (for children). 1954.
A Pictorial History of the American Indian. 1956; edition for children, as *The American Indian,* 1960.
Behind the Mountains. 1956.
Santa Fe: The Autobiography of a Southwestern Town, with Arthur N. Morgan. 1959.
The Man with the Calabash Pipe: Some Observations, edited by Winfield Townley Scott. 1966.

Editor, *Introduction to American Indian Art.* 1931.
Editor, with Jay Bryan Nash, *The New Day for the Indians: A Survey of the Working of the Indian Reorganization Act of 1934.* 1938.
Editor, *The Changing Indian.* 1942.

Translator, *A Mans Place,* by Ramon Sender. 1940.

*

Critical Studies: *La Farge* by Everett A. Gillis, 1967; *Indian Man: A Life of La Farge* by D'Arcy McNickle, 1971; *La Farge* by T. M. Pearce, 1972; "Oliver La Farge" by Everett A. Gillis, in *A Literary History of the American West,* 1987; "Oliver La Farge, Writer and Anthropologist" by Philip A. Dennis, in *Literature and Anthropology* edited by Dennis and Wendell Aycock, 1989; *Modern Writers in New Mexico: Charles Lummis, Oliver La Farge, D.H. Lawrence, Willa Cather, and the Quest for Purpose and Place in the Southwest* (dissertation) by Michael Oren Smedshammer, 1998.

*   *   *

Of the more than twenty books by Oliver La Farge, nearly half are scientific or historical and one-third are fiction. Yet he is generally known as the author of but one book, his first novel, *Laughing Boy.*

It is not surprising that his histories are virtually unknown. Of those concerning Indians, his most important is *A Pictorial History of the American Indian,* which offers a wealth of material about the various tribes to a public aware of the minority question. Other histories, however—about World War II, the city of Santa Fe, the events of La Farge's own life—are too specialized to be of general interest.

For a similar reason, his scientific work is all but unknown. Not only has the subsequent accumulation of knowledge dwarfed his contributions to ethnology, but as he notes in his personal history, *Raw Material,* the details that absorb the scientist are unlikely to interest more than a handful of fellow scientists. The accounts of his expeditions to Central America—*Tribes and Temples, The Year Bearers People, Santa Eulalia*—are highly readable, but too narrowly concerned with the Indian to interest the public for which they were intended.

On the other hand his second novel, *Sparks Fly Upward,* using the same Indian material, was a bestseller. This and *The Enemy Gods,* dealing with the Navajos in the southwest, reveal the plight of the Indian caught between two cultures. The theme is also explored in a collection of short stories, *All the Young Men.*

With his fifth novel, *The Copper Pot,* La Farge attempted to avoid being typecast as a writer about Indians. This story of an artist in New Orleans is more an affectionate memoir than a novel. Two short story collections, *A Pause in the Desert* and *The Door in the Wall,* use other than Indian material, as does *The Long Pennant,* a novel about the aftermath of piracy by a New England vessel.

Yet it is La Farge's knowledgeable use of Indian material that distinguishes his fiction. A symbiotic relationship exists between the scientific and the creative in his work, the former providing it with substance and originality. Although a first-rate storyteller, he exhibits no particularly original turn of mind. He breaks no new ground in his use of language or fictional techniques. As he makes plain in his newspaper columns, collected in *The Man with the Calabash Pipe,* he wished to preserve traditional values, in language and elsewhere—an attitude reflected in his lifelong involvement with the Indian.

This attitude and his unique material are most happily met in his two finest novels, *Laughing Boy* and *The Enemy Gods.* The latter is considered superior, presenting more information and dealing with weightier problems. Yet it is unremittingly melancholy and gray compared with *Laughing Boy,* whose young lovers in an Indian Eden are likely to continue to make it the book by which La Farge will be known.

—Robert F. Richards

L'AMOUR, Louis (Dearborn)

Pseudonym: Also wrote as Tex Burns; Jim Mayo. **Born:** Louis Dearborn LaMoore in Jamestown, North Dakota, 28 March 1908. **Military Service:** Served in U.S. Army, 1942-46, lieutenant. **Family:** Married Katherine Elizabeth Adams in 1956; one son and one daughter. **Career:** Worked as prizefighter, deckhand on a tugboat, lumberjack, prospector and miner, deputy sheriff, longshoreman, fruit picker, and elephant handler. **Awards:** Spur award from the Western Writers of America, 1969; Theodore Roosevelt Rough Rider award, 1972; American Book award, 1980 and 1981; Buffalo Bill award, Distinguished Newsboy award, and National Genealogical Society award, all in 1981; Congressional Gold Medal, 1983; Presidential Medal of Freedom, 1984. L.L.D: Jamestown College, 1972; North Dakota State University, 1981; University of Laverne, 1981; and Pepperdine University, 1984. **Died:** 10 June 1988.

PUBLICATIONS

Novels

Westward the Tide. 1950.
"Hopalong Cassidy" series:

Hopalong Cassidy and the Riders of High Rock. 1951.
Hopalong Cassidy and the Rustlers of West Fork. 1951.
Hopalong Cassidy and the Trail to Seven Pines. 1951.
Hopalong Cassidy, Trouble Shooter. 1952.
Hondo (novelization of screenplay, adapted from short story "The Gift of Cochise"). 1953.
Showdown at Yellow Butte. 1953.
Crossfire Trail. 1954.
Utah Blaine. 1954.
Kilkenny. 1954.
Heller with a Gun. 1955.
To Tame a Land. 1955.
Guns of the Timberlands. 1955.
The Burning Hills. 1956.
Silver Canyon. 1956.
Last Stand at Papago Wells. 1957.
The Tall Stranger. 1957.
Sitka. 1957.
Radigan. 1958.
The First Fast Draw. 1959.
Taggart. 1959.
Flint. 1960.
"The Sacketts" series:
The Daybreakers. 1960.
Sackett. 1961.
Lando. 1962.
Mojave Crossing. 1964.
The Sackett Brand. 1965.
Mustang Man. 1966.
The Sky-Liners. 1967.
The Lonely Men. 1969.
Galloway. 1970.
Ride the Dark Trail. 1972.
Treasure Mountain. 1972.
Sackett's Land. 1974.
To the Far Blue Mountains. 1976.
The Warrior's Path. 1980.
Ride the River. 1983.
Jubal Sackett. 1985.
Shalako. 1962.
Killoe. 1962.
High Lonesome. 1962.
How the West Was Won (novelization of screenplay). 1963.
Fallon. 1963.
Catlow. 1963.
Dark Canyon. 1963.
Hanging Woman Creek. 1964.
Kiowa Trail. 1964.
The High Graders. 1965.
The Key-Lock Man. 1965.
Kid Rodelo. 1966.
Kilrone. 1966.
The Broken Gun. 1966.
Matagorda. 1967.
Brionne. 1968.
Chancy. 1968.
Down the Long Hills. 1968.
The Empty Land. 1969.
Conagher. 1969.
Reilly's Luck. 1970.
The Man Called Noon. 1970.

Under the Sweetwater Rim. 1971.
Tucker. 1971.
"The Chantrys" series:
  North to the Rails. 1971.
  The Ferguson Rifle. 1973.
  Over on the Dry Side. 1975.
  Borden Chantry. 1978.
  Fair Blows the Wind. 1978.
Callaghen. 1972.
The Man from Skibbereen. 1973.
The Quick and the Dead. 1974.
The Californios. 1974.
"The Talons" series:
  The Man from the Broken Hills. 1975.
  Rivers West. 1975.
  Milo Talon. 1981.
Where the Long Grass Blows. 1976.
The Rider of Lost Creek. 1976.
The Mountain Valley War. 1978.
Bendigo Shafter. 1979.
The Iron Marshal. 1979.
The Proving Trail. 1979.
Lonely on the Mountain. 1980.
Comstock Lode. 1981.
The Cherokee Trail . 1982.
The Shadow Riders. 1982.
The Lonesome Gods. 1983.
Son of a Wanted Man. 1984.
The Walking Drum. 1984.
Passin' Through. 1985.
Last of the Breed. 1986.
The Haunted Mesa. 1987.

Short Stories

War Party. 1975.
The Strong Shall Live. 1980.
Yondering. 1980.
Buckskin Run. 1981.
Bowdrie. 1983.
Law of the Desert Born. 1983.
The Hills of Homicide. 1983.
Bowdrie's Law. 1984.
Dutchman's Flat. 1986.
Riding for the Brand. 1986.
The Trail to Crazy Man. 1986.
The Rider of the Ruby Hills. 1986.
Night over the Solomons. 1986.
West from Singapore. 1987.
Lonigan. 1988.
Long Ride Home. 1989.
The Outlaws of Mesquite. 1990.

Plays

Screenplays: *East of Sumatra* with Frank J. Gill, Jr., and Jack
  Natteford, 1953; *Four Guns to the Border,* with George Van
  Marter and Franklin Coen, 1954; *Treasure of the Ruby Hills,*
  with Tom Hubbard and Fred Eggers, 1955; *Stranger on Horse-*
  back, with Herb Meadow and Don Martin, 1955; *Kid Rodelo*
  with Jack Natteford, 1966.

Poetry

Smoke from This Altar. 1939.

Prose

Frontier (essays), photographs by David Muench. 1984.
A Trail of Memories: The Quotations of Louis L'Amour, edited
  by Angelique L'Amour. 1988.
The Sackett Companion: A Personal Guide to the Sackett Novels.
  1988.
Education of a Wandering Man (autobiography). 1989.

*

Bibliography: "Louis L'Amour" in *Fifty Western Writers: A Bio-
Bibliographical Sourcebook,* 1982; *The Work of Louis L'Amour:
An Annotated Bibliography and Guide* by Halbert W. Hall, 1995.

Critical Studies: *Critical Essays on the Western American Novel*
edited by William T. Pilkington, 1980; "Last of the Breed: Louis
L'Amour's Survivalist Fantasy" by Philip G. Terrie, in *Journal of
Popular Culture,* vol. 25, 1992; "History and Louis L'Amour's
Cowboy" by Darin Cozzens, in *Journal of American Culture,* vol.
14, 1991; "Louis L'Amour" by Robert Lee Gale, in *Updating the
Literary West,* 1997.

*   *   *

Louis L'Amour is undoubtedly the most widely read and best-
selling western author ever. His domination of the popular western for nearly half a century has helped to develop the genre,
which continues to fascinate readers of all ages and from all walks
of life.

L'Amour worked at a number of hard scrabble jobs in his youth,
served in the U.S. Army during World War II, and published short
stories throughout this early period. These tales of action portray
soldiers, cowboys, and sailors, and they served as a kind of apprenticeship for his later productivity as a novelist. His first novel,
Westward the Tide, was published in England in 1950 and was
virtually ignored. This first effort contains many of the elements
L'Amour is famous for—heroes back from war, valiant heroines,
plenty of bad guys, and lots of action.

His next publication found a receptive audience and began his
long run of fame. *Hondo,* a novelization of a screenplay based on
an earlier short story, "The Gift of Cochise," was published in
1953 and features the tough L'Amour hero that became a standard in so many of his books. All the classic western elements are
here: conflicted hero, pioneer damsel in distress, gunplay with Indians and frontier toughs, and the struggle between settling down
and remaining independent. The publications for the next fifteen
years or so depict cowboys and world adventurers in a variety of
settings, mostly frontier ones. *The Daybreakers,* published in
1960, begins his epic of the Sackett family, following them from
England on their westward journey. His other two epic families,
the Chantrys and the Talons, were likewise slated for an extensive westward chronicle, showing the history of America through
the families' experiences, but L'Amour's death cut short the
completion of this saga. So extensive was this twenty-five-volume
story of the Sacketts that late in his life, L'Amour published a guide-
book to the family he created. In addition to several screenplays on

which L'Amour collaborated and the almost fifty movies and television shows made from his works, the Sackett series was adapted for television as the wildly popular miniseries starring Sam Elliott.

His last novel, *The Haunted Mesa,* culminates a long and successful writing career and weaves New Age mythology with ancient Anasazi prehistory and other modern-day elements. In fact, continually setting the standard for the popular western, L'Amour was always interested in including various innovations, such as telephones and automobiles as well as his growing fascination and sympathy with Indian cultures and the environment, in his novels throughout the 1960s, 1970s, and 1980s. Just prior to his death, L'Amour wrote his autobiography, casting himself in the role of wanderer. Despite the limitations of the genre he helped to mold and the hurried editing of pulp publication, L'Amour's characters were never stock or stereotypes. Always heavy on laconic stoicism, fierce courage, staunch independence, and male-dominated patriotism, L'Amour's West is a memorable landscape whose influence will be felt in western writing, popular culture, and American literature well into the twenty-first century.

—Jay Ann Cox

LANIER, Sidney

Born: Macon, Georgia, 3 February 1842. **Education:** A private academy in Macon, and at Oglethorpe University, near Milledgeville, Georgia, 1857-60, graduated 1860. **Military Service:** Served with the Macon Volunteers in the Confederate forces during the Civil War, 1861-65: prisoner-of-war, 1864-65. **Family:** Married Mary Day in 1867; four sons. **Career:** Worked in his father's law office and as a hotel clerk and teacher, Macon, 1865-73; musician from an early age: flute player in the Peabody Orchestra, Baltimore, from 1873; lecturer in English, Johns Hopkins University, Baltimore, 1879-81. **Died:** 7 September 1881.

PUBLICATIONS

Collections

The Works (includes letters), edited by Charles R. Anderson and others. 10 vols., 1945.
Selected Poems, edited by Stark Young. 1947.

Poetry

The Centennial Meditation of Columbia, music by Dudley Buck. 1876.
Poems. 1877.
Poems, edited by Mary Day Lanier. 1884; revised edition, 1891, 1916.
Poem Outlines. 1908.

Fiction

Tiger-Lilies. 1867.

Other

Florida: Its Scenery, Climate, and History. 1875.
Some Highways and Byways of American Travel, with others. 1878.

The Science of English Verse. 1880.
The English Novel and the Principle of Its Development, edited by William Hand Browne. 1883; edited by Mary Day Lanier, 1897.
Music and Poetry: Essays upon Some Aspects and Inter-Relations of the Two Arts, edited by Henry Wysham Lanier. 1898.
Retrospects and Prospects: Descriptive and Historical Essays, edited by Henry Wysham Lanier. 1899.
Letters of Lanier: Selections from His Correspondence 1866-1881, edited by Henry Wysham Lanier. 1899.
Bob: The Story of Our Mocking-Bird, edited by Henry Wysham Lanier. 1899.
Shakespeare and His Forerunners: Studies in Elizabethan Poetry and Its Development from Early English, edited by Henry Wysham Lanier. 2 vols., 1902.

Editor, *The Boys Froissart, Being Sir John Froissart's Chronicles.* 1879.
Editor, *The Boy King Arthur, Being Sir Thomas Malory's History of King Arthur and His Knights of the Round Table.* 1880.
Editor, *The Boys Mabinogion.* 1881.
Editor, *The Boys Percy, Being Old Ballads of War, Adventure, and Love.* 1882.

*

Bibliography: in *Bibliography of American Literature* by Jacob Blanck, 1969; *Lanier, Henry Timrôd, and Paul Hamilton Hayne: A Reference Guide* by Jack De Bellis, 1978.

Critical Studies: *Lanier: A Biographical and Critical Study* by Aubrey H. Starke, 1933; *Lanier, Poet and Prosodist* by Richard Webb and Edwin R. Coulson, 1941; *Lanier: The Man, The Poet, The Critic* by Edd Winfield Parks, 1968; *Lanier* by Jack De Bellis, 1972; *A Living Minstrelsy: The Poetry and Music of Lanier* by Jane S. Gabin, 1985; "Looking for Sidney" by R. S. Gwynn, in *Shenandoah,* summer, 1989.

*   *   *

The life of Sidney Lanier is an odyssey from a small southern city to the great cultural centers of America; from a law desk in a Georgia office to a prominent place in a major professional orchestra; from an aesthetically restrictive tradition to an existence totally imbued with the arts. Throughout his career, from the time he was deciding whether to defy southern tradition in favor of art, through the period in which he was totally devoted to art, music seems to have been in competition with poetry for his time and attention. But there was never any conflict in the negative sense, for without his musical experiences Lanier could never have arrived at the type of poetry he was finally to create.

The story of Lanier is both inspiring and pathetic. It is a series of thwarted plans, shattered hopes, incomplete projects. Lanier spent most of his life dreaming of entering artistic circles, but when he finally decided to devote himself wholeheartedly to this end he was able to reach only slightly beyond the periphery. He was forever not quite reaching his goals. He aimed for the *Atlantic Monthly,* the country's arbiter of literary taste, but reached *Lippincott's;* he vowed to play only for Theodore Thomas's orchestra in New York, but instead worked with Asger Hamerik at the Peabody Conservatory; he craved acclaim in New York City, but had to find it in Baltimore. True, what he did accomplish was of no little consequence—*Lippincott's* was also one of the nation's leading publications, Hamerik a conductor of international reputation, and Baltimore a thriving and respected center of culture. But they were all second choices for Lanier, and represent the disappointment that underlay all his successes.

Yet considering Lanier's background, he accomplished miracles. He came from a genteel southern tradition that scorned the arts as a profession. His education was removed from the main currents of American academic life, and he had very little formal musical training. Constantly hounded by poverty after the Civil War, he was forced to write pot-boilers in order to support his family, wasting precious creative energy. Tuberculosis had attacked him when he was 22; by the time he finally determined to pursue an artistic career, he had only seven years to live, and of this time had to spend weeks and months away from his work in desperate search of a cure.

It is remarkable that Lanier managed to do so much in so little time. He played first flute in a conservatory orchestra; delivered successful and popular lectures on Shakespeare and on the English novel; wrote numerous essays on music and about literature; edited collections of legends and tales for children; produced a guidebook to Florida that is still popular in that state; composed numerous musical works; wrote one of the best studies of English prosody (*The Science of English Verse* is a musical analysis of poetry); and in the midst of all these activities wrote dozens of poems, some of which are the most beautifully original in American literature.

His poetic style is a unique result of an attempt to convey musical impression in verse; this stems from his lifelong interest in the unity of poetry and music. His creative technique is original, and Lanier arrived at it through music. One has only to compare the early, naive, and sentimental lyrics of his 1868 song "Little Ella" and the intricately textured poem of 1880, "Sunrise," to see the revolutionary development of Lanier's verse. This change was brought about by music, and it is music that made Lanier a poet. Without it, his verse would have remained pretty and lyrical, but simple in structure, texturally unimaginative, and tied to the limiting song-concept. But Lanier's best works, his later poems, reflect the influence of larger musical forms, the blending of voices, lines, and timbre characteristic of the symphony. If he had never played Berlioz's *Symphonie Fantastique,* he might never have written his best poem, "The Marshes of Glynn." To Lanier, music and poetry were two different, but intimately related, media through which he expressed one ideal. This ideal is most notably expressed at the end of the poem "The Symphony": "Music is Love in search of a word." Lanier believed that man could come to terms with the problems of his civilization only through the redeeming powers of faith and love of art.

The most creative periods of Lanier's life—and the happiest— were those in which he was musically most active. Lanier's friends were, in the main, musical, not literary. He found enthusiastic applause for his flute-playing—which is supposed to have been of astonishing virtuosity—a compensation for the rejection-slips he received for his poetry. His writing, because it was so original, often came under harsh attack, but his musical performances never earned an unfavorable review.

Lanier is a unique figure—or rather phenomenon—in American literature; and since he is one of the rare American poets who was also a professional musician, his poetry's qualities are determined by practical experience. Lanier was an innovator whose possible further accomplishments can only be subjects of wistful speculation; but he is generally acknowledged by critics of the late twentieth century to be a significant figure in early modern literature.

—Jane S. Gabin

LARDNER, Ring(gold Wilmer)

Born: Niles, Michigan, 6 March 1885. **Education:** Niles High School, graduated 1901; Armour Institute of Technology (now Illinois Institute of Technology), Chicago, 1901-02. **Family:** Married Ellis Abbott in 1911; four sons. **Career:** Freight clerk, bookkeeper, and employee of Niles Gas Company, 1902-05; reporter, South Bend *Times,* Indiana, 1905-07; sportswriter, *Inter Ocean,* Chicago, 1907, Chicago *Examiner,* 1908, and Chicago *Tribune,* 1908-10; managing editor, *Sporting News,* St. Louis, 1910-11; sports editor, Boston *American,* 1911, Chicago *American,* 1911-12, and Chicago *Examiner,* 1912-13; columnist ("In the Wake of the News"), Chicago *Tribune,* 1913-19; moved to Long Island, New York, 1919; columnist ("Weekly Letter"), 1919-27, and wrote *You Know Me Al* comic strip, 1922-25, both for the Bell Syndicate; radio reviewer, *The New Yorker,* 1932-33. **Died:** 25 September 1933.

PUBLICATIONS

Collections

The Lardner Reader, edited by Maxwell Geismar. 1963.
The Best of Lardner, edited by David Lodge. 1984.
Ring around the Bases: The Complete Baseball Stories, edited by Matthew J. Bruccoli. 1992.
The Annotated Baseball Stories of Ring W. Lardner, 1914-1919. 1995.

Short Stories

Gullible's Travels. 1917.
How to Write Short Stories (with Samples). 1924.
The Love Nest and Other Stories. 1926.
Round Up: The Stories. 1929; as *Collected Short Stories,* 1941.
Some Champions: Sketches and Fiction, edited by Matthew J. Bruccoli and Richard Layman. 1976.

Novels

You Know Me Al: A Busher's Letters. 1916.
Own Your Own Home. 1919.
The Real Dope. 1919.
The Big Town. 1921.

Plays

Zanzibar, music and lyrics by Harry Schmidt (produced 1903). 1903.
Elmer the Great (produced 1928).
June Moon, with George S. Kaufman, from the story "Some Like Them Cold" by Lardner (produced 1929). 1930.
M*A*S*H*: The Screenplay. 1994.

Screenplay: *The New Klondike,* with Tom Geraghty, 1926.

Verse

Bib Ballads. 1915.

Other

My Four Weeks in France. 1918.
Treat 'em Rough: Letters from Jack the Kaiser Killer. 1918.
Regular Fellows I Have Met. 1919.
The Young Immigrunts. 1920.
Symptoms of Being 35. 1921.
Say It with Oil: A Few Remarks about Wives, with *Say It with Bricks: A Few Remarks about Husbands,* by Nina Wilcox Putnam. 1923.
What of It? 1925.
The Story of a Wonder Man. 1927.
Lose with a Smile. 1933.
First and Last. 1934.
Shut Up, He Explained, edited by Babette Rosmond and Henry Morgan. 1962.
Ring Around Max: The Correspondence of Lardner and Max Perkins, edited by Clifford M. Caruthers. 1973.
Letters from Ring, edited by Clifford M. Caruthers. 1979; revised as *Letters of Ring Lardner,* 1995.
Lardner's You Know Me Al: The Comic Strip Adventures of Jack Keefe. 1979.

Editor, with Edward G. Heeman, March 6th, 1914: *The Home Coming of Charles A. Comisky, John J. McGraw, James J. Callahan.* 1914.

*

Bibliography: *Lardner: A Descriptive Bibliography* by Matthew J. Bruccoli and Richard Layman, 1976.

Critical Studies: *Lardner: A Biography* by Donald Elder, 1956; *Lardner* by Walton R. Patrick, 1963; *Lardner* by Otto A. Friedrich, 1965; *Lardner and the Portrait of Folly* by Maxwell Geismar, 1972; *The Lardners: My Family Remembered* by Ring Lardner, Jr., 1976; *Ring: A Biography of Lardner* by Jonathan Yardley, 1977; *Lardner* by Elizabeth Evans, 1979; *Small Town Chicago: The Comic Perspective of Finley Peter Dunne, George Ade, and Lardner* by James DeMuth, 1980; "The Barber of Civility: The Chief Conspirator of 'Haircut'" by Hal Blythe and Charlie Sweet, in *Studies in Short Fiction,* fall 1986; "Lardner's 'Haircut'" by Nathan Cervo, in *Explicator,* winter 1989; "Ring Lardner's Dual Audience and the Capitalist Double Bind" by Douglas Robinson, in *American Literary History,* summer 1992; "The Reader's Role in Ring Lardner's Rhetoric" by Brian T. Cowlishaw, in *Studies in Short Fiction,* spring 1994, pp. 207-16; "Ring Lardner, Jr.: American Skeptic" by Barry Strugatz and Pat McGilligan, in *Backstory 3: Interviews with Screenwriters of the 1960s* edited by Pat McGilligan, 1997.

*   *   *

Ring Lardner wrote in the tradition of a long line of American popular journalists and humorists who exploited slang and the illiteracies of vernacular speech for comic ends. In doing so, he transmuted what was initially a stock comic device into something much more, an instrument of satire. At the same time, he was, however unwittingly, one of those writers, of whom **Mark Twain** is the great exemplar, whose sensitivity to the value of the spoken word helped to liberate American prose from the artificial diction that marked so much nineteenth-century writing.

Beginning as a sports writer on an Indiana paper, in 1913 he took over the "In the Wake of the News" column in the Chicago *Tribune.* Meanwhile, the Jack Keefe letters were appearing in magazines, purporting to be written by an oafish, semi-literate baseball player who, through his own words, unconsciously exposes himself in all his obnoxiousness. Published as an epistolary novel, *You Know Me Al,* the letters brought Lardner to the attention of a wider public and *How to Write Short Stories,* the title of which has been seen as typical of Lardner's inability to believe that he was a serious writer, brought critical acclaim. **Edmund Wilson,** for example, commenting on the discrepancy between the matter of the hook and the jokey way in which it was presented, wrote, "what one finds in *How to Write Short Stories* is a series of studies of American types almost equal in importance to those of **Sherwood Anderson** and **Sinclair Lewis.**"

Among the stories appearing in the volume were "Some Like Them Cold," an exchange of letters, wonderfully funny in their dead-pan way, between an aspiring popular song-writer on the make in New York City and a girl he has met by chance in the LaSalle Street railway station in Chicago, and "The Golden Honeymoon," in which an aging middle-class man from Trenton, New Jersey, father-in-law of "John H. Kramer, the real estate man," recounts the holiday he and his wife spent in Florida to celebrate their golden wedding.

These stories illustrate two things. The first is that Lardner, as Wilson pointed out in his *Dial* review, had "an unexcelled, a perhaps unrivalled, mastery" of the American language, that he knew equally well the language of the popular-song writer and the "whole vocabulary of adolescent cliches of the middle-aged man from New Jersey," and that he understood the difference between the spoken language of these types and the language they used for writing. The other thing is that, as all his critics have pointed out, Lardner's is nothing if not a reductive art. His characters expose themselves unerringly in their speech and letters in all the grossness of their complacency and self-regard. No element of affection or compassion is allowed to creep into their delineation. It measures the difference between Lardner's art and Sinclair Lewis's on the one hand and Sherwood Anderson's on the other.

In other words, Lardner was essentially a satirist, and increasingly since his death he has been seen as one of the major American satirists. In this respect he has, perhaps, been overrated. In his 1924 review Wilson, who had put Lardner forward as in some sense a latter-day Mark Twain, asked: "Will Ring Lardner then, go on to his *Huckleberry Finn* or has he already told all he knows?" The appearance of *The Love Nest and Other Stories* two years later, though it contained the merciless "Haircut," showed in effect that he had already told us all he knew. Admirable as his satire is, it seems time once again to emphasize the part he played in the liberation of American prose by bringing back into it the rhythms of native speech.

—Walter Allen

See the essay on "Haircut."

LAURENTS, Arthur

Born: Brooklyn, New York, 14 July 1918. **Education:** Cornell University, Ithaca, New York, B.A. 1937. **Military Service:** Served in the U.S. Army, 1940-45: sergeant; radio playwright, 1943-45 (Citation, Secretary of War, and *Variety* radio award, 1945). **Career:** Stage director. Director, Dramatists Play Service, New York, 1961-66. Council member, Dramatists Guild, from 1955. **Awards:** American Academy award, 1946; Sidney Howard Memorial award, 1946; Tony award, for play, 1967, for directing, 1984; Vernon Rice award, 1974; Golden Globe award, 1977; Screenwriters Guild award, 1978; Sydney Drama Critics award, for directing, 1983; best directing awards, *La Cage aux Folles*, Australian production, 1985, London production, 1986. **Member:** P.E.N., Authors League, Theatre Hall of Fame. **Residence:** New York City.

PUBLICATIONS

Plays

Now Playing Tomorrow (broadcast 1939). In *Short Plays for Stage and Radio*, edited by Carless Jones, 1939.
Western Electric Communicade (broadcast 1944). In *The Best One-Act Plays of 1944*, edited by Margaret Mayorga, 1944.
The Last Day of the War (broadcast 1945). In *Radio Drama in Action*, edited by Erik Barnouw, 1945.
The Face (broadcast 1945). In *The Best One-Act Plays of 1945*, edited by Margaret Mayorga, 1945.
Home of the Brave (produced 1945; as *The Way Back*, produced 1949). 1946.
Heartsong (produced 1947).
The Bird Cage (produced 1950). 1950.
The Time of the Cuckoo (produced 1952). 1953.
A Clearing in the Woods (produced 1957). 1957; revised edition, 1960.
West Side Story, music by Leonard Bernstein, lyrics by Stephen Sondheim (produced 1957). 1958.
Gypsy, music by Jule Styne, lyrics by Stephen Sondheim, from a book by Gypsy Rose Lee (produced 1959). 1960.
Invitation to a March (produced 1960). 1961.
Anyone Can Whistle, music by Stephen Sondheim (produced 1964). 1965.
Do I Hear a Waltz? music by Richard Rodgers, lyrics by Stephen Sondheim (produced 1965). 1966.
Hallelujah, Baby!, music and lyrics by Jule Styne, Betty Comden, and Adolph Green (produced 1967). 1967.
The Enclave (produced 1973). 1974.
Scream (produced 1978).
The Madwoman of Central Park West, with Phyllis Newman, music by Peter Allen and others (produced 1979).
A Loss of Memory (produced 1981).
Nick and Nora, music by Charles Strouse, lyrics by Richard Maltby (produced 1991).
Jolson Sings Again (produced 1994).
The Radical Mystique (produced 1995).
My Good Name (produced 1997).

Screenplays: *The Snake Pit*, with Frank Partos and Millen Brand, 1948; *Rope*, with Hume Cronyn, 1948; *Anna Lacasta*, with Philip Yordan, 1949; *Caught*, 1949; *Anastasia*, 1956; *Bonjour Tristesse*, 1958; *The Way We Were*, 1973; *The Turning Point*, 1977.

Radio Plays: *Hollywood Playhouse, Dr. Christian, The Thin Man, Manhattan at Midnight*, and other series, 1939-40; plays for *The Man behind the Gun, Army Service Force Presents* and *Assignment: Home* series, 1943-45; *This Is Your FBI* series, 1945.

Television Script: *The Light Fantastic*, 1967.

Fiction

The Way We Were. 1972.
The Turning Point. 1977.

*

Theatrical Activities:
Director: **Plays**—*Invitation to the March*, New York, 1960; *I Can Get It for You Wholesale* by Jerome Weidman, New York, 1961; *Anyone Can Whistle*, New York, 1964; *The Enclave*, Washington, D.C., and New York, 1973; *Gypsy*, London, 1973, New York, 1974 and 1989; *My Mother Was a Fortune Teller* by Phyllis Newman, New York, 1978; *Scream*, Houston, 1978; *The Madwoman of Central Park West*, Buffalo and New York City, 1979; *So What Are We Gonna Do Now?* by Juliet Garson, New York, 1982; *La Cage aux Folles* by Jean Poiret, adapted by Harvey Fierstein, Boston and New York, 1983, Sydney, 1985, London, 1986; *Birds of Paradise* by Winnie Holtzman and David Evans, New York, 1987; *Nick and Nora*, New York, 1991; *Jolson Sings Again*, 1993; *The Radical Mystique*, 1995; *My Good Name*, 1997.

*   *   *

Brooklyn-born, Hollywood-bred, Arthur Laurents is best known for his work in the two most successful American art forms, the Broadway musical and the Hollywood film. His films include *Caught* and *The Snake Pit* and versions of two of his stage plays, *Home of the Brave* and *The Time of the Cuckoo* (filmed as *Summertime*). All tend to prove Samuel Beckett's thesis: "We are all born mad. Some remain so." Psychology, especially self-realization, is Laurents' major interest and it runs through all of his work, even his musicals.

His musicals are *West Side Story* (*Romeo and Juliet* updated), *Gypsy* (based on the life of stripper Gypsy Rose Lee), *Do I Hear a Waltz?* and *Hallelujah, Baby!* These musicals show all the inventiveness and commercial savvy one would expect from a writer whose work ranges from adapting Marcel Maurette's TV play *Anastasia* for Ingrid Bergman's return to the screen, to a modern version of the Sleeping Beauty legend in which the heroine refuses to tread boring conventional paths and takes off with a plumber (*Invitation to a March*). Laurents attempted to make Broadway musicals in some way more serious. He didn't always succeed. As Walter Kerr put it in *Thirty Plays Hath November*, "if a musical is going to be as serious as *Do I Hear a Waltz?* it has got to be more serious than *Do I Hear a Waltz?* . . . . Half measures taken toward sobriety tend to leave us all half-hearted, torn between an elusive passion on the one hand and a lost playfulness on the other." Shall we settle for the ersatz, typically Broadway idea of the serious (especially in diversions such as *A Chorus Line*) and not strive for reality?

Laurents's plays are a strange combination of realism and self-irony. The stories of so many petty little lives are presented in an atmosphere resembling that "magic realism" that the "innocent" reader/spectator finds hard to accept because of its contradiction in terms. It is, however, the reality of the characters' inner lives, the history of all their failures, which they haven't yet learned to disguise as sacrifices for which they can later blame somebody else.

The irony of his plays reflects the alienation within American society itself. Disoriented couples faced too early with the idea of a permanent commitment, lonely women living their lives of "quiet desperation," men looking for "the perfect love" outside their not very successful marriages, all seem to meet in a No Man's Land of elusive hope, traveling to foreign countries in pursuit of their long-lasting ideals.

Laurents' plays do make a serious effort at seriousness: in a sense they are religious, if psychology is the New Religion. In *The Bird Cage* downtrodden employees of a dictatorial employer fly their nightclub cage. In *A Clearing in the Woods* a woman yearns "to rise in the air just a little, to climb, to reach a branch, even the lowest" and this bird learns to accept herself as "an imperfect human being," thus escaping the cage of her past. Can it be that Laurents, for all his interest in psychology, is telling us that we should avoid all the psychiatrists who want to adjust us, and achieve "mental health" just by learning to be happy with our craziness, accepting ourselves as "imperfect human beings?" In *Home of the Brave* an Army shrink copes with Coney, a soldier who learns that though he is Jewish he is just another "imperfect human being" like Mingo and everyone else who is secretly glad that it was The Other Guy who got killed, regardless of race, color, or creed. In *The Time of the Cuckoo* the uptight New England spinster Leona Samish has to work out for herself the appropriate reactions to a brief encounter in Venice with a dashing (but married) Italian. Predictably, "those louses/ Go back to their spouses" (as *Diamonds Are a Girl's Best Friend* teaches) and Leona realizes, reviewing her Puritan code, that he was not such a nice man, after all.

The Time of the Cuckoo is a play about solitude and misunderstanding, a comedy of deception in which characters strongly believe that a change in the landscape (a trip to Italy, in this case) will bring a change for the better in their lives. A painter who cannot paint anymore, and his too loving companion—a woman in search of the right person and in desperate need for someone to love—spend a summer in Italy, perpetually hoping for change. When nothing happens, they blame the strangeness of the place, the foreign language, fate itself, everything except themselves. "Something happens to this city at night," says Leona, the lonely woman, when she realizes that she is unable to deal with the love story she has always longed for. "The wonderful, mystical, magical miracle" that she wishes for cannot happen, because Leona, with her Puritan upbringing, has not been taught to enjoy life. "Relax and life is beautiful" seems to be an Italian concept. "You are too complicated, carra," observes Signor Di Rossi, "and *the feeling* is gone."

This psychologizing may not be as broad as a barn door, nor so deep as a well, but it will serve the theater, where **Thornton Wilder** once summed up all of Freud in a single sentence: "We're all just as wicked as we can be."

—Leonard R.N. Ashley, updated by Dayana Stetco

LAWSON, John Howard

Born: New York City, 25 September 1894. **Education:** Halstead School, Yonkers, New York; Cutler School, New York, graduated

1910; Williams College, Williamstown, Massachusetts, 1910-14, B.A. 1914. **Military Service:** Served in the American Ambulance Service in France and Italy during World War I. **Family:** Married 1) Kathryn Drain in 1919 (divorced 1923), one son; 2) Susan Edmond in 1925, one son and one daughter. **Career:** Cable editor, Reuters Press, New York, 1914-15; lived in Paris for two years after the war; director, New Playwrights Theatre, New York, 1927-28; film writer in Hollywood, 1928-47. Council member, Authors League of America, 1930-40; founding president, 1933-34, and member of the executive board, 1933-40, Screen Writers Guild. One of the Hollywood Ten: served a one-year sentence for contempt of the House Un-American Activities Committee, 1950-51. **Died:** 11 August 1977.

PUBLICATIONS

Plays

Servant-Master-Lover (produced 1916).
Standards (produced 1916).
Roger Bloomer (produced 1923). 1923.
Processional: A Jazz Symphony of American Life (produced 1925). 1925.
Nirvana (produced 1926).
Loudspeaker (produced 1927). 1927.
The International (produced 1928). 1928.
Success Story (produced 1932). 1932.
The Pure in Heart (produced 1934). In *With a Reckless Preface*, 1934.
Gentlewoman (produced 1934). In *With a Reckless Preface*, 1934.
With a Reckless Preface: Two Plays. 1934.
Marching Song (produced 1937). 1937.
Algiers (screenplay), with James M. Cain, in *Foremost Films of 1938*, edited by Frank Vreeland. 1939.
Parlor Magic (produced 1963).

Screenplays: *Dream of Love,* with others, 1928; *The Pagan,* with Dorothy Farnum, 1929; *Dynamite,* with Jeanie Macpherson and Gladys Unger, 1929; *The Sea Bat,* with others, 1930; *Our Blushing Brides,* with Bess Meredyth and Helen Mainard, 1930; *The Ship from Shanghai,* 1930; *Bachelor Apartment,* with J. Walter Rubin, 1931; *Success at Any Price,* with others, 1934; *Blockade,* 1938; *Algiers,* with James M. Cain, 1938; *They Shall Have Music,* with Irmgard Von Cube, 1939; *Four Sons,* with Milton Sperling, 1940; *Earthbound,* with Samuel C. Engel, 1940; *Sahara,* with others, 1943; *Action in the North Atlantic,* with others, 1943; *Counter-Attack (One Against Seven),* 1945; *Smash-Up—The Story of a Woman,* with others, 1947.

Other

Theory and Technique of Playwriting. 1936; revised edition, as *Theory and Technique of Playwriting and Screenwriting,* 1949.
The Hidden Heritage: A Rediscovery of the Ideas and Forces That Link the Thought of Our Time with the Culture of the Past. 1950.
Film in the Battle of Ideas. 1953.
Film: The Creative Process: The Search for an Audio-Visual Language and Structure. 1964; revised edition, 1967.

*

Critical Studies: *Drama and Commitment: Politics in the American Theatre of the Thirties* by Gerald Rabkin, 1964; "Friendship Won't Stand That: John Howard Lawson and John Dos Passos's Struggle for an Ideological Ground to Stand On" by Townsend Ludington, in *Literature at the Barricades: The American Writer in the 1930s* edited by Ralph F. Bogardus and Fred Hobson, 1982; *The Left Side of Paradise: The Screenwriting of Lawson* by Gary Carr, 1984; *Artist to Reactionary: The Evolution of John Howard Lawson's Aesthetic Vision and Political Commitment, 1923-1937* (dissertation) by Jonathan Lee Chambers, 1996.

*   *   *

John Howard Lawson was one of the Hollywood Ten who went to jail rather than implicate others before the House Un-American Activities Committee. HUAC need not have summoned him; they could have read his plays or seen his movies. Whether he belonged to the Communist Party or not is basically none of our business. That his work is imbued with Marxism and that he is characteristic of a period in which (as the garment workers' musical *Pins and Needles* put it) many sang "Sing Me a Song of Social Significance," is abundantly clear. In his time, it gave him strength. In the late twentieth century it makes all but a few of his film works look impossibly dated.

Servant-Master-Lover, Standards, and *Roger Bloomer* gave him his start, and with *Processional* his left-wing sympathies were expressed in the story of "the West Virginia coal fields during a strike" told in "this new technique . . . essentially vaudevillesque in character." The theory is adumbrated in a preface (more of his interesting ideas appear in prefatory material to *The Pure in Heart* and *Gentlewoman* and in the excellent textbook *Theory and Technique of Playwriting*) and illustrated in a series of scenes that recall the Living Newspaper of the depression, the propaganda techniques of agitprop, and other attempts at "an immediate emotional response across the footlights." All the force and all the faults of the left-wing theater tracts of the 1920s and 1930s, "the fervent years" as Harold Clurman calls them, are here: the party-line dogmatism and narrow vision; the confusion of tragedy and pathos; the axe-to-grind earnestness, where comedy (and everything else that relates to a sense of proportion) perishes; and so on, down to the stereotyped characters: Cohen the Jewish comedian, Rastus the minstrel clown, the hard-boiled Sheriff, the city-slicker newspaperman Phillpots, the woman called Mrs. Euphemia Stewart Flimmins, even a Man in a Silk Hat.

George Abbott played Dynamite Jim in *Processional,* but only in the last act did he soar for a moment above what Stark Young called "antagonisms, bad taste and crass thinking." The critics thought it basically an amateur play "conceived with varying degrees of taste, intelligence, insight and imagination." When it is good it is very, very good—Stark Young risked "streaked with genius"—and when it is bad it's as foolish as Odets without his primitive charm. It is not that the characters are unrealistic—"Mr. Lawson," reported *Contemporary Drama,* "says that he can find vaudeville characters on every street corner, whereas the so-called realistic characters he sees on the stage he never meets in life"—but that the politics distort the truth.

Processional was produced by the Theatre Guild and ran 96 performances in 1925 and 81 more when the Federal Theatre revived it in 1937. In the late twentieth century it would not run any more than would *Nirvana, Loudspeaker, The International* (a musical), *Success Story, Marching Song,* or other Lawson efforts.

"All great art and literature," boomed Shaw, "is propaganda," but that does not mean that all propaganda is great art.

Some of Lawson's films have survived better. Very typical are, say, *Blockade* and *Smash-Up.* The cinema was more congenial to Lawson's talents, though *Theory and Technique of Playwriting* amply demonstrates that, as Theophile Gautier said of drama critics and eunuchs in harems, those who see it done every night may know all about it but be quite unable to do it themselves.

—Leonard R.N. Ashley

LEE, Manfred B. *See* **QUEEN, Ellery.**

LEE, William. *See* **BURROUGHS, William S(eward).**

LEE, Willy. *See* **BURROUGHS, William S(eward).**

LEONARD, Elmore

Born: New Orleans, Louisiana, 11 October 1925. **Education:** University of Detroit, Ph.B. 1950. **Family:** Married 1) Beverly Cline in 1949 (divorced 1977), three sons and two daughters; 2) Joan Shepard in 1979 (died 1993); 3) Christine Kent in 1993. **Career:** Copywriter, Campbell-Ewald Advertising Agency, Detroit, Michigan, 1950-61; freelance copywriter, 1961-63; head of Elmore Leonard advertising agency, 1963-66. Beginning 1967 full-time writer. **Awards:** Edgar Allan Poe award, 1984; Michigan Foundation of the Arts award, 1985; Mystery Writers of America, Grand Master award, 1992. Honorary degree: Florida Atlantic University, 1996.

PUBLICATIONS

Novels

The Bounty Hunters. 1953.
The Law at Randado. 1955.
Escape from 5 Shadows. 1956.
Last Stand at Saber River. 1957.
Hombre. 1961.
The Big Bounce. 1969.
The Moonshine War. 1969.
Valdez Is Coming. 1970.
Forty Lashes Less One. 1972.
Mr. Majestyk. 1974.
Fifty-Two Pickup. 1974.
Swag. 1976.
Unknown Man. 1977.
The Hunted. 1977.
The Switch. 1978.
Gunsights. 1979.
City Primeval: High Noon in Detroit. 1980.
Gold Coast. 1980.
Split Images. 1981.

Cat Chaser. 1982.
Stick. 1983.
LaBrava. 1983.
Glitz. 1985.
Bandits. 1987.
Touch. 1987.
Freaky Deaky. 1988.
Killshot. 1989.
Get Shorty. 1990.
Maximum Bob. 1991.
Rum Punch. 1992.
Pronto. 1993.
Riding the Rap. 1995.
Out of Sight. 1996.
Cuba Libre. 1998.
The Tonto Woman and Other Western Stories. 1998.
Be Cool. 1999.

Screenplays: *The Moonshine War,* 1970; *Joe Kidd,* 1972; *Mr. Majestyk,* 1974; *High Noon, Part 2: The Return of Will Kane,* 1980; *Stick,* 1985; *52 Pick-Up,* 1986; *The Rosary Murders,* 1987; *Desperado,* 1988; *Cat Chaser,* 1989.

*   *   *

Elmore Leonard began his career writing Westerns, the most famous being *Hombre,* which was successfully filmed with Paul Newman. However, he joined the contemporary scene in 1969 with *The Big Bounce* and became known primarily as a writer of thrillers. He subsequently achieved fame with *Glitz* (1985), though many of his best novels—*The Switch, City Primeval, Stick,* and *La Brava*—were written earlier.

Fast moving, complexly plotted, and driven as much by dialogue as by action, Leonard's novels chart a world in which murder can be as casual as lighting a cigarette, one peopled by ex-cons, prostitutes, and men and women of ambiguous morals. His settings range from Detroit to Miami, from New Orleans to Las Vegas or Los Angeles, but the ambiance is essentially the same in each novel. His most sympathetic characters negotiate this world as best they can, struggling to establish who are the bad guys and who are the good guys or even whether there is any difference between them.

The urban world to which he turned his attention was hardly different from the lawless West of the previous century. The analogy emerges most clearly in *City Primeval.* Lieutenant Raymond Cruz is described by an interviewer as trying to look like a young Wyatt Earp—"the no-bullshit Old West lawman." Cruz watches in frustration as the psychopath Clement Mansell, who has boasted to him of killing nine people, evades the law. At the end he takes Mansell on in a personal duel. The situation is redolent with irony. Cruz locks Mansell away in an underground vault but refuses to abandon him to starvation. On the other hand, when Mansell reaches into his jacket, Cruz shoots him three times, but then Cruz discovers that Mansell was only looking for a bottle opener. The subtitle of the novel, "High Noon in Detroit," tells it all.

The hero of *Pronto* is another Old West lawman. Raylan Givens, a U.S. marshal, wears a cowboy hat and is referred to as a cowboy by the other characters. Another agent mockingly asks him if he wears the hat when he sits down to eat.

The Australian thriller writer and critic John Carroll has argued that "there are no debates about right or wrong in Leonard's kill-

or-be-killed world, no complicated moral choices; decisions always come swiftly and cleanly from the barrel of a gun, without histrionics." Carroll's words contain a good deal of truth but are not entirely the case. Most of Leonard's novels portray psychopaths or people with clear moral deficits. He seems especially obsessed with right-wing, neo-Nazi fanatics like Big Boy in *Rum Punch* and Richard Edgar Monk in *The Switch.* These novels feature gun running, drug dealing, bombings, bank robberies by the score, and car thefts by the hundreds. Murders are frequent and are committed in a matter-of-fact way. On the face of it, Leonard seems to portray an amoral world. In *Rum Punch,* Ordell calmly shoots his friend Louis because he had not noticed a witness when his money was being delivered. This occurs immediately after Louis shoots his accomplice Melanie merely because she won't stop talking: "Bam. Shot her again to make sure and because it felt good."

At the same time, Leonard's characters think often about who the good guys and bad guys are, however ambiguous their status. "You look around, I'll tell you," says bank robber Louis Gara in *The Switch,* "you're not sure who's side anybody's on." And, though a lowlife himself, Louis is the only character prepared to defend the life of the woman he has helped kidnap. Similarly, in *City Primeval* Mansell, the psychopathic killer, suggests his essential similarity to the cop who is pursing him, Raymond Cruz: "You don't set out to uphold the law any more'n I set out to break it." But the novel shows this to be fundamentally untrue. Cruz plays by his own code of ethics, refusing to leave Mansell to die in his underground vault. *Bandits,* Leonard's most explicitly political novel, depicts an ex-nun trying to raise money for the lepers in Nicaragua. In the process, she raises the political consciousness of the novel's hero, Jack Delaney.

Leonard's humor is grim and sardonic to the point of being almost sadistic. In *Rum Punch* the police raid three jackboys loading guns. The boys turn their rocket loaders on the police but fail to harm them because they cannot read the instructions properly. One detective tells them, "You should never've dropped out of school." The young female victim of an attempted rape lies there wondering, "What would Susan Brownmiller do?"

Leonard's dialogue is authentic. After spending three months with the Detroit police, he has been able to allow his characters to tell more of their stories in their own words. Leonard has also been able to achieve authenticity through research into and knowledge of his chosen world—of guns, bombs, and police techniques.

–Laurie Clancy

LEVERTOV, Denise

Born: Ilford, Essex, England, 24 October 1923; moved to the U.S. in 1948; became citizen in 1955. **Education:** Educated privately. **Military Service:** Served as a civilian nurse at St. Luke's Hospital, London, during World War II. **Family:** Married the writer Mitchell Goodman in 1947 (divorced 1972); one son. **Career:** Worked in antique shop and bookshop, London, 1946; nurse at British Hospital, Paris, Spring 1947; teacher at the YM-YWHA Poetry Center, New York, 1964, City College of New York, 1965, and Vassar College, Poughkeepsie, New York, 1966-67; visiting professor, Drew University, Madison, New Jersey, 1965, University of California, Berkeley, 1969, Massachusetts Institute of

Technology, Cambridge, 1969-70, Kirkland College, Clinton, New York, 1970-71, University of Cincinnati, Spring 1973, and Tufts University, Medford, Massachusetts, 1973-79; Fannie Hurst professor (poet-in-residence), Brandeis University, Waltham, Massachusetts, 1981-83; beginning 1982 professor of English, Stanford University, California. Poetry editor, *The Nation,* New York, 1961, 1963-65, and *Mother Jones,* San Francisco, 1975-78; honorary scholar, Radcliffe Institute for Independent Study, Cambridge, Massachusetts, 1964-66. **Awards:** Longview award, 1961; Guggenheim fellowship, 1962; Harriet Monroe prize, 1964; Inez Boulton prize, 1964; American Academy grant, 1966, 1968; Lenore Marshall prize, 1976; Bobst award, 1983; Shelley Memorial award, 1984; Robert Frost medal, 1990; NEA Senior fellowship, 1990; Lannan award, 1993. D.Litt.: Colby College, Waterville, Maine, 1970; University of Cincinnati, 1973; Bates College, Lewiston, Maine, 1984; St. Lawrence University, Canton, New York, 1984; Allegheny College, 1987; St. Michael's College, 1987; Massachusetts College of Art, 1989; University of Santa Clara, 1993. **Member:** American Academy, 1980; Corresponding Member, Mallarmé Academy, 1983. **Died:** 1997.

PUBLICATIONS

Poetry

The Double Image. 1946.
Here and Now. 1956.
Overland to the Islands. 1958.
5 Poems. 1958.
With Eyes at the Back of Our Heads. 1960.
The Jacob's Ladder. 1961.
O Taste and See: New Poems. 1964.
City Psalm. 1964.
Psalm Concerning the Castle. 1966.
The Sorrow Dance. 1967.
Penguin Modern Poets 9, with Kenneth Rexroth and William Carlos Williams. 1967.
A Tree Telling of Orpheus. 1968.
A Marigold from North Viet Nam. 1968.
Three Poems. 1968.
The Cold Spring and Other Poems. 1969.
Embroideries. 1969.
Relearning the Alphabet. 1970.
Summer Poems 1969. 1970.
A New Years Garland for My Students, MIT 1969-1970. 1970.
To Stay Alive. 1971.
Footprints. 1972.
The Freeing of the Dust. 1975.
Chekhov on the West Heath. 1977.
Modulations for Solo Voice. 1977.
Life in the Forest. 1978.
Collected Earlier Poems 1940-1960. 1979.
Pig Dreams: Scenes from the Life of Sylvia. 1981.
Wanderer's Daysong. 1981.
Candles in Babylon. 1982.
Poems 1960-1967. 1983.
Oblique Prayers: New Poems with 14 Translations from Jean Joubert. 1984.
El Salvador: Requiem and Invocation. 1984.
The Menaced World. 1984.

Selected Poems. 1986.
Poems: 1968-1972. 1987.
Breathing the Water. 1987.
Seasons of Light, with Peter Brown. 1988.
A Door in the Hive. 1989.
Lake, Mountain, Moon. 1990.
Evening Train. 1993.
Sands of the Well. 1996.
New Poems. 1996.
The Field. 1996.
Feet (limited edition). 1997.
The Life Around Us: Selected Poems on Nature. 1997.
The Stream and the Sapphire: Selected Poems on Religious Themes. 1997.
This Great Unknowing: Last Poems. 1999.

Fiction

In the Night. 1968.

Other

The Poet in the World (essays). 1973.
Conversation in Moscow. 1973.
Levertov: An Interview, with John K. Atchity. 1980.
Light Up the Cave (essays). 1981.
New and Selected Essays. 1992.
Tesserae: Memories and Suppositions. 1995.
The Letters of Denise Levertov and William Carlos Williams. 1998.
Conversations with Denise Levertov. 1998.

Editor, *Out of the War Shadow: An Anthology of Current Poetry.* 1967.
Editor and translator, with Edward C. Dimock, Jr., *In Praise of Krishna: Songs from the Bengali.* 1967.
Editor, *The Collected Poems of Beatrice Hawley.* 1989.

Translator, *Selected Poems,* poems by Guillevic. 1969.
Translator, *Black Iris,* poems by Jean Toubert. 1988.
Translator, *White Owl and Blue Mouse* (children's story) by Jean Toubert. 1990.

*

Bibliography: *A Bibliography of Levertov* by Robert A. Wilson, 1972; *Levertov: An Annotated Primary and Secondary Bibliography* by Liana Sakelliou-Schultz, 1988.

Critical Studies: *Levertov* by Linda W. Wagner, 1967, and *Levertov: In Her Own Province* edited by Wagner, 1979; *The Imagination's Tongue: Levertov's Poetic* by William Slaughter, 1981; *Revelation and Revolution in the Poetry of Levertov* by Peter Middleton, 1981; *Understanding Levertov* by Harry Marten, 1988; "Revolutionary Love: Levertov and the Poetics of Politics" by Sandra M. Gilbert in *Conversant Essays: Contemporary Poets on Poetry,* edited by James McCorkle, 1990; *Critical Essays on Levertov* edited by Linda Wagner Martin, 1990; Levertov issue of *Twentieth-Century Literature* vol. 38, no. 3, edited by Ronald R. Janssen, fall 1992; *Denise Levertov: Selected Criticism,* edited by Albert Gelpi, 1993; *Denise Levertov: The Poetry of Engagement* by Audrey T. Rodgers, 1993; *Poetics of the Feminine: Authority* *and Literary Tradition in William Carlos Williams, Mina Loy, Denise Levertov, and Kathleen Fraser* by Linda A. Kinnahan, 1994; *Spirit in the Poetry of Denise Levertov,* 1998.

*   *   *

By her own admission, Denise Levertov began writing as a "British Romantic with almost Victorian background" and has since become one of the powerful probing voices of contemporary American poetry. Levertov's poetic development reflects her own evolution from a strictly lyric poet to a more experimental political poet. Her outspoken advocacy of the women's movement, her opposition to the Vietnam War, and her adherence generally to the values of the political left came about through the gradual transformations of awareness since publishing *Here and Now* in 1957.

Raised and educated in a literary household in England, Levertov published a first book of poems, *The Double Image,* in 1946. In 1948 she emigrated to the United States with her American husband, the novelist Mitchell Goodman, whose friendship with **Robert Creeley** led to her association with the Black Mountain movement and the journal *Origin,* which began publishing her work. Her early poems show the influence of **William Carlos Williams** and **Charles Olson** in their diction and form, but by the middle of the 1950s, **Robert Duncan** encouraged her to experiment more boldly with mythic perception of her identity and circumstances. She has since explained her own poetic in the essay "Organic Form," which distinguishes between a free verse of disjointed statements and organic poetry, where "form," all facets of technique, is "a revelation of content." But her poems retain traditional verse conventions, and she has occasionally attacked the improvisational mode of other poets.

In her first substantial work, *With Eyes at the Back of Our Heads,* her poems moved to frank self-disclosures in an effort to grasp a personal identity underlying sexual stereotype. In "The Goddess," one of the finest poems of the volume, she dramatized her awakening to an inner nature after her expulsion from "Lie Castle," where she has been flung

> across the room, and
> room after room (hitting the walls, re-
> bounding—to the last
> sticky wall—wrenching away from it
> pulling hair out!)
> til it lay
> outside the outer walls!
> There in the cold air
> lying still where her hand had thrown me,
> I tasted the mud that splattered my lips
> the seeds of a forest were in it,
> asleep and growing! I tasted
> her power!

O Taste and See pursues the implications of "The Goddess" by boldly reaching into the feminine psyche to discover its raw vitality.

Beginning with *Relearning the Alphabet,* Levertov moved beyond purely personal issues to larger political concerns, war resistance, women's rights, poverty, and oppression in the Third World. In *Relearning the Alphabet,* Levertov reconstructs and recreates the alphabet, redefining each letter to give it a responsible, political, joyful connotation. Throughout this volume of poetry,

Levertov concerns herself with the nature of political change and revolution:

> Revolution: a crown of tree
> raises itself out of the heavy
> flood.
> A branch lifts
> under null skies' weight
> pushes against
> walls of air, flashing
> clefts in it.
> . . .
> Maybe what seems
> evanescent is solid.

This focus on political responsibility continues in Levertov's writings. The poems of *To Stay Alive* and *Footprints,* many taking a longer, serial form, follow her increasingly activist participation in various social movements of the last three decades.

Life in the Forest represents a deflation of all the intensity of Levertov's earlier political poetry during the Vietnam war years; as its title implies, the focus has shifted to the not-I, to the languors and diffusions of lyric focus to be found in "Cesar Pavese's poems of the '30s," according to her prefatory note. The poems are not as dense or electric here, but show the poet's flexibility with new subjects and rhythms, as she makes sense of her middle life and of peacetime. But in *Candles in Babylon* Levertov returned to the main theme of her canon, alienation in the modern age, and her poems are defenses against the torpor and discord of contemporary reality. These tighter, more argumentative poems are the true voice of the poet; her candor and perspicuity as a critic are to be found in the critical collection *Levertov: In Her Own Province* and in *Light Up the Cave,* which collects her recent essays and occasional prose. In her later works of the 1980s and 1990s like *Oblique Prayers, Breathing the Water,* and *Lake, Mountain, Moon,* Levertov explored a personal spirituality that emphasizes the search for vision and faith in the modern world. In her later poetry serenity and inner peace, not revolution or social upheaval, serve as the primary subjects and focus.

Although some critics felt that Levertov's late work lacked the inventiveness of her earlier material, her final poems reveal a consistent engagement with spiritual and aesthetic concerns as they pertain to an aging consciousness. In "For Those Whom the Gods Love Less," for example, from the 1996 collection *Sands of the Well,* she began by asking, "Have I outlived my vocation? Said already all that was / mine to say?" She answered the question directly, by acknowledging its terror and then focusing her attention on the example of other artists who continued to create into old age:

> . . . Each life in art
> goes forth to meet dragons that rise from their bloody
> scales
> in cyclic rhythm: Know and forget, know and forget.
> It's not only
> the passion for getting it right (though it's that, too)
> it's the way
> radiant epiphanies recur, recur,
> consuming, pristine, unrecognized—

until remembrance dismays you. And then, look,
some inflection of light, some wing of shadow
is other, unvoiced. You can, you must
proceed.

When Levertov died in late 1997, she left a notebook of finished poems that were published in the posthumous collection
In This Great Unknowing. In this last book, Levertov found
unvoiced revelations in a meeting with a homeless man, the experience of nature, the contemplation of the divine. The last
lines of "Immersion" could be said to describe her entire body
of work: "God's abstention is only from human dialects. The
holy voice / utters its woe and glory in myriad musics, in signs
and portents. / Our own words are for us to speak, a way to
ask and to answer."

In *The Poet in the World,* Levertov observed that poetry can
serve as "a revolutionary stimulus, awaken[ing] us from our
sloth." For Levertov poetry is itself a powerful force in the
world, capable of initiating powerful social, cultural, political,
and (as we see in her later poetry) spiritual changes. Indeed,
for Levertov, writing politically responsible and politically conscious poetry is imperative for, as she explained in *Poets in
the World,* if the poet "does not struggle against war and oppression, he will negate whatever his words may say, and will
soon have no world to say them in." As a spokesperson for
women's rights, as an opponent of American imperialism, and
as a politically conscious poet, Levertov raised a powerful voice
in contemporary American poetry.

—Paul Christensen, updated by Allison Hersh and Elizabeth
Shostak

LEWIS, (Harry) Sinclair

Born: Sauk Centre, Minnesota, 7 February 1885. **Education:** Sauk
Centre High School; Oberlin Academy, Ohio, 1902-03; Yale University, New Haven, Connecticut (editor, *Yale Literary Magazine*),
1903-06, 1907-08, A.B. 1908. **Family:** Married 1) Grace
Livingstone Hegger in 1914 (divorced 1928), one son; 2) the journalist Dorothy Thompson in 1928 (separated 1937; divorced,
1942), one son. **Career:** Janitor at Upton Sinclair's socialist community Helicon Home, Englewood, New Jersey, 1906-07; assistant editor, *Transatlantic Tales,* New York, 1907; reporter, Waterloo *Daily Courier,* Iowa, 1908; worked for charity organization,
New York, 1908; secretary to Alice MacGowan and Grace
MacGowan Cooke, Carmel, California, 1909; writer, San Francisco *Evening Bulletin,* 1909, and Associated Press, San Francisco,
1909-10; staff member, *Volta Review,* Washington, D.C., 1910;
manuscript reader, Frederick A. Stokes, publishers, 1910-12, assistant editor, *Adventure,* 1912, editor for Publishers' Newspaper Syndicate, 1913-14, and editorial assistant and advertising
manager, George H. Doran, publishers, 1914-15, all New York;
full-time writer from 1916; columnist ("Book Week"), *Newsweek,*
New York, 1937-38, and *Esquire,* New York, 1945. Writer-in-Residence, University of Wisconsin, Madison, Autumn 1942. **Awards:**
Pulitzer prize, 1926 (refused); Nobel prize for Literature, 1930.
Litt.D.: Yale University, 1936. **Member:** National Institute of Arts
and Letters, 1935, vice president, 1944; American Academy, 1938.
Died: 10 January 1951.

PUBLICATIONS

Collections

*The Man from Main Street: Selected Essays and Other Writings
1904-1950,* edited by Harry E. Maule and Melville H. Cane.
1953.
If I Were Boss: The Early Business Stories of Sinclair Lewis. 1997.

Fiction

Hike and the Aeroplane (for children). 1912.
Our Mr. Wrenn. 1914.
The Trail of the Hawk. 1915.
The Job. 1917.
The Innocents. 1917.
Free Air. 1919.
Main Street. 1920.
Babbitt. 1922.
Arrowsmith. 1925; as *Martin Arrowsmith,* 1925.
Mantrap. 1926.
Elmer Gantry. 1927.
The Man Who Knew Coolidge. 1928.
Dodsworth. 1929.
Ann Vickers. 1933.
Work of Art. 1934.
Selected Short Stories. 1935.
It Can't Happen Here. 1935.
The Prodigal Parents. 1938.
Bethel Merriday. 1940.
Gideon Planish. 1943.
Cass Timberlane. 1945.
Kingsblood Royal. 1947.
The God-Seeker. 1949.
World So Wide. 1951.
I'm a Stranger Here Myself and Other Stories, edited by Mark
Schorer. 1962.

Plays

Hobohemia, from his own story (produced 1919).
Jayhawker, with Lloyd Lewis (produced 1934). 1935.
It Can't Happen Here, from his own novel (produced 1936). 1938.
Angela Is Twenty-Two (produced 1938).
Storm in the West (screenplay), with Dore Schary. 1963.

Other

John Dos Passos' "Manhattan Transfer." 1926.
*Cheap and Contented Labor: The Picture of a Southern Mill Town
in 1929.* 1929.
The American Fear of Literature. 1931.
From Main Street to Stockholm: Letters of Lewis 1919-1930, ed-
ited by Harrison Smith. 1952.

*

Bibliography: *The Merrill Checklist of Lewis* by James Lundquist,
1970; *Lewis: A Reference Guide* by Robert E. Fleming, 1980;
*Sinclair Lewis: A Descriptive Bibliography: A Collector's and
Scholar's Guide to Identification* by Stephen R. Pastore, 1997.

Critical Studies: *Lewis: An American Life,* 1961, and *Lewis,* 1963, both by Mark Schorer, and *Lewis: A Collection of Critical Essays* edited by Schorer, 1962; *Lewis* by Sheldon Norman Grebstein, 1962; *Dorothy and Red* by Vincent Sheean, 1963; *The Art of Lewis* by D.J. Dooley, 1967; *Lewis* by James Lundquist, 1973; *The Quixotic Vision of Lewis* by Martin Light, 1975; *A Lewis Lexicon* by Hiroshige Yoshida, 1976; *Critical Essays on Lewis* edited by Martin Bucco, 1986, and *Main Street: The Revolt of Carol Kennicott* by Bucco, 1988; *Sinclair Lewis Remembered* by Isabel Lewis Agrell, 1996; *The Rise of Sinclair Lewis, 1920-1930* by James M. Hutchisson, 1996.

*   *   *

Sinclair Lewis, the first American Nobel Laureate in Literature, was recognized with justice by the Nobel Prize committee for the accuracy and the detail with which he portrayed American life. He applied the concepts of critical realism as they had been developed in the nineteenth century to the subject of the American Midwest, and, using a gift for satiric caricature and a remarkable skill at mimicry, created a vivid picture of middle-class America and its values, ideals, and assumptions in the early twentieth century. He portrayed with devastating satiric power and sardonic force the lack of beauty, dignity, and value in America's materialistic culture. Lewis, although he was hailed in his own day as the spokesman of a new literary movement, was actually a culmination of the movement of critical realism that had begun in the decades immediately after the Civil War. He came as the summarizing expression of moods and methods typical of the Midwestern "revolt from the village" that had produced such writers as **Hamlin Garland, E.W. Howe,** and **Edgar Lee Masters.** Like many other Midwest writers, Lewis moved from the Midwest to the East—in his case from Minnesota to Connecticut and New York—and then used the land of his childhood as his chief subject and often his principal target.

Between 1914 and 1920 he published five novels, the best being *The Job* and *Free Air,* and a number of short stories in popular periodicals. Critical hindsight shows us that these early works, although clearly in the tradition of the popular fiction of their time, also adumbrated in theme, treatment, and character the major work that was to come. In 1920 he published *Main Street,* a coruscating picture of the dullness, drabness, conformity, and materialism of a small Midwestern town. With it his career was brilliantly launched to the acclaim of the nation and the world. He followed it with *Babbitt,* a portrayal of a petit-bourgeois businessman in a middle-sized Midwestern city, a weak man who vainly attempts to break out of the pattern of conformity that shapes his days and to understand himself and achieve his own freedom. This plot pattern was to be recurrent in most of Lewis's work. *Babbitt,* perhaps his most satisfactory single work, was the first of a long series of novels each of which examined a specific business or profession. After publishing it, he started collecting material for a novel on the labor movement, but that book was never written. *Arrowsmith,* written with the aid of the biologist Paul DeKruif, and in its own time regarded by many as his finest work, studied the profession of medicine and contrasted it with the idealized view of scientific research. Lewis pointed his satiric guns at the Protestant ministry in *Elmer Gantry,* a howling comedy of extravagant and slashing satire; and he sympathetically portrayed the American businessman abroad and satirized the cultural pretensions of his wife in *Dodsworth.* This novel begins Lewis's signifi-

cant shift from the harsh treatment of his middle-class American subjects to a steadily growing sympathy for them.

In 1930, he received the Nobel Prize for literature and in his acceptance speech attacked Howells, whose critical movement he was himself the product of, and praised a group of young writers, such as **Thomas Wolfe** and **Ernest Hemingway,** who were soon to be important in advancing novelistic innovations that quickly dated his own work. In the 1920s Lewis had defined America, or at least important aspects of it, for itself and had produced vital, lively, original, and important satiric portraits of America's middle-class failings. The Nobel Prize crowned one of the major accomplishments in the social novel ever achieved by an American. But it came when that accomplishment was virtually complete. For following 1930, Lewis's career seems almost to be a search for subject matter.

In *Ann Vickers,* a book much influenced by his admiration for and exasperation with his second wife, the famous journalist Dorothy Thompson, Lewis examined the career woman, but with clearly mixed feelings. He turned his attention to the hotel industry in *Work of Art,* the first of his "major" works that was, as Mark Schorer declared, "completely without distinction." *It Can't Happen Here* re-established an important position for him with the American public. This study of the potentiality for American fascism seemed to be a political warning that spoke directly and responsibly to major issues in American life. In the late twentieth century, however, it seems thin and surprisingly conservative. That Lewis was indeed becoming increasingly conservative despite his attacks upon fascism was evident in *The Prodigal Parents,* a book about radical and irresponsible children, in which he draws what is almost a comic strip view of communism. Its protagonist, Fred Cornplow, whom Lewis admires, is essentially the same middle-class businessman he had earlier satirized as Babbitt and the denizens of *Main Street. Bethel Merriday* is the story of the education of a young actress in summer stock and touring companies. It is embarrassingly sentimental. *Gideon Planish* is an attack on organized philanthropy. More like *Elmer Gantry* than any book Lewis had written since 1927, it is angry and intemperate, an example of slashing satire and violent comedy; yet it is so overdrawn that it seems almost a parody of Lewis's earlier work. *Cass Timberlane* is an account of American marriage. *Kingsblood Royal* takes up the issue of race in a mechanical and unconvincing parable. *The God-Seeker* is a historical novel set in Minnesota in the days of its early settlement. Although it can be considered the first novel in an unfinished panel of labor books, it is too much like costume romance to be taken seriously. In *World So Wide,* published posthumously in 1951, the year of his death, Lewis returns to the theme of the American in Europe in a book that is virtually a rewriting of *Dodsworth,* though now the satiric edge is gone, and the European culture that he once supported has become the target of his attack. The characters in this last sad work seemed, as **Malcolm Cowley** said, "survivors from a vanished world."

Lewis's work falls easily into three periods—the early apprenticeship work, followed by the great accomplishment of the 1920s in which in five novels he gives a vigorous and emphatic picture of his world, followed by a long, sad, groping for suitable subjects. Few American writers have had a greater impact on their world than Lewis during his ten great years, 1920-29. As Schorer said, "He gave us a vigorous, perhaps unique thrust into the imagination of ourselves." But after this great success he was increasingly removed from the materials that were his primary subject matter, and he wrote out of memory rather than direct experience, so that his later novels were increasingly memorials to a world and an age that was past. He was a very good social novelist but not a truly great writer. Nevertheless, it was appropriate that the first American Nobel Laureate in Literature should have been a man intimately committed to using literature to portray his fellow countrymen and to instruct them through satiric portraiture.

—C. Hugh Holman

See the essay on *Main Street.*

LIM, Genny

Born: Genevieve Lim, 15 December 1946, in San Francisco, California. **Education:** Columbia University, certificate of completion in broadcast journalism program 1974; San Francisco State University, B.A. in creative writing 1977; M.A. in English, emphasis on creative writing 1988. **Family:** Two daughters. **Career:** Member of the rock band Glass Mountain during 1960s; freelance writer/reporter, television producer and commentator, 1973-81; performing member of Unbound Feet (theater collective), 1979-81; project investigator, Chinese Women of America Historical Project, San Francisco, 1981-83; visiting lecturer in creative writing, Asian-American Studies Department, University of California, Berkeley, 1983-85; producing artistic director of XX Theatre, beginning 1987; poet-in-residence, curator of Poets-in-the-Galleries, De Young Museum, San Francisco, beginning 1989; coordinator of performance program, New College of California, San Francisco, beginning 1989; teacher, University of Creation Spirituality. **Awards:** Robert Frost award for poetry, San Mateo County Fair, 1980; Before Columbus Foundation American Book award, 1982; *Downtown Villager* award for best new play, 1982; Mayor of San Francisco's Certificate of Honor in Appreciative Recognition of Distinction and Merit, 1985; Asian Community Mental Health Services award of Appreciation for valuable contributions in developing community mental health for Asians, 1986; Association of Asian Pacific American Actors James Wong Howe award, 1986; California Arts Council Multicultural Entry Grant Program fellowship, 1986-89; Zellerbach Family Fund Community Arts Program Grant, 1987, 1988; San Francisco State University Department of Creative Writing Lawrence and Lee First Prize Playwriting award, 1987; California Arts Council New Genre fellowship, 1988; *San Francisco Bay Guardian* Goldie award, Rockefeller Foundation grant and New Langton arts grant, all 1991. **Member:** National Asian American Telecommunications Association; San Francisco Arts Commission, beginning 1991; Alliance for Cultural Democracy.

PUBLICATIONS

Poetry

Winter Place. 1989.

Plays

Paper Angels (produced 1980; produced as Public Broadcasting Service "American Playhouse" teleplay, 1985). In *Two Plays by Genny Lim,* 1991.

Pigeons (one-act play; produced 1983; adapted for film and produced as *Fei Tein*). 1983.
The Pumpkin Girl (produced 1987). 1987.
Bitter Cane (produced 1989). In *Two Plays by Genny Lim,* 1991.
The Magic Brush (produced 1990). 1990.
Pins and Noodles (produced 1993).
This Poetry Thang: Voices from the Next Generation, with others (produced 1997).

Prose

Island: Poetry and History of Chinese Immigrants on Angel Island, 1910-1940, with Him Mark Lai and Judy Yung. 1980.
Wings for Lai Ho. 1982.

Other

Daughter of Han (performance piece; produced 1983). 1983.
I Remember Clifford (performance piece; produced 1983). 1983.
XX (performance piece; produced 1987). 1987.
Winter Place (epic jazz poem performance piece; produced 1989). 1989.
Faceless (performance art collaboration piece; produced 1989). 1989.
SenseUs: The Rainbow Anthems (music and poetry), with others. 1990.
La China Poblana (performance collaboration; produced 1991). 1991.

Editor, *The Chinese-American Experience: Papers from the Second National Conference on Chinese-American Studies.* 1984.
Editor, *Through Our Voices: An Anthology.* 1990.

Recordings: *Who Sane, Who Sane,* 1992; *America Fears the Drum,* 1992; *Arkaeology,* 1993; *Immigrant Suite* and *Devotee,* 1997.

*

Critical Study: "Paper Angels" in *Unbroken Thread: An Anthology of Plays by Asian American Women* edited by Roberta Uno, 1993.

*　*　*

Genny Lim, a native of San Francisco, is an acclaimed Chinese-American poet and playwright. Lim grew up as the youngest of seven children in a household with only one son. Lim's father, Edward Lim, was born in China and came to the United States when he was very young. He went back to China to get married and returned to America with his Chinese bride, Lin Sun, who was a native of Guangdong, China. Lim's father became a merchant, running a small sewing factory in San Francisco's Chinatown. Her mother worked as a seamstress and Lim was raised working for her parents' business.

Even though her parents did not encourage her to be an artist, they loved the Chinese theater and operas, and Lim often accompanied them to these productions. She decided to become an actor and studied theater and liberal arts at San Francisco State University. During the political and social turmoil in the 1960s, she became a singer with a rock band called Glass Mountain. After moving to New York in 1969, she graduated from the School of Journalism at Columbia University in 1973.

Lim began writing her best-known work, the play *Paper Angels,* in 1978 when she noted a lack of authentic representation of Asian American history and experience. Her interest in that history was sparked by the discovery in 1970 of dozens of calligraphic poems inscribed on the walls of the Angel Island immigrant detention center in San Francisco Bay, which were written by Chinese immigrants awaiting processing. Lim, with Chinese-American scholars Him Mark Lai and Judy Yung, began translating the poems in 1976. The scope of the project grew as the three talked to immigration officials and Chinese-Americans who had passed through the island. The interviews and poems formed the basis for the 1980 work, *Island: Poetry and History of Chinese Immigrants on Angel Island, 1910-1940.*

Paper Angels, first produced in 1980, again focuses on the immigrants of Angel Island. The play examines the whole of the immigrant experience details the efforts of seven Chinese people, four men and three women, to gain admittance to the United States. In *Unbroken Thread* Roberta Uno wrote that the work "explores a world peopled by those courageous individuals who in defiance of discriminatory immigration laws came to America in search of a better life."

Lim believes that gender and race are two of the biggest issues of our time, and she continues to explore racial and gender relations in her work. Her major plays deal not only with the history of racism against persons of color but also with the male and female identity and how the characters' sex affect or force their lives. While Lim illustrates the Chinese immigrants' struggle and loss of humanity on Angel Island—and their courageous confrontation with the discriminatory immigration laws—she focuses on tragic human relations, especially racial and gender relations of Chinese laborers and how the Chinese immigrants were exploited in the 1880s by the white owners of sugarcane plantations in Hawaii. In *Paper Angels* and *Bitter Cane,* Lim not only explores the issues of cultural awareness, racial identity, and ancestral roots but also reveals the tragic truth of American dreams that the Chinese immigrants believed. Seeking paradise and economic success, the Chinese characters as well as whites are forced to lose their self-respect, and ultimately, their dreams. *Paper Angels* and *Bitter Cane* are Lim's criticism of the discriminatory legislation that targeted a specific nationality and the system that denied the humanity of the early Asian immigrants. In *Unbroken Thread,* Uno observes that even though "the characters of *Paper Angels* are victimized by circumstance they are not victims." Addressing this topic, Lim, quoted by Uno, has stated that "For Westerners to become a hero you have to win or beat up or kill . . . . My characters are strong but they don't function like Western heroes."

As a writer who seeks her ancestral history and roots, Lim honestly presents oppression, struggle, and the unforgettable past of Asian Americans in the United States. Lim notes in an interview with Velina Hasu Houston, included in Houston's *The Politics of Life* (1993), that for her history is "the repository of the memory, the memory of where we've been as a people . . . . I feel that if we can examine history closely, we can learn from our mistakes and move on to firmer ground, otherwise, like the cat chasing its own tail, we'll be doomed to doing the same."

—Miseong Woo

LIN Tai-yi

Pseudonyms: Anor Lin; Wu-shuang Lin. **Born:** Peking, China, 1 April 1926; daughter of Lin Yutang. **Education:** Columbia University, 1946-49. **Family:** Married R. Ming Lai, 1949; one daughter and one son. **Career:** Instructor in Chinese at Yale University, 1945-1946; editor-in-chief of Chinese edition of *Reader's Digest,* Hong Kong, 1964-1987; author and translator. **Residence:** Arlington, Virginia.

PUBLICATIONS

Novels (in English)

War Tide. 1943.
The Golden Coin. 1946.
The Eavesdropper. 1958.
The Lilacs Overgrown. 1960; revised edition published in Chinese as *Dingxiang bianye,* 1965.
Kampoon Street. 1964; revised edition published in Chinese as *Jinpan jie,* 1979.

Novels (in Chinese)

Chunlei chunyu. 1991.
Mingyue jishiyou. 1992.

Prose

Our Family, with Adet Lin, introuction by Pearl S. Buck. 1939.
Dawn over Chungking, with Adet Lin and Meimei Lin. 1941.
Lin Yutang Chuan. 1989.

Other

Translator, with Adet Lin, *Girl Rebel,* by Ping-ying Hsieh, introduction by Lin Yutang. 1940.
Translator, *Flowers in the Mirror.* 1965.

Editor, *Chinese Selection from the Reader's Digest.* 1984.
Editor, *Chinese Literature in the Reader's Digest.* 1987.
Editor, with Lai Ming, *The New Lin Yutang Chinese-English Dictionary.* 1987.

*   *   *

As the daughter of **Lin Yutang,** one of the greatest modern Chinese writers, Lin Tai-yi has been under the influence of her father throughout her writing career. In her preface to *Lin Yutang Chuan,* she admitted that she was always introduced as "the daughter of Lin Yutang." Certainly, Lin Tai-yi's early living experiences in the United States, her precocious awareness of her Chinese identity, her education, as well as her later deep concern for the life and fate of the Chinese people, are all tied to some extent to the life and thought of Lin Yutang. Thus, despite the fact that Lin Tai-yi had published several books at an early age, she did not achieve distinction as an individual novelist until the publication of *Kampoon Street* in 1964 and its Chinese revision in 1979. Basically, the accomplishment of Lin Tai-yi as a creative writer lies in her exploration of the Chinese experiences during and after the second World War. Usually set against a realistic social context, her stories cover the experiences of the Chinese in Hong Kong, mainland China, Taiwan, and the United States. The political and social agitation of China as well as the struggle of Chinese individuals in such a historical context forms the central theme of Lin Tai-yi's best novels.

Lin Tai-yi's awareness of her Chinese identity and her interest in the people and culture of China developed from an early age. The Lin family first left China in 1936, when Tai-yi was only ten years old, and they left the United States in 1940 to return to China. No doubt Lin Tai-yi's many years in America had a great influence on her. In *Our Family,* the diary of Lin Tai-yi and her sister Adet during their sojourn in the United States, Lin Tai-yi demonstrates her strong sensitivity to the problems of race, identity, and the Chinese experience in America. In the entry "Why Am I Me?," she poses a series of questions about her identity. In "The Short History of My Name," she recounts the origin of her English name "Anor" and launches a comparison between the Chinese and Western methods of naming a person. With a precocious consciousness of self, she hated people to mispronounce her Chinese name. She pronounces her dislike for a traditional Western name because of the ridiculousness of any Chinese woman to bear a name like Violet, Rose, or Evelyn. Lin Tai-yi's awareness of and her resistance to the stereotypical image of Chinese in America are most poignantly revealed in "What They Ask Me About China." By the age of thirteen, Lin Tai-yi had correctly exposed white racism against the Chinese. Talking about the questions that Americans often ask about China, she states:

> Sometimes they hurt our feelings to think of what they think of China. Those questions are just silly, that's all. And I wonder how they dare to ask. It seems to me that they take these Chinese not as human beings but just as something strange and curious to know.

Here, Lin Tai-yi wanted not only to disrupt the stereotypical image of the Chinese but also to argue for the value of Chinese culture and people. Ideologically and emotionally tied to anything Chinese, Lin Tai-yi utters her homesickness for China in the final entry of *Our Family* without any reservations:

> My country that is different from the west. All the things in China. The land, the people, the food, the custom! I long for CHINA.

This deep concern for China and the Chinese runs through Lin Tai-yi's later works. Her favorite theme—the struggle and the interior growth of an individual in an age of social and political disturbance—appears as early as in *Dingxiang bianye (The Lilacs Overgrown).* Set against the background of China after the second World War, *Dingxiang bianye* explores the growth of two young sisters in a society of agitation. Like most of the novels of Lin Tai-yi, *Dingxiang bianye* is marked by intertwined story-plots and complex interactions between the characters from different social classes, but, in a sense, Lin Tai-yi as a thinker came to maturity much earlier than she did as a novelist; the thematic concern of this story was not developed with proper artistic subtlety until Lin Tai-yi rewrote *Dingxiang bianye* into *Chunlei chunyu,* which better demonstrates authorial mastery over the tools of writing.

Kampoon Street is one of Lin Tai-yi's most celebrated novels. Set in Hong Kong after the Communist takeover of mainland China, the novel recounts the experiences of the Zuo family, thus bringing to light the poverty, the dream, and the struggle of the Chinese refugees from Communist China. Lin Tai-yi's strength in this novel is still her realistic delineation of her characters' inner and outer experiences, the interaction between people in different social classes, as well as the callousness, the cruelty, the humanity, and the compassion of Hong Kong society toward struggling individuals.

A later work, *Mingyue jishiyou,* perhaps her best novel so far, expands the author's interests: the novel includes experiences of the overseas Chinese, the Chinese in Hong Kong, the memory of the Cultural Revolution, the Tiananmen Square Protest in 1989, as well as the apprehension of the people in Hong Kong who are destined to have their city taken over by Mainland China. The complexity of the politics is mingled in the story with the intricacy of the relationships between each character. For example, the familial emotions and obligations of the central character Hu Dayu, a professor of Asian Languages and Cultures at a university in the United States and also a famous writer about the Chinese experiences are intertwined with his love for a Hong Kong actress, Cui-cui. Here, the Chinese experiences—their struggles for survival, for love, for life accomplishments, and their sense of uncertainty in an age of disorder—all receive vivid investigation.

Lin Tai-yi as a novelist is never free from her preoccupation with the fate of China and the Chinese people living throughout the world. This deep concern for modern Chinese people and history distinguishes Lin Tai-yi from other contemporary Chinese American writers.

—Hsiu-chuan Lee

LIN Yutang

Born: Longxi, Fujian Province, China, 10 October 1895. **Education:** The Protestant College of Amoy (Xiamen); St. John's College, Shanghai, 1911-16, B.A. 1916; Harvard University, M.A. 1920; University of Leipzig, Germany, Ph.D. 1923. **Family:** Married Cuifeng Liao in 1919; three daughters. **Career:** Professor of English, Qinghua University, Beijing, 1916-19, and Beijing University, 1923-26; chair of English department, Beijing Normal University for Women, 1926; dean of College of Arts, Xiamen University, 1926-27; secretary of the Ministry of Foreign Affairs, Revolutionary Government of China, Wuhan, 1927; research fellow in philology at Academia Sinica and English editor for Kaiming Bookstore, 1930-35; founder and editor of *Lunyu banyuekan* (Analects Fortnightly), 1932-35, *Renjianshi* (This Human World Fortnightly), 1934-35, and *Yuzhoufeng* (The Cosmic Wind), 1934-36; contributing editor, *China Critic,* beginning 1927, *T'ien Hsia Monthly,* beginning 1936; freelance writer, 1936-66, New York and elsewhere; head of arts and letters division, United Nations Economic, Social, and Cultural Organization (UNESCO), Paris, 1948-49; chancellor, Nanyang University, Singapore, 1954-55; president, Chinese PEN, beginning 1969, and vice president, International PEN, 1975-76. **Died:** 26 March 1976.

PUBLICATIONS

Collections

Jianfuji (title means "Essays of Skirmishes"). 1928.
Yuyanxue lunji (title means "Philological Essays"). 1933.
Dahuangji (title means "The Lone Wayfarer"). 1934.
Wodehua (title means "It Seems to Me"). 2 volumes, 1934, 1936.
Yutang wenchun (title means "A Collection of Lin Yutang"). 1941.
Wusuobutan (title means "Free Talk"). 2 volumes, 1965, 1967.
Lin Yutang: The Best of an Old Friend, edited by A. J. Anderson. 1975.

Novels

Moment in Peking: A Novel of Contemporary Chinese Life. 1939.
Leaf in a Storm: A Novel of War-Swept China. 1941.
Vigil of a Nation. 1944.
Chinatown Family. 1948.
Miss Tu. 1950.
Widow Chuan. 1952.
The Vermilion Gate. 1953.
Looking Beyond. 1955; published in England as *Unexpected Island,* 1955.
Lady Wu: A True Story. 1957; published as *Lady Wu: A Novel,* 1965.
The Red Peony. 1961.
Juniper Loa. 1963.
The Flight of the Innocents. 1964.

Play

Confucius Saw Nancy, and Essays about Nothing. 1935.

Prose

Kaiming English Grammar. 1930.
China's Own Critics, with Hu Shih. 1931.
Letters of a Chinese Amazon: And, War-Time Essays. 1934.
The Little Critic: Essays, Satires and Sketches on China. 1935.
My Country and My People. 1935; revised edition, 1937; second revised edition, 1939; new edition, 1962.
A History of the Press and Public Opinion in China. 1937.
The Importance of Living. 1937.
The Birth of a New China: A Personal Story of the Sino-Japanese War. 1939.
With Love and Irony. 1940.
Between Tears and Laughter. 1943.
Chinese Ideal of Life. 1944.
Gay Genius: Life and Times of Su Tungpo. 1947.
On the Wisdom of America. 1950.
Peace Is the Heart. 1950.
The Secret Name. 1958; published in England as *The Secret Name: The Soviet Record, 1917-1958.* 1959.
From Pagan to Christian. 1959.
The Chinese Way of Life. 1959.
Farewell to Fear, with Toni Keitlen. 1960.
Imperial Peking: Several Centuries of China. 1961.
The Pleasure of a Non-Conformist. 1962.
Bashi zixu (Memoirs of an Octogenarian). 1980.

Other

Hongloumeng renming suoyin (An Index to the Characters' Names in *The Dream of the Red Chamber*). 1976.

Compiler, *Readings in Modern Journalistic Prose.* 1931.
Compiler, *The Chinese Theory of Art.* 1967.
Compiler, *Chinese-English Dictionary of Modern Usage.* 1972.

Translator, *Six Chapters of a Floating Life,* by Shen Fu. 1935.
Translator, *A Nun of Taishan and Other Translations,* by Liu E. 1936.
Translator, *Mao Tse-Tung's "Democracy": a Digest Bible of Chinese Communism.* 1947.
Translator and adapter, *Widow, Nun, and Courtesan.* 1951.
Translator, *Chuang-tzu.* 1955.
Translator, *The Importance of Understanding.* 1960; new edition published as *Translations from Chinese (The Importance of Understanding).* 1963.

Editor, *The Wisdom of China and India.* 1942.
Editor, *The Wisdom of India.* 1942.
Editor and translator, *Tales of Old China.* 1943.
Editor and translator, *The Wisdom of Confucius.* 1943.
Editor, *Gems from Chinese Literature.* 1947.
Editor and translator, *The Wisdom of Laotze.* 1948.
Editor, *Famous Chinese Stories.* 1952.
Editor and translator, *Famous Chinese Short Stories Retold.* 1952.

*

Bibliography: "Lin Yutang: A Bibliography of His English Writings and Translations" by Arthur James Anderson in *Bashi zixu* ("Memoirs of an Octogenarian") by Lin Yutang, 1980.

Critical Studies: *Our Family* by Adet Lin and Anor Lin, 1939; *Picture Book of Famous Immigrants* by Evelyn Lowenstein, 1962; "Golden Mountain: Chinese Versions of the American Dream in Lin Yutang, Louis Chu, and Maxine Hong Kingston" by Cheng Lok Chua, in *Ethnic Groups* vol. 4, nos. 1-2, 1982; "Three Novels on Singapore's Past: Description as a Narrative Form" by Arthur Yap, in *The Writer's Sense of Past: Essays on Southeast Asian and Australian Literature* edited by Kirpal Singh, 1987; "Lin Yutang: A Bundle of Contrasts" by Yi-chin Fu, in *Fu Jen Studies: Literature and Linguistics* vol. 21, 1988; *The Life and Times of Lin Yutang* by Diran John Sohigian, 1992; *Lin Yutang: Negotiating Modernity between East and West* (dissertation) by Jun Qian, 1996.

*   *   *

Lin Yutang is a success story of writing in one's second language. In his long career as an essayist, translator, editor, scholar, novelist, and lexicographer in China and the United States, Lin left a literary legacy that simultaneously juggles two modes of thought, the Eastern and the Western. Writing in his native language, Lin first established his name in China as one of the most influential advocates of Western ideas in the ongoing transformation of Chinese literature, particularly in popularizing humorist prose as a worthy literary genre. Later, in his sojourn of more than thirty years in the United States, Lin produced an incredible amount of nonfiction and fiction in English with the purpose of bringing Chinese wisdom to Western readers. The best of Lin's works not only have changed the Western perception of China for the better but have also in many ways become a permanent part of the American mind.

Lin's initial contact with the West came from his Christian family, particularly his father, a progressive Protestant priest, who borrowed money to send Lin to St. John's College in Shanghai, so that he could have the best possible education in English and other Western subjects in China at the time. From 1919 to 1923, Lin studied comparative literature at Harvard and modern linguistics in Germany. Following the years after his return to China, Lin held various teaching and editorial posts in universities and publishing houses. Meanwhile, he became known as the author of a best-selling grammar book on English and the editor of several successful literary magazines. Lin's concern for a modern China ridden with political corruption and social instability matched that of most reform-minded intellectuals. Lin wrote many poignant essays in order to honestly and frankly criticize China's diseases, and he even had a brief stint as a secretary for the short-lived Wuhan revolutionary government. But Lin was no revolutionist. His humanist orientation led him to oppose a cultural radicalism that increasingly became the tune of his time. By 1935, Lin's continuous advocacy of humor and character-building had alienated him from the dominant left-leaning writers led by Lu Xun, and his literary magazines ran into financial troubles due to internal disputes. When the American writer **Pearl S. Buck** invited him to write a book about China for Western readers, Lin jumped at the opportunity.

My Country and My People, published in 1936, was a runaway best-seller. In the same year, Lin moved his family to the United States at the urging of Pearl Buck. Two years later, Lin published his most widely-read book, *The Importance of Living.* These and a series of "wisdom books" in the following years firmly established Lin as an authoritative interpreter of Chinese philosophy in the West. These books filled a vacuum left by the unapproachable works of traditional sinologists and by missionaries' overwhelmingly negative portrait of Chinese society, which formed the Western perception of China since the nineteenth century. From the Confucian concept of humanity blended with Laotzian passivity, Lin extracts a philosophy of self-content that is supposed to govern the Chinese way of living. Often critical of certain aspects of the Chinese national character, Lin nevertheless holds a set of values such as detachment and high-mindedness, which guarantees intense joy in living, as essentially distinctive from the Western philosophy of life. Writing in a lively and witty style aided by a mastery of idiomatic English, Lin's prose emits a sense of humor that is both endearing and persuasive to its Western readers.

Lin is less well-known in the English world as a fiction writer. Only after he established himself as a phenomenal writer of English prose did he try his hand at fiction. All of his novels are written in English and when they were translated into Chinese—in many cases without his permission—Lin acquired a greater name as a novelist with the Chinese readers than with the English ones. The best of his novels are *Moment in Peking, Leaf in a Storm,* and *The Vermilion Gate,* which have come to be known as the "Lin Yutang Trilogy." *Moment in Peking* was completed during the Lins' extended vacation in France from 1938 to 1939. Structured as a close imitation of the great Chinese novel *The Dream of the Red Chamber,* the novel depicts the odyssey of two prominent Peking (Beijing) families in the first half of the twentieth century, a time marked by constant warfare. The narrative centers on Yao Mulan, one of the "daughters of a Taoist" who struggles against the ruinous effect of war on her personal and family life. The story culminates in a self-reckoning for inner peace that is profoundly Taoist. Some characters from this novel reappear in *Leaf in a Storm,* which explores the relationship between people and war in a humanist light. The story evolves around the disentangling of two triangular love affairs with the Anti-Japanese War in the background, and it is resolved by the protagonist's heroic exit in the name of love. In this novel, Lin demonstrates a more convincing characterization and the ability to handle delicate emotional conflicts. Unlinked in plot with the other two, *The Vermilion Gate* is a love story set against the backdrop of a family feud. That good will triumph over evil and love will prevail against all adversity reflect Lin's dearly held philosophical optimism.

Chinatown Family is Lin's only novel about the Chinese American experience. The success story of the Fongs in New York's Chinatown in the 1930s embodies Lin's vision for Chinese America: the initial conflict between the Chinese family ideal and the America dream will give way to an easy synthesis of the best of both. This synthesis is incarnated in Tom Fong, the third son of the family, in whom the American reality only increases his Chinese consciousness, which is guided by Taoist enlightenment and reinforced by his marriage to Elsie, a teacher of the Chinese tradition and a bearer of wisdom. Lin's own experience as a sojourner in the United States must have been the grounds for his theme of assimilation in the novel, but unlike other Chinese American writers at the time, this assimilation is met with a positive resistance by the Chinese values, a resistance that proves to be beneficial to the making of a Chinese American identity in *Chinatown Family.*

Over the years with his diligent literary production Lin came to be known in the United States and the West as the very personification of the Chinese wisdom that he wrote about, and in the words of one critic, Lin "has become completely one of us" (*Atlantic,* February 1938). But in 1966 Lin suddenly ended his sojourner's life and settled down in Taiwan. He began to write in Chinese again after writing in English for thirty years, and he was warmly received by his Chinese readers. Lin's fame has reached an international scale. His works have been translated into more than fifteen languages including his native Chinese. In the 1960s, Lin had several world tours in which he continued to expound on the "Lyrical Philosophy" of China. In 1975 he was elected the Vice President of the International PEN and was nominated as a candidate for the Nobel Prize for Literature. Lin's last significant work is his widely acclaimed *Chinese-English Dictionary of Modern Usage.* Lin spent the final decade of his life completing this project, a goal that had originated in his early training as a linguist. The dictionary is the most appropriate conclusion to a remarkable career of this bilingual writer.

—Li Dian

LINDSAY, (Nicholas) Vachel

Born: Springfield, Illinois, 10 November 1879. **Education:** Hiram College, Ohio, 1897-1900; studied for the ministry; studied art at Chicago Art Institute, 1901, and New York Art School, 1905. **Family:** Married Elizabeth Conner in 1925; one son and one daughter. **Career:** Pen and ink designer, 1900-10; lecturer on art history, 1905-10; also traveled through the United States living by reciting his poems, 1906-12; after 1912 became known for his verses and was thereafter in demand as lecturer and reader; teacher, Gulf Park College, Mississippi, 1923-24. **Award:** Litt.D.: Hiram College, 1930. **Member:** American Academy. **Died:** (suicide) 5 December 1931.

PUBLICATIONS

Collections

Selected Poems, edited by Mark Harris. 1963.
Letters, edited by Marc Chenetier. 1979.
The Poetry, edited by Dennis Camp. 2 vols., 1984-85.

Poetry

The Tramp's Excuse and Other Poems. 1909.
Rhymes to Be Traded for Bread. 1912.
General William Booth Enters into Heaven and Other Poems. 1913.
The Congo and Other Poems. 1914.
The Chinese Nightingale and Other Poems. 1917.
The Golden Whales of California and Other Rhymes in the American Language. 1920.
The Daniel Jazz and Other Poems. 1920.
Going-to-the-Sun. 1923.
Collected Poems. 1923; revised edition, 1925.
Going-to-the-Stars. 1926.
The Candle in the Cabin: A Weaving Together of Script and Singing. 1926.
Johnny Appleseed and Other Poems (for children). 1928.
Every Soul Is a Circus. 1929.
Selected Poems, edited by Hazelton Spencer. 1931.

Other

The Village Magazine. 1910.
Adventures While Preaching the Gospel of Beauty. 1914.
The Art of the Moving Picture. 1915; revised edition, 1922.
A Handy Guide for Beggars, Especially Those of the Poetic Fraternity. 1916.
The Golden Book of Springfield, Being a Review of a Book That Will Appear in 2018. 1920.
The Litany of Washington Street (miscellany). 1929.
Letters to A. Joseph Armstrong, edited by Armstrong. 1940.
The Progress and Poetry of the Movies: A Second Book of Film Criticism. 1995.

*

Critical Studies: *Lindsay: A Poet in America* by Edgar Lee Masters, 1935; *The West-Going Heart: A Life of Lindsay* by Eleanor Ruggles, 1959; *Lindsay* by Raymond Purkey, 1968; *Lindsay: Fieldworker for the American Dream* by Ann Massa, 1970; *The Vision of This Land: Studies of Lindsay, Edgar Lee Masters, and Carl Sandburg* edited by John E. Hallwas and Dennis J. Reader, 1976; *Poetry and Community* by Balz Engler, 1990; "Vachel Lindsay's Crusade for Cultural Literacy" by Lisa Wooley, in *Midamerica,* 1995, pp. 83-88; "Laughed Off: Canon, Kharakter, and the Dismissal of Vachel Lindsay" by T.R. Hummer, in *The Kenyon Review,* Spring 1995, pp. 56-96.

*　　*　　*

Vachel Lindsay was a man out of phase with his time. He was also a writer who had the misfortune to be judged solely on the basis of his poetry, even though he produced a sizeable corpus of prose, work that he felt to be ultimately more important than his poetry. While it is true that he has begun to receive the critical appreciation and interpretation he deserves, it is equally true that he is still considered by many to be a writer (and reciter) of verse—a twentieth-century troubadour who toured the country reciting his poems to hugely enthusiastic audiences, a propagandist for America whose exhortations were clothed in bombast, naivete, sentimentality, and theatrics, a phenomenon whose time had already come and gone. His role as social critic was unrecognized and such prose works as *Adventures While Preaching the Gospel of Beauty, The Art of the Moving Picture, A Handy Guide for Beggars,* and *The Golden Book of Springfield* were virtually ignored.

Lindsay's early books of verse, *General William Booth Enters into Heaven and Other Poems* and *The Congo and Other Poems,* established his reputation as a herald of the New Poetry. They mark a dramatic break with the genteel, derivative verse that then dominated the American literary scene, while marking a continuity with the Whitmanesque mode. His best poems ring with genuine music and vibrate with energy, and Lindsay's theatrical recitation of them established his reputation as an entertainer. But the latter reputation eclipsed the former and clung to him throughout the remainder of his life. His problem was two-fold: his superb qualities as an entertainer and the public's refusal to accept his definition of the role of the poet.

Lindsay felt poetry should serve the masses; that art for art's sake had no place on the American scene; that elitism in poetry was a negative and destructive force; and that Americans had to be awakened to the fact that they were allowing their country's true destiny to slip away. Lindsay considered his poetry to be the best means by which he could jolt the people into an awareness of what was happening; when they were made aware of it they would then fall in line behind him and join his efforts to recapture and restore to America its original promise.

But Lindsay's vision of America was not the vision of the American majority. Moreover, his pessimism and fundamentalist viewpoint (both of America's problems and of the solutions to them) were anathema to political, social, and literary arbiters of the day. And finally, since Lindsay believed poetry to be a social as opposed to artistic instrument (content should take precedence over style), he was not part of the imagist movement that influenced the course of twentieth-century American poetry from his day to the present.

Lindsay never recovered from the realization that the people wanted only entertainment from him and that his crusade for "religion, equality and beauty," his "gospel," was doomed. He died by his own hand, a bitter and psychotic man, "Staking his last strength and his final fight/That cost him all, to set the old world right" ("Litany of the Heroes").

—Catherine Seelye

LINNEY, Romulus

Born: Philadelphia, Pennsylvania, in 1930. **Education:** Oberlin College, Ohio, A.B. 1953; Yale University School of Drama, New Haven, Connecticut, M.F.A. 1958. **Military Service:** Served in the U.S. Army, 1954-56. **Career:** Actor and director in stock for 6 years; stage manager, Actors Studio, New York, 1960; has taught at the Manhattan School of Music, University of North Carolina, Chapel Hill, University of Pennsylvania, Philadelphia, Brooklyn College, Princeton University, New Jersey, Columbia University, New York, Hunter College, New York, and Connecticut College, New London. Teacher at The New School University, New York. **Awards:** National Endowment for the Arts grant, 1974; Obie award, 1980, for sustained achievement, 1992; Guggenheim fellowship, 1980; Mishima prize, for fiction, 1981; American Academy award, 1984; Rockefeller fellowship, 1986; American Theater Critics Association award, 1988, 1990; Helen Hayes award, 1990. Honorary degrees: Oberlin College, Ohio, 1994; Appalachian State University, 1996; Wake Forest University, 1998. **Member:** Dramatists Guild; fellowship of Southern Writers; American Academy of Arts and Letters. **Residence:** New York City.

PUBLICATIONS

Plays

The Sorrows of Frederick (produced 1967). 1966.
The Love Suicide at Schofield Barracks (produced 1972). With *Democracy and Esther*, 1973; one-act version (produced 1984), in *The Best Short Plays 1986*, edited by Ramon Delgado, 1986.
Democracy and Esther, adaptation of the novels by Henry Adams (as *Democracy*, produced 1974; revised version produced 1975). With *The Love Suicide at Schofield Barracks*, 1973; as *Democracy*, 1976.
Holy Ghosts (produced 1974). With *The Sorrows of Frederick*, 1977.
Appalachia Sounding (produced on tour 1975).
Old Man Joseph and His Family (produced 1977). 1978.
Childe Byron (produced 1977; revised version produced 1981). 1981.
Just Folks (produced 1978).
The Death of King Philip, music by Paul Earls (produced 1979). 1984.
Tennessee (produced 1979). 1980.
El Hermano (produced 1981).1981.
The Captivity of Pixie Shedman (produced 1981). 1981.
Goodbye, Howard (produced 1982). Included in *Laughing Stock*, 1984.
F.M. (produced 1982). Included in *Laughing Stock*, 1984.
April Snow (produced 1983). Included in *Three Plays*, 1989.
Laughing Stock (includes *Goodbye, Howard*; *F.M.*; *Tennessee*; produced 1984). 1984.
Wrath, in *Faustus in Hell* (produced 1985).
Sand Mountain (includes *Sand Mountain Matchmaking* and *Why the Lord Come to Sand Mountain*; produced 1986). 1985.
A Woman Without a Name (produced 1986). 1986.
Pops (includes *Can Can*, *Claire de Lune*, *Ave Maria*, *Gold and Silver Waltz*, *Battle Hymn of the Republic*, *Songs of Love*; produced 1986). 1987; *Ave Maria* produced as *Hrosvitha* in *Three Poets*, 1989.

Heathen Valley, adaptation of his own novel (produced 1986). 1988.
Yancey (produced 1988). Included in *Three Plays*, 1989.
Juliet (produced 1988). Included in *Three Plays*, 1989.
Pageant, with others, music and lyrics by Michael Rice (produced 1988).
Precious Memories, adaptation of a story by Chekhov (also director: produced 1989); as *Unchanging Love* (produced 1991). 1991.
Three Plays (includes *Juliet*, *Yancey*, *April Snow*). 1989.
Three Poets (includes *Komachi*, *Hrosvitha*, *Akhmatova*; also director: produced 1989). 1990.
2 (produced 1990). Included in *Six Plays*, 1993.
Ambrosio (produced 1992). Included in *Seventeen Short Plays*, 1992.
Seventeen Short Plays (includes *Ambrosio*; *The Love Suicide at Schofield Barracks*; *Sand Mountain Matchmaking*; *Why the Lord Come to Sand Mountain*; *Komachi*, *Hrosvitha*; *Akhmatova*; *Can Can*; *Claire de Lune*; *Gold and Silver Waltz*; *Songs of Love*; *Juliet*, *Yancey*; *The Death of King Philip*; *El Hermano*; *The Captivity of Pixie Shedman*; *Goodbye*; *Howard*). 1992.
Six Plays (includes *F.M.*; *Childe Byron*; *Tennessee*; *2*;*April Snow*; *Heathen Valley*). 1993.
Spain (produced New York, 1993). 1994.
Shotgun (produced 1995).
Oscar over Here (produced 1995).
True Crimes (produced 1996). 1996.

Television Plays: *The 34th Star*, 1976; episodes for *Feelin' Good* series, 1976-77.

Novels

Heathen Valley. 1962.
Slowly, By Thy Hand Unfurled. 1965.
Jesus Tales. 1980.

Other

Ten Plays for Radio. 1954.

Editor, with Norman A. Bailey and Domenick Cascio, *Radio Classics*. 1956.

*

Manuscript Collection: Lincoln Center Library for the Performing Arts, New York.

Critical Studies: "An Interview with Romulus Linney" by Don B. Wilmeth, in *Studies in American Drama, 1945-Present*, 1987, pp. 71-84; "Romulus Linney" by John L. DiGaetani, in *A Search for a Postmodern Theatre: Interviews with Contemporary Playwrights* edited by John L. DiGaetani, 1991; "The Low-Down on a High Place: Family Matters in Heathen Valley" by D.F. Hurley, in *Appalachian Journal: A Regional Studies Review*, winter 1993, pp. 176-81; "Storyteller in the Wilderness: The American Imagination of Romulus Linney" by James F. Schlatter, in *The Southern Quarterly: A Journal of the Arts in the South*, winter 1994, pp. 63-78; "Romulus Linney" by Don B. Wilmeth, in *Speaking on Stage: Interviews with Contemporary American Playwrights*, 1996.

Theatrical Activities:
Director: **Plays**— *F.M.*, 1982; *Sand Mountain Matchmakers*, 1989; *Love Suicide at Schofield Barracks*, 1991; *True Crimes*, 1996.

*   *   *

Romulus Linney has worked at the writer's trade as playwright, novelist, and television scriptwriter. His dramatic writing has garnered many national awards for playwriting and has resulted in more than 30 plays produced off Broadway and in regional theatre. Widely ranging in subject matter and structure, Linney's plays are largely drawn from either historical subjects or the mountain folks of Appalachia. They show him to be a writer of uncommon literacy.

Linney often develops in his dramas a pattern of action in which his protagonists enter into or mature in environments where they confront values repressive of their own worth as individuals. The pattern is evident in at least six plays: *The Love Suicide at Schofield Barracks, Democracy, Holy Ghosts, A Woman Without a Name, Tennessee*, and *The Sorrows of Frederick. The Love Suicide at Schofield Barracks*, Linney's only Broadway production, reveals through the testimony of witnesses at a military inquiry the events behind the ritualistic double suicide of an army general and his wife in Hawaii in 1970. Testimony describes a patriotric military officer whose beliefs are so shattered by Vietnam that he seizes upon suicide in the guise of a classic Japanese drama to protest his disapproval of the war. The play, as well as its equally powerful one-act version, makes a strong, tension-building statement about individual responsibility for national morality. *Democracy*, a combined dramatization of two Henry Adams novels, provocatively examines the virtues of nineteenth-century American democracy through the characters of two richly drawn, intelligent women who enter Washington's 1865 society at the time of the corruption-ridden U.S. Grant administration. The women are individually charmed and proposed to by two attractive, highly positioned men whose beliefs they abhor and courageously reject. Set in the Southern Appalachian highlands, *Holy Ghosts* is the story of an abused runaway wife who finds sanctuary with a Fundamentalist sect of snake handlers. The sect seeks redemption from self-loathing through surviving snake bites. When her boorish husband comes to reclaim his newly converted wife and lets his low self-esteem turn him into a cult convert, she realizes her own self-worth and leaves. *Holy Ghosts*, Linney's most frequently produced drama, intriguingly and colorfully recreates a rural southern milieu with its dispossessed. Also rising above domestic strife and despairing self-doubt by achieving self-recognition is the title character of *A Woman Without a Name*, adapted from Linney's novel *Slowly, by Thy Hand Unfurled*. An uneducated, small-town southern wife and mother records memories of family experiences and unfair calumny as characters come forward to reenact events and interact with her as a participant. She becomes progressively liberated and guilt-free in this imaginatively conceived portrait of feminine endurance and self-discovery. Similarly effective is the Obie-winning *Tennessee*, portraying an elderly 1870s widow who recalls her youth and realizes that her husband cheated her of independence within the stern service of a frontier marriage. The richly rounded protagonist creates a definitive world of the past with parallels to the present. (Appearing in a short-play trilogy entitled *Laughing Stock, Tennessee* accompanies two amusing comedies: *Goodby, Howard*, about the confused deathwatch of three sisters over a brother;

and *F.M.*, focusing on a talented creative writing student who shocks dilettante classmates.)

Each of Linney's three novels have been effectively adapted into plays. In addition to *Slowly, by Thy Hand Unfurled, Heathen Valley* generated a play by the same name, the narrator-protagonist of which disavows church dogmatism and hierarchy in a remote mountain town to champion his community's need for social goodness. Also *Jesus Tales*, which delightfully satirizes stories from the New Testament Apocrypha, is the source for *Old Man Joseph and His Children*.

Linney's range of historical subjects is diverse. Representative examples are Prussia's philosopher-king Frederick the Great in *The Sorrows of Frederick*, Oscar Wilde in *Oscar Over Here*, Lord Byron in *Childe Byron*, the title protagonist of *The Death of King Philip*, and Herman Goring in *2*. The title character of *The Sorrows of Frederick* forsakes great artistic and intellectual gifts as a king to pursue power only to sadly find himself a victim of his life. Enriched by elevated language and finely etched characterization, the drama reiterates Linney's concern with those who resolve their destinies through their choice of values. *2* thoughtfully examines Goring during the 1945-1946 Nuremberg Trials as he reveals the self-deception and intolerant prejudices existing within all nations and would-be world conquerors.

Two collections of short plays, *Sand Mountain* and *Pops*, admirably demonstrate Linney's penchant for comedy, romance, varied dramaturgical structure, and the one-act form. Strong in homespun humor, *Sand Mountain* encompasses two southern folklore yarns about, respectively, a discriminating young widow rejecting a band of eligible men for a truth-telling widower, and the visit of Jesus and Saint Peter in human disguise to a mountain family. *Pops*, six comedic one-acts for six actors, treats forms of love, with mood-underscoring music accompanying each play. One of the collection's funniest works tells the story of a romance between oldsters that is opposed by their progeny *(Songs of Love)*. In a more serious vein, a short-play trio entitled *Three Poets* perceptively delineates three women from different centuries who fearlessly struggle for their lives and their art: a Non heroine in *Komachi*, a tenth-century nun in *Hrosvithe*, and a twentieth-century Russian poet in *Akhmatova*. Another short-play trio collection entitled *Spain* forcefully compels a probative look at religiosity and crises of conscience in the fifteenth and twentieth centuries. Also deftly touching concerns with crises of faith is the short work *Amtrosio* adapted from Matthew Lewis's *The Monk*.

Two full-length dramas of the 1990s set in the rural world of Appalachia reflect a dark mood. *Unchanging Love* (formerly entitled *Precious Memories*), based on an Anton Chekhov story, starkly exposes the lack of honesty and social compassion within a merchant family. *True Crimes*, adapted from Leo Tolstoy's *The Power of Darkness*, details the degradation of a shiftless backwoods youth motivated by greed, lust, and murderous maternal advice. He beds a married neighbor, poisons her husband, impregnates his future stepdaughter, and kills the offspring. He rejects guilt and confession for fear of endangering a profitable marriage. Reservedly supportive of the play, critics praised Linney for never turning his folk characters into caricatures of sentimentalized pastels.

A widely produced and critically supported playwright, Linney's plays crackle with substantive issues and effective theatricality and evince through the range of their structural variety an imaginative craftsman. Linney has been a highly noted and effective contemporary American playwright-spokesman for the folk of Appalachia. The prolific author of more than 36 plays and 3 novels, he stands as a major talent among dramatists of his time.

—Christian H. Moe

LOCKE, Alain (Le Roy)

Born: Arthur Locke in Philadelphia, Pennsylvania, 13 September 1886. **Education:** Central High School and the Philadelphia School of Pedagogy; Harvard University, Boston, Massachusetts, 1904-07 and 1916-17, B.A. (honors) 1907 and Ph.D. 1917; Oxford University, England, 1907-10. **Career:** Taught at Howard University, Washington, D.C., taking occasional leave to research or to lecture in Haiti, 1912-43; Fisk University, Nashville, Tennessee, 1927-28; the University of Wisconsin, Madison, 1945-46; the New School for Social Research, New York City, 1947; City College of New York; and the Salzburg Seminar in American Studies, Austria. **Awards:** Rhodes scholarship, 1907-10; Honor Roll of Race Relations, 1942. **Member:** International Institute of African Languages and Culture; American Negro Academy; American Philosophical Association; League of American Writers; Associates in Negro Folk Education; Conference on Science, Philosophy, and Religion; Society for Historical Research; National Order of Honor and Merit. **Died:** 9 June 1954.

PUBLICATIONS

Collections

The Critical Temper of Alain Locke, edited by Jeffrey C. Stewart. 1983.

Prose

The New Negro: An Interpretation. 1925.
Four Negro Poets. 1927.
The Negro in America. 1933.
Frederick Douglass: A Biography of Anti-Slavery. 1935.
The Negro and His Music. 1936.
Negro Art: Past and Present. 1936.
Americans All: Immigrants All. 1939.
The Negro in Art. 1940.
When Peoples Meet, with Bernhard J. Stern. 1942.
Le Role du Negre dans la culture des Ameriques. 1943.
The Negro Artist Comes of Age. 1945.
The Negro in American Culture, completed by Margaret Just Butcher. 1956.

Other

Race Contacts and Interracial Relations. 1916.
Plays of Negro Life, with Montgomery Gregory (sourcebook). 1927.
A Decade of Negro Self-Expression (annotated bibliography). 1928.
World View on Race and Democracy. 1943.

*

Bibliography: by Robert E. Martin, in *The New Negro Thirty Years Afterward,* 1955; *Alain Locke: A Research Guide* by Jeffrey C. Stewart, 1988.

Critical Studies: *The Legacy of Alain Locke* by Eugene C. Holmes, 1963; *Alain Locke: Reflections on a Modern Renaissance Man* edited by Russell J. Linnemann, 1982; *Alain Locke and Philosophy: A Quest for Cultural Pluralism* by Johnny Washington, 1986; *The Philosophy of Alain Locke: Harlem Renaissance and Beyond* edited by Leonard Harris, 1989; "Vindication As a Thematic Principle in Alain Locke's Writings" by Paul Joseph Burgett, in *The Harlem Renaissance: Revaluations,* 1989; "Community and Cultural Crisis" by Everett H. Akam, in *American Literary History,* summer 1991.

*   *   *

A discussion about Alain Le Roy Locke has been almost certain to begin with his noted anthology *The New Negro: An Interpretation* (1925), but that does not necessarily have to be the case. Without a doubt, Locke wrote prolifically on issues of race, and with the publication of *The New Negro,* had a powerful influence upon how the Harlem Renaissance has come to be perceived, but his career spans a range that includes philosophy, anthropology, art, music, literature, education, political theory, sociology, and African studies. Locke began his intellectual career, in fact, as a philosopher.

Locke referred to himself as a Socratic midwife. His philosophy was influenced by his relationship with **John Dewey** and other American Pragmatists, but his perspective departed from Pragmatism in significant ways. Locke rejected the emphasis the Pragmatists placed upon scientific methodology and its ability to confirm or dismiss cultural beliefs. The dependence upon science seemed to Locke to rely too heavily upon American ideals of individualism, promoting divisiveness rather than demonstrating the interdependency of communities. In contrast, Locke's notion of philosophy and the ways it comes to know and influence culture is defined through an understanding of attitudes. Philosophy, for Locke, has a communal foundation, a premise that situates him in the philosophic tradition of African American scholars such as **W. E. B. DuBois, Booker T. Washington,** and Martin Luther King, Jr. Locke's deep concern about moral dilemmas facing both the black community and American society more generally solidified his commitment to the need for a practical and social philosophy.

As an African American, Locke was very disturbed by the political injustices that were afflicting the nation. It seemed to Locke that since the United States of America is founded upon diversity, the country's government must face the challenge of its cultural heritage. He believed that democracy should not, either in theory or in practice, consistently silence the voices of the minority under the principle of majority rule. Using the term "cultural pluralism" coined by Horace Kallen near the turn of the century, Locke explored the possibilities offered by democracy for liberation and freedom. For this exploration, Locke utilized the work of Dewey and **William James** as a framework. Locke concluded in his essays "Democracy Faces a World Order" (1942) and "The Unfinished Business of Democracy" (1942) that democracy's failings relate to institutionalized racial segregation, or to what DuBois had identified as the problem of the color line.

Although he died only a month after the 1954 ruling on *Brown v. The Board of Education of Topeka, Kansas,* which decided in favor of desegregation of the public school system, Locke must have viewed the decision as a triumph. Locke had dedicated much of his career to studying the issue of segregation. Locke's essay "Negro Education Bids for Par" (1925) demonstrates his early interests in this subject. Desegregation simply for the sake of integration was not important to Locke when he considered higher education. In fact, he believed that black educators should take advantage of the system's opportunities by seeking administrative positions at private historically black institutions. In this manner, Locke suggested, blacks could design curricula that might reflect the cultural legacies of the student body in order to promote positive self-images. Locke also asserted that predominantly white colleges and universities should be forced legally to enroll a certain number of black students. When he wrote "The Dilemma of Segregation" (1935), however, Locke had turned his attention to the primary and secondary public school system, and he is vehement about the need for integration. For Locke, segregation among primary and secondary schools, instituted during Reconstruction, was an anachronism that had long ago lost its usefulness.

Locke's contributions to art criticism are also quite significant. Locke presented African art to the scholarly community as a discipline that warranted serious consideration. He believed that Africa's artistic tradition needed to be studied because of its rich cultural and classical contributions. Although Locke's speculations on the connections between African Americans and Africans were sometimes grounded in mythology as much as more objective data, Locke insisted that serious scholarship on African art and music held the key to demystifying European art, particularly for African Americans. In essays like "The Legacy of the Ancestral Arts" (1925), Locke documented the influence African art had upon European artists such as Matisse, Picasso, Derain, Modigliani, and Utrillo. But by 1927, with the publication of "A Collection of Congo Art" and "African Art: Classic Style," Locke had stopped comparing African and European art and demanded that African art be considered on its own terms.

Despite Locke's prolific career, he remains best known for the anthology *The New Negro* (1925), which appeared during the Harlem Renaissance. This work was particularly significant because it called attention to the tremendous wealth of talented African Americans who had begun congregating in New York City early in the twentieth century. It is this work more than any other that has secured Locke's position as a noteworthy scholar because it gave name and voice to previously overlooked artists.

—Valerie Sweeney Prince

LOCKRIDGE, Ross

Born: Bloomington, Indiana, 25 April 1914. **Education:** Indiana University, Bloomington 1931-35, B.A. (summa cum laude) in English 1935 (Phi Beta Kappa); post-graduate study, Harvard University, Cambridge, Massachusetts, 1940-41. **Family:** Married Vernice Baker in 1937; four children. **Career:** Instructor in English, Indiana University, 1936-40 and Simmons College, Boston, 1941-45. **Died:** (suicide) 6 March 1948.

PUBLICATIONS

Fiction

Raintree County. 1948.

*

Critical Studies: *Ross and Tom: Two American Tragedies* by John Leggett, 1974; "Raintree County and the Critics of '48" by Ray Lewis White, in *Midamerica: The Yearbook of the Society for the Study of Midwestern Literature,* vol. 11, 1984; "Habits of the Heart in Raintree County" by Park Dixon Goist, in *Midamerica: The Yearbook of the Society for the Study of Midwestern Literature,* vol. 8, 1986; *Shade of the Raintree: The Life and Death of Ross Lockridge, Jr., Author of Raintree County* by Laurence S. Lockridge, 1995.

*   *   *

Ross Lockridge's one published work, the sprawling thousand-page novel *Raintree County,* was a huge popular and critical success in 1948. Praised as "a novel of rare stature," the first American epic since *Moby Dick,* then increasingly disparaged as "an amalgam of undigested Wolfe, murky Faulkner, and watery Whitman," it is rarely read or mentioned in the late twentieth century. Periodically literary historians try to restore it to prominence, even eminence, but with lean results, perhaps because the novel's sunny optimism, frontier humor, and abiding faith in the American dream are not congenial to contemporary readers. On all its many layers, *Raintree County* is an exuberant Fourth of July festival of Americana.

On the Fourth of July, 1892, in the small town of Waycross, Indiana, the townspeople join together for a holiday of celebration, oratory, and reminiscence, as observed by John Wickliff Shawnessy, a 53-year-old schoolteacher reunited with his boyhood friends—a sleek senator, an ailing railroad tycoon, a wry journalist. Flashbacks re-create their common past, which eventuates in montage: structurally, events in John's life contrast with national events (his wedding is counterpointed with John Brown's execution, the birth of his son with the firing on Fort Sumter), and stylistically each event is viewed in the contrasting styles of fictitious newspaper accounts, old diaries and letters, blustering gossips and salty frontiersmen. The montages build into a panoramic view of American history and a critique of the nineteenth-century corrosion of the Declaration of Independence. The omniscient, disillusioned, but still hopeful narrator implies that the second American Revolution was the Civil War, epic atonement for slavery, and that the third was the Rail Strike of 1877, epic industrialism and enslavement of the poor. The urbane, witty journalist (a fine comic character) is the hero's Darwinian alter ego, cosmopolitan theoretician of the American experiences that Hoosier Johnny must undergo and struggle to understand—such as soldiering against the South, watching the first trains arrive in the Midwest. The hero himself, a Jeffersonian idealist, is also America's fledgling poet, the modern Johnny Appleseed restoring the national earth with his words, his ideals, and his faith. Ringed with comic Bunyanesque characters and somber Lincolnesque tragedies, Johnny is in many ways the incorruptible soul of epic America, and his life documents the century's "contest for my soul." On multiple levels of historical and literary allusion, each level complete with its contrapuntal movements of personal and national life, Lockridge weaves a kaleidoscopic epic, striving to be myth, that owes obvious debts to Joyce, Melville, and Whitman. Lockridge's America is "mancreated," "greatchested," "buntinghung." Though the symbolism is sometimes muddled, and the sentiment sometimes saccharine, Lockridge's gigantesque conception and his technical virtuosity were perhaps unparalleled in America until Pynchon's *Gravity's Rainbow*. There is ample reason to consider *Raintree County* an important novel for its era and a substantial achievement.

—Jan Hokenson

LOGAN, Jake. *See* **SMITH, Martin Cruz.**

LONDON, Jack

Born: John Griffith London, San Francisco, California, 12 January 1876. **Education:** Attended a grammar school in Oakland, California; Oakland High School, 1895-96; University of California, Berkeley, 1896-97. **Family:** Married 1) Bessie Maddern in 1900 (separated 1903; divorced 1905), two daughters; 2) Charmian Kittredge in 1905, one daughter. **Career:** Worked in a cannery in Oakland, 1889-90; oyster "pirate," then member of the California Fisheries Patrol, 1891-92; sailor on the *Sophia Sutherland,* sailing to Japan and Siberia, 1893; returned to Oakland, wrote for the local paper, and held various odd jobs, 1893-94; tramped the United States and Canada, 1894-96; arrested for vagrancy in Niagara Falls, New York; joined the gold rush to the Klondike, 1897-98, then returned to Oakland and became a full-time writer; visited London, 1902; war correspondent in the Russo-Japanese War for the San Francisco *Examiner,* 1904; moved to a ranch in Sonoma County, California, 1906; attempted to sail around the world on a 45-foot yacht, 1907-09; war correspondent in Mexico, 1914. **Died:** 22 November 1916.

PUBLICATIONS

Collections

Short Stories, edited by Maxwell Geismar. 1960.
(*Works*; Fitzroy Edition), edited by I.O. Evans. 18 vols., 1962-68.
The Bodley Head London, edited by Arthur Calder-Marshall. 4 vols., 1963-66; as *The Pan London,* 2 vols., 1966-68.
Novels and Stories (Library of America), edited by Donald Pizer. 1982.
Novels and Social Writings (Library of America), edited by Donald Pizer. 1984.
The Complete Short Stories of Jack London. 1993.
Jack London: Stories. 1994.
The Portable Jack London. 1994.

Short Stories

The Son of the Wolf: Tales of the Far North. 1900; as *An Odyssey of the North,* 1915.

The God of His Fathers and Other Stories. 1901; as *The God of His Fathers: Tales of the Klondike,* 1902.
Children of the Frost. 1902.
The Faith of Men and Other Stories. 1904.
Tales of the Fish Patrol. 1905.
Moon-Face and Other Stories. 1906.
The Apostate (story). 1906.
Love of Life and Other Stories. 1907.
The Road. 1907.
Lost Face. 1910.
When God Laughs and Other Stories. 1911.
South Sea Tales. 1911.
The Strength of the Strong (story). 1911.
The House of Pride and Other Tales of Hawaii. 1912.
A Son of the Sun. 1912; as *The Adventures of Captain Grief,* 1954.
Smoke Bellew. 1912; as *Smoke and Shorty,* 1920.
The Dream of Debs (story). 1912(?).
The Night-Born . . . . 1913.
The Strength of the Strong (collection). 1914.
The Turtles of Tasman. 1916.
The Human Drift. 1917.
The Red One. 1918.
On the Makaloa Mat. 1919; as *Island Tales,* 1920.
Dutch Courage and Other Stories. 1922.
Tales of Adventure, edited by Irving Shepard. 1956.
Stories of Hawaii, edited by A. Grove Day. 1965.
Great Short Works, edited by Earle Labor. 1965.
Goliah: A Utopian Essay. 1973.
Curious Fragments: London's Tales of Fantasy Fiction, edited by Dale L. Walker. 1975.
The Science Fiction of London, edited by Richard Gid Powers. 1975.
The Unabridged London, edited by Lawrence Teacher and Richard E. Nicholls. 1981.
London's Yukon Women. 1982.
Young Wolf: The Early Adventure Stories, edited by Howard Lachtman. 1984.
In a Far Country: London's Western Tales, edited by Dale L. Walker. 1986.
To Build a Fire and Other Stories. 1995.
The Scarlet Plague and Other Stories. 1995.
Northland Stories. 1997.

Novels

The Cruise of the Dazzler. 1902.
A Daughter of the Snows. 1902.
The Kempton-Wace Letters, with Anna Strunsky. 1903.
The Call of the Wild. 1903.
The Sea-Wolf. 1904.
The Game. 1905.
White Fang. 1906.
Before Adam. 1907.
The Iron Heel. 1908.
Martin Eden. 1909.
Burning Daylight. 1910.
Adventure. 1911.
The Abysmal Brute. 1913.
John Barleycorn. 1913; as *John Barleycorn; or, Alcoholic Memoirs,* 1914.
The Valley of the Moon. 1913.

The Mutiny of the Elsinore. 1914.
The Scarlet Plague. 1915.
The Jacket (The Star Rover). 1915, as *The Star Rover,* 1915.
The Little Lady of the Big House. 1916.
Jerry of the Islands. 1917.
Michael, Brother of Jerry. 1917.
Hearts of Three. 1918.
The Assassination Bureau Ltd., completed by Robert L. Fish. 1963.

Plays

The Great Interrogation, with Lee Bascom (produced 1905).
Scorn of Women. 1906.
Theft. 1910.
The Acorn-Planters: A California Forest Play . . . . 1916.
Daughters of the Rich, edited by James E. Sisson. 1971.
Gold, with Herbert Heron, edited by James E. Sisson. 1972.

Other

The People of the Abyss. 1903.
The Tramp. 1904.
The Scab. 1904.
London: A Sketch of His Life and Work. 1905.
War of the Classes. 1905.
What Life Means to Me. 1906.
The Road. 1907.
London: Who He Is and What He Has Done. 1908(?).
Revolution. 1909.
Revolution and Other Essays. 1910.
The Cruise of the Snark. 1911.
London by Himself. 1913.
London's Essays of Revolt, edited by Leonard D. Abbott. 1926.
London, American Rebel: A Collection of His Social Writings . . . ., edited by Philip S. Foner. 1947.
Letters from London, Containing an Unpublished Correspondence Between London and Sinclair Lewis, edited by King Hendricks and Irving Shepard. 1965.
London Reports: War Correspondence, Sports Articles, and Miscellaneous Writings, edited by King Hendricks and Irving Shepard. 1970.
London's Articles and Short Stories in the (Oakland) High School Aegis, edited by James E. Sisson. 1971.
No Mentor But Myself: A Collection of Articles, Essays, Reviews, and Letters on Writing and Writers, edited by Dale L. Walker. 1979.
Revolution: Stories and Essays, edited by Robert Barltrop. 1979.
London on the Road: The Tramp Diary and Other Hobo Writings, edited by Richard W. Etulain. 1979.
Sporting Blood: Selections from London's Greatest Sports Writing, edited by Howard Lachtman. 1981.
London's California: The Golden Poppy and Other Writings, edited by Sal Noto. 1986.
The Letters of Jack London, edited by Earle Labor and others. 3 vols. 1988.
The Yukon Writings of Jack London. 1996.

*

Bibliography: *London: A Bibliography* by Hensley C. Woodbridge, John London, and George H. Tweney, 1966, supplement by Woodbridge, 1973; in *Bibliography of American Literature* by Jacob Blanck, 1969; *The Fiction of London: A Chronological Bibliography* by Dale L. Walker and James E. Sisson, 1972; *London: A Reference Guide* by Joan R. Sherman, 1977.

Critical Studies: *London: A Biography* by Richard O'Connor, 1964; *London and the Klondike: The Genesis of an American Writer* by Franklin Walker, 1966; *The Alien Worlds of London* by Dale L. Walker, 1973; *London* by Earle Labor, 1974; *White Logic: London's Short Stories* by James I. McClintock, 1975; *London: The Man, The Writer, The Rebel* by Robert Barltrop, 1976; *Jack: A Biography of London* by Andrew Sinclair, 1977; *London: Essays in Criticism* edited by Ray Wilson Ownbey, 1978; *London: An American Myth* by John Perry, 1981; *Solitary Comrade: London and His Work* by Joan D. Hedrick, 1982; *The Novels of London: A Reappraisal* by Charles N. Watson, Jr., 1983; *Critical Essays on London* edited by Jacqueline Tavernier-Courbin, 1983; *London* by Gorman Beauchamp, 1984; *London: An American Radical?* by Carolyn Johnston, 1984; *California Writers: Jack London, John Steinbeck; The Tough Guys* by Stoddard Martin, 1985; *London, Adventures, Ideas, and Fiction* by James Lundquist, 1987; *American Dreamers: Charmian and London* by Clarice Stasz, 1988; *Jack London: A Definitive Chronology* by Russ Kingman, 1992; *Standing Room Only: Jack London's Controversial Career As a Public Speaker* by Mark E. Zamen, 1993; *Call of the Wild: A Naturalistic Romance* by Jacqueline Tavernier-Courbin, 1994; *Jack London: A Life* by Alex Kershaw, 1997; *Complicity and Resistance in Jack London's Novels: From Naturalism to Nature* by Christopher Gair, 1997.

* * *

Jack London was a talented writer so caught up in certain myths that they were part of what destroyed him. The illegitimate son of an impoverished spiritualist, Flora Wellman, he early learned self-reliance. Although he attended high school and, briefly, college, he was largely self-educated. London's university was the world he experienced and subsequently wrote about: San Francisco Bay, first as an oyster pirate and then as a member of the State Fish Patrol; the Pacific, the Orient, and the Bering Sea as an able seaman on a schooner hunting seals; the nation, across which he tramped as a vagabond; Alaska, where he prospected for gold; and California, where eventually he was a wealthy landowner burdened by the problems of maintaining a large ranch. London saw himself as an exemplar of the rags-to-riches story, an Anglo-Saxon superman who succeeded because of his superior intelligence and physical prowess, who took pride in his individualism, yet sympathized with the masses and believed that some form of socialism was the cure for the inequities of capitalist society.

To assert that his deprived childhood and his personal adventures were central to his development is not to deny that he was profoundly influenced by what he read as a young man. Early in his adolescence he delved into the seminal thinkers of the nineteenth century; his biographer Andrew Sinclair writes that during a winter in the Alaskan Klondike London absorbed "the books that became the bedrock of his thought and writing, underlying even the socialism which was his faith." Among London's readings that winter were the works of Darwin, Thomas Huxley, Spencer, and Kipling. "Charles Darwin and Herbert Spencer, messiahs of the new creed, became his intellectual mentors, along with Frederick Nietzsche and Karl Marx," Charles Child Walcutt wrote in a pamphlet about London, declaring that the author's struggles came to seem to himself "an epitome of the Darwinian Struggle for Existence, his success an example of the Spencerian Survival of the Fittest." Natural laws governed everything, London decided, so his problem became to reconcile the unimportance of the individual in a Darwinian universe and the Marxist certainty of social revolution with his equal certainty that he had the force and intelligence to rise above his fellow men.

His writing constantly reflects these contradictory beliefs, sometimes emphasizing one, sometimes another. In a succession of essays, short stories, novels, plays, travel books, and autobiographical tracts—during his forty years of life he wrote more than fifty books, too many for them all to be good—he portrayed the immutable laws of nature and man's need for community, while at the same time creating heroic figures who dominated both people and environment. As London's success grew, he heeded his socialist beliefs less, ultimately in his fiction painting what he liked to think were self-portraits of supermen defying the forces of nature and the demands of capitalism or of the masses. At his best London was able to hold these contradictions in balance; and technically his work, as **H.L. Mencken** wrote in *Prejudices: First Series,* contained "all the elements of sound fiction: clear thinking, a sense of character, the dramatic instinct, and, above all, the adept putting together of words—words charming and slyly significant, words arranged, in the French phrase, for the respiration and the ear." But finally his techniques could not sustain work that had lost its thematic equilibrium. He was an individualist, not a socialist. His lip service to socialism, wrote Walcutt, was a "protest against his early poverty"; London, he added, never dwelled on what might be the benefits of socialism.

London's heroes and heroines are individualists who survive the challenges of nature and society if they are strong enough, or are defeated if they are not—or, one might add, if London was pained by his socialist conscience. Thus in what is perhaps his best and best known story, *The Call of the Wild,* the powerful dog Buck, snatched from an easy life and submitted to brutal treatment and a harsh environment in the Klondike, survives because he is the superior individual. Buck, returned to the world of his ancestors, eventually runs with a pack of wolves, but he is at their head, where his intelligence and strength have put him. Wolf Larsen, the superman figure of *The Sea-Wolf,* both attracts and repels the beautiful, fragile poetess Maud Brewster and the effete Humphrey Van Weyden, whom Larsen rescues aboard his ship, the *Ghost.* Antagonized by Larsen, the two escape to an island, only to have him reappear aboard the wrecked *Ghost.* The arrogant individualist Larsen eventually dies, but it is his strength and skill that are admirable; the other two survive because they become strong like Wolf, yet lack his utter egotism. London would later assert that his point had been that a Wolf Larsen could not survive in modern society; but clearly he empathized with the arch-individualist, and Van Weyden's victory comes only after he has assimilated Larsen's qualities.

Another of London's heroes, Martin Eden, would die because of his individualism, but his death by suicide seems gratuitous, not, as London claimed, the result of Eden's believing in nothing and not accepting the socialism the author professed to favor. London could not portray a socialist state even before he abandoned socialism, which he did in his fiction when—as in the novels *Burning Daylight, The Valley of the Moon,* and *The Little Lady of the Big House*—he blatantly espoused Aryan superman and escape from the urban masses. His socialist novel *The Iron Heel* takes the form of a text discovered long after socialism has triumphed. What the novel describes, however, is not a socialist utopia, but the violent rise of a repressive totalitarian state opposed by small cadres of insurgents led by a blond superman, Ernest Everhard. By 1914, when London reported for *Collier* magazine on the revolution in Mexico, he "no longer spoke as the compassionate revolutionary," notes Andrew Sinclair, "but as the racist and jingoist supporter of the American oil interests—a man of property, a man used to servants, who was echoing the views of other men used to property and servants."

London died in 1916, by then severely ill and depressed by the recognition that he could not live out the myths he portrayed in his fiction. Still, he had not failed; his best work is vivid and dramatic; and his hyperbole, if annoying, nevertheless tells the reader much about United States culture.

—Townsend Ludington

See the essay on *The Call of the Wild.*

LONGFELLOW, Henry Wadsworth

Born: Portland, Maine, 27 February 1807. **Education:** Bowdoin College, Brunswick, Maine, 1822-25, graduated 1825. **Family:** Married 1) Mary Potter in 1831 (died 1835); 2) Frances Appleton in 1843 (died 1861), two sons and four daughters. **Career:** Appointed to new chair of modern languages, Bowdoin College on condition he study abroad for a further three years: sent by trustees to Europe, 1826-29; taught at Bowdoin College, 1829-35; sent to Germany by Harvard University, Cambridge, Massachusetts, 1835; Smith Professor of Modern Languages, Harvard University, 1836-54; visited Europe, 1842 and 1868-69. **Awards:** Honorary degrees: Cambridge University, 1868; Oxford University, 1869. **Died:** 24 March 1882.

PUBLICATIONS

Collections

The Works and Final Memorials, edited by Samuel Longfellow. 14 vols., 1886-87.
Works. 10 vols., 1909.
The Essential Longfellow, edited by Lewis Leary. 1963.
Letters, edited by Andrew Hilen. 6 vols., 1966-83.

Poetry

Voices of the Night. 1839.
Ballads and Other Poems. 1842.
Poems on Slavery. 1842.
Poems. 1845.
The Belfry of Bruges and Other Poems. 1845.
Evangeline: A Tale of Acadie. 1847.
Poems, Lyrical and Dramatic. 1848.
The Seaside and the Fireside. 1849.
The Golden Legend. 1851.
The Song of Hiawatha. 1855.
Poetical Works. 1858.

The Courtship of Miles Standish and Other Poems. 1858.
Tales of a Wayside Inn. 1863.
Noel (in French). 1864.
Household Poems. 1865.
Flower-de-Lace. 1867.
The New England Tragedies. 1868.
Poetical Works. 1868.
The Divine Tragedy. 1871.
Three Books of Song. 1872.
Christus: A Mystery (includes *The Divine Tragedy, The Golden Legend, The New England Tragedies*). 1872.
Poetical Works. 1872; revised edition, 1875, 1880, 1883.
Aftermath. 1873.
The Hanging of the Crane. 1874.
The Masque of Pandora and Other Poems. 1875.
Keramos and Other Poems. 1878.
The Early Poems, edited by Richard Herne Shepherd. 1878.
Ultima Thule. 1880; *In the Harbor: Ultima Thule—Part II,* 1882.
Michael Angelo. 1884.
Boyhood Poems, edited by Ray W. Pettengill. 1925.

Play

The Spanish Student (produced 1895). 1843.

Fiction

Hyperion: A Romance (includes verse). 1839.
Kavanagh: A Tale. 1849.

Other

Syllabus de la Grammaire Italienne. 1832.
Outre-Mer: A Pilgrimage Beyond the Sea, numbers 1-2. 2 vols., 1833-34; vol. 2, 1835; revised edition, 1851.
Prose Works. 2 vols., 1857.
Complete Works, revised edition. 7 vols., 1866.

Editor, *Manuel de Proverbes Dramatiques.* 1830; revised edition, 1830, 1832.
Editor and Translator, *Elements of French Grammar,* by Lhomond. 1830.
Editor, *French Exercises.* 1830.
Editor, *Novelas Espanolas.* 1830.
Editor, *Le Ministre de Wakefield,* by Oliver Goldsmith, translated by T.E.G. Hennequin. 1831.
Editor, *Saggi de' Novellieri Italiani d'Ogni Secolo.* 1832.
Editor, *The Waif: A Collection of Poems.* 1845.
Editor, *The Poets and Poetry of Europe.* 1845; revised edition, 1871.
Editor, *The Estray: A Collection of Poems.* 1846.
Editor, with George Nichols and John Owen, *The Works of Charles Sumner.* 10 vols., 1870-83.
Editor, *Poems of Places: England,* 4 vols.; *Ireland,* 1 vol.; *Scotland,* 3 vols.; *France,* 2 vols.; *Italy,* 3 vols.; *Spain,* 2 vols.; *Switzerland,* 1 vol.; *Germany,* 2 vols.; *Greece,* 1 vol.; *Russia,* 1 vol.; *Asia,* 3 vols.; *Africa,* 1 vol.; *America,* 6 vols.; *Oceanica,* 1 vol. 31 vols., 1876-79.

Translator, *Coplas de Don Jorge Manrique.* 1833.
Translator, *The Divine Comedy,* by Dante. 3 vols., 1867.

*

Bibliography: in *Bibliography of American Literature* by Jacob Blanck, 1969.

Critical Studies: *The Life of Longfellow, with Extracts from His Journals and Correspondence* by Samuel Longfellow, 2 vols., 1886; *Young Longfellow (1807-1843)* by Lawrance Thompson, 1938; *Longfellow and Scandinavia: A Study of the Poet's Relationship with the Northern Languages and Literature* by Andrew Hilen, 1947; *Longfellow: A Full-Length Portrait,* 1955, *Longfellow: Portrait of an American Humanist,* 1966, and *Longfellow,* 1985, all by Edward Wagenknecht; *Longfellow: His Life and Work* by Newton Arvin, 1963; *Longfellow* by Cecil B. Williams, 1964; *Longfellow* by Edward L. Hirsch, 1964; *Longfellow Reconsidered: A Symposium* edited by J. Chesley Mathews, 1970; *Semiotics, Romanticism, and the Scriptures* by Jacques Chevalier, 1990; *A Victorian American: Henry Wadsworth Longfellow* by Herbert S. Gorman, 1992; "A Social Necessity: The Friendship of Sherwood Bonner and Henry Wadsworth Longfellow" by Lisa Pater Faranda, in *Patrons and Protegees: Gender, Friendship, and Writing in Nineteenth-Century America* edited by Shirley Marchalonis, 1994; "References in Longfellow's Journals (1856-1882) to Charles Dickens" by Edward L. Tucker, in *Dickens Studies Annual,* 1996, pp. 197-214; "Mars in Petticoats: Longfellow and Sentimental Masculinity" by Eric L. Haralson, in *Nineteenth Century Literature,* December 1996, pp. 327-56.

*   *   *

Some writers survive for the wrong reasons, like nostalgia or derision; some survive despite their defects, like prolixity or sentimentality; some survive—or deserve to—because of a small body of modest work culled long after the 'fact of popularity. Henry Wadsworth Longfellow belongs in all three categories.

No American writer was so admired, even revered, during his life; no writer has been so ridiculed subsequently. From 1839, when "A Psalm of Life" first moved his readers—as heavily influenced as the poem itself by Victorian and Puritan attitudes—to embrace its homilies ("Heart within, and God o'erhead!"), until his death in 1882, the decorous optimism of Longfellow's lyrics and the monotonous drone of his narrative poems stood him in high esteem. **Oliver Wendell Holmes** may have best defined Longfellow's appeal to his contemporaries: "a soft voice, a sweet and cheerful temper, a receptive rather than aggressive intelligence . . . ." This may, however, be a more damning indictment of the limitations of popular taste than of the poet's achievement. Longfellow's sympathetic biographer, Newton Arvin, proposed that we "agree, once for all that he was a minor writer." Still, in the classroom at least, the myth of Longfellow's significance persists, and probably rather more than fewer students have turned away from poetry because of some educator's insistence on perpetuating the lie.

Longfellow's lack of variety and seeming inability either to escape conventional metrics or to bring any originality to them always hampered him; moreover, he did not easily judge the prosody best suited to his materials. At the age of thirteen, he had published his first poem in the Portland *Gazette,* "The Battle of Lovell Pond," hammered out in anapestic couplets with mathematical regularity. He never really advanced far in technical proficiency after that. His earliest successes—"The Skeleton in Armour," "The Wreck of the Hesperus," and the quintessential "Excelsior"— suffer from this limitation. When, as in the last poem, the subject is "inspirational," he invites derision; and "higher" in its Latin comparative form is easily translated into shredded packing material— and not only by schoolboys who do not know their Latin. Longfellow was technically endowed to write light verse, had he possessed the sense of humor to do so, for he is not without extraordinary invention in manipulating syntax to suit his rhythms; and his inexhaustible command of rhyme, if employed for amusement, might not so easily undermine the content. At the zenith of his career, Longfellow beat his *Evangeline* into submission in jiggling dactylic hexameters. This popular narrative traces the wanderings of a girl from Acadia (Nova Scotia) in search of her lost lover. Finally, after many remarkable adventures, she becomes a kind of nun in Pennsylvania in her old age, only to meet her lover on his death bed. This "first genuine . . . fount which burst from the soil of America," called by one critic "one of the decisive poems of the world," sold 36,000 copies in its first ten years. *The Song of Hiawatha* did even better: 30,000 copies in six months. This pseudo-epic traces the development of an American Indian from birth to immortality: fathered by the West Wind; educated by nature and animals; loved by the beautiful Minnehaha; given mythic significance in his killing of an underwater monster, with the assistance of a helpful squirrel; sobered and matured by the deaths of Minnehaha (for whom he mourns seven days and seven nights) and his best friend (for whom he mourns seven times longer); and, finally, brought to a kind of metaphysical suicide— he simply gets in his canoe and starts paddling west—by the inevitable coming of the white race. Longfellow cramped this really promising material into 164 pages of four-trochee lines, likened by Oliver Wendell Holmes to the "normal rhythm of breathing" and by more than one high school student to tom-toms. At least *Hiawatha* didn't rhyme.

Longfellow wrote two inferior novels, *Hyperion* and *Kavanagh,* which offer some insight into his private life and attitudes toward religion, politics and literature. His single play, *The Spanish Student,* about a gypsy dancer named Preciosa (who turns out to be the long-lost daughter of a wealthy nobleman) and her chaste beau, suffers all the usual limitations of nineteenth-century melodrama. Although Longfellow had a successful career in education—he was one of the first modern language teachers, first at Bowdoin, then for 18 years at Harvard—his critical prose is distinguished by clarity rather than ingenuity or originality.

In spite of these several reservations, however, Longfellow wrote a number of valuable poems. In the sparse landscape of nineteenth-century American poetry, they grow sturdily. "Mezzo Camin," written in 1842 but not published until after his death, is a fine sonnet in which he laments his lack of significant poetic accomplishment. "The Cross of Snow," also unpublished during his life, and also a sonnet, is a touching tribute to his wife after her early death. Despite an insufferable circuitous dependent clause taking up all of its octet, the sonnet "Nature" ends superbly. A mother puts her child to bed: "So nature deals with us, and takes away/ Our playthings one by one, and by the hand/ Leads us to rest so gently, that we go/ Scarce knowing if we wish to go or stay,/ Being too full of sleep to understand/ How far the unknown transcends what we know." Its sustained imagery invites comparison with Whitman's "Goodbye, My Fancy," Emerson's "Terminus," and other epitaphic poems of the period. His ode to old age, "Morituri Salutamus," is especially valuable during the recent movement in America to recognize the oldest generation. "The Tide Rises, The Tide Falls" clearly anticipates Robert Frost's "Stopping by Woods on a Snowy Evening," even if less powerful

a poem. Finally, his less well-known "The Jewish Cemetery at Newport" deserves attention. Its inhabitants, "Taught in the school of patience to endure/ The Life of anguish and the death of fire," now abide in American soil, "not neglected; for a hand unseen,/ Scattering its bounty, like a summer rain,/ Still keeps their graves and their remembrance green." Probably there are other poems as well by this mild man that reflect, not without some distinction, the age of restraint and decorum for which they were written. Further, a skeleton in armor, a village smithy, a midnight ride by Paul Revere, even an arrow shot into the air, may introduce some beginning readers to some of the pleasures in poetry.

—Bruce Kellner

LONGSTREET, Augustus Baldwin

Born: Augusta, Georgia, 22 September 1790. **Education:** Waddell Academy, Willington, South Carolina, 1808-11; Yale University, New Haven, Connecticut, 1811-13, graduated 1813; studied law in Litchfield, Connecticut, 1813-14: admitted to Virginia bar, 1815. **Family:** Married Frances Eliza Parke in 1817 (died 1867); one son and two daughters. **Career:** Lawyer, Greensboro, Georgia, from 1817; member, Georgia Legislature, 1821; circuit judge, Superior Court of Georgia, 1822-25; moved to Augusta, Georgia, 1827; contributor, *Southern Recorder,* Milledgeville, Georgia, and various other newspapers, 1827-30; founding editor, *States Rights Sentinel,* Augusta, 1834-36; ordained Methodist minister, 1838; president, Emory College, Oxford, Georgia, 1839-48, Centenary College, Jackson, Louisiana, 1849, University of Mississippi, Oxford, 1849-56, and South Carolina College (now University of South Carolina), Columbia, 1857-65. Lived in Mississippi after 1865. **Awards:** LL.D.: Yale University, 1841. D.D.: University of Mississippi. **Died:** 9 July 1870.

PUBLICATIONS

Fiction and Sketches

Georgia Scenes, Characters, and Incidents, etc. 1835.
Master William Mitten; or, A Youth of Brilliant Talents Who Was Ruined by Bad Luck. 1864.
Stories with a Moral, Humorous and Descriptive of Southern Life a Century Ago, edited by Fitz. R. Longstreet. 1912.

Other

A Voice from the South (letters). 1847.

*

Bibliography: in *Bibliography of American Literature* by Jacob Blanck, 1973.

Critical Studies: *Judge Longstreet: A Life Sketch* by O.P. Fitzgerald, 1891 (includes letters and unpublished material); *Longstreet: A Study of the Development of Culture in the South* by John Donald Wade, 1924, edited by M. Thomas Inge, 1969; *Longstreet* by Kimball King, 1984; *The Tall Tale in American Folk-*

lore and Literature by Carolyn S. Brown, 1987; *Augustus Baldwin Longstreet's Georgia Scenes Complete: A Scholarly Text* (dissertation) by David Andrew Rachels, 1996; "Negotiating Community in Augustus Baldwin Longstreet's *Georgia Scenes*" by Scott Romine, in *Style,* Spring 1996, pp. 1-27; "Origins of American Literary Regionalism: Gender in Irving, Stowe, and Longstreet" by Marjorie Pryse, in *Breaking Boundaries: New Perspectives on Women's Regional Writing* edited by Sherrie Innes and Diana Royer, 1997.

*   *   *

Augustus Baldwin Longstreet's reputation rests primarily on *Georgia Scenes,* a collection of sketches and tales about life in Middle Georgia in the early nineteenth century. *Georgia Scenes* contrasted with the plantation literary tradition, which focused on wealthy slave-holding landowners. As a circuit-court judge, Longstreet visited many rural communities and collected humorous stories and anecdotes of rough but colorful country people. Their simple amusements such as barn dances, horse-swapping, and shooting matches are affectionately recorded, along with a slightly more brutal side of life (gander-pulling, fights, and political disputes). Overt cruelty and violence are generally overlooked. For example, in "The Fight" the maiming of the combatants is treated in an almost slapstick vein. In his close attention to physical details and settings and in his attempts to write colloquial dialogue, Longstreet anticipated the local color writers of the post-Civil War period. His best works, such as "Turn-Out," in which unruly country boys playfully "force" their schoolmaster to give them a day's vacation, are based on folk traditions and rituals and possess an archetypal power. Poe praised Longstreet because he was anxious to see American writers use native materials in their stories.

Longstreet was forty before he turned his hand to fiction. First his legal career, then his work as newspaper owner and editor, and later his ministry in the Methodist church took precedence over authorship. He sometimes feared his comic sketches were undignified; in fact, everything he wrote expressed firm religious beliefs and conservative political views. In *Georgia Scenes* his narrator, Hall, describes rural escapades, while the character Baldwin ridicules the affectations of newly rich townspeople. Both are aloof and frequently disapproving, like the author. Blacks, although they seldom appear in the stories, are treated comically or with contempt. Later essays, such as those collected in *A Voice from the South,* were devoted to defending slavery.

In his own day Longstreet was best known as the president of four different southern universities. Some of his experiences with students are included in his only novel, *Master William Mitten.* As a record of the times this neglected work is as informative as *Georgia Scenes;* and the author's characterizations of William and William's mother and uncle reveal a surer sense of satire and of the dynamics of family life than one finds in the earlier work. His essays on religious and political subjects and the posthumously collected tales in *Stories with a Moral* are elegantly phrased but discursive and tedious. He eventually considered himself more of a moral guide or social historian than a storyteller. Although some critics consider Longstreet a frontier humorist, he is primarily a southern writer, highly didactic, constructing a value system unique to his region.

—Kimball King

LOPEZ, Barry Holstun

Born: Port Chester, New York, 6 January 1945. **Education:** University of Notre Dame, A.B. (cum laude) 1966, M.A.T. 1968; University of Oregon, 1969-70. **Family:** Married Sandra Landers in 1967. **Career:** Beginning 1970 full-time writer. Associate at Gannett Foundation Media Center, New York City, 1985-; Distinguished Visiting Writer, Eastern Washington University, Cheney, Washington, 1985; Ida Beam Visiting Professor, University of Iowa, Iowa City, 1985; Distinguished Visiting Naturalist, Carleton College, Northfield, Minnesota, 1986; W. Harold and Martha Welch Visiting Professor, University of Notre Dame, 1989. Correspondent, *Outside* magazine, beginning 1982. **Awards:** John Burroughs Medal for distinguished natural history writing, Christopher Medal for humanitarian writing, and Pacific Booksellers award for excellence in nonfiction, and American Book award nomination, all for *Of Wolves and Men,* all 1980; Distinguished Recognition award, Friends of American writers, 1981; National Book award for nonfiction, Christopher Book award, Pacific Northwest Booksellers award, National Book Critics Circle nomination, *Los Angeles* book award nomination, American Library notable book citation, and American Library Association "Best Books for Young Adults" all for *Arctic Dreams: Imagination and Desire in a Northern Landscape,* all 1986; Award in Literature from American Academy and Institute of Arts and Letters, 1986; Parents' Choice award, for *Crow and Weasel,* 1990; Lannan Foundation award in nonfiction, for body of work, 1990; Governor's Award for Arts, 1990; Best Geographic Educational Article, National Council for Geographic Education, 1990; Award in fiction, pacific Northwest Booksellers, 1995. Honorary degrees: University of Portland, 1994.

PUBLICATIONS

Prose

Desert Notes: Reflections in the Eye of a Raven. 1976.
Giving Birth to Thunder, Sleeping with His Daughter: Coyote Builds North America. 1978.
Of Wolves and Men. 1978.
River Notes: The Dance of Herons. 1979.
Desert Reservation. 1980.
Winter Count. 1981.
Arctic Dreams: Imagination and Desire in a Northern Landscape. 1986.
Crossing Open Ground. 1988.
Crow and Weasel, illustrated by Tom Pohrt. 1990.
The Rediscovery of North America. 1991.
Field Notes: The Grace of the Canyon Wren. 1994.

*   *   *

"I want . . . to contribute to a literature of hope," Barry Lopez wrote in the introduction to his third collection of essays, *About This Life.* He found this hope in the infinite complexity and order of nature. Fascinated since boyhood by the landscape around him, Lopez has made it his life's work to reveal the vast wonder of the natural world—its majesty, beauty, and terror—to a culture that he believes is rapidly losing this knowledge.

In his personal essays and full-length works of nonfiction, Lopez combines a lucid interpretation of scientific information with a rare sense of wonder, never allowing his tone to become merely didactic. His meticulous research establishes a solid foundation for far-ranging explorations of moral and philosophical themes. In *Of Wolves and Men* (1978), for example, Lopez provided a comprehensive examination of the relationship between wolves and human societies. In addition to thorough scientific data, he included a wealth of references to folk and literary traditions that show how Western cultures project their own ambivalence onto these unjustly feared animals. In this way, Lopez argued, human beings have misunderstood wildlife and justified its abuse, sometimes to the point of extinction.

He broadened and deepened this theme in the acclaimed *Arctic Dreams: Imagination and Desire in a Northern Landscape* (1986). Here Lopez considered the meaning of an entire ecosystem—one that, to the untrained eye, might appear barren and devoid of interest. Yet, by comparing and contrasting the austere Arctic with the fecund tropics, where rainforests support huge numbers of species, Lopez showed a surprising reality. "Arctic ecosystems have the same elegant and Byzantine complexities, the same wild grace, as tropical ecosystems," he wrote. "[Their] complexities . . . lie not with, say, esoteric dietary preferences among 100 different kinds of ground beetle making a living on the same tropical acre, but with an intricacy of rhythmic response to extreme ranges of light and temperature. With the seasonal movement of large numbers of migratory animals. And with their adaptation to violent, but natural, fluctuations in their population levels." Lopez ruminated at length on each of these features, considering the dramatic physical and spiritual effects wrought by changes in amounts and types of light; the grandeur of icebergs, which he likened to gothic cathedrals; and the lives of the birds, seals, caribou, narwhals, and polar bears that live in or travel through the region. He considered, as well, the prospects for sustaining this wilderness against business interests—often ignorant of Arctic history or ecology—that seek to exploit the region's rich reserves of oil and gas. By giving as full an account of the Arctic landscape as possible, Lopez made it impossible for readers to revert to their previous misconceptions of the region as a frozen wasteland.

An awareness of the violence in nature is one of Lopez's important themes, for without it, he believes, a person's experience of the natural world is necessarily false, mitigated, and sentimentalized. This is part of the reason he is so fascinated by the Eskimo. "When I have thought about the ways in which they differ from people in my own culture," he wrote in *Arctic Dreams*, "I have realized that they are more afraid than we are. On a day-to-day basis, they have more fear. . . . They are afraid because they accept fully what is violent and tragic in nature." Yet Lopez was careful not to romanticize Eskimo attitudes. He pointed out that "there is murder and warfare and tribal vendetta in their history," as well as more contemporary problems such as alcohol and financial greed; nevertheless, he insisted that "a good reason to travel with Eskimo hunters in modern times is that . . . one feels the constant presence of people who know something about surviving."

His appreciation for distinct ecosystems and his respect for indigenous cultures has prompted Lopez to travel widely. He has explored undersea regions and deserts, has hunted and fished, and has accompanied both scientific expeditions and commercial pilots as they crossed the globe. Lopez has recounted these adventures in personal essays distinguished by their reverence for the natural world. In "Apologia," for example, collected in *About This Life*, Lopez described his compulsion to stop for dead animals he finds along the road: "I carry each one away from the pavement into a cover of grass or brush out of decency, I think. And worry. Who are these animals, their lights gone out? What journeys have fallen apart here?" Using an east-bound car trip as the essay's structural device, Lopez described his grief for the loss of animal life: "In Idaho I hit a young sage sparrow—*thwack* against the right fender in the very split second I see it . . . I rest the walloped bird in my left hand, my right thumb pressed to its chest. I feel for the wail of the heart. Its eyes glisten like rain on crystal. Nothing but warmth. I shut the tiny eyelids and lay it beside a clump of bunchgrass . . . I nod before I go, a ridiculous gesture, out of simple grief."

Similar themes also inform Lopez's short stories, many of which are based on the mythology of Native American cultures. But even stories with contemporary settings often feature encounters with the natural world. In "The Negro in the Kitchen," for example, included in *Field Notes,* the narrator finds an articulate, educated African American in his kitchen one morning. This man explains that he has walked across the United States. "I needed to see the breadth of the land," he tells his host. "To be in it. To hold it and be held by it." "The Entreaty of the Wiideema" is the story of an anthropologist's encounter with an ancient Australian hunting culture. In contrast to the ironic tone and the emphasis on characterization found in much contemporary fiction, these pieces share elements more typical of folklore or myth.

Describing the process through which his own writing developed, Lopez remembers the advice he once gave an aspiring novice: "Read. Find out what you truly believe. Get away from the familiar." The effects of this counsel are evident in the erudition, moral conviction, and far-ranging experience that Lopez brings so consistently to his work.

—Elizabeth Shostak

LORDE, Audre (Geraldine)

Pseudonym: Rey Domini. **Born:** New York City, 18 February 1934. **Education:** National University of Mexico, 1954; Hunter College (now Hunter College of the City University of New York), B.A. 1960; Columbia University, New York City, M.L.S. 1962. **Family:** Married Edwin Ashley Rollins in 1962 (divorced 1972); one son, one daughter. **Career:** Librarian, Mount Vernon Public Library, Mount Vernon, New York, 1961-63; head librarian, Town School Library, New York City, 1966-68; lecturer in creative writing, City College, New York City, 1968; lecturer in education department, Herbert H. Lehman College, Bronx, New York, 1969-70; associate professor of English, John Jay College of Criminal Justice, New York City, beginning 1970; professor of English, Hunter College, New York City, 1981-87, Thomas Hunter Professor, 1987-92. Visiting professor, Tougaloo University, Tougaloo, Mississippi, and Atlanta University, Atlanta, Georgia, both 1968. Visiting lecturer throughout the United States, Europe, Africa, and Australia. Founder, Kitchen Table: Women of Color Press and Sisterhood in Support of Sisters in South Africa. Poetry editor, *Chrysalis* and *Amazon Quarterly.* Contributor of short fiction to *Venture* magazine as Rey Domini. **Awards:** National Endowment for the Arts grants, 1968, 1981; Creative Artists Public Service grant, 1972, 1976; National Book award nominee, 1974; American Library Association Gay Caucus Book award, 1981, for *The Cancer Journals;* Borough of Manhattan President's award, 1987, for literary excellence; Before Columbus Foundation's American Book award, 1989; Triangle Publications Group's Bill Whitehead award for lifetime contribution to literature, 1990; Sappho award for contribution to literature on multicultural lesbian identity, 1990; Fund for Free Expression award, 1991; named New York State Poet Laureate, 1992. Honorary doctorates: Oberlin College; Haverford College; State University of New York at Binghampton. **Died:** 20 November 1992.

PUBLICATIONS

Collection

The Collected Poems of Audre Lorde. 1997.

Poetry

The First Cities. 1968.
Cables to Rage. 1970.
From a Land Where Other People Live. 1973.
The New York Head Shop and Museum. 1974.
Coal. 1976.
Between Our Selves. 1976.
The Black Unicorn. 1978.
Chosen Poems, Old and New. 1982; revised as *Undersong: Chosen Poems Old and New,* 1992.
Our Dead behind Us. 1986.
The Marvelous Arithmetics of Distance: Poems, 1987-1992. 1993.

Essays

Sister Outsider: Essays and Speeches. 1984.
A Burst of Light: Essays. 1988.

Other

Uses of the Erotic: The Erotic as Power. 1978.
The Cancer Journals (personal diary). 1980.
Zami: A New Spelling of My Name. 1982.

*

Bibliography: *Modern American Woman Poets* by Jean Gould, 1985.

Critical Studies: "Nothing Safe: The Poetry of Audre Lorde" by Joan Larkin, in *Margins* August 1975; "On the Edge of the Estate" by Sandra M. Gilbert, in *Poetry,* 1977; "Interview with Audre Lorde" by Anita Cornwell, in *Sinister Wisdom,* Fall 1977; interview with Deborah Wood, in *In the Memory and Spirit of Frances, Zora, and Lorraine: Essays and Interviews on Black Women and Writing,* 1979; interview with Karla M. Hammond, in *Denver Quarterly,* Spring 1981; "The Re-Vision of the Muse: Unnaming and Renaming in the Poetry of Audre Lorde, Pat Parker, Sylvia Plath, and Adrienne Rich" by Pamela Annas, in *Hudson Review,* Summer 1983; "No More Buried Lives: The Theme of Lesbianism in Lorde, Naylor, Shange, Walker" by Barbara Chris-

tian, in *Feminist Issues,* Spring 1985; "The Black Woman as Artist and Critic: Four Versions" by Margaret B. MacDowell, in *Kentucky Review,* Spring 1987; *Women Reading Women Writing: Self-Invention in Paula Gunn Allen, Gloria Anzaldúa, and Audre Lorde* by AnaLouise Keating, 1996.

*   *   *

One of the most extraordinary facets of the explosion of gay and lesbian literature since the Stonewall Riots in 1969 is the multitude of ways in which the common experiences of the community have been drawn, sung, and celebrated in poetry and prose. Of less prominence, until later, has been that body of writing addressing the needs, dreams, and hopes of gay men and lesbians outside mainstream homosexual culture. While some of this exclusion has been the result of a conscious choice on the part of group members—such as adherents of the Radical Faerie philosophy— often this marginalization is due to the reflection, within the homosexual world, of attitudes and trends prevalent in society at large. The most powerful of these have been racism and discrimination against women—as challengers of social limits and often on the basis of their status and sexual orientation. While writings by openly gay black men have eventually become a recognized part of the literature (with such anthologies as Joseph Beam's *In the Life,* for example), black women have possessed a visible and active presence in the creation of the current homosexual world almost from its birth through both their willingness to challenge accepted liberationist philosophies and the power of their individual and collective voices. One of the first and most influential of these voices was that of Audre Lorde.

Lorde was born in New York City in 1934; she was raised to fit the mold of many young women maturing in that metropolitan area. She enrolled at the National University of Mexico in 1954 and continued her postsecondary education at Hunter College and Columbia University, where she received her bachelor's degree and her professional certification in the field of librarianship in 1961. Lorde joined the staff of the Mount Vernon Public Library, the first in a series of positions that over the next three decades would expose her to the disparate influences of Saint Clare's School of Nursing, Lehman College, City College of the City University of New York, and the John Jay College of Criminal Justice. Her marriage to Edward A. Rollins in 1962 completed the matrix out of which her public sharing of private insights, griefs, and fierce joys would soon begin to arise in her first book of verse. The diversity of her creative gifts would prove to be well matched to the breadth of issues facing the communities of lesbians, women, and African Americans that she would address in her personal essays, journals, and especially in her vital and intense poetry.

To understand a written work, the reader must have a clear picture of its author's vision—of the private road he or she has followed in developing both as an artist and a human being. Lorde presents a particularly complex picture due to the wide variety of causes and environments she experienced. Nowhere in her work is this more openly presented than in her 1982 volume *Zami: A New Spelling of My Name.* In an interview with Mari Evans for the 1984 publication *Black Women Writers: A Critical Evaluation,* Lorde noted that she began to write because there was no visible source to channel the pain that accompanied her gradual comprehension of the world. *Zami* is perhaps the most coherent expression of this, telling a dual story of her life from childhood in Harlem before World War II to her completion of higher education in 1962 and the coalescence of her identities as both lesbian and aware black woman in America. Lorde's characterization of the text as a new species of writing, a "biomythography," is in keeping with her adoption of—and seeking for—traditional ancestral beliefs and symbols from prior generations of women.

This search had a particularly personal aspect for her, a granddaughter of the Caribbean island of Grenada, as she recalled the tales her mother told her of the ways of the offshore island of Carriacou where she had been raised prior to immigrating to New York City. In some ways, the key to Lorde's entire career as a writer and activist lies in a description of her mother's island home on the opening page of *Zami.* "This is the country of my foremothers, my fore-bearing mothers, those Black island women who defined themselves by what they did." Self-definition through chosen actions and open admittance of the joys and sorrows of making those choices is a thread common to much of Lorde's work. Even the title reflects her choice to claim her heritage; as Lorde writes in the book, "Zami" is "a Carriacou name for women who work together as friends and lovers," a beautifully apt term for the fusion and fashioning of diverse cultures evident in all her works. The book is also representative of a more limited group of lesbian autobiographies, foreshadowing later works such as Holly Near's 1990 work *Fire In the Rain, Singer in the Storm* and *Long Time Passing: Lives of Older Lesbians,* a collection published in 1986.

Lorde's two volumes of essays and speeches, *Sister Outsider* and *A Burst of Light,* provide the reader with both a window into the continuing growth of her consciousness as lesbian and activist and a bridge into the deepening power of her poetic voice. The first, *Sister Outsider,* contains fifteen selections written or delivered between 1976 and 1983, including an extended interview and self-analysis conducted with fellow lesbian poet Adrienne Rich. Of the essays, the text of a paper given at the Modern Language Association's December 1977 meeting in Chicago as part of the "Lesbian and Literature" panel is particularly valuable for comprehension of Lorde's deeply personal visions. Other papers touch upon topics such as the creative uses to which anger can be put as a generator of change, the concept of "the personal as political," and eroticism as a source of power for women. *Sister Outsider*'s 1988 successor, *A Burst of Light,* presents five shorter essays dealing with Lorde's first three years of living with cancer, her views on the discussion of sadomasochism within the lesbian community (represented by such writers as Pat Califia), frank and moving opinions on being a lesbian mother, and the comparative situation of African Americans and the blacks of South Africa under apartheid. Readers of black lesbian and gay writings of any political slant will find the third essay "I Am Your Sister: Black Women Organizing across Sexualities" valuable for the links it establishes with other major writers such as **Langston Hughes**, Alice Dunbar-Nelson, and Angelina Weld Grimke and the perspective it provides on the emergence of contemporary male poets such as Essex Hemphill and Assoto Saint.

Lorde's encounters with the pain of cancer and mastectomy may also be traced through the pages of the 1980 prose collection *The Cancer Journals,* which she termed "a piece of meaning words on cancer as it affects my life and my consciousness as a woman, a black lesbian feminist mother." Recognition of the place of such a testament in lesbian literature came with the designation of *The Cancer Journals* as the American Library Association's Gay Task Force Book of the Year for 1981.

The truest voice of Lorde will, however, be found in her poetry, for as she stated in the opening line of her 1977 essay *The*

Transformation of Silence into Language and Action: "I have come to believe over and over again that what is most important to me must be spoken, made verbal and shared, even at the risk of having it bruised or misunderstood." Beginning with her earliest book, 1968's *The First Cities*—written while she was the recipient of a grant from the National Endowment for the Arts—she focused a sharp eye of language on life and love, including her lesbian relationships. Three of her collections, *Cables to Rage, From a Land Where Other People Live,* and *New York Head Shop and Museum* were published in the 1970s by Detroit's Broadside Press, one of the centers of publication for new African American poets such as **Nikki Giovanni**. It would be these editions of Lorde's work that would begin to bring her influence to the wider audience of black lesbian writers, as exemplified by the early writings of California lesbian poet Pat Parker. The imagery in *The First Cities* and *Cables to Rage* is a blend of uniquely spicy twists of language and topics central to life as a black person in America at that time. These works would come to be recognized as some of the most vital contributions to the black arts movement, and the poems of these first volumes would later be collected and published under the title *Coal* in 1976. Perhaps most significant for the history of modern black gay and lesbian poetry is "Martha," which one critic noted as "the first poetic expression of Lorde's homosexuality."

A Creative Artists Public Service grant in 1972 provided the basis for generating her third book of poetry, *From a Land Where Other People Live,* published in 1973. Its lines express a maturation of the anger over injustices that had been present in *Cables to Rage,* as well as addressing more fully the author's identity as an African American woman and differing dimensions as mother, sister, and teacher. A nomination for the National Book Award for poetry for the year also served to further widen public awareness of Lorde as a leading feminist voice. Her fourth book, the 1974 *New York Head Shop and Museum,* is perhaps the most overtly political, using her visions of New York City as a matrix to explore her radical political views, foretelling the depth and power of such volumes as 1978's *The Black Unicorn.* Through her founding of Kitchen Table: Women of Color Press and work as poetry editor of *Chrysalis* and *Amazon Quarterly,* Lorde attempted to provide the rising generations of women writers who would follow her the venue she had not been able to find for the literary reflection of her inner selves.

Indefatigable in both claiming her life and cherishing her many-faceted insights, Lorde's honors included being named poet laureate of New York State in 1992. She died at her home on St. Croix in the Virgin Islands in late November 1992, a victim of the liver cancer she had lived with for more than a decade.

—Robert B. Marks Ridinger

LOVECRAFT, H(oward) P(hillips)

Born: Providence, Rhode Island, 20 August 1890. **Education:** Educated by tutors at home, at a local elementary school, and Hope Street High School, Providence, 1904-05, 1907-08. **Family:** Married Sonia Greene in 1924 (divorced 1929). **Career:** Freelance writer from 1908, working as a ghostwriter and, after 1918, a revisionist; astrology columnist, Providence *Evening News,* 1914-18; active in the amateur journalism movement from 1914: published

The Conservative, 1915-19, 1923, and President of the United Amateur Press Association, 1917-18, 1923; regular contributor to *Weird Tales* after 1923. **Died:** 15 March 1937.

PUBLICATIONS

Collections

Collected Poems. 1963; abridged edition, as *Fungi from Yuggoth and Other Poems,* 1971.
Selected Letters 1911-1937, edited by August Derleth and Donald Wandrei. 5 vols., 1965-76.
The Dream Cycle of H.P. Lovecraft: Dreams of Terror and Death. 1995.
The Transition of H.P. Lovecraft: The Road to Madness. 1996.

Short Stories

The Shunned House. 1928.
The Battle That Ended the Century. 1934.
The Cats of Ulthar. 1935.
The Shadow over Innsmouth. 1936.
The Outsider and Others, edited by August Derleth and Donald Wandrei. 1939.
The Weird Shadow over Innsmouth and Other Stories of the Supernatural. 1944.
The Best Supernatural Stories of Lovecraft, edited by August Derleth. 1945; revised edition, as *The Dunwich Horror and Others,* 1963.
The Dunwich Horror. 1945.
The Dunwich Horror and Other Weird Tales. 1945.
The Lurking Fear and Other Stories. 1947; as *Cry Horror!,* 1958.
The Haunter of the Dark and Other Tales of Horror. 1951.
The Case of Charles Dexter Ward. 1952.
The Curse of Yig. 1953.
The Dream Quest of Unknown Kadath. 1955.
The Survivor and Others, with August Derleth. 1957.
The Larking Fear and Other Stories (not same as 1947 book). 1964.
At the Mountains of Madness and Other Novels. 1964.
The Colour Out of Space. 1964.
Dagon and Other Macabre Tales, edited by August Derleth. 1965.
The Dark Brotherhood and Other Pieces, with others, edited by August Derleth. 1966.
3 Tales of Horror. 1967.
The Shadow Out of Time and Other Tales of Horror, with August Derleth. 1968; abridged edition, as *The Shuttered Room and Other Tales of Horror,* 1970.
Ex Oblivione. 1969.
The Tomb and Other Tales. 1969.
The Horror in the Museum and Other Revisions (ghostwriting), edited by August Derleth. 1970; abridged edition, 1975.
Nyarlathotep. 1970.
What the Moon Brings. 1970.
The Dream-Quest of Unknown Kadath (not same as 1955 book), edited by Lin Carter. 1970.
Memory. 1970.
The Shadow over Innsmouth and Other Tales of Horror. 1971.
The Shuttered Room and Other Tales of Terror, with August Derleth. 1971.

The Doom That Came to Sarnath, edited by Lin Carter. 1971.
The Lurking Fear and Other Stories (not same as 1947 and 1964 books). 1971.
The Watchers Out of Time and Others, with August Derleth. 1974.
The Horror in the Burying Ground and Other Tales. 1975.
Herbert West Reanimator. 1977.
Collapsing Cosmoses. 1977.
Bloodcurdling Tales of Horror and the Macabre: The Best of Lovecraft. 1982.
The Dunwich Horror and Others (original versions), edited by S.T. Joshi. 1985.

Poetry

The Crime of Crimes. 1915.
A Sonnet. 1936.
H.P.L. 1937.
Fungi from Yuggoth. 1941.
A Winter Wish, edited by Tom Collins. 1977.

Other

Looking Backward. 1920(?).
The Materialist Today. 1926.
Further Criticism of Poetry. 1932.
Charleston. 1936.
Some Current Motives and Practices. 1936(?).
A History of The Necronomicon. 1938.
The Notes and Commonplace Book, edited by R.H. Barlow. 1938.
Beyond the Wall of Sleep, edited by August Derleth and Donald Wandrei. 1943.
Marginalia, edited by August Derleth and Donald Wandrei. 1944.
The Lurker at the Threshold (novel), with August Derleth. 1945.
Supernatural Horror in Literature. 1945; revised edition, 1975.
Something about Cats and Other Pieces, edited by August Derleth. 1949.
The Lovecraft Collectors Library, edited by George T. Wetzel. 5 vols., 1952-55.
The Shuttered Room and Other Pieces, with others, edited by August Derleth. 1959.
Dreams and Fancies. 1962.
Autobiography: Some Notes on a Nonentity. 1963.
Hail, Klarkash-Ton! 1971.
Ec'h-Pi-El Speaks: An Autobiographical Sketch. 1972.
Medusa: A Portrait. 1975.
The Occult Lovecraft. 1975.
Lovecraft at Last (correspondence with Willis Conover). 1975.
To Quebec and the Stars, edited by L. Sprague de Camp. 1976.
Writings in The United Amateur 1915-1925, edited by Marc A. Michaud. 1976.
First Writings: Pawtuxet Valley Gleaner 1906, edited by Marc A. Michaud. 1976.
The Conservative: Complete 1915-1923, edited by Marc A. Michaud. 1977.
Memoirs of an Inconsequential Scribbler. 1977.
Writings in The Tryout, edited by Marc A. Michaud. 1977.
The Californian 1934-1938. 1977.
Uncollected Prose and Poetry, edited by S.T. Joshi and Marc A. Michaud. 1978.
Science versus Charlatanry: Essays on Astrology, with J.F. Hartmann, edited by S.T. Joshi and Scott Connors. 1979.

H.P. Lovecraft in the Argosy: Collected Correspondence from the Munsey Magazines. 1994.

Editor, *The Poetical Works of Jonathan E. Hoag.* 1923.
Editor, *White Fire,* by John Ravenor Bullen. 1927.
Editor, *Thoughts and Pictures,* by Eugene B. Kuntz. 1932.

*

Bibliography: *The New Lovecraft Bibliography* by Jack L. Chalker, 1962, revised edition, with Mark Owings, as *The Revised Lovecraft Bibliography,* 1973; *A Catalog of Lovecraftiana* by Mark Owings and Irving Binkin, 1975; *Lovecraft and Lovecraft Criticism: An Annotated Bibliography* by S.T. Joshi, 1981; *Lovecraft: The Books, Addenda* and *Auxiliary* by Joseph Bell, 1983.

Critical Studies: *In Memoriam Lovecraft: Recollections, Appreciations, Estimates* edited by W. Paul Cook, 1941; *H.P.L: A Memoir,* 1945, and *Some Notes on Lovecraft,* 1959, both by August Derleth; *Rhode Island on Lovecraft* edited by Donald M. Grant and Thomas P. Hadley, 1945; "Lovecraft Issue" of *Fresco,* spring 1958; *Lovecraft: A Look behind the Cthulhu Mythos* by Lin Carter, 1972; *Lovecraft: Dreamer on the Nightside* by Frank Belknap Long, 1975; *Essays Lovecraftian* edited by Darrell Schweitzer, 1976, and *The Dream Quest of H.P Lovecraft,* 1978, and *Discovering Lovecraft,* 1986, both by Schweitzer; *The Lovecraft Companion* by Philip A. Schreffler, 1977; *The Major Works of Lovecraft* by John Taylor Gatto, 1977; *The Roots of Horror in the Fiction of Lovecraft* by Barton Levi St. Armand, 1977; *Lovecraft: Four Decades of Criticism* edited by S.T. Joshi, 1980, *Lovecraft* by Joshi, 1982, and *An Epicure in the Terrible: A Centennial Anthology of Essays in Honor of H.P. Lovecraft* edited by Joshi and David E. Schulz, 1991; *Lovecraft: A Critical Study* by Donald R. Burleson, 1983; *A Subtler Magick: The Writings and Philosophy of H.P. Lovecraft* by S.T. Joshi, 1996; *The Philosophy of H.P. Lovecraft: The Route to Horror* by Timo Airaksinen, 1998.

*   *   *

H.P. Lovecraft's reputation depends not so much on any particular one of the more than sixty fantastic stories that he published, mostly in the pulp magazine *Weird Tales,* but rather on the way in which most of these stories contribute to what has become known since the author's death as the "Cthulhu Mythos." Although the stories are not consistent with each other and although Lovecraft never codified his cosmology (he was a visionary, not a blueprint-maker), the basic construct of the Mythos is that, in the days before mankind, this planet was inhabited by a group of fish-like beings called the "Old Ones," who worshiped Cthulhu, represented in "The Call of Cthulhu" as a gigantic, gelatinous form. Apparently because their culture decayed, the "Old Ones" were driven from the earth by man; but they were not destroyed. Led by the apparently immortal Yog-Sothoth, they retreated to the remote, dark planet Yogguth, where they still conspire to regain control of Earth. Sometimes, as in "The Whisperer in Darkness," they contemplate an attack on a decadent mankind; but more often, as in Lovecraft's longest work, "The Case of Charles Dexter Ward," they seek, through unspeakable rites of black magic, to mate with human beings through the connivance of dissolute human collaborators.

The generally suppressed knowledge of the Cthulhuites is hinted at only in the forbidden *Necronomicon* of the mad Arab Abdul Alhazred, one Latin copy of which is preserved at Miskatonic University in Arkham, a moldering New England seaport that is the setting of many of Lovecraft's tales. When the plots of the "Old Ones" are foiled, the earthly invaders or fishy-looking half-breeds dissolve, leaving behind only a pool of noxious-smelling, jelly-like material. Characters who are willfully or inadvertently involved in the conspiracies—like those in "The Dunwich Horror" and "The Color Out of Space"—usually face madness and inevitable destruction. The Mythos, despite vagueness and inconsistencies, is a remarkable fictional manifestation of the mentality that has produced many conspiratorial theories about local and extra-terrestrial threats to human societies.

At first Lovecraft had difficulty finding readers, but he found his advocate to the world in 1926 when he attracted the attention of August Derleth. Derleth expanded and regularized the mythos, kept it in print, and even invited others to contribute to it; and Lovecraft attracted a small but fanatical band of cultists in the United States and abroad, especially in France.

Ordinary critical standards are irrelevant to such an enterprise. Lovecraft's fables were often awkwardly plotted and obscurely worded, but so are many "scriptures." Critics complained that he did not write novels, but, like Poe, his visions were best suited to shorter forms. Although many find his fantasies preposterous, he did create one of the most remarkable imaginative constructs of the twentieth century—an original myth that arises from a child's enormous fascination with sex and his repressive fear of it. Lovecraft's uniqueness lies in his ability to preserve—if perhaps only through dreams—and to articulate in adulthood the fantasies that provide a child's internal defense against inscrutable threats.

—Warren French

LOWELL, Amy (Lawrence)

Born: Brookline, Massachusetts, 9 February 1874. **Education:** Privately educated. **Career:** Lived in Europe for several years; associated with the Imagists in London, 1913, and thereafter promoted their work in America. Lecturer, Brooklyn Institute of Arts and Sciences, 1917-18. **Awards:** Pulitzer prize, 1926. Litt.D.: Baylor University, Waco, Texas, 1920. **Died:** 12 May 1925.

PUBLICATIONS

Collections

The Complete Poetical Works. 1955.
A Shard of Silence: Selected Poems, edited by Glenn Richard Ruihley. 1957.

Poetry

A Dome of Many-Coloured Glass. 1912.
Sword Blades and Poppy Seed. 1914.
Men, Women, and Ghosts. 1916.
Can Grande's Castle. 1918.
Pictures of the Floating World. 1919.

Legends. 1921.
Fir-Flower Tablets: Poems Translated from the Chinese by Florence Ayscough, English Versions by Lowell. 1921.
A Critical Fable. 1922.
What's O'Clock, edited by Ada Dwyer Russell. 1925.
East Wind, edited by Ada Dwyer Russell. 1926.
The Madonna of Carthagena. 1927.
Ballads for Sale, edited by Ada Dwyer Russell. 1927.

Play

Weeping Pierrot and Laughing Pierrot, music by Jean Hubert, from a work by Edmond Rostand. 1914.

Fiction

Dream Drops; or, Stories from Fairy Land, with Elizabeth Lowell and Katherine Bigelow Lowell. 1887.

Other

Six French Poets: Studies in Contemporary Literature. 1915.
Tendencies in Modern American Poetry. 1917.
John Keats. 2 vols., 1925.
Poetry and Poets: Essays, edited by Ferris Greenslet. 1930.
Florence Ayscough and Lowell: Correspondence of a Friendship, edited by Harley Farnsworth MacNair. 1946.

Editor, *Some Imagist Poets.* 3 vols., 1915-17.

*

Critical Studies: *Lowell: A Critical Appreciation* by Bryher, 1918; *Lowell: A Chronicle, with Extracts from Her Correspondence* by S. Foster Damon, 1935; *Lowell: Portrait of the Poet in Her Time* by Horace Gregory, 1958; *Lowell* by Frank C. Flint, 1969; *The Thorn of a Rose: Lowell Reconsidered* by Glenn Richard Ruihley, 1975; *Amy: The World of Lowell and the Imagist Movement* by Jean Gould, 1975; *American Aristocracy: The Lives and Times of James Russell, Amy, and Robert Lowell* by C. David Heymann, 1980; *Lowell* by Richard Benvenuto, 1985; *"Myself Was Formed—A Carpenter—": The House in the Poetry of Three New England Women* (dissertation) by Susan Lee Maccallum-Whitcomb, 1994.

*   *   *

Even more than is commonly the case with rebel poets and personalities, Amy Lowell was subjected to heavy-handed abuse as well as uncritical admiration in her own lifetime. But there was little or no understanding of the nature of her work, and, following her untimely death in 1925, a shift in poetic fashions all but obliterated the memory of her unusual achievements. The reasons for that eclipse lie both in the poet and in her audience. Lowell was very prolific and very uneven. Because so much of her poetry was bad, it was easy to judge her harshly. Moreover, her best and most characteristic poetry was very puzzling to conventional readers and remains so to this day. The language of these poems is chiefly pictorial, with the result that she was dismissed as a writer who touched only the physical surfaces of the world and so failed to illuminate any of its deeper meanings. As for the

defects in her audience, the misreading of the poet was due to the ignorance and superficiality of the literary journalists of her day. After her death, the misunderstanding was perpetuated by the "new critics" who scorned writers who fell outside the pale of the poetry of wit and cultural memory promoted by **T.S. Eliot** and **Ezra Pound**. Though Lowell, at her best, is a writer of extraordinary verve, freshness, and beauty of expression, she is little better understood sixty years after her death than she was in 1912 when she published her first book of poems, *A Dome of Many-Coloured Glass.*

This book was rightly criticized for its feebleness and conventionality of expression; but it has one merit unnoticed by the interpreters of her poetry. The poems are written in a late Romantic style of direct statement and they chart with unusual thoroughness all of the facets of Lowell's idealistic and mystical thought. After 1912, as suggested above, Lowell expressed herself imagistically. To a poet concerned with extra-rational areas of experience, the new style was a great advance over the confines of logical statement, but it also led to failures of communication. However, study of the poems in *A Dome* enables us to know precisely the content of her thought and the beliefs she had adopted, as a substitute for Christianity, to explain her own insights into reality.

The most important of these concerns the existence of a transcendent power that permeates the world and accounts for the divinity that Lowell sensed in all created things. In her poem "Before the Altar," a lonely and penniless worshiper offers his life and being as sacrifice to this power, which Lowell also celebrated in "The Poet," another early poem. Moved by the awesome splendors of creation, the poet is urged, she says, to forsake the ordinary pleasures of life to pursue the ideality symbolized by the "airy cloudland palaces" of sunset. Such a person, she says, "spurns life's human friendships to profess Life's loneliness of dreaming ecstasy." In much of Lowell's most admirable imagistic poetry, this mystical conception of reality is rendered by means of her "numinous landscape" or scene, as in the poems "Ombre Chinoise" and "Reflections," where the physical objects concerned are presented with a kind of divine nimbus.

The realm of ideality envisioned in these four poems is sometimes perceived as a solution to the painful incompletions of life. This is the second major theme in Lowell's poetry, and the incompletion is most tragic in the case of the denial of love. Such denial is a spiritual malaise, in her view, because she identifies love not with sex but with inner emotional development. "Patterns," Lowell's most famous poem, dramatizes the withering of spirit resultant on the death of the heroine's lover. The poem is highly voluptuous and insists on the physical beauties of lover and lady and the formal, spring-time garden where the poem is set, but the heroine's decision to live a loveless, celibate life calls attention to the deeper meaning of the relationship.

The spirituality that is implicit in romantic attachments includes recognition of an element of divinity in the beloved. The achievement of love as sacred rite is a third principal theme in Lowell's writings and it occurs in many of her most striking poems, beginning with a loose effusion in *A Dome* but ending with the sublimity of "In Excelsis" and her six sonnets written to Eleonora Duse. The loved one as sacred presence or, at the least, a part of an all-encompassing divinity is consistent with the poet's preoccupation with a transcendent reality and completes the circle of her themes by returning her thought to its starting place. In terms of individual poems, Lowell's treatment of these themes is so varied and intermixed with nearly all the other issues of life that only a long survey can do them justice. But it is important to note that Lowell approached life as a mystic at a profound, intuitive level, and the imagistic mode in which she cast her poems was the one best suited to her gifts and the visionary character of her poetry. As poet her contribution is a revivification of the human sense of the beauties and mysteries of existence.

In addition to the solitary, contemplative role of poet that she adopted for herself, Lowell fulfilled another dynamic "political" role in the far-reaching effort she made to obtain public acceptance of the "new poetry" that appeared in America in 1912. The role she played was political in that the new poetry, seemingly odd and irregular in its form, challenged nearly all established social norms and ideals. Through her critical writings as well as her countless public appearances as lecturer and reader, Lowell assumed leadership of this movement and was responsible for a large measure of its success in creating a new poetic taste and awareness in America.

—Glenn Richard Ruihley

LOWELL, James Russell

Born: Cambridge, Massachusetts, 22 February 1819. **Education:** Harvard College, Cambridge, 1834-38, A.B. 1838, and Harvard Law School, 1838-40, L.L.B. 1840; admitted to Massachusetts bar, 1840. **Family:** Married 1) Maria White in 1844 (died 1853), three daughters and one son; 2) Frances Dunlap in 1857 (died 1885). **Career:** Editor, with Robert Carter, *The Pioneer: A Literary and Critical Magazine,* Boston, 1843; editorial writer, *Pennsylvania Freeman,* Philadelphia, 1845; corresponding editor, *National Anti-Slavery Standard,* 1848; lived in Europe, 1851-52; delivered Lowell Lectures, Boston, 1855; Smith Professor of Modern Languages, 1855-86, and professor emeritus, 1886-91, Harvard University; first editor, *Atlantic Monthly,* Boston, 1857-61; editor, with Charles Eliot Norton, *North American Review,* Boston, 1864-72; visited Europe, 1872-75; delegate, Republican National Convention, and member of the Electoral College, 1876; U.S. Ambassador to Spain, 1877-80, and to Great Britain, 1880-85. **Awards:** D.C.L.: Oxford University, 1872. LL.D.: Cambridge University, 1874; University of Edinburgh, 1884. **Died:** 12 August 1891.

PUBLICATIONS

Collections

Poetical Works, edited by Horace E. Scudder. 1897; revised edition, edited by Marjorie R. Kaufman, 1978.
The Complete Writings, edited by Charles Eliot Norton. 16 vols., 1904.
Essays, Poems, and Letters, edited by William Smith Clark II. 1948.

Poetry

Class Poem. 1838.
A Years Life and Other Poems. 1841.
Poems. 1844.

Poems: Second Series. 1848.
A Fable for Critics. 1848.
The Biglow Papers. 1848; edited by Thomas Wortham, 1977.
The Vision of Sir Launfal. 1848.
Poems. 2 vols., 1849.
The Biglow Papers. Second Series. 3 vols., 1862.
Ode Recited at the Commemoration of the Living and Dead Soldiers of Harvard University. 1865.
Under the Willows and Other Poems. 1869.
Poetical Works. 1869.
The Cathedral. 1870.
Three Memorial Poems. 1877.
Under the Old Elm and Other Poems. 1885.
Heartsease and Rue. 1888.
Lust Poems, edited by Charles Eliot Norton. 1895.
Four Poems. 1906.
Uncollected Poems, edited by Thelma M. Smith. 1950.
Undergraduate Verses: Rhymed Minutes of the Hasty Pudding Club, edited by Kenneth Walter Cameron. 1956.

Play

Il Pesceballo: Opera Seria, with Francis J. Child. 1862; edited by Charles Eliot Norton, 1899.

Other

Conversation on Some of the Old Poets. 1845.
Fireside Travels. 1864.
Among My Books. 2 vols., 1870-76.
My Study Windows. 1871.
Democracy and Other Addresses. 1887.
Political Essays. 1888.
The English Poets, Lessing, Rousseau: Essays. 1888.
Books and Libraries and Other Papers. 1889.
The Writings. 10 vols., 1890; 2 additional vols. edited by Charles Eliot Norton, 1891-92.
American Ideas for English Readers (lectures). 1892.
Letters, edited by Charles Eliot Norton. 2 vols., 1894.
Lectures on English Poets, edited by S.A. Jones. 1897.
Impressions of Spain, edited by Joseph B. Gilder. 1899.
Early Prose Writings. 1902.
The Anti-Slavery Papers, edited by William Belmont Parker. 2 vols., 1902.
The Round Table. 1913.
The Function of the Poet and Other Essays, edited by Albert Mordell. 1920.
New Letters, edited by M.A. De Wolfe Howe. 1932.
The Pioneer (magazine), edited by Sculley Bradley. 1947.
Representative Selections, edited by Harry Hayden Clark and Norman Foerster. 1947.
The Scholar-Friends: Letters of Francis James Child and Lowell, edited by M.A. De Wolfe Howe and G.W. Cottrell, Jr. 1952.
Literary Criticism, edited by Herbert F. Smith. 1969.

Editor, *The Poems of Maria Lowell.* 1855.
Editor, *The Poetical Works of Dr. John Donne.* 1855.
Editor, *The Poetical Works of Andrew Marvell.* 1857.

*

Bibliography: in *Bibliography of American Literature* by Jacob Blanck, 1973; "James Russell Lowell" by Robert A. Rees, in *Fifteen American Authors before 1900: Bibliographical Essays on Research and Criticism* edited by Earl N. Harbert and Robert A. Rees, 1984.

Critical Studies: *Lowell: A Biography* by Horace E. Scudder, 2 vols., 1901; *Lowell* by Richmond Croom Beatty, 1942; *Victorian Knight-Errant: A Study of the Early Literary Career of Lowell* by Leon Howard, 1952; *Lowell* by Martin Duberman, 1966; *Lowell* by Claire McGlinchee, 1967; *Lowell: Portrait of a Many-Sided Man* by Edward Wagenknecht, 1971; *American Aristocracy: The Lives and Times of James Russell, Amy, and Robert Lowell* by C. David Heymann, 1980; "James Russell Lowell" by Thomas Wortham, in *The Transcendentalists: A Review of Research and Criticism* by Joel Myerson, 1984; *Genteel Rhetoric: Writing High Culture in Nineteenth-Century Boston* by Dorothy C. Broaddus, 1998.

*   *   *

Of all the schoolroom poets, James Russell Lowell was easily the most talented, clearly the most versatile, and probably the one who strove hardest to achieve poetic excellence. Yet in the late twentieth century his poetry is less critically valued and read than the verses of his contemporaries **Holmes, Longfellow,** and **Whittier.** Some explanation for the disparity between his ability and accomplishments resides in the very nature of his life and talents. Among other things he was poet, essayist, journalist, editor, critic, linguist, teacher, reformer, and diplomat. In 1848, before his thirtieth birthday, he published *A Fable for Critics, The Biglow Papers,* and *The Vision of Sir Launfal* to secure his poetic reputation. Ten years later he assumed the first editorship of the *Atlantic Monthly* and by his critical judgment and taste made it the finest literary journal in America. In his later years he became ambassador to Spain, and from 1880 to 1885 he served as ambassador to Britain. To highlight these few achievements from so many illustrates part of Lowell's problem: his brilliance, erudition, and versatility constantly led him to new tasks and dissipated the control and self-discipline needed for artistic excellence. In addition his responsiveness to the tradition of public oratory and imitations of older writers made his serious verse declamatory and derivative. Dated by forgotten issues and lacking a significant form, much of his longer poetry remains unreadable.

Despite these critical problems, Lowell wrote good poetry and in selected pieces well deserves his place among American poets. His *A Fable for Critics* occupies a central place among the few critical pronouncements written by nineteenth-century American authors. Its mocking, casual humor perfectly balances shrewd critical insights, while its taut epigrams still surprise and delight. Lowell called **Edgar Allan Poe** "two-fifths sheer fudge," depicted **William Cullen Bryant** as "quiet, as cool, and as dignified, / As a smooth, silent iceberg, that never is ignified," and noted that **James Fenimore Cooper**'s females were "All sappy as maples and flat as a prairie." Even his own shortcomings were catalogued: "There is Lowell, who's striving Parnassus to climb / With a whole bale of *isms* tied together with rhyme." Both series of his *Biglow Papers* display a mastery of "down-east" humor, Yankee dialect and caricature. Though their contemporary subject matter and grotesque mixture of moral aphorisms with political observations render them uneven, individual pieces like "The Courtin'" and

"Sumthin' in the Pastoral Line" demonstrate Lowell's rare gift for native idiom and folk humor. His exploration of these New England materials produced his finest poem, "Fitz Adam's Story," a 632-line saga about the essential traits of a Yankee world. Though its central story concerns the attempts of a crusty Deacon Bitters to outsmart the devil, the poem's rich digressions on religion, back-country types, and rural descriptions constitute its main pleasure.

Among his longer, more serious poems, "Agassiz," *Ode Recited at the Commemoration of the Living and Dead Soldiers of Harvard University, The Cathedral,* and a few others deserve continued reading and examination. In these poems Lowell's deeply felt thoughts were elaborately and skillfully presented, while the form, that of the familiar verse essay, perfectly suited his penchant for rhymed declamation and long digressions. "Agassiz," a moving tribute to the great Harvard scientist, cleverly blends the tradition of the pastoral elegy with contemporary images as the telegraph wire announces Agassiz's death. Throughout the poem Lowell balances his personal sorrow with a tenuous, yet affirmative, hope that such a nature as Agassiz's must exist somewhere "perfected and conscious." In the *Ode* Lowell uses the occasion of the Civil War to present a rhymed meditation on the complex oppositions of song and deed, war and truth, death and the ideal. The poem's conclusion and didactic tone prove acceptable because of the poem's careful development of basic images and firm structure. Perhaps Lowell's most successful longer poem is *The Cathedral.* Like Tennyson's *In Memoriam* it deals with a quest for religious certainty by a man imbued with his age's disbelief. The magnificent stone monument of Chartres Cathedral serves as the focus for the poem's imagery and structure. Its four main sections examine natural, religious, and even democratic responses to the spiritual, and build to the hesitant but honest suggestion that the commonplace of miracles is available for every age.

What Lowell achieved is best seen in a poem like *The Cathedral.* If his verse lacked the mighty choral power of Whitman and only fitfully imitated Emerson's grandeur, it deserves its own place among the American traditions of vernacular poetry, satiric verse, and rhymed public oratory. As Henry James once noted upon re-reading Lowell, "He looms, in such a renewed impression, very large and ripe and sane . . . . He was strong without narrowness; he was wise without bitterness and bright without folly. That appears for the most part the clearest ideal of those who handle the English form, and he was altogether in the straight tradition."

—John B. Pickard

See the essay on *The Cathedral*

LOWELL, Robert (Traill Spence, Jr.)

Born: Boston, Massachusetts, 1 March 1917. **Education:** Schools in Washington, D.C., and Philadelphia; Brimmer School, Boston; Rivers School; St. Mark's School, Southboro, Massachusetts, 1930-35; Harvard University, Cambridge, Massachusetts, 1935-37; Kenyon College, Gambier, Ohio, 1938-40, A.B. (summa cum laude) 1940 (Phi Beta Kappa); Louisiana State University, Baton Rouge, 1940-41. **Military Service:** Conscientious objector during World War II: served prison sentence, 1943-44. **Family:** Married 1) Jean Stafford, in 1940 (divorced 1948); 2) the writer Elizabeth Hardwick in 1949 (divorced 1972), one daughter; 3) the writer Caroline

Blackwood in 1972, one son. **Career:** Editorial assistant, Sheed and Ward, publishers, New York, 1941-42; teacher at the University of Iowa, Iowa City, 1950, 1953, and Kenyon School of Letters, Gambier, Ohio, 1950, 1953; lived in Europe, 1950-52; teacher at Salzburg Seminar on American Studies, 1952, University of Cincinnati, 1954, Boston University, 1956, Harvard University, 1958, 1963-70, 1975, 1977, and New School for Social Research, New York, 1961-62; professor of literature, University of Essex, Wivenhoe, Colchester, 1970-72. Consultant in Poetry, Library of Congress, Washington, D.C., 1947-48; Visiting Fellow, All Souls College, Oxford, 1970. **Awards:** Pulitzer prize, 1947; American Academy grant, 1947; Guggenheim fellowship, 1947, 1974; Harriet Monroe Poetry award, 1952; Guinness prize, 1959; National Book award, 1960; Ford grant, for poetry, 1960, for drama, 1964; Bollingen Poetry Translation prize, 1962; New England Poetry Club Golden Rose, 1964; Obie award, for drama, 1965; Sarah Josepha Hale award, 1966; Copernicus award, 1974; National Medal for Literature, 1977. **Member:** American Academy. **Died:** 12 September 1977.

PUBLICATIONS

Collections

The Collected Prose, edited by Robert Giroux. 1987.
Robert Lowell: Interviews and Memoirs, edited by Jeffrey Meyers, 1988.
Collected Poems. 1997.

Poetry

Land of Unlikeness. 1944.
Lord Weary's Castle. 1946.
Poems 1938-1949. 1950.
The Mills of the Kavanaughs. 1951.
Life Studies. 1959; augmented edition, 1959.
Imitations. 1961.
For the Union Dead. 1964.
Selected Poems. 1965.
The Achievement of Lowell: A Comprehensive Selection of His Poems, edited by William J. Martz. 1966.
Near the Ocean. 1967.
The Voyage and Other Versions of Poems by Baudelaire. 1968.
Notebook 1967-1968. 1969; augmented edition, as *Notebook,* 1970.
The Dolphin. 1973.
For Lizzie and Harriet. 1973.
History. 1973.
Poems: A Selection, edited by Jonathan Raban. 1974.
Selected Poems. 1976; revised edition, 1977.
Day by Day. 1977.

Plays

Phaedra, from the play by Racine (produced 1961). In *Phaedra and Figaro,* 1961.
The Old Glory (Benito Cereno and My Kinsman, Major Molineux) (produced 1964). 1964; expanded version, including *Endecott and the Red Cross* (produced 1968), 1966.
Prometheus Bound, from a play by Aeschylus (produced 1967). 1969.
The Oresteia of Aeschylus. 1978.

Other

Editor, with Peter Taylor and Robert Penn Warren, *Randall Jarrell 1914-1965.* 1967.

Translator, *Poesie,* by Eugenio Montale. 1960.

*

Bibliography: *Lowell: A Reference Guide* by Steven Gould Axelrod and Helen Deese, 1982; *The Robert Lowell Papers at the Houghton Library, Harvard University: A Guide to the Collection,* n.d., compiled by Patrick K. Miehe.

Critical Studies: *The Achievement of Lowell 1939-1959,* 1960, and *The Poetic Themes of Lowell,* 1965, both by Jerome Mazzaro, and *Profile of Lowell* edited by Mazzaro, 1971; *Lowell: The First Twenty Years* by Hugh B. Staples, 1962; *Lowell: A Collection of Critical Essays* edited by Thomas Parkinson, 1968; *Lowell* by Richard J. Fein, 1970, revised edition, 1979; *The Autobiographical Myth of Lowell* by Phillip Cooper, 1970; *The Public Poetry of Lowell* by Patrick Cosgrove, 1970; *Lowell: A Portrait of the Artist in His Time* edited by Michael London and Robert Boyers, 1970; *Lowell* by Jay Martin, 1970; *Critics on Lowell* edited by Jonathan Price, 1972; *The Poetic Art of Lowell* by Marjorie G. Perloff, 1973; *The Poetry of Lowell* by Vivian Smith, 1974; *Lowell* by John Crick, 1974; *Pity the Monsters: The Political Vision of Lowell* by Alan Williamson, 1974; *Circle to Circle: The Poetry of Lowell* by Stephen Yenser, 1975; *Lowell: Life and Art* by Steven Gould Axelrod, 1978, and *Robert Lowell: Essays on the Poetry* edited by Axelrod and Helen Deese, 1989; *American Aristocracy: The Lives and Times of James Russell, Amy, and Robert Lowell* by C. David Heymann, 1980; *Lowell* by Burton Raffel, 1981; *Lowell: A Biography* by Ian Hamilton, 1982; *Lowell: Nihilist as Hero* by Vereen M. Bell, 1983; *Lowell: An Introduction to the Poetry* by Mark Rudman, 1983; *Lowell: The Poet and His Critics* by Norma Procopiow, 1984; *Robert Lowell's Language and Self* by Katharine Wallingford, 1988; *The Years of Our Friendship: Robert Lowell and Allen Tate* by William Doreski, 1990; *Lost Puritan: A Life of Robert Lowell* by Paul L. Mariani, 1994; *Robert Lowell and the Sublime* by Henry Hart, 1995; *A Different Poem: Rainer Maria Rilke's American Translators Randall Jarell, Robert Lowell, and Robert Bly* by Hartmut Heep, 1996.

*   *   *

Robert Lowell has been described as "a poet of restlessness without repose" (John Crick). His career is a history of violent changes in subject matter and in manner, which often annoyed and confused his critics. Even after his death, there is little general agreement about his stature. But perhaps, even in this, Lowell is a representative figure: the years in which Lowell was publishing (1944-77) witnessed a fragmentation of culture that denies us the sorts of certainty about the status that it was once possible to accord to Eliot, or to Yeats. This period will never, one suspects, be accepted as "The Age of Lowell." Individual poets seem no longer capable of this sort of centrality of significance.

But if any poet in this period—perhaps sometimes with too earnest a deliberateness—lived through, proved upon his pulses, the central concerns, preoccupations, and pains of his time, it was Lowell. The career may, conveniently, be seen in three parts: the early poetry of Lowell's Catholicism that embraces *Land of Un-likeness, Lord Weary's Castle,* and *The Mills of the Kavanaughs;* the mid-period poetry of personal breakdown and political concern that includes *Life Studies, For the Union Dead,* and *Near the Ocean;* and the final period that saw the various attempts to create a larger, freer form through the subsequent stages of *Notebook, History, For Lizzie and Harriet,* and *The Dolphin,* a period concluding with the sustained elegiac note of *Day by Day.*

On the face of it, the three phases of the career seem to have little in common, apart from certain stylistic tics—most notably, and often irritatingly, Lowell's penchant for the triple adjective and the attention-seeking oxymoron. Some insight into an underlying continuity in Lowell's "one life, one writing" may be provided by remarking on his exceptional insistence on revising himself in public. One of the most upsetting aspects of *Notebook,* for many of its reviewers, was the shock of coming across familiar Lowell lines either in very different contexts, or procrusteanly racked into the uniform regularity of the book's "sonnets." Lowell's apparently cavalier freedom with his own published work suggests not so much a desire to do a little better what he has done brilliantly before, but rather a deep-seated impatience with his own enormous talent and with poetry itself. In the poem "Tired Iron" in *The Dolphin,* there is an almost Beckettian dismissal of the work, even as he is engaged on it—"I can't go on with this, the measure is gone." It is possible to see in Lowell, as in some of the greatest artists of the second half of the twentieth century, a radical dissatisfaction with art itself, with its consolations, its sense of order, its morality. What gives Lowell's dissatisfaction its unique savor is his refusal of the obvious alternative of a bleak nihilism in favor of a worried, guilty commitment to a traditional New England liberalism. The oddity of Robert Lowell's sensibility is perhaps suggested in a shorthand way by pointing to the poems in *Notebook* and *History* dedicated to Eugene McCarthy and Robert Kennedy: an existential absurdist clinging precariously to sanity celebrates the pragmatic politics of liberal capitalism.

Dissatisfaction, restlessness, unease: these are the signatures of Lowell's work. The early formalist poetry nominally takes its cue from **Allen Tate** and the southern Fugitives. In fact, the formal majesty of the poems is everywhere disturbed by a raucous alliterative bellowing; the Catholicism is everywhere collapsed into savage heresy and blasphemy:

O Mother, I implore
Your scorched, blue thunderbreasts of love to pour
Buckets of blessings on my burning head.

If this is rhetoric, it is a rhetoric of desperation. Even in the more tender poems—"The Quaker Graveyard in Nantucket" and "Mother Marie Therese"—Lowell's sonic boom threatens his formal perfection. His dissatisfaction compels him almost to wring the neck of his magnificent rhetoric. Such dissatisfactions led to a long silence during "the tranquillized Fifties," a silence during which the dissatisfactions of his personal life involved periods in mental hospitals. The silence was broken only at the end of the decade by the publication of *Life Studies,* a book in an entirely different mode and manner; Lowell was now so dissatisfied with his earlier work that he attempted almost its polar opposite, a poetry close to Chekhovian prose. This is the one work of Lowell's about which almost all critics agree: it was the book of its time, following, with total assurance, a direction more hesitantly beginning to be taken by some of his contemporaries, profoundly influential in its dis-

covery of a new sort of personal voice. It signals, in "Beyond the Alps," Lowell's break with Catholicism, and it proceeds to worry out, "confessionally," the psychic disturbances and extremities of his harrowing personal experience. This is a poetry resolutely committed to walking naked; but the voice is moving and desperate and rises to a unique and instantly recognizable "Lowellian" pathos:

A car radio bleats,
'Love, O careless Love . . .' I hear
my ill-spirit sob in each blood cell,
as if my hand were at its throat
I myself am hell,
nobody's here—.

But, unlike that of some poets who crawled in under the mantle of "confessional" poetry, Lowell's writing refuses the temptations of an easy solipsism. Christopher Ricks, in a *New Statesman* review of *For the Union Dead* (26 March 1965), maintained that "The singular strength of Robert Lowell's poetry has always been a matter of his power to enforce a sense of context." The work after *Life Studies* evidences a desire to speak, out of personal pain and catastrophe, about society and politics, and about literature, religion, and history, the sustaining "outer contexts" of our lives. Restlessly moving away from the "prose" style of *Life Studies,* Lowell wrote, in the central poems of *Near the Ocean*—especially, perhaps, in "Walking Early Sunday Morning"—the greatest elegies for a generation that suffered the Vietnam war and the threat of nuclear extinction, and he wrote them, with his casually characteristic refusal of the obvious, in a finely judged, perfectly achieved neoclassical form that recalls that other poet of the barbarities of which a "civilized" society is capable, Andrew Marvell:

Pity the planet, all joy gone
from this sweet volcanic cone;
peace to our children when they fall
in small war on the heels of small
war—until the end of time
to police the earth, a ghost
orbiting forever lost
in our monotonous sublime.

In *For the Union Dead,* the forms are again free, though the relatively uncluttered simplicity of these poems belies a carefully crafted subtlety of association, allusion, and symbolism. These haunted, nostalgic poems begin in a consideration of the joys and pains of personal relationship but extend themselves into the troubles of political life. The volume's title-poem relates private and public breakdown in a muted poetry of understatement, working by implication and suggestion. The poem's final stanza is as devastating as anything in Lowell, but the devastation comes across quietly, hesitantly, thrown off almost parenthetically compared with the aggressive climaxes of the poems in *Lord Weary's Castle:*

The Aquarium is gone. Everywhere,
giant finned cars nose forward like fish;
a savage servility
slides by on grease.

The ability to relate his own trouble to the trouble of his times is the impulse behind *Notebook.* This, and the works that grew out of it, are the most ambitious of Lowell's writing: he is attempting a large, inclusive form, a form for all occasions, in the manner of Pound's *Cantos,* of Berryman's *Dream Songs.* In the poems in the sequence—all irregular fourteen-liners—that deal with "history," there is too often the feeling of formal monotony, rhythmic inertia, a tired, mechanical repetitiveness. The lack of a real voice and the absence of anything but the most straightforward chronology to serve as "plot" render *History* a generally wearying experience. The failure derives, perhaps, from Lowell's refusal to admit that a sonnet sequence, or its equivalent, is really capable of handling only limited types of material. The larger successes of *For Lizzie and Harriet* and *The Dolphin* are perhaps the result of their being more traditionally plotted around the themes and occasions of personal love and marriage. The idea of writing "history" as a sequence of sonnets has an almost wilful perversity about it, as though Shakespeare had decided to put the material of the history plays, as well as the story of his "two loves," into a sonnet sequence.

But such perversity, and the overall failure of a single book, are perhaps the inevitable price of an heroic refusal to repeat himself, a nervous, restless desire to define and re-define the protean self. "We are words," Lowell insists in a poem in *History* addressed to Berryman, "John, we used the language as if we made it." The claim is large; it is characteristic of Lowell's proud ambition that he should make it for himself; but in the formal variety, the technical ingenuity, and the inventiveness of his poems—and of his translations and plays—he comes, at the very least, close to justifying it.

—Neil Corcoran

See the essay on *Life Studies.*

LYTLE, Andrew (Nelson)

Born: Murfreesboro, Tennessee, 26 December 1902. **Education:** Sewanee Military Academy, Tennessee; Exeter College, Oxford, 1920; Vanderbilt University, Nashville, 1921-25, B.A. 1925 (Phi Beta Kappa); Yale University School of Drama, New Haven, Connecticut, 1927-28. **Family:** Married Edna Langdon Barker in 1938 (died 1963); three daughters. **Career:** Actor in and around New York, 1929-30; professor of history, Southwestern College, Memphis, Tennessee, 1936; professor of history, University of the South, Sewanee, Tennessee, and managing editor, *Sewanee Review,* 1942-43; lecturer, 1946-48, and acting head, 1947-48, University of Iowa School of Writing, Iowa City; lecturer in creative writing, University of Florida, Gainesville, 1948-61; lecturer in English, 1961-67, professor of English, 1968-73, and beginning 1973 professor emeritus, University of the South; editor, *Sewanee Review,* 1961-73; teacher, University of Kentucky, Lexington, 1977. **Awards:** Guggenheim fellowship, 1940, 1941, 1960; National Endowment for the Arts grant, 1966; Lyndhurst Foundation prize, 1985. Litt.D.: Kenyon College, Gambier, Ohio, 1965; University of Florida, 1970; University of the South, 1973. D.H.L.: Hillsdale College, Michigan, 1985. **Died:** 12 December 1995.

Publications

Fiction

The Long Night. 1936.
At the Moon's Inn. 1941.

A Name for Evil. 1947.
The Velvet Horn. 1957.
A Novel, a Novella and Four Stories. 1958.
Alchemy. 1979.
Stories: Alchemy and Others. 1984.

Other

I'll Take My Stand: The South and the Agrarian Tradition, with others. 1930.
Bedford Forrest and His Critter Company (biography). 1931; revised edition, 1960.
Who Owns America? A New Declaration of Independence, with others, edited by Herbert Agar and Allen Tate. 1936.
The Hero with the Private Parts: Essays (literary criticism). 1966.
Editor, *Craft and Vision: The Best Fiction from The Sewanee Review.* 1971.
A Wake for the Living: A Family Chronicle. 1975.
The Lytle-Tate Letters, edited by Thomas Daniel Young and Elizabeth Sarcone. 1987.
Southerners and Europeans: Essays in a Time of Disorder. 1988.
From Eden to Babylon, (essays). 1990.
Kristin: A Reading by Andrew Lytle. 1992.

*

Bibliography: *A Lytle Checklist* by Jack De Bellis, 1960; *Lytle: A Bibliography 1920-1982* by Stuart Wright, 1982; *Lytle, Walker Percy, Peter Taylor: A Reference Guide* by Victor A. Kramer, 1983.

Critical Studies: "Lytle Issue" in *Mississippi Quarterly* fall 1970; *The Form Discovered: Essays on the Achievement of Lytle* edited by M. E. Bradford, 1973; "The Novelist as Historian: Andrew Lytle's Forrest" by Walter Sullivan in *American Letters and the Historical Consciousness: Essays in Honor of Lewis P. Simpson* edited by Gerald J. Kennedy and Daniel Mark Fogel, 1987; "The Velvet Horn and Andrew Lytle's Roving Point of View" by Elizabeth Sarcone in *Horns of Plenty: Malcolm Crowley and His Generation* vol. 3, no. 1, 1990.

*   *   *

Andrew Lytle's family on both sides was prominent in middle Tennessee and, in fact, Murfreesboro, the town where he was born, was founded on land given by his ancestor. His family chronicle, *A Wake for the Living,* traces the course of their history for almost two centuries. Lytle's movement into the writing of fiction was gradual. His undergraduate years at Vanderbilt University coincided with the heyday of the Fugitive group, and the friendships he formed with these poets led him into his own literary career. His main interest during the 1920s, however, was theater; he studied playwriting at the Yale School of Drama, and in New York he had a brief career as an actor.

Even before he left New York he had begun the research on his first book, *Bedford Forrest and His Critter Company.* He thus followed his friends **Allen Tate** and **Robert Penn Warren,** whose first prose works were likewise Civil War biographies. In 1930 these men and nine of their friends, led by their former teacher **John Crowe Ransom,** published *I'll Take My Stand: The South and the Agrarian Tradition.* This famous symposium inaugurated the Agrarian movement, to which Lytle was passionately committed. He was indeed about the only Agrarian who actually practiced farming during the 1930s, and for a few years he attempted to combine this with the literary profession. His great interest in the history of his region led to his first novel, *The Long Night*, a tragedy of revenge set against the background of the Civil War.

Although Lytle is usually identified with Tennessee, where three of his four novels are set, he is keenly aware of the larger clash of cultures. *At the Moon's Inn* brings the Spanish explorer De Soto to his fate in North America as he attempts to overcome the vast wilderness through an act of will. The short novel *Alchemy* likewise has Pizarro confronting the Inca world of Peru. In the foreword to *A Novel, a Novella, and Four Stories* Lytle comments that "the westward movement of Europeans, beginning with Columbus, not only shattered the narrow physical boundaries of Christendom but, like all extension, weakened it by reducing a union composite of spiritual and temporal parts to the predominance of material ends." This statement might serve as the theme that links all of Lytle's books. His third novel, *A Name for Evil*, uses the fictional convention of the ghost story to tell of a modern Southerner who brings ruin upon himself and his family in an abortive effort to restore the past. *The Velvet Horn*, which is set in the Cumberland Mountains soon after the Civil War, involves a boy's initiation into manhood and an extraordinary tangle of family relationships. It is the richest of Lytle's books and one of the masterpieces of Southern fiction.

Lytle has not, however, devoted his literary energies only to fiction. In addition to early critical works such as *I'll Take My Stand,* he has published two volumes of essays: *Southerners and Europeans: Essays in a Time of Disorder* in 1988 and, in 1990, *From Eden to Babylon,* where he examines the impact upon the South of the changes which followed the Civil War. Among these changes are the "decline and fall" of the "country gentleman" (plantation owner); the deterioration of the South's agrarian society; and the decline of the independent craftsman—all of which he blames on the rise of industrialism. Lytle asserts in these essays that the industrial revolution also ushered in the rise of materialism, which he believes is "erasing from the common memory and the formal instructions in schooling and church" the truth about the human condition. Further, Lytle argues these changes are actually resulting in a change in human nature. Under the guidance of materialism, he writes, man has come to assume that "the body of the world . . . is reducible to man's will"—a tenant the Southern farmer knew all too well was inaccurate.

Now in his 90s, Lytle continues to contribute to the literary world, though he seems to venture away from his Southern roots less and less, both physically and in his writings. As some of his champions have observed, Lytle continues to patiently sit upon his mountain considering the fallen South and occasionally issuing an insightful observation.

—Ashley Brown, updated by Craig Bryson

M

MacARTHUR, Charles (Gordon)

Born: Scranton, Pennsylvania, 5 November 1895. **Education:** Wilson Memorial Academy, Nyack, New York. **Military Service:** Served as a trooper in the 1st Illinois Cavalry, on the Mexican border, 1916; in the 149th Field Artillery, U.S. Army, 1917-19: private; assistant to the chief of the Chemical Warfare Service, Washington, D.C., 1942-45: lieutenant colonel. **Family:** Married 1) Carol Frink in 1920 (divorced 1926); 2) the actress Helen Hayes in 1928, one daughter and one adopted son, the actor James MacArthur. **Career:** Reporter, *Oak Leaves,* Oak Park, Illinois, 1915, Chicago *City Press,* 1915-16, Chicago *Examiner,* 1919-21, and Chicago *Tribune,* 1921-24; writer, New York *American,* 1924-27, and for *New Yorker* and *International Magazine;* screenwriter, producer, and director from 1929; formed a production company with Ben Hecht, 1934-36; editor, *Theatre Arts* magazine, New York, 1948-50. **Awards:** Academy award (Oscar), 1936. **Died:** 21 April 1956.

Publications

Collections

The Stage Works (includes *Lulu Belle; Salvation; The Front Page; Twentieth Century; Ladies and Gentlemen; Swan Song; Johnny on a Spot; Stag at Bay,* with Nunnally Johnson), edited by Arthur Dorlag and John Irvine. 1974.

Plays

My Lulu Belle, with Edward Sheldon (as *Lulu Belle,* produced 1926). 1925; in *Stage Works,* 1974.
Salvation, with Sidney Howard (produced 1928). In *Stage Works,* 1974.
The Front Page, with Ben Hecht (produced 1928). 1928; in *Stage Works,* 1974.
Twentieth Century, with Ben Hecht (produced 1932). 1932; in *Stage Works,* 1974.
Jumbo, with Ben Hecht, music by Richard Rodgers, lyrics by Lorenz Hart (produced 1935). 1935.
Ladies and Gentlemen, with Ben Hecht, from a play by Ladislas Bus-Fekete (produced 1939). 1941; in *Stage Works,* 1974.
Fun to Be Free: Patriotic Pageant, with Ben Hecht (produced 1941). 1941.
Johnny on a Spot, from a story by Parke Levy and Alan Lipscott (produced 1942). In *Stage Works,* 1974.
Wuthering Heights (screenplay), with Ben Hecht, in *Twenty Best Film Plays,* edited by John Gassner and Dudley Nichols. 1943.
Swan Song, with Ben Hecht, from a story by Ramon Romero and Harriett Hinsdale (produced 1946). In *Stage Works,* 1974.
Stag at Bay, with Nunnally Johnson (produced 1976). In *Stage Works,* 1974.

Screenplays: *Billy the Kid,* with Wanda Tuchock and Laurence Stallings, 1930; *The King of Jazz,* with others, 1930; *Way for a Sailor,* with others, 1930; *The Girl Said No,* with Sarah Y. Mason and A.P. Younger, 1930; *Paid,* with Lucien Hubbard, 1931; *The Unholy Garden,* with Ben Hecht, 1931; *The New Adventures of Get-Rich-Quick Wallingford,* 1931; *The Sin of Madelon Claudet (The Lullaby),* 1931; *Rasputin and the Empress,* 1932; *Twentieth Century,* with Ben Hecht, 1934; *Crime without Passion,* with Ben Hecht, 1934; *The Scoundrel,* with Ben Hecht, 1935; *Barbary Coast,* with Ben Hecht, 1935; *Once in a Blue Moon,* with Ben Hecht, 1935; *Soak the Rich,* with Ben Hecht, 1936; *Wuthering Heights,* with Ben Hecht, 1939; *Gunga Din,* with others, 1939; *I Take This Woman,* with James Kevin McGuinness, 1940; *The Senator Was Indiscreet,* with Edwin Lanham, 1947; *Lulu Belle,* with Everett Freeman, 1948; uncredited collaborations—*The Front Page,* 1931; *The President Vanishes (The Strange Conspiracy).* 1934.

Other

A Bug's-Eye View of the War. 1919.
War Bugs. 1929.

Film Director: *Crime without Passion,* 1934, *The Scoundrel,* 1935, *Once in a Blue Moon,* 1935, and *Soak the Rich,* 1936, all with Ben Hecht.

*

Critical Studies: *Charlie: The Improbable Life and Times of MacArthur* by Ben Hecht, 1957; *Front Page Marriage: Helen Hayes and Charles MacArthur* by Jhan Robbins, 1984.

*   *   *

The young Charles MacArthur was a reporter in Chicago, worked on the New York *American,* and contributed to Hearst's *International Magazine* and other journals. From their Chicago journalism experience, but chiefly from Jed Harris traditions of Broadway melodrama, MacArthur and **Ben Hecht** created the famous play *The Front Page.* The *New York Times* (15 August 1928) liked this sensational and sentimental, if somewhat raucous and callous hymn to the antics of the working press. It said the play opened the season "noisily": "By superimposing a breathless melodrama upon a good newspaper play the authors and directors [actually **George S. Kaufman**] of 'The Front Page' . . . have packed an evening with loud, rapid, coarse and unfailing entertainment . . . have told a racy story with all the tang of front-page journalism . . . [and] convey the rowdy comedy of the pressroom, the whirr of excitement, of nerves on edge . . . in the hurly-burly of a big newspaper yarn."

MacArthur's unaided work (such as the forced farce of *Johnny on a Spot*) was undistinguished, but in collaboration he did well: he wrote *Lulu Belle* with **Edward Sheldon,** *Salvation* with **Sidney Howard,** and *Twentieth Century* with Hecht. All were solid Broadway vehicles. With Hecht he also wrote the spectacular *Jumbo,* *Ladies and Gentlemen, Swan Song,* and several film scripts.

MacArthur married as his second wife Helen Hayes, later to be queen of the legitimate stage, but professionally after 1928 he was more or less married to the movies. He began with several scripts in 1930, but hit the jackpot with a vehicle for Helen Hayes, *The Sin of Madelon Claudet*. Later films include *Rasputin and the Empress* (with the Barrymores), *Crime without Passion* (writer, producer, director), *The Scoundrel, Gunga Din*, and *Wuthering Heights*. When he died he was working with Anita Loos on a vehicle for Hayes. He was by then one of Hollywood's most respected writers.

His service with the Rainbow Division in France in World War I led to *A Bug's-Eye View of the War* and *War Bugs*. It is too bad he did not do more humorous prose. He brought together a nice combination of sentiment and wit and a touch of irony with a raucous sense of fun and irreverence. All these elements are at their best in *The Front Page*. Brooks Atkinson wrote that *"The Front Page* is to journalism what *What Price Glory?* is to the Marines—rudely realistic in style but romantic in its loyalties, and also audaciously profane." Actually, the "baldest profanity and most slatternly jesting as has ever been heard on the public stage" (as the New York *Times* had it in 1928) sounds rather tame late in the twentieth century—and the play is not as realist as it seemed then. But some reporters still at least attempt to sound like MacArthur-Hecht characters (for nature imitates art), and *The Front Page* still has life in it, while *Five Star Final, Press Time, The Squeaker, Freedom of the Press*, and *Kiss the Boys Goodbye*, and a host of other newspaper plays are long dead.

—Leonard R.N. Ashley

MACDONALD, Anson. *See* **HEINLEIN, Robert Anson.**

MACDONALD, Ross

A pseudonym for Kenneth Millar. **Born:** Los Gatos, California, 13 December 1915; brought up in Canada. **Education:** The Kitchener-Waterloo Collegiate Institute, Ontario, graduated 1932; University of Western Ontario, London, 1933-38, B.A. (honors) 1938; University of Toronto, 1938-39; University of Michigan, Ann Arbor, 1941-44, 1948-49 (graduate fellow, 1941-42; Rackham fellow, 1942-43), M.A. 1942, Ph.D. in English 1951. **Military Service:** Served in the U.S. Naval Reserve, in the Pacific, 1944-46: lieutenant junior grade. **Family:** Married Margaret Sturm (i.e., the writer Margaret Millar) in 1938; one daughter. **Career:** Teacher of English and history, Kitchener-Waterloo Collegiate Institute, 1939-41; teaching fellow, University of Michigan, 1942-44, 1948-49. Book reviewer, San Francisco *Chronicle*, 1957-60. **Awards:** Crime Writers Association Silver Dagger, 1965; University of Michigan Outstanding Achievement award, 1972; Mystery Writers of America Grand Master award, 1973; Popular Culture Association award of Excellence, 1973; Private Eye Writers of America Life Achievement award, 1981. **Member:** Mystery Writers of America, board of directors, 1960-61, 1964-65, and president, 1965. **Died:** 11 July 1983.

PUBLICATIONS

Fiction

The Dark Tunnel. 1944; as *I Die Slowly*, 1955.
Trouble Follows Me. 1946; as *Night Train*, 1955.

Blue City. 1947.
The Three Roads. 1948.
The Moving Target. 1949; as *Harper*, 1966.
The Drowning Pool. 1950.
The Way Some People Die. 1951.
The Ivory Grin. 1952; as *Marked for Murder,* 1953.
Meet Me at the Morgue. 1953; as *Experience with Evil,* 1954.
Find a Victim. 1954.
The Name Is Archer (stories). 1955.
The Barbarous Coast. 1956.
The Doomsters. 1958.
The Galton Case. 1959.
The Ferguson Affair. 1960.
The Wycherly Woman. 1961.
The Zebra-Striped Hearse. 1962.
The Chill. 1964.
The Far Side of the Dollar. 1965.
Black Money. 1966.
The Instant Enemy. 1968.
The Goodbye Look. 1969.
The Underground Man. 1971.
Sleeping Beauty. 1973.
The Blue Hammer. 1976.
Lew Archer, Private Investigator (stories). 1977.

Other

On Crime Writing. 1973.
A Collection of Reviews. 1979.
Self-Portrait: Ceaselessly into the Past, edited by Ralph B. Sipper. 1981.

Editor, *Great Stories of Suspense.* 1974.

*

Bibliography: *Millar/Macdonald: A Descriptive Bibliography* by Matthew J. Bruccoli, 1983.

Critical Studies: *Dreamers Who Live Their Dreams: The World of Macdonald's Novels* by Peter Wolfe, 1976; *Macdonald* by Jerry Speir, 1978; *Macdonald/Millar* by Matthew J. Bruccoli, 1984; *The Hard-Boiled Explicator: A Guide to the Study of Dashiell Hammett, Raymond Chandler, and Ross Macdonald* by Robert E. Skinner, 1985; Ross Macdonald issue of *South Dakota Review*, Winter 1988; *Hard-boiled Heretic: The Lew Archer Novels of Ross Macdonald* by Mary S. Weinkauf, 1994.

*   *   *

Ross Macdonald is one of the central authors of his time and place. Inheriting a wide variety of influences from a number of different sources, his works provide an accurate and fascinating chronicle of the major preoccupations of contemporary America. It seems likely that future generations will read his fiction as we read, for example, Conan Doyle—to discover some important facts and truths about a bygone age. The complicated elements of his complicated books reveal a spider web of connections with literature and history, with the cultures of past and present, and with some timeless themes and patterns of human behavior.

As all readers of detective fiction must know, Macdonald's novels initially grew out of the hard-boiled fiction of the 1920s and 1930s, more specifically, from the powerful traditions established by **Dashiell Hammett** and **Raymond Chandler**. He named his private detective Lew Archer, after Sam Spade's murdered partner in *The Maltese Falcon,* and endowed him with some of the wit and compassion of Chandler's Philip Marlowe. Although his early books displayed some interesting prose, a sure sense of scene and atmosphere, and an ability to sketch out character, Macdonald came into his own when he stopped trying merely to improve upon Hammett and Chandler and began to stake out new territory in detective fiction. His humor and toughness always had the forced, false ring of a toy telephone and his style sometimes bordered on the self-consciously literary; what changed Macdonald was his own recognition of his real strengths—complexity and sorrow.

Starting—by his own reckoning—with *The Galton Case,* Macdonald began Lew Archer's long and troubled exploration of the tangled wilderness of the human heart that he embodies in the landscape of southern California. (In reality, his themes are at least roughly adumbrated in such early books as *Blue City* and *The Three Roads*.) His novels began to depart radically from the tough fiction of his original inspiration in their curiously static sense of action; instead of representing human behavior in moments of sequential violence, they generally demonstrate the continuing mysteries of the past. The most notable element in all of Macdonald's fiction is its obsessive preoccupation with the sources of human evil. Lew Archer invariably discovers that whatever crime or problem he confronts in the present has its real meaning in some previous—almost always perverse or shocking—event many years before. The immensely complicated plots of the Macdonald novels are not so much chronicles of actions as retracings of interlocking histories and personalities.

In their profuse ramifications, the plots—along with other important aspects of his fiction—demonstrate the author's significant links with a variety of writers and modes far removed from the usual backgrounds of detective stories. Like his illustrious predecessors in the form, he creates yet another version of the chivalric romance, which has always been submerged but visible beneath the dark waters of the private-eye novel. Like that of previous American writers, Hawthorne and Melville in particular, his chief concern is not so much with the fact of crime as with its causes and effects. Like Dickens, whom he resembles in his penchant for intricate stories and surprising connections, he frequently builds his work around the image and reality of a betrayed, neglected, abandoned, and suffering child.

Out of his knowledge of psychology, his scholar's training in literature, and his interest in such figures as Homer, Sophocles, Coleridge, and Freud, and out of the painful personal life that he occasionally discussed with interviewers, Macdonald made perhaps the most powerful use of the normal materials of detective fiction. With a structure and texture derived from folklore, fairy tale, romance, and myth, he confronts the age-old problems that also, quite unsurprisingly, turn out to be the major difficulties of our time: paternity, identity, the iron chains forged by violence, by sex, by blood, by guilt. The body of his fiction forms a complex picture, then, of our world and its tensions and anxieties.

Those who see his work as a sort of southern California pop sociology miss the point; that is merely the location where his subject surfaces. Those who consider him a useful reporter of the rapid changes in contemporary American society catch a bit more, but all the descriptions of aimless youths, drug users, the decadent rich and the corrupted bourgeoisie, and the destruction of the environment provide only the necessary context for more permanent concerns. Those who read his works in the future may find some accurate creation of a special time and place, but it is more likely that in Macdonald's fiction they will be instructed in the harsh lessons of an inner reality. They will discover in the novel of crime, violence, and detection a sense of the mystery and sadness of human action, a dark and troubled picture of a dark and troubled age. Macdonald not only inherited a form and a central figure from Hammett and Chandler; he also acquired the sense of mission to continue and improve their advances in making the detective novel a significant and powerful literary form.

Macdonald's own place in the continuum of American detective fiction is as solid as that of Hammett and Chandler. His influence on later writers, beyond the superficial levels of the host of writers who imitate some of his mannerisms and themes, is more difficult to determine. Though contemporary detective fiction is littered with sensitive private eyes, it remains to be seen if the form will truly learn from Macdonald's work in the ways he learned from that of Hammett and Chandler; his present imitators do not seem promising. What cannot be doubted is that Macdonald's greatest influence has been to add to the literary richness and possibility of his form.

—George Grella

MacKAYE, Percy (Wallace)

Born: New York City, 16 March 1875; son of the dramatist Steele MacKaye. **Education:** Harvard University, Cambridge, Massachusetts, A.B. 1897; University of Leipzig, 1898-1900. **Family:** Married Marion Homer Morse in 1898 (died 1939); two daughters and one son. **Career:** Teacher, Craigie School for Boys, New York, 1900-04; full-time writer from 1904; Fellow in Poetry, Miami University, Ohio, 1920-24; advisory editor, *Folk-Say* journal, from 1929; teacher of poetry and folk backgrounds, Rollins College, Winter Park, Florida, 1929-31; visiting professor of drama, Sweet Briar College, Virginia, 1932-33; director, White Top Mountain Folk Festival, Virginia, 1933; folklore researcher in the Appalachian Mountains, 1933-35, and in Switzerland and the British Isles, 1936-37. Founding member, Phi Beta Kappa Associates, 1941; president, Pan American Poets League of North America, 1943; founder, Marion Morse-Percy MacKaye Collection at Harvard University Library, 1943. **Awards:** Shelley Memorial award, 1943; Academy of American Poets fellowship, 1948. M.A.: Dartmouth College, Hanover, New Hampshire, 1914. Litt.D.: Miami University, 1924. **Member:** American Academy. **Died:** 31 August 1956.

<small>PUBLICATIONS</small>

Plays

Kinfolk of Robin Hood (as *Inhabitants of Carlysle,* produced 1901). 1924.
The Canterbury Pilgrims (produced 1903). 1903; revised version, music by Reginald DeKoven, 1916.

Fenris the Wolf. 1905.
St. Gaudens Masque-Prologue (produced 1905). 1910.
Jeanne d'Arc (produced 1906). 1906.
Sappho and Phaon (produced 1907). 1907.
Mater: An American Study in Comedy (produced 1908). 1908.
The Scarecrow, from the story "Feathertop" by Hawthorne (produced 1908). 1908.
A Garland to Sylvia: A Dramatic Reverie. 1910.
Anti-Matrimony (produced 1910). 1910.
Hannele, with Mary Safford, from a play by Gerhart Hauptmann (produced 1910).
A Masque of Labor. 1912.
Tomorrow (produced 1913). 1912.
Yankee Fantasies (includes *Chuck, Gettysburg, The Antick, The Cat-Boat, Sam Average*). 1912.
Chuck (produced 1912). In *Yankee Fantasies,* 1912.
Sam Average (produced 1912). In *Yankee Fantasies,* 1912.
Gettysburg (produced 1912). In *Yankee Fantasies,* 1912.
The Antick (produced 1915). In *Yankee Fantasies,* 1912.
Sanctuary: A Bird Masque (produced 1913). 1914.
A Thousand Years Ago: A Romance of the Orient (produced 1913). 1914.
St. Louis: A Civic Pageant, with Thomas Wood Stevens (produced 1914). 1914.
The Immigrants, music by Frederick Converse. 1915.
The New Citizenship: A Civic Ritual (produced 1916). 1915.
Caliban, By the Yellow Sands (produced 1916). 1916.
The Evergreen Tree (produced 1917). 1917.
Sinbad the Sailor. 1917.
The Roll Call: A Masque of the Red Cross (produced 1918). 1918.
The Will of Song: A Dramatic Service of Community Singing, music by Harry Barnhart (produced 1919). 1919.
Washington, The Man Who Made Us (produced 1920). 1919; shortened versions published as *George Washington,* 1920, *Washington and Betsy Ross,* 1927, and *Young Washington at Mt. Vernon,* 1927.
Rip Van Winkle, music by Reginald DeKoven (produced 1920). 1919.
The Pilgrim and the Book. 1920.
This Fine-Pretty World (produced 1923). 1924.
Kentucky Mountain Fantasies (includes *Napoleon Crossing the Rockies, The Funeralizing of Crickneck, Timber*). 1928; revised edition, 1932.
The Sphinx. 1929.
Wakefield: A Folk-Masque of America, music by John Tasker Howard (produced 1932). 1932.
The Mystery of Hamlet, Prince of Denmark; or, What We Will: A Tetralogy (produced 1949). 1950.

Fiction

Tall Tales of the Kentucky Mountains. 1926.
Weathergoose Woo! 1929.

Poetry

Johnny Crimson: A Legend of Hollis Hall. 1895.
Ode on the Centenary of Abraham Lincoln. 1909.
Poems. 1909; as *The Sistine Eve and Other Poems,* 1915.
Uriel and Other Poems. 1912.
The Present Hour. 1914.

Dogtown Common. 1921.
The Skippers of Nancy Gloucester. 1924.
April Fire. 1925.
Winged Victory. 1927.
The Gobbler of God: A Poem of the Southern Appalachians. 1928.
Songs of a Day. 1929.
William Vaughn Moody, Twenty Years After. 1930.
Moments en Voyage: Nine Poems for the Harvard Class of 1897. 1932.
In Another Land, with Albert Steffen. 1937.
The Far Familiar. 1938.
Poem-Leaflets in Remembrance of Marion Morse Mackaye. 1939.
My Lady Dear, Arise! Songs and Sonnets in Remembrance of Marion Morse MacKaye. 1940.
What Is She? A Sonnet of Sonnets to Marion Morse. 1943.
Rememberings 1895-1945: Four Poems. 1945.
The Sequestered Shrine. 1950.
Discoveries and Inventions: Victories of the American Spirit. 1950.

Other

The Playhouse and the Play, and Other Addresses Concerning the Theatre and Democracy in America. 1909.
The Civic Theatre in Relation to the Redemption of Leisure. 1912.
A Substitute for War. 1915.
Poems and Plays. 2 vols., 1916.
Epoch: The Life of Steele Mackaye. 2 vols., 1927.
American Theatre-Poets. 1935.
Poesia Religio. 1940.
Poog's Pasture: The Mythology of a Child: A Vista of Autobiography. 1951.
Poog and the Caboose Man: The Mythology of a Child: A Vista of Autobiography. 1952.

Editor, *Letters to Harriet,* by William Vaughn Moody. 1935.
Editor, *An Arrant Knave and Other Plays,* by Steele MacKaye. 1941.

Translator, *The Canterbury Tales of Chaucer: A Modern Rendering into Prose of the Prologue and Ten Tales.* 1904.
Translator, with John S.P. Tatlock, *The Modern Reader's Chaucer: Complete Poetical Works Now First Put into Modern English.* 1912; selection as *Canterbury Tales,* edited by Carl W. Ziegler, 1923.

*

Critical Studies: *MacKaye: A Sketch of His Life with Bibliography of His Works,* 1922; *Dipped in Sky* by Frank A. Doggett, 1930; *Annals of an Era: Percy MacKaye and the MacKaye Family* edited by E.O. Grover, 1932; in *American Playwrights, 1880-1945: A Research and Production Sourcebook* edited by William W. Demastes, 1995.

*   *   *

As the son of Steele MacKaye, Percy MacKaye might have been expected to show an interest in experimental drama. And he did, beginning with his graduation speech from Harvard in 1897 entitled "The Need of Imagination in the Drama of Today." Early in his career he added his efforts to the work of a small group of poetic dramatists—**William Vaughn Moody**, Josephine Peabody Marks, George Cabot Lodge—who were attempting to offset the excess of realism on the American stage with something of the artistry that Yeats and Maeterlinck were creating abroad. MacKaye's poetic dramas, however—*The Canterbury Pilgrims, Jeanne d'Arc, Sappho and Phaon*—were minor contributions to the genre.

It was with pageant drama and community theater that MacKaye trod most successfully in the steps of his father, generally celebrating America's heritage on the grand scale his father envisioned. As a crusader for community theater he wrote several books and numerous articles—*The Playhouse and the Play, The Civic Theatre.* One of his most successful pageants—allegorical masques is a more accurate descriptive term: he called his work "poetry for the masses; the drama of democracy"—was *St. Louis: A Civic Pageant,* which had a cast of 7,500 and attracted more than half a million people to its five performances. *Caliban, By the Yellow Sands,* produced on the 300th anniversary of Shakespeare's death, was an elaborate pageant using various scenes from Shakespeare's plays to humanize Caliban, to suggest, as MacKaye explained, "the slow education of mankind through the influences of cooperative art." His other pageants included *The Roll Call,* requested by the American Red Cross, and *Wakefield,* in which he attempted to dramatize the effect of "the Folk-Spirit of America" on American freedom.

For the historian of American drama one of MacKaye's particular contributions is *Epoch,* his definitive two-volume biography of his father, a man Percy worshiped and with whom he shared the dream of creating drama for the people. As a poet and a dramatist, MacKaye's best and most enduring work was his dramatization of **Nathaniel Hawthorne**'s "Feathertop," which he called *The Scarecrow.* Created before the audience's eyes with a display of imagination and theatrical skill, the scarecrow comes to life as Lord Ravensbane and achieves a considerable sense of humanity before it succumbs to the wiles of mankind and its own artificial construction. It is a fine example of MacKaye's commentary on the "need of imagination" and still retains its theatrical magic for modern audiences.

—Walter J. Meserve

MacLEISH, Archibald

Born: Glencoe, Illinois, 7 May 1892. **Education:** Schools in Glencoe; Hotchkiss School, Lakeville, Connecticut, 1907-11; Yale University, New Haven, Connecticut (editor, *Yale Literary Magazine*), 1911-15, A.B. 1915 (Phi Beta Kappa); Harvard Law School, Cambridge, Massachusetts, 1915-17, 1919, LL.B. 1919. **Military Service:** Served in the U.S. Army, 1917-19: captain. **Family:** Married Ada Hitchcock in 1916; one daughter and three sons. **Career:** Lecturer in Government, Harvard University, 1919-21; attorney, Choate Hall and Stewart, Boston, 1920-23; lived in Paris, 1923-28; editor, *Fortune* magazine, New York, 1929-38; curator, Niemann Foundation, Harvard University, 1938; Librarian of Congress, Washington, D.C., 1939-44; director, U.S. Office of Facts and Figures, assistant director, Office of War Information, 1942-43, and Assistant Secretary of State, 1944-45, Washington, D.C.; Chair of the U.S. Delegation to the UNESCO drafting conference, London, 1945, and member of the executive Board, UNESCO,

1946. Rede Lecturer, Cambridge University, 1942; Boylston Professor of Rhetoric and Oratory, Harvard University, 1949-62; Simpson Lecturer, Anmherst College, Massachusetts, 1963-67. **Awards:** Shelley Memorial award, 1932; Pulitzer prize, for verse, 1933, 1953, for drama, 1959; New England Poetry Club Golden Rose, 1934; Bollingen prize, 1952; National Book award, 1953; Sarah Josepha Hale award, 1958; Tony award, 1959; National Association of Independent Schools award, 1959; Academy of American Poets fellowship, 1965; Oscar, for documentary, 1966; Presidential Medal of Freedom, 1977; National Medal for Literature, 1978; American Academy Gold Medal for Poetry, 1979. M.A.: Tufts University, Medford, Massachusetts, 1932. Litt.D.: Wesleyan University, Middletown, Connecticut, 1938; Colby College, Waterville, Maine, 1938; Yale University, 1939; University of Pennsylvania, Philadelphia, 1941; University of Illinois, Urbana, 1947; Rockford College, Illinois, 1952; Columbia University, New York, 1954; Harvard University, 1955; Carleton College, Northfield, Minnesota, 1956; Princeton University, New Jersey, 1965; University of Massachusetts, Amherst, 1969; York University, Toronto, 1971. LL.D.: Dartmouth College, Hanover, New Hampshire, 1940; Johns Hopkins University, Baltimore, 1941; University of California, Berkeley, 1943; Queen's University, Kingston, Ontario, 1948; University of Puerto Rico, Rio Piedras, 1953; Amherst College, Massachusetts, 1963. D.C.L.: Union College, Schenectady, New York, 1941; L.H.D.: Williams College, Williamstown, Massachusetts, 1942; University of Washington, Seattle, 1948. Commander, Legion of Honor (France); Commander, el Sol del Peru; President, American Academy, 1953-56. **Died:** 20 April 1982.

PUBLICATIONS

Collections

Letters 1907-1982, edited by R.H. Winnick. 1983.

Poetry

Songs for a Summer's Day (A Sonnet Cycle). 1915.
Tower of Ivory. 1917.
The Happy Marriage and Other Poems. 1924.
The Pot of Earth. 1925.
Streets in the Moon. 1926.
The Hamlet of A. MacLeish. 1928.
Einstein. 1929.
New Found Land: Fourteen Poems. 1930.
Before March. 1932.
Conquistador. 1932.
Frescoes for Mr. Rockefeller's City. 1933.
Poems 1924-1933. 1933; abridged edition, as *Poems,* 1935.
Public Speech. 1936.
Land of the Free—U.S.A. 1938.
Dedication: Motet for Six Voices, music by Douglas Stuart. 1938.
America Was Promises. 1939.
Freedom's Land, music by Roy Harris. 1942.
Actfive and Other Poems. 1948.
Collected Poems 1917-1952. 1952.
Songs for Eve. 1954.
New York. 1958.
Collected Poems. 1963.

The Wild Old Wicked Man and Other Poems. 1968.
The Human Season: Selected Poems 1926-1972. 1972.
New and Collected Poems 1917-1976. 1976.
On the Beaches of the Moon. 1978.

Plays

Nobodaddy. 1926.
Union Pacific (ballet scenario), music by Nicholas Nabokoff (produced 1934). In *The Book of Ballets*, 1939.
Panic: A Play in Verse (produced 1935). 1935.
The Fall of the City: A Verse Play for Radio (broadcast 1937). 1937.
Air Raid: A Verse Play for Radio (broadcast 1938). 1938.
The States Talking (broadcast 1941). In *The Free Company Presents*, edited by James Boyd, 1941.
The American Story: Ten Broadcasts (includes *The Admiral; The American Gods; The American Name; Nat Bacon's Bones; Between the Silence and the Surf; Discovered; The Many Dead; The Names for the Rivers; Ripe Strawberries and Gooseberries and Sweet Single Roses; Socorro, When Your Sons Forget*) (broadcast 1944). 1944.
The Trojan Horse (broadcast 1952). 1952.
This Music Crept by Me upon the Waters (broadcast 1953). 1953.
J.B.: A Play in Verse (produced 1958). 1958.
The Secret of Freedom (televised 1959). In *Three Short Plays*, 1961.
Three Short Plays: The Secret of Freedom, Air Raid, The Fall of the City. 1961.
Our Lives, Our Fortunes, and Our Sacred Honor (as *The American Bell*, music by David Amram, produced 1962). In *Think*, July-August 1961.
Herakles: A Play in Verse (produced 1965). 1967.
An Evening's Journey to Conway, Massachusetts: An Outdoor Play (produced 1967). 1967.
The Play of Herod (produced 1968).
Scratch, from *The Devil and Daniel Webster* by Stephen Vincent Benét (produced 1971). 1971.
The Great American Fourth of July (produced 1975). 1975.
Six Plays (includes *Nobodaddy, Panic, The Fall of the City, Air Raid, The Trojan Horse, This Music Crept by Me upon the Waters*). 1980.

Screenplays (documentaries): *Grandma Moses*, 1950; *The Eleanor Roosevelt Story*, 1965.

Radio Plays: *The Fall of the City*, 1937; *King Lear*, from the play by Shakespeare, 1937; *Air Raid*, 1938; *The States Talking*, 1941; *The American Story* series, 1944; *The Son of Man*, 1947; *The Trojan Horse*, 1952; *This Music Crept by Me upon the Waters*, 1953.

Television Play: *The Secret of Freedom*, 1959.

Other

Housing America, with others. 1932.
Jews in America, with others. 1936.
The Irresponsibles: A Declaration. 1940.
The Next Harvard, As Seen by MacLeish. 1941.
A Time to Speak: The Selected Prose. 1941.

The American Cause. 1941.
American Opinion and the War: The Rede Lecture. 1942.
A Time to Act: Selected Addresses. 1943.
Poetry and Opinion: The Pisan Cantos of Ezra Pound: A Dialog on the Role of Poetry. 1950.
Freedom Is the Right to Choose: An Inquiry into the Battle for the American Future. 1951.
Art Education and the Creative Process. 1954.
Poetry and Journalism. 1958.
Emily Dickinson: Three Views, with Louise Bogan and Richard Wilbur. 1960.
Poetry and Experience. 1961.
The Dialogues of MacLeish and Mark Van Doren, edited by Warren V. Bush. 1964.
The Eleanor Roosevelt Story. 1965.
A Continuing Journey. 1968.
The Great American Frustration. 1968.
Champion of a Cause: Essays and Addresses on Librarianship, edited by Eva M. Goldschmidt. 1971.
Riders on the Earth: Essays and Recollections. 1978.
Reflections, edited by Bernard A. Drabeck and Helen E. Ellis. 1986.

Editor, with E.F. Prichard, Jr., *Law and Politics: Occasional Papers of Felix Frankfurter 1913-1938.* 1962.

Other journalism pieces, lectures, and pamphlets published.

*

Bibliography: *A Catalogue of the First Editions of MacLeish* by Arthur Mizener, 1938; *MacLeish: A Checklist* by Edward J. Mullaly, 1973; *Archibald MacLeish: A Selectively Annotated Bibliography* by Helen E. Ellis, 1994; *Descriptive Catalog of the Archibald MacLeish Scrapbooks* by Margaret E.C. Howland, 1996.

Critical Studies: *MacLeish* by Signi Lenea Falk, 1965; *MacLeish* by Grover Smith, 1971; "MacLeish Revisited" by William H. Pritchard, in *Poetry*, February 1983; *Archibald MacLeish: Reflections* edited by Bernard A. Drabeck and Helen E. Ellis, 1988, and *The Proceedings of the Archibald MacLeish Symposium, May, 1982* edited by Drabeck, Ellis, and Seymour Rudin, 1988; *Archibald MacLeish: An American Life* by Scott Donaldson, 1992; "Prelude to War: The Interventionist Propaganda of Archibald MacLeish, Robert E. Sherwood, and John Steinbeck" by Peter Buitenhuis, in *Canadian Review of American Studies*, Winter 1996, pp. 1-30; "Archibald MacLeish: 'Ars Poetica' and Other Observations" by John Haislip, in *Poetics in the Poem: Critical Essays on American Self-Reflexive Poetry* edited by Dorothy Z. Baker, 1997.

*   *   *

By 1940 Archibald MacLeish had written numerous books of poems and was a well-known writer. He was also the target of adverse criticism. His early work is too derivative. It abounds with the distracting influence of **T.S. Eliot** and **Ezra Pound**, among others. MacLeish writes on the same subjects as Eliot and Pound and from exactly their point of view, but his early long poems proved very weak. His most famous one is *Conquistador*, which won him the first of three Pulitzer Prizes. It is a verbose, unqualified glorification of Spain's slaughter and enslavement of Mexican natives, and is, at best, unthinkingly adolescent. Other works in this period are marred by the confusing about-face MacLeish executes concerning the role of the poet. In his "Invocation to the Social Muse," he criticizes those who would urge the poet to concentrate on social issues. These issues, however, soon become central to his own work. MacLeish proceeds to sermonize, harangue—and produce much poor poetry, especially in *Public Speech* and his plays for radio.

Yet, despite the inferior work written in these decades, MacLeish was beginning to compile an outstanding body of lyric poetry. Some of the short poems in *Streets in the Moon* and *New Found Land* hold up very well. "L'an trentième de mon age" is a superior presentation on the subject of the lost generation. Other fine poems include "Eleven," "Immortal Autumn," and "Memorial Rain." "Ars poetica" develops the stimulating idea that "A poem should not mean / But be." Perhaps the best of all is "The End of the World," a dramatization of the belief that the universe is basically meaningless. *Poems 1924-1933* brought together such superior lyrics as "Pony Rock," "Unfinished History," and "Lines for an Interment."

What became increasingly apparent in the 1940s and thereafter was that MacLeish's primary strength as a writer resided in the lyric form. In fact, MacLeish did most of his best work after the age of fifty.

Even some of MacLeish's later plays and long poems, two genres he never really excelled at, rise above the mediocre. The full-length play *J.B.*, despite its bland poetry and tepid main character, effectively dramatizes the tragedies that engulf that character and offers a frequently rousing debate between Mr. Zuss (representing orthodox religion) and Nickles (representing a pragmatic outlook). The one-act play *This Music Crept by Me upon the Waters* is also successful. The main characters, Peter and Elizabeth, are interesting; the plot builds in suspense; and the poetry and the theme (a preference for the present over the past) are powerful. *Actfive* is MacLeish's best long poem. The first section, which delineates modern man's basic predicament, is quite absorbing.

Still, it is MacLeish's lyric poetry that will be remembered the longest. Starting with the poems collected in 1948, the number of excellent lyrics mounts steadily, rendering unjust the critical neglect of MacLeish in the late twentieth century. These later lyrics center on three sometimes overlapping subjects. One presents the poet's increasing awareness of the mystery that permeates human experience. Earlier in his life, MacLeish wrote several poems that spoke confidently, if not cockily about setting out on explorations; now he writes "Voyage West," a sensitive expression of the uncertainty involved in a journey. Significantly, "Poet's Laughter" and "Crossing" are full of questions, while "The Old Man to the Lizard" and "Hotel Breakfast" end with questions, not answers. MacLeish sums up his sense of the mysterious in "Autobiography" when he says, "What do I know of the mystery of the universe? I Only the mystery."

He also wrote several tender eulogies and epitaphs. Two such poems about his mother are "The Burial" and "For the Anniversary of My Mother's Death." A pair of even finer poems, "Poet" and "Hemingway," have **Ernest Hemingway** for their subject. Other outstanding poems in this vein include "Edwin Muir," "Cummings," and "The Danger in the Air."

Finally, MacLeish wrote a host of fine poems about old age. The difficulty of creativity when one is no longer young is described in "They Come No More, Those Words, Those Finches." Tiredness is poignantly depicted in "Walking" and "Dozing on

the Lawn." "Ship's Log" records the narrowing awareness of the old: "Mostly I have relinquished and forgotten / Or grown accustomed, which is a way of forgetting." Yet " 'The Wild Old Wicked Man'" presents an old person's wisdom and passion. In the two poems concerning "The Old Gray Couple," MacLeish offers the reader a moving portrait of the final, deepest stage of human love. Lastly, using Odysseus as narrator, MacLeish chooses human love (symbolized by the aging wife) and mortal life over love for the abstract (symbolized by the goddess Calypso) and the metaphysical in his lovely poem "Calypso's Island": "I long for the cold, salt, / Restless, contending sea and for the island / Where the grass dies and the seasons alter."

—Robert K. Johnson

MADHUBUTI, Haki R.

Pseudonym: Don L. Lee. **Born:** Little Rock, Arkansas, 23 February 1942. **Education:** Attended Wilson Jr. College; Roosevelt University, Chicago; University of Iowa, Iowa City, M.F.A. 1984. **Military Service:** Served in the U.S. Army, 1960-63. **Family:** Married Safisha (Carol D. Easton) in 1974; three sons and two daughters. **Career:** Apprentice curator for the DuSable Museum of African American History, Chicago, 1963-67; stock department clerk for Montgomery Ward, 1963-64; clerk for the U.S. Post Office, Chicago, 1964-65; junior executive for Spiegels, Chicago, 1965-66; publisher and editor of Third World Press, Chicago, beginning 1967; founding member of Organization of Black American Culture, Writers' Workshop, 1967-75; writer-in-residence at Cornell University, Ithaca, New York, 1968-69; cofounder with Safisha of Institute of Positive Education, Chicago, 1969, director 1969-1992; poet-in-residence at Northeastern Illinois State College, Chicago, 1969-1970; lecturer at University of Illinois, Chicago, 1969-70; writer-in-residence at Howard University, Washington, D.C., 1970-78; cofounder with Safisha of the New Concept Development Center, Chicago, 1972; writer-in-residence at Morgan State College, Baltimore, Maryland, 1972-73; professor of English at Chicago State University, since 1984. Past executive council, Congress of African People; vice chair, African Liberation Day Support Committee, 1972-73; president, African-American Publishers, Booksellers, and Writers Association, 1990-1993; founding member, National Association of Black Book Publishers, 1993. Editor, *Black Books Bulletin,* winter 1993-94. **Awards:** National Endowment for the Humanities grant, 1969, 1982; American Book Award for Publisher and Editor, 1991; Illinois Association of Teachers of English award, 1991.

PUBLICATIONS

Collections

Directionscore: Selected and New Poems. 1971.
Earthquakes and Sunrise Missions: Poetry and Essays of Black Renewal, 1973-83. 1984.

Poetry

Think Black. 1967.

Back Again, Home. 1968.
Black Pride. 1968.
For Black People (and Negroes Too). 1968.
One Sided Shoot-out. 1969.
Don't Cry, Scream. 1969.
We Walk the Way of the New World. 1970.
Book of Life. 1973.
Killing Memory, Seeking Ancestors. 1987.
GroundWork: New and Selected Poems of Don L. Lee/Haki R. Madhubuti, from 1966-1996. 1996.
Heartlove: Wedding and Love Poems. 1998.

Prose

Kwanzaa. 1942.
Dynamite Voices I: Black Poets of the 1960s. 1971.
The Need for an African Education. 1972.
From Plan to Planet. 1973.
Black People and the Coming Depression, with Jawanza Kunjufu. 1975.
Enemies: The Clash of Races. 1978.
Black Men: Obsolete, Single, Dangerous? 1990.
Claiming Earth. 1994.
African-Centered Education: Its Value, Importance, and Necessity in the Development of Black Children. 1994.

Other

Editor, with Pat L. Brown and Francis Ward, *To Gwen with Love.* 1971.
Editor, *Say That the River Turns* (essays and poems). 1987.
Editor, *Confusion by Any Other Name* (essays). 1992.
Editor, *Why L.A. Happened: Implications of the '92 Los Angeles Rebellion* (essays). 1993.

Recordings: *Rappin' and Readin,'* 1970; *Rise Vision Comin'* (with the African Liberation Arts Ensemble), 1976; *Mandisa* (with the African Liberation Arts Ensemble), n.d.; *Haki R. Madhubuti Reads Poetry* (videocassette), 1988.

*

Critical Studies: "Poetry in the Sixties" by Paul Breman in *Black American Writer* edited by C.W.E. Bigsby, 1969; "Don Lee" by David Llorens in *Ebony,* March 1969; "The Motif of Dynamic Change in Black Revolutionary Poetry" by A. Russell Brooks, "The Poetry of Three Revolutionists: Don L. Lee, Sonia Sanchez, and Nikki Giovanni" by R. Roderick Palmer, and "New Black Poetry: A Double-Edged Sword" by Bernard Bell, all in *CLA,* September 1971; "From a Black Perspective: The Poetry of Don L. Lee" by Paula Giddings in *Amistad,* vol. 2, 1971; *New Directions from Don Lee* by Marlene Mosher, 1975; "Haki R. Madhubuti: Prescriptive Revolution" by D.H. Melhem in *Heroism in the New Black Poetry,* 1990; interview by Stephanie Stokes Oliver in *Essence,* July 1991; "Humanistic Protest in Recent Black Poetry" by Richard K. Barksdale in *Praisesong of Survival,* 1992; "Builders of a New Concept" by Barbara Kensey in *N'Digo,* December 1993; *The X-Factor Influence on the Transformed Image of Africa in the Poetry of Haki Madhubuti and Sonia Sanchez: Issues of Re(re)Naming and Inversion* (dissertation) by Regina B. Jennings, 1993.

*   *   *

Haki R. Madhubuti's scholarly response to the volatile social eruptions in Los Angeles, California, a collection of essays entitled *Why L.A. Happened: Implications of the '92 Los Angeles Rebellion* (1993), is in keeping with his persistent focus on national occurrences that negatively impact upon the black community. As a commentary on the communal rage that followed the brutal beating of motorist Rodney King, Madhubuti gathered a concerned group of authors, activists, and educators to address the "chain of injustice" reaffirmed by the acquittal of King's "uniformed assailants." Difficult questions permeate Madhubuti's work, as also evident in his *Black Men: Obsolete, Single, Dangerous?* (1990), a series of essays which offers analyses, guidance, and solutions on the critical dilemmas that assail black men in particular, and thus threaten to destroy the black family. In a January 7, 1990, Chicago *Sun-Times* interview with Patricia Smith, Madhubuti stated his concerns: "Black men in the United States are virtually powerless, landless and moneyless in a land where white manhood is measured by such acquisitions . . . They find themselves unable to fit into a service-oriented and information-gathering economy." *Black Men* has sold over 200,000 copies, helping make Madhubuti one of the world's best selling authors of poetry and nonfiction, with more than 3,000,000 copies of his works in circulation. Madhubuti is also in demand internationally as a lecturer.

Born Don Luther Lee, the fiery political poet of the 1960s published *Think Black* (1967), *Black Pride* (1968), *Back Again, Home* (1968), and *Don't Cry, Scream* (1969) in rapid succession and to mixed reviews. In "Poetry into the Sixties" in *The Black American Writer* (1969), David Breman expressed irritation with what he called Lee's "largely unreadable work" and "all-out ranting," which Breman felt had become rapidly outdated. But David Llorens offered a contrasting assessment of the tone of Lee's poetry in a March 1967 *Ebony* article: "The voice of Don Lee is faithful to its master, resonant, haunting, leaving in the distance all manner of half-truths. Transcending customs. Niceties. Platitudes. Seeking no approval. No applause. No contest. Just making people hear their own silence. A disquieting experience." And in the introduction to Lee's *Don't Cry, Scream,* poet **Gwendolyn Brooks** summed up Lee's work in a concise statement: "Lee's poetry is— necessarily: imperatively— capable of an awful fang and of a massive beautifully awful supersedure."

In *Enemies: The Clash of Races* (1978), Madhubuti admitted that he was not a "born or trained" writer, and that for him writing was a "weapon" in the war to "raise the consciousness" of himself and his people. He discussed the dire poverty of his youth and the early awakenings that occurred on Chicago's Westside and Detroit's lower East side, "amidst acute poverty and death." The toll of single-parenthood reduced his mother to alcoholism and an early death at age thirty-five, following a futile battle for survival through menial jobs as janitor, building caretaker, and barmaid. In an early autobiographical poem, "The Death Dance, (for Maxine)," the poet addresses her paradoxical legacy of strengths and weaknesses that provided the explosive seed of her son's self-growth. As she talked "funny sadtalk," she would remind him "son you is a man, a black man," until he "began to dance dangerous steps, / warrior's steps."

Madhubuti's early works of poetry are a clarion call to his black cultural community to wake up and confront the racial realities of America. In the introduction to *Think Black,* he announced, "I was born into slavery in Feb. of 1942," and forcefully introduced himself: "Black. Poet. Black Poet am I. This should leave little doubt in the minds of anyone as to which is first." In poems like "Re-act for Action, for brother H. Rap Brown," Madhubuti demanded: "react / NOW niggers / & you won't have to / act / false-actions / at / your / children's graves." One of the most articulate and intense voices of the black arts movement of the 1960s, Madhubuti was persistent in his questioning of America's treatment of black people, yet equally unsparing when he directed his piercing irony, understatement, and sarcasm to those black people and "Negroes" who were slow to assess the barrier of inequality preventing their access to the American Dream. The opening poem of *Black Pride,* "The New Integrationist," succinctly captures his defining statement in the goal of cultural unity: "I / seek / integration / of / negroes / with / black / people." But the razor-sharp slashes of his well-targeted words were not limited to his community; he inflicted the same scrutiny upon his own actions that he did upon others. In "The Self-hatred of Don L. Lee," he admits to being lulled into the cozy assimilationist web of America's mythical "melting pot" and eagerly accepting the "tokenism" of being "the only one" and "our negro," based upon his light skin color. But in poems like "BACK AGAIN, HOME (confessions of an ex-executive)," he emphatically denounces participation in the "whi-te" establishment:

He resigned, we wonder why;
let his hair grow—a mustache too,
out of a job—broke and hungry,
friends are coming back—bring food,
not quiet now—trying to speak,
what did he say?

"Back Again,

BLACK AGAIN,

Home."

In his early career, poetry afforded Madhubuti the tool he needed to capture the attention of a black cultural constituency often accused of not reading books. Along with **Amiri Baraka** (Leroi Jones), Sonia Sanchez, and **Nikki Giovanni**, Madhubuti hammered home his meaning by manipulating graphic visualization, rhythmic repetitions, and jazz musical forms. As though the classic stylistic devices of anaphora, polyptoton, and metonymy would mar his message of militancy if used in their familiar rhetorical guises, he stretched them taut to issue his cultural community a call to action in a "highly recognizable musical form." In his third book of poetry, *Don't Cry, Scream,* the poems virtually vibrate with quick staccato beats of jazz phrasing set against the wheezing bursts of sounds emanating from the frenzied horn of John Coltrane. The title poem is dedicated "(for John Coltrane/ from a black poet / in a basement apt. crying dry tears of 'you ain't gone.')," with poems like "communication in whi-te" also acting out the sound of high powered weaponry to jazz renditions:

allllllllllll allll llllllll deathtoallllllll alllllllll
alllllllleeeeeeee

te te te te te te te/te/te/te/te/te/tetetetetetetetetete
tetetetetetete:

the Paris peace talks, 1968.

Madhubuti insistently links black poetry to music and sees the black poets of the sixties striving to reach people in a shared language. In *Dynamite Voices I* (1971), he wrote, "We heard them, [the poets] quietly screaming to a black world that needed a new music." And in his *Sun-Times* interview with Smith, he stated: "To me, poetry represents black secular music, the music most people call jazz. That would be close to what Europeans call classical music. In terms of language, poetry is our classical language. If it works at all, it's got to capture us the way a piece of music does."

In 1973, when Don L. Lee changed his name to Haki R. Madhubuti, meaning "precise" and "accurate" in Swahili, there was a perceptible shift in the tone, form, expression, and maturity of his work. Although he continued to publish some poetry, his dominant literary form became and remains the essay as a means of projecting his maturing views and distinctive voice. Madhubuti follows legions of African-American writers, notably, **W.E.B. Du Bois**, Marcus Garvey, **Ralph Ellison**, and **James Baldwin**, who also mastered the essay form as a tool for the critical evaluation of African- American cultural life in America, and acknowledges them as literary predecessors in dedications to much of his work.

In the introduction to *From Plan to Planet* (1973), Madhubuti recognizes the fact that knowledge does not "develop in a vacuum" and pays homage to the generations of writers who paved the way for work which is "motivated toward the working and building of African minds and institutions that will deal systematically and sensibly with the problems of African people."

He directs his attention to the survival of black people by asserting the critical need for African centered educational institutions and introduces the concepts necessary for the survival of the black community. Madhubuti plants the seed of cultural responsibility as he reaffirms his support of the system of "Kawaida," created by Maulana Karenga in 1966, as a means of teaching the cultural values, defined customs, and traditions in the "Nguzo Saba" (the Seven Principles of Blackness). Born of a need to construct a Black Family Value System, the principles of Unity (Umoja), Self-Determination (Kujichagulia), Collective Work and Responsibility (Ujima), Co-operative Economics (Ujamaa), Purpose (Nia), Creativity (Kuumba), and Faith (Imani) culminate in an annual holiday season known as Kwanzaa (December 26-January 1).

In his next two books of essays, *Enemies* and *Black Men,* Madhubuti persistently probes the dilemma of inequality for black people in America, the need for black people to build their own cultural institutions, and the critical function of an African centered educational system. In both books his Pan African worldview is thrust to the forefront of discussion as he illuminates the continuing struggle for survival in the community, the responsibilities of black leadership, the necessity of extended family support, and the rationale for black institution building. In his December 1993 *N'Digo* interview with Barbara Kensey, Madhubuti addresses the questions he had posed to himself as a poverty-stricken youth: "'Why am I so poor?' 'Why was my education so deficient?' and 'What do conscious people do about that?'" His response to this self-directed interrogation was: "I felt if we were to survive and develop in this country, we would have to be institution-based. We have to move from a beggar philosophy to a producer philosophy."

In 1967, with the assistance of Johari Amini (Jewel Latimore) and Carolyn Rodgers, both well-known poets, Madhubuti founded Third World Press Publishing Company in the basement of his southside apartment in Chicago. Currently, it is the oldest, continually operating, black-owned book publishing company in the country, publishing in all genres. In 1969 he founded the Institute of Positive Education (IPE), a community-based nonprofit organization with a part-time facility for the cultural enrichment of children. In 1972, he cofounded, with his wife Dr. Safisha Madhubuti, an educator, writer, lecturer, and scholar, an expansion of IPE, the New Concept Development Center (NCDC), a fully-accredited primary and elementary school, which was expanded into a full-time educational facility in 1974, teaching levels from preschool to the sixth grade. In 1979, continuing the spirit of institution-building, Madhubuti founded the African American Book Center. In addition to his activities as author, publisher, and educator, he worked to establish the Gwendolyn Brooks Center for Black Literature and Creative Writing at Chicago State University and currently serves as its director. In his *Sun-Times* interview, Madhubuti addresses the cultural commitment that makes him center his energies on the southside of Chicago: "Even though I consider my work universal, my aim was always to cultivate the community I'm a part of. I will always be where my people are. That's where the real need is."

—B.J. Bolden

MAILER, Norman (Kingsley)

Born: Long Branch, New Jersey, 31 January 1923. **Education:** Boys' High School, Brooklyn, graduated 1939; Harvard University, Cambridge, Massachusetts (associate editor, *Harvard Advocate*), 1939-43, S.B. (cum laude) in aeronautical engineering 1943; the Sorbonne, Paris, 1947. **Military Service:** Served in the U.S. Army, 1944-46; sergeant. **Family:** Married 1) Beatrice Silverman in 1944 (divorced 1951), one daughter; 2) Adele Morales in 1954 (divorced 1961), two daughters; 3) Lady Jeanne Campbell in 1962 (divorced 1963), one daughter; 4) Beverly Bentley in 1963 (divorced 1979), two sons; 5) Carol Stevens in 1980 (divorced 1980); 6) Norris Church in 1980, one son. **Career:** Cofounder, 1955, and columnist, 1956, *Village Voice*, New York; columnist ("Big Bite"), *Esquire*, New York, 1962-63, and *Commentary*, New York, 1962-63. Member of the Executive Board, 1968-73, and beginning 1984, President, 1984-86, PEN American Center. Independent Candidate for Mayor of New York City, 1969. **Awards:** American Academy grant, 1960; National Book award, for nonfiction, 1969; Pulitzer prize, for nonfiction, 1969, 1980; MacDowell Medal, 1973; National Arts Club Gold Medal, 1976; Emerson-Thoreau Medal, for lifetime literary achievement, 1989. D.Litt.: Rutgers University, New Brunswick, New Jersey, 1969. **Member:** American Academy, 1985. **Residence:** Brooklyn, New York.

PUBLICATIONS

Fiction

The Naked and the Dead. 1948.
Barbary Shore. 1951.
The Deer Park. 1955.
New Short Novels 2, with others. 1956.

An American Dream. 1965.
The Short Fiction. 1967.
Why Are We in Vietnam? 1967.
A Transit to Narcissus, edited by Howard Fertig. 1978.
The Short Fiction (not same as 1967 book). 1981.
Ancient Evenings. 1983.
Tough Guys Don't Dance. 1984.
Harlot's Ghost. 1991.
The Executioners Song. 1993.
The Gospel According to the Sun. 1997.

Plays

The Deer Park, from his own novel (produced 1960; revised version, produced 1967). 1967.
A Fragment from Vietnam (as *D.J.,* produced 1967). In *Existential Errands,* 1972.
Maidstone: A Mystery (screenplay and essay). 1971.

Screenplays: *Wild 90,* 1968; *Beyond the Law,* 1968; *Maidstone,* 1971; *The Executioner's Song,* 1982; *Tough Guys Don't Dance,* 1987.

Poetry

Deaths for the Ladies and Other Disasters. 1962.
Huckleberry Finn, Alive at One Hundred. 1985.

Other

The White Negro. 1957.
Advertisements for Myself. 1959.
The Presidential Papers. 1963.
Cannibals and Christians. 1966.
The Bullfight. 1967.
The Armies of the Night: The Novel as History. History as a Novel. 1968.
Miami and the Siege of Chicago: An Informal History of the Republican and Democratic Conventions of 1968. 1968.
The Idol and the Octopus: Political Writings on the Kennedy and Johnson Administrations. 1968.
Of a Fire on the Moon. 1971; as *A Fire on the Moon,* 1971.
The Prisoner of Sex. 1971.
The Long Patrol: 25 Years of Writing, edited by Robert F. Lucid. 1971.
King of the Hill: On the Fight of the Century. 1971.
Existential Errands. 1972.
St. George and the Godfather. 1972.
Marilyn: A Novel Biography (on Marilyn Monroe). 1973.
The Faith of Graffiti, with Mervyn Kurlansky and Jon Naar. 1974; as *Watching My Name Go By,* 1975.
The Fight. 1975.
Some Honorable Men: Political Conventions 1960-1972. 1976.
Genius and List: A Journey Through the Major Writings of Henry Miller, with Henry Miller. 1976.
The Executioner's Song: A True Life Novel (on Gary Gilmore). 1979.
Of Women and Their Elegance, photographs by Milton H. Greene. 1980.
The Essential Mailer. 1982.
Pieces and Pontifications (essays and interviews). 1982.

Conversations with Norman Mailer, edited by J. Michael Lennon. 1988.
Marilyn: The Classic. 1989.
Oswald's Tale: An American Mystery. 1996.
Portrait of Picasso As a Young Man. 1996.
The Time of Our Time. 1998.

Film director: *Wild 90,* 1968; *Beyond the Law,* 1968; *Maidstone,* 1971; *Tough Guys Don't Dance,* 1987.

*

Bibliography: *Mailer: A Comprehensive Bibliography* by Laura Adams, 1974.

Critical Studies: *Mailer* by Richard Foster, 1968; *The Structured Vision of Mailer* by Barry H. Leeds, 1969; *Sexual Politics* by Kate Millett, 1970; *Mailer: The Man and His Work* edited by Robert F. Lucid, 1971; *Mailer* by Richard Poirier, 1972; *Mailer: A Collection of Critical Essays* edited by Leo Braudy, 1972; *Down Mailer's Way* by Robert Solotaroff, 1974; *Mailer: A Critical Study* by Jean Radford, 1975; *Existential Battles: The Growth of Mailer* by Laura Adams, 1976; *Mankind in Barbary: The Individual and Society in the Novels of Mailer* by Stanley T. Gutman, 1976; *Mailer* by Philip Bufithis, 1978; *Mailer* by Robert Merrill, 1978; *Mailer: The Radical as Hipster* by Robert Ehrlich, 1978; *Mailer's Novels* by Sandy Cohen, 1979; *Mailer, Quick-Change Artist* by Jennifer Bailey, 1979; *Acts of Regeneration: Allegory and Archetype in the Work of Mailer* by Robert J. Begiebing, 1980; *An American Dreamer: A Psychoanalytic Study of the Fiction of Mailer* by Andrew M. Gordon, 1980; *Mailer: A Biography* by Hilary Mills, 1982; *Mailer: His Life and Times* by Peter Manso, 1985; *Mailer's America* by Joseph Wenke, 1987; *Toward a New Synthesis: John Fowles, John Gardner, Norman Mailer* edited by Robert J. Begiebing, 1989; *Radical Fictions and the Novels of Norman Mailer* by Nigel Leigh, 1990; *Journalistic Technique in American Fiction–Norman Mailer* by Chitra Sharma, 1995; *Norman Mailer* by Michael K. Glenday, 1995; *The Courtroom As Forum: Homicide Trials by Dreiser, Wright, Capote, and Mailer* by Ann M. Algeo, 1996; *The Last Party: Scenes from My Life with Norman Mailer* by Adele Mailer, 1997; *Mailer: A Biography* by Mary V. Dearborn, 1999; *Ex-Friends: Falling Out with Allen Ginsberg, Lionel and Diana Trilling, Lillian Hellman, Hannah Arendt, and Norman Mailer* by Norman Podhoretz, 1999.

*   *   *

Norman Mailer's career embraces the whole of what we might call contemporary American literature—from his brilliant debut with *The Naked and the Dead* to the long-awaited, much ballyhooed *Ancient Evenings.* Indeed, it would be hard to think of another American writer who has so dominated "the scene" by his words and by his presence. If he is the enfant terrible personified, as exasperating as he is controversial, he is also central. For better or worse, his private obsessions have become our cultural facts.

Mailer's themes—whether they express themselves in his novels or his non-fiction, on television or the lecture circuit—remain the same: violence, sex, power. The configurations may change, but Mailer remains convinced that these are the dark threads of America's cultural tapestry.

The Naked and the Dead, a mercilessly realistic World War II novel set in the Pacific, was at one and the same time a breathtak-

ing debut for 25-year-old Mailer and an albatross of expectation he has had to wear ever since. Great wars ought to produce great literature—World War I (e.g., **Hemingway**'s *A Farewell to Arms;* **E.E. Cummings**'s *The Enormous Room;* Erich Maria Remarque's *All Quiet on the Western Front*) certainly did. Until **Joseph Heller**'s *Catch-22* came along in 1961, *The Naked and the Dead* had virtually no competition as the World War II novel.

In retrospect, the very realism that had so impressed its first, and second, generation of readers—the decaying corpses, the nearly overpowering sense of jungle stench—seems as strained as its aesthetics seems dated. But in the confrontations between General Cummings and Lieutenant Hearn—as well as those that pit one GI against another—Mailer was pointing to concerns that would continue to riddle him, and us, in the decades after World War II: the fate of the individual in a world increasingly filled with crushing institutions; the price of courage versus the costs of cowardice; and perhaps most important of all, what power game will prevail in contemporary America.

For Mailer, this quest took the shape of novels—or more correctly, the grand vision of novels—that would test out how a hero fit for our time might look and, more important, *act.* As Mailer imagined it, the "Napoleonic" plan—consisting of an eight-part epic work—would carry his mythic hero, Sergius O'Shaugnessy, through the eight stages of his dream life. It was an ambitious scheme, but Mailer proved himself no James Joyce, nor was his novel likely to be mentioned in the same breath as *Finnegan's Wake.* The best Mailer could do by way of O'Shaugnessy—after devoting nearly all of the 1950s to the project—was *The Deer Park* (essentially a Hollywood novel, in the mold of **Nathanael West**'s *The Day of the Locust*) and two short stories: "The Man Who Studied Yoga" and "The Time of Her Time."

What Mailer discovered, however, is that nothing succeeds in American letters like "failure." In 1959, he published *Advertisements for Myself,* a collection of reprinted material and candid, even "confessional," introductions that were as revealing, and as riveting, about Mailer as **F. Scott Fitzgerald**'s "Crack Up" essays had been about him.

That Mailer did not develop as a novelist *per se* began to seem less important than his roles as national dreamer, public gadfly, talk show "personality." *An American Dream* represented Mailer's capacity for dream at its novelistic best. Stephen Rojack, yet another of Mailer's heroes who is destined to push against all limitations, all that would repress, and then deaden the psyche. It is a novel of tests, and of extremes, but for all its dizzying heights of violence and absurdity, there was a disturbing sense that Mailer had seen contemporary American life steady and whole.

Nonetheless, the Novel seemed more limited in the 1960s than it did when Mailer, writing *The Naked and the Dead,* imagined the genre capable of enormous power. Increasingly, Mailer turned his attention to that hybrid form known as the "New Journalism," and in works like *The Armies of the Night* and *The Prisoner of Sex* and most spectacularly in *The Executioner's Song* he was able to bring his formidable skills as a novelist to the turf usually occupied by newspaper reporters. Along with **Truman Capote** and **Tom Wolfe**, Mailer revolutionized the ground rules, and our expectations. Not surprisingly, there were those who felt that such works ducked the imaginative requirements of fiction, as well as the responsibilities of journalism.

Ancient Evenings was the big novel Mailer had been promising for some three decades. If **T.S. Eliot** mined the anthropology of Frazer's *The Golden Bough* for eventual use in a Christian view of tragedy, Mailer used the mythology surrounding Isis and Osiris as a testing ground for his pet theories about existential hipness (see, for example, "The White Negro" in *Advertisements for Myself*) and further investigations into the polymorphous perverse. *Ancient Evenings* is an extended odyssey through the Land of the Dead (indeed, Mailer's principle piece of research seems to be *The Egyptian Book of the Dead*), with all its terrors and violence and general unpleasantness.

To be sure, Mailer means to use this material as both an instruction manual on behalf of a healthy Ka, or shadow self, and as a cautionary tale for those whose lives are not yet worthy of reincarnation. Menenhetet, the novel's protagonist, is a wanderer, a quester of his elusive identity through four lifetimes. The result makes for a complicated plot, full of wooden talk about "how an existential man should live." At bottom, though, what Mailer tries mightily to beat is the death question. Earlier in his controversial career, he had claimed that cancer signified a life badly lived; with *Ancient Evenings,* he seems to suggest that death itself is what happens to those who are afraid of life.

Harlot's Ghost is Mailer's epic novel, and the first installment of a longer work. Here the author attempts to examine the inner workings of the Central Intelligence Agency and to explain the agency's effect on American foreign policy. Narrated by Harry Hubbard, a ghost writer for the C.I.A., the novel travels the world and spans that time from the end of World War II through the Bay of Pigs and the Cuban missile crisis to the assassination of John F. Kennedy. Mailer's key themes—as well as his obsessions—are reiterated in *Harlot's Ghost.*

About Mailer nobody is neutral. But even those who do not count themselves among his ardent supporters must admit that he will figure prominently when the history of contemporary American letters is written. He has all the elements that make for sticking power: ambition, scope, and a willingness to explore the darker side of the psyche's uncharted vistas.

—Sanford Pinsker, updated by Denise Wiloch

MALAMUD, Bernard

Born: Brooklyn, New York, 26 April 1914. **Education:** Erasmus Hall High School, New York; City College of New York, 1932-36, B.A. 1936; Columbia University, New York, 1937-38, M.A. 1942. **Family:** Married Ann de Chiara in 1945; one son and one daughter. **Career:** Teacher, New York high schools, evenings 1940-49; instructor to associate professor of English, Oregon State University, Corvallis, 1949-61; member of the division of languages and literature, Bennington College, Vermont, 1961-86; visiting lecturer, Harvard University, Cambridge, Massachusetts, 1966-68. President, PEN American Center, 1979-81. **Awards:** Rosenthal award, 1958; Daroff Memorial award, 1958; Ford fellowship, 1959, 1960; National Book award, 1959, 1967; Pulitzer prize, 1967; O. Henry award, 1969, 1973; Jewish Heritage award, 1977; Vermont Council on the Arts award, 1979; Brandeis University Creative Arts award, 1981; American Academy Gold Medal, 1983; Bobst award, 1983; Mondello prize (Italy), 1985. **Member:** American Academy, 1964; American Academy of Arts and Sciences, 1967. **Died:** 18 March 1986.

Pᴜʙʟɪᴄᴀᴛɪᴏɴs

Collection

The Complete Stories. 1997.

Short Stories

The Magic Barrel. 1958.
Idiots First. 1963.
Rembrandt's Hat. 1973.
Two Fables. 1978.
The Stories. 1983.
The People, and Uncollected Short Stories, edited by Robert Giroux. 1990.

Novels

The Natural. 1952.
The Assistant. 1957.
A New Life. 1961.
The Fixer. 1966.
Pictures of Fidelman: An Exhibition. 1969.
The Tenants. 1971.
Dubin's Lives. 1979.
God's Grace. 1982.

Other

A Malamud Reader. 1967.
Conversations with Malamud, edited by Lawrence Lasher. 1991.
Talking Horse: Bernard Malamud on Life and Work. 1996.

*

Bibliography: *Malamud: An Annotated Checklist,* 1969, and *Malamud: A Descriptive Bibliography,* 1991, both by Rita N. Kosofsky; *Malamud: A Reference Guide* by Joel Salzburg, 1985.

Critical Studies: *Malamud* by Sidney Richman, 1967; *Malamud and Philip Roth: A Critical Essay* by Glenn Meeter, 1968; *Malamud and the Critics,* 1970, and *Malamud: A Collection of Critical Essays,* 1975, both edited by Leslie A. and Joyce W. Field; *Art and Idea in the Novels of Malamud* by Robert Ducharme, 1974; *Malamud and the Trial by Love* by Sandy Cohen, 1974; *The Fiction of Malamud* edited by Richard Astro and Jackson J. Benson, 1977 (includes bibliography); *Rebels and Victims: The Fiction of Richard Wright and Malamud* by Evelyn Gross Avery, 1979; *Malamud* by Sheldon J. Hershinow, 1980; *The Good Man's Dilemma: Social Criticism in the Fiction of Malamud* by Iska Alter, 1981; *Understanding Malamud* by Jeffrey Helterman, 1985; *Theme of Compassion in the Novels of Malamud* by M. Rajagopalachari, 1988; *Malamud: A Study of the Short Fiction* by Robert Solotaroff, 1989; *The Heart's Essential Landscape: Bernard Malamud's Hero* by Kathleen G. Ochshorn, 1990; *Bernard Malamud Revisited* by Edward A. Abramson, 1993; *Experimental Essays on the Novels of Bernard Malamud: Malamud's People* by Phillip Davis, 1995; *The Short Stories of Bernard Malamud: In Search of Jewish Post-Immigrant Identity* by Begoña Sio-Castiñeira, 1998.

*   *   *

Bernard Malamud, one of the most popular contemporary writers of Jewish-American fiction, contributed significantly to the growth in ethnic consciousness in American letters. He raised serious questions about the American dream and the American tradition. The luckless and bungling heroes that populate his fiction are twentieth-century replies to the supernatural powers of Natty Bumppo, the heroic stature of Captain Ahab, and the moral development of Isabel Archer.

Malamud's short stories and novels derived from two essential aspects of his life: his Jewish upbringing and his secular education. The Jewish past provided Malamud with much surface detail (setting, dialect) and with the ironic tone and biting humor of much of his fiction. But Malamud was also a careful student of the Western Christian literary tradition, which was often a source for symbols and literary parallels. It even colored his theme of redemption through suffering to the extent that his characters appear more as Christian martyrs than as Yiddish-speaking immigrants.

Malamud's first novel, *The Natural,* is his most ingenious adaptation of Christian legend. The story of the baseball hero, Roy Hobbs, it is a conflation of the American myth of the sports hero, specifically the baseball hero, and the medieval legends of the Fisher King and the Grail. A natural athlete, Roy is plagued by false goddesses and unworthy goals. In the end, when promised the opportunity to redeem the dry land, the unsuccessful team, Roy fails morally. He helps fix the game.

The Assistant, also a novel of striving after new gods, is one of Malamud's most oppressive, but it is not a story of hopelessness. Frank Alpine, a Gentile who participates in the robbery of Morris Bober's grocery and rapes Helen Bober, learns to repent. An admirer of St. Francis, Frank is redeemed through his suffering—he becomes a Jew like his former employer Norris Bober. One of the most effective aspects of this novel is its vividly evoked setting. The Bobers are living a life of poverty and desperation, but into this darkened vision beams the light of Frank's love for Helen and his gradual salvation through the laws of self-sacrifice.

A New Life, a barely disguised *roman à clef* of Malamud's years at Oregon State University, chronicles the growth of Sam Levin from loser to family man. He arrives at a first teaching position; he is approaching thirty, anxious to please, filled with aspirations. Only after he arrives at Cascadia College does he discover that it is not a liberal arts school but a technical institute. This is only the first of a series of disappointments and reversals. In his first year he has an affair with the wife of the chairman of the English Department and is forced to leave Cascadia and the profession of teaching. He takes with him a pregnant woman whom he no longer loves, her two adopted children, and a mature vision of the responsibility of the individual.

In *The Fixer* Malamud turns from the American landscape to the Russian countryside. The plot is based on the Mendel Belis case of the early twentieth century, but the character Yakov Bok is wholly Malamud's creation. A simple, irreligious Jew, Yakov attempts to escape the *shtetl,* Jewishness, and an unfaithful wife by slipping out of the Pale of Settlement. He is discovered living in a Christian area and accused of the ritual murder of a Gentile boy. The development of his Jewish and humanitarian consciousness is a direct result of his torture in the Russian prison. His victory over disease, death, and insanity is more than a physical one and more than an individual one.

In *Pictures of Fidelman,* a picaresque novel, Arthur Fidelman travels to Italy, first to study art, then to paint, finally simply to become human. Three of the episodes collected in this novel had been previously published as short stories. By collecting them into a single volume and adding new episodes, Malamud rounds out the bungling and lost character that is Fidelman. In this foreign setting, an American innocent, like many American innocents before him, learns what Europe has to offer. But, more than that, he learns what his own inadequacies are.

The Tenants, an experimental novel, suggests some of the complexities of the relationship between blacks and Jews in mid-twentieth-century America. Malamud's ambivalence about this relationship is apparent in the three suggested endings to the novel. Added to the problems of black-white interaction are the deprived atmosphere of the setting (an abandoned tenement house) and the jealousy of competitors (both main characters are novelists). As the conflict intensifies between Harry Lesser and Willie Spearmint, Malamud develops the social, sexual, political, and even aesthetic implications of their argument. In the end, they represent also the struggle between the formalist writer and the Marxist writer. Another writer—this time a biographer—is the central character of *Dubin's Lives.*

Malamud's tales run the gamut from painful reality to sheer fantasy. (Fantasy, surprisingly, is the tone of his final novel, *God's Grace,* an apocalyptic and allegorical beast fable.) The short stories are most often peopled by the Jews of Malamud's experience—immigrants and second-generation Americans. Even in the most fantastic of the tales, the quality of the Yiddish past filters through—in the turn of a phrase, detail of a setting, background of a character, or in a thematic concern with the holiness of intellectuality.

In the best of Malamud's short fiction the main characters share more with the Yiddish past than do their counterparts in the novels. Whether the hero be an unfeeling yeshiva student ("Magic Barrel"), a father protecting an idiot son ("Idiots First"), a modern-day Job confronted by a black Jewish angel ("Angel Levine"), a talking bird ("The Jewbird"), a guilty son duped by a fake miracle rabbi ("The Silver Crown"), a frightened American in Russia accosted by a censored writer ("Man in the Drawer"), or a talking horse ("The Talking Horse"), each of these individuals is clearly indebted to the Jewish past in the Diaspora. Each is specifically indebted to the ambivalent feelings of chosenness that has been the lot of the Jew in Europe since the first century.

—R. Barbara Gitenstein

See the essay on *The Assistant.*

MAMET, David

Born: Chicago, Illinois, 30 November 1947. **Education:** Goddard College, Plainfield, Vermont, B.A. in English 1969; attended Neighborhood Playhouse School of the Theatre, 1968-69. **Family:** Married 1) actress Lindsay Crouse in 1977, one daughter; 2) actress Rebecca Pidgeon in 1991, two children. **Career:** Actor, New England summer theater productions, 1969; drama instructor, Marlboro College, Marlboro, Vermont, 1970; artist-in-residence and drama instructor, Goddard College, 1971-73; director, *Beyond the Horizon,* St. Nicholas Theatre, Chicago, 1974; visiting lecturer, University of Chicago, 1975-76, and 1979; contributor, *Oui* magazine, 1975-76; teaching fellow, Yale School of Drama, New Haven, Connecticut, 1976-77; director, *The Woods,* St. Nicholas Theatre, 1977; associate artistic director, Goodman Theatre, Chicago, 1978-84; director, "The Sancity of Marriage," " Dark Pony," and "Reunion," in *Reunion,* Circle Repertory Theatre, New York City, 1979; director, *Twelfth Night,* Circle Repertory Theatre, 1980; director, *A Sermon,* Ensemble Studio Theatre, New York City, 1981; visiting lecturer, New York University, New York City, 1981; director, "Litko" in *Litko* and *Shoehorn,* Hartley House Theatre, New York City, 1984; associate director, New Theatre Company, Chicago, 1985; film work: director, *House of Games,* Orion, 1987; director, *Things Change,* Columbia, 1988; associate professor of film, Columbia University, 1988. Also worked in a canning plant, a truck factory, at a real estate agency, and as a window washer, office cleaner, taxi driver, short-order cook, and telephone salesman. Founder and artistic director, St. Nicholas Theatre Company, Plainfield, 1972; faculty member, Illinois Arts Council, 1974; founder and director, St. Nicholas Players, Chicago, 1974-76; cofounder, Dinglefest Theatre. **Awards:** Joseph Jefferson award, 1975, 1976; Obie award, 1976, 1983; Children's Theatre grant, New York State Council on the Arts, 1976; Rockefeller grant, 1976; Columbia Broadcasting System fellowship in creative writing, 1976; New York Drama Critics Circle award for best American play, 1977, 1984; Outer Critics award, 1978; Society for West End Theatre award, 1983; Pulitzer prize, 1984; Hull-Warriner award, Dramatists Guild, 1984; American Academy and Institute of Arts and Letters award for Literature, 1986; Golden Globe award nomination, best screenplay, 1988; Tony award for best play, for *Speed-the-Plow,* 1988. **Member:** Dramatists Guild, Writers Guild of America, Actors Equity Association, PEN, United Steelworkers of America, Randolph A. Hollister Association. **Residence:** Chicago, Illinois.

Publications

Plays

Lakeboat (produced 1970; revised version produced 1980). 1981.
Duck Variations (produced 1972). In *Sexual Perversity in Chicago and Duck Variations,* 1978.
Sexual Perversity in Chicago (produced 1974). In *Sexual Perversity in Chicago and Duck Variations,* 1978.
Squirrels (produced 1974). 1982.
American Buffalo (produced 1975, 1976; revised version 1977). 1977.
Reunion (produced 1976). 1979.
The Woods (produced 1977). 1979.
All Men Are Whores (produced 1977). In *Short Plays and Monologues,* 1981.
A Life in the Theatre (produced 1977). 1978.
The Revenge of the Space Pandas, or Binky Rudich and the Two-Speed Clock (produced 1977). 1978; in *Three Children's Plays,* 1986.
The Water Engine: An American Fable and Mr. Happiness (broadcast 1977; produced 1977). 1978.
Dark Pony (produced 1977; in *Reunion,* 1979). 1978.
The Poet and the Rent: A Play for Kids from Seven to 8:15 (produced 1984). In *Three Children's Plays,* 1977.
The Sanctity of Marriage (produced in *Reunion,* 1979). 1982.
Lone Canoe, or the Explorer (produced 1979).
Shoeshine (produced 1979). In *Short Plays and Monologues,* 1981.

A Sermon (produced 1981, 1987). In *Short Plays and Monologues,* 1981.
Donny March (produced 1981).
Litko (produced 1984). In *Short Plays and Monologues,* 1981.
Edmond (produced 1982, 1985). 1983.
The Disappearance of the Jews (produced 1983).
Five Unrelated Pieces, includes "Two Conversations," "Two Scenes," "Yes, But So What" (produced 1983). In *Dramatic Sketches and Monologues,* 1985.
Glengarry Glen Ross (produced 1983). 1984.
The Dog (produced 1983). In *Dramatic Sketches and Monologues,* 1985.
Film Crew (produced 1983). In *Dramatic Sketches and Monologues,* 1985.
4 A.M. (produced 1983). In *Dramatic Sketches and Monologues,* 1985.
Vermont Sketches, includes "Pint's a Pound the World Around," "Deer Dogs," "Conversations with the Spirit World," and "Dowsing" (produced 1984). In *Dramatic Sketches and Monologues,* 1985.
The Frog Prince (produced 1984). In *Three Children's Plays,* 1986.
The Shawl and *Prairie du Chien* (produced together 1985). 1985.
The Spanish Prisoner (produced 1985).
Vint, based on Chekov's short story (produced under the title of "Orchards" together with six other one-act plays based on Chekov's short fiction, 1985). In *Orchards,* 1986.
The Cherry Orchard, adaptation of Chekov's play (produced 1985). 1987.
Speed-the-Plow (produced 1988). 1988.
Where Were You When It Went Down? (produced 1988).
Uncle Vanya, adaptation of Chekov's play. 1989.
Goldberg Street. 1989.
Bobby Gould in Hell (produced with Shel Silverstein's *The Devil and Billy Markham,* 1989).
Five Television Plays: A Waitress in Yellowstone; Bradford; The Museum of Science and Industry Story; A Wasted Weekend; We Will Take You There. 1990.
The Three Sisters, adaptation of Chekov. 1992.
Oleana. 1993.
A Life with No Joy in It and Other Plays and Pieces. 1994.
Plays One (includes *Dark Variations*; *Sexual Perversity in Chicago*; *Squirrels*; *American Buffalo*; *The Water Engine*; *Mr. Happiness*). 1994.
The Cryptogram (also director: produced 1994). 1995.
The Old Neighborhood: Three Plays (includes *The Disappearance of the Jews*; *Jolly*; *Deeny*). 1998.
The Spanish Prisoner and the Winslow Boys: Two Screenplays. 1999.
Jafsie and John Henry: Essays. 1999.

Screenplays: *The Postman Always Rings Twice,* 1981; *The Verdict,* 1982; *House of Games,* 1987; *The Untouchables,* 1987; *Things Change,* with Shel Silverstein, 1988; *We're No Angels,* 1989; *Homicide,* 1992; *Glengary Glen Ross,* 1992; *The Water Engine,* 1992; *Hoffa,* 1992; *Texan,* 1994; *Oleanna,* 1994; *Vanya on 42nd Street,* 1994; *American Buffalo,* 1996; *The Spanish Prisoner,* 1997; *The Edge,* 1997; *Wag the Dog,* adaptation of novel *American Hero* by Larry Beinhart, 1997.

Television scripts: for *Hill Street Blues* series, 1987.

Novels

The Village. 1994.
The Old Religion: A Novel. 1997.

Poetry

The Chinaman: Poems. 1999.

Other

Warm and Cold, with illustrations by Donald Sultan. 1984.
The Owl (with Lindsay Crouse). 1987.
Writing in Restaurants (essays). 1987.
Some Freaks (essays). 1989.
On Directing Film. 1992.
Homicide. 1992.
The Cabin: Reminiscence and Diversions. 1993.
A Whore's Profession: Notes and Essays. 1994.
Passover (for children). 1995.
The Duck and the Goat (for children, with illustrations by Maya
    Kennedy). 1996.
Make-Believe Town: Essays and Remembrances. 1996.
True and False: Heresy and Common Sense for the Actor. 1997.
3 Uses of the Knife: On the Nature and Purpose of Drama. 1998.
On Acting. 1999.
Bar Mitzvah. 1999.
Henrietta. 1999.

*

Critical Studies: *David Mamet: Language as Dramatic Action* by
Anne Dean, c. 1990; "Jewish Aphoria: The Rhythm of Talking in
Mamet" by Toby Silverman Zinman in *Theatre Journal*, May 1992;
"Every Fear Hides a Wish: Unstable Masculinity in Mamet's Drama"
by Carla McDonough in *Theatre Journal*, May 1992; *David Mamet
and Film: Illusion/disillusion in a Wounded Land* by Gay Brewer,
1993; *Dark Visions of America: David Mamet's Adaptation of Novels
and Plays for the Screen* (dissertation) by Sonya Yvette Alvarado,
1997; *Rites of Passage in the Plays of David Mamet* (dissertation) by
Ira Schaeffer, 1998; *Weasels and Wisemen: Ethics and Ethnicity in the
Work of David Mamet* by Leslie Kane, 1999.

*   *   *

It is difficult to say whether the reviewers of *Writing in Restaurants,* David Mamet's collection of essays published in 1987,
adopt a condescending, slightly amused, and partially negative attitude towards the book because they are (as they claim to be)
disappointed with the stylistic quality of the writing itself or because Mamet's critique of American theater and society is rather
difficult to accept. "We live in an illiterate country," Mamet writes,
" . . . in a world ruined by Reason . . . in a very confusing time."

Influenced by the ideals of "poor" theater and Eastern European dramatic philosophy, Mamet wishes for times when actors
"who bring to the stage or screen generosity, desire, organic life,
actions performed freely—without desire for reward or fear of
either censure or misunderstanding" are once again "cherished and
rewarded. . . ." That, says Mamet, "will be one of the first signs
that the tide of our introverted, unhappy time has turned and that
we are once again eager and prepared to look at ourselves."

As Andrew Hislop put it in his review of *Writing in Restaurants*, "Mamet's book brings out clearly the incongruities of a curious relationship between American dramatic 'realism' and Eastern European philosophy of the theater." The American playwright
is actually requiring less desire of commercial success and more
substance of truth on the stage as well as on screen.

A successful playwright whose productions have acquired critical recognition for the past twenty years, Mamet brings to the
stage that particular "flavor" of everyday speech that makes his
characters so humane and so easy to identify with. With an ear
for the vernacular, Mamet is a master of dialogue who writes plays
that are each "a microcosmic view" of the American experience.

Although associated with names like Samuel Beckett and Harold
Pinter, David Mamet succeeds in maintaining a unique position in
the American theater. A "language playwright," Mamet never forgets that the characters on the stage engage in more or less painful
relationships in order to prove their humanity. There is something
more to his plays than a mere impossibility of communication.
Beyond silence or walls of language that each impede on the characters' ability to communicate, Mamet's protagonists are restless,
insecure individuals.

According to Jack Kroll, "Mamet is the first playwright to create a formal and moral shape out of the undeleted expletives of
our foul-mouthed time." "Our time" seems to be Mamet's main
concern. *American Buffalo,* his first national success, portrays a
petty world of material and spiritual failure. *American Buffalo* was
first produced in Chicago in 1975 and then in several regional theaters (and it is worthwhile mentioning here that Mamet believes
more in regional theaters than in the Broadway syndrome), as well
as three productions in New York.

In 1984, with *Glengarry Glen Ross,* Mamet won the Pulitzer
Prize and the New York Drama Critics' Circle award for best
American play. Convinced that the public prefers a mystery to
an explanation, Mamet says very little about his characters. There
is an economy of language in *Glengarry Glen Ross* that increases
the dramatic tension and presents an ironic vision of the American Dream. The American way of making a living, of selling and
buying, is critiqued in the play through the image of a real estate
agency. There are no dreams and no illusions for the characters in
Glengarry Glen Ross. Their existence is reduced to a parody and
their rage turned into bitter laughter.

In *Oleanna* (1993), Mamet confronts the pitfalls and fallacies of political correctness and the brutality of sexual and intellectual power. In the protected, upwardly mobile world of
university life, John, a professor, attempts to hold a worldly
power over his student Carol, who is as versed in pragmatism
as he is in the uses of language. She ultimately undermines him
and, as she does, she illustrates the spoiling power of envy
when it is disguised as political correctness. "Words are acts,"
Mamet has written, and *Oleanna* reveals how the authority of
position and knowledge can make the gaps between people almost unbridgeable.

The Cryptogram (1995), a play in three concise scenes, turns
toward the resonance of contradictory and puzzling emotional in-
tensities of family life. Mamet concentrates on the charged, unspoken frustration that can produce emotional static and, in turn,
produce the moment that the child sees that parental embrace can
collapse. Again the playwright is concentrating, through characteristic oblique dialogue, on illuminating the sources of cruelty and
faithlessness that his characters find in the world. Coded speech,
which cloaks meaning, is the only kind of speech that comprises

the dialogue between child and grown-up; it is what cloaks the emotional life of the child. The ground of the play is constantly shifting, never stable. Cruelty and faithlessness are what these Mamet characters find in the world, and the aftershock of the play—much like the aftershock of these life events—is its resonance.

Mamet uses a three-act structure in *The Old Neighborhood* to study dislocation between characters, namely the dislocation in a marriage between a Gentile and a Jew. Characters live in the fantasy that they can abandon the frames of life they've chosen and cultivated. Instead of the terse dialogue that is a more common trademark of Mamet, these three acts are linked by one character who mainly listens. Nostalgia and rage are the poles between which the sufferer can navigate in order to exist, and emotion is barely squeezed out between the acts of speech.

Mamet is also a successful screenplay writer. Given in 1979 the opportunity to write a screenplay for the film remake of James M. Cain's novel *The Postman Always Rings Twice* and in 1982 for *The Verdict*, Mamet considers both to have been interesting learning experiences. It is now that the playwright realizes the difference between dialogue and characters on a stage and dialogue, characters, and actions in film. "I always thought I had a talent for dialogue and not for plot," says Mamet," but it's a skill that can be learned. Writing for the movies is teaching me not to be so scared about plots." In *The Spanish Prisoner*, as in the shadowy *House of Games* and *Homicide*, the looming institutions in the background of the characters' angst remain unnamed and vague. Transactions are casual but suspect and contribute to a slow but sure sense of paranoia. Modern capitalism is critiqued in a way that leaves it seeming like a Kafkaesque netherworld of empty and dogged repetition; real communication and survival is impossible.

It is not surprising, under the circumstances, that Mamet's books of essays *Writing in Restaurants* and *Some Freaks* (published in 1989) met a certain resistance. Mamet is clearly a more talented playwright than he is an essayist, but what is seen as "preaching" about the theater in these two volumes is of a deeper substance. As one of the "freaks" of which he writes (those who are privileged to live in the world of arts), Mamet suggests a return to the humanity of the theater. As Hislop wrote in his review of *Some Freaks*, "Running through the book is the idea that the purpose of theater is truth but that the decadence of American society, television, and the materialism of Broadway are undermining not just the economic basis but the disciplines and dedication necessary for true theater."

What is the meaning of "true theater" for Mamet? Maybe that "adoration of the evanescent" he mentions in his essays, which Hislop considers, along with other metaphors and theories "of collective dreams," a forced connection between theory and culture, and most of the time not a very successful one. Is Mamet's image of the theater artificial? Possibly, taking into account the commercial face of American theater today and its preference for well-made plays and superficial musical comedies. But in substance, the playwright's ideals could merge into a new age of the American theater, an age whose main purpose would be to reveal the truth and to make sense of a spiritually impoverished but nevertheless hopeful existence.

—Dayana Stetco, updated by Martha Sutro

See the essay on *American Buffalo*.

MARKHAM, Edwin

Born: Charles Edward Anson Markham in Oregon City, Oregon, 23 April 1852. **Education:** San José Normal School, California; Christian College, Santa Rosa, California. **Family:** Married 1) Annie Cox in 1875 (divorced 1884); 2) Carolyn E. Bailey in 1887; 3) Anna Catherine Murphy in 1898; one son. **Career:** Schoolteacher: headmaster, University Observation School, Oakland, California, for 10 years. Lived in New York and New Jersey from c. 1900: lecturer and editor. **Awards:** Academy of American Poets prize. Honorary degrees: Baylor University, Waco, Texas; Syracuse University, New York; New York University. Honorary President, Poetry Society of America. **Member:** American Academy, 1930. **Died:** 7 March 1940.

PUBLICATIONS

Collections

Poems, edited by Charles L. Wallis. 1950.

Poetry

The Man with the Hoe and Other Poems. 1899.
Lincoln and Other Poems. 1901.
The Shoes of Happiness and Other Poems. 1915.
Gates of Paradise and Other Poems. 1920.
Funeral of Adam Willis Wagnalls. 1924.
New Poems: Eighty Songs at Eighty. 1932.
The Star of Araby. 1937.

Other

Modern Poets and Christian Teaching, with Richard Watson Gilder and E.R. Sill. 1906.
The Burt-Markham Primer: The Nature Method, with Mary Burt. 1907.
Children in Bondage: A Presentation of the Anxious Problem of Child Labor, with Benjamin B. Lindsey and George Creel. 1914.
California the Wonderful. 1914.
Archibald Henderson: An Appreciation of the Man. 1918.
Campbell Meeker. 1925.

Editor, *The Real America in Romance.* 15 vols., 1909-27.
Editor, *Foundation Stones of Success.* 10 vols., 1917.
Editor, *The Book of Poetry.* 3 vols., 1926.
Editor, *Songs and Stories of California.* 1931.
Editor, *The Book of English Poetry.* 1934.
Editor, *Poetry of Youth.* 1935.

*

Critical Studies: *Markham* by William L. Stidger, 1933; *The Unknown Markham: His Mystery and Its Significance* by Louis Filler, 1966; *Markham: The Poet for Preachers* by George Truman Carl, 1977.

*   *   *

Edwin Markham, best known for a single poem, "The Man with the Hoe," produced five published collections of verse in his lifetime as well as a few other poetic attempts, in addition to a series of articles on the injustices of child labor and on various other Progressive/Reform causes. As a poet he was an unsophisticated traditionalist (hence, a mainstream writer, as **Emily Dickinson**, **Walt Whitman**, **Wallace Stevens**, **e.e. cummings**, and **William Carlos Williams** could never be). He strove, generally with the aid of regular rhythms and conventional rhymes, to promote brotherhood, love, and all the other standard virtues. A strong sense of Christian "awareness" runs throughout his work, which reflects not only his sensitive conscience in the face of man's inhumanity to man, but his spiritual commitment: an ongoing manifesto of the need for good works and the security of faith.

A series of unlikely circumstances combined to make "The Man with the Hoe" (based on the painting by the Barbizon artist Jean-Francois Millet) one of America's most famous poems of all time: deeper and more suggestive than its subject, in almost a subliminal, inexpressible way. Millet's painting of course must be kept in mind here; then the opening lines of the poem: "Bowed by the weight of centuries he leans / Upon his hoe and gazes on the ground, The emptiness of ages in his face, / And on his back the burden of the world." That this poem and no other quite like it could profoundly affect an entire nation, was proven by the general neglect accorded Markham's comparable poem (likewise predicated on a Millet painting of a poor peasant), "The Sower" (in Lincoln and Other Poems): "He is the stone rejected, yet the stone / Whereon is built metropolis and throne."

Markham's "Lincoln, The Man of the People" was well received, with its image of the fallen president suggesting the fall of "a lordly cedar," leaving "a lonesome place against the sky." A good deal of comment and speculation were provoked by his poem "Virgilia" (in *The Shoes of Happiness and Other Poems*). With its companion-piece, "The Crowning Hour," it spoke of a mysterious lost love and the poet's determination to undertake a cosmic quest in order to find her; here again one can sense, despite all the changes in fashion and style since the poem was written, the basis for strong reader identification: "Our ways go wide and I know not whither, / But my song will search through the worlds for you, / Till the Seven Seas waste and the Seven Stars wither / And the dream of the heart comes true."

Staid, ultra-conventional though Markham's poems were, he himself was a deeply passionate man and a much more complicated person than he is generally regarded as being. School superintendent and principal, writer of popular poems and verses, public lecturer and anthologist of popular verse—these job designations do not begin to explain him, any more than do the facts of his unhappy childhood and his tormented relationship with his neurotic mother, or his being a product of the Oregon-California coastal region. A restless, driven man, he lived an inner life quite at variance with his outward appearance of majestic, assured, bearded dignity; this is borne out, for example, by the nightmare poem "The Ballad of the Gallows Bird" (printed originally in 1926).

—Samuel Irving Bellman

MARQUAND, John P(hillips)

Born: Wilmington, Delaware, 10 November 1893. **Education:** Newburyport High School, Massachusetts; Harvard University, Cambridge, Massachusetts, 1912-15, A.B. 1915. **Military Service:** Served in the Massachusetts National Guard in the Mexican Border Service, 1916; student, Camp Plattsburg, 1917; commissioned 1st lieutenant in the U.S. Field Artillery, and served in the 4th Brigade in France, 1917-18; special consultant to the secretary of war, Washington, D.C., 1944-45; war correspondent for the U.S. Navy, 1945. **Family:** Married 1) Christina Davenport Sedgwick in 1922 (divorced 1935), one son and one daughter; 2) Adelaide Hooker in 1937 (divorced 1958), two sons and one daughter. **Career:** Assistant magazine editor, Boston *Transcript*, 1915-17; with the Sunday magazine department, New York *Tribune*, 1919-20; advertising copywriter, J. Walter Thompson Company, New York, 1920-21. Member, board of overseers, Harvard University; member of the editorial board, Book-of-the-Month Club, 1944-60. **Awards:** Pulitzer prize, 1938; Sarah Josepha Hale award, 1957. Litt.D.: University of Maine, Orono, 1941; Rochester University Rochester, New York, 1944; Yale University, New Haven, Connecticut, 1950. D.H.L.: Bates College, Lewiston, Maine, 1954. **Member:** American Academy. **Died:** 16 July 1960.

PUBLICATIONS

Fiction

The Unspeakable Gentleman. 1922.
Four of a Kind (stories). 1923.
The Black Cargo. 1925.
Do Tell Me, Doctor Johnson. 1928.
Warning Hill. 1930.
Haven's End. 1933.
Ming Yellow. 1935.
No Hero. 1935; as *Mr. Moto Takes a Hand*, 1940; as *Your Turn, Mr. Moto*, 1963.
Thank You, Mr. Moto. 1936.
The Late George Apley: A Novel in the Form of a Memoir. 1937.
Think Fast, Mr. Moto. 1937.
Mr. Moto Is So Sorry. 1938.
Wickford Point. 1939.
Don't Ask Questions. 1941.
H.M. Pulham, Esquire. 1941.
Last Laugh, Mr. Moto. 1942.
So Little Time. 1943.
Repent in Haste. 1945.
B.F.'s Daughter. 1946; as *Polly Fulton*, 1947.
Point of No Return. 1949.
It's Loaded, Mr. Bauer. 1949.
Melville Goodwin, USA. 1951.
Sincerely, Willis Wayde. 1955.
North of Grand Central (omnibus). 1956.
Mr. Moto's Three Aces (omnibus). 1956.
Stopover: Tokyo. 1957; as *The Last of Mr. Moto*, 1963; as *Right You Are, Mr. Moto*, 1977.
Life at Happy Knoll (stories). 1957.
Women and Thomas Harrow. 1958.

Play

The Late George Apley, with George S. Kaufman, from the novel by Marquand (produced 1944). 1946.

Other

Prince and Boatswain: Sea Tales from the Recollections of Rear-Admiral Charles E. Clark, with James Morris Morgan. 1915.
Lord Timothy Dexter of Newburyport, Mass. 1925.
Federalist Newburyport; or, Can Historical Fiction Remove a Fly from Amber? 1952.
Thirty Years (miscellany). 1954.
Timothy Dexter Revisited. 1960.

*

Bibliography: *Bibliography of American Fiction 1919-1988* edited by Matthew J. Bruccoli and Judith S. Baughman, vol. 1, 1991.

Critical Studies: *Marquand* by John J. Gross, 1963; *Marquand* by C. Hugh Holman, 1965; *The Late John Marquand* by Stephen Birmingham, 1972 (includes bibliography); *Marquand: An American Life* by Millicent Bell, 1979.

*   *   *

John P. Marquand was a popular professional writer who—having whetted his skills of realistic and gently satiric writing to a very fine edge in several popular novels and scores of short stories in the mass circulation magazines—set out in 1937 to employ these skills with affectionate irony on affluent upper-middle-class America in its seats of influence and power. For the twenty years that followed he was not only a practiced portrayer of American life but also one of the most popular novelists that America has produced.

The Late George Apley, which in 1937 broke the pattern of Marquand's popular fiction, is a parody of "collected letters with commentary" of distinguished people. It is a satiric picture of a very proper Bostonian and the ways in which the constraints of his society kept him in line and made him a good but stuffy and frustrated man. It received the Pulitzer Prize and launched Marquand's career as an important American social novelist. It was the first of three novels in which Marquand explored in contrasting panels aspects of the life of Boston. *Wickford Point* is the story of a decaying family loosely bound to the Transcendentalists, a comic picture of the diminishment of greatness and the sadness of the Indian summer of the spirit, and *H.M. Pulham, Esquire* is a self-portrait by a contemporary Bostonian, a post-World War I businessman, and the account of his ineffectual revolt against his class and its customs. These three novels form a triptych of New England life and use a variety of satiric skills, largely resulting from ironic points of view and the extensive use of flashbacks.

Like **Sinclair Lewis,** whom he greatly admired, Marquand moved on, after his complex portrait of Boston, to other cities and other professions in his growing list of studies of American life. *So Little Time* explores the vulgarly opulent world of West Coast moviemakers. It is set during World War II, and suggests the inexorable passage of time. His other wartime novel, *B.F.'s Daughter,* deals with big business and the Washington bureaucracy, and is only a limited success. (A short novel, *Repent in Haste,* also deals with the war, but it is very slight.) *Point of No Return* is, after *The Late George Apley,* Marquand's best novel. It is the story of a banker who explores his New England small-town roots in an effort to find bases for a decision he must make, only to

discover that all the decisions have already been made without his being aware of it, and that he has passed "the point of no return," a conclusion that most Marquand protagonists reach after painfully reviewing their lives. In addition to many amusing social caricatures, the book contains a serious examination of the sociology of New England towns, and to some degree of New York City. It and the Boston trilogy are Marquand's works that seem most likely to survive.

Melville Goodwin, USA is a portrayal of a general seen through the admiring eyes of a popular journalist. The journalist himself is a devastating portrait of the shallowness of the view of man held by the popular media, but, at the time the book was published, few critics recognized the novel's irony; most mistakenly assumed that Marquand approved of the general and his decisions. After *The Late George Apley* this novel represents Marquand's most complex use of narrative point of view for satire, and indicates that his use of technical devices and his skill as a satiric novelist continued to grow through much of his long career. *Sincerely, Willis Wayde* is that Marquand novel most obviously like Sinclair Lewis's novels of the 1920s. It is a devastating portrait of a big business promoter, a man utterly without character. In 1958 Marquand published what he declared in advance would be his last novel, *Women and Thomas Harrow,* the story of a very successful playwright and his three marriages. This novel is a kind of self-consciously ironic *Tempest* to John P. Marquand's career.

Marquand is particularly notable for the double vision, through which he could be in his world and still see it and himself from the vantage point of a detached onlooker. The result was that his portraits of American citizens, their frustrations, the extent to which their lives had already been determined by a structure of social decisions made by others without their awareness, and the sort of quiet desperation in which they lived out their days were particularly powerful. The reader who sees himself in some of his more absurd actions and postures in Marquand's novels has the feeling that he is also seeing Marquand as well. Like Sinclair Lewis he is the chronicler of men who make ineffectual revolts, of men who lack the stature of character and mind to be in any significant sense heroes; thus his ultimate view is comic. He examined the social conditions of American lives with irony and grace, and his "badgered American male" captures in his recurrent problems and poses not only how we behave, but also how hollow our lives often are at the core. He speaks both to our social-historical sense and to an unslaked spiritual thirst that our aridity creates. He never was capable of poetic soaring, but to his own age, at least, he spoke with ease and skill, with irony and wit, but, above all, with the authority of unsentimental knowledge.

—C. Hugh Holman

MARQUIS, Don(ald Robert Perry)

Born: Walnut, Illinois, 29 July 1878. **Education:** Walnut High School to age 15; Knox College, Galesburg, Illinois, one term; Corcoran School of Art, Washington, D.C., 1899-1900. **Family:** Married 1) Reina Melcher in 1909 (died 1923), one son and one daughter; 2) the actress Marjorie Vonnegut in 1926 (died 1936). **Career:** Worked in a pharmacy, on a chicken farm, on the railroad, and as a schoolteacher, late 1890s; clerk, U.S. Census Bureau, and reporter, Washington *Times,* 1900-02; journalist in Philadelphia, 1902; associate editor, Atlanta *News,* 1902-04; editorial writer, Atlanta *Journal,* 1904-07; associate editor to Joel Chandler Harris, *Uncle Remus's* magazine, Atlanta, 1907-09; reporter, New York *American,* and Brooklyn *Daily Eagle,* 1909-12; staff member, 1912, and columnist ("The Sun Dial"), 1912-22, New York *Sun;* columnist ("The Lantern"), New York *Tribune* (later *Herald Tribune*), 1922-25; screenwriter in Hollywood, 1928-29 and intermittently, 1931-36; founding publisher, *Column,* 1933. **Member:** American Academy, 1923. **Died:** 29 December 1937.

PUBLICATIONS

Collections

The Best of Marquis, edited by Christopher Morley. 1946.
Archyology II: The Final Dig—The Long Lost Tales of Archy and Mehitabel. 1998.

Fiction

Danny's Own Story. 1912.
The Cruise of the Jasper B. 1916.
Carter and Other People (stories). 1921.
Pandora Lifts the Lid, with Christopher Morley. 1924.
When the Turtles Sing and Other Unusual Tales. 1928.
A Variety of People (stories). 1929.
Off the Arm. 1930.
Chapters for the Orthodox (stories). 1934.
Sun Dial Time (stories). 1936.
Sons of the Puritans (unfinished novel). 1939.

Plays

The Old Soak (produced 1922). 1926.
The Dark Hours: Five Scenes from a History (produced 1932). 1924.
Words and Thoughts. 1924.
Out of the Sea (produced 1927). 1927.
Everything's Jake (produced 1930). 1978.
Master of the Revels. 1934.

Screenplay: *Skippy,* with others, 1931.

Poetry

Dreams and Dust. 1915.
Noah an' Jonah an' Cap'n John Smith. 1921.
Poems and Portraits. 1922.
Sonnets to a Red-Haired Lady (from a Gentleman with a Blue Beard) and Famous Love Affairs. 1922.
The Awakening and Other Poems. 1924.
The Lives and Times of Archy and Mehitabel. 1940.
　Archy and Mehitabel. 1927.
　Archy's Life of Mehitabel. 1933.
　Archy Does His Part. 1935.
Love Sonnets of a Cave Man and Other Verses. 1928.
An Ode to Hollywood. 1929.
The Archy and Mehitabel Omnibus: Archy and Mehitabel, with Archy's Life of Mehitabel. 1998.

Other

Hermione and Her Little Group of Serious Thinkers. 1916.
Prefaces. 1919.
The Old Soak, and Hail and Farewell. 1921.
The Revolt of the Oyster. 1922.
Mr. Hawley Breaks into Song. 1923.
The Old Soak's History of the World. 1924.
The Almost Perfect State (essays). 1927.
Her Foot Is on the Brass Rail. 1935.

*

Critical Studies: *O Rare Don Marquis: A Biography* by Edward Anthony, 1962; *Marquis* by Lynn Lee, 1981.

*　　*　　*

Don Marquis is remembered as a humorist, but he wrote both humorous and serious plays, poetry, and fiction. His last novel, *Sons of the Puritans,* is serious. Although unfinished, this autobiographical narrative about a boy who grows to manhood in a small Midwestern town presents greater depth of feeling and complexity of character and situation than Marquis's earlier, lighter novels. Like most of his work, it is well written and interesting. Like his serious short stories, plays, and poetry, however, it is unique without being very different from good books by other authors on the same subject.

His serious poetry in particular sounds like the well-written, graceful verse of other poets on the same well-worn themes. Yet his first collection of serious poems, *Dreams and Dust,* served a purpose; for the effect of much of his later comic verse—*Love Sonnets of a Cave Man,* for example—depends upon his sure knowledge of such themes in just such terms. Even his parodies of free verse, over the name of "Archy the Cockroach," occasionally contain poems that are comic largely on account of their sprightly elegant meter and rhyme.

Marquis is remembered chiefly for his creation of Archy, whose ideas and adventures first filled his newspaper columns and then were collected in books. Other columns, collected in *The Almost Perfect State,* deal lightly, humorously, sometimes seriously, with Marquis's notions concerning that state. Still other columns resulted in books about "The Old Soak," who became the central character in Marquis's only successful play.

The Old Soak, Archy the Cockroach, and Mehitabel the Cat reveal Marquis's comic capabilities at their best. As Archy, Marquis views life from the underside, that is, the side from which it appears ridiculous and therefore not to be taken seriously. So the incongruities, discrepancies, paradoxes involved in this view—whether of man's morality and politics, Mehitabel's social and artistic pretensions, or any other matter—strike the reader as comic. Further, Archy's literary efforts make him ridiculous in turn, both because he is a cockroach and because he has the quite human soul of a free verse poet. For his broken typographic lines, without punctuation or capital letters, could not have been written by a cockroach and should not have been written by a poet. The comic effect is increased by the mockery of free verse and its maker.

Similarly, the Old Soak cannot be taken seriously. His views of history, the Good Book, and prohibition, together with his misspellings and malapropisms, expose his ignorance and turn him

into a figure of fun. For good reason, the play about him succeeded, banal as it is, whereas Marquis's more serious plays—
mainly derived from legend and history—failed. Marquis was constantly depressed because he had to do what he called hack work
for a living, and believed his serious work had greater literary value.
Yet his strength lies not in development of character, but in "characters," not in suspenseful action, but in absurd situations. These
express his real gift, rare and rewarding in literature, the truly comic
angle of vision.

—Robert F. Richards

MARSHALL, Paule

Born: Brooklyn, New York, 9 April 1929. **Education:** Brooklyn
College (now of the City University of New York), B.A., 1953.
Hunter College, 1955. **Family:** Married 1) Kenneth E. Marshall
in 1950 (divorced 1963), one son; 2) Nourry Menard in 1970.
Career: Worked as a free-lance writer and librarian in the New
York Public Libraries 1950-53; staff writer of *Our World;* lecturer
on African-American literature at colleges and universities including Oxford University, Columbia University, Michigan State University, Lake Forest College, Cornell University, and Yale University; professor of English at Virginia Commonwealth University.
Awards: Guggenheim fellowship, 1960; Rosenthal award from the
National Institute of Arts and Letters, 1962; Ford Foundation grant,
1964-65; National Endowment for the Arts grant, 1967-68; Before Columbus Foundation American Book award, 1984. **Residence:** Richmond, Virginia.

PUBLICATIONS

Novels

Brown Girl, Brownstones. 1959; reprinted with afterword by Mary
    Helen Washington, 1981.
The Chosen Place, the Timeless People. 1969.
Praisesong for the Widow. 1983.
Daughters. 1991.

Short Stories

Soul Clap Hands and Sing. 1961.
Reena and Other Stories. 1983; as *Merle: A Novella and Other
    Stories.* 1985.

Play

Television Play: *Brown Girl, Brownstones.* 1960.

Nonfiction

Language Is the Only Homeland: Bajan Poets Abroad. 1995.

*

Critical Studies: "Sculpture and Space: The Interdependency
of Character and Culture in the Novels of Paule Marshall" by Bar-

bara Christian in *Black Woman Novelists: The Development of a
Tradition, 1892-1976,* 1980, and "Paule Marshall: A Literary Bi-
ography" and "Ritualistic Process and the Structure of Paule
Marshall's *Praisesong for the Widow*" by Christian in *Black Femi-
nist Criticism: Perspectives on Black Women Writers,* 1985; "The
Closing of the Circle: Movement from Division to Wholeness in
Paule Marshall's Fiction" by Eugenia Collier in *Black Women Writ-
ers (1950-1980)* edited by Mari Evans, 1984; "And Called Every
Generation Blessed: Theme, Setting, and Ritual in the Works of
Paule Marshall" by John McCluskey, Jr., in *Black Women Writers (1950-1980)* edited by Mari Evans, 1984; "Paule Marshall's
Praisesong for the Widow: The Reluctant Heiress, or Whose Life
Is It Anyway?" by Keith A. Sandiford in *Black American Literature Forum* vol. 21, no. 4, 1986; "The Widow's Journey to Self
and Roots: Aging and Society in Paule Marshall's *Praisesong for
the Widow*" by Barbara Frey Waxman in *Frontiers* vol. 9, no. 3,
1987; "Describing Arcs of Recovery: Paule Marshall's Relationship to Afro-American Culture" by Susan Willis in *Specifying:
Black Women Writing the American Experience,* 1987; "Politics
and Metaphors of Materialism in Paule Marshall's *Praisesong for
the Widow* and Toni Morrison's *Tar Baby*" by Angelita Reyes in
*Politics and the Muse: Studies in the Politics of Recent American
Literature* edited by Adam J. Sorkin, 1989; "Paule Marshall's Bajan
Women in *Brown Girl, Brownstones*" by Helene Christol in *Women
and War: The Changing Status of American Women from the 1930s
to the 1950s* edited by Maria Diedrich, 1990; interview with Daryl
Cumber Dance in *The Southern Review* vol. 28, no. 1, 1992; *To-
ward Wholeness in Paule Marshall's Fiction* by Joyce Owens
Pettis, 1995; *Bridging the Americas: The Literature of Paule
Marshall, Toni Morrison, and Gayl Jones* by Stelamaris Coser, 1995;
Places of Silence, Journeys of Freedom: The Fiction of Paule Marshall
by Eugenia C. DeLamotte, 1998; *Caribbean Waves: Relocating Claude
McKay and Paule Marshall* by Heather Hathaway, 1999.

*   *   *

Paule Marshall has stated that her goal as a writer is "to create
a body of work that will offer young black women . . . a more
truthful image of themselves in literature." Such a literature,
Marshall said in *Southern Review*, "is an empowering force. It
gives us the sense of our right to 'be' in the world, and once you
have that sense of your right to be in the world, all positive things
follow from that." With the publication of her first novel, *Brown
Girl, Brownstones,* in 1959, Marshall began to achieve her desire, providing a younger generation of African American women writers—
Alice Walker, Gloria Naylor, Terry McMillan, and others—with
a model that Marshall never found in her vast reading as a child.
    Marshall's fiction situates her characters not just in America but
in the larger world inhabited by the African diaspora—Latin
America, the Caribbean, and North America—and in a time that
includes the past and present. Marshall identifies two major
themes in her writing: connection and reconciliation. She creates
characters who must connect and be reconciled to their racial history, to their own personal pasts, to their communities (in Brooklyn, the American South, the West Indies, Africa, and Brazil), and
to one another. She is especially concerned that her works show
"all o' we is one," as the Carnival motto claims in *The Chosen
Place, The Timeless People.* Marshall's career as a writer started
when she was a child listening to her mother and the other immigrant women from Barbados talking in the kitchen, just as the protagonist of her first novel does. Though an avid reader as a child,

Marshall writes, "No grade school literature teacher of mine had ever mentioned Dunbar or James Weldon Johnson or Langston Hughes. I didn't know that Zora Neale Hurston existed . . . Nor was I made aware of people like Frederick Douglass and Harriet Tubman." She read whatever she could find at the Brooklyn Public Library, from Jane Austen to Thomas Hardy to **Zane Grey.** However, she says, "I never saw me" in anything she read until she came across the poetry of **Paul Laurence Dunbar.** His writing convinced her of two things: that dialect or "nonstandard" English, the language she heard and spoke at home, had a place in great literature; and that, since it was written about in books, her life as an African American had value. Her mentors, then, became the women in the kitchen, who "didn't just sit around the kitchen table and tell a story 'in any old kinda way,'" as she told Sabine Brock; instead, their stories displayed a clear sense of structure, characterization, and drama. Most importantly, as those women— who worked all day scrubbing white women's floors, cooking other people's food, and serving as live-in maids for rich white families—talked about their neighbors, their children, and "home," they also discussed the economy, FDR, and Marcus Garvey. The young Marshall began to see them and herself in a larger context— as part of a larger world of dark people. And when she came upon **Gwendolyn Brooks's** novel *Maud Martha,* she saw reflected there the lives of ordinary dark-skinned women. Maud is not like the stereotypical black women found in the works of **Mark Twain** and **William Faulkner,** not Topsy or the maids in *Gone With the Wind.* Brooks gave Marshall literary permission to write about the lives of her community, a community particularly of women spread around the world from Brooklyn to the Sea Islands to Barbados to Brazil.

Brown Girl, Brownstones (1959) was a critical though not a financial success. Reprinted in 1981, it has since become a standard in the African American and women's literature canon. The story of a Brooklyn family with roots in Barbados, the novel focuses on two characters: the adolescent Selina Boyce and her hardworking mother Silla, who, both in their own ways, attempt to find a bridge between two worlds—West Indian immigrant culture and American culture. Silla's way is through the acquisition of real estate. Cleaning offices and other people's houses, she buys the American Dream, a Brooklyn brownstone. In the process, however, she drives away her husband, silences her already reticent older daughter, and creates an irreparable divide between herself and her youngest daughter. Selina inherits her mother's strength, which she uses to navigate her world, exploring her identity and her awakening sexuality as well as American jazz and Bajan customs. Battling Silla's intimidating force also gives Selina the stamina to make her own way from the Flatbush and childhood to Barbados and adulthood.

Central to Marshall's next two works—her collection of four short stories, *Soul Clap Hands and Sing* (1961), and her novel *The Chosen Place, The Timeless People* (1969)—is the issue of identity as shaped by history, culture, race, and class. The four stories in her collection, entitled "Barbados," "Brooklyn," "British Guiana," and "Brazil," represent a postcolonial world in which men nearing the ends of their lives struggle to know where they belong and who they are. Marshall uses as a basis for her stories the political climate of the 1950s, a time of newly acquired independence in the West Indies and political persecution in Joseph McCarthy's America. As Stelamaris Coser observes, in these stories "the old structure, like the protagonists, is patriarchal and decadent, but young people and new ideals may announce change."

Saul Amrow of *The Chosen Place* is a Jewish American anthropologist married to a rich Philadelphia socialite-turned-researcher, Marion Shippens, whose family fortunes can be traced to the colonial period's triangular West Indian slave trade. Employed by a U.S. foundation intent on bringing a multimillion-dollar development to the West Indies, Saul comes to Bourne Island confident that his scholarly insights will lead to economic well-being for the island's poor inhabitants—only to discover that he understands nothing about this place and people. The light-skinned, educated elite of the island have no confidence in the future for the dark-skinned poor. When Saul's affair with the English-educated mulatta Merle Kinbana and Marion's recognition of her family's responsibility in the slave trade lead to the latter's suicide, Saul is transformed. Convinced that the investment scheme will destroy the poor of Bournehill, who live a marginal existence dependent on sugar cane, Saul is removed from the project but stays on to do anthropological work that will improve the lives of the poor. A crucial part of the novel is the island's celebration of Carnival, a time, according to Coser, that "helps unmask the hypocrisy hidden in the development scheme, as well as the contradictions within each individual"—a catharsis that can and does, on the one hand, lead to catastrophe but, on the other, presents the possibility of interracial unity and community.

Praisesong for the Widow (1983) is Marshall's most critically acclaimed work and perhaps her best. It is an account of sixty-year-old Avey Johnson's journey of self-discovery, one that requires her to consider the price she and her husband paid for their middle-class status. She must remember what she had long forgotten—her family, her history, and her African heritage. Aboard the luxury cruise liner *Bianca Pride,* making its way from one Caribbean tourist spot to the next, Avey dreams of her old great-aunt Cuney, the family matriarch with whom the little girl Avey spent her summers in the Georgia-Carolina Sea Islands. Aunt Cuney told Avey stories of the Ibos brought from Africa, noble people who saw the slavery that awaited them in this country and decided to walk back across the water to Africa rather than wear chains. Avey's uneasiness subsequent to dreaming drives her from the ship to Grenada to await the next flight home to New York. Among the islanders, whose faces and voices remind her of the West Indians with whom she grew up in Harlem, Avey dreams again, this time of her husband, the man whose passion for her, for jazz, and for African American poetry was replaced by ambition and a desire for money. In her dream Jerome Johnson chastises his wife for throwing away her boat passage and wasting money. She awakens, remembering only now, three years after his death, that she never cried at her husband's funeral. She realizes that *Jay* Johnson, the husband she loved, died years ago when the respectable Masonic Lodge member *Jerome* Johnson took his place. Avey wanders up the Grenadan beach into the rum shop of Lebert Joseph. When he tries to convince her to accompany him on the Carriacou Excursion, an annual pilgrimage to pay homage to the island's forebears, she hesitates until he asks her, "And what you is?" She cannot answer what nation she comes from— Arada, Cromanti, Yarraba, Temne, Banda, Moko. Despite her name, upon which Aunt Cuney had insisted—"Avatara," the incarnation of all who went before her—Avey cannot recall her nation until she makes the difficult trip to Carriacou. There she participates in the Dance of Nations and joins in the dance called the Carriacou Tramp, a variation of the Ring Shout she saw in the South with her great-aunt. Participation in this communal act allows Avey to discover her identity as a member of the African diaspora.

Daughters, Marshall's 1991 novel, examines another member of that diaspora, one who lives in two cultures—in contemporary urban New York and on the Caribbean island of Triunion. In the novel Marshall is interested in both personal and political issues. The central character, Ursa MacKenzie, is daughter to Triunion's prime minister, a man whose youthful idealism has been compromised by age, petty local politics, and "First World" control of "Third World" countries. Having thrown off colonialism, the newly independent West Indian countries find their leaders repeating old patterns of corruption and exploitation. Ursa recognizes the same sort of corruption in New Jersey city politics, which she is privy to as a researcher and one-time true believer in political reform. The city's new black mayor betrays his supporters in favor of politics as usual; white men in suits who have money hold more sway than poor black constituents. Returning home for her father's last election, Ursa and her father's former supporters abandon him in hope of the people's true political autonomy. She knows her father's young opponent, Ursa's poor childhood "fowl-yard" playmate, has the idealism and energy needed to move Triunion forward.

Daughters is also about personal autonomy. Marshall has remarked that "daughters" in the title refers to all the women who make Ursa who she is: her mother Estelle, the American daughter of a long line of Tennessee schoolteachers and social workers, who met and married Primus MacKenzie in Connecticut and who emigrates to Triunion to aid in his nation building; Astral Forde, Primus MacKenzie's "keep-miss," his mistress, who runs his motel and holds towels and juice after each of Ursa's childhood Sunday swims; Celestine Bellgarde, one of Primus's mother's "fowl-yard" children, eight years his elder, who provides young Primus with his first sexual experience and remains his trusted servant and a second mother to Ursa all her life; and, finally, Congo Jane, the mythical slave woman who, with Will Cudjoe, led a slave rebellion and is commemorated with a statue on the island, providing Ursa with one of her earliest memories as her mother lifts her up to touch the toes of this great woman's figure. On the shoulders of all these women, Ursa is able to leave her pointless relationship with the fastidious Lowell Carruthers, who cannot commit to Ursa. She can now help her mother bring her father's political career to an end and begin an independent life with a clear sense of her own identity.

Paule Marshall is an extraordinary writer whose vision of African American experience is not confined to this continent. She places the members of the diaspora in the larger world from which they come and must return—through history, memory, storytelling, and culture—in order to arrive at self-knowledge and self-acceptance. Marshall has said, "All of my novels and stories come out of questions I'm always putting to myself . . . Writing novels and stories is my way of seeking answers." The questions she poses and the answers she finds are ones that inform and delight all of us.

—Laura Weiss Zlogar

MARVEL, Ik. *See* **MITCHELL, Donald Grant.**

MASO, Carole

Education: Vassar College, B.A. 1977. **Career:** Distinguished writer-in-residence, Illinois State University, 1991-92; Jenny McKeon Moore writer-in-residence, George Washington Univer-

sity, 1992-93; associate professor of writing, School of the Arts, Columbia University, New York City, 1993. Since 1995 professor of English and director of creative writing, Brown University. **Awards:** CAPS Grant for fiction, 1983; W.K. Rose fellowship in the creative arts, 1985; New York Foundation for the Arts grant, 1987; National Endowment for the Arts Emerging Artist Reading grant, 1987; National Endowment for the Arts Literature grant, 1988; Lannan Literary fellowship for fiction, 1993.

PUBLICATIONS

Novels

Ghost Dance. 1987.
The Art Lover. 1990.
Ava. 1993.
The American Woman in the Chinese Hat. 1994.
Defiance. 1996.

Screenplay: *Pandora's Box,* 1993.

*

Critical Study: "Carole Maso: An Introduction and an Interpellated Interview" by V.F. Harris, in *Review of Contemporary Fiction,* 1997.

*   *   *

The failure to include Carole Maso in many standard reference works devoted to contemporary writers underscores both the rarefied nature of her writing and the difficulty the literary establishment has appreciating and accommodating work published by alternative presses. Defying the logic of conventional narrative that, she believes, "reassures no one," Maso writes a fiction in which "form takes as many risks as the content." She takes a similarly iconoclastic approach to language. Helene Cixous's call for a language that extends rather than limits possibility and that "heals as much as it separates" is central to Maso's erotically as well as aesthetically inclined writing. Hers is an art which evokes and alludes rather than makes explicit: an art of tenuous, fragile connections rather than reductive causal relationships in which the limited and limiting goal of the work of art as a finished product is supplanted by the open-endedness of the work-in-progress and (in Roland Barthes's terms) the pleasures (*jouissance*) of the writerly text.

Ghost Dance offers an excellent as well as accessible introduction to Maso's major preoccupations. Vanessa Wing, the daughter of a famous poet and a Princeton philosopher, tries to deal with the loss (disappearance) of her parents and brother by trying to remember them. Drawn to "the order of libraries," as well as the golden ratio and the sacred hoop, Vanessa follows the twin paths of imagination and philosophy in her search for peace, for the elusive missing piece that will restore her to wholeness. Setting down the things she knows out of scraps of memory—sometimes just a line, sometimes more—she fashions a narrative that proves both disjunctive and elegiac.

These qualities are more apparent in Maso's more formally innovative second novel, *The Art Lover.* Here Caroline Chrysler's need to name, order, and arrange is far greater following the death of her father, an art historian. While settling his estate, Caroline carries on a dialogue with her dead father that incorporates, or is interspersed with, a vast array of materials at once distinct from the main narrative yet in their own way pertinent to it: poems, fliers concerning lost pets, text and illustrations from art history books, "Skywatch" columns from the *New York Times*, photos, letters, prayers, and lines from the *Baltimore Catechism*. The sensibility veers sharply from **T. S. Eliot's** shoring of fragments against the ruin in this highly personal *Waste Land* to **William Carlos Williams's** loving attention to the thing itself. Caroline is "the lover of detail" "trying to regain analytic perspective" by an act, and art, which seeks simultaneously to restore a lost world and to keep that world at bay by turning to, and turning it into, art. However, in Maso's fiction, art and life intertwine like lovers. The necessity of turning life into art and vice versa—and, via art, of keeping the dead alive as well as at an aesthetically safe distance—is especially apparent when Caroline's story gives way first to the story she is writing about a character not unlike herself and, finally, to Maso's own story of love and loss. One can ultimately say of all three stories, of *The Art Lover* as a complex whole, and of Maso's work in general what the novel says of "Van Gogh in the wheat field lifting his brush to forestall collapse"–"to resist disintegration."

In *The American Woman in the Chinese Hat*—the fourth of her published novels but third in order of composition—Maso continues her preoccupation with or meditation on the relationship between art and loss while expanding on fiction's erotic possibilities. Catherine's success as a writer has resulted in a falling out with her lover. While hoping that her lover will join her in France, Catherine writes about waiting and the several lovers she takes. In this reimagining of Thomas Mann's "Death in Venice," Catherine's "sad stories"—"stories of love and love taken away"—are played out against her belief that "Nothing is ever forgotten. Everything comes back." The erotic energy of language and life is pressed further in *Aureole*. In this "story of the woman who wants," the line separating the narrative from the lyrical, between one story or character and another, is not so much blurred as obliterated in a novel of "glimpses" linked solely by desire.

Interesting as *The American Woman* and *Aureole* are, however, it is the novel Maso wrote between them, *Ava*, that is her masterwork. Ava Klein is another of Maso's sensuous and highly cultivated female protagonists, a thirty-nine-year-old professor of comparative literature, a "rare bird" dying of a rare blood disease. The novel follows Ava, or rather her mind, during her last day ("Morning," "Afternoon," "Night") as she wanders over the course of her life. Part *Arabian Nights* and part "Song of Myself," *Ava* brilliantly gives emotional and aesthetic substance to the cliché "her whole life flashed before her eyes" and the kitschiness of *The Sound of Music* song "My Favorite Things." This "story without a message," as Maso has described it, "throbs" and "pulses" with life. It joyously rather than sadly savors a life lived so fully, sensuously, and sensitively, but once again it is set against that awareness of loss that gives Maso's writing both its power and its poignancy.

Defiance differs from Maso's earlier novels in two important ways. It is the first issued by a major commercial publisher since the 1987 paperback reprint of *Ghost Dance* and the first to deal with eroticism's dark side. Bernadette O'Brien, a physics professor at Harvard, seeks in equations what Maso's other protagonists seek in art. What most distinguishes her from her predecessors in Maso's work is her working-class Irish Catholic background.

In a world of sexual repression and intellectual stultification, she is made to feel a misfit, which is what she becomes when she kills two of her most brilliant students, the first by design ("this highly stylized, preposterous exorcism"), the second by chance. In her life the erotic becomes the demonic, passion turns into perversion. In the journal she writes in prison, the sexually charged prose of the earlier novels becomes the fierce, defiant language of her "death book." Far from being a foray into the lurid and sensational, *Defiance* offers a harrowing depiction of death-obsessed Puritan America in which "the obsessive fear of our own erotic [and imaginative] power has done us in, yes."

—Robert Morace

MASON, Bobbie Ann

Born: Mayfield, Kentucky, 1 May 1940. **Education:** University of Kentucky, Lexington, B.A. 1962; State University of New York at Binghamton, M.A. 1966; University of Connecticut, Storrs, Ph.D. 1972. **Family:** Married Roger B. Rawlings (a magazine editor and writer) in 1969. **Career:** Writer for the *Mayfield Messenger* in Kentucky, 1960; writer for magazines including *Movie Stars, Movie Life,* and *T.V. Star Parade,* New York City, 1962-63; assistant professor of English, Mansfield State College, Pennsylvania, 1972-79; writer, beginning 1979. **Awards:** National Book Critics Circle nomination, 1982; American Book award nomination, 1982; PEN-Faulkner nomination, 1983; Ernest Hemingway Foundation award, 1983; National Endowment for the Arts fellowship, 1983; Pennsylvania Arts Council grant, 1983; Guggenheim fellowship, 1984; American Academy and Institute for Arts and Letters award, 1984; Southern Book award, 1993. **Residence:** Kentucky.

PUBLICATIONS

Collections

Shiloh and Other Stories. 1982.
Love Life: Stories. 1989.

Novels

In Country. 1985.
Spence + Lila. 1988.
Feather Crowns. 1993.

Short Stories

Landscapes, with Martha Bennett Stiles. 1984.
With Jazz. 1996.
Still Life with Watermelon. 1998.

Other

Nabokov's Garden: A Guide to Ada. 1974.
The Girl Sleuth: A Feminist Guide. 1974.
Clear Springs: A Memoir. 1999.

Recordings: selections from *In Country,* 1985; *Spence + Lila,* 1989.

*

Critical Studies: "Private Rituals" by Albert E. Wilhelm, in *Midwest Quarterly,* winter 1987; "The Freak Endures" by Linda Adams Barnes, in *Since Flannery O'Connor,* 1987; interview by Albert E. Wilhelm, in *Southern Quarterly,* winter 1988; "The Function of Popular Culture in Bobbie Ann Mason's *Shiloh and Other Stories* and *In Country*" by Leslie White, in *Southern Quarterly,* summer 1988; "Dispatches from Ghost Country" by Thomas Meyers, in *Genre* vol. 21, no. 4, 1988; "Minimalism and the American Dream" by Barbara Henning, in *Modern Fiction Studies,* winter 1989; "Narrative Strategies in Recent Vietnam War Fiction" by Marilyn Durham, and "Men, Women, and Vietnam" by Milton J. Bates, both in *America Rediscovered,* 1990; "Decentered Authority in Bobbie Ann Mason's *In Country*" by Barbara T. Ryan, in *Critique,* spring 1990; "Bobbie Ann Mason and the Recovery of Mystery" by Richard Giannone, in *Studies in Short Fiction,* fall 1990; "Gender Issues in Bobbie Ann Mason's *In Country*" by Ellen A. Blais, in *South Atlantic Review,* May 1991; interview by Bonnie Lyons and Bill Oliver in *Contemporary Literature,* winter 1991; "Use to the Menfolks Would Eat First" by Darlene Reimers Hill, in *Southern Quarterly,* winter-spring 1992; interview by Dorothy Combs Hill in *Southern Quarterly,* fall 1992; "Humping the Boonies" by Katherine Kinney, and "Realism, Verisimilitude, and the Depiction of Vietnam Veterans in *In Country*" by Matthew C. Stewart, both in *Fourteen Landing Zones,* 1992; "Remembering Vietnam" by Joanna Price, in *Journal of American Studies,* August 1993; "History As Her Story: Adapting Bobbie Ann Mason's *In Country* to Film" in *Vision/Revision: Adapting Contemporary American Fiction by Women to Film* by Barbara Tepa Lupack, 1996.

*   *   *

Bobbie Ann Mason, author of two short-story collections and three novels, is one of contemporary American fiction's most promising authors. Known for her portrayal of blue collar southern life, Mason draws on her observations of life in rural Kentucky, where she was born and raised. Mason attended a country school and then went to Mayfield High School, where she won a scholarship to the University of Kentucky. There, she majored in journalism and wrote for the school paper. Mason subsequently moved to New York City and worked as a writer for fan magazines. Following graduate studies in New York and Connecticut, she taught English at Mansfield State College in Pennsylvania.

In 1979 Mason left her academic post to devote her time and energy to her fiction. After submitting twenty short stories to the *New Yorker,* Mason got her first story accepted and published in 1980. *Shiloh and Other Stories,* Mason's first major collection, was published only two years later. Mason won the Ernest Hemingway Foundation award in 1983 for *Shiloh* and received nominations for other prestigious awards. Mason's success stems from her ability to create rural atmospheres peopled with engaging but problem-ridden characters who attempt to survive in the Wal-mart culture that pervades Mason's work. Her characters are "regular" people—busboys, housewives, clerks at Kroger, truck drivers, high school dropouts—rather than romantic heroes. She uses references to popular culture to draw her readers into close identification with her characters. Instead of distant caricatures of

rednecks or hillbillies, Mason creates three-dimensional country people who struggle to find a place for themselves in the modern world.

Many of Mason's characters have to deal with changes in their lives that catch them by surprise. In *Shiloh and Other Stories,* Mason writes about husbands and wives in marriages that break up, a father who attempts to keep up with his college-age daughter by reading her textbooks when she comes home, and families who live together but who cannot cross the generation gaps separating them. These divisions and changes add depth of emotion to these stories, which are deceptively simple on the surface. The humor stemming from popular culture references turns in on itself as Mason shows how these characters are representative of larger issues that human beings face: death, divorce, loss of love.

Mason's first novel, *In Country,* continues her exploration of characters who live in rural Kentucky. Samantha (Sam), the novel's protagonist, represents America's struggle to resolve the aftermath of the Vietnam War. Fresh out of high school (class of 1984), she spends the summer on a quest to learn more about her father, who was killed in Vietnam before Sam was born. Sam turns to her mother, Irene, and her uncle, Emmett, to help her on her journey, but neither source proves very cooperative. Irene is remarried and has started another family. Emmett, a Vietnam veteran himself, has to struggle to maintain his own equilibrium and is not interested in reviving memories of the war. Mason uses her trademark popular culture references and humor throughout the novel to engage readers in the story. *In Country*'s climax is Sam's trip to the Vietnam Veterans Memorial, where she finds both her father's name and her own. Warner Bros. made *In Country* into a feature film starring Bruce Willis as Emmett and Emily Lloyd as Sam in 1989.

Spence + Lila, Mason's second novel, is the story of a Kentucky couple who live on a farm and have been married for more than forty years. The novel alternates between their memories of the past and scenes where they confront the pain of the present, particularly Lila's upcoming surgery. The strength of this short novel is Mason's continuing use of realistic detail and dialogue to vivify her characters.

But it is Mason's third novel, *Feather Crowns,* that promises to secure her reputation as a powerful novelist. This story is set in Hopewell, Kentucky, the same town in *In Country,* but the time is the turn of the century. Christie and James Wheeler live in hard economic times. However, the birth of their quintuplets renders everything else in their lives insignificant, and changes Christie's entire outlook on life. The outside world becomes interested in the Wheeler babies, and Christie becomes interested in the world. Mason maintains her use of authentic details and period dialogue to underscore the realities of her characters' lives.

Mason's unique blend of humor and realism with elements of popular culture makes her stories both accessible and powerful. Readers of her work cannot help but see parts of themselves in her characters grappling with elusive concepts like hope and happiness. It is this ability to represent humanity at its most vulnerable that makes Mason such an important voice in contemporary American literature.

—Deanna E. Ramey

MASTERS, Edgar Lee

Born: Garnett, Kansas, 23 August 1868; brought up in Lewistown, Illinois. **Education:** Schools in Lewistown; Knox

College, Galesburg, Illinois, 1889; studied law in his father's law office; admitted to Illinois bar, 1891. **Family:** Married 1) Helen M. Jenkins in 1898 (divorced 1925), three children; 2) Ellen Coyne in 1926. **Career:** Lawyer in Chicago, 1891-1921; then full-time writer in New York. **Awards:** Twain Medal, 1927; Academy of American Poets fellowship, 1946. **Died:** 5 March 1950.

PUBLICATIONS

Collections

Selected Poems, edited by Denys Thompson. 1972.
The Enduring River: Edgar Lee Master's Uncollected Spoon River Poems, edited by Herbert K. Russell. 1991.

Poetry

A Book of Verses. 1898.
The Blood of the Prophets. 1905.
Songs and Sonnets. 2 vols., 1910-12.
Spoon River Anthology. 1915; revised edition, 1916.
The Great Valley. 1916.
Songs and Satires. 1916.
Toward the Gulf. 1918.
Starved Rock. 1919.
Domesday Book. 1920.
The Open Sea. 1921.
The New Spoon River. 1924.
Selected Poems. 1925.
The Fate of the Jury: An Epilogue to Domesday Book. 1929.
Lichee Nuts. 1930.
The Serpent in the Wilderness. 1933.
Invisible Landscapes. 1935.
The Golden Fleece of California. 1936.
Poems of People. 1936.
The New World. 1937.
More People. 1939.
Illinois Poems. 1941.
Along the Illinois. 1942.
The Harmony of Deeper Music: Posthumous Poems, edited by Frank K. Robinson. 1976.

Plays

Maximilian. 1902.
Althea. 1907.
The Trifler. 1908.
The Leaves of the Tree. 1909.
Eileen. 1910.
The Locket. 1910.
The Bread of Idleness. 1911.
Lee: A Dramatic Poem. 1926.
Jack Kelso: A Dramatic Poem. 1928.
Gettysburg, Manila, Acoma. 1930.
Godbey: A Dramatic Poem. 1931.
Dramatic Duologues (includes *Henry VIII and Ann Boleyn, Andrew Jackson and Peggy Eaton, Aaron Burr and Madam Jumel, Rabelais and the Queen of Whims*). 1934.
Richmond: A Dramatic Poem. 1934.

Fiction

Mitch Miller. 1920.
Children of the Market Place. 1922.
Skeeters Kirby. 1923.
The Nuptial Flight. 1923.
Mirage. 1924.
Kit O'Brien. 1927.
The Tide of Time. 1937.

Other

The New Star Chamber and Other Essays. 1904.
Levy Mayer and the New Industrial Era: A Biography. 1927.
Lincoln, The Man. 1931.
The Tale of Chicago. 1933.
Vachel Lindsay: A Poet in America. 1935.
Across Spoon River: An Autobiography. 1936.
Whitman. 1937.
Mark Twain: A Portrait. 1938.
The Sangamon (on the Sangamon River). 1942.

Editor, *The Living Thoughts of Emerson.* 1940.

*

Bibliography: *Masters: Catalogue and Checklist* by Frank K. Robinson, 1970.

Critical Studies: *The Chicago Renaissance in American Letters* by Bernard Duffey, 1954; *The Vermont Background of Masters* by Kimball Flaccus, 1955; in *America's Literary Revolt* by Michael Yatron, 1959; *Spoon River Revisited* by Lois Hartley, 1963; *Masters: The Spoon River Poet and His Critics* by John T. Flanagan, 1974; *The Vision of This Land: Studies of Vachel Lindsay, Masters, and Carl Sandburg* edited by John E. Hallwas and Dennis J. Reader, 1976; *Masters: A Biographical Sketchbook* by Hardin Wallace Masters, 1978; *Beyond Spoon River: The Legacy of Masters* by Ronald Primeau, 1981; *Last Stands: Notes from Memory* by Hilary Masters, 1982; *Masters* by John H. and Margaret M. Wrenn, 1983; "Two Unpublished Edgar Lee Masters Manuscripts" by Howard A. Wilson, in *Great Lakes Review: A Journal of Midwest Culture,* fall 1984; "Revolt from the Grave: Spoon River Anthology by Edgar Lee Masters" by K. Narayana Chandran, in *Midwest Quarterly: A Journal of Contemporary Thought,* summer 1988; "Meditations on *Spoon River Anthology:* The Epitaph As Life" by Emilio Timoneda, in *American Notes & Queries,* summer 1997, pp. 45-47.

* * *

One of the ancient Greek poets has written: "No man knows happiness; all men / Learn misery who live beneath the sun," thereby anticipating the spirit of Edgar Lee Masters's *Spoon River Anthology.* Though the book was brilliantly successful, the road to it was a long and arduous one. Seventeen years earlier Masters's first book of poems was an ignominious failure. The next few books were also unsuccessful. By this date the poet was a well-known lawyer, a robust man about town in Chicago who had made an unsuitable marriage but never allowed matrimony to interfere with his libertine instincts. The contrast between the poems, classic in form and hackneyed in thought, and their lusty author led one literary friend of Masters, the editor of *Reedy's Mirror,* to nudge him in the direction of a more original subject-matter. In any case, at the age of 45, Masters had failed at poetry, the one great passion of his life, and in his personal life. His one transcendent gift, fascination with human nature and insight into its workings, had found expression only in his legal career where he had espoused the cause of working-class victims of capitalist greed.

This was the situation in May 1914, when the poet's mother arrived to visit him. According to Masters, this lady was witty, acutely observant, and "full of divinations" into the lives of the townspeople they had known in Petersburg and Lewistown, Illinois. Mother and son reviewed these lives, reviving emotions and interests that had long been dormant in the poet's mind. The result was the sudden eruption of his latent gifts as chronicler of a whole community of inter-related lives. Between May and December, though under heavy pressure from his legal duties, Masters composed the 214 epitaphs that were published that year in Reedy's Mirror. Other than the memory of his neighbors, the chief sources of inspiration were the polished epigrams of the Greek Anthology and the stimulus of the American free verse revolt that had just burst on a startled, genteel reading public. These three sources, along with the sobering reflections on human mortality induced by his mother's visit, produced "the most read and talked of volume of poetry that has ever been written in America."

Five years after the publication of *Spoon River,* Masters retired from the law and devoted himself to the writing of thirty or more books of poetry, novels, biographies, and Illinois history and geography. Though he showed a dogged determination to succeed, he never caught fire again. His first great achievement was his last, and the remaining 35 years of his life were an embarrassing anticlimax as his first 45 were a despairing preparation. Masters's own life, which he includes in his book under the name Webster Ford, was one of the most curious and ironical of the tales he tells there.

The anthology, as expanded and republished in 1916, contains a short prologue, "The Hill," and 243 individual epitaphs. The verses, of a marvelous conciseness and vitality, relate only the most essential features of the speakers' lives. Each soul, speaking for himself from the grave, bares his innermost nature and the secrets of his life, his own self-portrait being qualified by the words of those with whom his fate was interlocked, so that nineteen separate story lines are developed. Each epitaph has its own tone and style; each speaker treats the climactic experiences or insights of his life. Depending on the character of the speaker, the language varies from mystical utterance downwards to sonorous rhetoric and racy colloquialism. The criticism that the style is prosy and flat, made by **Floyd Dell** and others when the book first appeared, is traceable to the lack of conventional prettiness in meter and rhyme. Though rarely "pretty," many of the poems are written in a highly imaginative metaphoric style, all are freshly conceived on the basis of a unifying rhetorical design with ample use of every form of verbal patterning, many are haunting, and some contain images of real beauty.

Without the power of its language, *Spoon River* would never have aroused its readers as it did. But its essence is in its portraiture. As few other authors have done, and no other author, perhaps, in the compass of a single book, Masters produced a "summation" and "universal depiction of life." Every variety of human nature is represented: celebrants at life's feast and neurasthenics, rowdies and lovers, pious Christians and atheists, rapists and whores, society women and laundresses, scientists and factory hands, clairvoyants, preachers, and a stable boy who sees the face of God. One of the largest groups is the philosophers. Masters was a zealous scholar and had read widely in several languages. Along with the anti-Christian and libertarian elements in his make-up, there was also the social idealist, the cosmic optimist, and the mystic that he counted as his essential self. The epitaphs of the philosophers are usually limited to one strand of thought from which one may infer their life and character, and their reflections are framed in such a way that they are as dramatic as the life histories.

Two criticisms of Masters should be considered here. The first is that the poet is preoccupied with sex, and much of the anthology is sordid and obscene. This charge, originating with **Amy Lowell** and others, is curious because there are only a dozen poems that are chiefly concerned with sex, none of these is salacious, and they tend to show that the wages of sin are death. The basis of the complaint lies in the candor with which Masters treats sex wherever it appears in life. Readers had been conditioned to literature in which the subject-matter was not actual life but a given writer's conception of it so that much of the earth and roots had been removed—as well as the uppermost reaches of branches that were beyond the interests of a workaday world. One of the novelties of Masters's treatment was to eliminate authorial censorship and to allow his characters, based as they were on real-life persons, to speak honestly of their lives. Though this was not his intention, the result was the first expose of village life, which set a new pattern for literature, while the poet's views are said to have influenced subsequent writing between the two world wars.

According to the second objection, the poet falsified the American Midwestern town by presenting an overly sensationalistic and pessimistic account of its life. It is true that the incidence of crime and sudden death is greater than one would normally find, but Masters was not writing a sociological report. The epitaphs taken together form a highly patterned comical tragedy that represents life as it works on the human imagination. At some moment all of these disasters actually happen to someone, but the book, as Alice Henderson remarked, is also steeped in a "flaming idealism." There are many heroes and noble souls, and the final impression that it makes is of the dignity, stoic courage, and resilience of humanity in its hapless "fool's errand" to the grave. In writing these portraits, Masters creates the bond of understanding and sympathy with a many-faced humanity that motivated his own legal work for luckless victims of circumstances.

—Glenn Richard Ruihley

MATHER, Cotton

Born: Boston, Massachusetts, 12 February 1663; son of the clergyman and writer Increase Mather. **Education:** Home and at Boston Latin School; Harvard University, Cambridge, Massachusetts, 1675-78, A.B. 1678; studied medicine, 1679-80, M.A. 1681. **Family:** Married l) Abigail Phillips in 1686 (died 1702), nine children; 2) Elizabeth Clark Hubbard in 1703 (died 1713), six children; 3) Lydia Lee George in 1715. **Career:** Assistant, 1680-85 (ordained 1685), teacher, 1685-1723, and minister, 1723-28, 2nd Congregational Church (Old North Church), Boston. A leader in colony's rebellion against British governor Sir Edmund Andros, 1689. Fellow, Harvard University, 1690-1703: appointed president of Harvard, 1703, but appointment overruled; involved with Connecticut College (later Yale University): appointed president, 1721 (declined). D.D.: University of Glasgow, Scotland, 1710. **Member:** Royal Society (London), 1713 (first American-born member). **Died:** 13 February 1728.

PUBLICATIONS

Collections

Selections, edited by Kenneth B. Murdock. 1926.
Selected Letters, edited by Kenneth Silverman. 1971.

Works (selection)

A Poem Dedicated to the Memory of Urian Oakes. 1682.
The Boston Ephemeris: An Almanack. 1683.
An Elegy on Nathaniel Collins. 1685.
The Call of the Gospel. 1686.
Military Duties Recommended to an Artillery Company. 1687.
Early Piety Exemplified. 1689.
The Declaration of the Gentlemen. 1689.
Work upon the Ark. 1689.
Memorable Providences, Relating to Witchcrafts and Possessions. 1689; in *Narratives of the Witchcraft Cases 1648-1706,* edited by George Lincoln Burr, 1914.
The Present State of New-England. 1690.
A Companion for Communicants. 1690.
The Way to Prosperity. 1690.
The Wonderful Works of God Commemorated. 1690.
Little Flocks Guarded against Grievous Wolves. 1691.
Some Considerations on the Bills of Credit. 1691.
The Triumphs of the Reformed Religion in America. 1691; as *The Life and Death of the Renowned Mr. John Eliot,* 1691.
Blessed Unions. 1692.
Fair Weather. 1692.
A Midnight Cry. 1692.
Preparatory Meditations upon the Day of Judgment, with Great Day of Judgment, by Samuel Lee. 1692.
Ornaments for the Daughters of Zion. 1692.
The Return of Several Ministers (on the Salem witchcraft trials). 1692.
The Wonders of the Invisible World (on the Salem witchcraft trials). 1692; in *Narratives of the Witchcraft Cases 1648-1706,* edited by George Lincoln Burr, 1914.
Winter-Meditations. 1693.
The Short History of New-England. 1694.
Early Religion Urged. 1694.
Durable Riches. 1695.
Brontologia Sacra. 1695.
Johannes in Eremo. 1695.
Piscator Evangelicus; or, The Life of Mr. Thomas Hooker. 1695.
Things for a Distressed People to Think Upon. 1696.
Songs of the Redeemed: A Book of Hymns. 1697.
Humiliations Followed with Deliverances. 1697.
Pietas in Patriam: The Life of His Excellency Sir William Phips. 1697; as *The Life of Sir William Phips,* edited by Mark Van Doren, 1929.
The Bostonian Ebenezer: Some Historical Remarks on the State of Boston. 1698.

Eleutheria; or, An Idea of the Reformation in England. 1698.
Decennium Lactuosum. 1699; in *Narratives of the Indian Wars 1675-1699,* edited by Charles Henry Lincoln, 1913.
Pillars of Salt: An History of Some Criminals Executed in This Land for Capital Crimes. 1699.
A Family Well-Ordered. 1699.
A Pillar of Gratitude. 1700.
The Everlasting Gospel. 1700.
The Religious Mariner. 1700.
An Epistle to the Christian Indians. 1700.
A Monitory and Hortatory Letter to Those English Who Debauch the Indians by Selling Strong Drink unto Them. 1700.
A Warning to the Flocks. 1700.
Reasonable Religion. 1700.
A Collection of Some of the Many Offensive Matters Contained in The Order of the Gospel Revived. 1701.
An Advice to the Churches of the Faithful. 1702.
Christianus per Ignem. 1702.
Proposals for the Preservation of Religion in the Churches. 1702.
Magnalia Christi Americana; or, The Ecclesiastical History of New-England. 1702; edited by Thomas Robbins, 2 vols., 1853-55; books 1-2 edited by Kenneth B. Murdock, 1977.
Wholesome Words. 1702(?).
A Faithful Man Described and Rewarded (on Michael Wigglesworth). 1705.
Family-Religion Excited and Assisted. 1705.
Hatchets to Hew Down the Tree of Sin. 1705.
A Letter about the Present State of Christianity among the Christianized Indians. 1705.
Lex Mercatoria; or, Just Rules of Commerce Declared. 1705.
The Negro Christianized. 1706.
Good Fetched Out of Evil (captivity narratives). 1706.
The Best Ornaments of Youth. 1707.
A Memorial of the Present Deplorable State of New England. 1707.
Frontiers Well-Defended. 1707.
A Golden Curb for the Mouth. 1707.
The Soldier Told What He Shall Do. 1707.
Corderius Americanus: An Essay upon the Good Education of Children. 1708.
The Deplorable State of New-England. 1708.
Winthropi Justa. 1708.
The Sailor's Companion. 1709.
Nehemiah: A Brief Essay on Divine Consolations. 1710.
Theopolis Americana. 1710.
Bonifacius: An Essay upon the Good. 1710; as *Essays to Do Good,* edited by George Burder, 1807; edited by David Levin, 1966.
Christianity Demonstrated. 1710.
Dust and Ashes: An Essay upon Repentance. 1710.
Elizabeth in Her Holy Retirement. 1710.
The Heavenly Conversation. 1710.
Orphanotrophium; or, Orphans Well-Provided For. 1711.
Persuasions from the Terror of the Lord. 1711.
A Letter about Good Management under the Distemper of Measles. 1713.
Duodecennium Lactuosum. 1714.
A New Offer to the Lovers of Religion and Learning. 1714(?).
The Stone Cut Out from the Mountain/Lapis e Monte Excisus. 1716.
Fair Dealing Between Debtor and Creditor. 1716.
Malachi. 1717.

Victorina. 1717.

Psalterium Americanum. 1718.

A Voice from Heaven. 1719.

Concio ad Populum. 1719.

Virgilius. 1719.

Mirabilia Dei. 1719.

News from Robinson Cruso's Island (possibly not by Mather). 1720.

The Christian Philosopher. 1720.

The Accomplished Singer. 1721.

Silentiarius. 1721.

India Christiana. 1721.

Some Account of Inoculating the Small Pox, with Zabdiel Boylston. 1721.

The Angel of Bethesda. 1722; edited by Gordon W. Jones, 1972.

Friendly Debate, with Isaac Greenwood. 1722.

A Father Departing. 1723.

Coelestinus: A Conversation in Heaven. 1723.

The Voice of God in a Tempest. 1723.

Parentator (on Increase Mather). 1724.

The Words of Understanding. 1724.

Une Grande Voix du Ciel a la France. 1725.

The Palm-Bearers. 1725.

El-Shaddai. 1725.

Vital Christianity. 1725.

A Proposal for an Evangelical Treasury. 1725.

Zalmonah. 1725.

Manuductio ad Ministerium. 1726.

Fasciculus Viventium. 1726.

Ratio Disciplinae Fratrum Nov Anglorum: A Faithful Account of the Discipline Professed and Practiced in the Churches of New-England. 1726.

The Vial Poured Out upon the Sea: A Remarkable Relation of Certain Pirates. 1726.

A Good Old Age. 1726.

Hatzar-Maveth. 1726.

The Instructor. 1726.

Some Seasonable Advice unto the Poor. 1726.

Suspiria Vinctorum. 1726.

Terra Beata. 1726.

Agricola; or, The Religious Husbandman. 1727.

The Terror of the Lord: Some Account of the Earthquake That Shook New- England. 1727.

Boanerges: A Short Essay to Preserve and Strengthen the Good Impressions Produced by Earthquakes. 1727.

Christian Loyalty. 1727.

The Balance of the Sanctuary. 1727.

Baptismal Piety. 1727.

Hor-Hagidgad. 1727.

Signatus. 1727.

The Mystical Marriage. 1728.

Diluvium Ignis. 1730.

Diary 1681-1724, edited by Worthington Chauncey Ford. 2 vols., 1911-12.

The Diary for the Year 1712, edited by William R. Manierre II. 1964.

Paterna: The Autobiography, edited by Ronald A. Bosco. 1976.

The Threefold Paradise of Cotton Mather: An Edition of Triparadisus. 1995.

*

Bibliography: *Mather: A Bibliography of His Works* by Thomas J. Holmes, 3 vols., 1940.

Critical Studies: *The Mathers: Three Generations of Puritan Intellectuals 1596-1728* by Robert Middlekauff, 1971; *Mather: The Young Life of the Lords Remembrancer 1663-1703* by David Levin, 1978; *Mather* by Babette Levy, 1979; *The Life and Times of Mather* by Kenneth Silverman, 1984; *Mather and Benjamin Franklin: The Price of Representative Personality* by Mitchell Robert Breitwieser, 1984; *Cotton Mather's Verse in English* edited by Denise D. Knight, 1989; "Cotton Mather Published Abroad" by D.N. Deluna, in *Early American Literature* vol. 26, 1991; "Authority and Witchery: Cotton Mather's *Ornaments* and Mary English's *Acrostic*" by William J. Scheick, in *Arizona Quarterly: A Journal of American Literature, Culture, and Theory,* spring 1995, pp. 1-32.

*   *   *

Cotton Mather was viewed as a stereotyped New England puritan before the stereotype existed. A Harvard student at age eleven, already proficient in Latin, Greek, and Hebrew, he was regarded as a prig by his fellow students. His congregants and acquaintances in later life were largely in agreement with this early assessment of his character, for while respected as a worthy and learned heir to New England's most illustrious dynasty of scholars and divines, that dynasty's mission of creating in New England a New Jerusalem was fading in the light of new commercial concerns and eighteenth-century rationalism. More receptive to the new thinking than is usually recognized, Mather was still very much aware of what was expected of him and strove, perhaps too hard, to compensate for a speech impediment, a melancholy disposition, and a number of personal tragedies, in carrying out the role in which God had cast him.

As one on whom heredity had placed the mantle of a prophet to the chosen in the new Israel of Massachusetts, Mather spoke with a prophet's self-assurance, and he spoke often. He published more than 400 works and left volumes of manuscripts that have never seen print. Indeed, some critics have suggested that his position in American letters is owed less to the quality of his work than to the quantity; so much from so famous a name could not but have some effect on colonial American culture and therefore at least an indirect influence on the generations that followed. Criticism in the late twentieth century has treated him somewhat more kindly. To be sure, most readers still remember the infamous *The Wonders of the Invisible World,* a treatise on witchcraft largely supportive of the Salem witch trials. The last gasp of the superstitious horror that had plagued Europe for centuries, Mather's book should at least be credited for its insistence on careful evidence rather than torture in such proceedings.

Certainly the work that has received the most critical attention is *Magnalia Christi Americana,* a monumental history of the first century of the Massachusetts colony. Even this, his major literary effort, has attracted such adjectives of critical praise as bigoted, ponderous, pompous, and superstitious. It is all of these, but its flaws are somewhat less glaring if approached as something other than history. As a historian, Mather did not weigh the significance of his material. Witches, church leaders, even criminals appear in equal prominence; folklore bleeds into fact, and the facts are too often just plain wrong. Moreover, the whole is an expression of the long-ago discarded theory of history as the working out of God's will. As a reliable record of the American puritan theocracy, the *Magnalia* fails. Modern critics, then, have had to consider whether it can stand, as a few supposedly factual narratives can, as a work of imaginative literature. Viewed as an allegorical epic on the theme of a new dispensation, a divine covenant with a new Israel that will prepare the world for the Messiah's reappearance, the *Magnalia* fares better. The elements of the narrative need not be weighed on the scale of mundane human significance; the episodes are not significant as facts. The *Magnalia* is a cloud of exempla revolving around the single, grand theme of the old covenant renewed.

Mather liked the ornate style popular in the seventeenth century, and often he is pompous for pomposity's sake, but the high style of the *Magnalia* seems less inappropriate when heard as an epic rather than historical voice. Mather was a great appreciator of Milton; passages from *Paradise Lost* are quoted and adapted for the *Magnalia*. Critics have had trouble with Milton's style too, but considering the grandeur of the theme, decorum has argued for the forgiveness of his linguistic excesses. However, Milton's theme, on close scrutiny protestant and puritan to be sure, was still catholic enough to fit into the context of general Christianity. Mather's theme of a new Israel in America, while grand too, was tied to the destiny of a particular people in a particular time and place. Milton dealt with God in the universe; Mather put Him in New England, and in narrowing the thematic focus, so diminished the need for the style he chose that in the view of most critics intended magnificence still rings as pomposity and even bombast.

Some mention should be made of Mather as a writer of sermons, for two-thirds of his published works are of this genre. Considerably less baroque than the *Magnalia,* they became all but unread. While reflective of traditional puritan themes, the sermons read in the context of Mather's own diary are more personal than might at first be suspected and depict the same earthly concerns in conflict with spiritual aspirations that the moody and imaginative author experienced throughout his life. As he coped with his own doubts by deliberately accentuating in thought and conduct the puritan ideals of which he was the last and greatest spokesman, so the sermons echo with a conscious and too often dull self-righteousness that renders them even less readable as literature than the histories.

In 1963 the *Magnalia* was chosen as one of 1800 books from America's literary history to make up a White House library for Presidents. It sits there, one supposes, not so much as a book really to be read as a monument to a period in American history that modern students view with very mixed feelings. The literary career of that book's author is itself a monument to enormous effort on behalf of an ideal that was fading even then and like most monuments is acknowledged now only in passing.

—William J. Heim

MAYO, Jim. *See* **L'AMOUR, Louis (Dearborn).**

McCARTHY, Mary (Therese)

Born: Seattle, Washington, 21 June 1912; sister of the actor Kevin McCarthy. **Education:** Forest Ridge Convent, Seattle; Annie Wright Seminary, Tacoma, Washington; Vassar College, Poughkeepsie, New York, A.B. 1933 (Phi Beta Kappa). **Family:** Married 1) Harold Johnsrud in 1933 (divorced 1936); 2) Edmund Wilson in 1938 (divorced 1946), one son; 3) Bowden Broadwater in 1946 (divorced 1961); 4) James Raymond West in 1961. **Career:** Editor, Covici Friede publishers, New York, 1936-38; editor, 1937-38, and drama critic, 1937-62, *Partisan Review,* New York, and New Brunswick, New Jersey; instructor, Bard College, Annandale-on-Hudson, New York, 1945-46, and Sarah Lawrence College, Bronxville, New York, 1948; Northcliffe Lecturer, University College, London, 1980; President's Distinguished Visitor, Vassar College, 1982; Stevenson Chair in Literature, Bard College, 1986. **Awards:** Guggenheim fellowship, 1949, 1959; American Academy grant, 1957; National Medal for Literature, 1984; MacDowell Medal, 1984; First Rochester Literary award, 1985; nomination for book of the year award, National Book Critics Circle, 1986. D.Litt.: Syracuse University, New York, 1973; University of Hull, Yorkshire, 1974; Bard College, 1976; Bowdoin College, Brunswick, Maine, 1981; University of Maine, Orono, 1982. LL.D.: University of Aberdeen, 1979. **Member:** American Academy, National Institute of Arts and Letters. **Died:** 25 October 1989.

PUBLICATIONS

Fiction

The Company She Keeps. 1942.
The Oasis. 1949; as *A Source of Embarrassment,* 1950.
Cast a Cold Eye (stories). 1950.
The Groves of Academe. 1952.
A Charmed Life. 1955.
The Group. 1963.
Birds of America. 1971.
Cannibals and Missionaries. 1979.
The Hounds of Summer and Other Stories. 1981.

Other

Sights and Spectacles 1937-1956. 1956; as *Sights and Spectacles: Theatre Chronicles 1937-1958,* 1959; augmented edition, as *Theatre Chronicles 1937-1962,* 1963.
Venice Observed: Comments on Venetian Civilization, 1956.
Memories of Catholic Girlhood. 1957.
The Stones of Florence. 1959.
On the Contrary (essays). 1961.
The Humanist in the Bathtub (essays). 1964.
Vietnam. 1967.
Hanoi. 1968.
The Writing on the Wall and Other Literary Essays. 1970.
Medina. 1972.
The Mask of State: Watergate Portraits. 1974.
The Seventeenth Degree. 1974.
Can There Be a Gothic Literature? (lecture). 1975.
Ideas and the Novel. 1980.
La Traviata (story adaptation), music by Verdi. 1983.
Occasional Prose: Essays. 1985.
How I Grew. 1987.
Intellectual Memoirs: New York, 1936-1938. 1993.
Between Friends: The Correspondence of Hannah Arendt and Mary McCarthy, 1949-1975. 1995.

Translator, *The Iliad; or, the Poem of Force,* by Simone Weil. 1948.
Translator, *On the Iliad,* by Rachel Bespaloff. 1948.

*

Bibliography: *McCarthy: A Bibliography* by Sherli Goldman, 1968; *McCarthy: An Annotated Bibliography* by Joy Bennett and Gabriella Hochmann, 1992.

Critical Studies: *McCarthy* by Barbara McKenzie, 1966; *The Company She Kept* by Doris Grumbach, 1967; *McCarthy* by Irvin Stock, 1968; *McCarthy* by Willene Schaefer Hardy, 1981; *Fictions in Autobiography: Studies in the Art of Self-Invention* by Paul John Eakin, 1985; "An American Woman of Letters" by Sonya Rudikoff, in *The Hudson Review* vol. 42, no. 1, spring 1989; *Conversations with McCarthy* edited by Carol Gelderman, 1991; *Writing Dangerously: McCarthy and Her World* by Carol Brightman, 1992; "From Autobiography to Infinity: Mary McCarthy's *Memories of a Catholic Girlhood* and *How I Grew*" by Lynn Domina, in *Auto-Biography Studies,* fall 1995, pp. 68-86; "Reliable Narrators and Unreliable Memories: The Case of Mary McCarthy's *Memories of a Catholic Girlhood*" by Barbara Kraus, in *Blurred Boundaries: Critical Essays on American Literature, Language, and Culture* edited by Klaus H. Schmidt and David Sawyer, 1996; *Twenty-four Ways of Looking at Mary McCarthy: The Writer and Her Work,* 1996.

*   *   *

Mary McCarthy belongs to that set of modern American authors who appear at first to be circumscribed by their own times. Her first novel, *The Company She Keeps,* is the most charming and vigorous of her novels in spite of being almost too conscious of the political and social milieu of Greenwich Village. *The Company She Keeps* is a daring experiment, containing six chapters, which differ from one another in time and place, with one common personality to hold the stories together. The strength of that personality, of the viewing eye, and the consistency of vision and perspective that that eye provides, form the only cohesion in the "novel." It has about it the feel of the early experiments in surrealist fiction and at the same time the freshness and youthful vitality in the early stories of **F. Scott Fitzgerald**. McCarthy has captured, through details, the spirit of her generation just as surely. In the socio-historical context, one learns more from writers like McCarthy and Fitzgerald than from our more "literary" writers. McCarthy chronicles an age as well as the complex sentiments of that age in her fiction. *The Company She Keeps* also offers a fascinating glimpse of McCarthy's powers as a journalist.

McCarthy's critical essays are collected in *On the Contrary, The Writing on the Wall, Ideas and the Novel, Occasional Prose,* and *How I Grew.* Her *Theatre Chronicles,* begun in the 1930s, offers the same strong command and vigor, as well as a truly original understanding and analysis of the theater. Her essay on Macbeth in *The Writing on the Wall* demonstrates the skill with which McCarthy perceives connections between literature and contemporary culture by emphasizing the modern relevance of Shakespeare's play.

Her essays show what kind of professor she must have been: funny, inventive, clever, determined to catch at the sparkling threads of every idea. With *The Groves of Academe,* she created a small scandal with a biting portrait of a college president strug-

gling with the politics of his English department. *The Groves of Academe* and her fourth novel, *A Charmed Life,* are probably meant to be allegories—the former of Senator Joseph McCarthy's communist witch-hunts, and the latter of a moral and philosophical sort where generalizations meant to apply to all of us are drawn out of a small community. *A Charmed Life* is a magnificent book—unlimited by time or political boundaries, it concerns what happens to people who retire from the world to devote themselves to art. It is a gentle but shocking reminder that we cannot hide from the world out of dedication, commitment, or devotion to an unworldly goal. Life, McCarthy seems to assert, remains dangerous even outside of its conventional parameters. The characters in this novel come to life more thoroughly than the eight heroines who attend Vassar in *The Group,* McCarthy's most famous novel. *The Group* was a great success when it appeared, although quite controversial for its sexual content: its vision of life affected an entire generation. McCarthy's autobiography, *Memories of a Catholic Girlhood,* is a beautiful, classic, searching piece of writing that chronicles McCarthy's coming of age in Seattle and her struggles with the Catholic faith and its precepts. Along with *A Charmed Life, Memories of a Catholic Girlhood* is the best showcase for her prose.

McCarthy has always walked a delicate line between her knowledge that the modern novel is plotless and between her love for the world and its myriad details. *The Company She Keeps* is a carefully plotted novel, but it does not follow a timeline; *The Groves of Academe* has a traditional novelistic conception but, lacking the freewheeling movement of *Company,* is less successful; *A Charmed Life* is positioned insecurely but brilliantly on the line between the Dickensian novel of action and detail and the plotless modern impressionistic novel that dramatizes the conflict between clashing ideas and philosophies; *The Group* represents McCarthy's return to a novel form that is more disjointed but richer of plot.

Mary McCarthy has been, at various times in her life, a novelist, a short story writer, a critic, a journalist, an essayist, and an art historian. Her contribution to literature is particularly notable for its frankness, its energy, and its insight into the cultural milieu of its subject. For McCarthy, writing is itself an exercise in distilling truth. In a description of her plans for *The Groves of Academe,* McCarthy has explained, "One's purpose in sitting down to any project is to find how much of specific knowledge or general truth this material will yield, what, so to speak, there is *in* it, and one's purpose as an artist more generally is to continue to do this again and again to different areas of experience." In her exploration of experience, particularly the experience of American intellectual circles of the late 1940s and 1950s, McCarthy's vision and insight remain unsurpassed.

—Brady Nordland, updated by Allison Hersh

McCULLERS, (Lula) Carson

Born: Lula Carson Smith, Columbus, Georgia, 19 February 1917.
Education: Columbus High School, graduated 1933; attended classes at Columbia University, New York, and New York University, 1934-36. **Family:** Married James Reeves McCullers, Jr. in 1937 (divorced 1941); remarried in 1945 (died 1953). Lived in Charlotte, 1937-38, and Fayetteville, 1938-39, both North Caro-

lina, and in New York City, 1940-44, and Nyack, New York, after 1944. **Awards:** Bread Loaf Writers Conference fellowship, 1940; Guggenheim fellowship, 1942, 1946; American Academy grant, 1943; New York Drama Critics Circle award, 1950; Donaldson award, for drama, 1950; Theatre Club Gold Medal, 1950; University of Mississippi grant, 1966; Bellamann award, 1967. **Member:** American Academy, 1952. **Died:** 29 September 1967.

PUBLICATIONS

Short Stories

The Member of the Wedding (novella). 1946.
The Ballad of the Sad Café: The Novels and Stories of McCullers.
    1951; as *Collected Short Stories,* 1961; as *The Shorter Novels and Stories of McCullers,* 1972.
Seven. 1954.

Novels

The Heart Is a Lonely Hunter. 1940.
Reflections in a Golden Eye. 1941.
Clock without Hands. 1961.

Plays

The Member of the Wedding, from her own novel (produced 1949).
    1951.
The Square Root of Wonderful (produced 1957). 1958.

Television Plays: *The Invisible Wall,* from her story "The So-journer," 1953; *The Sojourner,* from her own story, 1964.

Poetry

The Twisted Trinity, music by David Diamond. 1946.
Sweet as a Pickle and Clean as a Pig (for children). 1964.

Other

The Mortgaged Heart (uncollected writings), edited by Margarita G. Smith. 1971.

*

Bibliography: *Katherine Anne Porter and McCullers: A Reference Guide* by Robert F. Kiernan, 1976; *McCullers: A Descriptive Listing and Annotated Bibliography of Criticism* by Adrian M. Shapiro, Jackson R. Bryer, and Kathleen Field, 1980.

Critical Studies: *McCullers: Her Life and Work* by Oliver Evans, 1965, as *The Ballad of McCullers,* 1966; *McCullers* by Lawrence Graver, 1969; *McCullers* by Dale Edmonds, 1969; *The Lonely Hunter: A Biography of McCullers* by Virginia Spencer Carr, 1975; *McCullers* by Richard M. Cook, 1975; *McCullers' The Member of the Wedding: Aspects of Structure and Style* by Eleanor Wikborg, 1975; *McCullers* by Margaret B. McDowell, 1980; "The Work of Carson McCullers," in *Pembroke Magazine* vol. 20, 1988; "Adverbials, Direct Objects and the Style of Carson McCullers" by John M. Dienhart, in *The Twain Shall Meet: Danish Ap-*proaches to English Studies *edited by Jorgen Erik Nielsen, 1992;* Wunderkind: The Reputation of Carson McCullers, 1940-1990 *by Judith Giblin James, 1995;* Critical Essays on Carson McCullers, 1996.

*　　*　　*

Although severe illness—strokes, heart disease, paralysis, and eventually cancer—limited Carson McCullers's productivity after the age of thirty, she had already achieved both critical and popular acclaim in several genres—the novel, the novella, the short story, and the drama. Her first three novels appeared in six years, each selling more than half a million copies. Her play based on *The Member of the Wedding* ran for more than a year on Broadway and then became a successful film, as did her first two novels.

McCullers regarded all her major works as southern, maintaining that authors always reflect the place of their birth and cannot escape from its "voices and foliage and memory." All her novels are set in Georgia. Though she repeatedly returned to the south, she retained an antagonism toward it as a region where one might be regarded as worth "no more than a load of hay": her treatment of southern life, thus, is never sentimental. Her most effective use of southern folklore occurs in the blending of realism and fantasy in *The Ballad of the Sad Cafe.* Problems of unemployed transients and of workers in southern textile mills loom in the background of *The Heart Is a Lonely Hunter* and *The Ballad of the Sad Cafe.* **Richard Wright** praised her treatment of southern blacks in *The Heart Is a Lonely Hunter.* Her portrayal of Berenice and her black friends and relatives in *The Member of the Wedding* brought wide acclaim. In her last novel, *Clock without Hands,* she less effectively portrayed Sherman Pew, a blue-eyed black homosexual. However, even in this novel, her depiction of Sherman Jones's execution; the police action in the death of Grown Boy, a retarded adolescent; and the plight of the legless beggar, Wagon, provide a striking contrast between the struggles of southern blacks and the mindlessness of segregationist Judge Clane.

Because she is southern, some have assumed that the bizarre situations and grotesque characters in *Reflections in a Golden Eye* and *The Ballad of the Sad Cafe* categorize McCullers as a writer of sensational and comic southern Gothic. Actually her serious implications of uncontrollable evil link these works instead with the Gothic tales of the Danish Isak Dinesen, greatly admired by McCullers, and with the fiction of D. H. Lawrence that explores the psychic origins of deviant or irrational behavior. In McCullers's novels, military regimentation, athletic prowess, police cruelty, imprisonment, and even executions cannot change the course of perverse human nature or mindless fate.

Though a master of the realistic, McCullers moved always toward symbolic, allegorical, and philosophical ramifications as she analyzed the elemental realities confronting her characters. She repeats a few central themes: the individual's frustrated love for a less worthy person; the universality of loneliness; love pursued as the only cure for loneliness; love as the intensifier of loneliness; the rare existence of selfless love; the evanescence of even the most affectionate relationship; and the connection between isolation and evil. In nearly every work conflict occurs within an individual who longs for close identification with others, but at the same time struggles for freedom, lack of responsibility, and self-centered control of outside forces. Such conflict is most forcefully presented in Frankie Addams in *The Member of the Wed-*

ding and Miss Amelia in *The Ballad of the Sad Cafe.* Related to this conflict is the agonizing loneliness that most of McCullers's characters experience and their inability to communicate their deep feelings. In *The Heart Is a Lonely Hunter,* two deaf-mutes symbolize such inability in all the other characters. Elgee Williams, the silent soldier in *Reflections in a Golden Eye,* functions similarly as he lurks in the night staring in the window at the sleeping wife of an army officer. In *The Member of the Wedding,* Frankie looks toward a perfect intuitive and wordless understanding in the three-person wedding she envisions that will unite her with her brother and his bride. Berenice looks back toward her perfect marriage, with the now dead Ludie, where words of love were not needed. Frankie and Berenice have occasional moments of perfect wordless communication but ordinarily speak in parallel monologues rather than to one another. In *Clock without Hands,* Malone suffers needlessly alone for months because he cannot share the news of his impending death with his family.

Ultimately, the universality of music pervasively informs metaphor and background in McCullers's work more than does a sense of her geographical region. Her eight hours of daily piano practice in childhood and adolescence surely intensified McCullers's persistent sense of being different from others, as it isolated her from her peers. She clearly implies this in her first story, "Wunderkind," written when she was sixteen. The other two young girls in her novels—Mick Kelly in *The Heart Is a Lonely Hunter* and Frankie in *The Member of the Wedding*—lack McCullers's prodigious musical talent, but both are almost obsessively preoccupied with music. Mick hides under windows in the dark to hear music from her neighbors' radios and listens to the phonograph owned by a tenant in her mother's boarding house. She builds a violin from a cigar box, and she grieves about having to quit school, mainly because she can no longer try to play the piano in the empty gym. Frankie complains about "sweet sleazy music" on the kitchen radio; she fears she will go mad when the piano tuner fails to finish a scale and when a trombonist in a neighboring house interrupts a compelling phrase in a blues song. She finds comfort in the rhythm of a small motor she has salvaged for her room. McCullers assumed a connection between her work and her musical understanding. Her first novel was outlined for the publisher completely in musical, rather than literary, terms, as if it were a symphony. She insisted that *The Member of the Wedding*—both as novel and stage play—had to possess "precision and harmony." Because of this, she was able to present effectively the subtleties of the separate personalities warring within both Frankie and Berenice and project the internal action and philosophical implications demanded by the drama for which **Tennessee Williams** had paved the way in the theaters of the 1950s.

—Margaret B. McDowell

See the essay on *The Member of the Wedding.*

McKAY, Claude

Born: Festus Claudius McKay in Sunny Ville, Clarendon Parish, Jamaica, 15 September 1889. **Education:** A grammar school in Jamaica; Tuskegee Institute, Alabama, 1912; Kansas State College, Manhattan, 1913-14. **Family:** Married Eulalie Imelda Edwards in 1914 (separated 1914); one daughter. **Career:** Ap-

prentice cabinet-maker and wheelwright, 1907-08; joined Jamaican Constabulary, 1909, and policeman in Spanish Town, Jamaica, 1911-12; moved to New York, worked at various jobs and opened a restaurant, 1914; staff member, *Workers' Dreadnought* communist newspaper, London, 1919-20; associate editor, 1921-22, and coeditor, 1922, *Liberator,* New York; lived in the Soviet Union, 1922-23, and Europe (mainly France) and Tangier, 1923-34; laborer in welfare camp, New York, 1934-35; writer for the Works Progress Administration until 1939; worked in a shipbuilding yard, 1943; joined Catholic Church, 1944, and worked for National Catholic Youth Organization, Chicago, 1944-48. **Awards:** Harmon prize, 1929. **Died:** 22 May 1948.

PUBLICATIONS

Collections

Selected Poems. 1953.
The Passion of McKay: Selected Poetry and Prose 1912-1948, edited by Wayne Cooper. 1973.
My Green Hills of Jamaica, and Five Jamaican Short Stories, edited by Mervyn Morris. 1979.

Poetry

Constab Ballads. 1912.
Songs of Jamaica. 1912.
Spring in New Hampshire and Other Poems. 1920.
Harlem Shadows. 1922.
The Dialect Poetry. 1972.

Fiction

Sud Linchom (in Russian). 1925; translated as *Trial by Lynching: Stories about Negro Life in North America,* edited by A.L. McLeod, 1977.
Home to Harlem. 1928.
Banjo: A Story without a Plot. 1929.
Gingertown (stories). 1932.
Banana Bottom. 1933.

Other

Negry v Amerike (in Russian). 1923; translated as *The Negroes in America,* edited by A.L. McLeod, 1979.
A Long Way from Home (autobiography). 1937.
Harlem: Negro Metropolis. 1940.

*

Bibliography: by Manuel D. Lopez in *Bulletin of Bibliography,* October-December 1972.

Critical Studies: *Roots of Negro Racial Consciousness: Three Harlem Renaissance Authors* by Stephen H. Bronz, 1964; *The West Indian Novel and Its Background* by Kenneth Ramchand, 1970; *McKay: The Black Poet at War* by Addison Gayle, Jr., 1972; *McKay* by James R. Giles, 1976; *McKay: Rebel Sojourner in the Harlem Renaissance* by Wayne F. Cooper, 1987; *Claude McKay:*

A Black Poet's Struggle for Identity by Tyrone Tillery, 1992; "McKay's Tragic Confusion: An African's Comments on Tyrone Tillery's Claude McKay" by Femi Ojo Ade, in *Literary Griot: International Journal of Black Expressive Cultural Studies,* fall 1994, pp. 54-59; "Claude McKay's *Banana Bottom:* A Black Response to Late-Nineteenth and Early-Twentieth-Century White Discourse on the Meaning of Black Reality" by H. Nigel Thomas, in *Nationalism Versus Internationalism: (Inter)National Dimensions of Literatures in English* edited by Wolfgang Zach and Ken L. Goodwin, 1996; "The Clothes Make the Woman: The Symbolics of Prostitution in Nella Larsen's *Quicksand* and Claude McKay's *Home to Harlem*" by Kimberly Roberts, in *Tulsa Studies in Women's Literature,* spring 1997, pp. 107-30.

*   *   *

Claude McKay attempted throughout his career to resolve the complexities surrounding the black man's paradoxical situation. A widely traveled man, he lived for twelve years (1922-1934) in Britain, Russia, Germany, France, Spain, and Morocco. It is during these years that a new wave of Afro-American writing, which became widely known as the Harlem Renaissance, spread across America. McKay is generally credited with having inspired the Renaissance with his militant poem "If We Must Die" (1919) when the nation was gripped with a red scare and race riots in the Northern cities. Later, however, the self-exiled McKay developed an ambivalent relationship with the New Negroes of the 1920s; he did not share the "social uplift" philosophy of **Alain Locke** and **W.E.B. Du Bois** although he had affinities as writer with **Jean Toomer**, **Langston Hughes** and **Zora Neale Hurston**. McKay is also considered a pioneer in the development of West Indian fiction, though he never returned to the land of his birth, Jamaica, having left it at age twenty-three. In the late twentieth century, many regard his fiction as his most valuable contribution, but McKay also published four collections of poems, an autobiography, many essays, and a sociological study of Harlem.

It is as a poet that McKay first won attention in both the West Indies and the United States. In 1912, before he went to Kansas as an agriculture student (hoping to become the prophet of scientific farming on his return home!), he had published two volumes of dialect verse, *Songs of Jamaica* and *Constab Ballads,* and won himself a reputation as "the Jamaican Bobby Burns." Soon, he was made aware of the intricacies of American racial prejudice and he decided to cast his lot with working-class Afro-Americans. McKay was both stimulated and angered by the American environment—"Although she feeds me bread of bitterness /. . . I love this cultured hell that tests my youth!" ("America"). His background in the Jamaican society where the blacks formed a majority often gave him an edge as poet-observer over black American artists whose careers were sometimes wrecked by a debilitating bitterness. In his poems of personal love and racial protest, McKay gave strong expression to joy and anger, pride and stoicism. "If We Must Die," although not his best poem, won him great popularity because it powerfully evoked, in lines charged with emotion, the militant mood of Afro-American communities over the treatment meted out to black soldiers returning from World War I. The poem achieved a kind of universality in spite of its trite diction, as was well-demonstrated when Winston Churchill related it to the Allied cause by reading it to the House of Commons during World War II.

McKay's influence on later black poetry is measured better by the power of his sentiment than by any innovations in form, style or diction. McKay empathizes with the sufferings of working-class blacks in the many poems of *Harlem Shadows,* but he succeeds best when he focuses on an individual's tragedy to protest against the forces of oppression. This is evident in poems such as "The Harlem Dancer," where a young female dancer is surrounded by a crowd of "wine-flushed, bold-eyed boys" that has no inkling of her soulful pride. In "Baptism," he expresses a Victorian stoicism that asserts the individual's victory through the harshest of tests. McKay often tried his hand at the sonnet form, using irregular rhyme and meter to achieve his own poetic ends. "One Year After," dealing with interracial love in a two-sonnet sequence, anticipates contemporary black attitudes in attributing the failure of a black-white relationship not to society's pressures but to the lover's black pride: "Not once in all our days of poignant love / Did I a single instant give to thee / My undivided being wholly free." McKay also wrote many poems about love and sex that had little to do with racial conflict and in some of these (e.g., "Flower of Love" and "A Red Flower")—as often in his fiction, especially in *Home to Harlem*—he creates erotic effects through suggestive portrayals of sexual pleasure. Yet McKay's link to later black literature is based primarily on his protest poems and his three novels.

McKay wrote both short stories and novels. *Gingertown,* his only collection of short stories, is important mainly as a source of clues and parallels to his development as novelist-thinker. The three novels—*Home to Harlem, Banjo,* and *Banana Bottom*—together form a thematic trilogy exploring the black man's special situation against the Manichean opposition between "instinct" and "intellect." *Home to Harlem* and *Banjo,* both essentially plotless novels, raise issues relating to the black's alleged primitivism, and its possible uses in an age when the fear of standardization is obsessive. The two protagonists—Jake and Banjo respectively—are rollicking roustabouts, taking life and women as they come. Their life of instinctive simplicity is, however, not without a Hemingway-like code. If they would not scab against a fellow worker, they would not be gullible enough to join a union either. As lovers, they do not permit themselves to become pimps or demean themselves to satisfy their women's masochistic desires. In the sexual metaphor that is McKay's lens in all the three novels, sexual deviations and perversions symbolize the pernicious influence of white values on black lives. In *Banana Bottom* there is a tentative resolution of these conflicts in the character of Bita Plant who (like McKay himself) despite self-hatred cannot reject native traditions completely even as she continues to find uses in her life for Western thought. Bita is, in some ways, a dramatization of the tangled thoughts on the significance of race and heritage in modern life that McKay filtered through the character of Ray, who appears in both *Home to Harlem* and *Banjo.*

There is no hint in either his autobiography, *A Long Way from Home,* or his sociological study, *Harlem: Negro Metropolis,* of McKay's conversion in 1944 to Roman Catholicism, an astonishing turnabout by any standards. McKay's autobiography is unusual in not giving any details of his personal life, although useful as a mirror to his independence in the midst of stimulating encounters with issues, places, and people (including Frank Harris, H.G. Wells, Isadora Duncan, **Sinclair Lewis**). The section on his Russian visit is particularly valuable in determining a phase of his uneasy relationship with the leftist movement, from the days of his association with Max Eastman and the *Liberator* to the anti-

Communist sentiments of his final years. *Harlem: Negro Metropolis* offers a scathing view of Harlem's community life and the obsessive fight of its leaders against segregation. The reviewers criticized the book justifiably for its frequent failures in objectivity. Although McKay never became an apologist for capitalist imperialism, he did try in his last years to vindicate his conversion to Catholicism in his essay "On Becoming a Roman Catholic" and in many letters to his life-long friend, Max Eastman. One cannot, however, help feeling that a tired McKay surrendered his difficult search for the positive meanings of black life by giving in to the traditional discipline of the Roman Church. As he himself put it in a letter (16 October 1944) to Eastman: "It seems to me that to have a religion is very much like falling in love with a woman. You love her for her . . . Beauty, which cannot be defined."

—Amritjit Singh

McMILLAN, Terry

Born: Port Huron, Michigan, 18 October 1951. **Education:** The University of California-Berkeley, B.S. in journalism 1979; studied screenwriting at Columbia University in New York, M.F.A. 1979; participated in creative writing workshops in the Harlem Writer's Guild of New York, the MacDowell Colony, 1983. **Family:** One son. **Career:** Instructor at the University of Wyoming at Laramie, 1987-90; professor at the University of Arizona, Tucson, 1990-93. Beginning 1993 full-time writer. **Awards:** National Endowment for the Arts fellowship, 1988; New York Women in Communications Matrix award, 1993. **Residence:** Danville, California.

PUBLICATIONS

Novels

Mama. 1987.
Disappearing Acts. 1989.
Waiting to Exhale. 1992.
How Stella Got Her Groove Back. 1996.

Short Stories

"Men Who Are Good with Their Hands." *Esquire,* July 1988.

Other

Editor, *Breaking Ice: An Anthology of Contemporary African-American Fiction.* 1990.

Recording: *I've Got a Feeling,* 1993.

*

Critical Studies: "Profile of a First Novelist: Terry McMillan and *Mama*" by Helen Eisenbach in *Writer's Digest,* October 1987; interview with Wendy Smith in *Publishers Weekly,* 11 May 1992; "Chilling Out in Phoenix" by Susan Isaacs in *New York Times Book Review,* 31 May 1992; "Looking for Mr. Right" by John Boudreau

in *Los Angeles Times,* 19 June 1992; "McMillan's Millions" by Daniel Max in *New York Times Book Review,* 9 August 1992; interview with Quincy Troupe in *Emerge.* October 1992; "Terry McMillan Waiting to Inhale" by Audrey Edwards in *Essence,* October 1992; "Possessing the Secrets of Success" by Karen Grigsby Bates in *Emerge,* October 1992; interview with Laura B. Randolph in *Ebony,* May 1993; *Terry McMillan: An Unauthorized Biography* by Diane Patrick, 1999; *Terry McMillan: A Critical Companion* by Paulette Richards, 1999.

*   *   *

Terry McMillan accomplished a major literary feat when she dismantled a long-standing myth that black Americans do not buy or read books. When she published her third novel, *Waiting to Exhale* (1992), McMillan ignited the fires of literary curiosity that caused a multi-ethnic mix of readers to storm local bookstores and gain insight into what she had to say about relationships between black men and women. In an interview with Audrey Edwards of *Essence* magazine, McMillan stated: "Seriously, I just don't get it; I really don't." McMillan added: "I keep thinking, I got to go back and read this book." In real terms, the success of McMillan's novel can be measured by the eight hundred thousand sales of hardback copies prior to the purchase of the paperback rights. Pocketbook Publishers paid a stunning $2.64 million for reprint rights to *Waiting to Exhale,* an amount surpassed only by the auction of Scott Turow's 1987 *Presumed Innocent* for a reported $3.3 million. As an added impetus to the continuing success of *Waiting to Exhale,* Hollywood's Twentieth Century-Fox created a film version of the novel.

McMillan's energetic jaunts around the country illuminate the astounding diversity of audience for her realistic portrayal of the complexities in the romantic lives of contemporary black professional women. John Boudreau of the *Los Angeles Times* noted the hordes of supporters patiently waiting for a booksigning at Marcus Brothers bookstore in Oakland, California, one of the oldest African American bookstores in the nation. As McMillan told Boudreau: "There is a real strong identity with some of the things these women are experiencing, and not just among black women. I'm hearing a lot from white women." McMillan continued: "There are millions of women out here now in America between the ages of 30 and 40 who are well-educated, attractive, self-sufficient and having a hell of a time finding Mr. Right." The broad scope of McMillan's appeal is also evident in the demand for her appearance on talk shows like *Oprah* and *The Today Show* and the articles and interviews published in *Emerge, Essence, Ebony, Publishers Weekly,* and *New York Times Book Review.*

Yet, in contrast to the massive audience of supporters who have been captivated by McMillan's realistic portrayal of four frustrated black women, whose lives are complicated by men unwilling to make commitments, are critics who are highly offended by the liberal seasoning of spicy language in the dialogue of Savannah, Bernadine, Robin, and Gloria. Boudreau noted the blunt opinion of Charles R. Larson, a professor of literature at American University: "It's as if we're listening to four foul-mouthed stand-up comedians—all of them lashing out blindly at men." In a *Publishers Weekly* interview with Wendy Smith, McMillan responded to her critics: "Basically, the language that I use is accurate . . . . That's the way we talk. And I want to know why I've never read a review about the language that male writers use!" In addition to charges leveled against McMillan's brazen use of racy language is the criticism of her limited character profiles of males in the novel. But the reality is that the novel is more about the strengths in the sisterhood built by a community of black women than it is about the men they want to love. McMillan remarked in the Smith interview: "The men are on the periphery, they're not the focus of this story, therefore they don't get the three-dimensionality that the women do."

McMillan is no novice to critical commentary, nor to the controversies generated by her personal, and often intimate, approach to writing. She insists that *Waiting to Exhale* is not an autobiographical work, yet conceded in an *Essence* interview with Audrey Edwards that "there are bits and pieces of me" in the novel. However, she readily admits that her second novel, *Disappearing Acts* (1989), was created from the seeds of her own personal experiences; so much so that a former lover, Leonard Welch, father of her son, Solomon, sued her and Viking publishers for defamation of character, based on what he viewed as a nearly identical depiction of him in the book. Ultimately, his $4.75 million libel suit was dismissed by the New York Supreme Court in a decision that protects the artist's creative license. The main character of *Disappearing Acts* is Franklin, an unschooled blue-collar construction worker whose intense emotional somersaults and increasing insecurities play havoc with his ability to sustain a positive relationship with the equally insecure Zora Banks, a college-educated music teacher and aspiring singer. As with *Waiting to Exhale,* critics of *Disappearing Acts* blasted McMillan's penchant for the raunchy language that spills from the mouths of her characters. *Publishers Weekly* reviewer Sybil Steinberg noted that McMillan "bombards readers with four-letter words"; the critic then asked: "Do we want to read a novel with such relentlessly scatological dialogue?" McMillan resists such criticism and persists in producing narratives in what Edwards maintains is "a tough, new urban voice."

Admirers of McMillan's work build an equally strong case for her compelling rendition of the male voice in Franklin's characterization. Franklin speaks in the gritty voice of an urban ghetto man who is defined by his daily battle for survival against a rockslide of oppression. *Cosmopolitan* reviewer Louise Bernikow noted that "the stunning achievement here is the creation of Franklin, whose voice on the page rings with authenticity, whose intimidation, anger, even violence are unforgettable." The final measure of success for *Disappearing Acts* is the sale of the movie rights to Metro-Goldwyn-Mayer studios, with McMillan commissioned to write the screenplay.

Written on an equally personal and autobiographical level, McMillan's first novel, *Mama* (1987), revels in the hilarious sledgehammer approach to life of a feisty mother of five, Mildred Peacock, who singles out every opportunity to live her own life to the fullest, while securing educational opportunities for her rambunctious brood. What started out as a short story of a female factory worker who tosses her drunken husband out and opts to raise her children alone stretched into a novel when McMillan spent brief writing stints under the auspices of the Harlem Writer's Guild and the MacDowell Colony in 1983. Not satisfied with merely writing a novel that met with solid critical acclaim, McMillan, with her customary kinetic energy, masterminded a new-age publicity campaign when she wrote over three thousand letters to bookstores and universities inviting them to stock copies of her book, then embarked upon her own promotional tour. Her independent efforts produced sales of over five thousand and a third printing in the sixth week of publication.

McMillan's preparation for her seemingly rapid-fire literary success began at the age of sixteen when she took a $1.25 per hour job shelving books at the local library in her small blue-collar factory town of Port Huron, Michigan. To her amazement, the face of **James Baldwin** appeared on the cover of a book, shocking her into an awareness of an African American tradition in literature. McMillan was unable to comprehend the possibility that Baldwin's literary skills might equal, or even surpass, those of the major white writers she had studied; unable to confront this newfound fear, she shied away from reading Baldwin. Yet, ultimately, her sense of security in reading **Henry David Thoreau, Ralph Waldo Emerson, Louisa May Alcott, Nathaniel Hawthorne, Ernest Hemingway**, and **William Faulkner** yielded to the pressure of her new intellectual appetite for black writers. She enrolled in an introductory course on African American literature at Los Angeles Community College and became passionate over the works of **Zora Neale Hurston, Countée Cullen, Ann Petry, Langston Hughes, Jean Toomer, Ralph Ellison, Richard Wright**; finally, she read James Baldwin. The exposure to writers of her own cultural community opened the door to McMillan's own poetic instincts, and shortly thereafter, she published her first love poem. In 1976, while majoring in journalism at the University of California at Berkeley, she published her first short story, "The End," with the assistance of writer Ishmael Reed and his creative outlet for ethnic writers, the Before Columbus Foundation. The passionate relationship McMillan developed with black writers over the years culminated with her decision to compile an updated anthology of writings by black authors. She published *Breaking Ice: An Anthology of Contemporary African-American Fiction* (1990) after discovering the omission of black writers in recent anthologies of the "best" stories. In the introduction to *Breaking Ice,* she wrote: "I was appalled as I snatched every last one of these anthologies off my bookshelf, and could literally count on one hand the number of African-American writers who were in the table of contents."

McMillan's intense love affair with writing continued unabated as she relocated to New York to pursue a master's degree in screenwriting at Columbia University. But her lingering dissatisfaction over the rigid discipline of the Berkeley program and the tense racist atmosphere at Columbia finally caused McMillan to drop out of the screenwriting program and take a job with a New York law firm. About the same time, McMillan was trying to extricate herself from a devastating romantic liaison that fed on the most vulnerable aspects of her personality. Her mother had suffered poverty and abuse at the hands of her alcoholic husband and divorced him when McMillan was thirteen years old. McMillan's live-in-lover, Leonard Welch, was an unemployed construction worker who began dealing drugs. It was in the throes of her three-year drug and alcohol-induced stupor that McMillan decided to end the volatile relationship and save her own life. She abruptly stopped using drugs just after her thirtieth birthday in October of 1981 and opted for a ninety-day Alcoholic's Anonymous program that has left her sober since February 22, 1983. In an *Ebony* magazine interview with Laura B. Randolph, McMillan revealed the "life-changing" decisions that freed her from potential drug addition and alcoholism to finally "own" herself: "I mean feeling good about what I'm doing, how I've done it, the changes and struggles I've been through. That's what I mean when I say there are certain things I own. Now, I own me."

The astonishing success McMillan has garnered with the publication of three novels, an anthology, and contributions to essay collections was forecast by reviewers with a keen eye for talent. In *Cosmopolitan* magazine, Louise Bernikow ended her review of

Disappearing Acts with: "Watch Terry McMillan. She's going to be a major writer." *New York Times Book Review* critic Valerie Sayers noted: "Terry McMillan has the power to be an important contemporary novelist." Indeed McMillan has joined the ranks of black women writers who have achieved literary acclaim by their relentless pursuit of narrative voices that are informed by their self-defined artistic integrity. As Karen Grigsby Bates wrote in *Emerge*, "The success of **[Toni] Morrison**, **[Alice] Walker** and McMillan may have begun another renaissance for black authors— which in turn may result in more black bookstores and even publishing houses, which can only benefit all of mainstream publishing." Literary divas Morrison and Walker forged a Women's Renaissance in the 1970s that etched out an artistic path for newer women writers like **Gloria Naylor**, Marita Golden, and Bebe Moore Campbell. Terry McMillan has emerged to take her place among these highly esteemed writers, equally brilliant, yet determined to speak to her contemporary audience in her own "tough, new urban voice."

—B.J. Bolden

McMURTRY, Larry (Jeff)

Born: Wichita Falls, Texas, 3 June 1936. **Education:** Archer City High School; North Texas State College (now University), Denton, Texas, B.A. in English 1954; Rice University, Houston, Texas, M.A. in English 1960; additional study at Stanford University, Palo Alto, California, 1960. **Family:** Married Josephine Ballard in 1959 (divorced 1966); one son. **Career:** Instructor, Texas Christian University, Fort Worth, Texas, 1961-62; lecturer in English and creative writing, Rice University, 1963-69; visiting professor, George Mason University, Fairfax, Virginia, 1970, and American University, 1970-71; contributor, essayist, and reviewer for *Houston Post*, *New York Times Book Review*, *American Film*, *Atlantic*, *Gentleman's Quarterly*, *Saturday Review*, and *Washington Post*. Contributing editor to *American Film* beginning 1975; screenwriter for various projects; book dealer and rare book scout; co-owner of Booked Up, Inc., rare book store, Washington, D.C., beginning 1971, with branches in Texas and Arizona. President of PEN American Center beginning 1989. **Awards:** Wallace Stegner Fellowship, 1960; Jesse H. Jones award from Texas Institute of Letters, 1962; Guggenheim fellowship, 1964; Academy of Motion Picture Arts and Sciences award (Oscar), for screenplay, 1972; Barbara McCombs/Lon Tinkle award, 1986; Pulitzer prize for fiction, 1986; Western Writers of America Spur award, 1986; Southwestern Booksellers Association Texas Literary award, 1986. **Member:** Texas Institute of Letters. **Residence:** Texas, Virginia, and Tucson, Arizona.

PUBLICATIONS

Novels

Horseman, Pass By. 1961; as *Hud*, 1963.
Leaving Cheyenne. 1963.
The Last Picture Show. 1966.
Moving On. 1970.
All My Friends are Going to Be Strangers. 1972.

Terms of Endearment. 1975.
Somebody's Darling. 1978.
Cadillac Jack. 1982.
The Desert Rose. 1983.
Lonesome Dove. 1985.
Texasville. 1987.
Anything for Billy. 1988.
Some Can Whistle. 1989.
Buffalo Girls. 1990.
The Evening Star. 1992.
The Streets of Laredo. 1993.
The Late Child. 1995.
Pretty Boy Floyd. 1996.
Zeke and Ned. 1998.
Duane's Depressed. 1999.
Crazy Horse. 1999.

Plays

Screenplays: *The Last Picture Show.* 1970; *The Ballad of Mary Phagan.* 1988; *Texasville.* 1990.

Nonfiction

In a Narrow Grave: Essays on Texas. 1968.
It's Always We Rambled: An Essay on Rodeo. 1974.
Film Flam: Essays on Hollywood. 1987.
Splendors and Miseries of Being an Author-Bookseller. 1995.

*

Bibliography: "A McMurtry Bibliography" in *Western American Literature* vol. 3, 1968; "McMurtry" in *Southwestern American Literature: A Bibliography* edited by John Q. Anderson, Edwin W. Gaston, Jr., and James W. Lee, 1980.

Critical Studies: *McMurtry* by Thomas Landess, 1969; *The Ghost Country: A Study of the Novels of McMurtry* by Raymond L. Neinstein, 1976; *McMurtry* by Charles D. Peavy, 1977; *McMurtry: Unredeemed Dreams* edited by Dorey Schmidt, 1978; "McMurtry" in *Talking with Texas Writers: Twelve Interviews* by Patrick Bennett, 1980; *McMurtry's Texas: Evolution of the Myth* by Lera Patrick Tyler Lich, 1987; *Taking Stock: A McMurtry Casebook* edited by Clay Reynolds, 1989; *Larry McMurtry and the Victorian Novel* by Roger Walton Jones, 1994; *Larry McMurtry and the West: An Ambivalent Relationship* by Mark Busby, 1995; *Larry McMurtry and the Western: The Rhetoric of Novelization* (dissertation) by S. Renee Dechert, 1997; *Telling Western Tales: From Buffalo Bill to Larry McMurtry* by Richard W. Etulain, 1999.

*   *   *

Larry McMurtry has described himself as the sensitive, bookish son of a North Texas ranch family, starved for books until going off to college in 1954. Once there, he began a life that revolves around books—reading them, writing them, buying and selling them, all with distinction. The career path that would eventually lead him to become a rare book dealer and Pulitzer Prize winning novelist would also lead him back to Texas in his life and his fiction, striking a constant chord of leaving home, self-isolation, and the transformation of frontier to urban culture. A common thread in his work has been this tension between moving from home and back again and the emotional fallout of leaving a life behind that disappears before one can get back to it. Many of his best works have an elegiac mood that has translated successfully to visual media.

McMurtry has said that he begins a novel with some concept of a culminating scene: "Often this scene will refine itself in fairly high definition before I write a word . . . . I know what the last words are going to be, and I know that something's ended . . . . The final scene contains, sort of, the thematic resolutions of whatever story you're telling." This technique has served him well from the very beginning. His first novel, *Horseman, Pass By,* written from the viewpoint of a seventeen-year-old grandson, focuses on the independent cattleman Homer Bannon, forced to slaughter his herd, and thus his very existence, due to a devastating screwworm infestation. The novel was later produced as the critically acclaimed film *Hud.* Another of these elegiac, final scenes became the novel *The Last Picture Show,* which depicts small-town life with the satiric revenge of a skilled novelist once forced to live in such a place, now able to see the human dramas there as well. *Leaving Cheyenne,* published between these two novels, portrays a more modern culture of working and running ranches from three intertwined viewpoints. Some have categorized these novels as the Thalia trilogy, since that fictional town modeled on Archer City, Texas (not the actual Texas Panhandle town), figures peripherally if not predominantly in all of them. The later *Texasville* has confounded this idea of a trilogy.

McMurtry's next several novels are often referred to as his city novels. Much critical attention was paid to the fact that he had abandoned old Texas as a subject for his fiction, until the best-selling, Pulitzer Prize winning *Lonesome Dove* was published in 1985. In fact, his essays provide interesting commentary and background to the novels of this period. In *In a Narrow Grave: Essays on Texas,* McMurtry is openly critical of Texas as a literary subject and claims to be more interested in writing about the transition so many were making to city life, a much more animate subject than the old days of ranching, roping, and trail driving.

On a whole, this transition never seems complete as the characters in *Moving On, All My Friends, Terms of Endearment,* and *Cadillac Jack* move pointlessly around the country, or, in *Somebody's Darling,* adopt the restless Hollywood lifestyle of shallow roots and endless movement along the freeways. His last novel of this series is *The Desert Rose,* a story about an aging show girl whose daughter's star is rising as hers is waning. In terms of the theme of movement from country to city, the novel is poised between the two. Harmony has not yet left the glitter of the Las Vegas stages but sees the handwriting on the wall and is preparing for that day when she will retire to her peacock farm in the desert. Similarly, McMurtry seems to have been at a turning point with this novel, lingering lovingly on this character that he claims is his favorite of them all.

His next series of books, published at a rate of almost one per year, took him back to Texas and the rich myths of the West. *Lonesome Dove* follows out-of-work Texas Rangers on a last trail drive before the trains and fences put trail drivers out of business too. Winning several prizes and garnering McMurtry national attention primarily as a novelist, *Lonesome Dove* returns to Texas and to its prevalent romantic myths but instead shows the impossibility of this way of life. Its sequel, *The Streets of Laredo,* and his other old West novels, *Buffalo Girls* and *Anything for Billy,* continue the bleak vision of what the old West had and would

become in the eyes of wild west shows, dime novelists, and the former rangers and cowboys who had helped "tame" it by turning it into a sideshow.

Although set in modern Texas, several novels reprise characters who are grappling with the bewildering changes in Texas. *Texasville* returns to Thalia thirty years later to find the teenagers of *The Last Picture Show* victims of aging, a busted oil boom, and the pervasive disillusionment of a postmodern, decidedly nonmythic Texas. McMurtry revives Danny Deck for *Some Can Whistle* and, perhaps his most popular character, Aurora Greenway, in *The Evening Star,* marking an important new phase in McMurtry's career. While not even attempting to embrace the dusty myths of Texas and the old West, McMurtry can be praised for returning to these subjects and characters with a fresh perspective, taking inventory and reexamining them with the gentle eye of a native son and the skill of an experienced writer.

McMurtry has also been a successful screenwriter, sharing an Academy award for his adaptation of *The Last Picture Show* with Peter Bogdanovich. He was a part of the writing team for *Hud* and wrote the screenplay for the movie production of *Texasville.* The 1983 Academy Award for Best Picture (in addition to four other Oscars) was given to *Terms of Endearment.* James L. Brooks adapted McMurtry's novel, adding characters and deleting others. The result, however, retains the heart and soul of McMurtry's story about a young woman and her mother coping with an unfaithful husband, a fickle ex-astronaut lover, and the agony of the daughter's early death from cancer. None of these films can hold a candle in popularity to the critically acclaimed, blockbuster miniseries *Lonesome Dove,* which aired in 1988 and starred Tommy Lee Jones and Robert Duvall among other big stars. Although McMurtry did not work on the teleplay, the six-hour format allowed the writers and producers to include many of McMurtry's finest touches and remains true to the grand sweep of the last trail drive. (It is interesting to note briefly that the television sequel, *Return to Lonesome Dove,* was panned by critics and received fairly low ratings. Wisely, McMurtry had nothing to do with this miniseries; he had already written *The Streets of Laredo* as a sequel.)

McMurtry divides his time between writing—he claims to write five pages almost every day he is working on a novel—and his book stores in Dallas and Washington, D.C., and the duties of his presidency of the PEN American Center.

His novels place him in the Texas pantheon of novelist-gods and have earned him a firm spot in the American literary canon. Throughout his writing, McMurtry chronicles a Texas and an America that is passing away but that can be felt in the restless and unsettled spirits of those who populate his novels.

—Jay Ann Cox

McNICKLE, (William) D'Arcy

Born: St. Ignatius, Montana, 18 January 1904; used stepfather's name, Dahlberg, for college publications. **Education:** Schools in Montana and Washington and at Indian boarding school in Chemawa, Oregon, 1913-16; University of Montana, 1921-25; Oxford University, England, 1925-26; University of Grenoble, France, summer 1931. **Family:** Married 1) Joran Birkeland in 1926 (divorced 1938), one daughter; 2) Roma Kauffman in 1939 (divorced 1967), one daughter; 3) Viola Pfrommer in 1969 (died 1977). **Career:** Worked for various publishers and trade journals in New York, 1926-35, and Philadelphia, 1929; joined the Federal Writers Project in Washington D.C., 1935-36; worked for the Bureau of Indian Affairs, 1936-52; director, American Indian Development, Inc., Bolder, Colorado, 1952-66; taught in the Anthropology Department, University of Saskatchewan Regina Campus, 1966-71; program director, Center for the History of the American Indian at The Newberry Library, Chicago, Illinois, 1972-77. **Awards:** Guggenheim fellowship, 1963; honorary Doctor of Science from the University of Colorado, 1966. **Member:** Charter member of the National Congress of American Indians; fellow of the American Anthropological Association. **Died:** October 1977.

Publications

Collections

The Hawk Is Hungry & Other Stories, edited by Birgit Hans. 1992.

Novels

The Surrounded. 1936.
Runner in the Sun: A Story of Indian Maize (for children). 1954.
Wind from an Enemy Sky. 1978.

Other

They Came Here First: The Epic of the American Indian. 1949.
Indians and Other Americans: Two Ways of Life Meet, with Harold E. Fey. 1959.
Native American Tribalism: Indian Survivals and Renewals. 1962.
Indian Man: A Life of Oliver La Farge. 1971.

*

Critical Studies: *D'Arcy McNickle* by James Ruppert, 1988; "Textual Perspectives and the Reader in *The Surrounded,*" in *Narrative Chance: Postmodern Discourses on Native American Indian Literatures* edited by Gerald Vizenor, 1989; "The Red Road to Nowhere: D'Arcy McNickle's *The Surrounded* and 'The Hungry Generations'" by Louis Owens, in *American Indian Quarterly* vol. 13, no. 3, 1989; *Word Ways: The Novels of D'Arcy McNickle* by John Purdy, 1990; *Singing an Indian Song: A Biography of D'Arcy McNickle* by Dorothy R. Parker, 1992; "Re-Visions: An Early Version of *The Surrounded*" by Birgit Hans, in *Studies of American Indian Literatures* vol. 4, no. 2-3, 1992; *Singing an Indian Song: A Biography of D'Arcy McNickle* by Dorothy R. Parker, 1994; *The Legacy of D'Arcy McNickle: Writer, Historian, Activist* edited by John Lloyd Purdy, 1996.

*   *   *

D'Arcy McNickle was the first important Native American writer; his fiction anticipated the award-winning novels of **N. Scott Momaday** and **Leslie Marmon Silko** by thirty years. In his first novel, *The Surrounded,* he rejected the then prevalent idea that the tribal peoples of America had to give up their own cultures completely and assimilate, becoming a part of white culture. McNickle showed that the Flathead culture of his main char-

acter was a living culture even in the twentieth century and that its loss meant the spiritual and physical decline of the individual and the tribe.

McNickle was an enrolled member of the Salish Kootenai Confederated Tribes (Flathead). His mother married a white man, William McNickle, who was, among other things, a farmer. Even at age seventy, McNickle remembered with some bitterness the problems of growing up as a mixed-blood child in Montana and on the Flathead Reservation; he felt that he was not accepted by either the white community or the Native American community. After his parents' divorce in 1913, McNickle had to attend the Indian boarding school in Chemawa, Oregon, for three years. In this government school teachers still insisted that Native American cultures would disappear. Native Americans had to become white people. When McNickle left the school, he must have been more determined than ever to become a white man. He had certainly achieved this goal when he returned from England in 1925 and settled in New York City. Not only was he a part of the busy life of the city, he was also writing early versions of *The Surrounded* that expressed the need for complete assimilation. However, unlike other early Native American writers—such as Mourning Dove and **John Joseph Mathews**—McNickle managed to leave his early training behind and to take pride in his Native American culture.

Several events caused McNickle to re-think his Indian heritage and to change his mind about assimilation. The growing economic pressures of the Great Depression led him to question two basic values of Euroamerican life: the emphasis on the individual and on material success. In addition, he re-established contact with his mother and, through her, those years of growing up that he had deliberately left behind. He also accepted a position in the Bureau of Indian Affairs in 1936, two years after the federal government had stated in the Indian Reorganization Act that Native Americans had a right to self-government and that tribal cultures were important even in the twentieth century. After sixteen years in the Bureau of Indian Affairs, McNickle left the government service. He continued his work with tribal peoples by organizing summer workshops and community programs for American Indian Development, Inc., teaching at the University of Saskatchewan, lecturing extensively, writing numerous articles and three very well received non-fiction books about Indian-white relations. Finally, as director of the Center for the History of the American Indian at The Newberry Library in Chicago, McNickle trained tribal historians. McNickle was respected by tribal peoples and Euroamericans alike and his unexpected death at age seventy-three came as a shock to both communities.

McNickle's best-known novel is *The Surrounded,* which was reviewed rather favorably by literary critics but did not prove a commercial success. The realistic portrayal of contemporary life on the Flathead Reservation was not what Euroamerican readers were looking for. They preferred the picturesque Indian of the past, the Noble Savage of literary tradition, to make them forget the problems the Great Depression was causing and to give them hope for a better life.

In *The Surrounded* McNickle tells the story of the half-blood Archilde who returns to the Flathead Reservation to say good-bye to his Flathead mother. He intends to leave the reservation forever in order to escape the Flathead part of his heritage. Instead of leaving though, he helps his estranged father with the harvest and takes his mother hunting. On the hunting trip, Archilde and his mother witness the killing of one of Archilde's criminal brothers by the game warden, who is killed in turn by Archilde's mother. Archilde hides the body of the game warden. At last his father realizes that this youngest mixed-blood son is different from his other sons who are always in trouble with the law. After a reconciliation with Archilde, the father dies. His mother renounces Catholicism and returns to her Flathead culture; she dies as well. At the end of the novel Archilde, who has learned much about Flathead culture, is arrested for the murder of the game warden.

There are two dominant themes in *The Surrounded:* the mixed-bloods and Catholicism. From the beginning of the novel the reader is aware that the mixed-bloods, those descendants of Euroamericans and Flathead people, are tainted; in fact, they seem to inherit the negative characteristics of both cultures. They are horse thieves, prostitutes, etc. Archilde is set apart in the beginning, because he had renounced his Flathead culture and feels nothing but contempt for it. However, as the novel progresses he learns about the oral tradition of the Flathead, the injustices that they have suffered and still suffer, and the continuity and strength of Flathead culture. He begins to respect the old Flathead people, among them his mother, and the things that they teach. In the end he may lose his freedom, but he has gained the cultural knowledge necessary to set him free spiritually. There is no longer a need to deny the Flathead part of his heritage.

Most contemporary Native American writers deal with the mixed-blood theme and the mixed-blood's ambiguous position in both communities. McNickle also deals with the rather sensitive subject of the missionary work of Catholic priests among the Flathead. One of the most remarkable characters of the novel is the old Jesuit priest who, though busy writing the history of the triumphs of early missionary work among the Flathead, has a sense that the church has been a destructive force among the Flathead. The church has made it possible for the white farmers to take the land and to dispossess the Flathead. However, the final indictment of the church comes from Catherine, Archilde's mother; Faithful Catherine, whose whole life has been devoted to obeying the priests and who has had to watch the destruction of her family, rejects Catholicism and returns to her traditional Flathead beliefs. Catherine, by the way, is only one of the strong women characters in the novel. Even though the novel employs juxtaposition and includes stories from Flathead oral tradition, the structure of *The Surrounded* does not have the complexity and richness of broken narratives that later Native American novels have. However, it foreshadows contemporary novels and remains important reading because of its characterizations and the portrayals of Flathead-Euroamerican relationships. The novel is also considered a fine example of western realism.

McNickle never returned to writing fiction full-time after joining the Bureau of Indian Affairs. In fact, except for a short story or two he did not publish any more adult fiction during his lifetime. His second novel, *Wind from an Enemy Sky,* was published posthumously in 1978, the year after his death. *Wind from an Enemy Sky* shows excellent literary craftsmanship but lacks the energy of *The Surrounded.* It is a polemic piece of writing; McNickle had a point to make about federal Indian policy and his fictional Little Elk people represent all tribes in the United States.

The novel focuses on two characters who are representatives of their communities. Superintendent Rafferty, who is willing to help the Little Elk people whom he respects, becomes hampered by the restrictive and dogmatic policies handed down by the Bureau of Indian Affairs and the fossilized church; and Bull, the traditional leader of the tribe, is willing to become a farmer if the stolen sacred bundle of his people, Feather Boy, is returned and,

thereby, the spiritual survival of the Little Elk people is assured. The hope that Bull will lead his people to a meaningful life in the twentieth century is destroyed at the end of the novel. Feather Boy has been destroyed by neglect in a museum. Bull shoots Rafferty and the representative of the museum and is himself killed by an Indian policeman.

Characters in *Wind from an Enemy Sky* are not as thoroughly developed as in *The Surrounded,* since federal Indian policies and their destructive nature are the focal points of the novel. The Catholic church is mentioned, but its representative lacks the redeeming human qualities of the old priest in *The Surrounded.* On the whole, it is a pessimistic novel that leaves the reader with the distinct impression that nothing has really changed in the relationship of the federal government and tribal peoples.

The Hawk Is Hungry is a collection of short stories that reflect McNickle's various experiences. Some deal with Indian life on the reservation, some with the experiences of the Euroamerican farmers in Montana, some with urban life in cities like New York and Paris. This short fiction shows McNickle at his best. The stories of the farmers' struggle with the land especially further his reputation as an accomplished western realist.

McNickle's writing career was bracketed by his two novels. When he applied to the Bureau of Indian Affairs, he said in his application that his writing was to deal with the history of the West. Fiction, then, could be used to write history. People and cultures could not simply be reduced to facts and statistics. After writing several books of traditional Euroamerican history, McNickle returned to fiction to write Indian history. It was McNickle's personal triumph that he could write the history of his people from a Native American point of view after his early training in assimilation and that he managed to do so thirty years earlier than other Native American writers.

—Birgit Hans

McPHERSON, James Alan

Born: Savannah, Georgia, 16 September 1943. **Education:** Morris Brown College, Atlanta, Georgia, 1961-63, 1965, B.A. in history 1965; Morgan State College, Baltimore, Maryland, 1963-64; Harvard University, Cambridge, Massachusetts, LL.B. 1968; University of Iowa, Iowa City, M.F.A. 1969. **Family:** Married in 1973 (divorced); one daughter. **Career:** Instructor, University of Iowa Law School, Iowa City, 1968-69; lecturer in English, University of California, Santa Cruz, 1969-70; assistant professor of English, Morgan State University, Baltimore, Maryland, 1975-76; associate professor of English, University of Virginia, Charlottesville, 1976-81; professor of English, University of Iowa, since 1981. Contributing editor, *Atlantic Monthly,* Boston, since 1969; guest editor of fiction issues of *Iowa Review,* Iowa City, 1984, and *Ploughshares,* Cambridge, Massachusetts, 1985, 1990. Staff writer, *Double-Take Magazine,* beginning 1994. Member, Rona Jaffe Foundation, Arts Outreach, Spencer, Iowa, 1995. **Awards:** *Atlantic Monthly* award, 1968; *Atlantic Monthly* grant, 1969; National Institute of Arts and Letters award, 1970; Rockefeller grant, 1970; Guggenheim fellowship, 1972; Pulitzer prize, 1978; MacArthur Foundation award, 1981; Award for Excellence in Teaching, University of Iowa, 1991; Green Eyeshades Award for Excellence in Print Commentary, The Society of Southern Journalists, 1994; Fellow, Center for Advanced Studies in the Behavioral Sciences, Stanford University, 1997-98. Honorary degree: Morris Brown College, Atlanta, Georgia. **Member:** American Academy of Arts and Sciences, 1995. **Residence:** Iowa City, Iowa.

PUBLICATIONS

Short Stories

Hue and Cry. 1969.
Elbow Room. 1977.

Other

Railroad: Trains and Train People in American Culture, with Miller Williams. 1976.
Crabcakes. 1998.

Editor, with Miller Williams, *Railroad.* 1976.
Editor, *One Hundred Years After Huck: Fiction by Men in America,* special issue of *Iowa Review.* Winter 1984.
Editor, *Fathering Daughters,* with Dewitt Henry. 1998.

*

Bibliography: *American Ethnic Literatures: Native American, African American, Chicano/Latino and Asian American Writers and Their Backgrounds* by David R. Peck, 1992.

Critical Studies: "Developing a Sense of Self: The Androgynous Ideal in McPherson's *Elbow Room*" by Mary A. Gervin, in *CLA Journal,* vol. 26, no. 2, 1982; interview with Bob Shacochis, in *Iowa Journal of Literary Studies,* vol. 4, no. 1, 1983; "James McPherson" by Patsy B. Perry, in *Dictionary of Literary Biography* vol. 38, 1985; "Antaeus Revisited: James A. McPherson and *Elbow Room*" by Ruthe T. Sheffey, in *Amid Visions and Revisions* edited by Burney J. Hollis, 1985; "Negotiations: The Quest for a Middle Way in the Fiction of James Alan McPherson and Ernest Gaines," in *Fingering the Jagged Grain* by Keith E. Byerman, 1985; interview in *Finding the Words* by Nancy Bunge, 1985; "The Voices of Misery and Despair in the Fiction of James Alan McPherson" by William Domnarski, in *Arizona-Quarterly,* Spring 1986; "I Yam What You Is and You Is What I Yam: Rhetorical Invisibility in James Alan McPherson's 'The Story of a Dead Man'" by Herman Beavers, in *Callaloo,* Fall 1986; "Interracial Relationships in Three Short Stories by James Alan McPherson" by Edith Blicksilver, in *CEA-Critic,* Winter/Summer 1987-88; "The Politics of Style in Three Stories by James Alan McPherson," in *Modern Fiction Studies,* Spring 1988, and "The Story Behind the Story in James Alan McPherson's *Elbow Room,*" in *Studies in Short Fiction,* Fall 1988, both by Jon Wallace; *Wrestling Angels into Song: The Fictions of Ernest J. Gaines and James Alan McPherson* by Herman Beavers, 1995.

*   *   *

In twenty-five years of writing essays and short fiction, editing books and journals, and teaching writing, James Alan McPherson has established himself as an important voice in American literature. Recognition of his achievements has come in the form of numerous literary awards, including the *Atlantic Monthly* "Firsts" award in 1968, an *Atlantic Monthly* grant in 1969, an award for *Hue and Cry* from the National Institute of Arts and Letters in 1970, a Rockefeller grant in 1970, a Guggenheim fellowship during 1972 and 1973, the Pulitzer prize for *Elbow Room* in 1978, and a MacArthur Foundation award in 1981. In addition, McPherson's short stories appear in several "year's best" or annual prize story collections as well as in literature textbooks. Noteworthy, too, is the fact that he has received generally positive critical evaluations from American, British, and Japanese reviewers, who praise his artistic perception of human nature, his understanding of painful insensitivities and betrayals, and his timeless, universal characters, with whom the exploited and disenfranchised of all races, classes, and ethnic groups can identify.

McPherson was born on September 16, 1943, in Savannah, Georgia. His parents struggled to maintain a stable home, but their efforts were thwarted by the fact that McPherson, Sr., a master electrician, suffered repeated, unjust denials of an electrician's license. Forced to work as a common laborer, he turned to alcohol, a major cause of his death in 1961 at the age of forty-eight.

Though McPherson grew up in lower-class black neighborhoods and attended Savannah's segregated public schools, he witnessed the shift from segregation to integration in public education, public accommodations, and housing. From his various jobs as a grocer's helper, railroad worker, and janitor, he noticed subtle variations of change in American life. In addition, during his college and university experiences in both the South and North, he absorbed the many resistances to change, the tensions surrounding change, and the reluctant individual and institutional accommodations to change which characterize the decades of the 1960s and 1970s.

McPherson received a National Defense Student Loan and studied at Morris Brown College in Atlanta from 1961 to 1963. During 1963 and 1964 he was enrolled at Morgan State College in Baltimore, Maryland, but returned to Morris Brown, graduating in 1965 with a B.A. degree in history. Already beginning to demonstrate exceptional talent, he won a creative writing contest sponsored by the United Negro College Fund and *Reader's Digest* in 1965. Unfortunately this entry, his first short story, was lost. Also during 1965 McPherson was recruited by Harvard Law School, and "Gold Coast," his second short story, won an *Atlantic Monthly* first prize. Here began associations with two New England institutions, which resulted in McPherson's earning an LL.B degree from Harvard Law School in 1968 and his continuing relationship with *Atlantic Monthly.* "Gold Coast" was published in the November 1968 issue of *Atlantic Monthly;* the January 1969 issue reported his 1968 Atlantic "Firsts" distinction and the $750 cash award for "Gold Coast"; the February 1969 issue announced his Atlantic grant for *Hue and Cry;* the March 1969 issue advertised and the May issue published his exclusive study on "The Blackstone Rangers and the Chicago Police"; and the June 1969 issue named him as a contributing editor—a position he has continued to hold.

From 1968 to 1969 McPherson studied and taught at the University of Iowa, earning a master of fine arts degree in 1969 and serving as a writing instructor in the Law School. He has continued to balance a schedule of teaching and writing, and, of course, some of his best teaching can be found in his brilliant collections of short stories. McPherson opens *Hue and Cry* with a passage from Pollock and Maitland's *History of English Law* which states that "the hue and cry . . . should be raised" when a felony is committed. He then demonstrates numerous offenses against individuals and groups, the subtle tactics that the offended use when protesting, and the lessons that all, including the reader, can learn from each experience. Without bitterness and often with understatement and irony, McPherson guides his characters toward greater understanding of themselves and others. He is convinced, as he states in an interview with Nancy Bunge, that "indirection persuades people more effectively than direct statement."

For example, McPherson's excellent stories of life on the railroad, "On Trains" and "A Solo Song: For Doc," vividly underscore the differences between learned rules and instinctive behavior while depicting various degrees of racial intolerance and exploitation. There is great irony in Doc Craft's having built the railroad with his "fine moves" that, codified in a book of rules, were used later to force him into retirement. Similarly, in "A Matter of Vocabulary," Thomas, the thirteen-year-old grocer's helper, finds that his supervisors refuse to recognize his intelligence and competence. If he is to keep his job, he must perform according to the stereotype of African American youth. This truth is made clear to him when his brother Eddie, having used the word "evidently," angers Miss Feinberg and quits his job rather than demean himself to fit her image of him as incapable of superior language skills. Vocabulary is again important as McPherson concludes the story with Thomas's discovery of "a big word, that made good sense of [the Barefoot Lady's] sound and the burning feeling thing he felt inside himself . . . She came always in the night to scream because she, like himself, was in misery, and did not know what else to do." This painful initiation into what it means to be black, rejected, and miserable is even more poignant because Thomas's one-way window at the grocery store holds no promise for real communication. It seems to suggest, instead, that we as readers may see Thomas's future in Doc Craft's experiences. Frustrated ambition, loneliness and isolation, broken contracts, obstructed justice, near madness, and approaching death mark the stories in *Hue and Cry.*

Including in *Elbow Room* a variety of contemporary American relationships, institutions, and cultural realities, McPherson portrays characters as they negotiate new territories. He presents his personae as conscious—sometimes as near-equal—contestants as they confront individuals who would impose limits based on sex, race, class, or region. For example, the Southern-born black narrator of "Why I Like Country Music" confesses that he enjoys square dancing and country music despite the association of these forms with white people. Additionally, "Problems of Art" and "A Sense of Story" provide excellent demonstrations of individuals who defy the stereotypical notions of what they represent. In "Widows and Orphans" and in the title story "Elbow Room," McPherson's characters emphasize movement toward higher levels of being and understanding. The goal is to acknowledge and accept many styles and values, to allow for many different ways of viewing the world, to make "elbow room."

Indeed, McPherson has suggested that African American writers make "elbow room" for themselves as writers—that they free themselves from sociological boundaries within which they have protested racial discrimination as a major theme. In his essay "On Becoming an American Writer," McPherson records what he calls "the model I was aiming for in my book of stories, . . . a synthesis of high and low, black and white, city and country, provincial and universal." He has achieved this aim while, at the same time, giving an insider's view of African American life in loving and unforgettable portraits.

One of McPherson's most memorable portraits is of himself in *Crabcakes: A Memoir* (1998). After two decades of near silence, he describes his torturous journey from "the black compartment" back to "being openly human." Very important to the completion of this journey are his memory and subsequent dream of "a trail of seafood, along the path [his] life had taken, from the crabs and shrimp of Savannah to the cod and lobsters of Boston to the crabcakes of Baltimore and to the *fugu* of Japan."

As subject and narrator of *Crabcakes,* McPherson is meditative and philosophical. He speaks of "extraordinary pressures for well over ten years" and of having grown, for some sixteen years, "painfully cautious and aware of [himself] as a black American male." In addition, in *Contemporary Authors Autobiography Series,* he describes the "deep fear . . . back in Charlottesville in the immediate aftermath of receiving a MacArthur Fellowship." Whether his silence resulted from the writer's block which sometimes follows a major award, a general fear and distrust of humanity, or some combination of these or other reactions, McPherson suffered deeply before heeding his own admonition to "Run," to remove himself "from the field of battle." In the 1990s he traveled in Japan, discovering there a "natural," supportive culture. But, predictably, it was through introspection that he was able to renew himself. According to *Crabcakes,* he practiced "kiting of the imagination"—imagining the possibilities of the future in order to survive the present. Aptly titled, *Crabcakes,* the Maryland delicacy and a metaphor for all that is good in life, can be anticipated and re-created for sustenance. McPherson explains that "one can always focus on the future enjoyment of a Maryland crabcake. Such exercises of the imagination keep hope alive." Further, he shares the rediscovery of his inner "*deepness . . . two simultaneous awarenesses,*" or the coexistence of past and present, of the Self and the Other of which the self is a part. In these two life-affirming revelations, he recognizes the end of his journey within himself.

Always complex and multi-dimensional in his use of language, relationships, and events, McPherson moves from the opening half of the book—a narrative of his activities in Baltimore, Maryland; Charlottesville, Virginia; and Iowa City, Iowa—to the closing half, composed of a series of letters to his Japanese friend Kiyo. The two parts are loosely connected by frequent evocations of crabcakes. Told in a circular, elliptical style, and heavy with Japanese philosophy, *Crabcakes* nonetheless repays careful reading as a means of charting McPherson's journey beyond people, places, and events into the realm of the human spirit.

—Patsy B. Perry

MELVILLE, Herman

Born: New York City, 1 August 1819. **Education:** New York Male School; Albany Academy to age 12. **Family:** Married Elizabeth Knapp Shaw in 1847; two sons and two daughters. **Career:** Worked from age 12 as clerk, farmhand, and schoolteacher; ship's boy on the *St. Lawrence,* bound for Liverpool, 1839-40; traveled in Midwest, 1840; ordinary seaman on the whaler *Achushnet,* 1841 until he jumped ship in the Marquesas, 1842; left the islands on the Sydney whaling barque *Lucy Ann,* and jumped ship in Tahiti, 1842; harpooner on whaler *Charles and Henry,* from Nantucket, in southern Pacific, 1842-43; clerk and bookkeeper in general store,

Honolulu, 1843; shipped back to Boston on U.S. Navy frigate *United States,* 1843-44; writer from 1844; lived in New York, 1847-50, and Pittsfield, Massachusetts, 1850-63; traveled in Near East and Europe, 1856-57; on lecture circuits in the United States, 1857-60; lived in Washington, D.C., 1861-62, and in New York after 1863; district inspector of customs, New York, 1866-85. **Died:** 28 September 1891.

PUBLICATIONS

Collections

Works. 16 vols., 1922-24.
Collected Poems, edited by Howard P. Vincent. 1947.
The Portable Melville, edited by Jay Leyda. 1952.
Selected Poems, edited by Hennig Cohen. 1964.
Great Short Works, edited by Warner Berthoff. 1966.
Writings, edited by Harrison Hayford, Hershel Parker, and G. Thomas Tanselle. 1968—.
Selected Poems, edited by Robert Penn Warren. 1970.
Typee, Omoo, Mardi (Library of America), edited by G. Thomas Tanselle. 1982.
Redburn, White-Jacket, Moby Dick (Library of America), edited by G. Thomas Tanselle. 1983.
Pierre, Israel Potter, The Confidence-Man, Tales and Billy Budd (Library of America), edited by Harrison Hayford. 1985.
The Essential Melville, edited by Robert Penn Warren. 1987.
The Complete Shorter Fiction, edited by Harrison Hayford, Alma McDougall, G. Thomas Tanselle, and others. 1997.

Short Stories

The Piazza Tales. 1856.
The Apple-Tree Table and Other Sketches. 1922.
Billy Budd and Other Prose Pieces, edited by Raymond M. Weaver, in *Works.* 1924.

Novels

Narrative of Four Months' Residence among the Natives of a Valley in the Marquesas Islands; or, A Peep at Polynesian Life. 1846; as *Typee,* 1846; revised edition, 1846.
Omoo: A Narrative of Adventures in the South Seas. 1847.
Mardi, and a Voyage Thither. 1849.
Redburn, His First Voyage. 1849.
White Jacket; or, The World in a Man-of-War. 1850; as *White-Jacket,* 1850.
The Whale. 1851; as *Moby Dick; or, The Whale,* 1851.
Pierre; or, The Ambiguities. 1852.
Israel Potter, His Fifty Years of Exile. 1855.
The Confidence-Man, His Masquerade. 1857.

Poetry

Battle-Pieces and Aspects of the War. 1866; edited by Hennig Cohen, 1963.
Clarel: A Poem, and Pilgrimage in the Holy Land. 1876; edited by Walter E. Bezanson, 1960.
John Marr and Other Sailors, with Some Sea-Pieces. 1888.
Timoleon Etc. 1891.

Other

Journal up the Straits October 11, 1856-May 5, 1857, edited by Raymond M. Weaver. 1935; as *Journal of a Visit to Europe and the Levant,* edited by Howard C. Horsford, 1955.
Journal of a Visit to London and the Continent 1849-1850, edited by Eleanor Melville Metcalf. 1948.
Letters, edited by Merrell R. Davis and William H. Gilman. 1960.

*

Bibliography: *The Merrill Checklist of Melville* by Howard P. Vincent, 1969; in *Bibliography of American Literature* by Jacob Blanck, 1973; *Melville: An Annotated Bibliography 1: 1846-1930,* 1979, and *Melville: A Reference Guide, 1931-1960,* 1987, both by Brian Higgins; *Melville and the Critics: A Checklist of Criticism 1900-1978* by Jeanetta Boswell, 1981; *Melville's Foreign Reputation: A Research Guide* by Leland R. Phelps, 1983.

Critical Studies: *Melville: The Tragedy of Mind* by William E. Sedgwick, 1944; *Call Me Ishmael: A Study of Melville* by Charles Olson, 1947; *The Trying-Out of Moby Dick* by Howard Vincent, 1949; *Melville* by Richard Chase, 1949; *Melville* by Newton Arvin, 1950; *The Melville Log: A Documentary Life of Melville 1819-1891* by Jay Leyda, 2 vols., 1951, revised edition, 1969; *Melville: A Biography* by Leon Howard, 1951; *Melville's Quarrel with God* by Lawrance Thompson, 1952; *The Fine-Hammered Steel of Melville* by Milton R. Stern, 1957; *Melville's Billy Budd and the Critics* edited by William T. Stafford, 1961, revised edition, 1968; *The Example of Melville* by Warner Berthoff, 1962; *A Reader's Guide to Melville* by James E. Miller, Jr., 1962; *Melville* by Tyrus Hillway, 1963, revised edition, 1979; *Ishmael's White World: A Phenomenological Reading of Moby-Dick* by Paul Brodtkorb, Jr., 1965; *Melville's Thematics of Form: The Great Art of Telling the Truth* by Edgar A. Dryden, 1968; *Plots and Characters in the Fiction and Narrative Poetry of Melville* by Robert L. Gale, 1969; *Melville: The Ironic Diagram* by John D. Seelye, 1970; *Moby Dick As Doubloon: Essays and Extracts 1851-1970* edited by Hershel Parker and Harrison Hayford, 1970; *An Artist in the Rigging: The Early Works of Melville,* 1972, *Melville's Short Fiction,* 1977, and *Melville's Later Novels,* 1986, all by William B. Dillingham; *Melville: The Critical Heritage* edited by W.G. Branch, 1974; *The Early Lives of Melville* by Merton M. Sealts, Jr., 1974, and *Pursuing Melville 1940-1980* edited by Sealts, 1982; *Melville* (biography) by Edwin Haviland Miller, 1975; *The Method of Melville's Short Fiction* by R. Bruce Bickley, Jr., 1975; *Twentieth-Century Interpretations of Moby Dick* edited by Michael T. Gilmore, 1977; *New Perspectives on Melville* edited by Faith Pullin, 1978; *The Body Impolitic: A Reading of Four Novels by Melville* by R.M. Blau, 1979; *Melville* by Edward H. Rosenberry, 1979; *Exiled Waters: Moby Dick and the Crisis of Allegory* by Bainard Cowan, 1982; *Subversive Genealogy: The Politics and Art of Melville* by Michael Paul Rogin, 1983; *Melville: Reassessments* edited by A. Robert Lee, 1984; *Melville* edited by Harold Bloom, 1986; *A Companion to Melville Studies* edited by John Bryant, 1986; *New Essays on Moby Dick* edited by Richard H. Brodhead, 1987; *Melville's Reading* by Merton M. Sealts, Jr., 1987; *Mourning, Gender, and Creativity in the Art of Melville* by Neal L. Tolchin, 1988; *Melville's Sources* by Mary K. Bercaw, 1988; *Melville's Marginalia* by Walker Cowen, 2 vols., 1988; *On Melville: The Best from "American Literature"* edited by Edwin H. Cody and Louis Budd, 1989;

Empire for Liberty: Melville and the Poetics of Individualism by Wai-chee Dimock, 1989; *Some Other World To Find: Quest and Negation in the Works of Melville* by Bruce L. Grenberg, 1989; *Reading Billy Budd* by Hershel Parker, 1990; *The Hawthorne and Melville Friendship* edited by James C. Wilson, 1991; *After the Whale: Melville in the Wake of Moby Dick* by Clark Davis, 1995; *Melville's Muse: Literary Creation & the Form of Philosophical Fiction* by John Paul Wenke, 1995; *Cosmopolis and Truth: Melville's Critique of Modernity* by Bernhard Radloff, 1996; *Sounding the Whale: Moby Dick As Epic Novel* Christopher Sten, 1996; *Melville and His Circle* by William B. Dillingham, 1996; *The Weaver-God, He Weaves: Melville and the Poetics of the Novel* by Christopher Sten, 1996; *Strike through the Mask: Herman Melville and the Scene of Writing* by Elizabeth Renker, 1996; *Melville and the Visual Arts: Ionian Form, Venetian Tint* by Douglas Robillard, 1997; *Herman Melville's Religious Journey* by Walter Donald Kring, 1997; *The Sign of the Cannibal: Melville and the Making of a Postcolonial Reader* by Geoffrey Sanborn, 1998; *American Palestine: Melville, Twain, and the Holy Land Mania* by Hilton Obenzinger, 1999; *Essays on Fiction–Dickens, Melville, Hawthorne, and Faulkner* by Thomas Edmund Connolly, 1999.

*   *   *

What characterizes Herman Melville's novels from *Typee* through *Moby Dick* is the sense of an immanent personality, the author through his narrator, examining himself, his experiences, and the world about him. This personality seeks categorical answers and finds none, and, when his quest fails, seeks ways to survive in an inscrutable universe. In these novels the theme of the autobiographical quest is signaled by the presence of a first-person narrator and by the easy identification of setting and events with the facts of Melville's life as a sailor. If the writings after *Moby Dick* seem less autobiographical, it is because Melville places more distance between himself and his stories. Their subjects are more obviously interior, spiritual voyages to less romantic places, and an omniscient author, skeptical though compassionate, has displaced the roving, questing youth who spins high-spirited tales of his travels.

Soon after he returned from his voyage to the Pacific, Melville began to write. His first books, *Typee* and *Omoo*, are sailor's yarns based on his adventures in the Marquesas Islands and Tahiti after he jumped ship to sojourn with cannibals, to comb the beaches, and, when his Polynesian paradise began to pall, to go back to the sea. Hindsight reveals hints of themes that were to preoccupy him later, such as man's capacity for evil, appearance and reality, or the dubious blessings of both civilization and its opposite, primitivism; for it was typical of Melville to present another side of the question as a way of stating the complexity and uncertainty of things. They also show a capacity for quiet comedy, delight in word play, and penchant for social criticism. But in the main these books are light-hearted, colorful adventure, mildly fictionalized. Actually, *Typee* follows the facts closely, exploiting the potentiality for suspense in the uncertainty of the Typee's eating habits, the temptations of the narrator's situation as their petted prisoner, and the accumulating pressure to escape from being culturally if not physically consumed by them. An Australian whaler in need of hands rescues him, and he sails off toward the horizon. At this point the sequel, Omoo (the name means "wanderer"), begins. The captain proves incompetent and the mate a drunkard,

so the sailors refuse duty. They are confined to a casually kept jail in Tahiti from which the young narrator wanders to a nearby island. After more wanderings of a picaresque sort, he goes back to sea.

Such open-endedness suggests uncertainty, or at least open-mindedness, and it encourages sequels. By this time Melville had been taken up by Evert and George Duyckinck, influential New York editors. He began to imbibe their ideas on literary nationalism and liberal politics and to borrow from their extensive collection of Renaissance books, reading Rabelais, Montaigne, Burton, Browne, and the Renaissance dramatists. This was heady stuff, and along with the chagrin he felt because publishers and critics questioned the authenticity of his realistic narratives, it caused him to try another tack. His third narrative, *Mardi*, begins realistically. On board a whaler in the South Seas two sailors contemplate desertion. However, theirs soon becomes "a chartless voyage" among allegorical islands of a mythical archipelago. The sailor-narrator rescues a symbolically provocative white captive, loves her, loses her, and pursues her beyond the ends of the earth. He is as relentless as Ahab in quest of the white whale and as self-destructive, but the search is put aside from time to time for intervals of philosophizing, rhapsodizing, and satirizing on topics of contemporary political, theological, artistic, and scientific interest. Mardi is a thing of patches, some of which presage the bravura passages of *Moby Dick* and *The Confidence-Man*. Melville's family and friends advised that he forego his mental traveling, and to the accompaniment of grumbling about financial necessities, he restrained himself in *Redburn* and *White Jacket*.

Redburn recalls Melville's first voyage, a summer's service on a trader carrying cotton to Liverpool. *White Jacket* reflects his experiences as an ordinary seaman on a "homeward bound" American frigate. Both novels contributed to his bank account and reputation. In *Redburn* the titular narrator is a callow lad who grows up, discarding his social pretension, encountering misery and evil about which he can do little, yet learning to stand on his own. *White Jacket* is likewise an initiation story, but more. Its titular character is named for a non-regulation pea jacket he is issued, which distinguishes him in a way that he first finds flattering yet proves so disadvantageous that the plot concerns his efforts to rid himself of it. His ship is treated as a microcosm of his nation, a professedly democratic state but one sustained by an authoritarian hierarchy that abuses "the people," as the ratings are called, and that is corrupt or inept. Despite this irony, *White Jacket*, with its emphasis on the brotherhood of the common seaman and the prospect that "Our Lord Admiral" above will right earthly wrongs, is Melville's most optimistic book.

Apparently *Moby Dick* was conceived in the pattern of its predecessors—a sailor recalling, in a realistic and casual way, his experiences aboard a whaler on a Pacific cruise. But it grew from narrative to novel, encompassing drama and epic and a number of lesser genres (e.g.. sermon, natural history, tall tale, technical manual); expanding its tonal range to include low comedy, high wit, and lofty tragedy; and posing questions both metaphysical and pragmatic. If the theme of this leviathanic book must be simplistically stated, one could say that it is a quest for a way to live with dignity in a world in which the only certainty is uncertainty. Superficially, it is the melodramatic tale of the search for an albino whale by a mad sea captain whom it had maimed, but the book is so rich that it encourages many interpretations. Indeed this seems the intention of the author, supporting its essential nature as an epistemological quest.

Pierre is a departure from Melville's six sea narratives. It opposes an Edenic countryside and a postlapsarian city, settings in which *Pierre,* an idealistic young patrician, attempts to attack the evil he discovers, the sin of his father, with the weapons of Christian rectitude. In a memorable analogy, Melville suggests that clocks on earth are only relatively accurate because they must be made applicable to earthly contours. Absolutely perfect time is obtained in heaven alone. Pierre's attempt to apply celestial time to earth is disastrously out of joint. Badly received, *Pierre* compels, in the words of its subtitle, by means of "the ambiguities" laid bare through its psychological and ethical probing.

Melville now turned magazinist. *Israel Potter,* the fictionalized biography of a soldier during the Revolutionary War and later adrift in London, explores the endurance of the common man. The magazine stories were collected in *Piazza Tales.* It is distinguished for "Bartleby," an account of the response of a worldly lawyer whose copyist gently declines to exist; "Benito Cereno" the Gothic adventure of a good-natured American sea captain who encounters a ship deviously controlled by its cargo of slaves; and "The Encantadas," sketches of the Galapagos Islands, a volcanic waste in the thrall of an evil spell. The last prose fiction Melville published, *The Confidence-Man,* is a darkly comic work of such originality of concept, technique, and verbal dexterity that it seems a prototype of the modern American novel. The setting is a Mississippi River steamboat on April Fool's Day. The action involves a series of confidence men (though perhaps only one, variously guised) in ritualistic confrontation with their marks who are vulnerable because of their faith, hope, and charity. The book satirizes American types and deflates American beliefs through the device of the confidence man who preaches trust apparently for some selfish reason. But one is never sure. This, Melville's most ingenious book, was a failure. Thereafter he never attempted to write for a popular audience.

Always a self-taught student, Melville studied poetry. Near the end of the Civil War he undertook a verse sequence, *Battle-Pieces,* which sought to comprehend this national tragedy. It begins with "The Portent," on the hanging of the abolitionist firebrand John Brown, and ends with elegies to the dead of both sides. **Walt Whitman**'s *Drum-Taps* is the only comparable body of verse. A decade later he published *Clarel,* an ambitious narrative poem about a party of "pilgrims" of diverse background and persuasion who tour the Holy Land. The framework permits discussions of science, religion, and the future of the New World. While on the whole they do not lift the spirits and the tetrameter couplets grow wearisome, the poem has a stony integrity and curious, digressive cantos on such subjects as Piranesi's prison etchings and the Hindu god Rama. His shorter verses, issued privately, draw from his early life as a sailor, his travels in Europe and the Levant, and his literary explorations. They are uneven, but the most flawed are not without interest for their tensions, juxtapositions, and sense of tragedy, for what they attempt rather than what they achieve.

Melville's last work is a short novel, *Billy Budd.* A handsome sailor on a warship strikes down a petty officer. There are mitigating circumstances, but he is hanged so that the discipline of the crew might be assured. The tale is sensitive to every complexity and delicately controlled, but as always with Melville its emphasis is on questions rather than answers.

—Hennig Cohen

MENCKEN, H(enry) L(ouis)

Born: Baltimore, Maryland, 12 September 1880. **Education:** Knapp's Institute, 1935. **Career:** Reporter, *Herald,* 1899-1901; editor, *Sunday Herald,* 1901-03; city editor, *Morning Herald,* 1903-04, and *Evening Herald,* 1904-05; editor-in-chief, *Herald,* 1906; news editor, *Evening News,* 1906; editor, *Sunday Sun,* 1906-10, and editor and columnist ("The Free Lance"), *Evening Sun,* 1910-16, all in Baltimore; war correspondent in Germany, 1916-18; columnist, New York *Evening Mail,* 1917-18; columnist and political correspondent, *Baltimore Sunpapers,* 1919-41, 1948. Literary critic, 1908-23, and editor with George Jean Nathan, 1914-23, *Smart Set,* New York; founder, with Nathan, *Parisienne, Saucy Stories,* and *Black Mask* pulp magazines, late 1910s; founder, with Nathan, 1923, co-editor, 1924-25, and sole editor, 1925-33, *American Mercury,* New York; contributor, Chicago *Tribune,* 1924-28, and *New York American,* 1934-35; contributing editor, *The Nation,* New York, 1931-32. Literary adviser, Knopf publishers, New York, from 1917. **Awards:** American Academy Gold Medal, 1950. **Died:** 29 January 1956.

PUBLICATIONS

Collections

Letters, edited by Guy J. Forgue. 1961.
The American Scene: A Reader, edited by Huntington Cairns. 1965.

Fiction

Christmas Story. 1946.

Plays

The Artist (produced 1927). 1912.
Heliogabalus: A Buffoonery, with George Jean Nathan. 1920.

Poetry

Ventures into Verse. 1903.

Other

George Bernard Shaw: His Plays. 1905.
The Philosophy of Friedrich Nietzsche. 1908.
What You Ought to Know about Your Baby, with Leonard Keene Hirshberg. 1910.
Men Versus the Man: A Conversation Between Robert Rives La Monte, Socialist, and Mencken, Individualist. 1910.
Europe after 8:15, with George Jean Nathan and Willard Huntington Wright (travel). 1914.
A Little Book in C Major. 1916.
A Book of Burlesques. 1916; revised edition, 1920.
A Book of Prefaces. 1917.
Pistols for Two, with George Jean Nathan. 1917.
Damn! A Book of Calumny. 1918; as *A Book of Calumny,* 1918.
In Defense of Women. 1918; revised edition, 1922.
The American Language: A Preliminary Inquiry into the Development of English in the United States. 1919; revised edition, 1921, 1923, 1936; supplement, 1945, 1948.

Prejudices, First Series. 1919; *Second Series,* 1920; *Third Series,* 1922; *Fourth Series,* 1924; *Selected Prejudices,* 2 vols., 1926-27; *Fifth Series,* 1926; *Sixth Series,* 1927; *Prejudices: A Selection,* edited by James T. Farrell, 1958.

The American Credo, with George Jean Nathan. 1920.

Notes on Democracy. 1926.

James Branch Cabell. 1927.

Treatise on the Gods. 1930; revised edition, 1946.

Making a President: A Footnote to the Saga of Democracy. 1932.

Treatise on Right and Wrong. 1934.

The Sunpapers of Baltimore 1837-1937, with others. 1937.

A Choice of Days (selections from autobiography), edited by Edward L. Galligan. 1980.

> *Happy Days 1880-1892.* 1940.
> *Newspaper Days 1899-1906.* 1941.
> *Heathen Days 1890-1936.* 1943.

A Mencken Chrestomathy. 1949.

The Vintage Mencken, edited by Alistair Cooke. 1955.

Minority Report: Mencken's Notebooks. 1956.

A Carnival of Buncombe (essays), edited by Malcolm Moos. 1956; as *On Politics,* 1960.

The Bathtub Hoax and Other Blasts and Bravos from the Chicago Tribune, edited by Robert McHugh. 1958.

Mencken on Music, edited by Louis Cheslock. 1961.

Smart Set Criticism, edited by William H. Nolte. 1968.

The Young Mencken: The Best of His Work, edited by Carl Bode. 1973.

A Gang of Pecksniffs and Other Comments on Newspaper Publishers, Editors, and Reporters, edited by Theo Lippman, Jr. 1975.

Mencken's Last Campaign: Mencken on the 1948 Election, edited by Joseph C. Goulden. 1976.

The New Mencken Letters, edited by Carl Bode. 1977.

Letters from Baltimore: The Mencken-Cleator Correspondence, edited by P. E. Cleator. 1982.

The Diary of H.L. Mencken, edited by Charles A. Fecher. 1989.

Do You Remember?: The Whimsical Letters of H.L. Mencken and Philip Goodman. 1994.

In Defense of Marion: The Love of Marion Bloom and H.L. Mencken. 1996.

Editor, *A Doll's House, Little Eyolf,* by Ibsen. 2 vols., 1909.

Editor, *The Gist of Nietzsche.* 1910.

Editor, *The Free Lance Books.* 5 vols., 1919-21.

Editor, *Americana.* 1925.

Editor, *Menckeniana: A Schimpflexicon.* 1928.

Editor, *Essays,* by James Huneker. 1929.

Editor, *The American Democrat,* by James Fenimore Cooper. 1931.

Editor, *Southern Album,* by Sara Haardt. 1936.

Editor, *A New Dictionary of Quotations on Historical Principles.* 1942.

Translator, *The Antichrist,* by Nietzsche. 1920.

*

Bibliography: *H.L.M.: The Mencken Bibliography* by Betty Adler and Jane Wilhelm, 1961, and *The Mencken Bibliography: A Ten-Year Supplement 1962-1971* by Adler, 1971; *Bibliographic Checklist* by Vincent Fitzpatrick, in *Menckeniana: A Quarterly Review,* winter, 1992; *H.L. Mencken: A Descriptive Bibliography* by Richard J. Schrader, 1998.

Critical Studies: *Life of Mencken* by William Manchester, 1951, revised edition, 1986, as *The Sage of Baltimore,* 1952; *Mencken: A Portrait from Memory* by Charles Angoff, 1956; *Mencken: Literary Critic* by William H. Nolte, 1966; *Mencken* by Philip Wagner, 1966; *The Constant Circle: Mencken and His Friends* by Sara Mayfield, 1968; *Mencken* by Carl Bode, 1969; *Mencken: Iconoclast from Baltimore* by Douglas C. Stenerson, 1971; *Serpent in Eden: Mencken and the South* by Fred C. Hobson, Jr., 1974; *Mencken* by W.H.A. Williams, 1977; *Mencken: A Study of His Thought* by Charles A. Fecher, 1978; *Mencken: Critic of American Life* by George H. Douglas, 1978; *On Mencken* edited by John Dorsey, 1980; *The Sage in Harlem: Mencken and the Black Writers of the 1920's* by Charles Scruggs, 1984; *Mencken and the Debunkers* by Edward A. Martin, 1984; "The Diary of H.L. Mencken" by Thomas Yoseloff, in *The Literary Review: An International Journal of Contemporary Writing,* winter 1991; *H.L. Mencken Revisited* by W.H.A. Williams, 1998.

*   *   *

H.L. Mencken's reputation was etched by the acidic wit that characterized his commentary on the American culture of his day. Trained as a newspaperman, Mencken reached the height of his powers in the 1920s when, as an associate of the *Sun* papers in Baltimore and an editor first of the *Smart Set* and then of the *American Mercury,* he became one of the nation's most influential critics.

A prodigious writer, he published some twenty-five books—not to mention literally thousands of articles, essays, stories, editorials, book reviews—during the course of his career, beginning curiously with the now-forgotten *Ventures into Verse* in 1903 and moving in 1905 and 1908 respectively to the more representative *George Bernard Shaw: His Plays* and *The Philosophy of Friedrich Nietzsche.* Throughout, however, his style and his messages were those found in *Prejudices,* his most representative work, a six-volume collection of opinion published between 1919 and 1927. The messages were intensely iconoclastic: American culture had become stultified by its rigid adherence to a peculiarly "Puritan" form of Christian morality, and the quality of American politics—and, indeed, of American life—was being compromised by a foolish but persistent belief in egalitarianism. These messages and their many corollaries he published again and again, employing a style that became his particular signature, a style whose ingredients were the acerbic allusion, the caustic joke, the unusual word, the irreverent comparison. However, a story like "The Girl from Red Lion, P.A." is essentially a good-natured look at an ignorant country girl, with more than a hint of compassion.

With the advent of the 1930s Depression, the popularity of Mencken's social commentary waned. In 1919, however, he had published *The American Language,* a book that he revised and supplemented at various times until 1948. In *The American Language* Mencken sought, as he said in his subtitle, to inquire "into the development of English in the United States." The volume was quickly accepted by linguists, and continues in the late twentieth century as a standard reference work in the field. Indeed, it may well account for Mencken's fame long after his other work has become dated and been forgotten.

—Bruce A. Lohof

MÉNDEZ M., Miguel

Born: Bisbee, Arizona, 15 June 1930. **Education:** Government schools for six years in El Claro, Sonora, Mexico. **Family:** Married Maria Dolores Fontes in 1969; one son and one daughter. **Career:** Agricultural and construction worker in Tucson, Arizona, 1946-70; instructor in Spanish, creative writing, and Hispanic literature, Pima Community College, 1970-86. Beginning 1986 professor, University of Arizona. **Awards:** José Fuentes Mares National Award of Mexican Literature from Universidad Autónoma de Ciudad Juarez, 1991. **Residence:** Tucson, Arizona.

PUBLICATIONS

Short Stories

Cuentos para niños traviesos. 1979.
Tata Casehua y otros cuentos. 1980.
De la vida y del folklore de la frontera. 1986.
Cuentos y ensayos para reír y aprender. 1988.
Que no mueran los sueños. 1991.

Novels

Peregrinos de Aztlán. 1974, translated as *Pilgrims in Aztlán,* 1993.
El sueño de Santa María de las Piedras. 1986, translated as *The Dream of Santa Maria de las Piedras,* 1989.
From Labor to Letters: A Novel Autobiography. 1997.

Verse

Los criaderos humanos y sahuaros. 1975.

*

Bibliography: *Chicano Perspectives in Literature: A Critical and Annotated Bibliography* by Francisco A. Lomelí and Donaldo W. Urioste, 1976; *A Selected and Annotated Bibliography of Chicano Studies* by Charles M. Tatum, 1979; *A Bibliography of Criticism of Chicano Literature* by Ernestina Eger, 1982.

Critical Studies: "Méndez" in *Chicano Authors: Inquiry by Interview* by Juan Bruce-Novoa, 1980; "Méndez" in *La Palabra* vol. 3, nos. 1-2, 1981; "Méndez y el compromiso con el pueblo" in *La novela chicana escrita en español: cinco autores comprometidos* by Salvador Rodríguez del Pino, 1982; "Méndez" in *Dictionary of Literary Biography,* 1989; "Social and Magical Realism in Méndez's *El sueño de Santa María de las Piedras*" in *America's Review* by Roland Walter, 1990.

*   *   *

Miguel Méndez M. is a self-taught construction worker with a sixth-grade education who has become a prolific writer, a deft manipulator of language, and a chronicler of a socioeconomic class of which he is a member and advocate. Of course, since garnering an honorary Ph.D., an appointment as a full professor at the Uni-

versity of Arizona, and being lauded as a masterful writer by Spain's Nobel laureate, Camilo José Cela, Méndez M. does not belong to the working class anymore. Nevertheless, as an intellectual and a member of the academic community, his writings continue to expose man's inhumanity to man, and his stories reflect the rich cultural heritage of the Hispanic Southwest.

Méndez M.'s baroque and poetic prose along with his virtuoso manipulation of Spanish dialects from the Southwest have made his writings almost impossible to translate. His first novel, *Peregrinos de Aztlán,* published in 1974, was finally translated by David Foster and published in 1993, almost twenty years after its first publication. However, most of his short stories have been published in a bilingual format, giving English readers access to his writings and his world.

Méndez M. was born in Bisbee, Arizona, a small mining town close to the Mexican border. His parents were Mexican immigrants from the neighboring Mexican state of Sonora who had moved to Bisbee in search of work in the mines. However, with the coming of the Great Depression, his parents moved back to El Claro, an ejido (government-owned land) within a community of Yaqui Indians in Sonora. When the first public school was opened in El Claro, Méndez M. had already been taught how to read by his mother who encouraged him to attend the six years of elementary school available to him. But Méndez M.'s education was expanded and enriched by the stories he heard and learned from the elders of the Yaqui communities in which he had roots. He soon left his family and headed back to Arizona where he worked as an itinerant farmworker and finally settled down in Tucson where he worked as a bricklayer until 1970.

During those years as a construction worker, Méndez M. became a voracious reader and wrote stories by candlelight after work. His unpublished stories, based on the people and situations he encountered while working throughout the Southwest, began to pile up. It wasn't until the Chicano Movement reached Arizona in the late sixties that Méndez M. realized his stories might find a wider audience. He sent one of his stories, "Tata Casehua," to *El Grito,* the literary magazine in Berkeley, California, which was the first such magazine to publish Chicano literature. When *El Grito* published Méndez M.'s story in 1968, it became an instant hit.

"Tata Casehua" is written in poetic language and tells the story of an old Yaqui chief who wanders the Sonoran desert looking for an heir in whom to deposit the old stories from his people. Méndez M.'s critics wondered how an author with a six-year education could manipulate the Spanish language like a consummate writer. Other stories soon followed, and Méndez M. received invitations from literary circles and universities to lecture on his works. In 1970, he was offered the post of instructor in Spanish by Pima Community College in Tucson where he finished his GED. He was subsequently awarded an honorary degree and was granted the position of full professor by the University of Arizona in 1984.

His first novel, *Peregrinos de Aztlán,* published in Guadalajara, Mexico, in 1974, did not disappoint his critics. In this novel Méndez M. plays with the Spanish language, moving between the jargons and dialects of Chicano Spanish and the most sophisticated and poetic variations of literary Spanish. *Peregrinos,* according to some critics, is a social document, an indictment of man's behavior in contemporary society. Set in the border town of Tijuana, the novel deals with the wretched human condition created and bred by two unjust socioeconomic systems that, as

Méndez M. puts it, "condemn humans because of their sins of being poor, dark and Indians." Written with a strong dose of social realism, the novel rescues the stories of these people through the feverish mind of Loreto, an old car-washer who once rode with Pancho Villa himself and now walks the streets of Tijuana looking for tourist cars to wash and recreating the stories of the people he meets along the way. Through Loreto, all the classic characters that populate the border city, which Méndez M. personifies as attracting these types of people, come to life. There are pimps, whiteslavers, corrupt officials, prostitutes, wetbacks, the oppressed, the oppressors: all pilgrims towards the illusory American Dream.

In his second novel, *The Dream of Santa María de las Piedras*, Méndez M. goes from social realism to magic realism in the tradition of the Latin American masters of that style: Juan Rulfo and Gabriel García Márquez. Again, Méndez M. reconstructs the history and characters of Santa María de las Piedras through the recollections of some old-timers who come together in the town's square to reminisce and tell their versions of the past. Santa María de las Piedras (St. Mary of the Stones) is a small town near the Mexican border whose location is hard to pinpoint since it tends to appear and disappear due to the reverberations, mirages or just plain sunstroke of those trying to find it in the desert. The old-timers fight each other as each one recollects the past from a different perspective. Thus the reader listens to different accounts of the discovery of gold in Santa María, or when the first whorehouse came to town. Many colorful characters from the town's past come to life, and the novel ends with the return of Timoteo Noragua to Santa María. Noragua has been on an odyssey on the other side of the border, searching for "wachusey" ("what'd you say?"), who he believes has built a great civilization. Noragua finally finds "wachusey" on the day of his burial. Working his way through the funeral ceremony and pageant, Noragua lifts the lid of the coffin only to find his own image in the face of "wachusey."

Méndez M.'s short stories are mostly about characters indigenous to the border and northern Mexico: the undocumented farmworker, the homeboy, the revolutionary, the misfit. However, some of his most celebrated stories are a transposed retelling of the old Spanish stories from the *Calila et Dimna*. These stories were taken from old Persian and Hindu tales brought by the Moors to Spain and translated during the Middle Ages. Méndez M. transposes them to the Southwest where they are sprinkled with Chicano spice and given a new life in Southwestern folklore. These stories are in *Cuentos para niños traviesos (Stories for Mischievous Children)*.

Despite his success in his novels and short stories, Méndez M. believes that his great accomplishment has been his mostly ignored *Los criaderos humanos y sahuaros (The Human Breeding Grounds and Saguaros)*. This work is an epic poem about the oppressed Indians and dark people of the Southwest and the institutions that oppress them. Méndez M. believes that this work is his greatest indictment against injustice in America.

Méndez M. continues to write in Spanish, a trait that separates him from those who combine Spanish and English in their works. In this way Méndez M. does not only contribute to American literature but also to Latin American letters. His vision and perspective of the American Southwest and its four hundred years of Hispanic heritage adds to and complements the reality of a multicultural America—an America which would not be complete without his and other Chicano writers' contributions.

—Salvador Rodriguez del Pino

MERRILL, James (Ingram)

Born: New York City, 3 March 1926. **Education:** Lawrenceville School; Amherst College, Massachusetts, B.A. 1947. **Military Service:** Served in the U.S. Army, 1944-45. **Awards:** National Book award, 1967, 1979; Bollingen prize, 1973; Pulitzer prize, 1977; National Book Critics Circle award, 1984; Bobst award, 1984; National prize in poetry, 1990. **Member:** American Academy, 1971. **Died:** 6 February 1995.

PUBLICATIONS

Poetry

Jim's Book: A Collection of Poems and Short Stories. 1942.
The Black Swan and Other Poems. 1946.
First Poems. 1951.
Short Stories. 1954.
A Birthday Cake for David. 1955.
The Country of a Thousand Years of Peace and Other Poems. 1959; revised edition, 1970.
Selected Poems. 1961.
Water Street. 1962.
The Thousand and Second Night. 1963.
Violent Pastoral. 1965.
Nights and Days. 1966.
The Fire Screen. 1969.
Two Poems. 1972.
Braving the Elements. 1972.
Yannina. 1973.
The Yellow Pages: 59 Poems. 1974.
Divine Comedies. 1976.
Metamorphosis of 741. 1977.
Mirabell: Books of Number. 1978.
Ideas, etc. 1980.
Scripts for the Pageant. 1980.
The Changing Light at Sandover. 1982.
Marbled Paper. 1982.
Peter. 1982.
Santorini: Stopping the Leak. 1982.
From the First Nine: Poems 1947-1976. 1982.
From the Cutting Room Floor. 1982.
Souvenirs. 1984.
Bronze. 1984.
Late Settings. 1985.
The Inner Room. 1988.
Selected Poems, 1946-1985. 1993.
Self-portrait in Tyvek Windbreaker (limited edition). 1995.
A Scattering of Salts. 1995.
Selected Poems. 1996.

Plays

The Bait (produced 1953). In *Artists' Theatre: Four Plays,* edited by Herbert Machiz, 1960.
The Immortal Husband (produced 1955). In *Playbook: Plays for a New Theatre,* 1956.
The Image Maker. 1986.

Fiction

The Seraglio. 1957.
The (Diblos) Notebook. 1965.

Other

Recitative, edited by J.D. McClatchy. 1986.
A Different Person: A Memoir. 1993.

Editor, *The Singing Underneath,* by Jeffrey Harrison. 1988.

*

Bibliography: by Jack W.C. Hagstrom and George Bixby in *American Book Collector,* November-December 1983.

Critical Studies: *Merrill* by Ross Labrie, 1982; *Merrill: Essays in Criticism* edited by David Lehman and Charles Berger, 1983; *Merrill: An Introduction to the Poetry* by Judith Moffett, 1984; *Merrill* edited by Harold Bloom, 1985; *The Consuming Myth: The Work of Merrill* by Stephen Yenser, 1987; *Critical Essays on James Merrill* edited by Guy L. Rotella, 1996; *James Merrill's Poetic Quest* by Don Adams, 1997.

*   *   *

James Merrill's books of poems are like the rings of a tree: each extends beyond the content, expression, outlook, and craft of the previous work. Merrill has patiently, even doggedly, pursued his craft, giving each poem, however short or terse or ephemeral, a certain lapidary sheen and hardness. Merrill's complete output of verse, fiction, and plays is characterized by an absorption with technique and difficulty.

But his earliest poems are overworked with rhyme scheme, metric pattern, enameled diction. Merrill came onto the literary scene during the vogue of revived metaphysical poetry, verse wrought in a traditional manner with high polish and much verbal flourishing under formal restraint. Such is the poetry of his first major book, *The Country of a Thousand Years of Peace,* with its elegant experiences, its widely cultivated tastes, its voice of leisured travel and gracious living—the poetry, in other words, of an American aristocrat. *Water Street* continues this elegant discourse on the vicissitudes of life, love, travel, the perennially chilly rooms and beds of his daily life.

But with *The Fire Screen* a new dimension to the persona comes into view: his life in Greece, where the warm sun, the old culture, the intimacy of life release a deeper self-awareness into his poems. Instead of the isolated, inward existence of New England, here the speaker is thrust into a more primal and assertive culture where his passions and convictions are awakened. There are also poems of return to the northeastern United States, lyrics of resignation and quiet regrets. In the American edition is the long verse narrative "The Summer People," with its obvious irony. *Braving the Elements* is both freer in its verse forms and more open and intimate in its content. Instead of the choppy quality of his earlier, too tightly wrought lines, there is now a smooth, conversational rhythm in his three- or four-line stanza structures. "Days of 1935," "18 West 11th Street" (which laments the death of young anti-war radicals), and "Days of 1971" are open, intimate revelations of the poet's mind.

Merrill's progress is toward a compromise between rigid formalism and the open poem, where craft would continue to discipline the choice and assembly of language but where the content would be free to take its own course. That balance is reached in the long sequence "The Book of Ephraim" in *Divine Comedies.* The twenty-six alphabetically ordered parts are interwoven through a leisurely plot where the poet and his lover communicate, through the Ouija board, with the spirit of Ephraim, whose insight and wit make life seem a mere changing room in a vast spiritual universe. In discovering this broader realm, Merrill is dazzling as a conversational poet. Ephraim's reckless honesty about the other side enables the speaker to unravel a complex plot of lives and after-lives, including his own father's, in a humorous, novel-like progression of poems. The verse never impedes the narrative; it enhances it with its exuberance of puns, amazing condensations of ideas and observations, feats of beautiful lyric sound.

With the appearance in 1982 of *The Changing Light at Sandover* an ambitious project begun in *Divine Comedies* came to completion. Though critical assessments are still only preliminary on this newest of the century's long poems, it is indisputable that this 560-page verse narrative must be ranked among the epic masterworks of the modern age. Though its range and intellectual intentions are smaller than those of earlier long poems, Merrill's opus is a tour de force of technical virtuosity comparable to Lowell's sonnet cycle, *History.* Its central device of a Ouija board, through which to weave many arguments connecting spiritual and material realms, puts it in the mainstream of contemporary art. *Late Settings* is a small gathering of poems written after the ardors of *The Changing Light at Sandover,* and is a quiet, gentle series of reflections on mortality.

With the issuance of *Recitative* (with its compassionate and insightful introduction by J.D. McClatchy), the memoir *A Different Person* and *The Inner Room* a fuller picture of Merrill's self-construction as a writer is emerging. For one thing, there is more prose, and as Merrill concedes in his brief "Foreword" to *Recitative,* "There are after all things to be said for prose. I still read it, often with more profit than I do poetry." And *The Inner Room,* though subtitled "Poems," contains something called "Prose of Departure": a series of vignettes drifting in and out of haiku and other verse forms, loosely structured by an underlying travelogue-narrative of a visit to Japan and a series of philosophical meditations on mortality and the death of friends. Also present are the dramatic masque "The Image Maker" and lyrics that range from the carefully subdued and cosmopolitan to the openly clever and playful.

—Paul Christensen, updated by Joseph O. Aimone

MERWIN, W(illiam) S(tanley)

Born: New York City, 30 September 1927. **Education:** Princeton University, New Jersey, A.B. in English 1947. **Family:** Married 1) Diana Whalley in 1954; 2) Paula. **Career:** Tutor in France and Portugal, 1949, and to Robert Graves's son in Mallorca, 1950; freelance translator, London, 1951-54; Playwright-in-Residence, Poets' Theatre, Cambridge, Massachusetts, 1956-57; poetry editor, *The Nation,* New York, 1962; associate, Theatre de la Cite, Lyons, France, 1964-65. **Awards:** Yale Series of Younger Poets award, 1952; *Kenyon Review* fellowship in poetry, 1954; American Academy grant, 1957; Arts Council of Great Britain bursary, 1957; Rabinowitz research fellowship, 1961; Bess Hokin prize, 1962; Ford grant, 1964; Chapelbrook award, 1966; Harriet Monroe Memorial prize, 1967; PEN translation prize, 1969; Rockefeller grant, 1969; Pulitzer prize, 1971; Academy of American Poets fellowship, 1974; Shelley Memorial award, 1974; National Endowment for the Arts grant, 1978; Bollingen prize, 1979. **Member:** American Academy. **Residence:** Haiku, Hawaii.

PUBLICATIONS

Poetry

A Mask for Janus. 1952.
The Dancing Bears. 1954.
Green with Beasts. 1956.
The Drunk in the Furnace. 1960.
The Moving Target. 1963.
The Lice. 1967.
Three Poems. 1968.
Animae. 1969.
The Carrier of Ladders. 1970.
Signs: A Poem. 1971.
Writings to an Unfinished Accompaniment. 1974.
The First Four Books of Poems. 1975.
Three Poems. 1975.
The Compass Flower. 1977.
Feathers from the Hill. 1978.
Finding the Islands. 1982.
Opening the Hand. 1983.
Selected Poems. 1988.
The Rain in the Trees. 1988.
Travels. 1992.
The Second Four Books of Poems. 1993.
The Vixen: Poems. 1997.
Flower and Hand: Poems, 1977-1983. 1997.
East Window: The Asian Translations. 1999.

Plays

Darkling Child, with Dido Milroy (produced 1956).
Favor Island (produced 1957).
Eufemia, from the play by Lope de Rueda, in *Tulane Drama Review.* 1958.
The Gilded West (produced 1961).
Turcaret, from the play by Alain Lesage, in *The Classic Theatre 4,* edited by Eric Bentley. 1961.
The False Confession, from a play by Marivaux (produced 1963), in *The Classic Theatre 4,* edited by Eric Bentley. 1961.
Yerma, from the play by Garcia Lorca (produced 1966).
Iphigenia at Aulis, with George E. Dimock, Jr., from a play by Euripides (produced 1982). 1982.

Other

A New Right Arm (essay). N.d.
Selected Translations 1948-1968. 1968.
The Miner's Pale Children. 1970.
Houses and Travellers. 1977.

Selected Translations 1968-1978. 1979.
Unframed Originals: Recollections. 1982.
Regions of Memory: Uncollected Prose 1949-1982. 1987.
The Lost Upland: Stories of Southwest France. 1989.

Editor, *West Wind: Supplement of American Poetry.* 1961.
Editor, *The Essential Wyatt.* 1989.

Translator, *The Poem of the Cid.* 1959.
Translator, *The Satires of Persius.* 1961.
Translator, *Some Spanish Ballads.* 1961; as *Spanish Ballads,* 1961.
Translator, *The Life of Lazarillo de Tormes: His Fortunes and Adversities.* 1962.
Translator, *The Song of Roland,* in *Medieval Epics.* 1963; published separately, 1970.
Translator, *Transparence of the World: Poems of Jean Follain.* 1969.
Translator, *Products of the Perfected Civilization: Selected Writings,* by Sebastian Chamfort. 1969.
Translator, *Voices: Selected Writings of Antonio Porchia.* 1969.
Translator, *Twenty Love Poems and A Song of Despair,* by Pablo Neruda. 1969.
Translator, with others, *Selected Poems: A Bilingual Edition,* by Pablo Neruda, edited by Nathaniel Tarn. 1969.
Translator, *Chinese Figures: Second Series.* 1971.
Translator, *Japanese Figures.* 1971.
Translator, *Asian Figures.* 1973.
Translator, with Clarence Brown, *Selected Poems of Osip Mandelstam.* 1973.
Translator, *Vertical Poems,* by Roberto Juarroz. 1977.
Translator, with J. Moussaieff Masson, *Sanskrit Love Poetry.* 1977; as *The Peacock's Egg: Love Poems from Ancient India,* 1981.
Translator, *Four French Plays.* 1984.
Translator, *From the Spanish Morning.* 1984.

*

Bibliography: "Seven Princeton Poets" in *Princeton Library Chronicle,* Autumn 1963.

Critical Studies: "Merwin Issue" of *Hollins Critic,* June 1968; *The Quest for Being: Theodore Roethke, Merwin, and Ted Hughes* by Daniel Liberthson, 1977; *W.S. Merwin* by Cheri Davis, 1981; *W.S. Merwin the Mythmaker* by Mark Christhilf, 1986; *What I Cannot Say: Self, Word and World in Whitman, Stevens and Merwin* by Thomas B. Byers, 1990; *Poetry as Labor and Privilege: The Writings of W.S. Merwin* by Edward J. Brunner, 1991; *Echoes and Moving Fields: Structure and Subjectivity in the Poetry of W.S. Merwin and John Ashbery* by Edward Haworth Hoeppner, 1994; *From Origin to Ecology: Nature and the Poetry of W.S. Merwin* by Jane Frazier, 1999.

*   *   *

W.S. Merwin's writing career erupted suddenly in 1952 with the publication of *A Mask for Janus.* Both it and *The Dancing Bears,* his second collection, are books of traditional formal poetry inspired by the work of **Ezra Pound** and allegorical in nature, stressing short, consciously crafted lines that move with densely worded statement. These early poems introduced

Merwin's abiding concern with mankind's relationship with nature. *The Dancing Bears,* slightly freer in form and showing more confidence in composition, is dry and bookish, but Merwin exercised his skill in these earliest volumes, and his intelligence and promise were evident throughout.

In *Green with Beasts* and *The Drunk in the Furnace* Merwin is in greater control of his imagination, and the experience in his lyrics is suddenly intense and compelling. The mythic content of *Green with Beasts* anticipates the bold explorations of subjectivity of later volumes. But sheer variety of tone and diction, clarity of image, leaps of thought and perception give *Green with Beasts* surges of power. *The Drunk in the Furnace* retreats slightly from the daring pursuit of the earlier volume, but the ordinary world is rediscovered here, especially in the title poem, in which the poet discovers a man living contentedly in an abandoned furnace. The landscape of these mature works is charged with magic and the fabulous, and the drunk rattling his bottle of liquor against the iron walls of his home is typical of the uncanny world in which Merwin has rooted his lyric.

By 1960, Merwin appears to have exhausted his interest in traditional English poetry, for in translating certain Spanish poets he discovered surrealist techniques that he incorporated in his own work. Merwin's verse embodied the melancholic mysteries of human life in a spare and surreal language. In these sometimes cryptic visions, he spoke of loss and pain with lyrical grace. The Pulitzer prize winning *The Carrier of Ladders* collects his best work from this period.

The problem with *The Moving Target,* however, is the emphasis given to a disembodied voice whose lyric statements arise from unstated situations and have little or no core of argument. There is a sameness to this poetry as each poem passes into the other with its silky array of words touching briefly on the particulars of life.

In his more recent volumes, Merwin has written what appears to be the stages of a spiritual progress. Each volume is intent to mine a deeper layer of the subjective mind, to test the limits of perception where it borders on fantasy and archetypal thought, to let merge the states of dream and waking. *The Lice* is composed in the soft, remote language of surrealist lyrics and offers a distant reflection of the turbulence of the 1960s, without indictment or direct reference to actual events. A sense of political terror and unrest pervades these somber poems. In *Writings to an Unfinished Accompaniment,* Merwin comes to an end of the disjunctive, loosely imagistic poem. A noticeable change of attention takes over in *The Compass Flower* where the quotidian is suddenly fresh and vital, and his poems come to crisp focus on objects of immediate experience.

Opening the Hand explores a personal terrain, reckoning with the poet's past, particularly the memory of his father, and of his own youth. Like other poets of his generation, Merwin is struggling to make reconciliations after the tumultuous and often rebellious work of youth; some of these poems make peace with a contentious nature, and seek to discover value in what was once dismissed as an arid sentimentality. The language abounds in images of light, mirrors, memories, as the past is relived and revalued.

Selected Poems is an overview of the stages of Merwin's poetic career since the 1950s, presenting examples of his work from the early formal verse to the surrealistic visions of the 1960s to his more recent interior explorations. Throughout, Merwin's examination of the proper relationship between man and nature is evident. *Selected Poems* provides a comprehensive introduction to a consistently engaging poet.

—Paul Christensen, updated by Denise Wiloch

MILLAY, Edna St. Vincent

Born: Rockland, Maine, 22 February 1892. **Education:** Camden High School, Maine, graduated 1909; Barnard College, New York, 1913; Vassar College, Poughkeepsie, New York, 1914-17, graduated 1917. **Family:** Married Eugen Boissevain in 1923 (died 1949). **Career:** Freelance writer, and occasionally actress, New York, 1917-21; associated with the Provincetown Players; contributor, 1920, and European correspondent, 1921-23, *Vanity Fair,* New York; lived in Austerlitz, New York, after 1925. **Awards:** Pulitzer prize, 1923. Litt.D.: Tufts University, Medford, Massachusetts, 1925; Colby College, Waterville, Maine; University of Wisconsin, Madison. L.H.D.: New York University. **Member:** American Academy. **Died:** 19 October 1950.

PUBLICATIONS

Collections

Letters, edited by Allan Ross Macdougall. 1952.
Collected Poems, edited by Norma Millay. 1956.
Early Poems. 1998.

Poetry

Renascence and Other Poems. 1917.
A Few Figs from Thistles. 1920.
Second April. 1921.
The Ballad of the Harp-Weaver. 1922.
The Harp-Weaver and Other Poems. 1923; as *Poems,* 1923. (*Poems*), edited by Hughes Mearns. 1927.
The Buck in the Snow and Other Poems. 1928.
Poems Selected for Young People. 1929.
Fatal Interview: Sonnets. 1931.
Wine from These Grapes. 1934.
Vacation Song. 1936.
Conversation at Midnight. 1937.
Huntsman, What Quarry? 1939.
Make Bright the Arrows: 1940 Notebook. 1940.
There Are No Islands Any More. 1940.
Collected Sonnets. 1941.
The Murder of Lidice. 1942.
Collected Lyrics. 1943.
Mine the Harvest: A Collection of New Poems, edited by Norma Millay. 1954.

Plays

Aria da Capo (produced 1920). 1921.
The Lamp and the Bell (produced 1921). 1921.
Two Slatterns and a King: A Moral Interlude (produced 1921). 1921.
Three Plays. 1926.

The King's Henchman (opera libretto), music by Deems Taylor
(produced 1927). 1927.
The Princess Marries the Page. 1932.

Other

Distressing Dialogues. 1924.
Fear. 1927(?).

Translator, with George Dillon, *Flowers of Evil,* by Baudelaire.
1936.

*

Bibliography: *A Bibliography of the Works of Millay* by Karl Yost,
1937; *Millay: A Reference Guide* by Judith Nierman, 1977; *Edna
St. Vincent Millay: Catalogue of a Collection* by Paulette Greene,
1994.

Critical Studies: *The Indigo Bunting: A Memoir of Millay* by
Vincent Sheean, 1957; *Restless Spirit: The Life of Millay* by Miriam
Gurko, 1962; *Millay* by Norman A. Brittin, 1967, revised edition,
1982; *Millay* by James Gray, 1967; *The Poet and Her Book: A
Biography of Millay* by Jean Gould, 1969; *Millay in Greenwich
Village* by Anne Cheney, 1975; "Edna St. Vincent Millay—Saint
of the Modern Sonnet" edited by Jean Gould, in *Faith of a
(Woman) Writer* edited by Alice Kessler-Harris and William
McBrien, 1988; "The Force of Flippancy: Edna Millay's Satiric
Sketches of the Early 1920s" by Will Brantley, in *Colby-Quar-
terly,* September 1991; *Millay at 100: A Critical Reappraisal* ed-
ited by Diane P. Freedman, 1995.

*   *   *

If it is true that "You cannot touch a flower without disturbing
a star," then the whole firmament must have been tremulous at
the birth of Edna St. Vincent Millay. A woman of pronounced
and strongly held convictions, she was catapulted to fame in 1920
by her book *A Few Figs from Thistles,* and became the prototype
of the "new, emancipated woman." The unheard of freedom that
Millay demanded—freedom in love, freedom of thought in matters of morality and religion, equality with men, and, above all,
the freedom to act out her own individuality unhampered by outworn social codes—was one that was needed to counteract the
deadening effects of Victorian proprieties. The rebellion that Millay
promoted opened many new paths for the adventuresome human
spirit, and she is not to be blamed if the new freedoms are often
abused. As she noted in one of her finest sonnets, "What rider
spurs him," civilization is a contest fought in the dark against tremendous obstacles and requires a continuous forward motion to
counteract the destructive and stultifying tendencies in human nature. It is curious that Millay, the proponent of new, creative designs for life, clothed her verse in traditional forms and language,
while **T.S. Eliot**, who harked to the past and worshiped authority as the solution to the world's ills, developed a new language
and style for poetry. His contribution was also a forward motion
for poetry, but the great admiration for Eliot among academics
served for many years to minimize the recognition of the achievements of lyrical poets such as Millay.

More, perhaps, than any other poet in English, Millay's stance
vis-a-vis the universe was one of a human being almost totally
absorbed in her own human situation, whose reactions to that situation, including, of course, the condition of the whole human race,
are nearly always of an immediate, personal character. She does
not stand outside herself but reports all the tumults of existence
as they reverberate in her own being. Since she was a personality
more than life-size and was gifted with "a high sense of drama,"
her personalist approach created poetry of great vitality and conviction. On the other hand, being caught in the cage of personal,
individual existence becomes suffocating, and, in her case, largely
excluded awareness of the strange Otherness of things, or any transcendent order of reality.

Such as it was, however, Millay's outlook produced a large body
of lyrical works of the highest distinction and expressiveness. It
is easy to understand Louis Untermeyer's hyperbolic statement
in 1923 that "Renascence," written when Millay was nineteen
years old, was "possibly the most astonishing performance of this
generation." Sentiments of great verve and freshness are given classic expression in a style that is always concise and musical. As
James Gray says, the content of her poetry is equally attractive
since it consists of her own version of the ageless contest between
life and death, in both the physical and spiritual senses, the raptures and failures of love, and the ever-present struggle between
the processes of decay and rebirth. There are times, as suggested
above, when the reader may feel oppressed by the weight of Millay's
tortured self-absorption, but this is a price worth paying for the
sharply etched and poignant account of her soul's turnings.

—Glenn Richard Ruihley

MILLER, Arthur

Born: New York City, 17 October 1915. **Education:** Abraham
Lincoln High School, New York, graduated 1932; University of
Michigan, Ann Arbor (Hopwood Award, 1936, 1937), 1934-38,
A.B. 1938. **Family:** Married 1) Mary Slattery in 1940 (divorced
1956), one son and one daughter; 2) the actress Marilyn Monroe
in 1956 (divorced 1961); 3) Ingeborg Morath in 1962, one daughter. **Career:** Worked in automobile supply warehouse, 1932-34;
member of the Federal Theatre Project, 1938; writer for CBS and
NBC Radio Workshops; associate professor of drama, University
of Michigan, 1973-74. International President, PEN, London and
New York, 1965-69. **Awards:** Theatre Guild award, 1938; New
York Drama Critics Circle award, 1947, 1949; Tony award, 1947,
1949, 1953; Pulitzer prize, 1949; National Association of Independent Schools award, 1954; American Academy gold medal,
1959; Brandeis University Creative Arts award, 1969; Peabody
award, for television play, 1981; Bobst award, 1983; Algur
Meadow award, Southern Methodist University, 1991. D.H.L.:
University of Michigan, 1956. Litt.D.: University of East Anglia,
Norwich, 1984. **Member:** American Academy, 1981. **Residence:**
Connecticut.

PUBLICATIONS

Plays

Honors at Dawn (produced 1936).
No Villains (They Too Arise) (produced 1937).

The Pussycat and the Expert Plumber Who Was a Man, and *William Ireland's Confession,* in *100 Non-Royalty Radio Plays,* edited by William Kozlenko. 1941.

The Man Who Had All the Luck (produced 1944). In *Cross-Section 1944,* edited by Edwin Seaver, 1944.

That They May Win (produced 1944). In *Best One-Act Plays of 1944,* edited by Margaret Mayorga, 1945.

Grandpa and the Statue, in *Radio Drama in Action,* edited by Erik Barnouw. 1945.

The Story of Gus, in *Radio's Best Plays,* edited by Joseph Liss. 1947.

The Guardsman, radio adaptation of a play by Ferenc Molnar, and *Three Men on a Horse,* radio adaptation of the play by George Abbott and John Cecil Holm, in *Theatre Guild on the Air,* edited by William Fitelson. 1947.

All My Sons (produced 1947). 1947.

Death of a Salesman: Certain Private Conversations in Two Acts and a Requiem (produced 1949). 1949.

An Enemy of the People, from a play by Ibsen (produced 1950). 1951.

The Crucible (produced 1953). 1953.

A View from the Bridge, and A Memory of Two Mondays: Two One-Act Plays (produced 1955). 1955; revised version of *A View from the Bridge* (produced 1956), 1957.

Collected Plays (includes *All My Sons, Death of a Salesman, The Crucible, A Memory of Two Mondays, A View from the Bridge*). 1957.

After the Fall (produced 1964). 1964.

Incident at Vichy (produced 1964). 1965.

The Price (produced 1968). 1968.

Fame, and The Reason Why (produced 1970). *Fame* in *Yale Literary Magazine,* March 1971.

The Creation of the World and Other Business (produced 1972). 1973; revised version, as *Up from Paradise,* music by Stanley Silverman (produced 1974).

The Archbishop's Ceiling (produced 1977; revised version, produced 1984). 1984.

The American Clock, from the work *Hard Times* by Studs Terkel (produced 1979). 1980.

Playing for Time, from a work by Fania Fenelon (televised 1980; produced 1986). In *Collected Plays 2,* 1981.

Collected Plays 2 (includes *The Misfits, After the Fall, Incident at Vichy, The Price, The Creation of the World and Other Business, Playing for Time*). 1981.

Up from Paradise, music by Stanley Silverman; a musical based on *The Creation of the World and Other Business,* 1984.

Two-Way Mirror (includes *Elegy for a Lady* and *Some Kind of Love Story;* produced 1982). 1984.

The Archbishop's Ceiling. 1984.

Danger: Memory! (produced 1987). 1986.

The Golden Years. 1990.

The Ride down Mount Morgan. 1991.

The Last Yankee. 1991.

The Ride Down Mount Morgan (produced 1991). 1991.

Broken Glass: A Play in Two Acts. 1994.

Plays: Two (includes *The Misfits; After the Fall; Incident at Vichy; The Price; The Creation of the World and Other Business; Playing for Time*). 1994.

Plays: Five (includes *The Last Yankee; The Ride Down Mount Morgan; Almost Everybody Wins*). 1995.

Mr. Peters' Connections. 1999.

Screenplays: *The Story of G.I. Joe* (uncredited), 1945; *The Witches of Salem,* 1958; *The Misfits,* 1961; *Everybody Wins,* 1990.

Television play: *Playing for Time,* 1980.

Fiction

Focus. 1945.

The Misfits (novelization of screenplay). 1961.

I Don't Need You Any More: Stories. 1967.

The Misfits and Other Stories. 1987.

Other

Situation Normal. 1944.

Jane's Blanket (for children). 1963.

In Russia, photographs by Inge Morath. 1969.

The Portable Miller, edited by Harold Clurman. 1971.

In the Country, photographs by Inge Morath. 1977.

The Theatre Essays of Miller, edited by Robert A. Martin. 1978.

Chinese Encounters, photographs by Inge Morath. 1979.

"Salesman" in Beijing. 1984.

Timebends: A Life. 1987.

Spain. 1987.

Conversations with Arthur Miller, edited by Matthew C. Roudane. 1987.

*

Bibliography: *"Miller: The Dimension of His Art: A Checklist of His Published Works,"* in *The Serif,* June 1967, and *Miller Criticism (1930-1967),* 1969, revised edition, as *An Index to Miller Criticism,* 1976, both by Tetsumaro Hayashi; *Miller: A Reference Guide* by John H. Ferres, 1979; *Studies in Miller's Drama: A Selected International Bibliography* by Charles A. Carpenter, 1982.

Critical Studies: *Miller,* 1961, and *Miller: A Study of His Plays,* 1979, revised edition, as *Miller the Playwright,* 1983, both by Dennis Welland; *Miller* by Robert Hogan, 1964; *Miller: The Burning Glass* by Sheila Huftel, 1965; *Miller: Death of a Salesman: Text and Criticism* edited by Gerald Weales, 1967; *Miller* by Leonard Moss, 1967, revised edition, 1980; *Miller, Dramatist* by Edward Murray, 1967; *Miller: A Collection of Critical Essays* edited by Robert W. Corrigan, 1969; *Psychology and Miller* by Richard I. Evans, 1969; *The Merrill Guide to Miller* by Sidney H. White, 1970; *Miller: Portrait of a Playwright* by Benjamin Nelson, 1970; *Miller* by Ronald Hayman, 1970; *Twentieth-Century Interpretations of The Crucible* edited by John H. Ferres, 1972; *Studies in Death of a Salesman* edited by Walter J. Meserve, 1972; *Critical Essays on Miller* edited by James J. Martine, 1979; *Miller: New Perspectives* edited by Robert A. Martin, 1982; *Miller* by Neil Carson, 1982; *Twentieth-Century Interpretations of Death of a Salesman* edited by Helene Wickham Koon, 1983; *Miller* by June Schlueter and James K. Flanagan, 1987; *Miller 1987, Miller's "All My Sons"* 1988, *Miller's "Death of a Salesman"* 1988, and *Willy Loman,* 1989, all edited by Harold Bloom; *Communists, Cowboys, and Queers: The Politics of Masculinity in the Work of Miller and Tennessee Williams* by David Savran, 1992; *The Crucible: Politics, Property, and Pretense* by James J. Martine, 1993; *Arthur Miller's Death of a Salesman* by Lloyd Cameron, 1995; *The*

Achievement of Arthur Miller: New Essays, edited by Steve Centola, 1995; *The Cambridge Companion to Arthur Miller,* edited by C.W.E. Bigsby, 1997; *Understanding The Crucible: A Student Casebook to Issues, Sources, and Historical Documents* by Claudia D. Johnson, 1998; *Arthur Miller's The Crucible,* edited by Harold Bloom, 1998; *Readings on The Crucible,* edited by Thomas Siebold, 1999.

*   *   *

In "On Social Plays," the introduction to the 1955 edition of *A View from the Bridge,* Arthur Miller expressed his dissatisfaction with the subjective play so popular on Broadway in the 1950s. At the same time, he rejected the customary definition of the social play ("an arraignment of society's evils") and identified his own work as "the drama of the whole man," an inextricable mixture of the social and the psychological. The emphasis on one side or the other varied over the years and his conception of the nature of man underwent a change in the 1960s, but his 1955 sense of his work is a useful description of the whole career of Miller as a social playwright.

In his student plays, his wartime one-acters, his early radio plays, even his first Broadway offering, *The Man Who Had All the Luck,* Miller can be seen working his way toward the theme that was to dominate his early plays. From *All My Sons* through *A View from the Bridge,* Miller places his protagonist in a setting in which society functions as a creator of images, and the hero-victim is destroyed because, as he says in the essay quoted above, "the individual is doomed to frustration when once he gains a consciousness of his own identity." Ironically, the destruction comes whether a man accepts or rejects the role that society asks or demands that he play. Joe Keller, in *All My Sons,* is a good man, a loving husband and father, a successful businessman who believes that his responsibility ends "at the building line"; when his son teaches him that neither the welfare of his family nor the self-protective impulse of conventional business ethics can excuse a shipment of faulty airplane parts, he commits suicide. Willy Loman, in *Death of a Salesman,* embraces the American dream, assumes that success is not only possible, but inevitable, and, faced with his failure, kills himself; the irony of the final suicide and the strength of the play is that Willy goes to his death, his dream still intact, convinced that the elusive success will be visited on his son, Biff, a man already crippled by society's neatly packaged ideas. In *The Crucible,* the victim becomes a romantic hero. John Proctor, guilty of adultery, confuses his accusing wife with an accusing society and admits to practicing witchcraft, but, finally unwilling to sign his name, he rejects society's demand for ritual confession, regains his identity, and dies, purely, in an act of defiance. Eddie Carbone, in *A View from the Bridge,* dies crying out for his name, too, but he wants a lie, the pretense that he has not violated the neighborhood ethic; like Joe Keller and Willy Loman, he accepts his society, but he breaks its rules when his desire for his niece and his attraction to her sweetheart threaten him with labels more frightening than informer. The explicit assumption of all these plays is that, win or lose, in contemporary society you can't win; the implicit assumption is that the individual is at his strongest, philosophically and dramatically, when the tensions between self and society are made manifest by a revealing crisis. The artistic result of the twin assumptions is a group of remarkably effective plays, reflecting Miller's theatrical skill as clearly as they do his moral concerns. In the best of them, *Death*

of a Salesman, Miller's social-psychological mix has given birth, in Willy Loman, to one of the richest characters in American drama.

Between 1956, when the revised version of *A View from the Bridge* appeared, and 1964, Miller was inactive in the theater. During those years he published a number of short stories, later collected in *I Don't Need You Any More,* including "The Misfits," which was the basis for the short novel and screenplay, written for his wife Marilyn Monroe. The most startling thing about the work is that in it Miller seems to be accepting the concept of the curative power of love in a way that recalls the prevailing cliche of Broadway in the 1950s; he had already given the idea explicit statement in two essays published a few years before the story-novel-film—the introduction to *Collected Plays* and "Bridge to a Savage World" (*Esquire,* October 1958).

When Miller returned to the theater with *After the Fall* and *Incident at Vichy,* he had put aside the momentary softness of *The Misfits,* but he had also discarded the concept of man as an admirable loser which marked his earlier plays. "The first problem," he wrote in "Our Guilt for the World's Evil" (*New York Times Magazine,* 3 January 1965), "is . . . to discover our own relationship to evil, its reflection of ourselves." Quentin in *After the Fall* learns to live and Von Berg in *Vichy* to die by the process of self-discovery already familiar in Miller's work, but identity is no longer individual. Miller, like the Salem of *The Crucible,* is now forcing an image of guilt on his characters. Finally in 1972, with *The Creation of the World and Other Business,* Miller makes obvious what has already been stated in the title *After the Fall,* that his post-1964 subject is original sin translated into the psychological commonplace that makes everyone responsible for "the World's Evil." Miller does not try to dramatize the corollary, that when everyone is guilty no one is, but it is possible—or so the autobiographical elements in *After the Fall* suggest—that the idea is working on the author if not within the play. One result of Miller's new concept of man is that the later plays have a schematic look to them; the characters lack the vitality of Miller's early protagonists and often appear to be simply figures in an exemplum.

The Price is the only one of the later plays that escapes the look of drama as demonstration. Ideologically one with the other post-1964 plays, it returns to the domestic setting familiar with Miller as far back as the time of his student work *They Too Arise.* Whether it is the inherent drama of two brothers at odds or the presence of the old furniture dealer, Miller's only successful comic figure, *The Price* escapes Significance with a capital S and finds theatrical validity. In *The Archbishop's Ceiling* Miller seems to have moved away from the ideological concerns that marked his drama from *After the Fall* to *The Creation of the World,* but the play is more intellectual than dramatic and the characters are more complex in conception than in presentation. In recent years his work has reflected diversity of material and form. This work includes *The American Clock,* which grew out of Studs Terkel's *Hard Times;* a number of short plays; *Playing for Time,* a television adaptation of Fania Fenelon's book about an orchestra composed of prisoners in a concentration camp; and still another revision of *Up from Paradise,* the musical version of *The Creation of the World* which he and Stanley Silverman have been working on since 1974.

Since Miller is a playwright of ideas, it is perhaps fitting to emphasize his themes in discussing his work, stopping occasionally to suggest that the ideational content of a play can interfere with the dramatic action or dehumanize character. These strictures are valid only to the extent that Miller is a realistic playwright in the American tradition, a dramatist who wants to create psychologically valid characters with whom audiences can identify directly. That is Miller's tradition, although he is one of a number of postwar American playwrights who recognize that that kind of character can exist outside a conventional realistic play. *Death of a Salesman* and *After the Fall* are examples of domesticated American Expressionism in which realistic scenes are played in an anti-realistic context. *The Crucible* is a romantic history play with a consciously artificial language, and Alfieri's stilted speeches in *A View from the Bridge,* which turn into free verse in the original version, are an attempt to impose the label tragedy on the play. *The Creation of the World* is an unhappy mixture of philosophical drama and Jewish low comedy. *Incident at Vichy* is a roundtable discussion and *The Price* is a debate of sorts with exits and entrances so artificially conceived that Miller surely means them to be seen as devices. The playwright's nearest approaches to traditional realism are *All My Sons* and the affectionate short play *A Memory of Two Mondays.*

Aside from his plays, Miller's work includes not only the short stories and screenplay mentioned above, but a novel, *Focus;* a report on Americans in training during World War II, *Situation Normal;* a children's book, *Jane's Blanket;* three volumes in which his text shares space with photographs by his wife Inge Morath, *In Russia, In the Country* and *Chinese Encounters;* his most impressive recent work, *"Salesman" in Beijing,* an account of his directing *Death of a Salesman* in China; and a great many articles and essays, most of them about the theater. The chief value of these works lies less in their specific generic virtues than in those analogies—in theme, in method—that heighten our appreciation of the plays. After all, Miller is pre-eminently a playwright, one of the best the American theater has produced.

In *The Ride down Mount Morgan* (1992) Miller returns to his early theme of an individual confronted with a crisis which puts him at odds with both himself and his family. Lyman Felt, a millionaire insurance executive, is seriously injured in a car accident, and must face the consequences when his two wives are summoned to the hospital. In the *Booklist* review, Ray Olson writes that *The Ride down Mount Morgan* "provocatively . . . psychodramatizes Lyman's life, exploring the male of the species' seemingly eternal internal conflict between desire and responsibility."

Miller's most recent play, *The Last Yankee,* revolves around carpenter Leroy Hamilton, one of George Washington's descendants, and his chance meeting with a rich businessman, Frick, at a public asylum where both of their wives are patients. The *New Yorker*'s Edith Oliver writes that a "discussion of Hamilton's natty clothes leads (needless to say) to a Miller lecture on the competitiveness of life in America, and other national attitudes that displease him."

In his 1987 autobiography, *Timebends,* Miller writes not only about his childhood, family, marriages, political views, and literary and social friendships, but considers the relationship between his life experiences and his art. Bruce Bawer writes in the *American Scholar* that the autobiography reveals that "the majority of his plays, by his account, did not grow out of characters, situations, or voices, but out of hankerings to make bold public statements." *Timebends*' insight and poetic sensibility, according to the *Booklist* reviewer, make it a "welcome addition to American letters." Similarly, *Publisher's Weekly* says *Timebends* "does with [Miller's] life story what nature does

with rock strata, folding it back on itself to achieve the effects of many-layered richness and simultaneity that he aims for in his plays."

—Gerald Weales, updated by Lisa C. Harper

MILLER, Henry (Valentine)

Born: Yorkville, New York City, 26 December 1891. **Education:** P.S. 85, Brooklyn, graduated 1907; City College, New York, 1909. **Family:** Married 1) Beatrice Sylvas Wickens in 1917 (divorced 1924), one daughter; 2) June Edith Smith in 1924 (divorced 1934); 3) Janina Martha Lepska in 1944 (divorced 1952), one daughter and one son; 4) Eve McClure in 1953 (divorced 1961); 5) Hiroko Tokuda in 1967 (separated 1970). **Career:** Worked for Atlas Portland Cement Company, New York, 1909; reporter in Washington, D.C., 1917; worked for Bureau of Economic Research, New York, 1919; employment manager, Western Union Telegraph Company, 1920-24; lived in Europe, mainly in France, 1930-40; proofreader, Chicago *Tribune* Paris edition, 1932; teacher, Lycee Carnot, Dijon, 1932; psychoanalyst, New York, 1935; editor, with Lawrence Durrell and Alfred Perles, *The Booster* (later *Delta*), Paris, 1937-38; European editor, *Volontes,* Paris, 1938-39, and *Phoenix,* Woodstock, New York, 1938-39; returned to the United States, 1940; lived in California from 1942. Also an artist: exhibitions of watercolors in New York, 1927, London, 1944, and Los Angeles, 1966. **Member:** American Academy, 1958; Officer, Legion of Honor (France), 1975. **Died:** 7 June 1980.

PUBLICATIONS

Collections

A Miller Reader, edited by John Calder. 1985.

Fiction

Tropic of Cancer. 1934.
Black Spring. 1936.
Tropic of Capricorn. 1939.
The Smile at the Foot of the Ladder. 1948.
The Rosy Crucifixion:
Sexus. 1949.
Plexus. 1953.
Nexus. 1960.
Nights of Love and Laughter (stories). 1955.
Quiet Days in Clichy. 1956.
Opus pistorum. 1983; as *Under the Roofs of Paris,* 1985.

Plays

Scenario: A Film with Sound. 1937.
Just Wild about Harry: A Melo-Melo in Seven Scenes (produced 1963). 1963.

Poetry

Reflections, edited by Twinka Thiebaud. 1981.

Other

What Are You Going to Do about Alf? 1935.

Aller Retour New York. 1935; selection, as *Reunion in Barcelona,* 1959.

Money and How It Gets That Way. 1938.

Max and the White Phagocytes. 1938.

Hamlet, with Michael Fraenkel. 2 vols., 1939-41; vol. 1 revised, 1943; both vols. revised, as *The Michael Fraenkel-Miller Correspondence,* 1962.

The Cosmological Eye. 1939.

The World of Sex. 1940; revised edition, 1957.

The Colossus of Maroussi; or, The Spirit of Greece. 1941.

Wisdom of the Heart (short stories and essays). 1941.

Murder the Murderer: An Excursus on War. 1944.

Varda: The Master Builder. 1944.

The Angel Is My Watermark. 1944.

Sunday after the War. 1944.

The Plight of the Creative Artist in the United States of America. 1944.

Semblance of a Devoted Past. 1944; unexpurgated edition, with *To Paint Is to Love Again,* 1968.

Echolalia: Reproductions of Water Colors by Miller. 1945.

Why Abstract?, with Hilaire Hiler and William Saroyan. 1945.

Miller Miscellanea. 1945.

The Air-Conditioned Nightmare. 1945; vol. 2, *Remember to Remember,* 1947.

Obscenity and the Law of Reflection. 1945.

The Amazing and Invariable Beauford De Laney. 1945.

Maurizius Forever. 1946; abridged edition, as *Reflections on the Maurizius Case,* 1974.

Patchen: Man of Anger and Light, with *A Letter to God,* by Kenneth Patchen. 1947.

Of by and about Miller: A Collection of Pieces by Miller, Herbert Read, and Others. 1947.

Portrait of General Grant. 1947.

The Waters Reglitterized: The Subject of Water Color in Some of Its More Liquid Phases (includes reproductions of pictures). 1950.

The Books in My life. 1952.

A Devil in Paradise: The Story of Conrad Moricand, Born Paris, 7 or 7:15pm, January 17, 1887, Died Paris, 10:30pm, August 31, 1954. 1956.

Argument about Astrology. 1956.

The Time of the Assassins: A Study of Rimbaud. 1956.

Big Sur and the Oranges of Hieronymus Bosch. 1957.

The Red Notebook. 1958.

Art and Outrage: A Correspondence about Miller between Alfred Perles and Lawrence Durrell, with an Intermission by Miller. 1959.

A Miller Reader, edited by Lawrence Durrell. 1959; as *The Best of Miller,* 1960.

The Intimate Miller. 1959.

Defence of the Freedom to Read. 1959.

To Paint Is To Love Again (includes reproductions of pictures). 1960.

Stand Still like the Hummingbird. 1962.

Watercolors, Drawings and His Essay "The Angel Is My Watermark." 1962.

Lawrence Durrell and Miller: A Private Correspondence, edited by George Wickes. 1963.

Books Tangent to Circle: Reviews. 1963.

Greece. 1964.

Miller on Writing. edited by Thomas H. Moore. 1964.

Letters to Anais Nin, edited by Gunther Stuhlmann. 1965.

Selected Prose. 2 vols., 1965.

Order and Chaos chez Hans Reichel. 1966.

Writer and Critic: A Correspondence, with William A. Gordon. 1968.

Collector's Quest: The Correspondence of Miller and J. Rives Childs, edited by Richard Clement Wood. 1968.

Entretiens de Paris, with Georges Belmont. 1970; translated as *Face to Face with Miller: Conversations with Georges Belmont,* 1971; as *Miller in Conversation,* 1972.

Insomnia; or, The Devil at Large. 1970.

My Life and Times, edited by Bradley Smith. 1971.

Reflections on the Death of Mishima. 1972.

On Turning Eighty, and Journey to an Antique Land. 1972.

The Immortal Bard (on John Cowper Powys). 1973.

First Impressions of Greece. 1973.

This Is Henry—Henry Miller from Brooklyn: Conversations, with Robert Snyder. 1974.

Letters of Miller and Wallace Fowlie, 1943-1972, edited by Fowlie. 1975.

The Nightmare Notebook. 1975.

J'suis pas plus con qu'un autre. 1976; as *Je ne suis pas plus con qu'un autre,* 1980.

Genius and Lust: A Journey through the Major Writings of Miller, with Norman Mailer. 1976.

Flash Back: Entretiens a Pacific Palisades, with Christian de Bartillat. 1976.

Miller's Book of Friends (memoirs). 1976; vol. 2, *My Bike and Other Friends,* 1978; vol. 3, *Joey: A Loving Portrait of Alfred Perles, Together with Some Bizarre Episodes Relating to the Other Sex,* 1979.

Four Visions of America, with others. 1977.

Sextet: Six Essays. 1977.

Mother, China, and the World Beyond. 1977.

Gliding into the Everglades and Other Essays. 1977.

An Open Letter to Stroker! 1978.

Miller: Years of Trial and Triumph 1962-1964: The Correspondence of Miller and Elmer Gertz, edited by Gertz and Felice Flanery Lewis. 1978.

The Theatre and Other Pieces. 1979.

The World of Lawrence: A Passionate Appreciation, edited by Evelyn J. Hinz and John J. Teunissen. 1980.

Notes on "Aaron s Rod" and Other Notes on Lawrence from the Paris Notebooks, edited by Seamus Cooney. 1980.

Correspondance privee 1935-1978, with Joseph Delteil, edited by F.-J. Temple. 1980.

The Paintings of Miller (includes essays), edited by Noel Young. 1982.

From Your Capricorn Friend: Miller and the Stroker 1978-1980 (letters). 1984.

Dear, Dear Brenda: The Love Letters of Miller to Brenda Venus, edited by Gerald Seth Sindell. 1986.

Conversations with Henry Miller. 1994.

Farewell from France: A Letter to Huntington Cairns April 30, 1939. 1995.

Henry Miller and James Laughlin: Selected Letters. 1996.

Henry Miller and Elmer Gertz: Selected Letters 1964-1975. 1998.

*

Bibliography: *Miller: A Chronology and Bibliography* by Bern Porter, 1945; *Bibliography of Miller* by Thomas H. Moore, 1961; *A Bibliography of Miller 1945-1961* by Maxine Renken, 1962; *Miller: A Bibliography of Secondary Sources* by Lawrence J. Shifreen, 1979; *A Certain Kind of Madness: Henry Miller and the Bibliography of Primary Sources,* 1994; *Henry Miller and the "Nudies": Bibliography for Readers and Collectors* edited by Roger Jackson, 1996; *The Personal Archive of Henry Miller,* 1997; *Henry Miller: A Bibliography of Watercolors: A List of 545 Published Watercolors, Cross Referenced by Title and Year of Completion,* 1997.

Critical Studies: *Miller* by Nicholas Moore, 1953; *My Friend Miller: An Intimate Biography by Alfred Perles,* 1956; *Miller, Expatriate* by Annette Kar Baxter, 1961; *Miller and the Critics* edited by George Wickes, 1963, and *Miller* by Wickes, 1966; *Miller* by Kingsley Widmer, 1963; *Miller* by F.J. Temple, 1965; *The Mind and Art of Miller* by William A. Gordon, 1967; *The Literature of Silence: Miller and Samuel Beckett* by Ihab Hassan, 1968; *Miller: Three Decades of Criticism* edited by Edward B. Mitchell, 1971; *Orpheus in Brooklyn: Orphism, Rimbaud and Miller* by Bertrand Mathieu, 1976; *Always Merry and Bright: The Life of Miller* by Jay Martin, 1978; *Miller* by J.D. Brown, 1986; *Miller: Full of Life* by Kathryn Winslow, 1986; *Henry Miller Down and Out in Paris* by George Wickes, 1994; *Henry Miller's Semblance of a Devoted Past: A Study in Censorship* edited by Bern Porter and Roger Jackson, 1995; *Passionate Lives: D.H. Lawrence, F. Scott Fitzgerald, Henry Miller, Dylan Thomas, Sylvia Plath—In Love* by John Tytell, 1995.

*   *   *

Henry Miller's name became known to a wider public than that of a fashionable, rather trendy literary elite largely as an unexpected result of the Allied forces in Paris after 1944. The soldiers and the civilians who accompanied them discovered his books— *Tropic of Cancer, Black Spring, Tropic of Capricorn*—most of which had been refused publication in English-speaking countries because of their blatantly sexual matter. But they were available in Paris published by Girodias's Obelisk Press, and were eagerly seized on by Americans and Britons, many of whom succeeded in smuggling their finds into their home countries.

Too often the books were large, inchoate, rambling works with an autobiographical thread. They passed rapidly, like a rushing, uncontrolled stream, from the rhapsodic to the sordid to the pornographic. Miller's freedom of language and subject had a deep influence on the thousands of writers who benefitted from the literary emancipation from censorship. Miller himself may have been influenced by much of the erotica of the ages. But he was influenced also by such American writers as **Walt Whitman** and **Robinson Jeffers**, by the back-to-nature animists such as **Henry David Thoreau** and D.H. Lawrence (about whom he wrote a study), and by all the European writers who in one way or another contributed to such movements as Dadaism and Surrealism. He praises such not always well-known writers as Celine, Cingria, Blaise Cendrars, Milosz, Knut Hamsun, and Rimbaud, whose *Season in Hell* he translated. He has a sort of American-Irish dislike of the British, except for Lawrence Durrell and John Cowper Powys (whose novels he claims to understand, but whose real virtue was that he had written *In Defence of Sensuality,* and sensuality was a habit to which Miller always gave a high priority).

Miller as a writer is for freedom in every possible sense, an indecent Shelley, a Tom Paine with the lid off. He expresses, too, a semi-mystical belief that everything links with everything else and that the Creator will arrange that "If there is a genuine need it will be met." Miller, indeed, himself had amazing luck in becoming a highly saleable writer. He always suffered from logorrhea— and, then he realized that he could earn real money by writing, from appalling over-production. He can be funny in a boisterous sort of way; he is a farceur; he can even convince one from time to time that he is genuinely perceptive, though the conviction seldom lasts long. He had a gift for assimilating trendy names and attitudes; Zen, Hokusai, the Essenes, Restif de la Bretonne, astrology, the occult, Milarepa the Tibetan monk. But paradoxically he can still react salutarily against the fashionable, against the claims, for example, of American medicine and the endless, self-defeating "don'ts" of urban Western societies—don't over-eat, don't walk if you can run, don't listen to the radio or watch television, don't get vaccinated or inoculated, don't get frightened if you are over or under weight. And, he concludes: "The great hoax which we are perpetuating every day of our lives is that we are making life easier, more comfortable, more enjoyable, more profitable. We are doing just the contrary. We are making life stale, flat and unprofitable every day in every way. . . ." His attitude is far from new. It is certainly as old as the time of the Romantic poets. Nor does it advance our perceptions to keep on saying these things. Miller is not a great writer, and he can en masse be a great bore.

His best literary work, written with skill and brio, is *The Colossus of Maroussi,* for it carries to us the whole flavor of Athens in the months immediately preceding World War II, and the sense of the Greek-ness of Greeks. In general his early works are much the best, for he was then really trying. *Tropic of Cancer* is a light-hearted, racy account of his life as a poor, hungry, always lustful, writer in the Paris suburbs, just as *Sexus* (part of *The Rosy Crucifixion* trilogy) does give a picture of the lower- middle-class, working-class, and prostitutes' life in New York in the years before World War I. There are some rather fine passages in these books— "Easter came in like a frozen hare—but it was fairly warm in bed." Nor can one deny he achieves at least novelty in his descriptions, sometimes quite comic, of sexual organs and of varieties of the sexual act. But the characters in his long autobiographical reminiscences are seldom visualized, except occasionally as extreme oddities when we see them like comic caricatures. There is little consideration of motives and less of psychology. The men and women move and act but we know only that it is because of the prime, crude instincts—sexual desire, and the desire for food of which Miller makes a great deal.

Miller was a copious letter writer all his life and an entertaining one. The correspondence between him and Durrell makes excellent reading, and there are vast stores of Miller letters in the archives of the University of California, Los Angeles.

—Kenneth Young

MILLER, Joaquin

A pseudonym for Cincinnatus Hiner Miller. **Born:** Liberty, Indiana, 10 March 1839; moved with his parents to Oregon, 1852. **Education:** Studied law in Oregon; admitted Oregon bar, 1861.

Career: Messenger in the gold mining district of Idaho, 1856-59; manager, Eugene *Democratic Register,* Oregon, 1863; lawyer in Canon City, Oregon, 1863-66; county court judge, Grant County, Oregon, 1866-70; lived in London and gained notoriety as the "frontier poet," 1870-71; returned to the United States and subsequently became a fruit grower: lived on his estate in Oakland, California, after 1887; Klondike correspondent, New York *Journal,* 1897-98. **Died:** 17 February 1913.

PUBLICATIONS

Collections

Poetical Works, edited by Stuart P. Sherman. 1923.
Selections (verse), edited by Juanita Joaquina Miller. 1945.
Selected Writings, edited by Alan Rosenus. 1977.

Poetry

Specimens. 1868.
Joaquin, et al. 1869.
Pacific Poems. 1871.
Songs of the Sierras. 1871.
Songs of the Sun-Lands. 1873.
The Ship in the Desert. 1875.
Songs of Italy. 1878.
Songs of Far-Away Lands. 1878.
Songs of the Mexican Seas. 1887.
In Classic Shades and Other Poems. 1890.
Songs of the Soul. 1896.
Complete Poetical Works. 1897; revised edition, 1902.
Chants for the Boer. 1900.
As It Was in the Beginning: A Poem Dedicated to the Mothers of Men. 1903.
Light: A Narrative Poem. 1907.
Panama: Union of the Oceans. 1912.

Plays

The Baroness of New York. 1877.
First Families in the Sierras. 1875; revised version, as *The Danites in the Sierras* (produced 1880), 1881.
Forty-Nine: A California Drama. 1882.
The Silent Man. 1883.
Tally-Ho!, music by John Philip Sousa. 1883.
An Oregon Idyll, in *Collected Works.* 1910.

Fiction

The One Fair Woman. 1876.
Shadows of Shasta. 1881.
'49: The Gold-Seeker of the Sierras. 1884.
The Destruction of Gotham. 1886.

Other

Life amongst the Modocs: Unwritten History. 1873; as *Paquita, The Indian Heroine,* 1881; revised edition, as *My Own Story,* 1890; as *Romantic Life amongst the Red Indians: An Autobiography,* 1890; as *Unwritten History,* edited by Alan Rosenus, 1972.

The Danites and Other Choice Selections, edited by A. V. D. Honeyman. 1878.
Memorie and Rime. 1884.
The Building of the City Beautiful. 1893.
An Illustrated History of the State of Montana. 2 vols., 1894.
The Battle of Castle Crags. 1894.
True Bear Stories. 1900.
Japan of Sword and Love, with Yone Noguchi. 1905.
Collected Works. 6 vols., 1909-10.
Trelawney with Shelley and Byron. 1922.
Overland in a Covered Wagon: An Autobiography, edited by Sidney G. Firman (based on *Introduction to Collected Works*). 1930.
California Diary 1855-1857, edited by John S. Richards. 1936.
Joaquin Miller's Charcoal Sketches. 2 vols, 1996.

*

Bibliography: in *Bibliography of American Literature* by Jacob Blanck, 1973; *Three Writers of the Far West: A Reference Guide* by Ray C. Longtin, 1980.

Critical Studies: *Miller: Literary Frontiersman* by Martin S. Peterson, 1937; *Splendid Poseur: Miller, American Poet* by M. Marion Marberry, 1953; *Miller* by O.W. Frost, 1967; *Miller* by Benjamin S. Lawson, 1980; "Joaquin Miller on New York; Presented to Professor Willem Schrickx on the Occasion of His Retirement" by Kristiaan Versluys, in *Elizabethan and Modern Studies* edited by J.P. Vander Motten, 1985; "Yone Noguchi's Poetry: From Whitman to Zen" by Yoshinobu Hakutani, in *Comparative Literature Studies,* spring 1985; "So Here Then Is a Little Journey to the House of Joaquin Miller" by James Williams, in *Jack London Journal,* 1996, pp. 74-81; "Joaquin Miller" by Benjamin S. Lawson, in *Updating the Literary West,* 1997.

*   *   *

Were it not for the outlandish image of himself that he deliberately cultivated, Cincinnatus Hiner Miller, better known as Joaquin Miller, after the Mexican bandit Joaquin Murietta, whose exploits he helped to popularize, would probably be forgotten in the late twentieth century. Dressed in western sombrero, boots, and buckskin britches, Miller proclaimed himself the poetic spokesman for the American West, and during his lifetime he came to symbolize, both in America and abroad, the spirit of freedom, adventure, and bravado that characterized the West in the popular imagination.

Ironically, Miller rose to fame not in America but in England, where he went to find a publisher for his book, *Pacific Poems,* and to make his presence felt in more sophisticated literary circles than those that America offered him. His earlier collections of poetry, *Specimens* and *Joaquin et al.,* had received scant recognition in America, and Miller shrewdly understood that he and his works might best appeal to a foreign audience unfamiliar with the stereotypes that he projected. Although Americans simply refused to take him seriously, Miller became something of a celebrity in Britain, where his rustic dress and primitive manners endeared him to the public and brought him to the attention of the leading literary figures of the day. From Britain, Miller's fame spread to America. His most famous book, *Songs of the Sierras,* first published in London, was issued the same year in Boston.

Most of Miller's works are vaguely autobiographical. He drew his themes from his own experiences, which he embellished or exaggerated according to the effects he wished to achieve. Nearly all of Miller's works are about the West. *Life amongst the Modacs* and *Memorie and Rime* are prose accounts of his early adventures in the mines and among the Indians of California. *Shadows of Shasta,* Miller's most successful novel, draws attention to the injustices done to the Indians, with whom Miller greatly sympathized. When he writes about the West, Miller is generally passionate and bold. He possessed the ability to make legend seem real and the real seem legendary. Miller possessed a flair for the dramatic and was especially effective as a playwright. His most popular play, *The Danites in the Sierras,* was acted before packed audiences, much to the chagrin of **Bret Harte** and **Mark Twain,** who envied Miller's dramatic talents. When he departed from western themes, however, as he did in the novels *The One Fair Woman* and *The Destruction of Gotham,* Miller's writing becomes forced and unconvincing.

Miller's poetry, while lacking in intrinsic merit, had a profound effect on the development of western American literature. For forms and techniques, Miller studied the British romantics and the American fireside poets. Like **Longfellow,** Miller was especially fond of rhymed iambic pentameter, and his western heroes bear a marked resemblance to those of Byron. In those poems where form matches content, Miller's verse possesses a haunting, rhythmic quality, reminiscent of Indian chants, and captures the spirit and vitality of his western themes. Miller is especially noted for his attempts to write poetry in the American vernacular. His most famous poem, "Columbus," has become a classic and is still recited by American schoolchildren, who see in it a primitive expression of the American Dream.

—James A. Levernier

MIRIKITANI, Janice

Born: Stockton, California, 5 February 1942. Incarcerated in Rohwer, Arkansas Concentration Camp during World War II. **Education:** University of California at Los Angeles, B.A. (cum laude) 1962; University of California at Berkeley, teaching credential 1963; San Francisco State University, California, graduate studies in creative writing. **Family:** Married Reverend Cecil Williams (pastor of Glide Memorial United Methodist Church, San Francisco); one daughter. **Career:** Teacher of English, Speech, and Dance for Contra Costa Unified School District, California, 1964-65; administrative assistant, Glide Church, 1966-69; program director, Glide Church/Urban Center, since 1969; choreographer and artistic director, Glide Dance Group, beginning 1973; guest choreographer, Asian American Dance Collective, San Francisco, 1983-85; president of the Glide Foundation, beginning 1982. Cofounder of Asian American Publications; member of Third World Communications (publishers); past board member of Vanguard Foundation; Grants for the Arts of the San Francisco Hotel Tax Fund; Asian American Media Center; Yerba Buena Cultural Board; California Poets in the Schools; Asian American Theatre Company; Asian American Dance Collective; board member of Zellerbach Community Arts Distribution Committee; United Tenderloin Community Fund; board of directors, Haight Ashbury Free Medical Clinic. **Awards:** Pacific Asian American Women Bay Area Coalition award, 1983; The Women's Foundation award, 1985; University of California at San Francisco Chancellor's medal of honor (with Cecil Will-

iams), 1988; 17th Assembly District, California, Woman of the Year award, 1988; Japanese Community Youth Council Outstanding Leadership award, 1990. **Residence:** San Francisco.

PUBLICATIONS

Collections (poetry and prose)

Awake in the River. 1978.
Shedding Silence. 1987.

Poetry

We, the Dangerous: New and Selected Poems. 1995.

Other

Editor, *Aion Magazine* vols. I and II. 1971, 1972.
Editor, *Third World Women.* 1973.
Editor, *Time to Greez!: Incantations from the Third World.* 1975.
Editor, *Ayumi: A Japanese American Anthology.* 1980.
Japanese-American Editor, *Making Waves: An Asian Women's Anthology.* 1988.
Editor, *Breaking Free: A Glide Songbook.* 1989.
Editor, *I Have Something to Say about This Big Trouble.* 1989.
Editor, *Watch Out! We're Talking.* 1993.

*

Bibliography: *The Third Woman: Minority Women Writers of the United States* edited by Dexter Fisher, 1980; *A Directory of American Poets and Fiction Writers: 1980-81 Edition,* 1981; *Breaking Silence: An Anthology of Contemporary Asian American Poets* edited by Joseph Bruchac, 1983.

Critical Studies: "Notes toward a New Multicultural Criticism: Three Works by Women of Color" by John F. Crawford in *A Gift of Tongues: Critical Challenges in Contemporary American Poetry* edited by Kathleen Aguero and Marie Harris, 1987; *Articulate Silences: Hisaye Yamamoto, Maxine Hong Kingston, Joy Kogawa* by King-Kok Cheung, 1993; "Embodied Language: The Poetics of Mitsuye Yamada, Janice Mirikitani, and Kimiko Hahn" in *Masking Selves, Making Subjects: Japanese American Women, Identity, and the Body* by Traise Yamamoto, 1999.

*   *   *

Like the early immigrants from China and the Philippines, early Japanese immigrants who came to the United States seeking a better economic life were subjected to legal repression and racism. Until the mid 1960s, the U.S. government regulated immigration of Asians coming to America, the nature of their employment, and segregation from the dominant society. During the second World War (after the Japanese attack on Pearl Harbor), the U.S. government relocated Japanese Americans in military prison camps, believing they were a threat to national security. Japanese American families were separated and properties were lost due to imprisonment. More importantly, the internment experience during World War II forced many Japanese Americans to consider what their racial identity meant, providing proof that they would never be fully accepted into American society. Janice Mirikitani is a sansei, third-generation Japanese American, who was born near the end of World War II and incarcerated at Rohwer, Arkansas. Although she was too young to recall camp life clearly, Mirikitani has attempted to reconstruct the Japanese American internment experience in the majority of her writings. Mirikitani is a seminal figure in Asian American literary history in that her poetry conveys the trauma of internment and the struggle against racism. Mirikitani's works are also crucial to the Asian American movement (which emerged in the early 1970s), for they urge readers to politically respond against all forms of social injustice.

Mirikitani has developed a number of characteristically Asian American themes in her poetry. The struggle between two worlds, Japanese and American, and their respective cultural values is one of those distinguishing features of Asian American writing. Mirikitani often depicts the "double bind" that many Asian Americans must face throughout their lives. For Mirikitani, this "double bind" has much to do with adhering to the Japanese idea of "silence" as constituting individual strength and empowerment, versus accepting the Western notion of "silence" as passive and disempowering. In her writings, Mirikitani has turned to the past, to the experiences of her parents and friends, as a means to interrogate these conflicting concepts of "silence."

Ultimately, Mirikitani's poetry advocates a rejection of traditional Asian ideas of "silence," arguing that racism and social injustices will only be abolished through active speech and protest. Mirikitani's poetic style is also a fusion of the two cultural traditions she has been raised with. Her poetry is clear and simple, reminiscent of classical Japanese haiku, allowing the language to speak for itself through its clear and concrete imagery. But, Mirikitani's poetry is not merely a set of aesthetic pieces to be admired and absorbed by the reader. Her critically acclaimed collections of poetry, *Awake in the River* and *Shedding Silence,* speak vividly, in a haunting, yet strong voice, of the disillusionment, pain, and suffering of oppressed peoples in America.

Mirikitani's experience of subjugation and racism within her own "homeland" provided a historical context with which to view other events taking place globally. The trauma of Japanese American internment, the nuclear devastations of both Hiroshima and Nagasaki, and U.S. imperialism in Southeast Asia are painful experiences that have shaped Mirikitani's poetry in *Awake in the River.* In this first collection, Mirikitani has turned her sense of history into a weapon, an active protest against racist ideology in America. The opening poem, "For My Father," reveals the dominant concerns and imagery of the rest of Mirikitani's work.

The author portrays her father in a contradictory light, as both hero and tragic persecutor of his children. However, Mirikitani unearths the roots of her father's paradoxical nature. The father denies his own children a sampling of the strawberries he has grown because of economic necessity. This poem is powerful in its depiction of the results of oppression. Mirikitani contrasts the wealthy white world to the isolated, impoverished, and oppressive world of the Japanese Americans. These distinctions are constructed in the poem by references to the internment experience of "Tule Lake" (the most severe military prison camp), and the bombings of Hiroshima and Nagasaki, where "Iron [is]/ in your eyes/ to shield/ the pain/ to shield desert-like wind." Thus, the desert, for Mirikitani, becomes a powerful metaphor for the exile of Japanese Americans during World War II and their continued struggle to emerge from the barren past. Another poem, "Loving from Vietnam to Zimbabwe," depicts American atrocities against the Vietnamese, fusing graphic images of life and death, and love

and pain. The final poem in this collection, "Awake in the River," is an explicit description of camp life, emphasizing themes of dignity and survival. The child narrator compares herself to a tortoise that has entered the camps. Mirikitani's message is clear in this poem: the children try to confine the tortoise, but the women urge them to set it free for "It is wrong to imprison any living thing." The last lines "Sleep in the desert/ Awake in the river," merge images of Japanese American prisoners waiting for the war to end and the tortoise searching for freedom.

But it is for her second volume, *Shedding Silence,* that Mirikitani will best be known. Mirikitani actively confronts the issue of "silence," attesting to the prevailing impulse of Asian Americans to forswear silence, an impulse that emerged along with the Asian American movement of the early 1970s. This collection reflects the strength of a literature that refuses to be subjugated and silenced. Mirikitani attempts to dispel the stereotype of "Orientals" as the "silent minority," as voiceless and passive in American culture and politics. The most powerful poem and the best representative of the volume is appropriately entitled "Breaking Silence," dedicated to the poet's mother and her testimony before the Commission on Wartime Relocation and Internment of Japanese Americans Civilians. Similar to the poems in *Awake in the River,* Mirikitani again incorporates the historical past—quoted excerpts from her mother's testimony, descriptions of camp life, disillusionment and rage—with an urgent message for the present. The poem begins with the Asian conception of silence: "We were told/ that silence was better/ golden like our skin,/ useful like." Mirikitani here articulates how verbal restraint, in most Asian communities, is reinforced as a survival strategy in the face of racism. However, the repeated intrusion of her mother's testimony immediately points to the inadequacy of this approach. Her mother's voice interrupts the poem's silent description: "Mr. commissioner . . . / But I exhume my past/ to claim this time./ My youth is buried in Rohwer . . . Words are better than tears,/ so I spill them./ I kill this, the silence . . . " Thus, Mirikitani employs her mother's testimony to both authenticate the tragedy of the past and to strengthen her message that racism and social injustice must be abolished. The poem is an uncovering of the trauma of internment, urging Asian Americans to "break" their "silence" against oppressive forces in America. The poem ends with an affirmation of the Japanese American community and a celebration of its emerging voice: "We hear everything./ We are unafraid./ Our language is beautiful."

Aside from her poetry, Mirikitani has edited anthologies including *Ayumi: A Japanese American Anthology,* and *Time to Greez!: Incantations from the Third World,* collections that carry on Mirikitani's work against racism and oppression in America. Similar to her poetry, these compilations of Asian American and ethnic American writings express the pain of concentration camps, government injustices, the void of the desert, and, more importantly, the voices of survival. It is Mirikitani's role as both artist and community representative that makes her an indispensable writer in the literary history of Asian Americans.

—Rowena Tomaneng

MITCHELL, Donald Grant

Pseudonym: Ik Marvel. **Born:** Norwich, Connecticut, 12 April 1822. **Education:** John Hall's School, Ellington, Connecticut, 1830-

37; Yale University, New Haven, Connecticut (editor, *Yale Literary Magazine*), 1837-41, graduated 1841. **Family:** Married Mary Frances Pringle in 1853. **Career:** Farmer and writer, New London County, Connecticut, 1841-43; clerk to the U.S. Consul, Liverpool, England, 1844-45; toured Europe, 1845-46; wrote for *Morning Courier* and *New York Enquirer* (correspondent in Paris, 1848), also studied law in the offices of John Osborne Sargent, New York, 1846-50; editor, *Lorgnette,* New York, 1850; full-time writer from 1850; U.S. Consul, Venice, 1853-54; lived in Paris, 1855; returned to the United States and settled on a farm, later called Edgewood, near New Haven, Connecticut. **Awards:** New York Agricultural Society silver medal, 1843; New England Association of Park Superintendents silver cup, 1904. **Died:** 15 December 1908.

PUBLICATIONS

Fiction

The Lorgnette; or, Studies of the Town by an Opera Lover. 1850; as *The Opera Goer,* 1852.
Reveries of a Bachelor; or, A Book of the Heart. 1850. *Dream Life: A Fable of the Seasons.* 1851.
Fudge Doings, Being Tony Fudge's Record of the Same. 1855.
Seven Stories, with Basement and Attic. 1864.
Dr. Johns, Being a Narrative of Certain Events in the Life of an Orthodox Minister of Connecticut. 1866.

Other

Fresh Gleanings; or, a New Sheaf from the Old Fields of Continental Europe. 2 vols., 1847.
The Battle Summer, Being Transcripts from Personal Observation in Paris 1848. 1849.
My Farm of Edgewood: A Country Book. 1863.
Wet Days at Edgewood, with Old Farmers, Old Gardeners, and Old Pastorals. 1865.
Rural Studies, with Hints for Country Places. 1867; as *Out-of-Town Places,* 1884.
Pictures of Edgewood, photographs by Rockwood. 1868.
About Old Story-Tellers, of How and When They Lived, and What Stories They Told. 1878.
A Report to the Commissioners on Lay-Out of East Rock Park. 1882.
Bound Together: A Sheaf of Papers. 1884.
English Lands, Letters, and Kings. 4 vols., 1889-97.
American Lands and Letters. 2 vols., 1897-99.
Looking Back at Boyhood. 1906.
Works. 15 vols., 1907.
Louis Mitchell: A Sketch, edited by Waldo H. Dunn. 1947.

Editor, with Oliver Wendell Holmes, *The Atlantic Almanac 1868.* 1867.
Editor, *The Atlantic Almanac 1869.* 1868.
Editor, with Alfred Mitchell, *The Woodbridge Record, Being an Account of the Descendants of the Rev. John Woodbridge.* 1883.
Editor, *Daniel Tyler: A Memorial Volume.* 1883.

*

Bibliography: in *Bibliography of American Literature* by Jacob Blanck, 1973.

Critical Studies: *The Life of Mitchell* by Waldo H. Dunn, 1922; "The Disappearance of Ik Marvel" by Arnold G. Tew and Allan Peskin, in *American Studies,* fall 1992.

*   *   *

There was perhaps no writer in nineteenth-century America who could more appropriately be labeled "genteel" than Donald Grant Mitchell. There was also perhaps no writer who more fully expressed the ambitions and mores of middle-class Americans. Like his contemporaries Richard Watson Gilder, Thomas Bailey Aldrich, and Richard Henry Stoddard, Mitchell addressed a middle-class audience that in both public and private life gave priority to "respectability," and nowhere was respectability more firmly entrenched than in the home. In a series of "country books" that included *My Farm of Edgewood, Wet Days at Edgewood,* and *Rural Studies,* Mitchell detailed an ideal respectable domestic life based on his own life at Edgewood, his home in rural Connecticut. The "country books" are long out of print, but for half a century they were highly regarded. At the time of Mitchell's death in 1908, surely few of his readers could have guessed that within a generation both Edgewood and its genial master would be forgotten.

Mitchell established his reputation in 1850 with the publication of *Reveries of a Bachelor*—a book utterly without original ideas but with a wealth of sentimental observations that gave it especial appeal for young women. Mitchell never disappointed his original audience; in book after book, they (and their husbands) found abundant sentiment and gentle advice. The formula extended even to his literary criticism, collected in, among other volumes, *American Lands and Letters.* Strictly speaking, it was not literary criticism but literary appreciation that he wrote.

Mitchell's genial, invariably pleasing writings deserve greater attention than they usually receive. As literature, they are of minor interest, yet as expositions of the aspirations and values of the genteel American they are invaluable. If a reader wishes to discover the ideal perimeters of life in middle-class America a century ago, Mitchell's books can show him.

—Edward Halsey Foster

MITCHELL, Langdon (Elwyn)

Born: Philadelphia, Pennsylvania, 17 February 1862; son of S. Weir Mitchell. **Education:** St. Paul's School, Concord, New Hampshire; studied for three years in Dresden and Paris, then studied law at Harvard Law School, Cambridge, Massachusetts, and Columbia University, New York; admitted to New York bar, 1886, but did not practice. **Family:** Married the actress Marion Lea in 1892; one son and two daughters. **Career:** Playwright and author from mid-1880s; lecturer in English, George Washington University, Washington, D.C., 1918-20; professor of playwriting, University of Pennsylvania, Philadelphia, 1928-30. **Member:** American Academy. **Died:** 21 October 1935.

PUBLICATIONS

Plays

Sylvian, in Sylvian: A Tragedy, and Poems. 1885.

George Cameron (produced 1891).
In the Season (produced 1892). 1898.
Ruth Underwood (produced 1892).
Deborah (produced 1892; as *The Slave Girl,* produced 1893).
Don Pedro (produced 1892).
Becky Sharp, from the novel *Vanity Fair* by Thackeray (produced 1899). Edited by J. B. Russak, in *Monte Cristo and Other Plays,* 1941.
The Adventures of Francoise, from a novel by S. Weir Mitchell (produced 1900).
The Kreutzer Sonata, from a work by Jacob Gordin based on novel by Tolstoy (produced 1906). 1907.
The New York Idea (produced 1906). 1908.
The New Marriage (produced 1911).
Major Pendennis, from the novel by Thackeray (produced 1916).

Fiction

Love in the Backwoods (stories). 1897.

Poetry

Sylvian: A Tragedy, and Poems. 1885.
Poems. 1894.

Other

Understanding America. 1927.

*

Critical Study: in *American Playwrights, 1880-1945: A Research and Production Sourcebook* edited by William W. Demastes, 1995.

*   *   *

Langdon Mitchell's reputation in American theater rests almost completely on one play—*The New York Idea.* His first published play, *Sylvian, A Tragedy* written partly in verse and more for the closet than the stage, appeared in a volume of verse in 1885. Among his ten other plays, *Becky Sharp,* a dramatization of Thackeray's *Vanity Fair,* was a successful vehicle for the American actress Minnie Madden Fiske. But only *The New York Idea,* which Arthur Hobson Quinn, the drama historian, termed a "sterling comedy," could be considered a contribution to the developing American drama. It also helped spread the work of American dramatists abroad, for it played in London, was produced in Germany as *Jonathans Tochter* under the direction of Max Reinhardt, and was translated into other European languages.

Something of a landmark in the progress of social comedy in America, *The New York Idea*—"New York is bounded on the North, South, East and West by the state of Divorce"—mixes farce-comedy with melodrama in delightful portions while Mitchell reveals his rather probing insights into the "state of Divorce" through witty and satirical comments. As a satire on marriage in New York society, the play defines marriage as "three parts love and seven parts forgiveness of sin." The fast-moving plot is determined by two divorced women each of whom plans to marry the other's ex-husband until one of them decides she really loves the man she has just divorced. Most of the characters are one-dimensional foils for the author's quick wit—the stuffy husband,

the insipid clergyman, the English fop intriguer. Contrived situations such as the wedding scene and the clubhouse episode make the play successful and show Mitchell's particular skills as a dramatist. With wit, irony, and carefully created incongruities, the play treats a serious issue with a modern touch that provides some distinction to early twentieth-century American drama.

Mitchell never repeated his success and, in fact, made only two more attempts to write for the theater, neither one successful. In related work he became, in 1928, the first occupant of the Chair of Playwriting founded by the Mask and Wig Club at the University of Pennsylvania, a position he held for two years. For the student or historian of American drama, he remains primarily the author of a single memorable play.

—Walter J. Meserve

MITCHELL, Margaret (Munnerlyn)

Born: Atlanta, Georgia, 8 November 1900. **Education:** Washington Seminary, Atlanta, 1914-18; Smith College, Northampton, Massachusetts, 1918-19. **Family:** Married 1) Berrien Kinnard Upshaw in 1922 (divorced); 2) John R. Marsh in 1925. **Career:** Feature writer and reporter, Atlanta *Journal and Constitution* and *Sunday Journal Magazine,* 1922-26. **Awards:** Pulitzer prize, 1937. M.A.: Smith College, 1939. **Died:** 16 August 1949.

PUBLICATIONS

Fiction

Gone with the Wind. 1936.

Other

Mitchell's "Gone with the Wind" Letters 1936-1949, edited by Richard Harwell. 1976.
Mitchell, A Dynamo Going to Waste: Letters to Allen Edee 1919-1921, edited by Jane Peacock. 1985.
Lost Laysen. 1996.

*

Critical Studies: *Mitchell of Atlanta* by Finis Farr, 1965; *The Road to Tara: The Life of Mitchell* by Anne Edwards, 1983; *Gone with the Wind as Book and Film* edited by Richard Harwell, 1983; "How Black Was Rhett Butler?" by Joel Williamson, in *The Evolution of Southern Culture* edited by Numan V. Bartley, 1988; "Matters of Canon: Reappraising Gone with the Wind" by Amy Levin, in *Proteus: A Journal of Ideas,* spring 1989; *Margaret Mitchell and John Marsh: The Love Story behind Gone with the Wind* by Marianne Walker, 1993; *The Irish Roots of Margaret Mitchell's Gone with the Wind* by David O'Connell, 1996; *Margaret Mitchell's Models in Gone with the Wind* by Sammy J. Hardman, 1996.

*   *   *

Margaret Mitchell wrote only one novel, *Gone with the Wind,* but it proved to be the most popular novel of her generation. At the time of her death in 1949, 3,800,000 copies were in print, and it continues to attract a large number of readers. *Gone with the Wind* was also made into a motion picture that at the time broke all box-office records and has since been regularly revived.

The continuing popularity of *Gone with the Wind* is not hard to account for. The tempestuous love affair of Scarlett O'Hara and Rhett Butler is in the great popular tradition. The Civil War background, the pathos of the South's defeat, the poverty and suffering (with its clear parallels to the 1930s depression) and eventual economic triumph of Scarlett, so cheering to readers with little to feel cheerful about, and then the "realistic" ending with its bittersweet parting of Rhett and Scarlett, contained more excitement than a dozen lesser novels. When one adds to the plethora of homely details about southern life, the humor, the dozens of colorful minor characters all presented in competent if somewhat florid prose, one understands how even a writer as discriminating as **F. Scott Fitzgerald** would be impressed with what Mitchell had been able to pull off.

Literary critics also found things to admire in *Gone with the Wind;* some even felt it deserved the Pulitzer Prize it won in 1937 by nosing out **George Santayana**'s *The Last Puritan.* In *Cavalcade of the American Novel,* Edward Wagenknecht praised it for undercutting the "futilitarianism" and "deflation of values" that had been so smart in the 1920s. One can see how a political message could be extracted from Scarlett O'Hara's willingness to do anything (exploit convict labor, seduce her sister's fiancé) to get the money to save the family plantation. Even more significant, however, is the contrast afforded between Mitchell's vision of southern history and **William Faulkner**'s, particularly Mitchell's pragmatism and Faulkner's traditionalism. If one considers Faulkner's Flem Snopes one side of the moral coin, on the other side of which is Scarlett O'Hara, Mitchell's pragmatic history takes on an even deeper significance.

—W.J. Stuckey

MITCHELL, S(ilas) Weir

Born: Philadelphia, Pennsylvania, 15 February 1829. **Education:** The University Grammar School, Philadelphia; University of Pennsylvania, Philadelphia, 1844-48, left because of illness without taking a degree, awarded a B.A. for Class of 1848, 1906; Jefferson Medical College, Philadelphia, M.D. 1850; studied medicine in Europe, 1850-51. **Military Service:** Served as a surgeon in the Union Army during the Civil War. **Family:** Married 1) Mary Middleton Elwyn in 1858 (died 1862), two sons, including Langdon Mitchell, *q.v.*; 2) Mary Cadwalader in 1875. **Career:** Practiced medicine in Philadelphia, initially as an assistant to his father, from 1851; staff member, Philadelphia Orthopaedic Hospital and Infirmary for Nervous Diseases for forty years, and professor at the Philadelphia Polyclinic and College for Graduates in Medicine; also a researcher: published extensively on pharmacological, physiological, and toxicological subjects, and, most notably, on his research into nervous diseases: pioneered the application of psychology to medicine; renowned for developing the theory of the "rest cure" as treatment for various mental diseases. Trustee, University of Pennsylvania, from 1875; trustee, Carnegie Institution, Washington, D.C.; first president, Franklin Inn (writer's club of Philadelphia), 1902-14. **Awards:** M.D.: University of Bologna, 1888. LL.D.: Harvard University, Cambridge, Massachusetts, 1886; University Of Edinburgh, 1895; Princeton University, New Jersey, 1896; University of Toronto, 1906; Jefferson Medical College, 1910. Fellow, American Academy of Arts and Sciences. **Died:** 4 January 1914.

PUBLICATIONS

Fiction

The Children's Hour (for children), with Elizabeth Stevenson. 1864.
The Wonderful Stories of Fuz-Buz and Mother Grabem the Spider (for children). 1867.
Hephzibah Guinness, Thee and You, and A Draft on the Banks of Spain. 1880.
In War Time. 1885.
Roland Blake. 1886.
Prince Little Boy and Other Tales out of Fairy-Land. 1888.
Far in the Forest. 1889.
Characteristics. 1892.
Mr. Kris Kringle: A Christmas Tale. 1893.
When All the Woods Are Green. 1894.
Philip Vernon: A Tale in Prose and Verse. 1895.
A Madeira Party. 1895.
Hugh Wynne, Free Quaker. 1897.
The Adventures of Francois, Foundling, Thief, Juggler, and Fencing-Master during the French Revolution. 1898.
The Autobiography of a Quack, and The Case of George Dedlow. 1900.
Dr. North and His Friends. 1900.
Circumstance. 1901.
The Autobiography of a Quack and Other Stories. 1901.
A Comedy of Conscience. 1903.
Little Stories. 1903.
New Samaria, and The Summer of St. Martin. 1904.
The Youth of Washington, Told in the Form of an Autobiography. 1904.
Constance Trescot. 1905.
A Diplomatic Adventure. 1906.
A Venture in 1777 (for children). 1908.
The Red City: A Novel of the Second Administration of President Washington. 1908.
The Guillotine Club and Other Stories. 1910.
John Sherwood's Ironmaster. 1911.
Westways: A Village Chronicle. 1913.

Play

Francis Drake: A Tragedy of the Sea. 1893.

Poetry

The Hill of Stones and Other Poems. 1883.
A Masque and Other Poems. 1888.
The Cup of Youth and Other Poems. 1889.
A Psalm of Deaths and Other Poems. 1891.
The Mother. 1891.
The Mother and Other Poems. 1893.
Collected Poems. 1896.

Ode on a Lycian Tomb. 1899.
The Wager and Other Poems. 1900.
Selections from the Poems. 1901.
Pearl, Rendered into Modern English Verse. 1906.
The Comfort of the Hills. 1909.
The Comfort of the Hills and Other Poems. 1910.
Complete Poems. 1914.

Other

Researches upon the Venom of the Rattlesnake. 1861.
Gunshot Wounds and Other Injuries of Nerves, with George R. Morehouse and William W. Keen. 1864.
Wear and Tear; or, Hints for the Overworked. 1871.
Injuries of Nerves and Their Consequences. 1872.
Fat and Blood, and How to Make Them. 1877; revised edition, 1878, 1884.
Lectures on Diseases of the Nervous System, Especially in Women. 1881; revised edition, 1885.
Researches upon the Venom of Poisonous Serpents, with Edward T. Reichert. 1886.
Doctor and Patient. 1888.
Two Lectures on the Conduct of the Medical Life. 1893.
The Composition of Expired Air and Its Effects upon Animal Life, with J.S. Billings and D.H. Bergey. 1895.
Clinical Lessons on Nervous Diseases. 1897.
A Brief History of Two Families: The Mitchells of Ayrshire and the Symons of Cornwall. 1912.
Some Recently Discovered Letters of William Harvey, with Other Miscellanea. 1912.
Works. 13 vols., 1913.

Editor, *Five Essays,* by John Kearsley Mitchell. 1859.

*

Bibliography: in *Bibliography of American Literature* by Jacob Blanck, 1973.

Critical Studies: *Mitchell: His Life and Letters* by Anna Robeson Burr, 1929; *Mitchell: Novelist and Physician* by Ernest Earnest, 1950; *Mitchell as a Psychiatric Novelist* by David M. Rein, 1952; *Mitchell, M.D.—Neurologist: A Medical Biography* by Richard D. Walker, 1970; *Mitchell* by Joseph P. Lovering, 1971; "The Weir Mitchell Rest Cure: Doctor and Patients" in *Women's Studies: An Interdisciplinary Journal* vol. 10, 1983, and "The Physician and Authority: Portraits by Four Physician-Writers," in *Literature and Medicine,* vol. 2, 1983, both by Suzanne Poirier.

*   *   *

S. Weir Mitchell enjoyed during his lifetime almost as wide an acclaim for his work as a physician as for his writing. The hand that produced hundreds of scientific medical treatises was no less prolific in this other imaginative area, as Mitchell viewed it, and he voluminously turned out novels, short fiction, and poetry. "He's a world-doctor for sure," but "I can't say that he's a world-author," said **Walt Whitman.** Contemporary praise that ranked one Mitchell novel with *The Scarlet Letter,* two others as superior to *Henry Esmond* and *A Tale of Two Cities,* and one of his poems as finer than "Lycidas" was sincere but excessive.

Preceding and then accompanying his novel writing, Mitchell's short fiction is noteworthy mainly for its foreshadowing and typifying. The tales of fantasy, a few O. Henryish pieces, and several Poe-esque stories of supernatural mystery are more distinctive, but traditional trappings prevail in others. Probably most memorable is "The Case of George Dedlow," the autobiography of a quadruple amputee whose legs return during a climactic seance.

Mitchell's primary success as a storyteller came from his "summer-born books," the thirteen novels that were largely vacation products of his last thirty years. More accurately labeled romances, these works reveal a pioneer physician but a literary conservative during the rise of American Realism. Mitchell made three distinct contributions to American fiction, each with important realistic implications but none with significant realistic achievement. Characterization grounded in the psychological knowledge of his clinical experience was first in time and remains first in import. His coup here, the obsessed, neurotic woman with a marked capacity for evil, is best seen in *Roland Blake, Circumstance,* and *Constance Trescot.* Mitchell chose his names carefully: Octopia Darnell is octopus-like in her demanding hold upon the Wynnes, Lucretia Hunter is an unscrupulous seeker of lucre, and Constance Trescot is relentless in driving her husband's killer to suicide. Mitchell rightly thought *Constance Trescot* the best of his novels. A second contribution was the creation of a convincing atmosphere of a definite past. His long works of historical fiction—*Hugh Wynne, Free Quaker,* a best-seller about the American Revolution; *The Adventures of Francois,* set during the French Revolution; and *The Red City,* a novel of Philadelphia in Washington's second administration—manifest the extensive research and historical immersion with which Mitchell prepared himself for their writing. His third contribution, like his first, is more suggestive than fully realized. *Characteristics* and its sequel, *Dr. North and His Friends,* have been called "conversation novels" and lauded for their experimental originality. Plainly autobiographical, they continue the tradition of **Oliver Wendell Holmes**'s autocratic *Breakfast-Table* series but look toward the more sophisticated use of conversation and complex interpersonal relationships in more serious fiction.

Mitchell was always serious about his poetry, but the judgment he hoped it would be given by time has not been forthcoming. His own nomination for immortality was the "Ode on a Lycian Tomb," inspired by the *Les Pleureuses* monument and his deep grief for the death of a daughter.

—Bert Hitchcock

MOHR, Nicholasa

Born: New York City, 1 November 1935. **Education:** The Art Students' League in New York City, 1953-56; New School for Social Research; Brooklyn Museum of Art School, 1959-66; Pratt Center for Contemporary Printmaking, 1966-69. **Family:** Married Irwin Mohr in 1957 (died); two children. **Career:** Fine arts painter in New York, California, Mexico, and Puerto Rico, 1952-62; printmaker in New York, Mexico, and Puerto Rico, beginning 1963; teacher in art schools in New York and New Jersey, beginning 1967; art instructor at Art Center of Northern New Jersey, 1971-73; MacDowell Colony, Peterborough, New Hampshire, writer in residence, 1972, 1974, and 1976; artist-in-residence with New York City public schools, 1973-74; State University of New

York at Stony Brook, lecturer in Puerto Rican studies, 1977; visiting lecture in creative writing, 1977-78; distinguished visiting professor at Queens College of the City University of New York, 1988-91; writer-in-residence/visiting scholar, Richmond College, The American University in London, 1994-95. **Awards:** *New York Times* Outstanding Book award in juvenile fiction, 1973; Jane Addams Children Book award, 1974; Society of Illustrators citation of merit for book jacket design, 1974; *New York Times* Outstanding Book award in teenage fiction, 1975; School Library Journal Best Book award, 1975; National Book award finalist, 1976; American Library Association Best Book award in young adult literature, 1977; Before Columbus Foundation American Book award, 1981; commendation from the Legislature of the State of New York, 1986; Edgar Allen Poe award, 1990; Lifetime Achievement award, National Congress of Puerto Rican Women, Philadelphia, 1996; 100 Hispanic Women award for Literary Achievement, 1997; 1997 Professional Achievement award in the Field of Arts and Culture, Boricua College, New York City, 1997; Hispanic Heritage award for Literature, 1997; Honoree for Dedication to Puerto Rican Heritage, 1998. Honorary doctorate of letters: State University of New York, Albany, 1989. **Residence:** Brooklyn, New York.

PUBLICATIONS

Fiction

Nilda. 1973.
El Bronx Remembered: A Novella and Stories. 1975.
In Nueva York. 1977.
Felita. 1979.
Going Home. 1986.
Jaime and the Conch Shell. 1987.
All for the Better: A Story of El Barrio. 1992.
The Song of El Coquí and Other Tales of Puerto Rico. 1995.
The Magic Shell (for children). 1995.
Old Letivia and the Mountain of Sorrows/La vieja Letivia y el monte de los pesares. 1996.
A Matter of Pride and Other Stories. 1997.

Plays

Screenplay: *The Artist,* with Ray Blanco, 1981.

Radio play: *Inside the Monster.* n.d.

Other

Rituals of Survival: A Woman's Portfolio. 1985.
Growing Up inside the Sanctuary of My Imagination (memoir). 1994.

*

Critical Studies: *Children's Literature* vol. 3, 1974; *Newsweek,* 4 March 1974; interview with Paul Janeczko, in *From Writers to Students: The Pleasures and Pains of Writing,* 1979; "An Interview with Nicholasa Mohr" by Roni Natov and Geraldin DeLuca, in *The Lion and the Unicorn: A Critical Journal of Children's Literature,* 1987; *Something about the Author Autobiography Series* (autobiographical essay), volume 8, 1989; "Latina Narrative and Politics of Signification: Articulation, Antagonism, and Populist Rupture" by Ellen McCracken, in *Critica: A Journal of Critical Essays,* Fall 1990.

*   *   *

As an impoverished youth, Nicholasa Mohr used her imagination as a temporary escape from her often shocking surroundings. As an adult, she employs this same creativity to relate her feelings as a woman and as an American Puerto Rican, presenting the reality of a people and expressing her artistic talent. Once an aspiring fine arts painter and printmaker, Mohr became a successful writer and illustrator of her own books. While her realistic novels and stories have won many awards and have garnered her a following among readers, Mohr has found satisfaction in being able to demonstrate her many talents while also assisting the people she cares about. She explained in an essay for *Something about the Author Autobiography Series* (*SAAS*): "As a writer I have used my abilities as a creative artist to strengthen my skills and at the same time in small measure have ventured to establish a voice for my ethnic American community and our children."

Mohr was born on 1 November 1935, to Pedro and Nicolasa (Rivera) Golpe. Her parents migrated from Puerto Rico during the Great Depression to a barrio in Manhattan, New York. Before long, the family moved to the Bronx. When Mohr was just eight years old, her father died. Often ill herself, Mohr's mother struggled to ensure that her family stayed together, and she constantly encouraged her children to develop their talents and work hard themselves. As the author related in *SAAS,* it was her mother who gave Mohr paper, a pencil, and some crayons—and with them, Mohr learned that "by making pictures and writing letters I could create my own world . . . like 'magic.'"

Although her mother died before Mohr began high school, her mother's influence did not. "My mother's strength and independence served as a strong role model for me," the author stated in her *SAAS* essay. "As I look back, she was the first feminist I knew." Upon graduation from high school, Mohr enrolled in the Arts Students' League. While engaged in her studies, she supported herself as a waitress, a clerical factory worker, and a translator.

Although she saved enough money to study art in Europe, Mohr decided to travel to Mexico City. There, at the Taller de Gráfica Popular, she studied the works of artist José Clemente Orozco, the murals of Diego Rivera, and the paintings of Rivera's wife, Frida Kahlo. Mohr admits to being influenced by the colors, figures, and methods that these artists used to express their feelings about their cultures. "The impact was to shape and form the direction of all my future work," she confided to *SAAS.*

After Mohr returned to New York City, she studied at the New School for Social Research. Mohr continued studying fine arts at the Brooklyn Museum of Art School, from 1959 to 1966, and then took up printmaking and silkscreening at the Pratt Center for Contemporary Printmaking from 1966 to 1969. With the help of a grant for Mohr's work, she moved with her husband and two sons to the suburb of Teaneck, New Jersey. There, Mohr worked in her huge art studio. According to Mohr's essay in *SAAS,* her prints are not "just . . . literal scenes of social injustices, . . . or aesthetically abstract . . . [they were] filled with bold figures, faces, and various symbols of the city . . . numbers, letters, words, and phrases . . . a kind of graffiti." Her bold innovations brought Mohr some measure of notoriety in the New York art scene. Mohr also began teaching at schools in New York and New Jersey.

As a successful artist with her own one-woman exhibitions and an agent, Mohr had never considered authorship until she was asked by a publisher to write about her life as a Puerto Rican American. Although she composed fifty pages of vignettes and the publisher liked the piece, it was rejected for publication. In an interview with Paul Janeczko, she recalled: "I think what she expected was something much more sensational, the sort of stereotypical ghetto person. So I told her that much to my embarrassment I had never stolen anything, taken hard drugs, been raped or mugged. So I guess she thought my life was uneventful."

Mohr put away her pen and continued to work as an artist until Harper and Row Publishers asked her to do a cover for one of their books. Instead, Mohr brought them her vignettes. She was encouraged to develop what she had written and was given a contract. She spent time writing at the MacDowell Colony in New Hampshire, and she finished her first book, *Nilda,* which appeared in 1973. Mohr recalled in her interview with Janeczko that she "fell very much in love with writing," although she was "a little bit nervous." While it was difficult for her to make the transition from being primarily an artist to becoming a writer, she remembered in the same interview that she "found that I could do certain things in writing and there was a crying need for what I had to say as a Puerto Rican, as someone living here, and as a woman." She found that she "could draw a picture with words, and it was extremely stimulating and eye-opening to realize what one could do with words."

While Mohr found herself intrigued with writing, readers expressed fascination with her work. They were touched and enlightened as they read *Nilda,* the autobiographical story of a poor Puerto Rican girl living in New York's Spanish Harlem. While the story is set during World War II, emphasis is given to the situation on the homefront. Puerto Ricans, already American citizens, were called "spics" and animals by the very people who were supposed to guide, uphold, and assist their youth. Teachers, social workers, nurses, and even police refer to Puerto Ricans as "you people" in the book, and the young girl's peers behave just as cruelly. Particularly effective are two scenes, one in which a very poor girl is taunted for her lack of a real suitcase at camp, and another in which a youth who has just given birth to a baby is denied entrance to her home by her own embarrassed mother. One child, who found this episode to be almost overwhelming, told *Newsweek:* "When I found out Petra was pregnant, I had to put down the book, get myself a glass of milk, turn up the heat and cuddle up in my quilt." The book was powerful in other ways, too; according to Mohr, it would demonstrate how one could escape reality through imagination. "Once there [in her imagination], she [Nilda], would also find relief from an environment she, in fact, is powerless to change in any other way," wrote the author in *SAAS.*

Nilda was a great success. Critics praised the story's fresh characters, content and style, as well as the cover and eight illustrations Mohr had provided. One critic, Donald B. Gibson, lauded the work in *Children's Literature:* "There is no pity here, for the author is too much aware of the humanity of her characters and of the other implications of pity to be in any way condescending." He wrote that *Nilda* was "what I would call a significant book, a touchstone by which others may be judged." Mohr's book received numerous honors, including the Jane Addams Children's Book Award.

After her experience with *Nilda,* Mohr felt impelled to write more. Her next book, a collection of short stories complete with a book jacket of her own creation, was published in 1975. The twelve tales and novella in *El Bronx Remembered* are set in postwar New York, and deal frankly with once-delicate subjects. One story, for example, features a doomed marriage between a pregnant teenager and an aging homosexual. Another narrative concerns a lonely, dying old Jewish man who is befriended by a Puerto Rican family. Other stories deal with racism, religion, as well as sexuality and death. All of the works, spiced with Spanish words, are realistic. "If there is any message at all in these stories, any underlying theme," wrote a critic in the *New York Times Book Review,* "it is that life goes on."

El Bronx Remembered also received many honors, including a National Book Award nomination in 1976. Bantam Books chose to publish Mohr's books in paperback form. Mohr realized that she could combine her love of art with her talent for writing and reach more people. She made the decision to continue writing, and did so as a writer-in-residence at the MacDowell Colony.

Mohr's third self-illustrated book, the children's novel *Felita,* published in 1979, relates the story of a Puerto Rican girl whose parents decide to move to a better part of town. Felita misses her old friends, and her new neighbors will not let their children befriend her. Discouraged by discrimination and harassment, Felita's family returns to their old neighborhood, and she is forced to readjust. *Felita,* well-received by critics, won an American Book Award from the Before Columbus Foundation in 1981.

From 1977 to 1980, Mohr attempted to contribute to her community through more than her writing and artwork. She lectured in Puerto Rican studies in 1977 at the State University of New York at Stony Brook and was a visiting lecturer in creative writing for various groups. She also served as the head creative writer and co-producer of the television series *Aqui y Ahora* ("Here and Now") and as a member of the New Jersey State Council on the Arts. A member of the board of trustees as well as a consultant for the Young Filmmakers Foundation, she also consults on bilingual media training for Young Filmmakers Video Arts.

When Mohr's husband died and her sons went to off to college, the author moved to a small townhouse in Brooklyn in 1980. In 1981, Mohr's brother Vincent, to whom she was very close, also died. Mohr did not publish another book until 1985. *Rituals of Survival: A Woman's Portfolio,* a collection of short stories and a novella written for adults, was published by Arte Público Press. For this work, Mohr was presented a Legislative Resolution from the State of New York, commending her for her "valuable contributions to the world of literature."

Mohr has a broad list of writing and teaching experience. She has had selections of her work published in *Family in Harmony and Conflict,* edited by Peter Reinke. Her short stories have appeared in *Children's Digest, Scholastic Magazine,* and *Nuestro.* She is a member of the board of contributing editors of *Nuestro,* and is a member of both the Authors Guild and the Authors League of America. She also has contributed to textbooks and anthologies such as *The Ethnic American Woman: Problems, Protests, Lifestyles,* which was edited by Edith Blicksilver. Finally, she wrote a piece for the radio entitled, "Inside the Monster," for the Latino Writers Symposium. Also, from 1988 to 1990, Mohr was a distinguished visiting professor at Queens College in New York City.

In her writing, Mohr strives to challenge readers of all ages to view the world with open eyes, to encourage them to alter their perception, and to entertain them. Mohr, who escaped reality as a child through her imagination, uses her creative talents to try to change reality through her readers.

—Ronie-Richele Garcia-Johnson

MOMADAY, N(avarre) Scott

Born: Lawton, Oklahoma, 27 February 1934. **Education:** High schools in New Mexico and Augusta Military Academy in Virginia; University of New Mexico, A.B. in political science 1958; Stanford University, M.A. in literature 1960, Ph.D. in literature 1963. **Family:** Married 1) Gaye Mangold in 1959 (divorced), three daughters; 2) Regina Heitzer in 1978 (divorced), one daughter. **Career:** Assistant professor, 1963-65, and associate professor, 1968-69, University of California, Santa Barbara; associate professor of English and comparative literature, University of California, Berkeley, 1969-73; professor, Stanford University, Stanford, California, 1973-82; visiting professor, Columbia University, New York City, 1979; professor, 1982-88, and Regents Professor in English and Comparative Cultural and Literary Studies, beginning 1989, University of Arizona, Tucson. Contributor, essayist and reviewer on books, travel, and native American issues, *New York Times*; narrator for numerous radio and television programs; painter, exhibited in various national and international galleries; consultant, National Endowment for the Humanities and National Endowment for the Arts, beginning 1970; trustee, Museum of the American Indian and Heye foundation. **Awards:** Academy of American Poets prize, 1962; Guggenheim Fellowship, 1966-67; Pulitzer prize for fiction, 1969; National Institute of Arts and Letters grant, 1970; Western Heritage award (with David Muench), 1974; Western Literature Association Distinguished Service award, 1983. **Member:** Gourd Dance Society of the Kiowa Tribe; PEN. **Residence:** Tucson, Arizona, and Santa Fe, New Mexico.

Publications

Collections

In the Presence of the Sun: Stories and Poems, 1961-1991, with illustrations by the author. 1992.
The Man Made of Words: Essays, Stories, Passages. 1997.

Novels

House Made of Dawn. 1968.
The Ancient Child. 1990.

Poetry

The Journey of Tai-Me (retold Kiowa Indian folktales), with etchings by Bruce S. McCurdy. 1967; as *The Way to Rainy Mountain,* with illustrations by Alfred Momaday, 1969.
Angle of Geese and Other Poems. 1974.
The Gourd Dancer, with illustrations by the author. 1976.

Plays

The Indolent Boys. n.d.

Screenplay: *The Man Who Killed the Deer* (adaptation of novel by Frank Waters). n.d.

Recording: *An Evening with N. Scott Momaday,* 1993.

Video: *The Way to Rainy Mountain: Scott Momaday Reads His Work.* 1995.

Other

Colorado, Summer/Fall/Winter/Spring. 1973.
The Names: A Memoir. 1976.
Circle of Wonder: A Native American Christmas Story. 1994.
Conversations with N. Scott Momaday. 1997.
In the Bear's House. 1999.

Editor, *The Complete Poems of Frederick Goddard Tuckerman.* 1965.

*

Critical Studies: *Four American Indian Literary Masters: N. Scott Momaday, James Welch, Leslie Marmon Silko, and Gerald Vizenor* by Alan Velie, 1982; "Who Puts Together" by Linda Hogan in *American Indian Literature: Critical Essays and Course Designs,* 1983; "Technology and Tribal Narrative" by Karl Kroeber in *Narrative Chance: Postmodern Discourse on Native American Indian Literatures,* 1989; *Landmarks of Healing: A Study of "House Made of Dawn"* by Susan Scarberry-García and Andrew Wiget, 1990; *"House Made of Dawn" and the Social Context of Contemporary Native American Literature* by Tommy Joe Arant, 1992; *Place and Vision: The Function of Landscape in Native American Fiction* by Robert M. Nelson, 1993; *Cultural Survival and the Oral Tradition in the Novels of D'Arcy McNickle and His Successors, Momaday, Silko, and Welch* (dissertation) by Lori Lynn Burlingame, 1995; *Poststructuralist Environmentalism and Beyond Ecoconsciousness in Snyder, Kingsolver, and Momaday* (dissertation) by Yong-ki Kang, 1996; *Momaday, Vizenor, Armstrong: Conversations on American Indian Writing* by Hartwig Isernhagen, 1999.

*　　*　　*

"The man made of words," a description from one of N. Scott Momaday's own essays, provides an accurate, suggestive moniker for the Pulitzer prize-winning novelist, painter, and poet. Of Kiowa, European, and Cherokee blood, Momaday is the most influential Native American writer of this century. His first novel, *House Made of Dawn,* sparked what has been called the Native American renaissance, encouraging many younger and important Native novelists, such as **James Welch, Leslie Marmon Silko, Simon J. Ortiz,** and Gerald Vizenor, and attracting a flood of critical attention to Native American literature and ethnic American literature in general. In addition to this groundbreaking novel, Momaday has published several books of poetry; numerous essays and articles for a wide variety of magazines, journals, and anthologies; and two remarkable books that might both be considered autobiographical, *The Way to Rainy Mountain* and *The Names.* In the latter of these, Momaday describes his early childhood, what it was like to imagine himself as an Indian, and what the lives of his Kiowa ancestors must have been.

Born in the Indian Hospital in Lawton, Oklahoma, to artists and teachers Alfred Morris and Natachee Scott Momaday, Momaday was taken to live in New Mexico, where his parents taught on the Navajo reservation and in Jemez pueblo. (Momaday's mother is also a writer; her books *The Owl in the Cedar Tree* and *American Indian Lives* are frequently attributed to her son). The rich Indian environment of his upbringing was further enriched by the stories and lives of his grandparents and other ancestors. *The Names* is a lyrical autobiography that explores the sacred business of naming and claiming, and taking the events of one's personal history as stories like those of his ancestors. By piecing together family photographs and anecdotes, Momaday connects the past and present into one dominant image, that of his Kiowa name, *Tsoai-talee,* or "Rock Tree Boy," which is taken from a story about a boy who turned into a bear. Thus, at the very heart of his autobiographical identity is both the absolute self-evidence of a name and its mythic connections brought into words.

"I think of all my work as being one story," Momaday has said. *The Way to Rainy Mountain* explores the connections between the ancestral heritage described in *The Names* and the traditions and stories of the Kiowa. In a three-part narrative designated by different typefaces, Momaday retells Kiowa legend from the "days when dogs could talk," relates anthropological and historical information, and narrates family stories. This powerful narrative explains the interwoven nature of storytelling, myth, and historical "facts" without losing any of the orality that is his trademark. Another element to *The Way to Rainy Mountain* is the collaboration between image and word, father and son; Momaday's father, an accomplished artist and a clear influence for Momaday's desire to become a painter himself, illustrated his son's text.

Much has been written on Momaday's first novel, *House Made of Dawn.* Its great critical acclaim and Pulitzer Prize attest as much to Momaday's gifts as to the recognition of a Native American literary tradition begun by **D'Arcy McNickle**, Mourning Dove, and some other, earlier writers. About *House Made of Dawn,* many parallels have been drawn between modernist fiction and influences such as **William Faulkner, Ernest Hemingway**, and D.H. Lawrence. Themes of displacement, expatriation, fragmentation, and the portrayal of pure evil are all clearly evident in his text, but of greater importance are the elements of Native American cosmology—the rituals and traditional paradigms that bring the protagonist, Abel, from a state of illness following his return from World War II to the healing reintegration that the novel's ending promises. The novel's careful manipulation of time, its references to the Navajo healing chants, and its circular, cyclical structure have all been found by scholars to add a previously unknown dimension to American literature. *House Made of Dawn* is clearly an important American novel; like other ethnic works that have challenged the literary canon, it incorporates the literary structures of its European influences with the cultural oral traditions of another America.

Momaday's writing career began with poetry in *The Journey of Tai-Me* and a longer, unpublished work that later became *House Made of Dawn.* He has continued to publish poetry and frequently illustrates his own books. "I see my poetry as being . . . cross-cultural . . . . I think probably that it's good for me to work across these boundaries." Again, this blending of form, medium, voice, and culture attest to Momaday's mixed-blood heritage and the all-important relationship of man to words.

For his 1990 novel, *The Ancient Child,* Momaday again draws heavily on the story central to his own identity. The main character, Set, is a painter who feels himself turning into a bear. He is also inexplicably drawn to a young woman, Grey, who herself feels drawn back in time to help Billy the Kid escape from the Lincoln County jail. Here, readers can see Momaday again syncretizing his love of painting, his fascination with the mythic old West (including the more typical West of gunslingers and desperados), and his affinity both for beautiful, powerful women and for bears. In the end, Set discovers and accepts his Native culture, successfully incorporating it into the effete world of the artist. As with most of Momaday's work, the crucial scenes revolve around a central archetype in Kiowa myth: the boy who turns into a bear and whose sisters become stars.

Momaday's other work is extensive and diverse. His painting and drawings have been exhibited in Switzerland, Germany, and the United States, and he travels extensively, speaking, telling stories, and teaching in a variety of capacities. Among other efforts are a screen adaptation of Frank Waters's novel *The Man Who Killed the Deer* and a stage play entitled *The Indolent Boys,* which Momaday has read to audiences at Harvard University.

The interweaving of oral and literary traditions, of written genres and visual images, and of the several cultures and tribes whose histories and lives have shaped him can all be found in Momaday's writing and art. Such skillful blending conveys the vantage point from which ethnic American writers view their heritage and, in Momaday's work, reveals the uniquely American experience of similar writers and their invaluable contribution to American letters.

—Jay Ann Cox

MONROE, Lyle. *See* **HEINLEIN, Robert Anson.**

MONTOYA, José

Born: On the ranch El Gallego near Escoboza, New Mexico, 28 May 1932. **Education:** Moved with family to Albuquerque in 1937 and to California in 1941, living in Delano and Oakland and then in Fowler, where he completed high school in 1951. Writing classes at University of California, Berkeley; San Diego City College, California, A.A. 1956; California College of Arts and Crafts, Oakland, B.A. 1962; California State University, Sacramento, M.A. 1971. **Military Service:** Joined United States Navy; served on minesweeper during Korean War. **Family:** Married; six children. **Career:** Teacher, Wheatland High School, 1962-70; assistant professor of art, California State University, Sacramento, 1970-74, associate professor 1974-81, full professor beginning 1981. Visiting professor, Universidad Anáhuac, Mexico City, Summer 1974, Deguanawidah-Quetzalcóatl University, Davis, California, Summer 1976. Founder, Rebel Chicano Art Front (RCAF), Sacramento, 1970; art exhibits in New York, Mexico City, Havana, Paris; organized musical group Trio Casindio, 1983. Founder, Mexican Concilio for Yuba-Sutter Counties, Marysville, California; board member, Washington Neighborhood Center, Sacramento, 1980-84. **Residence:** Sacramento, California.

PUBLICATIONS

Collections

InFormatioN, 20 Years of Joda. 1992.

Poetry

El sol y los de abajo and Other R.C.A.F. Poems, bound with Alejandro Murguía's *Oración a la mano poderosa.* 1972.

Prose

Pachuco Art, A Historical Perspective. 1977.
Thoughts on la Cultura, the Media, Con Safos and Survival. 1979.
Cultural and Ethnic Awareness Manual for Professionals Working with Mexican-American Migrant Families. 1980.

Other

"Portfolio 5" (black and white reproductions of eight paintings plus one poem, "I Paint Because") in *El Grito,* Spring 1969.

Recordings: *Casindio: Chicano Music All Day,* 1985.

*

Bibliography: *Chicano Perspectives in Literature: A Critical and Annotated Bibliography* by Francisco A. Lomelí and Donaldo W. Urioste, 1976; *Comprehensive Annotated Bibliography of Chicano Art, 1965-1981* by Shifra M. Goldman and Tomás Ybarra-Frausto, 1985.

Critical Studies: "Art in the Barrio: One Man's Commitment" by Sharon MacLatchie in *La Luz,* December 1974; "Art in Montoya's Resonant Valley" by Robert G. Lint in *La Luz,* March-April 1975; "Linguistic Structures in José Montoya's 'El Louie'" by Ignacio Orlando Trujillo in *Modern Chicano Writers* edited by Joseph Sommers and Tomás Ybarra-Frausto, 1979; interview in *Chicano Authors: Inquiry by Interview,* 1980, and "José Montoya's 'El Louie,'" *Chicano Poetry, A Response to Chaos,* 1982, both by Juan Bruce-Novoa; "Voces Chicanas: José Montoya" (videocassette), 1981; interview in *Partial Autobiographies: Interviews with Twenty Chicano Poets* edited by Wolfgang Binder, 1985; "Towards a Chicano Poetics: The Making of the Chicano Subject, 1969-1982" by Jose David Saldivar in *Confluencia,* Spring 1986; in *Four Trails to Valor* by Dorothy Cave, 1997.

*   *   *

José Montoya, poet and artist, began to write early in life, but it was not until 1969 that his first poems appeared in print. As reported by Juan Bruce-Novoa in his *Chicano Authors: Inquiry by Interview,* Montoya met Octavio Romano, the editor of *El Grito,* in 1968 at a Chicano art exhibit in San Francisco. There Romano mentioned that he "had heard that I wrote poetry, and he asked me for some for *El Grito.* He liked it and decided to hold it for *El Espejo,* the anthology. That's how I first got into print. *Espejo* came out and I started to be known, give readings and all that. But I had been writing for a long time before then."

Montoya has said that his writing has been influenced mostly by American authors. When he was in the Navy he read **John Steinbeck**'s *Tortilla Flat,* a novel that left him angered. But later, while at San Diego City College, he discovered some of Steinbeck's other works and was attracted by his style. The *El Espejo* poems, however, were written under the influence of **Walt Whitman**. In his interview with Wolfgang Binder in *Partial Autobiographies,* Montoya said that Whitman was the first poet to "to show me that you did not have to rhyme and meter, and I really, really liked him." The poem he dedicated to him, "Pobre viejo Walt Whitman" (Poor Old Walt Whitman)—the first of the nine appearing in *El Espejo/The Mirror* in 1969—was written at a time when Montoya was disillusioned with Whitman the man and his ideology, and therefore the poem reflects not admiration for Whitman, but "a lot of anger, a lot of anger."

At that time, Montoya was also very much attracted by another American poet, **William Carlos Williams**, whose works he had read at Berkeley. He told Bruce-Novoa: "The one I could relate to most was William Carlos Williams. I liked the way he wrote, so I made an effort to find his work." He also read the poetry of the beat poets, with whom he sympathized. However, he says, "They were so far out that it took the works of **Eliot** and **Pound** as well as Whitman and Williams to get me to accept their stuff early on. Now I consider them to have been an influence—especially Snyder and Ginsberg." At that time he also read French authors, among them Rimbaud, who impressed Montoya with his rebelliousness, and Camus's *The Myth of Sisyphus,* which to him became a symbol for the struggle of the Chicanos. "I thought that the Chicano really knew how to push that rock up there and let it roll down and enjoy the trip. The dealing with the search became, at that time in my life, very real."

Also included in *El Espejo* was one of Montoya's best known poems, "La Jefita" (Our Mother; literally, "The Little Boss"), in which he recreates the image of a representative Chicano mother as the master in her own house, striving to keep the household going and the family together. This image is vividly rendered by the use of onomatopoeic verses reflecting the never ending activities of the hard-working jefita. The use of English and Spanish in the same verse, a technique at which Montoya is a master, is quite effective in this poem:

When I remember the campos [fields]
Y las noches [and the nights] and the sounds

In "Los vatos" (The Dudes), also appearing in *El Espejo,* Montoya for the first time introduces a pachuco, a popular character in Chicano society of the late thirties, forties and fifties which later was to be the subject of his most famous poem, "El Louie." The most striking formal characteristics of the poem "Los vatos" are the longer verse form; the prose introduction (*"Back in the early fifties el Chonito and I were on the way to the bote [jail] when we heard the following dialogue"*); and the dramatic narrative structure: *"Below I sing of an unfortunate act of that epoch."*

"El Louie," Montoya's most successful poem, appeared in 1970—a year after "Los vatos"—in an obscure Oakland, California, periodical, *Rascatripas,* but was popularized in 1972 by Joseph Sommers and others in their anthology, *Chicano Literature: Text and Context.* Since that publication, the poem has been widely anthologized and analyzed. When Binder asked Montoya "How can you write about *pachucos,* you were too young," he replied, "Well, I was not writing about *pachucos.* I was writing about

'*Louie*,' and I was writing about '*Los vatos*.'" That statement underlines the main characteristic of Montoya's poetry: he writes about what he has experienced. "I can only write what I feel and have lived," he said in the Binder interviewer. He had known Louie, who was a *vato* from Fowler, California, named Louie Rodríguez. In the late sixties Montoya, as a poet, underwent a change. He decided to abandon models offered by Whitman and other learned poets and write in a popular vein, more like the beat poets, making a more extensive use of Spanish and the language of the Chicano people and giving more importance to social issues. The result was the poetry included in his first published book, *El sol y los de abajo* (The Sun and the Underdogs), a collection of twenty-four poems (three of them entirely in Spanish) which appeared in 1972. The tone of the seven-part title poem is characteristic of the rest of the poems in this collection, in which Montoya recreates a Chicano world from the perspective of an underdog, a person trying to find a way out of his miserable condition.

Twenty years were to pass before Montoya could collect all the poems he had written and publish them in a single volume, *InFormatioN, 20 Years of Joda,* a book also containing three portfolios of his own drawings. For the first time, the reader has the opportunity to observe Montoya's development as a poet, since the compositions appear in chronological order according to the date of publication or composition, from 1969 to 1989. Outstanding are those poems in which Montoya gives a voice to the downtrodden, presenting their plight in their own caló (barrio dialect), but without forgetting to express an underlying ray of hope.

As a graphic artist, Montoya has been influenced by the Mexican engraver José Guadalupe Posada, as well as the muralists Diego Rivera, José Clemente Orozco, and Alfaro Siqueiros. In 1975, with the collaboration of John M. Carrillo, Montoya wrote an unpublished paper about Posada in which he includes a comparative analysis of his work and that of the Chicano art movement, as well as some notes about the influence of Posada's calaveras (Day of the Dead cartoons) on Chicano art. In the poems and drawings collected in *InFormatioN,* however, it can be seen that Montoya is not a slavish imitator of the Mexican masters. In the poem "I paint because" he states his desire to innovate when he says

> I paint because I love Orozco and Shan.
> I paint to destroy Orozco and Shan.

In his paintings, as in his poetry, Montoya's subject matter is drawn from life in the barrio and from the experiences of the Chicano people in their struggle for a better life. His close association with the community has not only inspired him to express with pen and brush the sufferings and aspirations of the people he loves and knows so well, but also to transform this expression into action through his humanitarian service to the community.

—Luis Leal

MOODY, William Vaughn

Born: Spencer, Indiana, 8 July 1869. **Education:** New Albany High School, Indiana, graduated 1885; Riverview Academy, Poughkeepsie, New York, 1887-89; Harvard University, Cambridge, Massachusetts (editor, *Harvard Monthly*), 1889-94, A.B. 1893, A.M. 1894. **Family:** Married Harriet Tilden Brainard in

1909. **Career:** High school teacher, Corydon Pike, 1886, and Spencer, 1886-89, Indiana; instructor in English, Harvard University and Radcliffe College, Cambridge, Massachusetts, 1894-95; instructor in English and rhetoric, 1895-99, and non-teaching assistant professor of English, 1901-08, University of Chicago; full-time writer after 1908. **Awards:** Litt.D.: Yale University, New Haven, Connecticut, 1908. **Member:** American Academy, 1908. **Died:** 17 October 1910.

PUBLICATIONS

Collections

Selected Poems, edited by Robert Morss Lovett. 1931.

Plays

The Masque of Judgment: A Masque-Drama. 1900.
The Fire-Bringer. 1904.
The Great Divide (as *A Sabine Woman,* produced 1906; revised version, as *The Great Divide,* produced 1906). 1909.
The Faith Healer. 1909; revised version (produced 1910), 1910.

Poetry

Poems. 1901; as *Gloucester Moors and Other Poems,* 1909.

Other

A History of English Literature, with Robert Morss Lovett. 1902; revised edition, 1918; simplified edition, as *A First View of English Literature,* 1905; as *A First View of English and American Literature,* 1909.
Poems and Plays, edited by John M. Manly. 2 vols., 1912.
Some Letters, edited by Daniel Gregory Mason. 1913.
Letters to Harriet, edited by Percy MacKaye. 1935.

Editor, *The Pilgrim's Progress,* by Bunyan. 1897.
Editor, *The Rime of the Ancient Mariner by Coleridge and The Vision of Sir Launfal by Lowell.* 1898.
Editor, *The Lady of the Lake,* by Scott. 1899.
Editor, with Wilfred Wesley Cressy, *The Iliad of Homer,* books 1, 6, 22, 24, translated by Alexander Pope. 1899.
Editor, *The Complete Poetical Works of Milton.* 1899.
Editor, with George Cabot Lodge and John Ellerton Lodge, *The Poems of Trumbull Stickney.* 1905.
Editor, *Selections from De Quincey.* 1909.

*

Bibliography: in *Bibliography of American Literature* by Jacob Blanck, 1973.

Critical Studies: *Moody: A Study* by David D. Henry, 1934; *Moody* by Martin Halpern, 1964; *Estranging Dawn: The Life and Works of Moody* by Maurice F. Brown, 1973; in *American Playwrights, 1880-1945: A Research and Production Sourcebook* edited by William W. Demastes, 1995.

*　　*　　*

After William Vaughn Moody's early death, **Edwin Arlington Robinson**, his close friend and literary ally, wrote Harriet Moody, "Thank God he lived to do his work—or enough of it to place him among the immortals." While that assessment late seemed exaggerated, Moody's work, as a scholar, poet, and dramatist, is sufficient to give him a firm place in literary history. As the author of *The Great Divide,* he is considered the first playwright to provide the American stage with a serious, realistic, modern drama, thus ushering in the new age in American theater. Critics have speculated that had he lived to realize his full potential, his only rival would have been **Eugene O'Neill**.

Martin Halpern, in his critical biography of Moody, has suggested that his literary career falls into two periods: from 1890 until the publication of *The Masque of Judgment and Poems,* in 1900 and 1901 respectively, his primary interest was poetry; from then until his final illness debilitated him in 1909 he worked consciously as a practicing dramatist. Although *The Masque of Judgment* is the first part of a projected dramatic trilogy, it is a closet drama in verse. And while two of the four plays he wrote during the last decade of his life are also verse dramas, they were intended for the stage.

Moody's poems have few admirers in the late twentieth century, largely because they seem imitative of the English romantics in inflated diction and archaic subject matter. Some of his poems are innovative, however, notably his poems that involve social commentary or those that are conscious attempts to use the vernacular. "On a Soldier Fallen in the Philippines," for instance, is an ironic attack on American foreign policy. Perhaps his most celebrated poem has become "The Menagerie," a comic soliloquy in which the inebriated speaker speculates on how the animals in the zoo regard the putative fulfillment of the evolutionary process, man. The psychologically honest "The Daguerreotype," a tribute to his mother, and the ambiguous "I Am the Woman" are two disparate treatments of the symbolic and psychic implications of the feminine principle, an interest that informs "The Death of Eve." Generally his poems, like his poetic trilogy, are full of high seriousness, frequently devolving upon theological, especially eschatological, matters.

Moody's two prose plays successfully combine realistic and symbolic dramatic techniques. Originally produced as *A Sabine Woman* in Chicago, *The Great Divide* was a commercial as well as a critical success, playing for two years in New York. The play deals with the conflicting cultures of the eastern and western United States, symbolized by the abduction and eventual marriage of a woman from Massachusetts to a rough but honest man from Arizona. The less well-received *The Faith Healer* deals with the conflict between human and spiritual passions; the conflict is resolved when the protagonist discovers that his religious work is effective only when he has accepted human love.

Although *The Fire-Bringer,* Moody's verse play based on the Prometheus legend, and the fragment, *The Death of Eve,* were not produced commercially, critics have found them to be more artistically interesting than the prose plays. Moody was able to complete only one act of *The Death of Eve,* but the poem by the same title and his recorded plans for the play suggest that with it he might have achieved his dream of making verse drama a viable theatrical experience. Even so, his contribution to American drama and poetry is considerable.

—Nancy Carol Joyner

MOORE, Marianne (Craig)

Born: Kirkwood, Missouri, 15 November 1887. **Education:** Metzger Institute, Carlisle, Pennsylvania, 1896-1905; Bryn Mawr College, Pennsylvania, 1905-09, A.B. 1909; Carlisle Commercial College, Pennsylvania, 1909-10, diploma 1910. **Career:** Head of the Commercial Studies Department, U.S. Industrial Indian School, Carlisle, 1911-15; lived in Chatham, New Jersey, 1916-17; private tutor and secretary, New York, 1918-21; part-time librarian, Hudson Park Branch of New York Public Library, 1921-25; acting editor, 1925, and editor, 1926-29, *The Dial,* New York; lived in Brooklyn, 1929-65, and Manhattan after 1966; teacher, Cummington School, Massachusetts, 1942; visiting lecturer, Bryn Mawr College, 1953; Ewing Lecturer, University of California, 1956. **Awards:** Hartsock Memorial prize, 1935; Shelley Memorial award, 1941; Harriet Monroe Poetry award, 1944; Guggenheim fellowship, 1945; American Academy grant, 1946, and Gold Medal, 1953; Pulitzer prize, 1952; National Book award, 1952; Bollingen prize, 1953; Poetry Society of America Gold Medal, 1960, 1967; Brandeis University Creative Arts award, 1962; Academy of American Poets fellowship, 1965; MacDowell Medal, 1967; National Medal for Literature, 1968. Litt.D.: Wilson College, Chambersburg, Pennsylvania, 1949; Mount Holyoke College, South Hadley, Massachusetts, 1950; Rochester University, Rochester, New York, 1951; Dickinson College, Carlisle, 1952; Rutgers University. New Brunswick, New Jersey, 1955; New York University, 1967; St. John's University, Jamaica, New York, 1968; Princeton University, New Jersey, 1968; Harvard University, Cambridge, Massachusetts, 1969. L.H.D.: Smith College, Northampton, Massachusetts, 1950; Pratt Institute, Brooklyn, 1958. D.Litt.: Washington University, St. Louis, 1967. **Member:** American Academy, 1955. **Died:** 5 February 1972.

PUBLICATIONS

Collections

Complete Prose, edited by Patricia C. Willis. 1986.
Complete Poems. 1994.

Poetry

Poems. 1921.
Marriage. 1923.
Observations. 1924; revised edition, 1925.
Selected Poems. 1935.
The Pangolin and Other Verse. 1936.
What Are Years. 1941.
Nevertheless. 1944.
Collected Poems. 1951.
Like a Bulwark. 1956.
O to Be a Dragon. 1959.
Eight Poems. 1962.
The Arctic Ox. 1964.
Tell Me, Tell Me: Granite, Steele, and Other Topics. 1966.
The Complete Poems. 1967; revised edition, 1981.
Selected Poems. 1969.
Unfinished Poems. 1972.

Play

The Absentee, from a story by Maria Edgeworth. 1962.

Other

Predilections. 1955.
Idiosyncrasy and Technique: Two Lectures. 1958.
Letters from and to the Ford Motor Company, with David Wallace. 1958.
A Moore Reader. 1961.
Dress and Kindred Subjects. 1965.
Poetry and Criticism. 1965.
Answers to Some Questions Posed by Howard Nemerov (essay). 1982.
The Selected Letters of Marianne Moore. 1998.

Translator, with Elizabeth Mayer, *Rock Crystal: A Christmas Tale,* by Adalbert Stifter. 1945; revised edition, 1965.
Translator, *The Fables of La Fontaine.* 1954; *Selected Fables,* 1955.
Translator, *Puss in Boots, The Sleeping Beauty and Cinderella: A Retelling of Three Classic Fairy Tales,* by Charles Perrault. 1963.

*

Bibliography: *Moore: A Descriptive Bibliography.* 1977, and *Moore: A Reference Guide,* 1978, both by Craig S. Abbott.

Critical Studies: *The Achievement of Moore: A Biography 1907-1957* by Eugene P. Sheehy and Kenneth A. Lohf, 1958; *Moore* by Bernard F. Engel, 1964; *Moore* by Jean Garrigue, 1965; *Moore: An Introduction to the Poetry* by George W. Nitchie, 1969; *Moore* by Sister Mary Therese, 1969; *Moore: A Collection of Critical Essays* edited by Charles Tomlinson, 1969; *Moore: The Cage and the Animal* by Donald Hall, 1970; *Moore: Poet of Affection* by Pamela White Hadas, 1977; *Moore: The Poet's Advance* by Laurence Stapleton, 1978; *Moore: Imaginary Possessions* by Bonnie Costello, 1981; *Moore* by Elizabeth Phillips, 1982; *Reading and Writing Nature: The Poetry of Robert Frost, Wallace Stevens, Marianne Moore, and Elizabeth Bishop* by Guy Rotella, 1991; *Illusion Is More Precise Than Precision: The Poetry of Marianne Moore* by Darlene Williams Erickson, 1992; *The Web of Friendship: Marianne Moore and Wallace Stevens* by Robin G. Schulze, 1995; *Marianne Moore: Questions of Authority* by Cristanne Miller, 1995; *Marianne Moore and the Visual Arts: Prismatic Color* by Linda Leavell, 1995; *Modernism and the Other in Stevens, Frost, and Moore* by Andrew M. Lakritz, 1996; *Cultural Critique and Abstraction: Marianne Moore and the Avante-garde* by Elizabeth W. Joyce, 1998.

*   *   *

Marianne Moore seems the best woman poet to have written in the United States during the twentieth century. Her poetry is richer and more inclusive than that of **H.D.** or of **Elizabeth Bishop**, to name two who resemble her in their fastidious interest in natural history—Moore's predilection and habitual material. Herself of the modernist generation of **Stevens**, **Williams**, **Pound**, and **Eliot**, she knew Williams, Pound, and H.D. in her days at Bryn Mawr College; and in the 1920s she was associated with the New York magazine *The Dial,* becoming its editor from 1926 to 1929.

Like Williams, she was a naturalist in her subject-matter, and would not have disagreed with Pound's program for Imagism. Many of the American modernist poets learned to purge their beams at her empirical eye. Yet Eliot, who could not have accepted Williams's dictum "No ideas but in things," also admired Moore's poetry for the distinction of its language. In his preface to her *Selected Poems,* he judged that she was "one of those few who have done the language some service in my lifetime."

Moore appears at first an idiosyncratic writer. She chooses odd subjects and sees them from odd angles; she is miscellaneous in her subject matter and unpredictable in her reflections; she writes in a chopped prose in lines of spectacular irregularity, but with metrical distinctness and, surprisingly often, rhyme. Yet her style, for all its asymmetry, is rapid, clear, unself-concerned, flexible, and accurate, and her work gradually discloses her exceptional sanity, intelligence, and imaginative depth. Unmistakably modern, she has no modernist formlessness; curious and precise, she is too brave in her vision to be an old maid. Some of these paradoxical qualities appear in her openings, which demand attention by their directness, as in "The Steeple-Jack":

> Dürer would have seen a reason for living
> in a town like this, with eight stranded whales
> to look at; with the sweet sea air coming into your house
> on a fine day, from water etched
> with waves as formal as the scales
> on a fish.

or "Silence":

> My father used to say,
> "Superior people never make long visits,
> have to be shown Longfellow's grave
> or the glass flowers at Harvard.
> Self-reliant like the cat—
> that takes its prey to privacy,
> the mouse's limp tail hanging like a shoelace from its mouth—
> they sometimes enjoy solitude . .

or "To a Snail":

> If "compression is the first grace of style,"
> you have it. Contractility is a virtue
> as modesty is a virtue.

or "Poetry":

> I, too, dislike it.
> Reading it, however, with a perfect contempt for it, one discovers in
> it, after all, a place for the genuine.

This last is a complete poem, and unusually brief, although most of her poems are meditations of this characteristic briskness. "The Steeple-Jack" is a classic among her longer poems, as is "A Grave," which begins:

> Man looking into the sea,
> taking the view from those who have as much right to it as

you have to it yourself,
it is human nature to stand in the middle of a thing, but
you cannot
stand in the middle of this;
the sea has nothing to give but a well excavated grave.

The resonance of that last line states openly, with "an elegance of which the source is not bravado," the essential seriousness that Moore often took pains to bury deep in her bright-eyed concern with the external world, of which she was such a connoisseur. Like La Fontaine, whose Fables she translated, she was fundamentally a humane moralist, however passionate and fine her observation of animals, baseball players, and nature's remoter aspects; and she was fundamentally serious despite her turn for the smacking epigram.

Her career illuminated the American scene for an exceptionally long time, and to increasing recognition. Her powers did not diminish, but her idiosyncrasy and allusiveness intensified. Thoroughly American and modern, she demonstrated the possibility of a highly civilized and eclectic mind operating with discrimination and unsentimental enjoyment on the premise basic to so much modern American poetry, that everything that is human is material for poetry. "Whatever it is, let it be without / affectation" ("Love in America").

—M.J. Alexander

See the essay on "Poetry."

MORALES, Alejandro

Born: In the Simons Brick Company barrio in Montebello, California, 14 October 1944 of Mexican immigrant parents. **Education:** Simons and another local elementary school, Montebello Junior High School and Montebello High School; California State University at Los Angeles, 1963-67, B.A. 1967; Rutgers University, New Brunswick, New Jersey, 1969-75, M.A. 1971, Ph.D. 1975. **Family:** Married Helen Rohde in 1967; one son and one daughter. **Career:** Taught Spanish at Claremont High School, California 1968-69; teaching assistant, 1969-72, member of public relations staff of the E.O.P. Program, 1971-72, secretary to director of Junior Year Abroad in Mexico program, 1973-74, Rutgers University; assistant professor in department of Spanish and Portuguese, 1974-80, associate professor, 1980-84, professor, beginning 1984, University of California at Irvine; novelist; essayist; critic; lecturer; book reviewer for the *Los Angeles Times*. Has traveled extensively in Mexico. **Awards:** Ford Foundation fellowship, 1972-73; ITT International fellowship, 1973-74; Mexica Press contest finalist for *Caras viejas y vino nuevo*, 1975; Mellon Foundation fellowship; National Endowment for the Arts grant; California Arts Council grant; funding from UC-MEXUS. **Residence:** Santa Ana, California.

PUBLICATIONS

Novels

Caras viejas y vino nuevo. 1975; English translation as *Old Faces and New Wine* by Max Martínez, 1981.

La verdad sin voz (Spanish). 1979; English translation as *Death of an Anglo* by Judith Ginsberg, 1988.
Reto en el paraíso (bilingual). 1983; French translation, 1992; all-Spanish translation, 1993.
The Brick People. 1988.
The Rag Doll Plagues. 1992; Dutch translation as *Plager,* 1993.
Barrio on the Edge=Caras viejas y vino nuevo. 1998.

Other

Editor, with others, *Into the Storm: A Vietnam Odyssey*. 1989.

*

Bibliography: "Alejandro Morales" by Marvin A. Lewis, in *Dictionary of Literary Biography: Chicano Writers,* 1989.

Critical Studies: "*Caras viejas y vino nuevo:* Reverse Journey through a Disintegrating Barrio" by Erlinda Gonzales-Berry, in *Latin American Literary Review,* 1979; interview (Spanish) with José Monleón, in *Maize,* 1980-81; *La novela chicana escrita en español: Cinco autores comprometidos* by Salvador Rodríguez del Pino, 1982; "*Caras viejas y vino nuevo,* la tragedia de los barrios" by Willy O. Muñoz, in *Aztlán,* 1984; "State of Siege in *Old Faces and New Wine*" by Francisco A. Lomelí, in *Missions in Conflict: Essays on U.S.-Mexico Relations and Chicano Culture,* 1986; *Alejandro Morales: Fiction Past, Present, Future Perfect* edited by José Antonio, 1996; *Identities on the Margin: Perspectives on Cisneros, Conde, Crosthwaite, and Morales* (dissertation) by Jeffrey Norman Lamb, 1997.

* * *

Alejandro D. Morales has developed into one of the leading Chicano novelists due to his breadth and scope. From masterful depiction of a hard-core *barrio* to historically grounded narratives, he has explored timeless issues within a futuristic construct, and describes his work as "culturally multidimensional." His forte is his focus on craft, that is, the writing of a novel as a continuous experiment with language, structure, time, and theme. Besides delving into character and circumstance, and how these are ultimately conditioned by historical forces, his works become self-referential or self-conscious acts of writing. They serve to fill some of the gaps of a people who have been regarded as ahistorical or insignificant in a hostile social context. The result is a dynamic and internal view of Chicanos who have indeed played a key role in America's development, particularly in the Southwest.

Alejandro Morales first entered the Chicano literary scene in 1975 with a provocative and controversial portrayal of a hard-core *barrio* in *Caras viejas y vino nuevo* (*Old Faces and New Wine*). It reflects an attitude he later revealed in an interview: "Writing [is] my way out of a mess." The work defied the sensibilities of a Chicano nationalism that tended to idealize the *barrio*. Chicanos at the time were reclaiming a voice, a language and a place, but his work suggested that deeper questions had to be addressed. Romanticizing a people's condition was for him dishonest and unrealistic, or at least inadequate. Instead, he opted for a graphic depiction of a state of dehumanization marked by drugs, alcohol, sex, social degeneration and moral decay. Here characters age early in a sort of war zone that reduces them to creatures of instinct, immediate gratification, and apocalyptic tendencies. The novel's backdrop, ironically, is Christmas, a time of sharing and togetherness. What prevails is an acute violence that penetrates the very soul of the characters, leaving them defenseless and mutilated. Action, limited and stagnant, is confined by a hallucinogenic world where reality is either distorted or shaped by stimulants. Narrated in reverse order, the sensation is that the protagonist, Mateo, must seek answers from within as a way of conquering his demons. His *barrio* counterpart, Julian, lives on a collision course. Mateo aspires to be an example and guide for others out of this alienating environment, but dies of leukemia, succumbing to the forces of his environment.

Caras viejas y vino nuevo's experimental virtuosity entails a truncated language of fragmented meanings that pierce logic and rationality. The result is a deliberately convoluted style in Spanish that demands careful examination for its mode of capturing a social reality, much like a distorting camera. Confusion in the text reigns where narrators are at times unclear and perspectives blend into some ritualistic mass of incoherence. Here, people matter little and objects appear as if dismembered. The result is a tense atmosphere about to explode like a time-bomb, unveiling the underside of an American urban reality that is generally ignored and forgotten, thus forging a view of a hard-core existence where fate is social conditioning. Although not claiming the stance of a social protest narrative, *Caras viejas y vino nuevo* does present a troubling picture of a place in dire need of change. Morales dedicates the novel to his *barrio,* which he states "will be with me forever."

Morales' shattering bluntness did not create easy outlets for his works, forcing him to seek the publication of his first two works with Joaquín Mortiz in Mexico City. His second work, *La verdad sin voz* (*Truth without a Voice*), breaks new ground by concentrating on an Anglo doctor named Michael Logan, whose social idealism translates into action benefiting the downtrodden and disenfranchised. However, another story, that of Professor Morenito, who struggles against institutionalized racism and the traps of the tenure process, mirrors Logan's from a totally divergent perspective. *La verdad sin voz,* then, is about two characters who exist apart and marginalized from their respective social milieu. Much of the internal tension stems from these two stories that appear, on the surface, to have little contact or commonality, and from a less developed third story about Mexico and its contemporary Third world situation of social unrest, espionage, drug trafficking, and political intrigue. Dr. Logan seems consequential due to his convictions until dying at the hands of an Anglo policeman, Pistola Gorda; meanwhile, Morenito experiences humiliation in his academic environment but regains determination and becomes a writer. The theme revolves around alienation versus social commitment, but the work is also about what generates a novel. Much like the magician madman Melquiades in the Colombian author García Márquez's *Cien Años de Soledad* (*A Hundred Years of Solitude*), Morenito initiates the writing process at the end that will become the novel we just read, bringing to mind the clever manipulations of space and time in the Latin American New Novel. Therefore, the three stories have merged to give birth to a novel thanks to the creative process.

Morales is known for producing complex novels of intertwined and echoing events. Whereas *Caras viejas y vino nuevo* focuses on language and tone, *La verdad sin voz* explores contrasting situations. His third and most ambitious novel, *Reto en el paraíso* (*Defiance in Paradise*), shuffles numerous stories like a gigantic deck of cards, creating an epic novel in the form of a kaleidoscope. Spanning over four generations of the Coronel family, *Reto en el*

paraíso might be regarded as various novels in one given its multilayered storylines: historical (counterpoints patriarch Antonio Francisco Coronel with landgrabber James Lifford), existential (Dennis Berreyesa Coronel's identity search), social (an ambiance of conflict and racism), magical realism (the incredible and ordinary are juxtaposed) and mythic (Garden of Eden contrasted with Aztlán, or the Chicano homeland). These narratives weave a rich tapestry where the past and present interconnect, social groups (Mexicans and Anglos) clash, world views conflict, and individuals either become entrenched in their positions or begin to blur their differences. The novel offers historical breadth as well as unveiling personal struggles, such as Dennis' concept of himself, particularly in working as an architect for the Lifford Company that usurped his ancestors' land more than one hundred years ago. The central moral conflict emerges when he enjoys the material gains of a comfortable lifestyle while ignoring his complicity in upholding a questionable enterprise.

Reto en el paraíso aims to make a number of artistic and philosophical points. In part it traces the *Californios'* downfall, but it also shows how their descendants have been coopted without demanding historical vindication. On another level, the novel serves as a depository for Antonio Francisco Coronel's manuscript of the same name. In this way, his literary attempt lives on, functioning much like a conscience and becoming a full-fledged novel, thanks in part to the unwilling modern partner, Dennis, who becomes the convergent point between past and present. *Reto en el paraíso* then is as much about greed and ethics as it is a multi-stranded story narrated in two languages, and the world views those imply. Much like García Márquez's *Cien Años de Soledad* in its emphasis on a family's curse related to incest, genealogical duplications through names, history repeating itself, and magical realism (for example, a rain of butterflies), and Peruvian author Mario Vargas Llosa's *Guerra del fin del mundo* (*War of the End of the World*) and *Casa verde* (*Green House*) for the simultaneity of actions, shifting points of view, and sense of historicity, Morales creates a work that retells and reinvents history for the sake of delving into what might have been. Like these two authors and the Mexican writer Carlos Fuentes, Morales manages to replace history with myth, thereby demystifying the fabricated "history" of what became Southern California.

In *The Brick People* (1988) Morales recreates a specific place, the Simons *barrio* in the Los Angeles area, blending oral history and sociological biography with fiction, and including elements of magical realism. As a brick factory barrio, Simons is presented as a "benevolent" oasis where a working-class people experience material gains and maintain a strong sense of place, but sacrifice their spiritual contentment and freedom. There is a price to pay. Morales, contrasting the Revueltas and Simons families, interprets the official history of a specific locale, rewriting and replacing it with a version viable to those written out of it. In doing so, Morales undermines the ahistorical version of this people's existence while offering a narrative framework for better understanding their life experience.

Morales' interest in expanding Chicano fictional projects is noteworthy. Most of his works are well grounded in elements of fact, but another strong inclination is experimentation, particularly with perspective and language. *The Rag Doll Plagues* (1992) breaks down barriers in Chicano writing while emphasizing transculturation or the convergence of cultures. The novel's eeriness is partly attributed to its grotesque descriptions of incredible diseases of uncontainable proportions during three distinct eras: the end of eighteenth-century Mexico, the end of twentieth-century Southern California, and the latter part of the twenty-first century in a region called Lamex (a combination of the United States and Mexico). The contrasts are accentuated in terms of social evolution—from primitive to modern to futuristic—but they are also neutralized by the presence of mysterious plagues that reappear in cycles. In each case, humanity is reduced to its fragile condition of limitations and impotence while groping for answers.

As in other works by Morales, a novel-within-a-novel construct (an eighteenth-century doctor's manuscript) drives the narrative full circle. This text about the first plague serves as the cornerstone for subsequent medical inquiries on potential cures. Divided into three books, the novel repeats various elements: two spirits named Papa Damian and Gregorio inspire and sometimes instruct the protagonist in each respective section, who as a descendant and doctor feels predestined to act to save lives; the narrator-protagonists' names are always a variant of Gregory; under different names—La Mona, Aids, Blue Buster—the diseases mystify and obsess their contemporaries. Magical realism qualities are interspersed to balance the macabre qualities of the catastrophes. *The Rag Doll Plagues* marks a significant turn to new thematics in Chicano fiction.

Morales has a reputation of creating distinctive works that offer a totalizing view of a segment of American society as it relates to Chicanos, without limiting their perspective to them. His novels reflect serious experiments with craft as well as attempts to reinterpret official historical accounts by highlighting Chicano presence as a visible people with deep roots in the United States. In this way, Morales is able to reestablish Chicanos as a natural part of the landscape of American letters.

—Francisco A. Lomelí

MORLEY, Christopher (Darlington)

Born: Haverford, Pennsylvania, 5 May 1890. **Education:** Haverford College, 1906-10, B.A. 1910; New College, Oxford (Rhodes Scholar), 1910-13. **Family:** Married Helen Booth Fairchild in 1914; one son and three daughters. **Career:** Staff member, Doubleday, Page and Company, publishers, New York, 1913-17, *Ladies Home Journal*, New York, 1917-18, Philadelphia *Evening Public Ledger*, 1918-20, and New York *Evening Post*, 1920-23; a founder, 1924, and columnist ("The Bowling Green"), 1924-41, *Saturday Review of Literature*, New York. **Awards:** D.Litt.: Haverford College, 1933. **Member:** American Academy. **Died:** 28 March 1957.

PUBLICATIONS

Collections

Bright Cages: Selected Poems and Translations from the Chinese, edited by John Bracker. 1965.
Christopher Morley, Two Complete Novels. 1996.

Fiction

Parnassus on Wheels. 1917.

In the Sweet Dry and Dry, with Bart Haley. 1919.
The Haunted Bookshop. 1919.
Kathleen. 1920.
Tales from a Rolltop Desk. 1921.
Where the Blue Begins. 1922.
Pandora Lifts the Lid, with Don Marquis. 1924.
Thunder on the Left. 1925.
Pleased to Meet You. 1927.
The Arrow. 1927; augmented edition, as *The Arrow and Two Other Stories,* 1927.
Rudolph and Amina; or, the Black Crook. 1930.
Human Being. 1932.
Swiss Family Manhattan. 1932.
The Trojan Horse. 1937.
Kitty Foyle. 1939.
Thorofare. 1942.
The Man Who Made Friends with Himself. 1949.

Plays

Thursday Evening (produced 1921). 1922.
Rehearsal. 1922.
One Act Plays (includes *Thursday Evening, Rehearsal, Bedroom Suite, On the Shelf Wilt, East of Eden*). 1924.
Where the Blue Begins, with E.S. Colling. 1925.
Good Theatre. 1926.
Really, My Dear. . . . 1928.
In Modern Dress. 1929.
The Blue and the Gray; or, War Is Hell, from the play *Allatoona* by Judson Kilpatrick and J. Owen Moore. 1930.
The Rag-Picker of Paris; or, The Modest Modiste, from the play by Edward Stirling. 1937.
Soft Shoulders (produced 1940).
The Trojan Horse. 1941.

Screenplay: *You Will Remember,* with Lydia Hayward and Sewell Stokes, 1941.

Poetry

The Eighth Sin. 1912.
Songs for a Little House. 1917.
The Rocking Horse. 1919.
Hide and Seek. 1920.
Chimneysmoke. 1921.
Translations from the Chinese. 1922.
Parsons' Pleasure. 1923.
Toulemonde. 1928.
Poems. 1929.
Mandarin in Manhattan: Further Translations from the Chinese. 1933.
The Apologia of the Ampersand. 1936.
Footnotes for a Centennial. 1936.
The Middle Kingdom: Poems 1929-1944. 1944.
Spirit Level and Other Poems. 1946.
The Old Mandarin: More Translations from the Chinese. 1947.
Poetry Package, with William Rose Benet. 1950.
The Ballad of New York, New York, and Other Poems 1930-1950. 1950.
A Pride of Sonnets. 1951.
Gentlemen's Relish. 1955.

Other

Shandygaff. 1918.
Mince Pie: Adventures on the Sunny Side of Grub Street. 1919.
Travels in Philadelphia. 1920.
Pipefuls (essays). 1920.
Plum Pudding. 1921.
An Apology for Boccaccio. 1923.
Conrad and the Reporters. 1923.
Inward Ho! 1923.
The Powder of Sympathy. 1923.
Outward Bound. 1924.
Religio Journalistici. 1924.
Hostages to Fortune (miscellany). 1925.
Forty-four Essays. 1925; as *Safety Pins and Other Essays,* 1925.
Paumanok. 1926.
The Romany Stain. 1926.
I Know a Secret (for children). 1927.
The Case of Bouck White. 1927.
(Works). 12 vols., 1927.
The Tree That Didn't Get Trimmed. 1927.
Essays. 1928.
A Letter to Leonora. 1928.
Off the Deep End. 1928.
A Ride in the Cab of the Twentieth Century Limited. 1928.
The House of Dooner, with T. A. Daly. 1928.
The Worst Christmas Story. 1928.
Seacoast of Bohemia. 1929.
The Goldfish under the Ice (for children). 1930.
Apologia pro Sua Preoccupatione. 1930.
Born in a Beer Garden; or, She Troupes to Conquer: Sundry Ejaculations, with Ogden Nash and Cleon Throckmorton. 1930.
On the Nose. 1930.
Blythe Mountain, Vermont. 1931.
When We Speak of a Tenth—. 1931.
John Mistletoe (reminiscences). 1931.
Notes on Bermuda. 1931.
Ex Libris Carissimis (lectures). 1932.
Fifth Avenue Bus (miscellany). 1933.
Shakespeare and Hawaii (lectures). 1933.
Internal Revenue (essays). 1933.
"Effendi," Frank Nelson Doubleday 1862-1934. 1934.
Hasta la Vista; or, A Postcard from Peru. 1935.
Old Loopy: A Love Letter for Chicago. 1935.
Rare Books: An Essay. 1935.
Streamlines (essays). 1936.
Morley's Briefcase. 1936.
Morley's Magnum. 1938.
History of an Autumn. 1938.
No Crabb, No Christmas. 1938.
Letters of Askance. 1939.
Another Letter to Lord Chesterfield. 1945.
The Ironing Board (essays). 1949.
Barometers and Bookshops. 1952.
Prefaces without Books: Prefaces and Introductions to Thirty Books, edited by Herman Abromson. 1976.

Editor, *Record of the Class of 1910 of Haverford College.* 1910.
Editor, *American Rhodes Scholars, Oxford 1910-1913.* 1913.
Editor, *The Booksellers' Blue Book.* 2 vols., 1914.
Editor, *Making Books and Magazines.* 1916.

Editor, *Modern Essays.* 2 vols., 1921-24.
Editor, *The Bowling Green: An Anthology of Verse.* 1924.
Editor, *A Book of Days.* 1930.
Editor, *Ex Libris: A Small Anthology.* 1936.
Editor, with Louella D. Everett, *Bartlett's Familiar Quotations,* 11th edition. 1937; 12th edition, 1948.
Editor, *Walt Whitman in Camden: A Selection of Prose from Specimen Days.* 1938.
Editor, *Leaves of Grass,* by Walt Whitman. 1940.
Editor, *Sherlock Holmes and Dr. Watson: A Textbook of Friendship.* 1944.
Editor, *The Best of Don Marquis.* 1946.

Translator, *Two Fables,* by Alfred de Musset and Wilhelm Hauff. 1925.
Translator, *Mar and Moritz,* by Wilhelm Busch. 1932.

*

Bibliography: *A Bibliography of Morley* by Guy R. Lyle and H. Tatnall Brown, Jr., 1952.

Critical Studies: *Morley* by Mark I. Wallach and Jon Bracker, 1976; *Three Hours for Lunch: The Life and Times of Morley* by Helen McK. Oakley, 1976.

*   *   *

Christopher Morley was a distinguished and popular novelist, essayist, and poet whose intense literary passions and promotions, such as his sponsorship of the writings of Joseph Conrad and his organization (with his brothers) of the Baker Street Irregulars, combine with his writings to make him one of the few genuine American "men of letters."

Morley's earliest novels, *Parnassus on Wheels* and *The Haunted Bookshop,* are brief, simple stories of booksellers in World War I America, yet they set the tone for the more sophisticated works to follow, many of which also revolve around characters involved in the literary world. *Where the Blue Begins,* an allegory about the human quest for meaning in life, is written as a dog story and enjoyed considerable success in a children's edition, but is actually a profoundly and successfully serious book. *Thunder on the Left,* which followed, is a thoughtful and controversial fantasy about the problems of children trying to come to terms with adulthood.

Kitty Foyle, Morley's best-selling novel, is an ambitious interior monologue told by a working-class girl from Philadelphia. Kitty is an atypical Morley protagonist, neither intellectual nor literary, yet *Kitty Foyle* represents Morley at the peak of his style. Derived from Morley's experiences with the "new generation" of New York career girls in the 1920s and 1930s, Kitty nonetheless displays a striking degree of individuality. Although *Kitty Foyle* largely abandons Morley's usual "mission" of bringing literature to the common man, it paradoxically comes closest of all of Morley's works to being great literature itself.

Morley's last novel, *The Man Who Made Friends with Himself,* embodies much of what is weakest and strongest in his fiction: it is intensely personal, extravagantly allusive, and rich with quotation. Somewhat autobiographical, it is a complex and demanding book to read, but worth the effort for lovers of prose style.

While Morley is best remembered as a novelist, his frequent and polished essays in the *Saturday Review,* which he helped found in 1920, were perhaps as important in establishing his distinctive reputation among his contemporaries as a "man of letters." Collected into published volumes, such as *Streamlines* and *The Ironing Board,* many of these discuss people, places, and events with literary ties. While most are meant to be informative, Morley's essays always undertake the additional task of entertaining the reader, and are among his most enjoyable works.

Much of Morley's poetry reflects his predominant concern with literature. His earliest poems, however, following his marriage in 1914, are both domestic in subject and sentimental in tone, a blend Morley (with the concurrence of his critics) coined "dishpantheism." Perhaps his most important poetry is an original genre he called "Translations from the Chinese," which Morley first conceived as a burlesque of free verse, but later developed into a shrewd, ironic vehicle for social commentary. These "Translations" are among the most readable works of a writer who, while not of the first rank, was one of his era's most versatile and interesting literary figures.

—Mark I. Wallach

MORRIS, Wright (Marion)

Born: Central City, Nebraska, 6 January 1910. **Education:** Lakeview High School, Chicago; Crane College, Chicago; Pomona College, Claremont, California, 1930-33. **Family:** Married 1) Mary Ellen Finfrock in 1934 (divorced 1961); 2) Josephine Kantor in 1961. **Career:** Lecturer at Haverford College, Pennsylvania, Sarah Lawrence College, Bronxville, New York, and Swarthmore College, Pennsylvania; professor of English, California State University, San Francisco, 1962-75. Also a photographer. **Awards:** Guggenheim fellowship, 1942, 1946, 1954; National Book award, 1957; American Academy grant, 1960; Rockefeller grant, 1967; National Endowment for the Arts fellowship, 1976; Western Literature Association award, 1979; American Book award, 1981; Common Wealth award, 1982; Whiting award, 1985. Honorary degrees: Westminster College, Fulton, Missouri, 1968; University of Nebraska, Lincoln, 1968; Pomona College, 1973. **Member:** American Academy, 1970. **Died:** 1998.

PUBLICATIONS

Fiction

My Uncle Dudley. 1942.
The Man Who Was There. 1945.
The World in the Attic. 1949.
Man and Boy. 1951.
The Works of Love. 1952.
The Deep Sleep. 1953.
The Huge Season. 1954.
The Field of Vision. 1956.
Love among the Cannibals. 1957.
Ceremony in Lone Tree. 1960.
What a Way to Go. 1962.
Cause for Wonder. 1963.
One Day. 1965.
In Orbit. 1967.

Green Grass, Blue Sky, White House (stories). 1970.
Fire Sermon. 1971.
War Games. 1972.
A Life. 1973.
Here Is Einbaum (stories). 1973.
The Cat's Meow (stories). 1975.
Real Losses, Imaginary Gains (stories). 1976.
The Fork River Space Project. 1977.
Plains Song: For Female Voices. 1980.
The Origin of Sadness (story). 1984.
Collected Stories 1948-1986. 1986.
Three Easy Pieces. 1993.

Other

The Inhabitants (photo-text). 1946.
The Home Place (photo-text). 1948.
The Territory Ahead (essays). 1958.
A Bill of Rites, A Bill of Wrongs, A Bill of Goods (essays). 1968.
God's Country and My People (photo-text). 1968.
Morris: A Reader. 1970.
Love Affair: A Venetian Journal (photo-text). 1972.
About Fiction: Reverent Reflections on the Nature of Fiction with Irreverent Observations on Writers, Readers, and Other Abuses. 1975.
Structure and Artifacts: Photographs 1933-1954. 1975.
Conversations with Morris: Critical Views and Responses, edited by Robert E. Knoll. 1977.
Earthly Delights, Unearthly Adornments: American Writers as Image Makers. 1978.
Will's Boy: A Memoir. 1981.
Morris (portfolio of photographs). 1981.
Picture America, photographs by Jim Alinder, introduction by Ansel Adams. 1982.
Photographs and Words. edited by Jim Alinder. 1982.
The Writing of My Uncle Dudley (address). 1982.
Solo: An American Dreamer in Europe 1933-34. 1983.
Time Pieces: The Photographs and Words of Morris (exhibition catalogue). 1983.
A Cloak of Light: Writing My Life. 1985.
Time Pieces: Photographs, Writing, and Memory. 1989.
Wright Morris; Origin of Species: San Francisco Museum of Art (exhibition catalogue). 1992.
Writing My Life: An Autobiography. 1993.

Editor, *The Mississippi River Reader.* 1962.

*

Critical Studies: *Morris* by David Madden, 1965; *Morris* by Leon Howard, 1968; *The Novels of Morris: A Critical Interpretation* (includes bibliography) by G. B. Crump, 1978; *Morris: Memory and Imagination* by Roy K. Bird, 1985; "The Outsider as Sexual Center: Morris and the Integrated Imagination" by Carl A. Bredahl in *Studies in the Novel* vol. 18, no. 1, 1986; "Morris' *The Field of Vision*: A Re-Reading of the Scanlon Story" by Joe Hall in *Journal of American Culture* vol. 14, no. 2, 1991; *Wright Morris Revisited* by Joseph J. Wydeven, 1998.

*   *   *

Wright Morris, who has been called "the most major minor novelist in America," has had greater success with the critics than with the novel-reading public. He is also an important photographer: his "photo-text" books are interspersed among the many novels he has published since 1942. In addition, Morris's critical essays on the art of fiction, and its relation to life and the modern reader, are unusually candid and stimulating. In all of his fiction the characters are vivid Americans, their talk salty and often funny; but these people also struggle with the issues and problems that beset the modern world. Morris recognizes his estrangement from other novelists and novel readers, and the reasons for it: "In my use of language there is an element that the narrative novelist has no interest in, might even find obstructive. He would say, 'One of the things that is wrong with this novel is that it holds the reader up. He has to read too carefully.' I would agree."

The Nebraska plains of Morris's first nine years haunt his imagination, and his first five books (novels and photo-texts) all take him "home" again. Then, in his novels of the early 1950s, Morris portrays people cut off from the past (and often from love): they are monsters (like Mrs. Ormsby of *Man and Boy*), or suicidal (like Will Brady of *The Works of Love*). In *The Deep Sleep* the Porter house in suburban Philadelphia becomes a symbol of America, and the events in the novel become American experience in miniature. In the three "major" Morris novels that followed—*The Huge Season, The Field of Vision,* and *Ceremony in Lone Tree*—past and present are transformed through heroism, love, and the creative imagination.

In most of his fiction Morris contrasts old and young, and the revolution of the 1960s gave him exciting new matter. New frontiers of sex are explored in *Love among the Cannibals* and *What a Way to Go:* in both erotic love is overtly important. Although the action is focused upon the animal pound in a small California town in *One Day,* the day is November 22, 1963: Morris suggests, as he also does elsewhere, that nature might well abandon human civilization and make a new start with an animal (like the chipmunk in *The Huge Season*). In typical Morris fashion, too, the intellectual pessimism is leavened by his fascination with life, revealed most clearly through the hundreds of grotesque but vital characters that crowd his novels. *In Orbit* reveals age looking at youth: age sees the horrible but hopeful, living new day, envies and even admires. The prototypical motorcycle hoodlum rapes and pillages, albeit in a sometimes burlesque way; the victims, who are "upright citizens" of a small town, are unable—apparently unwilling—to identify the culprit. Then a tornado sweeps through the village, and the townspeople have no more hope of stopping the marauding youth than of halting the devastating wind storm. Both seem awful natural forces.

In *Fire Sermon* Morris returns to the picaresque auto trip of his first novel, *My Uncle Dudley;* the journey is still from California to the midwest, but the time has moved forward from the 1920s to the 1960s. Using a familiar Morris pair-up, *Fire Sermon* takes an old man and a boy back to Nebraska, plus two hitchhikers picked up on the way. This young hippie couple, totally free, inspire admiration in both the man and the boy; though it means the end of his day for the old man, he accepts the inevitable, natural succession of youth. *A Life* completes the story of the old man, who now seeks and achieves death at the hands of an Indian and thus fulfills a ritual requirement of nature.

Characters recur in Morris novels, sometimes (but not always) retaining the same names. Thus, Tom Scanlon first appears in *The World in the Attic,* is one of the central figures in *The Field of Vision,* and survives as the remaining inhabitant of Lone Tree, Nebraska, in *Ceremony in Lone Tree.* Taken together (and including his most recent novels, *The Fork River Space Project* and *Plains Song: For Female Voices*), Morris's works are intent on seeking out a usable past and its impact on the present, asserting the continuity of the American character, and positing the creative and vital forces in nature.

Like his photo-text books, the photographic exhibits Morris has staged also focus on the plains of the Midwest and the passage of time. A recent display at the San Francisco Museum of Modern Art (*Wright Morris: Origins of Species*, 1992) offered many of Morris's straightforward images of his native territory. Most of the photographs included in the exhibit were taken during a twenty-year period beginning in the mid-1930s and during which he travelled extensively in the region. Through these pictures, he froze in time some of the last faces of the determined optimism that marked the nation's period of westward expansion. Over the years, through interviews and writings (many compiled in *Time Pieces,* published in 1989) Morris went to great lengths to explain how he believes we should view his photographs. He tells us the origins of the photos, his intentions and, in some instances, their relationships to his autobiographical and fictional works. Collectively, Morris's body of photographic work serves to establish a real feel for a specific region and a specific time. Most of the photographs included in the exhibit at the San Francisco Museum of Modern Art appeared previously in Morris's photo-text volumes or exhibitions. This most recent collection, however, demonstrates a further attempt to present this image of that place and time, combined here, though, with fewer words than in past presentations—giving the impression that Morris wishes us to think of him, at least in this instance, primarily as a photographer.

—Clarence A. Glasrud, updated by Craig Bryson

MORRISON, Toni

Born: Chloe Anthony Wofford in Lorain, Ohio, 18 February 1931. **Education:** Howard University, Washington, D.C., B.A. 1953; Cornell University, Ithaca, New York, M.A. 1955. **Family:** Married Harold Morrison, 1958 (divorced 1964); two children. **Career:** Instructor of English at Texas Southern University, Houston, Texas, 1955-57, and Howard University, 1957-64; senior editor, Random House, New York, 1965-89; associate professor of English, State University of New York at Purchase, 1971-72; visiting professor, Yale University, New Haven, Connecticut, 1976-77; Schweitzer Professor of the Humanities, State University of New York at Albany, 1984-89; visiting professor, Bard College, 1986-88. Beginning 1989 Robert F. Goheen Professor of the Humanities, Princeton University, New Jersey. **Awards:** National Book award nomination, 1975; Ohioana Book award nomination, 1975; National Book Critics Circle award, 1977; American Academy award, 1977; New York State Governor's Art award, 1986; National Book award nomination, 1987; National Book Critics Circle award nomination, 1987; Pulitzer prize, 1988; Robert F. Kennedy award, 1988; Elizabeth Cady Stanton award from the National Organization for Women, 1988; Commonwealth award, 1989; Chianti Ruffino Antico Fattore International Literary prize, 1990; Nobel prize, 1993. **Member:** American Academy, National Council on the Arts. **Residence:** Princeton, New Jersey.

PUBLICATIONS

Novels

The Bluest Eye. 1969.
Sula. 1973.
Song of Solomon. 1977.
Tar Baby. 1981.
Beloved. 1987.
Jazz. 1992.
Paradise. 1997.

Plays

Dreaming Emmett (first produced in Albany, New York 1986). 1986.

Recordings: *Interview with Toni Morrison* with Kay Bonnetti, 1983; *Song of Solomon,* 1985; *Jazz,* 1992.

Other

Playing in the Dark: Whiteness and the Literary Imagination. 1992.
The Dancing Mind. 1996.
The Big Box (for children). 1999.

Editor, *The Black Book.* 1974.
Editor, *Race-ing Justice, En-Gendering Power: Essays on Anita Hill, Clarence Thomas, and the Construction of Social Reality.* 1992.

*

Bibliography: *Toni Morrison: An Annotated Bibliography* by David Middleton, 1987.

Critical Studies: *Critical Essays on Toni Morrison* edited by Nellie McKay, 1988; *The Crime of Innocence in the Fiction of Toni Morrison* by Terry Otten, 1989; *Toni Morrison* edited by Harold Bloom, 1990; "Toni Morrison issue" of *Callalo,* Summer, 1990; *Inspiring Influences* by Michael Awkward, 1991; *Fiction and Folkore: The Novels of Toni Morrison* by Trudier Harris, 1991; *Toni Morrison's Developing Class Consciousness* by Dorothea Drummond Mbalia, 1991; *Folk Roots and Mythic Wings in Sarah Orne Jewett and Toni Morrison: The Cultural Function of Narrative* by Marilyn Sanders Mobley, 1991; *The Novels of Toni Morrison* by Patrick Bryce Bjork, 1992; *Toni Morrison: Critical Perspectives, Past and Present* edited by Henry Louis Gates, Jr., and K.A. Appiah, 1993; *The Novels of Toni Morrison: The Search for Self and Place Within the Community* by Patrick Bryce Bjork, 1996; *Toni Morrison: Critical and Theoretical Approaches,* edited by Nancy J. Peterson, 1997; *The Novels of Toni Morrison: A Study in Race, Gender, and Class* by K. Sumana, 1998; *Critical Essays on Toni Morrison's Beloved,* edited by Barbara Solomon, 1998; *Toni Morrison: A Critical Companion* by Missy Dehn Kubitschek, 1998; *Toni Morrison's Beloved: A Casebook,* edited by William L. Andrews, 1999; *Silko, Morrison, and Roth: Studies in Survival* by Naomi R. Rand, 1999; *Toni Morrison and Womanist Discourse* by Aoi Mori, 1999.

*   *   *

While winning the 1993 Nobel Prize for literature gave Toni Morrison worldwide recognition as one of America's premier novelists, the support of popular talk show host Oprah Winfrey has brought Morrison her widest audience. Though Morrison's writing has long had a large and devoted audience, and her influence on American literature has extended to her an editorial backing for fellow African American women writers such as **Gayl Jones, Gloria Naylor,** and **Toni Cade Bambara,** the release of Winfrey's movie adaptation of Morrison's novel *Beloved* extended Morrison's vision to a new mass audience. Nonetheless, Morrison has maintained her demanding, lyrical prose and her ironic and often tragic artistic vision.

Morrison began her first novel, *The Bluest Eye,* while she was living in Syracuse, New York, and working for a textbook subsidiary of Random House. Begun as a short story about a young black girl who wanted blue eyes, the work evolved into an almost naturalistic study of the forces that assail Pecola Breedlove, a girl from a poor and dysfunctional family. Somewhat experimental in form and style, *The Bluest Eye* tells in its opening pages the story of Pecola's incestuous rape by her father, Cholly Breedlove, in part to subvert any salacious interest such a story might imply. Each section of *The Bluest Eye* is prefaced by a few lines from an imitation child's primer, highlighting the difference between the perfect, implicitly white world portrayed by American media and the real world of poor black children such as Pecola. Though Pecola is the central figure in the story, it is not so much a story about her as it is a story about conditions hostile to her. Pecola herself is a pitiable figure who sinks into madness after the rape.

Sula, Morrison's second novel, can be read as a complementary novel to *The Bluest Eye,* in that it presents a woman, Sula Peace, who grows up facing the same array of social forces as Pecola but develops a strong, forceful personality with whom the reader is by turns invited and challenged to identify. Like *The Blues Eye, Sula* is interested in presenting an entire way of life. The novel focuses on the black community of Medallion, Ohio, an area called the Bottom because the hill it was founded on was described to a freed slave as the bottom of heaven. Sula Peace is almost the exact opposite of Pecola Breedlove in that she is an audacious, proud woman who becomes a social outcast for challenging convention. The narrator invites readers to see Sula as a would-be artist without the discipline of an art form who, "like any artist with no art form became dangerous." Though the novel features a rich canvas of extraordinary characters, the central relationship in the book is the one between Sula and her childhood friend Nel. Not understanding why their childhood games of trading boyfriends should not extend into adulthood, Sula sleeps with Nel's husband, Jude. Only after years of estrangement and Sula's death does Nel come to realize how important Sula was to her, and she exclaims to her dead friend, "We was girls together. . . O Lord, Sula . . . girl, girl, girlgirlgirl." Though *Sula* would help to inspire a type of novel sometimes called the "girlfriend" novel, written for and about black women friends, Morrison told a *Paris Review* interviewer in 1993 that writing a novel about friendship was "a very radical thing when *Sula* was published." Taken together, *The Bluest Eye* and *Sula* are both novels about the destructive force of conventional society for black culture and black women in particular.

Though *Sula* was nominated for a National Book Award, it was Morrison's third novel, *Song of Solomon,* that won the award. The most overtly hopeful novel in Morrison's body of work, and perhaps her most popular (it became a bestseller in the 1990s when Winfrey made it one of the first selections in her "Oprah's Book Club"), it is also in part a fictional outgrowth of another project that Morrison was involved in the 1970s, the collection of historical documents about black life called *The Black Book*. *Song of Solomon*'s central character, Milkman Dead (born the same day as Morrison herself), is a pampered, middle-class black man whose quest for gold his father believes was lost down South turns into a quest for black history and, ultimately, self-discovery. The song of the title is a blues song his Aunt Pilate used to sing, about Solomon, a slave (also called Shalimar) who, according to the legends Milkman discovers, flew back to Africa. From the time of its publication, *Song of Solomon* was hailed by reviewers in such publications as the *New Yorker*, the *New York Times Book Review*, and *Time* (where Angela Wigan praised it for embodying an artistic vision "that encompasses both a private and a national heritage") as a major work by a major writer. It was selected as a Book-of-the-Month Club main selection and led to Morrison's appointment to the National Council on the Arts and her election to the American Academy and Institute of Arts and Letters.

When her fourth novel came out, it was a much-anticipated event that inspired a *Newsweek* cover story. *Tar Baby*, however, was not the critical success *Song of Solomon* had been. Set in the West Indies, *Tar Baby* focuses on Jadine, a black model who has studied in France and is cut off from black American culture, and Son, young black man from Florida who is critical of wealth. Using the story of Br'er Rabbit and the Tar Baby as a model, *Tar Baby* casts Son as both a rabbit-like trickster and a black figure who Jadine gets "stuck" to, forcing her to choose between him and the wealthy white man who has proposed to her. Though its publication was greeted as the work of a major writer, *Tar Baby* has proven to be the least critically popular of Morrison's novels. Her fifth novel, *Beloved*, however, is frequently cited alongside *Song of Solomon* as being Morrison's most significant works.

Written as the first in a trilogy of books that also includes *Jazz* and *Paradise*, *Beloved* and the two novels that followed are each inspired by a real-life killing, and they each investigate forms of love: the love of children, romantic love, and the love of God, respectively. Inspired by the story of Margaret Garner, an escaped slave who killed her infant daughter to protect her from a life of slavery, *Beloved* is a story about the violence of slavery and the quest for recovery. At the novel's beginning, Sethe and her daughter Denver are living after the Civil War in a house haunted by the ghost of the infant daughter Sethe killed. When Paul D, a former slave Sethe knew, shows up, the ghost disappears, but several days later a young woman appears who seems to be the age that Sethe's infant daughter would have been if she had lived, and who calls herself "Beloved," the one word that appears on the infant's tombstone. Tormented by the memories of slavery, experiences she was willing to kill her daughter to protect her from, Sethe holds tight to Denver and to Beloved, although Beloved becomes increasingly selfish and uncaring towards Sethe and Denver. It is only when Denver begins working outside the home that the black community around the area mobilizes to help Sethe. The ending is profoundly ambiguous in that Sethe has been forced to confront her past and may emerge healthier for it, but the fate of Beloved, who is expelled from the community and who may or may not be pregnant, is unclear.

A popular theory among Morrison's readers, though, is that she returns as Wild, the mother of Joe Trace, in *Jazz*. Inspired by the story of a young girl who was shot and who refused to name her killer, *Jazz* is set during the Harlem Renaissance of the 1920s and centers on Joe Trace, a black man who migrated to Harlem full of hope, and his shooting of Dorcas, a young girl he was in love with. The story of Joe, his wife Violet, and Dorcas is interwoven with a story of Joe and Violet's ancestors from the post-Reconstruction period in the South. These stories are told by a self-conscious narrator from Harlem who refers to herself and corrects herself at times, and seems indeed to be improvising parts of the narrative in the spirit of jazz performance. Jazz music, which played such a central role in the Harlem Renaissance and which relies largely upon improvisation, is the novel's central metaphor not only for the novel itself but for the lives of the Harlem "New Negro" residents who were trying to improvise new lives for themselves.

The last book in what has come to be known as the "*Beloved* trilogy" is *Paradise*. Beginning with the slaughter of wayward women in the home where they have collected, *Paradise* traces the history of Ruby, Oklahoma, a black town founded by refugees from a failed farming community called Haven. Ruby becomes the utopia of the World War II veterans who founded it, a town so perfect no one died there for years, but it has lost belief in itself. *Paradise* begins and ends with the assault on the convent, filling up the chapters in between with stories of the women who have taken refuge there, and of the town that is seventeen miles away. Inspired by a real-life attack on a girl's school in Brazil, Morrison has said that the seed of the novel was the question "How can they do that?" The answer, the novel implies, is that the men of Ruby are looking for scapegoats, unable to face the fact that the town has failed from within.

Praise for *Beloved*, *Jazz*, and *Paradise* has not been universal, but virtually all critics respect the careful language and the willingness to take risks and confront tough issues in these novels, and the ten years during which Morrison produced these works has been by far the most successful period in Morrison's professional life as a writer. It was *Beloved* that inspired her 1993 Nobel prize for literature, and the 1998 movie based on the book returned the novel to the bestseller list a decade after its initial publication. Additionally, *Paradise* was selected by Winfrey for her "Oprah's Book Club," and it, too, saw significant time as a bestseller, despite its challenging nature. Morrison has used her stature as a popular Nobel Laureate to edit many important books and to publish several short works about literature. The most influential of these has been *Playing in the Dark: Whiteness and the Literary Imagination*, a book that analyzes how presentations of race are used in works by white writers. *Playing in the Dark* has been frequently cited as a key text for understanding the construction of race in American literature.

That Toni Morrison has become one of the finest novelistic chroniclers of black life in America is beyond dispute. However, like Gabriel García Márquez and **William Faulkner,** fellow Nobel Laureates, she has produced a body of work of worldwide significance by focusing her writing on the stories, histories, and tragedies of a specific. Though her imagination is drawn to understand the violence in American culture, her keen eye for capturing the lyricism and hopefulness of African American life underscores the essential optimism propelling her work, so that even the horrific acts of violence—slavery, incest, slaughter—can be understood. Her work demands, though, that to understand humanity at its finest, we must also investigate it at its worst.

—Thomas Cassidy

MOWATT, Anna Cora

Pseudonym: Helen Berkley. **Born:** Anna Cora Ogden, Bordeaux, France, 5 March 1819, to American parents; lived in or near Bordeaux as a child; moved with her family to New York City, 1826. **Education:** Mrs. Okill's School, New York, 1826-28, and at a school in New Rochelle, New York, 1828-31. **Family:** Married 1) James Mowatt in 1834 (died 1851), three adopted children; 2) William Foushee Ritchie in 1854. **Career:** Traveled abroad for her health, 1837-38; returned to New York and began writing for the stage, 1839; appeared in recitals of poetry, New York and Boston, 1841-42, and thereafter wrote under the pseudonym Helen Berkley for *Godey's Lady's Book, Graham's,* and other magazines, and compiled books on cooking, etiquette, etc., for various publishers; made debut as actress, New York, 1845, and appeared, with E.L. Davenport as leading man, in New York and other American cities, London, and Dublin, 1846 until she retired in 1854; full-time writer from 1854; lived abroad after 1861, mainly in Florence. Active in the campaign to preserve Mount Vernon: vice-regent, Mount Vernon Ladies Association of the Union, 1858-66. **Died:** 21 July 1870.

PUBLICATIONS

Plays

Gulzara; or, The Persian Slave (produced 1840). In *The New World,* 1840.
Fashion; or, Life in New York (produced 1845). 1849.
Armand; or, The Peer and the Peasant (produced 1847). 1849.

Fiction

The Fortune Hunter; or, The Adventures of a Man about Town: A Novel of New York Society. 1842.
Evelyn; or, A Heart Unmasked. 1845.
Mimic Life; or, Before and behind the Curtain (stories). 1856.
Twin Roses. 1857.
Fairy Fingers. 1865.
The Mute Singer. 1866.
The Clergyman's Wife and Other Sketches. 1867.

Poetry

Pelayo; or, The Cavern of Covadonga. 1836.
Reviewers Reviewed: A Satire. 1837.

Other

Life of Goethe. 1844.
Etiquette of Courtship and Marriage. 1844.
The Management of the Sick Room. 1844.
The Memoirs of Madame d'Arblay. 1844.
Autobiography of an Actress; or, Eight Years on the Stage. 1853.
Italian Life and Legends. 1870.

*

Critical Studies: *Life and Letters* by Marius Blesi, 1952; *Anna Cora: The Life and Theatre of Mowatt* by Eric Wollencott Barnes,

1954, as *The Lady of Fashion,* 1955; "'The New Path': Nineteenth-Century American Women Playwrights" by Doris Abramson, in *Modern American Drama: The Female Canon* edited by June Schlueter, 1990; *Revelations of Self: American Women in Autobiography* edited by Lois J. Fowler and David H. Fowler, 1990; *The Rhetoric of Self-fashioning in the Works of Anna Cora Mowatt* (dissertation) by Kelly S. Taylor, 1994.

*   *   *

Mid-nineteenth-century American stage history records no more engaging figure than author-actress Anna Cora Mowatt, whose performances in her own and others' plays delighted audiences throughout the United States and Britain. Though known in the late twentieth century chiefly for her comedy *Fashion,* an amusing satire on middle-class pretentiousness, Mowatt's popularity during the 1850s derived from numerous other writings, but primarily from the many successful roles she brought to life in both English and American theaters. Her dual career marked a turning point, demonstrating that an American woman of genteel birth, given talent, perseverance, family support, and hard work, could achieve professional recognition in theatrical circles without sacrificing social respectability.

As her autobiography reveals, the story of Mowatt's dramatic experiences is still fascinating. Born in Bordeaux, the ninth of sixteen children of wealthy Americans, she enjoyed from early childhood such cultural advantages as extensive European travel; entree into the world of art, literature, and theater; familial stimulus and encouragement toward creative effort; and, above all, the guidance and support of her husband, James Mowatt, whom she married at fifteen. At sixteen she published a juvenile poetic romance entitled *Pelayo; or, The Cavern of Covadonga,* and then wrote an operetta, "The Gypsy Wanderer." These youthful effusions led to more mature essays, stories, and sketches appearing in leading American periodicals, and to her three plays, *Gulzara; or, The Persian Slave, Fashion,* and *Armand.* Other publications included three novels, two romantic tales of theatrical life under the title *Mimic Life; or, Before and behind the Curtain,* and the detailed account of her experiences in *Autobiography of an Actress*—in all, an impressive collection, written mainly between frequent illnesses and extended theatrical engagements.

Although Mowatt's stage performances were more widely heralded than her writings in the 1850s, throughout ensuing decades her reputation as the author of *Fashion* superseded that of her acting career. For the play not only scored immediate hits and enjoyed repeated, long-run performances in both England and America; it has continued, even in the late twentieth century, to attract more attention from producing groups than any other nineteenth-century American play except *Uncle Tom's Cabin.* Its enduring appeal is well deserved because no other play of its period captured so accurately or spoofed with such buoyant, satiric humor, characterization, and sprightly dialogue, the bourgeois aspirations of mid-century New York society.

—Eugene Current-Garcia

MUKHERJEE, Bharati

Born: Calcutta, India, 27 July 1940. Immigrated to Canada in 1968, became a naturalized citizen in 1972. Immigrated to the United

States in 1980, became a U.S. citizen in 1988. **Education:** An Anglicized Bengali school in Bellgune, 1944-48; in England and Switzerland, 1948-51; University of Calcutta, B.A. 1959; University of Baroda, India, M.A. 1959; University of Iowa, Iowa City, M.F.A 1963, Ph.D. 1969. **Family:** Married writer Clark Blaise in 1963; two sons. **Career:** Instructor in English at Marquette University, Milwaukee, Wisconsin, 1964-65; instructor, University of Wisconsin-Madison, 1965; lecturer, 1966-69, assistant professor, 1969-73, associate professor, 1973-78, full professor, 1978-79, McGill University, Montreal, Canada; visiting assistant professor of writing, University of Iowa, 1979, 1982; visiting assistant professor of English, Skidmore College, Saratoga Springs, New York, 1979-80, 1981-82; and Emory University, Atlanta, Georgia, 1983; associate professor, Montclair State College, New Jersey, 1984; professor, CUNY, 1987-89. Since 1990 professor, University of California, Berkeley. **Awards:** Grants from McGill University, 1968, 1970; Canada Arts Council, 1973-74 and 1977; Canadian Council of India, 1976; Guggenheim Foundation, 1978-79; National Endowment for the Arts, 1986; first prize from Periodical Distribution Association, 1980; National Magazine award second prize, 1981; National Book Critics Circle award for best fiction, 1988. Honorary degrees: Denison University, 1987; Williams College, 1989. **Member:** American Academy of Arts and Sciences, 1995.

PUBLICATIONS

Novels

The Tiger's Daughter. 1972.
Wife. 1975.
Jasmine. 1989.
The Holder of the World. 1993.
Leave It to Me. 1997.

Short Stories

Darkness. 1985.
The Middleman and Other Stories. 1988.

Screenplay: *Days and Nights in Calcutta,* with Clark Blaise. 1991.

Other

Kautilya's Concept of Diplomacy. 1976.
Days and Nights in Calcutta, with Clark Blaise. 1977; film script, 1989.
The Sorrow and the Terror, with Clark Blaise. 1987.
Political Culture and Leadership in India. 1991.
Regionalism in Indian Perspective. 1992.

*

Critical Studies: "Foreignness of Spirit: The World of Mukherjee's Novels" by Jasbir Jain in *Journal of Indian Writing in English,* July 1985; "An Interview with Mukherjee" by Geoff Hancock in *Canadian Fiction Magazine,* vol. 59, 1987; "Expatriates, Immigrants and Literature: Three South Asian Women Writers" by Roshni Rustomji-Kerns in *Massachusetts Review,* vol. 29, no. 4, 1988; "An Interview with Mukherjee" by Alison Carb in *Massachusetts Review,* vol. 69, no. 4, 1988; "Insider/Outsider Views of Belonging: The Short Stories of Mukherjee and Rohintan Mistry" by Amin Malik in *Short Fiction in New Literatures in English* edited by J. Bardolph, 1989; "Mukherjee" by Ammena Meer in *Bomb,* vol. 29, 1989; "Mukherjee's Darkness: Exploring the Hyphenated Identity" by Sudha Pandya in *Quill,* December 1990; interview by Michael Cornell, Jessie Greason and Tom Grimes in *Iowa Review,* Fall 1990; *Conquering America with Mukherjee* (videocassette) by Bill Moyers, 1990; "Kamala Markandaya, Mukherjee, and the Indian Immigrant Experience" in *Toronto South Asian Review,* Winter 1991, and *Mukherjee: Critical Perspectives,* 1993, both by Emmanuel S. Nelson; "New Englishes, New Discourses: New Speech Acts" by Cecil L. Nelson in *World Englishes,* Winter 1991; "Expatriates and Immigrants, Displacement and Americanization" by Liew-geok Leong in *International Literature in English* edited by Robert L. Ross, 1991; "Passages from India: Migrating to America in the Fiction of V.S. Naipaul and Mukherjee" by C.L. Chua and "South Asia/North America: New Dwellings and Past" by B.A. St. Andrews in *Reworlding: The Literature of the India Diaspora* edited by Emmanuel Nelson, 1992; "Co-Wanderers Kogawa and Mukherjee: New Immigrant Writers" by B.A. St. Andrews in *World Literature Today,* Winter 1992; "Refashioning the Self: Immigrant Women in Mukherjee's New World" by Arvindra Sant Wade and Karen Marguerite Radell in *Studies in Short Fiction,* Winter 1992; *Bharati Mukherjee: Critical Perspectives,* edited by Emmanuel S. Nelson, 1993.

*   *   *

There are no easy ways to categorize Bharati Mukherjee. Her life and her writing span East and West, past and present, tradition and change, hope and despair. Her remarkable skill in exploring through fiction her own position as an Indian woman in a foreign land has won her the highest critical praise. An additional delight, however, is her deftness in speaking in the voices of peoples who do not share her cultural position. Mukherjee's writing demonstrates that she is adept not only at asking her own questions but also the questions of others. Although *The Middleman and Other Stories,* for which she won a National Book Critic's Circle award, reveals the author's multivoiced competency the most obviously, all her fiction engages in dialogues of different voices, cultures, and pasts. Mukherjee is an important American author participating in the best tradition of American literature: the continual exploration of identity.

"There are no harmless, compassionate ways to remake oneself. We murder who we are so we can rebirth ourselves in the images of dreams," claims Jasmine, an Indian immigrant to the United States featured in Mukherjee's third novel. This phrase is important for the central characters of all of Mukherjee's fiction, particularly her novels. The central characters Tara *(The Tiger's Daughter),* Dimple *(Wife),* Jasmine *(Jasmine),* and Hannah *(The Holder of the World)* engage in cross-cultural exploration and assimilation as they attempt to find their place, their roles, in the new societies they encounter. The novels explore the condition of being between two countries, two cultures, and show how each woman must find her own method of facing the challenges and managing the pain of remaking herself as she encounters new worlds. The first three novels make for interesting comparisons. In *The Tiger's Daughter* fifteen-year-old Tara leaves her homeland, India, to study in the United States. She becomes dreadfully homesick yet returns later with a foreign husband and a new perspective. She finds reassimilation into the society of her childhood difficult, but it is her new distance which allows her to view her society from a more holistic position. For the first time Tara is forced to see beyond the protective veil of her class/caste privilege to the pain, corruption, and poverty facing her fellow citizens. Tara's transformation, during which she must abandon old beliefs for new, is more gradual and less dramatic than the rebirth of the next character, Dimple. Dimple, the Indian immigrant to the United States featured in *Wife,* endures a more dramatic remaking of the self that results ultimately in violence when she murders her traditional Indian husband. Some readers find Dimple's violent eruption indicative of psychological stresses resulting from an inability to master the metamorphosis from Indian to American woman. Others see Dimple's murder of her husband as a self-assertive though misguided act that allows her full rebirth into American society. Actually, both positions hold some truth. For Dimple to continue living in her present role as a subservient, obedient, self-denying Indian wife would mean denial of the possibility of becoming American. Breaking free from the past and the husband she has outgrown is a self-assertive act; however, her choice of murder over other alternatives such as divorce indicates the hold traditional India still has on her. The clash of the new freedom she desires and the old traditional thought patterns that keep her captive becomes too much, and she strikes out in frustration and rage.

In *Jasmine* Jasmine too learns to strike out, but she can distinguish appropriate from inappropriate expressions of her rage. Jasmine experiences a more gradual and balanced transformation than Dimple, which begins before her departure from India. Jasmine is the ideal immigrant, possessing a positive, open spirit which allows her to face new challenges, explore new worlds, and refuse to let defeat stop her pursuit of the American dream. When she is raped on her first day in the United States, she murders the man who has raped her rather than killing herself as her traditional values demand. Through this assertion of self, she is reborn. She no longer plans to burn herself on her husband's funeral pyre; instead, she begins a new life for herself. Eventually she learns to give herself permission to value her own happiness.

The Holder of the World is different from the three previous novels. The central character does not immigrate to the United States but is, conversely, a Puritan American who immigrates to India. The story is told by a narrator who is researching the life of Hannah, or the Salem Bibi, a Puritan resident of New Salem whose adventurous life leads her to the bedchamber of a Hindu Raja and the council chambers of the Mughal Emperor. The characters in the novel, therefore, confront many levels of difference. The narrator/researcher, Beigh Masters, is studying not only a time far distant from her own but two cultures, Puritan and Indian, different from her twentieth-century life. Beigh, like the woman she is researching, loves across cultural boundaries; she is married to an Indian computer scientist. Hannah goes further than Beigh, however, in that she learns to live within a new culture. Thus, in contrast to Mukherjee's previous narratives from the position of an Indian woman viewing, judging, and adopting the United States as her home, this story offers a view of India through the eyes of two American women.

Mukherjee's short stories have also received much notice. The short story collections *Darkness* and *The Middleman and Other Stories* explore themes similar to those presented in the novels. They differ, however, in their remarkable display of varied char-acters and points of view. One particularly chilling story presents a racist, violent man who rapes a young Indian girl in one of the rooms of her family's hotel. The rape of an Indian girl is a story Mukherjee has told before but not from the point of view of the rapist. While no information the narrator provides makes the rape justifiable, the story does give enough background material to help the reader understand the influences that have shaped this dangerous man. Another story addresses the issue of cross-cultural relationships from the perspective of an Italian-American young woman. Mukherjee's ability to speak in the variety of voices displayed in *The Holder of the World* is foreshadowed in these earlier stories.

Mukherjee has continued to make a considerable impression on the development of American literature. Few authors survey the realm of people who move between cultures with more sensitivity, insight, and skill. Her willingness to address difficult issues of race, class, and gender, her skill in asking the questions of others, and her mastery of the dialogue of difference place her on the cutting edge of literary progress. She, like many great American authors before her, explores the essential issues of cultural identity and asks the question, "What does it mean to be an American?"

Surely one of the most important aspects of American identity is the possibility for self-invention, and in her fifth novel, *Leave It to Me,* Mukherjee takes this theme to a comic-violent extreme. In the tradition of *The Adventures of Huckleberry Finn,* the young Debby DeMartino, a mixed-race foundling, lights out for the west coast to find her biological parents. The trip becomes a journey of self-transformation. "Just ask for me, Helena," she tells customers when she takes a telemarketing job, "Or depending on the mood of the day, Staci, Traci, Eva, Magda, Desiree." Unlike Twain's innocent character, however, Debby, who changes her name to Devi Dee in an allusion to the Indian goddess of vengeance, is bent on revenge against her former hippie mother and her "sex-guru serial killer" father, with whom she reunites in the book's apocalyptic climax. The novel's exaggerated violence, strong symbolism, and themes of fluid identity make *Leave It to Me* Mukherjee's most quintessentially American work but also her most controversial. Many critics found its plot unconvincing, its violence too absurd, its themes too strident. Others, however, read the novel as the logical culmination of the concerns informing Mukherjee's previous fiction. "Others who write stories of migration often talk of arrival at a new place as a loss . . .," Mukherjee wrote in a *Mother Jones* piece (January-February 1997). "I want to talk of arrival as gain." Though *Leave It to Me* remains a flawed work, Devi's insistence on deciding her own fate is the kind of personal gain that makes her a fully American character.

—Amy E. Hudock, updated by Elizabeth Shostak

MURFREE, Mary Noailles

Pseudonym: Charles Egbert Craddock. **Born:** Grantland, the family estate near Murfreesboro, Tennessee, 24 January 1850; became lame as a child; moved with her family to Nashville, Tennessee, 1856. **Education:** Nashville Female Academy; Chegary Institute, Philadelphia, 1867-69. **Career:** Writer from 1874; lived in St. Louis, 1881-90, and thereafter in Nashville. **Awards:** Honorary degree: University of the South, Sewanee, Tennessee, 1922. **Died:** 31 July 1922.

PUBLICATIONS

Fiction

In the Tennessee Mountains (stories). 1884.
Where the Battle Was Fought. 1884.
Down the Ravine. 1885.
The Prophet of the Great Smoky Mountains. 1885.
In the Clouds. 1886.
The Story of Keedon Bluffs. 1887.
The Despot of Broomsedge Cove. 1889.
In the "Stranger People's" Country. 1891.
His Vanished Star. 1894.
The Phantoms of the Foot-Bridge and Other Stories. 1895.
The Mystery of Witch-Face Mountain and Other Stories. 1895.
The Young Mountaineers: Short Stories. 1897.
The Juggler. 1897.
The Story of Old Fort Loudon. 1899.
The Bushwhackers and Other Stories. 1899.
The Champion. 1902.
A Spectre of Power. 1903.
The Frontiersmen (stories). 1904.
The Storm Centre. 1905.
The Amulet. 1906.
The Windfall. 1907.
The Fair Mississippian. 1908.
The Raid of the Guerilla and Other Stories. 1912.
The Ordeal: A Mountain Romance of Tennessee. 1912.
The Story of Duciehurst: A Tale of the Mississippi. 1914.

*

Bibliography: in *Bibliography of American Literature* by Jacob Blanck, 1973; "Murfree: An Annotated Bibliography" by Reese M. Carleton, in *American Literary Realism 1870-1910,* autumn 1974.

Critical Studies: *Craddock (Murfree)* by Edd Winfield Parks, 1941; *Murfree* by Richard Cary, 1967; "'The Visitants from Yesterday': An Atypical Previously Unpublished Story from the Pen of 'Charles Egbert Craddock'" by Franklin Benjamin Fisher IV, in *Tennessee Studies in Literature,* vol. 26, 1981; *Mary Noailles Murfree's Literary Treatment of Cherokee-Caucasian Relationships in Eighteenth-Century Tennessee* by Caffilene Allen, 1996.

*   *   *

Mary Noailles Murfree gained a deserved reputation in her day as an accurate and graphic local colorist. Her short stories and novels set in the mountains of Tennessee are distinguished for their accurate transcription of dialect and their vivid depictions of scenery. "I love to be particular," she stated, and in her attention to the detail of mountain background and speech she was indeed "particular."

The eight stories of *In the Tennessee Mountains,* published under the pseudonym of Charles Egbert Craddock, won immediate popularity and came to be regarded as significant contributions to the short story genre. In the books that followed, notably *Where the Battle Was Fought, The Prophet of the Great Smoky Mountains,* and *In the "Stranger People's" Country,* the meticulous portrayal of landscape and local color continued to be her forte.

Murfree's characterizations were sometimes stylized, and her lengthy descriptions occasionally impeded the flow of the narrative, especially in her novels. Her themes were in general restricted to a handful of set situations involving the legal tussles of mountainfolk and townspeople, the impact of the sophisticated stranger upon the mountain girl and her jealous lover, the complications that follow in the wake of the superstitious religious fanatic. Nonetheless, many of her characters achieved a high degree of verisimilitude: her beauties and crones, her fugitives from justice, her blacksmiths and preachers. In narrating their frustrated lives against the picturesque setting of the Tennessee Mountains, Murfree captured the public imagination and gained for herself a niche in regional literature.

Her style matched her vigorous themes. It was straightforward, forceful, and robust. Thus the revelation that Charles Egbert Craddock was the pseudonym of a woman astounded not merely her readers but her editor, Thomas Bailey Aldrich of the *Atlantic Monthly.*

Although Murfree experimented with other literary genres, including the historical novel and the romance, she is remembered primarily for these local color stories. Her work has been compared, in respect of its general portrayal of scenery and people, with that of other regional writers such as **Bret Harte, George Washington Cable,** and **Sarah Orne Jewett.**

—Madeleine B. Stern

N

NABOKOV, Vladimir

Pseudonym: V. Sirin (for works in Russian). **Born:** St. Petersburg, Russia, 23 April 1899; emigrated in 1919; became U.S. citizen, 1945. **Education:** Prince Tenishev School, St. Petersburg, 1910-17; Trinity College, Cambridge, 1919-22, B.A. (honors) 1922. **Family:** Married Véra Slonim in 1925; one son. Lived in Berlin, 1922-37, and Paris, 1937-40; moved to the United States, 1940. **Career:** Instructor in Russian literature and creative writing, Stanford University, California, summer 1941; lecturer in comparative literature, Wellesley College, Massachusetts, 1941-48; part-time research fellow, Museum of Comparative Zoology, Harvard University, Cambridge, Massachusetts, 1942-48; professor of comparative literature, Cornell University, Ithaca, New York, 1948-59; visiting lecturer, Harvard University, spring 1952; lived in Montreux, Switzerland, 1961-77. Translated or collaborated in translating his own works into English. **Awards:** Guggenheim fellowship, 1943, 1953; American Academy grant, 1951, and Award of Merit medal, 1969; Brandeis University Creative Arts award, 1953; National Medal for Literature, 1973. **Died:** 2 July 1977.

PUBLICATIONS

Collections

Sobranie sochinenii [Works]. 1987—.
The Stories of Vladimir Nabokov. 1995.
Vladimir Nabokov (Library of America edition). 1996.

Short Stories

Vozvrashchenie Chorba: Rasskazy I Stikhi [The Return of Chorb: Stories and Poems]. 1930.
Sogliadatai [The Spy] (novella). 1938; as *The Eye,* translated by the author and Dmitri Nabokov, 1965.
Nine Stories. 1947.
Vesna v Fial'te I drugie rasskazi [Spring in Fialta and Other Stories]. 1956.
Nabokov's Dozen: A Collection of 13 Stories. 1958.
Nabokov's Quartet. 1966.
A Russian Beauty and Other Stories, translated by the author, Dmitri Nabokov, and Simon Karlinsky. 1973.
Tyrants Destroyed and Other Stories, translated by the author and Dmitri Nabokov. 1975.
Details of a Sunset and Other Stories. 1976.
The Enchanter (novella), translated by Dmitri Nabokov. 1986.

Novels

Mashen'ka. 1926; as *Mary,* translated by the author and Michael Glenny, 1970.
Korol', Dama, Valet. 1928; as *King, Queen, Knave,* translated by the author and Dmitri Nabokov, 1968.
Zashchita Luzhina [The Luzhin Defense]. 1930; as *The Defense,* translated by the author and Michael Scammell, 1964.

Kamera Obskura. 1932; as *Camera Obscura,* translated by W. Roy, 1936; as *Laughter in the Dark,* revised and translated by the author, 1938.
Podvig' [The Exploit]. 1933; as *Glory,* translated by the author and Dmitri Nabokov, 1971.
Otchaianie. 1936; as *Despair,* translated by the author, 1937; revised edition, 1966.
Priglashenie na Kazn'. 1938; as *Invitation to a Beheading,* translated by the author and Dmitri Nabokov, 1959; revised edition in Russian, 1975.
The Real Life of Sebastian Knight. 1941.
Bend Sinister. 1947.
Dar. 1952; as *The Gift,* translated by the author and Michael Scammell, 1963.
Lolita. 1955; translated into Russian by the author, 1967; as *The Annotated Lolita,* edited by Alfred Appel, Jr., 1970.
Pnin. 1957.
Pale Fire. 1962.
Ada; or Ardor: A Family Chronicle. 1969.
Transparent Things. 1972.
Look at the Harlequins! 1974.

Plays

Smert' [Death], 1923, *Dedushka* [Grandad], 1923, *Agaspher* [Agasfer], 1923, *Tragediia Gospodina Morna* [The Tragedy of Mr. Morn], 1924, and *Polius* [The South Pole], 1924, all in *Rul'* [The Rudder] magazine.
Skital'tsy [The Wanderers], in *Grani II* [Facets II] magazine, 1923.
Chelovek iz SSSR [The Man from the USSR] (produced 1926). In *Rul'* [The Rudder] magazine, 1927.
Sobytie [The Event] (produced 1938). In *Russkie Zapiski,* 1938.
Izobretenie Val'sa (produced 1968). In *Russkie Zapiski,* 1938; translated as *The Waltz Invention* (produced 1969), 1966.
Lolita: A Screenplay. 1974.
The Man from the USSR and Other Plays, translated by Dmitri Nabokov. 1984.

Screenplay: *Lolita,* 1962.

Poetry

Stikhi [Poems]. 1916.
Dva Puti: Al'manakh [Two Paths: An Almanac]. 1918.
Gornii Put' [The Empyrean Path]. 1923.
Grozd' [The Cluster]. 1923.
Stikhotvoreniia 1929-1951 [Poems]. 1952.
Poems. 1959.
Poems and Problems. 1971.
Stikhi [Poems]. 1979.

Other

Nikolai Gogol. 1944.
Conclusive Evidence: A Memoir. 1951; as *Speak, Memory: A Memoir,* 1952; revised edition, as *Speak, Memory: An Autobiography Revisited,* 1966; as *Now Remember,* 1996.

Nabokov's Congeries: An Anthology, edited by Page Stegner. 1968; as *The Portable Nabokov,* 1977.

Strong Opinions (interviews and essays). 1973.

The Nabokov-Wilson Letters: Correspondence Between Nabokov and Edmund Wilson 1940-1971, edited by Simon Karlinsky. 1979.

Lectures on Literature, edited by Fredson Bowers. 1980.

Lectures on "Ulysses": A Facsimile of the Manuscript. 1980.

Lectures on Russian Literature, edited by Fredson Bowers. 1981.

Nabokov's Fifth Arc: Nabokov and Others on His Life's Work, edited by J.E. Rivers and Charles Nicol. 1982.

Lectures on Don Quixote, edited by Fredson Bowers. 1983.

Perepiska s sestroi [Correspondence with His Sister]. 1985.

Selected Letters 1940-1977, edited by Dmitri Nabokov and Matthew J. Bruccoli. 1989.

Editor and Translator, *Eugene Onegin,* by Alexander Pushkin. 4 vols., 1964; revised edition, 4 vols., 1976.

Translator, *Nikolka Persik* [Colas Breugnon], by Romain Rolland. 1922.

Translator, *Ania v Strane Chudes* [Alice in Wonderland], by Lewis Carroll. 1923.

Translator, *Three Russian Poets: Verse Translations from Pushkin, Lermontov, and Tyutchev.* 1945; as *Poems by Pushkin, Lermontov, and Tyutchev,* 1948.

Translator, with Dmitri Nabokov, *A Hero of Our Time,* by Mikhail Lermontov. 1958.

Translator, *The Song of Igor's Campaign: An Epic of the Twelfth Century.* 1960.

*

Bibliography: *Nabokov: Bibliographie des Gesamtwerks* by Dieter E. Zimmer, 1963, revised edition, 1964; *Nabokov: A Reference Guide* by Samuel Schuman, 1979; *Nabokov: A Descriptive Bibliography* by Michael Juliar, 1986.

Critical Studies: *Escape into Aesthetics: The Art of Nabokov* by Page Stegner, 1966; *Nabokov: His Life in Art—A Critical Narrative,* 1967, *Nabokov: His Life in Part,* 1977, and *VN: The Life and Art of Nabokov,* 1986, all by Andrew Field; *Nabokov: The Man and His Work* edited by L.S. Dembo, 1967; *Keys to Lolita* by Carl R. Proffer, 1968, and *A Book of Things about Nabokov* edited by Proffer, 1974; *Nabokov: Criticism, Reminiscences, Translations, and Tributes* edited by Alfred Appel, Jr., and Charles Newman, 1970, and *Nabokov's Dark Cinema* by Appel, 1974; *Nabokov* by Julian Moynahan, 1971; *Nabokov's Deceptive World* by W. Woodlin Rowe, 1971; *Crystal Land: Artifice in Nabokov's English Novels* by Julia Bader, 1972; *Nabokov's Garden: A Guide to Ada* by Bobbie Ann Mason, 1974; *Nabokov* by Donald E. Morton, 1974; *Reading Nabokov* by Douglas Fowler, 1974; *Nabokov* by L.L. Lee, 1976; *The Real Life of Nabokov* by Alex de Jonge, 1976; *Nabokov Translated: A Comparison of Nabokov's Russian and English Prose* by Jane Grayson, 1977; *Nabokov: America's Russian Novelist* by George Malcolm Hyde, 1977; *Fictitious Biographies: Nabokov's English Novels* by Herbert Grabes, 1977; *Nabokov: The Dimensions of Parody* by Dabney Stuart, 1978; *Blue Evenings in Berlin: Nabokov's Short Stories of the 1920's* by Marina Naumann, 1978; *Nabokov: His Life, His Work, His World—A Tribute* edited by Peter Quennell, 1979; *Nabokov and the Novel* by Ellen Pifer, 1980; *Nabokov: The Critical Heritage* edited by Norman Page, 1982; *Nabokov's Novels in English* by Lucy Maddox, 1983; *The Novels of Nabokov* by Laurie Clancy, 1984; *Nabokov: A Critical Study of the Novels* by David Rampton, 1984; *Critical Essays on Nabokov* edited by Phyllis A. Roth, 1984; *Problems of Nabokov's Poetics: A Narratological Analysis* by Pekka Tammi, 1985; *Nabokov: Life, Work, and Criticism* by Charles Stanley Ross, 1985; *Worlds in Regression: Some Novels of Nabokov* by D. Barton Johnson, 1985; *A Nabokov Who's Who* by Christine Rydel, 1986; *Nabokov* by Michael Wood, 1987; *Understanding Nabokov* by Stephen Jan Parker, 1987; *Nabokov: The Mystery of Literary Structures* by Leona Toker, 1989; *Nabokov: The Russian Years 1899-1940,* 1990, and *Nabokov: The American Years,* 1991, both by Brian Boyd; *Nabokov* by Tony Sharpe, 1991; *Nabokov's Otherworld* by Vladimir E. Alexandrov, 1991; *Social Semiotics As Praxis: Text, Social Meaning Making, and Nabokov's Ada* by Paul J. Thibault, 1991; *A Small Alpine Form: Studies in Nabokov's Short Fiction* edited by Charles Nicol and Gennady Barabtarlo, 1993; *The Magician's Doubts: Nabokov and the Risks of Fiction* by Michael Wood, 1994; *A Guide to Nabokov's Butterflies and Moths* by Dieter Zimmer, 1998.

*   *   *

The most fruitful way to approach the extensive and varied Vladimir Nabokov canon (verse, plays, short stories, autobiography, translations, critical articles, and works on chess and lepidoptery) is undoubtedly through the novels, particularly the earlier Russian ones that are frequently overlooked but that contain the fundamental themes and devices of the later works. For what is striking about Nabokov's art is the consistency with which it develops, structurally and thematically, from the initial exploration of nostalgia and émigré life of Berlin in *Mary* to the celebration of language and artifice and the treatment of time in *Ada.*

Nabokov's second novel, *King, Queen, Knave,* is the first to juxtapose crime and art for parodic purposes and leaves its hero, Franz, a myopic character (literally and figuratively), stranded outside the bliss of his criminal fictions. *The Eye,* a novella whose émigré narrator is beset with split perceptions of his self, is, according to Nabokov, the first work where he develops that "involute abode" of his later fiction. Of the other novels of this Berlin/Paris period, *Despair* is the most important, since Herman Karlovich is a recognizable (though very different) predecessor to *Lolita*'s Humbert Humbert. Herman is a wily, self-conscious villain who devises a complex crime involving the murder of his double, who, however, does not resemble Herman at all. Herman's "perfect crime," and his journal that records that crime, are flawed by the same misconception; he fails to realize that contingent reality cannot be manipulated and that "the invention of art contains far more truth than life's reality."

The Gift is important for its exploration of biography as a fictional form, an exploration that is also prominent in Nabokov's first English novel, *The Real Life of Sebastian Knight.* V., the narrator, attempts to write the biography of his brother, Sebastian Knight, but is foiled at every turn since Knight's life moves with that same obliqueness as the chess piece after which he is named. Ultimately, however, V.'s narrative approximates Sebastian's life by virtue of the dynamic character of the unfulfilled quest that uses parody as "a kind of springboard for leaping into the highest region of serious emotion."

Pnin is a warmly witty but sad portrait of Professor Timofey Pnin, an aging Russian exile attempting to master American language and culture at a New England university; the professorial politicking finally defeats him. Besides its preoccupation with cultural exile, the novel shows a self-consciousness of language, though never to the extent that we find in Nabokov's best-known novel, *Lolita.* In fact, given that Humbert Humbert, the narrator and hero, writes about his nympholeptic escapades with the twelve-year-old Lolita in prison where he has "only words to play with," language frames the entire novel and is the vehicle through which Humbert and Lolita are finally relegated to the "bliss of fiction." Humbert's sexual desire becomes a metaphor for the artistic desire to create, though not until Humbert learns the hard lesson that it is desire and not possession that is the transcendent reality. So when Humbert possesses Lolita in part I of the novel (the crime), he is forced to protect her jealously in a motel trek across America in part II (the getaway). He has violated the "intangible island of entranced time" that is established early in the novel with his childhood love, Annabel Lee. It is Annabel Lee in her "kingdom by the sea" who establishes the initial rift between desire and possession. Ultimately, Lolita is abducted from Humbert by Quilty, Humbert's double, and the final chase scene culminates in Quilty's murder, a comic, grotesque exorcism that allows Humbert some measure of grace in the "bliss of fiction."

Pale Fire is the most experimental and enigmatic of Nabokov's novels, since its structure entails a 999-line poem by John Shade and a foreword, commentary with footnotes, and index by Charles Kinbote, the poet's homosexual neighbor who is really an exile from the distant northern land of Zembla (Russia). Beyond the obvious parody of pedantic scholarship, the novel explores the interdependencies of multi-layered worlds, each reflecting and refracting the other: Shade tells his story in verse; Kinbote uses Shade's poem to reveal his Zemblan past; Gradus, a secret agent intent on killing Kinbote, murders Shade by mistake; and of course, stalking through the work there is Nabokov, the arch-inventor of them all. Because the narrative of each layer is invented and sustained by the other, the final effect is a spiral of artifice.

Ada, Nabokov's most ambitious fiction (although its status among critics remains uncertain), fuses the novelist's earlier themes and techniques with greater scope and linguistic dexterity. The opening three chapters present a baroque invocation, a fanfare of language for the core of the novel that chronicles the incestuous love affair of the precocious hero, Van Veen, and his sister, Ada. Van's obsession with the past and the novel's eroticism culminate in part in a long lecture on time and space. Here the past becomes an inseparable link to the present, making a "glittering 'now' that is the only reality of Time's texture." Erotic desire, the art of inventing, and the butterfly's life cycle are metaphors for the constant metamorphosis of the present, while the future is relegated to an unknowable realm of space. The narrative moves across an imaginary geography of overlapping Russian, European, and American landscapes, with an equally overlaid texture of language. All the familiar Nabokovian motifs and devices are heaped against the aristocratic setting of the "ardors and arbors of Ardis Hall": butterflies and botany, dreams and doubles, puns, word games, nostalgia, false leads, and eroticism. It is undoubtedly Nabokov's most festive celebration of language, artifice, and, what should not be overlooked, love.

Transparent Things is a novella bordering on the metaphysical as it deals with the transparency of objects in the present, and finally of life itself, as death, abetted by chance, brings Hugh Per-

son to a characteristic Nabokovian ending. *Look at the Harlequins!* is a first-person memoir of a writer whose life and works have disguised parallels with Nabokov's own. It is a fiction created out of fiction, a deepening of the labyrinth of inventing. And while these two works never surpass *Ada,* they do illustrate what has been evident in Nabokov from the start, namely, that fiction becomes the only sustained reality beyond contingent existence—even, no doubt, the sustenance of self.

—Brent MacLaine

See the essay on *Lolita.*

NASBY, Petroleum V(esuvius)

A pseudonym for David Ross Locke. **Born:** Vestal, near Binghamton, New York, 20 September 1833. **Education:** Schools in Marathon, New York, 1840-45. **Family:** Married Martha Hannah Bodine in 1855; three sons. **Career:** Apprentice printer, Cortland *Democrat,* Cortland, New York, 1845-50; printer, Corning *Journal,* Corning, New York, 1850-51, and Cleveland *Herald and Plain Dealer,* 1852; coowner and editor, Plymouth *Advertiser,* Ohio, 1853-55; publisher, Mansfield *Herald,* 1855-56, and Bucyrus *Journal,* 1856-61, both Ohio; publisher and editor, *Hancock Jeffersonian,* Findlay, Ohio, 1861-65 (wrote first Nasby letter for the paper, 1862); worked for a drag firm in Findlay, 1864-65; owner, Bellefontaine *Republican,* Ohio, 1864; editor, Toledo *Blade,* Ohio, 1865-88 (wrote Nasby letters for the paper until 1887); on lecture circuit in U.S., 1867-73; publisher and treasurer, New York *Evening Mail,* 1871-78; partner in advertising business, New York, 1873-75. Alderman from third ward, Toledo, 1886-88. **Died:** 15 February 1888.

PUBLICATIONS

Fiction and Sketches

The Nasby Papers. 1864.
Divers Views, Opinions, and Prophecies of Yours Trooly, Petroleum V. Nasby. 1866; abridged edition, as *Let's Laugh,* edited by Lloyd E. Smith, 1924.
Androo Johnson, His Life. 1866.
Swingin' round the Cirkle. 1867.
Ekkoes from Kentucky. 1868.
The Impendin Crisis uv the Democracy. 1868.
The Struggles (Social, Financial and Political) of Petroleum V. Nasby. 1872; revised edition, 1888; abridged edition, edited by Joseph Jones, 1963.
The Morals of Abou Ben Adhem. 1875.
Inflation at the Cross Roads. 1875.
The President's Policy. 1877.
A Paper City (novel). 1879.
The Democratic John Bunyan. 1880.
The Diary of an Office Seeker. 1881.
Nasby in Exile; or, Six Months of Travel. 1882.
The Demagogue (novel). 1891.
The Nasby Letters. 1893.
Civil War Letters, edited by Harvey S. Ford. 1962.

Plays

Inflation, with Charles Gayler (produced 1876).
Widow Bedott (produced 1879).

Poetry

Hannah Jane. 1882.

Other (temperance pamphlets)

Beer and the Body. 1884.
Prohibition. 1886.
High License Does Not Diminish the Evil. 1887.

*

Bibliography: by James C. Austin, in *American Literary Realism 4,* 1971.

Critical Studies: *Nasby* by James C. Austin, 1965; *The Man Who Made Nasby, David Ross Locke* by John M. Harrison, 1969; "The Platform Humorists: Comedy in One" by Kirk McManus, in *Performance of Literature in Historical Perspectives* edited by David W. Thompson, Wallace A. Bacon, Eugene Bahn, Lee Hudson, and Alethea S. Mattingly, 1983; "Civil War Politics in the Novels of Locke" by Ronald M. Grosh, in *Midamerica: The Yearbook of the Society for the Study of Midwestern Literature,* 1986.

*   *   *

Petroleum V. Nasby was the creation of David Ross Locke, one of America's greatest newspapermen. Beginning as a printer at the age of twelve and progressing successfully as writer, editor, and publisher of several New York and Ohio newspapers, he took over the Toledo, Ohio, *Blade* in 1865, and made it one of the most widely read papers in the Midwest. He had very little schooling, but he developed a rough but powerful editorial style that contributed to the course of American history. He supported the Republican Party from its beginnings. His opposition to the Confederacy during the Civil War encouraged the Union cause and President Lincoln personally. His insistence on the rights of blacks helped lead public opinion toward the Emancipation Proclamation and the Thirteenth, Fourteenth, and Fifteenth Amendments to the Constitution. His attacks on political corruption promoted Civil Service reform and the exposure of political fraud in the Gilded Age. He aided the causes of prohibition and women's rights that led long after his death to the Eighteenth and Nineteenth Amendments.

But his greatest and most lasting fame came from the Nasby letters—a series of newspaper columns written from 1862 until shortly before Locke's death in 1888. Petroleum Vesuvius Nasby, the fictitious writer of the letters, stood for everything that Locke was against. Nasby was an illiterate, drunken, bigoted, racist Democrat. The Nasby letters are considered part of the American tradition of crackerbox humor—journalistic humor expressed in a low-brow, rustic dialect and with a common-sense philosophy. But they are not humorous in a strict sense of the term; they are bitterly satirical, violently partisan, grossly concrete pictures of the American political scene. With the exception of Benjamin Franklin, Locke was probably America's greatest political satirist.

The best-known Nasby letters were collected in various books beginning in 1864. The best of these is *Divers Views,* which exposed blatantly the pro-Southern views of the Ohio Copperhead, Nasby, during the Civil War. But each collection included parts of the earlier material, and *The Nasby Letters* is the most complete, comprising a panorama of Republican thought and action during the most critical quarter-century of United States history.

The Nasby letters were but a part of Locke's literary activities. He was one of the most popular lecturers in America in an age when public lecturing was as important as television eventually became. His three famous lectures, delivered throughout the country under the pseudonym of Nasby, were small masterpieces on the issues of civil rights for blacks, women's rights, and political corruption. He was the author of two excellent political novels, *A Paper City* and *The Demagogue,* two plays, *Inflation* and *Widow Bedott,* the latter being performed continually into the twentieth century; a very popular, very sentimental poem, *Hannah Jane;* a number of quite creditable hymns; and an untold number of articles, editorials, stories, novels, verses, and essays in newspapers, magazines, and pamphlets.

Locke did not pretend to be a literary artist. He wrote for his times, and he believed that politics was the most important concern of a democracy. He was a significant editor and publisher. And his Nasby letters and his lectures deserve continued attention.

—James C. Austin

NASH, (Frederick) Ogden

Born: Rye, New York, 19 August 1902. **Education:** St. George's School, Newport, Rhode Island, 1917-20; Harvard University, Cambridge, Massachusetts, 1920-21. **Family:** Married Frances Rider Leonard in 1931; two daughters. **Career:** Teacher, St. George's School, 1922-23; bond salesman on Wall Street, New York, 1924; worked in advertising department of Doubleday, publishers, New York, 1925-31; editorial staff member, *New Yorker,* 1932, and regular contributor thereafter; screenwriter in Hollywood, 1936-42; panelist, *Masquerade* radio program, 1950s. **Awards:** Sarah Josepha Hale award, 1964. **Member:** American Academy. **Died:** 19 May 1971.

PUBLICATIONS

Collections

I Wouldn't Have Missed It: Selected Poems, edited by Linell Smith and Isabel Eberstadt. 1975.

Poetry

Hard Lines. 1931.
Free Wheeling. 1931.
Hard Lines and Others. 1932.
Happy Days. 1933.
Four Prominent So and So's, music by Robert Armbruster. 1934; as *Four Prominent Bastards Are We,* 1934.

The Primrose Path. 1935.
The Bad Parent's Garden of Verse. 1936.
Bon Voyage. 1936.
I'm a Stranger Here Myself. 1938.
The Face Is Familiar: Selected Verse. 1940; revised edition, 1954.
Good Intentions. 1942; revised edition, 1956.
The Nash Pocket Book. 1944.
Many Long Years Ago. 1945.
Selected Verse. 1946.
Nash's Musical Zoo, music by Vernon Duke. 1947.
Versus. 1949.
Family Reunion. 1950.
The Private Dining Room and Other New Verses. 1953.
You Can't Get There from Here. 1957.
Verses from 1929 On. 1959; as *Collected Verse from 1929 On,* 1961.
Scrooge Rides Again. 1960.
Everyone but Thee and Me. 1962.
Marriage Lines: Notes of a Student Husband. 1964.
The Mysterious Ouphe. 1965.
A Nash Omnibook. 1967.
Santa Go Home: A Case History for Parents. 1967.
There's Always Another Windmill. 1968.
Funniest Verses, edited by Dorothy Price. 1968.
Bed Riddance: A Posy for the Indisposed. 1970.
The Old Dog Barks Backwards. 1972.
Selected Poetry of Ogden Nash: 650 Rhymes, Verses, Lyrics, and Poems. 1995.
Under Water with Ogden Nash. 1997.

Plays

One Touch of Venus, with S.J. Perelman, music by Kurt Weill, from *The Tinted Venus* by F. Anstey (produced 1943). 1944.
Sweet Bye and Bye (lyrics only), book by S.J. Perelman and Al Hirschfeld, music by Vernon Duke (produced 1946).
Two's Company (lyrics only; revue) (produced 1952).
The Littlest Revue, with others (produced 1956).

Screenplays: *The Firefly,* with Frances Goodrich and Albert Hackett, 1937; *The Shining Hour,* with Jane Murfin, 1938; *The Feminine Touch,* with George Oppenheimer and Edmund L. Hartmann, 1941.

Other (for children)

The Cricket of Carador, with Joseph Alger. 1925.
Parents Keep Out: Elderly Poems for Youngerly Readers. 1951.
The Christmas That Almost Wasn't. 1957.
The Boy Who Laughed at Santa Claus. 1957.
Custard the Dragon. 1959.
A Boy Is a Boy: The Fun of Being a Boy. 1960.
Custard the Dragon and the Wicked Knight. 1961.
The New Nutcracker Suite and Other Innocent Verses. 1962.
Girls Are Silly. 1962.
The Adventures of Isabel. 1963.
A Boy and His Room. 1963.
The Untold Adventures of Santa Claus. 1964.
The Animal Garden. 1965.
The Cruise of the Aardvark. 1967.
The Scroobious Pip, by Edward Lear (completed by Nash). 1968.

Other

Born in a Beer Garden; or, She Troupes to Conquer: Sundry Ejaculations, with Christopher Morley and Cleon Throckmorton. 1930.

Editor, *Nothing but Wodehouse.* 1932.
Editor, *The Moon Is Shining Bright As Day: An Anthology of Good-Humored Verse.* 1953.
Editor, *I Couldn't Help Laughing: Stories* (for children). 1957.
Editor, *Everybody Ought to Know: Verses Selected and Introduced.* 1961.

*

Critical Studies: *An Index to the Poems of Nash* by Lavonne B. Axford, 1972; "'A Good Bad Poet': The Ogden Nash Collection" by George W. Crandell, in *Library Chronicle of the University of Texas,* 1981.

*   *   *

Ogden Nash's career as a writer of light verse began in the 1930s when he accepted defeat as a poet. Realizing that his serious verses were tongue-tied and sentimental, he began constructing a peculiar form of doggerel that broke all rules of symmetry and harmony in poetry. Lines grew as long as subway trains, capped by rhymes as outrageous as cocktail party chatter; philosophical questions were mocked by horse-sensical conclusions. "What is life? Life is stepping down a step or sitting on a chair, / And it isn't there." Though it wasn't great poetry, it made Nash America's most popular comic poet.

With these techniques, Nash was able to express poetically the plain-spoken American's frustration with poetic complication, as well as the conviction that, really, poetry is just prose that rhymes. (Or should be, Nash hints: "One thing that literature would be greatly the better for / Would be a more restricted use of simile and metaphor.") In the Introduction to the 1975 Nash collection *I Wouldn't Have Missed It,* **Archibald MacLeish** gave away the secret: "Nothing . . . suggests the structure of verse but the rhymes," which are used baldly to shoehorn sentences into what looks like verse. Basing his poems not on the poetic line, but on the sentence, Nash became (in his work) a "wersifier" painting men, women, and society from their poetic backsides.

Like his wersification, Nash's subjects come straight out of everyday life: summer colds and Monday mornings, leaky faucets and crashing bores. He is assailed by the mundane torments of living, perplexed by the oddities and failings of human nature, and mystified by women, just as they are by men. Yet no matter how disastrous life may be, Nash reassures us that perhaps it isn't so bad after all: "When I consider how my life is spent, / I hardly ever repent."

—Walter Bode

NATHAN, George Jean

Born: Fort Wayne, Indiana, 14 February 1882. **Education:** Taught privately by tutors; University of Bologna, 1897; University of

Paris, 1898; University of Heidelberg, 1899; Cornell University, B.A. 1904. **Family:** Married Julie Haydon in 1955. **Career:** Cub reporter, *New York Herald,* 1905; theatre critic, beginning 1905; drama department head, *Outing* and *Bohemian* magazine, 1906-08; theater critic, *Smart Set* magazine, 1909-23; cofounder and co-editor, *American Mercury,* 1924-30; cofounder, editor, and columnist, *American Spectator,* 1932-35. **Died:** 8 April 1958.

PUBLICATIONS

Prose

With H.L. Mencken and Willard Huntington Wright, *Europe after 8:15.* 1914.
Another Book on Theatre. 1915.
Bottoms Up: An Application of the Slapstick to Satire. 1917.
with H.L. Mencken, *Pistols for Two.* 1917.
A Book without a Title. 1918.
The Popular Theatre. 1918.
Comedians All. 1919.
with Mencken, *Heliogabalus: A Buffoonery in Three Acts.* 1920.
with Mencken, *The American Credo: A Contribution toward the Understanding of the National Mind.* 1920.
The Theatre, the Drama, the Girls. 1921.
The Critic and the Drama. 1922.
The World in Falseface. 1923.
Materia Critica. 1924.
The Autobiography of an Attitude. 1925.
The House of Satan. 1926.
Land of the Pilgrims' Pride. 1927.
The New American Credo: A Contribution toward the Interpretation of the National Mind. 1927.
Art of the Night. 1928.
Monks Are Monks: A Diagnostic Scherzo. 1929.
Testament of a Critic. 1931.
The Intimate Notebooks of George Jean Nathan. 1932.
Since Ibsen: A Statistical Historical Outline of the Popular Theatre Since 1900. 1933.
Passing Judgements. 1935.
The Theatre of the Moment: A Journalistic Commentary. 1936.
The Avon Flows. 1937.
The Morning after the First Night. 1938.
Encyclopedia of the Theatre. 1940.
The Bachelor Life. 1941.
The Entertainment of a Nation; or Three Sheets in the Wind. 1942.
Beware of Parents: A Bachelor's Book for Children. 1943.
The Theatre Book of the Year: A Record and an Interpretation. 1943-51.
The Critics' Prize Plays. 1945.
The World of George Jean Nathan. 1952.
The Theatre in the 'Fifties. 1953.
An Unhurried View of Erotica. 1958.
The Magic Mirror: Selected Writings on the Theatre. 1960.
A George Jean Nathan Reader. 1990.

*   *   *

For three decades—the 1920s, the 1930s, and the 1940s—George Jean Nathan was a force to be reckoned with in the American theatre. Witty, sophisticated, a man of learning and strong opinions, a theatre critic with something to say and a blazing literary style, Nathan terrorized many, insulted and infuriated more, and was a stabilizing and supporting friend to those he deemed worthy. A self-appointed critic's critic, Nathan denounced the "puffers" who dominated theatre criticism when he started his career in 1908. With a "raffish and egotistical writing style which brightened the pages of his reviews," according to the Boston critic Elliott Norton, Nathan struck furiously at playwrights, actors, producers, and even other critics whom he thought incompetent or fraudulent.

Although Nathan gained a reputation for "hating everything," it was not true, and throughout the hundreds of reviews he wrote he was seriously concerned with promoting a better theatre. If his means were questioned, his objectives were sustained by his peers, whom he eventually praised in *The Morning After the First-Night* (1938) for building up audiences and for changing in such ways as to promote a theatre to which one goes not to see life and nature but to see a "particular way in which life and nature happen to look to a cultivated, imaginative, and entertaining man who happens, in turn, to be a playwright." Theatregoers need a critic like George Jean Nathan, and when he or she does not exist, the theatre deteriorates. He was, if not always fair, creatively one-sided. Furthermore, he believed what he wrote, and his credentials were impressive.

Born to wealthy parents, Nathan grew up in the Midwest, graduated from Cornell University in 1904, and studied for a year in Europe before beginning his journalistic career with the *New York Herald* in 1906. Three years later he became drama critic for *Smart Set,* which he coedited (1914-1924) with **H. L. Mencken,** thus establishing himself as an irreverent iconoclast. With Mencken he founded the *American Mercury* in 1923 and served as its drama critic until 1932. That year, he founded the *American Spectator,* which he edited until 1935. At that point he became associated with several publications: *Newsweek, Theatre Arts, Saturday Review,* and *Esquire.* From 1943 to 1951 he published an annual *Theatre Book of the Year.* Never daunted by controversy or opposing reviews and able to express his ideas in a rich and pungent style, Nathan took his job of reviewing plays seriously and was one of the most probing theatre critics from the end of World War I through the middle of the twentieth century.

Early in his career Nathan published three plays by Eugene O'Neill in *Smart Set.* Ever afterward he promoted O'Neill's plays and was a close friend throughout the playwright's life. For his part, O'Neill dedicated *Ah, Wilderness!* to Nathan. Furious with the Theatre Guild for its indifference toward O'Neill—and toward many other American playwrights as well—Nathan became a consistent thorn in the side of the Guild, always pointing out its inadequacies and its preference for in-house plays and even suggesting in 1937 that its board of managers resign to be replaced by "a younger and more intelligent directorate." Others shared Nathan's views, and in 1935-1936 more than a dozen major drama critics, including Nathan, formed the Critics Circle with its subsequent awards.

During the last years of his life and after his death, Nathan's reputation as a critic was allowed to lie fallow in that vast terrain of theatre that changed some of its objectives and began to exhibit an arid perversity that encouraged few dramatic masterpieces. Perhaps Nathan was out of tune with the popular direction of American theatre. He considered *"musical comedy"* a misnomer: "It is not comic at all, but, on the contrary, highly lachrymose." And yet he reviewed even musical revues in all seriousness.

Historians frequently hark back to Nathan's commentary to define a contemporary vision of the theatre of his period. For his incisiveness and blisteringly correct vision, Nathan, with the "gusty force of a typhoon," is an extremely quotable critic. He described Eugene O'Neill's *Marco Millions* as "the sourest and most magnificent poke in the jaw that American business and the American businessman have ever got." There are two kinds of men, Nathan once wrote—those who like Vaudeville and those who can stand it when they are drunk. He described **Edward Sheldon's** *The Nigger* as one of the "ten dramatic shocks of the century." Sean O'Casey was "a Moliere full of Irish whiskey." Mary Ellen Chase's *Harvey* Nathan considered "the greatest intemperance document that the American Stage has ever offered." Few could resist the pungent style that made him one of the outstanding columnists of his generation and inspired Edith J. R. Isaacs to title her essay on Nathan in *Theatre Arts Magazine* "Critic as Showman."

—Walter J. Meserve

NAYLOR, Gloria

Born: New York City, 25 January 1950. **Education:** Brooklyn College of the City University of New York, B.A. in English 1981; Yale University, M.A. in Afro-American Studies 1983. **Career:** Missionary for Jehovah's Witnesses in New York, North Carolina, and Florida, 1968-75; worked for various hotels in New York City as a telephone operator, 1975-81; writer-in-residence, Cummington Community of Arts, 1983; visiting lecturer, George Washington University, Washington, D.C., 1983-84; cultural exchange lecturer, U.S. Information Agency, India, 1985; scholar-in-residence, University of Pennsylvania, 1986; visiting professor, New York University, New York City, 1986; visiting lecturer, Princeton University, Princeton, New Jersey, 1986-87; visiting professor, Boston University, Boston, Massachusetts, 1987; senior fellow, Cornell University Society for the Humanities, Ithaca, New York, 1988; Fannie Hurst Visiting Professor, Brandeis University, 1988; president, One Way Productions, New York City, beginning 1989. Executive board member of the Book of the Month Club, beginning 1989. **Awards:** American Book award, 1983; Distinguished Writer Award from Mid-Atlantic Writers Association, 1983; National Endowment for the Arts fellowship, 1985; Candace award from National Coalition of 100 Black Women, 1986; Guggenheim Fellowship, 1988; Lillian Smith award, 1989. **Residence:** New York City.

PUBLICATIONS

Novels

The Women of Brewster Place. 1982.
Linden Hills. 1985.
Mama Day. 1988.
Bailey's Cafe. 1992.

Other

Centennial. 1986.

Television plays: *The Women of Brewster Place* (adapted from Naylor's novel; produced 1989), 1984; *In Our Own Words* (unproduced), 1985.

*

Critical Studies: "The Ornamentation of Old Ideas: Gloria Naylor's First Three Novels" by James Robert Saunders in *Hollins-Critic,* April 1990; "Dominion and Proprietorship in Gloria Naylor's *Mama Day* and *Linden Hills*" by Nellie Boyd in *MAWA Review,* December 1990; "Gloria Naylor's Narrative: Looking Past the Losing" by Kazuko Inoue in *Language and Culture,* vol. 18 1990; "Black Feminism and Media Criticism: The Women of Brewster Place" by Jacqueline Bobo and Ellen Seiter in *Screen,* Autumn 1991; "Gothic and Intertextual Constructions in *Linden Hills*" by K.A. Sandiford in *Arizona Quarterly,* Autumn 1991; "The Fathomless Dream: Gloria Naylor's Use of the Descent Motif in *The Women of Brewster Place*" by Maxine L. Montgomery in *College Language Association Journal,* September 1992; *The Language of Rape: Sexual Violence in Novels by Faulkner, Naylor, and Morrison* (dissertation) by Pamela E. Barnett, 1996; *The Critical Response to Gloria Naylor,* 1997; *Understanding Gloria Naylor* by Margaret Earley Whitt, 1998; *Gloria Naylor's Early Novels,* edited by Margot Anne Kelley, 1999.

*   *   *

In the final scene of her first novel, *The Women of Brewster Place,* Gloria Naylor depicts a scene in which women, dependent on one another, are in "perfect unison." In the woman-centered world of Naylor's texts, the self-determination that her characters struggle to create, is fully realized. Naylor crafts the texture of her authorial voice from her literary ancestors, **Zora Neale Hurston** and **Toni Morrison.** Naylor, then, focuses on the lives of women, building upon the literary traditions established by African American women writers from the Harlem Renaissance to the present.

Naylor has developed themes around the issues of women, centering on the lives of other women. Just as Naylor's literary ancestors helped to shape her focus, her characters benefit from relationships with women who help them along the process of self-actualization. Naylor's women relate to other women sexually and through both filial and familial ties. They drive her fictional world as they share oppression, dreams, and desire in the telling of their stories. In her texts, community is figured through the relating of the histories of African American women. Naylor, in her insistence on creating fictional places that are often disconnected from the rest of the world, adds a spiritual dimension to her work.

Naylor's influence as a writer is suggested by how her texts shape women's identity. She has issued four novels, each of which has received literary acclaim. The first, *The Women of Brewster Place,* won the American Book award for first fiction in 1983. The work's characterizations proved so compelling that the novel was adapted into a miniseries in 1989, and in 1990 *The Women of Brewster Place* was produced as a weekly television series on ABC. The text focuses on the lives of women as lovers, friends, mothers, and wives in a society that is very much dominated by them. What is provocative about Naylor's characterizations is that she manages to create a woman-centered community relating across generations, social class, and sexual preference. Out of her examination of two kinds of female love, lesbian love and sisterhood, Naylor's community of women search for self-identity.

Her second novel, *Linden Hills,* seems initially to be a male-centered text. Situated in a community shaped by successive generations of the Nedeed family, the book depicts the oppression of women in male-dominated relationships in a community of middle- class blacks, many of whom have no sense of who they are. Through the experiences of two male poets, Naylor weaves portraits of women, successive generations of Nedeed wives, related by their shared oppression rather than by familial bonds.

Naylor again uses this generational motif in *Mama Day.* In her portrait of Cocoa, Naylor sculpts a character who must come to an understanding about how her ancestors shaped their own identities to spite the world dominated by male desire and slavery. Cocoa's story, complete with first-person narration, relates the history of Willow Springs, a mystical place that does not fall within the boundaries of any state. The legacy left to Cocoa by her great-grandmother reflects on her own story. Until she can name what was lost in past generations, Cocoa is unable to articulate her self. It is the presence of a woman guide, her great aunt Miranda, that enables Cocoa to embrace her history. Naylor's fourth book, *Bailey's Cafe* also centers on the necessity of sharing histories in a mystical place where social and temporal boundaries do not exist.

Naylor's focus on community, ancestry, and history is at the center of her depictions of African American women. In rendering their stories, she creates a mythical space where the search for self- actualization always remains possible.

—Sheila Smith-McKoy

NEAL, John

Born: Falmouth (now Portland), Maine, 25 August 1793. **Education:** Local schools. **Family:** Married Eleanor Hall in 1828; five children. **Career:** Clerk in a succession of shops in Portland then itinerant teacher of penmanship and drawing in various towns along the Kennebec River; settled in Baltimore; co-owner of dry goods store, 1814-16; studied law, while writing for a living; briefly editor of Baltimore *Telegraph;* contributed to *Portico;* assisted Paul Allen in compiling *A History of the American Revolution;* published novels, 1816-23; admitted to bar, 1819; lived in England, 1823-27; contributor to *Blackwood's* and other periodicals, and secretary to Jeremy Bentham; returned to the United States, 1827, settled in Portland, and practiced law there; editor, *Yankee,* 1828-29; later briefly editor of *New England Galaxy,* Boston, and a Portland newspaper; editor, *Brother Jonathan* (comic), New York, 1843; contributor to *North American Review, Harper's,* and *Atlantic Monthly,* from 1850. **Awards:** M.A.: Bowdoin College, Brunswick, Maine, 1836. **Died:** 20 June 1876.

PUBLICATIONS

Collections

Observations on American Art: Selections from the Writings, edited by Harold Edward Dickson. 1943.
The Genius of Neal: Selections, edited by Benjamin Lease and Hans-Joachim Lang. 1978.

Fiction

Keep Cool: A Novel, Written in Hot Weather. 1817.
Logan: A Family History. 1822.
Errata; or, The Works of Will Adams. 1823.
Randolph. 1823.
Seventy-Six. 1823.
Brother Jonathan; or The New Englanders. 1825.
Rachel Dyer: A North American Story. 1828.
Authorship: A Tale. 1830.
The Down-Easters. 1833.
True Womanhood: A Tale. 1859.
The White-Faced Pacer; or, Before and after the Battle. 1863.
The Moose-Hunter; or, Life in the Maine Woods. 1864.
Little Mocassin; or, Along the Madawaska: A Story of Life and Love in the Lumber Region. 1866.

Play

Otho. 1819.

Poetry

The Battle of Niagara. 1818; revised edition, 1819.

Other

One Word More: Intended for the Reasoning and Thoughtful among Unbelievers. 1854.
Account of the Great Conflagration in Portland. 1866.
Wandering Recollections of a Somewhat Busy Life: An Autobiography. 1869.
Great Mysteries and Little Plagues. 1870.
Portland Illustrated. 1874.
American Writers, edited by Fred Lewis Pattee. 1937.

*

Bibliography: in *Bibliography of American Literature* by Jacob Blanck, 1973.

Critical Studies: *A Down-East Yankee from the District of Maine* by Windsor Pratt Daggett, 1920; *That Wild Fellow Neal and the American Literary Revolution* by Benjamin Lease, 1972; *Neal* by Donald A. Sears, 1978; *A Right View of the Subject: Feminism in the Works of Charles Brockden Brown and Neal* by Fritz Fleischmann, 1983; "'A Likeness, Once Acknowledged': John Neal and the 'Ideosyncrasies' of Literary History" by Fritz Fleischmann, in *Myth and Enlightenment in American Literature* edited by Dieter Meindl and Friedrich W. Horlacher, 1985; "The Old World and the New in the National Landscapes of John Neal" by Francesca Orestano, in *Views of American Landscapes* edited by Mick Gigley and Robert Lawson-Peebles, 1989.

*   *   *

Strongly influenced by American nationalism following the War of 1812, John Neal developed a theory of literature that, put into practice in a series of unusual novels, has helped to win him a minor place in American literary history. Concerned that American writers like **Charles Brockden Brown**, **Washington Irving**, and **James Fenimore Cooper** were not sufficiently "American" in their writing, Neal sought to create an original body of fiction that would imitate no foreign models, and would accurately depict American persons and places and faithfully reproduce the American language. He constructed his works, moreover, on a psychological theory that placed great stress on the "heart" and the "blood," as opposed to the mind, a theory that led him to write rather formless fictions that frequently lapse into incoherence.

He turned to the American past for some of his novels—Indian conflicts in *Logan,* the American Revolution in *Seventy-Six* and *Brother Jonathan,* and the Salem witch trials in *Rachel Dyer*—and he drew American characters and reproduced American speech with considerable skill. At his best, Neal achieved a degree of realism uncommon in his time and occasionally reached a depth of psychological penetration suggestive of Poe. At his worst, however, he strained too much for effect, descended to Byronic posturing, indulged in both Gothic and sentimental absurdities, and fell into melodrama. All of Neal's books suffer to some degree from his excesses, and from his unwillingness—or inability—to give form to his novels. Only *Rachel Dyer,* perhaps his best book, exhibits a sustained authorial control but even it has a long and digressive passage in one of the courtroom scenes.

Neal's one significant contribution to American fiction is his style. Derived from the cadences of American speech, it ranges from local dialect through the more general vernacular to the biblical or prophetic. At its best, it gives a sense of immediacy to his work, whether the story is told, like *Seventy-Six,* by a common man who uses his natural language, or, like *Rachel Dyer,* by a narrative voice appropriately attuned to the seriousness of the action and theme. Neal was especially skillful in moving his story forward through the speech of his characters, and in some of his works, the reader will find page after page containing little more than conversation. In both style and narrative technique, therefore, Neal stands near the head of the vernacular tradition in American literature and dimly foreshadows the language of **Mark Twain**.

—Donald A. Ringe

NELSON, Richard

Born: Chicago, Illinois, 17 October 1950. **Education:** Hamilton College, Clinton, New York, 1968-72, B.A. 1972. **Family:** Married Cynthia B. Bacon in 1972; one daughter. **Career:** Literary manager, BAM Theater Company, Brooklyn, New York, 1979-81; associate director, Goodman Theatre, Chicago, 1980-83; dramaturg, Guthrie Theatre, Minneapolis, 1981-82. **Awards:** Watson fellowship, 1972; Rockefeller grant, 1979; Obie award, 1979, 1980; National Endowment for the Arts fellowship, 1980, 1985; Guggenheim fellowship, 1983; ABC award, 1985; Playwrights USA award, 1986; HBO award, 1986; *Time Out* award (London), 1986; Giles Cooper award for best radio play, for *Languages Spoken Here,* 1988; Lila Wallace Writers Award, Reader's Digest Fund, 1991-93; Tony award nomination, best play, 1992, for *Two Shakespearean Actors.*

PUBLICATIONS

Plays

The Killing of Yablonski (produced 1975).
Conjuring an Event (produced 1976). Included in *An American Comedy and Other Plays,* 1984.
Scooping (produced 1977).
Jungle Coup (produced 1978). Published in *Plays from Playwrights Horizons,* 1987.
The Vienna Notes (produced 1978). Published in *Wordplays 1,* 1980.
Don Juan, adaptation of a play by Molière (produced 1979).
The Wedding, with Helga Ciulei, adaptation of a play by Brecht (produced 1980).
The Suicide, adaptation of a play by Nikolai Erdman (produced 1980).
Bal (produced 1980). Included in *American Comedy and Other Plays,* 1984.
Rip Van Winkle; or, "The Works" (produced 1981). New York, Broadway Play Publishing, 1986.
Il Campiello, adaptation of the play by Goldoni (produced 1981). 1981.
Jungle of Cities, adaptation of a play by Brecht (produced 1981).
The Marriage of Figaro, adaptation of a play by Beaumarchais (produced 1982).
The Return of Pinocchio (produced 1983). Included in *An American Comedy and Other Plays,* 1984.
An American Comedy (produced 1983). Included in *An American Comedy and Other Plays,* 1984.
Accidental Death of an Anarchist, adaptation of a play by Dario Fo (produced 1984). 1987.
Three Sisters, adaptation of a play by Chekhov (produced 1984).
Between East and West (also co-director: produced 1984). Published in *New Plays USA 3,* edited by James Leverett and M. Elizabeth Osborn, 1986.
An American Comedy and Other Plays. 1984.
Principia Scriptoriae (produced 1986). 1986.
Chess (revised version), with Tim Rice, music by Benny Andersson, lyrics by Björn Ulvaeus (produced 1988).
Some Americans Abroad (produced 1989). 1989.
Eating Words (broadcast 1989). Published in *Best Radio Plays of 1989,* 1990.
Sensibility and Sense (televized 1990). 1989.
Two Shakespearean Actors (produced 1990). 1990.
Columbus and the Discovery of Japan (produced 1992). 1992.
Misha's Party, with Alexander Gelman (produced 1993).
Life Sentences (produced 1993).
New England (produced 1995).
The School for Husbands, adaptation of Moliere (produced 1995).
The Imaginary Cuckold, adaptation of Moliere (produced 1995).
The Father (produced 1996).
Plays by Richard Nelson: Early Plays. 1998.

Screenplay: *Ethan Frome,* 1993.

Radio Plays: *Languages Spoken Here,* 1987; *Roots in Water,* 1989; *Eating Words,* 1989; *Advice to Eastern Europe,* 1990; *The Unrequited Lovers' Manual; Hank Aaron's 715th; The Fall of Agnew; Watergate: An Audio Memory.*

Television Plays: *Sensibility and Sense,* 1990; *The End of a Sentence,* 1991.

Other

Making Plays: The Writer-Director Relationship in Theatre Today, with David Jones. 1995.

Editor, *Strictly Dishonorable and Other Lost American Plays.* 1986.

*

Critical Studies: "Richard Nelson" by Craig Gholson, in *BOMB,* Summer 1990, pp. 46-49; "Creating a Self, Personal and National, in Richard Nelson's *Trilogy*" by Robert J. Andreach, in *University of Mississippi Studies in English,* 1993-95, pp. 329-43.

Theatrical Activities:
Director: **Play**—*Between East and West* (co-director, with Ted D'Arms), Seattle, 1984.

*   *   *

A prolific playwright and exacting craftsman, Richard Nelson tried and rejected an array of dramatic formulas while still introducing many signature themes. *Conjuring an Event,* a two-act absurdist exercise, established his fascination with the social roles of writers. A journalist, by trying to improve his sense of smell, hopes simply to invoke newsworthy events, transcending historical reportage. In *Jungle Coup* the protagonist fabricates a bush war to justify a variety of journalistic platitudes. Nelson possesses a keen ear for cliché and professional jargon, and his characters demonstrate the misuses of language. Early characters inclined toward monologue, reducing moral positions to egocentric blather. In the long one-act *Bal,* the title character, a perversely aggressive, self-gratifying Everyman, contrasts with a quieter, self-effacing companion, a pairing that Nelson often employs.

The pre-socialized hedonist undergoes a conversion in Nelson's first pseudo-history play, *Rip Van Winkle,* a social parable written like Edward Bond's historical fables, complete with alienating violence, rambling plot, and juxtaposition of idealized agrarianism with evil industrialization. The play was staged by British director David Jones, whose professional relationship with Nelson extended over two decades and led to the Royal Shakespeare Company premiering over half a dozen Nelson plays. Nelson remains more popular in Britain, where reviewers praise him for developing serious ideas unlike the usual domestic fare of American drama.

Cultural conflict, a recurring theme, first emerges in the one-act play *The Return of Pinocchio,* where an adult, human Pinocchio, successful in Hollywood and spouting platitudes extolling American culture, returns to the harsh reality of post-World War II Italy. There women abort in the fields and villagers kill Pinocchio's father for underselling black market prices.

Nelson continues the theme of cultural displacement in *Between East and West,* a moving dramatization of the difficulty that an immigrant Czech director, Gregor, and his actress wife, Erna, have adapting to America. Characters use flawless English when they supposedly communicate in Czech, but heavy accents emerge whenever they speak English. At the climax Erna fails to eliminate her accent from a *Three Sisters* audition piece, and the long-

ing for Moscow of the sisters of the play's title accentuates her own homesickness. A frequent translator and adapter, Nelson had just finished *Three Sisters,* and *Between East and West* shows Anton Chekhov's influence. Language defines behavior in the play, and Nelson develops a more finely modulated, minimalist, understated, and oblique dialogue that persists in later plays.

Nelson's adaptations of the plays of Bertholt Brecht may have suggested experiments with disrupted narration. *Between East and West* begins at the end, then flashes to the beginning of the sequence of events. One scene appears twice, first as remembered by Gregor and then by Erna. *Sensibility and Sense* intermixes two time frames almost fifty years apart, with three characters each played by two actors, contrasting three 1930s radicals with the old people they become. Even when Nelson uses sequential plotting, scenes begin in the middle, which he says affirms the fluidity of a world without beginnings or endings. He uses projected titles, another Brechtian device, to help the audience maintain its bearings.

Principia Scriptoriae, Nelson's first London production, projects adages about writing principles behind scenes depicting the imprisonment and torture of two young writers, emphasizing the inadequate intersection of life and literature. The play also disrupts its chronology by jumping forward fifteen years in the second act, returning at the end to an omitted scene where the younger men undergo a mock execution.

The revolutionary fervor of the young American writer in *Principia Scriptoriae* emerges as bluster, and Nelson often depicts characters that he identifies as representatives of his own generation, baby boomers born too late to participate in the protests of the 1960s. *Roots in Water,* a collection of twelve vignettes set between 1976 and 1988, exposes the vacuousness of these characters; most have failed relationships and long for social commitment they cannot achieve.

Nelson's mature work divides into two related streams: dramatic symposia and large-cast history plays. *Some Americans Abroad* and *New England* both treat cultural displacement, the first with American academics conducting summer classes in England. Their unpleasant interpersonal dealings fail to reflect the qualities they purportedly admire in great literature. Nelson is not simply satirizing Americanism. *New England* depicts the reverse situation: English expatriates in America, contemptuous of the shallowness of their adopted country but unable to rise above pettiness in their own interactions. Both are dining room plays using group conversations, replete with non-sequiturs, extraneous arguments, and small talk. Sentences overlap, or remain unfinished, and subtext emerges from silences. The plays are very funny, but under the satire rests a concern for human loneliness and despair deeper than the comedy.

Royal Shakespeare Company's ability to field large casts enables Nelson to pursue his interest in historical drama. His revisionism that deflates great individuals and develops fringe characters resembles other contemporary British historical drama. *Columbus and the Discovery of Japan* and *The General from America,* about Benedict Arnold, are fairly standard costume dramas. But Nelson more successfully fuses historical material with themes of cultural conflict and social alienation in *Two Shakespearean Actors,* contrasting the American Edwin Forrest and British William Macready, in the context of the Astor Place Riots; *Misha's Party,* set against the 1991 Moscow coup attempt; and *Goodnight Children Everywhere,* a tight, realistic drama about English children sent to Canada and Wales during World War II.

The staging of *Columbus* exemplifies Nelson's treatment of historical material. Openings in enclosed spaces reveal larger exterior actions, exposing historical developments from confined personal perspectives. In *Two Shakespearean Actors*, Forrest and Macready privately share a vision of the superiority of theatrical fantasy while rioters die offstage. Nelson fuses two dramatic genres in *Misha's Party*, depicting large historical issues as dining room drama. Misha's sixtieth birthday dinner breaks up, reflecting the disintegration of Soviet society. His first wife represents the old regime, his second wife represents displaced emigrants of Brezhnev's era, and his young fiancée represents New Russia. On both a personal and a political level, momentous events occur behind the facade of banality. History in Nelson's world is always disruptive and personal.

—Richard H. Palmer

NEMEROV, Howard (Stanley)

Born: New York City, 1 March 1920; brother of the photographer Diane Arbus. **Education:** Fieldston School, New York, graduated 1937; Harvard University, Cambridge, Massachusetts (Bowdoin prize, 1940), A.B. 1941. **Military Service:** Served in the Royal Canadian Air Force, 1942-44: flying officer; and the U.S. Air Force, 1944-45; first lieutenant. **Family:** Married Margaret Russell in 1944; three sons. **Career:** Instructor in English, Hamilton College, Clinton, New York, 1946-48; member of the Literature Faculty, Bennington College, Vermont, 1948-66; professor of English, Brandeis University, Waltham, Massachusetts, 1966-69; Hurst Professor of English, 1969-76, and beginning 1976 Edward Mallinckrodt Distinguished University Professor, Washington University, St. Louis, Missouri; visiting lecturer, University of Minnesota, Minneapolis, 1958-59; writer-in-residence, Hollins College, Virginia, 1962-64; Consultant in Poetry, Library of Congress, Washington, D.C., 1963-64; associate editor, *Furioso*, Madison, Connecticut, later Northfield, Minnesota, 1946-51. **Awards:** Oscar Blumenthal prize, 1958; Harriet Monroe prize, 1959; American Academy grant, 1961; New England Poetry Club Golden Rose, 1962; Brandeis University Creative Arts award, 1963; National Endowment for the Arts grant, 1966; Theodore Roethke award, 1968; Guggenheim fellowship, 1968; St. Botolph's Club prize, 1968; Academy of American Poets fellowship, 1970; Frank O'Hara prize, 1971; Levinson prize, 1975; Pulitzer prize, 1978; National Book award, 1978; Bollingen prize, 1981; National Medal of Art, 1987. D.L.: Lawrence University, Appleton, Wisconsin, 1964; Tufts University, Medford, Massachusetts, 1969; Washington and Lee University, Lexington, Virginia, 1976; University of Vermont, Burlington, 1979; Cleveland State University; Hamilton College, Clinton, New York; McKendree College, Lebanon, Illinois. **Member:** Fellow, American Academy of Arts and Sciences, 1966; member, American Academy, 1976; Chancellor, Academy of American Poets, 1977; United States Poet Laureate, 1988-1990. **Died:** 5 July 1991.

PUBLICATIONS

Collections

The Collected Poems. 1977.

New and Selected Essays. 1985.
A Howard Nemerov Reader. 1991.

Poetry

The Image and the Law. 1947.
Guide to the Ruins. 1950.
The Salt Garden. 1955.
Small Moment. 1957.
Mirrors and Windows. 1958.
New and Selected Poems. 1960.
The Next Room of the Dream: Poems and Two Plays. 1962.
Five American Poets, with others, edited by Ted Hughes and Thom Gunn. 1963.
Departure of the Ships. 1966.
The Blue Swallows. 1967.
A Sequence of Seven. 1967.
The Winter Lightning: Selected Poems. 1968.
The Painter Dreaming in the Scholar's House. 1968.
Gnomes and Occasions. 1972.
The Western Approaches: Poems 1973-1975. 1975.
By Al Lebowitz's Pool. 1979.
Sentences. 1980.
Inside the Onion. 1984.
War Stories: Poems about Long Ago and Now. 1987.
Trying Conclusions: New and Selected Poems, 1961-1991. 1991.

Plays

Endor. 1962.
Tall Story. 1990.

Fiction

The Melodramatists. 1949.
Federigo; or, The Power of Love. 1954.
The Homecoming Game. 1957.
A Commodity of Dreams and Other Stories. 1959.
Stories, Fables, and Other Diversions. 1971.

Other

Poetry and Fiction: Essays. 1963.
Journal of the Fictive Life. 1965.
Reflexions on Poetry and Poetics. 1972.
Figures of Thought: Speculations on the Meaning of Poetry and Other Essays. 1978.
The Oak in the Acorn: On Remembrance of Things Past, and on Teaching Proust, Who Will Never Learn. 1987.
Ethics of Change: Humanistic Values vs. Technological Imperatives. 1989.

Editor, *Longfellow.* 1959.
Editor, *Poets on Poetry.* 1966.
Editor, *Poetry and Criticism,* by Marianne Moore. 1965.

*

Bibliography: *Elizabeth Bishop and Nemerov: A Reference Guide* by Diana E. Wyllie, 1983.

Critical Studies: *Nemerov* by Peter Meinke, 1968; *The Critical Reception of Nemerov: A Selection of Essays and a Bibliography* edited by Bowie Duncan, 1971; *The Shield of Perseus: The Vision and Imagination of Nemerov* by Julia A. Bartholomay, 1972; *The Stillness in Moving Things: The World of Nemerov* by William Mills, 1975; *Nemerov* by Ross Labrie, 1980; "Impressions of Nemerov" by Richard Holinger, in *The Southern Review,* winter 1987; *Howard Nemerov and Objective Idealism: The Influence of Owen Barfield* by Donna L. Potts, 1994.

*   *   *

Although Howard Nemerov has written a journal, two collections of short stories, three novels, and much fine criticism (including exceptionally insightful essays on **Wallace Stevens**, Dylan Thomas, **Vladimir Nabokov**, and Marcel Proust), his primary importance as a writer stems from his poetry. He is a superior craftsman, particularly skilled at blank verse. Moreover, the content of his poetry is quite penetrating. Perhaps the foremost reason for this richness in content is that Nemerov believes that a major function of the poet is to try to perceive reality precisely as it is. "The Private Eye" makes it clear that the artist should strip himself of preconceptions. In "Vermeer" Nemerov praises this painter for taking "what is, and seeing it as it is."

Despite the fact that reality contains patterns, Nemerov finds that, fundamentally, reality is primitive and chaotic. "The Town Dump" and "The Quarry" stress the relentless chaotic decay occurring in our world, while raw primitiveness is emphasized in "Lobsters." "The Goose Fish" reports that nature is also impenetrably enigmatic. No Dionysian oneness fusing man and nature is possible. Instead, nature is apt to paralyze the will, as it does the speaker's in "Death and the Maiden."

Humans, then, are very limited creatures, a main point in both of Nemerov's verse plays, *Endor* and *Cain.* For Nemerov the other major function of the artist is to create some kind of comforting order, even though this order is only temporary and subjective. Nemerov stresses this point in such poems as "Elegy for a Nature Poet" and "Lines and Circularities." He also reminds us, in "Monet" for example, that nature's beauty can stir us to create works of art celebrating that beauty. However, we must never think that human creations can "replace" reality—the warning given in "Projection." So, too, after meditating on reality, we must return to it, a theme in "The Sanctuary."

Because nature is ceaselessly changing, Nemerov suggests that we, too, should be flexible. "Lot Later" dramatizes this point. We should not let the past imprison us; for even sanctified history can later be proven false, the point in "To Clio, Muse of History." Nevertheless, we should not let ourselves be crippled by cynicism, as is the Minister in *Endor.*

Nemerov's poetry is valuable because it incisively presents us with a no-nonsense view of the world, a view that is stark, but not entirely negative. In "The View from an Attic Window" he declares that we live amid chaos, that our individual lives are short, and that, as a result, "life is hopeless," yet "beautiful"—and we should try to endure and to grow. We can summon the strength to cope with what haunts us late in life (described in "Insomnia I") and with our own death ("Last Things"). Throughout his work Nemerov maintains that our love of the physical world is not a foolish emotion. We gain sustenance from it and, as "Autumnal" states, from the love that can exist between two people.

Nemerov's last works reflect the need of an astute but weary scholar to reflect upon a writer's life, and then to present a sampling of representative works before departing. Both *War Stories* and *A Nemerov Reader* accomplish this feat. The first book reminds us that Nemerov was of that generation of poets for whom World War II was the event that both defined their early lives and gave them the forced "leisure" time to read and compose (Nemerov asserts in the introduction to *The Oak in the Acorn* that he could teach a *Remembrance of Things Past* only because as a pilot he had the time to read it—repeatedly—while waiting for bombing runs during the war). In "The Afterlife," for instance, the poet's military experiences inform his relationship with friends, with society stateside, and even with heaven: "The many of us that came through the war / Unwounded and set free in Forty-Five / Already understood the afterlife / We'd learned enough to wait for, not expect, / During the years of boredom, fear, fatigue." *A Howard Nemerov Reader* sums up the author's life with samplings from every genre, including a reprint in its entirety of the 1954 novel *Federigo, Or, The Power of Love.* The poet's *magnum opus* contains only sixty-eight pages of poetry, arguably the best gems from his more than a dozen books. Collected here for the first time is the poem that provides the title for his final book of selected poems, *Trying Conclusions.* The last lines would make an appropriate epitaph for this prominent American poet:

> What rational being, after seventy years,
> When Scripture says he's running out of rope,
> Would want more of the only world he knows?
> No rational being, he while he endures
> Holds on the inveterate infantile hope
> That the road ends but as the runway does.

—Robert K. Johnson, updated by Andrew O. Jones

NIN, Anaïs

Born: Paris, France, 21 February 1903; moved to the United States in 1914; later became U.S. citizen. **Education:** John Jasper Elementary School, New York, 1914-18. **Family:** Married Hugh Guiler (also called Ian Hugo) in 1924(?). **Career:** Fashion and artist's model, 1918-20; lived in Paris, 1930-40; established Siana Editions, Paris, 1935; moved to New York, 1940, and established Gemor Press. **Member:** American Academy. **Died:** 14 January 1977.

PUBLICATIONS

Collection

White Stains. 1998.

Short Stories

The Winter of Artifice (novellas). 1939.
Under a Glass Bell. 1944; augmented edition, as *Under a Glass Bell and Other Stories,* 1948.
This Hunger (novellas). 1945.
Waste of Timelessness and Other Early Stories. 1977.

The White Blackbird and Other Writings, with *The Tale of an Old Geisha and Other Stories* by Kanoko Okamoto. 1985.
A Model and Other Stories. 1995.
Stories of Love. 1996.

Novels

The House of Incest (prose poem). 1936.
Ladders to Fire. 1946.
Children of the Albatross. 1947.
The Four-Chambered Heart. 1950.
A Spy in the House of Love. 1954.
Solar Barque. 1958; expanded edition as *Seduction of the Minotaur*, 1961.
Cities of the Interior (collection). 1959; expanded edition, 1974.
Collages. 1964.
Delta of Venus: Erotica. 1977.
Little Birds: Erotica. 1979.

Other

D.H. Lawrence: An Unprofessional Study. 1932.
Realism and Reality. 1946.
On Writing. 1947.
The Diary, edited by Gunther Stuhlmann. 6 vols., 1966-76; as *The Journals*, 6 vols., 1966-77; *A Photographic Supplement*, 1974.
The Novel of the Future. 1968.
Unpublished Selections from the Diary. 1968.
Nuances. 1970.
An Interview with Nin, by Duane Schneider. 1970.
Paris Revisited. 1972.
Nin Reader, edited by Philip K. Jason. 1973.
A Woman Speaks: The Lectures, Seminars, and Interviews of Nin, edited by Evelyn J. Hinz. 1975.
In Favor of the Sensitive Man and Other Essays. 1976.
Aphrodisiac, with John Boyce. 1978.
Linotte: The Early Diary 1914-1920. 1978; *The Early Diary 1920-1931*, 3 vols., 1982-85.
Henry and June: From the Unexpurgated Diary. 1986.
A Literate Passion: Letters of Nin and Henry Miller 1932-1953, edited by Gunther Stuhlmann. 1987.
Incest: From a Journal of Love—The Unexpurgated Diary of Nin 1932-24. 1992.
Conversations with Anaïs Nin. 1994.
Fire: From a Journal of Love—The Unexpurgated Diary of Nin, 1934-37. 1995.
The Mystic of Sex and Other Writings. 1995.
Arrows of Longing: The Correspondence between Anaïs Nin and Felix Pollak, 1952-1976. 1998.

*

Bibliography: *Nin: A Bibliography* by Benjamin Franklin V, 1973; *Nin: A Reference Guide* by Rose Marie Cutting, 1978.

Critical Studies: *Nin* by Oliver Evans, 1968; *The Mirror and the Garden: Realism and Reality in the Writings of Nin* by Evelyn J. Hinz, 1971; *A Casebook on Nin* edited by Robert Zaller, 1974; *Collage of Dreams: The Writings of Nin* by Sharon Spencer, 1977; *Nin: An Introduction* by Benjamin Franklin V and Duane Schneider, 1979; *Nin* by Bettina L. Knapp, 1979; *Nin* by Nancy Scholar, 1984; *Anaïs, Art and Artists, a Collection of Essays* edited by Sharon Spencer, 1986, and "The Music of the Womb: Nin's 'Feminine' Writing" by Spencer, in *Breaking the Sequence: Women's Experimental Fiction* edited by Ellen G. Friedman and Miriam Fuchs, 1989; *Nin* by Linde Salber, 1992; *Anais: The Erotic Life of Anais Nin* by Nöel Riley Fitch, 1993; *Aesthetic Autobiography: From Life to Art in Marcel Proust, James Joyce, Virginia Woolf, and Anaïs Nin* by Suzanne Nalbantian, 1994; *Anaïs Nin: A Biography* by Deirdre Bair, 1995; *Anaïs Nin: An Understanding of Her Art* by Rochelle Lynn Holt, 1997; *Anaïs Nin: Literary Perspectives* edited by Suzanne Nalbantian, 1997; *Anaïs Nin and the Remaking of Self: Gender, Modernism, and Narrative Identity* by Diane Richard-Allerdyce, 1998.

*   *   *

Anaïs Nin's fiction may best be described as symphonic tone poems in prose, with their programmatic intermingling of similar themes and characters from one novel to another. Her characters are dancers, actresses, artists, musicians, and writers, all impelled by inner visions, illusions, or frustrations, who play their solo parts contrapuntally and always return as in the rondo form to the central female protagonist, with whom they all interact. Also characteristic of tone poems, Nin's style is psychologically discursive and impressionistic, with dreams and interior monologues substituting for the realism, dialogue, and clearly delineated plots of more traditional narratives. And her language is rhythmic, rich in sensuous imagery, and symbolic.

Nin's interests and opinions weave in and out of her novels like leitmotifs as contrapuntally as her characters do. Haunting all her fiction are evocations of music—jazz, opera, symphony—which Nin views as the inevitable preserver of memory and thus a barrier to all efforts to escape the past. Her faith in psychoanalysis as a tool for plumbing that past for constructive creative resources pervades all the novels, as does her belief in the permanency of art in contrast to the ephemerality of politics. Her fiction is totally apolitical; it focuses instead on the intricacies of intense physical and emotional relationships. Through these relationships, Nin also manifests her strong conviction in the fundamentally different sensibilities of men and women. Her men are usually unable to accept emotional responsibilities, are frustrated by their inability to act, and are drawn to the vision and sensitivity of nurturing women. Her women are seductive, submissive, and vulnerable because of their need for men; at the same time, they struggle to overcome this dependency on authority figures and to develop into independent human beings. Nin's depiction of women's search for a synthesis of these contrary facets of their personality along with her explicit rendering of female responses to sexual and emotional encounters—traditionally described from the male perspective—have made her novels attractive to a wide audience.

While her fiction need not be read in any particular order, there is a gradual evolution of control over the structure and language of her novels during the thirty years of their composition. Her craft developed from the earliest, *The House of Incest,* a random collection of poetic impressions, to later ones like *Collages* that are more complex in characterization and more ambitious in structure, artistically shaped cycles of portraits radiating from a central figure. If Nin's fiction is read chronologically and concurrently with her diaries of the same period, the essential function of the latter to her fictional mode becomes strikingly evident. It was from her experiences and the portraits delineated in her diaries that Nin drew the material for all her novels, sometimes rewritten, often lifted intact into them. And the characteristics of her diaries parallel those in her fiction: musically counterpointed themes and characters; mystical, sensual, and poetic prose; and an enduring faith in the artistic life, psychoanalysis, and the differing sensibilities of the male and the female.

—Estelle C. Jelinek

NORRIS, (Benjamin) Frank(lin, Jr.)

Born: Chicago, Illinois, 5 March 1870; moved with his family to San Francisco, 1884. **Education:** Belmont Academy, California, 1885-87; Boys' High School, San Francisco; studied art at Atelier Julien, Paris, 1887-89; attended University of California, Berkeley, 1890-94, and Harvard University, Cambridge, Massachusetts, 1894-95. **Family:** Married Jeannette Black in 1900; one daughter. **Career:** War correspondent for San Francisco *Chronicle* in South Africa during the Uitlander insurrection, 1895-96; editorial staff member, San Francisco *Wave*, 1896-97; Spanish-American War correspondent in Cuba for *McClure's* magazine, New York, 1898; reader for Doubleday, publishers, New York, 1899-1902; moved to San Francisco, 1902. **Died:** 25 October 1902.

PUBLICATIONS

Collections

Collected Writings. 10 vols., 1928.
The Letters, edited by Franklin Walker. 1956.
Novels and Essays (Library of America), edited by Donald Pizer. 1986.
The Best Short Stories of Frank Norris. 1998.

Fiction

Moran of the Lady Letty: A Story of Adventure off the California Coast. 1898; as *Shanghaied,* 1899.
McTeague: A Story of San Francisco. 1899; edited by Donald Pizer, 1977.
Blix. 1899.
A Man's Woman. 1900.
The Epic of Wheat:
    The Octopus: A Story of California. 1901; edited by Kenneth S. Lynn, 1958.
    The Pit: A Story of Chicago. 1903.
A Deal in Wheat and Other Stories of the New and Old West. 1903.
The Joyous Miracle. 1906.
The Third Circle (stories). 1909.
Vandover and the Brute, edited by Charles G. Norris. 1914.

Poetry

Yvernelle: A Legend of Feudal France. 1891.

Other

The Responsibilities of the Novelist and Other Literary Essays. 1903.

The Surrender of Santiago: An Account of the Historic Surrender of Santiago to General Shafter, July 17, 1898. 1917.
Two Poems and "Kim" Reviewed. 1930.
Norris of The Wave: Stories and Sketches from the San Francisco Weekly 1893 to 1897, edited by Oscar Lewis. 1931.
The Literary Criticism, edited by Donald Pizer. 1964.
A Novelist in the Making: A Collection of Student Themes and the Novels Blix and Vandover and the Brute, edited by James D. Hart. 1970.

*

Bibliography: *Norris: A Bibliography* by Kenneth A. Lohf and Eugene P. Sheehy, 1959; *The Merrill Checklist of Norris* by John S. Hill, 1970; in *Bibliography of American Literature* by Jacob Blanck, 1973; *Norris: A Reference Guide* by Jesse S. Crisler and Joseph R. McElrath, Jr., 1974; *Norris and The Wave: A Bibliography,* 1988, and *Frank Norris: A Descriptive Bibliography,* 1992, both by McElrath.

Critical Studies: *Norris: A Biography* by Franklin Walker, 1932; *Norris: A Study* by Eugene Marchand, 1942; *Norris* by Warren French, 1962; *The Novels of Norris* by Donald Pizer, 1966; *Norris* by Wilbur M. Frohock, 1969; *Norris: Instinct and Art* by William D. Dillingham, 1969; *The Fiction of Norris: The Aesthetic Context* by Don Graham, 1978, and *Critical Essays on Norris* edited by Graham, 1980; *Norris: The Critical Reception* edited by Joseph R. McElrath, Jr., and Katherine Knight, 1979, and *Norris Revisited* by McElrath, 1992; "Anti-Racist Strategies in Frank Norris' Fiction; Actes du G(roupe de) R(echerche et d') E(tudes) N(ord)-A(mericaines), 1981" by Andre Poncet, in *Les Americains et les autres* edited by Serge Ricard, 1982; "Norris" by William B. Dillingham, in *Fifteen American Authors before 1900: Bibliographical Essays on Research and Criticism* edited by Earl N. Harbert and Robert A. Rees, 1984; "Corporate Fiction: Norris, Royce, and Arthur Machen" by Walter Benn Michaels, in *Reconstructing American Literary History* edited by Sacvan Bercovitch, 1986, and "Frank Norris, Josiah Royce and the Ontology of Corporations" by Michaels, in *American Literary Landscapes: The Fiction and the Fact* edited by F. A. Bell and D. K. Adams, 1988; "Norris" by Don Graham, in *A Literary History of the American West,* 1987; *The Art of Frank Norris, Storyteller* by Barbara Hochman, 1988; *Writing Realism: Howells, James, and Norris in the Mass Market* by Daniel H. Borus, 1989; *A Biography of Frank Norris* (dissertation) by Donna A. Danielewski, 1997; *Harbingers of a Century: The Novels of Frank Norris* by Lawrence E. Hussman, 1998; *Deconstructing Frank Norris's Fiction: The Male-Female Dialectic* by Lon West, 1998.

*   *   *

Although Frank Norris never wrote a work that could be considered a masterpiece, he occupies an important place in American literary history. He is an early practitioner of naturalism, along with his contemporaries Crane and Dreiser; he is an example of the French influence on American letters; and he is a noteworthy creator of the fictional landscape of California. Norris was a very uneven writer and capable of writing popular magazine romance as well as serious fiction in the realistic/naturalistic tradition. Only two or three of his novels have demonstrated survival power.

As a young man Norris studied art in Paris, but there is no evidence that he read the French realists/naturalists at that time. He then was interested in romance, and his first work was a narrative poem, *Yvernelle: A Legend of Feudal France,* published while he was a student at the University of California. In 1894, when he entered Harvard as a special student of writing under Lewis Gates, he discovered Balzac, Flaubert, and especially Zola. He worked on his first novel, *McTeague,* during that year but didn't finish it until later after returning to California.

McTeague is a remarkable first novel, the most important piece of naturalism produced in America up to that time. It shows a strong Zola influence but is thoroughly naturalized in the United States. It is the story of a San Francisco dentist who is victimized by his inability to cope with marriage and complex social relationships. McTeague is a man of great strength but under the influence of alcohol loses his self-control. He is too stupid to cope with his wife, who becomes a miser, and a former friend, who causes him to lose his dental practice. The San Francisco locale is well done, and the disintegration of McTeague under the impact of forces he cannot control makes this a powerful naturalistic novel. The ending, unfortunately, is melodramatic and the symbolism far too obvious.

The Octopus, however, is a more mature work and is generally regarded as Norris's best achievement. It was the first of a projected trilogy to be called *The Epic of Wheat. The Octopus* deals with the growing of the wheat and is laid in the San Joaquin Valley of California. The ranching scenes, especially the planting of the wheat, are rendered with a good eye for local color. Although there are many characters and several subplots, the story basically concerns the struggle between the ranchers and the railroad (the octopus) over shipping rates and land prices. It is an unequal battle because the railroad holds all the trump cards, and in the climactic episode of the novel the ranchers are defeated in an armed confrontation with the railroad deputies. There are a good many romantic elements in the novel and it ends on a note of cosmic optimism, but the work falls mainly in the category of naturalism. After the railroad has won the struggle, the President of the company argues that the railroad is a "force born out of certain conditions." No man can stop or control it any more than anyone can stop the wheat from growing.

The second novel in the trilogy was *The Pit,* completed just before Norris's fatal appendectomy and published posthumously.

It depicts the trading of the wheat on the Chicago grain exchange, and while it is inferior to *The Octopus,* it tells an absorbing story of the protagonist's unsuccessful efforts to corner the wheat market. The third volume in the trilogy, which was to have been called *The Wolf* and was to deal with the distribution of the wheat in a famine-stricken Europe, was never written.

Another of Norris's novels that also deserves attention is *Vandover and the Brute,* a work that he wrote before *McTeague* but never could get published. It was issued with some cuts and perhaps some additions by his brother Charles, in 1914. The novel, a powerful study of disintegrating character, was too advanced for Doubleday, McClure and Co. in 1899. Vandover is weak-willed, indolent, badly brought up; after his father dies, leaving him a handsome legacy, he squanders his money, is victimized by a friend, and ends in abject degradation.

Norris is perhaps the most notable disciple of Zola in American literature. He praised Zola passionately and often reread his favorite novels, *L'Assommoir, La Terre, Germinal, La Bete humaine.* He researched his novels as Zola did, studying a manual of dentistry before writing *McTeague,* visiting a wheat farm while planning *The Octopus.* So pervasive was the influence that he joked about it in the inscription he wrote in the flyleaf of his wife's copy of *The Octopus:* "To my boss, Jeannette Norris, most respectfully . . . Mr. Norris (The Boy Zola)."

Although he was influenced by Zola, Norris never got over the original impulse towards romance. His critical views as outlined in *The Responsibilities of the Novelist* favor the spontaneous, improvising storyteller. He cites Dumas as an excellent example. He also believed that all good novels must have some significant pivotal event—such as the battle between the ranchers and the railroad deputies in *The Octopus.* It is no wonder that Norris is not a thorough-going naturalist. In addition, Norris never took himself very seriously. He wrote too fast and between *McTeague* and *The Octopus* there is much trash. He was torn between the Kipling-**Richard Harding Davis** tradition and Zola.

—James Woodress

See the essay on *The Octopus.*

NOVACK, Joseph. *See* **KOSINSKI, Jerzy (Nikodem).**

O

OATES, Joyce Carol

Pseudonym: Rosamond Smith. **Born:** Millersport, New York, 16 June 1938. **Education:** Syracuse University, New York, 1956-60, B.A. in English, 1960 (Phi Beta Kappa); University of Wisconsin, Madison, M.A. in English, 1961; Rice University, Houston, 1961. **Family:** Married Raymond J. Smith in 1961. **Career:** Instructor, 1961-65, and assistant professor of English, 1965-67, University of Detroit; member of the Department of English, University of Windsor, Ontario, 1967-78. Since 1978 writer-in-residence, and currently Roger S. Berlind Distinguished Professor, Princeton University, New Jersey. Since 1974 publisher, with Raymond J. Smith, *Ontario Review,* Windsor, later Princeton. **Awards:** National Endowment for the Arts grant, 1966, 1968; Guggenheim fellowship, 1967; O. Henry award, 1967, 1973, and Special Award for Continuing Achievement, 1970, 1986; Rosenthal award, 1968; National Book award, 1970; Rea Award, for short story, 1990; Alan Swallow award for fiction, 1990. **Member:** American Academy, 1978. **Residence:** Princeton, New Jersey.

PUBLICATIONS

Short Stories

By the North Gate. 1963.
Upon the Sweeping Flood and Other Stories. 1966.
The Wheel of Love and Other Stories. 1970.
Cupid and Psyche. 1970.
Marriages and Infidelities. 1972.
A Posthumous Sketch. 1973.
The Girl. 1974.
Plagiarized Material (as Fernandes/Oates). 1974.
The Goddess and Other Women. 1974.
Where Are You Going, Where Have You Been? Stories of Young America. 1974.
The Hungry Ghosts: Seven Allusive Comedies. 1975.
The Poisoned Kiss and Other Stories from the Portuguese (as Fernandes/Oates). 1975.
The Triumph of the Spider Monkey. 1976.
The Blessing. 1976.
Crossing the Border. 1976.
Daisy. 1977.
Night-Side. 1977.
A Sentimental Education. 1978.
The Step-Father. 1978.
All the Good People I've Left Behind. 1979.
The Lamb of Abyssalia. 1979.
A Middle-Class Education. 1980.
A Sentimental Education (collection). 1980.
Funland. 1983.
Last Days. 1984.
Wild Saturday and Other Stories. 1984.
Wild Nights. 1985.
Raven's Wing. 1986.
The Assignation. 1988.

Heat: And Other Stories. 1991.
Where Is Here? 1992.
Where Are You Going, Where Have You Been?: Selected Early Stories. 1993.
Haunted. 1994.
Will You Always Love Me? And Other Stories. 1996.
Demon and Other Tales. 1996.
The Collector of Hearts: New Tales of the Grotesque. 1998.

Novels

With Shuddering Fall. 1964.
A Garden of Earthly Delights. 1967.
Expensive People. 1968.
Them. 1969.
Wonderland. 1971.
Do with Me What You Will. 1973.
The Assassins: A Book of Hours. 1975.
Childwold. 1976.
Son of the Morning. 1978.
Cybele. 1979.
Unholy Loves. 1979.
Bellefleur. 1980.
Angel of Light. 1981.
A Bloodsmoor Romance. 1982.
Mysteries of Winterthurn. 1984.
Solstice. 1985.
Marya: A Life. 1986.
You Must Remember This. 1987.
Lives of the Twins (as Rosamond Smith). 1987.
Soul-Mate (as Rosamond Smith). 1989.
American Appetites. 1989.
Because It Is Bitter, and Because It Is My Heart. 1990.
I Lock My Door upon Myself. 1990.
The Rise of Life on Earth. 1991.
Black Water. 1992.
What I Lived For. 1994.
First Love: A Gothic Tale. 1996.
Tenderness. 1996.
Zombie. 1996.
Man Crazy: A Novel. 1997.
We Were the Mulvaneys. 1997.
My Heart Laid Bare. 1998.
Broke Heart Blues. 1999.

Plays

The Sweet Enemy (produced 1965).
Sunday Dinner (produced 1970).
Ontological Proof of My Existence, music by George Prideaux (produced 1972). Included in *Three Plays,* 1980.
Miracle Play (produced 1973). 1974.
Daisy (produced 1980).
Three Plays (includes *Ontological Proof of My Existence, Miracle Play, The Triumph of the Spider Monkey*). 1980.
The Triumph of the Spider Monkey, from her own story (produced 1985). Included in *Three Plays,* 1980.

Presque Isle, music by Paul Shapiro (produced 1982).
Lechery, in *Faustus in Hell* (produced 1985).
In Darkest America (*Tone Clusters* and *The Eclipse*) (produced 1990; *The Eclipse* produced 1990). 1991.
Twelve Plays (includes *Tone Clusters, The Eclipse, How Do You Like Your Meat?, The Ballad of Love Canal, Under/ground, Greensleeves, The Key, Friday Night, Black, I Stand before You Naked, The Secret Mirror, American Holiday*). 1991.
New Plays. 1998.

Poetry

Women in Love and Other Poems. 1968.
Anonymous Sins and Other Poems. 1969.
Love and Its Derangements. 1970.
Woman Is the Death of the Soul. 1970.
In Case of Accidental Death. 1972.
Wooded Forms. 1972.
Angel Fire. 1973.
Dreaming America and Other Poems. 1973.
The Fabulous Beasts. 1975.
Public Outcry. 1976.
Season of Peril. 1977.
Abandoned Airfield 1977. 1977.
Snowfall. 1978.
Women Whose Lives Are Food, Men Whose Lives Are Money. 1978.
The Stone Orchard. 1980.
Celestial Timepiece. 1980.
Nightless Nights: Nine Poems. 1981.
Invisible Woman: New and Selected Poems 1970-1982. 1982.
Luxury of Sin. 1984.
The Time Traveller: Poems 1983-1989. 1989.

Other

The Edge of Impossibility: Tragic Forms in Literature. 1972.
The Hostile Sun: The Poetry of D.H. Lawrence. 1973.
New Heaven, New Earth: The Visionary Experience in Literature. 1974.
Contraries: Essays. 1981.
The Profane Art: Essays and Reviews. 1983.
Funland. 1983.
On Boxing, photographs by John Ranard. 1987.
(Woman) Writer: Occasions and Opportunities. 1988.
Conversations with Joyce Carol Oates, edited by Lee Milazzo. 1989.
Come Meet Muffin (for children). 1998.

Editor, *Scenes from American Life: Contemporary Short Fiction.* 1973.
Editor, with Shannon Ravenel, *The Best American Short Stories 1979.* 1979.
Editor, *Night Walks: A Bedside Companion.* 1982.
Editor, *First Person Singular: Writers on Their Craft.* 1983.
Editor, with Boyd Litzinger, *Story: Fictions Past and Present.* 1985.
Editor, with Daniel Halpern, *Reading the Fights* (on boxing). 1988.
Editor, with Daniel Halpern, *The Sophisticated Cat: A Gathering of Stories, Poems, and Miscellaneous Writings about Cats.* 1992.
Editor, *The Oxford Book of American Short Stories.* 1992.
Editor, with R.V. Cassill, *The Norton Anthology of Contemporary Fiction.* 1998.

*

Bibliography: *Oates: An Annotated Bibliography* by Francine Lercangee, 1986.

Critical Studies: *The Tragic Vision of Oates* by Mary Kathryn Grant, 1978; *Oates* by Joanne V. Creighton, 1979; *Critical Essays on Oates* edited by Linda W. Wagner, 1979; *Dreaming America: Obsession and Transcendence in the Fiction of Oates* by G. F. Waller, 1979; *Oates* by Ellen G. Friedman, 1980; *Oates's Short Stories: Between Tradition and Innovation* by Katherine Bastian, 1983; *Isolation and Contact: A Study of Character Relationships in Oates's Short Stories 1963-1980* by Torborg Norman, 1984; *The Image of the Intellectual in the Short Stories of Oates* by Hermann Severin, 1986; *Oates: Artist in Residence* by Eileen Teper Bender, 1987; *Understanding Oates* by Greg Johnson, 1987; *Refusal and Transgression in Joyce Carol Oates' Fiction* by Marilyn C. Wesley, 1993; *Understanding Oates* by Greg Johnson, 1987; *Joyce Carol Oates: A Study of the Short Fiction* by Greg Johnson, 1994; *Lavish Self-divisions: The Novels of Joyce Carol Oates* by Brenda O. Daly, 1996; *The Critical Reception of the Short Fiction by Joyce Carol Oates and Gabriele Wohmann* by Sigrid Mayer, 1998; *Invisible Writer: A Biography of Joyce Carol Oates* by Greg Johnson, 1998; *Love Eclipsed: Joyce Carol Oates's Faustian Moral Vision* by Nancy Ann Watanabe, 1998.

*   *   *

In a 1982 *Contemporary Literature* interview with Leif Sjornberg, Joyce Carol Oates defined her standards for determining "what is important in literature": "Standards of greatness must encompass depth of vision; a breadth of actual work; a concern for various levels of human society; a sympathy with many different kinds of people; an awareness of and a concern for history, or at least contemporary history; a sense of the interlocking forces of politics, religion, economics, and the mores of society; concern with experimentation in forms and language; and above all a 'visionary sense'—the writer is not simply writing for his own sake, but to speak to others as forcefully as possible."

Oates has more than met her own measure. Her prodigious production of novels, short stories, plays, poetry, and literary and social commentary is legendary. She has published more than 1,000 separate pieces, including novels and novellas, volumes of short fiction, collections of poems, collections of plays, and compilations of literary criticism. Her works range from spiritual inquiry (*New Heaven, New Earth*) to the highly regarded book-length essay *On Boxing*. But the best measure of Oates's accomplishment has been the attainment of her own high standards—breadth of subject, sympathy for the human situation at many levels, an intelligent inquiry into the complex forces that shape human beings, and an abiding concern for the values that may save us.

The recurrent subject of Oates's work has been the desperation of people in a wide variety of contexts. Although her most frequent focus has been teenagers in troubled families (*With Shuddering Fall, them, Childwold, Marya,* and *Because It Is Bitter, Because It Is My Heart,* for example), she has also written about distressed adults in such works as *Solstice, Cybele,* and *American Appetites.* Her several series of novels also demonstrate the breadth of her subjects. Oates once commented on her "laughably Balzacian ambition to get the whole world into a book," a project well under way in novels that examine the professions: medicine in *Wonderland,* the law in *Do with Me What You Will,* religious vocation in *Son of the Morning,* and politics in *The Assassins.* The early novels *A Garden of Earthly Delights,* written about the plight of a migrant farm family, *them,* about the difficult lives of a family in urban Detroit, and *Expensive People,* about the vagaries of an unhappy suburban family, were conceived as a trilogy devoted to the consideration of three American economic classes.

Two later series combine an experimental interest in the forms of fiction with social concerns. *Bellefleur, A Bloodsmoor Romance,* and *Mysteries of Winterthurn* are parodic treatments of nineteenth-century popular genres that, according to Oates, "explore authentic crimes against women, children, and the poor in the guise of entertainment." Under the pseudonym Rosamond Smith she has published novels of suspense (*Lives of the Twins* and *Soul/Mate*) that are united by formal genre and thematic emphasis on the problem of contemporary identity.

There is much evidence of Oates's concern about the meaning of the collective experience of American life, from the so-called golden days of the 1850s through the challenges of the 1990s. Oates has remarked that the historical forces shaping her parents' experiences are as imaginatively available to her as those affecting her own life. Thus her works treat the experience of the Great Depression (*A Garden of Earthly Delights*) as well as the turmoil of the 1960s (*them* and *Wonderland*). *You Must Remember This,* one of her finest novels, captures the spirit of the Eisenhower years, while a frequent touchstone of her fiction is the assassination of John F. Kennedy, which precipitates the personal crisis at the conclusion of *Because It Is Bitter, Because It Is My Heart.* Works like *Angel of Light* and *American Appetites* treat the crisis in values in contemporary society. At the heart of her literature, Oates avers, is the predicament of characters who are "caught in the stampede of time."

This stampede is comprised of "interlocking forces"—political, economic, and ideological—that her characters can rarely name but always struggle to transcend. Jesse of *Wonderland,* perhaps Oates's most ambitious novel, is the victim of a father whose business failure precipitates the nearly successful attempt to murder the whole family. The surviving son's serial incarnations in successive American families is a study in the complex personal/social influences shaping a man's life. In *Marya,* a novel with the subtitle *A Life,* the protagonist's abandonment after the murder of her labor organizer father and her subsequent development as child, student, professor, and political analyst present a similar study of the influences shaping female experience.

Oates explained to interviewer Dale Boesky in "Correspondence with Joyce Carol Oates" that "I am always concerned with the larger social/political/moral implications of my characters' experiences," experiences that symbolize the problems of "our society in miniature." Her plots present the "desirable straining of a personality now outgrown or a social role too restrictive." The 1993 novel *Foxfire* typifies this general concern. In a blue-collar city in Oates's invented Eden County of upstate New York, charismatic "Legs" Sadovsky organizes an "outlaw" group of teenage girls committed to "true blood sisterhood" and the reclamation of the power that their situations in dysfunctional families and an uncaring community have denied them. More than the exploits of a "girl gang" of the 1950s, the novel is an inquiry in the revolutionary possibility of combining nurturance with agency. *Foxfire,* then, recapitulates the philosophical preoccupations of Oates's entire oeuvre: first, the failure of social institutions, especially the family, and, second, the necessity for the examination and restructuring of relationships of power in American society.

In *Heat,* Oates's 1991 collection of short stories, the stories range from psychological realism, her most typical form, to the folktale, the basic form of her tour de force gothic novel *Bellefleur,* to science fiction, a new genre in Oates's oeuvre. The constant formal experimentation that characterizes her career is paralleled by an insistence on visionary experimentation. Despite frequent critical misreadings of the bleakness and violence of her fiction, Oates insists on the capacity of literature to change the world. "It is my belief," she stated in the preface to *New Heaven, New Earth* (1974), "that the serious artist insists upon the sanctity of the world—even the despairing artist insists on the power of *his* art to transform what is given. It may be that his role, his function, is to articulate the very worst, to force into consciousness the most perverse and terrifying possibilities of the epoch, so that they can be dealt with and not simply feared." *What I Lived For* (1994) unravels the theme of the sins of the fathers being visited on subsequent generations. The novel chronicles the downfall of Corky Corcoran, who rose out of lower-class life but ultimately succumbs to his own narcissism and is unable to escape his past. In a suspenseful study of human vulnerability, Oates fully enters Corky's consciousness, capturing the thought process, speech patterns, and behavioral traits of a particular breed of macho male. The novella *First Love* (1996) confronts the consequential time in a girl's life when she understands that love is a two-sided coin. The notions of liberation and poignancy that come with first love are disrupted by the complications of emerging sexuality.

Will You Always Love Me?: And Other Stories (1996) reveals Oates's genius at opening with the seemingly mundane and then gradually escalating to a pitch of horrific revelation. Bodily disintegration is a menace to the characters in these stories, who endure tumors, palsies, strokes, a brain fissure, and child abuse. Oates's baroque imagination and her ability to convey the depths of violence and evil lying just below a thin veneer of civilization give these stories a chilling dimension. Vincent Canby, in a review of her play *The Truth-Teller,* observed that she has a "particular gift for locating the grotesque, the melancholy and the menacing within the resolutely commonplace." *Zombie* (1996) carries macabre imagination to the extreme. Presented as a diary of the character Quentin's pursuit of the perfect murder victim, the narrative incorporates crude drawings and typographic play to evoke the hermetic imagination of the psychopath. What results is a slim, sadistic reverie on human darkness and evil.

Certainly Oates's motifs of the frequently bloody assault by the world on the individual and the individual's counterattacks upon the world force our contemplation of that which may be feared. But Oates's ambition, as expressed in her criticism, extends beyond this achievement to the imagination of that which may be desired. In "The Death Throes of Romanticism" Oates argues that the competitive "I" projected by the romantic sensibility is a dangerous anachronism that must be replaced by the imaginative concept of "we." It is this constructive and collective possibility that Oates's disturbing protagonists struggle to introduce.

Oates's 1997 novel *We Were the Mulvaneys* traces the profound and darkly realistic chronicle of one family's hubristic heyday and of its fall from grace. More than a decade after the shattering events of the family crisis, there is a surprising denouement in which Oates delivers a guardedly optimistic vision of the future. Flashbacks help capture the same urgency of tone as the present narrative and contribute to the emotional power of the novel. In *My Heart Laid Bare* (1998) Oates picks up the tradition of her earlier historical gothic novels and explores Americans meeting the Fricks, Morgans and Rockefellers while facing the Roaring Twenties, the stock market crash, and the Great Depression. The novel investigates the relationship between deception and morality and in the process paints an alternative vision of the period.

In general, Oates's characters are victims of fate. Family traumas and human isolation are the sites of repeated study. The 27 macabre stories in *Collector of Hearts* present the cosmic predicaments of the individual that come to shape their narratives. As Oates navigates reality as well as its negative image, she presents stories that, at their most disturbing, push the limits of plausibility. In "The Hand Puppet" a ragged toy hideously alters a child's voice and behavior, to the terror of the unsuspecting mother. In "Death Mother" a woman recently released from a psychiatric ward attempts to reclaim her daughter, a college student who has never been able to escape traumatic memories. In the course of the stories Oates inhabits many different voices and psyches, often to the effect of an ominous, even blood-chilling, atmosphere.

There is no critical consensus on the meaning or value of Oates's work. Her central issues have been interpreted as tragedy, history, love, culture, and the power relations of the American family. She has been labeled a romantic and an antiromantic, a naturalist and a surrealist, and an antifeminist as well as a feminist. Her fictions have been both condemned as melodramatic and hailed for their sensitive portrayals. The volume of her production, the complexity of her style, and her philosophical dedication to open possibility make hers a literature that demands a great deal from her readers. What is generally agreed is that she is a consummate craftsman of the short story form and a gifted and intelligent novelist. What seems certain is that, when in years to come people mull over the meaning of American experience in all of its historical, moral, and social complexity, they will turn to the literature of Oates as among the most comprehensive, skillful, and visionary examinations the twentieth century provides.

—Marilyn C. Wesley, updated by Martha Sutro

O'BRIEN, (Michael) Fitz-James

Born: Ireland, probably in County Limerick, in 1828; immigrated to the United States, 1852. **Military Service:** Served in the Civil War in the 7th New York Regiment, 1861-62; aide-de-camp to General Lander; commissioned lieutenant, 1862; died of wounds. **Career:** Left Ireland for London, 1849; editor, *Parlour Magazine,* 1851; moved to New York, 1852; staff member, New York *Daily Times,* 1852-53; regular contributor to *Harper's Monthly,* 1853-62, and assistant editor and columnist ("Man about Town"), *Harper's Weekly,* 1857; drama critic, New York *Saturday Press,* 1858-59; press agent for actress Matilda Heron, 1859; columnist ("Here and There"), *Vanity Fair,* 1860. **Died:** 6 April 1862.

PUBLICATIONS

Collections

The Poems and Stories, edited by William Winter. 1881.
The Golden Ingot, The Diamond Lens, A Terrible Night, What Was It? 1921.

Collected Stories, edited by Edward J. O'Brien. 1925.
The Fantastic Tales, edited by Michael Hayes. 1977.

Plays

My Christmas Dinner (produced 1852).
A Gentleman from Ireland (produced 1854).
The Sisters, from a French play (produced 1854).
Duke Humphrey's Dinner (produced 1856).
The Tycoon; or, Young America in Japan, with Charles G. Rosenberg (produced 1860).

Poetry

Sir Brasil's Falcon. 1853.

*

Bibliography: in *Bibliography of American Literature* by Jacob Blanck, 1973.

Critical Studies: *O'Brien: A Literary Bohemian of the Eighteen-Fifties* by Francis Wolle, 1944 (includes bibliography); "Fitz-James O'Brien" by Thomas D. Clareson, in *Supernatural Fiction Writers: Fantasy and Horror, 2: A.E. Coppard to Roger Zelazny* edited by Everett Franklin Bleiler, 1985; "A Matter of Taste: Fitz-James O'Brien's 'The Diamond Lens' and Poe's Aesthetic of Beauty" by Michael Wentworth, in *American Transcendental Quarterly,* December 1988.

*   *   *

After education in Ireland and a short stint in London on the literary fringes, Fitz-James O'Brien immigrated to the United States and soon became a prominent member of New York's literary bohemia that frequented Pfaff's, the old Hone House, and Windust's. O'Brien contributed lavishly to a number of American periodicals over the next six years, among them the *American Whig Review, Putnam's, Harper's Weekly* and *Monthly, Vanity Fair, Atlantic Monthly,* and the *New York Times.* O'Brien was also the author of several plays, one, *A Gentleman from Ireland,* being presented successfully as late as 1895. His most imaginative story, "The Diamond Lens," appeared in 1858, winning him some fame, but at that point O'Brien's career as dandy author and bohemian faltered. He had acted as literary agent to M.L. Bateman, a theatrical director, and became involved with Matilda Heron, who appears to have had some responsibility for the collapse of O'Brien's fortunes. His splendid clothes, extensive library, elegant furnishings, soon disappeared; even his attractive personal appearance suffered a change for the worse with a broken nose from a professional pugilist. But he retained all his ebullience, and his end was brilliant. When the Civil War broke out, he joined the 7th Regiment of the National Guard of New York and won special mention for gallantry at the Battle of Bloomery Gap. A few days later he was wounded in the shoulder, indifferently nursed, and died of tetanus in 1862.

The general judgment on O'Brien is that he is more significant as personality than as author. Certainly, he wrote with unfortunate facility, and his verse is jaunty and negligible. Several of his stories, however, suggest a minor Poe with a dash of Hoffmann. O'Brien had an undisciplined but powerful Gothic imagination that ranged over such topics as abnormal psychology, mesmerism, magic, alchemy, and revenants, along with sharp flashes of prophetic imagination. "The Diamond Lens," a study of a mad microscopist, "The Wondersmith," with its aggressive manikin robots, and the ectoplasmic visitor of "What Was It?" retain some power to "electrify" the reader.

--Ian Fletcher

O'BRIEN, Tim(othy)

Born: Austin, Minnesota, 1 October 1946. **Education:** Macalester College, B.A. (Summa cum laude) 1968; Harvard University. **Military Service:** U.S. Army, served in Vietnam, 1968-70: sergeant; received purple heart. **Family:** Married in 1973. **Career:** Writer. National affairs reporter, Washington, DC, 1973-74. **Awards:** O. Henry Memorial awards, 1976 and 1978; National Book award, 1979; Vietnam Veterans award, 1987; Heartland prize, 1990.

PUBLICATIONS

Fiction

Northern Lights. 1975.
Going After Cacciato. 1978.
The Things They Carried. 1990.
In the Lake of the Woods. 1994.
Twinkle, Twinkle. 1994.
Tomcat in Love. 1998.

Other

If I Die in a Combat Zone, Box Me Up and Ship Me Home. 1973.

*

Critical Studies: *Questioning Truth: War and the Art of Writing in Ambrose Bierce, Stephen Crane, Michael Herr, and Tim O'Brien* (dissertation) by Dennis Keith Rudge, 1996; *Tim O'Brien's In the Lake of the Woods* by Iris Brewer, 1997; *Tim O'Brien* by Tobey C. Herzog, 1997; *Imagining the Truth: Narrative Structure and Technique in the Works of Tim O'Brien* (dissertation) by Michael A. Padelich, 1998.

*   *   *

With the exception of two books, Tim O'Brien has focused his writing on Vietnam. That country and conflict represent his loss of innocence and his growth as an artist. He is in fact always telling war stories, and he begins with *If I Die in the Combat Zone* (1973), a personal account heavily influenced by the new journalism of Michael Herr and **Norman Mailer.** The view of the war in *Combat Zone* is from the perspective of a young "grunt" who, with confusion and doubt, records his experience in order to understand the war. He recounts that, when they heard about his draft notice, his college friends told him, "No war is worth losing your life for." Early in his war experience O'Brien thinks of the

moral implications of soldiers' behavior; in *Combat Zone* he tells an Army chaplain, "a man cannot be fully a man until he acts in pursuit of goodness." The enormous evil of Vietnam thus stakes its claim in O'Brien's first book. Finally, O'Brien asks, "Can the foot soldier teach anything important about war, merely for having been there?" This question focuses on the fact that one can't "merely" have been there; to have been there was to be guilty. O'Brien has created stories that illustrate the conflict the horror of Vietnam generated within the individual soldier.

Going After Cacciato, winner of the 1979 National Book Award, illustrates the divided nature of O'Brien's response to the war. The novel has two points of view. The two views are not pro- and anti-war but rather realistic and surrealistic. O'Brien brings the experience of war for protagonist Paul Berlin to the fore then turns it into a fantasy about the escape of Cacciato, who has gone AWOL and run away to Paris. Imagining Cacciato's flight, Berlin is both in the war and outside of it, experiencing the war and creating the story that will take him away from the conflict. In "The Observation Post" chapters, Berlin is on duty during the middle-hour guard. He imagines the other story—the story of Cacciato, the young soldier who will lead him and his buddies "west through peaceful country, deep country . . . coaxing them step by step through rich and fertile country towards Paris." The fantasy of escape to Paris constitutes the other chapters of the novel. Berlin asks, "What, in fact, had become of Cacciato? . . . What part was fact and what part was extension of fact?" In his search for the answers about what happens to Cacciato, he probes human motivation. Like O'Brien, Berlin admits that he wants "just to live a normal life, to live to an old age."

O'Brien tried again to "tell a true war story" in *The Things They Carried* (1990). The book investigates O'Brien's responsibility for cowardice eighteen years before—"I was a coward, I went to war." In this book, dedicated to the men of Alpha Company, O'Brien tells how he did not run away to Canada, how he went to war—"I would go to the war I would kill and maybe die because I was too embarrassed not to." In the stories his buddies—Ted Lavender ("shot in the head on the way back from peeing"), Norman Bowker, Kiowa, Rat Kiley, Henry Dobbins, Curt Lemon—all "carried themselves with poise, a kind of dignity." It is that dignity that O'Brien honors with the assertion that "if at the end of a war story you feel uplifted . . . then you have been made the victim of a very old and terrible lie." Instead, he begins to understand that "you can tell a true war story by its absolute and uncompromising allegiance to obscenity and evil." The "uncompromising obscenity and evil" of war leads John Wade, the central character of "In the Lake of the Woods," to try to deny his part in the Vietnam tragedy. Having seen the massacre of My Lai, he has expunged himself from history. Watching the killing, he thinks, "This could not have happened. Therefore it did not." John Wade, also known as Sorcerer, leaves the war, trades his actual past for one he thinks people can love, and becomes a politician. He runs for the Senate. Near the end of the campaign his complicity in My Lai comes out, and he must run again from the guilt. John Wade's wife Kathy also vanishes; the mystery of her disappearance is never solved. Did she run away to Canada, as O'Brien wished he had? Has John Wade murdered her? There are no answers because life is a mystery and because guilt in America has always been kept secret. That secret guilt places "In the Lake of the Woods" next to **Hawthorne's** *Scarlet Letter* in its analysis of secret sin. In an interview for a Penguin Publishers "Reading Group Guide," O'Brien said, "We're all responsible for our actions in the world, and John Wade is responsible for his. Unfortunately, he can't own up to his sins . . . He not only hides them from others but from himself, as so many of us do." For O'Brien, the crime is in not telling the "true war story," and his novels and stories condemn America for not telling the truth about Vietnam.

O'Brien has also written *Northern Lights* (1974), another Vietnam fiction; *Nuclear Age* (1985), a novel that intersperses fantasy and reality in an attempt to deal with the possibility of nuclear annihilation; and *Tomcat in Love* (1998), a comedy about divorce, revenge, and true love. In all his work, a scarred and damaged man seeks some form of redemption through storytelling, and O'Brien himself finds the story the only way to deal with the horror of American history.

—Mary A. McCay

O'CONNOR, (Mary) Flannery

Born: Savannah, Georgia, 25 March 1925. **Education:** Peabody High School, Milledgeville, Georgia, graduated 1942; Georgia State College for Women (now Georgia College at Milledgeville), 1942-45, A.B. 1945; University of Iowa, Iowa City, 1945-47, M.F.A. 1947. **Career:** Writer; suffered from disseminated lupus after 1950. **Awards:** American Academy grant, 1957; O. Henry award, 1957, 1963, 1964; Ford Foundation grant, 1959; National Catholic Book award, 1966; National Book award, 1972. D.Litt.: St. Mary's College, Notre Dame, Indiana, 1962; Smith College, Northampton, Massachusetts, 1963. **Died:** 3 August 1964.

PUBLICATIONS

Collections

Complete Stories, edited by Robert Giroux. 1971.
Collected Works (Library of America), edited by Sally Fitzgerald. 1988.

Short Stories

A Good Man Is Hard to Find and Other Stories. 1955; as *The Artificial Nigger and Other Tales,* 1957.
Everything That Rises Must Converge. 1965.

Novels

Wise Blood. 1952.
The Violent Bear It Away. 1960.

Other

Mystery and Manners: Occasional Prose, edited by Sally and Robert Fitzgerald. 1969.
The Habit of Being: Letters, edited by Sally Fitzgerald. 1979.
The Presence of Grace and Other Book Reviews, edited by Carter W. Martin and Leo J. Zuber. 1983.
The Correspondence of O'Connor and the Brainard Cheneys, edited by C. Ralph Stephens. 1986.

Conversations with O'Connor, edited by Rosemary M. Magee. 1987.

Editor, *A Memoir of Mary Ann.* 1961; as *Death of a Child,* 1961.

*

Bibliography: *O'Connor and Caroline Gordon: A Reference Guide* by Robert E. Golden and Mary C. Sullivan, 1977; *O'Connor: A Descriptive Bibliography* by David Farmer, 1981.

Critical Studies: *O'Connor: A Critical Essay* by Robert Drake, 1966; *O'Connor* by Stanley Edgar Hyman, 1966; *The Added Dimension: The Art and Mind of O'Connor* edited by Melvin J. Friedman and Lewis A. Lawson, 1966, and *Critical Essays on O'Connor* edited by Friedman and Beverly L. Clark, 1985; *The True Country: Themes in the Fiction of O'Connor* by Carter W. Martin, 1969; *The World of O'Connor* by Josephine Hendin, 1970; *The Eternal Crossroads: The Art of O'Connor* by Leon Driskell and Joan T. Brittain, 1971; *The Christian Humanism of O'Connor* by David Eggenschwiler, 1972; *Nightmares and Visions: O'Connor and the Catholic Grotesque* by Gilbert Muller, 1972; *O'Connor: Voice of the Peacock* by Kathleen Feeley, 1972, revised edition, 1982; *Invisible Parade: The Fiction of O'Connor* by Miles Orvell, 1972, as *O'Connor: An Introduction,* 1991; *O'Connor* by Dorothy Walters, 1973; *The Question of O'Connor* by Martha Stephens, 1973; *O'Connor* by Preston M. Browning, Jr., 1974; *O'Connor* by Dorothy Tuck McFarland, 1976; *The Pruning Word: The Parables of O'Connor* by John R. May, 1976; *O'Connor's Dark Comedies: The Limits of Inference* by Carol Shloss, 1980; *O'Connor: Her Life, Library, and Book Reviews,* 1980, and *Nature and Grace in O'Connor's Fiction,* 1982, both by Lorine M. Getz; *O'Connor's South* by Robert Coles, 1980; *O'Connor's Georgia* by Barbara McKenzie, 1980; *The O'Connor Companion* by James A. Grimshaw, Jr., 1981; *O'Connor: The Imagination of Extremity* by Frederick Asals, 1982; *O'Connor: Images of Grace* by Harold Fickett and Douglas Gilbert, 1986; *O'Connor's Religion of the Grotesque* by Marshall Bruce Gentry, 1986; *O'Connor: A Study of the Short Fiction* by Suzanne Morrow Paulson, 1988; *O'Connor and the Mystery of Love* by Richard Giannone, 1989; *Flannery O'Connor: The Woman, the Thinker, the Visionary* by Ted Ray Spivey, 1995; *Understanding Flannery O'Connor* by Margaret Earley Whitt, 1995; *Writing Against God: Language As Message in the Literature of Flannery O'Connor* by Joanne Halleran McCullen, 1996; *Flannery O'Connor's Characters* by Laurence Enjolras, 1998; *Flannery O'Connor: A Proper Scaring* by Jill P. Baumgaertner, 1998; *Flannery O'Connor's Characters* by Laurence Enjolras, 1998; *Flannery O'Connor* edited by Harold Bloom, 1999.

*   *   *

Flannery O'Connor belongs to a small group of twentieth-century writers whose work is profoundly religious, not through direct statement or preachment but because its informing theme and structure are theological. O'Connor was raised as a Roman Catholic in the Protestant South, and she found in the "Christ-haunted" fundamentalist religious beliefs of that region much that awoke responsive chords in her, despite her basic theological differences with the Protestant faith. She brought to the portrayal of the people of her region a clear, hard, witty style, an unblinking eye, and a sense of both the divine and the ridiculous; and she used her violent portrayals of grotesque people to express a deep and unsentimental religious faith. Fairly early in her career, she developed lupus, an incurable disease that progressed inexorably to its conclusion in her death at the age of 39. Much of her work was produced after this disease had initially struck, and a great deal of her best fiction is concerned with death, and often with death as a release or means of salvation. Although this is a limited theme, and the range of her work often seems distressingly narrow, Flannery O'Connor worked within the limits of her art with great commitment, artistic integrity, high technical skill, and frequent success.

She is primarily a writer of short stories. The collection *A Good Man Is Hard to Find* and the posthumous *Everything That Rises Must Converge* contained nineteen examples of her best work in this form. *The Complete Stories* added twelve more. Her first novel, *Wise Blood,* was a weaving together of material originally written in short-story form. Her only other novel was *The Violent Bear It Away.* (She was working on a third novel at the time of her death but apparently without the expectation of ever completing it.) Despite excellent elements in both her novels, O'Connor will survive as a master of the short-story form. Her stories were based on what she called "anagogical vision . . . the kind of vision that is able to see different levels of reality in one image or one situation." It is this anagogical element that has led to very extensive examination of levels of meaning in her stories by many critics.

Wise Blood is the story of the preacher Hazel Motes, called, he believed, to preach "the Church without Christ," a man who is driven by acts of violent grace finally to accept the Jesus whom he had denied, to blind himself, and to die, and in his death to achieve a kind of salvation. *The Violent Bear It Away* is the record of the efforts of a boy, Francis Marion Tarwater, to escape the prophetic calling bequeathed to him by his dead great-uncle. A much more tightly organized work than *Wise Blood, The Violent Bear It Away* is really the harrowing chronicle of the struggle of cosmic forces, represented by the religious great-uncle and a very modern uncle, for the soul of Francis Tarwater. The great-uncle ultimately triumphs.

O'Connor's short stories deal with simple Georgia people, hungry with a passionate desire for a spiritual dimension that the nature of their lives and their beliefs denies them. The usual pattern in these stories is that of a desperate search through extreme, violent, and grotesque actions that usually culminate in the entry of divine grace through some instrumentality that bestows salvation in the moment of death. The frantic and misdirected struggles of these human beings result in a violent but comic representation that seems in many ways to reflect the long tradition of American Southwestern humor, with its extreme portrayals of grotesque people in violent and unusual situations. Her work is most like that of **Erskine Caldwell** in terms of the grotesqueness of her characters, the extravagance of her actions, the sharp and vigorous starkness of her prose, and her kind of pervasive comic sense. However, where Caldwell presents his characters as people distorted as a result of economic deprivation, O'Connor's world is the world of people rendered grotesque by their inability to satisfy their spiritual hungers. All of her characters can be explained in one sense in St. Augustine's phrase, "Our souls are restless till they find rest in Thee." Among her short stories of particular distinction are "A Good Man Is Hard to Find," "Good Country People," "The Artificial Nigger," "The Lame Shall Enter First,"

"Revelation," "Greenleaf," and the short novel "The Displaced Person."

In her short life O'Connor accomplished much in her intense art. Narrow though her range and subjects are, they are pursued with great distinction and great force. Ultimately she will remain a minor figure in American letters, but a minor figure of enormous challenge, subtlety, and accomplishment.

—C. Hugh Holman

See the essay on *Wise Blood.*

ODETS, Clifford

Born: Philadelphia, Pennsylvania, 18 July 1906; grew up in the Bronx, New York. **Education:** Morris High School, New York, 1921-23. **Family:** Married 1) the actress Luise Rainer in 1937 (divorced 1941); 2) Bette Grayson in 1943 (divorced 1951), one son and one daughter. **Career:** Actor on radio and on Broadway, 1923-28, and with Theatre Guild Productions, New York, 1928-30; cofounder, Group Theatre, New York, 1930; wrote for the stage from 1933; joined Communist Party, 1934 (resigned 1934); film writer and director. **Awards:** New Theatre League prize, 1935; Yale drama prize, 1935; American Academy Award of Merit Medal, 1961. **Died:** 14 August 1963.

PUBLICATIONS

Plays

Waiting for Lefty (produced 1935). In *Three Plays,* 1935.
Awake and Sing! (produced 1935). In *Three Plays,* 1935.
Till the Day I Die (produced 1935). In *Three Plays,* 1935.
I Can't Sleep: A Monologue (produced 1935). In *New Theatre 3,* 1936.
Paradise Lost (produced 1935). 1936.
Golden Boy (produced 1937). 1937.
Rocket to the Moon (produced 1938). 1939.
Six Plays. 1939.
Night Music (produced 1940). 1940.
Clash by Night (produced 1941). 1942.
The Russian People, from a play by Konstantin Simonov (produced 1942). In *Seven Soviet Plays,* edited by H.W.L. Dana, 1946.
None but the Lonely Heart (screenplay), in *Best Film Plays 1945,* edited by John Gassner and Dudley Nichols. 1946.
The Big Knife (produced 1949). 1949.
The Country Girl (produced 1950). 1951; revised version, as *Winter Journey* (produced 1952), 1955.
The Flowering Peach (produced 1954). 1954(?).
The Silent Partner (produced 1972).
Sweet Smell of Success (screenplay). 1998.

Screenplays: *The General Died at Dawn,* 1936; *Black Sea Fighters,* 1943; *None But the Lonely Heart,* 1944; *Deadline at Dawn,* 1946; *Humoresque with Zachary Gold,* 1946; *Sweet Smell of Success,* with Ernest Lehman, 1957; *The Story on Page One,* 1960; *Wild in the Country,* 1961.

Television Plays: *Big Mitch,* 1963, and *The Mafia Man,* 1964 (both for *The Richard Boone Show*).

Other

Rifle Rule in Cuba, with Carleton Beals. 1935.
1940 Journal. 1987.
Clifford Odets: In Hell and Why—Paintings on Paper from the 1940s and 1950s. 1996.

*

Bibliography: *Guide to the Clifford Odets Papers in the Lilly Library,* 1995.

Critical Studies: *Odets,* 1963, and "Clifford Odets and the Jewish Context" in *From Hester Street to Hollywood: The Jewish-American Stage and Screen* edited by Sarah Blacher Cohen, 1983, both by R. Baird Shuman; *Odets: The Thirties and After* by Edward Murray, 1968; *Odets, Humane Dramatist* by Michael J. Mendelsohn, 1969; *Odets the Playwright,* 1971, revised edition, 1985, and "Clifford's Children; Or, It's a Wise Playwright Who Knows His Own Father" in *Studies in American Drama, 1945-Present,* 1987, both by Gerald Weales; *Odets, Playwright-Poet,* 1978, and "Odets' Yinglish: The Psychology of Dialect as Dialogue" in *Studies in American Jewish Literature,* 1982, both by Harold Cantor; *Odets, American Playwright: The Years from 1906 to 1940* by Margaret Brenman-Gibson, 1981; "Clifford Odet's Musical World: The Failed Utopia" in *Studies in American Jewish Literature,* 1986, and "Waiting for Odets: A Playwright Takes a Stand" in *Politics and the Muse: Studies in the Politics of Recent American Literature* edited by Adam J. Sorkin, 1989, both by George L. Groman; *Odets* by Gabriel Miller, 1989.

*   *   *

Clifford Odets's first produced play was *Waiting for Lefty,* a one-act agitprop drama based on the New York City taxi strike of 1934. It is uncharacteristic Odets in both form and intention. A group of naturalistic dramatic sketches set within a union meeting, still visible while the more intimate scenes are being played, *Waiting for Lefty* is non-realistic theater that breaks the conventional frame to invite the audience to join in the final call for a strike. Aside from this play, Odets remained within the American realistic tradition even when he attempted to open the form with cinematic techniques (*Golden Boy*), visual and musical devices (*Night Music*), and Yiddish-biblical fantasy (*The Flowering Peach*). Although most of his plays, particularly the early ones like *Awake and Sing!* and *Paradise Lost,* have the mandatory optimistic ending decreed by the American Left in the 1930s, *Waiting for Lefty* is the only overt propaganda play Odets wrote, except for *Till the Day I Die,* an ineffective anti-fascist piece hastily written to fill out the bill when *Lefty* moved to Broadway. He did do a few sketches, like "I Can't Sleep," for benefit performances and he worked at two political plays, *The Cuban Play* and *The Silent Partner,* which he never got into final form. If *Waiting for Lefty* is uncharacteristic in some ways, it is also unmistakable Odets. Scenes like "Joe and Edna" and "The Young Hack and His Girl" show that Odets's political and social concerns look their best transformed into domestic conflict, and the language of those scenes set the tone for the Odets work to come. When Edna says, "Get

out of here!" meaning "I love you" and Sid, in affectionate exasperation, calls his brother "that dumb basketball player," we get a first taste of the Odets obliquity—the wisecrack as lament, slang as lyricism—that, trailing its Yiddish and urban roots, enriches *Awake and Sing!* and *Paradise Lost* before it peters out in the self-parody of some of the lines in the screenplay *Sweet Smell of Success.*

Although *Waiting for Lefty* introduced Odets to audiences and critics, it was not his first play. *Awake and Sing!* was already written and about to open when *Lefty* was produced. *Awake and Sing!,* Odets's most enduring work, is the American depression play, a still vital example of the 1930s conviction that, however terrible the situation, it could be rectified by an infusion of idealistic rhetoric administered at the final curtain. Although Odets was a Communist when he wrote it (and the play carries a few verbal indications of that fact), its optimism is more generalized, tied into the historical American penchant for possibility that, battered by the first years of the depression, had begun to revive with the election of Franklin D. Roosevelt in 1932. Not only is Odets hooked into the American ideational mainstream in *Awake and Sing!,* but he recalls earlier American drama in his choice of a family setting for his play and in his willing employment of melodramatic commonplaces—the suicide of Jacob, the pregnancy of Hennie. He transcends the structural weaknesses in the play with the creation of a milieu so real that an audience feels it can be touched; this texture—partly verbal, partly emotional—is probably a product not simply of Odets's talent but of the context in which the play was written. Odets was a member of the Group Theatre, an acting company that was a family of sorts, and his Bergers are an echo of the loving, quarreling Group company that was a home for Odets, one that—reacting like Ralph and Hennie to Bessie Berger's Bronx—he sometimes saw as a trap. All of his plays through *Night Music* were written for the Group actors, but *Paradise Lost,* which Odets once correctly described as "a beautiful play, velvety . . . gloomy and rich," and *Rocket to the Moon* come closest in texture to *Awake and Sing!*

When the success of *Awake and Sing!* was followed by the failure of *Paradise Lost,* Odets went to Hollywood to work on *The General Died at Dawn.* After that, he vacillated between Hollywood and New York, commerce and art, guilt and regeneration. These terms suit his view of the matter as reflected in *The Big Knife,* in which the Odets surrogate, the actor Charlie Castle, is destroyed as man and artist by the movie business. Despite this gloomy view of Hollywood Odets constantly returned to a suspicion that the movies too were an art, all the more attractive for the size of the audience. Ironically, the movies he worked on were conventional Hollywood products; even the two he directed as well as wrote, *None but the Lonely Heart* and *The Story on Page One,* are interesting primarily for their attempt at poetic verisimilitude, the visual equivalent of the sense of milieu created by other means in *Awake and Sing!* and *Paradise Lost.*

Odets's greatest commercial successes were *Golden Boy,* a parable in boxing gloves about the destructiveness of the American success ethic, and *The Country Girl,* an effective sentimental melodrama about an alcoholic actor's attempt to recover his career and his life. Both plays show Odets's theatrical skill, but his most attractive failures, *Paradise Lost* and *Night Music,* display a bumbling sweetness that is as important a part of Odets's talent as his technical proficiency. Both the staccato dialogue of *Golden Boy* and the rambling non sequiturs of *Paradise Lost* are aspects of the authentic Odets voice that can still be heard at its purest in *Awake and Sing!*

—Gerald Weales

See the essay on *Awake and Sing!*

OGDEN, H. B. *See* **ASIMOV, Isaac.**

O'HARA, Frank

Born: Francis Russell O'Hara in Baltimore, Maryland, 27 June 1926. **Education:** Privately educated in piano and musical composition, 1933-43; at New England Conservatory of Music, Boston, 1946-50, A.B. in English 1950; University of Michigan, Ann Arbor (Hopwood Award, 1951), M.A. 1951. **Career:** Served in the U.S. Navy, 1944-46. Staff member, 1951-54, fellowship curator, 1955-64, associate curator, 1965, and curator of the International Program, 1966, Museum of Modern Art, New York. Editorial associate, *Art News* magazine, New York, 1954-56; art editor, *Kulchur* magazine, New York, 1962-64. **Awards:** Ford fellowship, for drama, 1956. **Died:** 25 July 1966.

PUBLICATIONS

Collections

Collected Poems, edited by Donald Allen. 1971.
Selected Poems, edited by Donald Allen. 1974.
Selected Plays. 1978.
Poems Retrieved. 1996.

Poetry

A City Winter and Other Poems. 1952.
Oranges. 1953.
Meditations in an Emergency. 1956.
Harrigan and Rivers with O'Hara: An Exhibition of Pictures, with Poems. 1959.
Second Avenue. 1960.
Odes. 1960.
Featuring O'Hara. 1964.
Lunch Poems. 1964.
Love Poems: Tentative Title. 1965.
In Memory of My Feelings: A Selection of Poems, edited by Bill Berkson. 1967.
Two Pieces. 1969.
Odes. 1969.
Belgrade, November 19, 1963. 1973.
Hymns of St. Bridget, with Bill Berkson. 1974.
Early Poems 1946-1951, edited by Donald Allen. 1976.
Poems Retrieved 1951-1966, edited by Donald Allen. 1977.

Plays

Try! Try! (produced 1951; revised version, produced 1952). In *Artists' Theatre,* edited by Herbert Machiz, 1960.

Change Your Bedding (produced 1951).
Love's Labor: An Eclogue (produced 1960). 1964.
Awake in Spain (produced 1960). 1960.
The General Returns from One Place to Another (produced 1964). In *Eight Plays from Off-Off Broadway,* edited by Nick Orzel and Michael Smith, 1966.
Surprising J.A., with Larry Rivers, in *Tracks 1,* November 1974.
Kenneth Koch: A Tragedy, with Larry Rivers (produced 1982).

Screenplay: *The Last Clean Shirt.* N.d.

Other

Jackson Pollock. 1959.
Standing Still and Walking in New York, edited by Donald Allen. 1975.
Art Chronicles 1954-1966. 1975.
Early Writing, edited by Donald Allen. 1977.

Editor, *Robert Motherwell: A Catalogue with Selections from the Artist's Writings.* 1966.

*

Bibliography: *O'Hara: A Comprehensive Bibliography* by Alexander Smith, Jr., 1980.

Critical Studies: *O'Hara, Poet among Painters* by Marjorie G. Perloff, 1977; *Homage to O'Hara* edited by Bill Berkson and Joe LeSueur, 1978; *O'Hara* by Alan Feldman, 1979; "Franked Letters: Crossing the Bar" by Eleanor Honig Skoller, in *Visible Language: The Quarterly Concerned with All That Is Involved in Our Being Literate,* 1980; "Frank O'Hara's Poetics of Speech: The Example of 'Biotherm'" by Mutlu Konuk Blasing, in *Contemporary Literature,* 1982; "Frank O'Hara and His Poetry: An Interview with Kenneth Koch," in *American Writing Today* edited by Richard Kostelanetz, 1982; "'Alterable Noons': The 'poemes elastiques' of Blaise Cendrars and Frank O'Hara" by Marjorie Perloff, in *Yearbook of English Studies,* 1985; "Crossing the Delaware with Larry Rivers and Frank O'Hara: The Post-Modern Hero at the Battle of Signifiers" by Suzanne Ferguson, in *Word and Image: A Journal of Verbal Visual Enquiry,* 1986; *The Exploration of the Secret Smile: The Language of Art and of Homosexuality in Frank O'Hara's Poetry* by Alice C. Parker, 1989; "The 'Post-Anti-Esthetic' Poetics of Frank O'Hara" by John Lowney, in *Contemporary Literature,* 1991; *Politics and Form in Postmodern Poetry: O'Hara, Bishop, Ashbery, and Merrill* by Mutlu Konuk Blasing, 1995.

*   *   *

Frank O'Hara's status as an important poet of the post-World War II era was only established in the late twentieth century. During his lifetime he was known only to a circle of friends, many of them painters in New York whom he knew from his work as an associate curator of the Museum of Modern Art. But his canon is large and runs to more than five hundred pages of text in Donald Allen's edition of *The Collected Poems.*

O'Hara was cavalier about his reputation as a poet and reluctant to have his poetry in print. As a result, his work largely went unnoticed in the review columns; when his name did surface, he was taken lightly. It was only later that his work received serious critical attention; Marjorie Perloff's book vigorously argues his major status as an innovator of lyrical poetry. Perloff and others consider O'Hara to have had an influence on younger poets comparable to that of **Charles Olson**, **Robert Creeley**, and **Allen Ginsberg**.

O'Hara's poetry from 1951 to 1954 shows the influence of **Ezra Pound**, **William Carlos Williams**, and W.H. Auden. His early poems, collected in *A City Winter and Other Poems*, are lyrical and strive very deliberately for surprising effects. His friend the poet **John Ashbery** once commented that this was O'Hara's "French Zen period," which is an astute observation of the lushly surrealistic language of these poems. As he commented in an early poem, "Poetry":

> The only way to be quiet
> is to be quick, so I scare
> you clumsily, or surprise
> you with a stab. A praying
> mantis knows time more
> intimately than I and is
> more casual.

Auden once wrote to caution O'Hara against tiring the reader with an excess of surreal statements, and he appears to have heeded his counsel, for in the poetry of the later 1950s, gathered in *Meditations in an Emergency* and *Lunch Poems*, he exerted greater control over the structure of his poems and gave himself more intense freedom in brief, dazzling displays of lyrical exuberance.

In *Second Avenue* and other longer poems—"Easter," "In Memory of My Feelings," "Ode to Michael Goldberg('s Birth and Other Births)" and the late "Biotherm (for Bill Berkson)"—O'Hara, like Pushkin and Byron before him, created perhaps the essential hero of urban cultural life, a sophisticated romantic who thrives on the city's alien and exotic elements. His many shorter poems are briefer expressions of this same captivating persona.

O'Hara also succeeds in rendering consciousness and its fringe states with intense accuracy and daring in a style partly influenced by the methods and experiments of the Abstract Expressionist painters. O'Hara wrote several plays, and essays on contemporary painting collected in *Standing Still and Walking in New York* and *Art Chronicles 1954-1966*. Although not a theorist or trained critic of painting, his eye was sensitive to technique and his instinct sharp in discerning the great works of his time.

—Paul Christensen

O'HARA, John (Henry)

Born: Pottsville, Pennsylvania, 31 January 1905. **Education:** Fordham Preparatory School, Keystone State Normal School; Niagara Preparatory School, Niagara Falls, New York, 1923-24. **Family:** Married 1) Helen Petit in 1931 (divorced 1933); 2) Belle Mulford Wylie in 1937 (died 1954), one daughter; 3) Katharine Barns Bryan in 1955. **Career:** Reporter, Pottsville *Journal*, 1924-26, and Tamaqua *Courier*, Pennsylvania, 1927; reporter, New York *Herald-Tribune*, and *Time* magazine, New York, 1928; rewrite man, New York *Daily Mirror*, radio columnist (as Franey Delaney), New York *Morning Telegraph*, and managing editor, *Bulletin In-*

dex magazine, Pittsburgh, 1928-33; full-time writer from 1933; film writer, for Paramount and other studios, from 1934; columnist ("Entertainment Week"), *Newsweek*, New York, 1940-42; Pacific war correspondent, *Liberty* magazine, New York, 1944; columnist ("Sweet and Sour"), Trenton *Sunday Times-Adviser*, New Jersey, 1953-54; lived in Princeton, New Jersey, from 1954; columnist ("Appointment with O'Hara"), *Collier's*, New York, 1954-56, ("My Turn"), *Newsday*, Long Island, New York, 1964-65, and ("The Whistle Stop"), *Holiday*, New York, 1966-67. **Awards:** New York Drama Critics Circle award, 1952; Donaldson award, for play, 1952; National Book award, 1956; American Academy award of Merit Medal, 1964. **Member:** American Academy, 1957. **Died:** 11 April 1970.

PUBLICATIONS

Collections

Selected Letters, edited by Matthew J. Bruccoli. 1978.
Collected Stories, edited by Frank MacShane. 1985.
The Novellas of John O'Hara. 1995.

Fiction

Appointment in Samarra. 1934.
Butterfield 8. 1935.
The Doctor's Son and Other Stories. 1935.
Hope of Heaven. 1938.
Files on Parade (stories). 1939.
Pal Joey (stories). 1940.
Pipe Night (stories). 1945.
Here's O'Hara (omnibus). 1946.
Hellbox (stories). 1947.
All the Girls He Wanted (stories). 1949.
A Rage to Live. 1949.
The Farmers Hotel. 1951.
Ten North Frederick. 1955.
A Family Party. 1956.
The Great Short Stories of O'Hara. 1956.
Selected Short Stories. 1956.
From the Terrace. 1958.
Ourselves to Know. 1960.
Sermons and Soda Water (includes *The Girl on the Baggage Truck*, *Imagine Kissing Pete*, *We're Friends Again*). 3 vols., 1960.
Assembly (stories). 1961.
The Cape Cod Lighter (stories). 1962.
The Big Laugh. 1962.
Elizabeth Appleton. 1963.
49 Stories. 1963.
The Hat on the Bed (stories). 1963.
The Horse Knows the Way (stories). 1964.
The Lockwood Concern. 1965.
Waiting for Winter (stories). 1966.
The Instrument. 1967.
And Other Stories. 1968.
Lovey Childs: A Philadelphian's Story. 1969.
The O'Hara Generation (stories). 1969.
The Ewings. 1972.
The Time Element and Other Stories, edited by Albert Erskine. 1972.

Good Samaritan and Other Stories, edited by Albert Erskine. 1974.
The Second Ewings. 1977.
We'll Have Fun. 1996.

Plays

Pal Joey (libretto), music by Richard Rodgers, lyrics by Lorenz Hart, from the stories by O'Hara (produced 1940). 1952.
Five Plays (includes *The Farmers Hotel, The Searching Sun, The Champagne Pool, Veronique, The Way It Was*). 1961.
Two by O'Hara (includes *The Man Who Could Not Lose* and *Far from Heaven*). 1979.

Screenplays: *I Was an Adventuress,* with Karl Tunberg and Don Ettlinger, 1940; *He Married His Wife,* with others, 1940; *Moontide,* 1942; *On Our Merry Way* (episode), 1948; *The Best Things in Life Are Free,* with William Bowers and Phoebe Ephron, 1956.

Other

Sweet and Sour (essays). 1954.
My Turn (newspaper columns). 1966.
A Cub Tells His Story. 1974.
An Artist Is His Own Fault: O'Hara on Writers and Writings, edited by Matthew J. Bruccoli. 1977.

*

Bibliography: *O'Hara: A Checklist,* 1972, and *O'Hara: A Descriptive Bibliography,* 1978, both by Matthew J. Bruccoli.

Critical Studies: *The Fiction of O'Hara* by Russell E. Carson, 1961; *O'Hara* by Sheldon Norman Grebstein, 1966; *O'Hara* by Charles C. Walcutt, 1969; *O'Hara: A Biography* by Finis Farr, 1973; *The O'Hara Concern: A Biography* by Matthew J. Bruccoli, 1975; *The Life of O'Hara* by Frank MacShane, 1980; *O'Hara* by Robert Emmet Long, 1983; *Critical Essays on John O'Hara* edited by Philip B. Eppard, 1994.

* * *

John O'Hara's 374 short stories and 18 novels record the changing habits and values of the United States from World War I to the Vietnam War. O'Hara began writing as a reporter, editor, press agent, and script writer; he worked first in his native eastern Pennsylvania coal region (Pottsville—his fictional Gibbsville), and later in New York and Hollywood. His short stories began appearing in the *New Yorker* in 1928, and his first novel, *Appointment in Samarra,* identified him as a first-rate writer. His short stories range from short monologues, reminiscent of **Ring Lardner** (whose influence he acknowledged), to hundred-page novellas that may be his finest work: O'Hara has been called America's best short-story writer. Through his involvement with the New York theatrical world—plus an acknowledged mastery of dialogue—he tried to write for the stage. Even though his *Pal Joey* became a hit Rodgers and Hart musical, his *Five Plays* is a testament to his lack of success as a playwright.

As O'Hara's fame grew, it was often asserted that his first novel, *Appointment in Samarra,* was also his best. The fast pace and shifting point of view hold the reader until the suicide of Julian

English at the end, which is still being debated: did Gibbsville drive him to it (just after the Great Crash in 1929), or did the compulsion come from within him? Nearly all of O'Hara's stories hold the reader's interest in the same way: how will the characters develop and what will happen to them? O'Hara said he was picturing, as honestly as he could, how twentieth-century Americans were driven by money, sex, and a struggle for status—often to their own destruction. In 1935 O'Hara published *Butterfield 8,* his only *roman á clef.* The heroine, Gloria Wandrous, is much like the Jazz Age celebrity Starr Faithfull, whose body was washed up on a Long Island beach in 1931. The novel was a popular success and extended O'Hara's fictional domain from Pennsylvania to New York City. *Hope of Heaven* pushed his range much farther, to Hollywood. But there is a link between all three of the first novels: the protagonist-narrator (and Hollywood scriptwriter) of *Hope of Heaven* is Jimmy Malloy, a former Gibbsville reporter who has covered the Gloria Wandrous murder/suicide/accident.

More than a hundred short stories and sketches were published in *The Doctor's Son and Other Stories, Files on Parade,* and *Pipe Night.* These tightly written stories present character and situation satirically, but O'Hara is not callous about the loneliness, misery, and degradation he reveals—on Broadway or in Gibbsville. The best known of these stories are the heavily ironic monologues (in the form of letters) of Joey Evans, a night club master of ceremonies. *Pal Joey,* a collection of fourteen stories, became the Rodgers and Hart musical. Joey is a heel, an anti-hero, and the sexual innuendo was shocking in 1940; but *Pal Joey* also had a strong plot line and has been called the first realistic American musical.

A Rage to Live is the first of O'Hara's long and elaborately documented novels. The period is 1900 to 1920 and the locale is Fort Penn (Harrisburg, Pennsylvania), but the serious social history was obscured for many readers by his heroine's lack of sexual control. In *Ten North Frederick,* O'Hara moved the setting back to Gibbsville, where Joe Chapin earns great wealth and prestige with the help of his family name, a Yale law degree, and considerable intelligence. But Chapin aspires to be president of the United States: he attempts to buy the lieutenant governorship, is duped by an Irish politician, and drinks himself to death in "the quiet, gentlemanly, gradual way in which he had lived his life," as one critic wrote. *From the Terrace* is an even larger and more ambitious work: O'Hara tells the story of Alfred Eaton, a small-town Pennsylvania boy who goes to New York and Washington, becomes a great financier and government official, and finally discovers that his life is empty and meaningless. O'Hara regarded it as his masterpiece.

O'Hara wrote prodigiously in the last fifteen years of his life. *Ourselves to Know,* a big novel set in eastern Pennsylvania, uses a circular technique and shifting perspective in trying to understand and explain Robert Millhouser, who killed his wife and was acquitted in a murder trial. In the foreword to *Sermons and Soda Water,* three novellas all filtered through the consciousness of Jimmy Malloy, O'Hara explains why he used this unpopular and unprofitable form instead of expanding each of the stories into a 350-page novel:

> I want to get it all down on paper while I can. I am now fifty-five years old and I have lived with as well as in the Twentieth Century from its earliest days. The United States in this Century is what I know, and it is my business to write about it to the best of my ability,

with the sometimes special knowledge I have. The Twenties, the Thirties, and the Forties are already history, but I cannot be content to leave their story in the hands of the historians and the editors of picture books. I want to record the way people talked and thought and felt, and to do it with complete honesty and variety.

The Big Laugh is O'Hara's second Hollywood novel: his monologues of classic Hollywood types are bawdy, funny, and authentic. *Elizabeth Appleton* is an academic novel, focused on a weekend when the dean's wife sees her husband passed over for the presidency of a small Pennsylvania college. *The Lockwood Concern,* O'Hara's last major novel, is "a condensed big book" (400 pages): four generations of the family have lived in a small town near Gibbsville since 1840, but third-generation George Lockwood compulsively destroys the dynasty by driving his only son to a criminal career in California. Critics charged that O'Hara's protagonists often destroy themselves and their social fabric without explicable motivation.

There were three more novels to come. *The Instrument* explores the parasitism of playwright Yank Lucas: he deserts the star actress on opening night, writes a new play on their relationship, and she commits suicide. *Lovey Childs: A Philadelphian's Story* deals with a Main Line heiress and her playboy husband (Sky Childs), who became 1920s celebrities; after divorce she achieves a stable marriage with her proper Philadelphia cousin. This is O'Hara's weakest novel, but it aroused speculation about his interest in lesbianism. At his death in 1970 O'Hara had completed *The Ewings* and was at work on a sequel: better than the two previous novels, it is the story of a young Cleveland lawyer and his wife in the booming economy of World War I. Six short story collections appeared in the 1960s, and two more after O'Hara's death.

Before World War II an "official" view of O'Hara had been established. **John Peale Bishop** (1937) found him skillful but cynical, a post-Jazz Age follower of **Ernest Hemingway** and **F. Scott Fitzgerald. Edmund Wilson** (1940) recognized that O'Hara was a social commentator and that his writing was "of an entirely different kind from Hemingway's." O'Hara resembles Fitzgerald more than any other writer, and their friendship—O'Hara proof-read Fitzgerald's *Tender Is the Night*—was renewed during Fitzgerald's last bitter days in Hollywood. O'Hara was a staunch Fitzgerald champion when that was not a popular cause, and wrote the introduction to *The Portable F. Scott Fitzgerald* (1945). When the big O'Hara novels became best sellers in the 1950s and 1960s, critics objected to the "mere accuracy" of his dialogue and detail, to the "surface reality" of his American scenes, and to the social climbing and sexual conduct of his characters. But, even when they found him "a hack writer," critics continued to review his books, and **John Steinbeck** called O'Hara the most underrated writer in America. His work lives, no matter how unfashionably. Though some critics object that his characters are not worth writing about, O'Hara's readers do not agree; and they admire the clarity of his style even though the critics would like more complexity and ambiguity. The academic world objects to O'Hara's view of life and literature, but if future generations seek an American Balzac to lay bare life in the United States from 1900 to 1970, they will find John O'Hara the most complete, the most accurate, and the most readable chronicler.

—Clarence A. Glasrud

OLSEN, Tillie (née Lerner)

Born: In either Mead or Omaha, Nebraska, 14 January 1912 or 1913. **Education:** High school education. **Family:** Married Jack Olsen in 1943 (died); four daughters. **Career:** Has worked in the service, warehouse, and food processing industries, and as an office typist. Visiting professor, Amherst College, Massachusetts, 1969-70; visiting instructor, Stanford University, California, spring 1971; writer-in-residence, Massachusetts Institute of Technology, Cambridge, 1973; visiting professor, University of Massachusetts, Boston, 1974; visiting lecturer, University of California, San Diego, 1978; International Visiting Scholar, Norway, 1980; Hill Professor, University of Minnesota, Minneapolis, 1986; writer-in-residence, Kenyon College, Gambier, Ohio, 1987; Regents' Professor, University of California, Los Angeles, 1988; writer-in-residence Yeshiva University, 1998, University of Nebraska at Kearney, 1998, and Creighton University, 1998; creative writing fellow, Stanford University, 1956-57; fellow, Radcliffe Institute for Independent Study, Cambridge, Massachusetts, 1962-64. **Awards:** Ford grant, 1959; O. Henry award, 1961; National Endowment for the Arts grant, 1966, and senior fellowship, 1984; American Academy award, 1975; Guggenheim fellowship, 1975; Unitarian Women's Federation award, 1980; Bunting Institute fellowship, 1986. Doctor of Arts and Letters, University of Nebraska, Lincoln, 1979. Litt.D.: Knox College, Galesburg, Illinois, 1982; Albright College, Reading, Pennsylvania, 1986. L.H.D.: Hobart and William Smith Colleges, Geneva, New York, 1984; Clark University, Worcester, Massachusetts, 1985; Wooster College, Ohio, 1991; Amherst College, 1998. **Residence:** San Francisco, California.

PUBLICATIONS

Short Stories

Tell Me a Riddle: A Collection. 1961; enlarged edition, 1964.

Novel

Yonnondio: From the Thirties. 1974.

Other

Life in the Iron Mills. 1972.
Silences (essays). 1978.
Mothers and Daughters: That Special Quality: An Exploration in Photographs, with Julie Olsen-Edwards and Estelle Jussim. 1987.

Editor, *Mother to Daughter, Daughter to Mother: Mothers on Mothering.* 1984.

*

Manuscript Collections: Stanford University, Albin Berg Collection at the New York Public Library, and Anne Sexton archive, Ransom Humanities Center, Austin, Texas.

Critical Studies: *Olsen* by Abigail Martin, 1984; *Olsen and a Feminist Spiritual Vision* by Elaine Neil Orr, 1987; *Olsen* by Abby

Werlock and Mickey Pearlman, 1991; *Protest and Possibility in the Writing of Tillie Olsen* by Mara Faulkner, 1993; *The Critical Response to Tillie Olsen* edited by Kay Hoyle Nelson and Nancy Lyman Huse, 1994; *Better Red: The Writing and Resistence of Tillie Olsen and Meridel Le Sueur* by Constance Coiner, 1995; *Tillie Olsen: A Study of the Short Fiction* by Joanne S. Frye, 1995; *Three Radical Women Writers: Class and Gender in Meridel Le Sueur, Tillie Olsen, and Josephine Herbst* by Nora Ruth Roberts, 1996; *Women's Ethical Coming-of-Age: Adolescent Female Characters in the Prose Fiction of Tillie Olsen* by Agnes Toloczko Cardoni, 1998.

*   *   *

Tillie Lerner Olsen has come to represent a voice not frequently heard in literature: that of a politically active, working-class woman writer. It is a bitter irony and one of Olsen's major issues that the body of work responding to her texts is larger than her literary production. As she so frequently points out, the financial and emotional pressures on the woman writer in particular to raise and maintain a family often subsume the woman's ability to write.

Born in 1912 or 1913 in either Mead or Omaha, Nebraska (no birth certificate exists), Olsen learned the particular difficulties facing an intellectually capable but financially poor woman struggling to transform her beliefs into literature. Olsen's parents, Ida and Samuel Lerner, were Russian-born Jewish immigrants who fled to the United States after the failure of the Russian Revolution of 1905. The unmarried but cohabiting couple continued their political involvement in their adopted country; Samuel became secretary of the Socialist Party in Nebraska. Olsen's parents played an early and prominent role in the formation of her political consciousness. One of her earliest memories is of sitting on the lap of Eugene V. Debs (a Socialist Party and labor leader) in the living room as Debs and Olsen's parents discussed contemporary politics.

It was as a student at Central High School in Omaha that Olsen became aware of her intellectual capabilities as well as the prejudices directed against her as a member of the working class. Needed at home to look after her four younger siblings, she left school after completing the eleventh grade. Although she wrote a successful humor column for her high school newspaper, her writings subsequent to high school took on a decidedly political bent, combining her socialist and feminist interests into a number of skits and musicals she wrote for the Young People's Socialist League. At eighteen Olsen joined the Young Communist League, to which she remained dedicated for the next year and a half.

Olsen began her first, only, and never completed novel, *Yonnondio*, at age nineteen. The first chapter, "The Iron Throat," appeared in 1934 in *Partisan Review*. Although she received high acclaim for the novel's beginning, the birth of her first child and quick dissolution of her marriage diverted Olsen's attention away from her writing. She spent the following years participating in such political activities as the San Francisco Maritime strike in 1934 and a packing house strike, both of which led to her arrest and brief imprisonment. She wrote a number of short pieces such as "The Thousand Dollar Vagrant" (published in the *New Republic,* 1934), and "The Strike" (published in *Partisan Review,* 1934), and a couple of poems in response to her political experiences, but the time and resources to pursue longer literary projects remained elusive.

While she spent time in jail for vagrancy as a result of her participation in the Maritime strike, Random House editors were searching for the author of "The Iron Throat"; they hoped to convince her to complete the novel. Upon discovering Olsen, the editors offered to pay her an advance to produce a chapter a month. She left her daughter with relatives and began to write. Although she was free of the interruptions of raising a child alone and having to hold a job, she could not rid herself of the guilt she felt at leaving her daughter with relatives previously unknown to the girl. Olsen picked up her daughter and told Random House of her inability to fulfill the contract. Olsen's reputation as an important literary figure was not diminished by this incident, however. She was asked to attend the American Writers Conference in 1935.

Olsen bore three children by Jack Olsen before they married in 1943. As she raised her children amid frequent poverty and numerous short-lived jobs (both Tillie and Jack's names appeared on blacklists for their membership in the Communist Party), she continued her political involvement in such projects as forming a women's division of the International Longshoremen and Warehousers Union (Jack was a member), the public school system, and as president of the California CIO Women's Auxiliary. She wrote during this period, but most of her work was strictly political in nature.

In 1955 Stanford University granted Olsen the year-long Stegner Fellowship. Unencumbered again by the need to hold a job, she at last found the time to write. In this year she produced four highly acclaimed short stories collected under the title of the most highly regarded piece, "Tell Me A Riddle." While the rewards for that year's production (an O. Henry Award and inclusion of two of the pieces in *Best American Short Stories*) demonstrated Olsen's ability, after the fellowship expired Olsen's time quickly became consumed with her struggle to keep herself and her family financially solvent.

She did not publish again until 1971, when her novella *Requa* appeared in *Best American Short Stories*. In 1974 she stumbled across a portion of the novel she had begun at nineteen, *Yonnondio*. After forty years and five children, Olsen attempted again to finish her novel, of which there were seven chapters written. She soon discovered, however, that the young woman who had begun the novel and envisioned its direction no longer existed. Rather than force an ending, Olsen published *Yonnondio* in 1974, adding only a brief explanation of the text's history.

Told mostly through young Mazie's eyes, *Yonnondio* is the story of the Holbrook family's struggle to survive amidst the dirt, danger, and oppression of a coal mining town. The oppression the family faces in their struggle against poverty and their own physical and sexual abuse of one another is further compounded by the seeming helplessness of the Holbrooks to improve their condition. The family moves to the country to begin their lives anew away from the problems of the mining town. They quickly discover, however, that they have neither the resources nor the know-how to run a farm and subsequently move to yet another form of oppression in a mill town. Although the novel is bleak in its portrayal of this working-class family, Olsen is frequently cited as explaining that she had conceived of this novel as a "portrait of the artist as a young girl." Mazie and her brother Jim were to become labor leaders, while Mazie recorded the plight of the working class in her own stories.

Of her stories, "I Stand Here Ironing," often identified as Olsen's most autobiographical piece, portrays a mother's guilt and helplessness at not giving her daughter the attention the girl needed when young. Despite the mother's worry, however, the daughter demonstrates her ability to survive and, in fact, shows considerable talent as a mime and comedienne.

"Tell Me A Riddle" tells the story of a retired couple, married for forty-seven years, who argue bitterly over whether or not they should sell their house and move into a retirement home. Looking forward at last to having time alone, tending to no one (the couple has six children), Eva, the wife, increasingly withdraws from her family and husband, often remaining silent for days. As Eva removes herself, she joyfully recalls songs from her childhood in Russia, before she had children and before her marriage. Despite her desire to be alone in her own house, Eva dies at the home of one of her children, speaking only of her life before her family.

Requa tells the story of a thirteen-year-old boy who goes to live with his bachelor Uncle Wes, a junk dealer, after the death of his mother. Chronically sick, silent, and withdrawn, the boy slowly comes back to life at his uncle's frequently violent frustration with the boy's complacency. Eventually the boy revives completely, working in the junkyard, and learning how to fish, hunt, and love again.

Constance Coiner's *Better Red: The Writing and Resistance of Tillie Olsen and Meridel Le Sueur* (1995) explores not just Olsen's particular talents as a writer but also the more general history of the Left in the 1930s. Coiner discusses Olsen's complicated relationships with the Communist Party as an activist and a feminist. While the Communist Party never adequately addressed issues of feminism or even sexism within its own ranks, there were few organizations in which women felt they had a right to challenge sexism. Along with the more general political history of the 1930s and a number of chapters devoted specifically to Olsen's writings, Coiner includes a biography of Olsen as well as some provocative thoughts on a future direction for the literary canon based on Olsen's focus on working-class women.

—Kathleen Grimm Garrett

OLSON, Charles (John)

Born: Worcester, Massachusetts, 27 December 1910. **Education:** Classical High School, Worcester, graduated 1928; Wesleyan University, Middletown, Connecticut, 1928-32, B.A. 1932 (Phi Beta Kappa), M.A. 1933; Harvard University, Cambridge, Massachusetts, 1936-38. **Career:** Assistant Chief of Foreign Language Division, Office of War Information, Washington, D.C., during World War II. Teacher, Clark University, Worcester, and Harvard University, 1936-39; worked for Democratic Party, 1939-44, and adviser, Democratic National Committee, late 1940s; instructor and rector, Black Mountain College, North Carolina, 1948, 1951-56; teacher at State University of New York, Buffalo, 1963-65, and University of Connecticut, Storrs, 1969. **Awards:** Guggenheim grant (twice); Wenner-Gren Foundation grant, 1952; American Academy grant, 1966, 1968. **Died:** 10 January 1970.

Publications

Poetry

Corrado Cagli March 31 through April 19 1947. 1947.
Y & X. 1948.

Letter for Melville 1951. 1951.
This. 1952.
In Cold Hell, in Thicket. 1953.
The Maximus Poems 1-10. 1953.
Ferrini and Others, with others. 1955.
Anecdotes of the Late War. 1955.
The Maximus Poems 11-22. 1956.
O'Ryan 2 4 6 8 10. 1958; expanded edition, as *O'Ryan 12345678910,* 1965.
The Maximus Poems. 1960.
The Distances. 1960.
Maximus, from Dogtown I. 1961.
Signature to Petition on Ten Pound Island Asked of Me by Mr. Vincent Ferrini. 1964.
West. 1966.
Olson Reading at Berkeley, edited by Zoe Brown. 1966.
Before Your Very Eyes!, with others. 1967.
The Maximus Poems, IV, V, VI. 1968.
Reading about My World. 1968.
Added to Making a Republic. 1968.
Clear Shifting Water. 1968.
That There Was a Woman in Gloucester, Massachusetts. 1968.
Wholly Absorbed into My Own Conduits. 1968.
Causal Mythology. 1969.
Archaeologist of Morning: The Collected Poems outside the Maximus Series. 1970.
Maximus, to Himself. 1970.
New Man and Woman. 1970.
May 20, 1959. 1970.
The Maximus Poems, Volume Three, edited by Charles Boer and George F. Butterick. 1975.
The Horses of the Sea. 1976.
Some Early Poems. 1978.
Spearmint and Rosemary. 1979.
The Maximus Poems, edited by George F. Butterick. 1983.

Plays

The Fiery Hunt and Other Plays. 1977.

Fiction

Stocking Cap: A Story. 1966.

Other

Call Me Ishmael: A Study of Melville. 1947.
Apollonius of Tyana: A Dance, with Some Words, for Two Actors. 1951.
Mayan Letters, edited by Robert Creeley. 1953.
Projective Verse. 1959.
A Bibliography on America for Ed Dorn. 1964.
Human Universe and Other Essays, edited by Donald Allen. 1965.
Proprioception. 1965.
Selected Writings, edited by Robert Creeley. 1966.
Pleistocene Man: Letters from Olson to John Clarke during October 1965. 1968.
Letters for Origin 1950-1956, edited by Albert Glover. 1969.
The Special View of History, edited by Ann Charters. 1970.
Poetry and Truth: The Beloit Lectures and Poems, edited by George F. Butterick. 1971.

Additional Prose: A Bibliography on America, Proprioception, and Other Notes and Essays, edited by George F. Butterick. 1974.

The Post Office: A Memoir of His Father. 1974.

In Adullam's Lair (lecture). 1975.

Olson in Connecticut: Last Lectures As Heard by John Cech, Oliver Ford, Peter Rittner. 1975.

Olson and Ezra Pound: An Encounter at St. Elizabeths, edited by Catherine Seelye. 1975.

Muthologos: The Collected Lectures and Interviews of Olson, edited by George F. Butterick. 2 vols., 1976-79.

Olson/Den Boer: A Letter. 1979.

D.H. Lawrence and the High Temptation of the Mind. 1980.

Olson and Robert Creeley: The Complete Correspondence, edited by George F. Butterick. 5 vols., 1980-83.

*

Bibliography: *A Bibliography of Works by Olson* by George F. Butterick and Albert Glover, 1967.

Critical Studies: *What I See in the Maximus Poems* by Ed Dorn, 1960; *Olson/Melville: A Study in Affinity, 1968,* and *Olson: The Special View of History, 1970,* both by Ann Charters; *Olson in Connecticut* by Charles Boer, 1975; *A Guide to the Maximus Poems of Olson* by George F. Butterick, 1978; *Olson's Push: "Origin," Black Mountain, and Recent American Poetry* by Sherman Paul, 1978; *Olson: The Scholar's Art* by Robert von Hallberg, 1978; *Olson: Call Him Ishmael* by Paul Christensen, 1979; *Olson's Maximus* by Don Byrd, 1980; *To Let Words Swim into the Soul: An Anniversary Tribute to the Art of Olson* by Gavin Selerie, 1980; *Olson and Edward Dahlberg: A Portrait of a Friendship* by John Cech, 1982; *The Poetry of Olson: A Primer* by Thomas F. Merrill, 1982; *The Lyric and Modern Poetry: Olson, Creeley, Bunting* by Brian Conniff, 1988; "'To Get the Rituals Straight': The Poetics of Charles Olson's *The Maximus Poems*" by Lisa Pater Faranda, in *The Green American Tradition: Essays and Poems for Sherman Paul* edited by H. Daniel Peck, 1989; "The Topology of Being: The Poetics of Olson" by Judith Halden-Sullivan, 1991; "Olson: Against the Past" by Charles Doria, in *American Writing Today* edited by Richard Kostelanetz, 1991; "Fields of Spacetime and the 'I' in Olson's *The Maxiumus Poems*" by Steven Carter, in *American Literature and Science* edited by Robert J. Scholnick, 1992; *Charles Olson* by Eniko Bollobas, 1992; "Toward a Common Ground: Versions of Place in the Poetry of Charles Olson, Edward Dorn, and Theodore Enslin," in *Sagetrieb: A Journal Devoted to the Poets in the Imagist Objectivist Tradition,* winter 1996, pp. 243-61; "The William Bronk-Charles Olson Correspondence" by Burt Kimmelman, in *Minutes of the Charles Olson Society,* January 1998, pp. 2-29.

*   *   *

Although any final judgment regarding the work and influence of Charles Olson remains controversial, he must nevertheless be regarded as a seminal force in the reshaping of American poetry written since World War II. Olson showed little inclination to be a poet until his mid-thirties. Shortly after the death of Roosevelt, however, Olson left government and committed himself to a literary career. By then he had written only the draft of a short book on Melville, *Call Me Ishmael,* and several conventional poems published in popular magazines. From these unpromising beginnings,

Olson began writing in earnest in the late 1940s. With the help of **Edward Dahlberg,** a completely revised *Call Me Ishmael* was published in 1947; two years later, Olson composed "The Kingfishers," among the most innovative poems to have emerged since World War II. And in 1950, largely from the example of the techniques employed in "The Kingfishers," and ideas taken from a variety of sources, including **William Carlos Williams, Ezra Pound,** Dahlberg, and his close friend **Robert Creeley,** Olson synthesized the provocative and highly influential manifesto, "Projective Verse."

This essay established a new set of conventions for the short poem. In place of the old rules of repetitive measure, rhyme, and fixed stanza, Olson introduced the principle that "form is an extension of content," or that form is the result of allowing content to assume its own partly accidental shape during composition. Around this main principle are certain technical corollaries: for example, the poet, rather than treating his theme in an orderly progression of ideas, should instead rush from "perception to perception" until his argument is exhausted. The poet should allow the rhythm of his breath during composition to determine the length of each line, so that he has scored it for the reading voice. And in fitting words together in the line itself, the poet should let sound, rather than sense, determine syntax. A logic of the ear should take precedence over intellect in the fashioning of language.

Olson suggested that all of these new conventions were dependent on a new stance to experience, which he called Objectism. The poet should no longer consider his mind a clearing house of data, from which to select bits of information for his poems. Rather, the poet should include the rest of his organism in the act of perception and awareness, and should feel himself rush out of his private emotion into the realms of phenomena free of self-consciousness and inhibition. Objectism called for the poet to accept himself as merely another object inhabiting the phenomenal welter making up the world. The techniques advised in the first half of the essay, then, are all the means of making experience direct and unmediated for the poet who plunges fully into the phenomena around him.

"The Kingfishers" satisfies most of the conditions of composition set forth in the "Projective Verse" essay. Its form is the result of a rush of discourse on a series of loosely related topics, of experiments in combinations of sounds, and of the arrangement of words in clusters to show the changing shape of his thinking moment by moment. This striking poem creates the feeling of having kept pace with the random and shifting content of the poet's awareness.

Olson's projective methodology and the example of "The Kingfishers" are clearly efforts to explore and even to track the behavior of the imagination. More significant is the fact that Olson's poetic brings poetry into the general current of freeforming methods then being applied to the other arts: atonal, free-form jazz composition, abstract expressionism, improvisational theater, and kinetic sculpture.

Olson went on to refine the doctrine that became known as Objectism in subsequent essays and lectures, but his several collections of short poems and the long, sequential work *The Maximus Poems* are the basis of his reputation and influence as a poet. In 1953 Creeley published Olson's first full-length volume of poems, *In Cold Hell, in Thicket,* which contains not only "The Kingfishers" but many of Olson's boldest shorter poems. Many, but by no means all, of these shorter poems are composed in the projective mode; others are written in a more leisurely-paced free verse style. The whole work is concerned with the burdens of tradition and influence the poet must cast off to pursue his own direction. The poet argues, often petulantly, against Ezra Pound, whom Olson identifies as his spiritual father and arch rival.

Creeley later edited Olson's *Selected Writings,* further establishing Olson's reputation as a key figure of the new poetry. A more finished and elaborate poetry emerges in *The Distances,* but there is less bold experiment in these more mature lyrical poems. Olson had moved to less defined areas of awareness; many of the poems are startling reenactments of dreams, in which the supralogical narratives are skillfully and persuasively dramatized, and there is a greater interest in myth and the content and forms of consciousness.

But the primary text for judging Olson as poet rests with his central work, the long, epical *Maximus* sequence, begun in the late 1940s and sustained to the last months of his life. The work remains unfinished, although the final volume, found among the poet's papers, has been edited and published. The work in one way is a celebration of the seacoast town of Gloucester, Massachusetts, where communal spirit among the fishermen thrived before industry was established; in another, it is close scrutiny of life in America and a search for an alternative ideology rooted in new spiritual awareness.

In the first volume, *The Maximus Poems,* Olson's persona, Maximus, named after an itinerant Phoenician mystic of the fourth century A.D., surveys contemporary Gloucester and finds its citizenry in disarray and the local culture ugly and alien. This judgment prompts a systematic inquiry into the origins of Gloucester and of America, which takes up the remainder of the volume. In the second volume, *Maximus IV, V, VI,* the speaker widens his interests to include mythological lore, the history of human migration, religious literature, and the finer details of Gloucester's past, which seem to Maximus to re-enact certain of the myths and fables of the ancient world. The final volume, more somber in mood and subject, continues Maximus's intense survey of Gloucester and himself. A vision of a new cosmos is summoned in these poems, in the hope of redeeming and possibly reconstituting the communal ethos of Gloucester's past. But that hope gives way to remorse and disparagement of the reckless present and its deadening commercial enterprises.

The poem is among the more ambitious experiments in sustained narrative in the post-war period; it ranks in conception and execution with other verse epics of the modern period, including Pound's *Cantos,* Williams's *Paterson,* and **Hart Crane**'s *The Bridge.* Although Olson is less musical in his language, and at times a dry poet given to long quotation from historical documents, the sweep of his thought and the scope of his imaginative arguments distinguish him as a major American poet of the Whitman tradition.

—Paul Christensen

See the essay on *The Maximus Poems.*

O'NEILL, Eugene (Gladstone)

Born: New York City, 16 October 1888; son of the actor James O'Neill. Toured with his father as a child. **Education:** Catholic boarding schools, and at Betts Academy, Stamford, Connecticut; attended Princeton University, New Jersey, 1906-07, and George Pierce Baker's "47 Workshop" at Harvard University, Cambridge, Massachusetts, 1914-15. **Family:** Married 1) Kathleen Jenkins in 1909 (divorced 1912), one son; 2) Agnes Boulton in 1918 (divorced 1929), one son and one daughter; 3) the actress Carlotta Monterey in 1929. **Career:** Worked for New York-Chicago Supply Company, mail order firm, New York, 1907-08; gold prospector in Honduras, 1909; seaman on a Norwegian freighter to Buenos Aires, and advance agent and box-office man for his father's company, 1910-11; reporter, New London *Telegraph,* Connecticut, 1912; patient in a tuberculosis sanitarium, 1912-13; full-time writer from 1914; associated with the Provincetown Players, New York, and Provincetown, Massachusetts, as actor and writer, 1916-20; wrote for the Theatre Guild; manager, with Kenneth Macgowan and Robert Edmond Jones, Greenwich Village Theatre, New York, 1923-27; a founding editor, *American Spectator,* 1934; in ill-health from 1934; in later years suffered from Parkinson's disease. **Awards:** Pulitzer prize, 1920, 1922, 1928, 1957; American Academy of Arts and Letters Gold Medal, 1922; Nobel prize for Literature, 1936; New York Drama Critics Circle award, 1957. Litt.D.: Yale University, New Haven, Connecticut, 1926. **Member:** American Academy, 1923, and Irish Academy of Letters. **Died:** 27 November 1953.

PUBLICATIONS

Plays

Thirst and Other One Act Plays (includes *The Web, Warnings, Fog, Recklessness*). 1914.
Thirst (produced 1916). In *Thirst and Other One Act Plays,* 1914.
Fog (produced 1917). In *Thirst and Other One Act Plays,* 1914.
Bound East for Cardiff (produced 1916). In *The Moon of the Caribbees . . . ,* 1919.
Before Breakfast (produced 1916). 1916.
The Sniper (produced 1917). In *Lost Plays,* 1950.
In the Zone (produced 1917). In *The Moon of the Caribbees . . . ,* 1919.
The Long Voyage Home (produced 1917). In *The Moon of the Caribbees . . . ,* 1919.
Ile (produced 1917). In *The Moon of the Caribbees . . . ,* 1919.
The Rope (produced 1918). In *The Moon of the Caribbees . . . ,* 1919.
Where The Cross Is Made (produced 1918). In *The Moon of the Caribbees . . . ,* 1919.
The Moon of the Caribbees (produced 1918). In *The Moon of the Caribbees . . . ,* 1919.
The Moon of the Caribbees and Six Other Plays of the Sea. 1919.
The Dreamy Kid (produced 1919). In *Complete Works 2,* 1924.
Beyond the Horizon (produced 1920). 1920.
Anna Christie (as *Chris,* produced 1920; revised version, as *Anna Christie,* produced 1921). With *The Hairy Ape, The First Man,* 1922.
Exorcism (produced 1920).
The Emperor Jones (produced 1920). With *Diff'rent, The Straw,* 1921.
Diff'rent (produced 1920). With *The Emperor Jones, The Straw,* 1921.
The Straw (produced 1921). With *The Emperor Jones, Diff'rent,* 1921.
Gold (produced 1921). 1921.

The First Man (produced 1922). With *The Hairy Ape, Anna Christie*, 1922.

The Hairy Ape (produced 1922). With *The First Man, Anna Christie*, 1922.

Welded (produced 1924). With *All God's Chillun Got Wings*, 1924.

The Ancient Mariner: A Dramatic Arrangement of Coleridge's Poem (produced 1924).

S. S. Glencairn: Four Plays of the Sea (includes *Bound East for Cardiff, In the Zone, The Long Voyage Home, The Moon of the Caribbees*) (produced 1924). 1926.

All God's Chillun Got Wings (produced 1924). With *Welded*, 1924.

Desire under the Elms (produced 1924). In *Complete Works 2*, 1924.

Complete Works. 2 vols., 1924.

The Fountain (produced 1925). With *The Great God Brown, The Moon of the Caribbees*, 1926.

The Great God Brown (produced 1926). With *The Fountain, The Moon of the Caribbees*, 1926.

Marco Millions (produced 1928). 1927.

Lazarus Laughed (produced 1928). 1927.

Strange Interlude (produced 1928). 1928.

Dynamo (produced 1929). 1929.

Mourning Becomes Electra: A Trilogy (produced 1931). 1931.

Ah, Wilderness! (produced 1933). 1933.

Days without End (produced 1934). 1934.

The Iceman Cometh (produced 1946). 1946.

A Moon for the Misbegotten (produced 1947). 1952.

Lost Plays (includes *Abortion, The Movie Man, The Sniper, Servitude, A Wife for a Life*), edited by Lawrence Gellert. 1950.

Long Day's Journey into Night (produced 1956). 1956.

A Touch of the Poet (produced 1957). 1957.

Hughie (produced 1958). 1959.

More Stately Mansions (produced 1962). 1964.

Ten "Lost" Plays. 1964.

Children of the Sea and Three Other Unpublished Plays (includes *Bread and Butter, Now I Ask You, Shell Shock*), edited by Jennifer McCabe Atkinson. 1972.

The Calms of Capricorn (scenario by O'Neill, with completion by Donald Gallup). 1982.

Chris Christophersen (original version of *Anna Christie*). 1982.

Desire under the Elms and The Great God Brown. 1995.

Ten "Lost" Plays (includes *A Wife for Life, Thirst, The Web, Warnings, Fog, Recklessness, Abortion, The Movie Man, Servitude, The Sniper*). 1995.

Beyond the Horizon and The Emperor Jones. 1996.

Four Plays by Eugene O'Neill (includes *Beyond the Horizon, Emperor Jones, Anna Christie, Hairy Ape*). 1998.

Poetry

Poems 1912-1944, edited by Donald Gallup. 1980.

Other

Inscriptions: O'Neill to Carlotta Monterey O'Neill, edited by Donald Gallup. 1960.

O'Neill at Work: Newly Released Ideas for Plays, edited by Virginia Floyd. 1981.

The Theatre We Worked For: The Letters of O'Neill to Kenneth Macgowan, edited by Jackson R. Bryer. 1982.

*

Bibliography: *O'Neill and the American Critic: A Bibliographical Checklist* by Jordan Y. Miller, 1973; *O'Neill: A Descriptive Bibliography* by Jennifer McCabe Atkinson, 1974.

Critical Studies: *The Haunted Heroes of O'Neill* by Edwin A. Engel, 1953; *O'Neill and the Tragic Tension* by Doris V. Falk, 1958, revised edition, 1982; *O'Neill and His Plays: Four Decades of Criticism* edited by Oscar Cargill and others, 1961; *O'Neill* (biography) by Arthur and Barbara Gelb, 1962, revised edition, 1973; *The Tempering of O'Neill* by Doris Alexander, 1962; *O'Neill* by Frederic I. Carpenter, 1964, revised edition, 1979; *O'Neill: A Collection of Critical Essays* edited by John Gassner, 1964; *The Plays of O'Neill* by John Henry Raleigh, 1965; *Playwright's Progress: O'Neill and the Critics* by Jordan Y. Miller, 1965; *O'Neill* by John Gassner, 1965; *O'Neill's Scenic Images* by Timo Tiusanen, 1968; *O'Neill: Son and Playwright*, 1968, and *O'Neill: Son and Artist*, 1973, both by Louis Sheaffer; *A Drama of Souls: Studies in O'Neill's Super-naturalistic Techniques* by Egil Tornqvist, 1969; *O'Neill* by Horst Frenz, 1971, and *O'Neill's Critics: Voices from Abroad* edited by Frenz and Susan Tuck, 1984; *Contour in Time: The Plays of O'Neill* by Travis Bogard, 1972; *O'Neill: A Collection of Criticism* edited by Ernest Griffin, 1976; *Ritual and Pathos: The Theater of O'Neill* by Leonard Chabrowe, 1976; *Forging a Language: A Study of the Plays of O'Neill* by Jean Clothia, 1979; *O'Neill: A World View* edited by Virginia Floyd, 1980, and *The Plays of O'Neill: A New Assessment* by Floyd, 1984; *O'Neill's New Language of Kinship* by Michael Manheim, 1982; *O'Neill* by Normand Berlin, 1982; *The O'Neill Companion* by Margaret Loftus Ranald, 1984; *Critical Essays on O'Neill* edited by James J. Martins, 1984; *Final Acts: The Creation of Three Late O'Neill Plays* by Judith E. Barlow, 1985; *O'Neill's Century: Centennial Views on America's Foremost Tragic Dramatist* edited by Richard F. Moorton, Jr., 1991; *Provincetown as a Stage: Provincetown, the Provincetown Players, and the Discovery of Eugene O'Neill* by Leona Rust Egan, 1994; *The Inner Strength of Opposites: O'Neill's Novelistic Drama and the Melodramatic Imagination* by Kurt Eisen, 1994; *Staging Depth: Eugene O'Neill and the Politics of Psychological Discourse* by Joel Pfister, 1995; *Mimetic Disillusion: Eugene O'Neill, Tennessee Williams, and U.S. Dramatic Realism* by Anne Fleche, 1997; *Struggle, Defeat, or Rebirth: Eugene O'Neill's Vision of Humanity* by Thierry Dubost, 1997; *Eugene O'Neill and His Eleven-Play Cycle: "A Tale of Possessors Self-Dispossessed"* by Donald Gallup, 1998; *The Cambridge Companion to Eugene O'Neill* edited by Michael Manheim, 1998.

*   *   *

Ultimately recognized as America's greatest dramatist, Eugene O'Neill stumbled through several styles and subjects in his will to resurrect tragedy for the modern stage. In 1912, at age 24, having survived a suicide attempt and a bout with tuberculosis, he determined to become a playwright, and he spent the next three decades in dedication to that mission. Starting with variants on melodrama, he steered into realistic sea plays, then to expressionist agons, and finally to sprawling realistic plays with an epic dimension. O'Neill was haunted by death, but he gave dramatic life to America's history and geography, men and women, poets and stutterers, illusion and disillusion. Earnest of purpose, contemptuous of facility, O'Neill shaped his thought and torment into 46 (published) plays, destroying those that illness prevented him from completing.

O'Neill's early melodramas have survived by accident, and they are of interest mainly by contrast with *Bound East for Cardiff,* the first of the *S. S. Glencairn* sea plays. Astonishing is young O'Neill's graduation from literary imitation to experiential authenticity, from stilted dialogue to salty colloquialism, from exotic settings to the minutely observed ship, from climactic violence to aimless drifting, for already O'Neill converted his seagoing experience into a long day's dramatic journey into night.

Beyond the Horizon brought O'Neill beyond the horizon of Provincetown to New York. Spanning a decade in the lives of two brothers in love with the same woman, the play traces the irony of their fate; marriage yokes the dreamer Robert to domesticity, whereas practical Andrew goes to sea. The three major characters succumb to their destiny, but O'Neill's three-act tragedy was his first triumph. Such irony within and outside his plays colors O'Neill's whole career.

No sooner did O'Neill find his sea legs in realism than he reached out toward expressionism. In 1920 he worked almost simultaneously upon the experimental *The Emperor Jones* and the realistic *Ole Davil* (which became *Anna Christie*). The two dissimilar plays not only confirmed O'Neill's position as America's leading dramatist at that time; they also endure in many non-commercial productions to this day. O'Neill later said that he had attempted to create "original rhythms of beauty, where beauty apparently isn't" in four plays written between 1920 and 1924—*The Emperor Jones, The Hairy Ape, All God's Chillun Got Wings,* and *Desire under the Elms.*

The Emperor Jones is at once a gripping drama about an oppressed American black, a modern tragedy about a hero with a flaw, an expressionist quest play probing to the racial roots of the protagonist; above all, it is more highly theatrical than its European analogues, gradually quickening the tom-tom from normal pulse-rhythm, stripping away colorful costume to the naked man beneath, subordinating dialogue to innovative lighting in order to illuminate an individual and his racial heritage.

Another expressionist play, *The Hairy Ape,* dramatizes the quest of natural man in a mechanized world. And again the quest is a failure, ending in death. More ambitious scenically and symbolically, *The Hairy Ape* has not weathered as well as *The Emperor Jones,* and *All God's Chillun* is no longer performed at all. *Desire under the Elms,* by contrast, is not only frequently revived, it set O'Neill's feet firmly on hard realistic ground. Like the other three plays in which O'Neill felt he had created "original rhythms of beauty," *Desire under the Elms* dramatizes people at the bottom of the social ladder—in this case nineteenth-century New England farmers. In O'Neill's hands, however, these characters loom large—in part because the plot follows the Phaedra-Hippolytus-Theseus myth, in part because the indoor-outdoor setting permits visualization of the private-public resonances of that plot. Although marred by turgid dialogue and abuse of repetition, *Desire under the Elms* nevertheless achieves moments of passionate intensity that predict O'Neill's wholly functional final tragedies.

O'Neill, ever productive though he was, only gradually worked up to that summit. From the mid-1920s to the mid-1930s he cast about for non-realistic forms to contain his tragic vision. *Desire under the Elms*'s American background for Greek tragedy climbs the social ladder in *Mourning Becomes Electra*—a post-Civil War *Oresteia* in which the many specific details are credible at both the realistic and mythic levels. *Marco Millions* stages a picaresque and satirized Babbitt. O'Neill used masks to theatricalize an Apollonian-Dionysian conflict in *The Great God Brown.* Shortly afterwards O'Neill wrote his most ambitious play, *Lazarus Laughed,* which draws upon the Bible, Greek choruses, Elizabethan expansiveness, expressionist masks, crowd scenes with more than a hundred actors, and orchestrated laughter that damns materialism. Then, reverting to the twentieth century for *Strange Interlude,* O'Neill in his "woman play" resurrects the stage aside to reveal repressed desires. *Dynamo* deifies a dynamo in its final apocalyptic scene. Although it is customary to consider these plays unplayable today, a late-twentieth-century staging of *Strange Interlude* (with Glenda Jackson a memorable Nina Leeds) gives the lie to this custom. During O'Neill's lifetime, he never magnetized a consistently loyal director, but Jose Quintero faithfully directed the late realistic tragedies after the playwright's death.

In 1932, at age 44, O'Neill conceived the idea of a cycle of plays about several generations of an American family—"A Tale of Possessors Self-Dispossessed." By 1941, he noted in his Work Diary: "Idea was first 5 plays, then 7, then 8, then 9, now 11!—will never live to do it—but what price anything but a dream these days!" His prediction was accurate. Ill and unable to write, he salvaged only *A Touch of the Poet,* and *More Stately Mansions* was salvaged in spite of his wishes. Ironically, O'Neill's extracycle, extra-dream plays are his greatest—*The Iceman Cometh* and *Long Day's Journey into Night.* The two plays are similar in their return to surface realism, their concentration and specificity of place and time (the year 1912), their tender comedy that intensifies the tragic drive, their memorable characters that do not strain for, yet somehow attain mythic dimension. The differences between the two plays testify to O'Neill's final range and depth: a working-class saloon and an upper-middle-class country home; nineteen characters of diverse origin and four members of an Irish-American family; a plot that derives from the Bible and a bawdy joke and a plot grounded in O'Neill's own autobiography; the gentle savoring of illusory hope and the merciless exposure of pernicious illusion.

Finally, O'Neill lives in contradictions. The sheer bulk of his achievement is undermined by a relative paucity of contemporary production; his restless experimentation is subdued to realism; his obsession with tragedy is eroded by productions that stress comedy, stasis, or existential absurdity. The tragic fate that O'Neill pursues in play after play crystallizes at last in palpable moments of grace.

—Ruby Cohn

See the essays on *Long Day's Journey into Night* and *Strange Interlude.*

ORTIZ, Simon J(oseph)

Born: Albuquerque, New Mexico, 27 May 1941. Raised in McCartys (Deetseyamah), New Mexico, part of the Acoma Pueblo homeland. **Education:** Attended Fort Lewis College, 1961-62; the University of New Mexico, 1966-68; the University of Iowa, 1968-69. **Military Service:** Served in the U.S. Army, 1963-66. **Family:** Married 1) Roxanne Dunbar in 1976 (divorced 1981); 2) Marlene Foster, December 1981 (divorced 1984); **Career:** Worked as a uranium mill worker near Grants, New Mexico, 1960-61; in public relations at Rough Rock Demonstration School, Rough Rock, Arizona, 1969-70; as a newspaper editor for the National Youth Council, Albuquerque, New Mexico, 1970-73; instructor at San Diego State University, San Diego, California, 1974; at Institute of American Indian Arts, Santa Fe, New Mexico, 1974; Navajo Community College, Tsaile, Arizona, summer sessions 1975-77; College of Marin, Kentfield, California, 1976-79; University of New Mexico, Albuquerque, 1979-81; Sinte Gleska College, Mission, South Dakota, 1985-86; Lewis and Clark College, Portland, Oregon, 1990. Arts coordinator-liason for the Metropolitan Arts Commission in Portland, Oregon, 1990. **Awards:** National Endowment for the Arts Discovery award, 1969; NEA fellowship, 1981; honored poet in the White House Salute to Poetry and American Poets, 1980; Pushcart prize for poetry, 1982; Humanitarian award for Literary Achievement, New Mexico Humanities Council, 1989; the Returning the Gift award, 1993; Lila Wallace Reader's Digest Writer's award, 1997-99. **Residence:** Tucson, Arizona.

PUBLICATIONS

Collection

Men on the Moon: Collected Short Stories. 1999.

Poetry

Naked in the Wind. 1971.
Going for the Rain. 1976.
A Good Journey. 1977.
Fight Back: For the Sake of the People, for the Sake of the Land (poetry and prose). 1980.
A Poem Is a Journey. 1981.
From Sand Creek. 1981.
Woven Stone: A 3-in-1 Volume of Poetry and Prose. 1992.
After and before the Lightning. 1994.

Short Stories

Howbah Indians. 1978.
Fightin': New and Selected Stories. 1983.

Children's Literature

The People Shall Continue. 1977.
Blue and Red. 1981.
The Importance of Childhood. 1982.

Other

Editor, with others, *Califia: The California Poetry.* 1978.
Editor, with Rudolfo Anaya, *A Ceremony of Brotherhood.* 1980.
Editor, *Earth Power Coming.* 1983.
Editor, *Speaking for the Generations: Native Writers on Writing.* 1998.

*

Bibliography: *Simon Ortiz* by Andrew Wiget, 1986.

Critical Studies: "Old Voices of Acoma: Simon Ortiz's Mythic Indigenism" by Willard Gingerich, in *Southwest Review,* 1979;

"Coyote Ortiz: Canis Latrans in the Poetry of Simon Ortiz" by Pat Clark Smith, in *Minority Voices,* 1980, reprinted in *Studies in American Indian Literature* edited by Paula Gunn Allen, 1983; "The Now Day Indi'ns" in *Native American Renaissance* edited by Kenneth Lincoln, 1983; special issue on Simon Ortiz, *SAIL: Studies in American Indian Literature,* 1984; "The Killing of a New Mexican State Trooper: Ways of Telling an Historical Event" by Larry Evers, in *Wicazso Sa Review,* 1985, reprinted in *Critical Essays on Native American Literature* edited by Andrew Wiget, 1985; "Modern Poetry" by Andrew Wiget, in *Native American Literature,* 1985; *Simon Ortiz* by Andrew Wiget, 1986.

*   *   *

Simon J. Ortiz is highly regarded as both a poet and a short story writer. Born into an important Acoma Pueblo family in New Mexico in 1941, Ortiz reflects in his writing a groundedness in the experiences and perceptions of contemporary American Indians. Ortiz gained recognition in the late 1960s and early 1970s when the American public became interested in hearing American Indian voices. Ortiz was in the forefront of writers who began to articulate American Indian issues and concerns. Some of these issues had to do with establishing and maintaining identity in what many Indians regard as an alienating and dehumanizing American society. That identity, historically in peril from acculturating federal policies, is reaffirmed by writers like Ortiz, who see the formation of an Native American identity deeply tied to land, culture, and language.

Understanding the values of one's community and its relationship to the land is a central theme in Ortiz's writing, both his poetry and short prose fiction. But full understanding of these values is available only through their articulation in language. Language, for Ortiz, is the heart and soul of existence. In his essays, such as "Song, Poetry and Language," Ortiz explains how language provides us with consciousness, a measure of both our inner and outer lives.

Ortiz has written eloquently about his formation as a writer in the introduction to his volume *Woven Stone.* As a child growing up in a traditional Acoma family in which the primary source of knowledge is acquired through the spoken word, Ortiz did not imagine himself as a writer. That dream came later. But Ortiz had, nonetheless, an intense and interesting relationship to language. He tells here the story of a little boy, probably Ortiz himself, who will not talk. His sisters, out of love for the boy, ask their grandfather to teach him to speak. The family patriarch does so by speaking to the boy, telling the boy that he will speak when it is time; the grandfather says, "It is with language you will come about for yourself as a person . . . it is with knowledge and words that you will know and express love for yourself and your people." After this, the grandfather takes a brass door key out of his pocket, and inserting it into the boy's mouth he tells the boy, "Now, Grandson, you will speak."

Speaking the values, knowledge, history, and desires of Acoma people, and American Indian people generally, has been the principle aim of Ortiz's writing. Growing up in the 1960s, a decade of political consciousness-raising among U.S. minorities and Third World peoples throughout the world, Ortiz sees his writing as both politically and spiritually motivated. Writing, for Ortiz, is a way to resist a dominant society that would annihilate the small regional and ethnic cultures, such as the American Indian cultures that have held on and persisted in spite of forces of assimilation.

Coming into consciousness of himself as an Indian, as part of a despised minority, Ortiz began to feel the rage, loneliness, and desperation that has been expressed in many works by American Indian writers.

In his short story, "Woman Singing," included in his volume titled *Fightin'*, Ortiz writes about migrant farm workers, Southwestern Indians who find themselves picking potatoes in Idaho. In a life characterized by poverty and alcoholism, Ortiz evokes the loneliness of one Indian worker who falls in love with another man's wife because her singing makes him think of his homeland. Finding a way to make a song, his own song "like those of The People," is what gives the man the strength to leave the lonely and desperate life he has led and to go home. The song seems like a small consolation, but Ortiz is also convinced that those who are disenfranchised by poverty, neglect, and racism can overcome these circumstances: language can help us heal. Healing provides us with a way to continue in our humanity, allows us to grow as individuals and to understand our commitment to the people.

Ortiz often expresses this movement of consciousness as a journey, and language—as he says in a biographical note to *The Man to Send Rain Clouds*, "as a way of life which is a path, a trail which I follow in order to be aware as much as possible of what is around me and what part I am in that life." Language, and by extension, writing, thus inscribes a path of knowledge and self-knowledge. It enables a person to find a road for the individual to follow from inside oneself to the outside, and from outside oneself to inside. This journeying in and out can be compared to the journey Ortiz describes in his prologue to his first volume of poetry, *Going for the Rain*. Rain is a scarce but vital resource in the Southwest. In the high arid deserts of New Mexico and Arizona, its presence makes life possible. When Ortiz invokes the motif of rain and journeying, he is calling on a traditional source, the prayers, songs, and journeys that will insure the arrival of the shiwana, those spiritual entities that bring the rain, that insure survival and continuance of people, plants, and animals. Those who go forth in search of the shiwana are engaged in something vital. We can read this as metaphorical, but it is certainly more than that, for all those who go forth and return for the benefit of the people enact a belief in, and commitment to, the creative and generative forces that help Indians and—as Ortiz believes—all the oppressed survive.

—Janice Gould

OZICK, Cynthia

Born: New York City, 17 April 1928. **Education:** New York University, B.A. (cum laude) in English 1949 (Phi Beta Kappa); Ohio State University, Columbus, M.A. 1951. **Family:** Married Bernard Hallote in 1952; one daughter. **Career:** Instructor in English, New York University, 1964-65; Stolnitz Lecturer, Indiana University, Bloomington, 1972; distinguished artist-in-residence, City University, New York, 1982; Phi Beta Kappa Orator, Harvard University, Cambridge, Massachusetts, 1985. **Awards:** National Endowment for the Arts fellowship, 1968; Wallant award, 1972; B'nai B'rith award, 1972; Jewish Book Council Epstein award, 1972, 1977; American Academy award, 1973; Hadassah Myrtle Wreath award, 1974; Lamport prize, 1980; Guggenheim fellowship, 1982; Strauss Living award, 1983; Rea award, for short story,

1986; Lucy Martin Donnelly fellow, Bryn Mawr College, 1992; PEN/Spiegel-Diamonstem award for the Art of the Essay, 1997; Harold Washington Literary award, City of Chicago, 1997. L.H.D.: Yeshiva University, New York, 1984; Hebrew Union College, Cincinnati, 1984; Williams College, Williamstown, Massachusetts, 1986; Hunter College, New York, 1987; Jewish Theological Seminary, New York, 1988; Adelphi University, Garden City, New York, 1988; State University of New York, 1989; Brandeis University, Waltham, Massachusetts, 1990; Bard College, Annandale-on-Hudson, New York, 1991. **Member:** American Academy of Arts and Sciences; American Academy of Arts and Letters. **Residence:** New Rochelle, New York.

PUBLICATIONS

Collection

A Cynthia Ozick Reader. 1996.

Short Stories

The Pagan Rabbi and Other Stories. 1971.
Bloodshed and Three Novellas. 1976.
Levitation: Five Fictions. 1982.
The Shawl: A Story and a Novella. 1989.

Novels

Trust. 1966.
The Cannibal Galaxy. 1983.
The Messiah of Stockholm. 1987.
The Puttermesser Papers. 1997.

Other

Art and Ardor (essays). 1983.
Metaphor and Memory (essays). 1989.
What Henry James Knew and Other Essays on Writers. 1993.
Fame and Folly: Essays. 1996.

*

Bibliography: "A Bibliography of Writings by Ozick" by Susan Currier and Daniel J. Cahill, in *Texas Studies in Literature and Language,* Summer 1983.

Critical Studies: "The Art of Ozick" by Victor Strandberg, in *Texas Studies in Literature and Language,* Summer 1983; *Ozick* edited by Harold Bloom, 1986; *The Uncompromising Fictions of Ozick* by Sanford Pinsker, 1987; *Ozick* by Joseph Lowin, 1988; *Cynthia Ozick's Fiction: Tradition and Invention* by Elaine M. Kauvar, 1993; *Cynthia Ozick's Comic Art: From Levity to Liturgy* by Sarah Blacher Cohen, 1994; "The Transgression of Postmodern Fiction: Philip Roth and Cynthia Ozick" by Alfred Hornung, in *Affirmation and Negation in Contemporary American Culture,* edited by Gerhard Hoffmann and Alfred Hornung, 1994; "Cynthia Ozick: Prophet for Parochialism" by Sarah Blacher Cohen, in *Women of the World: Jewish Women and Jewish Writing,* edited by Judith R. Baskin, 1994; "Matrilineal Dissent: The Rhetoric of Zeal in Emma Lazarus, Marie Syrkin, and Cynthia Ozick" by

Carole S. Kessner, in *Women of the World: Jewish Women and Jewish Writing,* edited by Judith R. Baskin, 1994; "Jewish Jacobites: Henry James's Presence in the Fiction of Philip Roth and Cynthia Ozick" by Mark Krupnick, in *Traditions, Voices, and Dreams: The American Novel Since the 1960s,* edited by Melvin J. Friedman and Ben Siegel, 1995; "The Holocaust and the Witnessing Imagination" by S. Lillian Kremer, in *Violence, Silence, and Anger: Women's Writing as Transgression,* edited by Deirdre Lashgari, 1995; "Cynthia Ozick's Paradoxical Wisdom" by Marilyn Yalom, in *People of the Book: Thirty Scholars Reflect on Their Jewish Identity,* edited by Jeffrey Rubin Dorsky and Shelley Fisher Fishkin, 1996.

*   *   *

Cynthia Ozick professes that she began her first novel as an American writer but ended it as a Jewish writer. Since then she has been a firm believer in the ties of personal history to the creation of literature. Ozick feels that to ignore one's history, especially for a writer, is to perform "a kind of cultural autolobotomy." Although best known for her fiction, Ozick is an acclaimed essayist, poet, and critic as well. She manages a wide range of subjects, weaving philosophical and poetic prose with elements of Jewish folklore, pagan tales, comedy, and satire. Although Ozick admits in *Art and Ardor* that at one time "I was a worshipper of literature, literature was my single altar," the author is always concerned with the dangers of turning a love of literature into idol worship. "Her apprehension of the perilousness of idolatry, her allegiance to the judgements of history, her concept of tradition itself as innovation—these convictions have increasingly occasioned the speculation that Cynthia Ozick may eventually be judged our **T. S. Eliot**," writes Elaine M. Kauvar in the preface of *Cynthia Ozick's Fiction: Tradition and Invention.* Elisa New, in "The Timing of Cynthia Ozick," agrees: "Ozick is a writer who surveys waste, idolatry, compromise, and the meretricious; and, with Eliot, she is a writer who proposes a sterner, and an older, way."

The daughter of Russian-Jewish immigrants who ran a drugstore in the Bronx, Ozick says that her approach to writing is more inclusive than "American" literature. She insists that to be a Jew is "the expression of universalism." Her essays and short stories have been translated into 11 languages, including Hebrew, French, and Finnish. She has been called the leader of a movement of Jewish writers whose fiction proudly draws from the Jewish textual tradition. "Jewish-American writers are, of course, a representative case of the general condition [of humankind]," explains Sanford Pinsker in *The Uncompromising Fiction of Cynthia Ozick,* "albeit one writ large and in exclamation points."

Because her work comes from such a clearly defined religious tradition, Ozick is most often compared to T. S. Eliot, **Flannery O'Connor**, and **Grace Paley**. The writer who exerted the most influence on the young Ozick, however, was **Henry James**. At Ohio State University she wrote her master's thesis on James's fiction ("Parable in the Late Novels of Henry James"), and her first two novels (the first of which has not been published) unmistakably resemble the work of James.

Called by critics Ozick's "portrait of a lady," her first published novel, *Trust* (1966), involves the story of a wealthy American family. The tale grows out of a tradition as old as literature itself: the son's search for a father. But Ozick revises this tradition when she places a daughter's search for a father at the center of the novel. The nameless female narrator is motivated solely by the need to solve the riddle of her birth and, in turn, to discover who she is. True to the structure of a Jamesian novel, *Trust* takes the form of a quest; its themes are initiation and self-discovery, its characters are upper-middle-class citizens, and there is a juxtaposition of American and European settings and manners. When the heroine discovers that she is the illegitimate child of a pagan demigod, she begins to disavow her cultural heritage in favor of pantheism, and so begins the "Pan versus Moses theme" that propels so much of Ozick's fiction.

Ozick explains that she was influenced by the later writings of James and that she, like him, came to a point in her career when she was a worshiper of literature. Faced with the decision to choose real life over a wholehearted devotion to art, Ozick chose art. It is not surprising, therefore, that one of the most completely developed themes of Ozick's work concerns the potential (and perhaps immoral) dangers of turning a love of literature into idol worship. She makes clear that this is a special dilemma for a Jewish artist, for to be a Jew theologically means "one who shuns idols." Ozick reveals, however, that her craft requires the utmost concentration and devotion. She says that the first draft of her writing is usually the last draft, because she refuses to go on to a second sentence until she has perfected the first. And when she writes, she finds that she enters a sort of "trance"; in this world of language, she exists only on the page.

Further developing the ideas introduced in *Trust,* the award-winning short stories in *The Pagan Rabbi* and *Bloodshed* depict the competing ideas behind an inherited tradition and the betrayal of that tradition, thus continuing the dispute between the pagan world and the demands of Mosaic law. *The Pagan Rabbi* shows Pan battling Moses for the souls of a rabbi, a Yiddish poet, and an attorney. The stories make clear the "double life" of a Jew in America. The strife of dual perspectives resulting from Hebrew tradition saturates this volume of stories, while *Bloodshed* is wholly set on showing the consequences of repudiating that tradition. In the title stories of *Bloodshed* and *A Pagan Rabbi,* for instance, both the rabbi (whose name, Isaac Kornfeld, suggests both his Jewishness and gentleness) and Bleilip yearn to be "part of the society at large" (Bleilip even calls himself a "secularist"). Ozick reminds us in "Toward a New Yiddish" that "the secular Jew is a figment; when a Jew becomes a secular person he is no longer a Jew." In short, Kornfeld and Bleilip are in danger of having no identity at all. "Toward a New Yiddish" warns that, if the Jew "does not judge what he finds, if he joins it instead, he disappears."

Ozick's essays provide grounding for her fiction. Her two collections of essays *Metaphor and Memory* and *Art and Ardor* are made up of 25 years of journal contributions. Exploring the dilemmas of Jewish-American culture and what it means to be a "Jewish-American writer," the essays offer keen insights into Ozick's unique style of writing. In them she strives to uphold tradition in art and to connect the individual talent and life to that tradition. Many critics have taken as her credo the essay "Toward a New Yiddish," originally published in 1970. Arguing against the desire of Jewish-American writers to blur the uniqueness of their tradition by seeking universalism, Ozick rallies them to retain the distinction of their heritage by insisting that "literature does not spring from the urge to Esperanto but from the tribe."

While *Bloodshed* emphasizes the tribal, *Levitation: Five Fictions* emphasizes the nature of the artistic imagination. In fact, fantasy controls all of the five fictions. Kauvar has described the stories in *Levitation* as "five paintings hung in an imaginary gallery, portraits of artists in the act of imaginative creation." The title story is a "picture" of a married couple, the Feingolds, who are both novelists living in New York. It is a satire on a type of postmodern writing (writing that concerns itself with the act of writing) and a criticism of the Feingolds' novel writing, but it is ultimately about Jewish identity. As Lucy Feingold has a vision during a cocktail party about a rising room that levitates real Jews while those who do not share in the Holocaust remain on the ground floor, she feels the difference between her orthodox husband and herself magnified. The remaining stories of *Levitation* are concerned with identity, Jewish as well as feminine. And all of the stories depend on fantasies, sometimes as outlandish as Lucy's dream of the ascending Jews.

In 1980 Ozick paid a visit to the renowned scholar of Jewish mysticism Gershom Scholem in Jerusalem. She then produced two of the most "mystical" works of her career: *The Cannibal Galaxy* (1983) and *The Messiah of Stockholm* (1987). In *The Cannibal Galaxy* Ozick applies the idea of cannibal galaxies (a theory in which galaxies "devour smaller brother-galaxies") to human relationships. Once again the author endeavors to mix the contributions of Western culture with the legacy of Judaism. Joseph Brill, a Holocaust survivor and the principal of a school whose curriculum he has designed, attempts to unite Jewish with Western culture in a Jewish-American educational program. Brill has witnessed the Holocaust cannibalize his family, his fellow Jews, and his native France. And although it would seem that he would naturally have a dim view of humankind, he chooses for his school motto "ad astra" (reach for the stars). The motto is problematic, however, for as the melancholic Brill puts it, he is forever "consorting with the Middle." Although he was born in France, he quotes his father in Yiddish; although educated at the Sorbonne, "his vowels strive to be American." Brill sees himself "in the middle of ashen America, heading a school of middling reputation." At the center of the idea of cannibalism, however, lies the paradoxical idea that cannibalism creates as well as destroys. For in merging Jewish and Western cultures at his school, Brill may be destroying the very heritage he hopes to preserve in his curriculum.

The Messiah of Stockholm, like *The Cannibal Galaxy*, highlights an obsessive hero and centers around the mystery of creation. Lars Andemening puts his faith in the far-fetched idea that he is the lost son of the Jewish writer Bruno Schulz, an actual Polish author who was shot dead on a street of his hometown of Drohobycz by a Nazi SS agent in 1942. Lars becomes proficient in Polish and obsessively reads (and rereads) all of Schulz's tales until he feels himself caught in a confused fantasy that resembles the author's nightmarish stories. The story revolves around the possible existence of a lost manuscript of Schulz (it is rumored that the actual Schulz was working on a book called *The Messiah* at the time of his death) and the possibility of there being an unknown son of Schulz. *The Messiah of Stockholm* incorporates Ozick's favorite juxtapositions: the past (Drohobycz in the 1930s) and the present (Stockholm in the 1980s); East and West; Jews and gentiles; and, of course, biblical and mythological beliefs.

Secrecy and invisibility have been Ozick's great subjects; in fact, she writes late at night at an old Sears, Roebuck desk. She writes for, what reviewer James Wood calls, "the secret coaxing of sentences." Her 1996 collection of essays, *Fame and Fortune,* seeks the absence in public life, which is the place of the stylist. She contends with the biographies of those writers she admires—Jane Austen, T. S. Eliot, the Russian writer Isaac Babel, among others—and dissects the permutations between their private and public lives. She sees in these predecessors a fragile interplay between reward and failure, tracing their reactions to setbacks and their readiness to take their main chances.

In her 1997 collection of two stories and three novellas, *The Puttermesser Papers,* Ozick chronicles the life of a brilliant woman lawyer, Ruth Puttermesser, beginning with her entry into middle age and ending with her death at the threshold of old age. Puttermesser, even after she loses her job, does not lose her liberal convictions, among them the plight of Soviet Jews. The bureaucracy that tolerates sexism and rewards ineptitude works against Puttermesser's commitment and professionalism. When she dies, she is an isolated and forgotten figure. Throughout the stories Ozick is charmed by the obscure lore of the kabala, by the tales of the rabbis of medieval Spain and of Renaissance Prague, by the mystical powers locked inside the letters of the Hebrew alphabet. The works were written over more than two decades, and Ozick says that in *The Puttermesser Papers* she "wanted to try the experiment of writing a single chapter that would, in some way, contain the essence of a decade of human life—some imaginary adventure that would be expressive of the infrastructure of a mind."

Not only is Ozick a novelist, essayist, and short story writer, but she is also a poet and a translator who has been instrumental in recovering the work of other artists in the Jewish tradition. A premier translator of Yiddish poetry, Ozick has published her translations in *A Treasury of Yiddish Poetry* (1969) and the *Penguin Book of Modern Yiddish Verse* (1987). Ozick's own early poetry appeared in the *Literary Review* and the *Virginia Quarterly Review.* Her verse has also been circulated in important Jewish periodicals, including *Commentary, Judaism,* and *Midstream.* Some of her shorter works have been anthologized in *Voices within the Ark: The Modern Jewish Poets.* Although she is the niece of the Hebrew poet Abraham Regelson, Ozick herself has generally shied away from a career in poetry, preferring to stick to prose. A member of the American Academy and Institute of Arts and Letters since 1988, Ozick has been recognized as one of the greatest American writers of stories. Whether she is labeled a "blunt essayist," a "Jewish-American author," or a "Jewish fiction writer," her works have earned universal respect.

—Susan Bunn, updated by Martha Sutro

P-Q

PAGE, Thomas Nelson

Born: Oakland Plantation, Hanover County, Virginia, 23 April 1853. **Education:** Local schools, and at Washington College (later Washington and Lee University), Lexington, Virginia, 1869-72; read law with his father, 1872-73; studied law at the University of Virginia, Charlottesville, 1873-74, LL.B. 1874. **Family:** Married 1) Annie Seddon Bruce in 1886 (died 1888); 2) Florence Lathrop Field in 1893 (died 1921). **Career:** Lawyer in Richmond, Virginia, 1874-93; writer, 1884-1910; lived in Washington, D.C., after 1893; U.S. Ambassador to Italy, 1913-19. **Awards:** Litt.D.: Washington and Lee University, 1887; Yale University, New Haven, Connecticut, 1901; Harvard University, Cambridge, Massachusetts, 1913. LL.D.: Tulane University, New Orleans, 1899; College of William and Mary, Williamsburg, Virginia, 1906; Washington and Lee University, 1907. **Member:** American Academy, 1908. **Died:** 1 November 1922.

PUBLICATIONS

Fiction

In Ole Virginia; or, Marse Chan and Other Stories. 1887.
Two Little Confederates. 1888.
On Newfound River. 1891; revised edition, 1906.
Among the Camps; or, Young People's Stories of the War. 1891.
Elsket and Other Stories. 1891.
The Burial of the Guns. 1894.
Pastime Stories. 1894.
Unc' Edinburg: A Plantation Echo. 1895.
The Old Gentleman of the Black Stock. 1897.
Two Prisoners. 1898; revised edition, 1903.
Red Rock: A Chronicle of Reconstruction. 1898.
Santa Claus's Partner. 1899.
Gordon Keith. 1903.
Bred in the Bone (stories). 1904.
Under the Crust (stories). 1907.
Tommy Trot's Visit to Santa Claus. 1908.
John Marvel, Assistant. 1909.
The Land of the Spirit (stories). 1913.
The Stranger's Pew (story). 1914.
The Red Riders. 1924.

Poetry

Befo' de War: Echoes in Negro Dialect, with A. C. Gordon. 1888.
The Coast of Bohemia. 1906.

Other

The Old South: Essays Social and Political. 1892.
Social Life in Old Virginia before the War. 1897.
The Negro: The Southerner's Problem. 1904.
The Novels, Stories, Sketches, and Poems (Plantation Edition). 18 vols., 1906-12.

Robert E. Lee: The Southerner. 1908; as *General Lee,* 1909.
The Old Dominion: Her Making and Her Manners. 1908.
Mount Vernon and Its Preservation. 1910.
Robert E. Lee: Man and Soldier. 1911.
Italy and the World War. 1920.
Dante and His Influence: Studies. 1922.
Washington and Its Romance. 1923.
Mediterranean Winter—1906: Journal and Letters, edited by Harriet R. Holman. 1971.

Editor, *The Old Virginia Gentleman and Other Sketches,* by George W. Bagby. 1910.

*

Bibliography: by Theodore L. Gross, in *American Literary Realism 1,* 1967; in *Bibliography of American Literature* by Jacob Blanck, 1973; *Three Virginia Writers: A Reference Guide* by George C. Longest, 1978.

Critical Studies: *Page: A Memoir of a Virginia Gentleman* by Rosewell Page, 1923; *Patriotic Gore: Studies in the Literature of the American Civil War* by Edmund Wilson, 1962; *Page* by Theodore L. Gross, 1967; *The Literary Career of Page 1884-1910* by Harriet R. Holman, 1978; "Americanisms in the Writings of Page" by John McCluskey, in *American Speech: A Quarterly of Linguistic Usage,* 1982; "Red Rock: A Reappraisal" by Earl F. Bargainnier, in *The Southern Quarterly: A Journal of the Arts in the South,* 1984; "Page and Harry Stillwell Edwards" by Doris Lanier, in *Southern Studies: An Interdisciplinary Journal of the South,* 1990.

*   *   *

Thomas Nelson Page owed his popularity to the local color movement, the interest of Northern readers in the defeated South following the Civil War, and the growth of the family magazine. Although there were writers in the deep South and the mountain areas, the dominant literary image of the region was provided by accounts of life in the tidewater. Page and other writers in the plantation literary tradition increased the Southerner's pride in his past and dramatized his sense of victimization and self-sacrifice. Page's essays and dialect stories, published first in such magazines as *Scribner's* and *Century,* eulogized a civilization in which landlords abided by an almost medieval sense of *gentilesse,* women were exalted, and all the chivalric virtues prevailed. Sir Walter Scott's romances and stories by the Virginia writers George Bagby and Armistead Gordon influenced Page's style and themes. His protagonists were typically those who had survived the war and were faced with the task of adjusting to a new and alien culture. He attempted to evoke a world that lived only in memory, and nostalgia was, therefore, the dominant mood of his most successful work.

The favorable reception in both North and South of "Marse Chan," "Meh Lady," and the other stories of *In Ole Virginia* convinced Page that authorship would prove a surer path to fame than the legal profession. Consequently, after his first wife died and he married a wealthy widow, Page devoted himself to full-time writing. He wrote several novels in which he experimented with urban settings and satirical dialogue. Even in these works, however, Page described the impact of Southern values on the rest of the nation. Each of the major novels written in his middle years (*Red Rock, Gordon Keith,* and *John Marvel, Assistant*) concerns Southern "missionaries," Virginia gentlemen who preach their Southern ideals and convert Yankees in the process. Part of their doctrine was a distrust of industrialization, a belief that aristocratic paternalism could still combat the grosser aspects of democracy, and a wistful agrarianism. It was the first decade of the new century that brought Page to the peak of his literary fame. After 1910 he all but retired from writing and devoted his time to political affairs in Washington, D.C.; he was a personal friend of Theodore Roosevelt, and eventually became ambassador to Italy.

Few writers after Page described Southern institutions so uncritically. Of the later writers **Margaret Mitchell** came closer than most to sharing the elegant Virginian's views, while **Ellen Glasgow, James Branch Cabell, William Faulkner,** and their contemporaries perceived the ironies and injustices of the system Page had defended. At his best Page epitomized the plantation literary tradition, and the strengths and weaknesses of his prose provide an excellent illustration of a once popular literary genre.

—Kimball King

PAINE, Thomas

Born: Thetford, Norfolk, England, 29 January 1737. **Education:** Grammar school to age 13; then apprenticed in his father's trade of staymaker (corsets or possibly ships' cables). **Military Service:** Served in the Pennsylvania militia, 1776. **Family:** Married 1) Mary Lambert in 1759 (died 1760); 2) Elizabeth Ollive in 1771 (legally separated 1774; died 1808). **Career:** Went to sea on privateer, 1756; staymaker, London, 1756-57, and Dover, 1758, Sandwich, 1759, and Margate, 1760, all Kent; supernumerary excise officer, Thetford, 1761, Grantham, Lincolnshire, 1762-64, and Alford, Lincolnshire, 1764-65 (dismissed for neglect of duty); staymaker, Diss, Norfolk, 1766; usher, London, 1766-68; excise officer, Lewes, Sussex, 1768-74 (dismissed after leading move to gain pay rise); went to Philadelphia, 1774, with letters of introduction from Benjamin Franklin; journalist: editor, *Pennsylvania Magazine,* Philadelphia, 1775-76; secretary, Continental Congress committee to negotiate treaty with the Indians, 1777, and committee on foreign affairs, 1777-79; clerk, Pennsylvania Assembly, 1779-81; secretary on a mission to France to raise money for George Washington's army, 1781; lived in Bordentown, New Jersey, and on farm (confiscated from loyalists) given to him near New Rochelle, New York, and worked on design for single arch iron bridge (design approved by French Academy, 1787), 1783-87; lived in England and France from 1787; tried in absentia for treason (over *The Rights of Man*), and outlawed from England, 1792; made French citizen by Assembly, 1792; member of National Convention, for Pas de Calais, 1792, as part of Gironde group (supported banishment, not execution, of Louis XVI); at fall of Girondists deprived of French citizenship and imprisoned, 1793-94; resumed seat in Convention, 1795, and lived in Paris until 1802; lived in New Jersey, New Rochelle, and New York City, 1802-09. **Awards:** M.A., University of Pennsylvania, Philadelphia, 1780. **Died:** 8 June 1809.

PUBLICATIONS

Collections

Life and Works, edited by William M. Van der Weyde. 10 vols., 1925.
Representative Selections, edited by Harry Hayden Clark. 1944; revised edition, 1961.
Complete Writings, edited by Philip S. Foner. 2 vols., 1945.
The Unique Genius of Thomas Paine. 1994.
Collected Writings (Library of America). 1995.
Rights of Man; Common Sense; and Other Political Writings. 1995.

Works

Common Sense. 1776; revised edition, 1776.
The American Crisis. 13 vols., 1776-83; *The Crisis Extraordinary,* 1780; *A Supernumerary Crisis,* 2 vols., 1783.
Public Good. 1780.
Letter Addressed to the Abbe Raynal on the Affairs of North America. 1782.
Dissertations on Government: The Affairs of the Bank; and Paper-Money. 1786.
Prospects on the Rubicon. 1787; as *Prospects on the War and Paper Currency,* 1793.
The Rights of Man. 2 vols., 1791-92; edited by Henry Collins, 1969.
Letter Addressed to the Addressers. 1792.
The Writings. 1792(?).
The Case of the Officers of Excise. 1793.
Reasons for Wishing to Preserve the Life of Louis Capet (i.e., Louis XVI). 1793.
The Age of Reason. 2 vols., 1794-95.
Dissertation on First Principles of Government. 1795.
The Decline and Fall of the English System of Finance. 1796.
Letter to George Washington. 1796.
La justice agraire. 1797; as *Agrarian Justice,* 1797.
Letter to the People of France and the French Armies. 1797.
Discourse at the Society of Theophilanthropists. 1798; as *Atheism Refuted,* 1798.
Compact Maritime. 1801.
Letters to the Citizens of the United States. 1803.
To the Citizens of Pennsylvania, on the Proposal for Calling a Convention. 1805.
Examination of the Passages in the New Testament, Quoted from the Old, and Called Prophecies Concerning Jesus Christ. 1807.
Of the Causes of Yellow Fever, and the Means of Preventing It. 1807.
On the Origins of Free-masonry. 1810.
Miscellaneous Poems. 1819.
Six New Letters, edited by Harry Hayden Clark. 1939.
Selected Work, edited by Howard Fast. 1946.
Common Sense and Other Political Writings, edited by Nelson F. Adkins. 1953.

*

Critical Studies: *The Life of Paine* by Moncure Daniel Conway, 2 vols., 1892; *Man of Reason: The Life of Paine,* 1959, and *Paine's American Ideology,* 1984, both by Alfred Owen Aldridge; *Paine: His Life, Work, and Times* by Audrey Williamson, 1973; *Paine* by David Freeman Hawke, 1974; *Paine and Revolutionary*

America by Eric Foner, 1976; *Paine* by Jerome D. Wilson and William F. Ricketson, 1978; *Paine, The Greatest Exile* by David Powell, 1985; *A Concordance to Paine's Common Sense and The American Crisis* by Manfred Putz and Jon K. Adams, 1989; *Thomas Paine: Revolutionary Author* by Karin Clafford Farley, 1994; *Crisis in Representation: Thomas Paine, Mary Wollstonecraft, Helena Maria Williams, and the Rewriting of the French Revolution* by Steven Blakemore, 1997; *Thomas Paine: The Case of the King of England and His Officers of Excise* by George Hindmarch, 1998.

* * *

Few American writers have generated as much controversy as that surrounding Thomas Paine and his works. Revered as a folk hero during the American Revolution, Paine died in ignominy, an embarrassment to his former friends and an object of ridicule in the very country that his writings had done so much to establish. Nonetheless, his works are, as one critic explains, "unique as an example of English in action," placing him among the most successful persuasive writers of all times. Even Paine's most strident adversaries have been forced to admit that without him there might very well have never been an American Revolution.

Paine first rose to public prominence as a writer of pamphlets during the time of the Revolutionary War. Published anonymously in early January 1776, his essay *Common Sense* sold hundreds of thousands of copies and is credited with almost singlehandedly convincing the American colonies to enter into armed rebellion against Great Britain. In this work Paine popularized the Enlightenment concept that government is a "social contract" that exists by consent of the people for the protection of their "natural rights." Attacking the idea of monarchy, Paine catalogued the abuses that the British king had imposed upon his American subjects, and he called for the establishment of a new government, independent of Britain. Equally popular and equally effective was *The American Crisis,* an essay series published in thirteen parts (including an addendum) between 1776 and 1783. Issued at periods during the war when the patriot cause seemed desperate, *The American Crisis* lifted the morale of soldiers and civilians alike and helped secure the revenues and determination needed to see the conflict through to a successful conclusion. According to one scholar, the very history of the war "may be read in the blazing light of these mighty pamphlets." The first part opens:

> These are the times that try men's souls. The summer soldier and the sunshine patriot will, in this crisis, shrink from the service of their country; but he that stands it now deserves the love and thanks of man and woman. Tyranny, like hell, is not easily conquered; yet we have this consolation with us, that the harder the conflict, the more glorious the triumph.

After the war, in such works as *The Rights of Man* and *The Age of Reason,* Paine set out to accomplish for the world what he had already accomplished for America. Written in two parts, *The Rights of Man* defends the French Revolution against the attacks lodged against it by Edmund Burke in his *Reflections on the Revolution in France* and even goes so far as to call for a democratic revolution against the British monarchy. So fearful was the British crown that this work might indeed inspire rebellion that an order was issued for Paine's arrest, and he was forced to leave the country for France, where he was initially received as a hero but later imprisoned for his denunciation of the execution of Louis XVI.

Abandoned by three countries and embittered, Paine wrote *The Age of Reason* in the hopes of enlightening mankind concerning matters of religion. Far from the atheist tract that it was labeled by Paine's political detractors, *The Age of Reason* consists of little more than an educated attempt to popularize the ideas of scientific deism widely held during the late eighteenth century by individuals as respected as **Benjamin Franklin, Thomas Jefferson**, and George Washington. "My country is the world," wrote Paine, "and my religion is to do good." Nonetheless, it was this work, along with a letter critical of Washington, that led to Paine's vilification in the American popular imagination and that earned him the title of "filthy little atheist."

Although scholars have debated the exact nature of Paine's indebtedness to other writers, it is generally conceded that with few exceptions most of Paine's ideas were not original. His social and political theories, for example, are borrowed from such writers as Rousseau, Montesquieu, Locke, and Hobbes, and his religious views owe their origin to the theories set in motion by Newton and Diderot. Likewise, it is generally conceded that what distinguishes Paine from other writers of his time is his tremendous talent for persuasion.

Indeed, Paine has been called "one of the world's truly great practitioners of the art of persuasive writing," and although he sometimes ignored the niceties of conventional grammar and was capable of subverting logic to suit his ends, in the works of Paine can be seen a truly extraordinary grasp of the principles of effective rhetoric. Speaking with conviction as a common man in the idiom of the common man, Paine at his best could generate a unique sense of identification between himself and his audience. He is, as Quintilian would have said, an admirable man speaking to an equally admirable group of people.

Disavowing the complex neoclassical rhetoric of his day, Paine espoused instead a style that was forceful, direct, clear, and simple. Easily understood, his prose was carefully structured to move his audience to action. A master at the use of such rhetorical devices as parallelism, repetition, the apostrophe, the invective, the rhetorical question, the summary, and the ethical appeal, Paine was able, as one scholar has explained, to awaken "the lukewarm, hesitating, and indifferent, and turn them in great numbers to the support of the cause." As a result, lines such as those quoted above and "The sun never shined on a cause of greater worth" remain, as one analyst has pointed out, "as vibrant today as they were 200 years ago."

—James A. Levernier

See the essay on *Common Sense.*

PALEY, Grace

Born: Grace Goodside, New York City, 11 December 1922. **Education:** Evander Childs High School, New York; Hunter College, New York, 1938-39. **Family:** Married 1) Jess Paley in 1942, one daughter and one son; 2) the playwright Robert Nichols in 1972. **Career:** Has taught at Columbia University, New York, and Syracuse University, New York. Since 1966 has taught at Sarah Lawrence College, Bronxville, New York, and since 1983 at City

College, New York. New York State Author, 1986-88. **Awards:** Guggenheim grant, 1961; National Endowment for the Arts grant, 1966; American Academy award, 1970; Edith Wharton award, 1988, 1989; Rea award for short story, 1993; Vermont Governor's award for excellence in the arts, 1993; award for contribution to Jewish culture, National Foundation of Jewish Culture. **Member:** American Academy, 1980; American Institute of Arts and Letters. **Residence:** New York City.

PUBLICATIONS

Short Stories

The Little Disturbances of Man: Stories of Men and Women in Love. 1959.
Enormous Changes at the Last Minute. 1974.
Later the Same Day. 1985.
The Collected Short Stories. 1994.

Poetry

Leaning Forward. 1985.
New and Collected Poems. 1992.

Other

365 Reasons Not to Have Another War. 1989.
Long Walks and Intimate Talks (stories and poems). 1991.
Just As I Thought. 1998.

*

Critical Studies: *Paley: Illuminating the Dark Lives* by Jacqueline Taylor, 1990; *Paley: A Study of the Short Fiction* by Neil Isaacs, 1990; "Truth in Mothering: Grace Plaey's Stories" by Judith Arcana, in *Narrating Mothers: Theorizing Maternal Subjectivities,* edited by Brenda Daly, 1991; *Imagining a Past: Memory and History in the Fiction of Grace Paley, Alice Walker, Achy Obejas, and Joyce Carol Oates* (dissertation) by Andrea Rohlfs Wright, 1998.

*   *   *

William Blake taught that life is lived in "minute particulars" rather than in grand gestures. As though she took this as dictum, Grace Paley's sure and precise method is to illuminate the ordinary moments of humans in struggle and beauty. Her stories open and close without conventional beginning, middle, or end, demonstrating the continuum in which we live. The titles of her three major collections even describe that method: *The Little Disturbances of Man: Stories of Men and Women in Love, Enormous Changes at the Last Minute,* and *Later the Same Day.* The heightened moments of these fictions—the "little disturbances" that create a moment's "enormous change"—tend to begin in medias res, illuminate the personalities involved, and end with no resolution of the drama proscribed. In fact, lives can return to the center of attention or disappear, much as the personalities the reader might daily encounter. "Later the same day" is an effective tag for the method; as a title it suggests a chronicle in progress and continuing. Yet these struggles are so consistently

evocative and resonant that one after another the stories have been acclaimed as small classics of the storyteller's art, and Paley has achieved a reputation as a major writer from a relatively small body of work.

"A Conversation with My Father," an often anthologized story from *The Little Disturbances of Man,* illuminates Paley's method and her recognition of the power of storytelling. The subject of the conversation—or argument—between the narrator and her hospitalized father is storytelling. The daughter writes a story to please her father, who has requested a story of de Maupassant's simplicity. With willingness and a disarming earnestness, the daughter tries. In her story a woman becomes a junkie in order to find acceptance in her teenaged son's group of friends. She is left alone when the son moves out. When the daughter's one-paragraph outline is rejected by the father, the daughter elaborates the story into a fantastic and humorous two-page effort—heavy on the mock heroic and the absurd, answering all the questions posed by her father's classical probing for meaning. The father insists that he has been told a classic tragedy culminating in the fictive woman's fated doom, but the daughter insists that the abandoned mother in her story has hope. Continuing to write, she follows the life further to the woman's victory: finding personal worth through work in a neighborhood clinic.

The victories in "A Conversation with My Father" are twofold, for the narrator-daughter (who becomes empowered in the debate with her father about the nature of the human drama) as well as for the story she creates. These assertions are highly representative of Paley's world, where stories not yet told—of the marginalized and silent—become real and lively without being sentimentalized. The story also demonstrates a long-held concern of Paley's—that the dialogue of men and women differs. Paley's critics (notably Jacqueline Taylor) have commented that storytelling by women often strays from a dominant voice (male style) to empowering a number of voices to speak the narrative (female style). Paley, raised in the Bronx by immigrant parents who spoke Russian and Yiddish at home, hears a New York filled with Jewish, Puerto Rican, African American, Irish, Chinese, and other dialects, voices which speak freely and variously in a fiction that proceeds more by dialogue than by narrative. Almost all of Paley's stories are spoken rather than narrated, and the quirky obsessions and speech patterns of the speakers create the distinctive humor, color, and life of the tales.

Faith, a character much like the author, and her family recur in a number of stories throughout Paley's collections, which can be read singly or interpreted as a continuum of storytelling documenting an empathic community the author inhabits. Familiar characters age across the books but wrestle with familiar themes like bigotry, recovering from social meanness, and setting priorities within the challenges of everyday existence.

Throughout her career as a writer of stories, Paley has also been a poet with a profound appreciation of the greater literary tradition; Jane Cooper writes that Paley has taken a singular love in reading Milton out loud to her students. The rhythms of poetic speech and the making of a cultural language are very significant in the world she records; each story is an exercise in compression. "Friends," one of the most moving works in *Later the Same Day,* contains a novel's worth of interaction in a few pages. In this story a group of women discussing the nature of their commitments during a period of illness among members of their circle cover (with surprising depth) such topics as the bondedness of mothers to children, the recognition that children are only part of the lives that unfold, the culture and sociology of codependence, and the meaning of their bonds with each other.

Two volumes of Paley's verse show the same set of concerns with women's issues and social issues documented in the stories. The poetry photographs, as it were, the small ironies from which culture emerges. "A Warning," for example, translates Jewish liturgy into personal terms, reflecting on a visit to the Holy Land and interpreting immediate imagery in light of generations of antisemitism. "Illegal Aliens" documents prisoners at O'Hare Airport scheduled for deportation and sets the situation into the observer's moral framework. In eleven brief lines "The Boys from St. Bernard's" sketches snowball fighters from two parochial schools and invokes the methodology by which holy wars become invented.

Paley's method opens up in *Just As I Thought,* a political-literary memoir constructed by cobbling thirty years of reflections, essays, and articles together. A consistency of clarity, love, and philosophy inform these pages, which become an almanac of progressive embraces. Paley's topics of concern range comfortably between the personal and political as she meditates on the connections between her appreciations of women writers and statements on pacifism and the movements for human rights. "I've accumulated enough experience to be easy or difficult," she hazards, "whatever the provocation exacts."

The comedy, wit, and understatement of Paley's writing belie important topics. She achieves a simplicity without embracing easy sentiment. If her harshest critics say that little happens in these stories, she responds that the contrary is true, for hers is an art celebratory of the daily struggles within and across the urban culture in which she has lived her life.

—David Shevin

PARETSKY, Sara (N.)

Born: Ames, Iowa, 8 June 1947. **Education:** The University of Kansas, B.A. 1967; University of Chicago, M.B.A. 1977, Ph.D. 1977. **Family:** Married Courtenay Wright in 1976; three children. **Career:** Publications manager, Urban Research Corp., Chicago, Illinois, 1971-74; freelance business writer, 1974-77; manager of advertising and direct mail marketing programs, Continental National America Insurance Co., Chicago, 1977-85. **Awards:** Friends of American Writers award, 1985; Woman of the Year, *Ms.* magazine, 1987; Silver Dagger award, Crime Writers Association, 1988; fellowship, Wolfson College, Oxford, 1997. **Member:** Founder and president, Sisters in Crime, Chicago, 1986-88; member of Private Eye Writers of America; member of Authors Guild; member of Crime Writers Association; director, National Abortion Rights Action League, Illinois, beginning 1987. **Residence:** Chicago, Illinois.

PUBLICATIONS

Novels

Indemnity Only. 1982.
Deadlock. 1984.
Killing Orders. 1985.

Bitter Medicine. 1987.
Blood Shot. 1988; as *Toxic Shock.* 1988.
Burn Marks. 1990.
Guardian Angel. 1991.
Tunnel Vision. 1994.
Windy City Blues. 1995.
Ghost Country. 1998.
Hard Time. 1999.

Other

Editor, *A Woman's Eye.* 1991.
Editor, *Women on the Case.* 1996.

*

Critical Studies: "The Feminist Counter-Tradition in Crime: Cross, Grafton, Paretsky, and Wilson" by Maureen Reddy, in *The Cunning Craft: Original Essays on Detective Fiction and Contemporary Literary Theory,* 1990; "Paretsky, Turow, and the Importance of Symbolic Ethnicity" by Guy Szuberla, in *Midamerica,* 1991; "New Women Detectives: G Is for Gender-Bending" by Glenwood Irons, in *Gender, Language, and Myth: Essays and Popular Narrative,* 1992; "'Friends Is a Weak Word for It': Female Friendships and the Spectre of Lesbianism in Sara Paretsky" by Ann Wilson, in *Feminism in Detective Fiction* edited by Glenwood H. Irons, 1995.

*   *   *

In 1982 Sara Paretsky published *Indemnity Only,* the mystery novel that introduced her heroine, V.I. "Vic" Warshawski. One of several American women beginning to publish popular detective novels around the same time, Paretsky created Warshawski as a street-smart, feminist private investigator. Although the plots vary from book to book, *Indemnity Only* sets up some of the series' constants such as the white-collar crimes that lead to murder against the backdrop of Chicago. The series was generally well received; *Deadlock* won the Friends of American Writers Award in 1985, *Blood Shot* won the Crime Writers Association's Silver Dagger award in 1988, and Paretsky herself was named one of *Ms.* magazine's 1987 Women of the Year. Although Paretsky has placed her novels within the tradition of hard-boiled detective fiction, it is above all her ability to update and deviate from that standard that makes the Warshawski mysteries notable.

Born June 8, 1947, in Ames, Iowa, Sara Paretsky wrote her first story at age six. Despite the early interest in writing, Paretsky was never encouraged to consider a professional career in creative writing. In her family, talent and professions were reserved for the men, while women were expected to become housewives or, at most, secretaries. It was perhaps youthful frustration with traditional gender roles, voiced in her novels by different characters, but most consistently espoused by Lieutenant Bobby Mallory, that partly motivated the strong feminist tone her novels take.

Warshawski's feminism may also be a reflection of Paretsky's own political involvement. In the 1960s and 1970s, Paretsky became socially and politically active, especially in helping the lobby for abortion rights and later, after the passage of *Roe v. Wade,* becoming active in the National Abortion Rights Action League. Her commitment to women's reproductive freedom is most clearly represented in Warshawski's battles with pro-life groups in *Bitter*

Medicine. Certainly, social activism was at least partially responsible for Paretsky's, and thus for Warshawski's, Chicago residency. Paretsky first came to Chicago in the summer of 1966 as a college sophomore to help run an inner city summer camp. The experience made such an impression on her that after obtaining her B.A. from the University of Kansas in 1967, she moved to Chicago permanently, eventually setting all of her Warshawski novels in the city.

Paretsky attended the University of Chicago as a doctoral candidate during the 1970s. She also worked, while finishing her dissertation in history, as a publications manager for the Urban Research Corp. from 1971 until 1974 when the company dissolved, leaving her to seek an M.B.A. She received both her Ph.D. and M.B.A. from Chicago in 1977.

From 1977 through 1985, she worked as manager of advertising and direct mail marketing programs for Continental National America, an insurance company. Though successful, she was told she was too creative for a corporate career. While still working for CNA, Paretsky began working on a Raymond Chandler parody. Reversing the traditional genders, her detective, Minerva Daniels, was essentially a traditional male hard-boiled detective in drag. On New Year's Day in 1979, having realized this parody to be one of several false starts, Paretsky decided to write a book that year. At that point, she realized the need for a female character working, as she did, in a man's world.

That first Warshawski book, *Indemnity Only,* was completed in May, 1980, and clearly drew from topics with which Paretsky felt comfortable. Using Paretsky's expertise in the insurance business, *Indemnity Only* also involves a missing woman, unions, and, of course, murder. Paretsky expands the locations for her big business crimes in the later books. *Deadlock,* published in 1984, won Paretsky an award from the Friends of American Writers for its story of crime and violence centering around the Chicago shipping industry. Turning to the Catholic church and organized crime, *Killing Orders* (1985) has Warshawski solving both professional and personal mysteries concerning missing stock certificates and the secret behind a long-ago promise Warshawski made to her mother. In *Bitter Medicine* (1987), Warshawski investigates malpractice and murder in the medical profession, while *Blood Shot* (1988), winner of the Silver Dagger award, returns to big business for this mystery involving chemical companies and local politicians. Warshawski investigates the world of construction, contractors, and the homeless in *Burn Marks* (1990), and takes on lawyers and politicos in *Guardian Angel* (1992).

Although Warshawski is hired by a seeming stranger in the first novel, subsequent books usually have her pulled into the mysteries by someone she knows: a dead cousin in *Deadlock,* her aunt in *Killing Orders,* or a childhood friend in *Blood Shot.* Each novel, thus, expands and adds depth to her character. While it is clear from the beginning of the series that Warshawski is from the south side of Chicago, the daughter of an Italian opera singer and a Polish policeman, and an ex-lawyer, the later books fill in her background and flesh out the supporting characters, especially Lotty Herschel, Warshawski's best friend, and Mr. Contreras, her neighbor.

Indeed, this extended family of Lotty, Mr. Contreras, and Peppy, the dog, is one example of Paretsky's break from the strict hard-boiled detective genre in which she works. The tradition is also updated most significantly in the character of Warshawski herself. While Warshawski is as tough as any of her private investigator predecessors, she is not afraid of self-irony or doubt.

Paretsky also portrays Warshawski, an ex-lawyer, as grounded in logic, but not averse to using dreams or intuition to help her solve cases. Above all, Warshawski has a strict moral sense and a rigorous political agenda that guide her decisions.

Although Paretsky's books were reviewed positively, they have been criticized for displaying this political agenda too ostentatiously. Paretsky's response to some of this criticism was to turn it into dialogue for the next book. Despite these relatively minor objections, however, critics have long recognized Paretsky's work as well-written and an important update to popular detective fiction.

—Laura Wyrick

PARKER, Dorothy

Born: Dorothy Rothschild, West End, New Jersey, 22 August 1893. **Education:** Blessed Sacrament Convent, New York; Miss Dana's School, Morristown, New Jersey, 1907-11, graduated 1911. **Family:** Married 1) Edwin Pond Parker II in 1917 (divorced 1928); 2) Alan Campbell in 1933 (divorced 1947; remarried 1950; died 1963). **Career:** Played piano at a dancing school, New York, 1912-15; editorial staff member, *Vogue,* New York, 1916-17; staff writer and drama critic, *Vanity Fair,* New York, 1917-20; theater columnist, *Ainslee's,* 1920-33; book reviewer ("Constant Reader" column), *New Yorker,* 1925-27; columnist, *McCall's,* New York, late 1920s; book reviewer, *Esquire,* New York, 1957-62. Founder, with Robert Benchley, Robert E. Sherwood, and others, Algonquin Hotel Round Table, 1920. **Awards:** O. Henry award, 1929; Marjorie Peabody Waite award, 1958. **Died:** 7 June 1967.

PUBLICATIONS

Collection

The Poetry and Short Stories of Dorothy Parker. 1994.
The Best of Dorothy Parker. 1995.
Laments for the Living: Collected Stories. 1995.

Short Stories

Laments for the Living. 1930.
Here Lies: The Collected Stories. 1939.
Collected Stories. 1942.
Big Blonde and Other Stories. 1995.

Novel

After Such Pleasures. 1933.

Plays

Chauve-Souris (revue), with others (produced 1922).
Round the Town (lyrics only; revue) (produced 1924).
Close Harmony; or, The Lady Next Door, with Elmer Rice (produced 1924). 1929.
Business Is Business, with George S. Kaufman (produced 1925).
Sketches, in *Shoot the Works* (revue) (produced 1931).

The Coast of Illyria, with Ross Evans (produced 1949). 1990.
The Ladies of the Corridor, with Arnaud d'Usseau (produced 1953). 1954.
Candide (lyrics only, with Richard Wilbur and John LaTouche), book by Lillian Hellman, music by Leonard Bernstein, from the novel by Voltaire (produced 1956). 1957.

Screenplays: *Here Is My Heart* (uncredited), with others, 1934; *One Hour Late,* with others, 1935; *The Big Broadcast of 1936,* with others, 1935; *Mary Burns, Fugitive,* with others, 1935; *Hands Across the Table,* with others, 1935; *Paris in Spring,* with others, 1935; *The Moon's Our Home,* with others, 1936; *Lady Be Careful,* with others, 1936; *Three Married Men,* with Alan Campbell and Owen Davis, Sr., 1936; *Suzy,* with others, 1936; *A Star Is Born,* with others, 1937; *Sweethearts,* with Alan Campbell, 1938; *Trade Winds,* with others, 1938; *The Little Foxes,* with others, 1941; *Weekend for Three,* with Alan Campbell and Budd Schulberg, 1941; *Saboteur,* with Peter Viertel and Joan Harrison, 1942; *Smash-Up—The Story of a Woman,* with others, 1947; *The Fan,* with Walter Reisch and Ross Evans, 1949.

Television Plays: *The Lovely Leave, A Telephone Call,* and *Dusk before Fireworks,* from her own stories, 1962.

Poetry

Enough Rope. 1926.
Sunset Gun. 1928.
Death and Taxes. 1931.
Collected Poems: Not So Deep As a Well. 1936; as *Collected Poetry,* 1944.
Not Much Fun: The Lost Poems of Dorothy Parker. 1996.

Other

High Society, with George S. Chappell and Frank Crowninshield. 1920.
Men I'm Not Married To, with *Women I'm Not Married To,* by Franklin P. Adams. 1922.
The Portable Parker. 1944; as *The Indispensable Parker,* 1944; as *Selected Short Stories,* 1944; revised edition, as *The Portable Parker,* 1973; as *The Collected Parker,* 1973.
Constant Reader. 1970; as *A Month of Saturdays,* 1971.
The Sayings of Dorothy Parker. 1996.

Editor, *The Portable F. Scott Fitzgerald.* 1945.
Editor, with Frederick B. Shroyer, *Short Story: A Thematic Anthology.* 1965.

*

Critical Studies: *An Unfinished Woman: A Memoir* by Lillian Hellman, 1969; *You Might As Well Live: The Life and Times of Parker* by John Keats, 1970; *Parker* by Arthur F. Kinney, 1978; *The Late Mrs. Parker* by Leslie Frewin, 1986; *Parker: What Fresh Hell Is This?* by Marion Meade, 1988; "Making Love Modern: Parker and Her Public" by Nina Miller, in *American Literature: A Journal of Literary History, Criticism, and Bibliography,* 1992; *The Rhetoric of Rage: Women in Dorothy Parker* by Sondra Melzer, 1997; *Dorothy Parker, Revised* by Arthur F. Kinney, 1998.

*   *   *

Dorothy Parker's writings were aptly characterized by Alexander Woollcott as "a potent distillation of nectar and wormwood, of ambrosia and deadly nightshade." This assessment covers her perennially popular volumes of short stories, *Laments for the Living* and *After Such Pleasures.* It also encompasses her three best-selling volumes of wry, bittersweet verse (not serious "poetry," she claimed), *Enough Rope, Sunset Gun,* and *Death and Taxes*—mostly love lamentations. It could also apply to her crisp, tart book reviews for the *New Yorker;* she dismissed Milne's *The House at Pooh Corner* with "Tonstant Weader fwowed up."

Her book reviews for *Esquire* (1957-62) are skimpier and less successful. Her major play, *The Ladies of the Corridor* (with Arnaud d'Usseau), a slice-of-life portrayal of aging, pathetic women who have lost their central purpose for living (through departures of husbands, lovers, children) is better as dialogue than as drama.

Many of Parker's well-crafted short stories focus on upper-class Manhattan women of the 1920s and 1930s. The economic comfort of these women, whether young, middle-aged, or old, is counteracted by their superficial, pointless lives, barren of goals, meaningful activities, and inner resources. Although they are often physically attractive and elegantly dressed ornaments at the parties they live for, without such external social props they collapse.

Other people in Parker's stories do the real work; the men earn the money, the maids rear the children. So these women are bored, neurotic, unhappy, pampered parasites. Their fate is the fate of those who live through others, excessive emotional dependency: "Please, God, let him telephone me now." This cripples their potentiality for gaiety and charm and transforms them into shrill, malicious shrews who drink too much, talk too much, think too shallowly, and do too little. These characters are their own most pathetic victims; they seldom deceive others as they delude themselves.

Parker excels in economically incisive descriptions of personalities, settings, costumes: a honeymooning bride "looked as new as a peeled egg." Her dramatic monologues are devastating, ironic characterizations. Thus the hypocritical "Lady with a Lamp" offers cold comfort to her alleged friend, jilted and unhappily recuperating from a clandestine abortion: "I worry so about you, living in a little furnished apartment, with nothing that belongs to you, no roots, no nothing." Parker's dialogues capture the cadences of real speech and the subtle nuances of personality and values: "Good night, useless," says the spoiled mother to her firstborn infant.

The essence of such social satire is the author's implicit desire to reform these empty lives into significant existences. Her best story, "Big Blonde," which won the O. Henry Award in 1929, epitomizes Parker's mixture of love and anger, coalesced into an enduring work of art. Indeed, many of Parker's stories are memorable cameos, etched in acid and polished to gemlike luster.

—Lynn Z. Bloom

PARKMAN, Francis (Jr.)

Born: Boston, Massachusetts, 16 September 1823. **Education:** John Angier's school, Medford, Massachusetts, 1831-35; Gideon Thayer's school, Boston, 1835-40; Harvard University, Cambridge, Massachusetts, 1840-44, A.B. 1844 (Phi Beta Kappa); Dane Law School, Harvard University, 1844-46, LL.B. 1846. **Family:** Married Catherine Scollay Bigelow in 1850 (died 1858); two daughters and one son. **Career:** Traveled from St. Louis along Oregon Trail and spent some weeks with Sioux Indians, 1846; suffered from series of nervous ailments after 1846; professor of horticulture, Harvard University, 1871; overseer, 1868-71 and 1874-76, and fellow of the corporation, 1875-88, Harvard University; president, Massachusetts Horticultural Society, 2 years; founder, Archeological Institute of America, 1879; founder and first President, St. Botolph Club, Boston. **Awards:** LL.D.: McGill University, Montreal, 1879; Harvard University, 1889. **Died:** 8 November 1893.

PUBLICATIONS

Collections

Works, edited by John Fiske. 20 vols., 1897-98.
The Parkman Reader, edited by Samuel Eliot Morison. 1955; as *France and England in North America,* 1956.
Letters, edited by Wilbur R. Jacobs. 2 vols., 1960.

Fiction

Vassall Morton. 1856.

Other

The California and Oregon Trail, Being Sketches of Prairie and Rocky Mountain Life. 1849; revised edition, as *The Oregon Trail,* 1872; edited by David Levin, 1982.
History of the Conspiracy of Pontiac and the War of the North American Tribes Against the English Colonies. 2 vols., 1851; revised edition, 1868, 1870.
France and England in North America (Library of America), edited by David Lavin. 2 vols., 1983.
Pioneers of France in the New World. 1865; revised edition, 1886.
The Jesuits in North America in the Seventeenth Century. 1867.
The Discovery of the Great West. 1869; revised edition, as *La Salle and the Discovery of the Great West,* 1879.
The Old Regime in Canada. 1874; revised edition, 1894.
Count Frontenac and New France under Louis XIV. 1877.
    Montcalm and Wolfe (part 7). 1884.
    A Half-Century of Conflict (part 6). 1892.
The Book of Roses. 1866.
Some of the Reasons against Woman's Suffrage. 1883.
Our Common Schools. 1890.
Letters from Parkman to E. G. Squier, edited by Don C. Seitz. 1911.
Representative Selections, edited by Wilbur L. Schramm. 1938.
The Journals, edited by Mason Wade. 2 vols., 1947.
Francis Parkman and the Plains Indians. 1995.

*

Bibliography: *in Bibliography of American Literature* by Jacob Blanck, 1973.

Critical Studies: *Parkman, Heroic Historian* by Mason Wade, 1942; *Parkman's History: The Historian As Literary Artist* by Otis A. Pease, 1953; *History As Romantic Art: Bancroft, Motley,* *Prescott, and Parkman* by David Levin, 1959; *Parkman* by Howard Doughty, 1962; *Parkman* by Robert L. Gale, 1973; *The American Compromise: Theme and Method in the Histories of Bancroft, Parkman, and Adams* by Richard C. Vitzthum, 1974; "Modern Misjudgements of Racial Imperialism in Hawthorne and Parkman" by David Levin, in *Yearbook of English Studies,* 1983; "Francis Who? Thoughts on Parkman and New York State" by Richard W. Couper in *New York History,* 1983; "Parkman: A Brahmin among Untouchables" by Francis Jennings, in *The William and Mary Quarterly: A Magazine of Early American History and Culture,* 1985; "Parkman and the Male Tradition" by Kim Townsend, in *American Quarterly,* 1986; "Tracking the Pequod along The Oregon Trail: The Influence of Parkman's Narrative on Imagery and Characters in Moby-Dick" by Jack Scherting, in *Western American Literature,* 1987; "Cunning Corridors: Parkman's La Salle As Quest-Romance" by Daniel James Sundahl, in *Colby Library Quarterly,* 1989; "Narrative Voices in Parkman's Montcalm and Wolfe" by Ellen Donovan, in *CLIO: A Journal of Literature, History, and the Philosophy of History,* 1989; "Two Boston Fugitives: Dana and Parkman" by Daniel Aaron, in *American Literature, Culture, and Ideology: Essays in Memory of Henry Nash Smith* edited by Beverly R. Voloshin, 1990; "'Drunk with the Chase': The Influence of Parkman's *The California and Oregon Trail* upon Herman Melville's Moby-Dick, or the Whale" by Thomas L. Altherr, in *Journal of the American Studies Association of Texas,* 1990; "Willa Cather and Parkman: Novelistic Portrayals of Colonial New France" by Wilbur R. Jacobs, in *Willa Cather: Family, Community, and History* edited by John J. Murphy, Linda Hunter Adams, and Paul Rawlins, 1990; "Running Out of Bounds: The Search for Models of Bodily and Social Conduct in Francis Parkman's *The Oregon Trail*" by W.C. Harris, in *The Image of the Frontier in Literature, the Media, and Society* edited by Will Wright and Steven Kaplan, 1997.

*   *   *

Francis Parkman began his literary career in 1845 with four short stories and a poem, all published in *Knickerbocker Magazine.* All dealt with one of the themes of his writing, the conflict between whites and Indians in North America. He had dedicated himself at eighteen to write what he called "a history of the American forest" and these were the first literary results. Parkman was primarily a historian whose one attempt at a major literary work, the novel *Vassall Morton,* was not successful. But his history survives because of its literary qualities.

His most well-known work, *The Oregon Trail,* went through nine editions in his lifetime and remains in print. Its qualities explain Parkman's survival while fellow historians like Motley or Prescott have long since disappeared from publishers' lists. Parkman paid great attention to atmosphere, to introducing the reader to all the sights, sounds, and smells of described landscapes. He worked to integrate his historical characters into their worlds. His imaginative reconstructions have survived all attempts to question their authenticity, bearing witness to his qualities both as historian and literary figure.

Parkman's major literary influences were **James Fenimore Cooper,** Sir Walter Scott, and Lord Byron. He shared Scott's delight in reconstructing historical episodes and transforming them into literary vehicles, though he took no liberties with the facts. He responded to Cooper's fascination with the west and to Byron's interest in character especially as drawn out in *Childe Harold's*

Pilgrimage, which Parkman re-read throughout his life. Parkman's education introduced him to the literatures of Germany, France, and Spain, as well as that of ancient Greece, which had a particular influence on him. His *La Salle and the Discovery of the Great West* presents a man who would be familiar to all readers of Greek tragedy, brave, purposeful, self-absorbed—so fatally flawed, and in the end destroyed. Similarly the description of Pontiac, the central figure in *History of the Conspiracy of Pontiac,* owes much to Greek models.

Parkman was also influenced by French writers like Chateaubriand, who showed his fascination with man's interaction with Nature. Parkman is read in the late twentieth century partly because of the influence on him of another Frenchman, the ethnologist Joseph-Francois Lafitau who saved him from contemporary stereotypes of Indians. Parkman was no cultural relativist, but he did see the Indian on his own terms and disapproval only followed after understanding. Likewise Parkman was able to reject much of his Protestantism (he was a Mather on his mother's side) when dealing with the Jesuits of New France. A tour of Italy (1843-44) led him, he felt, to understand the functional importance of the Catholic Church and to be able to deal with it evenhandedly on the North American continent. He did, however, feel that Catholicism and despotism were closely connected, as were Protestantism and liberty, and, like many another teleologically-minded nineteenth-century observer, that the triumph of secularism was inevitable. This underlying process helped explain the triumph of Great Britain and the fall of France in North America, dealt with climactically in *Montcalm and Wolfe.*

Parkman's fascination with the heroic and with the individual has been criticized by a more democratically minded age. He was, like Cooper, fearful of democratic excess and believed in beneficent leadership by the educated. Too much should not be made of the social attitudes exhibited in *The Oregon Trail,* which is the work of a young man. It does not seem sensible to reject Parkman's West because he fails to dwell on frontiersmen. Frederick Jackson Turner admired Parkman's work though he did see him as "even greater as an artist than as an historian" because of his "dramatic insight." Parkman was fascinated by leadership, its demands and its destructiveness, and therefore generally ignored those who merely followed. The accent on the individual makes him seem old-fashioned in contemporary historiographical circles but does not detract from his literary merits. Since contemporary historiographical preoccupations are unlikely to be permanent it may be that such criticisms will in time become outdated.

Parkman understood the need to balance "dramatic interest" and "historic proportion," as he put it. His success in doing so explains his attractiveness to historian and literary critic alike. It is possible that his partial blindness made him particularly aware of the power of good descriptive writing, but it is also true that in the end his imagination was a limited one. Perhaps because of his historical training Parkman wrote best when he fleshed out historical incident, best of all when he decorated his own experiences as in those depicted in *The Oregon Trail.* Parkman needed sources before he could begin to write successfully, but this limitation brought rewards. Not many writers could expect to be praised by **Henry James** as both "solid and artistic."

—R.A. Burchell

PARKS, Suzan-Lori

Education: Mount Holyoke College, South Hadley, Massachusetts, B.A. in English and German literature (Phi Beta Kappa) 1985. **Career:** Drama studio, London, 1986. Guest lecturer, Pratt Institute, New York, 1988, University of Michigan, Ann Arbor, 1990; playwright-in-residence, Yale University, New Haven, Connecticut, and New York University, 1990-91; playwrighting professor, Eugene Lang College, New York, 1990; writer-in-residence, New School for Social Research, New York, 1991-92. **Awards:** Mary E. Woolley fellowship, 1989; Naomi Kitay fellowship, 1989; National Endowment for the Arts grant, 1990, and playwrighting fellowship, 1990, 1991; New York Foundation for the Arts grant, 1990; Rockefeller Foundation grant, 1990; Obie award, 1990.

PUBLICATIONS

Plays

The Sinner's Place (produced 1984).
Betting on the Dust Commander (produced 1987). 1990.
Imperceptible Mutabilities in the Third Kingdom (produced 1989).
Greeks (produced 1990).
The Death of the Last Black Man in the Whole World (produced 1990). Published in *Theatre,* summer/fall 1990.
The America Play (produced 1991).
Devotees in the Garden of Love (produced 1991).
Venus: A Play. 1998.

Screenplay: *Anemone Me,* 1990.

Radio Plays: *Pickling,* 1990; *The Third Kingdom,* 1990; *Locomotive,* 1991.

Video: *Poetry Spots,* 1989; *Alive from Off Center,* 1991.

Recording: *Imperceptible Mutabilities, The Last Black Man,* 1991.

*

Critical Studies: "Signifying on the Signifyin': The Plays of Suzan-Lori Parks" by Alisa Solomon, in *Theater,* Summer/Fall 1990, pp. 73-80; "Suzan-Lori Parks and Liz Diamond: Doo-a-Diddly-Dit-Dit" by Steven Drukman, in *The Drama Review: A Journal of Performance Studies,* Fall 1995, pp. 56-75; "Interview with Suzan-Lori Parks" by Shelby Jiggetts, in *Callaloo,* Spring 1996, pp. 309-17; "Body Parts: Between Story and Spectacle in *Venus* by Suzan-Lori Parks" by Elaine Brousseau, in *Staging Resistence: Essays on Political Theater* edited by Jeanne M. Colleran and Jenny Spencer, 1998.

*   *   *

When Shark-Seer, a choral voice from Suzan-Lori Parks's *Imperceptible Mutabilities in the Third Kingdom* (1986), incants, "My new Self was uh third Self made by the space in between," he speaks into being a new American theater centered in the crucial implications of Parks's first major production. From its initial premier at the BACA Downtown Theater in 1989, Parks's revolutionary dramaturgy and radical reorientation of the cultural function of theater as resistance has significantly envisioned a new direction in African American drama (though Parks herself is reluctant to racially categorize her work). More importantly her focus upon what Stuart Hall has termed the "politics of representation" has enacted a crucial link with other radical world theaters that since the 80s have been revisioning the space of theater as the nexus point for interrogating cultural systems of power and "re-membering" rituals of collective and individual experience. Developing the social realism of **James Baldwin** and the avant-garde theater of Adrienne Kennedy's *Funnyhouse of a Negro* (1964) and infusing the discursive reinventions of **Gertrude Stein** with the spectacular experimentation of Richard Foreman, Parks creates a drama that involutes the very act of theater itself, transforming the spectacle into the main actor on the stage and demanding that her audience question its own role in the ideological implications of cultural production—indeed, that they reify the "in between."

This liminal space of representation and ethos of an engaged theater permeates the major productions through which Parks has begun to construct a new American drama since that "Big Bang" (one of her subtitles). From the initial interrogations of *Imperceptible Mutabilities* to the "postmodern slave narrative" (so called by scholar Louise Bernard) of *Death of the Last Black Man in the Whole Entire World* (1989), to the archaeology of knowledge in the "Great Hole of History" in *The America Play* (1990-1993), to the culmination of her work, her deconstruction of the Victorian theatricalization of the Hottentot Venus in *Venus* (1994), Parks explores and explodes the act of signification, making her work a "signifying on the signifyin'" or what many critics term a metacritical theater. To do so, she literally and figuratively plays with language and with traditional languages of the theater and other sites of cultural imaging. Her "dreamscape," as scholar Alisa Solomon terms Parks's stage, is replete with a cacophony of voices and discourses, from the omnipresent "Voice on thuh Tee V" in *Death of the Last Black Man,* to the repetitive riff on Lincoln's assassination in *The America Play,* to a variety of stereotypical racial "dialects," to the voice of the objectified Venus declaring her own complicity in the imperialist program of the sideshow. Anything but merely absurdist, such heterophony indicates Parks's attempts to implicate the discursive spaces that constitute our identities in light of racialist, classist, colonialist, and patriarchal oppression. Hence her characters dialogue in what Parks terms "Repetition and Revision," a radical juxtaposition of vernacular voices echoing the musicality of Blues/Jazz variations with the official narratives of history and hegemony, making her work "dialogic poetry" (Louise Bernard) or as Parks has conjured it, "spells in our mouths." In similarly revolutionary technique Parks redirects the physicality of performance, punctuating her characters' lines with gutteral sounds, sighs, and teeth-suckings or merely with their silent presence on stage (Parks's style of scripting characters without dialogue). In the central moments of each play these perpetual dissonances and harmonies flow together into what has become Parks's *modus teatri:* the incantatory soliloquy that acts not as revelatory moment but instead—to continue the musical metaphor—as radicalizing bottom line. Such confluence resembles ritual insistence upon the importance of re-presenting as much as the content of her work insists upon the need, as 'Yes And Greens Blackeyed Peas Cornbread" mandates in *Death and the Last Black Man,* to signify the unofficial experiences of those erased and dispossessed:

> You should write it down because if you dont write it down then they will come along and tell the future that we did not exist . . . It will be of us but you should mention them from time to time so that in the future when they come along and know that they exist. You should hide it all under a rock so that in the future when they come along they will say that the rock did not exist. (Parks, *America Play*)

This tension between sign and signified, between mastery and erasure, between role and ideology becomes manifested in each of Parks's productions as the "in between" space of history and spectacle itself. Whereas *Imperceptible Mutabilities* treats this gap in terms of the Middle Passage, the plays that follow it transform the historical event with an increasing awareness of the role of theater in the act of cultural reinvention. Thus her most significant plays, *The America Play* and *Venus,* become explorations of the "lack" of essential identity at the same time that they expose the ways in which such invisibility is potentially liberating. Just as Venus will turn her gaze back upon the spectators in defiant pose, so too do most of Parks's characters end her productions in subversive reclamation of what Louise Bernard has termed "the displaced voices of history, thus filling in the hole." In this way Parks avoids the typical representations of the Other and elides the assumed binaries of discourses of Othering, creating in its place a metaphysics of hybrid, creolized identity, a new ritual of a third Self. It is in this connection to "others" that Parks's theater must be contextualized, for it represents finally a lateral identification between American theater and the 1980s movement worldwide toward a drama conjoining the past with the present and re-possessing the stage, the screen, the set.

In the 1990s, Parks's screenplay for Spike Lee's *Girl 6* engendered a crucial translation of her central tropes from stage to screen: the reality of the (black female) body and the theatricality of its images. Though *Girl 6* was not as well received as her other productions, the development of Parks's dramatic style into cinematic modes seemed not only logical but also a critical step in what Louise Bernard might term "a prophetic journey that acts as a libation to the ancestors and a call to present/future generations to carve out their histories, restore knowledge, and take their rightful place in the eternal struggle for representation."

—Rob Canfield

PATCHEN, Kenneth

Born: Niles, Ohio, 13 December 1911. **Education:** East Junior High School, 1924-26, and Warren G. Harding High School, 1926-29, both Warren, Ohio; Experimental College, University of Wisconsin, Madison, 1929-30; Commonwealth College, Mena, Arkansas, 1930. **Family:** Married Miriam Oikemus in 1934. **Career:** Farm worker, gardener, and janitor, throughout the United States and Canada, 1930-33; freelance writer from 1934; staff member, New Directions, publishers, Norfolk, Connecticut, 1939-40; moved to San Francisco, 1951, and to Palo Alto, California, 1956. Artist: individual show of books, graphics, and paintings, Corcoran Gallery, Washington, D.C., 1969. **Awards:** Guggenheim fellowship, 1936; Shelley Memorial award, 1954; National Endowment for the Arts grant, 1967. **Died:** 8 January 1972.

PUBLICATIONS

Poetry

Before the Brave. 1936.
First Will and Testament. 1939.
The Teeth of the Lion. 1942.
The Dark Kingdom. 1942.
Cloth of the Tempest. 1943.
An Astonished Eye Looks out of the Air, Being Some Poems Old and New against War and in Behalf of Life. 1945.
Outlaw of the Lowest Planet, edited by David Gascoyne. 1946.
Selected Poems. 1946; revised edition, 1958, 1964.
Pictures of Life and Death. 1947.
They Keep Riding down All the Time. 1947.
Panels for the Walls of Heaven. 1947.
A Letter to God, with *Patchen: Man of Anger and Light,* by Henry Miller. 1947.
CCCLXXIV Poems. 1948.
To Say If You Love Someone and Other Selected Love Poems. 1948.
Red Wine and Yellow Hair. 1949.
Fables and Other Little Tales. 1953.
The Famous Boating Party and Other Poems in Prose. 1954.
Poems of Humor and Protest. 1954.
Orchards, Thrones and Caravans. 1955.
Glory Never Guesses. 1956.
A Surprise for the Bagpipe Player. 1956.
When We Were Here Together. 1957.
Hurrah for Anything: Poems and Drawings. 1957.
Two Poems for Christmas. 1958.
Poem-scapes. 1958.
Pomes Penyeach. 1959.
Poems of Humor and Protest. 1960.
Because It Is: Poems and Drawings. 1960.
A Poem for Christmas. 1960.
The Love Poems. 1960.
Patchen Drawing-Poem. 1962.
Picture Poems. 1962.
Doubleheader. 1966.
Hallelujah Anyway. 1966.
Where Are the Other Rowboats?. 1966.
But Even So (includes drawings). 1968.
Love and War Poems, edited by Dennis Gould. 1968.
Selected Poems. 1968.
The Collected Poems. 1968.
Aflame and Afun of Walking Faces: Fables and Drawings. 1970.
There's Love All Day, edited by Dee Danner Barwick. 1970.
Wonderings. 1971.
In Quest of Candlelighters. 1972.
Still Another Pelican in the Breadbox, edited by Richard G. Morgan. 1980.

Plays

The City Wears a Slouch Hat (broadcast 1942). In *Lost Plays,* 1977.
Don't Look Now (produced 1959; as *Now You See It,* produced 1966). In *Lost Plays,* 1977.
Lost Plays, edited by Richard G. Morgan. 1977.

Radio Play: *The City Wears a Slouch Hat,* 1942.

Fiction

The Journal of Albion Moonlight. 1941.
The Memoirs of a Shy Pornographer: An Amusement. 1945.
Sleepers Awake. 1946.
See You in the Morning. 1948.

Other

Patchen: Painter of Poems (exhibition catalogue). 1969.
The Argument of Innocence: A Selection from the Arts of Patchen, edited by Peter Veres. 1976.
Patchen: The Last Interview, edited by Gene Detro. 1976.
What Shall We Do without Us? The Voice and Vision of Patchen. 1984.

*

Bibliography: *Patchen: An Annotated, Descriptive Bibliography* by Richard G. Morgan, 1978.

Critical Studies: *Patchen: A Collection of Critical Essays* edited by Richard G. Morgan, 1977; *Tribute to Patchen,* 1977; *Patchen* by Larry Smith, 1978; *Patchen and American Mysticism* by Raymond Nelson, 1984; *Patchen* by Carroll F. Terrell, 1986; "A Poet in the Depression: Letters of Patchen, 1934-1941" by Amos N. Wilder, in *Sagetrieb: A Journal Devoted to Poets in the Pound H.D. Williams Tradition,* 1986; "Patchen: Letter about Ezra Pound, 1946" by Larry Smith, in *The Epistolary Form and the Letter As Artifact* edited by Jim Villani, 1991; *The Problem of Words: Kenneth Patchen's Poetry, 1936-1954: Towards a Poetry Beyond Oppositions* (dissertation) by Jesse B. Powell, 1996.

*　　　*　　　*

Kenneth Patchen is in the tradition of American poets that descends from **Walt Whitman** through **William Carlos Williams** to the Black Mountain poets, and beyond them to such younger writers as **Galway Kinnell.** That is to say, Patchen is a "redskin" poet as opposed to a "paleface." His poems do not make use of European-inspired formal devices; his language is deliberately a "barbaric yawp" (Whitman's famous phrase from *Song of Myself;* and his subject matter is drawn from his own very American experiences. He is a poet of the open air and the open road, a hunter after experience, claiming a kind of mystical connection with the animals he kills (in this he is very like **Ernest Hemingway, James Dickey,** and, perhaps, **Robinson Jeffers**); his style is free-ranging, colloquial, wise-cracking, but also unembarrassedly ready with the big word, the huge emotion. In short, he sounds very like **Carl Sandburg.**

Yet Patchen is a self-conscious poet. He may play the cracker-barrel philosopher, but as Thomas Hardy said of William Barnes, "He sings his native woodnotes wild with a great deal of art." Look, for example, at so small a poem as "In Memory of Kathleen":

How pitiful is her sleep.
Now her clear breath is still.

There is nothing falling tonight,
Bird or man,
As dear as she.

Nowhere that she should go
Without me. None but my calling.

O nothing but the cold cry of the snow.

It is a very finely written poem of grief, and a subtle one. The play on "pitiful" is perhaps obvious; but the way in which "falling" anticipates the cry of the snow is not so obvious, yet entirely just; as is the extraordinary compacted "None but my calling." "None" comes from the earlier "nowhere," and it means that Patchen finds himself utterly alone: she has gone where he can't follow, there is only his calling, his voice to be heard. That, and the cry of the snow: whiteness, death, its falling reminding him that she, too, has fallen in death. Glanced over casually, this little poem may seem hopelessly slight; looked at more carefully, it emerges as the work of a considerable poet.

Patchen doesn't always write with this degree of tense urgency. It is characteristic of his kind of poetry that there should be a great deal of sprawl about it; and while one may salute the energy that led him to produce so many volumes of verse—he must be one of the most unflaggingly fertile of twentieth-century American poets—it is also possible to wish that some of his work had been more intensively worked over. There is, for instance, a wonderful idea, partly spoiled, in *First Will and Testament* that has at its core a play for voices, featuring a Mr. Kek and his brothel, to which come, in turn, a group of famous poets, Donne, Marvell, Jonson, etc.; and then jazzmen Beiderbecke, Armstrong, Allen; gangsters, sportsmen—all outsiders, all seeking warmth and love and a good time, and trying to escape "the enemy." Much of this is obviously borrowed from Auden, but it has some fizzing wit and a great deal of hard-hitting panache that are Patchen's own. The trouble is that it degenerates into **E.E. Cummings**-like sentimentality; all picaros are better than all lawmen; to be an artist you have to be on the outside, a society reject, a bum. In other words the play is written out of cliche, so that although it has local life it is finally soggy.

This criticism applies to a good deal of Patchen's work. Yet nothing said here is intended to detract from the vitality of his best writing, which can crop up anywhere, and is just as likely to show itself in a late volume, like *When We Were Here Together*, as in an early one, such as *Before the Brave*.

—John Lucas

PAULDING, James Kirke

Born: Great Nine Partners, now Putnam County, New York, 22 August 1778; grew up in Tarrytown, New York. **Education:** A local school. **Military Service:** Served in the New York militia, 1814: major. **Family:** Married Gertrude Kemble in 1818 (died 1841); several children. **Career:** Settled in New York City c. 1796; worked in a public office and continued his studies on his own; writer from c. 1805; contributor, *Analectic Magazine*, 1812; secretary, Board of Navy Commissioners, Washington, D.C., 1815-23; navy agent, Port of New York, 1823-38; secretary of the Navy, in the administration of Martin Van Buren, 1838-41; lived on a country estate near Hyde Park, New York, after 1846. **Died:** 6 April 1860.

PUBLICATIONS

Collections

Collected Works, edited by William I. Paulding. 4 vols., 1867-68.
The Letters, edited by Ralph M. Aderman. 1962.

Fiction

Salmagundi; or, The Whim-Whams and Opinions of Launcelot Langstaff, Esq., and Others, with Washington and William Irving. 2 vols., 1807-08; in *History, Tales and Sketches* (Library of America) by Washington Irving, edited by James W. Tuttleton, 1983; Second Series (by Paulding only), 2 vols., 1819-20.
The Diverting History of John Bull and Brother Jonathan. 1812; revised edition, 1813.
Koningsmarke: The Long Finne: A Story of the New World. 1823.
John Bull in America; or, The New Munchausen. 1825.
The Merry Tales of the Three Wise Men of Gotham. 1826.
Tales of the Good Woman. 1829.
Chronicles of the City of Gotham, from the Papers of a Retired Common Councilman. 1830.
The Dutchman's Fireside. 1831.
Westward Ho! 1832; as *The Banks of the Ohio,* 1833.
The Book of Saint Nicholas. 1836.
A Christmas Gift from Fairy Land. 1838; as *A Gift from Fairy Land,* n.d.
The Old Continental; or, The Price of Liberty. 1846.
The Puritan and His Daughter. 1849.
A Book of Vagaries (selections), edited by William I. Paulding. 1868.

Plays

The Lion of the West, revised by John Augustus Stone and William Bayle Bernard (produced 1831; as *The Kentuckian; or, A Trip to New York,* produced 1833). Edited by James N. Tidwell, 1954.
The Bucktails; or, Americans in England. In *American Comedies* by William I. Paulding, 1847.

Poetry

The Lay of the Scottish Fiddle: A Tale of Havre de Grace, Supposed to Be Written by Walter Scott, Esq. 1813.
The Backwoodsman. 1818.

Other

The United States and England. 1815.
Letters from the South. 2 vols., 1817.
A Sketch of Old England by a New England Man. 2 vols., 1822.
The New Mirror for Travellers, and Guide to the Springs. 1828.
Sketch of the Early Life of Joseph Wood, Artist. 1834.
Works. 15 vols., 1834-39.
A Life of Washington. 2 vols., 1835(?).
Slavery in the United States. 1836.

*

Bibliography: in *Bibliography of American Literature* by Jacob Blanck, edited by Virginia L. Smyers and Michael Winship, 1983;

"James Kirke Paulding: A Bibliographic Survey" by Michael John McDonough, in *Resources for American Literary Study*, autumn 1985.

Critical Studies: *Literary Life of Paulding* by William I. Paulding, 1867; *Paulding: Versatile American* by Amos L. Herold, 1926; "An Uncollected Letter of James Kirke Paulding" by David K. Jackson, in *Poe Studies*, December 1982; "Paulding's The Dutchman's Fireside and the Early American Romance" by Robert P. Winston, in *Studies in American Fiction*, spring 1983; *James Kirke Paulding* by Larry J. Reynolds, 1984; "Introduction to James Kirke Paulding, *The Dutchman's Fireside*" by Thomas F. O'Donnell, in *Upstate Literature: Essays in Memory of Thomas F. O'Donnell* edited by Frank Bergmann and Edwin H. Cady, 1985; "James Kirke Paulding and the Picturesque Tour: 'Banqueting on the Picturesque' in the 1820s and '30s" by Beth L. Lueck, in *University of Mississippi Studies in English*, 1991.

*   *   *

Through the 1830s James Kirke Paulding's popularity with American readers rivaled that of his somewhat younger contemporaries Washington Irving and **James Fenimore Cooper**. His name was also well known not only in Britain, but on the continent, where two of his novels—*The Dutchman's Fireside* and *Westward Ho!*—appeared in numerous translations. Although his audience dwindled sharply after 1845, he is still remembered as perhaps the most versatile, if not the most graceful, American author of the generation that matured between the two wars with Britain. During his long career Paulding won fame as a poet, novelist, essayist, biographer, playwright, and critic. He also wrote scores of short stories and sketches for both American and British periodicals. Most of his writing was done while he followed another career as public servant that culminated with his appointment in 1838 as Secretary of the Navy by President Martin Van Buren, a long-time friend whose ancestral roots lay, like Paulding's, in the Dutch-American Hudson River valley.

Paulding was always more concerned with ideas than with art. Unlike his friend Irving (to whom he was related by marriage and with whom he collaborated on *Salmagundi*), he never made peace with either England or the romantic movement, which he scorned as a British conspiracy designed to sap the fiber of sturdy new-world republicanism. In a series of satires, commencing with *The Diverting History of John Bull and Brother Jonathan* and concluding with *John Bull in America*, he vigorously defended his young country against printed attacks by British travelers and reviewers. During the same period he wrote *The Lay of the Scottish Fiddle*, a book-length parody of *The Lay of the Last Minstrel*, burlesquing not only Scott's verse but his copious notes, and *The Backwoodsman*, another lengthy, often clumsy poem in heroic couplets designed, according to Paulding, to inform young American writers of the "rich poetic resources" available to them on their native ground. His call for American literary independence continued in his best-remembered essay, "National Literature," which appeared in *Salmagundi, Second Series*.

Prompted by the success of Cooper's *The Spy* and *The Pioneers*, Paulding turned to the novel in 1823, with *Koningsmarke*. Here he continued his satirical attack on Scott and what he considered to be the excesses of romanticism. In this first novel, Paulding hoped to demonstrate that Fielding, rather than Scott, was the proper model for American novelists. When *Koningsmarke*

was misread and praised for the wrong reasons, Paulding abandoned satire and modified his attitude toward romanticism. *The Dutchman's Fireside,* set in the 1750s and in an area (upstate New York) that Cooper had already celebrated, was widely praised—not only by Cooper himself but by British readers, including an anonymous critic for the *Westminister Review* who praised Paulding for being "neither too elaborate like Irving, nor too diffuse like Cooper." Paulding's third novel, *Westward Ho!,* captured the sense of adventure that urged many of his contemporaries to move from a settled east to an unsettled and still dangerous west. A fourth novel, *The Old Continental,* is based on the Benedict Arnold episode of the American Revolution. This and *The Puritan and His Daughter* were poorly planned and awkwardly written; they deserve the neglect they received even in Paulding's time.

Although Paulding had great ambitions as a playwright, he wrote only two plays of note, both comedies that dramatized social tensions between England and America. The second of them, *The Lion of the West,* won him a national prize, and was successfully produced in America and in London. It is most memorable for the character of Nimrod Wildfire, who closely resembles the American frontier hero, Davy Crockett.

Paulding's greatest success as a biographer came with his *A Life of Washington,* a work that appeared in numerous editions until it was superseded by Washington Irving's.

—Thomas F. O'Donnell

PAYNE, John Howard

Born: New York City, 9 June 1791. **Education:** Berry Street Academy, Boston, to 1805; Union College, Schenectady, New York, 1806-08. **Career:** Clerk in the counting house of Grant and Bennet Forbes, New York, 1805-06; editor, *Thespian Mirror*, New York, 1805-06, and *Pastime,* Schenectady, 1807-08; began writing for the stage, 1806; made debut as an actor in New York in 1809 and enjoyed an immediate success throughout the United States; moved to England, 1813; acted in the provinces, 1814; thereafter earned his living in London by dramatic hackwork; secretary at Covent Garden, 1818-19; leased Sadler's Wells Theatre to produce his own plays, 1820, but went bankrupt: imprisoned for debt, Fleet Prison, 1820-21; moved to Paris to escape his creditors, 1821; lived in London, 1823-25 and 1826-32; editor and publisher of the weekly theatrical paper *Opera Glass,* 1826-27; returned to the United States, 1832; U.S. Consul, Tunis, 1842-45 and 1851-52. **Died:** 9 April 1852.

PUBLICATIONS

Collections

Life and Writings, edited by Gabriel Harrison. 1875; revised edition, as *Payne, His Life and Writings,* 1885.
Trial without Jury and Other Plays (includes *Mount Savage, The Boarding School, The Two Sons-in-Law, Mazeppa, The Spanish Husband*), edited by Codman Hislop and W. R. Richardson. 1940.
The Last Duel in Spain and Other Plays (includes *Woman's Revenge, The Italian Bride, Romulus the Shepherd King, The Black Man*), edited by Codman Hislop and W. R. Richardson. 1940.

Plays

Julia; or, The Wanderer (as *The Wanderer*, produced 1806). 1806.

Lovers' Vows, from versions by Mrs. Inchbald and Benjamin Thompson of a play by Kotzebue (produced 1809?). 1809.

The Magpie or the Maid?, from a play by L.C. Caigniez and J. Baudouin d'Aubigny (produced 1815). 1815; as *Trial without Jury; or, The Magpie and the Maid,* in *Trial without Jury and Other Plays,* 1940.

Accusation; or, The Family D'Anglade, from a play by Frederic du Petit-Mere (produced 1816). 1817.

Brutus; or, The Fall of Tarquin, music by Hayward (produced 1818). 1818.

Therese, The Orphan of Geneva, from a play by Victor Ducange (produced 1821). 1821.

Adeline, The Victim of Seduction, from a play by Pixerecourt (produced 1822). 1822.

Love in Humble Life, from a play by Scribe and Dupin (produced 1822). 1825.

Ali Pacha; or, The Signet-Ring, adapted by J.R. Planche (produced 1822). 1823.

Peter Smink; or, The Armistice (produced 1822; revised version, produced 1826). N.d.

The Two Galley Slaves, music by Tom Cooke and C.E. Horn (produced 1822). 1825.

Mount Savage, from a play by Pixerecourt (as *The Solitary of Mount Savage; or, The Fate of Charles the Bold,* produced 1822). In *Trial without Jury and Other Plays,* 1940.

Clari; or, The Maid of Milan, music by Henry Bishop (produced 1823). 1823.

Mrs. Smith; or, The Wife and the Widow (produced 1823). N.d.

Charles the Second; or, The Merry Monarch, with Washington Irving, from a play by Alexandre Duval (produced 1824). 1824; edited by Arthur Hobson Quinn, in *Representative American Plays.* 1917.

'Twas I; or, The Truth a Lie, from a French play (produced 1825). 1827.

The Fall of Algiers, music by Henry Bishop (produced 1825). 1825.

Richelieu: A Domestic Tragedy, with Washington Irving, from a play by Alexandre Duval (produced 1826; as *The French Libertine,* produced 1826). 1826.

The White Maid, from a play by Scribe, music by Adrien Boieldieu (produced 1827; also produced as *The White Lady*).

The Lancers (produced 1827). 1828(?).

Procrastination (produced 1829).

The Spanish Husband; or, First and Last Love, from a play by La Beaumelle (produced 1830). In *Trial without Jury and Other Plays,* 1940.

Fricandeau; or, The Coronet and the Cook (produced 1831).

Oswali at Athens (produced 1831).

Woman's Revenge (produced 1832). In *The Last Duel in Spain and Other Plays,* 1940.

Virginia (produced 1834).

Poetry

Juvenile Poems. 1813; revised edition, as *Lispings of the Muse,* 1815.

Other

Indian Justice: A Cherokee Murder Trial, edited by Grant Foreman. 1934.

Payne to His Countrymen, edited by Clemens de Baillou. 1961.

Editor, *Addresses Delivered before the Boston Federal Band.* 1805.

*

Bibliography: in *Bibliography of American Literature* by Jacob Blanck, edited by Virginia L. Smyers and Michael Winship, 1983.

Critical Studies: *The Early Life of Payne* by Willis T. Hanson, Jr., 1913; *Payne* by Rosa Pendleton Chiles, 1930; *America's First Hamlet* by Grace Overmyer, 1957; "A Romantic 'Impenitent' as Translator of French Romantic Poetry: Aspects of John Payne's Translations of Hugo, Baudelaire and Leconte de Lisle" by Jennifer Draskau, in *The Romantic Heritage: A Collection of Critical Essays* edited by Karsten Engelberg, 1983.

*   *   *

During the first half of the nineteenth century, theater audiences in both England and America enjoyed the strong, romantic rhetoric of poetic drama. In America the earliest dramatist to achieve success in this genre, and the most prolific, was John Howard Payne. A youthful prodigy, he attracted attention as an actor, a critic, and an editor of the *Thespian Mirror,* and as a playwright whose first work, *Julia; or, The Wanderer,* was performed at New York's Park Theatre in 1806. When his career as an actor did not reach the success he anticipated, however, he embarked in 1813 for what he felt would be the greener theatrical fields of England. In this he was seriously mistaken, for his acting engagements were few and soon relegated to the provinces. But chance and necessity offered him a new career.

In 1809, before going to England, Payne had published *Lovers' Vows,* a version of August von Kotzebue's *Das Kind der Liebe* that he had adapted from two English translations. Six years later while in Paris he translated the current French hit, *La Pie Voleuse,* as *The Magpie or the Maid?* for the Drury Lane management. This was the beginning of a career—adapting and translating comedy, melodrama, and romantic tragedy—in which his particular forte was his ability to recognize dramatic material and create a successful play from various sources. Like other prolific dramatists of his time, his talent was not in writing original plays, but he soon became the first American dramatist to enjoy a substantial reputation abroad.

Among his best works is *Brutus; or, The Fall of Tarquin.* Using five major sources he created a major acting vehicle for Edmund Kean; the subsequent cry of plagiarism was particularly ironic at a time when play pirating was a common sport. Another popular adaptation was *Clari; or, The Maid of Milan,* which contains the song for which most Americans will, if at all, remember Payne— "Home, Sweet Home." They would, however, readily recognize the name of his collaborator in his most successful comedy, *Charles the Second; or, The Merry Monarch*—**Washington Irving**. Before Irving tired of the drama they worked on six plays together.

Returning to America in 1832 Payne epitomized the plight of the dramatist during America's formative years. With considerable skill and abundant energy, he had created many successful plays and made money for everyone—actors, managers—but himself. Recognized by theater-goers and critics as a major contributor to American drama, he was never financially secure and became increasingly bitter over the treatment of American dramatists during the final years of his life, which were separated from the theater. His position in the history of American drama, however, is unquestionably secure.

—Walter J. Meserve

PERCY, Walker

Born: Birmingham, Alabama, 28 May 1916. **Education:** University of North Carolina, Chapel Hill, B.A. 1937; Columbia University, New York, M.D. 1941; intern at Bellevue Hospital, New York, 1942. **Family:** Married Mary Bernice Townsend in 1946; two daughters. **Career:** Contracted tuberculosis, gave up medicine and became a full-time writer, 1943. **Awards:** National Book award, 1962; American Academy grant, 1967; National Catholic Book Award, 1972; St. Louis Literary award, 1985. Fellow, American Academy of Arts and Sciences. **Member:** American Academy. **Died:** 10 May 1990.

PUBLICATIONS

Fiction

The Moviegoer. 1961.
The Last Gentleman. 1966.
Love in the Ruins: The Adventures of a Bad Catholic at a Time Near the End of the World. 1971.
Lancelot. 1977.
The Second Coming. 1980.
The Thanatos Syndrome. 1987.

Other

The Message in the Bottle: How Queer Man Is, How Queer Language Is, and What One Has to Do with the Other. 1975.
Lost in the Cosmos: The Last Self-Help Book. 1983.
Novel-Writing in an Apocalyptic Time. 1984.
Conversations with Percy (interviews), edited by Lewis A. Lawson and Victor A. Kramer. 1985.
State of the Novel: Dying Art or New Science. 1988.
Signposts in a Strange Land (interviews), edited by Patrick Samway. 1991.
More Conversations with Walker Percy (interviews), edited by Lewis A. Lawson and Victor A. Kramer. 1993.
A Thief of Peirce: The Letters of Kenneth Laine Ketner and Walker Percy. 1995.
The Correspondence of Shelby Foote and Walker Percy. 1997.

*

Bibliography: *Andrew Lytle, Walker Percy, Peter Taylor: A Reference Guide* by Victor A. Kramer, 1983; *Walker Percy: A Bibliography 1930-1984* by Stuart Wright, 1986; *Walker Percy: A Comprehensive Descriptive Bibliography* by Linda Whitney Hobson and Walker Percy, 1988.

Critical Studies: *The Sovereign Wayfarer: Percy's Diagnosis of the Malaise* by Martin Luschei, 1972; *Percy: An American Search* by Robert Coles, 1978; *The Art of Percy: Stratagems for Being* edited by Panthea Reid Broughton, 1979; *Percy: Art and Ethics* edited by Jac Tharpe, 1980, and *Percy* by Tharpe, 1983; *Percy's Heroes: A Kierkegaardian Self* by L. Jerome Taylor, 1984; *Percy and the Old Modern Age: Reflections on Language, Argument, and the Telling of Stories* by Patricia Lewis Poteat, 1985; *Percy: A Southern Wayfarer* by William Rodney Allen, 1986; *Modern Critical Views: Walker Percy* edited by Harold Bloom, 1986; *The Fiction of Walker Percy* by John Edward Hardy, 1987; *Understanding Walker Percy* by Linda Whitney Hobson, 1988; *Following Percy: Essays on Walker Percy's Work* edited by Lewis A. Lawson, 1988; *Critical Essays on Walker Percy* edited by Donald J. Crowley and Sue Mitchell Crowley, 1989; *Walker Percy: Novelist and Philosopher* edited by Jan Nordby Gretlund and Karl Heinz Westarp, 1991; *Walker Percy: Books of Revelation* by Gary M. Ciuba, 1991; *The House of Percy: Honor, Melancholy, and Imagination in a Southern Family* by Bertram Wyatt-Brown, 1994; *Departures: Journeys from the Margin(al) in the Fiction of Walker Percy, Eudora Welty, and Toni Morrison* by Kavin Charles Gibley, 1995; *Walker Percy: Prophetic, Existentialist, Catholic Storyteller* by Robert E. Lauder, 1996; *Walker Percy: The Last Catholic Novelist* by Kieran Quinlan, 1996; *Walker Percy: A Life* by Patrick H. Samway, 1997; *At the Crossroads: Ethical and Religious Themes in the Writings of Walker Percy* by John F. Desmond, 1997.

*   *   *

Walker Percy belongs to the movement in modern Southern writing that derives from **T. S. Eliot** and includes, among others, **Allen Tate, Caroline Gordon, Robert Penn Warren,** and **William Faulkner.** Percy was a traditionalist in reaction against what is perceived as the decay of moral standards, the loss of a sense of community and of shared values. His ideas are given rather full intellectual scope in his work of non-fiction, *The Message in the Bottle.* In his novels the issue is focused on sexuality, and the problem, as expressed in his fiction, is how to square sexual desire with traditional ideas of love and responsibility, complicated by the modern confusion of love and sex. What used to be regarded as sin and perversion is now acceptable to, even sanctioned by, church and state. The traditional concept of love is too idealistic to provide Percy's protagonists with a satisfactory pattern of behavior. Inevitably his novels involve the setting up of the problem and the working out of a solution, the protagonist wrestling with his moral confusion, then, finally, creating for himself a synthesis in which love and lust—giving and taking—are appropriately balanced.

His first novel, *The Moviegoer,* concludes with the protagonist, a lusty bachelor, failing in his latest sexual escapade and marrying a young woman of his own class, partly out of affection, but also because they share a sense of experienced responsibility. In *The Last Gentleman,* the hero, who suffers emotional detachment (which Percy sees as the chief modern malady) cures himself through his personal devotion to a dying youth and in turn helps cure a confused young woman and her cynical older brother. *Love in the Ruins,* set in the future "at a time near the end of the world," deals with the collapse of modern technology and concludes with the responsible marriage of the protagonist who tries to save his doomed world but, failing that, gives himself over to whiskey and lust for three beautiful women. At the novel's close he marries the most responsible and moral of the three and begins to live a simple, natural, and properly lustful life in the shadow of the remnants of the old Catholic Church.

In *Lancelot* the pessimism is deeper, the solution more tenuous. The hero, at first tolerant of his wife's sexual infidelity, finally kills her and her lover, is confined to a mental institution, is "cured" and then released into the world. For a time, he takes on responsibility for a young woman who has been raped and maimed by a gang of thugs, but is rebuffed by her in the language of radical feminism. This protagonist, then, stands alone against a world shown to be corrupt beyond redemption. A slight ray of final hope is that the woman may eventually join him in his exile. *The Second Coming* has the familiar problem and resolution: Will Barrett's death-in-life existence is resolved by a lusty love affair with a schizophrenic girl, and Barrett, a non-believer, nevertheless concludes that the girl, a "gift," must be a sign of the Lord, "the giver."

Percy's last novel, *The Thanatos Syndrome,* concerns the government's plan to build a utopia in the state of Louisiana. The public—to the dismay of the ruling class—is uncooperative and becomes increasingly restless and unhappy, refusing to adapt to the goals of the social engineers. To "ease" the growing crisis the authorities introduce a chemical solution into the area's water supply. This solution causes individual loss of identity and free will, while it facilitates docile acceptance of government plans to "improve the quality of life."

Percy's rendering of characters and scenes is striking, vivid, and bitingly satirical. He is a moral and, ultimately, a religious writer, but a perceptive novelist of manners as well. His sensitive and poetic style elevates material that less subtly treated might appear contrived and moralistic.

—W.J. Stuckey, updated by Denise Wiloch

PERELMAN, Bob

Born: Youngstown, Ohio, 2 December 1947. **Education:** University of Michigan, Ann Arbor, M.A. in classics 1969; University of Iowa, Iowa City, M.F.A. in poetry 1970; University of California, Berkeley, Ph.D. in English 1990. **Family:** Married Francie Shaw in 1975. **Career:** Beginning 1990 assistant professor, University of Pennsylvania, Philadelphia. Editor, *Hills* magazine, Berkeley, California, 1973-80.

PUBLICATIONS

Poetry

Braille. 1975.
Seven Works. 1978.
a.k.a. 1979.
Primer. 1981.
To the Reader. 1984.
The First World. 1986.
Face Value. 1988.
Captive Audience. 1988.

Virtual Reality. 1993.
Fake Dreams. 1996.
The Future of Memory. 1998.
Ten to One: Selected Poems. 1999.

Plays

The Alps (produced 1980). 1980.

Other

The Trouble with Genius: Reading Pound, Joyce, Stein, and Zukofsky. 1994.
The Marginalization of Poetry: Language Writing and Literary History. 1996.

Editor, *Writing Talks.* 1985.

*

Critical Studies: *Total Syntax* by Barrett Watten, 1984; *The New Sentence* by Ron Silliman, 1987; *Textured Politics and the Language Poets* by George Hartley, 1989; *A Poetics* by Charles Bernstein, 1992; *Double Reading: Postmodernism after Deconstruction* by Jeffrey T. Nealon, 1993.

*   *   *

The concept of literary genres, or distinct of types of literary discourse, is one that has fallen out of fashion in advanced circles. A variety of factors—ranging from the problematic hierarchy of value attached to certain genres to the mass media's omnivorous processing and regurgitation of almost any generic raw material—have contributed to this discredit. Nonetheless, as Bob Perelman's poetry suggests, the ghosts of these old generic categories continue to haunt both everyday experience and the activity of reading. Accordingly, the terminology and concept of genre figure broadly in his work, as a quick survey of titles from over twenty years of writing demonstrates. *Primer,* for example, was the title of his 1981 collection, while the individual poems carry such titles as "Essay on Style," "How to Improve," "An Autobiography," "Vienna: A Correspondence," "Philosophical Investigations," "How It's Done," "The History of Art," "A History Lesson," "A Prophecy," "Statement," "Novel," "Play," "Movie," "Cliff Notes," "Autobiography By Aphorism," "A Literal Translation of Virgil's Fourth Eclogue," "Fake Dreams," and "The Mask of Rhyme." Perelman, in short, makes reference to a myriad of genres, some quite conventional and central (*e.g.,* the novel, the autobiography, the how-to book), others arcane or outmoded (fake dreams, prophecies), still others largely academic (philosophical investigations, literal translations) or pedagogical (primers, study guides).

As frameworks for Perelman's poetry, of course, none of these genres retains its traditional shape. They are for Perelman the object of parody and pastiche, or else their realization in the poetry stands in ironic tension with the conventional functions and values attached to them in their normal use. In general, genres develop as ways of framing social and personal experience in works of art and literature. They allow the artist or writer to draw on a stock language to help bring about a predictable reaction from an audience, such as indignation from a scene of injustice or sympathy from a touching scene; they also constitute stereotyped backgrounds that may be manipulated by the artist to present less openly statable sentiments and views under the cover of the conventional. Perelman's use of genre draws on both functions. Some of his parodies or inappropriate references to genres seek to reveal how experience can be prepackaged, controlled, or petrified through stereotyped thinking, especially as promulgated by the mass media for political and commercial ends. Perelman often suggests how generic forms mask actual suffering or betray, through idealization, the difficulty and complexity of real life:

> Cuts heal, though children
> read their skin
> as a too-vivid fairy tale where, beneath the happy ending, the
> monster lives
> bright red, ready to surface at the slightest conflict
> to force a conclusion.

In other cases, however, he embraces the more off-beat or outmoded genre as a way of framing poetic statements in unfamiliar ways, rendering them striking or strange. In fact, in one of his programmatic works, the verse essay (an eighteenth-century genre) entitled "The Marginalization of Poetry," he suggests that the employment of a number of generic frames might be valuable in itself, if only because it increases the possible contexts in which a work might find an echo. "Strikingly original language," he writes, "/ is not the point; the degree / to which a phrase or sentence / fits into a multiplicity of contexts / determines how influential it will be." Similarly, in a series of aphorisms (or pseudo-aphorisms) entitled "Chapters of Verse," he offers the image of the writing poet's mind as "a mass of social individuals all using words at different times." An excellent example of Perelman's deft occupation of genres is the poem "Measure" from *Primer*. This poem takes off from the science-fiction premise of the "amazing shrinking man" movie of the 1950s, in which an average Joe one day realizes that a chance combination of chemical substances has caused him to shrink irreversibly. In Perelman's amusing reworking of this basic plot around a writer protagonist, language takes on a central role in the drama, both as a physical backdrop for his shrinking author-hero and as the prime agent in his disturbing fate. Thus, "wielding the club-sized pencil," his diminutive character "leaps across / Cracks between words": the cracks are both the relatively expanding white spaces that are physical engulfing the hero's body and the acrobatic moves he is forced to execute across Perelman's elliptical narrative. As the poem develops, it becomes clear that the poem and its sentences have become involved in the misfortune of its protagonist. Thus, when the shrinking man's wife leaves open a door and "in / Comes the killer cat," Perelman goes on to suggest that he alone controls, from outside, the strings of language that dictate the puppetlike character's actions: "The sentence will force / The author down to study syntax / In the basement." Nor is the cat immune to the power of language: "Intuition / Nags her, but logic / Requires that she abandon / The shivering, half-drowned homunculus." Yet in a disquieting twist, this authorial control appears at best illusory, as the poem's narrative maw devours author and character alike. The poet and the shrinking writer merge in the final disappearing act of the last line, suggesting the close kinship of Perelman's mutant poetic language, monstrously crossing lyric poem and B-grade flick, and the mutant body of his fictional character, fading towards nothingness.

"We're left with the disembodied voice," Perelman concludes—leaving his readers to ponder who speaks this line and where, if anywhere, this "disembodied voice" might be found.

—Tyrus Miller

PERELMAN, S(idney) J(oseph)

Born: Brooklyn, New York, 1 February 1904. **Education:** Schools in Providence, Rhode Island; Brown University, Providence, 1921-25, B.A. 1925. **Family:** Married Laura West (sister of Nathanael West) in 1929 (died 1970); one son and one daughter. **Career:** Writer and cartoonist, *Judge* magazine, 1925-29, and *College Humor* magazine, 1929-30; contributor to *New Yorker* from 1934; host of radio quiz show *Author, Author!*, 1939; lived in London, 1970-72. **Awards:** New York Film Critics award, 1956; Academy award for screenplay, 1957; Writers Guild West award, for screenplay, 1957; Special National Book award, 1978. **Member:** American Academy. **Died:** 17 October 1979.

PUBLICATIONS

Prose

Dawn Ginsbergh's Revenge. 1929.
Parlor, Bedlam and Bath, with Q.J. Reynolds. 1930.
Strictly from Hunger. 1937.
Look Who's Talking! 1940.
The Dream Department. 1943.
Crazy Like a Fox. 1944.
Keep It Crisp. 1946.
Acres and Pains. 1947.
The Best of Perelman. 1947.
Westward Ha! or, Around the World in Eighty Cliches. 1948.
Listen to the Mocking Bird. 1949.
The Swiss Family Perelman. 1950.
A Child's Garden of Curses (omnibus). 1951.
The Ill-Tempered Clavichord. 1952.
Hold That Christmas Tiger! 1954.
Perelman's Home Companion: A Collector's Item (the Collector Being S.J. Perelman) of 36 Otherwise Unavailable Pieces by Himself. 1955.
The Road to Miltown; or, Under the Spreading Atrophy. 1957; as *Bite on the Bullet,* 1957.
The Most of Perelman. 1958.
The Rising Gorge. 1961.
Chicken Inspector No. 23. 1966.
Baby, It's Cold Inside. 1970.
Monkey Business. 1973.
Vinegar Puss. 1975.
Eastward Ha! 1977.
The Last Laugh. 1981.

Plays

Sketches in *The Third Little Show* (produced 1931).
Sketches, with Robert MacGunigle, in *Walk a Little Faster* (produced 1932).

All Good Americans, with Laura Perelman (produced 1933).

Sketches in *Two Weeks with Pay* (produced 1940).

The Night before Christmas, with Laura Perelman (produced 1941). 1942.

One Touch of Venus, with Ogden Nash, music by Kurt Weill, from *The Tinted Venus* by F. Anstey (produced 1943). 1944.

Sweet Bye and Bye, with Al Hirschfeld, music by Vernon Duke, lyrics by Ogden Nash (produced 1946).

The Beauty Part (produced 1962). 1963.

Monkey Business (screenplay), with Will B. Johnstone, in *The Four Marx Brothers in Monkey Business and Duck Soup.* 1972.

Screenplays: *Monkey Business,* with Will B. Johnstone, 1931; *Horse Feathers,* with others, 1932; *The Miracle Man,* with others, 1932; *Sitting Pretty,* with Jack McGowan and Lou Breslow, 1933; *Florida Special,* with others, 1936; *Boy Trouble,* with others, 1939; *Ambush,* with Laura Perelman and Robert Ray, 1939; *The Golden Fleecing,* with others, 1940; *Around the World in Eighty Days,* with James Poe and John Farrow, 1956.

Television Scripts: for *Omnibus* series, 1957-59; *The Changing Ways of Love,* 1957; *Elizabeth Taylor's London,* 1963.

Other

Conversations with S.J. Perelman. 1995.

*

Bibliography: *Perelman: An Annotated Bibliography* by Steven H. Gale, 1985.

Critical Studies: *Perelman* by Douglas Fowler, 1983; *Perelman: A Life* by Dorothy Herrmann, 1986; "Che razza di mestiere fa questo tipo?" by Guido Almansi, in *Il recupero del testo: Aspetti della letteratura ebraico-americana* edited by Guido Fink and Gabriella Morisco, 1988; "'Lay Off the Muses—It's a Very Tough Dollar': Perelman Onstage" by James Magruder, in *Theater,* summer-fall 1992; *S.J. Perelman: Critical Essays* edited by Steven H. Gale, 1992.

*   *   *

As screenwriter, playwright, and, primarily, essayist, S.J. Perelman spent fifty years perfecting a unique and surrealistic style of humor marked by an uncontrollable imagination and an enormous, arcane vocabulary. Perhaps best described as a mixture of Groucho Marx (with whom he worked) and James Joyce (whom he called "the comic writer of the century"), Perelman is a roman candle of language, firing off metaphors where the untrained eye might see only an unloaded verb: "Carstairs exchanged a quizzical glance with his manservant, fitted it into an ivory holder and lit it abstractedly." At the extreme, Perelman's sentences leap from pillar to post with a sheerly linguistic logic, sneering at cliche: "On her dainty egg-shaped head was massed a crop of auburn curls; the cucumbers she had grown there the previous summer were forgotten in the pulsing rhythm of the moment." Perelman's distinguishing characteristic is his total imaginative control of the work, and consequently neither his film scripts nor his stage plays have the comic intensity of the meticulously crafted essays.

Perelman's distaste for the mediocrity of the everyday world manifested itself in a complete disdain for broad political and social satire. A large number of his essays take aim at popular movies, magazines, and novels, at newspapers, at advertising—soft prose and soft thinking of all stripes. Increasingly, however, he turned inward, spinning off exotic tales from the merest personal anecdotes. Perelman was pleased to call himself a *feuilletoniste,* a writer of lapidary prose, and a crank who wrote only when sufficiently enraged. He once summed up his interest in humor with these words (*New York Times Magazine,* 26 January 1969): "For me, its chief merit is the use of the unexpected, the glancing allusion, the deflation of pomposity, and the constant repetition of one's helplessness in a majority of situations."

—Walter Bode

PETRY, Anne (Lane)

Born: Old Saybrook, Connecticut, 12 October 1908. **Education:** Old Saybrook High School; Connecticut College of Pharmacy (now the University of Connecticut), 1925-31; Ph.D., 1931; Columbia University, New York, 1943-44. **Family:** Married George D. Petry in 1938; one child. **Career:** Worked as pharmacist in James' Pharmacy, Old Saybrook, 1931-38. Worked as writer and advertising saleswoman, *Amsterdam News,* New York, 1938-41; reporter and editor of woman's page, *People's Voice,* New York, 1941-44; fiction writer, New York, 1944-48. **Awards:** Houghton Mifflin Literary fellowship, 1945. Honorary degrees: Sulfolk University, Sulfolk, England, 1983; University of Connecticut, 1988; Mount Holyoke, Massachusetts, 1989. **Residence:** Old Saybrook, Connecticut. **Died:** 28 April 1997.

PUBLICATIONS

Novels

The Street. 1946.

Country Place. 1947.

The Drugstore Cat (for children). 1949.

The Narrows. 1953.

Harriet Tubman: Conductor on the Underground Railroad (for children). 1955.

Tituba of Salem Village (for children). 1964.

Legends of the Saints (for children). 1970.

Short Stories

Miss Muriel and Other Stories. 1971.

*

Critical Studies: *The Negro Novel in America* by Robert Bone, 1965; interview with John O'Brien in *Interviews with Black Writers* 1973; *Women and War: The Changing Status of American Women from the 1930s to the 1950s* edited by Maria Diedrich and Dorothea Hornung-Fischer, 1990; "The Ornamentation of Old Ideas: Gloria Naylor's First Three Novels" by James Robert Saunders in *Hollins Critic,* vol. 27, no. 2, April 1990; *Haunting* *the House of Fiction: Feminist Perspectives on Ghost Stories by American Women,* edited by Lynette Carpenter and Wendy K. Kolmar, 1991; "A Distaff Dream Deferred? Petry and the Art of Subversion" by Keith Clark in *African-American Review,* vol. 26, no. 3, Fall 1992; *The Subversion of Cultural Ideology in Ann Petry's The Street and Country Place* (dissertation) by Hazel Arnett Ervin, 1993; *Ann Petry: A Bio-bibliography* by Hazel Arnett Ervin, 1993; *Necessary Knocking: The Short Fiction of Ann Petry* (dissertation) by Muriel Wright Brailey, 1996; *Blackness and Value: Seeing Double* by Lindon Barrett, 1998.

*   *   *

The pages of publishing history will record that Ann Petry, with the release of her first novel, *The Street,* became the first black woman in America to boast of book sales of more than a million copies. This seminal achievement, combined with the impressive body of literature she subsequently produced, established Petry as a significant twentieth-century fiction writer.

As a young girl growing up in the small New England town of Old Saybrook, Connecticut, Petry, the product of the town's only black couple, was isolated from the harsh realities of deprivation and socio-economic strife that so devastated the lives of African Americans in the rural South and the urban ghettos of the 1940s and 1950s. As the daughter of an established pharmacist and a licensed chiropodist, Petry was steeped in the values of her Puritan environment. Like the three generations of family professionals who preceded her, the future author was taught to follow a path of thrift, hard work, moderation and rugged individualism, values which would find their way onto the pages of her short stories and novels. Later, as a young bride transplanted to the mean streets of Harlem in 1938, where she lived and worked as a cub reporter for the New York *Amsterdam News* and *People's Voice,* Petry saw her Puritan idealism challenged by the poverty, crime, racial discrimination and exploitation she saw prevailing in the lives of the resilient but downtrodden black city dwellers. It was perhaps the ironic impact of these contrasting life experiences that developed within Petry a deep sensitivity to the plight of Harlem's poor. The stories she covered provided her with the raw materials, but it was Petry's sensibility as an artist which prompted her to use fiction as a medium for exploring the complex lives of those who survived in these less-than-human conditions. This distinctive literary feature, coupled with a penchant for plot intricacy and vivid characterization, made Petry a major literary influence, and identified her as the forerunner of a long line of successful black female writers, who were destined to build on her literary legacy.

Petry develops a number of traditionally American themes in her writing. A fascination with the American Dream and all that the concept implies—power, money and material fulfillment—permeates her fiction and proves the undoing of many of her characters. In her short stories and at least two of her novels, Petry celebrates small town life in New England before the turn of the century. This nostalgic strain is also evident in the strength and vitality she gives her small, close-knit New England communities and the reverence she shows for their fictional inhabitants of all races who subscribe to the Puritan ethic. Some of the author's most memorable characters achieve almost heroic stature as they toil in factories, operate small businesses and raise families, leading ordinary lives and weaving their uniqueness into the fabric of American life.

Petry's shorter fiction brims with folk elements which link her to fellow New England writers. Stories of ghosts, witches and supernatural occurrences are characterized by an irony and an irrepressible humor which is part and parcel of the American landscape. But it is themes of a darker strain for which Petry's works are most remembered. The erosion of small town values in the path of an encroaching metropolis, African Americans' often uncritical acceptance of white, middle-class values and the corrosive effects of racism on the personal lives of blacks are themes to which she returns throughout her career as an author. Significant too is that Petry introduced into her fiction a previously unexplored theme in American literature: the abuse, subordination and exploitation of women and the intersection of class, race and gender as they impact on African-American women in particular. As Nellie Y. McKay noted in *Women and War: The Changing Status of American Women from the 1930s to the 1950s,* "[Petry] foreshadowed a later generation of women [writers] like **Toni Morrison, Alice Walker** and **Gloria Naylor** in sharing with them a complex vision of the place that gender roles and economics play in the lives of black people."

Nowhere is that complexity of gender, class and race more apparent than in Petry's best-known novel, *The Street,* published in 1946, near the end of the naturalistic period in American literature. Within months after her first short story, "On Saturday the Sirens Sounds at Noon," appeared in *Crisis* magazine, Petry was awarded a Houghton Mifflin literary fellowship on the strength of the first five chapters of her first novel. Set in Harlem in an atmosphere of poverty, crime and drugs, *The Street* chronicles Lutie Johnson's futile struggle to change the course of her life through hard work, discipline, thrift and ambition. Left to survive by her own wits after the untimely death of her mother and grandmother, Lutie unwisely hires herself out as a live-in maid to the wealthy Chandlers. Lutie's presence in the Chandler household brings her face to face with the alcoholism and adultery that lie beneath the surface of their glitzy, upper middle-class veneer and marks the beginning of her disillusionment with the American Dream. Left without the companionship and love of his wife and shattered by his own sense of failure, her husband, Jim, becomes involved with another woman and eventually abandons Lutie and their son. When Lutie severs ties with her husband and employer and moves to Harlem, she retreats even further from her dream of success, leaving herself more vulnerable than ever. Trapped in a world where slum conditions and racial discrimination are the norm, Lutie discovers that her efforts to qualify for civil service or to become a night club singer count for little. Offered only the most menial jobs, she finds herself trapped in the subhuman conditions of a steam laundry. Her vulnerability is increased by her beauty which does little more than identify her as a sex object worthy only of being exploited. The novel's other black female characters are Min, the building superintendent's physically abused live-in companion, and Mrs. Hedges, the madame, who earns her living through promoting prostitution and is the only self-sufficient, independent black woman in the novel. While Lutie rejects Mrs. Hedges' offer to capitalize on her youthful beauty, Lutie is not so successful at countering the sexual advances of the degenerate superintendent (Jones), the powerful white Harlem businessman (Junto), or his sidekick (Boots).

Near the end of the novel, Lutie kills Boots to ward off a sexual assault, but she is not successful in saving herself or her son, Bub, from the attending ugliness of the sordid world they must inhabit. At the conclusion of the novel, Petry suggests that Bub will probably go to reform school while Lutie boards a bus for Chicago, maintaining her hope of putting her life back together but no closer to the illusive dream. Lutie emerges as a heroic but tragic victim unable to control her own life.

Another major novel, *Country Place,* was hailed as a critical success for Petry at the time of its release. A selection of the British Book Club, the novel was named by Robert Bone in *The Negro Novel in America* as one of the eight major novels written by a black American. One of the few literary works written by a black writer using white characters, *Country Place* revolves around the lives of Johnnie Roane, a returning World War II veteran and his beautiful but unfaithful wife, Glory. Glory's involvement with the lustful Ed Barrell and Barrell's sexual liaison with Lillian, the daughter-in-law of Mrs. Gramby, the town pillar, set the stage for a tragic, climactic ending. The story ends on a note of despair with Barrell and Mrs. Gramby plunging to an accidental death and Johnnie Roane, the novel's only admirable character, leaving the past behind for an art career in New York. *Country Place* is a story of adultery, greed and ambition set against a backdrop of aristocratic respectability.

Unlike the black protagonists of her previous novels, Link Williams, the focal character in Petry's third book, *The Narrows,* is a product of a Dartmouth education and an entrepreneurial family. Yet these advantages neither guarantee him success nor shield him from the fatal price he must pay for an adulterous affair with a white New England heiress. Link's violent murder at the end of the novel anticipates the attention that would be given to a now familiar theme—the black man as victim—and foreshadows **Ralph Ellison**'s ironic suggestion that America denies success to its most talented and deserving native sons.

While Petry's achievement with the novel form is undisputed, several of her short stories qualify as first-rate pieces deserving of attention. "Like a Winding Sheet," a penetrating story of racism and its tragic effects on the personal lives of its victims, won Petry a place in Martha Foley's *Best American Short Stories of 1946.* There are occasional flashes of brilliance in her later collection, *Miss Muriel and Other Stories.* "The Witness" is a haunting story of initiation, rendered symbolically, which depicts a high school teacher's unexpected confrontation with human evil. Two other stories in the volume explore racial prejudice from both interracial and intraracial perspectives. "The Bones of Louella Brown" mocks the hypocrisy of segregated cemeteries, and "Has Anybody Seen Miss Dora Dean?" explores the counterproductive consequences of divisiveness within black families and communities.

Though eclipsed in her time by popular naturalists like **Richard Wright**, **Stephen Crane** and **Theodore Dreiser**, Petry will be remembered for the extent to which she transcended the limitations of naturalism by refusing to focus microscopically on a single character in her literary works. As Keith Clarke noted in the *African-American Review,* Petry's lens is "panoramic," a fact which positions her "closer to the tradition of African-American writers who view the black community in its totality." By recasting a dominant theme—the never-ending pursuit of the American Dream—in a decidedly female context, Petry carved out a place for herself in literary history and exerted an influence on major writers like Toni Morrison, Gloria Naylor and Alice Walker that continues to resonate through the pages of American literature.

—Sandra Carlton Alexander

PHILLIPS, David Graham

Born: Madison, Indiana, 31 October 1867. **Education:** Madison High School, graduated 1882; Asbury College (now DePauw University), Greencastle, Indiana, 1882-85; Princeton University, New Jersey, 1885-87, A.B. 1887. **Career:** Reporter, Cincinnati *Star Times,* 1888, and Cincinnati *Commercial Gazette,* 1889-90; editorial staff member, New York *Sun,* 1890-93; London correspondent, 1893, general reporter, 1893-95, feature writer, 1895-97, and editorial department member, 1897-1902, New York *World;* full-time writer from 1902; frequent contributor to various national magazines, especially *Saturday Evening Post,* Philadelphia, and *Cosmopolitan,* New York. **Died:** (murdered) 24 January 1911.

PUBLICATIONS

Fiction

The Great God Success. 1901.
Her Serene Highness. 1902.
A Woman Ventures. 1902.
Golden Fleece: The American Adventures of a Fortune Hunting Earl. 1903.
The Master-Rogue: The Confessions of a Croesus. 1903.
The Cost. 1904.
The Mother-Light. 1905.
The Plum Tree. 1905.
The Social Secretary. 1905.
The Deluge. 1905.
The Fortune Hunter. 1906.
The Second Generation. 1907.
Light-Fingered Gentry. 1907.
Old Wives for New. 1908.
The Fashionable Adventures of Joshua Craig. 1909.
The Hungry Heart. 1909.
White Magic. 1910.
The Husband's Story. 1910.
The Grain of Dust. 1911.
The Conflict. 1911.
The Price She Paid. 1912.
George Helm. 1912.
Degarmo's Wife and Other Stories. 1913.
Susan Lenox: Her Fall and Rise. 1917.

Play

The Worth of a Woman: A Play, Followed by A Point of Law: A Dramatic Incident (produced 1908). 1908.

Other

The Reign of Gilt. 1905.
The Treason of the Senate (essays). 1953.
Contemporaries: Portraits in the Progressive Era, edited by Louis Filler. 1981.

*

Bibliography: in *Bibliography of American Literature* by Jacob Blanck, edited by Virginia L. Smyers and Michael Winship, 1983.

Critical Studies: *Phillips: His Life and Times* by Isaac F. Marcosson, 1932; *Phillips* by Abe C. Ravitz, 1966; *Voice of Democracy: A Critical Biography of Phillips, Journalist, Novelist, Progressive* by Louis Filler, 1978; "David Graham Phillips, Robert Herrick and the Doctor: A Turn of the Century Dilemma" by William R. Higgins, in *American Transcendental Quarterly*, June 1988.

* * *

David Graham Phillips's first novel, *The Great God Success,* concerns a newspaperman who gains fortune and power by championing the cause of the people against "the interests," but who sells out when he begins to identify with the rich. In *The Deluge, Light-Fingered Gentry, The Master-Rogue,* and *The Grain of Dust* Phillips also dealt with the corrupting influence of capitalism on essentially good men.

While in college, Phillips roomed with Albert Beveridge, who was later to serve as senator from Indiana. They remained good friends for the rest of their lives, and Phillips used Beveridge as a model for his paragon of political virtues, Hampden Scarborough. In *The Cost,* Scarborough's career is contrasted with that of his rival in love, an evil industrialist named Dumont. Scarborough's legislation ultimately triumphs over the capitalist's trusts. In *The Plum Tree,* Scarborough becomes a foil to a dishonest political power-broker. In these, as in his other political novels, *The Fashionable Adventures of Joshua Craig* and *George Helm,* Phillips recommends a vague populism and a return to honesty as the answer to the enormous social and economic problems facing America. His interest seems to be in exposing corruption, not in solving problems.

In his two "economic" novels, Phillips was somewhat bolder. Victor Dorn, the hero of *The Conflict,* is a revolutionary who contends that Marx will dominate the next two thousand years as Christ has dominated the last two thousand. In *The Second Generation,* Phillips seems to recommend the abolition of inherited property because of the harm done to both society and property-owners themselves.

Yet Phillips's greatest achievement was in his novels dealing with women's place in modern society. In *A Woman Ventures, Old Wives for New, The Price She Paid,* and in his only play, *The Worth of a Woman,* he ridiculed the stereotypical weak, soft home-bodies and extolled the virtues of women who competed on equal terms with men. In *The Hungry Heart* he defended the rights of neglected women to seek sexual satisfaction outside of marriage. Phillips's most impressive novel, *Susan Lenox: Her Fall and Rise,* published posthumously, chronicles the life of a girl who is condemned by social forces beyond her control to a life of vice and crime. Nothing in **Theodore Dreiser** or **Upton Sinclair** can match the brutality of Phillips's pictures of slum life and the horrors of white slavery. Through all her degradation, Susan maintains her essential dignity. When she overcomes her poverty, she still rejects all offers of respectability and marriage.

When Roosevelt applied the term "Muckraker" to a certain kind of investigative reporting, he was specifically referring to Phillips and his *The Treason of the Senate,* and it is for his reporting, not his literary work, that history will remember him. Yet his novels provide a valuable insight into the hopeful, optimistic America of his era.

—William Higgins

PHILLIPS, Jayne Anne

Born: Buckhannon, West Virginia, 19 July 1952. **Education:** West Virginia University, B.A. (magna cum laude) 1974; University of Iowa, M.F.A. 1978. **Family:** Married Mark Brian Stockman. **Career:** Writer. Beginning 1982 adjunct professor of English, Boston University; Fanny Howe Chair of Letters, Brandeis University, Waltham, Massachusetts, 1986-87. **Awards:** Pushcart prize, for *Sweethearts,* 1979; Fels award in fiction, for *Sweethearts,* 1978; National Endowment of the Arts fellowship, 1978, 1985; St. Lawrence award for fiction, for *Counting,* 1979; Sue Kaufman award for first fiction, for *Black Tickets,* 1980; O. Henry award, for short story "Snow," 1980; Bunting Institute fellowship, 1981; National Book Circle award nomination, for *Machine Dreams,* 1984; American Library Association Notable Book citation, for *Machine Dreams,* 1984.

PUBLICATIONS

Short Stories

Sweethearts. 1976.
Counting. 1978.
Black Tickets. 1979.
How Mickey Made It. 1981.
Fast Lanes. 1984.

Novels

Machine Dreams. 1984.
Shelter. 1994.

*

Critical Studies: *Listen to Their Voices: Twenty Interviews with Women Who Write* by Mickey Pearlman, 1993; "Jayne Anne Phillips: The Mystery of Language" in *Passion and Craft: Conversations with Notable Writers* edited by Bonnie Lyons and Bill Oliver, 1998.

* * *

Black Tickets (1979), a collection of two dozen short fictions, ranging from conventional coming-of-age stories to experimental prose poems, was strong enough to make Nadine Gordimer praise Jayne Anne Phillips, who was in her late twenties at the time of publication, as the best short-story writer since Eudora Welty. Raymond Carver called the book a "crooked beauty."

Although the commercial success of *Black Tickets* may have had something to do with its graphic description of the late 1970s hippie lifestyle and its lyrical portrayal of female sexuality in such stories as "El Paso," "Lechery," and "Black Tickets" and such prose poems as "Stripper" and "Slave," the stories most favored by reviewers and anthologists are the three realistic accounts of a young woman returning home and coming to terms with her divorced parents: "Home," "The Heavenly Animal," and "Souvenir." Whereas the former stories derive from Phillips's youthful cross-country travels and her initial desire to become a poet, the latter, more conventional, stories are perhaps the result of her training in the famous University of Iowa writing program; all three combine realistic psychological motivation with an inevitable movement toward a final frozen moment of metaphoric revelation. For example, at the end of "Souvenir" a mother and daughter are suspended on the top of a ferris wheel, while "Home" concludes with a mother and daughter standing silently in front of a sink of steaming water.

Criticizing some of the shorter pieces in *Black Tickets* as self-consciously poetic and experimental, reviewers such as John Irving hoped that her next book would be a novel. But that novel, *Machine Dreams* (1984), although generally well-received, was criticized by some as a mistaken capitulation by a talented short-story writer to the more commercially successful, critically respectable novel. As opposed to her short stories, which are often poetically and metaphorically detached lyric meditations focused more on an evocative use of language than on plot or character, in her first novel, Phillips created the most predictable kind of novel, one that focuses on the varied perspectives of a disintegrating family to reflect the parallel disintegration of a society. Phillips singled out American society between the mythically significant World War II and the nightmarish fragmentation of Vietnam because it provided her with the historical context for exploring how all the old social, religious, and familial assurances were disappearing.

Phillips does not identify herself as a political writer, except in the sense that, as she says, "writing about so-called ordinary people is a political statement because it's talking about everyday life and why it's precious and why it's worth defending against whatever forces." Phillips' own description of the difference between her short stories in *Black Tickets* and her novel *Machine Dreams* is reflective of basic differences between the short story and the novel form. In the novel, she says, she was primarily interested in cause and effect, whereas in the short stories, she wanted to make the experience of the stories as immediate as possible. The novel was meant to be a work of character in which the language was subdued, whereas in the stories, the focus was on language itself. What you recall about the novel, she says, are the people, whereas in the stories it is the "sound of the stories themselves that one remembers."

Phillips' second collection of short stories, *Fast Lanes* (1984), did not substantially add to her reputation, however, for the stories, some of which had been published earlier in limited editions, were not equal to the powerful visceral impact of the pieces in *Black Tickets*. Because of her twin themes of drifting and family, Jay McInerney suggested that Phillips was becoming a regional writer and a family chronicler. But Phillips rejected the "regional" title, calling it a "silly term" used by people who have never lived outside New York City; her own work, she affirmed, was meant to deal not with a region but with the world.

Phillips' eagerly-awaited second novel, *Shelter* (1994), did not appear until eight years later, when it was released to almost universal rave reviews, with critics comparing her to Flannery O'Connor and William Faulkner. The dark, densely-written story focuses on children at a summer camp for girls in the fictitious county of Shelter, West Virginia, in the early 1960s. Instead of providing an equivalent of parental nurturing, Camp Shelter threatens to become the sow that eats its litter. Family is once again important, but this time because of its absence. Because of the ignorance or ineffectuality of parents and other adults, children must struggle to become their own source of justice and order. The central figures are four girl campers—most of whom are vic-

tims of molestation, abandonment, and neglect—who encounter a father who abuses his son, a fanatically religious loner who is his nemesis, and a right-wing reactionary who warns of communists under every bed but who is oblivious to real dangers. At the center of the danger, and much in need of parental protection, is the wild-child Buddy, preternaturally aware of the nightmares that hover around the camp.

Instead of focusing on historical context, as she did in *Machine Dreams*, in *Shelter* Phillips created a mythic world, inevitably compared to Faulkner's Yoknapatawpha County, in which she dealt with the universal themes of good and evil, innocence and experience. Once again, as she did so brilliantly in her early short stories, Phillips focused as much on the precision of the language as she did on the characters that populate her story. The result is a book so dark in atmosphere and so dense in language that it threatens to bog readers down in swampy dankness or engulf them in an hallucinatory nightmare world that becomes the only reality. Even as *Shelter* makes use of the conventions of Southern Gothic, it transmutes and transcends them with its complex structure and highly controlled poetic writing, to culminate in a climax both horrifying and satisfying at once.

—Charles E. May

PINSKY, Robert

Born: Long Branch, New Jersey, 20 October 1940. **Education:** Rutgers University, New Brunswick, New Jersey, B.A. 1962; Stanford University, M.A. 1965, Ph.D. 1966. **Family:** Married Ellen Bailey in 1961, three daughters. **Career:** Assistant professor, University of Chicago, 1966-67; professor of English, Wellesley College, 1967-80; visiting lecturer in English, Harvard University, 1980; professor of English, University of California, Berkeley, 1980-89. Beginning 1988 professor of English, Boston University. **Awards:** Woodrow Wilson fellowship, 1962 and 1966; Fulbright fellowship, 1965; Stegner fellowship in creative writing, 1965; National Endowment for the Humanities fellowship, 1974; Massachusetts Council for the Arts award, 1976; Oscar Blumenthal prize, 1979; American Academy and Institute of Arts and Letters award, 1980; Saxifrage prize, 1980; Guggenheim fellowship, 1980; Fanny Hurst Professor, Washington University, 1980; Eunice B. Tietjens prize, 1983; National Endowment for the Arts fellowship, 1984; William Carlos Williams prize, 1985; Joseph Warren Beach Lecturer, University of Minnesota, 1985; Morris Graves Lecture, Harvard University, 1988; National Book Critics Circle nomination in criticism, 1988; Landon prize in translation, 1995; Los Angeles Times Book award, 1995; Shelley Memorial award, 1996; Ambassador Book award in poetry, 1997; Poet Laureate of the United States, beginning 1997; Lenore Marshall prize in poetry for *The Figured Wheel*, 1997. **Member:** American Academy of Arts and Sciences, 1993. **Residence:** Boston, Massachusetts.

PUBLICATIONS

Poetry

Sadness and Happiness. 1975.
An Explanation of America. 1979.

History of My Heart. 1984.
The Want Bone. 1990.
The Figured Wheel: New and Collected Poems, 1966-1996. 1995.

Novel

Mindwheel. 1985.

Other

Landor's Poetry. 1968.
The Situation of Poetry: Contemporary Poetry and Its Traditions. 1977.
Poetry and the World. 1988.
The Sounds of Poetry. 1998.

Editor, *The Handbook of Heartbreak.* 1998.
Co-editor, *Americans' Favorite Poems.* 1999.

Translator, with Robert Hass, *The Separate Notebooks,* by Czeslaw Milosz. 1984.
Translator, *The Inferno of Dante.* 1994.

*

Manuscript Collection: Regenstein Library, University of Chicago.

Critical Studies: *The Didactic Muse* by William Spiegelman, 1989; "On Robert Pinsky" by James Longenbach, in *Salmagundi,* Summer 1994.

*   *   *

In 1999 Robert Pinsky was appointed to an unprecedented third term as poet laureate of the United States, a position to which he was originally nominated in 1997. Pinsky is a poet, critic, translator, and public figure. A member of the American Academy of Arts and Sciences, his books of poetry include *The Figured Wheel: New and Collected Poems 1965-1995, An Explanation of America, The Want Bone, Sadness and Happiness,* and *History of My Heart.* Pinsky wrote four books of criticism, including *Poetry and the World.* His translation of *The Inferno of Dante* won the Los Angeles Times Book award for poetry and the Howard Morton Landon prize for translation. He is a co-translator of Nobel prize winner Czes aw Mi osz's poems in *The Separate Notebook.*

The book *History of My Heart* (1984) contains a group of poems that recall Pinsky's mother ("History of My Heart"), his father's patients ("The Questions"), and his neighborhood ("The Street"). "The Figured Wheel" opens the collection and symbolizes the inexorable march of the wheel through space and time and across borders: "It separates and recombines all droplets and grains." The wheel accumulates symbols, messages, and devices. It even rolls over Pinsky and his loved ones, but since it is a "nothing-trans-figuring wheel," its effect is deflated. Pinsky is concerned in his work with death ("The Questions," "Dying") and near death ("The Saving"), and with the living ("The Living"). About sexual awakening, "History of My Heart" is a lengthy, important poem whose title also gives name to his collection. The poet remembers a "thin blonde girl" who makes him feel "desired," and "the heart yearns further into giving itself into the air." In this same poem he reminisces about his mother, his grandfather, and his music.

On a visit to a Krakow concentration camp in "The Unseen," the narrator wants to kill the Nazis and protests to God, "O discredited Lord of Host," but he accepts God's secrets regarding good and evil. "The Unseen" reads as an emotional poem that evokes a powerful response in the reader. A preponderance of poems in *History of My Heart* adopts two or three-line stanzas, reminiscent of Dante's terza rima, as in "The Living." Pinsky was awarded the William Carlos Williams prize of the Poetry Society of America for *History of My Heart.*

In another book of poetry, *Sadness and Happiness* (1975), the "Poem about People" focuses on the prejudice and distrust among diverse groups of people; Pinsky asserts, "Hate my whole kind, but me." Not all of Pinsky's poems are solemn. He writes a five-part poem on tennis and extols the desire to win. "Sadness and Happiness" is a long poem meditating on the sadness of past failures that "organize life," as well as happy events. People are fixed in the bosom of art and life, "desperate" to find sadness or happiness. Another group of poems fixes on "Persons" who have been special to Pinsky, including his father, his daughter, and an old woman. "The Beach Women" recollects women of an earlier day, and Pinsky reflects on the evolution of gender roles.

"Essay on Psychiatrists" is a long poem in which the poet tries to define psychiatrists and finds they have no characteristics that distinguish them from other human beings. After he examines Dionysus and Pentheus as classical harbingers of psychiatrists, Pinsky links psychiatrists with writers and dispels the notion that psychiatrists are unique after all. As Pinsky dissipates romanticism about writers and psychiatrists, he merges them with everyone.

In the collection *The Want Bone* (1990), the poem "From the Life of Jesus" is a fable about Jesus at the age of five, creating clay birds that turn into real ones and fly away. Jesus also makes another child "wither" because he destroys his tiny dam. The poem demonstrates both the miraculous power of Jesus at an early age and his fallible humanity. Another poem, "The Want Bone," describes in great detail the mouth bones of a dead beached whale, recalling the life force of the whale. "The Refinery" alerts the reader to the dangers of industrial progress.

An Explanation of America (1979) is a three-part epic, which the poet dedicates to his daughter in his attempt to explain to her what the country is about: "A country is the things it wants to see." Yet people everywhere want to see "the awful, trivial, and atrocious" in all countries.

Among Pinsky's newer poems, "Poem with Refrains" depicts Pinsky's mother's ambivalence over the death of her own mother. "The Ice Storm," in memory of Pinsky's friend Bernie Fields, meditates on the nature of human mortality and asks, "What is a life?"

Pinsky ranks among the leading American poets for his eclectic choice of subjects, sensitivity to human concerns, and depth of feeling. His is a discursive poetry that emphasizes daily experience. He deals with varied subjects from childhood memories to concentration camps. His meditative tone, wit, and inclusiveness are reminiscent of the works of **Randall Jarrell.**

—Shirley J. Paolini

PLATH, Sylvia

Born: Boston, Massachusetts, 27 October 1932. **Education:** Schools in Wellesley, Massachusetts; Smith College, Northampton,

Massachusetts (Glasscock Prize 1955), B.A. (summa cum laude) in English 1955 (Phi Beta Kappa); Newnham College, Cambridge (Fulbright Scholar) 1955-57, M.A. 1957. **Family:** Married the poet Ted Hughes in 1956 (separated 1962); one daughter and one son. **Career:** Guest editor, *Mademoiselle* magazine, New York, summer 1953; Instructor in English, Smith College, 1957-58; moved to England in 1959. **Awards:** Yaddo fellowship, 1959; Cheltenham Festival award, 1961; Saxon fellowship, 1961. **Died:** (suicide) 11 February 1963.

PUBLICATIONS

Collections

Collected Poems, edited by Ted Hughes. 1981.
Selected Poems, edited by Ted Hughes. 1985.

Poetry

A Winter Ship. 1960.
The Colossus. 1960.
Ariel, edited by Ted and Olwyn Hughes. 1965.
Uncollected Poems. 1965.
Wreath for a Bridal. 1970.
Million Dollar Month. 1971.
Fiesta Melons. 1971.
Crossing the Water, edited by Ted Hughes. 1971.
Crystal Gazer. 1971.
Lyonnesse: Hitherto Uncollected Poems. 1971.
Winter Trees, edited by Ted Hughes. 1971.
Child. 1971.
Pursuit. 1973.
Two Poems. 1980.
Two Uncollected Poems. 1980.

Play

Three Women: A Monologue for Three Voices (broadcast 1962; produced 1973). 1968.

Radio Play: *Three Women,* 1962.

Fiction

The Bell Jar. 1963.

Other

Letters Home: Correspondence 1950-1963, edited by Aurelia Schober Plath. 1975.
The Bed Book (for children). 1976.
Plath: A Dramatic Portrait (miscellany), edited by Barry Kyle. 1976.
Johnny Panic and the Bible of Dreams, and Other Prose Writings, edited by Ted Hughes. 1977; augmented edition, 1979.
The Journals, edited by Ted Hughes and Frances McCullough. 1982.
The It-Doesn't-Matter Suit. 1996.

Editor, *American Poetry Now: A Selection of the Best Poems by Modern American Writers.* 1961.

*

Bibliography: *A Chronological Checklist of the Periodical Publications of Plath* by Eric Homberger, 1970; *Plath and Anne Sexton: A Reference Guide* by Cameron Northouse and Thomas P. Walsh, 1974; *Plath: A Bibliography* by Gary Lane and Maria Stevens, 1978; *Plath: An Analytical Bibliography* by Stephen Tabor, 1986.

Critical Studies: *The Art of Plath: A Symposium* edited by Charles Newman, 1970; *The Savage God: A Study of Suicide* by A. Alvarez, 1971; *The Poetry of Plath: A Study of Themes* by Ingrid Melander, 1972; *A Closer Look at Ariel: A Memory of Plath* by Nancy Hunter Steiner, 1973; *Plath* by Eileen M. Aird, 1973; *Plath: Method and Madness* by Edward Butscher, 1976, and *Plath: The Woman and the Work* edited by Butscher, 1977; *Plath: Poetry and Existence* by David Holbrook, 1976; *Chapters in a Mythology: The Poetry of Plath* by Judith Kroll, 1976; *Plath* by Caroline King Barnard, 1978; *Plath and Ted Hughes* by Margaret Dickie Uroff, 1979; *Plath: New Views on the Poetry* edited by Gary Lane, 1979; *Plath: The Poetry of Initiation* by Jon Rosenblatt, 1979; *Protean Poetics: The Poetry of Plath* by Mary Lynn Broe, 1980; *Plath's Incarnations: Woman and Creative Process* by Lynda K. Bundtzen, 1983; *Critical Essays on Plath* edited by Linda W. Wagner, 1984, and *Plath: A Literary Biography* by Wagner, 1986; *Ariel Ascending: Writings about Plath* edited by Paul Alexander, 1985; *The Dialectics of Art and Life: A Portrait of Plath as Woman and Poet* by Sylvia Lohrer, 1985; "Sylvia Plath's Children's Poems" by Mary Cohen, in *Courage and Tools: The Florence Howe Award for Feminist Scholarship 1974-1989* edited by Joanne Glasgow and Angela Ingram, 1990; *Reflecting on The Bell Jar* by Pat MacPherson, 1991; "Sylvia Plath: Beyond the Biographical" by Rochelle Ratner, in *American Writing Today* edited by Richard Kostelanetz, 1991; *The Liberation of Sylvia Plath's Ariel: Psychosemantics and a Glass Sarcophagus* by Jennifer Draskau, 1991; *Sylvia Plath: Confessing the Fictive Self* by Toni Saldivar, 1992; *Sylvia Plath: Killing the Angel in the House* by Elaine Connell, 1993; *Reconstructed Vase: Sylvia Plath and New Critical Essays* by Vicki Graham, 1994; *Sylvia Plath: New Views on the Poetry* edited by Gary Lane, 1994; *The Silent Woman: Sylvia Plath and Ted Hughes* by Janet Malcolm, 1995; *Sylvia Plath: The Shaping of Shadows* by Al Strangeways, 1998.

*   *   *

The adolescent heroine of Sylvia Plath's only novel, *The Bell Jar,* has looked into her grave and seen a sobering and a maddening truth. Her suicidal hysteria, like that which finally took Plath herself, is the anguish of a being who has realized her own gratuitousness, "Factitious, artificial, sham." What she has called her "self," that unique and coddled ego, is no more than a nexus of donated being, a field of battle where the conflicting forces of her environment, her familial and social experience, clash, divide, and coalesce. Plath wrote of the poem "Daddy" as "spoken by a girl with an Electra complex. Her father died while she thought he was God. Her case is complicated by the fact that her father was also a Nazi and her mother very possibly Jewish. In the daughter the two strains marry and paralyze each other—she has to act out the awful little allegory before she is free of it." While the details hardly correspond accurately to Plath's own biography, their symbolic function in the emotional ecology of her work is clear. The title poem of *The Colossus* acknowledges such a condition: addressed to her dead father ("I shall never get you put together entirely") it is self-consciously post-Freudian and pre-Christian: "A blue sky out of the Oresteia / Arches above us"; if her father is now no more than a "Mouthpiece of the dead," this is equally true of all selves, whose "hours are married to shadow," the marionettes of an unconscious in whose formation they had no hand. "Poem for a Birthday" is a complex dramatic monologue in which a psyche struggles towards birth, in "the city of spare parts" that is the world. Its voice is a Cinderella or Snow-White princess in nightmare exile among incomprehensible and uncomprehending powers, feeling herself "Duchess of Nothing," "housekeep[ing] in Time's gut end" and "married [to] a cupboard of rubbish." It is a representative text.

The imagery of Plath's poems undergoes endless transformations, in which the links are often suppressed or arbitrary: sudden shifts of tack and emotion lead off in unexpected directions. Her poetic narratives fork and proliferate in this way because, in unfolding the implications of a sequence of images, she uncovers the complex and contradictory possibilities condensed within them, the infantile traumas lying treacherously beneath the surface of adult experience. The same image can be charged with quite contradictory emotional valencies. The bee, for example, a recurring motif (her father was an apiculturalist), stirs rich, ambiguous feelings. It is a female, a source of honey and creativity, but it has a male sting; the hive includes drudges and drones, but also that dark leonine queen at the core; in "The Swarm" and "The Arrival of the Bee-Box," bees are the collective "black, intractable mind" of a genocidal Europe and the "swarmy," "angrily clambering" impulsions of the individual unconscious. Such transitions express her own sense of the self, not as a hierarchically ordered pyramid, but as an ensemble of possibilities, in which none usurps precedence for long, and to which only a provisional coherence can be given, in the specifying of a name and image ("The Arrival of the Bee-Box," after toying with the starvation or release of the bees that threaten and fascinate, concludes, "The box is only temporary"). Self for Plath is either a rigid, false persona or an amorphous, uncongealed, and fluid congeries, like the bee-swarm itself, undergoing constant metamorphosis, continually dying and being reborn in the mutations of the imagery. In "Elm," the social self speaks as a tree, rooted in its context, wrenched violently by a wind that "will tolerate no bystanding." But such fixity is an illusion, for its roots reach down to the dissolute sea, its branches "break up in pieces that fly about like clubs," it is dragged by the moon (usually the image of a sterile maternal force), and it contains subversive lives that are part of itself yet frighteningly independent:

> I am inhabited by a cry.
> Nightly it flaps out
> Looking, with its hooks, for something to love.

> I am terrified by this dark thing
> That sleeps in me;
> All day I feel its soft, feathery turnings, its malignity.

Plath repeatedly sees relationships as predatory, exploitative, and destructive, yet desired and necessary, as in "The Rabbit-Catcher" ("And we too had a relationship, / Tight wires between us, / Pegs too deep to uproot, and a mind like a ring / Sliding shut on some quick thing, / The constriction killing me also"). In "Tulips," even the smiles of husband and children, in a photograph, "catch onto my skin, little smiling hooks," while identity itself, in "The Applicant," is seen as a collection of functions, answers to others'

questions, a poultice for their wounds, apple for their eyes, "A living doll" that is the accretion of artificial limbs and artificial commitments.

This aspect of her verse has made her co-option by the women's movement inevitable. But it is also just. Plath is, in fact, a profoundly political poet, who has seen the generic nature of these private catastrophes of the self, their public origin in a civilization founded on mass-manipulation and collective trickery. Esther Greenwood, in *The Bell Jar,* links her electric shock treatment with the electrocution that is the Rosenbergs' punishment for rebellion against the American way of life: she fears most of all being consigned to the charity wards, "with hundreds of people like me, in a big cage in the basement. The more hopeless you were, the further away they hid you." In a century that has shut away millions, in hospitals, concentration camps, and graveyards, where the self can be "wiped out . . . like chalk on a blackboard" by administrative diktat, Plath sees a deep correspondence between the paternal concern of the psychiatrist and the authority of the modern state, even in its most extreme variants: both presuppose the self as the victim, passive and compliant, as *sine qua non* of any "final solution." For Plath, concerned that "personal experience shouldn't be a kind of shut box and mirror-looking narcissistic experience," but "should be generally relevant, to such things as Hiroshima and Dachau and so on," the refusal to collaborate was a profoundly positive act, the assertion not of the nihilism of which she has been accused but of a more exacting and scrupulous conscience. If, in poems such as "Daddy" and "Lady Lazarus," she veers close to disintegration, she also promises a breakthrough into a resurrection that sheds the constricting husks of the past, a vengeful return that is only justice:

> So, so. Herr Doktor.
> So, Herr Enemy.
> I am your opus,
> I am your valuable,
> The pure gold baby

> That melts to a shriek.
> I turn and burn,
> Do not think I underestimate your great concern.

> Herr God, Herr Lucifer
> Beware
> Beware.

> Out of the ash I rise with my red hair
> And I eat men like air.

—Stan Smith

See the essay on *Ariel*.

POE, Edgar Allan

Born: Boston, Massachusetts, 19 January 1809; orphaned, and given a home by John Allan, 1812. **Education:** The Dubourg sisters' boarding school, Chelsea, London, 1816-17; Manor House School, Stoke Newington, London, 1817-1820; Joseph H. Clarke's School, Richmond, 1820-23; William Burke's School, Richmond,

1823-25; University of Virginia, Charlottesville, 1826; U.S. Military Academy, West Point, New York, 1830-31 (court-martialled and dismissed). **Military Service:** Served in the U.S. Army, 1827-29: sergeant-major. **Family:** Married his 13-year-old cousin Virginia Clemm in 1836 (died 1847). **Career:** Lived in Baltimore, 1831-35; assistant editor, 1835, and editor, 1836-37, *Southern Literary Messenger,* Richmond; lived in New York, 1837 and after 1843, and Philadelphia, 1838-43; assistant editor, *Gentleman's Magazine,* 1839-40, and editor, *Graham's Magazine,* 1841-42, both Philadelphia; sub-editor, New York *Evening Mirror,* 1844; editor and briefly proprietor, *Broadway Journal,* New York, 1845-46. Lecturer after 1844. **Died:** 7 October 1849.

PUBLICATIONS

Collections

Complete Works (Virginia Edition), edited by James A. Harrison. 17 vols., 1902.
Poems, edited by Floyd Stovall. 1965.
Collected Works, edited by Thomas Ollive Mabbott. 3 vols., 1969-78.
Short Fiction, edited by Stuart and Susan Levine. 1976.
Collected Writings, edited by Burton R. Pollin. 1981—.
Poetry and Tales (Library of America), edited by Patrick F. Quinn. 1984.
Essays and Reviews (Library of America), edited by G.R. Thompson. 1984.
Poetry, Tales, and Selected Essays (Library of America). 1996.
Complete Poems. 1998.

Short Stories

Tales of the Grotesque and Arabesque. 1840.
The Prose Romances 1: The Murders in the Rue Morgue, and The Man That Was Used Up. 1843.
Tales. 1845.

Novels

The Narrative of Arthur Gordon Pym of Nantucket. 1838.
The Literati: Some Honest Opinions about Authorial Merits and Demerits. 1850.

Poetry

Tamerlane and Other Poems. 1827.
Al Aaraaf, Tamerlane, and Minor Poems. 1829.
Poems. 1831.
The Raven and Other Poems. 1845.

Play

Politian: An Unfinished Tragedy, edited by Thomas Ollive Mabbott. 1923.

Other

The Conchologist's First Book; or, A System of Testaceous Malacology (textbook; revised by Poe). 1839; revised edition, 1840.

Eureka: A Prose Poem. 1848; edited by Richard P. Benton, 1973(?).
Letters, edited by John Ward Ostrom. 2 vols., 1948; revised edition, 2 vols., 1966.
Literary Criticism, edited by Robert L. Hough. 1965.
The Unknown Poe: An Anthology of Fugitive Writings, edited by Raymond Foye. 1980.
The Annotated Poe, edited by Stephen Peithman. 1981.
The Other Poe: Comedies and Satires, edited by David Galloway. 1983.
Poems and Essays on Poetry, edited by Charles Hubert Sisson, 1995.

*

Bibliography: *Bibliography of the Writings of Poe* by John W. Robertson, 1934; *A Bibliography of First Printings of the Writings of Poe* by Charles F. Heartman and James R. Canny, 1940, revised edition, 1943; *Poe: A Bibliography of Criticism 1827-1967* by J. Lesley Dameron and Irby B. Cauthen, Jr., 1974; *Poe: An Annotated Bibliography of Books and Articles in English 1827-1973* by Esther F. Hyneman, 1974; in *Bibliography of American Literature* by Jacob Blanck, edited by Virginia L. Smyers and Michael Winship, 1983.

Critical Studies: *Poe: A Critical Biography* by Arthur Hobson Quinn, 1941; *Poe As a Literary Critic* by John Esten Cooke, edited by N. Bryllion Fagin, 1946; *Life of Poe* by Thomas Holley Chivers, edited by Richard Beale Davis, 1952; *Poe: A Critical Study* by Edward H. Davidson, 1957; *The French Face of Poe* by Patrick F. Quinn, 1957; *Poe* by Vincent Buranelli, 1961, revised edition, 1977; *Poe: A Biography* by William Bittner, 1962; *Poe: The Man Behind the Legend* by Edward Wagenknecht, 1963; *Poe's Literary Battles: The Critic in the Context of His Literary Milieu* by Sidney P. Moss, 1963; *Poe as Literary Critic* by Edd Winfield Parks, 1964; *Poe* by Geoffrey Rans, 1965; *The Recognition of Poe: Selected Criticism since 1829* edited by Eric W. Carlson, 1966; *Poe: A Collection of Critical Essays* edited by Robert Regan, 1967; *Poe, Journalist and Critic* by Robert D. Jacobs, 1969; *Poe the Poet: Essays New and Old on the Man and His Work* by Floyd Stovall, 1969; *Plots and Characters in the Fiction and Poetry of Poe* by Robert L. Gale, 1970; *Twentieth-Century Interpretations of Poe's Tales* edited by William L. Howarth, 1971; *Poe Poe Poe Poe Poe Poe Poe* by Daniel Hoffman, 1972; *Poe: A Phenomenological View* by David Halliburton, 1973; *Poe's Fiction: Romantic Irony in the Gothic Tales* by G.R. Thompson, 1973; *Poe* by David Sinclair, 1977; *Building Poe Biography* by John Carl Miller, 1977; *The Tell-Tale Heart: The Life and Works of Poe* by Julian Symons, 1978; *The Extraordinary Mr. Poe* by Wolf Mankowitz, 1978; *The Rationale of Deception in Poe* by David Ketterer, 1979; *A Psychology of Fear: The Nightmare Formula of Poe* by David R. Saliba, 1980; *A Poe Companion: A Guide to the Short Stories, Romances, and Essays* by J.R. Hammond, 1981; *Poe* by Bettina L. Knapp, 1984; *The Genius of Poe* by Georges Zayed, 1985; *Poe: The Critical Heritage* edited by I.M. Walker, 1986; *Poe, Death and the Life of Writing* by J. Gerald Kennedy, 1987; *Fables of Mind: An Inquiry into Poe's Fiction* by Joan Dayan, 1987; *The Poe Log: A Documentary Life of Poe 1809-1849* by Dwight Thomas and David Jackson, 1987; *Poe: The Design of Order* by A. Robert Lee, 1987; *A World of Words: Language and Displacement in the Fiction of Poe* by Michael J. S. Williams, 1988; *Edgar Allan Poe and the*

Philadelphia Saturday News by Richard Kopley, 1991; *Poe: His Life and Legacy* by Jeffrey Meyers, 1992; *Poe: Mournful and Never-Ending Remembrance* by Kenneth Silverman, 1992; *Poe's Pym: Critical Explorations* edited by Richard Kopley, 1992; "An Intrinsic Luminosity: Poe's Use of Platonic and Newtonian Optics" by William J. Scheick, in *American Literature and Science* edited by Robert J. Scholnick, 1992; *Valery and Poe: A Literary Legacy* by Lois Davis Vines, 1992; *Grim Phantasms: Fear in Poe's Short Fiction* by Michael L. Burduck, 1992; *New Essays on Poe's Major Tales* edited by Kenneth Silverman, 1993; *Edgar Allan Poe's Biographies of Byron: Byrons Differed/Byrons Deferred in The Tales of the Folio Club* by Katrina Bachinger, 1994; *The Raven and the Whale: Poe, Melville, and the New York Literary Scene* by Perry Miller, 1997; *The Poe Encyclopedia*, 1997; *Rhetorical Deception in the Short Fiction of Hawthorne, Poe, and Melville* by Terry J. Martin, 1998.

*   *   *

Although Edgar Allan Poe wrote that for him "poetry has been not a purpose but a passion," he wrote only some fifty poems (excluding his album verses, jingles, and acrostics). Obliged to work at drudging journalism, he never realized his dream of founding a literary magazine of his own. While grinding out scores of reviews of some of the most forgettable books of the nineteenth century he wrote the tales, poems, and essays on which his posthumous renown is based. Aiming his work "not above the popular, nor below the critical, taste," he made use, as a professional magazinist must, of the fictional conventions of his day, turning to his own obsessive needs the Gothic horror story ("Ligeia," "The Fall of the House of Usher," "Berenice") and the tale of exploration ("A Descent into the Maelstrom," *The Narrative of Arthur Gordon Pym*). In "The Gold Bug," "The Murders in the Rue Morgue," and "The Purloined Letter," he virtually invented the modern detective story, and he set the mold upon science fiction with "Mesmeric Revelations," "The Facts in the Case of Monsieur Valdemar," and "The Balloon Hoax." He also wrote dozens of satirical sketches. His critical writings were the most systematic and intelligent produced in America until his time.

Despite the paucity of his productions as a poet, he proved a major influence upon Baudelaire, who translated several of his tales and wrote that if Poe had not existed, he would have had to invent him. Through Baudelaire, Poe's critical theories influenced the entire French Symbolist movement. Although Poe believed, with Tennyson, that imprecision of meaning was necessary for the creation of beauty, he also believed that the poet is a deliberate maker who devises all of his effects to contribute to the single aim of his poem. "The Philosophy of Composition," an essay purporting to demonstrate how Poe wrote "The Raven," presents the creative process as an interlocked series of conscious choices. Although this would seem the opposite of the Romantic view of the poet as inspired seer, Poe's systematic process is in fact determined by Romantic necessity and is derived from Coleridge's aesthetic. That necessity is the excitation of the soul through the contemplation of the most melancholy of subjects—the death of a beautiful woman. The complex interaction in this theory between obsessive emotional need and what Poe in his detective stories called "ratiocination" is characteristic of all of his best work.

It seems ironic and cruel that a writer whose tales of guilt and terror won him the admiration of Dostoevsky had to live a hand-to-mouth existence and, after his death, was defamed by a hostile editor and reviled by readers who took as autobiographical the characters in his tales who were opium fiends and necrophiliacs. **Allen Tate** (in his essay "The Angelic Imagination") identifies what it is in Poe's work that really set on edge Victorian sensibility: the lack of any God save impersonal force, a fictive world without Christian morality. Far more evocatively than in the naturalistic novels of fifty years later, Poe imagined the nightmare of a universe without the consolations of faith.

This visionary author's life was unmitigatedly wretched. His parents were itinerant actors; the alcoholic father deserted, leaving Elizabeth Arnold Poe with three infant children. A brother and sister of Edgar's were adopted by connections in Baltimore but she kept young Eddie by her as she acted the heroine in plays no more melodramatic than his life would be. Stricken by tuberculosis, she died a lingering death in Richmond, Virginia, attended by kindly local matrons, when Edgar was only three. The boy was taken into the home of John Allan, a prosperous tobacco factor who brought Edgar to England when his business took him there and sent the boy to the school so vividly remembered in "William Wilson." Allan sent Poe to the new University of Virginia where, on a niggardly allowance among the scions of wealthy families, he ran up gambling debts and was expelled. Mrs. Allan, like Poe's natural mother, died of tuberculosis, and Poe, who had no inclination for the tobacco business, quarreled with his "Pa" (he had discovered Allan's infidelities while his wife was still alive). Allan withheld love from Edgar and never adopted him, so Poe was cast adrift penniless to make his way as an author. Not even a hitch in the army or a later enlistment in the military academy at West Point mollified Allan. Poe, deciding to leave West Point, could not persuade "Pa" to intercede for his release and had to feign illness until he was expelled. By this time he had published two volumes of poems. One is dedicated to the Corps of Cadets.

Poe's career henceforth was as assistant or principal editor on several magazines in Richmond, Philadelphia, and New York. While so engaged, he wrote nearly 90 tales and sketches, countless critical columns and reviews, two novellas, and an astrophysical treatise on the nature of the universe, entitled *Eureka*, which he described as a poem.

Poe married his first cousin Virginia Clemm when she was thirteen and lived with her and her mother (his aunt) until Virginia, too, died of tuberculosis at 23. Thereafter Poe conducted frenzied courtships of several poetesses; at this time he well may have been mad with grief. He died in delirium, under unexplained circumstances, on a trip to Baltimore. Poe's biographers agree that he idealized women, and that sexual desire seems not to have had an overt part in any of his relationships.

Poe classified his own fiction into the categories of "Tales of the Grotesque and Arabesque." Borrowing these terms from Scott, Poe meant by them to describe satirical, bizarre, jocose writings on the one hand, and on the other the fictional equivalents of poems. These were his prose efforts to excite his readers' souls by the contemplation of beauty and terror. His review of **Nathaniel Hawthorne** outlines his theory of fiction. The tale, like the poem, must be all of a piece, each detail contributing to the desired unity of effect; symbolism (Poe, in the nomenclature of the day, calls it allegory) must be present as a "profound undercurrent" in the tale. His fiction will work by indirection.

In Poe's work there is a mysterious interpenetrability of the soul's excitation with subterranean dread. A *frisson* of honor runs through his most impassioned tales. The clue of Poe's contradictions may be in his sketch "The Imp of the Perverse," for the fiction frequently dramatizes its theme of man's irresistible urge toward self-destruction (a man is driven to commit a terrible crime, then to reveal his guilt). This connects also with the theme of double identity ("William Wilson," "The Cask of Amontillado") and Poe's strain of hoaxing, not entirely confined to his jocular productions. Poe delighted in tricking his readers. He would make them believe that his mesmerizer had really hypnotized a dying man so that the soul lingered and answered questions for months after the death of the body; or that his balloonists had actually crossed the Atlantic in three days, arriving in South Carolina. So too with fantastic descents into the maelstrom and journeys to the end of the earth and back. "The Philosophy of Composition" is in one respect such a hoax. Like his detective genius Monsieur Dupin, Poe demonstrates his intuitive intellectual superiority.

Although only in *Pym* did he write a successful fiction of more than thirty pages, Poe's significance is multifold. He is a systematic critic and theorist predictive of the Symbolist movement. His best poems and fictions embody his aesthetic intention that every part of the literary artifact must contribute to the unifying effect of the whole. His mastery of popular genres made him the unwitting godfather of much popular literature in the twentieth century, as well as a major influence on films. His poetic theory passed from the Symbolists back into American poetry through **T.S. Eliot** and its influence continues in Allen Tate and **Richard Wilbur**, among others. His fiction is widely translated and widely read. Poe's work indeed has reached both the popular and the critical taste.

—Daniel Hoffman

See the essays on "The Fall of the House of Usher" and "The Murders in the Rue Morgue."

PORTER, Katherine Anne

Born: Callie Russell Porter in Indian Creek, Texas, 15 May 1890. **Education:** Thomas School, San Antonio, Texas. **Family:** Married 1) John Henry Koontz in 1906 (separated 1914; divorced 1915); 2) Ernest Stock in 1925; 3) Eugene Dove Pressly in 1933 (divorced 1938); 4) Albert Russell Erskine, Jr., in 1938 (divorced 1942). **Career:** Journalist and film extra in Chicago, 1911-14; tuberculosis patient, Dallas and San Angelo, Texas, and New Mexico, 1915-17; worked with tubercular children in Dallas, 1917; staff member, Fort Worth *Critic,* Texas, 1917-18; reporter, 1918, and drama critic, 1919, *Rocky Mountain News,* Denver; lived in New York, 1919, and mainly in Mexico, 1920-31, and Europe in 1930s; copy-editor, Macauley and Company, publishers, New York, 1928-29; taught at Olivet College, Michigan, 1940; contract writer for MGM, Hollywood, 1945-46; lecturer in writing, Stanford University, California, 1948-49; guest lecturer in literature, University of Chicago, spring 1951; visiting lecturer in contemporary poetry, University of Michigan, Ann Arbor, 1953-54; Fulbright lecturer, University of Liège, Belgium, 1954-55; writer-in-residence, University of Virginia, Charlottesville, autumn 1958; Glasgow Professor, Washington and Lee University, Lexington, Virginia, spring 1959; lecturer in American literature for U.S. Department of State, in Mexico, 1960, 1964; Ewing Lecturer, University of California, Los Angeles, 1960; Regents' Lecturer, University of California, Riverside, 1961. Library of Congress Fellow in Regional American Literature, 1944; vice president, Na-

tional Institute of Arts and Letters, 1950-52; U.S. delegate, International Festival of the Arts, Paris, 1952; member, Commission on Presidential Scholars, 1964; consultant in poetry, Library of Congress, 1965-70. **Awards:** Guggenheim fellowship, 1931, 1938; New York University Libraries gold medal, 1940; Ford Foundation grant, 1959, 1960; O. Henry award, 1962; Emerson-Thoreau medal, 1962; Pulitzer prize, 1966; National Book award, 1966; American Academy gold medal, 1967; Mystery Writers of America Edgar Allan Poe award, 1972. D.Litt.: University of North Carolina Woman's College, Greensboro, 1949; Smith College, Northampton, Massachusetts, 1958; Maryville College, St. Louis, 1968. D.H.L.: University of Michigan, Ann Arbor, 1954; University of Maryland, College Park, 1966; Maryland Institute, 1974. D.F.A.: La Salle College, Philadelphia, 1962. **Member:** American Academy, 1967. **Died:** 18 September 1980.

PUBLICATIONS

Short Stories

Flowering Judas. 1930; augmented edition, as *Flowering Judas and Other Stories,* 1935.
Hacienda: A Story of Mexico. 1934.
Noon Wine (story). 1937.
Pale Horse, Pale Rider: Three Short Novels (includes *Noon Wine* and "Old Mortality"). 1939.
The Leaning Tower and Other Stories. 1944.
Selected Short Stories. 1945.
The Old Order: Stories of the South. 1955.
A Christmas Story. 1958.
Collected Stories. 1964; augmented edition, 1967.

Novel

Ship of Fools. 1962.

Poetry

Katherine Anne Porter's Poetry. 1996.

Other

My Chinese Marriage. 1921.
Outline of Mexican Popular Arts and Crafts. 1922.
What Price Marriage. 1927.
The Days Before: Collected Essays and Occasional Writings. 1952; augmented edition, as *The Collected Essays and Occasional Writings,* 1970.
A Defense of Circe. 1955.
The Never-Ending Wrong (on the Sacco-Vanzetti case). 1977.
Conversations with Porter, Refugee from Indian Creek, with Enrique Hank Lopez. 1981.
Porter: Conversations, edited by Joan Givner. 1987.
Letters, edited by Isabel Bayley. 1990.
The Strange Old World and Other Book Reviews by Porter, edited by Darlene Unrue. 1991.

Translator, *French Song-Book.* 1933.
Translator, *The Itching Parrot,* by Fernandez de Lizárdi. 1942.

*

Bibliography: *A Bibliography of the Works of Porter* and *A Bibliography of the Criticism of the Works of Porter* by Louise Waldrip and Shirley Ann Bauer, 1969; *Porter and Carson McCullers: A Reference Guide* by Robert F. Kiernan, 1976; *Porter: An Annotated Bibliography* by Kathryn Hilt and Ruth M. Alvarez, 1990.

Critical Studies: *The Fiction and Criticism of Porter* by Harry John Mooney, Jr., 1957, revised edition, 1962; *Porter* by Ray B. West, Jr., 1963; *Porter and the Art of Rejection* by William L. Nance, 1964; *Porter* by George Hendrick, 1965, revised edition, with Willene Hendrick, 1988; *Porter: The Regional Sources* by Winifred S. Emmons, 1967; *Porter: A Critical Symposium* edited by Lodwick Hartley and George Core, 1969; *Porter's Fiction* by M.M. Liberman, 1971; *Porter* by John Edward Hardy, 1973; *Porter: A Collection of Critical Essays* edited by Robert Penn Warren, 1979; *Porter: A Life* by Joan Givner, 1982, revised edition, 1991; *Porter's Women: The Eye of Her Fiction* by Jane Krause DeMouy, 1983; *Truth and Vision in Porter's Fiction,* 1985, and *Understanding Porter,* 1988, both by Darlene H. Unrue; *The Texas Legacy of Porter* by James T. Tanner, 1990; "The Ring or the Dove: The New Woman in Katherine Anne Porter's Fiction" by Esim Erdim, in *Women and War: The Changing Status of American Women from the 1930s to the 1950s* edited by Maria Diedrich and Dorothea Fischer-Hornung, 1990; *Strategies of Reticence: Silence and Meaning in the Works of Jane Austen, Willa Cather, Katherine Anne Porter, and Joan Didion* by Janis P. Stout, 1990; *Katherine Anne Porter and Texas: An Uneasy Relationship* edited by Clinton Machann and William Bedford Clark, 1990; "Katherine Anne Porter's Miranda: The Agrarian Myth and Southern Womanhood" by Mary Titus, in *Redefining Autobiography in Twentieth-Century Women's Fiction: An Essay Collection* edited by Janice Morgan, Colette T. Hall, and Carol L. Snyder, 1991; "The Louisiana's Katherine Anne Porter's Mind" by Merrill Skaggs, in *Louisiana Women Writers: New Essays and a Comprehensive Bibliography* edited by Dorothy H. Brown and Barbara C. Ewell, 1992; "Katherine Anne Porter and The Southern Review" by Darlene Harbour Unrue, in *'To Love So Well the World': A Festschrift in Honor of Robert Penn Warren* edited by Dennis L. Weeks, 1992; *Porter and Eliot: "Flowering Judas" and "Burbank-Bleistein"—Two Essays in Interpretation* by Thomas Meade Harwell, 1996; *Critical Essays on Katherine Anne Porter* edited by Darlene Harbour Unrue, 1997.

* * *

Katherine Anne Porter was probably the finest writer of short stories and novellas of her time in the United States. Her last work of fiction, *Ship of Fools,* suggests either that the novel as such was not her form or that the hatred and contempt aroused in her by German behavior under the Nazis had robbed her both of her usual skill and of her usual sense that life, in all its sadness and frustrations, is incurably poetic. Her collections of essays, *The Days Before,* however, is fascinating both in the excellence of its criticism and in the light it throws on her own work: "I am passionately involved with those individuals who populate all these enormous migrations, calamities, who fight wars and furnish life for the future." We see such an individual in Porter's own stories (in *The Leaning Tower,* for instance) as a quiet, imaginative, sad girl of old Southern family, aware of the past because of her grandmother and her old black servant, aware of the grotesque because of a visit to a circus whose clowns frighten her, and aware of death

and horror because of a brother who kills a pregnant rabbit and shows her the baby rabbits, who will now never be born in its womb. We see Miranda (in *Pale Horse, Pale Rider*) as a young girl who has married to flee from her family and yet in some ways is emotionally dried up. Other stories, like *Noon Wine,* evoke a sense of fatality, violence springing from heat and bewilderment.

Porter's great gift as a storyteller is to take material, particularly a wistfulness for the past, a sense of the strangeness, loneliness, cruelty, and treachery of life, the decay of love, or the failure to be able to love, and to avoid the twin temptations of treating this material with either sentimentality or a cheap cynicism. She evokes gravely and gracefully both the potential beauty and the bewildering lurking betrayal of life. Born in Texas in 1890, but maturing as a writer in the 1930s, she combined in an unusual way a solid sense of the past and the atmosphere of place with a fine sense of that ambivalence or complexity of attitude that we have in mind when we talk of "modernity" in fiction. Her proper readers will have the sense of reading in two ages at once, and of being presented with two possible standards of judgment, one the firm, exact, and unargued standard of the Old South, the other the modern standard that, more frighteningly, hands over the task of judgment to the reader.

—G.S. Fraser

See the essays on "Old Mortality" and *Ship of Fools.*

PORTILLO, Estela. *See* **PORTILLO TRAMBLEY, Estela.**

PORTILLO TRAMBLEY, Estela

Also referred to as Estela Portillo. **Born:** El Paso, Texas, 16 January 1936. **Education:** University of Texas, El Paso, B.A. 1957, M.A. 1977. **Family:** Married Robert D. Trambley in 1953; five daughters, one son. **Career:** Worked as a high school English teacher in El Paso, 1957-64; department chair, El Paso Technical Institute, 1965-69; resident dramatist, Community College, El Paso, 1970-75; affiliated with Department of Special Services, El Paso Public Schools, beginning 1977; hostess of "Estela Sez," talk show on Radio KIZZ, 1969-70, and "Cumbres," cultural television program on KROD-TV, 1971-72, both in El Paso. **Awards:** Quinto Sol award for literature, 1972; Outstanding Chicana award from the Bilingual League of the San Francisco Bay Area, 1973; first prize, Second Annual Women's Plays competition, 1984, for *Puente Negro* ("Black Bridge"); second prize, New York Shakespeare Festival's Hispanic American Playwright's competition, 1985, for *Blacklight.*

PUBLICATIONS

Novels

Trini. 1986.

Short Stories

Rain of Scorpions and Other Writings. 1976.

Poetry

Impressions. 1972.

Plays

The Day of the Swallows. 1971.
Morality Play (musical; produced 1974).
We Are Chicano, with others. 1974.
Blacklight (produced 1975, 1985).
El Hombre Cosmico (The Cosmic Man) (produced 1975).
Sun Images (musical; produced 1976).
Isabel and the Dancing Bear (produced 1977).
Sor Juana and Other Plays. 1983.
Puente Negro (Black Bridge) (produced 1984).

Radio Play: *The Burning* (produced 1983).

*

Critical Studies: Interview with Juan Bruce-Novoa in *Chicano Authors: Inquiry by Interview,* 1980; *Mexican American Biographies: A Historical Dictionary, 1836-1987* by Matt S. Meier, 1988; *Breaking Boundaries: Latina Writings and Critical Readings* by Asuncion Horno-Delgado, Eliana Ortega, Nina M. Scott, and Nancy Saporta Sternbach, 1989; *The Chicana Female Hero and the Search for Paradise: Estela Portillo-Trambley's Archetypal Discourse on Liberation* (dissertation) by George D. Eagar, 1996.

*   *   *

Estela Portillo Trambley was the first Chicana to be published during the Chicano/Chicana Renaissance, a social, cultural, and political movement that flowered during the late 1960s and the 1970s. The creative energies of resistance and celebration typified by this movement and the Chicana feminist movement that evolved from it find fictional expression in the many dramatic, poetic, and prose works of Portillo Trambley. She imaginatively explores and elaborates socio-political, psychological, emotional, and natural environments to liberate her protagonists from stifling conventions. By doing so she artistically undermines the poisonous effects of oppression on the human spirit, identity, and self will. Portillo Trambley grew up poor and surrounded by poverty, and relates to Juan Bruce-Novoa in *Chicano Authors: Inquiry by Interview* that "I am still poor, pero la pobreza nunca derriba el espíritu [but poverty never defeats spirit] . . . . A common suffering is a richness in itself." Commenting in this same interview on the Chicano humanism of her writings, she asserts: "There are so many features of the Chicano experience that are 100 percent eternal, that any people in the world can identify with. The strengths, our hopes, our family structure, our capacity to love, all the results of the closure of our society and what it has made us. This vital and human experience could actually find readers, aside from the Americans, readers in Italy, Spain . . . because it is a universal one. They have all been through the same thing historically."

The grandmother protagonist in her short story "The Paris Gown" illuminates for her admiring granddaughter the necessity of creating an autonomous and original Self, one that depends and survives on the aesthetic beauty reflected in art and life as much as it does on the creative capacity of personal design. Grandmother relates the story of her scrupulously planned escape to Paris from her Mexican father's arranged marriage. Unable to squelch his own desires for her future, she luxuriates in the exquisite fashioning of a gown she orders from Paris. But when the moment arrives for her engagement ball debut, she appears and descends the staircase un-gowned—stark naked—thus compelling her father to eventually send her away. This shocking, humorous, and vengeful act allows her "a kind of insanity finding its own method to fight what I considered a slavery."

Myth, magic, and ritual often course throughout her dialogues and narratives, fusing an ancient past with contemporary worlds. The inevitability of sacrifice, like that performed in Aztec culture in order to give life and movement to the cosmos, appears frequently in her work. In her story "The Burning," a woman healer, believed to be a witch, is burned at the stake while already dying of a high fever. In another, "The Apple Trees," a woman commits suicide after transforming herself into a power-hungry capitalist unsuitable to her family. Her play *The Day of the Swallows* pushes the mythical and ritualized timelessness of the village of San Lorenzo into horrifying and complex time-bound tragedies. Upon curtain's rising the loving and charitable main character, Dona Josefa, has cut out the tongue of a young boy who has witnessed her making love to her female companion. This act of violence silences the boy's act of witness, and situates Josefa's lesbian love defiantly outside the bounds of social codes rigorously programmed and enforced. She must also sacrificially commit suicide by play's end, but not without commentary on the multiple dramatic meanings of stasis, violence, and self-death.

—Janice L. Dewey

POUND, Ezra (Weston Loomis)

Born: Hailey, Idaho, 30 October 1885. **Education:** Chelten Hills School, Cheltenham Military Academy, and Cheltenham Township High School, all Philadelphia; University of Pennsylvania, Philadelphia, 1901-03 and 1907-08, M.A. in Romance languages 1906; Hamilton College, Clinton, New York, 1903-05, Ph.B. 1905. **Family:** Married Dorothy Shakespear in 1914; one daughter (by Mary Rudge) and one son. **Career:** Traveled in Spain, Italy, and France, 1906-07; member of the Department of Romance Languages, Wabash College, Crawfordsville, Indiana, 1907; lived in Venice, 1908, London, 1908-21, Paris, 1921-24, and Rapallo, Italy, 1924-46; regular reviewer, *New Age,* London, from 1911; English editor, *Poetry,* Chicago, 1912-19; literary editor, *New Freewoman* (later *The Egoist*), London, 1913-14; founder, with Wyndham Lewis, *Blast,* London, 1914; English editor, *Little Review,* 1917-19; drama and ballet critic, *Athenaeum,* London, 1920; Paris correspondent, *The Dial,* 1920-23; founding editor, *The Exile,* 1927-28; contributor, *Il Mare,* Rapallo, 1932-40, and *New English Weekly,* London, 1932-35; promoted "social credit" economic theories from late 1920s; met Mussolini, 1933, and visited his Salo Republic, 1943; broadcast over Rome Radio from 1940, and was arrested and jailed for these broadcasts by the U.S. Army, 1945; imprisoned near Pisa, found unfit to stand trial for treason, and committed to St. Elizabeths Hospital, Washington, D.C., 1946-58; returned to Italy, and lived mainly in Venice, 1958-72. **Awards:** Bollingen prize, 1949; Harriet Monroe award, 1962; Academy of American Poets fellowship, 1963; National Endowment for the Arts grant, 1966. Honorary degree: Hamilton College, 1939. **Died:** 1 November 1972.

PUBLICATIONS

Collections

Selected Prose 1909-1965, edited by William Cookson. 1973.
Selected Poems 1908-1959. 1975.
Early Poems. 1996.

Poetry

A Lume Spento. 1908.
A Quinzaine for This Yule. 1908.
Personae. 1909.
Exultations. 1909.
Provenca: Poems Selected from Personae, Exultations, and Canzoniere. 1910.
Canzoni. 1911.
Ripostes. 1912.
Lustra. 1916.
Lustra, with earlier poems. 1917.
The Fourth Canto. 1919.
Quia Pauper Amavi. 1919.
Hugh Selwyn Mauberley. 1920.
Umbra: The Early Poems. 1920.
Poems, 1918-21, Including Three Portraits and Four Cantos. 1921.
A Draft of XVI Cantos. 1925.
Personae: The Collected Poems. 1926; revised edition, 1949; as *Personae: Collected Shorter Poems,* 1952; as *Collected Shorter Poems,* 1968.
A Draft of the Cantos 17-27. 1928.
Selected Poems, edited by T.S. Eliot. 1928.
A Draft of XXX Cantos. 1930.
Eleven New Cantos: XXXI-XLI. 1934; as *A Draft of Cantos XXXI-XLI,* 1935.
Homage to Sextus Propertius. 1934.
Alfred Venison's Poems, Social Credit Themes. 1935.
The Fifth Decade of Cantos. 1937.
Cantos LII-LXXI. 1940.
A Selection of Poems. 1940.
The Pisan Cantos. 1948.
The Cantos. 1948; revised edition, 1965; revised edition, as *Cantos No. 1-117, 120,* 1970.
Selected Poems. 1949.
Seventy Cantos. 1950; revised edition, as *The Cantos,* 1954, 1964, 1976.
Section: Rock-Drill: 86-95 de los cantares. 1955.
Thrones: 96-109 de los cantares. 1959.
Versi prosaici. 1959.
A Lume Spento and Other Early Poems. 1965.
Canto CX. 1965.
Selected Cantos. 1967; revised edition, 1970.
Cantos, 110-116. 1967.
Drafts and Fragments of Cantos CX-CXVII. 1969.
Collected Early Poems, edited by Michael John King. 1976.

Other

The Spirit of Romance. 1910; revised edition, 1953.
Gaudier-Brzeska: A Memoir. 1916; revised edition, 1960.

"Noh" or Accomplishment: A Study of the Classical Stage of Japan, with Ernest Fenollosa. 1917; as *The Classical Noh Theatre of Japan.* 1959.
Pavannes and Divisions. 1918.
Instigations. 1920.
Indiscretions; or, Une Revue de Deux Mondes. 1923.
Antheil, and The Treatise on Harmony. 1924.
Imaginary Letters. 1930.
How to Read. 1931.
ABC of Economics. 1933.
ABC of Reading. 1934.
Make It New: Essays. 1934.
Social Credit: An Impact. 1935.
Jefferson and/or Mussolini. 1935; revised edition, as *Jefferson e Mussolini,* 1944.
Polite Essays. 1937.
Guide to Kulchur. 1938; as *Culture,* 1938.
What Is Money For? 1939.
Carta da visita. 1942; translated by John Drummond, as *A Visiting Card,* 1952.
L'America, Roosevelt, e le cause della guerra presente. 1944; translated by John Drummond, as *America, Roosevelt, and the Causes of the Present War,* 1951.
Oro e lavoro. 1944; translated by John Drummond, as *Gold and Labour,* 1952.
Introduzione alla natura economica degli S.U.A. 1944; translated by Carmine Amore, as *An Introduction to the Economic Nature of the United States,* 1950. *Orientamenti.* 1944.
If This Be Treason. 1948.
Patria Mia. 1950; with *The Treatise on Harmony,* 1962.
The Letters of Pound 1907-1941, edited by D.D. Paige. 1950.
The Translations of Pound. 1953; revised edition, 1970.
Secondo biglietto da visita. 1953.
Literary Essays, edited by T.S. Eliot. 1954.
Lavoro ed usura. 1954.
Pavannes and Divagations. 1958.
Impact: Essays on Ignorance and the Decline of American Civilization, edited by Noel Stock. 1960.
Nuova economia editoriale. 1962.
EP to LU: Nine Letters Written to Louis Untermeyer, edited by J. Albert Robbins. 1963.
Etre Citoyen Romain. 1965.
Pound/Joyce: The Letters of Pound to James Joyce, edited by Forrest Read. 1967.
The Caged Panther: Pound at St. Elizabeths (includes 53 letters), by Harry M. Meachum. 1967.
Rondondillas; or, Something of That Sort. 1968.
Dk: Some Letters of Pound, edited by Louis Dudek. 1975.
Certain Radio Speeches of Pound: From the Recordings and Transcriptions of His Wartime Broadcasts, Rome 1941-1943, edited by William Levy. 1975.
Sulla moneta. 1977.
Pound and Music: The Complete Criticism, edited by R. Murray Schaefer. 1977.
Pound Speaking: Radio Speeches of World War II, edited by Leonard W. Doob. 1978.
Letters to Ibbotson 1935-1952 (letters to Joseph Darling Ibbotson), edited by Vittoria I. Mondolfo and Margaret Hurley. 1979.
Pound and the Visual Arts, edited by Harriet Zinnes. 1980.
Lettere 1907-1958, edited by Aldo Tagliaferri. 1980.

From Syria: The Worksheets, Proofs, and Text, edited by Robin Skelton. 1981.

Pound's Cavalcanti: An Edition of the Translations, Notes and Essays, edited by David Anderson. 1982.

Pound/Ford: The Story of a Literary Friendship (letters to Ford Madox Ford), edited by Brita Lindberg-Seyersted. 1982.

Letters to John Theobald, edited by Donald Pearce and Herbert Schneidau. 1984.

Pound and Dorothy Shakespear: Their Letters 1909-1914, edited by Omar Pound and A. Walton Litz. 1985.

Pound/Lewis: The Letters of Pound and Wyndham Lewis, edited by Timothy Materer. 1985.

Letters to Tom Carter, edited by Andrew Kappel. 1985.

Pound and Japan, edited by Sanehide Kodama. 1986.

Burgos: A Dream City of Old Castile: An Early Travel Essay. 1994.

The Sayings of Ezra Pound. 1994.

Ezra Pound and James Laughlin: Selected Letters. 1994.

Ezra Pound and Senator Bronson Cutting—A Political Correspondence, 1930-1935. 1995.

"Dear Uncle George": The Correspondence between Ezra Pound and Congressman Tinkham of Massachusetts. 1996.

Machine Art and Other Writings: The Lost Thought of the Italian Years—Essays. 1996.

Pound/cummings: The Correspondence of Ezra Pound and e.e. cummings. 1996.

"I Cease Not to Yowl": Ezra Pound's Letters to Olivia Rossetti Agresti. 1998.

Ezra and Dorothy Pound: Letters in Captivity, 1945-1946. 1998.

Editor, *Des Imagistes: An Anthology.* 1914.

Editor, *Poetical Works of Lionel Johnson.* 1915.

Editor, *Catholic Anthology 1914-1915.* 1915.

Editor, *Passages from the Letters of John Butler Yeats.* 1917.

Editor, *Rime,* by Guido Cavalcanti. 1932.

Editor, *Profile: An Anthology.* 1932.

Editor, *Active Anthology.* 1933.

Editor, *The Chinese Written Character as a Medium for Poetry: An Ars Poetica,* by Ernest Fenollosa. 1936.

Editor, *De Moribus Brachmanorum, Liber Sancto Ambrosio Falso Adscriptus.* 1956.

Editor, with Marcella Spann, *Confucius to Cummings.* 1964.

Translator, *The Sonnets and Ballate of Guido Cavalcanti.* 1912; as *Pound's Cavalcanti Poems,* 1966.

Translator, *Cathay: Translations.* 1915.

Translator, with Ernest Fenollosa, *Certain Noble Plays of Japan.* 1916.

Translator, *Dialogues of Fontenelle.* 1917.

Translator, *The Natural Philosophy of Love,* by Remy de Gourmont. 1922.

Translator, *The Call of the Road,* by Edouard Estaunie. 1923.

Translator, *Ta Hio: The Great Learning,* by Confucius. 1928.

Translator, *Digest of the Analects,* by Confucius. 1937.

Translator, *Italy's Policy of Social Economics 1939-1940,* by Odon Por. 1941.

Translator, with Alberto Luchini, *Ta S'en Dai Gaku, Studio Integrale,* by Confucius. 1942.

Translator, *Ciung Iung, l'Asse che non vacilla,* by Confucius. 1945.

Translator, *The Unwobbling Pivot and The Great Digest,* by Confucius. 1947.

Translator, *Confucian Analects.* 1951.

Translator, *The Classic Anthology Defined by Confucius.* 1954; as *Shih-ching,* 1976.

Translator, *Moscardino,* by Enrico Pea. 1956.

Translator, *Women of Trachis,* by Sophocles. 1956.

Translator, *Rimbaud* (5 poems). 1957.

Translator, with Noel Stock, *Love Poems of Ancient Egypt.* 1962.

Translator, *Fancy Goods, and Open All Night,* by Paul Morand, edited by Breon Mitchell. 1984.

*

Bibliography: *Pound: A Bibliography* by Donald Gallup, 1983.

Critical Studies: *Pound: His Metric and Poetry* by T.S. Eliot, 1918; *Poetry and Opinion: The Pisan Cantos of Pound: A Dialog on the Role of Poetry* by Archibald MacLeish, 1950; *Pound: A Collection of Essays* edited by Peter Russell, 1950, as *An Examination of Pound,* 1950; *The Poetry of Pound,* 1951, and *The Pound Era,* 1971, both by Hugh Kenner; *Pound and the Cantos* by Harold H. Watts, 1952; *Motive and Method in the Cantos of Pound* edited by Lewis Leary, 1954; *A Primer of Pound* by M.L. Rosenthal, 1960; *Pound* by G.S. Fraser, 1960; *Pound* by Charles Norman, 1960, revised edition, 1969; *The Confucian Odes of Pound: A Critical Appraisal* by L.S. Dembo, 1963; *Pound: Poet as Sculptor,* 1964, and *Pound,* 1975, both by Donald Davie; *Pound's Poetics and Literary Tradition* by N. Christoph De Nagy, 1966; *The Influence of Pound* by K.L. Goodwin, 1966; *The Rose in the Steel Dust: An Examination of the Cantos of Pound* by Walter Baumann, 1967; *The Early Poetry of Pound* by Thomas H. Jackson, 1968; *The Poetry of Pound: Forms and Renewal 1908-1920* by Hugh Witemeyer, 1969; *New Approaches to Pound* edited by Eva Hesse, 1969; *The Barb of Time: On the Unity of Pound's Cantos* by Daniel Pearlman, 1969; *The Life of Pound* by Noel Stock, 1970, revised edition, 1982; *A ZBC of Pound* by Christine Brooke-Rose, 1971; *Pound* by Jeannette Lender, 1971; *Discretions* by Mary de Rachewiltz, 1971; *Pound and the Troubadour Tradition* by Stuart McDougal, 1972; *Pound: The Critical Heritage* edited by Eric Homberger, 1972; *Pound: An Introduction to the Poetry* by Bernetta Quinn, 1973; *Pound: A Collection of Critical Essays* edited by Grace Schulman, 1974; *Pound, The Last Rower: A Political Profile* by C. David Heymann, 1976; *The Genesis of Pound's Cantos* by Ronald Bush, 1976; *Time in Pound's Work* by William Harmon, 1977; *The Later Cantos of Pound,* 1977, and *The American Roots of Pound,* 1985, both by James J. Wilhelm; *Pound* by James F. Knapp, 1979; *Pound's Cantos: The Story of the Text* by Barbara Eastman, 1979; *A Student's Guide to the Selected Poems of Pound* by Peter Brooker, 1979; *End to Torment: A Memoir of Pound* by H.D., edited by Norman Holmes Pearson and Michael King, 1979 (includes poems by Pound); *The Poetic Achievement of Pound* by M.J. Alexander, 1979; *A Light from Eleusis: A Study of Pound's Cantos* by Leon Surette, 1979; *Pound and the Cantos: A Record of Struggle* by Wendy Stallard Flory, 1980; *A Companion to the Cantos of Pound* by Carroll F. Terrell, 2 vols., 1980-85; *The Formed Trace: The Later Poetry of Pound* by Massimo Bacigalupo, 1980; *The Tale of the Tribe: Pound and the Modern Verse Epic* by Michael Andy Bernstein, 1980; *Pound and the Pisan Cantos* by Anthony Woodward, 1980; *Pound and His World* by Peter Ackroyd, 1981; *Critic as Scientist: The Modernist Poetics of Pound* by Ian Bell, 1981, and *Pound: Tactics for Reading* edited by Bell, 1982; *Pound and William Carlos Williams* edited by

Daniel Hoffman, 1983; *A Guide to Pound's Selected Poems,* 1983, and *To Write Paradise: Style and Error in Pound's Cantos,* 1985, both by Christine Froula; *Cities on Hills: A Study of I-XXX of Pound's Cantos* by Guy Davenport, 1983; *The Roots of Treason: Pound and the Secret of St. Elizabeths* by E. Fuller Torrey, 1984; *Pound: The Prime Minister of Poetry* by Burton Raffel, 1984; *Pound and History* by Marianne Korn, 1985; *Pound's Cantos* by Peter Makin, 1985; *A Guide to the Cantos of Pound* by William Cookson, 1985; *Pound* by P.N. Furbank, 1985; *The Modernism of Pound: The Science of Poetry* by Martin Kayman, 1986; *Ezra Pound Criticism, 1905-1985: A Chronological Listing of Publications in English* edited by Volker Bischoff, 1991; *Pound's Epic Ambition: Dante and the Modern World* by Stephen Sicari, 1991; *The Political Aesthetic of Yeats, Eliot, and Pound* by Michael North, 1991; *Studies in Ezra Pound* by Donald Davie, 1991; "Ezra Pound and the Visual: Notations for New Subjects in The Cantos" by Norman Wacker, in *Image and Ideology in Modern/Postmodern Discourse* edited by David B. Downing and Susan Bazargan, 1991; "Excavating the Ideological Faultlines of Modernism: Editing Ezra Pound's Cantos" by Ronald Bush, in *Representing Modernist Texts: Editing As Interpretation* edited by George Bornstein, 1991; "Kenneth Patchen: Letter about Ezra Pound, 1946" by Larry Smith, in *The Epistolary Form and the Letter as Artifact* edited by Jim Villani, 1991; "Fascists of the Final Hour: Pound's Italian Cantos" by Robert Casillo in *Fascism, Aesthetics, and Culture* edited by Richard J. Golsan, 1992; *Ezra Pound* by Hand Christian Kirsch, 1992; *ABC of Influence: Ezra Pound and the Remaking of American Poetic Tradition* by Christopher Beach, 1992; *A Calculus of Ezra Pound: Vocations of the American Sign* by Philip Kuberski, 1992; *A Walking Tour in Southern France: Ezra Pound among the Troubadours* edited by Richard Sieburth, 1992; *Ezra Pound and America* edited by Jacqueline Kaye, 1992; *Ezra Pound As Critic* by G. Singh, 1994; *Ezra Pound's Epic Variations: The Cantos and the Major Long Poems* by Terri Brint Joseph, 1995; *Epic Reinvented: Ezra Pound and the Victorians* by Mary Ellis Gibson, 1995; *Ezra Pound, Popular Genres, and the Discourse of Culture* by Michael Coyle, 1995; *A New Approach to the Poetry of Ezra Pound: Through the Medieval Provencal Aspect* by Helen May Dennis, 1996; *Ezra Pound and China* by John J. Nolde, 1996; *Ezra Pound's Early Poetry and Poetics* by Thomas F. Grieve, 1997; *Ezra Pound and the Appropriation of Chinese Poetry: Cathay, Translation, and Imagism* by Ming Hsieh, 1998; *Consumption and Depression in Gertrude Stein, Louis Zukofsky, and Ezra Pound* by Luke Carson, 1998; *The Cambridge Companion to Ezra Pound* edited by Ira Bruce Nadel, 1998.

*   *   *

Ezra Pound is conventionally regarded as one of the fathers of modernism, the man who discovered **T.S. Eliot** and James Joyce and got them into print, and was in the vanguard of the modernist movement with his own poetic experiments before 1914, and his *Cantos* in the years following World War I. The reality was somewhat different. Pound was first and foremost a showman, an impresario who was expert (in his early years) at managing his own performance and that of his contemporaries. He championed and promoted modernism because it was the current movement, rather than because he had any deep-rooted modernist inclinations. Later he got bored with it, turned to an eccentric branch of economics, and drifted into political propaganda. In most people's eyes, he made a fool of himself in so doing; but at least he retained public attention until the end of his life, and this is probably what he wanted most of all.

He was descended from two old-established American families who had come down in the world. Brought up in a suburb of Philadelphia and educated at the University of Pennsylvania and at Hamilton College, he displayed no marked talent at anything except self-advertisement until, having failed to hold down a teaching job in a small Midwestern college, he departed precipitously for Europe in the spring of 1908, aged 22. During a summer in Venice he had his first book of poems, *A Lume Spento,* printed privately, and then set off for London, where he managed to attract the sympathetic notice of various figures in the British literary establishment, including W.B. Yeats. Only a matter of months after his arrival, *Punch* was guying him jocularly, and many reviewers felt they could perceive that an important new voice in poetry had arrived.

His early poems did have a lot of life in them, but it was the vigor of an antiquarian, an enthusiastic literary historian, rather than of a poet writing from personal experience and feeling. His first major passion was for the medieval French troubadours, and he wrote in what he believed to be their manner, though it usually came out as Pre-Raphaelite pastiche. Now and then he achieved a brilliant little poem of his own, such as "Portrait d'une Femme," or "The Return" (1912), which Yeats thought was the most accomplished piece of *vers libre* written to that date. But he made more splash as the leader of a new poetic movement, Imagism (typically, he invented the name before he knew what it really meant); and arguably he achieved more by championing the causes of others—James Joyce, the sculptor Gaudier-Brzeska, Wyndham Lewis, and the young T.S. Eliot—than in his own writing. His best work before 1920 did include the brilliant little *Cathay,* a set of loose translations from the Chinese, but his ambitious *Homage to Sextus Propertius* was widely pilloried for its erroneous renderings from the Latin (though it is a fine poem in itself), and his mannered, obscure *Hugh Selwyn Mauberley* is metrically brilliant but scarcely manages to communicate more than a set of nuances.

Pound's rebarbative character soon alienated him from London's editors and publishers, and by the end of 1920 he decided, with his English wife Dorothy, to abandon the British capital for the Continent, taking with him the beginnings of an "endless poem" that was to be all about everything, the *Cantos.* It emerged into print, section by section, from 1925 until the end of his life, eventually numbering somewhat over a hundred cantos (a precise figure cannot be given as it ends in fragments). The *Cantos* contain many passages of beauty, but only Pound's most convinced admirers can manage to persuade themselves that the work possesses any real structure, or is more than a fairly random set of statements about what happened to be interesting its author at a particular moment—subjects ranging from ancient Chinese history to American presidents and contemporary economic theory. Unfortunately, Pound chose to write no other form of poetry once he had begun the *Cantos,* burying his tremendous lyric gift (**William Carlos Williams** said his was the finest ear ever born to listen to language) beneath a mass of redundant, irrelevant detail.

Immensely long as the work is, the *Cantos* only represents a comparatively small part of Pound's literary output from the 1920s onwards. Towards the end of that decade, he became obsessed with the eccentric economic theories of one Major C. H. Douglas, and devoted most of the 1930s to evangelizing Douglas's doctrine of "Social Credit"—which few people have clearly understood, and of which (it may be suspected) Pound himself had only a shaky grasp. At times he seemed to have grown bored with literary activities. At other moments he would rush into print, in such books as *ABC of Reading* and *Guide to Kulchur,* telling the world what it should read and think—usually basing his instructions on an alarmingly narrow and esoteric range of ideas; he rejected most major poets (Shakespeare, Milton, Wordsworth, to name a few), exhorted his readers to study Confucius, and praised such obscure thinkers as Leo Frobenius (a German anthropologist) and Sylvio Gesell (another unorthodox economist). Much of *Guide to Kulchur* is devoted to proving that Aristotle's ethics are rubbish.

By the mid-1930s Pound had become an admirer of Mussolini (though he scarcely had any idea what Fascism meant), and he began to indulge in anti-Semitism, first in private letters, and then more openly in the newspaper columns of the British Union of Fascists. He was now living in Italy—Paris, his first Continental port of call, had proved as disappointing as London, and he shifted to Rapallo—and when war broke out he was content to remain behind enemy lines, and broadcast on the "American Hour" of the official Fascist radio. His radio talks were eccentric explosions of rage against Roosevelt, for being supposedly duped into a meaningless war; the real war, said Pound, was against the "usurers." The broadcasts were often—intentionally—comic; he read his scripts in a variety of exaggerated American crackerbarrel accents, and one might argue that there is more poetry in his performance at the microphone than in many stretches of the *Cantos.* But the American government did not take kindly to it, and when Italy was liberated in May 1945 Pound found himself under interrogation, on a treason charge. He was confined for several weeks in a cage in the open air, an experience that prompted the writing of *The Pisan Cantos* (his detention camp was at Pisa), the only section of the work in which personal experience and feeling is allowed to penetrate and bring to life the jumbled fragments in Pound's storehouse of literary memory.

His trial (in Washington, DC) was abandoned when a jury found him insane, a judgment that took no account of the fact that his behavior at the microphone was no different from how he had always behaved; he was no more (or less) insane in 1945 than he had been in 1908. But he was incarcerated in a federal mental asylum (St. Elizabeths Hospital, Washington), and it took his friends and supporters more than twelve years to get him out. During his internment he worked at two further sections of the *Cantos,* but failed to bring the enterprise towards any sort of conclusion; and when he left St. Elizabeths in 1958 and returned to Italy he began to suffer severe depression. Eventually, after bouts of illness, he sank into near silence—though typically he made himself the center of attention by so doing.

Terms like "flawed" or "patchy" are totally inadequate for the whole body of Pound's poetry. It is scarcely credible that the man who wrote *Cathay* could descend to some of the near-meaningless jumble of the John Adams Cantos (written at the end of the 1930s); and all through his oeuvre there are indications of laziness and total disregard for normal standards. Yet at his best, there is no one better. His good work has probably been more influential than Eliot's, for (as Yeats said) he was the first person in English to make free verse sound natural. But it is unwise to take him seriously (as some critics have done, at enormous length); rather, one should relish the whole absurd variety of the man and his work, and wonder at the spectacle of such a talented poet becoming bored, so quickly, with his own talent, and choosing instead

to be what Dudley Fitts called "the bad boy, strutting and shocking."

—Humphrey Carpenter

See the essay on the *Cantos.*

POWERS, J(ames) F(arl)

Born: Jacksonville, Illinois, 8 July 1917. **Education:** Quincy College Academy, Illinois; Northwestern University, Chicago campus, 1938-40. **Family:** Married Betty Wahl in 1946; three daughters and two sons. **Career:** Worked in Chicago, 1935-41; editor, Illinois Historical Records Survey, 1938; hospital orderly during World War II; teacher at St. John's University, Collegeville, Minnesota, 1947 and after 1975, Marquette University, Milwaukee, 1949-51, and University of Michigan, Ann Arbor, 1956-57. Writer-in-Residence, Smith College, Northampton, Massachusetts, 1965-66. **Awards:** American Academy grant, 1948; Guggenheim fellowship, 1948; Rockefeller fellowship, 1954, 1957, 1967; National Book award, 1963. **Member:** American Academy.

PUBLICATIONS

Fiction

Prince of Darkness and Other Stories. 1947.
The Presence of Grace (stories). 1956.
Morte d'Urban. 1962.
Look How the Fish Live (stories). 1975.
Wheat That Springeth Green. 1988.

*

Critical Studies: *Powers* by John F. Hagopian, 1968; *Powers* edited by Fallon Evans, 1968; "The Second Coming of J. F. Powers" by Carol Iannone in *Commentary,* January 1989.

*   *   *

J.F. Powers was frustrated trying to find work in Chicago during the Depression years 1935 through 1941. In the early years of World War II he met many social rebels in Chicago—workers, blacks, and European exiles—and became a pacifist: he was appalled equally by the destructive war and patriotic propaganda. His pacifism led him to the Catholic Church. Early in 1943 he was the only lay person to attend a priests' retreat at St. John's Abbey in Collegeville, Minnesota. Following a period of reading and introspection Powers wrote the story "Lions, Harts, Leaping Does," in which Father Didymus attains true holiness as he dies, holding to his faith along with a strong sense of unworthiness. Since this initial effort, Powers's work has continued to reflect his Catholic faith.

In *Prince of Darkness and Other Stories,* the best pieces have priest protagonists: the title story, "The Forks," "The Valiant Woman," and "Lions, Harts, Leaping Does." Among the eleven stories are three bitter tales about the plight of Chicago blacks; "Jamesie," a story of adolescence that is probably autobiographical; and "Renner," a story of anti-semitism. The critical reception of Powers's stories—especially among his fellow writers—was impressive. *The Presence of Grace* has nine stories, all but two of them about priests. The prevailing mood is mellow in these stories, and some reviewers found his clerical scenes deplorably picturesque instead of astringent.

Except for the story of Father Didymus, Powers used both humor and irony to expose priestly venality in his earlier stories: they reveal the dark side of "the endless struggle between religious idealism and selfish, worldly interests." Wit and subtle irony are still at work on priestly foibles in the nine stories of *The Presence of Grace,* but the absurdities seem less vicious and more forgivable. "Zeal" is a fair example: obtuse and bungling Father Early provokes his sophisticated bishop into a redeeming examination of his own soul.

Although mistakenly labelled a writer of Catholic stories, Powers tried to place his work above and in opposition to religion. As John Hagopian points out in his 1968 study, *Powers,* the writer was hopelessly trying to correct the false impression of his work as being predominantly religious. "Out of parochial materials he shapes subtle but highly charged human situations that capture the moral and emotional texture of modern life," notes Hagopian.

Powers has published only one novel, *Morte d'Urban,* which grew out of a short story he had begun fifteen years earlier. In "The Devil Was the Joker," the Order of St. Clement is a central concern; and some minor figures in the novel—Father Udovic, Monsignor Renton, and their Bishop—are the chief characters in "Dawn." For his novel Powers sets up two Minnesota dioceses, Great Plains and Ostergothenburg. Powers's own words best describe his intention: "The story is about Father Urban being sent to this foundation of the Order (Clementines) in Minnesota. He had been a big-time speaker, a poor man's Fulton Sheen. He was suddenly sent up here to this white elephant . . . as one of the boys . . . . That's my story . . . how he tried to put the place on its feet . . . . I thought it would be a nice little nut-brown novel, all kinds of irony." Though the critics reviewed *Morte d'Urban* favorably, most of them missed some levels of irony and even misinterpreted the point. Perhaps because parts of the novel had appeared in journals and Powers had an impressive reputation as a writer of short stories, many reviewers found *Morte d'Urban* episodic and lacking in unity as a novel. Powers's ironic unifying devices were possibly too subtle.

Look How the Fish Live is uneven: half of the stories are clearly below Powers's usual high quality. Several of these inferior pieces, including the title story and "Tinkers," are new in subject matter and technique; but they fall far short of five stories in this collection that match Powers's best. These are stories of young, emancipated curates devoted to their creature comforts and with callow notions of how the Church should modernize; middle-aged priestly operators who specialize in efficiency, public relations, and good housekeeping; and elderly priests and dying bishops who clearly belong to another era but survive preposterously and precariously in an alien world. Through the agency of such Roman Catholic clerics, Powers views the modern world humorously and seriously at the same time—but always ironically.

Powers has always been a painstaking writer, and critics often praised his technical expertise, his skill at rendering Midwestern dialects, and the authentic quality to his dialogue. The brilliant satire and subtle humor of *Morte d'Urban* have been recognized—though not widely enough; and Powers's use of the Arthurian matter has been variously interpreted and assessed. But one aspect of this and other Powers fiction has not been properly appreciated, perhaps because his Roman Catholic subject matter is probed so deeply and detailed so accurately. He uses the dilemma of Roman Catholicism in the middle years of the twentieth century to dramatize the impact of rampant materialism on a society trying to save—or find—its soul and sanity.

With a career begun in anger, Powers's evolution as a writer is rather surprising. His feelings of anger and initial perceptions of the world changed, and the frustration turned into the ability to see the comic side of life. Powers's irony is a benign one, however. His characters, although able to laugh at their own fate, will not forget a lifetime of humiliation.

—Clarence A. Glasrud, updated by Dayana Stetco

PURDY, James (Amos)

Born: Ohio, 17 July 1923. **Education:** University of Chicago, University of Madrid, and University of Puebla, Mexico. **Career:** Faculty member, Lawrence College (now University), Appleton, Wisconsin, 1949-53; interpreter in Latin America, France, and Spain; editor in Spain; United States Information Agency lecturer in Europe, 1982; taught fiction writing at New York University in 1980s. **Awards:** National Institute of Arts and Letters grant in literature, 1958; Guggenheim fellowship, 1958, 1962; Ford Foundation grant, 1961; PEN-Faulkner award nomination, 1985; Rockefeller Foundation grant; Morton Dauwen fiction award, American Academy of Arts and Letters, 1993; Oscar Willimas/Gene Durwood award, 1997. **Residence:** Brooklyn, New York.

PUBLICATIONS

Fiction

Don't Call Me By My Right Name and Other Stories. 1956; included in *63: Dream Palace: A Novella and Nine Stories,* 1957.
63: Dream Palace. 1956; as *63: Dream Palace: A Novella and Nine Stories,* 1957; uncensored edition with preface by Edith Sitwell, 1961.
Color of Darkness. 1956; as *Color of Darkness: Eleven Stories and a Novella,* 1957; with *Malcolm* and introduction by Tony Tanner as *Color of Darkness [and] Malcolm,* 1974; original edition reissued with foreword by Edward Albee as *63: Dream Palace and Other Stories,* 1981.
Malcolm. 1959; with foreword by Edward Albee, 1980.
The Nephew. 1960; 1961; with foreword by Edward Albee, 1980.
Children Is All (stories and plays). 1962.
Cabot Wright Begins. 1964.
Eustace Chisholm and the Works. 1967.
An Oyster Is a Wealthy Beast (story and poems). 1967.
Mr. Evening: A Story and Nine Poems. 1968.
On the Rebound: A Story and Nine Poems. 1970.
"Sleepers in Moon-Crowned Valleys" series:
    Jeremy's Version. 1970.
    The House of the Solitary Maggot. 1974.
I Am Elijah Thrush. 1972; with introduction by Paul Binding, 1986.

In a Shallow Grave, introduction by Jerome Charyn. 1976.
A Day after the Fair: A Collection of Plays and Short Stories. 1977.
Narrow Rooms. 1978.
Lessons and Complaints. 1978.
Sleep Tight. 1979.
Dream Palaces: Three Novels (contains *Malcolm, The Nephew,* and *63: Dream Palace*). 1980.
Mourners Below. 1981; 1984.
On Glory's Course. 1984.
The Candles of Your Eyes, illustrations by Ed Colker. 1985; as *The Candles of Your Eyes and Thirteen Other Stories,* 1987.
In the Hollow of His Hand. 1986.
The Candles of Your Eyes and Thirteen Other Stories. 1987.
Garments the Living Wear. 1989.
63: Dream Palace; Selected Stories, 1956-1987. 1991.
Out with the Stars. 1993.
Gertrude of Stony Island Avenue. 1997.
Epistles of Care, 1995.

Recordings: *Eventide and Other Stories,* Spoken Arts, 1968; *63: Dream Palace,* Spoken Arts, 1969.

Poetry

The Running Sun. 1971.
Sunshine Is an Only Child. 1973.
I Will Arrest the Bird That Has No Light. 1978.
Lessons and Complaints. 1978.
Don't Let the Snow Fall: A Poem; Dawn: A Story. 1984.
The Brooklyn Branding Parlors, edited by Josh Gosciak and Maurice Kenny, illustrated by Vassilis Vogils. 1986.
Are You in the Winter Tree? 1987.
Collected Poems. 1990.
Forbidden Poems. 1998.

Plays

Mr Cough and the Phantom Sex. 1960.
Cracks. 1963.
Wedding Finger. 1973.
Two Plays (contains *A Day at the Fair* and *True*). 1979.
Proud Flesh: Four Short Plays. 1981.
Scrap of Paper [and] The Berrypicker. 1981.
Foment. 1998.

*

Bibliography: "James Purdy" by George E. Bush, in *Bulletin of Bibliography* January/March 1971, pp. 5-6.

Critical Studies: *"The Not-Right House": Essays on James Purdy* by Bettina Schwarzchild, 1968; *City of Words* by Tony Tanner, 1971; *James Purdy* by Henry Chupack, 1975; *James Purdy* by Stephen D. Adams, 1976; *The Post-Modern Aura* by Charles Newman, 1985; "Interview with James Purdy" by Patricia Lear, in *Story Quarterly* no. 26, 1989; *The Gay Novel in America* by James Levin, 1991; "James Purdy" by James Morrison, in *Contemporary Gay American Novelists* edited by Emmanuel S. Nelson, 1992.

*   *   *

We're all alike in-
side, and we're all
connected.

You can't run away
from yourself. You
can run to the ends
of the earth, but
you'll be waiting for
yourself there.

James Purdy is a much-neglected writer who stands firm against the literary establishment that, as he has said, rejects his unconventional and often scalding portrayals of American society: "From the beginning my work has been greeted with a persistent and even passionate hostility." "The theme of American commercial culture," he adds, is "that man can be adjusted . . . that to be 'in' is to exist. My work is the furthest from this definition of reality." Despite his difficulties in gaining publication ("Had it not been for Dame Edith Sitwell, who prevailed upon a British publisher," states Purdy, "I would never have been published in America and never heard of"), when his works *Color of Darkness* and, later, *Malcolm* appeared, Purdy was recognized as a writer of extraordinary imagination, a fantasist who, while concerned with matters common to the writers of the Beat movement and the dramatists of the absurd—the isolation of youth from peers, parents, and society—brought to his form a unique style. Purdy combined surrealism with a meticulously rhetoric-free prose. He mixed realism, fairy tale, and allegory, and created an entirely new form; he transcribed and often poeticized American speech within brutal satiric forms; he illustrated the exquisite varieties of suffering that society imposes upon the innocent and the nonconformist.

In *63: Dream Palace, Color of Darkness, The Nephew,* and, perhaps his best-known work, *Malcolm,* Purdy portrayed the inevitable and lethal possessiveness within both heterosexual and homosexual love; the need and yet fear of human companionship; and the human failure in the struggle toward identity. Malcolm, typical of Purdy's orphaned heroes and prototype of all Purdy's men-children who long to belong and embrace an identity, becomes instead an appendage, an object, to be used, manipulated, brutalized, and ultimately discarded by the so-called caring people of his world. In *Children Is All, Cabot Wright Begins,* and *Eustace Chisholm and the Works,* Purdy remains frightening for his readers—indeed deeply troubling—as he treats in detail taboo subjects like homosexuality, abortion, rape, and incest, within ingenious frames. *Cabot Wright Begins,* which portrays an American automaton who can assert a human identity only through acts of rape, is one of the most savage and grotesque comedies in contemporary American literature. Purdy's tone remains defiant. As one of his earliest critics, Warren French, later wrote of *Eustace Chisholm,* in *A Season of Promise:* "I was scarcely prepared for the violently compressed power, the exhausting vehemence, the almost superhuman exorcism of the wanton evil that destroys many innocents that sets Purdy's new effort far apart from the whining and cocktail chatter that often passes for serious fiction."

Jeremy's Version and *The House of the Solitary Maggot,* the first two parts of Purdy's trilogy *Sleepers in Moon-Crowned Valleys,* combine his gift for realism with the erotic phantasmagorias of his more elliptical works. Again, scathing humor and caustic wit indict a society and its efforts to neuter the human spirit. Somewhat like Faulkner in *The Sound and the Fury,* Purdy here creates in a post-bellum family a parable of fallen America. He portrays in vivid detail a family whose growth and decline is underscored by excruciating pride and pain, where parents and children visit on one another an occasional kindness, but more often a persistent cruelty. Again, Purdy's subject is, on the one hand, the human struggle for love—specifically in the context of birthright and family—and on the other, the inevitable selfishness, violence, and destruction that are played out in parent (especially the mother) and child in payment for the secretive bond of incest.

In a Shallow Grave, about a war veteran whose horribly disfigured body is both the grave in which he must daily survive and the condition that he must submit to, was described by a *New York Times* reviewer as "a modern Book of Revelation," a gripping, imaginative, "powerful" novel "with prophecies, vision, and demonic landscapes." The remarkable *Mourners Below* combines Purdy's investigation into the fragile distance between the living and the dead with the initiation theme. After the delicate and young Duane Bledsoe learns that his two adored brothers have been killed, he retreats into a world of isolation and mourning. Their ghosts visit him, and he becomes the victim of their commands, participating in a series of violent and grotesque sexual acts, while somehow retaining his innocence. *On Glory's Course* further explores the pain of lovelessness, along with the power of guilt and greed, in a meticulously detailed 1930s Midwestern community. Comparing Purdy's work with that of his respected American contemporaries, a reviewer in the *Spectator* wrote: "Although he strikes me as a writer of far greater originality and power, . . . Purdy has only rarely received his due in his native America . . . I have always felt that a small, perpetually radioactive particle of genius irradiates the mass of the work he has produced . . . [in] his attempts to create a private American mythology."

In fact, what has been called Purdy's unremitting bitterness and grotesqueness of vision is ultimately transcended by an exquisite poetic prose and by the author's deep feeling for the human condition. Purdy's style, based upon, as he has said, "the rhythms and accents of American speech," has about it, as a *New York Times* reviewer noted, "briers in his voice, as if he meant to tear at his readers with a kind of harsh music . . . [a] deliberate scratching of the reader's ear," enabling the author "to mix evil and naivete without spilling over into melodrama and tedious morality plays." Remarkable, in addition, is Purdy's richly textured, compressed, seemingly simple and direct prose, which weaves together level upon level of symbol—often from nature as well as from classical and biblical sources.

Gertrude of Stony Island Avenue is one of Purdy's finest books because of its characterizations, breadth of passionate utterance, and unrelentingly somber yet sympathetic vision of the human condition. The novel takes place on Chicago's South side and, typically, as in his finest works *Malcolm* and *House of the Solitary Maggot,* Purdy captures with extraordinary skill the accents and cadences appropriate to his setting.

Gertrude is a renowned young artist who unexpectedly dies. Her mother is Carrie Kinsella, the wife of an ailing but overbearing man she calls "Daddy." Grief-stricken and nearly mad over the death of her estranged child, Carrie undertakes to finally understand the daughter she never knew. In this modernized quest of Demeter for Persephone, Carrie searches for the "real" Gertrude, reading her private journals, speaking to various people the girl knew, and visiting Gertrude's supposedly favorite haunts. Finally, the mother comes to understand the grim and empty reality of

her own life: "I had never, like other people lived . . . except in a kind of dream. . . . [I had never] even once been rapturously alive." She continues: "Being such a woman I had failed my only child," adding, "More importantly I had failed myself."

Typically, Purdy spares nothing in revealing the horrific reality and loneliness at the core of the human spirit, as his main character strips off all facades in gaining "the true sensation of a [personal and family] homecoming." In so doing, Purdy reiterates the potential—limited but palpable—for redemption, if only in self-knowledge. His basic themes remain constant: creativity and self-destruction are inevitable, parents and children are estranged, death may lead to love, and the distance between profound loss and renewal remains constant.

Finally, one is left with the author's profound compassion. Readers may often feel anger, horror, and even repulsion towards Purdy's sadistic, licentious, and greedy people, but at the same time they are haunted and overwhelmed by their loneliness and innocence. Purdy touches his readers on the deepest level, as he portrays, in everything he writes, human courage, dignity, and ultimate victory in the act of mere survival.

—Lois Gordon

PUZO, Mario

Born: New York City, 15 October 1920. **Education:** The New School for Social Research and Columbia University. **Military Service:** Served with the U.S. Army Air Forces during World War II; corporal. **Family:** Married Erika Lina Broske in 1946; three sons and two daughters. **Career:** Variously employed as messenger with New York Central Railroad, New York City, public relations administrator with U.S. Air Force in Europe, administrative assistant with U.S. Civil Service, New York City, and editor-writer with Magazine Management; in the interim, determined to become novelist and began publishing. **Awards:** Academy award, American Academy of Motion Picture Arts and Sciences, and Screen award, Writers Guild of America, West, Inc., 1972 and 1974; Golden Globe award for best screenplay, Hollywood Foreign Press Association, 1973 and 1990. **Died:** 2 July 1999.

PUBLICATIONS

Novels

The Dark Arena. 1955; revised edition, 1985.
The Fortunate Pilgrim. 1964.
The Godfather. 1969.
Fools Die. 1978.
The Sicilian. 1984.
The Fourth K. 1991.
The Last Don. 1996.

Plays

Screenplays: *The Godfather,* with Francis Ford Coppola, 1972; *The Godfather: Part II,* with Coppola, 1974; *Earthquake,* with George Fox, 1974; *Superman,* with others, 1978; *Superman II,* with others, 1981; *The Godfather: Part III,* with Coppola, 1990; *Christopher Columbus: The Discovery,* with others, 1992.

Other

The Runaway Summer of Davie Shaw (juvenile). 1966.
"The Godfather" Papers and Other Confessions (nonfiction). 1972.
Inside Las Vegas (nonfiction). 1977.

*

Critical Studies: "The Mythology of Crime and Its Formulaic Embodiments" by John G. Cawelti in his *Adventure, Mystery, Romance: Formula Stories as Art and Popular Culture*, 1976; *"The Godfather* as the World's Most Popular Novel" by Marianna De Marco Torgovnick in *South Atlantic Quarterly*, Spring 1988; "Ethnicity and the Literary Marketplace" by Thomas J. Ferraro in *The Columbia History of the American Novel*, edited by Emory Elliott, 1990, and "Blood in the Marketplace" in his *Ethnic Passages: Literary Immigrants in Twentieth-Century America*, 1993.

*   *   *

Mario Puzo was a novelist, screenwriter, and literary persona who was also, not incidentally, the most influential Italian-American writer of his generation and, arguably, of all time. Born in 1920 and raised in the Hell's Kitchen ghetto of Manhattan through the Depression, Puzo went on to defy fate three times: his mother had him slotted to be a railroad clerk, but the coming of World War II (he volunteered) leveraged him out of the neighborhood forever; employment in the armed services after the war brought him a modicum of mobility and opportunity, which he found the courage to abandon for a literary education (presumably on the G.I. Bill) at the New School for Social Research and Columbia University; with art-for-art's sake dedication, he produced two serious novels in fifteen years (*The Dark Arena* of 1955, *The Fortunate Pilgrim* of 1964) that were critically well received but left him penniless, at which time he determined to write himself into fame and fortune, which he did, to use his own idiom, with donnish vengeance.

The Godfather (1969) combined what Puzo knew from the Congressional "Valachi" hearings and library research with what he knew from Hell's Kitchen and his own cultural unconscious; the novel transformed the Little Caesar loner archetype of the gangster film into an ethnic super(family) man, and the southern Italian huddled masses of immigrant fiction (including his own) into the First Family of illegitimate entrepreneurial capitalism. *The Godfather* vaulted immediately into the bestselling novel of all time, where it is likely to remain. After *The Godfather,* he published three additional novels with populist ambitions—*Fools Die* (1978), *The Sicilian* (1984), *The Fourth K* (1991)—that were in fact mildly successful with general readers, although rarely with critics. But his subsequent hold on the public imagination has stemmed mainly from his screenplays, above all the three he wrote with Francis Ford Coppola for *The Godfather* trilogy (the original and *Part II* winning the Academy Award for best screenplay from another medium, 1972 and 1974), which launched a genre, but including also the first two *Superman* films (which are themselves immigrant sagas of a sort, depicting a very special "refugee" from Krypton).

Mario Puzo produced two masterpieces, one minor and acknowledged by ethnic literary specialists, the other major and awaiting for time to tell. *The Fortunate Pilgrim* and *The Godfather* have placed the United States and the world eternally in his debt: the United States, because *The Fortunate Pilgrim* is simply the finest account this country has in any genre (be it literature, scholarship, journalism, or film) of what the southern Italian struggle to establish itself in the Northeast industrial corridor characteristically entailed: the world, because *The Godfather* in its two aspects (the novel, the triptych of films) recasts the history of an immigrant few to one country into an epic of mythic resonance (the Japanese, for instance, love *The Godfather*): a phantasmagoric narration of the transformation from tradition to modernity—*by* and *for* the *family*—that is primally Italian-American in its imaginative origins yet speaks across nation-states and continents to the tragic process of the globalization of culture.

—Thomas J. Ferraro

PYNCHON, Thomas

Born: Glen Cove, New York, 8 May 1937. **Education:** Cornell University, Ithaca, New York, 1954-58, B.A. 1958. **Career:** Served in the U.S. Naval Reserve. Former editorial writer, Boeing Aircraft, Seattle. **Awards:** Faulkner award, 1964; Rosenthal Memorial award, 1967; National Book award, 1974; American Academy Howells medal, 1975.

PUBLICATIONS

Fiction

V. 1963.
The Crying of Lot 49. 1966.
Gravity's Rainbow. 1973.
Mortality and Mercy in Vienna (story). 1976.
Low-lands (story). 1978.
The Secret Integration (story). 1980.
The Small Rain (story). 1980(?).
Slow Learner: Early Stories. 1984.
Vineland. 1990.
Mason and Dixon. 1997.

*

Bibliography: *Three Contemporary Novelists: An Annotated Bibliography* by Robert M. Scotto, 1977; *John Barth, Jerzy Kosinski, and Pynchon: A Reference Guide* by Thomas P. Walsh and Cameron Northouse, 1977; *Thomas Pynchon: A Bibliography of Primary and Secondary Materials* by Clifford Mead, 1989.

Critical Studies: *Pynchon* by Joseph V. Slade, 1974; *Mindful Pleasures: Essays on Pynchon* edited by George Levine and David Leverenz, 1976; *The Grim Phoenix: Reconstructing Pynchon* by William M. Plater, 1978; *Pynchon: A Collection of Critical Essays* edited by Edward Mendelson, 1978; *Pynchon: Creative Paranoia in Gravity's Rainbow* by Mark Richard Siegel, 1978; *Pynchon: The Art of Allusion* by David Cowart, 1980; *The Rainbow Quest of Pynchon* by Douglas A. Mackey, 1980; *Pynchon's Fictions: Pynchon and the Literature of Information* by John O. Stark, 1980; *A Reader's Guide to Gravity's Rainbow* by Douglas Fowler, 1980; *Critical Essays on Pynchon* edited by Richard Pearce, 1981; *Pynchon: The Voice of Ambiguity* by Thomas H. Schaub, 1981;

Pynchon by Tony Tanner, 1982; *Signs and Symptoms: Pynchon and the Contemporary World* by Peter L. Cooper, 1983; *Approaches to Gravity's Rainbow* edited by Charles Clerc, 1983; *Ideas of Order in the Novels of Pynchon* by Molly Hite, 1983; *Understanding Thomas Pynchon* by Robert D. Newman, 1986; *The Fictional Labyrinths of Thomas Pynchon* by David Seed, 1988; *Beyond and Beneath the Mantle: On Thomas Pynchon's The Crying of Lot 49* by Georgiana M. Colvile, 1988; *Thomas Pynchon* by Joseph W. Slade, 1990; *Thomas Pynchon: Allusive Parables of Power* by John Dugdale, 1990; *New Essays on The Crying of Lot 49* edited by Patrick O'Donnell, 1991; *The Postmodernist Allegories of Thomas Pynchon* by Deborah L. Madsen, 1991; *Pynchon's Poetics: Interfacing Theory and Text* by Hanjo Berressem, 1993; *The Vineland Papers: Critical Takes on Pynchon's Novel,* 1994; *Shadows of Doubt: The American Historical War Novels of James Fenimore Cooper, Stephen Crane, and Thomas Pynchon* (dissertation) by Abagail Edna Disney, 1994; *Supreme Fictions: A Study of the Novels of Marcel Proust, James Joyce, and Thomas Pynchon* (dissertation) by Donald Matthew Brown, 1994.

*   *   *

Thomas Pynchon's novels *V., The Crying of Lot 49,* and *Gravity's Rainbow* have in common qualities that attract some readers and repel others. Both companies of readers are, however, likely to agree on what it is they respond to in the work of Pynchon. It is an unremitting brilliance of invention, accompanied by a wide range of knowledge. The knowledge embraces the major course of European history over the past century and often deviates into nooks and crannies of the entire course of Western experience. In this respect Pynchon has a novelist's plenty that makes him the peer of **John Barth, William Gaddis,** and others of his time. Consequently one has the sense not only of reading a novel but of progressing through pages from the Britannica torn out at random. "At random" is not entirely just. The assorted slices of erudition—scientific as well as cultural—are linked with Pynchon's often mad narrative sequences in ways that lead readers to think, at certain turns of a Pynchon novel, that they have come to the beating heart of the narrative. For throughout the tales are scattered clues that seem to lead from the witch's house of a particular novel—a place of confinement a la Hansel and Gretel—back to comprehension and mastery. But clues to meaning—to the intent and often the animus of the novels—are scattered so generously that each reader is likely to follow a solitary path from the witch's hut (the novel as experienced) to some safe edge of a forest (the act of personal judgment).

Yet certain judgments are not wholly solitary. Each novel has a strand of interest that threads through scenes of great comic and satiric effect. There is in *V.* a decades-long pursuit of a mysterious being; one can hardly call this being a woman since her eyes are glass, her dentures precious metal, and her feet detachable. And there is in *The Crying of Lot 49* the effort of Mrs. Oedipa Maas to discover whether an ancient European secret society for distributing mail is still alive and functioning in today's California. In *Gravity's Rainbow* events in England and Germany during the closing years of World War II are concerned with English efforts to frustrate buzz bombs and other missiles and with German efforts to launch those missiles. (A young American named Slothrop has a sexual activity that seems linked with the arrival of the bombs. But this is only a small part of a variegated story.) Such strands are obviously purloined from popular, facile tales of intrigue.

In Pynchon's novels the strands become enmeshed in displays of brilliant language and events both grotesque and, if one has missed a clue or so, gratuitous. The clues—if that is what certain passages come to—sometimes do point to the identity of V., or to the workings of the society that competes with the public mail systems of the world in *The Crying of Lot 49,* or to the crisis of world order in *Gravity's Rainbow.* At other times the clues are or seem to be self-subsistent rather than centers about which one can gather the motley contents of a novel. *V.,* for example, ranges from the 1910s to about 1956. European-based characters are touched by V. and "her" progress from human to an assemblage of inanimate elements wondrously animated. In contrast the American characters are known only in an immediate present; this is "The Crew," a collection of people united by their drinking and whoring and also by an uneasy but quite intermittent questioning of all they do. What is the relation between these two strands? Is the V. experience an account of the decadence that reached its terminus in Pynchon's boozy crew of young "Nueva Yorkers"? Similarly, is the Trystero group that Oedipa Maas pursues, come weal come woe, one that allures the heroine because it speaks, unclearly, of firm purpose asserting itself in a world where there is none? And is the action of the German rocket chief in *Gravity's Rainbow*—the launching of the body of his young lover inside one of the last rockets—a scream of despair for civilization or just one more comic incident among many such?

Pynchon's publication of five stories in *Slow Learner* begins with a relaxed, candid, twenty-page introduction providing a glimpse into the writer's sense of self. In this essay he criticizes the looming prose and foreboding tone of these early stories, all of which were written before *V.* Replete with absurdities and satire, they contain the comic elements that are Pynchonesque trademarks. Like those in his novels, the characters seek meaning in disordered lives, and the stories denounce the societies with which these characters must contend.

Vineland, unlike Pynchon's earlier novels, is less complex and ambitious. Set in contemporary California and peopled with aging 1960s radicals, it abounds in references to popular culture. More mainstream in flavor, *Vineland* has fewer allusions to historical, scholarly, or literary ideas; thus its portrait of what ails modern civilization is clear. While this novel differs in range and scope from the author's previous works, it contains Pynchon's trademark themes and is spiced with humor and wit. Pynchon—satiric and ironic at most times, moralistic in rare but intense passages—creates textures of narrative that distort but do not much misrepresent the society they mirror. Back and forth over this texture Pynchon's mind darts. It sometimes expresses an intellect that is disembodied and uninvolved. At other times there is acknowledgment of a link between the novelist and what he sets down; but such a link is no sooner noted than severed.

Seven years after the publication of *Vineland,* Pynchon returned to his encyclopedic, postmodern style in *Mason & Dixon,* a work that, like *V.* and *Gravity's Rainbow,* may overwhelm readers with its extraordinary tautological weight and plot complexities. Pynchon's imaginative approach to the retelling of history combines fact and fiction in a grotesquely comic rendering of colonial America and the two men who surveyed the legendary dividing line between the North and the South. The novel offers a score of characters whose stories within the main story about Charles Mason and Jeremiah Dixon create a pastiche of history, legend, humor, and fantasy told by one of the characters, the Reverend Wicks Cherrycoke, twenty years after Dixon's death.

The assortment of characters, as absurd as those in *V.* and *Gravity's Rainbow,* includes the ancestors of Pig Bodine from *V.,* preposterous camp hands, Jesuit cabalists, the extended family of Reverend Wicks Cherrycoke as audience and commentators, and even cameo appearances by George Washington, Thomas Jefferson, and Benjamin Franklin. Yet Pynchon's use of satire and farce—a defining characteristic in all his novels—serves to fully develop his two protagonists to a degree lacking in his previous novels. The result is a more emotionally stirring work. Amidst this miscellany the two main characters acquire a depth that reveals their strengths and weaknesses—Mason's need for family and Dixon's insecurities hidden by his conviviality. In its historical views, the book provides a critique of the eighteenth century, the Age of Reason, the delineation of the New World, and the institution of slavery as only Pynchon can, decked with travesty but supported by truths of a dark nature.

—Harold H. Watts, updated by Denise Wiloch and Martha Sutro

QUEEN, Ellery

A pseudonym for the cousins Frederic Dannay and Manfred B. Lee; also wrote as Barnaby Ross. **DANNAY, Frederic: Born:** Daniel Nathan in Brooklyn, New York, 20 October 1905; grew up in Elmira, New York. **Education:** Boys' High School, Brooklyn. **Family:** Married 1) Mary Beck in 1926 (died), two sons; 2) Hilda Wisenthal in 1947 (died 1972), one son; 3) Rose Koppel in 1975. **Career:** Writer and art director for advertising agency, New York, prior to 1931; full-time writer, with Lee, 1931-71, and on his own from 1971. Visiting professor, University of Texas, Austin, 1958-59. **Died:** 3 September 1982. **LEE, Manfred B(ennington): Born:** Manford Lepofsky in Brooklyn, New York, 11 January 1905. **Education:** Boys' High School, Brooklyn; New York University. **Family:** Married the actress Kaye Brinker (second wife), in 1942; four daughters and four sons. **Career:** Publicity writer for film companies, New York, prior to 1931; full-time writer, with Dannay, 1931-71. Justice of the Peace, Roxbury, Connecticut, 1957-58. **Died:** 3 April 1971. Dannay and Lee were under contract to film companies in the 1930s; they edited *Mystery League* magazine, 1933-34, and *Ellery Queen's Mystery Magazine,* from 1941 (Dannay the active editor); they wrote *The Adventures of Ellery Queen* radio series, 1939-48. Co-founders and co-presidents, Mystery Writers of America. **Awards:** Mystery Writers of America Edgar Allan Poe award, for radio play, 1945, for story, 1947, 1949, special award, 1951, 1968, and Grand Master award, 1960.

PUBLICATIONS

Fiction

The Roman Hat Mystery. 1929.
The French Powder Mystery. 1930.
The Dutch Shoe Mystery. 1931.
The Egyptian Cross Mystery. 1932.
The Greek Coffin Mystery. 1932.
The Tragedy of X: A Drury Lane Mystery. 1932.
The Tragedy of Y: A Drury Lane Mystery. 1932.

The Tragedy of Z: A Drury Lane Mystery. 1933.
Drury Lane's Last Case: The Tragedy of 1599. 1933.
The Siamese Twin Mystery. 1933.
The American Gun Mystery. 1933; as *Death at the Rodeo,* 1951.
The Chinese Orange Mystery. 1934.
The Adventures of Ellery Queen (stories). 1934.
The Spanish Cape Mystery. 1935.
Halfway House. 1936.
The Door Between. 1937.
The Four of Hearts. 1938.
The Devil to Pay. 1938.
The Dragon's Teeth. 1939; as *The Virgin Heiresses,* 1954.
The New Adventures of Ellery Queen (stories). 1940; with varied contents, as *More Adventures of Ellery Queen,* 1940.
Calamity Town. 1942.
There Was an Old Woman. 1943; as *The Quick and the Dead,* 1956.
The Case Book of Ellery Queen. 1945.
The Murderer Is a Fox. 1945.
Ten Days' Wonder. 1948.
Cat of Many Tails. 1949.
Double Double. 1950; as *The Case of the Seven Murders,* 1958.
The Origin of Evil. 1951.
Calendar of Crime (stories). 1952.
The King Is Dead. 1952.
The Scarlet Letters. 1953.
The Golden Summer (by Dannay only). 1953.
The Glass Village. 1954.
Q.B.I.: Queen's Bureau of Investigation. 1954.
Inspector Queen's Own Case: November Song. 1956.
The Finishing Stroke. 1958.
The Player on the Other Side. 1963.
And on the Eighth Day. 1964.
The Fourth Side of the Triangle. 1965.
Queens Full (stories). 1965.
A Study in Terror (novelization of screenplay). 1966; as *Sherlock Holmes Versus Jack the Ripper,* 1967.
Face to Face. 1967.
The House of Brass. 1968.
QED: Queen's Experiments in Detection. 1968.
Cop Out. 1969.
The Last Woman in His Life. 1970.
A Fine and Private Place. 1971.
The Best of Queen: Four Decades of Stories from the Mystery Masters, edited by Francis M. Nevins, Jr., and Martin H. Greenberg. 1985.

Plays

Danger, Men Working, with Lowell Brentano (produced 1936?).

Screenplays: *Closed Gates,* by Manfred B. Lee and Frances Guihan, 1927; *Ellery Queen, Master Detective,* with Eric Taylor, 1940.

Radio Plays: Most scripts for *The Adventures of Ellery Queen* series, 1939-48.

Other

The Detective Short Story: A Bibliography. 1942.

Queen's Quorum: A History of the Detective-Crime Short Story as Revealed by the 106 Most Important Books Published in This Field Since 1845. 1951; revised edition, 1969.

In the Queen's Parlor and Other Leaves from the Editors' Notebook. 1957.

Queen's International Case Book (true crime). 1964.

The Woman in the Case (true crime). 1966; as *Deadlier Than the Male,* 1967.

Editor, *Challenge to the Reader.* 1938.

Editor, *101 Years' Entertainment: The Great Detective Stories, 1841-1941.* 1941; revised edition, 1946.

Editor, *Sporting Blood: The Great Sports Detective Stories.* 1942; as *Sporting Detective Stories,* 1946.

Editor, *The Female of the Species: The Great Woman Detectives and Criminals.* 1943; as *Ladies in Crime: A Collection of Detective Stories by English and American Writers,* 1947.

Editor, *The Misadventures of Sherlock Holmes.* 1944.

Editor, *Best Stories from Ellery Queen's Mystery Magazine.* 1944.

Editor, *The Adventures of Sam Spade and Other Stories,* by Dashiell Hammett. 1944; as *They Can Only Hang You Once,* 1949; selection as *A Man Called Spade,* 1945.

Editor, *Rogues' Gallery: The Great Criminals of Modern Fiction.* 1945.

Editor, *The Continental Op,* by Dashiell Hammett. 1945.

Editor, *The Return of the Continental Op,* by Dashiell Hammett. 1945.

Editor, *To the Queen's Taste: The First Supplement to 101 Years' Entertainment, Consisting of the Best Stories Published in the First Five Years of Ellery Queen's Mystery Magazine.* 1946.

Editor, *Hammett Homicides,* by Dashiell Hammett. 1946.

Editor, *The Queen's Awards,* later as *Mystery Annuals and Anthologies* (from *Ellery Queen's Mystery Magazine*). 34 vols., 1946-81.

Editor, *Murder by Experts.* 1947.

Editor, *Dead Yellow Women,* by Dashiell Hammett. 1947.

Editor, *The Riddles of Hildegarde Withers,* by Stuart Palmer. 1947.

Editor, *Dr. Fell, Detective, and Other Stories,* by John Dickson Carr. 1947.

Editor, *The Department of Dead Ends,* by Roy Vickers. 1947.

Editor, *The Case Book of Mr. Campion,* by Margery Allingham. 1947.

Editor, *20th Century Detective Stories.* 1948; revised edition, 1964.

Editor, *Nightmare Town,* by Dashiell Hammett. 1948.

Editor, *Cops and Robbers,* by O. Henry. 1948.

Editor, *The Literature of Crime: Stories by World-Famous Authors.* 1950; as *Queen's Book of Mystery Stories,* 1957.

Editor, *The Creeping Siamese,* by Dashiell Hammett. 1950.

Editor, *The Monkey Murder and Other Hildegarde Withers Stories,* by Stuart Palmer. 1950.

Editor, *Woman in the Dark,* by Dashiell Hammett. 1951.

Editor, *Queen's 1960 Anthology,* and later volumes, including Mid-Year, Spring-Summer, and Fall-Winter editions. 43 vols., 1959-81.

Editor, *A Man Named Thin and Other Stories,* by Dashiell Hammett. 1962.

Editor, *12.* 1964.

Editor, *Lethal Black Book.* 1965.

Editor, *Poetic Justice: 23 Stories of Crime, Mystery and Detection by World-Famous Poets from Geoffrey Chaucer to Dylan Thomas.* 1967.

Editor, *The Case of the Murderer's Bride and Other Stories,* by Erle Stanley Gardner. 1969.

Editor, *Minimysteries: 70 Short-Short Stories of Crime, Mystery and Detection.* 1969.

Editor, *Murder—In Spades!* 1969.

Editor, *Shoot the Works!* 1969.

Editor, *Mystery Jackpot.* 1970.

Editor, *P as in Police,* by Lawrence Treat. 1970.

Editor, *The Golden 13: 13 First Prize Winners from Ellery Queen's Mystery Magazine.* 1971.

Editor, *The Spy and the Thief,* by Edward D. Hoch. 1971.

Editor, *Queen's Best Bets.* 1972.

Editor, *Amateur in Violence,* by Michael Gilbert. 1973.

Editor, *Kindly Dig Your Grave and Other Stories,* by Stanley Ellin. 1975.

Editor, *Magicians of Mystery.* 1976.

Editor, *Champions of Mystery.* 1977.

Editor, *How to Trap a Crook and 12 Other Mysteries,* by Julian Symons. 1977.

Editor, *Japanese Golden Dozen: The Detective Story World in Japan.* 1978.

Editor, *Secrets of Mystery.* 1979.

Editor, *The Amazing Adventures of Lester Leith,* by Erle Stanley Gardner. 1981.

Editor, *Eyes of Mystery.* 1981.

Editor, *Eyes of Mystery II.* 1981.

Editor, *Doors of Mystery.* 1981.

Editor, *Eyewitnesses.* 1981.

Editor, *More Eyewitnesses.* 1982.

Editor, *Maze of Mysteries.* 1982.

Editor, with Eleanor Sullivan, *Book of First Appearances.* 1982.

Editor, with Eleanor Sullivan, *Lost Ladies.* 1983.

Editor, with Eleanor Sullivan, *Lost Men.* 1983.

Editor, with Eleanor Sullivan, *Prime Crimes.* 1984.

Editor, *Circumstantial Evidence.* 1987.

Editor, *Faces of Mystery.* 1992.

*

Critical Studies: *Queen: A Double Profile* by Anthony Boucher, 1951; *Royal Bloodline: Queen, Author and Detective* by Francis M. Nevins, Jr., 1974 (includes bibliography).

*   *   *

Ellery Queen is both the pseudonym and the detective creation of two Brooklyn-born first cousins, Frederic Dannay and Manfred B. Lee. At the time they created Ellery Queen, Dannay was a copywriter and art director for a Manhattan advertising agency and Lee a publicity writer for the New York office of a film studio. The announcement of a $7500 prize contest for a detective novel catalyzed the cousins into literary action in 1928, and Ellery's first adventure was published the following year. Dannay's experience in advertising may have inspired the innovation of using the same name for the cousins' deductive protagonist and for their own joint byline—a device that, along with the excellence of the books themselves, turned Ellery Queen into a household name and his creators into wealthy men.

In the late 1920s the dominant figure in American detective fiction was S. S. Van Dine (Willard Huntington Wright), an erudite art critic whose novels about the impossibly intellectual aesthete-sleuth Philo Vance were consistent best-sellers. The early Ellery Queen novels, with their patterned titles and their scholarly dilettante detective forever dropping classical quotations, were heavily influenced by Van Dine, though superior in plotting, characterization, and style. Ellery is a professional mystery writer and amateur sleuth who assists his father, Inspector Richard Queen, whenever a murder puzzle becomes too complex for ordinary police methods. His first-period cases, from *The Roman Hat Mystery* (1929) through *The Spanish Cape Mystery* (1935), are richly plotted specimens of the Golden Age deductive puzzle at its zenith, full of bizarre circumstances, conflicting testimony, enigmatic clues, alternative solutions, fireworks displays of virtuoso reasoning, and a constant crackle of intellectual excitement. All the facts are presented, trickily but fairly, and the reader is formally challenged to solve the puzzle ahead of Ellery. Most of Queen's distinctive story motifs—the negative clue, the dying message, the murderer as Iagoesque manipulator, the patterned series of clues deliberately left at scenes of crimes, the false answer followed by the true and devastating solution—originated in these early novels. Perhaps the best works of the first period are *The Greek Coffin Mystery* and *The Egyptian Cross Mystery,* which both appeared in 1932, the same year in which, under the second pseudonym of Barnaby Ross, Dannay and Lee published the first and best two novels in the tetralogy dealing with actor-detective Drury Lane: *The Tragedy of X* and *The Tragedy of Y.*

By 1936 the Van Dine touches had left Queen's work and been replaced by the influence of the slick-paper magazines and the movies, to which the cousins had begun to sell. In second-period Queen the patterned titles vanish and Ellery gradually becomes less priggish and more human. In several stories of the period he is seen working as a Hollywood screenwriter, reflecting the cousins' brief stints at Columbia, Paramount, and MGM. Most of Queen's work in the late 1930s is thinly plotted, overburdened with "love interest," and too obviously written with film sales in mind, but the best book of the period, *The Four of Hearts,* is an excellent detective story as well as a many-faceted evocation of Hollywood in its peak years.

At the start of the new decade most of the cousins' energies went into writing a script a week for the long-running *The Adventures of Ellery Queen* radio series (1939-48) and accumulating a vast library of detective short stories. Out of this collection came *Queen's 101 Years' Entertainment,* the foremost anthology of the genre, and *Ellery Queen's Mystery Magazine,* which from 1941 until

his death was edited solely by Dannay. In 1942 the cousins returned to fiction with the superbly written and characterized *Calamity Town,* a seminaturalistic detective novel in which Ellery solves a murder in the "typical small town" of Wrightsville, U.S.A. Their third and richest period as mystery writers lasted sixteen years and embraced twelve novels, two short story collections and Dannay's autobiographical novel *The Golden Summer* (1953), published under his real name, Daniel Nathan. In third-period Queen the complex deductive puzzle is fused with in-depth character studies, magnificently detailed evocations of place and mood, occasional ventures into a topsy-turvy Alice in Wonderland otherworld reflecting Dannay's interest in Lewis Carroll, and explorations into historical, psychiatric, and religious dimensions. The best novels of this period are *Calamity Town* itself; *Ten Days' Wonder,* with its phantasmagoria of biblical symbolism; *Cat of Many Tails,* with its unforgettable images of New York City menaced by a heat wave, a mad strangler of what seem to be randomly chosen victims, and the threat of World War III; and *The Origin of Evil,* in which Darwinian motifs underlie the clues and deductions. Finally, in *The Finishing Stroke,* the cousins nostalgically recreated Ellery's young manhood in 1929, just after the publication of "his" first detective novel, *The Roman Hat Mystery.*

The cousins apparently meant to retire as active writers after *The Finishing Stroke.* Five years later, however, they launched a fourth and final group of Ellery Queen novels, from *The Player on the Other Side* (1963), the best book of the period, to *A Fine and Private Place* (1971), published in the year of Manfred Lee's death. The novels and short stories of period four retreat from all semblance of naturalistic plausibility and rely on what Dannay has called "fun and games"—heavily stylized plots and characterizations and the repetition of dozens of motifs from the earlier periods. But the reputation of Ellery Queen, author and detective, has long been assured. Of all America's mystery writers Queen is the supreme practitioner of that noble but now dying genre, the classic formal detective story.

—Francis M. Nevins, Jr., updated by Lisa C. Harper

QUINN, Martin. *See* **SMITH, Martin Cruz.**

QUINN, Simon. *See* **SMITH, Martin Cruz.**

R

RAND, Ayn

Born: Alice Rosenbaum in St. Petersburg, Russia, 2 February 1905; immigrated to the United States in 1926; naturalized 1931. **Education:** The University of Leningrad, degree in history, 1924. **Family:** Married Charles Francis O'Connor (Frank O'Connor) in 1929. **Career:** Screenwriter for Universal Pictures, Paramount Pictures, and Metro-Goldwyn-Mayer, 1932-34; freelance script reader for RKO Pictures and Metro-Goldwyn-Mayer, 1934-35; worked as a typist for Eli Jacques Kahn (architect in New York) doing research for *The Fountainhead*, 1937; script reader for Paramount Pictures, New York, 1941-43; screenwriter 1944-49; editor, *The Objectivist*, 1962-71; visiting lecturer at Yale University, 1960, Princeton University, 1960, Columbia University, 1960, 1962, University of Wisconsin, 1961, Johns Hopkins University, 1961, Harvard University, 1962, Massachusetts Institute of Technology, 1962. Coeditor, *The Objectivist Newsletter*, 1962-65; contributor, *The Objectivist*, 1966-71; writer and publisher, *The Ayn Rand Letter*, 1971-76; columnist, *Los Angeles Times*. **Awards:** Doctor of Humane Letters, Lewis and Clark College, Portland, Oregon, 1963. **Died:** 6 March 1982.

PUBLICATIONS

Collections

The Early Ayn Rand: A Selection from Her Unpublished Fiction, edited by Leonard Peikoff. 1984.
The Ayn Rand Letter. 1990.
The Ayn Rand Column: A Collection of Her Weekly Newspaper Articles, Written for the Los Angeles Times. 1990.

Novels

We the Living. 1936.
Anthem. 1938; revised edition, 1946.
The Fountainhead. 1943.
Atlas Shrugged. 1957.

Plays

Night of January 16th (produced as *Woman on Trial*, 1934; as *Night of January 16th*, 1935; as *Penthouse Legend*, 1973). 1936; revised edition, 1987.
The Unconquered, adaptation of her novel *We the Living* (produced 1940).

Screenplays: *You Came Along*, with Robert Smith, 1945; *Love Letters*, 1945; *The Fountainhead*, 1949.

Other

Textbook of Americanism. 1946.
Notes on the History of American Free Enterprise. 1959.
Faith and Force: The Destroyers of the Modern World. 1961.

For the New Intellectual: The Philosophy of Ayn Rand. 1961.
The Objectivist Ethics. 1961.
America's Persecuted Minority: Big Business. 1962.
Conservatism: An Obituary (lecture). 1962.
The Fascist "New Frontier." 1963.
The Virtue of Selfishness: A New Concept of Egoism. 1964.
Capitalism: An Unknown Ideal, with others. 1966; revised edition, 1986.
Introduction to Objective Epistemology. 1967; revised edition, 1990.
The Romantic Manifesto: A Philosophy of Literature. 1970; revised edition, 1971.
The New Left: The Anti-Industrial Revolution. 1971.
Philosophy: Who Needs It? 1982.
The Voice of Reason: Essays in Objectivist Thought. 1989.
Letters of Ayn Rand. 1995.
Ayn Rand's Marginalia: Her Critical Comments on the Writings of Over 20 Authors. 1996.
Journals of Ayn Rand. 1997.

*

Critical Studies: *Who Is Ayn Rand? An Analysis of the Novels of Ayn Rand*, 1962 and *Judgment Day: My Years with Ayn Rand*, 1989, both by Nathaniel Branden; *An Existential Ethics* by Hazel Estella Barnes, 1967; *Is Objectivism a Religion?* by Ellis Albert, 1968; *With Charity Toward None: An Analysis of Ayn Rand's Philosophy* by William O'Neill, 1971; *It Usually Begins with Ayn Rand* by Jerome Tuccille, 1972; *The Philosophic Thought of Ayn Rand* edited by Douglas Den Uyl and Douglas Rasmussen, 1984; *The Ayn Rand Companion* by Mimi Reisel Gladstein, 1984; *The Passion of Ayn Rand: A Biography* by Barbara Branden, 1986; *The Ayn Rand Lexicon: Objectivism from A to Z* edited by Harry Binswanger, 1986; *Ayn Rand: The Russian Radical* by Chris Matthew Sciabarra, 1995; *Without a Prayer: Ayn Rand and the Close of Her System* by John W. Robbins, 1997.

*   *   *

"In 1926, Ayn Rand was a twenty-one-year-old Russian immigrant to America struggling with her first story in English . . . . In 1938, a mere twelve years later, she was writing *The Fountainhead*, in full command of her distinctive philosophy, aesthetic approach, and literary style. A progression such as this represents an astonishing intellectual and artistic growth," remarked Leonard Peikoff in his introduction to *The Early Ayn Rand: A Selection of Her Unpublished Fiction.* An admirer and follower of Rand's work, Peikoff decided to publish her early stories in an attempt to show Rand's development as a writer and philosopher, as well as her struggle with a foreign language.

Even for her admirers, Ayn Rand remains an unsolved riddle: her stories, mostly romances, present to the reading public characters whose ideology is clearly defined. Rand's heroes never hesitate and never give up; they take life as it is, in a society incapable of understanding their "stubbornness"; they are fierce individualists, strong, purposeful, determined idealists; they accomplish their goals after an amazing display of strength and free will;

they have luminous souls and a clear conscience; they are perfect, self-confident, and talented human beings.

It is not surprising that Rand's novels became popular in a very short time, regardless of the critical opinion. Defying the cultural and political trends of the time, Ayn Rand established for herself a unique place in the history of American literature. Her experience with communism—with the collectivist political system in Russia—determined her philosophy and politics for life.

Ayn Rand's entire work is a protest against any individual submission. Her novels and stories are a defense of individual rights, of human creativity, of freedom of thought. Her defense of capitalism based on moral grounds is extremely articulate. "Capitalism," observed Ayn Rand, "has been called a system of greed—yet it is the system that raised the standard of living of its poorest citizens to heights no collectivist system has ever begun to equal."

While a student in Russia, Rand (then Alice Rosenbaum) decided to major in history, not being able to face the mystification of literature and philosophy imposed by the communist regime. She believed that being a writer in a country that professes the imprisonment of thought and spirit would be a never-ending compromise. Determined to write about a world of her imagination, free of any restriction, Ayn Rand created ideal heroes, detached from reality and living in their own universe, inspiring and optimistic.

Written in 1936, Rand's first novel, *We the Living*, was rejected by many publishing houses as dangerously anti-Soviet. Rand's writing was considered biased and too bitter, her views of communism too negative. Rand's implicit warning that communism—like any other collectivist system—destroys people's individuality, personality, and hope was not received well and certainly did not cast a favorable light on her career. The reading public, however, enjoyed her strong, colorful, dramatic style of writing, her tragic heroes sacrificed by a regime of terror, and her wish for a perfect world. Her readers understood that *We the Living* is not a story about Russia in particular but about the perils of dictatorship in general.

The Fountainhead is the first novel that portrays Rand's favorite type of character: the superhero, the human titan, the true artisan of the spirit. Howard Roark, the main character of the book, is an unusual architect. He dreams of constructions that defy basic laws of architecture and mainstream currents. He either builds as he wishes, or he refuses to build. Although Rand did a great deal of research in the field, Roark has little in common with any contemporary figure in architecture. *The Fountainhead* (published in 1943) is not intended as a book on architecture but it states its purpose clearly in Roark's stubborn war against stupidity, conservatism, and fright.

If *The Fountainhead* is a celebration of the self—a victory of individualism over collectivism—*Atlas Shrugged*, Rand's last novel, portrays the ideal, god-like man. Like Ayn Rand herself, John Galt, the hero of *Atlas Shrugged*, radiates "the kind of intensity that one could imagine changing the course of history," as Leonard Peikoff puts it. Like Ayn Rand, John Galt frees himself, and a number of other positive, self-centered followers, from an oppressive exploitation of mind and body.

It is interesting to notice that Ayn Rand never believed in the mind-body dichotomy. The philosophy that she proposed—Objectivism—rejects this distinction; as a consequence, her novels and plays are a mixture of emotions, reason, romance, suspense, moral principles, and idealism. Ayn Rand's books are a strange combination of propagandistic literature, popular romance, and philosophy. And it is this philosophy that, through the years, has gained an important number of followers and has influenced many careers.

When Leonard Peikoff, the future associate editor of *The Objectivist*, met Ayn Rand in 1951, he was a student in medicine. In his writings he described this meeting as an episode that changed the course of his life: "Ayn Rand was unlike anyone I had ever imagined. Her mind was utterly firsthanded. On intellectual issues, she said what no one else said or perhaps even thought, but she said these things so logically—so simply, factually, persuasively—that they seemed to be self-evident . . . . She convinced me . . . that philosophy is a science, with objective, provable answers to its questions; it is a science that moves the world, she argued, whether men acknowledge the fact or not. It did not take me long to give up medicine and decide on philosophy as a career."

Ayn Rand's intense personality influenced a whole generation of writers and thinkers. Her strong personality had an impact on both disciples and detractors of her work. A decade after her death, Objectivism is still a viable philosophical trend, while her literary superheroes continue to assert their uncompromising, pure, and stubborn views on a brave and better world.

—Dayana Stetco

RANSOM, John Crowe

Born: Pulaski, Tennessee, 30 April 1888. **Education:** Bowen School, Nashville, Tennessee, graduated 1903; Vanderbilt University, Nashville, 1903-04 and 1907-09, A.B. 1909 (Phi Beta Kappa); Christ Church, Oxford (Rhodes Scholar), 1910-13, B.A. 1913. **Military Service:** Served in the U.S. Army, 1917-19. **Family:** Married Robb Reavill in 1920; three children. **Career:** Schoolteacher in Mississippi, 1905, and Tennessee, 1906, in a private school, 1909-10, and at Hotchkiss School, Lakeville, Connecticut, 1913-14; instructor, 1914-16, assistant professor, 1919-26, and professor of English, 1927-37, Vanderbilt University; Carnegie Professor of Poetry, 1937-58, and professor emeritus, 1958-74, Kenyon College, Gambier, Ohio. Visiting lecturer in English, Chattanooga University, Tennessee, 1938; visiting lecturer in language and criticism, University of Texas, Austin, 1956. Member of the Fugitive group of poets: co-founder, *The Fugitive*, Nashville, 1922-25; editor, *Kenyon Review*, Gambier, Ohio, 1937-59. Honorary consultant in American letters, Library of Congress, Washington, D.C. **Awards:** Guggenheim fellowship, 1931; Bollingen prize, 1951; Loines award, 1951; Brandeis University Creative Arts award, 1958; Academy of American Poets fellowship, 1962; National Book award, 1964; National Endowment for the Arts award, 1966; Emerson-Thoreau medal, 1968; American Academy gold medal, 1973. **Member:** American Academy, and American Academy of Arts and Sciences. **Died:** 3 July 1974.

PUBLICATIONS

Collections

Selected Essays, edited by Thomas Daniel Young and John J. Hindle. 1984.
Selected Letters, edited by Thomas Daniel Young and George Core. 1985.

Poetry

Poems about God. 1919.
Armageddon, with *A Fragment* by William Alexander Percy, and
    Avalon by Donald Davidson. 1923.
Chills and Fever. 1924.
Grace after Meat. 1924.
Two Gentlemen in Bonds. 1927.
Selected Poems. 1945; revised edition, 1963, 1969.

Other

I'll Take My Stand: The South and the Agrarian Tradition, with
    others. 1930.
God Without Thunder: An Unorthodox Defense of Orthodoxy.
    1930.
*Shall We Complete the Trade? A Proposal for the Settlement of
    Foreign Debts to the United States.* 1933.
Who Owns America? A New Declaration of Independence, with
    others, edited by Herbert Agar and Allen Tate. 1936.
The World's Body. 1938; revised edition, 1968.
The New Criticism. 1941.
A College Primer of Writing. 1943.
Poems and Essays. 1955.
*Exercises on the Occasion of the Dedication of the New Phi Beta
    Kappa Hall* (in Williamsburg, Virginia). 1958.
American Poetry at Mid-Century, with Delmore Schwartz and John
    Hall Wheelock. 1958.
Beating the Bushes: Selected Essays 1941-1970. 1972.

Editor, *Topics for Freshman Writing: Twenty Topics for Writing,
    with Appropriate Materials for Study.* 1935.
Editor, *The Kenyon Critics: Studies in Modern Literature from
    the "Kenyon Review."* 1951.
Editor, *Selected Poems,* by Thomas Hardy. 1961.

*

Bibliography: *Ransom: An Annotated Bibliography* by Thomas
Daniel Young, 1982.

Critical Studies: *Ransom* by John L. Stewart, 1962; *The Poetry
of Ransom: A Study of Diction, Metaphor, and Symbol* by Karl F.
Knight, 1964; *The Equilibrist: A Study of Ransom's Poems 1916-
1963* by Robert Buffington, 1967; *Ransom: Critical Essays and a
Bibliography* edited by Thomas Daniel Young, 1968, and *Ransom,*
1971, and *Gentleman in a Dustcoat: A Biography of Ransom,* 1976,
both by Young; *Ransom* by Thornton H. Parsons, 1969; *Ransom:
Critical Principles and Preoccupations* by James E. Morgan, 1971;
The Poetry of Ransom by Miller Williams, 1972; "There Are Many
Wonderful Owls in Gambier" by Maureen Howard, in *Yale Re-
view,* Summer 1988; "John Crowe Ransom: As I Remember Him"
by Cleanth Brooks in *American Scholar,* spring 1989; *John Crowe
Ransom's Secular Faith* by Kieran Quinlan, 1989; "'Blue Girls'
and A Voyage to Pagany: A Note on William Carlos Williams and
John Crowe Ransom" by George Monteiro, in *Sagetrieb: A Jour-
nal Devoted to Poets in the Imagist Objectivist Tradition,* Spring/
Fall 1989; "Apparition Head versus Body Bush: The Prosodical
Theory and Practice of John Crowe Ransom" by Noralyn
Masselink in *Southern Quarterly: A Journal of the Arts in the
South,* Winter 1991; "The Colloquy between John Crowe Ran-

som and Robert Graves" by Kieran Quinlan, in *The Vanderbilt
Tradition: Essays in Honor of Thomas Daniel Young* edited by
Mark Royden Winchell, 1991; "Reviewing America: John Crowe
Ransom's *Kenyon Review*" by Gordon Hutner, in *American Quar-
terly,* March 1992; *The Unregenerate South: The Agrarian
Thought of John Crowe Ransom, Allen Tate, and Donald Davidson*
by Mark G. Malvasi, 1997.

*   *   *

As poet, teacher, critic, and editor, John Crowe Ransom was
one of the most influential men of his generation. Although scholars and critics have agreed that Ransom commands an eminent
position, they have disagreed on the precise nature of his contribution. The priorities Ransom established for his literary career
displeased some of his friends. He was, as **Allen Tate** once said,
"one of the great elegiac poets of the English language," who produced ten or twelve almost perfect lyrics that will be read as long
as poetry is regarded as a serious art. Yet the major portion of his
creative energies were devoted to the writing of poetry only for a
very brief period. During the remainder of a long and active literary career, much of his thought and most of his efforts were expended on speculations on the nature and function of poetic discourse; on the significance of religious myth, the need for an inscrutable God; and on discussions of the proper relations that
should exist between man, God, and nature.

Most of the poetry for which Ransom will be remembered was
written between 1922 and 1925 and published in *Chills and Fever* and *Two Gentlemen in Bonds.* During the winter of 1922 Ransom read at one of the Fugitive meetings his poem "Necrologi-
cal," which convinced Allen Tate that almost "overnight he had
left behind him the style of his first book [*Poems about God*]
and, without confusion, had mastered a new style." All of his best
poems are written in this "new style," what critics have come to
refer to as his "mature manner": the subtle irony, the nuanced ambiguities, the wit, and the cool detached tone. In these poems Ransom uses a simple little narrative as a means of presenting the
"common actuals"; an innocent character is involved in a common
situation and through this involvement he comes to have a fuller
understanding of his own nature. Few poets of his generation have
been able to represent with greater accuracy and precision the inexhaustible ambiguities, the paradoxes and tensions, the dichotomies and ironies that make up the life of modern man. His poetry
reiterates a few themes: man's dual nature and the inevitable misery and disaster that accompany the failure to recognize and accept this basic truth; mortality and the fleetingness of youthful
vigor and grace, the inevitable decay of feminine beauty; the disparity between the world as man would have it and as it actually
is, between what people want and need emotionally and what is
available for them, between what man desires and what he can
get; the necessity of man's simultaneous apprehension of nature's
indifference and mystery and his appreciation of nature's sensory
beauties; the inability of modern man to experience love.

Throughout his career, Ransom maintained that human experience can be fully realized only through art. In many of his critical
essays—some of which are collected in *The World's Body, The
New Criticism,* and *Beating the Bushes*—Ransom tries to define
the unique nature of poetic discourse, which functions to "induce
the mode of thought that is imaginative rather than logical," to
recover "the denser and more refractory original world which we
know loosely through our perceptions and memories." That which

we may learn from poetry is "ontologically distinct" because it is the "kind of knowledge by which we must know what we have arranged that we cannot know otherwise." Only through poetry, which is composed of a "loose logical structure with a good deal of local texture," can man recover the "body and solid substance of the world." The basic kind of data that science can collect reduces the "world to a scheme of abstract conveniences." Whereas science is interested only in *knowing,* art has a double function; it wants both to *know* and to *make.*

In many of his later essays, Ransom attempts to demonstrate how the critic should react in his efforts to define the nature of poetic discourse and to justify its existence in a society becoming more and more enamored of the quasi-knowledge and the false promises of science. In essay after essay he insists that the truths that poetry contains can be obtained only through a detailed analytical study of the poems themselves, and he repeats one theme: without poetry man's knowledge of himself and his world is fragmentary and incomplete.

—Thomas Daniel Young

RAWLINGS, Marjorie Kinnan

Born: Washington, D.C., 8 August 1896. **Education:** Western High School, Washington, D.C.; University of Wisconsin, Madison, 1914-18, B.A. 1918 (Phi Beta Kappa). **Family:** Married 1) Charles Rawlings in 1919 (divorced 1933); 2) Norton Sanford Baskin in 1941. **Career:** Editor, YWCA National Board, New York, 1918-19; assistant service editor, *Home Sector* magazine, 1919; staff member, Louisville *Courier Journal,* Kentucky, and Rochester *Journal,* Rochester, New York, 1920-28; syndicated verse writer ("Songs of a Housewife"), United Features, 1926-28; full-time writer in Florida from 1928. **Awards:** O. Henry award, 1933; Pulitzer prize, 1939. LL.D.: Rollins College, Winter Park, Florida, 1939. L.H.D.: University of Florida, Gainesville, 1941. **Member:** American Academy, 1939. **Died:** 14 December 1953.

PUBLICATIONS

Collections

The Rawlings Reader, edited by Julia Scribner Bigham. 1956.
Selected Letters, edited by Gordon E. Bigelow and Laura V. Monti. 1983.
Short Stories, edited by Rodger L. Tarr. 1994.

Fiction

South Moon Under. 1933.
Golden Apples. 1935.
The Yearling. 1938.
When the Whippoorwill— (stories). 1940.
Jacob's Ladder. 1950.
The Sojourner. 1953.

Poetry

Poems by Marjorie Kinnan Rawlings: Songs of a Housewife. 1997.

Other

Cross Creek. 1942.
Cross Creek Cookery. 1942; as *The Rawlings Cookbook,* 1961.
The Secret River (for children). 1955.

*

Bibliography: *Marjorie Kinnan Rawlings: A Descriptive Bibliography* by Rodger L. Tarr, 1996.

Critical Studies: *Frontier Eden: The Literary Career of Rawlings* by Gordon E. Bigelow, 1966; *Rawlings* by Samuel Irving Bellman, 1974; "In 'Mystic Company': The Master Storyteller in Marjorie Kinnan Rawlings's *The Yearling*" by Carol Anita Tarr, in *Marjorie Kinnan Rawlings Journal of Florida Literature,* vol. 2, 1988; "Marjorie Kinnan Rawlings: Woman, Writer, and Resident of Cross Creek" by Peggy Whitman Prenshaw, in *Rawlings Journal,* vol. 1, 1988; "Symbolic Divergence: Communication and Alienation in Marjorie Kinnan Rawlings's 'The Pelican Shadow'" by Robert L. McLaughlin and Sally E. Parry, in *Marjorie Kinnan Rawlings Journal of Florida Literature,* vol. 3, 1991; "The Otherness of Cross Creek" by Peggy Whitman Prenshaw, in *Marjorie Kinnan Rawlings Journal of Florida Literature*, vol. 4, 1992; "Nature, Spirituality, and Homemaking in Marjorie Kinnan Rawlings' *Cross Creek*" by Carolyn M. Jones, in *Homemaking: Women Writers and the Politics and Poetics of Home* edited by Catherine Wiley and Fiona R. Barnes, 1996.

*   *   *

Marjorie Kinnan Rawlings is a regional writer. Her work is inhabited by the simple people and natural settings of the Florida backwoods that she adopted as her home. Often paramount in her novels is the struggle against the vicissitudes of an uncertain existence by the poor white—the Florida cracker—commonly epitomized in an archetypical young protagonist with frontier virtues. These patterns are evident in her first four novels and in much of her short fiction.

South Moon Under depicts the difficulties of a hunter scratching out a living as a moonshiner in the Florida scrub country. The novel combines vividly descriptive scenes of rural existence with strong characterizations and an eventful plot. *Golden Apples* recounts the efforts of an orphaned and impoverished brother and sister to survive in late-nineteenth-century northern Florida. They "squat" on the estate of an exiled and embittered young Englishman whom they patiently regenerate. The resourceful protagonist is a more convincing figure than the vaguely sketched Englishman in this flawed but dramatically forceful novel. In the novella *Jacob's Ladder*, a rootless and destitute young cracker couple encounter adversities in luckless attempts to wrest a living from a bounteous but treacherous environment. The pair's deep mutual reliance and indomitable spirit are poignant and emotionally powerful.

Rawlings's internationally acclaimed novel *The Yearling* is her finest achievement. The hero is 12-year-old Jody Baxter, who lives with his parents in the Florida hammock country in the 1870s. As his family undergoes severe economic setbacks, Jody tames a fawn that becomes his forest-roaming companion. When, however, his pet cannot be restrained from eating the precious crops, it must be killed. The anguished boy feels betrayed by his father and severs their close relationship. Eventually they are reconciled. Tragedy has made a man of Jody. Throughout the story weave such themes as man's need to belong to the land that, in turn, belongs to those who lovingly cultivate it, and the inevitability of unfair and unexpected betrayal by man and nature. Rawlings's compellingly truthful portrait of a boy and his tender relationships is universally appealing. Her striking description of nature's elemental forces and the simple but significant events in the lives of people close to the land enrich an absorbingly ingenuous story. *The Yearling* is a classic of both adult and children's literature.

When the Whippoorwill—, a collection of Rawlings's major short fiction, is highlighted by three richly amusing cracker comedies often told in the vernacular ("Benny and the Bird Dogs," "Cocks Must Crow," and "Varmints"), and also contains a serious portrayal of a wife exploited by a shiftless backwoods bootlegger ("Gal Young 'Un") as well as the novella *Jacob's Ladder.* While the remaining stories are undistinguished, the overall collection displays the hand of an able storyteller. *The Sojourner,* an ambitious but imperfect novel, is a wooden family chronicle centering on a Job-like farmer toiling on a New York State farm owned by an unloving mother reserving her affection for his wandering elder brother. Notably absent are the Florida locales of her earlier fiction, which were also detailed with verve and warmth in the autobiographical *Cross Creek.*

Rawlings is a pastoral writer of percipience and power whose blaze on the tree of American regional literature has been cut deep enough to last.

—Christian H. Moe

RECHY, John (Francisco)

Born: El Paso, Texas, 10 March 1934. **Education:** Texas Western College, B.A. in English 1952; New School for Social Research, New York, 1954. **Military Service:** Served in the U.S. Army in Germany, 1952-54. **Career:** Conducted writing seminars at Occidental College and University of California, Los Angeles; teacher in the graduate school of the University of Southern California, 1983-96. **Awards:** Longfellow Foundation fiction prize, 1961; International Prix Formentor nominee for *City of Night;* National Endowment for the Arts grant, 1976; *Los Angeles Times* Book Award nomination, 1984; PEN-USA-West Lifetime Achievement award, 1999; Bill Whitehead Lifetime Achievement award in literature, 1999. **Member:** Texas Institute of Letters. **Residence:** Los Angeles, California.

PUBLICATIONS

Novels

City of Night. 1963.
Numbers. 1967.
This Day's Death. 1969.
The Vampires. 1971.
The Fourth Angel. 1973.
Rushes. 1979.
Bodies and Souls. 1983.
Marilyn's Daughter. 1988.
The Miraculous Day of Amalia Gomez. 1991.

Our Lady of Babylon. 1996.
The Coming of the Night. 1999.

Plays

Momma as She Became—Not as She Was (produced 1978).
Rushes; adaptation of his own novel (produced 1986).
Tigers Wild; adaptation of Rechy's novel *The Fourth Angel* (produced 1986).

Other

The Sexual Outlaw: A Documentary. 1977.

*

Critical Studies: *The Confusion of Realms* by Richard Gilman, 1963; "The Cities of Night: John Rechy's *City of Night* and the American Literature of Homosexuality" by Stanton Hoffman, in *Chicano Review,* no. 2-3, 1964; interview with James R. Giles and Wanda Giles, in *Chicago Review* no. 25, 1973; "In Search of the Honest Outlaw: John Rechy" by Juan Bruce-Novoa, "The Sexual Underworlds of John Rechy" by Charles M. Tatum, and "Odysseus in John Rechy's Tormented World" by Carlos Zamora, all in *Minority Voices,* vol 3, no. 1, 1979; "John Rechy's Tormented World" by Ben Satterfield, in *Southwest Review,* winter 1982; "Starless and Black: Alienation in Gay Literature" by Terry Woods, in *Lesbian and Gay Writing: An Anthology of Critical Essays,* 1990; interview in *Poets and Writers,* May-June 1992; "John Rechy" by Gregory W. Bredbeck, in *Contemporary Gay American Novelists,* 1993; *The Homophile Difference: Pathological Discourse and Communal Identity in Early Gay Novels* (dissertation) by Douglas J. Eisner, 1996; in *Show and Tell: Identity as Performance in U.S. Latina/o Fiction* by Karen Christian, 1997.

*   *   *

Since his literary debut in 1958, John Rechy has produced an impressive body of prose in the genres of fiction, reportage, and essays on a variety of subjects, but he is known mainly for his controversial treatments of homosexual themes, and gay prostitution in particular. His first novel, *City of Night,* has become a modern classic. This tale of a young man's initiation into the underground world of gay prostitution burst on the American literary scene in the years between the conservative 1950s and the liberal late-1960s. It scandalized a society not yet accustomed to the open depiction of sex, much less of the gay persuasion. The scandalous elements of Rechy's plots continually overshadow the considerable formal qualities of his writing.

Born and raised in El Paso, Texas, Rechy is a product of border culture. While both of his parents were Mexican, his father was of Scottish descent. His interest in the arts surfaced early. As a child he acted with a Mexican theater troupe; later he wrote voluminously and illustrated his writings with his own drawings. In high school he won awards for excellence in mathematics and finished first drafts of two lengthy novels. The *El Paso Times* awarded him a scholarship to attend Texas Western College, where he edited the college magazine and received a B.A. in English literature. He graduated at the precocious age of eighteen and, although offered help to attend Harvard, he accepted his draft notice. He got early release from his tour of duty in Germany to return to New York when Columbia University accepted him. At the invitation of Hiram Hayden, who conducted a novel-writing course, he attended the New School for Social Research. In his *Contemporary Authors Autobiography* essay he succinctly states what happened next to change his life: "Instead of Columbia, I went to Times Square."

While he places his first homosexual encounter in Paris a year earlier, it was in Times Square that his experimentation with gay prostitution began. There he learned the thrill of being desired, mixed with the need to hide both emotions and intelligence. The roll of indifferent observer masked his keen attention to detail, a quality that later served him well when he turned his experience into the raw material for his fiction. He gathered much first-hand knowledge traveling the gay underground circuit across the country, hustling in New York, Los Angeles, San Francisco, St. Louis, Chicago, and New Orleans, a route that traced the map of his first novel. He wrote a letter to a friend at this time, relating a crazed marathon of alcohol, drugs, and sex that took place during Mardi Gras in New Orleans. In doing so Rechy tapped back into his life's other obsession: writing.

That letter became "Mardi Gras," his first published story, which appeared in the *Evergreen Review,* perhaps the most prestigious avant-garde magazine in the country at the time. Rechy's photo appeared on the review's back cover among such luminaries as Samuel Beckett, Karl Jaspers, **H.D.**, and Antonin Artaud; sharing the space of the issue, but not meriting a cover photo, were Roland Barthes, **Jack Kerouac**, **Charles Olson**, Kenneth Koch, and **Denise Levertov**, among others. Amid this illustrious company, a caption proclaimed Rechy a "new American writer." In truth, Rechy began at the top, an auspicious start that bore fruit: "Mardi Gras" became the final section of *City of Night,* a voluminous novel published by Grove Press.

City of Night—written in first-person, eyewitness fashion and replete with graphic details of sexual encounters—is remembered most as a no-holds-barred expose of gay hustling. The narrator leads readers through a series of transcontinental adventures in which the voices of many social outlaws are recorded, the stories behind the facades revealed. The theme underlying them all is the conflict between social order and individual illusions. There is a common striving for fulfillment on their own terms against social and biological destiny. The protagonist's own version of this struggle is his fear of aging and death and his refusal to abandon the sex hunt in favor of a more stable lifestyle. He categorically rejects the world of respectability, represented in work, but also rejects the possibility of monogamous love relationships between men. The narrator sets the tone for Rechy's career: the relentless seeking out of intense sensations.

The thematic conflict is reflected in the writing. Rechy infuses his text with the pulsing rhythms of rock music, using punctuation not for grammatical ends, but for pace and intensity. Spelling and capitalization are similarly idiosyncratic. All of this underscores the characters' chaotic lives. Yet the content is structured into a balanced design of measured chapters; a system of leitmotifs ties the sections together. A key image, that of the arcade game Fascination, floats through the pages, a constant metaphor of the hustler's life of seemingly arbitrary combinations of "numbers" in which one player wins, becoming the focus of all the others' attention and envy, or loses—but only momentarily—because almost instantly the game starts anew.

Through the repeated playing out of the sex game, a cyclical pattern asserts its underlying presence, creating the sense of in-

exorable movement towards an end feared and resisted by those in the system. Players get more desperate as they pass from fresh novices to experienced professionals on their way to becoming pathetic, aged veterans. They fear the moment when they will go from being the object of desire to the desiring subject. Constant movement masks the dread of the set pattern of life. In the end, it is this tension between content and form, perfectly mirroring the thematic conflicts, that gives the novel its rhythmic dynamism.

Another key image in the novel is the window through which the narrator occasionally gazes out at the teaming life around him. Most of the time, however, he is on the street, moving in the swift stream, with the reader gazing through the lens of the prose as if safely behind a pane of glass. Rechy creates the camera-eye perspective for the voyeuristic pleasure of his audience. Yet, midway through the text, a mirror begins to replace the window as the theme of personal fulfillment versus societal destiny begins to point up the problems of not only a marginal group, but also the universal ills affecting the reader as well. It is this dimension that takes Rechy's writing beyond the limited parameters of a minority literature: the essential struggle for meaning as seen in the life of a gay hustler is shared by all of his mainstream contemporaries.

Numbers distills one element of *City of Night,* the sex hunt, into a dense, carefully paced crescendo, with the suspense of an adventure novel. Johnny Rio is on vacation from his orderly, controlled life. In Los Angeles he discovers the hustling preserve of Griffith Park and begins a game: to pick up thirty sex partners as quickly as he can. The novel can seem to be just that simple, but Rechy has more in mind. Behind the sex hunt, what is at stake is Johnny's sense of an ordered world in which life's vital impulses can be contained as if they were measurable merchandise. As long as he believes in the authority of that exterior order, his sex game is just that, a game he does not have to commit to in any real sense. Johnny eventually is seduced by the hunt, and he abandons himself to it, not as a game, but as a way of life. Like existential literature of the mid-twentieth century, Rechy's novel challenges the reader by presenting a case of absolute fidelity to life, fully lived, in contrast to mediocre, unfeeling existence. Rechy's Johnny is much like the epitome of the existential hero, the outlaw saint.

This Day's Death replays the same theme with a twist. This time the protagonist is mistakenly arrested for engaging in homosexual sex in Griffith park. The narrative alternates between his trial in Los Angeles and his tormented home-life in El Paso, Texas. In the end, when he is found guilty, the young man returns to the park to perform some act that will make the verdict true. At the same time he accepts his gay identity. Rechy says that *This Day's Death* is his only novel that he dislikes, criticizing his manipulation of the plot to prove a point. From a critical perspective the flaw might be that, in spite of himself, Rechy here affirms the legitimacy of the social system: in the end the law is right, its judgment actually revealing the protagonist's true self. This is as close as Rechy has ever come to granting authority to mainstream society. The novel is out of character for the author. However, it should be noted that it also contains one of the most incisive depictions of the mother-son relationship in U.S. Latino literature.

The Vampires is set on a Caribbean island where a group of people has gathered for an encounter of ambiguous psychological or spiritual significance. They share the bond of searching for symbolic victims whose sacrifice can purge the group's guilt. In the end, the youngest, apparently most innocent, are chosen. En route to the climax, each character reveals the hidden traumas that have determined their character. Rechy's fascination with this structure also can be found in *The Fourth Angel* in which a group of young people roam the streets in search of some act of violence capable of transporting them beyond the limits of their small lives. The narrative probes each character, presenting the facade and revealing the truth behind it. Although written more than a decade later, *Bodies and Souls* has a similar structure, but here the players in the ritual game are scattered over Los Angeles, strangers to each other, though fated to come together at a fatal climax. Each one's story is told, revealing what takes them to a certain freeway overpass at the tragic moment. There is much of *The Bridge of San Luis Rey* in *Bodies and Souls,* the same delving behind apparently arbitrary fate to discover the factors that have led people to their encounter with death.

Between *The Fourth Angel* and *Bodies and Souls,* Rechy produced two intricately related texts. *The Sexual Outlaw* has been called Rechy's finest achievement in that, while being a lengthy essay, the author shifts voices and points of view to achieve a multifaceted subject in the position of narrator who also sees himself as the object of a gaze that is his own writing. The book is autobiographical in the sense that Rechy makes his life as much the subject of the exposition as his ideas. He is concerned with social degradation, in particular with the rising violence among gays. As early as *City of Night* he had expressed his fascination with, but rejection of, sadomasochism, but here he takes a definite stand against the brutality of corporal violations. *Rushes* is the fictional twin of the essays. Yet another sinister parody of religious ritual, it plays off of both the Catholic Mass and its diabolic twin, the Black Mass. Set in a leather bar, with its sadomasochistic orgy room, the narrative mimics Catholic liturgy to relate the customers' ritual-like movements. Expectation is thick as the characters await, as in earlier novels, the sacrifice, the violent catharsis they have come to witness, or perhaps to incarnate in their own body. The end is punctuated with the horrifying fulfillment of those expectations. Rechy masterfully controls the prose, from the latinate vocabulary, to the parody of ritual, to the creation of a visceral sense of setting.

Marilyn's Daughter and *The Miraculous Day of Amalia Gomez* represent both a change and continuation: while in each the protagonist is female, they share with the previous works the search for a crowning, transcending event. The former tells the story a young woman who may or may not be Marilyn Monroe's daughter with Robert Kennedy. Her search for identity is swept up into the legend of her possible mother. The novel takes on the air of a detective story, with the search detoured through the Hollywood dream world of masks and costumes. Artifice becomes reality, if only the reality of filmland artifice. Characters recreate themselves, but always in terms of the dominant legends of stardom.

In *The Miraculous Day,* Hollywood is again the setting, but here it is the new Hollywood of the multi-ethnic poor, the trashy Hollywood of drug dealers and gangs. Amalia, like previous characters, searches for her personal miracle, but discovers along the way facts that destroy her illusions about herself and her family. The miraculous climax is full of Rechy's ironic juxtapositions of the transcendent ideal and degrading reality.

Despite his numerous publications, the obvious attention to craft, the intricate structures and meticulous selection of words and images, John Rechy is still the captive of his first and greatest success. Nothing he has written has shaken the fusion of the name Rechy and *City of Night,* a situation he laments. Yet, all things considered, to be known as the author of a legitimate modern classic places Rechy among a very elite group of writers—where he has been from the start.

—Juan Bruce-Novoa

REDDING, (Jay) Saunders

Born: Wilmington, Delaware, 13 October 1906. **Education:** Howard High School in Wilmington; Lincoln University, Pennsylvania, 1923-24; Brown University, Ph.D. 1928, M.A. 1932; Columbia University, graduate study, 1933-34. **Family:** Married Esther Elizabeth James in 1929; two sons. **Career:** Instructor at Morehouse College, Atlanta, Georgia, 1928-31, in Louisville, Kentucky, 1934-36, at Southern University, Baton Rouge, Louisiana, 1936-38, Hampton Institute, Virginia, 1943-66, and Cornell University, 1970-75; professor emeritus, Cornell University, 1975-88. Lectured in India, Africa, and South America; special consultant to U.S. Department of Health, Education, and Welfare, 1958-59, and National Endowment for the Humanities, 1970-88. **Awards:** Rockefeller Foundation fellowship, 1939-40; North Carolina Mayflower award, 1944; Guggenheim fellowship, 1944-45, 1959-60; Ford Foundation fellowship, Duke University, 1964-65; honorary conservator of American culture, Library of Congress, 1973-77. Honorary degrees from Virginia State College, 1963; Hobart College, 1964; University of Portland, 1970; Wittenberg University, 1977. **Member:** College English Association, Phi Beta Kappa. **Died:** 2 March 1988.

PUBLICATIONS

Books

To Make a Poet Black. 1939; with introduction by Henry Louis Gates, 1988.
No Day of Triumph. 1942.
Stranger and Alone. 1950; with foreword by Pancho Savery, 1989.
They Came in Chains. 1950; revised edition, 1973.
On Being Negro in America. 1951.
An American in India. 1954.
The Lonesome Road. 1958.
The Negro. 1967.
Of Men and the Writing of Books. 1969.
Negro Writing and the Political Climate. 1970.

Other

Editor, with Ivan E. Taylor, *Reading for Writing.* 1952.
Editor, with Arthur P. Davis, *Calvacade: Negro American Writing from 1760 to the Present.* 1971.

*

Bibliography: by Pancho Savery in foreword to *Stranger and Alone,* 1989.

*   *   *

In his introduction to the fiftieth anniversary edition of *To Make a Poet Black,* **Henry Louis Gates** calls Saunders Redding the veritable dean of African American literary critics. After his first book of criticism, Redding wrote social histories of the black race that emphasized personalities more than events. The theme of courage and achievement, followed at times by betrayal, constitutes a pattern in his major works, and his greatest influence may well be the impetus he gave to a proliferation of writings about black people where few existed before.

From the complexity of poems by the slave **Phillis Wheatley** to the folksy fiction of **Zora Neale Hurston**; from his stated admiration of **Frederick Douglass** and **W. E. B. Du Bois** and his lack of admiration for **Booker T. Washington**; from noting the frustration of **Paul Laurence Dunbar** as seen in "I Know Why the Caged Bird Sings" to the celebration of Harlem life in the works of **Langston Hughes** and the celebration of life everywhere in the writings of **James Weldon Johnson**; Redding offers critical insights and appraisals. In graceful, easy prose he writes chronicles of African American life—past and present.

A Rockefeller Foundation grant sponsored his second book, which later won a North Carolina Mayflower award. Graphic descriptions of what it was (and is) like to be black in America permeate *No Day of Triumph,* a first hand account of Redding's travels in the South in the early 1940s. Scenes of poverty, deprivation, and, occasionally, palpable fear leap from the pages. One false move in a Memphis police station, however innocent, would have cost him his life, Redding states. On the other hand, there are lighter moments, such as the wake of an old man famed for his tall tales. Redding listens to male relatives recount with gusto some of the old man's stories, while elsewhere in the house the female relatives and the minister are properly sedate and sad. Redding ends his book with a New Orleans Louis Armstrong dance concert where some of the white spectators cannot restrain themselves in their reserved section. They join the black people on the dance floor.

Stranger and Alone, Redding's sole novel, is a satire on a school system in the lower South from the 1920s through the 1940s. The main character, Sheldon Howden, is a bumbling college student, a loner, who is afraid to speak his mind. After graduation, he is hired by a self-serving black college president who cows his faculty and kowtows to the white establishment. Prior to a visit by the state's governor, the school head suspends classes while the faculty supervises students in window washing and other cleaning chores. The governor openly states that the purpose of his visit is to eat and to have fun, and he proceeds to tell racist jokes. Only one faculty member leaves in disgust. Howden is rewarded with a job as supervisor of the state's public school system for blacks. Following orders, he spies on meetings where civil rights discussions are held and reports to his white bosses. *Stranger and Alone* echoes situations Redding recounted earlier in his travels. Like the novel's lone teacher who would not tolerate indignities, Redding found himself teaching in a Southern college where he did not fit in and was called a radical. After three years at this school, he was fired.

They Came in Chains, first published in 1950 and revised in 1973, is one of Redding's most fully researched and indexed works. Recounting episodes of the black experience, the book begins with Pedro Alonzo, the black captain of the "Nina" on the 1492 voyage of Christopher Columbus, and ends with the death of Martin Luther King. The first section deals with the backgrounds of slavery and the breeding of slaves for sale. New information is given

about some of the individuals mentioned in Redding's first book—some of it sketchy, some detailed. Altogether, hundreds of persons from all walks of life are discussed. Briefly noted, for example, is the inventor Elijah McCoy—"the real McCoy." In writing of problems regarding the joblessness of free African American men in the North, Redding notes that some of these men turned to violence. He comments on certain Southern white men such as Tom Watson and Vardaman and the mob violence of the KKK. In conclusion, Redding states that while feelings of hopelessness and helplessness pervaded the ranks of a minority, the majority of black people were only "temporarily disheartened"; men and women of achievement in many endeavors almost crowd out writers in this book.

On Being Negro in America, Redding's most authentically autobiographical and philosophical book, deals in part with the ineptitude of communists who tried to recruit him, but more fully with racial encounters. He says flatly that there is sickness in America, and that he, too, is sick, despite his efforts to purge himself. He tells of his eight year old son, who happily played with a white boy the same age in the aisle of grocery store while the latter's maid shopped. When the white boy's father (who wore a Phi Beta Kappa key) showed up, Redding's son is told by the child that they can no longer play together because blacks are inferior—the child's father said so. When asked for an explanation by his son, Redding tells him that the white man is not a good man: he does not tell the truth. Elsewhere, Redding points out the ignorance and distortion of the facts of black life that prevail in many publications. As a Christian, he feels that the basic tenet of Christianity is that people must love one another in a manner that promotes dignity and brotherhood, and that this may be the cure for America's sickness. His theory of Christian love as a cure for ailing America is remarkably similar to that which Martin Luther King later espoused.

In 1952, the State Department sent Redding on a lecture tour of India, and *An American in India* is a report of what he found there. He was well received at most of the universities, but was challenged on occasions by students who spouted communist propaganda and who wanted to talk about the faults of America. Some Indians identified with his skin color, stating that it was the same as theirs, and that they, too, suffered under white arrogance. One educated Hindu woman said she would remain unmarried because she was too dark for the men whose caste she preferred. A young educated Moslem woman told him that she planned to spend the rest of her life in efforts to liberate Indian women. American women were already liberated, she said. A Jainist asked Redding to carry back the message that "materialism is polluting the soul" of America. Redding concluded in his final report that the American ambassador did not share his fears about communist propaganda. Nevertheless, the author left India a troubled man.

An especially engaging history in graceful prose that tells of black people who helped to shape America sums up *The Lonesome Road.* To some extent, Redding again repeats, with new information, some of the names he has previously spoken about. He never tires of extolling Du Bois, whether it is for his writing or his part in founding the National Association for the Advancement of Colored People (NAACP). This book retells the story of the 54th Massachusetts Regiment (celebrated in the motion picture *Glory*), and that of young Daniel Payne, the South Carolina freedman who was forbidden on pain of death to continue teaching ex-slaves to read. Payne left the state to become a Methodist bishop. Redding also writes of Daniel Hale Williams, the first surgeon to perform open heart surgery. This pioneering doctor was betrayed and almost destroyed by another black doctor who resented both his skill and near-white complexion. Others whose feats emblazon these pages are Marcus Garvey, Paul Robeson, and Robert S. Abbott, the publisher of *The Chicago Defender*. Added to these are stories of A. Phillip Randolph, a union organizer and organizer of the 1963 March on Washington, of boxer Joe Louis, and, finally, one of Thurgood Marshall.

Redding was a life long teacher as well as a writer. Who can determine when or where a great teacher's influence begins or ends? Redding was a modest person. Nevertheless, he took all facets of African American life to be his province. A long train of respectful writers and researchers continues to follow.

—Jean M. Bright

REED, Ishmael (Emmett Coleman)

Born: Chattanooga, Tennessee, 22 February 1938. **Education:** Attended high school in Tennessee; State University of New York at Buffalo, 1956-60. **Family:** Married 1) Priscilla Rose in 1960 (divorced 1970), one son and one daughter; 2) Carla Blank (a modern dancer), one daughter. **Career:** Teacher in prose workshop, St. Mark's in the Bowery, New York City, 1966; co-founder and director, Yardbird Publishing Company, Berkeley, California, 1971-75; co-founder, Reed, Cannon & Johnson Communications, Berkeley, 1973; co-founder, Before Columbus Foundation, Berkeley, 1976; co-founder, *Quilt* magazine, Berkeley, 1980. Guest lecturer, University of California at Berkeley, University of Washington, Seattle, State University of New York at Buffalo, Yale University, New Haven, Connecticut, Dartmouth College, Hanover, New Hampshire, Sitka Community Association, Columbia University, New York City, University of Arkansas at Fayetteville, Harvard University, Boston, Massachusetts; Regent's Lecturer at the University of California, Santa Barbara, 1988. **Awards:** Nominated for Pulitzer prize in poetry, 1973; National Endowment for the Arts writing fellowship, 1974; Guggenheim award, 1974; National Institute of Arts and Letters award, 1975; Lewis Michaux award, 1978; American Civil Liberties Union award, 1978; Pushcart prize, 1979; three New York State publishing grants for merit; three National Endowment for the Arts publishing grants for merit; California Arts Council grant. **Residence:** Oakland, California.

PUBLICATIONS

Novels

The Free-Lance Pallbearers. 1967.
Yellow Back Radio Broke-Down. 1969.
Mumbo Jumbo. 1972.
The Last Days of Louisiana Red. 1974.
Flight to Canada. 1976.
The Terrible Twos. 1982.
Reckless Eyeballing. 1986.
The Terrible Threes. 1989.
Japanese by Spring. 1993.

Poetry

catechism of d neoamerican hoodoo church. 1970.
Conjure: Selected Poems, 1963-70. 1972.
Chattanooga: Poems. 1973.
A Secretary to the Spirits. 1977.
New and Collected Poems. 1990.

Prose

Shrovetide in Old New Orleans. 1978.
God Made Alaska for the Indians: Selected Essays. 1982.
Writin' is Fightin': Thirty-Seven Years of Boxing on Paper. 1988.
Airing Dirty Laundry. 1993.

Plays

The Lost State of Franklin, with Carla Blank and Suzushi Hanayagi. 1976.
Savage Wilds. In *Action.* 1997.
The Preacher and the Rapper. In *Action.* 1997.

Other

Cab Calloway Stands In for the Moon. 1986.
Ishmael Reed: An Interview. 1993.
Conversations with Ishmael Reed. 1995.

Editor, *The Rise, Fall, and . . . ? of Adam Clayton Powell.* 1967.
Editor, *19 Necromancers from Now.* 1970.
Editor, *Yardbird Lives!* 1978.
Editor, *Calafia: The California Poetry.* 1979.
Editor, *The Before Columbus Foundation Poetry Anthology.* 1991.

Recordings: *Ishmael Reed Reading his Poetry,* 1976; *Ishmael Reed and Michael Harper Reading in the UCSD New Poetry Series,* 1977.

*

Bibliography: *Ishmael Reed: A Primary and Secondary Bibliography* by Elizabeth A. Settle and Thomas A. Settle, 1982.

Critical Studies: *Ishmael Reed and the New Black Aesthetic Critics* by Reginald Martin, 1987; "Ishmael Reed's Syncretic Use of Language: Bathos as Popular Discourse" by Reginald Martin in *Modern Language Studies,* Spring 1990; "Chango, el gran putas as Liberation Literature" by Ian I. Smart in *College Language Association Journal,* September 1991; interview by Kevin Bezner in *Mississippi Review* volume 20, numbers 1-2, 1991; "Postmodernism, Ethnicity and Underground Revisionism in Ishmael Reed" by David Mikics in *Postmodern Culture,* May 1991; "The Limbs of Osiris: Reed's *Mumbo Jumbo* and Hollywood's *The Mummy*" by Carol Siri Johnson in *MELUS,* Winter 1991-92; "Babaluaiye: Searching for the Text of a Pandemic" by Barbara Browning in *AIDS: The Literary Response* edited by Emmanuel S. Nelson, 1992; *Ishmael Reed: An Interview* by Cameron Northhouse, 1993; *Ishmael Reed and the Ends of Race* by Patrick McGee, 1997; *The Critical Response to Ishmael Reed,* edited by Dick Bruce, 1999.

* * *

There is a long history of American writers who have regarded their craft as a vehicle to recreate American life, rather than simply reflect it. In this context, Ishmael Reed pushes the envelope in singularly wild, unpredictable, and imaginative directions. His novels reflect a vaudeville and picaresque world where folk traditions inform the language and philosophy, where time sequences and chronology can be altered to prove argumentative points, where the absurd becomes routinely possible, all to reinterpret and analyze the nature of social and cultural structure. What the work achieves in sequences of fantastic situations, cartoon events and biting parody is a coherent investigation of historic motivations, pointing the reader toward a more humane analysis of our cultural journey.

Reed's vision of an egalitarian world suffers no fools gladly. Ever increasingly, his novels satirize every stripe of fanaticism. But from the early work forward, he pokes fun first at conventions of Western European, Christian culture. While *The Free-Lance Pallbearers* takes opportunists in black leadership to task, it is clearly the white power structure that has manufactured the conditions against which cynical power plays unfold. The second novel, *Yellow Back Radio Broke-Down,* begins pitting Christian traditions against HooDoo, Reed's representation of the secret forces of life. The novel's hero, in fact, is a timeless cosmic jester; The Loop Garoo Kid is a member of the divine family, a black cowboy who has existed at least since the ancient Egyptian civilization and who is being hunted by the Christian Goddess. Formally, *Yellow Back Radio Broke-Down* mimics the Old West dime novel. As the town of Yellow Back Radio is confronted with a murder, Loop Garoo and his traveling circus enter town. The town has, in desperation, appealed to the dreaded power monger, the rancher Drag Gibson. Gibson, rather than aiding the town, sends his cowhands to massacre the troupe and the town's children. From the dying circus members, Loop is bequeathed ever-greater supernatural powers, which he puts to use in battle with Drag Gibson and his putative cohort, Pope Innocent. Science fiction, religious epic and history mix in the epic events that follow. For example, when Loop's disobedience to religious and civil authority have led him to expect martyrdom, his deliverance arrives in the form of two children in a Chicken Delight truck, who announce the discovery of paradise. The novel's conclusion is a turn of the screw on the-town-at-peace-and-the-hero-rides-into-the-sunset. At the book's end, Yellow Back's survivors follow the children to paradise and the Amazon Warriors (earlier introduced to the plot's battle themes) reclaim a forest free from colonizing incursions, while Loop (astride his green horse) enters the sea to catch up to Pope Innocent's ship, returning to Rome. In this parody of popular novel and melodrama, Reed establishes an aesthetic in which past and present are not only inseparable, but intertwined in contiguous patterns.

The two mysteries involving Hoodoo detective Papa LeBas, *Mumbo Jumbo* and *The Last Days of Louisiana Red,* continue to build Reed's mythologies of heroic and mock-heroic reinterpretation of history—lampooning real historic figures, and undermining the motivations of powerful actors in a plastic, malleable American culture. *Flight to Canada* is arguably the most hopeful outcome for the playactors on Reed's stage. This novel, against a plot in which the slave Raven Quickskill flees his owner Massa Arthur Swille to Canada, posits the free land as both a political and spiritual entity enabling happiness.

The paired political satires *The Terrible Twos* and *The Terrible Threes* continue explorations of time and mythologies, but turn more explicitly to the political scene for their materials. In *The Terrible Twos,* Santa Claus is the agent of redistributing American wealth, and politicians are promoted on appearance alone. This stage of Reed's writing demonstrates so clear a process in creating an internal historic world that he drew comparison to Garcia Marquez's creations in Macondo. *Reckless Eyeballing* also addresses specific fronts in the social and political debate, satirizing both the literary marketplace and popular feminist analysis.

Japanese by Spring showcases Reed in a less fantastic and more allegorizing mode. The book tells the story of the unlikely rise of a frustrated black scholar, Chappie Puttputt, who suddenly finds himself elevated after being convinced he'd hit a solid glass ceiling at Jack London College. Now calling the shots, Puttputt's journey romps over such diverse topics as the "politically correct" canon, Japanophobia, and the nation's racial divide.

Factors inhibiting black advancement in American culture are an important backdrop in Reed's fictive world. They become the foreground in his work as essayist, journalist and poet. *Writin' Is Fightin'* sets out a number of proofs for the thesis of *Japanese by Spring* that, while no ideology has a monopoly on exclusivity and closed-mindedness, we grow strong and interesting at all of the points where our many cultures intersect. Expressions of culture from an interpretive black aesthetic (so often called "Hoodoo" or "Voodoo" in the novels) set the range for the poems, where the method is to contain a broad cultural catalogue within his own quirky dialectic.

Reed's versatility as a writer allows him to work in many formal genres. The vision is consistent enough that genre becomes more liberating than limiting; while a reader may predict a new Reed work to be inventive, fun, and bordering on the fantastic, the nature and quality of the invention will always be new. His effect may come close to that of **Kurt Vonnegut, Jr.**; Reed has every bit as idiosyncratic an attitude as his contemporary fantasist. If the experiment of American literature has given us any certainties thus far, one is that satire this strong endures.

—David Shevin

REEVE, Winnifred Eaton. *See* **EATON, Winnifred.**

REXROTH, Kenneth

Born: South Bend, Indiana, 22 December 1905. **Education:** Englewood High School and the Art Institute, both Chicago; Art Students' League, New York. **Family:** Married 1) Andree Dutcher in 1927 (died 1940); 2) Marie Kass in 1940 (divorced 1948); 3) Marthe Larsen in 1949 (divorced 1961), two daughters; 4) Carol Tinker in 1974. **Career:** Conscientious objector during World War II. Forest Service patrolman in Washington State, farm worker, factory hand, and seaman, 1920s; moved to San Francisco, 1927, and was active in libertarian and anarchist movements of 1930s and 1940s; orderly, San Francisco County Hospital, 1939-45; painter: individual shows in Los Angeles, New York, Chicago, San Francisco, and Paris; San Francisco correspondent, *The Nation,* New York, from 1953; columnist, San Francisco *Examiner,* 1958-68, *San Francisco Magazine,* and *San Francisco Bay Guardian,* from 1968; teacher, San Francisco State College, 1964, and University of Wisconsin, Madison; part-time lecturer, University of

California, Santa Barbara, from 1968. **Awards:** Guggenheim fellowship, 1948; Shelley Memorial award, 1958; Amy Lowell fellowship, 1958; American Academy grant, 1964; Fulbright fellowship, 1974; Copernicus award, 1975; National Endowment for the Arts grant, 1977. **Member:** American Academy. **Died:** 6 June 1982.

PUBLICATIONS

Collections

Selected Poems, edited by Bradford Morrow. 1984.
Sacramental Acts: The Love Poems of Kenneth Rexroth. 1997.

Poetry

In What Hour. 1940.
The Phoenix and the Tortoise. 1944.
The Art of Worldly Wisdom. 1949.
The Signature of All Things: Poems, Songs, Elegies, Translations, and Epigrams. 1950.
The Dragon and the Unicorn. 1952.
A Bestiary for My Daughters Mary and Katharine. 1955.
Poems. 1955.
In Defense of the Earth. 1956.
The Homestead Called Damascus. 1963.
Natural Numbers: New and Selected Poems. 1963.
Collected Shorter Poems. 1967.
Penguin Modern Poets 9, with Denise Levertov and William Carlos Williams. 1967.
The Heart's Garden, The Garden's Heart. 1967.
Collected Longer Poems. 1968.
The Spark in the Tinder of Knowing. 1968.
Sky Sea Birds Trees Earth House Beasts Flowers. 1970.
New Poems. 1974.
On Flower Wreath Hill. 1976.
The Silver Swan: Poems Written in Kyoto 1974-75. 1976.
The Morning Star: Poems and Translations. 1979.
Between Two Wars: Selected Poems Written Prior to the Second World War. 1982.

Plays

Beyond the Mountains (includes *Phaedra, Iphigenia, Hermaios, Berenike*) (produced 1951). 1951.

Other

Bird in the Bush: Obvious Essays. 1959.
Assays (essays). 1961.
An Autobiographical Novel. 1966.
Classics Revisited. 1968.
The Alternative Society: Essays from the Other World. 1970.
With Eye and Ear (literary criticism). 1970.
American Poetry in the Twentieth Century. 1971.
The Rexroth Reader, edited by Eric Mottram. 1972.
The Elastic Retort: Essays in Literature and Ideas. 1973.
Communalism: From Its Origins to the Twentieth Century. 1975.

Editor, *Selected Poems,* by D.H. Lawrence. 1948.
Editor, *The New British Poets: An Anthology.* 1949.

Editor, *Four Young Women: Poems.* 1973.
Editor, *Tens: Selected Poems 1961-1971,* by David Meltzer. 1973.
Editor, *The Selected Poems of Czeslaw Milosz.* 1973.
Editor, *The Buddhist Writings,* by Lafcadio Hearn. 1977.
Editor, *Seasons of Sacred Lust,* by Kazuko Shiraishi. 1978.

Translator, *Fourteen Poems,* by O.V. de L.-Milosz. 1952.
Translator, *100 Poems from the Japanese.* 1955.
Translator, *100 Poems from the Chinese.* 1956.
Translator, *30 Spanish Poems of Love and Exile.* 1956.
Translator, *100 Poems from the Greek and Latin.* 1962.
Translator, *Poems from the Greek Anthology.* 1962.
Translator, *Selected Poems,* by Pierre Reverdy. 1969.
Translator, *Love and the Turning Earth: 100 More Classical Poems.* 1970.
Translator, *Love and the Turning Year: 100 More Chinese Poems.* 1970.
Translator, *100 Poems from the French.* 1970.
Translator, with Ling O. Chung, *The Orchid Boat: Women Poets of China.* 1972.
Translator, *100 More Poems from the Japanese.* 1976.
Translator, with Ikuko Atsumi, *Burning Heart: The Women Poets of Japan.* 1977.
Translator, with Ling O. Chung, *Complete Poems,* by Li Ch'ing-chao. 1979.

*

Critical Studies: *Rexroth* by Morgan Gibson, 1972; *For Rexroth* edited by Geoffrey Gardner, 1980; "Rexroth Issue" of *Ark 14,* 1982; "Kenneth Rexroth" by Donald Hall, in *American Writing Today* edited by Richard Kostelanetz, 1982; "This Ancient Man Is I: Kenneth Rexroth's Versions of Tu Fu" by Ling Chung, in *A Brotherhood in Song: Chinese Poetry and Poetics* edited by Stephen C. Soong, 1985; *Revolutionary Rexroth: Poet of East-West Wisdom* by Morgan Gibson, 1986; *Kenneth Rexroth* by Lee Bartlett, 1988; *The Holiness of the Real: The Short Verse of Kenneth Rexroth* by Donald Gutierrez, 1996.

*   *   *

Kenneth Rexroth must be counted among the last of a distinguished and vanishing rank of writers in America, the true man of letters. He was acutely perceptive as a literary critic and historian; he was an active force in the San Francisco Renaissance through his editorial and teaching roles; he was an able translator and anthologist; above all, he possessed the enviable acuity of the polymath, with his attention focused on many centers of cultural activity at once, which he then brought to his poetry and various other writings. He has left his profound influence upon the quality and variety of literature produced in California since World War II. Final assessments of his contributions to American literary life will have to include his efforts in bridging the literature of modernism (1910-1925), especially the poetry of **Ezra Pound,** with that of post-modernism, the surge of experimental writing that began in the 1950s. Rexroth championed the work of America's primary innovators and taught their uses to younger writers. His work as a translator brought to American readers the international currents of modernism, thus helping to end the literary provinciality in the United States that had persisted well into mid-century.

Rexroth's longer poems resemble the casual narrative style of Auden, although comparisons should not be taken too far. In his polemic essays, his style and approach to the basic issues of American culture, industrial economy, depersonality in the mass population, and commerciality, are reminiscent of the early essays of **Edmund Wilson**, **Paul Goodman**, and **Edward Dahlberg**. Rexroth's poems on nature anticipated by many years the accurate, sensitive naturalist poems of **Gary Snyder**, who later in turn influenced Rexroth.

It is therefore difficult to isolate Rexroth from the stream of literature and ideas in which he fashioned his work. But an essential Rexroth is perceptible in his elegant love poems and landscape meditations, gathered in *Collected Shorter Poems*. These reveries and amorous lyrics present an unguarded, visionary persona unlike any other in American poetry, as in "Camargue":

Green moon blaze
Over violet dancers
Shadow heads catch fire
Forget forget
Forget awake aware dropping in the well
Where the nightingale sings
In the blooming pomegranate
You beside me
Like a colt swimming slowly in kelp
In the nude sea
Where ten thousand birds
Move like a waved scarf
On the long surge of sleep

The shorter poetry is brief, lyrical; touching on love, travels, and occasionally social comment. The strain of the didactic is strong in Rexroth's work, especially in the long travelogue poem, *The Dragon and the Unicorn*.

Rexroth's polemical criticism of American literature and ideology is contained in a number of volumes, *With Eye and Ear, The Alternative Society, Communalism*, and *American Poetry in the Twentieth Century*, in which he is intensely perceptive and iconoclastic. In the last he argued persuasively that American poetry should be traced not from Europe but from Native Indian cultures. As a figure central to most of the major phases of American writing throughout the century, Rexroth was a watershed of literary ideas and principles, and a writer who communicated a stubborn, wilful intellect in a century of increasing squeamishness and doubt.

—Paul Christensen

RICE, Elmer

Born: Elmer Leopold Reizenstein in New York City, 28 September 1892. **Education:** A high school in New York to age 14; earned high school diploma and studied law in night school, LL.B. (cum laude), New York Law School, 1912; admitted to New York bar, 1913. **Family:** Married 1) Hazel Levy in 1915 (divorced 1942), one son and one daughter; 2) the actress Betty Field in 1942 (divorced 1956), two sons and one daughter; 3) Barbara A. Marshall in 1966. **Career:** Claims clerk, Samstag and Hilder Brothers, New York, 1907; law clerk, 1908-14; began writing and producing for

the theater, 1914; dramatic director, University Settlement, 1915-16, and Chairman, Inter-Settlement Dramatic Society, New York; scenarist, Samuel Goldwyn Pictures Corporation, Hollywood, 1918-20; freelance writer for Famous Players, the Lasky Corporation, and Real Art Films, Hollywood, 1920; lived in Paris, 1928-30; returned to New York and organized the Morningside Players, with Hatcher Hughes; purchased and operated the Belasco Theatre, New York, 1934-37; regional director, Federal Theatre Project (Works Progress Administration), New York, 1935-36; founder, with Robert E. Sherwood, Maxwell Anderson, S.N. Behrman, Sidney Howard, and John F. Wharton, Playwrights Company, 1938; lecturer in English, University of Michigan, Ann Arbor, 1954; adjunct professor of English, New York University, 1957-58; president, Dramatists Guild, 1939-43, and Authors League of America, 1945-46; international vice president, and vice president of the New York Center, PEN, 1945-46. **Awards:** Pulitzer prize, 1929. Litt.D.: University of Michigan, 1961. **Member:** American Academy. **Died:** 8 May 1967.

PUBLICATIONS

Plays

On Trial (produced 1914). 1919.
The Iron Cross (produced 1917). 1965.
The Home of the Free (produced 1917). 1934.
For the Defense (produced 1919).
Wake Up, Jonathan, with Hatcher Hughes (produced 1921). 1928.
It Is the Law, from a novel by Hayden Talbot (produced 1922).
The Adding Machine (produced 1923). 1923.
The Mongrel, from a play by Hermann Bahr (produced 1924).
Close Harmony; or, The Lady Next Door, with Dorothy Parker (produced 1924). 1929.
Is He Guilty?, from play *The Blue Hawaii* by Rudolph Lothar (produced 1927).
Cock Robin, with Philip Barry (produced 1928). 1929.
Street Scene (produced 1929). 1929; revised version, music by Kurt Weill, lyrics by Langston Hughes (produced 1947), 1948.
The Subway (produced 1929). 1929.
A Diadem of Snow, in *One-Act Plays for Stage and Study 5*, edited by Rice. 1929.
See Naples and Die (produced 1929). 1930.
The Left Bank (produced 1931). 1931.
Counsellor-at-Law (produced 1931). 1931.
The House in Blind Alley. 1932.
Black Sheep (produced 1932). 1938.
We, The People (produced 1933). 1933.
The Gay White Way, in *One-Act Plays for Stage and Study 8*. 1934.
Judgment Day (produced 1934). 1934.
The Passing of Chow-Chow (produced 1934). 1934(?).
Three Plays Without Words (includes *Landscape with Figures, Rus in Urbe, Exterior*). 1934.
Between Two Worlds (produced 1934). In *Two Plays*, 1935.
Two Plays: Not for Children, and Between Two Worlds. 1935.
Not for Children (produced 1935; as *Life Is Real*, produced 1937). In *Two Plays*, 1935; revised version (produced 1951), 1951.
American Landscape (produced 1938). 1939.
Two on an Island (produced 1940). 1940.
Flight to the West (produced 1940). 1941.
A New Life (produced 1943). 1944.

Dream Girl (produced 1945). 1946.
Seven Plays. 1950.
The Grand Tour (produced 1951). 1952.
The Winner (produced 1954). 1954.
Cue for Passion (produced 1958). 1959.
Love among the Ruins (produced 1963). 1963.
Court of Last Resort. 1985.

Screenplays: *Help Yourself,* with others, 1920; *Rent Free,* with
    Izola Forrester and Mann Page, 1922; *Doubling for Romeo,* with
    Bernard McConville, 1922; *Street Scene,* 1931; *Counsellor-at-
    Law,* 1933; *Holiday Inn,* with Claude Binyon and Irving Berlin,
    1942.

Fiction

A Voyage to Purilia. 1930.
Imperial City. 1937.
The Show Must Go On. 1949.

Other

The Supreme Freedom. 1949.
The Living Theatre. 1959.
Minority Report: An Autobiography. 1963.

Editor, *One-Act Plays for Stage and Study 5.* 1929.

*

Bibliography: "Rice: A Bibliography" by Robert Hogan, in *Modern Drama,* February 1966.

Critical Studies: *The Independence of Rice* by Robert Hogan, 1965; *Rice* by Frank Durham, 1970; *Rice: A Playwright's Vision of America* by Anthony F. Palmieri, 1980; "The Courtroom Scene in Four Plays of Elmer Rice" by John T. Dorsey, in *Journal of the College of International Relations* February 1980; "Elmer Rice, Liberation, and the Great Ethnic Question" by Jules Chametzky, in *From Hester Street to Hollywood: The Jewish-American Stage and Screen* edited by Sarah Blacher Cohen, 1983; "Names and Numbers in The Adding Machine" by Russell E. Brown, in *Journal of the American Name Society,* September 1986; *Elmer Rice: A Research and Production Sourcebook* by Michael Vanden Heuvel, 1996.

*   *   *

Elmer Rice was one of the most prolific and technically proficient of the modern American dramatists, as well as, in many of his plays, an eclectic experimenter and an outspoken social critic. Although he graduated from law school cum laude and was admitted to the New York bar, he gave up law to write plays; one of his early pieces, a deftly constructed thriller entitled *On Trial,* achieved a rather spectacular success in 1914. For the next nine years Rice wrote two kinds of plays—commercial potboilers, some of which were produced, and experimental plays with social themes, which were generally not produced. In 1923, however, he had a critical success when the Theatre Guild staged his expressionistic satire about the automated modern world, *The Adding Machine.* This play is one of Rice's few to retain its popularity

and effectiveness over the years, and is considered one of the significant modern American plays. A companion piece, *The Subway,* did not receive a production until 1929; although somewhat dated, it has some remarkable strengths and has been unfairly neglected. Rice's other plays until 1929 were either adaptations or collaborations (one with **Dorothy Parker** and one with **Philip Barry**) of little importance.

In 1929, after much difficulty in finding a producer, Rice's *Street Scene* opened in New York, ran for 602 performances, and won the Pulitzer prize. The play is a realistic depiction of life on a segment of a New York street, with something of a melodramatic plot to tie its many diverse strands together. Its powerful impact was that of a "shock of recognition"; and only a huge cast requirement (more than eighty characters) has prevented its more frequent revival. Rice also directed this play, and was thereafter to direct all of his New York productions, as well as some by **S. N. Behrman** and **Robert E. Sherwood**. Also in 1929, Rice produced a trivial light comedy, *See Naples and Die,* and, in 1931, a somewhat more substantial study of American expatriates in Paris, *The Left Bank.* The same year saw one of Rice's most durable pieces, *Counsellor-at-Law.* Somewhat akin in tone and pace to *The Front Page,* the play is full of hectic activity and makes an excellent vehicle for a strong actor.

Three other plays of the 1930s show Rice's preoccupation with social issues. *We, The People* is a sprawling "panoramic presentation" of American life, specifically critical but generally affirmative. Its large cast and many issues make it thin in characterization and rather more akin to a film scenario than to a play: in the novels *Imperial City* and *The Show Must Go On* Rice was able to be fuller and more effective. In 1934 Rice acquired the Belasco Theatre in New York, intending to produce a season of his own work. The first play, *Judgment Day,* a serious melodrama based somewhat on the Reichstag fire trial, was an indictment of fascism; it was a failure in New York, but a distinct success in London. Rice's second play at the Belasco, *Between Two Worlds,* was even less successful with the New York critics, though a better play. It is a thickly drawn Chekhovian drama of ideas, containing some of Rice's best work. Set on an ocean liner and with the usual large cast, the play contrasts the values of capitalistic and communistic societies, and suggests that the best of two worlds must somehow be welded together. Rice was to have produced a third play, *Not for Children,* at the Belasco, but, disheartened by the critical response to the first two plays, he announced his disenchantment with the commercial stage and turned to travel and to writing a novel. The unproduced play (done some years later in an inferior revised version) is a richly droll, technically dazzling attack on the inadequacies and superficialities of the drama as an artistic form. Successful really only in its Dublin production at the Gate Theatre, the play remains a seriously neglected tour de force.

In 1938 Rice returned to the theater as a partner in the Playwrights Company. Most of the plays he wrote for the company were patriotic social commentaries, such as *American Landscape* and *Flight to the West;* thin work compared to the Belasco plays. One comedy, *Dream Girl,* which starred his second wife, Betty Field, was successful theater; and his panoramic paean to New York City, *Two on an Island,* contains some excellent satiric writing in a rather trite plot.

Rice's last commercially produced plays were less ambitious in scope, but more thoughtful in content. *The Grand Tour* and *The Winner* were about the relation of morality to money, and, although not his most memorable work and set on a much smaller scale, both were quite craftsmanlike. *Cue for Passion* was a psychoanalytic version of the Hamlet story, set in California, and is really too weak in characterization to be successful. *Love among the Ruins* is a thoughtful contemplation of the contemporary world, in which a group of American tourists in Lebanon look back on America. Rather more ambitious than *The Winner,* the play is also somewhat dull.

When Rice died in 1967, he had written more than fifty plays (of which about forty were published or produced), two long novels, a satire on the early movies, a knowledgeable book about the professional theater, and a long autobiography. He will, however, be remembered primarily as a playwright, as one of the men who transformed the American theater from the gentility of **Clyde Fitch** and the entertainment of **David Belasco** into a forum for the serious depiction of life, the critical social statement, and the broadening of technique. Not as powerful as **Eugene O'Neill**, sometimes deficient in character drawing, and often simplistic in statement, Rice nevertheless left a handful of plays that must be considered part of the permanent American repertory.

—Robert Hogan

RICH, Adrienne (Cecile)

Born: Baltimore, Maryland, 16 May 1929. **Education:** Radcliffe College, A.B. (cum laude) 1951. **Family:** Married Alfred Haskell Conrad in 1953 (died 1970); three children. **Career:** Conductor of workshops, YM-YWHA Poetry Center, New York City, 1966-67; visiting lecturer, Swarthmore College, Swarthmore, Pennsylvania, 1967-69; adjunct professor in writing division of Graduate School of the Arts, Columbia University, New York City, 1967-69; lecturer in SEEK English program, 1968-70, instructor in creative writing program, 1970-71, then assistant professor of English, 1971-72 and 1974-75, City College of the City University of New York, New York City; Fannie Hurst visiting professor of creative literature, Brandeis University, Waltham, Massachusetts, 1972-73; Lucy Martin Donelly fellow, Bryn Mawr College, Bryn Mawr, Pennsylvania, 1975; professor of English, Douglass College, Rutgers University, New Brunswick, New Jersey, 1976-78; A. D. White professor-at-large, Cornell University, 1981-86; Clark Lecturer and distinguished visiting professor, Scripps College, Claremont, California, 1983; Burgess lecturer, Pacific Oaks College, Pasadena, California, 1986; professor of English and feminist studies, Stanford University, Stanford, California, 1986-1993. **Awards:** Yale Series of Younger Poets award, 1951; Guggenheim fellowships, 1952 and 1961; Poetry Society of America's Ridgely Torrence Memorial award, 1955; Friends of Literature (Chicago) Thayer Bradley award, 1956; Phi Beta Kappa Poet, College of William and Mary, 1960, Swarthmore College, 1965, and Harvard University, 1966; National Institute of Arts and Letters award for poetry, 1961; Amy Lowell traveling fellowship, 1962; Bollingen Foundation translation grant, 1962; *Poetry* magazine's Bess Hokin prize, 1963; Bautibak Translation Center grant, 1968; *Poetry* magazine's Eunice Tietjens Memorial prize, 1968; National Endowment for the Arts grant, 1970; Poetry Society of America's Shelley Memorial award, 1971; Ingram Merrill Foundation grant, 1973-74; National Book award, 1974; National Gay Task Force Fund for Human Dignity award, 1981; Modern Poetry Association/American Council for the Arts Ruth Lilly Poetry prize, 1986; Brandeis University Creative Arts medal for poetry, 1987; National Poetry Association award, 1987; New York University's Holmes Bobst award for arts and letters, 1989; Lambda Literary award for lesbian poetry, 1992; Publishing Triangle's Bill Whitehead award for lifetime achievement in lesbian and gay literature, 1992; MacArthur fellowship, 1994–; Dorothea Tanning award, Academy of American Poets, 1996. Litt.D.: Wheaton College, 1967; Smith College, 1979; Brandeis University, 1987; and College of Wooster, 1988. **Member:** American Academy of Arts and Letters.

Publications

Poetry

A Change of World, foreword by W. H. Auden. 1951.
Poems. 1951.
The Diamond Cutters and Other Poems. 1955.
The Knight, after Rilke. 1957.
Snapshots of a Daughter-in-Law: Poems, 1954-1962. 1963.
Necessities of Life. 1966.
Focus. 1967.
Selected Poems. 1967.
Leaflets: Poems, 1965-1968. 1969.
The Will to Change: Poems, 1968-1970. 1971.
Diving into the Wreck: Poems, 1971-1972. 1973.
Poems: Selected and New, 1950-1974. 1974.
Adrienne Rich's Poetry: Texts of the Poems, The Poet on Her Work, Reviews and Criticism, edited by Barbara Charlesworth Gelpi and Albert Gelpi. 1975.
Pieces (previously published in *The Will to Change: Poems, 1968-1970*). 1977.
Twenty-one Love Poems. 1977.
The Dream of a Common Language: Poems, 1974-1977. 1978.
A Wild Patience Has Taken Me This Far: Poems, 1978-1981. 1981.
Sources. 1983.
The Fact of a Doorframe: Poems Selected and New, 1950-1984. 1984.
Your Native Land, Your Life. 1986.
Time's Power: Poems, 1985-1988. 1989.
An Atlas of the Difficult World: Poems, 1988-1991. 1991.
Collected Early Poems, 1950-1970. 1992.
Dark Fields of the Republic: Poems, 1991-1995. 1995.
Selected Poems, 1950-1995. 1996.
Midnight Salvage: Poems, 1995-1998. 1999.

Nonfiction

Of Woman Born: Motherhood As Experience and Institution. 1976.
Women and Honor: Some Notes on Lying (monograph). 1977.
On Lies, Secrets, and Silence: Selected Prose, 1966-1978. 1979.
Compulsory Heterosexuality and Lesbian Existence (monograph). 1981.
Blood, Bread, and Poetry: Selected Prose, 1979-1986. 1986.
Adrienne Rich's Poetry and Prose: Poems, Prose, Reviews, and Criticism. 1993.
What Is Found There: Notebooks on Poetry and Politics. 1995.

Other

Translator, with Aijaz Ahmad and William Stafford, *Poems by Ghalib,* edited by Aijaz Ahmad. 1969.
Translator, *Reflections* by Mark Insingel. 1973.
Translator, *De amor oscoro/Of Dark Love* by Francisco Alarcon. 1991.

Recordings: *Adrienne Rich Reading at Stanford.* Stanford, 1973; with others, *A Sign I Was Not Alone.* Out and Out, 1978.

*

Critical Studies: *Adrienne Rich's Poetry: A Norton Critical Edition* edited by Barbara Charlesworth Gelpi and Albert Gelpi, 1975; *Five Temperaments* by David Kalstone, 1977; *Reconstituting the World: The Poetry and Vision of Adrienne Rich* by Judith McDaniel, 1979; "The 'I' in Adrienne Rich: Individuation and the Androgyne Archetype" by Betty S. Flowers in *Theory and Practice of Feminist Literary Criticism* edited by Gabriela Mora and Karen S. Van Hooft, 1982; *Writing Like a Woman* by Alicia Ostriker, 1983; *An American Triptych: Anne Bradstreet, Emily Dickinson, Adrienne Rich* by Wendy Martin, 1984; *Reading Adrienne Rich: Reviews and Re-Visions, 1951-81* edited by Jane Roberta Cooper, 1984; *The Transforming Power of Language: The Poetry of Adrienne Rich* by Myriam Diaz-Diocaretz, 1984, and *Translating Poetic Discourse: Questions on Feminist Strategies in Adrienne Rich* by Diaz-Diocaretz, 1985; *The Aesthetics of Power: The Poetry of Adrienne Rich* by Claire Keyes, 1986; interview with David Montenegro, *Points of Departure: International Writers on Writing and Politics,* 1991; *The Dream and the Dialogue: Adrienne Rich's Feminist Poetics* by Alice Templeton, 1994; "Mapping the Air: Adrienne Rich and Jorie Graham" in *Soul Says: On Recent Poetry* by Helen Hennessy Vendler, 1995; *Adrienne Rich: Passion, Politics, and the Body* by Liz Yorke, 1997; *Fashioning the Female Subject: The Intertextual Networking of Dickinson, Moore, and Rich* by Sabine Sielke, 1997; *Stein, Bishop and Rich: Lyrics of Love, War, and Place* by Margaret Dickie, 1997.

*   *   *

Adrienne Rich's comments on her early poems offer the best insight into the shape of her career. In "When We Dead Awaken: Writing As Re-Vision" (1971) she notices that "beneath the conscious craft are glimpses of the split I even then experienced between the girl who wrote poems, who defined herself in writing poems, and the girl who defined herself by her relationships with men." In other contexts Rich extends her use of the term "splits" to explain the structure of all contemporary problems—artistic, psychological, and social. Insofar as she defines her poetry in terms of a response to splits within and without, Rich accepts the modernist premise that the poet begins his or her work in a fragmented world.

Rich's early poems in *A Change of World* and *The Diamond Cutters* use their mastery of formal elements to control and order the splits. The poems in *Snapshots of a Daughter-in-Law* continue the intense examination of experience, but they no longer insist on bringing all tensions under control by the end of the poem and risk very dearly bought defenses in order to get closer to the actual dynamics of experience. With this change of stance, her poems begin to confront the tensions she finds in the world with an eye toward changing the world or changing that part of herself that formerly had been intimidated by the tensions. Rather than protecting the self or the poet's voice from the tensions in the world, these poems begin the process of integrating the self in order to encounter the world in a full and direct attempt to overcome the limitations of experience or of that intimidating experience of the early poems. Thus, while speakers in the early poems take comfort and define success in closing shutters and other protective habits developed by experience, the speaker in "The Phenomenology of Anger" (1972) finds the simmering frustrations and tensions a source of energy and enjoys speculating on the shape of future experiences when the force of the anger breaks out from its containment.

Having begun this intense exploration of self and world, Rich finds a sense of wholeness in poems such as "Planetarium" (1971) and "Diving into the Wreck" (1973), which develop images that respect the integrity of conflicts within and without and still enable a holistic view of self and world. In one of Rich's longest poems, "From an Old House in America," she extends the possibilities of her sense of an integrated identity to social and political contexts. She not only finds a positive definition of self, as she had in "Diving into the Wreck," but she also finds a place in which the self can work and interact in a positive and effective fashion. The poems in *The Dream of a Common Language* extend the positive sense of self and world to social, political, and personal relationships, especially with other women, both contemporaries and predecessors, and with all women in all places. The problems of epistemological consistency and psychological comfort become occasions for discovery and new information in *The Dream of a Common Language* and in *A Wild Patience Has Taken Me This Far.* Her highly acclaimed 1986 collection *Your Native Land, Your Life* brings a shift in emphasis from the strictly feminist concerns to new subjects—ways to come to terms with age, physical pain, and the issue of racial heritage. Out of a self-inquisition emerges a wider sense of responsibility, so that Rich becomes not just a representative figure, a spokeswoman, but instead embodies an exemplar, an active agent in the service of the good. *Your Native Land, Your Life* represents an impulse toward an inclusive human commonality.

Time's Power (1989) shows Rich's fierce attention enlarge and deepen even further. She ranges backward through personal and international history, geographically from southern California to Vermont to the Golan. She confronts, by turns, what it means to be an American Jew in the time of the Palestinian-Israeli conflict; what a white woman can learn from, and give back to, the liberation struggles of people of color; how love changes in the face of pain, of historical exigency, and of death and how it changes them. She does not try to create a universal to contain and explain all of her specifics; she juxtaposes the specifics and leaves the conclusion to the reader. Her synthesis is often achieved through a cinematic or collagist technique. Narrative threads, dialogue, and quotations are intercut within the central interior monologue of the speaker, sometimes identified with the writer, at a crossroads in her personal history or taking stock of the import of past events.

Rich picks up and continues this thread in her 1991 collection *An Atlas of the Difficult World,* a historical work in which she confronts neglected portions of American history. For Rich the westward journey is a representation of national damage, a damage that is variously alluded to as a sea of indifference, foreclosed properties, and missiles, which in turn represent apathy, economic want, and fear, respectively. The title poem critically and consciously explores marginality, power, and powerlessness. "I am struck to earth," the poet says, as she reveals worlds of hatred, suffering, and violence that try the senses of light and darkness, beauty and love. One of the book's most heartrending poems, "Tattered Kaddish," is spoken on behalf of "all suicides" and, like all of the book's poems, has as its focal point "the *difficult* world"—as opposed to the other "worlds" the poet may have chosen.

In her 1995 collection of essays *What Is Found There,* Rich passionately interrogates herself, her medium, and her culture, exploring the difficulties of constructing connections between poetry, political conviction, and historical realities at a time when even poets can believe their work to be marginal or elitist. Many of the essays are designed around passages from the work of lesser-known poets of broadly varied backgrounds—Diane Glancy, Judy Grahn, Irena Klepfisz, and Jimmy Santiago Baca, among others. Rich convincingly illuminates the brilliance of the work that is being produced in an inhospitable cultural climate and testifies to the tenacity of those poets who refuse to disappear. Rich argues that poetry has the power to liberate imagination, creative desire, and the will for political change. It is an unsilenceable voice reminding you "when and where and how you are living and might live."

Dark Fields of the Republic (1995) takes over where *An Atlas of the Difficult World* left off, invoking the intersection of the personal and the historical. Rich takes on a parallel meditation on the questions confronting an affluent country at a time of momentous social change, discrediting the bitter cynicism of our own age. The poems chronicle our growing alienation from one another, stranded on islands of identity as women and men, rich and poor, gays and straights, blacks and whites, Asians, Jews, and Latinos. They also propose a global community that is all of ours to repair. *Midnight Salvage: Poems 1995-1998* moves in from the vast landscapes of *Dark Fields of the Republic* to smaller, more intimate spaces and urban snapshots—a New York subway, a Harvard restaurant, the house of a photographer, and a revolutionary, Tina Modotti. Her motivation, as it has been, is a need to make connections, whether it is to lost heroines, as in "Modotti," or to her own past self, as in "Seven Skins": "What a girl was then what a body / ready for breaking open like a lobster . . ." The book finds Rich more somberly reflective, less angry, than in her earlier works. She ponders the tension between the devotion to beauty and intimacy with incandescent honesty, writing in a way that encompasses all time and all people. In all of her work Rich not only finds a wholeness, but she also establishes a platform from which to move the world.

—Richard C. Turner, updated by Martha Sutro

RICHTER, Conrad (Michael)

Born: Pine Grove, Pennsylvania, 13 October 1890. **Education:** The Susquehanna Academy and Tremont High School, Pennsylvania, graduated 1906. **Family:** Married Harvena Achenbach in 1915; one daughter. **Career:** Teamster, farm laborer, bank clerk, and journalist, in Pennsylvania, 1906-08; editor, *Weekly Courier,* Patton, Pennsylvania, 1909-10; reporter, Johnstown *Leader,* Pennsylvania, and Pittsburgh *Dispatch,* 1910-11; private secretary in Cleveland, 1911-13; free-lance writer, in Pennsylvania, 1914-27; settled in New Mexico, 1928. **Awards:** New York University Society of Libraries Gold Medal, 1942; Pulitzer prize, 1951; American Academy grant, 1959; National Book award, 1960. Litt.D.:

Susquehanna University, Selinsgrove, Pennsylvania, 1944; University of New Mexico, Albuquerque, 1958; Lafayette College, Easton, Pennsylvania, 1966. LL.D.: Temple University, Philadelphia, 1966. L.H.D.: Lebanon Valley College, Annville, Pennsylvania, 1966. **Member:** American Academy. **Died:** 30 October 1968.

PUBLICATIONS

Fiction

Brothers of No Kin and Other Stories. 1924.
Early Americana and Other Stories. 1936.
The Sea of Grass. 1937.
The Awakening Land. 1966.
    The Trees. 1940.
    The Fields. 1946.
    The Town. 1950.
Tacey Cromwell. 1942.
The Free Man. 1943.
Smoke over the Prairie and Other Stories. 1947.
Always Young and Fair. 1947.
The Light in the Forest. 1953.
The Lady. 1957.
The Waters of Kronos. 1960.
A Simple Honorable Man. 1962.
The Grandfathers. 1964.
A Country of Strangers. 1966.
The Wanderer. 1966.
The Aristocrat. 1968.
The Rawhide Knot and Other Short Stories. 1978.

Other

Human Vibration: The Mechanics of Life and Mind. 1925.
Principles in Bio-Physics. 1927.
The Mountain on the Desert: A Philosophical Journey. 1955.
Over the Blue Mountain (for children). 1967.

*

Critical Studies: *Richter* by Edwin W. Gaston, Jr., 1965; *Richter* by Robert J. Barnes, 1968; *Richter's Ohio Trilogy: Its Ideas, Themes, and Relationship to Literary Tradition* by Clifford D. Edwards, 1970; *Richter's America* by Marvin J. LaHood, 1975; "Writing To Survive: The Private Notebooks of Conrad Richter" edited by Harvena Richter, in *South Dakota Review,* Autumn 1987; *Conrad Richter* by Edwin W. Gaston, Jr., 1989; *Settlement and Town Building in the Works of Four American Authors: James Fenimore Cooper, Caroline Kirkland, Herbert Quick, and Conrad Richter* (dissertation) by Jerry Steven Lance, 1995.

*   *   *

Conrad Richter is the latest and one of the best novelists of the American frontier, in the tradition of **James Fenimore Cooper** and **Willa Cather.** To this tradition he brings a deeper perspective and a more self-conscious artistry, as suggested by his choice of titles: his first novel was *The Sea of Grass,* and his second volume of short stories, *Early Americana.* But his best fiction, by far, is the trilogy *The Trees, The Fields,* and *The Town.* These three novels narrate the growth of an American family from its early struggle with the wilderness and the Indians, through its settlement and clearing of the fields, to the beginnings of an industrial America in the new town.

Perhaps the best and certainly the most original of these novels is *The Trees,* which follows the migration of Sayward Luckett and her family through the forests of western Pennsylvania to the Ohio frontier. But more powerful than any human protagonist is the brooding presence of the primeval trees, which shadow the lives of all those beneath, until "the woodsies" adopt their dark and often savage ways in order to survive. In this world tragedy is inevitable: Sayward's mother dies of fever, her huntsman father deserts (or disappears), and she is left to bring up her younger siblings. There is no room in this world for romance, and the novel ends with Sayward's strange marriage to a drunken young lawyer, a fugitive from his New England past. The later two novels of the trilogy continue the story of the new family into the modern world.

After this Ohio trilogy, Richter's most interesting novels are two that use autobiographical material to describe the conflict between a preacher father and his son. *The Waters of Kronos* tells of an early pioneer town that has been condemned to make way for a new reservoir, whose waters—like the waters of time—will drown the memory of its pioneer past. Underlying this is the ancient myth of Kronos, the titan father conquered by the son. A second novel, *A Simple Honorable Man,* describes the infinite complexity of the conflicts that create the "simple" character of the titular hero.

Richter's best early novel, *The Sea of Grass,* tells of the pioneer Southwest, as do many of his short stories. *The Light in the Forest* narrates the tragic conflict of a white boy, kidnaped and brought up by Indians, who tries to return to his own people. This same conflict informs *A Country of Strangers,* whose heroine had also been raised by Indians. Three novels, *Tacey Cromwell, Always Young and Fair,* and *The Lady,* describe heroines of different types who cope in different ways with the male-dominated society of the frontier. Finally, several volumes of non-fiction develop the philosophy that gives form to all Richter's creative writing. The best of these is *The Mountain on the Desert.*

—Frederic I. Carpenter

RIDING, Laura

Pseudonyms: Laura Riding Gottschalk; Mrs. Schuyler B. Jackson; Laura Riding Jackson. **Born:** Laura Reichenthal in New York City, 16 January 1901; took the surname Riding in 1926. **Education:** Girls' High School, Brooklyn; Cornell University, Ithaca, New York, 1918-21. **Family:** Married 1) Louis Gottschalk in 1920 (divorced 1925); 2) Schuyler B. Jackson in 1941 (died 1968). **Career:** Associated with the Fugitive group of poets; lived in Europe, 1926-39; with Robert Graves established the Seizin Press, 1928, and *Epilogue* magazine, 1935. **Awards:** Mark Rothko Appreciation award, 1971; Guggenheim fellowship, 1973; National Endowment for the Arts fellowship, 1979. **Died:** 1991.

PUBLICATIONS

Poetry

The Close Chaplet. 1926.
Voltaire: A Biographical Fantasy. 1927.
Love as Love, Death as Death. 1928.

Poems: A Joking Word. 1930.
Twenty Poems Less. 1930.
Though Gently. 1930.
Laura and Francisca. 1931.
The Life of the Dead (in French and English), illustrated by John Aldridge. 1933.
The First Leaf. 1933.
Poet: A Lying Word. 1933.
Americans. 1934.
The Second Leaf. 1935.
Collected Poems. 1938.
Selected Poems: In Five Sets. 1970.
The Poems. 1980.
A Selection of the Poems of Laura Riding. 1996.

Fiction

Experts Are Puzzled (stories). 1930.
No Decency Left, with Robert Graves. 1932.
14A, with George Ellidge. 1934.
Progress of Stories. 1936; revised edition, 1982.
Convalescent Conversations. 1936.
A Trojan Ending. 1937.
The World and Ourselves. 1938.
Lives of Wives (stories). 1939.
Description of Life. 1980.

Other

A Survey of Modernist Poetry, with Robert Graves. 1927.
A Pamphlet against Anthologies, with Robert Graves. 1928; as *Against Anthologies,* 1928.
Contemporaries and Snobs. 1928.
Anarchism Is Not Enough. 1928.
Four Unposted Letters to Catherine. 1930.
Pictures (pamphlet on painting). 1933.
Len Lye and the Problem of Popular Films. 1938.
The Covenant of Literal Morality. 1938.
The Left Heresy in Literature and Life, with Harry Kemp and others. 1939.
The Telling. 1972.
From the Chapter "Truth" in "Rational Meaning: A New Foundation for the Definition of Words," with Schuyler B. Jackson. 1975.
It Has Taken Long (selected writings), in "Riding Issue" of *Chelsea* 35, 1976.
How a Poem Comes to Be. 1980.
Some Communications of Broad Reference. 1983.
The Word "Woman" and Other Related Writings. 1993.
Rational Meaning: A New Foundation for the Definition of Words, and Supplementary Essays. 1997.

Editor, *Everybody's Letters.* 1933.
Editor, *Epilogue 1-3.* 3 vols., 1935-37.
Editor, *The World and Ourselves: Letters about the World Situation from 65 People of Different Professions and Pursuits.* 1938.

Translator, *Anatole France at Home,* by Marcel Le Goff. 1926.
Translator, with Robert Graves, *Almost Forgotten Germany,* by Georg Schwarz. 1936.

*

Bibliography: *Riding: A Bibliography* by Joyce Piell Wexler, 1981.

Critical Studies: *Riding's Pursuit of Truth* by Joyce Piell Wexler, 1979; "Riding's Poetry" by M. L. Rosenthal, in *The Southern Review,* Winter 1985; "Riding's Poems: A Double Ripeness" by Barbara Adams, in *Modern Poetry Studies,* vol. 11, 1987; *The Enemy Self: Poetry and Criticism of Riding* by Barbara Adams, 1990; "Riding's Essentialism and the Absent Muse" by Susan M. Schultz, in *Arizona Quarterly,* Spring 1992; "The Telling: Laura (Riding) Jackson's Project for a Whole Human Discourse" by James Odham, in *Reclaiming Rhetorica: Women in the Rhetoric Tradition* edited by Andrea A. Lunsford, 1995; "This Is Something Unlosable: Laura Riding's Compacting Sense" by Luke Carson, in *Texas Studies in Literature and Language,* Winter 1995, pp. 414-44; "Riding's Reason: An Introduction to Laura (Riding) Jackson and Schuyler Jackson, Rational Meaning: Toward a New Foundation of Words" by Charles Bernstein, in *College Literature,* October 1997, pp. 138-50; "We Are but We: Laura Riding's Geography of Difference" by Anatasia Anastasiadou, in *Women, Creators of Culture* edited by Ekaterini Georgoudaki and Domna Pastourmatzi, 1997.

*   *   *

Laura Riding is, according to **Kenneth Rexroth** in *American Poetry in the Twentieth Century,* "the greatest lost poet in American literature." The inaccessibility of her poetry, both in the literal and figurative sense, partially accounts for this lack of attention. Since the publication of her substantial *Collected Poems* in 1938, she has published sparingly and has rarely allowed her poems to be anthologized. Hence, her poetry is hard to find but, once found, quite rewarding to follow. Her brief poem "Grace" illustrates the complexity and grace of her writing style:

> This posture and this manner suit
> Not that I have an ease in them
> But that I have a horror
> And so stand well upright—
> Lest, should I sit and, flesh-conversing, eat,
> I choke upon a piece of my own tongue-meat.

The subject matter here is, quite typically, an examination of interior feeling, a self-conscious exploration of the division between the true self and the social persona, between the weight of reality and the burden of illusion.

Riding's definition of a poem in the preface to the *Collected Poems* is "an uncovering of truth of so fundamental and general a kind that no other name besides poetry is adequate except truth." This definition, if tautological, is indicative of Riding's strong commitment to purity in language. This strong belief impelled her eventually to abandon the writing of poetry, for she found that she could not reconcile the necessity to keep the language pure with the desirability of making the poems sensuously appealing to the readers.

Riding's use of repetition, verbal punning, and tautology in her poetry is reminiscent of **Gertrude Stein**'s prose. For example, in "Beyond," published in *Selected Poems,* Riding explores the incommunicability and the alienation of pain:

> Pain is impossible to describe

> Pain is the impossibility of describing
> Describing what is impossible to describe
> Which must be a thing beyond description
> Beyond description not to be known
> Beyond knowing but not mystery
> Not mystery but pain not plain but pain
> But pain beyond but here beyond

For Riding, as for Stein, poetic meaning can not only be found in words of the poem; it is also produced in the spaces between words, in the sparks that result from the collision of words and in the static created by the repetition of language.

In *Selected Poetry: Five Sets,* Riding offers her reader one prose poem about poetry, entitled "Poet: A Lying Word," which asserts, "It is a false wall, a poet: it is a lying word. It is a wall that closes and does not." Here Riding's use of paradox and contradiction helps to elucidate her accusation that poets characteristically traffic in the art of lying, even as they simultaneously strive to uncover truth. Riding's poetry typically sets up such contradictions, as she frequently invokes paradox as a means of understanding or achieving truth. By encouraging her reader to confront opposites, to recognize that objects and actions are neither singular nor self-evident, Riding creates a complicated and often gleefully self-contradictory poetic world.

Riding's undeservedly neglected fiction has received even less attention than her poetry. Her *Progress of Stories,* a collection marked by impressive variety and a somewhat flamboyant wit, is unlike her poetry in tone although it treats similar themes of truth, self, unity, and perfection. The comic sketch "Eve's Side of It," for instance, complements such feminist poems as "Divestment of Beauty" and "Auspice of Jewels." She has deliberately adopted a lighter vein for these stories, she explains in the preface, because she is tired of the accusation of obscurity and being made "a scape goat for the incapacity of people to understand what they only pretend to want to know."

Of her numerous theoretical studies, the two she wrote in collaboration with Robert Graves are best known. Their 1927 work *A Survey of Modernist Poetry* attempts to define the modernist idiom and offers a method of textual scrutiny that influenced and informed William Empson's *Seven Types of Ambiguity.* While the work of **e.e. cummings** most often provides examples for the book, Riding's poem "The Rugged Back of Anger" is also examined. To apply Riding's critical method to her poetry is helpful in understanding this austere, complicated, and significant poet. Riding and Graves's second collaboration produced *A Pamphlet against Anthologies,* which opposes the modern marketing trend of anthologizing poetry in such a manner as to distort the relationship between poems and poets. They especially reject the capitalistic motivations of anthologies, which they charge make poetry both profitable and useful.

As a poet, a novelist, and a literary critic, Riding is a literary force in the twentieth century who influenced many of her contemporaries, particularly **Wallace Stevens**, with her imaginative poetic style. In much of her writing, Riding is concerned with the aesthetics of truth and with the struggle to define identity. Towards the end of her life, Riding renounced poetry, arguing that poetry is itself incapable of achieving truth; she concluded rather starkly in *The Telling:* "There can be no literary equivalent to truth."

—Nancy Carol Joyner, updated by Allison Hersh

RILEY, James Whitcomb

Born: Greenfield, Indiana, 7 October 1849. **Education:** Local schools, and at Greenfield Academy, 1870. **Career:** House-and sign-painter, 1870-71; itinerant entertainer, giving readings and lectures, 1872-75, 1876; worked in his father's law office, 1875-76; lived in Indianapolis from 1879; journalist, Indianapolis *Journal*, 1879-88; gave annual reading tour of the United States, 1882-1903. **Awards:** American Academy gold medal, 1911. M.A.: Yale University, New Haven, Connecticut, 1902. D.Litt.: University of Pennsylvania, Philadelphia, 1904. D.L.: Indiana University, Bloomington, 1907. **Member:** American Academy, 1911. **Died:** 22 July 1916.

PUBLICATIONS

Collections

Letters, edited by William Lyon Phelps. 1930.
The Best of Riley, edited by Donald C. Manlove. 1982.
Little Orphant Annie, and Other Poems. 1994.

Poetry

The Old Swimmin'-Hole and 'leven More Poems. 1883; revised edition, as *Neighborly Poems,* 1891.
Afterwhiles. 1887.
Nye and Riley's Railway Guide, with Edgar W. Nye. 1888.
Old-Fashioned Roses. 1888.
Pipes o' Pan at Zekesbury. 1888.
Rhymes of Childhood. 1890.
The Flying Islands of the Night. 1891.
Green Fields and Running Brooks. 1893.
Poems Here at Home. 1893.
Armazindy. 1894.
The Days Gone By and Other Poems. 1895.
A Tinkle of Bells and Other Poems. 1895.
A Child-World. 1896.
Rubaiyat of Doc Sifers. 1897.
The Golden Year, edited by Clara E. Laughlin. 1898.
Love-Lyrics. 1899.
Home-Folks. 1900.
The Book of Joyous Children. 1902.
Nye and Riley's Wit and Humor, with Edgar W. Nye. 1902.
His Pa's Romance. 1903.
Out of Old Aunt Mary's. 1904.
A Defective Santa Claus. 1904.
Songs o' Cheer. 1905.
While the Heart Beats Young. 1906.
Morning. 1907.
The Boys of the Old Glee Club. 1907.
The Riley Baby Book. 1913; as *Baby Ballads,* 1914.
Songs of Friendship. 1915.
The Old Soldier's Story: Poems and Prose Sketches. 1915.

Fiction

Character Sketches: The Boss Girl: A Christmas Story, and Other Sketches. 1886; as *Sketches in Prose and Occasional Verses,* 1891.

Other

Poems and Prose Sketches (Homestead Edition). 16 vols., 1897-1914.
Complete Works (Biographical Edition), edited by Edmund Henry Eitel. 6 vols., 1913.

*

Bibliography: *A Bibliography of Riley* by Anthony J. and Dorothy R. Russo, 1944; in *Bibliography of American Literature* by Jacob Blanck, edited by Virginia L. Smyers and Michael Winship, 1983.

Critical Studies: *Commemorative Tribute to Riley* by Hamlin Garland, 1922; *Riley, Hoosier Poet* by Jeannette Covert Nolan, 1941, and *Poet of the People: An Evaluation of Riley* by Nolan, Horace Gregory, and James T. Farrell, 1951; *Hoosier Boy: Riley* by Minnie B. Mitchell, 1942; *Those Innocent Years: The Legacy and Inheritance of a Hero of the Victorian Era, Riley* by Richard H. Crowder, 1957; *Riley* by Peter Revell, 1970; "Poet as Entertainer: Will Carleton, James Whitcomb Riley, and the Rise of the Poet-Performer Movement" by Paul H. Gray, in *Literature in Performance: A Journal of Literary and Performing Art,* November 1984; "James Whitcomb Riley's Georgia Connection" by Doris Lanier, in *The Old Northwest: A Journal of Regional Life and Letters,* Fall/Winter 1985-86; *James Whitcomb Riley: The Poet As Flying Islands of the Night* by Thomas E.Q. Williams, 1997.

*   *   *

Although James Whitcomb Riley occasionally wrote prose, he was pre-eminently a poet—one of the most famous in turn-of-the-century America. Not exactly the household word he once was, Riley remains an important figure in American popular culture; schoolchildren continued to learn "Little Orphan Annie" and "The Raggedy Man" well through the 1930s and more than three quarters of a century after his death his work stays in print. He began to write verse in the 1870s, contributing primarily to Indiana newspapers, particularly the Indianapolis *Journal,* on the staff of which he served for years. His verse was widely reprinted and, as his reputation spread, new poems began to appear in newspapers and magazines far from his Indiana base. His first book, *The Old Swimmin'-Hole and 'leven More Poems,* was published in 1883 and new collections of his periodical verse quickly followed. He issued book-length poems only twice—*The Flying Islands of the Night,* a verse drama so uncharacteristic that his readers rejected it, and the more acceptable *Rubaiyat of Doc Sifers,* written in the Hoosier dialect used in his most popular poems.

He occasionally tried set forms—sonnets, for instance—but he ordinarily worked in rhymed couplets or quatrains, and the subject matter dictated the length of the poems. The stanza forms sometimes vary, and the meter is sometimes irregular, but in most cases these are designed to fit the speaking voice. Riley was as much performer as poet, traveling the country to give readings, and his admirers have always known that his verse fits better in the mouth than on the page. His dialect poems are much more effective than his other verse, which too easily succumbs to conventional poetic diction, as a comparison of "Knee-deep in June" with the sonnet beginning "O queenly month of indolent repose!" will show.

Riley wrote many happy poems—evocations of nature and rec-ollections of childhood—but popular taste has always been as lu-gubrious as it is sentimental, and Riley, whose own despondency found an answering chord in his audience, fills his work with bro-ken toys and broken hearts, dead children and cheerful cripples, lost days, lost joys, "lost sunshine / Of youth." He offers the consolation of Heaven or of time that lets one taste "the sweet / Of honey in the saltest tear." It is pain, not comfort, however, that gives Riley his best images, as in the old man who wants to "strip to the soul, / And dive off in my grave like the old swimmin'-hole" or the speaker in "A Summer's Day" who longs to "spread / Out like molasses on the bed, / And jest drip off the aidges in / The dreams that never comes ag'in." Riley's triumph as a popular poet is that he gave a great deal of pleasure to a great many people over a great many years, and all his readers know, as they wink back the happy tears, is that

the Gobble-uns'll git you
Ef you
Don't
Watch
Out!

—Gerald Weales

RINEHART, Mary Roberts

Born: Pittsburgh, Pennsylvania, 12 August 1876. **Education:** El-ementary and high schools in Pittsburgh; Pittsburgh Training School for nurses, graduated 1896. **Family:** Married Stanley Marshall Rinehart in 1896 (died 1932); three sons. **Career:** Full-time writer from 1903. Correspondent, *Saturday Evening Post,* during World War I; reported presidential nominating conventions. Lived in Pitts-burgh until 1920, in Washington, D.C., 1920-32, and in New York from 1932. **Awards:** Mystery Writers of America Special award, 1953. Litt.D.: George Washington University, Washington, D.C., 1923. **Died:** 22 September 1958.

Publications

Fiction

The Circular Staircase. 1908.
The Man in Lower Ten. 1909.
When a Man Marries. 1909.
The Window at the White Cat. 1910.
The Amazing Adventures of Letitia Carberry. 1911.
Where There's a Will. 1912.
The Case of Jennie Brice. 1913.
The After House. 1914.
The Street of Seven Stars. 1914.
K. 1915.
Tish. 1916.
Bab, A Sub-Deb. 1917.
Long Live the King! 1917.
The Altar of Freedom. 1917.
The Amazing Interlude. 1918.
Twenty-Three and a Half Hours' Leave. 1918.

Dangerous Days. 1919.
Love Stories. 1919.
A Poor Wise Man. 1920.
The Truce of God. 1920.
Affinities and Other Stories. 1920.
More Tish. 1921.
Sight Unseen, and The Confession. 1921.
The Breaking Point. 1922.
The Out Trail. 1923.
Temperamental People (stories). 1924.
The Red Lamp. 1925; as *The Mystery Lamp,* 1925.
Tish Plays the Game. 1926.
Nomad's Land (stories). 1926.
The Bat (novelization of play). 1926.
Lost Ecstasy. 1927; as *I Take This Woman,* 1927.
Two Flights Up. 1928.
This Strange Adventure. 1929.
The Romantics (stories). 1929.
The Door. 1930.
Miss Pinkerton. 1932; as *The Double Alibi,* 1932.
The Album . 1933.
Mr. Cohen Takes a Walk. 1934.
The State Versus Elinor Norton. 1934; as *The Case of Elinor Norton,* 1934.
The Doctor. 1936.
Married People (stories). 1937.
Tish Marches On. 1937.
The Wall. 1938.
The Great Mistake. 1940.
Familiar Faces: Stories of People You Know. 1941.
Haunted Lady. 1942.
Alibi for Isabel and Other Stories. 1944.
The Yellow Room. 1945.
The Curve of the Catenary. 1945.
A Light in the Window. 1948.
Episode of the Wandering Knife: Three Mystery Tales. 1950; as *The Wandering Knife,* 1952.
The Swimming Pool. 1952; as *The Pool,* 1952.
The Frightened Wife and Other Murder Stories. 1953.
The Best of Tish (stories). 1955.

Plays

Double Life (produced 1906).
Seven Days, with Avery Hopwood (produced 1909). 1931.
Cheer Up (produced 1912).
Spanish Love, with Avery Hopwood (produced 1920).
The Bat, with Avery Hopwood, from novel *The Circular Stair-case* by Rinehart (produced 1920). 1932.
The Breaking Point (produced 1923).

Screenplay: *Aflame in the Sky,* with Ewart Anderson, 1927.

Other

Kings, Queens, and Pawns: An American Woman at the Front. 1915.
Through Glacier Park: Seeing America First, with Howard Eaton. 1916.
The Altar of Freedom. 1917.
Tenting Tonight: A Chronicle of Sport and Adventure in Glacier Park and the Cascade Mountains. 1918.

Isn't That Just Like a Man! 1920.
My Story (autobiography). 1931; revised edition, 1948.
Writing Is Work. 1939.

*

Critical Studies: *Improbable Fiction: The Life of Rinehart* by Jan Cohn, 1980; "Mary Roberts Rinehart" by Jan Cohn, in *10 Women of Mystery* edited by Earl F. Bargainnier, 1981; "Spinsters in Jeopardy" by James C. Dance, in *Armchair Detective: A Quarterly Journal Devoted to the Appreciation of Mystery, Detective, and Suspense Fiction,* winter 1989; *Had She But Known: A Biography of Mary Roberts Rinehart* by Charlotte MacLeod, 1994.

*   *   *

Mary Roberts Rinehart, a successful writer of thrillers and of comic novels about the travels and adventures of a spinster, "Tish," modeled on herself and her friends, is one of the founding figures of the American mystery and suspense novel. From her successful first novel, *The Circular Staircase,* to a later work like *The Album,* she used the same pattern. The setting is usually in a more-or-less enclosed house, often a lodging house or block of houses deliberately shut off from the outer world. The heroine is usually either an inexperienced but bright young woman or a shrewd but eccentric spinster. By overhearing odd conversations or mysterious footsteps the heroine slowly tracks down a murderer, whose identity comes as a shock to her. But then a real detective, a minor character (he may have been posing as one of the lodgers), rescues her in time. Rinehart's novels are still popular, especially in America, and their period and oddly wholesome flavor (one never really believes that the heroine will suffer the fate looming over her) make them agreeable reading: they were jocularly christened novels of the "Had I but known . . ." school (they were always told in the first person). Mignon G. Eberhart was Rinehart's most distinguished successor.

—G.S. Fraser

RIVERA, Tomás

Born: Crystal City, Texas, 22 December 1935. **Education:** Crystal City, completing high school in 1954; Southwest Texas Junior College, Ubalde, A.A., 1956; Southwest Texas State University, San Marcos, B.A. in English, 1959, M.Ed., 1964; NDEA Seminar, Guadalajara, Mexico, 1962; University of Oklahoma, Norman, 1966-69, M.A., Ph.D., 1969. **Family:** Married Concepción Garza, 1958; two daughters, one son. **Career:** Teacher, San Antonio, Texas, public schools, 1958-60; teacher, League City, Texas, public schools, 1960-65; instructor, Southwest Texas Junior College, Ubalde, 1965-66; instructor in Spanish, University of Oklahoma, Norman, 1966-69; associate professor, Sam Houston State University, Huntsville, Texas, 1969-71; professor of Spanish, University of Texas, San Antonio, 1971-73; College of Multidisciplinary Studies, University of Texas, El Paso, associate dean, 1973-76, vice chancellor of administration, 1976-78, executive vice president Academic Affairs, 1978-79; chancellor, University of California, Riverside, 1979-84. Member of editorial board, MICTLA Publications, beginning 1971, and *El Magazin,*

beginning 1972; contributing editor, *El Grito,* beginning 1971, and *Revista Chicano-Riqueña,* beginning 1973; member of board of directors of the Pan American Student Forum, 1965. Appointed to the National Commission on Secondary Schooling for Hispanics and the President's Commission on a National Agenda for the Eighties. **Awards:** Premio Quinto Sol, 1970. Ed.D.: University of Santa Clara, San José, California. **Died:** 16 May 1984.

PUBLICATIONS

Collections

The Harvest; Short Stories/La cosecha; cuentos, edited by Julián Olivares. 1989.
The Searchers: Collected Poetry, edited by Olivares. 1990.
Tomás Rivera: The Complete Works, edited by Olivares. 1992.

Novels

" *. . . y no se lo tragó la tierra*" / " *. . . and the Earth Did Not Part*" bilingual edition, English translation by Herminio Ríos C. 1971; as *This Migrant Earth,* English translation by Rolando Hinojosa, 1985; English translation by Evangelina Vigil-Piñón, 1987.

Verse

Always and Other Poems. 1973.

Other

La ideología del hombre en la obra poética de León Felipe (nonfiction). 1969.

Contributor, *Songs and Dreams,* edited by Joseph Flores. 1972.
Contributor, *El Quetzal Emplumece,* edited by Leonardo Anguiano and Cecilio Garcia. 1976.
Contributor, *The Identification and Analysis of Chicano Literature,* edited by Francisco Jiménez. 1979.

Editor with Ed Simmen, *New Voices in Literature: The Mexican Americans.* 1972.

*

Critical Studies: "The Narrative: Focus on Tomás Rivera," in *Modern Chicano Writers: A Collection of Critical Essays* edited by Joseph Sommers and Tomás Ybarra-Frausto, 1979; interview by Juan Bruce-Novoa, in *Chicano Authors: Inquiry by Interview,* 1980; *International Studies in Honor of Tomás Rivera* edited by Julián Olivares, 1986; *Tomás Rivera 1935-1984: The Man and His Works* edited by Vernon E. Lattin, Rolando Hinojosa, and Gary Keller, 1988; "The Novel and the Community of Readers; Rereading Tomás Rivera's *Y no se lo tragó la tierra*" by Hector Calderon and "Chicano Border Narratives as Cultural Critique" by Jose David Saldivar, both in *Criticism in the Borderlands: Studies in Chicano Literature, Culture and Ideology* edited by Hector Calderon and Jose David Saldivar, 1991; "Cuando lleguemos/When We Arrive: The Paradox of Migration in Tomas Rivera's . . . *Y no se lo trago la tierra*" by Brooke Fredericksen, in *Binlingual Re-*

view, *La Revista Bilingue,* April-May 1994, pp. 142-50; "Character and Protagonist in . . . *and the Earth Did Not Part*" by Maria Jesus Sanchez-Manzano, in *REDEN: Revista Espanola de Estudios Norteamericanos,* 1996, pp. 43-50.

* * *

Tomás Rivera's success as a writer and university administrator was due to his philosophy of life, his well-defined objectives, and his strong interest in the welfare of his people. As a boy, he had been told by his maternal grandmother that writing and art were the most important things in life. As the son of migrant workers, however, he had to conquer tremendous odds in order to be able to fulfill his desire to become a writer. It was not until he was thirty-five years old that he succeeded in having his first important work published. In 1969 the editorial house Quinto Sol (Fifth Sun) of Berkeley, California, publishers of the Chicano periodical *El Grito,* in which some poems by Rivera had appeared that year, announced the establishment of an annual prize for the best book by a Chicano author, written in either English or Spanish. In 1970 Rivera submitted the manuscript of a novel in Spanish and won first prize. Translated into English by Herminio Ríos C., it appeared in a bilingual edition in 1971 under the title *" . . . y no se lo tragó la tierra" / . . . And the Earth Did Not Part"* and became an immediate success, making its author a celebrity among Hispanic readers.

The road to success had not been an easy one. As was customary in many Chicano families living along the Rio Grande, Rivera had to accompany his parents on the yearly journey to work in the fields. In his article "We Are All Immigrants" (*San Antonio Express-News* 7 September 1975), he explains: "The winter garden areas [of southern Texas] only provided work half the year so very early the migrant labor experience became regularized. The first years the family worked throughout Texas and during the depression there was a yearly migration to California or the Midwestern states." As can be observed in most of his fiction, those experiences made a strong impact on his life. But it was not until he had the opportunity to publish in Spanish that he was able to transform his experiences into meaningful stories. As he told Burt A. Folkart (*Los Angeles Times* 17 May 1984), what he wrote in English "didn't reach into my subconscious because English is a learned experience for me. But, when I learned that Quinto Sol . . . accepted manuscripts in Spanish, it liberated me. I knew that for the first time I could express myself exactly as I wanted."

His first known publication, which appeared during the Spring of 1967 in the Norman, Oklahoma periodical *Original Works: A Foreign Language Quarterly,* was the elegy "Me lo enterraron" ("They Have Buried Him") written upon the death of his father and in which the poetic voice establishes the relationship between the dead father and the living son. The poem is structured around the technique of remembrance. The son assumes that those who buried his father did not know his personal habits and characteristics as well as he, the son, did. He is sad to see his father buried by strangers and expresses his desire to have him at home to preserve the family unity and, especially, to repeat the daily rituals that had been part of his life. This poem, together with six others, appeared in the Fall 1969 issue of the periodical *El Grito,* and were reprinted in the second edition (1972) of the first Chicano literary anthology, *El Espejo/The Mirror.*

It was not, however, until his first novel appeared that Rivera was recognized as a significant writer. The reason for this was that in Tierra he gave expression to a vital theme for Chicanos

(the hardships endured by migrant workers), and also made use of a fragmented structure by means of which the apparently independent stories are integrated into a harmonious unity. In the first and last chapters of the novel, which serve to give the enclosed stories a narrative frame, the author introduces the theme of the lost individual in search of an answer. In the opening chapter, "El año perdido" ("The Lost Year"), the protagonist appears to be a confused person. His dream is a much more complex dream than that of Bunyan's Pilgrim. His dream is a dream inside a dream, a dream that can be confused with reality. This dream inside a dream is another form of the labyrinth, a motif common in Rivera's works.

For Tomás Rivera, one of the most important functions of literature is to help people maintain their culture. Literature accomplishes this function by creating a language that permits them to express their own psychology and their own attitudes towards life. At the same time it helps them to understand themselves. But Rivera was not only a theorist; he wrote poetry, fiction and essays demonstrating his literary principles. His literature has inspired a large number of Chicano writers, and will continue to do so in the future.

—Luis Leal

RIVERSIDE, John *See* HEINLEIN, Robert Anson.

ROBERTS, Elizabeth Madox

Born: Perryville, Kentucky, 30 October 1881. **Education:** Covington Institute, Springfield, Kentucky; Covington High School, Kentucky, 1896-1900; University of Chicago (Fiske prize, 1921), 1917-21, Ph.B. in English, 1921 (Phi Beta Kappa). **Career:** Private tutor and teacher in public schools, Springfield, 1900-10. **Awards:** O. Henry award, 1930. L.H.D.: Russell Sage College, Troy, New York, 1933. **Member:** American Academy, 1940. **Died:** 13 March 1941.

PUBLICATIONS

Fiction

The Time of Man. 1926.
My Heart and My Flesh. 1927.
Jingling in the Wind. 1928.
The Great Meadow. 1930.
A Buried Treasure. 1931.
The Haunted Mirror: Stories. 1932.
He Sent Forth a Raven. 1935.
Black Is My Truelove's Hair. 1938.
Not by Strange Gods: Stories. 1941.

Poetry

In the Great Steep's Garden. 1915.
Under the Tree (for children). 1922; revised edition, 1930.
Song in the Meadow. 1940.

*

Bibliography: "Elizabeth Madox Roberts: A Bibliographical Essay" by Linda Tate, in *Resources for American Literary Study* volume 18, 1992.

Critical Studies: *Roberts: A Personal Note* by Glenway Wescott, 1930; *Roberts: An Appraisal* by J. Donald Adams and others, 1938; *Roberts, American Novelist* by Harry Modean Campbell and Ruel E. Foster, 1956; *Herald to Chaos: The Novels of Roberts* by Earl Rovit, 1960; *Roberts* by Frederick P.W. McDowell, 1963 (includes bibliography); "Taken with a Long-Handled Spoon: The Roberts Papers and Letters" by William H. Slavick, in *The Southern Review,* autumn 1984; "The Poetry of Space in Elizabeth Madox Roberts' *The Time of Man*" by Anne K. McBride, in *Southern Literary Journal,* fall 1985; "Place in the Short Fiction of Elizabeth Madox Roberts" by Wade Hall, in *The Kentucky-Review,* fall/winter 1986; "Against the Chaos of the World: Language and Consciousness in Elizabeth Madox Roberts's *The Time of Man*" by Linda Tate, in *Mississippi Quarterly: The Journal of Southern Culture,* spring 1987; "Coming of Age and Domesticating Space in the Wilderness: Roberts's *The Great Meadow* and Cather's *Shadows on the Rock*" by John J. Murphy, in *Willa Cather Pioneer Memorial Newsletter,* fall 1989; "Comprehension, Composition, and Closure in Elizabeth Madox Robert's *The Time of Man*" by Stephen Bernstein, in *The Kentucky Review,* spring 1990; "Elizabeth Madox Roberts: A Bibliographical Essay" by Linda Tate, in *Resources for American Literary Study,* 1992, pp. 22-43; *The Truth of a Song: A Study of the Function and Meaning of Music in the Novels and Selected Writings of Elizabeth Madox Roberts* (dissertation) by Victoria V. Barker, 1996.

*   *   *

The philosophic idealism of Bishop Berkeley, the realistic conventions of regional fiction, and a poetic talent for rendering sensuous impressions are the unlikely ingredients that conjoin in the making of Elizabeth Madox Roberts's novels. Her characteristic way of harmonizing these disparate materials is through the focus of an introspective woman who serves as narrator-protagonist—a controlling consciousness that shapes the contours of her own growing personality and those of the outside world, interactively and simultaneously. Two of Roberts's novels, *The Time of Man* and *The Great Meadow,* attained considerable success when they were originally published. The first chronicles the sensibility of a Kentucky girl, Ellen Chesser, whose experience as a migrant farm wife is measured by the eternal cycles of poverty, labor, and the universal portions of grief, pain, joy, and love. Deliberately conceived on the model of the *Odyssey, The Time of Man* aims at a kind of epic quality in its unsentimental depiction of the struggle between creative life instincts and the implacable limitations of the human condition. *The Great Meadow* reworks this theme, but its heroine, Diony, is a more sophisticated consciousness; she is aware of herself and her role, and the journey motif is not the twenty-year wanderings of an impoverished farm family, but the great western trek from Virginia to the founding of Kentucky in the late eighteenth century. Both novels allowed Roberts to develop and display her strengths as a novelist: a supple, lyrical prose style, admirably suited to the particular feminine sensibility that she espoused; a sense of rhythmical narrative structure that moves in slow, undramatic accretions of episodic action; and an unforced, natural symbolism infusing the texture of events.

Although these two novels are regarded as Roberts's major achievements, *My Heart and My Flesh* and *He Sent Forth a Raven* are scarcely less accomplished. The first was meant to be an antithetical sequel to *The Time of Man,* the protagonist, in this case, being stripped of all buffers against adversity only to assert an indomitable will to live. The second is Roberts's most ambitious effort; *He Sent Forth a Raven* invokes the allegorical grandeur of the biblical story of Noah and of *Moby Dick,* and, although the novel is not entirely able to control its materials, it is rich in meaning and strangely powerful. Roberts also wrote three other novels, two collections of short stories, and three volumes of poetry. Her poems—fresh, vivid, and marked by their capacity to record a direct sensuous immediacy—are frequently anthologized in collections of verse for children.

—Earl Rovit

ROBERTS, Kenneth (Lewis)

Born: Kennebunk, Maine, 8 December 1885. **Education:** Schools in Malden, Massachusetts; Stone's School, Boston; Cornell University, Ithaca, New York (editor, *Cornell Widow*), 1904-08, A.B. 1908. **Military Service:** Served in the U.S. Army, in the intelligence section of the Siberian Expeditionary Force, 1918-19: captain. **Family:** Married Anna Seiberling Mosser in 1911. **Career:** Worked in leather business in Boston, 1908-09; reporter and columnist, Boston *Post,* 1909-18, and editor of *Sunday Post* humor page, 1915-18; editorial staff member, *Life* magazine, New York, 1915-18; correspondent, in Washington, D.C., and Europe, *Saturday Evening Post,* Philadelphia, 1919-28; thereafter a full-time writer; lived in Italy, 1928-37, then in Kennebunkport, Maine. **Awards:** Special Pulitzer prize, 1957. Litt.D.: Dartmouth College, Hanover, New Hampshire, 1934; Colby College, Waterville, Maine, 1935; Bowdoin College, Brunswick, Maine, 1937; Middlebury College, Vermont, 1938; Northwestern University, Evanston, Illinois, 1945. **Member:** American Academy. **Died:** 21 July 1957.

Publications

Fiction

Arundel. 1930.
The Lively Lady. 1931.
Rabble in Arms. 1933.
Captain Caution: A Chronicle of Arundel. 1934.
Northwest Passage. 1937.
Oliver Wiswell. 1940.
Lydia Bailey. 1947.
Boon Island. 1956; as *Boon Island: Including Contemporary Accounts of the Wreck of the Nottingham Galley,* 1996.

Plays

Panatella, with Romeyn Berry, music by T.J. Lindorff and others (produced 1907). 1907.
The Brotherhood of Man, with Robert Garland. 1934.

Other

Europe's Morning After. 1921.
*Sun Hunting: Adventures and Observations among the Native and
  Migratory Tribes of Florida.* 1922.
Why Europe Leaves Home. 1922.
The Collector's Whatnot, with Booth Tarkington and Hugh Kahler.
  1923.
Black Magic. 1924.
Concentrated New England: A Sketch of Calvin Coolidge. 1924.
Florida Loafing. 1925.
Florida. 1926.
Antiquamania. 1928.
For Authors Only and Other Gloomy Essays. 1935.
It Must Be Your Tonsils. 1936.
Trending into Maine. 1938; revised edition, 1944.
The Roberts Reader. 1945.
I Wanted to Write. 1949.
Don't Say That about Maine! 1951.
Henry Gross and His Dowsing Rod. 1951.
The Seventh Sense. 1953.
Cowpens: The Great Morale-Builder. 1957; as *The Battle of
  Cowpens,* 1958.
Water Unlimited. 1957.

Editor, *March to Quebec: Journals of the Members of Arnold's
  Expedition.* 1938; revised edition, 1940, 1953.
Editor and Translator, with Anna M. Roberts, *Moreau de St.
  Mery's American Journey (1793-1798).* 1947.

*

Bibliography: *Roberts: A Bibliography* by P. Murphy. 1975.

Critical Study: *A Century of American History in Fiction: Roberts' Novels* by Janet Harris, 1976.

*   *   *

Kenneth Roberts's reputation rests on his historical novels dealing with American history from the time of the French and Indian War to the War of 1812. These are long, character-and-action-packed novels that succeed admirably in bringing history to life. Roberts brought to the writing of fiction two decades of newspaper and magazine journalism and a passion for accurate detail, and his novels are noteworthy for their historical accuracy. His interest in historical fiction began with a curiosity about his own Maine ancestors who had been involved in the American Revolution.

Roberts researched his novels as though he were writing history. He borrowed trunk loads of books from the Library of Congress and historical societies and ransacked the shelves of antiquarian book dealers. When he could not find what he wanted in printed sources, he went to the archives. In researching *Northwest Passage,* for example, he found in the British Public Record Office a large collection of previously unused letters, petitions, and reports written by Major Robert Rogers himself, who was to be the protagonist of the novel. When he was writing *The Lively Lady* at his winter home off the coast of Tuscany he spent hours with Bowditch's *Navigator* and binoculars watching sailing ships in the harbor in order to master the details of sailing a brig.

Without the help of **Booth Tarkington**, his summer neighbor in Kennebunkport, Maine, however, Roberts might not have become a novelist. In 1928 Tarkington persuaded him to drop his journalism and begin his first novel. For the next fifteen years Tarkington talked over plans, encouraged him and then, when the novels were in rough draft, acted as adviser and editor. Night after night Roberts read aloud from manuscripts and gratefully accepted suggestions for deletions and revisions. Roberts's diary shows that in one three-month period in 1936 he spent 58 nights reading the first 51 chapters of *Northwest Passage.*

Arundel is the story of Benedict Arnold's disastrous expedition against Quebec in 1775, narrated by a Richard Nason from Arundel, Maine. Nason's son is the protagonist of Roberts's next novel, *The Lively Lady,* which deals with the operations of a privateer in the War of 1812. *Rabble in Arms* is also about men from Arundel who fight with Arnold, the hero of the novel, and ends with the Battle of Saratoga. *Captain Caution* is another sea story set at the time of the War of 1812. *Northwest Passage* is Roberts's most memorable work and depicts the fascinating career of Major Rogers, Indian fighter during the French and Indian War, who dreamed of finding the Northwest Passage to the Pacific, was governor of Michilimackinac, and was later court-martialed. *Oliver Wiswell* is a novel of particular interest because it tells the story of the American Revolution from the viewpoint of a loyalist.

—James Woodress

ROBINSON, Edwin Arlington

Born: Head Tide, Maine, 22 December 1869; grew up in Gardiner, Maine. **Education:** Gardiner High School, graduated 1888; Harvard University, Cambridge, Massachusetts, 1891-93. **Career:** Freelance writer in Gardiner, 1893-96; lived in New York City, 1897; secretary to the president of Harvard University, 1899; moved to New York, 1899, settled in Greenwich Village, and held various jobs, including subway-construction inspector, 1903-04; through patronage of Theodore Roosevelt, who admired his poetry, became clerk in the U.S. Customs House, New York, 1904-09; spent summers at the MacDowell Colony, Peterborough, New Hampshire, 1911-34. **Awards:** Pulitzer prize, 1922, 1925, 1928; American Academy Gold Medal, 1929. Honorary degrees: Yale University, New Haven, Connecticut, 1922; Bowdoin College, Brunswick, Maine. **Member:** American Academy. **Died:** 6 April 1935.

Publications

Collections

Collected Poems. 1937.
Selected Letters, edited by Ridgely Torrence and others. 1940.
Tilbury Town: Selected Poems, edited by Lawrance Thompson.
  1953.
Selected Early Poems and Letters, edited by Charles T. Davis. 1960.
Selected Poems, edited by Morton Dauwen Zabel. 1965.
Uncollected Poems and Prose, edited by Richard Cary. 1975.

Poetry

The Torrent and the Night Before. 1896; revised edition, as *The Children of the Night,* 1897.
Captain Craig. 1902; revised edition, 1915.
The Town Down the River. 1910.
The Man Against the Sky. 1916.
Merlin. 1917.
Lancelot. 1920.
The Three Taverns. 1920.
Avon's Harvest. 1921.
Collected Poems. 1921.
Roman Bartholow. 1923.
The Man Who Died Twice. 1924.
Dionysus in Doubt. 1925.
Tristram. 1927.
Collected Poems. 5 vols., 1927.
Sonnets 1889-1927. 1928.
Fortunatus. 1928.
Three Poems. 1928.
Modred: A Fragment. 1929.
The Prodigal Son. 1929.
Cavender's House. 1929.
The Glory of the Nightingales. 1930.
Matthias at the Door. 1931.
Poems, edited by Bliss Perry. 1931.
Nicodemus. 1932.
Talifer. 1933.
Amaranth. 1934.
King Jasper. 1935.
Hannibal Brown: Posthumous Poem. 1936.

Plays

Van Zorn. 1914.
The Porcupine. 1915.

Other

Letters to Howard George Schmitt, edited by Carl J. Weber. 1940.
Untriangulated Stars: Letters to Harry de Forest Smith 1890-1905, edited by Denham Sutcliffe. 1947.
Letters to Edith Brower, edited by Richard Cary. 1968.

Editor, *Selections from the Letters of Thomas Sergeant Perry.* 1929.

*

Bibliography: *A Bibliography of Robinson* by Charles Beecher Hogan, 1936; *Robinson: A Supplementary Bibliography* by William White, 1971; *Robinson: A Reference Guide* by Nancy Carol Joyner, 1978.

Critical Studies: *Robinson* by Mark Van Doren, 1927; *Robinson: A Biography* by Hermann Hagedorn, 1938; *Robinson* by Yvor Winters, 1946, revised edition, 1971; *Robinson* by Ellsworth Barnard, 1952, and *Robinson: Centenary Essays* edited by Barnard, 1969; *Robinson: The Literary Background of a Traditional Poet* by Edwin S. Fussell, 1954; *Where the Light Falls: A Portrait of Robinson* by Chard Powers Smith, 1965; *Robinson: A Poetry of the Act* by W.R. Robinson, 1967; *Robinson: A Critical Introduc-tion* by Wallace L. Anderson, 1967; *Robinson: The Life of Poetry* by Louis O. Coxe, 1968; *Robinson* by Hoyt C. Franchere, 1968; *Appreciation of Robinson* edited by Richard Cary, 1969, and *The Early Reception of Robinson: The First Twenty Years* by Cary, 1974; *Robinson: A Collection of Critical Essays* edited by Francis Murphy, 1970; "Time, Space, and Vision in E.A. Robinson's Tristram" by Gerald B. Kinneavy, in *The Language Quarterly,* spring/summer 1987; *Edwin Arlington Robinson* edited by Harold Bloom, 1988; "Edwin Arlington Robinson's Arthurian Poems: Studies in Medievalisms?" by Rebecca Cochran, in *Arthurian Interpretations,* fall 1988; "The Ambivalence of Stance in Edwin Arlington Robinson's Early Poems and Letters" by Anna Blumenthal, in *Style,* spring 1989; "Death, Darkness, Desolation: Negative House-Imagery in the Poems of E.A. Robinson" by Carol Cedar Amelinckx, in *University of Mississippi Studies in English* volume 8, 1990; "Edwin Arlington Robinson: Arthurian Pacifist" by Valerie M. Lagorio, in *King Arthur through the Ages* edited by Valerie M. Lagorio and Mildred Leake Day, 1990; "Edwin Arlington Robinson's Morgan Le Fay: Victim or Victimizer?" by Rebecca Cochran, in *Platte Valley Review,* spring 1991; "Robinson's The Sheaves" by A.R. Coulthand, in *Explicator,* summer 1996, pp. 226-29; *The New England Oblique Style: The Poetry of Ralph Waldo Emerson, Emily Dickinson, and Edwin Arlington Robinson* by Anna Sabol Blumenthal, 1998.

*   *   *

More than any other poet of his time, Edwin Arlington Robinson made poetry his career. He neither traveled nor taught, married nor made public appearances. Aside from a handful of prose pieces and two unsuccessful plays, he devoted himself exclusively to the writing of poetry, publishing many volumes of verse in a forty-year period. He suffered during the first half of his career from neglect and near impoverishment; he suffered during his last years from an excess of adulation. After the signal success of *Tristram,* for which he won his third Pulitzer Prize, he was hailed as America's foremost poet. Although his reputation has diminished since his death, he is nevertheless established as the most important poet writing in America at the turn of the century and has a firm place as one of the major modern poets.

He was, as Robert Frost noted in his preface to *King Jasper,* "content with the old way to be new." The old way was his unwavering insistence on traditional forms. His poems demonstrate his facility in an impressive variety of verse forms, from blank verse in most of the long narratives to Petrarchan sonnets and villanelles in his shorter work, but he was positively reactionary in his dismissal of the then current *vers libre* movement. In a letter, he once placed free verse along with prohibition and moving pictures as "a triumvirate from hell, armed with the devil's instructions to abolish civilization."

Robinson was new in his attitudes in and toward his poetry. He may be called an impersonal romantic, breaking with the nineteenth-century tradition by objectifying and dramatizing emotional reactions while at the same time emphasizing sentiment and mystical awareness. His combination of compassion and irony has become a familiar stance in modern poetry, and his celebrated advocacy of triumphant forbearance in the face of adversity anticipates the existentialist movement. In a letter to the *Bookman* in 1897, responding to the charge that he was pessimistic, he wrote, "This world is not a 'prison house,' but a kind of spiritual kindergarten where millions of bewildered infants are trying to spell God with the wrong blocks." While he was reluctant to be classified as an exponent of any formal philosophical or theological stance, he was entirely willing, in and out of his poetry, to condemn materialistic attitudes. Robinson's use of humor within his serious poetry, in *Amaranth* for instance, placed a new importance on the comic.

While Robinson frequently wrote poems on conventional topics, his subject matter was new in his heavy emphasis on people. Unlike other romantic poets, he generally avoided the celebration of natural phenomena, bragging to a friend about his first volume that one would not find "a single red-breasted robin in the whole collection." Many of his short poems are character sketches of individuals, anticipating **Edgar Lee Masters**'s *Spoon River Anthology*. All of the long narratives deal with complicated human relationships. Frequently they explore psychological reactions to a prior event, such as *Avon's Harvest,* Robinson's "ghost story" about a man destroyed by his own hatred, and *Cavender's House,* a dialogue between a man and his dead wife that deals with questions of jealousy and guilt. The people inhabiting Robinson's books include imaginary individuals; characters modeled on actual acquaintances, such as Alfred H. Louis in *Captain Craig;* figures from history, as in "Ben Jonson Entertains a Gentleman from Stratford," "Rembrandt to Rembrandt," and "Ponce de Leon"; and mythic figures, notably characters from the Bible and Arthurian legend.

Edwin S. Fussell, in his book on Robinson's literary background, devotes separate chapters to the English Bible and the Greek and Roman classics as significant influences on Robinson's work. English poets of particular importance to him were Shakespeare, Wordsworth, Kipling, Tennyson, and Robert Browning, although Robinson objected to the inevitable comparison between his character analyses and those of Browning. Among American poets Robinson found Emerson to be his most significant precursor. Because of his narrative impulse, Robinson's work is also compared to the fiction of Hawthorne and **Henry James**.

Robinson is best known for his earliest work, the short sketches of characters, chiefly failures, who reside in Tilbury Town, the name he uses for Gardiner, Maine. Partially because of their frequent appearance in anthologies, "Richard Cory," "Miniver Cheevy," and "Mr. Flood's Party" are his most famous poems. "Eros Turannos" has been singled out by Louis O. Coxe as the most impressive Tilbury poem. Also highly regarded are a few of the poems of medium length, notably "Isaac and Archibald" and "Aunt Imogen."

Not all of Robinson's poems are narratives, and some of the symbolic lyrics have been highly praised, particularly "For a Dead Lady" and the poem about which Theodore Roosevelt wrote, "I am not sure I understand 'Luke Havergal,' but I am sure that I like it." "The Man Against the Sky," the title poem of the first volume that received widespread critical approval, is an ironic meditation on the possibilities of adopting various philosophical attitudes. It has received a great deal of critical attention from both admirers and detractors. Robinson said that the poem "comes as near as anything to representing my poetic vision."

Critics have tended to neglect Robinson's long narratives, those thirteen book-length poems that occupied most of his attention during the second half of his career. According to his earliest biographer, Hermann Hagedorn, the difficulty Robinson had with *Captain Craig,* first in getting a publisher and then in the adverse critical reaction, was a devastating experience for the young poet. Until he issued his first *Collected Poems* in 1921, Robinson alternated his long poems with volumes of shorter, more readily accessible pieces. After he was thoroughly established, however, he

concentrated on the long narratives. Though these poems are sometimes verbose and repetitious, they nevertheless provided Robinson with his most congenial form, allowing him to unite his talents of narration, characterization, and symbolic discursiveness.

—Nancy Carol Joyner

ROETHKE, Theodore (Huebner)

Born: Saginaw, Michigan, 25 May 1908. **Education:** John Moore School, 1913-21, and Arthur Hill High School, 1921-25, Saginaw; University of Michigan, Ann Arbor, 1925-29, B.A. 1929 (Phi Beta Kappa), M.A. 1936; Harvard University, Cambridge, Massachusetts, 1930-31. **Family:** Married Beatrice O'Connell in 1953. **Career:** Instructor in English, 1931-35, director of public relations, 1934, and varsity tennis coach, 1934-35, Lafayette College, Easton, Pennsylvania; instructor in English, Michigan State College, East Lansing, fall 1935; instructor, 1936-40, assistant professor, 1940-43, and associate professor of English composition, 1947, Pennsylvania State University, University Park; instructor, Bennington College, Vermont, 1943-46; associate professor, 1947-48, professor of English, 1948-62, and honorary poet-in-residence, 1962-63, University of Washington, Seattle. **Awards:** Yaddo fellowship, 1945; Guggenheim grant, 1945, 1950; American Academy grant, 1952; Fund for the Advancement of Education fellowship, 1952; Ford grant, 1952, 1959; Pulitzer prize, 1954; Fulbright fellowship, 1955; Borestone Mountain award, 1958; National Book award, 1959, 1965; Bollingen prize, 1959; Poetry Society of America prize, 1962; Shelley Memorial award, 1962. D.H.L.: University of Michigan, 1962. **Died:** 1 August 1963.

PUBLICATIONS

Collections

On the Poet and His Craft: Selected Prose, edited by Ralph J. Mills, Jr. 1965.
Collected Poems. 1966.
Selected Letters, edited by Ralph J. Mills, Jr. 1968.
Selected Poems, edited by Beatrice Roethke. 1969.

Poetry

Open House. 1941.
The Lost Son and Other Poems. 1948.
Praise to the End! 1951.
The Waking: Poems 1933-1953. 1953.
Words for the Wind: The Collected Verse. 1957.
The Exorcism. 1957.
Sequence, Sometimes Metaphysical. 1963.
The Far Field. 1964.
Two Poems. 1965.
The Achievement of Roethke: A Comprehensive Selection of His Poems, edited by William J. Martz. 1966.

Other

I Am! Says the Lamb (for children). 1961.

Party at the Zoo (for children). 1963.

Straw for the Fire: From the Notebooks 1943-1963, edited by David Wagoner. 1972.

Dirty Dinky and Other Creatures: Poems for Children, edited by Beatrice Roethke and Stephen Lushington. 1973.

*

Bibliography: *Roethke: A Bibliography* by James R. McLeod, 1973; *Roethke's Career: An Annotated Bibliography* by Keith R. Moul, 1977.

Critical Studies: *Roethke* by Ralph J. Mills, Jr., 1963; *Roethke: Essays on the Poetry* by Arnold S. Stein, 1965; *Roethke: An Introduction to the Poetry* by Karl Malkoff, 1966; *The Glass House: The Life of Roethke* by Allan Seager, 1968; *Profile of Roethke* edited by William Heyen, 1971; *The Wild Prayer of Longing: Poetry and the Sacred* by Nathan A. Scott, 1971; *A Concordance to the Poems of Roethke* by Gary Lane, 1972; *Roethke's Dynamic Vision* by Richard Allen Blessing, 1974; *Roethke: The Garden Master* by Rosemary Sullivan, 1975; *The Echoing Wood of Roethke* by Jenijoy La Belle, 1976; *The Edge Is What I Have: Roethke and After* by Harry Williams, 1976; *Roethke: An American Romantic* by Jay Parini, 1979; *Roethke: Poetry of the Earth, Poet of the Spirit* by Lynn Ross-Bryant. 1981; *Roethke* by George Wolff, 1981; *Roethke: The Poetics of Wonder* by Norman Chaney, 1982; "Blake and Roethke: When Everything Comes to One" by Jay Parini, in *William Blake and the Moderns* edited by Robert J. Bertholf and Annette S. Levitt, 1982; *Roethke: The Journey from I to Otherwise* by Neal Bowers, 1983; *Roethke's Meditative Sequences: Contemplation and the Creative Process* by Ann T. Foster, 1985; *Theodore Roethke: The Poet and His Critics* by Randall Stiffler, 1986; "Theodore Roethke" by Kermit Vanderbilt, in *A Literary History of the American West*, 1987; *Understanding Theodore Roethke* by Walter B. Kalaidjian, 1987; *Theodore Roethke* edited by Harold Bloom, 1988; *Theodore Roethke's Far Fields: The Evolution of His Poetry* by Peter Balakian, 1989; "Theodore Roethke: The Darker Side of the Dream" by Karl Malkoff, in *American Writing Today* edited by Richard Kostelanetz, 1991; *Theodore Roethke: A Body with Motion of a Soul* by Mina Surjit Singh, 1991; *The Glass House: The Life of Theodore Roethke* by Allan Seager, 1991; *Theodore Roethke and the Writing Process* by Don Bogen, 1991; "Waltzing with Papa, Dancing with the Bears: Illness, Alcoholism and Creative Rebirth in Theodore Roethke's Poetry" by Timothy Rivinus, in *Beyond the Pleasure Dome: Writing and Addiction from the Romantics* edited by Sue Vice, Matthew Campbell, and Tim Armstrong, 1994; "Gentle Giant" by John Montague, in *The Southern Review*, summer 1996, pp. 561-71; "Roethke's Revisions and the Tone of 'My Papa's Waltz'" by John J. McKenna, in *ANQ: A Quarterly Journal of Short Articles, Notes, and Reviews*, spring 1998, pp. 34-38.

*   *   *

Theodore Roethke's posthumous collection, *The Far Field*, is a resume and retrospect of a lifetime's preoccupations, acknowledging its debt to those poets who have confronted the mystery of personal extinction—the later Eliot and Yeats and that "Whitman, maker of catalogues" whose "terrible hunger for objects" is repeated in these writings of a man who has "moved closer to death, lived with death." Roethke always felt "the sepa-

rateness of all things," the fragility of being. In "The Dream" he had written "Love is not love until love's vulnerable"; "The Abyss" adds a new, desperate urgency to the theme, poised on a dark stair that "goes nowhere," knowing the abyss is "right where you are— / A step down the stair." Yet if this last volume broods over childhood initiations into mortality, it also celebrates the spontaneous impulse towards life, light, growth in which he shares:

> Many arrivals make us live: the tree becoming
> Green, a bird tipping the topmost bough,
> A seed pushing itself beyond itself. . . .
>
> What does what it should do needs nothing more.
> The body moves, though slowly, towards desire.
> We come to something without knowing why.

Summoned once more to the field's end, in old age Roethke returned to "the first heaven of knowing," that second childhood of radical innocence that has always been the American visionary's home. If "Old men should be explorers," he replies to the Eliot of *Four Quartets*, "I'll be an Indian. /Iroquois," thus unashamedly assuming the role of the noble savage in retreat, whose "journey into the interior," into the heart of the continent, is also a "long journey out of the self," into the unconscious and preconscious, the elemental life of the planet.

There is a paradoxical resolution of stasis and motion throughout Roethke's work. "The Sententious Man" claims to "know the motion of the deepest stone"; in "The Far Field," imagery of dwindling, darkening, and decline shifts into sudden surges and spurts of life, as not only air, fire, and water but even earth take on the fluidity that leaves no ground secure: "the shale slides dangerously," dust blows, rubble falls, the arroyo cracks, the swamp is "alive with quicksand." Amid this movement the self floats unperturbed: "I rise and fall in the slow sea of a grassy plain" (the theological punning here recurs throughout his verse); "And all flows past. . . . I am not moving but they are," for the soul, preparing itself for death, has finally found that longed-for "imperishable quiet at the heart of form." Throughout his verse, the field is a complex metaphor: it is the green field of nature, the field of perception, and, at their intersection, a heraldic field in which matter blazons forth spirit, where "All finite things reveal infinitude" disclosing, in the words of one of his earliest poems, "skies of azure / The pageantry of wings the eyes' right treasure."

Movement from closure to openness, finitude to immensity, has been the characteristic rhythm of all Roethke's poetry. The title poem of *Open House* proclaims this:

> My secrets cry aloud. . . .
> My heart keeps open house,
> My doors are widely swung. . . .
> I'm naked to the bone
> With nakedness my shield.
> Myself is what I wear.

The Lost Son pokes around in origins, under stones, in drains and subsoil, to find the answer to his most basic question: "Where do the roots go?" Roethke felt himself at home amidst the abundant verminous life of a vegetable nature that (as in "Cuttings, *later*") strains like a saint to rise anew in "This urge, wrestle, resurrection of dry sticks"—a world to which he was introduced in his florist father's greenhouses, where he learned to "study the lives on a leaf: the little / Sleepers, numb nudgers"; and not only to study, but to find in them, as in the "Shoots [which] dangled and drooped, / Lolling obscenely" in "Root Cellar," an imagery of his own instinctual life. He was impressed by the stubborn persistence of this residual realm: "Nothing would give up life: / Even the dirt kept breathing a small breath."

His poems are rites of passage, exits and entrances where "the body, delighting in thresholds, / Rocks in and out of itself." *Praise to the End!* employs the bouncy rhythms and inconsequential surrealism of nursery rhyme and baby talk, used to such effect in his poems for children, to enact the birth or rebirth of the scattered psyche (Roethke suffered from periodic mental illness) out of a tangle of instinctual impulses—eating, touching, snuffling, sucking, licking—in all of which identity is constituted as lack ("I Need, I Need"), a fall from innocence into disenchantment that brings us to our proper selfhood, aware of time and consequence, and able to announce "I'm somebody else now." In "Give Way, Ye Gates," one line of six verbs charts the whole pilgrimage through need, mutuality, and loss into separated being: "Touch and arouse. Suck and sob. Curse and mourn." The technique of this volume is a riddling, exclamatory questioning, like that of an insistent child who neither expects nor receives an answer, wanting only confirmation of its own puzzling existence. Yet this catechism of the "happy asker" reveals a world of correspondences where everything is an answer to everything else, and the creatures sing their own richness and diversity: "A house for wisdom. A field for revelation. / Speak to the stones and the stars answer."

In his love poems this most physical of poets assumes a metaphysical lightness and delicacy, a clarity of syntax and almost allegoric translucence of imagery that recall Renaissance neoplatonism and the courtly love of the troubadours. His women (even the "woman lovely in her bones") are the Beatrices of a rarefied sensuality, "know[ing] the speech of light" and "cry[ing] out loud the soul's own secret joy"; but even here Roethke's playfulness is preserved in sudden unexpected carnalities of language ("pure as a bride . . . /And breathing hard, as that man rode / Between those lovely tits"). "The Renewal" shows love to be the force that moves the stars, reducing to a oneness knowing and motion, the dualities of his universe, just as "Words for the Wind," which provided the title for his collected verse, sees it as both the journey and the destination of the soul:

> I cherish what I have
> Had of the temporal:
>
> I am no longer young
> But the wind and waters are;
> What falls away will fall;
> All things bring me to love.

—Stan Smith

See the essay on "The Lost Son."

RØLVAAG, O(le) E(dvart)

Born: Donna Island, Helgeland, Norway, 22 April 1876; immigrated to the United States, 1896; became citizen, 1908. **Education:** Donna schools to age 14; Augustana College, Canton, South Dakota, 1899-1901; St. Olaf College, Northfield, Minnesota, 1901-05, B.A. 1905, M.A. 1910; University of Oslo, 1905-06. **Family:** Married Jennie Marie Berdahl in 1908; three sons and one daughter. **Career:** Fisherman in Norway, 1891-95; worked on his uncle's farm in South Dakota, 1896-99; professor of Norwegian language and literature, 1906-31, and head of the Norwegian department, 1916-31, St. Olaf College. Secretary, Norwegian-American Historical Association, 1925-31. **Awards:** Honorary degree, University of Wisconsin, Madison, 1929; Knight of the Order of St. Olaf, Norway, 1926. **Died:** 5 November 1931.

PUBLICATIONS

Fiction

Amerika-breve (Letters from America). 1912; translated by Ella Tweet and Solveig Zempel, as *The Third Life of Per Smevik,* 1971.
Paa Glemte Veie (On Forgotten Paths). 1914.
To Tullinger: Et Billede fra Idag (Two Fools: A Picture of Our Time). 1920; revised edition, translated by Sivert Erdahl and Rølvaag, as *Pure Gold,* 1930.
Laengselens Baat. 1921; translated by Nora O. Solum, as *The Boat of Longing,* 1933.
Giants in the Earth, translated by Lincoln Colcord and Rølvaag. 1927.
> *I de Dage: Fortaelling om Norske Nykommere I Amerika* (In Those Days: A Story of Norwegian Pioneering in America). 1924.
> *Ricket Grundlaegges* (The Founding of the Kingdom). 1925.
Peder Seier. 1928; translated by Rølvaag and Nora O. Solum, as *Peder Victorious,* 1929.
Den Signede Dag (The Blessed Day). 1931; translated by Trygve M. Ager, as *Their Fathers' God,* 1931.

Other

Ordforklaring til Nordahl Rolfsens Laesebok for Folkeskolen II. 1909.
Haandbok I Norsk Retskrivning og uttale til Skolebruk og Selvstudium, with P.J. Eikeland. 1916.
Norsk Laesebok, with P.J. Eikeland. 3 vols., 1919-25.
Omkring Faedrearven (essays). 1922.

Editor, *Deklamationsboken.* 1918.

*

Critical Studies: *Rølvaag: A Biography* by Theodore Jorgenson and Nora O. Solum, 1939; *Rølvaag: His Life and Art* by Paul Reigstad, 1972; *Prairies Within: The Tragic Trilogy of Ole Rølvaag* by Harold P. Simonson, 1987; "Rølvaag and Krause: Two Novelists of the Northwest Prairie Frontier" by Arthur R. Huseboe, in *A Literary History of the American West,* 1987; *Ole Edvart Rølvaag* by Ann Moseley, 1987; "The Function of the Mad Woman Episode in Rølvaag's *Giants in the Earth*" by Joseph F. Green, in *Platte Valley Review,* spring 1989; "Rølvaag's 'Roguish Smile' in *Peder Victorious*" by Dexter Martin, in *Western American Literature,* November 1989; "Rølvaag's Lost Novel" by Einar Haugen, in *Norwegian American Studies* volume 32, 1989; "Keillor and

Rølvaag and the Art of Telling the Truth" by Bruce Michelson, in *American Studies,* spring 1989; "'To Lose the Unspeakable': Folklore and Landscape in O.E. Rølvaag's *Giants in the Earth*" by April Schultz, in *Mapping American Culture* edited by Wayne Franklin and Michael Steiner, 1992.

*   *   *

O.E. Rølvaag's great achievement is *Giants in the Earth,* first published in Norway in 1924 and 1925, then translated into English by Rølvaag and Lincoln Colcord in 1927. The result is remarkable: to a bilingual reader the characters seem to be thinking and speaking in Norwegian patterns and cadence, even though the words are English and few Norwegian expressions are left untranslated. By common agreement, *Giants in the Earth* is America's best immigrant story, its great pioneering novel, and a towering documentary of the middle west.

The events Rølvaag describes in *Giants in the Earth* occurred 25 years before he arrived in America. But the setting is the South Dakota he came to in 1896 at the age of twenty, the characters his own kind of Norwegian immigrants, and the events a composite of many accounts he had heard from Dakota pioneers. Writing the book in the 1920s, Rølvaag relied especially on the memory of his father-in-law, Andrew Berdahl. Although the prairie he describes is a formidable adversary for his pioneers, Rølvaag's characters are even more remarkable, especially the hard-driving, inventive, and irrepressible Per Hansa: he is the very type of the ideal American pioneer, yet also very Norwegian. An even more moving character is Per's wife, Berit, who is neurotic, backward-looking, and fanatically religious. Rølvaag's pioneer has a dual struggle: against the unbroken prairie and a wife who thinks she has sinned unforgivably in disobeying her parents, in marrying Per Hansa, and in leaving Norway.

Per Hansa's story is heroic and tragic, rare qualities in twentieth century fiction. Berit lives on through the two sequels Rølvaag wrote—*Peder Victorious* and *Their Fathers' God*—and achieves a greatness of her own. The struggle to retain her Norwegian heritage in the new American settlements was a cause Rølvaag supported whole-heartedly. But the essential themes of the two later novels—assimilation and cultural clashes—lack the power and drama of the pioneering struggle. Of more interest is *Pure Gold,* a reworking of Rølvaag's 1920 novel *To Tullinger* (Two Fools): it is the stark tale of a pioneering couple who become monsters of greed. Rølvaag's own favorite was *Laengselens Baat,* which appeared in English translation as *The Boat of Longing* after his death. The strong note of pathos (perhaps pessimism) in this novel has two sources: Nils, a sensitive, artistic, young immigrant, encounters a materialistic America; and his Norwegian parents wait in vain for letters from their son.

Even though the greatness of *Giants in the Earth* was recognized at once, scholars and critics have been uneasy about assigning Ole Rølvaag a place in American literature: he wrote in Norwegian, not English. His psychological realism might owe something to **Sherwood Anderson,** but a greater influence stemmed from Knut Hamsun and Arne Garborg. As his correspondence reveals, Rølvaag wrote as fluently in English as in Norwegian. Working with translators in turning his novels into English, he weighed and considered each word and phrase. But Rølvaag taught Norwegian language and literature during most of his life in America. Despite Conrad's achievement in the English novel, Rølvaag thought that giving up his native language would require "a re-

making of soul." Such a "spiritual readjustment" he would not undertake.

—Clarence A. Glasrud

ROSE, Wendy (Bronwen Elizabeth Edwards)

Pseudonym: Chiron Khanshendel. **Born:** Oakland, California, 7 May 1948. **Education:** Cabrillo College, Aptos, California, and Contra Costa College, San Pablo, California; University of California, Berkeley, B.A. 1976, M.A. 1978. **Family:** Married Arthur Murata, 1976. **Career:** Instructor, Native American Studies/Ethnic Studies, University of California, Berkeley, 1979-83; instructor, California State University, Fresno, 1983-84; instructor and coordinator of American Indian Studies, Fresno City College. Formerly associated with the Women's Literature Project of Oxford University Press and the Smithsonian's Native Writers Series. Former member of board of directors, Coordinating Council of Literary Magazines; member, Modern Language Association's Commission on Languages and Literature of the Americas, National Association of Ethnic Studies, Association for the Study of American Indian Literatures. **Residence:** California.

PUBLICATIONS

Poetry

Hopi Roadrunner Dancing. 1973.
Long Division: A Tribal History. 1976; second edition, 1980.
Academic Squaw. 1977.
Builder Kachina: A Home-Going Cycle. 1979.
Lost Copper. 1980.
What Happened When the Hopi Hit New York. 1981.
The Halfbreed Chronicles. 1985.
Going to War with All My Relations: New and Selected Poems. 1993.
New: Bone Dance. 1994.
Now Poof She Is Gone. 1994.

Other

Aboriginal Tattooing in California (anthropology). 1979.

Multi-media (book, audio tape, and slides): *Poetry of the American Indian Series: Wendy Rose.* 1978.

*

Critical Studies: "Finding the Loss" by Kenneth Lincoln, in *Parnassus,* spring-summer 1982; interview with Carol Hunter, in *Coyote Was Here* edited by Bo Scholer, 1984; "Blue Stones, Bones and Troubled Silver," in *Studies in American Indian Literature,* spring 1983; "The Bones Are Alive: An Interview with Wendy Rose" by Joseph Bruchac, in *Survival This Way,* 1987; "Wendy Rose: Searching through Shards, Creating Life" by James Saucerman, in *The Wicazo Sa Review,* fall 1989; "Anthropological

Roles: The Self and Its Others in T.S. Eliot, William Carlos Williams and Wendy Rose" by Christoph Irmsher, in *Soundings,* winter 1992.

*   *   *

Wendy Rose, a Hopi-Miwok author of poetry, has built a career of college teaching and writing. She is also a social anthropologist who has sometimes found herself caught between the conflicting forces of science and art, of material and spiritual values, and, above all, of white and Indian heritages.

Rose is an urban Indian reared in Oakland, California, as a Roman Catholic without the experience of a reservation childhood and, except for stories from her father's Hopi people, without direct ties to either Miwok or Hopi heritage. This does not make her unique, but it does shape her poetry. Being an anthropologist does not make her unique either, but that academic experience drives many of her poems. Nonetheless, her cultural identity seems to come more from her artistic heritage than from the study of anthropology. Rose, as Indian woman anthropologist and poet, addresses the diverse confrontations of direct personal, professional, and tribal importance as she engages the more universal problems of fragmentation versus healing unity of her (and our) world.

In the preface to *Going to War with All My Relations* (1993), Rose writes that "the 'war' is everyone's war . . . [and that] our 'Relations' are each other, all that is alive, with the awareness that life is everywhere." Much of her poetry is a series of engagements in that war, wherein she fights the fragmentation and, through her art, attempts to recreate unity and wholeness. Many of her poems describe her sometimes uncomfortable role as anthropologist who, because she is Native American, was sometimes at first regarded with suspicion; other poems deal with the "academic squaw" syndrome, a term she uses ironically, of course, saying in a footnote that she would never use such a derogatory word except in ironic opposition to white usage that identifies a role almost thrust on her. She also fights the racism inherent in the habit of relegating all things Indian to anthropology, thus denying the aesthetic values of Indian literary art so important to her.

Other related poems focus on the desecration of graves of Native Americans and the subsequent dehumanizing of them as archaeological specimens, reduced to what she calls invoiced "ethnodata," or, even worse, the commercial marketing of skeletons (skulls especially) as artifacts to collectors. However, the movement in her poems is typically toward perceptions of identity and a healing unity. The first part of "Three Thousand Dollar Death Song," for instance, is filled with images of depersonalization, of once living beings "smattered into traces of rubble." By contrast, in the second half of the poem artifacts are imagined as rising like bears and marching together out of the museum door as "our bones rise to meet them," creating a scene reminiscent of the ghost dance days.

Other of Rose's poems engage personal and ethnic identity and her own creativity. Many of these poems are filled with images of mountain, rabbit, corn pollen, many-colored winds, and summer storms. However, the matrix from which she flakes the words, as she says in one poem, can be the modern city itself. In the poem "The Urban Child Listens" the storyteller, modern and urban, feels the need to preserve the culture through oral tales. In the absence of images of "corn-tassels," "sheep-fat candles," "silver spider web," and "thunderhead," she must pass on the stories to the children even in the midst of traffic noise and city buildings because "Coyote speeds through our lives anyway."

Although many of Rose's poems are polemic or militant, some of her poems are more mellow. In the short poem "Summer Evenings in Tucson Remembered," a sense of being is shaped in childhood like loaves of bread, round and brown. Still other poems of wholeness are restorations of identification with "her people," some of whom she knows but some of whom are mythic recreations of personal tribal experiences such as the title poem to *Hopi Roadrunner Dancing* or the "Happy Child Poem" from that same volume.

Rose's later poems have become less strictly Indian and more global. In the 1982 interview with Carol Hunter she stated "one thing . . . seems to be happening not just in my work, but in the work of a lot of people all at once, especially Indian people. Many of us are acknowledging and identifying with a world-wide perspective, identifying with the struggle of indigenous people the world over . . . . My work has become larger than Hopi or even Indian, too, and I've begun writing about El Salvador, about the Jewish holocaust, about the exploitation of 'circus freaks,' and so on. I've called this . . . work *The Halfbreed Chronicles.*"

Rose is not alone in her quest for order; however, her place in contemporary American literature is unique because of the conflicts she feels in being a Native American anthropologist and artist. Through two different moods of the same persona, Rose emerges from the fragmenting, depersonalizing effects of her professional experience in the dominant white urban society while locating her place within the Native part of American culture. Above all, hers is a healing voice whose art, graphic and literary, helps restore an almost lost spiritual past, one that cannot be recaptured but can be recreated in our present life through art.

—James R. Saucerman

ROTH, Henry

Born: Tysmenica, Austria-Hungary, 8 February 1906; brought to New York City, 1908. **Education:** DeWitt Clinton High School, New York, graduated 1924; City College, New York, 1924-28, B.S. 1928. **Family:** Married Muriel Parker in 1939; two sons. **Career:** Worked for the Works Progress Administration (WPA), 1939; substitute teacher, Roosevelt High School, New York, 1939-41; precision metal grinder in New York, Rhode Island, and Boston, 1941-46; teacher in Montville, Maine, 1947-48; attendant, Augusta State Hospital, Maine, 1949-53; waterfowl farmer, 1953-62; private tutor, 1956-65. **Awards:** American Academy grant, 1965; City College of New York Townsend Harris Medal, 1965; University of New Mexico D. H. Lawrence Fellowship, 1968. **Died:** 1995.

PUBLICATIONS

Fiction

Call It Sleep. 1934.
Mercy of a Rude Stream Volume 1: *A Star Shines Over Mt. Morris Park.* 1994.
A Diving Rock on the Hudson. 1995.
From Bondage. 1996.
Requiem for Harlem. 1998.

Other

Nature's First Green (memoir). 1979.
Great Violinists in Performance (bibliography). 1986.
Shifting Landscape: A Composite, 1925-1987, edited by Mario
    Materissi. 1987.

*

Critical Studies: *World of Our Fathers* by Irving Howe, 1976,
as *The Immigrant Jews of New York 1881 to the Present,* 1976;
Roth by Bonnie Lyons, 1977; "Linguistic Universes in Henry
Roth's *Call it Sleep*" by Naomi Diamont in *Contemporary Literature* vol. 27, no. 3, 1986; "Call it Irresponsible" by Donna Rifkind
in *The New Criterion* vol. 6, no. 6, 1988; "An American Messiah:
Myth in Henry Roth's *Call it Sleep*" by Lynn Altenbernd in *Modern Fiction Studies* vol. 35, no. 4, 1989.

*   *   *

Henry Roth had one of the most extraordinary careers in American letters. He arrived in the United States as a small boy around
1909 and lived first on the Lower East Side and later in Harlem.
In 1934 he published his masterpiece *Call It Sleep*, a closely autobiographical novel heavily influenced by James Joyce's *Ulysses*,
T. S. Eliot's *The Waste Land,* and the psychoanalytic theories of
Sigmund Freud, but it met at first with little critical attention. After that, Roth found himself unable to write fiction, and his reputation languished until 1963, when *Call It Sleep* was republished
to widespread acclaim as a paperback.

Whereas it seemed incongruous on its first appearance, in the
middle of an era dominated by realist and protest fiction and preoccupied with the widespread troubles caused by the Depression,
Call It Sleep has since come to be admired for its Joycean technique of interior monologue, its dense cluster of metaphors, and
its evocation of a crowded, impoverished city in which people of
many different nationalities and origins struggle to live together.

Its theme is familiar enough and has its roots in the works of
Charles Dickens. It deals with the inner conflict and psychological disturbance of a sensitive young boy, David Schearle, as he
struggles to come to terms with the meaning of his Jewish heritage and with the violence in the world he sees all around him.
The story is told from David's perspective, and it is a process
that ultimately ends in defeat. David does not experience the revelation he was seeking, the light he yearns for does not come, and
the unclean world that repulses him is not cleansed. David is impoverished in part by language. One of the things the novel does
in painfully comic scenes is to juxtapose the beauty, the idiomatic
richness, and the vitality of the natural Yiddish of David and his
mother against the appalling impoverishment of their broken English. It is an extremely powerful, if at times claustrophobic, novel.

Roth was seventy-three when, in 1979, he finally began writing fiction again, a mammoth sequence called *Mercy of a Rude
Stream*; the first volume, *A Star Shines Over Mt. Morris Park*,
appeared in 1994. Before that, and as a kind of preparation and a
reminder of his existence to the world, he had published a collection of short prose pieces, mainly interviews and uncollected short
stories, called *Shifting Landscape* (1987). Roth died in 1995, but
the books have continued to be published; four volumes, the first
part of *Mercy of a Rude Stream*, have now appeared. According
to a publishing note, what remains consists of five separate sections totaling 1,457 manuscript pages, which deal with the 1930s
and chronicle the relationship of Ira Stigman and M, the composer
with whom he falls in love and marries.

The first part of the sequence tells the story of Ira Stigman
from his arrival with his parents, and later many of his relatives,
in New York. Although the author warns us against taking the
story as autobiographical, the novels reflect closely what we know
of the circumstances of Roth's own life. It is a story largely of
Ira's defeat and humiliation, the loss of his self-confidence, the
theft of a pen that leads to his expulsion from school, and his
clandestine couplings first with his sister and then with a young
cousin. Some of the events and situations—the fierce beatings Ira
receives from his father, for example, or advances by a predatory
would-be lover of Ira's mother—echo those of *Call It Sleep.* The
main text is interspersed with reflections on the part of the narrator, writing in the present from the distanced viewpoint of some
seventy years later. He engages in a dialogue with his computer,
Ecclesias. He conveys the intensity of his love for M, whom he
sees as the prime healing influence in his life, and is shattered when
she dies before he does.

Frequently, the observations are ironical at Roth's own expense.
For example, at one point he quotes another writer's hatred of "generational novels." Looking back on his recollections of early childhood, the narrator comments, "It should have gone into a novel, several novels perhaps, written in early manhood, after his first—and
only—work of fiction. There should have followed novels written in
the maturity gained by that first novel. Well, salvage whatever you
can, threadbare mementos glimmering in recollection."

But in reality the extraordinarily ambitious enterprise represents
far more than "threadbare mementos." Through a prodigious feat
of memory, Roth goes back almost seventy years to recall and
evoke the sounds, sights, and smells of the Harlem area in which
he grew up. He recounts his rejection of his Jewish heritage, and
his guilt over that rejection, as well as his regrets that he did not
resist more firmly the aggression directed against him as a Jew.

Roth seems to blame his prolonged silence on his failure to stand
up for his Jewish heritage, and it is probably for this reason that
he turns violently on his former mentor Joyce, who, he claims,
did much the same with his Irish heritage. In his speculative passages Roth engages in a constant running battle with Joyce, saying of *Ulysses* that "the book was the work of a man who sought
to fossilize his country, its land, its people, to rob them of their
future, arrest their ebullient, coursing life, their traditions and aspirations." What Joyce needed was "a complete overhaul of the
haughty psyche that derided the very source of its identity, the
Irish folk." In contrast, the aged Ira enthusiastically embraces his
home land of Israel, even though he fears for its future.

Not surprisingly, Roth's alter ego Ira expresses frequent doubts
as to the worth of what he is doing: "His stuff was now old hat,
and for all he knew, stereotyped as well." It is perhaps too early
to pass judgment on the project, but whatever else, it represents
a remarkable feat of stamina and artistic integrity.

—Laurie Clancy

ROTH, Philip (Milton)

Born: Newark, New Jersey, 19 March 1933. **Education:**
Weequahic High School, New Jersey; Newark College, Rutgers

University, 1950-51; Bucknell University, Lewisburg, Pennsylvania (Phi Beta Kappa), 1951-54, A.B. 1954; University of Chicago, 1954-55, M.A. 1955. **Military Service:** Served in the United States Army, 1955-56. **Family:** Married 1) Margaret Martinson in 1959 (separated 1962; died 1968); 2) Claire Bloom in 1990 (divorced 1994). **Career:** Instructor in English, University of Chicago, 1956-58; visiting writer, University of Iowa, Iowa City, 1960-62; writer-in-residence, Princeton University, New Jersey, 1962-64; visiting writer, State University of New York, Stony Brook, 1966, 1967, and University of Pennsylvania, Philadelphia, 1967-80; distinguished professor, Hunter College, New York, 1988-92. General editor, Writers from the Other Europe series, Penguin, publishers, London, 1975-80. Member of the Corporation of Yaddo, Saratoga Springs, New York. **Awards:** Houghton Mifflin literary fellowship, 1959; Guggenheim fellowship, 1959; National Book award, 1960; Daroff award, 1960; American Academy grant, 1960; O. Henry award, 1960; Ford Foundation grant for drama, 1965; Rockefeller fellowship, 1966; National Book Critics Circle award, 1988; National Jewish Book award, 1988; PEN/Faulkner award, 1993; Pulitzer prize for fiction, for *American Pastoral,* 1998. Honorary degrees: Bucknell University, 1979; Bard College, Annandale-on-Hudson, New York, 1985; Rutgers University, New Brunswick, New Jersey, 1987; Columbia University, New York, 1987; Brandeis University, Massachusetts, 1991; Dartmouth College, New Hampshire, 1992. **Member:** American Academy, 1970.

PUBLICATIONS

Collections

A Roth Reader. 1980.

Novels

Letting Go. 1962.
When She Was Good. 1967.
Portnoy's Complaint. 1969.
Our Gang (Starring Tricky and His Friends). 1971.
The Breast. 1972; revised edition in *A Roth Reader,* 1980.
The Great American Novel. 1973.
My Life as a Man. 1974.
The Professor of Desire. 1977.
Zuckerman Bound: A Trilogy and Epilogue (includes "The Prague Orgy" epilogue). 1985; as *The Prague Orgy,* 1985.
    The Ghost Writer. 1979.
    Zuckerman Unbound. 1981.
    The Anatomy Lesson. 1983.
The Counterlife. 1987.
Deception. 1990.
Operation Shylock: A Confession. 1993.
Sabbath's Theater. 1995.
American Pastoral. 1997.
I Married a Communist. 1998.

Short Stories

Goodbye, Columbus, and Five Short Stories. 1959.
Novotny's Pain. 1980.

Plays

Television Play: *The Ghost Writer,* with Tristram Powell, from the novel by Roth, 1983.

Other

Reading Myself and Others. 1975; revised edition, 1985.
The Facts: A Novelist's Autobiography. 1988.
Patrimony: A True Story. 1991.
Conversations with Roth, edited by George J. Searles. 1992.

*

Bibliography: *Roth: A Bibliography* by Bernard F. Rodgers, Jr., 1974; revised edition, 1984.

Critical Studies: *Bernard Malamud and Roth: A Critical Essay* by Glenn Meeter, 1968; "The Journey of Roth" by Theodore Solotaroff, in *The Red Hot Vacuum,* 1970; *The Fiction of Roth* by John N. McDaniel, 1974; *The Comedy That "Hoits": An Essay on the Fiction of Roth* by Sanford Pinsker, 1975, and *Critical Essays on Roth* edited by Pinsker, 1982; *Roth* by Bernard F. Rodgers, Jr., 1978; "Jewish Writers" by Mark Shechner, in *The Harvard Guide to Contemporary American Writing* edited by Daniel Hoffman, 1979; introduction by Martin Green to *A Roth Reader,* 1980; *Roth* by Judith Paterson Jones and Guinevera A. Nance, 1981; *Roth* by Hermione Lee, 1982; *Reading Roth* edited by A. Z. Milbauer and D.G. Watson, 1988; *Understanding Roth* by Murray Baumgarten and Barbara Gottfried, 1990; *The Changing Mosaic: From Cahan to Malamud, Roth and Ozick,* edited by Daniel Walden, 1993; *Beyond Despair: Three Lectures and a Conversation with Philip Roth* by Aron Appelfeld, 1994; *The Imagination in Transit: The Fiction of Philip Roth* by Stephen Wade, 1996; *Philip Roth and the Jews* by Alan Cooper, 1996; *Silko, Morrison, and Roth: Studies in Survival* by Naomi R. Rand, 1998.

*   *   *

"Sheer Playfulness and Deadly Seriousness are my closest friends," Philip Roth once remarked in interview; "I am also on friendly terms with Deadly Playfulness, Serious Playfulness, Serious Seriousness, and Sheer Sheerness. From the last, however, I get nothing; he just wrings my heart and leaves me speechless." Roth's early work explored with a tense and exasperated earnestness "the whole range of human connections . . . between clannish solidarity . . . and exclusion or rejection"—the struggle of what he has called "the determined self" (in a double sense) against its contingent identity and environment. *When She Was Good* surprised his critics by delineating the self-deception and hypocrisy of small-town Gentile America with the same acid sharpness he brought to the anxieties, pieties, and suppressed hysteria of middle-class and metropolitan Jewry in *Goodbye, Columbus* and *Letting Go.* Roth's characters are usually painfully alert to the insistent and insidious dialogue of conscience with the unconscious; beneath the innocent and upright text of conversation and event lurks a subtext of amoral impulses, disclosed through Freudian slips and misprisions and by displacement, gesture, and "unintended" innuendo. With *Portnoy's Complaint* the libido came into its own, redefining the ironic, self-conscious wit that enlivened the earlier works as the evasive strategy of "people [who] wear the old unconscious on their *sleeves.*" Portnoy complains that he is "the son in the Jewish joke—*only it ain't no joke!*" and the book mischievously ends with a "punch line" that brackets the whole text as the protagonist's pre-analysis warm-up on the couch of his psychoanalyst, Dr. Spielvogel. (This same psychoanalyst returns in *My Life as a Man* as representative of a gray, reassuring normalcy that frames the novelist-hero's outrageously self-dramatizing "life.")

Portnoy's compulsive onanism, feted with Rabelaisian panache, provides a constant analogy for the art of fiction itself (a "complaint" is both physical disorder and literary device). Story-telling is also an autotelic act, a self-sufficient—and finally inconsequential—spilling of the beans. Thus, in *The Breast* the protagonist Kepesh wakes to find himself translated into the literary tradition he has been teaching, metamorphosed into a huge, almost self-enclosed mammary gland: "Beyond sublimation. I made the word flesh. I have outKafkaed Kafka." *The Great American Novel* (its very title self-reflexive) is a tissue of parody and pastiche that suggests that baseball is not only a theme but the supreme fiction of American culture (as Roth remarked in an essay, "The Literature of My Boyhood"). *My Life as a Man* has as its main text the "True Story" of the novelist Peter Tarnopol, preceded by two "Useful Fictions" that are his short-story variations on the crisis of marital breakdown and blocked creativity that dominates his in-any-case fictitious "Life." Roth plays further games with the reader, alluding to previous writings of Tarnopol's that inevitably and teasingly recall his own earlier work. But if here narcissism in "life" (*i.e.,* "content") becomes reflected in the autoreferentiality of the "text" (*i.e.,* "form"), the sheer exuberance of Roth's invention makes it clear that he is not fixated in the dead-end "Sheer Sheerness" of his fictive analogue. If Tarnopol is only tangentially affected by the great historic events of his era, Roth has written of them at length in *Our Gang* (settling accounts in advance with the Nixon mafia) and in the essays collected as *Reading Myself and Others.*

Kepesh, apparently normal, returns in *The Professor of Desire* (though the reader does not know whether he has escaped the dilemma of *The Breast,* has yet to face it, or exists in some parallel and unconnected life). Here too he perpetually balances anxious libido and angst-ridden literature, in a final grotesque dream sequence, set in the Prague of police repression and silenced writers, visiting Kafka's whore, who offers to show him her withered genitals in the interest of art (and money). The paralleling of textuality and sexuality from now on takes a darker turn, and Kafka is the lugubrious master of the later works.

In the 1973 essay "Looking at Kafka," Roth imagined being taught Hebrew as a boy by a Kafka who had escaped death and persecution in America. A similar fantasy animates *The Ghost Writer.* It is cast as a reminiscence, twenty years on, by the now successful Nathan Zuckerman, of a one-night visit to the aging novelist E. I. Lonoff, ensconced in the snow-bound Berkshires with a mysterious young woman. Nathan fantasizes that she is really Anne Frank, the diarist of Nazi persecution, who has accidentally survived the death camps to find a new life and father figure in America. Contrasted with her frank and artless narratives, Zuckerman's own artful novel *Carnovsky* (clearly a literary double of Roth's *Portnoy*) seems to him almost as the antisemitic tract it was accused of being by a scandalized Jewish middle class, who saw him doing the dirt on 4000 years of respectable suffering. *Zuckerman Unbound,* thirteen years on from the fictional time of *The Ghost Writer,* carries on this guilt-ridden postmortem. Ev-

erywhere, Zuckerman is mistaken for his fictional alter ego Carnovsky, lionized, reviled, and accosted in the streets, a prisoner of his own success. Even his own father's last word from his deathbed is "bastard." *The Anatomy Lesson* extends these tribulations. Here, Zuckerman's mother, having failed to recover from the shock of his book, is dying from a brain tumor that causes her, when asked her name, to write the word *holocaust.* Though she returns to haunt him not out of vengeance but only to check that he has not lost weight—a Jewish mother even in death—she perplexes Zuckerman with this inscription, from someone who never wrote down anything but recipes and knitting patterns. As he says ambiguously of the word (or the tumor): "It must have been there all the time without their even knowing." He broods about escaping "suffering that isn't semi-comical, the world of massive historical pain" symbolized by the Warsaw Ghetto.

Instead, he is afflicted by "this pain in the neck" that makes writing almost impossible and lovemaking complicated, generating novel (and novelish) terms of intercourse. The "anatomy lesson" itself is both Rembrandt's coldly clinical painting of a dissection and the chronic back pain that "teaches us who is boss" (just as Portnoy's sexual fixation had). Deciding to free himself from his "graphomania," he seeks "everything the word's in place of. The lowest of genres—life itself" by trying to redeploy as an obstetrician: "a new perspective on an old obsession . . . he owed it to women." He finds his guilt is assuaged by pretending, in casual conversations with strangers, to be a professional pornographer; once he professes his obsession as a crusading (and profitable) all-American business enterprise, he is accepted as a respectable citizen. His ultimate anatomy lesson is, however, the living death's head of an old woman who has for four years treated herself for cancer of the face, her jaw half eaten away and the bone exposed. The book's last sentence leaves him about to begin his initiation, its macabre pun on the word *corpus* as both book and body defining Roth's perennial dilemma: "as though he still believed that he could unchain himself from a future as a man apart and escape the corpus that was his."

Zuckerman is still present in Roth's 1987 novel *The Counterlife.* The dilemma of exile is cast between Zuckerman and his "uninteresting" brother Henry. The novel pursues the question of how brothers "know each other . . . as a kind of deformation of themselves." Roth, in this puzzle, is on his characteristic search for "the real wisdom of the predicament," a predicament that concerns some of his favorite dualities—impotence and its opposite, death and its opposite, and the cultivated self that barely exists outside the perceptions of others. The concept and puzzle of the paired thinker, the problem of the problem that is handled by two minds, is cast most vibrantly in *Operation Shylock: A Confession.* Here the main character, Philip Roth, meets Philip Roth, and the self-on-self relationship, at once comic and horrifying, is the central play of the novel's investigation. Instead of hanging tightly to a plot structure, it moves, as the parts of the self do, almost as an album, with a sense of assembled monologues and interviews.

In *Sabbath's Theater,* the comic Mickey Sabbath is the autonomous hero who, for the most part, manages to break free of his creator. The novel opens with Sabbath's dying lover asking him to renounce all other women and ends with his realization, a year after her death, that he can survive her loss. What happens in between is mostly retrospect. In the final section of the book, Sabbath goes "home" to New Jersey to arrange his own burial, and there he finds a solitary living relative and, amongst his brother's things, a Purple Heart. Both discoveries compel him against suicide. Whereas Roth's comedy typically takes aim at the hypocrisy of the American rabbinate for perpetuating a religion in whose purpose they no longer believe, in *Sabbath's Theater* he is addressing the loss that occurs when an entire culture, rebelling against moral distinctions deemed too narrow, fails to make any distinctions at all; he sees this as a universal madness.

For Roth the introversions of contemporary fiction reflect a wider, social dilemma: "Defying a multitude of bizarre projections, or submitting to them," he has said, "would seem to me at the heart of everyday living in America." Adapting Philip Rahv's division of American writers into "redskins" and "palefaces"—the one rumbustious and anarchic, the other stiff and priggish—he has proposed his own third category, a subversive synthesis of the two: the "redface." Roth's is the poetry of embarrassment and exposure; by making unease both theme and narrative technique, he has fused play and seriousness into a style inimitably his own, which is not easily rendered "speechless."

—Stan Smith, updated by Martha Sutro

ROWLANDSON, Mary (White)

Born: Probably in England, c. 1637; moved with her family to Lancaster, Massachusetts. **Family:** Married 1) Joseph Rowlandson c. 1656 (died 1678), three daughters and one son; 2) Samuel Talcott in 1679. **Career:** Captured (with three of her children, one of whom died) in raid on Lancaster by Wampanoag Indians during King Philip's War, 1676: held for 11 weeks, then ransomed. Lived in Boston, 1676, and Wethersfield, Connecticut, after 1677. **Died:** 5 January 1711.

PUBLICATIONS

Prose

The Soveraignty and Goodness of God, Together with the Faithfulness of His Promises Displayed; Being a Narrative of the Captivity and Restauration of Mrs. Mary Rowlandson. 1682; in *Narratives of the Indian Wars 1675-1699,* edited by Charles Henry Lincoln, 1913; as *The Captive: The True Story of the Captivity of Mrs. Mary Rowlandson Among the Indians and God's Faithfulness to Her in Her Time of Trial,* 1996.

*

Critical Studies: *Flintlock and Tomahawk: New England in King Philip's War* by Douglas Edward Leach, 1958; *Regeneration through Violence: The Mythology of the American Frontier 1600-1860* by Richard Slotkin, 1973; *The Indian Captivity Narrative: An American Genre* by Richard VanDerBeets, 1984; "New Light on Rowlandson" by David L. Greene, in *Early American Literature,* 1985; *American Puritanism and the Defense of Mourning: Religion, Grief, and Ethnology in Mary White Rowlandson's Captivity Narrative* by Michell Robert Breitwieser, 1990; *Bound and Determined: Captivity, Culture-Crossing and White Womanhood from Mary Rowlandson to Patty Hearst* by Christopher Castiglia, 1996; "Moving Targets: The Travel Text in *A Narrative of the*

Captivity and Restauration of Mrs. Mary Rowlandson" by Marilyn C. Wesley, in *Essays in Literature,* spring 1996, pp. 42-57; "Mary White Rowlandson Remembers Captivity: A Mother's Anguish, a Woman's Voice" by Parley Ann Boswell, in *Women's Life Writing: Finding Voice/Building Community* edited by Linda S. Coleman, 1997; "Mary Rowlandson and the Psalms: The Textuality of Survival" by Dawn Henwood, in *Early American Literature,* 1997, pp. 169-86.

*   *   *

Although she wrote only one book—*The Soveraignty and Goodness of God, Together with the Faithfulness of His Promises Displayed; Being a Narrative of the Captivity and Restauration of Mrs. Mary Rowlandson*—Mary Rowlandson is nonetheless remembered as one of the major writers of early America and one of only four women (the other three being **Anne Bradstreet, Phillis Wheatley**, and Sarah Kemble Knight) from the period to achieve prominence for their writings.

As the subtitle of her narrative indicates, *The Soveraignty and Goodness of God* is an account of its author's captivity among the Indians of New England at the time of King Philip's War (1675-78). Living with her family in the frontier outpost of Lancaster, Massachusetts, Rowlandson, along with her three children, was captured by a confederacy of Indians during a raid on her town in February 1676. Her youngest child, a girl of six, died shortly thereafter of wounds received during the attack. Although she had herself been wounded, Rowlandson remained with the Indians for nearly twelve weeks. Approximately thirty years old at the time of her capture, she was forced to march more than 150 miles in frigid weather and snow, and she was made to endure the privations of an Indian lifestyle during wartime.

On the day of the attack, Rowlandson's husband, a Harvard-educated Congregationalist minister, had been in Boston seeking military assistance for Lancaster. Eventually, he and the citizens of Massachusetts negotiated with Indian leaders for the release of his wife in early May 1676. Their remaining two children—a fourteen-year-old son, named Joseph after his father, and an eleven-year-old daughter, named Mary after her mother—were released within the next few weeks. While it was once thought that Rowlandson had died within a few years of her release, it became known that after the death of her husband in 1678 she married Captain Samuel Talcott, a leading citizen of Wethersfield, Connecticut, where she resided in prosperity until her death in 1711, more than thirty years later than had once been assumed.

Published in 1682, *The Soveraignty and Goodness of God* immediately became what has been termed America's first bestseller. In the first year of its publication alone, it went through four editions, including one published in England, and since then it has been reprinted more than forty times. Only four pages from the first edition survive because, as has been suggested, it was probably "read to pieces." The lasting popularity of the narrative is easy to understand. Written in a plain but vigorous style, it is an outstanding example of adventure writing at its best. During colonial times, when fear of Indian captivity was an imminent frontier reality, Rowlandson's captivity appealed to the emotions of generations of Americans interested in Indians and what **Washington Irving** later called "border romance." In more modern times, the vivid realism of Rowlandson's prose, the complexity of her psychology, and the heroism of her ordeal have kept her narrative alive.

In addition to the glimpse that it provides into the lifestyle of the Indians of New England before the wholesale invasion of their culture by the European colonists, Rowlandson's narrative provides insight into the workings of the Puritan American imagination, particularly with regards to the Indian, the wilderness, and the meaning of personal and cultural affliction. Interpreted within a typological context, the Indians are depicted as "murtherous wretches," "Barbarous Creatures," "merciless Enemies," and "hell-hounds," and the wilderness is described as "a lively resemblance of hell." Accordingly, Rowlandson's captivity is seen as a combination punishment and trial at the hands of God's enemies, whom he ultimately uses to instruct his servant and her contemporaries about the mysterious workings of providence.

Artfully written, *The Sovereignty and Goodness of God* is structured according to a series of what Rowlandson terms "Removes." Literally, these "removes" correspond to her physical removal, at the hands of the Indians, away from British civilization and the securities of culture and home. Psychologically and metaphorically, they create an aesthetic perspective not unlike the movement through hell in Dante's *Divine Comedy,* to which Rowlandson's narrative has been compared. Other literary analogues include John Bunyan's *Pilgrim's Progress* and the sermons, histories, and spiritual autobiographies of the day. While Rowlandson was probably not a highly educated woman, she possessed an instinctive grasp of literary structure and language, and she had no doubt read and internalized many of the staples of seventeenth-century Puritan literature.

Coming as it did at the beginning of a tradition of captivity stories that led in the nineteenth century to the novels of **James Fenimore Cooper, William Gilmore Simms, Robert Montgomery Bird,** and **Mark Twain,** *The Sovereignty and Goodness of God* is nonetheless considered the finest example of the form before it became appropriated by belletristic writers, and it should certainly be read by anyone interested in the literature and culture of early America.

—James A. Levernier

ROWSON, Susanna

Born: Susanna Haswell, Portsmouth, Hampshire, England, c. 1762; taken to Massachusetts, where her father, a naval officer, was stationed, c. 1767; deported with her Loyalist father to England, 1778. **Education:** Privately educated. **Family:** Married William Rowson in 1786. **Career:** Governess to children of Duchess of Devonshire, 1780s; actress, appearing with her husband, in Edinburgh, 1792-93; acted and wrote for New Theatre Company of Philadelphia, in Philadelphia, Baltimore, and Annapolis, Maryland, 1793-96, and Federal Street Theatre Company, Boston, 1796-97; founder and teacher, Young Girls' Academy, Boston, 1797-1822; editor, Boston *Weekly Magazine,* 1802-05. President, Boston Fatherless and Widows Association. **Died:** 2 March 1824.

Publications

Fiction

Victoria. 1786.
The Inquisitor; or, Invisible Rambler. 1788.
The Test of Honour. 1789.

Charlotte: A Tale of Truth. 1791; as *Charlotte Temple,* 1794; edited by Clara M. and Rudolf Kirk, 1964; edited by William S. Kable, in *Three Early American Novels,* 1970.
Mentoria; or, The Young Lady's Friend. 1791.
The Fille de Chambre. 1792; as *Rebecca,* 1814.
Trials of the Human Heart. 1795.
Reuben and Rachel; or, Tales of Old Times. 1798.
Sarah; or, The Exemplary Wife. 1813.
Charlotte's Daughter; or, The Three Orphans. 1828; as *Lucy Temple: One of the Three Orphans,* 1842(?).

Plays

Slaves in Algiers; or, A Struggle for Freedom. 1794.
The Female Patriot; or, Nature's Rights, from the play *The Bondman* by Philip Massinger (produced 1795).
The Volunteers: A Musical Entertainment, music by Alexander Reinagle (produced 1795).
Americans in England; or, Lessons for Daughters (produced 1797). 1796; as *The Columbian Daughter; or, Americans in England* (produced 1800), 1800.
The American Tar (produced 1796).
Hearts of Oak, from the work by John Till Allingham (produced 1810-11[?]).

Poetry

A Trip to Parnassus; or, The Judgment of Apollo on Dramatic Authors and Performers. 1788.
Poems on Various Subjects. 1789.
The Standard of Liberty: A Poetical Address. 1795.
Miscellaneous Poems. 1804.

Other

An Abridgement of Universal Geography, Together with Sketches of History. 1806.
A Spelling Dictionary. 1807.
A Present for Young Ladies (miscellany). 1811.
Youth's First Step in Geography. 1818.
Biblical Dialogues between a Father and His Family. 2 vols., 1822.
Exercises in History, Chronology, and Biography, in Question and Answer. 1822.

*

Bibliography: *Rowson, The Author of Charlotte Temple: A Bibliographical Study* by R.W.G. Vail, 1933; in *Bibliography of American Literature* by Jacob Blanck, edited by Virginia L. Smyers and Michael Winship, 1983.

Critical Studies: *Rowson, America's First Best-Selling Novelist* by Ellen B. Brandt, 1975; *In Defense of Women: Rowson* by Dorothy Weil, 1976; *The Life and Times of Charlotte Temple: The Biography of a Book* by Cathy N. Davidson, 1989; *The Happy Revolution: Colonial Women and the Eighteenth-Century Theater* by Mary Anne Schofield, 1990; *Susan Rowson: Feminist and Democrat* by Doreen Alvarez-Saar, 1991; "Female Captivity and the Deployment of Race in Three Early American Texts" by Maureen L. Woodward, in *Papers on Language and Literature: A Journal for Scholars and Critics of Language and Literature,* spring

1996, pp. 115-46; "Sisterhood Born from Seduction: Susanna Rowson's *Charlotte Temple* and Stephen Crane's *Maggie Johnson*" by Keith Fudge, in *Journal of American Culture,* spring 1996, pp. 43-50; "Playing with Republican Motherhood: Self-Representation in Plays by Susanna Haswell Rowson and Judith Sargent Murray, in *Early American Literature,* 1996, pp. 150-66; "America, Romance, and the Fate of the Wandering Woman: The Case of *Charlotte Temple*" by Kay Ferguson Ryals, in *Women, America and Movement: Narratives of Relocation* edited by Susan L. Roberson, 1998.

*   *   *

Because of the popularity, variety, and number of Susanna Rowson's books, she may properly be considered the foremost woman of letters of her generation in the United States. The phenomenal success on both sides of the Atlantic of her novel *Charlotte Temple* has tended to obscure her other considerable accomplishments, but she also wrote other novels and a large number of plays, poetry, textbooks, and miscellanies that defy classification. Her literary career is even more remarkable in light of her prominence in her other occupations, those of actress and educator. She has the distinction of being not only one of America's first professional women but also one of the first advocates of women's rights in the United States.

Charlotte: A Tale of Truth has gone through more than 200 editions since it was first published in 1791 and was, according to R.W.G. Vail, "the most popular of all early American novels." While detractors have dismissed it as sentimental and formulaic, supporters have accounted for its popularity by insisting on its forthright realism within the sentimental convention. Rowson herself claimed that the story of seduction and betrayal is an actual one, and in the early 1800s the gravestone of the purported model, Charlotte Stanley, was changed to "Charlotte Temple." It still may be seen in Trinity Churchyard in New York City. No other novel by Rowson approaches the popularity of this bestseller, but others were highly regarded, notably *The Fille de Chambre* and *Reuben and Rachel.*

One of her few extant plays, *Slaves in Algiers* is the first successfully produced play by a woman in America. A musical comedy, written in collaboration with Alexander Reinagle, it is of topical interest in that it was a protest against the capture of American ships off the Barbary coast from 1785 to 1794. The play is notable for its fervent nationalism and the insistence upon the equality of women in the new nation. Although it was well-received by playgoers, William Cobbett roundly attacked it for its feminist sentiments.

Rowson's poems and songs were not critically well-received, and in the late twentieth century they seem florid and derivative. Nevertheless many of them were immensely popular, especially "America, Commerce, and Freedom." Her textbooks and miscellanies eventually became of only historical interest. In spite of her significant contributions to American letters, little critical attention was paid her until the final quarter of the twentieth century, some 200 years after her career began. This attention is testimony to the enduring quality of her work.

—Nancy Carol Joyner

RUKEYSER, Muriel

Born: New York City, 15 December 1913. **Education:** Fieldston School, New York, 1919-30; Vassar College, Poughkeepsie, New York; Columbia University, New York, 1930-32. **Family:** Had one son. **Career:** Vice president, House of Photography, New York, 1946-60; teacher at Sarah Lawrence College, Bronxville, New York, 1946, 1956-57. Member of board of directors, Teachers-Writers Collaborative, New York, beginning 1967; president PEN American Center, 1975-76. **Awards:** Harriet Monroe award, 1941; American Academy award, 1942; Guggenheim fellowship, 1943; American Council of Learned Societies fellowship, 1963; Swedish Academy translation award, 1967; Copernicus award, 1977; Shelley Memorial award, 1977. D.Litt.: Rutgers University, New Brunswick, New Jersey, 1961. **Member:** American Academy. **Died:** 12 February 1980.

PUBLICATIONS

Collection

A Muriel Rukeyser Reader. 1994.

Poetry

Theory of Flight. 1935.
Mediterranean. 1937(?).
US. 1. 1938.
A Turning Wind. 1939.
The Soul and Body of John Brown. 1940.
Wake Island. 1942.
Beast in View. 1944.
The Children's Orchard. 1947.
The Green Wave. 1948.
Orpheus. 1949.
Elegies. 1949.
Selected Poems. 1951.
Body of Waking. 1958.
Waterlily Fire: Poems 1932-62. 1962.
The Outer Banks. 1967.
The Speed of Darkness. 1968.
29 Poems. 1972.
Breaking Open. 1973.
The Gates. 1976.
The Collected Poems. 1978.

Plays

The Middle of the Air (produced 1945).
The Colors of the Day (produced 1961).
Houdini (produced 1973).

Fiction

Orgy. 1965.

Other (for children)

Come Back Paul. 1955.
I Go Out. 1961.
Bubbles. 1967.
Mazes. 1970.
More Night. 1981.

Other

Willard Gibbs (biography). 1942.
The Life of Poetry. 1949.
One Life (biography of Wendell Wilkie). 1957.
Poetry and Unverifiable Fact: The Clark Lectures. 1968.
The Traces of Thomas Hariot. 1971.

Translator, with others, *Selected Poems of Octavio Paz.* 1963; revised edition, 1973.
Translator, *Sun Stone,* by Octavio Paz. 1963.
Translator, with Leif Sjoberg, *Selected Poems of Gunnar Ekelof.* 1967.
Translator, *Three Poems by Gunnar Ekelof.* 1967.
Translator, with others, *Early Poems 1935-1955,* by Octavio Paz. 1973.

*

Critical Studies: *The Poetic Vision of Rukeyser* by Louise Kertesz, 1980; *Who Is the Double Ghost Whose Head Is Smoke?: Women Poets on Aging* by Diana Hume-George, 1986; "Trans-Formations: Muriel Rukeyser's Ajanta" by Pramod K. Nayar, in *Indian Journal of American Studies,* winter 1994, pp. 55-59; "X-Ray Testimonials in Muriel Rukeyser" by David Kadlec, in *Modernism-Modernity,* January 1998, pp. 23-47.

*   *   *

Much has been said about the feminine voice in poetry, usually by critics. No one seems to know exactly what the "true" feminine voice is, except that somewhere between the despair and the joy of woman's second-class existence, a kind of experience is finally being written. **Sylvia Plath** wrote from this sensibility and a number of more recent women poets have missed the joy expressed between the lines, where Plath had made words that work together. The assumption that despair should somehow outweigh joy in serious poetry by women results from the Dickinson (and now, Plath) tradition.

Reading the work of Muriel Rukeyser, one quickly learns that feminism is not so easily defined. Once again, the near-answer is revealed for what it is, and we are thrown back to the poem itself. Rukeyser's work can be despairing, but her responses have larger potential. Even in moments of sad recollection, as in "Effort at Speech between Two People," Rukeyser's voice is not entirely despondent:

When I was three, a little child read a story about a rabbit
who died, in the story, and I crawled under a chair :
a pink rabbit : it was my birthday, and a candle
burnt a sore spot on my finger, and I was told to be happy.

Here, Rukeyser has successfully combined the elements of mature narrative with a verbal sense of what it was like to live through that third birthday. The poem is not cute, in any of its aspects, and in spite of succeeding lines ("I am unhappy. I am lonely. Speak to me.") never indulges in outright despondency. The hope for communication initially caused the poem and it survives, echoed by lively images, and imbues the poem ultimately with a sense of optimism.

Rukeyser's work is always tough, however, and never assumes the false authority that is so often mistaken for wisdom. She investigates nearly every aspect of life, from the desperate haircutting of a boy who needs work to "The Power of Suicide," one of her tight, excellent four-line poems:

The potflower on the windowsill says to me
In words that are green-edged red leaves:
Flowerflowerflowerflower
Today for the sake of all the dead   Burst into flower.

The simplicity of such a poem makes explication impossible: what gimmicks of "style" has the poet employed? One knows only that the poem is bound by a natural rhythm, and seems to relate a part of the poet's experience.

Some of Rukeyser's long poems, in particular "The Speed of Darkness," are among the finest we'll have to carry with us into the twenty-first century. Her vocabulary is truly of our generation, but she wrote poems of a longer endurance:

Whoever despises the clitoris despises the penis
Whoever despises the penis despises the cunt
Whoever despises the cunt despises the life of the child.

Resurrection music,   silence,   and surf.

In "Waterlily Fire," she curiously mixes hard consonant sounds with a softer, feminine voice:

We pray : we dive into each other's eyes
Whatever can come to a woman can come to me.
This the long body : into life from the beginning.

The toughness of these poems suggests that "feminine," with all its present connotations, is not the correct adjective for Rukeyser's work. The frankness of her love poems (read "What I See") combined with her muted optimism also makes for memorable poetry.

Rukeyser's poetry is feminine, but only because the poet is a woman. It is enduring because the poet retained all of her "seventeen senses," and used every one of them in her work.

—Geof Hewitt

RUNYON, (Alfred) Damon

Born: Manhattan, Kansas, 4 October 1880. **Education:** Schools in Pueblo, Colorado. **Military Service:** Served in the U.S. Army during the Spanish-American War, 1898-99: contributed to forces newspapers Manila *Freedom* and *Soldier's Letter.* **Family:** Married 1) Ellen Egan in 1911 (died), one son and one daughter; 2) Patrice del Grande in 1932 (divorced 1946). **Career:** Reporter, *Evening Press* and *Evening Post,* 1896-98, and *Chieftain,* 1900, all Pueblo; Colorado Springs *Gazette,* Denver *Post,* 1905-06, *Rocky Mountain News,* Denver, 1906-10, and San Francisco *Post,* 1910; sportswriter and columnist, New York *American* and *Sunday American,* 1911-37; correspondent for Hearst newspapers in Mexico, 1912, and in Europe, 1917-18; columnist and feature writer for King Features/International News Service, from 1918; columnist, New York *Daily Mirror,* late 1930s; producer at RKO and 20th Century-Fox studios, Hollywood, 1942-43. **Awards:** National Headliners Club prize, for journalism, 1939. **Died:** 10 December 1946.

PUBLICATIONS

Collections

A Treasury of Runyon, edited by Clark Kinnaird. 1958.
The Snatching of Bookie Bob and Other Stories. 1995.

Fiction (stories)

Guys and Dolls. 1931.
Blue Plate Special. 1934.
Money from Home. 1935.
More than Somewhat, edited by E.C. Bentley. 1937.
Furthermore, edited by E.C. Bentley. 1938.
The Best of Runyon, edited by E.C. Bentley. 1938.
Take It Easy. 1938.
My Old Man. 1939.
My Wife Ethel. 1939; as *The Turps,* 1951.
Runyon Favorites. 1942.
Runyon a la Carte. 1944.
The Three Wise Guys and Other Stories. 1946.
In Our Town. 1946.
Short Takes. 1946.
Trials and Other Tribulations. 1948.
Runyon First and Last. 1949; as *All This and That,* 1950.
Runyon on Broadway. 1950.
Runyon from First to Last. 1954.
Romance in the Roaring Forties and Other Stories. 1986.

Play

A Slight Case of Murder, with Howard Lindsay (produced 1935). 1940.

Poetry

The Tents of Trouble. 1911.
Rhymes of the Firing Line. 1912.
Poems for Men. 1947.

Other

Captain Eddie Rickenbacker, with Walter Kiernan. 1942.

*

Critical Studies: *Father's Footsteps* by Damon Runyon, Jr., 1954; *A Gentleman of Broadway* by Edwin P. Hoyt, 1964; *Runyonese: The Mind and Craft of Runyon* by Jean Wagner, 1965; *The World of Runyon* by Tom Clark, 1978; *The Men Who Invented Broadway: Runyon, Walter Winchell, and Their World* by John Mosedale, 1981; *Runyon* by Patricia Ward D'Itri, 1982; *A Horse Named Paul Revere: Damon Runyon on Film; Procedings of Fifth Annual Conference on Film at Kent State University* by Robert Nocera, 1987; "Damon Runyon at the Movies" by Guy Szuberla, in *Literature Film Quarterly,* 1993, pp. 71-79.

*   *   *

Damon Runyon belongs to that long line of American journalists who make copy out of the comic potentiality of life around them. Much of that comedy derives from the rich variety of speech patterns among the various immigrant communities spread across the United States: German, Dutch, Polish, Irish; and, in Runyon's case, the Jewish-Italian speech of the Bronx and other areas of New York. For what gives Runyon his special distinction is that he wrote about life in the big city, whereas previous journalist/fiction writers in his mold had largely confined themselves to small-town Midwestern communities.

Runyon's world is that of the seedy mafiosi, barflies, compulsive gamblers, womanizers, men who sport names such as "Society Max," "Harry the Horse," "Rusty Charlie," "Feet Samuels," "Dancing Dan." All the stories about these characters are written in the continuous present tense, as though Runyon himself is one of the barflies, spinning a yarn into his neighbor's ear, making a laughable anecdote out of his friends' misfortunes and misadventures. For example: "This Heine Schmitz is a very influential citizen of Harlem, where he has large interests in beer, and it is by no means violating any confidence to tell you that Heine Schmitz will just as soon blow your brains out as look at you. In fact, I hear sooner."

Once he had discovered this raffishly, down-at-heels, yet defiantly stylish world (or sub-world), and had discovered a style of narrating its doings, Runyon had no reason not to go on and on recounting anecdotes about it (much as Wodehouse, having invented Wooster and Jeeves, could set them in motion time after time). Runyon was, in fact, a prolific author. Quite apart from volumes of light verse, there were numerous collections of his short stories and a play. The verse and play need not detain us. They are lightweight, the verse reminiscent of poets like **James Whitcomb Riley** and **Eugene Field**, in that they tell folksy tales of lovable low-life characters, although in Runyon's case the characters were often of the city rather than of the country.

Of the volumes of short stories, perhaps the pick are *More Than Somewhat, Take It Easy, Furthermore,* and *My Old Man.* The best of the stories are hilarious, and Runyon manages effortlessly to capture a style of speech that, in its aping of "polite" or "standard" American English, tells one only too graphically of the difficulties immigrant communities had in learning a new tongue, while desperately—or naturally—keeping to modes of expression that belonged to their mother-tongue. Who can forget Nathan Detroit's anxious questioning of ever-loving Adelaide: "Would you say that some doll might fall for some guy which you would not think she would do so?" Or Joe the Joker's remark that "Only last night, Frankie Ferocious sends for Ropes and tells him he will appreciate it as a special favor if Ropes will bring me to him in a sack"?

One could, of course, object that the real world of the Mafia is so cynically immoral that laughter about it is indefensible. Perhaps. But against that it has to be said that Runyon's world is no more real than the world of the Woosters, or of Blandings. In its own way, however, it is just as funny.

—John Lucas

S

SALINGER, J(erome) D(avid)

Born: New York City, 1 January 1919. **Education:** McBurney School, New York, 1932-34; Valley Forge Military Academy, Pennsylvania (editor, *Crossed Sabres*), 1934-36; New York University, 1937; Ursinus College, Collegetown, Pennsylvania, 1938; Columbia University, New York, 1939. **Military Service:** Served in the 4th Infantry Division of the United States Army, 1942- 45; staff sergeant. **Family:** Married 1) Sylvia in 1945 (divorced 1946); 2) Claire Douglas in 1955 (divorced 1967), one daughter and one son. **Career:** Writer. **Residence:** New Hampshire.

PUBLICATIONS

Short Stories

Nine Stories. 1953; as *For Esme—With Love and Squalor and Other Stories,* 1953.
Franny and Zooey. 1961.
Raise High the Roof Beam, Carpenters, and Seymour: An Introduction. 1963.

Novel

The Catcher in the Rye. 1951.

*

Bibliography: *Salinger: A Thirty Year Bibliography 1938-1968* by Kenneth Starosciak, privately printed, 1971; *Salinger: An Annotated Bibliography 1938-1981* by Jack R. Sublette, 1984.

Critical Studies: *The Fiction of Salinger* by Frederick L. Gwynn and Joseph L. Blotner, 1958; *Salinger: A Critical and Personal Portrait* edited by Henry Anatole Grunwald, 1962; *Salinger and the Critics* edited by William F. Belcher and James W. Lee, Belmont, 1962; *Salinger* by Warren French, 1963, revised edition, 1976, revised edition as *Salinger Revisited,* 1988; *Studies in Salinger* edited by Marvin Laser and Norman Fruman, 1963; *Salinger* by James E. Miller, Jr., 1965; *Salinger: A Critical Essay* by Kenneth Hamilton, 1967; *Zen in the Art of Salinger* by Gerald Rosen, 1977; *Salinger* by James Lundquist, 1979; *Salinger's Glass Stories as a Composite Novel* by Eberhard Alsen, 1984; *In Search of Salinger* by Ian Hamilton, 1988; *The Catcher in the Rye: Innocence Under Pressure* by Sanford Pinsker, 1993; *J.D. Salinger,* edited by Harold Bloom, 1998.

*   *   *

Of his writings, J.D. Salinger has so far wished to preserve only a novel and thirteen short stories, all published between 1948 and 1959, mostly in the *New Yorker.* Despite this limited body of work, Salinger was, at least between 1951 and 1963, the most popular American fiction writer among serious young persons and many alienated adults because of the way in which he served as a spokesman for the feelings of his generation. Thus his work is of unique interest as evidence of the sensibility of those times.

Salinger had taken a short-story writing course under Whit Burnett, the influential editor of *Story,* which gave many important American fiction writers their start. Salinger's first published work, "The Young Folks," appeared there in 1940. Like much of his later work, this slight piece contrasted the behavior of, on one hand, shy, sensitive and, on the other, tough, flippant, unfeeling young upper-middle-class urbanites. During the 1940s, Salinger published (in *Story* and most of the popular slick magazines like *Collier's*) another nineteen stories that he has not allowed to be collected. Some of these, like "This Sandwich Has No Mayonnaise," are of interest for introducing a character named Holden Caulfield, who resembles the later protagonist of *The Catcher in the Rye,* but who dies during World War II. Most are very short, heavily ironic tales about troubled young people defeated by what Holden Caulfield would call "the phony world." The only one of great interest in the light of Salinger's later achievement is the longest, "The Inverted Forest," a cryptic tale about an artist's relationship to society. The lines quoted from the poetry of the central figure, Raymond Ford—"Not wasteland, but a great inverted forest / with all the foliage underground"—suggest that all beauties are internal, so that the artist is exempt from external responsibilities.

The question of the sensitive individual's responsibility to the world remains the focal question in all of Salinger's better known fiction. *The Catcher in the Rye* is the comically grotesque account of Holden Caulfield's two-and-a-half-day odyssey through the wasteland of New York City at Christmas time after he decides to quit his fashionable prep school. Holden dreams of escaping the city and going out West where he can build "a little cabin somewhere . . . and live there for the rest of my life . . . near the woods, but not right in them" (a description that foreshadows almost exactly the New England retreat where Salinger himself has lived for the past thirty years). In the speech that gives the novel its title, Holden tells his little sister Phoebe that the one thing he would like to do is stand guard over "all these little kids playing some game in this big field of rye and all" and "catch everybody if they start to go over the cliff." But Holden learns, when he sees obscenities scratched on the walls of Phoebe's elementary school, that "you can't ever find a place that's nice and peaceful, because there isn't any." And watching Phoebe ride the Central Park carousel, he realizes, "The thing with kids is, if they want to grab for the gold ring, you have to let them do it, and not say anything." Wiser but sadder, he decides that he must return home rather than take the responsibility for leading Phoebe astray.

Although Salinger is most often identified as the author of *The Catcher in the Rye,* Holden Caulfield, who finally compromises with his social responsibilities, is not the typical hero in Salinger's work. The stories that the author has chosen to preserve begin and end with accounts of the suicide of Seymour Glass, oldest son and spiritual guide to his six siblings of a New York Irish-Jewish theatrical family. In "A Perfect Day for Bananafish," the first story in the collection *Nine Stories,* the reader learns only the circumstances of Seymour's suicide in a Miami Beach hotel. In "Seymour: An Introduction," his brother and interpreter Buddy offers at last the explanation for the event: "The true artist-seer . . . is mainly dazzled to death by his own scruples, the blinding shapes and colors of his own sacred human conscience."

The eleven stories published between these two carry the reader from the account of the suicide to the illumination of its significance, and reflect along the way Salinger's increasing absorption in oriental philosophies, especially Zen Buddhism. Four stories in *Nine Stories*—"Uncle Wiggily in Connecticut," "The Laughing Man," "Just Before the War with the Eskimos," and "Pretty Mouth and Green My Eyes"—offer, like *The Catcher in the Rye*, depressing pictures of people trapped in the "phony" world but dreaming of a "nice" world. In four of the later stories, however, Salinger suggests that the grim situation might be ameliorated— "Down at the Dinghy" portrays Seymour's sister reconciling her small son to a threatening world; "For Esme—With Love and Squalor" is a triumphant epithalamion for a young girl who has done meaningful good in a warring world; "DeDaumier-Smith's Blue Period" is an amazingly successful description of a mystical experience that leads a young man to forsake aggressive ambitions; and the famous concluding story, "Teddy," presents a boy who has truly absorbed the Buddhist concept of the illusoriness of material life and is prepared to move serenely beyond it.

In the longer "Glass Saga" stories, Salinger focuses on Seymour's siblings and presents, in "Franny," the story of the youngest child's breakdown when confronted with the "ego" of the squalid world of college and theater. In "Zooey," her brother literally talks her out of her breakdown by assuming the voice of the departed Seymour, and counseling, "An artist's only concern is to shoot for some kind of perfection, and on his own terms, not anyone else's." "Raise High the Roof Beam, Carpenters" prefaces "Seymour: An Introduction" with Buddy's fond recollection of Seymour's violent responses to beauty and his supreme affront to the rituals of his urban caste when he persuades his intended to run off with him on their wedding day instead of submitting to a fancy ceremony.

Since these stories were collected in 1963, Salinger has published only "Hapworth 16, 1924," a labored account of seven-year-old Seymour's prodigious sexual and intellectual proclivities as revealed by a letter home from summer camp. In the one interview he has granted in recent years—to object to an unauthorized edition of his uncollected stories—Salinger protested that he is still writing constantly, but he denounced publication as "a terrible invasion" of his privacy.

—Warren French

SALTUS, Edgar (Evertson)

Born: New York City, 8 October 1855. **Education:** St. Paul's School, Concord, New Hampshire; studied at Yale University, New Haven, Connecticut, the Sorbonne, Paris, University of Heidelberg, and University of Munich, 1872-76; Columbia University Law School, New York, 1876-80, LL.B. 1880, but never practiced law. **Family:** Married 1) Helen Sturgis Read in 1883 (divorced 1891); 2) Elsie Welsh Smith in 1895 (separated 1901; died 1911), one daughter; 3) Marie Giles in 1911. **Career:** Lived in New York; writer from 1884; editor and compiler for P.F. Collier and Son, publishers, late 1890s. **Died:** 31 July 1921.

PUBLICATIONS

Fiction

Mr. Incoul's Misadventure. 1887.
The Truth about Tristrem Varick. 1888.
Eden. 1888.
A Transaction in Hearts. 1889.
The Pace That Kills. 1889.
A Transient Guest and Other Episodes. 1889.
Mary Magdalen. 1891; as *Mary of Magdala*, 1903.
Imperial Purple. 1892.
The Facts in the Curious Case of H. Hyrtl, Esq. 1892.
Madam Sapphira: A Fifth Avenue Story. 1893.
Enthralled: A Story of International Life. 1894.
When Dreams Come True: A Story of Emotional Life. 1895(?).
Purple and Fine Women. 1903.
The Perfume of Eros: A Fifth Avenue Incident. 1905.
Vanity Square: A Story of Fifth Avenue Life. 1906.
Daughters of the Rich. 1909.
The Monster. 1913.
The Paliser Case. 1919.
The Ghost Girl, edited by Marie Saltus. 1922.

Poetry

Poppies and Mandragora: Poems, with Twenty-Three Additional Poems by Marie Saltus, edited by Marie Saltus. 1926.

Other

Balzac. 1884.
The Philosophy of Disenchantment. 1885.
The Anatomy of Negation. 1886; revised edition, 1889.
Love and Lore. 1890.
Spain and Her Colonies. 1898.
Wit and Wisdom from Saltus, edited by G.F. Monkshood and George Gamble. 1903.
The Pomps of Satan (essays). 1904.
Historia Amoris: A History of Love Ancient and Modern. 1906; as *Love throughout the Ages*, 1908.
The Lords of the Ghostland: A History of the Ideal. 1907.
Oscar Wilde: An Idler's Impression. 1917.
The Gardens of Aphrodite. 1920.
The Imperial Orgy: An Account of the Tsars from the First to the Last. 1920.
Parnassians Personally Encountered, edited by Marie Saltus. 1923.
The Uplands of Dream (essays and poems), edited by Charles Honce. 1925.
Victor Hugo, and Golgotha: Two Essays, edited by Marie Saltus. 1925.

Editor, *The Capitals of the Globe.* 1893.
Editor, *The Lovers of the World.* 3 vols., 1896(?).
Editor, *The Great Battles of All Nations from Marathon to Santiago.* 2 vols., 1898.

Translator, *After-Dinner Stories from Balzac.* 1885; as *Tales from Balzac*, 1909.
Translator, *Tales Before Supper from Theophile Gautier and Prosper Merimee.* 1887.

Translator, *The Story without a Name,* by Jules Barbey d'Aurevilly. 1891.

*

Bibliography: in *The Uplands of Dream* by Saltus, edited by Charles Honce, 1925; in *Bibliography of American Literature* by Jacob Blanck, edited by Virginia L. Smyers and Michael Winship, 1983.

Critical Studies: *Saltus, The Man* by Marie Saltus, 1925; *Saltus* by Claire Sprague, 1968.

* * *

In 1884 Edgar Saltus began his literary career with *Balzac,* an introductory study that witnesses to his predominantly European interests. This was followed by his elegant popularizations of German contemporary pessimists, Schopenhauer and Hartmann, in *The Philosophy of Disenchantment* and *The Anatomy of Negation.* His first novel, *Mr. Incoul's Misadventure,* inaugurates the first, most successful phase of his fiction.

In 1891 Saltus published *Mary Magdalen,* reportedly originating in conversations with Oscar Wilde, the first of his impressionist quasi-histories. *Imperial Purple,* high-colored portraits of the Roman emperors from Caesar to Heliogabalus, was deservedly popular, but the attempted emulation in *Imperial Orgy,* which presented the Russian Czars from Ivan the Terrible to Nicholas "the last," is considerably less achieved.

Mr. Incoul's Misadventure, in fact, is typical of Saltus's novels, with its pessimism, self-conscious style, occasional authentic glimpses of upper-class life, melodramatic themes, and loose plotting: a millionaire coldly and ingeniously revenges himself on his wife and the man who loves her. *The Truth about Tristrem Varick* is more lucid in structure, with a "point of view" presented by the hero, though the incidents are hardly less melodramatic. *Eden* is less successful, but introduces us to what was to become Saltus's standard types of women: blonde Eve and darkly passionate, "fatal" Lilith. *A Transaction in Hearts* has an interesting "new" woman and a powerful storyline. *The Pace That Kills* has a suicidal villain-hero who is a less attractive version of Incoul, while *Enthralled* is an extravaganza owing something to Hugo and to Wilde's *The Picture of Dorian Gray.* In *When Dreams Come True,* a *Bildungsroman* of sorts, Saltus breaks through his own stereotypes—the "fatal woman" emerges as a witty and balanced wife—and produces his best novel. The relationship with his first wife, from whom he was divorced in 1891, underlies his virulent novel *Madam Sapphira.*

The later novels are less satisfying. *The Perfume of Eros,* the best of them, memorably portrays a slum child for whom the wages of sin are success; a charming flapper is killed off when her moral situation threatens to become too complex. *Vanity Square* promises that critique of a cultured and bored society Saltus was well endowed to write, but, though embodying entertaining discussion of ideas, disintegrates into fable. In *Daughters of the Rich,* Saltus moves from New York to southern California, but it is inhabited by the familiar Saltus types and situations: "new" women, murder, and misunderstandings in love. Incest, duels, two unconsummated marriages, theosophy, and mildly Wildean wit hardly redeem *The Monster. The Paliser Case* is a faded version of *The Perfume of Eros,* and *The Ghost Girl* a mediocre Gothic novel.

Saltus's sometimes amusing short stories were written largely for popular consumption and are more melodramatic in plot and exotic in setting than the novels. The poetry was collected in *Poppies and Mandragora;* chiseled in a Parnassian manner, it faintly recalls Heredia. The brief essay *The Gardens of Aphrodite,* which discusses the god of love as Eros-Don Juan, is interesting in itself and for the light it casts on Saltus's fiction. *The Lords of the Ghostland* examines the major religions of the world, introducing theosophy for the first time. *Oscar Wilde: An Idler's Impression* agreeably records a friendship, mainly through reported conversations. French literature is the subject of *Parnassians Personally Encountered* and *Victor Hugo, and Golgotha;* Saltus also translated Balzac, Merimee, and Gautier.

Saltus's importance is largely that of popularizer of European *fin de siecle* modes and topics in the United States. He produced no masterpiece, but his pessimism, determinism, use of fable, allegory, and paradox suggest a poor man's Oscar Wilde, a Wilde without the drama, but a dweller in a high, slightly flashy Bohemia.

—Ian Fletcher

SÁNCHEZ, Ricardo

Born: In El Barrio del Diablo (The Devil's Neighborhood) in El Paso, Texas, 29 March 1941. **Education:** Elementary and secondary schools in El Paso, dropped out of high school. Took extension courses from Alvin Junior College, 1965-69, earning a high school equivalency certificate in 1969; graduate work in American Studies at Union Graduate School at Cincinnati, Ohio, Ph.D. 1974. **Military Service:** Enlisted in the U.S. Army and then served sentences in Soledad Prison in California (paroled in 1963) and Ramsey I Prison Farm of the Texas Department of Corrections and Penitentiary System (paroled in 1969). **Family:** Married Maria Teresa Silva in November 1964. **Career:** Correspondent for *Richmond Afro-American Newspaper,* Richmond, Virginia, 1969; staff writer and instructor in School of Education at University of Massachusetts, Amherst, 1970; consultant, writer, and lecturer for Chicano Affairs Program and Teacher Corps & TTT Program, University of Texas at El Paso, 1971-72; community staff consultant and instructor for Social Welfare Teaching Center, New Mexico State University, Las Cruces, 1972-73; professor at El Paso Community College, El Paso, Texas, 1975; poet-in-residence under National Endowment for the Arts, 1975-76; visiting professor for Spanish-Speaking Outreach Institute, University of Wisconsin at Milwaukee, 1977; assistant professor at University of Utah, Salt Lake City, 1977-80; poet-in-residence, University of Alaska, Juneau, 1979; script writer for film *Entelequia,* 1979; psychiatric trainer, Brown Schools, Austin, Texas, 1982; founder and manager of Poets of Tejas Reading Series, San Antonio, Texas, 1982-83; director, Poetry Tejas International, San Antonio, 1983-84; owner and manager of Paperbacks y Mas, San Antonio, 1983-88; English as a second language (ESL) instructor, San Antonio Literacy Council, San Antonio, 1985-87; Sunday arts columnist, *San Antonio Express News,* 1985-88; poet/writer-in-residence, National Endowment for the Arts, Centro Cultural Aztlán, San Antonio, 1986-87; arts/culture columnist, *El Paso Herald-Post,* 1988-91; part-time instructor, El Paso Community College, 1991; associate professor, Washington State University, Pullman, beginning 1991; freelance writer, poet, journalist, consultant; developer of television programs and cassette recordings on Chicano culture and literature. Active in numerous literary, cultural, and arts organizations. Member of Texas Commission for the Arts, 1982-85; trustee of San Antonio Library System, 1985-87. **Awards:** Frederick Douglass fellowship in journalism, 1969; graduate fellow with Ford Foundation, Union Graduate School, 1973-75; named an outstanding faculty member by University of Utah Chicano Student Association, 1978-79. **Residence:** Pullman, Washington.

PUBLICATIONS

Poetry

Los cuatro (title means "The Four"), with Abelardo Delgado, Raymundo "Tigre" Pérez, and Juan Valdez (Magdaleno Avila). 1970.
Canto y grito mi liberación (y lloro mis desmadrazgos . . .); pensamientos, gritos, angustias, orgullos, penumbras poéticas, ensayos, historietas, hechizos almales del son de mi existencia . . . (title means "I Chant and Shout My Liberation (and I Cry My Zaniness . . .); Thoughts, Shouts, Anguish, Pride, Poetic Penumbras, Essays, Anecdotes, Soulful Spells of the Sound of My Existence . . ."). 1971.
HECHIZOspells. 1976.
Milhuas Blues and Gritos Norteños (title means "Milhuas Blues and Shouts from Northerners"). 1980.
Brown Bear Honey Madness: Alaskan Cruising Poems. 1981.
Amsterdam cantos (y poemas pistos . . .) (title means "Amsterdam Chants [and Loaded Poems . . .]"), forward by Paul Christensen. 1983.
Selected Poems. 1985.
Eagle-Visioned/Feathered Adobes: Manito Sojourns & Pachuco Ramblings. 1990.
Amerikan Journeys=Jornadas Americanas. 1994.
The Loves of Ricardo. 1997.

Chapbooks

Obras. 1971.
Perdido: A Barrio Story. 1985.
Bertrand & the Mehkgoverse: A Xicano Filmic Nuance. 1989.
The Northwest Cantos, Part 1. 1992.
Clearing the Labyrinth: From La Pinta to Macondo Via Aztlán (or Encounter with Cecil H. Green)—A Poetry Reading. 1993.

Editor

Los cuatro. 1970.
Mano a Mano (title means "Hand to Hand"). 1971.
Lemon Creek Gold: Journal of Alaskan Prison Literature. 1979.
NEXUS: Texas Writers' Newsletter. 1982.

Recordings: *Teaching Chicano Literature,* 1972; *Poets in the Struggle,* 1991.

*

Critical Studies: "El concepto del barrio en tres poetas chicanos: Abelardo, Alurista y Ricardo Sánchez" by Francisco A. Lomelí with Donaldo W. Urioste in *De Colores,* 1976; *World Literature* *Today* by Charles Tatum, 1976; "Ricardo Sánchez" in *Chicano Authors: Inquiry by Interview* by Juan Bruce-Novoa, 1980; "Forward" by Paul Christensen in *Amsterdam cantos (y poemas pistos . . .),* 1983; "Interview with Ricardo Sánchez" by Rafael Castillo in *Imagine: International Chicano Poetry Journal,* 1984; "Ricardo Sánchez" by Wolfgang Binder in *Partial Autobiographies: Interviews with Twenty Chicano Poets,* 1985; "Abelardo Delgado and Ricardo Sánchez" by Cordelia Candelaria in *Chicano Poetry: A Critical Introduction,* 1986; "Ricardo Sánchez: The Poetics of Liberation" by Yves Charles Grandjeat in *European Perspectives on Hispanic Literature of the United States,* 1988.

* * *

Ricardo Sánchez stands out as one of the most penetrating, pungent, and eloquent poets who pushed poetic discourse into new realms of expression during the peak of the Chicano Literary Renaissance of the 1970s. Charged with energy and determination, he turned poetry into a one-man show of performance and radical activism with the objective of promoting a cultural-political sense of self as a way to resist the dehumanizing elements of modern American society. His function and roles within the new awareness of identity varied much from ambassador to a pied piper troubadour, but most of all he was a conscience. His persona became equated with Chicano avant-garde writings of automatic and free expression that defied form and content, oftentimes writing his inspiration on napkins and diaries. He preferred to defy all and any conventionalism known in literature. He honored no limits and knew no bounds. In that sense, he presented a particular perspective of poetry as visceral, gut-wrenching, and a means for soul-searching. To Sánchez, poetry is not some abstract exercise in elitist manifestations of creating socially ungrounded beauty, but rather a means to probe into the very pulsations of existence. His poetry attempts to inscribe the dynamic elements of life speaking for those who remain silent. For Sánchez, poetry is breathing itself: highly testimonial and linked to power relations. Sánchez became an epicenter of creativity, a tornado of sensibility, and one of the most visible writers of what has been termed early Chicano Movement Poetry. As the radical zeal of the period waned, so did his popularity, but his intensity continues to be respected.

Sánchez's breakthrough in Chicano poetry occurred when he edited and contributed to *Los cuatro* in conjunction with Abelardo Delgado, Raymundo "Tigre" Pérez and Juan Valdez (Magdaleno Avila). Together they present a manifesto of angry nationalist poetry designed to criticize and attack what Americans consider sacred (i.e., democracy). Sánchez, in particular, flings out indictments and radically calls for the secession of the Chicano homeland (Aztlán) from the United States.

It is in *Canto y grito mi liberación (y lloro mis desmadrazgos . . .)* where Sánchez's poetics coalesces into a vibrant voice of well articulated protest and what he calls *desmadrazgos,* Mexican slang in part for madness, zaniness, and rage with a vengeance. The fierce denigration and alienation he experienced growing up in a hostile environment had haunted him: "Inside I felt an ever growing rage, a seething frustration which I could not overcome. I would finally explode in a near-suicidal series of robberies designed more to get me killed than anything else." Poetry became an outlet, his salvation and a cornerstone for recovering the essence of his being. In an existential search, he discovered falsehoods, contradictions and external trappings of a society that had shown him little acceptance. His main theme, understandably, addresses liberation and freedom as necessities for survival. In the process, he displays a verbal virtuosity of uncontainable divagations that freely oscillate between prose and poetry, mixing genres and languages with ease. While dialoguing with himself, he manifests an impassioned love for his people and all that was denied him, including simply being who he is.

Sánchez's iconoclastic spirit reaches its pinnacle in *HECHIZOspells,* a monumental collection of eight prosaic pieces that first set the spiritual-intellectual stage for the subsequent 98 poems. Each poem is dated and geographically placed to emphasize its testimoniality. Mesmerizingly truthful and authentic, an irreverent voice emerges to overwhelm complacency and blandness. Although he incorporates a wide range of feelings, an unflappable aggression flows with exuberance in an attempt at piercing comfort and uniformity. A zealousness pervades that leads him into various modes of expression: with an unbridled stream-of-consciousness, he soars into loftiness, penetrates infernos, unmasks timidness, remarks acerbically, and releases his demons in a process of poetic exorcism. Here he manages fully to develop and likewise transcend his poetics of rage and *desmadrazgos* by making it more socially redeemable. Originality rests in his blending any conceivable poetic tradition and remolding it. What might have seemed like graffiti in *Canto y grito mi liberación* now becomes a sophisticated interplay of codes, language nuances and variations, testimonials, Freudian explorations, and political diatribes. His voice becomes less desperate and more hopeful, crisscrossing every mood and state of mind: from indignation to tenderness, melancholy to paternalism, obsessiveness to philosophizing. A compulsive voice participates in an outpouring of his Chicanismo that begins existentially and results politically. Chaos and anguish are toyed with as a way of channeling a new conscience that can help his people. In the process, he resists vehemently any form of standardization that may undermine individual spontaneity and his creative meanderings. Anarchy is preferred but his plea for humanistic societal values intimates some amorphous order. What emerges is a picaresque character who answers to no one while exercising the absolute freedom to criticize, denounce, or deconstruct unquestioned beliefs. *HECHIZOspells* represents one of the most profound poetic eruptions of the human spirit. He sums up his poetic project thus: " . . . I have ever searched for a meaning beyond the superficialities of modern technocratized society. My raging poetry was part and parcel of a life undergoing turbulence, hate, fear, anomie, and dereliction."

After *HECHIZOspells,* it appeared that Sánchez was left momentarily gasping for another voice. In *Milhuas Blues and Gritos Norteños,* he continued with his humanizing poetry while giving homage to Chicano people as the reason for his spiritual recovery. Lyricism now prevails in a free-wheeling, socially committed expression, except that the explosiveness has become more meditative, even consoling. Anger gives way to remembrances and reconciliation. He also realizes his own mortality and finds refuge in humility and reflection. His biting incisiveness becomes less denunciatory as he prepares for a reconstructive phase. In one poem, he concludes: " . . . ya no/ puedo aceptar/ lo cinico/ que en un tiempo/ pretendi haber sido . . . " (I cannot accept how cynical I pretended to be at one time). This collection, then, marks a kind of rebirth of the spirit. He laments that the Movement has lost direction. The overall tone includes the sadness and melancholy of blues juxtaposed with the fiery shouts or public exclamations of Mexicans at a time of joy or uncontainable anguish.

The poet's restlessness and desire to experience new places led him to visit Alaska in 1979 from where emerged *Brown Bear Honey Madness: Alaskan Cruising Poems.* His introspection becomes accentuated as his lyricism turns laudatory of simple but meaningful things. His eruptiveness is checked and, as he states, "my words now come slower paced." The experience in Alaska allowed him again to denounce cultural interlopers who deny the Native American presence, but nonetheless he is more at peace with himself. A mature voice emerges to capture such a remote place as he also contemplates, through temporal distance, what the Chicano Movement accomplished and where it fell short. His previous militancy might be less exuberant but his incisive eye is that much sharper. Sánchez here discovers a new region and a new sensibility for his own development.

Sánchez's visit in 1978 to Amsterdam for the One World Poetry Festival rekindled some of his past flairs. The poetic result is contained in *Amsterdam cantos (y poemas pistos . . .).* The testimonial bent mixes autobiography with impressions and journalistic annotations with existential tidbits. He indulges in minute details about the Dutch, leaving his hostile baggage in the U.S.: "For the first time in 20 years/ I could simply/ just be/ me:/ a man sharing poetry." Freedom takes on new meaning as he struggles to redefine himself and his social context. Wittiness becomes his laser instrument to dissect falsehoods, contradictions, and ambivalences. In the process, his language shows a renewed vigor, almost a flighty bite to it, much like *HECHIZOspells* but lacking the rancor. This collection is as much about Sánchez's linguistic potency as it is about his rejuvenation as a poet among poets.

In 1985, Arte Publico Press published *Selected Poems,* a representative collection of Sánchez's writings that provides the evolution and thematic wanderings of the poet. In this poetic autobiography, the reader can follow Sánchez's personal trajectory as it parallels a Chicano conscience through memorable pieces.

As Sánchez returns to one of his spiritual homelands, New Mexico, in *Eagle-Visioned/Feathered Adobes: Manito Sojourns & Pachuco Ramblings,* he regains his impassioned bluntness while uncovering the facades and veneer of a commercialized (which he terms "contrived") pseudo-nativeness. He mocks and laments a loss of authenticity in this once enchanted land that promised a refuge: " . . . it did hurt/ to realize again/ that hispanics in the arts/ is a fantasy in nuevo mexico." His voice expresses confidence and wisdom as he speaks with experience and verve. The acerbic edge of *HECHIZOspells* is not as present but his incisive observations reveal the sharpness of a trenchant visionary.

Sánchez's poetry offers various significant landmarks in Chicano literature. He is recognized as a most prolific poet, as Nicolas Kanellos points out: "No Chicano poet has been more productive nor has seen his works published by the full gamut of the literary establishment: from Madison Avenue commercial houses to university presses and the smallest of the small presses." Ultimately, Sánchez's distinction lies in an uncontaminated honesty, clever word constructs, and a possessed spirit to express himself. He defies classification as his language emerges from the deepest corners of his soul, thus providing an x-ray of anguish, rage and disenchantment. His existential sojourn marks an uncompromising person whose poetry humanizes through protest, love, consolation, liberation and freedom, and, above all, vision. Sánchez is a poet's poet with a unique language—comprised of Spanish, English, barrio slang, and personal inventions—filled with pathos and heart.

—Francisco Lomelí

SANDBURG, Carl

Born: Galesburg, Illinois, 6 January 1878. **Education:** Lombard College, Galesburg (editor, *Lombard Review*), 1899-1902. **Military Service:** Served in the 6th Illinois Volunteers during the Spanish-American War, 1899: private. **Family:** Married Lilian Steichen in 1908; three daughters. **Career:** Staff member, *Tomorrow* magazine, Chicago, 1906; associate editor, *Lyceumite,* Chicago, 1907-08; district organizer, Social-Democratic Party, Appleton, Wisconsin, 1908; city hall reporter, Milwaukee *Journal,* 1909-10; secretary to Mayor of Milwaukee, 1910-12; city editor, Milwaukee *Social Democratic Herald,* 1911; staff member, Milwaukee *Leader* and Chicago *World,* 1912, and *Day Book,* Chicago, 1912-17; associate editor, *System: The Magazine of Business,* Chicago, 1913; Stockholm correspondent, 1918, and manager of the Chicago office, 1919, Newspaper Enterprise Association; reporter, editorial writer, and motion picture editor, 1917-30, and syndicated columnist, 1930-32, Chicago *Daily News;* lecturer, University of Hawaii, Honolulu, 1934; Walgreen Foundation Lecturer, University of Chicago, 1940; weekly columnist, syndicated by the Chicago *Daily Times,* from 1941. **Awards:** Poetry Society of America award, 1919, 1921; Friends of Literature award, 1934; Roosevelt Memorial Association prize, for biography, 1939; Pulitzer prize, for history, 1940, and for poetry, 1951; American Academy Gold Medal, 1952; National Association for the Advancement of Colored People award, 1965. Litt.D.: Lombard College, 1928; Knox College, Galesburg, Illinois, 1929; Northwestern University, Evanston, Illinois, 1931; Harvard University, Cambridge, Massachusetts, 1940; Yale University, New Haven, Connecticut, 1940; New York University, 1940; Wesleyan University, Middletown, Connecticut, 1940; Lafayette College, Easton, Pennsylvania, 1940; Syracuse University, Syracuse, New York, 1941; Dartmouth College, Hanover, New Hampshire, 1941; University of North Carolina, Chapel Hill, 1955; Uppsala College, New Jersey, 1959. LL.D.: Hollins College, Virginia, 1941; Augustana College, Rock Island, Illinois, 1948; University of Illinois, Urbana, 1953. **Member:** American Academy, 1940; Commander, Order of the North Star (Sweden), 1953. **Died:** 22 July 1967.

PUBLICATIONS

Collections

The Letters, edited by Herbert Mitgang. 1968.
Selected Poems. 1996.

Poetry

In Reckless Ecstasy. 1904.
The Plaint of the Rose. 1904(?).
Incidentals. 1904.
Joseffy. 1910.

Chicago Poems. 1916.
Cornhuskers. 1918.
Smoke and Steel. 1920.
Slabs of the Sunburnt West. 1922.

Other (for children)

Rootabaga Stories. 1922.
Rootabaga Pigeons. 1923.
Rootabaga Country. 1929.
Early Moon. 1930.
Potato Face. 1930.
Wind Song. 1960.
Not Everyday an Aurora Borealis for Your Birthday: A Love Poem. 1998.

Other

You and Your Job. 1908.
The Chicago Race Riot, July 1919. 1919.
Abraham Lincoln:
    The Prairie Years. 2 vols., 1926; selection (for children), as *Abe Lincoln Grows Up,* 1928.
    The War Years. 4 vols., 1939; revised abridgement, as *Storm over the Land,* 1942.
    The Prairie Years and the War Years (selection). 1 vol., 1954.
Steichen, The Photographer. 1929.
Mary Lincoln, Wife and Widow, with Paul M. Angle. 1932.
Home Front Memo. 1943.
The Photographs of Abraham Lincoln, with Frederick Hill Meserve. 1944.
Lincoln Collector: The Story of Oliver R. Barrett's Great Private Collection. 1949.
Always the Young Strangers (autobiography). 1953; selection (for children), as *Prairie-Town Boy,* 1955.
The Sandburg Range (miscellany). 1957.
Ever the Winds of Chance (autobiography). 1983.
Sandburg at the Movies: A Poet in the Silent Era 1920-1927 (film reviews), edited by Dale and Doug Fetherling. 1985.

Editor, *American Songbag.* 1927; *New American Songbag,* 1950.
Editor, *A Lincoln and Whitman Miscellany.* 1938.

Screen documentary: *Bomber,* 1945.

*

Bibliography: *Sandburg: A Bibliography* by Thomas S. Shaw, 1948.

Critical Studies: *Sandburg: A Study in Personality and Background* by Karl W. Detzer, 1941; *Sandburg* by Harry Golden, 1961; *Sandburg* by Richard H. Crowder, 1964; *The America of Sandburg* by Hazel Durnell, 1965; *Sandburg* by Mark Van Doren, 1969 (includes bibliography); *Sandburg: Lincoln of Our Literature* by North Callahan, 1970; *Sandburg, Yes* by W.G. Rogers, 1970; *Sandburg* by Gay Wilson Allen, 1972; *The Vision of This Land: Studies of Vachel Lindsay, Edgar Lee Masters, and Sandburg* edited by John E. Hallwas and Dennis J. Reader, 1976; *A Great and Glorious Romance: The Story of Sandburg and Lilian Steichen* by Helga Sandburg, 1978; *Sandburg Remembered* by William A. Sutton, 1979; *My Friend Sandburg: The Biography of a Friendship* by Lilla S. Perry, 1981; *Carl Sandburg: His Life and Works* by North Callahan, 1987; *From the Bottom Up: Three Radicals of the Thirties* by Adrian Oktenberg, 1987; *The Poet and the Dream Girl: The Love Letters of Lilian Steichen and Carl Sandburg* by Margaret Sandburg, 1987; *The Other Carl Sandburg* by Philip Yannella, 1996.

*   *   *

Harriet Monroe's magazine *Poetry* in 1914 gave conspicuous position to Carl Sandburg's early poems. Readers were drawn by his Whitman-like quality, now vigorous and rugged, now gentle and compassionate. His books *Chicago Poems* and *Cornhuskers* set the pace and established him as a leading American poet. His free verse lines were, at their best, musical and varied. His subject matter was generally quarried from the cities and countryside of the midwest. His themes were built on concern for the common man, concomitant with his interest in socialism. Out of the Depression came his book *The People, Yes,* consisting of folk sayings cemented together by optimistic prophecies to the effect that the ordinary man would eventually receive his due. Sandburg's last book of poems, *Honey and Salt,* continued to substantiate his thesis that the life of "the family of man" is not all sweet, that it is tempered by the sobering experience of everyday existence and even by tragedy. In this book the old poet, through his reliance on a proliferation of color images unusual in a writer at the end of his career, proved to be as vigorous as a tyro one-third his age.

The People, Yes had been a product of Sandburg's interest in folklore. His two edited collections of the songs of the people established him as something of an authority: *The American Songbag* and the expanded *New American Songbag.* In fact, for the twenty years preceding World War II Sandburg traveled widely singing these songs to large audiences, accompanying himself on the guitar.

In prose biography Sandburg showed a skillful hand. He wrote of his wife's brother in *Steichen, The Photographer* and of the wife of his life-long hero in *Mary Lincoln, Wife and Widow.* His most famous prose work remains his six-volume biography of Lincoln. If in this monumental work (without footnotes and index) he occasionally rearranged the chronology and indeed embroidered the facts, he nevertheless produced a rich and sensitive portrait, filled with incident, pointed up with insight, and made brilliant with poetic truth. His *Always the Young Strangers* tells the story of his own growing-up with a remarkable analytical objectivity in an enchanting style as engrossing as a novel.

Remembrance Rock was something else again. Commissioned by Metro-Goldwyn-Mayer to write a "great American novel" later to be made into a scenario for a moving picture, Sandburg turned out a wooden, repetitive piece of fiction, not only very long, but very tiresome. Like *The People, Yes* the book is packed with songs, proverbs, anecdotes, folk customs. Effective in a Depression poem, this subject matter was ill-suited to the novel form. In spite of the book's ineptness, however, Sandburg was continuing to show his integrity and generosity, his hatred of bigotry, his consuming love for his native country.

He was popular with children; his *Rootabaga Stories, Rootabaga Pigeons,* and *Potato Face* enjoyed wide readership. The fantasy, inventiveness, humor, and light-heartedness in these stories were similar to many of the traits in his poems, selections from which, indeed, were collected in anthologies intended for children.

Sandburg will long be remembered for his Lincoln biography and for many of his poems. The reader can recall the alternating robustness and pathos of "Chicago," the delicate imagism of "Fog," the loud anger of "To a Contemporary Bunkshooter," the wholesome aspiration of *The People, Yes.* Even though one cannot place him in the very top rank of American poets, it is possible to say that to have read Sandburg is to have been the companion of a deeply rooted and dedicated citizen of the United States and of a conscious craftsman skilled in communicating the basic emotions, especially as felt by the "ordinary" person. It must be emphasized that Sandburg was moved not just by the masses, what he lovingly called "the mob." True, he was sympathetic with his "people" as they struggled toward the stars (one of his early poems chanted, "I am the people, the mob"), but his many poems about individuals showed him to be actively aware of the inescapable fact that every man and woman experiences troubles and ecstasies (e.g., "The Hangman at Home," "Helga," "Ice Handler," "Mag"). Furthermore, though Sandburg is linked with **Vachel Lindsay** and **Edgar Lee Masters** as an Illinois poet, he is seen to be, on careful study, a poet of universals. If his most frequent subjects are the little people of his home state, his themes are nonetheless the concerns of all people everywhere.

—Richard H. Crowder

SANTAYANA, George (Agustin de)

Born: Madrid, Spain, 16 December 1863; immigrated with his family to the United States, 1872, but retained Spanish nationality. **Education:** The Brimmer School and the Latin School, both Boston; Harvard University, Cambridge, Massachusetts, 1882-86, A.B. 1886, A.M. (Walker Fellow in Germany and England), 1888, Ph.D. 1889; King's College, Cambridge, 1896-97. **Career:** Instructor, 1889-98, assistant professor, 1898-1907, and professor of philosophy, 1907-12, Harvard University; lived in England, France, and Rome, 1912-52. Hyde Lecturer, the Sorbonne, Paris, 1905-06; Spencer Lecturer, Oxford University, 1923. **Awards:** Royal Society of Literature (London) Benson Medal, 1928; Columbia University Butler Gold Medal, 1945. Honorary degree: University of Wisconsin, Madison, 1911. **Member:** American Academy. **Died:** 26 September 1952.

PUBLICATIONS

Collections

Works (Triton Edition). 15 vols., 1936-40.
Letters, edited by Daniel Cory. 1955.
Complete Poems, edited by William G. Holzberger. 1979.

Fiction

The Last Puritan: A Memoir in the Form of a Novel. 1935.

Plays

Lucifer: A Theological Tragedy. 1899; revised edition, 1924.
The Marriage of Venus, and *Philosophers at Court,* in *The Poet's Testament.* 1953.

Poetry

Sonnets and Other Verses. 1894; 2nd series, 1896.
A Hermit of Carmel and Other Poems. 1901.
Poems. 1923.
The Poet's Testament: Poems and Two Plays. 1953.

Other

Platonism in the Italian Poets. 1896.
The Sense of Beauty, Being the Outlines of Aesthetic Theory. 1896.
Interpretations of Poetry and Religion. 1900.
The Life of Reason; or, The Phases of Human Progress. 5 vols., 1905-06; revised edition, with Daniel Cory, 1954.
Three Philosophical Poets: Lucretius, Dante, and Goethe. 1910.
Winds of Doctrine: Studies in Contemporary Opinion. 1913.
Egotism in German Philosophy. 1915; as *The German Mind,* 1968.
Character and Opinion in the United States. 1920.
Little Essays, edited by Logan Pearsall Smith. 1920.
Soliloquies in England and Later Soliloquies. 1922.
Scepticism and Animal Faith. 1923.
The Unknowable. 1923.
Dialogues in Limbo. 1925; revised edition, 1948.
Platonism and the Spiritual Life. 1927.
The Realms of Being. 1942.
    The Realm of Essence. 1927.
    The Realm of Matter. 1930.
    The Realm of Truth. 1937.
    The Realm of Spirit. 1940.
The Genteel Tradition at Bay. 1931.
Some Turns of Thought in Modern Philosophy: Five Essays. 1933.
Obiter Scripta: Lectures, Essays, and Reviews, edited by Justus Buchler and Benjamin Schwartz. 1936.
Philosophy of Santayana, edited by Irwin Edman. 1936; revised edition, 1953.
Persons and Places (autobiography). 1963.
    The Background of My Life. 1944.
    The Middle Span. 1945.
    My Host the World. 1953.
The Idea of Christ in the Gospels; or, God in Man. 1946.
Atoms of Thought: An Anthology of Thoughts, edited by Ira D. Cardiff. 1950; as *The Wisdom of Santayana,* 1964.
Dominations and Powers: Reflections on Liberty, Society, and Government. 1951.
Essays in Literary Criticism, edited by Irving Singer. 1956.
The Idler and His Works, and Other Essays, edited by Daniel Cory. 1957.
Ten Letters and a Foreword. 1960.
Vagabond Scholar (letters and dialogues with Bruno Lind). 1962.
Animal Faith and Spiritual Life: Previously Unpublished and Uncollected Writings, edited by John Lachs. 1967.
The Genteel Tradition: Nine Essays, edited by Douglas L. Wilson. 1967.
Santayana's America: Essays on Literature and Culture, edited by James Ballowe. 1967.
Santayana on America, edited by Richard Colton Lyon. 1968.
Selected Critical Writings, edited by Norman Henfrey. 2 vols., 1968.
The Birth of Reason and Other Essays, edited by Daniel Cory. 1968.
Physical Order and Moral Liberty: Previously Unpublished Essays, edited by John and Shirley Lachs. 1969.

Lotze's System of Philosophy (1889 doctoral dissertation), edited by Paul Grimley Kuntz. 1971.

Translator, with others, *The Writings of Alfred de Musset,* revised edition, vol. 2. 1907.

*

Bibliography: *Santayana: A Bibliographical Checklist 1880-1980* by Herman J. Saatkamp, Jr., and John Jones, 1982.

Critical Studies: *The Philosophy of Santayana* edited by Paul Arthur Schilpp, 1940 (includes bibliography by Shonig Terzian); *Santayana and the Sense of Beauty* by Richard Butler, 1956; *Santayana's Aesthetics: A Critical Introduction* by Irving Singer, 1957; *Santayana: The Later Years* by Daniel Cory, 1963; *Santayana, Art, and Aesthetics* by Jerome Ashmore, 1966; *Santayana* by Willard E. Arnett, 1968; *Santayana* by Newton P. Stallknecht, 1971; *Santayana: An Examination of His Philosophy* by Timothy L.S. Sprigge, 1974; *Thresholds of Reality: Santayana and Modernist Poetics* by Lois Hughson. 1977; *Living in the Eternal: A Study of George Santayana* by Anthony Woodward, 1988; *A Philosophical Novelist: George Santayana and The Last Puritan* by Henry Tompkins Kirby-Smith, 1997.

*   *   *

Born in Spain of a Roman Catholic family, George Santayana was a philosopher, an atheist, and a materialist, but he retained a deep affection for the Roman Catholic Church and died in his old age, as an invalid, cared for by nuns in a convent hospital in Rome. His working life was spent at Harvard where his colleague, the optimistic pragmatist **William James**, disliked Santayana intensely and felt that his dry, cynical sadness was corrupting. Few philosophers of his time, if any (the possible rivals are F.H. Bradley and Henri Bergson) wrote with more charm and elegance. The defect of such a style in a philosopher, however, is that it lulls the reader who should be alert for logical flaws; as a result, it would be hard to summarize Santayana's thought. He might be described, perhaps, as a Platonizing materialist; only matter was eternal, man was mortal, but man could abstract from matter intellectual essences that (except that they were final products, not sources of being) resembled Plato's world of forms and ideas. Santayana is perhaps at his best as a thinker when he steps away from abstract thinking and applies his mind to literature, as in *Three Philosophical Poets,* or to a place that appealed to him, as in *Soliloquies in England.* In his novel, *The Last Puritan,* based on his knowledge of young Americans through his teaching at Harvard, he tries to do justice to the best sides of that American tradition that, with his innately hierarchical and conservative attitude, he on the whole rejected.

—G.S. Fraser

SANTOS, Bienvenido N(uqui)

Born: Tondo, Manila, Philippines, 22 March 1911; became naturalized U.S. citizen in 1976. **Education:** University of the Philippines, B.S. 1932; University of Illinois, M.A. 1942; Harvard University, 1945-46; University of Iowa, 1958-61. **Family:** Married Beatriz Nidea in 1933 (died 1981); three children. **Career:** Elementary and high school teacher in Philippines, 1932-41; public relations officer, Embassy of the Philippines, Washington, D.C., 1942-45; professor and vice president, Legazpi College, Legazpi City, Philippines, 1946-57, president, 1958; dean of College of Arts and Sciences, University of Nueva Caceres, Naga City, Philippines, 1961-66; lecturer at writers' workshop, University of Iowa, Iowa City, 1970-73; professor of creative writing and Distinguished Writer-in-Residence, 1973-82, and Professor Emeritus, beginning 1982, Wichita State University, Wichita, Kansas. Office of the President of the Philippines, Manila, member of textbook board, 1962-64, acting chair of board, 1964-65; visiting writer at Ohio State University, spring, 1983, Iowa State University, summer, 1984, University of the Philippines, Ateneo de Manila University, and Aspen Creative Writers Workshop, Aspen, Colorado, all in summer, 1985, and at De La Salle University, beginning 1986. **Awards:** First prize in Philippine section from *New York Herald Tribune*'s international short story contest, 1952; Rockefeller Foundation fellow, 1958-59; Guggenheim fellow, 1960; Republic Cultural Heritage Award in Literature, 1965; winner of *Philippine Free Press* annual short story contest, 1966; Medallion of Honor from City of Manila, 1971; fiction award from *New Letters,* 1977; Before Columbus Association Foundation American book award, 1981; National Endowment for the Arts fellowship, 1982; the X Award (Manila, Philippines), 1983; Manila Critics Circle award for fiction, 1983. Honorary degrees: University of the Philippines, 1981; Bicol University, Legazpi City, Philippines, 1981; Wichita State University, 1982; University of Nueva Caceres, Naga City, Philippines, 1983. **Residence:** The Philippines.

PUBLICATIONS

Short Stories

You Lovely People. 1955.
Brother My Brother. 1960.
Scent of Apples: A Collection of Stories. 1979.
Dwell in the Wilderness: Selected Short Stories: 1931-41. 1985.

Poetry

The Wounded Stag: 54 Poems. 1956.
Distances in Time. 1983.

Novels

Villa Magdalena. 1965.
The Volcano. 1965; revised edition, 1986.
The Praying Man. 1982.
The Man Who (Thought He) Looked Like Robert Taylor. 1983.
What the Hell for You Left Your Heart in San Francisco. 1987.

Other

The Day the Dancers Came: Selected Prose Works. 1967.
Memory's Fictions (autobiography). 1993.
Postscript to a Saintly Life. 1994.
Letters. 1995.

*

Critical Studies: *Asian American Literature: An Introduction to the Works and Their Social Context* by Elaine Kim, 1983; *The Empire Writes Back: Theory and Practice in Post-Colonial Literatures* by Bill Ashcroft and others, 1989; *Reading Asian American Literature: From Necessity to Extravagance* by Sau-ling Cynthia Wong, 1993.

*   *   *

After winning the Spanish-American War (1898) and the oft-forgotten Philippine-American War (1899-1901), the United States—a former colony itself—formally achieved colonizer status. As the boundaries and interests of the United States expanded to incorporate others, what constituted American literature necessarily expanded with it, though not necessarily at the same rate. The empire is still writing back and has begun to achieve recognition as a necessarily constitutive part of American culture and its literature.

One of the most important English-language literary figures emerging from these historical circumstances is Bienvenido N. Santos, a Filipino-born naturalized American citizen who has spent much of his life shuttling between America and the Philippines, America's former colony. Santos came to the United States in the 1940s and was a student at Columbia University. During World War II he was sent to Washington to work for the war effort, clipping news stories of the Philippines as a clerk in the Information Division of the Commonwealth Building. Over the next five decades, Santos would migrate between his homes in the Philippines and the United States, a migration usually in the service of the development of his career as a writer and a teacher and occasionally at the mercy of historical events, like martial law in the Philippines.

An appreciation of Santos and his writing demands a knowledge of this American history; much of Santos's best-known writing is a subtly impassioned call to remember and cherish these forgotten stories of Filipinos and the United States. In its sympathetic rendering of a forgotten past that crucially needs to be remembered and refigured because this past has been questionably represented or entirely absent from the dominant stories of America, Santos's writing does what perhaps only literature can do: communicate truly human stories.

For convenience's sake, historians break Filipino immigration down into three waves. First came the "manongs" (MAH-nongs), a group which consisted predominantly of male, migrant laborers to the western United States in the early part of this century. As is the recurring pattern in American labor history, these workers were often met with racial hostility, particularly from competing American laborers. Next were the "pensionados" (pen-see-yoh-NAH-dose) who came to the United States to go to universities and then return to the Philippines to live the good life. Government programs sponsored the early pensionados; the later pensionados followed the early pensionados' model, but without the funding. Consequently, many of these individuals were never able to return to the Philippines to live the good life; facing racial discrimination and with their educational plans unrealizable, they could only become menial laborers. The third wave consists of what are usually called "post-1965" immigrants who were permitted to come to the United States once the landmark Immigration Act of 1965, which abolished national origins quotas, was passed. Other candidates for Filipino immigration wave status include a group of 18th-century "Manilamen" who settled in Louisiana after serving on Spanish Galleons, and another consists of the many Filipinos who served in the United States military in World War II, usually in low-ranking positions, such as ship's stewards.

Though much of his writing does deal with the Philippines, Bienvenido Santos's writings that are known in the United States and would most conspicuously be deemed American literature, particularly his short stories, often fall somewhere between waves one and two. Understandably these stories' recurrent themes include exile, alienation, nostalgia, and diaspora. These much anthologized stories include "Immigration Blues," the story of a Filipino old-timer faced with an offer of a marriage of convenience to a Filipina, and "The Day the Dancers Came," the story of a couple of Filipino old-timers in Chicago, one of whom hopes to invite a touring Philippine dance troupe to his home for dinner. The latter story was even made into a short film. Both of these stories can be found in *Scent of Apples,* Santos's first book published in the United States. Of this book, Paul B. Phelps of the *Washington Post Book World* wrote: "Santos is a writer of deceptive simplicity, one whose graceful storytelling conceals considerable political commitment. He is determined to remind his countrymen of the price they are paying for economic development, and to record both the cultural riches they have already lost and the human misery that still remains. His stories capture with warmth and deep humility the pain of exile and the cost of progress."

"In a special sense, I, too, am an old timer," declares Santos in "Old Timers: Fact and Fiction" in *Amerasia.* Though his experiences are similar but not exactly the same as these old-timers, Santos "special sense" of being an old-timer is as the chronicler of these Filipinos: "I have sometimes been asked to explain the difference between the old timer as character in fiction and in real life. There is nothing to explain because there is no difference. If any, it is more in the manner of telling than in what is told. It is the difference between two extremes, of great fiction on the one hand and computerized statistics on the other. Statistics are mindless and without heart, and fiction is informed with mind, and, definitely, with heart. Through its language, fiction turns mere information into truth, truth that warms even as it may, occasionally, shock or cheer the reader into becoming a part of a living experience." For this quality alone, Santos's work remains a living and important part of American literature as his writing uniquely gives voice to unique American experiences. Alongside such early Filipino-American writers as Carlos Bulosan, N.V.M. Gonzalez, and Jose Garcia Villa, Bienvenido Santos's writings capture America's imperialist legacy from a human angle as this is where we all, whether we are directly related to the experiences or are concerned readers, can most acutely feel the costs of colonialism.

—Victor D.C. Bascara

SAROYAN, William

Born: Fresno, California, 31 August 1908. **Education:** Public schools in Fresno to age 15. **Military Service:** Served in the U.S. Army, 1942-45. **Family:** Married Carol Marcus in 1943 (divorced 1949; remarried 1951; divorced 1952); one son (the writer Aram Saroyan) and one daughter. **Career:** Worked as grocery clerk, vineyard worker, post office employee; clerk, telegraph operator, then office manager, Postal Telegraph Company, San Francisco, 1926-

28; cofounder, Conference Press, Los Angeles, 1936; founder and director, Saroyan Theatre, New York, 1942; writer-in-residence, Purdue University, Lafayette, Indiana, 1961. **Awards:** New York Drama Critics Circle award, 1940; Pulitzer prize, 1940 (refused); Academy award (for screenplay), 1944. **Member:** American Academy, 1943. **Died:** 18 May 1981.

PUBLICATIONS

Collections

My Name Is Saroyan, edited by James H. Tashjian. 1983.
The William Saroyan Reader. 1994.

Short Stories

The Daring Young Man on the Flying Trapeze and Other Stories. 1934.
Inhale and Exhale. 1936.
Three Times Three. 1936.
Little Children. 1937.
The Gay and Melancholy Flux: Short Stories. 1937.
Love, Here Is My Hat. 1938.
A Native American. 1938.
The Trouble with Tigers. 1938.
Peace, It's Wonderful. 1939.
3 Fragments and a Story. 1939.
My Name Is Aram. 1940.
Saroyan's Fables. 1941.
The Insurance Salesman and Other Stories. 1941.
48 Saroyan Stories. 1942.
Best Stories. 1942.
Thirty-One Selected Stories. 1943.
Some Day I'll Be a Millionaire: 34 More Great Stories. 1943.
Dear Baby. 1944.
The Saroyan Special: Selected Short Stories. 1948.
The Fiscal Hoboes. 1949.
The Assyrian and Other Stories. 1950.
The Whole Voyald and Other Stories. 1956.
Love. 1959.
After Thirty Years: The Daring Young Man on the Flying Trapeze (includes essays). 1964.
Best Stories of Saroyan. 1964.
My Kind of Crazy Wonderful People: 17 Stories and a Play. 1966.
An Act or Two of Foolish Kindness: Two Stories. 1977.
Madness in the Family, edited by Leo Hamalian. 1988.
The Man with the Heart in the Highlands and Other Early Stories. 1989.
Fresno Stories. 1994.

Novels

The Human Comedy. 1943.
The Adventures of Wesley Jackson. 1946.
The Twin Adventures: The Adventures of Saroyan: A Diary; The Adventures of Wesley Jackson: A Novel. 1950.
Rock Wagram. 1951.
Tracy's Tiger. 1951.
The Laughing Matter. 1953; as *A Secret Story,* 1954.
Mama I Love You. 1956.

Papa You're Crazy. 1957.
Boys and Girls Together. 1963.
One Day in the Afternoon of the World. 1964.

Plays

The Man with the Heart in the Highlands, in *Contemporary One-Act Plays,* edited by William Kozlenko. 1938; revised version, as *My Heart's in the Highlands* (produced 1939), 1939.
The Time of Your Life (produced 1939). In *The Time of Your Life* (miscellany), 1939.
The Hungerers (produced 1945). 1939.
A Special Announcement (broadcast 1940).
Love's Old Sweet Song (produced 1940). In *Three Plays,* 1940.
Three Plays: My Heart's in the Highlands, The Time of Your Life, Love's Old Sweet Song. 1940.
Subway Circus. 1940.
Something about a Soldier (produced 1940).
Hero of the World (produced 1940).
The Great American Goof (ballet scenario; produced 1940). In *Razzle Dazzle,* 1942.
Radio Play (broadcast 1940). In *Razzle Dazzle,* 1942.
The Ping-Pong Game (produced 1945). 1940; as *The Ping Pong Players,* in *Razzle Dazzle,* 1942.
Sweeney in the Trees (produced 1940). In *Three Plays,* 1941.
The Beautiful People (produced 1941). In *Three Plays,* 1941.
Across the Board on Tomorrow Morning (produced 1941). In *Three Plays,* 1941.
Three Plays: The Beautiful People, Sweeney in the Trees, Across the Board on Tomorrow Morning. 1941.
The People with Light Coming Out of Them (broadcast 1941). In *The Free Company Presents,* 1941.
There's Something I Got To Tell You (broadcast 1941). In *Razzle Dazzle,* 1942.
Hello, Out There, music by Jack Beeson (produced 1941). In *Razzle Dazzle,* 1942.
Jim Dandy (produced 1941). 1941; as *Jim Dandy: Fat Man in a Famine,* 1947.
Talking to You (produced 1942). In *Razzle Dazzle,* 1942.
Razzle Dazzle; or, The Human Opera, Ballet, and Circus; or There's Something I Got to Tell You: Being Many Kinds of Short Plays As Well As the Story of the Writing of Them (includes *Hello, Out There, Coming through the Rye, Talking to You, The Great American Goof, The Poetic Situation in America, Opera, Opera, Bad Men in the West, The Agony of Little Nations, A Special Announcement, Radio Play, The People with Light Coming Out of Them, There's Something I Got to Tell You, The Hungerers, Elmer and Lily, Subway Circus, The Ping Pong Players*). 1942; abridged edition, 1945.
Opera, Opera (produced 1955). In *Razzle Dazzle,* 1942.
Bad Men in the West (produced 1971). In *Razzle Dazzle,* 1942.
Get Away Old Man (produced 1943). 1944.
Sam Ego's House (produced 1947). In *Don't Go Away Mad and Two Other Plays,* 1949.
Don't Go Away Mad (produced 1949). In *Don't Go Away Mad and Two Other Plays.* 1949.
Don't Go Away Mad and Two Other Plays: Sam Ego's House; A Decent Birth, A Happy Funeral. 1949.
The Son (produced 1950).
The Oyster and the Pearl: A Play for Television (televised 1953). In *Perspectives USA,* Summer 1953.

A Lost Child's Fireflies (produced 1954).
Once around the Block (produced 1956). 1959.
The Cave Dwellers (produced 1957). 1958.
Ever Been in Love with a Midget (produced 1957).
The Slaughter of the Innocents (produced 1957). 1958.
Cat, Mouse, Man, Woman and *The Accident,* in *Contact 1,* 1958.
The Dogs; or, The Paris Comedy (as *The Paris Comedy; or The Secret of Lily,* produced 1960; as *Lily Dafon,* produced 1960). In *The Dogs; or, The Paris Comedy and Two Other Plays,* 1969.
Settled Out of Court, with Henry Cecil, from the novel by Cecil (produced 1960). 1962.
Sam, The Highest Jumper of Them All; or, The London Comedy (produced 1960). 1961.
High Time along the Wabash (produced 1961).
Ah Man, music by Peter Fricker (produced 1962).
Four Plays: The Playwright and the Public, The Handshakers, The Doctor and the Patient, This I Believe, in *Atlantic,* April 1963.
The Time of Your Life and Other Plays. 1967.
Dentist and Patient and Husband and Wife, in *The Best Short Plays 1968,* edited by Stanley Richards. 1968.
The Dogs; or, The Paris Comedy and Two Other Plays: Chris Sick; or, Happy New Year Anyway, Making Money, and Nineteen Other Very Short Plays. 1969.
The New Play, in *The Best Short Plays 1970,* edited by Stanley Richards. 1970.
Armenians (produced 1974).
The Rebirth Celebration of the Human Race at Artie Zabala's Off-Broadway Theatre (produced 1975).
Two Short Paris Summertime Plays of 1974 (includes *Assassinations* and *Jim, Sam, and Anna*). 1979.
Play Things (produced 1980).

Screenplays: *The Good Job* (documentary), 1942; *The Human Comedy,* with Howard Estabrook, 1943.

Radio Plays: *Radio Play,* 1940; *A Special Announcement,* 1940; *There's Something I Got to Tell You,* 1941; *The People with Light Coming Out of Them,* 1941.

Television Plays: *The Oyster and the Pearl,* 1953; *Ah Sweet Mystery of Mrs. Murphy,* 1959; *The Unstoppable Gray Fox,* 1962; *Making Money and Thirteen Other Very Short Plays,* 1970.

Ballet Scenario: *A Theme in the Life of the Great American Goof,* 1940.

Poetry

A Christmas Psalm. 1935.
Christmas 1939. 1939.

Other

Those Who Write Them and Those Who Collect Them. 1936.
The Time of Your Life (miscellany). 1939.
Harlem as Seen by Hirschfeld. 1941.
Hilltop Russians in San Francisco. 1941.
Why Abstract?, with Henry Miller and Hilaire Hiler. 1945.
The Bicycle Rider in Beverly Hills (autobiography). 1952.
The Saroyan Reader. 1958.

Here Comes, There Goes, You Know Who (autobiography). 1962.
A Note on Hilaire Hiler. 1962.
Me (for children). 1963.
Not Dying (autobiography). 1963.
Short Drive, Sweet Chariot (autobiography). 1966.
*Look at Us: Let's See: Here We Are: Look Hard: Speak Soft: I
    See, You See, We all See; Stop, Look, Listen; Beholder's Eye;
    Don't Look Now But Isn't That You? (us? U.S.?).* 1967.
Horsey Gorsey and the Frog (for children). 1968.
I Used to Believe I Had Forever; Now I'm Not So Sure. 1968.
Letters from 74 rue Taitbout. 1969; as *Don't Go But If You Must
    Say Hello to Everybody,* 1970.
Days of Life and Death and Escape to the Moon. 1970.
Places Where I've Done Time. 1972.
The Tooth and My Father (for children). 1974.
Famous Faces and Other Friends: A Personal Memoir. 1976.
Morris Hirshfield. 1976.
Sons Come and Go, Mothers Hang In Forever (memoirs). 1976.
Chance Meetings. 1978.
Obituaries. 1979.
Births. 1983.
Saroyan–Memoirs. 1994.

Editor, *Hairenik 1934-1939: An Anthology of Short Stories and
    Poems.* 1939.

*

Bibliography: *A Bibliography of Saroyan 1934-1964* by David I.
Kherdian, 1965.

Critical Studies: *Saroyan* by Howard R. Floan, 1966; *Last Rites:
The Death of Saroyan,* 1982, and *Saroyan,* 1983, both by Aram
Saroyan; *Saroyan: My Real Work Is Being* by David I. Stephen
Calonne, 1983; *Saroyan* by Edward Halsey Foster, 1984; *Saroyan:
A Biography* by Lawrence Lee and Barry Gifford, 1984; *Saroyan*
by Gerald W. Haslam, 1987; "William Saroyan and San Francisco:
Emergence of a Genius (Self-Proclaimed)" by Gerald Haslam, in
San Francisco in Fiction: Essays in a Regional Literature edited
by David Fine and Paul Skenazy, 1995.

*   *   *

William Saroyan is one of the striking paradoxes in twentieth-
century American literature. Dismissed by some for being nonliterary, he was praised by **Edmund Wilson** for his uncanny gift of
creating atmosphere: "Saroyan takes you to the bar, and he creates for you there a world which is the way the world would be if
it conformed to the feeling instilled by drinks. In a word, he
achieves the feat of making and keeping us boozy without the use
of alcohol and purely by the action of art."

Saroyan never went beyond high school and exemplifies the successful homespun writer. *The Daring Young Man on the Flying
Trapeze and Other Stories* was his first collection of short fiction,
and many consider it to be his finest. A breathtakingly prolific
writer (he produced about 500 stories between 1934 and 1940),
Saroyan wrote in several genres, but his claim to greatness rests
essentially on his plays like *My Heart's in the Highlands* and *The
Time of Your Life* and on his short stories. He has been criticized
for excessive sentimentality, but he replied that it is a very sentimental thing to be a human being. And to the charge that his style

is careless and sloppy, he responded: "I do not know a great deal
about what the words come to, but the presence says, Now don't
get funny; just sit down and say something: it'll be all right. Say
it wrong; It'll be all right anyway. Half the time I *do* say it wrong,
but somehow or other, just as the presence says, it's right anyway. I am always pleased about this."

One of his best stories, "The Daring Young Man on the Flying
Trapeze," is an interior monologue revealing the recollections of a
poor young writer who lives in the troubled present while achieving distance from it by reaching back into the past. Mostly unperturbed on the conscious level by his problems, occasionally
the writer is embittered by his need to sell his books to buy food.
Finally, one afternoon he returns to his room from his wanderings
and dies a sudden and painless death. Saroyan's identification with
his young protagonist is evident, despite the disclaimers. The story
is suffused with pathos, though there is clearly an attempt to hold
the sentimentality in check. Among his plays, *The Time of Your
Life* probably most fully reveals Saroyan the artist. It received
both the Drama Critics Circle award and the Pulitzer Prize, but
Saroyan refused the latter as an expression of his contempt for
commercial patronage of art. Despite its melodramatic plot, the
play, as Howard R. Floan admirably sums up, is "about a state of
mind, illusive but real, whose readily recognizable components are,
first, an awareness of America's youth—its undisciplined swag-
gering, unregulated early life—and, secondly, a pervasive sense of
America in crisis: an America of big business, of labor strife, of
depersonalized government, and, above all, of imminent war."

Saroyan's interest in the comedy-tragedy of life remained undiminished to the end of his writing career: "Living is the only thing.
It is an awful pain most of the time, but this compels comedy
and dignity." What made Saroyan stand out—especially among
American writers—was his optimism about life despite the world's
evidence to the contrary. His buoyancy certainly worked with his
considerable reading public, but the major appeal of his writing
comes from his characters, who are common people, and from his
heavily romantic emphasis on the individuality of human beings.

—J.N. Sharma

SARTON, (Eleanor) May

Born: Wondelgem, Belgium, 3 May 1912; brought to the United
States in 1916; became a naturalized United States citizen in 1924.
Education: Shady Hill School, Cambridge, Massachusetts, and
Institute Belge de Culture Française, Brussels, Belgium; graduated
from Cambridge High and Latin School, 1929. **Career:** Apprentice, Eva Le Gallienne's Civic Repertory Theatre, New York City,
1929-34; founder and director, Associated Actors Theatre, New
York City, 1934-37; scriptwriter, Overseas Film Unit, New York
City, 1941-52; Briggs-Copeland Instructor in English Composition, Harvard University, Cambridge, Massachusetts, 1949-52; lecturer, Bread Loaf Writer's Conference, Middlebury, Vermont, 1951-
53; lecturer, Boulder Writers' Conference, Boulder, Colorado, 1954;
lecturer in creative writing, Wellesley College, Wellesley, Massachusetts, 1960-64; poet-in-residence, Lindenwood College, St.
Charles, Missouri, 1965. Phi Beta Kappa visiting scholar, 1960;
visiting lecturer, Agnes Scott College, 1972. Fellow, American Academy of Arts and Sciences. **Awards:** New England Poetry Society
Golden Rose award, 1945; *Poetry* magazine Edward Bland Me-

morial prize, 1945; Poetry Society of America Reynolds Lyric award, 1952; Lucy Martin Donelly fellowship, Bryn Mawr College, 1953-54; Guggenheim fellow in poetry, 1954-55; Johns Hopkins University Poetry Festival award, 1961; Emily Clark Balch prize, 1966; National Endowment for the Arts grant, 1966; Sarah Josepha Hale award, 1972; College of St. Catherine Alexandrine medal, 1975; Deborah Morton award, 1981; Unitarian Universalist Women's Federation Ministry to Women award, 1982; Avon/COCOA Pioneer Woman award, 1983; Human Rights award, 1985; Fund for Human Dignity award, 1985; Before Columbus Foundation American Book award, 1985; Maryann University of Maine Hartman award, 1986; New England Booksellers Association New England Author award, 1990. Honorary doctorates from Clark University, 1975, Bates College, 1976, Colby College, 1976, University of New Hampshire, 1976, Thomas Starr King School of Religious Leadership, 1976, Nasson College, 1980, University of Maine, 1981, Bowdoin College, 1983, and Goucher College, 1985. Litt.D.: Russell Sage College, 1958, and New England College, 1971. **Died:** 1995.

PUBLICATIONS

Collections

Collected Poems: 1930-1973. 1974.
Sarton Selected: An Anthology of the Journals, Novels, and Poetry of May Sarton, edited and with an introduction by Bradford Dudley Daziel. 1991.
Collected Poems: 1930-1993. 1993.
May Sarton: Among the Usual Days: A Portrait: Unpublished Poems, Letters, Journals, and Photographs. 1993.
From May Sarton's Well: Writings of May Sarton. 1994.

Poetry

Encounter in April. 1937.
Inner Landscape. 1938.
The Lion and the Rose. 1948.
The Land of Silence. 1953.
In Time Like Air. 1958.
Cloud, Stone, Sun, Vine. 1961.
A Private Mythology. 1966.
As Does New Hampshire. 1967.
A Grain of Mustard Seed. 1971.
A Durable Fire. 1972.
Selected Poems. 1978.
Halfway to Silence. 1980.
Letters from Maine: New Poems. 1984.
The Silence Now: New and Uncollected Earlier Poems. 1988.
Coming into Eighty: And Earlier Poems. 1995.

Fiction

The Single Hound. 1938.
The Bridge of Years. 1946.
Shadow of a Man. 1950.
A Shower of Summer Days. 1952.
Faithful Are the Wounds. 1955.
The Fur Person. 1957.
The Birth of a Grandfather. 1957.

The Small Room. 1961.
Joanna and Ulysses. 1963.
Mrs. Stevens Hears the Mermaids Singing. 1965; revised edition, 1974.
Mrs. Pickthorn and Mr. Hare (fable). 1966.
The Poet and the Donkey. 1969.
Kinds of Love. 1970.
As We Are Now. 1973.
Punch's Secret (juvenile). 1974.
Crucial Conversations. 1975.
A Walk through the Woods (juvenile). 1976.
A Reckoning. 1978.
Anger. 1982.
The Magnificent Spinster. 1985.
The Education of Harriet Hatfield. 1989.

Nonfiction

I Knew a Phoenix: Sketches for an Autobiography. 1959.
Plant Dreaming Deep (autobiography). 1968.
Journal of Solitude. 1973.
A World of Light: Portraits and Celebrations. 1976.
The House by the Sea. 1977.
Writings on Writing. 1980.
Recovering: A Journal. 1980.
May Sarton: A Self-Portrait, edited by Marita Simpson and Martha Wheelock. 1982.
At Seventy: A Journal. 1984.
After the Stroke: A Journal. 1988.
Endgame: A Journal of the Seventy-Ninth Year. 1992.
Encore: A Journal of the Eightieth Year. 1993.
Among the Usual Days: A Portrait. 1993.
At Eighty-Two: A Journal. 1996.

Plays

Underground River. 1947.

Screenplays: *Toscanini: The Hymn of Nations,* 1944; *Valley of the Tennessee,* 1944.

Other

Punch's Secret. 1974.
A Walk through the Woods. 1976.
May Sarton: Selected Letters, 1916-1954. 1997.
Dear Juliette: Letters of May Sarton to Juliette Huxley. 1999.

*

Bibliography: *May Sarton: A Bibliography* by Lenora Blouin, 1978; "A Revised Bibliography" by Blouin in *May Sarton: Woman and Poet,* edited by Constance Hunting, 1982.

Critical Studies: *The Modern American Political Novel: 1900-1960* by Joseph Blotner, 1966; *May Sarton* by Agnes Silbey, 1972; "May Sarton's Women," in *Images of Women in Fiction* edited by Susan K. Cornillon, 1972; *Lesbian Images* by Jane Rule, 1975; "'Kinds of Love': Love and Friendship in the Novels of May Sarton" by Jane S. Bakerman in *Critique,* Number 20, 1979; *May Sarton: Woman and Poet* edited by Constance Hunting, 1982; "A

Note on May Sarton" by Margaret Cruikshank, in *Journal of Homosexuality,* May 1986; "The Passion of Friendship" by William Drake in *The First Wave: American Poets in America 1915-1945* edited by Drake, 1987; *May Sarton Revisited* by Elizabeth Evans, 1989; *The Gay Novel in America* by James Levin, 1991; "Paradox and Plenitude: A Grain of Mustard Seed" in *A House of Gathering: Poets on May Sarton's Poetry* edited by Marilyn Kallet, 1993; *Rewriting Selves, Rewriting Lives: The Serial Self-Writing of Lillian Helman, May Sarton, and Richard Rodriguez* (dissertation) by Laura Ilene Fina, 1994; *May Sarton: A Biography* by Margot Peters, 1997.

*   *   *

In a career that spanned more than fifty years, May Sarton wrote over fifty volumes of poetry, fiction, and nonfiction. Sarton is perhaps best known by a general reading public for her intensely powerful autobiographical writings, including *Plant Dreaming Deep* (1968), *Journal of a Solitude* (1973), *Recovering* (1980), and *At Seventy* (1984). The autobiographies explore her life-long quest to understand the precarious balance between living a life in connection with others (readers, friends, and lovers) and living as an artist in solitude, a necessary condition of the search to understand the mysteries of life.

Sarton's writings often explore the emotional, psychological, and physical dimensions of aging. She faces honestly and directly the issues our society seldom engages, a courageous act that endears her to the many readers who are caregivers for aging parents or grandparents, as well as those who recognize themselves standing with Sarton before "the doors opening out from old age to unknown efforts and surprises" (*Endgame*). She also has won the respect of healthcare professionals who work with the elderly and health science faculty who use her work to teach their students about aging. Spurred by a visit to a dying friend in a deplorable nursing home, Sarton wrote the novel *As We Are Now* (1973), a fictional memoir of Caro Spencer, who describes the nursing home in which she resides as "a concentration camp for the old." Although her life becomes a series of hostile, degrading, and dehumanizing encounters, Spencer fights heroically to maintain her strength and independence. Through most of the novel, her journal writing helps Spencer to keep a fragile hold on memory and life.

Sarton's own journals have similarly helped her to continue despite serious illness. *Endgame: A Journal of the Seventy-Ninth Year* (1992) and *Encore: A Journal of the Eightieth Year* (1993) stand as testimony to Sarton's love of life and enduring spirit in the face of overwhelming obstacles. She chronicles her own battles with constant pain and increasing frailty, never denying or minimizing the horror, yet creating two works that capture the essence of all that is valuable in living, including the love of friends and the ability to savor the moments. Sarton's posthumous work, *At Eighty-Two: A Journal* (1996), reveals a much more vulnerable spirit, suffering the limitations and indignities of "very old age." Here the poet's deteriorating garden, which she maintained for twenty years, serves as a metaphor for Sarton's own physical disintegration and emotional despair.

Despite her focus on self-reflection, personal experience, and solitude, Sarton stood very firmly in the larger world. Readers connect with her work because they see their own experiences, their own dreams, and their own fears reflected in hers. In addition, Sarton's work is as often about contemporary societal issues as it is about her own personal experience. The novel *Faithful are the Wounds* (1955) explores questions raised about loyalty and trust in the McCarthy era. Several poems are about the killings at Kent State and the Vietnam War. *Mrs. Stevens Hears the Mermaids Singing* (1965) as well as *The Education of Harriet Hatfield* (1989) include gay and lesbian characters forging their own identity. In the collection of poetry *The Silence Now*, Sarton wrote eloquently about the AIDS crisis, noting that "We are stretched to meet a new dimension / Of love, a more demanding range / Where despair and hope must intertwine." The move from despair to hope reverberates in the transformation of the line "Fear. Fear. Fear. Fear.": "The word is not fear, the word we live, / But an old word suddenly made new, / As we learn it again, as we bring it alive: / Love. Love. Love. Love."

Sarton thought of herself as a "maker of bridges." All of her writing emphasized the drive to understand ourselves and each other. In *Journal of a Solitude* she asserts that meaningful communication requires difficult, honest self-revelation: "If we are to understand the human condition, and if we are to accept ourselves in all the complexity, self-doubt, extravagance of feeling, guilt, joy, the slow freeing of the self to its full capacity for action and creation, both as human being and as artist, we have to know all we can about each other, and we have to be willing to go naked." Sarton held fast to that philosophy to the end. After her death on July 16, 1995, many of her "friends of the work" received a black-bordered announcement that Sarton had previously arranged. On it a brief excerpt from her poem "Coming into Eighty" read simply,

> Soon we must set sail
> On the last mysterious voyage
> Everybody takes
> Toward death.
> Without my ship there,
> Wish me well.

Marjorie Stelmach in *Paradox and Plenitude* credits Sarton as a "hero of the human journey," one who has "taught us how to live, how to find qualities in ourselves to love, how to stumble and get up gracefully, how to retire from a life's work, how to attend a death, how to guard our sense of integrity," and in so doing Sarton mapped life's journey for us all.

—Susan Swartzlander

SAUNDERS, Caleb. *See* **HEINLEIN, Robert Anson.**

SCHWARTZ, Delmore (David)

Born: Brooklyn, New York, 8 December 1913. **Education:** Townsend Harris High School; George Washington High School, New York, graduated 1931; University of Wisconsin, Madison, 1931-32; New York University (editor, *Mosaic*), 1933-35, B.A. in philosophy 1935; Harvard University, Cambridge, Massachusetts (Bowdoin prize, 1936), 1935-37. **Family:** Married 1) Gertrude Buckman in 1938 (separated 1943; divorced 1944); 2) Elizabeth Pollet in 1949 (separated 1955). **Career:** Briggs-Copeland Instructor in English Composition, 1940, instructor in

English, 1941-45, and assistant professor of English, 1946-47, Harvard University; lecturer, New School for Social Research and New York University, late 1940s; Gauss lecturer, 1949, and visiting professor, 1952, Princeton University, New Jersey; fellow, Kenyon School of English, Gambier, Ohio, summer 1950; visiting professor, Indiana School of Letters, Bloomington, 1951, University of Chicago, 1954, and University of California, Los Angeles, 1961; professor of English, Syracuse University, Syracuse, New York, 1962-66. Poetry editor, 1939, editor, 1943-47, and associate editor, 1947-55, *Partisan Review,* New York, later New Brunswick, New Jersey; associated with *Perspectives* magazine, New York, 1952-53; literary consultant, *New Directions,* publishers, New York, 1952-53; poetry editor and film critic, *New Republic,* Washington, D.C., 1953-57. **Awards:** Guggenheim fellowship, 1940; American Academy grant, 1953; Bollingen prize, 1960; Shelley Memorial award, 1960. **Died:** 11 July 1966.

PUBLICATIONS

Collections

Selected Essays, edited by Donald A. Dike and David H. Zucker. 1970.
What Is to Be Given: Selected Poems, edited by Douglas Dunn. 1976.
Letters, edited by Robert Phillips. 1984.

Poetry

In Dreams Begin Responsibilities (includes short story, and play *Dr. Bergen's Belief*). 1938.
Genesis: Book One (includes prose). 1943.
Vaudeville for a Princess and Other Poems (includes prose). 1950.
Summer Knowledge: New and Selected Poems 1938-1958. 1959.
Lust and Lost Poems, edited by Robert Phillips. 1979.

Plays

Choosing Company, in *The New Caravan,* edited by Alfred Kreymborg. 1936.
Shenandoah; or, The Naming of the Child. 1941.

Fiction

The World Is a Wedding and Other Stories. 1948.
Successful Love and Other Stories. 1961.
In Dreams Begin Responsibilities and Other Stories, edited by James Atlas. 1978.

Other

American Poetry at Mid-Century, with John Crowe Ransom and John Hall Wheelock. 1958.
I Am Cherry Alive, The Little Girl Sang (for children). 1979.
Portrait of Delmore: Journals and Notes 1939-1959, edited by Elizabeth Pollet. 1986.
The Ego Is Always at the Wheel: Bagatelles, edited by Robert Phillips. 1986.

Editor, *Syracuse Poems 1964.* 1965.

Translator, *A Season in Hell* (bilingual edition), by Arthur Rimbaud. 1939; revised edition, 1940.

*

Bibliography: in *Selected Essays,* 1970; *Delmore Schwartz: A Bibliographical Checklist,* in *American Book Collector* by Ronald Labuz, July-August 1983.

Critical Studies: *Schwartz* by Richard McDougall, 1974; *Schwartz: The Life of an American Poet* by James Atlas, 1977; *The Middle Generation: The Lives and Poetry of Delmore Schwartz, Randall Jarrell, John Berryman, Robert Lowell* by Bruce Bawer, 1986; *The Figure of the Film Critic as Virile Poet: Delmore Schwartz at the New Republic in the 1950s; Selected Papers* by Paul Bauer, 1991.

* * *

It is difficult, reading Delmore Schwartz, to disentangle the poetry from the legend. The darling of the group of American intellectuals associated with the *Partisan Review* in the 1930s and 1940s—to which he contributed as poet, critic, and short story writer, eventually becoming coeditor—Schwartz had a career worthy of the last *poete maudit.* A precociously brilliant first book, *In Dreams Begin Responsibilities,* was followed by a tragic decline into alcohol, insanity, and an early death, alone, in a seedy Manhattan hotel. Posthumously, Schwartz has undergone a literary "canonization" in one of the most heartbreaking sequences of **John Berryman**'s *Dream Songs* and as the eponymous "hero" of **Saul Bellow**'s *Humboldt's Gift.*

And Schwartz almost certainly saw himself in something like this role. The titles alone of some of his best known poems—"Do Others Speak of Me Mockingly, Maliciously?," "All of Us Always Turning Away for Solace"—suggest his fundamental view of the poet as one isolated from his tribe, cut off, as in the marvelous "The Heavy Bear Who Goes with Me," from contact even with his own body. The characteristic Schwartzian stance is apparent in his "Sonnet: O City, City": we live

> Where the sliding auto's catastrophe
> Is a gust past the curb, where numb and high
> The office building rises to its tyranny,
> Is our anguished diminution until we die.

In the same poem, however, he longs for an alternative human sympathy, "the self articulate, affectionate and flowing." Between these terms the course of his poetry runs.

It is a poetry that rarely loses touch with political and historical realities: "The Ballad of the Children of the Czar" and the verse play *Shenandoah* poignantly express Schwartz's understanding of his family's experience as Jewish immigrants to America. There is the larger feeling, in many poems, of human beings imprisoned in time, bearing the guilt of generations, and Schwartz probes at his guilts and anxieties in a way that occasionally, as in "Prothalamion," points forward to the "confessional" poetry to be written by his more famous contemporaries Berryman and **Robert Lowell**. The guardian angels of these poems, figures that haunt Schwartz's imagination and are returned to with obsessive insistence, are the heroic solitaries—Faust, Socrates, "Tiger Christ," "Manic-depressive Lincoln," and, above all, Hamlet.

But there is also in Schwartz, if less insistently, an energetically vibrant language and feeling, a kind of robust dandyism, as in "Far Rockaway":

> The radiant soda of the seashore fashions
> Fun, foam, and freedom. The sea laves
> The shaven sand. And the light sways forward
> On the self-destroying waves.

Douglas Dunn, in his introduction to *What Is to Be Given*, referred to Schwartz's "sometimes dispiriting ebullience," and it is this that many critics have objected to in the later work. A poem like "Seurat's Sunday Afternoon along the Seine" certainly needs to be read without the expectation of those judicious ironies on which most modern poetry thrives. But, *relaxed into*, the stretch and sweep, the sheer verbal intoxication of the poem, carry persuasive power.

Schwartz is a poet, and a critic, too little read and too little understood. Later republications, however, suggest that his work will survive, along with the best of his generation.

—Neil Corcoran

SEDGWICK, Catharine Maria

Born: Stockbridge, Massachusetts, 28 December 1789. **Education:** The district school and at boarding schools in Boston and Albany, New York; also received private instruction in several languages. **Career:** Lived in Albany and New York City, 1807-13; returned to Stockbridge, 1813; later lived in Lenox, Massachusetts, and New York; traveled in Europe, 1839-40, and in the Midwest, 1854. Active in the work of the Unitarian Church and the Women's Prison Association of New York. **Died:** 31 July 1867.

PUBLICATIONS

Fiction

A New-England Tale; or, Sketches of New-England Character and Manners. 1822; revised edition, as *A New England Tale, and Miscellanies,* 1852.
Mary Hollis. 1822.
Redwood. 1824; revised edition, 1850.
The Travellers (for children). 1825.
The Deformed Boy. 1826.
Hope Leslie; or, Early Times in the Massachusetts. 1827, revised edition, 1842.
Clarence; or, A Tale of Our Own Times. 1830; revised edition, 1849.
Home. 1835.
The Linwoods; or, "Sixty Years Since" in America. 1835.
Tales and Sketches. 2 vols., 1835-44.
The Poor Rich Man, and the Rich Poor Man. 1836.
Live and Let Live; or, Domestic Service Illustrated. 1837.
Stories for Young Persons. 1840.
The Boy on Mount Rhigi (for children). 1848.
Tales of City Life. 1850; as *The City Clerk and His Sister and Other Stories,* 1851.
The Irish Girl and Other Tales. 1853.

The Mysterious Story-Book; or, The Good Stepmother. 1856.
Married or Single? 1857.

Other

A Short Essay to Do Good. 1828.
Means and Ends; or, Self-Training (for children). 1839.
Letters from Abroad to Kindred at Home. 2 vols., 1841; revised edition, 1 vol., 1841.
Morals of Manners; or, Hints for Our Young People. 1846.
Facts and Fancies for School-Day Reading. 1847.
Memoir of Joseph Curtis, A Model Man. 1858.

Editor, with Katharine Sedgwick Minot, *Letters from Charles Sedgwick to His Family and Friends.* 1870.

*

Bibliography: in *Bibliography of American Literature* by Jacob Blanck, edited by Virginia L. Smyers and Michael Winship, 1983.

Critical Studies: *Life and Letters* edited by Mary E. Dewey, 1871; *Sedgwick* by Sister Mary Michael Welsh, 1937; *Three Wise Virgins* by Gladys Brooks, 1957; *Sedgwick* by Edward Halsey Foster, 1974; *A Plea for Fictional Histories and Old-Time "Jewesses"* by Alide Cagidemetrio, 1989; *Nineteenth-Century Autobiographies of Affiliation: The Case of Catharine Sedgwick and Lucy Larcom* by Carol Holly, 1991; *Catharine Maria Sedgwick's Hope Leslie: Radical Frontier Romance* by Carol J. Singley, 1992; *Sympathy As Strategy in Sedgwick's Hope Leslie* by Dana Nelson, 1992; "She Could Make a Cake As Well As Books ... Catharine Sedgwick, Anne Jameson, and the Construction of the Domestic Intellectual" by Maria LaMonaca, in *Women's Writing: The Elizabethan to Victorian Period,* 1995; "(Re)Writing the Frontier Romance: Catharine Maria Sedwick's *Hope Leslie*" by Cheri Louise Ross, in *College Language Association Journal,* March 1996, pp. 320-40; *Covenant and Republic: Historical Romance and the Politics of Puritanism* by Philip Gould, 1996; "Inscribing the 'Impartial Observer' in Sedgwick's *Hope Leslie*" by Douglas Ford, in *Legacy: A Journal of American Women Writers,* 1997, pp. 81-92.

*   *   *

The novels of Catharine Maria Sedgwick, the best of which include *Redwood* and *Hope Leslie*, are distinguished by close attention to realistic detail, especially regional customs and manners. They use American scenery, manners, customs, and materials, and are usually centered on moral circumstances of especially American interest. *Redwood*, for example, contrasts a Northern and a Southern family. *Hope Leslie* is set in Puritan New England, and aspects of New England history, scenery, and manners are finely detailed. In *The Linwoods*, the tensions that resulted in the American Revolution are dramatized in the conflicts between a family of colonists and a family of royalists. *Clarence* demonstrates the value of a natural aristocracy, an aristocracy of talent and virtue such as projected by **Thomas Jefferson**, over an aristocracy based solely on birth and wealth. *A New-England Tale*, the first of Sedgwick's novels, is partially a religious tract attacking the remnants of Calvinism in New England, and *Married or Single?* is one of the earliest feminist American pleas for socially equitable treatment of women.

Sedgwick's moral preoccupations are largely tied to the social and political concerns of her day, and while these moral concerns are in many instances of little interest in the late twentieth century (as well as obscure to readers without training in American social and political history), her novels have continuing literary value, being among the earliest and the best examples of regionalism in American writing. Sedgwick had an acute ear for American dialect and a fine sense of regional customs and manners. As a literary stylist, she was not especially remarkable, although superior to most of her contemporaries in America, but she was capable of detailing with precision regional characteristics, landscapes, and dialect. Furthermore, alone among American novelists of her time she created credible women in fiction. While it was common for American novelists to portray women as ideally (if improbably) passive and unambitious, Sedgwick's heroines are morally superior; all of her novels center on women whose superior moral judgment places them far above others—particularly men.

—Edward Halsey Foster

SEWALL, Samuel

Born: Bishopstoke, Hampshire, England, 28 March 1652; immigrated with his family to Boston, 1661. **Education:** Harvard University, Cambridge, Massachusetts, 1667-71, A.B. 1671, A.M. in theology 1674. **Family:** Married 1) Hannah Hull in 1676 (died 1717), 14 children; 2) Abigail Tilley in 1719 (died 1720); 3) Mary Gibbs in 1722. **Career:** Resident fellow (tutor), Harvard University, 1673-74; merchant and banker; made a freeman of the Massachusetts Bay Colony, 1679, and began political career; manager of Boston's printing press, 1681-84; deputy to general court for Westfield, Hampden county, and president of the general court, 1683; member of the colony's council, 1684-86, and (under new charter), 1691-1725; justice, superior court, 1692; appointed by Governor Sir William Phips as one of nine judges in Salem witchcraft cases, 1692 (19 persons were executed; Sewall publicly admitted errors of judgment, 1697, the only judge to do so); probate judge, Suffolk County, 1715-18; Chief Judge, Superior Court, 1718-28. **Member:** Ancient and Honorable Artillery Company, 1679, and Captain, 1701; commissioner, Society for the Propagation of the Gospel in New England, 1699. **Died:** 1 January 1730.

PUBLICATIONS

Prose

Phaenomena quaedam Apocalyptica; or, Some Few Lines Towards a Description of the New Heaven. 1697.
The Selling of Joseph. 1700; edited by Sidney Kaplan, 1969.
Proposals Touching the Accomplishment of Prophecies. 1713.
Diary 1674-1729. 3 vols., 1878-82; edited by M. Halsey Thomas, 2 vols., 1973; as *The Diary and Life of Samuel Sewall* (abridged version), 1998.
Letter-Book. 2 vols., 1886-88.
Letters of Samuel Lee and Sewall Relating to New England and the Indians, edited by George Lyman Kittredge. 1912.

*

Critical Studies: *Sewall and the World He Lived In* by Nathan H. Chamberlain, 1897; *Sewall of Boston* by Ola Elizabeth Winslow, 1964; *Sewall: A Puritan Portrait* by T.B. Strandness, 1967; *The Mental World of Samuel Sewall* by David D. Hall, 1984; "Between Hell and Plum Island: Samuel Sewall and the Legacy of the Witches, 1692-97" by David S. Lovejoy, in *New England Quarterly: A Historical Review of New England Life and Letters,* September 1997, pp. 355-67.

*   *   *

Samuel Sewall, whose nearly four score years bridged the seventeenth and eighteenth centuries, was a man of consequence in his New England Puritan world. Moses Coit Tyler's assertion that he was "great by almost every measure of greatness" suggests the legendary aura that continues to surround the Sewall name, even though the judgment invites qualification. Rejecting a call to the ministry for which he had prepared, Sewall's principal activities were in the secular world. Upon marrying into great wealth, he became an astute merchant and man of property and is sometimes judged critically for his questionable accommodation of religious ideas to pragmatic business procedures. It is true that he was a worldly and mercenary man; but he was also a man with intense religious convictions and a deep sense of justice, and he loyally served community, province, and colony.

Born in England in 1652, Samuel Sewall arrived in Boston at the age of nine. Under the tutelage of a local minister, he prepared for admission to Harvard College and was enrolled in the class of 1671. He stayed on following graduation to complete requirements for the master's degree in theology, and although he chose not to enter the ministry, his interest in theology pervaded his entire life. His public service was extensive. For a few years he managed the colony's printing press; one year in England he assisted Increase Mather in an unsuccessful effort to restore the colony's charter (1688-89); in 1683 he was elected to the Massachusetts General Court; and although he lacked formal legal training, he was appointed a judge of the Superior Court and later served as Chief Justice. More widely remembered is the fact that he was one of the magistrates selected to conduct the Salem witch trials in 1692. Later, in his personal petition of penitence read before his home congregation, he was the only magistrate to admit errors in judgment.

Obviously, the role of Sewall as public servant cannot be separated from history, but that temporal role pales when placed beside the lingering importance of Sewall as writer. Two works have special significance. In 1700, "dissatisfied with the Trade of fetching Negros from Guinea" and stimulated by the reading of biblical commentary, Sewall hastily prepared a statement, *The Selling of Joseph,* for presentation to the Council and General Court. The compelling piece, one of the earliest anti-slavery tracts published in America, continues to have historical interest. It is his remarkable diary, however, covering somewhat irregularly the years 1673 to 1729, for which Sewall is principally remembered. Often compared to the diary of the Englishman Samuel Pepys, but covering a longer span of time and lacking the "under the stairs" detail offered by Pepys, Sewall's diary is a major source of information not only of Sewall the man but also of the shifting texture of life among second- and third-generation Puritans in New England. Sewall's clearly secular tendencies, which he shared with the powerful men of his time, are tempered by the stern and honorable demeanor then conventional; his interest in material achievement and standing is juxtaposed with his devotion to the teachings of Calvin and his own almost obsessive interest in the sermons and religious writings of his day; the piety of his respected contemporaries is qualified by his casual notation of their eccentricities; his devotion to his beloved first wife, Hannah Hull, to whom he was married for forty-one years and whom he describes as "my most Constant Lover, my most laborious Nurse, a most tender mother," stands in sharp contrast to his meditated pursuit after her death of eligible widows whom he sought to attract with incongruous gifts such as sermons, shoebuckles, and raisins. At times the diary is an emotional record, responding to the joy of birth and the sadness of death; it is "edged in black," wrote T.B. Strandness, "illness and death on almost every page"—a factual reflection of the high mortality rate in both family and community, for Sewall himself lived to witness the deaths of two of his wives and all but three of his fourteen children. But it also exhibits the rational and sometimes troubled inquiry into the nature of justice and the necessity of reconciling Calvinistic dogma and secular advantage.

The highly personal diary remains vital reading, for it is a rich repository of vivid detail not only about the life of one man but also about the historical milieu that he in large measure epitomizes.

—Clayton L. Eichelberger

SEXTON, Anne (Gray)

Born: Anne Harvey, Newton, Massachusetts, 9 November 1928.
Education: Schools in Wellesley, Massachusetts, 1934-45; Rogers Hall, Lowell, Massachusetts, 1945-47; Garland Junior College, Boston, 1947-48; Radcliffe Institute, Cambridge, Massachusetts (Scholar), 1961-63. **Family:** Married Alfred M. Sexton in 1948 (divorced 1974); two daughters. **Career:** Fashion model, Boston, 1950-51; teacher, Wayland High School, Massachusetts, 1967-68; lecturer, 1970-71, and professor of creative writing, 1972-74, Boston University; Crawshaw Professor of Literature, Colgate University, Hamilton, New York, 1972. **Awards:** Bread Loaf Writers Conference Robert Frost fellowship, 1959; American Academy traveling fellowship, 1963; Ford grant, 1964; Shelley Memorial award, 1967; Pulitzer prize, 1967; Guggenheim fellowship, 1969. Litt.D.: Tufts University, Medford, Massachusetts, 1970; Regis College, Weston, Massachusetts, 1971; Fairfield University, Connecticut, 1971. Fellow, Royal Society of Literature (London). **Died:** (suicide) 4 October 1974.

PUBLICATIONS

Collections

The Heart of Sexton's Poetry, edited by Linda Gray Sexton and Lois Ames. 1977.
Complete Poems. 1981.

Poetry

To Bedlam and Part Way Back. 1960.
All My Pretty Ones. 1962.
Selected Poems. 1964.

Live or Die. 1966.
Poems, with Douglas Livingstone and Thomas Kinsella. 1968.
Love Poems. 1969.
Transformations. 1971.
The Book of Folly. 1972.
O Ye Tongues. 1973.
The Death Notebooks. 1974.
The Awful Rowing Toward God. 1975.
Words for Dr. Y: Uncollected Poems with Three Stories, edited by Linda Gray Sexton. 1978.

Play

45 Mercy Street (produced 1969). Edited by Linda Gray Sexton, 1976.

Other

Eggs of Things (for children), with Maxine Kumin. 1963.
More Eggs of Things (for children), with Maxine Kumin. 1964.
Joey and the Birthday Present (for children), with Maxine Kumin. 1971.
The Wizard's Tears (for children), with Maxine Kumin. 1975.
Sexton: A Self-Portrait in Letters, edited by Linda Gray Sexton and Lois Ames. 1977.
No Evil Star: Selected Essays, Interviews, and Poems, edited by Steven E. Colburn. 1985.

*

Bibliography: *Sylvia Plath and Sexton: A Reference Guide* by Cameron Northouse and Thomas P. Walsh, 1974.

Critical Studies: *Sexton: The Artist and Her Critics* edited by J.D. McClatchy, 1978; *Postmodernism and the Biographer* by Diane Wood-Middlebrook, 1990; *Anne Sexton's "Texas Foot"* by Joseph Colin-Murphey, 1992; *"Wild Animals Out in the Arena": Anne Sexton's Revisions for "All My Pretty Ones"* by Stephen Vinson, 1992; "What Prison Is This? Literary Critics Cover Incest in Anne Sexton's *Briar Rose*" by Dawn Skorczewski, in *Signs: Journal of Women in Culture and Society,* winter 1996; "There Are More Important Things Than Judgment Involved: James Dickey's Criticism of Anne Sexton and the Search for Self" by Carrie Martin, in *James Dickey Newsletter,* spring 1997; "Leading from 'You' to 'I' to 'We': Contemporary American Women's Poetry of Witness" by Cassie Premo Steele, in *Leadership Journal: Women in Leadership Sharing the Vision,* spring 1998, pp. 67-80.

*   *   *

Anne Sexton is known primarily for her remarkable imagery and apparent personal honesty in poems ranging from the formally structured early work (*To Bedlam and Part Way Back*) to the quasi-humorous prose poems of *Transformations* and the evocative free form poetry of *Love Poems*. Sexton had published much of her most mature work in the years immediately preceding her evident suicide, and her critical reputation has yet to acknowledge that last productive period.

Sexton was a model who married, reared two daughters, and came to poetry through a workshop at Boston University conducted by **Robert Lowell**. Influenced by Lowell and the writing of **W.D. Snodgrass** to break the restraint and intellectualism common to American poetry during the 1950s, Sexton wrote such moving personal poems as "The Double Image." Her consideration here of the relationship among a mother, daughter, and grandchild is important not only for the technical prowess with which she handled a possibly sentimental subject, but for the genuine insight into the women's condition. Encouraged by her friendship with **Sylvia Plath**, who also was a student in the Lowell workshop, Sexton mined areas of theme and image that were virtually unknown to contemporary poetry. "Those Times" recreates her own childhood as a time of torment; "Little Girl, My String Bean, My Lovely Woman" celebrates her joy in her daughter; "Flee on Your Donkey" plumbs the depths of personal despair; "Menstruation at Forty" questions the mortality image from a feminine view—most of Sexton's poems are adventurous in that she is writing not only about unconventional subjects, but her quick progression from image to image lends an almost surreal effect to the poetry.

Rather than simply describing Sexton's work as "confessional," the over-used label that attached itself to any writing that seemed autobiographical in origin (as what poetry is, finally, not?), readers should be aware that her work manages to distill the apparently autobiographical details into an imagistic whole that convinces any reader of its authenticity. The life in Sexton's poems is the life of the imagination, regardless of whether or not she has used the facts from her own existence in the re-creation of that life. Once the poems from the late collections have been assimilated with the earlier work, her continuous interest in religious themes and images will become as noticeable as her use of feminine psychology and concerns. Sexton's importance to American poetry will not rest simply on her mental stability or instability, her suicide, or her use of personal detail in her work; her importance will rest, finally, on her ability to craft poems that move the reader to the act of understanding.

—Linda Wagner-Martin

SHANGE, Ntozake

Born: Paulette Williams in Trenton, New Jersey, 18 October 1948; eldest child of Paul T. Williams (surgeon) and Eloise Williams (educator, psychiatric social worker); adopted Zulu name Ntozake ("she who comes with her own things") Shange ("who walks like a lion"), pronounced en-to-zaki shong-gay, in 1971. **Family:** Married 1) musician David Murray in 1977, one daughter (divorced); 2) John Guess. **Education:** Barnard College, New York City, majoring in American Studies with emphasis in African American music and poetry, B.A. *cum laude* 1970; University of Southern California, Los Angeles, M.A. in American Studies 1973. **Career:** Poet, performance and installation artist, author, playwright, dancer, violinist, weaver, director, actor; taught composition, Third World poetry and creative writing at Trenton State College, New Jersey, 1972; advanced composition, women's studies, and humanities at Sonoma State University, Rohnert Park, California, 1973–75; basic and advanced composition at University of California at Berkeley, 1973–75; African American studies and drama at Mills College, Oakland, California, 1975; creative writing at City College of New York, 1975; sociology of the black family at Medgar Evers Community College of the City University of New

York, 1975; African American studies and drama at Rutgers University, Newark, New Jersey, 1978; Rice University, Houston, Texas, 1983; playwrighting and creative writing at the University of Houston, Texas, 1986; artist-in-residence, Villanova University, Pennsylvania, 1990; performance art and African literature in the New World at the Maryland Institute, 1992. **Awards:** Outer Critics' Circle award, 1977; *Village Voice* Obie award, 1977 and 1980; Audelco award, 1977; *Mademoiselle Magazine* award, 1977; nominations for Tony, Grammy, and Emmy awards, 1977; Frank Silvera Writers' Workshop award, 1978; *Los Angeles Times* Book Review award for Poetry, 1981; Columbia University Medal of Excellence, 1981; National Endowment for the Arts creative writing award, 1981; New York State Council of the Arts award, 1981; Guggenheim fellowship, 1981; Taos (New Mexico) Poetry Circus World Heavyweight Champion, 1991; Lila Wallace *Readers' Digest* Writers' award, 1992. **Residence:** Philadelphia, Pennsylvania.

PUBLICATIONS

Plays

for colored girls who have considered suicide/ when the rainbow is enuf (produced 1976; PBS television adaptation produced 1981, aired 1982). 1977.

Mother Courage, adaptation of Bertolt Brecht's *Mother Courage and Her Children* (produced 1980).

Three Pieces: spell #7; a photograph: lovers in motion; boogie woogie landscapes. 1981.

Educating Rita, adaptation of Willy Russell's *Educating Rita* (produced 1983).

From Okra to Greens/ A Different Kinda Love Story: A Play/ With Music and Dance. 1985.

Three Views of Mt. Fuji: A Play (produced 1987).

"Daddy Says: A Play," in *New Plays for the Black Theatre,* edited by Woodie King, Jr. 1989.

Betsey Brown: A Rhythm and Blues Musical, for the Philadelphia, Pennsylvania American Music Theater Festival (produced 1989).

Performance Pieces

Where the Mississippi Meets the Amazon, with Jessica Hagedorn and Thulani Nkabinde Davis. 1977.

A Photograph: A Study in Cruelty. 1977.

A Photograph: Lovers in Motion. 1979.

From Okra to Greens. 1978.

Black & White Two-Dimensional Planes. 1979.

Mouths: A Daughter's Geography (A Performance Piece). 1981.

It Has Not Always Been This Way: A Choreopoem. 1981.

Dreamed Dwellings: An Installation & Performance Piece, with Wopo Holup. 1981.

Triptych & Bocas: A Performance Piece. 1982.

And How Shall We Know Him: Is This the Prince?, with Dianne McIntyre. 1982.

The Dancin' Novel: "Sassafrass, Cypress, & Indigo," with Dianne McIntyre and Rod Rodgers. 1982.

Ridin' the Moon in Texas. 1986.

Beneath the Necessity of Talking: A Performance Piece, with John Purcell and Jean-Paul Bourelly. 1989.

The Love Space Demands (A Continuing Saga). 1991.
Plays: *One* (includes *for colored girls who have considered suicide when the rainbow is enuf; Spell #7; I Heard Eric Dolphy in His Eyes; The Love Space Demands: A Continuing Saga*). 1992.

Poetry

Nappy Edges. 1972.
Some Men. 1981.
Matrilineal Poems. 1983.
Between the two of them: a painted poem, in limited edition. 1983.
from okra to greens: poems. 1984.
A Daughter's Geography. 1983.
Ridin' the Moon in Texas: Word Paintings. 1987.
The Love Space Demands (A Continuing Saga). 1991.
I Live in Music. 1994.

Novels

Sassafrass, novella. 1976.
Sassafrass, Cypress & Indigo. 1982.
Betsey Brown. 1985.
Liliane. 1994.

Essays

See No Evil: Prefaces, Essays & Accounts (1976-1983). 1984.
Whitewash. 1997.
If I Can Cook, You Know God Can. 1998.

*

Critical Studies: "Ntozake Shange Interviews Herself" in *Ms.,* December 1977; interview with Toni Morrison in *American Rag,* winter 1978; interview by James Early in *In the Memory and Spirit of Frances, Zora, and Lorraine: Essays and Interviews on Black Women and Writing* edited by Juliette Bowles, 1978; "Ntozake Shange" by Claudia Tate in *Black Women Writers at Work* edited by Tate, 1983; *Ntozake Shange's First Novel* by Reginald Martin, 1984; "'A Laying on of Hands'" by Carolyn Mitchell in *Women Writers and the City* edited by Susan Merrill Squier, 1984; "Black Feminism in *for colored girls who have considered suicide when the rainbow is enuf*" by Tobe Levin and Gwendolyn Flowers in *History and Tradition in Afro-American Culture,* 1984; interview with Stella Dong in *Publishers Weekly,* May 3, 1985; *Interviews with Contemporary Women Playwrights* edited by Kathleen Betsko and Rachel Koenig, 1987; "Rites and Responsibilities" by Helene Keyssar, and "Distraught Laughter" by Deborah R. Geis, both in *Feminine Focus: The New Women Playwrights* edited by Enoch Brater, 1989; interview with Kay Bonetti in *American Audio Prose Library,* 1989; "'The Poetry of a Moment'" by John Timpane in *Modern American Drama: The Female Canon* edited by June Schlueter, 1990; "If It's a Statistic, It's Not a Woman" by Helen Kidd in *Contemporary Poetry Meets Modern Theory* edited by Antony Easthope, 1991; "From Nice Colored Girl to Womanist" by Geta LeSeur in *Language and Literature in the African American Imagination* edited by Carol Aisha Blackshire-Belay, 1992; interview by Edward K. Brown II in *Poets & Writers,* May/June 1993; "Dancing Out of Form, Dancing into Self: Genre and Metaphor in Marshall, Shange, and Walker" by Barbara Frey Waxman, in *The Journal of the Society for the Study of the Multi-Ethnic Lit-*

erature of the United States, fall 1994, pp. 533-55; *Ntozake Shange: A Critical Study of the Plays* by Neal A. Lester, 1995; "Unmasking the Minstrel Mask's Black Magic in Ntozake Shange's *Spell #7*" by Karen Cronacher, in *Feminist Theater and Theory,* edited by Helene Keyssar, 1996; in *Black Women's Writing: Quest for Identity in the Plays of Lorraine Hansberry and Ntozake Shange* by Y.S. Sharadha, 1998.

*   *   *

When African American poet-playwright Ntozake Shange declared in her 1976-77 Broadway debut, *for colored girls who have considered suicide/ when the rainbow is enuf,* that "bein alive & bein a woman & bein colored is a metaphysical dilemma / i havent conquered yet," she assumed her role as "a war correspondent . . . in a war of cultural and esthetic aggression." Not only did Shange's staged presentation challenge Eurocentric ideals and violate prescribed boundaries of drama as a genre in its meshing of music, song, poetry, and dance as well as African elements of storytelling and movement into a single emotional moment, but her unabashed exaltation of black womanhood legitimized in a public arena experiences that were previously ignored or marginalized. Dealing with women's issues that transcend racial boundaries—loss of virginity, abortion, acquaintance rape—Shange presents a metaphoric "rainbow" of women struggling against racism and sexism. Their struggles become a black woman's song of inadequacy as she endeavors to mold herself into society's feminine ideal. Through redefinitions and revisions, *for colored girls* introduced Shange to a world curious about, intimidated by, and not easily willing to accept and respect the cultural and aesthetic terms of her own personal and political expression. This choreopoem form opened up possibilities for exploring the complex lives of women, black women, and peoples of color. Shange's writings in other genres affirm her steadfast commitment to documenting and challenging what she calls the three "fundamental flaws in the way our planet is run": sexism, racism, and capitalism.

While Shange had no intentions of seeing her poems performed as a "drama" when she read them singularly—sometimes accompanied by a dancer who moved to the rhythms and meanings of her words—in San Francisco Bay women's bars, the poems soon emerged as a unified piece with seven black female speakers sharing the pains and joy of collective black female experience. In addition to blurring genres, the choreopoem also presented black women whose language and behavior opposed a white feminine ideal of "lady." Shange's women talk about their lives honestly and without apology. As frustrated critics declared their failed efforts to categorize Shange's choreopoem as either "drama" or "poetry"—neither category alone adequately describes the piece—a public outcry arose from black males and not a few black women who insisted that Shange's celebration of black women was an attack on black men. They assumed that Beau Willie Brown, who drops his children from a fifth-story apartment window as their mother, his lover, looks on helplessly, is Shange's black Everyman. Closer examination reveals that this tragic moment at the end of the choreopoem results from the economic, social, and political "suffocation" both Beau and Crystal experience as they strive toward an ideal that ultimately works against them. Utterly powerless, both partners sacrifice their children as desperate demonstrations of individual power. With this final of a series of losses, the black women come to realize that their wholeness and their "holiness" come not from external sources—being a mother, lover, sister—but from within themselves: "i found god in myself / & i loved her / i loved her fiercely." These women recognize that the rainbow has always been inside them, and come to understand their potential for empowerment through self-realization.

Shange's second published choreopoem, *spell #7: geechee jibara quik magic trance manual for technologically stressed third world people (A Theater Piece),* celebrates blackness as *for colored girls* celebrates black womanhood. In this piece, nine professional artists assemble in a segregated Manhattan bar for a rap session on the impact of racism on their professional and personal aspirations. As actors debate with each other and among themselves whether not working at all is more noble than accepting stereotypical roles of pimps, prostitutes, and chauffeurs, the women in the group assert their own particular concerns that the men even in this race-conscious group do not respect their talent or intellect. Through improvisations that often stretch imagination to its limits, the characters demonstrate the power of creative imagination in liberating themselves from immediate and past limitations. The characters' final assertion is a conscious willing: "we gonna be / colored & love it."

Two important features of this presentation are Shange's use of a giant minstrel mask that hovers above the theater audience and a reversed minstrel show prologue—black characters/actors in blackface—as both literal and metaphorical (mis)representations of black people and their experiences. Debunking myths about black peoples' physicalities, behaviors, intellect, and creative possibilities, Shange shows how present racist notions emerge from past (mis)conceptions. She ultimately demonstrates the self-destructiveness of such notions when they are internalized and become negatively self-defining and limiting.

Shange's third choreopoem, *a photograph: lovers in motion,* is perhaps the more traditional of Shange's longer published theater pieces. It is also the first piece that features a male character in its lead role. Shange's educated and professional characters demonstrate the ambiguities of sexual identity. As three women and one man vie for the attentions and affections of photographer Sean David, Shange explores social and historical factors that define and confuse individuals' sense of who they are. Amid graphic discussions of sexuality, these characters never really resolve their frustrations. In this piece, dance, music and poetry are less in the foreground than the individual lives of these characters. The claim that Shange presents black men unsympathetically is disproven by her in-depth exploration of Sean's confused definitions of manhood and his unresolved tensions with his own deceased father.

boogie woogie landscapes, Shange's fourth published theater piece, is a companion to *for colored girls.* Here, Shange dissects the psyche of the "all-American colored girl." Using expressionist techniques, Shange presents Layla's fears and dreams as she realizes herself first as a black person and then as a woman. Layla's search for a life beyond a black and white two-dimensional plane ends as a confirmation of her existence. She learns with the help of night-life companions that she can define her existence on her own terms despite the physical, psychological, social, and political liabilities of her race and gender. Layla learns that she cannot rewrite the past or shield herself from future threats to her livelihood. Rather, she accepts that her life is defined by moments of self-actualization. This piece seems to address a fundamental issue in the formation of black female identity. Are black women black before they are women? Are they women before they are black? Shange demonstrates through Layla that black women's struggles with racism and sexism cannot be treated as separate battles since they occur simultaneously. Denying any dichotomy between race and gender for black women, she remarks in an interview with Edward Brown that "I have a vagina and skin at the same time . . . . I [can't] side with a racist or a sexist. I'm a feminist."

From Okra to Greens/ A Different Kinda Love Story: A Play/ With Music and Dance is perhaps Shange's clearest demonstration of the choreopoem form. Here, she takes poems almost verbatim from a previously published volume of poetry, *A Daughter's Geography,* and divides them into two voices—a black male (Greens) and a black woman (Okra). The choreopoem is structured as a love story between these characters, a love story that inverts the traditional (white) boy-meets-(white) girl story. That both characters are poets reflects Shange's distinct creative bias toward poets who make moments happen. As a feminist, Shange designs this piece as a learning experience for Greens, who is escorted by Okra through the landscapes of "a daughter's geography." That Greens is receptive to a black woman's feminist perspectives is Shange's affirmation that a man and a woman can exist in a mutually satisfying love relationship without power struggles.

Shange's novels, *Sassafrass, Cypress, and Indigo* and *Betsey Brown,* also explore the contours of black women's lives. In the first novel, set in Charleston, South Carolina, Shange examines the lives of three sisters (Sassafrass, a weaver and poet; Cypress, a dancer and journal keeper; and Indigo, a violinist) and their mother, and their individual relationships with the world and with each other, in a format that violates the boundaries of the traditional novel. Since these women enjoy cooking and experience creative powers through culinary cultural rituals, Shange scatters actual recipes throughout the novel. And since Sassafrass is a poet, Shange includes some of Sassafrass's poems. Shange also explores the "magic" she identifies as black womanhood, demonstrating strength in womanhood through ancient feminine rituals of spiritual healing, through folklore, and through storytelling. The lyricism and imagery of Shange's language evidence her identity as a poet even when writing a novel. *Betsey Brown* is Shange's semi-autobiographical novel of a thirteen-year-old middle-class black girl growing up in St. Louis, Missouri. It details Betsey's efforts to form her own racial and gender identity amid the social and political upheaval of the 1960s.

It is as a poet that Shange has most securely established her place in American literature and women's studies. Indeed, Shange continually identifies herself fundamentally as a poet whose task is to make words dance to her rhythms into readers' or listeners' emotional consciousness. She maintains that "a poem shd fill you up with something / cd make you swoon, stop in yr tracks, change yr mind, or make it up. a poem shd happen to you like cold water or a kiss." With language that is raw—to some offensive—and syntactically unpredictable and full of interpretative possibilities, Shange challenges the hegemony of Western patriarchy in her bold reconstruction of herself individually and collectively as a black woman. Her poetry stakes a territorial claim where she is empowered by folklore, popular culture, music, and rituals that legitimize and sustain women and peoples of color. Returning hopes, dreams, and legitimacy to those denied these because of slavery, racism, and sexism, Shange extols poetry as a communal language: "poetry is a collective experience it's the closest thing to the voice of the people you can get outside of the national anthem . . . the words and music [of poetry] allow us to offer a world that is more wholly the way we experience it." Race consciousness, strident feminism, American and world history, international and national politics, language and its myriad manifestations (both verbal and non-verbal) inform Shange's steadfast commitment to giving life to and preserving the livelihood of those most often denied voice.

—Neal A. Lester

SHAPIRO, Karl (Jay)

Born: Baltimore, Maryland, 10 November 1913. **Education:** University of Virginia, Charlottesville, 1932-33; Johns Hopkins University, Baltimore, 1937-39; Pratt Library School, Baltimore, 1940. **Military Service:** Served in the U.S. Army, 1941-45. **Family:** Married 1) Evalyn Katz in 1945 (divorced 1967), two daughters and one son; 2) Teri Kovach in 1967 (died 1982); 3) Sophie Wilkins in 1985. **Career:** Worked as a clerk in family business, mid-1930s; associate professor, Johns Hopkins University, 1948-50; visiting professor, University of Wisconsin, Madison, 1948, Loyola University, Chicago, 1951-52, University of California, Berkeley and Davis, 1955-56, and University of Indiana, Bloomington, 1956-57; professor of English, University of Nebraska, Lincoln, 1956-66, University of Illinois, Chicago Circle, 1966-68, and University of California, Davis, 1968-84. Beginning 1984 professor emeritus, University of California, Davis. Editor, *Poetry,* Chicago, 1950-56, *Newberry Library Bulletin,* Chicago, 1953-55, and *Prairie Schooner,* Lincoln, Nebraska, 1956-66. Consultant in Poetry, 1946-47, and Whittall Lecturer, 1964, 1967, Library of Congress, Washington, DC; lecturer, Salzburg Seminar in American Studies, 1952; State Department Lecturer, India, 1955; Elliston Lecturer, University of Cincinnati, 1959. **Awards:** Davis prize, 1942; Levinson prize, 1942; American Academy grant, 1944; Guggenheim fellowship, 1944, 1953; Pulitzer prize, 1945; Shelley Memorial award, 1946; Kenyon School of Letters fellowship, 1956, 1957; Tietjens prize, 1961; Blumenthal prize, 1963; Bollingen prize, 1968. D.H.L.: Wayne State University, Detroit, 1960. D.Litt.: Bucknell University, Lewisburg. Pennsylvania, 1972. Fellow in American Letters, Library of Congress. **Member:** American Academy of Arts and Sciences, American Academy. **Residence:** Davis, California.

PUBLICATIONS

Poetry

Poems. 1935.
Five Young American Poets, with others. 1941.
The Place of Love. 1942.
Person, Place and Thing. 1942.
V-Letter and Other Poems. 1944.
Essay on Rime. 1945.
Trial of a Poet and Other Poems. 1947.
Poems, 1940-1953. 1953.
The House. 1957.
Poems of a Jew. 1958.
The Bourgeois Poet. 1964.
Selected Poems. 1968.
There Was That Roman Poet Who Fell in Love at Fifty-Odd. 1968.
White-Haired Lover. 1968.

Auden (1907-1973). 1974.
Adult Bookstore. 1976.
Collected Poems, 1948-1978. 1978.
Love and War, Art and God. 1984.
Adam and Eve, edited by John Wheatcroft. 1986.
New & Selected Poems, 1940-1986. 1987.
The Old Horsefly. 1992.
Mountains and Rivers without End. 1996.
Finding the Space. 1996.
The Wild Card: Selected Poems, Early and Late. 1998.

Plays

The Tenor, with Ernst Lert, from a play by Wedekind, music by Hugo Weisgall (produced 1952). 1957.
The Soldiers Tale, from a libretto by C. F. Ramuz, music by Igor Stravinsky (produced 1968). 1968.

Fiction

Edsel. 1971.

Other

English Prosody and Modern Poetry. 1947.
A Bibliography of Modern Prosody. 1948.
Poets at Work, with others, edited by Charles D. Abbott. 1948.
Beyond Criticism. 1953; as *A Primer for Poets,* 1965.
In Defense of Ignorance (essays). 1960.
Start with the Sun: Studies in Cosmic Poetry, with James E. Miller, Jr., and Bernice Slote. 1960.
The Writer's Experience, with Ralph Ellison. 1964.
A Prosody Handbook, with Robert Beum. 1965.
Randall Jarrell. 1967.
To Abolish Children and Other Essays. 1968.
The Poetry Wreck: Selected Essays 1950-1970. 1975.
The Younger Son: Poet: An Autobiography in Three Parts, volume 1. 1988.
Reports of My Death: An Autobiography, volume 2. 1990.
A Place in Space: Ethics, Aesthetics, and Watersheds: New and Selected Prose. 1995.
Three on Community, with Wendell Berry and Carole Koda. 1996.

Editor, with Louis Untermeyer and Richard Wilbur, *Modern American and Modern British Poetry,* revised shorter edition. 1955.
Editor, *American Poetry.* 1960.
Editor, *Prose Keys to Modern Poetry.* 1962.
Editor, *Tryne,* by Cynthia Bates, Steve Ellzey, and Bill Lynch. 1976.

*

Bibliography: *Shapiro: A Descriptive Bibliography, 1933-1977* by Lee Bartlett, 1979.

Critical Studies: *Shapiro* by Joseph Reino, 1981; "Trying to Present America: A Conversation with Karl Shapiro" in *Southern Humanities Review* summer 1981; "An Interview with Karl Shapiro" by Andrea Gale Hammer in *Prairie Schooner* fall 1981; *Identity, Masculinity, and Femininity in the Poetry of Gary Snyder* (dissertation) by Maura Gage, 1997.

*   *   *

Karl Shapiro is a poet of great versatility who has a sophisticated command of prosody and a sharp ear for speech rhythms and verbal harmonies. He is a man of considerable erudition, though he never finished college, and a serious though good-humored social critic. Since his first volume of poems appeared in 1935, he has published continuously. As poet and critic he always has taken an iconoclastic stance. He attacks with great vigor intellectual poetry, poseurs, stuffed shirts, and the establishment, and as a result has been a controversial figure. As editor of *Poetry* and the *Prairie Schooner* for a total of sixteen years, he was a significant force in contemporary poetry, and as a professor he taught three decades of aspiring writers.

When Shapiro published *Selected Poems,* he ignored his first volume, about which he writes in "Recapitulations":

My first small book was nourished in the dark,
Secretly written, published, and inscribed.
Bound in wine-red, it made no brilliant mark.
Rather impossible relatives subscribed.

His first recognition came in 1941 when he appeared in *Five Young American Poets.* His next volume, *Person, Place and Thing,* contains excellent poems of social comment in traditional form. "The Dome of Sunday" comments in sharp, clear imagery cast in blank verse on urban "Row houses and row lives"; "Drug Store" observes youth culture satirically in unrhymed stanzas; "University [of Virginia]" mounts a low-keyed attack: "To hurt the Negro and avoid the Jew / Is the curriculum."

V-Letter and Other Poems contains some of the best poems to come out of World War II, some of which are "V-Letter," "Elegy for a Dead Soldier," "Troop Train," "The Gun," "Sunday: New Guinea," and "Christmas Eve: Australia." The form usually is rhymed stanzas, even terza rima, and here Shapiro's social comment finds a wider context. There also begin to be foreshadowings of later preoccupations: religious themes and attacks on intellectualism. "The Jew" anticipates *Poems of a Jew,* and "The Intellectual" ("I'd rather be a barber and cut hair / Than walk with you in gilt museum halls") looks toward attacks on **Ezra Pound** and **T.S. Eliot** in *In Defense of Ignorance.*

Although Shapiro does not write long poems (the exception is *Essay on Rime,* a youthful treatise on the art of poetry in which "Everything was going to be straightened out"), *Poems, 1940-1953* contains an evocative, seven-part sequence telling the story of Adam and Eve. (This interest in myth reasserts itself in *Adult Bookstore* in a poignant version in 260 lines of "The Rape of Philomel.") *Poems* also contains "Israel," occasioned by the founding of that country: "When I see the name of Israel high in print / The fences crumble in my flesh . . . . " As a boy Shapiro grew up in a Russian-Jewish family not particularly religious, and after his bar mitzvah "I lost all interest in what I had learned." But *Poems of a Jew* explores his Jewishness with pride, wit, and irony, beginning with "The Alphabet" ("letters . . . strict as flames," "black and clean," and bristling "like barbed wire").

As early as 1942, Shapiro had published a prose poem, "The Dirty Word," but in 1964 he turned to this form exclusively in *The Bourgeois Poet,* dropping the kind of verses he previously had thought best, "the poem with a beginning, a middle, and an end . . . that used literary allusion and rhythmic structuring and intellectual argument." He wanted a medium in which he could say anything he pleased—ridiculous, nonsensical, obscene, autobiographical, pompous. The individual pieces cover a wide variety of topics and, as earlier, they comment on persons, places, things. The longest, "I Am an Atheist Who Says His Prayers," which reminds one of Shapiro's enthusiasm for **Walt Whitman**, could have been called "Song of Myself." These prose poems (or free verse set as prose paragraphs) had a mixed reception. But **Adrienne Rich** noted that in his new style Shapiro was going through a "constant revising and purifying of his speech," as all poets must, and she thought parts of this volume were "a stunning success."

In *White-Haired Lover,* a cycle of middle-aged love poems, Shapiro returned to traditional forms, often the sonnet. This also is true of *Adult Bookstore,* a collection that ranges widely in subject. "The Humanities Building," "A Parliament of Poets," and the title poem show that Shapiro has not lost the wit, irony, and technique that have always characterized his work. "The Heiligenstadt Testament" is a splendid dramatic monologue of Ludwig van Beethoven's deathbed delirium, and among the poems occasioned by his move to California are "Garage Sale" ("This situation . . . / Strikes one as a cultural masterpiece") and a perfect Petrarchan sonnet on freeways and California suburbia.

Shapiro's last four books—two volumes of a three-part autobiography, a volume of selected poems, and a slim book of recent poetry titled *The Old Horsefly*—are all retrospective. The autobiographies catalog the poet's many love affairs, his various awards and academic posts, and enticing gossip on those literary figures prominent during the 1950s and 1960s. The "Interview in Verse" which concludes *The Old Horsefly* recounts a few of the poet's attitudes towards verse and the creative writing process, these being facets of the poet which are for the most part undiscussed in the two autobiographies. Regarding students of poetry, Shapiro says:

Get them to read the masters, let them
Learn some humility for art;
Let them copy, let them imitate,
Memorize models, learn languages,
Above all master their own. Sounds stuffy.

Sounding stuffy is exactly what Shapiro's own poetry avoids. Some of Shapiro's poems reflect the melancholy of a retired professor—in "Retirement" he ponders his state: "The word 'posthumous' pops into his head! / Has he joined some sect of the living dead?"—but most of the work in *The Old Horsefly,* which includes titles like "On Being Yanked from a Favorite Anthology" and "Gerard Manley Hopkins Mesmerizes a Duck," is meant to satirize and amuse.

The Poetry Wreck, which contains Shapiro's most important critical statements, throws light on his poetry, his sources, and his beliefs. The derogatory essays on Pound and Eliot are reprinted along with admiring appraisals of W.H. Auden ("Eliot and Pound had rid the poem of emotion completely . . . Auden reversed the process"), **William Carlos Williams**, "whose entire literary career has been dedicated to the struggle to preserve spontaneity and immediacy of experience," Whitman, Dylan Thomas, **Henry Miller**, and **Randall Jarrell**. Jarrell, whose "poetry I admired and looked up to most after William Carlos Williams," once said in a passage Shapiro quotes: "Karl Shapiro's poems are fresh and young and rash and live; their hard clear outline, their flat bold colors create a world like that of a knowing and skillful neo-primitive painting, without any of the confusion or profundity of atmosphere, or aerial perspective, but with notable visual and satiric force."

—James Woodress, updated by Andrew O. Jones

SHAW, Henry Wheeler

Pseudonym: Josh Billings. **Born:** Lanesboro, Massachusetts, 21 April 1818. **Education:** Lenox Preparatory School, Massachusetts; Hamilton College, Clinton, New York, 1833-34. **Family:** Married Zilpha Bradford in 1845; two daughters. **Career:** Worked at odd jobs in the Midwest, 1835-45, and in the east, 1845-54; auctioneer and realtor in Poughkeepsie, New York, 1854-66: alderman, 1858; contributor, Poughkeepsie *Daily Press* from 1860; lecturer, 1863-80; moved to New York, 1867; contributor, New York *Weekly*, 1867-85, and *Century Magazine*, 1884-85. **Died:** 14 October 1885.

Publications

Collections

Uncle Sam's Uncle Josh, edited by Donald Day. 1953.

Fiction

Josh Billings, Hiz Sayings. 1866; as *Josh Billings, His Book of Sayings,* 1866.
Josh Billings on Ice, and Other Things. 1868.
Josh Billings' Farmer's Allminax for the Year 1870. 1869 (and later volumes to 1879); 1 vol. edition, as *Old Probability: Perhaps Rain—Perhaps Not,* 1879; as *Josh Billings' Old Farmer's Allminax 1870-1879,* 1902.
Josh Billings' Wit and Humor. 1874; as *Everybody's Friend; or, Josh Billing's* (sic) *Encyclopedia and Proverbial Philosophy of Wit and Humor,* 1874.
Josh Billings: His Works, Complete. 1876.
Josh Billings' Trump Kards: Blue Grass Philosophy. 1877.
Josh Billings' Cook Book and Picktorial Proverbs. 1880; revised edition, as *Josh Billings Struggling with Things,* 1881.
Life and Adventures of Josh Billings. 1883.

Editor, *Josh Billings' Spice Box.* 1881(?).

*

Bibliography: in *Bibliography of American Literature* by Jacob Blanck, edited by Virginia L. Smyers and Michael Winship. 1983.

Critical Studies: *Billings, Yankee Humorist* by Cyril Clemens, 1932; *Shaw (Billings)* by David B. Kesterson, 1973; *The Platform Humorists: Comedy in One* by Kirk McManus, 1983.

*   *   *

Farmer, boatman, explorer, real-estate salesman, auctioneer, Henry Wheeler Shaw turned to writing in his middle age and leapt into national prominence in America with an "Essa on the Muel bi Josh Billings" ("The Muel is haf hoss and haf Jackass, and then kums to a full stop, natur diskovering her mistake"). He took a pen name but avoided the topical subjects of his contemporaries. Unfortunately for the modern reader, he did adopt the comic device of atrocious spelling, then considered in America to be a sure-fire laugh-getter. As with the Irish dialect of **Finley Peter Dunne**'s "Mr. Dooley," however, it is often worth the extra effort in reading for Josh Billings's cracker-barrel philosophy and "trump-kard" aphorisms are frequently hilarious. It's worth the trouble to meet characters such as Mehitable Saffron, "the virgin-hero ov wimmins' rights . . . she spoke without notes, at arms' length."

Max Eastman declared that Josh Billings was "the father of imagism" and found nothing in New England poetry before Billings's time "quite comparable to his statement that goats 'know the way up a rock as natural as woodbine,' which is Homeric." Certainly Billings is a primitive La Bruyere, a rustic La Rochefoucauld, and an aphorist with a moralistic rather than a cynical streak. "Most people repent ov their sins bi thanking God they ain't so wicked as their nabers." He stressed that "yu hav tew be wise before yu kan be witty" and there is plenty of wisdom in such comments as "There may cum a time when the Lion and the Lamb will lie down together—I shall be as glad to see it as enny body—but I am still betting on the Lion."

—Leonard R.N. Ashley

SHELDON, Edward

Born: Chicago, Illinois, 4 February 1886. **Education:** Harvard University, A.B. 1907, A.M. 1908. **Career:** Writer. Collaborated with other playwrights and aided in productions; stricken with debilitating arthritis and eventually confined to bed; after 1930 wrote no more plays, although continued to be active in the theater world. **Died:** 1 April 1946.

Publications

Plays

Salvation Nell (produced 1908). 1908.
The Nigger (produced 1909). 1910.
The Boss (produced 1911).
Princess Zim-Zam (produced 1911).
Egypt (produced 1912). 1912.
The High Road (produced 1912).
Romance (produced 1913). 1914.
The Garden of Paradise (produced 1914). 1915.
The Song of Songs (produced 1914).
The Jest (produced 1919).
The Lonely Heart (produced 1921).
The Czarina, adaptation of Melchior Lengyel (produced 1922).
Bewitched, with Sidney Howard (produced 1924).
Lulu Belle, with Charles MacArthur (produced 1926).
Jenny, with Margaret Ayer Barnes (produced 1929).
Dishonored Lady, with Margaret Ayer Barnes (produced 1930).

*

Critical Studies: *The Man Who Lived Twice: The Biography of Edward Sheldon* by Eric Wollencott Barnes, 1956; *Edward Sheldon* by Loren K. Ruff, 1982; "Miscegenation on Broadway: Hughes's *Mulatto* and Edward Sheldon's *The Nigger*" by Richard K. Barksdale, in *Critical Essays on Langston Hughes* edited by Edward J. Mullen, 1986.

*   *   *

Unlike most American playwrights, Edward Sheldon came from a wealthy and distinguished family and never lacked resources. His early passion for the theater, revealed in his writing and staging of plays during his youth, was encouraged by his doting mother. At Harvard College he enrolled in George Pierce Baker's English 47 Workshop for playwrights, where his strong humanitarian impulses fired the social realism of his early plays. Sheldon became a recognized force in the theater during the period between the two World Wars, when it was both a theater tradition and a mark of prestige to visit him in his New York apartment after a play opened on Broadway .

A self-appointed spokesman for the Progressive Era, Sheldon aspired to attract attention to social problems. He was not alone. The decade preceding World War I was a showcase for liberal-minded dramatists: Charles Klein, Eugene Walter, George Broadhurst, and **Rachel Crothers,** among many others. Sheldon's first professionally produced play was *Salvation Nell* (1908). Essentially a melodrama about a girl who works for, waits for, and wins to the right cause the man she loves, it was a direct outgrowth of a play entitled *A Family Affair* that Sheldon had written in 1906 for Professor Baker, who suggested revisions. Showing both his innate romantic idealism and his realistic if sentimental concern for the unfortunate, Sheldon visited big-city slums and then worked closely with Mrs. Fiske, who would play Nell, and Harrison Grey Fiske, who would produce the play. Their staging and casting emphasized the realism of the sordid world of Hell's Kitchen in Manhattan, where the play opens. The staged realism and socio-realistic thesis gave the youthful playwright a fine Broadway beginning.

Sheldon's next play, *The Nigger* (1909), was later described by New York theater critic George Jean Nathan, writing for the *Cosmopolitan* in November 1948, as one of the "ten dramatic shocks of the century." A play of social injustice, *The Nigger* dramatizes the plight of a southern governor who discovers that one of his grandparents was a black slave. Even before it opened, the play caused controversy when E. H. Sothern and Julia Marlowe resigned from the theater company rather than perform their assigned roles as the governor and his fiancée. Rumors spread, and Sheldon hastily published a letter explaining that the title of the play "reflects on the whites, not the blacks." Reviews of the production were mixed: "audacious," "ambitious," "fearless," and "truthful," yet "more lurid than learned" and a play that "shocks and nauseates." Premiering during the opening season of the ill-fated New Theater in New York, it closed after twenty-four performances but was then toured by three companies, rewritten as a novel in 1911 by W. Herrick, and made into a movie in 1915.

A third play, *The Boss* (1911), added to Sheldon's reputation as a precursor to the realistic playwrights of the 1920s. Using a labor-management struggle with its political agitations, Sheldon created a romantic situation ending with the breakdown and humanizing of a political and economic boss. Realistic in character, scene, and action, *The Boss* was based on the career of William James

"Fingy" Connors, a Buffalo, New York, politician. It had a fair run on Broadway before being toured across the country and eventually being made into a film in 1915.

After *The Boss* Sheldon's interest in romanticism began to dominate his plays, although both *The Princess Zimzim* (1911) and *Egypt* (1912), written for Margaret Anglin, were failures. With *The High Road* (1912) Sheldon wrote his final socio-realistic drama, this one concerned with women's liberation, political bribery, and a new morality for the heroine. *Romance* (1913), one of his most successful plays, told the story of a young American clergyman's grand passion for an Italian opera singer and preparation for the marriage of the clergyman's grandson to an actress. Perhaps Sheldon's romantic and poetic imagination is seen at its height in *The Garden of Paradise* (1914), a dramatization of Hans Christian Andersen's *The Little Mermaid.*

By 1915 Sheldon was beginning to suffer from serious health problems, which, although keeping him out of the action in World War I, did not interfere with his writing such plays as *The Jest* (1919) and *The Lonely Heart* (1921). He also began to collaborate with other playwrights—writing *Bewitched* (1924) with Sidney Howard and *Lulu Belle* (1926) with Charles MacArthur. But his physical deterioration spread quite rapidly. By 1922 he was bedridden, by 1928 his body was almost completely rigid, and by 1932 he was blind. Yet his friendship with the major people of the theater—actors and playwrights—and his influence upon these people persisted as he held court by his bedside in that New York apartment. Lillian Gish called him "the Pope of the Theater." Alexander Woollcott simply considered him "God."

—Walter J. Meserve

SHEPARD, Sam

Born: Samuel Shepard Rogers in Fort Sheridan, Illinois, 5 November 1943. **Education:** Duarte High School, California, graduated 1960; Mount San Antonio Junior College, Walnut, California, 1960-61. **Family:** Married O-Lan Johnson Dark in 1969 (marriage dissolved), one son; one daughter and one son with the actress Jessica Lange. **Career:** Worked as hot walker at the Santa Anita Race Track, stable hand, Connolly Arabian Horse Ranch, Duarte, herdsman, Huff Sheep Ranch, Chino, orange picker in Duarte, and sheep shearer in Pomona, all in California; actor with Bishop's Company Repertory Players, Burbank, California, and U.S. tour, 1962; car wrecker, Charlemont, Massachusetts; bus boy, Village Gate, 1963-64, waiter, Marie's Crisis Cafe, 1965, and musician with the Holy Modal Rounders, 1968, all in New York City; lived in England, 1971-74, and in California since 1974; playwright-in-residence, Magic Theatre, San Francisco, California; director of many of his own plays; film actor: roles in *Brand X,* 1970, *Days of Heaven,* 1978, *Resurrection,* 1981, *Raggedy Man,* 1981, *Frances,* 1982, *The Right Stuff,* 1983, *Country,* 1984, *Fool for Love,* 1985, *Crimes of the Heart,* 1986, *Baby Boom,* 1987, *Steel Magnolias,* 1989, *Hot Spot,* 1990, *Bright Angel,* 1991, and *Defenseless,* 1991. **Awards:** Obie award, 1967, 1970, 1973, 1975, 1978 (twice), 1980, 1984; Yale University fellowship, 1967; Rockefeller grant, 1967; Guggenheim grant, 1968; American Academy grant, 1974; Brandeis University Creative Arts award, 1976, 1985; Pulitzer prize, 1979; Theater Hall of Fame, 1994. **Member:** American Academy, 1992; American Institute of Arts and Letters, 1992.

PUBLICATIONS

Plays

Cowboys (produced 1964).
The Rock Garden (produced 1964; excerpt produced in *Oh! Calcutta!*, 1967). In *The Unseen Hand and Other Plays*, 1971.
Up to Thursday (produced 1965).
Dog (produced 1965).
Rocking Chair (produced 1965).
Chicago (produced 1965). In *Five Plays*, 1967.
Icarus's Mother (produced 1965). In *Five Plays*, 1967.
4-H Club (produced 1965). In *The Unseen Hand and Other Plays*, 1971.
Fourteen Hundred Thousand (produced 1966). In *Five Plays*, 1967.
Red Cross (produced 1966). In *Five Plays*, 1967.
La Turista (produced 1967). 1968.
Melodrama Play (produced 1967). In *Five Plays*, 1967.
Five Plays. 1967; as *Chicago and Other Plays*, 1982.
Cowboys #2 (produced 1967). In *Mad Dog Blues and Other Plays*, 1971.
Forensic and the Navigators (produced 1967). In *The Unseen Hand and Other Plays*, 1971.
The Holy Ghostly (produced 1969). In *The Unseen Hand and Other Plays*, 1971.
The Unseen Hand (produced 1969). In *The Unseen Hand and Other Plays*, 1971.
Operation Sidewinder (produced 1970). 1970.
Shaved Splits (produced 1970). In *The Unseen Hand and Other Plays*, 1971.
Mad Dog Blues (produced 1971). In *Mad Dog Blues and Other Plays*, 1971.
Cowboy Mouth, with Patti Smith (produced 1971). In *Mad Dog Blues and Other Plays*, 1971.
Back Bog Beast Bait (produced 1971). In *The Unseen Hand and Other Plays*, 1971.
The Unseen Hand and Other Plays. 1971.
Mad Dog Blues and Other Plays. 1971.
The Tooth of Crime (produced 1972). In *The Tooth of Crime, and Geography of a Horse Dreamer*, 1974.
Blue Bitch (televised 1972; produced 1973).
Nightwalk, with Megan Terry and Jean-Claude van Itallie (produced 1973).
Little Ocean (produced 1974).
Geography of a Horse Dreamer (produced 1974). In *The Tooth of Crime, and Geography of a Horse Dreamer*, 1974.
The Tooth of Crime, and Geography of a Horse Dreamer. 1974.
Action (produced 1974). In *Action, and The Unseen Hand*, 1975.
Action, and The Unseen Hand. 1975.
Killer's Head (produced 1975). In *Angel City and Other Plays*, 1976.
Angel City (produced 1976). In *Angel City and Other Plays*, 1976.
Angel City and Other Plays. 1976.
Suicide in B Flat (produced 1976). In *Buried Child and Other Plays*, 1979.
The Sad Lament of Pecos Bill on the Eve of Killing His Wife (produced 1976). In *Fool for Love, and The Sad Lament of Pecos Bill on the Eve of Killing His Wife*, 1983.
Curse of the Starving Class (produced 1977). In *Angel City and Other Plays*, 1976.
Inacoma (produced 1977).

Buried Child (produced 1978). In *Buried Child and Other Plays*, 1979.
Seduced (produced 1978). In *Buried Child and Other Plays*, 1979.
Tongues, with Joseph Chaikin, music by Shepard, Skip LaPlante, and Harry Mann (produced 1978). In *Seven Plays*, 1981.
Buried Child and Other Plays. 1979; as *Buried Child, and Seduced, and Suicide in B Flat*, 1980.
Savage/Love, with Joseph Chaikin, music by Shepard, Skip LaPlante, and Harry Mann (produced 1979). In *Seven Plays*, 1981.
True West (produced 1980). 1981.
Jackson's Dance, with Jacques Levy (produced 1980).
Four Two-Act Plays (includes *La Turista, The Tooth of Crime, Geography of a Horse Dreamer, Operation Sidewinder*). 1980.
Seven Plays (includes *Buried Child, Curse of the Starving Class, The Tooth of Crime, La Turista, True West, Tongues, Savage/Love*). 1981.
Superstitions (produced 1983).
Fool for Love (produced 1983). 1984.
Fool for Love, and The Sad Lament of Pecos Bill on the Eve of Killing His Wife. 1983.
Fool for Love and Other Plays. 1984.
A Lie of the Mind (produced 1985). 1987.
The War in Heaven (broadcast 1985; produced 1987). 1986.
Hawk Moon (produced 1989).
States of Shock (produced 1991).
Simpatico: A Play in Three Acts (produced 1994). 1995.
Plays: 2 (includes *True West; Buried Child; Curse of the Starving Class; The Tooth of Crime; La Turista; Tongues; Savage/Love*). n.d.
Plays: 3 (includes *A Lie of the Mind; States of Shock; Simpatico*). 1996.
Eyes for Consuela (produced 1998).

Screenplays: *Me and My Brother*, with Robert Frank, 1969; *Zabriskie Point*, with others, 1970; *Ringaleevio*, 1971; *Paris, Texas*, 1984; *Fool for Love*, 1985; *Far North*, 1988; *States of Shock, Far North, Silent Tongue*, 1993.

Television Play: *Blue Bitch*, 1972.

Other

Hawk Moon: A Book of Short Stories, Poems, and Monologues. 1973.
Rolling Thunder Logbook. 1977.
Motel Chronicles. 1982.
Letters and Texts 1972-1984, with Joseph Chaikin, edited by Barry V. Daniels. 1989.
Cruising Paradise: Tales. 1996.

*

Critical Studies: *American Dreams: The Imagination of Shepard* edited by Bonnie Marranca, 1981; *Shepard, Arthur Kopit, and the Off-Broadway Theater* by Doris Auerbach, 1982; *Inner Landscapes: The Theater of Shepard* by Ron Mottram, 1984; *Shepard* by Vivian M. Patraka and Mark Siegel, 1985; *Shepard* by Don Shewey, 1985; *Shepard: The Life and Work of an American Dreamer* by Ellen Oumano, 1986; *Essays on Modern American Drama: Williams, Miller, Albee, and Shepard* edited by Dorothy

Parker, 1987; *File on Shepard* edited by Simon Trussler,1989; *Sam Shepard* by David J. DeRose, 1992; *Sam Shepard on the German Stage: Critics, Politics, Myths* by Carol Benet, 1993; *Rereading Shepard: Contemporary Critical Essays on the Plays of Sam Shepard,* edited by Leonard Wilcox, 1993; *Sam Shepard and the American Theatre* by Leslie A. Wade, 1997; *The Theatre of Sam Shepard: States of Crisis* by Stephen J. Bottoms, 1998; *A Body Across the Map: The Father-Son Plays of Sam Shepard* by Michael Taay, 1999.

Theatrical Activities:
Director: **Plays**—many of his own plays. **Film**—*Far North*, 1988; *Silent Tongue,* 1992.
Actor: **Plays**—with Bishop's Company, Burbank, California; role in *Cowboy Mouth*, New York, 1971. **Films**—*Brand X*, 1970; *Days of Heaven,* 1978; *Resurrection,* 1981; *Raggedy Man,* 1981; *Frances,* 1982; *The Right Stuff,* 1983; *Country,* 1984; *Fool for Love,* 1985; *Crimes of the Heart,* 1987; *Baby Boom,* 1987; *Steel Magnolias,* 1989; *The Hot Spot,* 1990; *Defenseless,* 1991; *Voyager,* 1991; *Thunderheart,* 1992; *The Pelican Brief,* 1993; *Safe Passage,* 1994.

*　　*　　*

Playwright Sam Shepard is an imaginative original. Possibly wedded to paradox, Shepard is a movie star so suspicious of commercial theater that he will not allow his scripts to be mounted on Broadway and a Pulitzer prize winner whose plays are so outside the mainstream they often eschew development of consistent characters or a coherent plot. He is the creator of distinctively crafted monologues and dialogues acclaimed for their verbal skill, but who nevertheless puts words together improvisationally, with a spontaneity akin to that of the surrealists' "automatic writing." Although a writer especially concerned with father-son relationships, Shepard offended his father by dropping their family surname (Rogers) and left his own son in the care of his ex-wife. Many of his plays mock the movies, yet Shepard the actor has been nominated for an Oscar and is a recognized Hollywood box-office attraction. Although he debunks the American Dream in his drama, Shepard has fulfilled that dream in his life. Whereas he grew up on a ranch, dresses like a cowboy, and is at home on a horse, his plays disparage far more than they celebrate the macho Western type who is so often their subject.

A formative influence on Shepard's style was his early association with Joseph Chaikin's Open Theater, where he was exposed to acting exercises involving sudden, mid-scene character transformation. Cody in *Geography of a Horse Dreamer* becomes an Irishman, the New Yorkers in *Cowboys #2* move in and out of cowboy roles, Stu in *Chicago* periodically talks like an old lady, the characters in *Back Bog Beast Bait* turn into animals, and the boy in *La Turista* becomes both Kent's son and Kent himself before Kent escapes from the play as a movie monster. Another escape through transformation occurs when the Lobster Man in *Cowboy Mouth* is transmogrified into the rock-'n'- roll savior.

In *Curse of the Starving Class* Emma shifts from an A student to a delinquent, while Weston alters from a violent drunk to a model househusband, and Wesley, by donning his father's clothes, becomes Weston. In *Angel City* the contagion of Hollywood fantasy produces all sorts of transformations: the drummer turns into a child and a chef; the writer turns into a medicine man, a child, a newscaster, and a native; the secretary becomes an Irish nun and

a teenager; and one producer turns into a boxer and a teenager, the other producer into a lizard—until he and the writer switch roles, suggesting that the writer is the disaster in his own disaster movie. Blue Morphan and Sycamore likewise switch characters in *The Unseen Hand,* as do Pop and Ice in *The Holy Ghostly.* In *The Tooth of Crime* character transformations are a dueling technique, and in *Suicide in B Flat,* they serve as a vehicle for murder.

Shifts in who a given character may be are part of the dramatist's interest in the mutability of individual identity and, indeed, in the larger issue of ontology, or the nature of being. Shepard characters worry about disappearing, or they seem to be part of duplicated characters, as when two people in *Forensic and the Navigators* answer to the name Forensic or when Drake and Cisco dress like Duke in *Melodrama Play.* Human duality is also represented by opposites such as Lee and Austin in *True West* or Jake and Frankie in *A Lie of the Mind.* Both sets of brothers trade places. In *Simpatico* Carter and Vinnie, in the type of symbiotic American male relationship Shepard has virtually trademarked, play out the familiar contrast—Carter as the slick, successful achiever and Vinnie as the disheveled, disreputable loner who maintains the moral high ground. In their oppositional existences, the two complete each other. Just as Carter once swapped horses, at the end of the play he also wants to swap lives with Vinnie in an effort to achieve redemption. Lies of the mind, Shepard suggests, distort our identities, our natures, our beings.

Other subjects that recur in Shepard are the Old West, the family, and the plight of the creative artist. He has expressed ambivalent fascination with romantic myths of the frontier, beginning with his first play, *Cowboys,* and extending to later works such as *The Sad Lament of Pecos Bill on the Eve of Killing His Wife, True West, Fool for Love,* and *A Lie of the Mind.* Sometimes he kills off the mythic West—as in *Pecos Bill, Suicide,* and *The Holy Ghostly*'s patricide—but his heritage returns repeatedly to haunt him. The importance of father-son relations, though it surfaced in the early *The Rock Garden* and *The Holy Ghostly,* was not apparent until his five big family plays of the late 1980s and early '90s (together with his film *Paris, Texas*). These constitute a devastating examination of the Greek theme of *philos-aphilos,* or love mixed with hatred, as incest, bigamy, violence, murder, and oedipal and sibling rivalries stalk the stage. Finally, the plays that dramatize the artist facing commercial pressures to produce another hit are, with the exception of *True West,* not the domestic dramas but the more fanciful *Melodrama Play, The Tooth of Crime, Geography of a Horse Dreamer, Angel City,* and *Suicide in B Flat.*

Shepard as a pioneer in form is even more intriguing than Shepard as a commentator on his times, or as Edward Albee has said, "What Shepard's plays are about is a great deal less interesting than how they are about it." In addition to character transformations, absurdist disjunctions in the action, and Pinteresque menace (repeatedly evident), Shepard excels at visual theatricality, humor, and distinctive language.

Shepard's spectators carry away memorable images: Lobster Man cracking open in *Cowboy Mouth;* the headlights and fire and characters bouncing off the walls in *Fool for Love;* Stu clothed but sitting in a bathtub in *Chicago;* the giant catfish in *Pecos Bill;* Kent smashing through the set's back wall in *La Turista;* the two-headed pig-beast in *Back Bog Beast Bait;* monster scales and green ooze in *Angel City;* Hackamore covering himself with Kleenex in *Seduced;* the ghost, the witch, and the huge fire in *The Holy Ghostly;* or the Hopi costumes and ritual, the flashing blue lights, and the giant rattlesnake in *Operation Sidewinder.* Food imagery is plentiful, especially in the later plays. Who can forget, along with the muddy corpse in *Buried Child,* the piles of corn and carrots? Food farce occurs with Rice Krispies in *Forensic and the Navigators,* with apples in *4-H Club,* and later in two more plays set in kitchens: the toast popping out of a row of toasters in *True West* rivals the refrigerator stuffed with artichokes in *Curse of the Starving Class* as the archetypal Shepard symbols for both the raw hunger of libido and Americans' spiritual malnutrition.

Shepard's humor is nearly all nonverbal. Laughs grow from sight gags (Louis trying to kill himself with one hand and to save himself with the other in *Suicide,* or Becky making a pass at herself with one hand and trying to stop it with the other in *The Tooth of Crime*) or from situations (Mom walking into her house filled with debris and dead plants in *True West;* Shelly and later Father Dewis stranded with weirdos in *Buried Child;* Sycamore bewildered by the twentieth century in *The Unseen Hand*). Yet the dialogue, particularly in *Mad Dog Blues* and *Fool for Love,* sometimes yields a few delicious jokes.

Shepard's language is the argot of assorted male subcultures, including sports, the wild West, the music and movie businesses, the world of power brokers and that of ornery middle-Americans. He often interpolates long monologues into the action, and these speeches can be more narrative, expository, or descriptive than dramatic. Some speeches interrupt the action on the model of a jazz solo, a prose poem, or a virtuoso tap dance. Characters may seem not to be addressing one another, replying to what has gone before, or even listening. Yet the rhythms are insistent, the not surprising product of a writer who is also a rock drummer and often constructs his plays around music.

—Tish Dace, updated by Denise Wiloch and Martha Sutro

SHERWOOD, Robert E(mmet)

Born: New Rochelle, New York, 4 April 1896. **Education:** Milton Academy, Massachusetts, 1909-14; Harvard University, Cambridge, Massachusetts (editor, *Harvard Lampoon*), 1914-17, A.B. 1918. **Military Service:** Served in the Canadian Black Watch, 1917-19: wounded in action, 1918; served as special assistant to the Secretary of War, Washington, D.C., 1939-42; director, Overseas Branch, Office of War Information, 1942-44; special assistant to the secretary of the navy, Washington, D.C., 1945. **Family:** Married 1) Mary Brandon in 1922 (divorced 1934), one daughter; 2) Madeline Hurlock Connelly in 1935. **Career:** Drama editor, *Vanity Fair,* New York, 1919-20; film reviewer and associate editor, 1920-24, and editor, 1924-28, *Life* magazine, New York; literary editor, *Scribner's,* New York, 1928-30; full-time playwright from 1930; founder, with Elmer Rice, Sidney Howard, Maxwell Anderson, S.N. Behrman, and John F. Wharton, Playwrights Company, 1938. Founder, with Robert Benchley, Dorothy Parker, and others, Algonquin Hotel Round Table, 1920. Secretary, 1935, and president, 1937-40, Dramatists Guild; president, American National Theatre and Academy, 1940. **Awards:** Megrue prize, 1932; Pulitzer prize, 1936, 1939, 1941, and, for biography, 1949; American Academy Gold Medal, 1941; Oscar, for screenplay, 1946; Bancroft Prize, for history, 1949; Gutenberg award, 1949. D.Litt.: Dartmouth College, Hanover, New Hampshire, 1940; Yale University, New Haven, Connecticut, 1941; Harvard University, 1949. D.C.L.: Bishop's University, Lennoxville, Quebec, 1950. **Died:** 14 November 1955.

PUBLICATIONS

Plays

A White Elephant (produced 1916).
Barnum Was Right (produced 1918).
The Road to Rome (produced 1927). 1927.
The Love Nest, from the story by Ring Lardner (produced 1927).
The Queen's Husband (produced 1928). 1928.
Waterloo Bridge (produced 1930). 1930.
This Is New York (produced 1930). 1931.
Reunion in Vienna (produced 1931). 1932.
Acropolis (produced 1933).
The Petrified Forest (produced 1935). 1935.
Idiot's Delight (produced 1936). 1936.
The Ghost Goes West (screenplay), with Geoffrey Kerr, in *Successful Film Writing* by Seton Margrave. 1936.
Tovarich, from a play by Jacques Deval (produced 1936). 1937.
The Adventures of Marco Polo (screenplay), in *How to Write and Sell Film Stories* by Frances Marion. 1937.
Abe Lincoln in Illinois (produced 1938). 1939.
There Shall Be No Night (produced 1940). 1940.
An American Crusader (broadcast 1941). In *The Free Company Presents,* edited by James Boyd, 1941.
Rebecca (screenplay), with others, in *Twenty Best Film Plays,* edited by John Gassner and Dudley Nichols. 1943.
The Rugged Path (produced 1945). Shortened version in *The Best Plays of 1945-46,* edited by Burns Mantle, 1946.
Miss Liberty, music by Irving Berlin (produced 1949). 1949.
Second Threshold, completion of a play by Philip Barry (produced 1951). 1951.
Small War on Murray Hill (produced 1957). 1957.

Screenplays: *The Hunchback of Notre Dame,* with others, 1924; *The Lucky Lady,* with James T. O'Donohoe and Bertram Bloch, 1926; *The Age for Love,* 1931; *Around the World in Eighty Minutes with Douglas Fairbanks,* 1931; *Cock of the Air,* with Charles Lederer, 1932; *Roman Scandals,* with others, 1933; *The Scarlet Pimpernel,* with others, 1935; *The Ghost Goes West,* with Geoffrey Kerr, 1936; *Over the Moon,* with others, 1937; *Thunder in the City,* with others, 1937; *The Adventures of Marco Polo,* 1938; *The Divorce of Lady X,* with Lajos Biro, 1938; *Idiot's Delight,* 1939; *Abe Lincoln in Illinois,* 1940; *Rebecca,* with others, 1940; *The Best Years of Our Lives,* 1946; *The Bishop's Wife,* with Leonardo Bercovici, 1947; *Man on a Tightrope,* 1953; *Main Street to Broadway,* with Samson Raphaelson, 1953.

Radio Play: *An American Crusader,* 1941.

Television Writing: *The Backbone of America,* 1954.

Fiction

The Virtuous Knight. 1931; as *Unending Crusade,* 1932.

Other

Roosevelt and Hopkins: An Intimate History. 1948; revised edition, 1950; as *The White House Papers of Harry L. Hopkins,* 2 vols., 1948-49.

Editor, *The Best Moving Pictures of 1922-23, Also Who's Who in the Movies and the Yearbook of the American Screen.* 1923.

*

Critical Studies: *The Worlds of Sherwood: Mirror to His Times 1896-1939,* 1962, and *The Ordeal of a Playwright: Sherwood and the Challenge of War* edited by Norman Cousins, 1970, both by John Mason Brown; *Sherwood* by R. Baird Shuman, 1964; *Sherwood: Reluctant Moralist* by Walter J. Meserve, 1970; *Sherwood's "The Road to Rome": A Marxist Play by a Non-Marxian Playwright in the Twenties* in Panjab University Research Bulletin by Kshamanidhi Mishra, 1988; "Prelude to War: The Interventionist Propaganda of Archibald MacLeish, Robert E. Sherwood, and John Steinbeck" by Peter Buitenhuis, in *Canadian Review of American Studies,* winter 1996, pp. 1-30.

* * *

Though of a generation often described as "rootless" and "lost," Robert E. Sherwood was a romantic idealist with a liberal outlook whose plays embodied assumptions underlying the political philosophy of the Roosevelt administration and gave those assumptions powerful artistic expression. Alive to the need for creating an art imbued with a social and moral fervor, Sherwood believed that the one determining consideration for the future of the theater was "its ability to give its audiences something they can't obtain, more cheaply and conveniently, in the neighboring cinema palaces." The artist's lack of social purpose, he pointed out in his address to the PEN International Congress in 1950, gave him a guilty sense of inadequacy—the uneasy knowledge that reform, though needed, was not taking place. The supreme task of "all writers, young and old" was, therefore, to achieve a reconciliation of the "problems of the human heart with a world state of mind that appears to become increasingly inhuman."

Sherwood's apprehension of the threats posed by a world situation indifferent to finer human sentiments dominates his dramatic art. His realistic problem plays—whether set in Finland under Russian attack (*There Shall Be No Night*) or in a hotel in the Alps (*Idiot's Delight*) or in a gasoline station and lunch room in the Arizona desert (*The Petrified Forest*)—often relied on an extreme situation, a background of war or violence, to highlight the protagonist's search for ethical values. Sherwood's pacifism, though attuned to the feeling of many liberals during the Roosevelt era, was never parochial or chauvinistic and displayed dynamic, even militant, modulations over the years. His first play, *The Road to Rome,* dealing comically with Hannibal's decision to defer his march on Rome, represents a plea for absolute peace; his last important play, *There Shall Be No Night,* is characterized by the realization that freedom has to be defended even at the cost of endangering peace temporarily. In fighting the Russians in Finland, the scientist-protagonist of *There Shall Be No Night* fights for the emancipation of all men from oppression. *The Rugged Path* can be read, at one level, as an idealist's resolve to join the war in defense of peace and human dignity.

Several of Sherwood's plays exemplify his belief that the willingness to make personal sacrifice is the main moral test. In *The Petrified Forest* sacrifice appears as a necessary means of preventing Nature from "taking the world away from the intellectu-

als and giving it back to the apes." On the other hand, *Abe Lincoln in Illinois,* chronicling Lincoln's difficult years before his election to the presidency, sensitively focuses on the relationship between an individual's sacrifice and national interest. *There Shall Be No Night* returns to the same moral issue and implies, through the fate of its protagonist, that "There is no coming to consciousness without pain."

Sherwood is vulnerable to the charge of didacticism, but he understood his age and rarely suggested daring departures from opinions then current. As a result, the moralistic intentions behind his plays were so static that their appeal seldom extended beyond the topical. But it should be recognized that Sherwood's didacticism often became integral to the dramatic form: in Abe Lincoln in Illinois, for example, the curtain drops just as the farewell crowd, which is singing "John Brown's Body," reaches the line "His soul goes marching on." Also, Sherwood's use of comedy, as in *The Road to Rome* and *The Queen's Husband,* helps relieve the moralistic solemnity. Sherwood's ironic consciousness would not let him overlook the flaws in his own plays, flaws he recorded with rare candor. For instance, he found *The Road to Rome* defective because it employed "the cheapest sort of device—making historical characters use modern slang."

Sherwood wrote in other genres with mixed results. *The Virtuous Knight,* his early historical novel about the Third Crusade, was generally regarded as a failure, though in retrospect it does provide useful insights into the themes and techniques of his plays. His screenplay *The Best Years of Our Lives* won an Oscar in 1946, but his television show, *The Backbone of America,* was a dismal flop. The greatest success of his non-dramatic writing was his biography *Roosevelt and Hopkins,* based on his experience as special assistant to the secretary of war, director of the overseas branch of the Office of War Information, and, most important, as Roosevelt's favorite speechwriter and unofficial adviser. This book ranks among the finest histories of World War II written in the United States, and certainly deserved its Pulitzer Prize.

Immensely popular in his own lifetime, Sherwood is no O'Neill, Miller, or Williams. As time passes his plays seem increasingly dated. Still, his realistic problem plays, inspired as they were by his passion for freedom and peace, faithfully reflected the urges and anxieties of the American 1920s and 1930s and thereby have made a significant contribution to American drama.

—Chirantan Kulshrestha

SILKO, Leslie Marmon

Born: 1948. **Education:** Bureau of Indian Affairs schools, Laguna, New Mexico, and a Catholic school in Albuquerque; University of New Mexico, Albuquerque, B.A. (summa cum laude) in English 1969; studied law briefly. **Family:** Has two sons. **Career:** Taught for two years at Navajo Community College, Tsaile, Arizona; lived in Ketchikan, Alaska for two years; taught at University of New Mexico. Beginning 1978 professor of English, University of Arizona, Tucson. **Awards:** National Endowment for the Arts award, 1974; *Chicago Review* award, 1974; Pushcart prize, 1977; MacArthur Foundation grant, 1983. **Residence:** Tucson, Arizona.

PUBLICATIONS

Short Stories

Storyteller. 1981.

Novels

Ceremony. 1977.
Almanac of the Dead. 1991.
Gardens in the Dunes. 1999.

Plays

Lullaby, with Frank Chin, adaptation of the story by Silko (produced San Francisco, 1976).

Poetry

Laguna Woman. 1974.

Other

The Delicacy and Strength of Lace: Letters Between Silko and James A. Wright, edited by Anne Wright. 1986.

*

Critical Studies: *Silko* by Per Seyersted, 1980; *Four American Indian Literary Masters* by Alan R. Velie, 1982; *Narrative Chance: Postmodern Discourse on Native American Indian Literatures* edited by Gerald Vizenor, 1989; "Survival or Orality in a Literate Culture: Leslie Silko's Novel *Ceremony*" by Konrad Gross in *Modes of Narrative: Approaches to American, Canadian and British Fiction* edited by Reingard M. Nischik and Barbara Korte, 1990; "Tradition and Ceremony: Leslie Marmon Silko as an American Novelist" by C. W. Truesdale in *North Dakota Quarterly* vol. 59, no. 4, 1991; *Leslie Marmon Silko* by Gregory Salyer, 1997; *Leslie Marmon Silko: A Study of the Short Fiction* by Helen Jaskoski, 1998; *Leslie Marmon Silko: A Collection of Critical Essays,* edited by Louise K. Barnett and James L. Thorson, 1999.

*   *   *

Leslie Marmon Silko has attracted national and international attention for her writing about the Southwest and the Native American experience. Her 1977 novel *Ceremony* is considered one of the most influential works by a contemporary Native American writer. Silko's work has been widely analyzed to explore its inclusion of Laguna myth and culture and often discussed in the context of minority women's writing.

Growing up in Laguna Pueblo, by Route 66, in New Mexico, Silko was exposed to a web of various relatives, Natives, and non-Natives living on the edge of the pueblo. She soon learned that the stories about her family defined them in the reality of the community. As she grew, she perceived that oral tradition defined everyone in the pueblo. The stories told about an individual and his or her ancestors created an identity, assigned a role in the community.

Silko was also exposed to traditional Laguna stories. As she began to write, she used many of the stories she heard, often feeling as if she had lived the old stories, especially the Yellow Woman

stories. For Silko these stories transcended local detail and expressed a very deep level of human experience preserved in oral form. She perceives storytelling as a way of being, a way of perceiving and knowing the world.

Her first notice came through poetry. She won a National Endowment for the Arts Award, an award from the *Chicago Review*, and published *Laguna Woman*, a mixture of Laguna culture and personal experience. The publication of her poetry in *Carriers of the Dream Wheel* and her short stories in *The Man to Send Rain Clouds* brought her national attention. From the latter volume "The Man to Send Rain Clouds," "Tony's Story," and "Yellow Woman" are often anthologized. Much of Silko's material in both volumes employs traditional Laguna narratives and historical stories popular in her family and in the community.

Her novel *Ceremony* was published in 1977 to much acclaim, with the *New York Times Book Review* referring to her as "the most accomplished Indian writer of her generation." Silko's protagonist, Tayo, is a mixed-blood Laguna experiencing devastating difficulty with reintegrating himself back into his family and Laguna society after World War II. The deaths of his cousin in the war and of his Uncle Josiah back at the pueblo accentuate the disorientation he experiences upon returning home. The novel depicts his problems through a disjointed narrative that fractures chronological time and juxtaposes mythic elements with personal experience and verse with fiction. Tayo visits an unorthodox mixed-blood Navajo medicine man, Betonie, who performs a ceremony on him. But Betonie equates Tayo's illness with the larger universal illness of humankind. He foresees four elements of a journey that Tayo must make into the mountains above Laguna to perform his personal ceremony. During his journey, Tayo remembers many things from his past and understands their significance for his health and the health of Laguna Pueblo. He also meets a mysterious spirit woman who helps him see how his story, his ceremony, is part of a larger ceremony to defeat the forces of destruction and death. He rejects the vicious actions of some of his war buddies as they torture one of the returned veterans. Upon his return to the pueblo, he can help the community bring itself back into harmony. One of Silko's main themes is the important role in cultural change to be played by marginalized people. For Silko the ceremonies must keep changing or the life of the community dies, and the mixed-blood is in the position to assure that change leads to life-giving structures.

Silko includes verse material from the Laguna mythic tradition in *Ceremony*, intending the verse lines to be "heard" like oral performances. Her interest in bringing the oral into the written is also shown in the frame that she gives the novel. She starts by asserting that the story is taking place in Thought-Woman's mind. Thus this character from Laguna cosmology creates the reality experienced by the reader. Then she frames the body of the novel with the word "sunrise" as do certain Laguna prayers. These elements create a storytelling frame close to a religious function.

The function of the frame is to incorporate Tayo and the reader into a mythic vision of the world, or what she calls "the old, old, old way of looking at the world." Tayo must learn "the ear for the story, the eye for pattern." When he does that he realizes that there are no boundaries between time and space, only transitions. He has not been crazy, but has just seen the world as it truly is. Both Tayo and the reader are able to make sense of the disjointed elements of life, and the book as a whole is meant to represent a ceremony for the reader.

Silko's next book, *Storyteller*, contains family stories, traditional Laguna narratives, photographs of her family and the Laguna

Pueblo, uncollected short stories, poetry, and personal memories. While the book reveals some personal information about Silko and her family, it is more concerned with exploring a family and a community through the stories they tell. Some critics have seen this as an expression of a collective sense of self in the community. Silko has noted that one of her goals was to "clarify the relationship between the stories I heard and my sense of storytelling and language that had been given to me by the old folks, the people back home." To do this, she drops any chronological structure, opting for a juxtaposition of material from various sources to recreate something of the narrative background for her writing.

In 1991 Silko published her second novel, *Almanac of the Dead*. This ambitious novel intertwines the lives of a dozen or so characters into a series of interlocking narratives. The setting of the novel moves across North America from Alaska to Mexico and Central America. While placed in the near future, the novel evokes the history of European exploitation of the continent. Silko hypothesizes the existence of a Mayan almanac that tells of the epochs of the past and foretells of the future. Using the almanac structure allows Silko to experiment with juxtaposing narratives of the violent and spiritless lives of Euro-Americans with the story of a large, spiritually oriented peasant movement to regain the continent.

The almanac of the title prophesies the end of the era of the Dead-Eye Dog, which has dominated life in the Americas for the last five hundred years. With the start of the era of the Fire-Eye Macaw, many diverse forces converge on a convention of holistic healers in Tucson, Arizona. Eco-terrorists, homeless Vietnam veterans, oppressed descendants of African slaves, and displaced Native Americans are brought together by a barefoot Hopi prophet and Mexican Indian twin brothers, who are leading a revolt as Indian peasants swarm northward. Each dissident group hears the spirits of the Americas call out to reject the European desecration of North and South America. Spirits of the displaced African gods have united with the spirits of Native America. Fed by the bitterness and blood of millions, they seek revenge through various avenues, including catastrophic natural disasters. As one character concludes, "the Americas were full of furious, bitter spirits; five hundred years of slaughter had left the continents swarming with millions of spirits that never rested and would not stop until justice had been done."

Silko also has published *Delicacy and Strength of Lace,* a volume of her letters exchanged with **James Wright** prior to his death. In the letters Silko explores her life, her writing, and the role of storytelling. The 1993 volume *Yellow Woman* republished her well-known short story of the same name along with an interview and a variety of critical articles.

Sacred Water (1993) reveals Silko's love of book making. This special edition, hand-bound book was printed under her own imprint (Flood Plain Press) and unites autobiographical passages with graphic images. In 1996 she published a collection of essays and various writings entitled *Yellow Woman and a Beauty of the Spirit.* In this volume she gathers a number of pieces published previously in journals and anthologies along with new work. As she explores contemporary Native American experience, Silko weaves insights on Pueblo language and oral narratives with political and social commentary. Her style is personal and impassioned while firmly rooted in place, community, and family.

While not prodigious in her output, Silko has always experimented with new styles and forms, and her work solidly evidences her own Native American experience. Silko is one of the most important contemporary Native American writers and is arguably the Native writer most concerned with bringing the oral into the written, with the problems and potentials of that bridging, and with uniting the two world views that support those modes of expression.

—James Ruppert

SIMIC, Charles

Born: Belgrade, Yugoslavia, 9 May 1938; emigrated to the United States in 1954; naturalized, 1971. **Education:** Oak Park High School, Illinois: University of Chicago, 1956-59; New York University, 1959-61, 1963-65, B.A. in 1967. **Military Service:** United States Army, 1961-63. **Family:** Married Helen Dubin in 1964; one daughter and one son. **Career:** Proofreader, Chicago *Sun-Times*; member of department of English, California State College, Hayward, 1970-73. Beginning 1973 associate professor of English, University of new Hampshire, Durham. Editorial assistant, *Aperture* magazine, 1966-69. **Awards:** P.E.N. award, for translation, 1970, 1980; Guggenheim fellowship, 1972; national Endowment for the Arts fellowship, 1974, 1979; Edgar Allan Poe award, 1975; American Academy award, 1976; Harriet Monroe poetry award, 1980; Poetry Society of America de Castignola award, 1980; Fulbright fellowship, 1982; Pulitzer prize, 1990.

PUBLICATIONS

Poetry

What the Grass Says. 1967.
Somewhere among Us a Stone Is Taking Notes. 1969.
Dismantling the Silence. 1971.
White. 1972.
Return to a Place Lit by a Glass of Milk. 1974.
Biography and a Lament: Poems 1961-1967. 1976.
Charon's Cosmology. 1977.
Brooms: Selected Poetry. 1978.
School for Dark Thoughts. 1978.
Classic Ballroom Dances. 1980.
Shaving at Night. 1982.
Austerities. 1983.
Weather Forecast for Utopia and Vicinity: Poems 1967-82. 1983.
The Chicken Without a Head. 1983.
Selected Poems 1963-1983. 1985.
Unending Blues. 1986.
The World Doesn't End: Prose Poems. 1989.
In the Room We Share (includes prose). 1990.
The Book of Gods and Devils. 1990.
Hotel Insomnia. 1992.
A Wedding in Hell. 1994.
Walking the Black Cat. 1996.

Recording: *School for Dark Thoughts,* 1978.

Other

The Uncertain Certainty: Interviews, Essays, and Notes on Poetry. 1985.
Wonderful Words, Silent Truth. 1990.

Dimestore Alchemy. 1992.
Unemployed Fortune Teller. 1994.
Orphan Factory: Essays and Memoirs. 1997.

Editor, with Mark Strand, *Another Republic: 17 European and South American Writers.* 1976.
Editor, *The Essential Campion.* 1988.

Editor and translator, with C.W. Truesdale, *Fire Gardens,* by Ivan V. Lilac. 1970.
Editor and translator, *Four Yugoslav Poets: Ivan V. Lilac, Brank Milijkovic, Milorad Pavic, Ljubomir Simovic.* 1970.
Editor and translator, *Homage to the Lame Wolf: Selected Poems 1956-1975,* by Vasko Popa. 1979.

Editor and Co-translator, *Selected Poems of Tomaz Salamun.* 1988.

Translator, *Key to Dream According to Djordje.* 1978.
Translator, with Peter Kastmiler, *Atlantis: Selected Poems of Slavko Mihalic.* 1987.
Translator, *Roll Call of Mirrors: Selected Poems,* by Ivan V. Lilac. 1988.
Translator, *Some Other Wine and Light,* by Aleksander Ristovic. 1989.
Translator, *Bandit Wind,* by Slavko Janevski. 1991.
Translator, *The Horse Has Six Legs, an Anthology of Serbian Poetry.* 1992.
Translator, *Night Mail,* by Novica Tadic. 1992.

*   *   *

Born in Belgrade, Yugoslavia, in 1938, Charles Simic is one of the few American poets of his generation to have experienced war firsthand. In the memoir *In the Beginning* . . . he recalls listening to the radio ("Oslo, Lisbon, Moscow, Berlin, Budapest, Monte Carlo") through the night. "The nights of my childhood were spent," he writes, "in the company of that radio. I attribute my lifelong insomnia to its temptations." His insomnia may explain in part his prodigious output as a poet, translator from his native Serbian, and essayist. He remembers Belgrade and its inhabitants, natives and German soldiers alike, as gray and the war years as a perpetual autumn. His childhood was, he says, "a black and white movie."

There could be no better preparation for a poet than tuning in each night to the world's signals coming from imagined places. The war haunts Simic's poetry. It formed his grim, earthy, sardonic view of the world, one that accommodates in equal parts the real and the fantastic.

Simic arrived in the United States, by way of Paris, at age sixteen. On the first night his father, who had emigrated before his family did, took him to the jazz club Metropole on Times Square. Jazz and its roots, the blues, became for Simic an abiding source of pleasure and inspiration.

In Chicago, where he spent his late teens, Simic began to write poetry. Faced with the limitations of his English and with a poet's instinct that the conventional verse taught in high school was not for him, Simic began, after trial and error, to write a poetry of his own devising. Using spare, highly visual language, he wrote a sort of folk poetry about common objects—a spoon, his shoes, an ax. When published in his first book, *What the Grass Says,* these works had an immediate impact on the poets of his generation. By wedding a fairy-tale clarity with macabre images, Simic created an

American surrealism, as seen, for example, in his description of a fork: "It resembles a bird's foot / Worn around a cannibal's neck." As the title of Simic's book implies, he had listened to Walt Whitman's leaves of grass but had transformed what he heard through his European experience.

As his poetry evolved, Simic kept to everyday language and built his poems around startling images that presented deadpan, as if ants in Quaker hats, rats adept at calculus, and a child's head made from a heel of bread were the most natural things in the world. He favored the short lyric forms of **Emily Dickinson, William Carlos Williams**, and **Robert Creeley**, but he employed them to tell stories. The darker his poems became, the more sardonic his tone. In the celebrated poem "My Weariness of Epic Proportions" he begins, "I like it when / Achilles / Gets killed / And even his buddy Patroclus—." Then, after the gods "shut up," the poem shifts to imagine a young girl on her way along a "lovely little path" to a well. Simic contrasts the "important" savagery of heroes with an ordinary act, emphasizing that poetry is also, and profoundly, the voice of common things.

Between 1971, with the publication of *Dismantling the Silence,* and the appearance of his *Selected Poems* in 1983, Simic published seven books of poetry. Since then he has published seven more, including *Jackstraws* in 1999. He has also translated much Serbian poetry, most importantly the work of Vasko Popa, Ivan V. Lalic, and Aleksander Ristovic. American readers know twentieth-century Serbian poetry largely through Simic's efforts. In addition, he has produced three books of essays and a quirky and brilliant book on the artist Joseph Cornell. During this time Simic has earned his living as most of the American poets of his generation have done, by teaching, first in California and then for more than twenty-five years at the University of New Hampshire.

Simic has been well and widely rewarded for his labors. He has received a PEN International Award for translation, the Edgar Allan Poe Award, and the Harriet Monroe Award, and he has had fellowships from the Fulbright, Guggenheim, Ingram Merrill, and MacArthur foundations. In 1990 he received the Pulitzer Prize for *The World Doesn't End: Prose Poems.* He has read his frequently anthologized poetry throughout the United States and across Europe, and his poetry and prose have been translated into more than a dozen languages. Few American poets of his generation have been so celebrated.

Success has not altered Simic's essential outlook, however. He remains a poet of the dispossessed and eccentric, of the gypsies, street preachers, orphans, bums, madmen, and vaudeville characters in various guises who inhabit his works. He also retains a wary contempt for the figures of authority—dictators, statesmen, teachers, policemen, and philosophers—he writes about and who have proved to be so treacherous in the twentieth century. And yet Simic's black-and-white movie of our time is comic, and he writes as if he knows that fate's last laugh will be a horselaugh. His comedy is dark and often coarse, but it is nonetheless liberating, something Simic achieves by going against the prevailing ironic tone. The poet, who as a child was hurled out of bed and thrown across the room by the force of an exploding bomb, has an appetite for the grotesque. He knows that the world is not a safe place, but he is incapable of feeling sorry for others or for himself. "The Voice at 3 A.M.," the poem Simic placed first in *Jackstraws,* is emblematic: "Who put canned laughter / Into my crucifixion scene?"

—William Corbett

SIMMS, William Gilmore

Born: Charleston, South Carolina, 17 April 1806. **Education:** Public and private schools in Charleston; apprenticed to a pharmacist, 6 years; studied law: admitted to South Carolina bar, 1827. **Family:** Married 1) Anna Malcolm Giles in 1826 (died 1832), one daughter; 2) Chevillette Roach in 1836 (died 1863), 13 children. **Career:** Lawyer in Charleston, 1827-29; editor, *Southern Literary Gazette*, 1828, and Charleston *City Gazette*, 1830-32; visited the North, 1832, and formed friendship with William Cullen Bryant; lived in the North, 1833-34; returned to Charleston, 1835; lived at wife's family home, Woodlands Plantation, Barnwell County, and in Charleston, from 1836, and made annual trips to the North to look after his publishing interests; editor, *Magnolia*, 1842-43, *Southern and Western Magazine* (later *Simms's Magazine*), 1845, and *Southern Quarterly Review*, 1849-54; advocate of slavery: lectured in New York, 1856; editor of the newspapers Columbia *Phoenix*, 1865, *Daily South Carolinian*, 1865-66, and *Courier*, 1870; wrote serials for magazines in New York and Philadelphia from 1865. **Died:** 11 June 1870.

PUBLICATIONS

Collections

Works (Uniform Edition). 20 vols., 1853-59.
The Letters, edited by Mary C. Simms Oliphant, Alfred Taylor Odell, and T.C. Duncan Eaves. 5 vols., 1952-56; supplement, 1982.
Writings (Centennial Edition), edited by John C. Guilds. 1969—.

Fiction

Martin Faber: The Story of a Criminal. 1833; in *Writings 5*, 1974.
The Book of My Lady: A Melange (stories). 1833.
Guy Rivers: A Tale of Georgia. 1834.
The Yemassee: A Romance of Carolina. 1835; edited by J.V. Ridgely. 1964.
The Partisan: A Tale of the Revolution. 1835.
Mellichampe: A Legend of the Santee. 1836.
Martin Faber and Other Tales. 1837.
Richard Hurdis; or, The Avenger of Blood. 1838.
Pelayo: A Story of the Goth. 1838.
Carl Werner: An Imaginative Story, with Other Tales. 1838; as *Matilda*, 1846; in *Writings 5*, 1974.
The Damsel of Darien. 1839.
Border Beagles: A Tale of Mississippi. 1840.
The Kinsmen; or, The Black Riders of Congaree. 1841; as *The Scout*, 1854.
Confession; or, The Blind Heart: A Domestic Story. 1841.
Beauchampe; or, The Kentucky Tragedy. 1842; vol. 1 revised, as *Charlemont; or, The Pride of the Village*, 1856; vol. 2 revised, as *Beauchampe; or, The Kentucky Tragedy*, 1856.
The Prima Donna: A Passage from City Life. 1844; in *Writings 5*, 1974.
Castle Dismal; or, The Bachelor's Christmas: A Domestic Legend. 1844.
Helen Halsey; or, The Swamp State of Conelachita: A Tale of the Borders. 1844; as *The Island Bride*, 1869.
The Wigwam and the Cabin (stories). 2 vols., 1845-46; as *Life in America*, 1848.

Count Julian; or The Last Days of the Goth. 1845.
The Lily and the Totem; or, The Huguenots in Florida. 1850; as *The Huguenots in Florida*, 1884.
Flirtation at the Moultrie House. 1850; in *Writings 5*, 1974.
Katharine Walton; or, The Rebel of Dorchester. 1851.
The Golden Christmas: A Chronicle of St. John's, Berkeley. 1852.
As Good as a Comedy; or, The Tennesseean's Story. 1852; in *Writings 3*, 1972.
The Sword and the Distaff, or, "Fair, Fat and Forty." 1852; as *Woodcraft; or, Hawks about the Dovecote*, 1854; edited by Charles S. Watson, 1983.
Marie De Berniere (stories). 1853; as *The Maroon: A Legend of the Caribbees, and Other Tales*, 1855; as *The Ghost of My Husband*, 1866; in *Writings 5*, 1974.
Vasconselos: A Romance of the New World. 1853.
Southward Ho! A Spell of Sunshine. 1854.
The Forayers; or, The Raid of the Dog-Days. 1855.
Eutaw: A Sequel to The Forayers. 1856.
The Cassique of Kiawah. 1859.
Cavalier of Old South Carolina: Simms's Captain Porgy (selections), edited by Hugh W. Hetherington. 1966.
Voltmeier; or, The Mountain Men, edited by Donald Davidson and Mary C. Simms Oliphant, in *Writings 1*. 1969.
Paddy McGann; or, The Demon of the Stump, edited by Robert Bush, in *Writings 3*. 1972.
Joscelyn: A Tale of the Revolution, edited by Stephen Meats and Keen Butterworth, in *Writings 16*. 1975.

Plays

Norman Maurice; or, The Man of the People. 1851.
Michael Bonham; or, The Fall of Bexar. 1852.

Poetry

Monody on the Death of Gen. Charles Cotesworth Pinckney. 1825.
Lyrical and Other Poems. 1827.
Early Lays. 1827.
The Vision of Cortes, Cain, and Other Poems. 1829.
The Tri-Color; or, The Three Days of Blood in Paris. 1830.
Atalantis: A Story of the Sea. 1832; revised edition, 1848.
Southern Passages and Pictures. 1839.
Donna Florida. 1843.
Grouped Thoughts and Scattered Fancies: A Collection of Sonnets. 1845.
Areytos; or, Songs of the South. 1846.
Lays of the Palmetto. 1848.
Charleston and Her Satirists: A Scribblement. 2 vols., 1848.
The Cassique of Accabee, A Tale of Ashley River, with Other Pieces. 1849.
Sabbath Lyrics; or, Songs from Scripture. 1849.
The City of the Silent. 1850.
Poems: Descriptive, Dramatic, Legendary and Contemplative. 2 vols., 1854.
Poems: Areytos; or Songs and Ballads of the South, with Other Poems. 1860.

Other

Slavery in America, Being a Brief Review of Miss Martineau on That Subject. 1838; revised version, in *The Pro-Slavery Argument*, 1852.

The History of South Carolina. 1840; revised edition, 1842, 1860.

The Geography of South Carolina (for children). 1843.

The Social Principle: The True Source of National Permanence. 1843.

The Life of Francis Marion. 1844.

The Sources of American Independence. 1844.

Views and Reviews in American Literature, History and Fiction. 1846; 2nd series, 1847; 1st series edited by C. Hugh Holman, 1962.

The Life of Captain John Smith. 1847.

Self-Development. 1847.

The Life of Chevalier Bayard. 1848.

Father Abbot; or The Home Tourist. 1849.

South-Carolina in the Revolutionary War. 1853.

Egeria; or, Voices of Thought and Counsel for the Woods and Wayside. 1853.

The Spartanburg Female College. 1855.

Sack and Destruction of the City of Columbia, S.C. 1865; edited by A.S. Salley, 1937.

The Sense of the Beautiful. 1870.

Poetry and the Practical. 1996.

The Cub of the Panther: A Hunter Legend of the "Old North State." 1997.

Editor, *The Remains of Maynard Davis Richardson.* 1833.

Editor, *The Charleston Book: A Miscellany in Prose and Verse.* 1845.

Editor, *A Supplement to the Plays of William Shakespeare.* 1848.

Editor, *The Life of Nathanael Greene.* 1849.

Editor, *War Poetry of the South.* 1866.

*

Bibliography: *A Bibliography of the Separate Writings of Simms* by Oscar Wegelin, revised edition, 1941; *Pseudonymous Publications of Simms* by James E. Kibler, Jr., 1976, and *Simms: A Reference Guide* by Kibler and Keen Butterworth, 1980; in *Bibliography of American Literature* by Jacob Blanck, edited by Virginia L. Smyers and Michael Winship. 1983.

Critical Studies: *Simms* by William P. Trent, 1892; *Simms as Literary Critic* by Edd Winfield Parks, 1961; *Simms* by J.V. Ridgely, 1962; *The Politics of a Literary Man: Simms* by Jon L. Wakelyn, 1973; *The Poetry of Simms: An Introduction and Bibliography* by James E. Kibler, Jr., 1979; *Long Years of Neglect: The Work and Reputation of William Gilmore Simms: Essays in Honor of Thomas Cary Duncan Eaves*, 1988, and *Simms: A Literary Life*, 1992, both by John Caldwell Guilds; *The Edge of the Swamp: A Study of the Literature and Society of the Old South* by Louis D. Rubin, Jr., 1989; *William Gilmore Simms, Woodlands, and the Freedmen's Bureau* by Robert R. Singleton, 1996; *William Gilmore Simms and the American Frontier*, 1997.

*   *   *

The most versatile and representative southern writer of the nineteenth century and one of the more talented American writers of his period, William Gilmore Simms tried his hand at many literary forms and tasks. He published at least four biographies, the best of which, *The Life of Francis Marion,* is a consideration of sources and materials also used in several of his long fictions on the Revolution. He also wrote books on the geography and history of South Carolina.

Simms was early and late a journalist. He edited both newspapers and magazines and eventually possessed considerable influence, especially in the South, as editor and contributor of essays and criticism to such journals as the *Southern Literary Gazette, Southern Literary Messenger, Southern Literary Journal, Southern Quarterly Review,* and *Russell's Magazine.* He also contributed to many of the most consequential northern magazines, including the *Knickerbocker, Democratic Review, Graham's, Harper's New Monthly,* and *Lippincott's.* Some of his best periodical criticism is collected in *Views and Reviews,* but, as Edd Winfield Parks noted in *William Gilmore Simms as Literary Critic,* there is also important criticism in his prefaces and advertisements to the novels and in his letters. In the Advertisement to *The Yemassee* in 1835, for example, Simms elaborated on a distinction between the romance and the novel that allowed the writer of the former considerable latitude in the treatment of the possible and the probable. In long critical essays he discoursed learnedly on Cooper's writings in 1842 (and gave his chief American rival every bit of his due); in 1845 he dealt effectively with "Americanism in Literature"; and in letters in 1842 and thereafter he discussed perceptively the place of realism in fiction and fairly characterized Poe as magazinist, story writer, and poet. Simms's letters eventually assumed their rightful place in any study of his canon as a result of their publication in five volumes, with a sixth supplementary volume.

Simms also wrote a number of plays, including two in blank verse (*Norman Maurice* and *Michael Bonham*), and his view of his own merit as a poet is indicated in a remark in a letter of 24 November 1853 that his "poetical work exhibits the highest phase of the Imaginative faculty which this Country has yet exhibited, and the most philosophical in connection with it." Few, including his friends **Paul Hamilton Hayne** and **Henry Timrod**, agreed with him then or subsequently, but with *The Poetry of Simms* James E. Kibler, Jr., began laying the groundwork for a reappraisal of Simms's verse.

Over the years, however, most critics have agreed that Simms's chief contribution was to the novel. This is still largely the case when one considers the size and scope of his accomplishment in the seven books of the Revolutionary Romances (1835-56) or observes carefully the achievement in such individual works as *The Yemassee, Border Beagles, Katharine Walton, Woodcraft,* or *The Cassique of Kiawah.* But Simms was also a significant writer of short fiction, as John C. Guilds and Betty J. Strickland have demonstrated. Guilds maintains in his introduction to *Stories and Tales* (Volume 5 of the Centennial Edition) that the "short story or tale" is Simms's "best genre," and the contents of this edition plus the better-known tales of *The Wigwam and the Cabin* show that Simms did indeed make a consequential and varied contribution to short fiction.

Simms's versatility and prolixity, to say nothing of the adverse reaction of Northern readers to his political views during the Civil War and its aftermath, assuredly contributed to the decline in his literary reputation, which reached its nadir during World War II. However, with the studies of C. Hugh Holman in the late 1940s and thereafter, the edition of letters in the 1950s (including especially the critical evaluation of Simms's best work by Donald Davidson), the publication of the Centennial Edition, and the critical studies by Kibler and Mary A. Wimsatt, Simms's work is receiving some of the attention it has long merited.

—Rayburn S. Moore

SIMON, (Marvin) Neil

Born: New York City, 4 July 1927. **Education:** De Witt Clinton High School, New York, graduated 1943; New York University, 1944-45; University of Denver, 1945-46. **Military Service:** Served in the U.S. Army Air Force, 1945-46: corporal. **Family:** Married 1) Joan Baim in 1953 (died 1973), two daughters; 2) the actress Marsha Mason in 1973 (divorced 1983); 3) Diane Lander in 1987. **Career:** Radio and television writer, 1948-60. **Awards:** Emmy award, for television writing, 1957, 1959; Tony award, 1965, 1970, 1985, 1991; London *Evening Standard* award, 1967; Shubert award, 1968; Writers Guild of America West award, for screenplay, 1969, 1971, 1976; PEN Los Angeles Center award, 1982; New York Drama Critics Circle award, 1983; Outer Circle award, 1983, 1985; New York State Governor's award, 1986; Pulitzer prize, 1991; Peggy V. Helmerich Distinguished Author award, 1996. L.H.D.: Hofstra University, Hempstead, New York, 1981; Williams College, Williamstown, Massachusetts, 1984.

PUBLICATIONS

Plays

Sketches (produced 1952).
Sketches, with Danny Simon, in *Catch a Star!* (produced 1955).
Sketches, with Danny Simon, in *New Faces of 1956* (produced 1956).
Adventures of Marco Polo: A Musical Fantasy, with William Friedberg, music by Clay Warnick and Mel Pahl. 1959.
Heidi, with William Friedberg, music by Clay Warnick, adaptation of the novel by Johanna Spyri. 1959.
Come Blow Your Horn (produced 1960). 1961.
Little Me, music by Cy Coleman, lyrics by Carolyn Leigh, adaptation of the novel by Patrick Dennis (produced 1962). Included in *Collected Plays 2*, 1979.
Barefoot in the Park (as *Nobody Loves Me*, produced 1962; as *Barefoot in the Park*, produced 1963). 1964.
The Odd Couple (produced 1965; revised [female] version produced 1985). 1966.
Sweet Charity, music by Cy Coleman, lyrics by Dorothy Fields, based on the screenplay *Nights of Cabiria* by Federico Fellini and others (produced 1966). 1966.
The Star-Spangled Girl (produced 1966). 1967.
Plaza Suite (includes *Visitor from Mamaroneck*, *Visitor from Hollywood*, *Visitor from Forest Hills*) (produced 1968). 1969.
Promises, Promises, music and lyrics by Burt Bacharach and Hal David, based on the screenplay *The Apartment* by Billy Wilder and I.A.L. Diamond (produced 1968). 1969.
Last of the Red Hot Lovers (produced 1969). 1970.
The Gingerbread Lady (produced 1970). 1971.
The Prisoner of Second Avenue (produced 1971). 1972.
The Sunshine Boys (produced 1972). 1973.
The Comedy of Neil Simon (includes *Come Blow Your Horn*; *Barefoot in the Park*; *The Odd Couple*; *The Star-Spangled Girl*; *Plaza Suite*; *Promises, Promises*; *Last of the Red Hot Lovers*). 1972.
The Good Doctor, music by Peter Link, lyrics by Simon, adaptation of stories by Chekhov (produced 1973). 1975.
God's Favorite (produced 1974). 1975.
California Suite (includes *Visitor from New York*, *Visitor from Philadelphia*, *Visitor from London*, *Visitor from Chicago*; produced 1976). 1977.

The Goodbye Girl (screenplay 1977) stage version, music by Marvin Hamlisch, lyrics by David Zippel (produced 1992).
Chapter Two (produced 1977). 1979.
They're Playing Our Song, music by Marvin Hamlisch, lyrics by Carol Bayer Sager (produced 1978). 1980.
Collected Plays 2 (includes *The Sunshine Boys*, *Little Me*, *The Gingerbread Lady*, *The Prisoner of Second Avenue*, *The Good Doctor*, *God's Favorite*, *California Suite*, *Chapter Two*). 1979.
I Ought to Be in Pictures (produced 1980). 1981.
Fools (produced 1981). 1982.
Brighton Beach Memoirs (produced 1982). 1984.
Actors and Actresses (produced 1983).
Biloxi Blues (produced 1984). 1986.
Broadway Bound (produced 1986). 1987.
Rumors (produced 1988; revised version produced 1990). 1990.
Jake's Women (produced 1990; revised version produced 1992). 1993.
Lost in Yonkers (produced 1991). 1991.
Collected Plays 3 (includes *Sweet Charity*; *They're Playing Our Song*; *I Ought to Be in Pictures*; *Fools*; *The Odd Couple* [female version]; *Brighton Beach Memoirs*; *Biloxi Blues*; *Broadway Bound*). 1992.
Laughter on the 23rd Floor (produced 1993).
London Suite: A Comedy (produced 1993). 1996.
Neil Simon Monologues. 1996.
Proposals (produced 1997).
Collected Plays 4 (includes *Rumors*; *Lost in Yonkers*; *Jake's Women*; *Laughter on the 23rd Floor*; *London Suite*). 1998.

Screenplays: *After the Fox*, with Cesare Zavattini, 1966; *Barefoot in the Park*, 1967; *The Odd Couple*, 1968; *The Out-of-Towners*, 1970; *Plaza Suite*, 1971; *The Heartbreak Kid*, 1972; *The Last of the Red Hot Lovers*, 1972; *The Prisoner of Second Avenue*, 1975; *The Sunshine Boys*, 1975; *Murder by Death*, 1976; *The Goodbye Girl*, 1977; *The Cheap Detective*, 1978; *California Suite*, 1978; *Chapter Two*, 1979; *Seems Like Old Times*, 1980; *Only When I Laugh*, 1982; *I Ought to Be in Pictures*, 1982; *Max Dugan Returns*, 1983; *The Lonely Guy*, with Ed Weinberger and Stan Daniels, 1984; *The Slugger's Wife*, 1985; *Brighton Beach Memoirs*, 1987; *Biloxi Blues*, 1988; *The Marrying Man*, 1991; *Lost in Yonkers*, 1993; *Jake's Women*, 1996.

Radio plays: scripts for *Robert Q. Lewis Show*.

Television: *Phil Silvers Show*, 1948; *Tallulah Bankhead Show*, 1951; *Your Show of Shows*, 1956; *Sid Caesar Show*, 1956-57; *Jerry Lewis Show*; *Jackie Gleason Show*; *Red Buttons Show*; *Sergeant Bilko* series, 1958-59; *Garry Moore Show*, 1959-60; *The Trouble with People*, 1972; *Happy Endings*, with others, 1975; *Broadway Bound*, 1992.

Other

Rewrites: A Memoir. 1996.
The Play Goes On. 1999.

*

Bibliography: *Ten Modern American Playwrights* by Kimball King, 1982.

Manuscript Collection: Harvard University, Cambridge, Massachusetts.

Critical Studies: *Neil Simon* by Edythe M. McGovern, 1979; *Neil Simon* by Robert K. Johnson, 1983; "Neil Simon" by Michael Woolf, in *American Drama* edited by Clive Bloom, 1995; *Neil Simon's Laughter on the 23rd Floor* by John C. Carr, 1995; *Neil Simon: A Casebook* edited by Gary Konas, 1997.

*   *   *

Dramatists throughout American theatre history who have enjoyed overwhelming popular acclaim by their audiences during their lifetimes have consistently had difficulty finding appreciative acceptance and careful evaluation by critics and historians who consider themselves serious appraisers of dramatic art. It seems that the fact of attracting popular enthusiasm—an ability to entertain the masses—must be associated with superficiality and mediocrity of thought as well as the hocus-pocus of technical spectacle and a sense of the commonness of mankind that elite critics always view with contempt.

Neil Simon has paid a price for his great skill in pleasing America's theatre audiences. Like some of his predecessors in the American theatre—Dion Boucicault (1820-1890), **David Belasco** (1853-1931), **Clyde Fitch** (1865-1909), Owen Davis (1874-1956)—who were extremely popular with their contemporary audiences and who are now neglected, Simon, who successfully entertained theatregoers for nearly forty years and appropriately amassed a considerable fortune for his efforts, for a long time suffered from the facile commentary of critics who had preconceived expectations. But modern historians speak respectfully of Boucicault's criticism and of some of his plays; Belasco crowned his spectacular melodramas with *The Return of Peter Grimm* (1911); the prolific Fitch, with four plays in New York theatres during the 1901 season, died young; and Davis, after writing a hundred or more successful, violent melodramas, earned a Pulitzer Prize with *Icebound* in 1923. And Neil Simon finally received the critical acclaim he coveted for many years with *Lost in Yonkers* (1991), which received both a Pulitzer Prize and a Tony Award.

Simon has been quoted as saying that he knows few dramatists who are as successful as he is but a lot who are better writers. "It's just," he said, "that the things I write about appeal to a large number of people. In a way, I feel guilty about that." Perhaps! A native New Yorker, he served his apprenticeship writing comic material for radio and television personalities such as Phil Silvers. Before he became the most successful playwright of the 1960s, he cowrote sketches with his brother Danny for the Broadway shows *Catch a Star* (1955) and *New Faces of 1956*. With his first full-length comedy, *Come Blow Your Horn* (1961), in which he exploited the antics of two girl-crazy sons of a Jewish businessman, Simon created a spectacular Broadway hit and established his trademark as a writer of well-structured comic situations and exceedingly bright, fast repartee. Success followed success: musical farce *Little Me* (1962); *Barefoot in the Park* (1963), following the misadventures of newlyweds and featuring Robert Redford in his first major role; *The Odd Couple* (1965), illustrating the impossibility of the obsessively tidy Felix Ungar ever existing happily with a slovenly roommate like Oscar Madison; *Plaza Suite*, a combination of three one-act plays set in Suite 719 of New York's Plaza Hotel; and the musical *Promises, Promises* (1968). With *The Last of the Red Hot Lovers* in 1969, another hit, and four shows running simultaneously on Broadway, there could be no question of Simon's prowess nor of his success as a dramatist. Yet Simon clearly was not satisfied.

One review of Simon's next play, *The Gingerbread Lady* (1970), was titled "When the Funniest Writer Tries to be Serious." Audiences did not respond well to this play, which dealt honestly with alcoholism, because it did not show the playwright they thought they knew. But Simon was not to be deterred from his evident decision to write serious plays. His next plays, both produced in 1972—*The Prisoner of Second Avenue*, dealing with a character's mental breakdown when confronted with seeming futility, and *The Sunshine Boys*, underlining the self-destructive behavior of two retired Vaudeville performers—were bittersweet comedies. These were difficult years for Simon, whose wife died in 1973. *The Good Doctor*, adapted from stories written by Anton Chekhov, and *God's Favorite* (1976) were both failures. A remake of *Plaza Suite* called *California Suite* (1976) showed both Simon's move to California and some of his well-known wit. The tremendous effect on Simon of his wife's death and his eventual (and ill-fated) marriage to Marsha Mason appeared in *Chapter Two* (1977), which poignantly revealed a widower's bereavement. This play is generally regarded as a turning point in Simon's career and his finest work to date.

During the past twenty years, Neil Simon's career has been less spectacular but somehow more defining of his place in the history of American drama as the most successful writer of comedy in the last half of the twentieth century. Although his plays have not been consistent Broadway hits, his reputation for wit and cleverly contrived situations has been buttressed by his healthy use of sentiment and his sensitivity to the serious problems of mankind. A musical, *They're Playing Our Song* (1979), was popular; *I Ought to Be in Pictures* (1980) and *Fools* (1981) were not. Then Simon applied to his past the brash wit of his earlier plays, the wisdom of his maturity, and the charm of his newly acquired sense of well-being in *Brighton Beach Memoirs* (1983); *Biloxi Blues* (1985); and *Broadway Bound* (1986). Once again Simon captured Broadway, but not for long. In spite of Alan Alda's acting, *Jake's Women* (1990) could not draw audiences in 1992 to the New York theatre named for the playwright. But Simon had already received the award his plays so deserved in years past—in 1991, the Pulitzer Prize for *Lost in Yonkers*.

—Walter J. Meserve

SIMPSON, Louis (Aston Marantz)

Born: Jamaica, British West Indies, 27 March 1923. **Education:** Munro College, Jamaica, 1933-40, Cambridge Higher Schools Certificate, 1939; Columbia University, New York, B.S. 1948, A.M. 1950, Ph.D. 1959. **Military Service:** Served in the U.S. Army, 1943-45: Purple Heart and Bronze Star. **Family:** Married 1) Jeanne Claire Rogers in 1949 (divorced 1954), one son; 2) Dorothy Roochvarg in 1955 (divorced 1979), one son and one daughter; 3) Miriam Butensky Bachner in 1985 (divorced 1998). **Career:** Editor, Bobbs-Merrill Publishing Company, New York, 1950-55; instructor, Columbia University, 1955-59; professor of English, University of California, Berkeley, 1959-67; beginning 1967, professor of English, and beginning 1993 Distinguished Professor Emeritus, State University of New York, Stony Brook. **Awards:** American Academy in Rome fellowship, 1957; Edna St. Vincent Millay award, 1960; Guggenheim fellowship, 1962, 1970; American Council of Learned Societies grant, 1963; Pulitzer prize, 1964; Columbia University Medal for Excellence, 1965; American Academy award, 1976; Institute of Jamaica Centenary Award, 1980; National Jewish Book award, 1981; Elmer Holmes Bobst award for poetry, 1987; Harold Morton Landon award for translation, 1998. **D.H.L.**: Eastern Michigan University, Ypsilanti, 1977. Honorary degrees: Hampden-Sydney College, 1990; Adelphi University, 1997. **Residence**: Stony Brook, New York.

PUBLICATIONS

Poetry

The Arrivistes: Poems 1940-1949. 1949.
Good News of Death and Other Poems. 1955.
A Dream of Governors. 1959.
At the End of the Open Road. 1963.
Selected Poems. 1965.
Adventures of the Letter I. 1971.
Searching for the Ox. 1976.
Caviare at the Funeral. 1980.
The Best Hour of the Night. 1983.
People Live Here: Selected Poems 1949-1983. 1983.
Collected Poems. 1988.
In the Room We Share. 1990.
Jamaica Poems. 1993.
There You Are. 1995.

Play

The Breasts of Tiresias, from a play by Apollinaire, in *Modern French Theatre,* edited by Michael Benedikt and George E. Wellwarth. 1964; as *Modern French Plays,* 1965.

Fiction

Riverside Drive. 1962.

Other

James Hogg: A Critical Study. 1962.
Air with Armed Men (autobiography). 1972; as *North of Jamaica,* 1972.
Three on the Tower: The Lives and Works of Ezra Pound, T. S. Eliot, and William Carlos Williams. 1975.
A Revolution in Taste: Studies of Dylan Thomas, Allen Ginsberg. Sylvia Plath, and Robert Lowell. 1978; as *Studies of Dylan Thomas, Allen Ginsberg, Sylvia Plath, and Robert Lowell,* 1979.
A Company of Poets. 1981.
The Character of the Poet. 1986.
Selected Prose. 1989.
Ships Going into the Blue. 1994.
The King My Father's Wreck. 1995.

Editor, with Donald Hall and Robert Pack, *The New Poets of England and America.* 1957.
Editor, *An Introduction to Poetry.* 1986.

*

Bibliography: *Simpson: A Reference Guide* by William H. Roberson, 1980.

Critical Studies: *Louis Simpson* by Ronald Moran, 1972, and *Four Poets and the Emotive Imagination* by Moran and George S. Lensing, 1976; *On Louis Simpson: Depths beyond Happiness* by Hank Lazer, 1988.

*   *   *

Always more of a "paleface" than a "redskin" (to adopt Philip Rahv's famous categorization of American writers), Louis Simpson took some time to find his own poetic voice. His early poetry is heavily dependent on **John Crowe Ransom**, and much of the work of his first two volumes, *The Arrivistes* and *Good News of Death,* seems to derive from art rather than life. The exception comes with a remarkable group of war poems, especially "Carentan O Carentan" and "The Battle," which, with the exception of **Randall Jarrell**'s, are the best poems to have come from an American poet's confrontation with World War II.

A Dream of Governors is a tired, "literary" volume, full of echoes of such poets as Nemerov, Hecht, and Wilbur, all of them more polished performers than Simpson himself. Reading it, you feel that Simpson's talent is all but dead. But *At the End of the Open Road* achieves a remarkable breakthrough. Gone are the formal posturings—the conventional subjects, the making of poems out of poems—that featured so heavily in the earlier volumes. It is as though Simpson has suddenly found his true subject, and with it an answerable style. Instead of trying to be like other poets, he is content to be himself. He lets his Jewishness into the poetry, his sense of being something of an outcast, but an outcast who nevertheless knows he belongs to America, and who therefore sets out to celebrate his country, whenever he can find it and whatever it may prove to be. As the title of the volume hints, Simpson turns, as so many American poets have found themselves turning, to **Walt Whitman**. The Whitman he responds most deeply to is the poet who could embrace multitudes, engage contradictions, responsibly accept irresponsibility, whose gigantic achievement was to perceive the noble folly of American dreams. "All the grave weight of America / Cancelled! Like Greece and Rome. / The future in ruins." Those lines come from "Walt Whitman at Bear Mountain," one of Simpson's best poems.

Most of the poems of *At the End of the Open Road* are written in an informal, loose-limbed manner, which frees them to convey a more powerful and convincing personal voice than the earlier poems had managed to do. And where Simpson does return to a more formal mode, as in the extraordinarily fine, wittily melancholic "My Father in the Night Commanding No," he does it without leaning on any other poet. Some of the finest poems in this remarkable volume are ones in which Simpson broods on the inescapable fact of his Jewishness. He prods at it like an aching tooth, fascinated by it, yet fearing the pain it causes. The best of these is undoubtedly "A Story about Chicken Soup."

In *Adventures of the Letter I,* Simpson attempts to make further use of the style he had discovered for himself: musing, wryly observant, quizzical, contemplative; it is a volume marking time. There are no poems in it as good as the best in *At the End of the Open Road;* and yet it is an utterly readable, enjoyable piece of work by a poet who, having found his own voice, can be relied on not to bore.

Simpson's *Collected Poems* reveal the poet to be concerned, above all else, with what it is like to live in America. *Collected Poems* brings together work from four decades of Simpson's career and shows the extent to which the poet has reconciled himself to—in the words of *New York Times Book Review* contributor Edward Hirsch—the "diminished possibilities and dwindling hopes" of the American middle-class existence. Simpson writes in "In the Suburbs":

> There's no way out.
> You were born to waste your life.
> You were born to this middle-class life.
> As others before you
> Were born to walk in procession
> To the temple, singing.

Simpson, Hirsch noted, "has inherited the laurel from **Randall Jarrell** as the Chekhov of contemporary American poetry."

Simpson's cynical sympathy with the American experience shows through as well in his 1989 collection, *Selected Prose*. This sampling of autobiographical narratives, memoirs, and essays traces the developments in the poet's personal and aesthetic life, and finds Simpson offering insight into some of the best writers of the twentieth-century. "Mr. Simpson's passion and humility—openness to criticism, willingness to listen—shine through every lucid sentence of his prose," wrote *New York Times Book Review* contributor Anne Stevenson.

—John Lucas

SINCLAIR, Upton

Born: Baltimore, Maryland, 20 September 1878; moved with his family to New York, 1888. **Education:** City College, New York, 1893-97, A.B. 1897; Columbia University, New York, 1897-1901. **Family:** Married 1) Meta H. Fuller in 1900 (divorced 1911); 2) Mary Craig Kimbrough in 1913 (died 1961); 3) Mary Elizabeth Willis in 1961 (died 1967). **Career:** Writer from 1893; wrote Clif Faraday stories (as Ensign Clarke Fitch) and Mark Mallory stories (as Lieutenant Frederick Garrison) for various boys' weeklies, 1897-98; founded socialist community, Helicon Home, Englewood, New Jersey, 1906-07; Socialist candidate for Congress, from New Jersey, 1906; settled in Pasadena, California, 1915; Socialist candidate for Congress, 1920, for U.S. Senate, 1922, and for governor of California, 1926, 1930; moved to Buckeye, Arizona, 1953. **Awards:** Pulitzer prize, 1943; American Newspaper Guild award, 1962. **Died:** 25 November 1968.

Publications

Fiction

Springtime and Harvest: A Romance. 1901; as *King Midas,* 1901.
Prince Hagen. 1903.
The Journal of Arthur Stirling. 1903.
Manassas. 1904; revised edition, as *Theirs Be the Guilt,* 1959.
The Jungle. 1906.
A Captain of Industry. 1906.
The Industrial Republic. 1907.
The Metropolis. 1908.
The Moneychangers. 1908.
Samuel the Seeker. 1910.

Love's Pilgrimage. 1911.
Sylvia. 1913.
Damaged Goods. 1913.
Sylvia's Marriage. 1914.
King Coal. 1917.
Jimmie Higgins. 1918.
The Spy. 1919; as *100%: The Story of a Patriot,* 1920; excerpt, as *Peter Gudge Becomes a Secret Agent,* 1930.
They Call Me Carpenter. 1922.
The Millennium: A Comedy of the Year 2000. 1924.
Oil! 1927.
Boston. 1928; abridged edition, as *August 22nd,* 1965.
Mountain City. 1929.
The Wet Parade. 1931.
Roman Holiday. 1931.
Co-op: A Novel of Living Together. 1936.
The Gnomobile. 1936.
Little Steel. 1938.
Our Lady. 1938.
Marie Antoinette. 1939; as *Marie and Her Lover,* 1948.
World's End. 1940.
Between Two Worlds. 1941.
Dragon's Teeth. 1942.
Wide Is the Gate. 1943.
Presidential Agent. 1944.
Dragon Harvest. 1945.
A World to Win. 1946.
Presidential Mission. 1947.
One Clear Call. 1948.
O Shepherd, Speak! 1949.
Another Pamela; or, Virtue Still Rewarded. 1950.
The Return of Lanny Budd. 1953.
What Didymus Did. 1954; as *It Happened to Didymus.* 1958.
The Cup of Fury. 1956.
Affectionately Eve. 1961.
The Coal War: A Sequel to King Coal. 1976.

Plays

Prince Hagen, from his own novel (produced 1909). 1909. *Plays of Protest* (includes *Prince Hagen, The Naturewoman, The Machine, The Second-Story Man*). 1912.
Hell: A Verse Drama and Photo-Play. 1923.
The Pot Boiler. 1924.
Singing Jailbirds (produced 1930). 1924.
Bill Porter. 1924.
Wally for Queen! The Private Life of Royalty. 1936.
A Giant's Strength. 1948.
The Enemy Had It Too. 1950.
Three Plays (includes *The Second-Story Man, John D., The Indignant Subscriber*). 1965.

Poetry

Songs of Our Nation. 1941.

Other

The Toy and the Man. 1904.
Our Bourgeois Literature. 1905.
Colony Customs. 1906.

The Helicon Home Colony. 1906.

A Home Colony: A Prospectus. 1906.

What Life Means to Me. 1906.

The Overman. 1907.

Good Health and How We Won It, with Michael Williams. 1909; as *The Art of Health,* 1909; as *Strength and Health,* 1910.

War: A Manifesto Against It. 1909.

Four Letters about "Love's Pilgrimage." 1911.

The Fasting Cure. 1911.

The Sinclair-Astor Letters: Famous Correspondence between Socialist and Millionaire. 1914.

The Social Problem as Seen from the Viewpoint of Trade Unionism, Capital, and Socialism, with others. 1914.

Sinclair: Biographical and Critical Opinions. 1917.

The Profits of Religion. 1918.

Russia: A Challenge. 1919.

The High Cost of Living (address). 1919.

The Brass Check. 1919; excerpt, as *The Associated Press and Labor,* 1920.

Press-titution. 1920.

The Crimes of the "Times": A Test of Newspaper Decency. 1921.

Mind and Body. 1921; revised edition, 1950.

The McNeal-Sinclair Debate on Socialism. 1921.

Love and Society. 1922; revised edition, 4 vols., n.d.

The Book of Life. 1922.

The Goose-Step: A Study of American Education. 1922; revised edition, n.d.

Biographical Letter and Critical Opinions. 1922.

The Goslings. 1924; excerpt, as *The Schools of Los Angeles,* 1924.

Mammonart. 1925.

Letters to Judd. 1926; revised edition, as *This World of 1949 and What to Do about It,* 1949.

The Spokesman's Secretary. 1926.

Money Writes! 1927.

The Pulitzer Prize and "Special Pleading." 1929.

Mental Radio. 1930; revised edition, 1962.

Socialism and Culture. 1931.

Upton Sinclair on "Comrade" Rautsky. 1931.

American Outpost. 1932; as *Candid Reminiscences: My First Thirty Years,* 1932.

I, Governor of California, and How I Ended Poverty. 1933.

Upton Sinclair Presents William Fox. 1933.

The Way Out—What Lies Ahead for America? 1933; revised edition as *Limbo on the Loose: A Midsummer Night's Dream,* 1948.

EPIC Plan for California. 1934.

EPIC Answers: How to End Poverty in California. 1934.

Immediate EPIC. 1934.

The Lie Factory Starts. 1934.

A Sinclair Anthology, edited by I.O. Evans. 1934; revised edition, 1947.

Sinclair's Last Will and Testament. 1934.

We, People of America, and How We Ended Poverty: A True Story of the Future. 1934.

Depression Island. 1935.

I, Candidate for Governor, and How I Got Licked. 1935; as *How I Got Licked and Why,* 1935.

What God Means to Me: An Attempt at a Working Religion. 1936.

The Flivver King. 1937.

No Pasoran! (They Shall Not Pass). 1937.

Terror in Russia: Two Views, with Eugene Lyons. 1938.

Sinclair on the Soviet Union. 1938.

Expect No Peace! 1939.

Telling the World. 1939.

What Can Be Done about America's Economic Troubles? 1939.

Your Million Dollars. 1939; as *Letters to a Millionaire,* 1939.

Is the American Form of Capitalism Essential to the American Form of Democracy? 1940.

Peace or War in America? 1940.

Index to the Lanny Budd Story, with others. 1943.

To Solve the German Problem—A Free State? 1943.

A Personal Jesus: Portrait and Interpretation. 1952; as *Secret Life of Jesus,* 1962.

Radio Liberation Speech to the Peoples of the Soviet Union. 1955.

My Lifetime in Letters. 1960.

The Autobiography of Sinclair. 1962.

Editor, *The Cry for Justice: An Anthology of the Literature of Social Protest.* 1915.

*

Bibliography: *Sinclair: An Annotated Checklist* by Ronald Gottesman, 1973; *Upton Sinclair: A Descriptive, Annotated Bibliography* by John B. Ahouse, 1994.

Critical Studies: *Sinclair: A Study in Social Protest* by Floyd Dell, 1927; *This Is Sinclair* by James Harte Lambert, 1938; *The Literary Manuscripts of Sinclair* by Ronald Gottesman and Charles L.P. Silet, 1972; *Sinclair* by Jon A. Yoder, 1975; *Sinclair, American Rebel* by Leon Harris, 1975; *Critics on Upton Sinclair* edited by Abraham Blinderman, 1975; *Sinclair* by William A. Bloodworth, 1977; *Art for Social Justice: The Major Novels of Upton Sinclair* by R.N. Mookerjee; *Learning to Fight the Nazis: The Education of Upton Sinclair's Lanny Budd* by Sally E. Parry, 1992; *Upton Sinclair and "The Jungle": A Study of American Literature, Society, and Culture* by Suk Bong Suh, 1997; *Upton Sinclair: The Forgotten Socialist* by Ivan Scott, 1997.

*   *   *

No American author has produced more writing, had a greater influence on society, and received less serious critical attention than Upton Sinclair. The depository of Sinclair manuscripts, books, and letters at the Lilly Library, Indiana University, weighs more than eight tons. More than 250,000 letters are included in the collection, letters to Shaw, Gandhi, Trotsky, Roosevelt, Kennedy, and countless letters to readers and critics concerning his own work and that of others. The material is available for work that might lead to a reassessment of Sinclair similar to that which the discovery of the Malahide papers brought about in critical opinion concerning James Boswell.

Upton Sinclair wrote on more subjects than we can catalogue; he was interested in extrasensory perception, religion, economics, alcoholism, and much more. He wrote ninety books and many pamphlets, and without his work the social world in which we live would probably lack many of the benefits we take for granted. But of those books, only one, *The Jungle,* has survived as an American classic, and critics are divided as to whether it is a classic of imaginative literature or a classic work of propaganda. Even the once popular Lanny Budd series (eleven novels, 1940-53), one of which, *Dragon's Teeth,* won the Pulitzer Prize, is all but forgotten. The key critical issue apparent in the rather limited Sinclair scholarship is whether Upton Sinclair is a genuine novelist or a very skilled and effective propagandist for social and socialist reform. Most critics think the latter.

Van Wyck Brooks, in *The Confident Years*, acknowledged *The Jungle* as an outstanding example of muckraking literature; however, muckraking literature operates only on a level of social effect and falls short of serious art. *The Jungle* tells of the Lithuanian emigrant family of Jurgis Rudkus. Seeking the realization of the American Dream, the family settles in the Chicago of the early twentieth century. Jurgis goes to work in the stockyards (which provides Sinclair the opportunity to describe the filthy practices of the meat-packing industry) and the family moves into a ramshackle house, deceptively painted by the agent to appear new. There follows a series of tragedies and horrors as members of the family are killed or debased by a social system that cares nothing for the helpless people it exploits. Jurgis's futile attempts to strike back are rewarded with prison sentences. Finally, he learns of the socialist movement. He finds a job in a hotel managed by a socialist, and recaptures a sense of hope.

Despite certain well-constructed scenes of genuinely human life, such as the Lithuanian wedding of Jurgis and Ona, it is evident to most readers that Jurgis's family exists primarily as a means by which to gauge the failures of the social system that destroys them. They are acted upon; they do not act. Indeed, all we learn about human nature from *The Jungle*'s characters is that human nature can be perverted and debased by society. On the other hand, we learn a very great deal about the society. Readers in 1906 learned more than they imagined, and the conditions in the meat-packing industry, so well described by Sinclair, attracted the attention of reformers and presidents. The world of *The Jungle* is a naturalistic world, a world in which only the economically fit survive. Here, human lives are manipulated by an indifferent, if not hostile, scheme of things. But Sinclair's message is that the scheme can change. We have created or at least permitted the existence of the thing that oppresses us, and if enough are made aware of the full horror of that thing, the few who control and profit from it will have to surrender.

In *Upton Sinclair, American Rebel*, Leon Harris observes that successful propaganda must disappear. It seeks to make its ideas commonplace; it causes us to accept its message as the product of our own clear perception of the way things are. Then the actual organ of the propaganda fades in the glow of our self-satisfaction. Most of Sinclair's literature was intended to be, and was, just this kind of successful propaganda. Only on a very rare occasion does a piece of propaganda strike us with such impact that the work itself becomes part of the history that we study and remember, for it is dangerous to forget history. The result, as in the case of *The Jungle*, is a puzzle for critics who know that propaganda should fade away and novels should concern themselves with character development. Paradoxically, then, Sinclair at his best fails in both genres and creates a work that the literate world insists is a classic.

—William J. Heim

See the essay on *The Jungle*.

SINGER, Isaac Bashevis

Born: Icek-Hersz Zynger in Leoncin, Poland, 14 July 1904; immigrated to the United States, 1935; became citizen, 1943. **Edu-**cation: The Tachkemoni Rabbinical Seminary, Warsaw, 1921-22. **Family:** Married Alma Haimann in 1940; one son from earlier marriage. **Career:** Proofreader and translator, *Literarishe Bleter*, Warsaw, 1923-33; associate editor, *Globus*, Warsaw, 1933-35; journalist, *Vorwärts* (*Jewish Daily Forward*) Yiddish newspaper, New York, from 1935. **Awards:** Louis Lemed prize, 1950, 1956; American Academy grant, 1959; Daroff Memorial award, 1963; Foreign Book prize (France), 1965; two National Endowment for the Arts grants, 1966; Bancarella Prize (Italy), 1968; Brandeis University Creative Arts award, 1969; National Book award, for children's literature, 1970, and, for fiction, 1974; Nobel prize for literature, 1978; American Academy Gold Medal, 1989. D.H.L.: Hebrew Union College, Los Angeles, 1963. D.Lit.: Colgate University, Hamilton, New York, 1972. D.Litt.: Texas Christian University, Fort Worth, 1972; Ph.D.: Hebrew University, Jerusalem, 1973. Litt.D.: Bard College, Annandale-on-Hudson, New York, 1974, and Long Island University, Greenvale, New York, 1979. **Member:** American Academy, 1965; American Academy of Arts and Sciences, 1969; Jewish Academy of Arts and Sciences; Polish Institute of Arts and Sciences. **Died:** 24 July 1991.

PUBLICATIONS

Collections

A Singer Reader. 1971.

Short Stories

Gimpel the Fool and Other Stories, translated by Saul Bellow and others. 1957; as *Gimpel Tam un anderer Detailungen*, 1963.
The Spinoza of Market Street and Other Stories, translated by Elaine Gottlieb and others. 1961.
Short Friday and Other Stories, translated by Ruth Whitman and others. 1964.
Selected Short Stories, edited by Irving Howe. 1966.
The Séance and Other Stories, translated by Ruth Whitman and others. 1968.
A Friend of Kafka and Other Stories, translated by Isaac Bashevis Singer and others. 1970.
A Crown of Feathers and Other Stories, translated by Isaac Bashevis Singer and others. 1973.
Passions and Other Stories. 1975.
Old Love. 1979.
The Collected Stories. 1982.
The Image and Other Stories. 1985.
The Death of Methuselah and Other Stories. 1988.

Novels

Der sotn in Goray. 1935; as *Shoten an Goray un anderer Dertailungen* [Satan in Goray and Other Stories], 1943; as *Satan in Goray*, translated by Jacob Sloan, 1955.
Di Familie Mushkat. 1950; as *The Family Moskat*, translated by A. H. Gross. 1950.
The Magician of Lublin, translated by Elaine Gottlieb and Joseph Singer. 1960.
The Slave, translated by Isaac Bashevis Singer and Cecil Hemley. 1962.
The Manor, translated by Elaine Gottlieb and Joseph Singer. 1967.

The Estate, translated by Elaine Gottlieb, Joseph Singer, and Elizabeth Shub. 1969.
Enemies: A Love Story, translated by Alizah Shevrin and Elizabeth Shub. 1972.
Shosha, translated by Isaac Bashevis Singer and Joseph Singer. 1978.
Reaches of Heaven. 1980.
The Penitent. 1983.
The King of Fields, translated by Isaac Bashevis Singer, 1988.
Scum, translated by Rosaline Dukalsky Schwartz. 1991.
The Certificate, translated by Leonard Wolf. 1992.

Fiction (for children; translated by the author and Elizabeth Shub)

Zlateh the Goat and Other Stories. 1966.
Mazel and Shlimazel; or, The Milk of a Lioness. 1967.
The Fearsome Inn. 1967.
When Shlemiel Went to Warsaw and Other Stories, translated by Channah Kleinerman-Goldstein and others. 1968.
Joseph and Koza; or, The Sacrifice to the Vistula. 1970.
Alone in the Wild Forest. 1971.
The Topsy-Turvy Emperor of China. 1971.
The Fools of Chelm and Their History. 1973.
A Tale of Three Wishes. 1976.
Naftali the Storyteller and His Horse, Sus, and Other Stories, translated by Isaac Bashevis Singer and others. 1976.
The Power of Light: Eight Stories for Hanukkah. 1980.
The Golem. 1982.
Stories for Children. 1984.

Plays

The Mirror (produced 1973).
Shlemiel the First (produced 1974).
Yentl, The Yeshiva Boy, with Leah Napolin, from a story by Singer (produced 1974). 1979.
Teibele and Her Demon, with Eve Friedman (produced 1978). 1984.

Other (for children; translated by the author and Elizabeth Shub)

A Day of Pleasure: Stories of a Boy Growing Up in Warsaw (autobiographical), translated by Channah Kleinerman-Goldstein and others, photographs by Roman Vishniac. 1969.
Elijah the Slave: A Hebrew Legend Retold, illustrated by Antonio Frasconi. 1970.
The Wicked City. 1972.
Why Noah Chose the Dove. 1974.

Other

In My Father's Court (autobiography), translated by Channah Kleinerman-Goldstein, Elaine Gottlieb, and Joseph Singer, 1966.
The Hasidim: Paintings, Drawings, and Etchings, with Ira Moskowitz. 1973.
Love and Exile: The Early Years: A Memoir. 1984.
  A Little Boy in Search of God: Mysticism in a Personal Light, illustrated by Ira Moskowitz. 1976.
  A Young Man in Search of Love, translated by Joseph Singer. 1978.

Lost in America, translated by Joseph Singer. 1981.
Nobel Lecture. 1979.
Singer on Literature and Life: An Interview, with Paul Rosenblatt and Gene Koppel. 1979.
Conversations with Singer, with Richard Burgin. 1985.
Conversations: Singer, edited by Grace Farrell. 1992.

Translator (into Yiddish), *Pan,* by Knut Hamsun. 1928.
Translator (into Yiddish), *Di Vogler* [The Vagabonds], by Knut Hamsun. 1928.
Translator (into Yiddish), *In Opgrunt Fun Tayve* [In Passion's Abyss], by Gabriele D'Annunzio. 1929.
Translator (into Yiddish), *Mete Trap* [Mette Trap], by Karin Michäelis. 1929.
Translator (into Yiddish), *Roman Rolan* [Romain Rolland], by Stefan Zweig. 1929.
Translator (into Yiddish), *Viktorya* [Victoria], by Knut Hamsun. 1929.
Translator (into Yiddish), *Oyfn Mayrev-Front Keyn Nayes* [All Quiet on the Western Front], by Erich Maria Remarque. 1930.
Translator (into Yiddish), *Der Tsoyberbarg* [The Magic Mountain], by Thomas Mann. 4 vols., 1930.
Translator (into Yiddish), *Der Veg oyf Tsurik* [The Road Back], by Erich Maria Remarque. 1931.
Translator (into Yiddish), *Araber: Folkstimlekhe Geshikhtn* [Arabs: Stories of the People], by Moshe Smilansky. 1932.
Translator (into Yiddish), *Fun Moskve biz Yerusholayim* [From Moscow to Jerusalem], by Leon S. Glaser. 1938.

Editor, with Elaine Gottlieb, *Prism 2.* 1965.

*

Bibliography: by Bonnie Jean M. Christensen, in *Bulletin of Bibliography* 26, January-March 1969; *A Bibliography of Singer 1924-1949* by David Neal Miller, 1984.

Critical Studies: *Singer and the Eternal Past* by Irving Buchen, 1968; *The Achievement of Singer* edited by Marcia Allentuck, 1969; *Critical Views of Singer* edited by Irving Malin, 1969, and *Singer* by Malin, 1972; *Singer* by Ben Siegel, 1969; *Singer and His Art* by Askel Schiotz, 1970; *Singer, The Magician of West 86th Street* by Paul Kresh, 1979; *Singer* by Edward Alexander, 1980; *The Brothers Singer* by Clive Sinclair, 1983; *Fear of Fiction: Narrative Strategies in the Works of Singer* by David Neal Miller, 1985, and *Recovering the Canon: Essays on Singer* by Miller and E. J. Brill, 1986; *From Exile to Redemption: The Fiction of Singer* by Grace Farrell Lee, 1987; *Understanding Singer* by Lawrence Friedman, 1988; *Singer: A Study of the Short Fiction* by Edward Alexander, 1990; *Transgression and Self-Punishment in Isaac Bashevis Singer's Searches* by Frances Vargas Gibbons, 1995; *Isaac Bashevis Singer: A Life* by Janet Hadda, 1997; *Lost Landscapes: In Search of Isaac Bashevis Singer and the Jews of Poland* by Agata Tuszynska, 1998.

*   *   *

Isaac Bashevis Singer is an example of a strange phenomenon in American Jewish literature—a Yiddish writer who in his later years gained international fame through the English translation of his novels and short stories. The Yiddish audience for which Singer wrote was never a very large one; he did not cater to the nostalgic yearnings of one school of Yiddishists, or the socialist diatribes of the other.

Distancing himself from the latter group was especially difficult for the young Singer, for it implied a separation from his older brother, Israel Joshua, also an accomplished writer. This older brother was the first to open the door to secular education and to the questions that inevitably awakened Isaac to the narrowness of his father's world of Hasidism and the inadequacy of his mother's more rational, but nevertheless medieval, normative Judaism. But, unlike his brother, Isaac Bashevis was unwilling to discard his past altogether; he was unwilling to choose between mysticism and rationality, between past and present, or even between gothicism and realism. Singer's art is a marriage of these diverse elements in his past; they are what afford his fiction both its charm and its sophistication.

In his early years, Singer wrote solely for the Yiddish press, under several pseudonyms—for example, Varshavsky and Segal. Even his name Bashevis is a pseudonym in honor of his mother, Bathsheba. These early pieces included feuilletons, autobiographical sketches, short fiction, and novels. Some of these have been translated into English, but many remain unknown to the non-Yiddish-reading public. By 1950, Singer had begun the process that was to lead to his great fame in the next twenty years; he began to publish in English translation as well as in the original Yiddish.

The first major venture in this double publication was his epic novel *The Family Moskat,* which appeared simultaneously in English and Yiddish. The significant differences between the Yiddish original and the English translation reveal the problematic nature of Singer's identity as an English writer. In the English version, the main characters are left to their doom in Warsaw on the eve of the Nazi takeover. In the Yiddish version, a youthful remnant escapes to Israel. The symbolic significance of their escape and tenuous existence is not lost on the Yiddish writer Singer, nor the Yiddish reader.

As defined by Irving Malin, Singer's novels can be divided into two groups, open and closed. *The Family Moskat* is probably the best example of his open novels. It is a historical family chronicle; the scope of the tale is large and has significant sociological implication; the style is primarily realistic. For Singer, these chronicles are most often set in a time during which the confined *shtetl* life of the East European Jew is being questioned. Other novels in this manner include *The Manor* and *The Estate.*

Of the second (closed) type of Singer novel, *Satan in Goray* is probably the purest example. It is short, condensed in time; there is an aura of mystery and irrationality; the style, the characters, the setting are all symbolic. Set in the distressing era of the anti-Semitic pogromist Chmielnicki and the false messiah Shabbatai Zevi, this novel relates the disintegration of personality and community that resulted from these horrors of the Jewish past. Other closed novels include *The Magician of Lublin* and *The Slave.* (*Enemies: A Love Story* is hard to classify, but it is more closed than open.)

Singer's use of symbolism, which owes much to the structure and style of *kaballah,* is prominent in many of his short stories as well as the closed novels. In the best of the stories Singer suggests the complex dichotomies, the multiple levels of human existence, and the ambivalent nature of life itself by the use of name symbolism, the supernatural, and multiple narrators. Before the reader can with assurance interpret a story, he must note who

tells that story. The reader of "The Destruction of Kreshev" overlooks at his peril the fact that the narrator is Satan. If he reads the superstitious tale "Zeitl and Rickel," he must note that an uneducated old woman is speaking. The events in these tales are filtered through a perspective that colors subject, tone, and conclusion. Even in the masterpiece "Gimpel the Fool," readers must recognize that Gimpel himself tells the tale; his naivety and good nature determine the conclusion.

Another important type of narrator in Singer's fiction is semi-autobiographical. In the more belletristic of the tales, Singer uses this portrait of himself as a mirror reflecting another's story. In "A Friend of Kafka," Jacques Kohn tells the history of his peculiar life. But readers do not hear the tale directly; rather they hear it from a man bearing many similarities to the young Isaac Singer. He knew Jacques; Jacques told him a story, and he tells the readers.

The more simply autobiographical pieces are collected in two books (*In My Father's Court* and *A Day of Pleasure*). These sketches give a clear impression of the life of the young Singer, of his awakening experiences in life, love, and education, and of his movement away from his father's narrow past. However, it is 1976's *Little Boy in Search of God* that most tellingly reveals the intellectual ferment that troubled the young Singer and led him to the development of his twentieth-century mysticism.

Singer is modern in his vision of humanity: his treatment of sexuality and insanity alienated him from many of his Yiddish readers while enhancing his stature in the modern American mind. This rift has caused many English-language critics to overemphasize Singer's modernity. In so doing, they have overlooked the medieval method of symbolism that adds much of the depth and beauty to Singer's work. But such confusion is only a natural consequence of Singer's position as a Jewish-American writer, a man born in Poland but writing in New York, a man writing in Yiddish but being read in English, and a man looking toward the past to tell of the future.

—R. Barbara Gitenstein

SIRIN, V. *See* **NABOKOV, Vladimir.**

SMITH, Betty (Wehner)

Born: Brooklyn, New York, 15 December 1896. **Education:** P.S. 23 in Greenpoint, New York, through the eighth grade; as a special student at the University of Michigan, Ann Arbor (Avery Hopwood award, 1931), 1927-1930; at the Yale School of Drama, New Haven, Connecticut, 1931-1934. **Family:** Married 1) George H. E. Smith in 1924 (divorced 1938), two daughters; 2) Joseph Piper Jones in 1943 (divorced 1951); 3) Robert Finch in 1957 (died 1959). **Career:** Worked from age 14 as a clerk and factory worker in New York City; 1927-30, wrote one-act plays as well as feature columns for the newspaper syndicate NEA and the *Detroit Free Press;* actress and playwright for the Federal Theater Project, reader and editor for Dramatists Play Service, and radio announcer, 1931-34; from the mid-1930s visiting lecturer at the University of North Carolina at Chapel Hill in both the department of English and department of dramatic art; wrote novels and plays full time from 1943. **Awards:** Rockefeller fellowship in playwriting, 1931; Dramatists Guild Playwriting fellowship, 1938; silver cup from the Theater Guild for the best one-act play of 1938; Woman of the Year award, 1943; Sir Walter Raleigh award for fiction, 1958; Carolina Playmakers Alumni award, 1964. **Member:** American Academy, 1937. **Died:** 17 January 1972.

PUBLICATIONS

Novels

A Tree Grows in Brooklyn. 1943.
Tomorrow Will Be Better. 1948.
Maggie—Now. 1958.
Joy in the Morning. 1963.

Plays

Francie Nolan. 1930.
Folk Stuff (one-act), with Jay G. Sigmund. 1935.
His Last Skirmish (one-act), with Robert Finch. 1937.
Naked Angel (one-act), with Robert Finch. 1937.
Popecastle Inn (one-act), with Robert Finch. 1937.
Saints Get Together (one-act), with Jay G. Sigmund. 1937.
Trees of His Father (one-act), with Jay G. Sigmund. 1937.
Vine Leaves (one-act), with Jay G. Sigmund. 1937.
The Professor Roars (one-act), with Robert Finch. 1938.
Western Night (one-act), with Robert Finch. 1938.
Darkness at the Window (one-act), with Jay G. Sigmund. 1938.
Murder in the Snow (one-act), with Robert Finch. 1938.
Silvered Rope (one-act), with Jay G. Sigmund. 1938.
Youth Takes Over; Or, When a Man's Sixteen, with Robert Finch. 1939.
Lawyer Lincoln (one-act), with Chase Webb. 1939.
Mannequin's Maid (one-act). 1939.
They Released Barabbas (one-act), with Jay G. Sigmund. 1939.
A Night in the Country (one-act), with Robert Finch. 1939.
Near Closing Time (one-act), with Robert Finch. 1939.
Package for Ponsonby (one-act), with Robert Finch. 1939.
Western Ghost Town (one-act), with Robert Finch. 1939.
Bayou Harlequinade, with Clemon White. 1940.
Fun after Supper. 1940.
Heroes Just Happen, with Robert Finch. 1940.
Room for a King (one-act). 1940.
Summer Comes to the Diamond O (one-act), with Robert Finch. 1940.
To Jenny with Love (one-act), with Robert Finch. 1941.
Gander Sauce. 1942.
The Boy, Abe. 1944.
Young Lincoln. 1944.
Freedom's Bird. 1945.
The First in Heart (produced 1947).
A Tree Grows in Brooklyn (produced 1951), musical adaptation of her own novel, with George Abbott. 1951.
Durham Station (one-act). 1961.

Other

Editor, with Robert Finch and Frederick Henry Koch, *Plays for Schools and Little Theaters: A New Descriptive List.* 1937.
Editor, *25 Non-Royalty One-Act Plays for All-Girl Casts.* 1942.

Editor, *20 Prize-Winning Non-Royalty One-Act Plays.* 1943.
Editor, with others, *A Treasury of Non-Royalty One-Act Plays.* 1958.

*

Critical Studies: *American Women Writers* edited by Lina Mainiero, 1982; *Women Writers and the City* edited by Susan-Merrill Squier, 1984; "Smith, Betty" by Lynda Hart, in *Notable Women in the American Theater* edited by Alice M. Robinson, Vera Mowry Roberts, and Milly S. Barranger, 1989; *The Life and Works of Betty Smith, Author of "A Tree Grows in Brooklyn"* (dissertation) by Carol Siri Johnson, 1995.

*   *   *

Although best known as the author of *A Tree Grows in Brooklyn,* Betty Smith was a playwright with more than seventy plays to her credit before turning to the novel. The fame and wealth that her first novel brought all but overshadowed the rest of her professional and private life. She went on to write three subsequent books after *A Tree Grows in Brooklyn,* and though all of them sold well, they were panned by the critics for mining the same autobiographical ground as the first.

Elizabeth Wehner was born in the Williamsburg section of Brooklyn, New York, in 1896 to John and Catherine (Hummel) Wehner, both immigrants from Austria. One of three children, she was a bookish child and developed an early love for the theater, influenced by her actor father. Williamsburg was a poor but colorful area of Brooklyn, and the Wehners led a marginal existence, especially after the death of the father. Elizabeth, later known as Betty, had to quit school after the eighth grade and find work. Her mother remarried an Irish immigrant, Michael Keogh. It was a childhood and youth at once poor in material terms, but rich in experience.

Smith eventually fled Brooklyn for Ann Arbor, Michigan, where she enrolled in courses as a special student at the University of Michigan and where she also met and married a young law student, George Smith. It was at the university that she first began writing plays, winning the prestigious Avery Hopwood award for *Francie Nolan,* a play about growing up in the poverty of a Brooklyn slum out of which *A Tree Grows in Brooklyn* developed.

Many of Smith's plays were never published, written only for amateur theatricals. She collaborated for many years with the writer Robert Finch, later to be her third husband. Her themes ranged from comedy—*Popecastle Inn, Vine Leaves,* and *The Professor Roars*—to Christian teaching—*Room for a King* and *The Silvered Rope.* The latter group especially bears similarities to medieval miracle plays. Smith always strove for a strong, clearly expressed moral to her plays, often employing the artifice of the traveler or outsider who enables or sometimes forces the understanding of a moral. Whether it be redemption, as in *Western Night,* corrupt political practices, as in *Freedom's Bird,* or the Lincoln story, as in her cycle of plays *Lawyer Lincoln, The Boy, Abe,* and *First Sorrows,* Smith's plays maintained a parable-like simplicity along with richly conceived characters that make them ideal for amateur theater companies and school groups. Her one-act plays were never throw-aways; rather they strove to dig beneath the facade of life and give voice to social consciousness. Moving to New Haven, Connecticut, in 1931 to take a three-year course in playwriting at Yale under George Pierce Baker and Walter Prichard Eaton, Smith wrote scores of plays to scratch out a meager living. These, in addition to acting and editing, became her livelihood after the dissolution of her first marriage and her move to Chapel Hill, North Carolina, to take up a writing fellowship at the University of North Carolina.

By 1940 Smith had all but burned out on playwriting and decided to take a furlough to write a novel. What came of this vacation from plays was essentially eight hundred pages of dialogue and stage direction that she finally—by 1943—redrafted into a controllable novel entitled *A Tree Grows in Brooklyn.* The story of Francie Nolan, who grows up in the poor neighborhoods of Brooklyn but who retains a wonderfully hopeful view of life, was an overnight success. Following closely the path of Smith's own youth, the novel chronicles Francie's life through grade school, the loss of her lovable but heavy-drinking father, and the scramble for jobs just to stay afloat. But it also relates a brighter side: Francie's love of books, the wonderful cast of characters who inhabit Brooklyn, and the tree that grows in front of the family's tenement, the tree that Francie watches through the seasons and that—after being cut down—sprouts new growth from its trunk. As the critic Orville Prescott noted in the *Yale Review,* "[*A Tree Grows in Brooklyn*] is a first novel of uncommon skill, an almost uncontrollable vitality and zest for life, the work of a fresh, original and highly gifted talent." Others concurred. Rosemary Dawson, writing in the *Saturday Review of Literature,* found that the book "has the charm of accurately remembered details, set down simply and with feeling." The public response was tremendous: printing after printing sold out, making Smith wealthy and a celebrity overnight. The book has sold more than six million copies worldwide and has been translated into numerous languages. Two years after publication the novel was made into a movie, ensuring that Smith's name would become a household word. But not all the critics agreed on the literary merits of *A Tree Grows in Brooklyn.* Diana Trilling, writing in the *Nation,* was one of the first to question Smith's unabashedly sentimental style and plot: "Surely popular taste should be allowed to find its emotional level without being encouraged to believe that a 'heart-warming' experience is a serious literary experience." With Smith's following books, more critics would begin to voice this same doubt.

The success of her first novel allowed Smith the luxury of a real house for herself and her two daughters, and she also wed a second time, to a journalist from Chapel Hill, Joe Jones. Smith's second novel, *Tomorrow Will Be Better,* appeared in 1948. Set on the mean streets of Brooklyn among the poor, it features Margy Shannon as the young heroine battling poverty. But where Smith's first novel struck an honest chord with people around the world, *Tomorrow Will Be Better* fell flat. Walter Havighurst commented in the *Saturday Review of Literature* that "the novel leaves you remembering Brooklyn's folkways more vividly than its people." And G.E. Miles, in *Commonweal,* blasted the book, excluding it "from even the most summary of summer readings."

In 1949, theatrical rights to *A Tree Grows in Brooklyn* were acquired, and Smith began working—reluctantly at first—with George Abbott on the adaptation of the book into a musical. The play opened on Broadway on April 19, 1951, to instant success. The themes of poverty and struggle in the book were toned down for the musical, and a secondary character, Cissy, a cheerful trollop, became the focal point. Theater critic Brooks Atkinson noted in the *New York Times* that the musical was "one of those happy inspirations that the theater dotes on . . . a melodious frolic with all the pace and affluence of a happy musical show."

Smith returned to fiction and to the Brooklyn tenements with her third novel, *Maggie—Now,* chronicling the exploits of yet another Irish immigrant family. But reviewers and the public alike had grown weary of such tales. In 1963 with her fourth and last book, Smith moved on to new ground. Again writing autobiographically, she dealt with the first year of married life of a young couple. Set at a Midwestern college campus, *Joy in the Morning* details the adventures of a young Brooklyn girl who, with only a primary school education, manages to enter college, marry a young law student, and get her first writings published. But the sentimental writing was turning saccharine to many ears; the plots were all sounding familiar. Writing in the *New York Times Book Review,* Virgilia Peterson called the novel an "anachronism."

Smith went on to write several more plays, including *The First in Heart,* which premiered successfully at Yale and dealt with Mormonism in Illinois between 1840 and 1841. In her later years she became more concerned with watching her grandchildren grow up than with putting words on paper. At the age of seventy-two, Betty Smith died, leaving behind a body of work that paved new ground for dialogue and the realistic treatment of character and scene. With *A Tree Grows in Brooklyn,* Smith managed to give voice to the underclass, to give color and radiance to supposedly squalid environments. That her successive books drew too heavily on the same material does not erase the achievement of the first.

—J. Sydney Jones

SMITH, Lee

Born: Grundy, Virginia, 1 November 1944. **Education:** Hollins College, B.A. 1967; attended Sorbonne, University of Paris. **Family:** Married 1) James E. Seay in 1967 (divorced), one daughter and one son; 2) Hal Crowther in 1985. **Career:** Feature writer, film critic, and editor of Sunday magazine, *Tuscaloosa News,* Tuscaloosa, Alabama, 1968-69; seventh grade teacher, Harpeth Hall School, Nashville, Tennessee, 1971-73; teacher of language arts, Carolina Friends School, Durham, North Carolina, 1974-77; lecturer in creative writing, University of North Carolina, Chapel Hill, 1977-81. Beginning 1981 member of English department, North Carolina State University. **Awards:** Book-of-the-Month Club fellowship, for *The Last Day the Dogbushes Bloomed,* 1967; O. Henry award, 1979, 1981; Sir Walter Raleigh award, 1984; North Carolina award for literature, 1985.

PUBLICATIONS

Novels

The Last Day the Dogbushes Bloomed. 1968.
Something in the Wind. 1971.
Fancy Strut. 1973.
Black Mountain Breakdown. 1980.
Oral History. 1983.
Family Linen. 1985.
Fair and Tender Ladies. 1988.
The Devil's Dream. 1992.
We Don't Love with Our Teeth. 1994.
Saving Grace. 1995.

Novella

The Christmas Letters. 1996.

Short Stories

Cakewalk. 1980.
Me and My Baby View the Eclipse. 1990.
News of the Spirit. 1997.

Other

Appalachian Portraits, photographs by Shelby Lee Adams. 1993.

*

Critical Studies: *Rereading Agrarianism: Despoliation and Conservation in the Works of Wendell Berry, Lee Smith, and Bobbie Ann Mason* (dissertation) by Cynthia M. Howell, 1996; *Sexuality and Motherhood in the Novels of Lee Smith: A Divine Integration* (dissertation) by Linda Joyce Byrd, 1998; *Lee Smith: The Flesh, the Spirit, and the Word* (dissertation) by Sherry Lee Robinson, 1998.

*   *   *

Lee Smith is the storyteller of the Appalachian Mountains and has been instrumental in voicing the stories of Appalachian women. In her novels and short stories she deals in myth and oral history, in music and history. She has been compared with **William Faulkner, Flannery O'Connor,** and **Carson McCullers.** She has become the voice of the disempowered mountain women of North Carolina and Virginia. At the same time, however, Smith is never just a regional writer; like Faulkner, her focus on a single region reveals the universal truths of human lives. In *Southern Review* critic Virginia Smith claimed that Smith's novels "are tributes to memory, to the recovering and creating of family and cultural history." She also observed, "Smith's fiction springs from the minutiae of existence and the comic and poetic rhythms of speech."

Smith's novels usually deal with the trials and tribulations of women. Often these struggles end in deeper and richer understandings. Her novel *Black Mountain Breakdown* (1980) strays from this pattern in some remarkable ways. Crystal Spangler, unlike many of Smith's other female heroes, seems to live the perfect life in Black Rock. Crystal's external life is the stereotypical fairy tale; she is a popular, pretty cheerleader in high school, she earns good grades, she goes to college, she marries an up-and-coming politician—a "good" marriage. In essence, Crystal is the prototypical "good" girl, but, as her name implies, she is fragile. Contrary to the implications of her name, though, she is not transparent, is not "crystal" clear. She has a deep, dark, troubling stream rumbling beneath the surface, and the novel is the story of her "Black Mountain Breakdown."

In her novel *Oral History* (1983), Smith used unconventional narration to explore the stories of the mountain people. A relative from the city, Jennifer, has been assigned an oral history project by her professor, so she heads up to Hoot Owl Holler to discover her roots and to earn an A. She notes that the true benefits of this trip will be "from my new knowledge of my heritage and a new appreciation of these colorful, interesting folk. My *roots.*" Jennifer is not prepared for the stories she encounters. She is not prepared for the journey outside herself that she must take. Jennifer's definitions of history are altered, just as the reader's definitions are altered. Certainly one lesson to be learned from the novel is about stories and pride and point of view. The reader, along with Jennifer, is taught never to believe that simple folk are so simple. By the end of the novel Jennifer thinks, "They are really very primitive people, resembling nothing so much as some sort of early tribe. Crude jokes and animal instincts—it's the other side of the pastoral coin." She arrives on the mountain with little understanding and leaves with even less. The reader, however, has come to some deep and abiding understandings.

Some critics argued that Smith's female characters were too weak, too easily broken, like Crystal and Jennifer. No critic, however, could argue this after Ivy Rowe, the main character in *Fair and Tender Ladies* (1988), certainly one of Smith's strongest novels. This epistolary novel is told through the letters of Ivy Rowe, a mountain girl, and chronicles her life's journey from the age of twelve until her death as an old woman. The reader struggles with Ivy through a difficult, poverty-stricken childhood on Blue Star Mountain and through her sexual awakenings and marriage. In her letters, the reader learns of Ivy's affair with Honey Breeding, a magic man of the mountain who cures Ivy's black depression. The reader hears Ivy pass along her own knowledge to her child, and the reader is with Ivy as she passes on to another world. Ivy is not fragile like Crystal, nor is she as naive as the city cousin Jennifer. She is strong and resilient yet possesses an artist's temperament. She is a survivor.

Ivy remains one of Smith's deeper characters for reasons other than the strong narrative and effective epistolary style. Tanya Long Bennet argued in the *Southern Literary Journal* that "Ivy, unlike her predecessors in Smith's works, finds a way to see and to recognize a more substantial self." Ivy, in fact, becomes a mythic hero. In an interview published in *Southern Review* Smith claimed, "But I have always been interested in the notion of heroes and heroism, and I read a lot of Joseph Campbell. So I guess I wanted to create a woman who would have a heroic journey. But you had to put that journey in Ivy's terms and on her turf." *Fair and Tender Ladies* is a portrait of a woman who lives through historic events like the coming of electricity, yet her life remains timeless as she mixes with mythic characters like the Cline sisters and Granny Rowe, magic women of the mountain. Ivy's stories, despite her death, are tales of victory.

In *Saving Grace* (1995), Smith created yet another strong female character, Florida Grace, who must endure troubles and tragedies yet emerges on the other side with her own brand of salvation. Grace grows up in a family headed by a charismatic traveling preacher who is also a snake handler. Some of the snake scenes are grotesque and comic yet also compelling. As Grace ages, she marries an older man, again very religious. One day she snaps, flinging herself headlong into an adulterous affair. She must save her own life somehow, and she does. The novel is a vivid account of one woman's journey toward her salvation and grace.

Smith writes of her region, the Appalachian mountains, but she is not a regional writer. Her novels and stories evoke a specific time and place, yet they are also universal and timeless. Smith gives to her readers the people and music and stories of the mountains while still reaching where we all live.

—Jenny Brantley

SMITH, Martin Cruz

Pseudonyms: Nick Carter; Jake Logan; Simon Quinn; Martin Quinn; Martin Smith. **Born:** Martin William Smith in Reading, Pennsylvania, 3 November 1942. **Education:** The University of Pennsylvania, Philadelphia, B.A. 1964. **Family:** Married Emily Stanton Arnold in 1968; two daughters and one son. **Career:** Worked as a reporter for The Associated Press, 1965, and Magazine Management, 1966-68; traveled in former U.S.S.R., researching material for *Gorky Park*, 1973. **Awards:** British Crime Writers Association Gold Dagger, 1982; International Association of Crime Writers Hammett award, 1997. **Residence:** Mill Valley, California.

PUBLICATIONS

Novels

The Indians Won. 1971.
Gypsy in Amber. 1971.
The Analog Bullet. 1972.
Canto for a Gypsy. 1972
The Devil in Kansas. 1974.
His Eminence, Death. 1974.
The Last Time I Saw Hell. 1974.
Nuplex Red. 1974.
The Human Factor (novelization of screenplay). 1975.
Last Rites for the Vulture. 1975.
The Midas Coffin. 1975.
The Adventures of the Wilderness Family (novelization of screenplay). 1976.
North to Dakota. 1976.
Ride for Revenge. 1977.
Nightwing. 1977.
Gorky Park. 1981.
Stallion Gate. 1986.
Polar Star. 1989.
Red Square. 1992.
Rose. 1996.
Havana Bay. 1999.

Plays

Screenplay: *Nightwing*, with Steve Shagan and Bud Shrake. 1979.

*

Critical Studies: "Thinking Woman's Children and the Bomb" by Helen Jaskoski, in *The Nightmare Considered*, 1991.

*   *   *

Martin Cruz Smith writes crime fiction and is most widely known for the three novels, beginning with *Gorky Park*, that feature Moscow police investigator Arkady Renko. Before publication of *Gorky Park* in 1981, Smith had undertaken a ten-year apprenticeship in writing popular fiction, turning out a series of potboilers he kept at arm's length by using the pseudonyms Nick Carter, Jake Logan, Martin Quinn, and Simon Quinn. With the two Roman Grey novels, *Gypsy in Amber* and *Canto for a Gypsy*,

Smith began publishing his crime fiction under his own name, writing at first as Martin Smith. The gypsy books, while uneven in execution, introduce themes and strategies that characterize subsequent works. The detective-as-loner, a stock figure in American pulp fiction, is elaborated with the depiction of a whole marginalized group—in this case, the world of the Romany. In later works, Smith turns his attention to Native Americans, Siberians, Aleuts, and other marginalized communities. The other persistent thread in Smith's writing is a meticulous care for the details of crafts, trades, professions, or subcultures. The detailed information about the brotherhood of antique dealers in the gypsy books forecasts the attention later to minutiae of sable raising (*Gorky Park*), vampire bats and bubonic plague (*Nightwing*), or fish-cannery ships (*Polar Star*).

Veneration of craftspersonship and professional detail along with the development of a solitary, self-reliant masculine hero is an Ernest Hemingway formula, and Smith's best work resonates with Hemingway's themes. The character of Arkady Renko, Moscow police investigator, is cut from the same cloth as a Robert Jordan or Frederic Henry: these men are all honest, professionally expert, unlucky in love, and relatively powerless in a corrupt world. In *Gorky Park*, Renko, while reluctantly investigating the murder of two young Siberians and an American, is drawn into a labyrinth of duplicity, bribery, industrial espionage, black-market profiteering, trade wars, and pathological cruelty. The novel's villain is resplendently evil and a large cast of eccentric and fascinating characters moves the action forward, but the most gripping aspect of the story is Renko's continuing survival as, armed only with his training and native intelligence, he matches wits against antagonists belonging to a world permeated with violence and corruption. In *Polar Star*, the closed setting of the fish-cannery ship intensifies the suspense as Renko—now a sailor exiled from the Communist party, from Moscow, and from respectability—is once more unwillingly drawn into an investigation fraught with danger and uncertainty. Once again American and Soviet interests are entangled, although this time legally in the joint venture of the fishing company.

In *Red Square*, Renko has been rehabilitated as Moscow investigator. In this last of the three Renko stories, Smith sets up an interesting problem for the crime/mystery writer. It is often said that the mystery genre depends on the assumption of a stable, dependable social and moral order within which criminal or aberrant behavior can be clearly defined, investigated, disclosed, and corrected. In the chaos of post-Soviet Russia, however, behavior formerly stigmatized as criminal, like profit-making, becomes admirable, and former traitors are revived as heroes. As a result of this ambiguity of context, *Red Square* lacks the intensity of focus of *Gorky Park* and *Polar Star*; the investigation of murder and shady business dealings tends to fade into puzzled social observation.

Nightwing, the first novel published under the name Martin Cruz Smith, is replete with research on southwest Indian cultures (as well as scientific research on bats and bubonic plague). The plot is relatively straightforward, basically paralleling that of *Jaws* with plague-carrying bats in the shark's role and a development-obsessed Navajo entrepreneur (with fortuitous resemblance to a well-known tribal chairperson) as the antagonist. The novel does not integrate research into story as satisfactorily as the Russian-theme works do and may be faulted for its hostile vision of a vulnerable and endangered species, but it offers a view of native cultures as complex, vivid societies coping with twentieth-century reality.

Stallion Gate is of another order altogether, an ambitious work that critiques the Manhattan project by setting the development of atomic weapons against the traditional New Mexico Indian cultures where the project was carried out. Smith invents a fictitious pueblo and introduces into it the historical characters of J. Robert Oppenheimer, Claus Fuchs, and General Leslie Groves. The clash of values that permeates the novel sets the earth-centered, caretaking philosophy of the Pueblo people against the earth-dominating values of the scientists and their military backers. The story's protagonist, Joe Pena, is more interesting than the formula Hemingway hero: a man of integrity and wit, he is also something of an urban trickster, surviving by his wits and various scams (there is also a hint of the author in this character, as, like Smith's own parents, Pena's father is a musician). *Stallion Gate* is neither mystery nor suspense (the outcome of the Manhattan project not being in doubt), but naturalistic tragedy, an elegant, powerful meditation on intellectual and moral depravity, and Smith's best work to date.

—Helen Jaskoski

SMITH, Rosamond. *See* **OATES, Joyce Carol.**

SNODGRASS, W.D.

Pseudonym: S.S. Gardons. **Born:** Wilkinsburg, Pennsylvania, 5 January 1926. **Education:** Geneva College, Beaver Falls, Pennsylvania, 1943-44, 1946; University of Iowa, Iowa City, 1946-55, B.A. 1949, M.A. 1951, M.F.A. 1953. **Military Service:** Served in the U.S. Navy, 1944-46. **Family:** Married 1) Lila Jean Hank in 1946 (divorced 1953), one daughter; 2) Janice Wilson in 1954 (divorced 1966), one son; 3) Camille Rykowski in 1967 (divorced 1978); 4) Kathleen Brown in 1985. **Career:** Instructor in English, Cornell University, Ithaca, New York, 1955-57, University of Rochester, New York, 1957-58, and Wayne State University, Detroit, Michigan, 1959-67; professor of English and speech, Syracuse University, New York, 1968-77. Visiting teacher, Morehead Writers Conference, Kentucky, summer 1955, Antioch Writers Conference, Yellow Springs, Ohio, summers 1958-59, Narrative Poetry Workshop, State University of New York, Binghamton, 1977, Old Dominion University, Norfolk, Virginia, 1978-79, and University of Delaware, Newark, 1979-94. **Awards:** Ingram Merrill Foundation award, 1958; Longview award, 1959; Poetry Society of America Special Citation, 1960; Yaddo grant, 1960, 1961, 1965, 1976, 1977; American Academy grant, 1960; Pulitzer prize, 1960; Guinness award (UK), 1961; Ford fellowship, for drama, 1963; Miles award, 1966; National Endowment for the Arts grant, 1966; Guggenheim fellowship, 1972; Academy of American Poets fellowship, 1973; Centennial Medal (Romania), 1977. Honorary doctorate of letters: Allegheny College, 1991. **Member:** American Academy, 1972; PEN International; National Institute of Arts and Letters; fellow, Academy of American Poets, 1973. **Residence:** Erieville, New York.

PUBLICATIONS

Poetry

Heart's Needle. 1959.
After Experience: Poems and Translations. 1968.

Remains. 1970.
The Führer Bunker: A Cycle of Poems in Progress. 1977.
If Birds Build with Your Hair. 1979.
The Boy Made of Meat. 1983.
Magda Goebbels. 1983.
D.D. Byrde Calling Jennie Wrenn. 1984.
Heinrich Himmler: Platoons & Files. 1985.
The Kinder Capers. 1986.
Midnight Carnival. 1988.
The Death of Cock Robin. 1989.
Selected Poems, 1957-1987. 1993.
Each in His Season. 1993.
The Führer Bunker: The Complete Cycle. 1995.

Plays

The Führer Bunker (produced 1982).

Other

In Radical Pursuit: Critical Essays and Lectures. 1975.
Selected Translations. 1998.
After Images: Autobiographical Sketches. 1999.

Editor, *Syracuse Poems 1969.* 1969.

Translator, with Lore Segal, *Gallows Songs,* by Christian Morgenstern. 1967.
Translator, *Six Troubadour Songs.* 1977.
Translator, *Traditional Hungarian Songs.* 1978.
Translator, *Six Minnesinger Songs.* 1983.
Translator, *The Four Seasons.* 1984.

*

Bibliography: *Snodgrass: A Bibliography* by William White, 1960.

Critical Studies: *W.D. Snodgrass* by Paul L. Gaston, 1978; *The Poetry of W.D. Snodgrass: Everything Human* by Stephen Haven, 1993; *W.D. Snodgrass in Conversation with Philip Hoy, Between the Lines,* 1998; *Tuned and Under Tension: The Recent Poetry of W.D. Snodgrass* edited by Philip Raisor, 1999.

*   *   *

In his essay "A Poem's Becoming" (*In Radical Pursuit*), W.D. Snodgrass charts the evolution of his verse from the densely composed, ambiguous lyrics of his early years at the University of Iowa to a style of "becoming," in which a dramatic action unfolds through the speaker's intimate disclosures and self-revelations. But throughout his transition to a freer mode of lyric delivery, he has remained a technically conservative poet, writing mostly in tightly rhymed patterns and in set, metrical rhythms.

Although the craft of *Heart's Needle* and *After Experience* is at once lustrous and immaculate, Snodgrass is chiefly to be noted for having given voice to the inner life of the average middle-class American who came to maturity during World War II. Like **Robert Lowell,** under whom he studied, Snodgrass bases the speaker in his poems on his own life, from service in the war to graduate student days in Iowa to teaching posts around the country. His poems, however, are a careful selection of experiences that capture the disappointments, vicissitudes, and angst of a whole generation of Americans. The most emphatic theme of *Heart's Needle* and *After Experience* is a sense of an increasingly depersonalized identity as social life grows more rationalized.

Heart's Needle, which was awarded the Pulitzer Prize, begins with the disenchantments of returning veterans, who, in "Returned to Frisco, 1946," re-enter civilian life

> free to prowl all night
> Down streets giddy with lights, to sleep all day,
>
> Pay our own way and make our own selections;
> Free to choose just what they meant we should.

With this hint at authoritarianism, Snodgrass chronicles the life of the postwar American who carries pent-up, even violent, emotions under a carefully trained surface. Some of these poems have their speaker worry that he has grown too fearful and timid, as in "Home Town," where he has pursued, then eluded a bold young girl:

> Pale soul, consumed by fear
> of the living world you haunt,
> have you learned what habits lead you
> to hunt what you don't want;
> learned who does not need you;
> learned you are no one here?

The lovely, complex music of the final sequence, "Heart's Needle," captures this likeable, confused new Everyman as he struggles to remain parent to his young daughter. Snodgrass gives these ten poems his richest, most daringly metaphorical speech.

After Experience continues the Everyman chronicle of *Heart's Needle* but is less carefully structured and often less resonant in its language. Many of the poems take up themes of captivity, terror, potential violence, and disaster. Typical is "Lobsters in the Window," with its moving depiction of the near-frozen lobster seen through a restaurant window:

> He's fallen back with the mass
> Heaped in their common trench
> Who stir, but do not look out
> Through the rainstreaming glass,
> Hear what the newsboys shout,
> Or see the raincoats pass.

The closing section of the volume features skillful translations of a number of poets, particularly Rainer Maria Rilke.

The violence and turmoil that are subtexts of much of Snodgrass's poetry come to the surface in *The Führer Bunker,* which re-creates the last days of Adolf Hitler in his tunnels below the Reich Chancellory. Some of the scenes are harrowing indeed, and there are bold efforts to widen the poet's technical repertoire to include dramatic strategies, many of which are successfully deployed in the poems. Yet Snodgrass remains true to the confessional project of his earlier work, for these poems investigate the most painful complicity of his era (the Nazi atrocities), humanizing without exculpating the speakers of these fascist monologues. This humanization comes from an identification with the speakers, to work out issues of personal and universal psychic guilt. In an *American Poetry Review* interview with Elizabeth

Spires, Snodgrass said: "They may be more autobiographical than my first poems."

Painting (as well as music) has been a lasting fascination in Snodgrass's work, from the poems on Claude Monet, Edouard Manet, Vincent van Gogh and others in *After Experience,* to the Cock Robin poems inspired by DeLoss McGraw's paintings. McGraw, who had been reading Snodgrass's poems, began including a "W.D. Snodgrass" character in his paintings and sent slides to the poet, who in turn began writing poems based on the paintings. These poems, while sometimes medievally dark, exhibit a playfulness of language that results in a self-conscious, satiric mordancy. Snodgrass described the series to Spires as "a comic version of Orpheus."

—Paul Christensen, updated by Joseph O. Aimone

SNYDER, Gary (Sherman)

Born: San Francisco, California, 8 May 1930. **Education:** Lincoln High School, Portland, Oregon, graduated 1947; Reed College, Portland, 1947-51, B.A. in anthropology 1951; Indiana University, Bloomington, 1951; University of California, Berkeley, 1953-56; studied Buddhism in Japan 1956, 1959-64, 1965-68. **Family:** Married 1) Alison Gass in 1950 (divorced 1951); 2) the poet Joanne Kyger in 1960 (divorced 1964); 3) Masa Uehara in 1967, two sons. **Career:** Seaman, logger, trail crew member, and forest lookout, 1948-56; lecturer in English, University of California, Berkeley, 1964-65. Beginning 1986 professor, University of California, Davis. **Awards:** Bollingen grant, for Buddhist studies, 1966; American Academy prize, 1966; O'Hara prize, 1967; Levinson prize, 1968; Guggenheim fellowship, 1968; Pulitzer prize, 1975; Before Columbus Foundation award, 1984. **Residence:** California.

PUBLICATIONS

Collections

The Gary Snyder Reader: Prose, Poetry, and Translations, 1952-1998. 1999.

Poetry

Riprap. 1959.
Myths and Texts. 1960.
Hop, Skip, and Jump. 1964.
Nanao Knows. 1964.
The Firing. 1964.
Across Lamarack Col. 1964.
Riprap, and Cold Mountain Poems. 1965.
Six Sections from Mountains and Rivers without End. 1965; augmented edition, 1970.
Dear Mr. President, with Philip Whalen. 1965.
Three Worlds, Three Realms, Six Roads. 1966.
A Range of Poems. 1966.
The Back Country. 1968.
The Blue Sky. 1969.
Sours of the Hills. 1969.

Regarding Wave. 1969; augmented edition, 1970.
Anasazi. 1971.
Manzanita. 1971.
Plute Creek. 1971.
Clear Cut. N.d.
Manzanita (collection). 1972.
The Fudo Trilogy: Spell against Demons, Smokey the Bear Sutra, The California Water Plan. 1973.
Turtle Island. 1974.
All in the Family. 1975.
Song for Gaia. 1979.
True Night, illustrated by Bob Giorgio. 1980.
Axe Handles. 1983.
Left out in the Rain: Poems 1947-1984. 1986.
No Nature: New and Selected Poems. 1992.
Finding the Space. 1996.
Mountains and Rivers without End. 1996.

Other

Earth House Hold: Technical Notes and Queries to Fellow Dharma Revolutionaries. 1969.
Four Changes. 1969.
On Bread and Poetry: A Panel Discussion, with Lew Welch and Philip Whalen. 1977.
The Old Ways: Six Essays. 1977.
He Who Hunted Birds in His Father's Village: The Dimensions of a Haida Myth. 1979.
The Real Work: Interviews and Talks 1964-1979, edited by Scott McLean. 1980.
Passage through India. 1984.
The Practice of the Wild. 1990.
A Place in Space: Ethics, Aesthetics, and Watersheds: New and Selected Prose. 1995.

Editor, with Gutetsu Kanetsuki, *The Wooden Fish: Basic Sutras and Gathas of Rinzai Zen.* 1961.

*

Bibliography: *Snyder* by Katherine McNeil, 1983.

Critical Studies: "Snyder Issue" of *In Transit,* 1969; *The Tribal Dharma: An Essay on the Work of Snyder* by Kenneth White, 1975; *Snyder* by Bob Steuding, 1976; *Snyder* by Bert Almon, 1979; *Critical Essays on Gary Snyder* edited by Patrick D. Murphy, 1990, and *Understanding Gary Snyder* by Murphy, 1992; *Gary Snyder: Dimensions of a Life* edited by Jon Halper, 1991; "The Poetry of Gary Snyder" by Thomas Parkinson in *American Writing Today,* 1991; *Gary Snyder and the American Unconscious* by Tim Dean, 1991; *Identity, Masculinity, and Femininity in the Poetry of Gary Snyder* (dissertation) by Maura Gage, 1997.

*   *   *

Gary Snyder's writing is the chronicle of an itinerant visionary naturalist. His poetry contains few technical innovations but consolidates the Imagist ideas of **Ezra Pound** and **William Carlos Williams** and the free forms of Olson and the Beat poets. The poetry is wholly absorbed in the chronicle of the poet's wander-ings, his religious training in Japan, and his mythic and cultural perception of nature and experience.

Snyder organizes most of his poetry according to experience rather than theme. In *Riprap,* the crisp, taciturn Imagist poems narrate his days as "look out" and "choker" in the remote reaches of the American northwest and later his first trip to Japan on merchant tankers. The charm of these poems lies in the frank, modest, often tender lyric nature of the young observer, as in "Piute Creek":

> No one loves rock, yet we are here.
> Night chills. A flick
> In the moonlight
> Slips into Juniper shadow:
> Back there unseen
> Cold proud eyes
> Of cougar and Coyote
> Watch me rise and go.

Cold Mountain Poems contains translations of the Chinese poet, Han-shan, in which Snyder shows skill as an interpreter and cunning in the choice of a poet like himself in vision and inclination. Han-shan was a mountain recluse, whose regard for the mystery of nature is intense but not ponderous.

Myths and Texts, written before *Riprap* but not published until 1960, is the best orchestrated and developed of his works. By dividing the book into three parts, "Logging," "Hunting," and "Burning," Snyder creates an initiation ritual for his persona, who enters nature as destroyer (working for logging companies), then as hunter who must understand his prey to succeed, and who returns from these encounters awed by the power and will of nature. The themes of Snyder's early books establish the lines of development of his succeeding works. In *The Back Country,* he narrates experience from early years in Washington and Oregon, his departure for Japan in 1956, his later return to California. The volume has some notational lyrics, but the concision and intensity of most of the poems are deeply effective and dramatic.

Earth House Hold, a collection of prose, powerfully states the depth of his regard for the natural world and shows the maturing intellectual and spiritual subtlety of his mind over the twenty years the work records. Snyder, who became a cult figure of the ecology movement, carefully traces the evolution of his thought from jottings of natural phenomena to notes for the making of tribal culture in the post-industrial era. An able prose writer, Snyder is in command of both the facts and the theories of a new pastoral ideology.

Regarding Wave and *Turtle Island* continue the chronicle of the poet through family life and residence in the United States, where environmental abuse has stirred him to a lyricism of greater and greater activism. The final passages of *Turtle Island* are a series of prose tracts on conservation addressed directly to the reader. Snyder's subsequent book of poems, *Axe Handles,* pushes his poetic position to its limit of simplicity and directness of address. The language is shorn of all but the essential speech of daily life, and depends for its poetic effects strictly upon the assumptions and conclusions that are implicit in its delicate brevity. The title refers to the fact that one fashions the new handle from the old, and the human tool from the natural object, principles which Snyder himself exhibits with cunning throughout this collection.

Snyder's most recent collection of poetry, *No Nature,* and of essays, *The Practice of the Wild,* have re-established him as the foremost poet-philosopher of the modern deep-ecology movement, a movement whose tenets Snyder has incorporated in his writings with his interests in Eastern religions, indigenous peoples, bioregionalism, and feminism. Although Snyder asserts that nature should have a right to exist for its own sake, his essays reveal that he is most interested in humans' relationship with the natural world. Like **Henry David Thoreau** and Aldo Leopold, Snyder wonders aloud how simplicity and a study of the world around us can help us to reveal and understand the wilderness, as well as our own interior "wildness." Snyder's discussions of language, of politics, and of culture always return him to a contemplation of wilderness-as-place, to something palpable and real, as well as to a place where one can "more easily be touched by a larger-than-human, larger-than-personal view."

Although followers of Beat literature may associate Snyder with Japhy Ryder of **Jack Kerouac**'s *The Dharma Bums* (1958), or perhaps the cultural revolutions of the sixties and seventies, a close examination of the thirty-five years of writing contained in *No Nature* reveals Snyder to be a poet whose primary goal is to write from a native's knowledge of his home—whether it be a Zen monastery in Japan, a tent in rural Alaska, or his permanent home in California's Northern Sierras. Gary Snyder's poetry reveals a thinker who is far more than the sum of his eclectic influences; rather, Snyder as a poet evades all such limits, and, like Whitman, invites the reader to learn from the natural world with him:

> We are free to find our own way
> Over rocks—through the trees—
> Where there are no trails. The ridge and the forest
> Present themselves to our eyes and feet
> Which decide for themselves
> In their old learned wisdom of doing
> Where the wild will take us. (from "Off the Trail")

—Paul Christensen, updated by Andrew O. Jones

SONTAG, Susan

Born: New York City, 16 January 1933; took stepfather's name, c. 1945. **Education:** North Hollywood High School, Los Angeles, California; University of California at Berkeley, 1948-49; University of Chicago, 1949-51, B.A. in philosophy 1951; Harvard University, Cambridge, Massachusetts, 1952-57, M.A. in English 1954, M.A. in philosophy 1955, doctoral candidate in philosophy 1955-57; St. Anne's College, Oxford, England, 1957; University of Paris, 1957-58. **Family:** Married Philip Rieff in 1950 (divorced 1958); one son. **Career:** Worked as an English instructor at the University of Connecticut, Storrs, 1953-54; teaching fellow in philosophy at Harvard University, 1956-57; studied in England and Paris, 1957-58; moved to New York City and worked as an editor at *Commentary* magazine, 1959; lecturer in philosophy, City College of New York and Sarah Lawrence College, Bronxville, New York, 1959-60; instructor in religious studies, Columbia University, New York City, 1960-64; writer-in-residence, Rutgers University, New Brunswick, New Jersey, 1964-65; traveled to North Vietnam, 1968; traveled to Sweden to write and direct the film *Duet for Cannibals,* 1969; traveled to Sweden to write and direct the film *Brother Carl,* 1971; traveled to Israel to write and direct the documentary *Promised Lands,* 1974; co-organizer of the 48th

Congress of PEN International, New York City, 1986. **Awards:** American Association of University Women grant to study in England and Paris, France, 1957; Rockefeller Foundation fellowship, 1966, 1974; Guggenheim Memorial Foundation fellowship, 1966, 1975; George Polk Memorial award, 1966; National Book award nomination, 1966; Brandeis University Creative Arts award, 1975; National Institute and American Academy award for literature, 1976; Ingram Merrill Foundation award, 1976; National Book Critics Circle award, 1977; National Book Critics Circle award, 1978. **Member:** PEN American Center, president, 1987; American Academy of Arts and Letters; New York University Institute for the Humanities. **Residence:** New York City and Paris, France.

PUBLICATIONS

Collections

Against Interpretation and Other Essays. 1966.
Styles of Radical Will. 1969
On Photography. 1977.
Under the Sign of Saturn. 1980.
A Susan Sontag Reader, edited with an introduction by Elizabeth Hardwick. 1982.

Short Stories

I, etcetera. 1978.

Novels

The Benefactor. 1963.
Death Kit. 1978.
The Volcano Lover. 1992.
In America. 1999.

Plays

Alice in Bed (produced 1993). 1993.
Lady from the Sea, adaptation of Ibsen (produced 1997). In *Theater,* 1999.

Screenplays: *Duet for Cannibals,* produced 1969, published 1970; *Brother Carl,* produced 1971, published 1974; *Promised Lands,* 1974; *Unguided Tour* (adapted from Sontag's short story), 1983.

Prose

Trip to Hanoi. 1968.
Illness as Metaphor. 1978.
AIDS and Its Metaphors. 1989.
Cage, Cunningham, Johns: Dancers on a Plane, with Richard Francis. 1990.

Other

Editor and author of introduction, *Selected Writings,* by Antonin Artaud. 1976.
Editor and author of introduction, *A Roland Barthes Reader.* 1981.
Editor, *Best American Essays.* 1992.

*

Critical Studies: "Susan Sontag's Aesthetic" by P.R. Kher, in *Osmania Journal of English Studies* vol. 15, 1980; "The Noise of Decomposition: Response to Susan Sontag" by Steve Light, in *Sub-stance* vol. 26, 1980; "Sociology and Susan Sontag" by Joanne L. Finkelstein, in *Women's Studies International Quarterly* vol. 4, no. 2, 1981; "In a Gulf of Her Own" by Walter Kendrick, in *The Nation,* 23 October 1982; "Anti-Communism and the Sontag Circle" by Hilton Kramer, in *New Criterion* vol. 5, no. 1, 1986; *Susan Sontag: The Elegiac Modernist* by Sohnya Sayres, 1990; *Susan Sontag: Mind As Passion* by Liam Kennedy, 1995; *Conversations with Susan Sontag* edited by Leland A. Poague, 1995; *Discussion Notes on Susan Sontag's The Volcano Lover* by Lynne Strahan, 1996; in *Women Writers at Work: The Paris Review Interviews* edited by George Plimpton, 1998.

*   *   *

Since the publication in 1966 of her seminal collection of essays, *Against Interpretation and Other Essays,* Susan Sontag has generated an array of critical responses, ranging from adulation to bewilderment. Associated with both 1960s radicalism and arcane European intellectualism, Sontag has been labeled at various times as "the sensational Susan Sontag," "the high prophetess of high fashion," "Miss Camp," "the new dark lady of American letters," and even "Susie Creamcheese" by one baffled detractor. Sontag's work consistently has resisted facile comprehension or orderly categories. With her emphasis on high modernism, her repudiation of realism, and her privileging of aesthetic difficulty, Sontag espouses an aesthetic value derived from modern philosophers such as Theodor Adorno, Roland Barthes, and Jean-Paul Sartre.

Known primarily for her essays and reviews, Sontag has also authored three novels, written and directed four feature-length films, composed numerous short stories, and penned several plays. Sontag returns frequently in her writing to the question of the position of art and the role of the artist in what Sontag often views as a shattered, moribund, and deranged world. In her essay "The Pornographic Imagination," Sontag asserts that "most people in this society who aren't utterly mad are, at best, reformed or potential lunatics." In her critical study on Sontag, Sohnya Sayres contends that Sontag's intellectual heritage stems from the fusion of two cultures: the intellectual postmodernism associated with writers, artists, and philosophers such as Robbe-Grillet, Sarraute, Bataille, Artaud, Genet, Sartre, Lukács, and Barthes, and what has been called America's first intelligentsia. That is, the "quarrelsome, vigorous, politically committed," writers of New York, primarily those writers affiliated with journals such as *Partisan Review, Commentary, Politics,* and *Dissent.*

Born in New York City in 1933, Sontag (whose birth name remains a mystery, although it may have been Jacobson) was raised by relatives while her parents worked in the fur trade in Tianjin, China. Upon the death of Sontag's father in China from tuberculosis, Sontag's mother returned from abroad and took Sontag and her younger sister to live in Arizona. In 1945, Sontag's mother married Captain Sontag, whose surname Sontag adopted. The family then moved to Canoga Park, California, a suburb of Los Angeles located in the San Fernando Valley. Sontag has described her years in Los Angeles as ones of intellectual exile. A precocious student, Sontag graduated from North Hollywood High School at the age of fifteen and attended the University of California at Berkeley for one year before transferring to the University of Chicago. At seventeen, following a ten-day courtship, Sontag married

the sociologist Philip Rieff. After obtaining her B.A. in philosophy from the University of Chicago, Sontag moved to Boston with Rieff where she enrolled as a graduate student at Harvard University and acquired masters degrees in both English and philosophy. She then worked for several years towards a doctoral degree from Harvard in philosophy, but stopped short of completing her dissertation. During this time, Sontag also studied abroad at Cambridge University and the University of Paris. Following her return from Europe, Sontag divorced her husband and moved with her son David to New York City to begin her career as a freelance writer and novelist.

Sontag's first novel, *The Benefactor,* was published with acclaim in 1963. In a review article for *Book Week,* James R. Frakes determines that Sontag writes with "grace, with firmness, economy, and irony." Set in Paris, it focuses on the bizarre *pas de deux* of its two protagonists, Hippolyte, a 61-year-old dreamer, and Jean-Jacques, a professional boxer, novelist and prostitute. Sohnya Sayres reads *The Benefactor* as a *roman á clef* involving the French writers Antonin Artaud and Jean Genet as models for Hippolyte and Jean-Jacques. Ambitious and experimental, *The Benefactor* is reminiscent of the plays and novels of Samuel Beckett, a writer whose work Sontag characterizes as "delicate dramas of the withdrawn consciousness—pared down to essentials."

While *The Benefactor* was well-received critically, Sontag first attracted national attention with her essay "Notes on 'Camp'," written in 1964 for the *Partisan Review.* Here Sontag delineates the phenomenon of "camp" sensibility, a sensibility that celebrates the "artifice" of art with irony and whimsy. "Notes on 'Camp'" marked Sontag as an intellectual who was nonetheless intimate with the bizarre and the forbidden in modern culture. Sontag's tone of confidante and cognoscento in a concealed and tabooed world of art helped to transform her criticism, as Hilton Kramer writes in the *Atlantic,* into "a medium of intellectual scandal." And it was this, Kramer asserts, that won Sontag celebrity.

"Notes on 'Camp'" was republished in 1966 in Sontag's first collection of essays *Against Interpretation.* The ground-breaking title essay and its companion piece, "On Style," set up the intellectual parameters for the essays in *Against Interpretation,* which includes writings on Albert Camus, Michel Leiris, Georg Lukács, Jean Paul Sartre, Nathalie Sarraute, and Norman O. Brown. "Against Interpretation" and "On Style" read as manifestos for change as Sontag critiques American critical practice of the early and mid-1960s, which she argues consists of either reductive Freudianism or prescriptive aesthetics. Sontag feels that such approaches do violence to the works of art they purport to describe because they evince a desire to replace the work itself with the interpretation. Sontag feels that this is an instance of "the compliment which mediocrity often pays to genius," and she calls for a new formalism such as that practiced by literary critics like Roland Barthes, Walter Benjamin, and **Northrop Frye**. Ultimately, Sontag wants critics and viewers of art to stay focused on the materiality of the work of art and to develop an "erotics" of art. "What is important now is to recover our senses," writes Sontag. "We must learn to see more, to hear more, to feel more."

In her subsequent collections of essays, *Styles of Radical Will, On Photography,* and *Under the Sign of Saturn,* Sontag writes in a rebellious, political voice: a voice critical of racism in America, United States foreign policy, and, especially, the war in Vietnam. In her essay "What's Happening in America?," Sontag asserts that nothing can "redeem what this particular civilization has wrought upon the world." Although her political positions have shifted over the years, from enthusiastic support for Maoism in the 1960s to a controversial repudiation of all forms of Marxist governments in 1982 during a rally at the Town Hall in New York City, Sontag consistently has critiqued the status quo and argued in defense of the disenfranchised and the politically oppressed.

It was during the drafting of *On Photography* that Sontag was diagnosed with breast cancer, and her experience with cancer led her to write one of her most acclaimed works, *Illness as Metaphor.* Here Sontag delineates the metaphors used to describe illness, particularly tuberculosis, cancer, and insanity. These metaphors, Sontag argues, distort the event of the illness and involve the patient in a system of symbolic meaning that expands far beyond the occurrence of the disease itself. In *AIDS and its Metaphors,* written in 1989, Sontag extends her reflection on the persistent, and often deleterious, metaphors used by Western culture to think about disease.

Although Sontag's fame has come to be increasingly based on her nonfiction prose, she has continued to compose novels, short stories, screenplays, and plays. Indeed, in one interview Sontag asserts that she considers herself primarily a creative writer. Sontag's three novels, *The Benefactor, Death Kit,* and *The Volcano Lover,* have been highly lauded, but it is her short stories that have garnered the most unalloyed critical enthusiasm. Published in various periodicals including the *New Yorker* and the *Partisan Review,* Sontag gathered eight of her stories for her collection *I, etcetera,* which appeared in 1978. In a review article written for *Ms.* magazine, Laurie Stone writes that "Sontag's prose is especially supple and beautiful in [the story "Debriefing"]. It is a complaint, an elegy, a dialogue between two vivid personalities, one lost, the other uncertain of where to go."

Sontag's incisive, pugnacious, and elegant prose has had a profound impact on American letters. In an article written for the *Nation,* Walter Kendrick posits that Sontag exists in a "gulf of her own"—that is, the gulf between the American academy and the common reader. "The absence of an American intelligentsia makes Susan Sontag possible . . . . She has spent more than twenty years introducing us to that exotic creature, the European intellectual." Hilton Kramer writes of the "remarkable air of confidence" Sontag has brought to the "task of defending and codifying the values implicit in [the] movement to strip the arts of what she herself described as 'moral sentiment.'" In *Time,* Robert Hughes writes that "there are perhaps half a dozen critics in America whose silence would be a loss to writing itself, and Sontag is one of them."

—Catherine Judd

SOTO, Gary

Born: Fresno, California, 12 April 1952. **Education:** Roosevelt High School, Fresno, 1967-70; California State University, Fresno 1972-74, B.A. (magna cum laude) 1974; University of California, Irvine, 1974-76, M.F.A. 1976. **Family:** Married Carolyn Sadako Oda in 1975; one daughter. **Career:** Lecturer, fall 1977, assistant professor of English and Chicano Studies, 1979-84, associate professor, 1985-92, senior lecturer, 1992-95, University of California, Berkeley; Elliston Poet, University of Cincinnati, 1988; Martin Luther King/César Chávez/Rosa Parks Visiting Professor of English, Wayne State University, Detroit, Michigan, 1990. Juror:

National Endowment for the Arts, 1984-85, and PEN West Literary Prize, 1990. **Awards:** Academy of American Poets prize, 1975; *Nation* prize, 1975; International Poetry Forum United States award, 1976; *Poetry* Bess Hokin prize, 1978; Guggenheim fellowship, 1979-80; National Endowment for the Arts creative writing fellowship, 1981; *Poetry* Levinson Prize, 1984; Before Columbus Foundation American Book award, 1985; California Arts Council fellowship, 1988; California Library Association Beatty award, 1991, 1996. **Residence:** Berkeley, California.

PUBLICATIONS

Collection

New and Selected Poems. 1995.

Poetry

The Elements of San Joaquin. 1977.
The Tale of Sunlight. 1978.
Where Sparrows Work Hard. 1981.
Black Hair. 1985.
A Fire in My Hands. 1988.
Who Will Know Us? 1990.
Home Course in Religion. 1991.
Neighborhood Odes (for young adults). 1992.
Canto Familiar. 1995.
Junior College. 1997.
A Natural Man. 2000.

Prose

Living up the Street: Narrative Recollections. 1985.
Small Faces. 1986.
The Cat's Meow (for children). 1987.
Lesser Evils: Ten Quartets. 1988.
Baseball in April (for young adults). 1990.
A Summer Life. 1990.
Taking Sides (for young adults). 1991.
Pacific Crossing (for young adults). 1992.
Local News (for young adults). 1993.
Petty Crimes. 1998.
Buried Onions. 1998.

Plays

Novio Boy. 1997.
Nerdlandia. 1999.

Other

Editor, *California Childhood: Recollections and Stories of the Golden State.* 1988.
Editor, *Pieces of the Heart: New Chicano Fiction.* 1993.

*

Critical Studies: *Chicano Poetry: A Response to Chaos* by Juan Bruce-Novoa, 1982; *Chicano Literature: A Reference Guide* edited by Francisco A. Lomelí and Julio A. Martínez, 1985, and

Dictionary of Literary Biography, second series, vol. 82: *Chicano Writers* edited by Lomelí and Carl R. Shirley, 1989.

*   *   *

The son of Americans of Mexican descent, Gary Soto is not kind when describing his upbringing. In an unpublished interview (25 May 1987), he stated, "I do not come from a culturally rich family in the academic sense or educational sense of the word. We had our own culture which was more like the culture of poverty, as I like to describe it." Such acute awareness of his socioeconomic background is what gives Soto's poetry and prose their aesthetic and political edge. Soto is a careful stylist of his storytelling voice and pays close attention to matters of "subject and craft," as he stated in the same interview. Consequently, in both poetry and prose, Soto has succeeded in developing a narrative poetics that balance political and aesthetic concerns and have catapulted his work into the canon of American literature. Among the critics of his work there is widespread agreement that, as Patricia De La Fuente phrased it in *Revista Chicano-Riquena,* "Soto displays an exceptionally high level of linguistic sophistication." Soto received the Academy of American Poets Prize in 1975, was nominated for a Pulitzer Prize in 1978, received a Guggenheim Fellowship in 1979, and has won awards for individual collections of poetry. His first book of poetry, *The Elements of San Joaquin,* won the United States Award of the International Poetry Forum. *The Tale of Sunlight,* his second poetry collection, was a finalist for the prestigious Lenore Marshall Prize for Poetry. In 1978, *Poetry* awarded him the Bess Hokin Prize and in 1984 the Levinson Prize, the highest honor the journal offers. His first prose work, *Living up the Street,* received the Before Columbus Foundation American Book Award. Soto has also turned his talents towards writing children's literature, once again successfully demonstrating the general appeal of his storytelling voice.

Soto was born in Fresno, California, on April 12, 1952, and it is to this geographical and urban space that he returns again and again in his stories. When he was five, he was struck by tragedy when his father, only twenty-seven years old, was killed in an accident at work. The part that this tragic event has had in shaping the literary craft of Gary Soto cannot be overestimated. When he reached eighteen and entered Fresno City College with the intention to study geography, his childhood pain surfaced with great power and literally led him to the craft of poetry. Looking through the stacks of the library at Fresno City College, Soto one day came across an anthology of American poetry in which he found Edward Field's poem "Unwanted." In Field's poem, Soto saw that his own experience with loss and lack was less an individual suffering and more, as he put it in the unpublished interview, "a human pain." Field's poem made Soto aware of the power of language in its poetic function to capture an aspect of experience that is not merely subjective and personal but general and even universal. In 1972 and 1973, Soto studied at California State University with poet Philip Levine, whom he describes in the unpublished interview as "a master of the nuts and bolts of how to read a poem—how to analyze and how to critique a poem." Under Levine's tutelage, Soto learned the concrete linguistic tools for shaping language into poetry and refined his sense of how to give the universal expression in the particular. When in 1976 Soto's *The Elements of San Joaquin* emerged as the winner of the International Poetry Forum Award, Soto demonstrated that he had learned the nuts and bolts of writing poetry well. Thereafter, the rapid appearance of *The Tale of Sunlight, Where Sparrows Work Hard,* and *Black Hair,* each work displaying an increasingly more mature and self-confident poetic diction, showed beyond any doubt that Soto's success was no accident and that his gift was truly in poetry. Subsequent poetical works like *Who Will Know Us?* and *Home Course in Religion* have helped to strengthen Soto's stature as a poet of the American landscape.

Furthermore, the prose volume *Living up the Street* is significant because its marks a turn in Soto's career towards the creation of a narrative poetics that cuts across the genres of poetry and prose. The autobiographical prose works *Living up the Street, Small Faces, Lesser Evils: Ten Quartets,* and *A Summer Life* bring poetic diction and the short autobiographical essay together. Characteristic of this experimentation is Soto's concern for showing rather than telling. Speaking of how he conceived the idea for *Living up the Street,* Soto stated in the unpublished interview that the work was meant to be "a set of narrative recollections with very little commentary. . . . I made a conscious effort not to tell anything but just present the stories and let the reader come up with assumptions about the book—just show not tell—which is what my poetry has been doing for years." It is from showing and not telling that Soto derives that quality in his stories his critics tend to identify with their ability to blend the universal with the particular. Critic Raymund Paredes wrote in the *Rocky Mountain Review:* "Soto establishes his acute sense of ethnicity, and, simultaneously, his belief that certain emotions, values, and experiences transcend ethnic boundaries and allegiances." It is Soto's commitment to both the universal and the particular of human experience that translates into the politics and aesthetics of his stories. This dual concern for art and politics is what makes Soto's narrative poetics part of the postmodern aesthetics that hold sway in the American literary scene. Writing for *Poetry,* critic Alan Williamson paid Soto a high compliment when he put him shoulder to shoulder with two other American poets, one his former mentor: "Soto may be the most exciting poet of poverty in America to emerge since **James Wright** and Philip Levine."

Soto's *oeuvre* is made up of roughly three branches: poetry, prose, and literature for young adults. The third branch is a relatively late development and includes *The Cat's Meow, Baseball in April, Taking Sides, Pacific Crossing, Neighborhood Odes,* and *Local News.* However, Soto's stature in the American literary canon stems chiefly from his literary production in the first two branches. From his first work of poetry, Soto has demonstrated that he is a poet of the American landscape. *The Elements of San Joaquin* brings to light a layer of history that is integral to the American experience. Divided into three sections, the book provides a multifaceted perspective on the currents of life that have characterized the Fresno, California, of Soto's youth. The first section opens with a collage of sharply and vividly drawn characters who act out their lives in a Fresno that is hostile and unkind to human life. The next section focuses on the San Joaquin Valley of California as Soto draws it with imagery from the four elements of the Greek philosophers: earth, air, water, and fire. Soto identifies closely with the land of his birth, and, in that identification, the political tone of his voice is evident when he writes, "Already I am becoming the valley, / a soil that sprouts nothing / for any of us." The closing section makes the Chicano experience that Soto's verses are illuminating more personal but no less political, chronicling as it does the demise of Braly Street, where Soto spent his formative childhood years.

The Tale of Sunlight, Soto's second book, puts an emphasis on Latin America that gives this work strong political overtones. Indeed, the final poem of section two, "How an Uncle Became Gray," is dedicated to Columbian writer Gabriel García Márquez, perhaps the best known practitioner of magical realism. In "The Map," Soto places his verses in solidarity with all Latin America. The final section of *The Tale of Sunlight,* with its strong flavor of magical realism, reinforces the political solidarity between Soto's Chicano verses and Latin America. It is for this work that critic Alan Williamson classes Soto with Levine.

In 1980, Soto published two chapbooks of poetry, *Father Is a Pillow Tied to a Broom* and *Como Arbustos de Niebla.* The former work vividly foregrounds the theme of the absent father. The latter is a bilingual English-Spanish edition of eight Soto poems translated into Spanish with an introduction by Ernesto Trejo. This work coincides with Soto's year in Mexico on a Guggenheim fellowship. *Where Sparrows Work Hard* contains the images, sounds, people, and urban settings of California and tells the many stories of particular people who live out their hard lives in those settings. Always enunciated as a part of the Chicano community, Soto's storytelling voice often speaks of those with whom he has worked, the attention to the details of their lives producing a discourse that once again merges the political with the aesthetic. What critic Bruce Weigl said of this work in *Poet Lore* attests to the growing maturity of Soto's verse: "*Where Sparrows Work Hard* represents a crystallization of the stripped down, clear observations that run throughout Soto's canon. Most of his lines are short, seldom more than three beats, and most are enjambed so that there is [a] shunting effect as we are forced to pound down through the poems which seem to accumulate power as they move to some chilling inevitability."

With *Black Hair,* Soto's poetic diction becomes mature and confident, the themes of death and childhood taking on deeper philosophical resonance. More than previous works, *Black Hair* seems more closely tied to the sociolinguistic context in which Soto grew up. The angry tone of *The Elements* here resurfaces transformed into a quiet unease, sharing discursive space with an equally strong sense of triumph and joy. This mood of unease mixed with a certain sense of joy is a trait characterizing the ensuing works of poetry *Who Will Know Us?* and *Home Course in Religion,* as well as the prose works. Celebrating the everyday life of California, both these works solidify Soto's position as a poet of the American landscape. *Who Will Know Us?* aims to unveil a broad panoramic view of California. The poem entitled "At the All-Night Cafe," with its opening clause declaring "America is at work," offers a description that is quintessential Americana—a diner, a waitress, customers, controlled mayhem. In the title poem of the book, Soto's poetic diction turns more abstract as his verses look to the craft of poetry for the possibility of life after death. Likewise, *Home Course in Religion* also displays a similar kind of secular faith. Through this collection of poetry, Soto shows himself concerned with his childhood Catholicism, even if he does not wholly embrace it. While a certain sense of joy accompanies many of the poems in this collection, propositionally Soto's verses refuse any facile conception of religious faith and opt for action over dogma. For instance, in "The Asking," Soto writes a poem about his work teaching karate to underprivileged children. Reminded of his own upbringing, and thinking that what these children need is love, Soto adds the poetic line, "Something like Christ but not Christ." Thus, the world Soto describes in his poetry, from *Elements* to *Home Course,* is an enigmatic one, where value is not easy to fix, often

hostile but never altogether devoid of a measure of hope. A similar thematics can be traced in Soto's prose works.

Living up the Street marks an important turn in Soto's career, signifying his experimentation with a postmodern mode of exposition, the petit récit. That is, Soto, conscious of the prescription not to mix the diction of poetry with that of prose, nevertheless begins to write in the short essay genre, using a highly stylized but economical syntax. The result of this stylistic shifting and change in genre has once again shown Soto's ability to bring politics and art together. Because the emphasis in *Living up the Street* is on showing not telling, describing and not explaining, Soto's politics come across as unobtrusive to the stories he has to tell. Because they are short and economical, the stories resist the impulse to want to say everything about the politics of the Chicano experience in California from the 1950s into contemporary times. The main story lines are simple in their mode of reference, bringing to the foreground the small day-to-day events of Soto's life as a young boy growing up among both the Chicano and Anglo poor of Fresno, California. As reviewer Geoffrey Dunn put it in the *San Francisco Review of Books,* "the twenty-one autobiographical short stories assembled here recall with amazing detail the day-to-day traumas, tragedies and occasional triumphs of growing up brown in the American Southwest." Soto has adopted essentially the same strategy with all his prose works, with equal success. Alicia Fields, in the *Bloomsbury Review,* wrote of *Small Faces:* "Although *Small Faces* contains stories about major events in the author's life . . . this is primarily a book about small but telling moments." *Lesser Evils: Ten Quartets,* with its allusion to **T.S. Eliot**'s "Four Quartets," adds a layer of complexity to the compositional strategy adopted in the earlier works. Like Eliot's long poem, *Lesser Evils* is concerned with things spiritual, Soto's Catholicism, the ephemeral and the invariant of human life. Unlike that work, however, Soto's *Quartets* is ambivalent toward the religious motif that structures it, closer to *Who Will Know Us?* and *Home Course in Religion* in its secular spirit. Taking note of this added complexity of composition, a reviewer for *Publisher's Weekly* summed up the strength of this work: "While much pleasure arises from Soto's poetic talent for capturing small, telling details of his life, the book's depth lies in its quartet structure."

Soto applies the same subtlety of compositional structure to the thematics of his text in *A Summer Life,* in which Soto works with the metaphor of the edge of the world to give his stories richer thematic coherence. That is, throughout the stories, the reader finds Soto, at various stages of his life, exploring the limits of his world and wondering what lies beyond those limits. The closing story, "The River," brings theme and structure together in such a way that the reader sees Soto at seventeen years of age yet unable to dream of the power of language to open new frontiers, with *A Summer Life* standing as a testament to what happens once he does.

—Hector Torres

SPENCER, Elizabeth

Born: Carrollton, Missouri, 19 July 1921. **Education:** Belhaven College, B.A. 1942; Vanderbilt University, M.A. 1943. **Family:** Married John Rusher in 1956. **Career:** Writer. Professor of creative writing, Concordia University, Montreal, 1976-86; professor of creative writing, University of North Carolina, Chapel Hill, 1986-92. **Awards:** Women's Democratic Committee award, 1949; national Institute of Arts and Letters award, 1952; Guggenheim fellowship, 1953; Rosenthal Foundation award from American Academy of Arts and Letters, 1956; Kenyon College fellow in fiction, 1957; McGraw-Hill fiction award, 1960; Bryn Mawr College Donnelly fellow, 1962; Henry Bellamann award for creative writing, Southwestern University, 1968; Award of Merit Medal for the Short Story, American Academy and Institute of Arts and Letters, 1983; senior award grant in literature, 1988; Dos Passos award for Fiction, 1992; Salem award for literature, 1992: North Carolina Governor's award for literature, 1994. D.L.: Concordia University, 1988.

PUBLICATIONS

Fiction

Fire in the Morning. 1948.
This Crooked Way. 1952.
The Voice at the Back Door. 1956.
The Light in the Piazza. 1960.
Knights and Dragons. 1965.
No Place for an Angel. 1967.
Ship Island and Other Stories. 1968.
The Snare. 1972.
The Stories of Elizabeth Spencer. 1981.
Marilee. 1981.
The Salt Line. 1984.
Jack of Diamonds and Other Stories. 1988.
The Night Travellers. 1991.
On the Gulf. 1991.

Play

For Lease or Sale (produced 1989).

Other

Conversations with Elizabeth Spencer. 1991.
Landscapes of the Heart: A Memoir. 1997.

*

Critical Studies: *Self and Community in the Fiction of Elizabeth Spencer* by Terry Roberts, 1994; "Elizabeth Spencer: The Development of a Writer" by Laurie Champion, in *The Mississippi Quarterly,* 1996.

*   *   *

Though perhaps best remembered for the Italian tales she wrote after she left the South in the 1950s, Elizabeth Spencer first made her reputation as the author of three acclaimed novels set in the Mississippi hill country of her youth. A native of Carrollton, Mississippi (pop.475), who grew up just south of Faulkner's own "postage stamp" of soil, Spencer began her career in the waning days of the southern literary renaissance, writing about family, race, and religion in novels that evoked the same "old verities and truths of the heart" that had inspired a generation of southern writers before her. Following the success of these early efforts, Spencer traveled abroad, first to Italy in the 1950s and then to Canada, where she lived the next three decades before returning home to the South. These experiences resulted in a body of work as far ranging as her travels—novels and stories that draw on the foreign and the familiar to evoke what she calls the "permanent landscape of the heart."

In Spencer's Mississippi novels the path to reconciliation inevitably leads to the past. How her characters respond to the burden of history—be it the long-standing blood feud between the Gerrard and Armstrong families in her first novel, *Fire in the Morning,* or the legacy of racial hatred handed down from father to son in *The Voice at the Back Door*—determines their survival as individuals and as a community. The protagonists of these early novels tend to be either tragic heroes or failed visionaries—men such as Duncan Harper, the ex-All-American football player in *The Voice at the Back Door,* whose fateful simplicity prevents him from seeing the evil around him, or Amos Dudley, the "self-styled saint" in *This Crooked Way,* whose religious fanaticism threatens to ruin his family and everyone around him. More memorable perhaps are those on the periphery—displaced southerners such as Kerney Woolbright, the Yale graduate and New South ideologue who knows the South mainly through Faulkner novels, and Marcia Mae Hunt, the prodigal daughter who returns home to a South different from the one she left.

Even in works with more cosmopolitan settings, Spencer maintains her southern focus on the community and the individual within it. In the panoramic novel *No Place for an Angel,* a cast of rootless jet-setters wanders from Washington to Texas to Italy on a "dangerous journey" through the moral wasteland of the 1960s. Adrift in a "grey world," where good and evil have lost all meaning, they languish in a kind of transcendental homelessness that only intensifies their preoccupation with the world they have left behind. In *The Light in the Piazza,* Spencer's "little tall tale" about the city of Florence, an American woman plays a "tricky game" with the father of her daughter's young Italian suitor. Though Margaret Johnson succeeds in marrying off the beautiful but feeble-minded Clara to the unsuspecting Naccarelli family, she cannot help but question in the end whether she has indeed done "the right thing." Like the light that suffuses her tale, shining with a brilliance that reveals everything and nothing, Spencer's fable obscures its truths with a blinding ambiguity.

In Spencer's tales of "ironic liberation," triumphs are not necessarily victories, and discoveries often go unrewarded. In *Knights and Dragons* Martha Ingram frees herself from the memory of her ex-husband only to find that her freedom is merely dissolution, a "line of dark across a field of sun." Once a captive to the past, she now stands alone in the definitive season of her life, a "friend . . . to any landscape" but with no place to come to. In *The Salt Line* Arnie Carrington battles storms real and metaphorical as he tries to rebuild his life on the Gulf Coast in the aftermath of his own "hurricane-blasted" past. Only after he relinquishes his hold on the island he loves does this aging Prospero find the "bright redemption of love" that he seeks.

Many of Spencer's characters are outsiders who find refuge in unexpected places. For Nancy Lewis, the Mississippi teen who swims mermaidlike beneath the surface of ordinary life in "Ship Island," that refuge is the sea, where she drifts alone beyond the reach of the shore, lulled to sleep in the waters off the coast. In *The Snare* Julia Garrett leaves her respectable life in Audubon Place for the mean streets of the New Orleans underworld, where she learns firsthand how "people draw life from the crooked world" around them. This interest in subterfuges and countercultures carries over into later works such as "Jean Pierre," a contemporary fable about French-Canadian separatism, and *The Night Travellers*, a novel that follows the lives of anti-Vietnam War activists in Canada as they carry out their underground campaign of resistance in the 1960s.

Whether writing about the South or regions beyond, Spencer has continued to draw on those "traditional Southern sources of family and history," which have long been the vital center of her work. If her years abroad taught her anything, it was, she has said, that "you could be southern . . . anywhere you found yourself." Only when we know who we are and where we have been, said Spencer, can we begin to appreciate "the human and the humane, the decency that struggles against the indecent, the values of love, fairness, and justice that cannot live unless they are lived."

—Brian Carpenter

STAFFORD, Jean

Born: Covina, California, 1 July 1915. **Education:** University of Colorado, Boulder, B.A. 1936, M.A. 1936; University of Heidelberg, 1936-37. **Family:** Married 1) Robert Lowell in 1940 (divorced 1948); 2) Oliver Jensen in 1950 (divorced 1953); 3) the writer A.J. Liebling in 1959 (died 1963). **Career:** Instructor, Stephens College, Columbia, Missouri, 1937-38; secretary, *Southern Review,* Baton Rouge, Louisiana, 1940-41; lecturer, Queens College, Flushing, New York, spring 1945; fellow, Center for Advanced Studies, Wesleyan University, Middletown, Connecticut, 1964-65; adjunct professor, Columbia University, New York, 1967-69. **Awards:** American Academy grant, 1945; Guggenheim fellowship, 1945, 1948; National Press Club award, 1948; O. Henry award, 1955; Ingram-Merrill grant, 1969; Chapelbrook grant, 1969; Pulitzer prize, 1970. **Member:** American Academy, 1970. **Died:** 26 March 1979.

PUBLICATIONS

Fiction

Boston Adventure. 1944.
The Mountain Lion. 1947.
The Catherine Wheel. 1952.
Children Are Bored on Sunday (stories). 1953.
New Short Novels, with others, edited by Mary Louise Aswell. 1954.
Stories, with others. 1956; as *A Book of Stories,* 1957.
Bad Characters (stories). 1964.
Selected Stories. 1966.
The Collected Stories. 1969.

Other

Elephi: The Cat with the High I.Q. (for children). 1962.
The Lion and the Carpenter and Other Tales from the Arabian Nights Retold (for children). 1962.
A Mother in History (on Marguerite C. Oswald). 1966.

*

Bibliography: *Stafford: A Comprehensive Bibliography* by Wanda Avila, 1983.

Critical Studies: *The Young Girl in the West: Disenchantment in Jean Stafford's Short Fiction* by Mary Ellen Williams-Walsh, 1982; *Stalking the Feline Female: The Significance of Hunting in the Cub of the Panther and the Mountain Lion* by Carol Steinhagen, 1990; *Jean Stafford: The Savage Heart* by Charlotte Margolis Goodman, 1990; *Jean Stafford: A Study of the Short Fiction* by Mary Ann Wilson, 1996.

*   *   *

The art of Jean Stafford is the art of the miniaturist—the quickly realized short story, told with economy and control, is her ideal form. Many of her stories were published in the *New Yorker* and the *Saturday Evening Post,* and it is easy to detect the economy and tautness that come from the pressures of journalistic publication. "Miss Bellamy was old and cold," begins "The Hope Chest," "and she lay quaking under an eiderdown which her mother had given her when she was a girl of seventeen." In a sense, the half-dozen pages that follow merely expand the implications of that sentence. Typically, the story is rooted in the old woman's memories of her childhood and years as a young woman: most of Stafford's writing deals with loneliness perceived by the child who suffers it or by the adult who was once the child.

Her own artistic eye, in fact, is that of the child poised on the brink of adult experience and focusing on the concrete details of surrounding life. Her most successful writing enlarges its range by suggesting wider experience through symbols such as the mountain lion of her second novel, which represents the untamed, authentic power of the natural world into which the two young children of the story are plunged. The horrific violence that concludes the novel comes not from the lion but from man; like many of the stories, the work simmers with a brooding though suppressed sense of the brutality of experience.

Stafford's other novels, *Boston Adventure* and *The Catherine Wheel,* are less successful, possibly because they lack such a convincing controlling symbol. As is often the case in Stafford's work, both novels are concerned with young people, but the world these young grow into suggests imprisonment and failure rather than fulfillment and enrichment. But although these are not her best works, their prose is as fine as in any of her stories.

—Patrick Evans

STAFFORD, William (Edgar)

Born: Hutchinson, Kansas, 17 January 1914. **Education:** University of Kansas, Lawrence, B.A. 1937, M.A. 1947; University of Iowa, Iowa City, Ph.D. 1954. **Military Service:** Conscientious objector during World War II; active in pacifist organizations, and beginning 1959 member, Oregon Board, Fellowship of Reconciliation. **Family:** Married Dorothy Hope Frantz in 1944; two daughters and two sons. **Career:** Member of the English department, 1948-54, 1957-80, and professor emeritus 1980-93, Lewis and Clark College, Portland, Oregon; assistant professor of English, Manchester College, Indiana, 1955-56; professor of English, San Jose State College, California, 1956-57; consultant in poetry,

Library of Congress, Washington, D.C., 1970-71; U.S. Information Agency lecturer in Egypt, Iran, Pakistan, India, Nepal, and Bangladesh, 1972. **Awards:** Yaddo fellowship, 1955; Oregon Centennial prize, for poetry and for short story, 1959; National Book award, 1963; Shelley Memorial award, 1964; American Academy award, 1966, 1981; Guggenheim fellowship, 1966; Melville Cane award, 1974; Poet Laureate of Oregon, 1975-93. D.Litt.: Ripon College, Wisconsin, 1965; Washington College, Chesterton, Maryland, 1981. L.H.D.: Linfield College, McMinnville, Oregon, 1970. **Died:** 28 August 1993.

PUBLICATIONS

Collection

The Way It Is: New and Selected Poems. 1998.

Poetry

Poems. 1959(?).
West of Your City. 1960.
Traveling through the Dark. 1962.
Five American Poets, with others, edited by Thom Gunn and Ted Hughes. 1963.
Five Poets of the Pacific Northwest, with others, edited by Robin Skelton. 1964.
The Rescued Year. 1966.
Eleven Untitled Poems. 1968.
Weather. 1969.
Allegiances. 1970.
Temporary Facts. 1970.
Poems for Tennessee, with Robert Bly and William Matthews. 1971.
Someday, Maybe. 1973.
That Other Alone. 1973.
In the Clock of Reason. 1973.
Going Places. 1974.
North by West, with John Haines, edited by Karen and John Sollid. 1975.
Late, Passing Prairie Farm. 1976.
Braided Apart, with Kim Robert Stafford. 1976.
Stories That Could Be True: New and Collected Poems. 1977.
The Design in the Oriole. 1977.
Two about Music. 1978.
All about Light. 1978.
Passing a Creche. 1978.
Tuft by Puff. 1978.
Around You, Your House; and A Catechism. 1979.
The Quiet of the Land. 1979.
Absolution. 1980.
Things That Happen When There Aren't Any People. 1980.
Sometimes Like a Legend. 1981.
A Glass Face in the Rain: New Poems. 1982.
Roving across Fields: A Conversation and Uncollected Poems 1942-1982, edited by Thom Tammaro. 1983.
Segues: A Correspondence in Poetry, with Marvin Bell. 1983.
Smoke's Way: Poems from Limited Editions (1968-1981). 1983.
Listening Deep. 1984.
Stories, Storms, and Strangers. 1984.
Brother Wind. 1986.
An Oregon Message. 1987.

You and Some Other Characters. 1987.
Annie Over. 1988.
Writing the World. 1988.
Fin, Feather, Fur. 1989.
A Scripture of Leaves. 1989.
The Kansas Poems of William Stafford, edited by Denise Low. 1990.
How to Hold Your Arms When It Rains. 1990.
History Is Loose Again. 1991.
Passwords. 1991.
The Long Sigh the Wind Makes. 1991.
Holding onto the Grass. 1992.
My Name Is William Tell. 1992.
The Animal That Drank Up Sound. 1992.
The Darkness around Us Is Deep: Selected Poems, edited by Robert Bly. 1993.
Listening to the River: Seasons in the American West, photographs by Robert Adams. 1994.
Learning to Live in the World: Earth Poems. 1994.
The Methow River Poems. 1995.
Even in Quiet Places: Poems. 1996.

Other

Down in My Heart (experience as a conscientious objector during World War II). 1947.
Friends to This Ground: A Statement for Readers, Teachers, and Writers of Literature. 1967.
Leftovers, A Care Package: Two Lectures. 1973.
Writing the Australian Crawl: Views on the Writer's Vocation. 1978.
You Must Revise Your Life (interview). 1987.
Getting the Knack: Twenty Poetry Writing Exercises, with Stephen Dunning. 1992.
Who Are You Really, Wanderer: Pages in the Language of Respect and Conciliation. 1993.
The Mozart Myths: A Critical Reassessment. 1993.
Crossing Unmarked Snow: Further Views on the Writer's Vocation. 1997.

Editor, with Frederick Candelaria, *The Voices of Prose.* 1966.
Editor, *The Achievement of Brother Antoninus: A Comprehensive Selection of His Poems with a Critical Introduction.* 1967.
Editor, with Robert H. Ross, *Poems and Perspectives.* 1971.
Editor, with Clinton F. Larson, *Modern Poetry of Western America.* 1975.
Editor, with Stanley Plumly and Bill Henderson, *The Pushcart Prize X.* 1985.
Editor, with Steven Lautermilch, *Meaning of No.* 1993.

Translator, with Aijaz Ahmad and Adrienne Rich, *Poems by Ghalib.* 1969.
Translator, *Window on the Black Sea: Bulgarian Poetry in Translation.* 1992.

Recordings: *Capturing People of the South Wind: On Creative Process,* 1972; *Troubleshooting,* 1984.

*

Critical Studies: "Stafford Issue" of *Northwest Review,* spring 1974, and of *Modern Poetry Studies,* spring 1975; *Four Poets and* *the Emotive Imagination* by George S. Lensing and Ronald Moran, 1976; *The Mark to Turn: A Reading of Stafford's Poetry* by Jonathan Holden, 1976; *William Stafford* by David A. Carpenter, 1986; *Theodore Roethke, William Stafford and Gary Snyder: The Ecological Metaphor as Transformed Regionalism* by Lavs Nordstrom, 1989; *Understanding William Stafford* by Judith Kitchen, 1989; *On William Stafford: The Worth of Local Things* edited by Tom Andrews, 1995; *Writing the World: Understanding William Stafford* by Judith Kitchen, 1999.

*   *   *

William Stafford's poetry exemplifies the best of what is left of American transcendentalism. Like **Ralph Waldo Emerson** and **Henry David Thoreau**, he regards the human imagination as "salvational," and many of his poems are about the capacity of the imagination to derive meaning and awe from the world. Like the transcendentalists, Stafford also regards the natural world as a possible model for human behavior:

> The earth says every summer have a ranch
> that's minimum: one tree, one well, a landscape
> that proclaims a universe—sermon
> of the hills, hallelujah mountain,
> highway guided by the way the world is tilted.

But, although in Stafford's poems Nature ("the landscape of justice") evinces both a glimmer of consciousness and a strict propriety of process, it contains few prescriptions definite enough to be useful guides to human behavior. It provides only distant analogues. Nor is Nature a comforting maternal presence. If there be any one lesson that the human species might draw from natural process, it is humility, to know one's place, to have local priorities. Stafford has an organic conception of poetry, which also recalls the transcendentalists. For him, poetry is a manifestation of the "deepest [truest] place we have":

> They call it regional, this relevance—
> the deepest place we have: in this pool forms
> the model of our land, a lonely one,
> responsive to the wind. Everything we own
> has brought us here: from here we speak.

Composition is thus, for Stafford, a means of bringing to light the dark processes of the self:

> I do tricks in order to know:
> Careless I dance,
> then turn to see
> the mark to turn God left for me.

The style of Stafford's poems is quiet and colloquial. Few of them are very long. Throughout his poetry, certain words recur with a symbolic meaning. The most prominent of these words are "dark," "deep," "cold," "far," "God," and "home." Many of his earlier poems are rhymed, some heavily, some with slant or touch rhyme. His earlier work shows a fondness for sprung rhythm rather than quantitative metric. Since 1960 his work has grown steadily more relaxed in form and more rhetorically inventive. Typical of such inventiveness is the poem "Important Things":

> Like Locate Knob out west
> of town where maybe the world
> began. Like the rusty wire
> sagged in the river for a harp
> when floods go by.
> Like a way of talking, the slur
> in hello to mean you and God
> still think about justice.
> Like being alone, and you are
> alone, like always.
> You always are.

—Jonathan Holden

STEELE, Wilbur Daniel

Born: Greensboro, North Carolina, 17 March 1886. **Education:** Germany, 1889-92, and at schools in Colorado, 1892-1900; University of Denver Preparatory School, 1900-03; University of Denver, 1903-07, B.A. 1907; Boston Museum School of Fine Arts, 1907-08; Academie Julian, Paris, 1908. **Family:** Married 1) Margaret Thurston in 1913 (died 1931), two sons; 2) Norma Mitchell in 1932 (died 1967). **Career:** Freelance writer; lived in Provincetown, Massachusetts, until 1929: co-founder, Provincetown Players, 1915; lived in Chapel Hill, North Carolina, 1929-32, Hamburg, Connecticut, 1932-56, and Old Lyme, Connecticut, 1956-64; in rest home and hospital after 1964. **Award:** D.Litt.: University of Denver, 1932. **Died:** 26 May 1970.

PUBLICATIONS

Fiction

Storm. 1914.
Land's End and Other Stories. 1918.
The Shame Dance and Other Stories. 1923.
Isles of the Blest. 1924.
Taboo. 1925.
Urkey Island (stories). 1926.
The Man Who Saw through Heaven and Other Stories. 1927.
Meat. 1928; as *The Third Generation,* 1929.
Tower of Sand and Other Stories. 1929.
Undertow. 1930.
Sound of Rowlocks. 1938.
That Girl from Memphis. 1945.
The Best Stories. 1945.
Diamond Wedding. 1950.
Full Cargo: More Stories. 1951.
Their Town. 1952.
The Way to the Gold. 1955.
Wilbur Daniel Steele: Stories. 1996.

Plays

Contemporaries (produced 1915).
Not Smart (produced 1916). In *The Terrible Woman.* 1925.
The Giants' Stair (produced 1924). 1924.
Ropes, in *The Terrible Woman. . . .* 1925.

The Terrible Woman and Other One Act Plays. 1925.
Post Road, with Norma Mitchell (produced 1934). 1935.
How Beautiful with Shoes, with Anthony Brown, from the story
by Steele (produced 1935).
Luck, in *One Hundred Nonroyalty Plays,* edited by William
Kozlenko. 1941.

*

Critical Studies: *Steele* by Martin Bucco, 1972; *Wilbur Daniel Steele's Influence on William Faulkner's Revision of "Beyond,"* in *Mississippi Quarterly: The Journal of Southern Culture* by Hassell A. Simpson, summer 1981.

*   *   *

Between World War I and the Depression, Wilbur Daniel Steele was America's recognized master of the popular short story. Many of his nearly 200 published stories (an unschematized history of certain values prevailing in America at the time) transcend the formulas and cliches of mass fiction. Steele submitted to his day's conventions, but, like **Edgar Allan Poe**, created a medley of dazzling variations. By wedding the "New Psychology" to his tight plots, melodramatic adventures, jagged coincidences, and surprise endings, he achieved a particular and celebrated perfection. But as magazines turned increasingly to social realism, sensational confession, and quicksilver style, demand for Steele's intricate stories declined.

Through exotic detail and vivid suggestion, *The Best Stories of Wilbur Daniel Steele* evokes the atmospheres of Cape Cod, the South, the Caribbean, North Africa, and the Middle East. With remarkable purity of concentration Steele exploits the temporality of literature, subordinates part to whole, and makes each yarn a gestalt. "Romantic" themes like suspected innocence, revenge and retribution, power of love and friendship, premonition, and return from the "dead" intertwine with such "realistic" ideas as heredity versus environment, law and conscience, divided self, quest for identity, and awakening. Sophoclean symmetry heightens the commonplace, but sometimes Steele's heavy-handed "chance" destroys his grim illusions. Still, his sinewy twists and shock endings (less meretricious then **O. Henry**'s) force us to re-see life's awesome ironies and literature's delightful ones.

"The Man Who Saw through Heaven," one of his most effective stories, dramatizes the physical and spiritual evolution of mankind in a tour de force of condensation. The classic "How Beautiful with Shoes" (also a Broadway play) renders the emotional awakening of a cloddish Appalachian girl abducted by a runaway psychotic. "When Hell Froze" is a memorable period piece. For sheer ingenuity and suspense, "Footfalls," a tale of paternal revenge, has few equals. "Conjuh," "Blue Murder," "Bubbles," "The Body of the Crime," "For They Know Not What They Do"—these stories and many others have received high praise.

Steele's Euclidian logic, detective imagination, and knotty style suited the shorter form far better than the novel. His longer fiction, labored and wooden, displays feeble narrative line, thematic fuzziness, clotted exegesis, and trite detail. Perhaps *Meat,* an early novel that boldly indicts the perpetuation of weakness, is his best.

In the late twentieth century Steele's radiant prize stories crop up in anthologies, and historians of the American short story ac-

knowledge his uniqueness, but he attracts little serious critical attention. An important transitional writer who bridges the Poe-O. Henry and the Anderson-Hemingway traditions, Steele was a marvelous technician who occasionally compelled his stories to the level of high art.

—Martin Bucco

STEGNER, Wallace (Earle)

Born: Lake Mills, Iowa, 18 February 1909. **Education:** University of Utah, Salt Lake City, A.B. 1930; University of Iowa, Iowa City, A.M. 1932, PhD. 1935; University of California, Berkeley, 1932-33. **Family:** Married Mary Stuart Page in 1934; one son. **Career:** Instructor, Augustana College, Rock Island, Illinois, 1933-34; University of Utah, Salt Lake City, 1934-37; and University of Wisconsin, Madison, 1937-39; Briggs Copeland Instructor of Composition, Harvard University, Cambridge, Massachusetts, 1939-45; professor of English, 1945-69, and director of creative writing program, 1946-71, and Jackson Eli Reynolds Professor of Humanities, 1969-71, Stanford University, Stanford, California; Bissell Professor of Canadian-U.S. Relations, University of Toronto, Toronto, Ontario, 1975; Tanner Lecturer, University of Utah, Salt Lake City, 1980; Montgomery fellow, Dartmouth College, Hanover, New Hampshire, 1980. Writer in residence, American Academy in Rome, 1960; Phi Beta Kappa visiting scholar, 1960-61. West coast editor, Houghton Mifflin Company, publishers, Boston, 1945-53. Assistant to the United States Secretary of the Interior, Washington, DC, 1961. Member, National Parks Advisory Board, Washington, DC, 1962-66, and chairman, 1965-66. Editor-in-chief, *American West* magazine, Palo Alto, California, 1966-68. **Awards:** Little Brown prize, 1937; O. Henry award, 1942, 1950, 1954; Houghton Mifflin Life in America award, 1945; Anisfield Wolf award, 1945; Guggenheim fellowship, 1949-51, 1959; Rockefeller fellowship, 1950; Wenner Gren grant, 1953; Center for Advanced Studies in the Behavioral Sciences fellowship, 1955; National Endowment for the Humanities senior fellowship, 1972; Pulitzer prize, 1972; Western Literature Association award, 1974; National Book award, 1977; *Los Angeles Times* Kirsch award, 1980; National Book Critics Circle Award nomination, 1987, 1993. D.Litt.: University of Utah, Salt Lake City, 1968; Utah State University, Logan, 1972. D.F.A.: University of California, 1969; D.L.: University of Saskatchewan, Regina, 1973. D.H.L.: University of Santa Clara, California, 1979; University of Wisconsin, Madison, 1986; Montana State University, Bozeman, 1987. **Member:** American Academy, American Academy of Arts and Sciences. **Died:** 13 April 1993.

PUBLICATIONS

Collections

The Sound of Mountain Water: The Changing American West (essays). 1969.
One Way to Spell Man (essays). 1982.
Collected Stories of Wallace Stegner. 1990.
Where the Bluebird Sings to the Lemonade Springs: Living and Writing in the West (essays). 1993.

Novels

Remembering Laughter. 1937.
The Potter's House. 1938.
On a Darkling Plain. 1940.
Fire and Ice. 1941.
The Big Rock Candy Mountain. 1943.
Second Growth. 1947.
The Preacher and the Slave. 1950; as *Joe Hill: A Biographical Novel*, 1969.
A Shooting Star. 1961.
All the Little Live Things. 1967.
Angle of Repose. 1971.
The Spectator Bird. 1976.
Recapitulation. 1979.
Crossing to Safety. 1987.

Short Stories

The Women on the Wall. 1950.
The City of the Living and Other Stories. 1956.
New Short Novels 2, with others. 1956.

Other

Mormon Country. 1942.
One Nation, with editors of *Look.* 1945.
Look at America: The Central Northwest, with others. 1947.
This I Believe, with others, compiled by Edward R. Murrow. 1952.
The Writer in America (lectures). 1952.
Beyond the Hundredth Meridian: John Wesley Powell and the Second Opening of the West. 1954.
The Romance of North America, with others, edited by H. Mosley. 1958.
Wolf Willow: A History, a Story, and a Memory of the Last Plains Frontier. 1962.
American Heritage Book of Great Natural Wonders, with others, edited by Alvin M. Josephy. 1963.
Four Portraits and One Subject: Bernard DeVoto, with others. 1963.
Literary History of the United States, 3rd edition, with others, edited by R.E. Spiller and others. 1963.
The Gathering of Zion: The Story of the Mormon Trail. 1964.
American Literary Masters, with others, edited by C. R. Anderson and others. 1965.
Teaching the Short Story. 1965.
Michael/Frank: Studies on Frank O'Connor, with others, edited by Maurice Sheehy. 1969.
Discovery!: The Search for Arabian Oil. 1971.
Variations on a Theme of Discontent. 1972.
Robert Frost and Bernard DeVoto. 1974.
The Uneasy Chair: A Biography of Bernard DeVoto. 1974.
American Places, with Page Stegner, photographs by Eliot Porter. 1981.
The Tanner Lectures on Human Values, Vol. II: 1981, with others, edited by Sterling M. McMurrin. 1981.
Conversations with Wallace Stegner on Western History and Literature, with Richard Etulain. 1983.
The American West as Living Space. 1987.
The Best of California: Some People, Places, and Institutions of the Most Exciting State in the Nation, as Featured in California Magazine, 1976-86, with others, edited by Harold Hayes. 1988.

On the Teaching of Creative Writing. 1989.
Wilderness Letter. 1995.
Stealing Glances: Three Interviews with Wallace Stegner. 1998.

Editor, with others, *An Exposition Workshop: Readings in Modern Controversy.* 1939.
Editor, with others, *Reading for Citizens at War.* 1941.
Editor, with Richard Scowcroft, *Stanford Short Stories 1946.* 1947, and other volumes.
Editor, with Richard Scowcroft and Boris Ilyin, *The Writer's Art: A Collection of Short Stories.* 1950.
Editor, *This Is Dinosaur: Echo Park and Its Magic Rivers.* 1955.
Editor, *The Exploration of the Colorado River of the West,* by J. W. Powell. 1957.
Editor, with Mary Stegner, *Great American Short Stories.* 1957.
Editor, *Selected American Prose, 1841-1900: The Realistic Movement.* 1958.
Editor, *The Adventures of Huckleberry Finn,* by Mark Twain. 1960.
Editor, *The Outcasts of Poker Flat,* by Bret Harte. 1961.
Editor, *Report on the Lands of the Arid Regions of the United States,* by J. W. Powell. 1962.
Editor, with others, *Modern Composition,* four volumes. 1964.
Editor, *The American Novel: From James Fenimore Cooper to William Faulkner.* 1965.
Editor, *The Big Sky,* by A. B. Guthrie, Jr. 1965.
Editor, with Richard Scowcroft, *Twenty Years of Stanford Short Stories.* 1966.
Editor, *Twice Told Tales,* by Nathaniel Hawthorne. 1967.
Editor, *The Letters of Bernard DeVoto.* 1975.

Recording: *A Sense of Place,* 1989.

*

Bibliography: *Wallace Stegner: A Descriptive Bibliography* by Nancy Colberg, 1990.

Critical Studies: *Wallace Stegner* by Merrill and Lorene Lewis, 1972; *Wallace Stegner* by Forrest G. and Margaret G. Robinson, 1977; *Critical Essays on Wallace Stegner* by Anthony Arthur, editor, 1982; *Wallace Stegner: His Life and Work* by Jackson L. Benson, 1996; *Why I Can't Read Wallace Stegner and Other Essays: A Tribal Voice* by Elizabeth Cook-Lynn, 1996; *Wallace Stegner: Man and Writer* edited by Charles E. Rankin, 1996; *Wallace Stegner and the Continental Vision: Essays on Literature, History, and Landscape* edited by Curt Meine, 1997; *Wallace Stegner: A Study of the Short Fiction* by Jackson L. Benson, 1998.

*   *   *

In and of the American West Wallace Stegner lived his remarkable life, fifty years of which was dedicated to the advancement of American letters. Upon hearing of Stegner's death in April 1993, Leslie Epstein, novelist and director of the Boston University writing program, responded to M.R. Montgomery of the *Boston Globe,* "If you had called me yesterday, I would have told you he was America's greatest living writer." In addition to producing an impressive body of work over his long career, including not only novels and short story collections but also seminal historical works, Stegner was instrumental in the development of other notable writers, having founded the creative writing program at Stanford University. Though one of the fallacies he hoped to expose of the West was its mythical inexhaustibility, Stegner himself was a vital source of inspiration from which other creative tributaries sprung to nourish the region that had so influenced him.

Born in Lake Mills, Iowa, in 1909, Stegner lived an itinerant childhood across the West, marking time in Utah, North Dakota, Washington, Montana, Wyoming, and Saskatchewan. At sixteen he entered the University of Utah, graduating in 1930; by 1935 he had earned his Ph.D. at the University of Iowa and begun his writing career. Stegner held teaching positions at the University of Utah, the University of Wisconsin at Madison, and Harvard University before settling at Stanford University, the school with which he is most commonly associated and which honors him with a prestigious writing fellowship in his name.

Though wide in scope and genre, Stegner's work unmistakably focused on the American West. He was careful, however, to distinguish between the West and the "western," a genre that had the tendency to mythologize the region as that ideal created by "dime novels, comic books, television and movies," and whose popularization led to many of the environmental problems the region faced in his lifetime. "There are more dentists in the West than cowboys," Stegner said, "but no one writes about the dentists." Not surprisingly, Stegner's unique vision of the West can be found most evidently within the pages of his books. His first novel, *Remembering Laughter,* won him the top prize of $2,500 in a contest sponsored by Little, Brown, and encouraged him to continue writing. His next three novels, *The Potter's House, On a Darkling Plain,* and *Fire and Ice,* share with his first similar themes of individualism and isolation, but also the need for community and belonging. This complexity of human emotion, characterization that defied categorization or simple explanation, would become a hallmark feature of Stegner's later, more expansive works.

Borrowing from the personal history of his family, Stegner published in 1943 the largely autobiographical novel *The Big Rock Candy Mountain,* his first popular and critical success. The title is taken from a traditional hobo song that tells of a place where "handouts grow on bushes," and "the sun shines every day"— key myths of the West that Stegner hoped to debunk before the environmental consequences grew too large. The novel parallels his own family life, especially that with his father, a man who migrated across the West, unsuccessfully "on the lookout for the big chance, the ground floor, the inside track," Stegner wrote in his introduction to *Where the Bluebird Sings to the Lemonade Springs.*

Stegner turned to teaching at Stanford after he feared he had used up most of his autobiographical material in his early productive years, and came to the realization that he needed "to quit writing or to grow." He was also disappointed with the mixed critical reception he received for his biographical novel on a labor organizer, *The Preacher and the Slave,* which followed *Second Growth.* His next decade was spent cultivating the Stanford Writing Program, contributing articles as a journalist, writing short stories and even a biography on the explorer John Wesley Powell. Stegner's talents at writing nonfiction proved no surprise, as he had already published in 1942 a well received work on the geography of Utah and its settlers, *Mormon Country.* His tribute to the early pioneers of that western state continued with *The Gathering of Zion: The Story of the Mormon Trail,* published in 1964. The objectivity of this book can be attributed to Stegner's own claim that he wrote "as a non-Mormon but not a Mormon hater."

Indeed, as Harold Watts mentions in *Contemporary Novelists,* Stegner was "the most nontheological of novelists," openly regarded to be an agnostic. Other nonfiction titles of note included *Wolf Willow: A History, a Story, and a Memory of the Last Plains Frontier* in 1962, and *The Uneasy Chair: A Biography of Bernard DeVoto* in 1974.

Stegner returned to prominence with *A Shooting Star,* whose protagonist Sabrina Castro was regarded as a convincing portrait of a woman under hardship; characterization of Castro and her mother revealed the author's gifted capacity for portraying the experiences of women. Along with *All the Little Live Things* and *The Spectator Bird,* the novel is set in California, a state that Stegner never truly considered western because of its vigor and wealth. In 1972 Stegner achieved his greatest critical success by winning the Pulitzer Prize for *Angle of Repose.* The novel, also set in California, concerns a retired professor, Lyman Ward, who has lost his leg to a degenerative arthritis and whose wife has left him. In reconstructing the lives of his pioneer grandparents through reading their letters, he comes to realize that their lives were not as idealistic as he had once believed them. In this novel, largely considered to be his finest, Stegner fuses the past and present of this family, allowing Ward to discover that his grandparents "were more bound by guilt than by affection," states Montgomery, "and this knowledge . . . gives him the slight comfort of learning that loyalty is not necessarily the moral superior to abandonment." Stegner's next novel, *The Spectator Bird,* won the National Book Award in 1976, sealing his reputation as one of America's finest novelists. In it, Joe Allston—a recurring figure from *All the Little Live Things*—an aging literary agent, conducts a similar search of his family's past, this time in Denmark. *Recapitulation* followed in 1979, and eight years passed before publication of Stegner's last novel, *Crossing to Safety,* which won huge popular and critical acclaim, nominated for a National Book Critics Circle Award in 1987.

An old fashioned realist, Stegner carved out a lasting reputation with perseverance and integrity in a literary world that took its time appreciating the majesty of his straightforward style. In this way, he can be likened to the landscape he so dearly loved. Recognition did not come too late for Wallace Stegner, and in his lifelong dedication to revealing the beauty of the West to the rest of the world, he offered these words of advice: "You have to get over the color green; you have to quit associating beauty with gardens and lawns; you have to get used to an inhuman scale." Yet his characters, though flawed, were human in every sense, in both their failings and triumphs they exhibited the best and most heroic virtues the West had to offer them: "fortitude, resolution, magnanimity." Consistent with this is Stegner's belief "that man, even Modern Man, has some dignity if he will assume it, and that most lives are worth living, even when they are lives of quiet desperation."

—David Shih

STEIN, Gertrude

Born: Allegheny, Pennsylvania, 3 February 1874; as a child lived in Vienna, Paris, and Oakland, California. **Education:** Schools in Oakland and San Francisco; Radcliffe College, Cambridge, Massachusetts, 1893-97; studied philosophy under William James, B.A.

(Harvard University), 1897; studied medicine at Johns Hopkins Medical School, Baltimore, 1897-1901. **Family:** Lived in Paris from 1903, with Alice B. Toklas from 1908; center of a circle of artists, including Picasso, Matisse, and Braque, and of writers, including Hemingway, and Fitzgerald; lived in Mallorca, 1914-16. **Career:** Worked with American Fund for French Wounded, 1917-18; founder, Plain Edition, Paris, 1930-33; lectured in the United States, 1934-35. **Died:** 27 July 1946.

PUBLICATIONS

Collections

Writings and Lectures 1911-1945 (selection), edited by Patricia Meyerowitz. 1967; as *Look at Me Now and Here I Am,* 1971.
Selected Operas and Plays, edited by John Malcolm Brinnin. 1970.
The Yale Stein: Selections, edited by Richard Kostelanetz. 1980.
Writings, 1932-1946. 1998.

Short Stories

Three Lives: Stories of the Good Anna, Melanctha, and the Gentle Lena. 1909.
Mrs. Reynolds, and Five Earlier Novelettes, edited by Carl Van Vechten. 1952.

Novels

The Making of Americans, Being a History of a Family's Progress. 1925.
A Book Concluding with As a Wife Has a Cow: A Love Story. 1926.
Lucy Church Amiably. 1931.
Ida: A Novel. 1941.
Brewsie and Willie. 1946.
Blood on the Dining Room Floor. 1948.
Things as They Are: A Novel in Three Parts. 1950.
A Novel of Thank You, edited by Carl Van Vechten. 1958.
Lifting Belly, edited by Rebecca Marks. 1989.

Plays

Geography and Plays. 1922.
A Village: Are You Ready Yet Not Yet. 1928.
Operas and Plays. 1932.
Four Saints in Three Acts, music by Virgil Thomson (produced 1934). 1934.
A Wedding Bouquet: Ballet, music by Lord Berners (produced 1936). 1936.
In Savoy; or, Yes Is for a Very Young Man (produced 1946). 1946.
The Mother of Us All, music by Virgil Thomson (produced 1947). 1947.
Last Operas and Plays, edited by Carl Van Vechten. 1949.
In a Garden, music by Meyer Kupferman (produced 1951). 1951.
Lucretia Borgia. 1968.
D. Faustus Lights the Lights (produced 1984).
Operas and Plays. 1987.

Verse and Prose Poems

Tender Buttons: Objects, Food, Rooms. 1914.

Have They Attacked Mary. He Giggled. 1917.
Before the Flowers of Friendship Faded Friendship Faded. 1931.
Two (Hitherto Unpublished) Poems. 1948.
Stanzas in Meditation and Other Poems (1929-1933), edited by Carl Van Vechten. 1956.

Other

Portrait of Mabel Dodge. 1912.
Composition as Explanation. 1926.
Descriptions of Literature. 1926.
An Elucidation. 1927.
Useful Knowledge. 1928.
An Acquaintance with Description. 1929.
Dix Portraits. 1930.
How to Write. 1931.
The Autobiography of Alice B. Toklas. 1933.
Matisse, Picasso, and Gertrude Stein, with Two Shorter Stories. 1933.
Portraits and Prayers. 1934.
Chicago Inscriptions. 1934.
Lectures in America. 1935.
Narration: Four Lectures. 1935.
The Geographical History of America; or, The Relation of Human Nature to the Human Mind. 1936.
Everybody's Autobiography. 1937.
Picasso. 1938.
The World Is Round (for children). 1939.
Prothalamium. 1939.
Paris France. 1940.
What Are Masterpieces. 1940.
Petits poèmes pour un livre de lecture (for children). 1944; translated as *The First Reader, and Three Plays,* 1946.
Wars I Have Seen. 1945.
Selected Writings, edited by Carl Van Vechten. 1946.
Four in America. 1947.
Kisses Can. 1947.
Literally True. 1947.
Two: Stein and Her Brother and Other Early Portraits (1908-1912), edited by Carl Van Vechten. 1951.
Bee Time Vine and Other Pieces (1913-1927), edited by Carl Van Vechten. 1953.
As Fine as Melanctha (1914-1930), edited by Carl Van Vechten. 1954.
Painted Lace and Other Pieces (1914-1937), edited by Carl Van Vechten. 1955.
Absolutely Bob Brown; or, Bobbed Brown. 1955.
To Bobchen Haas. 1957.
Alphabets and Birthdays, edited by Carl Van Vechten. 1957.
On Our Way (letters). 1959.
Cultivated Motor Automatism, with Leon M. Solomons. 1969.
Stein on Picasso, edited by Edward Burns. 1970.
A Primer for the Gradual Understanding of Stein, edited by Robert Bartlett Haas. 1971.
Fernhurst, Q.E.D., and Other Early Writings, edited by Leon Katz. 1971.
Sherwood Anderson/Stein: Correspondence and Personal Essays, edited by Ray Lewis White. 1972.
Reflection on the Atomic Bomb, edited by Robert Bartlett Haas. 1973.
Money. 1973.

How Writing Is Written, edited by Robert Bartlett Haas. 1974.
Dear Sammy: Letters from Stein to Alice B. Toklas, edited by Samuel M. Steward. 1977.
The Letters of Stein and Carl Van Vechten 1913-1946, edited by Edward Burns. 2 vols., 1986.
The Letters of Gertrude Stein and Thornton Wilder. 1996.
Paris, France. 1996.

*

Bibliography: *Stein: A Bibliography* by Robert A. Wilson, 1974; *Stein: An Annotated Critical Bibliography* by Maureen R. Liston, 1979; *Stein and Alice B. Toklas: A Reference Guide* by Ray Lewis White, 1984.

Critical Studies: *Stein: Form and Intelligibility* by Rosalind S. Miller, 1949; *Stein: A Biography of Her Work* by Donald Sutherland, 1951; *The Flowers of Friendship* (letters to Stein) edited by Donald Gallup, 1953; *Stein: Her Life and Work* by Elizabeth Sprigge, 1957; *The Third Rose: Stein and Her World* by John Malcolm Brinnin, 1959; *Stein* by Frederick J. Hoffman, 1961; *What Is Remembered* by Alice B. Toklas, 1963, and *Staying On Alone: Letters of Alice B. Toklas* edited by Edward Burns, 1973; *The Development of Abstractionism in the Writings of Stein,* 1965, and *Stein,* 1976, both by Michael J. Hoffman; *Stein and the Present* by Allegra Stewart, 1967; *Stein and the Literature of Modern Consciousness* by Norman Weinstein, 1970; *Stein in Pieces* by Richard Bridgman, 1970; *Stein: A Biography* by Howard Greenfield, 1973; *Charmed Circle* by James Mellow, 1974; *Stein: A Composite Portrait* edited by Linda Simon, 1974; *Everybody Who Was Anybody: A Biography of Stein* by Janet Hobhouse, 1975; *Exact Resemblance to Exact Resemblance: The Literary Portraiture of Stein* by Wendy Steiner, 1978; *Stein: Autobiography and the Problem of Narration* by Shirley C. Neuman, 1979, and *Stein and the Making of Literature* by Neuman and Ira B. Nadel, 1988; *A Different Language: Stein's Experimental Writing* by Marianne DeKoven, 1983; *The Structure of Obscurity: Stein, Language and Cubism* by Randa Dubnick, 1984; *Stein's Theatre of the Absolute* by Betsy Alayne Ryan, 1984; *The Making of a Modernist: Stein from Three Lives to Tender Buttons* by Jayne L. Walker, 1984; *Stein* edited by Harold Bloom, 1986; *The Public Is Invited to Dance: Representation, the Body and Dialogue in Stein* by Harriet Scott Shessman, 1989; *Stein Advanced: An Anthology of Criticism* edited by Richard Kostelanetz, 1990; *They Watch Me as They Watch This: Gertrude Stein's Metadrama* by Jane Palatini Bowers, 1991; *Gertrude and Alice* by Diana Souhami, 1992; *Rescued Readings: A Reconstruction of Gertrude Stein's Difficult Texts* by Elizabeth Fifer, 1992; *Disjunctive Poetics: From Gertrude Stein and Louis Zukofsky to Susan Howe* by Peter Quartermain, 1992; *(Sem)erotics: Theorizing Lesbian Writing* by Elizabeth Meese, 1992; *The Senses of Nonsense* by Alison Rieke, 1992; *A Tradition of Subversion: The Prose Poem in English from Wilde to Ashbery* by Margueritte S. Murphy, 1993; *The Trouble with Genius: Reading Pound, Joyce, Stein, and Zukofsky* by Bob Perelman, 1994; *Gertrude Stein Remembered* edited by Linda Simon, 1995; *Sister Brother: Gertrude and Leo Stein* by Brenda Wineapple, 1996; *Henry James, Gertrude Stein, and the Biographical Act* by Charles Caramello, 1996; *Stein, Bishop, and Rich: Lyrics of Love, War, and Place* by Margaret Dickie, 1997; *Gertrude Stein and Richard Wright: The Poetics and Politics of Modernism* by M. Lynn Weiss, 1998; *Prepare for Saints: Gertrude Stein, Virgil Thomson, and the Mainstreaming of American Modernism* by Steven Watson, 1998; *Gender and Genre in Gertrude Stein* by Franziska Gygax, 1998.

* * *

If Paul Cezanne, of whom Gertrude Stein wrote a "portrait" in 1911, broke with traditional forms (such as perspective) and traditional modes (such as pictorial replication), he did so by accenting the verticals, horizontals, and diagonals that he saw in nature. He moved painting towards geometric forms, towards the abstract, and developed new spatial patterns in which, by showing an object simultaneously from several viewpoints, planes and surfaces interacted visually on the canvas. His paintings are not of nature, but provide a visualization of the formal parts of what he saw. Cezanne said that he did not paint pictures; he painted paint. Stein does the same thing with words.

Her work is largely a systematic investigation of the formal elements of language (syntax, parts of speech, grammar, etymology, punctuation) or of the formal elements of literature (narrative, poetry, dialogue, fiction, drama), in which we see the skeleton of the writing or of the form rather than the burden it carries. Apparent nonsense, her work has been the subject of much ridicule (yet it has influenced three generations of writers). "Nobody knows what I am trying to do but I do and I know when I succeed," she said, in *As Fine as Melanctha.* **William Carlos Williams** praised her for "cleansing" the language, for "tackling the fracture of stupidities bound in thoughtless phrases, in our calcified grammatical constructions, and in the subtle brainlessness of our rhythms which compel words to follow certain others without precision of thought." Her concern is for writing (or reading) as movement; for literature, seen as something other than a body of reference work; for writing (reading) envisioned as the first concern of the immediate and attentive moment.

It is convenient to divide Stein's work into three more-or-less distinct groups. The first consists of such well-known and comparatively straightforward narratives as *The Autobiography of Alice B. Toklas, Wars I Have Seen,* and *Three Lives,* which includes the much-anthologized "Melanctha" in which we see (or, more accurately, hear) Melanctha simultaneously from several angles, as in a Cubist painting. Some of the dialogue between Melanctha and Jeff has an effect much like that of Marcel Duchamp's painting *Nude Descending a Staircase.* **Richard Wright** records reading the story to "a group of semiliterate Negro stockyard workers" who "slapped their thighs, howled, laughed, stomped, and interrupted me constantly to comment on the characters" (*PM,* 11 March 1945). It is the language of speech.

The second group contains Stein's critical and exegetical work, such as *Composition as Explanation, Narration, What Are Masterpieces,* and the celebrated *Lectures in America,* in which she discusses her own writing and, offering general reflections on the forms, genres, modes, and periods of English literature, explains the principles on which much of her own work is based. The fruit of protracted meditation on language, her exegeses are at times difficult to follow; as **Thornton Wilder** observed, "Miss Stein pays her listeners the high compliment of dispensing for the most part with that apparatus of illustrative simile and anecdote that is so often employed to recommend ideas." And when, in *Lectures in America,* she says "more and more one does not use nouns," she is pointing to the very plasticity of language one finds in the third group of her work, the overtly experimental and difficult writing.

Work in this group, such as *Tender Buttons, Stanzas in Meditation, An Acquaintance with Description,* or *How to Write,* may properly be thought of as "exemplary," since it demonstrates the principles enunciated in the exegetical work. While composing *How to Write,* Stein called *Tender Buttons* "my first conscious struggle with the problem of correlating sight, sound and sense, and eliminating rhythm;—now I am trying grammar and eliminating sight and sound" (*Transition* 14, 1928), while in *Lectures in America* she said that in *Tender Buttons* "I struggled with the ridding of myself of nouns. I knew that nouns must go in poetry as they had gone in prose if anything that is everything was to go on meaning something." A noun is the name of a thing, and "if you feel what is inside that thing you do not call it by the name by which it is known"; instead, like Whitman, you "mean names without naming them." Breaking syntax, forcing words into multiple grammatical functions, in *Tender Buttons* or *Stanzas in Meditation* Stein seeks to write a poem that, taken as a whole, becomes itself a noun. For example, as Meredith Yearsley points out, under the title "A Box" the poem acts a box out linguistically by the quadruple repetition of a particular construction. The closedness of the box is caught by use of grammatical constructions that force the reader to re-scan the sentence. Here, most clearly, Stein uses words the way Cezanne uses paint.

How to Write, originally entitled *Grammar, Paragraphs, Sentences, Vocabulary, Etcetera,* works similarly, through exploring the effect of semantic and syntactic anomalies in a prose that demands of the reader the expectation that words, the part of speech, will hold their conventional position and function in the sentence. In a sentence like "It is very well a date which makes each separate in a leaf in a dismissal," the major source of difficulty is not in the lack of punctuation so much as in the ambiguous functions of words and phrases. In other sentences from "Arthur a Grammar" the reader need only supply punctuation to render the sentence wholly intelligible: "There is a difference between a grammar and a sentence this is grammar in a sentence I will agree to no map with which you may be dissatisfied and therefore beg you to point out what you regard as incorrect in the positions of the troops in my two sentences." In each case, the sentence acts out its meaning.

In such ways Stein's words remove themselves from the context in which they (may have) originated and acquire a new context in which they can assert their meaning by demonstrating it. The world of Stein is one in which things are the cause rather than the content of language, and it is thus an interiorized world, where definitions are held in the process and in the moment of defining: Stein held that poetry is stasis, where the object, be it Melanctha or Roast Beef or Arthur a Grammar, fills all the available space, much as a Cubist object fills a crowded flat surface. The work is dense, and exuberant.

While the strength of Stein's personality might account for her influence on writers like **Ernest Hemingway** or **Sherwood Anderson**, it does not account for her later influence, or for her friendship with painters like Picasso or Juan Gris. Later readers of her work, like **Robert Duncan**, George Bowering, or B.P. Nichol, find themselves, imitating her writing, turning to their own childhood. This is in part because Stein's language is devoid of allusion, seems to have no past, and things seem to speak directly, perceived in immediacy.

—Peter Quartermain

See the essays on *The Autobiography of Alice B. Toklas* and *Three Lives.*

STEINBECK, John (Ernst)

Born: Salinas, California, 27 February 1902. **Education:** Salinas High School, graduated 1919; Stanford University, California, intermittently 1919-25. **Family:** Married 1) Carol Henning in 1930 (divorced 1942); 2) Gwyn Conger (i.e., the actress Gwen Verdon) in 1943 (divorced 1948), two sons; 3) Elaine Scott in 1950. **Career:** Worked at various jobs, including reporter for the New York *American,* apprentice hod-carrier, apprentice painter, chemist, caretaker of an estate at Lake Tahoe, surveyor, and fruit picker, 1925-35; full-time writer from 1935; settled in Monterey, California, 1930, later moved to New York City; special writer for U.S. Army Air Force during World War II; correspondent in Europe, New York *Herald Tribune,* 1943. **Awards:** New York Drama Critics Circle award, 1938; Pulitzer prize, 1940; King Haakon Liberty Cross (Norway), 1946; O. Henry award, 1956; Nobel prize for literature, 1962; Presidential Medal of Freedom, 1964; U.S. Medal of Freedom, 1964. **Member:** American Academy, 1939. **Died:** 20 December 1968.

PUBLICATIONS

Collections

The Essential Steinbeck. 1994.
Novels and Stories, 1932-1937. 1994.

Short Stories

The Pastures of Heaven. 1932.
Saint Katy the Virgin. 1936.
The Red Pony. 1937.
The Long Valley. 1938.
The Moon Is Down (novella). 1942.
Burning Bright: A Play in Story Form (novella). 1950.
The Short Novels. 1953.

Novels

Cup of Gold: A Life of Henry Morgan, Buccaneer, with Occasional Reference to History. 1929.
To a God Unknown. 1933.
Tortilla Flat. 1935.
In Dubious Battle. 1936.
Of Mice and Men. 1937.
The Grapes of Wrath. 1939; edited by Peter Lisca, 1972.
Cannery Row. 1945.
The Wayward Bus. 1947.
The Pearl. 1947.
East of Eden. 1952.
Sweet Thursday. 1954.
The Short Reign of Pippin IV: A Fabrication. 1957.
The Winter of Our Discontent. 1961.

Plays

Of Mice and Men, from his own novel (produced 1937). 1937.
The Forgotten Village (screenplay). 1941.
The Moon Is Down, from his own novel (produced 1942). 1942.

A Medal for Benny, with Jack Wagner and Frank Butler, in *Best Film Plays 1945,* edited by John Gassner and Dudley Nichols. 1946.

Burning Bright, from his own novel (produced 1950). 1951.

Viva Zapata! The Original Screenplay, edited by Robert E. Morsberger. 1975.

Screenplays: *The Forgotten Village* (documentary), 1941; *Lifeboat,* with Jo Swerling, 1944; *A Medal for Benny,* with Jack Wagner and Frank Butler, 1945; *La perla (The Pearl),* with Jack Wagner and Emilio Fernandez, 1946; *The Red Pony,* 1949; *Viva Zapata!,* 1952.

Other

Their Blood Is Strong. 1938.

Steinbeck Replies (letter). 1940.

Sea of Cortez: A Leisurely Journal of Travel and Research, with Edward F. Ricketts. 1941.

Bombs Away: The Story of a Bomber Team. 1942.

The Viking Portable Library Steinbeck, edited by Pascal Covici. 1943; abridged edition, as *The Steinbeck Pocket Book,* 1943; revised edition, as *The Portable Steinbeck,* 1946, 1958; revised edition, edited by Pascal Covici, Jr., 1971; 1946 edition published as *The Indispensable Steinbeck,* 1950, and as *The Steinbeck Omnibus,* 1951.

The First Watch (letter). 1947.

Vanderbilt Clinic. 1947.

A Russian Journal, photographs by Robert Capa. 1948.

The Log from the Sea of Cortez. 1951.

Once There Was a War. 1958.

Travels with Charley in Search of America. 1962.

Speech Accepting the Nobel Prize for Literature . . . . 1962(?).

America and Americans. 1966.

Journal of a Novel: The East of Eden Letters. 1969.

Steinbeck: A Life in Letters, edited by Elaine Steinbeck and Robert Wallsten. 1975.

The Acts of King Arthur and His Noble Knights, from the Winchester Manuscripts of Malory and Other Sources, edited by Chase Horton. 1976.

Letters to Elizabeth: A Selection of Letters from Steinbeck to Elizabeth Otis, edited by Florian J. Shasky and Susan F. Riggs. 1978.

Conversations with Steinbeck, edited by Thomas Fensch. 1988.

Working Days: The Journals of The Grapes of Wrath, 1938-1941, edited by Robert DeMott. 1989.

*

Bibliography: *A New Steinbeck Bibliography 1929-1971 and 1971-1981* by Tetsumaro Hayashi, 2 vols., 1973-83; *Steinbeck: A Bibliographical Catalogue of the Adrian H. Goldstone Collection* by Adrian H. Goldstone and John R. Payne, 1974; *Steinbeck Bibliographies: An Annotated Guide* by Robert B. Harmon, 1987; *Cannery Row: A Selected Fifty Year Bibliographic Survey* by Robert B. Harmon, 1995.

Critical Studies: *The Novels of Steinbeck: A First Critical Study* by Harry T. Moore, 1939, as *Steinbeck and His Novels,* 1939; *Steinbeck and His Critics: A Record of Twenty-Five Years* edited by E.W. Tedlock, Jr., and C.V. Wicker, 1957; *The Wide World of Steinbeck,* 1958, and *Steinbeck, Nature, and Myth,* 1978, both by Peter Lisca; *Steinbeck* by Warren French, 1961, revised edition,

1975, and *A Companion to The Grapes of Wrath* edited by French, 1963; *Steinbeck* by F.W. Watt, 1962; *Steinbeck: An Introduction and Interpretation* by Joseph Fontenrose, 1964; Steinbeck Monograph series, from 1972, *A Study Guide to Steinbeck: A Handbook to His Major Works,* 2 vols., 1974-79, *Steinbeck's "The Grapes of Wrath": Essays in Criticism,* 1990, and *Steinbeck's Literary Dimenson,* 1991, all edited by Tetsumaro Hayashi; *Steinbeck: A Collection of Critical Essays* edited by Robert Murray Davis, 1972; *Steinbeck and Edward F. Ricketts: The Shaping of a Novelist* by Richard Astro, 1973; *The Novels of Steinbeck: A Critical Study* by Howard Levant, 1974; *Steinbeck: The Errant Knight: An Intimate Biography of His California Years* by Nelson Valjean, 1975; *The Intricate Music: A Biography of Steinbeck* by Thomas Kiernan, 1979; *Steinbeck* by Paul McCarthy, 1980; *The True Adventures of Steinbeck, Writer: A Biography* by Jackson J. Benson, 1984, and *The Short Novels of Steinbeck: Critical Essays with a Checklist to Steinbeck Criticism* edited by Benson, 1990; *Steinbeck: The California Years* by Brian St. Pierre, 1984; *Steinbeck: Life, Work, and Criticism* by John Ditsky, 1985; *Steinbeck's New Vision of America* by Louis Owens, 1985; *Steinbeck, The Voice of the Land* by Keith Ferrell, 1986; *Steinbeck's Fiction: The Aesthetics of the Road Taken,* 1986, and *The Dramatic Landscape of Steinbeck's Short Stories,* 1990, both by John H. Timmerman; *Beyond "The Red Pony": A Reader's Companion to Steinbeck's Complete Short Stories,* 1987, and *Steinbeck: A Study of the Short Fiction,* 1989, both by R.S. Hughes; *New Essays on "The Grapes of Wrath"* edited by David Wright, 1990; *With Steinbeck in the Sea of Cortez* by Sparky Enea and Audry Lynch, 1992; *John Steinbeck: The War Years, 1939-1945* by Roy S. Simmonds, 1996; *Steinbeck's Typewriter: Essays on His Art* by Robert J. DeMott, 1997; *John Steinbeck* edited by Harold Bloom, 1998; *John Steinbeck: America's Author* by Donnë Florence, 1999.

*   *   *

John Steinbeck often puzzled critics during his lifetime because early in his career his style and subject matter seemed to change with each new story, and after World War II there was a generally acknowledged but puzzling decline in his artistic powers. Later, however, in a larger perspective we can see that underlying the apparent diversity of Steinbeck's work is a consistently developing vision of man's relation to his environment. This larger perspective is provided, in part, by the generally acknowledged end of the Age of Modernism, as described in Maurice Beebe's "What Modernism Was" (*Journal of Modern Literature,* July 1974). After offering a longer definition, Beebe approves Philip Stevick's observation that the modernist sensibility might almost be defined by "its irony, its implicit admiration for verbal precision and understatement." Marston LaFrance in *A Reading of Stephen Crane* (1971) traces this characteristic irony to Kierkegaard and describes its possessors as perceiving "a double realm of values where a different sort of mind would perceive only a single realm."

Steinbeck's varying works during the years of his greatest popularity and power in the 1930s were characterized by precisely this kind of irony. It is excellently illustrated by Sir Henry Morgan's speech at the end of Steinbeck's first novel, *Cup of Gold,* "Civilization will split up a character, and he who refuses to split goes under." Despite its importance in establishing Steinbeck's viewpoint, this apprentice work is strikingly different from his later books. A flamboyantly written historical costume drama about a Caribbean pirate who sacks the golden city of Panama to capture a legendary woman and then returns her to her husband for a ransom and sells out his piratical cohorts for high government position, *Cup of Gold* exudes the same disenchanted world-weariness as the abundant "Waste Land" literature of the 1920s.

A similar preoccupation with characters of mythical dimensions in a dying world colors one of Steinbeck's strangest novels, *To a God Unknown* (third published, it antedates the second). In this fantasy, Joseph Wayne—the leader among four brothers who allegorize lust, sanctimoniousness, animalism, and martyrdom—sacrifices himself to bring the needed rain to his parched valley. Here, as in the story-cycle called *The Pastures of Heaven,* Steinbeck discovers the beautiful, small valleys of his native California as the settings for his most powerful tales. But whereas *To a God Unknown* employs the same kind of baroque language and bizarre episodes as *Cup of Gold, The Pastures of Heaven* offers a lower-keyed, vernacular language and earthy tales of the defeat of good intentions in a naturalistic manner that emphasizes the irony of man's sufferings in a paradisically beautiful setting.

Steinbeck continues to employ this naturalistic viewpoint in his next works. *Tortilla Flat* seems at first glance much different from the others because of the archaic style arising from the effort to translate Malory's *Morte Darthur* into the language and actions of Mexican-American "paisanos" in Monterey, California; but beneath its surface of quaint humor, it, too, is an ironic fable of civilization "splitting up" a person: once the fabulous Danny abandons his "natural life" in the woods to become a property owner, he can never go back again and must die with a gesture of defiant despair. *In Dubious Battle,* which is often justifiably called the best American strike novel, deals realistically with tense labor problems among California apple growers and migrant pickers and ends as grimly as *Tortilla Flat,* with the disappearance of Doc Burton, the one man of objective good will in the story, and a murder that renders faceless a young labor organizer.

In *Of Mice and Men,* Steinbeck's first experiment in writing a play-novelette, Lennie, a tower of physical strength, must die because he has not the mentality to control his behavior and kills the soft things he loves to fondle. His death destroys also his protector George's dream of their one day finding security on a farm of their own. The stories collected in *The Long Valley* record similar helpless defeats—in the most familiar of them, "Chrysanthemums" and "Flight," we see first a love-starved woman exploited by a wily itinerant and then another young man, whose mind is not strong enough to control his behavior, driven to his death by shadowy pursuers. The collection concludes with one of Steinbeck's most popular and masterful works, *The Red Pony.* This four-story cycle depicts a sensitive boy's growing into maturity through his encounters on his father's ranch with the fallibility of man, the wearing out of man, the unreliability of nature, and the exhaustion of nature that leads to the extinguishing of man's dynamic urge for "Westering."

Steinbeck's next work after his success with *Of Mice and Men* was apparently planned as another ironic, defeatist tale entitled *L'Affaire Lettuceberg,* based on his observation of the outrageous plight of migrant workers who had fled the Midwestern Dust Bowl in hope of making a new start in California. During the writing, however, Steinbeck experienced a great change of heart, abandoned what he had written as "a smart-alec book," and, writing feverishly, recast his work as *The Grapes of Wrath,* his most popular and most critically acclaimed work.

The Grapes of Wrath alternates the story of the travails of the Joad family, share-croppers tractored out of Oklahoma who find only a hostile reception in the West, with inter-chapters that generalize this family history as a nation's tragedy. Through the inspiration of the martyred ex-preacher Jim Casy, the Joads at last learn the lesson of cooperation summed up by Ma's speech, "Use' ta be the fambly was fust. It ain't so now. It's anybody." Yet the novel is still modernist in sensibility, for the much discussed ending in which daughter Rose of Sharon offers breast milk intended for her own dead baby to a dying old man is ambiguous. The Joads have found temporary haven, but no security; the national tragedy can only be solved by the readers, not the writer. Steinbeck has, however, turned from characters who are helpless victims to those who learn to heighten their consciousnesses enough to transcend their afflictions.

After reshaping this key novel, Steinbeck would never revert completely to the ironical modernist point of view; but neither was he able consistently to contrive situations convincingly optimistic enough to provide an alternative. His two further play-novelettes, *The Moon Is Down*—written during World War II about the military occupation of a peaceful nation—and *Burning Bright*—a meditation on sterility that pleads that "the species must go staggering on"—suffered from "misplaced universalism." They were populated with two-dimensional allegorical figures from medieval morality plays. Other works like the very popular *The Pearl, The Wayward Bus,* and the script for Elia Kazan's film *Viva Zapata!*—like the earlier short film *The Forgotten Village*—take Mexicans from underprivileged backgrounds and turn them into folk-Messiahs, "natural saints." (The driver of *The Wayward Bus* even has the initials J.C.) Kino's gesture in *The Pearl* of casting away the fabulous jewel that has brought only misery rather than promised fortune and the tribute at the end of Kazan's film to Zapata's indomitable spirit have heartened audiences, but they are theatricalized indications that Steinbeck, instead of looking ahead, seeks—as such later non-fiction works as *America and Americans* and the "Letters to Alicia" make clear—a return to simple, folk values of the past.

Only in *Cannery Row,* where Steinbeck again universalizes the comic story he tells through "inter-chapters," does he succeed in creating, in his portrait of Doc (based on his good friend Ed Ricketts), a remarkable figure who has both the selflessness and the sophistication to transcend the trials and temptations of the materialistic world by escaping into "the cosmic Monterey" fragmentarily embodied in deathless art.

Steinbeck attempted to tell such a story of transcendence again in his most ambitious novel, *East of Eden,* by again alternating between two kinds of material, but this time they fail to fuse. The story of his own family returns to the lyrical naturalism of his work of the 1930s, but the narrative is so heavily ironic that it fails to produce an affirmation; he seeks this through the labored fictional pursuit of the meaning of the Hebrew word "Timshel," which animates another allegorical fable—this one spiced up with much sensational material—about a modern Adam, his errant wife, and his twin sons who re-enact the biblical account of man's first family.

Steinbeck's subsequent fiction was trivial. *Sweet Thursday* brought back Doc and other characters from *Cannery Row,* but reduced Doc to a confused sentimentalist ministered to principally by kindly whores. *The Short Reign of Pippin IV* was a very funny, timely attack on French politics and art during the years of Charles de Gaulle, but its sketchiness makes it dated. Finally in *The Winter of Our Discontent,* Steinbeck tried to make a fresh start by writing about a small Long Island town. The novel developed from a very funny short story, "How Mr. Hogan Robbed a Bank," but the humor disappeared in this account of Ethan Allen Hawley's struggles with his conscience about having been betrayed by others and betraying others. While the novel does not quite become simply another revelation of modernist alienation (Hawley makes the affirmative gesture of rejecting suicide in order to help his daughter live), he really makes for less selfish reasons the same kind of compromise that the pirate Henry Morgan makes in Steinbeck's first novel. Thus Steinbeck's fiction returns at last almost full circle to the point where it had begun after achieving but falling away from the triumphant visions of *The Grapes of Wrath* and *Cannery Row*.

—Warren French

See the essay on *The Grapes of Wrath*.

STEINER, K. Leslie. *See* **DELANY, Samuel R(ay Jr.)**.

STERN, Gerald

Born: Pittsburgh, Pennsylvania, 22 February 1925. **Education:** University of Pittsburgh, B.A. 1947; Columbia University, New York, M.A. 1949. **Military Service:** United States Army Corps. **Family:** Married Patricia Miller in 1952; one daughter and one son. **Career:** Instructor, Temple University, Philadelphia, 1957-63; professor, Indiana University of Pennsylvania, Indiana, 1963-67, and Somerset County College, Somerville, New Jersey, 1968-82. Faculty member, Writer's Workshop, University of Iowa, Iowa City, 1982-94. Visiting poet, Sarah Lawrence College, Bronxville, New York, 1977; visiting professor, University of Pittsburgh, 1978, Columbia University, 1980, Bucknell University, Lewisburg, Pennsylvania, spring 1988, and New York University, fall 1989; Distinguished Chair, University of Alabama, 1984; Fanny Hurst Professor, Washington University, St. Louis, fall 1985; Bain Swiggert Chair, Princeton University, New Jersey, fall 1989; poet-in-residence, Bucknell University, spring 1994. Beginning 1973 consultant in literature, Pennsylvania Arts Council, Harrisburg. **Awards:** National Endowment for the Arts grant, 1976, 1981, 1987; Lamont Poetry Selection award, 1977; State of Pennsylvania creative writing grant, 1979; Pennsylvania Governor's award, 1980; Guggenheim fellowship, 1980; Bess Hokin award (*Poetry,* Chicago), 1980; Bernard F. Connor award, 1981; Melville Caine award, 1982; Jerome J. Shestack prize, 1984; fellowship, American Academy of Poets, 1993.

PUBLICATIONS

Poetry

The Naming of Beasts and Other Poems. 1973.
Rejoicings. 1973.
Lucky Life. 1977.
The Red Coal. 1981.
Paradise Poems. 1984.
Lovesick. 1987.
Leaving Another Kingdom: Selected Poems. 1990.

Two Long Poems. 1990.
Bread without Sugar. 1992.
Old Mercy. 1995.
This Time: New and Selected Poems. 1998.

Recording: *Rotten Angel,* 1989.

*

Critical Studies: "Gerald Stern" issue of *Poetry East,* fall 1988; *Making the Light Come: The Poetry of Gerald Stern* by Jane Somerville, 1990.

*   *   *

Gerald Stern's poetry has roots in many traditions, but most important formally is his use of Old Testament cadences; this rhythm has prompted many critics to compare Stern's work with that of **Walt Whitman,** and certainly some aspects of Stern's work bear up to this pairing. But a major point of difference between the two is that Stern has no interest in constructing the grand, imposing self that Whitman strives toward. Rather, Stern's poetry is frequently intensely personal, grounded in his Jewish heritage. He is both a narrative and a lyric poet; *Lucky Life* and *The Red Coal* employ both of these methods. Stern has continued to write in both strains, although one of his most recent works, "Hot Dog," a long poem published in *Odd Mercy,* reveals a more discursive and meditative thread. Other important influences on his writing include **Theodore Roethke,** for his strong imagery and percussive rhythm; W. H. Auden, for his wit and ironical humor; **Robert Lowell,** for his autobiographical candor and emotional strength; and **John Berryman,** for his disrupted syntax and formal brilliance. Stern has insisted that he is a poet who has drawn from diverse traditions, and the range of writers with whom he can be compared certainly supports this claim. The use of multiple speakers in his poetry, even occasionally using the voice of an animal or inanimate object, is another aspect of Stern's various interests. But again and again, critics tie his work to Whitman and the Old Testament, and, because of the prophetic cadences of the work, these comparisons are largely accurate.

The title of *Odd Mercy* is indicative of the major thematic aspect of Stern's work. The poet is fascinated by what the French philosopher Simone Weil called "gravity and grace." The coexistence of joy and pain, pleasure and suffering, and kindness and cruelty are all compelling subjects for Stern's poetry. These explorations of duality frequently lead the speakers in the poems to an acceptance of, a sort of submission to, the "odd mercy" that governs the world. For example, consider these lines from "Hot Dog," published as the last part of the collection *Odd Mercy*:

> I remember the smell
> of dead birds when I lived in Pittsburgh, there was
> a certain rottenness, a sweetness.

Both decay and ebullience manifest themselves in the image of the dead birds, and it is easy to see the birds as aspects of the dualities that Stern has tried to reconcile throughout his career. His earliest work did not receive much attention; in fact, he published his first collection of poetry in his late forties after more than a decade and a half of placing poems in magazines and journals.

Besides the formal signatures of his work, readers frequently note the emphasis his poetry usually places upon memory, history, and nostalgia. For Stern, unraveling the past is a mission compelled both by the desire both to understand and to redeem. Several critics have found in Stern's work ties to early nineteenth-century Romantic poetry, and this finding has merit. In Stern's work the speakers frequently long to discover the significance of the past; these attempts to understand and interpret history give the speaker a means to understand the present. Hence, memory—finely detailed memory—is often an important element in Stern's poetry. Consider, for example, the opening of the poem "The Bull-Roarer":

I only saw my father's face in butchery
once—it was a horror—there were ten men
surrounding a calf, their faces were red, my father's
eyes were shining; there might have been fewer than ten,
some were farmers, some were my father's friends
down from the city. I was nine, maybe eight;
I remember we slept a few hours and left
at four in the morning, there were two cars, or three,
I think it was West Virginia.

Two elements here are characteristic of Stern: a hesitance in piecing together memories and the enjambed syntax that uses run-on sentences and lists. The poem continues,

I remember
the pasture, the calf was screaming, his two eyes
were white with terror, there was blood and slaver
mixed, he was spread-eagled, there was a rope
stilling hanging from his neck, they all had knives

Also characteristic is this vivid eye for detail and how the poem moves from this disturbing image to a redemptive end where the speaker remembers an Eastern European toy and ends the poem, "They call it Uranic, / a heavenly force, sometimes almost a voice, / locked up in that whirling stone, dear father."

Although Stern's work has sometimes been placed under the rubric of "confessional" poetry, that label does not seen satisfactory. His poems do not attempt to evoke pathos for the experiences they describe in the same way that most poetry associated with that category does. In fact, Stern is much more interested in elevating rather than documenting the injustices of history, revealing the odd ways in which mercy frequently unfolds in the world.

—Tod Marshall

STEVENS, Wallace

Born: Reading, Pennsylvania, 2 October 1879. **Education:** Harvard University, Cambridge, Massachusetts, 1897-1900; New York University Law School, 1901-03; admitted to New York bar, 1904. **Family:** Married Elsie V. Kachel in 1909; one daughter. **Career:** Reporter, New York *Herald Tribune,* 1900-01; lawyer in New York, 1904-16; joined the Hartford Accident and Indemnity Company, Connecticut, 1916, vice president, 1934-55. **Awards:** Harriet Monroe Poetry award, 1946; Bollingen prize, 1950; National Book award, 1951, 1955; Pulitzer prize, 1955. **Member:** American Academy, 1946. **Died:** 2 August 1955.

PUBLICATIONS

Collections

Letters, edited by Holly Stevens. 1967.
The Palm at the End of the Mind: Selected Poems and a Play, edited by Holly Stevens. 1971.
*Collected Poetry and Prose.*1997.

Poetry

Harmonium. 1923; revised edition, 1931.
Ideas of Order. 1935.
Owl's Clover. 1936.
The Man with the Blue Guitar and Other Poems. 1937.
Parts of a World. 1942.
Notes Toward a Supreme Fiction. 1942.
Esthetique du Mal. 1945.
Description without Place. 1945.
Transport to Summer. 1947.
Three Academic Pieces: The Realm of Resemblance, Someone Puts a Pineapple Together, Of Ideal Time and Choice. 1947.
A Primitive Like an Orb. 1948.
The Auroras of Autumn. 1950.
Selected Poems, edited by Dennis Williamson. 1952.
Selected Poems. 1953.
Collected Poems. 1954.

Plays

Carlos among the Candles (produced 1917). In *Opus Posthumous,* 1957.
Three Travelers Watch a Sunrise (produced 1920). In *Opus Posthumous,* 1957.
Bowl, Cat, and Broomstick, in *Quarterly Review of Literature 16,* 1969.

Other

Two or Three Ideas. 1951.
The Relations Between Poetry and Painting. 1951.
The Necessary Angel: Essays on Reality and the Imagination. 1951.
Raoul Duffy: A Note. 1953.
Opus Posthumous (miscellany), edited by Samuel French Morse. 1957.
Vassar Viewed Voraciously: 16 Pencil Sketches. 1995.

*

Bibliography: *Stevens: A Descriptive Bibliography* by J.M. Edelstein, 1973.

Critical Studies: *The Shaping Spirit: A Study of Stevens* by William Van O'Connor, 1950; *Stevens: An Approach to His Poetry and Thought* by Robert Pack, 1958; *Stevens* by Frank Kermode, 1960, revised edition, 1967; *The Achievement of Stevens* edited by Ashley Brown and Robert S. Haller, 1962; *The Comic Spirit of Stevens* by Daniel Fuchs, 1963; *The Clairvoyant Eye: The Poetry and Poetics of Stevens* by Joseph N. Riddel, 1965; *The Act of the Mind: Essays on the Poetry of Stevens* edited by Roy Harvey Pearce and J. Hillis Miller, 1965; *Stevens: Musing the Obscure* by Ronald Sukenick, 1967; *The Dome and the Rock: Structure in* *the Poetry of Stevens* by James Baird, 1968; *On Extended Wings: Stevens' Longer Poems*, 1969, and *Stevens: Words Chosen Out of Desire*, 1984, both by Helen Vendler; *Stevens: Poetry as Life* by Samuel French Morse, 1970; *Stevens: The Poem as Act* by Merle E. Brown, 1970; *Images of Stevens* by Edward Kessler, 1971; *Introspective Voyager: The Poetic Development of Stevens* by A. Walton Litz, 1972; *Stevens* by Lucy Beckett, 1974; *Stevens: The Poems of Our Climate* by Harold Bloom, 1977; *Souvenirs and Prophecies: The Young Stevens* by Holly Stevens, 1977; *Stevens: An Introduction to the Poetry* by Susan B. Weston, 1977; *Stevens: The Poet and His Critics* by Abbie F. Willard, 1978; *Stevens: The Making of the Poem* by Frank Doggett, 1980, and *Stevens: A Celebration* edited by Doggett and Robert Buttel, 1980; *Advance on Chaos: The Sanctifying Imagination of Stevens* by David M. La Guardia, 1983; *Stanza My Stone: Stevens and the Hermetic Tradition* by Leonora Woodman, 1983; *Parts of a World: Stevens Remembered: An Oral Biography* by Peter Brazeau, 1983; *The Transparent Lyric: Reading and Meaning in the Poetry of Stevens and Williams* by David Walker, 1984; *The Long Poems of Stevens: An Interpretative Study* by Rajeev S. Patke, 1985; *Stevens: The Critical Heritage* edited by Charles Doyle, 1985; *Stevens: A Mythology of Self* by Milton J. Bates, 1985; *Forms of Farewell: The Late Poetry of Stevens* by Charles Berger. 1985; *Stevens: The Poetics of Modernism* edited by Albert Gelpi, 1986; *Stevens: The Early Years 1879-1923* by Joan Richardson, 1986; *Stevens: A Poet's Growth* by George S. Lensing, 1986; *Reading and Writing Nature: The Poetry of Robert Frost, Wallace Stevens, Marianne Moore, and Elizabeth Bishop* by Guy Rotella, 1991; *Lyric Contingencies: Emily Dickinson and Wallace Stevens* by Margaret Dickie, 1991; *The Wallace Stevens Case: Law and the Practice of Poetry* by Thomas C. Grey, 1991; *Wallace Stevens and the Actual World* by Alan Filreis, 1991; *Wallace Stevens and Literary Canons* by John Newcomb, 1992; *The Senses of Nonsense* by Alison Rieke, 1992; *Wallace Stevens and the Feminine* edited by Melita Schaum, 1993; *Beyond Music: The Poetics of Wallace Stevens* by Theodore Sampson, 1995; *Wallace Stevens: A Critical Assessment* by Chetan Karnani, 1996; *Wallace Stevens: A Spiritual Poet in a Secular Age* by Charles M. Murphy, 1997; *Solid Objects: Modernism and the Test of Production* by Douglas Mao, 1998.

*   *   *

Wallace Stevens is a poet who combined a long poetic career with another career as a business executive. The career that concerns us here—that of poet—produced a large body of work that circles around a lifelong consideration from which all his best poems radiate. Each poem is one testimony to an encompassing vision of what Stevens judges to be the prime obligation of a modern poet. That obligation leaves its mark on comparatively brief and early poems like "Peter Quince at the Clavier," "Sunday Morning," and "Thirteen Ways of Looking at a Blackbird" and continues in later and quite extensive works like *Transport to Summer* and *Ideas of Order*. Stevens is, early and late, concerned with a purification of the human intellect and sensibility—in the first place, the intellect and the sensibility of the poet who is writing, and, in the second place, the intellect and sensibility of the reader who responds to what the poet has written.

The purification takes place as service to a set of ideas—"ideas of order" in Stevens's phrase—that are ignored or, at best, served badly and intermittently in the culture to which Stevens belongs. Our sensibility has been corrupted by habits of thought that se-

duce the poet and his readers from a prime duty. Poet and reader have the chance, if they but respond rightly to the world that constantly surrounds them and indeed bombards them with endless impressions, to take in special sensations (the colors of light on the sea, the taste of cheese and pineapple, a musical cadence) and set them down in words. These sensations are most pure at a special time of the year (summer) and in southern climes where light and color are most intense. The sensations are adulterated by many things, by winter and northern climes, for example. Even more crucial in Stevens's account are the betrayals that are built into human culture, the dogmas and traditions and forms of artistic expression that are conventional and hackneyed. Stevens can speak bitterly of "statues" that dominate public squares and inhibit the innocent and intense sensory responses of the people who walk there.

Implied by this emphasis is a psychology—a theory of human perception—that is basically nominalistic. What is real and worthy of reverence—the poet's reverence and his readers'—is, for example, the contact the eye makes with a certain slant of light that is never the equivalent of some past contact with a slant of light. It is a mistake to move from several such special moments to any general conception about "shades of light." Each moment of perception must be preserved in its uniqueness, and the poet must, ideally, move no further from that moment than the carefully selected set of words that allow him to make a verbal record. Stevens—a poet quite well-informed in such matters—is aware of the traps into which other poets and other human beings have fallen. In *Harmonium*, there is an "Invective against Swans." Stevens writes: "The soul, o ganders, flies beyond the parks / And far beyond the discords of the wind." Here the "soul" has a vertigo that takes it beyond "parks" (and their clusters of rare and unique sensations) and beyond the manifestly rich "discords of the wind." The "soul" treacherously detaches the human sensibility from its proper and health-giving ground: the never-ending moments of intense sensation. The "soul" carries the human sensibility into a context of religious and social ideas that have at best a tenuous connection with "parks" and "discords of the wind."

The positive aspect of Stevens's reiterated warning appears in such lines as these from "Credences of Summer" in *Transport to Summer*. Here, Stevens suggests, is sound belief: "The rock cannot be broken. It is the truth. / It rises from land and sea and covers them." That is, the rock is—and remains—the source of acute physical perception. It is a natural object, far removed from any piece of stone that human hands have chipped at and made into a "statue," a memorial of some past event or an expression of human dogmas. A few more lines refine this particular statement, one that resembles many others in Stevens's work. The "rock of summer" (a "rock of winter" is apparently inferior) is not "A hermit's truth nor symbol in hermitage." A "hermit's truth" is what the gander soul flutters toward. Stevens continues:

> It is the visible rock, the audible,
> The brilliant mercy of a sure repose,
> On this present ground, the vividest repose,
> Things certain sustaining us in certainty.

Brief annotation—and all of Stevens's work stimulates such effort—would indicate that it is the actual rock that is esteemed, not the idea, Platonic or otherwise, of "rock." From the visible rock the errant "soul" gains a sure and not a treacherous "repose." And the rock is a "present ground" and, as such, the source of the only certainty in which a poet and his reader can have confidence.

Such lines indicate a perspective that extends throughout Stevens's work like a prairie landscape, insistent and unaltering. The lines, elegant in expression and charged with authority, invite each person to be a "center" into which are gathered separate moments of "vividest repose." Not the ersatz "repose" of some religious or political certainty. Not, even, the "repose" that some poets, retreating from politics and dogma, try to discover in personal relations, intense and unshakable. For the fierce outcry that is Matthew Arnold's only comfort on the "darkling plain" of "Dover Beach"—"Ah, love, let us be true / To one another!"—Stevens would have scarcely more patience than he has for "statues." As he observes in *Parts of a World:*

> Words are not forms of a single word.
> In the sum of the parts, there are only the parts.
> The world must be measured by eye . . .

To the villainous "gander soul," the whole is always greater than the sum of its parts and testimony to principle, to some inclusive order that lies in a divine mind or, at least, at the very roots of things. The "single word" (or Word, as Christians would say) is a delusion. Words serve the eye, and the eye takes in what aspect a "rock of summer" has at a particular moment.

As Stevens's large body of work indicates, such labor can be lifelong. It can exclude—and does—elements of existence that have counted for other poets and that, from Stevens's point of view, have corrupted them and those who read them. Stevens's "center" (the poet's awareness and perhaps his readers') is a clear crystal that sensation reaches—reaches and passes through with as little refraction as possible.

—Harold H. Watts

See the essay on "Sunday Morning."

STICKNEY, (Joseph) Trumbull

Born: Geneva, Switzerland, 20 June 1874. **Education:** Spent his childhood in Europe; tutored by his father; Walton Lodge, Clevedon, Somerset, 1886; Cutler's School, New York, 1890; Harvard University, Cambridge, Massachusetts, 1891-95 (editor, *Harvard Monthly*), A.B. (magna cum laude) 1895; the Sorbonne, Paris, Doctorat es Lettres, 1903. **Career:** Instructor in Greek, Harvard University, 1903-04. **Died:** 11 October 1904.

PUBLICATIONS

Collections

Homage to Stickney (selected verse), edited by James Reeves and Sean Haldane. 1968.
The Poems, edited by Amberys R. Whittle. 1972.

Poetry

Dramatic Verses. 1902.
Poems, edited by George Cabot Lodge, John Ellerton Lodge, and William Vaughn Moody. 1905.

Other

Les Sentences dans la Poésie Grecque d'Homere à Euripide. 1903.

Translator, with Sylvain Levi, *Bhagavadgita.* 1938.

*

Critical Studies: *The Fright of Time: Stickney* by Sean Haldane, 1970; *Stickney* by Amberys R. Whittle, 1973.

* * *

One of that group of gifted Americans who came to early maturity in the 1890s only to have their lives end before the first decade of the new century was completed, Trumbull Stickney is memorable on several counts. As an accomplished Greek and Sanskrit scholar and one of the first intellectual cosmopolitans to attempt a career in American letters, he exhibited a cultural impulse that was later followed more extensively by writers like **Ezra Pound** and **T.S. Eliot**. Further, along with **William Vaughn Moody** and George Cabot Lodge, he aimed at resuscitating verse-drama, and his work in this genre (*Prometheus Pyrphoros* and two fragments based on the lives of the Emperor Julian and the young Benvenuto Cellini) points forward to later efforts in the century. And, powerfully under the influence of Browning, he produced a number of "dramatic scenes" ("Kalypso," "Oneiropolos," "Lodovico Martelli," "Requiescam," etc.), although his instincts for dramatic conflict and psychological subtlety seem less vigorous than his evident delight in historical reconstruction.

It is perhaps the lyrical quality of his writing that suggests the most promise in his work. Almost suffocated in the cloying rhetoric of the *fin de siècle,* heavy with twilight and rose-dust and a fatigued embrace of futility, Stickney's lyrics frequently manage a new, if wistful, vitality to the cliches of romantic decadence. In poems like "Chestnuts in November," "At Sainte-Marguerite," "Mt. Lykaion," and in isolated passages from "Eride," Stickney's tempered musicality sustains the conventional formal structures, raising these poems above the level of similar lamentations that the Mauve Decade manufactured in wholesale lots. And in poems like "With thy two eyes look on me once again," "Leave him now quiet by the way," and, especially, "Mnemosyne," a quiet strength joins with a precise sense of rhythmical phrasing to produce verse that possesses an autonomy of statement and genuine eloquence. It is futile to speculate on what might have been, but in half a dozen poems Stickney's success was authentic and undeniable. As graceful as Santayana's verse but more concretely sensual, with an intellectual structure as sturdy as the early Robinson's but more personal and direct in tone, Stickney's achievement illustrates the highest ambitions of his generation, while implying a technique that may compensate for the weaknesses of its gentility.

—Earl Rovit

STOUT, Rex (Todhunter)

Born: Noblesville, Indiana, 1 December 1886. **Education:** Topeka High School, Kansas; University of Kansas, Lawrence. **Military Service:** Served in the U.S. Navy as a yeoman on President

Theodore Roosevelt's yacht, 1906-08. **Family:** Married 1) Fay Kennedy in 1916 (divorced 1933); 2) Pola Hoffman in 1933; two daughters. **Career:** Office boy, store clerk, bookkeeper, and hotel manager, 1916-27; invented the banking system for schoolchildren; full-time writer from 1927. Founding director, Vanguard Press, New York; host, *Speaking of Liberty, Voice of Freedom,* and *Our Secret Weapon* radio programs, 1941-43. Chair of the Writers' War Board, 1941-46, and the World Government Writers Board, 1949-75; president, Friends of Democracy, 1941-51, Authors' Guild, 1943-45, and Society for the Prevention of World War III, 1943-46; president, 1951-55, 1962-69, and vice president, 1956-61, Authors League of America; treasurer, Freedom House, 1957-75; president, Mystery Writers of America, 1958. **Awards:** Mystery Writers of America Grand Master award, 1959. **Died:** 27 October 1975.

PUBLICATIONS

Fiction

How Like a God. 1929.
Seed on the Wind. 1930.
Golden Remedy. 1931.
Forest Fire. 1933.
Fer-de-Lance. 1934.
The President Vanishes. 1934.
The League of Frightened Men. 1935.
O Careless Love! 1935.
The Rubber Band. 1936; as *To Kill Again,* 1960.
The Red Box. 1937.
The Hand in the Glove. 1937; as *Crime on Her Hands,* 1939.
Too Many Cooks. 1938.
Mr. Cinderella. 1938.
Some Buried Caesar. 1939; as *The Red Bull,* 1945.
Mountain Cat. 1939; as *The Mountain Cat Murders,* 1943.
Red Threads. 1939.
Double for Death. 1939.
Over My Dead Body. 1940.
Where There's a Will. 1940.
The Broken Vase. 1941.
Alphabet Hicks. 1941; as *The Sound of Murder,* 1965.
Black Orchids (stories). 1942.
Booby Trap (stories). 1944.
Not Quite Dead Enough (stories). 1944.
The Silent Speaker. 1946.
Too Many Women. 1947.
And Be a Villain. 1948; as *More Deaths Than One,* 1949.
The Second Confession. 1949.
Trouble in Triplicate (stories). 1949.
Three Doors to Death (stories). 1950.
In the Best Families. 1950; as *Even in the Best Families,* 1951.
Murder by the Book. 1951.
Curtains for Three (stories). 1951.
Triple Jeopardy (stories). 1951.
Prisoners Base. 1952; as *Out Goes She,* 1953.
The Golden Spiders. 1953.
Three Men Out (stories). 1954.
The Black Mountain. 1954.
Before Midnight. 1955.
Might as Well Be Dead. 1956.

Three Witnesses (stories). 1956.
Three for the Chair (stories). 1957.
If Death Ever Slept. 1957.
Champagne for One. 1958.
And Four to Go (stories). 1958; as *Crime and Again,* 1959.
Plot It Yourself. 1959; as *Murder in Style,* 1960.
Three at Wolfe's Door (stories). 1960.
Too Many Clients. 1960.
The Final Deduction. 1961.
Gambit. 1962.
Homicide Trinity (stories). 1962.
The Mother Hunt. 1963.
Trio for Blunt Instruments (stories). 1964.
A Right to Die. 1964.
The Doorbell Rung. 1965.
Death of a Doxy. 1966.
The Father Hunt. 1968.
Death of a Dude. 1969.
Please Pass the Guilt. 1973.
A Family Affair. 1975.
Justice Ends at Home and Other Stories, edited by John McAleer. 1977.
Under the Andes. 1985.

Other

The Nero Wolfe Cook Book, with others. 1973.
Corsage (miscellany). 1977.

Editor, *The Illustrious Dunderheads.* 1942.
Editor, with Louis Greenfield, *Rue Morgue 1.* 1946.
Editor, *Eat, Drink, and Be Buried.* 1956; as *For Tomorrow We Die,* 1958.

*

Bibliography: *Stout: An Annotated Primary and Secondary Bibliography* by Guy M. Townsend, 1980.

Critical Studies: *Nero Wolfe of West Thirty-Fifth Street: The Life and Times of America Largest Private Detective* by William S. Baring-Gould, 1969; *Stout: A Biography* by John McAleer, 1977; *The Brownstone House of Nero Wolfe* by Ken Darby, 1983; *Rex Stout* by David R. Anderson, 1984; *At Wolfe's Door: The Nero Wolfe Novels of Rex Stout* by J. Kenneth Van Dover, 1993.

* * *

At the beginning of a career undertaken after he had earned enough money in business to permit full-time devotion to writing, Rex Stout published four critically acceptable but unpopular "straight" novels. Then, in the decade after he had committed himself to the detective genre with the publication of *Fer-de-Lance,* he developed a variety of sleuths: "Dol" Bonner and Sally Colt in *The Hand in the Glove,* Tecumseh Fox who appears in three novels, Alphabet Hicks in one novel bearing his name, Delia Brand in *Mountain Cat,* and Inspector Cramer of *Red Threads.* Stout is known, however, almost entirely because he was the creator of Nero Wolfe.

Like Sherlock Holmes, Stout's evident model for a Great Detective, Nero Wolfe so dominates the tales in which he appears that enthusiasts refer to them as though they were authorless—they are simply Nero Wolfe stories; and, again like his model and a small handful of other fictional detectives such as Charlie Chan or Sam Spade, Nero Wolfe—the enormously fat, eccentric genius-recluse—has achieved independence of the tales themselves. He is an autonomous figure in the popular imagination, familiar even to those with only the slightest literary knowledge of his exploits.

There can be no doubt it was Stout's intention to create a mythic detective. The constellation of traits attributed to Wolfe coupled with his mental infallibility are the formula of a character who dominates as well as presides, and the narrative voice of Archie Goodwin, though it is quite unlike Dr. Watson's, provides for the distancing that surrounds the solver of mysteries with his own aura of mystery. Moreover, Archie's speech develops the illusion of a case's history with the attendant suspense necessary to deflect our awareness that the only subject of the fiction is the detective.

It would be incorrect, however, to describe Stout only as an imitator of formulas pioneered by Arthur Conan Doyle, for Stout artfully manages the genre of detection fiction in his own way. It is just that his way involves simplification of the genre rather than the transgression of conventions we usually associate with innovation. A striking example of Stout's simplification is in the setting of the stories. Wolfe's household is central to every tale. He never goes abroad to the classic country house or to walk the city's mean streets; thus, in one stroke we get both ambience (W. 35th St. equals Baker St.) and intensification of the detective's prominence, since clients and aides with the guilty and innocent suspects must all subject themselves to the force of his orbit, their thoughts and acts entirely subordinate to Wolfe's interpretations.

Fundamentally, the plot of every tale of detection is epistemological. It progresses through scenes of a detective's methodical expansion of his knowledge of the reality of some mysterious events until it is concluded by a celebration of rationality in which all the secondary characters witness the detective's literal creation of truth through summary analysis of events and motives. In plot, too, Stout has simplified. With Wolfe working on cases in his own study—the consummate armchair detective—each scene prefigures the classical denouement, maintaining a dominance by Wolfe's mind over events that matches the supremacy of his personality.

The result of Stout's simplification of the detection story is to invest the saga of Nero Wolfe with an Augustan formality. The incidents of the stories and novels vary, but each repeats invariable movements extolling the nature of a Great Detective.

—John M. Reilly

STOWE, Harriet (Elizabeth) Beecher

Born: Litchfield, Connecticut, 14 June 1811. **Education:** Miss Sarah Pierce's school, Litchfield; Hartford Female Seminary, Connecticut, 1824. **Family:** Married Reverend Calvin Ellis Stowe in 1836 (died 1886); three daughters and four sons. **Career:** Teacher, Hartford Female Seminary, 1829-32, and Western Female Institute, Cincinnati, 1833-35; lived in Brunswick, Maine, 1850-51, Andover, Massachusetts, 1852-63, then in Hartford and Mandarin, Florida; famous and controversial as a writer after publication of *Uncle Tom's Cabin,* 1852; active in abolitionist movement; visited England three times and toured Europe; friend of Lady Byron, George Eliot, and Ruskin. **Died:** 1 July 1896.

PUBLICATIONS

Collections

The Writings. 16 vols., 1896.
Collected Poems, edited by John M. Moran, Jr. 1967.
Uncle Tom's Cabin, The Minister's Wooing, Oldtown Folks (Library of America), edited by Kathryn Kish Sklar. 1982.
The Oxford Harriet Beecher Stowe Reader. 1999.

Fiction

Prize Tale: A New England Sketch. 1834.
The Mayflower; or, Sketches of Scenes and Characters among the Descendants of the Pilgrims. 1843; augmented edition, 1855.
Uncle Tom's Cabin; or, Life among the Lowly. 1852; edited by Kenneth S. Lynn, 1962.
Uncle Sam's Emancipation (stories). 1853.
Dred: A Tale of the Great Dismal Swamp. 1856; as *Nina Gordon,* 1866.
The Minister's Wooing. 1859.
Agnes of Sorrento. 1862.
The Pearl of Orr's Island: A Story of the Coast of Maine. 1862.
The Daisy's First Winter and Other Stories. 1867.
Queer Little People. 1867; as *Queer Little Folks,* 1886.
Oldtown Folks. 1869; edited by Henry F. May, 1966.
My Wife and I; or, Harry Henderson's History. 1871.
Pink and White Tyranny: A Society Novel. 1871.
Sam Lawson's Oldtown Fireside Stories. 1872.
We and Our Neighbors; or, The Records of an Unfashionable Street. 1875.
Poganuc People: Their Loves and Lives. 1878.

Plays

The Christian Slave, from her novel *Uncle Tom's Cabin.* 1855.

Poetry

Religious Poems. 1867.

Other

Primary Geography for Children, with Catharine Beecher. 1833; revised edition, as *First Geography for Children,* 1855; as *A New Geography for Children,* 1855.
An Elementary Geography. 1835.
A Key to Uncle Tom's Cabin, Presenting the Original Facts and Documents upon Which the Story Is Founded. 1853.
Sunny Memories of Foreign Lands. 2 vols., 1854.
The Two Altars; or, Two Pictures in One. 1855.
Our Charley and What to Do with Him. 1858.
A Reply in Behalf of the Women of America. 1863.
The Ravages of a Carpet. 1865.
Stories about Our Dogs. 1865.
House and Home Papers. 1865.
Little Foxes. 1866.
The Chimney-Corner. 1868.
Men of Our Times. 1868; as *The Lives and Deeds of Our Self-Made Men,* 1872.

*The American Woman's Home; or, Principles of Domestic Science,
with Catharine Beecher.* 1869; revised edition, as *The New
Housekeeper's Manual,* 1873.
Little Pussy Willow (for children). 1870.
Lady Byron Vindicated. 1870.
Woman in Sacred History. 1873; as *Bible Heroines,* 1878.
Palmetto-Leaves. 1873.
Betry's Bright Idea. 1876.
Footsteps of the Master. 1877.
A Dog's Mission (for children). 1881.
Our Famous Women. 1884.

*

Bibliography: *Stowe: A Bibliography* by Margaret Holbrook
Hildreth, 1976; *Stowe: A Reference Guide* by Jean Ashton, 1977.

Critical Studies: *Life of Stowe from Her Letters and Journals*
edited by Charles Edward Stowe, 1889; *Life and Letters of Stowe*
edited by Annie A. Fields, 1897; *Crusader in Crinoline: The Life
of Stowe* by Forrest Wilson, 1941; *The Rungless Ladder: Stowe
and New England Puritanism* by Charles H. Foster, 1954; *Stowe*
by John R. Adams, 1963; *Stowe: The Known and the Unknown*
by Edward Wagenknecht, 1965; *The Novels of Stowe* by Alice C.
Crozier, 1969; *Stowe: A Biography* by Noel B. Gerson, 1976; *The
Building of "Uncle Tom's Cabin"* by E. Bruce Kirkham, 1977;
Stowe and American Literature by Ellen Moers, 1978; *Critical
Essays on Stowe* edited by Elizabeth Ammons, 1980; *The Religious Ideas of Stowe: Her Gospel of Womanhood* by Gayle
Kimball, 1982; "Class and the Strategies of Sympathy" by Amy
Schrager Lang, in *The Culture of Sentiment: Race, Gender, and
Sentimentality in Nineteenth Century America,* 1992; "Home as
Haven, Home as Hell: Uncle Tom's Canon" by Leslie Fiedler, in
Rewriting the Dream: Reflections on the Changing American Literary Canon, 1992; *Harriet Beecher Stowe: A Life* by Joan D.
Hedrick, 1994.

* * *

Uncle Tom's Cabin, Harriet Beecher Stowe's masterpiece, has been
said to have had a "social impact . . . on the United States . . . greater
than that of any book before or since." There is no doubt that it
is one of the few books to have changed the climate of public
opinion and helped swing the political pendulum. Although evaluations of the work in the late twentieth century tend to reveal in
it not less but more literary craftsmanship, any critical analysis
must consider this novel not so much as a literary production but
as an instrument that led to action.

Stowe grew up in "a kind of moral heaven, replete with moral
oxygen—fully charged with intellectual electricity," and much of
that "moral oxygen" and "intellectual electricity" was injected into
Uncle Tom's Cabin. The guiding principles of self-abnegation, spiritual regeneration, and Christian purpose inculcated in her early
training filtered into her writing. Coupled with her own high-minded interest in social reform, they were shaped into a powerful ethical weapon. The author had read of the atrocities of slavery, and, when the Fugitive Slave Law spurred her to action, she
was finally metamorphosed into the instrument of the Lord who
created an "epic of Negro bondage." This powerful narrative of
damnation and salvation, with its bold message that slavery destroys both the master and the slave, electrified the nation. While

Uncle Tom's Cabin is, on the one hand, a domestic novel, it is
also a forceful, vital, original, and daring moral instrument.

Although its characters are sometimes symbols and some of its
incidents are stylized, the figures of Simon Legree, Eliza, Mr. St.
Clare, Little Eva, and Uncle Tom have joined the parade of unforgettable literary characters that have become part of the national
consciousness. The author's reliance upon tact did not preclude
her recourse to realism. Just how powerfully Mrs. Stowe's timely
propaganda stirred the American conscience is revealed by its publishing history. Within a year of publication its sales topped
300,000, and before the Civil War the figure reached three million.
It made its author famous overnight, inspired a spate of anti-Uncle
Tom novels, and won the praise of such diverse critics as **Henry
Wadsworth Longfellow** and **Henry James.** According to one reviewer: "The mightiest princes of intellect, as well as those who
have scarcely harbored a stray thought . . . friends of slavery equally
with the haters of that institution . . . all . . . bend with sweating
eagerness over her magic pages." Emerson traced its power to the
universality of its message when he commented: "We have seen
an American woman write a novel of which a million copies were
sold in all languages, and which had one merit, of speaking to the
universal heart, and was read with equal interest to three audiences, namely, in the parlor, in the kitchen, and in the nursery of
every house." *Uncle Tom's Cabin* still has the power of stirring
conflicting emotions in its critics. **James Baldwin**'s attribution
of racial prejudice to the novel, for example, has met its effective
rebutters. Although the novel is no longer widely read, it is unlikely that it will ever be forgotten.

Stowe's earlier work consisted of sentimental and conventional
sketches that reflected her belief in the sanctity of the home and
woman's place in it. After the success of *Uncle Tom's Cabin* she
replied to objectors with *A Key to Uncle Tom's Cabin* and returned
to the theme of anti-slavery in *Dred.* Between 1862 and 1884,
she produced at least a book a year; most of them consisted of
essays on the home, domestic novels, stories of death and redemption, as well as a defense of Lady Byron.

In the late twentieth century Stowe has surprisingly been called
"the only major feminine humorist nineteenth-century America
produced," an attribution based less upon a sense of the jocular
than upon an ear for idiom and an eye for actuality. The books
that flowed from her tireless pen often reveal these qualities. They
also reveal her dissection of the Calvinist ethic, and despite their
sentimentality they provide considerable documentary insight into
the moral climate of nineteenth-century New England.

The aptest description of Stowe was made by the biographer
who dubbed her a "Crusader in Crinoline." For the most part, her
crinolines have turned into period pieces, and her crusade has become historic. Yet she helped to document and advance that crusade, and in *Uncle Tom's Cabin* she created a book that shook the
world.

—Madeleine B. Stern

See the essay on *Uncle Tom's Cabin.*

STRAND, Mark

Born: Summerside, Prince Edward Island, Canada, 11 April 1934;
came to United States in 1938. **Education:** Antioch College, Yel-

low Springs, Ohio, B.A. 1957; Yale University, New Haven, Connecticut (Cook prize and Bergin prize, 1959), B.F.A. 1959; University of Florence (Fulbright fellow), 1960-61; University of Iowa, Iowa City, M.A. 1962. **Family:** Married 1) Antonia Ratensky in 1961 (divorced 1973, one daughter; 2) Julia Rumsey Garretson in 1976, one son. **Career:** Instructor, University of Iowa, Iowa city, 1962-65; Fulbright Lecturer, University of Brazil, Rio de Janeiro, 1965-66; assistant professor, Mount Holyoke College, South Hadley, Massachusetts, 1967; visiting professor, University of Washington, Seattle, 1968, 1970; adjunct associate professor, Columbia University, New York, 1969-72; visiting professor, Yale University, 1969; associate professor, Brooklyn College, New York, 1970-72; Bain-Swiggett lecturer, Princeton University, New Jersey; Hurst Professor, Brandeis University, Waltham Massachusetts; visiting professor, University of Virginia, Charlottesville, California State University Fresno, 1977, University of California, Irvine, 1978, Wesleyan University, Middleton, Connecticut, 1979, Harvard University, Cambridge, Massachusetts, 1980; visiting professor, University of Utah, Salt Lake City, beginning 1981. Beginning 1994 Elliot Coleman Professor of Poetry, The Writing Seminars, Johns Hopkins University, Baltimore, Maryland. **Awards:** Ingram Merrill Foundation fellowship, 1966; National Endowment for the Arts grant, 1976, 1977, 1986; Rockefeller award, 1968; Guggenheim fellowship, 1974; Edgar Allan Poe award, 1974; American Academy award, 1975; Academy of American Poets fellowship, 1979; MacArthur Foundation fellowship, 1987; United States Poet Laureate, 1990-91; Utah Governor's Award in Arts, 1992; Bobbitt National prize for Poetry, 1992; Bollingen prize for poetry, 1993. **Member:** American Academy.

Publications

Poetry

Sleeping with One Eye Open. 1964.
Reasons for Moving. 1968.
Darker: Poems. 1970.
The Story of Our Lives. 1973.
The Sargentville Notebook. 1974.
Elegy for My Father. 1978.
The Late Hour. 1978.
Selected Poems. 1980.
The Continuous Life. 1990.
New Poems. 1990.
The Monument. 1991.
Reasons for Moving, Darker, and The Sargentville Notebook. 1992.
Dark Harbor: A Poem. 1993.
Blizzard of One: Poems. 1998.

Short Stories

Mr. and Mrs. Baby and Other Stories. 1985.

Other

The Planet of Lost Things (for children). 1978.
The Night Book (for children). 1985.
Rembrandt Takes a Walk (for children). 1986.
Prose. 1987.
William Bailey. 1987.
Hopper. 1994.

Editor, *The Contemporary American Poets: American Poetry Since 1940.* 1969.
Editor, *New Poetry of Mexico.* 1972.
Editor and Translator, *The Owl's Insomnia: Selected Poems of Rafael Alberti.* 1973.
Editor and Translator, *Souvenir of the Ancient World: Selected Poems of Carlos Dummond de Andrade.* 1976.
Editor, with Chalres Simic, *Another Republic: 17 European and South American Writers.* 1976.
Editor, *Art of the Real: Nine American Figurative Painters.* 1983.
Editor, with Thomas Colchie, *Traveling in the Family: Selected Poems of Carlos Drummond de Andrade.* 1986.
Editor, with David Lehman, *The Best American Poetry 1991.* 1991.
Editor, *the Golden Ecco Anthology.* 1994.

Translator, *18 Poems from the Quechua.* 1971.
Translator, *Texas* by Jorge Luis Borges. 1975.

*

Manuscript Collection: Lilly Library, University of Indiana, Bloomington, Indiana.

Critical Studies: "Mark Strand: *Darker*" by James Crenner, in *Seneca Review,* April 1971; "Dark and Radiant Peripheries: Mark Strand and A.R. Ammons" by Harold Bloom, in *Southern Review,* winter 1972; "Entry to the Unaccounted For: Mark Strand's Fantastic Autism" by Lance Olsen, in *The Poetic Fantastic: Studies in an Evolving Genre,* 1989; *Mark Strand and the Poet's Place in Contemporary Culture* by David Kirby, 1990; "Mark Strand" by Harold Bloom, in *The Gettysburg Review,* spring 1991; "Poetry Chronicle: Amy Clampitt, Louise Gluck, Mark Strand" by Charles Berger, in *Rartian: A Quarterly Review,* winter 1991; "The Anxiety of Dedication: Joseph Brodsky's Kvintet/Sextet and Mark Strand" by John Givens, in *Russian, Croatian, Serbian, Czech and Slovak Polish Literature,* 1995; "Reading As Poets Read: Following Mark Strand" by Charles Berger, in *Philosophy and Literature,* April 1996.

*   *   *

Through nine poetry collections, beginning in 1968, Mark Strand has gone about building his reputation with the cunning of a chameleon. Even with his early, more energetic poems in the volumes *Moving* and *Darker,* Strand had a tendency to become invisible between the dramatically different writing styles of a tight club of poet-friends: the literary pyrotechnics of **Charles Simic** and **James Tate** at one end, and the meditative, at times opaque ruminations of Charles Wright and the late William Matthews at the other. Perhaps not surprisingly, an at times unbearable anxiety permeates the poems:

> In a field
> I am the absence
> of field.
> This is
> always the case.
> Wherever I am
> I am what is missing.

This vision of cynical self-absorption and eerie delight is reinforced by minimal attention to line and phrasing. It is almost as if the writer is insisting that the reader provide the additional insights and discoveries one would need to fill in the blanks, to populate the void. This method succeeds in creating a reciprocal anxiety in the careful reader, which spreads to cover the arc of Strand's career.

More than other poets of his generation, Strand has adapted his own writing to suit what he perceives to be prevailing currents in poetry. In the sixties his verses mimicked the irreverence of the Beats and **Louis Simpson;** in the seventies he often sounded like Simic, or Tate, or both; by the late eighties, after a younger generation had inspired a resurgence in narrative poetry, he laid claim to having always been a narrative poet; in the nineties, his poetry has become increasingly diffuse, strangely echoing, at times, his old nemesis, **John Ashbery.**

But through the permutations of style, Strand's one subject has always been the Self. It is not the Self made whole, or yearning for completion and greater awareness; it is the Self dissembling, the proud Self both preening in a mirror and refusing obligation by ducking out of the receiving line. It is the Self most interested in every aspect of itself:

I cannot decide whether or not to stroll
Through the somber garden where the grass in the shade
Is silver and frozen and where the general green

Of the rest of the garden is dark except
For a luminous patch made by the light of a window.
I cannot decide, and because it is autumn

When the sadness of gardens is greatest, I believe
That someone is already there and is waiting
For the pale appearance of another.

The anxiety of the earlier poems has been replaced by an attitude of world-weariness. It is as if the poet has come to the conclusion that every thought bears equal weight, that every idea is ephemeral, disposable. Note how the narrator speaks with the coldness of stones, how the author's early, gnomic utterances have given way to longer, Ashberyesque, prepositional phrasing, either creating multiple opportunities for indirection, or emotional and spiritual evasion.

Either way, ennui constitutes the increasingly dominant tone of Strand's compositions. In an era when American poetry has opened up to so many multicultural voices and small revolutions in style, Strand's concise, distant, and bloodless manner, in language and in theme, stands out from the frenetic activity going on all around him. Many contend that this alone makes Strand the perfect point person, in a dark time, for a marginal art. But others question the truth, substance, and ultimate staying power of such work.

—Robert McDowell

STRIBLING, T(homas) S(igismund)

Born: Clifton, Tennessee, 4 March 1881. **Education:** Clifton Masonic Academy; Southern Normal College, Huntingdon, Tennessee, 1898-1900; Normal College, Florence, Alabama, 1902-03, graduated 1903; studied law at the University of Alabama, Tuscaloosa, LL.B. 1905. **Family:** Married Lou Ella Kloss in 1930.

Career: Editor, *Clifton News,* 1900-02; teacher, Tuscaloosa High School, 1903-04; lawyer in Florence, 1906-07; staff member, *Taylor-Trotwood Magazine,* Nashville, Tennessee, 1907-08; full-time writer from 1908; wrote moral stories for Sunday school magazines; lived in South America and Europe, 1908-16; reporter, *Chattanooga News,* 1917; stenographer, Aviation Bureau, Washington, D.C., 1918; instructor in creative writing, Columbia University, New York, 1936, 1940; lived in Clifton after 1959. **Awards:** Pulitzer prize, 1933. LL.D.: Oglethorpe University, Atlanta, 1936. **Died:** 10 July 1965.

PUBLICATIONS

Fiction

The Cruise of the Dry Dock. 1917.
Birthright. 1922.
Fombombo. 1923.
Red Sand. 1924.
Teeftallow. 1926.
Bright Metal. 1928.
East Is East. 1928.
Clues of the Caribbees, Being Certain Criminal Investigations of Henry Poggioli, Ph.D. 1929.
Strange Moon. 1929.
Backwater. 1930.
The Forge. 1931.
The Store. 1932.
Unfinished Cathedral. 1934.
The Sound Wagon. 1935.
These Bars of Flesh. 1938.
Best Dr. Poggioli Detective Stories. 1975.

Play

Rope, with David Wallace, from the novel *Teeftallow* by Stribling (produced 1928).

Other

Laughing Stock: The Posthumous Autobiography of Stribling, edited by Randy K. Cross and John T. McMillan. 1982.

*

Critical Studies: *Stribling* by Wilton Eckley, 1975; "No More 'Treachy Sentimentalities': The Legacy of T.S. Stribling to the Southern Literary Renascence," in *Southern Studies: An Interdisciplinary Journal of the South,* spring 1981, "Selected Letters of T. S. Stribling, 1910-1934," in *Mississippi Quarterly: The Journal of Southern Culture,* fall 1985, and "Through a Lens Darkly: T.S. Stribling's Representation of the Past in His Alabama Trilogy," in *Southern Literary Journal,* fall 1990, all by Edward J. Piacentino.

*   *   *

T.S. Stribling, who began as a writer of moral adventure tales for Sunday school magazines and then moved on to the pulps and finally to serious fiction, is remembered chiefly for *The Store,* which won him the Pulitzer Prize in 1933. It is the second volume of his trilogy (*The Forge* and *Unfinished Cathedral* are the other two) dealing with the fortunes of the Vaiden family, particularly with the rise of Miltaides Vaiden from poor man to rich landowner and cotton planter in the antebellum South. In this trilogy, as in his other serious novels (*Birthright, Teeftallow, Bright Metal, The Sound Wagon, These Bars of Flesh*), Stribling is a social satirist and local colorist. His strong point is his gift of observation, of setting down in credible language the look and feel of a natural landscape and the poor whites and blacks who inhabit it. His weaknesses are his themes (which tend to be simplistic), his plots (melodramatic), and his style (often crudely pretentious). Like **Sinclair Lewis**, Stribling is a social critic and debunker, his locale the middle South (Tennessee, Alabama), and his chief concern prejudice against blacks and the general narrow-mindedness of ingrown southern communities. In *Birthright,* he deals with a Harvard-educated black from Tennessee forced to live the stereotyped role of an uneducated black laborer. But he also debunked the American scene of lawyers and businessmen (*The Sound Wagon*) and the American education college (*These Bars of Flesh*). Much of his fiction is hackwork, quickly turned out melodrama with a slight satirical edge. *Fombombo, Red Sand,* and *Strange Moon* mix satire, South American politics, business, and romance. Stribling also wrote detective stories (*Clues of the Caribbees*).

Stribling is an "objective" observer who sees history as a mechanical process, individuals as pawns in the grip of economic and social forces. His fiction is interesting to the literary historian for the way he blends popular stereotypes with old-fashioned liberal political and social ideas, and for the contrast offered between his mechanistic histories of the South and **William Faulkner**'s mythical histories, a contrast that helps make clear not only Stribling's appeal to liberal critics in the 1930s but also the reason Faulkner was disliked and undervalued.

—W.J. Stuckey

STYRON, William

Born: Newport News, Virginia, 11 June 1925. **Education:** Christchurch School, Virginia; Davidson College, North Carolina, 1942-43; Duke University, Durham, North Carolina, 1943-44, 1946-47 (Phi Beta Kappa), B.A. 1947; New School for Social Research, New York, 1947. **Military Service:** Served in the U.S. Marine Corps, 1944-45, 1951; 1st lieutenant. **Family:** Married Rose Burgunder in 1953; three daughters and one son. **Career:** Associate editor, McGraw-Hill, New York, 1947; advisory editor, *Paris Review,* Paris and New York, beginning 1952; fellow, Silliman College, Yale University, New Haven, Connecticut, beginning 1964; member of editorial board, *American Scholar,* Washington, DC, 1970-76; honorary consultant in American Letters, Library of Congress, Washington, DC. **Awards:** American Academy Rome prize, 1952, and Howells Medal, 1970; Pulitzer prize, 1968; American Book award, 1980; Connecticut Arts award, 1984; Cino del Duca Prize, 1985. Litt.D.: Duke University, 1968; National Medal of Arts, 1993. **Member:** American Academy of Arts and Letters; American Academy of Arts and Sciences; Commander, Order of Arts and Letters (France); Commander, Legion of Honor (France). **Residence:** Roxbury, Connecticut.

PUBLICATIONS

Fiction

Lie Down in Darkness. 1951.
The Long March. 1956.
Set This House on Fire. 1960.
The Confessions of Nat Turner. 1967.
Shadrach (story). 1979.
Sophie's Choice. 1979.
A Tidewater Morning. 1993.
The Long March; and In the Clap Shack. 1993.

Plays

In the Clap Shack (produced 1972). 1973.

Other

The Four Seasons, illustrated by Harold Altman. 1965.
Admiral Robert Penn Warren and the Snows of Winter: A Tribute. 1978.
The Message of Auschwitz. 1979.
Against Fear. 1981.
As He Lay Dead, A Bitter Grief. 1981.
This Quiet Dust and Other Writings. 1982.
Conversations with Styron (interviews), edited by James L.W. West III. 1985.
Darkness Visible: A Memoir of Madness. 1990.
Inheritance of Night: Early Drafts of "Lie Down in Darkness." 1993.

Editor, *Best Short Stories from the Paris Review.* 1959.

*

Bibliography: *Styron: A Descriptive Bibliography* by James L.W. West III, 1977; *Styron: A Reference Guide* by Jackson R. Bryer and Mary B. Hatem, 1978, and *William Styron: A Bibliography* by Bryer, 1981; *Styron: An Annotated Bibliography of Criticism* by Philip W. Leon, 1978.

Critical Studies: *Styron* by Robert H. Fossum, 1968; *Styron* by Cooper R. Mackin, 1969; *Styron* by Richard Pearce, 1971; *Styron* by Marc L. Ratner, 1972; *Styron* by Melvin J. Friedman, 1974; *The Achievement of Styron* edited by Irving Malin and Robert K. Morris, 1975, revised edition, 1981; *Critical Essays on Styron* edited by Arthur D. Casciato and James L.W. West III, 1982; *The Root of All Evil: The Thematic Unity of Styron's Fiction* by John K. Crane, 1985; *William Styron* by Judith Ruderman, 1987; *William Styron's Sophie's Choice: Crime and Self-Punishment* by Rhoda Sirlin, 1990; *William Styron's Darkness Visible* by Virgina Ross, 1991; *The Critical Response to William Styron* edited by Daniel Ross, 1995; *The Novels of William Styron: From Harmony to History* by Gavin Cologne-Brookes, 1995; *William Styron: A Life* by James L.W. West, III, 1998.

*   *   *

During the decades in which William Styron's fiction from *Lie Down in Darkness* to *Sophie's Choice* appeared, the Southern Renaissance went into a sad decline, suffering a loss of authority and coherence. To be sure, **Robert Penn Warren** and **Eudora Welty** continued to write and **Flannery O'Connor** and **Walker Percy** made substantial contributions to fiction, but the triumphs of the New Criticism, which owed so much to the South, the poetry that came from it, and the vision of **William Faulkner** were not matched. Styron is emblematic of this decline, both in his ambiguous relationship to the South and in the intrinsic quality of his work.

There is no question about a "southern" cast to Styron's fiction. It derives, above all, from the influence of Faulkner, and of Warren and **Thomas Wolfe** as well. All share an appetite for powerful rhetoric; in Styron's case the rhetoric is often turgid and undisciplined. In *Lie Down in Darkness* and *The Confessions of Nat Turner,* Styron uses the matter of the South and deals with those problems of sin, dissolution, and decadence that southern history has thrust upon the imagination of many southern writers. In this respect he is a traditionalist in subject matter and in values as well. But he is unaware of the cost of the ethical and humanistic orthodoxies that he has accepted. After his first novel, where the principal thrust is nihilistic, his fiction depends upon ideas of a viable self, the dignity of man, the reality of guilt and the possibility of redemption (religious concepts secularized in his work), the recognition and rejection of decadence, the need for love, the desirability of freedom, and the possibility of tragic magnitude and nobility. These constitute the intellectual and ethical furniture of the traditional novelist and seem particularly appropriate to a writer of the South, where tradition is cherished.

Like most writers who take these positions in the postwar world, Styron knows that great forces are at work everywhere to destroy him. He senses the morbidity of contemporary life and feels the presence of anarchic murder in the air. He knows that the machine age has damaged the South and attacked Old Testament fundamentalism there. His response to these destructive forces is, paradoxically, to deny allegiance to the South and dissociate himself from the southern school of letters. But analysis of his work will show that he has not escaped the South any more than he has neglected the Bible, which in fact he acknowledges as an influence upon him. Surely, both the South and the Bible helped him to frame those traditional values and attitudes that appear in his fiction.

That confusion about the impact of the South upon his literary consciousness is of a piece with his unselfconscious acceptance of the ideas of truth and reality, which are both metaphysical and technical constituents of his fiction. He agrees, for example, with Georgy Lukács's proposition that the writer should reproduce the complex and ramifying totality of the past with historical faithfulness. He seems to think that a single reality existed in the past, that it is "true," and that novelists can capture it, presumably by imitating "reality." He appears unaware of the challenge to literary realism made by the modernists. He appears naive in asserting that he tries to make his characters round, when modernists have called into question the very concept of character. He thinks the progression of time is one of the novelist's difficult problems, but they tend to believe that the idea of linear time may have been shattered by contemporary science. It is acceptable enough that the theory of fiction governing his practice of fiction be old-fashioned and conventional, but it is damaging that he can bring no vitality of deep understanding to the tradition, that he does not make the old new.

Lie Down in Darkness, derived from Faulkner and Freud, dramatizes the collapse into decadence and chaos of ceremony and ritual, of family, marriage, love, and religion. Styron deals here with the dissolution of a Virginia family in such a way as to show that the sins of the father are visited upon the daughter. Styron tries to broaden the impact of his novel by using the Freudian interpretation of the Electra myth and by linking the suicide of his protagonist to the dropping of the atomic bomb on Hiroshima. The novel ends bleakly in an affirmation of nihilism that does not appear in Styron's subsequent work.

The Long March, a largely successful novelette, embraces possibilities in human endurance and of triumph over absurdity. Peyton, naked at the end of the first novel, is nothingness; Mannix, the hero of this book, stripped to the skin at the end, is man, chastened but alive, with a regained sense of his own humanity. This guarded optimism also characterizes *Set This House on Fire,* which ends in a **Norman Mailer**-like regeneration through violence that restores the protagonist's creative capacities and in a successful quest for expiation. Unfortunately, this novel is pretentious and prolix; it strains for parallels to Greek tragedy, but in its banalities emerges as more like Italian opera.

The Confessions of Nat Turner also treats regeneration through violence, but here Styron's difficulties do not arise from a melodramatic treatment of his materials. Styron has other problems. He cannot reconcile Turner's dedication to both biblical ideals and murderous rebellion or even create a satisfying and believable tension in these ambivalences. Further, he slights the values of freedom and social justice implicit in these religious ideals and in the issue of slavery itself. Finally, as a white Southerner who cannot "know" the black man, he creates more difficulties for himself than he can resolve by making Nat the narrator of the novel. The novel aims at affirmation arising out of tragic failure, but Styron does not render this paradox convincing, making *The Confessions of Nat Turner* a failed affirmation.

In the melodrama of *Sophie's Choice,* Styron uses an exaggerated rhetoric to explore the idea of evil. He turns for help, in a not fully successful way, to Hannah Arendt, Simone Weil, and George Steiner, whose notions he does not adequately integrate into his fiction. The novel combines autobiographical and detective story methods. It deals with the terror and madness of the Nazis, which persuade the narrator that absolute evil can never be "extinguished from the world," a conclusion that cannot be squared with the unearned optimism with which Styron ends the book.

This Quiet Dust, Styron's first book of nonfiction, is, according to his prefatory note, "a very personal book" that includes essays about the writing of his fiction, writers he admires (Wolfe, Faulkner, **F. Scott Fitzgerald**), his friends, his childhood, his travels, and his political and moral concerns. Although, as Thomas R. Edwards of the *New York Times Book Review* points out, Styron "often calls on eloquence and passion to do the work of thought," *This Quiet Dust* still "holds considerable interest for readers of Mr. Styron's novels." Throughout the essays, Styron appears as an "appealing literary presence" as much for the trouble he has living up to his intentions as for the passion of his writing. Edwards writes that "death and loss" emerge as Styron's "major subjects, nostalgia and grief the moods that most powerfully stir his rhetorical powers." Ultimately, for the reviewer, the essays illuminate the novels—"often loose and murky but illuminated by flashes of impressive passion and humanity—that remain his chief claim on our attention."

Darkness Visible is Styron's intense autobiographical account of his mental illness, clinical depression. Victoria Glendinning writes in the *New York Times Book Review* that the book has some "tremendous writing" and "the rhythmic beat of some sentences demand that they be read aloud." Styron told Laurel Graeber, also in the *New York Times Book Review,* that he was "chagrined to discover how many people had a total misapprehension of what this illness is" and that his "need to communicate overrode the risks of self-exposure." *Publishers Weekly* considers the book's virtues to be twofold: as a "pitiless and chastened record of a nearly fatal human trial far commoner than assumed" and as a "literary discourse on the ways and means of our cultural discontents, observed in the figures of poets." *Darkness Visible,* while providing a poignantly accurate description of the sufferings and manifestations of mental illness, warns against the drugs that Styron thinks are too freely prescribed for the clinically depressed. Ultimately, Styron recovered, and, as Glendinning notes, we give "thanks for his sake and for the sake of American writing."

—Chester E. Eisinger, updated by Lisa C. Harper

SUCKOW, Ruth

Born: Hawarden, Iowa, 6 August 1892. **Education:** Grinnell College, Iowa, 1910-13; Curry Dramatic School, Boston, 1914-15; University of Denver, 1915-18, B.A. 1917, M.A. 1918. **Family:** Married Ferner Nuhn in 1929. **Career:** Editorial assistant, *The Midland,* Iowa City, 1921-22; owner and manager, Orchard Apiary, Earlville, Iowa, 1920s; spent winters in New York, 1924-34; lived in Cedar Falls, Iowa, 1934-52, and Claremont, California, from 1952. **Awards:** M.A.: Grinnell College, 1931. **Died:** 23 January 1960.

PUBLICATIONS

Fiction

Country People. 1924.
The Odyssey of a Nice Girl. 1925.
Iowa Interiors (stories). 1926; as *People and Houses,* 1927.
The Bonney Family. 1928.
Cora. 1929.
The Kramer Girls. 1930.
Children and Older People (stories). 1931.
The Folks. 1934.
Carry-Over. 1936.
New Hope. 1942.
Some Others and Myself: Seven Stories and a Memoir. 1952.
The John Wood Case. 1959.

*

Bibliography: "Ruth Suckow: A Critical Checklist" by Roger N. Casey, in *Bulletin of Bibliography,* December 1989.

Critical Studies: *Suckow* by Leedice McAnelly Kissane, 1969; *Suckow: A Critical Study of Her Fiction* by Margaret Stewart Omrcanin, 1972; *Suckow* by Abigail Ann Hamblen, 1978; "*The Folks:* Anatomy of Rural Life and Shifting Values" by Abigail Ann Martin, in *North Dakota Quarterly,* fall 1985; "A Book of Resolutions: Ruth Suckow's *Some Others and Myself*" by Fritz Oehlschlaeger, in *Western American Literature,* August 1986; "An Iowa Woman's Life: Ruth Suckow's *Cora*" by Mary Jean DeMarr, in *Midamerica: The Yearbook of the Society for the Study of Midwestern Literature* vol. 18, pp. 80-96.

*   *   *

In the 1920s Ruth Suckow was considered a major talent, destined to write novels and short stories of distinction, possibly a great American writer. **H.L. Mencken** published her short fiction in his *Smart Set* and *American Mercury,* and praised her extravagantly. Suckow's stories seemed to fit somewhere between those of **Willa Cather** and **Sinclair Lewis**, but to many she was more honest and straightforward than either. Sixty years later Suckow is considered a minor figure: a good Iowa regionalist, an uncompromising, unsentimental realist who wrote about the ordinary, middle-class people of the American heartland at the beginning of the automotive age.

After the 1920s the literary standing of Cather and Lewis was eclipsed by **Hemingway**, **Dos Passos**, **Steinbeck**, **Fitzgerald**, and **Faulkner**. Literary fashion turned against Suckow, but more important factors were responsible for her decline in stature. Her quiet, uneventful accounts worked best in short stories, but novels were more profitable and more prestigious. Her most ambitious novel, *The Folks* (727 pages), was a Literary Guild selection in 1934. More than twenty years elapse in this account of an Iowa small-town banker and his wife, and the start in life of their four children. The action extends to New York and San Diego, but the point of view is always Iowa small-town. Departing from her earlier practice, in this novel Suckow interprets and comments on the actions and motivations of her characters. But though people, places, and events ring true, there is too little drama, conflict, or interest in the people to sustain the long story. Two later novels—*New Hope* and *The John Wood Case*—drew little critical attention.

The Folks reveals Suckow's shortcomings. The same weaknesses are found in her earlier novels: *Country People, The Odyssey of a Nice Girl, The Bonney Family, Cora,* and *The Kramer Girls.* The last two of this group reveal her new interest in feminism; the earlier novels reveal the texture of small-town life in Iowa seen through the eyes of a young girl.

The short stories of *Iowa Interiors* and *Children and Older People* are Suckow's best work. The stories in a third volume, *Some Others and Myself,* are admittedly inferior—more reflective and contemplative, less objective. As in her longer fiction, the point of view in these stories is restricted and revealing: as a daughter of a small-town clergyman, Suckow saw many lonely, elderly couples and frustrated spinsters. She describes the countless family gatherings and church affairs she had been a part of, not social, political, and economic machinations. There is no explicit sex, no violence, no drama or suspense.

In his *Midwestern Farm Novel* Roy Meyer finds Suckow unsatisfactory because she sees Iowa farms—their people and problems—from the point of view of a small-town preacher's daughter who occasionally went out to visit those farms. A fellow Iowan, the socialist Josephine Herbst, objected to Suckow's blindness to social implications. A comparison with her slightly older contemporary, **Sherwood Anderson**, is revealing: like Suckow's, Anderson's short stories are far better than his novels, but the psychological insights in Anderson's stories contrast sharply with the flatness and simplicity of her honest realism.

—Clarence A. Glasrud

SWITHEN, John. *See* **KING, Stephen (Edwin).**

SYMMES, Robert Edward. *See* **DUNCAN, Robert.**

T

TAN, Amy (En-Mai)

Born: Oakland, California, 19 February 1952. **Education:** San Jose State, B.A. 1973, M.A. 1974; University of California, Berkeley, postgraduate study 1974-76. **Family:** Married Lou DeMattei. **Career:** Worked as consultant to programs for disabled children, 1976-81; reporter, managing editor, and associate publisher for *Emergency Room Reports* (now *Emergency Medicine Reports*), 1981-83; free-lance technical writer, 1983-87; full-time writer from 1987; screenplay writer, film producer, 1993. **Awards:** Commonwealth Club gold award for fiction, 1989; Bay Area Book Reviewers award for best fiction, 1989; American Library Association's best book for young adults award, 1989. **Residence:** San Francisco.

PUBLICATIONS

Novels

The Joy Luck Club. 1989.
The Kitchen God's Wife. 1991.
The Hundred Secret Senses. 1995.

Plays

Screenplays: *The Joy Luck Club,* with Ron Bass, 1993.

Other

The Moon Lady (for children). 1992.
The Chinese Siamese Cat (for children). 1994.

Recordings: *The Joy Luck Club.* 1989.

*

Critical Study: "Generational Differences and the Diaspora in *The Joy Luck Club*" by Walter Shear in *Critique* vol. 34, no. 3, 1993; *Amy Tan: A Critical Companion* by E.D. Huntley, 1998; *In Her Mother's House: The Politics of Asian American Mother-Daughter Writing* by Wendy Ho, 1999.

* * *

Amy Tan is noted for her depiction of the complicated relationships between Chinese immigrant mothers and their American-born daughters. In her first two novels, *The Joy Luck Club* and *The Kitchen God's Wife,* Tan portrays the nuances of the mother-daughter bond, such as maternal love and expectations, generational and cultural conflicts, and reconciliation, with the sensibility and precision stemming from her personal experiences.

Born to Chinese immigrant parents, Tan experienced her first traumatic loss at fifteen when her father died of a brain tumor. Tan's mother moved the family to Europe in hopes of changing the family luck. Unfortunately, Tan's sixteen-year-old brother also died of a brain tumor six months later. The pain of losing parents is clearly at the background of both *The Joy Luck Club* and *The Kitchen God's Wife.* The character Jing-mei's sense of failure in *The Joy Luck Club* also has an autobiographical origin. Tan felt that she had disappointed her mother when she dropped out of medical school and became an English major. All these personal elements are skillfully interwoven into Tan's dramatic stories of death and consolation, loss and reunion, disappointment and hope.

Tan started writing fiction to cure her compulsive working habit and professional ennui as a technical writer. After a failed attempt at psychoanalytic counseling, she joined a writers' group and began writing short stories. These stories eventually developed into *The Joy Luck Club* (1989) and launched Tan into a brilliant literary career.

The Joy Luck Club was an instant success. It remained on the *New York Times* best-seller list for nine months, and in 1993 the novel was adapted into a critically acclaimed motion picture, with Tan co-authoring the screenplay. The novel consists of four segments preceded by four vignettes narrated by the mothers. Each segment includes four individual stories told by the four Chinese immigrant mothers and their American daughters. Together, these sixteen stories are carefully arranged to represent the Joy Luck mothers' past and present and the daughters' stories of development.

The major theme of *The Joy Luck Club* is the difference and lack of understanding between mothers and daughters caused not only by generational gaps but also by the immigrant experience. The name Joy Luck, for example, signifies a hope for happiness despite misfortunes and oppression for the mothers. As related in the story, the character Suyuan Woo started the first Joy Luck Club in China during the Sino-Japanese War: four women played mah-jongg and held weekly parties in the middle of mass destruction. As Suyuan tells June, "each week, we could hope to be lucky. That hope was our only joy." The same spirit of hope prompted Suyuan to organize another Joy Luck Club in San Francisco. The daughters, on the other hand, fail to understand the significance of Joy Luck and regard it as "a shameful Chinese custom." Suyuan's daughter, Jing-mei, comes to understand the fear of her Joy Luck aunts after her mother's death: "They see that joy and luck does not mean the same to their daughters, that to these closed American-born minds 'joy luck' is not a word, it does not exist." To bridge the gap, the American-born daughters open their minds to their maternal cultural heritage. Tan provides the bridge through her skillful storytelling. *The Joy Luck Club* ends with a reunion of Suyuan's two Chinese daughters and Jing-mei, emblematic of the unification of the mother's Chinese past and American present that will create a Chinese American future for all of the daughters.

Tan's second novel, *The Kitchen God's Wife* (1991), was again a *New York Times* best-seller and confirmed her literary talent. Unlike the divided narrative in *The Joy Luck Club, The Kitchen God's Wife* focuses on a single mother and daughter pair, Winnie and Pearl, and the female friendship that supports Winnie through her nightmarish first marriage. Both Winnie and Pearl keep secrets from each other. Winnie attempts to cover up the identity of Pearl's biological father, and Pearl tries to hide her multiple sclerosis. The secrecy hinders their mutual understanding. Most of the novel consists of Winnie's first-person narrative of how she evolves from

Jiang Weili, the daughter of a wealthy Shanghai merchant, to Winnie Louie, the widow to a Chinese American minister and flower shop proprietor in Chinatown. Winnie's narrative of her past opens Pearl's eyes to her mother's trauma as an abandoned child, her psychological and sexual abuses by her first husband, her pain over losing three children, and her courage to escape her bondage. By setting her story during the Sino-Japanese War, Tan invests Winnie's life story with historical and cultural significance and moves it beyond the scope of personal tragedy.

The novel also pays tribute to the importance of female friendship. Winnie's life-long friendship with Helen (Hulan), although not without competition and resentment, sustains Winnie through her trials of abuse and loss. Auntie Du, whose funeral brings Winnie and Pearl physically together at the beginning of the novel, provides Winnie with maternal tenderness that somewhat relieves her pain of being abandoned by her own mother at age six.

In her most recent book, *The Hundred Secret Senses*, Tan presents a thoughtful work about what it means to be an orphan, drawing into focus the experience of two Chinese American half-sisters, Kwan and Olivia Yee. Kwan has "yin eyes," or second sight, and talks of relating to ghosts as an everyday experience. She has spent the first eighteen years of her life in rural China but easily accepts being uprooted to join her dead father's new family in San Francisco. Her half-sister Olivia, raised in San Francisco, is nearing divorce from her husband, Simon. Together with Kwan, Olivia and Simon set off for China. Although always irritated by Kwan's oddities, Olivia is entranced by her half-sister's eerie dreams. When they visit Kwan's former home in Changmian, Olivia realizes that the dreams are memories from past lives. Kwan, in her belief that she must help Olivia and Simon reunite, asserts that she will fix a broken promise from a previous incarnation. The effort is emblematic of one of Tan's favorite themes: hope for the future, embodied in family bonds.

Like the writing of **Maxine Hong Kingston**, Amy Tan's novels bring the experiences of Chinese immigrants and Chinese Americans into American literature. Her popularity among the general reading public represents a great personal and professional triumph. Her success also encourages other ethnic American writers to continue to write about multicultural experiences.

—Pin-Chia Feng, updated by Martha Sutro

TARKINGTON, (Newton) Booth

Born: Indianapolis, Indiana, 29 July 1869. **Education:** Phillips Exeter Academy, New Hampshire; Purdue University, Lafayette, Indiana, 1888-89; Princeton University, New Jersey, 1891-93. **Family:** Married 1) Laurel Louisa Fletcher in 1902 (divorced 1911), one daughter; 2) Susannah Robinson in 1912. **Career:** Writer from 1893; also an artist: illustrated *Character Sketches* by James Whitcomb Riley and other works; member of the Indiana House of Representatives, 1902-03; in later life also lived in Kennebunkport, Maine. **Awards:** Pulitzer prize, 1919, 1922; American Academy Gold Medal, 1933, and Howells Medal, 1945; Boy Scouts of America Silver Buffalo, 1935; Roosevelt Distinguished Service Medal, 1942. A.M.: Princeton University, 1899. Litt.D.: Princeton University, 1918; De Pauw University, Greencastle, Indiana, 1923; Columbia University, New York, 1924. L.H.D.: Purdue University, 1939. **Member:** American Academy. **Died:** 19 May 1946.

PUBLICATIONS

Collections

The Gentleman from Indianapolis: A Treasury of Tarkington, edited by John Beecroft. 1957.

Fiction

The Gentleman from Indiana. 1899.
Monsieur Beaucaire. 1900.
The Two Vanrevels. 1902.
Cherry. 1903.
In the Arena: Stories of Political Life. 1905.
The Beautiful Lady. 1905.
The Conquest of Canaan. 1905.
His Own People. 1907.
The Guest of Quesnay. 1908.
Beasley's Christmas Party. 1909.
The Flirt. 1913.
Penrod: His Complete Story (revised version). 1931.
    Penrod. 1914.
    Penrod and Sam. 1916.
    Penrod Jashber. 1929.
Growth. 1927.
    The Turmoil. 1915.
    The Magnificent Ambersons. 1918.
    The Midlander. 1923.
Seventeen. 1916.
The Spring Concert (story). 1916.
Harlequin and Columbine and Other Stories. 1918.
Ramsey Milholland. 1919.
Alice Adams. 1921.
Gentle Julia. 1922.
The Fascinating Stranger and Other Stories. 1923.
Women. 1925.
Selections from Tarkington's Stories, edited by Lilian Holmes Strack. 1926.
The Plutocrat. 1927.
Claire Ambler. 1928.
Young Mrs. Greeley. 1929.
Mirthful Haven. 1930.
Mary's Neck. 1932.
Wanton Mally. 1932.
Presenting Lily Mars. 1933.
Little Orvie. 1934.
Mr. White, The Red Barn, Hell, and Bridewater. 1935.
The Lorenzo Bunch. 1936.
Rumbin Galleries. 1937.
The Heritage of Hatcher Ide. 1941.
The Fighting Littles. 1941.
Kate Fennigate. 1943.
Image of Josephine. 1945.
The Show Piece (unfinished). 1947.
Three Selected Short Novels (includes *Walterson, Uncertain Molly Collicut,* and *Rennie Peddigoe*). 1947.

Plays

The Guardian, with Harry Leon Wilson. 1907; as *The Man from Home* (produced 1908), 1908; revised version, 1934.

Cameo Kirby, with Harry Leon Wilson (produced 1908).
Foreign Exchange (produced 1909).
If I Had Money (produced 1909)
Springtime (produced 1909).
Your Humble Servant, with Harry Leon Wilson (produced 1909).
Beauty and the Jacobin: An Interlude of the French Revolution (produced 1912). 1912.
The Man on Horseback (produced 1912).
The Ohio Lady, with Julian Street. 1916; as *The Country Cousin* (produced 1921), 1921.
Mister Antonio (produced 1916). 1935.
The Gibson Upright, with Harry Leon Wilson (produced 1919). 1919.
Up from Nowhere, with Harry Leon Wilson (produced 1919)
Poldekin (produced 1920). In *McClure's,* March-July 1920.
Clarence (produced 1921). 1921.
The Intimate Strangers (produced 1921). 1921.
The Wren (produced 1922). 1922.
The Ghost Story (for children) [produced 1922]. 1922.
Rose Briar (produced 1922).
The Trysting Place (produced 1923). 1923.
Magnolia (produced 1923).
Tweedles, with Harry Leon Wilson (produced 1924). 1924.
Bimbo, The Pirate (produced 1926). 1926.
The Travelers (produced 1927). 1927.
Station YYYY (produced 1927). 1927.
How's Your Health?, with Harry Leon Wilson (produced 1930). 1930.
Colonel Satan (produced 1932).
The Help Each Other Club (produced 1933). 1934.
Lady Hamilton and Her Nelson (produced 1945). 1945.

Screenplays: *Edgar and the Teacher's Pet,* 1920; *Edgar's Hamlet,* 1920; *Edgar's Little Saw,* 1920; *Edgar, The Explorer,* 1921; *Get Rich Quick Edgar,* 1921; *Pied Piper Malone,* with Tom Geraghty, 1924; *The Man Who Found Himself,* with Tom Geraghty, 1925.

Radio Plays: *Maud and Cousin Bill* series, 1932-33 (75 episodes).

Other

Works (Autograph Edition). 27 vols., 1918-32.
Works (Seaweed Edition). 27 vols., 1922-32.
The Collectors Whatnot, with Hugh Kahler and Kenneth Roberts. 1923.
Looking Forward and Others (essays). 1926.
The World Does Move (reminiscences). 1928.
Some Old Portraits: A Book about Art and Human Beings. 1939.
Your Amiable Uncle: Letters to His Nephews. 1949.
On Plays, Playwrights, and Playgoers: Selections from the Letters of Tarkington to George C. Tyler and John Peter Toohey 1918-1925, edited by Alan S. Downer. 1959.

Translator, *Samuel Brohl and Company,* with Victor Cherbuliez. 1902.

*

Bibliography: *A Bibliography of Tarkington* by Dorothy Ritter Russo and Thelma L. Sullivan, 1949, supplement in *Princeton University Library Chronicle 16,* 1955.

Critical Studies: *Tarkington: Gentleman from Indiana* by James Woodress, 1955; *Tarkington* by Keith J. Fennimore, 1974; *My Amiable Uncle: Recollections about Tarkington* by Susanah Mayberry, 1983; "Failure and the American Mythos: Tarkington's *The Magnificent Ambersons*" by Marcia Noe, in *Midamerica: The Yearbook of the Society for the Study of Midwestern Literature,* 1988; in *From Ben-Hur to Sister Carrie: Remembering the Lives and Works of Five Indiana Authors* by Barbara Olenyik Morrow, 1995; in *Being a Boy Again: Autobiography and the American Boy Book* by Marcia Ann Jacobson, 1996.

*   *   *

Although Booth Tarkington was a very popular author during his lifetime, his reputation has dimmed since his death, and in the late twentieth century few of his works are read. Yet he was an excellent fictional craftsman and a first-rate storyteller, and his best novels are absorbing. Though there is no sexual titillation and little tragedy in his books, he has a sense of humor and observes and records the human comedy with a clear eye. His significance lies in his depiction of urban, midwestern, middle-class America during the decades of intensely rapid growth in the late nineteenth and early twentieth centuries, and in his stories of children. He writes in the tradition of commonplace realism as pioneered by **William Dean Howells**.

His trilogy published under the collective title *Growth* is important. These novels study the social and economic life of a medium-sized midwestern city that may be identified as Indianapolis. *The Turmoil,* which contains a very contemporary-sounding indictment of air pollution and civic neglect in the pursuit of the dollar, is the story of an ascending family, the first-generation makers of the new industrial wealth. *The Magnificent Ambersons,* winner of a Pulitzer Prize, deals with an old family whose money was made in the Gilded Age. The family is engulfed by the encroaching industrialism of the twentieth century, and the wealth is dissipated by the second and third generations. *The Midlander,* which comes as close as Tarkington ever came to tragedy, is the unhappy story of a promoter-developer of urban growth. Similar in subject and theme to the *Growth* trilogy is *Alice Adams,* perhaps Tarkington's best novel. This novel, which deserves to be better known, is a poignant comedy of manners that details the unsuccessful efforts of a girl of modest circumstances to catch a socially prominent husband. Character, plot, and the theme of social mobility are skillfully blended in this novel, which won Tarkington a second Pulitzer Prize.

Tarkington's second major accomplishment lies in his stories of boyhood, *Penrod, Penrod and Sam,* and *Penrod Jashber.* These distinguished tales in the realistic tradition begun by **Mark Twain** in *Tom Sawyer* appeal to both children and adults, are rich in authentic detail and dialogue, and may turn out to be the author's most enduring work. Tarkington also was adroit in depicting adolescents, but the vast change in teenage mores since *Seventeen* appeared in 1916 makes this once-popular novel a period piece rather than a story of perennial interest.

Tarkington was a playwright as well as a novelist, and any history of American drama must accord him some attention for his two dozen plays. *The Man from Home,* which he wrote with Harry Leon Wilson, enjoyed a long run on Broadway, and *Clarence,* which starred Alfred Lunt and Helen Hayes at the beginning of their careers, was a memorable success. Few

American novelists have mastered the play form as well as Tarkington.

—James Woodress

TATE, (John Orley) Allen

Born: Winchester, Kentucky, 19 November 1899. **Education:** Georgetown Preparatory School, Washington, D.C.; Vanderbilt University, Nashville, Tennessee, 1918-22, B.A, 1923. **Family:** Married 1) Caroline Gordon in 1924 (divorced and remarried 1946; separated 1955; divorced 1959), one daughter; 2) the poet Isabella Stewart Gardner in 1959 (separated 1965; divorced 1966); 3) Helen Heinz in 1966, twin sons. **Career:** Member of the Fugitive group of poets: cofounder, *The Fugitive,* Nashville, 1922-25; high school teacher, Lumberport, West Virginia, 1924; assistant to the editor, *Telling Tales* magazine, New York, 1925; lived in Patterson, New York, 1926-27, Paris, 1928-29, Clarksville, Tennessee, 1930-31, and France, 1932-33; lecturer in English, Southwestern College, Memphis, Tennessee, 1934-36; professor of English, The Woman's College, Greensboro, North Carolina, 1938-39; poet-in-residence, Princeton University, New Jersey, 1939-42; consultant in poetry, Library of Congress, Washington, D.C., 1943-44; editor, *Sewanee Review,* Tennessee, 1944-46; editor, *Belles Lettres* series, Henry Holt, publishers, New York, 1946-48; lecturer in humanities, New York University, 1948-51; from 1951, professor of English, University of Minnesota, Minneapolis; Regents' Professor, 1966, professor emeritus, 1968. Visiting professor in the humanities, University of Chicago, 1949; Fulbright Lecturer, Oxford University, 1953, University of Rome, 1953-54, and Oxford and Leeds universities, 1958-59; Department of State Lecturer at universities of Liege and Louvain, 1954, Delhi and Bombay, 1956, the Sorbonne, Paris, 1956, Nottingham, 1956, and Urbino and Florence, 1961; visiting professor of English, University of North Carolina, Greensboro, 1966. and Vanderbilt University, 1967. Fellow, 1948, and senior fellow, 1956, Kenyon School of English, Kenyon College, Gambier, Ohio (now Indiana University School of Letters, Bloomington); member, Phi Beta Kappa Senate, 1951-53. **Awards:** Guggenheim fellowship, 1928, 1929; American Academy grant, 1948; Bollingen prize, 1957; Brandeis University Creative Arts award, 1960; Dante Society Gold Medal (Florence), 1962; Academy of American Poets fellowship, 1963; National Medal for Literature, 1976. Litt.D.: University of Louisville, Kentucky, 1948; Coe College, Cedar Rapids, Iowa, 1955; Colgate University, Hamilton, New York, 1956; University of Kentucky, Lexington, 1960; Carleton College, Northfield, Minnesota, 1963; University of the South, Sewanee, Tennessee, 1970. **Member:** American Academy, 1964; chancellor, Academy of American Poets, 1964; American Academy of Arts and Sciences, 1965; president, National Institute of Arts and Letters, 1968. **Died:** 9 February 1979.

<small>PUBLICATIONS</small>

Poetry

The Golden Mean and Other Poems, with Ridley Wills. 1923.
Mr. Pope and Other Poems. 1928.

Ode to the Confederate Dead, Being the Revised and Final Version of a Poem Previously Published on Several Occasions: To Which Are Added Message from Abroad and The Cross. 1930.
Three Poems. 1930.
Poems 1928-1931. 1932.
The Mediterranean and Other Poems. 1936.
Selected Poems. 1937.
Sonnets at Christmas. 1941.
The Winter Sea: A Book of Poems. 1944.
Poems 1920-1945: A Selection. 1947.
Fragment of a Meditation. 1947.
Poems 1922-1947. 1948.
Two Conceits for the Eye to Sing, If Possible. 1950.
Poems. 1960.
The Swimmers and Other Selected Poems. 1970.
Collected Poems 1919-1976. 1977.

Plays

The Governess, with Anne Goodwin Winslow (produced 1962).

Fiction

The Fathers. 1938; revised edition, 1960.
The Fathers and Other Fiction. 1977.

Other

Stonewall Jackson: The Good Soldier: A Narrative. 1928.
Jefferson Davis: His Rise and Fall: A Biographical Narrative. 1929.
I'll Take My Stand: The South and the Agrarian Tradition, with others. 1930.
Who Owns America? A New Declaration of Independence, with others, edited by Herbert Agar and Tate. 1936.
Reactionary Essays on Poetry and Ideas. 1936.
Reason in Madness: Critical Essays. 1941.
Invitation to Learning, with Huntington Cairns and Mark Van Doren. 1941.
Recent American Poetry and Poetic Criticism: A Selected List of References. 1943.
Sixty American Poets 1896-1944: A Preliminary Checklist. 1945.
On the Limits of Poetry: Selected Essays 1928-1948. 1948.
The Hovering Fly and Other Essays. 1948.
The Forlorn Demon: Didactic and Critical Essays. 1953.
The Man of Letters in the Modern World: Selected Essays 1928-1955. 1955.
Collected Essays. 1959.
Christ and the Unicorn: An Address. 1966.
Essays of Four Decades. 1969.
Mere Literature and the Lost Traveller. 1969.
The Translation of Poetry. 1972.
The Literary Correspondence of Donald Davidson and Tate, edited by John Tyree Fain and Thomas Daniel Young. 1974.
Memoirs and Minions 1926-1974. 1975; as *Memories and Essays: Old and New 1926-1974,* 1976.
The Republic of Letters in America: The Correspondence of John Peale Bishop and Tate, edited by Thomas Daniel Young and John J. Hindle. 1981.
The Poetry Reviews of Tate 1924-1944, edited by Ashley Brown and Frances Neel Cheney. 1983.

Cleanth Brooks and Allen Tate: Collected Letters, 1933-1976. 1998.

Editor, with others, *Fugitives: An Anthology of Verse.* 1928.
Editor, with Herbert Agar, *Who Owns America? A New Declaration of Independence.* 1936.
Editor, with A. Theodore Johnson, *America through the Essay: An Anthology for English Courses.* 1938.
Editor, *The Language of Poetry.* 1942.
Editor, *Princeton Verse between Two Wars: An Anthology.* 1942.
Editor, with John Peale Bishop, *American Harvest: Twenty Years of Creative Writing in the United States.* 1942.
Editor, *A Southern Vanguard: The John Peale Bishop Memorial Volume.* 1947.
Editor, *The Collected Poems of John Peale Bishop.* 1948.
Editor, with Caroline Gordon, *The House of Fiction: An Anthology of the Short Story.* 1950; revised edition, 1960.
Editor, with David Cecil, *Modern Verse in English, 1900-1950.* 1958.
Editor, with John Berryman and Ralph Ross, *The Arts of Reading* (anthology). 1960.
Editor, *Selected Poems of John Peale Bishop.* 1960.
Editor, with Robert Penn Warren, *Selected Poems,* by Denis Devlin. 1963.
Editor, *T. S. Eliot: The Man and His Work.* 1966.
Editor, *The Complete Poems and Selected Criticism of Edgar Allan Poe.* 1968.
Editor, *Six American Poets: From Emily Dickinson to the Present: An Introduction.* 1972.

Translator, *The Vigil of Venus/Pervigilium Veneris.* 1943.

*

Bibliography: *Tate: A Bibliography* by Marshall Fallwell, Jr., 1969.

Critical Studies: *The Last Alternatives: A Study of the Works of Tate* by R.K. Meiners, 1962; *Tate* by George Hemphill, 1964; *Tate* by Ferman Bishop, 1967; *Rumors of Morality: An Introduction to Tate* by M.E. Bradford, 1969; *Tate: A Literary Biography* by Radcliffe Squires, 1971, and *Tate and His Work: Critical Evaluations* edited by Squires, 1972; *Tate and the Augustinian Imagination: A Study of the Poetry* by Robert S. Dupree, 1983; *Tate and the Poetic Way* edited by J. Larry Allums, 1984; *The Years of Our Friendship: Robert Lowell and Allen Tate* by William Doreski, 1990; *Exiles and Fugitives: The Letters of Jacques and Raissa Maritain, Allen Tate, and Caroline Gordon* edited by John M. Dunaway, 1992; *Mumford, Tate, Eiseley: Watchers in the Night* by Gale H. Carrithers, Jr., 1992; *The Unregenerate South: The Agrarian Thought of John Crowe Ransom, Allen Tate, and Donald Davidson* by Mark G. Malvasi, 1997.

*   *   *

Allen Tate is always associated with the Fugitives, the small group of Southern poets who were led by **John Crowe Ransom** at Vanderbilt University in Nashville during the early 1920s. But Tate was always his own man, and as a young Fugitive he found it necessary to reject much in the South; by 1924 he was living in New York City. Certainly Southern literary culture offered nothing that he could imitate directly, though his sense of the age led

him to the French symbolists and hence back to **Edgar Allan Poe**, about whom he was to write three of his most important essays. His best poem before 1925 is his version of Baudelaire's "Correspondences." This seems as important as his friendship with his first master, Ransom, because it allowed him access to the mainstream of modern poetry.

In New York City, married to the novelist **Caroline Gordon**, Tate was on close terms with many writers of his generation, especially **Hart Crane**, and he could easily be put among the second generation of modernists (if we put **T.S. Eliot**, **Ezra Pound**, and James Joyce in the first generation). It may well be that his regional sense was sharpened by his residence in the East and then Paris for six years. At any rate, by 1926 he was writing the first version of his most ambitious early poem, "Ode to the Confederate Dead." The correspondence between Tate and his Fugitive friend **Donald Davidson** shows him at that time occupying a kind of intermediary position between Davidson, who was writing *The Tall Men,* a long poem about Tennessee, and Crane, who was working on *The Bridge,* a visionary poem about America. Almost by instinct Tate shunned the "epical" treatment of experience. Where his Southern quality emerges most convincingly is in the elevation of tone that was characteristic of the rhetoricians of this region. In a sense the Old South was organized by the voices of the preacher and the politician, and this legacy of public speaking descended to many of the writers of the modern Southern Renaissance.

The 1930s was the Agrarian period for the old Fugitive group, and Tate was frequently involved in the controversies that grew out of this movement, which coincided with an extraordinary outburst of literary achievement in the South. But his main energy went into his poetry, and his *Selected Poems* is one of the best collections of poetry in the decade. This volume contains the final version of the "Ode to the Confederate Dead," a distinguished meditative poem called "The Mediterranean," and a dozen shorter poems of great power and considerable range, such as "Emblems," "The Cross," and "The Wolves."

Meanwhile Tate was becoming one of the most important American critics; his first volume, *Reactionary Essays on Poetry and Ideas,* fully established his position. As critic he always took a large view of literary culture, but many of his influential early essays were written about such contemporaries as Crane, **Archibald MacLeish**, and **John Peale Bishop**. Certain theoretical essays have become classics of modern criticism: "Tension in Poetry," "Techniques of Fiction," "The Hovering Fly," and "A Southern Mode of the Imagination." These generated as much discussion as anything written during their period in the United States. Perhaps Tate's finest essays are two on **Edgar Allan Poe** and Dante, "The Angelic Imagination" and "The Symbolic Imagination," published in 1951 at a time when he was writing some outstanding poems. Tate's criticism, in fact, is very much the work of a poet and often provides the setting for his verse.

Another work in prose that is closely related to Tate's verse of the 1930s is his novel *The Fathers,* which has been even more admired in later years than it was when it was first published. Influenced in its technique by Ford Madox Ford's *The Good Soldier* ("the masterpiece of British fiction in this century"), the novel dramatizes with a great poetic intelligence the destruction of a Virginia family at the beginning of the Civil War. Tate's biographer, Radcliffe Squires, has shown the extent to which Tate drew on the history of his own family for the subject.

The last phase of Tate's poetry started during the early 1940s, though it was long anticipated. It includes the splendid satire "Ode to Our Young Pro-Consuls of the Air," an attack on the modern religion of the state; his very title proposes an analogy between America and Rome. This in a sense was preparatory for the long poem "Seasons of the Soul" and a later group of poems in *terza rima,* including "The Swimmers" and "The Buried Lake," his most impressive work of all. In these late poems Tate set his experience (his own, his family's, his region's) against a background of Christian experience represented most fully by Dante, and "imitated" Dante's verse more closely than any other American poet has done. Brilliant and sometimes restless, Tate was more than a fine poet: he helped to set the standards for the literary community in the United States.

—Ashley Brown

TATE, James

Born: Kansas City, Missouri, 8 December 1943. **Education:** University of Missouri, Kansas City, 1963-64; Kansas State College, Pittsburgh, B.A. 1965; University of Iowa, Iowa City, M.F.A. 1967. **Career:** Visiting lecturer, University of Iowa, Iowa City, 1965-67, and University of California, Berkeley, 1967-68; assistant professor, Columbia University, New York, 1969-71, and Emerson College, Boston, 1970-71. Beginning 1971 member of English department, University of Massachusetts, Amherst. Since 1967, poetry editor, *Dickinson Review,* North Dakota; associate editor, Pym Randall Press, Cambridge, Massachusetts, and Barn Dream Press; consultant, Coordinating Council of Literary Magazines. **Awards:** Yale Series of Younger Poets award, 1966; National Endowment for the Arts grant, 1968, 1969; American Academy award, 1974; Guggenheim fellowship, 1976; National Endowment for the Arts fellow, 1980; Pulitzer prize for poetry, for *Selected Poems,* 1992; National book award for poetry, for *Worshipful Company of Fletchers,* 1994; Tanning prize, Academy of American Poets, 1995.

PUBLICATIONS

Poetry

Cages. 1966.
The Destination. 1967.
The Lost Pilot. 1967.
The Torches. 1968.
Notes of Woe. 1968.
Mystics in Chicago. 1968.
Camping in the Valley. 1968.
Row with Your Hair. 1969.
Is There Anything. 1969.
Shepherds of the Mist. 1969.
The Oblivion Ha-Ha. 1970.
Amnesia People. 1970.
Deaf Girl Playing. 1970.
Are You Ready Mary Baker Eddy?, with Bill Knott. 1970.
The Immortals. 1970.
Wrong Songs. 1970.
Hints to Pilgrims. 1971.
Nobody Goes to Visit the Insane Anymore. 1971.
Absences: New Poems. 1972.
Apology for Eating Geoffrey Movius' Hyacinth. 1972.
Viper Jazz. 1976.

Riven Doggeries. 1979.
The Land of Little Sticks. 1981.
Constant Defender. 1983.
Just Shades. 1985.
Reckoner. 1986.
Distance from Loved Ones. 1990.
Selected Poems. 1991.
Worshipful Company of Fletchers: Poems. 1994.

Novel

Lucky Darryl, with Bill Knott. 1977.

Short Stories

Hottentot Ossuary. 1974.

Other

The Route As Briefed. 1999.

*

Manuscript Collection: Humanities Research Center, University of Texas, Austin.

*   *   *

At the heart of James Tate's poetry is the father he never knew. The poet's most direct statement that this is so must be the elegy "The Lost Pilot." The poem, which lends its title to Tate's winning book in the 1967 Yale Series of Younger Poets competition, is a tender address, in concise tercets, to the war pilot who died in 1944, the year after the poet's birth.

> I feel dead. I feel as if I were
> the residue of a stranger's life,
> that I should pursue you.
>
> My head cocked toward the sky,
> I cannot get off the ground,
> and, you, passing over again,
>
> fast, perfect, and unwilling
> to tell me that you are doing
> well, or that it was a mistake
>
> that placed you in that world,
> and me in this; or that misfortune
> placed these worlds in us.

Men who never know, or barely know, their fathers firsthand often are unusually focused people. The need to discover and settle on one's life's work—filling the void of an absent role model—afflicts the individual with uncommon urgency. Self-directed, self-motivated, such people often become early over-achievers. Certainly, Tate may be described in this way.

In a career now spanning thirty-two years, Tate has pursued and realized book and magazine publication with almost manic glee. From 1967 to 1973, for example, he published more than a dozen books. In fact, given his admission that he uses magazines to test nearly everything he writes, he may be America's most widely published poet during this period.

From the beginning, Tate's style has been declarative, crisp, and inclined toward the surprising point of view. Writing out of what he has called "the tradition of the impurists," Tate is descended from the traditions of Walt Whitman, **William Carlos Williams,** Pablo Neruda, and the French Surrealists. He can appear to be the American version of André Breton, a stand-up comic (Tate, and the poet Russell Edson, have written America's funniest poems in the second half of the twentieth century), a petulant, icy observer, a smart guy, a messenger of doom. All of these stances arise from the poet's encounter with the mysteries of intimacy and communication as illustrated by moments of intense improbability. In the poem "Today I Am Falling" the poet desires complete surrender to a benevolent, drug-induced, dream-rich natural world:

> A sodium pentothal landscape
> a bud about to break open—
> I want to be there, ambassador
> to the visiting blossoms, first
> to breathe their smothered secret
> odors. Today I am falling, falling,
> falling in love, and desire
> to leave this place forever.

In "Poem," the poet is thwarted again by the assumption that, no matter how promising the setting and circumstances, the ultimate, intimate connection will be denied.

> He did the handkerchief dance all alone.
> O Desire! It is the beautiful dress
> for which the proper occasion
> never arises.
> O the wedding cake and the good cigar!
> O the souvenir ashtray!

In the sonnet-like sequence "The Blue Canyon," Tate's on-the-surface transitions are razor-sharp:

> "I caught you," he cried. "See, I'm swimming
> out here off the end because a single
> hmmmm can magnolia, the years dotted
> with drooling cries, hopelessly broken . . ."

Humor has always worked best when tragedy is so thick and so near that one feels it through the laughter. It is no different in poetry. If, in the last fifteen years, especially, James Tate may be accused of writing and publishing too much, or of repeating his early, successful formulas, he must also be seriously read for the stylish innovations he has brought to poetry. Few poets have so consistently probed the loss of the father and other exquisitely painful losses that, after all, make up our shared humanity.

—Robert McDowell

TAYLOR, Bayard

Born: Kennett Square, Chester County, Pennsylvania, 11 January 1825. **Education:** Bolmar's Academy, West Chester, Penn-

sylvania, 1837-40; Unionville Academy, Pennsylvania, 1842. **Family:** Married 1) Mary Agnew in 1850 (died 1850); 2) Marie Hansen in 1857, one daughter. **Career:** Teacher, Unionville Academy, 1842; apprenticed to the printer of the West Chester *Village Record,* 1842-44; traveled in Europe as correspondent for *Saturday Evening Post* and *United States Gazette,* Philadelphia, and New York *Tribune,* 1844-46; publisher, *Pioneer* newspaper, Phoenixville, Pennsylvania, 1846-47; columnist, *Literary World,* New York, 1847-48; manager of the literary department, New York *Tribune,* 1848, and covered the California gold rush for the *Tribune,* 1849; traveled in the Middle and Far East, 1851-53, and lectured on his travels throughout the United States, 1854-56; traveled in Europe, 1856-58; settled on a farm, Cedarcroft, near Kennett Square, 1858; Washington correspondent, *Tribune,* 1862; secretary, later charge d'affaires, American Legation, St. Petersburg, Russia, 1862-63; returned to Cedarcroft, and worked on his translation of *Faust,* 1863-70; non-resident professor of German, Cornell University, Ithaca, New York, 1870-77; U.S. Ambassador to Germany, 1878. **Died:** 19 December 1878.

PUBLICATIONS

Collections

Dramatic Works. 1880.
Poetical Works. 1880.

Poetry

Ximena; or, The Battle of Sierra Morena and Other Poems. 1844.
Rhymes of Travel, Ballads, and Poems. 1848.
A Book of Romances, Lyrics, and Songs. 1851.
Poems of the Orient. 1854.
Poems of Home and Travel. 1855.
Poems. 1856.
The Poets Journal. 1862.
The Poems. 1864.
The Picture of St. John. 1866.
The Golden Wedding: A Masque. 1868.
The Ballad of Abraham Lincoln (for children). 1870.
Lars: A Pastoral of Norway. 1873.
Home Pastorals, Ballads, and Lyrics. 1875.
The National Ode. 1877.

Plays

The Masque of the Gods. 1872.
The Prophet: A Tragedy. 1874.
Prince Deukalion: A Lyrical Drama. 1878.

Fiction

Hannah Thurston. 1863.
John Godfrey's Fortunes. 1864.
The Story of Kennett. 1866; edited by C.W. La Salle, II, 1973.
Joseph and His Friend. 1870.
Beauty and the Beast, and Tales of Home. 1872.

Other

Views A-Foot; or, Europe Seen with Knapsack and Staff. 1846.

Eldorado; or, Adventures in the Path of Empire. 1850.
A Journey to Central Africa. 1854.
The Lands of the Saracen. 1854.
A Visit to India, China, and Japan in the Year 1853. 1855; revised edition, edited by G.F. Pardon, 1860.
Northern Travel. 1857.
Travels in Greece and Russia. 1859.
At Home and Abroad. 2 vols., 1859-62.
Colorado: A Summer Trip. 1867.
By-Ways of Europe. 1869.
A School History of Germany. 1874.
Egypt and Iceland in the Year 1874. 1874.
The Echo Club and Other Literary Diversions. 1876.
Boys of Other Countries: Stories for American Boys. 1876.
Studies in German Literature. 1879.
Critical Essays and Literary Notes, edited by Marie Hansen-Taylor. 1880.
Life and Letters, edited by Marie Hansen-Taylor and Horace E. Scudder. 2 vols., 1884.
Unpublished Letters in the Huntington Library, edited by John R. Schultz. 1937.
The Correspondence of Taylor and Paul Hamilton Hayne, edited by Charles Duffy. 1945.
Selected Letters of Bayard Taylor. 1997.

Editor, with George Ripley, *Hand-book of Literature and Fine Arts.* 1852.
Editor, *Cyclopaedia of Modern Travel.* 1856.
Editor, *Frithiof's Saga.* by Esaias Tegher, translated by William Lewery Blackley. 1867.
Editor, *Travels in Arabia.* 1871.
Editor, *Japan in Our Day.* 1872.
Editor, *Travels in South Africa.* 1872.
Editor, *The Lake Regions of Central Africa.* 1873.
Editor, *Central Asia.* 1874.
Editor, *Picturesque Europe.* 1877.

Translator, *Faust, by Goethe.* 1870-71; edited by Stuart Atkins, 1972.
Translator, *A Sheaf of Poems,* edited by Mary Taylor Kiliani. 1911.

*

Critical Studies: *Taylor* by Albert H. Smyth, 1896 (includes bibliography); *Taylor: Laureate of the Gilded Age* by Richmond Croom Beatty, 1936; *The Genteel Circle: Taylor and His New York Friends* by Richard Cary, 1952; *Taylor and German Letters* by John T. Krumpelmann, 1959; *Taylor* by Paul C. Wermuth, 1973, and "'My Full, Unreserved Self': Bayard Taylor's Letters to Charles Melancthon Jones" by Wermuth, in *Resources for American Literary Study* vol. 17, no. 2, 1991; "The Hiawatha Saga: Bayard Taylor's Possible Contribution" by David W. Berry, in *Colby Library Quarterly,* December 1981.

*   *   *

Although he wished to be remembered for his poetry, Bayard Taylor supported himself by writing travel literature, and it is for these works, as well as for his translation of *Faust,* that we remember him in the late twentieth century. The titles of his many travel books, most of which were widely read during the nineteenth century, reveal the vast extent of Taylor's travels: *A Jour-*

ney to Central Africa, The Lands of the Saracen, A Visit to India, China, and Japan, Northern Travel, Travels in Greece and Russia, and *Egypt and Iceland,* among numerous other works. Ironically, however, Taylor was at his best when writing about his homeland. His book on the California gold rush, *Eldorado,* which he wrote for Horace Greeley's *New York Times,* is one of the earliest and most engaging accounts of its subject; and *Colorado,* which he wrote while on a summer trip to the West, is a classic of American overland adventure. Rarely controversial, always factual, and seldom boring, Taylor's books appealed to the sensibilities of a largely female nineteenth-century American audience that was eager to learn more about foreign culture and exotic lands, including the American West.

With the onset of the Civil War, the market for travel literature declined, and, to earn a living, Taylor began writing novels. His models were Dickens and Thackeray, and his plots were overly melodramatic and excessively contrived, but, despite their conventionality, Taylor's novels provide a valuable insight into the tastes and spirit of the times that demanded felicitous endings, purity from its heroines, and a proper respect for social decorum. They also bridge the gap between the romanticism of the first half of the nineteenth century and the realism of the second. *Hannah Thurston,* for example, is about a bluestocking suffragette turned homemaker and mother who finds true happiness and freedom in the values of the home; and *The Story of Kennett,* with its quaint and descriptive portrayal of life in a rural Pennsylvania town, anticipates the local color movement of the 1870s, 1880s, and 1890s.

Taylor's poems, like his travel books and novels, demonstrate more than a modicum of literary talent but suffer from a self-conscious desire to please. He had an astute ear for music, and his verse is technically quite proficient, but it lacks the universal tensions that make for good poetry, and it also tends to be overly sentimental, overly ornate, and overly derivative, particularly of Shelley and the British romantics. Nonetheless, his most famous poem, "The Bedouin Song," is far from his best; and such poems as "The Summer Camp," "Hylas," "Daughter of Egypt," and "Hassan and His Mare" deserve more recognition than they have received. *The Poets Journal* and *The Picture of St. John* are especially deserving of attention because they constitute Taylor's attempt to write long narrative verse about his own experiences, vaguely disguised. His most popular collection of poetry, *Poems of the Orient,* displays a refreshing and aesthetically pleasing sense of the exotic. A collected edition of Taylor's poems was published during his lifetime; his masques and closet dramas were published after his death.

Throughout his life, Taylor maintained a genuine admiration for German culture. His second wife was German, and he was non-resident professor of German literature at Cornell University. Taylor's interest in Germany appears in many of his works, especially in *Studies in German Literature,* which was for many years one of the best introductions to the field, and in his translation of *Faust,* whose copious scholarly annotations and faithful reproduction of the meter of the original make it to this day one of the finest translations of Goethe's masterpiece.

—James A. Levernier

TAYLOR, Edward

Born: Sketchley, Leicestershire, England, in 1642(?). **Education:** Lost a teaching position in Bagworth, Leicestershire, for failing to subscribe to the Act of Uniformity, 1662; may then have attended Cambridge University; immigrated to Massachusetts Bay Colony, 1668; attended Harvard University, Cambridge, Massachusetts, 1668-71, A.B. 1671. **Family:** Married 1) Elizabeth Fitch in 1674 (died 1689), eight children; 2) Ruth Wyllys in 1692, six children. **Career:** Congregational minister, Westfield, Massachusetts, 1671-1725. **Awards:** A.M.: Harvard University, 1720. **Died:** 24 June 1729.

PUBLICATIONS

Collections

The Poetical Works, edited by Thomas H. Johnson. 1939.
The Poems, edited by Donald E. Stanford. 1960; *Selection,* 1963.
Unpublished Writings, edited by Thomas M. and Virginia L. Davis. 3 vols., 1981.

Poetry

Metrical History of Christianity (transcript), edited by Donald E. Stanford. 1962.

Other

Christographia (sermons and meditations), edited by Norman S. Grabo. 1962.
The Diary, edited by Francis Murphy. 1964.
Treatise Concerning the Lords Supper (sermons), edited by Norman S. Grabo. 1966.

*

Bibliography: *Taylor: An Annotated Bibliography 1668-1970* by Constance J. Gefvert, 1971.

Critical Studies: *Taylor* by Norman S. Grabo, 1961; *Taylor* by Donald E. Stanford, 1965; "Taylor Issue" of *Early American Literature,* vol. 4, no. 3, 1969-70; *The Will and the Word: The Poetry of Taylor* by William J. Scheick, 1974; *The Example of Taylor* by Karl Keller, 1975; *Saint and Singer: Taylor's Typology and the Poetics of Meditation* by Karen E. Rowe, 1986; *Gracious Laughter: The Meditative Wit of Edward Taylor* by John Gatta, 1989; *Gifts and Works: The Post-Conversion Paradigm and Spiritual Controversy in Seventeenth- Century Massachusetts* by Michael Schuldiner, 1991; *A Reading of Edward Taylor* by Thomas M. Davis, 1992; *Edward Taylor: Fifty Years of Scholarship and Criticism* by Jeffrey A. Hammond, 1993; *The Tayloring Shop: Essays on the Poetry of Edward Taylor in Honor of Thomas M. and Virginia L. Davis,* 1997.

*   *   *

It should be remembered as we read the poetry of Edward Taylor that he was for more than fifty years the village parson of a small New England frontier town, Westfield, in western Massachusetts. The ministry was his vocation; poetry was his avocation. The religious experience of the Puritan Calvinist was his abiding concern as a preacher and it was the subject matter of all his extant poems. His library, impressive for its time and place, had

many religious books, some of them rare and expensive, but only one volume of verse in English, the poems of **Anne Bradstreet**. Yet Taylor wrote poetry all of his mature life, and in the late twentieth century he is considered the major poet of New England Calvinistic Congregationalism just as **Jonathan Edwards**, who lived two generations later, is considered its paramount preacher, and this position Taylor has attained in spite of the fact that he published nothing during his lifetime.

Taylor's reputation as a poet rests on (to quote verbatim his own title page as it appears on his undated manuscript) *Gods Determinations Touching His Elect: and The Elects Combat in Their Conversion, and Coming up to God in Christ Together with the Comfortable Effects Thereof* and on his (to quote Taylor's manuscript page again) *Preparatory Meditations before My Approach to the Lords Supper Chiefly upon the Doctrin Preached upon the Day of Administration.*

The manuscript of *Gods Determinations* was prepared with particular care and may have been intended for publication, a supposition strengthened by the aim and content of the work. *Gods Determinations* is a series of poems in the form of dramatic dialogues interspersed with narrative and expository passages that explain and justify God's ways in bringing a few selected men (the elect) to salvation. Its purpose, apparently, was to convert those members of the Puritan community who felt themselves unable to accept full communion in the church because they had not experienced the reception of God's saving grace. Hence a great deal of the poem is taken up with a dramatization of the various ways in which God's grace operates among sinning men.

Gods Determinations opens with a preface that describes the creation in Calvinistic terms. The physical universe as well as all its inhabitants, including man, was created out of nothing by an Omnipotent God who may return it to nothing if he pleases. "The Effects of Mans Apostacy" follows, describing the Fall and the terror of natural man when he finds God his enemy. The tone of the verse and the theology are similar to that of Jonathan Edwards's later famous sermon *Sinners in the Hands of an Angry God.* With the third poem, a dialogue between Justice and Mercy, personified attributes of God, the dramatic struggle for the redemption of the elect begins with Justice playing the role of divine avenger who punishes and terrifies man, and Mercy playing the role of divine comforter who offers salvation to those who confess their sins and come into the church. Satan and Christ join the struggle and the ensuing action is seen as a series of military engagements in which Satan is eventually defeated by the combined efforts of Justice and Mercy. At the end of the poem the elect are depicted as riding to Glory in Christ's coach.

Much of the poem, in style and content, is dated. However, Satan's methods of tempting the sinner to abandon hope, methods derived in part from William Ames's *Cases of Conscience,* are subtle and sophisticated, and they reveal an understanding of the psychology of guilt that is still of interest to the modern reader. Also, there are passages written in a vigorous, colloquial, and highly figurative style that are worth noting, particularly the famous query in the opening lines referring to the creation: "Who in this Bowling Alley bowld the Sun?"

The *Preparatory Meditations* is a body of remarkable devotional verse consisting of more than two hundred poems written over a period of more than forty years, from 1682 to 1725. Because of their style, which is reminiscent of the Metaphysical Poets (particularly Herbert but also occasionally Donne, Crashaw, and Vaughan), they have in later years attracted the attention of scholars, for in the age of Pope, Taylor was writing like Donne. But his *Meditations* are of more than mere historical interest. His recurrent and moving expression of the experience of Saving Grace establishes him as the most important religious poet in American literature and worthy of comparison not only with Donne and Herbert but also with Gerard Manley Hopkins.

The purpose of each meditation was to prepare the pastor for administering the Lord's Supper, a sacrament by means of which the soul of the participant is united to Christ; therefore a number of the *Meditations* express the almost mystical exaltation of the union of the human with the divine, as in "The Experience":

> Most strange it was! But yet more strange that shine
> Which filld my Soul then to the brim to spy
> My Nature with thy Nature all Divine
> Together joyn'd in Him thats Thou, and I.

The structure of the poems varies, but more frequently it is three-fold with the opening lines expressing despairing personal awareness of original sin followed by joyful contemplation of Saving Grace made possible through faith in Christ and concluding with the hope that the poet will be one of the elect who will achieve salvation. These poems are in the tradition of the Christian meditative practice of self-examination best exemplified among the Roman Catholics by Loyola, but by the seventeenth century common among Protestant divines such as Richard Baxter, author of *The Saints Everlasting Rest* (1650), a book with which Taylor was probably familiar and which may have influenced his own meditative methods. The meditant fixes his attention on some point of doctrine, analyzes it by means of his understanding, and as a result of comprehending it is moved by feelings of love, hope, joy, etc. The doctrine in Taylor's *Meditations* is usually stated in a biblical text that is quoted in the title of the poem, the favorite source of quotation for Taylor being the *Song of Songs* or, as Taylor called it, *Canticles*. Taylor frequently makes use of Christian allegory, symbolism, typology, and a figurative style derived chiefly from the Bible (especially from the *Song of Songs* and *Revelation*) and from Herbert. A widely variant vocabulary is employed with words ranging from the humble life of the farmer— "I'le Wagon Loads of Love, and Glory bring" to abstruse theological terminology. Complicated conceits with terms and images from widely disparate fields of experience are juxtaposed and yoked by violence together in the metaphysical style (as defined by Samuel Johnson). At its best the style is direct and forceful, but at its worst bizarre, over-rhetorical, and rhythmically awkward. Yet in reading the *Preparatory Meditations* as a whole, one gains the impression that they were written by a humble, extremely pious, sincere Puritan for whom the experience of God's grace was profound and overwhelming.

Taylor composed and preached innumerable sermons during his long pastorate but the manuscripts of only a few have survived, the more important being available in *Christographia,* a series of fourteen sermons preached in Westfield from 1701 to 1703 on the mystery of the union of the divine and human natures of Christ, and in *Treatise Concerning the Lords Supper* (eight sermons preached in 1694), in which he argues that the Lord's Supper should be confined to the regenerate elect only. These sermons are, then, an attack on the practice of Solomon Stoddard (the grandfather of Jonathan Edwards), who in his Northampton Church was using the sacrament as a converting ordinance and inviting all who led a Christian life to partake. In this as in other matters Taylor ex-

pressed the views of the conservative faction of the Congregational Church of New England.

Taylor also wrote a number of occasional poems, the most interesting of which are the charming "Upon a Wasp Child with Cold" and the striking "Upon the Sweeping Flood." He composed a long poem of more than twenty thousand lines and of doubtful literary merit on the persecutions and martyrdoms of the Christians from the earliest times through the reign of Queen Mary of England, *Metrical History of Christianity.* He also wrote elegies on his contemporaries, the best being those on his first wife and on Samuel Hooker, pastor of the church of Farmington, Connecticut. But by far his best poetry is to be found in *Gods Determinations* and in the *Preparatory Meditations.*

—Donald E. Stanford

See the essay on *Gods Determinations.*

TEASDALE, Sara

Born: St. Louis, Missouri, 8 August 1884. **Education:** Privately educated. **Family:** Married Ernst B. Filsinger in 1914 (divorced 1929). **Career:** Traveled to Europe, 1912; moved to New York, 1916. **Awards:** Columbia Poetry prize (later Pulitzer prize), 1918. **Died:** (suicide) 29 January 1933.

PUBLICATIONS

Collections

Collected Poems. 1937.
Mirror of the Heart: Poems of Teasdale, edited by William Drake. 1984.

Poetry

Sonnets to Duse and Other Poems. 1907.
Helen of Troy and Other Poems. 1911; revised edition, 1922.
Rivers to the Sea. 1915.
Love Songs. 1917.
Vignettes of Italy: A Cycle of Nine Songs for High Voice. 1919.
Flame and Shadow. 1920; revised edition, 1924.
Dark of the Moon. 1926.
Stars To-Night: Verses New and Old for Boys and Girls. 1930.
Country House. 1932.
Strange Victory. 1933.

Other

Editor, *The Answering Voice: One Hundred Love Lyrics by Women.* 1917; revised edition, 1928.
Editor, *Rainbow Gold: Poems Old and New for Boys and Girls.* 1922.

*

Bibliography: by Vivian Buchan, in *Bulletin of Bibliography 25,* 1967.

Critical Studies: *Teasdale: A Biography* by Margaret Haley Carpenter, 1960; *Sara Teasdale: Woman and Poet* by William Drake, 1979; "Sara Teasdale: Fitting Tunes to Everything" by Mary Ann Mannino, in *Turn of the Century Women,* Summer/Winter 1990; "Saintly Singer or Tanagra Figurine? Christina Rossetti through the Eyes of Katharine Tynan and Sara Teasdale" by Diane D'Amico, in *Victorian Poetry,* Autumn-Winter 1994, pp. 387-407.

*   *   *

Sara Teasdale, whose verse suggests, in her own phrase, "a delicate fabric of bird song," was one of America's most charming lyrists. Well-received and popular for some fifteen years after *Love Songs* (1917) won the Pulitzer Prize for poetry, she was posthumously, and unjustly, somewhat underrated by the time *Collected Poems* appeared in 1937.

Teasdale's first book of consequence was her third, *Rivers to the Sea,* in which signs of the mature poet became evident. Happily, the best of her early work was incorporated into the body of *Love Songs,* whose seemingly artless musicality informs a lucid lyricism. *Flame and Shadow* marks, if anything, an advance in emotional depth and "natural falterings"; but *Dark of the Moon,* while gracefully competent, appears somewhat anticlimactic in its minor accents: the book of a "woman seemingly poured empty." The first posthumous collection, *Strange Victory,* has, however, some of Teasdale's most memorable pieces—"All That Was Mortal," "Grace Before Sleep," "Advice to a Girl" and others.

Teasdale's verse, repeatedly concerned with the stars, often reflective of her travels, always simple in technique and form and natural in statement, dewlike and fragile in quality, and gentle in its acceptance of sorrow (though never bathetic), poses no intellectual problems. Constantly preoccupied with beauty, as idea and as evocation, it offers instead quietly ironic but joyful acceptance of life, exquisiteness of feminine perception, and delicate artistry; all of which does not deny that Teasdale occasionally "reached into the black waters whose chill brings wisdom," poems like "Wood Song" and numerous others being the memorable evidence.

—George Brandon Saul

THEROUX, Paul

Born: Medford, Massachusetts, 10 April 1941. **Education:** University of Maine, 1959-60; University of Massachusetts, B.A. 1963; Syrcuse University, 1963. **Family:** Married Anne Castle in 1967 (divorced 1993); two sons. **Career:** Lecturer in English, Soche Hill College, Limbe, Malawi, 1963-65; lecturer in English, Makerere University, Kampala, Uganda, 1965-68; lecturer in English, University of Singapore, 1968-71. Beginning 1971 professional writer. **Awards:** Robert Hamlet one-act play award, 1960; *Playboy* editorial award, 1971, 1976; *New York Times Book Review* "Editor's Choice" citation, 1975; American Academy and Institute of Arts and Letters award, 1981. Honorary degrees: Trinity College, 1980; Tufts University, 1980; University of Massachusetts, Amherst, 1988.

PUBLICATIONS

Collection

Sunrise with Seamonsters: A Paul Theroux Reader. 1985.

Novels

Waldo. 1967.
Fong and the Indians. 1968.
Girls at Play. 1969.
Murder in Mount Holly, 1969.
Jungle Lovers. 1971.
Saint Jack. 1973.
The Black House. 1974.
The Family Arsenal. 1976.
Picture Palace. 1978.
The Mosquito Coast. 1982.
Doctor Slaughter. 1984.
Half Moon Street: Two Short Novels. 1984.
O-Zone. 1986.
My Secret History. 1989.
Chicago Loop. 1991.
Millroy the Magician. 1994.
My Other Life. 1996.
Kowloon Tong. 1997.
The Collected Short Novels. 1999.

Short Stories

Sinning with Annie and Other Stories. 1972.
The Consul's File. 1977.
World's End and Other Stories. 1980.
The London Embassy. 1982.
The Collected Stories. 1997.

Plays

White Man's Burden. 1987.

Other

V.S. Naipaul: An Introduction to His Works. 1972.
The Great Railway Bazaar: By Train through Asia. 1975.
A Christmas Card (for children). 1978.
London Snow: A Christmas Story (for children). 1979.
The Old Pantagonian Express: By Train through the Americas. 1979.
Sailing through China. 1984.
The Kingdom by the Sea: A Journey around Great Britain. 1985.
The Imperial Way: By Rail from Peshawar to Chittagong. 1985.
Sunrise with Seamonsters: Travels and Discoveries 1964-1984. 1985.
Pantagonia Revisited, with Bruce Chatwin. 1986.
Riding the Iron Rooster: By Train through China. 1989.
Travelling the World. 1990.
The Happy Isles of Oceania: Padding the Pacific. 1992.
The Pillars of Hercules: A Grand Tour of the Mediterranean. 1995.
Sir Vidia's Shadow. 1998.

*

Critical Study: "Punctuating Travel: Paul Theroux and Bruce Chatwin" by Tim Youngs, in *Literature and History,* 1997.

* * *

Although probably best known for his travel books, Paul Theroux has also written some twenty fictional works, ranging widely in mode and setting. His early work is primarily satiric. Writing about his first novel, *Waldo,* Theroux mentions the influence of **Nathanael West** and **James Purdy.** Purdy's black humor especially is apparent, but this tale of a student who discovers that he wants to be a writer has an arbitrariness in its satire of America that finally dissipates its energy.

His following novels, written after he had gone to live in Africa as a member of the Peace Corps, are better structured, and *Fong of the Indians* in particular is very funny. But it was with *Saint Jack* that Theroux began to make his reputation. Jack Flowers is an American who has worked in Singapore for fourteen years, mostly as a pimp. Though the title might seem ironical, Jack in a curious way regards himself as a moralist. In the highly affirmative ending, he is paid a large sum of money to spy on a U.S. general, but when he discovers that the man is not doing anything he disapproves of he withholds the information against him.

An English setting begins to make its way into Theroux's work with *The Black House,* though the purpose of the novel seems to be to compare African and English mores. *The Consul's File* and *The London Embassy* are both collections of stories linked by common characters, settings, and events. The narrator of *Picture Palace* is Maud Coffin Pratt, a world-famous photographer now in her seventies. On the eve of a retrospective of her work in the Guggenheim Museum, she looks back over her life. She has been in love with her beautiful brother Orlando all her life but eventually discovers that he and her sister are probably lovers. The preoccupation with incest is perhaps the beginning of Theroux's later interest in various forms of deviant behavior and with characters who are very much on the outskirts of conventional society.

Mosquito Coast, Theroux's best known and arguably most accomplished novel, is the story of a brilliant but egotistical man named Allie Fox. Disgusted with the quality of life in the United States, he takes his family to Honduras to get back to an earlier, more natural civilization where they can live self-sufficiently. Only slowly do his wife and children begin to see and understand his megalomania, and the novel reaches its spectacular conclusion. Allie is the strangest and most frightening of Theroux's protagonists, a man who denies the existence of God only to attempt eventually to take the place of God.

In *O-Zone,* an inventive, intelligent, but unattractive novel set in the future, a group of New Yorkers decide to spend the New Year in the O(uter)-Zone, an area in Missouri that has been ruined because nuclear waste stored there has leaked, with disastrous effects. There they discover what they consider "aliens," although the inhabitants are actually human beings. The United States becomes marked by vast inequities between the aliens and the "owners." New York is choked with security checks and dangerous organizations. The rich people recreate a "natural" atmosphere indoors, while the outdoors becomes a wilderness. At the same time, the novel offers nostalgic reminders of the way the world used to be.

Doctor Slaughter and *Dr. DeMarr* are companion novellas that continue Theroux's interest in dysfunctional characters. These works include clever variations on the doppelganger theme, which is one form taken by Theroux to investigate the question of iden-

tity. *Chicago Loop* is an almost clinical investigation of the variety of psychological drives that impel human beings to satisfy their lust for the slaughter of their fellows. A happily married father and successful architect, Parker Jagoda secretly places advertisements for single women and eventually murders one of them in a horrendous way. We are offered a wealth of explanations for Parker's psychic disorder, particularly his suppressed homosexuality, which he finds more and more difficult to keep in check.

Written in the first person, *My Secret History* is the story of André Parent, from his days as an altar boy in Boston to the novel's enigmatic conclusion in India. Theroux dismisses the notion that the book is autobiographical. Much of the same material appears in some of his short stories, while one section has much in common with Theroux's savage portrait of his former mentor V. S. Naipaul in *Saint Vidia's Shadow.* The title of the final part, "Two of Everything," suggests and makes more explicit the pervading metaphor of the secret life. It is one of his most impressive achievements.

Although Theroux tends to deal with unpleasant people in unpleasant situations—strangers in an alien society who question their own identity—his novels and stories surprisingly often end on a note of epiphany for his characters. Theroux has insisted on the importance of change in his life, and the various experiments he has made in fiction testify to this. He seems to adopt one mode in fiction only to abandon it immediately after he feels he has mastered it.

—Laurie Clancy

THOREAU, Henry David

Born: David Henry Thoreau in Concord, Massachusetts, 12 July 1817. **Education:** Miss Wheeler's school and Center School, both Concord; Concord Academy, 1828-33; Harvard University, Cambridge, Massachusetts, 1833-35 and 1836-37, graduated 1837. **Career:** Teacher in Canton, Massachusetts, 1835-36, and at Center School, 1837 (resigned); worked in his father's pencil factory, 1837-38, 1844, 1849-50 (in 1853 business changed to supplying lead to printers); took over Concord Academy with his brother, and taught there, 1838-41; secretary and curator, 1838-40, and curator, 1842-43, Concord Lyceum, and regular lyceum lecturer from 1848; contributor to the Transcendentalist periodical *The Dial,* Concord, 1840-44 (editor of April 1843 issue); lived with Ralph Waldo Emerson, 1841-43, and with Emerson's family, 1847; tutor to William Emerson's sons, Staten Island, New York, 1843; lived in a cabin at Walden Pond, near Concord, 1845-47; jailed for refusing to pay poll tax (on anti-slavery and anti-war principles), 1846; visited Maine, 1846, 1853, and 1857, and Canada, 1850; worked at various odd jobs, including gardening and building work; land surveyor from 1848. **Died:** 6 May 1862.

PUBLICATIONS

Collections

Complete Works, edited by Harrison G.O. Blake. 5 vols., 1929.
Collected Poems, edited by Carl Bode. 1943; revised edition, 1964.

The Correspondence, edited by Walter Harding and Carl Bode. 1958.

Writings (includes *Journal,* edited by John C. Broderick, 1981—), edited by William L. Howarth. 1971—.

Thoreau's Vision: The Major Essays, edited by Charles R. Anderson. 1973.

Selected Works, edited by Walter Harding. 1975.

A Week on the Concord and Merrimack Rivers, Walden, The Maine Woods, Cape Cod (Library of America), edited by Robert Sayre. 1985.

Prose

A Week on the Concord and Merrimack Rivers. 1849.

Walden; or, Life in the Wood. 1854; *The Variorum Walden,* edited by Walter Harding, 1962.

Excursions, edited by Ralph Waldo Emerson. 1863.

The Maine Woods, edited by Sophia Thoreau and William Ellery Channing. 1864.

Cape Cod, edited by Sophia Thoreau and William Ellery Channing. 1865.

Letters to Various Persons, edited by Ralph Waldo Emerson. 1865.

A Yankee in Canada, with Anti-Slavery and Reform Papers (includes "Civil Disobedience"), edited by Sophia Thoreau and William Ellery Channing. 1866; *The Variorum Civil Disobedience* edited by Walter Harding. 1967; *Reform Papers* edited by Wendell Clark, in *Writings,* 1973.

Early Spring in Massachusetts. 1881; *Summer,* 1884; *Autumn,* 1888; *Winter,* 1892.

Miscellanies. 1894.

The Service, edited by Frank B. Sanborn. 1902.

Sir Walter Raleigh, edited by Henry Aiken Metcalf. 1905.

The First and Last Journeys of Thoreau, edited by Frank B. Sanborn. 2 vols., 1905.

Journal, edited by Bradford Torrey. 14 vols., 1906; edited by Francis H. Allen, 1949; *Selected Journals* edited by Carl Bode, 1967, as *The Best of Thoreau's Journals,* 1971.

The Moon. 1927.

Consciousness at Concord: The Text of Thoreau's Hitherto Lost Journal (1840-41), edited by Perry Miller. 1958.

Thoreau's Minnesota Journey: Two Documents, edited by Walter Harding. 1962.

Literary Notebook, edited by Kenneth Walter Cameron. 1964.

Over Thoreau's Desk: New Correspondence 1838-1861, edited by Kenneth Walter Cameron. 1965.

Fact Book, edited by Kenneth Walter Cameron. 2 vols., 1966.

Canadian Notebook, edited by Kenneth Walter Cameron. 1967.

Huckleberries (lecture), edited by Leo Stoller. 1970.

The Indians of Thoreau: Selections from the Indian Notebooks, edited by Richard F. Fleck. 1974.

The Winged Life: The Poetic Voice of Thoreau, edited by Robert Bly. 1986.

Faith in a Seed: The Dispersion of Seeds and Other Late Natural History Writings. 1993.

Selections from the Journals. 1995.

Uncommon Learning: Thoreau on Education. 1999.

Other

Translator, *The Transmigration of the Seven Brahmans,* edited by Arthur E. Christy. 1932.

Translator, *Seven Against Thebes,* by Aeschylus, edited by Leo Max Kaiser. 1960.

*

Bibliography: *A Bibliography of the Thoreau Society Bulletin Bibliographies 1941-1969: A Cumulation and Index* by Jean Cameron Advena, edited by Walter Harding, 1971; *The Literary Manuscripts of Thoreau* by William L. Howarth, 1974; *Thoreau and the Critics: A Checklist of Criticism 1900-1978* by Jeanetta Boswell and Sarah Crouch, 1981; *Thoreau: A Descriptive Bibliography* by Raymond R. Borst, 1982; *The Thoreau Secondary Bibliography: Supplement One (1830-1900): With an Appendix of Commentary and Documents* by Kenneth Walter Cameron, 1997.

Critical Studies: *Thoreau, The Poet-Naturalist* by William Ellery Channing, 1873, revised edition, 1902; *Thoreau: A Critical Study* by Mark Van Doren, 1916; *The Concord Saunterer* by Reginald Cook, 1940, revised edition, as *Passage to Walden,* 1949; "From Emerson to Thoreau" by F.O. Matthiessen, in *American Renaissance: Art and Expression in the Age of Emerson and Whitman,* 1941; *Thoreau* by Joseph Wood Krutch, 1948; *A Thoreau Gazetteer* by Robert F. Stowell, 1948, revised edition, edited by William L. Howarth, 1970; *Thoreau: The Quest and the Classics* by Ethel Seybold, 1951; *The Making of Walden* by J. Lyndon Shanley, 1957; *After Walden: Thoreau's Changing Views on Economic Man* by Leo Stoller, 1957; *The Shores of America: Thoreau's Inward Exploration* by Sherman Paul, 1958, and *Thoreau: A Collection of Critical Essays* edited by Paul, 1962; *A Thoreau Handbook,* 1959, revised edition, as *The New Thoreau Handbook* with Michael Meyer, 1980, *The Days of Thoreau: A Biography,* 1965, revised edition, 1982, both by Walter Harding, and *The Thoreau Centennial* edited by Harding, 1964; *Companion to Thoreau's Correspondence* by Kenneth Walter Cameron, 1964; *Emerson and Thoreau: Transcendentalists in Conflict* by Joel Porte, 1966; *Twentieth-Century Interpretations of Walden* edited by Richard Ruland, 1968; *The Recognition of Thoreau: Selected Criticism since 1848* edited by Wendell Glick, 1969; *Thoreau* by Leon Edel, 1970; *Thoreau as Romantic Naturalist* by James McIntosh, 1974; *Thoreau and the American Indians* by Robert F. Sayre, 1977; *Young Man Thoreau,* 1977, and *Thoreau's Seasons,* 1984, both by Richard Lebeaux; *Thoreau's Redemptive Imagination* by Frederick Garber, 1977; *Several More Lives to Live: Thoreau's Political Reputation in America* by Michael Meyer, 1977; *Thoreau in the Human Community* by Mary E. Moller, 1980; *Thoreau: What Manner of Man?* by Edward Wagenknecht, 1981; *Dark Thoreau* by Richard Bridgman, 1982; *The Book of Concord: Thoreau's Life as a Writer* by William L. Howarth, 1982; *Thoreau: A Naturalist's Liberty* by John Hildebidle, 1983; *Thoreau's Psychology: Eight Essays* edited by Raymond D. Gozzi, 1983; *Writing Nature: Thoreau's Journal* by Sharon Cameron, 1985; *Thoreau: A Life of the Mind* by Robert D. Richardson, Jr., 1986; *Henry Thoreau, Bachelor of Nature* by Leon Bazalgette, 1992; *Essays on Henry David Thoreau: Rhetoric, Style, and Audience* by Richard Dillman, 1993; *Life of Henry David Thoreau* by Henry S. Salt, 1993; *Reimagining Thoreau* by Robert Milder, 1994; *The Environmental Imagination: Thoreau, Nature Writing, and the Formation of American Culture* by Lawrence Buell, 1995; *The Tran-*

scendental Saunter: Thoreau and the Search for Self by David
C. Smith, 1997; *Thoreau's Doctrine of Simplicity* by Kenneth
Walter Cameron, 1997; *My Friend, My Friend: The Story of
Thoreau's Relationship with Emerson* by Harmon L. Smith, 1999.

*   *   *

Henry David Thoreau was long remembered in his native town
of Concord in Massachusetts as a quirky man, and indeed he was,
but he was also a bold economist. "The mass of men," he said,
"lead lives of quiet desperation," so intent on earning a living that
they have no time to live. How much better, he thought, was one
day of work and six days at more profitable occupation than six
days of labor and one day of rest. Thoreau's work was for a brief
period that of school teacher, for a longer time that of a helper in
his father's pencil-making business, and latterly that of a surveyor.
His occupation was that of an observer and recorder of nature,
and of man's proper relation to the world in which he lived. Punning on the correct pronunciation of his name, he called himself a
thorough man, and that he was, thoroughly attentive to his daily
task of walking, observing, recording, and then painstakingly transcribing into his journals the profits that each day brought. These
journals were his storehouse containing materials from which his
writings were drawn, and remain a storehouse in which readers
discover quizzical nudgings toward truths.

For to Thoreau truths were not to be captured by declarative
frontal attack. Thoreau felt that they must be warily approached,
as any wild thing must be approached, circled cautiously, lest in
fear they take flight, or, if sprung on too suddenly become caged
in words that inevitably distort. "In wildness," Thoreau announced,
"is the preservation of the world." But wildness did not mean
wilderness. He was shocked to fear by wind-swept mountain tops,
so like primordial chaos. Nature was better with man in it. Thoreau
preferred the woodlands, swamplands, and waterways of a man-
centered universe. He thought of himself as a "self-appointed inspector of snow-storms and rainstorms," a "surveyor, if not of
highways, then of forest paths and across-lots routes," faithfully
minding, he said, "my own business."

He had a large sense of drama. He dramatized himself, and he
dramatized the world of nature. Though others have been imprisoned for the cause of conscience, Thoreau is remembered as the
one who spent a night in jail for refusal to pay taxes to support a
tainted war, and who then wrote the essay "Civil Disobedience,"
which still remains a handbook for young rebels. When he retired
in 1845 to a cabin beside Walden Pond, he chose the 4th of July,
the anniversary of America's Declaration of Independence, as the
day to take residence there in token of his own independence. He
was a supreme egotist, vauntingly unashamed of eccentricities of
dress and deportment. His mission was, he said, to crow like Chanticleer, to wake his neighbors up.

He went to his cabin in the woods not in surly withdrawal from
a workaday world. Indeed, he often walked into town, if only to
feast on his mother's delicious pies. While officially in residence
beside Walden Pond, he took time off for an excursion to Mount
Katahdin in Maine. But ordinarily he remained in residence, an
eccentric man making daily eccentric pilgrimages around and beyond the still waters of the pond, his evenings spent in recording
his daily adventures, culling from them and earlier recordings materials to be made into books or essays. For, like any sensible
writer, he sought in his pond-side retreat the quiet and solitude
necessary for writing.

While there, again dramatically for exactly two years, two
months, and two days, he completed one book and the draft of
another. The first was a reminiscent account of a two-week excursion that he and his brother, now deceased, had taken during the
summer of 1839, traveling through waterways in a boat of their
own construction to the White Mountains in New Hampshire. In
composing *A Week on the Concord and Merrimack Rivers,*
Thoreau telescoped those two weeks to one and limited himself
almost entirely to river adventures. By many, *A Week* is considered Thoreau's most lively book, filled with youthful verve and
somber remembrances, and with observations on men and nature
and books, and the livening power of each. "A basket," Thoreau
later called it, "of delicate texture," the weaving so fine that, as a
basket, its strands fall apart to shower a reader with whimsical
wisdom and insightful perceptions.

But *A Week* was not well-received when it appeared in 1849.
Of an edition of a thousand copies more than seven hundred were
returned to him by its publisher unsold. Meanwhile, Thoreau, in
residence now in Concord, continued on small excursions, to Cape
Cod, again to Maine, but mostly through the outskirts of his native town. He lectured occasionally, but not comfortably nor out-
standingly well. He published accounts of his excursions and "Civil
Disobedience," first titled "Resistance to Civil Government." But,
most importantly, he puttered over revisions of the second book
that had occupied him during his residence beside Walden Pond.

When it appeared in 1854, *Walden; or, Life in the Woods* was
better received than *A Week* had been, but the reception was not
always enthusiastic, indeed was more than often mocking: who is
this humbug, pretending to be a hermit, who has the insolence to
tell us how we should live? But no book written in the nineteenth
century, except perhaps Karl Marx's *Das Kapital,* has become
more of a scripture, a guide, a handbook. Its long first chapter on
"Economy" was often reprinted as a tract used by advocates of
labor reform on both sides of the Atlantic. Other people built,
and still build, secluded small hideaways where work may be done,
in art, literature, or contemplation. Many a busy, work-impris-
oned person has lived vicariously in an imaginary pond-side retreat of his own. William Butler Yeats is said to have modeled his
Innisfree on recollections of Walden. W.H. Hudson proclaimed
Thoreau "without master or mate . . . in the foremost ranks of the
prophets."

Thoreau condenses his more than two-year residence beside
Walden Pond into the four seasons of a single year, joyously
through New England's brief summer for twelve chapters, then a
single chapter on autumn and three more on winter, an exultant
penultimate chapter on spring, moving toward a conclusion that
gives final coherence to the cycle, which is not only seasonal but
diurnal—day, evening, night, and morning—and which also suggests the ages of man through youth, manhood, old age, death,
and finally, with spring and morning, resurrection. Though repri-
manding people for work-filled sloth, Walden is also a compelling, ecstatic book, a manual of affirmation, confidently asserting
in its final sentences, "There is more day to dawn. The Sun is but
a morning star."

To most people Thoreau is *Walden,* and *Walden* Thoreau. But
there was more life to live and record, more excursions to make,
more writing to be meticulously done. In his journals he made
notes for a Book of the Seasons, which remains in embryo, never
put together except by other people who have mined the journals
for seasonal lore. When Thoreau died in his mid-fifties, he left
sheaves of manuscript as his principal worldly legacy. Most of

them have been variously edited by friends or admirers. *Excursions* in 1863 was made up of essays, many of them previously published. *The Maine Woods* in 1864 told of three excursions into the northern wilderness. *Cape Cod* in 1865 and *A Yankee in Canada* in 1866, though not without occasional delicately phrased insights, were, like most of *The Maine Woods,* narratives of travel rather than testaments to an ideal. Thoreau's journals have been published, though not in their entirety, and other people have culled books from them; his letters have been gathered, his poems and translations from the Greek, and his juvenile writings, often neither complete nor completely correct. In 1971 the Princeton University Press inaugurated a new meticulous edition of his writings.

Thoreau represents many things to many people. To some he is the ultimate nonconformist who brings comfort to those who relish nonconformity in lifestyle or dress. To others, he is an escapist, unhindered by familial responsibilities. Still others suspect that his bachelorhood resulted from fear or distrust of women, or of himself. Naturalists have found him inexpert in identification of species. Ecologists claim him as a pioneer. Civil rebels, from Gandhi to Martin Luther King and beyond have found him a spark igniting them to action. He was perhaps each of these, but was in total more than the sum of them all. He was a writer, a stylist quite equal to any who in his time or since has managed the flexible complexities of our language. The delicacy of the web that his words construct is too fine to provide the comfort of didacticism. His words fly free to allow each reader to pattern them to dimensions of his own. Everyone, it has been said, gets the Thoreau that he deserves.

—Lewis Leary

See the essay on *Walden* and *Civil Disobedience.*

THORPE, Thomas Bangs

Born: Westfield, Massachusetts, 1 March 1815. **Education:** Schools in Albany, New York, and New York City; studied painting with John Quidor, New York, 1830-33; attended Wesleyan University, Middletown, Connecticut, 1834-36. **Military Service:** Served in the military government of New Orleans, 1862-64: colonel. **Family:** Married 1) Anne Maria Hinckley in 1838 (died 1855), two daughters and one son; 2) Jane Fosdick in 1857. **Career:** Painter in Louisiana 1837-54; lived in New York, 1840, then moved to St. Francisville, Louisiana; editor, *Southern Sportsman* magazine, 1843, and the Whig newspapers *Concordia Intelligencer,* Vidalia, 1843-45, New Orleans *Commercial Times,* 1845-46, New Orleans *Daily Tropic,* 1846 (war correspondent in Mexico), Baton Rouge *Conservator,* 1846-47, and New Orleans *National,* 1847; postmaster, Vidalia, 1844-45; lived in Baton Rouge, 1848-54; moved to New York, 1854; member of the editorial staff, *Leslie's Illustrated Newspaper,* 1857; lawyer, 1858-60; co-owner and co-editor, *Spirit of the Times,* New York, 1859-61; surveyor, Port of New Orleans, 1862-63; city surveyor, New York, 1865-69; chief of the warehouse department, New York Customs House, 1869-78. Delegate, Louisiana Constitutional Convention, 1864. **Awards:** M.A.: Wesleyan University, 1847. **Died:** 20 September 1878.

PUBLICATIONS

Fiction and Sketches

The Mysteries of the Backwoods; or Sketches of the Southwest. 1845.
The Hive of the Bee-Hunter: A Repository of Sketches. 1854.
The Masters House: A Tale of Southern Life. 1854.

Other

Our Army on the Rio Grande. 1846.
Our Army at Monterey. 1847.
The Taylor Anecdote Book: Anecdotes and Letters of Zachary Taylor. 1848.
Reminiscences of Charles L. Elliott, Artist. 1868.

*

Critical Studies: *Thorpe, Humorist of the Old Southwest* by Milton Rickels, 1962; "Thomas Bangs Thorpe in the Gilded Age: Shifty in a New Country" by Stanton Garner, in *Mississippi Quarterly: The Journal of Southern Culture,* Winter 1982-83; "The Common Doom: Thorpe's 'The Big Bear of Arkansas'" by Alice Hall Petry, in *The Southern Quarterly: A Journal of the Arts in the South,* Winter 1983; "Thomas Bangs Thorpe's Backwoods Hunters: Culture Heroes and Humorous Failures" by David C. Estes, in *University of Mississippi Studies in English,* vol. 5; *Reframing Culture and Criticism in Grotesque Laughter: The Sublime Excremental Vision of Thomas Bangs Thorpe, Humorist of the Old Southwest* (dissertation) by Kim Johnson-Bogart, 1993.

*   *   *

Thomas Bangs Thorpe, a Northerner who loved the South and lived in Louisiana for many years, is one of the finest writers in the group known as old Southwestern humorists. At his best Thorpe was able to relinquish a formal, educated, fashionable mode of writing for an informal, ungrammatical, humorous view of the old Southwest. Indeed, Thorpe's great talent was his ability to render frontier speech and humor vividly.

In 1839 Thorpe, a portrait painter by trade, achieved national and international attention with his first essay about the frontier. "Tom Owen, The Bee-Hunter" described an eccentric whom Thorpe had met in the backwoods of Louisiana, a man whose primary interest in life was fearlessly pursuing bees and taking their honey. Unfortunately, in this essay Thorpe used a highly literary language, hardly the language of the frontier, and he thereby held himself and his readers at a considerable distance from his subject.

This problem of authorial distance was completely solved, however, in Thorpe's masterpiece "The Big Bear of Arkansas," published in 1841. Although he began this tale with a predominantly formal description of the "heterogeneous" passengers on a Mississippi steamboat and ended it in an equally formal style, Thorpe permitted a rather uncouth passenger to tell a tall tale within this frame. Jim Doggett, an Arkansas frontiersman, speaks throughout most of "The Big Bear" and his language is far from literary. His pronunciation (as suggested by misspellings), the rhythms of his speech, his grammatical errors, the idioms and metaphors he uses are all appropriate to the Western roarer, and form a purposeful, telling contrast to the relatively dull-frame style. This contrast is intensified by the exaggerated nature of Jim's frontier humor: Jim reports that in Arkansas beets grow as large as cedar stumps and wild turkeys grow too fat to fly. But the primary exaggeration in this story is not particularly humorous. Doggett says that the big bear seems to raid his farm at will, to have almost supernatural powers, and to loom as large as a "black mist." None of these details sets one laughing. They do, however, suggest that this "creation bar," like **William Faulkner**'s bear, is a symbol of a once vast wilderness that itself is doomed. Indeed, Thorpe's bear seems to recognize his inevitable doom and to die, though at Jim's hands, only because "his time come." There is, nevertheless, a joke embedded within this rather melancholy strain. When the bear decides his time has come, he surprises Doggett at a most inopportune moment— the Arkansas hunter is literally caught with his "inexpressibles" down.

Thorpe never equaled this tale. His "second finest frontier story" (according to Milton Rickels), "Bob Herring, The Arkansas Bear Hunter," is certainly of interest. Though Bob Herring is not the ring-tail roarer that Jim Doggett is, he is a realistic frontiersman and his language is both amusing and authentic. Yet the structure of this story lacks the technical brilliance of "The Big Bear." While "The Big Bear" encloses Jim's yarn within a frame, "Bob Herring" rather awkwardly juxtaposes two bear hunts told from different perspectives. Moreover, the latter story relies extensively upon an imaginative but gentlemanly narrator, and one longs to hear the voice of Bob Herring more pervasively.

Thorpe subsequently published two collections of stories and essays, edited a number of newspapers, wrote a history of the Mexican War, composed a mediocre reform novel, and contributed many articles to national periodicals. But his single most creative product came early in his career and was not to be matched by later works. "The Big Bear of Arkansas" was Thorpe's greatest achievement, one that abetted the rise of realism, dealt with the nature of the frontier, and guaranteed its author a place in American literary history.

—Suzanne Marrs

THURBER, James (Grover)

Born: Columbus, Ohio, 8 December 1894. **Education:** Ohio State University, Columbus, 1913-14, 1915-18. **Family:** Married 1) Althea Adams in 1922 (divorced 1935), one daughter; 2) Helen Wismer in 1935. **Career:** Code clerk, American Embassy, Paris, 1918-20; reporter, Columbus *Dispatch,* 1920-24, Paris edition of Chicago *Tribune,* 1925-26, and New York *Evening Post,* 1926-27; editor, 1927, writer, 1927-38, then freelance contributor, *The New Yorker;* also an illustrator from 1929: several individual shows. **Awards:** Litt.D.: Kenyon College, Gambier, Ohio, 1950; Yale University, New Haven, Connecticut, 1953. L.H.D.: Williams College, Williamstown, Massachusetts, 1951. **Died:** 2 November 1961.

PUBLICATIONS

Collections

Vintage Thurber: A Collection of the Best Writings and Drawings. 2 vols., 1963.

People Have More Fun than Anybody: A Centennial Celebration of Drawings and Writings of James Thurber. 1995.
Writings and Drawings. 1996.

Short Stories and Sketches (illustrated by the author)

The Owl in the Attic and Other Perplexities. 1931.
The Seal in the Bedroom and Other Predicaments. 1932.
My Life and Hard Times. 1933.
The Middle-Aged Man on the Flying Trapeze: A Collection of Short Pieces. 1935.
Let Your Mind Alone! and Other More or Less Inspirational Pieces. 1937.
Cream of Thurber. 1939.
The Last Flower: A Parable in Pictures. 1939.
Fables for Our Time and Famous Poems Illustrated. 1940.
My World—and Welcome to It. 1942.
Men, Women, and Dogs: A Book of Drawings. 1943.
The Thurber Carnival. 1945.
The Beast in Me, and Other Animals: A New Collection of Pieces and Drawings about Human Beings and Less Alarming Creatures. 1948.
The Thurber Album: A New Collection of Pieces about People. 1952.
Thurber Country: A New Collection of Pieces about Males and Females, Mainly of Our Own Species. 1953.
Thurber's Dogs: A Collection of the Master's Dogs, Written and Drawn, Real and Imaginary, Living and Long Ago. 1955.
A Thurber Garland. 1955.
Further Fables for Our Time. 1956.
Alarms and Diversions. 1957.
Lanterns and Lances. 1961.
Credos and Curios. 1962.
Thurber and Company. 1966.

Fiction (for children)

Many Moons. 1943.
The Great Quillow. 1944.
The White Deer. 1945.
The 13 Clocks. 1950.
The Wonderful O. 1955.

Plays

The Male Animal, with Elliott Nugent (produced 1940). 1940.
A Thurber Carnival, from his own stories (produced 1960). 1962.

Wrote the books for the following college musical comedies: *Oh My! Omar,* with Hayward M. Anderson, 1921; *Psychomania,* 1922; *Many Moons,* 1922; *A Twin Fix,* with Hayward M. Anderson, 1923; *The Cat and the Riddle,* 1924; *Nightingale,* 1924; *Tell Me Not,* 1924.

Other

Is Sex Necessary? or, Why You Feel the Way You Do, with E.B. White. 1929.
Thurber on Humor. 1953.
The Years with Ross. 1959.
Selected Letters, edited by Helen Thurber and Edward Weeks. 1981.

Conversations with Thurber, edited by Thomas Fensch. 1989.
Collecting Himself: Thurber on Writing and Writers, Humor, and Himself, edited by Michael J. Rosen. 1989.

*

Bibliography: *Thurber: A Bibliography* by Edwin T. Bowden, 1968; *Thurber: An Annotated Bibliography of Criticism* by Sarah Eleanora Toombs, 1987.

Critical Studies: *Thurber* by Robert E. Morsberger, 1964; *The Art of Thurber* by Richard C. Tobias, 1969; *Thurber, His Masquerades: A Critical Study* by Stephen A. Black, 1970; *The Clocks of Columbus: The Literary Career of Thurber* by Charles S. Holmes, 1972, and *Thurber: A Collection of Critical Essays* edited by Holmes, 1974; *Thurber: A Biography* by Burton Bernstein, 1975; *Thurber's Anatomy of Confusion* by Catherine McGehee Kenney, 1984; *James Thurber* by Robert Emmet Long, 1988; *Remember Laughter: A Life of James Thurber* by Neil A. Grauer, 1995; *James Thurber: His Life and Times* by Harrison Kinney, 1995.

*   *   *

James Thurber, who was not destined to be one of America's celebrated poets, first turned up in the pages of the *New Yorker* on 26 February 1927 with two forgettable bits of verse. His third contribution (5 March 1927) was more indicative of what was to come. Called "An American Romance," it is the account of a "little man in an overcoat that fitted him badly," who stations himself in a revolving door, defying a number of authority figures, and stays there until he is rewarded with instant celebrity. An ur-Walter Mitty, then, caught in an American landscape that Thurber would eventually view more sardonically, almost a fable for our time.

Thurber had worked on the Columbus *Dispatch* and the Paris edition of the Chicago *Tribune* and as a freelance contributor to a number of publications before he arrived at the *New Yorker,* but it was with that magazine that his reputation both as writer and cartoonist was made, a reputation that he sometimes saw as limiting to his artistic aspirations. He served on the staff until 1938 and remained a contributor until 1961; eventually he tried to define the quality of the place and his own ambiguous attachment to it in *The Years with Ross,* which **E.B. White** called "a sly exercise in denigration, beautifully concealed in words of sweetness and love."

Thurber's first book was a collaboration with White, the parody volume *Is Sex Necessary?* His second, *The Owl in the Attic,* initiated the practice of collecting his magazine pieces, which he would follow for the rest of his writing life. Sometimes—*My Life and Hard Times, Let Your Mind Alone!, The Years with Ross*—the group of essays was obviously conceived as a book; in most cases, the mixture is fortuitous, although occasionally, as in *Thurber's Dogs,* held together by a common subject matter. Of his early books, *My Life and Hard Times,* a marvelously funny mock biography, is the most impressive, the more so when one considers that Thurber returned to the same Ohio home ground to do the completely different and equally successful *Thurber Album.*

There are many Thurbers: the playwright (*The Male Animal, A Thurber Carnival*); the author of children's books, of which *The White Deer* and *The 13 Clocks* are the happiest inventions; the adult fabulist of *Fables for Our Time* and *Further Fables;* the ca-

nine celebrant (*Thurber's Dogs*); the social observer who could write so well about soap opera ("Soapland" in *The Beast in Me, and Other Animals*); the perceptive critic who could work through parody or direct comment; and the concerned artist who defended humor from outside attack and inside timidity in the repressive atmosphere of the 1950s. Through all these, there is a persistent Thurber, the dark humorist who, one way or another, kept asking, as the moral of one of the *Further Fables* puts it, "Oh, why should the shattermyth have to be a crumplehope and a dampenglee?"

—Gerald Weales

See the essay on "The Secret Life of Walter Mitty."

TIMROD, Henry

Born: Charleston, South Carolina, 8 December 1828. **Education:** German Friendly Society School and Cotes's School, Charleston, 1836-40; Franklin College (later University of Georgia), 1845-46; read law in the office of James L. Petigru, Charleston, 1847-49. **Military Service:** Served in the Confederate Army during the Civil War, 1862 (discharged for health reasons, 1862). **Family:** Married Kate Goodwin in 1864; one son. **Career:** Schoolmaster and tutor for various Southern plantation families, 1850-61; assistant editor, *Charleston Mercury,* 1863; associate editor, and part owner, Columbia *South Carolinian,* 1864 until 1865 when Sherman's troops sacked the town; assistant private secretary to Governor J.L. Orr, 1864. **Died:** 7 October 1867.

PUBLICATIONS

Collections

The Essays, edited by Edd Winfield Parks. 1942.
The Collected Poems: A Variorum Edition, edited by Edd Winfield Parks and Aileen Wells Parks. 1965.

Poetry

Poems. 1859.
The Poems, edited by Paul Hamilton Hayne. 1873.
The Uncollected Poems, edited by Guy A. Cardwell. 1942.

Other

The Last Years of Timrod 1864-1867: Including Letters to Paul Hamilton Hayne and Letters about Timrod by William Gilmore Simms, John R. Thompson, John Greenleaf Whittier, and Others, edited by Jay B. Hubbell. 1941.

*

Bibliography: *Sidney Lanier, Timrod, and Paul Hamilton Hayne: A Reference Guide* by Jack De Bellis, 1978.

Critical Studies: *Timrod* by Edd Winfield Parks, 1964; "Henry Timrod: Poetic Voice of Southern Nationalism" by John Budd in

Southern Studies: An Interdisciplinary Journal of the South, winter 1981; "The Artistic Design of Societal Commitment: Shakespeare and the Poetry of Henry Timrod" by Christina Murphy in *Shakespeare and Southern Writers: A Study in Influence,* 1985.

*   *   *

Had it not been for the Civil War, Henry Timrod, although the best southern poet of his time except for **Edgar Allan Poe**, could be almost unknown today. In view of his reputation as chief of the southern poets of the War—he is characterized in such rebarbative phrases as "Laureate of the Confederacy" and "Harp of the South"—his life and thought are rich in ironies.

There was nothing of the Cavalier about his ancestry, and he was not a zealous propagandist for the region or for slavery. Like a number of other antebellum southern writers, he was often at odds with his section and its culture; a strain of astringent candor ran through his excellent essays. Although Charleston was the publishing center of the South, Timrod describes the region as a literary backwater, archaic in taste, unformed in judgment, materialistic, prosaic, uninterested in intellectual and poetic knowledge. He opposed southernism in literature and emphasized that poetry must belong to the world.

To some of the older generation of Charleston literary men, Timrod seemed extravagantly avant-garde: his principal heroes and models were William Wordsworth and Alfred Lord Tennyson. His theory and practice were tempered, however, by classicist ideas and habits. He insisted that after inspiration must come artistry; that excessive subjectivity spoils verse; and that poetry must be true and ethical. His apprentice verses show him industriously experimenting in forms and meters, and variant versions of mature poems indicate that he was an assiduous reviser. **Sidney Lanier** wrongly held that Timrod possessed a dainty artless art but never had time to learn the craft of the poet. His lyricism is most successful when most considered: his verse lacks spontaneity, intensity, and figurative imagination; his ideas and metrics are unoriginal. He was in a large sense an occasional poet whose delight in words and skill with meters could produce simply structured, controlled verses remarkably free of the sentimental verbosity and crudity of form that are characteristic of his southern contemporaries.

Amative and nature poetry make up the bulk of Timrod's verse, but the critical consensus is right in judging his war poetry, most of which stresses the losses and sorrows of the conflict, to be his best. Most memorable are "Ethno-genesis," "The Cotton Boll," "Carolina," "A Cry to Arms," "Charleston," and his Magnolia Cemetery ode.

Nearly all of Timrod's verses were first published in southern newspapers and magazines, usually for no pay. The *Southern Literary Messenger,* of Richmond, and *Russell's Magazine,* of Charleston, were the most important of the miscellanies to which he made regular contributions. Friends guaranteed the costs of the one slim volume of his verse that appeared during his lifetime. Posthumous collections more than double the number of poems contained in that first volume.

—Guy A. Cardwell

TOLSON, Melvin B(eaunorus)

Born: Moberly, Missouri, 6 February 1898. **Education:** Lincoln High School, Kansas City, Missouri, graduated 1918; Fisk Uni-

versity, Nashville, Tennessee, 1918-20; Lincoln University, Oxford, Pennsylvania, 1920-23, B.A. 1923; Columbia University, New York, 1930-31, M.A. 1940. **Family:** Married Ruth Southall in 1922; three sons and one daughter. **Career:** Teacher at Wiley College, Marshall, Texas, 1924-47; professor of English and drama, Langston University, Oklahoma, 1947-66; Avalon Professor of Humanities, Tuskegee Institute, Alabama, 1965. Columnist ("Caviar and Cabbage"), *Washington Tribune,* 1937-44; mayor of Langston, 1954 (re-elected 1954, 1956, 1958). **Awards:** American Academy award, 1966. D.L., 1954, and D.H.L., 1965, Lincoln University. Order of the Star of Africa (Liberia), 1954. **Died:** 29 August 1966.

PUBLICATIONS

Collection

Harlem Gallery and Other Poems of Melvin B. Tolson. 1999.

Poetry

Rendezvous with America. 1944.
Libretto for the Republic of Liberia. 1953.
Harlem Gallery: Book 1, The Curator. 1965.
A Gallery of Harlem Portraits, edited by Robert M. Farnsworth. 1979.

Play

The Fire in the Flint, from the novel by Walter F. White (produced 1952).

Other

Caviar and Cabbage: Selected Columns from the Washington Tribune 1937-1944, edited by Robert M. Farnsworth. 1982.

*

Critical Studies: introduction by Karl Shapiro to *Harlem Gallery,* 1965; *Tolson* by Joy Flasch, 1972; *Tolson's Harlem Gallery: A Literary Analysis* by Mariann Russell, 1980, and "Evolution of Style in the Poetry of Melvin B. Tolson" by Russell, in *Black American Poets between Worlds, 1940-1960,* 1986; *Tolson: Plain Talk and Poetic Prophecy* by Robert M. Farnsworth, 1984; "The Poetry of Melvin B. Tolson (1898-1966)" by Melvin B. Tolson, Jr., in *World Literature Today: A Literary Quarterly of the University of Oklahoma,* Summer 1990; "Melvin B. Tolson and the Deterritorialization of Modernism" by Aldon L. Nielsen, in *African American Review,* Summer 1992.

*   *   *

On the basis of his first volume of poetry, *Rendezvous with America,* it would hardly have been possible to predict the kind of poet Melvin Tolson was to be a decade later. A poet who writes "I gaze upon her silken loveliness / She is a passionflower of joy and pain / On the golden bed I came back to possess" does not show particular promise. Likewise the lines "America is the Black Man's country / The Red Man's, the Yellow Man's / The Brown

Man's, the White Man's" are not suggestive of the great lines yet to come.

There are, however, certain characteristics of the earlier poetry that were to develop and become hallmarks of the later poetry, more its essence than ornament. The second stanza, for example, of "An Ex-Judge at the Bar" is in style and content very much like a good deal of the later poetry and untypical of the rather commonplace character of much of the first volume. That stanza, "I know, Bartender, yes. I know when the Law / Should wag its tail or rip with fang and claw. / When Pilate washed his hands, that neat event / Set for us judges a Caesarean precedent," is in tone typically Tolsonian. The juxtaposition of the formal and the informal, the classical and the contemporary, the familiar and the unusual accounts in large measure for the unique character of Tolson's best poetry.

Such juxtapositions are more pronounced in *Libretto for the Republic of Liberia,* where, in addition, the "gift for language" noted in **Allen Tate**'s introduction to the volume becomes apparent. The effect of the juxtaposition of the learned encyclopedia references and the most abstruse vocabulary with commonplace references, vocabulary, and rhyme, all managed within a highly traditional form, is pyrotechnic. The occurrence in the same context of French, German, Latin, Hebrew, Swahili, Arabic, Spanish, and Sanskrit references with everyday activities, occupations, and events created a system of tensions not unlike the dynamic of forces holding an atom or a galaxy together. Each element threatens to go off on its own; yet as long as the balance of forces remains constant, the system functions. Tolson, by virtue of an extraordinary mind and intelligence, keeps a vast array of disparate elements in constant relationship. His poetry is, therefore, coherent, and its primary effect is of the containment and control of vast reserves of energy.

This bears on **Karl Shapiro**'s controversial statement in his introduction to *Harlem Gallery,* Tolson's final volume, that "Tolson writes in Negro." It is not at bottom the language that prompted Shapiro's observation. Rather, it is the intellectual disposition of the tension between two worlds that finds its manifestation in the language. Tolson belongs (and this distinguishes him from Eliot, Pound, and Hart Crane, whom he read avidly) to an Afro-American world and an American-European world, and he knows these worlds in intricate detail. The balance he sustains between them is the source of his power. Few understand him because few know both worlds as well, and few are as totally committed as he to such a high universal standard of values.

—Donald B. Gibson

TOOMER, Jean

Pseudonym: Nathan Eugene Toomer. **Born:** Washington, D.C., 26 December 1894. **Education:** High schools in Brooklyn, New York, and Washington, D.C.; University of Wisconsin, Madison, 1914; Massachusetts College of Agriculture; American College of Physical Training, Chicago, 1916; New York University, Summer 1917; City College, New York, 1917. **Family:** Married 1) Margery Latimer in 1931 (died 1932), one daughter; 2) Marjorie Content in 1934. **Career:** Taught physical education in a school near Milwaukee, 1918; clerk, Acker Merrall and Conduit grocery company, New York, 1918; shipyard worker, New York; worked at Howard

Theatre, Washington, D.C., 1920; studied at Gurdjieff's Institute in Fontainebleau, France, 1924, 1926: led Gurdjieff groups in Harlem, 1925, and Chicago, 1926-33; lived in Pennsylvania after 1934. **Died:** 30 March 1967.

PUBLICATIONS

Collections

The Wayward and the Seeking: A Collection of Writings by Toomer, edited by Darwin T. Turner. 1980.
Collected Poems, edited by Robert B. Jones and Margery Toomer Latimer. 1988.

Fiction

Cane (includes stories and verse). 1923; edited by Darwin T. Turner, 1988.

Play

Balo, in *Plays of Negro Life,* edited by Alain Locke and Montgomery Gregory. 1927.

Other

Essentials (aphorisms). 1931.
An Interpretation of Friends Worship. 1947.
The Flavor of Man. 1949.

*

Bibliography: "Toomer: An Annotated Checklist of Criticism" by John M. Reilly, in *Resources for American Literary Study,* Spring 1974.

Critical Studies: *In a Minor Chord (on Toomer, Cullen, and Hurston)* by Darwin T. Turner, 1971; *The Merrill Studies in Cane* edited by Frank Durham, 1971; *The Grotesque in American Negro Fiction: Toomer, Wright, and Ellison* by Fritz Gysin, 1975; *Toomer* by Brian Joseph Benson and Mabel Mayle Dillard, 1980; *Toomer, Artist: A Study of His Literary Life and Work 1894-1936* by Nellie Y. McKay, 1984; *The Lives of Toomer: A Hunger for Wholeness* by Cynthia Earl Kerman and Richard Eldridge, 1987; *Toomer's Years with Gurdjieff: Portrait of an Artist 1923-1936* by Rudolph P. Byrd, 1990; *To Make a New Race: Gurdjieff, Toomer, and the Harlem Renaissance* by Jon Woodson, 1998; *Jean Toomer and the Terrors of American History* by Charles Scruggs, 1998.

*   *   *

In a startling image of fulfillment Jean Toomer likened the descendants of slaves among whom he sought poetic motive to "purple ripened plums," the seed of one becoming "An everlasting song, a singing tree, / Caroling softly souls of slavery. What they were, and what they are to me." The lyric containing this image, "Song of the Son," serves as one of the impressionistic epigraphs uniting *Cane* into a symbolic account of Toomer's effort to reconcile the technical sophistication of Harlem Renaissance art with folk life. His assertion that black rural life in Georgia provided him with the soil for a living literature ratified the cultural nationalism of the Renaissance, while the experimental form of this book demonstrated its kinship with literary modernism. For contemporaries, then, *Cane* promised a vitally new art.

Each of the stories, sketches, and poems making up *Cane* examines the possibility of intuitive self-fulfillment. In the first part of the book, set in the South, a series of female characters achieve momentary redemption through expression of spontaneous feelings. The second part, set in Washington, D.C., variously represents characters whose feelings are blocked by social artifice. The whole concludes with a story-play in which the central figure, Kabnis, has internalized the violence and repression of caste relations so effectively that he is terrified of opening his senses at all. The complex intermingling of impressionism, expressionism, and generic forms in *Cane,* therefore, constitutes an argument for the spontaneity associated with "primitivism."

The tension between sophistication and spontaneity remained a dynamic source for Renaissance writers, but not for Toomer. Shortly after *Cane* was published he met Gurdjieff, had a mystical experience, and turned his life-long need for meaning toward a search for a transcendent principle of unity. One consequence was denial of the significance of racial identity. Another was production of writing increasingly distant from the sensual style of *Cane.* Toomer, once a harbinger of new art, became an enigmatic historical figure.

Only a small portion of his later writings was published. For critics the most notable piece is "Blue Meridian," a long, visionary poem about a new American race, which at its best resonates with the inspiration of **Walt Whitman**. One must conclude that in Toomer biographical experience overwhelmed creative imagination. A search for identity became so compelling that he could no longer gain the distance needed to convert the motive of his life into the substance of successful literature.

—John M. Reilly

TOURGÉE, Albion W(inegar)

Born: Williamsfield, Ohio, 2 May 1838. **Education:** Kingsville Academy, Ohio, 1854-59; Rochester University, Rochester, New York, 1859-61, B.A. 1862; studied law; admitted to Ohio bar, 1864. **Military Service:** Served in the 27th New York Volunteers, 1861; wounded at the first Battle of Bull Run, 1861; lieutenant in the 105th Ohio Regiment, 1862-64; prisoner of war, 1863. **Family:** Married Emma L. Kilbourne in 1863; one daughter. **Career:** Assistant principal of a school in Wilson, New York, 1861; taught and wrote for a newspaper in Erie, Pennsylvania, 1864-65; settled in Greensboro, North Carolina, 1865; practiced law; entered politics for "carpetbagger" interests, 1866; founded *Union Register,* which failed, 1867; delegate to the "carpetbag" conventions, 1868, 1875; judge, Superior Court of North Carolina, 1868-75; writer from 1874; pension agent, Raleigh, North Carolina, 1876-78; moved to New York, 1879, and settled in Mayville, 1881; editor, *Our Continent,* Philadelphia, 1882-84; regular contributor to the *Daily Inter Ocean,* Chicago, 1885-98; founded *The Basis: A Journal of Citizenship,* Buffalo, New York, 1895-96; U.S. Consul-General, Bordeaux, France, 1897-1905. **Died:** 21 May 1905.

PUBLICATIONS

Fiction

Toinette. 1874; as *A Royal Gentleman,* 1881.
Figs and Thistles: A Western Story. 1879.
A Fool's Errand. 1879; revised edition, incorporating *The Invisible Empire,* 1880; edited by John Hope Franklin, 1961.
Bricks Without Straw. 1880; edited by Otto H. Olsen, 1969.
'Zouri's Christmas. 1881.
John Eax and Marmelon; or, The South Without the Shadow. 1882.
Hot Plowshares. 1883.
Button's Inn. 1887.
Black Ice. 1888.
With Gauge and Swallow, Attorneys. 1889.
Murvale Eastmas, Christian Socialist. 1890.
Pactolus Prime. 1890.
'89. 1891.
A Son of Old Harry. 1892.
Out of the Sunset Sea. 1893.
An Outing with the Queen of Hearts. 1894.
The Mortgage on the Hip-Roof House. 1896.
The Man Who Outlived Himself (stories). 1898.

Play

A Fool's Errand, with Steele MacKaye, from the novel by Tourgée, edited by Dean H. Keller. 1969.

Other

The Code of Civil Procedure of North Carolina, with Victor C. Barringer and Will B. Rodman. 1878.
An Appeal to Caesar. 1884.
The Veteran and His Pipe (essays). 1886.
Letters to a King. 1888.
The War of the Standards: Coin and Credit Versus Coin Without Credit. 1896.
The Story of a Thousand, Being a History of the 105th Volunteer Infantry, 1862 to 1865. 1896.
A Civil War Diary, edited by Dean H. Keller. 1965.

*

Bibliography: "A Checklist of the Writings of Tourgée" by Dean H. Keller, in *Studies in Bibliography 18,* 1965.

Critical Studies: *Tourgée* by Roy Floyd Dibble, 1921; *Tourgée* by Theodore L. Gross, 1963; *Carpetbagger's Crusade: The Life of Tourgée* by Otto H. Olsen, 1965; "Tourgée's *Bricks without Straw:* History, Fiction and Irony" by Robert O. Stephens, in *Southern-Quarterly: A Journal of the Arts in the South,* Summer 1989; *A Fool's Errand and The Invisible Empire* edited by Theodore L. Gross, 1991; "Reconstructing Reconstruction: Region and Nation in the Work of Albion Tourgée" by Peter Caccavari, in *Regionalism Reconsidered: New Approaches to the Field* edited by David Jordan, 1994; "A Trick of Meditation: Charles Chesnutt's Conflicted Literary Relationship with Albion Tourgée" by Peter Caccavari, in *Literary Influence and African-American Writers,* edited by Tracy Mishkin, 1996; "Edmund Wilson Refights the Civil War: The Revision of Albion Tourgée's Novels" by Everett Carter, in *American Literary Realism,* Winter 1997, pp. 68-77.

*   *   *

Albion W. Tourgée's views on the art of the novel and his own practice as a novelist carry the unmistakable stamp of his active involvement as a journalist, polemicist, and judge in the political and public issues of the Reconstruction period. His unreserved preference for historical veracity and social purpose (as implied in his criticism of **Henry James**) always took precedence over subtleties of technique and nuances of character. Observing no separation between the role of the novelist and that of the historian, Tourgée conceived of the novel essentially as a frame for "a possible life . . . in a true environment," insisting that the test of artistic success was inevitably the consistency with which such a life related to its milieu and to the dominant predispositions of the age. Interestingly enough. such a conviction did not bring him any closer to the writers of a realist and naturalist persuasion whose treatment of human depravity and poverty he found crude and repulsive. His admiration, sometimes carried to uncritical extremes, was for the realism of **James Fenimore Cooper**'s descriptions, for there he found the ideals of love, truth, and purity that were worthy of emulation by the citizen of a new republic. As the author of *The Code of Civil Procedure of North Carolina* and the editor of the *Union Register,* a newspaper firmly committed to radical reform, he promoted these ideals in practical ways.

Tourgée's best novels, *A Fool's Errand,* recounting a carpetbagger's grim struggle to work for the cause of equality and pacifism in the South, and *Bricks Without Straw,* concerned with an uneducated but enlightened black man's attempt to achieve selfhood, amplify and illustrate his fictional themes and moral concerns—the possibility of social amelioration, the problem of vindicating one's cherished beliefs in a hostile society, the responses evoked by the tender and redemptive sentiment of love, sympathy for blacks, and the selflessness of the Republican set against the cupidity of the Southern white supremacist intent on denying political and civil rights to blacks. To these are added a preacher's zeal and intensity, a penchant for melodrama, a forceful style, and a penetrating if occasionally biased reading of the political climate in the South in the 1860s and 1870s. Tourgée's commitment to such themes and values places him securely, in **Edmund Wilson**'s incontestable judgment, in the "second category of writers who aim primarily at social history. His narrative has spirit and movement; his insights are brilliantly revealing, and they are expressed with emotional conviction."

The inwardness of the imagination that Tourgée sought to exploit in his later fiction on his return to the North in 1879 produced disappointing results. The absence of concrete historical, political, and social contexts often led him to write sentimental romantic tales abounding with improbable coincidences and permeated by an impractical ethical and religious humanitarianism: in *Black Ice* a somnambulist, who has climbed to the top of a snowy mountain in search of her baby's grave, is heroically rescued; in *Button's Inn* the hero, an ex-murderer, is redeemed by conversion to Mormonism. The relative success of *'89,* in which Tourgée returned to his earlier themes in the original Southern setting, showed that he obviously was at ease in the comforts of a familiar environment and that he wrote

most competently when called upon to provide a kind of fictional apologia for radical republicanism.

—Chirantan Kulshrestha

TRAVEN, B.

A pseudonym for a writer whose identity has not been established; most frequently identified with Hermann Albert Otto Maximilian Feige; also used name Hal Croves; adopted name Traven Torsvan after moving to Mexico. **Born:** Swiebodzin, Poland, 28 February 1882. **Family:** Married Rosa Elena Luján in 1957. **Career:** Worked as apprentice locksmith for 4 years; adopted name Ret Marut and worked as actor in Germany, 1907-15; political activist: published journal *Der Ziegel Brenner,* 1917-22; press minister in brief left-wing government in Munich, 1919; arrested and escaped; left Germany for England, 1923 (jailed as illegal alien, 1923-24); moved to Mexico; government photographer on expedition to Chiapas, 1926; became Mexican citizen, 1951. **Died:** 26 March 1969.

PUBLICATIONS

Fiction

Das Totenschiff. 1926; as *The Death Ship,* 1934.
Der Wobbly. 1926; as *Die Baumwollpflücker,* 1929; as *The Cotton-Pickers,* 1956.
Der Schatz der Sierra Madre. 1927; as *The Treasure of the Sierra Madre,* 1934.
Der Busch (stories). 1928; revised edition, 1930.
Die Brücke im Dschungel. 1929; as *The Bridge in the Jungle,* 1938.
Die weisse Rose. 1929; as *The White Rose,* 1965.
Der Karren. 1931; as *The Carreta,* 1935.
Regierung. 1931; as *Government,* 1935.
Der Marsch ins Reich der Caoba: Ein Kriegsmarsch. 1933; as *March to Caobaland,* 1961; as *March to the Monteria,* 1964.
Die Rebellion der Gehenkten. 1936; as *The Rebellion of the Hanged,* 1952.
Die Troza. 1936.
Ein General kommt aus dem Dschungel. 1940; as *General from the Jungle,* 1954.
Macario (in German). 1950.
Aslan Norval (in German). 1960.
Stories by the Man Nobody Knows: Nine Tales. 1961.
The Night Visitor and Other Stories. 1966.
Maze of Love. 1967.
The Kidnapped Saint and Other Stories, edited by Rosa Elena Luján and Mina C. and H. Arthur Klein. 1975.
Das Frühwerk (as Ret Marut). 1977.
Khundar: Ein deutsches Märchen (as Ret Marut). 1977.
To the Honourable Miss S— and Other Stories (as Ret Marut), translated by Peter Silcock. 1981.

Other

Lund des Frühlings (on Mexico). 1928.
Sonnen-Schöpfung: Indianische Legende. 1936; as *The Creation of the Sun and the Moon,* 1968.

*

Bibliography: "A Checklist of the Works of Traven and the Critical Estimates and Biographical Essays on Him" by E.R. Hagemann, in *Papers of the Bibliographical Society of America 53,* 1959; *B. Traven: A Bibliography* by Edward N. Treverton, 1999.

Critical Studies: *Anonymity and Death: The Fiction of Traven* by Donald O. Chankin, 1975; *Traven: An Introduction* by Michael L. Baumann, 1976; *Das Traven Buch* edited by Johannes Beck and others, 1976; *The Mystery of Traven* by Judy Stone, 1977; *My Search for Traven* by Jonah Raskin, 1980; *The Man Who Was Traven* by Will Wyatt, 1980, as *The Secret of the Sierra Madre,* 1980; *B. Traven: Life and Work* edited by Ernst Schurer and Philip Jenkins, 1987.

                              *   *   *

B. Traven kept his identity a closely guarded secret and never gave interviews to the press. He had Marxist leanings, wrote usually in German, and died in Mexico City. He knew Mexico well: his novel *General from the Jungle* tells the story of a rebellion of Indians against a Mexican dictator. Among adventure writers he deserves a high place—on the same level as **Jack London**—while some of his themes bring to mind Joseph Conrad.

In all his fiction Traven is concerned with the problem of Mammon. "Gold is the devil," says one of the characters in *The Treasure of the Sierra Madre*—a book on which John Huston based the successful film. Traven's most famous novel, and his finest, is *The Death Ship.* When it first came out in the mid-1930s in Germany, it sold more than 200,000 copies before it was banned. Subtitled "The Story of an American Sailor," it might be better described as the story of a hero without a name, for the author regards the sailor on a death ship as a gladiatorial hero whose Emperor is Mammon. Death ships are those that carry contraband, with ammunition and rifles hidden in crates labeled "Toys" or "Cocoa" or "Corned Beef." The crews are enlisted from men on the run—no names, no questions—or from seamen who have lost their papers and so have no status. This is what happens to Traven's hero, who is informed by the American consul in Paris: "I doubt your birth as long as you have no certificate of birth. The fact that you are sitting in front of me is no proof of your birth."

Later the hero, after a series of adventures with the Belgian and Dutch police and a short spell in a prison in Toulouse, finds himself aboard the *Yorikke,* a death ship that has put into Barcelona. Taken on as a fireman, he is made to work as a coal-shoveler. In a ship as old and patched up as the *Yorikke,* there is a constant danger that he may be burnt by the darts of scalding steam that continually escape from the pipes. He has to learn to slither from point to point like a snake. "Only the best snake dancers survived . . . . Others who had tried and failed were no longer alive." (In another novel, *March to Caobaland,* Traven writes: "Indian mahogany workers can be fed as royally as the stokers and oilers of a death ship where, as a rule, the food is of the lowest quality possible.")

The Nazis banned *The Death Ship* because they thought it communist; some critics have said the same about Traven's other books. But this is to misinterpret them. Traven's fiction is as much an attack on bureaucrats, whatever their political creed, as it is a protest against the dictatorial power that money can invest in one man over another. Labor camps, no less than sweated labor, are both a part of the world of Mammon.

                                                —Neville Braybrooke

TRILLING, Lionel

Born: New York City, 4 July 1905. **Education:** Columbia University, New York, B.A. 1925, M.A. 1926, Ph.D. 1938. **Family:** Married Diana Rubin (i.e., the writer Diana Trilling) in 1929; one son. **Career:** Editorial assistant, *Menorah Journal,* New York, 1923-31; instructor in English, University of Wisconsin, Madison, 1926-27, and Hunter College, New York, 1927-32; instructor, 1932-38, assistant professor, 1939-45, associate professor, 1945-48, professor of English, 1948-70, Woodberry Professor of Literature and Criticism, 1965-70, university professor, 1970-74, and university professor emeritus, 1974-75, Columbia University. George Eastman Visiting Professor, Oxford University, 1964-65; Norton Visiting Professor of Poetry, Harvard University, Cambridge, Massachusetts, 1969-70; visiting fellow, All Souls College, Oxford, 1972-73. Cofounder and senior fellow, Kenyon School of English, Kenyon College, Gambier, Ohio (now Indiana University School of Letters, Bloomington). **Awards:** Brandeis University Creative Arts award, 1968. D.Litt.: Trinity College, Hartford, Connecticut, 1955; Harvard University, 1962; Case Western Reserve University, Cleveland, 1968; Durham University, England, 1973; Leicester University, England, 1973. L.H.D.: Northwestern University, Evanston, Illinois, 1963; Brandeis University, Waltham, Massachusetts, 1974; Yale University, New Haven, Connecticut, 1974. **Member:** American Academy, 1951; American Academy of Arts and Sciences, 1952. **Died:** 5 November 1975.

PUBLICATIONS

Collection

Works (Uniform Edition), edited by Diana Trilling. 12 vols., 1978-80.

Fiction

The Middle of the Journey. 1947.
Of This Time, Of That Place and Other Stories, edited by Diana Trilling. 1979.

Other

Matthew Arnold. 1939; revised edition, 1949.
E.M. Forster. 1943; revised edition, 1965.
The Liberal Imagination: Essays on Literature and Society. 1950.
The Opposing Self: Nine Essays in Criticism. 1955.
Freud and the Crisis of Our Culture. 1956; revised version, in *Beyond Culture,* 1965.
A Gathering of Fugitives. 1956.
The Scholar's Caution and the Scholar's Courage. 1962.
Beyond Culture: Essays on Literature and Learning. 1965.
Sincerity and Authenticity. 1972.
Mind in the Modern World. 1973.
Prefaces to The Experience of Literature. 1979.
The Last Decade: Essays and Reviews, edited by Diana Trilling. 1979.
Speaking of Literature and Society, edited by Diana Trilling. 1980.

Editor, *The Portable Matthew Arnold.* 1949; as *The Essential Matthew Arnold,* 1969.

Editor, *Selected Letters of John Keats.* 1951.
Editor, with Steven Marcus, *The Life and Work of Sigmund Freud,* by Ernest Jones. 1961.
Editor, *The Experience of Literature: A Reader with Commentaries.* 1967.
Editor, *Literary Criticism: An Introductory Reader.* 1970.

*

Critical Studies: *Three American Moralists: Mailer, Bellow, Trilling* by Nathan A. Scott, Jr., 1973; *Trilling: Negative Capability and the Wisdom of Avoidance* by Robert Boyers, 1977; *Art, Politics, and Will: Essays in Honor of Trilling* edited by Quentin Anderson and others, 1977; *Three Honest Men: Edmund Wilson, F.R. Leavis, Trilling: A Critical Mosaic* by Philip French, 1980; *Trilling: Criticism and Politics* by William M. Chace, 1980; *Trilling* by Edward Joseph Shoben, Jr., 1981; *Trilling and the Fate of Cultural Criticism* by Mark Krupnick, 1986; *Lionel Trilling* by Stephen L. Tanner, 1988; *Explorations: The Twentieth Century* edited by Maurice W. duQuesnay and James A. Marino, 1989; *The Beginning of the Journey: The Marriage of Diana and Lionel Trilling* by Diana Trilling, 1993; *Lionel Trilling and the Critics: Opposing Selves,* edited by John Rodden, 1999; *Ex-Friends: Falling Out with Allen Ginsberg, Lionel & Diana Trilling, Lillian Hellman, Hannah Arendt, and Norman Mailer* by Norman Podhoretz, 1999.

*   *   *

Lionel Trilling was one of America's most distinguished literary critics. His first two books were on Matthew Arnold and E.M. Forster, and these were followed by a number of essays in which, like Arnold and Forster, he tried to show how liberal cultural values fostered by the study of literature could help civilization. In some of his later works, especially perhaps in *Beyond Culture,* this liberal stance, though aggressively stated, is maintained with a good deal of pessimism.

Keenly interested in politics in the early 1950s, Trilling seemed optimistic then about the fruitful interplay between politics and literature. Later, with the failure of the campus revolts of the 1960s and the retreat of literary criticism into its own peculiar jargon-ridden fortress, he became less confident, although *Sincerity and Authenticity* still maintains a high moral tone and is still written with the same sinewy elegance as the earlier works. The range of Trilling's criticism is very wide; he wrote brilliantly on John Keats, and James Joyce and Sigmund Freud, two writers not noted for sweetness or light, are treated at length and with perception. Trilling founded no critical movement, and his wish to see, like Arnold, things steadily and whole, may seem unfashionable, but truth does not cease to be truth merely because people have ceased to believe it.

An early short story, "Of This Time, Of That Place," first published in *Partisan Review* in 1943, is curiously prophetic. It shows how a university teacher, Joseph Howe, deals with two students, the brilliant but mad Tertan, and the amoral and philistine Blackburn. Tertan fails and Blackburn succeeds in spite of Howe's good intentions.

An equal pessimism is found in Trilling's one novel, *The Middle of the Journey.* The central character of this novel, John Laskell, recovering from a serious illness, visits his friends the Crooms in a Connecticut village. He finds himself involved with a woman in the village, Emily Caldwell, whose husband, Duck, works for the Crooms. A fleeting affair with Emily has little chance of success as her daughter Susan dies, attacked by the drunken Duck, though she has a weak heart and her death is accidental. The Crooms, who are presented unsympathetically, maintain that it is society, not Duck, who is responsible, whereas another friend of Laskell's, Gifford Maxim, a renegade communist who has adopted a Christian stance and whose defection is bitterly resented by the Crooms, thinks that Duck is guilty. Laskell takes up an indeterminate position, but does not feel that the rejection of the dogmatism of his friends is particularly effective, any more than his gesture of paying for Susan's funeral achieves anything. Written before the McCarthy witch-hunts had brought the issue of communism in America into the limelight, *The Middle of the Journey* may seem a confusing novel at a time when McCarthy himself is virtually forgotten. But it is not just a novel about communism versus Christianity, as it might seem to be at first sight; it is, perhaps a little too obviously, a novel that strives to assert the liberal values of Forster and Arnold in an unsympathetic world, and as such, should take its place with Trilling's critical works.

—T.J. Winnifrith

TRUMBULL, John

Born: Westbury, Connecticut, 24 April 1750. **Education:** Yale University, New Haven, Connecticut (Berkeley Scholar), 1763-70, B.A. 1767, M.A. 1770; studied law in John Adams's office in Boston, 1773; admitted to Connecticut bar, 1773. **Family:** Married Sarah Hubbard in 1776; seven children. **Career:** Schoolteacher and law student, Wethersfield, Connecticut, 1770-71; contributed essays (as "The Correspondent") to Connecticut Journal, 1770-73; tutor, Yale University, 1772-73; lawyer in New Haven, 1774-77, Westbury, 1777-81, and Hartford, Connecticut, 1781-1825; treasurer, Yale University, 1776-82; member, Hartford City Council, 1784-93; state attorney for Hartford, 1789-95; member, General Assembly of Connecticut, 1792, 1800-01; judge, Connecticut Superior Court, 1801-19, and Supreme Court of Errors, 1808-19; lived in Detroit, Michigan, 1825-31. Literary leader of the "Hartford Wits" in the 1780s and 1790s. **Award:** LL.D.: Yale University, 1818. **Member:** American Academy of Arts and Sciences, 1791. **Died:** 11 May 1831.

PUBLICATIONS

Collections

The Works, edited by Theodore Sizer. 1950; supplement, *The Autobiography,* 1953.
The Satiric Poems, edited by Edwin T. Bowden. 1962.

Poetry

An Elegy on the Death of Mr. Buckingham St. John. 1771.
The Progress of Dulness. 3 vols., 1772-73.
M'Fingal: A Modern Epic Poem, Canto First. 1775 (?); *M'Fingal in Four Cantos,* 1782; edited by Benson J. Lossing. 1864.
The Poetical Works. 2 vols., 1820.
The Anarchiad: A New England Poem, with others, edited by Luther G. Riggs. 1861.

Other

An Essay on the Use and Advantages of the Fine Arts. 1770.
Biographical Sketch of the Character of Governor Trumbull.
    1809.
"The Meddler" (1769-70) and "The Correspondent" (1770-73),
    edited by Bruce Granger, 1985.

*

Critical Studies: *Trumbull, Connecticut Wit* by Alexander Cowie,
1936 (includes bibliography); *Trumbull* by Victor E. Gimmestad,
1974; *Poetry and Ideology in Revolutionary Connecticut* by William C. Dowling, 1990; "Print, Poetry, and Politics: John Trumbull
and the Transformation of Public Discourse in Revolutionary
America" by Christopher Grasso, in *Early American Literature,*
1995, pp. 5-31.

*   *   *

John Trumbull is best remembered as spokesman for the group
of writers known as the "Connecticut" or "Hartford Wits." This
group, which included **Joel Barlow, Timothy Dwight,** and David
Humphreys, among others, was active during the years following
the Revolutionary War. Most of its members, Trumbull included,
were educated at Yale and were extremely conservative in their
political and literary views. They appreciated neoclassical decorum, and, from their center at Hartford, Connecticut, they used
their literary talent to exert pressure on the nation to stem the
rise of Jeffersonian democracy and to create a strong federal government, themes that the group collaboratively explored in *The
Anarchiad,* written in 1786 and 1787.

A lawyer by profession, Trumbull was also devoted to the arts.
He composed verses at the age of four and passed the entrance
exam to Yale when he was only seven. He possessed a keen mind
and a shrewd wit, which he used to his advantage when he wrote
satire. He was a master of the octosyllabic line, and delighted in
writing hudibrastic verse. For poetic models, Trumbull emulated
the works of Pope, Swift, and Dryden. More concerned with ideas
than with emotions, Trumbull valued restraint and disliked sentiment. Needless to say, he did not appreciate the Romantics, especially Wordsworth and Coleridge, who he felt placed expression before reason and subjectivity before objectivity.

Trumbull possessed a genuine gift for humor: he was at his best
when writing burlesque or satire, and found more serious verse
difficult to sustain. Like his contemporaries, he considered the ode
and the elegy superior in literary merit to satire, and although he
frequently tried to write in these forms, his "Ode to Sleep: An
Elegy on the Times," and *An Elegy on the Death of Mr. Buckingham
St. John* are among his least interesting poems. More engaging is
The Progress of Dulness, a three-part satirical epic, written while
Trumbull was studying for his masters degree at Yale, which ridicules outmoded educational practices and calls for a more useful
system of instruction than that experienced by Trumbull as an
undergraduate.

His most famous poem, *M'Fingal,* earned Trumbull the title of
"Poet of the Revolution." Written in the tradition of Dryden's
Mac Flecknoe, it is a mock heroic epic about the raucous adven-
tures of a Tory squire patterned after a British General, Thomas
Gage, but named M'Fingal, who tries to prevent a group of patri-
ots from giving further support to the Revolutionary War and is

himself tarred and feathered in the process. During the Revolutionary War, *M'Fingal* was used to stir up popular sentiment
against the British, and it was even printed in England, where
its literary merit drew the praise of critics who were impartial
enough to disassociate their political allegiances from their critical pronouncements. In America, the popularity of *M'Fingal*
continued long after it ceased to be useful as anti-British propaganda. In the late twentieth century it is recognized as one
of the finest political verse satires written in America prior to
the Civil War.

Trumbull is also remembered for his essays. Like his verse, they
are best when they satirize institutions and events. Favorite targets are education, the clergy, and, of course, the British, whom
he never really despised but was always ready to satirize. He patterned his prose style, which is witty and extremely polished,
after that of Joseph Addison and Sir Richard Steele, whom he
very much admired.

—James A. Levernier

TUCHMAN, Barbara W(ertheim)

Born: New York City, 30 January 1912. **Education:** Radcliffe
College, Cambridge, Massachusetts, B.A. 1933. **Family:** Married
Lester R. Tuchman, 1940; three daughters. **Career:** Research and
editorial assistant, Institute of Pacific Relations, New York City,
1933-35; foreign correspondent and staff writer, 1935-37, posted
as correspondent in Madrid, Spain, 1937, and as correspondent
in the United States, 1939, *Nation,* New York City; editor, Office
of War Information, New York City, 1943-45; lecturer at Harvard
University, Cambridge, Massachusetts; United States Naval War
College, Annapolis, Maryland; University of California; and other
institutions; trustee, Radcliffe College, 1960-72; Jefferson Lecturer,
National Endowment for the Humanities, 1980. **Awards:** Pulitzer
prize, 1963, 1972; American Academy of Arts and Sciences gold
medal for history, 1978; State University of New York Regent
Medal of Excellence, 1984; Union League Club Abraham Lincoln
Literary award, 1985; Sarah Josepha Hale award, 1985; Belgian
Order of Leopold. D.Litt.: Yale University; Columbia University;
New York University; Williams College; University of Massachu-
setts; Smith College; Hamilton College; Mount Holyoke College;
Boston University; Harvard University. **Member:** American Acad-
emy of Arts and Letters, president, 1979; American Academy of
Arts and Sciences. **Died:** 6 February 1989.

PUBLICATIONS

Collections

Practicing History: Selected Essays. 1981.

Prose

The Lost British Policy. 1938.
Bible and Sword. 1956.
The Zimmermann Telegram. 1958.
The Guns of August. 1962; in England as *August, 1914,* 1962.
The Proud Tower. 1966.

Stillwell and the American Experience in China, 1911-1945. 1971; in England as *Sand against the Wind: Stillwell and the American Experience in China, 1911-1945,* 1971.
Notes from China. 1972.
A Distant Mirror. 1978.
The March of Folly: From Troy to Vietnam. 1984.
The First Salute. 1989.

Screenplay: *The Guns of August.* 1964.

Other

Foreword, *Give Me Combat: The Memoirs of Julio Alvarez del Vayo.* 1973.
Foreword, *Who Makes War,* by Jacob K. Javits. 1973.
Foreword, *They Could Not Trust the King,* by Stanley Tretick. 1974.
Foreword, *Iphigene,* by Susan W. Dryfoos. 1981.
The Book. 1988.
Preface, with Anne Wertheim Werner, *Degas to Matisse,* by John O'Brian. 1988.

*

Bibliography: *Barbara Wertheim Tuchman: A Chronological Checklist, 1935-1984* by John Griffin, 1985.

Critical Studies: "Barbara Wertheim Tuchman" in *Current Biography,* 1963; "Barbara Tuchman . . . A Closer Mirror" by Catherine R. Stimpson in *Humanities,* March-April 1980; "The Mirrors of History: Barbara Tuchman's Fourteenth Century" by Charles Moorman in *Texas Review* spring 1980; *Bestsellers 89,* 1989.

*   *   *

Perhaps the only way to explain what could have motivated two-time Pulitzer Prize-winning historian Barbara Wertheim Tuchman to have produced such a voluminous output of literature during her lifetime is to understand why she thought that written history was so important. In an article published in *Proceedings of the American Academy of Arts and Letters and National Institute of Arts and Letters,* Tuchman lamented that oral history was metaphorically like a vacuum cleaner, sucking up facts, trash, and trivia indiscriminately, intermingling and confusing them all. Thus, she felt that history must be written down to accurately preserve it for posterity and devoted her life to so doing. From her beginnings as a journalist and foreign correspondent in the 1930s to her international renown as a historian beginning in the late 1950s, Tuchman was to constantly and consistently write readable and accurate historical accounts that appealed to scholars and laymen alike. Because of this ability to make history readable, Tuchman was without a doubt the preeminent American popular historian of the twentieth century.

Surprisingly, Tuchman never earned a Ph.D. or even an M.A. in history. She was glad that she did not, feeling that a higher degree might have been detrimental to the development of her easily readable writing style. Eschewing technical jargon and the countless footnotes that characterize academic writing, Tuchman chose instead to present narratives that can be read and understood by anyone, which undoubtedly accounted for her great popularity.

Her early experiences as a journalist unquestionably helped her develop her informal writing technique, and likewise her travels as a foreign correspondent helped broaden her perspective in regard to world history. By the time she began writing her first books, she had actually walked the famous countries and battlefields about which she would later write.

In her early books, *The Lost British Policy* and *Bible and Sword,* she honed her style while laboring in relative anonymity. With the publication of *The Zimmermann Telegram,* Tuchman finally began to gain worldwide recognition. The volume discusses the telegram that Germany sent to Mexico during World War I in an attempt to induce Mexico to declare war on the United States. The United States learned of the telegram's existence, however, and this discovery became a key factor in eventually bringing the Americans into the war. A best-seller, the book placed Tuchman at the forefront of historical writers.

Tuchman's next book, *The Guns of August,* was also a best-seller, and in it she looks at the first days of World War I. The book garnered Tuchman her first Pulitzer Prize and was adapted for the screen in 1964. Her next best-seller, *The Proud Tower,* also covers the period prior to World War I. *Stillwell and the American Experience in China,* which followed in 1971, is about the experiences of Joseph Warren Stillwell, an American officer whose service in China allowed him to witness the great changes during his lifetime in that country. For this volume, Tuchman was awarded her second Pulitzer Prize.

After *Notes from China,* Tuchman wrote *A Distant Mirror,* which was somewhat of a departure for her in that it chronicles events in the fourteenth century. *The March of Folly* encompasses mankind's proclivity for armed conflict from ancient times up until Vietnam. The book was also more theoretical in nature than Tuchman's other works, and as such it concentrated more on the political ideology that determines the course of history. As a result, *The March of Folly* was indisputably Tuchman's most controversial book and received more unfavorable reviews than any of her other books. Tuchman's last book, *The First Salute,* about the American Revolution, did not attempt to be as comprehensive as her previous publication and was received more favorably.

It is difficult to sum up a career as honored and influential as Tuchman's. Aside from her books, she wrote over one hundred articles, reviews, and editorials. She testified as an expert witness before Congress on at least half a dozen occasions and also had a substantial and important career as a university lecturer. Given her numerous best-sellers and international fame, she is undeniably one of the most influential popular historians that America has produced.

—James R. Simmons, Jr

TUCKERMAN, Frederick Goddard

Born: Boston, Massachusetts, 4 February 1821. **Education:** Bishop Hopkins' School, Burlington, Vermont, 1833-37; Harvard University, Cambridge, Massachusetts, 1837-38, and Harvard Law School, 1839-42; admitted to Suffolk County, Massachusetts, bar, 1844. **Family:** Married Hannah Lucinda Jones in 1847 (died 1857); three children. **Career:** Briefly practiced law; lived in Greenfield, Massachusetts, 1847-73. **Died:** 9 May 1873.

Collections

The Complete Poems, edited by N. Scott Momaday. 1965.

Poetry

Poems. 1860.

*

Critical Studies: *Tuckerman* by Samuel A. Golden, 1966; "Alone with God and Nature: The Poetry of Jones Very and Tuckerman" by David Seed, in *Nineteenth-Century American Poetry* edited by A. Robert Lee, 1985; "'A Monument of Labor Lost': The Sonnets of Frederick Goddard Tuckerman" by Andrew Hudgins, in *Chicago Review,* Winter 1990; *Shooting the Void: The Life and Work of Frederick Goddard Tuckerman* (dissertation) by Catherine Ann Wilcoxson, 1993.

*   *   *

Because Frederick Goddard Tuckerman's poetry was rescued from near-oblivion only in the later part of the twentieth century, a natural temptation for the critic is to fan the excitement generated by that rescue by overstating the value of the poetry. This temptation should be avoided, for much of Tuckerman's poetry is pedestrian.

Tuckerman's narrative poems are often merely inflated anecdotes. Many poems are maimed by tepid sermonizing. Sometimes Tuckerman's diction is ornate and tediously archaic, and his syntax awkward, even puzzling. Several sonnets are poorly constructed; the climax is followed by a number of distractingly anticlimactic lines. In his perceptive book on Tuckerman, Samuel A. Golden summarizes part of Tuckerman's world view. For the poet, "man's certainty rests in God." Unfortunately, Tuckerman's expressions of his religious faith are almost always inadequately documented and, as a result, are verbally bland, and quite unconvincing.

Nonetheless, the excitement caused by the rediscovery of Tuckerman's work is justified. Five sonnet sequences and "The Cricket"—all inspired by the death, after childbirth, of Tuckerman's wife—represent his finest efforts. Both the content and the form of these poems are, at their best, of a high quality.

In the nineteenth century most American poets regarded nature from a wholly sentimental point of view. Tuckerman tempered this view. As his sonnets make clear, he, too, believed that nature was a part of God's cosmic scheme, but, unlike his contemporaries, he did not proceed to interpret nature for the benefit of his readers. Instead, he admitted that he did not comprehend the ways of nature. Nor did nature provide Tuckerman with an all-encompassing comfort. "The Cricket" and the sonnets report that he gained solace from nature only after severely qualifying the degree of solace he hoped to gain.

Although Tuckerman—like his Transcendentalist peers—sometimes yearned to merge with nature, he chose to resist this impulse. In fact he came to realize that it was impossible to fulfill such an impulse. While the Transcendentalists found nature (indeed, the whole universe) to be wondrously like their own personalities, Tuckerman found nature to be quixotic, contradictory, enigmatic, and fundamentally separate from himself.

In "The Cricket" and the first two sonnet sequences especially, Tuckerman's stylistic weaknesses are far outweighed by many fine phrases, metaphors, and long descriptive passages enhanced by skillful rhythms, and rhyming. In "The Cricket," for instance, Tuckerman speaks of dead friends with "faces where but now a gap must be" and of death as the "crowning vacancy." He describes a night of love in terms of "wringing arms . . . / Closed eyes, and kisses that would not let go." His best sonnets also display a superb blending of form and content.

—Robert K. Johnson

TWAIN, Mark

A pseudonym for Samuel Langhorne Clemens. **Born:** Florida, Missouri, 30 November 1835; moved to Hannibal, Missouri, 1839. **Family:** Married Olivia Langdon in 1870 (died 1904); one son and three daughters. **Career:** Printer's apprentice and typesetter for Hannibal newspapers, 1847-50; helped brother with Hannibal *Journal,* 1850-52; typesetter and printer in St. Louis, New York, and Philadelphia, for Keokuk *Saturday Post,* Iowa, 1853-56, and in Cincinnati, 1857; apprentice river pilot, on the Mississippi, 1857-58; licensed as pilot, 1859-60; went to Nevada as secretary to his brother, then on the staff of the governor, and also worked as goldminer, 1861; staff member, Virginia City *Territorial Enterprise,* Nevada, 1862-64 (first used pseudonym Mark Twain, 1863); reporter, San Francisco *Morning Call,* 1864; correspondent, Sacramento *Union,* 1866, and San Francisco *Alta California,* 1866-69: visited Sandwich (i.e., Hawaiian) Islands, 1866, and France, Italy, and Palestine, 1867; lecturer from 1867; editor, *Express,* Buffalo, New York, 1869-71; moved to Hartford, Connecticut, and became associated with Charles L. Webster Publishing Company, 1884; invested in unsuccessful Paige typesetter and went bankrupt, 1894 (last debts paid, 1898); lived mainly in Europe, 1896-1900, New York, 1900-07, and Redding, Connecticut, 1907-10. **Awards:** M.A.: Yale University, New Haven, Connecticut, 1888. Litt.D.: Yale University, 1901; Oxford University, 1907. LL.D.: University of Missouri, Columbia, 1902. **Member:** American Academy, 1904. **Died:** 21 April 1910.

Collections

The Writings (Definitive Edition), edited by Albert Bigelow Paine. 37 vols., 1922-25.
The Portable Twain, edited by Bernard De Voto. 1946.
The Complete Short Stories, edited by Charles Neider. 1957.
Selected Shorter Writings, edited by Walter Blair. 1962.
The Complete Novels, edited by Charles Neider. 2 vols., 1964.
Twain Papers, edited by Robert H. Hirst. 1967—.
Works (Iowa-California Edition), edited by John C. Gerber and others. 1972—.
Mississippi Writings (Library of America), edited by Guy A. Cardwell. 1982.
The Innocents Abroad and Roughing It (Library of America), edited by Guy A. Cardwell. 1984.
The Science Fiction of Twain, edited by David Keterer. 1984.

Twain at His Best, edited by Charles Neider. 1986.
Collected Tales, Sketches, Speeches, and Essays (Library of America), edited by Lewis J. Budd. 2 vols., 1992.
Essays and Sketches of Mark Twain, edited by Stuart Miller. 1995.
The Oxford Mark Twain, edited by Shelley Fisher Fishkin. 1996.
The Unabridged Mark Twain, edited by Lawrence Teacher and Kurt Vonnegut. 1997.

Short Stories and Sketches

The Celebrated Jumping Frog of Calaveras County and Other Sketches, edited by Charles Henry Webb. 1867.
A True Story and the Recent Carnival of Crime. 1877.
Date 1601: Conversation as It Was by the Social Fireside in the Time of the Tudors. 1880; as *1601*, edited by Franklin J. Meine, 1939.
The Stolen White Elephant. 1882.
Merry Tales. 1892.
The £1,000,000 Bank-Note and Other New Stories. 1893.
Tom Sawyer Abroad. 1894.
Tom Sawyer Abroad, Tom Sawyer, Detective, and Other Stories. 1896; as *Tom Sawyer, Detective, as Told by Huck Finn, and Other Tales*, 1896.
The Man That Corrupted Hadleyburg and Other Stories and Essays. 1900.
A Dog's Tale. 1904.
The $30,000 Bequest and Other Stories. 1906.
Extract from Captain Stormfield's Visit to Heaven. 1909; revised edition, as *Report from Paradise*, edited by Dixon Wecter, 1952.
The Mysterious Stranger: A Romance (novella). 1916; *Mysterious Stranger Manuscripts*, edited by William M. Gibson, 1969.
The Curious Republic of Gondour and Other Whimsical Sketches. 1919.
The Mysterious Stranger and Other Stories. 1922.
A Boy's Adventure. 1928.
The Adventures of Thomas Jefferson Snodgrass, edited by Charles Honce. 1928.
Jim Smiley and His Jumping Frog, edited by Albert Bigelow Paine. 1940.
A Murder, A Mystery, and a Marriage. 1945.
The Complete Humorous Sketches and Tales, edited by Charles Neider. 1961.
Satires and Burlesques, edited by Franklin R. Rogers. 1967.
Twain's Hannibal, Huck, and Tom, edited by Walter Blair. 1969.
Twain's Quarrel with Heaven: Captain Stormfield's Visit to Heaven and Other Sketches, edited by Roy B. Browne. 1970.
Early Tales and Sketches, edited by Edgar M. Branch and Robert H. Hirst. 2 vols., 1979-81.
Wapping Alice. 1981.
Huck Finn and Tom Sawyer among the Indians and Other Unfinished Stories, edited by Dahlia Armon and Walter Blair. 1989.

Novels

The Innocents Abroad; or, The New Pilgrims' Progress. 1869.
The Innocents at Home. 1872.
The Gilded Age: A Tale of Today, with Charles Dudley Warner. 1873; The *Adventures of Colonel Sellers, Being Twain's Share of The Gilded Age*, edited by Charles Neider, 1965; complete text, edited by Bryant Morey French, 1972.
The Adventures of Tom Sawyer. 1876.

A Tramp Abroad. 1880.
The Prince and the Pauper. 1881.
The Adventures of Huckleberry Finn (Tom Sawyer's Comrade). 1884; as *Adventures of Huckleberry Finn*, 1885; edited by Sculley Bradley and others, 1977.
A Connecticut Yankee in King Arthur's Court. 1889; as *A Yankee at the Court of King Arthur*, 1889; edited by Allison R. Ensor, 1982.
The American Claimant. 1892.
Pudd'nhead Wilson. 1894; augmented edition, as *The Tragedy of Pudd'nhead Wilson, and The Comedy of Those Extraordinary Twins*, 1894; edited by Sidney E. Berger, 1980.
Personal Recollections of Joan of Arc. 1896.
A Double Barrelled Detective Story. 1902.
Extracts from Adam's Diary. 1904.
Eve's Diary. 1906.
A Horse's Tale. 1907.
Simon Wheeler, Detective, edited by Franklin R. Rogers. 1963.
Twain at His Best, edited by Charles Neider. 1986.
The Diaries of Adam and Eve. 1996.

Plays

Ah Sin, with Bret Harte (produced 1877). Edited by Frederick Anderson, 1961.
Colonel Sellers as a Scientist, with William Dean Howells, from the novel *The Gilded Age* by Twain and Charles Dudley Warner (produced 1887). In *Complete Plays of Howells*, edited by Walter J. Meserve, 1960.
The Quaker City Holy Land Excursion: An Unfinished Play. 1927.

Poetry

On the Poetry of Twain, with Selections from His Verse, edited by Arthur L. Scott. 1966.

Other

Twain's (Burlesque) Autobiography and First Romance. 1871.
Memoranda: From the Galaxy. 1871.
Roughing It. 1872.
A Curious Dream and Other Sketches. 1872.
Screamers: A Gathering of Scraps of Humour, Delicious Bits, and Short Stories. 1872.
Sketches. 1874.
Sketches, New and Old. 1875.
Old Times on the Mississippi. 1876; as *The Mississippi Pilot*, 1877.
An Idle Excursion. 1878.
Punch, Brothers, Punch! and Other Sketches. 1878.
A Curious Experience. 1881.
Life on the Mississippi. 1883.
Facts for Twain's Memory Builder. 1891.
How to Tell a Story and Other Essays. 1897; revised edition, 1900.
Following the Equator: A Journey Around the World. 1897; as *More Tramps Abroad*, 1897.
Writings (Autograph Edition). 25 vols., 1899-1907.
The Pains of Lowly Life. 1900.
English as She Is Taught. 1900; revised edition, 1901.
To the Person Sitting in Darkness. 1901.
Edmund Burke on Croker, and Tammany. 1901.
My Début as a Literary Person, with Other Essays and Stories. 1903.

Twain on Vivisection. 1905(?).

King Leopold's Soliloquy: A Defense of His Congo Rule. 1905; revised edition, 1906.

Editorial Wild Oats. 1905.

What Is Man? 1906.

On Spelling. 1906.

Writings (Hillcrest Edition). 25 vols., 1906-07.

Christian Science, with Notes Containing Corrections to Date. 1907.

Is Shakespeare Dead? From My Autobiography. 1909.

Speeches, edited by F.A. Nast. 1910; revised edition, 1923.

Queen Victoria's Jubilee. 1910.

Letter to the California Pioneers. 1911.

What Is Man? and Other Essays. 1917.

Letters, edited by Albert Bigelow Paine. 2 vols., 1917.

Moments with Twain, edited by Albert Bigelow Paine. 1920.

Europe and Elsewhere. 1923.

Autobiography, edited by Albert Bigelow Paine. 2 vols., 1924.

Sketches of the Sixties by Bret Harte and Twain . . . from The Californian 1864-67. 1926; revised edition, 1927.

The Suppressed Chapter of "Following the Equator." 1928.

A Letter from Twain to His Publisher, Chatto and Windus. 1929.

Twain the Letter Writer, edited by Cyril Clemens. 1932.

Works. 23 vols., 1933.

The Family Twain (selections). 1935.

The Twain Omnibus, edited by Max J. Herzberg. 1935.

Representative Selections, edited by Fred L. Pattee. 1935.

Notebook, edited by Albert Bigelow Paine. 1935.

Letters from the Sandwich Islands, Written for the Sacramento Union, edited by G. Ezra Dane. 1937.

The Washoe Giant in San Francisco, Being Heretofore Uncollected Sketches, edited by Franklin Walker. 1938.

Twain's Western Years, Together with Hitherto Unreprinted Clemens Western Items, by Ivan Benson. 1938.

Letters from Honolulu Written for the Sacramento Union, edited by Thomas Nickerson. 1939.

Twain in Eruption: Hitherto Unpublished Pages about Men and Events, edited by Bernard De Voto. 1940.

Travels with Mr. Brown, Being Heretofore Uncollected Sketches Written for the San Francisco Alta California in 1866 and 1867, edited by Franklin Walker and G. Ezra Dane. 1940.

Republican Letters, edited by Cyril Clemens. 1941.

Letters to Will Bowen, edited by Theodore Hornberger. 1941.

Letters in the Muscatine Journal, edited by Edgar M. Branch. 1942.

Washington in 1868, edited by Cyril Clemens. 1943.

Twain, Business Man, edited by Samuel Charles Webster. 1946.

The Letters of Quintus Curtius Snodgrass, edited by Ernest E. Leisy. 1946.

Twain in Three Moods: Three New Items of Twainiana, edited by Dixon Wecter. 1948.

The Love Letters, edited by Dixon Wecter. 1949.

Twain to Mrs. Fairbanks, edited by Dixon Wecter. 1949.

Twain to Uncle Remus 1881-1885, edited by Thomas H. English. 1953.

Twins of Genius: Letters of Twain, Cable, and Others, edited by Guy A. Cardwell. 1953.

Twain of the Enterprise, edited by Henry Nash Smith and Frederick Anderson. 1957.

Traveling with the Innocents Abroad: Twain's Original Reports from Europe and the Holy Land, edited by Daniel Morley McKeithan. 1958.

The Autobiography, edited by Charles Neider. 1959.

The Art, Humor, and Humanity of Twain, edited by Minnie M. Brashear and Robert M. Rodney. 1959.

Twain and the Government, edited by Svend Petersen. 1960.

Twain-Howells Letters: The Correspondence of Samuel L. Clemens and William Dean Howells 1872-1910, edited by Henry Nash Smith and William M. Gibson. 2 vols., 1960; abridged edition, as *Selected Twain-Howells Letters,* 1967.

Your Personal Twain. . . . 1960.

Life as I Find It: Essays, Sketches, Tales, and Other Material, edited by Charles Neider. 1961.

The Travels of Twain, edited by Charles Neider. 1961.

Contributions to The Galaxy 1868-1871, edited by Bruce R. McElderry. 1961.

Twain on the Art of Writing, edited by Martin B. Fried. 1961.

Letters to Mary, edited by Lewis Leary. 1961.

The Pattern for Twain's "Roughing It": Letters from Nevada by Samuel and Orion Clemens 1861-1862, edited by Franklin R. Rogers. 1961.

Letters from the Earth, edited by Bernard De Voto. 1962.

Twain on the Damned Human Race, edited by Janet Smith. 1962.

The Complete Essays, edited by Charles Neider. 1963.

Twain's San Francisco, edited by Bernard Taper. 1963.

The Forgotten Writings of Twain, edited by Henry Duskus. 1963.

General Grant by Matthew Arnold, with a Rejoinder by Twain (lecture), edited by John Y. Simon. 1966.

Letters from Hawaii, edited by A. Grove Day. 1966.

Which Was the Dream? and Other Symbolic Writings of the Later Years, edited by John S. Tuckey. 1967.

The Complete Travel Books, edited by Charles Neider. 1967.

Letters to His Publishers 1867-1894, edited by Hamlin Hill. 1967.

Clemens of the Call: Twain in California, edited by Edgar M. Branch. 1969.

Correspondence with Henry Huttleston Rogers 1893-1909, edited by Lewis Leary. 1969.

Man Is the Only Animal That Blushes—or Needs To: The Wisdom of Twain, edited by Michael Joseph. 1970.

Fables of Man, edited by John S. Tuckey. 1972.

Everybody's Twain, edited by Caroline Thomas Harnsberger. 1972.

A Pen Warmed Up in Hell: Twain in Protest, edited by Frederick Anderson. 1972.

What Is Man? and Other Philosophical Writings, edited by Paul Baender, in *Works.* 1973.

The Choice Humorous Works of Twain. 1973.

Notebooks and Journals, edited by Frederick Anderson and others. 1975—.

Letters from the Sandwich Islands, edited by Joan Abramson, 1975.

Twain Speaking, edited by Paul Fatout. 1976.

The Mammoth Cod, and *Address to the Stomach Club.* 1976.

The Comic Twain Reader, edited by Charles Neider. 1977.

Interviews with Clemens 1874-1910, edited by Louis J. Budd. 1977.

Twain Speaks for Himself, edited by Paul Fatout. 1978.

The Devil's Race-Track: Twain's Great Dark Writings: The Best from "Which Was the Dream" and "Fables of Man," edited by John S. Tuckey. 1980.

Selected Letters, edited by Charles Neider. 1982.

Plymouth Rock and the Pilgrims, and *Other Salutary Platform Opinions,* edited by Charles Neider. 1984.

Twain Laughing: Humorous Stories by and about Clemens, edited by P.M. Zall. 1985.

Letters (1853-1866), edited by Edgar M. Branch and others. 1987.

Letters (1867-1868), edited by Harriet Elinor Smith and Richard Bucci, 1990.

Mark Twain on Writing and Publishing, edited by Kathy Kiernan. 1994.

Letters (1872-1873), edited by Harriet Elinor Smith and Lin Salamo. 1997.

Translator, *Slovenly Peter* (Der Struwwelpeter). 1935.

*

Bibliography: *A Bibliography of the Works of Twain* by Merle Johnson, revised edition, 1935; in *Bibliography of American Literature* by Jacob Blanck, 1957; *Twain: A Reference Guide* by Thomas Asa Tenney, 1977; *Twain International: A Bibliography and Interpretation of His Worldwide Popularity* edited by Robert H. Rodney, 1982; *Mark Twain: A Descriptive Guide to Biographical Sources* by Jason Gary Horn, 1999.

Critical Studies: *My Twain: Reminiscences and Criticisms* by William Dean Howells, 1910, edited by Marilyn Austin Baldwin, 1967; *Twain: A Biography* by Albert Bigelow Paine, 3 vols., 1912, abridged edition, as *A Short Life of Twain,* 1920; *The Ordeal of Twain* by Van Wyck Brooks, 1920, revised edition, 1933; *Twain's America,* 1932, and *Twain at Work,* 1942, both by Bernard De Voto; *Twain: The Man and His Work* by Edward Wagenknecht, 1935, revised edition, 1961, 1967; *Twain: Man and Legend* by De Lancey Ferguson, 1943; *The Literary Apprenticeship of Twain* by Edgar M. Branch, 1950; *Twain as a Literary Artist* by Gladys Bellamy, 1950; *Twain and Huck Finn* by Walter Blair, 1960; *Twain* by Lewis Leary, 1960, and *A Casebook on Twain's Wound* edited by Leary, 1962; *Twain and Southwestern Humor* by Kenneth S. Lynn, 1960; *The Innocent Eye: Childhood in Twain's Imagination* by Albert E. Stone, 1961; *Twain: Social Philosopher,* 1962, and *Our Twain: The Making of a Public Personality,* 1983, both by Louis J. Budd, and *Critical Essays on Twain 1867-1910,* 1982, *Critical Essays on Twain 1910-1980,* 1983, and *New Essays on Adventures of Huckleberry Finn,* 1985, all edited by Budd; *Twain: The Development of a Writer* by Henry Nash Smith, 1962, and *Twain: A Collection of Critical Essays* edited by Smith, 1963; *Discussions of Twain* edited by Guy A. Cardwell, 1963; *Mr. Clemens and Mark Twain: A Biography,* 1966, and *Twain and His World,* 1974, both by Justin Kaplan; *Twain: The Fate of Humor* by James M. Cox, 1966; *Twain as Critic* by Sydney J. Krause, 1967; *Twain: God's Fool* by Hamlin Hill, 1973; *Plots and Characters in the Works of Twain* by Robert L. Gale, 2 vols., 1973; *The Dramatic Unity of Huckleberry Finn* by George C. Carrington, Jr., 1976; *The Art of Twain* by William M. Gibson, 1976; *Twain: A Collection of Criticism* edited by Dean Morgan Schmitter, 1976; *Twain as a Literary Comedian* by David E.E. Sloane, 1979; *Twain's Last Years as a Writer* by William R. Macnaughton, 1979; *Critical Approaches to Twain's Short Stories* edited by Elizabeth McMahan, 1981; *Twain's Escape from Time: A Study of Patterns and Images* by Susan K. Harris, 1982; *Writing Tom Sawyer: The Adventures of a Classic* by Charles A. Norton, 1983; *Twain* by Robert Keith Miller, 1983; *The Authentic Twain: A Biography of Clemens* by Everett Emerson, 1984; *One Hundred Years of Huckleberry Finn* edited by Robert Sattelmeyer and J. Donald Crowley, 1985; *The Making of Twain* by John Lauber, 1985; *Huck Finn among the Critics: A Centennial Selection* edited by M. Thomas Inge, 1985;

On Twain: The Best from "American Literature" edited by Louis J. Budd and Edwin H. Cady, 1987; *A Reader's Guide to the Short Stories of Twain* by James D. Wilson, 1987; *Twain* by John C. Gerber, 1988; *The Man Who Was Twain: Images and Ideologies* by Guy Cardwell, 1991; *Comedic Pathos: Black Humor in Twain's Fiction* by Patricia M. Mandia, 1991; *Getting To Be Mark Twain* by Jeffrey Steinbrink, 1991; *Mark and Livy: The Love Story of Twain and the Woman Who Almost Tamed Him* by Resa Willis, 1992; *Persona and Humor in Mark Twain's Early Writings* by Don Florence, 1995; *Mark Twain: The Ecstasy of Humor* by Louis J. Budd, 1995; *The Trouble Begins at Eight: Mark Twain's Lecture Tours* by Frederick William Lorch, 1995; *Mark Twain on the Loose: A Comic Writer and the American Self* by Bruce Michelson, 1995; *The Courtship of Olivia Langdon and Mark Twain* by Susan K. Harris, 1996; *Dreaming Mark Twain* by Bennett Kravitz, 1996; *"Littery Man": Mark Twain and Modern Authorship* by Richard S. Lowry, 1996; *Mark Twain in the St. Louis Post-Dispatch, 1874-1891* by Jim McWilliams, 1997; *Mark Twain's Ethical Realism: The Aesthetics of Race, Class, Gender* by Joe B. Fulton, 1997; *Inventing Mark Twain: The Lives of Samuel Langhorne Clemens* by Andrew Jay Hoffman, 1997; *The Jim Dilemma: Reading Race in Huckleberry Finn* by Jocelyn Chadwick-Joshua, 1998; *Mark Twain and the Novel: The Double-Cross of Authority* by Lawrence Howe, 1998; *Achilles and the Tortoise: Mark Twain's Fictions* by Clark Griffith, 1998; *Mark Twain: The Contemporary Reviews* edited by Louis J. Budd, 1999.

*   *   *

Samuel Langhorne Clemens, better known as Mark Twain, remains one of America's most widely read authors. To a great extent his popularity has rested upon his humor. It would be a mistake, however, to think of him simply as a humorist. To do so is to overlook the sharpness of his observation, the penetration of his social criticism, the depth of his concern for human suffering, and the clarity and extraordinary beauty of his style.

Storytelling came easily to Twain because he grew up in the little town of Hannibal on the Mississippi river where the telling of tall tales was one of the chief pastimes. Even as a boy he developed a reputation for yarnspinning, a reputation he strengthened while a pilot on the Mississippi and a newspaperman in Nevada and California. Before he left California for the East in 1867 he had begun to deliver humorous lectures, a practice that he continued on and off until almost the end of his life. Oral storytelling was immensely useful to him as a writer, for it taught him the value of such stylistic elements as point of view, proportion, timing, climax, concreteness, and dialogue that suggests real talk. He learned that the ear can catch much that the eye will miss; before finishing *Huckleberry Finn,* for example, he read it aloud over and over to make sure that it sounded right.

It should not be thought, however, that Twain was an untutored genius who became a fine writer simply because he could tell a good tale. To be sure he had only a few years of formal schooling. But he worked in newspaper offices under some of the finest journalists of the time. More importantly he was a steady reader. A limited list of his reading would include American newspaper humor; popular fiction, as well as juvenile fiction; parodies and burlesques; travel books; the novels of such writers as Cervantes and Dickens (whom he admired) and Austen and Scott (whom he did not admire); history, biography, and autobiography; scientific works; and the writings of such persons as **Thomas**

Jefferson, Hobbes, Bentham, Paine, Macaulay, Darwin, Carlyle, and especially W.E.H. Lecky. Most of Twain's important works are a blend of his reading and his personal experience given form by his imagination.

Naturally enough he began his literary career by writing humorous sketches for Midwestern and western newspapers. These apprentice pieces are derivative, satiric, and often gamey. About the only one that shows Twain's real promise as a literary figure is "The Celebrated Jumping Frog of Calaveras County." Significantly he wrote it for eastern instead of western publication. Van Wyck Brooks has argued that an eastern wife and eastern literary friends stunted Twain's artistic growth, even emasculated it. But most critics agree with Bernard De Voto that Twain would probably have remained little more than a newspaper humorist without the influence of eastern readers and writers. One fact is certain: once Twain began writing for an eastern audience he dropped the gaminess that had characterized his earlier work. Mrs. Clemens has been criticized for being too much of the moral censor, but the facts seem to indicate that Twain censored himself far more than did his wife or any of his friends. Ribald in some of his speeches at men's banquets and in a few works meant only for male readers (e.g., *1601*) he rarely in his major works alludes even to romance between the sexes except in conventional Victorian ways.

Twain continued to write short humorous sketches all through his life. His first longer works were travel books: *The Innocents Abroad* and *Roughing It*—followed later by *A Tramp Abroad, Life on the Mississippi,* and *Following the Equator.* Actually, the shift from short sketches to travel books was minimal since Twain's travel works were simply series of sketches, tales, and anecdotes strung together by loose chronological threads. Based largely on letters he wrote for the *Alta California, The Innocents Abroad* relates episodes from a trip Twain took to the Holy Land in 1867. It is not a tightly constructed book but a literary vaudeville show in which the reader's pleasure comes from the variety rather than the cohesion. As narrator, Twain shifts his role back and forth from a superior person (e.g., a gentleman or a teacher) to an inferior person (e.g., a simpleton or a sufferer) with unexpected and hilarious results. The appeal of *The Innocents Abroad* lies mainly in its humor, but in its time it also satisfied a growing curiosity in America about foreign lands, and in treating European culture without the customary deference it gave Americans an opportunity to feel less inferior about their own culture. Sold from door to door by agents of the American Publishing Company, a subscription house that published Twain's early books, it was an extraordinary success even though the times were hard.

Roughing It was even more successful and has continued to be one of Twain's best sellers. It is an account of his experiences in Nevada, California, and the Hawaiian Islands from 1861 through 1866. A somewhat more coherent account than *The Innocents Abroad,* it is still primarily a series of sketches, actual and imagined, salted with old anecdotes and folklore. Although as narrator he again plays a variety of roles for comic effect, there is in *Roughing It* a basic consistency as Twain shows himself developing from a callow greenhorn to the experienced old-timer. *A Tramp Abroad* recounts a trip with Joseph Twichell, a Hartford minister, through parts of Germany, Switzerland, and Italy in 1878. It also contains such famous set-pieces as "Baker's Blue-Jay Yarn" and "The Awful German Language." *Life on the Mississippi* is the most disconnected of the travel books. The best portion, chapters IV-XVII, was published in seven installments in the *Atlantic Monthly* in

1875 under the title "Old Times on the Mississippi." These chapters offer comic glimpses of Twain's experience as an apprentice pilot. The remainder of the book, sprinkled with many irrelevancies, tells of a trip down and up the Mississippi from New Orleans to St. Paul taken in 1882. *Following the Equator* narrates the story of the around-the-world lecture tour Twain took in 1895-96 with Mrs. Clemens and his daughter Clara in an attempt to recoup some of the fortune he had just lost. Financially the trip was a success, but it was hard on his health and ended in misery when news came to them in England that their oldest daughter, Susy, was dying of meningitis. The book, Twain said, was written to forget.

Twain collaborated with Charles Dudley Warner in writing his first novel, *The Gilded Age.* The work is poorly constructed and in places reads like the worst of sentimental novels, but it contains one of Twain's most memorable characters—Colonel Sellers, the incurable optimist—and some of his finest satire. His attacks on current get-rich-quick schemes and on political corruption were so trenchant that it is hardly an accident that the post Civil War period in America has been called the Gilded Age.

Next came the great books about boys. *The Adventures of Tom Sawyer* is his best constructed work since in it Twain manages to keep three narrative strands carefully interwoven: the family complication involving Tom and Aunt Polly; the love story between Tom and Becky; and the murder plot involving Tom, Huck, and Injun Joe. *Tom Sawyer* has been called "an idyll of boyhood," and as such it has never been surpassed. *The Prince and the Pauper,* the story of a mix-up in identity between Edward VI and the ragamuffin Tom Canty, was a happy addition to the children's literature of the time. *Adventures of Huckleberry Finn,* however, was an addition to the world's classics. This picaresque narrative is a modified frame story with Tom Sawyer being the focal center in the first three chapters and the last ten, and Huck and Jim being the center of interest in the middle 29 chapters dealing with the journey down the river on a raft. Episodic in nature, the story nevertheless holds together because of the river, the constant presence of Huck as narrator, and perhaps especially because of Huck's growing awareness of Jim's humanity. The emotional climax of the book occurs when Huck resolves to save Jim from slavery even if he must go to hell for doing so. Many readers believe that the book goes downhill from that point to the end. Despite its humor and picturesque qualities the work is at bottom an unrelenting indictment of Mississippi river society in the 1840s—and of humanity in general at any time. But probably the most notable aspect of *Huckleberry Finn* is its style. Letting Huck tell the story forced Twain to do what he did best: report concrete happenings in colloquial language. The result is what can properly be called folk poetry. It was this colloquial style that caused **Ernest Hemingway** to say that modern American literature began with Huckleberry Finn.

A Connecticut Yankee in King Arthur's Court begins as a spoof of Malory's *Morte Darthur* but quickly turns into an indictment of human tyranny: political, religious, and economic. As the sixth-century "boss," the nineteenth-century Yankee mechanic has one comic experience after another, but the work is essentially social satire, not so much of English history as contemporary industrialized society. The Yankee becomes less and less interesting as Twain uses him increasingly as a mouthpiece for his own views, especially the view that we are all the products of our training. The book is prophetic in its suggestion at the end that technology renders us insensitive to human suffering.

In the last twenty years of his life Twain's work fell off artistically though his political and social concerns continued to expand. In a work of potential greatness, *Pudd'nhead Wilson,* he confronted for the first time the more brutal aspects of slavery. His *Personal Recollections of Joan of Arc* is embarrassingly sentimental but more accurate in depicting the political forces at work than many other biographies of Joan. Shorter pieces attack such issues of the time as American imperialism, Christian Science, the role of the Western powers in the Boxer Rebellion, King Leopold's treatment of the Congolese, and the lynching of blacks in the Southern states. *The Mysterious Stranger,* a work that Twain started at least three times and never finished, exhibits his philosophy of mechanical determinism and his growing belief that life is only a dream. *What Is Man?,* a dialogue in which an elderly cynic invariably bests a young idealist, argues that man is a machine and that choice is only an illusion. There is no doubt that the pessimism and bitterness, latent in Twain throughout most of his life, finally surfaced in these last twenty years. Financial difficulties and the deaths of his wife and two daughters seemed at times to be more than he could bear. Nevertheless his perceptions remained sharp and his writing controlled. Besides, he was sustained by honors from home and abroad such as no other American writer had ever enjoyed.

Much that Twain wrote was topical and overwrought and is sliding into oblivion. But his best works remain unrivaled in their depiction of the comic and the pathetic in life—and of the inevitable relation between the two. **William Dean Howells,** Twain's best friend for forty years, composed a fitting epitaph when he wrote that Mark Twain was "sole, incomparable, the Lincoln of our literature."

—John C. Gerber

See the essays on *The Adventures of Huckleberry Finn, The Adventures of Tom Sawyer,* and "The Man That Corrupted Hadleyburg."

TYLER, Anne

Born: Minneapolis, Minnesota, 25 October 1941. **Education:** High school in Raleigh, North Carolina; Duke University, Durham, North Carolina, B.A. 1961; Columbia University, New York City, 1961-62. **Family:** Married Taghi Modarressi in 1963; two daughters. **Career:** Russian bibliographer, Duke University Library, Durham, NC, 1962-63; assistant to the librarian, McGill University Law Library, Montreal, Canada, 1964-65. **Awards:** *Mademoiselle* award, 1966; American Academy and Institute of Arts and Letters award for Literature, 1977; Janet Heidinger Kafka prize, 1981; American Book award nomination, 1982, 1983; PEN/Faulkner award, 1983; Pulitzer prize nomination, 1983, 1985; National Book Critics Circle award, 1985; Pulitzer prize, 1989. **Member:** American Academy and Institute of Arts and Letters. **Residence:** Baltimore, Maryland.

Publications

Collections

Anne Tyler: Four Complete Novels. 1990.

Anne Tyler: A New Collection: Two Complete Novels. 1991.

Novels

If Morning Ever Comes. 1964.
The Tin Can Tree. 1965.
A Slipping-Down Life. 1970.
The Clock Winder. 1972.
Celestial Navigation. 1974.
Searching for Caleb. 1976.
Earthly Possessions. 1977.
Morgan's Passing. 1980.
Dinner at the Homesick Restaurant. 1982.
The Accidental Tourist. 1985.
Breathing Lessons. 1988.
Saint Maybe. 1991.
Ladder of Years. 1995.
A Patchwork Planet. 1998.

Fiction (for children)

Tumble Tower. 1993. Pictures by Mitra Modarressi.

Other

Editor and author of introduction, with Shannon Ravenel, *Best American Short Stories 1983.* 1983.

*

Bibliography: "An Anne Tyler Checklist, 1959-1980" by Stella Nesanovich in *Bulletin of Bibliography,* April-June 1981; "A Bibliography of Writings by Anne Tyler" by Elaine Gardiner and Catherine Rainwater in *Contemporary American Women Writers* edited by Catherine Rainwater and William J. Scheick, 1985.

Critical Studies: "Maggie Moran, Anne Tyler's Madcap Heroine: A Game-Approach to *Breathing Lessons*" by Gene Koppel in *Essays in Literature,* fall 1991; "Cooking as Mission and Ministry in Southern Culture" by Angeline Godwin Dvorak in *Southern Quarterly,* winter-spring 1992; "Watching through Windows: A Perspective on Anne Tyler" by Patricia Rowe Willrich in *Virginia Quarterly Review,* summer 1992; "Complicate, Complicate: Anne Tyler's Moral Imperative" by Barbara Harrell Carson in *Southern Quarterly,* fall 1992; "Rewriting the Family during *Dinner at the Homesick Restaurant*" by Caren J. Town in *Southern Quarterly,* fall 1992; "Bright Books of Life: The Black Norm in Anne Tyler's Novels" by Alice Hall Petry in *Southern Quarterly,* fall 1992; "The Accidental Therapist: Intrapsychic Change in a Novel" by Barbara R. Almond in *Literature and Psychology* vol. 38, 1992; "America Tyler Style: Surrogate Families and Transiency" by Julie Persing Papadimas in *Journal of American Culture,* fall 1992; *Critical Essays on Anne Tyler* edited by Alice Hall Petry, 1992; *Moving On: The Heroines of Shirley Ann Grau, Anne Tyler, and Gail Godwin* by Susan S. Kissel, 1996; *Anne Tyler: A Critical Companion,* edited by Paul Bail, 1998; *Through the Window, Out the Door: Women's Narratives of Departure, from Austin and Cather to Tyler, Morrison, and Didion* by Janis P. Stout, 1998.

*   *   *

The author of fourteen novels and over four dozen stories, Anne Tyler demonstrates in her fiction an indebtedness to the American literary tradition, with characters and situations that recall Emerson, Thoreau, Welty, and Faulkner. At the same time, Tyler's fiction depicts the everyday details of southern life without the gothic overtones reminiscent of southern predecessors such as Flannery O'Connor. Tyler's characters are situated within the family, and their struggles are provoked by the stresses of living with other people. Critics note that her characters are frequently in conflict over the desire to stay at home, be united with other characters, and yet be autonomous. Often, they run away from home, return, and ultimately make some kind of accommodation to the world and other people. Tyler has admitted that she herself has experienced these conflicting desires: to remain at home united to something secure, while at the same time longing to break away.

In many of the early novels, characters seem unable to escape the bonds of family and/or patriarchy. The strings binding them to societal expectations are wound too tightly, and these novels often end with the characters merely accommodating society or compromising with it somehow. Ben Joe Hawkes of *If Morning Ever Comes,* Tyler's first novel, cannot enjoy being away at law school for worrying about what is happening back home. Yet when he spends only one day at home he begins to feel oppressed by the weight of his perceived duties. As the only man in a family of women, the role assigned to Ben Joe is protector, worrier, substitute father. Even though he longs to be free of the burden of his patriarchal role, he cannot completely suppress his feeling of duty, and consequently is dissatisfied.

Elizabeth Abbott of *The Clock Winder* is another character trapped in prescribed roles. Although at the beginning of the novel Elizabeth has left home and family expectations to work in a traditionally male job, she is not able to escape tradition. Working as a gardener and handyman for the Emerson family, Elizabeth tries to forge a new life for herself. The name of the family she joins, however (a name that recalls Thoreau), indicates how deeply entrenched in tradition even her "escape" is. Her life with the Emersons gains her the admiration of the Emerson sons, who are attracted to this competent woman who can fix things and perform unfeminine chores. After an abortive attempt to escape the Emersons, Elizabeth returns to nurse Mrs. Emerson, who has had a stroke. Elizabeth is refitted for a traditional woman's place as wife to Matthew, mother to a brood of little Emersons, and caretaker of the extended family.

In *The Tin Can Tree* characters are similarly stuck in their roles—even clinging to them for security. Joan Pike lives in the bedrooms of other people's houses, a position she attempts unsuccessfully to escape during the course of the novel. A single woman without her own space, Joan is expected to be unobtrusive, helpful, and quiet, the same behavior expected of single Victorian women (considered "redundant" since they contributed neither as wives nor mothers) living in the homes of relatives. Joan's attempts to confine her belongings to her assigned room signify the constraints imposed upon her by the culture, restrictions she attempts to escape when she buys a bus ticket to go back home to her parents. However, along the way she decides not to continue. She is, after all, just going to another location where her status will be the same. Joan returns, having decided that she needs the people she was trying to escape.

Cultural expectations also surround Evie Decker, the main character of *A Slipping-Down Life,* but unlike Joan, Evie takes disruptive action. An overweight, unattractive adolescent, Evie tries valiantly to fit into society's expectations of a young woman. She desires to be pretty, to have a boyfriend, to get married, but all her efforts seem thwarted. As a short, chubby, dull-looking girl, Evie lacks one basic requirement for success: she is not pretty. To gain recognition, she carves the name of a local rock singer in the flesh of her forehead, thereby assuring herself an identity and place in patriarchal culture. This mark of devotion increases the popularity of the singer, and ends by securing Evie's position: she eventually marries the singer, who desires not Evie's person, but her function as good publicity for his act.

After these early and somewhat simplistic explorations of characters' relationships with their home life, Tyler addresses more complex issues in her later works. *Dinner at the Homesick Restaurant* is the chronicle of a dysfunctional family whose children keep returning to the site of their childhood abuse. Despite their recognition of the problems caused by their runaway father and overburdened, abusive mother, they continue to reenact unfinished and unsatisfactory family dinners at the "Homesick Restaurant" established by Ezra, the stay-at-home son who wants to provide for others the kind of nurturing family environment he lacked as a child. In this novel, which has been compared to Faulkner's *As I Lay Dying,* Tyler suggests that family patterns are almost impossible to escape; even when one escapes the actual location of home, one rarely escapes or outgrows its influence.

Although some of Tyler's characters challenge traditional gender roles and lead eccentric lives, her fiction cannot be classified as feminist or political in intention. In her later novels, characters adopt behaviors that disrupt patriarchal expectations and resist tradition more directly than characters in the earlier works, but they still are unable to escape traditional structures. Tyler's women, competent managers who desire independence, inevitably assume the traditional roles of wife and mother. Her men are typically even less adventurous than the women—Jeremy of *Celestial Navigation* is an agoraphobic artist who never leaves his studio, and Macon of *The Accidental Tourist* writes travel guides that teach people how to travel without realizing they have ever left home. In these novels, women provide the links to more complete life. In *Breathing Lessons* as well, Ira Moran's practical and reserved disposition is balanced by wife Maggie's whimsical, impulsive, and highly romantic spirit. Though Tyler often focuses on male-female relationships, there is little overt sexuality in the fiction, and she has sometimes been criticized for her sanitized version of twentieth-century life.

In *Saint Maybe* Tyler extends her theme of characters' desire both to escape and remain at home to include an examination of the guilt often associated with family relationships. Ian, consumed with guilt because he fears he has contributed to his brother's death, finds penance and comfort in raising his brother's orphaned children. His domestic life often stifles him, but ultimately this nurturing man who loves children finds happiness by marrying and having a child of his own. Tyler suggests that the rewards of domestic life outweigh its restrictions.

In *Ladder of Years,* Tyler's forty-year-old female protagonist fulfills the fantasy of many Tyler characters, walking away from her family while on vacation, assuming a new name, and beginning a new life. Although she ultimately returns to her husband and her three nearly grown children, Delia finds fulfillment and contentment in her new life. In *A Patchwork Planet,* Barnaby Gaitlin, a thirty-year-old employee of Rent-a-Back, a business devoted to helping its elderly customers with household chores, has already left his home, but still struggles to free himself from early self-perceptions. Always interested in the lives and possessions of others, Barnaby channels his early predilection for breaking into homes and looking through mail, diaries, and souvenirs into a job that enables him to deal with other people's belongings on a daily basis. Although he is a model employee whom all his customers love, he has difficulty seeing himself as anything more than the juvenile delinquent he once was. But like Ian in *Saint Maybe*, Barnaby finally sees himself as a man who can be trusted.

Tyler is most often praised for her sympathetic portrayal of eccentric individuals and her ability to inject irony and humor into ordinary situations. Tyler manages to make both laughable and loveable the woman who alphabetizes her groceries as she puts them away in *The Accidental Tourist* and the man who wears a different costume and pretends to be a different person every day in *Morgan's Passing*. The good-natured and amusing quality of Tyler's narration has helped her novels gain considerable popularity. Four have been made into movies: *The Accidental Tourist, Breathing Lessons, Saint Maybe,* and *Earthly Possessions.* Tyler's canon has a good deal of consistency: a tone of amused detachment, an interest in domestic life, and a sympathetic portrayal of eccentric characters uncannily similar to most readers' relatives. This consistency also assures her a loyal and appreciative audience.

—Karen Wilkes Gainey

TYLER, Royall

Born: William Clark Tyler in Boston, Massachusetts, 18 July 1757. **Education:** Harvard University, Cambridge, Massachusetts, 1772-76, A.B. 1776, A.M. 1779; honorary B.A., Yale University, New Haven, Connecticut, 1776; studied law in the office of Francis Dana in Cambridge; admitted to Massachusetts bar, 1780. **Military Service:** Commanding major, Independent Company of Boston, in the Continental Army, serving as aide to General Sullivan in the Battle of Rhode Island, 1778; later served as aide to General Benjamin Lincoln and participated in the suppression of Shays' Rebellion, 1787. **Family:** Married Mary Hunt Palmer in 1794; eight sons and three daughters. **Career:** Lawyer in Falmouth, Massachusetts, Portland, Maine, and Braintree, Massachusetts, 1780-85, Boston, 1785-91, and Guilford, Vermont, 1791-1801; collaborated with Joseph Dennie (as Colon and Spondee), 1794, and wrote satirical verse and prose for periodicals; state's attorney, Windham County, Vermont, 1794-1801; associate judge, 1801-07, and Chief Justice, 1807-13, Supreme Court of Vermont; professor of jurisprudence, University of Vermont, Burlington, 1811-14; registrar of probate, Brattleboro, Vermont, after 1815. **Died:** 26 August 1826.

PUBLICATIONS

Collections

Verse and Prose, edited by Marius B. Peladeau. 2 vols., 1968-72.
The Verse of Royall Tyler, edited by Marius B. Peladeau. 1997.

Plays

The Contrast (produced 1787). 1790; edited by James B. Wilbur, 1920.

May Day in Town; or, New York in an Uproar (produced 1787).
The Georgia Spec; or, Land in the Moon (produced 1797; as *A Good Spec,* produced 1797).
Four Plays (includes *The Island of Barrataria, The Origin of the Feast of Purim, Joseph and His Brethren, The Judgement of Solomon*), edited by Arthur Wallace Peach and George Floyd Newbrough. 1941.

Fiction

The Algerine Captive. 1797.
The Bay Boy; or, The Autobiography of a Youth of Massachusetts Bay: Sketches from an Unpublished Novel, edited by Martha R. Wright. 1978.

Poetry

The Origin of Evil. 1793.
The Chestnut Tree; or, A Sketch of Brattleborough at the Close of the Twentieth Century. 1931.

Other

The Trial of Cyrus B. Dean. 1808.
The Yankey in London. 1809.
Reports of Cases Argued and Determined in the Supreme Court of Vermont (for 1800-03). 2 vols., 1809-10.
A Book of Forms (law forms). 1845.

*

Critical Studies: *Tyler* by G. Thomas Tanselle, 1967; *Tyler* by Ada Lou Carson and Herbert L. Carson, 1979; "Class Positioning and Shays' Rebellion: Resolving the Contradictions of *The Contrast*" by Richard S. Pressman, in *Early American Literature,* Fall 1986; "Narrative Irony and National Character in Royall Tyler's The Algerine Captive" by John Engell, in *Studies in American Fiction,* Spring 1989; "Nationalizing the American Stage: The Drama of Royall Tyler and William Dunlap as Post-Colonial Phenomena" by Gary A. Richardson, in *Making America/Making American Literature* edited by A. Robert Lee and W.M. Verhoeven, 1996.

*   *   *

With the presentation of *The Contrast* in New York City on 16 April 1787, Royall Tyler, identified by the evening's drama critics as "a man of genius," entered the history of American drama, becoming the first known native American writer of comedy to be professionally produced. At a time when the new nation was struggling for identity, Tyler showed his particular genius in his choice of material and the manner of his expression. Creating a typical Yankee character, and generally fostering the "just pride of patriotism" that Washington would later emphasize in his Farewell Address, Tyler wrote a popular play for his time. He was never able to do it again, and perhaps once was enough. He also had other interests to pursue.

Tyler was that inspired person who could combine the joys of literary creation with a professional career, and as a lawyer he eventually rose in his profession to serve as Chief Justice of Vermont's Supreme Court. As a writer, however, he was attracted by all genres. With Joseph Dennie, essayist, critic, and editor of the *Port Folio,* he wrote a large number of amusing and satirical essays, sketches, and verses. Signing themselves as "Colon & Spondee" they provided light and topical commentary on society, literature, and politics until 1811. Poetry, particularly in a light and satiric vein, interested Tyler throughout his life. His only novel, an episodic work stimulated by the activity of the Barbary Coast pirates, was *The Algerine Captive.* Other than *The Contrast,* however, he was at his best in essay or short sketch. The collection called *The Yankey in London* best illustrates his work: a sprightly style, a reverence for America, and a varied subject matter.

It was with *The Contrast* that he gained his reputation as a writer. Although it lacks much of a plot and is a talky play imitative of eighteenth-century British sentimental comedy, it is clearly distinguished by an originality in thought and character. From the prologue—"Exult each patriot heart!"—to the climax all aspects of the play emphasize the new nationalism. Although they may be caricatures, the characters' distinctive qualities delight the reader and viewer. And everywhere there is satire—on fashion, theater, the English, gossip—superimposed on the contrast—a contrast between the people of England and those of America, between affectation and straightforwardness, between city and country, between hypocrisy and sincerity, between foreign fraud and native worth. It was a play well-designed to meet the demands and tastes of the new country.

Tyler continued to write more plays, but without great success. *May Day in Town; or, New York in an Uproar* appeared in a New York theater a month after *The Contrast* but was not repeated. Four of Tyler's plays are published in the *America's Lost Plays* series. *The Island of Barrataria* is based on an episode in *Don Quixote;* the others have biblical sources. Only *The Island of Barrataria* deserves more critical attention than it has received. All, as might be expected of a lawyer, treat concepts of law, government, and justice. For Tyler, however, playwriting was only an avocation, though a pleasant one; he earned his living as a lawyer and justice. For the historian of American letters he is remembered mainly as the author of a single play.

—Walter J. Meserve

See the essay on *The Contrast.*

U–V

UPDIKE, John (Hoyer)

Born: Shillington, Pennsylvania, 18 March 1932. **Education:** Public schools in Shillington; Harvard University, Cambridge, Massachusetts, A.B. (summa cum laude) 1954; Ruskin School of Drawing and Fine Arts, Oxford (Knox fellow), 1954-55. **Family:** Married 1) Mary Pennington in 1953 (marriage dissolved), two daughters and two sons; 2) Martha Bernhard in 1977. **Career:** Staff reporter, *The New Yorker*, 1955-57. **Awards:** Guggenheim fellowship, 1959; Rosenthal award, 1960; National Book award, 1964; O. Henry award, 1966; Foreign Book prize (France), 1966; New England Poetry Club Golden Rose, 1979; MacDowell medal, 1981; Pulitzer prize, 1982, 1991; American Book award, 1982; National Book Critics Circle award, for fiction, 1982, for criticism, 1984; Union League Club Abraham Lincoln award, 1982; National Arts Club Medal of Honor, 1984; National Medal of the Arts, 1989; National Book Critics Circle award, 1990; Howells medal, 1995; National Book Foundation Lifetime Achievement award, 1998. **Member:** American Academy, 1976. **Residence:** Beverly Farms, Massachusetts.

PUBLICATIONS

Short Stories

The Same Door. 1959.
Pigeon Feathers and Other Stories. 1962.
Olinger Stories: A Selection. 1964.
The Music School. 1966.
Penguin Modern Stories 2, with others. 1969.
Bech: A Book. 1970.
The Indian. 1971.
Museums and Women and Other Stories. 1972.
Warm Wine: An Idyll. 1973.
Couples: A Short Story. 1976.
Too Far to Go: The Maples Stories. 1979; as *Your Lover Just Called: Stories of Joan and Richard Maple*, 1980.
Problems and Other Stories. 1979.
Three Illuminations in the Life of an American Author. 1979.
The Chaste Planet. 1980.
The Beloved. 1982.
Bech Is Back. 1982.
Getting Older. 1985.
Going Abroad. 1987.
Trust Me. 1987.
The Afterlife. 1987.
Brother Grasshopper. 1990.
Baby's First Step. 1992.
Love Factories. 1993.
The Afterlife and Other Stories. 1994.
Scenes from the Fifties. 1995.
Bech at Bay. 1998.
The Women Who Got Away. 1999.

Novels

The Poorhouse Fair. 1959.
Rabbit, Run. 1960.
The Centaur. 1963.
Of the Farm. 1965.
Couples. 1968.
Rabbit Redux. 1971.
A Month of Sundays. 1975.
Marry Me: A Romance. 1976.
The Coup. 1978.
Rabbit Is Rich. 1981.
The Witches of Eastwick. 1984.
Roger's Version. 1986.
S. 1988.
Rabbit at Rest. 1990.
Memories of the Ford Administration. 1992.
Brazil. 1994.
In the Beauty of the Lilies. 1996.
Toward the End of Time. 1997.

Plays

Three Texts from Early Ipswich: A Pageant. 1968.
Buchanan Dying. 1974.

Poetry

The Carpentered Hen and Other Tame Creatures. 1958; as *Hoping for a Hoopoe*, 1959.
Telephone Poles and Other Poems. 1963.
Verse. 1965.
Dog's Death. 1965.
The Angels. 1968.
Bath after Sailing. 1968.
Midpoint and Other Poems. 1969.
Seventy Poems. 1972.
Six Poems. 1973.
Query. 1974.
Cunts (Upon Receiving the Swingers Life Club Memberships Solicitation). 1974.
Tossing and Turning. 1977.
Sixteen Sonnets. 1979.
An Oddly Lovely Day Alone. 1979.
Five Poems. 1980.
Spring Trio. 1982.
Jester's Dozen. 1984.
Facing Nature. 1985.
A Pear Like a Potato. 1986.
Two Sonnets. 1987.
Recent Poems, 1986-1990. 1990.
Collected Poems, 1953-1993. 1993.
Poem Begun on Thursday, October 14, 1993, at O'Hare Airport, Terminal 3, around Six o'clock P.M. 1994.
In the Cemetery High above Shillington. 1995.
A Helpful Alphabet of Friendly Objects, with David Updike. 1995.
January. 1997.

Other

The Magic Flute (for children), with Warren Chappell. 1962.
The Ring (for children), with Warren Chappell. 1964.
Assorted Prose (includes stories). 1965.
A Child's Calendar (for children). 1965.
On Meeting Authors. 1968.
Bottom's Dream: Adapted from William Shakespeare's "A Mid-summer Night's Dream" (for children). 1969.
A Good Place. 1973.
Picked-Up Pieces (includes story). 1975.
Hub Fans Bid Kid Adieu. 1977.
Talk from the Fifties. 1979.
Ego and Art in Walt Whitman. 1980.
People One Knows: Interviews with Insufficiently Famous Americans. 1980.
Invasion of the Book Envelopes. 1981.
Hawthorne's Creed. 1981.
Hugging the Shore: Essays and Criticism (includes stories). 1983.
Confessions of a Wild Bore (essay). 1984.
Emersonianism (lecture). 1984.
The Art of Adding and the Art of Taking Away: Selections from Updike's Manuscripts, edited by Elizabeth A. Falsey. 1987.
Self-Consciousness: Memoirs. 1989.
Just Looking: Essays on Art. 1989.
Odd Jobs: Essays and Criticism (includes stories). 1991.
The Twelve Terrors of Christmas. 1993.
Golf Dreams. 1996.
More Matter. 1999.

Editor, *Pens and Needles,* by David Levine. 1970.
Editor, with Shannon Ravenel, *The Best American Short Stories 1984.* 1984; *The Year's Best American Short Stories,* 1985.
Editor, *A Century of Arts and Letters.* 1998.
Editor, *The Best Short Stories of the Century.* 1999.

*

Bibliography: *Updike: A Bibliography* by C. Clarke Taylor, 1968; *An Annotated Bibliography of Updike Criticism 1967-1973,* and *Checklist of His Works* by Michael A. Olivas, 1975; *Updike: A Comprehensive Bibliography with Selected Annotations* by Elizabeth A. Gearhart, 1978; *John Updike: A Bibliography, 1967-1993* by Jack De Bellis, 1994.

Critical Studies: interviews in *Life* 4, November 1966, *Paris Review,* Winter 1968, and *New York Times Book Review,* 10 April 1977; *Updike* by Charles T. Samuels, 1969; *The Elements of Updike* by Alice and Kenneth Hamilton, 1970; *Pastoral and Anti-Pastoral Elements in Updike's Fiction* by Larry E. Taylor, 1971; *Updike: Yea Sayings* by Rachael C. Burchard, 1971; *Updike* by Robert Detweiler, 1972, revised edition, 1984; *Updike: A Collection of Critical Essays* edited by David Thorburn and Howard Eiland, 1979; *Updike* by Suzanne H. Uphaus, 1980; *The Other Updike: Poems/Short Stories/Prose/Play* by Donald J. Greiner, 1981; *Updike's Images of America* by Philip H. Vaughan, 1981; *Married Men and Magic Tricks: Updike's Erotic Heroes* by Elizabeth Tallent, 1982; *Critical Essays on Updike* edited by William R. Macnaughton, 1982; *Updike* by Judie Newman, 1988; *John Updike: A Study of the Short Fiction* by Robert M. Luscher, 1993; *New Essays on Rabbit Run* edited by Stanley Trachtenberg, 1993;

Updike and the Patriarchal Dilemma: Masculinity and the Rabbit Novels by Mary O'Connell, 1996; *John Updike's Rabbit at Rest: Appropriating History* by Dilvo Ristoff, 1998; *John Updike Revisited* by James A. Schiff, 1998.

*   *   *

The successes of John Updike are linked with those of the *New Yorker,* a magazine on which he was once a staff member and to which he has remained a frequent contributor. But many of his novels go beyond the limits of interest that are frequently attributed to the magazine: a well-bred skepticism as to what is possible for human sensibility in our time. It is true that Updike's novels and, even more, his short stories sometimes conform to these limits that see all human effort as subject to the ironies of cross-purpose. But Updike's sensibility, particularly as it unfolds in his longer works, is not that of a writer who has fully acquiesced to the general decay and uncertainty of an era. Rather Updike takes shape as a writer who keeps circling around the modern detritus with a sharp eye for some fragmented persistence of meaning and order. He is a moralist out of season. The time for confident reading of meaning may be over, but the desire for such activity persists in much of Updike's work.

This may not be immediately apparent to some readers who can doubt that there is any link between a continuing moral curiosity and the many passages in the novels that give explicit accounts of sexual success and sexual impotence. Yet the sexual adventures of the minister in *A Month of Sundays* are no more exactly set down than are the "spiritual" aspirations that lead the minister to compose discourses that link the presence of sexuality with the advent of Grace. For Updike is not the kind of Stoic moralist common in the eighteenth century and elsewhere who seeks to detect and defend a purely humanistic code of excellence. The code of excellence that reveals itself intermittently in the Updike novels is one that has its roots in the *O altitudos* that had their traditional expression in the transports of mystics and in the teaching of the New Testament itself. The minister in *A Month of Sundays* thinks of **Barth** and Tillich when he is not fornicating and sometimes when he is. Updike provides some of his novels with epigraphs from the New Testament and Pascal. He provides flickers of light and inchoate illuminations that direct attention beyond traditional common sense and the current doubt that there is any sense whatever to the lives that a novelist may at present describe.

There is, in several of the novels, a central figure who sums up the moral situation in which modern persons live and make their Updike-sponsored effort to enjoy their lives and understand them. In *The Centaur* Updike speaks of a sequence—priest, teacher, and artist—that links the present to the past. The central figure in *The Centaur* is a frustrated teacher of science in a high school; his prototype is the ancient centaur, Chiron, who tried to reveal to his recalcitrant pupils the wisdom that had come to the early Greek oracles and the priests of holy places. The ancient centaur was mocked and wounded by his pupils; so also is the high school teacher by his students. But the modern centaur's son, Peter, responds to the harassed and comic nobility of his father. And when that son becomes an artist—when he leaves his father behind him—the son wonders whether his service of aesthetic excellence continues or cancels the pursuits of his father. (Earlier, the father had wondered about the relation of his teaching activity to his father's career as a clergyman.) Is the artist son the last link in a chain that extends backwards in time and moral-religious experience? Or is he a link that is independent of the earlier ones, a servant of a good that has no contact with the earlier excellences to which his father and grandfather were devoted?

This is a question that much of Updike's work raises but does not answer. The question is not asked monotonously. In his first novel, *The Poorhouse Fair*, Updike contrasts the humanitarian Connor, the director of the poor house, with a ninety-year-old man who maintains touch with older sources of moral illumination. In *Rabbit, Run, Rabbit Redux, Rabbit Is Rich*, and *Rabbit at Rest*, the center of awareness is Harry (Rabbit) Angstrom, an ill-educated and adulterous printer and, later, thanks to a useful marriage, a prosperous car salesman. He is a man who would, it seems, be singularly cut off from "priest" and "teacher." Yet Rabbit Angstrom is subject to malaises that have only a feeble source in his parents and that rather rise from his changes of partners, his unfulfilled obligations to his son, and his contact with a rebellious African American. In the midst of a life that is badly broken up, Angstrom demands not only sexual gratification but moral illumination from persons who are as confused as he is. The illumination is transient and is usually lost in a subsequent catastrophic event. But the event that is more than event—that is illumination—has occurred. This is all that Updike can report in his *Rabbit* narratives and elsewhere. In *Marry Me* Updike leads his chief character, who is about to dissolve a "good" marriage, to observe that we are in the midst of "the twilight of the old morality, and there's just enough to torment us, and not enough to hold us in." *Memories of the Ford Administration* is another novel that uses marriage to investigate the intersection of public and private. It links the wife swapping and bedroom adventuring of Americans during the Ford Administration with a meditation on the life and times, over a hundred years earlier, of America's fifteenth President, James Buchanan, a fussy, priggish, and repressed man.

Such are most of Updike's novels: clever tales that move from narrative to meditation. A book like *The Witches of Eastwick* is an excellent example of the usual Updike blend of mockery and seriousness. A company of modern New England witches—women isolated, feckless, and bitter—work their black magic and do little to alter themselves. *Bech at Bay* is another book in which Updike seems to be entertaining himself; it has the feel of a good travel book, where the writer, who discovers himself in alien contexts, finds himself to be more inadequate than the people he meets. Bech is constantly confronted by the suspicion that he is a fraud, an "experiment," as Updike puts it, "whose chemicals were about to be washed down the drain." Only in a book like *The Coup* does Updike make a rare foray beyond usual boundaries and direct his comic intelligence on human beings unfamiliar to him; the hero of *The Coup* is the dictator of an African state and falls foul of matters political, marital, and economic in ways that make him, at the very least, a distant cousin of Rabbit Angstrom.

Similarly, in *Brazil* Updike temporarily left behind his established subject matter. The story, based on the legend of Tristan and Iseult, follows the twenty-two-year relationship of Tristao, a black street kid, and Isabel, a bored white beauty from a well-to-do Carioca family. Brazil's tropical location and extravagant sexual freedoms, so un-American for this most American of authors, suggest a kind of Eden. Updike does not seek liberation from the spiritual crampedness of modern bureaucratic life, however, or from the anonymity of mass consumerism, but from his own upper-middle-class American liberalism. *Brazil* is Updike seeming to desire a vacation from being himself, the self that moralizes, the self

that is always "right." When he comes back home, he publishes, in 1994, *The Afterlife and Other Stories*, his first collection of stories in seven years. In these stories Updike reveals characters who sustain the value of seeing themselves, even in their suffocating Americanness, from the distances of England, Ireland, Italy, the Greek Islands. These are characters who lazily await a kind of transformation and optimistically believe they can get it.

In the Beauty of the Lilies describes a Presbyterian minister's loss of faith. Reverend Clarence Wilmot suffers his abandonment and announces his crisis in Paterson, New Jersey, in 1910. Unable to find decent work, he spends the rest of his life as an encyclopedia salesman and a movie devotee. This is the trajectory of the religious crisis of the novel, the movement from God to gods, and from the sacrament to the sacramentalized, the aesthetic. This seems to be Updike's concern in the last years of the century.

Updike has never been interested in little books. His narratives are those of an idea novelist, and his imagination has always made its aim that of exemplifying, interpreting, and re-forming the larger social world. Always well-crafted, well-thought-out, and well-driven, his stories and novels succeed in the effort to help us explain ourselves to ourselves.

—Harold H. Watts, updated by Martha Sutro

URISTA, Alberto H. *See* **ALURISTA.**

VAN DOREN, Mark (Albert)

Born: Hope, Illinois, 13 June 1894. **Education:** Elementary and high schools in Urbana, Illinois; University of Illinois, Urbana, A.B. 1914, A.M. 1915; Columbia University, New York, Ph.D. 1920. **Military Service:** Served in the U.S. Army Infantry, 1917-18. **Family:** Married Dorothy Graffe in 1922; two sons. **Career:** Instructor, 1920-24, assistant professor, 1924-35, associate professor, 1935-42, and professor of English, 1942-59, Columbia University; lecturer, St. John's College, Annapolis, Maryland, 1937-57. Literary editor, 1924-42, and film critic, 1935-38, *The Nation*, New York; panelist on the radio program *Invitation to Learning*, 1940-42. Visiting professor of English, Harvard University, Cambridge, Massachusetts, 1963. **Awards:** Pulitzer prize, 1940; Columbia University Alexander Hamilton Medal, 1959; Hale award, 1960; National Conference of Christians and Jews Brotherhood award, 1960; Huntington Hartford award, 1962; Emerson-Thoreau Medal, 1964. Litt.D.: Bowdoin College, Brunswick, Maine, 1944; University of Illinois, 1958; Columbia University, 1960; Knox College, Galesburg, Illinois, 1966; Harvard University, 1966; Jewish Theological Seminary of America, New York, 1970. L.H.D.: Adelphi University, Garden City, New York, 1957; Mount Mary College, Milwaukee, Wisconsin, 1965. Honorary M.D.: Connecticut State Medical Society, 1966. **Member:** American Academy. **Died:** 10 December 1972.

PUBLICATIONS

Collections

Essays, edited by William Claire. 1980.

Poetry

Spring Thunder and Other Poems. 1924.
7 P.M. and Other Poems. 1926.
Now the Sky and Other Poems. 1928.
Jonathan Gentry. 1931.
A Winter Diary and Other Poems. 1935.
The Lost Look and Other Poems. 1937.
Collected Poems 1922-1938. 1939.
The Mayfield Deer. 1941.
Our Lady Peace and Other War Poems. 1942.
The Seven Sleepers and Other Poems. 1944.
The Country Year. 1946.
The Careless Clock: Poems about Children in the Family. 1947.
New Poems. 1948.
Humanity Unlimited: Twelve Sonnets. 1950.
In That Far Land. 1951.
Mortal Summer. 1953.
Spring Birth and Other Poems. 1953.
Selected Poems. 1954.
Morning Worship. 1960.
Collected and New Poems 1924-1963. 1963.
Narrative Poems. 1964.
That Shining Place: New Poems. 1969.
Good Morning: Last Poems. 1973.

Plays

The Last Days of Lincoln (produced 1961). 1959.
Never, Never Ask His Name (produced 1965). In *Three Plays,* 1966.
Three Plays (includes *Never, Never Ask His Name, A Little Night Music, The Weekend That Was*). 1966.

Fiction

The Transients. 1935.
Windless Cabins. 1940.
Tilda. 1943.
The Short Stories. 1950.
The Witch of Ramoth and Other Tales. 1950.
Nobody Say a Word and Other Stories. 1953.
Home with Hazel and Other Stories. 1957.
Collected Stories. 3 vols., 1962-68.

Other

Henry David Thoreau: A Critical Study. 1916.
The Poetry of John Dryden. 1920; revised edition, 1931; as *John Dryden: A Study of His Poetry,* 1946.
American and British Literature since 1890, with Carl Van Doren. 1925; revised edition, 1939.
Edwin Arlington Robinson. 1927.
Dick and Tom: Tales of Two Ponies (for children). 1931.
Dick and Tom in Town (for children). 1932.
Shakespeare. 1939.
Studies in Metaphysical Poetry: Two Essays and a Bibliography, with Theodore Spencer. 1939.
The Transparent Tree (for children). 1940.
Invitation to Learning, with Huntington Cairns and Allen Tate. 1941.
The New Invitation to Learning. 1942.

The Private Reader: Selected Articles and Reviews. 1942.
Liberal Education. 1943.
The Noble Voice: A Study of Ten Great Poems. 1946; as *Great Poems of Western Literature,* 1966.
Nathaniel Hawthorne. 1949.
Introduction to Poetry. 1951.
Joseph and His Brothers. 1956.
Don Quixote's Profession. 1958.
Autobiography. 1958.
The Happy Critic and Other Essays. 1961.
The Dialogues of Archibald MacLeish and Van Doren, edited by Warren V. Bush. 1964.
Somebody Came (for children). 1966.
Carl Sandburg. 1969.
In the Beginning, Love: Dialogues on the Bible, with Maurice Samuel, edited by Edith Samuel. 1973.
The Book of Praise: Dialogues on the Psalms, with Maurice Samuel, edited by Edith Samuel. 1975.

Editor, *Samuel Sewall's Diary.* 1927.
Editor, *A History of the Life and Death, Virtues and Exploits of General George Washington,* by Mason Locke Weems. 1927.
Editor, *An Anthology of World Poetry.* 1928; revised edition, 1936; selection, as *An Anthology of English and American Poetry,* 1936.
Editor, *The Travels of William Bartram.* 1928.
Editor, *Nick of the Woods; or, The Jibbenainosay: A Tale of Kentucky,* by Robert Montgomery Bird. 1928.
Editor, *A Journey to the Land of Eden and Other Papers,* by William Byrd H. 1928.
Editor, *An Autobiography of America.* 1929.
Editor, *Correspondence of Aaron Burr and His Daughter Theodosia.* 1929.
Editor, with Garibaldi M. Lapolla, *A Junior Anthology of World Poetry.* 1929.
Editor, *The Life of Sir William Phips,* by Cotton Mather. 1929.
Editor, with Garibaldi M. Lapolla, *The World's Best Poems.* 1932.
Editor, *American Poets, 1630-1930.* 1932; as *Masterpieces of American Poets,* 1936.
Editor, *The Oxford Book of American Prose.* 1932.
Editor, with John W. Cunliffe and Karl Young, *Century Readings in English Literature,* 5th edition. 1940.
Editor, *A Listener's Guide to Invitation to Learning, 1940-41, 1941-42.* 2 vols., 1940-42.
Editor, *The Night of the Summer Solstice and Other Stories of the Russian War.* 1943.
Editor, *Walt Whitman.* 1945.
Editor, *The Portable Emerson.* 1946.
Editor, *Selected Poetry,* by William Wordsworth. 1950.
Editor, *Introduction to Poetry.* 1951; as *Enjoying Poetry,* 1951.
Editor, with others, *Riverside Poetry: 48 New Poems by 27 Poets.* 1956.
Editor, with others, *Insights into Literature.* 1965.
Editor, *100 Poems.* 1967.

Critical Study: *Mark Van Doren* by J.T. Ledbetter, 1996.

*   *   *

Mark Van Doren's poetry, which consists of more than a thousand poems in *Collected and New Poems* and other volumes, including a posthumous collection, *Good Morning,* constitutes one of the more prolific and accomplished bodies of work by an American poet in the twentieth century. While the sheer bulk has often astonished and sometimes dismayed critics, it represents, as Richard Howard has observed, "not so much an embarrassment as an embodiment of riches."

Van Doren was originally hailed by **T.S. Eliot** and others as a master of rural verse and conveniently placed in the tradition of **Robert Frost**. He soon demonstrated, however, a distinctive voice that deepened through a sustained middle period culminating in his first *Collected Poems* (1939) and that grew in variety of subject matter and range for over three more decades after he received the Pulitzer Prize in 1940. Influenced by John Dryden as a young scholar, Van Doren belongs in a group that might include Hardy, early Yeats, Graves and, in specifically American ways, **Emily Dickinson**, **Edwin Arlington Robinson**, and Frost. Allen Tate once wisely concluded, after also suggesting "a trace of William Browne (epigrams and *Britannia's Pastorals,* 1613), traces of Ben Jonson, more than a trace of **Robert Herrick**" that all of them might "add up to Mark Van Doren who is like nobody else."

Singularly devoid of the common French influences in modern verse, Van Doren also eschewed confessional or analytic tendencies. He treated his principal subjects, the cosmos, love, finality, family matters, and particularly children, animals, paradox, and knowledge in a lucid manner that transcends simplistic notions of modernity and personal sensibilities. There is a passionate intelligence lurking behind many of the poems that somehow never intrudes. Indeed, it is a subtle presence that calls forth different interpretations on subsequent readings, though there is never intentional obscurity.

His poetic corpus contains an intricate world of pleasures, observations, and intellectual insights. As a master craftsman, Van Doren would make an excellent case study for the continuity of English lyric and narrative verse. He also personifies a humanistic and metaphysical approach that is American at its core, a kind of Emersonian individualism with contemporary concerns. Taken together, his work over a half-century, which included substantial accomplishments in other literary fields, illustrates the American literary presence at its best with a poetry that, as one critic observed, never having been in fashion, will never go out of fashion.

—William Claire

VAN DRUTEN, John (William)

Born: London, England, 1 June 1901; moved to the United States, 1926; became citizen, 1944. **Education:** University College School, London, 1911-17; worked in a law office and studied law: LL.B., University of London, 1922; qualified as solicitor, 1923. **Career:** Special lecturer in English law and legal history, University College of Wales, Aberystwyth, 1923-26; full-time writer from 1926; also stage director: directed *The King and I,* New York, 1951, and several of his own plays. **Awards:** American Academy award of Merit Medal, 1946; New York Drama Critics Circle award, 1952. **Member:** American Academy, 1951. **Died:** 19 December 1957.

PUBLICATIONS

Plays

The Return Half (produced 1924).
Young Woodley (produced 1925). 1926.
Chance Acquaintance (produced 1927).
Diversion (produced 1928). 1928.
The Return of the Soldier, from the novel by Rebecca West (produced 1928). 1928.
After All (produced 1929; revised version, produced 1930). 1929.
London Wall (produced 1931). 1931.
Sea Fever, with Auriol Lee, from a play by Marcel Pagnol (produced 1931).
There's Always Juliet (produced 1931). 1931.
Hollywood Holiday, with Benn Levy (produced 1931). 1931.
Somebody Knows (produced 1932). 1932.
Behold, We Live (produced 1932). 1932.
The Distaff Side (produced 1933). 1933.
Flowers of the Forest (produced 1934). 1934.
Most of the Game (produced 1935). 1936.
Gertie Maude (produced 1937). 1937.
Leave Her to Heaven (produced 1940). 1941.
Old Acquaintance (produced 1940). 1941.
Solitaire, from the novel by Edwin Corle (produced 1942).
The Damask Cheek, with Lloyd R. Morris (produced 1942). 1943.
The Voice of the Turtle (produced 1943). 1944.
I Remember Mama, from the stories in *Mama's Bank Account* by Kathryn Forbes (produced 1944). 1945.
The Mermaids Singing (produced 1945). 1946.
The Druid Circle (produced 1947). 1948.
Make Way for Lucia, from novels by E.F. Benson (produced 1948). 1949.
Bell, Book, and Candle (produced 1950). 1951.
I Am a Camera, from *The Berlin Stories* by Christopher Isherwood (produced 1951). 1952.
I've Got Sixpence (produced 1952). 1953.
Dancing in the Chequered Shade (produced 1955).

Screenplays: *Young Woodley,* with Victor Kendall, 1930; *I Loved a Soldier,* 1936; *Parnell,* with S.N. Behrman, 1937; *Night Must Fall,* 1937; *The Citadel,* with others, 1938; *Raffles,* with Sidney Howard, 1940; *Lucky Partners,* with Allan Scott, 1940; *My Life with Caroline,* with Arnold Belgard, 1941; *Johnny Come Lately (Johnny Vagabond),* 1943; *Old Acquaintance,* with Lenore Coffee, 1943; *Forever and a Day,* with others, 1944; *Gaslight,* with Walter Reisch and John L. Balderston, 1944; *The Voice of the Turtle,* 1948.

Fiction

Young Woodley. 1929.
A Woman on Her Way. 1930.
And Then You Wish. 1936.
The Vicarious Years. 1955.

Other

The Way to the Present: A Personal Record. 1938.
Playwright at Work. 1953.
The Widening Circle (autobiography). 1957.

*

Critical Studies: *As They Appear* by John Mason Brown, 1953; *Theatre Chronicles 1937-1962* by Mary McCarthy, 1963.

*   *   *

A prolific writer—best known for his plays but also recognized as a novelist, screenwriter, and autobiographer—John Van Druten delighted audiences for more than thirty years with his polished, urbane comedies. The persistent tone in his works is warm and gentle; his style has been praised for its convincing naturalness and controlled simplicity.

Van Druten's plots are often loosely structured, imitative, and readily forgettable. *I Remember Mama,* one of his most popular works, for example, is structured as a series of vignettes linked together by tone and characters, but scarcely more unified than the collection of Kathryn Forbes's short stories on which it was based.

When there is a developed plot in either his original works or his adaptations, it is usually one of two variations on the same basic action: two people meet, have or contemplate having an affair, discover that they love each other, and then joyfully renounce wantonness and move toward a thoroughly conventional marriage (as in *There's Always Juliet; The Distaff Side; Bell, Book, and Candle; The Damask Cheek;* and *The Voice of the Turtle*); or, sadly, discover that their age, circumstance, or character prevents such a marriage (as in *Young Woodley, Old Acquaintance, The Mermaids Singing,* and *I Am a Camera*). In developing these plots, van Druten moves perilously close to the brink of sentimentality and heavy-handed moralism; but his wit and determination to master "the difficult art of sincerity" keep him, with rare exceptions, from plunging headlong into the abyss.

Indeed, Van Druten's plays were consistently praised for their fresh dialogue, their unforced cleverness, and their sophisticated repartee. His fiction and autobiographies, too, are natural and eminently readable.

His awareness of the importance of style and his concern that his works be well-written are reflected both in his commentary on his own works and in his evaluation of the works of others. For example, he criticizes bad writing, which he describes as that which is filled with bathos, facetiousness, and an endless flow of shop-worn phrases that "produce no effect save that of total weariness." He states that only the immature taste can appreciate great sweetness or a "mustard and vinegar sharpness," which the experienced palate would disdain. And in his own works, from the beginning, he attempted to avoid these excesses.

Van Druten's artistry in writing dialogue brings his characters to life. They are unforgettable. Sally Bowles, the complex, misguided, comical, pathetic American expatriate in *I Am a Camera,* who leads the life of the grasshopper as the deadly threat of the Third Reich moves forward; Marta, the warm, clever, protective, stable foundation of her family in *I Remember Mama;* Gillian Holroyd, the thoroughly human witch in *Bell, Book, and Candle*—these are only three who clearly rise above the ordinary to the distinctive.

This ability to create memorable characters, and thus major roles, was early recognized by Hollywood, where Van Druten wrote dialogue, adapted his own works and those of others, and collaborated on screenplays for major actors from virtually every important studio. He was largely responsible, for instance, for creating

the role of Paula Alquist in *Gaslight,* a role for which Ingrid Bergman won an Oscar in 1944. It is on such success that Van Druten's reputation rests.

—Helen Houser Popovich

VAN VECHTEN, Carl

Born: Cedar Rapids, Iowa, 17 June 1880. **Education:** Cedar Rapids High School; University of Chicago, 1899-1903, Ph.B. 1903. **Family:** Married 1) Anna Elizabeth Snyder in 1907 (divorced 1912); 2) the actress Fania Marinoff in 1914. **Career:** Composer and journalist; reporter, *Chicago American,* 1903-05; assistant music critic, 1906-07, 1910-13, and Paris correspondent, 1908-10, *New York Times;* author of program notes for the Symphony Society of New York, 1910-11; drama critic, *New York Press,* 1913-14; editor, *Trend,* New York, 1914; portrait photographer from 1932; individual exhibitions from 1942. Member of the Board of the Cosmopolitan Symphony Orchestra, and the W.C. Handy Foundation for the Blind; founder, 1941, and honorary curator, 1946, James Weldon Johnson Memorial Collection of Negro Arts and Letters, Yale University Library, New Haven, Connecticut; literary executor of Gertrude Stein, and editor of the Yale University Press Stein Edition, from 1946. **Awards:** Yale University Gold Medal, 1955. D.Litt.: Fisk University, Nashville, Tennessee, 1955. **Member:** American Academy, 1961. **Died:** 21 December 1964.

PUBLICATIONS

Fiction

Peter Whiffle, His Life and Works. 1922.
The Blind Bow-Boy. 1923.
The Tattooed Countess. 1924.
Firecrackers. 1925.
Nigger Heaven. 1926.
Spider Boy: A Scenario for a Moving Picture. 1928.
Parties: Scenes from Contemporary New York Life. 1930.

Other

Music after the Great War and Other Studies. 1915.
Music and Bad Manners. 1916.
Interpreters and Interpretations. 1917; revised edition, as *Interpreters,* 1920.
The Merry-Go-Round. 1918.
The Music of Spain. 1918.
In the Garret. 1920.
The Tiger in the House. 1920.
Red: Papers on Musical Subjects. 1925.
Excavations: A Book of Advocacies. 1926.
Feathers. 1930.
Sacred and Profane Memories (essays). 1932.
James Weldon Johnson, with Sterling A. Brown and A.B. Spingarn. 1941(?).
Libris, in *Dance Index* (triple issue). 1942.
Fragments from an Unwritten Autobiography. 2 vols., 1955.
The Dance Writings, edited by Paul Padgette. 1975.

With Formality and Elegance (on photography). 1977.
Portraits (photographs), edited by Saul Mauriber. 1978.
Keep a-Inchin' Along: Selected Writings about Black Art and Letters, edited by Bruce Kellner. 1979.
The Dance Photography, edited by Paul Padgette. 1981.
The Letters of Gertrude Stein and Van Vechten 1913-1946, edited by Edward Burns. 2 vols., 1986.

Editor, *Lords of the Housetops: Thirteen Cat Tales.* 1921.
Editor, *My Musical Life,* by Nikolay Rimsky-Korsakoff, translated by Judah A. Joffe. 1923; revised edition, 1942.
Editor, *Gertrude Stein: Selected Writings.* 1946.
Editor, *Last Operas and Plays,* by Gertrude Stein. 1949.
Editor, *Unpublished Writings of Gertrude Stein.* 8 vols., 1951-58.

*

Bibliography: *Van Vechten: A Bibliography* by Klaus W. Jonas, 1955; *A Bibliography of the Work of Van Vechten* by Bruce Kellner, 1980.

Critical Studies: *Van Vechten and the Twenties,* 1955, and *Van Vechten,* 1965, both by Edward Lueders; *Van Vechten and the Irreverent Decades* by Bruce Kellner, 1968; *Carl Van Vechten and the Harlem Renaissance: A Critical Assessment* by Leon Coleman, 1998.

*   *   *

Carl Van Vechten's personal flamboyance in manner and dress, as well as his frequent enthusiasm for both the avant garde and the patently old-fashioned, labeled him a dilettante in his own time. The range and foresight in several distinct careers, however, mark him a unique and underestimated American writer.

A partial list of his discoveries is staggering. As a newspaper critic he endorsed the first performances in America of Isadora Duncan, Anna Pavlova, Mary Garden, Feodor Chaliapin, and Sergei Rachmaninoff, and he was the earliest American admirer of the music of Erik Satie, Richard Strauss, and Igor Stravinsky. In a series of volumes of musical and literary criticism—*Interpreters* and *Excavations* are particularly rewarding—his perceptions are startlingly fresh. He advocated musical scores for films by serious composers, the value of popular music and ragtime, ballet, Spanish music—all far in advance of other writers. He was one of the first to rediscover **Herman Melville**, and Ronald Firbank and Arthur Machen owe their American reputations to him. Van Vechten's tireless efforts on behalf of **Gertrude Stein** are well known; he was instrumental in placing the first books of **Wallace Stevens** and **Langston Hughes**; he fostered the careers of George Gershwin, Ethel Waters, Paul Robeson among musicians, and **James Purdy** among writers. His book about cats, *The Tiger in the House,* is seminal. He was largely responsible for the popular recognition of the Negro as a creative artist during the Harlem Renaissance.

Van Vechten was probably too analytical and discursive, too involved with amassing and cataloging outre material, to have written fiction of the first order, although all seven of his novels are variously engaging. Few books catch the charm of New York and Paris before World War I so well as *Peter Whiffle.* None serves as such a good introduction to Harlem during the 1920s as *Nigger Heaven. The Tattooed Countess* criticizes small-town life at the

turn of the century with a gently cheerful malice denied more resolute realists. Three novels document Van Vechten's "splendid drunken Twenties," as he called the period: *The Blind Bow-Boy, Firecrackers,* and *Parties* form a serious social trilogy in the disguise of buffoonery and farce, written with slinky elegance and wit.

Van Vechten gave up writing in favor of photography to document the century's celebrities for various collections he established: the **James Weldon Johnson** Memorial Collection of Negro Arts and Letters, at Yale, and the George Gershwin Memorial Collection of Music and Musical Literature, at Fisk, among others.

His work has dated very little; since he wrote from the perspective of middle age. Van Vechten's evaluations of the 1920s are perhaps more solidly grounded than those of several more celebrated younger writers of the period.

—Bruce Kellner

VERY, Jones

Born: Salem, Massachusetts, 28 August 1813; spent much of his childhood at sea with his father, a ship's captain. **Education:** Fisk Latin School, Salem, 1832-34; Harvard University, Cambridge, Massachusetts, 1834-36 (Junior and Senior Bowdoin Prize), A.B. 1836. **Career:** Tutor in Greek at the university 1836-38; entered Harvard Divinity School, 1836; forced to resign because of erratic behavior caused by his mystical experiences, 1838; spent a month in McLean Asylum, Somerville, Massachusetts, 1838; associate of Emerson, late 1830s; licensed to preach as Unitarian minister by Cambridge Association of Ministers, 1843: held temporary pastorates in Eastport, Maine, and North Beverly, Massachusetts; lived in Salem after 1848. **Died:** 8 May 1880.

PUBLICATIONS

Collections

Selected Poems, edited by Nathan Lyons. 1966.

Other

Essays and Poems, edited by Ralph Waldo Emerson, 1839; revised edition, edited by James Freeman Clarke, as *Poems and Essays,* 1886; edited by Kenneth Walter Cameron, as *Poems,* 1965.

*

Critical Studies: *Very: Emerson's "Brave Saint"* by William Irving Bartlett, 1942 (includes bibliography); *Very: The Effective Years 1833-1840* by Edwin Gittleman, 1967; "Jones Very" by David Robinson, in *The Transcendentalists: A Review of Research and Criticism* edited Joel Myerson, 1984; "Alone with God and Nature: The Poetry of Very and Frederick Goddard Tuckerman" by David Seed, in *Nineteenth-Century American Poetry* edited by A. Robert Lee, 1985; *The Angelic Sins of Jones Very* by Sarah Turner Clayton, 1999.

*   *   *

A curious example of single-minded Quietism, Jones Very occupies a special place in nineteenth-century American poetry. He wrote more than 700 poems, most of these produced between 1833 and 1840—the tumultuous years in which Very resolved his youthful religious doubts and reconciled himself to the eccentricities of his dominating mother and the loss of his sea captain father. Dramatically realizing the Transcendentalist equation of self-reliance with God-reliance, Very experienced a transfiguring conversion in which he attained a second birth through the agency of the Holy Spirit. True, most of these poems tend to be repetitive, conventional in thought and expression, tedious, and oblivious to drama, the play of language, humor, or the ambiguities of human experience. In his best poems, however, Very's voice can be as piercing as a knife-blade. Writing from the perspective of one who knows himself to be the passive instrument of a Higher Will, Very triumphs in lean enunciations of Being rather than explorations of Becoming. Characteristically using mild variations on the form of the Shakespearean sonnet and deeply imbued with the diction and syntax of the Bible, his utterance sometimes rises above its own awkwardness and penchant for bland abstractions to achieve an intense purity of religious awareness. Even though his successful poems are overly dependent on the Christian paradox of total submission as a condition of total fulfillment, the results are unsentimental and wholly persuasive.

His "nature poetry" and his literary essays could perhaps have been written by any gifted young man swept up in the enthusiasm of Channing's Unitarianism and **Ralph Waldo Emerson**'s *Nature*. But some dozen or so meditational sonnets (e.g., "The Hand and Foot," "The Absent," "Morning," "The Presence," "The Journey," "The Eagles") succeeded in translating literally the Transcendentalist exhortations to discover an inner divinity into spiritual declarations of considerable power. At first extravagantly praised by Emerson, Bronson Alcott, Margaret Fuller, and Elizabeth Peabody, Very became something of an embarrassment due to the fanatic rigidity with which he judged all deviations from his way to salvation as well as the monochromatic mediocrity of much of his verse. From 1843 until his death, his literary production was almost entirely restricted to not particularly distinguished sermons.

—Earl Rovit

VIDAL, (Eugene Luther) Gore

Pseudonym: Edgar Box. **Born:** At U.S. Military Academy, West Point, New York, 3 October 1925. **Education:** Los Alamos School, New Mexico, 1939-40; Phillips Exeter Academy, New Hampshire, 1940-43. **Military Service:** Served in the United States Army, 1943-46: warrant officer. **Career:** Editor, E. P. Dutton, New York, 1946; lived in Antigua, Guatemala, 1947-49; Democratic Party candidate for Congress in the Twenty-ninth District of New York, 1960; member of President's Advisory Committee on the Arts, 1961-63; host of television program *Hot Line,* 1964; lived in Italy, 1967-76; co-founder of New Party, 1968-71; co-chair of People's Party, 1970-72; ran for nomination as Democratic Party senatorial candidate in California, 1982; writer and lecturer; appears frequently on television and radio talk shows. **Awards:** Mystery Writers of America Edgar Allan Poe award for television drama, 1955; Screen Writers Annual award nomination, 1964; Cannes Crit-

ics prize for screenplay, 1964; National Book Critics Circle award for criticism, 1982; named honorary citizen of Ravello, Italy, 1983; Prix Deauville, 1983; National Book award for nonfiction, for *United States: Essays, 1952-1992,* 1993; Chevalier de l'Ordre des Arts et des Lettres, France, 1995.

PUBLICATIONS

Collections

Three: Williwaw; A Thirsty Evil: Seven Short Stories; Julian, the Apostate. 1962.
The Essential Vidal. 1998.
Gore Vidal, Sexually Speaking: Collected Sex Writings. 1999.

Novels

Williwaw. 1946.
In a Yellow Wood. 1947.
The City and the Pillar. 1949; revised edition, 1965.
The Season of Comfort. 1949.
A Search for the King: A Twelfth Century Legend. 1950.
Dark Green, Bright Red. 1950.
The Judgment of Paris. 1953; revised edition, 1965.
Messiah. 1954; revised edition, 1965.
Julian. 1964.
Washington, D.C. 1967.
Myra Breckinridge. 1968; excised edition, 1968.
Two Sisters: A Novel in the Form of a Memoir. 1970.
Burr. 1973.
Myron. 1974.
1876. 1976.
Kalki. 1978.
Creation. 1981.
Duluth. 1983.
Lincoln. 1984.
Myra Breckenridge [and] *Myron.* 1986.
Empire. 1987.
Hollywood: A Novel of America in the 1920s. 1990.
Live from Golgotha. 1992.
The Smithsonian Institute. 1998.

Short Fiction

A Thirsty Evil: Seven Short Stories. 1956.

Essays

Rocking the Boat. 1962.
Sex, Death, and Money. 1968.
Reflections upon a Sinking Ship. 1969.
Homage to Daniel Shays: Collected Essays, 1952-1972. 1972; as *Collected Essays, 1952-1972,* 1974; as *On Our Own Now,* 1976.
Matters of Fact and of Fiction: Essays, 1973-1976. 1977.
With others, *Great American Families.* 1977.
With Robert J. Stanton, *Views from a Window: Conversations with Gore Vidal.* 1980.
The Second American Revolution and Other Essays. 1982.
Armageddon?: Essays, 1983-1987. 1987.

At Home: Essays, 1982-1988. 1988.
Screening History. 1992.
United States; Essays, 1951-1991. 1992.
Palimpsest: A Memoir. 1995.
Virgin Islands: A Dependency of United States: Essays 1992-1997. 1997.
The American Presidency. 1998.

Plays

Visit to a Small Planet: A Comedy Akin to a Vaudeville (produced 1957). 1957; revised edition, 1959.
The Best Man: A Play of Politics (produced 1960). 1960; revised edition, 1977.
On the March to the Sea: A Southron Comedy (adaptation of television play *Honor;* produced 1961).
Three Plays. 1962.
Romulus: A New Comedy (adapted from work by Freidrich Duerrenmatt; produced 1962). 1962.
Weekend: A Comedy in Two Acts (produced 1968). 1968.
With others, *An Evening with Richard Nixon* (produced 1972). 1972.

Screenplays: *The Catered Affair,* 1956; *I Accuse,* 1958; *The Scapegoat,* with Robert Hamer, 1959; *Suddenly Last Summer,* with Tennessee Williams, 1959; *The Best Man* (based on play of same title), 1964; *Is Paris Burning?,* with Francis Ford Coppola, 1966; *The Last of the Mobile Hotshots,* 1970; *The Sicilan,* 1970.

Television Plays: *Barn Burning,* 1954; *Dark Possession,* 1954; *Smoke,* 1954; *Visit to a Small Planet,* 1955; *The Death of Billy the Kid,* 1955; *Dr. Jekyll and Mr. Hyde,* 1955; *A Sense of Justice,* 1955; *Summer Pavilion,* 1955; *The Turn of the Screw,* 1955; *Stage Door,* 1955; *Honor,* 1956; *Portrait of a Ballerina,* 1956; *The Indestructible Mr. Gore,* 1959; *Dear Arthur,* 1960; *Dress Gray* (adaption of novel by Lucian Truscott), 1986; *Gore Vidal's "Billy the Kid,"* 1989.

Mystery Novels (as Edgar Box)

Death in the Fifth Position. 1952.
Death Before Bedtime. 1953.
Death Likes It Hot. 1954.
Three by Box: The Complete Mysteries of Edgar Box. 1978.

Other

Visit to a Small Planet and Other Television Plays. 1974.
A Conversation with Myself. 1974.
Vidal in Venice, edited by George Armstrong, photographs by Tore Gill. 1985.
The Best Man: A Screen Adaptation of the Original Play. 1989.
Who Owns the U.S.? 1992.

Editor, *Best Television Plays.* 1965.

Recordings: *An Evening with Richard,* 1973.

*

Manuscript Collection: University of Wisconsin, Madison.

Bibliography: *Gore Vidal: A Primary and Secondary Bibliography* by Robert J. Stanton, 1978.

Critical Studies: "Gore Vidal: The Search for a King" by John W. Aldridge in *After the Lost Generation: A Critical Study of the Writers of Two Wars,* 1951; *Gore Vidal* by Ray Lewis White, 1968; *The Apostate Angel: A Critical Study of Gore Vidal* by Bernard F. Dick, 1974; interview with Vidal in *Gay Sunshine,* Winter 1975; "Narrative Patterns in the Novels of Gore Vidal" by David Barton in *Notes on Contemporary Literature,* September 1981; *Gore Vidal* by Robert F. Kiernan, 1982; "Gore Vidal: The Writer as Citizen" by Claudia Dreifus in *Progressive,* September 1986; "Gore Vidal" by Mark Matousek in *Interview,* June 1987; "Gore Vidal" by David Sheff in *Playboy,* December 1987; "Tug of War" by Colin Wright in *New Statesman and Society,* 3 November 1989; "Gore Vidal: A Grandfather's Legacy" by Marvin J. LaHood in *World Literature Today,* Summer 1990; *Gay Fictions Wilde to Stonewall: Studies in a Male Homosexual Literary Tradition* by Claude J. Summers, 1990; *The Gay Novel in America* by James Levin, 1991; "My O My O Myra" by Catherine R. Stimpson in *New England Review,* Fall 1991; *Gore Vidal: Writer against the Grain* edited by Jay Parini, 1992; "Gore Vidal" by Joel Shatzky in *Contemporary Gay American Novelists,* edited by Emmanuel S. Nelson, 1993; "First Person Singular I: The Importance of Being Gore" by Andrew Kopkind, in *Nation,* July 1993, pp. 16-20; "Gore Vidal and the Erotics of Masculinity" by Robert J. Corber, in *Western Humanities Review* (Salt Lake City, Utah), Spring 1994, pp. 30-52; "Gore Vidal's Satire" by M.D. Fletcher and Kate Feros, in *Studies in Contemporary Satire* (Kearney), 1996, pp. 160-64; *Gore Vidal: A Critical Companion* by Susan Baker, Westport, Connecticut, 1997; *Gore Vidal: A Biography* by Fred Kaplan, 1999.

*   *   *

Of all the critical overviews of the wide-ranging work of Gore Vidal, his own appraisal may be as straightforward as one could desire. In a foreword to the 1956 collection *Visit to a Small Planet and Other Television Plays,* he writes: "I am at heart a propagandist, a tremendous hater, a tiresome nag, complacently positive that there is no human problem which could not be solved if people would simply do as I advise." There is a determined strain of social criticism—always articulate, often vituperative, and sometimes just bitchy—at the center of most of his fiction, drama, and film scripts, especially in his most recent work. Consumed by American political history, Vidal has fashioned characters and situations that often serve as mouthpieces for his heretical suspicions about the past and his unrelieved cynicism with regard to the future. Fortunately, there is almost always evidence of his considerable literary skill as well.

Since the publication of *Williwaw* when he was twenty-one, Vidal has prompted enthusiasm from critics lauding his "promise." Whether that promise has been fulfilled after forty years of work in popular American literature is still the central question for most Vidal commentators. What is certain is that he has managed to keep his name in contention the whole time. He found popular and critical success in fiction—first with *Williwaw,* then with best-sellers like *The City and the Pillar; Julian; Washington, D.C.; Myra Breckinridge; Burr; 1876;* and *Lincoln.* He turned to television in its formative years, in the era of live tele-drama, and produced well-received plays for *Omnibus, Studio One,* and *Philco Television Playhouse* (including the highly praised *Visit to a Small Planet*). *The Best Man,* produced on Broadway in 1960, was a major success, encouraging a film adaptation in 1964, followed by other film adaptations (including *Suddenly Last Summer,* written with Tennessee Williams) and original screenplays.

Critics familiar with Vidal's entire range of work seem to think that his real talent lies with the perfection of the essay, however. Indeed, the 1977 publication of a collection of his essays—*Matters of Fact and Fiction*—was greeted with widespread praise, even if some reviewers had reservations. Vidal's affinity for the essay form may account for the frequently heard criticism that his other work is too polemical. It may well be, as Vidal himself has suggested informally, that at the heart of his dramatic and fictional efforts there beats an essay, which sometimes overwhelms the conventions of the form that seeks to contain it.

The elements of Vidal's creative polemic seem to be characterized by his gift for language, his "wit" (in the classical sense), and his strong reactionary instincts. This last tendency seems puzzling at first, given his well-known liberalism in social and political affairs (television networks have used him as a representative "liberal intellectual," and he has run for office on suicidally liberal platforms). But the contradiction might be a natural consequence of being Gore Vidal, grandson of T. P. Gore, a respected Senator from Oklahoma, and son of a much-admired college athlete who was an instructor at West Point when Vidal was born. The reactionary strain might be a case of his natural predispositions—based upon his aristocratic origins, his attraction to money and power, and his unshakable suspicions about the stupidity of the American public overwhelming whatever ideological hopes he claims.

What emerges, in the words of P. N. Furbank (in a 1974 piece in the *Listener*), is "a sort of patriotic gloom." Rooted as he was in the schoolbook traditions of American history and its institutions, Vidal seems to have been particularly embittered by the unflattering lessons of his historical scholarship and his personal experience.

His 1992 novel *Live from Golgotha* fulfills Vidal's impulse to satirize one of these institutions — Christianity. At the end of the twentieth century, the major texts of the religion, stored on magnetic tape, have been "hacked" by a computer wizard, so the television networks are trying to capture the Crucifixion on a live broadcast. At the same time, Timothy, a surviving disciple of St. Paul, is urged by another network broadcaster to write his own version of the Gospel. Vidal stretches the capacities of technology beyond the wildest dreams of gods past and present; it includes the power to wipe the whole screen—both the public one and the private one of memory—clean. Reviewers praised Vidal's funny treatment of St. Paul, but criticized the predictability of the satire, in part because it rested on a superficial America, the kind derivable from CNN broadcasts. It does seem that this novel is Vidal's attempt to steer away from the staleness of grievances at which he arrives so frequently in his essays.

Screening History, which Vidal also published in 1992, nearly serves as a companion volume to his earlier American history novels. The book is a collection of lectures Vidal gave at Harvard and centers mainly on his lifelong love of the movies. In spite of his affection for Hollywood, however, Vidal does not miss most opportunities to ruminate and reference his family and his pedigree, a tendency that illustrates his continued association of culture with family.

Ultimately, Vidal is stuck with the residue of his expectations about American innocence and morality and confounded by what he knows about political history. In order to do justice to both the dream and the informed reality, he has developed an articulate, even lyrical, cynicism about the direction of modern letters and the final collision of the Republic with the world and the cultural tendencies it has, in part, created.

—Lawrence R. Broer, updated by Martha Sutro

VILLANUEVA, Alma Luz

Born: Lompoc, California, 4 October 1944. **Education:** Norwich University, Vermont College, Northfield, Vermont, M.F.A. 1984. **Family:** 1) Married at fifteen (marriage dissolved), three children; 2) Wilfredo Castano (separated), one child. **Career:** Held writer-in-residence positions at Cabrillo College, University of California-Santa Cruz, University of California-Irvine, Stanford University, San Francisco State College, Naropa Institute, Boulder, Colorado. Served on the National Endowment for the Arts fiction panel. **Awards:** Humanities, Hispanic Women Making History, 1986; Third Chicano Literary prize, University of California-Irvine, 1987; American Book award, 1989; Pen Fiction award, 1994; Latin American Writer's Institute award, 1994. **Residence:** Santa Cruz, California.

PUBLICATIONS

Novels

The Ultraviolet Sky. 1993.
Naked Ladies. 1994.

Short Stories

La Llorona/Weeping Woman. 1994.

Poetry

Bloodroot, introduction by James Cody. 1977.
Mother, May I? 1978.
Life Span. 1984.
La Chingada. In *Five Poets of Aztlan,* edited by Santiago Daydi-Tolson, 1985.
Planet, with *Mother, May I?* 1993.
Desire. 1998.

*

Critical Studies: "Terra Mater and the Emergence of Myth in Poems by Alma Villanueva" by Alejandro Morales, in the *Bilingual Review/La Revista Bilingüe,* vol. 7, no. 3, 1980; *Chicano Literature: A Critical History* by Charles Tatum, 1982; "Soothing Restless Serpents: The Dreaded Creation and Other Inspirations in Chicana Poetry" by Tey Diana Rebolledo, in *Third Woman,* vol. 2, no. 1, 1984; *Contemporary Chicana Poetry: A Critical Approach to an Emerging Literature* by Marta E. Sánchez, 1985, and "The Birthing of the Poetic 'I' in Alma Villanueva's *Mother, May I?:* The Search for a Feminine Identity" by Sánchez, in *Beyond Stereotypes: The Critical Analysis of Chicana Literature* edited by Maria Herrera-Sobek, 1985; "Demeter, Kore, and the Birth of the Self: The Quest for Identity in the Poetry of Alma Villanueva, Pat Mora, and Cherríe Moraga," in *Monographic Review/Revista Monografica,* vol. 6, 1990; "Chicana Poets: Re-Visions from the Margin" by Carmen M. Del Rio, in *Revista Canadiense de Estudios Hispanicos,* vol. 14, no. 3, 1990; "Body, Spirit, and the Text: Alma Villanueva's *Life Span*" by Elizabeth J. Ordonez, in *Criticism in the Borderlands: Studies in Chicano Literature, Culture, and Ideology* edited by Hector Calderon and Jose David Saldivar, 1991; "An Appreciation of Alma Luz Villanueva's *Life Span*" by Cesar A. Gonzalez-T., in *Confluencia: Revista Hispanica de Cultura y Literatura,* vol. 6, no. 2, 1991; "Leave-Taking and Retrieving in *The Road to Tamazunchale* and *The Ultraviolet Sky*" by Genevieve Fabre, in *The Bilingual Review/La Revista Bilingüe,* vol. 16, nos. 2 and 3, 1991.

*   *   *

Female identity, nature, unity, autobiography, and myth are terms critics frequently use to describe Alma Villanueva's writings. Themes that recur in her work are the female self and its discovery and affirmation, transformation and change, and the unity of all beings within nature. Her list of influences includes **Anaïs Nin, Sylvia Plath,** Pablo Neruda, Herman Hesse, Federico Garcia Lorca, **Anne Sexton,** Doris Lessing, D.H. Lawrence, and **Adrienne Rich.**

The ancient Native American view of humanity's oneness with nature is prevalent in her poetry collection, *Bloodroot.* In his introduction to this collection, James Cody compared the author to **Walt Whitman,** stating that she has that "extended line that is warp and woof of the prose-like weaving that proceeds from, is, nature itself." In Villanueva's view it is women who maintain a unity with nature, not men.

Villanueva's 1978 verse publication, *Mother, May I?,* is a short collection of sometimes angry autobiographical pieces that portray a woman's development as she strides a path towards wholeness, love, hope, and life. In the twenty-six poems in *Life Span,* the poetic voice is more sure, self- aware, and mature. There is an even closer relationship to nature, and many of the pieces take on an almost mystical tone. *La Chingada* takes a wider view of women; there is much more symbolism and myth here than in Villanueva's previous collections. Other works portray Chicano and Mexican figures, such as *La Malinche* ("The Bad Woman") and *La Llorona* ("The Weeping Woman"), that are well-known to most Mexican-Americans and emblematic of female history and the plight of contemporary Chicanas. *Planet* (published in one volume with a reissue of *Mother, May I?*) is dedicated "To the Earth, who I worship, and to all Native People of the planet." The poems here are sometimes personal, sometimes philosophical, and occasionally political. Many treat themes and topics found in nature.

Villanueva's 1988 novel, *The Ultraviolet Sky,* explores relationships between men and women through a protagonist named Rosa, who is a painter. In a constant quest to paint a perfect sky, Rosa experiences a life in turmoil—a ruined marriage, an adolescent son's sexual awakening, a failure in her relationship with a long-time friend, and a surprise pregnancy. It can be read as an "everywoman's" story of life in contemporary American society. Nineteen ninety-four's *Naked Ladies,* a title taken from the name of a wildflower, portrays the lives of four quite different women and examines relationships between and among the many peoples living in modern American society—African Americans, Anglos,

Chicanos, Native Americans, and Asian Americans. Throughout lives of turbulence and trouble, the women, like their wildflower counterparts, remain strong in the face of life's adversities and vicissitudes. Both novels contain passages that are highly lyrical and others that are filled with realistic and sometimes crude detail. Both contain themes previously seen in Villanueva's poetry but with the addition of war and social protest and some playful and more personal commentary. The voice here is mature, polished, and secure.

Villanueva's poetry and prose are at once personal and universal. Her feminist perspective, her reverence for all forms of life, and her artistic portrayals of the many passions of existence are significant contributions to contemporary Chicano literature in particular and American literature in general.

—Carl R. Shirley

VILLARREAL, José Antonio

Born: Los Angeles, California, 30 July 1924. **Education:** The University of California, Berkeley, B.A., 1950; graduate study, 1958. **Military Service:** Served in the U.S. Navy, 1942-46. **Family:** Married Barbara Gentles in 1953, two sons and one daughter. **Career:** Worked as a consultant, senior technical editor, proposal writer, and speech writer, Lockheed Aircraft Corp., Palo Alto, Sunnyvale, and Redlands, California, 1960-68; supervisor of technical publications and public relations, Ball Brothers Research Corp., Boulder, Colorado, 1968-71; assistant professor of English, University of Colorado, Boulder, 1971-72; assistant professor of English and writer-in-residence, University of Texas at El Paso, 1972-73; editor-in-chief, *Now in Mexico,* Mexico City, Mexico, 1973-74; translator and newscaster, XHRA-FM Radio, Guadalajara, Mexico, 1974-75; writer-in-residence and professor of English and creative writing, University of Santa Clara, Santa Clara, California, 1975-76; professor of literature of the Southwest, Texas A & I University, Laredo, 1976; freelance writer, Zacatecas, Mexico, 1976-77; professor of literature and composition, University of the Americas, Mexico City, Mexico, 1977-78; professor of English, American School Foundation, Mexico City, 1977-82; teacher of English as a second language, Centro de Estudios Universitarios, San Angel, Mexico, summer, 1977; Regents Lecturer and professor, University of California, Riverside, 1978; professor of English, School of Chemistry, Universidad Autónoma de México, Mexico City, 1978-79; instructor in English, Pan American University, Edinburg, Texas, 1982-84; professor of literature, 1985, professor of composition and advanced writing, 1985-86, California State University, Los Angeles; counselor at juvenile correctional institutions.

PUBLICATIONS

Novels

Pocho. 1959.
The Fifth Horseman: A Novel of the Mexican Revolution. 1974.
Clemente Chacón. 1984.

*

Critical Studies: "Contemporary Chicano Prose Fiction: A Chronicle of Misery" in *Latin American Literary Review*, vol. 1, no. 2, Spring 1973, and *Chicano Literature*, 1982, both by Charles M. Tatum; "An Interview with José Antonio Villarreal" by Francisco Jiménez in *Bilingual Review/Revista Bilingüe*, vol. 3, no. 1, January-April 1976; "*Pocho* as Literature" in *Aztlán*, vol. 7, no. 1, Spring 1976, and *Chicano Authors: Inquiry by Interview* both by Juan Bruce-Novoa, 1980; *The Identification and Analysis of Chicano Literature* edited by Francisco Jiménez, 1979; *Portraits of the Chicano Artist as a Young Man: The Making of the "Author" in Three Chicano Novels* edited by Arnold C. Vento, José Flores Peregrino, et al, 1979; "The Chicano Novel and the North American Narrative of Survival" by Joe D. Rodríguez in *Denver Quarterly*, vol. 16, no. 3, Fall 1981; *Chicano Literature: A Reference Guide* edited by Julio A. Martínez and Francisco A. Lomelí, 1985; "Villarreal's *Clemente Chacón* (1984): A Precursor's Accomodationist Dialogue" by Manuel de Jesús Hernández G. in *Bilingual Review/Revista Bilingüe*, vol. 16, no. 1, January-April 1991; "Language and Style in *Pocho*" by Inma Minoves Myers in *Bilingual Review/Revista Bilingüe*, vol. 16, no. 2-3, May-December 1991; *The Hispanic Condition: Reflections on Culture and Identity in America* by Ilan Stavans, 1994.

*　　*　　*

José Antonio Villarreal is among the founding fathers of Latino fiction in general, and Chicano literature in particular, in the United States. His novel *Pocho,* originally published in 1959, is widely considered a cornerstone of English-written Hispanic letters north of the Rio Grande. In a review in the *Nation,* John Bright found the book "notable not only for its own intrinsic virtues, but as a first voice from a people new in our midst who up to now have been almost silent." Early critics praised its style and structure, suggesting it was the very first fictional account of growing up Mexican American in the Southwest. But subsequent scholars have pointed out the book's flaws, describing it as a foundational work easily surpassed by later literary generations. Before Villarreal, scores of narrative memoirs by Chicanos and Anglo-Saxons dealt with the aftershock of the 1848 Guadalupe Hidalgo Treaty by which Mexico's Generalísimo Antonio López de Santa Ana sold Mexican territories including parts of California, Texas, Arizona, and New Mexico to the United States for $15 million. Writers also dealt with the Sleepy Lagoon and the Zoot Suit riots in California. In 1928, Felipe Alfau, a Spanish émigré, wrote a Pirandello-like work of fiction, *Locos: A Comedy of Gestures* in English. Although published in 1936, the novel was not widely read until the late 1980s; and thus Villarreal stands as the writer who opened up the door to Latino fiction in the United States. However, since the beginning, his readership has been largely composed of non-Hispanics and academic specialists.

Widely reviewed in the late 1950s and then more or less forgotten until its paperback reprint several decades later, *Pocho* is unquestionably a bildungsroman. ("Pocho" is a term used north of the Rio Grande to describe Mexican Americans.) At center stage is Richard Rubio, a young second-generation Mexican American in California during the 1930s. Richard faces a number of sexual, emotional, and intellectual challenges as he tries to discover his role as an American citizen of Mexican descent. Villarreal begins the story by offering an unrelated panoramic view of the Mexican Revolution in which Richard's father, inclined to macho tantrums, fought and from which he is forced to escape to survive. A book-ish adolescent, Richard struggles to understand his father's idiosyncratic behavior, which he compulsively idealizes. In a milieu in which women are increasingly asking to be respected as equals, Richard's mother, apparently better suited to life in a non-Hispanic environment, finally throws her womanizing and abusive husband out of the house and asks for Richard's support, which he reluctantly gives.

As Charles M. Tatum and others have suggested, Richard is not an altogether convincing character, especially in his boyhood philosophical musings. He seems to have an intellectual maturity that is well beyond his years. The novel also feels unbalanced. The first segment on the Mexican Revolution has little bearing to the rest of the narrative, and the end, in which Richard must decide between an education and the army, is abrupt. Ultimately, the protagonist and the novel fail to awaken the reader's sympathy and become unmemorable creations.

Villarreal is also the author of other novels less important in nature, tone, and impact. *The Fifth Horseman,* which stands as the background for *Pocho* and seems predictable and disengaging, focuses on the Mexican Revolution, an armed struggle in which the writer's father was active before emigrating to the United States. Its protagonist is Heraclio Inés, an exploited *peón* who joins Pancho Villa's army and eventually grows disenchanted. In an introduction to the work, the critic Luis Leal talks about the novel's literary antecedents, relating it to works by Juan Rulfo (*Pedro Páramo*), Carlos Fuentes (*The Death of Artemio Cruz*), Martín Luis Guzmán (*The Eagle and the Serpent*), Mariano Azuela (*The Underdogs*), and Agustín Yáñez (*On the Water's Edge*), among many others. Notwithstanding, Villarreal's book stands on its own in that it was published some seventy years after the peasants' struggle and, even more strikingly, unlike all precursors, it was originally written in English. In that sense it is closer to **John Dos Passos'** *The 42nd Parallel,* which includes a chapter ("The Camera Eyes, Newsreel XVII") dedicated to revolutionary Mexico, as well as Stirling Dickinson's *Death Is Incidental* and titles by Malcolm Wheeler-Nicholson, Carleton Beals, and Richard Carroll.

The author's third novel, *Clemente Chacón,* standing as a possible sequel or extremity to *Pocho,* follows a young Mexican who becomes successful as a businessman in the United States. While it attracted little attention when published in 1984, critics like Tomás Vallejos claim it is Villarreal's most accomplished work of fiction, with a display of characters who are, though not quite noteworthy, at least better-rounded.

Villarreal's importance as a Latino writer is double-faceted. First, like **Rolando Hinojosa-Smith**, the Chicano author of *Becky and Her Friends,* Villarreal was among the earliest writers to switch from Spanish to English to reach a wider audience. In an interview in *Contemporary Authors* he said, "As [a child] I knew only Spanish. It was not until my second year at school that I began to write and converse in English, and by the fifth grade, although I read and wrote in Spanish and spoke Spanish exclusively within our home, the idiom had become my second language. By then I knew that I wished to be a writer and attempted to write vignettes about my people. When I was perhaps thirteen years old, I realized that the non-Mexican population in my country did not know about us, did not know we existed, had no idea that we could be part of the mainstream of America and contribute to what I believe is the melting pot. I resolved then that I would write about my people. I wished that the American public would know of us. I believed, and still do, that I could best accomplish this through fiction."

Second, Villarreal opened up a new narrative field by introducing a distinctly Mexican-American perspective. Shortly after *Pocho* appeared, **John Rechy**'s explosive *City of Night* about gays, hustlers and Mexican Americans in the border region appeared, followed by Richard Vásquez's epic *Chicano,* and **Tomás Rivera**'s *y no se lo tragó la tierra/And the Earth Did Not Part.* And yet subsequent Latino, and particularly Chicano, authors in the United States have not looked at Villarreal for inspiration. Successors like Richard Rodríguez, **Sandra Cisneros**, Julia Alvarez, **Gary Soto**, and others have found affinities in other minority figures, often seeing *Pocho* as a traditional work of fiction by a boring realist. Many have not even read his work. In Mexico where Villarreal lived for some time, he is totally unknown because his work never was translated into Spanish, which means his significance and literary standing remain the sole property of U.S. scholars and researchers.

—Ilan Stavans

VOGEL, Paula (Anne)

Born: Washington, D.C., 16 November 1951. **Education:** Bryn Mawr College, Pennsylvania, 1969-72; Catholic University, Washington, D.C., 1972-74, B.A. 1974; Cornell University, Ithaca, New York, 1974-77, A.B.D. **Family:** Domestic partner Anne Fausto-Sterling beginning 1989. **Career:** Lecturer in women's studies and theater, Cornell University, Ithaca, New York, 1977-82; artistic director, Theater with Teeth, New York, 1982-85; production supervisor, theater on film and tape, Lincoln Center, New York, 1983-85; professor and director of graduate playwriting program, 1984-99 and professor-at-large, 1999-2000, Brown University, Providence, Rhode Island. **Awards:** Heerbes-McCalmon award, 1975, 1976; American College Theatre Festival award, 1976; Samuel French award, 1976; American National Theatre and Academy-West award, 1977; National Endowment for the Arts fellowship, 1980, 1991; MacDowell Colony, 1981, 1989; Bunting fellowship, 1990; Yaddo fellowship, 1992; McKnight fellowship, 1992; Bellagio fellowship, 1992; AT&T award, 1992; Governor's Award for the Arts, 1992; Obie award, 1992, 1997; Guggenheim fellow, 1995; Lucille Lortel award, 1997; Drama Desk Outer Critics Circle award, 1997; New York Drama Critics award, 1997; George and Elizabeth Morton award, 1997; The Fund for New American Plays, 1997; Robert Chesley Award in Playwrighting, 1997; Pew Charitable Trust Senior Residency award, 1997; Rhode Island Pell Award in the Arts, 1998; Pulitzer prize, for drama, 1998, for *How I Learned to Drive.* **Member:** New Dramatists. **Residence:** Providence, Rhode Island.

PUBLICATIONS

Plays

Meg (produced 1977). 1977.
The Last Pat Epstein Show Before the Reruns (produced 1979).
Desdemona (produced 1979). 1995.
Bertha in Blue (produced 1981).
The Oldest Profession (produced 1981).
And Baby Makes Seven (produced 1986).

The Baltimore Waltz (produced 1992).1992.
Hot 'n' Throbbing (produced 1992).
The Baltimore Waltz and Other Plays. 1997.
The Mineola Twins (produced 1996). 1997.
How I Learned to Drive (produced 1997). 1997.
The Mammary Plays (includes *The Mineola Twins; How I Learned to Drive*) . 1998.

Screenplays: *The Unmasking of O,* 1997; *The Oldest Profession,* 1999.

Television Plays: *On Common Ground,* 1999.

*

Critical Studies: "Time to Laugh" by Kathy Sova, in *American Theatre,* February 1997.

*   *   *

Paula Vogel is perhaps best defined as a modern American feminist/lesbian playwright with an incisive eye for contemporary social issues. This contemporaneity is combined with a unique voice for exposing both the ridiculous and tragic elements within her characters and society. The emphasis upon the tragicomic elements of modern American existence is clear in *How I Learned to Drive,* Vogel's 1997 Pulitzer Prize-winning drama. Here, sexual abuse and pedophilia are refracted through the testimony of the victim, Li'l Bit, and the corrupter, her Uncle Peck. In Vogel's play these characters are never stereotypical; rather, they are nuanced, humorous, and vulnerable. Li'l Bit is not the prototype of the youthful victim of unwanted amorous advances but is instead a flirtatious, tacitly complicit partner in the sexual exchange. And while Vogel never attempts to defend Peck's predatory actions, her depiction of him is entirely believable, even-handed, and strangely sympathetic. As a result, his tragic fall at the play's conclusion is presented as the inevitable self-destruction of a charming, yet entirely weak, individual.

While focusing upon such politically volatile topics as domestic violence and abortion, Paula Vogel maintains that "my writing isn't guided by issues . . . I only write about things that directly impact my life. . . . People see *Baltimore Waltz* as a play about AIDS, I see it as a way of talking to my dead brother." *The Baltimore Waltz* (1991) is an imaginary memory play, a funny yet deeply moving travelogue of a journey with her brother. Vogel has said, "My plays are reflecting at a deeper level a . . . sense of yearning and mourning," and *The Baltimore Waltz* is the clearest example of these emotions in Vogel's oeuvre. The play imagines a European tour, but this holiday is eventually revealed to be only a fantasy. In fact, the action never ventures from the hospital bedside of the dying man. *The Baltimore Waltz* pays homage to grief, while also emphasizing the realization that with loss comes redemption. And while concentrating upon individual loss, Vogel succeeds in making the spiritual rewards of love, loss, and despair seem both universal and particular.

In her more comic and ribald plays Vogel continues her exploration of life's confusions, contradictions, and near-tragic absurdities. In *The Mineola Twins* (1997) she creates a comic book-like milieu for a satirical examination of the American suburban landscape since the Eisenhower years. Through the characters of twin sisters from Mineola, Long Island—Myrna (described in Vogel's text as "the 'good' twin. Stacked.") and Myra ("the 'evil' twin. Identical to Myrna, except in the chestal area.")—Vogel confronts issues of the masculine gaze, the suburban mentality, political activism, Christian fundamentalism, and abortion rights, all in a tone that the playwright advises her performers should be perceived as "a constant state of hormonal excitement."

In *Desdemona: A Play About a Handkerchief* (1979) Vogel populates her stage exclusively with the female characters from Shakespeare's *Othello*—Desdemona, Emilia, and Bianca—in order to fashion a broad, farcical examination of female sexuality. Vogel writes the play in a manner reminiscent of one of Bertolt Brecht's intercalary scenes, those acting exercises Brecht created to provide imaginary given circumstances before such Shakespearean moments as the Romeo and Juliet balcony scene or Hamlet's "to be or not to be" soliloquy. In *Desdemona: A Play About a Handkerchief*, the bawdy and farcical events conclude just as Shakespeare's play turns tragic, and Desdemona prepares herself for bed, awaiting Othello's fateful arrival. Yet the most significant difference between Vogel's play and Shakespeare's is that Vogel's Desdemona is in fact exactly what the imagination of Shakespeare's Othello most fears. Vogel's Desdemona is a sensuous young libertine, one who takes advantage of her husband's trust in order to escape from the malaise of her May-December marriage and indulge in clandestine liaisons of pleasure and passion. Her murder by her husband will thus be the result of the young woman's audacity in defying society's norms by openly flouting her sexuality. This is a repeated emphasis in Vogel's work: the subversion of that theatrical and literary tradition in which women are penalized for not behaving according to the role that society has dictated for them.

Vogel has acknowledged the impact upon her work of three contemporary playwrights: **John Guare**, **Maria Irene Fornes**, and Caryl Churchill. Like those seminal dramatists, Vogel has achieved her success by uncovering a darker, more sinister world just below the surface of reality, in which confusion and hysteria are liable to reign but in which characters and themes are mocked, celebrated, exploited, and occasionally liberated.

—Arthur Horowitz

VONNEGUT, Kurt, Jr.

Born: Indianapolis, Indiana, 11 November 1922. **Education:** Cornell University, Ithaca, New York, 1940-42, 1945; Carnegie Institute, Pittsburgh, 1943; University of Chicago, 1945-47, M.A. in anthropology 1971. **Military Service:** Served in the U.S. Army Infantry, 1942-45: purple heart. **Family:** Married 1) Jane Marie Cox in 1945 (divorced 1979); one son, two daughters, and three adopted sons; 2) Jill Krementz in 1979. **Career:** Police reporter, Chicago City News Bureau, 1946; public relations writer, General Electric Company, Schenectady, New York, 1947-51; since 1951, free-lance writer; after 1965, teacher, Hopefield School, Sandwich, Massachusetts. Visiting lecturer, writers workshop, University of Iowa, Iowa City, 1965-67, and Harvard University, Cambridge, Massachusetts, 1970-71; visiting professor, City University, New York, 1973-74. **Awards:** Guggenheim fellowship, 1967; American Academy grant, 1970. Litt.D.: Hobart and William Smith Colleges, Geneva, New York, 1974. **Member:** American Academy, 1973, and vice president, 1975. **Residence:** New York City.

PUBLICATIONS

Fiction

Player Piano. 1952; as *Utopia 14*, 1954.
The Sirens of Titan. 1959.
Canary in a Cat House (stories). 1961.
Mother Night. 1962.
Cat's Cradle. 1963.
God Bless You, Mr. Rosewater; or, Pearls before Swine. 1965.
Welcome to the Monkey House: A Collection of Short Works. 1968.
Slaughterhouse-Five; or, The Children's Crusade. 1969.
Breakfast of Champions; or, Goodbye, Blue Monday. 1973.
Slapstick; or, Lonesome No More! 1973.
Jailbird. 1979.
Deadeye Dick. 1982.
Galapagos. 1985.
Bluebeard. 1987.
Hocus Pocus; or, What's the Hurry, Son? 1990.
Timequake. 1993.
Bagombo Snuff Box: Uncollected Short Fiction. 1999.

Plays

Happy Birthday, Wanda June (as *Penelope,* produced 1960; revised version, as *Happy Birthday, Wanda June,* produced 1970). 1970.
The Very First Christmas Morning, in *Better Homes and Gardens,* December 1962.
Between Time and Timbuktu; or, Prometheus-5: A Space Fantasy (televised 1972; produced 1976). 1972.
Fortitude, in *Wampeters, Foma, and Granfalloons,* 1974.
Timesteps (produced 1979).
God Bless You, Mr. Rosewater, from his own novel (produced 1979).
The Lie, edited by Vaughn McBride. 1992.
Miss Temptation. 1993.
Slaughter-house-Five. 1996.

Television Play: *Between Time and Timbuktu,* 1972.

Other

Wampeters, Foma, and Granfalloons: Opinions. 1974.
Sun Moon Star. 1980.
Palm Sunday: An Autobiographical Collage. 1981.
Nothing Is Lost Save Honor: Two Essays. 1984.
Conversations with Kurt Vonnegut, edited by William Rodney Allen. 1988.
Who Am I This Time?: For Romeos and Juliets. 1990(?).
Fates Worse Than Death: An Autobiographical Collage of the 1980s. 1991.

*

Bibliography: *Vonnegut: A Descriptive Bibliography and Annotated Secondary Checklist* by Asa B. Pieratt, Jr., and Jerome Klinkowitz, 1974.

Critical Studies: *Vonnegut* by Peter J. Reed, 1972; *Vonnegut: Fantasist of Fire and Ice* by David H. Goldsmith, 1972; *The Vonnegut Statement* edited by Jerome Klinkowitz and John Somer,

1973, *Vonnegut in America: An Introduction to the Life and Work of Kurt Vonnegut* edited by Klinkowitz and Donald L. Lawler, 1977, and *Kurt Vonnegut* by Klinkowitz, 1982; *Vonnegut* by Stanley Schatt, 1976; *Kurt Vonnegut* by James Lundquist, 1977; *Vonnegut: A Preface to His Novels* by Richard Giannone, 1977; *Vonnegut: The Gospel from Outer Space* by Clark Mayo, 1977; *Vonnegut's Duty-Dance with Death: Theme and Structure in Slaughterhouse-Five* by Monica Loeb, 1979; *Happy Birthday, Kurt Vonnegut: A Festschrift* edited by Jill Krementz and others, 1982; *Critical Essays on Kurt Vonnegut* edited by Robert Merrill, 1990; *Understanding Kurt Vonnegut* by William Rodney Allen, 1991; *The Survivor in Contemporary American Fiction: Saul Bellow, Bernard Malamud, John Updike, Kurt Vonnegut, Jr.* by Sukhbir Singh, 1991; *The Critical Responses to Kurt Vonnegut,* edited by Leonard Mustazza, 1994; *Chaos, Theory, and the Interpretation of Literary Texts: The Case of Kurt Vonnegut* by Kevin A. Boon, 1997; *The Short Fiction of Kurt Vonnegut* by Peter J. Reed, 1997; *Wholeness Restored: Love of Symmetry As a Shaping Force in the Writings of Henry James, Kurt Vonnegut, Samuel Butler, and Raymond Chandler* by Ralf Norrman, 1998.

*   *   *

In *Slaughterhouse-Five,* Kurt Vonnegut summarizes a science-fiction novel by Kilgore Trout in which a time traveler goes back to the Crucifixion and, with a stethoscope, listens to Christ's heart. The Savior, alas, is dead, stone dead. Trout is a character in several of Vonnegut's books, but his novel might well have been written by Vonnegut, for, like it, Vonnegut's novels satirically portray a world in which there is no hope, no purpose, no salvation for the universe. Vonnegut is a moralist but one who begins with the premise that morality, like civilization, merely expresses wishful thinking and chance. In this universe, divine intention is only imagined; it does not really exist.

Vonnegut's novels describe a deterministic, mechanistic world— a world of cause and effect with no overriding purpose or goal. The major novels and other works center on innocents like Billy Pilgrim (in *Slaughterhouse-Five*) and Dwayne Hoover (in *Breakfast of Champions*) who are victims both of other people, and,

more particularly, of an inability to meaningfully affect their own lives. For Vonnegut, civilization's problem is not that people don't, strictly speaking, take responsibility for their lives, but that they can't. *Breakfast of Champions* suggests that art offers at least temporary salvation, but it is more characteristic of Vonnegut's books to suggest that if there is any salvation for men, it lies in their innocence or their stupidity—and consequently their inability to understand how totally they are the product of circumstance, not free will.

Vonnegut's early reputation was largely among readers of science fiction. His books emphasize the obvious, if often overlooked, fact that the elaborate theoretical structures devised by modern technology and science have important moral implications. Since these structures tend to be entirely deterministic, they suggest that objective views of the universe have no room for chance or inspiration: everything has its immediate, ascertainable cause. True moral choice is, therefore, impossible.

In *Slapstick* Vonnegut argues that, at the least, "common decency" should characterize human relations. This conclusion may make his bleak moral view palatable to some readers, but it is also deeply sentimental. Vonnegut can appear sentimental even in his best work, but it may be this, together with his comic sense, that allows his work to escape the bitterness, if not the resignation, that his bleak view of experience would encourage.

Vonnegut's fiction has often centered on "privileged" Americans—i.e., Americans with the right genealogy, connections, or opportunities. But success in Vonnegut's world is without traditional moral dimensions, of course, and even Walter F. Starbuck, the "jailbird" in the novel of that name, eventually acquires respectability. What can one do with such a world? Vonnegut solves that problem in *Deadeye Dick* with a nuclear explosion. However much he may plead for "common decency," one senses a remorseless nihilism throughout his fiction. Vonnegut's *Galapagos* argues in effect that the universe is too often shaped by chance, sheer randomness, for anyone seriously to accept Darwin's orderly, logical conception of evolution, the survival of the fittest. In *Galapagos* the fittest never survive, and the book is finally as bleak and resigned as any Vonnegut has published.

—Edward Halsey Foster

WALKER, Alice (Malsenior)

Born: Eatonton, Georgia, 9 February 1944. **Education:** Spelman College, Atlanta, 1961-63; Sarah Lawrence College, Bronxville, New York, 1963-65, B.A. 1965. **Family:** Married Melvyn R. Leventhal in 1967 (divorced 1976); one daughter. **Career:** Voter registration and Head Start program worker, Mississippi, and with New York City Department of Welfare, mid-1960s; teacher, Jackson State College, 1968-69, and Tougaloo College, 1970-71, both Mississippi; lecturer, Wellesley College, Cambridge, Massachusetts, 1972-73, and University of Massachusetts, Boston, 1972-73; associate professor of English, Yale University, New Haven, Connecticut, after 1977; Fannie Hurst Professor, Brandeis University, Waltham, Massachusetts, Fall 1982. Distinguished writer, University of California, Berkeley, Spring 1982. Cofounder and publisher, Wild Trees Press, Navarro, California, 1984-88. **Awards:** Bread Loaf Writers Conference scholarship, 1966; *American Scholar* prize, for essay, 1967; Merrill fellowship, 1967; MacDowell fellowship, 1967, 1977; Radcliffe Institute fellowship, 1971; Lillian Smith award, for poetry, 1973; American Academy Rosenthal award, 1974; National Endowment for the Arts grant, 1977; Guggenheim grant, 1978; American Book award, 1983; Pulitzer prize, 1983; O. Henry award, 1986; Langston Hughes award, 1989; Nora Astorga Leadership award, 1989; Fred Cody award for lifetime achievement, Bay Area Book Reviewers Association, 1990; Freedom to write award, PEN West, 1990; California Governor's Arts award, 1994; Literary Ambassador award, University of Oklahoma Center for Poets and Writers, 1998. Ph.D.: Russell Sage College, Troy, New York, 1972. D.H.L.: University of Massachusetts, Amherst, 1983. **Residence:** San Francisco.

PUBLICATIONS

Novels

The Third Life of Grange Copeland. 1970.
Meridian. 1976.
The Color Purple. 1982.
The Temple of My Familiar. 1989.
Possessing the Secret of Joy. 1992.
Everyday Use. 1994.
By the Light of My Father's Smile: A Story of Requited Love, Crossing Over, and the Sexual Healing of the Soul. 1998.

Poetry

Once. 1968.
Five Poems. 1972.
Revolutionary Petunias and Other Poems. 1973.
Good Night, Willie Lee, I'll See You in the Morning. 1979.
Horses Make a Landscape Look More Beautiful. 1984.
Her Blue Body Everything We Know: Earthling Poems 1965-1990. 1991.

Short Stories

In Love and Trouble: Stories of Black Women. 1973.
You Can't Keep a Good Woman Down. 1981.
The Complete Stories. 1995.

Other

Langston Hughes, American Poet (biography for children). 1974.
In Search of Our Mothers' Gardens: Womanist Prose. 1983.
To Hell with Dying (for children), illustrated by Catherine Deeter. 1988.
Living by the Word: Selected Writings 1973-1987. 1988.
Finding the Green Stone (for children), illustrated by Catherine Deeter. 1991.
Warrior Marks: Female Genital Mutilation and the Sexual Blinding of Women. 1993.
Alice Walker Banned. 1996.
Anything We Love Can Be Saved: A Writer's Activism. 1997.

Editor, *I Love Myself When I am Laughing . . . and Then Again When I Am Looking Mean and Impressive: A Zora Neale Hurston Reader.* 1979.
Editor, *The Same River Twice: Honoring the Difficult: A Meditation of Life, Spirit, Art, and the Making of the Film "The Color Purple," Ten Years Later.* 1996.

*

Bibliography: *Walker: An Annotated Bibliography 1968-1986* by Louis H. Pratt and Darnell D. Pratt, 1988; *Walker: An Annotated Bibliography 1968-1986* by Erma Davis Banks and Keith Byerman, 1989.

Critical Studies: *Callaloo* (special Walker issue), Spring 1989; "Walker: The Achievement of the Short Fiction" by Alice Hall Petry, in *Modern Language Studies,* Winter 1989; "Tradition in Walker's 'To Hell with Dying'" by Michael Hollister, in *Studies in Short Fiction,* vol. 21, Winter 1989; *Alice Walker's The Color Purple* by Dina Benevol, 1995; *Alice Walker* by Caroline Evensen Lazo, 1999; *Critical Essays on Alice Walker,* edited by Ikenna Dieke, 1999.

*   *   *

Alice Walker's poems are direct and exuberant, but they are a minor achievement in comparison with her prose. Her main impulse in writing fiction, she has said, is to record history—"and the history of my family, like that of all black Southerners, is one of dispossession."

Dispossession, emotional and material, is the theme of her first novel, *The Third Life of Grange Copeland.* Grange, in his "first life," is brutalized by his labors in the field and by the humiliation of his deference to the white overseer. He abandons his son, Brownfield, listlessly named after the autumn colors of the Georgia cotton fields, and Brownfield becomes, in his turn, a sadistic brute. Grange spends his "second life" in New York and returns to spend his "third life" caring for Brownfield's youngest daughter Ruth, whom he can ultimately protect only by murdering Brownfield, "a beast Grange himself had created." The weakness of the novel is that Grange's crucial spiritual regeneration is unconvincing; its strength is in its vivid evocation of the Georgia countryside and of the intricate miseries of the suppression of hope and love.

Meridian, published in 1976, is the fragmented, unchronological story of Meridian Hill and her political and spiritual development, as she moves through marriage and motherhood at seventeen, a repressive college education, and traumatic experiences as a civil rights worker, into something approaching sainthood. It is also the story of Lynne Rabinowitz, a white girl from the North, married to and rejected by Meridian's black civil rights colleague Truman Held. Although Lynne is satirized for her self-indulgent reaction to the life of Southern blacks as "the same weepy miracle that Art always was for her," she is presented with great sympathy, and is a far more developed character than Truman. *Meridian* is a series of brilliant episodes rather than a unified whole.

The Color Purple (1982) is told through the letters of two black sisters, Celie and Nettie. Nettie's letters, written from Africa where she is a missionary, are tedious and banal, but Celie's letters, at first poignant in their poverty of expression, become marvelously rich as she gradually struggles against the effects of her stepfather's cruelty and against her husband's indictment: "You black, you pore, you ugly, you a woman . . . you nothing at all." The color purple comes to stand for Celie's affirmation of beauty and happiness; as Shug Avery, the woman who becomes her friend and lover, tells her: "I think it pisses God off if you walk by the color purple in a field somewhere and don't notice it." The optimism of the story's resolution, however, still seems contrived and inconsistent, and Sofia, a minor, tragic, figure, is the most impressive character in the novel.

Walker's art is peculiarly suited to the short story. Outstanding are "Everyday Use" and "Strong Horse Tea" from *In Love and Trouble* and "Nineteen Fifty-Five" and "The Abortion" from *You Can't Keep a Good Woman Down.* "Everyday Use" is narrated by the mother of Dee, who has become a sophisticated Black Muslim, and Maggie, her awkward and ignorant sister. The story turns on the old family quilts, which Dee wants to hang up to display her "heritage" and which, as she complains, Maggie would put to "everyday use." The mother, in a rare surge of feeling for Maggie, gives her the quilts, and Dee drives angrily away. "Strong Horse Tea" describes the pathetic and futile attempts of a poor black woman to save the life of her baby boy. Like "Everyday Use," its power is in the subtle economy of its rapidly shifting perspectives.

"The Abortion" is the sharp, witty account of a complex tangle of politics, sexuality, and sentimentality. "Nineteen Fifty-Five" is often considered Walker's best story. It is narrated by an old blues singer, Gracie Mae Still, who sells one of her songs to Traynor, a character obviously based on Elvis Presley. Over the years, Traynor becomes more and more oppressed by his failure to understand the song, even though he has made it a huge commercial success. He and Gracie Mae also get fatter and fatter. Her bulk is hilariously described, but eventually she realizes that "my fat is the hurt I don't admit, not even to myself." The story ends with Traynor's televised funeral, his ignorantly blubbering fans, and Gracie Mae's comment: "One day this is going to be a pitiful country, I thought."

Some of Walker's stories in *You Can't Keep a Good Woman Down*—"Coming Apart," for example—are very close to being essays, and her book of essays, *In Search of Our Mothers' Gardens,* contains many narratives, including several pieces of auto-

biography. The essays are lively, opinionated, and demonstrate her generous appreciation of other writers. Her essay collections *Living by the Word: Selected Writings 1973-1987* (1988), *The Same River Twice: Honoring the Difficult* (1996) (in which she discusses the film version of *The Color Purple*), and *Anything We Love Can Be Saved: A Writer's Activism* (1997) have contributed to Walker's rapidly accelerating prominence as a celebrity sage.

The novel *The Temple of My Familiar* (1989), described by Walker herself as "a romance of the last 500,000 years," is a complex fantasy that opens in social realism but soon becomes a polemic against every kind of tyranny from slavery to the hegemony of television. *Possessing the Secret of Joy* (1992) has a much narrower focus, concentrating its crusading ardor on a minutely detailed attack on the practice of female genital mutilation. Both these novels have narrative connections with *The Color Purple,* and indeed *Possessing the Secret of Joy* can be read almost as a sequel, but they have a didactic element that is far less prominent in Walker's earlier fiction. Her latest novel, *By the Light of My Father's Smile* (1998), is recognizably in this same tradition, but has a new playfulness, particularly on the topics of sex and life after death, which for Walker are closely associated.

Alice Walker is a figure of major contemporary importance whose work, like that of Toni Morrison, is celebrated not only for its artistic merit but for its part in establishing the central role of African American literature in American culture.

—Mary Condé

WALKER, Margaret (Abigail)

Born: Birmingham, Alabama, 7 July 1915. **Education:** Northwestern University in Evanston, Illinois, A.B. 1935; University of Iowa, M.A., 1940; Ph.D. 1965. **Family:** Married Firnist James Alexander in 1943 (deceased); two daughters and two sons. **Career:** Worked as a volunteer with the Works Progress Administration (WPA), 1934; employed for pay as a writer on the WPA Writer's Project in Chicago, 1939-1940s; taught English at Livingstone College, Salisbury, North Carolina, 1941-42 and 1945-46, West Virginia State College, Institute, West Virginia, 1942-43, and Jackson State College, Jackson, Mississippi, 1949-79; director of Institute for the Study of the History, Life, and Culture of Black Peoples, 1968; visiting professor in creative writing, Northwestern University, Chicago, spring 1969; staff member, Cape Cod Writers Conference, Craigville, Massachusetts, 1967 and 1969. **Awards:** Yale Series of Younger Poets award, 1942; Rosenthal fellowship, 1944; Ford fellowship for study at Yale University, 1954; Houghton Mifflin Literary fellowship, 1966; Fulbright fellowship, 1971; grant from National Endowment for the Humanities, 1972. D. Litt.: Northwestern University, 1974. D. Letters: Rust College, 1974. D. Fine Arts: Dennison University, 1974. D. Humane Letters: Morgan State University, 1976. **Died:** November 1998.

PUBLICATIONS

Collections

How I Wrote Jubilee and Other Essays on Life and Literature, edited by Maryemma Graham. 1989.

On Being Female, Black, and Free: Essays by Margaret Walker, 1932-1992. 1997.

Novels

Jubilee. 1965.

Poetry

For My People. 1942.
Ballad of the Free. 1966.
Prophets for a New Day. 1970.
October Journey. 1973.
For Farish Street Green. 1986.
Apparitions, with John Warner. 1987.
This Is My Century: New and Collected Poems. 1988.

Prose

A Poetic Equation: Conversations between Nikki Giovanni and Margaret Walker, with Nikki Giovanni. 1974; reprinted with new postscript, 1983.
How I Wrote Jubilee. 1977.
Richard Wright: Daemonic Genius. 1988.

*

Critical Studies: "Margaret Walker: Black Woman Writer of the South" by Joyce Pettis in *Southern Women Writers: The New Generation,* 1990; "From Uncle Tom's Cabin to Vyry's Kitchen: The Black Female Folk Tradition in Margaret Walker's *Jubilee*" by Charlotte Goodman in *Tradition and the Talents of Women,* 1991; "An Interview with Margaret Walker Alexander" by Kay Bonetti in *The Missouri-Review,* vol. 15, no. 1, 1992; *Womanist and Feminist Aesthetics: A Comparative Review* by Tuzyline Jita Allan, 1995; *Trumpeting a Fiery Sound: History and Folklore in Margaret Walker's Jubilee* by Jacqueline Miller Carmichael, 1998.

*   *   *

Margaret Walker's career as a writer was launched in 1942 with the publication of her first book of poems, *For My People.* Poet, novelist, essayist, literary scholar, and teacher, she has made a significant impact on American literature in general and African American literature in particular. *For My People* and the award-winning novel *Jubilee* are the primary publications on which Walker's literary reputation rests.

Walker's poems illustrate an indebtedness to Southern folk culture, particularly its oral tradition and the traditions of protest in the African American experience. Ten poems in *For My People* tell the deeds of black folk heroes, among them "Big John Henry" and "Bad-Man Stagolee," who actually lived, and "Molly Means," a fictional character who represents the African tradition of voodoo in the Southern community. Many of Walker's poems acknowledge the South as the poet's much-loved homeplace but not without recognition of its attendant racial hostility. "For My People," which has emerged as her signature poem, acknowledges the diversity of the black community brought together through its need for trenchant political and economical change. The image of children playing "in the clay and dust and sand of Alabama / backyards playing baptizing and preaching and doctor" is balanced by

"lost disinherited dispossessed, and happy / people filling the cabarets . . . and other people's pockets" in Chicago, New York, and New Orleans. For these and others, the last stanza proclaims, "Let a new earth rise," a sentiment that underscores other poems in the collection.

In addition to content, "For My People" is critically praised for its technical proficiency. It consists of nine stanzas of free verse marked by parallelism and paradox that depend on the tenth stanza for their completed idea. Its tone evokes the sound of black Southern pulpit rhetoric in an effective joining of content and form.

The latent rebellion that is recognizable in "For My People" is overt in *Prophets for a New Day* (1970), Walker's collection of twenty-two poems about the civil rights era. Comparisons between biblical prophets and leaders of the 1960s animate the fulfillment of prophecy and the expectation of change. Earlier revolutionaries and prophets such as Nat Turner, Gabriel Prosser, and Denmark Vesey are recognized in this volume alongside the new workers of the 1960s such as Goodman, Schwerner, and Chaney, killed in Mississippi in 1964.

Jubilee, the only novel in Walker's canon, has its genesis in the oral history communicated to the writer from her grandmother. As Walker has written in *How I Wrote Jubilee,* she structures the presentation of black slave life not only through family stories but also through years of extensive scholarly research in order "to undergird the oral tradition" and to produce a realistic depiction of that era. The novel loosely traces the growth of Vyry from childhood to womanhood against the panorama of antebellum years in Georgia, the Civil War strife, and resettlement during the Reconstruction era. Vyry falls in love with Randall Ware, through whom Walker treats the plight of the free black person in the South. Because the novel has an extensive cast of characters, some of them are necessarily presented as literary types. Walker's goal, however, is an authentic depiction of black folk culture during slavery, a goal she admirably achieves through the use of proverbs, songs, sermons, and folk healing in the daily life of the characters. Although other historical fiction by black authors preceded the publication of *Jubilee,* Walker's novel is distinguished by its development of the daily life and folklore of the black slave community.

Although Walker's fiction and poetry reflect her Southern roots, she lived in Chicago during the Depression era, where she worked briefly for the Works Progress Administration (WPA). She met fledgling writer **Richard Wright** there, and they became literary cohorts. Their friendship (irreparably damaged through misunderstanding) and Walker's aid in assisting Wright in some of the settings of his famous novel *Native Son* are part of the motivation for *Richard Wright: Daemonic Genius,* a critical portrait of both the man and his fiction. In this book, as in her critical essays, Walker demonstrates her expertise as a trained scholar. She analyzes Wright's works while simultaneously juxtaposing the author and his cultural milieu with his compositions. She also discusses Wright within American and African American literary traditions. The chronological structure of the study begins with Wright's developmental years in Mississippi from 1908 to 1927, which, Walker says, were "a veritable hell," and defines each significant period in his life—the ten years in Chicago, New York, and Paris, and his final two years, 1958 to 1960.

This Is My Century: New and Collected Poems contains Walker's previously published volumes of poetry along with new poems written after her retirement. Like many of the earlier compositions, these poems reflect her response to events and persons of history. She acknowledges the epoch in which she has come of age and the events that have shaped her, and she pays homage in several poems to influential world thinkers, such as Albert Einstein, Sigmund Freud, Karl Marx, Soren Kierkegaard, **W. E. B. Du Bois**, Marcus Garvey, Martin Luther King, Jr., **Frederick Douglass**, and Malcolm X. This volume places the private history of the poet within the wider historical context of its time, encountering many undesirable situations expressed through poems such as "Inflation Blues," "Money, Honey, Money," "Birmingham, 1963," and "I Hear a Rumbling." Walker does not sugarcoat the century in which the civil rights struggle occurred, with its brutality and deaths, and in which advance and defeat in the black community have seemingly counterbalanced each other.

Two collections of essays were published before Walker's death in November 1998. *How I Wrote Jubilee and Other Essays on Life and Literature* (1990) reprints the author's account of how *Jubilee* occupied her imagination for thirty years and includes texts of numerous speeches and essays. *On Being Female, Black, and Free* (1997), a compilation of essays spanning the years 1932 to 1992, is particularly insightful for the author's thoughts about being a black, politically conscious woman and author whose experiences spanned segregation, the civil rights era, and its aftermath. These two collections affirm Walker's considerable abilities as thinker, activist, and essayist.

For My People and *Jubilee* are the cornerstones of Walker's canon. Each adds a redirective component to its genre. In assessing Walker, it is significant to note that her writing career has been but one part of her professional existence. She eloquently notes the juggling dexterity required in balancing college teaching, motherhood, research, and creative writing and being black and female in the essay "On Being Black, Female, and Free." The black female writer "must arm herself with a fool's courage, foolhardiness, and serious purpose and dedication to the art of writing . . . because the odds are always against her." Walker's successes confirm her transcendence of such odds. Perhaps her successes may be attributed to her ability to look beyond narrow selfish concerns to the greater issues of the African American community in its interaction with the world.

—Joyce Pettis

WALLACE, Lew(is)

Born: Brookville, Indiana, 10 April 1827; moved with his family to Indianapolis, 1837. **Education:** Studied law in his father's office in Indianapolis: admitted to Indiana bar, 1849. **Military Service:** Raised a company, and served as a 2nd lieutenant in the U.S. Army Infantry in the Mexican War, 1846-47; appointed Adjutant General of Indiana at the beginning of the Civil War: served as a colonel in the 11th Indiana Volunteers; promoted to Brigadier general, 1861, and major general, 1862; prepared the defense of Cincinnati, 1863; given command of the Middle Division and VIII Army Corps, with headquarters at Baltimore, 1863; fought battle of Monocracy, and saved Washington, D.C., from capture, 1864; member of the court that tried Lincoln's assassins, and president of the court that tried the commandant of the Andersonville prison; mustered out, 1865. **Family:** Married Susan Arnold Elston in 1852. **Career:** Edited a free soil paper in Indianapolis, 1848; lawyer in Indianapolis, 1849; moved to Covington, 1850: prosecut-

ing attorney, 1850-53; moved to Crawfordsville, 1853; member, Indiana State Senate, 1856; returned to Crawfordsville and his law practice after the Civil War; Republican candidate for an Indiana seat in the U.S. House of Representatives, 1870; writer from 1870, also an illustrator; Governor of the New Mexico Territory, 1878-81; U.S. Minister to Turkey, 1881-85, then returned to Crawfordsville. **Died:** 15 February 1905.

PUBLICATIONS

Fiction

The Fair God; or, The Lust of the 'Tzins: A Tale of the Conquest of Mexico. 1873.
Ben-Hur: A Tale of the Christ. 1880.
The Boyhood of Christ. 1888.
The Prince of India; or, Why Constantinople Fell. 1893.

Play

Commodus. 1876.

Poetry

The Wooing of Malkatoon, Commodus. 1898.

Other

Life of General Ben Harrison. 1888.
An Autobiography. 2 vols., 1906.
Smoke, Sound, and Fury: The Civil War Memoirs of Major-General Lew Wallace, U.S. Volunteers. 1998.

Editor, *Famous Paintings of the World.* 1894.

*

Critical Studies: *"Ben-Hur" Wallace* by Irving McKee, 1947; *Wallace: Militant Romantic* by Robert E. and Katharine M. Morsberger, 1980; "'My God, Did I Set All of This in Motion?': General Lew Wallace and Ben-Hur" by Lee Scott Theisen, in *Journal of Popular Culture,* Fall 1984; *From Ben-Hur to Sister Carrie: Remembering the Lives and Works of Five Indiana Authors* by Barbara Olenyik Morrow, 1995; *Realism and Spectacle in Ben-Hur* (dissertation) by Theodore Hoyet, 1995.

*   *   *

Though famous in his day as a soldier, governor, lawyer, and diplomat, Lew Wallace is mainly remembered as the author of *Ben-Hur,* one of the three best-selling American novels of the nineteenth century. Indeed, the novel is known by many who could not name the author. *Ben-Hur* occupies a unique place in American cultural history; subtitled "A Tale of the Christ," it was the first and in some cases the only novel to be read by many puritanical fundamentalists who considered other fiction to be a sinful and idle waste of time. Dramatized in 1899 by William Young, *Ben-Hur* was an immense success for 20 years as a stage spectacle complete with chariot race run on treadmills. The play further broke down puritan inhibitions by introducing many to the theater, and a colossal 1925 film version accomplished the same feat for the movies. Wallace wrote two other successful historical novels, *The Fair God* and *The Prince of India;* a blank verse drama, *Commodus;* a long narrative poem, *The Wooing of Malkatoon,* about the founder of the Ottoman Empire; a campaign biography of Benjamin Harrison; an account of Fort Donelson for *Battles and Leaders of the Civil War;* and an autobiography completed by his wife after his death in 1905.

Though the reading public considered *Ben-Hur* a supplement to sacred scripture and went to the dramatizations as to a passion play, Wallace was not a churchgoer, and the novel is closer in spirit to Jacobean revenge tragedy than to the New Testament. Wallace claimed, however, that he wrote it in part to refute the agnosticism of Robert Ingersol, and that during its composition he became convinced of the divinity of Jesus. All his novels deal with the clash of religions and cultures: *The Fair God* with the conflict of Aztecs and Catholic conquistadors; *The Prince of India* with Moslem and Christian rivals during the fall of Constantinople; and *Ben-Hur* with Jewish, pagan Roman, and Christian adversaries. Wallace's heroes are an Aztec prince, a prince of Judea, and a Turkish Sultan—all unusual for a nineteenth-century Anglo-Saxon to champion. A thorough researcher and a careful stylist, Wallace blended exotic romanticism with realistic detail. Though his own life was as dramatic as any of his fiction, he felt himself in some ways a failure and wrote about the romantic past as an escape from the routine of the law, the army, and political and diplomatic posts.

—Robert E. and Katharine M. Morsberger

WALLACE, Naomi

Born: Prospect, Kentucky, 17 August 1960. **Education:** Hampshire College, Amherst, Massachusetts, B.A. in 1982; University of Iowa, M.F.A. in poetry 1986; M.F.A. in playwrighting 1993. **Family:** Three children. **Career:** Graduate instructor, University of Iowa, 1991-93; playwright-in-residence, Illinois State University, Norman, Illinois, fall, 1994; guest speaker, Yale University, 1994; invited speaker, Grinnell College, 1995. **Awards:** Eugene O'Neill National Playwright's Festival, 1989; *The Nation's* Discovery award for poetry, 1990; Jane Chamber's student playwrighting award, 1992; winner, National Poetry competition, 1993; British National Poetry Competition, 1994; Mobil playwrighting award, 1994; Susan Smith Blackburn Award, 1995, 1996; AT&T award for new plays, 1996; fellowship of southern writers Bryan family award for playwrighting, 1996; Kesselring prize for drama, 1996; Obie award, for best play, 1997.

Publications

Plays

In the Fields of Aceldama (produced 1991).
The War Boys (produced 1993).
The Fish Story. In *Monologues by Women for Women,* edited by T. Haring-Smith, Heinemann Press, 1994.
The Girl Who Fell through a Hole in Her Sweater, with Bruce McLeod (for children; produced 1994).
In the Heart of America (produced 1994). In *Staging Gay Lives: An Anthology of Gay Male Theater,* edited by John Clum, 1995; in *American Theater,* March 1995.

Slaughter City (produced 1994). 1996.
One Flea Spare (produced 1995). 1997.
Birdy (produced 1996). 1997.
Collected Plays. 1997.
The Testle at Pope Lick Creek (produced 1998).

Screenplay: *Lawn Dogs,* 1998.

Poetry

To Dance a Stony Field. 1995.

*

Critical Studies: "Forging Links" by John Istel, in *American Theatre,* March 1995, p. 26.

*   *   *

Naomi Wallace's plays use a brutal, poetic lyricism and a heightened, sometimes surreal theatricality to expose the complex nexus of sex, race, social class, and politics in postindustrial capitalist society. In her best work, such as *One Flea Spare,* set during a seventeenth-century plague, the characters transcend their roles as depictions of class struggle and power negotiations, and their yearnings and passions startle audiences and induce an uneasy empathy. On the other hand, the characters in efforts like *The War Boys,* in which three men prowl the Mexican border for illegal immigrants and play macho games, seem heavy-handed, groaning noisily under the symbolic freight with which they are laden.

The discomfort of American audiences with overtly political drama may partly explain why, like her friend and mentor **Tony Kushner,** Wallace has had most of her plays first produced in Britain and has received greater critical acclaim there. Besides Kushner, few other contemporary American dramatists match Wallace's marriage of poetics and politics. (Other influences would have to include Bertolt Brecht and Edward Bond.) Her plays are structurally adventurous, with characters jumping around in time. The panoramic *In the Heart of America,* for example, centers on an Arab-American woman's search for the fate of her gay brother in the military during the Persian Gulf War, but the cast also includes Lue Ming, the ghost of a Vietnamese victim of the My Lai massacre, destined to haunt all American "conflicts," in her search for Lieutenant Calley. *Slaughter City,* a play set in a slaughterhouse in Louisville, Kentucky, has characters from the industrial past mingle with contemporary American workers; Cod claims that his mother died in the Triangle Shirtwaist Factory fire, and a sausage grinder symbolizes industrialists through the ages. Wallace uses fluidity of time to suggest that the exploitation of labor—for war or for capitalist gain—is grounded in historical circumstances that transcend any present-day conflagration. Likewise, her dialogue often jumps styles within a play, moving from gritty naturalism to heightened poetic outbursts, stylized song, or the occasional archaic usage. In almost all of her scripts the playwright requests a design scheme to match, recommending a minimal setting that is in no way "realistic."

Within these fluid structures Wallace, who is a published poet, often creates startling, haunting stage images to embody her themes. In *The Trestle at Pope Lick Creek* a mother's hands are permanently died blue from working in a china plate factory; in *One Flea Spare* the quarantined child Morse trades an orange for a favor and tosses it into the air as the lights black out to end the play. More often the images find vibrancy in the very viscera of the human body. Although most obvious in *Slaughter City*, in all of Wallace's plays the characters' bodies, victimized by the twin evils of war and oppressive industrialization, bleed, piss, and suppurate.

Yet Wallace's plays are all love stories at heart, revealing her fascination with the way in which the human body can experience both exquisite desire and acute pain. Her characters literally eviscerate or penetrate one another in paroxysms of lust, love, or disgust. A Persian Gulf War soldier from *In the Heart of America* recalls stepping into the rib cage of an enemy infantryman and proclaiming, "Hey, boys, now I'm really standing in Iraq." In *One Flea Spare* the aristocratic Mrs. Snelgrave rediscovers her sensuality thanks to a scurvy sailor with whom she's been quarantined; their foreplay includes a moment when she squiggles her fingers in his festering wound. Likewise, in *The Trestle at Pope Lick Creek*, a tragic tale of teenage love set during the end of the Great Depression in rural America, the eccentric Pace recalls her father sticking her hand in a bucket of frogs. Later, a character claims, "The only way to love someone is to kill them." In *One Flea Spare* that is just what the young girl Morse does; following the orders of Mrs. Snelgrave, who has become a kind of foster mother to the orphan, the girl plunges a knife into the woman's heart. In Wallace's stage adaptation of William Wharton's novel *Birdy*, Al feeds his psychotic would-be feather friend by chewing food and regurgitating it into his mouth.

One can find the genesis of many of Wallace's plays in her volume of poetry, *To Dance a Stony Field*. *In the Heart of America* evolved from the poem "Kentucky Soldier in Saudi Arabia on the Eve of War"; *Slaughter City* reiterates the theme and emotional tone of "Meat Strike," a monologue in which a scab worker lyrically describes his relationship to the slabs of meat he hacks at in order to feed his family. In fact, Wallace's poems are as theatrical as her plays are lyrical. Many are first-person monologues by an assortment of characters: a woman working in a morgue; a man about to be executed in Nicaragua by the Contras; a farm woman who has murdered her child; an old man dreaming of Cuba; a sixteenth-century woman being burned at the stake for adultery. Just as often, Wallace channels the voice of well-known figures, fictional and historical: Hester Prynne, Judas, the Devil. For all these flights of fantasy, the imagery in Wallace's poems, as in her plays, is rooted in the minutiae of domestic and bodily concerns, with lust and love leaking through the brutality of the most hideous situations, always seeking to assert the hope of a civilized response to the most primitive savagery that marks human existence.

Wallace mines humanity's inability to escape its own physicality, no matter how heightened the poetry or brutal the battle. While puncturing the myth that America is a classless society and delineating the toll industrialization takes on our bodies, she reminds us that our common genetic code can be found in the armpit and the groin as well as in the heart.

—John Istel

WALLANT, Edward Lewis

Born: New Haven, Connecticut, 19 October 1926. **Education:** University of Connecticut, Storrs, 1944, 1946; Pratt Institute, New York, 1947-50; studied writing at New School for Social Research,

New York, 1954-55. **Military Service:** Served in the U.S. Navy, 1944-46. **Family:** Married Joyce Fromkin in 1948; two daughters and one son. **Career:** Graphic designer for various advertising agencies, New York, 1950-62; became art director for McCann-Erickson Agency. **Awards:** Bread Loaf Writers Conference fellowship, 1960; Daroff Memorial award, 1961; Guggenheim fellowship, 1962. **Died:** 5 December 1962.

PUBLICATIONS

Fiction

The Human Season. 1960.
The Pawnbroker. 1961.
The Tenants of Moonbloom. 1963.
The Children at the Gate. 1964.

*

Bibliography: by Nicholas Ayo, in *Bulletin of Bibliography 28,* 1971.

Critical Studies: *The Landscape of Nightmare: Studies in the Contemporary American Novel* by Jonathan Baumbach, 1965; *Wallant* by David Galloway, 1979; "A Prophet in the Labyrinth: The Urban Romanticism of Edward Lewis Wallant" by Sanford E. Marovitz, in *Modern Language Studies,* fall 1985; "The Grace of Suffering: The Fiction of Edward Lewis Wallant" by John G. Parks, in *Studies in American Jewish Literature* vol. 5, 1986; "From Buchenwald to Harlem: The Holocaust Universe of *The Pawnbroker*" by S. Lillian Kremer, in *Literature, the Arts, and the Holocaust* edited by Sanford Pinsker and Jack Fischel, 1987; "Images of Central Europe in the Fiction of Edward Lewis Wallant" by William V. Davis, in *Images of Central Europe in Travelogues and Fiction by North American Writers* edited by Waldemer Zacharasiewicz, 1995.

*   *   *

Edward Lewis Wallant died at 36, just as he was becoming known as a promising novelist. The four novels of his brief career center around two dominant motifs: the quest for family connections and the search for a viable religious-philosophical position. In *The Tenants of Moonbloom,* a spokesman comments, "There is a Trinity of survival, and it consists of Courage, Dream, and Love . . . he who possesses all three, or two, or at least one of these things wins whatever there is to win . . . . " All four of Wallant's protagonists become winners, in these terms, but first they must go through painful rebirths or births.

Joe Berman, a middle-aged plumber whose wife has just died in *The Human Season,* Wallant's first novel, curses his Jewish God for a time but then loses his belief in an anthropomorphic deity. In place of this, he comes to insist on the importance of the human capacity for wonder and love and to accept his own failings in family relationships. Thus he lays to rest the ghosts of his godlike father, whom he loved too well, and his son, whom he feels he did not love enough. *The Pawnbroker,* Wallant's second novel, presents Sol Nazerman, whose wife and children died in a Nazi concentration camp, where he was a subject of experimental surgery. Nazerman affects total cynicism and a harshness comparable to that of his Nazi tormentors, but his protective shell is broken by his young assistant in the pawnshop, Jesus Ortiz, who, with three other black men, plans to rob Sol. During the attempted robbery, Jesus, who has developed a confused filial love for Sol, takes the bullet intended for the pawnbroker, and Sol is spiritually reborn. This is not, however, an easy or sentimental resolution. Nazerman's rebirth is into "the crowding filth" of humanity, wherein he feels "hopeless, wretched, strangely proud."

Though published last due to an arrangement Wallant made before he died, The *Children at the Gate* was written third and is transitional. Here the protagonist, Angelo DeMarco, at eighteen, has never been emotionally alive. The agent of his awakening is a Jewish hospital orderly, a benevolent drug pusher and comic Christ figure whose symbol is the bedpan rather than the cross. The characters in this novel tend to be overdrawn, and the humor is sometimes forced, but the book provides a bridge to *The Tenants of Moonbloom.* Norman Moonbloom is another character in the process of becoming. After a protracted, cocoon-like education, his first job is as rental agent for his brother, owner of four tenement houses. Norman begins to empathize with the miserable tenants, and, though knowing it will do no real good, he sets out to repair everything in the tenements, as an act of personal affirmation. Norman's labors are preparatory to birth, and, as is the case in the other novels, coming to life includes recognition of death's inevitability, but for Norman this is not important. Through ritual initiation he has become identified with humanity and has thus achieved a kind of immortality.

In these novels, Wallant progressed from family concerns and questions of Jewish belief to Moonbloom's identification with the human family and an affirmation of the worldly value of the most inclusive religious ritual, the initiation rite. He progressed, also, from the rather grim acceptance of the first novel through reluctant affirmation in the second and third to joyful and comic belonging in the last, in which Moonbloom, at 33, loses his virginity and learns to laugh. Near that last novel's end, Norman Moonbloom, covered with filth from a bathroom wall he is repairing, shouts, "I'M BORN!"

—James Angle

WARD, Artemus

A pseudonym for Charles Farrar Browne. **Born:** Waterford, Maine, 26 April 1834. **Education:** Norway Liberal Institute, Maine. **Career:** Apprentice printer, *Lancaster Weekly Democrat,* New Hampshire, 1847-48; freelance compositor and reporter on various New England newspapers and in Boston, 1850-53; contributor to the humor magazine *Carpet-Bag,* 1852-53; printer in Ohio, 1853-57; local editor and columnist (as Artemus Ward), *Cleveland Plain Dealer,* 1858-60; managing editor, *Vanity Fair,* New York, 1860-62; performed selections of his own works in Ohio, 1860, Boston and New York, 1861, Washington, D.C., 1862, California and Nevada, 1863, New York and Canada, 1864, and London, 1866-67; contributor, *Punch,* London, 1866-67. **Died:** 6 March 1867.

PUBLICATIONS

Collections

Complete Works. 1870; revised edition, 1898.
Selected Works, edited by Albert Jay Nock. 1924.

Prose

Artemus Ward, His Book. 1862.
Artemus Ward, His Travels. 1865; revised edition, 1865.
Artemus Ward among the Fenians. 1866.
Artemus Ward in London and Other Papers. 1867.
Artemus Ward's Lecture, edited by T.W. Robertson and E.P. Hingston. 1869; as *Artemus Ward's Panorama,* 1869.
Letters of Artemus Ward to Charles E. Wilson 1858-1861. 1900.

*

Bibliography: in *Bibliography of American Literature* by Jacob Blanck, 1955.

Critical Studies: *Ward: A Biography and Bibliography* by Don C. Seitz, 1919; *Ward* by James C. Austin, 1964; *Comic Relief: The Life and Laughter of Ward* by John J. Pullen, 1983; "Who Wrote 'The World's Best Book Review'?" by John J. Pullen, in *New England Quarterly: A Historical Review of New England Life and Letters,* June 1986.

*   *   *

Charles Farrar Browne, better known as Artemus Ward, the Yankee humorist, is a foremost representative of native American humor. During the 1850s and 1860s he was so phenomenally popular that he became the national jester of the Civil War period. He reached national prominence with his Artemus Ward pieces, which first appeared in his column in the *Cleveland Plain Dealer* in 1858, and as editor of *Vanity Fair* he became the unofficial dean of American humor. Finally, he turned to lecturing and founded the comic lecture as an enduring American institution.

Browne's literary reputation rests largely on the humor he published in the *Plain Dealer* and *Vanity Fair.* Basic to the technique of this humor is his use of Artemus Ward, an old side-showman and rascal, as his alter ego. Using the sideshow-man's point of view and colloquial language, Browne commented on a great variety of subjects, usually by means of the anecdote and the mock letter to the editor. His favorite humorous device was misspelling, and he used it expertly.

The Artemus Ward pieces generally treat national figures, subjects, and issues; few significant aspects of mid-nineteenth-century culture escaped his scrutiny. Reformers and cultists caught Browne's attention early, and he directed some of his most pungent satire at the fanatics among them. He satirized militant feminists, zealous temperance advocates, Mormons, Shakers, and proponents of free love; his biggest guns, however, he reserved for unceasing war on the abolitionists. A strong Northern Democrat, Browne commented extensively on national politics. During the Civil War he repeatedly attacked Congress, the inept leadership of the Union Army, draft-dodgers, profiteers, and pseudo-patriots.

Browne also expressed freely his socioeconomic views, generally those of the Democratic Party. He was critical of questionable business practices, the mania for making money, speculation, and the excesses of capitalism in general. In all cases his targets were the false ideals of his age. In a number of his burlesques of the popular romance, for example, he satirized not only the style of the genre itself, but also the sentimentality, questionable values, and superficial moralism pervading popular culture.

Basically burlesques of the serious lyceum lecture, Browne's lectures were pure popular entertainment. By careful planning and cautious experimentation he succeeded in appealing to a large segment of the American people, and, at the end of his career, to British audiences as well. By making comic lecturing both respectable and profitable he paved the way for Mark Twain and the numerous other literary comedians who followed him. His best and most famous lecture was "Artemus Ward among the Mormons."

For almost two decades Browne held the attention, affection, and respect of countless Americans, including Abraham Lincoln. He not only entertained his fellow citizens, but, pleading for sanity, common sense, and moderation, he helped to shape public opinion during a critical period in American life. Finally, his success abroad helped to bring about a reappraisal by Americans of their native humorists.

—John Q. Reed

WARNER, Charles Dudley

Born: Plainsfield, Massachusetts, 12 September 1829; moved with his family to Charlemont, Massachusetts, 1837, and Cazenovia, New York, 1841. **Education:** Oneida Conference Seminary, Cazenovia; Hamilton College, Clinton, New York, B.A. 1851; studied law at the University of Pennsylvania, Philadelphia, 1856-58, LL.B. 1858. **Family:** Married Susan Lee in 1856. **Career:** Railway surveyor in Missouri, 1853-54; in business partnership, Philadelphia, 1855; lawyer in Chicago, 1858-60; moved to Hartford, Connecticut, 1860, and established partnership with Joseph R. Hawley: assistant editor to Hawley, 1860, then editor, 1861-67, of Hawley's *Evening Press;* editor and proprietor, with Hawley, of the *Courant* (which consolidated with the *Press*), 1867-1900; columnist ("The Editor's Drawer," 1884-98, and "The Editor's Study," 1894-98), *Harper's* magazine, New York; editor, *American Men of Letters* series, from 1881; co-editor, *Library of the World's Best Literature,* 1896-97. **Member:** Hartford Park Commission, and Connecticut State Commission on Sculpture; Vice-President, National Prison Association; President, American Social Science Association, and American Academy. **Died:** 20 October 1900.

PUBLICATIONS

Collections

Complete Writings, edited by Thomas R. Lounsbury. 15 vols., 1904.

Fiction

The Gilded Age: A Tale of Today, with Mark Twain. 1873; edited by Bryant Morey French, 1972.
A Little Journey in the World. 1889.
The Golden House. 1895.
That Fortune. 1899.

Other

My Summer in a Garden. 1871.
Saunterings (travel). 1872.

Backlog Studies. 1873.
Baddeck and That Sort of Thing (travel). 1874.
My Winter on the Nile, Among the Mummies and Moslems. 1876.
In the Levant. 1877.
In the Wilderness. 1878.
Being a Boy. 1878.
Washington Irving (biography). 1881.
Captain John Smith (1519-1631), Sometime Governor of Virginia, and Admiral of New England. 1881.
A Roundabout Journey. 1883.
A Study of Prison Reform. 1886.
Their Pilgrimage. 1887.
On Horseback: A Tour of Virginia, North Carolina, and Tennessee. 1888.
A-Hunting of the Deer and Other Essays. 1888.
Studies in the South and West, with Comments on Canada. 1889.
Our Italy. 1891; as *The American Italy,* 1892.
As We Were Saying. 1891.
As We Go. 1893.
The Relation of Literature to Life. 1896.
The People for Whom Shakespeare Wrote. 1897.
Fashions in Literature and Other Literary and Social Essays and Addresses. 1902.
Charles Dickens: An Appreciation. 1913.

Editor, *The Book of Eloquence.* 1851.
Editor, *The Warner Classics.* 4 vols., 1897.
Editor, *Dictionary of Authors, Ancient and Modern, and Synopsis of Books, Ancient and Modern.* 2 vols., 1910.

*

Critical Studies: *Warner* by Annie Fields, 1904; *Nook Farm: Mark Twain's Hartford Circle* by Kenneth R. Andrews, 1950; "'Everybody Chases Butterflies': The Theme of False Hope in The Gilded Age" by Jerry O'Brien, in *Journal of American Culture,* Spring 1983; in *Being a Boy Again: Autobiography and the American Boy Book* by Marcia Ann Jacobson, 1994.

*   *   *

Charles Dudley Warner was a competent essayist and editor whose high reputation from 1870 to 1900 is matched by an equally undeserved neglect in the twentieth century. About half of his books are pot-boilers, especially the ten travel books that dealt first with Europe and the Near East and later with America. For example, *Our Italy* was subsidized to encourage travel to California. Only through his collaboration with **Mark Twain** in *The Gilded Age* is Warner known to readers in the late twentieth century. But his 1904 biographer dismissed *The Gilded Age:* "With all its ingenuities and cleverness, the book can hardly be called a literary success." The three novels Warner published from 1889 to 1899—*A Little Journey in the World, The Golden House,* and *That Fortune*—were also passed over without much attention.

But in the late-twentieth-century years these novels have been reprinted as the value of their commentary on American society has been recognized. In the trilogy, a great fortune is built up and finally lost, an indictment of the new American plutocracy that accumulated wealth and sacrificed values. Warner knew the threat posed by the robber barons in the period called the "Gilded Age," but he had confidence in the eventual triumph of New England-based morality and middle-class idealism. These novels are the culmination of Warner's observations, and are his most serious studies of American society. As fiction they are less notable: Warner was an essayist, not a novelist.

Warner's literary criticism reflects conservative American cultural attitudes at the end of the nineteenth century. His two biographies are workmanlike: *Washington Irving* was his own volume in the "American Men of Letters" series that he edited in the 1880s; and *Captain John Smith* was written as a semi-humorous contribution to the abortive "Lives of American Worthies" planned by a rival publisher. With his brother, he edited *Library of the World's Best Literature*, volumes that later served only to document the literary taste of another day.

Although Warner's literary output was varied, his point of view remained consistent throughout his career. He was genial, idealistic, and temperate, a conservative in morals, literary tastes, and business matters. He was a thoroughly professional journalist-literary man, at his natural best in the personal essay. When his modest newspaper pieces, collected in *My Summer in a Garden*, made a tremendous success, he published the more elaborate *Backlog Studies* and was called a fit successor to Charles Lamb and **Washington Irving**. *In the Wilderness* and *Their Pilgrimage* are travel books about the Adirondacks and fashionable resorts, but more notable for their essays on manners. *As We Were Saying* and *As We Go* are collections of Warner's *Harper's* essays: American individuality is threatened by materialism and refinement. *Being a Boy* is his nostalgic memoir of a farm in the Berkshires in the 1830s. This reminiscence and *My Summer in a Garden* are worth seeking out and ought to be reprinted: Warner's unpretentious style and mellow mood are still charming.

—Clarence A. Glasrud

WARREN, Mercy

Born: Mercy Otis, West Barnstable, Massachusetts, 25 September 1728; sister of the political activist James Otis. **Education:** Privately educated. **Family:** Married James Warren in 1754 (died 1808); five sons. **Career:** Settled in Plymouth, Massachusetts, 1754; became active poet and historical apologist for the American cause in the pamphlet war preceding the Revolutionary War; friend of John Adams and other American patriots. **Died:** 19 October 1814.

PUBLICATIONS

Collections

Plays and Poems, edited by Benjamin Franklin V. 1980.

Plays

The Adulateur. 1773.
The Defeat, in *Boston Gazette*. 1773.
The Group. 1775.
The Sack of Rome and *The Ladies of Castile*, in *Poems*. 1790.

Poetry

Poems, Dramatic and Miscellaneous. 1790.

Other

Observations on the New Constitution. 1788.
History of the Rise, Progress, and Termination of the American Revolution. 3 vols., 1805.
A Study in Dissent: The Warren-Gerry Correspondence, edited by C. Harvey Gardiner. 1968.

*

Critical Studies: *Warren* by Alice Brown, 1896; *First Lady of the Revolution: The Life of Warren* by Katharine Anthony, 1958; "Mercy Otis Warren: Playwright, Poet, and Historian of the American Revolution" by Joan Hoff Wilson and Sharon L. Bollinger, in *Female Scholars: A Tradition of Learned Women before 1800* edited by J.R. Brink, 1980; "Mercy Otis Warren: Dramatist of the American Revolution" by Jean B. Kern, in *Curtain Calls: British and American Women and the Theater, 1660-1820* edited by Mary Anne Schofield and Cecilia Macheski, 1991; "Heroic Drama for an Uncertain Age: The Plays of Mercy Warren" by Cheryl Z. Oreovicz, in *Early American Literature and Culture: Essays Honoring Harrison T. Meserole* edited by Stodola Derounian and others, 1992; *A Woman's Dilemma: Mercy Otis Warren and the American Revolution* by Rosemarie Zagarri, 1995; *Gender Roles, Literary Authority, and Three American Women Writers: Anne Dudley Bradstreet, Mercy Otis Warren, Margaret Fuller Ossoli* by Theresa Freda Nicolay, 1995.

*   *   *

Under normal circumstances, Mercy Warren would probably have restrained her literary impulse to private correspondence, elegant letters with, now and then, a poem enclosed. By birth and marriage, however, she was allied to the anti-Tory faction in Massachusetts and, as a matron in her forties, she emerged as a voice in the pamphlet war that preceded America's Revolutionary War for Independence. Unlike her brother, James Otis, whose passionate but closely reasoned pamphlets were so influential in the 1760s, Warren chose to write satirical dramatic sketches. In *The Adulateur*, to which some other hand added a high-rhetoric account of the Boston Massacre, *The Defeat*, and *The Group*, she introduced caricatures of her political opponents who, in waspish blank verse, condemned themselves and their colleagues. However interesting as eighteenth-century agitprops, Warren's satires are minimally dramatic and have no characters in the complex sense of the word. Since the plays were published anonymously, as so much of the pamphlet literature was, later scholars decided that Warren was the author of a number of unsigned satirical plays. *The Blockheads; or, The Affrighted Officers* (1776) and *The Motley Assembly* (1779) are still assigned to her by some editors, but they are so different in tone and style from anything else that she published that it is highly unlikely that she wrote them. One anonymous work, the pamphlet *Observations on the New Constitution*, a vigorous statement of the anti-federalist position in the ratification fight of 1787-88, is now rightly recognized as hers.

Aside from her political writings, Warren wrote occasional verse, sometimes satirical, more often philosophic. Written in rhymed couplets, her poems were conventional in sentiment, vocabulary, and imagery, although they often embodied the austere, anti-deist, Christian morality that was so important to Warren's life and thought. She wrote two verse tragedies, *The Ladies of Castile* and

The Sack of Rome, which used historical material with contemporary overtones; like so many minor British plays of the eighteenth century, they substituted declamation for dramatic action. Her *History of the Rise, Progress, and Termination of the American Revolution,* thirty years in the making, is her most lasting work, although it is interesting in the late twentieth century not as an objective history but for the "Biographical, Political, and Moral Observations" the title page promises. Her work as a whole is less important as a literary oeuvre than as a vehicle that gives the reader a glimpse of a tough-minded American woman who reflected and in some ways transcended the political and social context in which she wrote.

—Gerald Weales

WARREN, Robert Penn

Born: Guthrie, Kentucky, 24 April 1905. **Education:** Guthrie High School; Vanderbilt University, Nashville, Tennessee, 1921-25, B.A. (summa cum laude) 1925; University of California, Berkeley, M.A. 1927; Yale University, New Haven, Connecticut, 1927-28; Oxford University (Rhodes Scholar), B. Litt. 1930. **Family:** Married 1) Emma Brescia in 1930 (divorced 1950); 2) the writer Eleanor Clark in 1952, one son and one daughter. **Career:** Assistant professor, Southwestern College, Memphis, Tennessee, 1930-31, and Vanderbilt University, 1931-34; assistant and associate professor, Louisiana State University, Baton Rouge, 1934-42; professor of English, University of Minnesota, Minneapolis, 1942-50; professor of playwriting, 1950-56, professor of English, 1962-73, and professor emeritus, 1973-89, Yale University. Member of the Fugitive group of poets: cofounder, *The Fugitive,* Nashville, 1922-25; founding editor, *Southern Review,* Baton Rouge, Louisiana, 1935-42; advisory editor, *Kenyon Review,* Gambier, Ohio, 1942-63. Consultant in poetry, Library of Congress, Washington, D.C., 1944-45; Jefferson Lecturer, National Endowment for the Humanities, 1974. **Awards:** Caroline Sinkler award, 1936, 1937, 1938; Houghton Mifflin fellowship, 1939; Guggenheim fellowship, 1939, 1947; Shelley Memorial award, 1943; Pulitzer prize, for fiction, 1947, and, for poetry, 1958, 1979; Screenwriters Guild Meltzer award, 1949; Foreign Book prize (France), 1950; Sidney Hillman prize, 1957; Edna St. Vincent Millay Memorial prize, 1958; National Book award, for poetry, 1958; Bollingen prize, for poetry, 1967; National Endowment for the Arts grant, 1968, and lectureship, 1974; Bellamann award, 1970; Van Wyck Brooks award, for poetry, 1970; National medal for literature, 1970; Emerson-Thoreau medal, 1975, Copernicus award, 1976; Presidential Medal of Freedom, 1980; Common Wealth award, 1981; MacArthur fellowship, 1981; Brandeis University Creative Arts award, 1983. D.Litt.: University of Louisville, Kentucky, 1949; Kenyon College, Gambier, Ohio, 1952; Colby College, Waterville, Maine, 1956; University of Kentucky, Lexington, 1957; Swarthmore College, Pennsylvania, 1959; Yale University, 1960; Fairfield University, Connecticut, 1969; Wesleyan University. Middletown, Connecticut, 1970; Harvard University, Cambridge, Massachusetts, 1973; Southwestern College, 1974; University of the South, Sewanee, Tennessee, 1974; Monmouth College, Illinois, 1979; New York University, 1983; Oxford University, 1983. LL.D.: Bridgeport University, Connecticut, 1965; University of New Haven, Connecticut, 1974; Johns Hopkins University, Baltimore, 1977. **Member:** American Academy, American Academy of Arts and Sci-

ences; Chancellor, Academy of American Poets, 1972; U.S. Poet Laureate, 1986. **Died:** 15 September 1989.

PUBLICATIONS

Collections

The Collected Poems of Robert Penn Warren. 1998.

Short Stories

Blackberry Winter. 1946.
The Circus in the Attic and Other Stories. 1948.

Novels

Night Rider. 1939.
At Heaven's Gate. 1943.
All the King's Men. 1946.
World Enough and Time: A Romantic Novel. 1950.
Band of Angels. 1955.
The Cave. 1959.
Wilderness: A Tale of the Civil War. 1961.
Flood: A Romance of Our Time. 1964.
Meet Me in the Green Glen. 1971.
A Place to Come To. 1977.

Plays

Proud Flesh (in verse, produced 1947; revised [prose] version, produced 1947).
All the King's Men, from his own novel (as *Willie Stark: His Rise and Fall,* produced 1958; as *All the King's Men,* produced 1959). 1960.

Poetry

Thirty-Six Poems. 1936.
Eleven Poems on the Same Theme. 1942.
Selected Poems 1923-1943. 1944.
Brother to Dragons: A Tale in Verse and Voices. 1953; revised edition, 1979.
To a Little Girl, One Year Old, in a Ruined Fortress. 1956.
Promises: Poems 1954-1956. 1957.
You, Emperors, and Others: Poems 1957-1960. 1960.
Selected Poems: New and Old 1923-1966. 1966.
Incarnations: Poems 1966-1968. 1968.
Audubon: A Vision. 1969.
Or Else: Poem/Poems 1968-1974. 1974.
Selected Poems 1923-1975. 1977.
Now and Then: Poems 1976-1978. 1978.
Two Poems. 1979.
Being Here: Poetry 1977-1980. 1980.
Love. 1981.
Rumor Verified: Poems 1979-1980. 1981.
Chief Joseph of the Nez Perce. 1983.
New and Selected Poems 1923-1985. 1985.

Other

John Brown: The Making of a Martyr. 1929.

I'll Take My Stand: The South and the Agrarian Tradition, with others. 1930.

Who Owns America? A New Declaration of Independence, with others, edited by Herbert Agar and Allen Tate. 1936.

Understanding Poetry: An Anthology for College Students, with Cleanth Brooks. 1938; revised edition, 1950, 1960, and 1976.

Understanding Fiction, with Cleanth Brooks. 1943; revised edition, 1959, 1979; abridged edition, as *The Scope of Fiction,* 1960.

A Poem of Pure Imagination: An Experiment in Reading, in *The Rime of the Ancient Mariner,* by Samuel Taylor Coleridge. 1946.

Modern Rhetoric: With Readings, with Cleanth Brooks. 1949; revised edition, 1958, 1970, 1979.

Fundamentals of Good Writing: A Handbook of Modern Rhetoric, with Cleanth Brooks. 1950.

Segregation: The Inner Conflict in the South. 1956.

Selected Essays. 1958.

Remember the Alamo! (for children). 1958; as *How Texas Won Her Freedom,* 1959.

The Gods of Mount Olympus (for children). 1959.

The Legacy of the Civil War: Meditations on the Centennial. 1961.

Who Speaks for the Negro? 1965.

A Plea in Mitigation: Modern Poetry and the End of an Era (lecture). 1966.

Homage to Theodore Dreiser. 1971.

John Greenleaf Whittier's Poetry: An Appraisal and a Selection. 1971.

A Conversation with Warren, edited by Frank Gado. 1972.

Democracy and Poetry (lecture). 1975.

Warren Talking: Interviews 1950-1978, edited by Floyd C. Watkins and John T. Hiers. 1980.

Jefferson Davis Gets His Citizenship Back. 1980.

A Warren Reader. 1987.

Portrait of a Father. 1988.

New and Selected Essays. 1989.

Cleanth Brooks and Robert Penn Warren: A Literary Correspondence. 1998.

Editor, with Cleanth Brooks and John Thibaut Purser, *An Approach to Literature: A Collection of Prose and Verse with Analyses and Discussions.* 1936; revised edition, 1952, 1975.

Editor, *A Southern Harvest: Short Stories by Southern Writers.* 1937.

Editor, with Cleanth Brooks, *An Anthology of Stories from the Southern Review.* 1953.

Editor, with Albert Erskine, *Short Story Masterpieces.* 1954.

Editor, with Albert Erskine, *Six Centuries of Great Poetry.* 1955.

Editor, with Albert Erskine, *A New Southern Harvest.* 1957.

Editor, with Allen Tate, *Selected Poems,* by Denis Devlin. 1963.

Editor, *Faulkner: A Collection of Critical Essays.* 1966.

Editor, with Robert Lowell and Peter Taylor, *Randall Jarrell 1914-1965.* 1967.

Editor, *Selected Poems of Herman Melville.* 1970.

Editor and part author, with Cleanth Brooks and R. W. B. Lewis, *American Literature: The Makers and the Making.* 2 vols., 1973.

Editor, *Katherine Anne Porter: A Collection of Critical Essays.* 1979.

Editor, *The Essential Melville.* 1987.

*

Bibliography: *Warren: A Reference Guide* by Neil Nakadate, 1977; *Warren: A Descriptive Bibliography 1922-79* by James A. Grimshaw, Jr., 1981.

Critical Studies: *Warren: The Dark and Bloody Ground* by Leonard Casper, 1960; *Warren* by Charles H. Bohner, 1964, revised edition, 1981; *Warren* by Paul West, 1964; *Warren: A Collection of Critical Essays* edited by John Lewis Longley, Jr., 1965; *A Colder Fire: The Poetry of Warren,* 1965, and *The Poetic Vision of Warren,* 1977, both by Victor Strandberg; *Web of Being: The Novels of Warren* by Barnett Guttenberg, 1975; *Twentieth-Century Interpretations of All the King's Men* edited by Robert H. Chambers, 1977; *Warren: A Vision Earned* by Marshall Walker, 1979; *Warren: A Collection of Critical Essays* edited by Richard Gray, 1980; *Critical Essays on Warren* edited by William B. Clark, 1981; *Warren: Critical Perspectives* edited by Neil Nakadate, 1981; *The Achievement of Warren* by James H. Justus, 1981; *Then and Now: The Personal Past in the Poetry of Warren* by Floyd C. Watkins, 1982; *Homage to Warren* edited by Frank Graziano, 1982; *Warren* by Katherine Snipes, 1983; *A Southern Renascence Man: Views of Warren* edited by Walter B. Edgar, 1984; *In the Heart's Last Kingdom: Warren's Major Poetry* by Calvin Bedient, 1984; *Warren and American Idealism* by John Burt, 1988; *The Braided Dream: Warren's Late Poetry* by Randolph Runyon, 1990; *Warren and the American Imagination* by Hugh M. Ruppersburg, 1990; *'To Love So Well the World': A Festschrift in Honor of Robert Penn Warren* edited by Dennis L. Weeks, 1992; *After the Fall: Tragic Themes in the Major Works of Nathaniel Hawthorne and Robert Penn Warren* by Yong-ok, Yi, 1993; *Robert Penn Warren's Modernist Spirituality* by Robert S. Koppelman, 1995; *Robert Penn Warren: A Biography* by Joseph Leo Blotner, 1997; *Sleeping with the Boss: Female Subjectivity and Narrative Pattern in Robert Penn Warren* by Lucy Ferriss, 1997; *The Blood-Marriage of Earth and Sky: Robert Penn Warren's Later Novels* by Leonard Casper, 1997; *Robert Penn Warren's Novels: Feminine and Feminist Discourse* by Cecilia S. Donohue, 1997; *Robert Penn Warren's Novels: Feminine and Feminist Discourse* by Cecilia S. Donohue, 1999.

*   *   *

Robert Penn Warren was a distinguished writer in at least three genres: the novel, poetry, and the essay. Although he left the South in 1942, he so consistently wrote novels, essays, and poetry on southern subjects, in southern settings, and about southern themes that he must be regarded still as a southern writer. Over much of his work there is a typically southern brooding sense of darkness, evil, and human failure, and he employs a gothicism of form and an extravagance of language and technique of a sort often associated with writing in the southeastern United States. Warren was a profoundly philosophical writer in all aspects of his work. Writing of Joseph Conrad, he once said, "The philosophical novelist, or poet, is one for whom the documentation of the world is constantly striving to rise to the level of generalization about values . . . for whom the urgency of experience . . . is the urgency to know the meaning of experience." The description fit him well.

In Warren's principal work in the novel and poetry, there is a persistent obsession with time and with history, a sense of man's imperfection and failure, and an awareness that innocence is always lost in the acts of achieving maturity and growth. His characters are usually men who destroy themselves through seeking an absolute in a relative universe. From John Brown, the subject of his first book, a biography, to Percy Munn, the protagonist of *Night Rider,* to Willie Stark of *All the King's Men,* to Jeremiah

Beaumont of *World Enough and Time,* to Lilburn Lewis in the poem-play *Brother to Dragons,* to Jed Tewksbury in *A Place to Come To*—Warren's protagonists repeat this pattern of the obsessive and ultimately self-destructive search for the impossible ideal.

His work usually rests on actual events from history or at least on actual historical situations—*Night Rider* on the Kentucky tobacco wars; *At Heaven's Gate* on a Nashville political murder; *All the King's Men* on the career of Huey Long; *World Enough and Time* on an 1825 Kentucky murder; *Band of Angels* and *Wilderness* on the Civil War; *The Cave* on Floyd Collins's cave entombment; *Flood* on the inundating of towns by the Tennessee Valley Authority; *A Place to Come To* on his own experiences as a college teacher, although the story can hardly be considered autobiographical. The poem *Brother to Dragons* is based on an atrocious crime committed by **Thomas Jefferson**'s nephews. This concern with history and the individual implications of social and political events is also present in Warren's nonfiction, such as *Segregation: The Inner Conflict in the South, The Legacy of the Civil War,* and *Who Speaks for the Negro?* These works, too, deal with fundamental issues of southern history.

In order to present the philosophical meaning of his novels and poems, Warren used highly individualized narrators, such as Jack Burden in *All the King's Men;* special techniques of narrative point of view, as in *World Enough and Time;* frequently a metaphysical style; the illumination of events through contrast with enclosed and frequently recollected narratives, as in *Night Rider* and *All the King's Men;* and highly melodramatic plots which become elaborate workings out of abstract statements, as in *Band of Angels.*

Warren's poetry reiterates essentially the same view of man. He began as an undergraduate at Vanderbilt University writing poetry with the Fugitive poetry group—**John Crowe Ransom, Allen Tate,** and **Donald Davidson**—and he continued to write a relatively fixed form, tightly constructed, ironic lyric verse until about 1943. Between 1943 and 1953 he concentrated predominantly on the novel. With *Brother to Dragons* he returned to poetic expression, and from that time to his death wrote extensively in both poetic and novelistic forms. The verse forms that he used since 1953 were much looser, marked by broken rhythms, clusters of lines arranged in patterns dictated by emotion, and frequent alternations in the level of diction. Behind his poetry, as behind his fiction, there is usually an implied, if not explicit, narrative pattern. This narrative pattern is often historical, as in "The Ballad of Billy Potts," *Brother to Dragons,* or *Audubon.* In the verse from the end of his career, Warren contrasts man's weaknesses and imperfections with the enduring stars, with time, and with eternity.

As a critic and a teacher, Warren had a profound influence on the study and criticism of literature. His textbook *Understanding Poetry,* written with Cleanth Brooks, a presentation of poetry in New Critical terms emphasizing the poem as an independent work of art, went a long way toward creating a revolution in how literature was taught in American colleges. He wrote many other textbooks and critical studies such as his *Homage to Theodore Dreiser, John Greenleaf Whittier's Poetry,* and *Democracy and Poetry.*

Warren was still very active, especially as a poet, up until his death in 1989. His work in all genres is marked by a high concern with language, a depth of philosophical statement, a firm and rigorous commitment to a moral-ethical view of man, and a willingness to experiment often beyond the limits of artistic safety with the forms in which he worked. Warren was a peculiarly indigenous

American writer of great intelligence and of significant accomplishment.

—C. Hugh Holman, updated by Theresa A. James

WASHINGTON, Booker T(aliaferro)

Born: Hale's Ford plantation, Franklin County, Virginia, 5 April 1856; worked in a Malden, West Virginia, salt-furnace and coal mine in childhood, and also as a domestic servant in home of furnace and mine owner. **Education:** Attended elementary school in Malden from 1865; Hampton Institute, Virginia, 1872-75, graduated with honors; Wayland Seminary, Washington, D.C., 1878-79. **Family:** Married 1) Fannie N. Smith in 1882 (died 1884), one daughter; 2) Olivia A. Davidson in 1885 (died 1889), two sons; 3) Margaret James Murray in 1893. **Career:** Hotel waiter, Connecticut, 1875; schoolteacher, Malden, 1875-78; teacher and secretary to principal, Hampton Institute, 1879-81; founder and first principal, Tuskegee Normal School (Tuskegee Institute from 1893), Alabama, 1881-1915. Frequent speaker on education and race relations from 1884; established numerous rural extension programs at Tuskegee Institute; founder, National Negro Business League, 1900; organizer, National Negro Health Week, 1914. **Awards:** A.M.: Harvard University, Cambridge, Massachusetts, 1896. LL.D.: Dartmouth College, Hanover, New Hampshire, 1901. **Died:** 14 November 1915.

PUBLICATIONS

Collections

Papers, edited by Louis R. Harlan. 1972—.

Prose

Daily Resolves. 1896.
Black-Belt Diamonds: Gems from the Speeches, Addresses, and Talks to Students, edited by Victoria Earle Matthews. 1898.
The Future of the American Negro. 1899.
A New Negro for a New Century, with N.B. Wood and Fannie Barrier Williams. 1900.
Some European Observations and Experiences. 1900.
Sowing and Reaping. 1900.
The Story of My Life and Work. 1900; as *An Autobiography,* 1901.
Up from Slavery: An Autobiography. 1901.
Character Building. 1902.
Working with the Hands. 1904.
Putting the Most into Life. 1906.
Frederick Douglass (biography). 1907.
The Negro in Business. 1907.
The Negro in the South: His Economic Progress in Relation to His Moral and Religious Development, with W.E.B. Du Bois. 1907; as *The American Negro* (Southern States), 1909.
The Story of the Negro. 2 vols., 1909.
My Larger Education, Being Chapters from My Experience. 1911.
The Man Farthest Down: A Record of Observation and Study in Europe, with Robert E. Park. 1912.
The Story of Slavery. 1913.

Selected Speeches, edited by E. Davidson Washington. 1932.
Quotations, edited by E. Davidson Washington. 1938.

Other

Editor, *The Negro Problem.* 1903.
Editor, *Tuskegee and Its People: Their Ideals and Achievements.* 1905.

*

Bibliography: in *Eight Negro Bibliographies* by Daniel T. Williams, 1970.

Critical Studies: *Washington, Educator and Interracial Interpreter* by Basil Mathews, 1948; *Washington and His Critics: The Problem of Negro Leadership* edited by Hugh Hawkins, 1962; *Washington* edited by E.L. Thornbrough, 1969; *Washington: The Making of a Black Leader 1856-1901,* 1972, and *Washington: The Wizard of Tuskegee 1901-1915,* 1983, both by Louis R. Harlan; "The Founding Fathers: Frederick Douglass and Booker T. Washington" by James Olney, in *Slavery and the Literary Imagination* edited by Deborah E. McDowell and Arnold Rampersad, 1989; "Booker T. Washington as Literary Trickster" by Frederick McElroy, in *Southern Folklore* vol. 49, no. 2, 1992; *Wealth Building Lessons of Booker T. Washington for a New America* by T.M. Pryor, 1995; *Booker T. Washington–Interpretive Essays* edited by Tunde Adeleke, 1998.

* * *

A reluctant author, persuaded to write by his admirers, Booker T. Washington is not a natural stylist. His books reflect the main concern of his life in the outside world—namely, the "raising up" of his fellow black Americans by means of land ownership and a thorough education, with emphasis on the mastery of skilled trades. Thrift and industry are the solutions he preaches, the familiar nineteenth-century gospel of self-help given substance by his own success at Tuskegee, the college largely built and supervised by Washington, his staff, and students. As much propaganda as literature, his works launch themselves at the consciousness of the reader with the immediacy of speech. Polemics, exhortations in writing from one of the greatest public speakers of his time, each of them delves deep into the personal experience of the man who wrote them. This experience sustains their author in the alien terrain of "literature." Washington's books impress by simplicity of utterance, by a telling use of anecdotes in the building of arguments, above all by their grasp of practical detail. As he states, "I have great faith in the power and influence of facts."

The improving intention behind his works is usually self-evident. *Character Building* and *My Larger Education* stress the importance of learning, the latter describing Washington's pioneering efforts in "project" education. *Working with the Hands* reaffirms the significance of manual laboring skills as a means of self-betterment. With the more ambitious *The Story of the Negro,* Washington attempts to correct the established mythology of his day, which regarded the black race as lacking in historic and cultural achievement. Some of his findings are questionable, and the book itself somewhat pedestrian, but if Washington knows little of his ancestry, he was surely right to trust the instinct that told him "A race which could produce as good and gentle and loving a woman as my mother must have some good in it that the geographers had failed to discover."

More impressive in many respects is *The Man Farthest Down,* inspired by a tour of Europe not long before the writer's death. In this detailed study Washington examines the lifestyles of European peasants and compares their lot with that of his black fellow-countrymen. It is typical of his positive vision that he claims his compatriots to be more fortunate than their white laboring counterparts. The great popularizer of industrial education also sees in the prosperity of Danish farmers proof of his own maxims in support of land ownership and agricultural labor. While his view of the black American's position at the turn of the century is perhaps over-optimistic, *The Man Farthest Down* remains a valid and intriguing social document.

Up from Slavery is Washington's masterpiece, outlining in simple but effective words the magnitude of the achievement that led him from childhood on a slave plantation to leadership of his people. Considering the random, fragmentary manner in which it was compiled, the work retains a remarkable unity and coherence. Laced with stories and humorous aphorisms, *Up from Slavery* embodies the broad vision of its author, together with his insistence on neatness and personal hygiene. It also stresses that policy of cooperation with the Southern whites that Washington campaigned for all his life, and for which he was so often criticized by his fellow blacks.

Washington's famous speech at the Atlanta Exposition of 1895, contained in the book, remains the most controversial and quotable of all his public utterances. His conciliatory approach, urging both sides to "Cast down your bucket where you are!" and work together, has been construed by some as a betrayal of his own people. Washington's claim that "In all things purely social we can be as separate as the fingers, yet one as the hand in all things essential to mutual progress" certainly implies acceptance of the black's inferior status, and he appears willing to forfeit political rights in return for blacks owning their own land. Nevertheless, it must be remembered that his gradualist message gained more for black Americans in his time than racial protest by his critics. Nor should his conciliatory efforts be misread as cowardice. *Up from Slavery* contains numerous examples of Washington speaking out against racial injustice, notably his impassioned outbursts condemning the Ku Klux Klan and the white lynch mobs. His written work bears witness to a cautious but shrewd pragmatism based on an awareness of what could be accomplished. This quality, together with the sincerity of its author, helps to make *Up from Slavery* one of the classic American autobiographies.

Throughout his writings, one is made aware of Washington's humanity, the genuine concern for his fellows that informs every page. Undoubtedly a man of strongly held opinions, he seems incapable of malice ("No man shall drag me down by making me hate him"). Self-taught himself, he never loses his close affinity with the black working man, whose respect he clearly retained. While it can be argued that his books give insufficient emphasis to higher education and political rights, there is truth in his claim that "No race can prosper till it learns that there is as much dignity in tilling a field as in writing a poem . . . Nor should we permit our grievances to overshadow our opportunities."

Washington was not a great writer; what is beyond doubt is that he was a great man. The best of his works are fitting testimony to the heroic nature of his achievement.

—Geoff Sadler

WATANNA, Onoto. *See* **EATON, Winnfred.**

WATERS, Frank (Joseph)

Born: Colorado Springs, Colorado, 25 July 1902. **Education:** Attended Colorado College, Colorado Springs, 1922-25. **Military Service:** Served in the United States Army, 1941-43. **Family:** Married 1) Lois Moseley in 1944 (divorced 1946); 2) Jane Sommervell in 1947 (divorced 1955); 3) Rose Marie Woodell in 1962 (divorced 1965); 4) Barbara Hayes in 1978. **Career:** Visited Navaho Reservation, New Mexico, with father, 1911; engineer in Los Angeles, Riverside, and Imperial Valley, Southern California Telephone Company, 1926-35; visited United States-Mexico border and interior Mexico 1925-29; propaganda analyst, Office of Inter-American Affairs, Washington, D.C., 1943-46; editor, *El Crepusculo* newspaper, Taos, New Mexico, 1949-51; book reviewer, *Saturday Review of Literature,* New York, 1950-56; information adviser, Los Alamos Scientific Laboratory, New Mexico, 1952-56; writer, C.O. Whitney Motion Picture Co., Los Angeles, 1957; visited Hopi Reservation, 1950s; writer-in-residence, Colorado State University, Fort Collins, 1966; director, New Mexico Arts Commission, Santa Fe, 1966-68. **Awards:** Commonwealth Club of California silver medal, 1942; Rockefeller grant, 1970; Western Heritage award, 1972; New Mexico Arts Commonwealth Literary award, 1975. D.Litt.: University of Albuquerque, New Mexico, 1973; Colorado State University, 1973; New Mexico State University, Las Cruces, 1976; University of New Mexico, Albuquerque, 1978; Colorado College, 1978; University of Nevada, Las Vegas, 1981; University of Colorado, Boulder Springs, 1982. **Died:** 3 June 1995.

PUBLICATIONS

Collections

Frank Waters: A Retrospective Anthology, edited by Charles L. Adams. 1985.

Novels

Fever Pitch. 1930; as *The Lizard Woman,* 1984.
The Wild Earth's Nobility: A Novel of the Old West. 1935.
Below Grass Roots. 1937.
The Dust within the Rock. 1940.
People of the Valley. 1941.
The Man Who Killed the Deer. 1942.
River Lady, with Houston Branch. 1942.
The Yogi of Cockroach Court. 1947.
Diamond Head, with Houston Branch. 1948.
The Woman at Otowi Crossing. 1966; revised edition, 1987.
Pike's Peak: A Mining Saga (a redaction of *The Wild Earth's Nobility, Below Grass Roots,* and *The Dust within the Rock*). 1971.
Flight from Fiesta. 1986.

Prose (nonfiction)

Midas of the Rockies: The Story of Stratton and Cripple Creek. 1937.
The Colorado. 1946.
Masked Gods: Navajo and Pueblo Ceremonialism. 1950.
The Earp Brothers of Tombstone: The Story of Mrs. Virgil Earp. 1960.

Book of the Hopi. 1963.
Leon Gaspard. 1964.
Pumpkin Seed Point. 1969.
To Possess the Land: A Biography of Arthur Rochford Manby. 1973.
Mexico Mystique: The Coming Sixth World of Consciousness. 1975.
Mountain Dialogues. 1981.
Brave Are My People: Indian Heroes Not Forgotten. 1993.
Of Time and Change: A Memoir. 1998.

Other

Editor, *Rocks and Minerals.* 1971.
Editor, with Charles L. Adams, *Cuchama and Sacred Mountains,* by W. Y. Evans-Wentz. 1981.
Editor, *Eternal Desert* (photographs by David Muench). 1990.

*

Bibliography: *Frank Waters: A Bibliography* by Terence A. Tanner, 1983.

Critical Studies: *Frank Waters* by Martin Bucco, 1969; *Conversations with Frank Waters* edited by John R. Milton, 1971; *Frank Waters* by Thomas J. Lyon, 1973; *Studies in Frank Waters* vols. 1-13, 1978-91; "Frank Waters" by Charles L. Adams in *A Literary History of the American West,* 1987; *Sundays in Tutt Library with Frank Waters* edited by Katherine Scott Sturdevant, 1988; interview by Charles Adams in *This Is about Vision: Interviews with Southwestern Writers* edited by William Balassi and others, 1990; *A Sunrise Brighter Still: The Visionary Novels of Frank Waters* by Alexander Blackburn, 1991; *Frank Waters: Man and Mystic,* edited by Vine Deloria, 1993; *The Control of Water and Land: Dams and Irrigation in Novels by Mary Hallock Foote, Mary Hunte Austin, Frank Waters, and D'Arcy McNickle* (dissertation) by Joan Elizabeth Thompson, 1994.

*   *   *

Frank Waters is often referred to as an author of "Westerns" rather than as an author of "western" literature. However, his work is not in the Western genre; rather, it is literature of the West. His career spans seven decades and includes more than twenty-five books of fiction and non-fiction dealing with the American Southwest. Two of his novels, *People of the Valley* and *The Man Who Killed the Deer,* rank as classics of Southwestern American literature, and *Deer* enjoys a secure place in Native American studies, especially study of the Pueblos. Additionally, Waters holds the distinction of being a nominee for the Nobel Prize for literature. As a boy growing up in Colorado in the early twentieth century, Waters became familiar with his father's Indian heritage, visiting the Navaho Reservation in New Mexico for several months when he was nine years old. His own mixed ancestry and exposure to other cultures along with his closeness to the land helped shape his interests. His later travels in Mexico and his association with his grandfather's mining ventures added to his interest in the land and form some of the bases for his work.

In an essay entitled "Roots and Literary Influences" in *Old Southwest/New Southwest,* Waters asserts that a writer "must attune his antennae to new views on old ideas, to new people and situations, to the land itself." His adherence to these criteria leads him to examine that which connects people to each other and to their world. These connections appear as a part of the sense of place in his works, and place becomes more than locale and more than the environment of the Southwest. It includes the land, humankind's reaction to the land, and the land's capacity to affect people's view of the self and the world. Waters extends his work beyond the land by exploring the possibility of racial and cultural reconciliation in the Southwest's pluralistic society of American Indians, Hispanic-Americans, and Anglos. He also considers the ramifications of gender in addressing the human potential for intellectual and spiritual fulfillment.

Both very early in his career and later as a more mature author, Waters employs the theme of a relationship to the land—sometimes harmonious, sometimes less than harmonious—in the creation of characters and the presentation of place to produce novels wherein the characters are inextricably linked to the land. His first novel, *Fever Pitch* (republished as *The Lizard Woman*) effectively uses as characters the desert and a mountain formation that resembles a giant lizard with a woman's face. Cultural variances come to the fore as the Anglo prospector, Lee Marston, fails to understand the Mexican desert, and the mixed-blood characters (Indian-Mexican) use their knowledge of the desert to survive. Marston ultimately comes to understand the importance of environment and its connection to his physical, psychological, and spiritual being. The realization, however, occurs in the negative land of the Lizard Woman and precludes spiritual harmony with nature and the universe.

The classic *People of the Valley* presents Maria del Valle, Waters's best-drawn character, as completely in tune with the land. Maria's heritage and growth reflect a direct connection to the land. Her mixed-blood ancestry (Indian-Mexican) provides her an understanding of the land as changeless and enduring that the arriving Anglos do not possess. Waters creates Maria and place as one; she embraces all of life both intellectually and spiritually as she reconciles issues of race, gender, and life's meaning through her relationship to the land.

While Maria del Valle maintains a constant relationship with the land from her birth to her death, Martiniano, the young Pueblo man in Waters's best-known work, *The Man Who Killed the Deer,* experiences personal and tribal conflict when he fails to recognize his inseparable connection to the earth. The conflict centers on Martiniano's unfamiliarity with Pueblo ways and his knowledge of white ways acquired at the government school. His development requires that he face internal dualities of racial and cultural origin and bring these polarities into reconciliation. Martiniano's progress is enabled by his wife, a strong female character who recognizes her connection to the other members of the tribe and all of nature.

While earlier novels present a spirit of place that involves the land, the spirit of place in *The Yogi of Cockroach Court* reflects a social environment. The setting for *Yogi* is a Mexican-American border town where prostitution, gambling, and the sale of drugs affect the lives of the characters and contribute to their destruction. Those conditions prevent the characters from knowing and accepting the land. The theme of dualities in racial and cultural heritage continues, but the characters fail to recognize the need for or possibility of reconciliation. The central character, Tai Ling, tries to escape his own ego and the world around him through meditation. He tries to deny any connection to the larger world and the suffering of the other characters. All too late, after transcending "self" and escaping the desires of the body, Tai Ling understands that he cannot fully separate himself from the rest of nature.

Helen Chalmers, the central character of *The Woman at Otowi Crossing,* bypasses conflict and struggle and arrives at her universal understanding of the world almost without effort. In the place of Otowi Crossing, Waters combines features of the industrial world and the pastoral mountains that surround the Crossing. The atomic bomb is being developed at the nearby Los Alamos laboratory at the same time that Helen is experiencing a terminal illness. The parallel destructive forces blend in Helen's realization of her connection to the land and the universe as she perceives the basic unity of all the natural world. In striking contrast to Tai Ling, Helen Chalmers achieves resolution and synthesis, aided in large part by a Pueblo Indian. Her sudden awakening—her mystical insight—is comparable to an atomic explosion that depends upon understanding of the atom, the core of physical structure. Waters uses the natural facts of atomic science to explain the spiritual facts of Helen's awakening. Land, culture, and spirit combine to produce full reconciliation.

In *Pike's Peak,* an autobiographical novel depicting Waters and his grandfather, the mountain environment is neither hostile nor beneficent; it is, however, the focus of Joseph Rogier's efforts to come to terms with the land and with himself. The mountain draws Rogier from the instant he first glimpses it, and he responds to it for the rest of his life. Although Rogier's quest to conquer and understand the mountain consumes his life, he ultimately comes to terms with the land. Rogier never really overcomes his basic cultural conflict—his Anglo desire to conquer the mountain—and he never understands his relationship to nature. Two generations later, the cultural dualities are reconciled through Rogier's grandson.

Waters's characters face individual conflicts stemming from heritage, both personal and cultural, that can lead to reconciliation and harmony. Whether their relationships to it appear negative or positive, his characters are linked to the land; place and mind become one. Avoiding formula in his continuing examination of environment, culture, and spirit, Waters's work reflects a broad conceptual view of humankind and the universe.

—Gary W. Rogers

WELCH, James

Born: Browning, Montana, 1940. **Education:** The University of Montana, Missoula, B.A.; attended Northern Montana University, Havre. **Career:** Poet and novelist. **Awards:** National Endowment for the Arts grant, 1969; *Los Angeles Times* prize, 1987. **Residence:** Missoula, Montana.

PUBLICATIONS

Novels

Winter in the Blood. 1974.
The Death of Jim Loney. 1979.
Fools Crow. 1986.
The Indian Lawyer. 1990.

Poetry

Riding the Earthboy 40. 1971; revised edition, 1975.

Other

James Welch, edited by Ron McFarland, 1986.
Killing Custer: The Battle of the Little Big Horn and the Fate of the Plains Indians. 1994.

Author of introduction, *Death and the Good Life,* by Richard Hugo. 1991.

Editor, with Ripley S. Hugg and Lois M. Welch, *The Real West Marginal Way: A Poet's Autobiography,* by Richard Hugo. 1986.

*

Critical Studies: *Four American Indian Literary Masters: N. Scott Momaday, James Welch, Leslie Marmon Silko, and Gerald Vizenor* by Alan R. Velie, 1982; *James Welch* by Peter Wild, 1983; "Closing the Distance: Critic, Reader, and the Works of James Welch" by Kathleen M. Sands in *MELUS: The Journal of the Society for the Study of the Multi-Ethnic Literature of the United States,* vol. 14, no. 2, Summer 1987; "I Just Kept My Eyes Open: An Interview with James Welch" by Joseph Bruchac in *Survival This Way: Interviews with American Indian Poets,* 1987; "Variations on a Theme: Traditions and Temporal Structure in the Novels of James Welch" by Roberta Orlandini in *South Dakota Review,* vol. 26, no. 3, Autumn 1988; "Now That the (Water) Buffalo's Gone: James Welch and the Transcultural Novel" by John Scheckter in *Entering the 90s: The North American Experience* edited by Thomas Schirer, 1991; *Place and Vision: the Function of Landscape in Native American Fiction* by Robert M. Nelson, 1993; *Tribal Selves: Subversive Identity in Asian American and Native American Literature* (dissertation) by Sharon S. Suzuki-Martinez, 1996; *Beyond Bounds: Cross-Cultural Essays on Anglo, American Indian and Chicano Literature* by Robert Gish, 1996; "James Welch: Alienation and Broken Narrative in *Winter in the Blood*" by Cecilia Sims, in *Critical Perspectives on native American Fiction,* edited by Richard F. Fleck, 1997.

*   *   *

It is unfortunate that James Welch often is first considered as a Native American writer. This consideration distracts both readers and critics who approach Welch's work expecting to find complex anthropological and sociological comment implied in his prose. Such features may or may not be there, depending on the readers's interpretation, but the emphasis draws attention away from Welch's main achievement and what should be the primary consideration: his fine writing.

Born in Montana of mixed Blackfeet and Gros Ventre ancestry, Welch indeed uses his background in all his books. Yet in the handling of this material the writer shows that he is opposing current fashion by not using his Indian-related subject matter as an easy ploy to gain readers' sympathy and interest. Rather, with great respect both for his own intelligence and for his art, he draws on the lives and landscapes he knows best as a vehicle for his talent. That ability is so intriguingly various that the result often is a near virtuoso performance. However, his is not a confusing many-

sidedness. It is quite the opposite. Two seemingly opposing features mark most of Welch's writing, and because he is able to make them work in tandem, playing one against the other, his writing gains the tension, playfulness, and intellectual charm of alchemy.

Welch's prose swings between the two poles of naturalism and the imagination. This first involves artistic distance from the subject, a near scientific remove. Going along with this is a lack of value judgment and a willingness to take into the prose whatever is found in the situation, however incongruent. The result is the sharp-edged realism of Welch's books. Welch balances this realism with his whimsical humor and his attraction to absurdity for its own sake, as if he believes that since we live in a world of doomed fools, we might as well enjoy ourselves. Adding to the humorous quality is his innate playfulness with words and the related willingness to take risks in his stories' development, surprising readers with how well the unexpected works.

Such features fit well with Welch's persona of a bewildered Indian caught between the two worlds of white and Native—between change and tradition—and unable to make much sense of either. Often musing on his own undeserved suffering and on his own foolishness, Welch attains a measure of victory in his novels by finally understanding that the roots of his problem lie both within himself and in the outside situation he can do nothing about. Thus he makes headway in mastering his romantic immaturity. By accepting the circumstances in which he is caught, he overcomes them to a degree that is livable, even enjoyable. These are, then, coming-of-age novels, and by working through their complexities Welch shows us more than the alienated antihero, the standard rendition of the victimized Indian. The persona, though particularized as an Indian, emerges not simply as another abused Native American but as a person struggling with the contradictions common to all of us and common to all of humanity.

Though the successful pattern changes from book to book, its basics can be seen throughout Welch's work, beginning with his first volume, *Riding the Earthboy 40.* In this collection of poems, the touch can be light, describing a skunk as it "swaggers," or impressionistic, shading off into the surreal as with "babies / blue from the waist down. / Their heads are cheese." Yet, almost always, the counterpoint of a dark world underlies the situations. "The Man from Washington," perhaps the best piece in the book, describes an Indian agent arriving from Washington in comical terms, "a slouching dwarf with rainwater eyes." But as with many dwarves in literature, he is far more grotesque than comical, for he is a powerful fraud betraying the people he is supposed to protect.

As is seen more clearly in *Winter in the Blood,* a remarkably accomplished first novel, Welch is not a racist any more than he is a devotee of the Cult of the Noble Savage. He does not point a finger of blame at white men's depredations on the innocent. Rather, evil exists in all people, and the agony of a culture overwhelmed by invaders is more of a recurring fact of history, unfortunate but to be accepted, than a morality play. In Welch, evil also can be something besides the raw material he works into artistic tragicomedies.

The main character in *Winter in the Blood* comes stumbling home, beat-up and hung-over, to his mother's ranch on the reservation. His girlfriend has left him, and his bad knee aches. He is unemployed. He is so ill-starred that, as part of the wry irony crackling through the book and balancing its very real human misfortunes, the writer does not deign to give this ne'er-do-well the dignity of a name. Worse, the main character is in psychological shock, so pained that his emotions have shut down; he is detached and unfeeling about his situation and the people around him. The emotional distance established in the book's early pages becomes the pivot of the story, for as the novel progresses, the detachment changes from a negative to a positive force and becomes the young man's saving grace.

Alternately working on his mother's ranch and going off to haunt the bars in town searching for the wayward girl, he suffers further indignities. Yet his slow realization that his romantic hopes are futile and that he inhabits a world that makes no sense marks not an ending but a beginning. Accepting such circumstances as givens, he gradually sheds his earlier self-indulgent *Weltschmerz*. He begins looking around him, and by gaining an understanding of his family and his ancestry, he overcomes his former malaise to better understand who he is and how he fits into his context. Thus, the novel is an evolution from nihilism to a personal, if limited, triumph, a journey from immaturity to a state approaching adulthood.

Welch's second novel, *The Death of Jim Loney,* again takes place in small-town Montana. As with the earlier protagonist, Jim Loney is a down-and-out Indian. A part-time agricultural worker, he spends much of his time in an alcoholic daze, sorting through his fractured past. Yet this time there is no redemption. Both Rhea, an idealistic English teacher from a wealthy Texas family, and Jim's sister, Kate, compete in their attempts to rescue Jim from his downward spiral. But unlike the main character of *Winter in the Blood,* Jim continues to unravel. The book, far less whimsical and more darkly cynical, ends when Jim goes on an alcoholic rampage, fulfilling his self-destructive urges when he provokes lawmen and is killed by their return fire. Lacking the counterbalance of humor and hope, *The Death of Jim Loney* swings into melodrama as Welch documents a pathetic figure's downward skid, and since there is little chance to avoid Loney's bleak and all but foreordained fate, the novel is less satisfying than Welch's first.

An historical work, *Fools Crow* shifts Welch's pattern in time and characterization. Set in Montana in the 1870s, this third novel follows the life of Fools Crow at a time when the whites were encroaching on Blackfeet territory. Therefore, the young warrior's problem is not from within but from without. He and his tribe are doomed by an impossible situation. Despite their best efforts, their traditional ways fail under the strain of new circumstances imposed upon them. This long novel suffers somewhat from its episodic nature and from its attempt to capture the Indians' descriptive language, as in calling a snake "crawls-along-the-ground." This language does not fit smoothly with some of the conventional Latinate language of the narrative. Nonetheless, *Fools Crow* is a rich anthropological tableau and a convincing study of painful cultural change.

The Indian Lawyer addresses the reverse of the problem found in Welch's previous work, that is, of the Indian who is successful in white society. Yellow Calf is an up-and-coming Montana lawyer. The local politicos realize that he would make a fine candidate for Congress, acceptable to whites and Indians alike. His name, however, is the same as that of the aged traditional Indian in *Winter in the Blood,* and in this lies an irony. The new Yellow Calf has entered the white world to such a degree that his Indianness is but a nostalgic connection to the past, albeit a powerful one. When caught in a compromise, Yellow Calf loses his taste for political acclaim and resigns from his congressional race in fear of being publicly exposed. He thereafter performs legal work for his people. Again, a Welch character has found his way by

struggling toward self-knowledge, though in this case it includes reduced expectations and a minor victory before an uncertain future.

Killing Custer originated as a script for the documentary film *Last Stand at Little Big Horn.* Welch writes nonfiction in a way that reflects his complex use of prose, the balance or union of naturalism and imagination. In *Killing Custer* Welch produces a work both solidly historical and personally impressionistic. He records his visits to locations, recounts incidents of the filming, and reflects on the historical record he presents. Through these, he places himself into the historic and contemporary geography of the Custer myth, the American ethos in which it grew, and the larger tragic structure of the Plains Indians' existence and struggle, past and present. *Killing Custer* begins where *Fools Crow* ends, the January 1870 Massacre at the Marias where cavalry troops killed 173 peaceful Pikunis. The book has its figurative and literal center on a well-documented and evocative account of the June 25, 1876, Battle at the Little Bighorn. It ends in December 1890 with a detailed description of the killing of Sitting Bull and a reference to the Wounded Knee Massacre. Welch informs these incidents with the social, anthropological, and economic forces at work in the United States at the time. By establishing himself in the landscape of this history, Welch makes the entire book an authentic expression of history and of his story, a working out of the internal need to come to grips with external reality. In that process, Welch abolishes clichés and achieves the humanization of the Plains Indians. As a recorder of history and as an artist of merit, he treats Custer and all other participants as fully human as well. *Killing Custer* demonstrates Welch's ability to use artistic concerns and accomplishments in fiction to address directly the often harsh realities of Native America and of life itself.

—Peter Wild, updated by Laurence Cohen

WELLMAN, Mac (John McDowell)

Born: Cleveland, Ohio, 7 March 1945. **Education:** University School, Shaker Heights, Ohio, graduated 1963; School of International Service, American University, Washington D.C., B.A. in international relations and organization 1967; University of Wisconsin, Madison, M.A. in English literature 1968. **Career:** Associate professor of English, Montgomery College, Rockville, Maryland, 1969-72; playwright-in-residence, New York University, 1981-82, Yale University School of Drama, New Haven, Connecticut, 1992, and Princeton University, New Jersey, 1992-93; teacher of playwrighting, Mentor Playwrights' Project at the Mark Taper Forum, Los Angeles, University of New Mexico, Albuquerque, New York University, Iowa Playwright's Lab, Iowa City, Brown University, Providence, Rhode Island, and New Dramatists, New Voices, Boston, Massachusetts, 1984-92; resident, Bellagio Study and Conference Centre, the Rockefeller Foundation, Bellagio, Italy, 1991; PNM distinguished chair in playwrighting, University of New Mexico, Albuquerque, 1991; master artist, Atlantic Center for the Arts, New Smyrna, Florida, 1991. **Awards:** New York Foundation for the Arts fellowship, 1986, 1990; McKnight fellowship, 1989; Rockefeller fellowship, 1989; Guggenheim fellowship, 1990; National Endowment for the Arts fellowship, 1990, 1995; Obie award, 1990 (three times), 1991; Outer Circle Critics award, 1990; Bessie award, for *7 Blowjobs,* 1992; American Theater Critics Association award, 1992; Commission for the McCarter Theatre, Princeton, 1994; resident at Yaddo, 1995, 1998; Lila Wallace-Reader's Digest Writers' award, 1996; honored in *A Horizontal Avalanche: The Mac Wellman Festival*, October 1997–March 1998. **Residence:** New York, New York.

PUBLICATIONS

Plays

Fama Combinatoria (broadcast 1973).
The Memory Theatre of Giordano Bruno (broadcast 1976).
Opera Brevis. 1977.
Starluster (produced 1979). Published in *Wordplays 1*, edited by Bonnie Marranca, 1980.
Dog in the Manger, adaptation of a play by Lope de Vega (produced 1982).
The Self-Begotten (produced 1982).
Phantomnation, with Constance Congdon and Bennett Cohen, music by James Ragland (produced 1983).
The Professional Frenchman (produced 1984). Published in *Theatre of Wonders*, edited by Wellman, 1985.
Bodacious Flapdoodle (produced 1984). 1987.
Harm's Way, music by Bob Jewett and Jack Maeby (broadcast 1984). 1984.
Energumen (produced 1985). Published in *Women with Guns*, edited by Christopher Gould, 1986.
The Bad Infinity (produced 1985). Published in *7 Different Plays*, edited by Wellman, 1988.
1951, with Anne Bogart and Michael Roth (produced 1986).
The Nain Rouge, music by Michael Roth (produced 1986).
The Distance to the Moon, music by Melissa Shiftlett (produced 1986).
Cleveland (produced 1986). Published in *Short Plays for Young Actors*, edited by Craig Slaight and Jack Sharrar, 1996.
Dracula, adaptation of the novel by Bram Stoker (produced 1987).
Albanian Softshoe (produced 1988).
Peach Bottom Nuclear Reactor Full of Sleepers (produced 1988).
Cellophane (produced 1988). 1988; in *Plays for the End of the Century*, edited by Bonnie Marranca, 1996.
Without Colors, adaptation of *Cosmicomics* by Italo Calvino, music by Melissa Shiftlett (produced 1989).
Whirligig (produced 1989). Published in *Plays in Process*, vol.10, no.7, 1989.
Bad Penny (produced 1989). 1990.
The Ninth World (produced 1989).
Terminal Hip (also director: produced 1989). Published in *Performing Arts Journal*, no. 40, 1992.
Crowbar (produced 1990).
Sincerity Forever (produced 1990).
7 Blowjobs (produced 1991). Published in *Theater Forum*, no. 1, 1992.
A Murder of Crows (produced 1991). Published in *Plays in Process*, 1992.
Tallahassee, adaptation of Ovid's *Metamorphoses*, with Len Jenkin, (produced 1991).
Coathanger (produced 1992).
Strange Feet (produced 1993).
The Land of Fog and Whistles (produced 1993). Published in *Theater*, vol. 24, no. 1, pp. 52-8, March/April 1993.

Three Americanisms (produced 1993). Published in *50: A Celebration of Sun and Moon Classics*, 1995.
The Hyacinth Macaw (produced 1994).
Why the Y? (In Ybor) (produced 1994).
The Land Beyond the Forest: Dracula and Swoop. Los Angeles, Sun and Moon Press, 1995.
Swoop (produced 1994).
Absence of Mallets, with David Van Tieghem (produced 1994).
tigertigertiger (produced 1995).
The Sandalwood Box (produced 1994; with *The Damned Thing* 1998). Published in *The Best American Short Plays*, edited by Howard Stein and Glenn Young, 1996.
London (In 10 Cities) (produced 1996).
Second-Hand Smoke (produced 1996).
Infrared (produced 1996).
Fnu Lnu (produced 1996).
The Lesser Magoo (produced 1997).
My Old Habit of Returning to Places (produced 1997).
The Porcupine Man and *Three Other Plays* (*No Smoking Piece, the Distance to the Moon,* and *Eyes of the Panther;* produced 1998).
I Don't Know Who He Was and I Don't Know What He Said (produced 1998).
The Difficulty of Crossing a Field (produced 1998).
Cat's Paw (produced 1998). Published with *The Difficulty of Crossing a Field* in *Theater*, vol. 27, nos. 2 &3, pp. 65-137, May 1997.

Radio Plays: (all broadcast in The Netherlands): *Nobody*, 1972; *Fama Combinatoria*, 1973; *Mantices*, 1973; *Two Natural Drummers*, 1973; *The Memory Theatre of Giordano Bruno*, 1976; *Harm's Way*, 1984.

Novels

The Fortuneteller. 1991.
Annie Salem. 1996.

Poetry

In Praise of Secrecy. 1977.
Satires. 1985.
A Shelf in Woop's Clothing. 1990.

Other

Breathing Space: An Anthology of Sound-Text Art. 1977.

Editor, *Theatre of Wonders.* 1985.
Editor, *7 Different Plays.* 1988.
Editor, *Slant Six.* 1990.
Editor, with Douglas Messerli, *From the Other Side of the Century II: A New American Drama 1960-1995,* 1998.

*

Critical Studies: "Mac Wellman's Horizontal Avalanches" by Eric Overmyer, in *Theater*, summer/fall 1990, pp. 54-56; "Seven Avenues Towards the Heart of a Mystery" by Carey Perloff, in *Theater*, vol. 27, nos. 2 & 3, spring 1997, pp. 61-63; "Werewolves,

Fractals and Forbidden Knowledge: An Interview with Mac Wellman" by Shawn Garrett, in *Theater*, vol. 27, nos. 2 & 3, spring 1997, pp. 87-95.

Theatrical Activities: Director: **Play**—*Terminal Hip*, New York, 1990.

*   *   *

Perhaps the best summation of Mac Wellman's work, if such a feat is possible, would be his own dedication to *The Bad Infinity,* the fifth and final installment in a series of plays that began with *Energuman* in the late 1970s: "*The Bad Infinity* is dedicated to the proposition that the theatrical body and soul of the world are not to be found in propositions per se, but in the subtle dialectic of gesture and spirit, parable and pratfall, dialogue and dance." Everything Wellman writes—and he has penned dozens of plays, musical librettos and lyrics, two novels, and several volumes of poetry—seems geared for such collisions, collapsing notions of high and low art with wit and humor while conflating the physical and the metaphysical, the miraculous and the mundane.

To parse the plays of Wellman is to take a meat cleaver to the ephemeral phantasms that make up his poetic creations. Characters often talk in tape loops of doggerel or in non sequiturs lathered in satire and menace. Whether the plays are domestic drama-mysteries like *A Murder of Crows* and *The Hyacinth Macaw*; the jazz-pop verse monologue *Terminal Hip*; the farcical, sexed-up *Dracula*; a historical, site-specific ghost story like *Crowbar*; or his political comedies in honor of Senator Jesse Helms and other censorious Republicans (*Sincerity Forever* and *7 Blowjobs*), Wellman combines a steady sense of the theatricality of language with the fluency of the language of the theater.

His plays often contain hip-hop choruses that lend sardonic descants on the main story line, if one is evident. In one of his most traditional narrative efforts, *Dracula*, a trio of "Vampirettes" vamp on his psychosexual satire of the familiar gothic tale. *Harm's Way* features a chorus as well as a character dubbed "Pop Star" who croons tacky ballads. The choruses are Wellman's particular Brechtian reverse alienation effect, using pop and cultural referents to release any hint of pomposity or self-righteousness and to create a bond with often bewildered audiences. A sense of self-importance seems the only sin in Wellman's dramatic lexicon.

Although many Wellman plays have memorable characters, a number might have come straight out of a bad film noir or from Alfred Jarry and other early dadaists, surrealists, and fantasists. A dog smokes a cigar in *Dracula*; a dead Santa appears in *The Bad Infinity,* as do a dog and a man named John Sleight, "alias Sam, a master of many identities"; and in *7 Blowjobs,* Bobbob Junior is described as "an idea of Surveillance" who in some madcap way is related to the central character, Senator Bob.

Such characters speak a Wellmanesque lingo that, not unlike Walt Whitman's, contains multitudes. Yet Wellman turns sanctimony on its head with a comic, vaudevillian sense of humor. *Terminal Hip* is inundated with this:

> Dodging pandas, the Fridge pops a long one, blacks
> out, blows cover, mesmerizes alien popover,
> hotdogs after half a sack, names the name,
> denies the Christ, heaves a Hail Mary, gambles
> for His garment at the foot of the cross,
> bails out, and buys some time with slo-mo

> mystic rendition of Old Man time with
> tweezers twixt his pointy ear flaps, doing
> the warty ham on rye, and no beanbag.

Much of Wellman's poetry runs in a similar vein. The title of the collection *A Shelf in Woop's Clothing* speaks volumes about his infatuation with wordplay. Imagine a writer who makes the imaginative leaps of **John Ashbery** and the surreal connections of **Mark Strand** or **James Tate** and who revels in the minutiae of punctuation as does **e.e. cummings**. The tendency to link diverse influences to explain Wellman's unique sensibility is contagious. One critic described his novel *Annie Salem,* about odd and idiosyncratic lower-class characters in America's heartland, thusly: "Part trenchant social commentary, part love story, part inscrutable sci-fi yarn, the novel reads a little like *Goodbye, Columbus* as rewritten by Kurt Vonnegut and Sherwood Anderson."

Wellman, like other playwrights he has inspired (**Suzan-Lori Parks** and Erik Ehn, to name two), is best enjoyed aloud, performed by a high-caliber cast able to navigate his vocabulary, puns, and nonnarrative structures. In the theater such dense verbosity only carries audiences so far, however, and his most mesmerizing works are his adaptations (*Dracula*) and his site-specific commissions like *Crowbar, Bad Penny,* and *Fnu Lnu.*

In *Crowbar,* written for En Garde Arts and performed in the prerenovated, dilapidated Victory Theater in Times Square, Wellman's flights of fancy are harnessed to a haunting, elliptical ghost story involving the spirits of David Belasco, Oscar Hammerstein I, and the original performers of **James A. Herne**'s early twentieth-century play *Sag Harbor,* which opened the theater. The audience, seated onstage, watched the actors roam through the decaying house (it has since been beautifully restored) as they declaimed bits of history, imagined domestic squabbles and cast conflicts, and sections of the play itself.

Likewise, Wellman's *Fnu Lnu,* a commissioned piece that investigates the smoky past of Ybor City, Florida, wittily plays off that town's cigar-rolling history. Any such rooting in reality lends a tenuous hold to Wellman's insistence on the beauty inherent in the illogical.

—John Istel

WELTY, Eudora (Alice)

Born: Jackson, Mississippi, 13 April 1909. **Education:** Mississippi State College for Women, Columbus, 1925-27; University of Wisconsin, Madison, B.A. 1929; Columbia University School for Advertising, New York, 1930-31. **Career:** Part-time journalist, 1931-32; publicity agent, Works Progress Administration (WPA), 1933-36; staff member, *New York Times Book Review,* during World War II; Honorary Consultant in American Letters, Library of Congress, Washington, D.C., 1958. **Awards:** Bread Loaf Writers Conference fellowship, 1940; O. Henry award, 1942, 1943, 1968; Guggenheim fellowship, 1942, 1948; American Academy grant, 1944, Howells medal, 1955, and Gold medal, 1972; Ford fellowship, for drama; Brandeis University Creative Arts award, 1965; Edward MacDowell medal, 1970; National Book award nomination, 1971; Christopher Book award, 1972; Pulitzer prize, 1973; National Medal for Literature, 1980; Presidential Medal of Freedom, 1980; American Book award, for paperback, 1983; Bobst award, 1984; Common Wealth award, 1984; Mystery Writers of America award, 1985; National Medal of Arts, 1987; Chevalier de l'Ordre des Arts et Lettres, France, 1987. D.Litt.: Denison University, Granville, Ohio, 1971; Smith College, Northampton, Massachusetts; University of Wisconsin, Madison; University of the South, Sewanee, Tennessee; Washington and Lee University, Lexington, Virginia. **Member:** American Academy, 1971. **Residence:** Jackson, Mississippi.

PUBLICATIONS

Collections

The Collected Stories. 1980.

Fiction

A Curtain of Green and Other Stories. 1941.
The Robber Bridegroom. 1942.
The Wide Net and Other Stories. 1943.
Delta Wedding. 1946.
Music from Spain (story). 1948.
The Golden Apples (stories). 1949.
Selected Stories. 1954.
The Ponder Heart. 1954.
The Bride of Innisfallen and Other Stories. 1955.
Thirteen Stories, edited by Ruth M. Vande Kieft. 1965.
Losing Battles. 1970.
The Optimist's Daughter. 1972.
Moon Lake and Other Stories. 1980.
Retreat (story). 1981.
Morgana: Two Stories from 'The Golden Apples.' 1988.
Why I Live at the P.O. and Other Stories. 1995.
The First Story. 1999.

Poetry

A Flock of Guinea Hens Seen from a Car. 1970.

Other

Short Stories (essay). 1949.
Place in Fiction. 1957.
Three Papers on Fiction. 1962.
The Shoe Bird (for children). 1964.
A Sweet Devouring (on children's literature). 1969.
One Time, One Place: Mississippi in the Depression: A Snapshot Album. 1971.
A Pageant of Birds. 1975.
Fairy Tale of the Natchez Trace. 1975.
The Eye of the Story: Selected Essays and Reviews. 1975.
The Little Store (memoir). 1975.
Ida M'Toy (memoir). 1979.
Miracles of Perception: The Art of Willa Cather, with Alfred Knopf and Yehudi Menuhin. 1980.
One Writer's Beginnings. 1984.
Conversations with Welty (interviews), edited by Peggy Whitman Prenshaw. 1984.
Photographs. 1989.
The Eye of the Story: Selected Essays and Reviews. 1990.

A Worn Path (children's story). 1991.
Monuments to Interruption (book reviews). 1994.
A Writer's Eye (book reviews). 1994.
More Conversations with Eudora Welty. 1996.
Stories, Essays, and Memoir. 1998.

Editor, with Ronald Sharp, *The Norton Book of Friendship.* 1991.

*

Bibliography: by Noel Polk, in *Mississippi Quarterly,* Fall 1973; *Welty: A Reference Guide* by Victor H. Thompson, 1976; *Welty: A Critical Bibliography 1936-1958* by Bethany C. Swearington, 1984; *The Welty Collection: A Guide to the Welty Manuscripts and Documents at the Mississippi Department of Archives and History* by Suzanne Marrs, 1988; *Eudora Welty: A Bibliography of her Work* by Noel Polk, 1993.

Critical Studies: *Welty* by Ruth M. Vande Kieft, 1962, revised edition, 1986; *A Season of Dreams: The Fiction of Welty* by Alfred Appel, Jr., 1965; *Welty* by Joseph A. Bryant, Jr., 1968; *The Rhetoric of Welty's Short Stories* by Zelma Turner Howard, 1973; *A Still Moment: Essays on the Art of Welty* edited by John F. Desmond, 1978; *Welty: Critical Essays* edited by Peggy Whitman Prenshaw, 1979; *Welty: A Form of Thanks* edited by Ann J. Abadie and Louis D. Dollarhide, 1979; *Welty's Achievement of Order* by Michael Kreyling, 1980; *Welty* by Elizabeth Evans, 1981; *A Tissue of Lies: Welty and the Southern Romance* by Jennifer L. Randisi, 1982; *Welty's Chronicle: A Story of Mississippi Life* by Albert J. Devlin, 1983; *With Ears Opening Like Morning Glories: Welty and the Love of Storytelling* by Carol S. Manning, 1985; *Sacred Groves and Ravaged Gardens: The Fiction of Welty, Carson McCullers, and Flannery O'Connor* by Louise Westling, 1985; *Welty* edited by Harold Bloom, 1986; *Welty: A Life in Literature* by Albert J. Aevlin, 1987; *Critical Essays on Welty* edited by W. Craig Turner and Lee Emling Harding, 1989; *Serious Daring from Within: Female Narrative Strategies in Welty's Novels* by Franziska Gygax, 1990; *Welty: Eye of the Storyteller* edited by Dawn Trouard, 1990; *The Heart of the Story: Welty's Short Fiction* by Peter Schmidt, 1991; *Welty: Two Pictures at Once in Her Frame* by Barbara Harrell Carson, 1992; "Eudora Welty Issue" in *The Southern Quarterly,* Fall 1993; *Eudora Welty's Aesthetics of Place* by Jan Nordby Gretlund, 1994; *Daughter of the Swan: Love and Knowledge in Eudora Welty's Fiction* by Gail L. Mortimer, 1994; *The Still Moment: Eudora Welty, Portrait of a Writer* by Paul Binding, 1994; *Eudora Welty and Virginia Woolf: Gender, Genre, and Influence* by Suzan Harrison, 1997; *Eudora Welty: A Writer's Life* by Ann Waldron, 1998; *Prophets of Recognition: Ideology and the Individual in the Novels by Ralph Ellison, Toni Morrison, Saul Bellow and Eudora Welty* by Julia Eichelberger, 1999; *Understanding Eudora Welty* by Michael Kreyling, 1999.

*   *   *

Eudora Welty is a part of the great outpouring of fiction that is often referred to as the Southern Renaissance, the discovery of solid traditions and uneasy tensions that color the work of **William Faulkner, Katherine Anne Porter, Caroline Gordon, William Styron,** and others. Welty's terrain overlaps with that of Faulkner, the state of Mississippi. But it offers a contrasting appearance—indeed, a predominantly sunny one despite the shadows of ancient pain, present injustice, and future uncertainty that both Faulkner and Welty discover in their part of the South. But Welty's imaginative world maintains its special rules: rules of civility and of affection that protect the continuance of human meaning and human dignity. It is a continuance that may well be a "losing battle," but it is never really a lost battle. The majority of Welty's characters reel under blows that chance, inheritance, and environment deal them, but they rise to hope and love another day. The compulsions they face and partly master are less awesome than those many a Faulkner character meets. There is guilt, but the guilt is personal rather than collective, accrued over the course of several generations. There are also distinct authoritative patterns of life. These patterns, in contrast to those of Faulkner, are familiar and easily identifiable rather than occult and mysterious. There is no "bear" or any other symbol of aboriginal compulsion moving back and forth in the delta and the hill country which Welty recollects and recreates in her short stories and her novels. Her characters—rednecks, cotton aristocrats, and the "just folks" of small county seats—are challenged by the events that overtake them, but they always manage to endure.

This can be seen in the many short stories, simple of surface but calculating in their approach to a revelatory conclusion. The story "Keela, The Outcast Indian Maiden," in *A Curtain of Green,* seems, for most of its course, to be a study of the guilt a young man feels for his share in the exploitation of a black midget who has been kidnapped and exhibited as a freak in a sideshow. But by the end of the story the young man has made a sort of expiation of his share of guilt. Suddenly, attention shifts to the little black man who is only amused by the antics of his visitor and sits down to supper with his children. Out of abasement and debasement the black man has won a minor victory.

The reversals of fate and complexities of life that Welty contemplates are the stuff of her many stories. Such reversals and complexities also furnish out the longer works, with the possible exception of Welty's early novel, *The Robber Bridegroom,* which is a pious salute to the violent times when Mississippi land was being invaded by white men, farmers, riverboat men, and robbers who attacked travellers on the Natchez Trace. This narrative has the willed simplicity of folk tale, as indeed do many of the short stories. But it is a simplicity that appears only intermittently in the longer novels, where the writer's imagination engages itself with a more or less contemporary milieu and the sensibilities educated there. *Delta Wedding* is a salute to the cotton aristocrats and their experience of power and complacency in the 1920s. Some characters in the novel enjoy their privileges and others try to measure them and test them. The careless "lose" their battle; the thoughtful attain to an uneasy survival and a profound comprehension of their situation. It is a comprehension that typically has to be recast from day to day.

This recasting is, in *Delta Wedding,* complex and difficult to express in a phrase. So it continues to be in shorter novels like *The Ponder Heart* and *The Optimist's Daughter,* two tales of matrimonial misadventures which are observed and studied by women, distinct centers of awareness in each novel, who are sufficient vehicles for Welty's own discriminations. A more difficult book is *Losing Battles.* In this long account of a family reunion up in the Mississippi hills, the novelist for the most part dispenses with the fairly refined and privileged observers of her other novels. She also gives up the comic discriminations of *Delta Wedding* and *The Ponder Heart. Losing Battles* is, in sheer event, not far removed from the farce of Li'l Abner's Dogpatch; there are mad car acci-

dents, watermelon fights, and gargantuan feastings. Nor does Welty allow her own prose to reproduce the thoughts of her mostly backcountry characters. The interminable conversations, fashioned from rural cliches, nevertheless become transparent envelopes through which appear the nature of redneck existence with a range of sensitivity almost as complex as that which is represented in *Delta Wedding.*

In an interview in *Conversations with Eudora Welty,* Welty explains the influence of the South on her writing: "I was very fortunate to grow up here [in Mississippi]. I think anyone who grew up in the South was fortunate, particularly writers. In the South the story is an integral part of life. Stories are just told. You get a sense of narrative. One of the most marvelous things is hearing all these stories and getting a sense of family and continuity. It is the world of memory." Indeed, Welty's fiction is deeply concerned with the nature of storytelling and narrative as it impacts upon southern life. Welty recreates a homey southern style of storytelling in her own fiction, creating novels and short stories ripe with the joys as well as the sorrows of experience, boldly celebrating the richness of life itself.

Welty is notable not only as an author but as a photographer as well. Her photographs of the post-depression Deep South are remarkable for the way in which they capture the people and the landscape of the American South. Welty's photographs, like her fiction, reflect a strong sense of place and reveal a sensitivity to and a profound understanding of the people of the South. Her photography is often compared to that of Walker Evans, who also photographed southern subjects in the wake of the depression, but Welty's photographs have a distinctive intimacy that stands in stark opposition to the more distant, detached perspective of Evans. In *One Time, One Place,* Welty articulates the connection between her photography and her fiction writing: "I learned quickly enough when to click the shutter, but what I was becoming aware of more slowly was a story-writer's truth: the thing to wait on, to reach there in time for, is the moment in which people reveal themselves." Indeed, neither the subjects of Welty's photography nor the characters in her fiction seem artificially constructed, either by the lens or the pen. Rather, they seem to "reveal themselves" and their deepest secrets to Welty's creative eye, which perhaps explains the intimacy which is so distinctive in Welty's work.

In short, Welty has a wide range of artistic talents as a novelist, a short story writer, and a photographer, but regardless of her medium, Welty seems predominantly concerned with how people respond to their opportunity to live and how they are able to survive in a world which is alternately, or perhaps simultaneously, brutal and blissful. Welty's fiction and her photography are each grounded deeply in the South and are concerned primarily with the nature of individual and communal identity in southern culture. By combining the domestic and the tragic in unlikely ways, Welty's fiction presents us with a world in which revelations may be found in the most unlikely places.

—Harold H. Watts, updated by Allison Hersh

WESCOTT, Glenway

Born: Kewaskum, Wisconsin, 11 April 1901. **Education:** The University of Chicago (president of the Poetry Society), 1917-

19. **Career:** Full-time writer from 1921; lived in France and Germany, 1925-33. **Awards:** D.Litt.: Rutgers University, New Brunswick, New Jersey, 1963. **Member:** National Institute of Arts and Letters, 1947, president, 1959-62. **Died:** 22 February 1987.

PUBLICATIONS

Fiction

The Apple of the Eye. 1924.
. . . Like a Lover (stories). 1926.
The Grandmothers: A Family Portrait. 1927; as *A Family Portrait,* 1927.
Good-bye Wisconsin (stories). 1928.
The Babe's Bed (story). 1930.
The Pilgrim Hawk: A Love Story. 1940.
Apartment in Athens. 1945; as *Household in Athens,* 1945.

Poetry

The Bitterns: A Book of Twelve Poems. 1920.
Native of Rock: Poems 1921-1922. 1925.

Other

Elizabeth Madox Roberts: A Personal Note. 1930.
Fear and Trembling (essays). 1932.
A Calendar of Saints for Unbelievers. 1932.
12 Fables of Aesop, Newly Narrated. 1954.
Images of Truth: Remembrances and Criticism. 1962.

Editor, *The Maugham Reader.* 1950.
Editor, *Short Novels of Colette.* 1951.

*

Bibliography: by Sy Myron Kaain, in *Bulletin of Bibliography* 22, 1956.

Critical Studies: *Wescott* by William H. Rueckert, 1965; *Wescott: The Paradox of Voice* by Ira Johnson, 1971; "Glenway Wescott, 1901-1987" by Bruce Brawer, in *The New Criterion,* May 1987; "Glenway Wescott: The Poetic Career of a Novelist" by Jerry Rosco, in *Chicago Review,* Winter 1990; "In a Thicket: Glenway Wescott's Pastoral Vision" by Jennifer Jordan Baker, in *Studies in Short Fiction,* Spring 1994, pp. 187-95; *Glenway Wescott: The Dialogic Tension of Realism and Modernism in Wescott's Novels* (dissertation) by Ted Wojtasik, 1998.

*   *   *

Glenway Wescott, a classmate of **Yvor Winters** and Vincent Sheean, was president of the Poetry Society at the University of Chicago. His imagist lyrics appeared in *Poetry* and were later printed privately in two small volumes. Then he turned away from poetry, and because of ill health left the university in 1919; for six restless years he lived briefly in New Mexico, the Berkshires, New York City, England, and Germany, usually with his lifelong friend Monroe Wheeler. Wescott's precocity, striking appearance (tall, blond), and cultivated British accent marked him during his expatriate years from 1925 to 1933, when he lived in Paris, at Villefrance-sur-Mer, and in Germany. In *The Autobiography of Alice B. Toklas,* **Gertrude Stein** records his first visit: "Glenway impressed us with his English accent. **Hemingway** explained. He said, when you matriculate at the University of Chicago, you write down just what accent you will have and they give it to you when you graduate." In the 1920s Wescott published impressive critical reviews (chiefly in the *Dial* and the *New Republic*), two novels, and a collection of short stories, though he published very little in the succeeding 50 years.

Wescott was 23 when *The Apple of the Eye* was published. The story of Hannah Madoc, a Wisconsin farm woman, is told from various perspectives. It is a novel of initiation and of revolt against the hostile environment of farm and town—especially against repressive Puritanism. *The Grandmothers* was Wescott's greatest popular success. Alwyn Tower, reliving in France his Wisconsin childhood, is "a participating narrator, identical to the author's second (artistic) self" (Ira Johnson). His curiosity aroused by an old family album, the young man pieces together the story of his three grandmothers (one grandfather married twice). Cadenced prose and high sensitivity present the pioneer experience, always focused on Wescott's major themes of love and the self.

An introductory essay lent its title to *Good-bye Wisconsin,* a short story collection. The ten stories, and *The Babe's Bed,* a slightly longer short story published in a limited Paris edition, show Wisconsin as hostile to the realization of the self. Wescott published only five more short stories, from 1932 to 1942, none of them noteworthy. He is often classified as a Midwestern realist and regionalist, and these stories obviously connect him with the "Revolt from the Village" writing of **Edgar Lee Masters,** **Sherwood Anderson,** and **Sinclair Lewis.** But Wescott's fiction also demonstrates his abandonment of realism, regionalism, and the provincial Midwest for a European aesthetic existence and artistic ideal. Among his friends were Ford Madox Ford, Jean Cocteau, Elly Ney, and Rebecca West.

Wescott's current reputation as a stylist is based primarily on *The Pilgrim Hawk: A Love Story,* which first appeared in two issues of *Harper's* and has been reprinted and anthologized. Alwyn Tower, now in America, recounts a day's incident in France in 1940 that involves Irish and American expatriates and their servants. Tower's nostalgic reminiscence is heavily ironic, and the falcon is central to the love story Tower narrates. In addition to the two physical love triangles, a third appears to perceptive readers, a subtle examination of the conflict between appetite and control; as James Korges puts it (in *Contemporary Novelists*), "The reader is not told about the conflict of love and art; instead he receives it, as a powerful undercurrent in the story of an Irish couple and a hawk, which is also a story about love and art, freedom and captivity."

Wescott considered *Apartment in Athens* his contribution to the war effort. A German officer is billeted in the apartment of a Greek middle-class intellectual. "The cramped physical and moral conditions, the readjustments in the relationships of the family, the whole distortion of the social organism by the unassimilable presence of the foreigner—all this is most successfully created" (**Edmund Wilson**). The novel, however, is marred by its ending, a long letter smuggled out of the prison cell of the condemned Greek father, and the anti-Nazi editorializing violates the fictional illusion.

Images of Truth collects the critical essays Wescott had published since 1939. His long essays on **Katherine Anne Porter,** **Elizabeth Madox Roberts,** Mann, Colette, Maugham, and **Thornton Wilder** are highly personal expressions of Wescott's own idiosyncratic views on life and literature. Wescott's imagist poetry, which he abandoned early, has been long forgotten. His essentially lyric talent found expression in his prose.

—Clarence A. Glasrud

WEST, (Mary) Jessamyn

Born: North Vernon, Indiana, 18 July 1902. **Education:** Union High School, Fullerton, California, graduated 1919; Whittier College, California, 1919-20, 1921-23, B.A. in English, 1923; Fullerton Junior College, 1920-21; Oxford University, England, 1929; University of California at Berkeley, 1929-31. **Family:** Married Harry Maxwell McPherson in 1923; one foster daughter. **Career:** Worked as school secretary and teacher in Hemet, California, 1924-29; taught at Bread Loaf Writers Conference at Middlebury College, Vermont, and other writing programs at Antioch College, Yellow Springs, Ohio; Indiana University, Bloomington; University of Notre Dame, Indiana; Colorado State University, Fort Collins; University of Utah, Salt Lake City; Washington State University, Pullman; Stanford University, California; University of Montana, Missoula; Portland University, Oregon; University of Kentucky, Lexington; and Loyola University, Los Angeles, California. Visiting professor at Wellesley College, University of California at Irvine, Mills College in Oakland, California, and Whittier College; visiting lecturer at numerous other colleges. **Awards:** Indiana Author's Day award, 1956; Thermod Monsen award, 1958; California Commonwealth Club award, 1970; California Literature Medal, 1971; Janet Kafka prize, 1976; Indiana Arts Commission award for Literature, 1977. D.Litt.: Whittier College; Mills College; Swarthmore College, Pennsylvania; Indiana State University, Terre Haute; Indiana University; Western College for Women, Oxford, Ohio; Wheaton College, Norton, Massachusetts; Juniata College, Huntingdon, Pennsylvania; Wilmington College, Ohio. Fellow, University of California at Berkeley. Posthumous honor: Dedication of Jessamyn West Park, Yorba Linda, California, 1984. **Member:** American Civil Liberties Union; National Association for the Advancement of Colored People; Whittier College Board of Trustees, 1970-83, honorary member, 1983-84. **Died:** 23 February 1984.

PUBLICATIONS

Short Stories

The Friendly Persuasion. 1945.
Cress Delahanty. 1953.
Love, Death, and the Ladies' Drill Team. 1955; in England as *Learn to Say Goodbye,* 1957.
Except for Me and Thee: A Companion to The Friendly Persuasion. 1969.
Crimson Ramblers of the World, Farewell. 1970.
A Story of a Story & Three Stories. 1982.
Collected Stories of Jessamyn West. 1986.

Novels

The Witch Diggers. 1951.
Little Men (in *Star Short Novels*). 1954; as *The Chilekings,* 1967.

South of the Angels. 1960.
A Matter of Time. 1966.
Leafy Rivers. 1967.
The Massacre at Fall Creek. 1975.
The Life I Really Lived. 1979.
The State of Stony Lonesome. 1984.

Nonfiction

The Reading Public (essay). 1952.
To See the Dream (autobiography). 1957.
Love Is Not What You Think (essay). 1959.
Hide and Seek: A Continuing Journey (autobiography). 1973.
The Woman Said Yes: Encounters with Life and Death (memoir). 1976; in England as *Encounters with Death and Life,* 1978.
Double Discovery: A Journey (autobiography). 1980.

Plays

Screenplays: *Friendly Persuasion,* with Robert Wyler, uncredited, based on story collection *The Friendly Persuasion* (produced 1956); *The Big Country,* with Robert Wyler, based on novel by Donald Hamilton (produced 1958); *Stolen Hours,* remake of *Dark Victory* (produced 1963).

Opera libretto: *A Mirror for the Sky,* music by Gail Kubik (first performed 1957). 1948.

Poetry

The Secret Look. 1974.

Other

Editor, *The Quaker Reader.* 1962.

*

Bibliography: *Jessamyn West: A Descriptive and Annotated Bibliography* by Ann Dahlstrom Farmer, 1998.

Critical Studies: *Jessamyn West* by Alfred S. Shivers, 1972, revised edition, 1992; *Jessamyn West* by Ann Dahlstrom Farmer, 1982.

*   *   *

Jessamyn West is best known for *The Friendly Persuasion* and *Cress Delahanty.* All but two of the chapters in these books appeared first as short stories in a variety of magazines, and a number of them continued to be reprinted in anthologies and short-story collections for four decades, thereby creating West's reputation as a writer of gentle stories about Quakers and adolescents. Despite this image, West's work is considerable in amount and scope: some twenty-four separate full-length publications and innumerable uncollected shorter works in a variety of genres.

Becoming a writer was an unthinkable goal for a woman born into a Quaker household in rural Indiana in 1902. West was raised on a citrus ranch in a fledgling community in southern California and educated at a small, Quaker-founded college where female students at that time were expected to become teachers, missionaries, or wives and mothers, even though her propensity for language and her love of words surfaced early and remained constant. As she stated in *The Woman Said Yes,* she remembered crying at the age of three or four because "I knew that I was born to read and write, and . . . could not make out the words in the book I was holding." At twelve, she began keeping scrapbooks of interesting words and ways the stories she read began and ended. In 1929, having married the summer after graduating from Whittier College and then teaching school, she veered closer to her unspoken goal by enrolling in Oxford University's Summer Meeting and then undertaking a doctoral program in English at the University of California at Berkeley. Two years later, with all of her Berkeley class work completed and her orals only days away, she suffered a lung hemorrhage that was subsequently diagnosed as far-advanced bilateral tuberculosis.

West was one of only five percent who ever recovered after such a diagnosis. In *The Woman Said Yes,* West credited her mother with not only saving her life after two years of sanitarium treatments had failed but in giving her the beginnings of her writing life by sharing memories of her own Indiana girlhood. Once West was able to return to her own home, she began creating stories from those memories as well as from her own memories of life in the sanitarium. Still partially bedridden and in her late thirties, she was free at last to write because she could do little else. Most of West's earlier major works are set in the Midwest of the 1800s; most of the later ones are placed in southern California during the first half of the 1900s.

The Friendly Persuasion covers a forty-year span in the life of Indiana Quaker nurseryman Jess Birdwell and his family. Some of the chapters are primarily humorous: for example, Jess's un-Quakerly longing for music and his love of fast horses, his wife's court appearance to win back a pet goose, and a neighbor's aversion to bath water. Others are more serious, such as Jess and Eliza's grieving for a dead child and the testing of the family's pacifist beliefs in the Civil War. *Except for Me and Thee,* which followed twenty-four years later, is another collection of Birdwell stories. Here for the first time are details of Jess and Eliza's courtship and the family's move to southern Indiana, the Birdwells' involvement with the Underground Railroad and their encounter with a dying Rebel soldier, the infatuation of a spinster seamstress for one of the Birdwell sons, and family birthdays and Christmas celebrations.

The Witch Diggers, West's first novel, is considerably darker than the Birdwell stories and combines two recurring themes in her work, emerging self-awareness and acceptance of that self. Here, amid the strange inmates of an Indiana Poor Farm, which her father manages and where her family lives, eighteen-year-old Cate Conboy comes to fear and deny her emotional and sexual selves, thereby losing the man she really loves and ultimately causing his death. *Leafy Rivers* is also set in the nineteenth-century Midwest and also features the coming of age of a young girl, in this case the title character. Leafy's journey to maturity coincides with the journey she undertakes to drive the family's hogs cross-country by herself when her husband is injured. Leafy, unlike Cate, has the courage to accept the self she discovers, and thus avoids tragedy. West's final work with a Midwestern setting is *The Massacre at Fall Creek.* For the first and only time, West created a story based on an actual historical event, the first known conviction, sentencing, and execution of whites for killing Indians. There are no heroes or villains here, only vulnerable human beings caught in a many-layered web of circumstances two hundred years in the making.

Cress Delahanty is West's first work set in southern California. Like *The Friendly Persuasion, Cress's* sixteen chapters were originally written as short stories, but they involved at least eight different adolescent heroines instead of members of a single family. West eliminated the inconsistencies and organized them into tales about one girl from the ages of twelve through sixteen. The stories are generally lighthearted looks at growing up, from Cress's delight in dreaming away an afternoon at home alone to her purchase of an entirely unsuitable hat with which to impress a boy. But there are more somber stories as well: her infatuation with a man critically ill with tuberculosis, her discovery that her music teacher has used her presence to cover up an illicit liaison, and a chilling evening spent with a school acquaintance and her sinister father.

South of the Angels, West's first California novel, involves nine months in the lives of the first settlers on a tract of undeveloped land that closely resembles the Yorba Linda of West's youth. Although some critics found the novel unsatisfactory because of its large cast of characters, this book is notable for its treatment of the emerging communities surrounding Los Angeles in the early 1900s, an area seldom described in fiction. *A Matter of Time,* also set in southern California, focuses on two sisters, very different in their looks and lifestyles, who conspire together to end the life of the younger one when the pain of terminal cancer becomes unendurable. Ten years later, West revealed in *The Woman Said Yes* that although the events in the sisters' early lives were products of her imagination, the circumstances of the sisters' collusion were exactly as she and her sister Carmen lived them.

Of all of West's fiction, *The Life I Really Lived* is the most remote from West's own life or the life of her family, but it is the one readers feel is the most autobiographical because it is told so convincingly. Like West, Orpha Chase leads a crucial second life, the one committed to paper in her journals and her books, but there the similarity ends. Orpha's real life is far different and far more turbulent than her creator's, from the violent early years in a rural Kentucky community fraught with incest, rape, and suicide, to the years in California during her faith-healer brother's trial for murder, her affair with the lead in the film based on one of her books, and the discovery that her daughter is one of the other women in his life. West's final novel, *The State of Stony Lonesome,* which was published after her death, is a return to West's own past, to a place very much like Yorba Linda, to a young girl very like herself with parents like Grace and Eldo West, and to a bond between the young girl and an uncle very much like West's own relationship with her favorite uncle.

West's specific contributions to American literature have been a host of memorable characters and landscapes, particularly several of the areas of southern California outside metropolitan Los Angeles and Hollywood. The characters are memorable because they are individualized and hence seem as real as ourselves and the landscapes because they are integral to the lives of her characters and have the vividness of actual places. Although Robert Kirsch of the *Los Angeles Times* is speaking about *The Life I Really Lived,* his estimate accurately describes West's entire literary output: "It is time . . . to recognize Jessamyn West as one of the treasures of this state's literature and, in fact, of the nation's . . . . she has written a masterpiece, turned tables on the conventional views, made universal the materials, the vocabulary of the southern California experience, done it with such zest and laughter and tears that readers will love it—and come back to thinking of what it says about writing, about courage, faith, love and death."

—Ann Dahlstrom Farmer

WEST, Nathanael

Born: Nathan Weinstein in New York City, 17 October 1903; changed name, 1926. **Education:** DeWitt Clinton High School, New York; Tufts College, Medford, Massachusetts, 1921; Brown University, Providence, Rhode Island, 1922-24, Ph.B. 1924. **Family:** Married Eileen McKenney in 1940. **Career:** Worked for his father in real estate business, 1924-25; lived in Paris, 1926-27; night manager, Kenmore Hall Hotel and Suffolk Club Hotel, New York, 1927-31; associate editor, to William Carlos Williams, for *Contact: An American Quarterly,* 1931-32; writer for Columbia, 1933, 1938, Republic, 1936-38, Universal, 1938, and RKO, 1938-40, all in Hollywood, California. **Died:** 22 December 1940.

PUBLICATIONS

Collections

Complete Works. 1957.

Fiction

The Dream Life of Balso Snell. 1931.
Miss Lonelyhearts. 1933.
A Cool Million: The Dismantling of Lemuel Pitkin. 1934.
The Day of the Locust. 1939.

Plays

Good Hunting: A Satire, with Joseph Shrank (produced 1938).

Screenplays: *The Presidents Mystery,* with Lester Cole, 1936; *Follow Your Heart,* with others, 1936; *Ticket to Paradise,* with others, 1936; *It Could Happen to You,* with Samuel Ornitz, 1937; *Rhythm in the Clouds,* with others, 1937; *Gangs of New York* (uncredited), 1938; *Orphans of the Street* (uncredited), 1938; *Born to Be Wild,* 1938; *Five Came Back,* with others, 1939; *I Stole a Million,* with Lester Cole, 1939; *Spirit of Culver,* with others, 1939; *Men Against the Sky,* with John Twist, 1940; *Let's Make Music,* 1940.

*

Bibliography: *West: A Comprehensive Bibliography* by William White, 1975; *West: An Annotated Bibliography of the Scholarship and Works* by Dennis P. Vannatta, 1976.

Critical Studies: *West: An Interpretive Study* by James F. Light, 1961, revised edition, 1971; *West* by Stanley Edgar Hyman, 1962; *West: The Ironic Prophet* by Victor Comerchero, 1964; *The Fiction of West* by Randall Reid, 1967; *West: The Art of His Life* by Jay Martin, 1970, and *West: A Collection of Critical Essays* edited by Martin, 1971; *West: A Critical Essay* by Nathan A. Scott, 1971; *West's Novels* by Irving Malin, 1972; *West: The Cheaters*

and the Cheated edited by David Madden, 1973; *West* by Kingsley Widmer, 1982; *West* by Robert Emmet Long, 1985; *Vanguard Desires: Sex, Machines, and Revolution in the Novels of Evgenii Zamiatin, John Dos Passo and Nathaniel West* (dissertation) by Mathew Roberts, 1994.

*   *   *

While many of the writers of the 1930s found in the naturalistic tradition a form that would directly express their protest at what seemed to be the collapse or corruption of the American Dream, Nathanael West developed an oblique vision that may prove more lasting than the products of many of his contemporaries. A statement by his painter-protagonist, Tod Hackett (*The Day of the Locust*), provides a reasonable thematic definition of West's artistic intentions: "It is hard to laugh at the need for beauty and romance, no matter how tasteless, even horrible, the results of that are. But it is easy to sigh. Few things are sadder than the truly monstrous." Focusing relentlessly on the radical disparity between the romantic expectations pandered to by the mass media and the actual limited portion that is the human lot, West's talent is to delineate "the truly monstrous" in a grotesque world that hovers ambiguously between the hilarious and the heartbreaking. Accepting more or less the same premises that underlie **T.S. Eliot**'s *The Waste Land,* West's work is equally hallucinatory and probably more pessimistic, as well as more comic. It is partly indebted to the techniques of surrealism that West absorbed in a brief post-college sojourn in Paris where he wrote his first novel (*The Dream Life of Balso Snell*), and its energy derives from a deep moral exasperation that could be a result of his youthful training in Judaism. Relatively overlooked when it was published, West's fiction brought the sub-genre of "Black Humor" into prominence after World War II when it served as a model of encouragement for such writers as **Carson McCullers, James Purdy, Flannery O'Connor,** and **John Hawkes.**

Although West wrote four novels in his abruptly ended career, he is remembered primarily for *Miss Lonelyhearts* and *The Day of the Locust.* In both novels West cultivates a stripped cinematic style, advancing his narrative in a spastic sequence of intense and fragmented scenes. As a Hollywood screenwriter for the last years of his life, West clearly found the discipline of the film compatible with his own penchant for constructing stories out of dominantly visual images, and *The Day of the Locust* is generally regarded as the premiere "Hollywood novel" in American fiction.

In *Miss Lonelyhearts,* the un-named protagonist is a bachelor newspaper columnist assigned to the job of giving advice to the lovelorn. Worn down by the barrage of unabated and insoluble misery that pours in on him and bedeviled by the savage nihilism of his city editor, Shrike, he finds himself unable even to imagine palliative possibilities for those who write to him. Further, his defensive cynicism and detachment erode as he begins to recognize his own condition in the broken human beings who are his suppliants. Killed finally in a ludicrous comedy of errors, he becomes a futile immolated Christ whose death is merely another addition to the crumpled heap of frustrated hopes that the novel assembles. West's dark mockery is pointed in all directions. The manipulators are as crippled and impotent as the manipulated; nor does the novel permit any sociopolitical resolution of the problems it presents. Lacking a sane religious option for satisfying "the need for beauty and romance," the frenetic improvisations of the spiritually dispossessed can only be freakishly monstrous and sad.

The Day of the Locust displaces a greater imaginative volume, just as its setting—Hollywood at the time when it was dream-factory to the world—is a larger milieu than the newspaper office and bars of *Miss Lonelyhearts*. Here West places his artist-protagonist on the margins of the action and structures the novel on what might be termed the principle of "an image within an image." Tod Hackett is engaged in painting *The Burning of Los Angeles*, a giant canvas that he intends to be prophetic in the Old Testament sense; and the novel as a whole duplicates on a greatly magnified screen his apocalyptic vision of a holocaust. Unlike the multitude of victims in *Miss Lonelyhearts*, the grotesques of *The Day of the Locust*, mindless as lemmings, purposeless as falling rain, seek vengeance for the rootlessness, disappointment, and excruciating boredom of their lives in random unprovoked destruction. If the keynote of *Miss Lonelyhearts* is a profound sadness wrested out of grotesque comedy, *The Day of the Locust* re-orchestrates that sadness with chords of terror. And the bitter humor of the earlier novel takes on accents of insane laughter in the later one.

—Earl Rovit

See the essay on *The Day of the Locust*.

WHARTON, Edith (Newbold)

Born: Edith Jones, New York City, 24 January 1862. Traveled in Italy, Spain, and France as a child. **Education:** Educated privately. **Family:** Married Edward Wharton in 1885 (divorced 1913). Lived in Newport, Rhode Island, after her marriage, and in Europe from 1907; close friend of Henry James, q.v. **Career:** Helped organize the American Hostel for Refugees and the Children of Flanders Rescue Committee, during World War I. **Awards:** Pulitzer prize, 1921; American Academy gold medal, 1924. Litt.D.: Yale University, New Haven, Connecticut, 1923. Chevalier, Legion of Honor (France), 1916, and Order of Leopold (Belgium), 1919. **Member:** American Academy, 1930. **Died:** 11 August 1937.

PUBLICATIONS

Collections

A Wharton Reader, edited by Louis Auchincloss. 1965.
Collected Short Stories, edited by R.W.B. Lewis. 1968.
Novels (Library of America; includes *The House of Mirth, The Reef, The Custom of the Country,* and *The Age of Innocence*), edited by R.W.B. Lewis. 1986.
The Stories, edited by Anita Brookner. 2 vols., 1988-89.
The Muse's Tragedy and Other Stories (Library of America), edited by Candace Waid. 1990.
Novellas and Other Writings (Library of America), edited by Cynthia Griffin Wolff. 1990.
Edith Wharton: Three Complete Works of Love, Morals, and Manners. 1996.
New York Novels (Modern Library edition; includes *The House of Mirth, The Custom of the Country,* and *The Age of Innocence*). 1998.

Short Stories

The Greater Inclination. 1899.
Crucial Instances. 1901.
The Descent of Man and Other Stories. 1904.
Madame de Treymes (novella). 1907.
The Hermit and the Wild Woman, and Other Stories. 1908.
Tales of Men and Ghosts. 1910.
Ethan Frome (novella). 1911; edited by Blake Nevius, 1968.
Xingu and Other Stories. 1916.
Summer (novella). 1917.
Old New York: False Dawn (The 'Forties). The Old Maid (The 'Fifties). The Spark (The 'Sixties). New Year's Day (The 'Seventies). 1924.
Here and Beyond. 1926.
Certain People. 1930.
Human Nature. 1933.
The World Over. 1936.
Ghosts. 1937.
Fast and Loose: A Novelette, edited by Viola Hopkins Winner. 1977.
Roman Fever and Other Stories. 1997.
The Reckoning and Other Stories. 1999.

Novels

The Touchstone. 1900; as *A Gift from the Grave,* 1900.
The Valley of Decision. 1902.
Sanctuary. 1903.
The House of Mirth. 1905; edited by Elizabeth Ammons, 1990.
The Fruit of the Tree. 1907.
The Reef. 1912.
The Custom of the Country. 1913.
The Marne. 1918.
The Age of Innocence. 1920.
The Glimpses of the Moon. 1922.
A Son at the Front. 1923.
The Mother's Recompense. 1925.
Twilight Sleep. 1927.
The Children. 1928; as *The Marriage Playground,* 1930.
Hudson River Bracketed. 1929.
The Gods Arrive. 1932.
The Buccaneers. 1938.

Plays

The Joy of Living, from a play by Hermann Sudermann (produced 1902). 1902.
The House of Mirth, with Clyde Fitch, from the novel by Wharton (produced 1906). Edited by Glenn Loney, 1981.

Poetry

Verses. 1878.
Artemis to Actaeon and Other Verse. 1909.
Twelve Poems. 1926.

Other

The Decoration of Houses, with Ogden Codman, Jr. 1897.
Italian Villas and Their Gardens. 1904.

Italian Backgrounds. 1905.

A Motor-Flight through France. 1908.

Fighting France: From Dunkerque to Belfort. 1915.

Wharton's War Charities in France. 1918.

L'Amérique en Guerre. 1918.

French Ways and Their Meaning. 1919.

In Morocco. 1920.

The Writing of Fiction. 1925.

A Backward Glance (autobiography). 1934.

Letters, edited by R.W.B. and Nancy Lewis. 1988.

Letters 1900-1915, with Henry James, edited by Lyall H. Powers. 1989.

Edith Wharton Abroad: Selected Travel Writings, 1888-1920. 1995.

Editor, *Le Livre des sans-foyer.* 1915; as *The Book of the Homeless: Original Articles in Verse and Prose,* 1916.

Editor, with Robert Norton, *Eternal Passion in English Poetry.* 1939.

*

Bibliography: *Wharton: A Bibliography* by Vito J. Brenni, 1966; *Wharton and Kate Chopin: A Reference Guide* by Marlene Springer, 1976; *Wharton: A Descriptive Bibliography* by Stephen Garrison, 1990; *Wharton: An Annotated Secondary Bibliography* by Kristin O. Lauer and Margaret P. Murray, 1990.

Critical Studies: *Wharton: A Study of Her Fiction* by Blake Nevius, 1953; *Wharton: Convention and Morality in the Work of a Novelist* by Marilyn Jones Lyde, 1959; *Wharton,* 1961, and *Wharton: A Woman in Her Time,* 1971, both by Louis Auchincloss; *Wharton: A Collection of Critical Essays* edited by Irving Howe, 1962; *Wharton and Henry James: The Story of Their Friendship* by Millicent Bell, 1965; *Wharton: A Critical Interpretation* by Geoffrey Walton, 1971, revised edition, 1982; *Wharton: A Biography* by R.W.B. Lewis, 1975; *Wharton and the Novel of Manners* by Gary Lindberg, 1975; *Wharton* by Margaret B. McDowell, 1976, revised edition, 1991; *Wharton* by Richard H. Lawson, 1977; *A Feast of Words: The Triumph of Wharton,* 1977, and *Wharton's Prisoners of Shame: A New Perspective on Her Neglected Fiction,* 1991, both by Cynthia Griffin Wolff; *The Frustrations of Independence: Wharton's Lesser Fiction* by Brigitta Lüthi, 1978; *Wharton's Argument with America* by Elizabeth Ammons, 1980; *The Female Intruder in the Novels of Wharton* by Carol Wershoven, 1982; *Wharton: Orphancy and Survival* by Wendy Gimbel, 1984; *Wharton: Traveller in the Land of Letters* by Janet Goodwyn, 1989; *Wharton and the Art of Fiction* by Penelope Vita-Finzi, 1990; *Verging on the Abyss: The Social Fiction of Kate Chopin and Wharton* by Mary E. Papke, 1990; *The House of Mirth: A Novel of Admonition* by Linda Wagner-Martin, 1990; *Wharton and the Unsatisfactory Man* by David Holbrook, 1991; *Wharton's Letters from the Underworld: Fictions of Women and Writing* by Candace Waid, 1991; *Discussion Notes on Edith Wharton's The Age of Innocence* by M.J. Roennfeldt, 1994; *Edith Wharton's The House of Mirth* by Dawn Keeler, 1995; *Edith Wharton: Matters of Mind and Spirit* by Carol J. Singley, 1995; *Edith Wharton: A House Full of Rooms, Architecture, Interiors, and Gardens* by Theresa Craig, 1996; *The End of the Age of Innocence: Edith Wharton and the First World War* by Alan Price, 1996; *Edith Wharton's Italian Gardens* by Vivian Russell, 1997; *Edith Wharton's Travel Writing: The Making of a Connoisseur* by Sa-

rah Bird Wright, 1997; *Edith Wharton A to Z: The Essential Guide to the Life and Work* by Sarah Bird Wright, 1998; *Edith Wharton: Matters of Mind and Spirit* by Carol J. Singley, 1998; *Displaying Women: Spectacles of Leisure in Edith Wharton's New York* by Maureen E. Montgomery, 1998; *Edith Wharton: Beyond the Age of Innocence* by Ruth Turk, 1998; *The Art of Dying: Suicide in the Works of Kate Chopin, Edith Wharton, and Sylvia Plath* by Deborah S. Gentry, 1998; *Edith Wharton in Context: Essays on Intertextuality,* 1999; *A Forward Glance: New Essays on Edith Wharton,* 1999; *Solitude and Society in the Works of Herman Melville and Edith Wharton* by Linda Costanzo Cahir, 1999.

*   *   *

Edith Wharton was a versatile as well as a prolific writer. She published more than forty books, including some twenty novels, ten collections of short stories, books of verse, the pioneer work in interior design (with Ogden Codman, Jr.) *The Decoration of Houses,* several books of travel, an autobiography, and books on Italian villas, France, and fictional theory. It is by her fiction, however, that her importance as a writer must be judged. Wharton was an admirer and close friend of **Henry James.** Because of that friendship and because of certain parallels between their lives (both New Yorkers, both expatriates) and between their fictions (both with an interest in the manners of the rich, and in Americans living abroad), as well as the aesthetic principles Wharton appears to have got from "the master," she has been called a disciple of James, a judgment that has obscured significant differences between them. James was a metaphysical writer, Wharton a novelist of manners. James's method was to remove his characters from the effects of social forces and to locate his story in the minds of his characters, Wharton's was to deal with the impact of social and moral forces on the lives of her protagonists. Conflict in James is usually internal. In Wharton, it is almost always external, involving a superior individual in a struggle with the representatives of a social world with which the individual is fundamentally at odds.

The grand exception is *The Reef,* Wharton's most Jamesian novel. Here the action is confined almost exclusively to a chateau in France and the issue narrowed to a psychological struggle in the mind of the heroine, Anna Leath, who discovers that the man she has agreed to marry has had an affair with the young woman who is about to marry her stepson. Despite the economy, the tightness, the remoteness from the usual social forces that move through Wharton's pages, the conflict is much like that to be found in other Wharton novels, except that here it is treated as a psychological problem rather than a social and moral struggle. Anna Leath, the protagonist, cannot accept her fiancé's promiscuity nor can she give him up; and so, at the end of the novel, she is reduced to a state of tormented indecision.

In the first of her major novels, *The House of Mirth,* Lily Bart, a young woman from an old New York family ruined by financial reverses and extravagance, is caught between her love of beauty and luxury and her moral fastidiousness. If she should marry the man she loves she would live in what to her would be physical squalor; if she marries a man she does not love in order to get the material things essential to her sense of well-being, she would violate her deepest nature. She manages to salvage her moral integrity but slides into poverty and, then, death, and a pathetic moral triumph.

Ethan Frome, a short novel that differs in some ways (a New England setting, impoverished rural characters) from Wharton's typical fiction, nonetheless deals with an issue similar to the one that confronts Lily Bart: the conflict between social and moral conventions and the deep desires of the individual. Ethan Frome, married to a homely neurasthenic woman several years older than himself, falls in love with his wife's pretty cousin. Although he contemplates eloping with the girl, Mattie Wills, social pressures win out. Ethan and Mattie's attempt to escape their fate through suicide ends with them maimed for life and left in the care of the grim woman they had tried to foil.

Both *Ethan Frome* and *Summer,* another short New England novel, give fuller rein to sexual passion than other Wharton novels. Ethan and Mattie have to pay for their passion in a cruelly ironic way; Charity Royal, protagonist of *Summer,* is allowed a kind of idyllic bliss in the arms of her lover before the score is reckoned and she is obliged to marry her elderly guardian, a good, solid man who will give her a respectable place in the town of North Dormer and a name for her unborn child, but a passionless marriage.

In *The Age of Innocence,* the last of Wharton's important novels, the same issue is dealt with in a lightly ironic way. Newland Archer has two choices: he can marry the conventional young woman to whom he is engaged or he can break with her and live with Ellen Olenska, a Europeanized American shown to be emotionally and aesthetically more attractive to Archer. The choice is between what is socially acceptable to old New York society and what most engages Archer's deepest feelings. Again, convention triumphs. Archer marries May. Ellen returns to Europe. Years later, in a kind of wistful epilogue, Archer visits Europe and, with his wife dead, might reestablish his relationship with Ellen. Archer fails to visit Ellen, however, and takes comfort from the knowledge that his life with May has had its compensations. Thus, it seems, Wharton has made a kind of peace with the vexing conflict between personal desire and social obligation.

The Custom of the Country, which appeared in 1913, strikes a note that was to be echoed increasingly after 1920. It is Wharton's major satire on American life and it lays out in a manner that anticipates the cruder satires of **Sinclair Lewis** the rise of vulgar Americans from the West. Undine Sprague is the feminine version, Elmer Moffat the male. With neither taste nor moral scruple, they assail the old-monied New York aristocracy, conquer it, and move on to Europe and repeat their triumph. Undine marries and divorces Ralph Marvel of New York, marries and divorces a French aristocrat and, then, marries Elmer Moffat who is now a multimillionaire settled in Europe and buying up rare antique art. In this novel Wharton's usual theme—the impingement of social and economic forces on the lives of sensitive individuals—is relegated to a minor role. Ralph Marvel's suicide (precipitated by Undine's greed) is but one of the brutal blows inflicted by Undine during her upward scramble.

After 1920 the satirical note predominated in novels such as *Twilight Sleep, The Children, Hudson River Bracketed,* and *The Gods Arrive.* In all of these novels there was a decided falling off both of artistic integrity and of imaginative energy. The brilliant, lucid style of the early work was scarcely visible now, except in *The Mother's Recompense* and in the nonsatirical parts of *The Children. The Glimpses of the Moon* was not much above the level of soap opera, and *Twilight Sleep* was a broader and less convincing satire on current representatives of American women than *The Custom of the Country. Hudson River Bracketed* and *The Gods*

Arrive deal with the career of an American novelist, Vance Weston, tracing his rise from obscurity in Euphoria, Illinois, to international fame in London and Paris, but they fail to bring his story into significant focus. In *The Buccaneers* Wharton returned once more to the scene of her earlier and best triumphs, old New York before the turn of the century, but the novel remained unfinished at her death.

Among Wharton's seventy or so published short stories at least a dozen appear to have enduring quality, including "The Other Two," "Xingu," "Kerfol," "The Bunner Sisters," "The Triumph of Night," "Bewitched," "A Bottle of Perrier," "After Holbein," "Mr. Jones," "Pomegranate Seed," "Roman Fever," "Joy in the House," and "The Eyes."

In 1934 Wharton published her autobiography, an engaging though carefully selective account of her life, which referred only briefly to her disastrous marriage and dealt humorously and ironically with her eminent friend Henry James. Even before her death in 1937 Wharton's literary reputation had begun to decline. It is only in the late twentieth century that interest in her work has revived, partly as the result of the new feminist consciousness. Still, even now, her novels and stories are not so highly regarded as they once were nor as seriously treated by literary critics as they deserve to be. What were once regarded as her strengths— her firm grasp of the social realities of her time and place, and her ready accessibility—now appear to be her chief limitations. However, her two novels about New England life, *Ethan Frome* and *Summer,* along with *The House of Mirth, The Reef* and *The Age of Innocence,* are among the best novels of their time and constitute an impressive body of work.

—W.J. Stuckey

See the essay on *The House of Mirth* and *The Age of Innocence.*

WHEATLEY, Phillis

Born: Africa, possibly Senegal, c. 1753; sold as a slave to the John Wheatley family in Boston, 1761. **Education:** Educated by the Wheatley family. **Family:** Married John Peters, a freed slave, in 1778; three children. **Career:** Sent to England for her health, 1773, and was received in London society; returned to Boston to care for Mrs. Wheatley, 1773; manumitted by the Wheatleys, 1774, and separated from the loyalist Wheatleys by the Revolutionary War; lived in Wilmington, Massachusetts, 1779-83, and Boston after 1783. **Died:** 5 December 1784.

Publications

Collections

Poems (includes letters), edited by Julian D. Mason, Jr. 1966.
Wheatley and Her Writings, edited by William H. Robinson. 1984.

Poetry

On Messrs. Hussey and Coffin. 1767.
An Elegiac Poem on the Death of George Whitfield. 1770.
To Mrs. Leonard. 1771.

To the Rev. Mr. Pitkin. 1772.
To Thomas Hubbard. 1773.
Poems on Various Subjects, Religious and Moral. 1773.
An Elegy to Mary Moorhead. 1773.
Phillis's Reply to the Answer in Our Last by the Gentleman in the Navy. 1775.
An Elegy to Samuel Cooper. 1784.
Liberty and Peace. 1784.
To Mr and Mrs.——, on the Death of Their Infant Son. 1784.

*

Bibliography: *Wheatley: A Bio-Bibliography* by William H. Robinson, 1981.

Critical Studies: *Wheatley: A Critical Attempt and Bibliography* by Charles F. Heartman, 1915; *Bid the Vassal Soar* by Merle A. Richmond, 1974; *Wheatley in the Black American Beginnings* by William H. Robinson, 1975, and *Critical Essays on Phillis Wheatley* edited by Robinson, 1982; "Phillis Wheatley and Oliver Goldsmith: A Fugitive Satire" by William J. Scheick, in *Early American Literature,* Spring 1984, and "Phillis Wheatley's Appropriation of Isaiah" by Scheick, in *Early American Literature,* vol. 27, 1992; "The Difficult Miracle of Black Poetry in America; or, Something Like a Sonnet for Phillis Wheatley" by June Jordan, in *Massachusetts Review,* Summer 1986; "'An Elegy on Leaving—': A New Poem by Phillis Wheatley" by Mukhtar Ali Isani, in *American Literature,* December 1986; "A Slave's Subtle War: Phillis Wheatley's Use of Biblical Myth and Symbol" by Sondra O'Neale, in *Early American Literature,* Fall 1986; "Phillis Wheatley's Methodist Connection" by Samuel J. Rogal, in *Black American Literature Forum,* Spring/Summer 1987; "Milton and Afro-American Literature" by Carolivia Herron, in *Re-Membering Milton: Essays on the Texts and Traditions* edited by Mary Nyquist and Margaret W. Ferguson, 1987; "Anglo-American Racism and Phillis Wheatley's 'Sable Veil,' 'Length'ned Chain,' and 'Knitted Heart'" by David Grimsted, in *Women in the Age of the American Revolution* edited by Ronald Hoffman and Peter J. Albert, introduction by Linda K. Kerber, 1989; *The Poems of Phillis Wheatley* by Julian D. Mason, Jr., 1989; "Phillis Wheatley and the New England Clergy" by James A. Levernier, in *Early American Literature,* vol. 26, 1991; "From Wheatley to Douglass: The Politics of Displacement" by Henry Louis Gates, Jr., in *Frederick Douglass: New Literary and Historical Essays* edited by Eric J. Sundquist, 1991; "The Rhetoric and Politics of Marginality: The Subject of Phillis Wheatley" by Helen M. Burke, in *Tulsa Studies in Women's Literature,* Spring 1991; "Phillis Wheatley and Literary Americanization" by Phillip M. Richards, in *American Quarterly,* June 1992; "Classical Tidings from the Afric Muse: Phillis Wheatley's Use of Greek and Roman Mythology" by Lucy K. Hayden, in *College Language Association Journal,* June 1992; "Phillis Wheatley's Subversive Pastoral" by John C. Shields, in *Eighteenth-Century Studies,* Summer 1994, pp. 631-47; "Subjection and Prophecy in Phillis Wheatley's Verse Paraphrases and Scripture" by William J. Scheick, in *College Literature,* October 1995, pp. 122-30; "The Tongues of the Learned Are Insufficient: Phillis Wheatley, Publishing Objectives, and Personal Liberty" by Christopher Felker, in *Texts and Textuality: Textual Instability, Theory and Interpretation* edited by Philip Cohen, 1997; "Other Questions: Phillis Wheatley and the Ethics of Interpretation" by Robert Kendrick, in *Cultural Critique,* Winter 1997-98, pp. 39-64; "Wheatley's *On the Affray in King Street*" by Antonio T. Bly, in *Explicator,* Summer 1998, pp. 177-80.

*　　　*　　　*

Phillis Wheatley's poetry is characterized by its adherence to form, in particular the heroic couplet, and conformity to neoclassical ritual in language and content. Thematically, she wrote to God's goodness, as opposed to His wrath, and she stressed that salvation is the most important goal in life. Her exposure to history, classical literature, and myths is obvious in her poetry.

Wheatley's verses were didactic, pious, conventional, and predictable in that she wrote a significant number of occasional poems—for commemorating an event, perhaps, or for lamenting a death. Her tone fits the poems, however, and there is revealed in them a genuine adaptation to the subject at hand. She incorporates the Popean politeness into her verses as well as other features of his style—antithesis, the mid-line pause, and apostrophe. Underneath the instructive tone and religious themes is the note of genuine religious joy based on her salvation from "The land of errors . . . those dark abodes." Some critics have argued that Wheatley lost contact with her blackness; rather, she accommodated her blackness to a form she selected freely to use for expressing herself artistically—the heroic couplet.

She did, however, condemn the hypocrisy of liberals who professed Christian charity towards blacks but also held slaves. In the 11 March 1774 *Connecticut Gazette* Wheatley published a letter that would be reprinted many times. She wrote: "In every human Breast, God has implanted a Principle, which we call Love of Freedom . . . God grant Deliverance in his own Way and Time, and get him honour upon all those whose Avarice impels them to countenance and help forward the Calamities of their fellow Creatures. This I desire not for their Hurt, but to convince them of the strange Absurdity of their Conduct whose Words and Actions are so diametrically opposite."

In nearly all of Wheatley's poetry, however, there rings affirmation of life, even when she clearly identifies her race in what seems to be shame for her past enslavement. Her efforts to project herself away from the individual to the universal were part of the artistic detachment imposed by the form of poetry she loved, and the Puritan world in which she lived and believed. She paid close attention to the requirements of good manners that were a part of the upper-class milieu in which she lived during her first fourteen years in America (she was about 7 when she came with other slaves in 1761).

Wheatley's total output seems small only if one forgets her origins, her brief life, and the possibility that her husband sold or lost many of her works after her death. From poverty and slavery emerged a remarkable poet who sang "What songs should rise, how constant, how divine!"

—Margaret Perry

WHEELWRIGHT, John (Brooks)

Born: Boston, Massachusetts, 9 September 1897. **Education:** St. George's School, Newport, Rhode Island; Harvard University, Cambridge, Massachusetts, 1916-20; studied architecture at Massachusetts Institute of Technology, Cambridge, late 1920s. **Ca-**

reer: Briefly worked in architectural partnership in Boston; joined Socialist Party of Massachusetts, 1932, and became poetry editor of the party journal *Arise*; founding member of Trotskyist Socialist Workers Party, 1937; editor, *Poems for a Dime* series, Boston, 1934-37. **Member:** Officer, New England Poetry Society. **Died:** 15 September 1940.

PUBLICATIONS

Collections

Collected Poems, edited by Alvin H. Rosenfeld. 1972.

Poetry

North Atlantic Passage. 1925.
Rock and Shell: Poems 1923-1933. 1933.
Masque with Clowns. 1936.
Mirrors of Venus: A Novel in Sonnets 1914-1938. 1938.
Political Self-Portrait. 1940.
Selected Poems. 1941.

Other

Editor, *A History of the New England Poetry Club 1915-1931.* 1932.

*

Critical Studies: *New England Saints* by Austin Warren, 1956; *The Revolutionary Imagination: The Poetry and Politics of Wheelwright and Sherry Mangan* by Alan M. Wald, 1983; "'Revising what we have done amisse': John Cotton and John Wheelwright, 1640" by Sargent Bush, Jr., in *William and Mary Quarterly,* October 1988, and "John Wheelwright's Forgotten Apology: The Last Word in the Antinomian Controversy" by Bush, in *New England Quarterly,* March 1991.

*   *   *

John Wheelwright published three collections during his lifetime, but none received sufficient notice to give him a reputation while alive. Wheelwright was not the average socialist scribbler of the Depression era, but a "proper Bostonian" of impeccable ancestry: on his father's side, he claimed his radical blood from the first Wheelwright, an emigré from England in 1636, who preached religious tolerance until he was banished from the Bay Colony. On his mother's side, he descended from John Brooks, an early governor of Massachusetts.

The contradictions explicit in such ancestry, radicalism and political authority, were manifest in Wheelwright's own character and poetry. He taunted Boston Brahmins with his eccentric behavior in public and declared his allegiance to the proletariat, whose Depression plight he championed in many poems. All the while he accepted his upper-class status and remained much of his life an official of the doughty New England Poetry Society.

Wheelwright was an erratic craftsman in his poems, even though he emphasized his technique in long prose commentaries that accompanied his three published books. Many poems are long-winded, prosaic, and loosely framed. But occasionally his poems

spring out with unanticipated lyric genius, as in "Train Ride" (*Political Self-Portrait*). His "sonnet novel" *Mirrors of Venus,* generally overwrought, includes his masterful elegy "Father":

> Come home. Wire a wire of warning without words.
> Come home and talk to me again, my first friend. Father,
> come home, dead man, who made your mind my home.

Wheelwright's work often takes the form of rambling poetic tracts, where he is an interpreter of what he felt to be the reshaping of America. As he wrote at the end of *Political Self-Portrait,* "The main point is not what noise poetry makes, but how it makes you think and act,—not what you make of it; but what it makes of you." Although this is unfair to the musical grace of much of his language, it is pointed and correct essentially about his intentions for his poetry.

Rock and Shell shows the poet searching for some premise of unity in his experience, especially in the powerful opening poem, "North Atlantic Passage," which joins prose and poetry together. Spiritual loneliness is followed by sexual loneliness in this carefully plotted book. *Mirrors of Venus* is, as one critic described it, his *In Memoriam* to his friend Ned Couch, but sags generally from its weight of technical embellishments.

Political Self-Portrait is Wheelwright's best book; here he has found a balance between the wrought textures of language and loosely plotted ideological arguments. The poems are longer, more discursive, but intensely dramatic as they register a diffident, sensitive conscience faced with social upheaval and coming war. The poems are rich in imagery, raw in angry, direct language, but dignified overall by the depth of the speaker's convictions. Some of these poems have lost their edge now, but many, including "Collective Collect," "Bread-Word Giver," and "Train Ride," are lasting expressions of faith in humanity. "Dusk to Dusk," included in *Collected Poems,* has an even shriller tone of indignation than *Political Self-Portrait,* and its structure is fragmented by the unleashed energies of this unusual poet.

—Paul Christensen

WHITE, E(lwyn) B(rooks)

Born: Mount Vernon, New York, 11 July 1899. **Education:** Mount Vernon High School, graduated 1917; Cornell University, Ithaca, New York (editor, *Cornell Daily Sun,* 1920-21), 1917-21, A.B. 1921. **Military Service:** Served in the U.S. Army, 1918: private. **Family:** Married Katharine Sergeant Angell in 1929 (died 1977); one son. **Career:** Reporter, *Seattle Times,* 1922-23; advertising copywriter, Frank Seaman Inc. and Newmark Inc., New York, 1924-25; contributing editor, *New Yorker,* from 1926; columnist ("One Man's Meat"), *Harper's* magazine, New York, 1938-43. **Awards:** National Association of Independent Schools award, 1955; American Academy Gold Medal, for essays, 1960; Presidential Medal of Freedom, 1963; American Library Association Wilder award, for children's books, 1970; National Medal for Literature, 1971; Pulitzer Special Citation, 1978. Litt.D.: Dartmouth College, Hanover, New Hampshire, 1948; University of Maine, Orono, 1948; Yale University, New Haven, Connecticut, 1948; Bowdoin College, Brunswick, Maine, 1950; Hamilton College, Clinton, New York,

1952; Harvard University, Cambridge, Massachusetts, 1954. L.H.D.: Colby College, Waterville, Maine, 1954. Fellow, American Academy of Arts and Sciences, 1973; **Member:** American Academy. **Died:** 1 October 1985.

PUBLICATIONS

Sketches and Prose

Is Sex Necessary? or, Why You Feel the Way You Do, with James Thurber. 1929.
Alice through the Cellophane. 1933.
Every Day Is Saturday. 1934.
Farewell to Model T. 1936.
Quo Vadimus?, or The Case for the Bicycle. 1939.
One Man's Meat. 1942; augmented edition, 1944.
World Government and Peace: Selected Notes and Comment 1943-1945. 1945.
The Wild Flag: Editorials from the New Yorker on Federal World Government and Other Matters. 1946.
Here Is New York. 1949.
The Second Tree from the Corner. 1954.
The Elements of Style, by William Strunk, Jr., revised by White. 1959; revised edition, 1972, 1979.
The Points of My Compass: Letters from the East, the West, the North, the South. 1962.
A White Reader, edited by William W. Watt and Robert W. Bradford. 1966.
Essays. 1977.

Fiction (for children)

Stuart Little. 1945.
Charlotte's Web. 1952.
The Trumpet of the Swan. 1970.

Poetry

The Lady Is Cold. 1929.
The Fox of Peapack and Other Poems. 1938.
Poems and Sketches. 1981.

Other

Letters, edited by Dorothy Lobrano Guth. 1976.

Editor, *Ho Hum: Newsbreaks from the New Yorker.* 1931.
Editor, *Another Ho Hum: More Newsbreaks from the New Yorker.* 1932.
Editor, with Katharine S. White, *A Subtreasury of American Humor.* 1941.
Editor, *Onward and Upward in the Garden,* by Katharine S. White. 1979.

*

Bibliography: *White: A Bibliography* by A.J. Anderson, 1978; *White: A Bibliographic Catalogue of Printed Materials in the Department of Rare Books, Cornell University Library* by Katherine R. Hall, 1979.

Critical Studies: *White* by Edward C. Sampson, 1974; "Magic in the Web: Time, Pigs, & E.B. White" by Helene Solheim, in *South Atlantic Quarterly,* Autumn 1981; "Strunk and White and Grammar as Morality" by Berel Lang, in *Soundings,* Spring 1982; "'Pattern of Life Indelible': E.B. White's 'Once More to the Lake'" by Leonard G. Heldreth, in *CEA Critic,* November 1982; "*Charlotte's Web:* Flaws in the Weaving" by Marilyn Apseloff, in *Children's Novels and the Movies* edited by Douglas Street, 1983; "The Sparrow on the Ledge: E.B. White in New York" by Thomas Grant, in *Studies in American Humor,* Spring 1984; *White: A Biography* by Scott Elledge, 1984; "Text as Teacher: The Beginning of Charlotte's Web" by Perry Nodelman, in *Children's Literature,* vol. 13, 1985; "E.B. White at the *New Yorker*" by William Howarth, in *Sewanee Review,* Fall 1985; "E.B. White's *Charlotte's Web:* Caught in the Web" by Sonia Landes, in *Touchstones: Reflections on the Best in Children's Literature, Volume One* edited by Nodelman, foreword by Jill P. May, 1985; "The Real Miracle of *Charlotte's Web*" by Norton D. Kinghorn, in *Children's Literature Association Quarterly,* Spring 1986; "E.B. White, Dark & Lite" by Joseph Epstein, in *Commentary,* April 1986; "Nonfiction in the Classroom: E.B. White's 'Once More to the Lake'" by Richard Cox, in *Conference of College Teachers of English Studies,* September 1987; "'Once More to the Lake': A Mythic Interpretation" by Roger S. Platizky, in *College Literature,* Spring 1988; "E.B. White and the Theory of Humor" by Stephen L. Tanner, in *Humor,* vol. 2, 1989; "Stylistics and the Study of Twentieth-Century Literary Nonfiction" by Dennis Rygiel, in *Literary Nonfiction: Theory, Criticism, Pedagogy* edited by Chris Anderson, 1989; "Satire and the Evolution of Perspective in Children's Literature: Mark Twain, E.B. White, and Louise Fitzhugh" by J.D. Stahl, in *Children's Literature Association Quarterly,* Fall 1990; "The Reproduction of Mothering in *Charlotte's Web*" by Lucy Rollins, in *Children's Literature,* vol. 18, 1990; "'The Miracle of the Web': Community, Desire, and Narrativity in *Charlotte's Web*" by Ashraf H.A. Rushdy, in *The Lion and the Unicorn,* December 15, 1991; *Critical Essays on E.B. White* edited by Robert L. Root, 1994; *E.B. White: The Children's Books* by Lucien L. Agosta, 1995; *E.B. White: The Emergence of an Essayist* by Robert L. Root, 1999.

*   *   *

In an editorial headnote in *Letters,* E.B. White refers to the "squibs and poems" that he began submitting to the *New Yorker* shortly after it was founded in 1925. He joined the staff of the magazine two years later and retained a real, if sometimes tenuous, connection with it for the rest of his writing life. His poems are conventional light verse, rather weak examples of a genre that tends toward wry sentiment, easy irony, and even easier rhyme. His important literary work is the care and feeding of the "squib," its transformation from fragile sketch to full-bodied essay. One of the tools in effecting that change was the discipline involved in writing the unsigned editorials, the "Notes and Comments" that he once called "my weekly sermon," samples of which have been collected in *Every Day Is Saturday* and *The Wild Flag.* It was the signed pieces, the "casuals" to use the *New Yorker* term, for which White became best known. As with most of the *New Yorker* humorists, he worked in a variety of styles (including the parody volume *Is Sex Necessary?* that he wrote with **James Thurber**), but he is at his most characteristic sketching ordinary incidents with affection and mild surprise, colored occasionally by outright fantasy. Most of his early work never escaped the pages of the magazine for which it was written, but the best of these pieces can be found in *Quo Vadimus?*

As early as 1929, in a letter to his brother, he wrote, "I discovered a long time ago that writing of the small things of the day, the trivial matters of the heart, the inconsequential but near things of this living, was the only kind of creative work which I could accomplish with any sincerity or grace." Although he never ceased to be concerned with "the small occasions," as he once called them, he came to know that the trivial and the inconsequential are inextricably bound with the vital, to write about everyday life with the awareness that it involved everyday death. The deepening tone in White's work began with "One Man's Meat," the monthly essay he started contributing to *Harper's* in 1937; it can be heard in later volumes like *The Second Tree from the Corner* and *The Points of My Compass.* In *Essays,* a retrospective gathering of more than forty years, White can be found at his saddest, his richest, his finest.

There is another White, but the author of the books for children is simply a gentler variation on the man who wrote *Essays,* as can be seen in the death of Charlotte and the rebirth made explicit in the arrival of all those baby spiders. *Charlotte's Web* is the most complex of White's children's books, placing a fantasy rescue in a realistic setting, using artifice to celebrate natural processes. Both *Stuart Little* and *The Trumpet of the Swan* are quest stories; the first of these is probably White's most enduring book for children, not simply for the charm of its hero, but because it has an ending that does not end, a close that leaves Stuart—like White, like any good writer—still in search of beauty.

—Gerald Weales

WHITMAN, Walt(er)

Born: West Hills, Huntington, Long Island, New York, 31 May 1819. **Education:** Schools in Brooklyn, New York, 1825-39. **Career:** Office boy/clerk in a lawyer's office, a doctor's office, and, in 1830, a printing office; worked on *Long Island Patriot* and for printers Worthington, 1831, and Spooner, 1832-34; schoolteacher on Long Island, 1836-41; founding editor, *Long Islander,* Huntington, 1838-39; compositor, *Long Island Democrat,* 1839; journalist in New York from 1841; editor, *Aurora,* 1842, *Evening Tattler,* 1842, *Statesman,* 1843, and *Democrat,* 1844; staff member, *Long Island Star,* 1845; editor, Brooklyn *Daily Eagle,* 1846-48; New Orleans *Crescent,* 1848, and Brooklyn *Freeman* (Free Soil Party paper), 1848-49; lived with his parents, writing poetry and working part-time as carpenter, 1850-54; freelance journalist, 1855-62; editor, Brooklyn *Daily Times,* 1857-59; served as a nurse in the Civil War, at hospitals in Washington, D.C., 1862-65; clerk, army paymaster's office, 1863, and Bureau of Indian Affairs, 1865, and staff member, Attorney-General's office, 1865-73, all in Washington, D.C.; suffered paralytic stroke, 1873, and lived with his brother in Camden, New Jersey; traveled in the western United States and Canada, 1879-80; lived in Camden after 1884. **Died:** 26 March 1892.

PUBLICATIONS

Collections

Complete Poems and Prose 1855-1888. 1888.
Complete Prose Works. 1892.

Complete Writings, edited by Richard Maurice Bucke and others. 10 vols., 1902.
Uncollected Poetry and Prose, edited by Emory Holloway. 2 vols., 1921.
Collected Writings, edited by Gay Wilson Allen and Sculley Bradley. 1961.
Complete Poems, edited by Francis Murphy. 1975.
Poetry and Prose (Library of America), edited by Justin Kaplan. 1982.
Civil War Poetry and Prose. 1995.

Poetry

Leaves of Grass. 1855; revised edition, 1856, 1860, 1866, 1871, 2 vols. 1876, 1881, 1889, 1892, 1897; manuscripts edited by Fredson Bowers, 1955, and Arthur Golden, 2 vols., 1968; *A Textual Variorum of the Printed Poems* edited by Sculley Bradley. 3 vols., 1980.
Drum-Taps. 1865; with *Sequel to Drum-Taps,* 1865.
Poems, edited by W. M. Rossetti. 1868.
Passage to India. 1871.
After All, Not to Create Only. 1871.
As a Strong Bird on Pinions Free. 1872.
November Boughs (includes prose). 1888.
Good-Bye My Fancy. 1891.
Pictures: An Unpublished Poem, edited by Emory Holloway. 1927.

Fiction

Franklin Evans; or, The Inebriate. 1842; edited by Emory Holloway, 1929.
The Half-Breed and Other Stories, edited by Thomas Ollive Mabbott. 1927.

Other

Democratic Vistas. 1870.
Memoranda during the War. 1876; edited by Roy P. Basler, 1962.
Specimen Days and Collect. 1882; revised edition, as *Specimen Days in America,* 1887.
Autobiographia. 1892.
In Re Walt Whitman, edited by Horace L. Traubel and others. 1893.
Calamus (letters), edited by Richard Maurice Bucke. 1897.
The Wound Dresser (letters), edited by Richard Maurice Bucke. 1898.
Notes and Fragments, edited by Richard Maurice Bucke. 1899.
An American Primer, edited by Horace L. Traubel. 1904.
Diary in Canada, edited by William Sloane Kennedy. 1904.
Lafayette in Brooklyn. 1905.
Criticism: An Essay. 1913.
The Gathering of the Forces (journalism and essays), edited by Cleveland Rodgers and John Black. 2 vols., 1920.
Rivulets of Prose: Critical Essays, edited by Carolyn Wells and Alfred F. Goldsmith. 1928.
Whitman's Workshop, edited by Clifton Joseph Furness. 1928.
A Child's Reminiscence, edited by Thomas Ollive Mabbott and Rollo G. Silver. 1930.
I Sit and Look Out (editorials), edited by Emory Holloway and Vernolian Schwarz. 1932.
Whitman and the Civil War: A Collection of Original Articles and Manuscripts, edited by Charles I. Glicksberg. 1933.

New York Dissected (essays), edited by Emory Holloway and Ralph Adimari. 1936.

Backward Glances, edited by Sculley Bradley and John A. Stevenson. 1947.

Faint Clews and Indirections: Manuscripts of Whitman and His Family, edited by Clarence Gohdes and Rollo G. Silver. 1949.

Whitman Looks at the Schools, edited by Florence Bernstein Freedman. 1950.

Whitman of the New York Aurora, edited by Joseph Jay Rubin and Charles H. Brown. 1950.

The Eighteenth Presidency!, edited by Edward F. Grier. 1956.

Whitman's Civil War, edited by Walter Lowenfels. 1960.

Whitman's New York: From Manhattan to Montauk (essays), edited by Henry M. Christman. 1963.

Camden Conversations, edited by Walter Teller. 1973.

Poet at Work: Recovered Notebooks from the Thomas Biggs Harned Walt Whitman Collection. 1998.

The Journalism, 1834-1846. 1998.

*

Bibliography: by Oscar Lovell Triggs, in *Complete Writings 10,* 1902; *A Concise Bibliography of the Works of Whitman* by Carolyn Wells and Alfred Goldsmith, 1922; *Whitman's Journalism: A Bibliography* by William White, 1969; *Whitman and the Critics: A Checklist of Criticism 1900-1978* by Jeanetta Boswell, 1980; *Whitman 1838-1939: A Reference Guide* by Scott Giantvalley, 1981; *Whitman 1940-1975: A Reference Guide* by Donald D. Kummings, 1982; *Walt Whitman: An Encyclopedia* edited by J.R. LeMaster and Donald D. Kummings, 1998.

Critical Studies: *Whitman* by Frederik Schyberg, translated by Evie Allison Allen, 1951; *The Solitary Singer: A Critical Biography,* 1955, revised edition, 1967, *A Reader's Guide to Whitman,* 1970, and *The New Whitman Handbook,* 1975, all by Gay Wilson Allen; *Whitman Reconsidered,* 1955, and *Whitman,* 1961, both by Richard Chase; *Leaves of Grass One Hundred Years After,* 1955, and *Whitman: The Critical Heritage,* 1971, both edited by Milton Hindus; *The Evolution of Whitman* by Roger Asselineau, 2 vols., 1960-62; *The Presence of Whitman* edited by R.W.B. Lewis, 1962; *Whitman: A Collection of Critical Essays* edited by Roy Harvey Pearce, 1962; *Whitman,* 1962, and *The American Quest for a Supreme Fiction: Whitman's Legacy in the Personal Epic,* 1979, both by James E. Miller, Jr.; *A Century of Whitman Criticism* edited by Edwin H. Miller, 1969, and *Whitman's Poetry: A Psychological Journey* by Miller, 1969; *The Structure of Leaves of Grass* by Thomas E. Crawley. 1971; *The Historic Whitman* by Joseph Jay Rubin, 1973; *The Foreground of Leaves of Grass* by Floyd Stovall, 1974; *Whitman's Journeys into Chaos: A Psychoanalytic Study of the Poetic Process* by Stephen Ames Black, 1975; *Whitman: A Life* by Justin Kaplan, 1980; *Whitman and the Body Beautiful* by Harold Aspiz, 1980; *Emerson, Whitman, and the American Muse* by Jerome Loving, 1982; *Language and Style in Leaves of Grass* by C. Carroll Hollis, 1983; *Critical Essays on Whitman* edited by James Woodress, 1983; *Whitman: The Making of a Poet* by Paul Zweig, 1984; *Disseminating Whitman: Revision Corporeality in Leaves of Grass* by Michael Moon, 1991; *Whitman in His Own Time: A Biographical Chronicle of His Life, Drawn from Recollections, Memoirs, and Interviews by Friends and Associates* edited by Joel Myerson, 1991; *Whitman and the American Idiom* by Mark Bauerlein, 1991; *The Teachers & Writ-*

ers Guide to Walt Whitman edited by Ron Padgett, 1991; *Whitman's Presence: Body, Voice, and Writing in Leaves of Grass* by Tenney Nathanson, 1992; *With Walt Whitman in Camden, July 7, 1890-February 10, 1891; Volume 7* by Horace Traubel, edited by Jeanne Chapman and Robert Macisaac, 1992; *Masculine Landscapes: Walt Whitman and the Homoerotic Text* by Byrne R.S. Fone, 1992; *The Continuing Presence of Walt Whitman: The Life after the Life* edited by Robert K. Martin, 1992; *The Frailest Leaves: Whitman's Poetic Technique and Style in the Short Poem* by John E. Schwiebert, 1992; *Walt Whitman* by Bettina L. Knapp, 1993; *Walt Whitman's Native Representations* by Ed Folsom, 1994; *Poet-Chief: The Native American Poetics of Walt Whitman and Pablo Neruda* by James Nolan, 1994; *Walt Whitman's America: A Cultural Biography* by David S. Reynolds, 1995; *Walt Whitman: Critical Assessments* edited by Graham Clarke, 1995; *Whitman, Slavery, and the Emergence of Leaves of Grass* by Martin Klammer, 1995; *Strange Meetings: Walt Whitman, Wilfred Owen and Poetry of War* by Keith V. Comer, 1996; *Whitman, the Political Poet* by Betsy Erkkila, 1996; *Walt Whitman: The Contemporary Reviews* edited by Kenneth M. Price, 1996; *The Strange Sad War Revolving: Walt Whitman, Reconstruction, and the Emergence of Black Citizenship, 1865-1876* by Luke Mancuso, 1997; *Walt Whitman: A Gay Life* by Gary Schmidgall, 1997; *Walt Whitman and 19th-Century Reformers* by Sherry Ceniza, 1998; *Walt Whitman: The Song of Himself* by Jerome Loving, 1999.

*   *   *

The life and work of Walt Whitman are in some measure a metaphor for America. Whitman began sounding his "barbaric yawp" over the roofs of the world when the youthful United States was a power of little consequence among nations. He was scorned or ignored at first, but gradually his *Leaves of Grass* compelled attention to its democratic message. By the time Whitman died his poetry had become a force to reckon with in the world.

Whitman's considerable apprenticeship as a newspaper writer and editor before 1855 gives no warning of a major poet in the making. His early poetry is undistinguished, and his prose is only competent journalism. But somehow Whitman found his inspiration and his vocation as poet. **Ralph Waldo Emerson** was probably the dominant influence, for in his essay "The Poet" he had called for a great American poet: "I look in vain for the poet whom I describe." And he added that "we have yet had no genius in America" who "knew the value of our incomparable materials." Whitman, for his part, later said: "I was simmering, simmering, simmering; Emerson brought me to a boil."

In response to a presentation copy of the first edition of *Leaves of Grass* in 1855, Emerson wrote Whitman: "I find it the most extraordinary piece of wit and wisdom that America has yet contributed . . . I greet you at the beginning of a great career." The first edition was a slender volume of 95 pages that Whitman had had to publish himself, but it contained one of the great poems of the English language, the long, untitled poem that later, after revisions and additions, was called "Song of Myself." What Emerson had read when he opened the volume to the beginning of the poetry was

I celebrate myself, And what I assume you shall assume,
    For every atom belonging to me as good belongs to you.

Thus began Whitman's mystic vision of equality, national purpose, and international brotherhood, "hoping to cease not till death," as he added in a line written later. The work did go on as long as he lived, and preparations for the final edition of his lifetime, arranged in the way he wanted his literary executors to print future editions, were in progress at the time he died.

The first edition is the work of the somewhat brash, 36-year-old Brooklyn carpenter-poet. But by the time the third edition appeared in 1860, Whitman had matured and deepened his human sympathies. Also the book had grown from the original 12 poems to 100 and contained the so-called "sex poems" that made Whitman anathema to proper Victorians. These are the "Children of Adam" poems dealing with heterosexual love and the "Calamus" poems treating homosexual affection. Many of them are tender, beautiful poems worth close study. But the most important new poem was "Out of the Cradle Endlessly Rocking," one of Whitman's greatest lyrics. It blends theme, symbol, and reminiscence in a free-verse form that Whitman had absolutely mastered. This edition, moreover, gives us a clear insight into Whitman's growth as a poet. It is an articulated whole, with a beginning, middle, and end, and one can begin to see the shape of *Leaves of Grass* in its final form. The most prominent themes of the third edition are love and death; both appear in the first two editions, but here they take on a tragic significance, and in Whitman's struggle with these themes he becomes a major poet.

Whitman's experiences in Washington as a volunteer nurse and his visits to Virginia battlefields during the Civil War provided the material for *Drum-Taps,* later incorporated into *Leaves of Grass.* This is the best collection of war poetry produced by any American writer on the Civil War. "Come up from the Fields, Father" and "Vigil Strange I Kept on the Field One Night" are vivid, poignant examples. Shortly after *Drum-Taps* appeared, Lincoln's assassination inspired Whitman's memorable elegy "When Lilacs Last in the Dooryard Bloom'd." This poem employs the symbols of star (Lincoln), lilac (love), and bird (poet's soul) in 16 stanzas of beautiful free verse and begins:

> When lilacs last in the dooryard bloom'd,
> And the great star early droop'd in the western sky in the
> night,
> I mourn'd, and yet shall mourn with ever-returning spring.

But at the end the poet is reconciled to the loss of the wartime leader. The star, the lilac, and the bird singing in the swamp will remind him annually of "the dead I loved so well."

The fifth edition of *Leaves of Grass* came out in 1871, and in it the main order of the book became settled. It opens with the "Inscriptions," follows with "Starting from Paumanok" and ends with "Songs of Parting." Published as an annex to this edition was another of Whitman's best-known poems, "A Passage to India," a poem in which his vision of universal fraternity is clearly shown. It begins by celebrating the joining of east and west by the transcontinental railroad, the Suez Canal, and the Atlantic cable and goes on to envision these engineering feats as part of "God purpose" for "The people to become brothers and sisters."

An edition of 1881 was to have been brought out by James R. Osgood and Co. of Boston, but the district attorney of Boston threatened prosecution and Whitman was forced to find another publisher. A bolder Philadelphia firm issued the book without incident, for by this time Whitman, "The good gray poet," as his friend William O'Connor had dubbed him during the Washington years, was becoming a national figure and living down the early notoriety. In this edition the poems received their final revisions and titles ("Song of Myself" appears here for the first time) and

permanent positions. Whitman continued to write until he died, but later editions print the later poems as annexes.

Although Whitman's poetry is the reason for his literary stature, he also wrote a considerable body of prose. The preface to the 1855 edition is an important statement; also noteworthy is the preface to *As a Strong Bird. Democratic Vistas,* however, is his major prose work. It is a collection of essays that are more a glimpse into the future of democracy than an analysis of the present. It tempers Whitman's usual buoyant optimism with a frank admission that the American democracy of 1871 (the period of the Grant Administration and the "Gilded Age") was not perfect. But he did not lose his faith in the ultimate success of the American experiment. Another prose work of interest is the informal autobiography that he published under the title *Specimen Days.*

Whitman was the first American poet to achieve a truly international reputation. Although Baudelaire discovered **Edgar Allan Poe** before anyone had ever heard of Whitman, the Pre-Raphaelites in England soon discovered Whitman, and William Michael Rossetti edited an edition of *Leaves of Grass* in 1868. British interest in Whitman helped to convince Americans that the poet was not a charlatan, and from that modest beginning his reputation has spread like eddies from a rock dropped in still water. Jan Christian Smuts wrote a book on him in 1895, a study of his prosody was published in Italy in 1898, and an important French study appeared in 1908.

Although Whitman claimed he was not interested in technique, the sizable number of extant manuscripts show that he labored over his poems, making many cuts, additions, emendations. The variant readings of successive editions likewise reveal the poet as reviser. His form, however, has given critics trouble over the years. He said: "My form has strictly grown from my purports and facts, and is the analogy of them." His purpose was to present his vision and his experience, and it is not surprising that some readers have seen in his work the raw material of poetry rather than finished poems. The chief structural device is parallelism: repetition of idea, repetition of syntax, repetition of sound. Some 41 percent of the 10,500 lines of *Leaves of Grass* contain initial reiteration. One notes also that run-on lines are a rarity, and the first person singular is used extensively.

The influences on Whitman's free verse seem to have been public address, the Bible, and music. Not only was Emerson an inspiration in Whitman's finding his vocation as poet, but Emerson's essays, written as lectures, contain many of the same rhetorical devices that Whitman used. Whitman as a young man wrote speeches and at one time had thought of making a career as a public speaker. The parallelism and coordinate structure of the Bible, which Whitman knew well, also may have influenced his style, though this is hard to document. Finally, the impact of music must be accorded a place in Whitman's development. The repetition of themes, the use of recitative and aria support Whitman's own statement: "But for the opera I could never have written *Leaves of Grass.*"

—James Woodress

See the essay on *Leaves of Grass.*

WHITTIER, John Greenleaf

Born: Near Haverhill, Massachusetts, 17 December 1807. **Education:** Local schools; studied art at Haverhill Academy, 1827.

Career: Editor of various country newspapers, 1826-32, and of *American Manufacturer,* Boston, 1829-31; teacher, Haverhill Academy, 1827-28; delegate to the founding convention of the American Anti-Slavery Society, 1833, and edited and wrote for abolitionist and reform journals, 1833-60; representative for Haverhill in Massachusetts Legislature, 1835; editor, *Pennsylvania Freeman,* Philadelphia, 1838; contributing editor, *National Era,* Washington, D.C., 1847-57; regular contributor, *Atlantic Monthly,* Boston, after 1857. Lived in Amesbury after 1836, and Danvers after 1876, both Massachusetts. **Died:** 7 September 1892.

PUBLICATIONS

Collections

The Writings, edited by Horace E. Scudder. 7 vols., 1888-89; revised edition, 1894.
The Poetical Works, edited by W. Garrett Horder. 1919.
Letters, edited by John B. Pickard. 3 vols., 1975.

Poetry

Moll Pitcher. 1831; revised edition, 1840.
Mogg Megone. 1836.
Poems Written during the Progress of the Abolition Question, 1830-1838. 1837.
Poems. 1838.
Moll Pitcher, and The Minstrel Girl. 1840.
Lays of My Home and Other Poems. 1843.
The Song of the Vermonters. 1843.
Miscellaneous Poems. 1844.
Ballads and Other Poems. 1844.
The Stranger in Lowell. 1845.
Voices of Freedom. 1846.
Poems. 1849.
Songs of Labor and Other Poems. 1850.
Poetical Works. 1853.
The Chapel of the Hermits and Other Poems. 1853.
A Sabbath Scene. 1854.
The Panorama and Other Poems. 1856.
The Sycamores. 1857.
The Poetical Works. 2 vols., 1857.
Home Ballads and Other Poems. 1860.
In War Time and Other Poems. 1864.
National Lyrics. 1865.
Snow-Bound: A Winter Idyl. 1866.
The Tent on the Beach and Other Poems. 1867.
Among the Hills and Other Poems. 1869.
Poetical Works. 2 vols., 1870.
Ballads of New England. 1870.
Miriam and Other Poems. 1871.
The Pennsylvania Pilgrim and Other Poems. 1872.
Hazel-Blossoms. 1875.
Mabel Martin: A Harvest Idyl. 1876.
Favorite Poems. 1877.
The Vision of Echard and Other Poems. 1878.
The King's Missive and Other Poems. 1881.
The Bay of Seven Islands and Other Poems. 1883.
Early Poems. 1885.
Saint Gregory's Guest and Recent Poems. 1886.

Poems of Nature. 1886.
Narrative and Legendary Poems. 1888.
At Sundown. 1890.
Legends and Lyrics. 1890.
A Legend of the Lake. 1893.
The Demon Lady. 1894.

Fiction

Leaves from Margaret Smith's Journal. 1849.

Other

Legends of New England. 1831.
Justice and Expediency. 1833.
Narrative of James Williams, An American Slave. 1838.
The Supernaturalism of New England. 1847; edited by Edward Wagenknecht, 1969.
Old Portraits and Modern Sketches. 1850.
Literary Recreations and Miscellanies. 1854.
Prose Works. 2 vols., 1866.
Works. 1874.
Complete Works. 1876.
Whittier on Writers and Writing: The Uncollected Critical Writings, edited by Edwin Cady and Harry Hayden Clark. 1950.

Editor, *The Journal of John Woolman.* 1871.
Editor, *Child Life: A Collection of Poems.* 1873.
Editor, *Child Life in Prose.* 1874.
Editor, *Songs of Three Centuries.* 1876; revised edition, 1877.

*

Bibliography: *A Bibliography of Whittier* by Thomas Franklin Currier, 1937; *Whittier: A Comprehensive Annotated Bibliography* (secondary works) by Albert J. von Frank, 1976.

Critical Studies: *Life and Letters of Whittier* by Samuel T. Pickard, 1894, revised edition, 2 vols., 1907; *A Study of Whittier's Apprenticeship As a Poet* (includes uncollected poetry) by Frances M. Pray. 1930; *Quaker Militant* by Albert Mordell, 1933; *Whittier: Bard of Freedom* by Whitman Bennett, 1941; *Whittier: Friend of Man* by John A. Pollard, 1949; *Whittier* by Lewis Leary, 1961; *Whittier: An Introduction and Interpretation* by John B. Pickard, 1961, and *Memorabilia of Whittier* edited by Pickard, 1968; *Whittier: A Portrait in Paradox* by Edward Wagenknecht, 1967; *Whittier's Poetry: An Appraisal and a Selection* by Robert Penn Warren, 1971; *Lowell, Whittier, Very and the Alcotts among Their Contemporaries: A Harvest of Estimates, Insights and Anecdotes from the Victorian Literary World and an Index* by Kenneth Walter Cameron, 1978; *Critical Essays on Whittier* edited by Jayne K. Kribbs, 1980; *Mori to Rohen* by Koichi Ikeda, 1980; "Barnes and Whittier, Early Folklorists" by Charlotte Lindgren, in *Tennessee Folklore Society Bulletin,* June 1981; "Whittier's Leaves from Margaret Smith's Journal" by William J. Kimball, in *New England Quarterly,* June 1982; "John Greenleaf Whittier" by Karl Keller, in *Fifteen American Authors before 1900: Bibliographical Essays on Research and Criticism* edited by Earl N. Harbert and Robert A. Rees, 1984; "The Immortalizing Power of Imagination: A Reading of Whittier's Snow-Bound" by E. Miller Burdick, in *ESQ,* 2nd quarter, 1985; *The Parkman Dexter Howe Library, V: The John*

Greenleaf Whittier Collection by John Benedict Pickard, edited by Sidney Ives, 1987; "John Greenleaf Whittier—Poet of Rural New England: Telling the Bees" by Anne M. Witmer, in *Amerikanische Lyrik: Perspektiven und Interpretationen* edited by Rudolf Haas, 1987; "John Greenleaf Whittier in *The Critic,* 1881-1892" by Arthur Sherbo, in *Studies in Bibliography,* vol. 43, 1990; "Fire in the Ashes of Puritanism: The Conflict of Discourse between John Greenleaf Whittier and Reverend George Ellis" by Michael Vella, in *American Transcendental Quarterly,* December 1991; "John Greenleaf Whittier and the Washington Territory" by Jeanne Moskal, in *New England Quarterly,* March 1992; *John Greenleaf Whittier and Ebenezer Elliott* by Joanne Moskal, 1994.

*   *   *

In the "Proem," a poem that introduced his collected works, John Greenleaf Whittier scrutinized his life and poetic achievement in these lines:

> The rigor of a frozen clime,
> The harshness of an untaught ear,
> The jarring words of one whose rhyme
> Beat often Labor's hurried time,
> Or Duty's tugged march, through storm and strife, are here.

The honesty of these sparse lines is characteristic. Raised as a poor farm boy in a non-conformist Quaker faith, he had little education and was primarily a sectional romantic poet in his early years. Fortunately his enlistment in the abolitionist cause in 1833 converted the aspiring young lyricist into a radical propagandist, politician, and part-time editor whose verses championed the rights of slaves and democratic principles. The twenty years of abolitionist work reforged Whittier's vapid sentimentalism into a powerful weapon for the oppressed and strengthened his regard for moral action. By the 1850s Whittier's reform work was over, and in his remaining years his writing showed him as a religious humanist, striving for moral perfection and inner spirituality rather than social and political reform.

Like those of most of the "schoolroom" poets, **Henry Wadsworth Longfellow, James Russell Lowell, Oliver Wendell Holmes**, and others, Whittier's themes were few and limited: the value of domestic emotions, the innocence of childhood, the necessity of social equality, and the nobility of ethical action. However, unlike these other popular poets, Whittier drew upon his native roots for inspiration. In his best poems Whittier displayed a mastery of local color techniques, a competent use of rural imagery, and the everyday language of the Merrimack farmer. His instinctive handling of native materials conveyed his inner love for the environment that molded, and his understanding of the traditions that inspired, him. Still his poetry suffered from the diffusion and sentimentality inherent in the tradition of public rhetoric in which he wrote. Perhaps no other established nineteenth-century American poet wrote so much poor verse, but the miracle is that by the most exacting poetical standards his best remains so good.

Aside from a few nature poems like "The Last Walk in Autumn," an occasional abolitionist poem like "Ichabod," and selections from his religious poems, Whittier's ballads and genre pieces represent his finest poetical achievement. They contain some of the best examples of native folklore written in America. His bal-

lads, especially, express his lifelong interest in colonial history, the Quakers, local legends, and folk superstitions; and they are remarkably true to the graphic realism and dramatic intensity of traditional folk balladry. His best ballads take incidents like a skipper who had betrayed his own townspeople, a witch who prophesied death, or the terrifying actions of specter warriors, bed-rocks them with exact physical detail, and then concentrates on the dramatic moment of conflict. "Telling the Bees" skillfully handles a local superstition with childlike detail to hide the chilling reality of nature's destruction; "The Garrison of Cape Anne," "The Palatine," and "The King's Missive" rework historical incidents; "Amy Wentworth," "The Countess," and "The Witch of Wenham" narrate pastoral romances; while the often-parodied "Barbara Frietchie" was accepted by a war-wearied nation as an expression of their personal conviction that the Union must be preserved. Whittier's finest ballad, "Skipper Ireson's Ride," was based on an old Marblehead song about women tarring and feathering a fishing boat captain. The ballad opens in medias res, plunging directly into the wild tumult and chaos of mob action as the skipper is pushed through Marblehead. Finally Ireson cries out his remorse, and with "half scorn, half pity" the women free him. The final refrain changes "Old" Floyd Ireson to "Poor" Floyd Ireson and becomes a mournful dirge forever accusing and dooming Ireson, besides emphasizing the hollowness of the women's revenge.

Similarly, Whittier's genre poems elevated the ordinary details of Essex County life into a universal expression of boyhood innocence, agrarian simplicity, and pastoral romance that caught the pathos and beauty of a dying rural tradition. In poems like "Maud Muller," "In School-Days," "Among the Hills," and "Memories," Whittier idealized and typified the district school days, the harvest-filled autumn days, and the barefoot-boy days to capture the romantic aspirations of a responsive American public. "Cobbler Keezar's Vision," "Abraham Davenport," "To My Old Schoolmaster," and others contain some of Whittier's best rustic anecdotes as well as realistic and humorous sketches of the Yankee character. Whittier's particular skill in recreating the past is seen most fully in his one sustained triumph, *Snow-Bound*. In this poem Whittier expresses the value of family affections by the symbolic development of a fire-snow contrast and by the skillful interweaving of present reality with past memories. His artistic handling of structure, careful development of the fire image, and graphic depiction of the family and outside visitors make this a minor masterpiece of nineteenth-century poetry. In this poem Whittier captured the essence of the New England mind and placed himself in the direct line of American expression that stretches from **Anne Bradstreet** to **Robert Frost**.

Although Whittier's poems fall far short of the poetic imagination and philosophical depth of major American poets such as **Walt Whitman, Edgar Allan Poe, Emily Dickinson**, and **Ralph Waldo Emerson**, his verses exhibit more spiritual illumination and downright "grit" than the polished verses of **Longfellow** and the other minor poets. Despite the severe criticism of his poetry in the twentieth century, Whittier's place in American literature seems secure. He will continue to be read and enjoyed as long as people respond to their traditions and demand honest expression of their fundamental democratic and religious feelings.

—John B. Pickard

See the essay on *Snow-Bound.*

WIDEMAN, John Edgar

Born: Washington, D.C., 14 June 1941. **Education:** Peabody High School, Pittsburgh; University of Pennsylvania, Philadelphia (Benjamin Franklin Scholarship, creative writing prize, Phi Beta Kappa) B.A. 1963; New College, Oxford, England (Rhodes Scholar, 1963, Thouron Fellow, 1963-66) B. Phil. 1966; University of Iowa Writers' Workshop, Iowa City (Kent Fellow), 1966-67. **Family:** Married Judith Ann Goldman in 1965; three children. **Career:** Professor of English, University of Pennsylvania, Philadelphia, 1967-74, assistant basketball coach, 1968-72, director of Afro-American studies program, 1971-73; professor of English, University of Wyoming, Laramie, 1974-86; USIS lecturer, 1976; professor of English, University of Massachusetts, Amherst, 1986—; Phi Beta Kappa regional lecturer. Member, board of directors, Association of American Rhodes Scholars; National Humanities Faculty; American Studies Association Council, 1980-81; Chair, Modern Language Association Commission on Literature and Languages of America, 1882-83; National Endowment for the Arts Fiction Panel, 1985; President's Commission on White Fellows. **Awards:** National Endowment for Humanities grant; Young Humanist fellowship, 1975; PEN/Faulkner award for fiction, 1984 and 1990; DuSable Museum Prize for Non-fiction, 1985; National Book Critics Circle Nomination, 1985; Longwood College, Virginia, John Dos Passos Prize for Literature, 1986; National Magazine Editors Prize for Short Fiction, 1987; Lannan award, 1991; MacArthur fellow, 1993. D.Litt.: University of Pennsylvania, 1986; Rutgers University, New Brunswick, New Jersey, 1990. **Member:** American Academy of Arts and Sciences, since 1992. **Residence:** Amherst, Massachusetts.

PUBLICATIONS

Collections

The Homewood Trilogy. 1985.
The Homewood Books. 1992.
The Stories of John Edgar Wideman. 1992; as *All Stories Are True*, 1993.

Novels

A Glance Away. 1967.
Hurry Home. 1970.
The Lynchers. 1973.
Hiding Place. 1981.
Sent for You Yesterday. 1983.
Reuben. 1987.
Philadelphia Fire. 1990.
Identities: Three Novels. 1994.
The Cattle Killing. 1996.
Two Cities. 1998.

Short Stories

Damballah. 1981.
Fever. 1989.

Other

Brothers and Keepers (memoris). 1984.
Fatheralong: A Meditation on Fathers and Sons, Race and Society. 1994.
Conversations with John Edgar Wideman. 1998.

*

Bibliography: "The Pain of Being Two" by James Marcus in *Nation,* October 4, 1986.

Critical Studies: *Interviews with Black Writers* edited by John O'Brien, 1973; "The Novels of Wideman" by Kermit Frazier in *Black World,* 1975; conversation with Wilfred Samuels in *Callaloo,* February 1983; *Afro-American Literature in the Twentieth Century* by Michael G. Cooke, 1984; *Exorcizing Blackness* by Trudier Harris, 1984; "Beyond Discourse: The Unspoken versus Words in the Fiction of Wideman" by Jacqueline Berben in *Callaloo,* Fall 1985; "Going Back Home: The Literary Development of Wideman" by James W. Coleman in *CLA Journal,* March 1985; "The Shape of Memory in Wideman's *Sent for You Yesterday*" by John Bennion in *Black American Literature Forum,* Spring-Summer 1986; *The Afro-American Novel and Its Tradition* by Bernard W. Bell, 1987; *Blackness and Modernism* by James William Coleman, 1989; interview with Charles H. Rowell in *Callaloo,* Winter 1990; review of *Fever* by Randall Kenan in *Nation,* January 1, 1990; "Listening to the Secret Mother: Reading Wideman's *Brothers and Keepers*" by Margot C. Hennessy in *American Women's Autobiography,* 1992; interview with Jessica Lustig in *African American Review,* Fall 1992; *John Edgar Wideman: Reclaiming the African Personality* by Doreatha D. Mbalia, 1995; *Damballah: Voice as Ground in John Wideman's Fiction* by Thomas W. Banks, 1996; *The Black Nationalist Aesthetic and the Early Fiction of John Edgar Wideman* by Raymond E. Janifer, 1997; *Stories of Resilience in Childhood: The Narrative Strategies of Maya Angelou, Maxine Hong Kingston, Richard Rodriguez, John Edgar Wideman, and Tobias Wolff* by Daniel D. Challener, 1997; *John Edgar Wideman: A Study of the Short Fiction* by Keith Eldon Byerman, 1998.

*   *   *

My writing is what it is because it did not follow a particular path. I blundered into dead ends, made mistakes, had infatuations at one point or another, models that I imitated without really understanding what I was imitating. But that kind of trial and error and back and forth is what learning to write is all about, and that's how I visualize progress in art, not linear but circular, mysteriously wrapped up in time's mysterious unfolding. (*Callaloo,* Winter 1990)

John Edgar Wideman launched his writing career at the age of twenty-six with the novel *A Glance Away* (1967), and has since published twelve volumes of fiction that prove him to be a remarkably provocative and always evolving writer whose work is characterized by its literary experimentation. Wideman constructs his social commentary through experiments with dialogue, character, stream-of-consciousness and non-linear narration, philosophical exposition and a poetic voice that delves into the interior world of his characters and their often futile struggle in life.

While Wideman's earlier fiction maintains a distance from his black upbringing, his latter works take on this subject. Born in 1941 to working-class parents, Wideman spent his childhood in the African American community of Homewood in Pittsburgh, Pennsylvania. It was not until his parents moved to Shadyside, a middle class, predominantly white neighborhood in Pittsburgh, and Wideman attended Peabody High School, that the impact of a segregated America was revealed to him. But Wideman's introduction into this other America was cushioned by his academic and athletic success. An honor student and star of the basketball team, Wideman was popular and graduated valedictorian of his class. Even at this early age, his life was split between the white world of affluence, to which he had access through his academic achievement, and the black working-class community of Homewood, to which his parents eventually returned.

Wideman was soon immersed in the white world and assimilated its values and norms. Upon graduation from high school, he was awarded a Benjamin Franklin Scholarship for scholastic and athletic achievement and attended the University of Pennsylvania, first majoring in psychology, then in English. In 1963 Wideman won a Rhodes scholarship to study at Oxford University, becoming only the second African American male in over fifty years to win the award. At Oxford, Wideman wrote his thesis on the eighteenth-century novel.

Wideman's return to the United States in the late sixties was marked by socio-political upheaval, yet his education and lifestyle placed him at the periphery of those epochal changes. After spending a year as a Kent Fellow at the University of Iowa's renowned Writers' Workshop, Wideman accepted a post at the University of Pennsylvania, where he became the first African American tenured professor. Despite his apparent removal from the drastic, sometimes violent, changes wrought by African Americans on U.S. society, Wideman found himself drawn into the social movement. It was at that prestigious university that Wideman would have his baptism in the study of African American writing. At the request of some black students on campus, Wideman found himself teaching a course in African American literature. When first approached, he attempted to evade the request by pointing out that he did not specialize in that field; but, after some reflection, he felt obligated to address the needs of the students. For the first time in his academic career, Wideman read African American literature and researched its culture, surprising himself at the extent to which he had strayed from the group to which he belonged. Wideman's commitment to that field of inquiry led him, between 1972 and 1973, to chair the University of Pennsylvania's first African American Studies program. That decision has had a profound and long-lasting effect on Wideman's life as well as on his writing career.

Wideman's *A Glance Away* garnered comparison to European modernist writers such as **T.S. Eliot**, James Joyce, and Albert Camus, Wideman's major influences at this stage in his career. Nonetheless, African American writers such as **Richard Wright** and **James Baldwin** give perspective on Wideman's position within the African American canon. While the works of Wright, Baldwin and Wideman certainly differ from each other stylistically and in content, their novels all can be placed within a "protest tradition" that articulates the frustrating and futile existence that often closes in on working-class African American people.

Although the protagonist of *A Glance Away* is an anglo-English professor named Robert Thurley, Wideman's engagement in the African American protest tradition is revealed in his treatment of a black man with whom Thurley engages in a casual homosexual affair. The return from a drug rehabilitation program of the main African American character, Eddie Lawson, is marred by his mother's death, which throws him into despair. Wideman's portrayal of African American life is bleak and hopeless; the novel's ending signals defeat rather than any possible victory or redemption.

The theme of alienation is not new to the African American literary tradition. In *Hurry Home* (1970), Wideman's second novel, he focuses on the schism between an African American intellectual and the working-class community that spawned him. Cecil Braithwaite, a law school graduate, attempts to flee his community and his wife by traveling to Spain and Africa, but he is drawn back home and reluctantly takes his place within American society. Wideman offers a poignant and sensitive portrayal of the alienation of African American intellectuals. Although Cecil's education and intimacy with anglo culture prevent him from identifying with his community, he cannot readily find a niche within anglo society. Comparable themes of alienation are explored in African American works such as **Amiri Baraka**'s (**LeRoi Jones**'s) *Dutchman* (1964), **Toni Morrison**'s *Tar-Baby* (1981), **Gloria Naylor**'s *Linden Hills* (1985), and George C. Wolfe's *The Colored Museum* (1988).

Wideman continues to explore such dilemmas in his third novel, *The Lynchers* (1973). Here, the historical atrocities to which African Americans were subjected provide the motivation for Littleman, the pseudo-intellectual who plans to make cultural amends by murdering a white policeman in a ritualized lynching. Wideman's technique in this text merits comment, and approaches what can be characterized as an African American aesthetics. His use of the black vernacular is new, and he writes in a collective, multi-vocal mode of narration that is somewhat reminiscent of the black church. The surreal, dream-like quality that pervades the text gives the aura of a ritual possession. *The Lynchers'* content is so grave that its style and form mediate between the hopeless world of the novel and the reader's perspective.

Like so many of Wideman's protagonists, Littleman has little contact with the community. He invests his plan with so much of his ego and his need for personal triumph that it undermines his desire to perform an act of collective retribution. Although Littleman manages to get three others to agree to join him, these men cannot be effective because they share his isolation from the community and have not resolved their own personal failings. Thomas Wilkerson, who has more formal education that Littleman, is a coward who would rather think about acting than carry through any plan. Graham Rice, the other conspirator, has eked out an existence on the edge of society for so long that his suspicion manages to foil the plan. The fourth member of this band, Leonard Saunders, is so thwarted by his dysfunctional background that he anesthetizes himself to other people's pain. Littleman's plan is destined to fail; Wideman portrays these African American men as being so ineffectual that they are unable to salvage even themselves. *The Lynchers* is a sad exposé of African Americans' deferred dreams, and Littleman's predicament makes it clear that if African Americans remain oblivious to their historical connections, they will not be able to save their lives from destruction.

Almost ten years elapsed before Wideman published his fourth novel, *Hiding Place* (1981). This period of silence coincided with his move to the University of Wyoming. Perhaps being in that immense setting afforded Wideman the opportunity to reflect on his past and to return to his childhood roots. *Hiding Place* is the first in the Homewood Trilogy, in which Wideman draws extensively on his personal and familial myths and stories, as well as on characters from Homewood. Tommy, the protagonist, is a relative of Bess, who seeks her out after he is accused of murder. Bess refuses to help him at first because, after the death of her husband, she has a crisis of faith and goes into seclusion. Bess is the family storyteller and the guardian of its history. She locates Tommy in the family history, and it is through her interactions with him that she is reminded of her own joys, her family and her place in the community. Tommy also benefits from their relationship. He confronts himself, and grows confident with the support and love of a family. At the novel's conclusion, Bess makes plans to rejoin the community, and Tommy decides to confront the charges, even if it means going to jail. With Bess, Wideman finally achieves the voice of the African American storyteller.

Bess is such a richly developed character that she comes alive off the page. This intimate quality no doubt stems from the source and inspiration for Bess and other characters like her—Wideman's aunts and other family members. In *Hiding Place* and the two books of the trilogy that follow, Wideman draws on and modifies his family stories. Moreover, the setting of these works is the community where Wideman grew up. As such he functions as a symbolic griot, a West African historian and storyteller. Gone is the alienation evident in his earlier work. In *Hiding Place, Damballah* (1981) and *Sent for You Yesterday* (1983), Wideman portrays a community with strong and intact family ties that act as a buffer against a harsh society.

In *Damballah,* the second book in the trilogy, Wideman's series of stories embraces the African diaspora, as suggested by the title. Damballah is the god of fertility, whose sign is the snake, and who originates in Dahomey. This collection of short stories is dedicated to Robby, Wideman's incarcerated younger brother. Wideman seems to evoke the god in an attempt to break Robby free from the bars that entrap him. This is a desire that has its roots in the commonly held belief that the voodoo deities helped the Haitian people to free themselves from the bonds of slavery in 1803 and become the first nation of blacks in the new world to gain its freedom. Wideman features himself in these stories that connect him to his family. While he is not at ease or as lucid as his Aunt May, he nonetheless affirms his connection and claims the power of his maternal ancestor. In these interrelated stories, Wideman no longer uses imaginary characters to work through his isolation; rather, he inserts his own voice and honestly explores his place within his family and the Homewood community.

In *Sent for You Yesterday* (1983), the last book in the trilogy, the intellectual Doot returns to the community and, through his creation of a myth of Homewood, situates himself within that community. The oral tradition, most evident in African American music, serves as the center of this mythological creation. In addition, Wideman collapses time and space, has the dead interacting with the living, and fuses dialogue so that the past and the present merge as one unending yarn that connects African American people.

In *Brothers and Keepers* (1984), Wideman combines journalistic reporting, personal essays, social commentary and fiction in an attempt to understand the events leading up to the imprisonment for murder of his younger brother, Robby. In this text, Wideman takes himself to task by tracing how his education re-

moved him from the desperation and drugs that stalked Robby and ultimately led to Robby's conviction and life-sentence. Wideman does not let himself off the hook for drifting away from his community and his family. He writes, "That day six years later, I talked with Robby three hours, the maximum allotted for weekday visits with a prisoner. It was the first time in life we'd ever talked that long." In this work Wideman comes full circle and reunites himself both emotionally and spiritually to the African American community. It is a candid exposé of personal guilt and grief.

Subsequently, in his novel *Reuben* (1987), Wideman portrays a character who is an intellectual and a lawyer but maintains a longstanding relationship with the underclass African Americans of Homewood. Although Reuben does not believe he can control his destiny, he creates fiction to empower his African American clients so they do not feel so besieged and at the mercy of an irrational, arbitrary world. Reuben's stories serve as armor for the community.

Wideman's next work, *Fever* (1989), is a collection of stories that portray the yellow fever epidemic that wreaked havoc in Philadelphia in 1793. It is a chilling work in which a free African American preacher risks his life to help save whites who deny him full citizenship. Wideman tells the same story from several vantage points. Some of the stories in this collection are narrated by individuals, others from a collective third person perspective. In his review of *Fever,* Randall Kenan observes that "Wideman's true mission appears to be to replace the *I* at the center of all his stories, to make it subject to an internal order of things rather than to external structures and limitations" (*Nation,* 1 January 1990).

It is this external structure that Wideman takes on in *Philadelphia Fire* (1990), which is based on the 1985 bombing of MOVE headquarters in Philadelphia. At the time, five children and eleven adult members of this organization were killed, and dozens of homes were destroyed as the uncontrollable fire raged. As with his other works, *Philadelphia Fire* is not limited to a linear narration of plot. Cudjoe, a journalist armed with Aretha Franklin songs and poetry, wanders though the city looking for a boy who was seen escaping the fire. The disjointed narrative documents African Americans' precarious position in urban cities. As in *The Homewood Trilogy,* Wideman identifies with the black community's position and personalizes the narrative. He demonstrates the ways in which circumstances in his own life parallel the destruction met by his characters by inserting an essay in the middle of the text that explores the events which led to his younger son serving a life-sentence for stabbing to death his roommate while on a camping trip. Tragedy confronts tragedy, fiction intersects with reality.

John Edgar Wideman is unafraid to experiment with many voices. He has pushed his fiction to embrace both European and African American aesthetic traditions. Some aspect of his life is at the center of all of his works. He probes, relentless in his attempt to understand the social machine that seems so controlling and leaves so many people feeling powerless. While Wideman's experimental techniques might not always provide clarity, his works nonetheless cause one to look beyond the surface. As a writer and a man, Wideman has confronted the demons and is now joined by his community and family in an endless struggle for answers and stories to buoy them across rough waters. Thus, it is fitting to end with Wideman's view on his art, as he stated in *Callaloo* in 1990:

Writing for me is an expressive activity, so it's as intimate as my handwriting, or the way I dance, or the way I play basketball .... Writing for me is a way of opening up, a way of sharing, a way of making sense of the world, and writing's very appeal is that it gives me a kind of hands-on way of coping with the very difficult business of living a life.

—Opal Palmer Adisa

WIGGLESWORTH, Michael

Born: England, probably in Yorkshire, 18 October 1631; immigrated with his parents to the Massachusetts Bay Colony, 1638, and settled in New Haven, Connecticut. **Education:** Harvard University, Cambridge, Massachusetts, A.B. 1651, A.M. 1653. **Family:** Married 1) Mary Reyner in 1655 (died 1659), one daughter; 2) Martha Mudge in 1679 (died 1690), five daughters and one son; 3) Sybil Sparhawk Avery in 1691, one son. **Career:** Tutor, Harvard University, 1652-54; ordained minister of Puritan church, 1656; minister to the church at Malden, Massachusetts, 1656-63 and with assistants because of ill-health, 1663-86; sole minister again after 1686; also studied and practiced medicine, Freeman, Massachusetts Bay Colony, 1680; fellow, Harvard University, 1697-1705. **Died:** 10 June 1705.

PUBLICATIONS

Collections

The Day of Doom with Other Poems, edited by Kenneth B. Murdock. 1929.

Poetry

The Day of Doom. 1662(?); revised edition, 1666.
Meat out of the Eater. 1670; revised edition, with *Riddles Unriddled,* 1689.
Riddles Unriddled; or, Christian Paradoxes. 1689.

Other

The Diary 1653-1657, edited by Edmund S. Morgan. 1965.

*

Critical Studies: *Sketch of the Life of Wigglesworth, to Which Is Appended a Fragment of His Autobiography, Some of His Letters, and a Catalogue of His Library* by John W. Dean, 1863, revised edition, as *Memoir of Wigglesworth,* 1871; *No Featherbed to Heaven: A Biography of Wigglesworth* by Richard H. Crowder, 1962; "'Our Cursed Natures': Sexuality and the Puritan Conscience" by Kathleen Verduin, in *New England Quarterly,* June 1983; "'Ladders of Your Own': The Day of Doom and the Repudiation of 'Carnal Reason'" by Jeffrey A. Hammond, in *Early American Literature,* Spring 1984; "Petrus Ramus and Michael Wigglesworth: The Logic of Poetic Structure" by Allan H. Pope, in *Puritan Poets and Poetics: Seventeenth-Century American Poetry in Theory and Practice* edited by Peter White, 1985; "'Day of Doom': La Rhetorique de la fin des temps dans la Nouvelle-Angleterre du XVIIe siécle" by Pierre Petillon, in *Age d'or et apocalypse* edited by Robert Ellrodt and Bernard Brugiere, 1986; "Night Pollution and the Floods of Confession in Michael Wigglesworth's Diary" by Eva Cherniavksy, in *Arizona Quarterly,* Summer 1989; "Alexander Richardson and the Ramist Poetics of Michael Wigglesworth" by John C. Adams, in *Early American Literature,* vol. 25, 1990; "'Meat out of the Eater': Panic and Desire in American Puritan Poetry" by Walter Hughes, in *Engendering Men: The Question of Male Feminist Criticism* edited by Joseph A. Boone and Michael Cadden, 1990; "Wigglesworth's *The Day of Doom*" by Gary Sloan, in *Explicator,* Winter 1998.

*   *   *

Michael Wigglesworth's first major publication, *The Day of Doom*—a best-seller for a century—was a jeremiad of 224 eight-line stanzas presenting in vivid detail the Calvinist notion of the events of the Final Judgment. The writer's purpose was not to write fine poetry but to provide uncomplicated facts in easy rhyme. For generations children recited from memory the entire poem, which devotes a few stanzas to the rewards of the saved but many more to the pleas, sentencing, and punishment of the damned. In the same volume with *The Day of Doom* Wigglesworth published several other poems setting forth Puritan doctrine, pleading with the reader to turn from wickedness and avoid everlasting punishment (e.g., "A Short Discourse on Eternity" and "Vanity of Vanities"), verses couched in sermonic phrases, jogging along in well-worn meters without much variety. The imagery, already familiar to his churchgoing readers, was nevertheless vigorously pictorial as the poet strove to convert the sinners.

Another jeremiad, "God's Controversy with New-England," showed the reader that because of the general evil-doing of the colonists God was right in inflicting illness and drought on the region. The verse forms here change from ballad structure ("fourteeners") to six-line iambics to quatrains as Wigglesworth pleads the cause for spiritual renewal.

The other large work he called *Meat out of the Eater,* a series of ten meditations and "A Conclusion Hortatory" demonstrating "the Necessity, End, and Usefulness of Afflictions." "Riddles Unriddled," clusters of verses constituting nine paradoxes, uses a little more variety in verse form in an attempt to fit structure to meaning. For example, the first paradox, "Light in Darkness," consists of ten "Songs," some in the form of medieval debates. The poet moves from ballad form in one "Song" to six-syllable lines in couplet rhyme in another. The other paradoxes likewise are composed of a number of separate poems, illustrating such themes as "Strength in Weakness" and "In Confinement Liberty."

In a twelve-year span (1662-73)—during a period when he was physically too weak to preach from his Malden pulpit—Wigglesworth wrote nearly all his extant poetry, and in a surprising variety of forms: lyric, dramatic, narrative, descriptive, didactic and hortatory, and autobiographical. Though not a major poet, he made a serious contribution to Puritan Calvinist doctrine, preserving in not unreadable verse the ideas that his readers were hearing from the pulpit Sunday after Sunday.

Wigglesworth's diary was edited by Edmund S. Morgan. He transcribed and made available to modern readers the frequent passages in shorthand. The diary fully discloses the poet's constant struggle with his conscience, his soul warring against powerful drives inside his frail flesh. A couple of college orations (including "The Praise of Eloquence") have been preserved and are sometimes anthologized. Written in "plain style," they are obviously class assignments discussing the elements of effective oratory.

—Richard H. Crowder

WILBUR, Richard (Purdy)

Born: New York City, 1 March 1921. **Education:** Amherst College, Massachusetts, B.A. 1942; Harvard University, Cambridge, Massachusetts, A.M. 1947. **Military Service:** Served in the U.S. Army, 1943-45; sergeant. **Family:** Married Charlotte Ward in 1942; one daughter and three sons. **Career:** Member of the Society of Fellows, 1947-50, and assistant professor of English, 1950-54, Harvard University, Cambridge, Massachusetts; associate professor of English, Wellesley College, Wellesley, Massachusetts, 1955-57; professor of English, Wesleyan University, Middletown, Connecticut, 1957-77; writer-in-residence, Smith College, Northampton, Massachusetts, 1977-86. General editor, Laurel Poets series, Dell Publishing Company, New York. State Department cultural exchange representative to the U.S.S.R., 1961. **Awards:** Guggenheim fellowship, 1952, 1963; American Academy in Rome fellowship, 1954; Pulitzer prize, 1957, 1989; National Book award, 1957; Edna St. Vincent Millay Memorial award, 1957; Ford fellowship for drama, 1960; Melville Cane award, 1962; Bollingen prize, 1963 for translation, 1971 for verse; Sarah Joseph Hale award, 1968; Brandeis University Creative Arts award, 1970; Henri Desfeuilles Prize, 1971; Shelley Memorial award, 1973; Harriet Monroe award, 1978; PEN translation award, 1983; Drama Desk award for translation, 1983. L.H.D.: Lawrence College, Appleton, Wisconsin, 1960; Washington University, St. Louis, 1964; Williams College, Williamstown, Massachusetts, 1975; Rochester University, Rochester, New York, 1976; Carnegie Mellon University, Pittsburgh, 1980. D.Litt.: Amherst College, 1967; Clark University, Worcester, Massachusetts, 1970; American International College, Springfield, Massachusetts, 1974; Marquette University, Milwaukee, 1977; Wesleyan University, 1977; Lake Forest College, Illinois, 1982. **Member:** American Academy of Arts and Sciences; president, 1974-77, and chancellor, 1977-78, 1981, American Academy of Arts and Letters; chancellor, Academy of American Poets; Chevalier, Ordre National des Palmes Academiques, 1983. **Residence:** Cummington, Massachusetts.

PUBLICATIONS

Poetry

The Beautiful Changes and Other Poems. 1947.
Ceremony and Other Poems. 1950.
Things of This World. 1956; one section reprinted as *Digging to China.* 1970.
Poems 1943-1956. 1957.
Advice to a Prophet and Other Poems. 1961.
The Poems. 1963.
The Pelican from a Bestiary of 1120. 1963.
Prince Souvanna Phouma: An Exchange Between Wilbur and William Jay Smith. 1963.

Complaint. 1968.
Walking to Sleep: New Poems and Translations. 1969.
Seed Leaves: Homage to R.F. 1974.
The Mind-Reader: New Poems. 1976.
Verses on the Times, with William Jay Smith. 1978.
Advice from the Muse. 1981.
Seven Poems. 1981.
New & Collected Poems. 1989.
Bone Key and Other Poems. 1998.

Plays

The Misanthrope, from the play by Moliere (produced 1955). 1955; revised version, music by Margaret Pine (produced 1977).
Candide (lyrics only, with Dorothy Parker and John LaTouche), book by Lillian Hellman, music by Leonard Bernstein, from the novel by Voltaire (produced 1956). 1957.
Tartuffe, from the play by Moliere (produced 1964). 1963.
School for Wives, from a play by Moliere (produced 1971). 1971.
The Learned Ladies, from a play by Moliere (produced 1977). 1978.
Andromache, from the play by Racine. 1982.
Phaedre, from a play by Racine. 1990.
The School for Husbands, from a play by Moliere. 1990.
The Imaginary Cuckold, from a play by Moliere. 1993.
Amphitryon, from a play by Moliere. 1995.
Don Juan, from a play by Moliere. 1998.

Other

Emily Dickinson: Three Views, with Louise Bogan and Archibald MacLeish. 1960.
Loudmouse (for children). 1963.
Opposites (for children), drawings by the author. 1973.
Responses: Prose Pieces 1953-1976. 1976.
The Whale and Other Uncollected Translations. 1982.
On My Own Work. 1983.
Conversations with Richard Wilbur, (interviews). 1990.
More Opposites (for children). 1991.
The Catbird's Song. 1997.
A Game of Catch (for children). 1997.
The Disappearing Alphabet (for children). 1998.

Editor, with Louis Untermeyer and Karl Shapiro, *Modern American and Modern British Poetry,* revised shorter edition. 1955.
Editor, *A Bestiary* (anthology). 1955.
Editor, *Complete Poems of Poe.* 1959.
Editor, with Alfred B. Harbage, *Poems of Shakespeare.* 1966; revised edition, as *The Narrative Poems and Poems of Doubtful Authenticity.* 1974.
Editor, *Selected Poems,* by Witter Bynner. 1978.

Translator, *The Funeral of Bobo,* by Joseph Brodsky. 1974.

*

Bibliography: *Wilbur: A Bibliographical Checklist* by John P. Field, 1971; *Richard Wilbur: A Reference Guide* by Frances Bixler, 1991.

Critical Studies: *Wilbur* by Donald L. Hill, 1967; *Wilbur* by Paul F. Cummins. 1971; *Wilbur's Creation* edited by Wendy Salinger,

1983; *Wilbur's Poetry* by Bruce Michelson, 1991; *A Reader's Guide to the Poetry of Richard Wilbur* by Rodney S. Edgecombe, 1995.

*   *   *

Richard Wilbur's first volume of poems surprised its early readers in 1947: there is none of the standard theorizing about history or large "modern" issues and only occasional reflections of the poet's experiences in the war; instead, the poet of *The Beautiful Changes* speaks openly of beauty, unabashedly expressing his delight in the sights and sounds and movements of the world and demonstrating a dazzling virtuosity at re-creating them in his verse. He also reveals his delight in wit, imaginative play, and even games. One of the poems is entitled simply "&," and his delights are joined in some lines from "Grace":

> One is tickled again, by the dining-car waiter's absurd
> Acrobacy—tipfingered tray like a wind-besting bird
> Plumblines his swinging shoes, the sole things sure
> In the shaken train.

In addition to the high spirits, the poems often almost exemplify elegance, poise, and good manners.

A number of those qualities and subjects came to seem even more startling in the years that followed. From the beginning, Wilbur's poetry has shown notable continuities. He has remarked that in his later poems he tends to move toward "a plainer and more straightforward" way of writing and, also, from poems that use a "single meditative voice balancing argument and counter-argument, feeling and counter-feeling" to more "dramatic" ones (such as "Two Voices in a Meadow" or "The Aspen and the Stream") that may use two opposing voices. Readers also may detect a general deepening of feeling and a clearer personal voice as well as some unpredictable developments. But most of the earlier qualities remain, and there continue to be signal exclusions: no confessional poetry and no free verse (Wilbur wrote that in the fairy story about the genie that could be summoned out of a bottle, he had always assumed that the genie gained his strength from being *in* the bottle).

It is unlikely that anyone could have predicted, however, that the poet who showed an almost Keatsian responsiveness to the sensuous should become the translator of Moliere into extraordinary English couplets. In retrospect, it is clearer that Moliere represents part of what Wilbur is, as well as what he admires: a humane voice of uncommonly rational common sense; a user of language that is both familiar and chaste; a witty enemy of the pompous, the gross, and the fanatic; and a juggler, a master of poise and point. (That he later became the translator of Racine—*Andromache*—may still seem surprising.) Nor could one have anticipated "Junk," the liveliest re-creation of Anglo-Saxon meters and feeling since **Ezra Pound,** or the scathing Miltonic sonnet to Lyndon Johnson, or the tenderness of the translations from Charles d'Orleans, Voltaire, and Francis Jammes, or the effectiveness of "A Christmas Hymn," or the moving elegy for Dudley Fits.

Neither could one have quite anticipated "Walking to Sleep," an extraordinary exploration of the paths, stratagems, surprises, and terrors that lie between waking and sleep, nor "The Mind-Reader," although both long poems extend one of Wilbur's most persistent themes in his more obviously personal lyrics: the processes, reflections, and creations of the mind. Wilbur once re-

marked, "A good part of my work could, I suppose, be understood as a public quarrel with the aesthetics of **Edgar Allan Poe.**" His continuous concern is evidenced by his edition of Poe's poems and a number of substantial essays on both the prose and the verse: three of the sixteen provocative and lucid essays in *Responses: Prose Pieces 1953-1976* concern Poe. He once wrote, "There has never been a grander conception of poetry [than Poe's], nor a more impoverished one." As that sentence suggests, the quarrel continues because Wilbur finds it so difficult to make a decision once and for all. His ambivalence is the theme of a number of his best poems. At its simplest level this ambivalence arises from his fascination with the intellectual, the perfectly beautiful and purely harmonious, and his almost simultaneous reaction away from such an ideal in an acceptance and love for the imperfect human and material reality that we can know here and now. "A World Without Objects Is a Sensible Emptiness" is one of many that move from a moment of the soul's ascension toward the empyrean to a rejoicing in the body and its world. Wilbur's poetry often seems that of a natural Platonist who keeps learning to accept the Incarnation. "The Writer" movingly recognizes that the literary "flight" has its origins as well as final resting place in human suffering and love.

If **Robert Frost** has an authentic living heir, it is probably Wilbur—particularly as the poet of the short lyric in strict and familiar meters who speaks in the middle voice, wittily and movingly, to a wide audience. There are, however, important differences: Wilbur's voice usually is more obviously that of an urban man in contrast to the characteristic voice of the countryman that Frost so carefully crafted; and Frost never devoted such care to the attempt to translate, self-effacingly, the poetry of others, nor did he write for the public theater. But the most important difference is probably in their spirits. Frost did not share with anything like Wilbur's conviction the notion that "Love Calls Us to the Things of This World?" It may have been, in part at least, that conviction that enabled Wilbur to make imaginatively convincing his early "Advice to a Prophet" concerning how we might be persuaded not to destroy our earth.

In his latest work he has continued to search out the subtle in the everyday, the puzzling in the obvious, preoccupied with the natural inclination to contrariety in human thought and feeling—as he puts it in "Advice from the Muse": "That slight uncertainty that makes us sure." And he has continued his interest in the playful: riddles, a fable, gnomics, light subjects (such as his wife buying a new dress) treated wryly. Even his "On Freedom's Ground," words for a cantata by William Schuman written to commemorate the bicentennial of the Statue of Liberty, reflect this attitude: Wilbur describes it in the introduction to *New and Collected Poems* as "an effort to say something clear and acceptable, yet not wholly predictable, on a national occasion."

But finally, Wilbur's work is about less outward concerns. A poem about a dream of riding a horse ("The Ride") becomes a poignant eruption of metaphysical nostalgia, a longing for everything in the past, for the moment of creation, for the career of writing. A reflection on "Hamlen Brook" becomes the occasion for enunciating the inevitable incompletion of joy, in an obliquely Keatsian moment rendered in canny colloquial speech:

> Joy's trick is to supply
> Dry lips with what can cool and slake,
> Leaving them dumbstruck also with an ache
> Nothing can satisfy.

Here joy is the project of poetry, one with which Wilbur's poetry perpetually entangles itself, even in its darkest utterances.

—Joseph H. Summers, updated by Joseph O. Aimone

WILDER, Thornton (Niven)

Born: Madison, Wisconsin, 17 April 1897. **Education:** Thacher School, Ojai, California, 1912-13; Berkeley High School, California, graduated 1915; Oberlin College, Ohio, 1915-17; Yale University, New Haven, Connecticut, 1917, 1919-20, A.B. 1920; American Academy in Rome, 1920-21; Princeton University, New Jersey, 1925-26, A.M. 1926. **Military Service:** Served in the U.S. Coast Artillery Corps, 1918; in the U.S. Army Air Intelligence, rising to the rank of lieutenant-colonel, 1942-45: honorary M.B.E. (Member, Order of the British Empire), 1945. **Career:** French teacher, 1921-25, and house master, 1927-28, Lawrenceville School, New Jersey. Full-time writer from 1928. Part-time Lecturer in Comparative Literature, University of Chicago, 1930-36; visiting professor, University of Hawaii, Honolulu, 1935; Charles Eliot Norton Professor of Poetry, Harvard University, Cambridge, Massachusetts, 1950-51. U.S. Delegate: Institut de Cooperation Intellectuelle, Paris, 1937; International PEN Club Congress, England, 1941; UNESCO Conference of the Arts, Venice, 1952. **Awards:** Pulitzer prize, for fiction, 1928, for drama, 1938, 1943; American Academy Gold Medal, 1952; Freedom prize (Frankfurt), 1957; Brandeis University Creative Arts award, 1959; MacDowell Medal, 1960; Presidential Medal of Freedom, 1963; National Medal for Literature, 1965; National Book award, for fiction, 1968. D.Litt.: New York University, 1930; Yale University, 1947; Kenyon College, Gambier, Ohio, 1948; College of Wooster, Ohio, 1950; Northeastern University, Boston, 1951; Oberlin College, 1952; University of New Hampshire, Durham, 1953; Goethe University, Frankfurt, 1957; University of Zurich, 1961. LL.D.: Harvard University. 1951. **Member:** Chevalier, Legion of Honor (France), 1951; Order of Merit (Pern); Order of Merit (Germany), 1957; honorary member, Bavarian Academy of Fine Arts; Mainz Academy of Science and Literature; American Academy. **Died:** 7 December 1975.

PUBLICATIONS

Collection

The Collected Short Plays of Thornton Wilder. 1998.

Fiction

The Cabala. 1926.
The Bridge of San Luis Rey. 1927.
The Woman of Andros. 1930.
Heaven's My Destination. 1934.
The Ides of March. 1948.
The Eighth Day. 1967.
Theophilus North. 1973.

Plays

The Trumpet Shall Sound (produced 1926). In *Yale Literary Magazine*, October-December 1919, January 1920.
The Angel That Troubled the Waters and Other Plays (includes *Nascuntur Poetae, Proserpina and the Devil, Fanny Otcott, Brother Fire, The Penny That Beauty Spent, The Angel on the Ship, The Message and Jehanne, Childe Roland to the Dark Tower Came, Centaurs, Leviathan, And the Sea Shall Give up Its Dead, Now the Servant's Name Was Malchus, Mozart and the Gray Steward, Hast Thou Considered My Servant Job?, The Flight into Egypt*). 1928.
The Long Christmas Dinner (produced 1931). In *The Long Christmas Dinner and Other Plays*, 1931; libretto for opera version, as *Das Lange Weihnachtsmal*, music by Paul Hindemith (produced 1961), libretto published, 1961.
The Happy Journey to Trenton and Camden (produced 1931). In *The Long Christmas Dinner and Other Plays*, 1931; revised version, as *The Happy Journey*, 1934.
Such Things Only Happen in Books (produced 1931). In *The Long Christmas Dinner and Other Plays*, 1931.
Love and How to Cure It (produced 1931). In *The Long Christmas Dinner and Other Plays*, 1931.
The Long Christmas Dinner and Other Plays in One Act. 1931.
Queens of France (produced 1932). In *The Long Christmas Dinner and Other Plays*, 1931.
Pullman Car Hiawatha (produced 1962). In *The Long Christmas Dinner and Other Plays*, 1931.
Lucrece, from a play by Andre Obey (produced 1932). 1933.
A Doris House, from a play by Ibsen (produced 1937).
Our Town (produced 1938). 1938.
The Merchant of Yonkers, from a play by Johann Nostroy, based on *A Well-Spent Day* by John Oxenford (produced 1938). 1939; revised version, as *The Matchmaker* (produced 1954), in *Three Plays*, 1957.
The Skin of Our Teeth (produced 1942). 1942.
Our Century (produced 1947). 1947.
The Victors, from a play by Sartre (produced 1949).
Die Alkestiade (as *A Life in the Sun*, produced 1955; as *Die Alkestiade*, music by Louise Talma, produced 1962). 1960; as *The Alcestiad; or, A Life in the Sun, and The Drunken Sisters: A Satyr Play*. 1977.
The Drunken Sisters (produced 1970). 1957.
Three Plays. 1957.
Bernice, and The Wreck of the 5:25 (produced 1957).
Plays for Bleecker Street (includes *Infancy, Childhood*, and *Someone from Assisi*) (produced 1962). *Childhood* and *Infancy* published, 2 vols., 1960-61.

Screenplays: *We Live Again*, with others, 1934; *Our Town*, with Frank Craven and Harry Chandlee, 1940; *Shadow of a Doubt*, with others, 1943.

Other

The Intent of the Artist, with others. 1941.
Kultur in einer Demokratie. 1957.
Goethe und die Weltliteratur. 1958.
American Characteristics and Other Essays, edited by Donald Gallup. 1979.

The Journals 1939-1961 (includes unfinished play *The Emporium*), edited by Donald Gallup. 1985.
The Letters of Gertrude Stein and Thornton Wilder. 1996.

*

Bibliography: *Wilder: A Bibliographical Checklist of Works by and about Wilder* by Richard Goldstone and Gary Anderson, 1982.

Critical Studies: *Wilder* by Rex Burbank, 1961, revised edition, 1978; *Wilder* by Helmut Papajewski, 1961, translated by John Conway, 1968; *Wilder* by Bernard Grebanier, 1964; *The Art of Wilder* by Malcolm Goldstein, 1965; *The Plays of Wilder: A Critical Study* by Donald Haberman, 1967; *Wilder: The Bright and the Dark* by Mildred Christophe Kuner, 1972; *Wilder: An Intimate Portrait* by Richard Goldstone, 1975; *Wilder: His World* by Linda Simon, 1979; *A Vast Landscape: Time in the Novels of Wilder* by Mary Ellen Williams, 1979; *Wilder and His Public* by Amos Wilder, 1980; *The Enthusiast: A Life of Wilder* by Gilbert A. Harrison, 1983; *Wilder* by David Castronovo, 1986; "The Way We Come Back into *Our Town*" by Mariana Net, in *Cahiers Roumains d'Etudes Litteraires,* vol. 1, 1988; "Thornton Wilder's *Adam und Messias*" by Franz Link, in *Paradeigmata: Literarische Typologie des Alten Testaments* edited by Link, 1989; "Alcestis: How Myth Means and Functions" by Rebecca Rovit, in *Text and Presentation* edited by Karelisa Hartigan, 1989; "Errors in Thornton Wilder's *The Eighth Day*" by Michael V. Williams, in *English Language Notes,* March 1990; "The Politics of Thornton Wilder's *The Ides of March*" by Peter G. Christensen, in *Classical and Modern Literature,* Fall 1991; *Conversations with Thornton Wilder* edited by Jackson Bryer, 1992; "A Further Case of the 'Detective Novel Unbound': Thornton Wilder's *The Eighth Day* and the Mystery Novel" by Raimund Borgmeier, in *Telling Stories: Studies in Honour of Ulrich Broich on the Occasion of His 60th Birthday* edited by Elmar Lehmann and Bernd Lenz, 1992; *Wilder Rediscovered,* 1997; *Readings on Thornton Wilder* edited by Katie De Koster, 1998; *Thornton Wilder: New Essays,* 1999.

*   *   *

Many American writers have written both plays and fiction, but no other has achieved such a distinguished reputation for both as Thornton Wilder. He is distinguished also for the uniqueness of his works: each is a fresh formal experiment that contributes to his persistent conception of the artist's reinventing the world by revivifying our perceptions of the universal elements of human experience.

Wilder's earliest published works in *The Angel That Troubled the Waters and Other Plays* are short pieces presenting usually fantastic situations in an arch, cryptic style employed by such favored writers of the 1920s as **Elinor Wylie.** A number of the plays deal with the special burden that falls upon persons who discover that they possess artistic gifts, and most of them demand staging too complex for actual performance.

Before he became a successful playwright, Wilder was a novelist. His first novel, *The Cabala,* displays much the same preciosity as the early plays. It describes through loosely linked episodes the effort of an aspiring young American writer to be accepted by the Cabala, "members of a circle so powerful and exclusive that . . . Romans refer to them with bated breath." These elegant figures turn out to be contemporary embodiments of the ancient Roman gods, and the veiled point of the work is that the U.S. is to succeed a decaying Rome as the next abiding place of these gods.

This fantasy did not attract many readers, but Wilder achieved an astonishing success with his next short novel, *The Bridge of San Luis Rey,* which became a surprise bestseller. This episodic story about the perishability of material things and the endurance of love is exquisitely structured. It tells the stories of the five persons who die in the collapse of a famous Peruvian bridge. The framework of the novel is provided by the narrative of a Brother Juniper, who investigates the accident to learn whether "we live by accident and die by accident, or live by plan and die by plan?" For his efforts, both he and his book are publicly burned. The last sentence stresses that the only bridge that survives is love.

Wilder's third novel, *The Woman of Andros,* was attacked by socially-minded critics of the 1930s for evading present realities and retreating to the classical world; but this subtle fictionalization of Terence's Andria actually relates closely to Wilder's own seemingly dying world through its presentation of the death of the Greek world at the time of the coming of Christ because its commercial and artistic communities had become alienated. With his next novel, *Heaven's My Destination,* Wilder returned to contemporary America to create one of his most beguiling characters, George Brush, a high-school textbook salesman in the Midwest, who fails comically and pathetically in his constant efforts to uplift other people and who recovers his faith only when he realizes that he must remain an isolated wanderer, happy only in the world that he makes for himself.

The world that we make for ourselves is the subject again of one of Wilder's most admired works and his major contribution to a myth of American community, the play *Our Town.* Wilder explained in *The Intent of the Artist* that he turned from the novel to the stage in the 1930s because "the theater carries the art of narration to a higher power than the novel or the epic poem." He was impatient, however, with the elaborate stage settings of the naturalistic theater, and he had already sought in short plays like *The Long Christmas Dinner* to tell a fundamental human story with only the simplest of props. His culminating experiment with this technique was *Our Town,* a chronicle of the value of "the smallest events in our daily life" in a traditional New England village.

Wilder next experimented with updating a nineteenth-century farce that had been popular in both English and German versions as *The Merchant of Yonkers.* Unsuccessful when first ponderously presented by Max Reinhardt, the play in a revised version entitled *The Matchmaker* was a popular success that subsequently provided the basis for the enormously popular musical comedy, *Hello, Dolly!* Wilder did enjoy great immediate success with his third major play, *The Skin of Our Teeth,* an expressionist fantasy about man's struggles for survival through the Ice Age, the Flood, and the Napoleonic Wars as symbolized by the travails of the Antrobus family. Again Wilder's timing was superb. A world reduced to doubt and despair by World War II responded enthusiastically to this affirmative vision of man's possible survival despite his destructive propensities.

Wilder served with American intelligence units in Italy during World War II, and for his first post-war work returned to the novel and to a classical Roman setting for *The Ides of March.* This pseudo-history, which Malcolm Goldstein compares to "a set of bowls placed one within another," centers on the assassination of

Julius Caesar, but traces through four overlapping sections an ever widening circle of events in order to present "the tragic difference between Caesar's idealistic visions and the sordid events for which they are finally responsible"—a subject fraught with implications for the mid-twentieth century.

After the comparatively cool reception of this work, Wilder published little for twenty years. Although his plays remained popular, he was generally too lightly regarded after World War II when existential angst dominated literary criticism. His writings were felt to be too affirmative and optimistic, and his long silence caused him to be regarded as an artist whose time had passed. Literary mandarins were startled, therefore, by the appearance in 1967 of his longest and most complex work, *The Eighth Day*. This novel jumps back and forth in time as it resurrects the events relating to a murder in a southern Illinois coal town early in the twentieth century, the false conviction of a man who escapes, and the eventual solution of the cunning crime. This mystery plot, however, provided only a backdrop for Wilder's observation that all history is one "enormous tapestry" and that "there are no Golden Ages and no Dark Ages. There is the ocean-like monotony of the generations of men under the alternations of fair and foul weather." At the center of the work stands the falsely accused John Ashley, who avoids succumbing to despair over this inescapable cycle by "inventing" afresh such fossilized institutions as marriage and fatherhood as he also invents small practical objects to make man's work easier. An old woman whom he meets sums up the sensibility that informs the novel, "The human race gets no better. Mankind is vicious, slothful, quarrelsome, and self-centered . . . [But] you and I have a certain quality that is rare as teeth in a hen. We work. And we forget ourselves in our work."

The Eighth Day triumphantly capped Wilder's "re-invention" of mankind, but he had one final delight for readers. Perhaps to complement James Joyce's and others' portraits of the artist as a young man by a young man, Wilder presented in his last published work, *Theophilus North*, an episodic novel about the artist as a young man by an old man. The seemingly loosely connected tales are actually—as in his other works—parts of an intricate mosaic that discloses against a background of the "nine cities" of Newport, Rhode Island, the nine career possibilities that a young man explores before discovering that being a writer will encompass all of them.

—Warren French

See the essay on *Our Town*.

WILLIAMS, John A(lfred)

Pseudonym: J. Dennis Gregory. **Born:** Jackson, Mississippi, 5 December 1925. **Education:** Central High School, Syracuse, New York; Syracuse University, English and Journalism, A.B. 1950; graduate study, English, 1950-51. **Military Service:** Served in the U.S. Navy, 1943-46. **Family:** Married 1) Carolyn Clopton in 1947 (divorced), two sons; 2) Lorrain Isaac, 5 October 1965, one son. **Career:** Worked as a supermarket clerk after college graduation; case worker for Onondaga County Welfare department, Syracuse, 1950-52; member of public relations agency, Doug Johnson Associates, Syracuse, 1952-54, and later with Arthur P. Jacobs Com-

pany; publicity, CBS Hollywood and New York City, 1954-55; publicity director, Comet Press Books, New York City, 1955-56; publisher and editor, *Negro Market Newsletter*, New York City, 1956-57; assistant to the publisher, Abelard-Schuman, New York City, 1957-58; director of information, American Committee on Africa, New York, 1958; European correspondent for *Ebony* and *Jet* magazines, 1958-59; special events announcer, WOV Radio, New York City, 1959; contributing editor, *Herald Tribune Book Week*, 1963-65; Africa correspondent, *Newsweek*, 1964-65; columnist, stringer, special assignment, and/or staff, various black newspapers, periodicals and news agencies, including the *National Leader, Progressive Herald, Age, Defender, Post-Standard, Tribune, Courier*, and the Associated Negro Press, 1965-66; narrator and co-producer of programs, National Education Television, 1965-66; interviewer for *Newsfront* program, 1968; lecturer in Afro-American Literature, College of the Virgin Islands, summer 1968; lecturer in creative writing, City College of the City University of New York, 1968-69; guest writer at Sarah Lawrence College, Bronxville, New York, 1972-73; contributing editor, *American Journal*, 1972-74; Regents Lecturer, University of California, Santa Barbara, 1973; distinguished professor of English, La Guardia Community College, City University of New York, 1973-78; visiting professor, University of Hawaii, summer 1974; contributing editor, *Politicks*, 1977; visiting professor, Boston University, Massachusetts, 1978-79; Exxon Visiting Professor of English, New York University, New York City, 1986-87; professor of English, 1979-90, Paul Robeson Professor of English, 1990 to retirement in 1993, Rutgers University, Newark, New Jersey. Member of editorial board, *Audience*, 1970-72; member of board of directors, *Journal of African Civilizations*, 1979-84; member of board of directors, New York State Council on the Arts; member of board of directors, Rabinowitz Foundation; member of Coordinating Council of Literary Magazines (later renamed Council of Small Presses and Literary Magazines), 1983-85, chair, 1984. **Awards:** National Institute of Arts and Letters award, 1962; Syracuse University Centennial Medal for Outstanding Achievement, 1970; National Endowment for the Arts grant, 1977; Rutgers University Lindback award for distinguished teaching, 1982; Before Columbus Foundation, American Book award for *!Click Song*, 1983, for *Safari West*, 1998. D.Litt.: Southeastern Massachusetts University, North Dartmouth, 1978. D.L.H.:Syracuse University, 1995. **Residence:** Teaneck, New Jersey.

PUBLICATIONS

Novels

The Angry Ones. 1960; as *One for New York*, 1975.
Night Song. 1961.
Sissie. 1963; as *Journey out of Anger*, 1968.
The Man Who Cried I Am. 1967.
Sons of Darkness, Sons of Light: A Novel of Some Probability. 1969.
Captain Blackman. 1972.
Mothersill and the Foxes. 1975.
The Junior Bachelor Society. 1976.
!Click Song. 1982.
The Berhama Account. 1985.
Jacob's Ladder. 1987.
Clifford's Blues. 1999.

Prose (nonfiction)

Africa: Her History, Lands and People. 1962.
The Protectors, with Harry J. Anslinger. 1964.
This Is My Country Too. 1964.
The Most Native of Sons. 1970.
The King God Didn't Save. 1970.
Flashbacks: A Twenty Year Diary of Article Writing. 1973.
Minorities in the City. 1975.
If I Stop I'll Die, with Dennis A. Williams. 1991.

Plays

Last Flight from Ambo Ber (produced 1981). 1984.
August Forty-five (produced 1991).
Vanqui, libretto, music by Leslie Buens (produced 1998).

Poetry

Safari West. 1998.

Television Scripts: *The History of the Negro People: Omowale—The Child Returns Home,* 1965; *The Creative Person: Henry Roth,* 1966.

Other

Editor, *The Angry Black.* 1962.
Editor, *Beyond the Angry Black.* 1967.
Editor, with Charles F. Harris, *Amistad I and II.* 2 vols., 1970-71.
Editor, *Yardbird No 1.* 1979.
Coeditor, with Gilbert H. Muller, *Introduction to Literature.* 1985.
Coeditor, with Gilbert H. Muller, *Bridges: Literature across Cultures.* 1993.
Coeditor, with Gilbert H. Muller, *Introduction to Literature.* 1994.
Coeditor, with Gilbert H. Muller, *Ways In: Approaches to Reading and Writing about Literature.* 1994.
Editor, *Street Guide to African Americans in Paris.* 1996.

*

Critical Studies: *The Evolution of a Black Writer: John A. Williams* by Earl Cash, 1975; *John A. Williams* by Gilbert H. Muller, 1984; "John A. Williams' *Sissie*" by Ralph Reckley, Sr., in *MAWA Review,* June 1990.

*   *   *

John A. Williams, one of the most prolific African American writers of the twentieth century, has been internationally acclaimed for his mastery of a wide array of literary genres, including novels, plays, science fiction, children's books, short stories, literary criticism, and journalism. Williams remains best known for the ten novels so vibrantly and indelibly imprinted by his life experiences, including *The Man Who Cried I Am, Captain Blackman,* and *!Click Song.* This frequently autobiographical fiction often alludes to or thematically incorporates issues linked to the impact of twentieth-century publishers' biases on African American writers. And though African American writers and professors populate Williams's fiction, they represent only one of several autobiographical components in his work. Settings closely resembling

the Syracuse of his childhood; recreations of racist incidents that too often circumscribed his Navy, college and professional careers; African American contributions to the U.S. military; political conspiracies; and the adventures of African American expatriates in Europe and Africa are topics that reoccur in his novels in much the same way that they have punctuated Williams's life. Williams has excelled as a chronicler of the dreams, pathos and frustrations of his peers, and his ability to simultaneously reveal both the heterogeneity of the African American community and the universality of oppression's pain is unique.

Though born in his parents' home in Jackson, Mississippi, the oldest of John Henry and Ola Williams's two girls and two boys, Williams was reared and educated in the northern city of Syracuse, New York. In 1943, during the course of World War II, Williams interrupted his high school education to join the Navy. Following an honorable discharge in 1946, Williams returned to his hometown, married, and enrolled at Syracuse University. Upon graduating in 1950, he pursued his studies in the graduate school at Syracuse. By now the father of two sons, he held jobs that ran the gamut from foundry work to clerking in a supermarket.

In this regard, Williams was typical of his college-educated peers, whose career aspirations were often constrained by segregation and discrimination. In his book entitled *John A. Williams,* Earl Cash recalls an interview in which Williams observed that "Loblaw's Supermarket on Adams Street . . . must have had the most intellectual group of clerks in the city. They were trying to do something, I suppose, democratic. But all of the black people there had at least a Bachelor's degree and some had Master's." Subsequent jobs included social work and insurance sales. Then, in 1954, after his marriage fell apart, Williams moved to Los Angeles. A year of job hunting resulted in a dead-end insurance sales position, and a disillusioned Williams departed for home.

His return to New York marked the beginning of a haphazard, often frustrating, and frequently impoverished career as a writer. Free-lance articles, magazine assignments, stints on Madison Avenue, and other writing jobs provided an erratic income during the early years. In the *Flashbacks* essay "Career by Accident," Williams recalls that when *The Angry Ones* (*One for New York*) was accepted for publication, he had vowed to quit writing if he couldn't sell that third draft. By the time the book was published, his advance had long since been spent. Then, in the space of a week, he contracted for three books, two novels, and a nonfiction work. These events marked the advent of his since uninterrupted commercial success. By 1961, in addition to numerous articles and short stories, he had published two novels, and his first nonfiction volume, *Africa: Her History, Lands and People,* was nearing completion. For the rest of the decade, while juggling a schedule that included extensive traveling, lecturing, and writing in several genres, Williams managed to average at least one major book per year.

It was during this period that Williams became embroiled in an unforgettable controversy. After he was named 1961 recipient of the prestigious American Academy of Arts and Letters fellowship to Rome, Williams's award was mysteriously withdrawn. His suspicion that racial discrimination was the culprit was confirmed when Alan Dugan, the poet who eventually received the award, made a courageous public disclosure affirming Williams's hunch. In the wake of the ensuing scandal, the American Academy prize for literature was discontinued for a time. Although this was a painful and disheartening experience, Williams used the incident in *The Man Who Cried I Am.* Like many other indignities, this became grist for the novelist's mill.

This autobiographical element of Williams's fiction is quite evident in his first novel, which opens as thirty-year-old publicist Stephen Hill, a World War II veteran who was the first in his family to attend college, relocates from Los Angeles to New York. The insensitivity and pandering to stereotypes exhibited by the unethical vanity press editor for whom Hill works are based upon Williams's firsthand experience. Published in 1960, and originally titled *One for New York,* the book was released as *The Angry Ones* when the publisher insisted that "anger" would sell more books. Williams, eager to have a novel published, reluctantly agreed to the change.

Night Song probes the elusive world of the black jazz musicians whose lives and songs are both in and of the night. The narrative evolves around three virtually co-equal protagonists. David Hillary, an unemployed alcoholic professor, is haunted by his possible responsibility for the auto accident that killed his wife. As the book opens, Hillary meets Eagle, a drug-addicted musical genius whose life is loosely patterned after that of Charlie "Yardbird" Parker, in a pawnshop. In pawning a wedding band and saxophone, respectively, each has metaphorically "sold himself to the devil." They head downtown—seeking oblivion in the "night" of New York's jazz scene—on a journey akin to Dante's. Whereas Eagle ultimately rescues Hillary, it is Keel Robinson, the Harvard seminary-trained former preacher, who acts as Eagle's "guardian angel." As owner of a coffee house catering to jazz musicians, this dropout from both Christianity and Islam serves as foil to both Hillary and Eagle.

Sissie, Big Ralph, Ralph, Jr., and Iris Joplin, the primary characters of *Sissie,* are survivors. It is through their survival strategies that Williams deconstructs the era's popular myths regarding black families. The kinship, strength, hope and love evidenced in this story are Williams's tribute to his own family. Based in part upon the Williamses of Syracuse, these characters reappear (individually and/or collectively) in *The Man Who Cried I Am, The Junior Bachelor Society,* and *!Click Song.* For Williams, the Joplins become an archetypal domestic grouping.

Between 1960 and 1963, Williams published the trilogy of *The Angry Ones, Night Song,* and *Sissie.* Each traced the problems faced by blacks in a white society. The world of publishing explored in *The Angry Ones,* the New York jazz scene of *Night Song,* and the pain and celebration of *Sissie*'s Joplin family were initially considered part of a canon of protest writing framed by moral outcry and reformist solutions. However, many later critics noted that Williams's educated, middle-class characters embraced the same postwar expectations as the African American populace of the time, who had faith in the promises of both integration and assimilation. Although each book highlights ways that institutionalized racism limits the characters' educational, employment, and housing prospects, those setbacks are repeatedly contrasted to an inner fortitude that seemingly strengthens them. With this referent, Stephen Hill's sense of hope after quitting the vanity press job can be interpreted as in accord with the early 1960s spirit of optimism. Nonetheless, the fact remains that the nonviolent, apolitical, often ahistorical characters of Williams's early novels share dreams of success and fulfillment that are repeatedly thwarted. In this regard, their aspirations and experiences merely mirror those of the working and middle-class blacks of Williams's world.

Not surprisingly, as the apocalyptic events of the late 1960s radically altered the worldview and politics of many African Americans, the themes of Williams's fiction also changed. The militancy and black nationalism of the era, refracted by Williams's military service and travels in the American South, Europe, and Africa, end up shaping Williams's second trilogy, *The Man Who Cried I Am, Sons of Darkness, Sons of Light,* and *Captain Blackman,* in much the same way that the "meism" of the late 1970s and early 1980s would place its imprint upon *Mothersill and the Foxes, The Junior Bachelor Society,* and *!Click Song.*

Williams's second trilogy has been referred to as the "Armageddon" novels. The disenchantment with racial progress, the political overtones, and the apocalyptic conclusions of these works brought Williams unprecedented international fame and commercial success. The adventures of expatriate writers Max and Harry, their discovery of the U.S. government's genocidal "King Alfred Plan," *Sons of Darkness, Sons of Light*'s conspirators, and Abraham Blackman's dreamed participation in every U.S. military initiative exemplify the shift in tone and narrative that Bernard Bell, in *The Afro-American Novel and Its Tradition,* refers to as "a shift from an appeal to white conscience to black consciousness."

Mothersill and the Foxes, with its search for rural peace, marks the beginning of a third phase, in which Williams rejects the political urgency of his 1960s and 1970s novels for more introspective themes. In *The Junior Bachelor Society,* we discover a group of nine men in their late forties returning to Central City for the seventieth birthday of their high school coach. Among this group of troubled men seeking reaffirmation is Ralph Joplin, Jr., now a successful playwright. Ultimately, the novel becomes one of celebration, as the bachelors discover that in spite of the hardships they've endured, there's still reason to hope. In *!Click Song,* Williams reverts to a plot involving the careers of two writers, as he had in *The Man Who Cried I Am.* Cato Douglass is the black writer whose experiences the author contrasts to those of his Jewish classmate Paul Cummings. In a highly autobiographical work, Williams uses Cato Douglass as the prism through which the lives of all black artists can be seen. Douglass, unable to overcome the racism of the publishing industry, is in many ways Williams's reminder to his readers that in the thirty years since his portrayal of Stephen Hill, little had changed.

In *Jacob's Ladder,* Williams returns to two favorite topics—Africa and politics. Set in the pre-Vietnam era, this novel of international intrigue finds Chuma Fasseke, president of a small fictitious African nation, trying to block U.S. intervention while he finishes a nuclear reactor. The ensuing diplomatic negotiations are led by the newly appointed U.S. ambassador, a childhood friend of Fasseke's named Jake Henry, who ultimately realizes that the CIA has lied to him and plans to destroy the nuclear reactor and assassinate his friend. By returning to the political thriller format that brought him such success during the 1970s, Williams, perpetual chronicler of his times, also affirms both the mainstream American 1980s shift in focus from "me" to "we" and the renewed black American interest in Africa.

Williams's writings, in addition to their notable artistic and literary merit, perhaps offer the clearest window into the lives of highly educated twentieth-century African Americans. Williams ultimately shows that for this group, as for the African American community as a whole, the "American Dream" has remained elusive.

—Gloria H. Dickinson

WILLIAMS, Tennessee

Born: Thomas Lanier Williams in Columbus, Mississippi, 26 March 1911. **Education:** The University of Missouri, Columbia, 1929-31; Washington University, St. Louis, 1936; University of Iowa, Iowa City, 1938, A.B. 1938. **Career:** Clerical worker and manual laborer, International Shoe Company, St. Louis, 1934-35; held various jobs, including waiter and elevator operator, New Orleans, 1939; teletype operator, Jacksonville, Florida, 1940; worked at odd jobs, New York, 1942, and as screenwriter for Metro-Goldwyn-Mayer (MGM), Hollywood, 1943; full-time writer from 1944; Distinguished Writer-in-Residence, University of British Columbia, Vancouver, 1980. **Awards:** Rockefeller fellowship, 1940; American Academy grant, 1944, and Gold Medal, 1969; New York Drama Critics Circle award, 1945, 1948, 1955, 1962; Sidney Howard award, 1945; Donaldson award, 1945, 1948; Pulitzer prize, 1948, 1955; London Evening Standard award, 1958; Brandeis University Creative Arts award, 1964; Medal of Freedom, 1980. L.H.D.: Harvard University, Cambridge, Massachusetts, 1982. **Member:** American Academy, 1976. **Died:** 25 February 1983.

PUBLICATIONS

Collections

Collected Stories. 1985.

Plays

Cairo, Shanghai, Bombay!, with Doris Shapiro (produced 1935).
The Magic Tower (produced 1936).
Headlines (produced 1936).
Candles to the Sun (produced 1937).
Fugitive Kind (produced 1937).
Spring Song (produced 1938).
The Long Goodbye (produced 1940). In *27 Wagons Full of Cotton and Other One-Act Plays,* 1946.
Battle of Angels (produced 1940). 1945; revised version, as *Orpheus Descending* (produced 1957), published as *Orpheus Descending, with Battle of Angels,* 1958.
This Property Is Condemned (produced 1942). In *27 Wagons Full of Cotton and Other One-Act Plays,* 1946.
You Touched Me!, with Donald Windham, from the story by D. H. Lawrence (produced 1943). 1947.
The Glass Menagerie (produced 1944). 1945.
27 Wagons Full of Cotton and Other One-Act Plays (includes *The Purification, The Lady of Larkspur Lotion, The Last of My Solid Gold Watches, Portrait of a Madonna, Auto-da-Fe, Lord Byron Love Letter, The Strangest Kind of Romance, The Long Goodbye, Hello from Bertha,* and *This Property Is Condemned*). 1946; augmented edition (includes *Talk to Me Like the Rain and Let Me Listen* and *Something Unspoken*), 1953.
Portrait of a Madonna (produced 1946). In *27 Wagons Full of Cotton and Other One-Act Plays,* 1946.
Moony's Kid Don't Cry (produced 1946). In *American Blues,* 1948.
The Last of My Solid Gold Watches (produced 1947). In *27 Wagons Full of Cotton and Other One-Act Plays,* 1946.
Lord Byron's Love Letter (produced 1947). In *27 Wagons Full of Cotton and Other One-Act Plays,* 1946; revised version, music by Raffaello de Banfield (produced 1964); libretto published, 1955.

Auto-da-Fe (produced 1947). In *27 Wagons Full of Cotton and Other One-Act Plays,* 1946.
The Lady of Larkspur Lotion (produced 1947). In *27 Wagons Full of Cotton and Other One-Act Plays,* 1946.
Stairs to the Roof (produced 1947).
A Streetcar Named Desire (produced 1947). 1947.
Summer and Smoke (produced 1947). 1948; revised version, as *The Eccentricities of a Nightingale* (produced 1964), published as *The Eccentricities of a Nightingale, and Summer and Smoke,* 1965; revised version (produced 1976).
American Blues: Five Short Plays (includes *Moony's Kid Don't Cry; The Dark Room; The Case of the Crushed Petunias; The Long Stay Cut Short; or, The Unsatisfactory Supper;* and *Ten Blocks on the Camino Real*). 1948.
The Rose Tattoo (produced 1951). 1951.
Ten Blocks on the Camino Real, in *American Blues,* 1948; revised version, as *Camino Real* (produced 1953). 1953.
The Purification (produced 1954). In *27 Wagons Full of Cotton and Other One-Act Plays,* 1946.
27 Wagons Full of Cotton (produced 1955). In *27 Wagons Full of Cotton and Other One-Act Plays,* 1946.
Something Unspoken (produced 1955). In *27 Wagons Full of Cotton and Other One-Act Plays,* 1953.
Cat on a Hot Tin Roof (produced 1955). 1955; revised version (produced 1973), 1975.
Three Players of a Summer Game (produced 1955).
Sweet Bird of Youth (produced 1956). 1959.
Baby Doll: The Script for the Film, Incorporating the Two One-Act Plays Which Suggested It: 27 Wagons Full of Cotton and The Long Stay Cut Short; or, The Unsatisfactory Supper. 1956.
The Case of the Crushed Petunias (produced 1957). In *American Blues,* 1948.
Garden District: Something Unspoken, Suddenly Last Summer (produced 1958). 1958.
The Fugitive Kind: Original Play Title: Orpheus Descending (screenplay). 1958.
Period of Adjustment: High Point over a Cavern: A Serious Comedy (produced 1958), 1960.
Talk to Me Like the Rain and Let Me Listen (produced 1958). In *27 Wagons Full of Cotton and Other One-Act Plays,* 1953.
The Enemy: Time, in *Theatre,* March 1959.
The Night of the Iguana (produced 1959; revised version, produced 1961). 1962.
I Rise in Flame, Cried the Phoenix: A Play about D. H. Lawrence (produced 1959). 1951.
Hello from Bertha (produced 1961). In *27 Wagons Full of Cotton and Other One-Act Plays,* 1946.
To Heaven in a Golden Coach (produced 1961).
The Milk Train Doesn't Stop Here Anymore (produced 1962; revised versions, produced 1963, 1964, 1968). 1964.
The Dark Room (produced 1966). In *American Blues,* 1948.
Slapstick Tragedy (The Mutilated and *The Gnadiges Fraulein)* (produced 1966). 2 vols., 1967; revised version of *The Gnadiges Fraulein,* as *The Latter Days of a Celebrated Soubrette* (produced 1974).
The Two-Character Play (produced 1967; revised version, produced 1969). 1969; revised version, as *Out Cry* (produced 1971), 1973; revised version (produced 1974).
Kingdom of Earth, in *Esquire* (New York), February 1967; (revised version, as *The Seven Descents of Myrtle,* produced 1968), published as *Kingdom of Earth (The Seven Descents of Myrtle).* 1968.

At Liberty (produced 1968). In *American Scenes,* edited by William Kozlenko, 1941.

In the Bar of a Tokyo Hotel (produced 1969). 1969.

The Strangest Kind of Romance (produced 1969). In *27 Wagons Full of Cotton and Other One-Act Plays,* 1946.

Confessional (produced 1970). In *Dragon Country,* 1970; revised version, as *Small Craft Warnings* (produced 1972), 1972.

The Frosted Glass Coffin (produced 1970). In *Dragon Country,* 1970.

Senso, with Paul Bowles, in *Two Screenplays,* by Luigi Visconti. 1970.

Dragon Country: A Book of Plays (includes *In the Bar of a Tokyo Hotel; I Rise in Flame, Cried the Phoenix; The Mutilated; I Can't Imagine Tomorrow; Confessional; The Frosted Glass Coffin; The Gnadiges Fraulein; A Perfect Analysis Given by a Parrot*). 1970.

A Streetcar Named Desire (screenplay), in *Film Scripts 1,* edited by George Garrett, O. B. Hardison, Jr., and Jane Gelfman. 1971.

The Long Stay Cut Short; or, The Unsatisfactory Supper (produced 1971). In *American Blues,* 1948.

The Theatre of Williams: 1. *Battle of Angels, A Streetcar Named Desire, The Glass Menagerie.* 1972. 2. *The Eccentricities of a Nightingale, Summer and Smoke, The Rose Tattoo, Camino Real.* 1972. 3. *Cat on a Hot Tin Roof, Orpheus Descending, Suddenly Last Summer.* 1972. 4. *Sweet Bird of Youth, Period of Adjustment, Night of the Iguana.* 1972. 5. *The Milk Train Doesn't Stop Here Anymore; Kingdom of Earth,* revised version; *Small Craft Warnings; The Two Character Play,* revised version. 1976. 6. *27 Wagons Full of Cotton and Other One Act Plays* (includes *The Unsatisfactory Supper, Steps Must Be Gentle, The Demolition Downtown: Count Ten in Arabic*). 1981. 7. *Dragon Country, Lifeboat Drill, Now the Cats with Jewelled Claws, Now the Peaceable Kingdom.* 1981.

The Red Devil Battery Sign (produced 1975; revised version, produced 1976).

This Is an Entertainment (produced 1976).

Demolition Downtown: Count Ten in Arabic—Then Run (produced 1976). In *The Theatre of Williams 6,* 1981.

A Perfect Analysis Given by a Parrot (produced 1976). 1958.

I Can't Imagine Tomorrow (televised 1970; produced 1976). In *Dragon Country,* 1970.

Vieux Carre (produced 1977). 1979.

Tiger Tail (produced 1978).

A Lovely Sunday for Creve Coeur (as *Creve Coeur,* produced 1978; as *A Lovely Sunday for Creve Coeur,* produced 1979). 1980.

Lifeboat Drill (produced 1979). In *The Theatre of Williams 7,* 1981.

Kirche, Kuchen, und Kinder (produced 1980).

Clothes for a Summer Hotel (produced 1980). 1983.

Will Mr. Merriwether Return from Memphis? (produced 1980).

Tennessee Laughs: Three One-Act Plays (*Some Problems for the Moose Lodge; A Perfect Analysis Given by a Parrot; The Frosted Glass Coffin*) (produced 1980; revised version of *Some Problems for the Moose Lodge,* as *A House Not Meant to Stand,* produced 1981, revised version, 1982). *The Frosted Glass Coffin* and *A Perfect Analysis Given by a Parrot* in *Dragon Country,* 1970.

Something Cloudy, Something Clear (produced 1981).

Stopped Rocking and Other Screenplays. 1984.

Screenplays: *Senso* (*The Wanton Countess;* English dialogue, with Paul Bowles), 1949; *The Glass Menagerie,* with Peter Berneis, 1950; *A Streetcar Named Desire,* with Oscar Saul, 1951; *The Rose Tattoo,* with Hal Kanter, 1955; *Baby Doll,* 1956; *Suddenly Last Summer,* with Gore Vidal, 1959; *The Fugitive Kind,* with Meade Roberts, 1960; *Boom,* 1968.

Television Plays: *I Can't Imagine Tomorrow,* 1970; *Stopped Rocking,* 1975.

Fiction

One Arm and Other Stories. 1948.

The Roman Spring of Mrs. Stone. 1950.

Hard Candy: A Book of Stories. 1954.

Three Players of a Summer Game and Other Stories. 1960.

Grand (stories). 1964.

The Knightly Quest: A Novella and Four Short Stories. 1967; augmented edition, as *The Knightly Quest: A Novella and Twelve Short Stories,* 1968.

Eight Mortal Ladies Possessed: A Book of Stories. 1974.

Moise and the World of Reason . 1975.

It Happened the Day the Sun Rose and Other Stories. 1982.

Poetry

Five Young American Poets, with others. 1944.

In the Winter of Cities. 1956.

Androgyne, Mon Amour. 1977.

Other

Memoirs. 1975.

Letters to Donald Windham 1940-1965, edited by Windham. 1976.

Where I Live: Selected Essays, edited by Christine R. Day and Bob Woods. 1978.

Conversations with Williams (interviews), edited by Albert J. Devlin. 1986.

*

Bibliography: *Williams: A Bibliography* by Drewey Wayne Gunn, 1980; *The Critical Reputation of Williams: A Reference Guide* by John S. McCann, 1983.

Critical Studies: *Williams* by Signi Lenea Falk, 1961, revised edition, 1978; *Williams: The Man and His Work* by Benjamin Nelson, 1961; *Williams, Rebellious Puritan* by Nancy Tischier, 1961; *The Dramatic World of Williams* by Francis Donahue, 1964; *Williams and Friends* by Gilbert Maxwell, 1965; *The Broken World of Williams* by Esther Jackson, 1965; *Williams* by Gerald Weales, 1965; *A Look at Williams* by Mike Steen, 1969; *Williams: A Moralist's Answer to the Perils of Life* by Ingrid Rogers, 1976; *Williams: A Tribute* edited by Jac Tharpe, 1977; *Williams: A Collection of Critical Essays* edited by Stephen S. Stanton, 1977; *The World of Williams* edited by Richard Freeman Leavitt, 1978; *Williams: The Tragic Tension* by Emmanuel B. Asibong, 1978; *A Portrait of the Artist: The Plays of Williams* by Foster Hirsch, 1979; *Williams* by Felicia H. Londre, 1980; *Williams: An Intimate Biography* by Dakin Williams and Shepherd Mead, 1983; *The Glass Menagerie: A Collection of Critical Essays* edited by R.B. Parker, 1983; *Dictionary of Literary Biography Documentary Series 4* edited by Margaret A. Van Antwerp and Sally Johns, 1984; *Tennes-*

see: Cry of the Heart: An Intimate Memoir of Williams by Dotson Rader, 1985; *The Kindness of Strangers: The Life of Williams* by Donald Spoto, 1985; *Williams on File* edited by Catherine M. Arnott and Simon Trussler, 1985; *As If: A Personal View of Williams* by Donald Windham, 1985; *Williams* by R. Boxill, 1986; *Williams: A Portrait in Laughter and Lamentation* by Harry Rasky, 1986; "The Fox's Cubs: Lillian Hellman, Arthur Miller, and Tennessee Williams" by Charlotte Goodman, and "Loneliness and Longing in Selected Plays of Carson McCullers and Tennessee Williams" by Mary McBride, in *Modern American Drama: The Female Canon* edited by June Schlueter, 1990; "Tennessee Williams: *The Glass Menagerie* and *A Streetcar Named Desire*" by Mark Lilly, in *Lesbian and Gay Writing: An Anthology of Critical Essays* edited by Lilly, 1990; "The South, Tragedy, and Comedy in Tennessee Williams's *Cat on a Hot Tin Roof*" by M. Thomas Inge, in *The United States South: Regionalism and Identity* edited by Valeria Lerda and Tjebbe Westendorp, 1991; "A Streetcar Named Misogyny" by Kathleen Margaret Lant, in *Violence in Drama* edited by James Redmond, 1991; "The Fox and the Phoenix: Tennessee Williams's Strong Misreading of D.H. Lawrence" by Lydia Blanchard, in *D. H. Lawrence's Literary Inheritors* edited by Keith Cushman and Dennis Jackson, 1991; *Communists, Cowboys, and Queers: The Politics of Masculinity in the Work of Arthur Miller and Tennessee Williams* by David Savran, 1992; *Tennessee Williams and Elia Kazan: A Collaboration in the Theatre* by Brenda Murphy, 1992; *The Faces of Eve: A Study of Tennessee Williams's Heroines* by Gulshan Rai Kataria, 1992; "'Something Cloudy, Something Clear': Homophobic Discourse in Tennessee Williams" by John M. Clum, in *Homosexual Themes in Literary Studies* edited by Wayne R. Dynes and Stephen Donaldson, 1992; "South toward Freedom: Tennessee Williams" by W. Kenneth Holditch, in *Literary New Orleans: Essays and Meditations* edited by Richard S. Kennedy, 1992; *Critical Essays on Tennessee Williams* edited by Robert A. Martin, 1997; *Dramatizing Dementia: Madness in the Plays of Tennessee Williams* by Jacqueline O'Connor, 1997; *The Cambridge Companion to Tennessee Williams* edited by Matthew Charles Roudané, 1997; *Tennessee Williams: A Guide to Research and Performance* edited by Philip C. Kolin, 1998; *The Politics of Reputation: The Critical Reception of Tennessee Williams' Later Plays* by Annette J. Saddik, 1999.

*   *   *

Shortly before *Vieux Carre* opened on Broadway in 1977, Tennessee Williams wrote an article for the *New York Times* that began, "Of course no one is more acutely aware than I that I am widely regarded as the ghost of a writer." So, at that time, he was. The name Tennessee Williams still conjures up the flamboyant plays of the 1940s and 1950s—*A Streetcar Named Desire, Cat on a Hot Tin Roof, Suddenly Last Summer.* But except for a period in the mid-1960s when he suffered mental and physical collapse, Williams was a remarkably busy ghost. In the mid-1970s new plays were staged in London, San Francisco, and New York, and he published a novel (*Moise and the World of Reason*), a book of short stories (*Eight Mortal Ladies Possessed*), a book of poems (*Androgyne, Mon Amour*), and *Memoirs.* Artistically and personally, he became an advertisement for the theme that obsessed him ever since Amanda Wingfield tried to hold her disintegrating family together in *The Glass Menagerie*—survival.

When *Vieux Carre* opened, the critics did treat it as a ghost play, a nostalgic look at the New Orleans of Williams's youth,

full of echoes of characters, situations, themes relentlessly familiar to Williams admirers. In the *Times* article, in *Memoirs,* in any number of interviews, Williams attempted to explain how he was transformed from America's most popular serious playwright into an historical figure, inexplicably still active in the real world. His plays through *The Night of the Iguana,* he suggested, shared a similarity of style—"poetic naturalism" he called it—which became so identified with him that when he made a shift into new styles, his audiences could not or would not follow him. It is true that there are great stylistic similarities among the Williams plays through *The Night of the Iguana* and it is also true that he lost the large audiences that had once flocked to his work, but the new styles had their roots in his earlier work.

He was never a realistic playwright, which may be what the phrase poetic naturalism is supposed to suggest, but he was always capable of writing a psychologically valid scene in the American realistic tradition—the breakfast scene in *The Glass Menagerie,* for instance, or the birthday dinner in *A Streetcar Named Desire.* His characters are able to claim the allegiance of audiences who continue to identify with them even after they become larger than life (Big Daddy in *Cat on a Hot Tin Roof,* Alexandra Del Lago in *Sweet Bird of Youth*) or when the use of significant names (Val Xavier in *Orpheus Descending,* Alma in *Summer and Smoke*) turn them into myth or symbol. However grounded in realistic surface, the events in Williams's plays, particularly the violent events, take on meaning that transcends psychological realism ("Here is your God, Mr. Shannon," says Hannah when the storm breaks in *The Night of the Iguana*), and when the violence moves off stage—the cannibalism in *Suddenly Last Summer,* the castration in *Sweet Bird of Youth*—the non-realistic implications of the event are heightened by its transformation into narrative (*Summer and Smoke*) or promise (*Sweet Bird of Youth*). From the glass menagerie through the dressmaker's dummies in *The Rose Tattoo* to the costumes, ritually donned by Shannon and Hannah in *The Night of the Iguana,* Williams always used sets, props, dress as devices whose significance runs deeper than the verisimilitude required by realism. When Williams deserted old forms—or thought he did—he brought two decades of nonrealistic theater with him. *Slapstick Tragedy* may have suggested absurdist drama to some of its viewers, but Polly and Molly, the grotesque comedy team whose voices sustain *The Gnadiges Fraulein,* are variations on Dolly and Beulah, who introduce *Orpheus Descending,* and Flora and Bessie, the "female clowns" of *The Rose Tattoo* and *A Perfect Analysis Given by a Parrot.* When each of the characters in *Small Craft Warnings* takes his place in the spotlight to sound his sorrow—a mechanism that suggests that the title of an earlier version of the play, *Confessional,* is more apt—we have at most an intensification of the device Williams used extensively in his earlier plays, most notably in Maggie's opening speech in *Cat on a Hot Tin Roof* and the soliloquies of Chance and Alexandra in *Sweet Bird of Youth.*

Stylistically, then, the later Williams plays grow out of the early ones. Nor are there surprising shifts in theme. The similarities between the pre- and post-*The Night of the Iguana* plays can best be seen in the recurrence of characters. The Blanche of *A Streetcar Named Desire,* whose variants people *Summer and Smoke, Camino Real, Sweet Bird of Youth,* and *The Night of the Iguana,* is still visible in Isabel in *Period of Adjustment,* Miriam in *In the Bar of a Tokyo Hotel,* and, bizarrely, in the fish-trapping heroine of *The Gnadiges Fraulein.* Amanda—or at least her comic toughness—is apparent in Flora Goforth in *The Milk Train Doesn't Stop*

Here Anymore, Myrtle in *Kingdom of Earth,* and Leona in *Small Craft Warnings.* Laura, the frightened daughter of *The Glass Menagerie,* is present in characters as different as One in *I Can't Imagine Tomorrow* and Clare in *Out Cry.* Further, Blanche, Amanda, and Laura are three aspects of the perennial Williams character, the fugitive kind, who, male and female, was the playwright's concern from his very early one-act plays to *Vieux Carre.* At first, his characters were simply outsiders, set off from the rest of society by a recognizable difference of one kind or another—Laura's limp, Blanche's defensive sexuality, Alma's pseudo-artistic sensitivity. It became increasingly clear—even as the forces that opposed his protagonists became more violent— that all men are outsiders. The murderous Jabe in *Orpheus Descending* is set apart by the disease that is killing him as obviously as Val is by his priapic aura, his guitar, and his snake skin jacket, as Lady is by being Italian, as Carol Cutrere is by her unconsoling wealth and self-lacerating sex, as Vee Talbot is by her painting and her religious visions. Chance calls Alexandra "nice monster" in *Sweet Bird of Youth,* and she calls him "pitiful monster," and both are "Lost in the beanstalk country . . . the country of the flesh-hungry, blood-thirsty ogre," but the play's ogre, Boss Finley, is supposed to be monster-ridden too, and Williams kept revising the play in the hopes that that point would emerge. The enemy is no longer the ugly other, but a surrogate self, or time (note all those age-obsessed Williams characters, like Mrs. Stone who wanted a Roman spring), or a godless universe. This last is presented most clearly in two plays, *Suddenly Last Summer* and *The Night of the Iguana,* which come closest to making specific theological statements. Man, as Williams sees him—as Williams embodies him—is a temporary resident in a frightening world in an indifferent universe. The best he can hope is the transitory consolation of touching and the best he can do is hang on for dear (and only) life.

In the *Times* article quoted above Williams mentioned his "private panic:" his dreams "full of alarm and wild suspicion" that made him want to "cry . . . out to all who will listen," and his continued revision of *Out Cry* emphasized his urgency. But that cry always echoed through his work—his novels, his short stories, his poetry, his autobiography, and all his plays. In the hope that the cry would come through more clearly, he continually revised and rewrote, turning short stories into plays, short plays into long ones, full-length plays into other full-length plays, as *Battle of Angels* became *Orpheus Descending,* and *Summer and Smoke* became *The Eccentricities of a Nightingale.* Audiences withdrew from Williams, I suspect, not because his style changed or his concerns altered, but because in his desperate need to cry out he turned away from the sturdy dramatic containers that once gave the cry resonance and settled for pale imitations of familiar stage images; he built on the direct address of the early soliloquies and the discursiveness of plays like *The Night of the Iguana* and substituted lyric argument for dramatic language. It is a measure of his stature as a playwright and the importance of his central theme that each new play carried the promise of old vigor in new disguise. If that promise was not fulfilled for audiences when Williams's later plays were first performed, new strengths may still be discovered with the revaluations that are sure to come since the playwright has died. In the meantime, admirers of Williams will continue to turn back to his more celebrated works, works that have become contemporary classics.

—Gerald Weales

See the essays on *The Glass Menagerie* and *A Streetcar Named Desire.*

WILLIAMS, William Carlos

Born: Rutherford, New Jersey, 17 September 1883. **Education:** A school in Rutherford, 1889-96; Chateau de Lancy, near Geneva, Switzerland, and Lycée Condorcet, Paris, 1897-99; Horace Mann High School, New York, 1899-1902; University of Pennsylvania, Philadelphia, 1902-06, M.D. 1906; intern at hospitals in New York City, 1906-08; post-graduate work in pediatrics, University of Leipzig, 1908-09. **Family:** Married Florence Herman in 1912; two sons. **Career:** Practiced medicine in Rutherford, 1910 until he retired in the mid-1950s; editor, *Others,* 1919; editor, with Robert McAlmon, *Contact,* 1920-23; editor, *Contact: An American Quarterly,* 1931-33. Appointed consultant in poetry, Library of Congress, Washington, D.C., 1952, but did not serve. **Awards:** Loines award, 1948; National Book award, 1950; Bollingen prize, 1952; Academy of American Poets fellowship, 1956; Brandeis University Creative Arts award, 1958; American Academy gold medal, 1963; Pulitzer prize, 1963. LL.D.: State University of New York, Buffalo, 1956; Fairleigh Dickinson University, Teaneck, New Jersey, 1959. Litt.D.: Rutgers University, New Brunswick, New Jersey, 1948; Bard College, Annandale-on-Hudson, New York, 1948; University of Pennsylvania, 1952. **Member:** American Academy. **Died:** 4 March 1963.

PUBLICATIONS

Collections

The Williams Reader, edited by M. L. Rosenthal. 1966.
Selected Poems, edited by Charles Tomlinson. 1976.
Collected Poems, edited by A. Walton Litz and Christopher MacGowan. 2 vols., 1987-88.
Asphodel, That Greeny Flower and Other Love Poems. 1994.

Short Stories

A Novelette and Other Prose 1921-1931. 1932.
The Knife of the Times and Other Stories. 1932.
Life along the Passaic River. 1938.
Make Light of It: Collected Stories. 1950.
The Farmers' Daughters: The Collected Stories. 1961.

Novels

A Voyage to Pagany. 1928.
White Mule (first part of trilogy). 1937.
In the Money (second part of trilogy). 1940.
The Build-Up (third part of trilogy). 1952.

Poetry

Poems. 1909.
The Tempers. 1913.
Al Que Quiere! 1917.
Kora in Hell: Improvisations. 1920.

Sour Grapes. 1921.
Spring and All. 1923.
Go Go. 1923.
The Cod Head. 1932.
Collected Poems, 1921-1931. 1934.
An Early Martyr and Other Poems. 1935.
Adam & Eve & the City. 1936.
The Complete Collected Poems 1906-1938. 1938.
The Broken Span. 1941.
The Wedge. 1944.
Paterson, Book One. 1946; *Book Two,* 1948; *Book Three,* 1949;
    Book Four, 1951; *Book Five,* 1958; *Books I-V,* 1963.
The Clouds. 1948.
The Pink Church. 1949.
Selected Poems. 1949.
The Collected Later Poems. 1950; revised edition, 1963.
The Collected Earlier Poems. 1951.
The Desert Music and Other Poems. 1954.
Journey to Love. 1955.
Pictures from Brueghel and Other Poems. 1962.
Penguin Modern Poets 9, with Denise Levertov and Kenneth
    Rexroth. 1967.

Plays

Betry Putnam (produced 1910).
A Dream of Love (produced 1949). 1948.
Many Loves (produced 1958). In *Many Loves and Other Plays,*
    1961.
Many Loves and Other Plays: The Collected Plays (includes *A
    Dream of Love; Tituba's Children; The First President,* music
    by Theodore Harris; *The Cure*). 1961.

Other

The Great American Novel. 1923.
In the American Grain. 1925.
The Autobiography. 1951.
Williams' Poetry Talked About, with Eli Siegel. 1952; revised edi-
    tion, edited by Martha Baird and Ellen Reiss, as *The Williams-
    Siegel Documentary,* 1970, 1974.
Selected Essays. 1954.
John Marin, with others. 1956.
Selected Letters, edited by John C. Thirlwall. 1957.
*I Wanted to Write a Poem: The Autobiography of the Works of a
    Poet,* edited by Edith Heal. 1958.
Yes, Mrs. Williams: A Personal Record of My Mother. 1959.
Imaginations: Collected Early Prose, edited by Webster Schott.
    1970.
A Beginning on the Short Story (lecture). 1974.
The Embodiment of Knowledge, edited by Ron Loewinsohn. 1974.
Interviews with Williams: Speaking Straight Ahead, edited by Linda
    W. Wagner. 1976.
A Recognizable Image: Williams on Art and Artists, edited by Bram
    Dijkstra. 1978.
Something to Say: Williams on Younger Poets, edited by James E.
    B. Breslin. 1985.
Williams and James Laughlin: Selected Letters, edited by Hugh
    Witemeyer. 1990.
*The Last Word: Letters Between Marcia Nardi and William Carlos
    Williams.* 1994.

*Pound/Williams: Selected Letters of Ezra Pound and William Carlos
    Williams.* 1996.
The Letters of Denise Levertov and William Carlos Williams. 1998.
*William Carlos Williams and Charles Tomlinson: A Transatlantic
    Connection.* 1998.

Translator, *Last Nights of Paris,* by Philippe Soupault. 1929.
Translator, with others, *Jean sans terre/Landless John,* by Yvan
    Goll. 1944.
Translator, with Raquel Hélène Williams, *The Dog and the Fever,*
    by Francisco de Quevedo. 1954.

*

Bibliography: *A Bibliography of Williams* by Emily Wallace
Mitchell, 1968; *Williams: A Reference Guide* by Linda W. Wagner,
1978.

Critical Studies: *Williams* by Vivienne Koch, 1950; *Williams: A
Critical Study* by John Malcolm Brinnin, 1963; *The Poems of Wil-
liams,* 1964, and *The Prose of Williams,* 1970, both by Linda W.
Wagner; *The Poetic World of Williams* by Alan Ostrom, 1966; *Wil-
liams: A Collection of Critical Essays* edited by J. Hillis Miller,
1966; *An Approach to Paterson* by Walter Scott Peterson, 1967;
The Music of Survival by Sherman Paul, 1968; *Williams' Pater-
son: Language and Landscape* by Joel Connarroe, 1970; *Williams:
An American Artist* by James E.B. Breslin, 1970; *Williams: The
American Background* by Mike Weaver, 1971; *A Companion to
Williams's Paterson* by Benjamin Sankey, 1971; *Williams: The
Later Poems* by Jerome Mazzaro, 1973; *The Inverted Bell: Modernism and the Counterpoetics of Williams* by Joseph N. Riddel,
1974; *Williams* by Kenneth Burke and Emily H. Wallace, 1974;
Williams: The Knack of Survival in America by Robert Coles,
1975; *Williams: Poet from Jersey* by Reed Whittemore, 1975; *Wil-
liams: The Poet and His Critics,* 1975, and *Williams: A New World
Naked,* 1981, both by Paul L. Mariani; *The Early Poetry of Will-
iams* by Rod Townley, 1976; *Williams and the American Scene
1920-1940* by Dickran Tashjian, 1978; *Williams's Paterson: A
Critical Reappraisal* by Margaret Glynne Lloyd, 1980; *Williams:
The Critical Heritage* edited by Charles Doyle, 1980, and *Will-
iams and the American Poem* by Doyle, 1982; *Williams and the
Painters 1909-1923* by William Marling, 1982; *Williams: Man and
Poet* by Carroll F. Terrell, 1983; *Williams: A Poet in the American
Theatre* by David A. Fedo, 1983; *Ezra Pound and Williams* ed-
ited by Daniel Hoffman, 1983; *Williams and Romantic Idealism*
by Carl Rapp, 1984; *The Visual Text of Williams* by Henry M.
Sayre, 1984; *American Beauty: Williams and the Modernist
Whitman* by Stephen Tapscott, 1984; *The Transparent Lyric:
Reading and Meaning in the Poetry of Stevens and Williams* by
David Walker, 1984; *Williams and the Meanings of Measure* by
Stephen Cushman, 1985; *A Poetry of Presence: The Writing of Wil-
liams* by Bernard Duffey, 1986; *Williams and the Maternal Muse*
by Kerry Driscoll, 1987; *Virgin and Whore: The Image of Women
in the Poetry of Williams* by Audrey T. Rodgers, 1987; *The Early
Politics and Poetics of Williams* by David Frail, 1987; *The Early
Prose of Williams, 1917-1925* by Geoffrey H. Movius, 1987; *Wil-
liams: The Art, and Literary Tradition* by Peter Schmidt, 1988;
Williams and Autobiography: The Woods of His Nature by Ann
W. Fisher-Wirth, 1989; *Williams: A Study of the Short Fiction* by
Robert F. Gish, 1989; *Soundings: On Shakespeare, Modern Po-
etry, Plato, and Other Subjects* by Albert Cook, 1991; "Editing

William Carlos Williams" by A. Walton Litz and Christopher MacGowan, in *Representing Modernist Texts: Editing as Interpretation* edited by George Bornstein, 1991; *A Tradition of Subversion: The Prose Poem in English from Wilde to Ashbery* by Margueritte S. Murphy, 1992; *The Letters of William Carlos Williams & Charles Tomlinson* edited by Barry Magid and Hugh Witemeyer, introduction by Hugh Kenner, preface by Charles Tomlinson, 1992; *Critical Essays on William Carlos Williams* edited by Steven Gould Axelrod and Helen Deese, 1994; *Ideas in Things: The Poems of William Carlos Williams* by Donald W. Markos, 1994; *William Carlos Williams and Alterity: The Early Poetry* by Barry Ahearn, 1994; *The Writings of William Carlos Williams: Publicity for the Self* by Daniel Morris, 1995; *Orientalism and Modernism: The Legacy of China in Pound and Williams* by Zhaoming Qian, 1995; *Approaching Authority: Transpersonal Gestures in the Poetry of Yeats, Eliot, and Williams* by Anthony Flinn, 1997; *Countries of the Mind: The Poetry of William Carlos Williams* by Stanley Koehler, 1998; *Money and Modernity: Pound, Williams, and the Spirit of Jefferson* by Alec Marsh, 1998; *My Toughest Mentor: Theodore Roethke and William Carlos Williams (1940-1948)* by Robert Kusch, 1999.

*   *   *

William Carlos Williams is one of the leading figures of American modernist poetry whose critical recognition supports the impact his poems and fiction had throughout the modern and contemporary periods. Williams was a writer's writer in that his reputation existed chiefly among other writers—**Ezra Pound, H. D., Marianne Moore, Hart Crane, Wallace Stevens, John Dos Passos, Ernest Hemingway**—at least until New Directions began publishing his work in the late 1930s. Most of Williams's first dozen books were privately printed or subsidized. Some were collections of poems; others were an innovative mixture of poetry and prose, or of prose-poem form. Regardless of apparent genre, Williams wrote consistently in a mode based on the rhythms of the speaking voice, complete with idiomatic language, colloquial word choice, organic form and structure, and an intense interest in locale as both setting and subject.

This most American of poets was born of mixed parentage, and part of his fascination with the identification of—even the definition of—the American character may have stemmed from his own feeling of dislocation. His short early poems as well as his collection of essays on American historical figures, *In the American Grain,* present personae and scenes germane to the United States: "a young horse with a green bed-quilt/on his withers shaking his head?" "A big young bareheaded woman/ in an apron, Flowers through the window / lavender and yellow / changed by white curtains." The fact that these scenes and characters are presented with neither apology nor psychological justification emphasized the aesthetic position that the thing was its own justification. Whether echoing **John Dewey**, Henri Bergson, or **William James**, Williams's innate pragmatism led him to a concentration on the unadorned image (as a means to universal understanding, truth) that opened many new directions in modern poetry. Williams did not use the image as symbol, a substitute for a larger idea; he was content to rest with the assumption that the reader could duplicate his own sense of importance for the red wheelbarrows and green glass between hospital walls, and thereby dismiss the equivocation of symbolism. As he said so succinctly in *Paterson,* "no ideas but in things."

Allied with the notion of presentation was the corollary that the author was to be as invisible as possible, so as not to dilute the effect of the concrete object or character. Not until his later poems did Williams change that tenet, but the strikingly personal "The Desert Music" and "Asphodel, That Greeny Flower" benefit from his use of a more personal stance toward the materials. Through the writing of his five-book epic poem, *Paterson,* from the 1940s to 1958, Williams was moving toward a kind of self-revelation, albeit unevenly. The epic concerns a poet-doctor-city persona named Paterson, tracing some events of the poet-doctor's life through an intense juxtaposition of scene, image, and memory. The technique of placing one image or scene against another, often without verbal transition, resembled the montage effect in the art contemporary with Williams; troubling as it was to his readers thirty years ago, it became the *modus operandi* for many contemporary writers, a way of increasing speed, of covering more images and sources of imagery, in the context of a rapidly moving poem.

Williams established many new principles in the writing of his poetry—his confidence that the common American was an apt source of character, his joy in re-creating natural speech, his experimentation with a structure and line that would allow the flexible and fluid pace of speech to be presented—but his prose was also influential. From the 1923 *Spring and All,* when he combined aesthetic theory with such famous poems as "The Red Wheelbarrow," "To Elsie?," and "At the Ballgame," to the trilogy of a family establishing itself in American business culture (the Stetchers in *White Mule, In the Money,* and *The Build-Up*), Williams turned away from the established conventions in order to present sharply, idiomatically, the gist of his drama. Much of his prose is carried through dialogue that makes Hemingway's seem contrived and redundant; most of his fiction has no ostensible plot. Moving as far from artifice as possible, his prose was criticized repeatedly for being artless; but contemporary readers have found the organic emphasis on language-structure-character an important direction for their own writing. "The Burden of Loveliness?" "Jean Beicke," "The Use of Force" are stories often anthologized, provocative in their presentation of convincing characters whose human conditions proceed without drama, but—in Williams's handling—always with sympathy.

That Williams was a practicing physician until the mid-1950s adds some interest to his use of apparently real people in his fiction and poetry. The authenticity of his knowledge about people is undeniable, and he speaks movingly in his autobiography about the reciprocity between being a doctor (a pediatrician by specialization, but a general practitioner for all intents) and a writer. Working from insights that a more reclusive person might not have had, Williams was able to portray accurately many elements of the American culture that had not been treated in the literature of the twentieth century (**T.S. Eliot**'s Prufrock would not have come to Williams's New Jersey office). Disturbed as he often was about his lack of time to write, he nevertheless acknowledged that his busy life was a rich one; and his writing after his retirement (chiefly because of a severe stroke) frequently returned to subjects and characters from that more active life. The stories about Williams's writing during his rushed days as physician are apocryphal: pulling his car off the road while on his way to make a house call so that he could scribble a poem on a prescription blank; equipping his office desk with a hidden typewriter so that he could flip the machine in place between patients. His production as writer in the midst of his full days as doctor is amazing, but what made that production possible was his personal intent: he considered himself primarily a poet; his aim and direction in life were toward success in writing. No hurried schedule could prevent his implementing that dream.

Williams's poems are not all affirmative pictures of American character and scene; in fact, much of his writing during the 1930s and 1940s is bleak and despairing. and the early books of *Paterson* reflect that disillusionment with what had earlier appeared to be inexhaustible American promise. The late books of *Paterson,* however, supply Williams's own hard-won answers: love, even if foolhardy; virtue; knowing oneself; doing what one can; creating. These are hardly new answers, but their lack of innovation does not lessen their impact. Like Dante traveling through the Inferno, Williams takes us into blind alleys of Paterson (his poems are realistic because we see wrong answers as well as right ones, and sometimes no answers at all), only to move up through Limbo to a kind of modern-day heaven, a place with the answers at least implied in passages like:

> Through this hole
> at the bottom of the cavern
> of death, the imagination
> escapes intact.
> It is the imagination
> which cannot be fathomed.
> It is through this hole
> we escape.

From this resolution, it is only a step to the gentle poise of the last poems. One of the most striking poems of his Pulitzer Prize-winning book, *Pictures from Brueghel,* is "Asphodel," the love poem to his wife of nearly fifty years, which speaks of "love, abiding love." "Death is not the end of it," Williams writes, comparing love to "a garden which expands . . . a love engendering gentleness and goodness." Williams contrasts the quiet assurance of this love with "Waste, waste! dominates the world. It is the bomb's work." And his love is broadened to include his total response to life, as he declares proudly toward the end of the poem:

> Only the imagination is real!
> I have declared it
> time without end.
> If a man die
> it is because death
> has first
> possessed his imagination . . . .
> But love and the imagination
> are of a piece
> swift as the light
> to avoid destruction . . . .

Williams's impact on modern American poetics might appear to have been largely technical, for all the discussion of his use of the local, the triadic line, the idiom; but ultimately readers and fellow writers probably respond as well to the pervasive optimism of the doctor-poet's view, and to the openness with which he shared his life and his reactions with his readers. One may forget the rationale for Williams's triadic line division; but one does not forget his candor and his affirmation.

—Linda Wagner-Martin

See the essay on *Paterson.*

WILLIS, Nathaniel Parker

Born: Portland, Maine, 20 January 1806. **Education:** Boston Latin School; Phillips Academy, Andover, Massachusetts; Yale University, New Haven, Connecticut, 1823-27, graduated 1827. **Family:** Married 1) Mary Stace in 1835 (died 1845); 2) Cornelia Grinnell in 1846, three daughters and two sons. **Career:** Became known as a writer while still an undergraduate; edited 2 issues of *The Legendary,* 1828, and an annual *The Token,* 1829; founding editor, *American Monthly Magazine,* Boston, 1829-31; coeditor, 1831-33, and correspondent in Europe, 1833-36, and the United States, 1836-39, New York *Mirror;* founding coeditor, *Corsair,* New York, 1839; co-owner and editor, *New Mirror,* 1843, and *Weekly* and *Evening Mirror,* 1844-45; visited Europe, 1845; co-owner and editor, *National Press* (later *Home Journal*), 1846-64, and sole owner and editor, 1864-67; lived in Idlewild, New York, after 1853. **Died:** 20 January 1867.

PUBLICATIONS

Collections

Prose Writings, edited by Henry A. Beers. 1885.
Poetical Works. 1888.

Fiction

Inklings of Adventure. 1836.
Loiterings of Travel. 1840.
Romance of Travel (stories). 1840.
Dashes at Life with a Free Pencil. 1845.
People I Have Met (stories). 1850.
Life Here and There (stories). 1850.
Fun-Jottings; or, Laughs I Have Taken a Pen To (stories). 1853.
Paul Fane; or, Parts of a Life Else Untold. 1857.

Plays

Bianca Visconti; or, The Heart Overtasked (produced 1837). 1839.
Tortesa; or, The Usurer Matched (produced 1839). 1839.

Poetry

Sketches. 1827.
Fugitive Poetry. 1829.
Poem Delivered before the Society of the United Brothers, with Other Poems. 1831.
Melanie and Other Poems. 1835.
The Sacred Poems. 1843.
Poems of Passion. 1843.
The Lady Jane and Other Poems. 1843.
Poems Sacred, Passionate, and Humorous. 1845; revised edition, 1849.
Poems of Early and after Years. 1848.

Other

Pencillings by the Way. 3 vols., 1835; revised edition, 1844; reprinted in part as *Summer Cruise in the Mediterranean,* 1853.

A l'Abri; or, The Tent Pitched. 1839; revised edition, as *Letters from under a Bridge, and Poems,* 1840.
American Scenery, drawings by W. H. Bartlett. 2 vols., 1840.
Canadian Scenery Illustrated, drawings by W. H. Bartlett. 2 vols., 1842.
The Scenery and Antiquities of Ireland, with J. Stirling Coyne, drawings by W. H. Bartlett. 2 vols., 1842.
Lectures on Fashion. 1844.
Complete Works. 1846.
Prose Works. 1849.
Rural Letters and Other Records of Thought at Leisure. 1849.
Hurry-Graphs; or, Sketches of Scenery, Celebrities, and Society. 1851.
Memoranda of the Life of Jenny Lind. 1853.
Health Trip to the Tropics. 1854.
Famous Persons and Places. 1854.
Out-Doors at Idlewild. 1855.
The Rag-Bag: A Collection of Ephemera. 1855.
The Convalescent. 1859.

Editor, *The Legendary.* 1828.
Editor, *Trenton Falls, Picturesque and Descriptive.* 1851.
Editor, with George Pope Morris, *The Prose and Poetry of Europe and America.* 1857.

*

Critical Studies: *Willis* by Henry A. Beers, 1885 (includes bibliography); *The World of Washington Irving* by Van Wyck Brooks, 1944; *Willis* by Cortland P. Auser, 1969; "Bayard Taylor and the Boston Millionaire: An Unpublished Letter" by Albert J. VonFrank, in *Resources for American Literary Study,* Autumn 1980; "American Theatrical Taste As Class Warfare" by Warren Kliewer, in *South Dakota Review,* Spring 1984; *Sentiment and Celebrity: Nathaniel Parker Willis and the Trials of Literary Fame* by Thomas Nelson Baker, 1998.

*   *   *

Nathaniel Parker Willis was in his day the most famous recorder of the details of social life and customs in America. In a sense, he was to his age what **Tom Wolfe** is to ours, but he was, in a way that Wolfe is not, sympathetic to most of the signs of status that he found around him—the resorts, homes, clothes, and so forth.

Willis seldom dealt with old established families. He generally concerned himself with the newly rich in search of the means through which they could express their status. He provided them with newspaper and magazine columns describing exactly the things they wanted to know and collected his observations in a series of volumes that were quite popular at the time. His books about fashionable life can be divided into three categories: books dealing with fashionable life abroad (a subject of endless fascination for newly rich Americans who, as a measure of their recently acquired status, adopted European standards, customs, and even diction—although few such people had crossed the Atlantic); books concerning fashionable life in America, especially in New York City and in such watering-places as Saratoga Springs, New York; and, most significantly, books detailing rural, middle-class life. *Pencillings by the Way* is an excellent account of his observations abroad, and *Hurry-Graphs* is typical of his volumes on life in America. His books on rural life include *A l'Abri, Out-Doors at Idlewild,* and *The Convalescent* and are of major importance to social as well as cultural historians as three of the earliest and most influential expressions of middle-class obsession with rural and suburban life. Willis, together with the essayist and landscape gardener Andrew Jackson Downing, was among the first to popularize this way of life in America. He also worked with the picturesque painter W. H. Bartlett.

Willis was also a poet (albeit a minor one), a playwright, a novelist, and a short story writer. His short stories, such as those collected in *Dashes at Life with a Free Pencil,* have from time to time attracted critical attention, and his novel *Paul Fane* has been considered a forerunner of **Henry James**'s international novels, but it was as a journalist, critics generally agree, that he was most successful: Willis will be remembered for his documents of fashionable life.

—Edward Halsey Foster

WILSON, August

Born: Pittsburgh, Pennsylvania, 27 April 1945. **Education:** Quit school at age sixteen and worked menial jobs while successfully submitting poetry to black publications. **Family:** Married Judy Oliver, 1981 (divorced); one child. **Career:** Became active in the theater; founder of the Black Horizons Theatre Company, St. Paul, Minnesota, 1968; script writer for the Science Museum of Minnesota, 1979. **Awards:** New York Drama Critics' Circle Best Play of the Year, 1984, 1987, 1988, 1990, 1996; American Theatre Critics Outstanding Play award, 1986; Whiting Writers' award, 1986; *Chicago Tribune* Artist of the Year, 1987; Outer Critics Circle John Gasner award, 1987; Antoinette Perry (Tony) award for best play, 1987; Drama Desk award, 1987, 1990; Literary Lion award, New York public library, 1988; Pulitzer prize for drama, 1987, 1990. **Residence:** St. Paul-Minneapolis, Minnesota.

PUBLICATIONS

Collections

August Wilson: Three Plays. 1991.

Plays

The Homecoming. 1979.
The Coldest Day of the Year. 1979.
Fullerton Street. 1980.
Black Bart and the Sacred Hills. 1981.
Jitney (produced 1982).
Ma Rainey's Black Bottom (produced 1984, Broadway 1984). 1981.
Fences (produced 1985, Broadway 1987). 1986.
Joe Turner's Come and Gone (produced 1986, Broadway 1988). 1986.
The Piano Lesson (produced 1987, Broadway 1990). 1990.
Two Trains Running (produced 1990, Broadway 1992). 1992.
Three Plays (includes *Ma Rainey's Black Bottom; Fences; Joe Turner's Come and Gone*). 1991.
Seven Guitars (produced 1996). 1996.

Musical: Book for stage musical about jazz musician Jelly Roll Morton.

Other

Introduction, *Breath of Blood & Milk,* by Amir Rashidd. 1989.
Introduction, *Romance Rhythm & Revolution: Selected Poetry of Rob Penny.* 1990.

*

Critical Studies: "Wrestling against History" by Mei-Ling Ching, and "Two Notes on August Wilson: The Songs of a Marked Man," by Margaret Glover, both in *Theater,* Summer-Fall, 1988; "August Wilson's America: A Conversation with Bill Moyers" (PBS videocassette), 1989; "August Wilson's Blues Poetics" by Paul Carter Harrison, 1991; "From Lorraine Hansberry to August Wilson: An Interview with August Wilson" by Sandra Shannon in *Callaloo,* Winter, 1991; "Reclaiming the Past: Narrative and Memory in August Wilson's *Two Trains Running*" by Lisa Wilde in *Theater,* Winter 1990-91; "August Wilson: A New Approach to Black Drama" by Yvonne Shafer in *Zeitschrift für Anglistik und Amerikanistik,* vol. 39, no. 1, 1991; "Hymns of Sedition: Portraits of the Artist in Contemporary African-America Drama" by James C. McKelly in *Arizona Quarterly,* Spring 1992; *An African American Odyssey: Self-Authentication in the Plays of August Wilson* by Kim Pereira, 1994; *May All Your Fences Have Gates: Essays on the Drama of August Wilson,* edited by Alan Nadel, 1994; *August Wilson and the African-American Odyssey* by Kim Pereira, 1995; *The Dramatic Vision of August Wilson* by Sandra Garrett Shannon, 1995; *I Ain't Sorry for Nothin' I Done: August Wilson's Process of Playwrighting* by Joan Herrington,1998; *August Wilson: A Research and Production Sourcebook* by Yvonne Shafer, 1998; *Understanding August Wilson* by Mary L. Bogumil, 1998; *August Wilson* by Peter Wolfe, 1999.

*   *   *

In his review of the Yale Repertory Theatre production of *Ma Rainey's Black Bottom* in 1984, the *New York Times* critic Frank Rich hailed August Wilson as a "major find for the American Theatre." Within the next eight years, this endorsement was emphatically underscored as Wilson won Pulitzer prizes (for *Fences* and *The Piano Lesson*), Antoinette Perry (Tony) awards, and numerous other theater accolades. His artistic goal of writing a play for every decade of the twentieth century promises to become a dramatic testament not only to the experiences of African Americans but to the history of all Americans. After a childhood of poverty in Pittsburgh, Pennsylvania, a city that became the setting for many of his plays, Wilson quit school at the age of sixteen and began working at menial jobs, during which time he undoubtedly garnered insights into the black working class that later produced such rich characters as Troy Maxson, the garbage collector protagonist of *Fences,* and Boy Willie, the visionary in *The Piano Lesson.* Despite dropping out of school—an act partly prompted by the refusal of a history teacher to accept his word that his essay was not plagiarized—Wilson continued to pursue a literary career by successfully submitting poems to black publications at the University of Pittsburgh Press. In 1968, he founded the Black Horizons Theatre Company in St. Paul, Minnesota. There he wrote his first play, *Jitney,* a realistic drama set in a Pittsburgh taxi sta-

tion. It was accepted for workshop production at the O'Neill Theatre Center's National Playwrights Conference in 1982, and was followed by another play, *Fullerton Street.* His reputation as an important playwright was secured only after his third play, *Ma Rainey's Black Bottom,* was produced at the Yale Repertory Theatre under the direction of Yale Drama School's artistic director, Lloyd Richards, who also directed several other plays by Wilson. This partnership was considered one of the most fruitful artistic collaborations between playwright and director in the history of the American theatre.

Ma Rainey's Black Bottom is the real beginning of Wilson's dramatic documentation of the experiences of African Americans; in particular, their struggle to gain a foothold within the social context of twentieth-century America by reinventing themselves within the cultural and mythological dimensions of their African roots. Migration, separation, and reunion are among the major themes that sustain this odyssey of self-authentication. In *Ma Rainey,* which is set in a Chicago studio in 1927, where the blues singer Ma Rainey and her sidemen are gathered for a recording session, these themes materialize through stories and reminiscences by the characters. The main conflict occurs between Levee, the brash young trumpeter who favors the new style of swing, and the other musicians, including Ma Rainey, who are proponents of the older blues. Sturdyvant, the white producer, has promised Levee a recording contract for the swing arrangements of his songs, and this motivates the young musician to belittle the blues songs of Ma and her other sidemen. To view Levee simply as a bitter and cynical young man who has suffered a terrible ordeal—as a child, he watched his mother being raped by four white men—is to miss the deeper significance of his actions. Wilson has imbued his character with a rebellious, individualistic streak that finds validation in African mythology: Levee is a cultural descendent of Eshu, the Yoruban trickster deity reincarnated in the persona of Brer Rabbit in the slave tales and related to such other religious and mythological figures as the Dahomean Legba, the Hindu Krishna, the Greek Hermes, and the Native American Coyote. These characters embody the creative rhythms that inveigh against restrictive authority; in them are sanctioned the artistic impulses that seek new forms. Unfortunately for Levee, this same trickster tradition that authenticates his actions also contains a destructive element—the trickster, bent on survival, is blind to the deeper truths of the traditions he debunks. In pursuit of his own musical career, Levee disavows the roots of his music—he fails to perceive the understructure of the blues in the swing that he so avidly embraces. Alienated from his roots and his people, he plunges into self-destruction. When Sturdyvant reneges on a promise to give him a recording contract, Levee finds himself without a job—he has just been fired by Ma Rainey—and with no musical future. At this point, the slightest provocation ignites the simmering rage that he has been carrying around for a lifetime—Toledo, a fellow musician, steps on his new shoes, and Levee murders him.

Levee's fury stems from experiences similar to the discrimination and thwarted hopes that fuel Troy Maxson's bitterness in *Fences.* A former baseball player who was denied the opportunity to play in the major leagues because of his race, Troy now works for a garbage collection company. Caught in an exhausting routine of work just to make ends meet and filled with acrimony because of his missed chances, Troy refuses to let his son, Cory, accept a football scholarship to college, claiming that athletics will never provide blacks with real opportunities to excel. Having migrated North to escape a tyrannical father, Troy finds himself in a similar situation with his own son, with the roles now reversed. Despite the changing times—*Fences* is set in 1957 and Jackie Robinson has already broken into the major leagues—Troy is determined to keep Cory as far away from sports as he can. In doing so he alienates the boy, who runs away from home—just as Troy himself had done—and joins the marines. Migration from South to North—a theme dealt with in greater detail in *Joe Turner's Come and Gone*—psychological separation between father and son, husband and wife (Troy has an affair and a child with another woman), and reunion as the estranged seek reconciliation with each other are integral to the action of this play. Caught in a hostile social climate, these characters must fashion for themselves the means for survival. In some cases, this leads to over-protection; in others, it leads to betrayal, as Troy, seeking relief from the mirthless routine of providing for his family, finds himself having an affair with another woman, thus jeopardizing his relations with the very family he strives to protect. Finally, all the characters realize that the only way they can survive is through each other; they have to put aside their differences and find solace and comfort in communal and familial unity.

Joe Turner's Come and Gone follows the efforts of an ex-slave to find his wife. Herald Loomis was kidnapped by Joe Turner, the brother of the Governor of Tennessee, held for seven years, and then released. With his daughter, Zonia, he arrives at Seth Holly's inn in Pittsburgh in 1911, looking for his lost wife. At the inn are a host of other migratory characters—among them are Jeremy, a blues guitarist who is looking for female companionship; Mattie, who wants to bring back her estranged husband; and Mollie, an adventurous woman heading North. Helping all of them is a rootworker called Bynum—the People Binder—who is also involved in his own quest: he seeks validation of his life's work from the Shiny Man who once appeared to him in an apocryphal vision. While *Fences* portrays the effects of this migration forty years later—the continuing struggle to find jobs and hold together disintegrating families and homes—*Joe Turner's Come and Gone* returns to the beginning of the southern exodus and explores the genesis of what was really a journey towards self-affirmation. It depicts the influence of the migration on the identity of each character, how their quests for lost loves and new loves reflect a deeper search for themselves. It raises fundamental questions about the nature of the black experience in America, probing the fascinating blend of two cultures that have informed the sensibilities of black Americans—their African heritage and the Christian tradition into which they were thrust. It investigates their poignant yearnings for meaningful relationships and their struggle to sing the song of their true identity. In both plays, the path to self-discovery lies in a reunion with the past, a solution Wilson continues to explore and advocate in his subsequent play.

In *The Piano Lesson*, Wilson introduces a new variation on the old theme of migration. Boy Willie is the first Wilson character to claim the South as his home. The play is set in Pittsburgh in 1936, in the home of Doaker Charles, uncle to Boy Willie, and of his sister Berniece, who also lives there. Boy Willie arrives one morning from Mississippi and tries to convince Berniece to sell the old piano that stands in the living room. This piano had originally been traded for Boy Willie's great-grandmother and her son by Mr. Sutter, their owner. To keep their memory alive, Boy Willie's great-grandfather, the first Boy Willie, carved on the piano the images of his separated wife and child and later added other events in the family's history—portraits, weddings, funerals, slave sales—

which imbued the piano with a totemic aura, for it now represented the struggle of this family to survive slavery and sharecropping. Boy Willie wants to sell the piano so that he can buy the farm on which several generations of his family had been slaves. It is a proposal of double significance: one, it seeks to reverse the position of his family from ex-slaves to owners, and two, it asserts emphatically that blacks will stay to claim the South as their home. But Berniece will not sell so precious a family heirloom, even though she cannot bring herself to play it. Their great struggle culminates in Boy Willie's fight with the ghost of their former owner and Berniece's invocation—at the piano—to her dead ancestors. At that moment brother and sister are finally reconciled and brought to the realization that their parents, grandparents, and great-grandparents died trying to preserve the familial bonds that they are now in danger of severing.

In Wilson's next play, *Two Trains Running*, the perseverance, hope, and struggle for survival continues in the turbulent period of the sixties. The four earlier plays cover a period of about fifty years. Their chronological sequence—from the 1911 of *Joe Turner* to the 1957 of *Fences*—spans a half century of struggle that yielded only a few grudging concessions to black Americans in their quest for self-authentication. The prevailing sense that the changes came very slowly—a full century to achieve the recognition promised by the Emancipation Proclamation—is sifted through the themes of migration and separation, which stretch the plays beyond their immediate locales in the twentieth century to the eras of slavery and Reconstruction. The theme of reunion propels them further back, into the real and mythological dimensions of the characters' African pasts.

Essential to an understanding of Wilson's plays is recognizing the importance of black music, particularly the blues. In some instances, the blues is an integral part of the subject (*Ma Rainey*); in others, it takes on a more symbolic role (*The Piano Lesson*). The blues, storytelling, gospel music, and black sermons are part of a dramatic tradition that inspired such black playwrights as **Langston Hughes** and are vital to the form and structure of much black drama, for in them are theatrically codified the experiences and cultural impulses of black Americans. Wilson is an exciting new voice in a long tradition of black playwrights and, like other great playwrights, his plays resonate beyond cultural boundaries.

—Kim Pereira

WILSON, Edmund

Born: Red Bank, New Jersey, 8 May 1895. **Education:** Hill School, Pottstown, Pennsylvania, 1909-12; Princeton University, New Jersey (member of the editorial staff, 1913-15, and managing editor, 1915-16, *Nassau Literary Magazine*), 1912-16, A.B. 1916. **Military Service:** Served in the U.S. Army Intelligence Corps, 1917-19. **Family:** Married 1) Mary Blair in 1923 (divorced 1928), one daughter; 2) Margaret Canby in 1930 (died 1932); 3) Mary McCarthy in 1938 (divorced 1946), one son; 4) Elena Thornton in 1946, one daughter. **Career:** Reporter, New York *Evening Sun*, 1916-17; managing editor, *Vanity Fair*, New York, 1922-23; contributing editor, 1925-26, and associate editor, 1926-31, *New Republic*, New York; book reviewer, *New Yorker*, 1944-47, and occasionally thereafter. **Awards:** Guggenheim fellowship, 1935; American Academy Gold medal, for nonfiction, 1955; Presidential Medal of freedom, 1963; MacDowell medal, 1964; Emerson-Thoreau medal, 1966; National medal for literature, 1966; Aspen award, 1968; Nice Book Festival Golden Eagle, 1971. **Died:** 12 June 1972.

PUBLICATIONS

Collections

Letters on Literature and Politics 1912-1972, edited by Elena Wilson. 1977.
The Portable Wilson, edited by Lewis M. Dabney. 1983.
From the Uncollected Edmund Wilson. 1995.
The Edmund Wilson Reader. 1997.

Fiction

I Thought of Daisy. 1929; revised edition, with *Galahad,* 1967.
Memoirs of Hecate County (stories). 1946; revised edition, 1958.
Galahad, with I Thought of Daisy. 1967.
The Higher Jazz. 1998.

Plays

The Evil Eye, lyrics by F. Scott Fitzgerald, music by P. B. Dickey and F. Warburton Guilbert (produced 1915). 1915.
The Crime in the Whistler Room (produced 1924). In *This Room and This Gin and These Sandwiches,* 1937.
Discordant Encounters: Plays and Dialogues. 1926.
This Room and This Gin and These Sandwiches: Three Plays (includes *The Crime in the Whistler Room, A Winter in Beech Street,* and *Beppo and Beth*) (produced 1978). 1937.
The Little Blue Light (produced 1950). 1950.
Five Plays: Cyprian's Prayer, The Crime in the Whistler Room, This Room and This Gin and These Sandwiches, Beppo and Beth, The Little Blue Light. 1954.
The Duke of Palermo and Other Plays, with an Open Letter to Mike Nichols (includes *Dr. McGrath and Osbert's Career; or, The Poet's Progress*). 1969.

Poetry

The Undertaker's Garland, with John Peale Bishop. 1922.
Poets, Farewell! (poems and essays). 1929.
Note-Books of Night (poems, essays and stories). 1942.
The White Sand. 1950.
Three Reliques of Ancient Western Poetry Collected by Wilson from the Ruins of the Twentieth Century. 1951.
Wilson's Christmas Stocking: Fun for Young and Old. 1953.
A Christmas Delerium. 1955.
Night Thoughts. 1961.
Holiday Greetings 1966. 1966.

Other

Axel's Castle: A Study in the Imaginative Literature of 1870-1930. 1931.
The American Jitters: A Year of the Slump (essays). 1932; as *Devil Take the Hindmost,* 1932.
Travels in Two Democracies (dialogues, essays, and story). 1936.

The Triple Thinkers: Ten Essays on Literature. 1938; augmented edition, as *The Triple Thinkers: Twelve Essays on Literary Subjects,* 1948.
To the Finland Station: A Study in the Writing and Acting of History. 1940.
The Boys in the Back Room: Notes on California Novelists. 1941.
The Wound and the Bow: Seven Studies in Literature. 1941.
Europe without Baedeker: Sketches among the Ruins of Italy, Greece, and England. 1947; revised edition, 1966.
Classics and Commercials: A Literary Chronicle of the Forties. 1950.
The Shores of Light: A Literary Chronicle of the Twenties and Thirties. 1952.
Eight Essays. 1954.
The Scrolls from the Dead Sea. 1955; revised edition, as *The Dead Sea Scrolls 1947-1969,* 1969; as *Israel and the Dead Sea Scrolls,* 1978.
A Literary Chronicle 1920-1950. 1956.
Red, Black, Blond, and Olive: Studies in Four Civilizations: Zuni, Haiti, Soviet Russia, Israel. 1956.
A Piece of My Mind: Reflections at Sixty. 1956.
The American Earthquake: A Documentary of the Twenties and Thirties. 1958.
Apologies to the Iroquois. 1960.
Patriotic Gore: Studies in the Literature of the American Civil War. 1962.
The Cold War and the Income Tax: A Protest. 1963.
The Bit between My Teeth: A Literary Chronicle of 1950-1965. 1965.
O Canada: An American's Notes on Canadian Culture. 1965.
A Prelude: Landscapes, Characters, and Conversations from the Earlier Years of My Life. 1967.
The Fruits of the MLA. 1968.
Upstate: Records and Recollections of Northern New York. 1971.
A Window on Russia for the Use of Foreign Readers. 1972.
The Devils and Canon Barham: Ten Essays on Poets, Novelists, and Monsters. 1973.
The Twenties [The Thirties, The Forties, The Fifties]: From Notebooks and Diaries of the Period, edited by Leon Edel. 4 vols., 1975-86.
The Nabokov-Wilson Letters: Correspondence between Vladimir Nabokov and Wilson 1940-1971, edited by Simon Karlinsky. 1979.

Editor, *The Last Tycoon: An Unfinished Novel by F. Scott Fitzgerald, Together with The Great Gatsby and Selected Writings.* 1941.
Editor, *The Shock of Recognition: The Development of Literature in the United States Recorded by the Men Who Made It.* 1943; enlarged edition, 1955.
Editor, *The Crack-up: With Other Uncollected Pieces, Note Books, and Unpublished Letters,* by F. Scott Fitzgerald. 1945.
Editor, *The Collected Essays of John Peale Bishop.* 1948.
Editor, *Peasants and Other Stories,* by Anton Chekhov. 1956.

*

Bibliography: *Wilson: A Bibliography* by Richard David Ramsey. 1971.

Critical Studies: *Wilson: A Study of the Literary Vocation in Our Time* by Sherman Paul, 1965; *Wilson* by Warner Berthoff, 1968;

Wilson by Charles P. Frank, 1970; *Wilson* by Leonard Kriegel, 1971; *A Wilson Celebration* edited by John Wain, 1978, as *Wilson: The Man and His Work,* 1978; *Three Honest Men: Wilson, F.R. Leavis, Lionel Trilling: A Critical Mosaic* by Philip French, 1980; *Wilson's America* by George H. Douglas, 1983; *Wilson* by David Castronovo, 1984; "The Vexations of Modernism: Edmund Wilson's *Axel's Castle*" by James W. Tuttleton, in *The American Scholar,* Spring 1988; "La Corrida Nabokov/Wilson" by Gilles Barbedette, in *L'Infini,* Spring 1988; "The Green Tradition: Found and Lost in Edmund Wilson's *I Thought of Daisy* and *Memoirs of Hecate County*" by James Guimond, in *The Green American Tradition: Essays and Poems for Sherman Paul* edited by Daniel H. Peck, 1989; "The Shy Little Scholar of Holder Court: Edmund Wilson at Princeton" by Lewis M. Dabney, in *The American Scholar,* Summer 1990, and "Edmund Wilson" by Dabney, in *American Writing Today* edited by Richard Kostelanetz, 1991; "Edmund Wilson en Oxford" by Isaiah Berlin, in *Revista de Occidente,* January 1991; "Fitzgerald's Third Regret: Intellectual Pretense and the Ghost of Edmund Wilson" by Milton A. Cohen, in *Texas Studies in Literature and Language* Spring 1991; "Mary McCarthy: At Home with Edmund Wilson" by Carol Brightman, in *Salmagundi,* Spring/Summer 1991; "Scott Fitzgerald and Edmund Wilson: A Troubled Friendship" by Jeffrey Meyers, in *The American Scholar,* Summer 1992; "Edmund Wilson and the Problem of Marx: History, Biography, and *To the Finland Station*" by Stanley Corkin, in *CLIO,* Winter 1993; *Edmund Wilson: Centennial Reflections,* 1997; *Edmund Wilson Revisited* by David Castronovo, 1998.

*   *   *

The life and work of Edmund Wilson place him in a quintessentially American literary tradition, somewhere between the pragmatic tinker role of **Benjamin Franklin** and the omnivorous man of letters stance of **Henry James**. While the concept of an author who works in many genres may seem quite European— only a few contemporary Americans such as **Thornton Wilder,** **Robert Penn Warren, Norman Mailer,** or **John Updike** fit such a definition—Wilson's literary craft is not as broad or deep as it may seem. True, he wrote literary criticism, poetry, drama, short stories, novels, reportage, anthropological studies, history, memoirs, diaries. Also true, he mastered many languages and political positions, from Russian to Hebrew, from cool mandarin to engaged leftist. But Wilson was fundamentally a writer fascinated by a sort of prose narrative one might call critical characterizations. He wrote a great, continuing novel about figures in the cultural landscape, characters in action—as poets, soldiers, religious thinkers, novelists, ethnics, revolutionaries. But all his subjects share one quality with their chronicler: they all create.

Although Wilson commenced his career as an occasional poet— his first published book, written with **John Peale Bishop,** *The Undertaker's Garland,* appeared in 1922, and he continued to write light verse and modestly introspective short poems throughout his career until *Night Thoughts* (1961)—and short story writer as well as closet dramatist, his formally creative efforts seem to strike a minor chord. The novel *I Thought of Daisy* does evoke a sense of being young and in lust in the *New York* of the 1920s; the notorious (banned in Boston) *Memoirs of Hecate County* is remarkable mostly for the lyric power of "The Princess with the Golden Hair" and the story a clef "The Man Who Shot Snapping Turtles." And Wilson wrote nearly a dozen plays from *The Crime in the*

Whistler Room (produced by Provincetown Players in New York) to his apocalyptic *The Little Blue Light.* His creative efforts, however, unlike those of other artist-critics such as Eliot or **Ezra Pound,** serve largely to exemplify Wilson's willingness to attempt a variety of genres and his skills in writing adequate and intelligent poems, stories, and plays.

Wilson's reputation as a literary critic, as opposed to journalist or reviewer, depends on three seminal books that—as was most often the case—collect essays first published in journals such as the *New Republic* or the *New Yorker. Axel's Castle: A Study in the Imaginative Literature of 1870-1930* treats in a combination of concise biography and richly inspired readings the basic works of those authors enshrined as the giants of modernism: Yeats, Valéry, Eliot, Proust, Joyce, **Gertrude Stein,** and Rimbaud. Unabashedly describing writer and text with the confidence of a firm biographer and superb reader, Wilson releases his genuinely creative talent; these portraits are clear and tough-minded, not vague and impressionistic, studies of complexly vital characters and forcefully difficult texts. While he never condescends to his readers, still, Wilson has the popularizer's zest as he energetically describes symbolism and stream of consciousness as if they are parts of the contemporary reader's cultural baggage, and enlivens the authors as if they are psychologically valid characters. *The Triple Thinkers* is more wide-ranging, more a collection of occasional pieces on Pushkin, Housman, Flaubert, Butler, and Shaw; two of the essays, on John Jay Chapman and on the ambiguity of Henry James, are among Wilson's finest, and the last, "Marxism and Literature," points the way to his socially involved writing. *The Wound and the Bow* may be Wilson's critical masterpiece. Taking as a point of departure the myth of Philoctetes who compensated for a wound by his fine archery, Wilson in a Freudian mode attends to Casanova and **Edith Wharton, Ernest Hemingway** ("The Gauge of Morale," a brilliant early appreciation) and Joyce ("The Dream of H. C. Earwicker"); and in Wilson's views of Dickens ("The Two Scrooges") and the "unknown" Kipling for the first time establishes the ways the childhood wounds of blacking factory and parental desertion, when understood, help to account for the anger in the novels and stories. Generations of scholars have drawn on these insights. Wilson's strength comes from his novelistic ability to make the real figures of Dickens and Kipling appealing and remarkable as characters without reducing their works to psychological exempla.

As the United States moved into social and political traumas during the 1930s, Wilson turned his attention first to documentary writing then to historical studies. *The American Jitters* gathers his reportage on travels through Depression-stunned America before the Roosevelt era's attempts to help the poor and jobless: the book is angry, informed, topical, radical, and personalized. Both Wilson the reporter and American working- and middle-class figures become embittered characters in a starkly realized landscape. Much of the book is superbly evoked description, ordered and impassioned. Also traveling to the Soviet Union, studying the history of socialist thought, Wilson started to publish his major historical work *To the Finland Station* as chapters in the *New Republic* in 1934. By the time the book appeared in 1940, it combined most of Wilson's literary gifts: it is a report on how socialism grew as an idea from the nineteenth century to the moment in 1917 when Lenin made his dramatic return to Russia; the book is very much a literary study, describing and commenting on key texts from Michelet, Vico, and Marx; and *To the Finland Station* bids fair to gain consideration as an historical epic, peopled with marvelously drawn characterizations of Marx, Lenin, and Trotsky, among others. Here Wilson the journalist, the literary critic, the social historian, and the creator of character joins his techniques in a manner established by Thomas Carlyle's best writing in *The French Revolution.*

The next thirty years of Wilson's writing career followed the pattern defined in the first two decades. He continued to attend to literature, most steadily in his role as book reviewer for the *New Yorker,* from whence came *Classics and Commercials: A Literary Chronicle of the Forties.* Wilson also kept up his special brand of travel writing—on Italy, Greece, and England after the war (*Europe without Baedeker*); on the Zuni and Iroquois tribes, on Haiti, on Israel (*Red, Black, Blond, and Olive*). At times anthropological, at times scholarly and historical, Wilson remained a popularizer, largely because of his flexible and persuasive narrative style; thus, *The Scrolls from the Dead Sea* (for which he mastered Hebrew) was both fare for *New Yorker* readers and acceptable to biblical scholars.

Finally, Wilson concentrated on American literature and history. In 1943 he edited *The Shock of Recognition,* a brilliantly articulated collection of writers' responses to each other's achievements that highlights American authors as personalities; he also edited his friend **F. Scott Fitzgerald**'s literary remains in *The Crack-up.* This looking backward inspired Wilson to follow three strands of American writing that took up his later career. First, he began to collect and rework his own previous writings; *The Shores of Light,* for example, is subtitled "A Literary Chronicle of the Twenties and Thirties." Even posthumously, under the dedicated editing of Leon Edel, Wilson's letters and journals of the decades continue to provide revisits to his published essays. Second, he become more fascinated with his own life and that of his family, as well as his home in Talcottville, New York, culminating in a powerful memoir, *Upstate.* And third, for more than ten years he worked on what many consider his greatest achievement, *Patriotic Gore,* certainly a valuable American companion to his earlier work on European history. A remarkable study, part literary criticism, part a reading of history, part character analysis, the book responds to Wilson's lifelong need to draw, in ways that eluded him as writer of formal fiction or drama, American characters. By using the great fratricidal moment in American history, the Civil War, as foreground and watershed, Wilson provided portraits of American political and literary heroes and heroines that are concise yet probing. By critically understanding their rhetoric, Wilson enlivens old names such as **Harriet Beecher Stowe** and Julia Ward Howe, such as the fiction writers **John William De Forest** and **Ambrose Bierce,** such as the anti-heroes Jefferson Davis and Alexander Stephens, such as Wilson's heroes, Abraham Lincoln and **Oliver Wendell Holmes,** and many other figures. Evocative and concerned, *Patriotic Gore* displays Wilson at his creative best, a novelist as historian, a lyricist as critic.

—Eric Solomon

WINNEMUCCA, Sarah

Also known as Sarah Winnemucca Hopkins. **Born:** c. 1844 into the Northern Paiute tribe. **Education:** Received no formal education. **Family:** Married 1) Lieutenant Edward C. Bartlett in 1871 (divorced 1876); 2) Joseph Satwaller in 1878 (divorced 1878); 3)

Lewis H. Hopkins in 1881. **Career:** Served as scout and interpreter for U.S. Army in 1868. Worked intermittently as interpreter at the Malheur Reservation from 1875 to 1880 and lecturer on tribal life. Traveled to Washington, D.C., in 1880 to plead for land rights of Paiutes. Worked again as interpreter, 1880 to 1882. Returned to East Coast for lecture tour, 1882 to 1884, in which she protested against Federal Indian policy. Returned to Nevada and started Peabody Indian School in 1885. Because of lack of funding and her ill health, school failed in 1887. Moved to Idaho to live with sister, Elma, in 1889. **Died:** 1891.

PUBLICATIONS

"The Pah-Utes," in *The Californian.* 1882.
Life among the Piutes: Their Wrongs and Claims. 1883.

*

Bibliography: *American Indian Women: A Guide to Research* by Gretchen Bataille and Kathleen Mullen Sands, 1991.

Critical Studies: *Sarah Winnemucca: Most Extraordinary Woman of the Paiute Nation* by Katherine Gehm, 1975; "Sarah Winnemucca, Northern Paiute, 1844-1891" by Catherine S. Fowler, in *American Indian Intellectuals* edited by Margot Liberty, 1978; *Sarah Winnemucca of the Northern Paiutes* by Gae Whitney Canfield, 1983; *American Indian Women: Telling Their Lives* edited by Gretchen M. Bataille and Kathleen Mullen Sands, 1984, and "Indian Women's Personal Narrative: Voices Past and Present" by Sands, in *American Women's Autobiography: Fea(s)ts of Memory* edited by Margo Culley, 1992; *American Indian Autobiography* by H. David Brumble, 1988; "Three Nineteenth-Century American Indian Autobiographers" by A. LaVonne Brown Ruoff, in *Redefining American Literary History* edited by Ruoff and Jerry W. Ward, Jr., 1990; "Story, Take Me Home: Instances of Resonance in Sarah Winnemucca Hopkins's *Life among the Piutes*" by William C. Strange, in *Entering the 90s: The North American Experience,* 1991; *Performing Indianness: Strategic Utterance in the Works of Sarah Winnemucca, Zitkala-Sa, and Mourning Dove* (dissertation) by DeLinda Day Wunder, 1997; "Sarah Winnemucca Hopkins (1844-1891)" by Shelle C. Bryant and Patrick W. Bryant, in *Nineteenth-Century American Women Writers: A Bio-Bibliographical Critical Sourcebook* edited by Denise D. Knight and Emmanuel S. Nelson, 1997; "Only an Indian Woman: Sarah Winnemucca and the Heroic Protagonist" by Lee Schweninger, in *Native American Women in Literature and Culture* edited by Susan Castillo and Victor M.P. DaRosa, 1997.

*   *   *

Sarah Winnemucca was born into an important family in the Northern Paiute tribe in about 1844 on the brink of a period of tremendous change for her people. Gold was discovered in California soon after her birth, bringing tides of immigrants through her people's native homelands in Nevada. Contact with white civilization changed the tribe forever, and Winnemucca's family played a significant role in shaping that contact. Her grandfather, Truckee, who served with General Fremont in California, counseled his tribe to accommodate the white settlers and soldiers, believing it would be to the benefit of both peoples to practice peace. As U.S. government policy toward the Paiutes became harsher, peaceful relations were more tenuous; even so, Winnemucca's father, Chief Winnemucca, believed in avoiding conflict with white settlers and the military, keeping his people away from areas where conflict might arise. Winnemucca inherited a leadership role, serving as translator, interpreter, lecturer, lobbyist, and spokesperson for her people for much of her adult life. Her autobiographical work, *Life among the Piutes: Their Wrongs and Claims* (1883), in many ways amplifies that role.

Life among the Piutes documents the history of contact and reveals a series of betrayals and broken promises that frequently marked Native American and white relations. Although most of the Northern Paiutes did not resist their removal to a reservation in the 1850s, little was offered them in exchange for their traditional nomadic way of life that included seasonal hunting and gathering. Rather, the best of the arable land set aside for them was frequently occupied by white squatters, and the government agents who were in charge of the reservations often profited by leasing portions of the reservation to white ranchers, by selling the government goods designated for the tribe, and by not paying tribal members for their agricultural labor. Winnemucca describes these injustices and reserves her harshest criticism of white society for these corrupt government agents. Decimated by hunger, disease, and attacks by white settlers, the Paiute tribe saw its population dwindle during the years of Winnemucca's adulthood.

By the time she was twenty-four, Winnemucca was working as a scout for the U.S. army and an interpreter for Camp McDermitt, an army post in Nevada. Because of her grandfather's influence, she had spent her early teenage years living and working with a white family in Genoa, Nevada, learning to speak fluent English, and apparently, although little is known about her education, to read and write. Because she also knew the languages of the neighboring tribes—Shoshone and Bannock—Winnemucca was extremely valuable to the army as an interpreter. Her skills made her equally valuable to her own people, as frequent misunderstandings and conflicts arose between the government agents and her tribe. At one point, as she relates in the text, one of her tribesmen begs her to speak for them, saying, "[Y]ou are the only one that is always ready to talk for us." The Paiutes respected the absolute truthfulness of a person's word, written or spoken, thus the importance of Winnemucca being chosen to speak for her tribe.

Winnemucca's willingness to "talk for" her tribe led her to lecture publicly about the Paiutes in the hope of changing the white perception that her people were "savages" and remedying the injustices they experienced. Tapping into white curiosity about Indian royalty, she billed herself as "Princess Sarah" and spoke before audiences in San Francisco. In a less theatrical position, she also traveled to Washington, D.C., in 1880, with her father, her brother, and other important members of her tribe to negotiate a more safe and stable life for her people. Winnemucca returned to the East Coast for a lecture tour in 1883, already a well-known personality. Her cause had been taken up by two sympathetic Boston sisters, Elizabeth Peabody and Mary (Peabody) Mann, who had been abolitionists, and who, because of their connections, were very helpful in guiding Winnemucca's public life.

While Winnemucca's lectures were successful, she felt that what she said was frequently incomplete, and so, with the editorial assistance of Mary Mann, she wrote *Life among the Piutes: Their Wrongs and Claims* in 1883. The profits from both the lectures and the book went toward a fund for a school that Winnemucca had envisioned, teaching Paiute children English and white skills,

but in the Paiute way. Winnemucca eventually returned to Nevada after raising enough money and started a school at her brother's ranch. Although the school was briefly successful, financial problems and conflicts with the government, which insisted that Paiute students attend a government-run boarding school in Colorado, forced the school to close. After the death of her husband, Lewis Hopkins, in 1887, Winnemucca lived with her widowed sister on her ranch in Howard's Lake, Idaho. There, she died quietly in 1891.

As with her lectures, Winnemucca's audience for her autobiography was largely educated and liberal, former abolitionists in some cases, reformers of various sorts, and, frequently, women. By demonstrating to this audience that both she, as an individual, and the Paiutes, as a people, were human beings deserving their sympathy, Winnemucca hoped that her audience would rally to her support and intervene as citizens to the extent that they could in shaping a sympathetic government policy toward the tribe. Such goals inevitably shaped the tone and, to some degree, the structure of the text. Winnemucca frequently appeals directly to her audience within her narrative, as when she exclaims, "Oh, my dear good Christian people, how long are you going to stand by and see us suffer at your hands?" Repeatedly, she demonstrates that the Paiutes share the virtues of civilized culture, but few of its vices. Winnemucca insists that the failure of the Paiutes to adapt to white ways has little to do with their ability or willingness, but has more to do with the corruption of the Indian agents who refuse to make such an assimilation possible.

In a letter Winnemucca wrote to the U.S. government in 1870, collected in Helen Hunt Jackson's *A Century of Dishonor* (1885), she summarizes her hopes for her people: "[I]f the Indians have any guarantee that they can secure a permanent home on their own native soil, and that our white neighbors can be kept from encroaching on our rights, after having a reasonable share of ground allotted to us as our own, and giving us the required advantages of learning, I warrant that the savage (as he is called today) will be a thrifty and law-abiding member of the community fifteen or twenty years hence." Clearly, Winnemucca saw adaptation to white ways as the best means of survival for her tribe.

While her assimilationist attitude has earned her much criticism, readers need to keep in mind that she was writing for an audience who, by and large, believed that the Indians would die out if they failed to assimilate. Few, if any, whites at the time recognized any tribe as having a coherent culture of their own, especially hunter-gatherer tribes like the Paiutes, who had not developed a warrior culture, like some of the tribes of the plains, nor a pueblo culture, like some of the tribes of the Southwest, both of whom had values recognizable to white society. Known as "diggers," the Northern Paiutes were perceived as remnants of the stone age, at best, not likely to survive in an era of railroads and developing technologies. Winnemucca recognized the need to create empathy with her readers on the basis of a common humanity and strove to emphasize her people's similarities to, rather than differences from, the dominant culture: hence, the assimilationist tone of her text.

As a personal chronicle and the first autobiography of an American Indian woman, the narrative is charged with the personality of an exceptionally dynamic individual. Winnemucca, more than other nineteenth-century women autobiographers, focuses on her public life rather than her private life. Having a public life and an outspoken voice meant going against the conventions of female behavior in white society, and Winnemucca often received the condemnation of white women for her behavior. She demonstrates within the text, however, that Paiute women often played public roles, as when she describes the operations of the tribal council: "The women know as much as the men do, and their advice is often asked." Leadership roles were not unusual for Paiute women, nor were they expected to defer to the voices of men.

It is instructive to compare Winnemucca's autobiography to slave narratives, like that of **Harriet Jacobs**'s *Incidents in the Life of a Slave Girl* (1861), because both were writing for a largely sympathetic audience who, nonetheless, might have judged the lives of women of another race. Like Jacobs, Winnemucca represents herself as an example of the humanity of her people by sharing her experiences and the emotions they evoked. But she also represents herself as a woman who should not be judged by the standards of white society, because she comes from a culture where women have different responsibilities and because she was rarely offered the rights and protections granted to white women. Winnemucca attempts to bridge cultural differences and find common ground in a shared humanity. Appealing to her audience as "only an Indian woman," Sarah Winnemucca succeeds in distilling a life that defies both the conventions of white culture and exceeds the traditions of her tribe in her efforts to speak for her people.

—Anna Carew-Miller

WINTERS, (Arthur) Yvor

Born: Chicago, Illinois, 17 October 1900; grew up in Eagle Rock, California. **Education:** The University of Chicago, 1917-18; University of Colorado, Boulder, 1923-25, B.A. and M.A. in Romance languages 1925; Stanford University, California, Ph.D., 1934. **Family:** Married the writer Janet Lewis in 1926; one daughter and one son. **Career:** Patient in tuberculosis sanatorium, Santa Fe, New Mexico, 1919-21. Schoolteacher, Madrid and Los Cerillos, New Mexico, 1921-22; instructor in French and Spanish, University of Idaho, Pocatello, 1925-27; instructor, 1927-37, assistant professor, 1937-40, associate professor, 1941-48, professor, 1948-51, and Albert Guerard professor, 1961-66, Stanford University. Founding editor, with Howard Baker and Janet Lewis, *Gyroscope*, Palo Alto, California, 1929-30; regional editor, *Hound and Horn*, Portland, Maine, 1932-34; fellow, Kenyon School of English, Gambier, Ohio, 1948-50. **Awards:** American Academy grant, 1952; Brandeis University Creative Arts award, 1959; Harriet Monroe Poetry award, 1960; Bollingen prize, 1961; National Endowment for the Arts grant, 1967. **Member:** American Academy of Arts and Sciences. **Died:** 25 January 1968.

PUBLICATIONS

Collections

Collected Poems, edited by Donald Davie. 1978.
The Uncollected Poems of Yvor Winters, 1919-1928. 1997.
The Selected Poems of Yvor Winters. 1999.

Poetry

The Immobile Wind. 1921.

The Magpie's Shadow. 1922.
The Bare Hills: A Book of Poems. 1927.
The Proof. 1930.
The Journey and Other Poems. 1931.
Before Disaster. 1934.
Poems. 1940.
The Giant Weapon. 1943.
To the Holy Spirit: A Poem. 1947.
Three Poems. 1950.
Collected Poems. 1952; revised edition, 1960.
The Early Poems 1920-28. 1966.

Fiction

The Brink of Darkness (story). 1947.

Other

The Case of David Lamson: A Summary, with Frances Theresa Russell. 1934.
Primitivism and Decadence: A Study of American Experimental Poetry. 1937.
Maule's Curse: Seven Studies in the History of American Obscurantism. 1938.
The Anatomy of Nonsense. 1943.
Edwin Arlington Robinson. 1946; revised edition, 1971.
In Defense of Reason. 1947; revised edition, 1960.
The Function of Criticism: Problems and Exercises. 1957.
On Modern Poets. 1959.
The Poetry of W.B. Yeats. 1960.
The Poetry of J.V. Cunningham. 1961.
Forms of Discovery: Critical and Historical Essays of the Forms of the Short Poem in English. 1967.
Uncollected Essays and Reviews, edited by Francis Murphy. 1973.
Hart Crane and Winters: Their Literary Correspondence, edited by Thomas Parkinson. 1978.

Editor, *Twelve Poets of the Pacific.* 1937.
Editor, *Selected Poems,* by Elizabeth Daryush. 1948.
Editor, *Poets of the Pacific, Second Series.* 1949.
Editor, with Kenneth Fields, *Quest for Reality: An Anthology of Short Poems in English.* 1969.

Translator, *The Last Sonnets of Pierre de Ronsard,* with *Diadems and Fagots,* by Olavo Bilac, translated by John Meem. c. 1921.

*

Bibliography: *Winters: An Annotated Bibliography 1919-1982* by Grosvenor Powell, 1983.

Critical Studies: *The Complex of Winters' Criticism* by Richard Sexton, 1973; *Language As Being in the Poetry of Winters* by Grosvenor Powell, 1980; *An Introduction to the Poetry of Winters* by Elizabeth Isaacs, 1981; "Winters Issue" of *Southern Review,* October 1981; "Charters and Poets: Winters, Swallow, Drummond" by Martin Bucco, in *Western American Literature,* February 1982; *Wisdom and Wilderness: The Achievement of Winters* by Dick Davis, 1983; *Revolution and Convention in Modern Poetry* by Donald E. Stanford, 1983; "Winters's Melville" by Helen Trimpi, in *Melville Society Extracts,* May 1984; "Wallace

Stegner and Yvor Winters As Teachers" by Edward Loomis, in *South Dakota Review,* Winter 1985; *In Defense of Winters* by Terry Comito, 1986; "Melville and the Myths of Modernism" by Kingsley Widmer, in *A Companion to Melville Studies* edited by John Bryant, 1986; "The Western-ness of Yvor Winters's Poetry" by Shyamal Bagchee, in *South Dakota Review,* Winter 1986; "Advances on Chaos: The Poetry and Esthetics of Stevens, Williams and Winters" by Terry Whalen, in *Canadian Review of American Studies,* Winter 1986; "Yvor Winters, Wallace Stevens, and 'Thanatopsis'" by Richard Elman, in *Under Open Sky: Poets on William Cullen Bryant* edited by Norbert Krapf, 1986; "Yvor Winters and *In Defense of Reason*" by Jerome Mazzaro, in *Sewanee Review,* Fall 1987; "Strategies of Knowing: The Proof Sonnets of Yvor Winters" by Richard Hoffpauir, in *English Studies in Canada,* March 1997, pp. 73-88; "The Seriousness of Ivor Winters" by David Yezzi, in *New Criterion,* June 1997, pp. 26-33.

* * *

The poetry of Yvor Winters falls into two phases, the imagist phase (1920-28), and the post-symbolist phase (1929-68). During the first period Winters was writing markedly cadenced, imagistic free verse under the influence of **William Carlos Williams**, **Ezra Pound**, **Glenway Wescott**, **H. D.**, and American Indian poetry. The influence was technical: that is, Winters learned to write his free verse by studying carefully selected poems he admired by these authors, but his own poems were not merely imitative. He developed a style of his own of great emotional intensity, brilliantly perceptive and even hypersensitive to the point of being hallucinatory. The literary and autobiographical background of these early years is described by Winters in his introduction to *The Early Poems,* in which he states that his philosophical position at that time was solipsistic and deterministic, a position that he later rejected. Some of the most remarkable of these verses are evocative of the life and landscape of New Mexico where Winters was recuperating from tuberculosis. At the same time, Winters was studying the mechanics of the image and how it was most effectively employed not only by the imagists but by Coleridge, Browning, Hopkins, **Edwin Arlington Robinson**, **Wallace Stevens**, **Ralph Waldo Emerson**, and the French symbolists.

In his late twenties Winters became impatient with the limitations of so-called free verse; he began to suspect that he could gain a greater emotional and intellectual range by the employment of the conventional iambic line as it occurs in the heroic couplet, the sonnet, in tetrameter and pentameter quatrains, and in other forms. *The Proof,* though it opens with poems written in the imagist manner, contains in the closing pages a number of verses in traditional iambic meters. The eight poems in *The Journey* are all in heroic couplets that show the influence not only of Dryden and Pope but also of the freely run-over couplets of Charles Churchill. One of the best of these, "On a View of Pasadena from the Hills," was directly influenced by Robert Bridges's 1899 poem in iambic pentameter couplets, "Elegy: The Summer-House on the Mound."

In his early thirties Winters was re-reading the poetry of Bridges, Hardy, Robinson, Stevens, Paul Valéry, and T. Sturge Moore with increasing admiration. All these poets (including Stevens in his best poem, "Sunday Morning") wrote in conventional prosody, a fact that strengthened Winters's conviction that free verse and imagism were temporary aberrations from the main tradition of Anglo-American verse. At this time he was forming

the tastes and principles to be found in his critical essays, which were to attract considerably more attention than his poetry. In *Primitivism and Decadence* he analyzed the technical innovations of the "new poetry," and, although he admired a few free verse poems by H. D., Williams, Stevens, and **Marianne Moore**, he concluded that on the whole the experimentalist movement had been a failure. By the time he was writing the poetry that appeared in *The Giant Weapon* and in the *Collected Poems of 1952* he had developed his critical theory concerning the nature of poetry, applied in a series of essays eventually published under the titles *In Defense of Reason, The Function of Criticism,* and *Forms of Discovery.* The gist of his theory is that a successful poem is a statement in words about human experience that communicates by means of verse—as distinct from prose, which is less precisely rhythmical than verse and therefore less effective in expressing emotion—appropriate feeling motivated by an understanding of the experience. In this kind of poetry full use is made of both the denotative and connotative significance of words. This theory is obviously operating in all of the poetry of Winters's mature years.

Late in his career Winters began referring to what he called the post-symbolist style of the best American poetry of the twentieth century. In his essay "Poetic Styles Old and New" (1959), after a discussion of the two major styles of the Renaissance, the plain and the ornamental, he said in describing post-symbolism, "It ought to be possible to embody our sensory experience in our poetry in an efficient way, not as ornament, and with no sacrifice of rational intelligence." Sensory experience communicated by fresh and original imagery charged with rational significance occurs in Winters's best poems from about 1930 on, including "The Slow Pacific Swell" (1931), "Sir Gawaine and the Green Knight" (1937), and "A Summer Commentary" (1938).

A few dominant and closely related themes, explored in Winters's verse from the beginning of his career until the end, give to his work a remarkable coherence and unity. Among these are a recurrent examination of the relationship between the rational mind and the poetic sensibility that may enrich it or destroy it, a theme that derives from his own experience and also from the poetry of T. Sturge Moore. In his earliest verse the sensibility is dominant to the point of rational disintegration, and even as late as 1955 Winters was writing in his "At the San Francisco Airport": "The rain of matter upon sense Destroys me momently." Achievement of balance between intellect and sensibility is the subject of "A Summer Commentary" and "Sir Gawaine and the Green Knight"; it is implicit in his allegorical poems on Greek subjects such as "Heracles," "Theseua," "Orpheus," and others. His concern with threats to the preservation of one's identity motivated a number of poems on death and the ravages of time, the most powerful of which are "For My Father's Grave," "To the Holy Spirit," "The Cremation," "A Leave-Taking," and "Prayer for My Son."

Winters is considered one of the most intellectual of all American poets. Yet he was keenly alive to the beauties of the sensory world as well as to its dangers. His purpose was "To steep the mind in sense / Yet never lose the aim." Consequently much of his poetry is remarkable for its freshly perceived descriptive detail of the natural world as in "The California Oaks" and "Time and the Garden." Finally it should be noted that Winters is the only twentieth-century poet of consequence who mastered the technique of free verse as practiced by the imagists and then abandoned it for conventional prosody, although he did not abandon what he had learned about the effective use of imagery. His poetry and his criticism present a significant case history of revolution and counter-revolution in modern poetry.

—Donald E. Stanford

WISTER, Owen

Born: Germantown, Philadelphia, Pennsylvania, 14 July 1860. **Education:** Schools in Hofwyl, Switzerland, 1870-71, and England, 1871-72; Germantown Academy, 1872; St. Paul's School, Concord, New Hampshire, 1873-78; Harvard University, Cambridge, Massachusetts, 1878-82, B.A. (summa cum laude) in music 1882; studied music in Paris, 1882-83; attended Harvard Law School, 1885-88, LL.B. 1888; admitted to Pennsylvania bar, 1889. **Family:** Married his second cousin Mary Channing Wister in 1898 (died 1913); three sons and three daughters. **Career:** Worked at Union Safe Deposit Vaults, Boston, 1884-85; lawyer in Philadelphia, 1889-91; thereafter a full-time writer; moved to Charleston, South Carolina, 1902. Overseer, Harvard University, 1912-18, 1919-25. **Member:** American Academy; Honorary Member, Society of Letters (Paris); Honorary Fellow, Royal Society of Literature (London). **Died:** 21 July 1938.

PUBLICATIONS

Collections

The West of Wister: Selected Short Stories, edited by Robert L. Hough. 1972.

Fiction

The New Swiss Family Robinson. 1882.
The Dragon of Wantley. 1892.
Red Men and White (stories). 1896; as *Salvation Gap and Other Western Classics,* 1999.
Lin McLean. 1897.
The Jimmyjohn Boss and Other Stories. 1900.
The Virginian: A Horseman of the Plains. 1902.
Philosophy 4: A Story of Harvard University. 1903.
A Journey in Search of Christmas (story). 1904.
Lady Baltimore. 1906.
How Doth the Simple Spelling Bee. 1907.
Mother. 1907.
Members of the Family. 1911.
Padre Ignacio (stories). 1911.
When West Was West. 1928.

Plays

Dido and Aeneas, Music by Wister (produced 1882).
Watch Your Thirst: A Dry Opera. 1923; revised version, as *The Honeymoon Shiners,* in *Writings,* 1928.
The Vain, with Kirke La Shelle. 1958.

Poetry

Done in the Open, illustrated by Frederic Remington. 1903.

Indispensable Information for Infants; or, Easy Entrance to Education. 1921.

Other

Ulysses S. Grant. 1900.
Musk-Ox, Bison, Sheep, and Goat, with Caspar W. Whitney and George Bird Grinnell. 1904.
The Seven Ages of Washington: A Biography. 1907.
The Pentecost of Calamity (essay). 1915.
A Straight Deal; or, The Ancient Grudge (essay). 1920.
Neighbors Henceforth. 1922.
Writings. 11 vols., 1928.
Roosevelt: The Story of a Friendship 1880-1919. 1930; as *Theodore Roosevelt,* 1930.
Two Appreciations of John Jay Chapman. 1934.
My Father, Owen Wister, and Ten Letters . . . to His Mother during His First Trip to Wyoming in 1885, by Frances Kemble Wister Stokes. 1952.
Wister out West: His Journals and Letters, edited by Fanny Kemble Wister. 1958.
My Dear Wister: The Frederic Remington-Wister Letters, edited by Ben Vorpahl. 1972.
That I May Tell You: Journals and Letters of the Wister Family, edited by Fanny Kemble Wister. 1979.

*

Bibliography: by Dean Sherman, in *Bulletin of Bibliography 28,* 1971; "Wister: An Annotated Bibliography of Secondary Material" by Sanford E. Morovitz, in *American Literary Realism 7,* 1974.

Critical Studies: *The Eastern Establishment and the Western Experience: The West of Frederic Remington, Theodore Roosevelt, and Wister* by G. Edward White, 1968; *Wister* by Richard W. Etulain, 1973; "How the Western Ends: Fenimore Cooper to Frederic Remington" by Christine Bold, in *Western American Literature,* August 1982; "*The Virginian* and Antonia Shimerda: Different Sides of the Western Coin" by John J. Murphy, in *Women and Western American Literature* edited by Helen Winter Stauffer and Susan J. Rosowski, 1982; "Home by Way of California: The Southerner As the Last European" by Lewis P. Simpson, in *Southern Literature in Transition: Heritage and Promise* edited by Philip Castille and William Osborne, 1983; "Owen Wister's Achievement in Literary Tradition" by John D. Nesbitt, in *Western American Literature,* Fall 1983; *Owen Wister* by John L. Cobbs, 1984; "The Western: Can It Be Great?" by J. Bakker, in *Dutch Quarterly Review of Anglo-American Letters,* vol. 14, 1984; "Unseemly Realities in Owen Wister's Western/American Myth" by Sanford E. Marovitz, in *American Literary Realism, 1870-1910,* Autumn 1984; *Wister: Chronicler of the West, Gentleman of the East* by Darwin Payne, 1985; "Humor and Society in the Frontier Novels of the Americas: Wister, Guiraldes, and Amado" by Nina M. Scott, in *Proceedings of the Xth Congress of the International Comparative Literature Association* edited by Anna Balakian, James J. Wilhelm, Douwe W. Fokkema, Claudio Guillen, and M. J. Valdes, 3 vols., 1985; "*The Virginian* and Molly in Paradise: How Sweet Is It?" by Forrest G. Robinson, in *Western American Literature,* May 1986; "'When You Call Me That . . . ': Tall Talk and Male Hegemony in *The Virginian*" by Lee Clark Mitchell, in *PMLA,*

January 1987; "'I'm Not an Old Fogey and You're Not a Young Ass': Owen Wister and Ernest Hemingway" by Alan Price, in *The Hemingway Review,* Fall 1989; "Owen Wister: Wyoming's Influential Realist and Craftsman" by Leslie T. Whipp, in *Great Plains Quarterly,* Fall 1990; "Transatlantic Twins: Rudyard Kipling and Owen Wister" by J.C. Furnas, in *The American Scholar,* Autumn 1995, pp. 599-606; "The Western Hero As Logos; or, Unmaking Meaning" by Susan J. Rosowski, in *Western American Literature,* Fall 1997, pp. 269-92.

*   *   *

Although he never gave himself fully to the American West, the West was the making of Owen Wister as a man and as a writer. Born into an aristocratic Philadelphia family, educated in eastern schools and abroad, Wister initially sought a career in music. His practical father encouraged a business career, then law. Uncertain of himself, Wister took the advice of his physician in 1885 and went to Wyoming for the summer. Then and in succeeding summers in the West, he found health, and a frontier and cowboy milieu that he knew was about to end and deserved to be put into fiction. Wister saw great romantic possibilities in the cowboy, at that time known to fiction only in dime novels.

Wister had published a burlesque of *Swiss Family Robinson* the year he graduated from Harvard. Shortly thereafter he and a cousin wrote a novel, but he took the advice of **William Dean Howells,** who found the book too bold, and did not submit it for publication. Wister's instinct was for the actual and the concrete, and he might have been a better writer had he not acquiesced repeatedly to the genteel tradition. The habit of writing ingrained, he kept detailed journal entries on his western summers—the factual basis for many of his stories. The journals, published twenty years after Wister's death, are well worth reading.

In 1891 Wister wrote "Hank's Woman," his first western story. *Harper's* accepted it and encouraged Wister to write about the West. His stories were full of local color interest when the local color movement was still important in American literature. *Red Men and White,* his first short story collection, was published in 1896, followed by *Lin McLean.* The cowboy McLean gave some unity to the hook, but it is hardly a novel. *The Virginian,* the novel that is Wister's most important achievement, was likewise based on earlier published stories. It, too, has problems of point of view. The eastern tenderfoot who arrives in Wyoming and "grows up" there, could not possibly know all the material he relates. The novel's structure is episodic. The contrast of East and West, however, gave embodiment to Wister's sense of the romantic possibility of the cow-puncher, possibilities that became legion in western novels and movies. Wister's hero is a natural aristocrat who is capable of showing his inner fiber in a land with its own rules for law and order. Wister was not particularly interested in portraying the inside of ranch life; rather, he wished to show his hero grow and adjust to the closing frontier, proving himself worthy of the aristocratic Molly Stark Wood of Vermont, who has come to Wyoming to teach school. Later, Wister described *The Virginian* as the embodiment of "the best thing the Declaration of Independence ever turned out."

However attractive the West might be for summer hunting and adventure, Wister became increasingly pulled to the East and to Europe, and to the South. He had moved to Charleston, South Carolina, in 1902, where the Southern aristocratic codes were congenial to his temperament. *Lady Baltimore* is Wister's Jamesian

comedy of manners. The Jamesian narrator comes from the North to Kings Port (Charleston) to engage in genealogical research. The love story he narrates, and plays a part in, enables Wister to juxtapose culture against culture. The novel is pleasant reading, convincing in its portrayal of Southern attitudes of the time, and indicative of the reservations Wister had about the cruder West. Thereafter, Wister wrote other stories about the West, but he ceased to visit it, and by the time of World War I his main concern was his family, Europe, and politics.

—Joseph M. Flora

WOLFE, Thomas (Clayton)

Born: Asheville, North Carolina, 3 October 1900. **Education:** The Orange Street grade school, Asheville, 1905-12; North State Fitting School, Asheville, 1912-16; University of North Carolina, Chapel Hill (editor, *Tar Heel* magazine), 1916-20, B.A. 1920; Harvard University, Cambridge, Massachusetts, where he studied playwriting in George Pierce Baker's "47 Workshop," 1920-23, M.A. in English 1922. **Career:** Part-time Instructor in English, Washington Square College, New York University, 1924-30; full-time writer from 1930; made several trips to Europe and lived briefly in London; traveled in the Pacific Northwest, 1938: contracted pneumonia. **Awards:** Guggenheim fellowship, 1930. **Member:** American Academy. **Died:** 15 September 1938.

PUBLICATIONS

Collections

The Letters, edited by Elizabeth Nowell. 1956; selection, 1958.
The Wolfe Reader, edited by C. Hugh Holman. 1962.
Complete Short Stories, edited by Francis E. Skipp. 1987.

Fiction

Look Homeward, Angel: A Story of the Buried Life. 1929.
Of Time and the River: A Legend of Man Hunger in His Youth. 1935.
From Death to Morning (stories). 1935.
The Web and the Rock, edited by Edward C. Aswell. 1939.
You Can't Go Home Again, edited by Edward C. Aswell. 1940.
The Hills Beyond (stories), edited by Edward C. Aswell. 1941.
The Short Novels, edited by C. Hugh Holman. 1961.
A Prologue to America, edited by Aldo P. Magi. 1978.
K-19: Salvaged Pieces, edited by John L. Idol, Jr. 1983.
The Train and the City, edited by Richard S. Kennedy. 1984.
The Lost Boy: A Novella. 1992.

Plays

The Return of Buck Gavin (produced 1919). In *Carolina Folk-Plays,* second series, 1924.
The Third Night (produced 1919). In *The Carolina Play Book,* September 1938.
The Mountains (produced 1921), edited by Pat M. Ryan. 1970.
Welcome to Our City (produced 1923), edited by Richard S. Kennedy. 1983.

Gentlemen of the Press (produced 1928). 1942.

Mannerhouse. 1948; edited by Louis D. Rubin, Jr., and John L. Idol, Jr., 1985.

The Streets of Durham, edited by Richard Walser. 1982.

Poetry

A Stone, A Leaf, A Door, edited by John S. Barnes. 1945.

Other

The Crisis in Industry. 1919.

The Story of a Novel. 1936.

A Note on Experts: Dexter Vespasian Joyner. 1939.

Wolfe's Letters to His Mother, Julia Elizabeth Wolfe, edited by John Skally Terry. 1943.

The Years of Wandering in Many Lands and Cities. 1949.

A Western Journal: A Daily Log of the Great Parks Trip, June 20-July 2, 1938. 1951.

The Correspondence of Wolfe and Homer Andrew Watt, edited by Oscar Cargill and Thomas Clark Pollock. 1954.

Wolfe's Purdue Speech, "Writing and Living," edited by William Braswell and Leslie A. Field. 1964.

The Letters of Wolfe to His Mother, Newly Edited from the Original Manuscripts, edited by C. Hugh Holman and Sue Fields Ross. 1968.

The Notebooks, edited by Richard S. Kennedy and Paschal Reeves. 2 vols., 1970.

My Other Loneliness: Letters of Wolfe and Aline Bernstein, edited by Suzanne Stutman. 1983; supplement, as *Holding on for Heaven: The Cables and Postcards of Wolfe and Aline Bernstein,* edited by Stutman, 1985.

The Autobiography of an American Novelist (includes *The Story of a Novel* and "Writing and Living"), edited by Leslie Field. 1983.

Beyond Love and Loyalty: The Letters of Wolfe and Elizabeth Nowell, edited by Richard S. Kennedy. 1983.

Wolfe Interviewed 1929-1938, edited by Aldo P. Magi and Richard Walser. 1985.

*

Bibliography: *Of Time and Thomas Wolfe: A Bibliography with a Character Index,* 1959, and *Wolfe: A Checklist,* 1970, both by Elmer D. Johnson; *Wolfe: A Reference Guide* by John S. Phillipson, 1977; *Thomas Wolfe: An Annotated Critical Bibliography* by John Earl Bassett, 1996.

Critical Studies: *Wolfe* by Herbert J. Muller, 1947; *Thomas Wolfe: A Critical Study* by Pamela Hansford Johnson, 1947, as *Hungry Gulliver: An English Critical Appraisal of Wolfe,* 1948, as *The Art of Wolfe,* 1963; *The Enigma of Wolfe* edited by Richard Walser, 1953, and *Wolfe: An Introduction and Interpretation,* 1961, and *Wolfe: Undergraduate,* 1977, both by Walser; *Wolfe: The Weather of His Youth* by Louis D. Rubin, Jr., 1955, and *Wolfe: A Collection of Critical Essays* edited by Rubin, 1973; *Wolfe's Characters* by Floyd C. Watkins, 1957; *Wolfe: A Biography* by Elizabeth Nowell, 1960; *Wolfe, 1960,* and *The Loneliness at the Core: Studies in Wolfe,* 1975, both by C. Hugh Holman, and *The World of Wolfe* edited by Holman, 1962; *The Window of Memory: The Literary Career of Wolfe* by Richard S. Kennedy, 1962; *Wolfe as I Knew Him and Other Essays* by Vardis Fisher, 1963; *Wolfe* by Bruce R. McElderry, Jr., 1964; *Wolfe* by Andrew Turnbull, 1968; *Wolfe: Three Decades of Criticism* edited by Leslie A. Field, 1968; *Wolfe's Albatross: Race and Nationality in America* by Paschal Reeves, 1969, and *Wolfe: The Critical Reception* edited by Reeves, 1974; *Wolfe* by Elizabeth Evans, 1984; *Critical Essays on Wolfe* edited by John S. Phillipson, 1985; *Look Homeward: A Life of Wolfe* by David Herbert Donald, 1987; *The Art of Fact: Contemporary Artists of Nonfiction* by Barbara Lounsberry, 1990; *The Aristocracy of Art in Joyce and Wolfe* by Margaret Mills Harper, 1990; *Conversations with Tom Wolfe* edited by Dorothy Scura, 1990; *The Critical Response to Tom Wolfe* edited by Doug Shomette, 1992; *Of Time and the Artist: Thomas Wolfe, His Novels, and the Critics* by Carol Ingalls Johnston, 1995; *Thomas Wolfe: Voice of the Mountains* by Richard Cooper, 1997; *Thomas Wolfe: A Writer's Life* by Ted Mitchell, 1997; *The Death of Thomas Wolfe: A 60 Year Retrospective* by S. Robert Lathan, 1998.

*   *   *

With the publication in 1929 of Thomas Wolfe's *Look Homeward, Angel,* American fiction was invested with a fresh talent quite unlike that of any writer of the past. On its narrative level, it was a story of maturation, covering the first twenty years in the life of a youth in conflict with his family and his small North Carolina town, but it was no novel in the usual sense, rather a loose chronicle held together with an assemblage of some memorable characters. Noticeable throughout were vestiges of thwarted careers in playwriting and poetry, careers he would have preferred. Availing himself of the titanism then permitted in American fiction, and gifted with a Proustian power of nearly total recall of sights and sounds, Wolfe lacquered the narrative of *Look Homeward, Angel* with dithyrambic luxuriance and a sensuous Whitmanesque prose, twisting easily from the rhetorical to the dramatic. At his command, too, was a gift for caricature, even burlesque, and satire. His comic exaggeration in depicting characters was never understood by those acquainted with the models on whom they were based. Symbols—the angel, the ghost, trains, mountains, and those images in the haunting refrain "a stone, a leaf, an unfound door"—underscored Wolfe's intent in characterization and meaning.

A sequel, *Of Time and the River,* took Wolfe's autobiographical hero, Eugene Gant, to Harvard, New York, and Europe. For his thesis, Wolfe appropriated the Joycean wanderer's search for the father, and imposed an epic framework upon the narrative by intoning names from Greek legends. In such a novel as this, Wolfe became, according to one ecstatic comment, "our closest approach to Homer." Allied with the search for the father was an attempt to discover America's greatness through the intensity of one man's experience, and to reveal to Americans as totally as possible the loneliness and transiency of their lives. In order to accomplish this, the hero was provided with a Faustian hunger, an obsessive and unquenchable desire for achievement and knowledge. There must be, he proclaimed, "never an end to curiosity! . . . I must think. I must mix it all with myself and with America." *The Story of a Novel,* Wolfe's confessional monograph of how *Of Time and the River* was written, tells of a "great black cloud" within him that poured forth "a torrential and ungovernable flood" about "night and darkness in America." The result was a novel of apparent formlessness, but it was an intentional formlessness, symbolically parallel to the formlessness of life itself and of his native land.

Though Wolfe's second book was a great success, so sensitive was he to charges of excessive emotional energy and lyricism that for his third, *The Web and the Rock,* he promised to write an "objective" account of his hero, now named George Webber. Webber was given a somewhat different background and young manhood, but in midstream Webber took on the familiar traits of Eugene Gant—that is to say, Thomas Wolfe himself. A love affair with a woman much older than Webber led directly into *You Can't Go Home Again,* by the end of which Wolfe's promise of objectivity was realized, his understanding of social problems effected, and his transformation completed: from romantic egocentricity to a clearer vision of the realities of life, from chaos to order, from uncertainty to assurance, from self, in short, to mankind. In the development of a social consciousness, Wolfe's hero was propelled into a rejection of a number of youthful ambitions. No longer sufficient were success and fame and romantic love; of ultimate primacy was one's belief "that America and the people in it are deathless, undiscovered, and immortal, and must live."

After the publication of *Look Homeward, Angel,* Wolfe lived only another nine years. Since he was resolved on a one-man vision of life, everything was part of the "single" book, including his early plays, two volumes of letters, his notebooks, two collections of short stories, the excerpts and essays, and *A Western Journal.* That he produced such an abundance in so short a time was due to a compulsion to write almost continuously. He rarely took vacations, was annoyed by intrusions, and was committed wholly to his "work," as he called it. It has been argued that Wolfe's works should be read in isolated segments, as tone poems perhaps, or as short novels where his control can easily be observed. His books, according to another view, were rather a "fictional thesaurus," composed of many diverse elements—theatrical dialogue, choral ode, essay, travelogue, biography, oratory, lyric poetry, dramatic episode. Though his four major books were no more autobiographical than many single works by **Herman Melville** and **Mark Twain, F. Scott Fitzgerald** and **Ernest Hemingway,** his persistent chronological continuum affronted some readers and critics in a way the practices of other novelists had not.

As an American writer—and he may turn out to be the most American writer—Wolfe was in the tradition of **Ralph Waldo Emerson, Henry David Thoreau,** Melville, Twain, **Theodore Dreiser, Carl Sandburg,** and **Sherwood Anderson.** He shared the idealism of **Thomas Jefferson** and **Walt Whitman,** especially in their projection of the American Dream in which lay the hopes of young men and women everywhere to do the best that was within them to do. His pages were often a sheer symbolic poetry of time and the river, of the web and the rock. Yet his greatest attainment was a fiction of scenes and characters remarkably vital, bountiful, and rich.

—Richard Walser

See the essay on *Look Homeward, Angel.*

WOLFE, Tom(as Kennerly, Jr.)

Born: Richmond, Virginia, 2 March 1930. **Education:** St. Christopher's Episcopal prep school; Washington and Lee University, B.A. 1951; Yale University, Ph.D. (American Studies) 1957. **Career:** Reporter and correspondent for *Springfield Union,*

1956-59, *Washington Post,* 1959-62, and *New York Herald Tribune,* 1962-66. Writer for *New York Sunday* magazine (now *New York* magazine), 1962-66; *New York World Journal Tribune,* 1966-67. Contributing editor for *New York* magazine, 1968-76; *Esquire* magazine, 1977—; *Harper's* magazine, 1978-81. **Family:** Married Sheila Berger (art director of *Harper's* magazine), 1978; one daughter and one son. **Awards:** Front Page awards for humor and foreign news reporting, Washington Newspaper Guild, 1961; Award of Excellence, Society of Magazine Writers, 1970; Virginia Laureate for literature, 1977; American Book award, 1980; Columbus Journalism award, 1980; National Book Critics Circle award in nonfiction, 1980; John Dos Passos award, 1984; Washington Irving Medal for literary excellence, Nicholas Society, 1986; St. Louis Literary award, Quinnipiac College, 1990; President award, 1993. **Residence:** New York City.

PUBLICATIONS

Collections

The Purple Decades: A Reader (collection). 1982.

Nonfiction

The Kandy-Kolored Tangerine-Flake Streamline Baby (self-illustrated). 1965.
The Electric Kool-Aid Acid Test. 1968.
The Pump House Gang (self-illustrated). 1968; published in England as The *Mid-Atlantic Man and Other New Breeds in England and America,* 1969.
Radical Chic and Mau-Mauing the Flak Catchers. 1970.
The Painted Word (self-illustrated). 1975.
Mauve Gloves and Madmen, Clutter and Vine (self-illustrated). 1976.
The Right Stuff. 1979.
In Our Time (self-illustrated). 1980.
From Bauhaus to Our House. 1981.

Novels

The Bonfire of the Vanities. 1987.
A Man in Full. 1998.

Other

The New Journalism, edited by Tom Wolfe and E.W. Johnson. 1973.

*

Critical Studies: *The New Fiction: Interviews with Innovative American Writers* by Joe David Bellamy, 1974; *The Reporter As Artist: A Look at the New Journalism Controversy* edited by Ronald Weber, 1974; special issue on The New Journalism, *Journal of Popular Culture,* Summer 1975; *The Mythopoeic Reality: The Postwar American Nonfiction Novel* by Mas'ud Zavarzadeh, 1976; *Fact and Fiction: The New Journalism and the Nonfiction Novel* by John Hollowell, 1977; *The Literature of Fact: Nonfiction in American Writing* by Ronald Weber, 1980; *Fables of Fact: The New Journalism as New Fiction* by John Hellmann, 1981; "An Exploration of Power: Tom Wolfe's Acid Test" by Carl A. Bredahl in *Critique*, Winter 1981-1982; *Style as Argument: Contemporary American Nonfiction* by Chris Anderson, 1987; *The Art of Fact: Contemporary Artists of Nonfiction* by Barbara Lounsberry, 1990; *Conversations with Tom Wolfe* edited by Dorothy Scura, 1990; special issue on Tom Wolfe, *Journal of American Culture*, Fall 1991; *A Sourcebook of American Literary Journalism: Representative Writers in an Emerging Genre* edited by Thomas B. Connery, 1992; *Literary Selves: Autobiography and Contemporary American Nonfiction* by James N. Stull, 1993; *Tom Wolfe* by William McKeen, 1995.

*   *   *

After writing nonfiction pieces for *New York* magazine, *Esquire,* and other popular-interest periodicals throughout much of the 1960s, Tom Wolfe emerged as one of the chief practitioners of the "New Journalism," a form of literary nonfiction in which novelistic techniques are used to reconstruct and dramatize journalistic fact. In his introduction to *The New Journalism,* Wolfe explains that an ambitious journalist could use these techniques to write nonfiction works similar in scope to the social realism of Dickens, Balzac, Thackeray, and other nineteenth-century writers. Over the last two decades, Wolfe has backed up his claim by writing vivid journalistic and historical accounts of the space program, the drug culture, New York society, the city of Las Vegas, and many other aspects of American life.

Though Wolfe's works chronicle the rich and changing tapestry of contemporary American life, specific themes and a recognizable ideology are found in most of his nonfiction. Like the writings of his literary colleague John McPhee, Wolfe's books reveal a fascination with both the contemporary American male hero and charismatic leaders who use (or abuse) power in their relations with disciples and other group members. As the word "disciples" suggests, Wolfe often interprets membership within exclusive social groups, whether it is the Merry Pranksters or the world of custom cars, as a form of secular religion. When Wolfe writes about these subcultures and other exclusive societies, which he calls "status spheres," he typically focuses on symbolic details— forms of dress, language, hair styles—because he believes they are the signs that best reveal personal identity. In *Mauve Gloves and Madmen, Clutter and Vine* Wolfe maintains that "every person's 'real self,' his psyche, his soul, is largely the product of fashion and other outside influences on his status." In an interview with Joe David Bellamy, Wolfe was asked if his exploration of status was the primary subject of his works. He noted that it is "really more of an analytical tool than a subject per se. It's just so fundamental to everything that people do that it's going to come up. That's the first thing I always look for." In *The Kandy-Kolored Tangerine-Flake Streamline Baby* (1965), *The Pump House Gang* (1968), and other collections of nonfiction Wolfe profiles, for example, specific status groups and individuals—Hugh Hefner, California surfers, rock stars, and other cultural impresarios—who built monuments to their styles of life as a result of the post-World War II economic boom. Even when Wolfe writes about marginal, even adversarial, groups, he proposes an economic interpretation of culture that depoliticizes experience and suggests that all individuals are status conscious and preoccupied with their position in the socio-economic pecking order. Wolfe often emphasizes the interaction—and confrontation—between these status groups and reveals culture as a kind of game, with implied and stated rules, in which social players compete for a share of the economic pie and promote their own idiosyncratic versions of reality.

In *The Electric Kool-Aid Acid Test* Wolfe describes how a countercultural group, the charismatic **Ken Kesey** and his Merry Pranksters, define a social and psychic reality that is quite different from the one experienced by most mainstream Americans. Like many other important works of American literature, Wolfe's chronicle is a frontier tale embedded in the form of a quest narrative that features the Merry Pranksters venturing east to the New York World's Fair in a bus painted in a swirl of psychedelic colors. Though description of this journey makes up only a portion of the book, the physical movement serves as a symbolic affirmation of the Pranksters' attempt to explore their psychic frontiers and create a secular religion with the use of hallucinogenic drugs. The Pranksters' experiments with LSD were commonly known as Acid Tests, and they often occurred at large communal gatherings that included a psychedelic light show and the music of the Grateful Dead, a San Francisco-based rock band closely associated with the counterculture. Wolfe's commitment to in-depth ("saturation") reporting is evident in his vivid reconstruction of the Pranksters' lifestyle. In addition to describing their clothing and living conditions, he captures their psychedelic experiences and cognitive reality by using interior monologue, stream of consciousness, repetition, onomatopoeia, typography, and a cornucopia of other techniques that have made *Acid Test* one of Wolfe's most enduring works.

In *Radical Chic and Mau-Mauing the Flak Catchers* (1970) Wolfe continued to profile other "status spheres"—blacks and ethnic groups—as they confronted a white America during a time of racial turbulence and social unrest. "Radical Chic," the more important piece, first appeared as a long essay in *New York* magazine. Wolfe describes and satirizes the evening in which a group of liberal New York socialites and the Black Panthers gathered together at Leonard and Felicia Bernsteins' penthouse apartment for a fund-raiser that would help the twenty-one Panthers who had been arrested for conspiring to blow up five department stores in New York City. Wolfe lampoons the Bernsteins and their liberal friends for their fashionable slumming, mixing with people from a lower socio-economic class and simultaneously congratulating themselves on their concern with less fortunate others. Unlike many other social critics, Wolfe acknowledges the ironic and playful nature of this and other symbolic confrontations of the era. Critics have noted, however, that Wolfe refused to consider the partygoers' political commitments as a bona fide attempt to ameliorate racial differences. While Wolfe attempts to individualize his characters, particularly when he enters their minds and uses interior monologue or stream-of-consciousness in an attempt to portray their subjective reality, he devotes too much attention to describing status details and distinctions. When he describes, for example, the dress and language of the Panthers—a black idiom punctuated with "sees" and "you knows"—they are often reduced to stereotypes and become, in Morris Dickstein's words, "butts of social satire." Wolfe's attempt to acknowledge cultural diversity and pluralism is generally subverted by his tendency to describe all experience using a strikingly similar language that ultimately reveals his own preoccupation with status and power. This is perhaps most evident in works like *The Painted Word* (1975) and *From Bauhaus to Our House* (1981), in which he resorts to consensus history and emphasizes how competition and status jockeying figure as prominently in the world of art as in other arenas of life.

Wolfe avoided these kinds of generalizations when he wrote his most popular work of nonfiction, *The Right Stuff*, which won both the National Book Critics Circles Award and the American Book Award for nonfiction in 1980. As in many other works of literary nonfiction, Wolfe humorously chides reporters for their institutional allegiances and their inability to act independently of one another, a phenomenon commonly known as "pack journalism." The New Journalist, Wolfe would have us believe, is more of a literary cowboy who covers a story on his own idiosyncratic terms and is ultimately privy to a world hidden from less creative journalists. In *The Right Stuff*, for example, Wolfe chronicles the history of the American space program and profiles a group of reticent individualists—test pilots and astronauts—whose private lives have been hidden from public scrutiny. Though Wolfe often deflates his subjects by describing anti-heroic moments—getting an enema, for example—his goal was to write a story that celebrates the ambiguity of American heroism. Wolfe emphasizes his subjects' competitive nature and criticizes them for their unreflective bravery. Yet he also admires some of the vices—drinking, driving fast cars, and chasing women—that are associated with male camaraderie and chauvinism. Wolfe humorously reveals the pilots' success as another form of social climbing and status competition when he describes the rivalries and conflicts both within and between different hierarchal groups: test pilots and astronauts, doctors and astronauts, and among the astronauts themselves. Though Wolfe used in-depth interviews and archival information to personalize and individualize his subjects, he often defines them, perhaps inadvertently, by a few superficial traits and phrases: John Glenn is identified as the "good Presbyterian," for example, and Gus Grissum is frequently referred to as "gruff Gus." As a whole, Wolfe's characters tend to be one-dimensional. This appropriately identifies their own narrow vision and preoccupation with success (as pilots or astronauts), but it also reveals Wolfe's inability to portray his subjects as psychologically individuated selves. Part of this problem resulted from writing about events that occurred between ten and twenty years before *The Right Stuff* was published. Some of his subjects could not recall what they were thinking or how they felt, and others refused to be interviewed. These obstacles reveal how difficult it is for Wolfe and other literary journalists to fully portray the subjective reality of their characters.

After the popular and critical success of *The Right Stuff*, Wolfe focused on writing a novel, *Bonfire of the Vanities*, which was published serially in *Rolling Stone* magazine and later as a book in 1987. The novel focuses on the fall of Sherman McCoy, a smug Yale graduate and wealthy Wall Street bond trader, who finds himself in circumstances he cannot control when he is accused of killing Henry Lamb, a young black man, in a hit-and-run accident in the Bronx. The incident becomes a preoccupation for a large ensemble of characters, including an alcoholic journalist, a black minister, and a district attorney running for re-election, who use it as a vehicle to achieve either personal or political success. Wolfe's extensive research and "legwork"—riding the Bronx subway and investigating the Bronx court system—resulted in a novel characterized by reportorial authenticity and the realistic social details of an elaborately plotted Dickensian novel. Despite its panoramic sweep and genuine and often humorous dialogue, his self-serving and unlikable characters are too narrowly drawn and often defined almost exclusively by their status consciousness, social maneuvering, and the stereotypes associated with specific types of people, such as militant blacks, Jewish politicians, and WASP bond traders. Moreover, Sherman McCoy's ambiguous redemption and the open-ended conclusion suggest that Wolfe could successfully entertain his readers for over six hundred pages but was unable to bring his intricately structured novel to a convincing close.

Sherman McCoy's character seems somewhat reincarnated in the character of Charlie Croker, the aging, arrogant protagonist of Wolfe's novel *A Man in Full*, (1998). Though Wolfe readers have waited over ten years for the new book, which, at 742 pages, is his heftiest, they will find that Wolfe's concerns here are similar to those in *Bonfire*. Both McCoy and Croker are high-flying corporate types who have trouble living within their lives of plenty; racial tension, devoid—as Wolfe will have it in the 1990s, of liberal sentimentality—drives the plot forward, and the unceasing calculation of status is the obsession of every character. As the novel opens, Croker's life of conquest and football-hero machismo is becoming unmanageable: he cannot keep up with the demands of his trophy wife, he needs to keep impressing friends at his Georgia plantation, and his real estate empire is threatened by the bank. The world of Atlanta, in which the novel takes place, is a place where blacks, whites, and Asians co-exist, but it is because of a black Georgia Tech running back's alleged rape of the daughter of one of Atlanta's most prominent businessmen that Croker's luck turns. Ultimately, the football player, Fareek Fanon, finds himself in a California jail—Wolfe's social world distilled into a place where social status is measured completely by male sexual agression. Wolfe seems to see himself more as a sociobiologist at times in *A Man in Full* than as a novelist, and at times his hyper-realistic approach to his characters and scenes can pull them into states of photographic schizophrenia. Vanity, status, and competition are the driving forces behind every character's motives, and in *A Man in Full* America amounts to a very loud collage of vanity, trash, and noise.

Despite the immense popularity of *Bonfire of the Vanities* and *A Man in Full*, some critics are not convinced that they are "serious" works of literature. Wolfe will surely be remembered, of course, as one of America's chief writers of literary nonfiction. In order to be eulogized as a novelist, however, Wolfe must prove he can write about topics other than status and be willing to more thoroughly explore the psychological reality of his subjects.

—James N. Stull, updated by Martha Sutro

WOLFF, Tobias (Jonathan Ansell)

Born: Birmingham, Alabama, 19 June 1945. **Education:** Hill School, 1964; Oxford University, B.A. 1972, M.A. 1975; Stanford University, California, M.A. 1977. **Military Service:** Served in the U.S. Army, 1964-68: lieutenant. **Family:** Married Catherine Dolores Spohn in 1975; two sons and one daughter. **Career:** Jones Lecturer in creative writing, Stanford University (Stegner fellow), 1975-78. Beginning 1980 Peck Professor of English, Syracuse University, New York. **Awards:** National Endowment fellowship, 1978, 1985; Rinehart grant, 1979; O. Henry award, for short story, 1980, 1981, 1985; St. Lawrence award, 1981; Guggenheim fellowship, 1982; PEN/Faulkner award, 1985; Rea award, for short story, 1989; Whiting Foundation award, 1990; Lila Wallace-Reader's Digest award, 1994; Lyndhurst Foundation award, 1994; Esquire-Volvo-Waterstone's award, 1994.

PUBLICATIONS

Short Stories

In the Garden of the North American Martyrs. 1981; as *Hunters in the Snow*, 1982.
The Barracks Thief (novella). 1984.
Back in the World. 1985.
The Night in Question: Stories. 1996.

Other

Ugly Rumours. 1975.
This Boy's Life: A Memoir. 1989.
In Pharaoh's Army: Memories of the Lost War. 1994.
Two Boys and a Girl (for children). 1996.

Editor, *Matters of Life and Death: New American Short Stories.* 1983.
Editor, *The Short Stories of Anton Chekhov.* 1987.
Editor, *Best American Short Stories, 1994.* 1994.
Editor, *The Vintage Book of Contemporary American Short Stories.* 1994.

*

Critical Studies: *Tobias Wolff: A Study of the Short Fiction* by James Hannah, 1996; "Tobias Wolff: Citizens and Outlaws" in *Passion and Craft: Conversations with Notable Writers* edited by Bonnie Lyons and Bill Oliver, 1998; in *Story, Story, Story: Conversations with American Authors* by Jim Schumock, 1999.

*   *   *

Tobias Wolff has probably been most popularly known as the author of the memoir *This Boy's Life* (1989), an account of his youthful struggles with a sadistic stepfather, which was made into a film starring Robert DeNiro and Leonardo DiCaprio. However, his critical reputation rests largely on his three collections of short stories. The first collection, *In the Garden of the North American Martyrs* (1981), was well received by critics, and several stories have become favorites in anthologies read widely by university students. "All my stories are autobiographical," Wolff has said. "In fact, you could say that all of my characters are reflections of myself, in that I share their wish to count for something and their almost complete confusion as to how this is supposed to be done."

The title story of Wolff's first collection centers on a female history professor who goes for a job interview only to find out that she has been invited merely to satisfy an affirmative action requirement. When she presents a public lecture as part of the interview, she ignores a prepared paper and launches into a passionate account of how the Iroquois once captured two Jesuit priests in the area, including graphic descriptions of the tortures they suffered. She quotes one of the priests, who, just before his agonizing death, tells his torturers, "Mend your lives. You have deceived yourselves in the pride of your hearts." When the professorial audience tries to shout her down, she continues to exhort them, turning off her hearing aid so she will not be distracted. "Turn from power to love. Be kind. Do justice. Walk humbly." The story exemplifies what Wolff calls "winging it," which he describes as a "kind of lifting off, letting go, listening to the voice within and speaking with the magic of that voice."

Wolff's most famous example of "winging it" is the concluding story in *In the Garden of the North American Martyrs.* "The Liar" describes a boy similar to the Wolff persona in *This Boy's Life*, who creates his own fictional world. Wolff once told an interviewer, "I was a liar myself when I was a kid. I'm still a liar, really." The title refers to a sixteen-year-old boy whose lying is precipitated by the death of his father, a man who also coped with his fears by telling lies. The story ends with a poetic scene on a bus trip to Los Angeles, during which the boy tells his fellow passengers that he worked with refugees from Tibet. When a woman asks him to speak some Tibetan, the other passengers lean back in their seats and close their eyes while the boy, who knows no Tibetan, sings to them "in what was surely an ancient and holy tongue." The story is a fiction writer's manifesto, a lyrical evocation of the human need to create an imaginative reality that binds people together even as it asserts one's unique identity.

The Barracks Thief (1984), Wolff's only novel, focuses on three young soldiers on an American military base trying to find ways to identify themselves as men and bond with each other in a world dominated by stereotyped masculine roles. Treated as children by the more experienced soldiers, the three feel the need to prove themselves. However, a showdown over a threatened ammunition dump, an encounter with a homosexual, and a beating for stealing a wallet provide the vehicles for Wolff's suggestion that what it means to be a "man among men" is complex and always potentially ironic. The book received little attention until it won the PEN/Faulkner Award for fiction in 1985, after which it was praised as an important moral drama about the Vietnam era.

In Wolff's second collection of stories, *Back in the World* (1985), "Soldier's Joy" focuses on the search for camaraderie in the army, with one character insisting that the Vietnam War was a fulfilling experience: it provided a home where he felt he was with friends. Being back in the states ("back in the world"), he says, lacks order or meaning. Wolff has said that the final story in the collection, "The Rich Brother" (also frequently anthologized), is the closest thing to a fable that he has ever written. In the story, the prodigal brother Donald is humane and generous but a financial failure; older brother Pete is successful but unfeeling and dissatisfied. Pete comes to rescue Donald as he has before, but he gives up on him when Donald once again throws away his money on foolish fantasies and the needs of others. However, the story ends with a redemptive change of heart. Writer Russell Banks has called the story a "small classic about family life in America, what's left of it."

Wolff's collection *The Night in Question* (1996), which received stronger reviews than *Back in the World,* once more includes stories about the challenge of being a buddy in the Vietnam War, as well as such lyrical pieces as "Powder," in which a boy feels safe with his father who drives him safely home after a snow storm. In "Firelight" Wolff continues to explore a favorite theme, the substitution of imaginative reality for an unsatisfactory or unworthy real one. A boy and his mother play fantasy shopping games, trying on clothes they know they cannot afford. When the boy finds out his mother once turned down a marriage proposal from an all-American football player, he scolds her, complaining that they could be rich now.

This Boy's Life ends with Wolff's escape from his harsh stepfather by falsifying records to get into a prep school. At the beginning of Wolff's second memoir, *In Pharaoh's Army: Memories of the Lost War* (1994), Wolff is kicked out of the school when his charade is discovered, and he becomes a lieutenant in Vietnam.

Rather than recounting firefights, however, Wolff focuses on mundane but revealing realities of war. In "Thanksgiving Special" he steals a television so he can watch a double episode of "Bonanza" in color. At the end of the book, Wolff is studying at Oxford, preparing himself to become a man of letters that he indeed became.

—Charles E. May

WOOLSON, Constance Fenimore

Born: Claremont, New Hampshire, 5 March 1840; while still an infant moved with her family to Cleveland. **Education:** Miss Hayden's School, Cleveland, and the Cleveland Female Seminary; Madame Chegaray's School, New York, graduated 1858. **Career:** Regular contributor to *Harper's, Atlantic Monthly,* and other periodicals. Lived in Cleveland after 1858, and for part of each year in the Carolinas and Florida, 1873-79; lived in Italy, 1879-83, England, 1883-86, Florence, 1887-89, Oxford, 1891-93, and Venice, 1893-94. Close friend of Henry James from 1880. **Died:** 24 January 1894.

PUBLICATIONS

Collections

The Old Stone House (for children). 1872.
Castle Nowhere: Lake-Country Sketches. 1875.
Rodman the Keeper: Southern Sketches. 1880.
Anne. 1882.
For the Major. 1883.
East Angels. 1886.
Jupiter Lights. 1889.
Horace Chase. 1894.
The Front Yard and Other Italian Stories. 1895.
Dorothy and Other Italian Stories. 1896.

Poetry

Two Women: 1862. 1877.

Other

Mentone, Cairo, and Cob. 1895.

*

Bibliography: by Rayburn S. Moore, in *A Bibliographical Guide to Midwestern Literature* edited by Gerald Nemanic, 1981.

Critical Studies: *Woolson: Literary Pioneer* by John D. Kern, 1934; *Henry James: The Conquest of London 1870-1881,* and *Henry James: The Middle Years 1882-1895* both by Leon Edel, 1962; *Woolson* by Rayburn S. Moore, 1963; "'Always, Your Attached Friend': The Unpublished Letters of Constance Fenimore Woolson to John and Clara Hay" by Alice Hall Petry, in *Books at Brown,* vols. 29-30, 1982; "In Anticipation of the Fiftieth Anniversary of Woolson House," in *Legacy,* Fall 1985, "'Miss Grief'

by Constance Fenimore Woolson" in *Legacy,* Spring 1987, and *Constance Fenimore Woolson: The Grief of Artistry,* 1989, all by Cheryl B. Torsney; "Constance Fenimore Woolson and the Genre of Regional Fiction" by Harry Forrest Lupold, in *Ohioana Quarterly,* Winter 1986; "Henry James and the Artist-Heroine in the Tales of Constance Fenimore Woolson" by Mary P. Edwards Kitterman, in *Nineteenth-Century Women Writers of the English-Speaking World* edited by Rhoda B. Nathan, 1986; "Women Artists As Exiles in the Fiction of Constance Fenimore Woolson" by Joan Myers Weimer, in *Legacy,* Fall 1986; "Constance Woolson's Southern Sketches" by Sharon L. Dean in *Southern Studies,* Fall 1986; "Island Fortresses: The Landscape of the Imagination in the Great Lakes Fiction of Constance Fenimore Woolson" by Victoria Brehm, in *American Literary Realism,* Spring 1990.

* * *

Although Constance Fenimore Woolson contributed verse to magazines and published a long poem, wrote a children's story, and collected some of her travel sketches for a volume that appeared posthumously, she was best known in her own day as a writer of fiction, and to one Boston critic at least as the "novelist laureate" of America. Such a characterization is likely to strike present-day readers as a bit off the mark, but in the late nineteenth century her stories and novels struck many reviewers and critics, including **Henry James**, as important contributions to literature.

Even readers of the late twentieth century must concede that Woolson made a contribution to the short fiction of her period. Her best stories—"The Lady of Little Fishing," "Rodman the Keeper," "King David," "The Front Yard," and "A Transplanted Boy," among others—demonstrate her capacity to deal with scenes as varied as the Great Lakes country, the South, and Europe with universally valid characters. She was not an innovator in technique, but her best tales suggest that she was mindful of the work of George Eliot, Turgenev, and Henry James.

As a novelist she was less successful. Though the scenes and characters are, as in the short stories, handled ably, the structure of her novels (except *Horace Chase*) seems episodic and infrequently functional. This weakness in structure is ironically pointed up by her success with *For the Major,* her only novella, a minor classic in many ways, and her most successful sustained piece of fiction. Still, each novel has its individual merits and *East Angels,* as James maintained in *Harper's Weekly* in 1887, "is a performance which does Miss Woolson the highest honour."

Her best work belongs to the development of realism in America, as regards both local color and the psychological analysis of character, and it offers, as I have noted in *Constance Fenimore Woolson,* "a sympathetic understanding and treatment of character in authentic surroundings by one whose vision was broad enough and whose insight was deep enough to include not only her own country but Europe as well."

—Rayburn S. Moore

WRIGHT, James (Arlington)

Born: Martins Ferry, Ohio, 13 December 1927. **Education:** Kenyon College, Gambier, Ohio, B.A. 1952; University of Vienna

(Fulbright Fellow), 1953; University of Washington, Seattle, M.A. 1954, Ph.D. 1959. **Family:** Married Edith Anne Runk; two sons from previous marriage. **Career:** Teacher at University of Minnesota, Minneapolis, 1957-64, Macalaster College, St. Paul, Minnesota, 1963-65, and Hunter College, New York City, 1966-80. **Awards:** American Academy grant, 1959; Guggenheim fellowships, 1964, 1978; Brandeis University Creative Arts award, 1970; Academy of American Poets fellowship, 1971; Melville Cane award, 1972; Pulitzer prize, 1972. **Member:** American Academy, 1974. **Died:** 25 March 1980.

PUBLICATIONS

Collections

Collected Prose, edited by Annie Wright. 1982.

Poetry

The Green Wall. 1957.
Saint Judas. 1959.
The Lion Tail and Eyes: Poems Written out of Laziness and Silence, with Robert Bly and William Duffy. 1962.
The Branch Will Not Break. 1963.
Shall We Gather at the River. 1968.
Collected Poems. 1971.
Two Citizens. 1974.
Moments of the Italian Summer. 1976.
Old Booksellers and Other Poems. 1976.
To a Blossoming Pear Tree. 1977.
The Journey. 1981.
This Journey. 1982.
The Temple in Nimes. 1982.

Other

The Summers of James and Annie Wright. 1980.
With the Delicacy and Strength of Lace: Letters between Leslie Marmon Silko and Wright, edited by Annie Wright. 1986.

Editor and Translator, *Poems,* by Hermann Hesse. 1970.

Translator, with Robert Bly, *Twenty Poems of Georg Trakl.* 1961.
Translator, with Robert Bly and John Knoepfle, *Twenty Poems of Cesar Vallejo.* 1962.
Translator, *The Rider on the White Horse,* by Theodor Storm. 1964.
Translator, with Robert Bly, *Twenty Poems of Pablo Neruda.* 1968.
Translator, with Robert Bly and John Knoepfle, *Neruda and Vallejo: Selected Poems.* 1971.

*

Bibliography: "Wright: A Checklist" by Belle M. McMaster, in *Bulletin of Bibliography 31,* 1974; *James Wright: An Annotated Secondary Bibliography* by James B. Keegan, 1994.

Critical Studies: *Four Poets and the Emotive Imagination* by George S. Lensing and Ronald Moran, 1976; "Wright Issue" of *Ironwood 10,* 1977; *The Pure Clear Word: Essays on the Poetry of Wright* edited by Dave Smith, 1982; "How Dignified Can We Be?" by Laurel Speer, in *Black Warrior Review,* Spring 1989; "James Wright at Kenyon" by E.L. Doctrow, in *Gettysburg Review,* Winter 1990; "A Special Feature on James Wright," in *Gettysburg Review,* Winter 1990; *The Poetry of James Wright* by Andrew Elkins, 1991; "Give-Down and Outrage: The Poetry of the Last Straw" by James Dickey, in *Southern Review,* Spring 1991; "Wright's Lyricism" by Nathan A. Scott, Jr., in *Southern Review,* Spring 1991; "Protest and the Individual Talents of Three Black Novelists" by Kalu Ogbaa, in *College Language Association Journal,* December 1991; "A Listening to Walt Whitman and James Wright" by George Yatchisin, in *Walt Whitman Quarterly Review,* Spring 1992; *A Dangerously Religious Man: The Mystic Quest of James Wright* (dissertation) by Richard S. Wilson, 1996; *Three Citizens: Postmodern Identity in the Poetry of Amiri Baraka (Leroi Jones), Adrienne Rich, and James Wright* (dissertation) by Joseph Heithaus, 1996.

*   *   *

James Wright's poems are notable for their range of intense emotions and for the way both form and theme develop in the work. Wright's early style was characteristic of the 1950s in its rhetorical literariness and use of traditional English meters, often with exact rhymes. Titles such as "A Girl in a Window," "To the Ghost of a Kite" were formal too, almost announcing themselves as technical exercises and part of Wright's apprenticeship as a poet. His first book, *The Green Wall,* included the notable and characteristic "On the Skeleton of a Hound":

> Nightfall, that saw the morning-glories float
> Tendril and string against the crumbling wall,
> Nurses him now, his skeleton for grief,
> His locks for comfort curled among the leaf.

That skillfully formed poem, exhibiting a near perfect surface elegance and finish helped Wright in his next book, *Saint Judas,* to advance his impressive range of techniques in order to express the reality of human suffering. "In Shame and Humiliation," "Old Man Drunk," and "At the Executed Murderer's Grave" all express powerful emotions. The biblical Judas, in the title poem of the collection, heading off to commit suicide, runs to the aid of a man set on by a mob:

> Banished from heaven, I found this victim beaten,
> Stripped, kneed, and left to cry. Dropping my rope
> Aside, I ran, ignored the uniforms:
> Then I remembered bread my flesh had eaten,
> The kiss that ate my flesh. Flayed without hope,
> I held the man for nothing in my arms.

A profound, somewhat tortured humanity is to be found throughout Wright's poetry. This was its first appearance and perhaps the most moving of all.

When Wright published his *Collected Poems* in 1971 he interposed a number of translations from Juan Ramon Jiminez, Jorge Guillen, Pablo Neruda, Georg Trakl, Cesar Vallejo, Pedro Salinas, and Goethe between the poems of *Saint Judas* and those of his next book to indicate the introduction of something new in the progression. Wright's knowledge of other languages and his translations from the Spanish of Neruda and Vallejo introduced new rhythms into his poems, extending their tone and feel far beyond the technical restraint of his earlier iambic meters. **Robert Bly**, himself an important translator and a friend of Wright's, published these influential translations during the 1960s. Wright was also to publish a selection from the poems of Hermann Hesse in 1970. The extent to which these translations opened up the forms of American poetry has never properly been acknowledged.

Wright, Bly, and William Duffy each contributed poems to *The Lions Tail and Eyes*. This book demonstrated the development brought about in Wright's poems by his translations and also his use of the so-called "deep-image" style of writing, whereby each poem focused solely on one central image. The poems, reprinted with others in Wright's next book—and surely his very best— *The Branch Will Not Break*, are spare, delicate, original, and sensitive in their use of the new rhythm. As in "Lying in a Hammock at William Duffy's Farm in Pine Island, Minnesota" where the poet meditates on the natural life around him concluding: "I lean back, as the evening darkens and comes on. A chicken hawk floats over, looking for home. I have wasted my life." The mood creates the rhythm and, as a consequence, convinces the reader that the final line is a natural associative conclusion to what has gone before. The poem has what Herbert Read called "organic unity," a quality enabling Wright unobtrusively to express personal feeling, as again in the second part of "Two Hangovers":

In a pine tree,
A few yards away from my window sill,
A brilliant blue jay is springing up and down, up and down,
On a branch.
I laugh, as I see him abandon himself
To entire delight, for he knows as well as I do
That the branch will not break.

Nothing could be further from the formal grandeur of Wright's first book. Wright had learned how to pare away inessential verbiage to arrive at the heart of the poem, the essence of what should be expressed. The book includes poems of subtle political comment, and also poems on the suffering of individuals; but it is chiefly memorable for an overall acceptance of life, whereby suffering is complemented by happiness.

If *The Branch Will Not Break* is about acceptance and the possibility of happiness, *Shall We Gather at the River*, Wright's next book, returns anew to the theme of isolation and unhappiness, expressed this time in more fluid organic rhythms. Old people, the poor, mourners, prostitutes, an illiterate black soldier hiding in a church, lone animals such as a brown cricket and a dead swan, are the subjects of the poems. The book seems to come out of a period of trouble, and it expresses isolation honestly, without self-consciousness and in a profoundly moving way. Suffering is accepted with equanimity, even quiet humor, in the title "In Terror of Hospital Bills," a poem containing the affirmation "But my life was never so precious / To me as now."

Wright's *Collected Poems* marked him out as one of the most original contemporary American poets. His ability to express the deepest emotions in a simple manner was a welcome antidote to the shrill imitators of "confessional poetry" much in evidence at the time. The books after the *Collected Poems: Two Citizens, To a Blossoming Pear Tree*, and *This Journey* (posthumously published after his early death in 1980), continued to express in fluid rhythms and deceptively unadorned language the deepest human emotions. But, although each contained fine poems, it is true to say that none exceeded the excellence of *The Branch Will Not Break*. This is not to say that Wright's powers declined. To the end his poems celebrate beauty, the animal kingdom, landscape, places, people: Wright's warmth and empathy for isolated individuals or animals are continually present.

One other posthumous publication that should not be overlooked is Wright's *Collected Prose* edited by his widow Annie Wright. This book is essential reading for anyone who wants to find out more about the man who wrote the poems. It reveals Wright as a first-rate critical intelligence, and contains essays and reviews on Dickens, **Walt Whitman**, **Gary Snyder**, **Robert Penn Warren**, Thomas Hardy, Georg Trakl, **Robert Frost**, and many other writers. It also includes "Some Notes on Chinese Poetry," the text of a sermon, and four interviews. In the 1972 interview with Michael Andre, Wright talks of the poet Edward Thomas: "A holy man, I believe, a saintly man, Edward Thomas, without any great public reputation, but one of the secret spirits who help keep us alive . . . This is all we have, is it not? We have our internal life. Our external life is usually asinine . . . ." Words that we may equally well apply to the poetry of Wright himself, cutting, as it so often does, through all the niceties of literature to speak on our behalf of the essential things of life.

—Jonathan Barker

WRIGHT, Richard (Nathaniel)

Born: Near Natchez, Mississippi, 4 September 1908; brought up in an orphanage. **Education:** Local schools through junior high school. **Family:** Married 1) Rose Dhima Meadman in 1938; 2) Ellen Poplar; two daughters. **Career:** Worked in a post office in Memphis, Tennessee, at age 15; later moved to New York; worked for Federal Writers Project, 1937, and Federal Negro Theatre Project; Harlem editor, *Daily Worker,* New York; lived in Paris from 1947. **Awards:** Guggenheim fellowship, 1939; Spingarn medal, 1941. **Member:** Communist Party, 1932-44. **Died:** 28 November 1960.

PUBLICATIONS

Collections

The Wright Reader, edited by Ellen Wright and Michel Fabre. 1978.

Short Stories

Uncle Tom's Children: Four Novellas. 1938; augmented edition, 1940.
Eight Men. 1961.
The Man Who Lived Underground (story; bilingual edition), translated by Claude Edmonde Magny, edited by Michel Fabre. 1971.

Novels

Native Son. 1940.
The Outsider. 1953.

Savage Holiday. 1954.
The Long Dream. 1958.
Lawd Today. 1963.

Plays

Native Son (The Biography of a Young American), with Paul Green, from the novel by Wright (produced 1941). 1941; revised version, 1980.
Daddy Goodness, from a play by Louis Sapin (produced 1968).

Screenplay: *Native Son,* 1951.

Other

How Bigger Was Born: The Story of "Native Son." 1940.
The Negro and Parkway Community House. 1941.
Twelve Million Black Voices: A Folk History of the Negro in the United States. 1941.
Black Boy: A Record of Childhood and Youth. 1945.
Black Power: A Record of Reactions in a Land of Pathos. 1954.
Bandoeng: 1.500.000.000 Hommes, translated by Hélène Claireau. 1955; as *The Color Curtain: A Report on the Bandung Conference,* 1956.
Pagan Spain. 1957.
White Man, Listen! 1957.
Letters to Joe C. Brown, edited by Thomas Knipp. 1968.
American Hunger (autobiography). 1977.

*

Bibliography: *Wright: A Primary Bibliography* by Charles T. Davis and Michel Fabre, 1982; *A Wright Bibliography: Fifty Years of Criticism and Commentary, 1933-1983* by Keneth Kinnamon, 1988.

Critical Studies: *Wright: A Biography* by Constance Webb, 1968; *Wright* by Robert Bone, 1969; *The Art of Wright* by Edward Margolies, 1969; *The Most Native of Sons: A Biography of Wright* by John A. Williams, 1970; *Twentieth-Century Interpretations of Native Son* edited by Houston A. Baker, Jr., 1972; *The Emergence of Wright: A Study of Literature and Society,* 1972, *New Essays on Native Son,* 1990, and "How Native Son Was Born," in *Writing the American Classics* edited by James Barbour and Tom Quirk, 1990, all by Keneth Kinnamon; *Wright* by David Bakish, 1973; *The Unfinished Quest of Wright* by Michel Fabre, translated by Isabel Barzun, 1973, *The World of Wright,* 1985, and *Wright: Books and Writers,* 1990, both by Fabre; *Wright: Impressions and Perspectives* edited by David Ray and Robert M. Farnsworth, 1973; *Wright's Hero: The Faces of a Rebel-Victim* by Katherine Fishburn, 1977; *Wright: The Critical Reception* edited by John M. Reilly, 1978; *Rebels and Victims: The Fiction of Wright and Bernard Malamud* by Evelyn Gross Avery, 1979; *Wright* by Robert Felgar, 1980; *Wright: Ordeal of a Native Son* by Addison Gayle, Jr., 1980; *The Daemonic Genius of Wright* by Margaret Walker, 1982; *Critical Essays on Wright* edited by Yoshinobu Hakutani, 1982; *Wright: A Collection of Critical Essays* edited by Richard Macksey and Frank E. Moorer, 1984; *Wright's Art of Tragedy* by Joyce Ann Joyce, 1986; *Wright,* 1987, *Wright's Native Son,* 1988, and *Bigger Thomas,* 1990, all edited by Harold Bloom; *Wright, Daemonic Genius* by Margaret Walker, 1988; *Voice of a*

Native Son: The Poetics of Wright by Eugene E. Miller, 1990; *Telling Lies in Modern American Autobiography* by Timothy Dow Adams, 1990; *Creative Revolt: A Study of Wright, Ellison, and Dostoevsky* by Michael F. Lynch, 1990; "Negating the Negation As a Form of Affirmation in Minority Discourse: The Construction of Richard Wright As Subject" by Abdul R. JanMohamed, in *The Nature and Context of Minority Discourse* edited by JanMohamed and David Lloyd, 1990; *Native Son: The Emergence of a New Black Hero* by Robert Butler, 1991; *Politics in the African American Novel: James Weldon Johnson, W.E.B. Du Bois, Richard Wright, and Ralph Ellison* by Richard Kostelanetz, 1991; "On Richard Wright's *Native Son*" by Caesar R. Blake, in *Rough Justice: Essays on Crime in Literature* edited by M. L. Friedland, 1991; "Beneath My Father's Name" by James M. Cox, in *Home Ground: Southern Autobiography* edited and introduced by J. Bill Berry, 1991; "Rape and Resignation: Silencing the Victim in the Novels of Morrison and Wright" by Kimberly Drake, in *Lit: Literature Interpretation Theory,* 1995, pp. 63-72; "Wright's *Native Son*" by Sharon Hamilton, in *Explicator,* Summer 1997, pp. 227-29.

*   *   *

Richard Wright's career can be described in terms of three reputations he has earned: the realist protesting racial oppression, the typifier of the experience of entry into modern history, and the author who makes his themes seem inevitable by his artistry. In the best late-twentieth-century criticism these three reputations coalesce, and the different levels of significance in his writing are explored. But while Wright was alive the fact of his race and his dissent from the culture of his native land, first as radical, then as expatriate, concentrated attention upon the thematic burden of his works.

Wright served a literary apprenticeship made harsh because of his poverty and the restrictions of Jim Crow laws but otherwise similar to other American authors'; yet he seemed to leap into literary prominence when his collection of stories, *Uncle Tom's Children,* won first prize in a contest sponsored by *Story* magazine for writers on the Federal Writers Project. The four novellas in that volume are arranged to depict the struggles of Southern black peasants in resistance to a caste system dependent upon lynch violence for its sanction and efficacy. For most reviewers the book was a shocking rendition of the facts of racial conflict in an affecting narrative, its distinction not so much that the author was black, though reviews made as much of that as they did of the prize the book had won, but rather that *Uncle Tom's Children* told its stories from within the black experience. The book brought news that blacks could effectively articulate their victimization.

As though to match horror with horror, Wright's first published novel, *Native Son,* carried the story of racial conflict to the North where Bigger Thomas, Chicago-born and bred, acts out his role in the American racial drama by his murder of a white woman. At the risk of fulfilling racist expectations in his portrayal of Bigger, Wright completed his inversion of the stereotype of the black victim by showing violence as the necessary prelude to self-realization for his protagonist. Again Wright had written a book that brought news to its audience; *Native Son* was a cautionary tale for whites.

With the popular success of *Native Son* Wright became a public figure called upon to lecture and write as a spokesman for African Americans. He was qualified for the role not only by literary success but also by a childhood in Mississippi and an adulthood in Northern cities similar in pattern to the life of thousands of other black migrants, so it was appropriate that he organize that experience in literature: first with *Twelve Million Black Voices,* a documentary history of black peasants transplanted into urban life told in the poetic prose of a collective first-person narration, and then with his own autobiography, *Black Boy.*

It is unusual for a person not yet forty to write an autobiography and to end the story even before he had established himself in adulthood, but Wright justifies his book by presenting it as at once his own and his people's story. For many other blacks this latter point was dubious. They charged that he had been extremely selective by omitting any positive portrayal of black cultural and family life. The point has justice, but *Black Boy* enhanced Wright's reputation as the realist who showed more profoundly than anyone before him the human waste that is the heritage of North American slavery.

There can be no doubt Wright felt personally threatened by racism in a way that literary success could not alleviate. It was the motive for his move to Paris in 1947. Though objectively different, Wright's experience in the Communist Party (described in a portion of the original manuscript of *Black Boy,* cut from the book on advice of editors, published separately in 1944, and issued in the excised section of autobiography titled *American Hunger* in 1977) seems to have been psychologically as problematic as racism, so that when he exiled himself from America he was also without the political commitment that had informed his work until 1944.

The first book he wrote in exile enhanced Wright's second reputation. *The Outsider* portentously invites reading as philosophical fiction. Cross Damon seizes upon the accident of a false report of his death to embark upon a life free of contingency, where action is self-sanctioned and alienation grants a perception of mankind in a world of dead myths. Cross, however, can neither escape anguish nor achieve disalienation in his version of freedom. In that respect his problem reflects the author's. Wright described himself in publicity for the novel as a man without ideological burdens for the first time in his life, but his own characteristic feeling of alienation produced an interesting novel undermined by its nihilism.

Wright needed new premises for his writing and found them in the Third World. The four nonfictional books he published from 1954 to 1957 derive from Wright's belief that his own experience was being repeated in the history of Africans and Asians moving from a pre-industrial, traditional society into a modern, mass world. Out of this felt congruity he wrote accounts of Ghana, the Bandung Conference, Spain—which represented the world not yet touched by modernism—and the lectures published as *White Man, Listen!* All blend reportage and subjective response to show Wright looking at, feeling with the world in change, and defining himself again as typical, though this time on a worldwide stage.

Wright's exile has sometimes been described as though it were the fag end of his career. In fact, it was a creative period twice as long as he had in the United States. Besides his nonfictional reports, he published three novels and compiled a collection of short stories, *Eight Men,* issued posthumously. One of the novels, *Savage Holiday,* extends Wright's interest in extreme narrative situations to the plight of a white man trapped by psychosis and an accidental death for which he feels responsible. *The Long Dream,* meant to open a trilogy tracing the movement of a young man from Mississippi into life in Europe, is a tightly written *Bildungsroman* neatly synthesizing Wright's conception of the psychological trauma of social experience in the person of "Fish" Tucker.

None of Wright's exile writings, however, received the critical or popular acclaim of his first works. There may be a number of explanations for this, besides the possibility of their lesser quality, but a leading reason for the slump in his popular reputation must be that he no longer wrote as the realistic bringer of news about America and that his performance in the role of typifier of modern life had less authority than the writing by acknowledged "experts." Nevertheless, the exile works alert us to the importance of Wright as an artist.

Examining *The Outsider* and *Savage Holiday,* for instance, we find that their structures are inversions and parodies of the thriller genre, that the expressionistic parable "The Man Who Lived Underground," as well as the stories in *Eight Men,* include experiments in narrative stripped down to bare dialogue. Intrigued by these findings, we return to the early writings and find that they, too, are constructed so that transgression of the conventions of genre constitute meaning, with imagery and controlled narrative voice accounting for the impact of such stories as *Native Son* which we read at first without awareness of literary craft, and that the mediations of ideology in *Uncle Tom's Children* and the portrait of the artist in *Black Boy* are masterfully subordinated in character and plot. In short, we complete the survey of Wright's career by recognizing that the themes that won him fame as a realist and attention as an intellectual are the products of art. So, now we are ready to study Richard Wright in earnest.

—John M. Reilly

See the essay on *Native Son.*

WYLIE, Elinor (Morton)

Born: Elinor Hoyt, Somerville, New Jersey, 7 September 1885. **Education:** Miss Baldwin's School, Bryn Mawr, Pennsylvania, 1893-97; Mrs. Flint's School, 1897-1901, and Holton-Arms School, 1901-04, both Washington, D.C. **Family:** Married 1) Philip Hichborn in 1906 (died 1912), one son; 2) Horace Wylie in 1916 (separated 1921; divorced 1923), one son; 3) William Rose Benét, in 1923. Eloped with Horace Wylie in 1910, and moved with him to England as Mr. and Mrs. Waring; returned to the United States in 1915; moved to New York, 1921. **Career:** Poetry editor, *Vanity Fair,* New York, 1923-25; editor, *Literary Guild,* New York, 1926-28; contributing editor, *New Republic,* New York, 1926-28. **Awards:** Julia Ellsworth Ford prize, 1921. **Died:** 16 December 1928.

PUBLICATIONS

Collections

Collected Poems, edited by William Rose Benét. 1932.
Collected Prose. 1933.

Poetry

Incidental Numbers. 1912.
Nets to Catch the Wind. 1921.
Black Armour. 1923.

Angels and Earthly Creatures (collection). 1929.
Nadir. 1937.
Lust Poems, edited by Jane D. Wise. 1943.

Fiction

Jennifer Lorn: A Sedate Extravaganza. 1923.
The Venetian Glass Nephew. 1925.
The Orphan Angel. 1926; as *Mortal Image,* 1927.
Mr. Hodge and Mr. Hazard. 1928.

*

Bibliography: "Elinor Wylie: A Bibliography" by Kathryn Hilt, in *Bulletin of Bibliography,* March 1985; *Bibliography of American Literature,* vol. 9: *Edward Noyles Westcott to Elinor Wylie* compiled by Jacob Blanck, edited by Michael Winship, 1991.

Critical Studies: *Wylie: The Portrait of an Unknown Lady* by Nancy Hoyt, 1935; *Wylie* by Thomas A. Gray, 1969; *Wylie, A Life Apart: A Biography* by Stanley Olson, 1979; "Elinor Wylie, Edna St. Vincent Millay, and the Elizabethan Sonnet Tradition" by Judith Farr, in *Poetic Traditions of the English Renaissance* edited by Maynard Mack and George deForest Lord, 1982; *The Life and Art of Wylie* by Judith Farr, 1983; "Amatory Sonnet Sequences and the Female Perspective of Elinor Wylie and Edna St. Vincent Millay" by Phyllis M. Jones, in *Women's Studies,* vol. 10, 1983; "Cabell As Prospero, Wylie As Miranda in Richmond-in-Virginia" by Edgar E. Macdonald, in *Kalki,* vol. 8, 1983; "Wylie's 'Beauty'" by Thomas Allan Hoagwood, in *Explicator,* Fall 1984, "Wylie's 'The Crooked Stick'" by Hoagwood, in *Explicator,* Spring 1986, and "'Wild Peaches': Landscapes of Desire and Deprivation" by Hoagwood and Anna Shannon Elfenbein, in *Women's Studies,* vol. 15, 1988.

*   *   *

Elinor Wylie's prestigious social background, striking personality, beauty, elegance, and conversational gifts, with the romantic aura of her daring break with conventional society when she eloped with Horace Wylie, made her a symbolic figure to many persons caught up in the "American poetic renaissance." Consequently, judgments of her writings were for some years infused with feelings about the writer. Thomas A. Gray's monograph of 1969 discusses widely differing views of her achievement.

In the essay "Jewelled Bindings" (1923), Wylie saw herself and a few other contemporary lyric poets as "enchanted by a midas-touch or a colder silver madness into workers in metal and glass . . . in crisp and sharp-edged forms." They choose "short lines, clear small stanzas, brilliant and compact." Such standards produced her most widely known poems: the 3-quatrain "Let No Charitable Hope" that climaxes with "In masks outrageous and austere / The years go by in single file; But none has merited any fear, / And none has quite escaped my smile"; "The Eagle and the Mole," with its fastidious trimeter: "Avoid the reeking herd . . . "; the art-for-art's-sake poem "Say not of Beauty she is good, / Or aught but beautiful"; and the exquisite "Velvet Shoes": "Let us walk in the white snow / In a soundless space."

This preference for the delicately sensuous or even impalpable characterized many of her poems—"I love the look, austere, immaculate, / Of landscapes drawn in pearly monotones"—and her first two "novels." *Jennifer Lorn: A Sedate Extravaganza* appealed to a public that was seeking relief from the ugly realities. Set in the late eighteenth century in the realms of aristocracy and wealth in England and India, it is a long catalogue of lovely, delicate objects; what plot it has concerns the fragile, fainting Jennifer and—the spine of the story—her husband Gerald, the exact, cool aesthete. It has been compared to a tapestry, and among the mille fleurs are many phrases and lines from eighteenth-century literature. Wylie's wide reading in this period showed itself also in the amusing *The Venetian Glass Nephew.* Her long and perhaps abnormal admiration for Shelley brought about *The Orphan Angel,* in which the libertarian poet is rescued from drowning and accompanies a Yankee sailor to America and across the continent. This trend toward more realistic treatment continued in *Mr. Hodge and Mr. Hazard,* a satirical allegory on the stifling of the late romantics by the Victorians.

Mary Colum, who described Wylie as "one of the few important women poets in any literature," observes, "She seemed to write little out of a mood or out of a passing emotion, but nearly always out of complex thought (*Life and the Dream,* 1947). Many found her poems cold; the fastidious speaker seeks isolation and death. A last group of sonnets, however, shows a capacity for love: "And so forget to weep, forget to grieve, / And wake, and touch each other's hands, and turn / Upon a bed of juniper and fern." Another critic found her not a "great" poet but a "rare" poet: "Refinement is her essential characteristic as an artist."

—Alice R. Bensen

Y-Z

YERBY, Frank (Garvin)

Born: Augusta, Georgia, 5 September 1916. **Education:** Paine College, Augusta, A.B., 1937; Fisk University, Nashville, Tennessee, M.A., 1938; University of Chicago, 1939. **Family:** Married 1) Flora Helen Claire Williams in 1941 (divorced), two sons and two daughters; 2) Blanca Calle Perez in 1956. **Career:** Instructor at Florida Agricultural and Mechanical College, Tallahassee, 1938-39, and Southern University and A&M College, Baton Rouge, Louisiana, 1939-41; laboratory technician, Ford Motor Company, Dearborn, Michigan, 1941-44; Magnaflux inspector, Ranger (Fairchild) Aircraft, Jamaica, New York, 1944-45; full-time writer from 1945; moved to Madrid, Spain, 1954. **Awards:** O. Henry award, 1944. **Died:** Madrid, Spain, 29 November 1991.

PUBLICATIONS

Fiction

The Foxes of Harrow. 1946.
The Vixens. 1947.
The Golden Hawk. 1948.
Pride's Castle. 1949.
Floodtide. 1950.
A Woman Called Fancy. 1951.
The Saracen Blade. 1952.
The Devil's Laughter. 1953.
Benton's Row. 1954.
Bride of Liberty. 1954.
The Treasure of Pleasant Valley. 1955.
Captain Rebel. 1956.
Fairoaks. 1957.
The Serpent and the Staff. 1958.
Jarrett's Jade. 1959.
Gillian. 1960.
The Garfield Honor. 1961.
Griffin's Way. 1962.
The Old Gods Laugh: A Modern Romance. 1964.
An Odor of Sanctity. 1965.
Goat Song: A Novel of Ancient Greece. 1967.
Judas, My Brother: The Story of the Thirteenth Disciple. 1969.
Speak Now. 1969.
The Dahomean. 1971; in England as *The Man from Dahomey,* 1971.
The Girl from Storyville: A Victorian Novel. 1972.
The Voyage Unplanned. 1974.
Tobias and the Angel. 1975.
A Rose for Ana Maria. 1976.
Hail the Conquering Hero. 1977.
A Darkness at Ingraham's Crest. 1979.
Western: A Saga of the Great Plains. 1982.
Devilseed. 1984.
McKenzie's Hundred. 1985.

*

Critical Studies: "The Guilt of the Victim: Racial Themes in Some Yerby Novels" by Jack B. Moore, in *Journal of Popular Culture,* Spring 1975; "A Harrowing Experience: Frank Yerby's First Novel to Film" by Phyllis R. Klotman, in *College Language Association Journal* vol. 31, no. 2, 1987; "An Interview with Frank Garvin Yerby" by James L. Hill, in *Resources for American Literary Study,* 1995, pp. 206-39.

*   *   *

Readers of his many best-selling romances are still amazed to discover that Frank Yerby began his career as a militant writer of black protest fiction. Perhaps a more surprising activity of his early years was his poetry writing. The careful and painstaking construction of sonnets does not seem a practice this supposedly inartistic teller of racy, swashbuckling tales would spend much time on. But Yerby was a writer and a person filled with curious complexities, and the more one studies his career, the more one observes a fascinating and paradoxical phenomenon.

His first published short stories in the 1940s were outspoken and bitter works about the predicament of contemporary black Americans. "Homecoming" (*Common Ground,* 1946) ironically portrays the return to his home in the rural South of a young black veteran who has lost a leg defending democracy. His white neighbors view him as just another "uppity nigger" too big for his britches, and instead of receiving a hero's welcome he is almost lynched. "Health Card" (*Harper's,* May 1944), another early story, won an O. Henry Award. The work relates the humiliation a black soldier and his wife are forced to face in the South during World War II: it is assumed in the camp town where the protagonist is stationed that any black woman seen with a black man is probably a whore needing a "health card."

Around the time World War II ended, Yerby's life as a writer took a totally unpredictable turn. He had written an apparently realistic novel about black life but no publisher was interested in it. And so, according to a very cynical article he wrote for *Harper's* in 1959, he set out, quite coolly and rationally, to become a popular author. He studied those novels that had high sales over a period of years and derived from them what almost amounts to a formula to ensure popularity. He would create escapist costume novels containing no dominating social problems. He would construct relatively tightly plotted stories about strong, sexy men and vivacious, sexy women.

Obviously, few writers who attempt to write racy, adventurous novels become best-sellers. But Yerby succeeded in an unprecedented fashion. Since his first published novel and smash popular success, *The Foxes of Harrow,* Yerby wrote hit after hit, becoming one of the most popular writers of the 1940s and 1950s. Many of his novels were made into films. Around the mid-1950s his popularity began to decline. It has been claimed that eight of his novels made the best-seller lists, a record that at one time placed him second only to **Mary Roberts Rinehart**, whose popular novels were often serialized in periodicals such as the *Saturday Evening Post*. This achievement seems even more remarkable when it is considered that after the 1960s his novels were rarely reviewed in the major mass-circulation magazines. The audience he built up apparently needed no stimulation beyond his books themselves.

The few critics who have taken his work seriously point out that he wrote something closer to anti-romance than romance. Both his heroes and heroines are more apt to be cunning opportunists than virtuous aristocrats. The fantasy worlds in which his characters operate—the Spanish Main, the Holy Land, the reconstruction South—are rather dirty and unglamorous places as Yerby describes them. Moreover, the frequently stated charge that he had turned his back on his race (in *Anger and Beyond,* for example, **Saunders Redding** claims that in ignoring his racial heritage Yerby was revealing "pathological overtones" in his fiction) is absolutely false. In many of his most popular novels, such as *Griffin's Way* or *A Woman Called Fancy,* Yerby dealt quite accurately with the oppressive treatment of blacks in the South. *A Darkness at Ingraham's Crest* not only attacks slavery but presents an aristocratic African hero, Hwesu ("Wes"), who views and treats most Southern whites as uncivilized savages. *McKenzie's Hundred* upends a number of Civil War myths, depicting many members of the Southern gentry as cowards or louts with barnyard sexual appetites and reports in detail on the infamous New York City Draft Riots of 1863, in which free blacks including women and children were hounded and slaughtered by rampaging whites. The novel's hero, Rose McKenzie, rambles far from the traditional pedestal of Southern womanhood and romps lustily like a picaro from battle camp to bedroom with great spirit, though not too much intelligence, among mainly doltish or brutal males. In his later years, Yerby differentiated between his serious works (such as *Speak Now*) and his entertainments (practically any of his early hits) and claimed that he was going to concentrate on serious fiction. Certainly his sardonic and academic "A Note to the Reader" prefacing *A Darkness at Ingraham's Crest* openly declares the book's political message that slavery in the South was more an absolute evil than the crimes of Nazi Germany.

The distinction between his serious and entertaining work seems something of an apology, however, and perhaps an unnecessary one. Though his characterizations are rarely subtle and sometimes it is difficult to determine what is parodic and what is tritely formulaic in his dialogue and plotting, for several decades Yerby was the most popular novelist in America addressing the racial theme. In all, he wrote thirty-three novels during the course of his career. From the mid-1940s to the mid-1950s, he turned out approximately one novel a year, with his total book sales topping sixty-two million copies. On November 29, 1991, Yerby died of heart failure in Madrid, Spain, at the age of 76. His death went largely unnoticed. This was due in part to the fact that his wife kept the news of her husband's death secret for nearly two months, but it also testifies to Yerby's diminished literary stature in his later years.

—Jack B. Moore, updated by Craig Bryson

YEZIERSKA, Anzia

Born: Plinsk, Poland, c. 1883. Immigrated to the United States c. 1890 and lived with her parents, her three brothers, and her three sisters in New York City's Lower East Side. **Education:** Attended night school while working as a servant and in a sweatshop; lived in the Clara de Hirsch Home for working girls, 1890; attended Teachers College of Columbia University, 1904, received certificate to teach domestic science, 1904; attended a seminar at Columbia University taught by philosopher John Dewey, 1917. **Family:** Married 1) Jacob Gordon in 1910 (marriage annulled 1910); 2) Arnold Levitas in 1911 (separated 1916); one daughter. **Career:** Awarded movie contract by Samuel Goldwyn following publication of first story collection and lived in Hollywood for several months, 1920; lived in New York City, except for 1929-30, when she held a Zona Gale fellowship at the University of Wisconsin, and 1931-32, when she lived in Arlington, Vermont; worked for Federal Writers Project of the Works Projects Administration (WPA), 1935; wrote book reviews for the *New York Times,* 1950-54. **Awards:** Edward J. O'Brien award for best short story of 1919; Zona Gale fellowship, University of Wisconsin, 1931-32. **Died:** 21 November 1970.

PUBLICATIONS

Collections

The Open Cage: An Anzia Yezierska Collection, edited by Alice Kessler Harris. 1979.
How I Found America: Collected Stories of Anzia Yezierska. 1991.

Short Stories

Hungry Hearts. 1920.
Children of Loneliness. 1923.

Novels

Salome of the Tenements. 1923.
Bread Givers. 1925.
Arrogant Beggar. 1926.
All I Could Never Be. 1932.
Red Ribbon on a White Horse. 1950.

*

Critical Studies: "Introduction" by Alice Kessler-Harris to *Bread Givers* by Yezierska, 1975; "Daughters of Loneliness" by Babbette Ingleheart, in *Studies in American Jewish Fiction,* Winter 1975; *Anzia Yezierska* by Carol B. Schoen, 1982; *Love in the Promised Land: The Story of John Dewey and Anzia Yezierska* by Mary V. Dearborn, 1988; *Anzia Yezierska: A Writer's Life* by Louise Levitas Henriksen, 1988; "Hunger and Hatred in Anzia Yezierska, Ellen Glasgow, and Edith Summers Kelley" by Elizabeth Ammons, in *Conflicting Stories: American Women Writers at the Turn into the Twentieth Century,* 1991; "Looking at Yezierska" by Laura Wexler, in *Women of the Word* edited by Judith R. Baskin, 1994; "The Image of the City in Yezierska's *Bread Givers*" by Edith C. Weinthal, in *Studies in American Jewish Literature,* 1994, pp. 10-13; "The Ultimate Shaygets and the Fiction of Anzia Yezierska" by Ann R. Shapiro, in *MELUS,* Summer 1996, pp. 79-88; "Lady Liberty's *Colonization* and Anzia Yezierska's *Bread Givers*" by Lisa Muir, in *Centennial Review,* Fall 1997, pp. 635-43; "Administered Identities and Linguistic Assimilation: The Politics of Immigrant English in Anzia Yezierska's *Hungry Hearts*" by Delia Caparoso Konzett, in *American Literature: A Journal of Literary History, Criticism, and Bibliography,* September 1997, pp. 595-619.

* * *

During the 1920s Anzia Yezierska was a well-known American writer. Her autobiographical short stories and novels focus on the experiences of immigrant American Jewish women such as herself. Yezierska's career was launched when her short story "The Fat of the Land," was chosen by Edward J. O'Brien, editor of the *Best Short Stories* series, as the best short story of 1919. The following year, when her first short story collection, *Hungry Hearts,* was published, she was awarded a Hollywood film contract by Samuel Goldwyn and dubbed "the sweatshop Cinderella" by Goldwyn's publicist. Although she published another volume of short stories, *Children of Loneliness,* in 1923, and four novels, *Salome of the Tenements* in 1923, *Bread Givers* in 1925, *Arrogant Beggar* in 1926, and *All I Could Never Be* in 1932, by the time her last autobiographical novel, *Red Ribbon on a White Horse,* was published in 1950, her other work virtually had been forgotten. Due to the efforts of Alice Kessler-Harris, however, Yezierska's best novel, *Bread Givers,* was reissued in 1975, and *The Open Cage,* a collection of Yezierska's short stories edited by Kessler-Harris, appeared in 1979. Also responsible for a revival of interest in Yezierska's work were studies of contexts relevant to a consideration of her fiction, such as Irving Howe's study of the American Jewish experience in *The World of Our Fathers,* Elizabeth Ammons's analysis of American women writers in *Conflicting Stories,* and Mary V. Dearborn's discussion of gender and ethnicity in American culture, *Pocahontas's Daughters.* Reflecting a renewed interest in the work of Yezierska, a number of literary anthologies published in the 1980s and 1990s, including *The Norton Anthology of Literature by Women,* featured her work.

"No Don Quixote ever went fighting windmills more wholly unprepared than I as a writer," Yezierska wrote to the publicity department of Houghton Mifflin in 1920 when they were about to publish her first volume of short stories, *Hungry Hearts.* Feeling that she lacked a proper formal education, she insisted nevertheless, "If I can't get a chance to learn the American English, I'll write in immigrant English . . . —but write I must!" In truth, she was fully capable of writing standard English by the time she submitted her first short story, "Soap and Water," for publication in 1915, but instead she deliberately chose to render her fiction in the rhythms and inflections of immigrant European Jews like herself, whose native tongue was Yiddish rather than English. Her own imperative, like that of the narrator of her "America and I," was to "build a bridge of understanding" between her world and that of the "American-born." As her narrator explains, "Since their life was shut out from such people as me, I began to open up my life and lives of my people to them. In only writing about the Ghetto I found America." Praising her for having so movingly portrayed the life of Jewish immigrants, Dr. Frank Crane, a syndicated columnist for the Hearst newspapers who helped to establish her literary reputation, wrote after reading *Hungry Hearts,* "From a sweatshop worker to a famous writer! All because she dipped her pen in her heart!"

Yezierska's prototypical female protagonist is a feisty immigrant who struggles to escape the strictures of poverty, parochialism, and patriarchy. Sara Smolinsky, the rebellious first person narrator of *Bread Givers,* for example, is determined to find a job, acquire an education, and rent a room so that she can leave forever the overcrowded tenement apartment in which she lives with her domineering father and her overburdened mother. When Sara eventually succeeds in becoming a teacher, she moves to a room where, finally, she can be alone, celebrating its "clean, airy emptiness." One of the fictional female city dwellers whom Blanche Gelfant describes in *Women Writing in America* as "hungry" women, Sara is starved not only for food more substantial than her daily ration of "herring and pickle over dry bread," but for knowledge. Sara declares: "I want to learn something. I want to do something. I want some day to make myself for a person and come among people."

A formidable antagonist in Sara's quest for autonomy is her father, Reb Smolinsky, a pious, impoverished scholar who is supported by the meager income his wife and daughters are able to generate from menial labor while he spends his days studying holy Jewish texts. When Sara insists on her right to obtain an education rather than being married off as her three older sisters had been, this raging patriarch, a "tyrant from the Old World where only men were people," rants, "Woe to America where women are let free like men."

In a number of Yezierska's novels and short stories, the figure of an autocratic Old World patriarch, modeled on Yezierska's own father, is contrasted with that of an intellectual American male who becomes a mentor and in some cases a lover of the female protagonist. Such a character is Sara Reisel's teacher in "The Miracle," who says to her, "We Americans are too much on earth. We need your power to fly." Scholars Carol B. Schoen, Mary V. Dearborn, and Yezierska's daughter, Louise Levitas Henriksen, all have pointed out the resemblance between this figure and American philosopher **John Dewey**, whom Yezierska met in 1917, when she was about thirty-five and Dewey was fifty-eight. Infatuated with the volatile, attractive, and intellectually-insatiable Yezierska, Dewey not only served as her mentor but wrote a number of poems about her that were discovered after his death and later included in *The Poems of John Dewey.* The miraculous event referred to in the title of Yezierska's "The Miracle" occurs at the story's conclusion, when Sara Reisel's teacher kisses her passionately and declares his love for her. Louise Levitas Henriksen claims, however, that though Yezierska was drawn to Dewey, when he kissed her, she repelled his sexual advances, causing him great embarrassment. Saying he was too busy to see her when she came to his office the following day, he asked her to return the letters he had sent her. Soon afterward Dewey left for a lecture tour in China. Ten years later, when she made an appointment to see him, he was coldly polite, and she was much chagrined to discover on his shelf a copy of *Hungry Hearts* whose pages had never been cut.

Another important issue that is dramatized in Yezierska's fiction is the feeling of dislocation and alienation experienced by American immigrants who have succeeded in escaping from the ghetto. This is the theme of her prize-winning story, "The Fat of the Land," whose protagonist, Hannah Breineh, once a poor resident of the Lower East Side, is installed by her now affluent children in an elegant but sterile apartment on Riverside Drive. When she flees the "marble sepulcher" of her uptown apartment and goes to visit her old friend Mrs. Pelz in the ghetto, Hannah realizes that even though she herself feels isolated and lonely uptown, she also can "no longer endure the sordid ugliness" of her former neighborhood. As Yezierska reveals in her most autobiographical novel, *Red Ribbon on a White Horse,* she experienced Hannah Breineh's feeling of dislocation whenever she chose to separate herself from the familiar world of her youth. The two times Yezierska left New York City for an extended time period—in 1920 when she went to Hollywood and in 1931 when she moved briefly to rural Arlington, Vermont—she felt isolated and rootless. Seeing herself as an outsider both within the immigrant community and in the world beyond its confines, seeking the solitude she found necessary to pursue her writing career yet lamenting the fact that without intimate family relationships to sustain her she was desperately lonely, Yezierska was never at peace. ·

The isolation Yezierska experienced after she left home as a youth was compounded in her later years by her own growing infirmity. During the last two decades of her life, she wrote a number of short stories about old women that depict the daily indignities inflicted on the elderly and the rage they experience as a result of their limiting circumstances. In "A Chair in Heaven," she focuses on a rich old woman who has been all but abandoned by her children; in "A Window Full of Sky," her narrator is a solitary old woman afflicted with neuritis who is trying to decide whether to move into a "narrow coffin" of a room in a home for the aged or to "die alone" in the room she now occupies from whose windows she can glimpse the Hudson River; in "Take up Your Bed and Walk," the narrator is a forgotten elderly writer who feels invigorated when a young student expresses interest in her work; and in the posthumously published "The Open Cage," an elderly tenant in an overcrowded rooming house, identifying herself with a bird that gets trapped in her room, exults when the bird is set free by a neighbor.

In her essay, "Writing As a Woman and a Jew in America," Norma Rosen—who also published a novel called *John and Anzia: An American Romance*—conjectures that when she herself was a young woman during the 1950s, it might have helped her if she had "known about a Jewish-American writer named Anzia" and about "her burning desire to become an educated woman and a writer." In the 1990s Yezierska's best novel, *Bread Givers,* and many of her short stories are in print once again. Though Yezierska's range as a writer is somewhat narrow, and though her work in the aggregate suffers from repetition, some of her short stories and her female Bildungsroman, *Bread Givers,* are memorable works of fiction that deserve to reach a wider audience. Supplementing the visions of the American Jewish experience provided in the works of writers such as **Abraham Cahan**, Michael Gold, **Henry Roth**, **Saul Bellow**, **Bernard Malamud**, and **Philip Roth**, Yezierska movingly depicts the failures and triumphs of American Jewish women in the New World.

—Charlotte Margolis Goodman

YORK, Simon. *See* **HEINLEIN, Robert Anson.**

ZUKOFSKY, Louis

Born: New York City, 23 January 1904. **Education:** Columbia University, M.A. 1924. **Family:** Married Celia Thaew in 1939; one son. **Career:** Instructor in English, University of Wisconsin, Madison, 1930-31; assistant then associate professor, Polytechnic Institute of Brooklyn, New York City, 1947-66. Visiting professor, Colgate University, summer 1947; writer-in-residence, San Francisco State College, 1958. **Awards:** Lola Ridge Memorial award, Poetry Society of America, 1949; Longview Foundation award, 1961; Union League Civic and Arts Foundation prize, *Poetry* magazine, 1964; Oscar Blumenthal/Charles Leviton prize, *Poetry* maga-

zine, 1966; National Endowment for the Arts *American Literary Anthology* awards, 1967 and 1968; awards from National Institute and American Academy. **Died:** 12 May 1978.

PUBLICATIONS

Collections

All: The Collected Short Poems 1923-1958. 1965.
All: The Collected Short Poems, 1956-1964. 1966.
Prepositions: The Collected Critical Essays of Louis Zukofsky. 1967.
All: The Collected Short Poems, 1923-1964. 1971.
Collected Fiction. 1990.
Complete Short Poetry, foreword by Robert Creeley. 1991.

Poetry

First Half of "A" 9. 1934.
55 Poems. 1941.
Anew. 1946.
Some Time: Short Poems. 1956.
Barely and Widely. 1958.
"A" 1-12. 1959.
It Was. 1959.
Louis Zukofsky: 16 Once Published. 1962.
I's (Pronounced Eyes). 1963.
Found Objects: 1962-1926. 1964.
After I's. 1964.
An Unearthing. 1965.
Iyyob. 1965.
I Sent Thee Late. 1965.
Finally a Valentine: A Poem. 1965.
"A" 9. 1966.
"A" 14. 1967.
From Thanks to the Dictionary. 1968.
Ferdinand, Including "It Was." 1968.
The Gas Age. 1969.
"A" 13-21. 1969.
Autobiography, with music by C. Zukofsky. 1970.
Initial. 1970.
An Era. 1970.
"A" 24. 1972.
"A" 22 and 23. 1975.
A. 1978.
80 Flowers. 1978.

Play

Arise, Arise (produced 1965). 1973.

Criticism

Le Style Apollinaire, with Rene Taupin. 1934.
A Test of Poetry. 1948.
Bottom: On Shakespeare, with C. Zukofsky. 1963.

Other

"A" Libretto. 1965.

Little: A Fragment For Careenagers. 1969; expanded version *Little; for Careenagers,* 1970.
Pound-Zukofsky: Selected Letters of Ezra Pound and Louis Zukofsky, edited by Barry Ahearn. 1987.

Editor, *An "Objectivists" Anthology.* 1932.

Translator, with C. Zukofsky, *Catullus Fragmenta,* music by Paul Zukofsky. 1968.

*

Manuscript Collections: Humanities Research Center, University of Texas, Austin; Beinedke Library, Yale University, New Haven, Connecticut.

Bibliography: *A Bibliography of Louis Zukofsky* by Celia Thaew Zukofsky, 1969.

Critical Studies: "Song? After Bread: Notes on Zukofsky's A 1-12" by Robert Kelly, in *Kulchur,* Winter 1963 (entire issue); "Louis Zukofsky" by William Carlos Williams, in *Agenda,* December 1964, pp. 1-4; *Louis Zukofsky: Objectivists Poetics and the Quest for Form* by L. S. Dendo, 1972; *Louis Zukofsky in the Twenties* by John Stanley Tomas, 1991; *Niedecker and the Correspondence with Zukofsky, 1931-1970* by Jenny Lynn Penberthy, 1993; *The Trouble with Genius: Reading Pound, Joyce, Stein, and Zukofsky* by Bob Perelman, 1994; *Louis Zukofsky and the Transformation of a Modern American Poetics* by Sandra Kumamoto Stanley, 1994; *Apocalypse and After: Modern Strategy and Postmodern Tactics in Pound, Williams, and Zukofsky* by Bruce Comens, 1995; *Consumption and Depression in Gertrude Stein, Louis Zukofsky, and Ezra Pound* by Luke Carson, 1998; *Louis Zukofsky and the Poetry of Knowledge* by Mark Scroggins, 1998; *The Practice of Poetry: Reconsiderations of Louis Zukofsky's A Test of Poetry* by Cid Corman, 1998.

*   *   *

Louis Zukofsky's poetry usually is associated with the Objectivist Movement, which originated in the early 1930s and was highly influenced by **Ezra Pound** and **William Carlos Williams**; other Objectivist poets included Charles Reznikoff, Lorine Niedecker, and George Oppen. Each of these poets wrote quite distinct work, though, and thus the label is more for convenience than to describe a formal literary movement. However, what the group shared is a profound interest in the relationship between language and reality. To borrow from Pound's description of the Imagist Movement, a movement with which the Objectivists shared many affinities, one question that obsessed the Objectivists was how a writer could directly treat the object and somehow render its reality in poetry. Or, more specifically, how could the writer get "the thing" (object, experience, or person) onto the page? Each of these writers explored different answers to this question. Of the poets associated with the movement, Zukofsky was the most interested in the intersection between poetry and music. In his essay "An Objective," Zukofsky writes, "The order of all poetry is to approach a state of music wherein the ideas present themselves sensuously and intelligently and are of no predatory intention." Although admitting that poetry may not ever achieve the isolation of sound from sense, Zukofsky's desire to somehow

divorce sound from meaning or, at least, place sound over meaning was to become a primary force behind his work, culminating in the fugue-like intricacies of his long poem *A.*

His early work, though, is akin to Williams's poetry. Consider, for example, this short excerpt from the poem, "Ferry":

> Gleams, a green lamp
> In the fog:
> Murmur, in almost
> A dialogue
>
> Siren and signal
> Siren and signal
> Parts the shore from the fog.

Although Williams would surely resist the playful rhymes of this poem, the attention to the particular objects—the lamplight and horns in the fog—contribute to a strong visual and tactile texture. The last line of the poem reads, "Plash. Night. Plash. Sky," again illustrating an attraction to onomatopoeia and the ways that language can somehow vividly represent the world. Other early lyrics show a similar imagistic compulsion; in this early work Zukofsky seems to be hovering between his attraction to the mandates of Imagism, embodied by the early work of Williams and Pound, and his desire to somehow shape a more musically oriented poetry.

Zukofsky began writing *A* in 1927. The poem was influenced by the work of Pound and contains a playfulness with language that is similar to that of James Joyce, as well as Zukofsky's musical interests; in fact, and not surprisingly, the composer Johann Sebastian Bach is a central figure in the piece. Essentially, the poem articulates a search for order, a way to make sense of time and one's place in it. Sometimes autobiographical, sometimes historical, and frequently both, the poem takes the reader on a tour through many of the events of the twentieth century; however, content, in some ways, is overshadowed by the formal innovations of the poem. In some sections of the poem, mathematical formulas govern the distribution of certain letter sounds; in others, Zukofsky puts together excerpts from brochures on musical awards. Other sections read as fugue-like manipulations of language, devoid of referent sense and immersed in the sound quality of repeated words. The poem is diverse and difficult, the embodiment of a life's work devoted to unraveling the high modernist attraction to autotelic form. Twenty-four movements in length, completed in 1974, *A* certainly stands alongside Pound's *Cantos,* **T. S. Eliot**'s *Four Quartets,* Williams's *Paterson,* **John Berryman**'s *The Dream Songs,* and **H.D.**'s *Trilogy* as one of the most interesting long poems of the century; whether it is as accomplished or as engaging as these other works is debatable.

Critical reaction to Zukofsky's experiments with form is mixed; some see the musical structure as an innovative and invigorating exploration of how poetry can embrace and make use of other art forms, notably, music; others have praised its frank autobiographical elements. Others have found it merely indulgent of a sensibility far too attracted to aesthetic concerns and lacking in genuine artistic merit. Regardless, the poem's formal accomplishment is undeniable, and several of the autobiographical sections, especially those concerning his fears and hopes for his son, are quite stirring.

Zukofsky also wrote a significant collection of prose, *Prepositions.* In this book he considers several contemporary poets and

Shakespeare, and offers several of his theories regarding poetry. His career was long and varied, eventually evolving in the later parts of *A* beyond the heavy influence of Pound and Williams to use a more autobiographical mode that engages important historical events of the middle of the twentieth century, including the civil rights movement and the assassination of John F. Kennedy. Although grouped with the Objectivist poets, especially his lover and correspondent Lorine Niedecker, it is probably unjust to pigeonhole Zukofsky in such a manner; his career was wide-ranging, and his work shows a similar attraction to eclectic fields of writing. Throughout, however, Zukofsky articulates a profound concern with the musicality of poetry, which separates him from the other poets of his generation and distinguishes him from the other Objectivist writers. Connected to this concern, though, are the weaknesses of his verse. His poetry, even when at its formal best, frequently lacks emotional engagement. But Zukofsky has moments where his work exceeds this criticism, and his poetry is valuable both for these occasional moments and for its technical brilliance.

—Tod Marshall

WORKS

ABSALOM, ABSALOM!
Novel by William Faulkner, 1936

Although often considered William Faulkner's best novel, *Absalom, Absalom!* is also his most involved. First of all, the narrative is related by mostly unreliable narrators years after the events described. The basic details upon which the story is based are few and easily related, but as they pass through the consciousnesses of the narrators who relate them, they become not only complicated and involved but at many points contradictory. Each narrator has a different version of what happened and often varying opinions of the effects of what occurred to the inhabitants of Jefferson.

In 1833 Thomas Sutpen came to Jefferson riding a thoroughbred horse and wearing two well-oiled and carefully cared-for pistols. After a few days at the hotel, he left and returned a few weeks later, bringing with him a wagon, a few tools, some half-wild slaves, and a French architect. The rumor spread that Sutpen had acquired some land from the Chickasaws, and he was doing no less than establishing the largest and best plantation in Yoknapatawpha County. After his return little was seen or heard of Sutpen, although he did occasionally invite some of the men from Jefferson out to hunt. On these outings he would often join several of his slaves in a pit about twenty feet wide and five feet deep where they would "fight, stomp, and gouge" until there was only one man left conscious and standing, and that man was usually Sutpen. The visitors would always note the progress Sutpen was making as he attempted to bring his wilderness under control and how the mansion the French architect was building for him was developing.

One day Sutpen passed through the town again. When he returned this time he brought with him furniture and furnishings finer than anyone in Yoknapatawpha County had ever seen. He was making the mansion into a showplace. Then he began his quest for the accoutrements that would make him a southern gentleman in one generation, a station the Compsons, Sartorises, and McCaslins had reached only after many years. First, he named his place Sutpen's Hundred and married Ellen Coldfield, daughter of one of the leading families in Jefferson. In due time he had the required son and heir, Henry, and a daughter, Juliet.

Henry eventually entered the law school of the University of Mississippi, the law being one of the acceptable professions for a southern gentleman. There he met Charles Bon, who was rumored to be Sutpen's son by his first marriage, which he had dissolved as soon as he discovered his wife was part black. Henry and Charles become good friends and Henry brings Charles home with him. Charles and Juliet fall in love, but before they can marry, Henry, Charles, and Sutpen go off to the Civil War, with Sutpen as second in command of the cavalry unit raised by Colonel John Sartoris. Soon the men in the unit become convinced Colonel Sartoris is exposing them to unnecessary danger and elect Sutpen as their commanding officer. Charles and Henry fight side-by-side throughout the war. During their years together Henry has learned of Charles's true identity, and all the way home he begs Charles to tell him what he is going to do about the engagement. Charles will not reveal his intentions. As they come in sight of the house, Henry says, you cannot marry my sister because you are my half-brother. "No, I'm not," Charles replies, "I'm the nigger that's going to marry your sister." Almost before the words are out of his mouth, Henry kills him and leaves home. (He later returns half-crazy, and Juliet hides him in the house.) Sutpen returns to find his slaves gone, his buildings ruined, and his land grown up in weeds. His "design" is destroyed. He is later killed by Wash Jones because Sutpen mistreats his daughter, Millie (because the illegitimate child he has by her is a girl). He wants a boy so that he can reestablish his "design" and become an aristocrat.

Like many other great novels, this one has been subjected to many interpretations. The reading offered here is based upon the following hypothesis: 1) there is no reliable narrator, so except for a few basic facts we do not know what happened and why it occurred; 2) the Quentin Compson who appears as a character and narrator in *Absalom, Absalom!* is the same youth who had the disturbing and destroying experiences related in *The Sound and the Fury;* and 3) the narrative he "creates" in *Absalom* is mostly influenced by the experience of that novel (to understand fully *Absalom,* one must first read *The Sound and the Fury*). Quentin is the principal agent in the creation of a legend that gives him temporary relief from the powerful emotional disturbances (found in *The Sound and the Fury*) that will destroy him: his inability to punish Dalton Ames, his sister's seducer (as Henry punished "the nigger" who was going to marry *his* sister), and his failure to accept the incestuous feelings he has for his sister (as Thomas is able to accept his feeling toward Judith). The "real legend" of Thomas Sutpen is the one Quentin creates because in relating it to his roommate he receives the strength that allows him to bear, for a short time, his own overwhelming burdens.

—Thomas Daniel Young

THE ADVENTURES OF HUCKLEBERRY FINN
Novel by Mark Twain, 1884

Mark Twain conceived of what became *Adventures of Huckleberry Finn* in the summer of 1875, began to write the following summer, and after long interruptions completed a manuscript with a rush in 1883. It was to be a boys' book, a sequel to *The Adventures of Tom Sawyer;* yet even the first reviewers saw some ambiguity about its proper audience. What Twain himself seems never fully to have understood is the extent to which the book moved during composition towards the adult and the serious or how superior it is to his other works.

Appealing to a broad spectrum of readers, the book gained an immediate popular success. Although several reviewers objected to its violence and to the bad models it set for boys, most liked it for his comedy, characters, and pictures of life in the Mississippi Valley of about 1840. It was easy to feel sympathy in the mid-1880s for Twain's praise of freedom and condemnation of slavery. Industrial capitalism had brought tensions; images of peace, individual liberty, dozing villages, and harmony with Nature had general appeal. The myth of the West was potent everywhere.

More recently, optimistic readings have declined, and emphasis has been placed on themes and thematic images that run counter to primary American ideologies and *mentalités* of the past century. The book now appears to imply more than a distaste for a slave society: the Old South is metonymic. All society is coercive; men are greedy. The novel subverts the assumptions of all religion and of all socially inspired morality.

A certain gravity was built into the novel from its first conception: it had to do with slavery and hypocrisy. The southwestern humorists whom Twain learned from wished to do more than amuse; they intended to capture for posterity regional oddities of life and speech, to record manners, customs, and characters. They did not, however, write jeremiads. Twain's book as published is crowded with images of fog and night, violent death, difficult rebirth, unfreedom, and shifting identity. Counter images of peace, freedom, generosity, loving companionship, and cosmicity tend to blur.

Twain's chief characters have maintained their appeal. As Twain wrote later, in Huck "a sound heart & a deformed conscience come into collision & conscience suffers defeat." By passing a series of moral tests, Huck, a Rousseauistic Child of Nature, separates himself from a tainted society. Tom, who helps open the book with his childish fantasizing, reappears in Chapter 33, and Huck slips back into something resembling his original state. Sophisticated readers often judge Tom to be the novelistic villain of the piece: he lives by false conventions; he diminishes the book's seriousness. The treatment accorded Jim has repeatedly raised the issue of racism. Jim begins and ends as a minstrel-show darkey; but in the book's center he furnishes authentic pathos, achieves full humanity, and joins Huck as an archetypal figure. In this central section the River becomes (in **T.S. Eliot**'s phrase) "a strong brown god" and the equivalent of a character. A gallery of lesser figures who provide comedy and tragedy populate the Shore or irrupt upon the majestic River.

The structure of the novel has been much discussed. That the book is, to an extent, picaresque has always been recognized. It has also been described as a romance, a social novel, a realistic novel, a symbolic novel, and a psychological novel. Polysemous possibilities encourage hermeneutic fecundity. Loose organization and awkward, mechanical plotting are typical of Twain; but more subtle unifying elements than plot have been found. The voice of Huck as narrator is of first importance: his moral development gives the book the configuration of a *Bildungsroman*. The River, too, plays an organizing role; and rhythmic patterns develop, as in shifts from burlesque to genre passages to tragedy, from low-vernacular to vernacular-sublime. Contrapuntal themes (life-death; freedom-slavery; individual-society) are elaborated and fortified by illustrative symbols and images.

The principal flaw in the novel is reputed to be its final section, beginning with Chapter 33, where Tom Sawyer reappears; but even that section has distinguished champions. **Lionel Trilling** and Eliot have defended the ending on technical grounds: it has a formal aptness, is appropriate for a romance and for Huck—a hero who by his nature can have no beginning and no end.

Adverse criticism charges the last chapters with destroying the credibility of Huck's moral maturation; he loses sight of his discovery that men are often vicious and hypocritical, and he fails to demonstrate any reasonable accommodation with society. Just as Huck loses his grasp of the realities of the human condition, so Jim loses his dignity, accepts degradation, and becomes again the eye-rolling pawn that he was in the beginning. The major theme of freedom is thus obscured and made trivial. The imagination of Tom, who supplants Huck as hero, seems conventional and puerile, the comedy that he initiates to be interminably, tediously slap-

stick. The two much-praised final sentences, in which Huck proposes to "light out for the Territory" so that Aunt Sally cannot adopt and "sivilize" him, yield only a glint of hope. Civilization and community may not, it is felt, be dismissed so lightly.

In praising the novel, critics have often isolated one or two of its aspects as responsible for its greatness. Eliot wrote that "the Boy and the River" gave the book distinction. Others have concentrated attention on Twain's choice of the first-person point of view and on Huck, a speaker of richly colloquial English, as his narrative persona. Yet it may be observed that although Twain used approximately the same formula later, he was notably unable to repeat his triumph.

It is to grant to *Huckleberry Finn* too much novelty and influence to suggest, as have Lionel Trilling and others, that in this volume Twain established for writers the virtues of American colloquial speech. Twain has, nevertheless, been exceptionally influential through his effective representation of the colloquial. Contrary to the opinion of many critics, Huck's voice does not carry without lapse throughout the book, nor does Twain give us with exactness the colloquial and dialectal speech of the Missouri region. The author's mask slips at many places; Huck's voice falters. It may well be argued, however, that Twain improved on conventional renderings and did what was artistically necessary to give the impression of living speech.

Critics see Huck's vernacular as true to the culture, vivid, and flexible—a touchstone for exposing the falsities of "genteel" speech and "literary" rhetoric. This impression may be enhanced for readers by their acceptance of the pervasive image of Twain as a hero of the folk. Huck's presence as narrator placed useful constraints on Twain's tendencies towards excess in the direction of buffoonery and sentimentality and forced the writer to dramatize. But no matter how important, Huck is not the sole savior of the book: its towering reputation is properly attributable to the combination of many elements, some planned, some fortuitous. At this time, it would seem that no other American novel has been so suspected and so controverted, and perhaps that no other has maintained its eminence so well.

—Guy A. Cardwell

THE ADVENTURES OF TOM SAWYER
Novel by Mark Twain, 1876

In his preface to *The Adventures of Tom Sawyer* Mark Twain writes that "most of the adventures recorded in this book really occurred; one or two were experiences of my own, the rest of boys who were schoolmates of mine." Twain's memories of his boyhood in Hannibal, Missouri, form the basis of the novel and give it its idyllic, often nostalgic tone of celebration of lost childhood; Twain called the book "simply a hymn, put into prose form to give it a worldly air."

Tom Sawyer is not the complex masterpiece that its successor *Adventures of Huckleberry Finn* is, but it is well worth reading in its own right. The novel lives on because of its humor and its memorable evocation of the world of childhood. The novel takes place in a transformed, eternal-summer version of Hannibal called St. Petersburg (Saint Peter's burg, a kind of Heaven). *Tom Sawyer* is full of lavish lyrical descriptions of the summer world as it is experienced by those who can appreciate it best—children. The novel also remembers the nightmare side of childhood; grave-robbing, murder, revenge, and grisly death are also part of St. Petersburg.

As he wrote and revised the book, Twain could not make up his mind whether he was writing a book for children or adults. In his preface, Twain expresses a double purpose: "Although my book is intended mainly for the entertainment of boys and girls, I hope it will not be shunned by men and women on that account, for part of my plan has been to try to pleasantly remind adults of what they once were themselves." Although the point of view is Tom's most of the time, the narrator leading us into Tom's experience is clearly an adult—amused, superior, and nostalgic by turns—who expects readers to see more than Tom does, to laugh at him and admire him from a perspective of adulthood.

Tom Sawyer is in part a reaction against the "Sunday-school literature" abounding in 19th-century America, which featured relentlessly good children who were rewarded and naughty children who came to bad ends. Comic writers like Thomas Bailey Aldrich and B.P. Shillaber parodied this moralistic school. Before *Tom Sawyer* Twain wrote burlesques entitled "The Story of the Bad Little Boy Who Didn't Come to Grief" and "The Story of the Good Little Boy Who Did Not Prosper," but in *Tom Sawyer* he went a step further and told the story of a "bad" (i.e., normal) boy who will clearly become a good man.

In the opening chapters of the novel, Tom displays all the faults of the "bad child" of the moralists: he lies, plays hooky, steals, and generally considers the respectable adult world his natural enemy. He cannot learn a single Bible verse, but he can memorize the most minute details of the adventures of Robin Hood. It never occurs to him to apply himself in school, but he can be patient, careful, and untiringly diligent in pursuit of childhood arts like whistling and in his sentimental courtship of Becky Thatcher. Like that earlier Tom, Tom Jones, this imprudent boy is naturally goodhearted; in *Tom Sawyer* Twain is willing to believe in a natural goodness of heart, however much he may distrust such a notion elsewhere.

Tom lives in a private world of gorgeous theatrical dreams, sagas of pirates, robbers, and buried treasure, all starring himself. He successfully transforms dusty everyday life in St. Petersburg into dramas in which he holds center stage, most spectacularly when he attends his own funeral. He is an inspired schemer and entrepreneur, as readers learn in one of the first incidents in the book, the famous whitewashing scene.

Twain himself said that the book had "no plot" and critics since his time have called *Tom Sawyer* everything from "utterly formless and shapeless" to "a most ingeniously plotted novel." Three related plotlines intertwine. The first is Tom's relationship with Aunt Polly, and by extension with the confining "respectable" adult world; this relationship is loving but elaborately hedged with comic plotting on both sides. The second strand is Tom's courtship of Becky Thatcher, and the third is his involvement with the murder, the buried treasure, and the horrific Injun Joe. During the course of these adventures Tom begins to mature; at the end, while Huck remains the natural and innocent escapee from "civilization," Tom edges closer to it.

But is "civilized" St. Petersburg worth joining? From the narrator's wider perspective, we can perceive the narrowness and hypocrisy of the worthies of the little country town. Much of the book's humor comes from the disparity between what the inhabitants of St. Petersburg "officially" think and feel and what they actually think and feel. But Twain does not condemn this world as he condemns the river society of *Huck Finn,* and *Tom*

Sawyer does not taste of the bitter pessimism of Twain's later works. Tom's increasing "civilization" is not a cause for alarm; he will be a good man in a good, if parochial world.

—Mollie Sandock

THE AGE OF INNOCENCE
Novel by Edith Wharton, 1920

The Age of Innocence, a reminiscent but satiric account of the time, place, and society in which Edith Wharton grew up, won for the author a 1921 Pulitzer Prize and was a bestseller when it appeared. Wharton had earlier taken up the topic of the society of the old New York—in which her wealthy parents played important roles—in novels such as *The House of Mirth* and *The Custom of the Country.* But, written after Wharton had experienced the horror and destruction of World War I, in a time during which old systems of beliefs and customs seemed to be collapsing, *The Age of Innocence* looks back to a time of apparent stability—a time in which the forms and conventions were understood, if sometimes repressive. The novel is typically read as a discussion of the conflict between the individual and society, and between the safety and order of old, familiar ways and the possible chaos and uncertainty of new ways. Thus the conflict is crystallized in Newland Archer's choice between May and Ellen, a choice that represents the split between the society of old New York, in which his family holds a respectable place, and that of the newly wealthy invaders of his society that were rising to prominence after the Civil War. Because *The Age of Innocence* subtly censures the values and actions of both respectable old New York society and the fashionable newcomers, it is generally considered among Wharton's finest works.

Although the title of the novel literally refers to a 1788 Sir Joshua Reynolds portrait of a little girl, the title can be interpreted in several ways. The innocent age might be the condition of New York society in 1872, the year in which most of the action of the novel takes place. This is a society that refuses to discuss any of the unpleasant facts of life, such as divorce, extramarital affairs among its members, or the possibility of marriages made for financial gain. At the same time, society insists upon the absolute innocence, purity, and ignorance of all sexual matters in its unmarried women. Newland's spinster sister Janey is the monstrous outcome of this insistence—an adult who is perpetually forced to pretend a childish innocence. May Welland is another product of such an upbringing, and even her husband-to-be believes in her complete innocence; when observing his fiancee watching the seduction scene in the opera *Faust,* Newland boasts to himself that May "doesn't even guess what it's all about." But while May participates in presenting herself as an innocent maiden, she shows by her actions later in the novel that she understands the facts of life that motivate men and women—both in operas and in real life. Newland begins to suspect that his bride is not as shallow as he had suspected when he finds that she has lied to Ellen about being certain of her pregnancy in order to keep her marriage intact. Later, Newland finds that May has told their son on her deathbed that Newland gave up the thing he wanted most (Ellen) when May asked him to. "She never asked me," Newland recalls.

But the title *The Age of Innocence* could also refer to Newland's own youthful belief that love between a man and a woman is all that is needed to secure their happiness. When he voices his desire to Ellen that they might live happily outside of all social constraints, Ellen replies that such a life is not possible since too many other people would be hurt by their actions. Newland's process of coming to terms with the realities of relationships is an education of irony. When he is called upon by his family to counsel Ellen not to seek a divorce, he states the case in terms of family responsibility: "The individual, in such cases, is nearly always sacrificed to what is supposed to be the collective interest: people cling to any convention that keeps the family together—protects the children, if there are any . . . . It's my business, you know, to help you to see these things as the people who are fondest of you see them. The Mingotts, the Wellands, the van der Luydens, all your friends and relations: if I didn't show you honestly how they judge such questions, it wouldn't be fair of me, would it?" But, ironically, it is these same reasons that Ellen forces Newland to consider when he later urges her to leave the stifling New York society to live in a world where such ugly designations as mistress and adultery do not exist. "Oh, my dear—where is that country? Have you ever been there?" Ellen asks Newland, attempting to make him realize that his dream is impossible.

May and Ellen represent different types of women to Newland. Even before becoming involved with Ellen he becomes interested in "the case of the Countess Olenska" rather than in Ellen as an individual. Since he is unaware of the depth of May's mind, Newland sees his fiancee and Ellen as contrasts, with May representing all that is safe, secure, and known in his society, while Ellen embodies all that is unknown and exotic in European society. May and Ellen can be read as the traditional light and dark heroines of literature, since Wharton portrays May as a wholesome blonde and Ellen as a seductive brunette. Newland thinks of May as representing "a Civic Virtue or a Greek Goddess"; her skill at archery reminds Newland of the goddess Diana. He notices May's eyes repeatedly as being transparent, serious, pale, limpid, and blue—all reminders of the extreme innocence he believes she possesses. In contrast, Ellen plays the role in Newland's mind as an exotic, European femme fatale who represents the threat of disorder that is descending upon old New York society. Her hands, described as being fragile and decorated with rings, are one of her most attractive attributes to Newland. The most sensual scene between Ellen and Newland is the one in which he takes off her glove in the carriage to kiss her hand. Newland learns few actual facts about Ellen's unhappy marriage and subsequent life, but is attracted by her mystery. Ellen is unconventional because of her desire to get a divorce from her cruel husband, her scandalous and shadowy past, her choice to live in a Bohemian section of New York, and her open friendships with men who are married or engaged. But while Newland mistakenly sees only the roles he ascribes to both May and Ellen, they are actually much more complex than these simple characterizations.

Although Wharton was perhaps more like Ellen than any other character in the novel (both are at once inside and outside of fashionable New York society, divorce their husbands, leave America to live in Paris, and greatly value stimulating conversation), the novel is more Newland's story than either May's or Ellen's. Just as Wharton did, Newland becomes interested in anthropology and is able to view his own society as an outsider and think critically of its rules and values. Wharton describes in detail the tribal rites that go on prior to a marriage between old New York families; May and Newland's schedule of prenuptial visits to relatives and friends follows a specific pattern. Even the decision to move up their wedding date must be approved by the family matriarch,

Granny Mingott. In the opening scene of the novel Wharton refers to both Lawrence Lefferts, old New York's authority on form, and Sillerton Jackson, old New York's authority on family. But we see the hypocrisy of society since even Lefferts, a crusader for morality, has extramarital affairs. As Newland takes up the study of anthropology and begins to see such incongruities in his own society, he feels the impulse to break free from what he sees as stifling and meaningless conventions. However, Ellen's actions to save her cousin's marriage, May's maneuvers to keep Newland with her, and Newland's own inertia keep him from acting against his family's traditions.

By the end of the novel, when Newland's respectable son is about to marry the illegitimate daughter of Julius Beaufort, it is obvious that time and the invaders of old New York society have caused changes. Although little is mentioned of the twenty-six years between Newland's engagement to May and the closing scenes of the novel, we understand that he and his family have benefited from his (forced) decision to give up Ellen. Wharton depicts both the good and the bad sides of renunciation; the family is made stronger, although the individual suffers from wondering what might have been. But since society has changed in spite of Newland's actions to maintain the old standards, it is clear that the suffocating old ways could not last.

—Jennifer A. Hynes

ALL THE KING'S MEN
Novel by Robert Penn Warren, 1946

Robert Penn Warren's *All the King's Men* was published in 1946 and received the Pulitzer Prize. It is the most celebrated of a series of novels that was initiated by *Night Rider*, and that continues through such books as *The Cave and Flood.* In general, the novels are centered on an awareness that is more sensitive and discriminating than those which surround it; it is an awareness that would like to make sense of the mixture of good and evil in society and in each person but is usually unable to do so. One could say that Warren's alter egos in the novels—Jack Burden in *All the King's Men*—aspire to philosophic utterance but are often distracted by the diversity and sheer disorder of the life in which they are immersed. The result—in *All the King's Men,* at least—is a series of arresting insights, but insights the outlines of which are recurrently made obscure by the malice of other persons and the sheer jumble of event, of chance, that makes a thinker doubt the general relevance of an insight he has just framed. An early comment by Diana Trilling noted this "largeness of intention." "Mr. Warren's study of a political leader is intended to investigate the moral relativism inherent in the historical process. One might describe it as a fictional demonstration of Hegel's philosophy of history."

As just noted, the "thinker" in *All the King's Men* is a middle-aged man named Jack Burden, who is the product of a privileged southern environment and a good education. At one point Burden had tried to base a university dissertation on the journal of a Civil War ancestor named Cass Mastern. But Burden abandoned this work to become a newspaperman. It was work that moved him away from the assessment of human values that, perhaps, comes naturally to a student of history. And Jack Burden—of Burden's Landing—moves still further away from thought and often becomes lost in the sheer welter of event when he becomes an administrative assistant to a southern politician named Willie Stark.

It is Willie Stark from whom radiates the confusion that haunts Burden. It is Willie Stark, incidentally, who assured the contemporary celebrity of the novel. Any reader of the mid-1940s could recognize that Willie Stark was at least suggested to Warren by the career of the Louisiana governor of the 1930s, Huey Long; to some an unscrupulous rabble-rouser and plunderer of the public till, and to others (chiefly the poor and the uneducated) a knight on a white horse.

With Long as a point of departure (but no more) Warren elaborates the figure that holds Jack Burden in bondage; the guile of Stark exerts esthetic fascination at the same time that it arouses moral repugnance. Burden again and again tries to tear himself loose from the low-brow corruption of Willie but is set free only when Willie is shot to death. Only then is Burden—Warren's assessor of meaning—able to embrace his true loves: a woman named Anne Stanton and the life of thought and analysis that is natural to him.

A film version of the novel and popular discussion of it of course placed Willie Stark at the center of the stage. But the book is more justly read with Jack Burden's preoccupations in command, as indeed they are in Warren's book. For Burden is actually surrounded by many other persons just as essential to him as Willie. One and all, these persons compose the seed-bed of evil which, as Burden sees the matter, is the only terrain from which good can grow. Among the persons are Willie's hangers-on, as corrupt as Willie but less clever, less charismatic. There is Sadie Burke, Willie's secretary and one-time mistress; she is the ultimate planner of Willie's death. There is Tiny Duffy, a venal operator who helps set up the actual slaying of Willie to protect his own interests. And from outside the state house circle comes the actual assassin, Adam Stanton, a noble scientist whom Willie outrages on two counts: Willie's new mistress is Adam's sister Anne (she is also Jack Burden's ultimate beloved), and Willie also seems to be using Adam Stanton as a respectable "front" in the construction of a hospital.

When Jack Burden often draws away from all this—to catch his breath, as it were—he finds Burden's Landing no purer in fact than Willie Stark's state house. For human betrayal is also endemic in Jack's childhood town, and he is often more aware of the seed-bed of evil there than he is of the love and affection he has met in the village.

A great interest in the novel is Burden's alternation between resigned connivance with corruption and his passionate revolt against it: a revolt made in the name of goodness, purity of intent, and all those traditional values lost in the southern shuffle of the novel. Two long sections of the novel are typical withdrawals from the unending depiction of the "real world."

First, there is Burden's study of his ancestor's Civil War journal. Cass Mastern emerges from that record as a man antique and curious: curious at least to Burden. For Mastern is a man who breaks the moral code and can say clearly to himself that he has broken the code that holds society together. In contrast, Jack Burden, his descendant, wants to pass similar judgments on himself and others, but is often unable to do so. So Burden's study of the ancestral journal puts before him a noble sinner whom he cannot imitate.

Then there is Burden's auto trip to California, during which he has a revelation that is cynical and easier for him to appropriate. At moments of course. For no appropriation of Burden's is final. Two phrases dominate the Burden mind at times. There is the Great Sleep, which amounts to a resignation from the entire human project, evil or good. And there is the annunciation of an alternate deity: alternate to the one ancestor Cass Mastern knew.

This deity is the Great Twitch: briefly, reflex and conditioning as shaping forces in human life. (The novel was written at the time when Pavlov and his dogs were barking.)

Readers who wish to make final sense of *All the King's Men* will move beyond the limits of the novel itself and will leave Burden behind enjoying the only security he can trust: the arms of his boyhood sweetheart, Anne Stanton, once the mistress of Willie Stark and, at the end of the novel, Burden's solace—if not his key to inclusive meaning. As Diana Trilling observed in 1946, it is perhaps "the low quality of Burden's moral awareness" that qualifies the impact of *All the King's Men.* Jack Burden (if not Warren himself) cannot really rise above his version of the Hegelian ebb-and-flow.

—Harold H. Watts

THE AMBASSADORS
Novel by Henry James, 1903

The Ambassadors was the first written of Henry James's three late "major phase" novels. James himself regarded it "as, frankly, quite the best, 'all round,' of my productions" (Preface). After the shorter "experimental" fiction of the 1890s, experimenting with technique and treating English themes, James returns here to a large-scale novel treating the theme of international confrontation with which he originally established his reputation. His middle-aged hero, Lambert Strether, is a recognizable Jamesian type sometimes referred to as "the poor sensitive gentleman," who combines sensibility, integrity, and a capacity for growth, with naivety and relative powerlessness in worldly terms. Strether is the first of the ambassadors designated in the title, and the novel concerns the gradual evolution of his insights and attitudes.

He arrives in Europe from Woollett, Massachusetts, as the representative of his patron and provisional fiancee, Mrs. Newsome, assuming that it is his unequivocal duty to rescue her son Chad from a French mistress and from the dissipations of Paris. But he discovers an immensely improved and civilized Chad, and a lady, Madame de Vionnet, whose gentility is unquestionable and whose sophistication and grace both captivate and intimidate Strether himself. Strether's gradual awakening to the pleasures, beauty, style, and nuance of Paris is epitomized in the first of the two great recognition scenes of the novel, that of the sculptor Gloriani's garden party in Book V. Here Madame de Vionnet makes her first appearance in her representative character of *femme du monde,* accompanied by her exquisite young daughter Jeanne, as quintessential *jeune fille.* Strether must now speculate anew on what holds Chad in Paris. Moreover, he is overwhelmed by the sense of his own social ineptitude, middle age, and lost opportunities, and this sense culminates in the speech which James designates in his Preface as the origin of the novel, Strether's enjoinder to a young man present to "Live all you can; it's a mistake not to."

In this ecstatic embrace of Parisian possibilities Strether finds himself altogether at odds with the Woollett point of view, and by the end of Book VI, the exact midpoint of the novel, he reverses his original position. It would be wrong for Chad to desert a world and a person who have recreated him as a civilized man. Hence the need for Mrs. Newsome to despatch the second ambassador alluded to in the title, her thin-lipped, humorless, narrowly judgmental daughter, Sarah Pocock, accompanied by Sarah's husband Jim, who thinks that Paris is the Folies Bergere. The arrival of the Pocock ménage therefore sets off the imaginative distance Strether has traversed, his spiritual evolution from the moralistic Woollett pole of values toward the aesthetic Parisian pole of values. But the structure of the novel was devised by James as that of an hourglass, and its second half now reverses the first. Having cast all his allegiance with Madame de Vionnet and Paris, and effectively resigned his Woollett ambassadorship, Strether is now gradually subjected to a more intimate view of Paris, the seamy underside of his own original impression. Chad, he discovers, is superficially refined but not intrinsically changed and is, therefore, susceptible to the bait of a pretty girl back home and an advertising career in Woollett. Madame de Vionnet and not Jeanne fears for the loss of him. In the second great recognition scene of the novel, in Book XI, Strether accidentally discovers Chad and Madame de Vionnet boating together in the countryside during a weekend excursion and must recognize, after all, that this is the old Parisian story of an adulterous love affair. This moment of discovery indisposes his moral stomach and he must retreat to Woollett to maintain his own integrity, yet his vision of a richer, more beautiful life in Paris and his own affection and pity for Madame de Vionnet have unfitted him for Woollett, too.

The Ambassadors is representative of James in this sort of unresolved, bleak ending in which loss figures largely; in its counterpointing of aesthetic and moral values, sophistication and naivety, against one another in association with European and American points of view; and in its suggestion that the fusion of aesthetic and moral sensibility exists as an ideal bought at great price by his supersubtle protagonists. *The Ambassadors* is also representative in technique, for example, in its architectonic crafting, manifest in the hourglass structure and in the counterbalancing of the recognition scenes in Books V and XI, and also in its dramatization of intense inward subjective experience. To this end James utilizes functional characters ("*ficelles*") such as Maria Gostrey, a Europeanized American resident in Paris, and Waymarsh, a staunch New Englander and Mrs. Newsome's spy, to engage and challenge Strether and thereby to draw out and dramatize his states of mind. Likewise, settings and symbolic metaphors project character and mental attitudes, for the story is primarily one of inward evolution rather than outer events.

—Jean Frantz Blackall

AMERICAN BUFFALO
Play by David Mamet, 1975

American Buffalo hints at many influences. Its style is traditionally naturalistic. Like the mise-en-scène of two of his most notable playwriting influences, Samuel Beckett and Harold Pinter, Mamet's setting for *American Buffalo* is uncompromisingly spare. The language is stylized, and Mamet has pointedly alluded to its classical structure, saying, "It's divided into two acts. It takes place in twenty-four hours and adheres to all the unities." In a sense *American Buffalo* is also an autobiographical memory/morality play. In his essay, "Gems from a Gambler's Notebook," Mamet writes:

> For years I played cards every day. The game was held in an old junk store on the North Side of Chicago. The junk store was a front for a fence, and the fence ran a game every day of the year from noon till eight P.M., and I was there every day.

In *American Buffalo* Mamet re-creates that junk shop as the location for his play, a microscopic examination of three small-time crooks, Don, Bob, and Teach, who are plotting to steal a coin collection. Yet, beneath its grimy surface location, *American Buffalo* also assesses American business practices, the lexicon of power politics, and the inability of language to accurately communicate basic human wants and needs.

The underlying theme of *American Buffalo* may well be symbolized by the piece of pig iron stolen before the play begins by the off-stage character of Fletch.

> DON: He didn't steal it, Bob.
> BOB: No?
> DON: No.
> BOB: She was *mad* at him . . .
> DON: Well, that very well may be, Bob, but the fact remains that it was *business*. That's what business is.
> BOB: What?
> DON: People taking *care* of themselves. Huh?

The pig iron thus serves as metaphor for the compulsion to bully and destroy the opposition by whatever means necessary. *American Buffalo* is a refraction of America's moral decay caused by capacious greed and society's willful justification of rapacity, all reduced to the street value of a buffalo nickel.

Mamet's themes are expressed through his timing, which rivals that of a stand-up comic. What has often been called his great ear for dialogue is more accurately defined as an indication of the innate emptiness of his characters, reflected in their fragmented syntax, self-contradiction, and use of repetition, with obscenity disguised as non sequitur. The American language of the late twentieth century becomes the lifeline of Mamet's characters. Indeed, based upon the playwright's insistence that "there's no such thing as character," this Aristotelian playwriting element is replaced in *American Buffalo* by the characters' repetitions, rhythms, and by what passes for their actions: their almost farcically inept attempt at a robbery. Their failure leads to mutual suspicion, accusations of betrayal, physical violence, and ultimately estrangement. In *American Buffalo* the three characters expose their inadequacy through self-contradiction and negation. Teach's self-contradiction is most telling: his language says "I am calm. I'm just upset," while Mamet's stage action dictates, "[he] picks up the dead pig-sticker and starts trashing the junk shop."

At first Mamet's use of repetition is comic, but eventually the repetitions reveal the insecurities of the characters. Mamet has said: "I'm fascinated by the way the language we use, its rhythms, actually determines the way we behave, rather than the other way around." Mamet is also intrigued by coded language—language that allows the participants in a conversation to set themselves apart from eavesdroppers. In his essay "Make-Believe Town," Mamet writes: " I love and have always loved jargon, the secret symbols, the fraternal hailing-signs, the codes of the personals column . . . The codes mean to me that something of surpassing interest was in progress . . . ." In *American Buffalo* the encoded language of the petty criminal, the card game, and the lunch counter fascinate and enthrall the eavesdropping listener even while it isolates and entraps the speakers.

In the play Mamet carefully examines the American system of values, revealing its betrayal and its subversion. The characters are infused with contemporary society's values—or rather, perhaps, its lack thereof. Don, Teach, and Bob strive for material success, hoping to achieve the "big score," even as their actions and speech expose these values as inauthentic and insubstantial. They are trapped within stereotypical attitudes of machismo, misogyny, and bluster, which they articulate with comic incoherence.

—Arthur Horowitz

ANATOMY OF CRITICISM
Criticism by Northrop Frye, 1957

Most literary critics agree—some more reluctantly than others—that Northrop Frye's *Anatomy of Criticism* is the single most important work of literary criticism in the twentieth century. Although based on formalist modes of analysis, *Anatomy* originated the breakup of New Criticism's hold on literary study by urging a comparative, theoretical method; consequently, it prepared the ground for the Anglo-American discovery of 1920s Russian Formalism and the invasion of European structuralism, Formalism's linguistic heir. *Anatomy* argues lucidly and forcefully that criticism does not consist merely of explications or subjective evaluations of individual literary works, or of some external conceptual framework from history, sociology, or psychology applied to the study of literature. Rather, criticism deals with literature in terms of a specific conceptual framework that is not literature itself but not outside of literature either.

One cannot "learn" literature, insists Frye; what one learns is the criticism of literature, which is based on the assumption that literature is not a piled aggregate of works but rather a unified order of words spread out in conceptual space from some kind of center that only criticism can locate. Frye says that the repugnance some critics feel for any schematization of literature is based on a failure to distinguish between the unified body of knowledge known as criticism and one's individual experience of literature. The skill developed from studying literature, he says, is a special skill, like playing the piano, "not the expression of a general attitude toward life, like singing in the shower."

In the first essay in *Anatomy*, "Historical Criticism: A Theory of Modes," Frye develops five categories based on the relationship between the hero of the work and the ordinary human being. If the hero is superior in kind, he is a divine being and the mode is myth; if he is superior in degree, he is a leader and thus a hero of the high mimetic mode of epic and tragedy; if he is not superior, he is one of us and the hero of the low mimetic mode of comedy and most realistic fiction; finally, if he is inferior in power or intelligence, he belongs to the ironic mode.

In the second essay, "Ethical Criticism: Theory of Symbols," Frye uses the word "ethical" to refer to "ethos," or the "internal social context" of the work. He emphasizes his conviction that poems are not imitations of nature but imitations of other poems, asserting one of his most controversial statements: "Poetry can only be made out of other poems; novels out of other novels." Too often, Frye says, our romantic tendency to elevate the individual above his society leads us to underestimate the importance of conventions. Literature, he reiterates, comes from literature, not from life.

The third essay, "Archetypal Criticism: Theory of Myths," is the most sweeping and influential section of the book. Using the analogy of painting, Frye argues that the critic must "stand back" from a close analysis of details of the work, thereby enabling the overall design of the work, its archetypal organization, to become clear. For example, if we stand back from the beginning of the fifth act of *Hamlet*, we see a grave into which the hero, his enemy, and the heroine descend, followed by a fatal struggle in the upper world. Frye aligns myths with the seasons in a cyclical pattern: identifying comedy with spring, romance with summer, tragedy with autumn, and irony and satire with winter.

In one of the most frequently anthologized sections of the book, the discussion of the forms of prose fiction in the fourth essay, "Rhetorical Criticism: Theory of Genres," Frye distinguishes between the novel and the romance based on the concept of character. Frye says the romancer does not try to create real people, but rather, stylized figures who expand into psychological archetypes. The novelist, however, deals with personality, with characters wearing their social masks. Thus, the novelist needs the framework of a stable society, whereas the romancer deals with characters idealized by revery.

Although Frye aroused the scorn of Marxist and other social and cultural theorists by arguing that the "imaginative element in works of art" elevates them "from the 'bondage of history,'" *Anatomy of Criticism* truly initiated what has been called an era of theory in literary criticism.

—Charles E. May

ANGELS IN AMERICA
Play by Tony Kushner, 1991

In interviews dramatist Tony Kushner has confessed his love for "big, splashy, juicy plays." He has also spoken about what it means to be a gay Jewish socialist with a commitment to trying to tell the truth. That stage-show aesthetics and social critique can be effective partners has not always been clear to theatergoers in the United States, but the astounding success of Kushner's *Angels in America: A Gay Fantasia on National Themes* generated some new thinking about the possibilities of activist drama. Both parts of this ambitious seven-hour production, *Millennium Approaches* and *Perestroika,* received prestigious prizes; Kushner's work garnered a Pulitzer Prize, two Tony awards, two Drama Desk awards, and a host of other citations in the United States and abroad. And critical acclaim was matched by popular appreciation—standing ovations, extended runs, repeat attendance.

What is *Angels in America* about? The traditional narrative summary is not especially useful when addressing the content of this play. (Reviewer Harry Cherkinian described the Broadway opening in these terms: "The play featured graphic language, nudity, and sexual situations, amid themes of AIDS, family, betrayal, politics, religion, gender identity, and Mormons. And an angel crashed through the roof of a bedroom.") Those seeking easy labels have characterized *Angels* as an "AIDS play." But in an article in the *Harvard Gay and Lesbian Review,* Kushner explained that, contrary to widespread belief, his purpose was not to write a play about AIDS: "I set out to write a play about what it was like to be a gay, Jewish, Leftist man in New York City in mid-80's Reagan America." The plot of *Angels,* correspondingly, is complicated, discontinuous, and surreal. To speak of relationships, instead of plot, is somewhat more helpful. *Angels in America* features two troubled partnerships. The first comes apart as Louis, a word processor who works for the Second Circuit Court of Appeals, cannot face living with his AIDS-infected lover, Prior. Unable to tolerate the grimmer aspects of his partner's illness, Louis abandons him. But Prior is not to suffer his ordeal alone. His former lover, Belize (now a nurse), offers solicitous support and understanding (and later warns Louis about the consequences of violating "the hard law of love"). As the play develops, Louis becomes ever more guilty and self-destructive, while Prior, although anguished, acquires what might be called a cosmic understanding.

The play's second partnership involves a married couple. Joe, a chief clerk in the Second Circuit Court of Appeals (and a devout Mormon and ardent Reaganite), separates from his Valium-addicted wife, Harper, after acknowledging his long-denied homosexuality and the disaster his denial has made of their lives. Joe's mentor, Roy Cohn (a fictional version of the McCarthy-era villain turned successful lawyer and power broker), counsels him in an ethics of selfishness while trying to manipulate him to personal advantage. As Joe attempts to find happiness as a selfish gay Republican, Harper, who has partially withdrawn into a world of hallucinations and imaginary friends, has a series of strange revelations. When the unhappy Joe attempts to resume the marriage, she has learned enough to say no and to leave her miserable past behind. But much of the power of *Angels in America* derives from events and characters that at first seem incidental to the story of these failing relationships (for example, speeches by rabbis and Bolsheviks; the well-intentioned efforts of Joe's mother, Hannah) and from the periodic abandonment of realism for over-the-top fantasy (the haunting of Roy Cohn by the ghost of the executed spy Ethel Rosenberg; a Mormon visitor's center diorama that, magically, comes to life). Most spectacular, of course, are the angels that literally come crashing into Prior's bedroom—and, later, into his hospital room—challenging him mentally, physically, and spiritually. In combination with a campy and defiantly foul-mouthed humor, the play's pathos and extravagant theatricality work surprisingly well. Ultimately, *Angels in America* is about those things we are told not to address in polite company: sex, politics, religion. It is about passion and the dangers of not knowing who we are. It is about taking ethical responsibility in reactionary times. It is about human suffering, human compassion, and capitalist opportunism. It is about loss and recovery, weakness and strength. It is about the possibility of transformation. From a critic's point of view, *Angels* is an embarrassment of riches: any attempt to mine its themes and significance must prove embarrassingly inadequate.

The success of this big, splashy, juicy play, darkly comic in its confrontation of American homophobia, may usher in a new era of social theater, may encourage more playwrights to challenge powerful ideologies. At the least, this drama has pointed the way. And it stands on its own as a clear moment of social truth.

—Janis Butler Holm

ANNIE ALLEN
Poems by Gwendolyn Brooks, 1950

Annie Allen won a Pulitzer Prize for Gwendolyn Brooks in 1950, making her the first black person to receive a Pulitzer in any field. This second collection of Brooks's poems, some of which previously won the Eunice Tietjens Memorial Prize in 1949, actually consists of one long narrative prose-poem, "The Anniad," and several shorter poems depicting the lives of black women.

The work begins with "Notes from the Childhood and the Girl-hood" and speaks of Annie's parents, Maxie and Andrew Allen, and her childhood; her mother chastises the late sleeping Annie: "Get a broom to whish the doors or get a man to marry." Proud Annie thinks, "never men so many chief enough to marry me." In the epic poem "The Anniad," however, this "sweet and chocolate" black woman, "all her harvest buttoned in," must choose only domesticity, a man, a "Paladin" to love, to marry, to be her all. Her lover, the unnamed "tan man" appears, consumes her, and then marches off to war leaving Annie to wait alone. When he returns from the drama of war to a powerless existence in the ghetto, he rejects the meek Annie for a lighter-skinned "maple banshee." Annie, the "little lady who lost her fur, shivers in her thin hurrah" and gives all her energy to her children. When the "tan man" returns spent and diseased, "she folds his rust and cough in the pity old and staunch." He dies, and alone again, Annie, a young but old "hay-colored" twenty-four is "almost derelict and dim and done," "kissing in her kitchenette the minuets of memory." Thus ends the sad story of a proud black woman brought down by poverty and a racist, sexist society.

Brooks named this poem "The Anniad" to evoke the classical epics the *Aeneid* and the *Iliad*, only this time the central character is a woman, and her life, unlike those of the ancient Greek and Roman heroes, is more inward than outward. As Ann Stanford writes, "'The Anniad' adopts the character of an epic to appropriate the genre for an investigation into the process by which gender formation and sexual relationships are . . . at least powerfully shaped by the material culture out of which they arise." Claudia Tate's observation that "commonplace characters and events have been elevated in a ceremonious manner by using lofty diction and complicated techniques" responds to earlier critiques of Brooks's experimentation, namely, that it often led to obtuseness. Yet the precise attention Brooks pays to each word is necessary to convey both the romanticism and the realism of her indelible images of black life. In her autobiography, *Report from Part One*, she wrote that she wanted "every phrase to be beautiful, and yet to contribute sanely to the whole."

In the last section of the book, "The Womanhood," the poems are written in the first-person words of black mothers, such as Annie, who try to give their poor children, "adjudged the leastwise of the land," protection, teachings, and warnings on how to survive—"to carry hate in front . . . and harmony behind"—and advice on how to die.

This section also includes poems filled with irony that tell of those whites who sit in little booths at Benvenutis and stare at the "colored people" and of the poor blacks who gaze at the homes of the rich and say, "it is only natural that it should occur to us how much more fortunate they are than we are."

The poetry cycle ends with a plaintive though passionate and life-affirming stanza for Brooks's—and Annie's—people, "There are no magics or elves or timely godmothers to guide us. We are lost, must wizard a track through our own screaming weed." As George Kent concludes in his 1990 *Life* of Brooks, her representation of the human condition allows "engagement with the contradictoriness and complexity of experience."

Surprisingly, scholarly critiques of Brooks's work, including *Annie Allen*, were few until the 1990s. Among the most notable of these is the book entitled *On Gwendolyn Brooks: Reliant Contemplation* (1996), which includes essays on *Annie Allen* by Harvey Curtis Webster, **Stanley Kunitz**, and **J. Saunders Redding**. Kunitz comments on Brooks's facility with the sonnet form in "The Children of the Poor," five related sonnets in *Annie Allen*, "where the tightness of the form forces her to consolidate her energies and to make a disciplined organization of her attitudes and feelings."

In *Annie Allen* Brooks employs a circular rhythm to construct not only the life of one black woman but, in her graceful yet pointed words, the dignity of all women. This is why *Annie Allen* continues to compel readers to search for its true meaning.

—Jacquelyn Marie

ARIEL
Poems by Sylvia Plath, 1965

Sylvia Plath's best-known collection of poetry, *Ariel,* was published posthumously in 1965. It was assembled from the work left at her death in early 1963, and included most of the poems written during the fall of 1962 (the so-called "October" poems such as "Lady Lazarus," "Daddy," "Cut," and the bee sequence) and those from early 1963, "Edge," "Words," "Totem," and "Kindness." The poems from *Ariel* have more recently been published in *The Collected Poems,* which appeared in 1981 and was awarded the Pulitzer Prize for Poetry in 1982. In that book, they are arranged by the date in which they were written, according to Plath's records.

The effect of this slim volume of poetry—both in England, where it first appeared, and then in the United States, where it carried an introduction by **Robert Lowell**—was one of shock mingled with admiration for the strange brilliance of the poetry. The shock stemmed from the seemingly harsh anger underlying many of the poems, sometimes treated with comedy, again expressed as vituperation. Except for **Allen Ginsberg**'s long poem *Howl* in the mid-1950s, very few American poems had treated such powerful emotion; to find such feeling in poetry by a woman was especially surprising. From the beginning, Plath's work was considered an anomaly, as well as a conundrum: what was the furor behind her writing? What was a well-educated American woman living in London doing writing poems such as these?

Readers quickly adopted her as an important poet, and—perhaps more central to many lives—a representative of a culture where unspoken anger was understood: the women's movement quoted her work; people interested in depression and suicide; other poets whose lives had also been spent trying for new effects in a highly competitive art. She quickly became a staple of poetry anthologies, and a few key poems became the Plath poems that everyone recognized. It was as if she had managed to express the social angers and angst that was to become pervasive a few years later, in the disillusioned 1960s and 1970s.

Plath's poem "Lady Lazarus" was a mocking monologue, spoken by a woman who divided her lifetime into suicide attempts: "I have done it again. / One year in every ten / I manage it—" The wry comedy of this poem, punctuated with horrifying comments like "Dying / Is an art, like everything else. / I do it exceptionally well," was set in surprising juxtaposition to the raw seriousness of its theme. Her poem "Daddy" worked in the same manner: to move the reader from an expected response (in this case, a perhaps maudlin but certainly sentimental evocation of the daughter's memories of her father) to a sharply contrasted mood. The venom of the speaker's reminiscence in "Daddy" seems inexplicable, until the key psychological fusion—that the husband who has recently left her and the father figure are one and the same, the authoritative male—is clarified:

I made a model of you,
A man in black with a Meinkampf look

And a love of the rack and the screw.
And I said I do, I do. . . .

Marriage fares badly in *Ariel,* most bitterly in "The Applicant," a funny poem about a woman's qualifications for the lifework of marrying a man, but motherhood is caught vividly and with sympathy. "You're," the series of metaphors describing the unborn child, is a sprightly and winning poem; "The Night Dances," the beautiful "Morning Song" ("Love set you going like a fat gold watch"), "Balloons," and "Kindness," with its poignant "The blood jet is poetry, / There is no stopping it. / You hand me two children, two roses," are each masterful poems expressing the mother's enjoyment in her children.

The majority of Plath's *Ariel* poems, however, are darkly foreboding, from the 1961 "Tulips" with its long, weary lines to the sinister "A Birthday Present," "Elm," "Getting There," and "Death & Co." The oppressive weight of the knowledge of death recurs in poems like "Berck-Plage" and "The Bee Meeting," even though the other four poems in what is known as the "bee sequence" are more affirmative. "Stings," for example, pictures the achieving woman as the old, wily queen bee, still in control, still winning ("They thought death was worth it, but I / Have a self to recover"). Many of Plath's late poems set this image of victory against the omnipresent tone of defeat: "Wintering," "Little Fugue." "Fever 103°," and especially the title poem, "Ariel," in which the speaker rides a triumphant horse into the sun, "the red / Eye, the cauldron of morning." Throughout these striking poems, Plath has managed to weave imagery from anthropology and dream, as well as from women's lives, to evoke truly wide-ranging responses. The *Ariel* poems must not be read as rational statements. They are the best of contemporary poetry, drawing on all the poet's resources, and demanding that panoply of resources as well from the reader.

Because Plath's estranged husband, Ted Hughes, edited the book *Ariel* for its publication, changing it dramatically from the manuscript Plath had left ready for the press, readers should check the information about the book as Plath had planned it in *The Collected Poems,* where all the late poems now appear. There, its identity as the words of the androgynous, and ultimately triumphant, spirit from Shakespeare's *The Tempest* rises above the sense of depression that dominates the collection as it was published in 1965. In Plath's own arrangement, the book began with the word "Love" and ended with "Spring," and was a memorable progression of emotion, from affirmation through depression to further affirmation.

—Linda Wagner-Martin

THE ASSISTANT
Novel by Bernard Malamud, 1957

Alfred Kazin has written of Bernard Malamud's fiction: "The scene is always the down-at-heel grocery, the winter street, the irreversible hardness of the modern city. Malamud has caught at once the guttural toughness of big city speech and the classic bitterness of Jewish dialogue" (*Contemporaries,* 1962). But, he goes on, this harshness is always linked with another quality: "the otherworldly feeling." Nowhere is this truer than of *The Assistant.*

Malamud, Kazin says, gives us "the talk of people who are not merely on edge but who live really on the edge." In *The Assistant* this is not merely the edge of economic marginality. **Philip Roth** observed of Malamud in "Writing American Fiction" that "his people live in a timeless depression and a place-less Lower East Side," and indeed it would be difficult, without comparing commodity prices in Morris Bober's store, to work out in which of several decades in this century the novel is set. Bober's grocery store is certainly down at heel, in a declining neighborhood. The Jewish idiom of his wife Ida catches the irony of his perpetual bad-timing: "You should sell long ago the store." But if Bober's luck is always wrong, "he could not escape his honesty, it was bedrock; to cheat would cause an explosion in him, yet he trusted cheaters." He gets up every morning at six a.m. for a single customer, the old anti-semitic Polish woman who buys a three cent roll—not just for the money but out of a sense of obligation. One of the people who cheats him is Frank Alpine, the young Italian American down-and-out drifter, another anti-semite, who first with a friend mugs and robs Bober for a few dollars from the till and then, found starving and unrecognized by Bober in his cellar, comes to work as his assistant. Another person whose luck has always evaded him, Frank obscurely hopes to pay Morris back by stinting himself, falling in love with Bober's daughter Helen while barely daring to speak to her, but weakly unable to resist spying on her in the shower, until he finds himself once more with his hand in the till.

Frank transgresses another margin, between love and lust, when he first rescues Bober's daughter Helen from a rapist and then rapes her himself. Both these crimes, of robbery and rape, in a sense actually consummate the blood relation between Alpine and the Bober family. Like so many of Malamud's characters, Alpine is on edge with a spiritual restlessness and anxiety, a sense of failure before even starting out, and, an orphan, he feels that his true, authentic life, has eluded him. "Life renews itself," Helen says to him after he tells her of his failure in one earlier attempt to "look for a better life": "My luck stays the same," he replies. It is this belief in an external "luck" which is the heart of his problem. What Alpine comes to realize is that "his luck had so often curdled, because he had the wrong idea of what he really was and had spent all his energy trying to do the wrong things." But finding who he really is is not so easy. For Frank, it involves conversion to that Jewishness he once despised as a religion of suffering and acquiescence.

The edge these characters finally approach is that between life and death. Bober dies after falling while, still sick, he insists on clearing snow outside the store. Frank, losing his footing on the crumbling edge of Bober's grave, actually tumbles in, but in doing so he begins his rebirth, taking on himself for the first time the weight of responsibilities Bober has now renounced.

In the end, the edge of which Kazin speaks is that between two dimensions of moral being—the this-worldly cynicism and brutality in which Alpine has been reared, and the other-worldly realm towards which he aspires, represented by his patron saint, St. Francis, whose self-chosen poverty becomes the symbol of a different way of living. This other world makes itself felt in Frank's repeated moral urge towards atonement, his desire to justify and redeem himself in the eyes of some surrogate for the father he never had, which is the deepest impulse of his being. Frank had confused renewal with running away. Like all Malamud's heroes, he learns in the end that the new life is found where he is, in a new mode of relation to his life and those around him. Strug-

gling to make himself worthy of Helen, he takes over Morris's role after his death, working to make the shop profitable and send Helen to college. Helen, still keeping him at a distance in the closing pages of the book, nevertheless notices the change:

> She had despised him for the evil he had done, without understanding the why or aftermath, or admitting that there could be an end to the bad and a beginning of good. It was a strange thing about people—they could look the same but be different. He had been one thing, low, dirty, but because of something in himself—something she couldn't define, a memory perhaps, an ideal he might have forgotten and then remembered—he had changed into somebody else, no longer what he had been. . . . What he did to me was wrong, she thought, but since he has changed in his heart he owes me nothing.

Helen has changed, too, moving towards Christian forgiveness as he moves towards a Jewish sense of atonement (the language of debt and credit common to both religions). In the last moments of the book he consummates this change by undergoing circumcision ("The pain enraged and inspired him. After Passover he became a Jew") thereby redeeming his own casual anti-semitism and accidental criminality by an act of deliberate choice and commitment. Alpine's conversion is not the renunciation of one religion for another—a kind of flight. Rather it is the bringing to fruition of the messianic hope concealed in both: the rebirth of the other-worldly within the flesh of this world. It is a token of that release from historical contingency which is also a release into his own true life and identity, finding a new life and testament within the old. Significantly, Malamud prefaces this symbolic gift of the foreskin to Jehovah with a different gift, conceived of in terms of Frank's Catholicism. In a reverie, Frank dreams of St. Francis retrieving from the garbage where Helen had thrown it the wooden rose Frank had carved for her. In the saint's hands, it turns into a real flower and, from him, Helen accepts the gift. The sexual symbolism is as real and as persuasive as the spiritual one. For Malamud, the "different life" all the characters seek is to be found, at last, not in some other-worldly place, but by making the sordid and actual world they inhabit flower with a human, and humane, significance.

—Stan Smith

THE AUTOBIOGRAPHY OF ALICE B. TOKLAS
Memoir by Gertrude Stein, 1933

If a casual reader picked up either the gray cloth first edition of *The Autobiography of Alice B. Toklas,* published by Harcourt Brace in 1933, or the black cloth edition, published by the Literary Guild that same year, he or she would be inclined to believe that the book was indeed by Alice B. Toklas, as Gertrude Stein's name does not appear on the binding or the title page. Yet the book was written by Stein, who, writing as Toklas, says on the last page: "About six weeks ago Gertrude Stein said, it does not look to me as if you are ever going to write that autobiography . . . . I am going to write it for you . . . . She has and this is it."

As such this "autobiography" is autobiographical only in the sense that much of it chronicles Stein's life, as Toklas, who was Stein's longtime companion, gives way to Stein about five pages into the work, and so for a good third of the book the reader is treated to a narrative detailing Stein's life and experiences. As such, the book is in reality a biography/autobiography of both Toklas and Stein, and this is underscored by the fact that in reality Toklas had little to do with the composition of the work, and her primary contribution to the book was an occasional comment that she inserted as she typed it.

It is not advisable to classify the work as simply a standard account of the lives of two people, however, for in addition to the biographical aspects of the book, the narrative introduces the reader to many of the twentieth century's most important figures in the arts and literature. **Ernest Hemingway**, **F. Scott Fitzgerald**, **Sherwood Anderson**, **Ezra Pound**, James Joyce, **T.S. Eliot**, and **Louis Bromfield** are but a few of the literary figures encountered, and among the artists we find personages no less famous than Picasso and Matisse, both of whom are often discussed in the narrative. Along with a first hand look at so many important figures, the reader is acquainted with the Cubist movement, World War I, the Rosseau banquet, and the inner-workings and literary exchanges of the American expatriates in Paris during the 1920s, to whom Stein attached the still frequently used appellation "The Lost Generation."

Recognizing the great potential of a work so broad in scope, Stein's agent in Paris, William Aspenwall Bradley, quickly sold the American publishing rights to Harcourt Brace, and the English rights to Bodley Head. The book became the Literary Guild selection for September 1933, and Stein realized one of her greatest desires when *Atlantic Monthly* serialized the book in four installments beginning in May 1933. Stein, who had published over a dozen books prior to 1933, saw her fame and recognition expand greatly after the publication of *The Autobiography of Alice B. Toklas,* and her work gained a much wider acceptance from that point on. In that respect, *The Autobiography of Alice B. Toklas* became a touchstone for her career, as she was thereafter recognized as a literary force as opposed to being merely a literary personality.

Critics then as well as now have found the book difficult to classify in relation to Stein's other work, as it is uncharacteristic of her in comparison to her overall literary output. **Edmund Wilson**, writing in "Gertrude Stein Old and Young: 27, rue de fluerus" in 1933, called it "an instructive and entertaining book," and said that although it may not have been "Stein's most important book, it is likely to prove her most popular." In "Gertrude Stein," Francis Russell wrote in 1954 that Stein's recollections have "a sprightliness about them that is a welcome relief to what has gone before," but that the book "gives her away, exposes her shallowness, [and] her flaccid impervious mind." In 1975, Richard Kostelanetz wrote in "Gertrude Stein: The New Literature" that although *The Autobiography of Alice B. Toklas* is often taught because it is one of her "simpler books," it is not one of her "extraordinary ones—those whose special qualities have never been exceeded."

Overall, although *The Autobiography of Alice B. Toklas* may not be Stein's most representative work, it may well be the one that is most often read. Interesting not only for what it tells us about Stein and Toklas, it also provides a good but admittedly selective look as some of the most important figures in literature and art in the early part of the twentieth century. For this reason if no other, *The Autobiography of Alice B. Toklas* is a work that is indispensable to students seeking to learn more not only about Gertrude Stein, but about any number of great writers and artists that have

since come to be regarded as a highly formative part of our present cultural and intellectual makeup.

—James R. Simmons, Jr.

AWAKE AND SING!
Play by Clifford Odets, 1935

The social and economic environment of the depression dominates Clifford Odets's classic play *Awake and Sing!* in a curiously ambiguous way. The survival ethic that, in one way or other, governs all members of the Bronx Jewish family means that in places a heroic defiance enshrines human stature, even in some of its meanest gestures. On the other hand, the depression context also operates like the melodramatic hand of fate, arbitrarily making and breaking, so that individuality seems a transitory commodity. Economic survival becomes a lottery, cushioning some characters, driving others to suicide, and a similar pattern of arbitrary causation invades other aspects of characters' lives, as when the daughter finds she is pregnant to a (non-appearing) commercial traveller. Microcosmically, the family absorbs the national fraud, through the father's faith that "the government ain't gonna allow everything to be a fake." The naivety of this view is exposed by the lodger, who has learned a line of pragmatism from his experience as a war cripple: "It's all a racket-from horse racing down. Marriage, politics, big business—everybody plays cops and robbers." For some characters, the lesson is picaresque: they learn what their mother has known from the start, that they cannot afford morality. But, however vague, the principles of regeneration and transcendence echo from the title to lift other characters through adversity towards a better (revolutionary) future.

Because most of the events are presented as the product not of personality, but rather of superhuman forces, the mechanics of the action may seem contrived or propagandist. The play, however, is quite distinct from the mainstream of melodrama because the characters' existence is quite remote from audience norms. The Berger family seems to be lower middle class (Odets may even have conceived them as proletarian), and so the characters' mobility is actually in the direction of the audience. This means that not only does an upper-middle-class theater audience fail to share the Bergers' dreams, but an intense irony is generated because the characters' fantasies fall short of audience commonplace. When Jacob, the economic messiah, commits suicide so that his grandson may inherit his insurance money, $3,000, the audience simply shudders at a drama that is pivoting on principles of extrinsic value. His life's worth seems to correlate precisely with the Caruso records which, broken, drain much of the lyricism out of the title.

The first version of the play, entitled *I Got the Blues,* was found by the Group Theatre's director, Harold Clurman, to have a "masochistically pessimistic ending." This was partially remedied in the produced version by the substitution of an ambivalent ending (in which pessimism is an available interpretation), and by an enormous reduction in the explicit Yiddishkeit in the dialogue. No close study of any version of the play, however, can ignore the fact that all the characters suffer from an intense feeling of cultural dislocation, and are groping for a twentieth-century promised land. In need of a liberator in the mold of Gideon, one character pins his hopes on Teddy Roosevelt, another on Popeye the Sailor—who, eating spinach and knocking out "four bums," seems the closer to the legendary judges of Israel. Similarly, several characters articulate a notion of paradise, within the sordid constraints of twentieth-century life. Cultural dislocation also generates a nervous assertiveness. As a settled American Jew, with a matriducal empire tentatively established, Bessie feels an intense antagonism towards a recently arrived "foreigner" who, though also Jewish, lacks her expertise in American english. It is, similarly, important to her husband to lecture his son on "an American father's duty."

The brittleness of a family structure grounded on such premises is considerable, especially when both female characters perjure themselves in their dealings with their men, without being pushed to an extreme situation. That at least some of the characters have some constancy is shown when the grandfather, a Marxist Jew who quotes the title passage from *Isaiah,* commits suicide by jumping from the tenement roof; this is generally interpreted as a means of exploiting an insurance company, but it may also imply a realization of that eschatological section of the *Isaiah* prophecy (ch. 26-7). Such matters were alluded to extensively in the first version, but in the final text are reduced to stage directions as vague as "Quotes two lines of Hebrew."

Awake and Sing! is unquestionably important for its political and cultural content, and the terms of its social realism are striking beside other plays which Group audiences were at the time responding warmly to, such as **Sidney Kingsley**'s absurd medical melodrama, *Men in White.* Odets's play, however, also has a strong claim for critical attention on dramaturgic grounds, in that it exploits subtextual energies much more extensively than any other American play of the 1930s. Partly, this is through Yiddish mannerisms, but it also emerges through "wiseguy" talk from characters whose insecurity in human relationships leads them to a sonorous commercial rhetoric, the basis of which in reality is often impossible to determine.

—Howard McNaughton

THE AWAKENING
Novel by Kate Chopin, 1899

Like most of Kate Chopin's stories, *The Awakening,* set in the late- nineteenth-century Creole society of the New Orleans area, features a strong local ambiance and a richly symbolic texture; but thematically it transcends regional writing. Critics have frequently noted its close connections to the French work of Maupassant and Flaubert, especially Flaubert's *Madame Bovary. The Awakening* is the story of a young woman's quest for freedom; and the discoveries she makes along the way, including the ultimate realization that the complete freedom for which she yearns is not available to her in mortal life, constitute her awakening.

During her summer dalliance with one Robert Lebrun, Edna Pontellier becomes increasingly aware of the restrictiveness of her conventional marriage, and almost by chance discovers, simultaneously with her learning to swim, that the drive toward self-determination should be just as appropriate for women as it traditionally has been for men. It occurs to her that tradition has placed restraints on women by establishing societal modes (the structure of the family, patterns of social conduct) and by dictating concepts of morality (primarily through the church). Acting on her new realization that since tradition has been created by people it can also be set aside by people, she defies her husband and her father, sends her children to the country, moves out of the family home into her own small cottage, and in an illicit rela-

tionship with one Alcée Arobin flaunts her rebellion against moral propriety.

At first pleased with her escape from tradition, she soon discovers that she is less free than she had expected to be. Her sensual attraction to Arobin teaches her that sex and love are not equivalent, that sex is a separate, instinctive, fundamental force of nature that attracts men and women to each other and, as Per Seyersted asserts in his Chopin biography, "spurs us blindly on toward procreation." Edna's relationship with Arobin, combined with her smoldering love for Robert and her presence at the travail of her friend Adéle, the conventional biblical mother, leads Edna to understand that free love is not free, that the connection between love-making and the pain of childbirth is firmly established within the context of natural law by which all people are bound and from which there is no escape. But, although she understands all this and although she feels intensely the loneliness and the sense of separation which inevitably accompany the attempt to create one's own destiny, Edna is not willing to relinquish her quest.

Still driven by the need for self-determination, by the urgent longing for total freedom, and unwilling to accept the natural role which she sees as an inevitable succession of lovers before her, she returns to the gulf to recapture the sense of freedom that exhilarated her by signalling her independence when, early in the novel, she learned to swim. Alone, ignoring warnings intended for her well-being, she swims out too far and tires. Flawed by her own mortality, like the bird with the broken wing, she falters— "her strength was gone." Kaleidoscopic images of the past flash through her mind reminding her of cast-off traditional connections, but they do not draw her back. Informed by her recent discoveries, she realizes it is too late for all that—"the shore was far behind her." Assuming the role of the courageous soul, one who "dares and defies," she indicates no desire to return or to be rescued. Like Taji in Melville's *Mardi,* when he was unable to find ultimate beauty in this world, Edna moves out through "the circumvallating reef" into the unknown regions beyond, thus extending her search into eternity. Her realization that the ideal she so desperately desires is not available to her as a mortal is her final discovery, the final phase of her awakening.

Whether the denouement of the novel is read literally as the renunciation of the unacceptable restrictions of mortal life or interpreted as a symbolic extension of the quest for ultimate freedom, the existential choice of self-determination is implicit.

—Clayton L. Eichelberger

BECAUSE I COULD NOT STOP FOR DEATH
Poem by Emily Dickinson, written 1863

According to Thomas H. Johnson, whose indispensable 1955 edition of Emily Dickinson's poetry established both canon and chronology, "Because I could not stop for Death" (J.712) was written in 1863, one of the three of those astonishingly prolific years in which she produced over one-third of the 1775 poems in the collection. Also included in the first collection of the poems in 1890, it was given a title, "The Chariot," and suffered other emendations by Thomas Wentworth Higginson, who deleted stanza four entirely and made such changes in diction as substituting "played" for "strove" in line nine: "where Children strove / At Recess—in the Ring—." It is the most famous of her proleptic poems (i.e., the persona speaks beyond the grave) and is typical of her work in that it fuses two of her most prevalent themes, death and courtship, and represents her major strategy, using the simple ballad stanza and natural or domestic images for elliptical and complex statement.

The six quatrains can be summarized as follows: 1) Death in the personification of a suitor calls on the speaker and takes her for a carriage ride, along with one other passenger named Immortality; 2) they ride slowly because Death is not in a hurry and the speaker has politely put aside both her work and play in order to go with him; 3) they pass familiar sights: schoolchildren, a field of grain, the sunset; 4) the temperature drops and the speaker becomes aware of her inadequate clothing; 5) they pause near an underground dwelling; 6) the centuries that have passed since then seem less long than the day the carriage ride began.

Neither this nor any other paraphrase can do justice to the multiplicity of interpretations inherent in the poem. Death may be construed as a courtly lover or a false seducer. Similarly, the speaker may be understood to be a willing or unwilling partner. The clothes imagery of the fourth stanza, a gown made of gossamer and a tippet of tulle, suggests both a bridal dress and a nun's habit. Most intriguing of all are the concluding lines:

> Since then—'tis Centuries—and yet
> Feels shorter than the Day
> I first surmised the Horse's Heads
> Were toward Eternity-

These might imply that the speaker is remembering the day of her death from beyond the grave, or that her escort has betrayed her by keeping her riding in limbo, or that she is expressing a death wish, or that she merely distinguishes between finitude ("the Day") and timelessness, or that she finds the human's lot of the realization of death to be so overwhelming that it makes time stand still.

Interpreters have remained constant in focusing attention on this poem, even as critical styles and emphases have changed. A 1932 essay by **Allen Tate**, calls it "one of the perfect poems in English" and praises it for its ambiguity. In 1960, Charles R. Anderson concentrated on the necessarily metaphoric language to express the inexpressible and saw the poem "flawless to the last detail." Sharon Cameron, in her 1979 study, *Lyric Time,* provides a post-structural reading, emphasizing the shifting back and forth between temporality and timelessness. Vivian R. Pollak (*Dickinson: The Anxiety of Gender,* 1984) and Jane Donahue Eberwein (*Dickinson: Strategies of Limitation,* 1985) offer feminist readings, one arguing that the speaker represents the poet, the other that the speaker is imaginary. According to Richard B. Sewall's highly respected biography, the impulse for this poem might derive from Dickinson's hearing that an acquaintance, Olivia Coleman, died suddenly of tuberculosis while riding in a carriage. Eberwein reminds us that Dickinson wrote Abiah Root in 1846: "I almost wish there was no Eternity. To think that we must live forever and never cease to be." These biographical hints shed some light on the provenance and philosophical stance of the poem.

Technically, the poem is typical of Dickinson's eccentric style. Within the ballad form she is presumed to have adopted from familiar hymns, she incorporates here slant rhyme, unconventional capitalization, punctuation consisting almost entirely of dashes, syntactical peculiarities, puns ("Civility" and "gazing grain"), and elaborate personification. One atypical attribute is the colorlessness of its imagery. Ordinarily Dickinson uses color lavishly, as

she does in the "Blue—uncertain, stumbling Buzz" of a companion proleptic poem, "I heard a Fly buzz—when I died" (J.465). The lack of color in J.712 is underscored by the filmy, ghost-like quality of "gossamer" and "tulle," and in turn underscores the cool, detached tone of one of the several masterpieces of this extraordinary poet.

—Nancy Carol Joyner

BELOVED
Novel by Toni Morrison, 1987

Beloved, Toni Morrison's fifth novel, originated from a nineteenth-century newspaper article she read while doing research in 1974. The article focused on a fugitive slave, Margaret Garner, who had run away with her four small children sometime in 1856 from a plantation in Kentucky. Using the Underground Railroad, she had travelled to Ohio, where she lived with her mother-in-law. When her Kentucky owner arrived in Ohio to take Margaret and the four children back, she tried to murder her children and herself. She managed to kill her two year-old daughter and severely injure the remaining three children before she was arrested and jailed. *Beloved* reinvents Garner's life by selectively developing two related themes: the destructive potential of a mother's love for her children, her man, and other relatives; and the impossibility of the former slaves ever forgetting their experiences in bondage.

The novel's fragmentary and repetitive form reflects the duality of the central characters, who live both in the present, Ohio in 1873, and, through memory, in the past, Kentucky in the 1850's. The mother, Sethe, lives with her one remaining child, a daughter named Denver, in her deceased mother-in-law's house. This house is occupied by one other person, a spiteful ghost believed to be that of the two-year-old daughter Sethe had murdered eighteen years earlier. In the beginning of the story, Paul D, one of the men who had lived on the Kentucky plantation with Sethe, arrives in Ohio and manages to rout the ghost before he moves in with Sethe and Denver. The relationship between Sethe and Paul is threatened by her intense devotion to Denver and to her recurring memory of having murdered the daughter she posthumously named Beloved. Given his past experiences with violent white slave owners, Paul D temporarily moves out of Sethe's life when he learns of the murder.because of his conviction that black people neither could or would do such a thing.

A twenty year old woman, calling herself Beloved, arrives at the house one day and proceeds to nearly destroy each of the three central characters. As the physical manifestation of Sethe's murdered daughter, Beloved seeks reparations from her mother and competes with Denver for this attention. Denver devotes herself at first to granting Beloved's every wish because she was lonely for a companion. Once Denver understands Beloved's intentions to deplete Sethe's physical and emotional strength as an act of revenge, she takes the steps necessary to rejoin the black community from which she has been isolated all of her life by her mother's actions. Beloved disrupts the relationship between Sethe and Paul D by first making him feel unwanted in the three-woman household, and then by luring him into a sexual encounter out in a back-yard shed. As they each deal with Beloved and the problematic situations that she initiates, Sethe, Denver, and Paul D learn to face truths about their individual and collective past.

Reviewers hailed *Beloved* as Morrison's best novel to date because of its profound exegesis of slavery in America and the emotional ramifications that extended long after its supposed abrupt halt in 1865. Literary critics noted *Beloved*'s similarity to nineteenth-century slave narratives in its use of memory to make the slave experience more accessible to contemporary readers. Some have placed the novel in the American literary tradition along with Stowe's *Uncle Tom's Cabin,* and compared the circular narrative strategies to those of William Faulkner. Awarded the Pulitzer Prize in 1988, Toni Morrison's *Beloved,* places her in the first ranks of American literature.

—Alice A. Deck

THE BIG SLEEP
Novel by Raymond Chandler, 1939

In "The Simple Art of Murder" Raymond Chandler poured scorn on the stylized decadence of "logic-and-deduction" detective stories, all exhibiting "the same old fussing around with timetables and bits of charred paper and who trampled the jolly old flowering arbutus under the library window." During the 1930s, beginning in the hard-boiled fiction of the pulp magazines, the crime novel was displacing the detective story. When at fifty Chandler wrote *The Big Sleep,* his first novel, he cannibalized whole chunks from several of the twenty short stories he had already written for the pulps.

Chandler, with literary ambitions, wanted to shift the emphasis from plot to character and style. Character sketches, not plot, make the opening hook for the reader. But character remains largely stereotype; style is Chandler's triumph. Out went ratiocination and the body in the library, in came tough talk, mean streets, fast violent action, and—in Marlowe—a hero whose idealism and sentimentality hides behind self-deprecating irony and wit. Marlowe is the man with a code of behavior, the familiar figure of the frontier translated to the modern city. Originally called Mallory, he remained a knight: his search for damsels to rescue is figured in the stained-glass entrance of the Sternwood house on *The Big Sleep*'s first page. But Carmen, the novel's naked damsel, is to Chandler not worth saving. The irony is aimed not at knights but at a world which doesn't deserve them: "it wasn't a game for knights," Marlowe admits later.

Eddie Mars is the god behind most of the private wars. Marlowe cannot stop him, fails to clean up society, and in that sense is an anti-hero. There is also an absent hero, Rusty Regan, dead before the narrative begins, emphasizing the futility of Marlowe's quest. Regan and Marlowe brought joy and salvation to the Sternwoods and were to be thanked by being dumped in the sump, the source of their oil-rich wealth. In the depression of 1932 Chandler had been sacked from his oil company job for alcoholism; in the novel Carmen, not Marlowe, has the exotic drink problem. Marlowe and his oil-millionaire employer get on well when they meet man to man. This is Chandler's fantasy of revenge and self-justification. It is also a parable of the individualistic ethic and its contradictions. By living on his wits Marlowe escapes wage-slavery, yet must still seek employment: "I'm selling what I have to sell to make a living." Ideology as much as style makes for Chandler's appeal to intellectuals.

"Down these mean streets a man must go who is not himself mean, who is neither tarnished nor afraid," wrote Chandler of his hero. Marlowe may throw more wisecracks than punches, but in one way he is worse than mean: "Women made me sick." Part baby, part sexual predator, Carmen is the familiar schizoid stereotype of romanticism. Her "small corrupt body," her threatening sexuality, are the novel's signs of murderous insanity. Her sister Vivian ("She'd make a jazzy weekend, but she'd be wearing for a steady diet") is little better, for Chandler equates them when they both offer themselves to Marlowe in quick succession. There must be more to hate than this, but Marlowe's loves are no more plausible. Mona Mars, his obsession at the end, is a metal woman, with a wig "so platinumed that her hair shone like a silver fruit bowl" and a "silvery voice" with a "tiny tinkle" in it. He calls her "Silver-Wig," never using her name. In complete contrast, when Bogart played Marlowe his easy empathy with women became the driving force of the film. But in the book male attractiveness throws Marlowe as much as female, and the strident disgust at "fags," "queens," and "pansies," plus the mistrust of women, have led some to discern a savage repression of the homosexual element in Marlowe-Chandler. Going to bed with women is "letting them down." Chandler's English public-school attitudes are showing. Thankfully, some of the women get their own back in kind: when Marlowe asks the dumb blonde Agnes whether he hurt her head, she replies, "You and every other man I ever met."

This novel's "mean streets" are hardly mean at all. Chandler loved the city, and Marlowe evokes it memorably as the coffee shop smell and the soot from the oil burners of the hotel drift in at his window. The streets are never cozier than when drenched by Chandler's insistent rain. Marlowe snuggles down in his car and watches the policemen in their rubber slickers which "shone like gun barrels" having fun carrying giggling girls through puddles. It is the suburbs, canyons, and empty country beyond the city which are this Marlowe's heart of darkness. Houses lurk low down behind their trees and shrubs. The imaginative deaths happen out of the city: Regan rotting in the lonely sump; Owen Taylor drowned off Lido pier; Geiger in his dark exotic house with the square box hedge masking the door completely and "no solid ground" around it. The book's two climaxes, the confrontations with Canino and with Carmen, have equally lonely settings. This jungle, not urban but "natural," is prefigured in the opening chapters with the "uncomfortable" line of the foothills and the orchids of Sternwood's conservatory, "nasty things" with flesh "too much like the flesh of men." Nature becomes comfortable only when tamed like the "flawless lines of the orange trees" which go "wheeling away like endless spokes into the night" as Marlowe drives to face Canino.

Later Chandler works were sometimes more perfect, sometimes more hesitant, than this fast-paced first novel. Though it is memorable for its action and for Marlowe talking out of the left side of his heart, it is this other aspect of style—the imagery of nature, the city, mirrors, rain, and the images of color in the opening chapters—which truly constitutes the novel's imaginative intensity.

—R.J.C. Watt

BIG TWO-HEARTED RIVER
Story by Ernest Hemingway, 1925

"Big Two-Hearted River" is one of the great American short stories, although long by Ernest Hemingway's standards. It relates a single day's fishing excursion by a young man in Michigan's secluded upper peninsula. Nick Adams is the only character, and, as the reader comes to recognize, the real drama takes place in his psyche. Nevertheless, while Hemingway creates a memorable landscape (he had Cézanne in mind) of the far north country, he appeals to all of our senses (sight, touch, smell, taste, and sound) as he relates Nick's walk to the river, his preparation of camp, and his fishing for trout.

Often anthologized, the story is the first Hemingway writing that many readers encounter. Such readers will find much to admire and to intrigue them, but they will discover more of the story's complexity if they read it in the context of *In Our Time* (1925, revised 1930), Hemingway's first major book, an experimental work that confirmed his genius. Hemingway conceived of the story as the culmination to that work, which he thought of as much more than a gathering of his short stories. The book has, he insisted, a special unity.

"Big Two-Hearted River" returns the reader to Nick Adams, the character who figures prominently in the first several stories of *In Our Time,* stories that carry Nick in chronological order from his boyhood to the risky time when he lights out on his own, as he does in "The Battler," a story written especially for *In Our Time.* After that story, Nick seems to disappear from the work. Then Hemingway boldly focuses attention on him in "Cross-Country Snow," the last in a group of four stories about young married people; there we learn that Nick has taken his place among the married, though earlier his friend Bill advised that marrying meant that a man was "absolutely bitched."

But no wives are mentioned in "Big Two-Hearted River." If Nick is not married in "Big Two-Hearted River," then that story departs from the chronological pattern that governs *In Our Time.* It is important to remember that although there are parallels between Nick's life and Hemingway's, there are also many differences. Though this story is based on a trip Hemingway took the year before his marriage to Hadley Richardson, material that he excised from "Big Two-Hearted River" indicates that he had thought of Nick there as a married man. In any case, memories of women are, by design, kept minimal. Women mean complexities, Nick learned, and his fishing trip is an effort to simplify his life. Despite a shaky beginning to his journey, things begin to go better simply because he is a disciplined traveler. "Nick felt he had left everything behind, the need for thinking, the need to write, other needs." Although the story is pronouncedly a male affair (even the trout Nick catches are male), the context of *In Our Time* suggests that Nick has to work through numerous problems, many of them having to do with women. There is the mother he rejects ("The Doctor and the Doctor's Wife"), the ruined romance with Marge ("The End of Something"), and possibly a greater trauma suggested by the rejection of the unnamed protagonist by Luz in "A Very Short Story" near the middle of *In Our Time.* This experience suggests the turning point, perhaps the most important loss Nick had yet experienced.

Interchapter VI, juxtaposed tightly against "A Very Short Story," suggests another major trauma. The chapter commences "Nick sat against the wall of the church," where he has been carried after being badly wounded in shelling on the Italian front. The interchapters of the first half of *In Our Time,* all concerned with war, have acted as counterpart to the cluster of stories about Nick's youth that begin the book. Although the book contains no stories about Nick's war experiences, "Big Two-Hearted River" reveals a young man still coming to terms with the destruction of the war and his own close brush with death. In "Big Two-Hearted

River" Nick returns to a place removed from the late conflict, but he remembers it as he passes through the ruins of Seney, Michigan, burned to the ground. Life contains many destructions.

For a time Nick is stunned as he surveys the burnt-out country in and around Seney. But he slowly rallies, finding in nature abiding values that enable him to carry a heavy load to a well-earned rest as night falls. He rises refreshed the next morning to test his nerves in the drama of trout fishing, not wishing to rush his sensations or even to catch many fish. He looks to make small gains so that he can later make big gains—perhaps even to write the stories about the war that are not found in *In Our Time.* We catch a vision of the challenge Nick faces through the image of the dark swamp. Nick wisely refrains from entering it now: "In the swamp fishing was a tragic adventure. Nick did not want it. He did not want to go down the stream any further today." He will save that psychic journey for another time.

The "Big Two-Hearted River" comes to symbolize the stream-of-life—its challenges, its affirmations and its denials, and finally the reality of death. Although the Nick who goes fishing in it has a specific history (evoked most concretely in the story through memories of his friend Hopkins near the end of the first part of the two-part story), Nick also becomes archetypal. As he walks through the forest toward "the good place" that he seeks, he is like John Bunyan's Pilgrim, who shoulders a heavy load before finding a satisfactory rest. And Nick Adams is never more Adamic than he is in this story. He experiences anew the innocence he had earlier lost, finds the primal energy that will enable him to pursue again the challenge of creation. Although many of Hemingway's stories deal with loss, he ended *In Our Time* with a story of affirmation and hope, but not of false promise. "There were plenty of days when he could fish the swamp."

—Joseph M. Flora

BILLY BUDD
Novel by Herman Melville, 1924 (written 1888–91)

Billy Budd is a classic because it deals with universal themes with the insight and artistry of a great writer. The themes are the timeless questions: What is the source of evil? Is there ultimate justice? What is the worth of the individual? What philosophy can an honest man accept? In his masterpiece, *Moby-Dick* (1851), Herman Melville explored these issues through the first-person narrator, Ishmael (symbol of all the spiritually disinherited). In the end, everyone except the philosophizing narrator goes down with the whale (symbol of a cruelly impersonal universe). Thus the author judges Romanticism's "noble savage," Humanism's "superman," and Christianity's "first mate" inadequate. He is left clinging to partial truths drifting on an ocean of doubt. Forty years later, in a style equally rich in symbolism and allusion, Melville reduces the scale of setting and characters but deepens his perceptions of the major truths.

In *Billy Budd,* instead of primeval forces or a megalomaniac, tragedy is introduced through the credible villainy of a petty officer. The "noble savage" is no longer a Pacific Island prince with power over life and death but an illiterate British seaman. The Christian is no longer the cautious first mate of a New England whaler but the noble captain of a British man-o'-war and a learned gentleman. The author no longer speaks through a youthful critic of society but as the author, sympathetic to all facets of the drama. Thus he finds Claggart's evil baffling but concedes the man is powerless to resist it. He acknowledges the brutality of war but approves the character of the naval chaplain and justifies Vere's decision to sacrifice one for the good of all.

By historical incident, reasoned argument, symbolism, and allusion Melville argues that this life is an ironic mixture of good and evil that will be set right by the "Last Assizes" (Final Judgment). The Great Mutiny was a "monstrous" evil, but it led to good. Vere (truth) reminds the drumhead court that a decision based on compassion for Billy risks mutiny, a tragedy for many. When the ship (society) engages the enemy, the Athéiste (atheist), it defeats it but at terrible cost, for Vere is mortally wounded. However, he dies with Billy's name on his lips, not in remorse but in the conviction that they are to be reunited. Other allusions support this basically Christian position. Of Claggart's death Vere exclaims, "It is the divine judgment of Ananias" (Acts 5:1-5). Vere's farewell to Billy is likened to that of Abraham about to sacrifice his son, Isaac, a test of obedience to God. Billy and the crew call out "God bless Captain Vere"; Billy's hanging becomes an Ascension (victory over death), and chips of the spar from which he was hanged become as pieces of the Cross to his shipmates (lasting influence for good).

Attention to the wealth of allusion and symbolism reveals Melville's perception of the complexity of this life and the spiritual universe it imperfectly reflects. For example, Billy is described as "young Adam before the Fall," but is, of course, living in the world after the Fall. His appearance implies that his mother was "eminently favored by Love and the Graces," but these gifts were used to produce a "foundling." Billy's tan (seagoing experience) has subdued the lily (purity) but not the rose (passion) in him. The Dansker, an "old sea-Chiron" (tutor to Achilles and Hercules) names Billy "Baby Budd," identifying his fatal immaturity. Captain Graveling calls him a "peacemaker," saying a "virtue went out of him" (as in Jesus's healing); Lieutenant Ratcliffe replies, "blessed are the peace-makers [Matt. 5:9], especially the fighting peacemakers." The *Rights of Man* loses Billy to the demands of society's survival, but while he loses some of his rights, he gains opportunity to prove his worth (Vere was about to recommend him to the captaincy of the mizentop).

Perhaps the most significant symbol is speech, a paramount achievement of civilized man. Its skillful use is essential to most of society's functions. It is also a major indicator of the individual's mental, emotional, and spiritual condition. Thus Vere uses it successfully to command his ship and to win the trust and affection of Billy. He perceives its misuse by Claggart, urges its careful use upon Billy. Billy's failure to use it under inner stress is the crucial evidence of his immaturity.

Melville wrote his earlier sea tales during a period of rapid expansion in America's size, wealth, and power, but, like his friend **Nathaniel Hawthorne**, he challenged the popular optimism by portraying the tragic aspects of Nature, Society, and Individualism. As the biographical nature of his material gave way to his increasingly painful spiritual struggles, his work grew richer but darker. In this final work the gloom is dissipated by acceptance of concepts that restore beauty to youth, honor to leadership, value to society, and victory to goodness.

—Esther Marian Greenwell Smith

BLACK ELK SPEAKS
Autobiography by Black Elk as told to John G Neihardt, 1932

Originally published in 1932, John G. Neihardt's *Black Elk Speaks* may yet prove to be the last half of the twentieth century's most controversial work of Native American literature. The book is venerated by some critics as much more than the sketchy astold-to autobiography of a Sioux visionary and medicine man that it initially appears to be; they claim Neihardt's text weaves a bold religious tapestry out of a Sioux life rich in myths and symbols of universal appeal. Meanwhile, other critics question the book's merit as non-fiction and as a trustworthy record of Sioux life, religious and otherwise. Certain of Black Elk's tales have proven to be heavily edited by Neihardt, while outright authorial invention elsewhere has sparked serious debate concerning the book's historical authenticity. Regardless, *Black Elk Speaks* remains an achievement lavish in Native American biography, anthropology, history, and anecdote.

The book opens with Black Elk's offering of the peace pipe, and the reader is immediately introduced to a world where little exists that separates this world from the spirit world. After a pipe ceremony Black Elk, medicine man and visionary, begins the narrative of his life as a Lakota of the Ogalala band. Born "in the Moon of the Popping Trees (December) on the Little Powder River in the Winter When Four Crows Were Killed (1863)," Black Elk spends little time on his early childhood, except as it alludes to the first of several visions he has over the course of his life. Nine years old when his first and most elaborate vision comes to him, Black Elk doesn't immediately understand the role it seems to dictate for him as a savior of his people.

Black Elk's gradual understanding of this vision is an odyssey woven throughout the remainder of the Lakota's tales. Some of the more humorous tales recount such Sioux traditions as buffalo hunts and courting rituals, while others deal seriously with the ever encroaching white man's hold on Sioux land. The retelling of the battles of Little Big Horn and Wounded Knee, the murder of Crazy Horse, and Black Elk's trip to Europe as a player in a traveling show put on by Buffalo Bill present an important first-hand account of key points in Native American history. The narrative comes to an end just after the battle at Wounded Knee in 1890, as the medicine man who has tried so hard to defend his people finally acknowledges their inevitable fate, as women and children are butchered because of the white man's greed for the "yellow metal" and Sioux land.

John G. Neihardt's role in documenting Black Elk's spiritual and historical odyssey often generates the book's most ardent criticism. Black Elk's son, Ben, served as translator between the author and the medicine man, while Neihardt's stenographer daughter took notes during the many hours of interviews. Yet, transcriptions of the un-edited interview reveal a second Black Elk, one of much greater expression than the deliberately Indian-sounding Black Elk of the book. More misleading than Neihardt's rough colloquialisms are the words critics say the author put in Black Elk's mouth. Particularly the much idealized Crazy Horse has proven to be derived from something other than Black Elk's tales. Neihardt invented the book's Crazy Horse from a conglomeration of written sources, so that the Ogalala leader comes to represent a man with an otherworldly presence. Similarly, never does Black Elk in the original transcripts describe the spirit world in which he believes as casting a shadow on this real world, as he does in a moving passage of the book. Such obvious discrepancies have led critics to question Neihardt's motives and the historical merits of *Black Elk Speaks.*

Regardless of the vast critical interest in the Black Elk, who has come to light in other sources, there is no denying that Neihardt's 1932 text was a remarkable publication for its day. *Black Elk Speaks* will continue to be an important introductory text into a world less like our own with each passing minute, if only because Black Elk, both the man and mystic, is one of our literature's greatest heroes.

—Brian Beatty

THE BRIDGE
Poem by Hart Crane, 1930

In his essay "Modern Poetry" (1930) Hart Crane argued that "unless poetry can absorb the machine, i.e., *acclimatize* it as naturally and casually as trees, cattle, galleons, castles and all other human associations of the past, then poetry has failed of its full contemporary function." In fact, Crane seems to have done more than simply "acclimatize" the machine as a subject for poetry. It would seem that in a sense he created poems as machines are created, and perhaps in turn the machine is useful as a metaphor to understand how Crane's poem achieves its objective.

The Bridge, like the structure it celebrates, is a work of creative engineering. In a remarkable letter which Crane wrote to his patron Otto Kahn while *The Bridge* was in progress, he discusses his work on the poem as dryly and objectively as an engineer might detail his plans for a new kind of engine or a new road. It is clear that Crane quite consciously developed his metrical and symbolic patterns and strategies for the poem on the basis of his close study of French symbolism and the metrics of the Elizabethans, Donne, and other early English poets. Traditional prosody was as immutable to his poetic sensibility as the laws of physics which dictated the essential form of the Brooklyn Bridge. Crane used that prosody to realize his poem in much the way that John Fitch, John Stevens, and other early American engineers used the steam engine to make new forms of transportation: one adapted one's vision to whatever means—metrical or mechanical—were available.

The poetic vision at the center of *The Bridge*—a vision of the American spirit as endowed with quasi-divine strength and purpose—came largely from **Walt Whitman**, but Crane seems to have had little interest in, or at least understanding of, Whitman's prosody. For Whitman it was essential to develop a new poetics, a new way of speaking, in order to express his special vision of the American spirit; the language and the vision are not in fact separate or separable. For Crane, however, prosody and vision were not at all the same; the second was in effect a device at the service of the first.

Crane's very conservative poetics obviously set off *The Bridge* from the work of older modernist poets such as **William Carlos Williams** and **Marianne Moore**, and the Whitmanesque optimism which much of the poem embodies was largely at odds with much serious poetry being published. (It was at this time, after all, that **T.S. Eliot**'s *The Waste Land* was having its impact on the sensibilities of new poets.) But if the great optimism of *The Bridge* is seldom found in the work of subsequent poets, the influence of Crane's synthesis of traditional English poetics, French symbolism, and American subjects can be clearly seen in the work of such "academic" poets as **Robert Lowell**, notably in "The Quaker Graveyard in Nantucket."

The Bridge is divided into eight sections, preceded by "To Brooklyn Bridge," eleven tightly shaped, metrically precise, rhymed quatrains which show Crane's symbolist technique at its most intense and in which the bridge is poetically raised to divine significance: "Unto the lowliest sometime sweep, descend / And of the curveship lend a myth to God." With its powerful mixture of sublime conviction and absolute metrical control, "To Brooklyn Bridge" is among Crane's most impressive achievements, and several of the poems which follow are also of an equally high order. Among the best certainly are "Atlantis," "The River," "Ave Maria," and "Cape Hatteras," in which the poet confronts his mentor, Whitman.

In "Cape Hatteras" the airplane serves Crane as the equivalent of the railroad in "Passage to India," Whitman's celebration of technology. Later in "The Tunnel" the poet meets **Edgar Allan Poe** ("Your eyes like agate lanterns") in the dark, violent world of the subway—also, of course, a railroad but, unlike Whitman's, one suggesting discord, anger, and fear. Crane takes Whitman's vision but expands it with moral and emotional complexities that his predecessor could not, or would not, acknowledge. Poe's nightmare sensibility cannot be excluded from Crane's America, but it does not finally weaken or damage the sublime Whitmanesque optimism that is at the center of *The Bridge.* The poem ends with the same ecstatic affirmation of its vision as that with which it began.

In spite of that ecstatic affirmation, however, one senses that it is less the Whitmanesque vision itself than the poet's own will which fuses his poem into a single effective unit. Read separately, parts of *The Bridge,* particularly "Indiana," seem weak and sentimental. But behind even the weakest parts, Crane's determination to unify *The Bridge* can be felt. It is that determination and fixed delight in making things, in engineering things, that may be seen as the ultimate motivating power in *The Bridge* and perhaps the chief reason it continues to astonish us.

—Edward Halsey Foster

THE CALL OF THE WILD
Novel by Jack London, 1903

In the Soviet Union, Jack London is regarded as one of the greatest of American writers, chiefly because of such sentiments as are found in now-obscure works of his such as "A Night with the Philomaths." There he has a firebrand orating about a revolution of the proletariat

> twenty-five millions strong . . . to make rulers and ruling classes pause and consider. The cry of this army is: No quarter! We want all that you possess. We want in our hands the reins of power and the destiny of mankind . . . . We are going to take your governments, your palaces, and all your purpled ease away from you, and in that day you shall work for your bread even as the peasant in the field or the starved and runty clerk in your metropolises . . . . You have failed in your management of society, and your management is to be taken away from you . . . . This is the revolution, my masters. Stop it if you can.

However, the early poverty and struggle that drew London to Marx and to communist or socialist ideology as he read books in the Klondike winter were followed by success and belief, according to Charles Child Walcutt, in himself as "an epitome of the Darwinian Struggle for Existence, his success an example of the [Herbert] Spencerian Survival of the Fittest." He had also read Nietzsche, and he came to people his prolific output of fiction with supermen, heroes who could succeed without or in spite of either communism or democracy, heroes that were not so much self-sacrificing socialists as rapacious capitalists of the spirit. They conquered by force of will and indomitable courage rather than by cleverness. In the great American tradition, they "hung in there"; and when the going got tough, they got tougher. London liked to think of himself as one of these semi-divine heroes. A newspaper reporter once noticed that his Korean houseboy called London "Mr. God." The reporter added, "Jack liked it."

In London's most popular novel, *The Call of the Wild,* the hero is a dog—the story is told entirely from the dog Buck's point of view—and even when ill treatment causes him to revert to the "dominant primordial beast" he is a symbol of what man can do to overcome obstacles and become the leader of his fellows. A mongrel, a cross between a German Shepherd and a St. Bernard, Buck is uprooted, stolen from his comfortable California home, and sold for work as a sled dog in the Gold Rush of 1897. Then he becomes the companion and eventually the savior of a young prospector. Finally he becomes the leader of a wild pack, and the book ends with these triumphant and famous words:

> When the long winter nights come on and the wolves follow their meat into the lower valleys, he may be seen running at the head of the pack through the pale moonlight or glimmering borealis, leaping gigantic above his fellows, his great throat a-bellow as he sings a song of the younger world, which is the song of the pack.

In some sense Buck is a representation of the author as he would like to see himself. An illegitimate child of a spiritualist (who later married John London, not his father), London quit school at 14, worked in a cannery, became a pirate on the ship *Razzle Dazzle* in San Francisco Bay at 16 and a sailor to Siberia and Japan at 17, tramped around, and went to the Klondike in 1897. There he found more adventure, opportunity for the will to power, risk and challenge and self-fulfillment, freedom from civilization's restraints—the life suited to a man who once said "morality is only an evidence of low blood pressure."

London returned from the Klondike without gold but with a rich vein of wilderness experiences which he industriously mined thereafter. *The Call of the Wild* is but one of his tales of heroism and violence in circumstances of danger. Where **Bret Harte** told the story of "A Yellow Dog" that became a snob in the gold fields and Eric Knight was to sentimentalize canine faithfulness in *Lassie Come-Home,* London told the tale of a dog who went from snob to superdog. London's was a rousing tale that had a message as well as a love for mankind.

London, who always had more drive than deftness in writing, was extremely clever to focus on Buck rather than on the human world around him. Judge Miller, by whose Santa Clara, California, fireside the young Buck lay in innocence and peace before he was "dognapped," has more of a function than a character in the book. John Thornton, the strong, silent, noble type to whom Buck becomes attached in the Yukon, is a stereotype: we provide his qualities from other reading rather than discover them in the novel.

"Black" Burton and other bad guys are also stock characters. So are the greenhorns and the French-Canadians and the other humans. The animals, however, are sufficiently humanized, and if they, too, are stereotypes we are more impressed with the personalities they are given than with their lack of depth. Pike (the thief), Dub (the clumsy one), Dave and Sol-leks (the sled dogs who are dedicated "professionals"), Curly (the amiable Newfoundland dog) who "made advances to a husky dog the size of a full-grown wolf" and was "ripped open from eye to jaw" in an instant—these animals each have their place in the story and can be said to be characters in the fiction in a sense in which the humans are not. Among the dogs are the "bully" personalities so beloved of the Teddy Roosevelt period of American history. Among them is clearly shown "the law of club and fang": "So that was the way. No fair play. Once down, that was the end of you." Among them, also, there are treachery and nobility, faithfulness unto death, and a conviction that moral nature is "a vain thing and a handicap in the ruthless struggle for existence." They learn that "kill or be killed, eat or be eaten, was the law." Towering above all is Buck. "When he was made, the mould was broke," says Pete. And in awkward dialect Hans affirms: "Py jingo! I t'ink so mineself."

That a good deal of the book is given to describing the feelings of the animals is an advantage in the light of London's clumsiness with cliche ("Every animal was motionless as though turned to stone") and dialogue ("Plumb tuckered out, that's what's the matter"). The action moves swiftly; we are seldom aware of the "stoppages" of the sleds or that characters are "lessoned," of the awkward prolepsis or the literary infelicities, as the melodramatic tale unfolds of how Buck "put his name many notches higher on the totem pole of Alaskan fame." We discover that sentiment can exist without a love story; Mercedes, the only woman in the book, is a shadow. Popular writers discover that a riveting story, as of the "kidnapped king" tried in the furnace and emerging pure gold (or "a yellow metal," as London would say), is enough.

Those who want more can see London as a racist, fascist, Social Darwinist; as a predecessor of **Jack Kerouac** and other "on the road" writers; as a tough-guy writer in the tradition developed by **John Dos Passos**, **Ernest Hemingway**, and **Norman Mailer**, though perhaps best exemplified in **Dashiell Hammett** and other writers of crime fiction; as a writer about animals (such as Buck and the wolf-dog that seeks civilization in *White Fang*) foreshadowing George Orwell's *Animal Farm* in using them as metaphors of humanity; as a giant in his time—in 1913 the most popular and best-paid writer in the world—who was denigrated in later times; as (to note Andrew Sinclair's argument) a path-finder in areas as different as the boxing novel and sociobiology of the school of Lorenz, Ardrey, and Desmond Morris.

In the biography *Jack* (1977), Sinclair makes a gallant effort to rescue London from too close identification with the message that "a man with a club was a law-giver, a master to be obeyed" and the view of "nature red in tooth and claw." Sinclair does much to bring him to serious consideration as much more than a once-popular author, an author of juvenile literature, the master of the dog story. Nonetheless, London's place in literary history depends now and always will depend on the appeal of *The Call of the Wild.*

—Leonard R.N. Ashley

THE CANTOS
Poems by Ezra Pound, from 1925

The Cantos of Ezra Pound are a work of 802 pages in the current Faber 1975 edition (reprinted from the earlier New Directions editions). They are the chief product of the author's very active writing life, the continuous though not the sole project of the years 1909-59. He always wanted to write an epic ("a poem containing history" and "the tale of the tribe"); the result is his greatest achievement, *pace* those who prefer his earlier poems or even his criticism. The ostensible purpose of the *Cantos* is to show the history of the West from its mythical origins in the world of the *Odyssey,* through various ideal societies, through its eventual perversion in the triumph of mercantile avarice in an industrial society run by presbyterian bankers—to its final crash in 1914. There are 117 cantos, issued in ten volumes between 1925 and 1969, a canto being a sequence of between two and twenty pages in length. Each is devoted to a single subject often presented dramatically and from sharply opposed angles. The mode of presentation is dramatic and lyrical rather than discursive or analytic, and the author's views are not stated, though it is clear, for example, that he is against usury (Canto 45) and in favor of the founding fathers of the American republic. The technique is frequently of a moving tableau or montage of images, a concentrated style developed for shorter poems in the period of imagism.

The result is full of historical "piths and gists," of magically evocative landscapes and crucial moments. The lack of a unified narrative and of an explicit discourse makes the reading of the *Cantos* a disconnected experience, especially after *The Pisan Cantos* (1948), a dramatic monologue from the poet's cell in the U.S. Army camp outside Pisa in 1945: "from the rains of Europe, *ego scriptor.*" Thereafter the poem, though chiefly concerned with periods of pre-modern history, becomes increasingly, though sometimes unwittingly, an intellectual autobiography, as the guide nears the end of his guided tour. As well as an Odyssean exploration of cultural experience, the *Cantos* are intermittently modelled on a Dante-like ascent from hell through purgatory to heaven, though the steps are not obvious and Aquinas's map useless to a humanist. Hell and purgatory are full of usurers, war-profiteers, and newspapers; heaven is a mythical Mediterranean landscape of ideal city states run by just rulers and full of cafés, nymphs, temples, and goddesses, where farmers, craftsmen, and artists can flourish. Pound preferred Italy to Philadelphia, the old world to the new, and being looked at by Beatrice to listening to Virgil. His own political ideals are various, from the Confucius, who in Canto XIII says "When the prince has gathered about him / All the savants and artists, his riches will be fully employed," to the lawgivers of Byzantium and medieval England, to the reformist founders **Thomas Jefferson** and Napoleon, and to unorthodox men of will and destiny such as Sigismundo Malatesta of Rimini and Benito Mussolini. Pound wants a just society by good government in the interests of the more productive of the people, in a curious combination of a Ruskinian medieval organic society (such as one sees in Ambrogio Lorenzetti's fresco of Good Government in the Palazzo Pubblico at Siena), with a free American individualism which seems at odds with so harmonious a vision. Though Pound advocated Social Credit economics in the middle cantos, practical political contradictions do not have to be resolved because the *Cantos* work by the juxtaposition of fragments in a way Pound called "ideogrammic," contrasting various kinds of good government or individual conduct with their opposites rather than by

articulating the relations of various social goods. Though full of actualities and documented facts, the *Cantos* are primarily concerned with these as instances of ideals in action. Their moments of splendid coherence are lyrical rather than systematic. Pound's *Cantos* are the greatest, as well as the longest, long poem in English of this century; only David Jones's *The Anathemata* bears comparison. Pound's epic is greatest in ambition and in achievement, and in its radical challenge to received cultural history; in scope, range, and variety, and in voice, image, music, and finesse. The chief disadvantage of the poem is not its difficulty of reference but its scale and structure, and its serial production. In their ventriloquism, allusiveness, and multicultural fragmentariness the *Cantos* resemble *The Waste Land* (for which the first seven cantos prepared the way). Pound, having cut *The Waste Land* severely, described it as "19 pages, and let us say the longest poem in the English langwidge" (sic). The *Cantos* are forty times as long as *The Waste Land,* and organized less visibly. Joyce's *Ulysses* eventually becomes more unreadable than the *Cantos,* but it did appear in one volume.

The first thirty cantos center on the individualist world of Italian Renaissance princes, their lust for beauty and order in art in contrast with their lust for power in their lives; here the successful rebel Sigismundo Malatesta is Pound's hero. A second contrast, between the Quattrocento and a perverted modern world, is insisted upon; and the economic theme becomes strident in the middle cantos, counterpointed with paradisal visions of Chinese and Mediterranean historical epochs and landscapes. From Canto 42 onwards the enlightened eighteenth-century republics of Siena and the United States are presented, with a Confucian digest of the history of China. *Cantos* 71-2, in Italian, defending the Italian republic of Mussolini, do not appear in English editions. The Pisan cantos articulate a seared vision of a world seen from the "death cells" at Pisa. Thereafter the personal and visionary parts of the poem are markedly more successful than the chunks of "objective" historical celebration of ideal states and just cities. The fragmentariness of the units of composition increases as the poem goes on, but so does the poet's refinement of skill in creating a vocal weave and a musical organization for his perceptions, his nuggets of historical and actual fact, and his memories. The *Cantos* are not, as extracts may suggest, a lecture with a machine-gun, but a sustained conversation with the reader. Pound is a great talker in verse, often with a self-ironic or interrogative note, as well as a lyric celebrant of the world of eye and ear.

—M.J. Alexander

CATCH-22
Novel by Joseph Heller, 1961

Joseph Heller's *Catch-22* is essentially a postmodern war novel. It recreates and mocks, simultaneously, the tradition of ironic and grim war fiction that culminated in the separate peace sought by **Ernest Hemingway**'s characters. And Heller's book deconstructs all wars and establishments: ostensibly about World War II, but written after Korea, and published during Vietnam, *Catch-22* parodies the American business, religious, and political hegemonies that the military echelons reflect.

The humor of *Catch-22* appeared to Philip Toynbee to resemble a Marx brothers film as Kafka might have conceived it. The novel is apocalyptic and lunatic, illogical and post-Christian. And very funny. A work also of black humor, *Catch-22* has a hero in Yossarian who not only perceives the system's venality and corruption but ultimately makes an existential choice for freedom. To leave the insane war—where men are suborned to bomb their own units for business purposes, where pilots are sacrificed for their superior officers' records, where the good and the innocent become victims—is not to desert in the face of the enemy but to refuse to help this enemy within; as Walt Kelly's Pogo remarked, "We have met the enemy, and he is us."

Heller has admitted that his novel is "about the contemporary regimented business society" and satirizes oil claims, public relations, psychiatry, racism, loyalty oaths, and security trials as well as larger American idealistic constructs such as sportsmanship, success, patriotism, and abstract morality: the Protestant Ethic and the American Dream. Heller writes of war in terms of contemporary philosophy, raising matters of time's indeterminacy, phenomenology, alienation, and illogic. Like a Swift, Heller apologizes for his soldiers' revolts because in the absurd world of war, the men revolt against what is revolting. And Heller's vision is such that in doing so they convert revolutionary anger into sardonic comedy.

There are four basic character divisions in this novel that traces a bomber squadron's missions during the Italian campaign; their drunken and sex-obsessed leaves in Rome; their absorption into the business enterprises of the madly corrupt mess officer Milo Minderbinder who cheats and steals to the motto "What's good for M & M Enterprises is good for the country," even to the extent of arranging to bomb American bases and steal their morphine; their attempts to stop the ever-increasing numbers of missions to be flown before the pilots can go home; their disappearances and deaths. First, there are the purely corrupt, ambitious men who use their fellow humans: the Colonels Cathcart and Korn, Generals Dreedle and Peckham, and officers who accept the system, Cargill, Scheisskopf, Black, Whitcomb, Aarfy; they are all, like Aarfy, murderers. At the opposite end of the spectrum are the outsiders, good men trapped in and mostly wiped out by this system: Nately, Chief White Halfoat (whose family history as a Native American is appallingly awful and humorous), Hungry Joe, McWatt, Danby, Dunbar, the Chaplain. Yossarian is one of them, and momentarily their leader, for in refusing to fly any more missions, he saves the remnant. While the third character group is predatory, too, each is so outrageously comic and so self-aware of rapacity, that the individuals are only evil in the sense of a Groucho Marx or W.C. Fields persona: Milo, ex-Pfc Wintergreen, Doc Daneeka, even Clevinger, Major Major Major, and Major _____ de Coverly. Fourth, there are those who carry the novel's serious subtext, the dead who never were alive in the book: the unknown soldier Mudd who did not officially get on the roster, Kraft, the invisible soldier in the hospital, and, crucially, Snowden, whose ghastly death in Yossarian's arms over Avignon recurs again and again in a **T.S. Eliot**-like litany that raises the overwhelming question, What is Man? (Just matter, entrails). In categories of their own are the women nurses who are only objects of lust, and Orr, the wise squirrel of a pragmatist who tries to teach Yossarian how to crash and escape by raft to Sweden.

In many important ways the novel is deeply religious as it moves from portraying Yossarian as a mock-savior eschewing false gods of violence and business—Heller stated that he was depicting business society "against the background of universal sorrow and inevitable death"—to showing his paranoia become valid when he makes a terrible night journey through a devastated Rome where "The night was filled with horrors, and he thought he knew how Christ must have felt as he walked through the world . . . . "Heller asserts that the comic world of American bomber squadrons is a function of the tragic world of beaten children and murdered whores. Thus, Yossarian's refusal to be tempted by the Colonels who would save him at the price of betrayal of his fellow pilots, his commitment to himself, to the young sister of a dead whore, to Sweden—freedom—turn *Catch-22* from a war novel of despair to a universal fiction that ends in hope, in the admission of the protagonist's humanity, into a leap for freedom and responsibility (just as **Ralph Ellison**'s Invisible Man will rise from underground), in the acceptance of contingency and a war against war. All this and marvelous comic writing too make *Catch-22* one of the great war novels of this century.

—Eric Solomon

THE CATCHER IN THE RYE
Novel by J.D. Salinger, 1951

When J.D. Salinger published *The Catcher in the Rye* in 1951, it met with mixed reviews but soon became a tremendous success among young people, who felt that Salinger was speaking to them directly. The novelist **Joan Didion** reports meeting a typical Salinger fan in 1956, a young woman from Sarah Lawrence who declared that Salinger was the only person in the world capable of understanding her. In the 1960s members of the youth culture who read Salinger's later stories hoping to find enlightenment in the conversations of the Glass family continued to read *Catcher* as a testament to the emptiness of the "establishment." Today the novel is more often assigned in English courses than passed from friend to friend, but it continues to find a number of enthusiastic readers outside the classroom.

The Catcher in the Rye has been read both as the story of a neurotic who cannot make the "adjustments" necessary to adult life and as the story of an outsider who can see clearly, with the vision of a child or a saint, the horrors of mid-century American life which are not visible to those comfortably ensconced within it. The novel is a long monologue by Holden Caulfield, who tells the story of "this madman stuff that happened to me around last Christmas," the events of three days in a bleak, loveless New York City, where Holden has fled after flunking out of his third prep school. He is in flight from what he sees as the unbearably "phony" world of prep school snobbery, stupidity, and cruelty, and from a future in which he can do no more than "make a lot of dough and play golf and play bridge and buy cars and drink Martinis and look like a hot-shot."

Holden is an outcast like Huck Finn, and like Huck he tells his story in his own idiom. Holden's voice is not merely a virtuoso re-creation of contemporary adolescent speech. His profanity reflects his experience of a "goddam"-ed life, a "hell." He repeatedly insists that he is telling the truth ("I really did," "It really is") because in his experience and by his rigorous standards, most people do *not* speak the truth. He prefaces his revelations with "if you really want to hear about it," "if you really want to know," and "if you want to know the truth," because he has found that few people *do* want to know the truth.

Holden feels a scathing, harrowing disgust for the "phoniness" he senses so acutely all around him. It makes him literally ill. He is repulsed not only by the insincerity and self-promotion of the "phonies," "hot-shots," "jerks," "bastards," and "morons," but by the phoniness that is excellence corrupted: Holden's brother D.B., the Lunts, and Ernie the piano player are corrupted by the success of what they do well. Holden himself is implicated in the pretense that so disgusts him; we see him do those things for which he castigates others, and he is half-aware of the fact. But in the midst of his revulsion he is moved by pity and forgiving love for the people who appall him.

His story is full of failed attempts to communicate, messages never delivered, uncompleted phone calls, overtures not taken up, appeals repulsed. **William Faulkner**, who praised the novel, said that when Holden "attempted to enter the human race, there was no human race there." In his great trouble, Holden attempts to address serious questions to Mr. Spencer, to Sally Hayes, to Carl Luce, to Mr. Antolini; no one can really hear him. All interchanges prove sour and barren. When Holden despairs of ever getting through to anybody, he decides in furious disgust to run away and stop trying: "I thought what I'd do was, I'd pretend I was one of those deaf-mutes. That way I wouldn't have to have any goddam stupid useless conversations with anybody."

One literal message does get delivered: Holden's note to his little sister Phoebe, significantly, does reach her. Phoebe receives the message, and she is the only one who listens to him. And it is Phoebe, finally, who brings Holden back to some unresolved relationship with the world he is fleeing. At his lowest point in the novel, alone in the defaced mummies' tomb in the museum, he ascends to find her dragging a heavy suitcase, begging to run away with him; he finds that he cannot be responsible for taking her away from what she finds hopeful and good even in the world he so distrusts.

Holden wishes that Phoebe could remain safe in beautiful and innocent childhood; this feeling is allied to his grief for his brother Allie who died at ten, Phoebe's age. He wants what is "nice" to be proof against change; he dreams of saving children from falling "over the cliff" into the adult world, so much of which disgusts him. Phoebe's redeeming love makes him realize that he cannot keep her from "falling": "The thing with kids is, if they want to grab for the gold ring, you have to let them do it . . . . If they fall off, they fall off . . . ." It is not at all clear whether Holden can (or should) compromise with the life expected of him, but he will not lure Phoebe into total retreat, and she saves him from it.

—Mollie Sandock

THE CATHEDRAL
Poem by James Russell Lowell, 1870

James Russell Lowell's *The Cathedral* is a neglected major American poem. First printed in 1869 and given final revised form for an edition of Lowell's collected works in 1890, it is richly representative of Lowell as poet, and profoundly reflective of his historical time and nationality. It is no less revealingly and impressively the product of a timeless human struggle.

How God is to be defined or man to fix his relationship to Him—the old question of faith—is the burden of *The Cathedral*. Consisting of 813 lines of blank verse in 21 unnumbered sections, it is an extended meditation, a verse essay. Historically it is important as a transitional work between romanticism and modernism. While its diction, syntax, and rhetoric may sometimes convey the flavor of a static nineteenth-century poetic product, its

dominant, modernist impact is of a shared process, of experiencing an individual mind in search of answers.

The Cathedral was inspired by a visit to Chartres when Lowell was in France in the summer of 1855. The day of his visit was "clear and lucent," truly "superb," he reported to a friend at the time, and the Chartres cathedral was "wonderful," "very grand." Never, he wrote, had he "heard finer music than the wind made among the stone chords of the spire"; the cathedral was almost enough in itself for a lifetime." Fourteen years later a poem based upon the experience "wrote itself"—just "all of a sudden it was there," Lowell claimed. "I hope it is good," he said in a letter just after the intense period of the poem's creation, "for it fairly trussed me at last and bore me up as high as my poor lungs will bear into the heaven of invention." "It is a kind of religious poem . . . ."

Its original title of *A Day at Chartres* indicates the germinal, concentrated personal experience out of which *The Cathedral* was written and which remains a powerful emotional factor and the narrative, structural framework of the finished poem. It is with the memory of this particular day that the poem opens—a day "Cloudless of care, down-shod to every sense, / And simply perfect from its own resource"—but transition is quickly made through other "such days" to general philosophical considerations, classically Romantic in concept and Transcendental in assertion ("I find my own complexion everywhere"). In this concern with memory and experience, thought and Fancy, Nature and Self, the presence of a distinct individual is strong, and is straightforwardly accounted for: "I know not how it is with other men / Whom I but guess, deciphering myself." Introduced into the poem, then, before the return to "a day at Chartres" in line 179 are the themes of loss and doubt, and a sense of individual struggle with questions that are personal because they are universal.

Visiting the cathedral, which is "Imagination's very self in stone," the poet is visited by major questions about supernatural faith. Although he tries to believe himself "a happy Goth," he realizes that he is a "child of an age that lectures, not creates," of an "age that blots out life with question-marks." "Ancient faith" is "irrecoverable," he concludes; "each age must worship its own thought of God." In the cathedral and elsewhere "where others worship," the poet can "but look and long," and yet, reaching a tentative resolution, he is thankful that "seeing where God *has* been," it may be possible to "trust in Him."

Such respite from doubt is short-lived, however, for Time and Change and an overwhelming sense of the present return to dominate the poet's thoughts. An American, he seizes upon Democracy and its New World Man as perhaps the hope, the answer, of the future. But this belief, this hope, cannot be sustained either. The poet walks saddened from the cathedral, and in his turning, parting look gets a hint of a solution from seeing sparrow-hawks above sparrows on the cathedral. Moving from interpreting this sight to another natural analogy of root and tree-top, the poet finds consoling "evidence of Thee so far above / Yet in and of me!" His final fear, the expression of which concludes *The Cathedral,* is not of God's non-existence or His withdrawal from man, but of "seeing, to know Thee not," of himself and other men's failing to recognize God "in the commonplace of miracle." This conclusion, as a modern commentator has noted, should be "seen as hope rather than as homily," "an appropriate and valiant ending to a challenging poem."

The Cathedral invites comparison, looking back, to Tennyson's *In Memoriam* and Matthew Arnold's "Stanzas from the Grande Chartreuse" and, looking forward, to **Henry Adams**'s *Mont-Saint-*

Michel and Chartres and *The Education of Henry Adams* and **T.S. Eliot**'s *Four Quartets*. John Ruskin found its "main substance" "most precious," "its separate lines some-times unbetterable."

The change of title to *The Cathedral* is significant, adding to the poem's meaning and emphasizing inspired human art. Lowell wrote that in his work he could see "a bit of clean carving here and there, a solid buttress or two, and perhaps a gleam through painted glass." Indeed, there are parallels between what he created and the building that inspired it, including the grotesque that results in the poem from coexistence of the humorous, down-to-earth, very-consciously-American Lowell and the learned Harvard-professor, very-consciously-European Lowell. But Lowell's craftsmanship often impresses itself upon a reader, particularly in individual lines. And if, philosophically and spiritually, solid buttresses are harder to come by, they do exist in *The Cathedral*. About, metaphorically, its providing at least "a gleam through painted glass," there can be no doubt.

—Bert Hitchcock

CATHEDRAL
Short story by Raymond Carver, 1983

"Cathedral," Raymond Carver's most admired and frequently anthologized story, marked a shift from the so-called "grim" minimalism of his first two major collections to the more "generous" realism of the next two. The story centers on a blind man's visit to the home of an old friend and her husband, the narrator, a cynical man who is prepared to dislike the blind man not only because of his wife's previous friendship but because his only idea of blindness comes from the movies, where blind people never laugh and move slowly. After eating dinner and sharing a marijuana cigarette, the two men watch a show on public television about cathedrals. Robert, the blind man, asks the narrator to describe a cathedral for him, but the narrator cannot, saying that he is not religious and cathedrals do not mean much to him. At Robert's suggestion, he gets pens and paper, and while Robert holds his hand over the narrator's hand, the two men begin to draw a simple boxlike structure with a roof and some spires. As the blind man encourages the narrator, saying, "Never thought anything like this could happen in your lifetime, did you, bub?" the narrator becomes more and more involved in the process, closing his eyes while Robert guides his hand across the paper. "It was like nothing else in my life up to now," the narrator says. The story ends with him still sitting on the floor, his eyes closed, thinking that although he knows he is in his house, he did not feel as if he was inside anything.

"Cathedral" contains more exposition, information, and clarification than Carver's earlier stories, which focused primarily on a mysterious situation detached from any social or contextual background. The first section of the story recounts the narrator's knowledge of his wife's previous marriage and her friendship with the blind man and even of the blind man's wife, who has recently died. Although this information bears little thematic relevance to the final epiphanic revelation of the story, it reveals the narrator to be an insensitive character with many prejudiced notions.

"Cathedral" is less experimental and innovative, more explicit and conventionally optimistic and moral than Carver's earlier stories. Obviously, the narrator reaches some sort of traditional revelation at the end; ironically, whereas he was morally blind before, he is now able to see. An account of a spiritual experience, the story is about the narrator's final ability to identify with the blind man, the two men blending together into one entity. It is much more "talky" than Carver's earlier stories, in part because it is a first-person narrative in which the narrator's personality, not an ambiguous encounter, is the thematic heart of the story, but also because Carver seems to feel he has arrived at an explanation for things that he did not try to account for previously.

The narrator of "Cathedral" is not completely unfeeling and unsympathetic; his initial inability to identify with the blind man is somewhat understandable, as he has never known any blind people himself. The story suggests, however, that there is something lacking within him: his wife remarks that he has no friends, and he reveals that he smokes dope every night and then has bizarre dreams from which he awakes with his heart "going crazy." He is clearly a man in need of some spiritual awakening.

The challenge of identifying with another person is a recurring theme in Carver's stories. Such earlier stories as "Neighbors," "Why Don't You Dance," and "Fat" focus on encounters in which characters intuitively sense some potential identification with a mysterious "other," but either because they view the other voyeuristically at a distance or because they are unable to translate their vague longings into any kind of meaningful action, the stories conclude with a sense of inarticulate frustration. By focusing on the religious metaphor of the cathedral, the shamanistic aura of the blind man, and the communal sharing of an imaginative act, Carver creates in "Cathedral" a moment of union and transcendence with a more confident sense of meaning and moral closure than can be found in many of his earlier works.

—Charles E. May

CEREMONY
Novel by Leslie Marmon Silko, 1977

Leslie Marmon Silko's first novel, *Ceremony,* received much praise when it was published in 1977. It continues to be one of the most widely read and studied works in contemporary Native American literature. Part of its appeal can be explained by the way Silko mediates between modern literary conventions from the psychological and naturalistic novel and the stories of the Laguna Pueblo people. The novel is able to satisfy a variety of readers' expectations while moving them to new insights about the Native American worldview.

The novel begins by establishing a frame in which Thought-Woman, the creator in Laguna oral tradition, is thinking the story of the novel into reality. Silko establishes the importance of the stories to fight off illness and death, emphasizing the continuing and growing role of the stories in defining the ritual struggle against evil. This frame introduces the idea that the story of Tayo has a role in a ceremony described in the novel and that the novel has a role in a larger emerging ceremony. Indeed, beginning and ending the novel proper with the word "Sunrise" turns the book into a prayer, as if coming from one of the religious societies of the Laguna.

Silko's protagonist, Tayo, is a mixed-blood Laguna raised by his aunt after his mother abandons him. His position in the family and in the community has always been that of an outsider. He has been raised as a brother to his cousin, Rocky. The two young men served together in the Pacific during World War II. When ordered to kill Japanese prisoners, Tayo has a vision that one of them is really his wise Uncle Josiah. Josiah, who has befriended Tayo, actually dies about this time. Later, Rocky is mortally wounded and the two are taken prisoners. Tayo, broken by his war experience, is returned to a military hospital. Psychological therapy seems not to help him and he is returned to his family in Laguna, New Mexico.

Following the traditions of the psychological novel, Silko creates a narrative style that mirrors Tayo's psychological state. She merges past and present with little warning to the readers so that they are moved into Tayo's swirling, shattered state of mind; to enhance this, Silko uses no chapter breaks. Against this prose, Silko juxtaposes lines of what appear to be poetry. However, initially these lines present Laguna mythic stories about drought, returns to tradition, and emergence. She spreads these out over the length of the novel not only to comment on the action in the prose, but also to provide a mythic pattern in which Tayo's story gains meaning. Thus Silko implies that mundane reality finds more inclusive meaning in a mythic view of the world.

When Tayo does not respond to his family's care and to traditional Laguna practices for returned warriors, he is encouraged to see a mixed-blood Navajo medicine man, Betonie. Betonie makes his home on the edge of the reservation on a hill overlooking Gallup. His hogan is packed with traditional ceremonial paraphernalia as well as miscellaneous items like calendars and phone books necessary to chart the movements of the modern Euro-American world. His unorthodox healing ceremonies are distrusted by many Navajos because he creates new ceremonies for a new shape of evil in the world.

During Betonie's ceremony, Tayo learns that his illness is part of some larger evil that is infecting the world. He understands that there are no real boundaries separating time and space. There is only a lack of perception of the true nature of the world. This essentially mythic vision allows Tayo to realize he has not been crazy, only perceiving the world as it really is. His problem was that he began to disbelieve the old stories that explained this reality. He is now able to place his story in the story of worldwide witchery created by the Destroyers. Betonie directs Tayo on his personal ceremony that will hold off the forces of destruction. Betonie's vision is of a mountain, some cattle, a woman, and a specific constellation of stars.

Rejecting his meaningless life of drinking and wandering with fellow returned veterans, Tayo begins a trip up Mount Taylor in search of some cattle Josiah purchased years ago. He finds the cattle and meets a spirit woman named Ts'eh. Through Tayo and Ts'eh's lovemaking, Silko emphasizes the necessity of love in combating the evils of the world. Ts'eh instructs Tayo on his role in making the story end correctly as well as the appropriate loving, respectful relationship toward the spiritual and natural world. He now can perceive the world as timeless, the artificial boundaries of time and space falling away.

As Tayo returns from the mountain he is tempted by Emo, a returned veteran who is acting as an unwitting tool of the Destroyers. When Emo tortures to death another returned vet, Tayo resists the desire to rush down and kill Emo. Ts'eh and Betonie have warned him against joining into the violence of the witchery. His task is to see that the story ends properly on the mythic plane. He ends the story/ceremony watching the rising sun on equinox morning as the forces of the universe balance in one large sandpainting. Tayo's renewal is acknowledged by the elders of the pueblo, and he is welcomed into the religious center of the community to guide its renewal.

In Silko's narrative, Tayo realizes that his actions have immense meaning on a mythic plane. Now that he understands the struggle against the witchery, he must act responsibly. However, readers are placed in a similar position. They can discover the overriding significance of the novel in its revelation of the story of the Destroyers. The readers are now part of the story and have a responsibility to struggle against the forces of death and destruction.

—James Ruppert

CIVIL DISOBEDIENCE
Essay by Henry David Thoreau, 1849

After its presentation as an oration at the Concord Lyceum on January 26, 1848, Thoreau's essay "Resistance to Civil Government" was published the following spring in *Aesthetic Papers,* edited by Elizabeth Peabody. The title "Civil Disobedience" was first attached to a reprint of essay after Thoreau's death, and although it is the more widely known title, it does not reflect the author's intention. That Thoreau's text is an explicit refutation of William Paley's essay on "The Duty of Submission to Civil Government" is emphasized not only by the original title but by the author's citation of Paley in the text.

"Resistance to Civil Government" is a highly polemical piece, aiming to move the reader to more than mere aesthetic or moral appreciation: it contains a clear call to action in the service of principle, and indeed argues that mere conviction without action is worthless. The contemporary issues that engaged Thoreau's moral outrage at the time were American military aggression in Mexico and the legality of slavery in the United States. In seeking a way for the conscientious individual to deal with such issues, Thoreau offers a meditation on timeless and absolute principles that, he feels, should guide the moral person. The substance of the author's argument is that each person has a duty to follow conscience rather than law when the two are in conflict, and further has a duty to oppose unjust laws by taking action against them.

The argument is developed through a set of assertions describing the individual's relation to the state in terms of mutually exclusive oppositions. One of the main sets of contrasting terms is principle or conscience opposed to expediency. Thoreau repeatedly characterizes government as operating according to expediency, whereas the individual citizen is capable of acting according to a higher principle, that of morality or conscience. In advising that the individual has not merely the right but the duty to resist unjust laws, Thoreau postulates a higher, spiritual, law that supersedes civil or constitutional law. Conscience instructs the individual in this higher law, according to Thoreau, and must be obeyed even at the cost of sacrificing material possessions or liberty. Underlying and supporting this abstract opposition of conscience versus expediency is a metaphor that repeatedly characterizes the individual as animate and the state as inanimate. Thoreau's consistent figure for government or the state is a machine, while the citizen is always a living being. The trope supports the contention explicitly stated in Thoreau's argument that the individual is superior to the state both in moral character and in actual strength. The individual who has the courage to act on principle can overcome the tyranny of the majority.

At the heart of the essay is an anecdote Thoreau relates of his own experience in resisting the state. About two-thirds of the way through his discussion he narrates a brief account of his arrest and night spent in Concord jail because of his refusal to pay a poll tax. Thoreau felt that the tax supported armed aggression in Mexico and followed his conscience in refusing to pay it. He was arrested but spent only a single night in jail, as another person (who has never been definitively identified) paid the tax for him and secured his release. The anecdote does not dwell on the details of Thoreau's arrest nor the actual refusal to the tax collector, but rather on the memorable night spent in the jail.

The experience was not particularly unpleasant: his cellmate was affable and kind, the quarters were spartan but clean, and the ambience seems to have been that of a family visit almost as much as an incarceration. During the night, Thoreau relates, his mind was given over to a rather extravagant flight of fancy, in which he imagined himself in a medieval lock-up, and the town of Concord a village on the Rhine peopled with knights and burghers. The experience also afforded him a paradoxical, unprecedented intimacy with the town, as he was made an involuntary eavesdropper on all the business in the kitchen of the inn next door to the jail.

This new view of his townspeople contrasts with the narrator's attitude in the first part of the essay, in which Thoreau sets the conscientious person apart from the "mass of men" who share the inanimacy of the state they compliantly serve: the majority are "wooden men" who serve the state "as machines" with their bodies only, as contrasted with the man of character who lives a spiritual life. After his night in jail, Thoreau offers a mellower view of his neighbors, along with a more optimistic vision of the possibilities of government. Whereas the opening paragraphs of the essay contain the famous dictums regarding the superiority of no government at all to an improved government, at the end of the essay, after telling the story of his night in jail, the author resumes his argument but allows for a vision of an ideal state, supportive of the highest aspirations of its citizens.

"Resistance to Civil Government" draws on several sources in Thoreau's reading and in turn has been influential on following thinkers. The Bible, of course, is an inspiration for this New England heir of the puritans. There is also a suggestion that Thoreau developed the idea of a higher law with superior claims on conscience from his reading of Sophocles' play *Antigone,* in which the heroine resists the law of the land and obeys the command of the gods to bury her traitorous brother in opposition to the authority of the state. Thoreau also quotes Confucius in his essay and, like fellow transcendentalist **Ralph Waldo Emerson**, was influenced by the spirituality of Eastern thought. A series of important writers and activists have been influenced by "Resistance to Civil Government," applying its principles to similar situations. Notable among these are Gandhi, who first read the essay while a young man in South Africa and who published an analysis of it early in his career, and Martin Luther King, Jr., who drew on both Thoreau and Gandhi in developing principles of nonviolent resistance to unjust laws.

—Helen Jaskoski

THE COLOR PURPLE
Novel by Alice Walker, 1982

In *The Souls of Black Folk* (1903), African American scholar W. E. B. Du Bois uses the term "double consciousness" to describe the struggle of a person who is caught in "his twoness—an American, a Negro, two souls, two thoughts, two unreconciled strivings . . . longing to attain self-conscious manhood." What the statement does not describe, however, is the uniqueness of African American women's experience which demonstrates that intracultural conflicts are capable of producing equally detrimental effects on a person's sense of selfhood and dignity. Indeed, to compare African American male writers' works and those by African American female writers is to discover a divergence in focus: whereas many African American male writers are interested in exploring inter-cultural conflict, the thematic power of African American female writers' works is often generated by their eagerness to engage both sexism and racism.

In 1982, the publication of Alice Walker's *The Color Purple* helped initiate a movement to reclaim African American women's sense of history and identity. In *The Color Purple,* the main character Celie's experience epitomizes the growth of a person from what Walker describes in her essay, "In Search of Our Mothers' Gardens," as a physically and psychologically abused black woman to a new black woman, a "womanist," who can freely recreate herself out of the legacy of her maternal ancestors.

Celie has two role models in *The Color Purple:* Sofia and Shug Avery. Sofia is physically strong; she commands respect and is willing to fight to protect her dignity. But it is from her close friend, Shug, that Celie has learned that to emancipate herself physically from the entrapment of an abusive relationship, she will have to grow mentally strong. Under Shug's influence, Celie has matured into a person who has developed enough self-awareness and self-confidence to challenge tradition's hegemonic impulse: if her decision to leave her husband demonstrates Celie's determination to break away from the old mold of life, her starting a business to make pants for women suggests her readiness to create a new life for herself, regardless of what social norm dictates (women were not supposed to wear pants in the 1930s).

Celie's achievement of knowledge and understanding of herself is paralleled in *The Color Purple* by her sister Nettie's newly developed religious beliefs. Nettie represents what Walker in "In Search of Our Mothers' Gardens" calls an exceptional black woman, a woman torn by "contrary instincts" who, in order to try to fulfill her creativity, is forced to repress the sources from which it comes. In appearance, Nettie had a better education and lives a better life than Celie does. But readers do not feel as emotionally close to Nettie as they do to Celie, partly because the kind of formal and "refined" English Nettie uses in her letter correspondence with Celie seems to create a linguistic barrier between her innermost feelings and the reader, and partly because of the role Nettie plays in being a missionary in Africa. Nevertheless, the experience in Africa helped Nettie realize the necessity to change some of her religious beliefs, as she confides in Celie: "God is different to us now, after all these years in Africa. More spirit than ever before, and more internal. Most people think he has to look like something or someone—a roofleaf or Christ—but we don't. And not being tied to what God looks like, frees us." Nettie also tells Celie after she comes back to America that she wants to "found a new church in our community that has no idols in it whatsoever, in which each person's spirit is encouraged to seek God directly."

What both Celie and Nettie's lives prove positively is also accentuated in *The Color Purple* by several male characters' blunders. Both Celie's husband, whom she addresses as Mr. _____, and his son Harpo, for instance, display their inability to live their own lives under the influence of traditions which have, for centuries, endorsed sexism and prevented African American women from achieving self-realization. Harpo sincerely cares for his wife, Sofia. Given a choice, he would be quite content playing the kind of role he wanted to play in his relationship with Sofia. But Harpo is pressured by people around him to be a "man" and the "master" at home. His "voracious" appetite for food obviously results from Mr. _____'s advice: "Wives is like children. You have to let 'em know who got the upper hand. Nothing can do that better than a good sound beating," and from his awareness that he is not as physically strong as Sofia.

Mr. _____ himself, by the same token, functions only as an instrument and mouthpiece for what he has learned from his father. Mr. _____'s reaction to Sofia's telling him about her pregnancy, for instance, was not very much different from how his father reacted when Shug told him about the children she had with Mr. _____: both men were suspicious of who the real father was. Because both Mr. _____ and Harpo are unable to break away from moribund traditions, they become but a pair of merry-go-round fixtures in a vicious circle.

The tone of *The Color Purple*'s ending is reconciliatory and positive. Mr. _____'s willingness to help Celie sew and Celie's addressing Mr. _____ by his first name, Albert, all point to the beginning of a new relationship, a relationship that is built on mutual understanding and respect. The optimistic tone reflects one of Walker's beliefs which is stated in the poem under the title, "These Days": "Surely the earth can be saved/by all the people/Who insist on love."

In *The Color Purple*, Walker is faithful in following the conventional practice of the epistolary novel. The form of letter correspondence, the intimate tone, and the use of anonymous characters, misidentities, discoveries, and a happy ending all work cohesively with Walker's thematic preoccupations with her characters' search for identity and their struggle to achieve self-realization. What is interesting to notice, however, is that by successfully using a conventional literary form to deal with issues which are as timeless as they are topical, Walker is able to emphasize both the possibility and the necessity of change. The use of the form in *The Color Purple*, therefore, not only reveals, but also reinforces Walker's thematic concerns.

In *The Color Purple*, Walker consciously celebrates the African American cultural heritage. Her use of African American English underlines the writer's deep identification with her gender and race. It is intended to democratize the American literary voice by (re)presenting the mis(sing)-represented and by giving voice to the "voiceless." To appreciate *The Color Purple* is, therefore, to recognize the cause for the sufferings of those who are caught in both inter-cultural and intra-cultural conflicts, to respond to their call for understanding and change, and to value the culturally diverse nature of American society.

—Qun Wang

COMMON SENSE
Essay by Thomas Paine, 1776

Thomas Paine's little pamphlet *Common Sense* is one of those books that changed the world. Like *Uncle Tom's Cabin, The Communist Manifesto,* or *The Origin of Species,* it had the effect of altering men's minds with consequences that were far-reaching and long-lasting. No one could have predicted such a work from the pen of Paine, who had come to America only in 1774 at the age of 37 after a very undistinguished career in England. He was a born propagandist, however, and the cause of American independence fueled his imagination and inspired his writing. Of all the thousands of political pamphlets that have been forgotten since the invention of printing this is one that has survived. Written as an ephemeral tract, it has remained one of the important documents of American history.

The pamphlet appeared on 10 January 1776, less than six months before the signing of the Declaration of Independence. At the time it was published Americans were very much divided in their attitude towards Britain. The struggle for home rule had been going on for years and was gradually intensifying, but only a few Americans then favored separation from England. The Continental Congress was called in 1774 in an effort to head off a radical solution. **Benjamin Franklin**, in London, said in March 1775 that he had never heard anyone in America, drunk or sober, advocate independence. George Washington told a friend in May 1775 that if the friend ever heard of Washington joining the movement for separation, he had his leave to set him down for everything wicked. **Thomas Jefferson** wrote in July 1775 that he was looking with fondness towards reconciliation with Great Britain.

Then the next January Paine's pamphlet, with title supplied by Benjamin Rush, burst on the colonies, and nothing was ever the same afterwards. Although leaders like Washington, Samuel Adams, Franklin, Richard Henry Lee, and others were beginning to work quietly for independence by that time, no one before Paine had come out flatly in print for separation. Paine's pamphlet swept through the colonies, and since there was no copyright law, anyone could reprint it. Perhaps 100,000 copies were in circulation by the time the Declaration was signed, and it has been estimated that probably every literate person in the thirteen colonies had read it. While most writers of political pamphlets were intellectuals writing for other intellectuals, Paine wrote a prose that anyone could read, farmers, mechanics, tradesmen, laborers. Paine committed every logical fallacy in his argument, but the brilliance of his journalism was overwhelming, and it had a catalytic effect in moving public opinion in favor of independence.

Washington wrote to Joseph Reed: "By private letters which I have lately received from Virginia, I find *Common Sense* is working a powerful change there in men's minds." Charles Lee, who became a general in the continental army, wrote Washington: "I never saw such a masterly, irresistible performance. It will . . . give the *coup-de-grace* to Great Britain." Franklin and others also testified to the prodigious effects of the pamphlet, and the *American Annual Register . . . for the Year 1796* recalled: "When the first copies arrived in the American camp at Cambridge, they were perused with transport. An officer in that army observed lately that a reinforcement of five thousand men would not have inspired the troops with equal confidence as this pamphlet did." Of course, the Revolution would have occurred whether or not Paine had existed, but *Common Sense* did prepare people's minds for the break with England.

Where Paine got the ideas that he put into his pamphlet is moot. He was not a reader, and he no doubt picked up his notions here and there, perhaps from conversations with friends like Franklin and Rush. He always prided himself on the originality of his ideas, but his thoughts on government and natural rights were widely current in the Enlightenment, as perhaps are the ideas of Freud today among people who never have read him. The idea with which Paine opened his pamphlet, that "government, even in its best state, is but a necessary evil; in its worst state an intolerable one" was held by many liberal theorists of the time. After this preliminary statement, Paine went for the jugular in attacking the British Constitution and undermining American loyalty to the Crown. Americans already were at odds with Parliament over the issue of taxation without representation, but they did not blame the king for their grievances. Paine attacked monarchy, hereditary succession, and the divine right of kings with eminently quotable language. As for the divine right of William the Conqueror to rule England: "A French bastard, landing with an armed banditti and establishing himself king of England against the consent of the natives is in plain terms a very paltry rascally original."

Then Paine moved on to "Thoughts on the Present State of American Affairs," in which he offered "nothing more than simple facts, plain arguments, and common sense." He answered the argument that because America had flourished under British rule it should remain under it by saying: "We may as well assert that because a child has thrived on milk, that it is never to have meat." And later he even called on astronomy to buttress his case: " . . . there is something absurd in supposing a continent to be perpetually governed by an island. In no instance hath nature made the satellite larger than its primary planet." So he went on, arguing sometimes logically, sometimes illogically, arguing by analogy, begging the question, but always phrasing his brief in memorable language. He ended this section with a peroration for freedom: "O ye that love mankind! Ye that dare oppose not only the tyranny but the tyrant, stand forth! Every spot of the old world is overrun with oppression . . . . Europe regards her [freedom] like a stranger, and England hath given her warning to depart. O receive the fugitive, and prepare in time an asylum for mankind." Then he ended the final chapter of the pamphlet with a call for a "DECLARATION FOR INDEPENDENCE."

—James Woodress

THE CONTRAST
Play by Royall Tyler, 1787

Although *The Contrast* first appeared anonymously, reviews indicate that Royall Tyler (1757-1826) was recognized as the author. It is presumed that it was because he wrote the part of Jonathan for Thomas Wignell that Tyler gave the copyright of the play to Wignell, who eventually arranged the first printing of the play in 1790. From that point on *The Contrast* was an integral part of American dramatic literature. In the theater, however, the play was successful only by the standards of the day. From 1787 to 1804 there is evidence of thirty-eight performances in New York City, Baltimore, and Philadelphia by the Old American Company. Other theater companies produced the play in Boston and in smaller cities in Virginia, Maryland, and South Carolina. In these latter versions songs were added, changes made, and the title revised to *The Contrast; or, the American Son of Liberty*. Changing tastes seem to have ruled out performance of the play during most of the nineteenth century: there were no productions from 1804 to 1894, when it was revived by the American Academy of Dramatic Art. In 1912 and 1917 the play was again produced, and after World War II, it occasionally appeared on college and university stages, as the study of American literature became popular and programs in American studies were established. Given this academic emphasis, it may have been inevitable that in the fall of

1972, *The Contrast* opened in New York City as a musical, adapted by Anthony Stimac, with music by Don Pippin and lyrics by Steve Brown.

The Contrast lacks much of a plot and tends to be a talky play with little action, but it has many compensating strengths. Though imitative of the eighteenth-century British sentimental comedy, any consequent dullness is relieved by an originality in thought and in character presentation that distinguishes this play above all other comedies in eighteenth-century America. Structurally, it follows the traditional five-act pattern, while, in keeping with its thesis of "contrast," each act divides into two scenes that provide contrast in form as well as in content. Tyler was both well-read and talented, and the play shows his familiarity with traditional dramatic techniques, idiosyncratic language, and literature of the period.

Basically, the play satisfied all the demands of the theatre audience of 1787. The prologue ("Exult each patriot heart!"), the characterizations of Jonathan and Colonel Manly, and the dialect, issues, and final line of the play—all emphasize the new nationalism. Although they may be caricatures, the characters have distinctive qualities that delight the reader and viewer. Charlotte, for example, is a charming flirt, witty and full of life: "Scandal," she observes, "is but amusing ourselves with the faults, foibles, follies, and reputations of our friends." Colonel Manly, her brother, is a stiff and sentimental bore, but a patriotic bore. Jonathan, in the tradition of the Yankee character born almost a generation before *The Contrast,* provides good farcical humor that, with his rural eccentricities and "down East" dialect, makes him theatrically attractive, "a true blue son of Liberty," as he describes himself. Dimple is the typical fop, affecting the manners of the English and offending the American sense of manhood by not minding the main chance and by being careless with money and deceptive with women. As a strong moral was another sine qua non of American drama of the period, Tyler provided it generously in the actions of Manly, in the filial duty of Maria, and in the final scene of the play, where Charlotte repents and Manly explains what probity, virtue, and honor can accomplish. Complementing the light wit of Charlotte is the farcical humor between Jonathan and Jessamy, Dimple's steward. Finally, there is the satire that American audiences had always enjoyed: satire on fashion, the theater, the English, and gossip. Additionally, to enliven the play there were songs, while superimposed on all elements was contrast—contrast between the people of England and those of America, between affectation and straightforwardness, between city and country, between hypocrisy and sincerity, and between foreign fraud and native worth.

With all these characteristics assembled with a certain natural talent and an abundance of wit, it would have been surprising had *The Contrast* not appealed to Americans. Tyler in his youthful exuberance must have enjoyed ridiculing the stuffy romancing of Manly and Maria and the girlish gossip of Charlotte, as well as the backcountry innocence of Jonathan contrasted with the hypocrisy of those tainted by English manners. Yet, with all the fun, a strain of honesty runs through the American characters. Tyler surely believed them, as he contrasted their unaffected manners with the affectations he despised. Although as a dramatist he was interested in provoking laughter, Tyler included nationalistic sentiments that he expected the audience of his day to take seriously. One presumes that they did.

—Walter J. Meserve

THE COUNTRY OF THE POINTED FIRS
Novel by Sarah Orne Jewett, 1896

Sarah Orne Jewett's *The Country of the Pointed Firs,* which many fellow writers (Kipling was one, **Willa Cather**, less surprisingly, another) have considered a small masterpiece, belongs not so much to a genre as to a certain infrequent kind which seems, by its nature, to have a curious lasting appeal. Its nearest English likeness is Mrs. Gaskell's *Cranford* (1853): but more on this presently. Not quite autobiography (the narrator is nameless, uninvolved), neither novel nor nouvelle (it has linked episodes rather than central plot), *The Country of the Pointed Firs* recreates a scene and a people at a late point in their own time. Each character might be a painting (Dutch master? American primitive?) suddenly touched into life. Strange personal tales are there, sometimes partly caught, in teasing or haunting fragments—but so it is in life. The strong wild landscape, dark woods and cliffs, the rocky shore, the sweet-smelling herbs and grasses, the abiding sea and wind, are present on every page.

"One evening in June a single passenger landed upon the steamboat wharf." So the narrator (a writer wanting rustic quiet) steps into the orderly frugal life of this dwindling, aging community on the coast of Maine. The people she comes to know are solitaries, widows of seamen, seamen widowers, with their working days and emotional upheavals behind them; but memories and secrets can be summoned for the narrator's hearing. The visitor—she is an event, and welcome—is the medium through which we know these people. But—good listener, observer, and companion as she is sometimes called on to be—she is deliberately underplayed in the book; we know nothing of her name, her looks, and this is as it should be. Her story, if any, lies elsewhere.

In one sense, then, we are in a haven of ordered peace, where the smallest event has quality, and the only wildness is in the elements. We meet no rebellious or troubled adolescents. The child inhabitants of the little schoolhouse that the narrator rents as a workplace in the vacation are nowhere visible in the book. But no character is without a private drama, something not so tranquil. Mrs. Almira Todd, with whom the narrator lodges, herb-gatherer and herbal healer, spirit of goodness, the book's central figure indeed, still feels sharp grief not only for her drowned young husband Nathan, but for the real love of her youth, prevented from marrying by his parents. "My heart was gone out o' my keeping before ever I saw Nathan; though he loved me well and made me real happy." It was, in the narrator's words, "an absolute archaic grief. She might have been Antigone alone on the Theban plain." We hear of "Poor Joanna," who felt that she had "committed the unpardonable sin" (jilted just before her marriage, she had allowed herself to feel a wrath towards God), and had spent the rest of her life totally alone on a little island several miles from the coast. We also meet the dignified old woman whose hard life had been cheered by the thought that she was Queen Victoria's twin, born on the same day, giving her children the same names. We share the narrator's pleasure in discovering the secret courtship of quiet William and his shepherdess, both in their sixties and toilworn, seeing each other scarcely once a year.

Most memorable of all, though, is the story told to the narrator by Captain Littlepage, a man of worn and troubled refinement with a head full of classical poetry and a tale of Coleridgean awe. Wrecked in the arctic regions, he was given rough shelter by an old seaman, Gaffett, lone survivor of a polar exploring expedition. "There is a strange sort of country," Gaffett told him, "way up north beyond the ice, and strange folks living in it . . . shapes of folks, all blowing gray figures."

Gaffett believed that it was the next world to this. He said that he and another man came near one of the fog-shaped men that was going along slow with the look of a pack on his back, among the rocks, an' they chased him; but, Lord! he flittered away out o' sight like a leaf the wind takes with it, or a piece of cobweb. They would make as if they talked together, but there was no sound of voices.

"Say what you like," Gaffett assured him, "'twas a kind of waiting place between this world and the next."

Did Jewett know *Cranford*? It hardly matters; each of the works is essentially of its author's kind. Still, the likenesses and differences are of interest. Both use an under-stressed narrator as viewer and recorder. Both are episodic. Both are based on long-known places and people. Both centre affectionately on the middle-aged and old. You can't really choose between them. But the Jewett book has the tremendous asset of the natural scene itself. This scene is an essential part of the book's fabric. So is the meticulous and moving detail (Joanna's gingham dress, for instance; the bonnet of the angry old woman, paralysed by a stroke); so too is the speech of its characters with its quaint, almost Elizabethan turn of phrase. As for the story element, you would call the work open-ended; no tale is brought to a final close. If the test of a book's quality is that it can be read again and again with unfailing interest, there is no doubt of this book's high place.

—Naomi Lewis

THE CRYING OF LOT 49
Novel by Thomas Pynchon, 1966

The Crying of Lot 49, Thomas Pynchon's second novel, was published and short-listed for the National Book Award in 1966, three years after Pynchon's *V.* won the Faulkner Prize for best first novel. Popular and academic interest in *The Crying of Lot 49* remained high until his third novel, *Gravity's Rainbow,* regarded by many as one of the finest works in American literature, won the National Book Award in 1973. Since then, although regard for *The Crying of Lot 49* has diminished somewhat in light of Pynchon's subsequent works, it remains an excellent primer for Pynchon's writing, in part because its brevity—less than one hundred and fifty pages—makes it more accessible and easier to study than his other, much longer novels.

Although brief, *The Crying of Lot 49* is neither simple nor simplistic. Many have noted the encyclopedic qualities of Pynchon's novels, which often include a grab bag of eclectic allusions and references, ranging, as Pynchon himself suggests, "from high magic to low puns," from literary and scientific theory to classical music and literature to popular music, movies, and comics. *The Crying of Lot 49* is no exception, taking shape from references to such disparate fields as Egyptian mythology, Jacobean revenge tragedy, epic, philately, information theory, spectrum analysis, Latin American painting, European history, psychoanalytic theory, and early 1960s American pop culture. Moreover, Pynchon's scientific allusions often refer to counterintuitive, frequently paradoxical concepts in modern science such as entropy, the Heisenberg uncertainty principle, Schrodinger's cat, Maxwell's Demon, and so on. On one level, Pynchon weaves these seemingly unrelated elements into an open-ended narrative form analogous to a postmodern mystery or detective story; on another, he provides not only an encyclopedic survey of ways to communicate but also a complex philosophical critique of the relationship between information and knowledge.

The novel is loosely structured around what may be described as a quest motif. Oedipa Maas, a California housewife and wife of disc-jockey and former used car salesman Wendell "Mucho" Maas, has been named executrix of the will of her late boyfriend, real estate tycoon and entrepreneur Pierce Inverarity. As Oedipa sets out to execute the will along with Metzger (Inverarity's lawyer and a former child actor known as Baby Igor), she is initially daunted by the task of assembling the bits and pieces of Inverarity's vast financial empire. However, a few seemingly unrelated details—graffiti on a bathroom wall and references to the presence of human bones in charcoal-filtered cigarettes—lead Oedipa to see patterns that she comes to regard as more than mere coincidence. The accumulation of such coincidences results in her discovery of an alternative mail system known as W.A.S.T.E., whose icon is a muted post horn (an instrument used by mail-coach guards in earlier centuries). Eventually, Oedipa sees this icon everywhere, and she begins to suspect a vast, mysterious international underground network known as Tristero.

Most of the novel thus moves from apparent randomness and chaos to total paranoia and Oedipa's sense that everything is somehow connected. This trajectory is fueled by the presence of actual and fictitious transnational corporations that, here and in Pynchon's other work, always signal international conspiracy. Thus Oedipa finds that Inverarity was involved with the Beaconsfield Tobacco Company, which plans to use human bones to make charcoal for cigarette filters; its partners in this enterprise include Yoyodyne, a former toy company turned defense contractor, the Cosa Nostra; and the Thurn and Taxis mail system, long thought to be defunct. Eventually, with the help of Randolph Dribblette, director of the Jacobean drama *The Courier's Tragedy,* Oedipa traces the connections further and further back in western European history. She comes to believe that Tristero has not only been in existence since the fourteenth century but also that it has had a significant though hidden role in shaping many of the more nefarious and unsavory features of Western culture.

Although the mood of paranoia and conspiracy remains strong until the end of the novel, Pynchon's ending undercuts the sense of closure inherent and traditional in those literary forms he imitates, such as mystery and detective fiction and the epic. First, the people associated with Oedipa earlier in the novel either disappear or are marginalized in her life; Mucho withdraws into an LSD-induced haze; Metzger runs off with a fifteen-year old; Dribblette commits suicide; and so on. Then, with the aid of Genghis Cohen, a well-known philatelist and her sole remaining human contact, Oedipa comes to believe that the key to her quest is somehow connected both to Inverarity's stamp collection—identified as Lot 49 in the auction of his personal effects—and to the mysterious, anonymous collector who has expressed, through an agent, interest in buying the collection. Finally, as the novel ends with Oedipa waiting for the auction to begin, Pynchon presents the reader with a wonderful, multivalent ontological still point that projects beyond the end of the text. Through this unfulfilled ending, Pynchon leaves the reader with a powerful image of the uncertainty and anxiety that characterize not only his other works

but also mid-to- late-twentieth-century American life—and literature as well.

—Terry Reilly

THE DAMNATION OF THERON WARE
Novel by Harold Frederic, 1896

The literary sensation of 1896 was Harold Frederic's *The Damnation of Theron Ware,* published in England as *Illumination.* One of the oddities in this book about a Methodist minister who strays from the fundamentals of his religion is that no one, neither Theron Ware himself nor the Catholic priest Father Forbes, seems to believe in God. Religion is, rather, a profession and a social institution, and the motto of the book might well be Alice Ware's disappointed remark when her husband is not awarded the pastorate he had longed for: "Don't talk to me about the Lord to-night; I can't bear it!" The novel concerns just such petty people unable to bear (surely that verb has a mock heroic ring to it in the context of Alice's petulance) petty disappointments, empty men and women who yearn for the status symbols of the middle class. In materialistic America at the end of the 19th century, with old-time religion under attack as never before by the new science, damnation no longer signifies alienation from God and the good, as it had for Jonathan Edwards or Lorenzo Dow. Now damnation means the failure to achieve wealth, success, and power, or, from Frederic's point of view, the failure to achieve true self-knowledge. Theron Ware is indeed cursed by his own self-deception, by alienation from himself.

When the Methodist elders deny Theron Ware the pulpit at Tecumseh he had so much coveted and assign him instead to Octavius ("render unto Caesar the things that are Caesar's"), he finds himself the minister of a tight-fisted fundamentalist congregation. His salvation, like Hester Prynne's in *The Scarlet Letter* (a book upon which Frederic drew heavily, as he did also upon "Young Goodman Brown" and "Ethan Brand" among other stories), involves accepting a point of view initially presented as unattractive in the extreme. Certain that no one in his new audience will appreciate the oratorical powers upon which he had built his hopes for the Tecumseh pastorate, Theron rejects the townspeople's fundamentalism and gravitates instead toward the Darwinian Doctor Ledsmar, the comparative mythology of Father Forbes, and, above all, the self-styled Hellenism of Celia Madden, spoiled daughter of the richest Roman Catholic in town. Theron's religious training identifies all Catholics with the Antichrist, while his ideas about the Irish come largely from the political cartoons of Thomas Nast. He sees them as bestial and sensual, but will not acknowledge to himself that for just those reasons—that is, for her sensuality and supposed accessibility—he is attracted toward Miss Madden. That his prurience is altogether of an adolescent or even infantile variety becomes clear in the scene in the forest during the Catholic picnic when he buries his head in the folds of Celia's clothes and imagines himself a small boy again, being mothered. Later he follows Celia and Father Forbes to New York, stalking them like a detective he remembers from a favorite juvenile fiction and hoping to detect them in a re-enactment of the primal scene, thereby establishing (in his own mind) their absolute guilt and his own unimpeachable innocence and integrity.

Celia Madden is not the only woman in the novel with whom Theron Ware fantasizes an ambiguous relationship, part infantile and part sexual. Both his own wife, Alice, and the debt-raiser Sister Soulsby serve also as surrogate mothers (and symbols of power and influence), and both also inspire Theron's sexual curiosity. He sees himself as a figure of irresistible virility, like the circuit riders from the early days of muscular Christianity, and there is more than a little irony involved in Levi Gorringe's comparing him with Henry Ward Beecher, central figure in a notorious scandal and trial for adultery. For adultery is what, in his darkest heart, Theron dreams of committing with Celia and Sister Soulsby, even as he seems incapable of entering into any normal sexual relationship with women.

In addition to such psychological themes centering on Theron's sexuality but possessing as well implications for 19th-century American culture, there are numerous other themes in *The Damnation of Theron Ware* that command the interest of the reader. These include the book's treatment of the impact of Darwinian thought upon articles of basic religious faith; the city (New York) and the country (Theron's boyhood home, among other rustic locales) as symbols of America's past and future; and European complexity (the Roman Catholic culture and religion) in conflict with American simplicity. These themes are treated ambiguously, as, indeed, are all the major ideas in the novel. But the book is most engaging, finally, in its portrayal of Theron's inability to understand his own motivations, to take himself at anything other than face value and as anything other than the finest of fellows, cruelly misunderstood and betrayed. The great future that he sees before him at the end of the novel is, like so much of the rest of his life as chronicled in the book, a fictional construction, a grand illusion, but Theron never loses faith in his own fictions.

—Robert D. Arner

DARKER
Poems by Mark Strand, 1968

Mark Strand's third book of poems, *Darker,* reveals a self that suffers from a psychic fissure and that attempts, through various stances, continuations, and dispersals, to reconcile its divisions: "Wherever I am / I am what is missing." The self is detachedly charted, even as it fragments and rejoins, blurs, and converges. Strand, along with Charles Simic and Robert Bly, is responsible for bringing the influences of European surrealism to American poetry in the 1960s. Throughout *Darker* Strand moves in and out of surrealist gestures, at times rebelling against sense. Although there are moments when the poems manage to strive for hope, they are mainly figured by a terrible, even surprised despair so assuredly drawn that it can seem strangely comforting; all that remains are the efforts to stun an ever-existent fear of death. The poems are luminous as particular arrivals appear, but ultimately the darknesses—psychic, physical, material—are the determinants of realization: "I have a key / so I open the door and walk in. / It is dark and I walk in. / It is darker and I walk in." Residues of darkness stain every effort to relinquish what is known of the self and to stain the nothingness out of which they ultimately occur: "I empty myself of my life and my life remains." Strand's aperture is the aperture of darkness instead of light. The poems are spare, clear, and disarmingly coherent, and the confrontations of death, rebirth, and streams of consciousness happen in a space that is temporally inconsequent and materially thin. This is so even when time and matter are conjured in an apparent mass, as

they are in "Giving Myself Up" and in the two poems titled "From a Litany."

In the first section of the book, "Giving Myself Up," the fourteen poems strive for a complete relaxation of the will, with the movement of the poems simultaneously drifting and decisive as if, out of this paradoxical state, the self might dissolve in order to regain and clarify itself. In "Breath" this place is where "breath is the beginning again, that from it all resistance falls away, as meaning falls away from life, or darkness falls from light." The vision of this and other poems in the first section is the vision of attaining "the self no longer belonging to me, but asleep / in a stranger's shadow, now clothing / the stranger, now leading him off." The frail tether holding past self to present self, familiar self to stranger, adult self to child is continually thinned; at moments of imminent rupture the extraordinary, and at times the terrible, is possible.

In "Giving Myself Up," one of the most impressive poems in the collection, the parts of the body are systematically relinquished, some with a parodying tone, some wistfully, some tragically, even hauntingly: "I give up my clothes which are walls that blow in the wind / and I give up the ghost that lives in them." Ultimately there is nothing left but the voice chiming, "I give up. I give up." It all seems to be an exhausted urge to reach the moment at which emptiness will yield to a new substance, at which "already I am beginning again without anything." At the end of the section a completion resonates in "Coming to This." "This" is the place of uneven reconciliation that self must negotiate with self: "Coming to this / has its rewards: nothing is promised, nothing is taken / away." The arrivals, after the kinds of waiting that are suspended even from themselves, feel invisible, distrusting of their locus, drawn only by the certainty that there is "no place to go, no reason to remain."

"Black Maps," the second and most lyrical section of the book, picks up at this moment of stasis and strives, through nine comparatively vigorous, searching, and extensive poems, to sharpen and demand more from the physicality of recognition. Instead of pervasive, atmospheric darkness, the poems use repetitions of images that involve the sharp and hard, the immortal—bones, the moon, keys, stones, and stars. In the momentous, magically immediate poem "The Recovery," the bones of the speaker's father are "laid out on the ground" as if they could help the speaker break his expectation of recociliation and immediately confront his memory of his father. Instead, everything remains at a distance: "the doctors wave from the deck of a boat / that steamed from port, their bags open, / their instruments shining like ruins under the moon, / and it was no more than anyone might have expected." The withdrawal from consequence and from reconciliation marks the active poems in this section. They strive toward exultation, though it is fleeting, though it offers only momentary and conditional rejuvenation: "I praise the motive of praise by which I shall be reborn." For Strand the cartography of the self, the maps of the search, are permanently black, not to be studied or understood, because "if they are studied at all / it is only to find, / too late, what you thought / were concerns of yours / do not exist." In "Black Maps" the self is locked in a kind of imminent potential, in a struggle to permit itself to vocalize.

Since the publication of *Darker,* Strand has edited a wide variety of anthologies, primarily of European, Mexican, and South American writers, and the surrealism that marks the poems in *Darker* seems colored by the fantastic, not unlike the fantastical textures in South American poetry. In the final section of the book, "My Life by Somebody Else," the poet sees himself from the outside, often in a state that borders on mockery. In "My Life," the poem that begins the section, the first line states, "The huge doll of my body / refuses to rise. / I am the toy of women." The poems are populated by other characters—the poet's mother and father, his wife, and an anonymous "you." The exhaustion and excruciation of offering himself to everything yields this: the condensation of postmodern fragmentation, in which an endless stream of images and unresolved encounters inhabit a place where life in its paradoxes and absurdities, like "the wooden sleep of the moon," is all that remains.

—Martha Sutro

THE DAY OF THE LOCUST
Novel by Nathanael West, 1939

Nathanael West's *The Day of the Locust* is a realistic novel about an unreal city. Centered in Hollywood and the world of movie-making, the story avoids the glitter of stardom to concentrate on the life of the disenchanted. It presents the disillusioned, those who find themselves cheated of the glamour their fantasies promised and the movies provided. The novel emphasizes the spiritual and moral death of the city, symptomatic of the condition within the country as a whole. Focusing on the despair of out-of-work bit actors, the illusions of romantic but untalented actresses, the unhappiness of once-successful vaudeville comics, the paralysis of those who journey to the coast, the novel stresses the death of dreams and culminates in a fiery riot of frenzied movie fans at a Hollywood premiere. This scene, which ends the novel, embodies the efforts of the protagonist, Tod Hackett, to finish his panoramic painting recording life in the city which he titles *The Burning of Los Angeles.* With the Old Testament allusions of its title and its apocalyptic ending by fire, the novel stands as a unique indictment of romance and its destruction in modern America. This intensely moral work, displaying characters entrapped between their idealism and corruption, initiates a series of Hollywood novels which extend West's satire. **F. Scott Fitzgerald**'s *The Last Tycoon,* Budd Schulberg's *What Makes Sammy Run?,* and **Joan Didion**'s *Play It As It Lays* are three distinguished examples.

The principal themes of *The Day of the Locust* are the tension between disillusionment and romance and the reaction to recognizing the absurdity of everyday life. The clearest demonstration of the conflict occurs in chapter 18 when Tod Hackett wanders about a studio lot in quest of Faye Greener, the lustful but elusive *femme fatale* he has met earlier in the book. Believing she is an extra in an epic entitled *Waterloo*—the title itself symbolic of the imminent downfall of Hollywood—he follows a group of *cuirassiers* heading for the set in search of her. He quickly loses them but encounters in succession a painted ocean liner, a papier-mâché sphinx, a desert, a western saloon, a jungle, a Paris street, a Romanesque courtyard, a waterfall, a campy resort, and a Greek temple where the god of Eros "lay face downward in a pile of old newspapers and bottles." Such is the fate of love in the novel— lost, discarded, and impotent. Before he actually witnesses the literal collapse of a cardboard Mont St. Jean when hundreds of soldiers enter a mock battle but unexpectedly crash through canvas, cardboard, and plaster, Tod glimpses an adobe fort, a wooden horse of Troy, a set of baroque palace stairs, a Dutch windmill, and the bones of a dinosaur. In this pivotal chapter, West emphasizes the riot of scenes and fraudulent quality of history when

placed in the hands of the image makers. But the chapter also echoes the illusionary lives all the characters lead in a city that is itself a jumble of architectural and life styles and which values masquerade over authenticity. In Hollywood, West emphasizes, the natural is the artificial.

The unusual characters in the novel parallel the melange of styles and values depicted. A dwarf, a painter, a bookkeeper, a family of Eskimos, a cowboy, a vaudeville comedian, and an untalented actress/prostitute are the principals. But their mixture expresses the frustration rather than achievement of talents. The life of these extras, movie fans, would-be stars, screenwriters, and hangers-on is one of boredom, suffering, and impotence repeated thematically and symbolically throughout the novel. Sordid rooms, sterile landscapes, and dead-end streets project the empty lives in Los Angeles. Promised romance and stardom, adventures and sex, the figures discover only the artificial world of make-believe. And for West's characters, resentment at this discovery unleashes violence. Not surprisingly, the original title of the novel was *The Cheated.*

Faye Greener, the heroine, embodies many of the contradictions of the city. Pursued by all, obtained by none, she is a kind of bitch goddess (like success) who will be possessed only by those who can pay for her. But like the image on a screen, she remains untouchable, a fantasy. She becomes a phantom bride not only for Tod Hackett and Homer Simpson, the retired bookkeeper, but also for the seedy cowboy actor Earle Shoop and the brutal but sexual Mexican Miguel. Faye remains elusive, the dream of love that is unattainable for the nation but which it continues to desire. "Her invitation wasn't to pleasure," West writes, "but to struggle, hard and sharp, closer to murder than to love."

The Day of the Locust is relentless in its exposure of the decay and violence that comes from the betrayal of dreams. Yet West exhibits supreme control in the telling of his story, despite the continued division between the idealism and actuality of Hollywood life. Adjusting to the discrepancy between the imagined and the real, Hackett becomes both an artist fashioning a new future and a Jeremiah predicting doom. The novel is a remarkable satire of America and its dreams, providing a disturbing portrait of its fantasies evoked through language, symbol, and character. And at the core of these desires is violence which for West is idiomatic in America. When the masses discover that "they haven't the mental equipment for leisure, the money nor the physical equipment for pleasure," their only recourse is to destroy. Boredom and disappointment make them savage, as Hackett experiences when he is caught in the mob scene at Kahn's Persian Palace Theatre which ends the novel. But the event paradoxically allows him a vision of his completed painting which he has been unable to finish until that moment.

Just before the climactic riot, Hackett remarks that "at the sight of their heroes and heroines, the crowd would turn demonic." The frustrations beneath the surface of wish-fulfillment and dream-seeking sharpen the theme of middle-class dissatisfaction, creating a startling work of fiction. In its presentation of divided characters, split between their desires and actions, in its rendering of anguish-ridden romantics surrounded by indifferent pragmatists, the work conveys the dilemma of the modern American psyche. And in its accuracy in showing "all those poor devils who can only be stirred by the promise of miracle and then only to violence," the novel has a remarkable contemporary quality. For West, life as illusion masks discontent, although awareness of this condition ironically intensifies the need for fantasy. Difficult to control and uncertain in their goals, the masses feel threatened by their idols and are prepared to destroy them when they fail to gratify their dreams. In the neo-Gothic world of his California, West creates a riveting but profoundly disturbing fiction.

—I.B. Nadel

DEATH OF A SALESMAN
Play by Arthur Miller, 1949

Published and first produced in 1949, Arthur Miller's *Death of a Salesman* won the Pulitzer Prize and other major awards, and in 1985 demonstrated its continuing dramatic power in Dustin Hoffman's extraordinary made-for-television production. Critics have differed widely over whether the play is a tragedy or not, whether it is chiefly social criticism, and if so about what, whether Linda or Willy should be considered the chief character, and whether Willy has or lacks the stature to be a tragic hero. Some see it in the classical Marxist, or existential tradition, while others see it as Biff's story, or an Oedipal ritual. Then is the "Requiem" tearful or not, is it intended as such by Miller, and what does its ironic nature say about the rest of the play? Is Willy Everyman, or merely shallow?

Phyllis Hartnoll states the play depicts the destructive power of illusion (related to Ibsen's conception of the "saving lie" in reverse?) shown in Willy Loman's refusal to face the failure of his own career as a salesman or the failure of his family relationships. Family and friends, in the play, declare him a "prince," yet surely not Machiavelli's, who never lets emotion interfere with reason, who does only that which works. Lee A. Jacobus contends that the play concerns Willy's acceptance of the idea that his success as a person must be measured in terms of his success as a businessman, and should be read as an attack on the "commercialization of society . . . and the confusion of human and monetary values"; this critic also feels the play can indeed be classified as a tragedy—the only one written by a contemporary dramatist.

Miller himself ("Tragedy and the Common Man") declared that "the common man is as apt a subject for tragedy in its highest sense as kings were," a point likely to be granted by most, but not meeting, necessarily, the two criteria generally held to be needed for achieving tragic status: 1) a hero with enough stature to make his suffering significant; and 2) a course of action that produces enlightenment. Other critics declare the play an indictment following the American Marxist line of the 1930s, undermining the "idyll of suburbia." The play becomes the tragedy of a man with noble traits inarticulately expressed; his choice of "the appointed death" makes it his own no less truly than Othello's or Antony's, though there is exultation—perhaps not shared by the audience—in Willy's preparing to join Ben in that dark land loaded with diamonds, so Biff can once more pass Bernard with the $20,000 in the mail from Willy's life insurance, "the last deception" (Allison, Carr, and Eastman, *Masterpieces of the Drama*).

Defining Willy's pathetic faith, "that he is beloved of buyers and that to be loved is to be a success," the *New York Times* wrote that Miller seized an essential feature of American psychology but felt that England, despite its national taste for games, would continue to believe that it took more than being well liked to gain diamonds, especially since Willy's worshipfully encouraged "sports" of sons became "seedy seducer" and "drifting lawbreaker." Perhaps Beckett's Vladimir and Estragon while waiting for Godot, and Camus's Sisyphus rolling that rock in hell, would

have understood about games as opposed to reality, the need to stay busy so you don't realize your responsibilities to others, or the torment demolishing you, or, in Willy's case, the real world about you. Perhaps we have an existential negative parable, a modern day rendering of dramatic irony worsened by Willy's lack of spiritual values and/or his unwillingness to examine those he might have. Existentially speaking, man is free but responsible, required to try to lift the quality of life not only for himself but also for everyone else every time he acts—and he must act. He is not free to run because compassionate actions may be difficult or dangerous, or to die to escape responsibility. Willy appears to see death as a means of avoiding the consequences of actions with which he can no longer cope, a means of escaping difficult decision-making, in addition to benefiting Biff financially. He spells "success" $u¢¢e$$, is extremely image-conscious, determined to succeed "out front with a shine and a smile," and is going through motions no longer effective, with strength he no longer has. Lonely on the road, with no spiritual vision to sustain him, he is vulnerable to predatory Boston females, some of those "good people" in his "New England paradise."

The Marxist view of an old worker tossed away when he no longer produces cannot fully explain the catastrophe. What we do see in Act II is Willy's being torn apart right before our eyes, figuratively speaking, an excruciatingly painful blend of his Boston adultery exposure scene and his crushing defeat in New York City immediately following his being fired and Biff's failure to get a loan from Oliver for the latest fairy tale get-rich-and-famous-quickly project. The boys leave Willy babbling in a toilet while they plan and leave for an evening's sex orgy, even denying at one point he's their father. As the Boston scene crashes Biff, and the New York scene Willy, the limp audience, drained of pity and terror, falls strangely quiet during the "Requiem." Charley survived because "I never took any interest in anything," doubtless playing the benevolent Machiavel, and offered Willy a paying job, which he refused. Willy, crushed, was no high-tragedy glorious failure—glorious because of spiritual victory, failure because of death. "Enter Here Only the Well-Liked" was not inscribed over his gate to heaven. Personality has lost the day. All he wanted was love and respect, freedom to work with his hands, success based on popularity in business . . . and Biff's love.

—Louis Charles Stagg

THE DEATH OF THE HIRED MAN
Poem by Robert Frost, 1914

Robert Frost's "The Death of the Hired Man" vividly illustrates a primary feature of his poetry: his preoccupation with conflict. As the poem opens, we learn that Silas, a now feeble old man who periodically worked for Warren and Mary, has returned to their farm. Mary has fed him and left him in the kitchen. When Warren comes home, she informs him of Silas's return and makes one of the key thematic statements in the poem; she says to Warren, "Be kind." Warren gruffly protests that he has never been anything but kind to Silas.

This exchange leads to the major development in the poem. Pressured to decide what to do about Silas, Mary and Warren present their outlooks on life. These viewpoints, like those of the two men in "Mending Wall," are distinctly different, but do not prove to be antipodal. Because Silas has failed to live up to Warren's high standards, Warren declares he will not allow Silas to remain on the farm. Warren bases his judgment on the fact that in the past Silas was undependable, going off when Warren needed him the most and (an important point with Warren) going off not even for the purpose of bettering himself. Significantly, Mary does not dispute what Warren says. Her reply makes it clear, though, that due to Silas's weak physical condition, she believes that any discussion about him must center not on usefulness, but on life and death. Because Silas, like Warren, judges men primarily according to their value as workers, he had insisted to Mary that he could still help with farm chores. Mary knows this illusion springs from Silas's attempt to maintain a modicum of self-respect—for which she admires him. When Mary tells Warren that Silas rambled on regretfully about his quarrels with the temperamentally different Harold Wilson, who also used to work on the farm, we realize this conflict counterpoints the one between Mary and Warren.

Mary's report about Silas stirs Warren to praise Silas's skill at building a load of hay and, so, to soften his attitude toward the old man. In this same sequence, Mary's summation of Silas's present situation indicates that Frost has created an Everyman figure in Silas. She describes him as someone with "nothing to look backward to with pride, / And nothing to look forward to with hope." Mary herself becomes an archetypal mother figure. Frost writes that Mary stares at the moon, which pours its light "softly in her lap." She touches the "morning-glory strings" hanging above the "garden bed." As Fritz H. Oehlschlaeger points out in his article in *Essays in Literature,* "The passage links Mary to three symbols of fertility" and shows she is "in touch with the cosmic rhythms of birth and death." Warren represents many fathers. When Mary tells him that Silas "has come home to die," Warren stresses justice and duty in his definition of home as a "place where, when you have to go there, / They have to take you in." Mary's definition of home as "Something you somehow haven't to deserve" stresses mercy, compassion, and an acceptance of man as frail.

Mary's words do not, however, end the debate. Warren states that Silas's brother could help out. Mary agrees, just as she tacitly agreed earlier with Warren that Silas was often irresponsible. Mary, then, is by no means non-judgmental. She is merely a kinder judge than her husband is. Warren resists Mary's viewpoint in another way—a way that saves the poem from any taint of mawkishness. When Mary risks saying that Silas's "working days are done," Warren quickly replies, "I'd not be in a hurry to say that." He does not want to surrender the hope that he can still get some practical use out of Silas. Mary simply tells him to go see Silas. Warren does and discovers that Silas is dead.

Silas and Harold Wilson always remained at odds. So, too, in many of Frost's other poems, such as "Home Burial," "The Hill Wife," and "A Servant to Servants," reconciliations to conflicts are not achieved. Indeed, human conflicts could cause the end of civilization, as Frost points out in "Fire and Ice." But in "The Death of the Hired Man," Warren and Mary finally come closer to each other. When Warren returns to say Silas is dead, he gently takes Mary's hand in his.

Reconciliations are of central importance to Frost because they provide one of the few sources of sustenance in a stark world where God is inscrutable and not always benevolent. Despite his skepticism regarding society and government, Frost did not believe people could stand alone and thrive. Although they should maintain their individuality, people need each other. And they can live together successfully—but only if they are not completely

unyielding and allow their individuality to be subsumed by love. As Frost states in "Birches," earth is "the right place for love"—because that is where love is needed the most.

—Robert K. Johnson

THE DREAM SONGS
Poems by John Berryman, from 1964

John Berryman began writing his "dream songs" in 1955 and continued—by habit, he said—until his death 17 years later. They are his principal achievement as a poet. 432 have been published, and hundreds more are in manuscript. *77 Dream Songs* was published in 1964, and an additional 308 appeared in *His Toy, His Dream, His Rest* in 1968. Two were included in *Delusions, Etc.* (1972) and another 45 in *Henry's Fate and Other Poems* (1977). The last of these volumes was not edited by Berryman, and there is some feeling that many of the songs published in it are inferior to the general level of those which had appeared earlier.

Most of the songs contain three stanzas of six lines, variously rhymed and metered. Berryman created a special language for his songs, in part formal and in part idiomatic and vernacular. They are marked as well by sudden syntactical inversions and nervous, jagged, clipped, at times frantic rhythms that reflect the tensions of their principal speaker and subject.

That speaker is "Henry" (not, as some have insisted, the poet himself), a man who, in Berryman's words, "has suffered an irreversible loss" (apparently the death of his father by suicide). Henry's personality is complex but marked essentially by anger, self-loathing, depression, fear, and other black moods and emotions. At times he can be very amusing, but the humor is ironic, bitter, or self-defensive. Although he is apparently a man of considerable learning, he has few passionate interests—or at least few that satisfy him. He travels widely, is obsessed with women, and has achieved some fame or celebrity as a writer, but nothing, except his children, seems to make him happy, and there are few songs that are not deeply touched by his private anguish.

Henry's private hell is made worse by the failure of any traditional means of release—spiritual, intellectual, emotional, sexual—to help him in any final way. He looks for salvation of any kind and finally finds it in anger, which allows him at least to speak with intensity and to find, for the moment, a source for his pain—something he can point to and name rather than live always in a swirl of seemingly causeless anguish. The most powerful of the songs are those in which Henry's emotional turbulence suddenly resolves itself into a redemptive, righteous anger—153 and 384 are among the best of these—or at least into sudden terrifying insight into the nature of his condition such as happens in the unnumbered dream song "Henry's Understanding," published in *Delusions.*

As John Haffenden's biography of Berryman (1982) demonstrated, there are considerable similarities between the facts of Henry's life and what we know of Berryman's, but Robert Phillips and others who have read the songs as autobiographical confession have missed the essential point. Berryman was writing songs, not autobiography, and his task was to force music out of a modern sensibility trapped in the psychological hell of anguish, depression, and despair. In the best of the dream songs, there is a lyric intensity that moves with precision and grace in spite of the depressive weight. Henry finds redemption in anger, but a much greater redemption lies in the fact that, in the midst of his personal horror, he is still able to sing.

The Dream Songs, according to 293, are structured "according to / Henry's / nature," but any sense of progression from one to the next is on occasion difficult or impossible to locate. Berryman insisted that the songs were not independent units but parts of a larger conception though "admittedly more independent than parts usually are." One way to approach them is as a series of modulations of sensibility and tone, but even so, at points the ordering seems entirely haphazard. The poem is also open-ended; it appears to lead to no inevitable conclusion, and had Berryman lived, he might well have continued writing songs as long as he wished. The variations which his subject and method allow seem infinite.

In many ways, *The Dream Songs* may remind us of **Walt Whitman**'s "Song of Myself"—also a series of modulations of sensibility and tone seemingly capable of infinite expansion. Whitman's poem ends essentially because the poet says it does, certainly not because it has said all that it has to say; if that were the case, Whitman would not have felt the need repeatedly to revise and expand it or, for that matter, add to *Leaves of Grass* such poems as "Song of the Open Road," which are in effect extended footnotes to the original poem. Berryman's Henry shares Whitman's infinite expansiveness and inclusiveness, but while the ability to accept everything and not bring things to an end is a source of much power for Whitman's poetic vision, it is another source of Henry's anguish: he is in pain because the past will not let him go, because he cannot ignore what is happening and what has happened to him, because he cannot forget. Whitman's expansiveness led to a new poetic line, a new kind of singing, free from the restrictions of traditional prosody. Henry, on the other hand, can transform his hell into song only by electing a formal and altogether arbitrary verse pattern. If his songs were to expand with the grand, arching lines of Whitman's verse, the pain would expand unbearably with them. It is only by keeping the poetic form constrained and tight that Henry is able to hold in his pain, survive it, and transform it into redemptive song. *The Dream Songs,* begun exactly a hundred years after the first edition of *Leaves of Grass,* is Berryman's dark inversion of Whitman's "Song of Myself."

—Edward Halsey Foster

THE EDUCATION OF HENRY ADAMS: AN AUTOBIOGRAPHY 1907

When the Massachusetts Historical Society published *The Education of Henry Adams* in 1918 it gave the world a work that had been written in 1905 and privately printed in 1907, intended for a small band of readers, one hundred in number. The publishers added the subtitle *An Autobiography,* something that decreases the intimacy of the original and suggests both an end and a beginning, whereas Adams had deliberately failed to bring the work to a conclusion. Two questions may be asked, first, whether *The Education* is to be read as the record of the historical Henry Adams, and second, whether it is to be taken as merely pursuing one theme.

Adams's preface speaks not of the man but of the "manikin" "on which the toilet of education is to be dropped." What he terms "the Ego," he says, has steadily tended to efface itself over 150 years. It would be easier to see *The Education* as the autobiography of a disappointed man were it not for the introduction of

this passive, lifeless figure and the extent to which Adams suggests his supposed sense of failure. Many critics have argued that this had a single origin, the failure to achieve high political office, yet it is difficult to find any definition of success within the work, while neither his friends for whom he wrote nor the less well connected reader would find it easy to see his life as lacking in achievement. Indeed the author may protest too much.

The Education proceeds chronologically but does not cover the twenty years between 1871 and 1892. Some critics have maintained that even Adams could not detach himself from the events leading up to and following on the suicide of his wife Marian in 1885. Whatever the reason the result is to emphasize that this is a record of a search for intellectual not emotional stability. It may be that Boston and Quincy, to use Adams's own figures, would not have allowed him to discuss feeling, the Puritan heritage demanding self-control, but whatever the reason this is an autobiography omitting much that is dear to 20th-century curiosity.

The search for intellectual stability becomes more marked, even more frantic, as *The Education* proceeds. Adams, as befits a man who complained that the formal education at Harvard gave him no knowledge of either Comte or Marx, hoped as they did to find some general explanation, particularly as a historian, for a meaning behind the passage of time. Unlike most historians he felt that this might come through an understanding of natural science and its rules, and the final chapters of *The Education* show his attempts to use its units of measurement to discover what he terms the "formula." This, as he argued, would not be possible without establishing a point of origin which led him, even as he was conceiving *The Education,* to publish *Mont-Saint-Michel and Chartres: A Study of Thirteenth-Century Unity.* He intended to fix a point from which he might better see his own position. According to Adams, the subtitle to *The Education* would have been *A Study of Twentieth-Century Multiplicity* and his purpose thus to see how multiplicity had grown from unity.

The Education, however, appears less interested in multiplicity than unity. Though it is debatable how much unity Adams believed the European mind of the period 1150-1250 possessed, it is clear that he would have welcomed the chance to resurrect its integrity. His desire was so strong that it led him to the paradox that unity was chaos at one point. It is arguable that all of *The Education,* even the earlier, more historical chapters, exhibits the drive to comprehend, to discover "some great generalization which would finish one's clamor to be educated," as he said, and that even the episode in England during the Civil War, fascinating as it is as an insider's account of the travails of the Northern delegation, might best be seen in terms of the lesson it taught Adams the historian that there was no single way of properly interpreting the actions of the British cabinet.

In this sense *The Education* was not the record of a disappointed man, for Adams felt able in the end to give a meaning to the passage of time, described in the chapter "A Law of Acceleration (1904)." The problem with the idea was the cataclysmic undertone, for as he said, "Prolonged one generation longer, it would require a new social mind." This followed from his assumption that there was an integral process stretching from 1200 to 1900, something that might suggest that the Ego was not as effaced as he said it was, for it is at least remarkable that he used all the past to explain his own present. Nonetheless the failure to provide the one great truth scarcely damns the account of one of the great intellectual odysseys of not merely the 19th century but also of the American mind. Adams begins by referring to Rousseau and **Benjamin Franklin** as models; he ends by joining their select company.

—R.A. Burchell

ETHAN BRAND
Story by Nathaniel Hawthorne, 1850

"Ethan Brand" by Nathaniel Hawthorne is an imperfect work of art about an extremely potent idea. Subtitled "A Chapter from an Abortive Romance," it does not develop its title character in much depth and merely synopsizes most of his life. Ethan is seen from the perspective of a lime-burner and his son; from their kiln, he had started on his search for the Unpardonable Sin, and to it he has returned, having found that the sin resides in his own heart. To the lime-burner, he defines it with perverse pride as "The sin of an intellect that triumphed over the sense of brotherhood with man and reverence for God, and sacrificed everything to its own mighty claims!"

Much of the story consists of conversation among the rustics about the mysterious Ethan Brand, and we learn that one of his activities was the ruin of a young girl and perhaps the annihilation of her soul in a cold and remorseless psychological experiment. Brooding in despair, Ethan recalls the tenderness, love, and sympathy for humanity with which he had begun his experiments, during the course of which "ensued that vast intellectual development which . . . disturbed the counterpoise between his mind and heart." In consequence, "He had lost his hold on the magnetic chain of humanity . . . . he was now a cold observer, looking on mankind as the subject of his experiment . . . . from the moment that his moral nature had ceased to keep the pace of improvement with his intellect," he had become a fiend.

Despite his proud statement that he would unshrinkingly reenact the sin, Brand is in such torment that he leaps into the lime-kiln, embracing the "deadly element of Fire," and is consumed, all but his hard heart.

As a story, "Ethan Brand" strains credulity and is guilty of what Poe called "the heresy of the didactic." One problem is that we see only the consequences of the Unpardonable Sin, not the sin itself. It is defined clearly enough, but Hawthorne does not dramatize it. His concept of the Unpardonable Sin is extremely perceptive and timeless, but readers may fail to grasp its significance because the author has not embodied it in an adequate narrative. Like many of Hawthorne's tales, "Ethan Brand" resembles a legend or fairy tale. On one level this quality gives the tales a timelessness, but it also removes such stories as "The Bosom Serpent," "The Man of Adamant," "Rappaccini's Daughter," and "The Birthmark" from reality. We read them as allegories rather than as plausible events. Hawthorne has to spell out for us what the sin is, because he has not dramatized it in Ethan. The crime of having experimented upon a young girl and ruined her life is too vague and is tossed off in a sentence.

Thus D.H. Lawrence's statement in his essay on Hawthorne is particularly applicable to "Ethan Brand": "You *must* look through the surface of American art and see the inner diabolism of the symbolic meaning. Otherwise it is all mere childishness." Likewise, **Herman Melville** wrote that "Young Goodman Brown" sounds like "a simple little tale . . . . Whereas it is as deep as Dante; nor can you finish it, without addressing the author in his own words: 'It is yours to penetrate, in every bosom, the deep mystery of sin.'" This statement applies equally to "Ethan Brand."

Since the story fails to incarnate the Unpardonable Sin in a sufficiently sinister form, we must apply Hawthorne's definition of it to history. There it is more than amply exemplified, in any figures for whom ideas are more important than individuals, abstractions, orthodoxies, and ideologies count for more than people, who for the sake of some elusive utopia or idea of purity will torture, brainwash, purge, enslave, or execute the individual. Examples before Hawthorne's time include the Spanish Inquisition, which tormented the bodies of alleged heretics in order to purify their souls and burned them at the stake to keep them from infecting the orthodox community; the revolutionary French ideologues who enacted a reign of terror to bring about liberty, equality, and fraternity via the guillotine; witch hunting in Hawthorne's own birthplace, Salem; and even the Puritan god of wrath and vengeance who, according to Calvinism, was so pure that He considered humans totally depraved and damned most of them to everlasting torment for being less pure than Himself.

Many other characters in Hawthorne's fiction are guilty of the Unpardonable Sin and suffer its punishment of solitary alienation from the chain of humanity. Roger Chillingworth falls into it in his obsessive revenge upon Dimmesdale; Aylmer, in "The Birthmark," commits it when he brings about his wife's death rather than tolerate the birthmark that symbolizes her imperfect humanity; Dr. Rappaccini commits it when he makes his daughter the subject of a poisonous experiment; and Hollingsworth in *The Blithedale Romance* is guilty of it when he puts his obsession with prison reform ahead of love and friendship: "By and by, you . . . grew drearily conscious that Hollingsworth had a closer friend than ever you could be; and this friend was the cold, spectral monster which he had himself conjured up, and on which he was wasting all the warmth of his heart, and of which at last . . . he had grown to be the bond slave. It was his philanthropic theory."

Profoundly influenced by Hawthorne, Melville rewrote *Moby-Dick* under that influence, transforming it from a fairly simple narrative into a complex symbolic work that explores the "mystery of iniquity." In it, Captain Ahab is guilty of the Unpardonable Sin in being so obsessed with revenge that he has withdrawn from human fellowship and risks the bodies and souls of his crew to fulfill his obsession.

Writers after Hawthorne did not use the term the Unpardonable Sin, but many of them expressed the same idea, and subsequent history certainly illustrated it. Several of Dostoevsky's characters are guilty of it. Raskolnikov, murdering an expendable old pawnbroker so her money can start him on the road to being a great humanitarian, learns that unless every life has value, no life does. Ivan, the intellectual Karamazov brother, argues a syllogistic amorality that if there is no God, all things are lawful, including murder, which the terrorists of *The Possessed* commit for political ideology. Terrorism and totalitarian regimes perfectly exemplify the Unpardonable Sin, whereby ideology is more important than humanity. One could go on multiplying examples—the Nazi doctors and scientists, the politicians and scientists who make chemical weapons and other horrors of modern warfare: and most of Hawthorne's unpardonable sinners are scientists. The point is that Hawthorne's seemingly simple tale is acutely perceptive, and its central concept has a long pedigree and an extensive progeny.

—Robert E. Morsberger

THE FALL OF THE HOUSE OF USHER
Story by Edgar Allan Poe, 1839

Generally acknowledged as Edgar Allan Poe's finest tale, "The Fall of the House of Usher" has attracted a good deal of negative criticism from some of the major literary figures of the 20th century, including **T.S. Eliot**, Cleanth Brooks, **Robert Penn Warren**, and **Allen Tate**. Most commonly, objections have been raised to Poe's heavily ornamented style and lack of concern for action and character development. The story has but one character, Roderick; Madeline, the narrator, the house are simply other versions of him, and Roderick does nothing. He neither acts nor is acted upon but merely exists for a few pages in an atmosphere created by style. Of course, these are the objections of post-World War I realism to romanticism in general.

Much, much more has been said about Poe's few pages of characterless inaction; indeed, in variety and volume of critical response, "The Fall of the House of Usher" is one of the most interpreted stories in the English language. Critics like to make precise what artists make vague, and Poe's tale is a masterpiece of ambiguity and imprecision. The story might be read as the reliable account of an encounter with a madman who buried his sister alive. It may be a quite literal account of a brush with the supernatural, a vampire tale perhaps, for certainly Madeline's escape from the vault described by the narrator could be accomplished by nothing human. "The Fall of the House of Usher" has inspired several film versions. Jean Epstein won acclaim with a French production in 1929; most famous is Roger Corman's American International version of 1960. The literal interpretation obviously works best for the filmmakers. The strength of their medium is its power to establish visual reality, but this it gains at the expense of the ambiguity available to the writer. Audiences will believe their eyes, but they may well doubt what they are told by an unreliable source, and here the literal interpretation meets a problem. There is little question but that Roderick Usher is mad, but as events unfold, the narrator, impressionable from the start, comes increasingly under Roderick's influence and even admits to the weakening of his own capacity for rational objectivity. He comes to accept without critical comment Roderick's impression of what is happening. As Madeline approaches, Roderick deliriously talks seemingly to himself and applies the epithet "madman," which ironically might now address the only other person present, the narrator. Thus, "The Fall of the House of Usher" can be read as the effusion of an irrational mind not only about the loss of sanity but itself an example of that theme.

With the narrator rejected as a reliable relater of facts, the way is opened for a variety of critical approaches that seek symbolic significance for characters and events. Perhaps Poe has written an allegory on the artistic process. Roderick, after all, is not really inactive, as some critics have charged. Whatever the real nature of the events that have led him to his present state, Roderick has painted them as abstractions so fantastic and powerful as to cause the narrator to reject his own senses and reason and accept the artist's vision as a truer account of reality. Andre Malraux said, "The modern artist's supreme aim is to subdue all things to his style." Roderick certainly does this in his paintings, in his "Haunted Palace" poem, and, in a larger sense, in the story itself. Of course, Malraux's "all things" must include the darker elements of the universe that the artist cannot explore without risk of passing a point of no return to reason. Roderick passed that point.

Poe's tale also lends itself very well to Freudian interpretation. Here, the entire story—just like the "Haunted Palace" poem it frames—is a symbolic image of a human mind. Roderick is the ego or consciousness which attempts to bury the primitive impulses of the id, Madeline. The narrator in this reading functions as the superego, an awareness of standards and conventions that mediates between the twins. The attempt to repress the force of the id is unsuccessful; Madeline breaks out of her tomb and emerges to the level of the waking consciousness precipitating the total mental breakdown of the organism.

Critics have commonly remarked on the tight unity of the tale; character, setting, and action are bound into a single image of ruin by a style carefully wrought for the purpose. Unity, however, is more than an effect in "The Fall of the House of Usher"; it is actually a theme, a central theme in Poe's work that found its definitive expression in *Eureka* (1848). Poe theorized that all creation emanated from a single point, and, despite cosmic diffusion, it is still a part of the Godhead. Ultimately this universe will cease to expand and bend back upon itself in a cycle of contraction resulting in final reunification with the source that must annihilate things as they now exist. Such ideas, long present in several mystical systems, resemble the Big Bang theory of modern theoretical physics. Poe's story is about fragments coming together. The narrator is drawn to the house; Roderick and Madeline, both at one with the house, are at last drawn violently and fatally together, and all is sucked into the black hole of the tarn. Poe's finest tale, then is about the end of things, which D.H. Lawrence, writing on Poe, remarked is part of the dual rhythm of "American art-activity" and prerequisite to the "forming of a new consciousness underneath."

—William J. Heim

THE FEDERALIST
Essays by Alexander Hamilton, James Madison, and John Jay, 1788

Written by Alexander Hamilton, James Madison, and John Jay, *The Federalist* consists of 85 essays (later combined and numbered as 84), most of which were originally published in New York newspapers between 27 October 1787 and 16 August 1788.

Initially, at least, these essays were intended for immediate ends and, it is believed, were meant only for local distribution. According to current scholarship, most of the essays were hurriedly written and only hastily revised. As one scholar has explained, although it now enjoys the status of "a great political classic," at the time of its publication "*The Federalist* was at bottom an electioneering pamphlet written to persuade contemporary New Yorkers to vote right." Responding to a groundswell of anti-Federalist sentiment in the New York press, Hamilton thought it necessary to generate additional popular support for the Constitution in New York. Pressed by numerous other commitments, he enlisted the assistance of his colleagues, John Jay and James Madison, and writing under the pseudonym of "Publius," they announced the publication of "a series of papers" in support of the Constitution. William Duer, Gouverneur Morris, and possibly Rufus King are also thought to have been approached, but they either declined or their work was rejected.

Roughly half the essays (1-36) that followed deal with the inadequacy of the Confederation of States as it then existed; the other half (37-85) deal with the need for a strong, centralized, federal government such as that proposed in the Constitution recently drafted at the convention for that purpose in Philadelphia. After the publication of these essays in two volumes in 1788, *The Federalist,* as the project then came to be called, received relatively wide circulation throughout the states even after ratification of the Constitution was assured, and it eventually became almost as important among early analysts of the Constitution as that document itself.

Even today *The Federalist* is generally considered "the most significant contribution Americans have made to political philosophy," and it is read and studied by scholars and students of both literature and history as "the classic interpretation of the American Constitution." As one commentator has explained, "Taken singly many of the papers still invite close study for what they say about federalism, representative government, checks and balances, judicial reviews, and guarantees of human rights. Altogether they have been taken as seminal writings of the founders, ranking just after the Declaration of Independence and the Constitution itself as explanations of the shape of American politics and institutions." Particularly singled out for analysis in this regard is *Federalist* 10, in which it is argued that an extended republic of the kind presented in the Constitution would preserve individual liberties by encouraging so many factions that no single group could ever gain an advantage over the others.

Regrettably, because *The Federalist* was published pseudonymously, the exact nature of the collaboration among its authors remains difficult to reconstruct, and despite vigorous scholarly efforts to do so, no one has been able successfully to identify the precise authorship of many of the essays in the project. In general, scholars concur that Hamilton assumed responsibility for writing 1, 6-9, 11-13, 21-36, 59-61, and 65-85; Madison for 10, 14, and 37-48; and Jay for 2-5 and 64. At issue are 18-20, 49-58, and 62-63, with internal evidence supporting Madison as the primary author for all but 49 and 53, which are generally attributed to Hamilton. Because of the furious pace at which the essays were published, there was probably little time for the authors to circulate their work among themselves. Most certainly, however, they discussed at the onset the ideas they intended to develop in their parts of the project, and evidence exists to suggest that the authors may have exchanged notes and research. Jay wrote the fewest of the essays because shortly after undertaking the endeavor he became incapacitated by illness.

It is, however, the general opinion of scholars that the success and overall brilliance of *The Federalist* reside less with any individual writer than with the combined expertise and good-will that all three authors brought to the series. At the conclusion of the Constitutional Convention, both Hamilton and Madison emerged with profound doubts about the efficacy of the document they had helped to create, and, moreover, each objected to it for radically different reasons. Distrustful of the laboring classes, Hamilton wanted a far stronger federal government than that proposed by the Constitution. Madison, on the other hand, feared that the Constitution gave too much centralized power to a federal authority, and he worried about the possibilities of tyranny and the loss of regional control by the states. In later life, Hamilton and Madison would once again come to odds over these issues, but at the time when they wrote *The Federalist* they realized that without some type of effective federal union anarchy and dissolution would inevitably erupt among the states and that the consequences for the future of North America would indeed be dire. For this reason,

they put aside their differences, joined forces under the banner of "Publius," and in a spirit of unique goodwill argued the prospective merits of a federal union of the kind outlined in the Constitution. The result of this decision was what one scholar has termed a richly textured interplay of opinion and a model of decorum that the readers of *The Federalist,* who themselves were divided by suspicions and factional interests, could appreciate, emulate, and eventually embrace.

In dividing up the essays, each writer took primary responsibility for those areas he was most suited to discuss. Jay, for example, with his extensive diplomatic experience, focused on the subject of foreign relations. As a former military officer, Hamilton devoted much of his attention to military and executive concerns. By far the most scholarly of the three, Madison is considered to have been the world's foremost expert on the strengths and weaknesses of historical republics, and hence he directed much of his energy to analyzing the potential advantages and disadvantages of the proposed union. All three writers brought to their discussions a familiarity with the most current political and social theorists of the day, including Locke, Hobbes, Montesquieu, and Hume.

As a literary artifact, *The Federalist* deserves attention for its remarkable clarity of expression, precision of argument, lucidity of style, and mastery of organization. Although it belongs in that genre of literature known as the "political pamphlet," a form that in America can be traced back to the published debates between Roger Williams and John Cotton, *The Federalist* avoids the excesses of vituperation so often found in such works during the 18th century. For their style and tone the writers of *The Federalist* turned to the essays of Joseph Addison, but they nonetheless managed to avoid the cleverness of phrasing and rhetorical embellishments popular among many 18th-century essayists. In many ways, the style of *The Federalist* is unique. As one critic has pointed out, in writing *The Federalist* the authors seemed to have adhered to the very modern theory of rhetoric that they articulated in *Federalist* 37: "The use of words is to express ideas. Perspicuity, therefore, requires not only that the ideas should be distinctly formed, but that they should be expressed by words distinctly and exclusively appropriate to them." By applying this theory to their own writing, the authors of *The Federalist* fashioned "a literary monument to one of [their] country's greatest achievements." In the words of one commentator, "a literary craftsman can hardly do more."

—James A. Levernier

THE FISH
Poem by Elizabeth Bishop, 1946

With the possible exception of "Man-Moth," "The Fish" is Elizabeth Bishop's best-known poem, frequently reprinted in anthologies. It was part of Bishop's first collection of poems, *North & South* (1946).

It is a poem of seventy-six relatively short lines, in free verse, spoken by a first-person narrator who, in one sense, tells a very simple story. The first line of the poem reads, "I caught a tremendous fish . . ." The last line reads, "And I let the fish go." The poem, however, focuses much more on how the narrator sees the fish than on what he or she does to it.

Between the catching and the letting go, the other seventy-four lines chiefly record a disinterested but intense observation of the fish, giving no hint that "he" will be released. (The poem provides the gender of the fish but not of the narrator.) At no point does the narrator betray any sense of sympathy for the fish.

Briefly, the narrator provides general information: The fish had not "fought at all," is "battered," "venerable," and "homely." There follows an abundance of physical detail about the fish's skin, which is compared to wallpaper; his coloring (mostly brown, with shapes like "full-blown" roses); his ailments and burdens (sea-lice, barnacles, and weeds); his previous struggles, as evidenced by four different hooks-and-lines hanging from his mouth; his eyes, gills, mouth, jaw, and face; and even his bones, flesh, and innards, which the narrator imagines. We are not told what kind of fish it is, but it is probably a species of salmon.

Out of this concentrated description, an implicit homage gradually emerges, as the narrator admits, "I admired his sullen face." Despite this admiration, the narrator never yields to the kind of sentiment expected in a more conventional account of a person capturing, then liberating, a wild creature. Nonetheless, late in the poem, an epiphany occurs. As a result of the exhaustive observation of the fish, the narrator begins to see the world differently: "I stared and stared / and victory filled up / the little rented boat . . . ."

This is a crucial moment in the poem. The narrator turns away from the fish but in doing so does not relax or become occupied with ordinary tasks, appearing instead to experience a revelation. And for the first time, a mysterious word appears in the poem: "victory." The reader need not be frustrated by the word and what it may mean, need not force a literal interpretation suggesting that the narrator is victorious in having caught a "tremendous" fish or that the fish has triumphed over the narrator's desire to keep him. While accepting the mystery and ambiguity of the word, the reader might speculate that what the narrator has won—has earned by means of the exacting observation of the fish—is a heightened perception of the world. Thus, the narrator continues to stare at the boat "until everything / was rainbow, rainbow, rainbow! / And I let the fish go." This is an ecstatic moment, the rainbow a familiar symbol of a metaphysical presence—of good luck, God, a path to spiritual fulfillment, or some other great prize. Bishop, however, rescues the symbol from cliché and convention by linking it specifically to the transformed image of the boat and by having her narrator "earn" the rainbow, so to speak, by taking an arduous journey of observation. Because the narrator has paid such careful attention to the world (the fish), the rainbow becomes an appropriate reward.

Moreover, it might be said that since the narrator has "earned the rainbow," there is no need to keep the fish. While letting this "tremendous" and "venerable" fish go seems appropriate, the liberation is not an act of pity or necessarily even a gesture involving the fish himself. Instead, the liberation seems to reverse the biblical idea of gaining the world and losing one's soul: because the narrator has gained, has earned, a new soul—a restored, blessed way of seeing—the narrator need not symbolically keep the world by literally holding on to the fish.

"The Fish," then, can be seen as a wry improvisation on that American folk tradition, the "fish story." Also, if read against the backdrop of the most famous American fish story, *Moby Dick*, the poem implicitly critiques Melville's epic study of good and evil and obsessive quest. For we may read "The Fish" as implying that "victory" comes not through a willful quest but through surrender, through stepping outside of oneself, looking at the world, and abandoning the myopic greed that drives humans to

possess and, in the end, possesses them. In this regard "The Fish" can also be compared with Hemingway's great fish narrative, *The Old Man and the Sea*, in which the old man triumphs even though sharks devour his extraordinary catch. A key difference obtains, however: Bishop's narrator does not need to catch the fish and lose it in order to learn a spiritual lesson. Her narrator simply lets the fish go, having learned just through seeing, not through ironic or tragic loss. One might consider Bishop's poem to be a feminist "fish story," then, because it does not depend upon agony, tragedy, combat, or quest.

In the context of Bishop's contemporaries, the poem's rich imagery and precise phrasing call to mind the poetry of **William Carlos Williams**, **Marianne Moore**, **Karl Shapiro**, **Theodore Roethke**, and **Randall Jarrell**. Insofar as "The Fish" represents a search for meaning in a comparatively ordinary natural encounter, it also anticipates the work of poets from subsequent generations, including John Haines, David Wagoner, **Gary Snyder**, and Mary Oliver.

—Hans Ostrom

GIFTS OF THE MAGI
Story by O. Henry, 1905

Considered from a non-traditional perspective, O. Henry's best-loved story, "Gifts of the Magi," published in the 10 December 1905 issue of the New York *Sunday World Magazine,* is much more than a sentimental Christmas morality. Though it has often been taken as the latter and is tagged with one of his conspicuous, ironic twists of plot, it is actually one of the strangest and most haunting stories he ever wrote. (The story is more familiar as "The Gift of the Magi." the title given it for its book publication in *The Four Million.*)

There is a succession of curious, provocative features, a layered pattern of fact and implication, relating to the story's composition and to the author's obscure intentions. First, the feature of subject matter and writer: "Gifts of the Magi" emphasizes the felicity of domestic relations and the sacramental nature of a married couple's exchange of Christmas presents. But it was written by a man who cared neither for marriage nor for religion. His two attempts at matrimony were egregious failures, largely because of his individualistic lifestyle and his lack of concern for the spouse. As for religion, his pagan outlook had been remarked on in his own day. Commenting on this, his biographer Richard O'Connor states, "He wasn't against religion, he simply ignored it."

Next there is the business of literary creation. Hobbled by bad work habits and a helter-skelter mode of bohemian-bachelor existence, O. Henry ground out his fiction pieces under the nagging pressure of crowding editorial deadlines and (what were for him) skimpy finances. He always found writing to order difficult, and the brief that led to "Gifts of the Magi" was especially irksome: he was to produce a newspaper fiction work scheduled for the Christmas issue, and having "something to do with Christmas, something at least faintly religious." His initial problem was lack of inspiration regarding the assignment; this was compounded by repeated delays in just getting down to work; but the result was a literary gem hurriedly conveyed to the newspaper office shortly before the paper went to press.

A young, struggling couple in an eight-dollar-per-week furnished flat have sold their most prized possessions—Jim Young, the gold watch that had come down from his father and his grandfather; his wife Della, her long beautiful tresses—so each could buy an appropriate Christmas gift for the other: a set of combs for Della and a watch fob-chain for Jim. Significantly, "Gifts of the Magi" evokes the biblical account of Samson and Delilah; in this instance the woman, whose name clearly suggests "Delilah," ravishes her own hair. This brings us to the biblical magi referred to by O. Henry, and to the gifts they bring to the Babe in the manger—gold, frankincense, and myrrh—gifts which O. Henry regards somewhat dubiously.

When Della tells Jim what she has done to her hair and why, she asks him to understand, saying that no one could ever measure her love for him. The author indicates that there is no way to put a monetary value on the rental of their flat—presumably because of the love it holds. In his illustration, neither mathematicians nor wits nor magi could explain the difference between what the Youngs pay for rent, and a million a year. Valuable as the magi's gifts to the Babe in the manger were, the ability to reduce love to monetary figures was not one of their gifts. This leads O. Henry to conclude that the magi doubtless gave the Babe wise gifts, possibly *exchangeable* "in case of duplication." But these "two foolish children" were the wisest of all giftgivers and receivers—because for their gifts they had "most unwisely sacrificed" their "greatest treasures"; people like them are the wisest of all—the (real-life) magi. Still, there is an elusive something in this strange amalgam of tenement romance and Bible sampler that nags at the reader's mind.

The last curious feature of "Gifts of the Magi" has to do with Jim Young, his watch, and conventional time. Before he sold his paternal heirloom watch, Jim had been accustomed to taking it out and admiring it. Della, before she learned that he had sold the watch, had told him that he would presently have to look at it a hundred times each day—in wifely fashion anticipating the effect of her gift, and reinforcing O. Henry's point that Jim had been very conscious of time. But with Jim's Christmas sacrifice of his timepiece, the old order of time ended. Yet, though he and Della will not be living under a new temporal order—symbolically, a timeless limbo—the possibility of redemption in an ultimate order of time remains. Jim, to Della: "let's put our Christmas presents away and keep 'em a while. They're too nice to use just at present." Thus, with *her* hair slowly beginning to grow back, and the (implied) possibility that Jim's watch might somehow, someday be bought back, there is good reason for these two self-sacrificing "magi" so deeply in love to await the glorious birth of a new age of unlimited possibility.

If O. Henry's ironic story-line suggests irony beyond irony, it may be stated in the form of a question: had he been a devout churchgoer and a good and proper husband, could O. Henry have written a more effective, meaningful story with the same original ingredients?

—Samuel Irving Bellman

THE GLASS MENAGERIE
Play by Tennessee Williams, 1944

Tennessee Williams first developed the characters and situation of *The Glass Menagerie* in a short story, "Portrait of a Girl in Glass" (published later in 1948), and an unproduced screenplay, *The Gentleman Caller,* before his first major success came with its award-winning Broadway stage production starring Laurette Taylor as Amanda. The autobiographical nature of his characters is evident. The playwright dramatizes his youthful self in Tom Wingfield, a would-be poet trapped by family obligations with a dull Depression-days job in a shoe factory, and in the maturing merchant seaman-narrator recalling for the audience with a mixture of guilt and sentimentality the memory of a mother, whom he self-tormentingly appreciates; an absent father (represented only by a grinning photograph which lights up on cue) from whom he is estranged; and a sister to whom he is strongly attached. Amanda, the charmingly overbearing mother, clings to the memory of being a southern belle in a genteel past that conflicts unkindly with her present straitened circumstances in a dingy city apartment. She neither understands her son's need for adventure and self-fulfillment nor accepts the extent of her daughter's reclusiveness. Tom's painfully shy and physically crippled sister Laura hides in a fantasy world of tiny glass animals. The characters are variations, excepting a younger brother, of Williams's own family: his mother, a Mississippi minister's daughter who experienced difficult circumstances while raising a family and forced a separation from the playwright's mostly absent father, a hard-drinking salesman not understanding of his quiet and bookish older son; his schizophrenic sister Rose; and the playwright himself whose experience parallels that of Tom Wingfield.

More significant, however, than the play's autobiographical base is its demonstration of Williams's early ability to write theatrically effective scenes that artfully intermixed the comic and the tragic and made telling use of symbolism (the drama's title is a prime example) to evoke mood and meaning, to compose lyrically rich dialogue reflecting a gifted poetic temperament and an ear for the rhythmic speech patterns of his native south, and to create finely sculpted characters who anticipate both his emerging view of the human condition and the nature of major characters yet to walk in subsequent works. Persons with the streak of sensitivity, gentility, or romanticism in Williams's world are confronted with a harsh, unkind reality which either destroys them as victims, rejects them as outcasts, or serves as a battleground on which they tenaciously struggle to emerge as survivors. While Amanda Wingfield clutches the romantic recollection of a gentle era when she entertained 17 gentlemen callers in one afternoon she also resiliently and feistily copes with life's stern reality for her own survival and that of her family. Laura, after abortive encounters with life including a climactic one with a "gentleman caller," reveals herself as too fragile—like her glass unicorn whose horn is broken by the caller's clumsiness—to pursue outside reality and thus becomes instead its victim retreating into her own fantasy world. Tom Wingfield refuses to accept commonplace life's proscriptive obligations and strictures and becomes therefore an outcast and wanderer. These figures are images that will appear again on the playwright's other dramatic canvases. Unusual in Williams's work is this tender family portrait, in sharp contrast to the far less gentle works which followed.

The play presents its people within the framework of eight scenes, essentially realistic in style but augmented by symbolic overtones and nonrealistic theatrical devices. Strong in theatricality and emotional power, the scenes, summoned up by the narrator who steps in and out of them as observer and participant, lead to the action's major incident: the arrival and aftermath of the gentleman caller, the unimaginative warehouse worker Jim O'Connor whom Laura recognizes as a secretly loved former high school hero. In a poignant scene, the caller unwittingly raises romantic expectations in Laura only to dash them when he confesses his engagement to another girl. His swift departure leaves a desolate Laura who retreats back with finality to her world of figurines, and an angry Amanda whose unfair upbraiding of Tom drives him to a pre-planned final departure. The action's climax and resolution are both moving and compelling. The play limns a portrait of the poet as a young man who must be free to follow his art and commemorates his escape from a family, the memory of which will pursue him on his journey as a writer.

Generally accepted as one of Williams's masterpieces, this work represents the start of his strongest creative period, lasting to *The Night of the Iguana* in 1961. Since its first New York production, *The Glass Menagerie* has been continually produced throughout the world. Its long-lasting success is well deserved.

—Christian H. Moe

GO TELL IT ON THE MOUNTAIN
Novel by James Baldwin, 1953

On occasion in his fiction James Baldwin wears the mask of the passionate priest, a medieval monk who has seized the pen in order to inscribe the legends, the chronicles, and the martyrdoms of his people. Indeed, his first novel, *Go Tell It on the Mountain,* reveals Baldwin in this role as monkish chronicler, setting forth in miniature the history of his people as they move from bondage and seek the promised land. And the religious ambience of this novel is consistent with a view of it as a formalized version of black legend.

It is not systematic or intellectual history, but folk history, episodic in character, made up of typical and representative actions which rest upon a commonly held body of belief and assumption and so carry wide-ranging implications. Minor examples will quickly illustrate this kinship with medieval literature. Florence, the aunt of John Grimes, the protagonist, flees the south when her employer threatens to make her his concubine. Deborah, the first wife of Gabriel, John's father, was raped by white men when she was sixteen years old. A nameless black soldier is mutilated and killed by a white mob. These actions are presented as typical, not unique, experiences. Baldwin is fulfilling a pattern for a literary exercise as highly stylized as the sermon or the legend: he is treating what might be called, after the medieval practice, the matter of the south. The reader in tune with Baldwin understands his heuristic purpose and can construct from his suggestive episodes the whole history of a suffering race.

Much of the novel deals with the emergence of the Grimes family from the south and especially with the struggle of Gabriel, the father and a preacher, to reach a state of grace, despite the obstacles that society puts in his way and despite his own violent and sinning nature. His marriage to Deborah, made in good part because she had been raped, and his marriage to Elizabeth, who had had an illegitimate son, are actions taken deliberately in search of expiation for his own sins. His hopes for Roy, the only living son of his loins, are the hopes of a patriarch for a successor who shall fulfill the destiny of his people. Baldwin persuades the reader to feel the weight of Gabriel's anguish as he makes his fateful choices and struggles with his exaggerated sense of sin. Gabriel is a more human figure than any other character in the chronicle, a man in whom passion and faith collide. And, as the lineaments of humanity appear in him, he is removed from his conventional role

as Patriarch, Leader of his Tribe. Nevertheless, in the largest sense, the story of the Grimes family as Baldwin conceives it is a formalized chronicle, a history of escape from a land of oppression to a new place where, after suffering, freedom and salvation may come, some time in the future, as deserved rewards.

This account of the suffering of the black people and the search for salvation, capsulized in the career of Gabriel Grimes, is treated in a series of flashbacks in the novel, while the action in the present takes place at a service in the Temple of the Fire Baptized church in Harlem. The flashback technique gives that sense of distance in time which creates the aura appropriate to legend, and in the singing and praying, the service lends ritual amplitude to the legend.

Baldwin plays his role as monkish chronicler well, in the sense that he faithfully records stereotypical characters and situations. He brings some originality and vitality to the other important aspect of this novel, the maturation of John Grimes, Gabriel's stepson and bastard of Elizabeth. The fourteen-year-old John is clearly an autobiographical figure, as Baldwin has said elsewhere, who is seeking to find his way out of adolescence. He must cope with a tyrannical father, an evangelical and puritanical religion, and exaggerated sense of sin, and a Harlem environment pregnant with violence as he seeks the road to maturity and identity. In the crucial experience of his life thus far, he frees himself from all the tyrannies in his life—the father, the guilt over his sins, the ghetto—by embracing religion and being embraced by it, by knowing that he must climb the mountain of faith and place his destiny in the hands of the Lord. John, the rejected son—it has been argued that he is Ishmael to Gabriel's Abraham—frees himself from his father, partly by rising above him in purity and zeal, when he gives himself into bondage to faith; at least some of the tensions between them are washed away in the new moral and spiritual assurance that comes to John after his ecstatic experience. Like Gabriel, John had suffered from a conflict between the narrow morality of his church and the awakening sexual demands of his body. This conflict is submerged if not resolved in that access of spirit which comes to John. The church also offers a refuge from the violence and degeneracy of Harlem which represent both the conditions of black life and the conception of it held by others. The church frees John from his father's tyranny and self-righteousness, from guilt over sin, from shame and terror at being black in the midst of black corruption. At the same time it defines the conditions of his search for maturity and identity. At the end of *Go Tell It on the Mountain* John accepts religion and Christianity because they free him from the problems he faces in the world; they free him to grow within the limits they set.

—Chester E. Eisinger

GODS DETERMINATIONS
Poem by Edward Taylor, written 1680s (?)

Gods Determinations touching his Elect: and The Elects Combat in their Conversion, and Coming up to God in Christ together with the Comfortable Effects thereof, which was probably written in the 1680s when the Stoddard controversy was just beginning, is the first of two major works by the American puritan poet and congregationalist minister Edward Taylor, the other being the *Preparatory Meditations* (1682-1725), a series of over 200 poems written as spiritual preparation for the pastor's administration of the Lord's Supper to his congregation in the church at Westfield, a small town in the western part of the Massachusetts Bay Colony. Although in fact only two stanzas of all of Taylor's poetic works were published in the poet's lifetime, Taylor may have at one time intended to publish *Gods Determinations.* The single extant manuscript of this poem of 2,101 lines was written in a very careful hand on numbered pages (the other pages in the Yale manuscript of the collected poems are not numbered) and placed just before the series of meditations. One has the impression that before he bound up *Gods Determinations* with other poems, he considered it as an independent work which he may well have carried with him to read from the pulpit or at prayer meetings. The poem is hortatory in nature. It is written with a definite audience in mind— first, perhaps, the members of his own congregation and by extension (if published) to any Christian reader who needed assurance that he was one of God's predestined elect and therefore eligible to be a full church member and participate in the sacred communion of the Lord's Supper. In the 1680s there was need of a spiritual awakening, for many puritans were under the so-called Half Way Covenant and uncertain of their spiritual fitness to become full members. At this time Solomon Stoddard, pastor of the church in the neighboring town of Northampton, was beginning to promulgate the doctrine that the Lord's Supper was a converting ordinance and that those who doubted their election might be converted to full assurance by accepting communion. Taylor attacked Stoddard in his letters, sermons, and poems. His position, the "orthodox" one, was that a person must be a converted "saint" before accepting communion. His task as a minister and (perhaps) as a poet was to convince the backward members of his congregation *before* communion that they were of the elect and could come to the communion table without fear of damnation. In *Gods Determinations* Taylor dramatically presents and explains God's mysterious ways in bringing his few chosen saints to salvation.

The doctrine of the poem is the orthodox Calvinism of the leading colonial ministers of Taylor's period including Increase and **Cotton Mather** and **Michael Wigglesworth**, author of the notorious poem *The Day of Doom:* predestination, the salvation of the elect few, the damnation of the many, the perseverance of the saints, the inefficacy of works to attain saving grace, justification and salvation by faith alone. Heaven and hell are seen as definite locations, not symbolic states of mind, and God, Christ, Satan, angels, and demons may take on the attributes of real persons. Gods Determinations is made up of a group of 35 poems in various meters and stanza forms. The poem as a whole has a threefold structure: l) The creation of the world and man, the fall of man, the damnation of the many, the salvation of the elect few through God's saving grace; 2) Satan's powerful attack on the elect and his failure to destroy them; 3) the joys of salvation.

Some of the best writing occurs in the Preface of part one. Taylor describes the beauties of the earth which God created out of "Nothing":

> Who made the Sea's its Selvedge, and it locks
> Like a Quilt Ball within a Silver Box?
> Who Spread its Canopy? Or Curtains Spun?
> Who in this Bowling Alley bowld the Sun?

God who is seen as all powerful ("Whose single Frown will make the Heavens shake / Like as an aspen leafe the Winde makes quake") creates "Nothing Man," giving him an eternal soul to glorify Him, but because of man's fall, this "Brightest Diamond" is

"grown / Darker by far than any Coalpit stone." The next four poems describe in detail man's fall and God's foresight in planning how, through the intervention of Christ's mercy, the elect will be saved. Part two, consisting of 23 individual poems, dramatically presents the spiritual combat between Satan and the elect. A very few of the elect escape the rigors of combat and are converted immediately by God into saints. The rest are divided into three ranks to lace the terrors of Satan's temptations. Satan becomes the most colorful character in the drama—a raging roaring beast intent on destroying his enemies at first by physical terror. The first rank, however, are soon comforted by Christ's intervention and, escaping Satan, begin their journey to heaven. Satan now, in a series of poems, but most interestingly in "Satan's Sophestry," attacks the remaining ranks with psychological warfare. In the most subtle of all his arguments he claims that if man is certain he is saved he (a poor sinner) is guilty of "presumption," that is, pride, which is a cardinal sin, and therefore he is damned. At last, however, the second and third ranks, with the help of God acting through saints already saved, become convinced they are truly of the elect and so escape Satan's wiles. Part three, which consists of seven poems, describes the ecstasy of the saints "while in Christs Coach they sweetly sing / As they to Glory ride therein."

The poem is in the spiritual combat tradition with scenes of martial warfare reminiscent of the Old Testament, and one is reminded also at times of Bunyan and Milton as well as of the medieval morality plays. Judged by literary standards, *Gods Determinations* cannot be compared with Milton's *Paradise Lost,* which also was written to "justify the ways of God to men." Nevertheless, because of its metrical and stylistic variety ranging from the colloquial diction of the colonial farmer to the exalted diction of such poets as Vaughan and Crashaw, it is far superior to Wigglesworth's *The Day of Doom* and more dramatic and intense than any of the longer poems of Anne Bradstreet. It is the best long poem of the 17th century written on what was to become United States soil.

—Donald E. Stanford

THE GRAPES OF WRATH
Novel by John Steinbeck, 1939

Today the *New York Review of Books* comments on social change: the roads are clogged with "retired farmers" who "leave for Florida in their fancy campers." John Steinbeck's *The Grapes of Wrath* records an earlier time, depression days of Dust Bowl farmers, their farms blown away, heading in jalopies for California's golden groves. If modern America has any idea of Okies and hard times, it is largely due to Steinbeck's greatest work.

In it, Steinbeck's "voice over" and vivid episodes create a kind of newsreel of a period when times got tough and the tough got going, westward as ever in their very American and indomitable flight to something better. It is that courage and determination "in the presence of this continent" that has made the book a classic of our literature, that gained it in its own day a great success despite its ignorant Okies (with their accents and even their customs all wrong), and its nasty union men (either venal or fanatic), and its sordid language, as some thought. ("Take the vulgarity out of this book," a shocked Oklahoma congressman told the House of Representatives in 1940, "and it would be blank from cover to cover.") Steinbeck outdid himself as he wrote about what some representative Americans of his time "are doing, thinking, wanting." He said: "It's all a writer knows. I have set down what a large section of our people are doing and wanting, and symbolically what all people of all time are doing and wanting. The migration is the outward sign of the want." He intensely admired the Okies "because they are brave, although the technique of their life is difficult and complicated, they meet it with increasing strength, because they are kind, humorous and wise, because their speech has the metaphor and flavor and imagery of poetry, because they can resist and fight back, and because I believe that out of these qualities will grow a new system and a new life which will be better than anything we have had before."

Steinbeck's faith seems to have been in something more like a Life Force than the strident socialism of his day; he had a sort of mystical belief in people, not a political belief in the proletariat. And so he wrote a work of art that went beyond the propaganda novel of police brutality and proletarian strikes, an angry and unorthodox New Testament of a religion of mankind. Critics differ as to whether Jim Casy is the Christ or the John the Baptist of this gospel and whether Tom Joad is the Christ or the St. Paul, but all must agree with the critic who wrote that what we have is "a re-enactment in modern times of events which occurred centuries ago," a story of man evicted from his garden that is far more successful as an allegory than *East of Eden.* The trials and tribulations show the sacrifice of a child to remove the curse of barrenness, the testing and the promise of salvation in the end, as well as the desert of despair and the water of life. God who provided the turtle with a shell can offer man no less protection. Run over, he will survive. Changes will have to come, but if brave Ma perishes then Rose of Sharon will be our Blessed Mother. This is a religious novel, not merely a socialist one, not merely a bitter comment on the sentimental "wagons westward" epics and the sociological diatribes. Steinbeck is more artist than activist, and he has woven of actual events and biblical allusions what has been rightly identified as "a pattern of dispossession; of nobility achieved by sacrifice necessitated by suffering; of wandering in the wilderness of exile; of struggle, defeat, hope, and eventual victory; of decadence and renewed struggles—here is an allegory of humanity itself."

This is the kind of message, if not exactly the kind of writing, that wins the Nobel Prize for Literature. This is the kind of theme that for once exactly fitted one of Steinbeck's basic limitations: he is not a great thinker and his characters are not, either. He specializes, our best American critic (**Edmund Wilson**) quickly noted, "not in those aspects of humanity in which it is most thoughtful, imaginative, constructive" but in simple human beings, "almost at the animal level," enduring or fighting to survive. His best subject is "the processes of life itself."

Steinbeck at his best, as in *The Grapes of Wrath*, writes of basic plights of mankind. Warren French perceptively writes: "If the Joads had not been caught up in the events of a particular time and place that had profoundly affected Steinbeck and troubled his public, we might more easily recognize that their story belongs with Shakespeare's *The Tempest* and other masterpieces of the travail and triumph of the human spirit."

"That is why Peter Lisca (who edited the 1972 edition of *The Grapes of Wrath,* in which the text appears with about a dozen essential critical documents of great value to the serious student) could write this at the beginning of his preface:

Very few of those who read *The Grapes of Wrath* in 1939 could have foreseen that this book, which dramatized the headlines and newsreels of the day, which seemed so intimately connected with them that its merits were debated not in literary terms but in those of sociological research and political ideology, would continue to be read long after the headlines had been forgotten . . . . What distinguishes this one novel is not only its greater authenticity of detail but also the genius of its author, who, avoiding mere propaganda, was able to raise those details and themes to the level of lasting art, while muting none of the passionate human cry against injustice . . . . In fact, the response of students leaves no doubt that as literature *The Grapes of Wrath* is generally experienced more completely today than it was in 1939, when it was much more difficult to dissociate the novel from current events or to see Steinbeck's bold technical experiments as something more than what one critic called "calculated crudities."

The novel also reads better today because many college students are, quite frankly, almost as unfamiliar with fine writing as they are with socialist theories or biologism or regional Oklahoma dialect (all of which take a beating in the book). They are moved by the tragedy of the Joads and the lilt of a "song of social significance" and they do not notice that this is one of those great American masterpieces (along with *Moby-Dick* and *An American Tragedy,* not to get too close to living writers) which is very awkwardly written. Edmund Wilson again: in 1948 he shrewdly summed up Steinbeck's novels, of which this is indisputably the most powerful, as marking "precisely the borderline between work that is definitely superior and work that is definitely bad."

The strong story line is well-known. The Joad family is driven from the Dust Bowl farm "house broke." Hardworking Grampa and religious Granma and lonely Uncle John join Ma (she's the one in charge) and Pa (he's a trifle confused by it all), stupid Noah, hotheaded Tom, Connie and Rose of Sharon (carrying a child), Al, Ruthie and Winfield—a motley crew joined in desperation and in hope. The trek will also involve Jim Casy (a sort of mix of the traditional preacher and the traditional village atheist). Some are lost on the way. Some desert. But the rest keep on: "There ain't nothin' else you can do." California is their dream but turns out to be a nightmare of evil sheriffs and worse. "The caravan winds up in a kind of concentration camp and the able-bodied are forced to pick fruit in a black-listed orchard, where they run into angry strikers. Leading the strikers is socialist Casy. He is killed, and Tom kills Casy's murderer and has to lie low. The others guard him, and pick cotton, and finally Ma sends Tom away. He goes to take up Casy's cudgels as a labor organizer, with a credo of helping the Little Man in need wherever he may be. Rose of Sharon's baby is born dead, but there is a hope of life going on: she suckles a starving man who "ain't et for six days." The men will organize and fight and the women will succour and bring new life. A little food, a dry place. Things will get better, somehow, some time. "We ain't gonna die out," says Ma. "People is goin' on . . . goin' right on." As the novel ends what is left of the group is hard-pressed indeed, but we are meant to believe that they will survive. It is, in fact, impossible to think otherwise.

This upbeat philosophy—and *The Grapes of Wrath* is bold to mix philosophy or even a secular theology with facts—is what the Nobel Prize chiefly honored in Steinbeck in 1962 when the Swedish Academy said:

His sympathies always go out to the oppressed, the misfits, and the distressed; he likes to contrast the simple joy of life with the brutal and cynical craving for money. But in him we find the American temperament also expressed in his great feeling for nature, for the tilled soil, the waste land, the mountains and the ocean coasts, all an inexhaustible source of inspiration to Steinbeck in the midst of, and beyond, the world of human beings.

Steinbeck liked the title *The Grapes of Wrath* "Because it is a march, because it is in our revolutionary tradition and because in reference to this book it has a large meaning." He added: "And I like it because people know the Battle Hymn [of the Republic] who don't know the Stars and Stripes." Others like the book because it is quintessentially American, and all the more so (perhaps) because though not "literary" it is one of our literary classics.

—Leonard R. N. Ashley

GRAVITY'S RAINBOW
Novel by Thomas Pynchon, 1973

Gravity's Rainbow, which *Time* found "funny, disturbing, exhausting, mind-fogging in its range and permutations," is Thomas Pynchon's masterpiece, the absurdist and apocalyptic story of the last days of World War II with dire significance for what we hope are not the last days of our nuclear age. It is the product of the rarest kind of American writer, the intellectual who keeps away from literary fads and pays no attention to contemporary authors or critical theories. It is that typically American everything-but-the-kitchen-sink construction and that almost unheard of American thing, the hilarious intellectual meditation. (Few Americans realize the truth of Borges's dictum that intellectual activity is always essentially ludicrous.) Critics, in the habit of reviewing personalities rather than real books, have hardly known how to react to a 900-page tome by an author who is practically anonymous, who (says *Saturday Review*) "has caught the inward movement of our time," and who writes about the most important things of our age in a way that is both dazzling and didactic.

The book is often overwhelming in language and structure. Not since James Joyce's *Finnegans Wake,* perhaps, has there been a major novel so extraordinary in its cinematographic construction and its mixtures and manipulation of languages. *Gravity's Rainbow,* too, is worthy of a "key" or a "key to the key" (or even an abridgement by Anthony Burgess, for it is as self-indulgent and extravagant in length as it is in everything else). Meanwhile we have to work it out for ourselves, supplying the history of the end of the Third Reich, brushing up on our German, Russian, French, Spanish, basic sciences, and more, picking our way through the intellectual minefields of the book and looking up lots of literary allusions, cheered by the fact that this is not "work in progress" but a finished product, loosely but carefully put together, depressing in its descriptions of war and pessimistic in its predictions of doom but laugh-out-loud funny and ultimately a hymn to man's ability to survive, even to survive the technological disasters he brings upon himself. Also, if man did not destroy himself, God would have to invent a destruction for him; *c'est son metier,* destroying as well as creating, and if The Firm or the military-industrial complex or some other bogeyman doesn't get

you (or, as more often happens, you don't like the way you have been getting yourself all along), then God and entropy, justice and gravity, will.

And what meaning does this complexity strive to express? As man rose from the clay, so he will end in it. God Who made the universe made this rule as well: everything that goes up must come down, whether priapic or ballistic. Life is your trajectory and your glory, the temporary triumph over extinction, the being that beats nothingness for five minutes with a rocket and maybe a little longer with an erection or an accomplishment. But Society if not God Himself wants to use and to use up anyone potent, especially the artist, and only for a brief span can one be "a system won," a burning (self-consuming) meteor or rocket "away from the feminine darkness, held against the entropies of lovable but scatter-brained Mother Nature." Women make babies to carry things on; men make technology to *get it up,* but neither time nor gravity waits for any woman or man. Rather, they lie in wait. So live while you can, and enjoy your arc. Gravity makes a nice parabolic rainbow in the sky of a destruction-laden V-2 rocket.

The plot resembles a detective or, better, espionage story: the antihero is in flight as in some John Buchan adventure, trying to make discoveries while he himself is being sought. It is also something of a political act, as all good novels are. Something of an anti-technology document, but written by a realist well aware that we can't blame our science for ourselves, because we made it before it started to remake us. Something of a love story, there being at least one character "in love, in sexual love, with his own death." Central in this picaresque and sometimes grotesque collection of (mostly) stereotypes with fictive names and firm functions in the book is the protagonist, Lt. Tyrone Slothrop, who can enjoy no excess of sloth because PISCES (Psychological Intelligence Scheme for Expediting Surrender) is after him. They have discovered that between his erections and the firing of German V-2s on London there is a "mean lag time" of four and a half days. He could be an instrument in the war effort! He wants to be a human being, not a tool, and he runs from Furies disguised as "The Firm," from the Authorities, from the ubiquitous Them—and he becomes just the runaway, the target, the Rocketman: another abstraction. He also is on an Orphic search in the Underworld: he has lost his harmonica down the toilet—the whole world is down the tubes, really—at Roseland. He meets a comic cast that would have done Fellini proud. (*Gravity's Rainbow* is also something of a Keystone Cop or Star Wars chase movie.)

In *Gravity's Rainbow* there is mention of Poisson's Distribution; it governs the random pattern of rocket strikes. Ours is a universe of laws (like gravity); so is the world of the novel. An iron rule of cohesion governs the wild and brilliant combinations of words, persons, places, things, ideas and digressions from them, in *Gravity's Rainbow.* As fully as in *Finnegans Wake,* as things fall apart the center holds, the author's personal genius keeps it all together. Perhaps not so much like a novelist as traditionally viewed, but more like that modern juggler who convulses and scares audiences as he juggles a weird assortment of bowling balls, sharp axes, oranges, and maybe a buzzsaw. It has the desire at once to entertain and to inculcate into audiences pride in humanity's skill in performance, acceptance of challenge, and final basic triviality. We run in search of ourselves and pursued by Them and in the long run it's the brief game that counts and not the victory.

There were few sensible reactions to *Gravity's Rainbow* when it was published some fifteen years ago, but there were some; and over the years the book that *Newsweek* greeted with caution ("it isn't plausible to call a novel great the week it's published, because the future will decide that") has become a classic, though that may mean simply a book everyone respects but has never read. Richard Poirier reviewed it elatedly: "the book is . . . a profound (and profoundly funny) historical meditation on the humanity sacrificed to a grotesque delusion—the Faustian illusion of the inequality of lives and the inequality of the nature of signs."

At the very worst, earth could start all over. If it cannot, at least it is *not a major planet.* And we had our innings, our brilliant "gravity's rainbow," or should have done, and if we haven't we have no one to blame but you-know-who, and it's not God.

—Leonard R. N. Ashley

THE GREAT GATSBY
Novel by F. Scott Fitzgerald, 1925

Influenced by Joseph Conrad, F. Scott Fitzgerald convinced his editor Maxwell Perkins, and most readers since, that *The Great Gatsby,* though barely fifty thousand words long, includes everything necessary to tell Gatsby's story. One reason Fitzgerald is able to accomplish this feat is his choice of point of view. The angle of narration is that of Nick Carraway, Gatsby's next-door neighbor on Long Island, who, like Gatsby, is a transplanted midwesterner. Nick can tell the story effectively and dramatically because he has information the reader does not have and since he is telling the story after the fact he realizes which of the events are important and the significance of each event. As he informs the reader on the second page of the novel: "When I came back from the East last Autumn I felt that I wanted to be in uniform and at a sort of moral attention forever; I wanted no more riotous excursions with privileged glimpses into the human heart." Jay Gatsby is the only character he wants exempted from his reaction because in Gatsby there was "something gorgeous . . . some heightened sensitivity to the promises of life."

The other reason Fitzgerald can get so much into such a compact novel, Perkins wrote him, is that "a vast amount is said by implication." Fitzgerald not only eliminates all unnecessary details but he maintains a unity of tone and texture: the reader knows all he needs to know of Tom Buchanan, the villain of the novel, from two or three lines of dialogue, including his Nazi-like theories of race. The spiritless inertia of the age is revealed by an abandoned dentist's sign and the wasteland environment around it, the rootlessness of the characters by the climactic action's occurring in an anonymous hotel room (almost as if none of the characters belongs anywhere). Gatsby's parties fall into perspective by the "old sports" he uses to recognize everyone, by the anonymous "long distance" telephone calls, by the "blue" cocktail music, the books in the library with their uncut pages, the unabashed pride with which he displays his vast horde of shirts. The values of Gatsby's world are indicated by the fact that almost all the images in the novel are sight images. Sounds, tastes, smells—those images more subtly associated with deep feelings—are conspicuously absent.

The story Nick tells is a version of the rags-to-riches tale so popular in American since Franklin's *Autobiography,* except in this case the hero does not get the girl. Jay Gatsby, whose real name is Gatz, comes from a poor midwestern family. As a young man he leaves home, becomes a protege of a wealthy goldminer and lives with him until the miner dies. Then, with some wealth of his own for the first time, he dreams of having more, but before he can get well underway, war is declared and he goes into the army. In uniform it is difficult to tell the rich from the poor so Gatsby begins to see the most popular girl in the town near his army post. From that time on he is determined to have the girl, Daisy. After the war he becomes involved in a drug ring and quickly gains wealth. When he next sees Daisy, however, she is married to Tom Buchanan and lives near him on Long Island. Gatsby begins to give parties, to which everyone is invited, in the hope Daisy will come to one of them. He discovers that Nick is a distant cousin of Tom's, and gets Nick to take him to see Daisy. He foolishly expects to resume his romance with Daisy exactly at the point where he had left it several years before. This is impossible, of course. In the end Gatsby is murdered by the man who thinks he has killed his wife, though actually Daisy has accidentally run over the woman in Gatsby's car.

Gatsby learns that he can neither recall the past nor shape the future. After Gatsby's death Nick comes to realize that, despite his unsavory reputation, he was the best of the lot. He was willing to take the blame for the death of Myrtle Wilson, Tom's mistress, even though Daisy had been driving the car. And Tom is responsible for Gatsby's death because he makes Wilson believe that Myrtle was Gatsby's mistress. At the end of the book Nick muses on the changes that have come to this "land of promise," since it had "flowered . . . for Dutch sailors' eyes—a fresh green breast of the new world."

—Thomas Daniel Young

HERZOG
Novel by Saul Bellow, 1964

In *Herzog,* one of the finest novels of ideas written by a 20th-century American, Saul Bellow makes serious use of comedy while demonstrating that human existence has value and worth. In the course of the novel Moses Herzog, a Jewish-American professor with a powerful intellectual attachment to Europe, analyzes and discards various intellectual formulations of pessimism or crisis ethics fashionable in the post-war period and comes in the end to a dependence upon faith in reason and intuitive feeling. Thus Bellow opts, as he had in earlier books, for a celebration of mind and life, even in the face of overwhelming evidence that "reality" is brutal, depraved, corrupt, violent. This defense of humanism, an unlikely blend of 18th-century rationalism and 19th-century Transcendentalism, is in the hands of an unheroic protagonist on the edge of psychic breakdown, an innocent like Candide who, for all his intelligence, acts like a schlemiel. The form of *Herzog* is an adaptation of the epistolary novel, a vehicle beautifully appropriate for the self-communing protagonist in a book which is largely a meditation; the story of an alienated intellectual imprisoned in the self needs a medium that promises privacy and turns in upon itself. The result is a book alive with ideas but deficient in action, written in a flexible, breathless, lively, energetic style which at the same time is restrained by the wry, skeptical, sometimes bitter expression with which Bellow endows Herzog.

These latter qualities are associated with what are regarded as typically Jewish modes of discourse. The "Jewish" aspects of the novel are also to be seen in the pattern of the alienated man and the Wandering Jew to which Herzog, like Joyce's Bloom, conforms. It can be argued that the strong family feeling; the schooling in grief; the ethnocentrism; the high value placed on education, intellectual achievement, and art; and even the rejection of despair and nihilism in favor of a humanistic faith in life, all present in the novel, do give the book, when taken together, a discernible Jewish flavor.

While Herzog's Jewish identity is clear enough, he is troubled because people do not perceive him as an American as well. But he had made a claim on his American heritage in high school, when he showed that he sprang from the faith and exuberance of Transcendentalism. As class orator, he had taken his text from Emerson, whose voice instructs and inspires him in the way of optimism, individualism, and the divinity of man.

This Jewish-American commands the intellectual riches of the European past as well. His model is the *philosophe;* he cares about creative reason, wisdom, the problems of belief, moral principles. He is also attached by lines of sympathetic understanding to the terrible plight of World War II Europe. He is a cosmopolitan, this new man, this American, and as such a distillation of the modern experience and a symbol of the modern condition, a man superbly and painfully conscious of the difficulties of being alive in our time. He teeters between sanity and destruction and carries the burden of his life precariously, and ineptly.

Opposed to 18th-century humanism, Transcendentalism, and the Jewish heritage, as Herzog conceives these, are the realities of the contemporary world and the philosophies of decline and negativism fashionable in his world. The disasters of his personal life bring him into the sordid company of lawyers, who represent themselves to him as Reality-Instructors and who regard him as an innocent whose troubles spring from a romantic conception of the world. Facts are nasty, they say; ergo, life is nasty. They open to Herzog the stunning power of corruption and cynicism in the "reality" of the external world and in human nature.

That notion of reality is confirmed by those intellectuals who believe in the disintegration and evil of mankind: Spengler and his decline of the West; Eliot and the spiritual aridities of the wasteland; Marx and others in their notions of alienation; Kierkegaard and the despair and absurdity of existentialism. But Herzog rejects all this, rejects the inauthenticity of despair, the passivity and humility of religion, the praise of suffering, the hopelessness of nihilism. Mankind, he asserts, is a subject too great for such weakness and cowardice. Herzog is a victim of history, of cultural disorder, of other people (and of his own ineptitude), who refuses to reconcile himself to victimhood. Everybody nowadays believes that man is a sick animal, he says, but he himself cannot feel spectacularly sick. He has experienced evil but he refuses to bow to it. He knows the limitations of reason, but he acts on faith and calls it reason. Obeying the deepest needs of his being, Herzog chooses an affirmative stance in life.

At the end, Herzog retires to his farm in the Berkshires, as Candide to his garden. He has brought himself under control. His psychic health is returning. Bellow does not suggest that Herzog has succeeded in making that synthesis of ideas which will yield him a final triumph over the intellectual, religious, and psychic fragmentations of contemporary life. But he has survived to deal with them, and at that point Bellow brings his story to a close. The ending is both abrupt and tentative, but Bellow is firmly clear about what he stands for and stands against. He is less sure about the coherence of his position or the eventual triumph of his ideas and values.

—Chester E. Eisinger

HOUSE MADE OF DAWN
Novel by N. Scott Momaday, 1968

House Made of Dawn takes its title from a translation of a Navaho song which is part of an extensive religious ceremony. The text of the translation is included in the novel as a song sung by one of the characters, Ben Benally, a Navajo man transplanted to Los Angeles by the federal policies of relocation and termination promoted in the 1950s. The house referred to has been identified as one of the prehistoric cliff dwellings along the upper Rio Grande, and the song alludes to it as home of the semi-divine personification of the dawn. Throughout the novel, important events and insights occur at dawn or sunrise. Also throughout the novel the author incorporates ceremonial, mythical and anthropological material from three different American Indian nations (Jemez Pueblo, Kiowa, and Navajo) into the texture of a contemporary story of psychological disintegration and renewal, as James Joyce incorporates Catholic religious and Irish political context along with classical Greek mythical parallels and allusions into works like *Ulysses* and *A Portrait of the Artist as a Young Man.*

House Made of Dawn is narratively complex, constructed on a principle of fragmentation and reconstitution somewhat like the modernist poems of **Ezra Pound** or **T.S. Eliot**. The story has a circular rather than linear or strictly chronological structure: the prologue that begins it actually depicts the closing event of the book, and within each section linear time is reshaped through the wandering thought patterns of the narrators and central consciousness. Moreover, within the story are inserted various non-narrative verbal forms: besides the translated poem text mentioned above, there is another translated poem, fragments purporting to be the diary of a priest, bits and pieces of bureaucratic/legal documents and testimony, and folk tales and legends. The reader's attention is repeatedly drawn away from the story and towards the author's literary devices.

The action of *House Made of Dawn* takes place between July 20, 1945, and February 28, 1952. The narration comprises an undated prologue and four dated portions set in the Jemez pueblo of Walatowa, New Mexico (Prologue and sections one and four), and the Los Angeles area (sections two and three).

After a brief prologue describing a young man running, the story proper opens on July 20, 1945, when a young man named Abel, an orphan raised by his traditionalist grandfather, Francisco, returns to Walatowa after serving in the second world war. Alienated and disorganized by war experiences (and also, it is suggested, by the early loss of his mother and brother and previous bouts of malaise), Abel is unable to make a meaningful reintegration into the life of the village. He takes a temporary job cutting wood for Angela St. John, a troubled, sensuous visitor to the area, and has an affair with her. He participates in a village festival and is singled out by a strange, ominous-appearing albino man. Meanwhile the omniscient narration follows a parallel line with the village priest, Father Olguin, as he studies the diary of his predecessor, Fray Nicolas. On August 1, Abel stabs the albino to death in a cornfield. This section of the story ends the next day, with Francisco again alone, hoeing in his fields.

The two parts of the second section are dated January 27 and 28, 1952; this part of the story takes place in Los Angeles and centers on the character of Tosamah, a Kiowa storefront preacher and priest of the peyote religion. The January 27 section contains the first of two sermons by Tosamah, a long discourse on a verse from the Gospel of John: "In the beginning was the Word."

Tosamah maintains that language has been debased by white people and its power lost or corrupted. At the time that Tosamah is giving this sermon, Abel appears to be lying miles away, barely conscious after having suffered a terrible beating that has disabled his hands. The omniscient narrator moves back and forth in time, presenting fragments of Abel's past: filling out forms in prison or afterwards, meetings with an earnest social worker named Milly with whom he has an affair, life in prison, testimony at his trial by Father Olguin and by one of his mates in the army. This section also contains a depiction of a peyote ceremony and introduces Benally, who will play a significant part in Abel's eventual apparent rehabilitation. The January 28 section is composed almost entirely of Tosamah's second sermon: this is a passage previously published in an essay in *Ramparts* magazine and later in *The Way To Rainy Mountain,* in which Momaday meditates on his Kiowa grandmother's life and the history and passing of the magnificent Kiowa culture.

The third section is dated February 20, 1952, and is narrated by Benally, who has relocated to urban Los Angeles. Benally's rambling narration includes references to more of Abel's life in Los Angeles: his job at a box-stapling factory, his encounters with a sadistic policeman named Martinez, his participation in the peyote services, their occasional socializing with Milly. Benally also recollects the recent encounter with Angela St. John, who visited Abel in the hospital as he was recovering from the beating that left his hands broken; Angela, now the mother of a son, told Abel a story with a heroic theme, intimating that he reminded her of the hero. Benally also recollects going with Abel to a "49" party in the hills outside the city on the night before Abel was to leave; Benally recalls that at this time, as previously, he sang traditional songs from Navajo healing ceremonies, including the verses beginning "House Made of Dawn" from the Night Chant.

The fourth section of *House Made of Dawn* is very brief, in two sections dated February 27 and February 28, 1952. Abel returns to Walatowa in time to perform the appropriate burial rituals for his grandfather. Having seen to this duty, he begins to run into the dawn. The novel has moved in a circle, returning to the event depicted in the prologue.

House Made of Dawn received the Pulitzer Prize for fiction in 1969. It was the first novel written by an American Indian author to be so recognized, and its publication along with the award initiated what has come to be called a Native American Renaissance of literature.

—Helen Jaskoski

THE HOUSE OF MIRTH
Novel by Edith Wharton, 1905

The House of Mirth, Edith Wharton's first major novel of manners, reflects her intimate knowledge of the elitist New York society into which she was born and her judgment of that society. Wharton draws her title from *Ecclesiastes* 7:4, "the heart of fools is in the house of mirth." It may be understood as a judgment either on her heroine, Lily Bart, or on Lily's social milieu, that of fashionable upper-middle-class New York City in the early 1900s. For Lily alternately succumbs to the materialistic values and empty lifestyle of her social world and, in fits of restiveness or moral recoil, despises the very things she aspires to. She is at once subject to and superior to her social environment.

The orphaned Lily's beauty and *savoir faire* are her working capital, together with the possibility of an inheritance. She has only to project agreeable images and to be useful to female patrons. This entails being a decorative object, an entertaining companion, an obliging social secretary, and an ingenue in the presence of likely suitors. Thus Lily should be able to make a marriage for place and for money, on which social power and a luxurious lifestyle depend. But Lily is unable to follow the prescribed course singlemindedly, and she is vulnerable as an unmarried and impecunious woman. Hence *The House of Mirth* becomes a naturalistic tragedy documenting a painful downward trajectory through socio-economic strata culminating in Lily's ambiguous death, a presumptive suicide.

"Inherited tendencies had combined with early training to make her the highly specialized product she was: an organism as helpless out of its narrow range as the sea-anemone torn from the rock. She had been fashioned to adorn and delight . . . . And was it her fault that the purely decorative mission is less easily and harmoniously fulfilled among social beings than in the world of nature? That it is apt to be hampered by material necessities or complicated by moral scruples? These last were the two antagonistic forces which fought their battle in her breast." The social Darwinism manifest in this passage, the detached scrutiny of Lily as an organism at the mercy of forces both hereditary and environmental, is characteristic of Wharton's attitudes and language. And yet like George Eliot, whom she greatly admired, Wharton holds her characters responsible for their behavior even as she documents their social entrapment and vulnerability as creatures.

Moral sentiment in Lily expresses itself in aesthetic terms. She is repelled by crudity and ugliness manifested either in physical objects, in a drab lifestyle, or in conduct. But she is capable under the duress of economic necessity and social ambition of postponing scrutiny of her own behavior. She accepts "loans" from Gus Trenor, a married man, without reckoning the potential cost. She allows herself to become a social intermediary for Simon Rosedale, a Jewish *nouveau riche.* And she allows Bertha Dorset to use her to entertain her husband while Bertha has an affair with Neddy Silverton. It is Lawrence Selden, whom Lily would love if circumstances permitted, who forces her into confrontations with herself. Selden enjoins Lily to be free in spirit, to extricate herself "from all the material accidents." To others he celebrates her beauty, and claims to believe that "the real Lily" is superior to her trivial world. Yet Selden is himself a male counterpart to Lily in his spiritual dividedness. They are products of the same society. If Lily cannot discard its economic norms, Selden is bound by the fiction that unmarried women must be ideal. He cannot trust his own judgment over the tarnished image reflected in the social mirror. Selden kneels at Lily's deathbed believing that, had she lived, they would have found each other, but the reader need not think so. Selden's aloof attitude of spectatorship, be it amused, admiring, or judgmental, is representative of various male figures in Wharton's fiction who stop short of full commitment to the women they profess to love. With characteristic irony Wharton makes Lily's last unambiguously willed act the burning of letters documenting Selden's own love affair with Bertha Dorset. Lily could have used these letters to blackmail Bertha into renewed social patronage and thereby cleared the way for her own social rehabilitation.

The closing scenes reflect a social terrain less familiar to Wharton, but equally characteristic of her interest. Destitute at last and living in a slum, Lily comes upon a working-class girl whom she had once patronized. Nettie has survived ill-health and a seduction because the man she later married accepted her as she was, another ironic reflection on Selden. Nettie comforts Lily and places her infant child in Lily's arms. Such empathic depiction of the very poor and the child as a symbol of hope are recurrent motifs in Wharton's fiction, as if she were reaching out imaginatively to worlds beyond her own experience.

—Jean Frantz Blackall

THE HOUSE ON MANGO STREET
Stories by Sandra Cisneros, 1984

This collection of short tales narrated by an adolescent girl emerged from sketches Sandra Cisneros was experimenting with in the late 1970s, influenced by Nabokov's memoirs. At the time she was searching for a literary "voice" that would distinguish her writing from that of her classmates in the graduate Creative Writing program at Iowa where she trained. It is an engaging book that has brought Cisneros much exposure and popularity, including a 1985 American Book Award. By the time the collection was published, however, Cisneros felt she had outgrown the voice of the narrator.

It is dedicated in English and Spanish "to the women," thus conveying that through these texts other women can empathize with the experiences recounted by the young narrator. The publication of this book coincides with several others by Chicana authors that give a fuller view of the Mexican-American *bildungsroman;* previous works by male authors had conveyed only a partial view of the Mexican-American population's life experiences.

The House on Mango Street shows a mounting progression in its forty-four short tales of how a young girl, on the threshold of womanhood, views and senses life around her. The narrator first identifies herself significantly through her home, its location and appearance; these elements are important in defining her, as descriptions of the house are crucial to the opening and closing stories of the collection. Next in importance to the narrator is her name, Esperanza: "In English my name means hope. In Spanish it means too many letters."

As Esperanza, in child-like language, recounts her life and impressions of events surrounding her, one sees her grow; the experiences are humorous and child-like in early stories, but they evolve later into brushes with sexuality and possible danger. For the several humorous stories about the "barrio" or Hispanic ghetto children—their games, nicknames, and even struggles, there are an even more significant number of stories that show Esperanza to be a keen observer of the female condition, of what options she may face in the near future. Humor and pathos are intermingled in the lighter stories, such as "A Rice Sandwich," where the schoolgirl protagonist yearns to eat with her friends in the school cafeteria, but has only a cold and greasy rice sandwich for her lunch because the family cannot afford lunch meat. One reads of young children trying on high heeled shoes as a form of vicariously experiencing adulthood, yet having to flee from the danger posed by a drunkard who wants to steal a kiss. Other stories tell of Esperanza's awkwardness at trying to dance with "chanclas" (old shoes) and feet that feel too big. "Hips" talks about how girl's bodies just open up, in case one someday decides to have kids.

But it is the stories that recount sad and sordid details of Esperanza's female neighbors, many of them young girls like her-self, which transmit the strong underlying message about the fate of poor Hispanic women. "Minerva is only a little bit older than me but already she has two kids and a husband who left." She attempts to write poems on small scraps of paper, but "her luck is unlucky." Rafaela sits home alone while her husband plays dominoes; he locks her up because she's too beautiful and may run away. Sally already knows the secrets of applying makeup and dressing all in black: skirt, shoes, and nylons; even her father says that "to be this beautiful is trouble." Everyone who sees her, including readers of the text, know that she indeed will find trouble. In "Sire" young Esperanza has to confront the sensuous and lustful gazes of young men who lean against neighborhood cars as she walks by. Tacitly understood in the title is the idea of "desire," which drives all the participants but scares Esperanza at the same time as it attracts her. In another tale, Esperanza accompanies her friend Sally to see some red clowns. This story is a startling awakening for the innocent narrator/protagonist who learns about love and lust in a tragic and violent way. Her brutal and physical experience is far from the fantasized ones of movies, romances and magazines. Esperanza is sullied and betrayed.

Every line of text in Cisneros' tales is carefully placed, studied, and reworked. Hers is the work of a poet, a painter with words, who relies on sounds, plural meanings, and resonances to produce rich and varied images in each reader's mind. The final stories bring one back to Mango Street and the author's house. As the young narrator outgrows this house, and the adolescent voice, so too does her inventor, Cisneros, who in later writing gives very mature portraits of women. The characters who inhabit the fictional house on Mango Street, and the books which Esperanza packs with her as she leaves, are part of the wealth that Cisneros also possesses. She is an author who left home, who both belongs yet does not want to belong, but who keeps returning to tell more stories.

—Eduardo F. Elías

HOWL
Poem by Allen Ginsberg, 1956

What **Jack Kerouac** hailed in *The Dharma Bums* as the beginning of the San Francisco Renaissance was a reading on 13 October 1955 at Six Gallery on Fillmore Street in the Marina that featured the west coast poets subsequently most prominently identified with the Beat Generation—Philip Lamantia, Michael McClure, **Gary Snyder**, and Philip Whalen. The high point of the evening, however, was the first public performance of a recently written long poem by a visitor from the east, Allen Ginsberg. His poem *Howl* was to provide the keynote for a growing countercultural movement. Respectable society at first ignored the outburst, but in March 1957 a second printing arriving from London was confiscated by U.S. Customs as obscene. These copies were released in May when a U.S. Attorney refused to proceed with the case, but the juvenile department of the San Francisco police took over and made the poem famous by arresting **Lawrence Ferlinghetti** for publishing and selling the work at his City Lights bookstore. A parade of famous reviewers and critics who testified for the defense attracted international attention to the work that trial judge Clayton Horn agreed he did not believe was "without the slightest redeeming social importance." His verdict for the defense inspired subsequent trials involving banned books and films that by 1969 virtually abolished governmental censorship in the United States.

Judge Horn's opinion—strongly influenced by Mark Schorer's testimony—still provides the most lucid and sensitive brief explication of the poem: "*Howl* presents a picture of a nightmare world; the second part is an indictment of those elements in modern society destructive of the best qualities of human nature . . . . The third part presents a picture of an individual who is a specific representation of what the author conceives as a general condition . . . . 'Footnote to *Howl*' seems to be a declaration that everything in the world is holy, including parts of the body by name. It ends in a plea for holy living . . . . "

Howl has indeed turned out to be, as some early reviewers predicted, *The Waste Land* of its generation; but an even more significant parallel, as **Robert Duncan** maintained during Ferlinghetti's trial, is with **Walt Whitman**'s *Leaves of Grass,* which had appeared exactly a century earlier. Ginsberg's feeling for Whitman is shown in "A Supermarket in California," one of five new poems collected with *Howl,* in which he addresses his predecessor as "dear father, graybeard, lonely old courageteacher." A centennial regeneration of Whitman's style and sentiments in language even he wouldn't have dared use, *Howl* proves that the most vital inspiration of the American bard remains Whitman's still unfulfilled vision of democracy, spirituality, and brotherhood.

Indeed, a problem that Ginsberg has posed his successors is that the opening line of *Howl* preempts the outraged charge that animates successive American countercultures: "I saw the best minds of my generation destroyed by madness, starving hysterical naked . . . angelheaded hipsters burning for the ancient heavenly connection." The rest of the long opening section follows Whitman's practice of reiterating initial reference pronouns to accumulate a graphic catalogue that many readers find shocking, identifying the practices by which the "best minds" would during the next two decades dramatically alter the American lifestyle through racial and sexual liberation movements.

The second section of the poem has been most aptly described by Judge Horn's listing of the destructive forces in modern culture as "materialism, conformity, and mechanization leading toward war," attributed by the repetition at the beginning of nearly every line to the Philistine god Moloch, whose worship involved the human sacrifice of children by the power hungry.

The third section is specifically addressed to Carl Solomon, whom Ginsberg had met while being treated at a psychiatric institution and to whom the whole poem is dedicated. The repeated lines beginning "I'm with you in Rockland" stress the point frequently made in many other modern social protests that those inside today's asylums are saner than their jailers, and the poem concludes—like Ginsberg's related "America"—by showing that the poet, again like Whitman, has not lost an affectionate faith in his often misguided native land: "we hug and kiss the United States under our bedsheets the United States that coughs all night and won't let us sleep."

Finally Judge Horn perceived better than many anthologists who have doubly missed *Howl*'s message by simply climbing on its bandwagon that "Footnote to *Howl*" is an inseparable part of the whole, which changes and counters the generally apocalyptic tone by evoking Whitman's vision of the holiness of a world that should glow with "the supernatural extra brilliant intelligent kindness of the soul!"

—Warren French

I KNOW WHY THE CAGED BIRD SINGS
Memoir by Maya Angelou, 1970

Telling a true story, especially one that represents the experience of a community and not just the individual speaker, is central to the African American autobiographical tradition. Such stories find their roots in antebellum slave narratives, tracing the narrators' movement from South to North, from slavery to freedom, from self-denial to self-affirmation. When she published *Incidents in the Life of a Slave Girl* in 1861, Harriet Jacobs explained in her preface that she was writing not to evoke pity for her own individual suffering, "but . . . to arouse the women of the North to a realizing sense of the condition of two millions of women at the South, still in bondage, suffering what I suffered, and most of them far worse."

Maya Angelou wrote *I Know Why the Caged Bird Sings* (1970) from a similar motive. She observes: "If growing up is painful for the Southern Black girl, being aware of her displacement is the rust on the razor. It is an unnecessary insult." *Caged Bird* is the story of a black girl's coming of age. It shows her moving from self-hatred to self-acceptance, from silence to a language and voice uniquely her own, from living in the small black town of Stamps, Arkansas, under the loving protection of her grandmother, to the world of brothels and bootleggers her mother inhabits in St. Louis, Missouri, and her father's world in 1940s Los Angeles. Finally, its shows her in World War II San Francisco, where, with the help of her mother, Angelou goes from child to woman, from a daughter and granddaughter to a teenaged mother. It is Angelou's story, an African American story, and an American story that she feels herself chosen to tell.

In the mid-1980s Angelou visited Stamps for the first time since having left the small town in her girlhood. In a televised interview with Bill Moyers, she stated that the suffering and self-loathing that the town's racism caused her still overwhelms her. "My God, what scars does that leave on somebody?" she asked. "I don't even dare to examine it myself. And when I reach for the pen to write, I have to scrape it across those scars to sharpen that point." *Caged Bird* records the scars. It is an account that, according to Pierre A. Walker, "reveals a sequence of lessons about resisting racist oppression, a sequence that leads Maya progressively from helpless rage and indignation to forms of subtle resistance, and finally to outright and active protest."

Children of divorced parents, Maya and her older brother Bailey are tagged and shipped by train from California to Arkansas to be raised by their grandmother, Annie Henderson, owner of the only black grocery store in town and a greatly respected woman in both the black and white communities. Despite the loving nurture of her grandmother, her handicapped uncle Willie, and the church, the little girl dreams of the day when she will wake up and "look like one of the sweet little white girls who were everybody's dream of what was right with the world." She must live in a world that does not value a black girl, one in which her beloved uncle is forced to hide in the store's potato bin all night long because the Klan intends to give trouble to any black man it can find, one in which Negro boxer Joe Louis's victory over the white fighter Primo Carnera spells real danger for any black person caught on the road alone that evening, one in which young children watch as a black man's bloated and mutilated body is retrieved from the river. Witness to the latter event, young Bailey asks, "Uncle Willie, why do they hate us so much?" Powerless, Maya must contain her rage or risk everything.

Even in St. Louis, the children are not safe. Raped at age eight by her mother's boyfriend, Mr. Freeman, Maya believes that her words are deadly. When she spoke his name, he died—at the hands of her mother's violent brothers. The little girl vows that she will speak to no one except her brother. Back in Stamps, she keeps her silence for three years, until the dignified black neighbor Mrs. Flowers puts Shakespeare, Dickens, and Poe in her hands and in her mouth. Through their words she finds her own once again.

Accompanying that voice is a strength of character that enables the adolescent Maya to begin to resist racist forces. When her employer Mrs. Cullinan refuses to call her by her proper name, Marguerite, and insists on calling her Mary, Maya cannot quit her job, but she can get herself fired. She breaks family heirloom dishes. When the other maid asks her whether "Mary" is the one responsible, Mrs. Cullinan barks, "Her name's Margaret, goddamn it, her name's Margaret!" The young woman can also glory in Henry Reed's valedictory speech, which transforms a moment of humiliation during her eighth grade graduation, when white school administrators consigned the proud young graduates to lives of domestic service and manual labor. Henry Reed's words and those of the "Negro National Anthem" raise them: "We were on top again. As always, again. We survived."

The last quarter of the book shows a young woman coming to accept herself as an African American and as a human being, a woman who develops the confidence to confront the racist culture that would deny her. Two events mark these crucial steps in her development. The first is the period Maya spends in a Los Angeles junkyard living in abandoned cars among other young people rejected by parents, communities, and society. Among a "collage of Negro, Mexican and white faces," she comes to a critical insight: "I was never again to sense myself so solidly outside the pale of the human race. The lack of criticism evidenced by our ad hoc community influenced me, and set a tone of tolerance for my life." In San Francisco Maya succeeds in her determination to become San Francisco's first "colored" streetcar conductorette.

I Know Why the Caged Bird Sings tells a true story of triumph. Through her use of "rhythmic language, lyrically suspended moments of consciousness, and detailed portraiture," as Joanne M. Braxton observes, Maya Angelou has written what may be considered one of the best autobiographical works in the American literary canon of the late twentieth century.

—Laura Weiss Zlogar

INVISIBLE MAN
Novel by Ralph Ellison, 1952

Anyone challenging Ralph Ellison's position in American literature because he has completed only one novel must recognize that *Invisible Man* is a hard act to follow. Arguably the most comprehensive fictional probing of the 20th-century American psyche, it is entitled to a place beside the 19th-century *Moby-Dick*. It is fitting that the novel is the work of a member of the nation's most consequential ethnic minority; yet its connection with the fashionable discovery of black writing has been a principal reason for often inadequate readings. Although deeply rooted in black experience, the implications of the unnamed narrator's tribulations are not basically racial in origin.

The invisible man's closing sentence addresses readers of any race, sex, or class: "Who knows but that, on the lower frequencies, I speak for you?" This is the story of anyone striving to establish a personal identity with dignity who learns that selfish forces seek to exploit others to advance themselves. When at the beginning of the novel the invisible man observes, "All my life I had been looking for something, and everywhere I turned someone tried to tell me what it was," he speaks for the human condition.

Another reductive error is viewing the novel as a modern picaresque, in which the protagonist's loosely linked misadventures parody Horatio Alger's myth of poor but honest and ambitious youngsters making their way to respectability in an America that offers unbounded opportunities. *Invisible Man* projects a far more complex and sophisticated vision of forces thwarting self-fulfillment.

Its structure resembles a series of nested boxes that an individual, trapped in the constricting center, seeks to escape, only to find each box within a bigger one that is more difficult to escape because it presents problems for which the captive figure's previous successes have not at all prepared him. Any summary of such a work must be oversimplified, but outlining the principal stages indicates the growing challenges each successively poses.

Ellison confines his shocking version of southern white middle-class exploitation of blacks to a brilliant first chapter in which the recent high school graduate, after being physically and intellectually humiliated, is condescendingly rewarded with a scholarship to a black college where he can learn to serve his people in a way approved by white supremacists. This melodramatic episode does nothing to prepare the naive youth for the tragedy to follow. He loves the college and daydreams of succeeding the Booker T. Washington-type President Bledsoe in this sanctuary, but his illusions are cruelly shattered when, in a controversial deviation from the conventions of black American fiction, Ellison shows how oppressed blacks can sometimes innocently and sometimes deceitfully exploit white benefactors. The narrator receives the most painful of many wounds when Bledsoe expels him permanently for not knowing how to lie to whites in order to protect the tiny empire Bledsoe has obsequiously created. Exiled to New York without recommendations, the narrator finally locates a menial job in a paint factory through a rich, sympathetic homosexual, whose more generous offers the narrator apparently does not comprehend. In his first encounter with industrial culture, he is trapped between the implacably opposed forces of an oldfashioned craftsman who fantasizes that *he* controls the business and a union seeking to organize the anonymous corporation. Expelled by a literal explosion, the narrator wakes up in the factory hospital, the subject of experiments by doctors who treat their patients the same way southern bigots did an "inferior" race.

The invisible man finds temporary refuge with Mary, the only person who treats him with genuine affection; but he must run out on her when her oversolicitousness might threaten the promising new career he accidentally launches when he makes an impassioned speech in support of an elderly black family that is being dispossessed. His talents bring him to the attention of two groups whose threats he fails to recognize until he is literally marked for execution. A white-controlled Brotherhood (resembling not just the Communist Party but any thought-control group) seeks to transform him into an unquestioning mouthpiece for its party line, but this work is resented by the black nationalist Ras, who vows to kill the narrator for betraying his race. The narrator tries to protect himself by emulating Rinehart, who successfully leads a double life as a numbers runner and "Spiritual Technologist" for a revivalist church; but the invisible man is never able to test the efficacy of this cynical pose, for while being pursued by Ras's assassins, he is literally swallowed up by the earth to become truly an invisible man living parasitically in an underground cavern illuminated by 1369 blazing electric lights.

Those who question the optimism of the narrator's final speculation that "there's a possibility that even an invisible man has a socially responsible role to play" should consider that Ellison's failure to produce a sequel to *Invisible Man* may mean that he has not been able to work out the nature of such a role in a society that has not changed much since the 1930s and 1950s that he mirrored.

—Warren French

JOHN BROWN'S BODY
Poem by Stephen Vincent Benét, 1928

"This poem is the most ambitious ever undertaken by an American on an American theme," **Allen Tate** wrote of *John Brown's Body* (*Nation,* 19 September 1928), although he did not believe that Stephen Vincent Benét's 1500 lines of verse about the Civil War constituted an epic. Yet for many reviewers and for thousands of readers, *John Brown's Body* was an American *Iliad.* Benét himself in his opening invocation to the American Muse said modestly that he had called "unsurely, from a haunted ground, / Armies of shadows and the shadowsound." Later in the poem he lamented his inability to write the "black-skinned epic" of the liberated slaves as well.

In spite of his very real humility, however, Benét was not unconscious of the genre, as shown by his invocation, his epic catalogue of ships (romantic sails metaphorically sunk by the ironclad "Monitor"), and his ride-past of the Southern chiefs and of the Northern regiments. Long metaphors fulfill the function of Homeric similes, and there are many allusions to the tale of Troy, sometimes ironic or satiric. For instance, Benét tells us that if Sarpedon fell in the Civil War, his limbs would not be laved in Scamander's streams, but buried in a "cumbered pit." Picnicking Congressmen watch the Battle of Bull Run "Like Iliad gods, wrapped in the sacred cloud" of bay-rum and cigars. A Southern soldier thinks "This is Virginia's *Iliad* . . . ." Lee's young aide-de-camp imagines his general in the chariot-rank with Agamemnon and Achilles, while Benét himself asks how to humanize this "marble man . . . / The head on the Greek coin." But humanize him he does, in what critics praised as the best historical portrait in the poem, although that of Stonewall Jackson is as effective.

For these and other historical characters and episodes, Benét read extensively, with a thirst for accuracy of detail. In certain passages, such as John Brown's last message or Lincoln's soliloquy, he quoted or adapted the man's own words. He showed realistically the terrible minutiae of army life and death, often with an implied analogy between the Civil War and World War I.

Critics such as Tate found *John Brown's Body* too episodic, told in "motion picture flashes," but Benét employed the film technique of montage to demonstrate America's diversity, already epitomized in his invocation. He eschewed panoramic effects except in the set battle pieces such as the "three long double miles / Of men and guns and horses . . ." at Gettysburg. Instead, he focussed briefly and vividly on successive characters, cutting rapidly from north to south, east to west, from owner to slave, "hider"

to volunteer, from Jefferson Davis to Abraham Lincoln. These are all connected by the war itself, by recurrent images of star, stone, and grain, and of Time and Phaeton, the letter also being the private symbol of Jack Ellyat, who represents the North. His Southern counterpart, Clay Wingate of Virginia, is characterized by his home Wingate Hall, which, like the South it represents, must tumble down, "a dream dissolving."

Wingate and Ellyat are the fictional centers of *John Brown's Body,* providing both insight and conventional romantic interest. Wingate hesitates between Sally, a French dancing-master's daughter, and Lucy, a proto-Scarlett O'Hara. Ellyat, escaping from his Southern captors, finds Melora Vilas, whose father has followed the wilderness stone. After an idyllic episode Ellyat is recaptured, and when Melora's child is born, she and her father go in search of him. To those who watch them pass by, Vilas is the Wandering Jew or John Brown's ghost; Melora becomes a folksong.

Indeed, legend and folksong are important motifs running through the poem. Benét refers to, quotes from, or adapts ballads, spirituals, and popular songs such as "Lord Randall," "Go Down, Moses," "Dixie," and "Jubilo." Their rhythms and those of Benét's own interpolated lyrics are part of the metrical variety of *John Brown's Body,* which consists primarily of unrhymed and irregularly iambic pentameters and hexameters, with occasional sections of much shorter or much longer lines. The Wingate episodes, however, dance and dash in a bouncing mixture of shorter couplets and quatrains. Sometimes there are even prose passages to link battle scenes and to paint a vignette of Walt Whitman, whose *Leaves of Grass* had a significant influence on Benét.

Yet it is John Brown who made this epic happen and who moves through it with his song as a shepherd, a fanatic, a ghost, and a legend, until, at the end of Book Eight, the bygone South and "the America we have not been" are buried in John Brown's grave. From his body grow, not the red rose of folk ballad, but "revolving steel, / . . . . / Rivet and girder, motor and dynamo . . . ." Originally Benét had intended to write a poem of twelve books (the number of the *Aeneid*), but he felt it had come to an end with eight. In a strangely low-key conclusion, he asks us neither to condemn nor adore the new America, but to say only, "'It is here.'" Perhaps these lines are also applicable to Benét's poem itself, overvalued and over-condemned by critics, but here—as 20th-century America's closest approach to an epic.

—Jane W. Stedman

THE JOY LUCK CLUB
Novel by Amy Tan, 1989

Amy Tan's first novel, *The Joy Luck Club,* is carefully structured around the stories of four pairs of Chinese immigrant mothers and their American-born daughters. The first and the last segments tell the mother's stories in China and in America. The middle two sections recall the daughters' experiences as children and as Chinese American women. The daughters' stories are embedded or "cradled" within the mothers' narratives. Through this formal device, Tan conveys a sense of mother-daughter interconnectedness that eventually resolves generational differences and conflicts.

The novel begins with stories of loss: Jing-mei "June" Woo tells of the death of her mother, Suyuan, and Suyuan's loss of her twin daughters during the Sino-Japanese War. This opening creates a sense of imminent loss which predominates the multiple stories of the entire novel. Unlike the other three Joy Luck mothers, Suyuan has no first-person narrative voice in the novel. June "replaces" her mother not only at the *mah-jongg* table but also in the act of storytelling. This duty of replacement burdens Jing-mei since she does not understand her mother and regards herself as a failure who always comes short of the mother's expectation of "best quality." At the end, however, Jing-mei realizes that she is the essence of hope for joy and luck to the mother, represented by the significance of Jing-mei's Chinese given name: the pure essence and the "best quality."

The basic conflict between Lindo Jong and her daughter Waverly also originates in the daughter's sense of inadequacy in front of the mother. Released herself from a pre-arranged marriage with a trickster's wisdom, Lindo teaches Waverly the manipulation of willpower in playing chess and in life. Throughout their stories, the mother and the daughter constantly engage in a battle of strong wills and become reconciled only when Waverly recognizes the similarities between them. They are, as Waverly admits, both "double-faced" and confront life's challenges with their mental power.

Obsessed with the death of her baby son during her abusive first marriage, Ying-Ying St. Clair loses her "*chi (qi),*" or spirit, in bad memories. Her daughter Lena is also trapped in a unloving marriage symbolized by the poorly designed end table in her impractical new house. By breaking the uneven table, Ying-Ying recollects her own tiger spirit and provides Lena a "clear reflection," as Ying-Ying's Chinese name suggests, of the daughter's marital problems. Courageously facing the past of her memories, Ying-Ying deploys her own pain to cut loose Lena's tiger spirit. Thus maternal love not only protects the daughter but also helps the mother toward spiritual regeneration.

An-mei Hsu also animates her daughter Rose with her own spirit and experiences during Rose's failing marriage. Both the mother and the daughter benefit from the grandmother's story. Victimized by Chinese traditions and forced to be a concubine of her rapist, the grandmother teaches An-mei the power of language and transforms her own silent victimization into victory with her spiteful suicide. As An-mei passes on this story of empowerment to her daughter, Rose finds her own voice, direction and selfhood buried by her marriage.

Significantly, *The Joy Luck Club* ends with a reunion of Suyuan's Chinese daughters, Chwun Yu (Spring Rain), Chwun Hwa (Spring Flower) and her Chinese American daughter Jing-mei "June." The names of the three sisters allude to a regenerative force that is associated with the seasonal metaphors of spring and summer. The lost mother is symbolically resurrected in the unification of her Chinese and American parts. Thus Tan tacitly explores the double meanings of Suyuan's Chinese name. Her "Long-Cherished Wish"—to have all of her daughters together—is fulfilled and her "Long-Held Grudge"—the involuntary abandonment of her Chinese daughters—is reconciled. This reunion also provides a missing piece in the development of Jing-mei. As she states, "And now I also see what part of me is Chinese. It is so obvious. It is my family. It is in my blood. After all these years, it can finally be let go." Suyuan's American daughter, who "grew up speaking only English and swallowing more Coca-Cola than sorrow," has finally recognized the "Chineseness" inside of her and come to terms with her hyphenated identity as a Chinese American woman.

The cycles of loss and reunion, death and regeneration, doubts and affirmation and the generational conflicts between the immigrant mothers and American daughters in *The Joy Luck Club* ex-

plain the novel's instant success. Tan's skillful storytelling not only provides culturally-specific experiences of Chinese-American women but also powerfully appeals to the universal emotions of general readers.

—Pin-Chia Feng

THE JUNGLE
Novel by Upton Sinclair, 1906

The Jungle, Upton Sinclair's one claim to a place in literary history, was not so much a novel as it was a tract for the times. Sinclair intended it not as a work of art but as an instrument for changing people's minds. He thought of it as an expendable round of ammunition in the battle for social justice. The novel is better judged as propaganda than as literature, but it has compelling power and interests readers today long after the circumstances under which it was written passed into history. Sinclair's considerable ability as a storyteller, coupled with the fierce indignation of a born reformer, made *The Jungle* perhaps the most memorable document of the muckraking movement. He was incensed by the appalling conditions he observed among the workers in the Chicago stockyards and was determined to do something to improve them.

Sinclair recalled the novel's provenance in 1946 when he wrote an introduction for a new edition. He remembered being sent in 1904 by the *Appeal to Reason,* a socialist magazine, to investigate conditions in the meat-packing industry. This was at a time when American business answered to no one for safety, sanitary conditions, product reliability, or working conditions. Unions were weak or non-existent, and business squeezed as much profit as it could from low wages. A good many magazines, chief of which was *McClure's,* were then busily publishing exposes of corruption and malpractice in both industry and government. After the scandal of lethal "embalmed beef" sold to the army during the Spanish-American War, the meatpacking industry seemed a prime subject for investigative reporting.

Sinclair spent seven weeks in Chicago living among and interviewing the stockyard workers and studying conditions in the packing plants. He found that he could go anywhere in the stockyards provided he wore old clothes and carried a lunch pail. One day outside the slaughter-houses he chanced upon a Lithuanian wedding supper and dance, spent the afternoon and evening watching and talking to the newly married couple and their relations, and realized that this immigrant group could provide his point of view for his propaganda novel. He invented Jurgis Rudkus and his family and depicted their lives in and about the stockyards. The story, which begins with the happy wedding scene, moves from joy to ever-increasing misery, as the Lithuanians are exploited inside the packing plant and cheated outside of it. The novel is never dull, at least the early chapters that involve the slaughter-house and life behind the stockyards are not. Here the novel has all the melodrama of a soap opera, and Jurgis suffers more disasters than the early Christian martyrs. Later Sinclair couldn't resist writing a polemic for the Socialist Party, and the novel even ends with a speech that Sinclair had delivered himself at a mass meeting in Chicago on behalf of Eugene V. Debs, the perennial socialist candidate for President in that era.

The Jungle was written in a one-room cabin outside Princeton, New Jersey. He offered the book to Macmillan, publisher of the romances he had written earlier, but that firm would not publish it unless some of the more lurid details about the packing industry were deleted. Meanwhile, it had been appearing in the *Appeal to Reason* where it was creating a sensation. Sinclair published the book himself with aid from Jack London and others, following which Doubleday Page took it over. Sinclair's purpose in writing the book was to improve the lot of the packinghouse workers, but his account of the lack of proper sanitation, the processing of spoiled and diseased meat, particularly the report of men who fell into the lard vats and were rendered into lard, shocked the public. Sinclair said of his book: "I aimed at the public's heart and by accident I hit it in the stomach."

No book ever published in the United States produced such an immediate response. Sinclair remembered being summoned to the White House by Theodore Roosevelt to tell his story, after which the President ordered an investigation of the Chicago slaughterhouses. Consumers shuddering over what they might be eating bombarded their senators and representatives with demands for action. Before the year was out Congress passed its first law to regulate the meat, food, and drug industries. No politician could ignore the outcry for reform produced by *The Jungle.*

The contemporary reader finds the socialist propaganda ladled generously into the novel hard to get through, and even the most dramatic chapters are written in a pedestrian style. The organization of the story, moreover, is loose and rambling. But despite its faults the novel has the air of truth and conveys a sense of terrible urgency. This, of course, is the result of its being true. Sinclair was writing a kind of work that might be called the reportorial novel or the novel of social protest, of which there have been many more recent examples. There is relatively little work of the creative imagination in *The Jungle,* for the bulk of it consists of closely observed detail and innumerable facts. Today the same material probably would be cast in the form of non-fiction, the sort of multi-part documentary that often appears in the *New Yorker.* Any student of American history and culture owes it to himself to read *The Jungle* in order to understand more clearly the impulse behind the labor movement, the drive for regulatory agencies, and the need for social conscience on the part of all citizens.

—James Woodress

THE LAST OF THE MOHICANS
Novel by James Fenimore Cooper, 1826

For more than a century after its publication in 1826, *The Last of the Mohicans* was by far the most widely read of any of the novels of James Fenimore Cooper. Nonetheless, while praised for its strong narrative interest, *The Last of the Mohicans* was generally disparaged as the least substantive of the Leatherstocking Tales, with *The Prairie, The Pioneers, The Pathfinder,* and *The Deerslayer* receiving far greater critical acclaim. According to its 19th-century critics, *The Last of the Mohicans* satisfied the popular demands of audiences that craved adventure, but it did so at the expense of both content and realism. Particularly objectionable was Cooper's depiction of Indians, whom reviewers found hopelessly romanticized and not at all historical. As one commentator explained, Cooper's Indians "have no living prototype in our forests. They may wear leggins and moccasins, and be wrapped in a blanket or a buffalo skin, but they are civilized men, not Indians." Even Francis Parkman, who found worth in Cooper's mythic dimensions, felt that the Indians of the Leatherstocking

Tales were "either superficially or falsely drawn." As a result, *The Last of the Mohicans* was for the most part dismissed as "almost pure adventure with slight social import."

Ironically, only in the 20th century, when the novel began to decline in popularity, did critical distinctions between novels of realism and novels of romance pave the way for scholars to discern in *The Last of the Mohicans* depths that had gone unnoticed for decades. To begin with, scholars attacked the notion that the novel lacked historical veracity. Research into Cooper's sources indicated that although he wrote the book in approximately four months he had researched his materials quite carefully. Among the many historical and anthropological sources attributed to the novel are Alexander Henry's *Travels and Adventures* (1809), Jonathan Carver's *Travels Through the Interior Parts of North-America* (1778), David Humphrey's *Life of Israel Putnam* (1788), Alexander Mackenzie's *Voyages from Montreal* (1802), and *The History. . . of Captains Lewis and Clark* (1814).

Additional research further determined that the Indian materials in the novel were derived from a careful reading of such works as John Heckewelder's *History, Manners, and Customs of the Indian Nations* (1818) and Cadwallader Colden's *History of the Five Indian Nations* (1727). Literary sources include *The Iliad, The Odyssey,* and *The Aeneid,* as well as *Paradise Lost* and the novels of Scott and Austen. Leatherstocking himself is thought to be based on John Filson's "Adventures of Col. Daniel Boone" (1784), and mistakes in historical accuracy, including the eloquent language of Cooper's Indians, are in general attributable to Cooper's sources, who at the time when they wrote were considered the foremost experts on the subjects they addressed. Even Cooper's landscape portraits, once thought to be hopelessly romantic backdrops to his fiction, came to be seen as complex symbolic structures that provide insight into the metaphysical foundations for a pre-Conradian analysis of the relationship between the wilderness and civilization.

Cooper himself said, however, that in writing *The Last of the Mohicans* he created a novel "essentially Indian in character," and it is in exploring what one analyst described as "the question of the relations between men of different races in the New World" that critics have found in the book a theme of "national, even hemispheric significance." Within this context, Cooper's vision of historical progress is seen as profoundly pessimistic and astutely prophetic. Extended into the wilderness setting of the novel, the rivalries between the French and English for control of the North American continent continue to propagate racial and nationalistic prejudices that the events of the narrative violently display. At the same time, the brutality of the Indians undercuts the romantic myth that in the wilderness of the New World the civilizations of the past will undergo a pastoral revitalization. Of the three characters in the novel capable of offering the possibility for moral renewal through a blending of the virtues of the Old and New Worlds, Cora and Uncas die, and Leatherstocking, described as a "man without a cross"—in other words, someone without preconceived prejudices who is open to the possibility of a new kind of moral order—remains childless and eventually vanishes into the wilderness. According to one critic, "In the bloodshed of William Henry the determining power of history is affirmed." People are seen as "incapable of change," and history becomes nothing more than "an endlessly repeating decimal" in which America's future will "necessarily recapitulate the European and the tribal past."

—James A. Levernier

LEAVES OF GRASS
Poems by Walt Whitman, 1855 (and later revisions)

In 1872, Walt Whitman wrote: "*Leaves of Grass* is, in its intentions, the song of a great composite *Democratic Individual, male or female*"; and this individual, he stated, was to be the prototype of a superlative "*Democratic Nationality*"; for the preeminent subject of Whitman's verse is the United States, which he considered to be "the greatest poem." His intentions were already evident in the opening poem (later named "Song of Myself") in the first (1855) edition of *Leaves of Grass*. The subject of this poem is much larger than one person; it deals, rather, with the human spirit in its relations with the physical and historical environment, the destiny of the race, and ultimately God. Discerning critics have recognized that "Song of Myself," like many other poems in *Leaves of Grass*, is a record of a mystical experience and the insights and visions that are revealed during it. Early in the poem, the poet describes how one "transparent summer morning" there

> Swiftly arose and spread around me the peace and knowledge that pass all the argument of the earth;
> And I know that the hand of God is the promise of my own,
> And I know that the spirit of God is the brother of my own, . . .

By definition a mystical experience involves the merging of the individual's soul, or consciousness, with some entity outside itself—God, the cosmos, all humanity, nature. Obviously, Whitman was not perpetually in a mystical state, but much of his writing was stimulated and colored by the lasting effects of an occasional mystical transport. The conviction that the mind under favorable conditions may have access to vast and unaccustomed areas of understanding and certainty has been held by some in all ages. In Whitman's day, the American transcendentalists (notably **Ralph Waldo Emerson** and **Henry David Thoreau**), among whom Whitman must be numbered, shared this conviction.

Leaves of Grass, beginning with the slim 1855 volume, underwent a steady growth in breadth and depth of content, as well as in size, through nine editions, the last (the so-called "deathbed edition") appearing in 1891-92. Over the years, Whitman added new poems, occasionally removed old ones, changed the position of some of them, and revised and rewrote extensively. If he published a set of poems separately, as with *Drum-Taps* (1865) or *Passage to India* (1871), he would soon incorporate its contents in the larger volume. The growth of *Leaves of Grass*, then, was organic; though continuously changing and expanding, it nevertheless remained the same entity.

Critics have attempted, with questionable success, to outline the structure of *Leaves of Grass*. There are, however, certain clusters of poems with similar themes. Among these are the groups titled "Children of Adam," celebrating "amativeness" or sexual love; "Calamus," celebrating "cohesiveness" or comradely love; "Sea-Drift," containing poems inspired by the sea. Most impressive of all the clusters are "Drum-Taps" and the related "Memories of President Lincoln." Among these poems are vivid renderings of war scenes ("By the Bivouac's Fitful Flame"); expressions of tender sympathy for wartime suffering ("Come Up from the Fields Father"); and the greatest of all of Whitman's poems, his elegy on Lincoln, "When Lilacs Last in the Dooryard Bloom'd."

Whitman's experience as a volunteer in the military hospitals in Washington during the Civil War exerted a spiritualizing influence on him and his writing for the rest of his life.

"I am the poet of the body and I am the poet of the soul," Whitman wrote; and he wrote of the body with a frankness that shocked most readers of his day. Again, he declared, "I am not the poet of goodness only, I do not decline to be the poet of wickedness also," and thus alienated even more readers and set himself apart from most of his fellow transcendentalists, who were reluctant to admit the existence of evil, except perhaps in its political expressions. Yet Whitman shared the transcendentalists' optimism concerning the future of humanity. The preponderance of his verse is a celebration of life in all its aspects as lived in the United States in his times. But he was a poet of death too, and had at one time planned to write, as a companion volume to *Leaves of Grass*, a book of poems in which he would "exhibit the problem and paradox of the same ardent and fully appointed personality entering the sphere of the resistless gravitation of Spiritual Law, and with a cheerful face estimating Death . . . as the entrance upon by far the greatest part of existence, and something that Life is at least as much for, as for itself." But Whitman did not need to produce this second volume; he had already done the job in *Leaves of Grass*. As early as 1855 he had written:

> And I know I am deathless,
> I know this orbit of mine cannot be swept by a carpenters compass,
> I know I shall not pass like a child's carlacue with a burnt stick at night.

"The knowledge of death" and "the thought of death," to use Whitman's phrases, pervade *Leaves of Grass* like leitmotivs and are the subject of several of his major poems. In "Out of the Cradle Endlessly Rocking" the poet, in some of his finest lyrical verse, recounts how as a boy he heard on the seashore alone at night a bird lamenting in song its dead mate, heard the waves lisping "the low and delicious word death," and knew years later that his "songs awakened from that hour." In "When Lilacs Last in the Dooryard Bloom'd" the hermit thrush sings of "*lovely and soothing death . . . dark mother . . . strong deliveress.*" In "Passage to India" a journey to that land of "budding bibles" via the newly built Suez Canal becomes a "Passage to more than India," a passage even to more than "primal thought," a passage, indeed, into death, as the poet exhorts:

> O my brave soul!
> O farther farther sail!
> O daring joy, but safe! are they not all the seas of God?
> O farther, farther, farther sail!

Though Whitman deplored organized religion as he knew it, he clearly shared belief in the immortality of the soul with most of the world's faiths.

Whitman, indeed, called for a "New Theology" and insisted that *Leaves of Grass* had a religious purpose. The "New Theology" apparently was to be based not only on a belief in the immortality of the soul but also on a conviction of a divine element in human beings and the consequent sacredness of life. Influenced by Emerson's essays "The Poet" and "The American Scholar," Whitman in the Preface to the 1855 edition of *Leaves of Grass* envisaged poets rather than priests as the spiritual leaders of the future. Again taking a cue from Emerson, he called for a poetry liberated from traditional rules and customs regarding subject matter and meter and rhyme. A new religion, a new people needed a new mode of literary expression. Thus Whitman developed a prosody suggestive of the *vers libre* of the next century. He eschewed rhyme and regular meter, letting, he hoped, the subject determine the form of the verse. As Emerson urged, he wrote of commonplace things and everyday events and situations, often resorting to pages-long lists in his effort to include in a poem a segment of life in America. In his style there are echoes of the Bible, Ossian, Shakespeare, oratory, and even opera, but he did create a style unprecedented in the poetry of the English language and one that has since found many admirers and imitators. For Whitman, largely scorned while alive, has long since gained the status of a world poet, perhaps the only one that America has produced.

—Perry D. Westbrook

THE LEGEND OF SLEEPY HOLLOW
Story by Washington Irving, 1820

"The Legend of Sleepy Hollow," Washington Irving's classic tale of the Hudson River Valley, with its late 18th-century Dutch villagers and its ghost legends (particularly that of the "headless horseman," the decapitated Hessian soldier left over from the Revolutionary War), has had an unusually wide appeal for readers of all ages. Spindly Ichabod Crane, hellraising Brom Bones, and "plump as a partridge" Katrina Van Tassel are supposed to be comic figures. Ichabod's getting knocked off his borrowed nag Gunpowder by the pumpkin Brom throws at him is taken as a high point in early American humor. Scholars have pointed out the story's various Germanic literary sources (Burger, Musaus, Otmar, etc.), in discussing Irving's sculpting and reworking a mass of folklore and legend, *and Americanizing it.* They have also considered the environmental influence of the Hudson River Valley on the imagination, Irving's joking and spoofing tendency, and his penchant (intensified by his travels in the German states, it would seem) for gothic tales and ghosts stories. Like youngsters exposed to the Walt Disney cartoon version of "The Legend of Sleepy Hollow," some of these much older readers have been smitten with the sensational plot element of the headless horseman, and they have traced its origins in Irving's reading, from Robert Burns's "Tam O'Shanter," back into obscure Germanic lore. An opinion often found in this latter group of academicians and critics is that there is a kind of regional-ethnic-ideological conflict in the case of Ichabod and his opponent. There is a suggestion that the Tarrytown-Sleepy Hollow region is well rid of Ichabod, and fortunate in having such a hero (Irving uses the word a number of times) in Brom Bones.

A different view of the story may be offered, but first it is necessary to state the bases given in the critical literature for the conventional view of the schoolmaster's and the bully's differences. Briefly, Ichabod is seen as the invading (Connecticut) Yankee, bringing his smart-aleckiness, book-learning, gluttony, and fortune-hunting opportunism into the peaceful agrarian Dutch community of industrious farm folk. Ichabod is also seen as having a kind of "imagination of disaster," with his head crammed full of **Cotton Mather**'s wonders of the invisible

world as well as a plethora of other spook stories and superstitions. In contrast to this oddball outlander, Brom is seen as belonging: a rough but good-natured local boy just having a little fun now and then with his buddies, while ripening toward the state of a proper Dutch farmer and landowner.

In fact, Irving's tale points up a viewpoint at variance with the conventional readings. It is odd that Ichabod, merely trying to get on in the world by means of his numerous talents (and what if he is a Yankee "handy-andy"?), seems by his very existence to arouse ridicule if not outrage in a number of the commentators, who resent his later prosperity in "a distant part of the country," through schoolteaching, practicing law, entering politics, and becoming a petty magistrate. Brom, so well accepted by the critics, is actually a lawless psychopath, a vandal, like many a village bully since time immemorial. Herculean and arrogant, he rules by force of might. Irving's description of the effect on the villagers when Brom and his crew ride into their midst reminds one of Ku Klux Klan doings or the western story in which the Bad Man and his gang periodically gallop into the helpless frontier town and shoot it up—for sport. Is there anything intrinsically funny about any of Brom's destructive capers, including the pumpkin-throw?

As for Katrina and her overall desirability as a wife: Irving's jocularity and playfulness (especially in his postscript) cannot hide his feelings in the matter. Katrina is described archly (and repeatedly) as a coquette. While this is a natural enough condition for such a spoiled little rich girl in a sleepy Dutch village, clearly she would not make the kind of wife Ichabod visualizes: a pioneer woman westering with her husband and a wagonload of children and belongings. Rather, she is one to lead any man a merry chase—unless he physically tames her and then intimidates her to keep her down. Irving mentions Brom's having selected her "for the object of his uncouth gallantries," compares Brom's "amorous toyings" with "the gentle caresses and endearments of a bear," and indicates that she somewhat encourages Brom's hopes. Did they live happily ever after? But then Katrina is affiliated with two groups that Irving openly disparages: women and the Dutch. The latter group is pictured as a simple, empty-headed lot (Brom Bones as hero is a playful contradiction in terms) living an utterly static existence. The former group is composed of creatures who cause "more perplexity to mortal man than ghosts, goblins, and the whole race of witches put together . . . ." Irving is telling us, finally: Ichabod is well out of it, and deucedly lucky not to have linked up with a girl of Katrina's tastes and inclinations.

Conventional readings of the story notwithstanding, the above view is set forth by Irving in the moral offered in the postscript. Far from being a mere joke or jest, the moral (stated by the story-teller) is true not only to the events of this story but to the meaning that a reasonable person would derive from the evidence in the text. It is stated as a pseudosyllogism: a) every situation can be taken advantage of, if we accept a joke on its own terms; b) running a race with a goblin trooper will mean rough riding; c) therefore, "for a country schoolmaster to be refused the hand of a Dutch heiress is a certain step to high preferment, in the state." One gathers that if Irving had any trickery in mind when he wrote this last, it was to so apply his gift of drollery that unwary readers (whose number has always been legion) would find truth, and mistake it for frolic.

—Samuel Irving Bellman

LIFE STUDIES
Poems by Robert Lowell, 1959

Robert Lowell's *Life Studies* is the best single volume of poetry in a movement known as confessional poetry, now regarded as an important contribution to the postmodernist rebellion against the impersonality of modernism. The name was first applied to *Life Studies* by M. L. Rosenthal, who, though praising Lowell, voiced a reservation: "it is hard not to think of *Life Studies* as a series of personal confidences, rather shameful, that one is honor-bound not to reveal." Lowell's pioneering in this direction was a surprise, since as the author of Pulitzer Prize winning *Lord Weary's Castle,* he had been seen as an important new voice in the impersonal literary modernism in vogue since the 1920s. What only Lowell's friends knew was that by 1953 he was seeking to break away, not only from a style that he had come to regard as symbol-ridden and unnecessarily obscure but from personal emotional restraints.

Lowell had developed a healthy respect for the sound of conversation in the poetry of **Robert Frost** and **William Carlos Williams** and sought to loosen up his own poetry by getting it closer to prose. But the specific model for a new subject matter was the poetry of a student at the Iowa Creative Writing Programs, **W.D. Snodgrass**, who was chronicling his divorce and painful separation from his daughter, later published as *Hearts Needle* (1959). Lowell began turning to the subject of four generations of his own family, existential versions of the social portraits in the early premodernist Boston poetry of **T.S. Eliot**. Following Williams, he provided for these family poems a "sense of place," Boylston Street, Dunbarton, Cape Cod, both to illuminate character and to portray the rapidly disintegrating world of the blueblooded Lowells and Winslows.

Life Studies is divided into four parts. In part I only "Beyond the Alps" is personal, describing a train ride from Rome to Paris, but metaphorically evoking Saint Augustine in order to see Lowell's own life journey as progressing from the "City of God" to Augustine's "Earthly City." Instead of continuing to confess to the clergy of God, Lowell will now address a laity of strangers.

Part II is Lowell's only long prose piece, "91 Revere Street," introducing his own unhappy childhood, focusing on the quarrels between his mother and his father but also evoking a sense of the decline of Boston society as the social register yielded to the cash register. Part III consists of four poems about tormented and spiritually exiled fellow artists—Ford Madox Ford, **George Santayana**, **Delmore Schwartz**, and **Hart Crane**.

Part IV is the "Life Studies" proper, eight time-obsessed poems marking a family sequence. The long poem "My Last Afternoon with Uncle Devereux Winslow" centers on Uncle Devereux, "dying of the incurable Hodgkin's disease," but Lowell also seeks to establish continuity with the past through remembered things. Two poems, "Dunbarton" and "Grandparents," dramatize the old order of his grandparents, "altogether otherworldly now." Three poems, "Commander Lowell," "Terminal Days at Beverly Farm," and "Father's Bedroom," further the account in "91 Revere Street" by reporting his father's last days and his death from a coronary. The last of these poems, "Sailing Home from Rapallo," records the death of his mother in Europe, shipped back home in the hold of the ship with her name on her coffin, misspelled "LOVEL."

The concluding poems, those on Lowell's own manic-depressive illness and on marriage, are the most personally confessional and the most emotionally intense. "During Fever" covers four generations of Lowells, his daughter in fever, his memories of conversations with his mother about his father, and her memories of her own father, "that old life of decency / without unseemly intimacy or quarrels." The final six poems feature Lowell as mental patient. "Waking in the Blue" views a mental hospital as a prison; in it Lowell confesses his fears of madness and death and presents a microcosm of the sickness of Boston society. "Home after Three Months Away" is an ironic poem of return—"Cured, I am frizzled, stale, and small." "Memories of West Street and Lepke" revisits the past once more to begin an evaluation of what it is to live "in the tranquilized fifties," a time "of lost connections," reminding him of the lobotomized Czar Lepke of Murder Inc.

The last poem, "Skunk Hour," is one of Lowell's best. Its setting evoking the loneliness and decadence at a resort area off season is appropriate for Lowell's frankest description of madness, an attempt to portray both a "dark night" of the soul and the hell of Milton's Satan—"I am myself hell"—while finding in a mother skunk searching for food for her children a reminder of the continuing will to live.

The controversy about the confessional nature of Lowell's *Life Studies* is long forgotten. The poems are rooted in the past and present of Lowell's personal life, contemplating the dark night of man's soul, never reaching any sort of transcendence, yet affirming painful endurance in Eliot's still present "waste land" of modern society. *Life Studies* is truly of its own time, the existential 1950s, but his aristocratic Boston Lowells and Winslows are as still relevant as **William Faulkner**'s Mississippi Sartorises and Compsons.

—Richard J. Calhoun

LITTLE WOMEN
Novel by Louisa May Alcott, 1868-69

The most famous work of Louisa May Alcott, *Little Women* (in two parts, 1868 and 1869), has remained a classic, in the sense that it has demonstrated remarkable staying power as a popular book, for nearly twelve decades. Although it does not command the wide audience it once did (for instance, in a 1927 survey American high school students listed *Little Women* as the book of most interest to them), it remains in print in several editions, and is considered a major work both in 19th-century fiction and in children's literature. From the outset *Little Women* was recognized as more than a children's book, however; in reviewing the first part of the novel the *Nation* wrote (October 1868): "Miss Alcott's new juvenile is an agreeable little story, which . . . may also be read with pleasure by older people." *Harper's* (August 1869) called the second part of *Little Women* "a rather mature book for the little women, but a capital one for their elders."

Alcott's purpose in writing *Little Women* was not to create a nostalgic portrait of an idyllic childhood, though the book is often read as such. She wrote it to make money. At first reluctant to agree to her publisher's wish for a "girl's book," she relented, and the writing became a cathartic process through which she could re-create her own difficult early years. At the time Alcott began this task she was 35 but looked older, and in constant pain as a result of the mercury poisoning she suffered while serving as a volunteer nurse during the Civil War. Her father, the philosopher Bronson Alcott, was lost in his own abstractions, as absent from his family mentally as Mr. March is absent physically during much of *Little Women.* Abigail May Alcott, the strong and long-suffering model for Marmee, had by now retreated into a preoccupation with her family history. For more than a decade Alcott had been augmenting the family income through writing, but most of her works were lurid "gothic" romances written under pseudonyms and filled with angry and tormented women. But in *Little Women* she created the loving March family whose four daughters—Meg, Jo, Beth, and Amy—were modelled after the Alcott girls. Though many elements in the story are based on actual events—family theatricals, the rebellious daughter's literary aspirations, the death of a beloved sister—*Little Women* transformed the troubling into the ideal. The Marches are not rich, but are much more prosperous than the Alcotts. Feast scenes in the book seem to compensate for the fact that at times the young Alcott did not have enough to eat. Jo cuts off her long hair to raise money to bring home her father, wounded in the war; in reality, Alcott lost her hair due to illness and poor medical treatment during her own wartime nursing experience.

Little Women therefore represents a psychologically helpful process for Alcott, a shift in her writing focus, and a clever response to the desires of the reading public. Her contemporary readers wanted tales of adventure, romance, piety, temperance, reform, travel, and the Civil War; Alcott gave them a stew of everything, but with her own flavoring. She was no hack, cranking out a simple plot with predictable characters. A number of statements in the book would have been considered unusual for the day, and illustrate Alcott's interest in unconventional ideas. For instance, Mrs. March removes Amy from a school in which there is corporal punishment, quite a departure in the "spare the rod and spoil the child" era. In a Protestant society, the book expresses an appreciation and approval of Catholic practices. The importance of dividing domestic labor is stressed; though the women do all the work in the March household, as in the Alcott home, peace comes to Meg and her husband John only after they divide housework and child care. *Little Women* also emphasizes the value of women working outside the home; Jo's lifestyle—up to a point—is a departure from the traditional feminine role, and she is happy and successful in her endeavors as a writer. She enjoys an exciting life because she refuses to fit the conventional mold of a "little woman," but eventually she does conform in some ways to the expected norms. Although Alcott herself would have preferred Jo to remain single, she allowed herself to be pressured by public opinion into having her marry. Still, Alcott demonstrates her strength: she insists upon expressing her own opinions while simultaneously keeping within the mainstream of popular thought. Books that alienated the reader, of course, would not sell, and *Little Women,* from the very first, sold exceptionally well. One mark of its success is that it was followed by several sequels, including *Little Men* and *Jo's Boys.*

In many ways *Little Women* is markedly superior to other books of its genre. While almost every other popular 19th-century novel had heavy-handed sermonizing, *Little Women* kept its homilies short and, appearing at natural intervals in the story, unobtrusive. In other books, villains were plainly villains and the virtuous were always clearly so. Alcott, more sophisticated, realized the complexities of the human character, and so created personalities with whose shortcomings and internal struggles readers could identify. Characters who are basically good do or contemplate things that are blameworthy: Jo, foreseeing an accident, still ignores Amy's cries for help when they are ice-skating; Amy burns Jo's books;

Laurie embarrasses Meg by forging a note from John. In *Little Women* human frailty is apparent—and believable. Descriptions are not overly sentimentalized and, again, readers could identify with many of the situations—comic, tragic, and tender—occurring in this story of a warm family dealing with realistic situations in a loving and positive way.

Although many of the events and circumstances are obviously dated, enough universality remains so that readers are still intrigued by the book. To the young reader of the 19th century, *Little Women* was a manual of social grace, illustrating how to overcome one's faults and problems on the pilgrimage toward maturity. To the modern reader, it is a charming portrayal of family relationships as well as a palatable study of 19th-century lifestyle, mores, and social structure.

—Jane S.Gabin

LOLITA
Novel by Vladimir Nabokov, 1955

The apparent subject of Vladimir Nabokov's *Lolita* is the titillating perversion of a madman who virtually kills his wife in order to make captive and lasciviously possess her 12-year-old daughter; and when the child, who has in fact seduced him, escapes him, running off with another man, he apparently kills that man. This lurid tale would seem to invite either a sensational or a moral response. The problem Nabokov deliberately sets for himself, however, is to persuade the reader to transcend the erotic content and eschew moral judgment in order to perceive his novel as an artistic creation and not as a reflection or interpretation of reality. *Lolita* is not immoral or didactic, he has said; it has no moral. It is a work of art. The apparent subject of the novel is Humbert Humbert's perverted passion for a nymphet. But we come closer to the real subject if we perceive that his passion is his prison and his pain, his ecstasy and his madness. His release from the prison of his passion and the justification of his perversion is in art, and that is the real subject of the novel: the pain of remembering, organizing, and telling his story is a surrogate for the pain of his life and a means of transcending and triumphing over it; art, as it transmutes the erotic experience, becomes the ultimate experience in passion and madness.

Late in the book Humbert says that unless it can be proved to him that it does not matter that Lolita had been deprived of her childhood by a maniac, then he sees nothing for the treatment of his misery but the palliative of articulate art. At the end of the novel, addressing Lolita, he says, I am thinking of angels, the secret of durable pigments, prophetic sonnets, the refuge of art. Here is the only immortality he and Lolita may share. Here is the only balm that will soothe. Here, in art, are the forms that will control the passionate furies while the music of the words cloaks it all in saving beauty.

Not that "reality" doesn't intrude. Nabokov sought and captured the way schoolgirls talk; he conveys the feel and the smell of American motel rooms in all their philistine vulgarity. But a major thrust of the novel is toward undermining and mocking the concepts of fact, reality, and truth in fiction, toward destroying, in short, the very bases of literary realism. Nabokov undercuts a firm conception of reality by involving Nabokov the "author," Humbert the "narrator," and John Ray the supposititious editor in the making of the book, creating an ambiguity and uncertainty about authorship, reliability, and authority which attack the validity of fact, reality, and truth: can we trust the criminally insane Humbert as the primary source of our knowledge of events and people, especially since "Humbert Humbert" is Humbert's own invention? And more especially since his diary, presumably the original source of the narrative, has been destroyed? Or the pompous Ray, who speaks of newspapers which carry the story of Humbert "For the benefit of old-fashioned readers who wish to follow the destinies of the 'real' people beyond the 'true' story . . . ," a man who asserts that the tale tends toward a moral apotheosis? The factitious factual character of the story that Ray emphasizes is only a device for encouraging our conventional expectations as readers of traditionally realistic fictions which make traditional moral judgments. Nabokov will disappoint these expectations just as he has deliberately confused the point of view and the identity and relationship of the characters. The techniques of the novel are forms of play for him, as art itself is play.

Writing his memoirs in prison, Humbert says, "Oh, my Lolita, I have only words to play with." It is the case that word play and pure sound are one source of the wit and joy of the novel, as Humbert imagines the nymphet he would coach in French and fondle in Humbertish. Nabokov uses language so that it draws attention to itself. It is frequently more important than the action of the novel. It is thus possible to argue that if Humbert had only words to play with, he never had a flesh and blood 12-year-old girl at all. She is a fantasy, imagined by a madman imprisoned as much in his cell as he is in his lust. Indeed the entire book may be a fantasy. When Humbert kills Clare Quilty, the playwright who abducted Lolita, the characters move as though they were under water or with that heavily retarded motion common to nightmare. Quilty may be as unreal as Lolita, Humbert's alter ego haunting him for his guilt in relation to the child. Lolita is thus an occasion for Humbert's fantasy of sex and Quilty for his fantasy of violence and revenge. It is as necessary to transmute the pain of one's fantasy life into art as it is the pain of one's conscious and quotidian life. Whether Lolita and Quilty are "real" or not, language will serve as a means of dealing with them.

It is not only through language that Lolita is removed from the "real" world. As a nymphet, she is nymphic, that is, daemonic. A nympholept like Humbert instantly recognizes and always burns for such a creature. When he gets her into bed, in an inn called appropriately enough for a magical, mythical experience The Enchanted Hunters, he thinks of her as an immortal daemon disguised as a female child. Thus it is possible to read Lolita as a daemonic spirit residing in the human id, that is, as an irrational, self-destructive force related to the primitive in man that will overwhelm his rationality with the frenzy of its appetite. The price of this ecstasy is its inevitable pain. And so we return to language, because only it, only art, will bring these demonic energies under control. And that is the essence of the entire novel: its primary if not its sole reality is language.

—Chester E. Eisinger

LONG DAY'S JOURNEY INTO NIGHT
Play by Eugene O'Neill, 1956

Composed in 1940, first produced in Stockholm in 1956, then in New York in 1957 and London in 1958, Eugene O'Neill's *Long Day's Journey into Night* won the Drama Critics Circle Award as

well as the first Pulitzer Prize ever awarded posthumously, and has been revived several times, notably with Laurence Olivier at London's National Theatre in 1971. It has been made into two excellent films—one with an all black cast starring Ruby Dee, and the other with an all white cast with Jason Robards and Katharine Hepburn. O'Neill dramatizes the "psychological trap in which his characters are caught by diminishing . . . the area of light in which his characters are permitted to move," beginning "in morning sunlight, but gradually, as the night comes and fog surrounds the house, the stage is reduced to a dim circle of light surrounded by darkness. O'Neill's last plays present "a bitter, uncompromising indictment of the failure of vision in a land of hope . . . the world beyond the fog, the unlighted cities, the source of terror that finally causes men to seek their reason for being, if not their salvation, by withdrawing into darkness, journeying into night" (Travis Bogard). James Tyrone's penuriousness intensifies the situation further as he forbids the family to burn more than one light bulb at a time, deepening the fog-induced darkness, so they will not make the electric company rich, as he all but turned out the light of Mary's and Edmund's lives by denying them crucial medical care, because of his intense fear of poverty, as he had "turned off" Mary's desire to break her morphine addiction because he refuses to make his house a home where a wife can be happy and children can develop normally. At best Mary Tyrone watches the family watch her, with little or no compassionate support offered to anyone by anyone.

Usually preferring expressionism, the language of poetic symbolism, and a faith in the dignity of man, O'Neill also enriched his art by an understanding of the "new psychology," an enlarged awareness of all conscious and unconscious realities—not merely Freudian—resulting in a "new depth of seriousness, a new vitality . . . and the free use, in stagecraft and acting, of experimental techniques which completely ignored the 'well-made' conventions, and called directly upon the subconscious responses of the audience" (*The American Tradition in Literature*). His analysis of the inner workings of human emotions in his characters, and the terror they can impose, has been compared to the best work of John Webster and Cyril Tourneur, 17th-century masters of terror. Such analysis, for O'Neill, constituted the essence of the dramatic, since he believed emotions, not the Greek gods of old, caused much of man's behavior, emotions which in most O'Neill plays produce a violent explosion by play's end. In addition to sound—the foghorn in *Long Day's Journey into Night*—to emphasize the hostile environment condemning man to loneliness, O'Neill also uses dialogue, especially that between Edmund and James Tyrone in Act IV. O'Neill's characters seem, frequently, to be making private, solitary utterances, not attempts to communicate, whether they use dialogue, monologue, soliloquy, or aside. Since no topic is "off limits" for the family members, and few, if any, wish to face the realities of daily life, especially the painful realities, the encounters are at times savage. Yet O'Neill tried to treat the characters— "his own dead"—with compassion and forgiveness. John Henry Raleigh contends that "old country" customs—part of Irish Catholic family culture—can account for much in characterization and action in *Long Day's Journey into Night:* Irish love poetry, the Judas-complex (a pathological obsession with it, in fact), national commitment to Roman Catholicism (with religious-blasphemous interaction), preoccupation with rhetoric and eloquence (loquaciousness), family relationships being non-communal, sexual chastity (specifically defined as not bothering good women), turbulence, drunkenness, sentimental and ironical feelings about love held simultaneously, tendency toward later marriage and young men living at home longer, and the difficult process of assimilating the Irish into American life.

The four haunted Tyrones reach spiritual self-realization seldom, and then only in the depths of despair: Mary who, if she dared, would take a lethal overdose, has now given up and decided to use morphine to send herself back to the safe, pure, and simplistic romantic time, before she met James Tyrone, when she thought she was either about to become a nun or a concert pianist; or James who realizes that he will never become the superior Shakespearean actor he could be because the possibility of making an incredible amount of money, plus the terror of devastating poverty, makes him prostitute his art and refuse to care for his family; or Jamie, who, in the depths of an incredibly intense drunk, warns Edmund of the love-hate feeling he has had for him all along, and states that he "taught him all he knew" merely to bring him down to his own level: the same Jamie who could not corrupt a pure woman and was as dedicated to the Virgin Mary as was Mary Tyrone, though the "Cynara" to whom he was faithful was Fat Violet, the prostitute about to be fired for being undesirable; or Edmund, who must have in terror and anger perceived what his family was doing to him, and admits he might have done better as a sea gull or a fish since his most memorable moments came when he was drunk with the beauty and singing rhythm of the sea, with no humans present.

Then there are the loneliness, and the alienation from nature, themselves, God, everything: Mary being forced to wait in cheap hotels or country houses for the drunken James Tyrone, Edmund waiting for death, James Tyrone waiting for poverty, Jamie waiting to conquer drink when Mary conquers dope, in a household run by a murderous Richard-III-at-Tewkesbury-father, and an Ophelia-run-mad-mother . . . as night deepens.

—Louis Charles Stagg

LOOK HOMEWARD, ANGEL
Novel by Thomas Wolfe, 1929

"Genius is Not Enough," the catchy title of Bernard De Voto's negative review of Thomas Wolfe's essay *The Story of a Novel*, was not written of *Look Homeward, Angel: A Story of the Buried Life*. Ever since the publication of Wolfe's first and unarguably best novel, it has been a target for critical attack and encomium. But the severest attacks Wolfe suffered were in reaction to his subsequent work. If Wolfe had never written anything else, *Look Homeward, Angel* would have more stature today. It has been dismissed as a "novel of youth," attractive only to teenagers; it has been excoriated as formless, verbose, shallow, and altogether too personal. While there is some truth in all of those accusations, the novel stands as a unique, perdurable monument of American literature. Richard Walser has called it "the most lyric novel ever written by an American," while Wolfe's principal British champion, Pamela Hansford Johnson, finds it the most "clear-sighted" of his novels, portraying his world "with an objectivity altogether remarkable." These traits of lyricism and realism, along with a Joycean complexity and exuberant good humor, are the most compelling qualities of the work.

An unabashedly autobiographical *Bildungsroman*, the book recounts the inner and outer life of the first twenty years (1900-20), of Eugene Gant. Eugene is the youngest of seven children of W. O. and Eliza Gant, a couple who live in the mountain village of Altamont. W. O., a Pennsylvanian with a penchant for rhetoric, alcohol, and prostitutes, owns a stonecutter's shop; his wife is a native of the area with a well-developed head for business and an interest in real estate. After a brief stint in 1904 in St. Louis, where one of her twins dies, she opens a boarding house in Altamont named Dixieland. The precocious Eugene starts school, aged five, against his mother's wishes. He spends his high school years in a private academy and at 15 enrolls in the university at Pulpit Hill. On his first summer vacation he has a brief romance with Laura James, a boarder at Dixieland. During the next summer he works as a laborer in Norfolk and that fall his favorite brother, Ben, dies of influenza. He graduates from college and leaves Altamont to study in the north.

All of the events of the preceding paragraph are exactly parallel to Thomas Wolfe's life. Only the names of the living characters and some place names have been changed. Altamont is the fictitious name for Asheville, North Carolina; Pulpit Hill is Chapel Hill. Floyd C. Watkins, after identifying 250 or 300 names of characters and places in *Thomas Wolfe's Characters*, maintains that there is not a single entirely fictional character or incident in the novel.

Anticipating negative reactions from the easily identifiable characters he portrays, Wolfe explains in a prefatory note that "all serious work in fiction is autobiographical" and that "he meditated no man's portrait here." Many of his readers did not accept that disclaimer, however, and were enraged when the book appeared (coincidentally in the same month as the stock market crash). That reaction is incorporated into his later work in two ways: fictionally in *You Can't Go Home Again* and factually in *The Story of a Novel*.

In *The Story of a Novel* Wolfe observed that "the quality of my memory is characterized . . . in a more than ordinary degree by the intensity of its sense impressions, its power to evoke and bring back the odors, sounds, colors, shapes, and feel of things with concrete vividness." Wolfe's special talent, then, is not a reportorial one but one which exercises almost total recall of sensory images. It is important to remember that he produced the bulk of his enormous manuscript, originally 350,000 words, while he was living in London during 1926-28. That he was far removed in space and time from the events he describes makes the sense of immediacy in his writing all the more impressive.

In spite of charges of formlessness, *Look Homeward, Angel* is carefully constructed. It attains unity and shape through the focus on Eugene, the chronological sequence of events, the preservation of the theme of the search for identity, and the balance, in Chapters 5 and 35, of the death scenes of the twins.

The tombstone in the form of an angel is a significant unifying device. "An angel poised upon cold phthisic feet, with a smile of soft stone idiocy" is first mentioned on the second page of the novel. It is the focus of Chapter 19, "The Angel on the Porch," an excellent vignette published in slightly different form in the August 1929 issue of *Scribner's Magazine*. A similar angel is present in the last scene of the book when Eugene has a conversation with his dead brother, Ben. As all symbols must, this one holds a multitude of meanings: death, remembrance, existence on a spiritual plane, W. O. Gant, and the stone-like quality of people in their inability to communicate with each other. When the original title of the novel, *O Lost*, was changed to the inspired borrowing from Milton's "Lycidas," the angel imagery was further strengthened.

Finally, one should not overlook the pervading humor of the novel. Bruce R. McElderry, Jr., in fact, has found it to be the funniest book in American literature since *Huckleberry Finn*. One manifestation of the humor may be seen in the comedic appeal of the characterizations—W. O.'s bombast, Luke's stuttering, Eliza's habit of pursing her lips and nodding her head. Another element of humor is found in the tone and timing. One instance involves the scene early on when the baby Eugene's face is stepped on by a dray-horse, Eugene having escaped from his yard into an adjoining alley and the driver of the encroaching wagon having fallen asleep. A physician is called: "'This looks worse than it is,' observed Dr. McGuire, laying the hero upon the lounge. . . . Nevertheless, it took two hours to bring him round. Everyone spoke highly of the horse."

Look Homeward, Angel was published in the same year as **William Faulkner**'s *The Sound and the Fury* and **Ernest Hemingway**'s *A Farewell to Arms*. While it does not currently enjoy the prestige of those other landmarks of American letters, it has never been out of print and continues to attract popular and critical attention. If Wolfe's genius was not enough to sustain a universally acclaimed writing career, it was ample for the creation of a genuine literary achievement.

—Nancy Carol Joyner

LOOKING BACKWARD 2000-1887
Novel by Edward Bellamy, 1888

The political and social impact of *Looking Backward 2000-1887* has been so great, the merits and deficiencies of the planned state it proposed so often and intensely debated, that the work's value as a product of the imagination has perhaps been unfairly minimized. Had not Edward Bellamy's novel been wrought with a craft appropriate to his polemical purposes it is doubtful that his idealistic document would have received such unusual attention. In Russia, Lenin's wife read it and Tolstoy made certain it was translated; in England the Fabians, including Bernard Shaw, discussed it; both Charles Beard and **John Dewey** listed it as second only to *Das Kapital* in its significance. Revealingly, it was a bestseller and within a decade of its publication more than a million copies were in circulation in the United States. Most of its readers were probably of the middle class, whose civic dreams the book's schemes so powerfully embodied that citizens formed over 150 political clubs inspired by Bellamy's plans, seeking to make them a fact not a fantasy of American life.

The character Ike in **John Dos Passos**'s *The 42nd Parallel* suggests the hope many gleaned from Bellamy's solid-seeming vision in a not completely accurate but heartfelt resume of the book's plot: "It's about a galoot that goes asleep an' wakes up in the year two thousand and the social revolution's all happened and everything's socialistic an' there's no jails or poverty and nobody works for themselves an there's no way anybody can get to be a rich bondholder or capitalist and life's pretty slick for the working class."

The central problems for which Bellamy sought solutions—unequal distribution of wealth, conflicts between classes, ruthless commercial competition, all those conditions that make life nasty, brutish, and short for so many and less rich and fulfilling for most—were of course not limited to any particular region. But his attack was rooted in the particular condition of post-Civil War

America, a time according to historian Russel Nye embodying "a great paradox. The nation's material prosperity was the envy of all Europe yet most of its social, cultural, and political institutions lagged far behind those of the advanced western countries. . . . In almost every sphere except the technological the nation's institutions cried out for modernization." Farmers found their profits drying up, powerful corporations in the oil, steel, coal, cotton, and sugar industries (to name a few) were turning into monopolies and trusts that corrupted politicians and controlled the lives of millions but with comparatively little control placed on them—indeed many businesses were larger in employees, revenues, and resources than some state governments. Gaps between workers, managers, and owners seemed to stretch into abysses, and industrial strife was increasingly common and violent. Daniel Boorstin refers to the time as "an age of revolution" in American life where "traditional politics could not cope with" the commercial institutions causing the revolution, "nor could traditional law harness them to social welfare."

Bellamy's Utopia in many ways flowed with the direction of force in America rather than opposed it. He presented an urban, industrial, technologically advanced society counter to the bucolic Brook Farms of earlier radicals. He imagined rather than one great union, one great trust. All monopolies merge into one, which blends into the state, ran presumably for the equitable benefit of all. This state clearly resembles a socialist or welfare state, though it is neither, precisely, at least according to Bellamy who studiously avoided using any form of the word socialism in explaining what he aimed at.

According to Bellamy the advanced state is achieved not through violent conflict or social Darwinian competition, but through humanity's increased awareness of its needs for cooperation. Underlying the social and political change in *Looking Backward* is Bellamy's "religion of solidarity," which declared that while an individual's badness was manifest in greed and selfishness, human goodness was a potentially greater counter-force leading toward a "passion for losing ourselves in others" and attaining a sense of "true self-interest" which was rational, and unselfish. The personal and selfish in humankind constituted a centrifugal force, whereas the willingness to join with others for common good was centripetal, drawing individuals together in communal harmony, not driving them apart and causing violence.

As the very reasonable Dr. Leete and sometimes his daughter Edith explain the good society of 2000 to Julian West, a 19th-century dilettante, its main features become crystal clear. Bellamy showed in his novels (for example, *The Duke of Stockbridge*) and his short stories that he was quite capable of adjusting the techniques of art to achieve various ends. Thus the book's undoubted success possibly results more from the craft of his seemingly simple narration than critics have generally admitted. However, it is the fullness of his picture and its clarity together with the many glimpses of a better life that is attainable that most compel interest. Describing a nation where all are employed, have access to good housing, can obtain a good and appropriate education, where none can accumulate or hoard or bequeath excessive profits, Bellamy can be very convincing. Less satisfactory are his reliance on a simplistic (though laudable) view of the essential goodness and reasonableness of mankind, and his failure to deal with some prickly contemporary problems such as minority rights. That he failed to perceive the dangers of state bureaucracies and the potentially dehumanizing effects of scientific management is lamentable but understandable.

Late in the book Julian dreams he has returned to Boston in 1887, and in a stunning, depressing passage the misery and woe of a degrading society are revealed to him as a nightmare which readers often recognize, cruelly enough, as their own real world. Henry George called *Looking Backward* "a castle in the air, with clouds for its foundation," but if so, it is also a construct that inspired utopian thinkers and common people alike to search for a better life in humanely conceived communities.

—Jack B. Moore

LOSING BATTLES
Novel by Eudora Welty, 1970

Eudora Welty has never belonged to any literary school. Her fiction explores life's mysteries rather than espousing any ideology, and it seldom falls into predictable patterns. The most distinguishing characteristics of Welty's fiction are its great variety and its consistent virtuosity—two qualities epitomized by the long novel *Losing Battles*. In this novel Welty deals with complex human relationships and a changing era, does so in both comic and tragic terms, and in the process fuses narrative method and her major concerns into a powerful whole.

Set in the 1930s during a family reunion in northeast Mississippi, *Losing Battles* presents two attitudes toward social change. On the one hand, the reunion participants—Granny Vaughn, her grandsons surnamed Beecham and granddaughter Beulah Beecham Renfro, their spouses, children, grandchildren, and in-laws—want to continue leading the traditional life of subsistence farmers. They worship the land on which they live, even when that land is parched and barren; they participate in a close-knit family life that "involves both a submerging and a triumph of the individual"; and they value the past—they know that the remembering and recounting of family stories are essential to a family's vitality. The retired schoolteacher Julia Mortimer, on the other hand, is a modernist who has never been a member of any reunion: she has faith in man's ability to harness or control nature; she emphasizes individual freedom and social duty as more desirable than family loyalty; and she believes in a philosophy of progress. Granny Vaughn and her descendants stand in sharp contrast to Julia Mortimer, but Welty does not choose between these viewpoints. Instead she presents two modes of survival in a world that resists systematization of any sort.

These unresolved conflicts between traditionalists and modernists follow both comic and tragic lines of development. Part 2 of *Losing Battles,* for instance, is the stuff of farce; Jack Renfro sets out to obey the will of his family reunion and to wreak vengeance on Judge Oscar Moody, the man who sentenced him to two years in Parchman Penitentiary. Jack hopes to force Moody's "luxurious" Buick into a ditch; instead when Jack's wife and daughter appear inopportunely in front of Moody's auto, Moody swerves to avoid hitting them and drives up Banner Top, the highest hill in Boone County. Jack, in gratitude, resolves to become Moody's savior, not his tormentor. Jack's love for his wife and child, his ability to defy his extended family without estranging himself from it, and his heart-felt recognition of human transience are all evident in his decision to save Moody. The plot is comic, but its import is quite serious. Yet not all of *Losing Battles's* serious concerns are conveyed through comedy. Julia Mortimer's individualistic battles with ignorance, her many losses, and the abuse which

plagues her final years reveal her heroic devotion to progress and the horrifying isolation to which such a life can lead. To label Julia's dark tale as tragic, however, is not to say it is nihilistic. Julia has known failure, but she has also produced many successful students. And Julia has come to realize that "From flat on your back you may not be able to lick the world, but at least you can keep the world from licking you. I haven't spent a lifetime fighting my battle to give up now. I'm ready for all they send me. There's a measure of enjoyment in it."

Whether the subject of Losing Battles is tragic or comic, Welty's method of narration and her major themes are complementary. *Losing Battles* consists primarily of short tales told by the Beechams and Renfros who have gathered to celebrate Granny Vaughn's 90th birthday, and their typically southern story-telling is central to the novel's deepest meaning. Welty has written that in the American south

> stories could be watched in the happening—lifelong and generation-long stories watched and participated in, first by one member of the family and then without a break by another, allowing the continuous and never-ending recital to be passed along in full course and to grow. The event and the memory and the comprehension of it and taking a role in it were scarcely marked off from the other in the glow of hearing it again, telling it anew, anticipating, knowing the whole thing by heart—and all right here where it happened.

The reunion of *Losing Battles* certainly is part of a "continuous and never-ending recital." The past is not gone for the clan. It comes alive at least once a year on Granny's birthday. Then the old stories are told, new stories are added to be retold in the future, and everyone participates in the telling—Percy with his "thready" voice, Etoyle who "embroiders," Aunt Beck with her "mourning dove's" voice, everyone. The death of Grandpa Vaughn is the reunion's newest story, and it is recounted with great sadness. Jack's rescue of the Moody's Buick will be a story that the next reunion can tell in high humor. The family members thus know that their lives are and will be part of the enduring family story, a story that seems to come alive in the telling. They feel a real continuity with the past. Yet this tendency to look backward in time also leads the family to resist or ignore innovative ideas, to refuse to plan for the future, and to face helplessly the decline of the agrarian south. The family is both blessed and encumbered by its reverence for the past, a reverence embodied in the storytelling which constitutes *Losing Battles.*

In *Losing Battles* Welty explores profoundly significant concepts and emotions, she refuses to simplify them, and she makes her method of narration a metaphor for her novel's central issues. As a result, Welty's description of great fiction seems a precise description of her own. "Great fiction," she writes, "is given to sprawling and escaping from bounds, is capable of contradicting itself, and is not impervious to humor. There is absolutely everything in great fiction but a clear answer. Humanity itself seems to matter more to the novelist than what humanity thinks it can prove." Though *Losing Battles* clearly investigates divergent ideas, no clear answers emerge from this investigation. And that fact may best explain the novel's powerful impact upon readers. The complexity, the humor and tragedy, the craftsmanship, and the humanity of *Losing Battles* combine to make it a major achievement in the rich and varied career of a major American writer.

—Suzanne Marrs

THE LOST SON
Poem by Theodore Roethke, 1951

"The Lost Son," Theodore Roethke's poem in five parts, is one of the essential American poetic sequences of the twentieth century. Published in the 1951 volume *Praise to the End!* "The Lost Son" arguably contains the poet's most coherent, compressed expression of pastoral style and romantic point of view.

Part one, the poem's longest section, evokes the narrator's childhood played out against the landscape of the woods, the garden, and the greenhouse. Roethke was a master of a dramatic phrasing that often echoes the Brothers Grimm:

> At woodlawn I heard the dead cry:
> I was lulled by the slamming of iron,
> A slow drip over stones,
> Toads brooding in wells.

Roethke's guileless narrator achieves such consummate immersion in The Moment that our self-limiting expectations fade away. Before he or she knows it, the reader is utterly with the narrator, wide-eyed, breathless, and vulnerable in the fields.

Coming of age so (for all great sequences are coming-of-age poems), the poet's personality takes shape from the rapid accumulation of directly observed phenomena ("All the leaves stick out their tongues . . . Nothing nibbled my line, / not even the minnows came"), the fractured, essential dialogue with the Other ("Voice, come out of the silence"), and the restorative power of language in poetry. It is a process of thorough engagement with the world, where doubt is freely admitted and poignantly articulated, where all questions are asked:

> Tell me:
> Which is the way I take;
> Out of what door do I go,
> Where and to whom?

For much of the twentieth century in American poetry, the sequence existed to disrupt narrative and make more personal the traditionally austere meditation. This can lead to small returns as trivia, inside jokes, and the poet's ego overwhelm the form. In "The Lost Son," none of this ever happens. Roethke's humanity and humility govern and shape the entire poem. A master of tone and pacing, he knows just when to veer from a linear storyline to evocative speculation. Often, with surprising, delightful results, he turns to the meters and rhythms of the nursery, of the pre-literate chant:

> The shape of a rat?
> It's bigger than that.
> It's less than a leg
> And more than a nose,
> Just under the water
> It usually goes.

The middle of the poem, bristling with such mirth, interrogation, and mystery-making, is bent on expressing a sheer delight in life itself. The quest that makes up a life's motion must inevitably descend to frightening depths, as we observe in part three: "The weeds whined, / The snakes cried, / The cows and briars / Said to me: Die." But the almost manic drive toward light, toward revelation, spins out of deepest darkness:

> All the windows are burning! What's left of my life?
> I want the old rage, the lash of primordial milk!
>
> Good-by, good-by, old stones, the time-order is going,
> I have married my hands to perpetual agitation,
> I run, I run to the whistle of money.
>
> Money money money
> Water water water
>
> How cool the grass is.

No poet has ever done this sort of thing better. The emotional ground covered in these few lines is immense, yet seems absolutely right and true.

As "The Lost Son" reaches its conclusion, winding back to the longer, relaxed lines and greenhouse days of childhood, the poem utters a plea for the patience and humility that begets wisdom:

> A lively understandable spirit
> Once entertained you.
> It will come again.
> Be still.
> Wait.

"The Lost Son" is an indispensable poem, a lyrical tour de force by one of the greatest American poets of the twentieth century.

—Robert McDowell

LOVE MEDICINE
Novel by Louise Erdrich, 1984; expanded 1993

At Easter time in 1981, June is on her way to catch a bus home for Easter to the Indian reservation after what has been a series of smothering relationships with men. A young white engineer beckons her into a bar and gives her a hard-boiled egg and a drink. She hopes maybe this man will be different. Later he drives her to a secluded place and attempts to make drunken love to her in his pickup. When he passes out she gets up and starts walking home. Her sense of direction is good, but her body freezes to death before she gets there. The pure and naked part of her goes on walking over the snow, however, and, as if she is walking on water, she comes home.

That is the opening segment of *Love Medicine*, a novel that burst onto the literary scene in 1984. It was by a young writer, then not yet 30, whom the world had scarcely heard of before that time. Drawing on her own mixed-blood heritage, Louise Erdrich explores in this novel some of the characters who surround June on and off the Chippewa Reservation in North Dakota. There is Lulu Nanapush, the loving and fecund woman who draws men as clover draws bees, who makes love with her brother-in-law Beverly in the tool shed the day her husband is buried, and who gives birth to Gerry—a man who will one day kick a cowboy in the balls and father a child with June. There is Marie Lazarre, who is beaten with a poker and scorched by a nun at the convent, who is seduced on her way home by a man carrying two geese, and who gives birth to a man named Gordie who eventually marries June and fathers a child with her. There is Henry Lamartine, Jr., who fights in Vietnam, who deflowers Albertine, and who drowns himself in a river. There is Nector Kashpaw, who reluctantly becomes tribal chairman, who has an affair with Lulu after delivering melting butter around the reservation with her, and who eventually chokes to death trying to swallow the love medicine of a raw turkey heart.

These are strange Indians doing strange things, yet Erdrich has us laughing and crying and caring and believing. Winner of the National Book Critics Circle Award for 1984 as well as four or five other major awards, *Love Medicine* gets readers thinking about such subjects as these: what is "love" and why does it need "medicine"?; has Catholicism helped or harmed Indians?; what role does alcohol play in Indian patterns of life, love, and dying?; is the fecund Lulu to be loved or despised for her promiscuity?; is the more responsible Marie to be loved or despised for her fidelity?; why does June, really a minor character who dies in the first chapter, so dominate this novel?; and what is the "home" to which this drunken prostitute walks across the water?

Love Medicine is a major work of fiction, the first of a series of novels about life on the Chippewa Reservation and in the imaginary nearby town of Argus, North Dakota. The other novels are *The Beet Queen* (1986), *Tracks* (1988), and *The Bingo Palace* (1994). The various white, Indian, and mixed-breed Indians in these novels interact in complex ways to give a fascinating picture of multicultural life in the twentieth century. Erdrich gives quiet but moving expression to the racial, feminist, social, and just plain human concerns that define the century. She writes in a prose so spare that it is almost anorexic, but a prose that carries us out of ourselves and into a robust world full of the thoughts and passions that matter most.

Readers have wondered ever since it was published whether *Love Medicine* is really a novel. After all, some of its "chapters" first appeared as stories, and the rest seem to cover such a wild variety of points of view, settings, and styles that it seems to be as much a collection of stories as a novel. These questions became more striking with the publication in 1993 of an "expanded" version of the book. This new work includes, interspersed among the old chapters (some of them slightly revised), four new chapters that Erdrich located in working on later novels in the series. We expect novelists to revise their work, but what do we do with a novel that is revised *after* publication? Readers who finally thought they had found unifying elements in the fourteen chapters of the earlier version will wonder what whether the eighteen chapters in the expanded version are still unified, or still unified in the same ways. Will we have to revise our notion of what a novel is so that it includes the notion of a work expanded throughout an author's lifetime? Perhaps so. After all, **Walt Whitman** revised and expanded *Leaves of Grass* for most of his life. Whatever we decide to do with our notions of definition and unity, Louise Erdrich's *Love Medicine* has earned an honored place for itself in the pantheon of American literature.

—Peter G. Beidler

THE LOVE SONG OF J. ALFRED PRUFROCK
Poem by T.S. Eliot, 1910-1911

As an undergraduate at Harvard in December 1908, Thomas Stearns Eliot happened upon a slender volume of critical essays that profoundly influenced both his personal life and the direction of twentieth-century English poetry. Arthur Symons's book *The Symbolist Movement in Literature* (1899) introduced him to the unique temperaments of French writers such as Charles Baudelaire, Arthur Rimbuad, and Jules Laforgue. Laforgue especially appealed to him, and once he was immersed in Laforgue's languishing moods and complaints of urban squalor, Eliot felt that he could transform his own impressions of growing up in the deteriorating industrial environment of St. Louis into poetry that would extend beyond the boundaries of traditional verse forms. Lyndall Gordon points out in *Eliot's Early Years* (1977) that the symbolists also taught him " . . . to broadcast secrets, to confess through the defeatist persona his own despair and, at the same time, to shield himself by playing voices against one another— the wry voice of the sufferer, the scathing or flippant voice of a commentator, the banal voice of a woman." Added to his interest in Dante, Elizabethan drama, and the subtleties of irony and detachment, Eliot was poised to do something new, something decisive. Two years later, he began "The Love Song of J. Alfred Prufrock" and completed it while studying at the Sorbonne in 1911. The poem stands as the major achievement of the first phase of his remarkable career, and when he showed it to **Ezra Pound** in 1914, Pound enthusiastically declared that Eliot had "modernized himself *on his own.*"

From quite early on, Eliot believed ("Tradition and the Individual Talent," 1919) that writing demanded an "escape from personality," which allowed the poet's mind to become a "medium" for impressions and feelings to "enter into new combinations." This enabled him to view his thoughts and emotions as objects for analysis, and he then worked to present them in concrete images and symbols that immediately would convey the diverse and obscure associations that were combining within him. Thus, when "Prufrock" was published by Harriet Monroe in *Poetry* in June 1915, it marked the advent of modernism and soon provoked a critical and academic enterprise because of its allusive complexity and its haunting details of decay and isolation. Often described as an interior monologue that uses stream-of-consciousness to draw readers into its private evocations, Eliot defended the poem as a dramatic monologue in which Prufrock is speaking to a male companion who remains silent. Accepting the poet's word, one can discern that Eliot adopts the mask of an disheartened middle age bachelor who is getting ready to attend an evening social gathering that he predicts will be sorely lacking in genuine vitality and meaning. Since he has made a practice of attending such events, Prufrock drags himself through each listless stage of a painful routine. He can anticipate the dingy streets, the sentimental digressions, and the eventual self-surrender, for he admits: "I have measured out my life with coffee spoons."

The title, epigraph, and opening segment establish the psychological tension of the poem. Prufrock's name indicates that he is a reticent and prudish individual who acquiesces to say and do what is expected of him. Since risk-taking is out of character, he speaks about himself in a rather self-mocking, ironic tone. For instance, he recognizes it is pointless to worry about inconsequential things like the starch in his collar, the part in his hair, and his arms and legs becoming thin, yet he is anxious about the criteria others will use to judge him. As his self-conscious musings develop, they do not comprise a "love song" in the customary sense of the phrase. He longs for the true affection of a loving relationship, but he has given up hope of ever attaining it. He still hears "mermaids singing each to each" on distant mythic waves, but he is convinced: "I do not think that they will sing to me." The epigraph from Dante's *Inferno* adds another despondent note. At the age of thirty-five (a fair estimate of Prufrock's age), Dante was lost in a Dark Wood, needing guidance to survive his personal abyss. In his descent into the Eighth *bolgia* of the Eighth Circle of Hell, Dante finds the Counsellors of Fraud like Guido da Montefeltro engulfed in tongue-like flames. Prufrock, too, is fraudulent. To disguise his contempt for the garish trappings of bourgeois society, he will allot himself time to "murder and create" a number of personas in order to "prepare a face" for others to meet. He is "politic, cautious, and meticulous" in his role of the genteel guest, to which he has become resigned. Even the details of his projected walk to the gathering signify he is in the grip of a spiritual malaise that approximates death. The evening is comatose, "Like a patient etherized upon a table." Soot falls from dirty chimneys; gutter water collects in stagnant drain pools. "Half-deserted" streets beguile him as he passes cheap hotels reminding him of lonely one-night sexual encounters that dissipate toward dawn. Cleanth Brooks in *Understanding Poetry* (1960) emphasizes: "Twilight is the atmosphere of the poem," in which "the quiet is not that of a natural sleep," but of an "ominous hush."

The pretentious universe of the drawing room into which he will step is fastidiously arranged, but among the porcelain, the teacups and the marmalade, Prufrock imagines being conspicuously out of place—an ageing aesthete at whom "Death" has begun to snicker. He is weary of the idle gossip and the name-dropping, of the women walking back and forth and "Talking of Michelangelo." He also is weary of the accusatory glances that formulate and pin him "wriggling on the wall" to be dissected. Though his attire is stylish, his physical appearance does not measure up; his nerves are tight. To Prufrock's discredit and dissatisfaction, he has lost faith in others and in himself. He aspires to break through the obvious triviality encircling him, yet he does not "dare" to confront others about their shallowness. Even if he had the courage to express himself, he would not know how "to presume" to state all that he feels. Sadly, he cannot persuade himself that the effort would even be worthwhile.

Of the many allusions Eliot includes to intensify Prufrock's questioning and hesitancy, his reference to Hamlet is the most often discussed and the most illuminating. Denmark is corrupted by incest and murder, and Hamlet's disgust for his mother and his uncle is so overpowering that it defies words. Though he contemplates suicide as a means of escape, Hamlet eventually acts against the circumstances that humiliate him. In contrast, Prufrock acknowledges: "I am not Prince Hamlet, nor was meant to be." He is aware that the malingering events of a late-afternoon get-together are insignificant in relation to the magnitude of those afflicting Hamlet. Nonetheless, he retreats from his moment of personal crisis. Rather than entrust his observations and emotions to a woman with whom he would like to be intimate, he resorts to posturing like a "ridiculous . . . Fool." In his self-imposed isolation, Prufrock concedes: "I should have been a pair of ragged claws / Scuttling across the floors of silent seas."

Unfulfilled desire makes Prufrock's life seem fragmentary and destitute. He ranks himself as one of the living dead who has seen his "head (grown slightly bald) brought in upon a platter." Fearing rejection, honesty and love elude him. Thus, Eliot intends for the closing tercet to convey a fatal message. He completes Prufrock's monologue by having him lament: "Till human voices wake us, and we drown." The fifth iamb in this metrical line requires a final stress on the verb "drown," which further accentu-

ates Prufrock's impending despair. Paradoxically, "human voices" have the potential to rescue him from his punishing thoughts, but the instant that he is lured into trivial conversation, he will "drown" in the meaningless superficiality that he so adamantly disdains.

The degree to which Eliot might be ridiculing Prufrock and to which Prufrock might be ridiculing himself are controversial topics that could affect one's final reading of the poem. There is no debate among critics, however, about the poem's forceful influence. For many, "The Love Song of J. Alfred Prufrock" is synonymous with modernism. Its ambitious techniques and themes set the foundation on which the movement is built. In fact, Prufrock has become an icon for the disillusioned, suffering intellectual struggling to endure at a fundamental level, as Eliot writes in "*Ulysses*, Order, and Myth" (1923), ". . . the immense panorama of futility and anarchy that is contemporary history."

—Joe Nordgren

MAIN STREET
Novel by Sinclair Lewis, 1920

"The history of a nation," Woodrow Wilson declared in 1900, "is only the history of its villages written large." Twenty years later, Sinclair Lewis infected millions with his large novelistic dose of the Village Virus in *Main Street: The Story of Carol Kennicott. Main Street* came to mean the smug, intolerant, dull conformity of the American small town. The book sold sensationally—nearly 300,000 copies the first year, another 100,000 copies before cheaper editions reached the masses—and provided timely ammunition for the cynical postwar generation. Lewis's apprenticeship novels—*Our Mr. Wrenn, Die Trail of the Hawk, The Job, The Innocents, Free Air*—reveal the realistic touches, satiric flashes, and small-town tintypes developed in *Main Street*. An heir of Charles Dickens and **Mark Twain**, of H.G. Wells and **H.L. Mencken**, Lewis wrote his explosive novel in the grubby-village tradition of **Edward Eggleston**, **E.W. Howe**, **Joseph Kirkland**, **Hamlin Garland**, **Harold Frederic**, **Edgar Lee Masters**, **Sherwood Anderson**, **Floyd Dell**, and **Zona Gale**. He first sketched his "Village Virus" expose in Sauk Centre, Minnesota, in 1905, when, as a Yale sophomore home on vacation, he read Garland's *Main Travelled Roads*. Knowing that magazine editors would expunge his slashing satire and gargantuan detail, Lewis fifteen years later refused to subject *Main Street*—as he had subjected his previous two novels—to serialization.

His panoramic novel of provincial life in the northern midwest from 1912 to 1920 documents in nearly 200 episodes the war between Carol Kennicott and Gopher Prairie. We first see Lewis's protagonist as a flighty Blodgett College idealist in Minneapolis in 1906, then as an earnest library student at a Chicago studio party, and later as a slightly weary librarian in St. Paul. Here beauty-minded Carol Milford meets competent, boyish Dr. Will Kennicott, who shows her photographs of his "darn pretty town." At year's end they marry, honeymooning in Colorado. On the gritty train to Gopher Prairie, Carol foresees in the scrawny trackside settlements the ugliness awaiting her. Seeking relief from her bridal home (a mildewed Victorian horror), Carol strolls around the whole disjointed hamlet in thirty-two minutes. Later, at dull parties in her honor, she raises prairie eyebrows by overplaying the Clever Little Bride from the Cities. Hikes, new furniture, her

Oriental housewarming party, winter sports, and a few confidants mitigate her unease, but young matrons of the Jolly Seventeen bridge club, among others, regard her as an affected snob. Her yearning to enlighten Will about poetry and to idealize his surgical dexterity prove as futile as her naive gestures to improve the town's architecture and culture through the la-di-da Thanatopsis Club. As the stagnant years pass, Carol, though devoted to her baby, draws further from her husband, imagining herself in love with a faun-like tailor. Thoroughly disillusioned with the peeping town, Carol decides to flee with her son to Washington, DC. There she attains the empty freedom of a government clerk. After thirteen months Will visits, begging her to return home. Having failed to transform her husband into Sir Launcelot and her town into the Vale of Arcady, Carol Kennicott—more mature and resigned after nearly two years in the capital (and feeling Will's second child stirring within her) returns to Main Street.

Even then, Carol, refusing to admit that her rebellion was wrong, resolves to continue questioning—with sympathy, not sarcasm. Leaving little unsaid, the discursive narrator explains that Carol "was a woman with a working brain and no work." No tragic figure, the high-strung Carol Kennicott, like Emma Bovary, is the type of the unfulfilled dreamer, the failed romantic, the female Quixote. Peopling Gopher Prairie are "humors" like the Good Influence, the Village Radical, the Big Cheese, the Gentleman Hen, the Loyal Servant, and the Street-corner Roue. Further, the novel is a guidebook of the seedy and the meretricious, a grammar of sectional slang and immigrant dialect. In truth, *Main Street* illustrates the author's own life-long ambivalence toward the Middle West and the middle class, the unsettled juxtaposition of the fantastic-pragmatic, the Carol-Will in himself.

Indeed, this inconsistency—Lewis's now uplifting, now undercutting of his main characters—bothered many critics. Yea-sayers saw Carol's battle as balanced, whole, and hallowed, but nay-sayers saw it as unfair, incomplete, and profane. Satire, of course, is never "fair." Like the caricaturist, the satirist startles us into recognition. Nor is he required to prescribe a "real" program of reform. So natural to Lewis were serial and slickstory engineering that even in *Main Street* he relies on a long series of contracted flights, installmentesque cliffhangers, and a swift, nervous style, flexible enough for popular fiction but never adequately rendering interior nuance. *Main Street*'s loose-jointed structure allowed the author to insert or delete his relentless catalogs of Gopher Prairieana. Lewis cut out 20,000 words before his manuscript went to press, but Main Street is still too long, its story simply too slender to support the freight of Lewis's around-the-clock carping.

Still, American popular fiction encouraged Lewis to look at the contemporary American scene. Sauk Centre, the town that once raged against its native son, raves about him now. Though *Main Street* might read like a period piece today, many young women still can identify with Carol—and some small towns with Gopher Prairie. For good or ill, many city people first learned to see the small town through Lewis's blazing camera-eyes. After *Main Street,* its author gained a reputation as more than a popular storyteller. After *Babbitt, Arrowsmith, Elmer Gantry,* and *Dodsworth,* this "fabulist" in 1930 was the first American to win the Nobel Prize in Literature. But for every reader who would elevate Lewis above George Eliot, no doubt there is another who would consign him to a place below James Whitcomb Riley. The influence of *Main Street* on major American writers like **Thomas Wolfe, Richard Wright,** and **William Faulkner** has been less direct than its im-

pact on such important regional writers as Edith Summers, **T.S. Stribling,** and Frederick Manfred.

—Martin Bucco

MAIN-TRAVELLED ROADS
Stories by Hamlin Garland, 1891

After three years reading, writing, and lecturing in Boston, Hamlin Garland in 1887 (after six years away from home) traveled to the old homestead in Iowa and then to South Dakota to visit his parents. Although Garland had grown up on frontier farms and rebelled against their drudgery, never before had he realized so fully their wretchedness. Guilt-ridden, depressed, and bitter about "the system," young Garland—disciple of **William Dean Howells,** Herbert Spencer, Henry George, and Eugene Veron— began a series of stories in the anti-idyllic tradition of **Edward Eggleston**'s *The Hoosier School-Master* (1871), **E.W. Howe**'s *The Story of a Country Town* (1883), and **Joseph Kirkland**'s *Zury* (1887). Four of the original six Mississippi valley stories in *Main-Travelled Roads* first appeared in the magazines *Harper's Weekly* and *Arena.* Garland added three stories to the 1899 edition and two more to the 1922 edition, but the first collection is historically the most important.

In "A Branch-Road," jealous Will Hannon, misunderstanding his sweetheart, flees his rural home. He returns seven years later, learns the truth, and begs her to abandon her bleak life with his former rival. In the end, Will leads mother and child out of their rustic hell. The last part of this story dramatically reverses the happy-to-sad structure of the first three parts. With his argument rising "to the level of Browning's philosophy," Garland's strong man does indeed sound like the great poet proposing to Elizabeth Barrett; as well, Will's early conviction that his sweetheart "gave herself too freely" echoes "My Last Duchess." Garland's impressionistic method recreates country scenes effectively, but his naive admixture of high-toned French and border dialect ("'biled chickun' formed the *piece de resistance*") is as bathetic as his lisping urchins.

Like "A Branch-Road," the next story is about return, but "Up the Coule" ends despondently. After successfully managing and acting in a theater troupe, elegant Howard McLane of New York returns to Wisconsin to discover that his mother, his brother, and his brother's family toil in poverty. Admitting his neglect, Howard heroically plans to buy back the old homestead for them, but his embittered brother, sensing that it is too late, refuses his brother's help. Garland describes well Howard's nostalgic mind, the images that rise up between the artificial world of his success and the natural world of his brother's failure. The dinner of milk, bread, and honey; the neighbors' surprise party; and the sister-in-law's revelations of despair are convincing. Less so is Howard's recital of a paragraph—indented—by the French painter Jean Francois Millet about domestic tragedy surrounded by natural glory.

The return home in "Among the Corn Rows" ends happily for Rob Rodemaker, a young outlander in need of a wife. An idealistic newspaperman looks upon Rodemaker ("road-maker") as an expanding Whitmanesque personality. Leaving his thriving South Dakota wheat field and joshing companions, Rob briefly backtrails to Wisconsin, where girls are "thicker 'n huckleberries." Among the hot corn rows there Julia Peterson, coincidentally, daydreams of a Yankee coming to rescue her. Although no particular tenderness existed between the former schoolmates, Rob now is affected "massively" by the swaying of Julia's powerful body. The eroticism, though oblique, is palpable. Julia's decision to escape from her hard Norwegian father triggers in her a flood of feeling for Rob. Late that night the pair come together like Romeo ("Rob!") and Juliet ("Julyie!"). To the song of katydids Rob indeed steals a hand, with only the harsher companion stories intimating their probable future.

"The Return of a Private" elevates Garland's father into the type of the Civil War veteran. His war with the south over, he must daily fight nature and injustice. Each scenic episode—the weary soldier's return, the wife's loneliness and dinner at Widder Gray's, the family reunion—builds to a dramatic resolution, only to be marred by Garland's metaphorical sentimentality: "They are fighting a hopeless battle, and must fight till God gives them furlough."

Also proud is Timothy Haskins, the moiling farmer in the highly compressed "Under the Lion's Paw," Garland's best-known story. Driven out of Kansas by grasshoppers, the Haskins family is befriended by an older farm couple. Haskins, however, is trapped by a speculator into paying double for the land that Haskins himself had doubled in value. Appropriately, the story ends abruptly, Haskins's head "sunk in his hands." Not forced to squeeze the luckless Haskins, the greedy Buller is more the villain of melodrama than himself the victim of economic determinism. The thumbnail sketch of Haskins's nine-year-old son slogging through his chores is Garland himself at that age.

The last story, "Mrs. Ripley's Trip," is flinty but less grim. Frugal Gran'ma Ripley fulfills her twenty-three-year promise to herself to visit her eastern birthplace—but not without feeling guilty for leaving her husband and young grandson even for a short time. The simple two-part story treats only what happens before and after the trip. The old couple's bittersweet b'gosh squabbling right down to the wife's last-minute instructions at the depot leads directly into Garland's sober picture of her trudging back home through the snow drifts. In response to her grandson's effusive welcome and her husband's restrained greeting, "She took up her burden again, never more thinking to lay it down."

In spite of obvious faults, *Main-Travelled Roads* is inherently and historically valuable. The author's combination of realism and impressionism effectively recreated the west of a particular time, place, and self. His essays in *Crumbling Idols* define his idea of *veritism*—"passion for truth and individual expression." Later, in his Rocky Mountain romances, Garland nourished rather than dispelled the myth of the west, but even in *Main-Travelled Roads*, as we have seen, Garland's ambivalence is obvious. But in both *Main-Travelled Roads* and the book which *Main-Travelled Roads* inspired **Sinclair Lewis** to write—*Main Street* (1920)—negative feelings predominate. Howard McLane's impressions of La Crosse could be Carol Kennicott's impressions of Gopher Prairie: "How poor and dull and sleepy and squalid it seemed! The one main street ended at the hillside at his left and stretched away to the north, between two rows of the usual village stores, unrelieved by a tree or a touch of beauty."

—Martin Bucco

THE MAMBO KINGS PLAY SONGS OF LOVE
Novel by Oscar Hijuelos, 1989

Receiving the Pulitzer Prize in 1989, *The Mambo Kings Play Songs of Love* made Oscar Hijuelos an instant celebrity. The fame of the author and his novel increased even more when the text was adapted for a feature film. *The Mambo Kings* was Hijuelos's second novel, his first being *Our House in the Last World* (1985), which was welcomed by the critics, although never a commercial success. It is obvious from this first novel that Hijuelos's main concern as a writer is a profound desire for an understanding of his parents' lives before he was born. *The Mambo Kings Play Songs of Love* is a continuation of Hijuelos's search for his parents' lives and culture, but this time he concentrates his artistic imagination on a fictionalization of a generation of Cubans in the 1950s in New York City.

One of the characters of *The Mambo Kings Play Songs of Love*, Eugenio, is a kind of alter ego of Hijuelos himself. Eugenio appears as the author of the prologue and epilogue of the novel, and there are some suggestions in the rest of the narration which indicate that Eugenio might have written the entire story of the Castillo brothers, Cesar and Nestor, and their musical accomplishments. Eugenio is the son of Nestor and the nephew of Cesar, Cuban immigrants who came to New York City from Havana in 1949, hoping to find success as musicians. A few months after their arrival in New York, Cesar and Nestor form the "Mambo Kings," an orchestra which was somewhat successful in night clubs along the East Coast. In 1954, the Castillo brothers appeared on the *I Love Lucy* television program after befriending fellow-Cuban Desi Arnaz, and this was their greatest accomplishment as entertainers. Nevertheless, neither their modest success with their orchestra nor their appearance in the *I Love Lucy* show were able to change the very sad experiences of their lives. For one, Nestor is never happy after leaving Cuba. He is always obsessed with the memory of a girlfriend named Maria who broke his heart back in Cuba. Actually, it is this tragic memory that inspires his composition "Beautiful Maria of My Soul," the Mambo Kings' most successful song. But Cesar is the central character of the novel, and it is he who undergoes a deep personal transformation. Cesar is the one who makes most of the decisions for the two brothers, including the very critical one to immigrate to New York from Cuba. His main obsessions are sex, drinking, and music, and this compulsive behavior allows him to appear happy in the first part of the novel (before Nestor's death). The critical moment of the narration is in 1957, when Nestor dies in a car accident while driving with Cesar to New Jersey. Cesar, despite being in the car when the accident happened, is not seriously injured, but his behavior from this point on reveals a deeply troubled personality. Cesar feels guilty for his brother's death, and this guilt brings up hidden problems within himself. It becomes clear that even his excessive womanizing is the product of a profoundly low self-esteem, which the novel tells us is due mainly to his father's abusive attitude towards him during his childhood in Cuba. At the end of his life, Cesar realizes that his obsession with sex was the paradoxical result of his low self-esteem and of his very good looks. It was only because of the way many women admired him that he temporarily felt he was worth something.

Nestor's character functions in the narration as the regressive force because he is always longing for what he no longer has. His personality is almost exclusively dominated by a sense of loss. But in spite of his regressive role, Nestor manages to marry a girl named Delores in New York, with whom he has two children: Eugenio and Leticia. Delores is a very interesting woman who, unlike Nestor and Cesar, is eager to study and attend school. She firmly believes that her role as a mother and wife is not in conflict with her impulse to learn from books.

After Nestor's death, she remarries a quiet man who seems to tolerate her aspirations.

Particularly important to the novel is the role of Desi Arnaz, a Cuban musician who came to the United States in the 1940s, and became the most well-known Cuban entertainer in the U.S. when he created the TV program *I Love Lucy* with his wife, Lucille Ball. In the novel, Desi is the symbol of the American Dream for Latin people in the U.S., especially Latin musicians. But at the very end of the novel, both Desi and Eugenio recall the past and express sorrow for a life that does not give any meaning to the act of dying.

The richness of *The Mambo Kings Play Songs of Love* relies not only on the story of the two immigrant brothers, but on the enormous amount of details and descriptions of life in New York City during the 1950s, 1960s, and 1970s. During the 1950s (the period given the most attention in the novel), Nestor and Cesar meet a great number of Latin musicians who were residing in the Big Apple at that time. The novel uses historical events and the real names of public figures of the time to recreate the ambiance of not only New York City, but also of Cuba; the events of the Cuban Revolution of 1959, for example, and the resulting waves of exiles from Cuba to the U.S. are an important part of the second section of the novel.

The story of the Castillo brothers and their Mambo Kings orchestra coincides with a new, world-wide interest in the Latin music and culture centered in New York City. This fact gives special importance to the events narrated in the novel because the music of the Castillo brothers introduces the reader to an important historical period in the relationship between the American society and Latin ethnic groups. With the growing popularity of their music and culture that began in the 1950s, Latin Americans, and particularly Cubans, assumed a more prominent role within American society and throughout the world. *The Mambo Kings Play Songs of Love* both exemplifies and continues this prominence.

—Emilio Bejel

THE MAN THAT CORRUPTED HADLEYBURG
Story by Mark Twain, 1899

In 1898, while living in Vienna, Mark Twain wrote "The Man That Corrupted Hadleyburg." First published in *Harper's Magazine* in 1899 and in book form in 1900, this story drew relatively little notice at the time of its publication. In recent years, however, it has been anthologized as the embodiment of themes and issues that preoccupied Twain during the last two decades of his life. It has also spurred vigorous critical debate while gathering praise as one of Twain's greatest achievements in short fiction, with some scholars naming it among the greatest short stories ever written.

In "The Man That Corrupted Hadleyburg" Twain depicts a self-righteous American town nationally renowned for its honest reputation. To gain revenge for an unnamed offence suffered at the hands of a Hadleyburg citizen, a stranger presents to the town an elaborate scheme whereby he exposes the community as a bastion of hypocrisy and greed. The stranger brings about the fall of Hadleyburg by tempting with prospects of wealth its nineteen principal inhabitants, including an elderly couple named Mary and Edward Richards, who become the focus of the narrative. Ironically, the temptation that the stranger introduces, a sack of gilded lead coins, is as false as the hypocritical facade of piety that he exposes. Disgraced, the town changes its name and motto, and its inhabitants vow never to be caught "napping again."

The plot of this carefully structured story breaks into four distinct sequences of action, each sequence initiated by a letter from the scheming stranger. As one critic notes, the result is a unity of plot more reminiscent of **Edgar Allan Poe** than of a man who said, "Narrative should flow as the brook down through the hills and the leafy woodlands." Inspiration for Twain's plot has been traced to such disparate sources as Dante's *Inferno,* Milton's *Paradise Lost,* and Poe's "The Cask of Amontillado," as well as to the classical myth of Baucis and Philomen. While Twain offers no clear geographical reference whereby the actual identity of Hadleyburg can be determined, scholars have argued persuasively for Fredonia, New York, where Twain's mother and sister once lived and where Twain himself became embroiled in several disputes and in a business venture that contributed to his bankruptcy.

Although critics divide over whether "The Man That Corrupted Hadleyburg" should be read as a deterministic allegory or a moralistic parable, the story clearly reflects themes that Twain repeated in most of his later works. In this narrative, as in many of these works, Twain attacks mankind, and America in particular, with a characteristically cruel satiric condemnation of the idealistic, romantic themes of democracy, religion, free will, and honesty prevalent in the popular culture and literature of his day. Developing these themes, Twain unmasks the ritual hypocrisy he saw in mankind, motivated by greed, ignorance, and vacuous pride. Virtually always read as satanic, the stranger in the tale echoes Twain's fascination in later life with Satan, who also functions prominently in such works as *The Mysterious Stranger* and *Letters from the Earth.*

On its most general level "The Man That Corrupted Hadleyburg" illustrates the maxims that money is the "root of all evil" and that "everyone has a price." On a deeper level, Twain attacks the concept of democracy. Instead of nurturing the common good, the citizens of Hadleyburg care only for their individual welfare, and at the end of the story, after their supposed regeneration from self-delusion and pride into virtue and moral responsibility, they elect Harkness (i.e., "Darkness"), the most sinister of the town's leaders, to the United States Congress, where he can practice his graft not just on Hadleyburg but on the nation as a whole. Moreover, there seems little indication that the citizens of Hadleyburg have come to revere the memory of Goodson, who is typically read as a Christ figure (i.e., "God's son"). Instead, they change the town motto from "Lead Us Not into Temptation" to "Lead Us into Temptation," thereby, as one critic has noted, rewriting Christ's words on how to pray and thus placing their own prideful confidence in themselves above the Bible and God.

Underscoring both these levels of meaning is a re-enactment of the myth of Eden in the environment of post-Enlightenment America. In Hadleyburg, where the town hall is "clothed," "festooned," and "swathed" with flags, where the nineteen leading citizens are known as "the incorruptibles," and where babies from the cradle are shielded from all temptation, Twain creates an ironic American Eden, an Eden founded on the Calvinistic principles of privilege and hypocrisy that Twain so reviled, one whose outward reputation was more important than its underlying values. Into this New World Eden again comes Satan, who, in the hopes of settling an ancient grudge, tempts mankind to sin anew.

According to Twain, people are always destined to choose evil over good because, as the stranger in the tale surmises, it is in both the nature of humanity and in the scheme of things for them to do so. Greed, selfishness, and pride—qualities engrained, Twain tells us, in the very essence of mankind since the beginning—are the motivating factors that determine the outcome of events in Hadleyburg, as they do in most of Twain's later fiction. Nonetheless, it should be noted that some critics view the story as a "sober affirmation" of free will. They point out that at each juncture in the narrative the citizens have the opportunity to make moral choices and that if they would choose to abide by the honest principles they profess the stranger's plan would fail. Within this context, Satan is seen as an ironic savior who forces the town to examine its sin and withstand future temptations.

In any event, in "The Man That Corrupted Hadleyburg" Twain pokes a cruel thorn in the side of humanity as a needling reminder that appearance is almost never reality. This fine story provides considerable insight into the workings of Twain's imagination during the final phase of his remarkable career.

—Thomas E. Hockersmith and James A. Levernier

MARGARET FLEMING
Play by James A. Herne, 1890

Margaret Fleming, written in 1890, is the result of author James A. Herne's desire to bring truth of character, setting, and idea to American drama and theatre. Realism was well established in nondramatic literature but, apart from local color, hardly existed in American drama at all.

Herne was a man of the theatre—at various times a leading actor, stage manager for the scenic-realist director David Belasco, director, and adapter of works by Dickens and other realist novelists and European playwrights. In his article "Art for Truth's Sake in the Drama" (*Arena,* February 1897), Herne says that the influence of Dickens and others made him prefer characters who reveal their human qualities most naturally and easily through realistic action and dialogue. He thought that the drama should emphasize humanity and show the common aspects of everyday life. Drama, said Herne, must deal with some large truth "which is not always beautiful, but in art for Truth's sake it is indispensable."

In *Margaret Fleming,* a comfortable and innocent middle-class young wife finds the strength both to confront the fact that her husband has had a child by another woman and to make him accept her knowledge of it. The action of the play opens in the office of her husband, Philip Fleming, owner of a mill. Herne describes the physical scene in realistic detail. It is sunny at the beginning of the scene, gradually turns dark, and ends with a storm outside—a reflection of the emotional action within the room. Philip is an easygoing, congenial man of about thirty who has both command of his business and warm relations with his employees. There is realistic talk of manufacturing and supply problems— the stuff of everyday life. Joe Fletcher, a former foreman in the mill who was brought down by alcohol and now peddles elixirs, arrives and is warmly welcomed by Philip. Their bantering conversation makes it clear that Philip was an active philanderer in his past. After Joe leaves, Dr. Larkin enters. He condemns Philip as a moral leper and tells him he is the father of a son by a young working woman, Lena Schmidt, who is dying as a result of the difficult birth. Herne introduces his theme of moral determinism when the doctor says, "The girl's not to blame. She's a product

of her environment. Under present social conditions, she'd probably have gone wrong anyhow." After the doctor's exit, the scene ends quietly with Philip and the mill manager dealing with business matters.

In scene 2 we meet Margaret Fleming and see her very comfortable home. Their baby's nurse, Maria, turns out to be the sister of Lena Schmidt, although Maria doesn't know of Philip's involvement with Lena. Philip arrives and we learn that he has made arrangements to ensure the financial security of Margaret and their baby daughter, Lucy. The act ends on a warm if ironic domestic note as Margaret fusses over Philip because he got chilled in the rain.

Act 2 opens with Dr. Larkin examining Margaret's eyes. Before leaving, he warns Philip that Margaret has glaucoma and that any great physical or mental suffering can lead to blindness. Maria begs Margaret to visit her dying sister, who has been asking about the Fleming household. Before Margaret leaves, there is warm domestic interplay with Philip. Leaving instructions with the cook, Margaret exits, "overflowing with fun and animation."

Act 3 is set in the cottage in which Lena Schmidt has been living. The landlady tells Dr. Larkin that Lena has died. Margaret arrives and refuses to obey the doctor's orders to leave. Maria confronts her and reads her a letter from Lena to Philip. Stunned at first, Margaret confronts the truth of the matter and sends for Philip. She does not carry on about feelings; there are none of the sentimental platitudes common in the melodramas so popular at the time. When Lena's baby cries with hunger, Margaret holds him and then "scarcely conscious of what she is doing, . . . she unbuttons her dress to give nourishment to the child, when the picture fades away into darkness."

Act 4 is again set in the Fleming home. Philip has been gone for seven days and Margaret is now blind. The two babies are fine and Margaret is cheery in spite of everything. Philip returns looking "weary and broken." He is ashamed, but Margaret assures him that "you're a man—people will soon forget." She has changed, however; the "wife-heart" has gone out of her. Margaret has grown through her pain: "the old Margaret is dead, the truth killed her," she says. She will raise Philip's baby son. She tells Philip to go back to work, that they must put the dead past behind them and face "the living future." She does not, however, sentimentally promise that their marriage will be restored. Philip swears that he will earn Margaret's respect and then win her back. In a direct echo from Ibsen's *A Doll's House,* Margaret says, "That would be a wonderful thing." The play ends as Philip steps into the garden to see the two children. Margaret "gazes into the darkness and a serene joy illuminates her face."

Margaret Fleming largely succeeds as a realistic play despite such melodramatic devices as Margaret's blindness and the rainstorm in the first act, and the worn comic device of Joe Fletcher. Measured against the standards set by Ibsen and other European realists working at the time, *Margaret Fleming* does not delve deeply into its subject. Nevertheless, a play that dealt openly with adultery and its results and which featured a woman about to breast-feed a baby was beyond the pale for American theatregoers. Herne was never able to get a producer to mount the play. When he produced it himself on three separate occasions, it met with neither critical nor popular success.

—Terry Browne

MARGRET HOWTH
Novel by Rebecca Harding Davis, 1862

Pioneer realist and sociological fiction writer, Rebecca Harding Davis was ahead of her times. But her times caught up with her. With sincerest intentions, she succumbed to prevailing literary tastes, and she is read today as a piece of literary history. An examination of her writing is a study of the unresolved conflict between well-wrought intentions and popular expediency. Her first and best-known novel, *Margret Howth,* is the key to the dilemma.

When originally published in the *Atlantic Monthly* (October 1861 to March 1862) the novel was entitled *A Story of To-Day.* It was meant to be timely. The action takes place within three consecutive days in October 1860 plus a conclusion of a few weeks in December. "Let me tell you a story of To-Day" are the opening words of the novel. "You want something," she says to her readers, "to lift you out of this crowded, tobacco-stained commonplace, to kindle and chafe and glow in you. I want you to dig into this commonplace, this vulgar American life, and see what is in it. Sometimes I think it has a new and awful significance that we do not see." "This vulgar American life" entails the drudgery of factory labor, unemployment, racism, economic inequality, anti-feminism, and class prejudice. These are the issues that were fermenting in the time of the election of Abraham Lincoln, November 1860, and the secession of South Carolina in December. Rebecca Blaine Harding (she married L. Clarke Davis in 1863) observed the issues with unsurpassed foresight and understanding.

Her setting too is timely—a mill town on the Wabash River in southwestern Indiana, where the industry of the East meets the feudalism of the South in the experimental democracy of the West. The author describes abundantly the sounds and smells of the woolen mills and the contrasting woods and prairies of the environs.

Further, the author shows an awareness of contemporary Republican, Socialist, Communist, Comtean, Federalist, Fourierite, and Fichtean social philosophies—as well as American Transcendentalism and Democracy. These she presents through the mouths of her characters. Most of the story is seen through the minds of these characters, as the author moves skillfully from the point of view of one to that of another. Margret Howth is the sweet but strong American woman; Stephen Holmes is the self-reliant individualist; Dr. Knowles is the would-be philanthropic reformer; old Mr. Howth is the southern conservative but pathetically weak; Joe Yare is the renegade ex-slave, gone wrong because of his social environment. And little Lois, Joe's daughter—patterned after Charles Dickens's Little Nell and **Harriet Beecher Stowe**'s Little Eva—is the catalytic model of innocent Christian charity in a deformed body and retarded mind. These characters are authentic American types, but they become humanly real through their reactions to their time and place.

But there is more than specific time and place to *Margret Howth*—more than local color. The ideological and social backgrounds that the author belabors are meant to show the Yesterday of which "To-Day" is the result. Not only through the characters and settings does the author show the influence of the past on the present; she also speaks directly as omniscient author to the reader. Furthermore, she is concerned not only with Yesterday and To-Day but with Tomorrow: its "new and awful significance that we do not see." Creeds, ideologies, and programs notwithstanding, we are too often "blind to the prophecy written on the earth since God first bade it tell thwarted man of the great To-morrow." The

human lot in life is to suffer, with the only hope being in heavenly salvation.

Such is the gloomy message of *Margret Howth.* But the message is diluted and sentimentalized by the feminine novelistic manner that the author felt compelled to follow. In fact, she was literally compelled by her editor, James T. Fields, to provide an ending more "sunny" than that she had originally submitted. After the climactic fire that burns down the mill at the end of Chapter VII, the novel deteriorates into authorial apologies and liberal Christian explanations. Stephen Holmes has a change of heart; Lois dies but with a profusion of tears and blessings; Joe Yare is not prosecuted for his villainy and remains free; and Margret marries her Stephen.

—James C. Austin

THE MAXIMUS POEMS
Poems by Charles Olson, from 1953

Charles Olson was perhaps more admired during the 1950s and 1960s for "Projective Verse" and his other essays on poetic theory than for *The Maximus Poems,* increasingly regarded now as one of the principal achievements of postmodernist American poetry. But, as Marjorie Perloff and others have shown, those essays owe more to the theories of other writers than Olson's supporters may have realized or at least were willing to admit. (Perloff found echoes of **Ezra Pound, William Carlos Williams,** and others in "Projective Verse.") Furthermore, Olson's poetry at times seems to have very little to do with the theories. He insisted, for example, that the breath should somehow provide the measure for the line, but whose breath he had in mind is a mystery—certainly in any case not his own as his recorded readings repeatedly testify.

Olson's supporters have felt that *Maximus* exemplifies the theories given in the essays and that in effect the essays are an introduction to the poems. In fact, it may be better to see essays and poems as complementing each other: both are the expressions of one of the most intense, assured, and compelling voices in contemporary American poetry. What matters is not whether the ideas in the essays and, for that matter, *Maximus* are derivative, poorly developed, or simply wrong: the voice which speaks them is what is interesting, and it has a fire, conviction, and apparent sophistication that experimental poets among Olson's generation rarely possessed.

Poets have, of course, traditionally sustained a poetic voice within self-imposed prosodic limits and the limits of the language itself, its vocabulary, syntax, and so forth. Olson in effect asserted the power of the voice over the language and the right to reject such limits. That he tried to bolster what he was doing poetically by arguing that these limits reduce language to a flat, linear process that denies the actual nature of experience is beside the point. The problem was not theoretical but practical: a poetic voice which, like **Walt Whitman**'s, required possibilities with language greater than, or at least very different from, any required by his predecessors. In his essays. Olson spoke as if he were reinventing poetry for the future, but that is simply another expression of his sublimely self-confident, expansive voice. In fact, the poetry he was reinventing was largely for himself.

In *Maximus* from time to time Olson simply suppresses traditional grammar, particularly connectives (something he had learned to do from Pound), and tries to establish new relationships between words. Within the English language, of course, only certain relationships—"and," "is," "seems," and so forth—can be indicated. The placement of words on the page—their proximity to, or distance from, each other—takes on special importance in *Maximus* as a way of suggesting the degree or the nature of relationship between terms. Even when the syntax looks most conventional, it is tempered by this visual fact, and Maximus cannot be read as Olson intended it should unless it is seen in the format, even in the particular typeface, in which the book appeared when its three sections were published in 1960, 1968, and 1975, respectively, and which they retain in the complete single-volume edition published in 1983. Clearly Olson rejected one set of prosodic and grammatical limits only to encumber himself with another, but within those new limits he was able to unleash a fury of linguistic invention that makes reading *Maximus* as exciting as any other masterwork of postmodernist poetry.

Much of Olson's book is dense with antiquarian knowledge about Gloucester, Massachusetts (in which the poem is set), as well as with references to Olson's rather esoteric and exotic readings in archeology, anthropology, and mythology, George F. Butterick's *A Guide to the Maximus Poems of Charles Olson* is an important companion to the work for that reason, but it is by no means essential to share Olson's antiquarian and scholarly interests in order to read *Maximus.* The book, like the essays, moves essentially according to the power of the poet's voice, not his interests. Indeed the interests seem fundamentally excuses for the poet to keep talking. Whatever it was Olson had to say in his essays and in *Maximus,* it was never as interesting as the voice with which it was said.

In the best way, good talk is what makes *Maximus* a great work. As "Letter 3" near the very beginning of the work concludes:

> Isolated person in Gloucester, Massachusetts, I, Maximus,
> address you
> you islands
> of men and girls

—Edward Halsey Foster

THE MEMBER OF THE WEDDING
Novel by Carson McCullers, 1946

The Member of the Wedding reflects such central Carson McCullers themes as the universality of isolation and the desperation arising from the unavailability of love and belonging. These themes are suggested, stated, and restated in the fashion of a sonata throughout the three distinct parts of the novella, a simple third-person story of a precocious and lonely girl's four-day initiatory journey from uneasy adolescence to young adulthood.

Akin to a sonata's first movement, Part 1 introduces the primary theme. Frankie Addams is a gawky, motherless, twelve-year-old tomboy rejected by her girlish friends, little attended to by a preoccupied father, and thrown on her own incoherent resources during school-less August days in a Georgia town near the end of World War II. Feeling like an "unjoined person," Frankie has spent the summer moping around the kitchen with her two sole companions, the only other major characters: John Henry, her six-year-old cousin, and Berenice Sadie Brown, the black cook. These two represent different refrains of Frankie's separateness. Frankie broodingly yearns to be a member of something, a "we" person. When her brother returns on wartime furlough to marry a local girl, Frankie seizes the notion of leaving and staying with them after the wedding. "They," she exclaims, "are the we of me." Thus Part I's ending rhythmically changes to a tempo of joyfulness.

McCullers perceptively details the three major characters with sympathy, humor, and detachment. Articulate, quick-witted Frankie uses language revealing her quality of mind and sensibility: words like "puzzling" and "curious," and literary affectations like "I am sick unto death." She longs for the future, impatient with John Henry's concern for the present and Berenice's for the past. She scrutinizes the human condition and yet also fantasizes fulsomely. Berenice, who claims to be 35, speaks with a deliberate cadence suggesting stoical wisdom earned from hard experience and uses an array of folk-sayings ("I believe the sun has fried your brains"), combining commonsensical earthiness with flowery metaphorical language. She fails with her loving, firm attempts to recall Frankie to the limitations of reality. Her four-marriage history and her blue false eye symbolize attempts at flight from the predestined conditions of her birth and betray a yet indefatigable romantic strain. She loved her first husband Ludie until his death and then married three worthless men in turn because each reminded her of "pieces" of Ludie. Berenice has learned that love cannot be repeated and hesitates to marry an importunate suitor because he does not make her "shiver." John Henry, the trio's third loving member, is still a child and cannot yet comprehend Frankie's feelings nor articulate his own. The trio's relationship is epitomized at one point when they join different songs in a wailing harmony suggesting the "we" of their separate lives, and exemplifying one of many moments when musical references are used to express the characters' often unarticulated emotions.

In Part II, the main theme further develops in a changed rhythm. Convinced that she is to be a member of the wedding and thereby "connected" to others, Frankie formally declares herself as "F. Jasmine Addams." The day before the wedding, she announces it in town to strangers and feels a kinship with the world. Her exuberant mood changes when she returns to her unchanged friends in the kitchen. Then she voices her problem: that everyone has a "caught" condition of spiritual isolation despite the urgent desire to be related to others: ". . . what is it all about? People loose and at the same time caught. Caught and loose. All these things and you don't know what ties them up." Berenice, being black and knowing life, responds that all of us are caught: "We born this way or that way and we don't know why." Confessing that with Ludie she didn't feel so "caught" Berenice accentuates the thesis: that love while it endures enables a person to escape the isolation of self and, paradoxically, to acquire self-identity by connecting with something outside.

In Part III, the novel's last "movement" are the climax and denouement. After the wedding, Frankie's dream of joining the couple ends predictably: she is pulled from the wedding car and hauled home. A "coda" concludes: some weeks later, Frankie (now called Frances) has turned 13, acquired a girlfriend, and forgotten her disillusionment. She has also forgotten John Henry, now dead from meningitis, and seems unconcerned that Berenice is leaving to marry a man who does not remind her of Ludie. Despite her new feelings of membership, Frankie remains an unjoined person out of touch with those who were closest to her. Yet the novella ends on a positive note: as adolescence passes, our individual aloneness is leavened by the recognition that human kinship is a fact of life.

This small, affecting portrait of adolescent angst skillfully recreates its compelling protagonist's mind and emotions through a simple plot and highly evocative poetical style. McCullers employs strong powers of narrative description and characterization to examine her theme, and communicates her vision directly, honestly, and lyrically.

—Christian H. Moe

MOBY-DICK
Novel by Herman Melville, 1851

"Is it I, God, or who, that lifts this arm," cries the mighty and suffering Ahab in his fearless pursuit of the white whale that has mutilated both his body and spirit. In Herman Melville's *Moby-Dick* Ahab would deprive himself of all human comfort and travel to the ends of the earth if he could just confront the seeming inscrutability of evil, that "malign thing that has plagued and frightened man since time began," that "mauls" and "destroys" and leaves man with half a body or half a soul. He is incapable of accepting the injustice of a godless and purposeless universe in which man plays no role in the distribution of good and evil.

Less noble yet courageous men accuse him of madness, egotism, and godlessness ("God, God is against thee, old man," cries the decent but prosaic Starbuck). Like his namesake, the wicked Old Testament king, and like Jonah, Ahab has defied the traditional godhead in his rejection of what is presumably the natural order. And early on, the character Elijah predicts a cursed voyage. But Ahab is not to be judged by ordinary standards or local superstition; he is already a man of exemplary reputation when the book begins, having enlisted an excellent crew from every corner of the world; later, under the greatest of extremities, each man remains loyal to him. Throughout, Melville describes him as spiritual heir of the greatest mythic and historical figures—Prometheus, Agamemnon, Oedipus, Job, Lear, Satan, Faust, Perseus, Adonis, and Jesus. Now, "old and bowed" and like "Adam, staggering beneath the piled centuries since Paradise," Ahab is magnificent in his rage for truth. He must understand his place in the scheme of things and demonstrate that man may indeed assert his will in the vast cosmos:

All visible objects . . . are but as pasteboard masks. But in each event . . . some unknown but still reasoning thing puts forth the moulderings of its features from behind the unreasoning mask. If man will strike, strike through the mask! How can the prisoner reach outside except by thrusting through the wall? To me, the white whale is that wall . . . . Sometimes I think there's naught beyond. But 'tis enough. He tasks me; he heaps me; I see in him outrageous strength, with an inscrutable malice sinewing it. That inscrutable thing is chiefly what I hate; and be the White Whale agent, or be the white whale principal, I will wreak that hate upon him. Talk not to me of blasphemy man; I'd strike the sun if it insulted me . . . . Fair play . . . . Who's over me? Truth hath no confines.

What Ahab comes to see, of course, is the "naught beyond."

The narrator with whom, interestingly, the reader also identifies, provides the means by which issues of evil, power, responsibility, and control—all the ethical issues relevant to Ahab's acts

and the universe at large—are evaluated; he is the obsessively moral and thinking mind, the meditative foil against which Ahab acts out his grand compulsion. From Ishmael come speculations on many subjects, and like his captain and the sea itself, Ishmael lives in a state of eternal transformation, in his own quest for truth. (His final vision must have been blasphemous to both the transcendental and orthodox views of Melville's day: "I have written a wicked book," Melville confessed to **Nathaniel Hawthorne**, "and feel as spotless as a lamb.")

An outsider and a loner, not unlike Ahab, Ishmael has his own quest. Is there, as he initially says, a pattern in the universe, where every act has a corresponding significance in nature, as well as in the higher realm of ultimates and absolutes: "O Nature, and O Soul of man! how far beyond all utterance are your linked analogies! Not the smallest atom stirs or lives on matter, but has its cunning duplicate in mind." We witness the love and trust Ishmael gives to the cannibal Queequeg and are seduced by his honesty and magical recordings of the plenitude and significance of life around him and, most importantly, his adoration of the captain. Always counterpointing his innocence and discourse, of course, are Ahab's increasing passion and single-minded goal. Melville maintains a subtle balance between Ishmael's book knowledge and Ahab's intuitive and experiential wisdom. Ishmael's small tome on the natural history of the genus whale is merely the formal classification of Ahab's vast understanding of the sea, including, for example, even the white whale's most secret swimming patterns.

What Ishmael comes to learn, or at least observe, and what Ahab will not accept is that evil and good, like order and disorder, exist both in man and in nature; furthermore, no purposive or malicious force marks the individual for either. Moby Dick, ubiquitous and eternal, scarred like Ahab and similarly majestic and terrible, is in fact the colorless neutrality of nature—beautiful, indifferent, massive, brutal, erotic, and protean, the color of death and atheism but also the color of purity and innocence, at one time all colors and a tabula rasa, the benign indifference of the universe, the universe without man or God, the rainbow without color, the absence of meaning. ("Is it that by its indefiniteness it shadows forth the heartless voids and immensities of the universe and stabs us from behind with the thought of annihilation, when beholding the white depths of the milky way?") To Ahab, this is unacceptable. There must be some way man may assert himself and touch or restore order to this world. To accept nature's moral neutrality is to rob it of both its majesty and terror. One ought to be able to place God on trial.

How, then, does one deal with Ahab's increasing madness, with his sacrifice of the crew, and with his willing denial of humanity—with, as Lewis Mumford expresses it, his battle against evil with "power instead of love," whereby he becomes the image of the thing he hates? Has Ahab actually lost his humanity in the very act of vindicating it? Or may one argue that Ahab is all the more magnificent for rejecting his humanity in order to fulfill his task?

Clearly, Ahab does not renounce all human connectedness, and the impersonality which he affects is accompanied by great pain. Melville makes it clear that he suffers for all mankind, "with crucifixion in his face," barely sleeping "with clenched hands . . . with his own bloody nails in his palms." At one of several points, when his feelings overwhelm his control, he "dropped a tear into the sea," about which Ishmael remarks, "nor did all the Pacific contain such wealth as that one wee drop."

Yet when Starbuck warns him to desist—"See Moby Dick seeks thee not. It is thou, thou that madly seekest him!"—Ahab acknowledges that renunciation of all human claims will alone serve his purpose. He speaks of the loneliness of his sacrifice, and he would save Starbuck and the ship:

> When I think of this life I have led; the desolation of solitude it has been; the . . . exclusiveness . . . oh weariness! heaviness! . . . Aye, I widowed that poor girl when I married her . . . . And then the madness, the frenzy . . . . Old Ahab has furiously, foamingly chased his prey . . . . Why this strife of the chase? . . . Hear, brush this old hair aside; it blinds me, that I seem to weep . . . . I feel deadly faint, bowed, and humped . . . . God! God!—crack my heart!—stave my brain!—mockery! mockery! bitter, bitter, biting mockery of grey hairs . . . Close! stand close to me . . . . I see my wife and my child in thine eye. No, no; stay on board, on board!—lower not when I do.

Like Jesus, Oedipus, Prometheus, and the many other figures with whom he is compared, Ahab knows that he cannot dissipate what must be superhuman will with human emotion. Neither can he reconcile himself to a fate he cannot understand, avoid, or control; he must fight every consolation if he is to retain the courage of his task and face that which he most fears. That he knows this claims his humanity and that he fully understands its consequences makes him superior to his fate: "I know that of me which thou knowest not of thyself, oh, thou omnipotent. . . . Through thee, thy flaming self, my scorched eyes do dimly see."

Ahab dies with self-knowledge and unmitigated hatred at the horror he has touched. He also knows that there is a pattern beyond human comprehension and that all of man's acts finally end in meaningless death: "We are turned round and round in this world, like yonder windlass, and Fate is the handspike. . . . We all sleep at last on the field . . . [and] rust amid greenness, as last year's scythes flung down, and left in the half-cut swaths."

There is a despair at the end of the novel, a sense of hopelessness beyond pain and feeling. As at the end of *The Sound and the Fury,* there is a kind of mindless serenity as the "orphan" Ishmael is picked up by the mourning-mother emblem, the ship Rachel, having borne witness to the majestic and demonic, to the futile effort of man's trying to understand his world, and the tale signifying nothing. Ishmael has seen Job in the whirlwind and will return victorious only in an art which, like that of the Ancient Mariner or Conrad's Marlow, will haunt and transfix his audience in some of our most magnificent language. Ishmael must forever relate Ahab's majestic reflections:

> But if the great sun move not of himself; but is as an errand-boy in heaven; nor one single star can revolve, but by some invisible power; how then can this one small heart beat; this one small brain think thoughts; unless God does that beating, does that thinking, does that living, and not I . . . . Look! see yon Albacore! who put it into him to chase and fang that flying fish! Where do murderers go, man! Who's to doom, when the judge himself is dragged to the bar! But it is a mild, mild wind, and a mild looking sky; and the air smells now, as if it blew from a far-away meadow . . . .

—Lois Gordon

MODERN CHIVALRY
Fiction by Hugh Henry Brackenridge, 1792-1805 (and later revisions)

Hugh Henry Brackenridge's *Modern Chivalry* is generally called a novel, but it stretches any accepted definition of that genre. Rather, it is a rambling, fictive diary of the development of democracy in the United States from the administration of George Washington to that of James Madison. It is also fine and sometimes raucous satire.

The structure of *Modern Chivalry* is simple on the one hand but loose and endless on the other. Simply, it is the story of the picaresque adventures of Captain John Farrago and his Irish servant Teague O'Regan. Patterned after Don Quixote and Sancho Panza, they travel geographically, politically, and socially around Brackenridge's western Pennsylvania. Teague gets into scrapes that the Captain has to help him out of. This leads to moral philosophizing by Farrago, followed by "reflections" and "observations" by the author Brackenridge himself. Such episodes, complete in themselves, are the format that the author repeated for 23 years. "Sir," Brackenridge is reported to have said in 1790, "I could set down and write a piece of humor for fifty-seven years without being in the least exhausted."

It is a matter of textual and bibliographical judgment even to establish the body of work that we can call *Modern Chivalry.* The best modern text (edited by Claude Milton Newlin, 1937) "is an exact reproduction of the first editions of the various parts of *Modern Chivalry,* except that it has been checked against the revised text of 1815 for the correction of misprints in the first editions." The "first editions" include seven volumes published separately between 1792 and 1815. The 1815 text is a collection containing revisions, deletions, and additions. The repetitive plot is similar to that of the comic strip or the soap opera. It can go on forever—a shaggy-dog story.

The formula permits the author to deal with all the topics of the times: law, education, religion, Indian treaties, marriage, romantic love, universities, racism, ethnicity, medicine, philosophical societies, the theater, popular oratory, social snobbery. He also deals with the mud and muck of the highways and the taverns of the everyday life of the times.

The consistent thesis is Madisonian democracy. Brackenridge was a classmate of James Madison at Princeton. *Modern Chivalry* should be required reading, after *The Federalist* papers, for any student of American government. "There is in every government a patrician class, against whom the spirit of the multitude naturally militates: And hence a perpetual war; the aristocrats endeavoring to detrude the people, and the people contending to obtrude themselves. And it is right it should be so; for by this fermentation, the spirit of democracy is kept alive."

Perhaps Brackenridge's greatest claim to fame is his literary style. In the Introduction to the first volume of *Modern Chivalry,* he boasts, with self-irony:

> It has always appeared to me, that if some great master of stile should arise, and without regarding sentiment, or subject, give an example of good language in his composition, which might serve as a model for future speakers and writers, it would do more to fix the orthography, choice of words, idiom of phrase, and structure of sentence, than all the Dictionaries and Institutes that have been ever made.

Brackenridge's style is brilliant. It is based on the classical Greek and Roman authors with whom he was proudly familiar, but even more it is based on the styles of Swift, Addison, and Fielding. "It may be said of satire, what was said of anger by some philosopher, It never pays the service it requires. It is your scratching, rump-tickling people, that get into place and power. I never knew any good come of wit and humor yet." It may be said of Brackenridge that his wit and humor are good today if we can take it.

—James C. Austin

MURDER IN THE CATHEDRAL
Play by T. S. Eliot, 1935

When, in the 1930s, T.S. Eliot decided to become a poet in (if not really of) the theatre, he started first with an "Aristophanic" fragment and a pageant. The relevance of *Sweeney Agonistes* (1932) and *The Rock* (1934) to *Murder in the Cathedral* has not been as much addressed as it ought to have been in the masses of criticism that have greeted *Murder in the Cathedral,* as (in fact) almost everything else by Eliot. In the long run his place in theatrical history will be for the children's book that served as the inspiration for the smash musical *Cats* and not for his imitation drawing-room comedies (*The Family Reunion, The Cocktail Party, The Confidential Clerk, The Elder Statesman*)—and for *Murder in the Cathedral,* which well may outlast all the rest of his drama because of its poetic rhythms (like *Sweeney Agonistes*) and for its pageantry (like *The Rock*).

First, rhythm. In 1936 Eliot gave a lecture in Dublin (not published until 1985 in the *Southern Review*), "The Tradition and the Practice of Poetry." It centered on the subject of rhythm and asserted that "the great revolutions of poetry are revolutions in the sense of rhythm." He said that "Wordsworth and Coleridge initiated a new age—not because their ideas were original, but because their rhythms were a departure from tradition." In *Sweeney Agonistes* he had given jazzy, modern, syncopated rhythms to his satirical comments on the lives of apenecks. In *Murder in the Cathedral* he perfected a kind of cadence of reason, a theatrical but philosophical-sounding rhythm of what one might call poetic-philosophical conversation. It gives a power to his play which puts it head and shoulders over *The Family Reunion* in theatrical effectiveness. Having experienced *Murder in the Cathedral* in performance, even those more or less baffled by the message will inevitably recall some of the impressive cadences of its great arias and exchanges. The rhythms lend it a kind of majesty, a quieter but also more dignified and intellectual evocativeness on the stage than even Marlowe's famous "mighty line." The verse gives a shape and a sound to the speeches (and they are speeches more than dialogue) that make the speakers larger and more memorable than ordinary people. Charwomen turn into Greek choruses, soldiers into philosophers, an archbishop into Everyman. It is all in the noble rhythms of their words. The play has a music that functions rather like the sound track of a film. It colors the words and interprets for us the situations. It assists in putting ideas into emotional contexts. As movie music often can make non-actors look as if they are acting, so the rhythms of the poetry often make *Murder in the Cathedral* seem to be happening, rather than simply being presented. The rhythms make a grand subject and grand historical figures grander, just as the archbishop in cope and mitre

looks like more than a man. Afraid of Eliot's reputation for profundity (or obscurity), audiences went to performances of *Murder in the Cathedral* dutifully and came away delighted. The rhythm of the verse, even more than any of the ideas, entranced audiences. They discovered *Murder in the Cathedral* is a musical. Like *Cats,* it has a vast and spectacular set and plenty of stimulating music.

The second point concerns not audiences but spectators. *Murder in the Cathedral* was initially meant to celebrate a church festival at Canterbury, to be a kind of super village pageant. What Eliot offered was far more than anyone could have expected, but it was and remains essentially more an historical pageant than a play. Like a High Mass, *Murder in the Cathedral* conveys messages through ritual and celebrates a martyrdom and salvation. It has a priest and acolytes, poetic chants and responses, and a sermon (Thomas à Becket's Christmas sermon, in prose). The sanctuary is the stage for a liturgical drama and all the Christian symbols are used to work on our visual sense while the poetry excites what Eliot called our "auditory imagination." Like an opera, the play has recitatives and arias, even verbal leitmotifs.

But it is more than a ceremony or a musical extravaganza. It is a well-ordered combination, within the overall religious setting which underlines the centrality of Christianity in western culture, of diverse dramatic traditions. It is a Greek tragedy, and the hubris of the hero is a central concern. It reminds us how the liturgy gave birth to the drama in Christian churches and later on pageant wagons. It resembles a medieval Morality play; its theme is the search for sainthood, and among its participants are embodiments of abstractions such as Worldly Pleasure, Temporal Power, Spiritual Power, and Eternal Glory, while St. Thomas is a more than usually self-examining Everyman, superior to other Morality protagonists in that he is no mere passive and unthinking victim. It is a problem play, with conflicted persons and reasons and rationalizations and a social message. It is a psychological drama that rises above mere didacticism or case study; at its center is a man torn between pride and humility, driven in some sense to suicide while of unsound mind and in another sense fully understanding even such subtleties as how one can do "the right deed for the wrong reason." It is a political play and a significant advance over closet drama in a direction more like that of Yeats than of such later proponents of the verbal pyrotechnic as (say) Christopher Fry. It is a true milestone in the poetic drama and also the drama of ideas, arguably the locus classicus of Eliot as "classicist in literature, royalist in politics, Anglo-Catholic in religion."

Murder in the Cathedral grapples with moral and spiritual values in a world where doubt has replaced dogma, in an Age of Anxiety which has replaced an Age of Faith. In this play Eliot is as Stephen Spender reports he always was in personal conversation: dogged and diffident at once, "gravely insistent." For once he seems able to be more outspoken as (to use Eric Thompson's phrase) a "philosophical poet in an age of disbelief," and, perhaps because his subject is a man examining his own belief and misgivings, he speaks out more clearly than he does in that marvelous poetry which (E.M. Forster once trenchantly remarked) Eliot wrote with his cards held too close to his chest, like a man who has seen something terrible but is not going to tell us, who will not let us "in" lest our presence increase the "barrenness" and desolation he suffers. Many of Eliot's other poetic works say to us that "that is not it, that is not it at all," and even when he promises to come back and tell us all, he does not. Harry Puckett, writing of Eliot's poetry in *New England Quarterly* (June 1971) says: "His people are surrounded by a world of talking birds, cryptic messages, telling images, and words unheard . . . knowledge latent, veiled, or hovering, often in some sense silent or unheeded, commonly available only through images."

For once, in his first important verse play, Eliot is able to deliver complex but clear messages to the eye and the ear, to improve the static into a tableau and make even the ancient fabric of Canterbury cathedral, or any church in whose sanctuary the play is mounted, speak to us. His own conflicts instead of preventing him from expressing himself straightforwardly rather contribute to the deep psychological soul-searching his characters undergo, and their attitudes toward self and certainty enrich the drama.

It is quite possible that J. B. Priestley was right when he criticized Eliot's devotion to a "Church that is timid and timeserving," but at least it produced in *Murder in the Cathedral* an honest and bold, timely and useful discussion of the place of faith in the modern world. If Shaw was right, we may not be ready for our saints. But in Becket as Eliot presents him we have as modern a man as anyone could wish, and questions that are timeless.

—Leonard R. N. Ashley

THE MURDERS IN THE RUE MORGUE
Story by Edgar Allan Poe, 1841

"The Murders in the Rue Morgue," published in *Graham's Magazine* in April 1841, was the first of what Edgar Allan Poe called his tales of ratiocination. It is now generally regarded as the first detective story. Both descriptions are somewhat misleading.

Poe fathered the detective story while engaged in something slightly different. Reading the tale in the light of subsequent detective fiction, we see so many features which were to become staples of the later genre—the locked-room mystery, the bungling police, the amateur investigator with his brilliant deductions and his marvelling companion—that it needs an effort to see that detection is almost a by-product of Poe's scheme, the point where two of his interests happen to coincide. The essential ingredients of "The Murders in the Rue Morgue" are an interest in logic and ratiocination on the one hand, and a fascination with the violent, sensational, and macabre on the other. When they combine, a mystery gets solved. But Poe's hero, Dupin, is not a detective as such, nor is that term used since detectives did not exist when the tale was written. And the elements which Poe called "grotesque and arabesque" contribute at least as much to the tale's impact as the element of ratiocination.

Poe begins with a disquisition on the analytical faculty which, though the "very soul and essence of method," brings about results so astonishing that they have the "air of intuition." In fact the tale which follows is the exact reverse: though the essence of imaginative invention, it has, as Poe cheerfully admitted elsewhere, an "*air* of method." Already we are being elaborately bamboozled.

More philosophical irony follows, and logic becomes the medium of mystification. Juggling with terms, the narrator argues the near-absurdity that chess taxes merely the attention, whereas draughts challenges the "higher powers of the reflective intellect." (The "higher powers" turn out to be the ability to fool an opponent.) We see the trick, but not how it is done; it has been well said that Poe's address to the reader is that of a hypnotist or a stage magician. Then comes an account of whist-playing, again in terms of gamesmanship. Central to all these—chess, draughts, whist—is the idea of a contest. Though they are offered as analogies for the tale which follows, nothing could be less appropriate: Dupin, the hero, will face no battle of wits with an antagonist. The analogies really point to the contest between Poe and his reader—a contest in which Poe holds all the cards as he dupes us into a sense of the uncanny and then springs his surprise explanation. Poe is aware of all this more acutely than some later practitioners of the story-written-backwards. As he said elsewhere, "where is the ingenuity of unravelling a web which you yourself (the author) have woven for the purpose of unravelling?" The tale mocks its readers' credulity and its own dubious methods.

After softening us up with discourse, Poe turns to narration. The scene shifts to Paris, the goal of many an American reader's cultural ambitions. The philosophical adept to whom we have listened now becomes a tyro dumbfounded by the brilliance of Dupin. And the familiar properties of gothic begin to take shape. Dupin and the narrator live in darkened rooms in their "grotesque" mansion and emerge at night, emphasizing their alienation from the social world. Interestingly, the murder victims, Madame L'Espanaye and her daughter, also live "an exceedingly retired life" in darkened rooms, and these parallels between hero and victims have encouraged allegorical and Freudian interpretations.

The episode where Dupin follows his silent companion's train of thought and then breaks in upon it is crucial in its appeal: what seems at first to be preternatural power of insight, compelling the reader's admiration, turns out when explained to be so simple that we all feel capable of it. Thus the promise of God-like power through the exercise of pure mind is held out to us all. But Dupin is called a "Bi-Part Soul . . . a double Dupin—the creative and the resolvent." The analytical rationalist is also the intuitive, visionary artist: in that sense Dupin is Poe himself, though a Poe translated into a fantasy society where his talents become all-powerful instead of superfluous.

The rest of the tale—the discovery of the mutilated corpses in the locked room, the evidence of witnesses, and Dupin's reasoning that the "criminal" is an escaped orang-outang—is a study in the refinements of the macabre. Poe used the orang-outang elsewhere. Here it is satisfying and necessary because when Dupin triumphantly reveals his deduction of its presence the grotesque and the rational coincide perfectly. The formal language of the inquest ("The head of the deceased was entirely separated from the body") and Dupin's appearance of inhuman rationality (he undertakes the investigation for "amusement") give a new twist to horror by narrating it deadpan. Critics have variously detected flaws in the details and logic of the story, but none of them matters much, especially when logic itself has already been so ironized: the illusion is all. Poe took pains to perfect it, revising details so as to make the ape's feat of swinging itself in at the window more credible.

Dupin was a central conception and Poe used him in further stories. Aristocratic, Romantic, alienated, Dupin was the progenitor of all those figures whose attraction to the intellectual reader consists in flattering the illusion that the reclusive thinking man can set the world to rights in occasional forays and can become what Conan Doyle calls Holmes, society's last court of appeal. And the choice of orang-outang as "villain" reduces crime to "natural" behavior, an irruption into an otherwise stable social order: violence is explained only to the extent of detecting the details of its occurrence, and any further social enquiry is closed off before it can begin. Poe's legacy to detective fiction was not taken up for three decades, but then, for good and ill, it became ubiquitous.

—R. J. C. Watt

MY ÁNTONIA
Novel by Willa Cather, 1918

The dual character of Willa Cather's *My Ántonia* is suggested by its title, for it is at once the story of Ántonia Shimerda, a Bohemian emigre to the state of Nebraska in the 1880s, and the story of the narrator character, who creates his own image of Ántonia. The novel is cast as Jim Burden's reminiscent re-creation of his childhood and youth. Ántonia figures both as a childhood companion and as a symbol of values that Jim retrospectively associates with the frontier experience that he has left behind. The novel changes character somewhat depending on whether one reads it as Ántonia's story or as Jim Burden's, but these threads merge initially in the depiction of the pioneering life shared by easterners removed to the frontier and by Scandinavian, Russian, and Bohemian emigres.

Jim Burden, orphaned in Virginia, arrives at Black Hawk (a fictional counterpart to Red Cloud, Nebraska) by the same train that brings the Shimerda family. The superb Book I of the novel counterpoints the more stable, established homesteading lifestyle of Burden's grandparents, a patriarchal lifestyle, against the animalistic grovelling struggle for survival of the penniless Shimerdas during their first winter in a sod hut. Cather depicts the hardships of the struggle to endure the weather and to master the land. She renders characters in silhouette against vast landscapes of undulating red grass and limitless horizons, or tunneling through snow to feed livestock. Animals are both competitors and companions to human beings in their solitude. Human and animal predators operate by the same rules. Suicide, murder, and madness are the lot of those least fit to survive. The quintessential grotesque image of the cost of the struggle is that of Ántonia's father's corpse, frozen to the ground in his own blood after he has shot himself, his coat and neckcloth and boots removed beforehand and carefully laid by for the survivors. Cather frequently uses a vivid episode or image such as this one to establish the mood of her story.

The dividedness between Jim's and Ántonia's fortunes becomes more explicit after their early childhood because of their disparate places in the social hierarchy. Removed from the farm to Black Hawk, the Burdens enter the establishment community, respectable, conventional, and dull in Jim's esteem, but the immigrants are hired girls, waitresses, and laundresses. It is characteristic of Cather to perceive the small-minded small town as the antagonist of individual enterprise and initiative, so that in Books II-IV the impulse to escape is a central motif of the novel. Jim flees to the university at Lincoln and eventually to Harvard and law school. Lena Lingard, a Norwegian girl, denigrates the farm and the family, and becomes a successful and celibate dressmaker in Lincoln. Tiny Soderball, who had worked in the hotel, makes her fortune feeding prospectors during the Klondike gold rush, and later invites Lena to join her in San Francisco. Even Ántonia has the prospect of escaping drudgery on the farm and domestic servitude in town through her romance with a railway conductor, but deceived and deserted in Denver, she returns to the farm and her taskmaster brother Ambrosch.

The land mastered, she must now overcome social opprobrium. Her success in doing so is celebrated by Jim in the concluding Book V of the novel, where he makes a nostalgic visit home and heroizes Ántonia as a sort of earth mother or fertility goddess. Twenty years have passed. Married within the Bohemian community, Ántonia has produced ten or eleven children and presides over a flourishing household: "She lent herself to immemorial human attitudes which we recognize by instinct as universal and true," Jim muses. "She was a battered woman now, not a lovely girl; but she still had that something which fires the imagination, could still stop one's breath for a moment by a look or a gesture that somehow revealed the meaning in common things. She had only to stand in the orchard, to put her hand on a little crab tree and look up at the apples, to make you feel the goodness of planting and tending and harvesting at last . . . . It was no wonder that her sons stood tall and straight. She was a rich mine of life, like the founders of early races." The adulatory retrospective attitude displayed here is typical of Jim's voice throughout the novel. Romantic, nostalgic, and unfulfilled in life, he celebrates the vitality and fruitfulness of the pioneering era as a lost Edenic world. In both the impulse to flee Black Hawk and the nostalgic retrospect in his enduring reverence for the pioneers, Jim's career and attitudes are indicative of Cather's own. But as a male character he has been perceived as being sexually ambivalent in his attitude toward the immigrant girls, escapist and regressive in the romanticizing of his own childhood.

—Jean Frantz Blackall

THE NAKED AND THE DEAD
Novel by Norman Mailer, 1948

Norman Mailer's *The Naked and the Dead* is a naturalistic novel remarkable for its critical examination of liberal-leftist ideology, and, oddly, for Mailer's discovery, as he wrote, that violence was more deeply appealing to him than politics. It is an impressive war novel, one to be grouped with the best written by Americans: *Guard of Honor, From Here to Eternity, Catch-22*.

The structure of the novel reveals more art than one might expect from a naturalistic writer's first book. As we know, the theory of naturalism dictates random movement governed by chance and inclusion of the totality of experience, but the practice of fiction imposes the task of selection and emphasis. Mailer shrewdly holds these mutually exclusive demands in equilibrium. He gives the appearance of random movement while at the same time imposing limitations that make for order. The accidental imperatives of combat seem to govern movement of the troops in the book; the focus shifts back and forth from men to officers for no apparent reason; and time shifts are abrupt. All this conveys the impression of planlessness. Yet the entire action takes place on an island, which means that, confined this way, the action is self-limiting. The story begins with the invasion of the Japanese-held island and ends with the defeat of the enemy and conquest of the island. This successfully completed campaign constitutes an action of classical unity. The random freedom of movement within the story turns out to be in fact movement defined and controlled by the setting and by the directed progress of the story from the beginning to the preordained end. That end is achieved not only in the ironic victory of General Cummings, in command of the American forces, but also in the victory of Cummings and Sergeant Croft over Lieutenant Hearn and Red Valsen. These pairings give us the ideological conflict in the novel which also provides a structural principle, the first two men representing militarism and proto-fascism and the second two liberalism and anti-authoritarianism. In his treatment of this conflict Mailer shows how thematic statement and an idea of order are mutually interdependent.

The naturalistic bias in the novel appears early in Mailer's conventional view of Mount Anaka, on the island, as indifferent to the designs of men. And throughout the novel nature is a barrier and obstacle to human purposes simply because it is indifferent. It is the motiveless malignancy of nature, in the form of jungle, hornets, mountain, that frustrates man's will and action, as the failed effort to climb Mount Anaka illustrates. This natural intransigence seems to indicate Mailer's belief in the absence of any benevolent guiding power in the cosmos.

Mailer's view of man, influenced by Marxist thought, is likewise naturalistic. Man in the mass, as in the army, is typical, not individual man upon whom social forces exert determining and conditioning forces. Martinez, the Mexican American sergeant specifically likened to Pavlov's dog, is conditioned to insecurity and fear by his status in American society. For Mailer, the quality of human existence produced by that society is rich in racial and religious tensions, haunted by the possibilities for fascism, scarred by economic insecurity, and rife with sexual frustrations.

These views, applied to the island war, give us a world in which nobody wins. General Cummings's victory is not the result of his brilliance but of the blundering effort of a stupid subordinate and of unanticipated Japanese weakness; in short, of accident. Effort, will, skill, mind, life itself are made to appear meaningless. But Cummings and Croft, the instrument of the General's theories, do win the ideological conflict. The General's army represents the concentration and apotheosis of power which kills individualism and arranges all men on the fear ladder. It induces anxieties, depersonalizes all men, and robs them of their beings. It is a paradigm for the authoritarian, stratified society that will emerge as postwar fascism in America. Opposed to these two are Hearn, whose liberalism is a compound of guilt and hesitation over commitment; whose egalitarianism is sentimental; and whose thinking is confused; and Valsen, who has only a romantic, rebellious anarchism to fall back upon. The organization of power represented by fascism first corrupts and then kills Hearn, and it breaks Valsen.

Mailer began the novel as a Marxist-influenced liberal-leftist who discovered, as he wrote, that he was responding to his characters at some point beneath the level of ideology. Sensing that his political ideology is bankrupt, he discovers in himself a terrifying appetite for violence. He faces the possibility that the worshipers of force, like Croft the war lover, will triumph in our world and that he may acquiesce in their victory. Thus Mailer engages in self-discovery, as he writes the novel, coming to terms with the deepest imperatives of his own being and anticipating the themes of his later books.

—Chester E. Eisinger

NATIVE SON
Novel by Richard Wright, 1940

If, as the black activist and educator **W.E.B. Du Bois** asserted, "the problem of the Twentieth Century is the problem of the color line," Richard Wright's *Native Son* is the central novel of the time—

at least in the United States—for it remains after its first, explosive appearance, the most powerful novel on the subject yet written. Writing of the book's social impact, the critic Irving Howe claimed in a well-known pronouncement that because of *Native Son* "American culture was changed forever . . . . It made impossible a repetition of the old lies." Wright had "brought out into the open, as no one ever had before, the hatred, fear, and violence that have crippled and may yet destroy our culture."

Not that the book has received unanimous critical approval. In fact, its enduring vitality is nowhere better demonstrated than by the critical controversy it still engenders along artistic and ideological lines: it has been attacked as being unfair to whites, and it has been criticized for its inadequacies in treating black life— though most frequently it is praised for the honesty and penetration of its vision of racial polarities. Some accused Wright of infusing the book too greatly with a left-wing perspective, while Ben Davis, Jr., an official of the Communist Party of America, wrote in a party publication that communism in the book was represented by atypical members with distorted ideas "which far from adequately" expressed Communist Party policy. Seemingly endless debate has focused on the merits (or shortcomings) of Wright's art, though increasingly few serious commentators question the novel's compelling drive and force.

Bigger Thomas represents in *Native Son* a black man (ultimately any human being) trapped under the oppressive weight of a history of cruelty, oppression, and violence that he had no role in creating. His ignorant, cowardly, hostile, and ultimately murderous behavior seems completely determined by the history of inequality and mutilated opportunity into which he is born. He is the worst-case product of an unjust society, and he seems as stuck in his character as a person's body would be fixed by something like a mine cave-in. Yet Bigger escapes his trap in the most shocking of ways: he kills two women (though tried only for the murder of the first, who is white), flees the police, is captured and convicted in racist proceedings—and accepts the responsibility for his acts. He does this because he discovers that they have liberated him from his passive, unknowing acceptance of fate. Therefore, he says, what he did must have been good. The killings, and what they came to mean to him, brought him to life.

Naturally this conclusion, its philosophic implications and worth, its suitability as a means of self-knowledge and assertion, have been examined from many angles. Wright was not, of course, crudely advocating murder as invariably a legitimate means of self-expression. But he did seem to advocate the necessity of violence after certain instances of extreme oppression to break the steel grip of determinism. It should be noted carefully, however, that Bigger's liberation, in terms of his finally coming to see who he was in the world and to take responsibility for his behavior, comes only after he has not just experienced but *contemplated* his crimes. His lawyer, Boris Max (patterned partly after Clarence Darrow, partly after the lawyer in **Theodore Dreiser**'s *An American Tragedy,* clearly one of Wright's major literary sources, along with Dostoevsky's *Crime and Punishment*), in a summation sometimes condemned as excessively rambling and vague, attempts to save Bigger's life through denying his responsibility and by pleading in effect that only by a shockingly nonviolent act—not destroying Bigger for the murder Max admits his client committed—can the cycle of oppression, violence, mutual fear, and counter violence be broken. But Bigger is executed. He goes to his death perhaps for the first time in his life seeing himself as a man, a human being, assuring Max he is "all right."

Though few critics have claimed that *Native Son* is tightly wrought, it is carefully conceived and forcefully orchestrated. Divided into three sections headed "Fear," "Flight," and "Fate," its texture and tone evolve as Bigger becomes at first more, then less and less of an animal. Crammed with realistic detail from its opening when an alarm clock's harsh clang and angry voices awaken Bigger's body (but not his mind), it proceeds relentlessly to another clang at the book's end when a steel door on death row shuts in Bigger but does not jail his now emancipated spirit. Particularly in the first two sections, the book abounds in painfully real and effectively symbolic scenes of black ghetto life, for example in the sequence where Bigger traps a panicked, vicious black rat as his mother prays to God for deliverance. Soon Bigger will be the rat. When in the street Bigger sees a plane, a symbol of impossible hope and futile escape, he wishes he could fly it so he could drop bombs. Other interwoven images of blindness, walls, and whiteness show how little people know of each other's realities, how thwarted and stifled life can be, how submerged black existence is in white society.

The book's last section is more discursive and less documentary as characters parade before Bigger like allegorical representations in a medieval drama, sometimes becoming less real people than representations of ideas. Wright also here employs expressionistic distortion of certain probabilities of life, the number and kinds of people who would be allowed in Bigger's cell, for example, to depict truths beneath the surface of reality. Flawed though it may be, *Native Son* is an inescapable accomplishment in American literature, and a revelation unbounded by time or region of what can happen when the human spirit is trapped.

—Jack B. Moore

NATURE
Essay by Ralph Waldo Emerson, 1836

Ralph Waldo Emerson's essay *Nature,* appearing in 1836 as a little booklet, is a landmark in American thought and literature. It is the archetypal statement of transcendentalism, one of the more extreme forms which European romanticism took in America. As one commentator has written, Emerson's "real purpose in *Nature* . . . was to find a scheme of unity into which God, the soul, and nature. . . could be fitted." In this ambitious purpose Emerson had been aided importantly by German idealist philosophy as interpreted to the English-speaking peoples by Samuel Taylor Coleridge in his *Aids to Reflection* (1825). Emerson was especially impressed by Coleridge's elucidation of the Kantian distinction between the Reason and the Understanding—a distinction basic not only in Emerson's writing but in transcendentalist thought generally. Coleridge explains the distinction as follows: "Reason is the power of universal and necessary conviction, the source and substance of truths above sense, and having their evidence in themselves . . . . Understanding is discursive"; it arrives at truth step by step and "in all its judgments refers to some other faculty (e.g., the senses) as its ultimate authority." Reason, then, closely resembles intuition. Understanding resembles what in everyday parlance is called reason. But as Emerson stated, Reason "never reasons; never proves, it simply perceives; it is vision."

 Emerson used this distinction as a starting point in formulating his concept of nature and its relation to humankind. Yet Emerson realized that his views and those of the idealist and transcenden-

talist philosophers had their origins far back in the history of human thought. As an epigraph in the first edition of *Nature,* he quoted from Plotinus: "Nature is but an image or imitation of wisdom, the last thing of the soul"; and as early as 1830 he included in his *Journals* this quotation from the *Mahabharata:* "The senses are nothing but the soul's instruments of action; no knowledge can get to the soul by this channel" and he noted that idealism (i.e., transcendentalism) is "a primeval theory."

Nature is one of the most carefully organized of Emerson's writings. He begins with a definition: Nature is that "great apparition that shines so peacefully around us." It is "the NOT ME," everything including one's body and human artifacts. Next, as an illustration of how truth may come to one, he describes a personal experience: "Crossing a bare common . . . at twilight . . . I become a transparent eyeball; I am nothing; I see all; the currents of Universal Being circulate through me." The Reason, or intuition, floods him with the profoundest of insights, as was the case with Wordsworth during moments of mystical revelation near Tintern Abbey.

Nature, Emerson continues, serves humanity in four ways: as commodity, as beauty, as language, as discipline. As commodity, it serves the body's needs. But "a nobler want is served by nature, namely, the love of Beauty"—especially moral beauty, which appeals to the sense of right and wrong as apprehended by the Reason. Nature also provides mankind with a language—all language, to Emerson, derives from the metaphorical use of natural objects—not only for everyday communication but for the loftiest poetic or philosophic utterances. Finally, nature serves as a teacher, or as discipline, most fundamentally in the exercise of the moral sense in the decisions and demands of daily life. "All things are moral," Emerson wrote, " . . . all things with which we deal preach to us. What is a farm but a mute gospel?"

Emerson speculates whether nature actually exists outside the mind, but reaches no conclusion. Yet he does insist that nature stands "as the apparition of God. It is the organ through which the universal spirit speaks to the individual as a plant upon the earth, so a man rests upon the bosom of God." Indeed the Reason is akin to the divine; Man, then, is actually a God, but "a God in ruins . . . the dwarf of himself." Once humans come to recognize the divinity within them, their potential for goodness and growth will prove to be infinite. Emerson's optimism was limitless.

Emerson in *Nature* and all his writings depended on striking epigrams and startling metaphors to goad his readers into thinking. The foregoing quotations illustrate this stylistic device. Other examples are: "A fact is the end or last issue of spirit"; or, "the whole of nature is a metaphor of the human mind." Whether one accepts or rejects such sweeping statements, they give one pause and, at least momentarily, stimulate thought.

—Perry D. Westbrook

THE OCTOPUS
Novel by Frank Norris, 1901

The Octopus was the sixth of the seven novels that Frank Norris wrote before his sudden death, at 32, in 1902. It is in most respects his best. In writing it, Norris was determinedly filling a gap in American literature: America had no adequate non-imitative "American novel" and no epic of the winning of the West.

By 1899 Norris had conceived an adequate subject: "the Wheat." Raised in the vast San Joaquin Valley of southern central California, it involved the labor of inhabitants of every ethnic and economic group. Then in "the Pit" in Chicago it was bought and resold to "the People" of the world. Finally, this product of American soil and labor sustained populaces of the farthest countries. *The Octopus* would be the first volume of a trilogy; *The Pit,* the second; and there would be a third, to have been called *The Wolf,* which Norris did not live to write.

The title *The Octopus* refers not, of course, to the wheat, but to the spoiling force, the railroad. The valley's fecundity gave rise to the railroad and made possible the abuses perpetrated by it. By the mid-1890s Norris had come to value and use various aspects of Zola's realism and naturalism—contemporary topics, careful documentation, close observation, recognition of natural forces—after a rather prolonged youthful period of captivation with medieval romance. The "Mussel Slough Massacre," the armed battle that had taken place between the agents of the Southern Pacific Railroad and the wheat farmers of Tulare County in May 1880, was the documented fact on which the action of *The Octopus* was based. In choosing to treat of the abuses of the railroad company, Norris was not taking a daring stand or even breaking new ground. The "unanimous hatred of the people of California toward the Southern Pacific Railway" already existed. The novel is more an epic than a work of propaganda.

The wheat and the need to transport it organize almost all of the action. The wheat grows on the new soil in generous abundance, ready to be used, but the railroad tycoons require farm machines to be moved by circuitous routes, raise rates prohibitively for small producers, cut wages despite high profits, fire those who protest, govern the local newspapers, and finally renege on the contracts made with the ranchers who have leased and improved the land. The company has bought the state government and the courts; the valley people are too disorganized to make a stand. Norris follows Zola in seeing the railroad as a living monster; it is a gigantic octopus with its tentacles clutching all.

Presley, an educated outsider and a poet, who has come to the West with the hope of writing a vaguely conceived grand romantic epic of the Indian and Spanish epochs, follows Norris's own development in jettisoning this plan and studying to depict the present valley situation. This observer is a friend of the young ranchers, drawn from friends of Norris: Harran Derrick, whose stately father Magnus had lost his bid for governorship rather than engage in corrupt politics; Annixter—truculent but admirable— the most fully presented character; the sophisticated Osterman. And there is Vanamee, an educated man, a strange mystic rover, temporarily a farm laborer, whose etherial sweetheart, Angele, raped by an intruder, had died in childbirth; his friendship with the old Spanish priest at the mission church sustains in the novel the Spanish background of the region. Many of the workmen are of Spanish or Portuguese descent. And there is the old German farmer, the anarchist bar-owner, and a scattering of womenfolk.

Memorable set scenes, Norris's forte, dramatize the life of those who tend the wheat: the big barn dance, the jackrabbit drive, the annual plowing: "The ploughs, thirty-five in number, each drawn by its team of ten, stretched in an interminable line, nearly a quarter of a mile in length . . . . Each of these ploughs held five shears, so that when the entire company was in motion, one hundred and seventy-five furrows were made at the same instant. At a distance, the ploughs resembled a great column of field artillery." Further animating the meticulous details of the scene is the metaphor of the earth—"the uneasy agitation of its members, the hidden tumult of its womb, demanding to be made fruitful, to reproduce,

to disengage the eternal renascent germ of Life that stirred and struggled in its loins."

The wheat is the living witness of the evolutionary force. When Annixter, after a night of internal struggle, finally recognizes his total love for Hilma—herself a type of Love—he sees in the dawn light the young wheat that has burst through the ground: "the Wheat, the Wheat . . . an exulting earth gleaming transcendent with the radiant significance of an inviolable pledge."

Though the struggle with the corrupt railroad causes the loss of Magnus Derrick's honor and the lives of Annixter, Harran, several other ranchers, and Hilma's baby, the promise of "life out of death" is sustained by the coming of the dead Angele's daughter the night of the first wheat, and by the unusually splendid harvest of the wheat itself. The book ends with an ambiguous passage in which the leading railroad tycoon justifies the railroad as itself being ruled by forces beyond it. Unambiguously, the railroad's local petty tyrant, S. Behrman, as he is exulting at seeing his wheat rushing down the chute into a ship for India, is himself caught into the downward rush.

Norris's exact descriptions, his recording, like Zola's, of scenes, sounds, and smells, produced a vibrant and memorable novel, despite some overwriting and unclear logic.

—Alice R. Bensen

OLD MORTALITY
Story by Katherine Anne Porter, 1938

"Old Mortality," like most of Katherine Anne Porter's fiction, is deeply rooted in its time. This is not to say that her stories lack originality or that they will fail to be of interest in the future, but rather, like the fiction of **Ernest Hemingway** and others of that generation, her stories grew out of and reflect the social and cultural upheavals that took place during and after World War I. There is a harking back to an earlier, innocent, more romantic time, but also simultaneously a fierce insistence on seeing life from what is felt to be a more honest modern point of view.

Part I: 1885-1902 of "Old Mortality" deals with the legends of the older generations; it captures the air of nostalgia and romance engendered by those legends while to some extent undercutting them by an ironic tone and by subjecting them, at times, to the doubtful questioning of two little girls, Miranda and her sister Maria. The girls are enchanted by their elders' stories, whether of a visit to the theater or of the larger than life actions of Aunt Amy and Uncle Gabriel, and they grow up with a sense of "a life beyond a life in this world" and have confirmed for them "the nobility of human feeling, the divinity of man's vision of the unseen, the importance of life and death, the depths of the human heart, the romantic value of tragedy." But even as they are charmed, Miranda and Maria have difficulty matching their grandmother's decaying keepsakes and the absurdly old-fashioned photographs of the dead heroes and heroines with the tales of high deeds and romantic adventure. These doubts and the pervasive tone of gentle mockery anticipate the disillusioning that is to come in Parts II and III.

Part I has an anecdotal richness; it ranges over several years and includes numerous episodes and characters, suggesting in method an old-fashioned way of storytelling. Part II: 1904, by contrast, has a decidedly modern ring. Whereas Part I recounted in leisurely fashion the legends of the old order, Part II narrowly focuses on the lives of two members of the younger generation, Maria and Miranda: it is limited to the events of one day during and after a visit to the racetrack. The limited scope, the constricted time and space, and, above all, the sordidness of detail and general air of deflation and repressed hope all give Part II a quality of modern "truth-telling" rather like that to be found in the stories of James Joyce's *Dubliners*. The point of this method of narration, however, is not merely modern truth-telling; it is a strategy for developing the theme of the story. The sordidness of Part II, which is in marked contrast to the romantic quality of Part I, is occasioned by the appearance at the racetrack of the girls' Uncle Gabriel who figured so prominently in Part I in the romantic legend of their Aunt Amy. The man the girls had been brought up to associate with gallant and romantic adventure turns out to be a "shabby fat man with bloodshot blue eyes, sad beaten eyes, and a big melancholy laugh, like a groan." Uncle Gabriel is a revelation, the meaning of which looks forward to Part III and to a fuller, more devastating revelation.

In Part III: 1912, Miranda is confronted by another figure out of the past, Cousin Eva Parrington, who, even in the stories told by Miranda's father, appeared as an unromantic, chinless spinster, suffragette, and teacher of Latin. Now, on the train carrying them both to Gabriel's funeral, she presents Miranda with her own myth of the past which, on the face of it, sounds plausible enough, perhaps even scientific. Cousin Eva dismisses all of the legendary claims about Amy's beauty and tragic nobility and provides a kind of economic and Freudian version of the past. All of those dances and parties, Cousin Eva claims, were a kind of marketplace for girls like Amy who were trying to cut the ground out from under each other. "It was just sex," Cousin Eva says, "their minds dwell on nothing else. They didn't call it that, it was all smothered under pretty names, but that's all it was, sex." Miranda briefly considers this new version of the past and then, wisely dismisses it. "Of course it was not like that. This is no more true than what I was told before, it's every bit as romantic."

Later, off the train, Miranda observes her father and cousin with their heads together, the old-fashioned romantic and the new Freudian, in cahoots over their common past, and she envies them their naturalness, their freedom from playing the role of son or daughter to an aged person. Then she rejects them and their love which requires that she see the world through their eyes "and yet could not tell her the truth, not in the smallest thing." Later, she thinks that although she can never know the truth about "the legend of the past, other people's memory of the past," she can at least know "the truth about what happens to" her. At that point the author steps in to comment: "making a promise to herself, in her hopefulness, her ignorance."

Although some readers may regard this comment as an unwarranted intrusion into the story, this final phrase provides a crucial insight. Miranda is able to recognize the falseness of the myths told by her father and her cousin, but she fails to understand the larger implications of the bond between them. Their easy acceptance of their past, despite their different versions of it, is the result of shared experience. For the truth about life, the conclusion of this story suggests, is not to be found in any words about it; such formulations are legends shaped by individual feeling and memory; the only reliable version of the past is the experience itself, the actual living of it.

—W. J. Stuckey

ON THE ROAD
Novel by Jack Kerouac, 1957

On the Road remains after thirty years not only the most popular novel by Jack Kerouac, but also the best-known prose work of the Beat Generation. It was not, however, Kerouac's personal favorite among his writings. He preferred *Visions of Cody* and considered *On the Road* as a superseded preliminary version of his efforts to transform his life "on the road" with Neal Cassady between 1947 and 1950 into part of the "Duluoz Legend," a projected fictionalization of his life. *On the Road* was, in fact, the first of four such preliminary efforts to be completed.

These attempts began in 1948, immediately after the completion of Kerouac's first novel, *The Town and the City,* while the events used in the new work were still in progress. Kerouac's estate has denied access to the manuscripts of the first two versions, but Tim Hunt has managed in *Kerouac's Crooked Road* (1981) to reconstruct them from Kerouac's correspondence and other unpublished materials. The third version, narrated by a teenaged black boy from North Carolina, provides most of the text for the posthumously published *Pic.*

The 175,000-word fourth version, typed on a single scroll of paper during three weeks in April 1951, was rejected by many publishers while it circulated with the title "The Beat Generation"; but finally, through the persistence of Malcolm Cowley, who suggested cuts and revisions, it was published by the prestigious Viking Press in 1957. As early as 1951, however, Kerouac, inspired by his discovery of "spontaneous prose," had begun to displace this text with the very different and much more experimental "Neal Book," which was not published in its entirety as *Visions of Cody* until after Kerouac's death. In it, the story line of *On the Road* is drastically condensed into the final fifth and its downbeat ending is replaced by a more optimistic one in which Ti-Jean Duluoz (Kerouac's alter ego) finally transcends the influence of Cody Pomeray (Neal Cassady's final avatar).

The formally traditional *On the Road* is thus a supplanted version of a work in progress that the author allowed to be published for financial reasons when even his friends considered the Joycean final version of his masterwork unmarketable. Possibly as a result of changes Malcolm Cowley suggested, *On the Road* is a much more carefully structured work than the published components of the "Duluoz Legend." Each of the four parts of this novel based on the experiences of Kerouac (Sal Paradise) and Cassady (Dean Moriarity) during their life on the road follows a repeated narrative pattern that foreshadows the brief fifth section. Each begins with Sal depressed by his sheltered life at home as he is writing his first novel. Energized by the example of Dean, Sal takes to the road four times and each time the action accelerates manically. As each frenzied episode reaches its climax, however, a disillusioning experience dashes Sal's hopes; and he slinks home, dejected and again depressed.

In Part One, Sal makes his first trip to San Francisco (largely by bus), where he ends up as a frustrated guard in a menacing security camp, "at the end of America" with "nowhere to go." During his trip home, Sal establishes with a Mexican girl the one satisfying romantic relationship depicted in the novel; but he abandons her because of what he later laments as his "white expectations." A year later in Part Two he travels with Dean to New Orleans and again San Francisco, where he envisions Dean, standing naked by a window, as someday "the pagan mayor" of the city; but Dean's energies run out, and Sal goes home not caring whether they ever meet again.

By the next spring, however, in Part Three, Sal is drawn back to San Francisco, where he offers to take his "brother" Dean to Italy and support them both, but on this, their wildest cross-country junket, in a borrowed car, Sal ruminates morbidly about his "raggedy travelings," and Dean becomes involved with so many wives and children that the trip abroad is called off. By spring 1950, however, Sal can still generate enthusiasm for a trip to Mexico City as "the most fabulous" one of all; but when Sal becomes seriously ill in Mexico, Dean deserts him and Sal realizes "what a rat" Dean is. The novel ends with a tableau that symbolizes the transparent but impenetrable wall between Sal and Dean. Back in New York Sal rides off to a Duke Ellington concert in a bookmaker friend's Cadillac, while Dean is left outside in the rain. Sal can only wave wordlessly through the back window before brooding that he can see no future but "the forlorn rags of growing old."

Thus, far from being the seductive promotional tract for an irresponsible threat to the traditional American way of life that it has been condemned as, *On the Road* is rather a defeatist cautionary tale about the "endless and beginningless emptiness" of what Sal calls "the senseless nightmare road." Its downbeat ending foreshadows better than Kerouac's preferred works his subsequent rejection of any responsibility for the counterculture that this novel helped inspire.

—Warren French

OUR TOWN
Play by Thornton Wilder, 1938

One of the most successful American plays of the 20th century, Thornton Wilder's *Our Town* owes its fame chiefly to the skill with which its author dramatizes the age-old theme of the importance of ordinary day-to-day human existence: namely, by means of a daring rearrangement of conventional stagecraft. To depict the supreme worth of savoring life fully while we possess it, Wilder drew upon such classic models as Homer's *Odyssey* and Dante's *Purgatorio,* both of which offer poignant contrasts between the fleeting beauty of the living and the dreary permanence of the dead, as in Achilles's dour comment in Hades that he would rather be a living slave than a dead king. In *Our Town* Wilder converted the universal message implicit in this scene into an allegory involving birth, marriage, and death in the United States of the 1930s. By his bold methods of staging his drama, his artful manipulation of time and place, he related the here and now of an insignificant New England village to the timeless concerns of human nature everywhere. His aim, he wrote, was "an attempt to find a value above all price for the smallest events in our daily life. I have made the claim as preposterous as possible, for I have set the village against the largest dimensions of time and place."

Wilder's two major innovations enabling him to fulfill his aim were the use of a bare stage and a centralizing character, the Stage Manager, a throwback to both the Chorus in classic Greek drama and the Property Man in Chinese theater. As a stand-in for author and director, he not only arranges stage props, but also initiates, controls, and interprets setting and action, explaining directly to the audience from the outset that they are going to witness a play about life in an ordinary little town in New Hampshire, Grover's Corners, beginning just before dawn on 7 May 1901. After pointing to some of its notable imaginary features, including the cemetery, he gives a brief history of the town, identifies some of its leading citizens, focusing on several members of the two neighboring families, the Webbs and the Gibbses, whose interrelationships will dominate the action from there on. As the Stage Manager develops their typical encounters with one another that day throughout Act One, he also offers further commentary from time to time, which illustrates the commonplaceness of routine in the Webb and Gibbs households, but also suggests its broader metaphysical significance. The blessed tie that binds Grover's Corners to the Universe and the Mind of God is then circuitously expressed in the colloquy between young George Gibbs and his sister Rebecca at the end of the first act.

Similar techniques are employed in the second and third acts to strengthen and clarify the union of theme and action. In Act II, which deals with the courtship and marriage of George Gibbs and Emily Webb three years later, the Stage Manager serves as both the minister who weds them and the commentator who disparages the glamour of the ceremony, which, he says, is interesting only "once in a thousand times." Nevertheless, as he muses on the fact that millions of folk since the dawn of time have celebrated such marriage rites as these, it becomes clear that the wedding of this particular young couple, however commonplace it appears, symbolizes a universal "fusion of nature's physical and spiritual purposes.

Again, in Act III Wilder boldly extends his basic analogy by literally juxtaposing life and death on the stage. Nine more years have elapsed, and some of the town's recent dead who were alive in Act II are now seated on chairs representing their graves in the cemetery, where they are witnessing the burial of Emily, who has just died in childbirth. As she joins them in the vacant chair next to her mother-in-law, she becomes the catalyst for the swift evocation of Wilder's deepest meaning. The granting of her desire to relive just a single day of her former life, her twelfth birthday, leads to her discovery that the living can neither appreciate nor understand the beauty of life till they have lost it. Crying "Oh, earth you're too wonderful for anybody to realize you," she is ready to return to the passionless Dead, whom the Stage Manager had described at the opening of the act as "waitin' for something they feel is comin'. Something important and great." The action has built up steadily throughout the play toward the dramatic revelation that human life, however painful, dreary, or inconsequential its quotidian events, is both a precious gift in itself as well as part of a mysterious plan that rests in the "Mind of God."

—Eugene Current-Garcia

PATERSON
Poem by William Carlos Williams, 1946-63

Paterson is among the half dozen or so long poems, including **Ezra Pound**'s *Cantos,* **T.S. Eliot**'s *Four Quartets,* **Hart Crane**'s *The Bridge,* **Charles Olson**'s *Maximus Poems,* and **Louis Zukofsky**'s *A,* that mark a resurgence of epic writing in the 20th century. Unlike their European counterparts of the middle ages, these American epics celebrate the unity of culture by means other than kings, heroes, saints, or religions, and speak of history in terms of ordinary life and personal experience, instead of wars, conquests, or high adventure. **Walt Whitman**'s *Leaves of Grass* (1855) was an early indication of the possibility of extended poetry in the industrial age, and subsequent long poems have drawn from it. But a more direct influence upon the modern long poem was James Joyce's *Ulysses* (1922), an Irish novel which draws parallels between Dublin life and the world of Homer's *Odyssey.* Joyce's novel seized upon the seeming disarray of contemporary life and thought and discerned principles of unity that not only related modernity to the past, but synthesized the fruits of the intellectual revolution of Darwin, Marx, Freud, and Einstein, from which a new vision of life was emerging.

William Carlos Williams did not conceive the project of a long poem until 1942, though *Eta in Hell* (1920) marks an early effort at writing an extended work, which his friend Pound liked but judged an imitation of the French poet Arthur Rimbaud. Williams's autobiographical novel *A Voyage to Pagany* portrays a writer seeking the experience that would lead him to a bold new form of writing, but who rejects the European culture other American writers had embraced as their subject. While Pound and Eliot wrote about European capitals in their own long poems, Hart Crane broke new ground in *The Bridge* (1930) with an extended verse treatment of the Brooklyn Bridge and of American life.

Paterson is divided into five books, which serve to structure the poem into a five-act drama in which a central figure, Mr. Paterson, seeks to dissolve boundaries between self and the city around him. His purpose is to incorporate the hidden nature of the city into his thought, to join the so-called objective or external world to his identity, and thus bring to mind an otherwise separate, alien reality. No one had tried to treat the American city from this vantage before—to make it an extension of self, an aspect of one's own nature, though in Whitman's "Song of Myself" a similar incorporation of the world to self is celebrated, but on a grander scale and without the struggle here dramatized. Indeed, the difficulties and reconciliations between Dedalus and Bloom in *Ulysses,* between lofty and sensuous extremes, is closer to the plotting of Williams's poem. In Book I of *Paterson* many things are set against each other, including the giant figures of Mr. Paterson, masculine intellect, and the feminine energies of the hills on which he stretches. Polarity must be overcome by patient dismantling of the closed self; each step gained is marked by a flow of sensuous identity and sympathy with the outside world. Book II contains the famous passage in which the central figure enters and liberates his own unconscious, with its confusion of experience resembling the vast stretches of terrain constituting Paterson. The Passaic river, which flows through Paterson, comes to represent the "stream of consciousness" of its citizenry, which the narrator articulates as his own voice. Various letters inserted in the text either accuse the protagonist of narcissism and self-indulgence, or praise his goals and intentions, thus monitoring the difficulties of his journey into the world.

Though conceived as early as 1942, the first four books of *Paterson* were not published as a single volume until 1958; the complete poem of five books, with notes and sketches for a sixth, was issued in 1963. Thus, the poem was written late in the author's life, but it marks Williams's richest period of composition, in which he also completed *Journey to Love* and *Pictures from Brueghel,* and such remarkable extended lyrics as "The Desert Music," written in 1951, and "Asphodel, That Greeny Flower," included in *Journey to Love.* The late work is characterized by greater frankness and intimacy, and by a more fluid phrasing, positioned on the page to suggest the pauses and rushes of thought during composition. These technical developments follow directly from the intentions of *Paterson,* in which a figure struggles to transcend his inhibitions and have free exchange with the life around him.

Paterson marks the point at which American poetry turned its attention away from Europe to its own culture, to domestic life and the travails of selfhood at home. Its treatment of a city as a living thing, in which a central intelligence articulates its character, pointed the way for subsequent treatments, most notably in the work of **Robert Lowell**, Charles Olson, and **Allen Ginsberg**, who made the cities of Boston, Gloucester, Massachusetts, and New York the subject of their poetry. Moreover, Williams's various strategies in *Paterson* for showing the interaction between personal and collective realms, a highly original program of devices that breaks up the flow of thought with intrusions from the outside, soon became the conventions of postmodern poetry. *Paterson,* together with Pound's *The Pisan Cantos* (1948), opened the way for a second surge of experiment in American poetry.

—Paul Christensen

PEREGRINOS DE AZTLÁN
A novel by Miguel Méndez M, 1974, English translation, 1993

Peregrinos de Aztlán, Miguel Méndez M.'s first novel, was a long awaited literary event in Chicano literature. Méndez M. had already achieved recognition through his short stories "Tata Casehua" and "Taller de imagenes: pase" (Shop of Images: Come In), which had been written in a very polished prose and innovative imagery in the Spanish language. *Peregrinos* came to verify the masterful use of language by a Chicano construction worker who had not finished high school and who, by reason of class, education, and resources, was considered incapable of writing literature. The novel did not disappoint anyone. Instead, it added new dimensions to the Spanish language by including apocryphus dialects such as Border Spanish, Chicano Spanish and "pachuco calo" (a hybrid street Barrio jargon) into a literary text. In other words, Méndez M. gave genuine expression to the different characters that inhabit the Mexican and Chicano world of "the Border."

The Border is a region where Méndez M. lived and experienced the injustice and oppression perpetrated by two political systems that converge and confront each other along one of the longest borders in the world: the U.S./Mexico border. The microcosm is Tijuana, a city on the California-Mexico border. Within this city one finds representatives of almost all suppressed classes as well as oppressors whose stories converge and confront each other by their need to be told. Méndez M. rescues these stories about ordinary people who are neither heroes, personalities, nor famous. These are stories about the downtrodden, the helpless, the poor, and the unwanted whose only crime seems to be their skin color and their Indian race.

Méndez M. employs a fragmented style of storytelling in order to include the many stories that the city harbors, and he anchors them in the feverish mind of Loreto, an old car washer, who retrieves them from oblivion by remembering them. The Anglo hippie, the white-slaver, the prostitute, the corrupt judge, the cynical bureaucrat, and the hapless undocumented worker are some of the characters that find voice through Méndez M., who lets them speak in their own language. Reading the text is a tour de force in linguistic expertise as the reader must be knowledgeable in various levels of Southwestern dialects in order to fully appreciate the richness of the text.

Méndez M. structures the novel in three parts: in the first part Loreto introduces the many characters to the reader as he meets these characters while walking the streets looking for cars to wash; the second part elaborates and details their stories and develops their personalities; and the third centers on Colonel Cuamea, an old Yaqui warrior, and Frankie Pérez, who dies in Vietnam. Revolution and war are the scenarios in the third part where the lives of Cuamea and Frankie are compared through a personal struggle of ideals.

The procession of deaths throughout the text, some of them tragic, others ironic, intensify the contrast of forgotten heroic stories with the uninspiring and useless lives of the people in power. Méndez M. creates here a novel of thesis where he indicts the perverse political systems converging on the border by rescuing stories that were never officially told or were too banal to be considered. One of these is the story of Pedro, the brother of Rosenda, who kills Mario Miller de Cocuch for selling his sister into prostitution. The local papers report the incident by presenting the vilest character in the novel as a "very distinguished citizen in city politics and business who is suddenly and without provocation assaulted and stabbed by an unknown evildoer who, without a word and driven by his criminal instinct, kills him and rapidly flees." The honor and dignity of the poor is constantly reviled by those in power who seem to be the only ones to command respect, by reason of wealth or political power. The stories succeed one another as Loreto guides us through the streets of the city introducing us to characters who seem to be invisible and insensible to the feelings of the foreign tourist or the wealthy passerby. The lives and histories of these city outcasts are retrieved from history's garbage pile and brought to life to remind us that their lives are also important and serve as counterparts to the stories of heroes and great persons that official history chooses, through a perverse system of values, as worthy of remembrance. Méndez M. reminds us that most of these outcasts and unwanted people are heroes themselves as the struggle for survival in the border is a heroic act in itself.

It took almost twenty years for *Peregrinos* to be translated into English. It was no easy task for translator David Foster to plunge himself into a linguistic labyrinth of converging dialects and levels of meanings and to come forth with a substantially good translation. While there may be detractors and critics who will find fault with it, they all have to agree that it was a difficult project and that its greatest achievement so far is that it made available, for the first time, an example of Chicano literature that had been kept away from English-speaking readers.

—Salvador del Pino

PERSONAL NARRATIVE
Autobiography by Jonathan Edwards, 1765

Jonathan Edwards's "Personal Narrative," although written around 1740, was not published until after his death. The personal narrative is a type of spiritual autobiography. Similar to other Puritans such as **William Bradford**, Winthrop, and **Cotton Mather**, Edwards is intensely concerned with religious introspection. In "Personal Narrative" Edwards traces his spiritual growth through childhood and adolescence. As in his well-known sermon "Sinners in the Hands of an Angry God," "Personal Narrative" reveals Edwards's belief in man's depravity and his need for spiritual awakening. Consistent with Puritan theology, Edwards accepts God's sovereignty "in showing mercy to whom He will show mercy and hardening and eternally damning whom He will."

"Personal Narrative" also reveals Edwards to be a proponent of the Enlightenment in America. Like Benjamin Franklin, a contemporary of his time, Edwards seeks to demystify the world around him. In his scientific essays "Of Insects" and "Of the Rainbow," Edwards observes and analyzes God's creation. Edwards is intrigued by Isaac Newton's concept that nature is composed of universal patterns forming a coherent system. To Edwards, conversion also contains such patterns within a system. Edwards seeks to examine his spiritual awakening empirically. He sees no contradiction between the rational and the religious, the scientific and the spiritual. Edwards wants to understand and experience conversion. Both intellectual and emotional acceptance of God's salvation are essential.

Edwards is greatly influenced by John Locke's emphasis on perception of the external world through the senses. Edwards recalls reading Locke's *An Essay Concerning Human Understanding* (1690) while a student at Yale College with more pleasure "than the greedy miser finds when gathering up handfuls of silver and gold, from some newly discovered treasure." Locke confirmed Edwards's belief that religion must be experienced before true understanding can be attained. Sensory language appears in "Personal Narrative," for Edwards, as with other individuals caught up in the "Great Awakening," realizes the importance of emotion in the conversion process. Only experience can lead man to true conviction of his sinfulness and his absolute need of God's grace.

In beginning "Personal Narrative," Edwards describes in detail his relapses back into sin after his early religious "seasons of awakening." Because he wants to understand his feelings of utter rejection and despair upon returning to sinfulness, Edwards graphically describes these experiences: "But in the process of time, my convictions and affections wore off; and I entirely lost all those affections and delights and left off secret prayer, at least to any constant performance of it, and returned like a dog to his vomit, and went on in ways of sin." Later after being seized with pleurisy and questioning the state of his soul, Edwards writes that God "brought me nigh to the grave, and shook me over the pit of hell."

Even more than expressing the misery of his fallen condition in "Personal Narrative," however, Edwards wants to share his unbridled joy when he undergoes true conversion. It was in his final year of college that Edwards writes, "I made seeking my salvation the main business of my life." From this point onward, Edwards ecstatically describes his religious experience with God. In this brief narrative, Edwards employs the words "sweet" and "delight" over fifty times. In addition, words such as "pleasant," "bright," "excellent," "lovely," "gentle," and "calm" appear frequently. God's sovereignty is characterized, for example, as "an exceedingly pleasant, bright, and sweet doctrine," and heaven is described as the place where "sweet, calm, and delightful love" reign.

Up until the 1700s, Puritans often used a "plain style" of language which appealed mainly to the intellect or understanding. Edwards seeks also to use language that is directed towards the emotions or feelings. Edwards writes that the religious delights of his childhood "never reached the heart." After his conversion, however, Edwards rejoices in experiencing God's glory and holiness. He wants to share his joy and demystify the process of spiritual awakening.

Edwards experiences this "sweet burning" in his heart most when he observes God's excellency in nature: the sun, moon, and stars; the clouds and blue sky; the grass, flowers, and trees; and the thunder and lightening. Like other Puritans such as **Anne Bradstreet**, Edwards views nature as God's second book. In nature he sees emblems which reflect God's character. Unlike other Puritans, however, Edwards responds emotionally when contemplating Christ while in nature. Edwards recounts an experience while riding through the woods on his horse in 1737. Upon meditating on Christ's grace and excellency, Edwards is overwhelmed by "a flood of tears and weeping aloud," a condition he remains in for an hour.

Edwards's sense of God's glory also leads him to see his own wickedness more vividly. Towards the end of "Personal Narrative," Edwards describes his sins as "infinite upon infinite." Edwards is not suggesting that he has rejected God as he did as a child. Although readers today may interpret such statements as displays of false humility, Edwards is actually expressing his own unworthiness and his need of God's grace.

"Personal Narrative" reveals Edwards's conviction that conversion is an essential process for those seeking salvation. Edwards views conversion as the most important event in one's life. He analyzes his own spiritual awakening, for he desires to intellectually understand and emotionally respond to this experience. Edwards's "Personal Narrative" reflects the religious maturation of a young man. It is a work which fuses Puritan theology with Enlightened thinking.

—John D. Battenburg

PICNIC
Play by William Inge, 1953

Although originally set in the 1930s, written in the late 1940s, and finally reproduced in a new version on Broadway in 1973, *Picnic* epitomizes the American 1950s and the smalltown midwest in which William Inge was born and bred.

In *Picnic* Inge creates a female world—insular, insecure, parochial, lonely, sexually unfulfilled—and agitates it by injecting a virile male presence. Set in two adjoining back yards during the end-of-summer Labor Day weekend—a time symbolizing fading youth and hopes for spinster teacher Rosemary, who boards with Madge, her sister Millie, and mother Flo—this realistic play employs as catalyst the sensual Hal Carter, who, while doing chores for Flo's neighbor Helen, sheds his shirt and arouses all the women, even tomboy Millie. Each of the women is carefully selected both for her potential vulnerability to Hal's charms and for the 1950s inhibitions likely to keep her forever sexually frustrated. Inge gives us varied portraits of tumescence curbed by propriety, for the 1950s presupposed the prohibition of sex outside marriage, and women took seriously their obligations to chastity—or guilt.

Inge's sympathies are entirely with this poignant female assortment: Helen Potts, doomed to care for the invalid mother who prevented Helen from consummating her marriage and had it annulled; Flo Owens, whose marriage was short and unfulfilling; Rosemary Sydney, whose hypocritical prudishness is designed to mask her longing for a man; young Millie, who feels too unattractive and ill at ease to try to please a man; and beautiful Madge, who, under maternal pressure to conform to social norms, has been doing what's expected of her in going out with a rich boy. Yet Madge—created by Janice Rule in her stage debut—also is a dreamer who wonders what the world might have in store for her if Alan—a sexually uncompelling fellow who, amazingly, was played by the young Paul Newman—weren't in her future and she took a train for someplace other than Kansas.

Inge constructs his second act around growing sexual excitement which builds in an impromptu, pre-picnic backyard dance. This mating ritual first foreshadows Hal and Madge's passion, then finds Rosemary (Eileen Heckart's role) throwing herself at Hal and, after her explosive disappointment has wounded Hal and provided Madge plenty of motive to comfort him, prompts Rosemary to demand romantic fulfillment from her own boyfriend: "I want to drive into the sunset, Howard! I want to drive into the sunset!" Left alone to bring the picnic baskets in their car, Hal instead lifts Madge in his arms and—in the culmination of the scene's erotic progression—announces "We're not goin' on no God-damn picnic."

Having thrust his two major women in forbidden sexual relations during the break between Acts II and III, Inge dramatizes the consequences of virgins yielding to their sexual needs. Rosemary may have given herself to Howard in order to trap him. Feeling trapped herself, stuck in her job teaching high school typing and shorthand and too old to have any more "chances," Rosemary repeatedly begs Howard to marry her. Responding to social pressures himself, Howard does what he "should" and accedes. Their marriage is the socially acceptable choice. The much younger Madge responds differently to a night of sexual and emotional fulfillment. Although she refuses Hal's importuning her to run off with him, once he's hopped a freight and she's had a few minutes to contemplate life without him, she hurries after her stud, jilting the man who offers a secure life in favor of her primal urges.

From their first meeting, Madge and Hal are strongly attracted to each other. Their eventually acting on their desire seems inevitable. Nevertheless, Inge himself was uncomfortable with Madge's following Hal—an ending which apparently evolved under director Joshua Logan's influence. He therefore reworked *Picnic* into *Summer Brave*.

Making many incidental and sometimes harmful changes, Inge particularly alters Hal's character. Some months before the action begins, in his efforts to go to Hollywood, Hal has stolen Alan's car, a precursor to his stealing Alan's girl. Inge improves his dramaturgy in one instance by giving Madge clearer choices in the third act. Despite Madge's having been bedded by his rival, Alan is still asserting his right to her when Madge refuses to go with Hal, saying she's going to marry Alan. Yet she does not bother to disguise from Alan her love for Hal, so she loses Alan. Madge regrets Hal's departure (but not Alan's), but she doesn't follow Hal. As the play ends, she appears resilient, already thinking of accepting a date from yet another fellow.

These changes have the curious effect of strengthening Madge (say, from a feminist viewpoint) yet trivializing all that has gone before, especially Madge and Hal's attraction—and their pain. The original inspires considerable compassion as well as admiration for Madge's courage in flouting convention and following her heart. *Summer Brave* substitutes for that a portrait—depending on how it is directed—either of impending sexual degeneracy or of a woman's maturation and independence.

In both versions, Inge created bittersweet roles for women, characters who live lives of not-so-quiet desperation. The older women are object lessons in female denial, suppression and repression, and the younger women—Millie who hopes to be a novelist and Madge who plans to be a wife and then surprises herself—become archetypes of 1950s women resisting the models their mothers set for them.

—Tish Dace

POETRY
Poem by Marianne Moore, 1919 (and later revisions)

"I, too, dislike it" is the startling opening statement of "Poetry," Marianne Moore's most famous poem. This landmark of 20th-century literature illustrates Moore's practice of extensive revision, her precision in language and syllabic consistency, her observation of zoological phenomena, her predilection for aesthetic enquiry and the work of contemporaneous poets, and her contrariness in her use of "anti-poetic" and paradoxical statements.

Bonnie Costello, in her 1981 *Marianne Moore: Imaginary Possessions,* says that revision "is a central part of Moore's aesthetic." Certainly the numerous revisions of "Poetry" are impossible to ignore. The original 30 lines of 1919 were reduced to 13 in 1924, but almost all of the original version, 29 lines, was restored in 1935. George W. Nitchie, in his comparison of the versions in his 1969 introduction to Moore's poetry, notes that this most often anthologized version is flawed technically in that the truncation destroys the consistency of the syllabic verse, which, in Moore's use, was a repetition of the number and arrangement of syllables in each stanza. The most drastic revision occurred in 1967, in what Moore whimsically chose to call *The Complete Poems:*

> I, too, dislike it.
> Reading it, however, with a perfect contempt for it, one discovers in
> it, after all, a place for the genuine.

In "To a Snail" Moore says that "contractility is a virtue." Apparently Moore found a virtue in presenting an imageless poem on poetry, but most of her critics have regarded this final "fiddling" a mistake, as does **Donald Hall** (*Marianne Moore: The Cage and the Animal,* 1970). At least the mistake is somewhat mitigated by her including the 1935 version in the notes to her final volume.

The argument of the poem is that poetry, though not especially important, is nevertheless "useful" insofar as it is intelligible and not restricted in subject matter, but that it must be written with skill and imagination. Poetry can only be worthwhile if it is written by "'literalists of the imagination'" who provide "'imaginary gardens with real toads in them.'" In her notes Moore identifies the first of the above quoted statements as Yeats's comment on Blake in *Ideas of Good and Evil.* "Imaginary gardens with real toads in them," the most notable image in the poem, also is enclosed in quotations, but it is not identified. Stanley Lourdeaux has written a note in the 1982 *Modern Philology* suggesting that the toad image comes from William Carlos Williams's "Romance Moderne," published in *Others* six months before "Poetry" appeared in that journal. Whatever the source, the line compellingly illustrates the theme of the poem and has attracted frequent explorations into the precise meaning of the metaphor.

The poem is amplified by other memorable and disjointed images, such as bats and baseball fans, statisticians and school-books. It proceeds through a series of contradictions and implications, raising both ontological and pragmatic questions about the worth of poetry. The apparent irony of the initial statement dissolves eventually to a consideration of its ambiguity, until the reader is finally convinced of the author's passionate restraint in dealing on both the abstract and concrete levels with the subject to which she devoted her life.

—Nancy Carol Joyner

THE PORTRAIT OF A LADY
Novel by Henry James, 1881

The Portrait of a Lady is the culminating work of Henry James's early period, a quintessential Victorian novel that yet adumbrates those particular qualities, architectonic and narrative, that James contributed to the development of the 20th-century novel.

The reader can perceive the older and newer impulses at work by comparing chapters 6 and 42. In chapter 6 a confidential narrator offers an analytic verbal portrait of Isabel Archer, enjoining the reader's indulgence and sympathy for a young heroine in whom theories may take the place of knowledge of the world, whose self-esteem may cause her to believe too much in her own opinion, and whose idealism and innocence may lead her into complexities she little anticipates. In short, "her errors and delusions were frequently such as a biographer interested in preserving the dignity of his subject must shrink from specifying." Not only the narrative manner in such a passage, but also James's theme, is Victorian, the marriage market and the relationship of money to marital options. Will money bring Isabel freedom of choice or make her an object of social predators? What effect has money upon her own imagination? In chapter 42, which James notes in his retrospective Preface as "obviously the best thing in the book," Isabel sits by the fire pondering what her husband has asked of her this evening, examining her marriage: "It was very well to undertake to give him a proof of loyalty; the real fact was that the knowledge of his expecting a thing raised a presumption against it. It was as if he had had the evil eye; as if his presence were a blight and his favor a misfortune. Was the fault in himself or only in the deep mistrust she had conceived for him? This mistrust was now the clearest result of their short married life; a gulf had opened between them over which they looked at each other with eyes that were on either side a declaration of the deception suffered." Here the action has moved inward, the point of view focused in the heroine's own consciousness, and the range of vision narrowed to what she herself can see and interpret. Question replaces answer, metaphor supersedes explicit statement, as Isabel searches for the similitude that will convey her intuitions and feelings. Such a passage is nearer to the late James in point of view and figurative language, and anticipates the 20th-century psychological novel which his own subtler experimentation fostered at the turn of the century.

The carefully crafted structure also looks to the later James. In his celebrated Preface to *The Portrait of a Lady,* written for the definitive New York Edition of his works, James has much to say about the architectonics of his novel, how he laid it brick by brick, building it outward from the initial perception of the character of Isabel Archer by devising those relations with other characters and those settings which would best reveal his heroine. "Such is the aspect that to-day *The Portrait* wears for me: a structure reared with an *'architectural'* competence . . . that makes it, to the author's own sense, the most proportioned of all my productions after *The Ambassadors*."

The Portrait of a Lady is also the crowning work, from his early period, in James's development of his theme of international contrast. Its plot is very simple and has been recognized as that of a fairy tale, in which the heroine must choose among three suitors; her fortunes must depend thereafter upon the wisdom of her choice. The first two suitors, Caspar Goodwood, an American business-man, and Lord Warburton, an English aristocrat, manifest national as well as personal characteristics, the dangers of ruthless self-assertiveness and of hereditary forms and obligations. Isabel's chosen suitor, Gilbert Osmond, is an American living abroad, who has absorbed effete and corrupt aspects of European civilization together with European aestheticism and sophistication. He becomes the principal foil for Isabel's new-world virtues of enthusiasm, innocence, and aspiration. Secondary characters, Mme. Merle, who betrays Isabel into this marriage, and Henrietta Stackpole, who remains her friend despite it, define similar polarities. Isabel's fate is left in the balance at the end. Having chosen wrongly, will she desert her husband or slavishly perpetuate the form of an empty marriage? Will she live by the memory of her deceased cousin Ralph Touchett, whom she now perceives as beloved? Or for the sake of her stepdaughter Pansy Osmond, to preclude a similar fate for her?

"The obvious criticism," James wrote in his *Notebooks*, "will be that it is not finished—that I have not seen the heroine to the end of her situation . . . . That is both true and false. The *whole* is never told; you can only take what groups together." Here again James analyzes his own salient qualities, his concern with form and the characteristic open-endedness of his fictions.

—Jean Frantz Blackall

A RAISIN IN THE SUN
Play by Lorraine Hansberry, 1959

African American dramatist Lorraine Hansberry was only twenty-nine when *A Raisin in the Sun* opened at the Ethel Barrymore Theatre on 11 March 1959. She was the first African American woman to have a play staged on Broadway and the youngest American to win the New York Drama Critics Circle Award. The play ran 538 successful performances and, later, a musical adapted from *A Raisin in the Sun* won a Tony Award as best musical of the year in 1974.

Like African American novelist **Toni Morrison** whose writings are intended not so much to find a language that can "transcend" the African American experience as to insist on the particular racial identities of her fictional people, Hansberry also believes that "one of the most sound ideas in dramatic writing is that, in order to create the universal, you must pay very great attention to the specific." *A Raisin in the Sun,* whose appeal and thematic power are generated by the commonality of its characters' struggles, stations itself firmly in the tradition of dramaturgical realism. The main conflict in *A Raisin in the Sun* revolves around how to spend the $10,000 dollars of insurance money Big Walter left for the family. The head of the family, Lena Younger (Mama), wants to buy a house in a suburban white neighborhood.

But Lena's two children, Walter Lee Younger and Beneatha Younger, have other dreams. Walter is in his middle thirties. Tired of working as a chauffeur and believing that the only way to pull himself from desperation and hopelessness as a slum resident in Chicago's Southside is to own his own business, Walter wants to use the money to buy a liquor store. Walter's sister, Beneatha, is a college student. At the age of twenty, she is free-spirited, idealistic, and eager to experiment "with different forms of expression." Beneatha's aspiration is to become a self-sacrificing doctor in Africa.

Following the conventional practice of realism, Hansberry uses a balanced approach in her portrayal of characters in *A Raisin in the Sun*. All the characters are ordinary individuals who possess both weaknesses as well as the capacity for heroism. Beneatha, for instance, is young and attractive. She is the self-appointed representative of the future. But, at the same time, the audience also confronts a Beneatha who is opinionated and self-centered. Her rejection of Lena's religion and lifestyle is tantamount to uprooting herself from the past and from her cultural heritage. Lack of a solid foundation is what turns the strength of Beneatha's impressionability into a display of vulnerability.

Walter, on the other hand, plays the traditional antithetical role against Beneatha. He is temperamental, demanding, and mercenary. After he loses the money Lena asks him to deposit in a bank to a swindler, Walter is eager to make a deal with a white man, Karl Lindner, who promises Walter money if he does not move into the all-white neighborhood. But when Lindner appears, Walter changes his mind. He rejects the proposal and declares: "we come from people who had a lot of pride. I mean—we are very proud people." After Lindner leaves, Lena proudly tells Walter's wife, Ruth: "He finally come into his manhood today, didn't he? Kind of like a rainbow after the rain . . . ."

What holds the family together is the matriarchal character, Lena Younger. Lena, who is in her early sixties, is both physically and mentally strong. She is religious, self-confident, optimistic, and proud. Even though Lena represents the family's link to the past and tradition, she is very supportive of her children's choices for the future. Her confidence in her children's ability to make the right decisions is underlined when she cautions Beneatha not to be so negatively judgmental of her brother: "When you start measuring somebody, measure him right, child, measure him right. Make sure you done taken into account what hills and valleys he come through before he got to wherever he is." When Lindner asks Walter to sign the deal, Lena insists that Travis, Walter and Ruth's ten-year-old son, stay in the room: "No. Travis, you stay right here. And you make him understand what you doing, Walter Lee. You teach him good. Like Willy Harris taught you. You show where our five generations done come to."

Hansberry's portrayal of the confrontation between mother and children and between brother and sister has brought critics such as Tom F. Driver in *New Republic* to the conclusion that *A Raisin in the Sun* is but another "domestic play," using formulas that are "old fashioned" and "over-worked." But Hansberry's thematic exploration of conflicts between the past and the present, dream and reality, human dignity and commercial success, elevates the play to a level that challenges what would be otherwise accepted as normal: it raises questions about the issue of social equality; it problematizes the study of social priorities by demanding individual involvement (as Lena says to Walter: "So now it's life. Money is life. Once upon a time freedom used to be life—now it's money"); it also helps us to redefine our relationship with the past, with tradition, and with our cultural heritage.

The title of *A Raisin in the Sun* is taken from African American poet Langston Hughes's poem "Harlem": "What happens to a dream deferred?/Does it dry up/Like a raisin in the sun?" In the article, "Lorraine Hansberry" in *Dictionary of Literary Biography* Volume 38, Professor Steven Carter posits that the title apparently points up "the bitterness of the social conditions that forcibly and continuously deferred the aspirations of the black family in the play." But the title suggests more than that: the image of a raisin in the sun, like that of Lena's "feeble little plant," also calls the audience's attention to the spirit and tenacity of a people who do not give up their dreams, who are determined to fight for what they deserve, and who are strong enough to triumph over adversity. The approach Hansberry uses in *A Raisin in the Sun* is, indeed, as dramatic as it is poetic.

—Qun Wang

THE RED BADGE OF COURAGE
Novel by Stephen Crane, 1895

The Red Badge of Courage is the most famous of all novels written about the Civil War. It is even more remarkable as the work of a young journalist of 24 who was not even born until six years after the conflict ended. When the novel appeared in 1895 it made Stephen Crane the most visible writer of his generation. The novel came at a time when the Civil War was a subject of great public interest. As the agonies of the war were forgotten and the bitter years of Reconstruction faded into memory, old soldiers began writing their memoirs, and historians found a public for their accounts of the old campaigns. There was, in addition, a great demand for historical romance in the 1890s, and Crane's novel appeared at an opportune time.

The Red Badge of Courage, however, is not historical romance, but rather a notable piece of realism with a certain amount of literary naturalism added. It belongs in the tradition of realism, such as **William Dean Howells** was urging on American novelists, and it anticipates the naturalism of **Theodore Dreiser** and **Frank Norris** inspired by the novels of Zola. Crane's novel also is notable for its impressionistic use of color, its streamlined unity (the story is told in 45,000 words), and its use of irony.

Crane worked very carefully from sources, though he manages to conceal background detail, and it takes close analysis to tie the novel to a specific engagement of the Civil War. Yet Crane used the three-day Battle of Chancellorsville, which took place 1-3 May 1863, as his setting. This was a Northern defeat that occurred just before the tide of war turned in favor of the Union armies. Crane may have heard about this battle when he was a boy, because some of the men who fought in it were from Port Jervis, New York, where he spend his childhood, but he also used *Battles and Leaders of the Civil War,* a book published in 1886, as a source.

Crane's chief interest in the novel is in the psychology of battle. He keeps a steady focus on his protagonist, Henry Fleming, the youth who enlists in the Union Army against his mother's wishes and leaves his New York farm. All unessential detail is pared away, and the reader stays constantly with Henry as his unit prepares for battle. There are no broad panoramas and no digressions. What takes place is what one private soldier can see and know from one small corner of the battlefield.

The three days of the Battle of Chancellorsville enabled Crane to examine Henry during three different phases. In the first part, which takes place before the battle and during the light fighting of the first day, Henry is tortured by doubt, wondering if he will run in the face of the enemy. During the second day when the fighting is heavy, he loses his nerve, drops his rifle, and bolts in panic towards the rear. Crane does a convincing job of creating a sense of terror, depicting the chaos and confusion of battle, during Henry's headlong flight. In this nightmarish scene Henry is hit on the head with a rifle butt by a crazed soldier and receives, ironically, his red badge of courage. When the confusion dies down, he returns sheepishly to his unit and receives the solicitous comfort of his buddies. The third and final day is Henry's triumph, as he leads the charge, captures the enemy flag, and becomes a hero.

Several aspects of Crane's style are of considerable interest. His use of epithets instead of names gives the illusion of universal war experience. He refers to Henry as the youth repeatedly, and it is not until the end of chapter II that the reader learns his name. Other soldiers are referred to similarly: the loud soldier, the tattered soldier, the tall soldier. To gain the psychological realism he wanted, Crane stays within the consciousness of his protagonist through much of the novel: Henry thinks, Henry feels, Henry contemplates. The reader experiences the war through Henry's mind. The technique is a sort of edited stream of consciousness, as opposed to the unedited sort that James Joyce uses in *Ulysses.*

Crane's use of color provides sharp, visual imagery, and the reader at the very outset sees the army camped along an amber-tinted river, and at night the red campfires of the enemy across the stream glow in the dark. When the army begins to march in the morning, their uniforms "glowed a deep purple hue." In the eastern sky "there was a yellow patch like a rug laid for the feet of the coming sun; and against it and patternlike, loomed the gigantic figure of the colonel on a gigantic horse." Besides the use of color, which has suggested to many readers a technique with words analogous to the brushwork of the impressionistic painters of Crane's day, Crane's novel abounds in animal imagery. The campfires of the enemy are not just red points across the river, they are red eyes shining in the dark, like those of predatory animals. When the battle begins Henry fights like a pestered animal worried by dogs, and on the third day he plunges like a mad horse at the Confederate flag.

The use of animal imagery helps convey the deterministic point of view of the literary naturalist, the idea that men are caught like animals in a world they cannot control. The naturalism is particularly clear in the flight chapters when Henry is running away in terror. When he retreats behind the lines and is no longer in danger, he rationalizes his act. Any creature has the right to self-preservation, he thinks. He throws a pine cone at a squirrel, which runs frightened up a tree. Henry feels exonerated: "Nature had given him a sign." The squirrel "did not stand stolidly baring his furry belly to the missile."

Crane, who is usually ironic, plants ironic barbs throughout the novel. The title, of course, is the supreme irony, but the battle itself is ironic, for after Henry's great display of bravery on the third day of battle, the army retreats and all the ground won at great cost is given up. Crane makes the sacrifices of war seem futile and the suffering not worth the cost. The moral, however, is implicit, for as the novel ends Henry feels great pride in himself: "He was a man."

—James Woodress

THE RISE OF SILAS LAPHAM
Novel by William Dean Howells, 1885

The Rise of Silas Lapham, the most widely read of William Dean Howells's many novels, is an excellent example of its author's theory of literary realism, which he set forth in his essay *Criticism and Fiction* (1891). Strongly influenced by such continental writers as Flaubert, Tolstoy, and Turgenev, Howells insisted on a distinction between the novel and the romance as two separate genres. The romance, in his view, serves for entertainment only, though its influence at times can be harmful. But the novel, he thought, is by definition serious, purposeful, and realistic; its emphasis is less on plot than on motivation, character, and ethical and social problems, though, he warned, it should not concern itself with what he called "illicit" love. It must, of course, be plausible in its presentation of events and situations. Howells, in his own realistic novels, was most successful in his close and accurate observation of the superficies of human behavior in the circumstances and interrelationships of everyday living. He was less effective when he attempted psychological or sociological analysis of motives and attitudes. He liked to place his characters in commonplace situations like a journey, an environment unfamiliar to them, or some social event, and examine their conduct, and he was fond of bringing together persons of different classes or backgrounds and describing their interaction.

The Rise of Silas Lapham is the story of a Vermont farmer who has discovered on his land minerals highly suitable for the manufacture of paint. Becoming wealthy, he moves to Boston with his wife and two daughters, Penelope and Irene, and there he struggles for acceptance by the upper, so-called Brahmin class. When Tom Corey, the son of an elite family, falls in love with one of the daughters and takes a position in Lapham's paint business, the goal of acceptance seems to have been reached, even though Lapham gets drunk and makes a fool of himself at a dinner party at the Coreys'. In the meantime, Lapham has been having a house built in a section of the city appropriate for a family with social standing.

But Lapham's luck does not hold. His business is threatened with failure, and his beloved house, almost completed, burns to the ground uninsured. His only chance to recoup his business losses is involving himself in a deal that would financially injure many innocent persons. His real "rise," as opposed to the social one, occurs when, after protracted agonizing, he turns down the deal, accepts failure, and returns to Vermont, where the ethical sense that prompted his honorable decision had presumably been bred into him. Howells implies that, in his crisis, Lapham's behavior is realistic in that it stems from a basic quality in his character—a decency that sets him apart from many, perhaps most, businessmen in a similar dilemma.

Howells employs a subplot in the novel to make another statement of his philosophy of realism, which he insists is applicable to actual living as well as to the writing of fiction. The Laphams have assumed that Tom Corey has been in love with the pretty but rather dull daughter, Irene; but it turns out that he actually loves the rather plain but witty Penelope. Irene is devastated by the discovery, and Penelope is prepared to sacrifice her happiness so that Irene may marry Tom after all. The problem is solved by a liberal clergyman, who points out that the choice is whether three people will be miserable, if Penelope rejects Tom, or only one, if she accepts Tom. The latter, realistic course is followed. The problem arose, according to Howells, because the girls had been reading romances, in which needless self-sacrifice is often presented as a supreme virtue. Had they been reading "realistic" novels, we are led to assume, the situation would never have occurred.

Thus, the novel is a vehicle for Howells's ideas on the value of realism both in literature and in life. But not to be overlooked is Howells's realism in the creation of character and physical and social setting. Howells knew his Boston well, and he acquaints his readers with many parts and aspects of it. His description of Lapham's sleigh-rides through the city on brisk winter days are a delight. His account of the dinner party at which the Coreys entertain the Laphams to the restrained amusement of the former and the self-consciousness of the latter is a masterpiece of the observation of manners. The characterization of brash, boastful, at times foolish, yet ultimately honest Lapham places him as one of the memorable figures in American fiction—a forebear of Babbitt, perhaps, but more likable. The unobtrusive sophistication of Tom and his dilettantish father, the grace with which they carry their wealth and their culture, softens any snobbishness that lies beneath the surface and makes them appear something more than mere representatives of their exclusive social class.

—Perry D. Westbrook

THE ROAD TO TAMAZUNCHALE
Novel by Ron Arias, 1975

The Chicano novel has diversified and flowered since the late 1960s, and *The Road to Tamazunchale* is an example of one of the finest. Its author, Ron Arias, is a journalist and a short story writer whose heritage, education and travels in Latin America have left their mark on his work, especially this, his only novel. *The Road to Tamazunchale* tells of the figurative and perhaps literal pilgrimage of a old, dying man named Fausto through the barrios of Los Angeles down to the border and on to the beautiful, mythical Tamazunchale in the mountains of Mexico. Arias blends the realism of the barrio with the magical realism of Latin American influences and the Faustian dance to create a uniquely Mexican-American fusion of death, renewal, and community.

Arias, the child of an Army family, won a press scholarship after high school and studied in Argentina, writing for the *Buenos Aires Herald* and the *New York Times.* During this time, he studied with Jorge Luis Borges at the National University. After a stint in the Peace Corps in turbulent Latin America in the 1960s, Arias pursued degrees in Spanish and journalism at UCLA. A prolific writer, Arias's short fiction, published in notable literary journals, culminates in the longer novel, *The Road to Tamazunchale.*

At the heart of *Road* is Fausto, an elderly man who is living his last four (or six—perhaps a deliberate confusion) days of his life. The novel even begins in ambiguity about whether or not Fausto is alive or dead: "Fausto lifted his left arm and examined the purple splotches . . . . He tugged at the largest one, near the wrist . . . . He tugged harder, expecting the tissue to tear . . . . Slowly it began to rip, peeling from the muscle. No blood." In the next paragraph, Carmela, his niece, asks him if he wants some more Kleenex when he offers her the piece of dead skin. Although his life and body have broken down, his mind and spirit obviously have not, which is not to say he is altogether lucid. But certainly, the dreams and inner realities of Fausto's mind are populated with many characters, real and magically real, whose disjointed Canterbury-esque tales provide Fausto a meaningful passage into death. In this novel, the distinctions between realities are marked only by the shift of a sentence, the introduction of a character, or more often, not at all.

Joining the "real" characters of Carmela and those who help her with Fausto are the other residents of the barrio, especially the group from the set piece of chapter seven. Drawn from the short story "Wetback" that won Arias the University of California Irvine Chicano Literary Award for fiction in 1975, David is a body found in a dry wash by children, his clothes soaking wet, an obvious victim of drowning. In a gently bizarre episode, Mrs. Rentería takes the young, handsome man as her suitor. After a few days, he restored to "his former self" by Fausto and left again in the wash. Joining David in the cast of magical characters is Marcelino Huanca, a Peruvian alpaca herder and flute player who accompanies Fausto on many of his forays south of the border, and Mario, the ever-shifting street-wise *pachuco*.

The male characters in this story form a host of shape-shifters that represent some traditional mythical figures: the trickster, the wise healer, and the romantic hero. Fausto imagines himself as the magician-healer, raising the dead, or at least reversing the decay, and as the hero, fighting wars, kissing the girl, and saving the village. His cohorts, Mario and Marcelino, are tricksters, manifested as *pachuco* and flute-playing shepherd, respectively. Mario, at first meeting, is described as "an apprentice wizard," who helps Marcelino and Fausto herd some sheep from the Los Angeles freeway. Sheep on the freeway is just one of the natural events with unnatural timing that make up this book. Others include a snowy day in Pacoima, the drowned David in the dry wash, an earthquake, a pageant and play in mythical Tamazunchale, and a funeral procession to the beach at the request of the already dead Fausto at the end of the novel.

Like other folk heroes, Fausto cheats death, or at least finds a way to mitigate its inevitability. The entire novel stands as a testament to the vitality of human imagination regardless of the state of the body. Part of Arias's gift is his skill at drawing from the world's literary, epic, and picaresque traditions—Faust, *Canterbury Tales* and *Don Quixote*—to create a universal journey from the barrio, not *to* death but *through* it. *The Road to Tamazunchale,* critically acclaimed in the Americas and Europe, stands as a wholly Chicano text with universal symbolic and aesthetic appeal.

—Jay Ann Cox

THE SCARLET LETTER
Novel by Nathaniel Hawthorne, 1850

There are reasons to call *The Scarlet Letter* the first modern novel. Certainly it has ancestors in the classic English gothic novel, in the popular sentimental novel, and in the divergent realism of Defoe and Fielding. Even more, it is a descendant of the historical romance of Walter Scott. But the heritage of these British models is transformed in the American offspring of Nathaniel Hawthorne. *The Scarlet Letter* is a modern novel in 1) its unity of plot, characterization, space, time, tone, and imagery; 2) its conscious use of symbolism; and 3) its serious moral-psychological theme.

The unity of *The Scarlet Letter* derives from the fact that Hawthorne was a short story writer and that he found an editor who realized that he had material for a self-sustaining book. Before 1850, Hawthorne had achieved a respectable reputation as a writer of short fiction. In fact, he made the short story an art form. *The Scarlet Letter* began as an extended short story, further expanded by editor James T. Fields's encouragement to a little over 250 uncrowded pages, not counting the 54-page introduction on the Salem, Massachusetts, Custom House (where Hawthorne worked as surveyor from 1846 to 1849). It was far shorter than the two- or three-volume English novels of the time. There was none of their rambling loquaciousness, designed to pass the hours of the bored upper-middle-class women and men who read novels both in England and America.

But Hawthorne's brevity is loaded. Though he could be chatty and timely in his essayistic style—as in the introductory "The Custom-House"—he exhibits the height of concentration in *The Scarlet Letter.* While Hawthorne followed Scott in style and in the romantic use of history, there are, in *The Scarlet Letter,* no subplots and no intrigues that require complicated explanations at the end. In fact, the physical action in the novel is minimal, most of it taking place before the novel begins. The opening and closing scenes at the scaffold are the only outwardly dramatic ones. Otherwise, the action proceeds in the minds and the words of the characters—with sufficient authorial narration and comment to direct the reader.

There are only four significant characters: Hester Prynne, Arthur Dimmesdale, Roger Chillingworth, and little Pearl. They are simplified types—indeed, archetypes—of American character. But they develop morally and psychologically through the novel, and are not, as they would be in a short story, transformed by a single event.

Each episode of *The Scarlet Letter* is set concretely and dramatically. The scenes move almost imperceptibly from chapter to chapter, and they are all within walking distance of the prison, the scaffold, the market-place, and the meeting-house in the early town of Boston between 1645 and 1653. References to the wide world, before and after the main action of the plot, are enough to suggest that Hester—and Hawthorne—transcend the place and time.

The whole drama is done in black and red, but with the quite important green and partly sunny chapters XIV to XIX, where Hester confronts each of the other characters in the natural settings of the seaside and the forest. Except for that pivotal interlude, the final tone of the novel is tragically bleak: "so somber is it, and relieved only by one ever-glowing point of light gloomier than the shadow:—'ON A FIELD SABLE, THE LETTER A, GULES.'"

Hawthorne's use of symbolism is simplistic on the one hand, yet infinitely complex. The letter A stands for adultery, the violation of the Seventh Commandment in the code of Puritan New England. But the letter A had more significance for Hawthorne and for subsequent readers. The letter A is the first letter of the alphabet. In the *New England Primer,* familiar to Hawthorne and to every schoolboy in New England since the 17th century, the letter was represented by the words: "In Adam's Fall/We sinned all"—with a woodcut of Adam and Eve on either side of a fruitful tree (of knowledge). We are all guilty, not of adultery, but of Adam's sin.

And the letter A can stand for more than adultery or Adam's fall. Hawthorne was not unaware of its implications, however much modern imagination may carry them to extremes. For example, A represents amour, art, ambiguity, allegory, America, and as far-fetched as these attributions appear, Hawthorne's open imagination would welcome them.

It is true that the letter A is overworked in the book, and the moral symbolism becomes wearisome. By the time the letter appears in the sky (or doesn't appear) in chapter XII, we have had enough of it, and its appearance (or non-appearance) on Dimmesdale's naked breast in the penultimate chapter is more than enough. Hawthorne was working with something that had not been fully exploited, and he felt compelled to make it clear to his readers—whether Puritan prudes or devourers of sentimental love stories—that he was concerned with more than surface.

By the time the letter appears in the sky, Hawthorne has evolved what has been called his "ambiguity device." Did the letter appear in the sky or was it an apparition of those who chose to believe? Was Hester guilty of anything beyond the transgression of the parochial beliefs of her immediate environment? Was her "sin" Christian and human love? Was she the noble heroine of a love story ordained in Heaven? Such ideas would be shocking—and were shocking—to many 19th-century readers. Hawthorne left them as questions.

The first chapter of *The Scarlet Letter,* entitled "The Prison Door," portends the whole. In the three short paragraphs of this chapter Hawthorne establishes the place and time of his narrative, fixing it in historical fact as well as in folklore. He sets the social-psychological mood of the people, the men in "sad-colored garments" assembled before the prison. He makes it visually real with concrete detail: "the wooden jail . . . already marked with weather-stains" and with "rust on the ponderous iron-work of its oaken door." The prevailing color imagery of the novel is forecast in reference to the prison as "the black flower of civilized society," one of the "earliest practical necessities" in the settlement of a new colony. The black is in contrast with the implied, but unstated, red of the wild rose bush next to the prison door.

This rose bush, by a strange chance, has been kept alive in history; but whether it had merely survived out of the stern old wilderness, so long after the fall of the gigantic pines and oaks that originally overshadowed it,—or whether, as there is fair authority for believing, it had sprung up under the footsteps of the sainted Ann Hutchinson, as she entered the prison-door,—we shall not take upon us to determine. Finding it so directly on the threshold of our narrative, which is now about to issue from that inauspicious portal, we could hardly do otherwise than to pluck one of its flowers and present it to the reader. It may serve, let us hope, to symbolize some sweet moral blossom, that may be found along the track, or relieve the darkening close of a tale of human frailty and sorrow.

That concluding paragraph of chapter I states the symbolic intent of the author. Yet it is carefully ambiguous. The "sweet moral blossom" of *The Scarlet Letter* is that good grows out of evil. Hester's sin was a violation of contemporary social values. Recognizing this, she rose to a humble heroism.

Hawthorne did not say that she ascended to heavenly bliss, nor did he say that she was condemned to the fiery hell of Puritan damnation. He was too aware of his own human frailty to arrogate final judgment. He left it to his readers to recognize their own sinful humanity and their redeeming brotherhood—and sisterhood—with their fellow humans.

—James C. Austin

THE SECRET LIFE OF WALTER MITTY
Story by James Thurber, 1939

Originally published in the *New Yorker* on 18 March 1939, "The Secret Life of Walter Mitty" is far and away James Thurber's most famous piece of fiction. The story features two themes, the war between men and women and the theme of psychological fantasy, long identified with Thurber, but in no other story has he brought them so successfully together. Though he was to write essays, stories, and casuals (those brief, anecdotal, and often autobiographical pieces favored by the *New Yorker* over formal short stories) for more than twenty years after this story appeared, in many ways "The Secret Life of Walter Mitty" represents the culmination of his career.

The war between men and women is fought on many fronts in Thurber's fiction: during cocktail parties and courtships; in bars, speakeasies, and saloons—wherever men and women come into each other's company. But it is waged most bitterly and insidiously by couples who are married, and for good reason. The special curse of marriage as an institution is that the prolonged intimacy it demands too often ends by estranging people from one another, reducing character to caricature and denying all privacies of personality. Over the years, husband and wife begin to believe that each knows the mind and spirit of the other, knows what and why the other thinks regardless of what words are being said. The process is essentially a fictionalizing one, substituting synecdoche and metonymy for the whole complex being, and it fictionalizes the self as well in response to the fiction of the other that has been created. "'I was thinking,'" Walter Mitty declares when his wife interrupts his fantasy for the fourth or fifth time. "'Does it ever occur to you that I am sometimes thinking?'" In marriages that have deteriorated into mere form, as the Mittys' marriage has, the answer to that question is, of course, that such an idea would never occur to Mrs. Mitty; it does not belong to the character of Mitty she has created, any more than the notion that Mitty's behavior is, indeed, a genuine cause for concern belongs to the image of his wife or himself with which Mitty lives. Mitty's astonished stare at his wife when she interrupts his first fantasy—she seemed, Thurber tells us, "grossly unfamiliar, like a strange woman who had yelled at him in a crowd"—may stand as a metaphor for the peculiar sense of estrangement that too often goes with marriages.

All of Mitty's fantasies involve gestures of renunciation and simple, unambiguous actions in a world of men, machines, and warfare. Mrs. Mitty responds with fictions of her own that cast her into the role of self-sacrificing, long-suffering mother of a sick child (the Mittys, significantly, appear to have no children): "'I'm going to take your temperature when I get you home.'" As much as her husband, in other words, though less obviously than he, Mrs. Mitty leads a fantasized existence, one that compensates for her husband's abdication of male responsibility and rewards her with his traditional power for having endured so cruel a mismatch.

The form of Thurber's story implicitly argues that no comfortable and absolute distinctions can be drawn between such mental constructions as Mitty's and his wife's and the supposed "real" world of physical events and activities. Mitty's first fantasy, for example, elaborates upon a few ascertainable facts (ascertainable, that is, within the context of a work of fiction): he is driving a car in weather that may be a bit inclement (recall Mrs. Mitty's command that he buy overshoes). But the fantasy also triumphantly transforms Mrs. Mitty's words, "You're not a young man any longer," into an heroic image of the naval commander, the "Old Man" idolized by the crew. Increasingly, moreover, one fantasy fertilizes another, and the "facts" upon which each new fantasy is built become more and more ambiguous. Mitty's broken arm in the courtroom fantasy, for instance, originates in his earlier determination to "wear my right arm in a sling" to prove that he couldn't possibly remove his own tire chains, and the melodrama of the trial itself comes from a newsboy's hawking cry about the "Waterbury trial." (As usual, Mitty's imagination transmutes this trial into something rich and strange, for the historical Waterbury trial was about political corruption and bribery, not murder.) The most poignant remark in the story, Mitty's vague and dream-like "'Things close in,'" is likewise born of two worlds, one conveniently labelled reality (Mrs. Mitty's sudden striking of his shoulder) and the other just as conveniently and arbitrarily called fantasy (the box-barrage as it closes in during Mitty's experiences as a World War I flying ace).

It is customary to regard Thurber's attitude toward Mitty as, finally, critical of the banal fantasies. Perhaps so. That, after all, is an aesthetic judgment with which most readers would concur. But they need also to admit that they, too, can become involved in the cliches of adventure literature, as they inevitably do when the story opens, and that they are unpleasantly awakened with Mitty to a different textual world from the one they thought they had entered: "'Not so fast! You're driving too fast!'" Such readers need also to recognize that, as habitual consumers of fiction, they regularly grant ontological status to works of sheer fantasy. Like all good parody, in short, Thurber's story subtly satirizes the reader, but out of that satire comes an increased awareness of the omnipresence of fantasy at the boundaries of any active mental life.

—Robert D. Arner

SELF-PORTRAIT IN A CONVEX MIRROR
Poem by John Ashbery, 1975

"Self-Portrait in a Convex Mirror" is one of the most significant long poems of John Ashbery, making it one of a handful of poems that have altered the course of contemporary American poetry. "Self-Portrait in a Convex Mirror" is a difficult piece; the poem owes clear debts to **Wallace Stevens** and pursues Stevens's obsession with the relationship between poetry and painting, art and epistemology, with intense energy. The title poem of Ashbery's 1975 collection, which garnered the triple crown of American literature (the Pulitzer Prize, the National Book Critics Circle Award, and the National Book Award), "Self-Portrait in a Convex Mirror" challenges readers to navigate a difficult meditation on visual and verbal representation, the past and present, and being and becoming.

Because, as Ashbery has intimated, "most of [his] poems are about the experience of experience," a reader needs to be aware that the poem's process of articulation, its movements toward and away from any sort of definitive position, is part of what Ashbery attempts to put down on the page. To put it another way, just as Stevens's "Thirteen Ways of Looking at a Blackbird" privileges none of the thirteen perceptions, Ashbery's poetry remains open to its own dismantling; in perfect postmodern fashion, Ashbery posits that the poem, like any position on reality, is provisional,

unstable, and undecidable. Keeping this in mind when looking at "Self-Portrait" allows a reader to see that the attempt to reach any sort of metaphysical, epistemological, or ontological conclusion—something one might expect in a poem that has such obviously discursive moments—is not undertaken in order to posit some conclusion; it is the attempt, the immersion in the process of what it is to make a self-portrait, that is important. Ashbery's poem asks what it is that the painter attempts to render. The answer: obviously, the self. Ashbery's poem reveals exactly how tricky such an attempt can be.

The poem begins with a description of the Parmigianino painting with the same title. Ashbery writes,

> As Parmigianino did it, the right hand
> Bigger than the head, thrust at the viewer
> And swerving easily away, as though to protect
> What it advertises.

These lines address a major impulse of the poem, the desire to reveal—"advertise"—through exploring the self, coupled with the desire to construct continuity through protection and recalcitrance. This dialectic between active inquiry and active resistance propels the poem. Later, when Ashbery writes, "the soul has to stay where it is," he is articulating that desire for contact with being, knowing that such a desire is fruitless, that becoming is all "our moment of attention" can reveal.

After the initial description of the painting, Ashbery departs on a series of explorations aimed at revealing exactly what can be known about the self. After asserting the momentary ability of the senses to reveal some aspect of the self, he begins the second verse paragraph (line 100) by metaphorically deflating this assertion. He writes, "The balloon pops, the attention / Turns dully away." This turn in the poem is toward undercutting our certainty of understanding any sort of essentialist self; in this section he examines the various ways that the self is constructed, both by forces of any given moment and in time through various historical forces. He writes,

> How many people came and stayed a certain time,
> Uttered light or dark speech that became part of you
> Like light behind windblown fog and sand,
> Filtered and influenced by it, until no part
> Remains that is surely you.

This assertion of an unknowable center, "eyes which . . . Dream but reveal nothing," returns Ashbery to the present in the third verse paragraph of the poem (line 151). Here the "moment of attention" is held with less confidence; subjectivity is more intensely interrogated, and Ashbery shows how we, by necessity, weed out so many particulars that the attention of any given moment has the capability of revealing very little. The particulars that we do register, however, are part of what gives us the hope of the opening of the poem—the hope of understanding some sense of self. Ashbery writes that the forms (these particulars) "were to nourish / A dream which includes them all"—in other words, a dream of some essentialist whole.

Verse paragraph four (ll. 213) returns to critical conceptions of the Parmigianino painting, ostensibly both to reveal the inadequacies of their responses to the work and to underscore once again the provisional nature of our subjective responses to the world. Verse paragraph five (line 252) returns to the question of historical constructs and the self, examining how time and place influence both viewer and viewed and further destabilize any essentialist notion of the self. And yet, for all of this doubt, verse paragraph six (ll. 311) swerves back toward the nagging, intuitive sense of the speaker that there must be some essentialist self behind all of these doubts, that the portrait—in this case both the painting and the poem—reveals. Ashbery writes,

> But it is certain that
> What is beautiful seems so only in relation to a specific
> Life, experienced or not, channeled into some form
> Steeped in the nostalgia of a collective past.

This form contributes to the "vague / Sense of something that can never be known," which is the intuitive sense of the transcendent, of the self, or, to borrow the language of the opening of the poem, of the soul. The longest section of the poem, this verse paragraph revolves around reconciling these various positions on subjectivity and the self. The poem arrives at the provisional conclusion that, like the moment captured in a self-portrait, we are allowed only interstitial glimpses of the whole, glimpses lost yet enduring "in cold pockets / Of remembrance, whispers out of time."

—Tod Marshall

SHIP OF FOOLS
Novel by Katherine Anne Porter, 1962

Twenty years in the writing, encompassing forty-five important characters of seven different nationalities, Katherine Anne Porter's only novel, *Ship of Fools,* spans twenty-seven days as it explores the moral landscapes of human beings journeying towards a future whose portents are grim. Drawing on her own 1931 voyage from Veracruz, Mexico, to Bremerhaven, Germany, and setting the book's action in that year, Porter began writing *Ship of Fools* in 1941 with the working title *No Safe Harbor.* The epigraphs heading each of the book's three divisions preserve the working title's suggestion of the theme of humanity's disappointed search for security and happiness. A quotation from Baudelaire heads art I, "Embarkation." Translated it reads "When shall we set sail toward happiness?," and it denotes humankind's longing belief in the possibility of achieving fulfillment, security, or some other avatar of happiness.

In the wake of this hopeful beginning follow the alienation and uncertainty suggested by part II's ("High Sea") epigraph, which translates "No house, no homeland . . . ." On the strength, or desperation, of their hope the travellers have set themselves adrift between the "true cross" (Veracruz) and the "broken haven" (Bremerhaven). But the epigraph heading part III, "The Harbors," foreshadows hope's ultimate sinking beneath successive waves of disillusionment as readers realize there is no homeland, no destination where truth or happiness or fulfillment resides: "For here have we no continuing city . . . ." Instead, passengers such as La Condesa arrive merely at a place of exile, the 876 migrant workers simply shift their miserable poverty from one country to another, and the hopeful Germans return to a nation already poisoning itself with crazed nationalistic racism, ready to strike even its own if they dissent, and slithering toward war. Thus the book's epigraphs and tripartite structure reinforce a bleak vision of humankind's condition: we are fools who deliberately drift through the world in a continual quest for that place of ultimate assurance and happiness—any place outside ourselves and distant from where we already are—and we find instead disappointment and impoverishment of soul.

Despite the grimness of such a view, *Ship of Fools* is not misanthropic in the sense of exhibiting any malice toward humanity. Porter explicitly includes herself among the passengers on board the *Vera,* and her compassion occasionally surfaces along with her severity. That she italicizes only one passage in the book, a passage sympathetically expressing humanity's child-like, blind yearning for love, is significant. It reads "What they were saying to each other was only, *Love me, love me in spite of all! Whether or not I love you, whether I am fit to love, whether you are able to love, even if there is no such thing as love, love me!*" One of the clearest thematic statements in the book, this plea born of human suffering extracts from the characters' numerous internal oppositions and struggles the unifying issue of the personal and societal consequences of humanity's failure or unwillingness to love. The novel proliferates with failures in love—the stale marriages of the Huttens, Baumgartners, and Lutzes; failures in amorous pursuits—Mrs. Treadwell and the purser, Pastora and Denny, Jenny and Freytag; and failures in commitment—Dr. Schumann and La Condesa, Jenny and David, Freytag and his absent wife Mary. In each case the failure exposes some form of unfulfilled personal need. Whether for survival (Pepe and Amparo), protection of identity (Jenny), independence (Mrs. Treadwell), fear (Frau Schmitt), or some other reason, the characters insulate themselves in an indifference both personally crippling and socially deadly. Mrs. Treadwell's indifference manifests itself as aloof self-possession, but her repressed needs for love and security burst forth in her frenzied, savage beating of Denny. Frau Schmitt's indifference takes the form of self-betrayal, for while she has previously registered her moral disapproval of Herr Rieber's proposal to place the unclean steerage passengers "in a big oven" with the gas on, she acquiesces to the Captain's similarly motivated displacement of Freytag, whose wife is Jewish, from the pure German company of his table. Other passengers are indifferent to the plight of the shop-keepers whose goods the zarzuela company raid and steal, and the whole ship is indifferent to Etchegaray's drowning. Reflecting on it all, Frau Schmitt concludes "she must be quiet, keep to herself, express no opinions, bear no witness . . . nobody cared, nobody cared, there was nobody." To indifference and a failure to love Porter attributes humankind's isolation, self-betrayal, and rage, and by extension she prefigures the individual's apathetic contribution to the rising tide of evil which would sweep over Hitler's Germany and shock the world.

In addition to provoking charges of misanthropy, *Ship of Fools* has aroused questions regarding whether it is merely post-World War II anti-German propaganda. Yet in it Porter negatively characterizes not only Germans, but also Americans, Spaniards, Swedes, Swiss, Cubans, and Mexicans. It is the individual's indifference, whatever his or her nationality, that colludes with evil by failing to oppose it. Dr. Schumann states this important theme clearly when he says "Our collusion with evil is only negative, consent by default, you might say . . . . Imagine if the human race were really divided into embattled angles and invading devils—no, it is bad enough as it is . . . with nine-tenths of us half asleep and refusing to be waked up." The evil of which Porter speaks through Dr. Schumann cuts across nationality, class, gender, and religion. The rise of Nazism is simply a dramatic case in point. Moreover, in an interview with Barbara Thompson published in the *Paris Review,* Porter acknowledged that *Ship of Fools* constitutes part of her effort, as articulated in her introduction to *Flowering Judas,* to understand the "majestic and terrible failure of the life of man in the Western world." Clearly this failure is unrestricted to Germans.

If the book can be said to have a climax, structured as it is around theme and character interaction rather than plot, that climax is the zarzuela troupe's fiesta in honor of Captain Thiele. A Walpurgisnacht of sex, violence, confusion, and drunkenness, the masked party conjures up many of the novel's themes and motifs: masks, self-delusion, appearance vs. reality, failed love, moral disorder, and collusion with evil. Underneath runs a strong current of sexuality, but here as throughout the novel sex is a source of frustration, violence, and guilt. Significantly, Porter juxtaposes all of the major characters' sexual encounters with strongly negative circumstances: both Pepe and Amparo and the Baumgartners preface their lovemaking with anger and violence, Ric and Rac raise the issue of incest, the Huttens make love in a context of discord and death, and Dr. Schumann and La Condesa mingle the ideas of sex, addiction, and guilt. Except for one, every sexual or romantic endeavor on the evening of the hellish fiesta fails. The very next morning brings us Porter's italicized version of humanity's forlorn cry for love. The despairing tone is inescapable. In a frenzy of frustrated efforts to obtain love and safety while maintaining guarded indifference, human beings drift, not towards a safe harbor, but towards despair and moral collapse.

Of note in this novel is Porter's universalizing these issues by creating male as well as female protagonists. Traditionally, she has focused on the female protagonist's struggle to balance her need for security in love and marriage with that need's concomitant call for sacrifice of identity or independence. But these are no longer exclusively women's issues; they are humanity's issues. If the setting on a ship does nothing else, it creates in microcosm a representative world peopled with different classes, ages, religions, nationalities, and genders. Indeed, in her preface Porter herself refers to "the ship of this world." She acknowledges the turmoil and suffering of men as well as women, locating the failures and internal conflicts in both. *Ship of Fools* is no polemic advocating a particular diagnosis or cure for humankind's "majestic and terrible failure." It is one artist's exploration of the universal problems human beings face. There are no conclusions, no solutions; indeed, there is *No Safe Harbor.*

—Margaret A. Loose

SISTER CARRIE
Novel by Theodore Dreiser, 1900

In *Sister Carrie* Theodore Dreiser went beyond the Hoosier romanticism of Meredith Nicholson's "Alice of Old Vincennes" (1900) and the genteel realism of **Booth Tarkington**'s *The Gentleman from Indiana* (1899). Growing up poor in Indiana, the daydreamy Dreiser envied the escape to the metropolis of his older brothers and sisters. Later, he drifted from one newspaper to another—Chicago, St. Louis, Pittsburgh. Charged with Balzac's *Comedie humaine,* Herbert Spencer's *First Principles,* and his own vivid memories, Dreiser began *Sister Carrie* in New York in 1899. The author based his first novel partly on his sister, Emma, who in 1886 had fled from the law with a saloon clerk. Because of the novel's sexual frankness, Dreiser's own publisher (Doubleday

Page) did not promote it; but the senior reader, the writer **Frank Norris**, zealously sent out review copies. When B.W. Dodge (in 1907) and Grosset and Dunlap (in 1908) reissued the controversial book, *Sister Carrie* reached a larger public.

The novel has an hourglass structure. Carrie Meeber—pretty, eighteen, penniless, full of illusions—leaves her dull Wisconsin home in 1889 for Chicago. On the train Charles Drouet, a jaunty traveling salesman, impresses her with his worldliness and affluence. In Chicago, Carrie lives in a cramped flat with her sister and brother-in-law. Her job at a shoe factory is physically and spiritually crushing. After a period of unemployment, she allows Drouet to "keep" her. During his absences, however, she falls under the influence of Drouet's friend, a suave, middle-aged bar manager. George Hurstwood deserts his family, robs his employers, and elopes with Carrie, first to Montreal and then, after returning most of the money, to New York, where they live together for several years. As Hurstwood declines, Carrie develops. To earn money, she goes on stage, rising from chorus girl to minor acting parts. When Hurstwood, failing to find decent work, becomes too great a burden, Carrie deserts him. In time, she becomes a star of musical comedies. Meanwhile, Hurstwood sinks into beggary and suicide. In spite of her freedom and success, Carrie is lonely and unhappy.

Critics have labeled the novel's biological-environmental determinism, graphic fidelity, and compassionate point of view as the work of, respectively, a "naturalist," a "realist," a "romanticist." Consistently, Dreiser intermingles the world-as-it-is, -seems, and -should-be. Like **Stephen Crane**, **Frank Norris**, and **Jack London**, he creates characters caught in the web of causation and chance. In one of his numerous philosophical asides, the narrator informs us that physico-chemical laws underlie all activity: "Now it has been shown experimentally that a constantly subdued frame of mind produces certain poisons in the blood called katastates, just as virtuous feelings of pleasure and delight produce helpful chemicals called anastates." To evoke the illusion of mechanical motion and spiritual drift, Dreiser relies on metaphor and symbol—Carrie attracted to the magnetic city, Carrie tossed about in the sea of humanity, Carrie rocking in a chair. Against baffling forces, she is a "half-equipped little knight," a "little soldier of fortune." And as fortune propels Carrie upward, so it spins Hurstwood downward. Though the narrator avows glorious reason at the end of human evolution, at the end of the novel he pictures a discontented Carrie—fated to remain in the clutch of her powerful opportunistic instincts.

Dreiser's network of dramatic contrasts, parallels, foreshadowings, and ironies (not to mention the cryptic chapter headings his publishers requested) help unify this episodic novel. The sheer mass of detail obscures the chiasmic symmetry of Carrie's rise and Hurstwood's fall, as it screens somewhat the improbability of Hurstwood's "accidental" theft of money and his calculated "abduction" of Carrie. Still, Hurstwood's destitution and matter-of-fact death seem less melodramatic than the tacked-on apostrophe sentimentalizing Carrie as no Saved Sinner or Lost Soul but rather as the Beautiful Dreamer. The awkwardness, repetition, and cliches of Dreiserian prose often grate on fine-tuned sensibilities—as when the narrator informs us that Carrie had "four dollars in money" or when a chapter begins: "The, to Carrie, very important theatrical performance was to take place at the Avery on conditions which were to make it more noteworthy than was at first anticipated." For all this, the author retains the power to endow his factories, hotels, department stores, slums, theaters, and restaurants with an extraordinary sense of life.

At first, *Sister Carrie* (in the 1901 abridged Heinemann edition) was better received in Britain than in America, though the myth of its "suppression" contributed to later interest both in America and abroad. Through *Sister Carrie* Dreiser led socio-literary novelists in the first decade of the 20th century into the creation of closer ties between American life and American literature. Although Dreiser did not receive the Nobel Prize, *Sister Carrie* and *An American Tragedy* are among the truly important novels in American literature. *Sister Carrie* is now available in the Pennsylvania edition (1981), which restores the novel as closely as possible to the author's more complex original manuscript. Whatever one might say about Dreiser's graceless genius, the raw integrity of *Sister Carrie* helped pave the way for the more candid, more crafted American masterpieces of the 1920s.

—Martin Bucco

THE SKY IS GRAY
Novella by Ernest J Gaines, 1963

"The Sky Is Gray" originally appeared in *Negro Digest* in 1963, and was reprinted in Ernest J. Gaines's collection of stories *Bloodline* in 1968. The thirteen-chapter novella is told from the point of view of eight-year-old James who, on the day of the story, is on his way to town with his mother to visit a dentist. In the course of his interior monologue the reader learns that his long-absent father has been drafted into the army and that James is the oldest child in a family suffering from severe poverty. The journey to town symbolically represents James's journey to manhood.

Octavia, his mother, may appear to others as cold and abusive. James is not supposed to put his arms around her because "she say that's weakness and that's cry-baby stuff, and she don't want no cry-baby 'round her." In a flashback, Octavia whips him for hesitating to kill two red birds. But James does not hate his mother; to the contrary, he admires and loves her. He knows that she is concerned for others. While waiting for the bus, he senses that Octavia is worrying about whether Auntie and the children will have enough wood to keep them warm while she's gone. He also understands why his Mama forced him to kill the red birds: if she were to die, responsibility for feeding and protecting the family would fall to him.

Monsieur Bayonne's prayerful attempts to exorcise the toothache prove futile and so, on this cold gray winter Louisiana day, Octavia carefully counts out her money and boards the segregated bus with her son for the fictional town of Bayonne where Dr. Bassett's waiting room allows James to observe some of the ideological conflicts within the black community. The preacher's religious resignation and political passivity is countered by the college student's skepticism and activism. The latter questions conventional wisdom: "The wind is pink; the grass is black," he asserts. He provokes people to think and James decides, "When I grow up I want be jest like him."

At the moment, though, James has his mother to believe in and emulate. When the dentist closes the office and tells them to return after lunch, Octavia and her son are thrown into the cold again. James appreciates his mother's ruse when she feigns interest in ax handles while he warms himself by the shopkeeper's heater. Having stretched their stay to the limit, they cross the tracks to the "back o'town where the colored people eat." In the black cafe, however, Octavia is accosted by a pimp—much to his peril.

She may be poor but she is proud; no price can be placed upon her dignity and integrity as the humiliated pimp discovers.

In the final (and longest) chapter of the story, James and his mother engage in a delicate dance of diplomacy with an elderly white woman, Helena, and her husband, "Alnest" (Ernest). The white couple have observed the black mother and son meandering through the cold streets of Bayonne and have prepared some food for them. But Octavia refuses to accept charity, which prompts the sensitive Helena to propose a quid pro quid: in exchange for James performing a few chores, Helena will feed them. Helena refuses James's help "unless you eat," she says, adding that "I'm old, but I have my pride, too, you know."

Alnest never emerges from his bedroom but his disembodied voice, full of concern, represents the hidden good within the white community. Helena more tangibly reifies the white forces of nurture and support in the South as when she encourages James to face the dentist bravely because there is "Nothing to be afraid of."

Helena's impulse, however, is perhaps to go too far in trying to right the social balance. When Helena attempts to give Octavia more than a quarter's worth of salt meat, James's mother starts to leave the old couple's store. She doesn't want more than she is entitled to. In response, Helena reduces the size of the purchase to more reasonably reflect the amount of Octavia's payment. With their dignity intact, both have accommodated themselves to the feelings and need of the other, and Octavia's philosophy—"You got to stand for yourself, by yourself"—has also undergone a subtle modification by the end of the story. Some of her coldness and reserve melts away as she says to Helena, "Your kindness will never be forgotten."

Back outside in the cold, Mama tells James to turn his collar back down because "You not a bum . . . you a man." Unlike Richard Wright's characters who become "almost a man" through acts of violence or whose manhood is discouraged by black mothers conditioning their sons to the menace of white society, James perceives his mother's actions through loving eyes. He sees the injustices of society (the family's penury, the confederate flag flying on top of the courthouse, inferior dental service for blacks, segregation in transportation and business) and appreciates his mother's determination, sacrifice, devotion, and strength. The trip into town has been a major learning experience for James.

Artistically, "The Sky Is Gray" draws from Gaines's Louisiana roots and the influence of **William Faulkner**. In addition to using the interior monologue form and creating a fictional locale, Gaines is attentive to dialect. "Pull-doos" refers to local birds, "jecked" translates into "jerked", "hist" stands for "hoist," "jugg" means "stuck," "blonks" is an elision of "belongs," etc. Making rich use of the vernacular, Gaines sifts potent images through the insightful mind of a sensitive youth well-launched on the road to maturity and manhood.

—Leonard Deutsch

SNOW-BOUND
Poem by John Greenleaf Whittier, 1866

The opening sequence of John Greenleaf Whittier's *Snow-Bound* introduces one of the poem's finest features—its descriptive details. Presenting the dreariness of the weather, these details make it clear that the poem will not be an overly sentimental depiction of New England in winter. The "cheerless" December sun gives the noon hour a "sadder light" than the "waning moon" would. The "thickening sky" warns of a storm; the bitter cold creates a "chill no coat" can "quite shut out." Early that evening comes "the swarm / And whirl-dance of the blinding storm." It will snow for two days and three nights. Yet even before the poet, a young lad at the time this storm occurred, goes to bed, he notes that the snowfall has already turned the clothes-line posts into "tall and sheeted ghosts." This detail introduces a major theme: the intermingling of the commonplace and the marvelous. Thus, the next morning the narrator remarks that "old familiar sights" took "marvelous shapes," that "strange domes and towers / Rose up where sty or corn-crib stood."

The "shrieking of the mindless wind" increases the isolation of the farmhouse inhabitants—a family and its boarders. Yet each "blast" makes the group feel more unified and more secure. The poet reports later that although snowflakes sifted through his bedroom's unplastered walls, he soon fell sound asleep. The sense of isolation builds to such an emotional intensity that the reader is not startled by the poem's sudden lyrical interludes. These outpourings, as Winfield Townley Scott remarks in "Something about *Snow-Bound*," rise "like songs from the narrative while remaining indigenous to the mood of the poem." The first "song" centers on the poet's acute awareness of time and change. A later, more effective one focuses on the poet's dead sisters. A good indication of Whittier's personality, this interlude's expression of hope for a familial reunion in the after-life is not based on theological reasoning, but on the poet's felt convictions, on truths "to flesh and sense unknown."

The pace of the action slows considerably at the end of the second day when the farmhouse inhabitants gather around the hearth to talk. The quality of the poem, however, does not decrease; for Whittier uses this scene to present vivid character delineations and interesting themes. Although the inhabitants are snow-bound, they roam far through their reminiscences. Yet intertwined with these realistic remembrances are reminders that physical reality also contains the mysterious. The father speaks of "witchcraft"; the mother, of a "gray wizard's conjuring book." These speakers illustrate Whittier's belief that physical reality is rich and multifold. So, too, the hearthside monologues stress the power of the imagination. The poet exclaims, "Forgotten was the outside cold."

The striking inclusiveness of the poet's view of the world becomes apparent. The world simultaneously contains the commonplace and the extraordinary, time present, past, and future, and physical reality and an eternal realm. Further, by means of his depiction of his uncle, a "simple" and "childlike" person, Whittier applauds traits that Wordsworth also honored. However, by means of his favorable portrait of the scholarly schoolteacher boarding at the farm, Whittier—unlike many Romantics—also praises the intellectual, seeing in him the justification for high hopes for America's future.

Then, just as the poem begins to sag toward sentimentality, Whittier introduces the other boarder—Harriet Livermore, a "half-welcome guest." His compelling portrait of this prickly, volatile woman evokes the darker, more dangerous side of life's mysterious forces. Indeed, the term "half-welcome" conveys the ambivalent feelings this powerful personality stirs in others. Because Whittier never understood this woman, she makes him humbly aware of how complicated human beings can be.

By the third morning, the storm has ceased, and the poem moves toward its conclusion. Awakened by shouts from teamsters breaking through the snow, the poet realizes that the storm has quickened human life in the whole region. In this lively section, variations of themes are offered. Inclusiveness, to cite one example, is celebrated again when the newspaper arrives with its fascinating world news. The intense isolation ends, and the poet declares that "all the world was ours once more!"

This would have been the best place for Whittier to end the poem. Instead, before concluding, he abandons his narrative base to sermonize. Still, the overall strengths of the poem decisively outweigh its weaknesses. Whittier took one pastoral incident, a snow storm, and skillfully used it to offer a vibrant variety of themes. As Edward Wagenknecht states in his book on the poet, Whittier also vividly recaptured past experiences and "revealed the beauty of common things." The result is a poem that easily passes the test of time.

—Robert K. Johnson

SOMEWHERE I HAVE NEVER TRAVELLED, GLADLY BEYOND
Poem by E.E. Cummings, 1931

The bulk of E.E. Cummings's poetry falls into three major categories. He is perhaps most famous for his satirical poems, such as "Plato told" and "My sweet old etcetera." "All ignorance tobaggans into know" is one of his many pieces that feature sweeping assertions. The third category consists of his poems of praise. He celebrates, for instance, the individualist in "My father moved through dooms of love"; the natural world in "This is the garden: colours come and go" and "In Just-"; the metaphysical world in "I will wade out"; and man's complexity in poems beginning "so many selves" and "but / he' i." Finally, "Somewhere i have never travelled, gladly beyond" exemplifies Cummings's many poems in praise of love. Because this poem also outlines Cummings's basic view of reality, it merits special attention.

The main reason the speaker in this love lyric values and praises his beloved so highly is introduced at the start of the poem when he states: "somewhere i have never travelled . . . your eyes have their silence." For this "silence" leads the speaker to a richer knowledge of reality than his previous experiences did. Because this knowledge is wholly positive, both the speaker and the woman he loves react to it "gladly" or joyously. A fundamental feature of this deeper reality is gentleness—but a gentleness far more powerful than brute force. For this reason the beloved's "most frail gesture" spurs the speaker to seek being enclosed within the realm of love. Though the woman is physically attractive, the gentleness her beauty embodies also spurs the speaker beyond the solely sensual—beyond what he could "touch"—to "things" essentially metaphysical. Yet the metaphysical permeates physical reality. As Norman Friedman points out, the true world for Cummings is both "the natural world" and "a timeless world of the eternal present."

Stanza two makes it clear that the love awakened in the speaker is inclusive as well as exclusive. Although the speaker, it is implied, had previously closed himself off from a corrupt and hostile society, the woman he loves, symbolized by "Spring," opens him (a "rose") "petal by petal"—sexually, emotionally, spiritually. "Spring," the only word capitalized in the poem, not only stands for the beloved, but also connotes the most important characteristics of the material world—life and resurrection (connoting, in turn, eternity). Furthermore, the springtime is described as skillful and mysterious, indicating that love and nature have enormous, but unfathomable, powers. In the third stanza's last two lines it is suggested again that the speaker's desire for exclusiveness is prompted by society's cruelty and crassness, represented by the snow "everywhere descending."

The penultimate stanza begins, "nothing which we are to perceive in this world equals / the power of your intense fragility." This fragility proves multifold, containing many "countries" or layers. The stanza's last line declares what was alluded to earlier. The power that resides within the woman renders "death and forever with each breathing." That is to say, quickened by love, the speaker intuits that physical reality and metaphysical reality are intertwined, and that the human spirit is immortal. Employing synesthesia in the last stanza, the speaker re-emphasizes that although it permeates the material world, the timeless world is beyond rational comprehension. The speaker can say only that "something in me understands / the voice of your eyes is deeper than all roses." In the poem's last line, rain is personified. But "nobody, not even the rain" has hands as "small" as his beloved's. For the speaker, nothing on earth matches the mysterious, delicate beauty of his beloved and of love.

"Somewhere i have never travelled, gladly beyond" is not a perfect representation of Cummings's poetry. It does not showcase the one original characteristic of his work, his experiments in word-coinage, punctuation, and typography—though he does in this poem use unconventional devices to prevent the punctuation from slowing down the rhythmic intensity. It is also true that Cummings's finest poems cannot hide the fact that his outlook on life became increasingly simplistic and intolerant. (In one poem he declares, "Humanity / i hate you.") However, "Somewhere i have never travelled, gladly beyond" does present Cummings's phrasing at its evocative best. Its content acknowledges life's painfulness but promises that if people open themselves to love, they will gain the courage to withstand cruelty and will perceive the universe's immeasurably positive richness. Lastly, the poem contains Cummings's typical dynamic intensity, an intensity that pulls the reader along line by line.

—Robert K. Johnson

SOULS OF BLACK FOLK
Essays by W.E.B. Du Bois, 1903

Souls of Black Folk, a collection of socio-political essays from the turn of the century, ranks among the great primal texts of black American literature. If **Booker T. Washington** may be seen as prefiguring Martin Luther King, W.E.B. Du Bois in these writings continues and intensifies a legacy of protest begun by **Frederick Douglass** and stretching forward to the present day. Both in form and content *Souls of Black Folk* stands as archetypal ancestor to works as disparate as **James Baldwin**'s *Notes of a Native Son,* Eldridge Cleaver's *Soul on Ice,* and some of the feminist essays of Angela Davis. The writer's attempt to penetrate the "Veil" of racial prejudice and show to his readers "the strange meaning of being black here at the dawning of the twentieth century" makes imaginative use of the essay form, welding a variety of short fragments into a coherent whole, whose theme is the black experience.

From beginning to end, the writing is impressive. Unlike his great rival Washington, Du Bois has a natural literary talent, and his force of expression is backed by a corresponding depth of thought. His prose style, occasionally ornate and high-flown in the manner of the day, is a potent weapon which manages to appear at once passionate and reasoned, its sober dignity matched by a fiery eloquence. It serves him well in *Souls of Black Folk,* ranging freely over the myriad aspects of black American life, and the barriers of discrimination that deny fulfillment to his people. Du Bois forces much into a short compass, sketching a brief history of his race's struggles since Emancipation, and the connivance of prejudice and political expedience that thwarted their freedom. The section best known to most readers is that in which he launches an attack upon Washington, then the most respected black leader in the country. Du Bois's criticism of his great contemporary, while carefully balanced, is remorseless in its logic, justly ridiculing the incompatible vision of a landowner who is also a second-class citizen shorn of voting rights. His thrusts are rendered more telling by the dignified restraint of his argument, honoring Washington's achievements while exposing the flaws in his "gospel of Work and Money." In this Du Bois clearly represents the voice of a growing black intelligentsia, based mainly in the north, who had come to regard Washington as an obstacle to progress.

If the attack on Washington is the best known of Du Bois's writings, it is by no means the most impressive. Some of the factual essays describing Du Bois's tours of the south, and in particular his work as a teacher there, blend literary mastery with the keen eye of the sociologist to bring a "problem" alive, the dry statistics taking on human form in a memorable and touching way. His searching analysis of a Georgia county laid waste by its reliance on the cotton crop is a brilliant piece of work, the breadth of the overview neatly balanced by thumbnail character sketches. Strong and penetrating in a different way are Du Bois's investigations of black religion and especially music as embodying the spiritual core of his people, their finest essence and at that time their sole means of fulfillment. If there is a weak point in the book, it comes towards the end, in the harrowing account of his child's death, and the grim—presumably fictional—parable, "Of the Coming of John." Understandably, period sentiment weighs rather too heavily in the former, while the latter cannot escape a certain touch of melodrama. Freed from the constraints of social analysis, Du Bois tends to grow self-indulgent, with the result that these essays impress themselves less upon the reader than their excellent companion pieces. Such minor flaws, however, serve only to highlight the virtues of the work as a whole, and to render it more striking.

Above all, *Souls of Black Folk* is a cry against injustice, the demand of a maligned race for its rights. The Du Bois of this period may be a world away from the Marxism of his later years—at one point he deplores "a cheap and dangerous socialism"—but his message is straightforward and admits of no compromise. "For this much all men know," he claims, "the Negro is not free," and concludes that: "the problem of the Twentieth Century is the problem of the color line." Du Bois asserts the qualities of his race, praising the elite of university graduates from a people thought incapable of learning, to which "Talented Tenth" he looks for future leadership. He exults in the cultural richness of black America, the supreme gift of the music of slave songs and spirituals. ("The Negro folk-song . . . stands not simply as the sole American music, but as the most beautiful expression of human experience born this side of the seas.") Recognizing this vast potential, he demands that the white world acknowledge it. The barriers which deny the black man his humanity must be dismantled, and he and his contemporaries will accomplish it. Invoking the Declaration of Independence, Du Bois declares: "By every civilized and peaceful method we must strive for the rights which the world accords to men."

As a social and political testament, *Souls of Black Folk* impresses; as a work of literature, it merits its classic status. A creation of vigorous youth which ensured the reputation of its author, it remains a landmark in American writing. Formerly, as with Washington, the black man made polite requests. Here, in memorable language, he stands proudly to demand the birthright that is his.

—Geoff Sadler

THE SOUND AND THE FURY
Novel by William Faulkner, 1929

When *The Sound and the Fury* was published in 1929, it was William Faulkner's fourth novel to see print, and sold the least well of any. Critical acclaim was loud, however, and the novelist Evelyn Scott was so moved by the convoluted story of the Compson family that she wrote a major essay for use in publicizing the book. Its creation was, according to Faulkner in an unpublished preface to the book, an experience of great emotional intensity, unparalleled in his writing career. "One day I seemed to shut a door between me and all publishers' addresses and book lists. I said to myself, Now I can write. Now I can make myself a vase like that which the old Roman kept at his bedside and wore the rim slowly away with kissing it."

Like other American modernists, Faulkner believed in the supreme value of the art object—whether it was a vase or a novel. He would be judged by his work; that was his only identity (and many of the tales he invented when asked about his personal life were evidence of the belief that his only existence rested in his fiction). The rare technical prowess of *The Sound and the Fury* attracted the admiration of writers, but it just as frequently confused the general reader.

Faulkner tells the story of the decaying Compson family and its southern home in a four-part structure. The first, told by the retarded Benjy, the youngest of the four children, recounts scenes and emotional understandings from the childhood of the four children—Quentin, Candace, Jason, and Benjy (formerly named Maury after his maternal uncle). Water fights in the branch, the death of their grandmother, Caddy's wedding, Benjy's castration, and Jason's misbehavior are woven into a modern-day narration that includes losing a quarter, celebrating Benjy's 33rd birthday, and arguments between the niece Quentin (Caddy's child) and her uncle, Jason. To simulate the flow of Benjy's consciousness, Faulkner used a remarkable stream-of-consciousness device. He asked that the text be set in eight different colors of type. Because the cost of doing this would have been prohibitive, the publisher used italic type, but to move into and out of italics does not do justice to the layers of narrative caught in Benjy's memory. One aid to placing events in time is the Gibson family, whose mother, Dilsey, has worked for the Compson family throughout their history; her children and grandchildren have, through the years, been responsible for caring for Benjy and their varying names aid the reader considerably.

The first part of the novel occurs on 7 April 1928, the Saturday of Easter weekend. The third, Jason's recounting, occurs the day before, on 6 April; and the fourth, told by a limited omniscient narrator, on Sunday, 8 April. The second, a striking counterpoint to the on-going 1928 story, is Quentin's monologue on the day of his suicide, 2 June 1910, as he plans his death by drowning and mulls over the various conflicts within his family. Moving back into the time of many of the events in Benjy's section intensifies the reader's reaction to those conflicts between mother and children, Caddy's sexuality and Quentin's modesty, Mr. Compson's cynicism and the need for innocence in children, and other of the dominant family patterns. Focus throughout is on Quentin's inability to deal with the realities of life, imaged in the character of his younger sister, Caddy. She, then, although she has no section of the book as her own, becomes a central figure in the development of each of her brothers.

Section three, the 1928 story as recounted by the middle child, Jason, currently a clerk in a local hardware store, is an ironic retelling of a Good Friday betrayal. Jason exemplifies the evil of conscious wrong-doing, and his treatment of his niece Quentin sets up the theft that closes the Easter weekend at the Compson home. That story occupies Easter Sunday, and though Dilsey takes her family and Benjy to a stirring service in the black church, Jason searches futilely, and almost meets his death in macabre fashion, for the last lost member of the Compson family, Quentin. The lineage of the Compson family ends in despair and emptiness, rather than fruition, and—as Faulkner said in the appendix which he wrote for the reprinting of the novel in 1945—the chief virtue of the tale is that the Gibson family, with its traditional values, including religion and respect for personhood and community, did endure.

Mirroring the tragedy of Shakespeare's *Macbeth,* from which the title is drawn, *The Sound and the Fury* conveys the bleak view of characters raised to believe in family, community, and established verities—and only in those values—without being equipped in any way to meet the changes that the modern age brought to southern life. For readers who had lived through World War I and knew the inevitability of change and what Faulkner called "flux," the sorrowful tale of the Compson family was universal rather than regional. It was moving as well as admonitory. It was also a skillful virtuoso performance by a writer whose equal was not to be found in modern American literature.

—Linda Wagner-Martin

STRANGE INTERLUDE
Play by Eugene O'Neill, 1928

The enormous success of Eugene O'Neill's *Strange Interlude* in its premiere season in 1928 astonished many critics almost as much as its popularity in revival right up to Glenda Jackson's performance in 1984, although in its remarkable production history it has also earned the verdict of "the worst play ever written by a major dramatist." As often with O'Neill, such extreme reactions reflect the audacity of his technical experimentation.

The story of this colossal, nine-act play is a Strindbergian saga of the sex war in which the dominant character is Nina, whose predatory sexual behavior is presented as a reaction to the loss of her fiance during World War I. Her first act of redemptive compensation consists in nursing crippled soldiers and sleeping with many of them (her relationship with her fiance was, she regrets, unconsummated). On the death of her father, a professor, she finds herself surrounded by three men: an oedipal, bisexual novelist, a coolly professional doctor, and a "guileless," boyish, hero-worshipper of her fiance, whom she marries. News of his family's congenital lunacy precipitates a secret abortion and the adulterous conception of a son by the doctor, in a context of (ostensibly) disinterested Darwinian debate. In the second part (final four acts), as in the second part of Strindberg's *Dance of Death,* much of the action is ironically duplicated in the next generation: Nina's son emulates the war hero fiance on the sports field, but by doing so attracts another Nina (Madeline) who wins the attentions of doctor and novelist and asks the obvious questions about the son's paternity, all of which are left hanging after Nina's husband's death at the end.

The play's chief distinction is in its dramaturgy, in the pervasive use of "thought asides," as O'Neill termed the (spoken) interior monologues which take up nearly half the published script. Obviously influenced to an extent by James Joyce's stream of consciousness and by popular psychoanalytical writings, the asides express thoughts which are often in conflict with dialogue utterances, and through them O'Neill generates more irony on a single page than many whole plays contain. All of the characters have asides (they are a well-established habit for Nina's son by the age of eleven) and so the audience's privileged insight penetrates the whole cast.

As a device for sustaining a contrapuntal tension, for constantly exposing the fabric of lies and half-truths that the characters trade as dialogue, the aside is an obviously valuable instrument. O'Neill, however, deployed it not just for verification, but as a means of dissolving the "masks" which, in his view, shield all behavior. Although his asides may simply undermine verbal behavior, they may alternatively corroborate it, embellish it, or reveal a subtextual dilemma which is scarcely hinted at in the dialogue. Their convenience for conveying exposition is evident, and O'Neill also develops them into a highly versatile means of generating momentum and suspense. Characters often ask questions of themselves and use the aside to articulate their uncertainty, in which case its informative value is nebulous. But, in another sense, every aside is virtually a disguised question, as it inevitably raises the possibility that its content may at some stage be translated into overt dialogue or action. The longer the play develops, the more extensive this subtextual minefield becomes, so that the final two acts are extremely intense, verging on a grand resolution and recognition scene which never quite occurs. It is particularly significant that most of the expressions of aggression and animosity in the play are contained in asides, never achieving realization.

O'Neill was well aware that various levels of consciousness might be in conflict within his characters, and the asides (to him, the most important part of the play) were deployed largely as a vehicle for this conflict; he judged his attempt successful "in so far as it concerns only surfaces and their immediate subsurfaces, but not where, occasionally, it tries to probe deeper." The stage directions which accompany the asides indicate that the controllability of the thoughts varies greatly; sometimes they are fantasies generated for consolation or self gratification, at other times they have an antagonistic energy of their own. Sometimes their effect on the thinker is presented as consolidating, but more often it is clearly divisive.

Plausibility is a criterion that has often been used against the characterization of Nina in particular; the way in which adolescent frustration escalates into a triumphant, Gargantuan voraciousness seems to indicate an authorial obsession about the nature of women. However, the yardstick of plausibility may less easily be applied to the thought asides, and the presentational style used in the theatre since the premiere should dismiss assumptions from realistic premises: throughout the thought asides, the actors freeze. In some productions, this has achieved the effect of embodying poetic crystallizations of fragments of the mind.

—Howard McNaughton

A STREETCAR NAMED DESIRE
Play by Tennessee Williams, 1947

What Walter Kerr designated "the finest single work yet created for the American theatre" packs such an emotional punch it can cut through a macho man's defenses. Well cast—as it has been on three occasions with the English actresses Jessica Tandy (Broadway), Vivien Leigh (London and the film), and Rosemary Harris (Broadway revival)—and well directed—as it was by Elia Kazan in a lyric production featuring jazz and a spotlight on Blanche DuBois—Tennessee Williams's *A Streetcar Named Desire* devastates spectators with those feelings engendered by tragedies, pity and fear.

Employing poetic symbolism but a frequently terse prose style, Williams creates compassion for a frightened, lonely, aging, southern belle, daughter of a patrician family, who is visiting her sister Stella and brother-in-law Stanley Kowalski in their cramped apartment in the French Quarter of New Orleans. Romance with a sensitive friend of Stanley's seems headed for marriage. But, as Blanche luxuriates in a hot bath offstage while singing "It wouldn't be make-believe if you believed in me," Stanley gives his wife the lowdown on her big sister who, after a disastrous marriage with a homosexual, has devoted her nights to casual sex. Stanley also tells Blanche's suitor the juicy details, thereby destroying her chance for a healing haven. Later, after he has issued the ultimatum that penniless Blanche must leave her refuge and as her mental stability is tottering, Stanley rapes Blanche. Her future destroyed, Blanche, like Williams's beloved sister Rose, is led off to an asylum.

Cleverly constructed around the seasons, *Streetcar* begins in springtime, a period when Blanche hopes she can salvage her life, progresses through a sweltering summer of explosive passions, and winds down in autumn, when not merely the days but Blanche's dreams will wane. *Streetcar's* remarkable economy of language is made possible by unobtrusive symbols: Stanley wears virile primary colors; Blanche, whose name means white, is garbed in that color because she's only technically impure. The family plantation, Belle Reve, was not a "beautiful dream" to live on but rather the scene of waking nightmares of death. The characters suggest the past versus the present in a changing South. Blanche soaks in a tub to keep herself dainty, in contrast to Stanley's body soaked in sweat. Streetcars named Desire and Cemeteries have brought Blanche to a road called Elysian Fields. (Previous Williams titles, *Blanche's Chair in the Moon* and *The Poker Night,* were not so evocative.) The colored paper lantern Blanche supplies to cover the light bulb serves to soften unpleasant truths about her age, her nerves, her situation. A Mexican woman sells "flores para los muertos" after we see Blanche's dreams of marriage to Mitch doomed.

Williams reveals Blanche's real prospects gradually. Blanche disguises her desperation with lies—about her drinking, her age, her reasons for coming to New Orleans, her sexual experience. Although she speaks of some of her losses early on—of the plantation and her relatives—only late in the play do we discover that she blames herself for her homosexual husband's suicide and that promiscuity much like his has cost her her reputation and her job.

Williams provides Stanley with many motives for hating Blanche. She drinks his hooch, patronizes him, sponges off him—while complaining because Stella has no maid. She has lost Belle Reve. Her presence interferes with Stanley and Stella's sex life. Blanche competes with Stanley for Stella, offering to rescue her from him. Crucial is Blanche's tirade about Stanley being a subhuman ape. The eavesdropping man is stung by her contempt.

Yet Blanche is rarely rude. Whereas Stanley is no gentleman, Blanche is a gentlewoman—refined, fragile, sensitive. Her sexual purity, like her jewelry, is imitation, but her gentility is genuine. Pitiable, but not pitiful, she is felled by a "common" Polish-American Apollo, a lusty barbarian, captain of the bowling team, an American version of Lady Chatterley's gardener. In part modeled on Williams's father, an aggressive, hard-drinking, poker player who damaged his son's self respect, Stanley is a stud who appeals to Williams but also repels him; he is not the character with whom the dramatist's greatest sympathies lie.

Williams appreciates Blanche's fears that her sexual "misconduct" will come to light because of his own early days as a closeted homosexual. Like Williams, Blanche has furtive sexual encounters but, though she does not repress her desires, she also cannot suppress her guilt. When she enters the French Quarter, which could accept her earthier side, she is prevented by the values she internalized in her youth from acknowledging the desire which brought her there.

One of the most difficult ways to grow up female in the United States early in this century was to do so in impoverished circumstances in the Deep South. Women of aristocratic lineage were expected to refrain from seeking most forms of employment—"A lady doesn't work"—although the teaching profession was an exception. And a lady must neither seek sex nor appear to enjoy it. As a woman of her period and place, Blanche was raised to trade upon her attractiveness. Yet when the marriage with which her allures are rewarded is destroyed by her conventional moral standards and then her own renegade sexuality flouts social strictures, she finds herself in turn the outcast who must deceive to survive. Williams may take a certain delight, of course, in seeing the easily shocked wife of a homosexual follow in his footsteps. On the other hand, Streetcar's original producer, Irene Selznick, as a woman, may have been touched by the power of the double standard to dictate that Blanche's father and grandfather could indulge in "epic fornications" and Stanley could be admired for his sexual prowess, but a woman of Blanche's class, once she has slipped off her pedestal, is fair target for rape.

Nowadays we regard rape not as a stud's right but as a reprehensible act of violence. We therefore can appreciate Stanley's attack on Blanche as completing the murder of her soul which he began when he decided to block her marriage to Mitch and throw her out of his home. (Sending her to the booby hatch afterwards is merely carting off the corpse to the cemetery to Stanley, although Stella and Mitch agonize at their complicity.) We can plainly see Blanche is terrified of Stanley, defends her honor with a broken bottle, is overpowered by him, and has a right to refuse him, whatever her sexual history may be.

Not so in December 1947. When Streetcar opened it received enthusiastic but misguided reviews from critics—all men, inciden-

tally—who regarded Blanche as a 19th-century fallen woman suffering punishment or, still worse, believed she went to bed with Stanley willingly. They described her as a prostitute or a nymphomaniac—a word not fashionable since women asserted their right to enjoy their sexuality—and spoke of her "affair" with Stanley and of the "strong attraction between them which is satisfied." Twenty-five years later few reviews misconstrued this event, and it was labeled rape.

Streetcar's early critics and its more recent interpreters likewise disagree about Blanche's sanity. Those writing in the late 1940s sometimes saw Blanche as deranged throughout the play. Now we are more likely to believe that until the play's end, when Blanche expects Shep Huntleigh, she does not confuse her pretenses with reality. She knows the difference, but prefers lies to her sordid surroundings and the looming abyss. A victim of romantic cliches about life, Blanche is one of "the fugitive kind" seeking solace in "magic." Her self-image as a lady may be at odds with the sleazier details of her past, but it is also the source of strength which allows her to survive. Knowing she has been raped, having lost her sister's protection because she has told the truth—an ironic downfall for a "fibber"—Blanche maintains dignity in defeat. "Please don't get up," she enjoins the poker players on her exit. She does not delude herself about their rising because a lady has entered the room, for rise they do. Perhaps heroism in a hopeless situation and madness are much the same thing.

An elegy from a chivalrous Mississippi playwright on the "civilized" South menaced by robust barbarians, Streetcar demonstrates in Williams's own words, "If we don't watch out, the apes will take over." As the author also remarked, "we are in the jungle with whatever we can work out for ourselves. It seems to me that the cards are stacked against us. The only victory is how we take it." So he sets up Blanche as a heart-wrenching sure loser, every card "stacked against" her, and she "takes it" with dignity as she is thrust once more upon "the kindness of strangers."

—Tish Dace

THE SUN ALSO RISES
Novel by Ernest Hemingway, 1926

Ernest Hemingway's first novel created a large and, generally, appreciative readership for the most modern fiction an American had, in 1926, yet produced. Spare dialogue, little description, and even less authorial interference made The Sun Also Rises seem an easy book to read, and its story of young Americans living abroad, disillusioned by the aftermath of World War I and people's reaction to it, was also accessible. Hemingway had earlier published poetry and short stories (vignettes or sketches, as some of the magazines that rejected them called them), and his short story collection In Our Time had been very well received. Working from these shorter modes, Hemingway brought to this full-length text some of the same techniques: images used to expand meaning, scenes that combined plot movement and characterization, laconic description of characters. The novel was innovative as well as shocking.

For the "hero" of The Sun Also Rises was a wounded newspaperman who spent much of his time drinking with his friends and expressing a disillusion with war, patriotism, mainstream American life, and whatever verities middle-class America held dear. Jake

Barnes was the center of a group of nomadic expatriates who lived from day to day, bed to bed, and drink to drink—none of his friends showed any more ambition or direction than he supposedly did. Yet *The Sun Also Rises* was, in Hemingway's words, a very moral novel. It showed the human values of friendship, understanding, and love in a different context, a different milieu, and convinced most readers that the postwar generation was in no way "lost."

Hemingway's mentor, Gertrude Stein, had quoted the author some words of a French auto mechanic, to the effect that the postwar generation was "lost," and Hemingway places that statement as the first quotation on his epigraph page. But below appears a long passage from Ecclesiastes, from which the novel's title comes, stating that life is cyclic: the sun rises and sets, the earth revolves, life goes on. Affirmation consequently follows negation, just as the values of Hemingway's characters evolve. From their disillusion comes a way to live in the disordered world.

Jake Barnes—despite his impotence from his wound—is the man Brett Ashley would like to spend her life with. Already engaged to Mike Campbell, she falls passionately in love with Pedro Romero, the young and noble Spanish bullfighter. In her decision to leave Romero, rather than ruin his promising career as a matador, Brett comes to understand morality in the postwar world. The active plot of the novel concerns Brett and her decisions; the meditative plot, which is a strong counterpart to the more active, concerns Jake as he fishes with his old friend Bill Gorton, tries to keep his friends together, and serves as a source of wisdom and comfort throughout the book. Rich with symbolism, *The Sun Also Rises* appears to be a racy account of friends moving from Paris to Spain, going on the holiday that gave the British edition of the book the title *Fiesta,* but Hemingway instead builds in intense meaning at every turn. Random conversations lead to important thoughts about relativity; Jake's visit to the monastery at Roncesvalles evokes the pageantry of past bravery; and the friendship of the aficionado understanding in Spain brings Jake himself to new realizations—among them that he and Brett cannot continue to be intimate.

The stark descriptions and laconic scenes, the heavy irony, and the sense of readers being a part of the sometimes secret meanings of the text mark the novel as particularly modern. Called a *roman a clef* because its characters and plot resembled the summer of 1925 in Spain, *The Sun Also Rises* presented as heroes people who did not live by accepted, middle-class codes of behavior. In doing so, it questioned those codes and values, just as had **F. Scott Fitzgerald**'s novel *The Great Gatsby* the year before. The question in both fictions remained, what was valued in American life, and what did the man who wanted to be successful in that culture have to do to be so considered? Very much a part of the 1920s atmosphere, *The Sun Also Rises* was in some ways more affirmative than other texts from that decade—**T.S. Eliot**'s *The Waste Land,* for example, or **Sinclair Lewis**'s *Main Street.* Hemingway showed his characters as acting, thinking human beings (for the most part; there is a heavy strain of antisemitism that is regrettable), who manage to make viable decisions even when faced with calamity, of whatever sort.

For 1926, *The Sun Also Rises* was no small accomplishment. Indeed, it prefigured many of the fictions to come during the 1930s, when all of America was called on to question its values in the midst of the devastating Depression. By that time, Hemingway had become famous with *A Farewell to Arms,* more stories, and his columns for *Esquire* and other magazines. The nucleus of nearly all of his later work, however, was the tough characterization and the rapid-fire action of *The Sun Also Rises.*

—Linda Wagner-Martin

SUNDAY MORNING
Poem by Wallace Stevens, 1923

"Sunday Morning" by Wallace Stevens was first published by Harriet Monroe in her magazine *Poetry* in November 1915. She impaired the quality of the original poem by omitting three stanzas and by rearranging the remaining five stanzas. Although the poem was not published as Stevens wrote it until the first edition of his first book *Harmonium,* in 1923, the Monroe version was sufficiently remarkable to establish 1915 as the year in which Stevens began his career as a major poet. "Sunday Morning" is today considered to be one of Stevens's most important poems, and many believe it to be the greatest poem written by an American in the 20th century.

It is a meditation on the loss of Christian faith, on what that loss meant to Stevens and, by implication, on what it meant to the Western world. As Stevens said in a letter in which he refers to the female protagonist of "Sunday Morning," "This is not essentially a woman's meditation on religion and the meaning of life. It is anybody's meditation." Loss of religious faith was a common subject of late Victorian and early 20th-century literature, but the poem itself is far from commonplace. Its importance lies in the power of its language. The beautifully cadenced and controlled blank verse with subtle and unobtrusive echoes of Shakespeare, Keats, Wordsworth, Milton, **William Cullen Bryant**, and Christian liturgy and with its significantly charged and freshly perceived imagery has seldom if ever been equalled in modern poetry.

In the opening stanza a woman amid the comfortable "Complacencies of the peignoir, and late / Coffee and oranges in a sunny chair" is disturbed by the thought of death and, because it is Sunday morning, specifically by the recollection of the crucifixion which, as will be made clear in the last stanza, she realizes is an actual physical and spiritual death. There is no resurrection, no transcendence, no immortality. The poem presents modern man face to face with absolute nihilism.

The woman's response to this "dark encroachment" is identical with Stevens's own—an aesthetic hedonism reminiscent of Walter Pater who wrote in his essay "Aesthetic Poetry": "One characteristic of the pagan spirit the aesthetic poetry has . . . the continual suggestion, pensive or passionate, of the shortness of life. This is contrasted with the bloom of the world, and gives new seduction to it." Stevens in a letter commenting on "Sunday Morning" wrote, "The poem is simply an expression of paganism."

In the second stanza the protagonist seeks consolation in the only paradise that for her exists, the earthly paradise:

Shall she not find in comforts of the sun,
In pungent fruit and bright green wings, or else
In any balm or beauty of the earth,
Things to be cherished like the thought of heaven?

And in this earthly paradise she may hold communion with the only divinity possible for her, her own emotions and the enjoyment of them. "Divinity must live within herself." The third stanza contrasts the hierarchical aristocratic pagan religions of the Graeco-Roman world (here personified by Jove) with the more democratic Christian religion. "The very hinds discerned it, in a star." The final lines look forward to a new paganism which will replace Christianity. This will be more fully defined in stanza seven. Stanza four is a melodious but melancholy (Pater would have called it "pensive") farewell to both the old pagan religions, "the golden underground" and "isle / Melodious where spirits gat them home," and Christianity, "the cloudy palm / Remote on heaven's hill." These are transitory and gone forever. Her own present earthly paradise seems to her more enduring.

In stanza five the thought of death again intrudes. Her response to it, "Death is the mother of beauty," is again reminiscent of Pater who wrote "the sense of death and the desire of beauty: the desire of beauty quickened by the sense of death." As Mario Praz has pointed out, the association of death with beauty is characteristic of what he called "the romantic agony." "Beauty and Death [were] looked upon as sisters by the Romantics . . . a beauty of which, the more bitter the taste, the more abundant the enjoyment." In Stevens's poem, new fruits are brought forth by the perishing of the old, and the maidens enjoy them amid images of death and decay: "The maidens taste / And stray impassioned in the littering leaves." Stanza six is a vision of a paradise similar to the earthly paradise but unchanging and eternal. Such a paradise would become tiresome and produce what Baudelaire called the greatest sin of all, ennui. Stanza seven describes the religion of the future, a new paganism in which men worship the physical universe, "the sun," of which they are a part and in which they had their origin. They shall believe in the brotherhood of man and they shall be aware that the lives of all men are temporary. "And whence they came and wither they shall go / The dew upon their feet shall manifest." Stevens's own gloss on these lines is "Life is as fugitive as dew upon the feet of men dancing in dew. Men do not either come from any direction or disappear in any direction. Life is as meaningless as dew." There is an interesting passage in D. H. Lawrence's *Apocalypse* (published several years after "Sunday Morning") in which Lawrence envisages a future religion exactly like that of Stevens. "We ought to dance with rapture that we should be alive and in the flesh, and part of the living incarnate cosmos. I am part of the sun as my eye is part of me. That I am part of the earth my feet know perfectly."

The beautifully written final stanza states that Jesus (God) is dead and that man must live alone, "unsponsored," on a transitory but lovely planet ("an old chaos of the sun"). In the last four lines the pigeons, symbolizing all life including man, are seen as accidental ("casual") components of a meaningless ("ambiguous") physical universe descending to death "on extended wings."

The structure of the poem is somewhat repetitious. As in music, a theme or an image such as the "wide water" is introduced, dropped, and then repeated, perhaps several times, and developed. It is this repetition, probably, that Monroe was trying to avoid when she first printed the poem with several stanzas deleted and the others rearranged. Most critics, however, consider the cumulative effect of the repeated themes and images to be successful. The poem as a whole is a striking example of what **Yvor Winters** defined as the post-symbolist method—the employment of associative rather than logical structure and the use of functional instead of merely ornamental imagery, each image being charged with a significance relevant to the poem as a whole.

—Donald E. Stanford

THE SWIMMER
Story by John Cheever, 1964

At the burial service for John Cheever in 1982, he was eulogized as "the leading fabulist of his generation . . . [who] wrote prose fiction in a manner more common with poets and their poetry." The speaker, **John Updike**, then added that the compactness of Cheever's rich, swift style was "always outracing expectation and keeping the thread between reader and writer taut." "The Swimmer" is a sparkling example of Cheever's best work, for it is a deftly condensed evocation of the classic Odyssean voyage, the heroic but abortive struggle of a modern middle-class wanderer to reach the safe haven of his home. But the story conveys much more than its surface events reveal.

Like most of Cheever's sizable body of fiction—especially his 130 or more short stories—"The Swimmer" presents a desolate yet sympathetic critique of 20th-century middle-class society in America by holding a mirror to the values and limitations of its members. Its emphatic but ominous tone is set in the bibulous scene at the Westerhazys' swimming pool in the opening paragraph: "We all *drank* too much." And as the youthful-looking but "far from young" Neddy Merrill sits beside the pool with one hand "around a glass of gin," both bravado and folly are implicit in the grandiose project he conceives and decides to undertake on this beautiful summer afternoon. He will swim and portage himself through some fourteen other pools at the homes of old friends and neighbors, which are strung out in a southwesterly dogleg direction from the Westerhazys' to his home in Bullet Park eight miles away.

Excitement and anticipation attend Merrill's jaunty take-off and initial progress as he makes his way easily, meeting conviviality and more good cheer along his watery course (now named the Lucinda River in his wife's honor) at the homes of the Grahams, Hammers, Lears, Howlands, and Bunkers, where an uproarious party is in full swing. But from here on gradual atmospheric changes and unexpected developments upset the rhythm of his quest and begin to dampen his enthusiasm for it. The Levys he finds temporarily absent and so drinks alone while sitting out a thunderstorm in their gazebo, but at the Welchers' he finds the house locked up and their pool dry. Then, having crossed his most difficult portage at route 424, where an empty beer can is thrown at him from the passing traffic, his sensibilities suffer increasingly greater indignities. For lack of a proper identification he is ejected from the crowded, stinking public pool at Lancaster; he receives foreboding news of his wife and daughters from their old friend, Mrs. Halloran and still bleaker disclosures from her daughter, Helen Sachs, who can offer no liquor to relieve his chill at her poolside next door; and finally he receives outright insults at the Biswangers' for crashing their party uninvited, as well as a shocking repudiation at the home of his former mistress, Shirley Adams. Wearied, shivering, and unstrung, Merrill can at last barely crawl through the last two pools and stagger under a darkened sky up the driveway to his own home—which he finds totally dark, locked, and empty!

To readers who follow Cheever's deepening tone carefully, this abrupt denouement may come as no great surprise, even though its shock value is unmistakable. They will have noted in the clues he drops progressively that his subtle allusions to discrepancies in time, to those of memory and forgetfulness, and to contrasts between warmth and chill, darkness and light, vigor and fatigue, all combine to form a pattern of meaning that transcends the merely structural account of a single imaginary exploit. Like one of **Nathaniel Hawthorne**'s best tales—let us say "Young Goodman Brown"—"The Swimmer" offers a dream vision of human life itself. The story shows why **Saul Bellow**, another literary friend at Cheever's memorial service, said that he strove "to give us the poetry of the bewildering and stupendously dreamlike world in which we find ourselves."

—Eugene Current-Garcia

THE TENTH MUSE
Poems by Anne Bradstreet, 1650

Anne Bradstreet's *The Tenth Muse Lately sprung up in AMERICA . . . By a Gentlewoman in those parts* is the first book of poems by an American poet and one of the first by a woman writing in English. Had Bradstreet not developed later into a poet of some importance, these would be about the only reasons for reserving a place for *The Tenth Muse* in literary history, for the poetry in this volume is generally undistinguished, with only a few flashes of originality or insight. Indeed, imitation and not originality was uppermost in Bradstreet's mind; she deliberately set herself the task of writing like her father, Thomas Dudley, and the French poet Guillaume du Bartas (as translated by Joshua Sylvester). She conceived of poetry as a vehicle for public rather than private sentiments and, like another of her models, Sir Walter Raleigh, saw the functions of poet and historian as complementary if not identical. The poems in *The Tenth Muse* are what they are largely because of Bradstreet's preconceptions concerning poetry, its nature and uses.

Yet *The Tenth Muse* is also the work of a craftswoman learning her trade, and as such it has a value larger than the merely historical. In it, Bradstreet begins the process of discovering her own voice and themes, both of which originate, finally, in her roles as wife and mother in American Puritan society. The limitations of such roles are obvious, but had her place in society not been so secure—had she not read Spenser and Sidney and maybe even Shakespeare *and* been encouraged in her writing by her family—she might never have written the poems for which she is remembered. By spiriting away her manuscript without her knowledge and arranging for its publication in London, her brother-in-law John Woodbridge may have embarrassed her as an artist, as she complained in a later poem entitled "The Author to Her Book," but that poem also makes clear that Woodbridge's act of benevolent piracy awakened her to a sense of artistic responsibility and self-awareness. She was to take her writing seriously thereafter, even to the extent of revising *The Tenth Muse.*

Following a cluster of dedicatory poems by Nathaniel Ward, Nicholas Henry, Benjamin Woodbridge, and other male writers, all of whom expressed playful (?) astonishment that a woman could write anything worth reading, *The Tenth Muse* commences with a poem inscribed to Bradstreet's father, and alluding to his poem, now lost, on the four parts of the world. It is likely that John Woodbridge got this and the next poem, "The Prologue," mixed up in the manuscript, for "To Her Most Honoured Father Thomas Dudley" clearly introduces "The Foure Elements" and the other Quaternions, while "The Prologue" just as clearly introduces the long "Four Monarchies"—patently a poem about wars and commonwealths and kings. In the book as Woodbridge assembled it, the reader must wait some sixty pages for the subject matter promised in "The Prologue."

It is, unfortunately, a wait without a reward. "The Four Monarchies" is so pedestrian that even Bradstreet grows impatient with it, taking Nathaniel Ward's favorite proverb about cobblers sticking to their lasts as her motto also and rushing through the Roman monarchy in five "tedious brief" pages. "The Prologue" in which she forewarns her readers about this tiresome poem, on the other hand, is probably the best piece in *The Tenth Muse.* In it, Bradstreet deftly contrasts humanistic with Christian and Calvinistic views of the capabilities of women and asserts at least a modest claim for herself as a poet: "Give wholesome Parsley wreath, I ask no Bayes" (this line, by the way, she later improved to "Give thyme or parsley wreath, I ask no bays"). In making her own femininity and the act of poetry itself the themes of this poem, Bradstreet anticipates attitudes that underlie her best and most memorable work.

Although some sprightly lines adorn "The Foure Ages of Man" and "The Foure Seasons of the Yeare," the most interesting of the remaining poems in *The Tenth Muse* are "A Dialogue between Old England and New" (for its topical references) and the elegies on Sir Philip Sidney (with whom she appears to claim remote kinship) and Elizabeth I. Elizabeth provides Bradstreet with a persona in whose name to claim worth for women: "Let such, as say our sex is void of reason, / Know 'tis a slander now, but once was treason." The final poem in the volume, "Of the vanity of all worldly creatures," restates as in a coda the themes of mutability, human frailty, and the inevitable demise of all earthly empires. reminding us at the end that Anne Bradstreet, America's first poet of note, produced her poetry in the context of an ideology that held, at best, a limited place for such frivolities.

—Robert D. Arner

THANATOPSIS
Poem by William Cullen Bryant, 1821

Anthologized in virtually every major collection of American poetry, "Thanatopsis" is William Cullen Bryant's most famous poem and is today considered a 19th-century American "classic." Begun when Bryant was not yet 18, "Thanatopsis" represents his youthful, yet remarkably sophisticated, attempts to confront his early doubts about life and his persistent fears about death. Taken from the Greek, the term "Thanatopsis" literally means "glimpse or view of death," and death is the subject of the poem.

Although from an early age onward Bryant wished to write a poem that would be remembered by future generations, "Thanatopsis" was originally published anonymously, without his knowledge or consent. While Bryant was away from home studying law, his father discovered unfinished versions of "Thanatopsis" and another poem, "Inscription for the Entrance to a Wood," and he sent both manuscripts to the *North American Review,* where in 1817 they were published together as one poem. Scholars debate the actual date when Bryant began writing the poem, but it is believed that he may have composed a first draft as early as 1811 and certainly not later than 1814. From numerous extant manuscripts we know that Bryant continued revising "Thanatopsis" until 1821, when it was published in its final form, with introductory and concluding stanzas substituting for the poem erroneously published as part of it in the 1817 version.

The complicated textual history of "Thanatopsis" is perhaps one explanation for the poem's tripartite structure. The poem begins with a 17-line introduction, spoken through a persona, who explains that nature's "visible forms" offer a variety of messages to anyone who "holds Communion with her." Specifically, the persona explains, nature offers a "healing sympathy" to those troubled by "bitter" thoughts of death. In the second section of the poem, extending in two stanzas from lines 18 to 72, nature itself speaks, attempting to console the individual who fears loss of personal identity in the general dissolution of the grave.

In response to these fears, nature offers two points of consolation. First, nature explains that death is a universal, if not an essentially democratic experience. Death, says nature, should not be taken personally; all of us are called to its "mysterious realm": "Thou shalt lie down / With patriarchs of the infant world—with kings, / The powerful of the earth— / The wise, the good." Second, nature explains that death is a natural and basically peaceful experience, part of the predictable cycles of life. Through death, explains nature, the individual simply blends forms with the "hills / Rock-ribbed and ancient as the sun,—the vales / Stretching in pensive quietness between," and the "venerable woods" and "rivers that move / In majesty" and "make the meadows green." Finally, in the last section of the poem, which extends for an additional nine lines, nature provides its now famous injunction to approach "the silent halls of death" not "like the quarry-slave at night, / Scourged to his dungeon" but with the "unfaltering trust" of "one who wraps the drapery of his couch / About him, and lies down to pleasant dreams."

While to the 20th-century reader, such ideas as these may seem didactic, sentimental, and even trite, it should be remembered that during the early-19th century, when religion provided the primary framework for any approach to death, they were far from conventional. Bryant's editors at the *North American Review,* for example, found "Thanatopsis" so original that they thought it could not have been written by someone "on this side of the water." Because its stoic approach toward death is totally devoid of religious consolation, one of Bryant's contemporaries publicly labelled "Thanatopsis" a "pagan" poem. Although Bryant was undoubtedly inspired to write "Thanatopsis" by the "graveyard" verses of the British poets Henry Kirke White, Bishop Beilby Porteous, Robert Blair, and Thomas Gray, among others, he refuses to succumb to either their neoclassical verse excesses or their piety. In fact, the language and diction of "Thanatopsis" is so restrained and so poignantly austere that the poem has been likened to a Puritan sermon and its language to the Puritan plainstyle.

Neither, however, does Bryant succumb to the equally facile and tempting romantic conclusion that death is desirable because it offers the harried individual a mystical fusion with nature's sublimity. Despite nature's encouraging message, Bryant views death not with anticipation, only with a stoic's sense of acceptance. While he hopes that death will bring with it "pleasant dreams," he possesses no illusions that death is preferable to life. Throughout the poem and even from the very voice of nature, bleak images of "melancholy waste," "sad abodes," the "sluggish clod," and the "oak" whose "roots" shall "pierce thy mold" remain ominously in the background.

In the end it is perhaps Bryant's stubborn refusal to dismiss the ultimate questions of life and death through conventional conclusions that creates the tensions and ambiguities that have attracted generations of readers to "Thanatopsis." No matter how easy it would be to reduce complex questions to simple answers, Bryant's intuitions inform him that life's more serious problems defy easy solutions. "Thanatopsis" remains true to those intui-

tions. It appeals to the haunting doubts in everyone that any single system of belief can totally quiet the ever present and unsettling reality "Of the stern agony, and shroud, and pall." If not a great work of art in the 20th-century sense of the term, "Thanatopsis" displays more than a little originality and certainly at least a spark of genius.

—James A. Levernier

THEIR EYES WERE WATCHING GOD
Novel by Zora Neale Hurston, 1937

Novelist and poet **Alice Walker**, in her foreword to Robert E. Hemingway's *Zora Neale Hurston: A Literary Biography,* has identified "racial health—a sense of black people as complete, complex, undiminished human beings" as the quality perhaps most characteristic of Zora Neale Hurston's work. Nowhere is this quality more evident than in *Their Eyes Were Watching God,* Hurston's timeless evocation of the first half of a remarkable woman's life. Here, rendered with a poet's lyrical sensibility, Hurston provides an absorbing narrative, while incorporating elements of both modernism and African American folklore. As the reader follows the adventures of the protagonist, Janie Mae Crawford, through three marriages and into middle age, the book addresses such large issues as the nature of love and service, of racism and intraracial relations, and of what constitutes a meaningful life.

Janie, raised by her grandmother, Nanny, on the grounds of a white family, doesn't realize her skin color sets her apart until she sees a photograph of herself: "before Ah seen de picture Ah thought Ah wuz just like de rest." Her ties to the white world, both of blood and of environment, continue to differentiate Janie throughout the novel. As a child she is called "Alphabet" ("'cause so many people had done named me different names'"), a name emblematic of the malleability that characterizes Janie as she adapts to fit in with many kinds of people along her path toward individuation.

Hurston creates an almost palpable sense of atmosphere in the early stages of the novel. We meet a sixteen year old Janie, on the brink of womanhood, intoxicated by spring:

> She was stretched on her back beneath the pear tree soaking in the alto chant of the visiting bees, the gold of the sun and the panting breath of the breeze when the inaudible voice of it all came to her. She saw a dust-bearing bee sink into the sanctum of a bloom; the thousand sister-calyxes arch to meet the love embrace and the ecstatic shiver of the tree from root to tiniest branch creaming in every blossom and frothing with delight . . . . She had been summoned to behold a revelation.

These images of fertility—pollen dust, blooming vegetation, the incredibly vivid living world—become motifs to which Hurston returns throughout the novel. Like the world she observes outside herself, Janie is in bloom, and Nanny, hoping to make Janie financially secure, marries her granddaughter off to the much older Logan Killicks. Having only once kissed a boy, Janie is now forced to consider the large questions involved in a marriage. To one of these—"Did marriage end the cosmic loneliness of the unmated?"—she receives an answer much later, at the very end of the novel.

Janie, not long after her marriage, presents her grandmother with a litany of complaints about her husband including the shape of his head, the size of his belly, his unwashed feet, and untrimmed toenails. Most tellingly, "He don't even never mention nothin' pretty." She finds herself in a marriage without romance. The language in this exchange is earthy and amusing. Nanny's advice is to appreciate her material advantages and count that enough. Nanny waxes philosophical about love:

> Pat's de very prong all us black women gits hung on.
> Pis love! Pat's just whut's got us uh pullin' and uh haulin'
> and sweatin' and doin' from can't see in de mornin' till
> can't see at night.

Janie bucks against this notion of love even as romantic love motivates the successive stages of her life. Her marriage with Logan Killicks has her in a state of "freezolity" and ripe for a new relationship when Joe Starks appears one day at her doorstep. Starks is another older man but with some education and an air of confidence and prosperity. Janie literally walks out of her marriage to strike out with Starks for a tiny all-black town, where he intends to be a "big voice."

It doesn't take long for Starks to install himself as mayor, in which position he expects certain rigid behaviors out of Janie, dictating how she should dress, wear her hair, and conduct herself in the store they run together. Upon Joe's being sworn in, Janie is invited to address the crowd. Joe abruptly cuts her off and then is "unconscious of her thoughts," a pattern that will come to typify their unhappy marriage. For Joe, Janie gains her identity via her husband and his social standing. He forbids her from taking part in the front porch discussions which provide the town's main source of communication and entertainment. Hurston savors the vitality and linguistic inventiveness of these front porch performances, the "big picture talkers . . . using a side of the world for a canvas." The many voices comment on the main characters and their activities in an African American version of the Greek chorus.

Janie learns to repress her thoughts and feelings in order to make a life with Joe, but when he needlessly insults her looks one day in the store, she doesn't hesitate to respond in kind, insisting "Ah'm uh woman every inch of me, and Ah know it." Her public criticism of her husband's fading sexuality leads to an irreparable rift. Even on his death bed, Joe, a man who has always worshiped "de works of his own hands," is unable to communicate effectively with his wife. His death effectually allows Janie to bloom once again.

A period of introspection follows during which Janie comes to understand that she must value people over things, realizing that she despises Nanny's overemphasis on material security: "She had been getting ready for her great journey to the horizons in search of people . . . . But she had been whipped like a cur dog, and run off down a back road after things." At this point in the novel Janie begins to allow her own personality to emerge and becomes ready "to walk where people could see her and gleam it around." She turns down a number of suitors before responding immediately to Virgible "Tea Cake" Woods, who proves to be the antithesis to Joe Starks. Tea Cake is playful, younger, a gambler. Most importantly, unlike Joe he credits Janie with intelligence and is genuinely interested in what she has to say. Janie links him to her archetypal "pear tree blossom in the spring"; for her, "He seemed to be crushing scent out of the world with his footsteps."

She decides to abandon the profitable store she has inherited from Joe to marry Tea Cake and run off to "the muck," a sugar cane growing area. Janie tells her friend Pheoby, "Ah wants tuh utilize mahself all over" and says of Tea Cake, "He done taught me de maiden language all over."

Their relationship continues to grow, allowing Hurston to survey the robust pleasures of the hard living people of the muck until a hurricane tests and finally provides a tragic end to their marriage. In rescuing Janie from a rabid dog, Tea Cake himself contracts the disease. In a horrible finale, Janie is forced to shoot the deranged Tea Cake in order to save herself. Cradling the dead Tea Cake's head in her lap, Janie "thanked him wordlessly for giving her the chance for loving service" and, by implication, for the opportunity to live life in a meaningful way. Janie is tried, ironically, for the murder of her husband by white lawyers, jury, and judge, of whom Hurston starkly observes, "none of them knew."

Hurston frames her novel with an imagined present that allows Janie to recount the central events of her life to her friend Pay. At the end of the novel we find Janie poised for the next phase of her life, coming to terms with the violence that ended her relationship with Tea Cake. She envisions her late great love "prancing" about the room: "Of course he wasn't dead. He could never be dead until she herself had finished feeling and thinking," she realizes, because "Here was peace."

—Robert Gaspar

THREE LIVES
Stories by Gertrude Stein, 1909

Written by Gertrude Stein during 1906, this collection of three long stories was published by a vanity press in 1909. The Grafton Press of New York took the project on after Stein, who had lived in Paris for nearly a decade, agreed to pay more than $600 for the book's publication. Hardly convinced that Stein was at the beginning of a stunning career as a leading modernist, the press sent a representative to her in Paris to ask if she wanted help with her English.

Originally titled *Three Histories*, the book included the narratives of "The Good Anna," "Melanctha," and "The Gentle Lena." Anna and Lena were German immigrant women who did housework and in Anna's case came to own and run her own boarding house. Their lives were reminiscent of those of thousands of white, usually European girls and women who were either first or second generation immigrants—the serving personnel in all households but Southern ones, who were drawn from the German, Italian, or Irish labor pool. In the South, black house servants were still the norm, although Stein's character of the African American Melanctha is higher-class than either Anna or Lena. Earning her own money seems of less importance to Melanctha. We see her various relationships, including the primary one with the black doctor Jeff Campbell, but we are seldom told what work she is doing.

The catalyst for *Three Lives* was partly the immense amount of fiction Stein was reading—particularly by realist writers Emile Zola, **Stephen Crane,** and Gustave Flaubert—and more directly her brother's suggestion that she translate from French to English Flaubert's story "Un Coeur Simple" (A Simple Heart), one of the stories from his book *Trois Contes*. While Stein undertook this task, she absorbed Flaubert's story of Felicite, the young serving girl, and her mind moved to her own servant, the German woman who had kept house for her and her brother when they were students at Johns Hopkins living in a rented house in Baltimore. Lena Lebender, loving and self-effacing—and controlling—became the model for the ostensibly "good" Anna Federner. Complex and somewhat older than either Lena or the Flaubertian model, the Anna in Stein's story lived discreetly and amiably—she was, after all, despite her "arduous and troubled life," characterized as "good"—but she managed in the midst of her duties to carve out a lesbian relationship for herself.

Stein reserved the name "Lena" for what was to be the third story in the book, the short tale of the young German maidservant who let herself be directed into an unsuitable and unwanted marriage—which led to her eventual death in childbirth. Stein wrote this story second, using it as a way to criticize well-intentioned, first-generation immigrant relatives in the States who saw no alternative to marriage for the young cousin they had brought to America. "The Gentle Lena" was Stein's attempt to discredit some of the gendered assimilationist attitudes in the States at the turn of the century. The question at the end of Lena's narrative was, why must all women marry? A more basic question was, why do women who are themselves settled into marriages try to coerce other women into the same pattern?

By the time she had written both "The Good Anna" and "The Gentle Lena," Stein had her prose method—of insistence, not mere repetition—firmly in hand. Her fiction was unlike any she had ever read; it was her attempt to make words fresh, even as she repeated information to an unusual degree. In her view the repetition forced readers to remember.

While her style in "Melanctha" may seem similar, there are important differences. First of all Pablo Picasso had begun painting Gertrude Stein's portrait. The painting required close to eighty sittings, and during them Picasso's mistress would talk with Stein or read to her in French. Stein gained a new appreciation for spoken language. Not only was she surrounded by the avant-garde in Picasso's studio; when she returned home to 27 Rue de Fleurus, she wrote "Melanctha" as she sat under Paul Cezanne's large "Portrait of Mme Cezanne." A few blocks away, her brother Mike Stein and his wife Sarah were collecting the most recent paintings of Henri Matisse. In "Melanctha" then, Stein's style became more extreme: her use of repetition intensified, her syntax grew more complex, and she seemed to see for the first time what the qualities of impressionist and modernist painting might have to do with writing, even with her own brand of realism.

Stein's presentation of the bisexual black Melanctha Herbert was more complicated and more sympathetic than her characterizations of Anna and Lena. Confident that her experience as a medical student working with blacks in Baltimore clinics had given her knowledge about African American culture that most whites did not have, Stein created a character that made her comparatively famous in the States. What little writing with black characters existed there was either autobiographical or "uplift"—fiction and poetry intended to reach out with a strong moral purpose. In such texts the morally right choices would be rewarded; motivated by both Christian and heterosexual belief systems, writers of uplift literature led readers into acceptable life paths. Stein's creation of a sexually experienced yet not socially "fallen" black woman—treated in a nonjudgmental manner—was unique to the time and the culture.

Thirty-five pages of "Melanctha" are spent describing all the character's early love affairs, the most important of them lesbian. Readers remember the novella, however, as an intricate philosophical dialogue between Dr. Jeff Campbell and Melanctha, a dialogue between the arbitrarily rational man and the purposefully inarticulate woman. These fifty pages are, indeed, difficult and memorable, particularly when Stein's later admission that she identified herself with the male speaker is folded in to readers' perceptions. Taken now as a double portrait of its author, "Melanctha" at the time appealed to white readers who saw black culture as exotic, interesting for its differences but lacking much relevance.

The portraits in *Three Lives* are usually said to be heavily "ironic," asking readers to see beneath the surface of the characters' lives to their somewhat hidden story. The literary epigraph of the published book, Jules Laforgue's line *donc je suis un malheureux et ce n'est ni ma faute ni celle de la vie* (Thus I am unhappy and this is neither my fault nor that of life), may have pointed readers toward the conventions of ironic modernism; but those conventions are less helpful when one considers how radical a writer Gertrude Stein considered herself to be. The overall frame of irony may be what critics have focused on—that for all the "goodness" and "gentleness" of Anna and Lena, qualities that should have brought them happiness in the Victorian world, both women died miserable, their only happiness coming from friendships with other women. Melanctha's situation is devastatingly similar. What readers recognized from the power of Stein's writing in *Three Lives* was, in the words of **William James,** her creation of a fine new kind of realism. Few of her readers felt a sense of identification with or admiration for the lives of Stein's three characters. Instead, readers wondered what they were to do with these unhappy protagonists, so far from heroic, so far from any optimistic view of what women's lives in the twentieth century could be like.

Linda Wagner-Martin

THE TUNNEL
Novel by William H. Gass, 1995

After twenty-five years of obsessively working, William H. Gass finally completed his monumental novel *The Tunnel* in 1995. Gass's admirers have praised the work as a poetic and philosophic masterpiece, comparable to James Joyce's *Finnegan's Wake*. But Gass's detractors have called it a bloated, self-indulgent compilation of the most deplorable vices of self-conscious postmodernism.

The central figure and narrative voice of *The Tunnel* is William Frederick Kohler, a history professor at a major Midwestern university. Kohler studied in Germany during the 1930s and was later a consultant during the famous Nuremberg Trials, after which he wrote a book that made many critics think he was not completely unsympathetic to the Nazis. At the beginning of *The Tunnel*, Kohler has just completed a magnum opus entitled *Guilt and Innocence in Hitler's Germany*. But when he tries to write a simple, self-congratulatory preface to the book, he finds himself blocked and begins to write about his own life. Instead of the carefully controlled historical writing for which he has an academic reputation, he composes a sprawling self-exploration filled with bitterness, hatred, lies, self-pity, and self-indulgence.

There is no physical action as such in this novel and no dramatized dialogue encounters. Instead, the entire book consists of

Kohler's psychic digging into his past. In *The Tunnel* everything that has happened to Kohler, everyone that he has encountered, is converted into consciousness. And Kohler's consciousness is the closed-in, claustrophobic world of the narrow-minded bigot. Long passages reveal his resentment toward his unforgiving, hard-fisted father and his self-pitying, alcoholic mother, his loathing for his fat and slothful wife, his contempt for his nondescript adolescent sons, and his scorn for his pedantic colleagues and his superficial lovers.

But it is not this rambling referential subject of *The Tunnel* that makes it Gass's most ambitious effort thus far; rather it is the highly polished prose, wonderfully sustained for over six hundred pages, and the philosophic exploration of the relationship between historical fascism and domestic solipsism that makes those who know and love Gass's work so enthusiastic about the novel. Gass continually breaks up the naive realist illusion that the subject of a novel—the territory it depicts—is identical with its map-like pattern or language. Kohler's first-person text is filled with references to the great works of history, philosophy, and literature, which he both honors and debunks, in what seems like a rambling, stream-of-conscious, free association, but which is really a carefully controlled aesthetic pattern so heavily loaded toward the metaphoric that readers cannot for a moment lose sight of the fact that it is language they are experiencing, not physical reality.

The Tunnel is one of those great narcissistic novels in which the only real person is the narrator himself; all others are merely grist for his mental mill. What it means to be human, the novel suggests, is to confront the hard truth that the self is the only subjectivity one can hope to grasp. Kohler knows that if one does not become pure subjective consciousness one runs the risk of being transformed into the consciousness of someone else. It is his solipsistic conviction that no one is as aware and real as he is that constitutes what Gass calls Kohler's inescapable "fascism of the heart."

Yet Kohler also knows that beneath the imposing self-created rhetorical illusion he is but a vulnerable lump of flesh subject to all manner of human weaknesses. Gass suggests, as Fedor Dostoevskii did in *Notes from Underground* a century before, that when one dares to burrow deep within, he or she always finds the same narcissistic egoism and the same shameful vulnerability. Gass's tunnel is an escape route out of the prison of the self and at the same time a gold mine in which the way to the treasure is itself the treasure. It is the entrance to the womb, the removal of all human restraints, and the reduction of the self to its most elemental.

—Charles E. May

THE TURN OF THE SCREW
Story by Henry James, 1898

Henry James was fascinated by the ghost story. He felt that to be truly effective, tales of the supernatural should not simply recount otherworldly "events" but instead should portray the effects of those events upon a sensitive observer. James acted upon this theory in writing *The Turn of the Screw* and created a tale which has horrified, and mystified, generations of readers. Few works of art have elicited such acerbic, polemical, and often fanciful critical debate.

The debate grows out of the ambiguities imposed by the way James limits point of view. From the moment that the governess's narrative takes over the story, our knowledge is strictly limited: all that we learn of the events at Bly, we learn through her. There is no omniscient narrator who can tell us directly what "really" happened or read the other characters' minds; all we have is the record of what the governess sees, or thinks she sees, and what she determines that others think and feel.

The governess tells a disturbing story. She, an inexperienced young woman, accepts a position as governess to two orphaned children who live on a remote country estate. Their uncle in London demands an unusual condition: she is never to report to him nor communicate with him in any way. She is to be head of the household and manage everything herself. The governess is charmed with her two small charges, eight-year-old Flora and ten-year-old Miles, although she is disturbed to find that Miles has been dismissed from school on mysterious grounds. All apparently goes well until the governess sees an unknown and quite horrifying man in one of the towers of the house and later at a window. She learns that the man she saw was surely Peter Quint, the master's former valet, but that Quint is dead!

It soon becomes clear to her that Quint and the previous governess, Miss Jessel (who is also dead), were "infamous" when alive, corrupted the children, and have now returned for them from beyond the grave; the seemingly innocent children welcome the demonic visitors. The frightened young woman struggles against this apparently invincible evil with no help but that of the unimaginative housekeeper, the aptly named Mrs. Grose, who cannot see the ghosts herself. The governess repeatedly doubts her own sanity and becomes nearly as eager to vindicate herself as to save the children. She does apparently save little Flora, but she saves Miles only in the most equivocal way: when she wrenches the boy's spirit away from Peter Quint, the "white face of damnation" at the window, he dies of the shock, "dispossessed."

But many readers have claimed that there is a second, hidden, story beneath the governess's narrative: the governess is mad, the ghosts are hallucinations, and the true horror of the story is that two innocent children are placed in the sole care of a madwoman, who literally frightens one of them to death.

These readers find support in the governess's nervous anxiety and insomnia, her romantic dreams about her employer, her father's reported "eccentricities," her confessed aptitude for sensing ghostly phenomena, and most of all in the fact that nobody else ever sees (or admits seeing?) the ghosts. These readers explain the children's growing uneasiness as a normal reaction to the peculiar behavior of their governess. And they point to the indisputable fact that the governess draws sweeping and horrifying inferences from very small and ambiguous pieces of evidence.

But, finally, any reader who claims that the evil spirits are merely the governess's hallucinations is left with an inexplicable kernel of "fact": how could the governess describe Peter Quint exactly, point by point, when she had never seen him nor heard of him, unless she really did see his "spirit"? Quint's is an unusual face, with attributes traditionally ascribed to the devil; the governess describes him minutely and Mrs. Grose recognizes the portrait at once. Furthermore, James himself wrote about the tale as a well-crafted ghost story, not simply a case study of madness.

James wrote that he wanted to "give the impression of the communication to the children of the most infernal imaginable evil and danger," and he wisely determined to leave the specifics of that evil to the imagination of each reader, only supplying hints that it was somehow sexual. "Only make the reader's general vision of evil intense enough, I said to myself . . . and his own experience, his own imagination, his own sympathy (with the children) and horror (of their false friends) will supply him quite sufficiently with all the particulars. Make him think the evil, make him think it for himself, and you are released from weak specifications." The question of the governess's sanity can be seen in this light: ambiguity is much more disturbing than specificity. The lingering ambiguities give yet another turn of the screw to the disquieting effect of this disturbing story.

—Mollie Sandock

UNCLE TOM'S CABIN
Novel by Harriet Beecher Stowe, 1852

If the greatness of a novel were based solely upon its popularity and sociological impact, then Harriet Beecher Stowe's *Uncle Tom's Cabin* would undoubtedly be one of the greatest American novels of all time. Originally published in the *National Era* between 5 June 1851 and 1 April 1852, Stowe's novel achieved unparalleled popularity and attention when it was eventually issued in two volumes by John P. Jewett, a fledgling publisher who worried that the tale might not sell because of its length and content.

Within two days of its release, the entire first edition had sold out, and after one year sales of the novel were estimated at more than 325,000 copies in America alone. Worldwide more than three million copies of the novel are thought to have been printed during Stowe's lifetime. According to one commentator, *Uncle Tom's Cabin* has been "translated into every civilized language from Welsh to Bengali," and it became, during the nineteenth century, "the world's second best seller, outranked only by the Bible." In terms of its effects on history, *Uncle Tom's Cabin* had equally sensational results. Abraham Lincoln himself is said to have referred to Stowe as "the little lady who wrote the book that made this big war," and Frederick Douglass described the novel as the flame that kindled "a million camp fires in front of the embattled hosts of slavery." No one, however, was more surprised at the success of the book than its author, who it is said had only hoped to earn enough from her first royalties to buy a new silk dress.

While detractors of *Uncle Tom's Cabin* have since the time of its publication been quick to point out its flaws in style, structure, and historicity, it is easy in retrospect to understand why the novel was such a sensation during the nineteenth century and why even today it continues to generate fierce critical debate. Simply put, it was, in the words of **Leslie A. Fiedler**, the "greatest of all novels of sentimental protest." Writing in response to the passage, in 1850, of the Fugitive Slave Law that forbade citizens of free states from in any way assisting in the flight of runaway slaves, Stowe explained that her primary motive in publishing the book was "to show the institution of slavery just as it existed." This she accomplished, forcefully and effectively, by constructing what she termed "a *living dramatic reality*" that "endeavored to show it [slavery] fairly, in its best and worst phases."

Accordingly, Stowe created some of the most memorable characters in all literature: Uncle Tom, the self-sacrificing slave who truly embodies the spirit of Christianity taught to him but not practiced by his white "masters"; Augustine St. Clare, the well-intentioned but ultimately ineffectual slave-holder who deplores the evils of slavery but despairs of how to remedy them; Topsy,

the slave child so miserably abused since birth that she believes herself incapable of doing good; and, of course, Simon Legree, the villainous embodiment of depravity who persists in tormenting and ultimately murdering Tom only because of Tom's goodness.

Although during the nineteenth century, Stowe was attacked as a rabid, unthinking, and untalented abolitionist who totally failed to research her novels and whose only goal was to vilify the South, scholarship has substantiated that most of the incidents and characters in the novel were based on carefully researched historical realities and that she did in fact attempt to provide a relatively "fair" depiction of slavery as it existed in America before the Civil War. Significantly, the southern slaveholder St. Clare is one of the most compassionate characters in the novel while the basest character in the book, Legree, was born and nurtured in the North, as was the New England reformer, Ophelia Sinclare, who outwardly professed an absolute abhorrence of slavery but who inwardly harbored prejudices that prevented her from so much as touching anyone of another race and whose solution to the problem of slavery was simply to transport the slaves back to Africa, out of "sight and smell."

Similarly, twentieth-century accusations that the novel encourages racist stereotyping and is devoid of artistry have been largely dispelled by scholars who have illustrated that *Uncle Tom's Cabin* is far more complex that it seems and is far more susceptible to rigorous aesthetic analysis than was once generally thought. Particularly noteworthy in this regard are analyses of Stowe's attitudes toward sexual roles, the law, and religion, as well as her pre-Marxist insights into the nature of class conflict and the millennial politics of her day.

Whatever controversies *Uncle Tom's Cabin* has engendered in the past or will continue to engender in the future, one thing remains certain: it will always be an important work for anyone interested in the literary and cultural development of the United States. As Charley Dudley Warner explained in 1896, "*Uncle Tom's Cabin* has the fundamental qualities, the sure insight into human nature, and the fidelity to the facts of its own time which have from age to age preserved works of genius."

—James A. Levernier

U.S.A.
Novels by John Dos Passos, 1930-36

John Dos Passos's *U.S.A.* (complete version, 1938) had as its goal the depiction of life and society in the United States during the first thirty years of the twentieth century. Actually *U.S.A.* comprises three novels, each published separately—*The 42nd Parallel, 1919,* and *The Big Money*. Dos Passos had already attempted a similar project, with considerable success, in *Manhattan Transfer,* a fictional representation of New York in all its complexity during the first two decades of the century. But *U.S.A.* was a vaster undertaking which challenged to the utmost the author's skill in developing new techniques suitable for his purpose. The manner and devices with which he met this challenge make him one of the most remarkable innovators in American literature. But before examining his methods, we need to know his attitude toward his subject.

Dos Passos was an idealistic liberal, if not a radical. As such, he was distressed by the materialism, the greed, the ruthlessness of business that he perceived as violating the promise of America.

U.S.A. is an angry book. In its first two novels it leans toward Marxism; in the last, *The Big Money,* the influence of Thorstein Veblen is dominant (a brief biography of Veblen, "The Bitter Drink," is included). While writing *U.S.A.* Dos Passos's political and economic philosophy was switching from the far left to the right, though it had not yet reached the conservatism of his later years.

The three novels in *U.S.A.* deal with three stages that Dos Passos discerns in the nation's economic and spiritual life. *The 42nd Parallel* describes pre-World War I confidence, an almost frontier type of brashness; but it also focuses on the labor troubles and other discontents of the period. Indeed the title of the book refers to a frequent meteorological storm path. *1919* has as its theme the moral and political disruptions immediately following the war. *The Big Money* presents a picture of spiritual bankruptcy on a national scale.

Dos Passos employs the same techniques in all three novels. The narrative elements, carried in 52 separate sections, revolve around the lives of twelve main characters who appear and reappear in one or more of the novels. Some of them, but not all, become involved with others of the twelve. These characters differ widely in background, education, goals, values, and competence; and each one may be perceived as a case history. To name several, Fenian McCreary is a printer and a worker in the I.W.W.; Charley Anderson, an ace in the air corps during the war, makes a fortune in business and in stocks, destroys his career and personal life with alcohol, and dies in an automobile crash; Mary French, a Vassar graduate, becomes involved in Communist-supported labor agitation; Margo Dowling is a star in the silent movies and temporarily Charley Anderson's mistress; J. Ward Morehouse, a public relations executive, succeeds in business but fails in his personal life.

Between the narrative sections are so-called Newsreels and Camera Eyes and biographical sketches of famous or notorious men and women of the era. There are biographies of Henry Ford (headed "Tin Lizzie"), William Randolph Hearst ("Poor Little Rich Boy"), Rudolph Valentino ("Adagio Dancer"), Isadora Duncan ("Art and Isadora"), Samuel Insull ("Power Superpower"), and President Wilson ("Meester Veelson"). In these and other sketches Dos Passos freely reveals his own feelings, which range from contempt to admiration. Most bitter of all is his sketch of the Unknown Soldier ("The Body of an American") at the end of *1919*. All of them serve in setting the tone and establishing the background in the sections of the trilogy in which they appear.

So also do the Newsreels, which are montages made up of snatches of newspaper articles, headlines, verses from popular songs, and advertisements. The Camera Eyes also serve the same purpose, but they are more subjective, for they record Dos Passos's own feelings in either private situations or in regard to public events in which he was involved. In a sense the Camera Eyes add an autobiographical dimension to the book. Though written as prose, they may be described as imagistic, impressionistic free verse. Most impressive in style and feeling is the Camera Eye beginning "walking from Plymouth to North Plymouth through the raw air of Massachusetts Bay," in which the author meditates on what he is sure is the wrong done to Bartolomeo Vanzetti, one of two Italian radicals executed in 1927 for a murder that liberals of the time considered unproved.

In writing *U.S.A.* Dos Passos drew to the limit from his talents as literary innovator. Like the Newsreels, the entire trilogy (almost 1500 pages) is a montage designed to create an inclusive impression (rather than a chronicle) of thirty years of a nation's and a people's existence. The impression is a disheartening one, which inevitably leaves the reader with the sense of profound loss, a feeling of ideals and values betrayed. Yet the fervor with which Dos Passos wrote indicates that he believed the loss might not be irretrievable. He wrote from imagination and outrage perhaps, but not total despair.

—Perry D. Westbrook

WALDEN
Prose by Henry David Thoreau, 1854

Walden; or, Life in the Woods by Henry David Thoreau is a major literary expression of New England transcendentalism. It records its author's experiences and thoughts while living for two years and two months in a hut that he had built on the wooded shores of Walden Pond near Concord, Massachusetts. A native of Concord and a graduate of Harvard College, Thoreau as a young man had become the protege of **Ralph Waldo Emerson**, the leading figure in transcendentalism and a resident of Concord. Thoreau had access to Emerson's library and for a time lived in the Emerson household, serving as handyman in return for room and board. Thus he became thoroughly imbued with transcendentalist thought and attitudes, equaling his mentor in enthusiasm and surpassing him in his determination to put his ideals and beliefs into practice.

On 4 July 1845 Thoreau moved into his hut at Walden, planning to write *A Week on the Concord and Merrimack Rivers,* but with the added purpose of putting to a test the transcendentalist view of life. "I went to the woods," he wrote in *Walden,* "because I wished to live deliberately, to front only the essential facts of life, and see if I could learn what it had to teach, and not, when I came to die, discover that I had not lived." The basic premise of transcendentalism was that reality lies in the worlds of thought and spirit; yet the world of things reflects intellectual and spiritual truths and hence merits close attention. "There seems to be a necessity in spirit to manifest itself in material forms," Emerson wrote; and Thoreau in one of his essays, echoed Emerson: "Let us not underrate the value of a fact; it will one day flow into a truth." However, both Emerson and Thoreau thought that material things were being vastly *over*rated in the America of their times. Believing that "our life is frittered away by detail," Thoreau at Walden Pond attempted to simplify his own existence to the utmost in order to free it from the conventions and concerns that in his opinion deadened the spirit.

In *Walden* Thoreau devotes his first chapter, titled "Economy," to a description of the way in which he rid his life of all but the most basic material demands. His living expenses for the first eight months at the pond came to exactly $61.99-3/4, including the cost of building his cabin. About half of this sum he had on hand; the rest he earned by day labor and by the sale of farm produce that he raised on a nearby field; his conclusion was that six weeks of physical work annually would maintain him in health; the remainder of the year he could spend in more important ways. Thus *Walden* is in part a repudiation of the Puritan work ethic, which required that one be constantly engaged in some productive occupation, whether for one's own profit or for the benefit of others.

Having arranged his life in this manner, Thoreau was ready for the spiritual "awakening" which he thought to be his due and that of every human being. "Awakening," in fact, is the central theme of *Walden,* and as he developed this theme, Thoreau revealed himself as a true poet both in the imagery and rhythms of his prose and in his use of metaphor. Thoreau agreed with Emerson that a function of nature is to provide language by which spiritual truths may be expressed. Consequently Thoreau's writing is always concrete, and he takes great pleasure in describing what he heard and saw and did at Walden, and he strives to bring his readers to a similar recognition of the beauty and significance of the world of nature. In the second chapter of *Walden,* "Where I Lived and What I Lived For," Thoreau declared, "I do not propose to write an ode to dejection, but to brag as lustily as chanticleer in the morning, standing on his roost, if only to wake my neighbors up"; and in what is virtually a hymn to dawn, he wrote: "The morning wind forever blows, the poem of creation is uninterrupted; but few are the ears that hear it . . . Morning is when I am awake and there is a dawn in me. Moral reform is the effort to throw off sleep." There is a potential dawn in everyone according to Thoreau. As the day unfolds, the fully "awake" person will discern new meanings in things and happenings previously taken for granted.

Thoreau occupied himself in many ways: walking, reading, talking with neighbors, writing, working—but always he was alert for meanings implicit in the objects and scenes and persons around him. The most remarkable of his days were those like the one described in the chapter "Sounds," in which he sat yogi-like (he was deeply read in the sacred books of the East) on the doorstep of his hut, listening to the sounds that impinged on the silence in which he was immersed. The critic Sherman Paul has written: "Silence and sound were Thoreau's grand analogy: silence was the celestial sea of eternity, the general, spiritual, and immutable: sound was the particular and momentary bubble on its surface." Silence was to Thoreau and Emerson a symbol of the Oversoul, or the "soul of the whole, the wise silence" (in Emerson's words), in which each individual person participates. Thus to Thoreau "all sound . . . produces one and the same effect, a vibration of the universal lyre." On days of such acute receptivity he said he grew in spirit "like corn in the night."

In "Sounds" Thoreau was describing what can only be taken as a mystical experience—the only one recorded in *Walden.* Elsewhere he focuses more on his daily life at the pond, always subjecting it to interpretations that go deeper than mere description or narrative. Thus, while the day from dawn to dusk symbolizes the awakening of the spirit to the reality beyond appearances, so too does the year. In *Walden* the succession of chapters follows the seasons from high summer through the spring of the following year—the two years and two months of residence at Walden Pond being telescoped into one year. Summer, of course, is the season of fullest spiritual awakening—the season of the chapter "Sounds."

The day and the year, then, served as symbols of the growth of the spirit to a full realization of itself. Another symbol, Walden Pond, is ever-present almost in symphonic counterpoint with those of the day and the year. First, the pond, which Thoreau had known from earliest childhood, typifies his profoundest self—the self that he shares with all humanity and which rests in the Oversoul. Local residents believed Walden Pond to be bottomless; Thoreau measured the depth and found it to be slightly over one hundred feet—still extraordinary for so small a pond and sufficient to represent the depths of the human spirit. Thus to Thoreau drifting in a boat on the pond's surface, with a fishline in the water, the tug of a biting fish was suggestive of the truths that one might pull from far beneath the surface of consciousness.

Thoreau conducted daily observations of the pond. In winter he made a chart of its depths, cutting holes in the ice through which to drop his leaded cod-line. He was interested when crews of men arrived to harvest ice, and he was delighted with the knowledge that much of the ice would be shipped as ballast to India and that there "the pure Walden water would mingle with the sacred water of the Ganges"—and this was Thoreau's way of saying that the insights and thoughts that his time at Walden had revealed to him were of the profoundest significance for all people and their birthright.

—Perry D. Westbrook

THE WASTE LAND
Poem by T.S. Eliot, 1922

When *The Waste Land* first appeared, in 1922, it was widely rejected as arid and incomprehensible, even as a tasteless joke at the expense of its readers. A more perceptive response shows it to be neither. T. S. Eliot's poem works through "a heap of broken images," the reflection of a world of fragments; but the aim is to weave these fragments into a harmony, which, however, is not to be imposed upon them, but must emerge—if at all—at the end of the creative process.

The first of the poem's five sections—*The Burial of the Dead*—opens with an evocation of springtime memories in which the month of rebirth becomes the month of deception, "breeding lilacs out of the dead land," tenuous intimations of life in "a heap of stony rubbish." In such a world certainty is sought in the ambiguous revelations of the medium Madame Sosostris, "known to be the wisest woman in Europe, / With a wicked pack of cards." She brings a series of sinister images—"the drowned Phoenician sailor," "Belladonna . . . The lady of situations," the Hanged Man—which will reappear in the course of the poem and which have in common a preoccupation with death under a variety of forms. This opening "movement" ends with a vision of the "Unreal City," where the crowds streaming each morning across London Bridge are seen as so many souls moving into Dante's Hell.

In the second section, *A Game of Chess,* the vision narrows to two sketches of vacancy and boredom in different "situations" of life. Both concern loveless "desire." A woman of leisure alternately addresses herself and her lover in tense staccato rhythms which answer to the emptiness and isolation stressed in an obsessive reiteration of the key word of the episode: "You know *nothing?* Do you see *nothing?* Do you remember / *Nothing?*" At this moment of rising tension a contrasting motif emerges in the form of an evocative echo from The Tempest: "Those are pearls that were his eyes." Two possible attitudes to death balance the sordid reality of "rat's alley" against the delicate beauty of Shakespeare's marine symbolism. A possible relationship between them may emerge by the end of the poem; but for the moment the sense of vacancy prevails in the return of the question "Are you alive or not? Is there nothing in your head?" and is underlined in a parallel episode by the gossip of two women in a working-class pub at the expense of a third who lives in fear of old age, unwanted children, and betrayal by her husband in search of "a good time" after demobilization. At the end of the "movement" the obsessive time-theme emerges in the final call of the barman—"Hurry up, please, it's time"—both as an urgent call to responsible choice and as an indication of the bleak reality which threatens to render it meaningless.

The third section, *The Fire Sermon,* is central to the entire conception. Against a background of the Thames, seen both in its commerce-stained modern aspect and in the more romantic light projected by the poets of the past, the pursuit of "desire" is embodied in the loveless seduction of a bored typist by "a small house agent's clerk." Seen through the eyes of a spectator, the blind seer Tiresias whose vision constitutes, as Eliot himself said, the substance of the poem, the episode marks the point at which its separate fragments begin to come together in a possible pattern. The Buddha and St. Augustine, representing ascetic tradition in East and West, are found to agree in presenting fire—the symbol of "desire"—as both consuming and purifying: "Burning burning burning burning / O Lord, thou pluckest me out." The first broken intimation of prayer prepares the way for as much positive resolution as the poem is prepared to offer.

After the short lyrical interlude *Death by Water,* which takes up a theme equivocally announced by Madame Sosostris and confirmed in the Shakespearean echo of *A Game of Chess,* the final "movement," *What the Thunder Said,* proposes a tentative ordering and recapitulation. Once more we are in the desert, the Waste Land; but the arid landscape is now associated with the Passion of Christ—the silence in the orchard, the red light on sweaty faces, the agony in stony places—and from it there emerges the vision (reality or illusion?) of the risen Savior on the road to Emmaus. The dryness of the desert leads to a descent into delirium as the absent water—symbol of life and restoration—becomes an obsessive presence in the imagination of the suffering pilgrim.

The hoped for relief, however, does not come. The moment of vision is replaced by an impression, equally conceived in delirium, of general ruin. The "falling towers" of the great cities of the past—London, Rome, Athens, Jerusalem—are, like the city of *The Burial of the Dead,* "unreal," and the voices evocative of past beliefs which emerge from them sing "out of empty cisterns and exhausted wells." Yet once again, and at the culminating moment of delirium, the vision changes. The voice of the cock is heard, heralding the long-awaited break in the drought. As a "damp gust" promises rain for the parched soil, the thunder affirms as much positive vision as can be available to those who dwell in the Waste Land.

"Thus spoke the Thunder." Its message is conveyed in a triple Sanskrit exhortation: "Give, Sympathize, Control." The three words answer to a logical progression. What must be "given" is "The awful daring of a moment's surrender": acceptance of the risk involved in the commitment by which alone our lives may become more than empty memories preserved in blank obituaries. To "give," in turn, is to aspire to "sympathize," to relate our isolation to that of our fellow human beings imprisoned in the private worlds of their own experience. Those who have accepted the risk of commitment and projected it into sympathy may, according to the third and final admonition, aspire to exercise "control" over their lives. The "boat" which they steer may be expected to respond "gladly," in joyful affirmation, to the hand now—and only now—"expert with sail and oar."

We note, however, that this sketch of a possible release remains tentative. The "boat" *would have responded:* the statement remains conditional rather than directly affirmative. As the poem ends its shadowy protagonist sits on the shore, with the "arid plain" still in sight, though now behind him, tentatively surpassed. The picture of human endeavor is still dominated by collapse and ruin, but the hope has emerged that the lives of individuals may be redeemed by the effort to achieve such personal order as may be within our reach. "Shall I at least set my lands in order?" To

this end the speaker has "shored" certain fragments of tradition against his "ruin": fragments which have been present through the poem in the form of "broken," disconnected images and which he may now aspire to relate positively to his developed experience. Though *The Waste Land* is not to be read as a poem of religious affirmation, it bears within itself implications of further progress.

—Derek A. Traversi

THE WEARY BLUES
Poems by Langston Hughes, 1926

Langston Hughes's first book was published in February 1926 almost simultaneously with his 24th birthday. The earliest poem in *The Weary Blues,* "When Sue Wears Red," was written when Hughes was 17 and still in high school. One of the most famous, "The Negro Speaks of Rivers," he composed at 18, shortly after his graduation. Yet this youthful volume contains some of Hughes's best-known and best-loved poetry.

Despite the book's title, it contains very few blues. Indeed, about half the book is lyric poems. Among these are some relatively traditional nature poems and poetry employing western images and conventions, such as *carpe diem* in several poems, the court fool—albeit black—in "The Jester," and the Pierrot figure in two poems. Yet even in such lyrics, Hughes employs amusing or startling imagery; the "March Moon" is joshed "Don't you know / It isn't nice to be naked?," and the "Caribbean Sunset" resembles "God having a hemorrhage, Blood coughed across the sky."

For every bit of artificial diction such as "thou" in "Poem to the Black Beloved" and "Song to the Dark Virgin," for every derivative cadence ("We buried him high on a windy hill, / But his soul went out to sea"), there are several verses of effective simplicity, such as the complete text of "Suicide's Note": "The calm, / Cool face of the river / Asked me for a kiss"; the close of "Sea Calm": "It is not good / For water / To be so still that way"; and the close of "Dream Variations": "Night coming tenderly / Black like me." What Hughes can do with the terse, reflective lyric may best be exemplified with one of the pieces known only as "Poem" and dedicated to "F. S.": "I loved my friend. / He went away from me. / There's nothing more to say. / The poem ends, / Soft as it began,— / I loved my friend."

If Hughes sometimes wrote of topics treated by bards of many another clime and time—death, the sea, love, dreams—and was influenced by other poets—particularly Carl Sandburg and Walt Whitman—he still generally chose as his focus his own people. If we have heard before something very like the refrain of "Harlem Night Song,"—"Come, / Let us roam the night together / Singing"—we have not heard this sung about roof tops in the ghetto. And so infused with his race are some of these early Hughes lyrics that they are truly original. The combination of historical perspective—"A queen from some time-dead Egyptian night / Walks once again"—and church shout—"Blow trumpets, Jesus!"—renders the teenage Hughes's tribute to Susanna Jones wearing red far above much verse by older writers.

This early influence of spirituals was only the first of many musical elements in Hughes's free verse. About a dozen of the book's poems reflect the form and mood of black music, the blues or jazz or both. Like most of *The Weary Blues*'s best poems, these love songs to Harlem are dramatic works, characterizing a person, describing a theatrical scene, telling a story, or addressing someone in monologue or dialogue. In "Jazzonia" "Six long-headed jazzers play"; in "Danse Africaine" the tom-tom being drummed to a jazz beat "Stirs your blood"; "Harlem Night Club" adjures the band "Play, PLAY, PLAY!," while the dancers in "Cabaret" whirl to a jazz-band which sobs, belying the form's apparent gaiety. "Lenox Avenue: Midnight" only tells us "The rhythm of life / Is a jazz rhythm," but "Negro Dancers"—one of Hughes's dialect poems—demonstrates this with its "Da da" imitation of the jazz instrumental. The greatest innovation in form, however, occurs in "The Cat and the Saxophone (2 A.M.)," which creates a verbal equivalent to syncopation with its interweaving of a lusty, liquor-swilling couple's conversation and a singer's wail. This extraordinary counterpoint is the poem about which Countee Cullen (who preferred to write and read bourgeois black verse) sneered—after questioning whether it was a poem—"I cannot say *This will never do,* but I feel that it ought never to have been done."

The same rhythmic risk-taking characterizes "Song for a Banjo Dance," an experiment which combines blues form and jazz riffs, one of many Hughes jive poems espousing a live-for-the-moment philosophy. Sexier is the blues "Strut and wiggle" of the "shameless gal" addressed in "To Midnight Nan at Leroy's," whereas the spirit of "Blues Fantasy" ranges from pain to laughter in a repertoire which reminds us that "I laugh to keep from crying" was a classic blues refrain before Hughes adapted it as a title for his fiction.

Most famous is the title poem about a blues pianist whose foot goes "Thump, thump, thump" on the floor, the "musical fool" who takes blues "from a black man's soul." Hughes had heard his Weary Blues refrain as a Kansas teenager, but it was his inner ear which created "Droning a drowsy syncopated tune, / Rocking back and forth to a mellow croon, / I heard a Negro play."

Because he dared to appropriate sensual, spontaneous music as his inspiration and to write about bohemian, urban types—dancers, lovers, musicians, and, repeatedly, prostitutes—Hughes was castigated by the black bourgeoisie. They would have preferred raceless rhymings of June and moon, and were more tolerant of "Aunt Sue's Stories" for a child than the earthy, hip, often funny blues and jazz poems.

Of Hughes's other specifically race-based poems, several eventually emerged—as it became more respectable for a black poet to acknowledge and even revel in his blackness—as major contributions to American literature. "I, too, sing America. / I am the darker brother," Hughes insisted when, while penniless in Genoa, he watched his white brothers easily hired by ships which denied him employment. "I looked upon the Nile and raised the pyramids above it" he exulted in "The Negro Speaks of Rivers," while contemplating the ancient and enduring black soul "grown deep like the rivers." "The South," his first protest poem, excoriates Ku Klux Klan territory, while "Lament for Dark Peoples" broadens the indictment to encompass white colonialism world-wide and "Cross" speculates on the fate of mulattoes "neither white nor black." In "Proem" (later reprinted as "Negro") and "My People" Hughes praises his race generally, whereas in "Mother to Son" the pride becomes a more personal injunction—in a maternal persona—not to give up when "it's kinder hard. / Don't you fall now— / For I'se still goin', honey, / I'se still climbin', / And life for me ain't been no crystal stair."

—Tish Dace

WHO'S AFRAID OF VIRGINIA WOOLF?
Play by Edward Albee, 1962

Savage and beautiful, cruel and compassionate, one of the funniest of modern plays, yet one of the most devastating, Edward Albee's *Who's Afraid of Virginia Woolf?* has been hailed by some as a tragedy and by others as a comedy; a smaller group—among them the Columbia University Trustees who denied it the 1963 Pulitzer Prize—simply regard it as a dirty play. For that reason, John Chapman's contemporary review was headlined "For Dirty Minded Females Only," while Robert Coleman insisted "No red-blooded American would bring his wife to this shocking play." Contrast these responses to Dorothy Kilgallen's judgment: "People who are reluctant to face life will be reluctant to face this play."

What so profoundly divides critics is a disturbing domestic drama which takes place on a sexual battleground. Choosing, like Strindberg as well as the Greek tragedians, the subject of philosaphilos, or the mixture of love and hatred expressed within families, Albee dissects two academic marriages. The hostilities occur during a long night in which huge quantities of booze are consumed and large numbers of obscenities are hurled about. These and the play's sexuality prompted Lord Chamberlain to demand extensive changes in the London production, beginning with the play's first words: "Jesus H. Christ" became "Mary H. Magdalen."

Taking his title—with Leonard Woolf's permission—from a Greenwich Village graffito which suggests the possibility of living without dependence on comforting illusions, Albee examines the ways we try to get through life, or at least the part of life involving sex and career. His characters, perhaps named after the Washingtons, are George, a history professor, and Martha, his wife, who return home after a party given by her father, the college president, whom George would one day replace if only he had administrative ability, or even the academic ability to make it to full professor. Soon they are joined by Nick and Honey, a younger academic couple whose revelations about their own marriage prove catalytic to George and Martha and vice versa. After they have had a try at humiliating one another, Martha unsuccessfully tries to seduce Nick, and Honey gets sick in the bathroom. George wins the war with Martha by killing off their imaginary son, and he exorcises a few of Nick and Honey's spooks in the bargain. Feisty Martha is reduced to frightened clinging to George, ironically the only man who ever made her happy, the only man she ever loved.

The play's sado-masochism—which prompted a *New York Times* critic to paraphrase Elizabeth Barrett Browning as "How can I hurt thee? Let me count the ways"—involves everyone wounding and wounded by everyone else. Frequently the weapons are words—what Norman Nadel terms Albee's "acetylene torch dialogue"—yet the immoral choices designed to damage others are far more telling. The "Fun and Games" (as Act I is called) which George sums up as "Good; better; best; bested," are mostly Martha having brutal fun at George's expense, as in her changing into sexy clothes, her "blue games for the guests," her account of George as a "bog" and a "flop," and her telling Honey she and George have a son—the latter a violation of the game-playing rules.

George retaliates first by taking aim at Martha with a short barreled trick shotgun, second, when hostilities escalate in the "Walpurgisnacht" section, by attempted strangulation when Martha has embarrassed him over his novel, and, still later, by feigned indifference to Martha's seduction of Nick. By that time, however, to Martha's attempts to bed Nick and bag George ("Hump the Hostess" and "Humiliate the Host") has been added

George's game of "Get the Guests." His efforts are made easier by Nick's surprising candor regarding his opportunistic marrying for money as well as Honey's honesty about her fear of pregnancy.

Spectators tend to accept the naivety with which Nick and Honey confide in George, along with their failure to leave the party as George and Martha's private war widens to include their guests. Although some critics have questioned the credibility of the younger couple's behavior, during the play's performance the psychological violence seems necessary and the son's symbolic murder in Act III—George's victory—inevitable. The masterful third act, dramatized with economy of words and actions, proves almost as devastating to an audience as to Martha. By the time George counterpoints Martha's speech on maternal protection with the requiem mass's "dies irae," we've inferred that this play—written by an adopted son—is about not one, but two childless couples.

If any thoughts intrude during the searing final minutes, they are likely to be comparisons of George's deliberate destruction of their solace in the fantasy son to the temporary loss of pipe dreams in *The Iceman Cometh* or the permanent replacement of illusion by confrontation with truth in *Long Day's Journey into Night* and *That Championship Season.* Although a few critics have delved for arcane symbols here—finding Khrushchev in Nick's character, representation of the American Dream in the son, or a figurative gay relationship in George and Martha's marriage—so lacerating and real is George and Martha's agonizing mutual dependence that anything which obscures it must be dismissed as extraneous to the play.

—Tish Dace

WINESBURG, OHIO
Stories by Sherwood Anderson, 1919

Winesburg, Ohio originated in observations of an actual place. Sherwood Anderson wrote, "I made last year a series of intensive studies of people of my home town, Clyde, Ohio" (letter, 14 November 1916). Yet the stories that comprise the finished work are so selectively developed according to a central theme that Winesburg must be understood as a mythical town populated by imaginary beings. That theme is announced in a prefatory sketch, "The Book of the Grotesque," which preserves the author's original title for his book and intimates his purpose. For *Winesburg* associates characters who resemble one another in being eccentric, ludicrous, absurd, persons who are in some way ridiculous.

In form the work is a cycle of stories, a genre which Anderson may have helped to popularize among American writers. "I have even sometimes thought that the novel form does not fit an American writer," he said, "that it is a form which had been brought in. What is wanted is a new looseness; and in *Winesburg* I had made my own form" (Memoirs). Such a form brings together individual stories which yet reflect upon and modify each other so as to create a total effect much richer and more complex than its parts. Anderson integrates his stories most obviously by their shared theme of the grotesque, but also by other insistently recurrent motifs, such as loneliness, isolation, the failure of communication, and frustrated or compromising sexual experience. Out of this reiteration of themes in a minor key a prevailing mood develops, a kind of autumnal mood of resignation, acceptance, reflectiveness:

"'What is the matter with me? I will do something dreadful if I am not careful,' she thought, and turning her face to the wall, began trying to force herself to face bravely the fact that many people must live and die alone, even in Winesburg" ("Adventure").

Another salient connective device is the reappearance of some characters in more than one story: Dr. Reefy, Kate Swift, Elizabeth Willard, and others. Most important among these is George Willard, an adolescent boy, whose work as the sole reporter for the Winesburg *Eagle* weekly newspaper places him in a pivotal position within the community. In this role George both seeks knowledge of the town and, because of his attitudes of curiosity and responsiveness, is sought by the grotesques in their efforts to communicate. Moreover, George aspires to be a writer, and this circumstance permits both the characters and the authorial persona to reflect upon the writer's vocation: "'You must not become a mere peddler of words. The thing to learn is to know what people are thinking about, not what they say'" ("The Teacher"). "'He is groping about, trying to find himself,' she thought. 'He is not a dull clod, all words and smartness. Within him is a secret something that is striving to grow. It is the thing I let be killed in myself'" ("The Mother").

The figure of the writer appears first in the prefatory sketch in the guise of an old man who has kept alive "the young thing within him," i.e., the imagination or inspiration or desire that causes him to envision "a long procession of figures before his eyes." This old man would seem to be an alter ego for George, the writer that he aspires to be or that he will become. For both are moved by pity for the grotesques. "The grotesques were not all horrible. Some were amusing, some almost beautiful." Here the voice of the authorial persona, speaking for the aged writer, guides the reader's response. This voice of the persona, which is in some sense that of the author, is yet another of the unifying principles of the book. It is a reflective, sympathetic, interpretive voice, speaking in a style that despite its seemingly colloquial effect, is highly contrived. Motif words and images supersede direct statement. Such motifs are dreams and dreaming, adventure, and, as we see above, words. The movements of hands, and the placing of hands upon the shoulders of another character, are gestures emblematic of the impulse to communicate; and looking out a window is a characteristic attitude of the passive grotesques. George Willard's own alternatives, to stay at home or to venture forth into the world, are intimated by images that masquerade as simple description: "[His room] had a window looking down into an alleyway and one that looked across railroad tracks to Biff Carter's Lunch Room facing the railroad station" ("The Thinker").

As these techniques suggest, Anderson's style has a poetic quality. He has been praised for his capacity to render the lyrical intensity of a captured moment of defiance, self-discovery, resignation, or the like. Stories in *Winesburg* that are particularly admired for this effect, sometimes compared to a Joycean epiphany, include "Hands," "The Strength of God," and "The Untold Lie."

—Jean Frantz Blackall

WINTER IN THE BLOOD
Novel by James Welch, 1974

"Again I felt that helplessness of being in a world of stalking white men," says the unnamed main character in *Winter in the Blood* as he sits bewildered by the street of a small Montana town.

"But," he adds, referring to a local bar, "those Indians down at Gable's were no bargain either. I was a stranger to both and both had beaten me." Earlier on in the novel, aging Yellow Calf had commented to the young visitor, "This earth is cockeyed." The two men would seem to agree in their sentiments that the world, both Indian and white, is out of joint. However, a telling difference marks their attitudes. Yellow Calf, a traditional Indian, still believes in the old mythology, for instance, that he can talk to deer, and from that he takes comfort. The younger man, caught between the modern and traditional Indian cultures, suffers a continuing malaise because he neither can believe in the old ways nor does he fit into the chaotic society of the whites. By novel's end, however, the youth finds that he, though he might not totally accept Yellow Calf's beliefs, at least has begun to understand them, and the younger man draws strength from that. He also slowly comes to accept the absurdity of the modern world. Through these two processes working together, the young Blackfeet begins to understand himself; he starts to abandon his youthful confusion and takes on the beginnings of wisdom.

The novel moves, then, from ignorance to knowledge, from instability to balance, and from nihilism to a measure of hope. It does so according to a traditional theme in literature: through suffering, the protagonist becomes strengthened and equipped to deal with the future. For this, *Winter in the Blood* is both a coming-of-age and a quest novel, in both cases involving a search for knowledge of the self.

James Welch accomplishes the transformation through what on the surface appears to be a simple plot. A young Indian down on his luck returns to his mother's ranch on the reservation and goes to town searching in the bars for the girlfriend who recently left him. Ironically, in a book full of ironies, this is a false search, for he has little chance of winning back the girl, but it is a search nevertheless, enabling him to find himself. As he goes back and forth to town, several other considerations come into play. Among them are the relationship between his mother and her new husband, Lame Bull; the fortunes of a white tourist called the "airplane man" that the main character meets in town; the main character's search for his native roots; and his piecing together the details of the death years ago of his brother, Mose. As disparate as such elements seem, they fit together well in a series of related parallels. The delusional white tourist, convinced he's on a secret mission, echoes the young Indian's confusion about his own goals. The young man's eventual understanding that Yellow Calf is his grandfather gives him the stability to deal with his brother's accidental death.

Many other apparently accidental events take place. However, in the world of doubt Welch creates, he goes beyond depicting humans as victims of the arbitrary events shaping their lives. Though on the surface *Winter in the Blood* may appear to be an absurdist novel, it is not. The deception and manipulation of readers' expectations, along with Welch's building of complexities behind the simple exteriors, is central to the pleasure one receives from watching the writer's skills unfold.

For instance, the novel opens and closes on notes of absurdity. On the first page the hung-over Indian walking home from a night in the bars stops to urinate in a ditch. The book ends on two, similar earthy scenes, with the rescue of a stupid cow from a slough and with a stumbling eulogy spoken over the fresh graveside of the Indian's grandmother. Between these opening and closing parentheses occur much that appears to be purely ridiculous for its own sake, writing by a man obsessed by lyrical hilarity. Yet the

absurd scenes serve as more than comic relief for the painful human issues of *Winter in the Blood*. Specifically, the opening and closing scenes signal the main character's contact with the earth, his return to reality. Elsewhere in this highly calculated writing, the senseless events confronting the main character also, and again ironically, have their positive aspects. They are teaching devices integral to the story. They either will defeat the Indian or, as happens here, they become the obstacles he faces and learns to live with and accept without rancor on his way to maturity.

The realization central to all this, that strength begins with a step-by-step coping with daily realities, rings of the psychoanalytical method. As the novel unfolds, conflicts are resolved when they are dredged up and dealt with directly. In a parallel process, the young Indian shifts from a romantic to an existential stance stiffening his resolve. For no apparent reason, a stranger in a restaurant keels over dead into his oatmeal. The Indian finds himself absurdly walking down the street carrying a purple teddy bear. As such things reflect, life may make no sense, yet by the end of the book the protagonist has shed his immature fixation on meaninglessness and at least shows signs of becoming able to function in a world of uncertainty. In this he expands the common figure of the alienated Indian in American literature to an Everyman coping with the doubts common to all of humanity.

Good literature often is polysemous, that is, open to various interpretations. This is because a master of words and plots can spin his material into intricate patterns. Readers and critics then see the artistic result from their own individual perspectives, seizing on the features reflecting their personal dispositions. As expected, some analyses of *Winter in the Blood* pick out the threads of women's issues running through the novel, while others probe beneath the surface of the piece, and by going to elaborate lengths they find Welch's use of traditional Blackfeet ceremonies lurking behind the events of a contemporary work of fiction. The variety of interpretive approaches, many of them well-argued, stands as a compliment to James Welch's success in persuading on multiple levels. The danger here, however, is that critics lose sight of the organic unity of the novel. They then begin judging the work on their own expectations and on what they know of the writer and his background. Whatever validity such approaches may or may not have, and whatever the provenance of the story and the intent of the storyteller, the overriding issue should not be lost sight of, that *Winter in the Blood* is a novel put together with a consummate writing talent.

—Peter Wild

WISE BLOOD
Novel by Flannery O'Connor, 1952

"For the author, Hazel's integrity lies in his not being able to get rid of the ragged figure who moves from tree to tree in the back of his mind." According to Flannery O'Connor's interpretation of *Wise Blood,* the ragged figure is Christ. She underlines the influence of her own convictions in the writing of the novel in the same note to the second edition: Hazel is a "Christian malgre lui"; the novel was written by an author for whom "the belief in Christ is a matter of life and death," and who believes that "free will does not mean one will, but many wills conflicting in one man. Freedom cannot be conceived simply. It is a mystery."

Can a man driven to kill another and to maim himself by his inability to get rid of the ragged figure really be called free? What choice can Hazel make, pursued as he is by the figure, with his back against the wall? He can turn his back to it, but there is only a wall ahead, and the figure is behind, hounding him. He does not have many wills, he has two wills, one for and one against, and he is fighting a Christ who has all the cards in his hands, who can turn coincidence into inevitability, accident into necessity, who can use the world for purposes that are so alien that whoever is being used is perceived as a monster. Even the clouds take shape—"the sky was . . . clear and even, with only one cloud in it, a large blinding white one with curls and a beard"—and change shape to underline the pervasiveness of the presence from which Hazel is trying to flee: "the blinding white cloud had turned into a bird with long thin wings and was disappearing in the opposite direction." Hazel is not free; that is the message that comes through loud and clear. Or rather, his only freedom comes from embracing the ragged figure, blinding himself and walking away from the wall hand in hand with it, wearing wire around his chest and stones in his shoes. What kind of freedom is that?

Hazel denies his call to Christianity with the same vehemence with which he would have embraced it, and acts with a violence towards himself and others that echoes in its particularity the violence in every manifestation of religious extremism, be it the primitive sacrificing of a life to the gods or a holy war or any ascetic's life down the ages. That is the mystery that seems to lie at the core of this novel: the mystery of the impulse towards holiness (which a Christian will call grace, but which is not the prerogative of Christianity), and the destructiveness of that impulse when carried to extremes. What is the necessity, in the eyes and in the will of a creative God, for such manifestations? What good do they do? Can it really, profoundly, be said that the necessity for such distortions—for what could in many cases be seen as a depravity—simply stems from the presence of sin in the world, that it is necessary to have those who act destructively from goodness, from rectitude, from integrity, to balance the mindless destructiveness of those who are evil? What good comes of it?

Certainly in *Wise Blood,* as in Dostoevsky's *The Idiot,* the result of goodness acting in the world is destructiveness, and although it is true that each character in *Wise Blood* has a moment when he or she could acknowledge the gnawing importance of Christ, and that this moment is brought about by Hazel's presence in their life, it is even more true that they all act with conspicuous lack of freedom, and that they seem simply instruments to drive Hazel to recognition and submission to the ragged figure. Who is "saved"? Not Enoch, last seen in a gorilla suit, staring "over the valley at the uneven skyline of the city." Not the false prophet, mowed down by an implacable Hazel, not Hawks or Onnie Jay Holy who disappear back into their lives of exploitation, not Sabbath who ends up in a detention home. Hazel, we suppose, is saved. But his inability to free himself of his religious impulse already guaranteed his salvation, and freedom and grace seem curiously spurious in his case.

There is only one person in the book who retains a human ambiguity in response to the call of religion and of Christianity and yet is transformed and converted by contact with Hazel and by sharing his (apparently) self-imposed martyrdom: the landlady, who on the last page "felt as if she had finally got to the beginning of something she couldn't begin." Can it be that in a world that moves, creates, and destroys itself through the conflict of wills, a God is fashioning human beings (those we call prophets), who have in fact no real choice, but are simply there as instruments to make the possibilities clearer to others? Can it be that Hazel's life and death make sense only to the extent that they led one, and only one, human being to a recognition of the essential mystery of life? Can it be that the apparently absurd convictions of the author of *Wise Blood* make sense to the extent that they lead us, in the reading, to the same recognition, and to gaze, with the landlady, into "the dark tunnel" until we too see "the pinpoint of light," even if it is "so far away that [we cannot] hold it steady in [our] mind"?

—M. J. Fitzgerald

THE WOMAN WARRIOR: MEMORIES OF A GIRLHOOD AMONG GHOSTS
Autobiography by Maxine Hong Kingston, 1975

Maxine Hong Kingston's *The Woman Warrior: Memoirs of a Girlhood Among Ghosts* has found an increasingly larger status in the literary canon since its first publication in 1975. It has been praised as a feminist text, and critics were delighted with the unique way in which Chinese and American culture is presented through descriptions incorporating both Chinese and English symbols and colloquial sayings. The book also received attention for the way it blurred distinctions between literary genres, "haunt[ing] a region somewhere between autobiography and fiction," according to *Time* critic Paul Gray. The text's classification as autobiography and Kingston's incorporation of first-person narration, myths, stories of relatives in China, multiple versions of stories, and a deep lyrical quality in the writing have all resulted in the inclusion of *The Woman Warrior* in a wide spectrum of academic courses, including offerings in English, literature, ethnic studies, women's studies, anthropology, sociology, history, and psychology. The text has been so widely used, in fact, that it has spawned a volume titled *Approaches to Teaching Maxine Hong Kingston's The Woman Warrior,* edited by Shirley G. Lim, in the Modern Language Association's "Approaches to Teaching World Literature" series.

It is no surprise, then, that hand-in-hand with its success in being incorporated into such a wide variety of courses, there is also some alarm with the prominence *The Woman Warrior* has achieved, especially over its reputation as a representative text of Chinese American culture. Scholar Sau-Ling Wong, in his essay "Autobiography As Guided Chinatown Tour," notes that "It is safe to say that many readers who otherwise do not concern themselves with Asian American literature have read [*The Woman Warrior*]." While other Chinese American texts have been published more recently and have similarly reached best-seller status, the debate among scholars of Asian American literature over the authenticity of *The Woman Warrior* continues to be a controversial topic. At issue is the text's classification as autobiography, which accounts for a large part of its inclusion in academic institutions.

Criticism of *The Woman Warrior* is usually directed at what appear to be Kingston's distortions of Chinese culture, which a few critics have claimed is an intentional move on Kingston's part to make her narrative appealing to mainstream American sensibilities and their appetite for the exotic. In particular, some readers are offended at how the tale of Fa Mu Lan (Hua MuLan), the woman warrior of the book's title, seems to unproblematically merge two well-known myths: Fa Mu Lan, the woman warrior similar to Joan of Arc, and Gnak Fei (Yue Fei), a male warrior who has letters symbolizing his loyalty to the Emperor carved into his back. Another point of the criticism is aimed at how American culture seems to be represented as less misogynistic, less barbaric, and generally superior to Chinese culture. Finally, the narrative ambiguity concerning what is fact (nonfiction) and what is fiction in Kingston's "talk-stories" (a term used to refer to a tradition of orally passing on stories) is seen by some critics as so indeterminable that labelling the text "autobiography" is a miscategorization.

Scholars Shirley Lim and Sau-Ling Wong have argued that while it is possible to find negative and contradictory messages on Chinese culture in the book, the text's value in terms of Chinese American representation is still recuperable. In "The Traditions of Chinese American Women's Life Stories," Lim states that "In taking a body of communal stories (the Chinatown family, legends, myths, and talk-stories) and rewriting these old narratives into new texts, books such as *The Woman Warrior* challenge us to read them as 'over-written' texts in which the written language figures as significantly as, if not more important than, the subject matter." Speaking to the criticism that Kingston assumes a position of a Chinese cultural authority, a status reminiscent of tour guides who lead tourists through the forced stereotypes of American Chinatowns, Wong, in "Autobiography As Guided Chinatown Tour," rejects such notions. "*The Woman Warrior* bespeak[s] a tentative groping toward understanding" of Chinese culture, Wong writes, also noting that "only a careless reader . . . would be able to conclude that Kingston's stance in *The Woman Warrior* is that of the trustworthy cultural guide." To support these views, Wong notes that the protagonist of *The Woman Warrior* expresses a naivete about Chinese holidays and other cultural elements.

Academic writing on *The Woman Warrior* often discusses the text's potential to challenge the traditional role of Chinese women, yet also affirms the narrator's identification with her mother and other women of her ethnic group. The protagonist is continually at odds with her mother, Brave Orchid, throughout the text, resisting her mother's injunctions to "not tell" family secrets and to be a traditional, submissive daughter, avoiding the "ghosts" that abound in their community. On the other hand, the narrator is also learning valuable lessons from her mother and the narrative has moments where admiration for Brave Orchid is expressed through the insight of the narrator's adult maturity. Scholar King-Kok Cheung notes in the essay "Don't Tell" that while "Brave Orchid predicts that Maxine will grow up to join the company of wives and slaves, she also teaches her the song of the woman warrior Fa Mu Lan, who excels in an area traditionally closed to women." Cheung also points out that Brave Orchid serves as a role model for nontraditional gender roles as she had worked as a doctor in China. Similarly, Lee Quinby in "The Subject of Memoirs" notes the power of breaking silence that is articulated through the protagonist's reinterpretation of Fa Mu Lan; the narrator, Quinby writes, is in "the predicament . . . of being caught between the imposition of muteness on women" and the "hysterical babbling," as the critic puts it, of the women in the Chinese American community. However, the protagonist comes to conclude that the insane people are the ones who couldn't explain themselves, and she then vows to be a "writer-warrior." At the conclusion of the "White Tigers" chapter, the narrator of *The Woman Warrior* relates: "The swordswoman and I are not so dissimilar . . . . What we have in common are the words at our backs . . . . The report-

ing is the vengeance . . . . And I have so many words—"chink" words and "gook" words too—that they do not fit on my skin."

Lim argues that the text contains both a racial and gendered consciousness. The voice that the protagonist uses to rebel against her mother is the same voice that she uses to stand up to a racist employer, although she is fired as a consequence. She also maintains a certain pride when druggist-ghosts, pitying what they presume to be her family's poverty, give her candy, which she does not eat. Silence is also not solely a Chinese phenomenon: "Normal Chinese women's voices are strong and bossy," Kingston writes. "We American-Chinese girls had to whisper to make ourselves American-feminine."

In sorting out the contradictions and critiques of both Chinese and American cultures, Wong states that "it is, in fact, essential to realize that the entire *Woman Warrior* is a sort of meditation on what it means to be Chinese American. To this end, the narrator appropriates whatever is at hand, testing one generalization after another until a satisfactory degree of applicability to her own life is found." Near the end of the text, the protagonist's rebellious attitude towards her mother begins to shift; having the benefit of leaving home and finally returning, the narrator warns, "Be careful what you say. It comes true. It comes true. I had to leave home in order to see the world logically . . . . I enjoy the simplicity. Concrete pours out of my mouth to cover the forests with freeways and sidewalks. Give me plastics, periodical tables, t.v. dinners with vegetables no more complex than peas mixed with diced carrots. Shine floodlights into corners: no ghosts." This realization helps to overcome her fears of China, "where I know they don't sell girls or kill each other for no reason," but there is also some vitality that is lost in the artificial and sterile atmosphere of American culture.

The text ends on a hopeful note, suggesting a seamless merging of bicultural identity; the final talk-story is one describing Tsai-Yen (Cai Yan), the poetess who is captured by barbarians and held for twelve years. She communicates through her song, which "translates well" once she returns to China. The talk-story is told by both Brave Orchid and the protagonist, and as the narrator relates "the beginning is hers," meaning Brave Orchid's, but "the ending, mine." In combining these stories, however, there is no distinguishable marker of transition between the two story tellers, an approach that signifies the unification of the protagonist's Chinese and American cultural heritages.

—Karen Chow

THE WONDERFUL WIZARD OF OZ
Novel by L. Frank Baum, 1900

The first of fabulist L. Frank Baum's books in his Oz series, *The Wonderful Wizard of Oz* is strong neither in literary style nor in grand design. Yet it is compelling and multi-layered enough to captivate children and gratify serious adult readers and critics.

Like earlier narratives of travel in exotic lands, *The Wizard of Oz* dispenses with the credible and gives us marvels: talking animals, artificial humans, and sorcerers. However, the protagonist is not the traditional masculine model of courage and enterprise, but a very young girl whose basic concern is finding a way of returning to her family. Whirled away from her home on the Kansas prairie by a cyclone and dumped down in the eastern region of the Land of Oz, Dorothy must cope with an array of unfamiliar creatures (some hazardous) and with a perilous obstacle course on alien soil before she can have any hope of returning to Kansas. She is aided to an extent by talismanic objects (a pair of magic slippers and a magic cap) and by a protective kiss from a good witch, but her hindrances are many, and the Wizard, on whom she relies for assistance, turns out to be a fraud.

An intriguing feature of *The Wizard of Oz* is its framework of allusions to American life. No one line of reasoning can be pushed very far, but a general if incomplete outline may be suggested. First, a necessary word on topography. The beautiful, jewel-rich Land of Oz, surrounded by an enormous desert, is divided into four zones. The North and South are each presided over by a good witch; the East and West (the latter a yellow-colored country of gold) are each dominated by a wicked witch. In the middle of Oz is the Emerald City, ruled by the Wizard himself, the Great Oz, in solitary splendor.

The cyclone drops Dorothy's house down on the wicked witch of the East killing her instantly. Thus, assuming that Baum was taking a populist view of the political-economic situation, we have the predatory Eastern capitalists ravaging American midwestern farmers, and laborers generally. Dorothy and her companions (Scarecrow, Cowardly Lion, Tin Woodman—symbols of the exploited classes) must follow the Yellow Brick Road (i.e., the current "gold standard") to find the Wizard and ask him to grant their wishes. But Dorothy has the dead witch's silver slippers to wear as amulets (the proposed "free silver" policy which would have brought economic relief to those oppressed by the federal government's single standard of gold for the national currency). These slippers, which will eventually carry her back to Kansas once she learns the appropriate ritual to use with them, would have taken her back home at any time, had she only known that ritual. The ineffective Wizard may represent one of the presidents of the 1890s—Benjamin Harrison, Grover Cleveland, William McKinley—or all three, or perhaps William Jennings Bryan, the repeatedly unsuccessful presidential candidate, advocate of "free silver." (A neatly argued political-economic interpretation that has been useful here is the 1964 study by Henry M. Littlefield.) North and South both appear as good—or at least safe—regions, but East and West suggest evil, until their witches are destroyed. Baum may have had something more in mind regarding the West (whose wicked witch Dorothy annihilates by dousing her with water) than the gold fever of 1849 and thereafter: namely, the ruinous freight rates imposed on western farmers by the railroad "octopus."

Psychological interpretations of *The Wizard of Oz* are also possible; Dorothy is removed from her proper authority figures— aunt and uncle (who remain safely behind in Kansas)—and is thrown among outsize *toy* figures for a strange interlude. Two temporary authority figures (witches) signify harm, but she suffers relatively little on their account; two others (also witches) are benevolent; and the leading authority figure in the land of her temporary exile (the Wizard) is actually a humbug. By the end of the story the small girl has been neither initiated nor transformed, just blissfully restored to her original guardians.

Underlying all other interpretations of *The Wizard of Oz* is a *pattern of substitutions* for coping with life's problems, real and imagined. Dorothy lives with substitute parents. Returning from Oz she finds that the old farmhouse the cyclone carried away has been replaced by a new one. The Wizard of her expectations becomes the con man of her experience, substituting special effects for the manifestations of himself that he wants others to believe in. He offers Dorothy's companions makeshift tokens (which they accept) for the things they want most: courage, brains, a heart. Dorothy's means of transportation back home should be the Wizard's balloon, but instead it is the magic slippers from the wicked witch of the East. Everywhere, forces of good seem to replace forces of evil. Even the Cowardly Lion displaces his evil counterpart—a giant tarantula terrorizing the creatures of the forest—so that he can assume his proper role as King of the Beasts. The one substitution that cannot endure—the desert-locked Land of Oz replacing Dorothy's poor, prairie-locked farm home in Kansas—at least serves a useful function in that it brings Dorothy and her surrogate parents even closer together than they were earlier. In addition it points up the eternal truth of the old adage: "North, South, East, or West—*home's* the best!"

—Samuel Irving Bellman

CHRONOLOGY

Abbreviations:

(f) fiction
(p) play
(pr) prose
(v) verse

Chronology prepared by Marshall Walker; updated by Charis Bower, Sallyann Ferguson, Amy Ling, and A. LaVonne Brown Ruoff.

DATE	AUTHOR AND TITLE	EVENT
1492		Christopher Columbus discovers West Indies, landing at San Salvador
1500		Formation of the Iroquois Confederacy
1502		Amerigo Vespucci sails down eastern seaboard of South America
1513		Florida discovered for Spain by Ponce de León
1558		Elizabeth I's reign (1558–1603)
1563		St. Augustine, the earliest settlement in North America, is founded in Florida by Spaniards
1585		Attempt under Sir Walter Ralegh to found colony in North Carolina; abandoned 1586
1588	Harriot, Thomas (c. 1560–1621): *A Brief and True Report of the New Found land of Virginia* (pr)	Defeat of Spanish Armada by English fleet
1603		James I's reign (1603–25)
1607		Colony of Virginia inaugurated at Jamestown by Captain John Smith
1608	Smith, John (1580–1631): *A True Relation* (pr)	
1611		King James Version of the Bible is published
1616	Smith, John: *A Description of New England* (pr)	
1620	*The Mayflower Compact* (pr)	Voyage of the *Mayflower*; settlement of Plymouth by Pilgrims
1624	Smith, John: *The Generall History of Virginia, New England and the Summer Isles* (pr)	
1625		Charles I's reign (1625–49)
1626		Dutch colony of New Amsterdam founded on Hudson River; Manhattan Island purchased from Indians for about 60 guilders' worth of cloth and trinkets

DATE	AUTHOR AND TITLE	EVENT
1629		Colony of Massachusetts Bay founded
1636		Harvard, first American university, founded
1637	Morton, Thomas (c. 1575–c. 1647): *New English Canaan* (pr)	
1638		First printing press in America established in Cambridge, Massachusetts
1640	*The Bay Psalm Book* (v) printed in Cambridge, Massachusetts; in use until 1773	
1641	Cotton, John (1584–1652): *The Way of Life* (pr)	
1643		Colonies of New England form New England Federation
1644	Cotton, John: *The Keyes of the Kingdom of Heaven* (pr) Williams, Roger (1603–83): *The Bloudy Tenent of Persecution, for Cause of Conscience* (pr)	
1649	Mather, Richard (1596–1669): *A Platform of Church Discipline* (pr) Winthrop, John (1588–1649): *History of New England* (pr) completed (published 1825–26)	Trial and execution of Charles I Commonwealth (1649–60)
1650	Bradford, William (1590–1657): *History of Plymouth Plantation* (pr) completed (published 1856) Bradstreet, Anne (c. 1612–72): *The Tenth Muse Lately Sprung Up in America* (v)	
1652	Williams, Roger: *The Bloudy Tenent Yet More Bloudy* (pr)	
1659	Hooker, Thomas (1586–1647): "A True Sight of Sin" (pr)	
1660		Restoration of monarchy Charles II's reign (1660–85)
1662	Wigglesworth, Michael (1631–1705): *The Day of Doom* (v)	
1664		English seize New Amsterdam, later renamed New York
1676		War against Indians in New England ends Destruction of Jamestown by Nathaniel Bacon and followers
1678	Bradstreet, Anne: *Severall Poems*	
1682	Rowlandson, Mary (c. 1637–1711): *The Soveraignty and Goodness of God. . . Being a Narrative of the Captivity and Restauration of Mrs. Mary Rowlandson* (pr)	
1685		James II's reign (1685–88)
1689		William III and Mary II's (d. 1694) reign (1689–1702)
1691		Plymouth Colony absorbed by Massachusetts

DATE	AUTHOR AND TITLE	EVENT
1692		Witchcraft trials in Salem, Massachusetts
1693	Mather, Increase (1639–1723): *Cases of Conscience Concerning Evil Spirits* (pr)	
1700	Sewall, Samuel (1652–1730): *The Selling of Joseph* (pr)	
1701		Foundation of Collegiate School of America, later Yale University
1702	Mather, Cotton (1663–1728): *Magnalia Christi Americana* (pr)	Anne's reign (1702–14) Asiento Guinea Company formed to develop slave trade between Africa and America
1704		The *News-Letter,* first continuously published weekly paper, founded by John Campbell of Boston
1708	Cooke (or Cook), Ebenezer (c. 1667–c. 1732): *The Sot-Weed Factor* (v)	
1714		George I's reign (1714–27)
1725	Franklin, Benjamin (1706–90): *A Dissertation on Liberty and Necessity, Pleasure and Pain* (pr)	
1727		George II's reign (1727–60)
1728	Byrd, William, II (1674–1744): *A History of the Dividing Line Run in the Year 1728* (between Virginia and North Carolina; pr; published 1841)	Vitus Bering discovers Straits between Asia and North America
1729	Sewall, Samuel completes his *Diary* (pr; published in 3 vols., 1878–82)	
1731		Building (to 1751) of State House, Philadelphia, later Independence Hall, designed by Alexander Hamilton Benjamin Franklin founds free public library in Philadelphia
1732	Franklin, Benjamin: first issue of *Poor Richards Almanack* (pr)	Founding of Georgia, last British colony in America
1733	Byrd, William, II: *A Journey to the land of Eden, A.D. 1733* (pr; published 1841)	Molasses Act: American trade with West Indies forbidden
1740	Edwards, Jonathan (1703–58): *Personal Narrative* (pr)	
1741		Jonathan Edwards preaches sermon *Sinners in the Hands of an Angry God* in Enfield, Connecticut
1745		Foundation of Philadelphia Academy, later (1789) University of Pennsylvania
1746		Princeton University and Library founded
1754		French and Indian War in North America; George Washington defeated at Great Meadows George II founds King's College, New York

DATE	AUTHOR AND TITLE	EVENT
1756		Start of Seven Years War
1760		George III's reign (1760–1820)
1763		Peace of Paris, ending Seven Years War
1764		Sugar Act levied
1765		Stamp Act; Patrick Henry's speech to Virginia House of Burgesses
1766		Stamp Act repealed; withdrawal of British troops from Boston Mason–Dixon Line marks boundaries between Pennsylvania and Maryland, separating free and slave regions
1767	Dickinson, John (1732–1808): *Letters from a Farmer in Pennsylvania to the Inhabitants of the British Colonies* (pr); first letters printed in Pennsylvania newspapers	
1770	Gronniosaw, James Albert Ukawsaw: *A Narrative of the Most Remarkable Particulars in the Life of James Albert Ukawsaw Gronniosaw, an African Prince, as Related by Himself* (pr)	Boston Massacre Repeal of American import duties except for that on tea
1772	Occom, Samson: *Sermon Preached at the Execution of Moses Paul* (pr), first Indian best seller	
1773		Boston Tea Party
1774	Woolman, John (1720–72): *Journal* (pr)	Parliamentary suppression of opposition to tea duty First meeting of Continental Congress in Philadelphia
1775	Wheatley, Phillis (1753?–84): *Poems on Various Subjects, Religious and Moral* (v)	Revolutionary War; Battle of Bunker's Hill; Paul Revere's ride; Battle of Concord and Lexington
1776	Jefferson, Thomas (1743–1826): *Declaration of Independence* (pr) Paine, Thomas (1737–1809): *Common Sense* (pr) and first of 13 pamphlets in *American Crisis* series (pr) Trumbull, John (1750–1831): *M'Fingal: A Modern Epic Poem*	Declaration of Independence from Britain
1780		American Academy of Sciences founded in Boston
1781	Freneau, Philip (1752–1832): *The British Prison-Ship* (v)	British under Cornwallis surrender to Washington at Yorktown
1782	Crèvecoeur Hector St. John de (1735–1813): *Letters from an American Farmer* (pr)	Bank of America established in Philadelphia
1783		Treaty of Paris ends Revolutionary War
1785	Dwight, Timothy (1752–1817): *The Conquest of Canaan* (v)	Dollar established as official U.S. currency
1786	Barlow, Joel (1754–1812), John Trumbull, and others: *The Anarchiad* (v; concluded 1787)	Daniel Shay's Rebellion in Massachusetts

DATE	AUTHOR AND TITLE	EVENT
1788	Hamilton, Alexander (1757–1804), James Madison (1751–1836), and John Jay (1745–1829): *The Federalist* (pr)	
1789	Brown, William Hill (1765–93): *The Power of Sympathy* (f) Equiano, Olaudah (1745–1797): *The Interesting Narrative of the Life of Olaudah Equiano, or Gustavus Vassa, the African* (p)	U.S. Constitution adopted George Washington administration (1789–97)
1791	Bartram, William (1739–1823): *Travels Through North and South Carolina, Georgia, East and West Florida* (pr) Franklin, Benjamin: *Autobiography* (pr)	Bill of Rights becomes law
1792	Brackenridge, Hugh Henry (1748–1816): *Modern Chivalry* (f; completed 1815)	Invention of the cotton gin by Eli Whitney U.S. Mint established
1797	Foster, Hannah Webster (1759–1840): *The Coquette* (f)	John Adams administration (1797–1801)
1798	Brown, Charles Brockden (1771–1810): *Wieland* (f)	
1799	Brown, Charles Brockden: *Ormond* (f), *Edgar Huntly* (f) *Arthur Mervyn* (f; publication completed 1800)	Death of George Washington
1800	Weems, Mason Locke (1759–1825): *The Life and Memorable Actions of George Washington* (pr)	Library of Congress established
1801		Thomas Jefferson administration (1801–09)
1803		Louisiana Purchase
1804		Alexander Hamilton killed in duel with Aaron Burr
1808		Importing of slaves forbidden by Federal Government
1809	Irving, Washington (1783–1859): *A History of New-York* (pr)	James Madison administration (1809–17) Sequoya (c. 1760–1843) begins to develop writing system for Cherokee Indians
1812		War of 1812
1813	Rowson, Susanna (c. 1762–1824): *Sarah, or, The Exemplary Wife* (f)	
1814	Key, Francis Scott (1779–1843): "The Star-Spangled Banner" (v)	Washington, D.C., burned by British troops
1817		James Monroe administration (1817–25)
1819	Irving, Washington: *The Sketch Book of Geoffrey Crayon, Gent.* (f; publication completed 1820) Willard, Emma (1787–1870): *A Plan for Improving Female Education* (pr)	
1820	Cooper, James Fenimore (1789–1851): *Precaution* (f)	Founding of Liberian Republic for freed slaves Missouri Compromise

DATE	AUTHOR AND TITLE	EVENT
1821	Bryant, William Cullen (1794–1878): *Poems* Cooper, James Fenimore: *The Spy* (f)	*Saturday Evening Post* begins publication Mexico acquires its independence from Spain
1823	Cooper, James Fenimore: *The Pilot* (f), *The Pioneers* (f)	Monroe Doctrine Bureau of Indian Affairs established
1825		John Quincy Adams administration (1825–29)
1826	Cooper, James Fenimore: *The Last of the Mohicans* (f)	
1827	Audubon, John James (1785–1851): first sections of *The Birds of America* (pr; completed 1838) Cooper, James Fenimore: *The Prairie* (f) Cusick, David: *Sketches of Ancient History of the Six Nations* (pr), earliest history published by an Indian Poe, Edgar Allan (1809–49): *Tamerlane and Other Poems* Sedgwick, Catharine Maria (1789–1867): *Hope Leslie* (f)	Disciples of Christ founded by Alexander Campbell
1828	Webster, Noah (1758–1843): *An American Dictionary of the English language* (pr)	Washington Square Park created in New York
1829		Andrew Jackson administration (1829–37)
1830	Smith, Joseph (1805–44): *Book of Mormon* (pr)	Debate in Congress between Daniel Webster and Robert Y. Hayne on the nature of the Union
1831	Bird, Robert Montgomery (1806–54): *The Gladiator* (p) Poe, Edgar Allan: *Poems*	Nat Turner's rebellion
1832	Irving, Washington: *The Alhambra* (f)	Anti–slavery Abolitionist Party founded in Boston
1835	Apess, William: *Indian Nullification of the Unconstitutional Laws of Massachusetts* (pr) Tocqueville, Alexis de (French; 1805–59): *Democracy in America,* vol. 1 (pr; vol. 2, 1840)	New York *Herald* founded Samuel Colt patents his revolver
1836	Emerson, Ralph Waldo (1803–82): *Nature* (pr)	
1837	Emerson, Ralph Waldo: "The American Scholar" (pr), Phi Beta Kappa address at Harvard Hawthorne, Nathaniel (1804–64): *Twice–Told Tales* (f)	Martin Van Buren administration (1837–41)
1838	Poe, Edgar Allan: *The Narrative of Arthur Gordon Pym* (f)	Underground railway organized by abolitionists
1839	Audubon, John James: *Ornithological Biography* (pr) Kirkland, Caroline Matilda Saintsbury: *A New Home— Who'll Follow?* (pr) Longfellow, Henry Wadsworth (1807–82): *Voices of the Night* (v)	10,000 Mormons settle at Nauvoo, Illinois (formerly Commerce)
1840	Cooper, James Fenimore: *The Pathfinder* (f) Poe, Edgar Allan: *Tales of the Grotesque and Arabesque* (f)	Transcendentalist magazine *The Dial* founded under editorship of Margaret Fuller (1810–50)
1841	Cooper, James Fenimore: *The Deerslayer* (f) Emerson, Ralph Waldo: *Essays* (pr)	William Henry Harrison administration (1841) John Tyler administration (1841–45) *New York Tribune* founded by Horace Greeley

DATE	AUTHOR AND TITLE	EVENT
1843	Prescott, William Hickling (1796–1859): *History of the Conquest of Mexico* (pr)	Joseph Smith authorizes Mormon polygamy
1845	Douglass, Frederick (1817–1895): *Narrative of the Life of Frederick Douglass, an American Slave Written by Himself* (p) Fuller, Margaret: *Woman in the Nineteenth Century* (pr) Mowatt, Anna Cora (1819–70): *Fashion; or, Life in New York* (p) Poe, Edgar Allan: *Tales* (f), *The Raven and Other Poems*	U.S. annexes Texas James K. Polk administration (1845–49) *Scientific American* begins publication
1846	Hawthorne, Nathaniel: *Mosses from an Old Manse* (f) Melville, Herman (1819–91): *Typee* (f) Whittier, John Greenleaf (1807–92): *Voices of Freedom* (v)	U.S. invades Mexico Mormons under Brigham Young set out for Utah Smithsonian Institution founded in Washington, D.C.
1847	Emerson, Ralph Waldo: *Poems* Longfellow, Henry Wadsworth: *Evangeline* (v) Melville, Herman: *Omoo* (f) Prescott, William Hickling: *History of the Conquest of Peru* (pr)	U.S. troops capture Mexico City Salt Lake City founded by Mormons Gold discovered in California More than 200,000 leave Ireland, many bound for U.S.
1848	Lowell, James Russell (1819–91): *The Biglow Papers,* first series (v/pr)	American Association for the Advancement of Science End of Mexican war First Chinese immigrants arrive in Gold Rush
1849	Parkman, Francis (1823–93): *The California and Oregon Trail* (pr) Thoreau, Henry David (1817–62): "Civil Disobedience" (pr), *A Week on the Concord and Merrimack Rivers* (pr)	Zachary Taylor administration (1849–50) William Hunt invents safety pin "Bloomers" introduced by Amelia Jenks Bloomer California Gold Rush
1850	Emerson, Ralph Waldo: *Representative Men* (pr) Hawthorne, Nathaniel: *The Scarlet Letter* (f) Melville, Herman: *White-Jacket* (f)	Millard Fillmore administration (1850–53) *Harpers New Monthly Magazine* founded Slave trade forbidden in District of Columbia *Raftsmen Playing Cards* (painting) completed by George Caleb Bingham Building of St. Patrick's Cathedral, New York (completed 1879) by James Renwick Chinese workers brought to Hawaii by sugar planters The Fugitive Slave Act passed
1851	Hawthorne, Nathaniel: *The House of the Seven Gables* (f) Melville, Herman: *Moby-Dick* (f) Parkman, Francis: *The Conspiracy of Pontiac* (pr)	First U.S. state prohibition law voted in Maine
1852	Hawthorne, Nathaniel: *The Blithedale Romance* (f) Melville, Herman: *Pierre; or, The Ambiguities* (f) Stowe, Harriet Beecher (1811–96): *Uncle Tom s Cabin* (f)	Wells, Fargo stagecoach company founded in New York Governor of California seeks land grants to encourage further Chinese immigration
1853	Brown, William Wells (1815–1884): *Clotel; Or, The President's Daughter* (f) Delany, Martin (1812–1855): *The Condition, Elevation, and Destiny of the Colored People of the United States* (p)	Franklin Pierce administration (1853–57)
1854	Howe, Julia Ward (1819–1910): *Passion-Flowers* (v)	Republican Party formally established

DATE	AUTHOR AND TITLE	EVENT
	Ridge, John Rollin: *Life and Adventures of Joaquin Murieta* (f), the first novel by an Indian Thoreau, Henry David: *Walden* (pr)	Yung Wing becomes first Asian to graduate from an American college
1855	Boker, George Henry (1823–90): *Francesca da Rimini* (p) Longfellow, Henry Wadsworth: *The Song of Hiawatha* (v) Whitman, Walt (1819–92): *Leaves of Grass* (v)	John Bartlett publishes his compilation, *Familiar Quotations*
1856	Melville, Herman: *The Piazza Tales* (f)	Osawatomie Massacre by John Brown
1857		James Buchanan administration (1857–61) *Atlantic Monthly* begins publication
1858	Holmes, Oliver Wendell (1809–94): *The Autocrat of the Breakfast-Table* (pr)	Central Park, New York, opened to the public
1859	Thoreau, Henry David: "A Plea for Captain John Brown" (pr) Wilson, Augusta Jane Evans (1835–1909): *Beulah* (f) Wilson, Harriet E.: *Our Nig; Or Sketches from the Life of a Free Black* (f)	*Thunderstorm with Rocky Mountains* (painting) by Albert Bierstadt *Old Kentucky Home* (painting) by Eastman Johnson After raid on federal arsenal at Harper's Ferry, John Brown hanged; song "John Brown's Body" attributed to T.B. Bishop (1835–1905)
1860	Emerson, Ralph Waldo: *The Conduct of Life* (pr)	Abraham Lincoln elected President South Carolina secedes from Union
1861	Holmes, Oliver Wendell: *Elsie Venner* (f) Jacobs, Harriet A. (Harriet Ann) (1813–1897): *Incidents in the Life of a Slave Girl Written by Herself* (p)	Abraham Lincoln administration (1861–65) Outbreak of Civil War
1862	Davis, Rebecca Harding (1831–1910): *Margret Howth* (f)	Battles of Shiloh, second Bull Run, Antietam (Sharpsburg), Fredericksburg Sioux rising in Minnesota suppressed
1863	Longfellow, Henry Wadsworth: *Tales of a Wayside Inn* (v)	Lincoln proclaims emancipation of slaves from 1 January Battles of Chancellorsville, Gettysburg, Vicksburg, Chattanooga *Symphony in White* (painting) by James McNeill Whistler
1864		Sherman's march through Georgia Ku Klux Klan organized in Pulaski, Tennessee
1865	Dodge, Mary Mapes (1830–1905): *Hans Brinker* (f) Whitman, Walt: *Drum-Taps* (v) and *Sequel to Drum-Taps* including "When Lilacs Last in the Dooryard Bloom'd" (v)	End of Civil War; Thirteenth Amendment abolishes slavery Lincoln assassinated by John Wilkes Booth Andrew Johnson administration (1865–69) *Prisoners from the Front* (painting) by Winslow Homer
1866	Melville, Herman: *Battle Pieces* (v) Whittier, John Greenleaf: *Snow-Bound* (v)	American Equal Rights Association founded
1867		Alaska ceded by Russia to U.S.
1868	Alcott, Louisa May (1832–88): *Little Women* (f; completed 1869) Alger, Horatio (1834–99): *Ragged Dick* (f) Ridge, John Rollin: *Poems* (v), first poetry book by an Indian	Fourteenth Amendment ratified

DATE	AUTHOR AND TITLE	EVENT
1869	Harte, Bret (1836–1902): "The Outcasts of Poker Flat" (f) Twain, Mark (1835–1910): *The Innocents Abroad* (f)	Ulysses S. Grant administration (1869–77) Union Pacific and Central Pacific railroads join in Utah; 110,000 Chinese workers completed much of the building American Woman's Suffrage Association started by Susan B. Anthony
1870	Lowell, James Russell: *The Cathedral* (v) Whitman, Walt: *Democratic Vistas* (pr)	
1871		Negotiations of treaties with Indians abandoned by the United States
1873	Twain, Mark, and Charles Dudley Warner (1829–1900): *The Gilded Age* (f)	Financial panic in U.S. caused by speculation and overproduction Remington Company produces typewriter
1875	Eddy, Mary Baker (1821–1910): *Science and Health* (pr) James, Henry (1843–1916): *Roderick Hudson* (f)	*The Gross Clinic* (painting) by Thomas Eakins
1876	Lanier, Sidney (1842–81): "The Symphony" (v) Twain, Mark: *The Adventures of Tom Sawyer* (f)	Telephone patented by Alexander Graham Bell Phonograph invented by Thomas Edison *Breezing Up* (painting) by Winslow Homer Custer's Battle at the Little Big Horn
1877	Jewett, Sarah Orne: *Deephaven* (f)	Rutherford B. Hayes administration (1877–81) Chief Joseph leads the Nez Perce outbreak
1878	Green, Anna K. (1846–1935): *The Leavenworth Case* (f)	
1880	Adams, Henry (1838–1918): *Democracy* (f) Cable, George Washington (1844–1925): *The Grandissimes* (f) Harris, Joel Chandler (1848–1908): *Uncle Remus: His Songs and His Sayings* (f)	
1881	James, Henry: *The Portrait of a Lady* (f)	James A. Garfield administration (1881) Garfield mortally wounded by assassin Chester A. Arthur administration (1881–85) Boston Symphony Orchestra founded
1882	Black Hawk, Sauk Chief (1767–1838): *Autobiography of Ma-ka-tai-me-she-kia-kiak, or Black Hawk* (pr)	Chinese Exclusion Act passed by Congress, prohibiting immigration from China
1883	Hopkins, Sarah Winnemucca: *Life among the Piutes* (pr), first autobiography written by an Indian woman (pr) Twain, Mark: *Life on the Mississippi* Wilcox, Ella Wheeler (1850–1919): *Poems of Passion*	New York Metropolitan Opera founded North Pacific Railroad constructed
1884	Twain, Mark: *The Adventures of Huckleberry Finn* (f; London edition)	Mergenthaler Linotype machine patented
1885	Howells, William Dean (1837–1920): *The Rise of Silas Lapham* (f) Riley, James Whitcomb (1849–1916): "Little Orphant Annie" (v)	Grover Cleveland first administration (1885–89)

DATE	AUTHOR AND TITLE	EVENT
1886	Carnegie, Andrew (1835–1919): *Triumphant Democracy* (pr) James, Henry: *The Bostonians* (f), *The Princess Casamassima* (f)	Statue of Liberty, New York, cast in copper: gift from France, designed by Frederick Auguste Bartholdi American Federation of Labor founded Geronimo and his band of Apaches surrender
1887	Phou, Lee Yan: *When I Was A Boy in China* (pr), first Asian American autobiography published in America	
1888	Bellamy, Edward (1850–98): *Looking Backward 2000–1887* (f)	"Kodak" box camera invented by George Eastman
1889	Larcom, Lucy: *A New England Childhood* (pr) Woolson, Constance Fenimore (1840–1894): *Jupiter Lights* (f)	Benjamin Harrison administration (1889–93)
1890	Dickinson, Emily (1830–86): *Poems* James, William (1842–1910): *The Principles of Psychology* (pr) Whittier, John Greenleaf: *At Sundown* (v)	Anti–trust law enacted Mississippi legislature institutes poll tax, literacy tests, etc., designed to restrict voting by blacks; other southern states follow example Massacre at Wounded Knee, Pine Ridge Reservation, South Dakota
1891	Callahan, Sophia Alice: *Wynema, a Child of the Forest* (f) Garland, Hamlin (1860–1940): *Main-Travelled Roads* (f) Gilman, Charlotte Perkins (1860–1935): "The Yellow Wallpaper" (f)	
1892	Whitman, Walt: *Leaves of Grass* (v; "Death–Bed Edition")	California earthquake disaster Antonin Dvorak (Czech) accepts directorship of National Conservatory of Music, New York
1893	Crane, Stephen (1871–1900): *Maggie, A Girl of the Streets* (f; revised edition 1896)	Grover Cleveland second administration (1893–97) Chicago World's Columbian Exposition *Struggle of the Two Natures of Man* (sculpture) by George Gray Barnard Symphony No. 9 ("From the New World") by Dvorak
1895	Crane, Stephen: *The Red Badge of Courage: An Episode of the American Civil War* (f) Johnson, Emily Pauline: *White Wampum* (v), first book of poetry published by an Indian woman	"Coca–Cola is now sold in every state of the Union"
1896	Dunbar, Paul Laurence (1872–1906): *Lyrics of Lowly Life* (v) Far, Sui Sin: "A Chinese Feud" (f), first Asian American short story published in America Frederic, Harold (1856–98): *The Damnation of Theron Ware* (f) Jewett, Sarah Orne (1849–1909): *The Country of the Pointed Firs* (f)	Louisiana "Jim Crow car law" upheld by Supreme Court William McKinley defeats William Jennings Bryan for presidency *Plessy v. Ferguson* Supreme Court decision upholds segregation
1897		William McKinley administration (1897–1901)
1898	James, Henry: *The Turn of the Screw* (f) Stanton, Elizabeth Cady (1815–1902): *Eighty Years and More* (pr)	Spanish–American War
1899	Chesnutt, Charles W. (1858–1932): *The Conjure Woman*	Scott Joplin's "Original Rag" and "Maple Leaf Rag" are

DATE	AUTHOR AND TITLE	EVENT
	(f)	first ragtime piano pieces published in sheet music form
	Chopin, Kate (1851–1904): *The Awakening* (f)	
	Dewey, John (1859–1952): *The School and Society* (pr)	
	Norris, Frank (1870–1902): *McTeague* (f)	
	Washington, Booker T.: *The Future of the American Negro* (pr)	
1900	Baum, L. Frank (1856–1919): *The Wonderful Wizard of Oz* (f)	Philadelphia Orchestra organized
	Dreiser, Theodore (1871–1945): *Sister Carrie* (f)	*The Sitwell Family* (painting) by John Singer Sargent
1901	Chesnutt, Charles Waddell: *The Marrow of Tradition* (f)	McKinley assassinated
	Norris, Frank: *The Octopus* (f)	Theodore Roosevelt administration (1901–09)
1902	Dunbar, Paul Lawrence: *The Sport of the Gods* (f)	U.S. coal strike (May–October)
	James, Henry: *The Wings of the Dove* (f)	Cuba declares its independence from the United States
	James, William: *The Varieties of Religious Experience* (pr)	
	Keller, Helen (1880–1968): *The Story of My Life* (pr)	
	Robinson, Edwin Arlington: *Captain Craig* (v)	
	Wister, Owen (1860–1938): *The Virginian* (f)	
1903	Du Bois, W.E.B. (1868–1963): *Souls of Black Folk* (pr)	New York Stock Exchange building completed
	James, Henry: *The Ambassadors* (f)	First immigrants from Korea come to the United States and Hawaii
	London, Jack (1876–1916): *The Call of the Wild* (f)	Wright brothers fly the first practical airplane
1905	Santayana, George (1863–1952): *The Life of Reason* (pr; completed 1906)	Big oil strike at "Tulsey Town," in Oklahoma, a prelude to "Tulsa" as "Oil Capital of the World"
	Wharton, Edith (1862–1937): *The House of Mirth* (f)	*Wrestlers* (painting) by George Benjamin Luks
1906	Henry, O. (1862–1910): *The Four Million* (f)	Pure Food and Drugs Act passed as result of Upton Sinclair's exposure in *The Jungle* of conditions in Chicago's stockyards
	London, Jack: *White Fang* (f)	San Francisco earthquake
	Sinclair, Upton (1878–1968): *The Jungle* (f)	
1907	Adams, Henry: *The Education of Henry Adams* (pr; private printing)	*The North American Indian,* vol. 1, published by photographer Edward Curtis
	James, William: *Pragmatism* (pr)	First immigrants from India come to the United States
1908	Fox, John, Jr.: *The Trail of Lonesome Pine* (f)	
	Rinehart, Mary Roberts: *The Circular Staircase* (f)	
1909	James, William: *A Pluralistic Universe* (pr)	William Howard Taft administration (1909–13)
	Pound, Ezra (1885–1972): *Personae* (v)	Henry Ford's Model T car
		Sigmund Freud lectures in U.S. on psychoanalysis
		Frank Lloyd Wright's prairie-style "Robie House" completed in Chicago
		NAACP founded
1910	Addams, Jane (1860–1935): *Twenty Years at Hull House* (pr)	Mexican Revolution begins; hundreds of thousands of people flee Mexico to the Southwestern United States
1911	Burnett, Frances Hodgson (1849–1924): *The Secret Garden* (f)	
	Washington, Booker T.: *My Longer Education* (pr)	
	Wharton, Edith: *Ethan Frome* (f)	
1912	Dreiser, Theodore: *The Financier* (f)	*Poetry* magazine (Chicago) founded by Harriet Monroe

DATE	AUTHOR AND TITLE	EVENT
	Grey, Zane (1872–1939): *Riders of the Purple Sage* (f) Johnson, James Weldon (1871–1938): *The Autobiography of an Ex-Colored Man* (f)	F.W. Woolworth Company incorporated by Frank Woolworth Woodrow Wilson defeats William Howard Taft and Theodore Roosevelt for presidency
1913	Cather, Willa (1873–1947): *O Pioneers!* (f) Frost, Robert (1874–1963): *A Boys Will* (v) Glasgow, Ellen (1873–1945): *Virginia* (f) Lindsay, Vachel (1879–1931): *General William Booth Enters into Heaven* (v) Williams, William Carlos (1883–1963): *The Tempers* (v)	Woodrow Wilson administration (1913–21) Armoury Show of post-Impressionist paintings in New York and Chicago Charlie Chaplin signs contract with filmmaker Mack Sennett
1914	Frost, Robert: *North of Boston* (v) Pound, Ezra (ed.): *Des Imagistes: An Anthology* (v) Stein, Gertrude: *Tender Buttons* (v)	World War I begins in Europe
1915	Masters, Edgar Lee (1868–1950): *Spoon River Anthology* (v) Pound, Ezra: *Cathay: Translations* (v)	D.W. Griffith's film *The Birth of a Nation* Start of the Great Migration of Southern blacks to the North
1916	Aiken, Conrad (1889–1973): *The Jig of Forslin* (v) Doolittle, Hilda (H.D.) (1886–1961): *Sea Garden* (v) O'Neill, Eugene (1888–1953): *Bound East for Cardiff* (p) Robinson, Edwin Arlington: *The Man Against the Sky* (v) Sandburg, Carl (1878–1967): *Chicago Poems*	*Saturday Evening Post* buys its first Norman Rockwell illustration
1917	Eliot, T.S. (1888–1965): *Prufrock and Other Observations* (v)	U.S. declares war on Germany and Austria–Hungary "The Darktown Strutters' Ball" recorded as first jazz record Congress passes the Immigration Act, imposing a literacy requirement on all immigrants
1918	Cather, Willa: *My Antonia* (f)	End of World War I Wilson's Fourteen Points Charlie Chaplin's *Shoulder Arms* (film)
1919	Anderson, Sherwood (1876–1941): *Winesburg, Ohio* (f) Cabell, James Branch (1879–1958): *Jurgen* (f) Mencken, H.L. (1880–1956): *The American Language* (pr)	Commodore Hotel opened in New York—the world's largest
1920	Fitzgerald, F. Scott (1896–1940): *This Side of Paradise* (f) Lewis, Sinclair (1885–1951): *Main Street* (f) Millay, Edna St. Vincent (1892–1950): *A Few Figs from Thistles* (v) O'Neill, Eugene: *The Emperor Jones* (p) Wharton, Edith: *The Age of Innocence* (f)	Prohibition of sales of alcoholic beverages (Eighteenth Amendment) Senate blocks U.S. entry into new League of Nations
1921		Warren G. Harding administration (1921–23)
1922	Eliot, T.S.: *The Waste land* (v) Lewis, Sinclair: *Babbitt* (f) McKay, Claude (1890–1948): *Harlem Shadows* (v)	First issue of *The Fugitive*
1923	Millay, Edna St. Vincent: *The Harp-Weaver and Other Poems* Rice, Elmer (1892–1967): *The Adding Machine* (p) Stevens, Wallace (1879–1955): *Harmonium* (v) Toomer, Jean (1894–1967): *Cane* (f)	Calvin Coolidge administration (1923–29) First issue of *Time* magazine

DATE	AUTHOR AND TITLE	EVENT
1924	Hearn, Lafcadio (1850–1904): *Creole Sketches* (f) Hurston, Zora Neale (1903–1960): *Isis* (f) Jeffers, Robinson (1887–1962): *Tamar and Other Poems* (v) Melville, Herman: *Billy Budd* (f; written 1888–91) Ransom, John Crowe (1888–1974): *Chills and Fever* (v)	Gentleman's Agreement with Japan limiting immigration from Japan Congress awards citizenship to all Indians First performance of "Rhapsody in Blue for Jazz Band and Piano" by George Gershwin
1925	Dos Passos, John (1896–1970): *Manhattan Transfer* (f) Dreiser, Theodore: *An American Tragedy* (f) Fitzgerald, F. Scott: *The Great Gatsby* (f) Glasgow, Ellen: *Barren Ground* (f) Pound, Ezra: *A Draft of XVI Cantos* (v)	Tennessee forbids teaching of human evolution in schools "Monkey Trial" of John D. Scopes The Harlem Renaissance
1926	Hemingway, Ernest (1899–1961): *The Sun Also Rises* (f) Hughes, Langston (1902–67): *The Weary Blues* (v) Parker, Dorothy (1893–1967): *Enough Rope* (v)	Dancer Martha Graham makes first solo appearance in New York Chicago bootlegger Al Capone's hotel headquarters sprayed with machine-gun fire by rival gang
1927	Cullen, Countee: *Copper Sun* (v) McKay, Claude: *Home to Harlem* (f)	Execution of Sacco and Vanzetti
1928	Barnes, Djuna (1892–1982): *The Ladies' Almanack* (f) and *Ryder* (f) Benét, Stephen Vincent (1898–1943): *John Brown's Body* (v) O'Neill, Eugene: *Strange Interlude* (p)	
1929	Faulkner, William (1897–1962): *Sartoris* (f), *The Sound and the Fury* (f) Hemingway, Ernest: *A Farewell to Arms* (f) Wolfe, Thomas (1900–38): *Look Homeward, Angel* (f)	Herbert Hoover administration (1929–33) Collapse of New York Stock Exchange begins world economic crisis
1930	Crane, Hart (1899–1932): *The Bridge* (v) Hammett, Dashiell (1894–1961): *The Maltese Falcon* (f)	More than four million unemployed in U.S.; more than 1300 banks close in U.S. *American Gothic* (painting) by Grant Wood
1931	Gamio, Manuel: *The Life Story of the Mexican Immigrant* (pr) Riggs, Lynn: *Green Grow the Lilacs* (f)	
1932	Caldwell, Erskine (1903–87): *Tobacco Road* (f)	
1933	Aiken, Conrad: *Great Circle* (f) Caldwell, Erskine: *Gods Little Acre* (f) Johnson, James Weldon (1871–1938): *Along This Way* (pr) Stein, Gertrude (1874–1946): *The Autobiography of Alice B. Toklas* (pr) West, Nathanael (1903–40): *Miss Lonelyhearts* (f)	Franklin D. Roosevelt administration (1933–45) Financial crisis continues; U.S. abandons gold standard IBM enters typewriter business End of Prohibition
1934	Behrman, S.N.: *End of Summer* (p) Fitzgerald, F. Scott: *Tender Is the Night* (f) Miller, Henry: *Tropic of Cancer* (f) O'Hara, John (1905–70): *Appointment in Samarra* (f) Saroyan, William (1908–81): *The Daring Young Man on the Flying Trapeze* (f)	*Partisan Review* begins publication First performance of "Symphony: 1933" by Roy Harris Gangster John Dillinger shot dead by F.B.I. agents
1935	Anderson, Maxwell (1888–1959): *Winterset* (p)	New Deal social security legislation

DATE	AUTHOR AND TITLE	EVENT
	Eliot, T.S.: *Murder in the Cathedral* (p) Odets, Clifford (1906–63): *Waiting for Lefty* (p), *Awake and Sing!* (p) Santayana, George: *The Last Puritan* (f) Steinbeck, John (1902–68): *Tortilla Flat* (f)	*Porgy and Bess* (opera) by DuBose Heyward and Ira and George Gershwin "Fallingwater" (Kaufmann House) by Frank Lloyd Wright, Bear Run, Pennsylvania
1936	Dos Passos, John: *U.S.A.* trilogy completed (f) Faulkner, William: *Absalom, Absalom!* (f) Mitchell, Margaret (1900–49): *Gone with the Wind* (f) Sandburg, Carl: *The People, Yes* (v)	Ford Foundation established Roosevelt re-elected, carrying 46 states First issue of *Life* magazine
1937	Hurston, Zora Neale (1903–1960): *Their Eyes Were Watching God* (f) Kang, Younghill: *East Goes West: The Making of an Oriental Yankee* (pr), first book by a Korean immigrant in the United States Marquand, J.P. (1893–1960): *The Late George Apley* (f) Stevens, Wallace: *The Man with the Blue Guitar* (v)	*Newsweek* magazine begins publication *Popular Photography* magazine begins publication *Snow White and the Seven Dwarfs* (film) by Walt Disney
1938	Cummings, E.E. (1894–1962): *Collected Poems* Schwartz, Delmore (1913–66): *In Dreams Begin Responsibilities* (v) Wilder, Thornton (1897–1975): *Our Town* (p)	*Billy the Kid* (ballet) by Aaron Copland
1939	Chandler, Raymond (1888–1959): *The Big Sleep* (f) Hellman, Lillian (1905?–1984): *The Little Foxes* (p) Steinbeck, John: *The Grapes of Wrath* (f) Thurber, James (1894–1961): *Cream of Thurber* (pr) Warren, Robert Penn (1905–89): *Night Rider* (f) West, Nathanael: *The Day of the Locust* (f)	World War II begins in Europe "Grandma Moses" (Anna M. Robertson) becomes famous in Unknown American Painters Exhibition
1940	Hemingway, Ernest: *For Whom the Bell Tolls* (f) McCullers, Carson (1917–67): *The Heart Is a Lonely Hunter* (f) Wilson, Edmund (1895–1972): *To the Finland Station* (pr) Wright, Richard (1908–60): *Native Son* (f)	U.S. unemployment more than eight million First Social Security payments made U.S. gives Britain 50 destroyers in return for eight bases in the Atlantic Roosevelt re-elected for unprecedented third term
1941	Agee, James (1909–55): *Let Us Now Praise Famous Men* (pr) with photographs by Walker Evans Ferber, Edna (1887–1968): *Saratoga Trunk* (f) Zukofsky, Louis (1904–78): *55 Poems*	Roosevelt and Churchill meet at sea and announce Atlantic Charter U.S. and Germany wage undeclared naval war in the Atlantic Japanese bomb Pearl Harbor; U.S. enters World War II *Citizen Kane* (film) by Orson Welles National Congress of American Indians established
1942	Villa, Jose Garcia (b. 1914): *Have Come, Am Here* (v), first Filipino poet published in U.S.	FDR signs Executive Order 9066, forcing more than 120,000 Japanese and Japanese Americans from the west coast and internment into interior concentration camps
1943	Bulosan, Carlos: *America Is in the Heart* (pr) Eliot, T.S.: *Four Quartets* (v)	"Zoot Suit" riots take place in southern California Chinese Exclusion Act repealed
1944	Bellow, Saul (b. 1915): *Dangling Man* (f) Williams, Tennessee (1911–83): *The Glass Menagerie* (p) Winsor, Kathleen (b. 1919): *Forever Amber* (f)	Supreme Court rules an American cannot be denied the right to vote because of color
1945	Wright, Richard: *Black Boy* (pr)	Roosevelt dies Harry S. Truman administration (1945–53)

DATE	AUTHOR AND TITLE	EVENT
		World War II ends in Europe
		U.S. drops atomic bombs on Hiroshima and Nagasaki; Japan surrenders
1946	Hersey, John (1914–93): *Hiroshima* (pr)	Returning veterans swell U.S. college enrollments to more than two million
	Lowell, Robert (1917–77): *Lord Weary's Castle* (v)	
	McCullers, Carson: *The Member of the Wedding* (f)	The first Puerto Rican governor, Jesús T. Piñero, is appointed by President Truman
	Merrill, James (1926–95): *The Black Swan* (v)	
	Warren, Robert Penn: *All the King's Men* (f)	
1947	Miller, Arthur (b. 1915): *All My Sons* (p)	Truman Doctrine of aid to countries to combat communism
	Williams, Tennessee: *A Streetcar Named Desire* (p)	
1948	Mailer, Norman (b. 1923): *The Naked and the Dead* (f)	Truman recognizes the State of Israel
	Merton, Thomas (1915–1969): *The Seven Storey Mountain* (pr)	House Committee on Un-American Activities begins round of anti-communist investigations
	Pound, Ezra: *The Pisan Cantos* (v)	*Number One* (painting) by Jackson Pollock
	Silko, Leslie Marmon: *Ceremony* (f)	
1949	Bowles, Paul: *The Sheltering Sky* (f)	
	Brooks, Gwendolyn (b. 1917): *Annie Allen* (v)	
	Hawkes, John: *The Cannibal* (f)	
	Miller, Arthur: *Death of a Salesman* (p)	
	Yamamoto, Hisaye (b. 1921): "Seventeen Syllables" (v)	
1950	Olson, Charles (1910–70): "Projective Verse" (pr)	Korean War begins
		United Nations Building, New York, completed
1951	Hughes, Langston: *Montage of a Dream Deferred* (v)	First performance of Symphony No. 2 by Charles Ives
	Jones, James (1921–77): *From Here to Eternity* (f)	CBS broadcasts color television
	Lowell, Robert: *The Mills of the Kavanaughs* (v)	U.S. Atomic Energy Commission builds first power-producing nuclear reactor
	Salinger, J.D. (b. 1919): *The Catcher in the Rye* (f)	
	Wouk, Herman (b. 1915): *The Caine Mutiny* (f)	
1952	Ellison, Ralph (1914–94): *Invisible Man* (f)	General Dwight D. Eisenhower nominated by Republicans to run for presidency against Democratic nominee Adlai Stevenson; Eisenhower wins election
	Hemingway, Ernest: *The Old Man and the Sea* (f)	
	Malamud, Bernard (1914–86): *The Natural* (f)	
	McCarthy, Mary (1912–89): *The Groves of Academe* (f)	
	Merwin, W.S. (b. 1927): *A Mask for Janus* (v)	
	O'Connor, Flannery (1925–64): *Wise Blood* (f)	
1953	Baldwin, James (1924–87): *Go Tell It on the Mountain* (f)	Dwight D. Eisenhower administration (1953–61)
	Bellow, Saul: *The Adventures of Augie March* (f)	Ethel and Julius Rosenberg executed for passing atomic secrets to Soviet agents
	Inge, William (1913–73): *Picnic* (p)	
	Miller, Arthur: *The Crucible* (p)	Eisenhower proposes "Atoms for Peace" program
	Olson, Charles: *The Maximus Poems 1–10* (v)	Korean War ends
	Roethke, Theodore (1908–63): *The Waking* (v)	*Playboy* magazine begins publication
	Shapiro, Karl (b. 1913): *Poems 1940–1953*	
	Warren, Robert Penn: *Brother to Dragons* (v; revised edition 1979)	
1954	De Vries, Peter (1910–93): *The Tunnel of Love* (f)	Vietnam divided into North and South
	Stevens, Wallace: *Collected Poems*	Lolita Lebron and associates injure congressmen in "Free Puerto Rico" demonstration
	Welty, Eudora (b. 1909): *The Ponder Heart* (f)	Senator Joseph R. McCarthy censured by Senate
		Supreme Court declares segregation in public schools unconstitutional

DATE	AUTHOR AND TITLE	EVENT

Hernández v. Texas recognizes that Hispanic Americans are not being treated as "whites"

Asians permitted to become U.S. citizens and are allowed to vote

1955
Donleavy, J.P. (b. 1926): *The Ginger Man* (f)
Gaddis, William (b. 1922): *The Recognitions* (f)
Nabokov, Vladimir (1899–1977): *Lolita* (f)

Rosa Parks, of Montgomery, Alabama, refuses to give up her seat on a bus to a white man

1956
Baldwin, James: *Giovanni's Room* (f)
Barth, John (b. 1930): *The Floating Opera* (f)
Bellow, Saul: *Seize the Day* (f)
Ginsberg, Allen (b. 1926): *Howl and Other Poems*
O'Neill, Eugene: *Long Day's Journey into Night* (p)

Supreme Court declares segregated seating in buses unconstitutional

My Fair Lady (musical) by Alan Jay Lerner and Frederick Loewe

1957
Cheever, John (1912–82): *The Wapshot Chronicle* (f)
Kerouac, Jack (1922–69): *On the Road* (f)
Malamud, Bernard: *The Assistant* (f)
Okada, John: *No–No Boy* (f), first Japanese American novel published in the United States
Singer, Isaac Bashevis (b. 1904): *Gimpel the Fool* (f)
Stevens, Wallace: *Opus Posthumous* (v/p/pr)

School integration disturbances in Little Rock, Arkansas
Civil Rights Commission established
First performance of Symphony No. 3 by Roger Sessions

1958
Capote, Truman (1924–84): *Breakfast at Tiffany's* (f)
Kunitz, Stanley (b. 1905): *Selected Poems 1928–1958*

John Birch Society founded
First U.S. earth satellite launched

1959
Albee, Edward (b. 1928): *The Zoo Story* (p)
Bellow, Saul: *Henderson the Rain King* (f)
Burroughs, William S. (1914–97): *The Naked Lunch* (f)
Faulkner, William: *The Mansion* (f)
Gelber, Jack (b. 1932): *The Connection* (p)

Hansberry, Lorraine (1930–63): *A Raisin in the Sun* (p)
Lowell, Robert: *Life Studies* (v)
Purdy, James (b. 1923): *Malcolm* (f)
Roth, Philip (b. 1933): *Goodbye, Columbus* (f)
Snodgrass, W.D. (b. 1926): *Hearts Needle* (v)
Updike, John (b. 1932): *The Poorhouse Fair* (f)

Alaska and Hawaii admitted to U.S. as 49th and 50th states
Eisenhower says nation's economy is "on a curve of rising prosperity"
Completion of Frank Lloyd Wright's Solomon R. Guggenheim Museum
Cuban revolution succeeds in overthrowing Batista regime

1960
Barth, John: *The Sot–Weed Factor* (f)
Hellman, Lillian: *Toys in the Attic* (p)
Kinnell, Galway (b. 1927): *What a Kingdom It Was* (v)
Lee, Harper (b. 1926): *To Kill a Mockingbird* (f)
O'Connor, Flannery: *The Violent Bear It Away* (f)
Plath, Sylvia (1932–63): *The Colossus* (v)
Sexton, Anne (1928–74): *To Bedlam and Part Way Back* (v)
Singer, Isaac Bashevis: *The Magician of Lublin* (f)
Updike, John: *Rabbit, Run* (f)

John F. Kennedy defeats Republican Vice–President Richard M. Nixon for presidency

1961
Baldwin, James: *Nobody Knows My Name* (pr)
Heinlein, Robert Anson: *Stranger in a Strange Land* (f)
Heller, Joseph (b. 1923): *Catch-22* (f)
Malamud, Bernard: *A New Life* (f)
Percy, Walker (1916–90): *The Moviegoer* (f)
Salinger, J.D.: *Franny and Zooey* (f)

U.S. severs relations with Fidel Castro's Cuba
John F. Kennedy administration (1961–63)
Bay of Pigs invasion; Khrushchev supports Cuba
Berlin Wall erected
First U.S. manned space expedition by Commander Alan B. Shepard, Jr.

DATE	AUTHOR AND TITLE	EVENT

1962
Albee, Edward: *Who's Afraid of Virginia Woolf?* (p)
Baldwin, James: *Another Country* (f)
Bly, Robert (b. 1926): *Silence in the Snowy Fields* (v)
Kesey, Ken: *One Flew over the Cuckoo's Nest* (f)
Porter, Katherine Anne (1890–1980): *Ship of Fools* (f)

Cuban missile crisis brings nuclear confrontation with U.S.S.R.
U.S. aids South Vietnamese against Vietcong guerrillas
United Farm Workers Organizing Committee founded by César Chávez, who later organizes strikes and national boycotts, including the successful Delano grape strike

1963
Friedan, Betty (b. 1921): *The Feminine Mystique* (pr)
McCarthy, Mary: *The Group* (f)
Plath, Sylvia: *The Bell Jar* (f)
Pynchon, Thomas (b. 1937): *V.* (f)
Vonnegut, Kurt, Jr. (b. 1922): *Cats Cradle* (f)
Williams, William Carlos: *Paterson, Books I–V* (v)

Kennedy assassinated in Dallas
Lyndon Baines Johnson administration (1963–69)
Martin Luther King, Jr., makes "I Have a Dream" speech at Civil Rights march in Washington, D.C.

1964
Baraka, Amiri (b. LeRoi Jones, 1934): *Dutchman* (p)
Bellow, Saul: *Herzog* (f)
Berger, Thomas (b. 1924): *Little Big Man* (f)
Berryman, John (1914–72): *77 Dream Songs* (v)
Condon, Richard (b. 1915): *An Infinity of Mirrors* (f)
Lowell, Robert: *For the Union Dead* (v)
Selby, Hubert, Jr. (b. 1926): *Last Exit to Brooklyn* (f)
Shepard, Sam (b. 1943): *Cowboys* (p)

U.S. bombs North Vietnamese bases
Race riots in Harlem and PhIladelphia
Student "free speech" demonstrations at University of California, Berkeley
Black Arts Movement
Civil Rights Act abolishes segregation in public accommodations throughout the south

1965
Kosinski, Jerzy (b. 1933): *The Painted Bird* (f)
Malcolm X (b. Malcolm Little, 1925–65): *The Autobiography of Malcolm X* (pr; with Alex Haley)
Plath, Sylvia: *Ariel* (v)
Warren, Robert Penn: *Who Speaks for the Negro?* (pr)
Wolfe, Tom (b. 1931): *The Kandy-Kolored Tangerine-Flake Streamline Baby* (pr)
Zukofsky, Louis: *All: The Collected Short Poems 1923–1958*

U.S. makes formal alliance with South Vietnam
Civil Rights demonstrations in Selma, Alabama, and Chicago
Race riots in Watts district of Los Angeles
Voting Rights Act provides guarantees for black voting in the south
Malcolm X shot dead
Early Bird put into orbit as world's first commercial satellite
Painting of a giant Campbell's Tomato Soup Can by Andy Warhol

1966
Baraka, Amiri: *Home: Social Essays* (pr)
Capote, Truman: *In Cold Blood* (pr)

James Meredith, University of Mississippi's first black graduate, shot from ambush
Race riots in Cleveland, Chicago, and Atlanta
National Organization for Women (NOW) is founded
Beginning of U.S. program to airlift Cubans to the United States, bringing more than 250,000 people, or 10% of Cuba's population, to the U.S. before Castro stopped the airlifts in 1973

1967
Baraka, Amiri: *Black Magic: Poetry 1961–1967*
Bly, Robert: *The Light Around the Body* (v)
Brautigan, Richard (1933–84): *Trout Fishing in America* (f)
Styron, William (b. 1925): *The Confessions of Nat Turner* (f)
Vidal, Gore (b. 1925): *Washington, D.C.* (f)

Anti-Vietnam War demonstrations, notably in New York, San Francisco, and Washington, D.C.
Race riots throughout country, worst in Newark and Detroit
Stokely Carmichael urges Black Power movement to be more militant

1968
Cleaver, Eldridge (b. 1935): *Soul on Ice* (pr)
Dickey, James (b. 1923): *Poems 1957–1967*
Giovanni, Nikki (b. 1943): *Black Judgement* (v)
Mailer, Norman: *The Armies of the Night* (pr)
Updike, John: *Couples* (f)
Vidal, Gore: *Myra Breckinridge* (f)
Wolfe, Tom: *The Electric Kool-Aid Acid Test* (pr)

My Lai Village massacre in South Vietnam
Senator Robert Kennedy assassinated
Martin Luther King, Jr., assassinated
Demonstrations and riots in Chicago, Boston, Kansas City and other cities
N. Scott Momaday's *House Made of Dawn* wins Pulitzer Prize; first by an Indian

DATE	AUTHOR AND TITLE	EVENT
		Students for a Democratic Society (SDS) promote strike action on many campuses
		Richard M. Nixon defeats Hubert Humphrey for presidency
1969	Cheever, John: *Bullet Park* (f)	Richard M. Nixon administration (1969–74)
	Jarrell, Randall (1914–65): *The Complete Poems*	Death of Mary Jo Kopechne at Chappaquiddick Island damages reputation of Senator Edward M. Kennedy
	Momaday, N. Scott (b. 1934): *Way to Rainy Mountains* (f)	U.S. moon landing
	Nabokov, Vladimir: *Ada* (f)	U.S. economic boom
	Roth, Philip: *Portnoy's Complaint* (f)	Woodstock Music and Art Festival, New York
	Vonnegut, Kurt, Jr.: *Slaughterhouse-Five; or The Children's Crusade* (f)	*Saturday Evening Post* ceases publication
1970	Brown, Dee (b. 1908): *Bury My Heart at Wounded Knee* (pr)	National Guardsmen fire on protesting students at Kent State University (Ohio), killing four
	Didion, Joan (b. 1934): *Play It as It Lays* (f)	Arabs blame U.S. for Israel's refusal to give up territory occupied since Six Day War (1967)
	Lowell, Robert: *Notebook* (v)	Voting Rights Act of 1970 prevents minority votes from being diluted in gerrymandered districts or through at-large elections.
	Millett, Kate (b. 1934): *Sexual Politics* (pr)	
	Toffler, Alvin (b. 1928): *Future Shock* (pr)	
	Welty, Eudora: *Losing Battles* (f)	
1971	Condon, Richard: *The Vertical Smile* (f)	Vietnam War increases rate of inflation
	Doctorow, E.L. (b. 1931): *The Book of Daniel* (f)	Excerpts from Pentagon Papers published in *New York Times*
	O'Hara, Frank (1926–66): *Collected Poems*	
	Wright, James (1927–80): *Collected Poems*	
1972	Ammons, A.R. (b. 1926): *Collected Poems 1951–1971*	Watergate affair begins; *Washington Post* investigates
	Barth, John: *Chimera* (f)	Nixon visits China and U.S.S.R.
	Shepard, Sam: *The Tooth of Crime* (p)	U.S. signs nuclear arms control agreement with U.S.S.R.
1973	Chin, Frank: *Chickencoop Chinaman* (p), first Asian American play produced in New York	Cease-fire in Vietnam, but bombing of Cambodia continues
	Jong, Erica (b. 1942): *Fear of Flying* (f)	*Skylab* astronauts photograph Comet "Kohoutek"
	Oates, Joyce Carol (b. 1938): *Do with Me What You Will* (f)	Senate holds hearings on Watergate affair
	Pynchon, Thomas: *Gravity's Rainbow* (f)	United Nations approves the right of Puerto Rican people to decide their own future as a nation
	Vidal, Gore: *Burr* (f)	
1974	Heller, Joseph: *Something Happened* (f)	World energy crisis deepens
	Lurie, Alison (b. 1926): *The War Between the Tates* (f)	Nixon resigns presidency as a result of Watergate affair
	Mamet, David (b. 1947): *Sexual Perversity in Chicago* (p)	Gerald Ford administration (1974–77)
	Roth, Philip: *My Life as a Man* (f)	Ford pardons Nixon
1975	Ashbery, John (b. 1927): *Self-Portrait in a Convex Mirror* (v)	Puerto Rican militants explode bombs in New York
	Doctorow, E.L.: *Ragtime* (f)	America's *Apollo 16* spacecraft docks in space with Russia's *Soyuz 19*
	Gaddis, William: *JR* (f)	North Vietnam conquers South Vietnam
	Wolfe, Tom: *The Painted Word* (pr)	Voting Rights Act Amendment of 1975 bans literacy tests
1976	Gardner, John (1933–82): *October Light* (f)	Bicentennial celebration
	Haley, Alex (1921–92): *Roots* (pr)	Congress passes law to admit women to military academies
	Kingston, Maxine Hong: *Woman Warrior* (pr)	*Viking II* spacecraft lands on Mars
	Merrill, James: *Divine Comedies* (v)	
1977	Ashbery, John: *Houseboat Days* (v)	Jimmy Carter administration (1977–81)
	Cheever, John: *Falconer* (f)	Gary Gilmore executed by firing squad

DATE	AUTHOR AND TITLE	EVENT

Coover, Robert (b. 1932): *The Public Burning* (f)
Miller, Arthur: *The Archbishop's Ceiling* (p)
Morrison, Toni (b. 1931): *Song of Solomon* (f)
Percy, Walker: *Lancelot* (f)
Warren, Robert Penn: *Selected Poems 1923–1975* (v),
    A Place to Come To (f)

Carter pardons draft–dodgers and supports production of neutron bomb
Department of Energy created

1978
Cheever, John: *The Stories*
Gordon, Mary (b. 1949): *Final Payments* (f)
Irving, John (b. 1942): *The World According to Garp* (f)
Merrill, James: *Mirabell: Books of Number* (v)
Updike, John: *The Coup* (f)
Williams, Tennessee: *A Lovely Sunday for Creve Coeur*
    (p)

More than 1000 Indians walk from California to Washington, D.C., to protest against legislation hostile to their treaty rights
Passage of American Indian Religious Freedom Act and Indian Child Welfare Act
U.S. announces intention to end diplomatic relations with Taiwan and to recognize China
U.S. agrees to yield control of Panama Canal to Panamanians in year 2000
Carter acts as broker in Camp David agreement between Egypt and Israel

1979
Barth, John: *Letters* (f)
Heller, Joseph: *Good as Gold* (f)
Mailer, Norman: *The Executioner's Song* (pr)
Malamud, Bernard: *Dubin's Lives* (f)
Roth, Philip: *The Ghost Writer* (f)

U.S. recognizes new government in Iran
Carter supports production of new MX super–missile
Sioux Indians awarded $17,500,000 in compensation for Black Hills of Dakota, confiscated in 1877, and judged to be entitled to interest of $105,000,000
U.S. hostages seized in Iran

1980
Doctorow, E.L.: *Loon Lake* (f)
Kingston, Maxine Hong: *China Men* (pr)
Levin, Harry (b. 1912): *Memories of the Moderns* (pr)
Lorde, Audre: *The Cancer Journals* (pr)
Toole, John Kennedy (1937–69): *A Confederacy of Dunces*
    (f)

After U.S.S.R. invades Afghanistan, Carter announces "Carter Doctrine" threatening military retaliation if Soviets invade Persian Gulf region
U.S. hostages continue to be held in Iran
A flotilla converges at Cuba's Mariel Harbor to pick up refugees. By year end, more than 125,000 "Marielitos" migrate to the United States

1981
De Vries, Peter: *Sauce for the Goose* (f)
Forché, Carolyn (b. 1950): *The Country Between Us* (v)
Irving, John: *The Hotel New Hampshire* (f)
Robinson, Marilynne (b. 1943): *Housekeeping* (f)
Updike, John: *Rabbit Is Rich* (f)

Ronald Reagan administration (1981–88)
U.S. hostages freed by Iranians during Reagan inauguration
Reagan hit by shot from would–be assassin
Columbia space shuttle into orbit
Sandra Day O'Connor appointed first woman member of Supreme Court

1982
Ammons, A.R.: *Worldly Hopes* (v)
Barth, John: *Sabbatical* (f)
Bellow, Saul: *The Dean's December* (f)
Kosinski, Jerzy: *Pinball* (f)
Mamet, David: *Edmond* (p)
Merrill, James: *The Changing Light at Sandover* (v)
Naylor, Gloria (b. 1950): *The Women of Brewster Place*
    (f)
Walker, Alice (b. 1944): *The Color Purple* (f)

Equal Rights Amendment defeated
U.S. unemployment more than 11 million (highest figure since 1940)
U.S. federal debt tops $1 trillion
Massive anti–nuclear demonstration in New York
Martin Luther King Day becomes national holiday

1983
Adler, Renata (b. 1938): *Pitch Dark* (f)
Clampitt, Amy (b. 1920): *The Kingfisher* (v)
Kennedy, William (b. 1928): *Ironweed* (f)
Mailer, Norman: *Ancient Evenings* (f)
Malamud, Bernard: *The Stories*
Mamet, David: *Glengarry Glen Ross* (p; London production)

Reagan proposes Strategic Defense Initiative (S.D.I.), which becomes known as "Star Wars"
U.S. invades island of Grenada and overthrows leftist regime
West European countries begin deployment of U.S.–made cruise missiles; U.S.S.R. protests by withdrawing from Geneva arms control talks

DATE	AUTHOR AND TITLE	EVENT

Oliver, Mary (b. 1935): *American Primitive* (v)
Ozick, Cynthia (b. 1928): *The Cannibal Galaxy* (f)
Roth, Philip: *The Anatomy Lesson* (f)
Van Dinh, Tran: *Blue Dragon, White Tiger: A Tet Story*
    (f), first novel by Vietnamese American
Warren, Robert Penn: *Chief Joseph of the Nez Perce* (v)

1984

Ashbery, John: *A Wave* (v)
Bellow, Saul: *Him with His Foot in His Mouth and Other*
    Stories
Gibson, William: *Neuromancer* (f)
Heller, Joseph: *God Knows* (f)
Rich, Adrienne (b. 1929): *The Fact of a Doorframe* (v)
Updike, John: *The Witches of Eastwick* (f)
Wright, Charles (b. 1935): *The Other Side of the River* (v)

Geraldine Ferraro is first woman to be nominated for the
    vice-presidency
Jesse Jackson is first black to mount serious bid for the
    presidency
Olympic Games held in Los Angeles
Reagan defeats Walter Mondale, carrying 49 states

1985

Auster, Paul (b. 1947): *City of Glass* (f)
DeLillo, Don (b. 1936): *White Noise* (f)
Hersey, John: *The Call* (f)
Irving, John: *The Cider House Rules* (f)
McMurtry, Larry (b. 1936): *Lonesome Dove* (f)
Roth, Philip: *Zuckerman Bound* (f)
Shepard, Sam: *A Lie of the Mind* (p)
Tyler, Anne (b. 1941): *The Accidental Tourist* (f)
Vonnegut, Kurt, Jr.: *Galápagos* (f)

U.S.S.R. returns to arms control talks despite Euromissile
    deployment
U.S. becomes net debtor nation for first time since 1914

1986

De Vries, Rachel: *Tender Warriors* (f)
Gordon, Mary: *Men and Angels* (f)
Hemingway, Ernest: *The Garden of Eden* (f)
Stone, Robert (b. 1937): *Children of Light* (f)
Wilson, August: *Fences* (p)

Challenger space shuttle explodes; seven astronauts perish
U.S. bombs Libya over terrorist links
Robert Penn Warren designated America's first official Poet
    Laureate
Reagan–Gorbachov summit at Reykjavik ends in failure to
    reach agreement on any issue
Arms sales to Iran controversy reduces Reagan's popularity

1987

Bellow, Saul: *More Die of Heartbreak* (f)
Fraser, Kathleen (b. 1937): *Notes Preceding Trust* (v)
Meridith, William: *Partial Accounts* (v)
Morrison, Toni: *Beloved* (f)
Wolfe, Thomas Kennerly, Jr. (b. 1931): *The Bonfire of*
    the Vanities (f)

Nearly 50,000 AIDS cases reported to federal Centers for
    Disease Control
Stock market loses 508 points on October 19—largest drop
    in history of market

1988

Auster, Paul: *In the Country of Last Things* (f)
Berry, Wendell (b. 1934): *Remembering* (f)
Bierds, Linda Louise (b. 1945): *The Stillness, the Dancing*
    (v)
Harris, Thomas (b. 1940): *The Silence of the Lambs* (f)
Hongo, Garrett (b. 1951): *The River of Heaven* (v)
Tyler, Anne: *Breathing Lessons* (f)
Voigt, Ellen Bryant (b. 1943): *The Lotus Flowers* (v)
Wasserstein, Wendy (b. 1950): *The Heidi Chronicles* (p)

David Henry Hwang's *M. Butterfly* is first play by Asian
    American to win a Tony Award
U.S. federal budget deficit reaches 3.2 trillion
George Bush defeats Michael Dukakis in U.S. presidential
    election

1989

Berry, Wendell: *The Wild Birds* (f)
Gage, Nicholas (b. 1939): *A Place for Us* (pr)
Hijuelos, Oscar (b. 1951): *The Mambo Kings Play Songs*
    of Love (f)
Powers, Tim: *The Stress of Her Regard* (f)
Tan, Amy (b. 1952): *The Joy-Luck Club* (f)
Walker, Alice: *The Temple of My Familiar* (f)

Federal judge upholds off–reservation fishing rights of
    Wisconsin Chippewa, guaranteed by treaties in 1837 and
    1842
George Bush administration (1989–1992)
Supertanker *Exxon Valdez* runs aground in Prince William
    Sound, fouling 1,100 miles of Alaskan shoreline
The Berlin Wall is torn down

DATE	AUTHOR AND TITLE	EVENT

1990   Baker, Nicholson (b. 1957): *Room Temperature* (f)
Bly, Robert: *Iron John* (pr)
Esteves, Sandra Maria: *Bluestown Mockingbird Mambo* (v)
Updike, John: *Rabbit at Rest* (f)
Wright Charles P. (b. 1935): *The World of the Ten Thousand Things* (v)

U.S. troops invade Panama and overthrow the government of Manuel Noriega
The 1990 U.S. Census reports an increase in homelessness and a population decline in cities

1991   Ellis, Bret Easton (b. 1964): *American Psycho* (f)
Fuentes, Carlos (b. 1928): *The Campaign* (f)
Momaday, N. Scott: *In the Presence of the Sun* (f/v)
Rich, Adrienne: *An Atlas of the Difficult World* (v)
Taylor, Richard (b. 1941): *Three Kentucky Tragedies* (f)

U.S. troops deployed in Persian Gulf War with Iraq
Collapse of Soviet Union

1992   Ackerman, Diane (b. 1948): *The Moon by Whalelight* (pr)
Christopher, Nicholas (b. 1951): *In the Year of the Comet* (v)
Guerrier, Edith (1870–1958): *An Independent Woman* (pr)
Hongo, Garrett (ed): *The Open Boat* (v), first Asian American poetry collection
Morrison, Toni: *Jazz* (f)
Pijoan, Theresa: *White Wolf Woman and Other Native American Transformation Myths* (pr)

Race riot sweeps across Los Angeles following the acquittal of 4 police officers charged with excessive force in the arrest of Rodney King
A U.N.-sanctioned military force, led by American troops, arrives in Somalia to ensure delivery of food to starving people

1993   Angelou, Maya (b. 1928): *Wouldn't Take Nothing for My Journey Now* (pr)
Brown, Rita Mae (b. 1944): *Venus Envy* (pr)
Kingsolver, Barbara (b. 1955): *Pigs in Heaven* (f)
Reed, Ishmael (b. 1938): *Japanese by Spring* (f)

North American Free Trade Agreement (NAFTA) between Mexico, the United States, and Canada is established
Toni Morrison becomes first African American to win Nobel Prize for Literature
Bill Clinton becomes the forty-second U.S. president

1994   Barth, John (b. 1930): *Once upon a Time* (f)
Bloom, Harold (b. 1930): *The Western Canon* (pr)
Erdrich, Louise (b. 1954): *The Bingo Palace* (f)
Forché, Carolyn (b. 1950): *The Angel of History* (v)
Tate, James (b. 1943): *Worshipful Company of of Fletchers* (v)

Republicans win both houses of Congress for the first time in forty years
United States and Russia agree to point their strategic missiles at oceans instead of each other
Former football star O.J. Simpson is charged with the murder of his former wife and her friend

1995   Ford, Richard (b. 1944): *Independence Day* (f)
Gass, William H. (b. 1924): *The Tunnel* (f)
Rich, Adrienne (b. 1929): *Dark Fields of the Republic* (v)
Stern, Gerald (b. 1925): *Old Mercy* (v)
Wilson, August (b. 1945): *Seven Guitars* (p)

Timothy McVeigh and Terry Nichols are charged with bombing a federal building in Oklahoma City
Black separatist Louis Farrakhan, head of the Nation of Islam, leads the "Million Man March," a demonstration in Washington, D.C, focusing on the concerns of black men
United States extends diplomatic recognition to Vietnam

1996   Dubus, Andre (b. 1936): *Dancing after Hours* (f)
Graham, Jorie (b. 1951): *The Dream of the Unified Field* (v)
Klein, Joe (b. 1946): *Primary Colors* (f)
Larson, Jonathan (b. 1960): *Rent* (p)
Snyder, Gary (b. 1930): *Mountains and Rivers without End* (v)

Bill Clinton defeats Bob Dole for a second term as president; Republicans maintain control of the House and Senate
Theodore Kaczynski, the so-called Unabomber, is arrested for mailing handmade explosives to academics and business executives
Summer Olympics are held in Atlanta

1997   Bellow, Saul (b. 1915): *The Actual* (f)
DeLillo, Don (b. 1936): *Underworld* (f)
Kenyon, Jane (b. 1947): *Otherwise: New and Selected Poems* (v)
Pynchon, Thomas (b. 1937): *Mason and Dixon* (f)
Vogel, Paula (b. 1951): *How I Learned to Drive* (p)

Poet Allen Ginsberg dies in New York City
Madeleine Albright becomes the first woman to hold the position of U.S. secretary of state
Flooding of the Red River causes extensive damage in the north-central United States, especially North Dakota
Women's National Basketball Association debuts

DATE	AUTHOR AND TITLE	EVENT

1998   Ashbery, John (b. 1927): *Wakefulness* (v)

        Hall, Donald (b. 1928): *Without* (v)
Irving, John (b. 1942): *A Widow for One Year* (f)
Johnson, Charles (b. 1948): *Dreamer* (f)
Strand, Mark (b. 1934): *Blizzard of One* (v)
Wolfe, Tom (b. 1930): *A Man in Full* (f)

U.S. House of Representatives impeaches President William Jefferson Clinton
   on articles of perjury and obstruction of justice
Mark McGuire of the St. Louis Cardinals hits seventy home runs in one season, breaking the previous record of sixty-one held by Roger Maris of the New York Yankees
U.S. government runs the first budget surplus in twenty-nine years; unemployment falls to 4.3 percent, also a twenty-nine-year low

1999   Ellison, Ralph (b. 1914-94): Juneteenth
Giovanni, Nikki (b. 1943) Blues: For All the Changes (p)
Hass, Robert (b. 1941): An Unnamed Flowing: The C
Mamet, David (b. 1947): The Chinaman: Poems (p)
Momaday, N. Scott (b. 1934): In the Bear's House
Oates, Joyce Carol (b. 1938): Broke Heart Blues (n)

The second impeachment trial in the history of the U.S. ends in the acquittal of President Clinton
NATO launches attack on Serbia
Columbine (Colorado) high school students Eric Harris and Dylan Klebold attack their school with guns and explosives, killing a teacher and twelve students before turning their guns on themselves.
U.S. retains smallpox virus sample, over protest of scientists and scores of nations demanding it be destroyed
John F. Kennedy, Jr., wife Caroline Bessette Kennedy, and sister-in-law Lauren Bessette die in small plane crash off the coast of Martha's Vineyard

TITLE INDEX

The following index includes the titles of all books listed in the Fiction, Verse, and Plays sections of the Publications lists. A few titles from other sections (Collections, Other prose, etc.) are included as part of the "other" category. Titles appearing in **bold** are subjects of individual essays in the Works section. The following abbreviations are used:

f	fiction
v	verse
p	play
scr	screenplay
radio	radio play/script
tv	television play/script
o	other

Adding Machine (pl Rice) 1923

Additional Prose: A Bibliography on America, Proprioception, and Other Notes and Essays (o Olson) 1974

Address on the Utility and Justice of Restrictions upon Foreign Commerce (o Brown) 1809

Address to the Good People of Ireland, on Behalf of America . . . 1778 (o Franklin) 1891

Address to the Government on the Cession of Louisiana to the French (o Brown) 1803

Adeline, The Victim of Seduction (pl Payne) 1822

Ades Fables (f Ade) 1914

Admiral Robert Penn Warren and the Snows of Winter: A Tribute (o Styron) 1978

Adolphus (po W. Benét) 1941

Adrea (pl Belasco) 1904

Adrienne Rich's Poetry: Texts of the Poems, The Poet on Her Work, Reviews and Criticism (po Rich) 1975

Adrift in New York (f Alger) 1903

Adrift in the City (f Alger) 1895

Adulateur (pl M. Warren) 1773

Adult Bookstore (po Shapiro) 1976

Adultery and Other Choices (f Dubus) 1977

Adventure (f London) 1911

Adventures and Letters (o Richard Davis) 1917

Adventures in Common Sense (o E. Howe) 1922

Adventures in the Alaskan Skin Trade (f Hawkes) 1985

Adventures of a Novelist (o Atherton) 1932

Adventures of a Young Man (f Dos Passos) 1939

Adventures of Ann: Stories of Colonial Times (o Freeman) 1886

Adventures of Augie March (f Bellow) 1953

Adventures of Captain Grief (f London) 1954

Adventures of Ellery Queen (f Queen) 1934

Adventures of Francois, Foundling, Thief, Juggler, and Fencing-Master during the French Revolution (f S. Mitchell) 1898

Adventures of Francoise (pl L. Mitchell) 1900

Adventures of Huckleberry Finn (f Twain) 1884

Adventures of Juan Chicaspatas (po Anaya) 1985

Adventures of Marco Polo (scr Sherwood) 1938

Adventures of Marco Polo (pl Sherwood) 1937

Adventures of Marco Polo: A Musical Fantasy (pl Simon) 1959

Adventures of My Freshman (o Richard Davis) 1884

Adventures of Robin Day (f Bird) 1839

Adventures of Sam Spade and Other Stories (f Hammett) 1944

Adventures of the Black Girl in Her Search for God (pl Isherwood) 1969

Adventures of the Letter I (po Simpson) 1971

Adventures of the Wilderness Family (f M. Smith) 1976

Adventures of Thomas Jefferson Snodgrass (f Twain) 1928

Adventures of Tom Sawyer (f Twain) 1876

Adventures of Wesley Jackson (f Saroyan) 1946

Adventures of Will Wizard! Corporal of the Saccarapa Volunteers (f Ingraham) 1845

Adventures While Preaching the Gospel of Beauty (o Lindsay) 1914

Advertisements for Myself (o Mailer) 1959

Advice (po Bodenheim) 1920

Advice from the Muse (po Wilbur) 1981

Advice to a Prophet and Other Poems (po Wilbur) 1961

Advice to a Young Man on Choosing a Mistress (o Franklin) 1930

Advice to Eastern Europe (radio Nelson) 1990

Advice to the Churches of the Faithful (o Mather) 1702

Advice to the Privileged Orders in the Several States of Europe (o Barlow) 1792-93

Aesop's Forest (f Coover) 1986

Affectionately Eve (f Sinclair) 1961

Affinities and Other Stories (f Rinehart) 1920

Aflame and Afun of Walking Faces: Fables and Drawings (po Patchen) 1970

Aflame in the Sky (scr Rinehart) 1927

Afloat and Ashore (f Cooper) 1844

Afloat and Ashore (f Cooper) vols. 3-4, 1844

Aforesaid (po Frost) 1954

Africa: Her History, Lands and People (o J. Williams) 1962

Africa in Battle against Colonialism, Racialism, Imperialism (o Du Bois) 1960

Africa in the World Democracy (o J. Johnson) 1919

Africa: Its Geography, People, and Products (o Du Bois) 1930

Africa: Its Place in Modern History (o Du Bois) 1930

African-Centered Education: Its Value, Importance, and Necessity in the Development of Black Children (o Madhubuti) 1994

African Garden (pl Childress) 1971

African Queen (scr Agee) 1951

African Romances (pl Dunbar) 1897

Afrikan Free School (o Baraka) 1974

Afrikan Revolution (po Baraka) 1973

After (f R. Anderson) 1973

After All (pl Van Druten) 1929

After All, Not to Create Only (po Whitman) 1871

After and before the Lightning (po Ortiz) 1994

After Business Hours (pl Daly) 1886

After Eros (pl Hwang) 1998

After Experience: Poems and Translations (po Snodgrass) 1968

After Henry (o Didion) 1992

After House (f Rinehart) 1914

After Ikkyu and Other Poems (po Harrison) 1996

After I's (po Zukofsky) 1964

After Lazarus: A Filmscript (f Coover) 1980

After 1903—What? (o Benchley) 1938

After Such Pleasures (f Parker) 1933

After the Fall (pl A. Miller) 1964

After the Fox (scr Simon) 1966

After the Stroke: A Journal (o Sarton) 1988

After the Thin Man (scr Hammett) 1936

After Thirty Years: The Daring Young Man on the Flying Trapeze (f Saroyan) 1964

Afterlife (f Updike) 1987

Afterlife and Other Stories (f Updike) 1994

Aftermath (f J. Allen) 1896

Aftermath (po Longfellow) 1873

Afternoon of a Pawnbroker and Other Poems (po Fearing) 1943

Afterwhiles (po Riley) 1887

Against Anthologies (o Riding) 1928

Against Fear (o Styron) 1981

Against Heavy Odds: A Tale of Norse Heroism (o Boyesen) 1890

Against This Age (po Bodenheim) 1923

Age (f Calisher) 1987

Age for Love (scr Sherwood) 1931

Age of Innocence (f Wharton) 1920

Age of Miracles: Stories (f Gilchrist) 1995

Age of Reason (o Paine) 1794-95

Agnes (f Arthur) 1848

Agnes of Sorrento (f Stowe) 1862

Agon: Toward a Theory of Revisionism (o Bloom) 1982
Agrarian Justice (o Paine) 1797
Agricola (o Mather) 1727
Ah Man (pl Saroyan) 1962
Ah Sin (pl Harte; Twain) 1877
Ah Sweet Mystery of Mrs. Murphy (tv Saroyan) 1959
Ah, Wilderness! (pl O'Neill) 1933
A-Hunting of the Deer and Other Essays (o Warner) 1888
Air Raid (pl MacLeish) 1938
Air Raid (radio MacLeish) 1938
Air with Armed Men (o Simpson) 1972
Airing Dirty Laundry (o Reed) 1993
Airplane Dreams: Compositions from Journals (po Ginsberg) 1968
Airport Music (pl Hagedorn) 1994
Airways, Inc (pl Dos Passos) 1927
Al Aaraaf, Tamerlane, and Minor Poems (po Poe) 1829
Al Que Quiere! (po W. Williams) 1917
Alabaster Box (f J. Allen) 1923
Alabaster Box, with Florence Morse Kingsley (f Freeman) 1917
Alarms and Diversions (f Thurber) 1957
Albanian Softshoe (pl Wellman) 1988
Albany Depot (pl Howells) 1891
Alberto Albertini (pl Dunlap) 1811
Album (pl H. James) 1894
Album (f Rinehart) 1933
Albuquerque (o Anaya) 1992
Alcestiad (pl Wilder) 1977
Alchemy (f Lytle) 1979
Alcuin: A Dialogue (o Brown) 1798
Aleck Maury, Sportsman (f Gordon) 1934
Alex and the Gypsy (f Elkin) 1977
Alex Katz (o Beattie) 1987
Alexander Hamilton and Jefferson: Representative Selections (o Jefferson) 1934
Alexander's Bridge (f Cather) 1912
Alfred Venison's Poems, Social Credit Themes (po Pound) 1935
Algerine Captive (f R. Tyler) 1797
Algiers (scr Cain; Lawson) 1938
Algiers (pl Cain; Lawson) 1939
Algren's Book of Lonesome Monsters (o Algren) 1964
Algy (pl Fitch) 1903
Alhambra (f W. Irving) 1832
Ali Pacha (pl Payne) 1823
Alibi for Isabel and Other Stories (f Rinehart) 1944
Alice (f Arthur) 1844
Alice Adams (f Tarkington) 1921
Alice, and The Lost Novel (f S. Anderson) 1929
Alice in Bed (pl Sontag) 1993
Alice May, and Bruising Bill (f Ingraham) 1845
Alice through the Cellophane (o White) 1933
Alice Walker Banned (o A. Walker) 1996
Alien Corn (pl S. Howard) 1933
Alison's House (pl Glaspell) 1930
Alixe (pl Daly) 1873
All about Light (po W. Stafford) 1978
All Day Long (scr Angelou) 1974
All Fall Down (scr Inge) 1962
All for the Best (f Arthur) 1850
All for the Better: A Story of El Barrio (f Mohr) 1992
All God's Children Need Traveling Shoes (o Angelou) 1986
All God's Chillun Got Wings (pl O'Neill) 1924

All Good Americans (pl S. Perelman) 1933
All Grass Isn't Green (f E. Gardner) 1970
All I Could Never Be (f Yezierska) 1932
All in the Family (po Snyder) 1975
All Men Are Whores (pl Mamet) 1977
All My Friends are Going to Be Strangers (f McMurtry) 1972
All My Pretty Ones (po Sexton) 1962
All My Sons (pl A. Miller) 1947
All of Us: The Collected Poems (po Carver) 1998
All Over (pl Albee) 1971
All Quiet on the Western Front (scr M. Anderson) 1930
All Shot Up (f Himes) 1960
All Summer Long (pl R. Anderson) 1952
All That Is Lovely in Men (po Creeley) 1955
All That Money Can Buy (pl S. Benét) 1943
All That Money Can Buy (scr S. Benét) 1941
All the Comforts of Home (pl Gillette) 1890
All the Conspirators (f Isherwood) 1928
All the Girls He Wanted (f J. O'Hara) 1949
All the Good People I've Left Behind (f Oates) 1979
All the King's Men (f R. Warren) 1946
All the King's Men (pl R. Warren) 1959
All the Little Live Things (f Stegner) 1967
All the Sad Young Men (f Fitzgerald) 1926
All the Troubles of the World (f Asimov) 1989
All the Young Men (f La Farge) 1935
All This and Moonlight (o C. Johnson) 1990
All This and That (f Runyon) 1950
All under Heaven (f Buck) 1973
All Watched Over by Machines of Loving Grace (po Brautigan) 1967
All We Need of Hell (f Crews) 1987
Allegiances (po W. Stafford) 1970
Allen Ginsberg: Shared Dreams, Some Roots and Later Leaves, Some Sources and Descendants (po Ginsberg) 1994
Alligator Bride (po Hall) 1968
Alligator Bride: Poems New and Selected (po Hall) 1969
All's Fair in Love: An Original Dramatic Story (pl Brougham) 1856
Alma Mater (pl Green) 1938
Almanac of the Dead (f Silko) 1991
Alms for Oblivion: Essays (o Dahlberg) 1964
Alnilam (f Dickey) 1987
Alnwick Castle with Other Poems (po Halleck) 1827
Aloneness (po Brooks) 1971
Along the Illinois (po Masters) 1942
Along the Trail: A Book of Lyrics (po Hovey) 1898
Along This Way (o J. Johnson) 1933
Alpha Centauri, the Nearest Star (o Asimov) 1976
Alphabet for Joanna (po Gregory) 1963
Alphabet for Writing the Navajo Language (o La Farge) 1936
Alphabet Hicks (f Stout) 1941
Alphabets and Birthdays (o Stein) 1957
Alpine Christ and Other Poems (po Jeffers) 1973
Alpine Roses (pl Boyesen) 1884
Alps (pl B. Perelman) 1980
Altar of Freedom (f Rinehart) 1917
Altar of Freedom (o Rinehart) 1917
Altered States (f Chayefsky) 1978
Altered States (scr Chayefsky) 1979
Alternate Asimovs (f Asimov) 1986
Althea (pl Masters) 1907

Altogether Lovely: Jonathan Edwards on the Glory and Excellency of Jesus Christ (o Edwards) 1997

Always and Other Poems (po Rivera) 1973

Always Young and Fair (f Richter) 1947

Amaranth (po Robinson) 1934

Amateur Benefit (pl B. Howard) 1881

Amateur Garden (f Cable) 1914

Amateurs (f Barthelme) 1976

Amazing Adventures of Lester Leith (f E. Gardner) 1981

Amazing Adventures of Letitia Carberry (f Rinehart) 1911

Amazing Interlude (f Rinehart) 1918

Amazons (f Delillo) 1980

Ambassadors (f H. James) 1903

Amber Empress (pl Connelly) 1916

Amber Princess (pl Connelly) 1917

Ambrose Bierce: Stories (f Bierce) 1994

Ambrose Holt and Family (f Glaspell) 1931

Ambrosio (pl Linney) 1992

Ambush (scr S. Perelman) 1939

Amen Corner (pl James Baldwin) 1968

America (po Creeley) 1970

America (po Dwight) 1780(?)

America and Americans (o Steinbeck) 1966

America and the Americans (o Cooper) 1836

America Eats (o Algren) 1992

America Is in the Heart (o Bulosan) 1946

America More of Less (pl Baraka) 1973

America More or Less (pl Chin) 1976

America Peek-a-Boo Kabuki, World War II and Me (pl Chin) 1985

America Play (pl Parks) 1991

America Was Promises (po MacLeish) 1939

American (pl Daly) 1876

American (f H. James) 1877

American (pl H. James) 1891

American Appetites (f Oates) 1989

American Articles (o Hearn) 1939

American Beauty (f Ferber) 1931

American Blues: Five Short Plays (pl T. Williams) 1948

American Born (pl Belasco) 1882

American Born (pl Cohan) 1925

American Buffalo (pl Mamet) 1975

American Buffalo (scr Mamet) 1996

American Childhood (o Dillard) 1987

American Citizen: Naturalized in Leadville, Colorado (po Boyle) 1944

American Claimant (f Twain) 1892

American Clock (pl A. Miller) 1979

American Comedy (pl Nelson) 1983

American Comedy and Other Plays (pl Nelson) 1984

American Composition and Rhetoric (o Davidson) 1939

American County Fair (o S. Anderson) 1930

American Credo (o Mencken) 1920

American Credo: A Contribution toward the Understanding of the National Mind (o Nathan) 1920

American Crisis (o Paine) 1776-83

American Crusader (radio Sherwood) 1941

American Crusader (pl Sherwood) 1941

American Democrat (o Cooper) 1838

American Dream (pl Albee) 1961

American Dream (f Mailer) 1965

American Dream Girl (f Farrell) 1950

American Duchess (pl Fitch) 1893

American Earthquake: A Documentary of the Twenties and Thirties (o E. Wilson) 1958

American Education Past and Future (o Dewey) 1931

American Essays (pl H. James) 1956

American Fairy Tales (o Baum) 1901

American Fear of Literature (o Lewis) 1931

American Fugitive in Europe (o W. Brown) 1855

American Gun Mystery (f Queen) 1933

American Hunger (o R. Wright) 1977

American Idea (pl Cohan) 1909

American Ideas for English Readers (o J. Lowell) 1892

American in India (o Redding) 1954

American Indian (o La Farge) 1960

American Italy (o Warner) 1892

American Jitters: A Year of the Slump (o E. Wilson) 1932

American Journal (po Hayden) 1978

American Lands and Letters (o D. Mitchell) 1897-99

American Landscape (pl Rice) 1938

American Language (o Mencken) 1919

American Liberty (po Freneau) 1775

American Lounger (f Ingraham) 1839

American Miscellany: Articles and Stories Now First Collected (o Hearn) 1924

American Negro (o Du Bois; Washington) 1909

American Notebooks (o Hawthorne) 1932

American Ones (po Coolidge) 1981

American Pastoral (f P. Roth) 1997

American People's Money (o Donnelly) 1895

American Poetry at Mid-Century (o Ransom; Schwartz) 1958

American Politician (f Crawford) 1884

American Primer (o Whitman) 1904

American Religion: The Emergence of the Post-Christian Nation (o Bloom) 1992

American Scene (pl H. James) 1907

American Scenery (o Willis) 1840

American Sense (o Creeley) 1965(?)

American Story: Ten Broadcasts (pl MacLeish) 1944

American Tar (pl Rowson) 1796

American Tragedy (f Dreiser) 1925

American Tropical (pl Ford) 1983

American Village (po Freneau) 1772

American Way (pl Hart; Kaufman) 1939

American Wives and English Husbands (f Atherton) 1898

American Woman in the Chinese Hat (f Maso) 1994

American Woman's Home (o Stowe) 1869

American Writers (o Neal) 1937

Americana (f Delillo) 1971

Americanization of Emily (scr Chayefsky) 1964

Americans (po Riding) 1934

Americans All: Immigrants All (o Locke) 1939

Americans in England (pl Rowson) 1796

America's Persecuted Minority: Big Business (o Rand) 1962

Amerikan Journeys=Jornadas Americanas (po Sánchez) 1994

Amicable Parting (pl Kaufman) 1957

Amiri Baraka/LeRoi Jones Poetry Sampler (po Baraka) 1991

Amnesia People (po J. Tate) 1970

Among My Books (o J. Lowell) 1870-76

Among the Ancestors (po Cofer) 1981

Among the Camps (f Page) 1891

Among the Hills and Other Poems (po Whittier) 1869

Among the Lost People (f Aiken) 1934
Among the Paths to Eden (tv Capote) 1967
Among the Usual Days: A Portrait (o Sarton) 1993
Among Thieves (pl Gillette) 1909
Among Those Present (f Ferber) 1923
Among Those Present (pl Kaufman) 1918
Amphitryon (pl Wilbur) 1995
Amphitryon 38 (pl Behrman) 1938
AM/TRAK (po Baraka) 1979
Amulet (f Murfree) 1906
Amy Lowell: Portrait of the Poet in Her Time (o Gregory) 1958
Anabasis: A Journey to the Interior (f Gilchrist) 1994
Analog Bullet (f M. Smith) 1972
Anarchiad: A New England Poem (po Barlow; Trumbull) 1861
Anarchism and Other Essays (o Goldman) 1910
Anarchism Is Not Enough (o Riding) 1928
Anasazi (po Snyder) 1971
Anastasia (scr Laurents) 1956
Anatomy Lesson (f P. Roth) 1983
Anatomy of Criticism: Four Essays (o Frye) 1957
Anatomy of Negation (o Saltus) 1886
Anatomy of Nonsense (o Winters) 1943
Ancestors (f Atherton) 1907
Ancestors of Peter Atherly and Other Tales (f Harte) 1897
Ancient Child (f Momaday) 1990
Ancient Evenings (f Mailer) 1983
Ancient Law (f Glasgow) 1908
Ancient Mariner: A Dramatic Arrangement of Coleridge's Poem
    (pl O'Neill) 1924
& (po Cummings) 1925
And As for the Ladies (pl Kopit) 1971
And Baby Makes Seven (pl Vogel) 1986
And Baby Makes Three (o S. Jackson) 1960
And Be a Villain (f Stout) 1948
And Four to Go (f Stout) 1958
—And I Work at the Writer's Trade (o Cowley) 1978
And in the Human Heart (po Aiken) 1940
And Now Tomorrow (scr Chandler) 1944
And on the Eighth Day (f Queen) 1964
And Other Stories (f J. O'Hara) 1968
And So Died Raibouchinska (tv Bradbury) 1988
And Still I Rise (pl Angelou) 1976
And Still I Rise (po Angelou) 1978
—And the Moon Be Still as Bright (tv Bradbury) 1990
And the Stars Were Shining (po Ashbery) 1994
And Then You Wish (f Van Druten) 1936
And What of the Night? (pl Fornés) 1989
Anderson: The Writer at His Craft (o S. Anderson) 1979
Anderson/Gertrude Stein: Correspondence and Personal Essays
    (o S. Anderson) 1972
André (pl Dunlap) 1798
Andrew the Lion Farmer (o Hall) 1959
Androgyne, Mon Amour (po T. Williams) 1977
Andromache (pl Wilbur) 1982
Androo Johnson, His Life (f Nasby) 1866
Andy Gordon (f Alger) 1905
Andy Grant's Pluck (f Alger) 1902
Anecdotes of Modern Art (o Hall) 1990
Anecdotes of the Late War (po Olson) 1955
Anemone Me (scr Parks) 1990
Anew (po Zukofsky) 1946

Angel Arms (po Fearing) 1929
Angel City (pl Shepard) 1976
Angel Fire (po Oates) 1973
Angel Intrudes (pl Dell) 1918
Angel of Bethesda (o Mather) 1722
Angel of History (po Forché) 1994
Angel of Light (f Oates) 1981
Angel That Troubled the Waters and Other Plays (pl Wilder) 1928
Angela Is Twenty-Two (pl Lewis) 1938
Angels (po Updike) 1968
Angels and Earthly Creatures (po Wylie) 1929
Angels in America, Part One (pl Kushner) 1992
Angels in America, Part Two (pl Kushner) 1992
Angels of Pompeii (po Bly) 1991
Angels over Broadway (scr Hecht) 1940
Anger (f Sarton) 1982
Angle of Ascent: New and Selected Poems (po Hayden) 1975
Angle of Geese and Other Poems (po Momaday) 1974
Angle of Repose (f Stegner) 1971
Angry Ones (f J. Williams) 1960
Angry Wife (f Buck) 1947
Animae (po Merwin) 1969
Animal Crackers (pl Kaufman) 1928
Animal Dreams (f Kingsolver) 1990
Animal Fairy Tales (o Baum) 1969
Animal Faith and Spiritual Life: Previously Unpublished and Un-
    collected Writings (o Santayana) 1967
Animal Kingdom (pl Barry) 1932
Animal That Drank Up Sound (po W. Stafford) 1992
Animals and Other People (o Bromfield) 1955
Animula (po Eliot) 1929
Ankor Wat (po Ginsberg) 1968
Ann Vickers (f Lewis) 1933
Anna Christie (pl O'Neill) 1920
Anna Karenina (scr Behrman) 1935
Anna Lacasta (scr Laurents) 1949
Anna Milnor, The Young Lady Who Was Not Punctual, and Other
    Tales (f Arthur) 1845
Anna Papers (f Gilchrist) 1988
Annabel (f Baum) 1906
Anne Boleyn (pl Boker) 1850
Anne of the Thousand Days (pl M. Anderson) 1948
Annie Allen (po Brooks) 1949
Annie Kilburn (f Howells) 1888
Annie Over (po W. Stafford) 1988
Annie Salem (f Wellman) 1996
Anniversary (f Auchincloss) 1998
Annotated "Gulliver's Travels" (o Asimov) 1980
Annotated Poe (o Poe) 1981
Annunciation (pl Fornés) 1967
Annunciation (f Gilchrist) 1983
Anonymous Sins and Other Poems (po Oates) 1969
Another America/Otra America (po Kingsolver) 1993
Another Book on Theatre (o Nathan) 1915
Another Country (f James Baldwin) 1962
Another Look (po Gregory) 1976
Another Pamela (f Sinclair) 1950
Another Part of the Forest (pl Hellman) 1946
Another Quarter Mile: Poetry (po King) 1979
Another Secret Diary 1739-1741 (o Byrd) 1942
Another Thin Man (scr Hammett) 1939

Another You (f Beattie) 1995
A'nque (po Alurista) 1979
Answered Prayers (f Capote) 1986
Answers to Some Questions Posed by Howard Nemerov (o Moore) 1982
Antelope Wife (f Erdrich) 1998
Ante-Mortem Statement (f E. Howe) 1891
Antepenultimata (o Bierce) 1912
Anthem (f Rand) 1938
Anthem Sprinters and Other Antics (pl Bradbury) 1963
Anthology of Another Town (o E. Howe) 1920
Anthropos (pl Cummings) 1945
Antick (pl MacKaye) 1912
Anti-Matrimony (pl MacKaye) 1910
Antiphon (pl Barnes) 1958
Antiquamania (o Roberts) 1928
Anti-Slavery Catechism (o Child) 1836
Anti-Slavery Papers (o J. Lowell) 1902
Anxiety of Influence: A Theory of Poetry (o Bloom) 1973
Anybody's Woman (scr Akins) 1930
Anyone Can Whistle (pl Laurents) 1964
Anything for Billy (f McMurtry) 1988
Anything We Love Can Be Saved: A Writer's Activism (o A. Walker) 1997
Apache Devil (f E. Burroughs) 1933
Apartment in Athens (f Wescott) 1945
Aperture (o Bowles) 1984
Aphrodisiac (o Nin) 1978
Apollonius of Tyana: A Dance, with Some Words, for Two Actors (o Olson) 1951
Apologia of the Ampersand (po Morley) 1936
Apologies to the Iroquois (o E. Wilson) 1960
Apology for Bad Dreams (po Jeffers) 1930
Apology for Eating Geoffrey Movius' Hyacinth (po J. Tate) 1972
Apostate (f London) 1906
Appalachia Sounding (pl Linney) 1975
Appalachian Elders: A Warm Hearth Sampler (o Giovanni) 1991
Apparition (pl Eberhart) 1951
Apparitions (po M. Walker) 1987
Appeal for the Indians (o Child) 1868
Appeal in Favor of That Class of Americans Called Africans (o Child) 1833
Appeal to Caesar (o Tourgée) 1884
Appendix to the Notes on Virginia Relative to the Murder of Logan's Family (o Jefferson) 1800
Apple Found in the Plowing (po Bly) 1989
Apple of the Eye (f Wescott) 1924
Apple-Tree Table and Other Sketches (f Melville) 1922
Applied Psychology: An Introduction to the Principles and Practices of Education (o Dewey) 1889
Appointment in Samarra (f J. O'Hara) 1934
Apprentice Fiction of Fitzgerald 1909-1917 (f Fitzgerald) 1965
April: A Fable of Love (f Fisher) 1937
April Fire (po MacKaye) 1925
April Fool (pl Harrigan) 1875
April Galleons (po Ashbery) 1987
April Hopes (f Howells) 1887
April Snow (pl Linney) 1983
April Twilights (po Cather) 1903
April Twilights and Other Poems (po Cather) 1923
April Weather (pl Fitch) 1893

April Witch (f Bradbury) 1987
Aqueduct (f Bradbury) 1979
Ara Vos Prec (po Eliot) 1920
Arabian Night in the Nineteenth Century (pl Daly) 1884
Aragon, Poet of Resurgent France (o Cowley) 1946
Ararat (po Glück) 1990
Archaeologist of Morning (po Olson) 1970
Archbishop's Ceiling (pl A. Miller) 1977
Archers (pl Dunlap) 1796
Archibald Henderson: An Appreciation of the Man (o Markham) 1918
Architectural Drawings (o Jefferson) 1960
Archy and Mehitabel (po Marquis) 1927
Archy Does His Part (po Marquis) 1935
Archy's Life of Mehitabel (po Marquis) 1933
Arctic Dreams: Imagination and Desire in a Northern Landscape (o Lopez) 1986
Arctic Ox (po Moore) 1964
Are You Hungry, Are You Cold (f Bemelmans) 1960
Are You in the Winter Tree? (po Purdy) 1987
Are You Insured? (pl Harrigan) 1885
Are You Listening Rabbi Löw? (f Donleavy) 1987
Are You Ready Mary Baker Eddy? (po J. Tate) 1970
Arethusa (f Crawford) 1907
Areytos (po Simms) 1846
Argonauts of North Liberty (f Harte) 1888
Aria da Capo (pl Millay) 1921
Ariel (po Plath) 1965
Arise, Arise (pl Zukofsky) 1973
Aristocracy (pl B. Howard) 1898
Aristocrat (f Richter) 1968
Aristocrats (f Atherton) 1901
Arizona Ames (f Grey) 1932
Arizona Clan (f Grey) 1958
Ark of Bones and Other Stories (f Dumas) 1970
Arkansas (o Fletcher) 1947
Arm Yrself or Harm Yrself (pl Baraka) 1967
Armageddon (po Ransom) 1923
Armand (pl Mowatt) 1849
Armazindy (po Riley) 1894
Armenians (pl Saroyan) 1974
Armies of the Night: The Novel as History. History as a Novel (o Mailer) 1968
Armourer's Escape (pl Barker) 1817
Army Alphabet (po Baum) 1900
Arnold (f Ingraham) 1844
Around Old Chester (f Deland) 1915
Around the World in Eighty Days (scr S. Perelman) 1956
Around the World in Eighty Minutes with Douglas Fairbanks (scr Sherwood) 1931
Around You, Your House; and A Catechism (po W. Stafford) 1979
Arrivistes: Poems 1940-1949 (po Simpson) 1949
Arrogant Beggar (f Yezierska) 1926
Arrow (f Morley) 1927
Arrow of Gold (f Ingraham) 1854(?)
Arrows of Longing: The Correspondence between Anaïs Nin and Felix Pollak, 1952-1976 (o Nin) 1998
Arrowsmith (scr S. Howard) 1931
Arrowsmith (f Lewis) 1925
Art (pl Fornés) 1986
Art and Ardor (o Ozick) 1983

Art and Artifice (pl Brougham) 1859
Art and Education (o Dewey) 1929
Art and Science: Investigating Matter (o Gass) 1996
Art as Experience (o Dewey) 1934
Art Chronicles 1954-1966 (o F. O'Hara) 1975
Art Lover (f Maso) 1990
Art of Adding and the Art of Taking Away: Selections from Updike's Manuscripts (o Updike) 1987
Art of Decorating Dry Goods Windows and Interiors (o Baum) 1900
Art of Fiction and Other Essays (pl H. James) 1948
Art of Living and Other Stories (f J. Gardner) 1981
Art of Swimming (o Franklin) 1816(?)
Art of the Essay (o Fiedler) 1958
Art of the Moving Picture (o Lindsay) 1915
Art of the Night (o Nathan) 1928
Art of the Novel: Critical Prefaces (pl H. James) 1934
Art of the Self. Essays a propos Steps (o Kosinski) 1968
Art of Travel: Scenes and Journeys in America, England, France, and Italy (pl H. James) 1958
Art of Worldly Wisdom (po Rexroth) 1949
Art Scene (pl Kingsley) 1969
Artemis to Actaeon and Other Verse (po Wharton) 1909
Artemus Ward among the Fenians (o Ward) 1866
Artemus Ward, His Book (o Ward) 1862
Artemus Ward, His Travels (o Ward) 1865
Artemus Ward in London and Other Papers (o Ward) 1867
Artemus Ward's Lecture (o Ward) 1869
Artemus Ward's Panorama (o Ward) 1869
Arthur Denwood (f Ingraham) 1846
Arthur Mervyn (f Brown) 1799-1800
Article 47 (pl Daly) 1872
Articulation of Sound Forms in Time (po S. Howe) 1987
Artie (f Ade) 1896
Artie (pl Ade) 1907
Artificial Nigger and Other Tales (f O'Connor) 1957
Artist (po Jeffers) 1928
Artist (pl Mencken) 1912
Artist (scr Mohr) 1981
Arundel (f Roberts) 1930
As a Strong Bird on Pinions Free (po Whitman) 1872
As Does New Hampshire (po Sarton) 1967
As Fine as Melanctha (1914-1930) (o Stein) 1954
As Good as a Comedy (f Simms) 1852
As He Lay Dead, A Bitter Grief (o Styron) 1981
As Husbands Go (scr Behrman) 1934
As Husbands Go (pl Crothers) 1931
As I Lay Dying (f Faulkner) 1930
As I Remember It: Some Epilogues in Recollection (o Cabell) 1955
As If (po Ciardi) 1955
As It Was in the Beginning: A Poem Dedicated to the Mothers of Men (po J. Miller) 1903
As James Said: Extracts from the Published Writings (o W. James) 1942
As Long as the Rivers Flow: The Stories of Nine Native Americans (o P. Allen) 1996
As Long as the Grass Shall Grow (o La Farge) 1940
As Now It Would Be Snow (po Creeley) 1970
As the Crow Flies (pl Hwang) 1986
As the Eye Moves: A Sculpture by Henry Moore (o Hall) 1970
As Thousands Cheer (pl Hart) 1933

As We Are Now (f Sarton) 1973
As We Go (o Warner) 1893
As We Know (po Ashbery) 1979
As We Were Saying (o Warner) 1891
As You Like It (pl Daly) 1890
As Young as You Feel (scr Chayefsky) 1951
Asbestos Phoenix (po Guthrie) 1968
Ascent of F6 (pl Isherwood) 1937
Ash-Wednesday (po Eliot) 1930
Asimov Laughs Again (po Asimov) 1993
Asimov on Astronomy (o Asimov) 1974
Asimov on Chemistry (o Asimov) 1974
Asimov on Numbers (o Asimov) 1977
Asimov on Physics (o Asimov) 1976
Asimov on Science: A Thirty Year Retrospective (o Asimov) 1989
Asimov on Science Fiction (o Asimov) 1981
Asimov's Annotated "Don Juan" (o Asimov) 1972
Asimov's Annotated "Paradise Lost" (o Asimov) 1974
Asimov's Biographical Encyclopedia of Science and Technology (o Asimov) 1964
Asimov's Chronology of Science and Technology (o Asimov) 1989
Asimov's Chronology of the World (o Asimov) 1991
Asimov's Guide to Earth and Space (o Asimov) 1991
Asimov's Guide to Halley's Comet (o Asimov) 1985
Asimov's Guide to Science (o Asimov) 1972
Asimov's Guide to Shakespeare (o Asimov) 1970
Asimov's Guide to the Bible (o Asimov) 1968-69
Asimov's Mysteries (f Asimov) 1968
Asimov's New Guide to Science (o Asimov) 1984
Asimov's Sherlockian Limericks (po Asimov) 1977
Ask a Policeman (f Hinojosa) 1998
Ask Me Tomorrow (f Cozzens) 1940
Ask Your Mama: 12 Moods for Jazz (po Hughes) 1961
Aslan Norval (f Traven) 1960
Aspern Papers, Louisa Pallant, The Modern Warning (f H. James) 1888
Aspirant (po Dreiser) 1929
Assassination Bureau Ltd. (f London) 1963
Assassins: A Book of Hours (f Oates) 1975
Assembly (f J. O'Hara) 1961
Assignation (f Oates) 1988
Assignment (pl Kopit) 1985
Assistant (f Malamud) 1957
Assommoir (pl Daly) 1879
Assorted Prose (o Updike) 1965
Assyrian and Other Stories (f Saroyan) 1950
Astonished Eye Looks out of the Air, Being Some Poems Old and New against War and in Behalf of Life (po Patchen) 1945
Astounding Crime on Torrington Road (f Gillette) 1927
Astraea: The Balance of Illusions (po Holmes) 1850
Astronomer and Other Stories (f Betts) 1966
Asylum (pl Kopit) 1963
At Dartmouth: The Phi Beta Kappa Poem 1839 (po Holmes) 1940
At Egypt (po Coolidge) 1988
At Eighty-Two: A Journal (o Sarton) 1996
At Fault (f Chopin) 1890
At Heaven's Gate (f R. Warren) 1943
At Home and Abroad (o B. Taylor) 1859-62
At Liberty (pl T. Williams) 1941
At Night the Salmon Move (po Carver) 1976
At Seventy: A Journal (o Sarton) 1984

At Sundown (po Whittier) 1890
At the Dim'crackr Convention (pl Baraka) 1980
At the Earth's Core (f E. Burroughs) 1922
At the End of the Open Road (po Simpson) 1963
At the Moon's Inn (f Lytle) 1941
At the Mountains of Madness and Other Novels (f Lovecraft) 1964
At the Roots of the Stars: The Short Plays (pl Barnes) 1995
At Your Service: The Way of Life in a Hotel (o Bemelmans) 1941
Atalantis: A Story of the Sea (po Simms) 1832
Atheism Refuted (o Paine) 1798
Atlanta (po Chivers) 1853
Atlanta Offering: Poems (po F. Harper) 1895
Atlantic City (scr Guare) 1980
Atlantis: The Antediluvian World (o Donnelly) 1882
Atlantis: Three Tales (f S. Delany) 1995
Atlas of the Difficult World: Poems, 1988-1991 (po Rich) 1991
Atlas Shrugged (f Rand) 1957
Atom: Journey Across the Subatomic Cosmos (o Asimov) 1991
Atoms of Thought: An Anthology of Thoughts (o Santayana) 1950
Atonement (f Auchincloss) 1997
Attack on Leviathan: Regionalism and Nationalism in the United States (o Davidson) 1938
Attic Where the Meadow Greens (po Bradbury) 1980
Attitudes toward History (o Burke) 1937
Aubade (pl Kopit) 1959
Auden (po Shapiro) 1974
Audubon: A Vision (po R. Warren) 1969
August Forty-five (pl J. Williams) 1991
August 22nd (f Sinclair) 1965
Aunt Fanny from Chautauqua (pl Ade) 1949
Aunt Jane's Nieces (f Baum) 1906-15
Aunt Jo's Scrap-Bag (f Alcott) 1872-82
Aunt Kipp (f Alcott) 1868
Aurora (po Brooks) 1972
Aurora (pl Fornés) 1974
Auroras of Autumn (po Stevens) 1950
Austerities (po Simic) 1983
Author of Beltraffio, Pandora, Georgina's Reasons, The Path of Duty, Four Meetings (f H. James) 1885
Authorship: A Tale (f Neal) 1830
Autobiographia (o Whitman) 1892
Autobiographical Memo (o J. Cooke) 1969
Autobiographical Sketch (1815-1842) (o Dana) 1953
Autobiographical Writings (o Franklin) 1945
Autobiography of a Play (o B. Howard) 1914
Autobiography of a Pocket Handkerchief (f Cooper) 1949
Autobiography of a Quack and Other Stories (f S. Mitchell) 1901
Autobiography of a Quack, and The Case of George Dedlow (f S. Mitchell) 1900
Autobiography of Alice B. Toklas (o Stein) 1933
Autobiography of an Actress (o Mowatt) 1853
Autobiography of an Attitude (o Nathan) 1925
Autobiography of an Ex-Colored Man (f J. Johnson) 1912
Autobiography of LeRoi Jones (o Baraka) 1984
Autobiography of Miss Jane Pittman (f Gaines) 1971
Autobiography: Some Notes on a Nonentity (o Lovecraft) 1963
Autobiograpy (o Creeley) 1990
Autocrat of the Breakfast-Table (o Holmes) 1858
Autocrat's Miscellanies (o Holmes) 1959
Auto-da-Fe (pl T. Williams) 1946

Autonomy (pl Barry) 1919
Autumn Garden (pl Hellman) 1951
Autumn People (f Bradbury) 1965
Autumnal Leaves: Tales and Sketches in Prose and Rhyme (f Child) 1857
Ava (f Maso) 1993
Avalanche (f Boyle) 1944
Avalanche: A Mystery Story (f Atherton) 1919
Avalon (po Davidson) 1923
Ave Maria (pl Linney) 1989
Ave, Roma Immortalis: Studies from the Chronicles of Rome (o Crawford) 1898
Avenging Brother (f Ingraham) 1869
Avenue Bearing the Initial of Christ into the New World: Poems 1946-1964 (po Kinnell) 1974
Avolio: A Legend of the Island of Cos (po Hayne) 1859
Avon Flows (o Nathan) 1937
Avon's Harvest (po Robinson) 1921
Awake and Rehearse (f Bromfield) 1929
Awake and Sing! (pl Odets) 1935
Awake in Spain (pl F. O'Hara) 1960
Awakening (f Chopin) 1899
Awakening and Other Poems (po Marquis) 1924
Awakening and Other Stories (f Chopin) 1970
Awakening and Selected Stories (f Chopin) 1984
Awakening Land (f Richter) 1966
Awakening of Helena Richie (f Deland) 1906
Away (po Creeley) 1976
Awful Rowing Toward God (po Sexton) 1975
Awkward Age (f H. James) 1899
Axe Handles (po Snyder) 1983
Axe to Grind (f E. Gardner) 1951
Axel's Castle: A Study in the Imaginative Literature of 1870-1930 (o E. Wilson) 1931
Ay, Compadre (pl Anaya) 1995
Ayn Rand's Marginalia: Her Critical Comments on the Writings of Over 20 Authors (o Rand) 1996
Azazel (f Asimov) 1988

B.F.'s Daughter (f Marquand) 1946
Bab, A Sub-Deb (f Rinehart) 1917
Babbitt (f Lewis) 1922
Babel to Byzantium: Poets and Poetry Now (o Dickey) 1968
Babel-17 (f S. Delany) 1966
Babe's Bed (f Wescott) 1930
Babes in Birdland (f Baum) 1911
Babes in the Wood (scr Baum) 1914
Baby Ballads (po Riley) 1914
Baby Cyclone (pl Cohan) 1929
Baby Doll (scr T. Williams) 1956
Baby Doll (pl T. Williams) 1956
Baby in the Icebox and Other Short Fiction (f Cain) 1981
Baby, It's Cold Inside (o S. Perelman) 1970
Babylon Revisited and Other Stories (f Fitzgerald) 1996
Baby's First Step (f Updike) 1992
Bachelor (pl Fitch) 1909
Bachelor Apartment (scr Lawson) 1931
Bachelor Life (o Nathan) 1941
Bachelor Party (tv Chayefsky) 1953
Bachelor Party (pl Chayefsky) 1957
Bachelor Party (scr Chayefsky) 1957

Bachelors Get Lonely (f E. Gardner) 1961
Back Again, Home (po Madhubuti) 1968
Back Bog Beast Bait (pl Shepard) 1971
Back Country (po Snyder) 1968
Back in the World (f Wolff) 1985
Back Roads to Far Places (po Ferlinghetti) 1971
Back to China (f Fiedler) 1965
Back to the Stone Age (f E. Burroughs) 1937
Backbone of America (tv Sherwood) 1954
Background of My Life (o Santayana) 1944
Backlog Studies (o Warner) 1873
Back-Stair Investigation (pl Ade) 1897
Backward Glance (o Wharton) 1934
Backward Glances (o Whitman) 1947
Backwards (po Creeley) 1975
Backwater (f Stribling) 1930
Backwoodsman (po Paulding) 1818
Bad Boys (po Cisneros) 1980
Bad Characters (f J. Stafford) 1964
Bad Children: A Play in One Act for Bad Children (pl S. Jack-
    son) 1959
Bad Infinity (pl Wellman) 1985
Bad Man (f Elkin) 1967
Bad Man From Bodie (f Doctorow) 1961
Bad Men in the West (pl Saroyan) 1942
Bad Parent's Garden of Verse (po Nash) 1936
Bad Penny (pl Wellman) 1989
Bad Samaritan (pl Ade) 1905
Bad Seed (pl M. Anderson) 1955
Baddeck and That Sort of Thing (o Warner) 1874
Baffling Means (po Coolidge) 1991
Bag of Bones (f King) 1998
Bagatelles from Passy (o Franklin) 1967
Bagombo Snuff Box: Uncollected Short Fiction (f Vonnegut) 1999
Bailey's Cafe (f Naylor) 1992
Bait (pl Merrill) 1953
Baker's Dozen of Emblems (po W. Benét) 1935
Bal (pl Nelson) 1980
Balance of the Sanctuary (o Mather) 1727
Balisand (f Hergesheimer) 1924
Ballad of Abraham Lincoln (po B. Taylor) 1870
Ballad of Beta-2 (f S. Delany) 1965
Ballad of Mary Phagan (scr McMurtry) 1988
Ballad of New York, New York, and Other Poems 1930-1950 (po
    Morley) 1950
Ballad of Remembrance (po Hayden) 1962
Ballad of the Brown Girl: An Old Ballad Retold (po Cullen) 1927
Ballad of the Brown King (pl Hughes) 1960
Ballad of the Burglar of Babylon (po E. Bishop) 1968
Ballad of the Duke's Mercy (po S. Benét) 1939
Ballad of the Free (po M. Walker) 1966
Ballad of the Harp-Weaver (po Millay) 1922
Ballad of the Sad Cafe (pl Albee) 1963
Ballad of the Sad Café: The Novels and Stories of McCullers (f
    McCullers) 1951
Ballad of William Sycamore 1790-1880 (po S. Benét) 1923
Ballades from the Hidden Way (po Cabell) 1928
Ballads and Other Poems (po Longfellow) 1842
Ballads and Other Poems (po Whittier) 1844
Ballads and Poems 1915-1930 (po S. Benét) 1931
Ballads for Sale (po A. Lowell) 1927

Ballads of New England (po Whittier) 1870
Ballywingle the Beloved (pl Gillette) 1873
Balo (pl Toomer) 1927
Baltimore Waltz (pl Vogel) 1992
Baltimore Waltz and Other Plays (pl Vogel) 1997
Balzac (o Saltus) 1884
Banana Bottom (f McKay) 1933
Band of Angels (f R. Warren) 1955
Band Wagon (pl Kaufman) 1931
Bandit of Hell's Bend (f E. Burroughs) 1925
Bandits (f Leonard) 1987
Bandoeng: 1.500.000.000 Hommes (o R. Wright) 1955
Bang! Bang! (f Ade) 1928
Banjo: A Story without a Plot (f McKay) 1929
Banker's Daughter (pl B. Howard) 1873
Banker's Wife (f Arthur) 1851
Bankrupt (pl Boker) 1855
Banks of the Ohio (f Paulding) 1833
Banquets of the Black Widowers (f Asimov) 1984
Baptism (pl Baraka) 1964
Baptism, and The Toilet (pl Baraka) 1967
Baptism of Desire (po Erdrich) 1989
Baptismal Piety (o Mather) 1727
Bar Ber Ous (pl Harrigan) 1876
Bar Harbor (o Crawford) 1896
Bar Sinister (f Richard Davis) 1903
BA-RA-KA (pl Baraka) 1972
Barbara Frietchie, The Frederick Girl (pl Fitch) 1900
Barbarous Barbers and Other Stories (f Hearn) 1939
Barbarous Coast (f Macdonald) 1956
Barbary Coast (scr Hecht; MacArthur) 1935
Barbary Shore (f Mailer) 1951
Bare Hills: A Book of Poems (po Winters) 1927
Barefoot in Athens (pl M. Anderson) 1951
Barefoot in the Park (pl Simon) 1962
Barefoot in the Park (scr Simon) 1967
Barefoot Saint (f S. Benét) 1929
Barely and Widely (po Zukofsky) 1958
Barker's Luck and Other Stories (f Harte) 1896
Barn Burning (tv Vidal) 1954
Barn Burning and Other Stories (f Faulkner) 1977
Barnum Was Right (pl Sherwood) 1918
Baron Rudolph (pl Belasco) 1887
Baron Rudolph (pl B. Howard) 1881
Baroness of New York (pl J. Miller) 1877
Barracks Thief (f Wolff) 1984
Barren Ground (f Glasgow) 1925
Barrier (pl Hughes) 1950
Barrio on the Edge=Caras viejas y vino nuevo (f Morales) 1998
Bar-Rooms at Brantley (f Arthur) 1877
Barty Crusoe and His Man Saturday (f Burnett) 1909
Baseball in April (po Soto) 1990
Bases of Artistic Creation: Essays (o M. Anderson) 1942
Basic Writings (o Jefferson) 1944
Basil and Josephine Stories (f Fitzgerald) 1973
Basket of Chips (pl Brougham) 1855
Bastard out of Carolina (f Allison) 1992
Bastion Saint-Gervais (radio M. Anderson) 1938
Bat (f Rinehart) 1926
Bat (pl Rinehart) 1932
Bath after Sailing (po Updike) 1968

Bathtub Hoax and Other Blasts and Bravos from the Chicago Tribune (o Mencken) 1958

Bats Fly at Dusk (f E. Gardner) 1942

Battle Cry (pl Faulkner) 1985

Battle in Greece (o S. Crane) 1936

Battle of Angels (pl T. Williams) 1940

Battle of Bunkers-Hill (pl Brackenridge) 1776

Battle of Castle Crags (o J. Miller) 1894

Battle of Cowpens (o Roberts) 1958

Battle of Lake Erie (o Cooper) 1843

Battle of Niagara (po Neal) 1818

Battle of the Aleutians (o Hammett) 1944

Battle of the Kegs (po Hopkinson) 1779

Battle of the Rafts and Other Stories (o Boyesen) 1893

Battle Summer, Being Transcripts from Personal Observation in Paris 1848 (o D. Mitchell) 1849

Battle That Ended the Century (f Lovecraft) 1934

Battlefields and Ghosts (f Bierce) 1931

Battle-Ground (f Glasgow) 1902

Battle-Pieces and Aspects of the War (po Melville) 1866

Baum's American Fairy Tales (f Baum) 1997

Baum's Juvenile Speaker (o Baum) 1910

Baum's Own Book for Children (o Baum) 1912

Bay Boy (f R. Tyler) 1978

Bay of Seven Islands and Other Poems (po Whittier) 1883

Bayou Folk (f Chopin) 1894

Bayou Harlequinade (pl B. Smith) 1940

Be Angry at the Sun (po Jeffers) 1941

Be Yourself (pl Connelly; Kaufman) 1924

Beaks of Eagles (po Jeffers) 1936

Bean Eaters (po Brooks) 1960

Bean Trees (f Kingsolver) 1988

Beasley's Christmas Party (f Tarkington) 1909

Beast in Me, and Other Animals: A New Collection of Pieces and Drawings about Human Beings and Less Alarming Creatures (f Thurber) 1948

Beast in View (po Rukeyser) 1944

Beastly Beatitudes of Balthazar B (pl Donleavy) 1981

Beastly Beatitudes of Balthazar B (f Donleavy) 1968

Beasts of Tarzan (f E. Burroughs) 1916

Beasts of the Southern Wild (f Betts) 1973

Beat the Devil (scr Capote) 1953

Beating the Bushes: Selected Essays 1941-1970 (o Ransom) 1972

Beatrice Hallam and Captain Ralph (f J. Cooke) 2 vols., 1892

Beatrice, The Goldsmith's Daughter: A Story of the Reign of the Last Charles (f Ingraham) 1847

Beau Brummell (pl Fitch) 1908

Beauchampe (f Simms) 1842

Beautiful and Damned (f Fitzgerald) 1922

Beautiful Changes and Other Poems (po Wilbur) 1947

Beautiful Lady (f Tarkington) 1905

Beautiful People (pl Saroyan) 1941

Beautiful Widow (f Arthur) 1847

Beauty and the Beast, and Tales of Home (f B. Taylor) 1872

Beauty and the Jacobin: An Interlude of the French Revolution (pl Tarkington) 1912

Beauty Part (pl Behrman; S. Perelman) 1962

Because I Was Flesh (f Dahlberg) 1964

Because It Is Bitter, and Because It Is My Heart (f Oates) 1990

Because It Is: Poems and Drawings (po Patchen) 1960

Because She Loved Him So (pl Gillette) 1898

Bech: A Book (f Updike) 1970

Bech at Bay (f Updike) 1998

Bech Is Back (f Updike) 1982

Beckonings (po Brooks) 1975

Becky and Her Friends (f Hinojosa) 1990

Becky Sharp (pl L. Mitchell) 1899

Bed Riddance: A Posy for the Indisposed (po Nash) 1970

Bedford Forrest and His Critter Company (o Lytle) 1931

Bedouins (o Huneker) 1920

Bedrooms Have Windows (f E. Gardner) 1949

Bedside Manner (o Benchley) 1952

Bedside Manners: A Comedy of Convalescence (pl Behrman) 1924

Bee Time Vine and Other Pieces (1913-1927) (o Stein) 1953

Bee-Hunter (f Cooper) 1848

Beer and the Body (o Nasby) 1884

Beet Queen (f Erdrich) 1986

Beetle Leg (f Hawkes) 1951

Befo' de War: Echoes in Negro Dialect (po Page) 1888

Before Adam (f London) 1907

Before and After the Election (f Arthur) 1853

Before Breakfast (pl O'Neill) 1916

Before Disaster (po Winters) 1934

Before March (po MacLeish) 1932

Before Midnight (f Stout) 1955

Before the Brave (po Patchen) 1936

Before the Curfew and Other Poems, Chiefly Occasional (po Holmes) 1888

Before the Flowers of Friendship Faded Friendship Faded (po Stein) 1931

Before the Gringo Came (f Atherton) 1894

Before Your Very Eyes! (po Olson) 1967

Beggar on Horseback (pl Connelly; Kaufman) 1925

Beginners of a Nation (o Eggleston) 1896

Beginning Again, Being a Continuation of "Work" (f Alcott) 1875

Beginning and the End (o Asimov) 1977

Beginning and the End and Other Poems (po Jeffers) 1963

Beginning of National Movement (o Baraka) 1972

Beginning of Wisdom (f S. Benét) 1921

Beginning on the Short Story (o W. Williams) 1974

Behind a Mask: The Unknown Thrillers (f Alcott) 1975

Behind Prison Walls (tv Capote) 1972

Behind the Mountains (o La Farge) 1956

Behind the Scenes (pl Harrigan) 1875

Behold My Wife (scr La Farge) 1934

Behold the Bridegroom (pl Kelly) 1928

Behold, We Live (pl Van Druten) 1932

Being a Boy (o Warner) 1878

Being and Race: Black Writing Since 1970 (o C. Johnson) 1988

Being Busted (o Fiedler) 1970

Being Geniuses Together 1920-1930 (o Boyle) 1968

Being Here: Poetry 1977-1980 (po R. Warren) 1980

Being There (f Kosinski) 1971

Being There (pl Kosinski) 1973

Being There (scr Kosinski) 1980

Bel Demonio (pl Brougham) 1870

Belfry of Bruges and Other Poems (po Longfellow) 1845

Belgrade, November 19, 1963 (po F. O'Hara) 1973

Bell, Book, and Candle (pl Van Druten) 1951

Bell in the Fog and Other Stories (f Atherton) 1905

Bell Jar (f Plath) 1963

Bell Martin (f Arthur) 1843

Bellamy Speaks Again! Articles, Public Addresses, Letters (o Bellamy) 1937

Bellarosa Connection (f Bellow) 1989

Bellefleur (f Oates) 1980

Belle's Stratagem (pl Daly) 1893

Bell-Ringer of Angel's and Other Stories (f Harte) 1894

Belly Song and Other Poems (po Knight) 1973

Beloved (f Morrison) 1987

Beloved (f Updike) 1982

Below Grass Roots (f Waters) 1937

Ben Barclay's Courage (f Alger) 1904

Ben Bruce: Scenes in the Life of a Bowery Newsboy (f Alger) 1901

Ben Logan's Triumph (f Alger) 1908

Ben, The Luggage Boy (f Alger) 1870

Benchley at the Theatre (o Benchley) 1985

Benchley Beside Himself (o Benchley) 1943

Benchley Lost and Found: 39 Prodigal Pieces (o Benchley) 1970

Benchley—or Else! (o Benchley) 1947

Benchley Roundup (o Benchley) 1954

Bend Sinister (f Nabokov) 1947

Bendigo Shafter (f L'Amour) 1979

Bending the Bow (po Duncan) 1968

Benefactor (f Sontag) 1963

Ben-Hur: A Tale of the Christ (f L. Wallace) 1880

Benigna Machiavelli (f Gilman) 1994

Ben's Nugget (f Alger) 1882

Benton's Row (f Yerby) 1954

Berg Goodman Mezey (po Goodman) 1957

Berhama Account (f J. Williams) 1985

Berkeley (f Ingraham) 1846

Berlin of Sally Bowles (f Isherwood) 1975

Berlin Stories (f Isherwood) 1946

Bernard Brook's Adventures: The Story of a Brave Boy's Trials (f Alger) 1903

Bernard Clare (f Farrell) 1946

Bernice (pl Glaspell) 1919

Bernice, and The Wreck of the 5:25 (pl Wilder) 1957

Bernice Bobs Her Hair and Other Stories (f Fitzgerald) 1996

Berryman's Sonnets (po Berryman) 1967

Bertha in Blue (pl Vogel) 1981

Bertha's Christmas Vision: An Autumn Sheaf (f Alger) 1856

Bertram Cope's Year (f Fuller) 1919

Bertrand (f Ingraham) 1845

Bertrand & the Mehkgoverse: A Xicano Filmic Nuance (o Sánchez) 1989

Best Dr. Poggioli Detective Stories (f Stribling) 1975

Best Hour of the Night (po Simpson) 1983

Best Letters (o Jefferson) 1926

Best Man (scr Vidal) 1964

Best Man: A Play of Politics (pl Vidal) 1960

Best Mysteries of Isaac Asimov (f Asimov) 1986

Best New Thing (f Asimov) 1971

Best of Bradbury (f Bradbury) 1976

Best of Isaac Asimov (f Asimov) 1973

Best of O. Henry (f Henry) 1929

Best of Perelman (o S. Perelman) 1947

Best of Queen: Four Decades of Stories from the Mystery Masters (f Queen) 1985

Best of Runyon (f Runyon) 1938

Best of Simple (f Hughes) 1961

Best of Thoreau's Journals (o Thoreau) 1971

Best of Times: An Account of Europe Revisited (o Bemelmans) 1948

Best of Tish (f Rinehart) 1955

Best Ornaments of Youth (o Mather) 1707

Best Science Fiction of Isaac Asimov (f Asimov) 1986

Best Short Stories of O. Henry (f Henry) 1945

Best Stories (f Freeman) 1927

Best Stories (f Steele) 1945

Best Supernatural Stories of Lovecraft (f Lovecraft) 1945

Best Things in Life Are Free (scr J. O'Hara) 1956

Best Times: An Informal Memoir (o Dos Passos) 1966

Best Years of Our Lives (scr Sherwood) 1946

Bestiary for My Daughters Mary and Katharine (po Rexroth) 1955

Bethel Merriday (f Lewis) 1940

Betrothal (pl Boker) 1850

Betry Putnam (pl W. Williams) 1910

Betry's Bright Idea (o Stowe) 1876

Betsey Brown (f Shange) 1985

Betsey Brown: A Rhythm and Blues Musical (pl Shange) 1989

Better Sort (f H. James) 1903

Betting on the Dust Commander (pl Parks) 1987

Betty Leicester: A Story for Girls (o Jewett) 1890

Betty Leicester's Christmas (o Jewett) 1899

Betty Leicester's English Xmas (o Jewett) 1894

Betty Zane (f Grey) 1903

Betty's Finish (pl Fitch) 1890

Between Dawn and Sunrise: Selections (o Cabell) 1930

Between East and West (pl Nelson) 1986

Between Friends: Letters of Cabell and Others (o Cabell) 1962

Between Friends: The Correspondence of Hannah Arendt and Mary McCarthy, 1949-1975 (o McCarthy) 1995

Between History and Poetry: The Letters of H.D. and Norman Holmes Pearson (o Doolittle) 1997

Between Our Selves (po Lorde) 1976

Between Planets (f Heinlein) 1951

Between the Dark and the Daylight: Romances (f Howells) 1907

Between the two of them: a painted poem (po Shange) 1983

Between Time and Timbuktu (pl Vonnegut) 1972

Between Time and Timbuktu (tv Vonnegut) 1972

Between Two Wars: Selected Poems Written Prior to the Second World War (po Rexroth) 1982

Between Two Worlds (pl Rice) 1934

Between Two Worlds (f Sinclair) 1941

Between Whiles (o H. Jackson) 1887

Beware of Parents: A Bachelor's Book for Children (o Nathan) 1943

Beware the Curves (f E. Gardner) 1956

Bewitched (pl S. Howard; Sheldon) 1924

Beyond Criticism (o Shapiro) 1953

Beyond Culture: Essays on Literature and Learning (o Trilling) 1965

Beyond Defeat: An Epilogue to an Era (f Glasgow) 1966

Beyond Desire (f S. Anderson) 1932

Beyond Life (f Cabell) 1919

Beyond the Bayou (f Chopin) 1996

Beyond the Farthest Star (f E. Burroughs) 1964

Beyond the Horizon (pl O'Neill) 1920

Beyond the Law (scr Mailer) 1968

Beyond the Mountains (pl Rexroth) 1951

Beyond the Wall of Sleep (o Lovecraft) 1943

Beyond Thirty (f E. Burroughs) 1955
Beyond This Horizon (f Heinlein) 1948
Bianca Visconti (pl Willis) 1839
Bib Ballads (po Lardner) 1915
Bible and Sword (o Tuchman) 1956
Bible Heroines (o Stowe) 1878
Bibliography of Modern Prosody (o Shapiro) 1948
Bibliography of the King's Book or, Eikon Basilike (po S. Howe) 1989
Bibliography on America for Ed Dorn (o Olson) 1964
Bicentennial Man and Other Stories (f Asimov) 1976
Bid Me to Live: A Madrigal (f Doolittle) 1960
Big and Little of It (pl Harrigan) 1871
Big As Life (f Doctorow) 1966
Big Ballad Jamboree: A Novel (f Davidson) 1996
Big Blonde and Other Stories (f Parker) 1995
Big Bonanza (pl Daly) 1884
Big Bounce (f Leonard) 1969
Big Box (o Morrison) 1999
Big Broadcast of 1936 (scr Parker) 1935
Big Clock (f Fearing) 1946
Big Deal (tv Chayefsky) 1953
Big Gold Dream (f Himes) 1960
Big Knife (pl Odets) 1949
Big Knockover (f Hammett) 1948
Big Land (f Grey) 1976
Big Laugh (f J. O'Hara) 1962
Big Money (f Dos Passos) 1936
Big Noise (scr Hecht) 1928
Big Rock Candy Mountain (f Stegner) 1943
Big Sea (tv Hughes) 1965
Big Sea: An Autobiography (o Hughes) 1940
Big Sleep (f Chandler) 1939
Big Sleep (scr Faulkner) 1946
Big Sleep (pl Faulkner) 1971
Big Sur (f Kerouac) 1962
Big Town (f Lardner) 1921
Big Wave (scr Buck) 1962
Big Woods (f Faulkner) 1955
Bigger They Come (f E. Gardner) 1939
Biglow Papers (po J. Lowell) 1848
Biglow Papers. Second Series (po J. Lowell) 1862
Bilingualism: Promise for Tomorrow (scr Anaya) 1976
Bill and Tony (scr W. Burroughs) 1966
Bill of Rites, A Bill of Wrongs, A Bill of Goods (o Morris) 1968
Bill Porter (pl Sinclair) 1924
Bill Sturdy (f Alger) 1887
Billy Bathgate (f Doctorow) 1989
Billy Budd and Other Prose Pieces (f Melville) 1924
Billy the Kid (scr MacArthur) 1930
Billy Woodhull (f Ingraham) 1844
Biloxi Blues (pl Simon) 1984
Biloxi Blues (scr Simon) 1988
Bimbo, The Pirate (pl Tarkington) 1926
Bingo (f R Brown) 1988
Bingo Palace (f Erdrich) 1994
Biochemistry and Human Metabolism (o Asimov) 1952
Biographical Sketch of the Character of Governor Trumbull (o Trumbull) 1809
Biographical Stories for Children (o Hawthorne) 1842
Biographies of Lady Russell, and Madame Guyon (o Child) 1832

Biographies of Madame de Stael, and Madame Roland (o Child) 1832
Biography (pl Behrman) 1933
Biography and a Lament: Poems 1961-1967 (po Simic) 1976
Birchbark House (o Erdrich) 1999
Bird Cage (pl Laurents) 1950
Bird Center: Cap Fry's Birthday Party (pl Ade) 1904
Bird in the Cage (pl Fitch) 1903
Bird's Nest (f S. Jackson) 1954
Birds of America (f McCarthy) 1971
Birds of Pompeii (po Ciardi) 1985
Birdy (pl N. Wallace) 1997
Birth (f Gale) 1918
Birth of a Grandfather (f Sarton) 1957
Birth of Galahad (pl Hovey) 1898
Birth of Reason and Other Essays (o Santayana) 1968
Birth of the United States, 1763-1816 (o Asimov) 1974
Birthday Cake for David (po Merrill) 1955
Birth-Day Song of Liberty: A Paean of Glory for the Heroes of Freedom (po Chivers) 1856
Birth-mark: Unsettling the Wilderness in American Literary History (o S. Howe) 1993
Birthright (f Stribling) 1922
Bishop's Wife (scr Sherwood) 1947
Bit between My Teeth: A Literary Chronicle of 1950-1965 (o E. Wilson) 1965
Bite on the Bullet (o S. Perelman) 1957
Bits of Gossip (o Rebecca Davis) 1904
Bits of Paradise: 21 Uncollected Stories (f Fitzgerald) 1973
Bits of Talk about Home Matters (o H. Jackson) 1873
Bits of Talk, in Verse and Prose, for Young Folks (o H. Jackson) 1876
Bits of Travel (o H. Jackson) 1872
Bits of Travel at Home (o H. Jackson) 1878
Bitter Cane (pl Lim) 1989
Bitter Creek (f Boyd) 1939
Bitter Lotus (f Bromfield) 1944
Bitter Medicine (f Paretsky) 1987
Bitterns: A Book of Twelve Poems (po Wescott) 1920
Bixby Canyon Ocean Path Word Breeze (po Ginsberg) 1972
Blabberhead, Bobbie-Bud & Spade (po Ciardi) 1988
Black Armour (po Wylie) 1923
Black Art (po Baraka) 1966
Black Bart and the Sacred Hills (pl A. Wilson) 1981
Black Beetles in Amber (po Bierce) 1892
Black Boy: A Record of Childhood and Youth (o R. Wright) 1945
Black Cargo (f Marquand) 1925
Black Cargoes: A History of the Atlantic Slave Trade, 1518-1865 (o Cowley) 1962
Black Christ and Other Poems (po Cullen) 1929
Black Dada Nihilismus (pl Baraka) 1971
Black Diplomat in Haiti: The Diplomatic Correspondence of U.S. Minister Douglass from Haiti 1889-1891 (o Douglass) 1977
Black Feeling, Black Talk (po Giovanni) 1968
Black Feeling, Black Talk and Black Judgement (po Giovanni) 1970
Black Ferris (tv Bradbury) 1990
Black Flame (f Du Bois) 1957
Black Folk Then and Now: An Essay in the History and Sociology of the Negro Race (o Du Bois) 1939
Black Hair (po Soto) 1985
Black House (f Theroux) 1974

Black Humor (o C. Johnson) 1970
Black Ice (f Tourgée) 1888
Black Is My Truelove's Hair (f Roberts) 1938
Black Judgement (po Giovanni) 1968
Black Light (f Kinnell) 1966
Black Love (po Brooks) 1982
Black Magic (o Roberts) 1924
Black Magic: A Pictorial History of the Negro in American Entertainment (o Hughes) 1967
Black Magic and Music: A Novelists Perspective of Bangor (o King) 1983
Black Magic: Poetry 1961-1967 (po Baraka) 1969
Black Man: His Antecedents, His Genius, and His Achievements (o W. Brown) 1863
Black Manhattan (o J. Johnson) 1930
Black Mass (pl Baraka) 1966
Black Men: Obsolete, Single, Dangerous? (o Madhubuti) 1990
Black Mesa (f Grey) 1955
Black Misery (o Hughes) 1969
Black Money (f Macdonald) 1966
Black Mountain (f Stout) 1954
Black Mountain Breakdown (f L. Smith) 1980
Black Music (o Baraka) 1968
Black Nativity (pl Hughes) 1961
Black North in 1901: A Social Study (o Du Bois) 1969
Black Orchids (f Stout) 1942
Black Oxen (f Atherton) 1923
Black People and the Coming Depression (o Madhubuti) 1975
Black Power: A Record of Reactions in a Land of Pathos (o R. Wright) 1954
Black Pride (po Madhubuti) 1968
Black Ralph (f Ingraham) 1844
Black Reconstruction in America: An Essay (o Du Bois) 1935
Black Riders and Other Lines (po S. Crane) 1895
Black Rock (po Fletcher) 1928
Black Sea Fighters (scr Odets) 1943
Black Sheep (pl Rice) 1932
Black Spring (scr Baraka) 1968
Black Spring (f H. Miller) 1936
Black Swan (scr Hecht) 1942
Black Swan and Other Poems (po Merrill) 1946
Black Tickets (f J. Phillips) 1979
Black Unicorn (po Lorde) 1978
Black Value System (o Baraka) 1970
Black Vote of Philadelphia (o Du Bois) 1905
Black Water (f Oates) 1992
Blackbeard (pl Green) 1922
Black-Belt Diamonds: Gems from the Speeches, Addresses, and Talks to Students (o Washington) 1898
Blackberry Winter (f R. Warren) 1946
Blackguard (f Bodenheim) 1923
Blacklight (pl Portillo Trambley) 1975
Blackmail (pl Richard Davis) 1913
Blacks (po Brooks) 1991
Blacks, Blues, Black (tv Angelou) 1968
Blade Runner: A Movie (f W. Burroughs) 1979
Blake; or the Huts of America (f M. Delany) 1859-62
Blake's Apocalypse (o Bloom) 1963
Blanche Talbot; or The Maiden's Hand: A Romance of the War of 1812 (f Ingraham) 1847
Bless Me, Ultima (f Anaya) 1972

Blessed Edmund Campion (o Guiney) 1908
Blessed Unions (o Mather) 1692
Blessing (f Oates) 1976
Blessing of Business (o E. Howe) 1918
Blessing Way (f Hillerman) 1970
Blessings (o Dubus) 1987
Bleter fun Mein Leben (o Cahan) 1926-31
Blind Alleys (tv Hwang) 1985
Blind Bow-Boy (f Van Vechten) 1923
Blind Boy (pl Dunlap) 1803
Blind Date (f Kosinski) 1977
Blind Lion (po P. Allen) 1974
Blind Man with a Pistol (f Himes) 1969
Blindman's World and Other Stories (f Bellamy) 1898
Blithedale Romance (f Hawthorne) 1852
Blix (f Norris) 1899
Blizzard of One: Poems (po Strand) 1998
Bloch and Bradbury (f Bradbury) 1969
Block (po Hughes) 1995
Blockade (scr Lawson) 1938
Blood and Grits (o Crews) 1979
Blood, Bread, and Poetry: Selected Prose, 1979-1986 (o Rich) 1986
Blood for a Stranger (po Jarrell) 1942
Blood Money (f Hammett) 1943
Blood of the Martyr (pl S. Crane) 1940
Blood of the Prophets (po Masters) 1905
Blood on the Dining Room Floor (f Stein) 1948
Blood Oranges (f Hawkes) 1971
Blood Pressure: Poems (o Gilbert and Gubar) 1988
Blood Seedling and Other Tales: The Uncollected Fiction of Hay (f Hay) 1972
Blood Shot (f Paretsky) 1988
Blood Wedding (pl Fornés) 1980
Bloodcurdling Tales of Horror and the Macabre: The Best of Lovecraft (f Lovecraft) 1982
Bloodline (f Gaines) 1968
Bloodrites (pl Baraka) 1970
Bloodroot (po Villanueva) 1977
Bloodshed and Three Novellas (f Ozick) 1976
Bloodsmoor Romance (f Oates) 1982
Bloodstream: River of Life (o Asimov) 1961
Bloody Chasm (f De Forest) 1881
Blue and the Gray (pl Harrigan) 1875
Blue and the Gray (pl Morley) 1930
Blue Beard: A Dramatic Romance (pl Dunlap) 1803
Blue Bitch (tv Shepard) 1972
Blue Bitch (pl Shepard) 1972
Blue City (f Macdonald) 1947
Blue Dahlia (scr Chandler) 1946
Blue Dahlia (pl Chandler) 1976
Blue Danube (f Bemelmans) 1945
Blue Estuaries: Poems 1923-1968 (po Bogan) 1968
Blue Grass (pl Daly) 1877
Blue Hammer (f Macdonald) 1976
Blue Hotel (pl Agee) 1960
Blue Jay's Dance: A Birth Year (f Erdrich) 1995
Blue Juniata (po Cowley) 1929
Blue Juniata: A Life: Collected and New Poems (po Cowley) 1985
Blue Mouse (pl Fitch) 1908
Blue Plate Special (f Runyon) 1934
Blue Ribbon (pl Harrigan) 1894

Blue Sky (po Snyder) 1969

Blue Swallows (po Nemerov) 1967

Blue Thunder (pl Green) 1928

Blue Voyage (f Aiken) 1927

Blue Wing Tilts at the Edge of the Sea: Selected Poems 1964-1974 (po Hall) 1975

Bluebeard (f Vonnegut) 1987

Blue-Eyed Buddhist and Other Stories (f Gilchrist) 1990

Blue-Grass Region of Kentucky and Other Kentucky Articles (o J. Allen) 1892

Blues: For All the Changes (po Giovanni) 1999

Blues for Mister Charlie (pl James Baldwin) 1964

Blues People: Negro Music in White America (o Baraka) 1963

Bluesman (o Dubus) 1993

Bluest Eye (f Morrison) 1969

Boanerges: A Short Essay to Preserve and Strengthen the Good Impressions Produced by Earthquakes (o Mather) 1727

Boarding House Blues (f Farrell) 1961

Boarding School (f H. Foster) 1798

Boat of Longing (f Rølvaag) 1933

Boat of Quiet Hours (po Kenyon) 1986

Bob Burton (f Alger) 1888

Bob: The Story of Our Mocking-Bird (o Lanier) 1899

Bobby Gould in Hell (pl Mamet) 1989

Bobby-Soxer (f Calisher) 1986

Bodacious Flapdoodle (pl Wellman) 1984

Bodies and Souls (f Rechy) 1983

Body (f Crews) 1990

Body of This Death (po Bogan) 1923

Body of Waking (po Rukeyser) 1958

Body Rags (po Kinnell) 1967

Bohemia (pl Fitch) 1896

Bold Hibernian Boys (pl Harrigan) 1876

Bolts of Melody: New Poems (po Dickinson) 1945

Bombing of Osage (scr Bambara) 1986

Bombs Away: The Story of a Bomber Team (o Steinbeck) 1942

Bon Voyage (po Nash) 1936

Bonaparte in England (pl Dunlap) 1803

Bonaventure: A Prose Pastoral of Acadian Louisiana (f Cable) 1888

Bondage (pl Hwang) 1992

Bondmaid (f Buck) 1949

Bone Key and Other Poems (po Wilbur) 1998

Bone Ring (pl Hall) 1987

Bonfield (f Ingraham) 1846

Bonfire of the Vanities (f Tom Wolfe) 1987

Bonifacius: An Essay upon the Good (o Mather) 1710

Bonjour Tristesse (scr Laurents) 1958

Bonney Family (f Suckow) 1928

Bonnybel Vane (f J. Cooke) 1883

Boob (po Duncan) 1966

Booby Trap (f Stout) 1944

Book (f Barnes) 1923

Book Class (f Auchincloss) 1984

Book Concluding with As a Wife Has a Cow: A Love Story (f Stein) 1926

Book of Americans (po S. Benét) 1933

Book of Burlesques (o Mencken) 1916

Book of Calumny (o Mencken) 1918

Book of Christmas (f Buck) 1974

Book of Common Prayer (f Didion) 1977

Book of Daniel (f Doctorow) 1971

Book of Dreams (f Kerouac) 1960

Book of During (po Coolidge) 1991

Book of Folly (po Sexton) 1972

Book of Gods and Devils (po Simic) 1990

Book of Joyous Children (po Riley) 1902

Book of Life (po Madhubuti) 1973

Book of Miracles (f Hecht) 1939

Book of Moments: Poems 1915-1954 (po Burke) 1955

Book of My Lady: A Melange (f Simms) 1833

Book of Nature 1910-1912 (po Fletcher) 1913

Book of Nightmares (po Kinnell) 1971

Book of Prefaces (o Mencken) 1917

Book of Queer Stories, and Stories Told on a Cellar Door (f Eggleston) 1871

Book of Repulsive Women: Eight Rhythms and Five Drawings (po Barnes) 1915

Book of Resemblances: Poems 1950-1953 (po Duncan) 1966

Book of Romances, Lyrics, and Songs (po B. Taylor) 1851

Book of Roses (o Parkman) 1866

Book of Saint Nicholas (f Paulding) 1836

Book of Stirs (po Coolidge) 1998

Book of Stories (f Cheever; J. Stafford) 1957

Book of the Dead: Poems (po Boker) 1882

Book of the Hamburgs: A Brief Treatise upon the Mating, Rearing, and Management of the Different Varieties of Hamburgs (o Baum) 1886

Book of the Homeless: Original Articles in Verse and Prose (o Wharton) 1916

Book of the Hopi (o Waters) 1963

Book of Vagaries (f Paulding) 1868

Book of Verses (po Masters) 1898

Book without a Title (o Nathan) 1918

Booker (tv C. Johnson) 1984

Booker T. Washington at Atlanta (radio Hughes) 1945

Books and Libraries and Other Papers (o J. Lowell) 1889

Boom (scr T. Williams) 1968

Boon Island (f Roberts) 1956

Borden Chantry (f L'Amour) 1978

Border Beagles: A Tale of Mississippi (f Simms) 1840

Border Comedy (po Hejinian) 1999

Border Legion (f Grey) 1916

Border States (o Kennedy) 1860

Borderers: A Tale (f Cooper) 1829

Borderlands—La Frontera: The New Mestiza (po Anzaldúa) 1987

Borderline (o Doolittle) 1930

Borgia (f Gale) 1929

Born of a Woman: New and Selected Poems (po Knight) 1980

Born to Be Wild (scr N. West) 1938

Bosoms and Neglect (pl Guare) 1979

Boss (pl Sheldon) 1911

Boston (f Sinclair) 1928

Boston Adventure (f J. Stafford) 1944

Boston Ephemeris: An Almanack (o Mather) 1683

Bostonian Ebenezer: Some Historical Remarks on the State of Boston (o Mather) 1698

Bostonians (f H. James) 1886

Boswell: A Modern Comedy (f Elkin) 1964

Both Your Houses (pl M. Anderson) 1933

Bottom Dogs (f Dahlberg) 1929

Bottom Dogs, From Flushing to Calvary, Those Who Perish, and Hitherto Unpublished and Uncollected Works (f Dahlberg) 1976

Bottom's Dream (o Updike) 1969

Bottoms Up: An Application of the Slapstick to Satire (o Nathan) 1917

Boulder Dam (f Grey) 1963

Bound East for Cardiff (pl O'Neill) 1916

Bound to Rise (f Alger) 1873

Bound Together: A Sheaf of Papers (o D. Mitchell) 1884

Bounty Hunters (f Leonard) 1953

Bourgeois Poet (po Shapiro) 1964

Bowdrie (f L'Amour) 1983

Bowdrie's Law (f L'Amour) 1984

Bowl, Cat, and Broomstick (pl Stevens) 1969

Box (pl Albee) 1968

Boy (po Creeley) 1968

Boy, Abe (pl B. Smith) 1944

Boy and Tarzan Appear in a Clearing (pl Baraka) 1981

Boy Fortune Hunters in Alaska (f Baum) 1908

Boy Fortune Hunters in Panama (f Baum) 1908

Boy Fortune Hunters in Egypt [China, Yucatan, the South Seas] (f Baum) 1908-11

Boy Made of Meat (po Snodgrass) 1983

Boy on Mount Rhigi (f Sedgwick) 1848

Boy Scout (f Richard Davis) 1914

Boy Trouble (scr S. Perelman) 1939

Boy Who Made Dragonfly: A Zuni Myth (f Hillerman) 1972

Boyhood in Norway: Stories of Boy-Life in the Land of the Midnight Sun (o Boyesen) 1892

Boyhood of Christ (f L. Wallace) 1888

Boyhood Poems (po Longfellow) 1925

Boys and Girls Together (f Saroyan) 1963

Boy's Adventure (f Twain) 1928

Boy's Fortune (f Alger) 1898

Boys in the Back Room: Notes on California Novelists (o E. Wilson) 1941

Boys of Other Countries: Stories for American Boys (o B. Taylor) 1876

Boys of the Old Glee Club (po Riley) 1907

Boys! Raise Giant Mushrooms in Your Cellar! (tv Bradbury) 1989

Boy's Will (po Frost) 1913

Bracebridge Hall (f W. Irving) 1822

Bradbury on Stage (pl Bradbury) 1991

Bradys (pl Harrigan) 1876

Braided Apart (po W. Stafford) 1976

Braille (po B. Perelman) 1975

Branch of Abingden (o Cabell) 1911

Branch Will Not Break (po J. Wright) 1963

Branches of Adam (po Fletcher) 1926

Branchiana (o Cabell) 1907

Brand New Life (f Farrell) 1968

Brant and Red Jacket (o Eggleston) 1879

Brass Monkey (pl Hoyt) 1888

Brat (scr Behrman) 1931

Brave and Bold (f Alger) 1874

Brave and Startling Truth (o Angelou) 1995

Brave Are My People: Indian Heroes Not Forgotten (o Waters) 1993

Bravery of Earth (po Eberhart) 1930

Braving the Elements (po Merrill) 1972

Bravo: A Venetian Story (f Cooper) 1831

Bravo! (pl Ferber; Kaufman) 1948

Brazil (f Updike) 1994

Brazil on the Move (o Dos Passos) 1963

Bread and Butter Come to Supper (pl Green) 1928

Bread and Roses (pl Hall) 1975

Bread Givers (f Yezierska) 1925

Bread of Idleness (pl Masters) 1911

Bread without Sugar (po Stern) 1992

Bread-Winners: A Social Study (f Hay) 1884

Breakdown (o Hammett) 1968

Breakers and Granite (po Fletcher) 1921

Breakfast at Tiffany's (pl Albee) 1966

Breakfast at Tiffany's: A Short Novel and Three Stories (f Capote) 1958

Breakfast of Champions (f Vonnegut) 1973

Breaking into Society (f Ade) 1904

Breaking of the Vessels (o Bloom) 1982

Breaking Open (po Rukeyser) 1973

Breaking Point (f Rinehart) 1922

Breaking Point (pl Rinehart) 1923

Breaking the Silence: Why a Mother Tells Her Son about the Nazi Era (o Boyle) 1962

Break-Up of Our Camp and Other Stories (f Goodman) 1949

Breast (f P. Roth) 1972

Breasts of Tiresias (pl Simpson) 1964

Breathing Lessons (f A. Tyler) 1988

Breathing the Water (po Levertov) 1987

Bred in the Bone (f Page) 1904

Brewsie and Willie (f Stein) 1946

Briar Rose (f Coover) 1997

Briary-Bush (f Dell) 1921

Brick People (f Morales) 1988

Brick Road (po Ammons) 1996

Bricks Without Straw (f Tourgée) 1880

Bridal Pond (f Gale) 1930

Bride Comes to Yellow Sky (pl Agee) 1960

Bride from Mantua (pl Eberhart) 1964

Bride of Innisfallen and Other Stories (f Welty) 1955

Bride of Liberty (f Yerby) 1954

Bride of the Mistletoe (f J. Allen) 1909

Bride Roses (pl Howells) 1900

Bridegroom Cometh (f Frank) 1938

Brides of the South Wind: Poems 1917-1922 (po Jeffers) 1974

Bridge (po H. Crane) 1930

Bridge Hand (pl Coover) 1981

Bridge in the Jungle (f Traven) 1938

Bridge of Lost Desire (f S. Delany) 1987

Bridge of San Luis Rey (f Wilder) 1927

Bridge of Years (f Sarton) 1946

Bridges of Binding (o Benchley) 1928

Brief History of Two Families: The Mitchells of Ayrshire and the Symons of Cornwall (o S. Mitchell) 1912

Brief Lives (po Hall) 1983

Brief Moment (pl Behrman) 1931

Brief Moment (scr Behrman) 1933

Briefings: Poems Small and Easy (po Ammons) 1971

Brigadier and the Golf Widow (f Cheever) 1964

Brigantine (f Ingraham) 1847

Brigham Young—Frontiersman (scr Bromfield) 1940

Bright Angel (scr Ford) 1991

Bright Metal (f Stribling) 1928

Bright Procession (f Buck) 1952

Bright Room Called Day (pl Kushner) 1991

Bright Shawl (f Hergesheimer) 1922
Bright Star (pl Barry) 1935
Brighton Beach Memoirs (pl Simon) 1982
Brighton Beach Memoirs (scr Simon) 1987
Bring! Bring! and Other Stories (f Aiken) 1925
Bring It Up from the Dark (po Duncan) 1970
Bring on the Girls (pl Kaufman) 1934
Bringing Jazz! (po Bodenheim) 1930
Brink of Darkness (f Winters) 1947
Brionne (f L'Amour) 1968
British Prison-Ship (po Freneau) 1781
Broadway Bound (pl Simon) 1986
Broadway Jones (pl Cohan) 1923
Broadway Melody of 1936 (scr Hart) 1935
Broke Heart Blues (f Oates) 1999
Broken Battalions (po Hayne) 1885
Broken Cord: A Family's Ongoing Struggle with Fetal Alcohol
    Syndrome (o Dorris) 1989
Broken Glass (pl A. Miller) 1994
Broken Gun (f L'Amour) 1966
Broken Necks and Other Stories (f Hecht) 1924
Broken Necks, Containing More 1001 Afternoons (f Hecht) 1926
Broken Promises: Four Plays (pl Hwang) 1983
Broken Span (po W. Williams) 1941
Broken Vase (f Stout) 1941
Broken Vessels (o Dubus) 1991
Broker of Bogota (pl Bird) 1834
Brontologia Sacra (o Mather) 1695
Bronwen, the Traw, and the Shape-Shifter (po Dickey) 1986
Bronze (po Merrill) 1984
Bronzeville Boys and Girls (po Brooks) 1956
Brook Evans (f Glaspell) 1928
Brooklyn Branding Parlors (po Purdy) 1986
Brooms: Selected Poetry (po Simic) 1978
Brother Carl (scr Sontag) 1971
Brother Grasshopper (f Updike) 1990
Brother Jonathan; or The New Englanders (f Neal) 1825
Brother My Brother (f Santos) 1960
Brother to Dragons: A Tale in Verse and Voices (po R. Warren)
    1953
Brother Wind (po W. Stafford) 1986
Brotherhood of Man (pl Roberts) 1934
Brotherhood of Men (po Eberhart) 1949
Brothers (radio Hughes) 1942
Brothers and Keepers (o Wideman) 1984
Brothers of No Kin and Other Stories (f Richter) 1924
Brown Bear Honey Madness: Alaskan Cruising Poems (po
    Sánchez) 1981
Brown Girl, Brownstones (f Marshall) 1959
Brownies and Bogles (o Guiney) 1888
Brownstone Eclogues and Other Poems (po Aiken) 1942
Browser's Dictionary and Native's Guide to the Unknown Ameri-
    can Language (o Ciardi) 1980
Brutus (pl Payne) 1818
Bryan Campaign for the American People's Money (o Donnelly)
    1896
Bubbles (o Rukeyser) 1967
Buccaneer (pl M. Anderson) 1925
Buccaneers (f Wharton) 1938
Buchanan Dying (pl Updike) 1974
Buck Fever Papers (o S. Anderson) 1971

Buck in the Snow and Other Poems (po Millay) 1928
Buckdancer's Choice (po Dickey) 1965
Buckskin Run (f L'Amour) 1981
Bucktails (pl Paulding) 1847
Buddha Bandits Down Highway 99 (po Hongo) 1978
Buddhist Writings (o Hearn) 1977
Buffalo Girls (f McMurtry) 1990
Buffalo Hunter (f Grey) 1977
Bug's-Eye View of the War (o MacArthur) 1919
Builder Kachina: A Home-Going Cycle (po Rose) 1979
Builders (f Glasgow) 1919
Building of the City Beautiful (o J. Miller) 1893
Build-Up (f W. Williams) 1952
Bulldog Drummond (scr S. Howard) 1929
Bullet Park (f Cheever) 1969
Bullfight (o Mailer) 1967
Bulwark (f Dreiser) 1946
Bunch of Keys (pl Hoyt) 1882
Bundle of Letters (f H. James) 1880
Bundle of Lies (pl Daly) 1895
Burglar of the Zodiac and Other Poems (po W. Benét) 1918
Burial of John Brown (po Channing) 1878
Burial of the Guns (f Page) 1894
Buried Child (pl Shepard) 1978
Buried Onions (po Soto) 1998
Buried Treasure (f Roberts) 1931
Burn Marks (f Paretsky) 1990
Burning (radio Portillo Trambley) 1983
Burning Bright (pl Steinbeck) 1951
Burning Bright: A Play in Story Form (f Steinbeck) 1950
Burning City (po S. Benét) 1936
Burning Daylight (f London) 1910
Burning Hills (f L'Amour) 1956
Burning House (f Beattie) 1982
Burning Mountain (po Fletcher) 1946
Burning-Glass (f Behrman) 1968
Burr (f Vidal) 1973
Burr Oaks (po Eberhart) 1947
Burst of Light: Essays (o Lorde) 1988
Burt-Markham Primer: The Nature Method (o Markham) 1907
Burton (f Ingraham) 1838
Bus Riley's Back in Town (scr Inge) 1965
Bus Stop (pl Inge) 1955
Bushwhackers and Other Stories (f Murfree) 1899
Business Is Business (pl Kaufman; Parker) 1925
Busy Man's Bible (o Cable) 1891
But Even So (po Patchen) 1968
But for Whom Charlie (pl Behrman) 1964
But Time and Chance: The Story of Padre Martínez of Taos, 1793-
    1867 (o Chávez) 1981
Butter and Egg Man (pl Kaufman) 1926
Buttered Side Down (f Ferber) 1912
Butterfield 8 (f J. O'Hara) 1935
Butterfly (f Cain) 1947
Butterfly House (f Freeman) 1912
Button's Inn (f Tourgée) 1887
Buy Jupiter and Other Stories (f Asimov) 1975
Buying Christmas Toys and Other Essays (o Hearn) 1939
By Al Lebowitz's Pool (po Nemerov) 1979
By Avon River (po Doolittle) 1949
By Liberal Things (o Frye) 1959

By Love Possessed (f Cozzens) 1957
By Shore and Sedge (f Harte) 1885
By the Candelabra's Glare (po Baum) 1898
By the Light of the Soul (f Freeman) 1907
By the Light of My Father's Smile: A Story of Requited Love, Crossing Over, and the Sexual Healing of the Soul (f A. Walker) 1998
By the North Gate (f Oates) 1963
By-Line: Hemingway. Selected Articles and Dispatches of Four Decades (o Hemingway) 1967
Bylow Hill (f Cable) 1902
By-Ways of Europe (o B. Taylor) 1869

Cabala (f Wilder) 1926
Cabaret for Freedom (pl Angelou) 1960
Cabbage Gardens (po S. Howe) 1979
Cabbages and Kings (f Henry) 1904
Cabin in the Cotton (scr Green) 1932
Cables to Rage (po Lorde) 1970
Cabot Wright Begins (f Purdy) 1964
Cadillac Jack (f McMurtry) 1982
Caesar's Column: A Story of the Twentieth Century (f Donnelly) 1890
Caesar's Gate: Poems 1949-1950 with Collages by Jess Collins (po Duncan) 1955
Caesarian Operations (pl Inge) 1972
Cage Keeper and Other Stories (f Dubus) 1989
Cages (po J. Tate) 1966
Cairo, Shanghai, Bombay! (pl T. Williams) 1935
Cake Upon the Waters (pl Akins) 1913
Cakewalk (f L. Smith) 1980
Calamity Town (f Queen) 1942
Calamus (o Whitman) 1897
Calavar (f Bird) 1834
Calaynos (pl Boker) 1848
Calendar (po Creeley) 1983
Calendar of Crime (f Queen) 1952
Calendar of Saints for Unbelievers (o Wescott) 1932
Calendar: Twelve Poems (po Creeley) 1984
Calhoun (f Algren) 1980
Caliban, By the Yellow Sands (pl MacKaye) 1916
Calico Shoes and Other Stories (f Farrell) 1934
California: An Intimate History (o Atherton) 1914
California and Oregon Trail, Being Sketches of Prairie and Rocky Mountain Life (o Parkman) 1849
California Diary 1855-1857 (o J. Miller) 1936
California Stories (f Harte) 1884
California Suite (pl Simon) 1977
California Suite (scr Simon) 1978
California the Wonderful (o Markham) 1914
Californian 1934-1938 (o Lovecraft) 1977
Californians (f Atherton) 1898
Californians (po Jeffers) 1916
Californios (f L'Amour) 1974
Call It Sleep (f H. Roth) 1934
Call Me Ishmael: A Study of Melville (o Olson) 1947
Call of the Canyon (f Grey) 1924
Call of the Gospel (o Mather) 1686
Call of the Wild (tv Dickey) 1976
Call of the Wild (f London) 1903
Callaghen (f L'Amour) 1972

Callahan the Detective (pl Harrigan) 1877
Calms of Capricorn (pl O'Neill) 1982
Camden Conversations (o Whitman) 1973
Cameo Kirby (pl Tarkington) 1908
Camera Obscura (f Nabokov) 1936
Camille (scr Akins) 1936
Camino Real (pl T. Williams) 1953
Campbell Meeker (o Markham) 1925
Camping in the Valley (po J. Tate) 1968
Camping Out (pl B. Howard) 1886
Can All This Grandeur Perish? and Other Stories (f Farrell) 1937
Can Grande's Castle (po A. Lowell) 1918
Can Such Things Be? (f Bierce) 1893
Can There Be a Gothic Literature? (o McCarthy) 1975
Can These Bones Live (o Dahlberg) 1960
Can Women Be Gentlemen? (o Atherton) 1938
Can You Hear, Bird: Poems (po Ashbery) 1995
Canadian Notebook (o Thoreau) 1967
Canadian Scenery Illustrated (o Willis) 1842
Canary in a Cat House (f Vonnegut) 1961
Cancer Journals (o Lorde) 1980
Candide (pl Hellman; Parker; Wilbur) 1956
Candle in the Cabin: A Weaving Together of Script and Singing (po Lindsay) 1926
Candle in the Wind (pl M. Anderson) 1941
Candle-Lightin' Time (po Dunbar) 1901
Candles in Babylon (po Levertov) 1982
Candles of Your Eyes (f Purdy) 1985
Candles of Your Eyes and Thirteen Other Stories (f Purdy) 1987
Candles to the Sun (pl T. Williams) 1937
Cane (f Toomer) 1923
Cannery Row (f Steinbeck) 1945
Cannibal (f Hawkes) 1949
Cannibal Galaxy (f Ozick) 1983
Cannibals and Christians (o Mailer) 1966
Cannibals and Missionaries (f McCarthy) 1979
Cannon Between My Knees (po P. Allen) 1981
Canolles: The Fortunes of a Partisan of '81 (f J. Cooke) 1877
Canterbury Pilgrims (pl MacKaye) 1903
Canto CX (po Pound) 1965
Canto Familiar (po Soto) 1995
Canto for a Gypsy (f M. Smith) 1972
Cantos (po Pound) 1948
Cantos, 110-116 (po Pound) 1967
Cantos LII-LXXI (po Pound) 1940
Cantos No. 1-117, 120 (po Pound) 1970
Canzoni (po Pound) 1911
Cap-a-Pie (pl Fornés) 1975
Cape Cod (o Thoreau) 1865
Cape Cod Lighter (f J. O'Hara) 1962
Capitalism: An Unknown Ideal (o Rand) 1966
Capote: Conversations (o Capote) 1987
Capsule Course in Black Poetry Writing (o Brooks) 1975
Captain Archer's Daughter (f Deland) 1932
Captain Blackman (f J. Williams) 1972
Captain Caution: A Chronicle of Arundel (f Roberts) 1934
Captain Craig (po Robinson) 1902
Captain Eddie Rickenbacker (o Runyon) 1942
Captain Jim's Friend, and The Argonauts of North Liberty (f Harte) 1889
Captain Jinks of the Horse Marines (pl Fitch) 1902

Captain John Smith (1519-1631), Sometime Governor of Virginia, and Admiral of New England (o Warner) 1881

Captain Kidd and Two Others (po S. Benét) 1997

Captain Kyd (f Ingraham) 1839

Captain Macklin, His Memoirs (f Richard Davis) 1902

Captain of Company K (f Kirkland) 1891

Captain of Industry (f Sinclair) 1906

Captain of the Gray-Horse Troop (f Garland) 1902

Captain Rebel (f Yerby) 1956

Captain Spike (f Cooper) 1848

Captains Courageous (scr Connelly) 1937

Captain's Youngest, Piccino and Other Child Stories (f Burnett) 1894

Captive Audience (po B. Perelman) 1988

Captive: The True Story of the Captivity of Mrs. Mary Rowlandson (o Rowlandson) 1996

Captives of the Desert (f Grey) 1952

Captives of the Flame (f S. Delany) 1963

Captivity of Pixie Shedman (pl Linney) 1981

Car (f Crews) 1972

Caras viejas y vino nuevo (f Morales) 1975

Career in C Major and Other Stories (f Cain) 1943

Career in C Major and Other Fiction (f Cain) 1986

Careful and Strict Enquiry into . . . Freedom of Will. . . (o Edwards) 1754

Careless Clock: Poems about Children in the Family (po Van Doren) 1947

Careless Love: Two Rhymes (po Ginsberg) 1978

Carl Werner: An Imaginative Story, with Other Tales (f Simms) 1838

Carlos among the Candles (pl Stevens) 1917

Carmen (pl Green) 1954

Carnal Myth: A Search into Classical Sensuality (o Dahlberg) 1968

Carnations: A One-Act Play (pl Carver) 1992

Carnival of Buncombe (o Mencken) 1956

Carol of the Brown King: Nativity Poems (po Hughes) 1998

Carolina (scr Green) 1934

Caroline Archer (f Ingraham) 1844

Carpentered Hen and Other Tame Creatures (po Updike) 1958

Carpenter's Gothic (f Gaddis) 1985

Carreta (f Traven) 1935

Carrie (f King) 1974

Carrier of Ladders (po Merwin) 1970

Carry-Over (f Suckow) 1936

Carson of Venus (f E. Burroughs) 1939

Carter and Other People (f Marquis) 1921

Carwin the Biloquist and Other American Tales and Pieces (f Brown) 1822

Casa Braccio (f Crawford) 1895

Casanova (pl S. Howard) 1924

Case Book of Ellery Queen (f Queen) 1945

Case of Charles Dexter Ward (f Lovecraft) 1952

Case of David Lamson: A Summary (o Winters) 1934

Case of Elinor Norton (f Rinehart) 1934

Case of Jennie Brice (f Rinehart) 1913

Case of Leon Trotsky: Report of the Hearings of the Charges Made against Him in the Moscow Trials (o Dewey) 1937

Case of the Amorous Aunt (f E. Gardner) 1963

Case of the Angry Mourner (f E. Gardner) 1951

Case of the Backward Mule (f E. Gardner) 1946

Case of the Baited Hook (f E. Gardner) 1940

Case of the Beautiful Beggar (f E. Gardner) 1965

Case of the Bigamous Spouse (f E. Gardner) 1961

Case of the Black-Eyed Blonde (f E. Gardner) 1944

Case of the Blonde Bonanza (f E. Gardner) 1962

Case of the Borrowed Brunette (f E. Gardner) 1946

Case of the Boy Who Wrote "The Case of the Missing Clue" with Perry Mason (o E. Gardner) 1959

Case of the Buried Clock (f E. Gardner) 1943

Case of the Calendar Girl (f E. Gardner) 1958

Case of the Careless Kitten (f E. Gardner) 1942

Case of the Careless Cupid (f E. Gardner) 1968

Case of the Caretaker's Cat (f E. Gardner) 1935

Case of the Cautious Coquette (f E. Gardner) 1949

Case of the Counterfeit Eye (f E. Gardner) 1935

Case of the Crimson Kiss (f E. Gardner) 1971

Case of the Crooked Candle (f E. Gardner) 1944

Case of the Crushed Petunias (pl T. Williams) 1948

Case of the Crying Swallow (f E. Gardner) 1971

Case of the Curious Bride (f E. Gardner) 1934

Case of the Dangerous Dowager (f E. Gardner) 1937

Case of the Daring Divorcee (f E. Gardner) 1964

Case of the Daring Decoy (f E. Gardner) 1957

Case of the Deadly Toy (f E. Gardner) 1959

Case of the Demure Defendant (f E. Gardner) 1956

Case of the Drowning Duck (f E. Gardner) 1942

Case of the Drowsy Mosquito (f E. Gardner) 1943

Case of the Dubious Bridegroom (f E. Gardner) 1949

Case of the Duplicate Daughter (f E. Gardner) 1960

Case of the Empty Pin (f E. Gardner) 1941

Case of the Fabulous Fake (f E. Gardner) 1969

Case of the Fan-Dancer's Horse (f E. Gardner) 1947

Case of the Fenced-In Woman (f E. Gardner) 1972

Case of the Fiery Fingers (f E. Gardner) 1951

Case of the Foot-Loose Doll (f E. Gardner) 1958

Case of the Fugitive Nurse (f E. Gardner) 1954

Case of the Gilded Lily (f E. Gardner) 1956

Case of the Glamorous Ghost (f E. Gardner) 1955

Case of the Golddigger's Purse (f E. Gardner) 1945

Case of the Green-Eyed Sister (f E. Gardner) 1953

Case of the Grinning Gorilla (f E. Gardner) 1952

Case of the Half-Wakened Wife (f E. Gardner) 1945

Case of the Haunted Husband (f E. Gardner) 1941

Case of the Hesitant Hostess (f E. Gardner) 1953

Case of the Horrified Heirs (f E. Gardner) 1964

Case of the Howling Dog (f E. Gardner) 1934

Case of the Ice-Cold Hands (f E. Gardner) 1962

Case of the Irate Witness (f E. Gardner) 1972

Case of the Lame Canary (f E. Gardner) 1937

Case of the Lazy Lover (f E. Gardner) 1947

Case of the Lonely Heiress (f E. Gardner) 1948

Case of the Long-Legged Models (f E. Gardner) 1958

Case of the Lucky Legs (f E. Gardner) 1934

Case of the Lucky Loser (f E. Gardner) 1957

Case of the Mischievous Doll (f E. Gardner) 1963

Case of the Moth-Eaten Mink (f E. Gardner) 1952

Case of the Murderers Bride and Other Stories (f E. Gardner) 1969

Case of the Musical Cow (f E. Gardner) 1950

Case of the Mythical Monkeys (f E. Gardner) 1959

Case of the Negligent Nymph (f E. Gardner) 1950

Case of the Nervous Accomplice (f E. Gardner) 1955

Case of the Officers of Excise (o Paine) 1793

Case of the One-Eyed Witness (f E. Gardner) 1950
Case of the Perjured Parrot (f E. Gardner) 1939
Case of the Phantom Fortune (f E. Gardner) 1964
Case of the Postponed Murder (f E. Gardner) 1973
Case of the Queenly Contestant (f E. Gardner) 1967
Case of the Reluctant Model (f E. Gardner) 1962
Case of the Restless Redhead (f E. Gardner) 1954
Case of the Rolling Bones (f E. Gardner) 1939
Case of the Runaway Corpse (f E. Gardner) 1954
Case of the Screaming Woman (f E. Gardner) 1957
Case of the Seven Murders (f Queen) 1958
Case of the Shapely Shadow (f E. Gardner) 1960
Case of the Shoplifter's Shoe (f E. Gardner) 1938
Case of the Silent Partner (f E. Gardner) 1940
Case of the Singing Skirt (f E. Gardner) 1959
Case of the Sleepwalker's Niece (f E. Gardner) 1936
Case of the Smoking Chimney (f E. Gardner) 1943
Case of the Spurious Spinster (f E. Gardner) 1961
Case of the Stepdaughter's Secret (f E. Gardner) 1963
Case of the Stuttering Bishop (f E. Gardner) 1936
Case of the Substitute Face (f E. Gardner) 1938
Case of the Sulky Girl (f E. Gardner) 1933
Case of the Sun Bathers Diary (f E. Gardner) 1955
Case of the Terrified Typist (f E. Gardner) 1956
Case of the Troubled Trustee (f E. Gardner) 1965
Case of the Turning Tide (f E. Gardner) 1941
Case of the Vagabond Virgin (f E. Gardner) 1948
Case of the Velvet Claws (f E. Gardner) 1933
Case of the Waylaid Wolf (f E. Gardner) 1960
Case of the Worried Waitress (f E. Gardner) 1966
Casebook of the Black Widowers (f Asimov) 1980
Cass Timberlane (f Lewis) 1945
Cassique of Accabee, A Tale of Ashley River (po Simms) 1849
Cassique of Kiawah (f Simms) 1859
Cast a Cold Eye (f McCarthy) 1950
Cast the First Stone (f Himes) 1952
Cast upon the Breakers (f Alger) 1974
Castaway (f Cozzens) 1934
Castle Dismal (f Simms) 1844
Cat and the Blackbird (po Duncan) 1967
Cat and the King (f Auchincloss) 1981
Cat Chaser (f Leonard) 1982
Cat Chaser (scr Leonard) 1989
Cat, Mouse, Man, Woman (pl Saroyan) 1958
Cat of Many Tails (f Queen) 1949
Cat on a Hot Tin Roof (pl T. Williams) 1955
Cat on the Scent (f R Brown) 1999
Cat That Jumped out of the Story (f Hecht) 1947
Cat Who Walks through Walls (f Heinlein) 1985
Catch-22 (f Heller) 1961
Catch-22 (pl Heller) 1973
Catch My Boy on Sunday (tv Chayefsky) 1953
Catcher in the Rye (f Salinger) 1951
catechism of d neoamerican hoodoo church (po Reed) 1970
Catered Affair (tv Chayefsky) 1955
Catered Affair (scr Vidal) 1956
Cathedral (f Carver) 1983
Cathedral (po J. Lowell) 1870
Cathedral Singer (f J. Allen) 1916
Cather in Europe: Her Own Story of the First Journey (o Cather) 1956

Catherine Carmier (f Gaines) 1964
Catherine Wheel (f J. Stafford) 1952
Catlow (f L'Amour) 1963
Cat's Cradle (f Vonnegut) 1963
Cat's Eye (scr King) 1984
Cat's Meow (f Morris) 1975
Cat's Meow (po Soto) 1987
Cats of Ulthar (f Lovecraft) 1935
Cat's Paw (pl Wellman) 1998
Cats Prowl at Night (f E. Gardner) 1943
Cattle (f Eaton) 1923
Cattle Killing (f Wideman) 1996
Caught (scr Laurents) 1949
Caught Wet (pl Crothers) 1931
Causal Mythology (po Olson) 1969
Cause for Wonder (f Morris) 1963
Cavalcade (scr Behrman) 1933
Cavalier (f Cable) 1901
Cavalier of Old South Carolina: Simms's Captain Porgy (f Simms) 1966
Cavanagh, Forest Ranger (f Garland) 1910
Cave (f R. Warren) 1959
Cave at Machpelah (pl Goodman) 1958
Cave Dwellers (pl Saroyan) 1957
Cave Girl (f E. Burroughs) 1925
Cavedweller (f Allison) 1998
Cavender's House (po Robinson) 1929
Caverns (f Kesey) 1989
Caves of Steel (f Asimov) 1954
Caviar and Cabbage: Selected Columns from the Washington Tribune 1937-1944 (o Tolson) 1982
Caviare at the Funeral (po Simpson) 1980
Cawdor and Other Poems (po Jeffers) 1928
Caxton Printers in Idaho: A Short History (o Fisher) 1944
Cecilia: A Story of Modern Rome (f Crawford) 1902
Cecilia Howard (f Arthur) 1844
Cedardale (f Arthur) 1852
Celebrated Hard Case (pl Harrigan) 1878
Celebrated Jumping Frog of Calaveras County and Other Sketches (f Twain) 1867
Celebration: A Novel (f Crews) 1998
Celebrity: An Episode (f Churchill) 1898
Celestial Navigation (f A. Tyler) 1974
Celestial Rail-Road (f Hawthorne) 1843
Celestial Timepiece (po Oates) 1980
Celia B. Moore, Master Tactician of Direct Action (scr Bambara) 1987
Cell (po Hejinian) 1992
Cellophane (pl Wellman) 1988
Centaur (f Updike) 1963
Centennial (o Naylor) 1986
Centennial Meditation of Columbia (po Lanier) 1876
Central Motion: Poems, 1968-1979 (po Dickey) 1983
Century of Dishonor: A Sketch of the United States Government's Dealings with Some of the Indian Tribes (o H. Jackson) 1881
Century's Ebb: The Thirteenth Chronicle (f Dos Passos) 1975
Ceremony (f Silko) 1977
Ceremony and Other Poems (po Wilbur) 1950
Ceremony in Lone Tree (f Morris) 1960
Certain Hour (f Cabell) 1916

Certain Measure: An Interpretation of Prose Fiction (o Glasgow) 1943

Certain People (f Wharton) 1930

Certain Things Last: The Selected Short Stories (f S. Anderson) 1992

Certificate (f Singer) 1992

Chainbearer (f Cooper) 1845

Chains: Lesser Novels and Stories (f Dreiser) 1927

Chains of Dew (pl Glaspell) 1922

Chains of the Heart (pl Dunlap) 1804

Chair Endowed (pl Green) 1954

Chalk Face (f Frank) 1924

Chamber Music and Other Plays (pl Kopit) 1969

Champagne for One (f Stout) 1958

Champion (f Murfree) 1902

Champion from Far Away (f Hecht) 1931

Chance Acquaintance (f Howells) 1873

Chance Acquaintance (pl Van Druten) 1927

Chancy (f L'Amour) 1968

Chandler and James M. Fox: Letters (o Chandler) 1979

Chandler Before Marlowe: Chandler's Early Prose and Poetry 1908-1912 (o Chandler) 1973

Chandler Speaking (o Chandler) 1962

Chandler's Unknown Thriller: The Screenplay of Playback (pl Chandler) 1985

Change (po Creeley) 1972

Change (po Ginsberg) 1963

Change of World (po Rich) 1951

Change Your Bedding (pl F. O'Hara) 1951

Changing Light at Sandover (po Merrill) 1982

Changing Status of Negro Labor (o J. Johnson) 1918

Channel Road (pl Kaufman) 1929

Chants for the Boer (po J. Miller) 1900

Chapel of the Hermits and Other Poems (po Whittier) 1853

Chapter Two (pl Simon) 1977

Chapter Two (scr Simon) 1979

Chapters for the Orthodox (f Marquis) 1934

Chapters of Erie and Other Essays (o Adams) 1871

Character and Opinion in the United States (o Santayana) 1920

Character Building (o Washington) 1902

Character of the Poet (o Simpson) 1986

Character Sketches: The Boss Girl: A Christmas Story, and Other Sketches (f Riley) 1886

Characteristics (f S. Mitchell) 1892

Characters and Events: Popular Essays in Social and Political Philosophy (o Dewey) 1929

Charity and Its Fruits (o Edwards) 1852

Charity Ball (pl Belasco) 1889

Charlemont (f Simms) 1856

Charles Blackford (f Ingraham) 1845

Charles Dickens: An Appreciation (o Warner) 1913

Charles Olson and Robert Creeley: The Complete Correspondence (o Creeley) 1980-83

Charles the Second (pl W. Irving; Payne) 1824

Charleston (o Lovecraft) 1936

Charleston and Her Satirists: A Scribblement (po Simms) 1848

Charlie Codman's Cruise (f Alger) 1866

Charlie in the House of Rue (f Coover) 1980

Charlie in the House of Rue (pl Coover) 1999

Charlie Smith and the Fritter Tree (tv C. Johnson) 1978

Charlie's Pad (tv C. Johnson) 1971

Charlotte: A Tale of Truth (f Rowson) 1791

Charlotte Temple (f Rowson) 1794

Charlotte's Daughter (f Rowson) 1828

Charlotte's Web (f White) 1952

Charm: Early and Uncollected Poems (po Creeley) 1968

Charmed Life (f McCarthy) 1955

Charms for the Easy Life (f Gibbons) 1993

Charnel Rose, Senlin: A Biography, and Other Poems (po Aiken) 1918

Charon's Cosmology (po Simic) 1977

Chase (scr Hellman) 1966

Chaste Adventures of Joseph (pl Dell) 1914

Chaste Planet (f Updike) 1980

Chatelaine of La Trinite (f Fuller) 1892

Chattanooga: Poems (po Reed) 1973

Chauve-Souris (pl Parker) 1922

Chávez: A Distinctive American Clan of New Mexico (o Chávez) 1989

Cheap and Contented Labor: The Picture of a Southern Mill Town in 1929 (o Lewis) 1929

Cheap Detective (scr Simon) 1978

Cheating the Kidnappers (pl Kaufman) 1935

Cheer Up (pl Rinehart) 1912

Cheerful, By Request (f Ferber) 1918

Cheers for Miss Bishop (scr S. Benét) 1941

Chekhov on the West Heath (po Levertov) 1977

Chelsea Rooming House (po Gregory) 1930

Chemicals of Life: Enzymes, Vitamins, Hormones (o Asimov) 1954

Chemistry and Human Health (o Asimov) 1956

Cherished and Shared of Old (f Glaspell) 1940

Cherokee Trail (f L'Amour) 1982

Cherry (f Tarkington) 1903

Cherry Orchard (pl Mamet) 1985

Chess (pl Nelson) 1988

Chessmen of Mars (f E. Burroughs) 1922

Chester Rand (f Alger) 1903

Chestnut Tree (po R. Tyler) 1931

Chevalier of Pensieri-Vani (f Fuller) 1890

Chicago (pl Shepard) 1965

Chicago and Other Plays (pl Shepard) 1982

Chicago: City on the Make (o Algren) 1951

Chicago Inscriptions (o Stein) 1934

Chicago Loop (f Theroux) 1991

Chicago Massacre of 1812 (o Kirkland) 1893

Chicago Poems (po Sandburg) 1916

Chicago Stories (f Ade) 1963

Chicano in China (o Anaya) 1986

Chicken Inspector No. 23 (o S. Perelman) 1966

Chicken Without a Head (po Simic) 1983

Chickencoop Chinaman (pl Chin) 1981

Chief Joseph of the Nez Perce (po R. Warren) 1983

Child (po Plath) 1971

Child and the Curriculum (o Dewey) 1902

Child Is Born (pl S. Benét) 1942

Child Is Born (radio S. Benét) 1942

Childe Byron (pl Linney) 1977

Childhood Is Not Forever and Other Stories (f Farrell) 1969

Childhood: The Biography of a Place (o Crews) 1978

Childish Jokes: Crying Backstage (pl Goodman) 1938

Children (po Creeley) 1978

Children (f Wharton) 1928

Children and Older People (f Suckow) 1931
Children and Others (f Cozzens) 1964
Children and the Machine Age (o Dell) 1934
Children Are Bored on Sunday (f J. Stafford) 1953
Children at the Gate (f Wallant) 1964
Children Coming Home (po Brooks) 1991
Children I Have Known (f Burnett) 1892
Children in Bondage: A Presentation of the Anxious Problem of
  Child Labor (o Markham) 1914
Children Is All (f Purdy) 1962
Children of God (f Fisher) 1939
Children of Loneliness (f Yezierska) 1923
Children of the Albatross (f Nin) 1947
Children of the Frost (f London) 1902
Children of the King (f Crawford) 1893
Children of the Levee (o Hearn) 1957
Children of the Market Place (f Masters) 1922
Children of the Night (po Robinson) 1897
Children's Hour (pl Hellman) 1934
Children's Hour (f S. Mitchell) 1864
Children's Hour (The Loudest Whisper) (scr Hellman) 1961
Children's Orchard (po Rukeyser) 1947
Child's Calendar (o Updike) 1965
Child's Garden of Curses (o S. Perelman) 1951
Child's Reminiscence (o Whitman) 1930
Childwold (f Oates) 1976
Child-World (po Riley) 1896
Chilekings (f J. West) 1967
Chill (f Macdonald) 1964
Chills and Fever (po Ransom) 1924
Chilly Scenes of Winter (f Beattie) 1976
Chimera (f Barth) 1972
Chimes (f Herrick) 1926
Chimney Corner Graduates (o J. Allen) 1900
Chimney-Corner (o Stowe) 1868
Chimneysmoke (po Morley) 1921
China Flight (f Buck) 1945
China Girl (scr Hecht) 1942
China, Japan and the U.S.A.: Present-Day Conditions in the Far
  East and Their Bearing on the Washington Conference (o
  Dewey) 1921
China Men (f Kingston) 1977
China Sly (f Buck) 1942
China to America (pl Buck) 1944
Chinaman Pacific & Frisco R. R. Co (f Chin) 1988
Chinaman: Poems (po Mamet) 1999
Chinatown Family (f Lin Yutang) 1948
Chinese Nightingale and Other Poems (po Lindsay) 1917
Chinese Orange Mystery (f Queen) 1934
Chinese Siamese Cat (o Tan) 1994
Chips Off the Old Benchley (o Benchley) 1949
Chiquita Banana (tv Hagedorn) 1972
Chita: A Memory of Last Island (f Hearn) 1889
Chivalry (f Cabell) 1909
Chocurua (pl Eberhart) 1981
Choice of Catastrophes: The Disasters That Threaten Our World
  (o Asimov) 1979
Choice of Days (o Mencken) 1980
Choir Invisible (f J. Allen) 1897
Choosing Company (pl Schwartz) 1936
Chopin Miscellany (o Chopin) 1979

Chopin: The Man and His Music (o Huneker) 1900
Chorus for Survival (po Gregory) 1935
Choruses from the Iphigenia in Aulis and the Hippolytus by
  Euripides (po Doolittle) 1919
Choruses from the Iphigenia in Aulis by Euripides (po Doolittle)
  1916
Chosen Country (f Dos Passos) 1951
Chosen Place, the Timeless People (f Marshall) 1969
Chosen Poems, Old and New (po Lorde) 1982
Chris Christophersen (pl O'Neill) 1982
Chris'mus Is A-Comin' and Other Poems (po Dunbar) 1905
Christ the Great Example of Gospel Ministers (o Edwards) 1750
Christian Loyalty (o Mather) 1727
Christian Philosopher (o Mather) 1720
Christian Slave (pl Stowe) 1855
Christianity Demonstrated (o Mather) 1710
Christianus per Ignem (o Mather) 1702
Christine (pl Buck) 1960
Christine (f King) 1983
Christmas: A Story (f Gale) 1912
Christmas Card (o Theroux) 1978
Christmas Carol (tv M. Anderson) 1954
Christmas Carol (pl M. Anderson) 1955
Christmas Carol (pl Kaufman) 1922
Christmas Comes to Hjalsen, Reno (po Clark) 1930
Christmas Delerium (po E. Wilson) 1955
Christmas Eve: A Morality Play (pl Hecht) 1928
Christmas Eve Service at Midnight at St. Michael's (po Bly) 1972
Christmas Gift from Fairy Land (f Paulding) 1838
Christmas Joys and Sorrows (pl Harrigan) 1877
Christmas Letters (f L. Smith) 1996
Christmas: May 10, 1970 (po Creeley) 1970
Christmas Memory (tv Capote) 1966
Christmas Memory (f Capote) 1966
Christmas 1939 (po Saroyan) 1939
Christmas Present, Christmas Presence! (po Duncan) 1967
Christmas Psalm (po Saroyan) 1935
Christmas Story (f Mencken) 1946
Christmas Story (f Porter) 1958
Christmas Tree (po Cummings) 1928
Christographia (o E. Taylor) 1962
Christopher Blake (pl Hart) 1947
Christopher Columbus: The Discovery (scr Puzo) 1992
Christopher Strong (scr Akins) 1933
Christus: A Mystery (po Longfellow) 1872
Christus Apollo (pl Bradbury) 1969
Chronicles of Cooperstown (o Cooper) 1838
Chronicles of the City of Gotham, from the Papers of a Retired
  Common Councilman (f Paulding) 1830
Chronicles of Wolfert's Roost and Other Papers (f W. Irving) 1855
Chrysanthemums (po Bly) 1967
Chuck (pl MacKaye) 1912
Church's Marriage to Her Sons and to Her God (o Edwards) 1746
Cider House Rules (f J. Irving) 1985
Cigarette-Maker's Romance (f Crawford) 1890
Cimarron (f Ferber) 1930
Cinderella and Other Stories (f Richard Davis) 1896
Cipango's Hinder Door (po Dahlberg) 1965
Cipher in the Plays and on the Tombstone (o Donnelly) 1899
Circuit Rider: A Tale of the Heroic Age (f Eggleston) 1874
Circular Staircase (f Rinehart) 1908

Circumstance (f S. Mitchell) 1901
Circus Day (f Ade) 1896
Circus in the Attic and Other Stories (f R. Warren) 1948
Circus World (The Magnificent Showman) (scr Hecht) 1964
Citadel (scr Van Druten) 1938
Cities of the Interior (f Nin) 1959
Cities of the Red Night: A Boy's Book (f W. Burroughs) 1981
Citizen Jefferson: The Wit and Wisdom of an American Sage (o Jefferson) 1994
Citizen of the Galaxy (f Heinlein) 1957
City: A Modern Play of American Life (pl Fitch) 1909
City and the Pillar (f Vidal) 1949
City Block (f Frank) 1922
City Chap (pl Ade) 1910
City Clerk and His Sister and Other Stories (f Sedgwick) 1851
City in Crisis (o Ellison) 1968
City Life (f Barthelme) 1970
City Looking Glass: A Philadelphia Comedy (pl Bird) 1933
City of a Thousand Suns (f S. Delany) 1965
City of Illusion (f Fisher) 1941
City of Night (f Rechy) 1963
City of the Living and Other Stories (f Stegner) 1956
City of the Silent (po Simms) 1850
City of Trembling Leaves (f Clark) 1945
City Primeval: High Noon in Detroit (f Leonard) 1980
City Psalm (po Levertov) 1964
City Streets (scr Hammett) 1931
City Wears a Slouch Hat (pl Patchen) 1942
City Wears a Slouch Hat (radio Patchen) 1942
City Winter and Other Poems (po F. O'Hara) 1952
Civil War Diary (o Tourgée) 1965
Civil War Letters (f Nasby) 1962
Claiming Earth (o Madhubuti) 1994
Claire Ambler (f Tarkington) 1928
Clara Howard (f Brown) 1801
Clara's Ole Man (pl Bullins) 1965
Clarel: A Poem, and Pilgrimage in the Holy Land (po Melville) 1876
Clarence (f Harte) 1895
Clarence (f Sedgwick) 1830
Clarence (pl Tarkington) 1921
Clarence Allen (f Ade) 1903
Clari (pl Payne) 1823
Clarice (pl Gillette) 1905
Clarion Call to Redeem the Race! (o Gilman) 1890
Clark Gifford's Body (f Fearing) 1942
Clark's Field (f Herrick) 1914
Clash by Night (pl Odets) 1942
Class Poem (po J. Lowell) 1838
Classic Ballroom Dances (po Simic) 1980
Classics and Commercials: A Literary Chronicle of the Forties (o E. Wilson) 1950
Clear Shifting Water (po Olson) 1968
Clear Springs: A Memoir (o Mason) 1999
Clearing in the Woods (pl Laurents) 1957
Clearing the Labyrinth (o Sánchez) 1993
Clemente Chacón (f Villarreal) 1984
Clergyman's Wife and Other Sketches (f Mowatt) 1867
Clerk's Journal (po Aiken) 1971
Cleveland (pl Wellman) 1986
Clew of the Forgotten Murder (f E. Gardner) 1935

!Click Song (f J. Williams) 1982
Cliff-Dwellers (f Fuller) 1893
Clifford's Blues (f J. Williams) 1999
Climate of Eden (pl Hart) 1953
Climate of Palettes (po Bradbury) 1989
Climbers (pl Fitch) 1906
Clinical Lessons on Nervous Diseases (o S. Mitchell) 1897
Clipper-Yacht (f Ingraham) 1845
Clippings from Denver Tribune 1881-1883 (o Field) 1909
Cloak of Light: Writing My Life (o Morris) 1985
Clock We Live On (o Asimov) 1959
Clock Winder (f A. Tyler) 1972
Clock without Hands (f McCullers) 1961
Clorindy (pl Dunbar) 1898
Close Chaplet (po Riding) 1926
Close Harmony (pl Parker; Rice) 1924
Close the Book (pl Glaspell) 1917
Closed Gates (scr Queen) 1927
Closing Time (f Heller) 1994
Clotel (f W. Brown) 1853
Cloth of the Tempest (po Patchen) 1943
Clothed with the Sun (po Chávez) 1939
Clothes for a Summer Hotel (pl T. Williams) 1980
Cloud Chamber (f Dorris) 1997
Cloud Nine (f Cain) 1984
Cloud, Stone, Sun, Vine (po Sarton) 1961
Clouds (pl Gale) 1936
Clouds (po W. Williams) 1948
Cloudy with Showers (pl Dell) 1931
Club Bedroom (pl Auchincloss) 1967
Club Room and Other Temperance Tales (f Arthur) 1845
Clues of the Caribbees, Being Certain Criminal Investigations of Henry Poggioli, Ph.D (f Stribling) 1929
C'mon Back to Heavenly House (pl Bullins) 1978
Coal (po Lorde) 1976
Coal War: A Sequel to King Coal (f Sinclair) 1976
Coast of Bohemia (f Howells) 1893
Coast of Bohemia (po Page) 1906
Coast of Illyria (pl Parker) 1990
Coast of Trees (po Ammons) 1981
Coat without a Seam: Sixty Poems 1930-1972 (po Kunitz) 1974
Coathanger (pl Wellman) 1992
Cobwebs from an Empty Skull (f Bierce) 1874
Cochise of Arizona: The Pipe of Peace Is Broken (o La Farge) 1953
Cock of the Air (scr Sherwood) 1932
Cock Pit (f Cozzens) 1928
Cock Robin (pl Barry; Rice) 1928
Cockpit (f Kosinski) 1975
Cocktail Party (pl Eliot) 1949
Cocoanuts (pl Kaufman) 1925
Cod Head (po W. Williams) 1932
Code of Civil Procedure of North Carolina (o Tourgée) 1878
Code of the West (f Grey) 1934
Coelestinus: A Conversation in Heaven (o Mather) 1723
Coffee Room (f Elkin) 1988
Coffee-House (pl Fuller) 1925-26
Coffin (tv Bradbury) 1988
Cohan Revue 1916 (pl Cohan) 1916
Cohan Revue 1918 (pl Cohan) 1918
Cold Air (pl Fornés) 1985

Cold of Poetry (po Hejinian) 1994
Cold Spring and Other Poems (po Levertov) 1969
Cold War and the Income Tax: A Protest (o E. Wilson) 1963
Cold Wind and the Warm (pl Behrman) 1959
Coldest Day of the Year (pl A. Wilson) 1979
Collages (f Nin) 1964
Collapsing Cosmoses (f Lovecraft) 1977
Collapsing Universe (o Asimov) 1977
Collected Essays of Leslie Fiedler (o Fiedler) 1972
Collected Essays of Robert Creeley (o Creeley) 1989
Collected Poems: Not So Deep As a Well (po Parker) 1936
Collected Stories of Jessamyn West (f J. West) 1986
Collection of Hayne Letters (o Hayne) 1944
Collection of Poems on American Affairs (po Freneau) 1815
Collection of Psalm Tunes (po Hopkinson) 1762
Collection of Reviews (o Macdonald) 1979
Collection of Some of the Many Offensive Matters Contained in
    The Order of the Gospel Revived (o Mather) 1701
Collection of the Familiar Letters and Miscellaneous Papers (o
    Franklin) 1833
Collector of Hearts: New Tales of the Grotesque (f Oates) 1998
Collector's Whatnot (o Roberts) 1923
College Primer of Writing (o Ransom) 1943
College Widow (pl Ade) 1924
Colonel Guiney and the Ninth Massachusetts: A Filial Apprecia-
    tion (o Guiney) 1932
Col. Ross of Piedmont (f J. Cooke) 1893
Colonel Satan (pl Tarkington) 1932
Colonel Sellers as a Scientist (pl Howells; Twain) 1887
Colonel Starbottle's Client and Some Other People (f Harte) 1892
Colonel Stonesteel and the "Desperate Empties" (tv Bradbury)
    1992
Colonel's Dream (f Chesnutt) 1905
Color (po Cullen) 1925
Color and Democracy: Colonies and Peace (o Du Bois) 1945
Color Curtain: A Report on the Bandung Conference (o R. Wright)
    1956
Color of Darkness (f Purdy) 1956
Color of Darkness: Eleven Stories and a Novella (f Purdy) 1957
Color Purple (f A. Walker) 1982
Color Struck (pl Hurston) 1926
Colorado (f Bromfield) 1947
Colorado (o Waters) 1946
Colorado: A Summer Trip (o B. Taylor) 1867
Colored People: A Memoir (o Gates) 1994
Colors Come from God-Just Like Me (o Forché) 1995
Colors of the Day (pl Rukeyser) 1961
Colossus (po Plath) 1960
Colour Out of Space (f Lovecraft) 1964
Coloured Baby Show (pl Harrigan) 1878
Columbia the Gem of the Ocean (pl Baraka) 1973
Columbiad (po Barlow) 1807
Columbian Daughter (pl Rowson) 1800
Columbus and the Discovery of Japan (pl Nelson) 1992
Columbus el Filibustero!! (pl Brougham) 1857
Come Along with Me: Part of a Novel, Sixteen Stories, and Three
    Lectures (o S. Jackson) 1968
Come and Get It (f Ferber) 1935
Come Back Charleston Blue (f Himes) 1967
Come Back, Dr. Caligari (f Barthelme) 1964
Come Back, Little Sheba (pl Inge) 1949

Come Back Paul (o Rukeyser) 1955
Come Blow Your Horn (pl Simon) 1961
Come Here (pl Daly) 1870
Come In and Other Poems (po Frost) 1943
Come Marching Home (pl R. Anderson) 1945
Come, My Beloved (f Buck) 1953
Comedian (pl Belasco) 1923
Comedians All (o Nathan) 1919
Comedy of Conscience (f S. Mitchell) 1903
Comfort of the Hills (po S. Mitchell) 1909
Comfort of the Hills and Other Poems (po S. Mitchell) 1910
Comfort Pease and Her Gold Ring (o Freeman) 1895
Comic Artist (pl Glaspell) 1928
Comic Tragedies Written by "Jo" and "Meg" and Acted by the
    "Little Women" (pl Alcott) 1893
Coming Forth by Day of Osiris Jones (po Aiken) 1931
Coming into Eighty: And Earlier Poems (po Sarton) 1995
Coming of Mrs. Patrick (pl Crothers) 1907
Coming of the Night (f Rechy) 1999
Comique Joker (o Harrigan) 1870
Command the Morning (f Buck) 1959
Commentary on the Writings of Henrik Ibsen (o Boyesen) 1894
Commodity of Dreams and Other Stories (f Nemerov) 1959
Commodus (pl L. Wallace) 1876
Common Faith (o Dewey) 1934
Common Glory: A Symphonic Drama of American History (pl
    Green) 1947
Common Glory Song-Book (po Green) 1951
Common Lot (f Herrick) 1904
Common Man (pl Hecht) 1944
Common Sense (o Paine) 1776
Common Way (o Deland) 1904
Commonplace Book of Jefferson: A Repertory of His Ideas on
    Government (o Jefferson) 1928
Compact Maritime (o Paine) 1801
Companion for Communicants (o Mather) 1690
Company (po Creeley) 1988
Company of Poets (o Simpson) 1981
Company She Keeps (f McCarthy) 1942
Compass Flower (po Merwin) 1977
Complaint (po Wilbur) 1968
Complete Anas (o Jefferson) 1903
Complete Humorous Sketches and Tales (f Twain) 1961
Complete Jefferson (o Jefferson) 1943
Composition and Rhetoric for Schools (o Herrick) 1899
Composition as Explanation (o Stein) 1926
Composition of Expired Air and Its Effects upon Animal Life (o
    S. Mitchell) 1895
Compromise (pl Ashbery) 1956
Compulsory Heterosexuality and Lesbian Existence (o Rich) 1981
Comrade X (scr Hecht) 1940
Comstock Lode (f L'Amour) 1981
Conagher (f L'Amour) 1969
Concentrated New England: A Sketch of Calvin Coolidge (o Rob-
    erts) 1924
Concerning a Woman of Sin and Other Stories (f Hecht) 1947
Concerning Children (o Gilman) 1900
Conchologist's First Book (o Poe) 1839
Concio ad Populum (o Mather) 1719
Concise American Composition and Rhetoric (o Davidson) 1964
Concord Hymn and Other Poems (po Emerson) 1996

Concrete Mixer (tv Bradbury) 1992
Condemned (scr S. Howard) 1929
Condensed Novels and Other Papers (f Harte) 1867
Conduct of Life (o Emerson) 1860
Conduct of Life (pl Fornés) 1986
Coney Island of the Mind (po Ferlinghetti) 1958
Confederacy: A Symphonic Outdoor Drama Based on the Life of
    General Robert E. Lee (pl Green) 1959
Confederate General from Big Sur (f Brautigan) 1965
Confession (f Simms) 1841
Confession of John Whitlock, Late Preacher of the Gospel (f E.
    Howe) 1891
Confessional (pl T. Williams) 1970
Confessions of a Housekeeper (f Arthur) 1852
Confessions of a Wild Bore (o Updike) 1984
Confessions of Dahlberg (o Dahlberg) 1971
Confessions of Nat Turner (f Styron) 1967
Confidence (f H. James) 1879
Confidence-Man, His Masquerade (f Melville) 1857
Confidential Clerk (pl Eliot) 1953
Confidential Letters to William Wirt (o Jefferson) 1912
Confidential Service (pl Cohan) 1932
Conflict (f D. Phillips) 1911
Confucius Saw Nancy, and Essays about Nothing (pl Lin Yutang)
    1935
Confusion (f Cozzens) 1924
Congo and Coasts of Africa (o Richard Davis) 1907
Congo and Other Poems (po Lindsay) 1914
Coniston (f Churchill) 1906
Conjure Woman (f Chesnutt) 1899
Conjure: Selected Poems, 1963-70 (po Reed) 1972
Conjuring an Event (pl Nelson) 1976
Connecticut Yankee in King Arthur's Court (f Twain) 1889
Conqueror, Being the True and Romantic Story of Alexander
    Hamilton (f Atherton) 1902
Conquest (Marie Walewska) (scr Behrman) 1937
Conquest of Canaan (po Dwight) 1785
Conquest of Canaan (f Tarkington) 1905
Conquest of Everest (pl Kopit) 1964
Conquest of Television (tv Kopit) 1966
Conquistador (po MacLeish) 1932
Conrad and Eudora (pl Chivers) 1834
Consciousness at Concord (o Thoreau) 1958
Conscript Mother (f Herrick) 1916
Conservation of Races (o Du Bois) 1897
Conservatism: An Obituary (o Rand) 1962
Conservative: Complete 1915-1923 (o Lovecraft) 1977
Considerable Speck (po Frost) 1939
Conspiracy of Kings (po Barlow) 1792
Constab Ballads (po McKay) 1912
Constance (po Kenyon) 1993
Constance Trescot (f S. Mitchell) 1905
Constant Defender (po J. Tate) 1983
Constant Reader (o Parker) 1970
Constantinople (o Crawford) 1895
Constantinople: The Forgotten Empire (o Asimov) 1970
Construction and Criticism (o Dewey) 1930
Consul (pl Richard Davis) 1911
Consul's File (f Theroux) 1977
Contemporaries (pl Steele) 1915
Contemporaries and Snobs (o Riding) 1928

Contemporaries: Portraits in the Progressive Era (o D. Phillips)
    1981
Context and Thought (o Dewey) 1931
Contexts of Poetry (o Creeley) 1968
Contexts of Poetry: Interviews 1961-1971 (o Creeley) 1973
Continental Op (f Hammett) 1945
Continuing Debate (o Fiedler) 1966
Continuous Life (po Strand) 1990
Contrast (pl R. Tyler) 1790
Convalescent (o Willis) 1859
Convalescent Conversations (f Riding) 1936
Convention (f Coover) 1982
Conversation (f Aiken) 1940
Conversation at Midnight (po Millay) 1937
Conversation on Some of the Old Poets (o J. Lowell) 1845
Conversation with Max (o Behrman) 1960
Conversations (o James Baldwin) 1989
Conversations in Rome: Between an Artist, A Catholic, and a Critic
    (po Channing) 1847
Conversations with Algren, with H.E.F. Donohue (o Algren) 1964
Conversations with Amiri Baraka (o Baraka) 1994
Conversations with Anaïs Nin (o Nin) 1994
Conversations with Capote (o Capote) 1985
Conversations with E.L. Doctorow (o Doctorow) 1999
Conversations with Elizabeth Spencer (o Spencer) 1991
Conversations with Ernest Gaines (o Gaines) 1995
Conversations with Hemingway (o Hemingway) 1986
Conversations with Jerzy Kosinski (o Kosinski) 1993
Conversations with John Edgar Wideman (o Wideman) 1998
Conversations with Kurt Vonnegut (o Vonnegut) 1988
Conversations with Louise Erdrich and Michael Dorris (o Erdrich)
    1994
Conversations with Malamud (o Malamud) 1991
Conversations with Malcolm Cowley (o Cowley) 1986
Conversations with Maya Angelou (o Angelou) 1988
Conversations with Morris: Critical Views and Responses (o Mor-
    ris) 1977
Conversations with Nikki Giovanni (o Giovanni) 1992
Conversations with Norman Mailer (o Mailer) 1988
Conversations with O'Connor (o O'Connor) 1987
Conversations with Paul Bowles (o Bowles) 1993
Conversations with Percy (o Percy) 1985
Conversations with Steinbeck (o Steinbeck) 1988
Conversations with Styron (o Styron) 1985
Conversations with Welty (o Welty) 1984
Conversations with William Faulkner (o Faulkner) 1999
Cool Million: The Dismantling of Lemuel Pitkin (f N. West) 1934
Co-op: A Novel of Living Together (f Sinclair) 1936
Cooper's Ward (f Alger) 1981
Cop-Out (pl Guare) 1968
Cop Out (f Queen) 1969
Cop-Out, Muzeeka, Home Fires (pl Guare) 1971
Copacetic (po Komunyakaa) 1984
Copernican Revolution (po Goodman) 1946
Copies of the Two Letters Cited by Rev. Mr. Clap (o Edwards)
    1745
Copper Pot (f La Farge) 1942
Copper Sun (po Cullen) 1927
Copperhead (f Frederic) 1893
Copperhead and Other Stories of the North During the American
    War (f Frederic) 1894

Cops and Robbers (f Henry) 1948

Cops on Campus and Crime in the Street (o E. Gardner) 1970

Copy-Cat and Other Stories (f Freeman) 1914

Coquette (f H. Foster) 1797

Coquettish Doll (f Field) 1995

Cora (f Suckow) 1929

Cordelia's Aspirations (pl Harrigan) 1883

Corderius Americanus: An Essay upon the Good Education of Children (o Mather) 1708

Cords of Vanity (f Cabell) 1909

Corleone (f Crawford) 1897

Corn Close (po Creeley) 1980

Corner (pl Bullins) 1968

Cornhuskers (po Sandburg) 1918

Coronado's Friars (o Chávez) 1968

Coronal. A Collection of Miscellaneous Pieces, Written at Various Times (f Child) 1832

Coronet of the Duchess (pl Fitch) 1904

Corrado Cagli March 31 through April 19 1947 (po Olson) 1947

Corregidora (f G. Jones) 1975

Correspondence (o S. Crane) 1988

Correspondence between Hart Crane and Waldo Frank (o H. Crane) 1998

Correspondence between Lydia Maria Child and Gov. Wise and Mrs. Mason, of Virginia (o Child) 1860

Correspondence Between Jefferson and Pierre Samuel du Pont de Nemours 1798-1817 (o Jefferson) 1930

Correspondence of Bayard Taylor and Hayne (o Hayne) 1945

Correspondence of Jefferson and Francis Walker Gilmer 1814-1826 (o Jefferson) 1946

Correspondence of O'Connor and the Brainard Cheneys (o O'Connor) 1986

Correspondence of Shelby Foote and Walker Percy (o Percy) 1997

Correspondence of Taylor and Paul Hamilton Hayne (o B. Taylor) 1945

Correspondence of William James (o W. James) 1998

Correspondence, Printed from the Originals in the Collections of William K. Bixby (o Jefferson) 1916

Corsage (o Stout) 1977

Corsair of Casco Bay (f Ingraham) 1844

Corsons Inlet (po Ammons) 1965

Cortez (f Bird) 1835

Cosmopolitan Greetings: Poems, 1986-1992 (po Ginsberg) 1994

Cost (f D. Phillips) 1904

Costumes by Eros (f Aiken) 1928

Cotton Candy on a Rainy Day (po Giovanni) 1978

Cotton Comes to Harlem (f Himes) 1965

Cotton-Pickers (f Traven) 1956

Couche dans le pain (f Himes) 1959

Counsellor-at-Law (pl Rice) 1931

Counsellor-at-Law (scr Rice) 1933

Count Bruga (f Hecht) 1926

Count Frontenac and New France under Louis XIV (o Parkman) 1877

Count Julian; or The Last Days of the Goth (f Simms) 1845

Count of Nine (f E. Gardner) 1958

Counter-Attack (One Against Seven) (scr Lawson) 1945

Counterfeit Presentment (pl Howells) 1877

Counterlife (f P. Roth) 1987

Counter-Statement (o Burke) 1931

Countess Gucki (pl Daly) 1895

Counting (f J. Phillips) 1978

Counting the Eons (o Asimov) 1983

Counting the Ways (pl Albee) 1976

Country Between Us (po Forché) 1981

Country By-Ways (f Jewett) 1881

Country Cousin (f Auchincloss) 1978

Country Cousin (pl Tarkington) 1921

Country Doctor (f Jewett) 1884

Country Girl (pl Daly) 1884

Country Girl (pl Odets) 1951

Country House (po Teasdale) 1932

Country of a Thousand Years of Peace and Other Poems (po Merrill) 1959

Country of Strangers (f Richter) 1966

Country of the Pointed Firs (f Jewett) 1896

Country People (f Suckow) 1924

Country Place (f Petry) 1947

Country Stores (f Harrison) 1993

Country Town Sayings: A Collection of Paragraphs from the Atchison Globe (o E. Howe) 1911

Country Year (po Van Doren) 1946

County Chairtan (pl Ade) 1924

Coup (f Updike) 1978

Couples (f Updike) 1968

Couples: A Short Story (f Updike) 1976

Courage to Be New (po Frost) 1946

Court of Last Resort (o E. Gardner) 1952

Court of Last Resort (pl Rice) 1985

Courts of Love: A Novella and Stories (f Gilchrist) 1996

Courtship of Miles Standish and Other Poems (po Longfellow) 1858

Cousin Billy (pl Fitch) 1905

Cousin Kate (pl B. Howard) 1897

Covenant of Literal Morality (o Riding) 1938

Covered Wagon and the West (f E. Howe) 1928

Cow with Golden Horns and Other Stories (o Freeman) 1884

Cowboy and the Lady (scr Behrman) 1938

Cowboy and the Lady (pl Fitch) 1908

Cowboy Mouth (pl Shepard) 1971

Cowboys (pl Shepard) 1964

Cowboys #2 (pl Shepard) 1967

Cowpens: The Great Morale-Builder (o Roberts) 1957

Cow's in the Corn (pl Frost) 1929

Coyote Waits (f Hillerman) 1990

Coyote's Daylight Trip (po P. Allen) 1978

Cozy Lion, as Told by Queen Crosspatch (f Burnett) 1907

Crabcakes (o McPherson) 1998

Cracks (pl Purdy) 1963

Cradle Song (scr Connelly) 1933

Craig's Wife (pl Kelly) 1926

Crane and Yvor Winters: Their Literary Correspondence (o H. Crane) 1978

Crane in the West and Mexico (o S. Crane) 1970

Crater (f Cooper) 1847

Crazy Horse (f McMurtry) 1999

Crazy Hunter and Other Stories (f Boyle) 1940

Crazy Hunter: Three Short Novels (f Boyle) 1940

Crazy Kill (f Himes) 1958

Crazy Like a Fox (o S. Perelman) 1944

Crazy Man (f Bodenheim) 1924

Cream of the Jest (f Cabell) 1917

Cream of Thurber (f Thurber) 1939
Creation (f Vidal) 1981
Creation of the New Ark (o Baraka) 1975
Creation of the Sun and the Moon (o Traven) 1968
Creation of the World and Other Business (pl A. Miller) 1972
Creative (o Creeley) 1973
Creative Intelligence: Essays in the Pragmatic Attitude (o Dewey) 1917
Creative Person: Henry Roth (tv J. Williams) 1966
Creatures in an Alphabet (po Barnes) 1982
Credos and Curios (f Thurber) 1962
Creeley Reads (po Creeley) 1967
Creeping Siamese (f Hammett) 1950
Creole (pl Belasco) 1876-77
Creole Sketches (o Hearn) 1924
Cress Delahanty (f J. West) 1953
Cressy (f Harte) 1889
Cretan Women (pl Jeffers) 1954(?)
Creve Coeur (pl T. Williams) 1978
Criers and Kibitzers, Kibitzers and Criers (f Elkin) 1966
Crime and Again (f Stout) 1959
Crime in the Whistler Room (pl E. Wilson) 1924
Crime of Crimes (po Lovecraft) 1915
Crime on Her Hands (f Stout) 1939
Crime without Passion (scr Hecht; MacArthur) 1934
Crimewatch (tv Capote) 1973
Crimson Ramblers of the World, Farewell (f J. West) 1970
Crisis (f Churchill) 1901
Crisis Extraordinary (o Paine) 1780
Crisis in Boston! (o Baraka) 1974
Crisis in Industry (o Thomas [Clayton] Wolfe) 1919
Crisis of the Film (o Fletcher) 1929
Criss-Cross (pl Crothers) 1904
Critic (pl Daly) 1874
Critic and the Drama (o Nathan) 1922
Critical Essays and Literary Notes (o B. Taylor) 1880
Critical Fable (po A. Lowell) 1922
Critical Year (pl Green) 1939
Critics' Prize Plays (o Nathan) 1945
Criticism: An Essay (o Whitman) 1913
Croakers (po Drake; Halleck) 1860
Cross and Sword: A Symphonic Drama of the Spanish Settlement of Florida (pl Green) 1966
Cross Creek (o Rawlings) 1942
Cross Creek Cookery (o Rawlings) 1942
Crossfire Trail (f L'Amour) 1954
Crossing (f Churchill) 1904
Crossing Open Ground (o Lopez) 1988
Crossing the Border (f Oates) 1976
Crossing the Water (po Plath) 1971
Crossing to Safety (f Stegner) 1987
Crossing Unmarked Snow: Further Views on the Writer's Vocation (o W. Stafford) 1997
Crow and Weasel (o Lopez) 1990
Crowbar (pl Wellman) 1990
Crown of Columbus (f Dorris; Erdrich) 1991
Crown of Feathers and Other Stories (f Singer) 1973
Crown Prince (pl Akins) 1927
Crows Can't Count (f E. Gardner) 1946
Crozart Story (f Fearing) 1960
Crucial Conversations (f Sarton) 1975

Crucial Instances (f Wharton) 1901
Crucible (pl A. Miller) 1953
Cruise of the Dazzler (f London) 1902
Cruise of the Dry Dock (f Stribling) 1917
Cruise of the Jasper B (f Marquis) 1916
Cruiser of the Mist (f Ingraham) 1845
Crusade Against Ignorance: Jefferson on Education (o Jefferson) 1961
Crusade of the Excelsior (f Harte) 1887
Crushed Actors (pl Harrigan) 1877
Crux (f Gilman) 1911
Cry and the Dedication (o Bulosan) 1995
Cry Horror! (f Lovecraft) 1958
Cry Killer! (f Fearing) 1958
Crying of Lot 49 (f Pynchon) 1966
Cryptogram (pl Mamet) 1994
Crystal Cup (f Atherton) 1925
Crystal Gazer (po Plath) 1971
Crystal Text (po Coolidge) 1986
Cub of the Panther: A Hunter Legend of the "Old North State." (o Simms) 1997
Cuba in War Time (o Richard Davis) 1897
Cuba Libre (o Baraka) 1961
Cuba Libre (f Leonard) 1998
Cuban and Porto Rican Campaigns (o Richard Davis) 1898
Cue for Passion (pl Rice) 1958
Cujo (f King) 1981
Culp (f Gass) 1985
Culprit Fay and Other Poems (po Drake) 1835
Cultivated Motor Automatism (o Stein) 1969
Cultivation of Christmas Trees (po Eliot) 1954
Culture and the National Will (o Frye) 1957
Culture's Garland, Being Memoranda of the Gradual Rise of Literature, Art, Music, and Society in Chicago and Other Western Ganglia (o Field) 1887
Cunts (po Updike) 1974
Cup of Fury (f Sinclair) 1956
Cup of Gold: A Life of Henry Morgan, Buccaneer (f Steinbeck) 1929
Cup of Youth and Other Poems (po S. Mitchell) 1889
Cupid and Psyche (f Oates) 1970
Cure for Dreams (f Gibbons) 1991
Cure of Flesh (f Cozzens) 1933
Curious Fragments: London's Tales of Fantasy Fiction (f London) 1975
Curious Republic of Gondour and Other Whimsical Sketches (f Twain) 1919
Currents and Counter-Currents in Medical Science, with Other Addresses and Essays (o Holmes) 1861
Currents of Space (f Asimov) 1952
Curse of Cain (pl Belasco) 1882
Curse of the Langston House (pl Fornés) 1972
Curse of the Starving Class (pl Shepard) 1977
Curse of Yig (f Lovecraft) 1953
Curtain of Green and Other Stories (f Welty) 1941
Curtains for Three (f Stout) 1951
Curve of the Catenary (f Rinehart) 1945
Custom of the Country (f Wharton) 1913
Cut Thin to Win (f E. Gardner) 1965
Cutie, A Warm Mamma (f Bodenheim; Hecht) 1924
Cybele (f Oates) 1979

Cycle of the Werewolf (f King) 1983
Cynic's Word Book (o Bierce) 1906
Cyrano de Bergerac (pl Daly) 1898
Cytherea (f Hergesheimer) 1922
Czarina (pl Sheldon) 1922

D. Faustus Lights the Lights (pl Stein) 1984
D.A. Breaks an Egg (f E. Gardner) 1949
D.A. Breaks the Seal (f E. Gardner) 1946
D.A. Calls a Turn (f E. Gardner) 1944
D.A. Calls It Murder (f E. Gardner) 1937
D.A. Cooks a Goose (f E. Gardner) 1942
D.A. Draws a Circle (f E. Gardner) 1939
D.A. Goes to Trial (f E. Gardner) 1940
D.A. Holds a Candle (f E. Gardner) 1938
D.A. Takes a Chance (f E. Gardner) 1948
D.D. Byrde Calling Jennie Wrenn (po Snodgrass) 1984
D.H. Lawrence and the High Temptation of the Mind (o Olson) 1980
D.H. Lawrence: An Unprofessional Study (o Nin) 1932
D.H. Lawrence's Sons and Lovers (o Gilbert and Gubar) 1965
Daddy (pl Bullins) 1977
Daddy Goodness (pl R. Wright) 1968
Daddy Long Legs (scr Behrman) 1931
Daddy's Gone A-Hunting (pl Akins) 1921
Dagger of the Mind (f Fearing) 1941
Dagon and Other Macabre Tales (f Lovecraft) 1965
Dahlberg Reader (o Dahlberg) 1967
Dahomean (f Yerby) 1971
Daily Notes of a Trip Around the World (o E. Howe) 1907
Daily Resolves (o Washington) 1896
Dain Curse (f Hammett) 1929
Daisy (f Oates) 1977
Daisy (pl Oates) 1980
Daisy Mayme (pl Kelly) 1927
Daisy Miller (pl H. James) 1883
Daisy Miller: A Study (f H. James) 1878
Daisy's First Winter and Other Stories (f Stowe) 1867
Dallas Galbraith (f Rebecca Davis) 1868
Dalva (f Harrison) 1988
Damaged Goods (f Sinclair) 1913
Damask Cheek (pl Van Druten) 1943
Damballah (f Wideman) 1981
Damn! A Book of Calumny (o Mencken) 1918
Damnation of Theron Ware (f Frederic) 1896
Damsel of Darien (f Simms) 1839
Dan the Newsboy (f Alger) 1893
Dan, The Detective (f Alger) 1884
Dance (pl Fornés) 1972
Dance and the Railroad (pl Hwang) 1981
Dance Hall of the Dead (f Hillerman) 1973
Dance of Death (f Bierce) 1877
Dance Photography (o Van Vechten) 1981
Dance Writings (o Van Vechten) 1975
Dances in Exile (pl Hwang) 1991
Dancing after Hours: Stories (f Dubus) 1996
Dancing Bears (po Merwin) 1954
Dancing Feather (f Ingraham) 1842
Dancing in the Chequered Shade (pl Van Druten) 1955
Dancing Mind (o Morrison) 1996
Dandelion Wine (f Bradbury) 1957

Dandelion Wine (pl Bradbury) 1977
Danger, Men Working (pl Queen) 1936?
Danger: Memory! (pl A. Miller) 1986
Dangerous Days (f Rinehart) 1919
Dangerous Ruffian (pl Howells) 1895
Dangerous Summer (o Hemingway) 1985
Dangerous Woman and Other Stories (f Farrell) 1957
Dangers of Intelligence and Other Science Essays (o Asimov) 1986
Dangling Man (f Bellow) 1944
Daniel (scr Doctorow) 1983
Daniel Jazz and Other Poems (po Lindsay) 1920
Danites and Other Choice Selections (o J. Miller) 1878
Danites in the Sierras (pl J. Miller) 1880
Danny's Own Story (f Marquis) 1912
Dan's Tribulations (pl Harrigan) 1884
Danse Macabre (o King) 1981
Dante (pl Baraka) 1961
Dante (po Duncan) 1974
Dante and His Influence: Studies (o Page) 1922
Danube (pl Fornés) 1982
Darby's Return (pl Dunlap) 1789
Dare-dare (f Himes) 1959
Dare's Gift and Other Stories (f Glasgow) 1924
Daring Twins (f Baum) 1911
Daring Young Man on the Flying Trapeze and Other Stories (f Saroyan) 1934
Dark Ages (o Asimov) 1968
Dark Angel (scr Hellman) 1935
Dark Arena (f Puzo) 1955
Dark at the Top of the Stairs (pl Inge) 1957
Dark Bridwell (f Fisher) 1931
Dark Brotherhood and Other Pieces (f Lovecraft) 1966
Dark Canyon (f L'Amour) 1963
Dark Carnival (f Bradbury) 1947
Dark City! and Its Bright Side (pl Daly) 1877
Dark Fields of the Republic: Poems, 1991-1995 (po Rich) 1995
Dark Green, Bright Red (f Vidal) 1950
Dark Half (f King) 1989
Dark Harbor: A Poem (po Strand) 1993
Dark Hours: Five Scenes from a History (pl Marquis) 1924
Dark Houses (po Hall) 1958
Dark Kingdom (po Patchen) 1942
Dark Lady (f Auchincloss) 1977
Dark Laughter (f S. Anderson) 1925
Dark Mother (f Frank) 1920
Dark of the Moon (po Teasdale) 1926
Dark People (o Bulosan) 1944
Dark Pony (pl Mamet) 1977
Dark Possession (tv Vidal) 1954
Dark Princess: A Romance (f Du Bois) 1928
Dark Room (pl T. Williams) 1948
Dark Summer (po Bogan) 1929
Dark Tower (pl Kaufman) 1934
Dark Tower II: Drawing of the Three (f King) 1987
Dark Tower III: The Waste Lands (f King) 1991
Dark Tower: The Gunslinger (f King) 1982
Dark Tunnel (f Macdonald) 1944
Dark Variations (pl Mamet) 1994
Dark Wind (f Hillerman) 1981
Darker Face of the Earth (pl Dove) 1994
Darker: Poems (po Strand) 1970

Darkling Child (pl Merwin) 1956
Darkness (f Mukherjee) 1985
Darkness and the Deep (f Fisher) 1943
Darkness around Us Is Deep: Selected Poems (po W. Stafford) 1993
Darkness at Ingraham's Crest (f Yerby) 1979
Darkness at Noon (pl Kingsley) 1951
Darkness at the Window (pl B. Smith) 1938
Darkness Visible: A Memoir of Madness (o Styron) 1990
Darkwater: Voices from within the Veil (o Du Bois) 1920
Darling of the Gods (pl Belasco) 1902
Dartmouth Lyrics (po Hovey) 1924
Das Frühwerk (f Traven) 1977
Das Totenschiff (f Traven) 1926
Dashes at Life with a Free Pencil (f Willis) 1845
Date 1601: Conversation as It Was by the Social Fireside in the Time of the Tudors (f Twain) 1880
Dateline: Toronto: The Complete Toronto Star Dispatches, 1920 to 1924 (o Hemingway) 1985
Daughter of Han (o Lim) 1983
Daughter of the Morning (f Gale) 1917
Daughter of the Philistines (f Boyesen) 1883
Daughter of the Snows (f London) 1902
Daughter of the Vine (f Atherton) 1899
Daughters (f Marshall) 1991
Daughters of Destiny (f Baum) 1906
Daughters of Nijo, a Romance of Japan (f Eaton) 1904
Daughters of the Rich (pl London) 1971
Daughters of the Rich (f Saltus) 1909
Daughter's Geography (po Shange) 1983
Daumier, Caricaturist (pl H. James) 1954
David Dubinsky: A Pictorial Biography (o Dewey) 1951
David Harum (scr Green) 1934
David Starr: Space Ranger (f Asimov) 1952
Dawn (pl Alurista) 1974
Dawn Ginsbergh's Revenge (o S. Perelman) 1929
Dawn O'Hara, The Girl Who Laughed (f Ferber) 1911
Dawn of a To-morrow (f Burnett) 1906
Dawn of a Tomorrow (pl Burnett) 1909
Dawn over Chungking (o Lin Tai-yi) 1941
Day after the Fair: A Collection of Plays and Short Stories (f Purdy) 1977
Day after Tomorrow (f Heinlein) 1951
Day and Other Poems (po Goodman) 1954(?)
Day Book (o Creeley) 1970
Day Book (po Creeley) 1972
Day by Day (po Lowell) 1977
Day for Surprises (pl Guare) 1970
Day in the Life of Old Japan (o Hearn) 1995
Day It Rained Forever (f Bradbury) 1959
Day It Rained Forever (pl Bradbury) 1966
Day It Rained Forever (tv Bradbury) 1990
Day of Deliverance (po W. Benét) 1944
Day of Doom (po Wigglesworth) 1662(?)
Day of the Beast (f Grey) 1922
Day of the Locust (f N. West) 1939
Day of the Swallows (pl Portillo Trambley) 1971
Day of Their Wedding (f Howells) 1896
Day Room (pl Delillo) 1987
Day the Dancers Came: Selected Prose Works (o Santos) 1967
Day the Money Stopped (pl M. Anderson) 1958

Day the Pig Fell into the Well (f Cheever) 1978
Day the Whores Came Out to Play Tennis (pl Kopit) 1965
Day We Went West (pl Harrigan) 1871
Daybreakers (f L'Amour) 1960
Days and Nights in Calcutta (o Mukherjee) 1977
Days and Nights in Calcutta (scr Mukherjee) 1991
Days Between (pl R. Anderson) 1965
Day's End (pl W. Benét) 1939
Days Gone By and Other Poems (po Riley) 1895
Days, Tangier Journal: 1987-89 (o Bowles) 1991
Days to Come (pl Hellman) 1936
Days without End (pl O'Neill) 1934
Dead End (scr Hellman) 1937
Dead End (pl Kingsley) 1935
Dead Father (f Barthelme) 1975
Dead Fingers Talk (f W. Burroughs) 1963
Dead Lecturer (po Baraka) 1964
Dead Muse: The Writer as Artist, the Artist as Writer (o Gass) 1997
Dead of Spring (f Goodman) 1950
Dead Reckoning (po Fearing) 1938
Dead Sea Scrolls 1947-1969 (o E. Wilson) 1969
Dead Seal near McClure's Beach (po Bly) 1973
Dead Yellow Women (f Hammett) 1947
Dead Zone (f King) 1979
Deadeye Dick (f Vonnegut) 1982
Deadline at Dawn (scr Odets) 1946
Deadlock (f Paretsky) 1984
Deaf Girl Playing (po J. Tate) 1970
Deal in Wheat and Other Stories of the New and Old West (f Norris) 1903
Dean Dunham (f Alger) 1890
Dean's December (f Bellow) 1982
Dear Adolf (radio S. Benét) 1942
Dear Arthur (tv Vidal) 1960
Dear Baby (f Saroyan) 1944
Dear John, Dear Coltrane (po M. Harper) 1970
Dear Judas and Other Poems (po Jeffers) 1929
Dear Juliette: Letters of May Sarton to Juliette Huxley (o Sarton) 1999
Dear Lovely Death (po Hughes) 1931
Dear Mr. President (po Snyder) 1965
Dear Old Darling (pl Cohan) 1935
Dear Rafe (f Hinojosa) 1985
Dear Sammy: Letters from Stein to Alice B. Toklas (o Stein) 1977
Dearly Beloved (f Fitzgerald) 1969
Death and Birth of David Markand: An American Story (f Frank) 1934
Death and Taxes (po Parker) 1931
Death at the Rodeo (f Queen) 1951
Death Before Bedtime (f Vidal) 1953
Death Comes for the Archbishop (f Cather) 1927
Death Dealers (f Asimov) 1958
Death Has Lost Its Charm for Me (po Bradbury) 1987
Death in the Afternoon (o Hemingway) 1932
Death in the Castle (f Buck) 1965
Death in the Family (f Agee) 1957
Death in the Fifth Position (f Vidal) 1952
Death in the Woods and Other Stories (f S. Anderson) 1933
Death Is a Lonely Business (f Bradbury) 1985
Death Kit (f Sontag) 1978

Death Likes It Hot (f Vidal) 1954
Death Notebooks (po Sexton) 1974
Death of a Child (o O'Connor) 1961
Death of a Doxy (f Stout) 1966
Death of a Dude (f Stout) 1969
Death of a Man (f Boyle) 1936
Death of a Salesman (pl A. Miller) 1949
Death of Bessie Smith (pl Albee) 1960
Death of Billy the Kid (tv Vidal) 1955
Death of Cock Robin (po Snodgrass) 1989
Death of General Montgomery at the Siege of Quebec (pl Brackenridge) 1777
Death of Jim Loney (f Welch) 1979
Death of King Philip (pl Linney) 1979
Death of Malcolm X (pl Baraka) 1969
Death of Methuselah and Other Stories (f Singer) 1988
Death of Nora Ryan (f Farrell) 1978
Death of the Kapowsin Tavern (po Hugo) 1965
Death of the Last Black Man in the Whole World (pl Parks) 1990
Death Ship (f Traven) 1934
Death, Sleep, and the Traveler (f Hawkes) 1974
Death Takes a Holiday (scr M. Anderson) 1934
Death to the Death of Poetry (o Hall) 1994
Death-Dealing Gold (f Arthur) 1890
Deaths for the Ladies and Other Disasters (po Mailer) 1962
Deborah (pl L. Mitchell) 1892
Debridement (po M. Harper) 1973
Debt of Honor: The Story of Gerald Lane's Success in the Far West (f Alger) 1900
Debtor (f Freeman) 1905
Debtor and Creditor (f Arthur) 1848
Debtor's Daughter (f Arthur) 1850
Decade of Negro Self-Expression (o Locke) 1928
Decennium Lactuosum (o Mather) 1699
Deception (f P. Roth) 1990
Declaration of Independence (o Jefferson) 1776
Declaration of the Gentlemen (o Mather) 1689
Déclassée (pl Akins) 1919
Decline and Fall of the English System of Finance (o Paine) 1796
Deconstruction and Criticism (o Bloom) 1979
Decoration of Houses (o Wharton) 1897
Decorative Plaques (o Freeman) 1883
Dedication: Motet for Six Voices (po MacLeish) 1938
Dedication: The Gift Outright (po Frost) 1961
Dedications and Other Dark Horses (po Komunyakaa) 1977
Deed from the King of Spain (pl James Baldwin) 1974
Deep Mrs. Sykes (pl Kelly) 1946
Deep Sleep (f Morris) 1953
Deep Tangled Wildwood (pl Connelly; Kaufman) 1923
Deeper Wrong (o Jacobs) 1862
Deephaven (f Jewett) 1877
Deer Park (f Mailer) 1955
Deer Park (pl Mailer) 1960
Deer Stalker (f Grey) 1949
Deerslayer (f Cooper) 1841
Defeat (pl M. Warren) 1773
Defective Santa Claus (po Riley) 1904
Defence of the Whigs (o Kennedy) 1844
Defenestration of Prague (po S. Howe) 1983
Defense (f Nabokov) 1964
Defiance (f Maso) 1996

Deformed Boy (f Sedgwick) 1826
Degarmo's Wife and Other Stories (f D. Phillips) 1913
DeGaulle Story (pl Faulkner) 1984
Degradation of the Democratic Dogma (o Adams) 1919
Delaplaine's Repository of the Lives and Portraits of Distinguished American Characters (o Barker) 1817
Delicacy and Strength of Lace: Letters Between Silko and James A. Wright (o Silko) 1986
Delicate Balance (pl Albee) 1966
Delicate Balance (scr Albee) 1976
Delicate Prey and Other Stories (f Bowles) 1950
Delicious (scr Behrman) 1931
Deliverance (f Dickey) 1970
Deliverance (scr Dickey) 1972
Deliverance (f Glasgow) 1904
Deliverance: A Screenplay (pl Dickey) 1981
Delta of Venus: Erotica (f Nin) 1977
Delta Wedding (f Welty) 1946
Deluge (f D. Phillips) 1905
Delusions, Etc (po Berryman) 1972
DeLuxe (pl Bromfield) 1934
Demagogue (f Nasby) 1891
Democracy (f Didion) 1984
Democracy (o Jefferson) 1939
Democracy (pl Linney) 1976
Democracy: An American Novel (f Adams) 1880
Democracy and Education: An Introduction to the Philosophy of Education (o Dewey) 1916
Democracy and Education in the World of Today (o Dewey) 1938
Democracy and Esther (pl Linney) 1974
Democracy and Other Addresses (o J. Lowell) 1887
Democratic John Bunyan (f Nasby) 1880
Democratic Vistas (o Whitman) 1870
Demolition Downtown: Count Ten in Arabic—Then Run (pl T. Williams) 1976
Demon and Other Tales (f Oates) 1996
Demon Lady (po Whittier) 1894
Denise (pl Daly) 1885
Dentist and Patient and Husband and Wife (pl Saroyan) 1968
Departure of the Ships (po Nemerov) 1966
Deplorable State of New-England (o Mather) 1708
Deputy Sheriff of Comanche County (f E. Burroughs) 1940
Der Busch (f Traven) 1928
Der Karren (f Traven) 1931
Der Marsch ins Reich der Caoba: Ein Kriegsmarsch (f Traven) 1933
Der Schatz der Sierra Madre (f Traven) 1927
Der Wobbly (f Traven) 1926
Derivations: Selected Poems 1950-1956 (po Duncan) 1968
Descansos: An Interrupted Journey (o Anaya) 1997
Descendant (f Glasgow) 1897
Descending Figure (po Glück) 1980
Descent of Man and Other Stories (f Wharton) 1904
Descent to the Dead: Poems Written in Ireland and Great Britain (po Jeffers) 1931
Description of Life (f Riding) 1980
Description of the Dismal Swamp and a Proposal to Drain the Swamp (o Byrd) 1922
Description without Place (po Stevens) 1945
Descriptions of Literature (o Stein) 1926
Desdemona (pl Vogel) 1979

Desert Gold (f Grey) 1913
Desert Incident (pl Buck) 1959
Desert Is Yours (o E. Gardner) 1963
Desert Music and Other Poems (po W. Williams) 1954
Desert Notes: Reflections in the Eye of a Raven (o Lopez) 1976
Desert of Wheat (f Grey) 1919
Desert Reservation (o Lopez) 1980
Desert Rose (f McMurtry) 1983
Deserter and Other Stories: A Book of Two Wars (f Frederic) 1898
Design for Living (scr Hecht) 1933
Design for Loving (tv Bradbury) 1958
Design in the Oriole (po W. Stafford) 1977
Desire (po Villanueva) 1998
Desire Me (scr Akins) 1947
Desire under the Elms (pl O'Neill) 1924
Desolation Angels (f Kerouac) 1965
Despair (f Nabokov) 1937
Desperado (scr Leonard) 1988
Desperation (f King) 1996
Despot of Broomsedge Cove (f Murfree) 1889
Dessins (o Bellow) 1960
Destination (po J. Tate) 1967
Destination Moon (scr Heinlein) 1950
Destinies of Darcy Dancer, Gentleman (f Donleavy) 1977
Destruction of Gotham (f J. Miller) 1886
Destruction of Jerusalem (pl Bannister) 1837
Desultory Days (po Creeley) 1978
Details of a Sunset and Other Stories (f Nabokov) 1976
Detective Story (pl Kingsley) 1949
Developing Imagination (o Frye) 1963
Device Out of Time (pl Bradbury) 1986
Devil and Daniel Webster (f S. Benét) 1937
Devil and Daniel Webster (pl S. Benét) 1939
Devil Catchers (pl Bullins) 1971
Devil Finds Work: An Essay (o James Baldwin) 1976
Devil in Kansas (f M. Smith) 1974
Devil Is a Woman (scr Dos Passos) 1935
Devil Take the Hindmost (o E. Wilson) 1932
Devil to Pay (f Queen) 1938
Devil Tree (f Kosinski) 1973
Devil's Advocate: A Bierce Readers (o Bierce) 1987
Devils and Angels (pl Eberhart) 1956
Devils and Canon Barham: Ten Essays on Poets, Novelists, and Monsters (o E. Wilson) 1973
Devil's Dictionary (o Bierce) 1911
Devil's Dream (f L. Smith) 1992
Devil's Laughter (f Yerby) 1953
Devil's Own Dear Son (f Cabell) 1949
Devil's Stocking (f Algren) 1983
Devilseed (f Yerby) 1984
Devotees in the Garden of Love (pl Parks) 1991
Dewey and Arthur F. Bentley: A Philosophical Correspondence 1932-1951 (o Dewey) 1964
Dewey: His Contribution to the American Tradition (o Dewey) 1955
Dewey on Education (o Dewey) 1959
Dhalgren (f S. Delany) 1975
Dharma Bums (f Kerouac) 1958
Diadem of Snow (pl Rice) 1929
Dialect Determinism (pl Bullins) 1965
Dialect Poetry (po McKay) 1972

Dialogue: James Baldwin and Nikki Giovanni (o James Baldwin; Giovanni) 1973
Dialogue with John Dewey (o Farrell) 1959
Dialogues in Limbo (o Santayana) 1925
Diamond As Big As the Ritz and Other Stories (f Fitzgerald) 1997
Diamond Cutters and Other Poems (po Rich) 1955
Diamond Head (f Waters) 1948
Diamond Wedding (f Steele) 1950
Diamonds (pl B. Howard) 1872
Diana Stair (f Dell) 1932
Diane (scr Isherwood) 1955
Diaries, 1936-41 (o S. Anderson) 1987
Diaries of Adam and Eve (f Twain) 1996
Diary (o Nin) 1966-76
Diary (o E. Taylor) 1964
Diary 1653-1657 (o Wigglesworth) 1965
Diary 1674-1729 (o Sewall) 1878-82
Diary and Life of Samuel Sewall (o Sewall) 1998
Diary in Canada (o Whitman) 1904
Diary of a Hackney Coachman (f Ingraham) 1844
Diary of a Man of Fifty, and A Bundle of Letters (f H. James) 1880
Diary of a Yuppie (f Auchincloss) 1987
Diary of an Office Seeker (f Nasby) 1881
Diary of Delia; Being a Veracious Chronicle of the Kitchen, with Some Side-Lights on the Parlour (f Eaton) 1907
Diary of H.L. Mencken (o Mencken) 1989
Diary: The Memoirs of a Dramatist, Theatrical Manager, Painter, Critic, Novelist, and Historian (o Dunlap) 1930
(Diblos) Notebook (f Merrill) 1965
Dick Gibson Show (f Elkin) 1971
Dictator (pl Richard Davis) 1904
Dictionary of Education (o Dewey) 1959
Did You Write My Name in the Snow? (pl Guare) 1963
Dido and Aeneas, Music by Wister (pl Wister) 1882
Dido, Queen of Hearts (f Atherton) 1929
Die Baumwollpflücker (f Traven) 1929
Die Brücke im Dschungel (f Traven) 1929
Die Rebellion der Gehenkten (f Traven) 1936
Die Troza (f Traven) 1936
Die weisse Rose (f Traven) 1929
Dien Cai Dau (po Komunyakaa) 1988
Different Person: A Memoir (o Merrill) 1993
Different Seasons (f King) 1982
Difficulty of Crossing a Field (pl Wellman) 1998
Diff'rent (pl O'Neill) 1920
Digby's Secretary (pl Gillette) 1884
Digging for Gold: A Story of California (f Alger) 1892
Diluvium Ignis (o Mather) 1730
Dimestore Alchemy (o Simic) 1992
Dinner at Eight (pl Ferber; Kaufman) 1932
Dinner at the Homesick Restaurant (f A. Tyler) 1982
Dinosaur Tales (f Bradbury) 1983
Dionysus in Doubt (po Robinson) 1925
Diplomacy (pl Gillette) 1914
Diplomatic Adventure (f S. Mitchell) 1906
Dirty Dingus Magee (scr Heller) 1970
Dirty Dinky and Other Creatures: Poems for Children (o Roethke) 1973
Dirty Eddie (f Bemelmans) 1947
Disagreeable Woman: A Social Mystery (f Alger) 1895

Disappearance of the Jews (pl Mamet) 1983

Disappearing Acts (f McMillan) 1989

Disappearing Man and Other Mysteries (f Asimov) 1985

Discarded Son (f Alger) 1981

Discordant Encounters: Plays and Dialogues (pl E. Wilson) 1926

Discourse at the Society of Theophilanthropists (o Paine) 1798

Discourse Concerning the Plague, With Some Preservations Against It (o Byrd) 1721

Discourse on the Life, Character, and Genius of Washington Irving (o Bryant) 1860

Discourses on Various Important Subjects (o Edwards) 1738

Discoveries and Inventions: Victories of the American Spirit (po MacKaye) 1950

Discovery of the Great West (o Parkman) 1869

Disengaged (pl H. James) 1894

Disfranchisement (o Du Bois) 1912

Dishonored Lady (pl Sheldon) 1930

Dismantling the Silence (po Simic) 1971

Disposal (pl Inge) 1968

Dispossessed (po Berryman) 1948

Disreputable Mr. Reagan (pl Richard Davis) 1895

Dissertation on Acute Pericarditis (o Holmes) 1937

Dissertation on First Principles of Government (o Paine) 1795

Dissertation on Liberty and Necessity, Pleasure and Pain (o Franklin) 1725

Dissertations by Mr. Dooley (o Dunne) 1906

Distaff Side (pl Van Druten) 1933

Distance (po Creeley) 1964

Distance from Loved Ones (po J. Tate) 1990

Distance to the Moon (pl Wellman) 1986

Distances (po Olson) 1960

Distances in Time (po Santos) 1983

Distant Episode: The Selected Stories (f Bowles) 1989

Distant Mirror (o Tuchman) 1978

Distant Stars (f S. Delany) 1981

Distinguishing Marks of a Work of the Spirit of God (o Edwards) 1741

Distortions (f Beattie) 1976

Distressing Dialogues (o Millay) 1924

District of Columbia (f Dos Passos) 1952

Diva's Ruby: A Sequel to Soprano and Primadonna (f Crawford) 1908

Divers Views, Opinions, and Prophecies of Yours Trooly, Petroleum V. Nasby (f Nasby) 1866

Diversifications (po Ammons) 1975

Diversion (pl Van Druten) 1928

Diverting History of John Bull and Brother Jonathan (f Paulding) 1812

Divine and Supernatural Light (o Edwards) 1734

Divine Comedies (po Merrill) 1976

Divine Gesture: A Fable (f Hemingway) 1974

Divine Passion (f Fisher) 1948

Divine Pilgrim (po Aiken) 1949

Divine Tragedy (po Longfellow) 1871

Diving into the Wreck: Poems, 1971-1972 (po Rich) 1973

Diving Rock on the Hudson (f H. Roth) 1995

Divisions and Other Early Poems (po Creeley) 1968

Divorce (pl Daly) 1884

Divorce of Lady X (scr Sherwood) 1938

Divorced Wife (f Arthur) 1850

Dix Portraits (o Stein) 1930

Do and Dare (f Alger) 1884

Do I Hear a Waltz? (pl Laurents) 1965

Do Tell Me, Doctor Johnson (f Marquand) 1928

Do These Bones Live (o Dahlberg) 1941

Do with Me What You Will (f Oates) 1973

Do You Remember?: The Whimsical Letters of H.L. Mencken and Philip Goodman (o Mencken) 1994

"Doc" Gordon (f Freeman) 1906

Doc' Horne (f Ade) 1899

Dock Ellis in the Country of Baseball (o Hall) 1976

Doctor (f Rinehart) 1936

Doctor and Patient (o S. Mitchell) 1888

Doctor Breen's Practice (f Howells) 1881

Dr. Bull (scr Green) 1933

Doctor Claudius (pl Crawford) 1897

Doctor Claudius: A True Story (f Crawford) 1883

Dr. Grimshaw's Secret: A Romance (f Hawthorne) 1883

Dr. Heidenhoff's Process (f Bellamy) 1880

Doctor Huguet (f Donnelly) 1891

Dr. Jameson's Raiders vs. the Johannesburg Reformers (o Richard Davis) 1897

Dr. Jekyll and Mr. Hyde (tv Vidal) 1955

Dr. Johns, Being a Narrative of Certain Events in the Life of an Orthodox Minister of Connecticut (f D. Mitchell) 1866

Dr Jonathan (pl Churchill) 1919

Dr. Kheal (pl Fornés) 1968

Dr. Lavendar's People (f Deland) 1903

Doctor Martino and Other Stories (f Faulkner) 1934

Dr. North and His Friends (f S. Mitchell) 1900

Doctor Sax: Faust Part Three (f Kerouac) 1959

Dr. Sevier (f Cable) 1884

Doctor Slaughter (f Theroux) 1984

Doctor Vandyke (f J. Cooke) 1872

Dr. Warrick's Daughters (f Rebecca Davis) 1896

Doctor Watts's Imitation of the Psalms of David, Corrected and Enlarged (po Barlow) 1785

Doctor's Christmas Eve (f J. Allen) 1910

Doctor's Son and Other Stories (f J. O'Hara) 1935

Dodsworth (scr S. Howard) 1936

Dodsworth (pl S. Howard) 1934

Dodsworth (f Lewis) 1929

Dog (pl Mamet) 1983

Dog (pl Shepard) 1965

Dog and Gun: A Few Loose Chapters on Shooting (f Hooper) 1856

Dog Beneath the Skin (pl Isherwood) 1936

Dog in the Manger (pl Wellman) 1982

Dog on the Sun: A Volume of Stories (f Green) 1949

Dogeaters (f Hagedorn) 1990

Dogeaters (pl Hagedorn) 1998

Dogs (pl Saroyan) 1960

Dogs Bark: Public People and Private Places (o Capote) 1973

Dog's Death (po Updike) 1965

Dog's Mission (o Stowe) 1881

Dog's Tale (f Twain) 1904

Dogtown Common (po MacKaye) 1921

Dokumenty walki o czlowieka (o Kosinski) 1955

Doll Master (pl Belasco) 1874-75

Dollars and Sense (pl Daly) 1885

Dolley: A Novel of Dolley Madison in Love and War (f R Brown) 1994

Dolliver Romance and Other Pieces (f Hawthorne) 1876
Dolly: A Love Story (f Burnett) 1877
Dolores Claiborne (f King) 1992
Dolphin (po Lowell) 1973
Dombey and Son (pl Brougham) 1849(?)
Dome of Many-Coloured Glass (po A. Lowell) 1912
Domesday Book (po Masters) 1920
Dominant City (po Fletcher) 1913
Dominations and Powers: Reflections on Liberty, Society, and
    Government (o Santayana) 1951
Domnei (f Cabell) 1920
Don Carlos (pl Dunlap) 1799
Don Juan (f Goodman) 1979
Don Juan (pl Nelson) 1979
Don Juan (pl Wilbur) 1998
Don Juan in Texas (pl Kopit) 1957
Don Orsino (f Crawford) 1892
Don Pedro (pl L. Mitchell) 1892
Donald Duk (f Chin) 1991
Done in the Open (po Wister) 1903
Donkey Inside (o Bemelmans) 1941
Donna Florida (po Simms) 1843
Donny March (pl Mamet) 1981
Donovans (pl Harrigan) 1875
Don't Ask Questions (f Marquand) 1941
Don't Call Me By My Right Name and Other Stories (f Purdy)
    1956
Don't Count on It: A Note on the Number of the 1001 Nights (o
    Barth) 1984
Don't Cry, Scream (po Madhubuti) 1969
Don't Go Away Mad (pl Ginsberg) 1968
Don't Go Away Mad (pl Saroyan) 1949
Don't Let the Snow Fall: A Poem; Dawn: A Story (po Purdy)
    1984
Don't Look Now (pl Patchen) 1959
Don't Neglect Your Wife (scr Atherton) 1921
Don't Say That about Maine! (o Roberts) 1951
Don't You Turn Back (po Hughes) 1969
Don't You Want to Be Free? (pl Hughes) 1937
Doodle Soup (po Ciardi) 1985
Doom That Came to Sarnath (f Lovecraft) 1971
Doomsters (f Macdonald) 1958
Doomswoman (f Atherton) 1893
Door (f Rinehart) 1930
Door Between (f Queen) 1937
Door in the Hive (po Levertov) 1989
Door in the Wall (f La Farge) 1965
Door into Summer (f Heinlein) 1957
Doorbell Rung (f Stout) 1965
Dora and the Great Wide World (tv Bradbury) 1992
Doris House (pl Wilder) 1937
Dormant Fires (f Atherton) 1922
Dorothy and the Wizard in Oz (f Baum) 1908
Dorothy Richardson: An Adventure in Self-Discovery (o Gregory)
    1967
Dostoevsky: A Screenplay (scr Carver) 1985
Dot and Tot of Merryland (f Baum) 1901
Double Alibi (f Rinehart) 1932
Double Axe and Other Poems (po Jeffers) 1948
Double Barrelled Detective Story (f Twain) 1902
Double Discovery: A Journey (o J. West) 1980

Double Double (f Queen) 1950
Double Dream of Spring (po Ashbery) 1970
Double for Death (f Stout) 1939
Double Image (po Levertov) 1946
Double Indemnity (scr Chandler) 1944
Double Indemnity (pl Chandler) 1946
Double Life (pl Rinehart) 1906
Double or Quits (f E. Gardner) 1941
Double Planet (o Asimov) 1960
Double Star (f Heinlein) 1956
Double Vision: American Thoughts Abroad (o Knowles) 1964
Doubleheader (po Patchen) 1966
Doubling for Romeo (scr Rice) 1922
Douglass on Women's Rights (o Douglass) 1976
Dove (pl Barnes) 1926
Down Broadway (pl Harrigan) 1878
Down in Dixie (pl Harrigan) 1876
Down in My Heart (o W. Stafford) 1947
Down the Long Hills (f L'Amour) 1968
Down the Ravine (f Murfree) 1885
Down There on a Visit (f Isherwood) 1964
Down Wind from Gettysbury (tv Bradbury) 1992
Down-Easters (f Neal) 1833
Downing Legends: Stories in Rhyme (po De Forest) 1901
Doyle Brothers (pl Harrigan) 1875
Dracula (pl Wellman) 1987
Draft of Cantos XXXI-XLI (po Pound) 1935
Draft of XVI Cantos (po Pound) 1925
Draft of the Cantos 17-27 (po Pound) 1928
Draft of XXX Cantos (po Pound) 1930
Drafts and Fragments of Cantos CX-CXVII (po Pound) 1969
Dragon (f Bradbury) 1988
Dragon and the Unicorn (po Rexroth) 1952
Dragon Country: A Book of Plays (pl T. Williams) 1970
Dragon Harvest (f Sinclair) 1945
Dragon of Wantley (f Wister) 1892
Dragon Seed (f Buck) 1942
Dragon's Teeth (f Queen) 1939
Dragon's Teeth (f Sinclair) 1942
Dramatic Verses (po Stickney) 1902
Dramatic Works (pl Dunlap) 1806-16
Dramatism and Development (o Burke) 1972
Dramatist and the Amateur Public (o Barry) 1927
Dream Department (o S. Perelman) 1943
Dream Drops (f A. Lowell) 1887
Dream Girl (pl Rice) 1945
Dream Life of Balso Snell (f N. West) 1931
Dream Lovers (pl Dunbar) 1898
Dream Maker (pl Gillette) 1921
Dream of a Common Language: Poems, 1974-1977 (po Rich) 1978
Dream of Debs (f London) 1912(?)
Dream of Governors (po Simpson) 1959
Dream of Love (scr Lawson) 1928
Dream of Love (pl W. Williams) 1948
Dream of Santa Maria de las Piedras (f Méndez M.) 1989
Dream of the Golden Mountains: Remembering the 1930s (o
    Cowley) 1980
Dream Palaces (f Purdy) 1980
Dream Quest of Unknown Kadath (f Lovecraft) 1955
Dream Songs (po Berryman) 1969
Dreamer (f C. Johnson) 1998

Dreaming America and Other Poems (po Oates) 1973

Dreaming Emmett (pl Morrison) 1986

Dreaming of Babylon: A Private Eye Novel 1942 (f Brautigan) 1977

Dream-Keeper and Other Poems (po Hughes) 1932

Dream-Quest of Unknown Kadath (f Lovecraft) 1955

Dreams and Dust (po Marquis) 1915

Dreams and Fancies (o Lovecraft) 1962

Dreamy Kid (pl O'Neill) 1919

Dred: A Tale of the Great Dismal Swamp (f Stowe) 1856

Dred; or The Dismal Swamp (pl Brougham) 1856

Dress and Kindred Subjects (o Moore) 1965

Dress Gray (tv Vidal) 1986

Drift Fence (f Grey) 1933

Drift from Two Shores (f Harte) 1878

Driftglass: Ten Tales of Speculative Fiction (f S. Delany) 1971

Drifting Apart (pl Herne) 1888

Drifting Down the Delta (o E. Gardner) 1969

Drink (pl Belasco) 1879

Drinks before Dinner (pl Doctorow) 1979

Driving Blind: Stories (f Bradbury) 1997

Drowning (pl Fornés), 1985

Drowning Pool (f Macdonald) 1950

Drowning with Others (po Dickey) 1962

Drug-Shop (po S. Benét) 1917

Drugstore Cat (f Petry) 1949

Druid Circle (pl Van Druten) 1948

Drumbeats in Georgia: A Symphonic Drama of the Founding of Georgia by James Edward Oglethorpe (pl Green) 1973

Drums (f Boyd) 1925

Drum-Taps (po Whitman) 1865

Drunk in the Furnace (po Merwin) 1960

Drunk with Love (f Gilchrist) 1986

Drunken Sisters (pl Wilder) 1957

Drury Lane Boys' Club (o Burnett) 1892

Drury Lane's Last Case: The Tragedy of 1599 (f Queen) 1933

Dry Salvages (po Eliot) 1941

Dry Season (po Cowley) 1941

Du Barry (pl Belasco) 1901

Duane's Depressed (f McMurtry) 1999

Dubin's Lives (f Malamud) 1979

Duck Variations (pl Mamet) 1972

Ducks (po Bly) 1968

Dude Ranger (f Grey) 1951

Duet for Cannibals (scr Sontag) 1969

Duffels (f Eggleston) 1893

Duke Herring (f Bodenheim) 1931

Duke Humphrey's Dinner (pl F. O'Brien) 1856

Duke of Palermo and Other Plays (pl E. Wilson) 1969

Duke of Stockbridge: A Romance of Shays' Rebellion (f Bellamy) 1900

Duke's Motto (pl Brougham) 1870

Dulcy (pl Connelly; Kaufman) 1921

Duluth (f Vidal) 1983

Dunne Family (f Farrell) 1976

Dunnigan's Daughter (pl Behrman) 1946

Dunwich Horror (f Lovecraft) 1945

Dunwich Horror and Other Weird Tales (f Lovecraft) 1945

Dunwich Horror and Others (f Lovecraft) 1963

Duodecennium Lactuosum (o Mather) 1714

Duplex: A Black Love Fable in Four Movements (pl Bullins) 1971

Durable Fire (po Sarton) 1972

Durable Riches (o Mather) 1695

Durham Station (pl B. Smith) 1961

Dusk of Dawn: An Essay Toward an Autobiography of a Race Concept (o Du Bois) 1940

Dust and Ashes: An Essay upon Repentance (o Mather) 1710

Dust Tracks on a Road: An Autobiography (o Hurston) 1942

Dust Which Is God: A Novel in Verse (po W. Benét) 1941

Dust within the Rock (f Waters) 1940

Dutch Courage and Other Stories (f London) 1922

Dutch Shoe Mystery (f Queen) 1931

Dutchman (pl Baraka) 1964

Dutchman (scr Baraka) 1967

Dutchman's Fireside (f Paulding) 1831

Dutchman's Flat (f L'Amour) 1986

Dutiful Dan, The Brave Boy Detective (f Alger) 1895

Duty of Disobedience to the Fugitive Slave Act: An Appeal to the Legislators of Massachusetts (o Child) 1860

Duveen (o Behrman) 1952

Duwamish Head (po Hugo) 1976

Dwarf (tv Bradbury) 1989

Dwell in the Wilderness: Selected Short Stories: 1931-41 (f Santos) 1985

Dwelling-Place of Light (f Churchill) 1917

Dying Gladiators and Other Essays (o Gregory) 1961

Dying Like a Gentleman and Other Stories (f E. Howe) 1926

Dynamite (scr Lawson) 1929

Dynamite Voices I: Black Poets of the 1960s (o Madhubuti) 1971

Dynamo (pl O'Neill) 1929

Each in His Season (po Snodgrass) 1993

Eagle Eye (f Calisher) 1973

Eagle in the Egg (o La Farge) 1949

Eagle-Visioned/Feathered Adobes: Manito Sojourns & Pachuco Ramblings (po Sánchez) 1990

Eagle's Heart (f Garland) 1900

Eagle's Mile (po Dickey) 1990

Eagle's Shadow (f Cabell) 1904

Earlier Stories (f Burnett) 1878

Early Americana and Other Stories (f Richter) 1936

Early Asimov (f Asimov) 1972

Early Autumn (f Bromfield) 1926

Early Critical Essays 1820-1822 (o Cooper) 1955

Early History of the University of Virginia (o Jefferson) 1856

Early Lays (po Simms) 1827

Early Martyr and Other Poems (po W. Williams) 1935

Early Moon (o Sandburg) 1930

Early Motion (po Dickey) 1981

Early Piety Exemplified (o Mather) 1689

Early Poems (po Whittier) 1885

Early Poems 1920-28 (po Winters) 1966

Early Poems 1946-1951 (po F. O'Hara) 1976

Early Prose and Poetry (o Faulkner) 1962

Early Prose Writings (o J. Lowell) 1902

Early Religion Urged (o Mather) 1694

Early Routines (f W. Burroughs) 1981

Early Spring in Massachusetts (o Thoreau) 1881

Early Stories (f Cather) 1957

Early Tales and Sketches (f Twain) 1979-81

Early Worm (o Benchley) 1927

Early Writing (o F. O'Hara) 1977

Early Writings (o S. Anderson) 1989

Earp Brothers of Tombstone: The Story of Mrs. Virgil Earp (o Waters) 1960

Earth House Hold: Technical Notes and Queries to Fellow Dharma Revolutionaries (o Snyder) 1969

Earth Is Room Enough (f Asimov) 1957

Earth Men (tv Bradbury) 1992

Earth Triumphant and Other Tales in Verse (po Aiken) 1914

Earthbound (scr Lawson) 1940

Earthly Delights, Unearthly Adornments: American Writers as Image Makers (o Morris) 1978

Earthly Possessions (f A. Tyler) 1977

Earthquake (scr Puzo) 1974

East and West (f Buck) 1975

East and West Poems (po Harte) 1871

East Coker (po Eliot) 1940

East Is East (f Stribling) 1928

East Is West (scr Eaton) 1930

East of Eden (f Steinbeck) 1952

East of Sumatra (scr L'Amour

East Wind (po A. Lowell) 1926

East Wind: West Wind (f Buck) 1930

East Window: The Asian Translations (po Merwin) 1999

Easter Bells (po H. Jackson) 1884

Easter Island: Island of Enigmas (o Dos Passos) 1971

Eastward Ha! (o S. Perelman) 1977

Easy Introduction to the Slide Rule (o Asimov) 1965

Eating the Honey of Words: New and Selected Poems (po Bly) 1999

Eating Words (pl Nelson) 1990

Eavesdropper (f Lin Tai-yi) 1958

Ec'h-Pi-El Speaks: An Autobiographical Sketch (o Lovecraft) 1972

Eccentricities of a Nightingale (pl T. Williams) 1964

Ecclesiastical Writings (o Edwards) 1994

Echo (po Hoffman) 1844

Echo Club and Other Literary Diversions (o B. Taylor) 1876

Echoes (po Ciardi) 1989

Echoes (po Creeley) 1982

Echoes from the Sabine Farm, Being Certain Horatian Lyrics (po Field) 1891

Echoes of the Foot-Hills (po Harte) 1874

Eden (f Saltus) 1888

Eden Rose (pl R. Anderson) 1949

Edgar and the Teacher's Pet (scr Tarkington) 1920

Edgar Huntly (f Brown) 1799

Edgar, The Explorer (scr Tarkington) 1921

Edgar's Hamlet (scr Tarkington) 1920

Edgar's Little Saw (scr Tarkington) 1920

Edge (scr Mamet) 1997

Edge of Tomorrow (f Asimov) 1985

Edgewater People (f Freeman) 1918

Edith Wharton (o Auchincloss) 1961

Edith Wharton Abroad: Selected Travel Writings, 1888-1920 (o Wharton) 1995

Edith Wharton: A Woman in Her Time (o Auchincloss) 1971

Editha's Burglar (pl Burnett) 1890

Editor's Troubles (pl Harrigan) 1875

Editorials from the Kobe Chronicle (o Hearn) 1913

Edmond (pl Mamet) 1982

Edna Ferber: Stories (f Ferber) 1996

Edsel (f Shapiro) 1971

Educated Imagination (o Frye) 1964

Education and the Social Order (o Dewey) 1934

Education of Harriet Hatfield (f Sarton) 1989

Education of Henry Adams: An Autobiography (o Adams) 1907

Education of Oscar Fairfax (f Auchincloss) 1995

Education Today (o Dewey) 1940

Educational Essays (o Dewey) 1910

Educational Frontier (o Dewey) 1933

Educational Situation (o Dewey) 1902

Edward Austin (f Ingraham) 1842

Edward Manning (f Ingraham) 1847

Edwin Arlington Robinson (o Winters) 1946

Efficiency Expert (f E. Burroughs) 1966

Egeria (o Simms) 1853

Egg and Other Stories (f S. Anderson) 1992

Eggs of Things (o Sexton) 1963

Ego and Art in Walt Whitman (o Updike) 1980

Ego Is Always at the Wheel: Bagatelles (o Schwartz) 1986

Ego-Tripping and Other Poems for Young People (po Giovanni) 1973

Egoist (pl Hecht) 1922

Egoists: A Book of Supermen (o Huneker) 1909

Egotism in German Philosophy (o Santayana) 1915

Egypt (pl Sheldon) 1912

Egypt and Iceland in the Year 1874 (o B. Taylor) 1874

Egyptian Cross Mystery (f Queen) 1932

Egyptians (o Asimov) 1967

Eight Cousins (f Alcott) 1875

Eight Men (f R. Wright) 1961

Eight Mortal Ladies Possessed: A Book of Stories (f T. Williams) 1974

1876 (f Vidal) 1976

Eighteenth Presidency! (o Whitman) 1956

Eighth Day (f Wilder) 1967

8th Ditch (pl Baraka) 1964

Eighth Sin (po Morley) 1912

80 Flowers (po Zukofsky) 1978

'89 (f Tourgée) 1891

Eileen (pl Masters) 1910

Ein General kommt aus dem Dschungel (f Traven) 1940

Einstein (po MacLeish) 1929

Einstein Intersection (f S. Delany) 1967

Ekkoes from Kentucky (f Nasby) 1868

El Bronx Remembered: A Novella and Stories (f Mohr) 1975

El Hermano (pl Linney) 1981

El Hombre Cosmico (pl Portillo Trambley) 1975

El Salvador: Requiem and Invocation (po Levertov) 1984

El Salvador: The Work of Thirty Photographers (o Forché) 1983

El sol y los de abajo and Other R.C.A.F. Poems (po Montoya) 1972

El-Shaddai (o Mather) 1725

Elbow Room (f McPherson) 1977

Elder Statesman (pl Eliot) 1958

Eldest: A Drama of American Life (pl Ferber) 1925

Eldorado (pl Kaufman) 1931

Eldorado (o B. Taylor) 1850

Eleanor Roosevelt Story (scr MacLeish) 1965

Eleanor Sherwood, The Beautiful Temptress! (f Ingraham) 1844

Election Machine Warehouse (pl Baraka) 1997

Electric Kool-Aid Acid Test (o Tom Wolfe) 1968

Electricity (pl Gillette) 1910

Electricity and Man (o Asimov) 1972
Electronic Nigger (pl Bullins) 1968
Elegiac Poem on the Death of George Whitfield (po Wheatley) 1770
Elegies (po Rukeyser) 1949
Elegy for My Father (po Strand) 1978
Elegy of the Late Titus Hosmer (po Barlow) 1782
Elegy on Nathaniel Collins (o Mather) 1685
Elegy on the Death of Mr. Buckingham St. John (po Trumbull) 1771
Elegy to Mary Moorhead (po Wheatley) 1773
Elegy to Samuel Cooper (po Wheatley) 1784
Elementals (pl S. Benét) 1940-41
Elementary Geography (o Stowe) 1835
Elements of San Joaquin (po Soto) 1977
Elements of Style (o White) 1959
Elephant and Other Stories (f Carver) 1988
Elephi: The Cat with the High I.Q (o J. Stafford) 1962
Eleutheria (o Mather) 1698
Elevator (pl Howells) 1885
Eleven Lady-Lyrics and Other Poems (po Chávez) 1945
Eleven New Cantos: XXXI-XLI (po Pound) 1934
Eleven Untitled Poems (po W. Stafford) 1968
Eleven Verse Plays 1929-1939 (pl M. Anderson) 1940
Eliot (po Channing) 1885
Elizabeth (pl Crothers) 1899
Elizabeth Appleton (f J. O'Hara) 1963
Elizabeth in Her Holy Retirement (o Mather) 1710
Elizabeth Madox Roberts: A Personal Note (o Wescott) 1930
Elizabeth the Queen (pl M. Anderson) 1930
Ellen Foster (f Gibbons) 1987
Ellen Glasgow (o Auchincloss) 1964
Ellen Hart (f Ingraham) 1844
Ellen Rogers (f Farrell) 1941
Ellery Queen, Master Detective (scr Queen) 1940
Ellie (f J. Cooke) 1855
Elmer Gantry (f Lewis) 1927
Elmer the Great (pl Lardner) 1928
Elsie Venner: A Romance of Destiny (f Holmes) 1861
Elsket and Other Stories (f Page) 1891
Elucidation (o Stein) 1927
E.M. Forster (o Trilling) 1943
Embargo (po Barker) 1808
Embarrassments (f H. James) 1896
Embezzler (f Auchincloss) 1966
Emblems of Fidelity: A Comedy in Letters (f J. Allen) 1919
Embodiment of Knowledge (o W. Williams) 1974
Embroideries (po Levertov) 1969
Emerald (f Barthelme) 1980
Emerald City of Oz (f Baum) 1910
Emersonianism (o Updike) 1984
Emily Dickinson's Open Folios (o Dickinson) 1995
Emily's Bread: Poems (o Gilbert and Gubar) 1984
Emissary (tv Bradbury) 1988
Emma McChesney & Co (f Ferber) 1915
Emperor Jones (pl O'Neill) 1920
Empire (f Vidal) 1987
Empire City (f Goodman) 1959
Empire Star (f S. Delany) 1966
Empire: A Visual Novel (f S. Delany) 1978
Empress of the Splendid Season (f Hijuelos) 1999

Empty Land (f L'Amour) 1969
Empty Mirror: Early Poems (po Ginsberg) 1961
Empty Purse: A Christmas Story (f Jewett) 1905
Enchanted Island of Yew (f Baum) 1903
Enchanted Isle (f Cain) 1985
Enchanted Maze: The Story of a Modern Student in Dramatic Form (pl Green) 1935
Enchanter (f Nabokov) 1986
Enclave (pl Laurents) 1973
Encore (f Deland) 1907
Encore: A Journal of the Eightieth Year (o Sarton) 1993
Encounter in April (po Sarton) 1937
Encounters with Chinese Writers (o Dillard) 1984
Encyclopedia of the Negro: Preparatory Volume (o Du Bois) 1945
Encyclopedia of the Theatre (o Nathan) 1940
End of a Sentence (tv Nelson) 1991
End of Desire (f Herrick) 1932
End of Eternity (f Asimov) 1955
End of Summer (pl Behrman) 1936
End of the Road (f Barth) 1958
End of the World (pl Kopit) 1984
End of the World: A Love Story (f Eggleston) 1872
End to Innocence: Essays on Culture and Politics (o Fiedler) 1955
End to Torment: A Memoir of Ezra Pound (o Doolittle) 1979
End Zone (f Delillo) 1972
Endgame: A Journal of the Seventy-Ninth Year (o Sarton) 1992
Endless Life: Selected Poems (po Ferlinghetti) 1981
Endor (pl Nemerov) 1962
Ends of the Earth: The Polar Regions of the World (o Asimov) 1975
Enemies: A Love Story (f Singer) 1972
Enemies: The Clash of Races (o Madhubuti) 1978
Enemy from Eden (o Dickey) 1978
Enemy Gods (f La Farge) 1937
Enemy Had It Too (pl Sinclair) 1950
Enemy of the People (pl A. Miller) 1951
Enemy: Time (pl T. Williams) 1959
Energies of Men (o W. James) 1908
Energumen (pl Wellman) 1985
Engineer of Moonlight (pl Delillo) 1979
England, A Dying Oligarchy (o Bromfield) 1939
England and Yesterday: A Book of Short Poems (po Guiney) 1898
England, with Sketches of Society in the Metropolis (o Cooper) 1837
English and Romantic Poets and Essayists (o Frye) 1957
English Hours (pl H. James) 1905
English Lands, Letters, and Kings (o D. Mitchell) 1889-97
English Notebooks (o Hawthorne) 1941
English Novel and the Principle of Its Development (o Lanier) 1883
English Poets, Lessing, Rousseau: Essays (o J. Lowell) 1888
English Prosody and Modern Poetry (o Shapiro) 1947
English Traits (o Emerson) 1856
Enigma (pl Dell) 1915
Enlarged Devil's Dictionary (o Bierce) 1967
Enlistment for the Farm (o Dewey) 1917
Enormous Changes at the Last Minute (f Paley) 1974
Enormous Radio and Other Stories (f Cheever) 1953
Enormous Room (f Cummings) 1922
Enough Rope (po Parker) 1926
Entertainment of a Nation; or Three Sheets in the Wind (o Nathan) 1942

Enthralled: A Story of International Life (f Saltus) 1894
Enthusiast (f Crews) 1981
Environments Out There (o Asimov) 1967
Eonchs of Ruby: A Gift of Love (po Chivers) 1851
Epic of Arkansas (po Fletcher) 1936
Epic of Wheat: (f Norris) 1901
Epilogos (po Duncan) 1967
Episode of Fiddletown and Other Sketches (f Harte) 1873
Episode of the Wandering Knife: Three Mystery Tales (f Rinehart) 1950
Episodes in Van Bibber's Life (f Richard Davis) 1899
Epistle to the Christian Indians (o Mather) 1700
Epistle to Walter Scott (po Brackenridge) 1811(?
Epistles of Care (f Purdy) 1995
Epitaph (po Dreiser) 1930
Epitaph for Willie (scr Bambara) 1982
Epitaphs of Our Times: The Letters of Dahlberg (o Dahlberg) 1967
Equality (f Bellamy) 1897
Equinox (f S. Delany) 1994
Era (po Zukofsky) 1970
Erie Train Boy (f Alger) 1890
Erik Dorn (f Hecht) 1921
Erminie (pl Connelly) 1921
Errand Boy (f Alger) 1888
Errata (o Hopkinson) 1763
Errata (f Neal) 1823
Escape (pl W. Brown) 1858
Escape from 5 Shadows (f Leonard) 1956
Escape on Venus (f E. Burroughs) 1946
Esmeralda (pl Gillette) 1881
Essay on Rime (po Shapiro) 1945
Essay on the Use and Advantages of the Fine Arts (o Trumbull) 1770
Essays (o White) 1977
Essays and Poems (o Very) 1839
Essays and Sketches (f W. Irving) 1837
Essays in Anglo-Saxon Law (o Adams) 1876
Essays in European and Oriental Literature (o Hearn) 1923
Essays in Experimental Logic (o Dewey) 1916
Essays in Literary Criticism (o Santayana) 1956
Essays in London and Elsewhere (pl H. James) 1893
Essays in Radical Empiricism (o W. James) 1912
Essays on American Literature (o Hearn) 1929
Essays on Faith and Morals (o W. James) 1943
Essays on German Literature (o Boyesen) 1892
Essays on Scandinavian Literature (o Boyesen) 1895
Essays, Speeches, and Public Letters (o Faulkner) 1966
Essays to Do Good (o Mather) 1807
Essence of Tragedy and Other Footnotes and Papers (o M. Anderson) 1939
Essential Faulkner (o Cowley) 1967
Essential Hemingway (f Hemingway) 1947
Essential Jefferson (o Jefferson) 1963
Essential Mailer (o Mailer) 1982
Essential Matthew Arnold (o Trilling) 1969
Essential Writings (o Dewey) 1977
Essential Writings (o W. James) 1971
Essentials (o Toomer) 1931
Estate (f Singer) 1969
Estelle (f Ingraham) 1844
Esther (f Adams) 1884

Esther (pl Hughes) 1957
Esthetique du Mal (po Stevens) 1945
Et Cetera: A Collector's Scrap-Book (o S. Crane) 1924
Etcetera: The Unpublished Poems (po Cummings) 1983
Eternal Lover (f E. Burroughs) 1925
Eternal Savage (f E. Burroughs) 1963
Ethan Frome (scr Nelson) 1993
Ethan Frome (f Wharton) 1911
Ethics (o Dewey) 1908
Ethics of Change: Humanistic Values vs. Technological Imperatives (o Nemerov) 1989
Ethics of Democracy (o Dewey) 1888
Etiquette of Courtship and Marriage (o Mowatt) 1844
Eufemia (pl Merwin) 1958
Eulogies (o Baraka) 1996
Eulogium of the Brave Men Who Have Fallen in the Contest with Great Britain (o Brackenridge) 1779
Eureka (pl Harrigan) 1874
Eureka: A Prose Poem (o Poe) 1848
Europe after 8:15 (o Mencken, Nathan) 1914
Europe of Trusts: Selected Poems (po S. Howe) 1989
Europe without Baedeker: Sketches among the Ruins of Italy, Greece, and England (o E. Wilson) 1947
Europe's Morning After (o Roberts) 1921
Europe's Two Frontiers (o Fletcher) 1930
Europeans: A Sketch (f H. James) 1878
Eustace Chisholm and the Works (f Purdy) 1967
Eutaw: A Sequel to The Forayers (f Simms) 1856
Evangeline: A Tale of Acadie (po Longfellow) 1847
Eve Effingham (f Cooper) 1838
Eve of St. Mark (pl M. Anderson) 1942
Evelyn (f Mowatt) 1845
Evelyn Brown: A Diary (pl Fornés) 1980
Even in Quiet Places: Poems (po W. Stafford) 1996
Even in the Best Families (f Stout) 1951
Even the Stars Look Lonesome (o Angelou) 1997
Evening Clothes (pl Gale) 1932
Evening Dress (pl Howells) 1893
Evening in the Country (po Ashbery) 1970
Evening Star (f McMurtry) 1992
Evening Train (po Levertov) 1993
Evening's Journey to Conway, Massachusetts: An Outdoor Play (pl MacLeish) 1967
Evening's Frost (pl Hall) 1965
Ever Been in Love with a Midget (pl Saroyan) 1957
Evergreen Tree (pl MacKaye) 1917
Everlasting Gospel (o Mather) 1700
Every Day Is Saturday (o White) 1934
Every Soul Is a Circus (po Lindsay) 1929
Everybody Does It (scr Cain) 1949
Everybody Wins (scr A. Miller) 1990
Everybody's Autobiography (o Stein) 1937
Everybody's Friend (f Shaw) 1874
Everyday (pl Crothers) 1921
Everyday Use (f A. Walker) 1994
Everyone but Thee and Me (po Nash) 1962
Everything in the Garden (pl Albee) 1967
Everything That Rises Must Converge (f O'Connor) 1965
Everything's Jake (pl Marquis) 1978
Everywhere I Roam (pl Connelly) 1938
Eve's Diary (f Twain) 1906

Fairylogue and Radio-Plays (scr Baum) 1908-09
Faith and Force: The Destroyers of the Modern World (o Rand) 1961
Faith and the Good Thing (f C. Johnson) 1974
Faith Doctor: A Story of New York (f Eggleston) 1891
Faith Healer (pl Moody) 1909
Faith in a Seed: The Dispersion of Seeds and Other Late Natural History Writings (o Thoreau) 1993
Faith of Aaron Menefee (tv Bradbury) 1962
Faith of Frances Craniford (f Churchill) 1917
Faith of Graffiti (o Mailer) 1974
Faith of Men and Other Stories (f London) 1904
Faith of Our Fathers (pl Green) 1950
Faithful Are the Wounds (f Sarton) 1955
Faithful Bull (o Hemingway) 1980
Faithful Man Described and Rewarded (o Mather) 1705
Faithful Narrative of the Surprising Work of God in the Conversion of Many Hundred Souls in Northampton (o Edwards) 1737
Fake Dreams (po B. Perelman) 1996
Falconberg (f Boyesen) 1879
Falconer (f Cheever) 1977
Falconer of God and Other Poems (po W. Benét) 1914
Fall of Algiers (pl Payne) 1825
Fall of America: Poems of These States 1965-1971 (po Ginsberg) 1972
Fall of the City (pl MacLeish) 1937
Fall of the Towers (f S. Delany) 1970
Fallen Man (f Hillerman) 1997
Falling in Place (f Beattie) 1980
Falling in with Fortune (f Alger) 1900
Falling, May Day Sermon, and Other Poems (po Dickey) 1981
Falling Upward (pl Bradbury) 1988
Fallon (f L'Amour) 1963
False Confession (pl Merwin) 1963
False Dawn: Women in the Age of the Sun King (o Auchincloss) 1984
False Entry (f Calisher) 1961
False Gods (f Auchincloss) 1992
False Kisses (scr Eaton) 1921
False Shame (pl Dunlap) 1798
False Youth—Four Seasons (po Dickey) 1983
Fam and Yam (pl Albee) 1960
Fama Combinatoria (pl Wellman) 1973
Fame (pl A. Miller) 1970
Fame and Folly: Essays (o Ozick) 1996
Fame and Fortune (f Alger) 1868
Familiar Faces: Stories of People You Know (f Rinehart) 1941
Familiar Poems Annotated (po Asimov) 1977
Family Affair (f Stout) 1975
Family Arsenal (f Theroux) 1976
Family Devotions (pl Hwang) 1981
Family Letters (o Jefferson) 1966
Family Linen (f L. Smith) 1985
Family Moskat (f Singer) 1950
Family Nurse; or Companion of The Frugal Housewife (o Child) 1837
Family Party (f J. O'Hara) 1956
Family Pictures (po Brooks) 1970
Family Portrait (f Wescott) 1927
Family Pride (f Arthur) 1844
Family Reunion (pl Eliot) 1939

Family Reunion (po Nash) 1950
Family Well-Ordered (o Mather) 1699
Family-Religion Excited and Assisted (o Mather) 1705
Famous Boating Party and Other Poems in Prose (po Patchen) 1954
Famous Old People, Being the Second Epoch of Grandfather's Chair (o Hawthorne) 1841
Famous Persons and Places (o Willis) 1854
Famous Sally (o S. Jackson) 1966
Fan (scr Parker) 1949
Fanatics (f Dunbar) 1901
Fanchette, by One of Her Admirers (f J. Cooke) 1883
Fancy Meeting You Again (pl Kaufman) 1952
Fancy of Hers (f Alger) 1981
Fancy Strut (f L. Smith) 1973
Fanny (pl Behrman) 1955
Fanny (pl Belasco) 1926
Fanny (po Halleck) 1819
Fanny Dale (f Arthur) 1843
Fanny H— (f Ingraham) 1843
Fanny Herself (f Ferber) 1917
Fanny with Other Poems (po Halleck) 1839
Fanshawe and Other Pieces (f Hawthorne) 1876
Fanshawe: A Tale (f Hawthorne) 1828
Fantastic Fables (f Bierce) 1899
Fantastic Voyage (f Asimov) 1966
Fantastic Voyage II: Destination Brain (f Asimov) 1987
Fantastics and Other Fancies (o Hearn) 1914
Fantazius Mallare: A Mysterious Oath (f Hecht) 1922
Fantine (pl B. Howard) 1864
Far and Near: Stories of Japan, China, and America (f Buck) 1948
Far as the Human Eye Could See (o Asimov) 1987
Far Country (f Churchill) 1915
Far Familiar (po MacKaye) 1938
Far Field (po Roethke) 1964
Far in the Forest (f S. Mitchell) 1889
Far North (scr Shepard) 1988
Far Rockaway of the Heart (po Ferlinghetti) 1997
Far Side of the Dollar (f Macdonald) 1965
Far-Away Melody and Other Stories (f Freeman) 1890
Faralitos of Christmas (pl Anaya) 1987
Farces: The Dictator, The Galloper, Miss Civilization (pl Richard Davis) 1906
Farewell, My Lovely (f Chandler) 1940
Farewell Sermon Preached at the First Precinct in Northampton (o Edwards) 1751
Farewell to Arms (scr Hecht) 1957
Farewell to Arms (f Hemingway) 1929
Farewell to Model T (o White) 1936
Farm (f Bromfield) 1933
Farm Book (o Jefferson) 1953
Farm Summer, 1942 (o Hall) 1994
Farmer (f Harrison) 1975
Farmer in the Sky (f Heinlein) 1950
Farmer Takes a Wife (pl Connelly) 1934
Farmers Hotel (f J. O'Hara) 1951
Farmers' Daughters: The Collected Stories (f W. Williams) 1961
Farnham's Freehold (f Heinlein) 1964
Farrell Case: A One Act Mystery (pl Cohan) 1919
Fasciculus Viventium (o Mather) 1726
Fascinating Stranger and Other Stories (f Tarkington) 1923

Fascist "New Frontier" (o Rand) 1963

Fashion (pl Mowatt) 1849

Fashionable Adventures of Joshua Craig (f D. Phillips) 1909

Fashions in Literature and Other Literary and Social Essays and Addresses (o Warner) 1902

Fast and Loose: A Novelette (f Wharton) 1977

Fast and Slow (po Ciardi) 1975

Fast Family (pl Belasco) 1879

Fast Lanes (f J. Phillips) 1984

Fat and Blood, and How to Make Them (o S. Mitchell) 1877

Fatal Interview: Sonnets (po Millay) 1931

Fatal Weakness (pl Kelly) 1947

Fate of a Crown (f Baum) 1905

Fate of the Jury: An Epilogue to Domesday Book (po Masters) 1929

Fate of Writing in America (o Farrell) 1946

Fates Worse Than Death: An Autobiographical Collage of the 1980s (o Vonnegut) 1991

Father (pl Dunlap) 1789

Father (pl Nelson) 1996

Father Abbot; or The Home Tourist (o Simms) 1849

Father Abraham (f Faulkner) 1984

Father Abraham's Speech (o Franklin) 1760

Father and Son (f Farrell) 1940

Father and the Boys (pl Ade) 1924

Father Bombo's Pilgrimage to Mecca 1770 (f Brackenridge, Freneau) 1975

Father, Dear Father (o Bemelmans) 1953

Father Departing (o Mather) 1723

Father Goose, His Book (po Baum) 1899

Father Goose's Year Book: Quaint Quacks and Feathery Shafts for Mature Children (po Baum) 1907

Father Hunt (f Stout) 1968

Father of an Only Child (pl Dunlap) 1806

Fatheralong: A Meditation on Fathers and Sons, Race and Society (o Wideman) 1994

Fathers (f A. Tate) 1938

Fathers and Other Fiction (f A. Tate) 1977

Fathers Playing Catch with Sons (o Hall) 1985

Faulkner at Nagano (o Faulkner) 1956

Faulkner at West Point (o Faulkner) 1964

Faulkner County (f Faulkner) 1955

Faulkner in the University (o Faulkner) 1959

Faulkner's MGM Screenplays (pl Faulkner) 1983

Faulkner-Cowley File: Letters and Memoirs, 1944-62 (o Cowley, Faulkner) 1966

Faust Foutu (pl Duncan) 1955

Faustina (pl Goodman) 1949

Favor Island (pl Merwin) 1957

Favorite Poems (po Whittier) 1877

Fear (po Ammons) 1995

Fear (o Millay) 1927(?

Fear and Trembling (o Wescott) 1932

Fear That Walks by Noonday (f Cather) 1931

Fearful Responsibility and Other Stories (f Howells) 1881

Fearful Responsibility and Tonnelli's Marriage (f Howells) 1882

Fearful Symmetry: A Study of William Blake (o Frye) 1947

Feast of Ortolans (pl M. Anderson) 1937

Feast of Snakes (f Crews) 1976

Feather Crowns (f Mason) 1993

Feathers (o Van Vechten) 1930

Feathers from the Hill (po Merwin) 1978

Featuring O'Hara (po F. O'Hara) 1964

February in Sydney (po Komunyakaa) 1989

Federalist Newburyport (o Marquand) 1952

Federigo (f Nemerov) 1954

Fee Fi Fo Fum (tv Bradbury) 1992

Fee-Gee (pl Harrigan) 1875

Feet (po Levertov) 1997

Fefu and Her Friends (pl Fornés) 1977

Felita (f Mohr) 1979

Fellow Countrymen: Collected Stories (f Farrell) 1937

Fellow Passengers (f Auchincloss) 1991

Female Patriot (pl Rowson) 1795

Feminine Touch (scr Nash) 1941

Fences (pl A. Wilson) 1986

Fennel and Rue (f Howells) 1908

Fenris the Wolf (pl MacKaye) 1905

Fer-de-Lance (f Stout) 1934

Ferdinand (po Zukofsky) 1968

Ferguson Affair (f Macdonald) 1960

Ferguson Rifle (f L'Amour) 1973

Fernanda (pl Daly) 1870

Fernhurst, Q.E.D., and Other Early Writings (o Stein) 1971

Ferrini and Others (po Creeley, Olson) 1955

Feud (pl M. Anderson) 1925

Fever (f Wideman) 1989

Fever Dream (f Bradbury) 1987

Fever Pitch (f Waters) 1930

Few Brass Tacks (o Bromfield) 1946

Few Figs from Thistles (po Millay) 1920

Fiasco Hall (po Hawkes) 1943

Fiction and Figures of Life (o Gass) 1970

Fidelity (f Glaspell) 1915

Fie! Fie! Fi-Fi! (pl Fitzgerald) 1914

Fiedler on the Roof: Essays on Literature and Jewish Identity (o Fiedler) 1991

Field (po Levertov) 1996

Field Book: Verses, Stories, and Letters (o Field) 1898

Field God (pl Green) 1927

Field Guide (po Hass) 1973

Field Notes: The Grace of the Canyon Wren (o Lopez) 1994

Field of Vision (f Morris) 1956

Field to Francis Wilson: Some Attentions (o Field) 1896

Fields (f Richter) 1946

Fields of Grace (po Eberhart) 1972

Fields of Wonder (po Hughes) 1947

Fiend's Delight (f Bierce) 1873

Fiery Hunt and Other Plays (pl Olson) 1977

Fiesta (f Hemingway) 1927

Fiesta Melons (po Plath) 1971

15 Poems with Time Expressions (po Goodman) 1936

Fifteen Selected Stories (f Farrell) 1943

Fifth Column (pl Hemingway) 1940

Fifth Column and Four Stories of the Spanish Civil War (f Hemingway) 1969

Fifth Column and the First Forty-Nine Stories (f Hemingway) 1938

Fifth Decade of Cantos (po Pound) 1937

Fifth Horseman: A Novel of the Mexican Revolution (f Villarreal) 1974

Fifth Sunday (f Dove) 1985

Fifty Literary Pillars: A Temple of Texts: An Exhibition to Inaugurate the International Writers Center (o Gass) 1991
Fifty Miles from Boston (pl Cohan) 1907
Fifty Stories (f Boyle) 1980
Fifty Years and Other Poems (po J. Johnson) 1917
Fifty-Two Pickup (f Leonard) 1974
52 Pick-Up (scr Leonard) 1986
Fight (o Mailer) 1975
Fight Back: For the Sake of the People, for the Sake of the Land (po Ortiz) 1980
Fight for Freedom: The Story of the NAACP (o Hughes) 1962
Fighting Caravans (f Grey) 1929
Fighting France: From Dunkerque to Belfort (o Wharton) 1915
Fighting Littles (f Tarkington) 1941
Fighting Man of Mars (f E. Burroughs) 1931
Fightin': New and Selected Stories (f Ortiz) 1983
Figs and Thistles: A Western Story (f Tourgée) 1879
Figure of Time (po Hayden) 1955
Figured Wheel: New and Collected Poems, 1966-1996 (po Pinsky) 1995
Figures in Black: Words, Signs, and the 'Radical Self' (o Gates) 1987
Figures of Capable Imagination (o Bloom) 1976
Figures of Earth (f Cabell) 1921
Figures of Thought: Speculations on the Meaning of Poetry and Other Essays (o Nemerov) 1978
Files on Parade (f J. O'Hara) 1939
Fille de Chambre (f Rowson) 1792
Film Crew (pl Mamet) 1983
Film Flam: Essays on Hollywood (o McMurtry) 1987
Film in the Battle of Ideas (o Lawson) 1953
Film: The Creative Process: The Search for an Audio-Visual Language and Structure (o Lawson) 1964
Fin, Feather, Fur (po W. Stafford) 1989
Final Deduction (f Stout) 1961
Final Poems of Philip Freneau (1827-1828) (po Freneau) 1979
Finally a Valentine: A Poem (po Zukofsky) 1965
Financier (f Dreiser) 1912
Find a Victim (f Macdonald) 1954
Finders-Keepers (pl Kelly) 1923
Finding a Form: Essays (o Gass) 1996
Finding a Fortune (f Alger) 1904
Finding a Girl in America (f Dubus) 1980
Finding an Old Ant Mansion (po Bly) 1981
Finding Moon (f Hillerman) 1995
Finding the Green Stone (o A. Walker) 1991
Finding the Space (po Shapiro, Shapiro) 1996
Finding the Space (po Snyder) 1996
Fine and Private Place (f Queen) 1971
Fine Clothes to the Jew (po Hughes) 1927
Fine Furniture (f Dreiser) 1930
Fine Wagon (pl Green) 1959
Finer Grain (f H. James) 1910
Finger (po Creeley) 1968
Finger Man and Other Stories (f Chandler) 1946
Finger Posts on the Way of Life (f Arthur) 1853
Finger: Poems 1966-1969 (po Creeley) 1970
Finishing Stroke (f Queen) 1958
Fir-Flower Tablets (po A. Lowell) 1921
Fire and Ice (f Stegner) 1941
Fire and Wine (po Fletcher) 1913
Fire in My Hands (po Soto) 1988

Fire in the Flint (pl Tolson) 1952
Fire in the Morning (f Spencer) 1948
Fire Next Time (o James Baldwin) 1963
Fire on the Moon (o Mailer) 1971
Fire Screen (po Merrill) 1969
Fire Sermon (f Morris) 1971
Fire: From a Journal of Love—The Unexpurgated Diary of Nin, 1934-37 (o Nin) 1995
Fire-Bringer (pl Moody) 1904
Firecrackers (f Van Vechten) 1925
Firefly (scr Nash) 1937
Fireman's Picnic (pl Cohan) 1918
Fireside Angel (f Arthur) 1853
Fireside Travels (o J. Lowell) 1864
Firestarter (f King) 1980
Firing (po Snyder) 1964
First American Gentleman (f Cabell) 1942
First and Last (o Lardner) 1934
First and Last Journeys of Thoreau (o Thoreau) 1905
First Blues: Rags, Ballads, and Harmonium Songs 1971-1974 (po Ginsberg) 1975
First Book in American History (o Eggleston) 1889
First Cities (po Lorde) 1968
First Decade: Selected Poems 1940-1950 (po Duncan) 1968
First Eagle (f Hillerman) 1999
First Encounter (f Dos Passos) 1945
First Families in the Sierras (pl J. Miller) 1875
First Family of Tasajara (f Harte) 1891
First Fast Draw (f L'Amour) 1959
First Flight (pl M. Anderson) 1925
First Four Books of Poems (po Glück) 1995
First Four Books of Poems (po Merwin) 1975
First Gentleman of America (f Cabell) 1942
First Gentleman of Europe (pl Burnett) 1897
First Geography for Children (o Stowe) 1855
First George Mills (f Elkin) 1981
First Half of "A" 9 (po Zukofsky) 1934
First in Heart (pl B. Smith) 1947
First Lady (pl Kaufman) 1935
First Leaf (po Riding) 1933
First Love (pl Akins) 1926
First Love: A Gothic Tale (f Oates) 1996
First Lover and Other Stories (f Boyle) 1933
First Man (pl O'Neill) 1922
First One (pl Hurston) 1927
First Person Singular (f W. Benét) 1922
First Poems (po Merrill) 1951
First Poems: 1946-1954 (po Kinnell) 1971
First Salute (o Tuchman) 1989
First Story (f Welty) 1999
First View of English Literature (o Moody) 1905
First View of English and American Literature (o Moody) 1909
First Watch (o Steinbeck) 1947
First Wife (pl Buck) 1945
First Wife and Other Stories (f Buck) 1933
First Will and Testament (po Patchen) 1939
First Winter of My Married Life (f Gass) 1979
First World (po B. Perelman) 1986
First Writings: Pawtuxet Valley Gleaner 1906 (o Lovecraft) 1976
Firstborn (po Glück) 1968
Fiscal Hoboes (f Saroyan) 1949

Fish or Cut Bait (f E. Gardner) 1963
Fish Story (pl N. Wallace) 1994
Fishing for Snakes (po Eberhart) 1965
Fitch and His Letters (o Fitch) 1924
Five Came Back (scr N. West) 1939
$500 (f Alger) 1890
Five Men and Pompey (pl S. Benét) 1915
Five Murderers (f Chandler) 1944
5 Numbers (po Creeley) 1968
Five Sinister Characters (f Chandler) 1945
Five Songs (po Duncan) 1981
Fixer (f Malamud) 1966
Fixin's (pl Green) 1924
Flag Flutter and U.S. Electric (po Coolidge) 1966
Flag Is Born (pl Hecht) 1946
Flagons and Apples (po Jeffers) 1912
Flags in the Dust (f Faulkner) 1973
Flame and Shadow (po Teasdale) 1920
Flappers and Philosophers (f Fitzgerald) 1920
Flash of Lightning (pl Daly) 1885
Flashbacks: A Twenty Year Diary of Article Writing (o J. Williams) 1973
Flattering Word (pl Kelly) 1919
Flavor of Man (o Toomer) 1949
Flea of Sodom (o Dahlberg) 1950
Fleming Field (f Ingraham) 1845
Flesh (scr Hart) 1932
Flies in the Web (pl Brougham) 1860
Flight from Fiesta (f Waters) 1986
Flight from Neveryon (f S. Delany) 1985
Flight into China (pl Buck) 1939
Flight of Pony Baker: A Boy's Town Story (f Howells) 1902
Flight of the Innocents (f Lin Yutang) 1964
Flight to Canada (f Reed) 1976
Flight to Lucifer: A Gnostic Fantasy (o Bloom) 1979
Flight to the West (pl Rice) 1940
Flights of Angels: Stories (f Gilchrist) 1998
Flint (f L'Amour) 1960
Flip and Other Stories (f Harte) 1882
Flirt (f Tarkington) 1913
Flirtation at the Moultrie House (f Simms) 1850
Floating Opera (f Barth) 1956
Flock of Guinea Hens Seen from a Car (po Welty) 1970
Flood of Blood (pl Chin) 1988
Flood: A Romance of Our Time (f R. Warren) 1964
Floodtide (f Yerby) 1950
Florence (pl Childress) 1949
Florence Bardsley's Story: The Life and Death of a Remarkable Woman (o Field) 1897
Florentine Dagger (f Hecht) 1923
Florida (o Roberts) 1926
Florida Days (o Deland) 1889
Florida Loafing (o Roberts) 1925
Florida Poems (po Eberhart) 1981
Florida Special (scr S. Perelman) 1936
Florida: Its Scenery, Climate, and History (o Lanier) 1875
Flow Chart (po Ashbery) 1998
Flow of the River (o Anaya) 1988
Flower and Hand: Poems, 1977-1983 (po Merwin) 1997
Flower and the Leaf: A Contemporary Record of American Writing Since 1941 (o Cowley) 1985

Flower Fables (f Alcott) 1855
Flower Herding on Mount Monadnock (po Kinnell) 1964
Flower in Her Hair (f Cozzens) 1974
Flower of Night (scr Hergesheimer) 1925
Flower of the Chapdelaines (f Cable) 1918
Flower-de-Lace (po Longfellow) 1867
Flowering Judas (f Porter) 1930
Flowering of the Rod (po Doolittle) 1946
Flowering Peach (pl Odets) 1954
Flowers of the Forest (pl Van Druten) 1934
Flowers of Virtue (pl Connelly) 1942
Floyd Dell: Essays from the Friday Literary Review, 1909-1913 (o Dell) 1995
Flush Times of Alabama and Mississippi (f Joseph G. Baldwin) 1853
Flush Times of California (f Joseph G. Baldwin) 1966
Flute and Violin and Other Kentucky Tales and Romances (f J. Allen) 1891
Flute Player (po Aiken) 1956
Fly on the Wall (f Hillerman) 1971
Flying Dutchman (pl Dunlap) 1827
Flying Girl [and Her Chum] (f Baum) 1911-12
Flying Islands of the Night (po Riley) 1891
Flying King of Kurio (o W. Benét) 1926
Flying Machine (pl Bradbury) 1986
F.M. (pl Linney) 1982
Fnu Lnu (pl Wellman) 1996
FOB (pl Hwang) 1979
Focus (f A. Miller) 1945
Focus (po Rich) 1967
Fog (pl O'Neill) 1914
Fog Horn (f Bradbury) 1987
Foghorn (pl Bradbury) 1975
Foghorn: Stories (f Atherton) 1934
Folk Stuff (pl B. Smith) 1935
Folks (f Suckow) 1934
Folks from Dixie (f Dunbar) 1898
Folline (pl Daly) 1874
Follow the Girl (pl Connelly) 1915
Follow Your Heart (scr N. West) 1936
Fombombo (f Stribling) 1923
Foment (pl Purdy) 1998
Fong and the Indians (f Theroux) 1968
Fool for Love (pl Shepard) 1983
Fool's Gold (po Fletcher) 1913
Foolish Notion (pl Barry) 1945
Fools (pl Simon) 1981
Fools Crow (f Welch) 1986
Fools Die (f Puzo) 1978
Fools Die on Friday (f E. Gardner) 1947
Fools in Time: Studies in Shakespearean Tragedy (o Frye) 1967
Foolscap Rose (f Hergesheimer) 1934
Fool's Errand (f Tourgée) 1879
Footloose (pl Akins) 1919
Footnotes for a Centennial (po Morley) 1936
Footprints (po Levertov) 1972
Footsteps of the Master (o Stowe) 1877
for colored girls who have considered suicide/when the rainbow is enuf (pl Shange) 1977
For a Time and Place (o Dickey) 1983
For Authors Only and Other Gloomy Essays (o Roberts) 1935

For Benny and Sabina (po Creeley) 1970
For Betsy and Tom (po Creeley) 1970
For Black People (po Madhubuti) 1968
For Doyle Fosco (po Ammons) 1977
For Esme—With Love and Squalor and Other Stories (f Salinger) 1953
For Farish Street Green (po M. Walker) 1986
For Illinois 1968: A Sesquicentennial Poem (po Brooks) 1968
For Instance (po Ciardi) 1979
For Joel (po Creeley) 1966
For Kurt Cobain (po Coolidge) 1995
For Lease or Sale (pl Spencer) 1989
For Lizzie and Harriet (po Lowell) 1973
For Love of Imabelle (f Himes) 1957
For Love: Poems 1950-1960 (po Creeley) 1962
For Me Myself (tv C. Johnson) 1982
For My Mother (po Creeley) 1973
For My People (po M. Walker) 1942
For Passion, For Heaven (f Fisher) 1962
For the Blood Is the Life: And Other Stories (f Crawford) 1996
For the Defense (pl Rice) 1919
For the Graduation (po Creeley) 1971
For the New Intellectual: The Philosophy of Ayn Rand (o Rand) 1961
For the Time Being (o Dillard) 1999
For the Union Dead (po Lowell) 1964
For Tomorrow We Die (o Stout) 1958
For Whom the Bell Tolls (f Hemingway) 1940
Forayers (f Simms) 1855
Forbidden Poems (po Purdy) 1998
Force of Calumny (pl Dunlap) 1800
Foregone Conclusion (f Howells) 1874
Foreign Correspondent (scr Benchley) 1940
Foreign Exchange (pl Tarkington) 1909
Foreign Language (pl Behrman) 1951
Forensic and the Navigators (pl Shepard) 1967
Forest Fire (f Stout) 1933
Forest Leaves (po F. Harper) 1845
Forest of the South (f Gordon) 1945
Forester's Daughter (f Garland) 1914
Foresters (pl Daly) 1892
Forever and a Day (scr Isherwood) 1943
Forever and a Day (scr Van Druten) 1944
Forever and the Earth (pl Bradbury) 1984
Forever Young (f Akins) 1941
Forfeits (pl M. Anderson) 1926
Forge (f Stribling) 1931
Forging Ahead (f Alger) 1903
Forgive Us Our Virtues: A Comedy of Evasions (f Fisher) 1938
Forgotten Village (pl Steinbeck) 1941
Fork River Space Project (f Morris) 1977
Forlorn River (f Grey) 1927
Form of Woman (po Creeley) 1959
Formative Years (o Adams) 1947
Forms of Discovery: Critical and Historical Essays of the Forms of the Short Poem in English (o Winters) 1967
Forrestal (f Ingraham) 1845
Fortitude (pl Vonnegut) 1974
Fortunate Pilgrim (f Puzo) 1964
Fortunatus (po Robinson) 1928
Fortune Heights (pl Dos Passos) 1933

Fortune Hunter (f Mowatt) 1842
Fortune Hunter (f D. Phillips) 1906
Fortunes of Ben Barclay (f Alger) 1896
Fortunes of Philippa Fairfax (f Burnett) 1888
Fortuneteller (f Wellman) 1991
45 Mercy Street (pl Sexton) 1969
Forty Lashes Less One (f Leonard) 1972
Forty Modern Fables (f Ade) 1901
Forty Stories (f Barthelme) 1987
Forty-Five Minutes from Broadway (pl Cohan) 1906
Forty-Nine: A California Drama (pl J. Miller) 1882
'49: The Gold-Seeker of the Sierras (f J. Miller) 1884
49ers (pl Connelly; Kaufman) 1922
XLI Poems (po Cummings) 1925
42nd Parallel (f Dos Passos) 1930
Forward the Foundation (f Asimov) 1993
Found Objects: 1962-1926 (po Zukofsky) 1964
Foundation (f Asimov) 1951
Foundation and Earth (f Asimov) 1986
Foundation and Empire (f Asimov) 1952
Foundation's Edge (f Asimov) 1982
Founders: A Symphonic Outdoor Drama (pl Green) 1957
Fountain (pl O'Neill) 1925
Fountain and Other Poems (po Bryant) 1842
Fountainhead (f Rand) 1943
Fountainville Abbey (pl Dunlap) 1795
4 A.M (pl Mamet) 1983
Four Baboons Adoring the Sun (pl Guare) 1992
Four Black Revolutionary Plays (pl Baraka) 1969
Four Changes (o Snyder) 1969
Four Dynamite Plays (pl Bullins) 1971
Four Guns to the Border (scr L'Amour) 1954
Four in America (o Stein) 1947
Four Million (f Henry) 1906
Four of a Kind (f Marquand) 1923
Four of Hearts (f Queen) 1938
Four Past Midnight (f King) 1990
Four Prominent Bastards Are We (po Nash) 1934
Four Prominent So and So's (po Nash) 1934
Four Ramages (po Bly) 1983
Four Saints in Three Acts (pl Stein) 1934
Four Seasons (o Styron) 1965
Four Sons (scr Lawson) 1940
Four Unposted Letters to Catherine (o Riding) 1930
Four Visions of America (o Boyle) 1977
Four Young Women: Poems by Jessica Tarahata Hagedorn, Alice Karle, Barbara Szerlip, and Carol Tinker (po Hagedorn) 1973
Four-Chambered Heart (f Nin) 1950
4-H Club (pl Shepard) 1965
Fourteen Hundred Thousand (pl Shepard) 1966
Fourteen Sisters of Emilio Montez O'Brien (f Hijuelos) 1993
14A (f Riding) 1934
Fourteenth Chronicle: Letters and Diaries (o Dos Passos) 1973
Fourth Angel (f Rechy) 1973
Fourth Canto (po Pound) 1919
Fourth K (f Puzo) 1991
Fourth Side of the Triangle (f Queen) 1965
Fox of Peapack and Other Poems (po White) 1938
Foxes of Harrow (f Yerby) 1946
Fragment (po Ashbery) 1969
Fragment from Vietnam (pl Mailer) 1967

Fragment of a Meditation (po A. Tate) 1947
Fragments from an Unwritten Autobiography (o Van Vechten) 1955
Fragments of a Disordered Devotion (po Duncan) 1952
Fragments: A Sit Around (pl Albee) 1993
Frame Structures: Early Poems, 1974-1978 (po S. Howe) 1996
France and Anderson: Paris Notebook 1921 (o S. Anderson) 1976
France and England in North America (o Parkman) 1983
Frances Waldeaux (f Rebecca Davis) 1897
Francesca da Rimini (pl Boker) 1855
Francesca da Rimini (pl Crawford) 1980
Franchise (f Asimov) 1989
Franchiser (f Elkin) 1976
Francie Nolan (pl B. Smith) 1930
Francis Drake: A Tragedy of the Sea (pl S. Mitchell) 1893
Francis Parkman and the Plains Indians (o Parkman) 1995
Frank and Fearless (f Alger) 1897
Frank Fowler, The Cash Boy (f Alger) 1887
Frank Hunter's Peril (f Alger) 1896
Frank Rivers (f Ingraham) 1843
Frank's Campaign (f Alger) 1864
Frankenstein: The True Story (scr Isherwood) 1972
Frankie and Johnny (scr Hart) 1936
Franklin and Catharine Ray Greene: Their Correspondence 1775-1790 (o Franklin) 1949
Franklin and the King (pl Green) 1939
Franklin Evans (f Whitman) 1842
Franklin Laughing: Anecdotes from Original Sources by and about Franklin (o Franklin) 1980
Franklin on Education (o Franklin) 1962
Franklin Reader (o Franklin) 1945
Franklin Sampler (o Franklin) 1956
Franklin; A New and Original Historical Drama (pl Brougham) 1856
Franklin's Contribution to Medicine (o Franklin) 1912
Franklin's Wit and Folly: The Bagatelles (o Franklin) 1953
Franny and Zooey (f Salinger) 1961
Franz Liszt (o Huneker) 1911
Fraternal Discord (pl Dunlap) 1809
Freaks: Myths and Images in the Secret Self (o Fiedler) 1978
Freaky Deaky (f Leonard) 1988
Freddy's Book (f J. Gardner) 1980
Frederick Douglass (o Chesnutt) 1899
Frederick Douglass (o Washington) 1907
Frederick Douglass: A Biography of Anti-Slavery (o Locke) 1935
Frederick Lemaitre (pl Fitch) 1890
Free Air (f Lewis) 1919
Free and Clear (pl R. Anderson) 1983
Free and Other Stories (f Dreiser) 1918
Free-Lance Pallbearers (f Reed) 1967
Free Man (f Richter) 1943
Free Wheeling (po Nash) 1931
Free-Trader (f Ingraham) 1847
Freedom and Culture (o Dewey) 1939
Freedom and Fame (po Knight) 1990
Freedom Drum (pl Childress) 1969
Freedom of the Poet (o Berryman) 1976
Freedom of the Will (o Edwards) 1969
Freedom's a Hard Bought Thing (pl S. Benét) 1941
Freedom's Bird (pl B. Smith) 1945
Freedom's Land (po MacLeish) 1942
Freedom's Plow (pl Hughes) 1943

Freeing of the Dust (po Levertov) 1975
Freeman and Other Poems (po Glasgow) 1902
Freemantle (f Ingraham) 1845
French Girls Are Vicious and Other Stories (f Farrell) 1955
French Governess (f Cooper) 1843
French Libertine (pl W. Irving, Payne) 1826
French Powder Mystery (f Queen) 1930
French Ways and Their Meaning (o Wharton) 1919
Frenchman Must Die (f Boyle) 1946
Frescoes for Mr. Rockefeller's City (po MacLeish) 1933
Fresh Gleanings (o D. Mitchell) 1847
Fresh Kill (scr Hagedorn) 1992
Fresno Stories (f Saroyan) 1994
Freud and the Crisis of Our Culture (o Trilling) 1956
Fricandeau (pl Payne) 1831
Friday (f Heinlein) 1982
Friday Book: Essays and Other Nonfiction (o Barth) 1984
Friend of Kafka and Other Stories (f Singer) 1970
Friendly Debate (o Mather) 1722
Friendly Persuasion (f J. West) 1945
Friends to This Ground: A Statement for Readers, Teachers, and Writers of Literature (o W. Stafford) 1967
Friendship (pl Cohan) 1931
Friendship Village (f Gale) 1908
Frightened Wife and Other Murder Stories (f Rinehart) 1953
Frisky Mrs. Johnson (pl Fitch) 1908
Frog (f Hawkes) 1996
Frog Prince (pl Mamet) 1984
Frolic of His Own (f Gaddis) 1993
from okra to greens: poems (po Shange) 1984
From a Land Where Other People Live (po Lorde) 1973
From an Altar Screen/El retablo: Tales from New Mexico (f Chávez) 1957
From Bauhaus to Our House (o Tom Wolfe) 1981
From Bed to Worse (o Benchley) 1934
From Bondage (f H. Roth) 1996
From Canal Boy to President (o Alger) 1881
From Death to Morning (f Thomas Wolfe) 1935
From Earth to Heaven (o Asimov) 1966
From Eden to Babylon (o Lytle) 1990
From Farm Boy to Senator, Being the History of the Boyhood and Manhood of Daniel Webster (o Alger) 1882
From Farm to Fortune (f Alger) 1905
From Flushing to Calvary (f Dahlberg) 1932
From Here to Eternity (f J. Jones) 1951
From Labor to Letters: A Novel Autobiography (f Méndez M.) 1997
From Main Street to Stockholm: Letters of Lewis 1919-1930 (o Lewis) 1952
From My Experience: The Pleasures and Miseries of Life on a Farm (o Bromfield) 1955
From Okra to Greens/A Different Kinda Love Story: A Play/With Music and Dance (pl Shange) 1985
From Plan to Planet (o Madhubuti) 1973
From Room to Room (po Kenyon) 1978
From Sand Creek (po Ortiz) 1981
From Sand Hill to Pine (f Harte) 1900
From Snow to Snow (po Frost) 1936
From Thanks to the Dictionary (po Zukofsky) 1968
From the Cutting Room Floor (po Merrill) 1982
From the First Nine: Poems 1947-1976 (po Merrill) 1982

From the Hidden Way (po Cabell) 1916
From the Other Side: Stories of Transatlantic Travel (f Fuller) 1898
From the Terrace (f J. O'Hara) 1958
Front Page (pl Hecht, MacArthur) 1928
Front Porch (pl Hughes) 1938
Frontiers II: More Recent Discoveries (o Asimov) 1993
Frontiers Well-Defended (o Mather) 1707
Frontiers: New Discoveries about Man and His Planet (o Asimov) 1991
Frontiersmen (f Murfree) 1904
Frost and Flower: My Life with Manic Depression So Far (o Gibbons) 1995
Frosted Glass Coffin (pl T. Williams) 1970
Frou-Frou (pl Daly) 1870
Frugal Housewife (o Child) 1829
Fruit at the Bottom of the Bowl (tv Bradbury) 1988
Fruit of the Tree (f Wharton) 1907
Fruits of the MLA (o E. Wilson) 1968
Fudge Doings, Being Tony Fudge's Record of the Same (f D. Mitchell) 1855
Fudo Trilogy: Spell against Demons, Smokey the Bear Sutra (po Snyder) 1973
Fugitive Kind (pl T. Williams) 1937
Fugitive Poetry (po Willis) 1829
Fugitive Trail (f Grey) 1957
Fugitive's Return (f Glaspell) 1929
Führer Bunker (pl Snodgrass) 1982
Full Cargo: More Stories (f Steele) 1951
Fullerton Street (pl A. Wilson) 1980
Fulton of Oak Falls (pl Cohan) 1936
Fun after Supper (pl B. Smith) 1940
Fun in a Green Room (pl B. Howard) 1882
Fun to Be Free: Patriotic Pageant (pl Hecht, MacArthur) 1941
Fun-Jottings (f Willis) 1853
Function of Criticism: Problems and Exercises (o Winters) 1957
Function of the Poet and Other Essays (o J. Lowell) 1920
Fundamentalism Versus Spiritualism: A Layman's Viewpoint (o J. Johnson) 1925
Funeral of Adam Willis Wagnalls (po Markham) 1924
Fungi from Yuggoth (po Lovecraft) 1941
Funk Lore: New Poems, 1984-1995 (po Baraka) 1996
Funland (f Oates) 1983
Funniest Verses (po Nash) 1968
Fur Person (f Sarton) 1957
Furies (pl Akins) 1928
Furious Seasons and Other Stories (f Carver) 1977
Furnace Trouble (scr Benchley) 1929
Further Criticism of Poetry (o Lovecraft) 1932
Further Fables for Our Time (f Thurber) 1956
Further Fridays (scr Barth) 1995
Further Poems (po Dickinson) 1929
Further Range (po Frost) 1936
Furthermore (f Runyon) 1938
Future Days: A Nineteenth-Century Vision of the Year 2000 (o Asimov) 1986
Future Is Ours, Comrade: Conversations with Russians (o Kosinski) 1960
Future of Memory (po B. Perelman) 1998
Future of the American Negro (o Washington) 1899
Future of the Novel: Essays on the Art of the Novel (pl H. James) 1956

Future of the Race (o Gates) 1996

Gaan Story (scr Harjo) 1979-84
Gabriel Conroy (f Harte) 1876
Gabrielle de Bergerac (f H. James) 1918
Galahad (f E. Wilson) 1967
Galapagos (f Vonnegut) 1985
Galatea (f Cain) 1953
Galilee Hitch-Hiker (po Brautigan) 1958
Gallantry (f Cabell) 1907
Gallegher and Other Stories (f Richard Davis) 1891
Gallery of Harlem Portraits (po Tolson) 1979
Gallery of Women (f Dreiser) 1929
Galloper (pl Richard Davis) 1905
Galloway (f L'Amour) 1970
Galton Case (f Macdonald) 1959
Gambit (f Stout) 1962
Gambler's Wife (pl Dunbar) 1890
Gambling (pl Cohan) 1929
Game (f London) 1905
Game of Adam and Eve (pl Bullins) 1966
Game of Love (pl Brougham) 1855
Gander Sauce (pl B. Smith) 1942
Gang of Pecksniffs and Other Comments on Newspaper Publishers, Editors, and Reporters (o Mencken) 1975
Gangster of Love (f Hagedorn) 1996
Garbage (po Ammons) 1993
Garbage Man: A Parade with Shouting (pl Dos Passos) 1925
Garden (po Glück) 1976
Garden District: Something Unspoken, Suddenly Last Summer (pl T. Williams) 1958
Garden of Adonis (f Gordon) 1937
Garden of Earthly Delights (f Oates) 1967
Garden of Eden (f Hemingway) 1986
Garden of Paradise (pl Sheldon) 1915
Gardenia (pl Guare) 1982
Gardens of Aphrodite (o Saltus) 1920
Gardens of This World (f Fuller) 1929
Garfield Honor (f Yerby) 1961
Gargoyles (f Hecht) 1922
Garland for Girls (f Alcott) 1887
Garland to Sylvia: A Dramatic Reverie (pl MacKaye) 1910
Garments the Living Wear (f Purdy) 1989
Garroters (pl Howells) 1886
Gary and Miami: Before and After (o Baraka) 1???
Gas Age (po Zukofsky) 1969
Gas-House McGinty (f Farrell) 1933
Gaslight (scr Van Druten) 1944
Gates (po Rukeyser) 1976
Gates of Paradise and Other Poems (po Markham) 1920
Gates of Wrath: Rhymed Poems 1948-1952 (po Ginsberg) 1972
Gather Together in My Name (o Angelou) 1974
Gather Ye Rosebuds (pl S. Howard) 1934
Gathering of Fugitives (o Trilling) 1956
Gathering of Old Men (f Gaines) 1983
Gathering of the Forces (o Whitman) 1920
Gathering the Tribes (po Forché) 1976
Gaulantus the Gaul (pl Bannister) 1836
Gay and Melancholy Flux: Short Stories (f Saroyan) 1937
Gay Old Dog (scr Ferber) 1919
Gay White Way (pl Rice) 1934

Gazette Publications (o Brackenridge) 1806

Gee, Pop! (pl Chin) 1974

Gehenna (f Aiken) 1930

Gemini (pl Kopit) 1957

Gemini: An Extended Autobiographical Statement of My First Twenty-five Years of Being a Black Poet (o Giovanni) 1971

Gems of American Poetry (o Hoffman) 1840

General Died at Dawn (scr Odets) 1936

General from the Jungle (f Traven) 1954

General Gage's Confession (po Freneau) 1775

General Gage's Soliloquy (po Freneau) 1775

General Hag's Skeezag (pl Baraka) 1992

General Lee (o Page) 1909

General Magazine and Historical Chronicle for All the British Plantations in America (o Franklin) 1741

General Returns from One Place to Another (pl F. O'Hara) 1964

General William Booth Enters into Heaven and Other Poems (po Lindsay) 1913

Generation without Farewell (f Boyle) 1960

Generous Heart (f Fearing) 1954

Genesis (po Ciardi) 1967

Genesis: Book One (po Schwartz) 1943

Genetic Code (o Asimov) 1963

Genetic Effects of Radiation (o Asimov) 1966

Genie in the Jar (po Giovanni) 1996

"Genius" (f Dreiser) 1915

Genius and List: A Journey Through the Major Writings of Henry Miller (o Mailer) 1976

Genteel Tradition at Bay (o Santayana) 1931

Gentle Furniture Shop (pl Bodenheim) 1917

Gentle Grafter (f Henry) 1908

Gentle Insurrection (f Betts) 1954

Gentle Julia (f Tarkington) 1922

Gentleman Caller (pl Bullins) 1969

Gentleman from Indiana (f Tarkington) 1899

Gentleman from Ireland (pl F. O'Brien) 1854

Gentleman of Lyons (pl Bannister) 1838

Gentlemen of the Press (pl Thomas [Clayton] Wolfe) 1928

Gentleman's Agreement (scr Hart) 1947

Gentleman's Alphabet Book (o Hall) 1972

Gentlemen, I Address You Privately (f Boyle) 1933

Gentlemen's Relish (po Morley) 1955

Gentlewoman (pl Lawson) 1934

Geographical History of America (o Stein) 1936

Geography and Plays (pl Stein) 1922

Geography III (po E. Bishop) 1977

Geography of a Horse Dreamer (pl Shepard) 1974

Geography of South Carolina (o Simms) 1843

Geology (po Coolidge) 1988

George Bernard Shaw: His Plays (o Mencken) 1905

George Cameron (pl L. Mitchell) 1891

George Carter's Legacy (f Alger) 1887

George Helm (f D. Phillips) 1912

George Jean Nathan Reader (o Nathan) 1990

George Mills (f Elkin) 1982

George Washington, Jr (pl Cohan) 1906

George Washington Slept Here (pl Hart, Kaufman) 1940

George's Mother (f S. Crane) 1896

Georgia, Georgia (scr Angelou) 1972

Georgia Scenes, Characters, and Incidents, etc (f Longstreet) 1835

Georgia Spec (pl R. Tyler) 1797

Georgie May (f Bodenheim) 1928

Gerald's Game (f King) 1992

Gerald's Party (f Coover) 1986

German Emigrants (pl Harrigan) 1871

German Mind (o Santayana) 1968

German Philosophy and Politics (o Dewey) 1915

Germantown Letters (o Jefferson) 1906

Gertie Maude (pl Van Druten) 1937

Gertrude of Stony Island Avenue (f Purdy) 1997

Gesualdo (po Hejinian) 1978

Get Away Old Man (pl Saroyan) 1943

Get Rich Quick Edgar (scr Tarkington) 1921

Get Shorty (f Leonard) 1990

Get-Rich-Quick Wallingford (pl Cohan) 1910

Getting Older (f Updike) 1985

Getting the Knack: Twenty Poetry Writing Exercises (o W. Stafford) 1992

Getting Up and Going Home (f R. Anderson) 1978

Gettysburg (pl MacKaye) 1912

Gettysburg, Manila, Acoma (pl Masters) 1930

Ghost Country (f Paretsky) 1998

Ghost Dance (f Maso) 1987

Ghost Girl (f Saltus) 1922

Ghost Goes West (pl Sherwood) 1936

Ghost of Dr. Harris (f Hawthorne) 1900

Ghost of My Husband (f Simms) 1866

Ghost of Yankee Doodle (pl S. Howard) 1938

Ghost Story (pl Tarkington) 1922

Ghost Town (f Coover) 1998

Ghost Volcano: Poems (o Gilbert and Gubar) 1995

Ghost Writer (f P. Roth) 1979

Ghosts (pl Kopit) 1982

Ghosts (f Wharton) 1937

Ghostway (f Hillerman) 1984

Giant (f Ferber) 1952

Giant Weapon (po Winters) 1943

Giant's Strength (pl Sinclair) 1948

Giants in the Earth (f Rølvaag) 1927

Giants' Stair (pl Steele) 1924

Gibbeted: Execution of a Youthful Murderer (o Hearn) 1933

Gibson Upright (pl Tarkington) 1919

Gideon (pl Chayefsky) 1962

Gideon Planish (f Lewis) 1943

Gideon's Band: A Tale of the Mississippi (f Cable) 1914

Gift (o Doolittle) 1982

Gift (f Nabokov) 1963

Gift from Fairy Land (f Paulding) 1???

Gift from the Grave (f Wharton) 1900

Gift of Black Folk: Negroes in the Making of America (o Du Bois) 1924

Gigolo (f Ferber) 1922

Gilded Age: A Tale of Today (f Twain, Warner) 1873

Gilded West (pl Merwin) 1961

Giles Corey, Yeoman (pl Freeman) 1893

Giles Goat-Boy (f Barth) 1966

Gillian (f Yerby) 1960

Gimpel the Fool and Other Stories (f Singer) 1957

Ginger Man (f Donleavy) 1955

Gingerbread Lady (pl Simon) 1970

Gingertown (f McKay) 1932

Gingham Dog and the Calico Cat: A Poem (po Field) 1994

Giovanni and the Other: Children Who Have Made Stories (f Burnett) 1892
Giovanni's Room (f James Baldwin) 1956
Gipsy Nurse (f Alger) 1981
Gipsy of the Highlands (f Ingraham) 1843
Girl (f Oates) 1974
Girl and the Judge (pl Fitch) 1901
Girl from Farris's (f E. Burroughs) 1965
Girl from Hollywood (f E. Burroughs) 1923
Girl from Storyville: A Victorian Novel (f Yerby) 1972
Girl I Left Behind Me; or The Country Ball (pl Belasco) 1893
Girl in the Coffin (pl Dreiser) 1916
Girl of the Golden West (pl Belasco) 1905
Girl Proposition (f Ade) 1902
Girl Said No (scr MacArthur) 1930
Girl Sleuth: A Feminist Guide (o Mason) 1974
Girl Who Fell through a Hole in Her Sweater (pl N. Wallace) 1994
Girl Who Has Everything (pl Fitch) 1906
Girl with the Green Eyes (pl Fitch) 1905
Girls (f Ferber) 1921
Girls (pl Fitch) 1908
Girls at Play (f Theroux) 1969
Girls at the Sphinx (f Farrell) 1959
Girls on the Run (po Ashbery) 1999
Give 'em the Ax (f E. Gardner) 1944
Give Your Heart to the Hawks and Other Poems (po Jeffers) 1933
Givers (f Freeman) 1904
Giving Birth to Thunder, Sleeping with His Daughter: Coyote Builds North America (o Lopez) 1978
Glad Day (po Boyle) 1938
Glad of It (pl Fitch) 1903
Gladiator (pl Bird) 1831
Glance Away (f Wideman) 1967
Glass Face in the Rain: New Poems (po W. Stafford) 1982
Glass House (tv Capote) 1972
Glass Key (f Hammett) 1931
Glass Menagerie (pl T. Williams) 1944
Glass Village (f Queen) 1954
Glaucus (pl Boker) 1940
Gleanings in Buddha-Fields: Studies of Hand and Soul in the Far East (o Hearn) 1897
Gleanings in Europe: England (o Cooper) 1837
Gleanings in Europe: Italy (o Cooper) 1838
Glengarry Glen Ross (pl Mamet) 1983
Glimpses of the Moon (f Wharton) 1922
Glimpses of Three Coasts (o H. Jackson) 1886
Glimpses of Unfamiliar Japan (o Hearn) 1894
Glinda of Oz (f Baum) 1920
Glitz (f Leonard) 1985
Gloria Mundi (f Frederic) 1898
Glory (f Nabokov) 1971
Glory in the Flower (pl Inge) 1959
Glory Never Guesses (po Patchen) 1956
Glory of Columbia: Her Yeomanry! (pl Dunlap) 1817
Glory of Hera (f Gordon) 1972
Glory of the Conquered (f Glaspell) 1909
Glory of the Nightingales (po Robinson) 1930
Glory Road (f Heinlein) 1963
Gloucester Moors and Other Poems (po Moody) 1909
Gluttony (pl Guare), 1985
Gnomes and Occasions (po Nemerov) 1972

Gnomobile (f Sinclair) 1936
Go Down, Moses, and Other Stories (f Faulkner) 1942
Go Go (po W. Williams) 1923
Go Tell It on the Mountain (f James Baldwin) 1953
Go to the Widow-Maker (f J. Jones) 1967
Goat for Azazel (f Fisher) 1956
Goat Song: A Novel of Ancient Greece (f Yerby) 1967
Goatfoot Milktongue Twinbird: Interviews, Essays, and Notes on Poetry 1970-6 (o Hall) 1978
Gobbler of God: A Poem of the Southern Appalachians (po MacKaye) 1928
Goblins and Pagodas (po Fletcher) 1916
God Bless Our Home (pl Barry) 1924
God Bless You, Mr. Rosewater (f Vonnegut) 1965
God Glorified in the Work of Redemption (o Edwards) 1731
God Knows (f Heller) 1984
God Made Alaska for the Indians: Selected Essays (o Reed) 1982
God of His Fathers and Other Stories (f London) 1901
God or Caesar? The Writing of Fiction for Beginners (o Fisher) 1953
God Rest You Merry Gentlemen (f Hemingway) 1933
God Without Thunder: An Unorthodox Defense of Orthodoxy (o Ransom) 1930
God's Country and My People (o Morris) 1968
God's Grace (f Malamud) 1982
God's Images: The Bible: A New Vision (o Dickey) 1977
God's Men (f Buck) 1950
God's Trombones: Seven Negro Sermons in Verse (po J. Johnson) 1927
God-Seeker (f Lewis) 1949
Godbey: A Dramatic Poem (pl Masters) 1931
Goddess (pl Chayefsky) 1958
Goddess Abides (f Buck) 1972
Goddess and Other Women (f Oates) 1974
Godfather (f Puzo) 1969
Godfather: Part II (scr Puzo) 1974
Godfather: Part III (scr Puzo) 1990
Gods Arrive (f Wharton) 1932
Gods of Mars (f E. Burroughs) 1918
Gods of the Lightning (pl M. Anderson) 1928
Gods Themselves (f Asimov) 1972
God's Favorite (pl Simon) 1974
Goethe and Schiller: Their Lives and Works (o Boyesen) 1879
Goin' a Buffalo: A Tragifantasy (pl Bullins) 1968
Going Abroad (f Updike) 1987
Going After Cacciato (f T. O'Brien) 1978
Going for the Rain (po Ortiz) 1976
Going Home (f Mohr) 1986
Going Home Again (pl Harrigan) 1874
Going Places (po W. Stafford) 1974
Going to Meet the Man (f James Baldwin) 1965
Going to the Territory (o Ellison) 1986
Going to War with All My Relations: New and Selected Poems (po Rose) 1993
Going-to-the-Stars (po Lindsay) 1926
Going-to-the-Sun (po Lindsay) 1923
Gold (pl O'Neill) 1921
Gold and Iron (f Hergesheimer) 1918
Gold Coast (f Leonard) 1980
Gold Comes in Bricks (f E. Gardner) 1940
Gold Diggers (f Creeley) 1954

Gold Hesperides (po Frost) 1935
Gold Piece (pl Hughes) 1921
Gold Rushes and Mining Camps of the Early American West (o Fisher) 1968
Gold through the Trees (pl Childress) 1955
Gold, with Herbert Heron (pl London) 1972
Goldberg Street (pl Mamet) 1989
Golden Apples (f Rawlings) 1935
Golden Apples (f Welty) 1949
Golden Apples of the Sun (f Bradbury) 1953
Golden Book of Springfield, Being a Review of a Book That Will Appear in 2018 o Lindsay) 1920
Golden Bottle (f Donnelly) 1892
Golden Bowl (f H. James) 1904
Golden Boy (pl Odets) 1937
Golden Calf (f Boyesen) 1892
Golden Calves (f Auchincloss) 1989
Golden Cherub (pl Guare) 1962(?)
Golden Child (pl Hwang) 1998
Golden Christmas: A Chronicle of St. John's (f Simms) 1852
Golden Coin (f Lin Tai-yi) 1946
Golden Curb for the Mouth (o Mather) 1707
Golden Door: The United States from 1865 to 1918 (o Asimov) 1977
Golden Fleece (po W. Benét) 1935
Golden Fleece of California (po Masters) 1936
Golden Fleece: The American Adventures of a Fortune Hunting Earl (f D. Phillips) 1903
Golden Fleecing (scr S. Perelman) 1940
Golden Gate (scr Hwang) 1993
Golden Gate Country (o Atherton) 1945
Golden Grains from Life's Harvest Field (f Arthur) 1850
Golden Hawk (f Yerby) 1948
Golden House (f Warner) 1895
Golden Legend (po Longfellow) 1851
Golden Mean and Other Poems (po A. Tate) 1923
Golden Peacock (f Atherton) 1936
Golden Remedy (f Stout) 1931
Golden Rooms (f Fisher) 1944
Golden Six (pl M. Anderson) 1961
Golden Spiders (f Stout) 1953
Golden Spike (f Dell) 1934
Golden Summer (f Queen) 1953
Golden Wedding: A Masque (po B. Taylor) 1868
Golden Whales of California and Other Rhymes in the American Language (po Lindsay) 1920
Golden Widow (pl Daly) 1889
Golden Year (po Riley) 1898
Golden Years (pl A. Miller) 1990
Golden Yesterdays (o Deland) 1941
Goldwyn Follies (scr Hecht) 1938
Golf Dreams (o Updike) 1996
Goliah: A Utopian Essay (f London) 1973
Gone with the Wind (scr S. Howard) 1939
Gone with the Wind (f M. Mitchell) 1936
Good as Gold (f Heller) 1979
Good Day to Die (f Harrison) 1973
Good Deed and Other Stories of Asia, Past and Present (f Buck) 1969
Good Doctor (pl Simon) 1973
Good Earth (f Buck) 1931

Good Earth (scr Connelly) 1937
Good Fellow (pl Kaufman) 1931
Good Fetched Out of Evil (o Mather) 1706
Good for the Soul (f Deland) 1899
Good Girl Is Hard to Find (pl Baraka) 1958
Good Help Is Hard to Find (pl Kopit) 1981
Good Hunting: A Satire (pl N. West) 1938
Good Intentions (po Nash) 1942
Good Journey (po Ortiz) 1977
Good Lion (f Hemingway) 1998
Good Luck in Cracked Italian (po Hugo) 1969
Good Luck, Miss Wyckoff (f Inge) 1971
Good Man Is Hard to Find and Other Stories (f O'Connor) 1955
Good Morning, Revolution: Uncollected Social Protest Writings (o Hughes) 1973
Good Morning: Last Poems (po Van Doren) 1973
Good Neighbor: An Interlude (pl Dunlap) 1814
Good News of Death and Other Poems (po Simpson) 1955
Good Night, Willie Lee, I'll See You in the Morning (po A. Walker) 1979
Good Old Age (o Mather) 1726
Good Place (o Updike) 1973
Good Samaritan and Other Stories (f J. O'Hara) 1974
Good Soldier: A Key to the Novels of Ford Madox Ford (o Gordon) 1963
Good Spec (pl R. Tyler) 1797
Good Taste (f Asimov) 1976
Good Theatre (pl Morley) 1926
Good Wives (o Child) 1833
Good Wolf (f Burnett) 1908
Good Woman (f Bromfield) 1927
Good Words to You (o Ciardi) 1987
Good-bye Wisconsin (f Wescott) 1928
Good-Bye My Fancy (po Whitman) 1891
Goodbye (pl Green) 1954
Goodbye, Columbus, and Five Short Stories (f P. Roth) 1959
Goodbye Girl (pl Simon) 1977
Goodbye, Howard (pl Linney) 1982
Goodbye Look (f Macdonald) 1969
Goodbye Sweetwater (f Dumas) 1988
Goodbye to Berlin (f Isherwood) 1939
Goody Two-Shoes and Other Famous Nursery Tales (o Freeman) 1883
Goose on the Grave, and The Owl: Two Short Novels (f Hawkes) 1954
Goose-Quill Papers (o Guiney) 1885
Gordon Keith (f Page) 1903
Gore Vidal's "Billy the Kid," (tv Vidal) 1989
Gorgeous Isle: A Romance: Scene, Nevis, B.W.I., 1842 (f Atherton) 1908
Gorilla, My Love (f Bambara) 1972
Gorky Park (f M. Smith) 1981
Gospel According to the Sun (f Mailer) 1997
Gospel Glow (pl Hughes) 1962
Gospel of Freedom (f Herrick) 1898
Gospel Singer (f Crews) 1968
Gossip (pl Fitch) 1895
Gotcha! (tv Bradbury) 1988
Gottschalk and the Grand Tarantelle (po Brooks) 1988
Gourd Dancer (po Momaday) 1976
Governess (pl A. Tate) 1962

Government (f Traven) 1935
Governor's Lady (pl Belasco) 1912
Governor's Son (pl Cohan) 1901
Goyescas (pl J. Johnson) 1915
Grace after Meat (po Ransom) 1924
Grace Notes (po Dove) 1989
Grace Weldon (f Ingraham) 1845
Graduation Dress (tv Faulkner) 1960
Graf Benyowsky (pl Dunlap) 1799
Graffiti (po Guthrie) 1959
Grain of Dust (f D. Phillips) 1911
Grain of Mustard Seed (po Sarton) 1971
Grammar of Motives (o Burke) 1945
Grand (f T. Williams) 1964
Grand Army Man (pl Belasco) 1907
Grand Design (f Dos Passos) 1949
Grand Duke's Opera House (pl Harrigan) 1877
Grand Mothers (po Giovanni) 1994
Grand Piano (f Goodman) 1942
Grand Tour (pl Rice) 1951
Grand'ther Baldwin's Thanksgiving with Other Ballads and Poems (po Alger) 1875
Grandfather's Chair: A History for Youth (o Hawthorne) 1841
Grandfathers (f Richter) 1964
Grandioso, Amoroso, Serioso, Verisoso, Polyglotte-Anglo-Italio-Americano Opera (pl Brougham) 1847
Grandissimes: A Story of Creole Life (f Cable) 1880
Grandma Moses (scr MacLeish) 1950
Grandma Never Lived in America: The New Journalism of Cahan (o Cahan) 1986
Grandmother of the Light: A Medicine Woman's Sourcebook (o P. Allen) 1991
Grandmothers: A Family Portrait (f Wescott) 1927
Grandmother's Pigeon (f Erdrich) 1996
Grandmother's Story of Bunker Hill Battle: As She Saw It from the Belfry (po Holmes) 1995
Grandpa and the Statue (pl A. Miller) 1945
Granite and Cypress (po Jeffers) 1975
Granny (pl Fitch) 1904
Granny Boling (pl Green) 1921
Grapes of Wrath (f Steinbeck) 1939
Grass from Two Years, Let's Leave (po Bly) 1975
Grass Harp (f Capote) 1951
Grass Harp (pl Capote) 1952
Gratitude to Old Teachers (po Bly) 1993
Graveyard for Lunatics: Another Tale of Two Cities (f Bradbury) 1990
Gravity's Rainbow (f Pynchon) 1973
Graysons: A Story of Illinois (f Eggleston) 1888
Great American Fourth of July (pl MacLeish) 1975
Great American Gentleman: Byrd of Westover in Virginia (o Byrd) 1963
Great American Goof (pl Saroyan) 1940
Great American Hoax (tv Chayefsky) 1957
Great American Novel (f P. Roth) 1973
Great American Novel (o W. Williams) 1923
Great Battles of the War (o S. Crane) 1901
Great Christian Doctrine of Original Sin Defended (o Edwards) 1758
Great Circle (f Aiken) 1933
Great Concern of a Watchman for Souls (o Edwards) 1743

Great Cryptogram: Francis Bacon's Cipher in the So-Called Shakespeare Plays (o Donnelly) 1888
Great Day (pl Hurston) 1932
Great Day in the Cows' House (po Hall) 1984
Great Days (f Barthelme) 1979
Great Days (f Dos Passos) 1958
Great Divide (pl Moody) 1909
Great Gatsby (f Fitzgerald) 1925
Great God Brown (pl O'Neill) 1926
Great God Success (f D. Phillips) 1901
Great Goodness of Life (A Coon Show) (pl Baraka) 1967
Great In-Toe-Natural Walking Match (pl Harrigan) 1879
Great Interrogation (pl London) 1905
Great Jones Street (f Delillo) 1973
Great Magoo (pl Hecht) 1932
Great Meadow (f Roberts) 1930
Great Mistake (f Rinehart) 1940
Great Mysteries and Little Plagues (o Neal) 1870
Great Praises (po Eberhart) 1957
Great Quillow (f Thurber) 1944
Great Railway Bazaar: By Train through Asia (o Theroux) 1975
Great Secession Winter of 1860-61 and Other Essays (o Adams) 1958
Great Short Works (f London) 1965
Great Sinner (scr Isherwood) 1949
Great Son (f Ferber) 1945
Great Stone Face (f Hawthorne) 1997
Great Taos Bank Robbery and Other Indian Country Affairs (o Hillerman) 1980
Great Tragic Revival (pl Brougham) 1858
Great Unknown (pl Daly) 1890
Great Valley (po Masters) 1916
Great Violinists in Performance (o H. Roth) 1986
Great Waltz (pl Hart) 1934
Great White Wall (po W. Benét) 1916
Great World and Timothy Colt (f Auchincloss) 1956
Greater Inclination (f Wharton) 1899
Greatest Western [Indian, Animal] Stories (f Grey) 1975
Greek Coffin Mystery (f Queen) 1932
Greeks (pl Parks) 1990
Greeks Had a Word for It (pl Akins) 1930
Greeks Had a Word for Them (scr S. Howard) 1932
Greeks Remember Marathon (radio M. Anderson) 1944
Greeks: A Great Adventure (o Asimov) 1965
Green Bay Tree (f Bromfield) 1924
Green Bough (po Faulkner) 1933
Green Centuries (f Gordon) 1941
Green Door (o Freeman) 1910
Green Fields and Running Brooks (po Riley) 1893
Green Fruit (po J. Bishop) 1917
Green Grass, Blue Sky, White House (f Morris) 1970
Green Hills of Africa (o Hemingway) 1935
Green Mile (f King) 1996
Green Pastures (scr Connelly) 1936
Green Pastures: A Fable Suggested by Roark Bradford's Southern Sketches "Ol' Man Adam an' His Chillun" (pl Connelly) 1929
Green Roller (o R. Bradford) 1949
Green Shadows, White Whale (f Bradbury) 1992
Green Wall (po J. Wright) 1957
Green Wave (po Rukeyser) 1948
Green with Beasts (po Merwin) 1956

Greenfield Hill (po Dwight) 1794

Greenwich Village as It Is (o Barnes) 1978

Greifenstein (f Crawford) 1889

Grendel (f J. Gardner) 1971

Grey, Outdoorsman: Best Hunting and Fishing Tales (f Grey) 1972

Greyslaer: A Romance of the Mohawk (f Hoffman) 1840

Griffin's Way (f Yerby) 1962

Griffith Gaunt (pl Daly) 1866

Grip (pl Harrigan) 1885

Groom Service (pl Dorris) 1993

Grossery of Limericks (po Asimov) 1981

Grossery of Limericks (po Ciardi) 1981

Grouch at the Game (f Ade) 1901

Ground We Stand On: Some Examples from the History of a Political Creed (o Dos Passos) 1941

Ground Work II: In the Dark (po Duncan) 1987

Ground Work: Before the War (po Duncan) 1984

GroundWork (po Madhubuti) 1996

Group (f McCarthy) 1963

Group (pl M. Warren) 1775

Grouped Thoughts and Scattered Fancies: A Collection of Sonnets (po Simms) 1845

Groves of Academe (f McCarthy) 1952

Growth (f Tarkington) 1927

Guard (po Hejinian) 1984

Guard of Honor (f Cozzens) 1948

Guardian (pl Tarkington) 1907

Guardian Angel (f Holmes) 1867

Guardian Angel (f Paretsky) 1991

Guest of Quesnay (f Tarkington) 1908

Guests (f Dorris) 1994

Guide (scr Buck) 1965

Guide, Grammar, Watch, and The Thirty Nights (po Hejinian) 1996

Guide to Research on North American Indians (o Dorris) 1984

Guide to the Ruins (po Nemerov) 1950

Guillotine Club and Other Stories (f S. Mitchell) 1910

Guillotine Party and Other Stories (f Farrell) 1935

Guilty Pleasures (f Barthelme) 1974

Gullible's Travels (f Lardner) 1917

Gulzara (pl Mowatt) 1840

Gunga Din (scr Hecht, MacArthur) 1939

Gunga Din Highway (f Chin) 1994

Gunnar: A Tale of Norse Life (f Boyesen) 1874

Guns of August (o Tuchman) 1962

Guns of the Timberlands (f L'Amour) 1955

Gunshot Wounds and Other Injuries of Nerves (o S. Mitchell) 1864

Gunsights (f Leonard) 1979

Guy Domville (pl H. James) 1894

Guy Rivers: A Tale of Georgia (f Simms) 1834

Guys and Dolls (f Runyon) 1931

Gypsy (pl M. Anderson) 1929

Gypsy (pl Laurents) 1959

Gypsy Days on the Delta (o E. Gardner) 1967

Gypsy in Amber (f M. Smith) 1971

Gypsy Wildcat (scr Cain) 1944

Gypsy's Curse (f Crews) 1974

Habit of Being: Letters (o O'Connor) 1979

Habitations of the World: Essays (o Gass) 1984

Hacienda: A Story of Mexico (f Porter) 1934

Hail and Farewell (tv Bradbury) 1989

Hail, Klarkash-Ton! (o Lovecraft) 1971

Hail the Conquering Hero (f Yerby) 1977

Hair o' the Chine (f Coover) 1979

Hairs: Pelitos (f Cisneros) 1994

Hairy Ape (pl O'Neill) 1922

Haiti (pl Du Bois) 1938

Half Gods (pl S. Howard) 1930

Half Moon Street: Two Short Novels (f Theroux) 1984

Half Portions (f Ferber) 1920

Half-Breed and Other Stories (f Whitman) 1927

Half-Century of Conflict (o Parkman) 1892

Half-Past Nation Time (o C. Johnson) 1972

Halfbreed Chronicles (po Rose) 1985

Halfway House (f Queen) 1936

Halfway to Silence (po Sarton) 1980

Hallelujah Anyway (po Patchen) 1966

Hallelujah, Baby! (pl Laurents) 1967

Hallelujah, I'm a Bum (Hallelujah, I'm a Tramp, Lazy Bones) (scr Behrman, Hecht) 1933

Hamlet (f Faulkner) 1940

Hamlet Had an Uncle (f Cabell) 1940

Hamlet of A. MacLeish (po MacLeish) 1928

Hamlin Garland: Stories (f Garland) 1994

Hammer and Rapier (f J. Cooke) 1870

Hammett Homicides (f Hammett) 1946

Hand in the Glove (f Stout) 1937

Hand of Siva (pl Hecht) 1920

Hand of the Potter (pl Dreiser) 1919

Hand That Cradles the Rock (po R Brown) 1971

Hand-Made Fables (f Ade) 1920

Hands Across the Table (scr Parker) 1935

Hands of Esau (f Deland) 1914

Handsome Cyril (f Ade) 1903

Handy Guide for Beggars, Especially Those of the Poetic Fraternity (o Lindsay) 1916

Hanging of the Crane (po Longfellow) 1874

Hanging Woman Creek (f L'Amour) 1964

Hangsaman (f S. Jackson) 1951

Hannah Jane (po Nasby) 1882

Hannah Thurston (f B. Taylor) 1863

Hannele (pl MacKaye) 1910

Hannibal Brown: Posthumous Poem (po Robinson) 1936

Hanoi (o McCarthy) 1968

Hans Christian Andersen (scr Hart) 1952

Happiness Machine (tv Bradbury) 1992

Happy Birthday, Wanda June (pl Vonnegut) 1970

Happy Days (po Nash) 1933

Happy Days 1880-1892 (o Mencken) 1940

Happy End (f Hergesheimer) 1919

Happy Ending: Collected Lyrics (po Guiney) 1909

Happy Grandmother. By Mrs. Child. To Which Is Added, The White Palfrey (f Child) 1835

Happy Isles of Oceania: Padding the Pacific (o Theroux) 1992

Happy Journey (pl Wilder) 1934

Happy Journey to Trenton and Camden (pl Wilder) 1931

Happy Man (po Hall) 1986

Happy Marriage (pl Fitch) 1909

Happy Marriage and Other Poems (po MacLeish) 1924

Harbinger: A May-Gift (po Holmes) 1833

Hard Candy: A Book of Stories (f T. Williams) 1954

Hard Facts (po Baraka) 1976

Hard Lines (po Nash) 1931

Hard Not to Be King (po Frost) 1951

Hard Time (f Paretsky) 1999

Harlem and Other Poems (po W. Benét) 1935

Harlem Gallery: Book 1, The Curator (po Tolson) 1965

Harlem Shadows (po McKay) 1922

Harlem: Negro Metropolis (o McKay) 1940

Harlequin and Columbine and Other Stories (f Tarkington) 1918

Harlot's Ghost (f Mailer) 1991

Harmonics (po Hovey) 1890

Harmonium (po Stevens) 1923

Harmony of Deeper Music: Posthumous Poems (po Masters) 1976

Harm's Way (pl Wellman) 1984

Harp-Weaver and Other Poems (po Millay) 1923

Harper (f Macdonald) 1966

Harriet Tubman: Conductor on the Underground Railroad (f Petry) 1955

Harrigan and Rivers with O'Hara (po F. O'Hara) 1959

Harry Harefoot (f Ingraham) 1845

Hart Crane and Winters: Their Literary Correspondence (o Winters) 1978

Hash Knife Oust (f Grey) 1933

Hasty-Pudding (po Barlow) 1796

Hat on the Bed (f J. O'Hara) 1963

Hatchets to Hew Down the Tree of Sin (o Mather) 1705

Hatzar-Maveth (o Mather) 1726

Haunted (f Oates) 1994

Haunted Bookshop (f Morley) 1919

Haunted Computer and the Android Pope (po Bradbury) 1981

Haunted Lady (f Rinehart) 1942

Haunted Mesa (f L'Amour) 1987

Haunted Mirror: Stories (f Roberts) 1932

Haunter of the Dark and Other Tales of Horror (f Lovecraft) 1951

Haunting of Hill House (f S. Jackson) 1959

Haunting of the New (tv Bradbury) 1989

Havana Bay (f M. Smith) 1999

Have a Heart (po Creeley) 1990

Have Space Suit, Will Travel (f Heinlein) 1958

Have They Attacked Mary (po Stein). 1917

Have You Seen These? (f Asimov) 1974

Have You Sold Your Dozen Roses? (scr Ferlinghetti) 1957

Haven's End (f Marquand) 1933

Haven't-Time and Don't-Be-in-a-Hurry and Other Stories (f Arthur) 1852

Hawai'i One Summer (o Kingston) 1987

Hawk Is Dying (f Crews) 1973

Hawk Moon (pl Shepard) 1989

Hawkes Scrapbook: A New Taste in Literature (o Hawkes) 1991

Hawkline Monster: A Gothic Western (f Brautigan) 1974

Hawks of Hawk-Hollow: A Tradition of Pennsylvania (f Bird) 1835

Hawkweed (po Goodman) 1967

Haworth's (f Burnett) 1879

Hawthorne's Creed (o Updike) 1981

Hazard of New Fortunes (f Howells) 1889

Hazardous Ground (pl Daly) 1868

Hazel Flagg (pl Hecht) 1953

Hazel-Blossoms (po Whittier) 1875

He and She (pl Crothers) 1912

He Married His Wife (scr J. O'Hara) 1940

He Sent Forth a Raven (f Roberts) 1935

He Who Hunted Birds in His Father's Village: The Dimensions of a Haida Myth (o Snyder) 1979

He Would Be a Mountebank (f Alger) 1888

Head and Heart of Thomas Jefferson (o Dos Passos) 1954

Head of the Family (pl Fitch) 1898

Head of the House of Coombe (f Burnett) 1922

Head-Deep in Strange Sounds: Free-Flight Improvisations from the UnEnglish (po Dickey) 1979

Heading West (f Betts) 1981

Headless Horseman (pl S. Benét) 1937

Headlines (pl T. Williams) 1936

Headsman (f Cooper) 1833

Healer (f Herrick) 1911

Healing Song for the Inner Ear: Poems (po M. Harper) 1985

Health Trip to the Tropics (o Willis) 1854

Hearing Out Farrell (o Farrell) 1985

Heart for the Gods of Mexico (f Aiken) 1939

Heart Is a Lonely Hunter (f McCullers) 1940

Heart of a Woman (o Angelou) 1981

Heart of Aztlán (f Anaya) 1976

Heart of Happy Hollow (f Dunbar) 1904

Heart of Hawthorne's Journal (o Hawthorne) 1929

Heart of Hyacinth (f Atherton, Eaton) 1903

Heart of Maryland (pl Belasco) 1895

Heart of Paddy Whack (pl Crothers) 1914

Heart of Rome: A Tale of the "Lost Water " (f Crawford) 1903

Heart of the West (f Henry) 1907

Heart's Garden, The Garden's Heart (po Rexroth) 1967

Heart's Highway: A Romance of Virginia in the Seventeenth Century (f Freeman) 1900

Heart's Kindred (f Gale) 1915

Heart-Histories and Life-Pictures (f Arthur) 1853

Heart-Shape in the Dust (po Hayden) 1940

Heartbreak Kid (scr Simon), 1972

Heartlove: Wedding and Love Poems (po Madhubuti) 1998

Hearts Come Home and Other Stories (f Buck) 1962

Hearts of Oak (pl Belasco, Herne) 1879

Hearts of Oak (pl Rowson) 1810-11(?)

Hearts of Three (f London) 1918

Heartsease and Rue (po J. Lowell) 1888

Heartsong (pl Laurents) 1947

Heart's Needle (po Snodgrass) 1959

Heat: And Other Stories (f Oates) 1991

Heat's On (f Himes) 1960

Heathcotes (f Cooper) 1854

Heathen Chinee (po Harte) 1870

Heathen Days 1890-1936 (o Mencken) 1943

Heathen Valley (f Linney) 1962

Heathens and Revolutionary Art: Poems and Lecture (o Baraka) 1994

Heaven and Other Poems (po Kerouac) 1977

Heaven's My Destination (f Wilder) 1934

Heavenly City, Earthly City (po Duncan) 1947

Heavenly Conversation (o Mather) 1710

Heavenly Host (f Asimov) 1975

Heavens and Earth (po S. Benét) 1920

HECHIZOspells (po Sánchez) 1976

Hector's Inheritance (f Alger) 1885

Hedgehog (f Doolittle) 1936

Hedylus (f Doolittle) 1928
Heidenmauer (f Cooper) 1832
Heidi (pl Simon) 1959
Heinrich Himmler: Platoons & Files (po Snodgrass) 1985
Heir of Gaymount (f J. Cooke) 1870
Heiress (f Arthur) 1845
Heiress of Red Dog and Other Sketches (f Harte) 1879
Held by the Enemy (pl Gillette) 1886
Held Up (pl Harte) 1903
Helen (radio Donleavy) 1956
Helen Ford (f Alger) 1866
Helen Halsey (f Simms) 1844
Helen in Egypt (po Doolittle) 1961
Helen of Troy and Other Poems (po Teasdale) 1911
Helen of Troy, New York (pl Connelly, Kaufman) 1923
Helen: A Courtship (po Faulkner) 1981
Heliodora and Other Poems (po Doolittle) 1924
Heliogabalus: A Buffoonery (pl Mencken) 1920
Hell of a Good Time and Other Stories (f Farrell) 1950
Hell: A Verse Drama and Photo-Play (pl Sinclair) 1923
Hellbox (f J. O'Hara) 1947
Heller with a Gun (f L'Amour) 1955
Hellman and Hammett: The Legendary Passion of Lillian Hellman
    and Dashiell Hammett (o Hammett) 1996
Hello, Broadway! (pl Cohan) 1914
Hello Charlie (tv Hecht) 1959
Hello from Bertha (pl T. Williams) 1946
Hello, Out There (pl Saroyan) 1941
Hello Towns! (o S. Anderson) 1929
Hello: A Journal, February 23—May 3, 1976 (po Creeley) 1978
Helmets (po Dickey) 1964
Help Each Other Club (pl Tarkington) 1933
Help Yourself (scr Rice) 1920
Helper (pl Bullins) 1970
Helpful Alphabet of Friendly Objects (po Updike) 1995
Helping Himself, or, Grant Thornton's Ambition (f Alger) 1886
Hemingway in Michigan (f Hemingway) 1966
Hemingway on Writing (o Hemingway) 1984
Hemingway Reader (o Hemingway) 1953
Hemingway: Cub Reporter; "Kansas City Star" Stories (o
    Hemingway) 1970
Hemingway: The Wild Years (o Hemingway) 1962
Hen Flower (po Kinnell) 1969
Henderson the Rain King (f Bellow) 1959
Henrietta (pl B. Howard) 1901
Henry Adams (o Auchincloss) 1971
Henry and June: From the Unexpurgated Diary (o Nin) 1986
Henry Gross and His Dowsing Rod (o Roberts) 1951
Henry Howard (f Ingraham) 1845
Henry James Year Book (pl H. James) 1911
Henry Moore: The Life and Work of a Great Sculptor (o Hall) 1966
Henry St. John, Gentleman, of "Flower of Hundreds" in the
    County of Prince George, Virginia: A Tale of 1774-75 (f J.
    Cooke) 1859
Henry's Fate and Other Poems 1967-1972 (po Berryman) 1977
Hephzibah Guinness, Thee and You, and A Draft on the Banks
    of Spain (f S. Mitchell) 1880
Her (f Doolittle) 1984
Her (f Ferlinghetti) 1960
Her Blue Body Everything We Know: Earthling Poems 1965-1990
    (po A. Walker) 1991

Her Fifth Marriage and Other Stories (f E. Howe) 1928
Her Great Match (pl Fitch) 1905
Her Husband's Affairs (scr Hecht) 1947
Her Majesty the Queen (f J. Cooke) 1873
Her Mountain Lover (f Garland) 1901
Her Own Enemy (pl Daly) 1884
Her Own Way (pl Fitch) 1907
Her Serene Highness (f D. Phillips) 1902
Her Sister (pl Fitch) 1907
Herakles: A Play in Verse (pl MacLeish) 1965
Herb Basket (po Eberhart) 1950
Herbert Carter's Legacy; or The Inventor's Son (f Alger) 1875
Herbert Selden (f Alger) 1981
Herbert West Reanimator (f Lovecraft) 1977
Here and Beyond (f Wharton) 1926
Here and Now (po Levertov) 1956
Here at Eagle Pond (o Hall) 1990
Here Come the Clowns (pl Barry) 1939
Here Is Einbaum (f Morris) 1973
Here Is New York (o White) 1949
Here Lies: The Collected Stories (f Parker) 1939
Here There Be Tygers (tv Bradbury) 1990
Here Today and Gone Tomorrow: Four Short Novels (f Bromfield)
    1934
Here's O'Hara (f J. O'Hara) 1946
Heritage of Dedlow Marsh and Other Tales (f Harte) 1889
Heritage of Hatcher Ide (f Tarkington) 1941
Heritage of the Desert (f Grey) 1910
Herland: A Lost Feminist Utopia (f Gilman) 1979
Herman de Ruyter (f Ingraham) 1844
Hermetic Definition (po Doolittle) 1972
Hermia, An American Woman (f Atherton) 1889
Hermia Suydam (f Atherton) 1889
HERmione (f Doolittle) 1981
Hermit and the Wild Woman, and Other Stories (f Wharton) 1908
Hermit of 69th Street (f Kosinski) 1986
Hermit of Carmel and Other Poems (po Santayana) 1901
Hermit Woman (f G. Jones) 1983
Hero (po Creeley) 1969
Hero (pl Kopit) 1964
Hero Ain't Nothin' but a Sandwich (f Childress) 1973
Hero of Santa Maria (pl Hecht) 1920
Hero of the World (pl Saroyan) 1940
Hero with the Private Parts: Essays (o Lytle) 1966
Heroes (pl Ashbery) 1952
Heroes Just Happen (pl B. Smith) 1940
Heroine in Bronze (f J. Allen) 1912
Herself (o Calisher) 1972
Herzog (f Bellow) 1964
Hesper (f Garland) 1903
Hetty's Strange History (f H. Jackson) 1877
Hey, Stay a While (pl Guare) 1984
Hi There! (po Creeley) 1965
Hidden Flower (f Buck) 1952
Hidden Heart of Baja (o E. Gardner) 1962
Hidden Heritage: A Rediscovery of the Ideas and Forces That Link
    the Thought of Our Time with the Culture of the Past (o
    Lawson) 1950
Hide and Seek (po Morley) 1920
Hide and Seek: A Continuing Journey (o J. West) 1973
Hiding Place (f Wideman) 1981

High Bid (pl H. James) 1908
High Graders (f L'Amour) 1965
High Hearts (f R Brown) 1986
High License Does Not Diminish the Evil (o Nasby) 1887
High Lonesome (f L'Amour) 1962
High Noon, Part 2: The Return of Will Kane (scr Leonard) 1980
High Place (f Cabell) 1923
High Road (pl Sheldon) 1912
High Society (o Parker) 1920
High Tide in Tucson: Essays from Now or Never (o Kingsolver)
   1995
High Time along the Wabash (pl Saroyan) 1961
High Tor (pl M. Anderson) 1937
High Window (f Chandler) 1942
High-Jinks of Baum (po Baum) 1959
Higher Jazz (f E. Wilson) 1998
Highest Bidder (pl Belasco) 1887
Highgate Road (po Ammons) 1977
Highland Call Song-Book (po Green) 1941
Highland Call: A Symphonic Play of American History (pl Green)
   1939
Hike and the Aeroplane (f Lewis) 1912
Hill of Stones and Other Poems (po S. Mitchell) 1883
Hillerman Country: A Journey through the Southwest with Tony
   Hillerman (o Hillerman) 1991
Hills Beyond (f Thomas Wolfe) 1941
Hills Grow Smaller (po Akins) 1937
Hills of Homicide (f L'Amour) 1983
Hilt to Hilt (f J. Cooke) 1869
Him (pl Cummings) 1927
Him with His Foot in His Mouth and Other Stories (f Bellow)
   1984
Hinge Picture (po S. Howe) 1974
Hints and Helps for the Home Circle (f Arthur) 1844
Hints to Pilgrims (po J. Tate) 1971
Hippolytus Temporizes (pl Doolittle) 1927
Hiram Elwood, The Banker (f Arthur) 1844
His Eminence, Death (f M. Smith) 1974
His Fortunate Grace (f Atherton) 1897
His Grace de Grammont (pl Fitch) 1894
His Grace of Osmonde (f Burnett) 1897
His Great Adventure (f Herrick) 1913
His Human Majesty (f Boyle) 1949
His Idea (po Creeley) 1973
His Last Skirmish (pl B. Smith) 1937
His Own People (f Tarkington) 1907
His Pa's Romance (po Riley) 1903
His Religion and Hers: A Study of the Faith of Our Fathers and
   the Work of Our Mothers (o Gilman) 1923
His Royal Nibs (f Eaton) 1925
His Thought Made Pockets & the Plane Buckt (po Berryman) 1958
His Toy, His Dream, His Rest: 308 Dream Songs (po Berryman)
   1968
His Vanished Star (f Murfree) 1894
Hist Whist and Other Poems for Children (po Cummings) 1983
Historia Amoris: A History of Love Ancient and Modern (o
   Saltus) 1906
Historia fun di Fareingte Shtaaten (o Cahan) 1910-12
Historical Essays (o Adams) 1891
Histories of the Dividing Line Betwixt Virginia and North Caro-
   lina (o Byrd) 1929

History (po Lowell) 1973
History Is Loose Again (po W. Stafford) 1991
History Is Your Own Heartbeat (po M. Harper) 1971
History of American Poetry 1900-1940 (o Gregory) 1946
History of Colonel Nathaniel Bacon's Rebellion in Virginia (po E.
   Cooke) 1731
History of England, 1765-95 (o Barlow) 1795
History of English Literature (o Moody) 1902
History of My Heart (po Pinsky) 1984
History of New York, for Schools (o Dunlap) 1837
History of Physics (o Asimov) 1984
History of Plymouth Plantation (o W. Bradford) 1912
History of South Carolina (o Simms) 1840
History of the American Theatre (o Dunlap) 1832
History of the Condition of Women, in Various Ages and Nations
   (o Child) 1835
History of the Conspiracy of Pontiac and the War of the North
   American Tribes Against the English Colonies (o Parkman) 1851
History of the Navy of the United States of America (o Cooper)
   1839
History of the Negro People: Omowale—The Child Returns Home
   (tv J. Williams) 1965
History of the New Netherlands, Province of New York, and the
   State of New York (o Dunlap) 1839-40
History of the Rise and Progress of the Arts of Design in the
   United States (o Dunlap) 1834
History of the Rise, Progress, and Termination of the American
   Revolution (o M. Warren) 1805
History of the United States of America during the Administra-
   tion of Jefferson and Madison (o Adams) 1889-91
History of the United States and Its People, for the Use of Schools
   (o Eggleston) 1888
History of the Work of Redemption (o Edwards) 1774
History of The Necronomicon (o Lovecraft) 1938
Hit-the-Trail Holliday (pl Cohan) 1916
Hither and Thither in Germany (f Howells) 1920
Hive of the Bee-Hunter: A Repository of Sketches (f Thorpe)
   1854
H.M. Pulham, Esquire (f Marquand) 1941
Hobohemia (pl Lewis) 1919
Hobomok, A Tale of Early Times (f Child) 1824
Hockey Poem (po Bly) 1974
Hocus Pocus (f Vonnegut) 1990
Hoffa (scr Mamet) 1992
Hogg (f S. Delany) 1996
Hold That Christmas Tiger! (o S. Perelman) 1954
Hold-Up Man (pl Hart) 1923
Holder of the World (f Mukherjee) 1993
Holding on for Heaven: The Cables and Postcards of Wolfe and
   Aline Bernstein (o Thomas Wolfe) 1985
Holding onto the Grass (po W. Stafford) 1992
Holding the Line: Women in the Great Arizona Mine Strike of
   1983 (o Kingsolver) 1989
Holes the Crickets Have Eaten in Blankets (po Bly) 1997
Holiday (pl Barry) 1929
Holiday (f Frank) 1923
Holiday Greetings 1966 (po E. Wilson) 1966
Holiday Inn (scr Rice) 1942
Holiday Song (tv Chayefsky) 1952
Hollywood Holiday (pl Van Druten) 1931
Hollywood Mystery! (f Hecht) 1946

Hollywood Pinafore (pl Kaufman) 1945
Hollywood: A Novel of America in the 1920s (f Vidal) 1990
Holy Food (radio Hagedorn) 1989
Holy Ghostly (pl Shepard) 1969
Holy Ghosts (pl Linney) 1974
Holy Grail and Other Fragments, Being the Uncompleted Parts
    of the Arthurian Dramas (pl Hovey) 1907
Holy the Firm (o Dillard) 1977
Holy-Cross and Other Tales (f Field) 1893
Homage to Mistress Bradstreet (po Berryman) 1956
Homage to Sextus Propertius (po Pound) 1934
Hombre (f Leonard) 1961
Home (f Sedgwick) 1835
Home as Found (f Cooper) 1838
Home Ballads and Other Poems (po Whittier) 1860
Home Boy (pl Bullins) 1976
Home Course in Religion (po Soto) 1991
Home Fires (pl Guare) 1969
Home, Its Work and Influence (o Gilman) 1903
Home of the Brave (pl Laurents) 1945
Home of the Free (pl Rice) 1917
Home on the Range (pl Baraka) 1968
Home Pastorals, Ballads, and Lyrics (po B. Taylor) 1875
Home Place (o Morris) 1948
Home Scenes and Home Influence (f Arthur) 1852
Home to Harlem (f McKay) 1928
Home to My Valley (f Green) 1970
Home Town (o S. Anderson) 1940
Home with Hazel and Other Stories (f Van Doren) 1957
Home: Social Essays (o Baraka) 1966
Home-Folks (po Riley) 1900
Home-Towners (pl Cohan) 1926
Homecoming (scr Kingsley) 1948
Homecoming (pl A. Wilson) 1979
Homecoming and Departure (po Goodman) 1937
Homecoming Game (f Nemerov) 1957
Homecoming: An Autobiography (o Dell) 1933
Homeland and Other Stories (f Kingsolver) 1989
Homely Lilla (f Herrick) 1923
Homespun of Oatmeal Gray (po Goodman) 1970
Homestead Called Damascus (po Rexroth) 1963
Homeward Bound (f Cooper) 1838
Homeward to America (po Ciardi) 1940
Homicide (scr Mamet) 1992
Homicide Trinity (f Stout) 1962
Hondo (f L'Amour) 1953
Honest John O'Brien (pl Cohan) 1916
Honest John Vane (f De Forest) 1875
Honeycomb (pl Green) 1972
Honeymoon Shiners (pl Wister) 1928
Honeymooners (pl Cohan) 1907
Honor (tv Vidal) 1956
Honor of the Family (pl Fitch) 1908
Honorable Amendments (po M. Harper) 1995
Honorable Men (f Auchincloss) 1986
Honorable Miss Moonlight (f Eaton) 1912
Honors at Dawn (pl A. Miller) 1936
Hoodlum Bard and Other Stories (f Harte) 1878
Hoosier Hand Book (f Ade) 1911
Hoosier School-Boy (f Eggleston) 1882
Hoosier School-Master (f Eggleston) 1871

Hop, Skip, and Jump (po Snyder) 1964
Hopalong Cassidy and the Trail to Seven Pines (f L'Amour) 1951
Hopalong Cassidy and the Rustlers of West Fork (f L'Amour)
    1951
Hopalong Cassidy and the Riders of High Rock (f L'Amour) 1951
Hopalong Cassidy, Trouble Shooter (f L'Amour) 1952
Hope Leslie (f Sedgwick) 1827
Hope of Heaven (f J. O'Hara) 1938
Hopeful Trout (po Ciardi) 1989
Hopi Roadrunner Dancing (po Rose) 1973
Hoping for a Hoopoe (po Updike) 1959
Hor-Hagidgad (o Mather) 1727
Horizon (pl Daly) 1885
Horn of Life (f Atherton) 1942
Horror in the Burying Ground and Other Tales (f Lovecraft) 1975
Horror in the Museum and Other Revisions (f Lovecraft) 1970
Horse Feathers (scr S. Perelman) 1932
Horse Heaven Hill (f Grey) 1959
Horse Knows the Way (f J. O'Hara) 1964
Horse-Shoe Robinson: A Tale of the Tory Ascendency (f Kennedy)
    1835
Horseman, Pass By (f McMurtry) 1961
Horses and Men (f S. Anderson) 1923
Horses Make a Landscape Look More Beautiful (po A. Walker)
    1984
Horses of the Sea (po Olson) 1976
Horse's Tale (f Twain) 1907
Hospital (scr Chayefsky) 1971
Hospital (f Fearing) 1939
Host with the Big Hat (o E. Gardner) 1970
Hot 'n' Throbbing (pl Vogel) 1992
Hot Day Hot Night (f Himes) 1970
Hot Iron (pl Green) 1926
Hot Plowshares (f Tourgée) 1883
Hotel Bemelmans (o Bemelmans) 1946
Hotel Insomnia (po Simic) 1992
Hotel Lautreamont (po Ashbery) 1992
Hotel New Hampshire (f J. Irving) 1981
Hotel Splendide (o Bemelmans) 1941
Hotel Universe (pl Barry) 1930
Hottentot Ossuary (f J. Tate) 1974
Houdini (pl Rukeyser) 1973
Hounds of Summer and Other Stories (f McCarthy) 1981
Hour, Gnats (po Eberhart) 1977
Hour Town (pl R. Anderson) 1938
Hours after Noon (f Bowles) 1959
House (po Shapiro) 1957
House and Home Papers (o Stowe) 1865
House Behind the Cedars (f Chesnutt) 1900
House by the Sea (o Sarton) 1977
House Divided (f Buck) 1935
House in Blind Alley (pl Rice) 1932
House Made of Dawn (f Momaday) 1968
House Not Meant to Stand (pl T. Williams) 1981
House of Blue Leaves (pl Guare) 1971
House of Brass (f Queen) 1968
House of Connelly (pl Green) 1931
House of Dust: A Symphony (po Aiken) 1920
House of Earth (f Buck) 1935
House of Fiction (pl H. James) 1957
House of Five Talents (f Auchincloss) 1960

House of Flowers (pl Capote) 1954
House of Games (scr Mamet) 1987
House of Incest (f Nin) 1936
House of Lee (f Atherton) 1940
House of Mirth (pl Fitch, Wharton) 1906
House of Pride and Other Tales of Hawaii (f London) 1912
House of Satan (o Nathan) 1926
House of Sleeping Beauties (pl Hwang) 1983
House of the Prophet (f Auchincloss) 1980
House of the Seven Gables: A Romance (f Hawthorne) 1851
House of the Solitary Maggot (f Purdy) 1974
House of Women (pl Bromfield) 1927
House on Jefferson Street: A Cycle of Memories (o Gregory) 1971
House on Mango Street (f Cisneros) 1983
House on Marshland (po Glück) 1975
House Party (pl Bullins) 1973
House VI Book (o Gass) 1980
House: An Episode in the Lives of Reuben Baker, Astronomer, and of His Wife Alice (f Field) 1896
Houseboat Days (po Ashbery) 1977
Housebreaker of Shady Hill and Other Stories (f Cheever) 1958
Household in Athens (f Wescott) 1945
Household Poems (po Longfellow) 1865
Hovering over Baja (o E. Gardner) 1961
How a Poem Comes to Be (o Riding) 1980
How Beautiful with Shoes (pl Steele) 1935
How Bigger Was Born: The Story of "Native Son" (o R. Wright) 1940
How Come Christmas: A Modern Morality (pl R. Bradford) 1930
How Do You Do? (pl Bullins) 1965
How Does a Poem Mean? (o Ciardi) 1960
How Doth the Simple Spelling Bee (f Wister) 1907
How His Ship Came Home (f Alger) 1887
How I Grew (o McCarthy) 1987
How I Learned to Drive (pl Vogel) 1997
How I Write 1 (o Hayden) 1972
How I Wrote Jubilee (o M. Walker) 1977
How Like a God (f Stout) 1929
How Mickey Made It (f J. Phillips) 1981
How One Friar Met the Devil and Two Pursued Him (f Field) 1900
How Stella Got Her Groove Back (f McMillan) 1996
How the Alligator Missed Breakfast (o Kinnell) 1982
How the West Was Won (f L'Amour) 1963
How to Enjoy Poetry (o Dickey) 1982
How to Have Europe All to Yourself (o Bemelmans) 1960
How to Hold Your Arms When It Rains (po W. Stafford) 1990
How to Read a Novel (o Gordon) 1957
How to Travel Incognito (o Bemelmans) 1952
How to Try a Lover (pl Barker) 1817
How to Write (o Stein) 1931
How to Write Short Stories (f Lardner) 1924
How To Enjoy Writing: A Book of Aid and Comfort (o Asimov) 1987
How We Think (o Dewey) 1910
How Well George Does It! (pl Gillette) 1936
How Writing Is Written (o Stein) 1974
How's the King? (pl Connelly) 1927
How's Your Health? (pl Tarkington) 1930
Howard (f Ingraham) 1843
Howbah Indians (f Ortiz) 1978

Howdy, Honey, Howdy (po Dunbar) 1905
Howl and Other Poems (po Ginsberg) 1956
H.P. Lovecraft in the Argosy: Collected Correspondence from the Munsey Magazines (o Lovecraft) 1994
H.P.L (po Lovecraft) 1937
Hub Fans Bid Kid Adieu (o Updike) 1977
Huck Finn and Tom Sawyer among the Indians and Other Unfinished Stories (f Twain) 1989
Huckleberries (o Thoreau) 1970
Huckleberry Finn, Alive at One Hundred (po Mailer) 1985
Hud (f McMurtry) 1963
Hudson River Bracketed (f Wharton) 1929
Hue and Cry (f McPherson) 1969
Huge Season (f Morris) 1954
Hugging the Shore: Essays and Criticism (o Updike) 1983
Hugh Selwyn Mauberley (po Pound) 1920
Hugh Wynne, Free Quaker (f S. Mitchell) 1897
Hughes in the Hispanic World and Haiti (o Hughes) 1977
Hughes Reader (o Hughes) 1958
Hughie (pl O'Neill) 1958
Hugo, The Deformed (f Alger) 1978
Hugo Weber (po Kerouac) 1967
Huguenots in Florida (f Simms) 1884
Human Being (f Morley) 1932
Human Body: Its Structure and Operation (o Asimov) 1963
Human Brain: Its Capabilities and Functions (o Asimov) 1964
Human Comedy (f Saroyan) 1943
Human Drift (f London) 1917
Human Factor (f M. Smith) 1975
Human Immortality: Two Supposed Objections to the Doctrine (o W. James) 1898
Human Nature (pl Dell) 1913
Human Nature (f Wharton) 1933
Human Nature and Conduct: An Introduction to Social Psychology (o Dewey) 1922
Human Season (f Wallant) 1960
Human Season: Selected Poems 1926-1972 (po MacLeish) 1972
Human Universe and Other Essays (o Olson) 1965
Human Wishes (po Hass) 1989
Human Work (o Gilman) 1904
Human Zero: The Science Fiction Stories (f E. Gardner) 1981
Humanist in the Bathtub (o McCarthy) 1964
Humanity Unlimited: Twelve Sonnets (po Van Doren) 1950
Humble Attempt to Promote Explicit Agreement and Visible Union of God's People in Extraordinary Prayer (o Edwards) 1747
Humble Inquiry into the Rules of the Word of God Concerning . . . Communion (o Edwards) 1749
Humble Romance and Other Stories (f Freeman) 1887
Humboldt's Gift (f Bellow) 1975
Humiliations Followed with Deliverances (o Mather) 1697
Humoresque with Zachary Gold (scr Odets) 1946
Humorous Poems (po Holmes) 1865
Humorous Stories (pl Brougham) 1858
Humors of Blood and Skin: A John Hawkes Reader (o Hawkes) 1984
Humpty Dumpty (f Hecht) 1924
Hunchback (pl Daly) 1893
Hunchback of Notre Dame (scr Sherwood) 1924
Hundred Camels in the Courtyard (f Bowles) 1962
Hundred Secret Senses (f Tan) 1995
Hundred White Daffodils (o Kenyon) 1999

Hunger (pl Fornés) 1988
Hungered One: Early Writings (f Bullins) 1971
Hungerers (pl Saroyan) 1939
Hungerfield and Other Poems (po Jeffers) 1954
Hungry Ghosts: Seven Allusive Comedies (f Oates) 1975
Hungry Heart (f D. Phillips) 1909
Hungry Hearts (f Yezierska) 1920
Hunt (po Hejinian) 1991
Hunted (f Leonard) 1977
Hunter Cats of Connorloa (f H. Jackson) 1884
Hunter's Moon (pl Connelly) 1958
Hunters in the Snow (f Wolff), 1982
Hunting Lost Mines by Helicopter (o E. Gardner) 1965
Hunting the Desert Whale (o E. Gardner) 1960
Huntsman, What Quarry? (po Millay) 1939
Hurrah for Anything: Poems and Drawings (po Patchen) 1957
Hurricanes (pl B. Howard) 1878
Hurry Home (f Wideman) 1970
Hurry-Graphs (o Willis) 1851
Husband's Story (f D. Phillips) 1910
Hyacinth Macaw (pl Wellman) 1994
Hydriotaphia (pl Kushner) 1987
Hymen (po Doolittle) 1921
Hymn to the Rising Sun (pl Green) 1936
Hymn—God Pray for Me (po Kerouac) 1959
Hymns (po Bryant) 1864
Hymns of St. Bridget (po F. O'Hara) 1974
Hyperion: A Romance (f Longfellow) 1839

I Accuse (scr Vidal) 1958
I Am a Barbarian (f E. Burroughs) 1967
I Am a Camera (pl Van Druten) 1952
I Am Cherry Alive, The Little Girl Sang (o Schwartz) 1979
I Am Elijah Thrush (f Purdy) 1972
I Am Lucy Terry (pl Bullins) 1976
I Am the Dog, I am the Cat (o Hall) 1994
I Am! Says the Lamb (o Roethke) 1961
I Apologize for the Eyes in My Head (po Komunyakaa) 1986
I Can't Imagine Tomorrow (pl T. Williams) 1970
I Can't Sleep: A Monologue (pl Odets) 1935
I Cannot Get You Close Enough (f Gilchrist) 1990
I Come as a Thief (f Auchincloss) 1972
I Could Never Be Lonely Without a Husband (o Barnes) 1987
I Die Slowly (f Macdonald) 1955
I Don't Need You Any More: Stories (f A. Miller) 1967
I Don't Know Who He Was and I Don't Know What He Said (pl
    Wellman) 1998
I, etcetera (f Sontag) 1978
I Go Out (o Rukeyser) 1961
I Greet the Dawn (po Dunbar) 1978
I Hate Actors! (f Hecht) 1944
I Have Moved to Dublin . . . (po Berryman) 1967
I Knew a Phoenix: Sketches for an Autobiography (o Sarton) 1959
I Knew Him When (f Ade) 1910
I Know My Love (pl Behrman) 1952
I Know Why the Caged Bird Sings (o Angelou) 1970
I Live in Music (po Shange) 1994
I Lock My Door upon Myself (f Oates) 1990
I Love You, I Love You, I Love You (f Bemelmans) 1942
I Loved a Soldier (scr Van Druten) 1936
I Married a Communist (f P. Roth) 1998

I Married a Witch (scr Connelly) 1942
I Marry You (po Ciardi) 1958
I Met a Man (po Ciardi) 1961
I Never Sang for My Father (pl R. Anderson) 1967
I Never Sang for My Father (scr R. Anderson), 1970
I Ought to Be in Pictures (pl Simon) 1980
I Ought to Be in Pictures (scr Simon), 1982
I Remember Clifford (o Lim) 1983
I Remember Mama (pl Van Druten) 1945
I Rise in Flame, Cried the Phoenix: A Play about D. H. Lawrence
    (pl T. Williams) 1951
I, Robot (f Asimov) 1950
I Sent Thee Late (po Zukofsky) 1965
I Shall Not Be Moved (po Angelou) 1990
I Sing the Body Electric! (f Bradbury) 1969
I Sit and Look Out (o Whitman) 1932
I Stole a Million (scr N. West) 1939
I Take This Woman (scr MacArthur) 1940
I Take This Woman (f Rinehart) 1927
I Thought of Daisy (f E. Wilson) 1929
I Wanted to Write (o Roberts) 1949
I Wanted to Write a Poem: The Autobiography of the Works of a
    Poet (o W. Williams) 1958
I Was an Adventuress (scr J. O'Hara) 1940
I Will Arrest the Bird That Has No Light (po Purdy) 1978
I Will Fear No Evil (f Heinlein) 1971
I Wonder as I Wander: An Autobiographical Journey (o Hughes)
    1956
I. Asimov: A Memoir (o Asimov) 1994
I'd Rather Be Right (pl Hart, Kaufman) 1937
I'll Take My Stand: The South and the Agrarian Tradition (o
    Davidson, Fletcher, Lytle, Ransom) 1930
I'm a Stranger Here Myself (po Nash) 1938
I've Got Sixpence (pl Van Druten) 1953
Iascaire (pl Harrigan) 1876
Icarus Montgolfier Wright (scr Bradbury) 1961
Icarus's Mother (pl Shepard) 1965
Ice Palace (f Ferber) 1958
Ice Palace and Other Stories (f Fitzgerald) 1998
Ice Storm (po Ashbery) 1987
Ice-Cream Headache and Other Stories (f J. Jones) 1968
Iceman Cometh (pl O'Neill) 1946
Iconoclasts: A Book of Dramatists (o Huneker) 1905
Ida M'Toy (o Welty) 1979
Ida: A Novel (f Stein) 1941
Idea of Christ in the Gospels (o Santayana) 1946
Ideal Bakery (f Hall) 1987
Ideal Wife (pl Crawford) 1912
Ideas and the Novel (o McCarthy) 1980
Ideas, etc (po Merrill) 1980
Ideas for Environment (o Burke) 1973-74
Ideas of Order (po Stevens) 1935
Identities: Three Novels (f Wideman) 1994
Ides of March (f Wilder) 1948
Idiosyncrasy and Technique: Two Lectures (o Moore) 1958
Idiot's Delight (pl Sherwood) 1936
Idiots First (f Malamud) 1963
Idler and His Works, and Other Essays (o Santayana) 1957
Idol and the Octopus: Political Writings on the Kennedy and
    Johnson Administrations (o Mailer) 1968
Idyll in the Desert (f Faulkner) 1931

Idylls of Norway and Other Poems (po Boyesen) 1882
Idylls of the Bible (po F. Harper) 1901
Idyls in Drab (f Howells) 1896
Idyls of the Foothills (f Harte) 1874
If Beale Street Could Talk (f James Baldwin) 1974
If Birds Build with Your Hair (po Snodgrass) 1979
If Blessing Comes (f Bambara) 1987
If Death Ever Slept (f Stout) 1957
If He Hollers, Let Him Go (f Himes) 1945
If I Can Cook, You Know God Can (o Shange) 1998
If I Die in a Combat Zone, Box Me Up and Ship Me Home (o T. O'Brien) 1973
If I Had Money (pl Tarkington) 1909
If I Stop I'll Die (o J. Williams) 1991
If It Please You (f Carver) 1984
If Men Played Cards Like Women Do (pl Kaufman) 1926
If Morning Ever Comes (f A. Tyler) 1964
If This Be I, As I Suppose It Be (o Deland) 1935
If You (po Creeley) 1956
Il Campiello (pl Nelson) 1981
Il Pesceballo: Opera Seria (pl J. Lowell) 1862
Il pleut des coups durs (f Himes) 1958
Ile (pl O'Neill) 1917
Ilka on the Hill-Top and Other Stories (f Boyesen) 1881
Ill-Tempered Clavichord (o S. Perelman) 1952
Illinois Poems (po Masters) 1941
Illumination (f Frederic) 1896
Illusion (pl Kushner) 1988
Illustrated History of the State of Montana (o J. Miller) 1894
Illustrated Man (f Bradbury) 1951
Illustrated Poems (po Holmes) 1885
Illustrated Temperance Tales (f Arthur) 1850
Image and Other Stories (f Singer) 1985
Image and the Law (po Nemerov) 1947
Image Maker (pl Merrill) 1986
Image of Josephine (f Tarkington) 1945
Images (o Edwards) 1948
Images of Kin: New and Selected Poems (po M. Harper) 1977
Images of Truth: Remembrances and Criticism (o Wescott) 1962
Imaginary Cuckold (pl Wilbur) 1993
Imagination (o Erdrich) 1980
Imaginations: Collected Early Prose (o W. Williams) 1970
Imbroglio Negro (f Himes) 1960
Imitations (po Lowell) 1961
Immigrants (pl MacKaye) 1915
Immobile Wind (po Winters) 1921
Immoral Proposition (po Creeley) 1953
Immortal Husband (pl Merrill) 1955
Immortal Marriage (f Atherton) 1927
Immortals (po J. Tate) 1970
Impendin Crisis uv the Democracy (f Nasby) 1868
Imperative Duty (f Howells) 1891
Imperceptible Mutabilities in the Third Kingdom (pl Parks) 1989
Imperfect Thirst (po Kinnell) 1994
Imperial City (f Rice) 1937
Imperial Orgy: An Account of the Tsars from the First to the Last (o Saltus) 1920
Imperial Purple (f Saltus) 1892
Imperial Way: By Rail from Peshawar to Chittagong (o Theroux) 1985
Imperial Woman (f Buck) 1956

Important Business (scr Benchley) 1944
Imported Bridegroom and Other Stories of the New York Ghetto (f Cahan) 1898
Impressions (po Portillo Trambley) 1972
Impressions of Soviet Russia and the Revolutionary World: Mexico, China, Turkey (o Dewey) 1929
Impressions of Spain (o J. Lowell) 1899
Improved Sunday School Record (o Eggleston) 1869
Improving Stories for the Young (f Arthur) 1847
In a Far Country: London's Western Tales (f London) 1986
In a Garden (pl Barry) 1926
In a Garden (pl Stein) 1951
In a Hollow of the Hills (f Harte) 1895
In a Marine Light (po Carver) 1987
In a Narrow Grave: Essays on Texas (o McMurtry) 1968
In a New World (f Alger) 1893
In a Shallow Grave (f Purdy) 1976
In a Yellow Wood (f Vidal) 1947
In Abraham's Bosom (pl Green) 1926
In Adullam's Lair (o Olson) 1975
In All Countries (o Dos Passos) 1934
In America (f Sontag) 1999
In Another Land (po MacKaye) 1937
In Aunt Mahaly's Cabin: A Negro Melodrama (pl Green) 1925
In Babel (f Ade) 1903
In Battle for Peace: The Story of My 83rd Birthday (o Du Bois) 1952
In Bed One Night and Other Brief Encounters (f Coover) 1983
In Case of Accidental Death (po Oates) 1972
In Classic Shades and Other Poems (po J. Miller) 1890
In Cold Blood: A True Account of a Multiple Murder and Its Consequences (o Capote) 1966
In Cold Hell, in Thicket (po Olson) 1953
In Colonial Times (f Freeman) 1899
In Connection with the De Willoughby Claim (f Burnett) 1899
In Country (f Mason) 1985
In Dahomey (pl Dunbar) 1903
In Darkest America (pl Oates) 1990
In Defense of Ignorance (o Shapiro) 1960
In Defense of Marion: The Love of Marion Bloom and H.L. Mencken (o Mencken) 1996
In Defense of Reason (o Winters) 1947
In Defense of the Earth (po Rexroth) 1956
In Defense of Women (o Mencken) 1918
In Dreams Begin Responsibilities (po Schwartz) 1938
In Dubious Battle (f Steinbeck) 1936
In Fact (po Ciardi) 1962
In Favor of the Sensitive Man and Other Essays (o Nin) 1976
In Fireworks Lie Secret Codes (pl Guare) 1979
In Ghostly Japan (o Hearn) 1899
In Her Day (f R Brown) 1976
In Joy Still Felt: The Autobiography of Isaac Asimov 1954-1978 (o Asimov) 1980
In London (po Creeley) 1970
In Love and Trouble: Stories of Black Women (f A. Walker) 1973
In Mad Love and War (po Harjo) 1990
In Memoriam Mrs. Katharine Donnelly (o Donnelly) 1895
In Memory of My Feelings: A Selection of Poems (po F. O'Hara) 1967
In Memory Yet Green: The Autobiography of Isaac Asimov 1920-1954 (o Asimov) 1979

In Modern Dress (pl Morley) 1929
In Morocco (o Wharton) 1920
In My Father's House (f Gaines) 1978
In New England Winter (pl Bullins) 1967
In Nueva York (f Mohr) 1977
In Old Plantation Days (f Dunbar) 1903
In Ole Virginia (f Page) 1887
In Orbit (f Morris) 1967
In Our Own Words (tv Naylor) 1985
In Our Terribleness: Some Elements and Meaning in Black Style (po Baraka) 1970
In Our Time (f Hemingway) 1924
In Our Time (o Tom Wolfe) 1980
In Our Town (f Runyon) 1946
In Pastures New (f Ade) 1906
In Pharaoh's Army: Memories of the Lost War (o Wolff) 1994
In Praise of Secrecy (po Wellman) 1977
In Pursuit of the Grey Soul (o Dickey) 1979
In Quest of Candlelighters (po Patchen) 1972
In Re Walt Whitman (o Whitman) 1893
In Reckless Ecstasy (po Sandburg) 1904
In Savoy (pl Stein) 1946). 1946
In Search of a Voice (o C. Johnson) 1991
In Search of Our Mothers' Gardens: Womanist Prose (o A. Walker) 1983
In Search of Treasure: The Story of Guy's Eventful Voyage (f Alger) 1907
In Service (pl Fornés) 1978
In That Far Land (po Van Doren) 1951
In the "Stranger People's" Country (f Murfree) 1891
In the Absence of Angels: Stories (f Calisher) 1951
In the American Grain (o W. Williams) 1925
In the Arena: Stories of Political Life (f Tarkington) 1905
In the Bar of a Tokyo Hotel (pl T. Williams) 1969
In the Beauty of the Lilies (f Updike) 1996
In the Beginning: Science Faces God in the Book of Genesis (o Asimov) 1981
In the Best Families (f Stout) 1950
In the Cage (f H. James) 1898
In the Carquinez Woods (f Harte) 1883
In the Cemetery High above Shillington (po Updike) 1995
In the Clap Shack (pl Styron) 1973
In the Clearing (po Frost) 1962
In the Clock of Reason (po W. Stafford) 1973
In the Closed Room (f Burnett) 1904
In the Clouds (f Murfree) 1886
In the Fields of Aceldama (pl N. Wallace) 1991
In the Fog (f Richard Davis) 1901
In the Fourth World (po Eberhart) 1983
In the Garden (o Burnett) 1925
In the Garden of the North American Martyrs (f Wolff) 1981
In the Garret (o Van Vechten) 1920
In the Great Steep's Garden (po Roberts) 1915
In the Heart of the Heart of the Country (f Gass) 1968
In the Heart of America (pl N. Wallace) 1994
In the Hollow of His Hand (f Purdy) 1986
In the Lake of the Woods (f T. O'Brien) 1994
In the Land of Dreamy Dreams (f Gilchrist) 1981
In the Levant (o Warner) 1877
In the Mecca (po Brooks) 1968
In the Midst of Life (f Bierce) 1892

In the Midst of Death (f Hecht) 1964
In the Money (f W. Williams) 1940
In the Night (f Levertov) 1968
In the North Woods (pl Harrigan) 1907
In the Palace of the Movie King (f Calisher) 1993
In the Palace of the King: A Love Story of Old Madrid (f Crawford) 1900
In the Red Room (o Bowles) 1981
In the Room We Share (po Simic, Simpson) 1990
In the Season (pl L. Mitchell) 1898
In the Service of My Country (radio Hughes) 1944
In the Sixties (f Frederic) 1897
In the Slammer (f Calisher) 1997
In the Stoneworks (po Ciardi) 1961
In the Suicide Mountains (f J. Gardner) 1977
In the Sweet Dry and Dry (f Morley) 1919
In the Tennessee Mountains (f Murfree) 1884
In the Time of Detachment, In the Time of Cold (po Brooks) 1965
In the Tradition: For Black Arthur Blythe (po Baraka) 1980
In the Valley (f Frederic) 1890
In the Valley and Other Carolina Plays (pl Green) 1928
In the Wilderness (o Warner) 1878
In the Wine Time (pl Bullins) 1968
In the Winter of Cities (po T. Williams) 1956
In the Zone (pl O'Neill) 1917
In This Our Life (f Glasgow) 1941
In This Our World (po Gilman) 1893
In Time Like Air (po Sarton) 1958
In Touch: The Letters of Paul Bowles (o Bowles) 1993
In Tragic Life (f Fisher) 1932
In War Time (f S. Mitchell) 1885
In War Time and Other Poems (po Whittier) 1864
In Watermelon Sugar (f Brautigan) 1968
In What Hour (po Rexroth) 1940
Inacoma (pl Shepard) 1977
Inadvertent Epic (o Fiedler) 1979
Incarnations: Poems 1966-1968 (po R. Warren) 1968
Incest: From a Journal of Love—The Unexpurgated Diary of Nin 1932-24 (o Nin) 1992
Incident at Vichy (pl A. Miller) 1964
Incident in the Park (pl Kopit) 1968
Incidental Numbers (po Wylie) 1912
Incidentals (po Sandburg) 1904
Incidents in the Life of a Slave Girl (o Jacobs) 1861
Incidents of the Insurrection in the Western Parts of Pennsylvania in 1794 (o Brackenridge) 1795
Incloser (o S. Howe) 1992
Inconstant (pl Daly) 1889
Increasing Purpose (f J. Allen) 1900
Indemnity Only (f Paretsky) 1982
Independence Day (f Ford) 1995
Indestructible Mr. Gore (tv Vidal) 1959
India Christiana (o Mather) 1721
Indian (f Updike) 1971
Indian Country: America's Sacred Land (o Hillerman) 1987
Indian Fighter (scr Hecht) 1955
Indian Giver (pl Howells) 1900
Indian Justice: A Cherokee Murder Trial (o Payne) 1934
Indian Lawyer (f Welch) 1990
Indian Princess (pl Barker) 1808
Indian Princess (o Eggleston) 1881

Indian Reform Letters of Helen Hunt Jackson, 1879-1885 (o H. Jackson) 1998

Indian Summer (f Howells, Knowles) 1886

Indians (pl Kopit) 1968

Indians and Other Americans: Two Ways of Life Meet (o McNickle) 1959

Indians in England (pl Dunlap) 1799

Indians of Thoreau: Selections from the Indian Notebooks (o Thoreau) 1974

Indians Won (f M. Smith) 1971

Indifferent Children (f Auchincloss) 1947

Indignations of Howe (o E. Howe) 1933

Indiscretion of an American Wife (scr Capote) 1954

Indispensable Information for Infants (po Wister) 1921

Indispensable Parker (o Parker) 1944

Individualism, Old and New (o Dewey) 1930

Individuals (po Hejinian) 1988

Indolent Boys (pl Momaday) 1???

Industrial Republic (f Sinclair) 1907

Infatuation and Other Stories of Love's Misfits (f Hecht) 1927

Infidel (f Bird) 1835

Infidel's Doom (f Bird) 1840

Inflation (pl Nasby) 1876

Inflation at the Cross Roads (f Nasby) 1875

Influence of Darwin on Philosophy and Other Essays in Contemporary Thought (o Dewey) 1910

Information to Those Who Would Remove to America (o Franklin) 1784(?)

Infrared (pl Wellman) 1996

Ing (po Coolidge) 1969

Ingenious Dr. Franklin: Selected Scientific Letters (o Franklin) 1931

Ingomar the Idiotic (pl B. Howard) 1871

Inhabitants (o Morris) 1946

Inhabitants of Carlysle (pl MacKaye) 1901

Inhale and Exhale (f Saroyan) 1936

Inheritance (scr James Baldwin) 1973

Inheritance of Night: Early Drafts of "Lie Down in Darkness." (o Styron) 1993

Inheritors (pl Glaspell) 1921

Initial (po Zukofsky) 1970

Injuries of Nerves and Their Consequences (o S. Mitchell) 1872

Injustice Collectors (f Auchincloss) 1950

Inklings of Adventure (f Willis) 1836

Inner Landscape (po Sarton) 1938

Inner Room (po Merrill) 1988

Innocence at Home (pl Harrigan) 1875

Innocence in Extremis (f Hawkes) 1985

Innocent (f Kim) 1968

Innocent Party (pl Hawkes) 1968

Innocents (scr Capote) 1961

Innocents (f Lewis) 1917

Innocents Abroad (f Twain) 1869

Innocents at Home (f Twain) 1872

Inquisitor (f Rowson) 1788

Inside Benchley (o Benchley) 1942

Inside of the Cup (f Churchill) 1913

Inside Out: Notes on the Autobiographical Mode (o Creeley) 1973

Inside the Atom (o Asimov) 1956

Inside the Onion (po Nemerov) 1984

Inside the Trojan Horse (po Ferlinghetti) 1987

Insomnia (f King) 1994

Inspector Queen's Own Case: November Song (f Queen) 1956

Instant Enemy (f Macdonald) 1968

Institute (f Cain) 1976

Instructor (o Mather) 1726

Instrument (f J. O'Hara) 1967

Insubordination: An American Story of Real Life (f Arthur) 1841

Insurance Salesman and Other Stories (f Saroyan) 1941

Insurrection (pl Baraka) 1969

Intellectual Memoirs: New York, 1936-1938 (o McCarthy) 1993

Intellectual Things (po Kunitz) 1930

Intellectual Vagabondage: An Apology for the Intelligentsia (o Dell) 1926

Intelligence in the Modern World: Dewey's Philosophy (o Dewey) 1939

Intelligent Man's Guide to Science (o Asimov) 1960

Interest and Effort in Education (o Dewey) 1913

International (pl Lawson) 1928

International Episode (f H. James) 1879

International Match (pl Daly) 1890

Interpretation of Friends Worship (o Toomer) 1947

Interpretations of Poetry and Religion (o Santayana) 1900

Interpretations: A Book of First Poems (po Akins) 1912

Interpreters (o Van Vechten) 1920

Interpreters and Interpretations (o Van Vechten) 1917

Interview with Nin (o Nin) 1970

Interviews (o Barnes) 1985

Interviews and Encounters with Stanley Kunitz (po Kunitz) 1993

Interviews with Williams: Speaking Straight Ahead (o W. Williams) 1976

Intervisions: Poems and Photographs (po Dickey) 1983

Intimate Notebooks of George Jean Nathan (o Nathan) 1932

Intimate Strangers (pl Tarkington) 1921

Intimations of Eve (f Fisher) 1946

Into the Stone and Other Poems (po Dickey) 1960

Introducing Irony: A Book of Poetic Short Stories and Poems (po Bodenheim) 1922

Introduction to Objective Epistemology (o Rand) 1967

Intruder in the Dust (f Faulkner) 1948

Invaders (f Frank) 1948

Invalid Corps (pl Harrigan) 1874

Invasion of the Book Envelopes (o Updike) 1981

Investigation (pl Harrigan) 1884

Invisible Landscapes (po Masters) 1935

Invisible Man (f Ellison) 1952

Invisible Swords (f Farrell) 1971

Invisible Wall (tv McCullers) 1953

Invisible Woman: New and Selected Poems 1970-1982 (po Oates) 1982

Invitation to a Beheading (f Nabokov) 1959

Invitation to a March (pl Laurents) 1960

Iola Leroy (f F. Harper) 1892

Ion (pl Doolittle) 1937

Iowa Interiors (f Suckow) 1926

Iowa, O Iowa! (po Garland) 1935

Iphigenia at Aulis (pl Merwin) 1982

Ireland vs. Italy (pl Harrigan) 1872

Irene the Missionary (f De Forest) 1879

Irish Emigrant (pl Harrigan) 1871

Irish Eye (f Hawkes) 1997

Irish Girl and Other Tales (f Sedgwick) 1853

Irish Triangle (pl Barnes) 1919
Irish Yankee (pl Brougham) 1856
Iron Cross (pl Rice) 1917
Iron Gate and Other Poems (po Holmes) 1880
Iron Heel (f London) 1908
Iron Horse (po Ginsberg) 1972
Iron Marshal (f L'Amour) 1979
Iron Petticoat (scr Hecht) 1956
Iron Woman (f Deland) 1911
Irradiations: Sand and Spray (po Fletcher) 1915
Irving Layton and Robert Creeley: The Complete Correspondence
   (o Creeley) 1990
Is 5 (po Cummings) 1926
Is Anyone There? (o Asimov) 1967
Is He Guilty? (pl Rice) 1927
Is Life Worth Living? (o W. James) 1896
Is Paris Burning? (scr Vidal) 1966
Is Sex Necessary? or, Why You Feel the Way You Do (o White)
   1929
Is There Anything (po J. Tate) 1969
Isaac Asimov Presents Superquiz (o Asimov) 1982
Isaac Asimov Presents: From Harding to Hiroshima (o Asimov)
   1988
Isaac Asimov's Book of Facts (o Asimov) 1979
Isaac Asimov's Library of the Universe. Index (o Asimov) 1990
Isaac Asimov's Limericks for Children (po Asimov) 1984
Isaac Asimov's Treasury of Humor (o Asimov) 1971
Isaac Asimov's Wonderful Worldwide Science Bazaar (o Asimov)
   1986
Isaac T. Hopper: A True Life (o Child) 1853
Isabel and the Dancing Bear (pl Portillo Trambley) 1977
Island (f Creeley) 1963
Island Bride (f Simms) 1869
Island Fire (f Hawkes) 1988
Island in the Atlantic (f Frank) 1946
Island Like You: Stories of the Barrio (o Cofer) 1995
Island of the Innocent (f Fisher) 1952
Island Tales (f London) 1920
Island: Poetry and History of Chinese Immigrants on Angel Is-
   land, 1910-1940 (o Lim) 1980
Islands in the Stream (f Hemingway) 1970
Isles of the Blest (f Steele) 1924
Isn't That Just Like a Man! (o Rinehart) 1920
Israel and the Dead Sea Scrolls (o E. Wilson) 1978
Israel Potter, His Fifty Years of Exile (f Melville) 1855
I's (po Zukofsky) 1963
It (po Creeley) 1989
It (f King) 1986
It Came from Outer Space (scr Bradbury) 1952
It Can't Happen Here (f Lewis) 1935
It Could Happen to You (scr N. West) 1937
It Had to Happen (f Bromfield) 1936
It Happened the Day the Sun Rose and Other Stories (f T. Will-
   iams) 1982
It Happened to Didymus (f Sinclair) 1958
It Happened to Them: Character Studies of New Testament Men
   and Women (o Davidson) 1965
It Has Come to Pass (o Farrell) 1958
It Has No Choice (pl Bullins) 1966
It Has Taken Long (o Riding) 1976
It Is the Law (pl Rice) 1922

It Must Be Your Tonsils (o Roberts) 1936
It Takes All Kinds (f Bromfield) 1939
It Was (po Zukofsky) 1959
It's a Mighty World (tv Hughes) 1965
It's a Wonderful World (scr Hecht) 1939
It's Always We Rambled: An Essay on Rodeo (o McMurtry) 1974
It's Loaded, Mr. Bauer (f Marquand) 1949
It's Nation Time (po Baraka) 1970
It's Such a Beautiful Day (f Asimov) 1985
Italian Backgrounds (o Wharton) 1905
Italian Ballet Master (pl Harrigan) 1876
Italian Father (pl Dunlap) 1810
Italian Holiday (o Bemelmans) 1961
Italian Hours (pl H. James) 1909
Italian Junkman (pl Harrigan) 1878
Italian Life and Legends (o Mowatt) 1870
Italian Villas and Their Gardens (o Wharton) 1904
Italy and the World War (o Page) 1920
Ivory, Apes, and Peacocks (o Huneker) 1915
Ivory Grin (f Macdonald) 1952
Ivory Tower (f H. James) 1917
Iyyob (po Zukofsky) 1965

Jack and Jill: A Village Story (f Alcott) 1880
Jack Kelso: A Dramatic Poem (pl Masters) 1928
Jack O'Lantern (Le Feu-Follet) (f Cooper) 1842
Jack of Diamonds and Other Stories (f Spencer) 1988
Jack Tier (f Cooper) 1848
Jack's Ward (f Alger) 1875
Jacket (f London) 1915
Jacklight (po Erdrich) 1984
Jackson Pollock (o F. O'Hara) 1959
Jackson's Dance (pl Shepard) 1980
Jacob's Ladder (po Levertov) 1961
Jacob's Ladder (f Rawlings) 1950
Jacobowsky and the Colonel (pl Behrman) 1944
Jacob's Ladder (f J. Williams) 1987
Jacques Duval (pl Kaufman) 1919
Jaglon and the Tiger Fairies (f Baum) 1953
Jailbird (f Vonnegut) 1979
Jaime and the Conch Shell (f Mohr) 1987
Jake's Women (pl Simon) 1990
Jalamanta, a Message from the Desert (f Anaya) 1996
Jamaica Poems (po Simpson) 1993
James and Robert Louis Stevenson: A Record of Friendship and
   Criticism (pl H. James) 1948
James Branch Cabell (o Mencken) 1927
James Dickey: The Selected Poems (po Dickey) 1998
James Hogg: A Critical Study (o Simpson) 1962
James on Psychical Research (o W. James) 1960
James Reader (o W. James) 1972
James Shore's Daughter (f S. Benét) 1934
James Welch (o Welch) 1986
James Weldon Johnson (o S. Brown, Van Vechten) 1941
Jamesons (f Freeman) 1899
Jane (pl Behrman) 1946
Jane Field (f Freeman) 1892
Jane Talbot (f Brown) 1801
Janet March (f Dell) 1923
Japan of Sword and Love (o J. Miller) 1905
Japan: An Attempt at Interpretation (o Hearn) 1904

Japan's Religions: Shinto and Buddhism (o Hearn) 1966
Japanese Blossom (f Eaton) 1906
Japanese by Spring (f Reed) 1993
Japanese Letters (o Hearn) 1910
Japanese Miscellany (o Hearn) 1901
Japanese Nightingale (f Eaton) 1901
Japanese Prints (po Fletcher) 1918
Jar (tv Bradbury) 1992
Jarl's Daughter and Other Stories (f Burnett) 1879
Jarrett's Jade (f Yerby) 1959
Jasmine (f Mukherjee) 1989
Jason and Medeia (f J. Gardner) 1973
Jason Edwards: An Average Man (f Garland) 1892
Java Head (f Hergesheimer) 1919
Jayhawker (pl Lewis) 1935
Jazz (f Morrison) 1992
Jazz and Other Stories of Young Love (f Hecht) 1927
J.B.: A Play in Verse (pl MacLeish) 1958
Jealous Gods: A Processional Novel of the Fifth Century B.C. (f
    Atherton) 1928
Jealous Woman (f Cain) 1950
Jealousy and Episode: Two Stories (f Faulkner) 1955
Jean Huguenot (f S. Benét) 1923
Jeanne d'Arc (pl MacKaye) 1906
Jed, The Poorhouse Boy (f Alger) 1900
Jeff Briggs's Love Story and Other Sketches (f Harte) 1880
Jefferson and Education in a Republic (o Jefferson) 1930
Jefferson and His Unknown Brother Randolph: Twenty-Eight Let-
    ters 1807 to 1815 (o Jefferson) 1942
Jefferson and the Foundations of American Freedom (o Jefferson)
    1965
Jefferson Himself: The Personal Narrative (o Jefferson) 1942
Jefferson in Love: Love Letters between Thomas Jefferson and
    Maria Cosway (o Jefferson) 1998
Jefferson on Democracy (o Jefferson) 1954
Jefferson Profile as Revealed in His Letters (o Jefferson) 1956
Jefferson's Garden Book 1766-1824 (o Jefferson) 1944
Jefferson's Ideas on a University Library: Letters from the Founder
    of the University of Virginia to a Boston Bookseller (o Jefferson)
    1950
Jefferson-Dunglison Letters (o Jefferson) 1960
Jeffersonian Principles (o Jefferson) 1928
Jefferson's Memorandum Books: Accounts, with Legal Records
    and Miscellany, 1767-1826 (o Jefferson) 1997
Jello (pl Baraka) 1970
Jemmy Daily (f Ingraham) 1843
Jennette Alison (f Ingraham) 1848
Jennie Gerhardt (f Dreiser) 1911
Jennifer Lorn: A Sedate Extravaganza (f Wylie) 1923
Jenny (pl Sheldon) 1929
Jeremy's Version (f Purdy) 1970
Jericho: The South Beheld (o Dickey) 1974
Jerico-Jim Crow (pl Hughes) 1963
Jerome, A Poor Many (f Freeman) 1897
Jerome: The Biography of a Poem (po Jarrell) 1971
Jerry of the Islands (f London) 1917
Jerry, The Backwoods Boy (f Alger) 1904
Jes Lak White Fo'ks (pl Dunbar) 1900
Jessie Hampton (f Arthur) 1852
Jest (pl Sheldon) 1919
Jest of Fate (f Dunbar) 1902

Jester's Dozen (po Updike) 1984
Jesuits in North America in the Seventeenth Century (o Parkman)
    1867
Jesus Came Again: A Parable (f Fisher) 1956
Jesus Tales (f Linney) 1980
Jew in Love (f Hecht) 1931
Jewel Merchants (pl Cabell) 1921
Jewels of Aptor (f S. Delany) 1962
Jig of Forslin: A Symphony (po Aiken) 1916
Jilts (pl Barry) 1923
Jim Black (pl Belasco) 1865
Jim Bludso of the Prairie Belle, and Little Breeches (po Hay) 1871
Jim Crow's Last Stand (po Hughes) 1943
Jim Dandy (pl Saroyan) 1941
Jim Dandy: Fat Man in a Famine (pl Saroyan) 1947
Jim Smiley and His Jumping Frog (f Twain) 1940
Jim's Book: A Collection of Poems and Short Stories (po Merrill)
    1942
Jimmie Higgins (f Sinclair) 1918
Jimmy's Blues: Selected Poems (po James Baldwin) 1983
Jimmyjohn Boss and Other Stories (f Wister) 1900
Jingling in the Wind (f Roberts) 1928
Jinny (f Harte) 1878
Jitney (pl A. Wilson) 1982
Jo's Boys and How They Turned Out (f Alcott) 1886
Joan of Arc (pl M. Anderson) 1948
Joan of Lorraine (pl M. Anderson) 1946
Joanna and Ulysses (f Sarton) 1963
Joaquin, et al (po J. Miller) 1869
Joaquin Miller's Charcoal Sketches (o J. Miller) 1996
Job (f Lewis) 1917
Job: A Comedy of Justice (f Heinlein) 1984
Jock o' Dreams (f Herrick) 1908
Joe Hill: A Biographical Novel (f Stegner) 1969
Joe Kidd (scr Leonard) 1972
Joe the Hotel Boy (f Alger) 1906
Joe Turner's Come and Gone (pl A. Wilson) 1986
Joe's Luck (f Alger) 1887
Joey and the Birthday Present (o Sexton) 1971
Joggin' Erlong (po Dunbar) 1906
Johannes in Eremo (o Mather) 1695
John (pl Barry) 1929
John Andross (f Rebecca Davis) 1874
John Barleycorn (f London) 1913
John Barry (f Fearing) 1947
John Brown (o Du Bois) 1909
John Brown and the Heroes of Harper's Ferry (po Channing) 1886
John Brown's Body (po S. Benét) 1928
John Bull in America (f Paulding) 1825
John Carter of Mars (f E. Burroughs) 1964
John Deth: A Metaphysical Legend, and Other Poems (po Aiken)
    1930
John Dos Passos' "Manhattan Transfer" (o Lewis) 1926
John Dough and the Cherub (f Baum) 1906
John Eax and Marmelon (f Tourgée) 1882
John Godfrey's Fortunes (f B. Taylor) 1864
John Gray: A Kentucky Tale of the Olden Time (f J. Allen) 1893
John Henry (f R. Bradford) 1931
John Henry Hammers It Out (radio Hughes) 1943
John J. Plenty and Fiddler Dan (po Ciardi) 1962
John Jackson's Arcady (f Fitzgerald) 1924

John Lothrop Motley: A Memoir (o Holmes) 1878
John March, Southerner (f Cable) 1894
John Marin (o W. Williams) 1956
John Marr and Other Sailors, with Some Sea-Pieces (po Melville) 1888
John Marvel, Assistant (f Page) 1909
John Randolph (o Adams) 1882
John Sherwood's Ironmaster (f S. Mitchell) 1911
John Smith U.S.A. (po Field) 1905
John Smith—Also Pocahontas (o Fletcher) 1928
John Ward, Preacher (f Deland) 1888
John Wood Case (f Suckow) 1959
Johnny Appleseed and Other Poems (po Lindsay) 1928
Johnny Come Lately (scr Van Druten) 1943
Johnny Crimson: A Legend of Hollis Hall (po MacKaye) 1895
Johnny Johnson: The Biography of a Common Man (pl Green) 1936
Johnny on a Spot (pl MacArthur) 1942
Johnny Pye and the Fool-Killer (f S. Benét) 1938
Johnson Girls (scr Bambara) 1972
John's Wife (f Coover) 1996
Jolson Sings Again (pl Laurents) 1994
Jonah (pl Goodman) 1950
Jonah's Gourd Vine (f Hurston) 1934
Jonathan Gentry (po Van Doren) 1931
Jonica (pl Hart) 1930
Jonoah and the Green Stone (f Dumas) 1976
Joscelyn: A Tale of the Revolution (f Simms) 1975
Joseffy (po Sandburg) 1910
Joseph and His Friend (f B. Taylor) 1870
Joseph Hergesheimer (o Cabell) 1921
Josephene (f Ingraham) 1853(?)
Josh Billings, His Book of Sayings (f Shaw) 1866
Josh Billings on Ice, and Other Things (f Shaw) 1868
Josh Billings Struggling with Things (f Shaw) 1881
Josh Billings: His Works, Complete (f Shaw) 1876
Josh Billings' Cook Book and Picktorial Proverbs (f Shaw) 1880
Josh Billings' Farmer's Allminax for the Year 1870 (f Shaw) 1869
Josh Billings' Old Farmer's Allminax 1870-1879 (f Shaw) 1902
Josh Billings' Trump Kards: Blue Grass Philosophy (f Shaw) 1877
Josh Billings' Wit and Humor (f Shaw) 1874
Jour de Chasse (po Hejinian) 1992
Journal (o Dana) 1968
Journal (o Thoreau) 14 vols., 1906
Journal from Ellipsia (f Calisher) 1965
Journal of a Novel: The East of Eden Letters (o Steinbeck) 1969
Journal of a Visit to Europe and the Levant (o Melville) 1955
Journal of a Visit to London and the Continent 1849-1850 (o Melville) 1948
Journal of Albion Moonlight (f Patchen) 1941
Journal of Arthur Stirling (f Sinclair) 1903
Journal of Solitude (o Sarton) 1973
Journal of the Fictive Life (o Nemerov) 1965
Journal up the Straits October 11, 1856-May 5, 1857 (o Melville) 1935
Journalism, 1834-1846 (o Whitman) 1998
Journals (o Nin) 6 vols., 1966-77
Journals (o Parkman) 1947
Journals of Ayn Rand (o Rand) 1997
Journey (po J. Wright) 1981
Journey and Other Poems (po Winters) 1931

Journey from Philadelphia to New-York (po Freneau) 1787
Journey in Search of Christmas (f Wister) 1904
Journey of Tai-Me (po Momaday) 1967
Journey of the Magi (po Eliot) 1927
Journey out of Anger (f J. Williams) 1968
Journey to Central Africa (o B. Taylor) 1854
Journey to Jerusalem (pl M. Anderson) 1940
Journey to Love (po W. Williams) 1955
Journey to the Land of Eden and Other Papers (o Byrd) 1928
Journeys between Wars (o Dos Passos) 1938
Joy in the Morning (f B. Smith) 1963
Joy Luck Club (f Tan) 1989
Joy of Living (pl Wharton) 1902
Joy to My Soul (pl Hughes) 1937
Joyous Miracle (f Norris) 1906
Joyous Season (pl Barry) 1934
J.P. Donleavy's Ireland in All Her Sins and Graces (tv Donleavy) 1993
J.P. Morgan: The Financier as Collector (o Auchincloss) 1990
JR (f Gaddis) 1975
Jubal Sackett (f L'Amour) 1985
Jubilee (pl Hart) 1935
Jubilee (radio Hughes) 1941
Jubilee (f M. Walker) 1965
Judas, My Brother: The Story of the Thirteenth Disciple (f Yerby) 1969
Judd Rankin's Daughter (f Glaspell) 1945
Judging of Jurgen (o Cabell) 1920
Judgment Day (f Farrell) 1935
Judgment Day (pl Rice) 1934
Judgment of Paris (f Vidal) 1953
Judgments in the Admiralty of Pennsylvania (o Hopkinson) 1789
Judith (f Farrell) 1969
Judith, the Daughter of Merari (pl Daly) 1864
Juggler (f Murfree) 1897
Julia (pl Payne) 1806
Julia Bride (f H. James) 1909
Julia France and Her Times (f Atherton) 1912
Julian (f Vidal) 1964
Juliet (pl Linney) 1988
Julip (f Harrison) 1994
Julius (f Alger) 1874
Jumbo (pl Hecht, MacArthur) 1935
Jumping Out of Bed (po Bly) 1973
June 30th, June 30th (po Brautigan) 1978
June Moon (pl Kaufman) 1929
June Moon (pl Lardner) 1930
Juneteenth (f Ellison) 1999
Jungle (f Algren) 1957
Jungle (f Sinclair) 1906
Jungle Coup (pl Nelson) 1978
Jungle Girl (f E. Burroughs) 1932
Jungle Lovers (f Theroux) 1971
Jungle of Cities (pl Nelson) 1981
Jungle Tales of Tarzan (f E. Burroughs) 1919
Junior Bachelor Society (f J. Williams) 1976
Junior College (po Soto) 1997
Juniper Loa (f Lin Yutang) 1963
Junkie: Confessions of an Unredeemed Drug Addict (f W. Burroughs) 1953
Junkies are Full of (SHHH. . .) (pl Baraka) 1970

Jupiter, the Largest Planet (o Asimov) 1973
Jurgen (f Cabell) 1919
Jurgen and the Censor (o Cabell) 1920
Jury of Her Peers (f Glaspell) 1927
Just a Little Simple (pl Childress) 1950
Just above My Head (f James Baldwin) 1979
Just and the Unjust (f Cozzens) 1942
Just Around the Corner (pl Hughes) 1951
Just As I Thought (o Paley) 1998
Just Before Dark: Collected Nonfiction (o Harrison) 1991
Just Folks (pl Linney) 1978
Just Give Me a Cool Drink of Water 'fore I Diiie (po Angelou) 1971
Just Looking: Essays on Art (o Updike) 1989
Just Out of College (pl Ade) 1924
Just Shades (po J. Tate) 1985
Just Wild about Harry: A Melo-Melo in Seven Scenes (pl H. Miller) 1963
Justice and Expediency (o Whittier) 1833
Justice Ends at Home and Other Stories (f Stout) 1977
Justin Harley: A Romance of Old Virginia (f J. Cooke) 1875
Justine's Lovers (f De Forest) 1878
Juvenile Poems (po Payne) 1813

K (f Rinehart) 1915
K-19: Salvaged Pieces (f Thomas Wolfe) 1983
Kabbalah and Criticism (o Bloom) 1976
Kaddish and Other Poems 1958-60 (po Ginsberg) 1961
Kalki (f Vidal) 1978
Kampoon Street (f Lin Tai-yi) 1964
Kandy-Kolored Tangerine-Flake Streamline Baby (o Tom Wolfe) 1965
Kansas Poems of William Stafford (po W. Stafford) 1990
Karate Is a Thing of the Spirit (f Crews) 1971
Karma (o Hearn) 1918
Kate (f B. Howard) 1906
Kate Beaumont (f De Forest) 1872
Kate Chopin's Private Papers (o Chopin) 1998
Kate Fennigate (f Tarkington) 1943
Kate's Experiences (f Ingraham) 1880
Katharine Lauderdale (f Crawford) 1894
Katharine Walton (f Simms) 1851
Kathleen (f Morley) 1920
Kathleen: A Love Story (f Burnett) 1878
Kautilya's Concept of Diplomacy (o Mukherjee) 1976
Kavanagh: A Tale (f Longfellow) 1849
Kawaida Studies: The New Nationalism (o Baraka) 1972
Kays (f Deland) 1926
Keep a-Inchin' Along: Selected Writings about Black Art and Letters (o Van Vechten) 1979
Keep Cool: A Novel, Written in Hot Weather (f Neal) 1817
Keep It Crisp (o S. Perelman) 1946
Keeping Up Appearances (f Arthur) 1847
Kempton-Wace Letters (f London) 1903
Kenneth Koch: A Tragedy (pl F. O'Hara) 1982
Kenny (f Bromfield) 1947
Kent Hampden (f Rebecca Davis) 1892
Kentons (f Howells) 1902
Kentuckian (pl Paulding) 1833
Kentucky Blue Grass Henry Smith (f Dahlberg) 1932
Kentucky Cardinal (f J. Allen) 1895

Kentucky Mountain Fantasies (pl MacKaye) 1928
Kentucky Warbler (f J. Allen) 1918
Kept Women Can't Quit (f E. Gardner) 1960
Keramos and Other Poems (po Longfellow) 1878
Key Largo (pl M. Anderson) 1939
Key to Uncle Tom's Cabin, Presenting the Original Facts and Documents upon Which the Story Is Founded (o Stowe) 1853
Key Word and Other Mysteries (f Asimov) 1977
Key-Lock Man (f L'Amour) 1965
Keys to the Caverns (po Coolidge) 1995
Khaled: A Tale of Arabia (f Crawford) 1891
Khundar: Ein deutsches Märchen (f Traven) 1977
Kicking the Leaves (po Hall) 1978
Kid (po Aiken) 1947
Kid (pl Coover) 1972
Kid Rodelo (f L'Amour) 1966
Kid Rodelo (scr L'Amour) with Jack Natteford, 1966
Kiddie (pl Crothers) 1909
Kidnapped Saint and Other Stories (f Traven) 1975
Kidnapped Santa Claus (f Baum) 1961
Kiki (pl Belasco) 1921
Kilkenny (f L'Amour) 1954
Killer in the Rain (f Chandler) 1964
Killer's Head (pl Shepard) 1975
Killing Custer: The Battle of the Little Big Horn and the Fate of the Plains Indians (o Welch) 1994
Killing Memory, Seeking Ancestors (po Madhubuti) 1987
Killing of Yablonski (pl Nelson) 1975
Killing Orders (f Paretsky) 1985
Killoe (f L'Amour) 1962
Killshot (f Leonard) 1989
Kilmourne (pl Baum) 1883
Kilrone (f L'Amour) 1966
Kincaid's Battery (f Cable) 1908
Kind of Act Of (po Creeley) 1953
Kind of Magic (o Ferber) 1963
Kinder Capers (po Snodgrass) 1986
Kinds of Love (f Sarton) 1970
Kinfolk (f Buck) 1949
Kinfolk of Robin Hood (pl MacKaye) 1901
King (f Barthelme) 1990
King Arthur's Socks (pl Dell) 1916
King Calico's Body Guard (pl Harrigan) 1875
King Carrot (pl Daly) 1872
King Coal (f Sinclair) 1917
King Coffin (f Aiken) 1935
King David (po S. Benét) 1923
King God Didn't Save (o J. Williams) 1970
King Is Dead (f Queen) 1952
King Jasper (po Robinson) 1935
King Midas (f Sinclair) 1901
King My Father's Wreck (o Simpson) 1995
King of Fields (f Singer) 1988
King of Folly Island and Other People (f Jewett) 1888
King of Jazz (scr MacArthur) 1930
King of Spain (po Bodenheim) 1928
King of the Hill: On the Fight of the Century (o Mailer) 1971
King, Queen, Knave (f Nabokov) 1968
King Was in His Counting House (f Cabell) 1938
King Who Saved Himself from Being Saved (po Ciardi) 1965
King's Henchman (pl Millay) 1927

King's Indian: Stories and Tales (f J. Gardner) 1974

King's Jackal (f Richard Davis) 1898

King's Missive and Other Poems (po Whittier) 1881

Kingdom by the Sea: A Journey around Great Britain (o Theroux) 1985

Kingdom Coming (f R. Bradford) 1933

Kingdom of Art: Cather's First Principles and Critical Principles 1893-1896 (o Cather) 1967

Kingdom of Earth (pl T. Williams) 1967

Kingdom of Evil: A Continuation of the Journal of Fantazius Mallare (f Hecht) 1924

Kingdom of the Sun (o Asimov) 1960

Kings, Queens, and Pawns: An American Woman at the Front (o Rinehart) 1915

Kingsblood Royal (f Lewis) 1947

Kinsmen (f Simms) 1841

Kiowa Trail (f L'Amour) 1964

Kirche, Kuchen, und Kinder (pl T. Williams) 1980

Kiss Kiss Kill Kill (scr Hagedorn) 1992

Kiss of Death (scr Hecht) 1947

Kisses Can (o Stein) 1947

Kissing Cousins (o Calisher) 1988

Kissing Sweet (pl Guare) 1969

Kit Brandon: A Portrait (f S. Anderson) 1936

Kit O'Brien (f Masters) 1927

Kitchen (po Creeley) 1973

Kitchen God's Wife (f Tan) 1991

Kitty Foyle (f Morley) 1939

Kitty's Choice (f Rebecca Davis) 1874(?)

Kitty's Class Day (f Alcott) 1868

Klail City (f Hinojosa) 1987

Knave and Queen (pl B. Howard) 1877

Knees of A Natural Man: The Selected Poetry of Henry Dumas (po Dumas) 1989

Knickerbocker Holiday (pl M. Anderson) 1938

Knife of the Times and Other Stories (f W. Williams) 1932

Knight, after Rilke (po Rich) 1957

Knight of Guadalquiver (pl Dunlap) 1800

Knight's Adventure (pl Dunlap) 1807

Knight's Gambit (f Faulkner) 1949

Knighting of the Twins and Ten Other Tales (f Fitch) 1891

Knightly Quest: A Novella and Four Short Stories (f T. Williams) 1967

Knights and Dragons (f Spencer) 1965

Knights of Seven Lands (f Ingraham) 1845

Knights of the Range (f Grey) 1939

Knocking the Neighbors (f Ade) 1912

Knockout Artist (f Crews) 1988

Knot Holes (pl Bodenheim) 1917

Knowing and the Known (o Dewey) 1949

Knoxville, Tennessee (po Giovanni) 1994

Kofi and His Magic (o Angelou) 1996

Kokoro: Hints and Echoes of Japanese Inner Life (o Hearn) 1896

Konigsmark: The Legend of the Hounds and Other Poems (po Boker) 1869

Koningsmarke: The Long Finne: A Story of the New World (f Paulding) 1823

Kora and Ka (f Doolittle) 1934

Kora in Hell: Improvisations (po W. Williams) 1920

Korean Love Songs from Klail City Death Trip (f Hinojosa) 1978

Kotto, Being Japanese Curios, with Sundry Cobwebs (o Hearn) 1902

Kowloon Tong (f Theroux) 1997

Kral Majales (po Ginsberg) 1965

Kramer Girls (f Suckow) 1930

Kreutzer Sonata (pl L. Mitchell) 1907

Kurzy of the Sea (pl Barnes) 1919

Kwaidan: Stories and Studies of Strange Things (o Hearn) 1904

Kwanzaa (o Madhubuti) 1942

Kyd the Buccaneer (f Ingraham) 1839

l'Abri (o Willis) 1839

L'Amérique en Guerre (o Wharton) 1918

La Belle Sauvage (pl Brougham) 1870

La Bonita Cigarera (f Ingraham) 1844

La Bonne Table (o Bemelmans) 1964

La Carte (pl Kelly) 1927

La China Poblana (o Lim) 1991

La Chingada (po Villanueva) 1985

La Conquistadora: The Autobiography of an Ancient Statue (o Chávez) 1954

La Gloire (o Auchincloss) 1996

La Llorona/Weeping Woman (f Villanueva) 1994

La perla (The Pearl) (scr Steinbeck) 1946

La Poesie d'Andre Fontainas (o Fletcher) 1919

La Salle and the Discovery of the Great West (o Parkman) 1879

La Traviata (o McCarthy) 1983

La Turista (pl Shepard) 1967

La verdad sin voz (f Morales) 1979

La Viuda (pl Fornés), 1961

Labor Spy: A Survey of Industrial Espionage (o S. Howard) 1921

LaBrava (f Leonard) 1983

Lad and the Lion (f E. Burroughs) 1938

Ladder of Years (f A. Tyler) 1995

Ladders to Fire (f Nin) 1946

Ladies Almanack (o Barnes) 1928

Ladies and Gentlemen (pl Hecht) 1939

Ladies and Gentlemen (pl MacArthur) 1941

Ladies and Gentlemen: A Parcel of Reconsiderations (o Cabell) 1934

Ladies of Castile (pl M. Warren) 1790

Ladies of the Corridor (pl Parker) 1954

Ladies' Fair (f Arthur) 1843

Lady (f Richter) 1957

Lady Baltimore (f Wister) 1906

Lady Be Careful (scr Parker) 1936

Lady Byron Vindicated (o Stowe) 1870

Lady from Dubuque (pl Albee) 1980

Lady from the Sea (pl Sontag) 1997

Lady from Toledo (f Chávez) 1960

Lady Hamilton and Her Nelson (pl Tarkington) 1945

Lady in Kicking Horse Reservoir (po Hugo) 1973

Lady in the Dark (pl Hart) 1941

Lady in the Lake (f Chandler) 1943

Lady Is Cold (po White) 1929

Lady Jane and Other Poems (po Willis) 1843

Lady of Larkspur Lotion (pl T. Williams) 1946

Lady of Lions (pl Harrigan) 1878

Lady of Luzon (pl Connelly) 1914

Lady of Quality (f Burnett) 1896

Lady of Rome (f Crawford) 1906

Lady of Secrets (scr Akins) 1936

Lady of Situations (f Auchincloss) 1990

Lady of the Aroostook (f Howells) 1879
Lady of the Gulf (f Ingraham) 1846
Lady of the Tropics (scr Hecht) 1939
Lady to Love (scr S. Howard) 1930
Lady Who Liked Clean Rest Rooms (f Donleavy) 1997
Lady Wu: A True Story (f Lin Yutang) 1957
Lady's Virtue (pl Crothers) 1925
Lafayette in Brooklyn (o Whitman) 1905
Lafcadio Hearn's Japan: An Anthology of His Writings on the Country and Its People (o Hearn) 1997
Lafitte, The Pirate of the Gulf (f Ingraham) 1836
Laguna Woman (po Silko) 1974
Lake (tv Bradbury) 1989
Lake Effect Country (po Ammons) 1983
Lake Gun (f Cooper) 1932
Lake, Mountain, Moon (po Levertov) 1990
Lakeboat (pl Mamet) 1970
Lam to the Slaughter (f E. Gardner) 1939
Lamb of Abyssalia (f Oates) 1979
Lament for Dark Peoples and Other Poems (po Hughes) 1944
Laments for the Living (f Parker) 1930
Lamp and the Bell (pl Millay) 1921
Lancelot (f Percy) 1977
Lancelot (po Robinson) 1920
Lancers (pl Payne) 1827
Land Beyond the Forest: Dracula and Swoop (pl Wellman) 1995
Land Is Bright (pl Ferber, Kaufman) 1941
Land of Canaan (o Asimov) 1971
Land of Fog and Whistles (pl Wellman) 1993
Land of Hidden Men (f E. Burroughs) 1963
Land of Little Sticks (po J. Tate) 1981
Land of Nod and Other Stories: A Volume of Black Stories (f Green) 1976
Land of Shorter Shadows (o E. Gardner) 1948
Land of Silence (po Sarton) 1953
Land of Terror (f E. Burroughs) 1944
Land of the Blue Flower (f Burnett) 1909
Land of the Free—U.S.A (po MacLeish) 1938
Land of the Pharaohs (scr Faulkner) 1955
Land of the Pilgrims' Pride (o Nathan) 1927
Land of the Spirit (f Page) 1913
Land of Unlikeness (po Lowell) 1944
Land Surveyor's Daughter (po Gilchrist) 1979
Land That Time Forgot (f E. Burroughs) 1924
Land Where My Father Died (f Dubus) 1984
Land's End and Other Stories (f Steele) 1918
Landlord at Lion's Head (f Howells) 1897
Landmark (f J. Allen) 1925
Lando (f L'Amour) 1962
Landor's Poetry (o Pinsky) 1968
Lands of the Saracen (o B. Taylor) 1854
Landscape of the Body (pl Guare) 1977
Landscape Painter (f H. James) 1919
Landscape West of Eden (po Aiken) 1934
Landscapes (f Mason) 1984
Landscapes of Living and Dying (po Ferlinghetti) 1979
Landscapes of the Heart: A Memoir (o Spencer) 1997
Langston Hughes, American Poet (o A. Walker) 1974
Language as Symbolic Action: Essays on Life, Literature and Method (o Burke) 1966
Language Is the Only Homeland: Bajan Poets Abroad (o Marshall) 1995

Language of Inquiry (po Hejinian) 1999
Languages Spoken Here (radio Nelson), 1987
Lani Maestro: Essays (o Forché) 1996
Lanterns and Lances (f Thurber) 1961
Lardner's You Know Me Al: The Comic Strip Adventures of Jack Keefe (o Lardner) 1979
Lark (pl Hellman) 1955
Larking Fear and Other Stories (f Lovecraft) 1947 1964
Lars: A Pastoral of Norway (po B. Taylor) 1873
Last Act Is a Solo (pl R. Anderson) 1991
Last Adam (f Cozzens) 1933
Last Analysis (pl Bellow) 1965
Last Carousel (f Algren) 1973
Last Christmas Tree: An Idyll of Immortality (f J. Allen) 1914
Last Circle: Stories and Poems (f S. Benét) 1946
Last Circus, and The Electrocution (f Bradbury) 1980
Last Clean Shirt (scr F. O'Hara) 1???
Last Day of the War (pl Laurents) 1945
Last Day the Dogbushes Bloomed (f L. Smith) 1968
Last Days (f Oates) 1984
Last Days of Lincoln (pl Van Doren) 1959
Last Days of Louisiana Red (f Reed) 1974
Last Decade: Essays and Reviews (o Trilling) 1979
Last Don (f Puzo) 1996
Last Egyptian (f Baum) 1908
Last Flight from Ambo Ber (pl J. Williams) 1981
Last Flower: A Parable in Pictures (f Thurber) 1939
Last Gentleman (f Percy) 1966
Last Go Round (f Kesey) 1994
Last Haiku (po Kerouac) 1969
Last Jew in America (f Fiedler) 1966
Last Laugh (o S. Perelman) 1981
Last Laugh, Mr. Moto (f Marquand) 1942
Last Night of Don Juan (pl S. Howard) 1925
Last of Mr. Moto (f Marquand) 1963
Last of Mr. Norris (f Isherwood) 1935
Last of My Solid Gold Watches (pl T. Williams) 1946
Last of the Breed (f L'Amour) 1986
Last of the Dandies (pl Fitch) 1901
Last of the Foresters (f J. Cooke) 1856
Last of the Hogans (pl Harrigan) 1891
Last of the Lowries (pl Green) 1920
Last of the Mobile Hotshots (scr Vidal) 1970
Last of the Mohicans: A Narrative of 1757 (f Cooper) 1826
Last of the Plainsmen (f Grey) 1908
Last of the Red Hot Lovers (pl Simon) 1969
Last Operas and Plays (pl Stein) 1949
Last Pad (pl Inge) 1972
Last Pat Epstein Show Before the Reruns (pl Vogel) 1979
Last Penny and Other Stories (f Arthur) 1852
Last Picture Show (f McMurtry) 1966
Last Poems (po Freneau) 1946
Last Puritan: A Memoir in the Form of a Novel (f Santayana) 1935
Last Refuge: A Sicilian Romance (f Fuller) 1900
Last Ride of Wild Bill and Eleven Narrative Poems (po S. Brown) 1975
Last Rites for the Vulture (f M. Smith) 1975
Last Song (po Harjo) 1975
Last Songs (po Hovey) 1900
Last Stand at Papago Wells (f L'Amour) 1957

Last Stand at Saber River (f Leonard) 1957

Last Thing He Wanted (f Didion) 1996

Last Time I Saw Hell (f M. Smith) 1974

Last Tycoon: An Unfinished Novel, Together with The Great Gatsby and Selected Writings (f Fitzgerald) 1941

Last Voyage of Somebody the Sailor (f Barth) 1991

Last Woman in His Life (f Queen) 1970

Last Word (pl Daly) 1891

Last Word: Letters Between Marcia Nardi and William Carlos Williams (o W. Williams) 1994

Last Words (f S. Crane) 1902

Last Words of Dutch Schultz: A Fiction in the Form of a Film Script (pl W. Burroughs) 1970

Last Worthless Evening (f Dubus) 1986

Last Yankee (pl A. Miller) 1991

Last Years of Timrod 1864-1867 (o Timrod) 1941

Late Child (f McMurtry) 1995

Late Christopher Bean (pl S. Howard) 1933

Late George Apley (pl Kaufman, Marquand) 1946

Late George Apley: A Novel in the Form of a Memoir (f Marquand) 1937

Late Hour (po Strand) 1978

Late, Passing Prairie Farm (po W. Stafford) 1976

Late Settings (po Merrill) 1985

Latent Heterosexual (pl Chayefsky) 1967

Later (po Creeley) 1978

Later Poetry of Charlotte Perkins Gilman (po Gilman) 1996

Later the Same Day (f Paley) 1985

Later: New Poems (po Creeley) 1979

Latin Deli: Prose & Poetry (o Cofer) 1993

Latin Women Pray (po Cofer) 1980

Latin Women Pray (pl Cofer) 1984

Latter Days of a Celebrated Soubrette (pl T. Williams) 1974

Laugh, Clown, Laugh! (pl Belasco) 1923

Laughable Poem (po Freneau) 1809

Laughing Boy (f La Farge) 1929

Laughing Gas (pl Dreiser) 1916

Laughing Matter (f Saroyan) 1953

Laughing Pioneer: A Sketch of Country Life (f Green) 1932

Laughing Stock (pl Linney) 1984

Laughing Stock: The Posthumous Autobiography of Stribling (o Stribling) 1982

Laughing to Keep from Crying (f Hughes) 1952

Laughter in the Dark (f Nabokov) 1938

Laughter of My Father (o Bulosan) 1944

Laughter on the 23rd Floor (pl Simon) 1993

Launcelot and Guenevere: A Poem in Dramas (pl Hovey

Laura (tv Capote) 1968

Laura and Francisca (po Riding) 1931

Laurel: An Ode to Mary Day Lanier (po Hovey) 1889

Law at Randado (f Leonard) 1955

Law for the Lion (f Auchincloss) 1953

Law Miscellanies (o Brackenridge) 1814

Law of the Desert Born (f L'Amour) 1983

Law unto Herself (f Rebecca Davis) 1878

Lawd Today (f R. Wright) 1963

Lawn Dogs (scr N. Wallace) 1998

Lawton Girl (f Frederic) 1890

Lawyer Lincoln (pl B. Smith) 1939

Lay Anthony (f Hergesheimer) 1914

Lay of the Scottish Fiddle (po Paulding) 1813

Lay the Marble Tea: Twenty-four Poems (po Brautigan) 1959

Lays of My Home and Other Poems (po Whittier) 1843

Lays of the Palmetto (po Simms) 1848

Lazarus Laughed (pl O'Neill) 1927

lbsen Revisited (pl Dell) 1914

Le Mouchoir: An Autobiographical Romance (f Cooper) 1843

Le Role du Negre dans la culture des Ameriques (o Locke) 1943

Leaf in a Storm: A Novel of War-Swept China (f Lin Yutang) 1941

Leafless American (o Dahlberg) 1967

Leaflets: Poems, 1965-1968 (po Rich) 1969

Leafy Rivers (f J. West) 1967

League of Frightened Men (f Stout) 1935

League of Frightened Philistines and Other Papers (o Farrell) 1945

Leah the Forsaken (pl Daly) 1863

Leaning Forward (po Paley) 1985

Leaning Tower and Other Stories (f Porter) 1944

Learned Ladies (pl Wilbur) 1977

Learning to Live in the World: Earth Poems (po W. Stafford) 1994

Least of These (pl Angelou) 1966

Leather and Silk (f J. Cooke) 1892

Leather Patch (pl Harrigan) 1886

Leather Stocking and Silk (f J. Cooke) 1854

Leatherstocking Tales (f Cooper) 1985

Leatherwood God (f Howells) 1916

Leave Her to Heaven (pl Van Druten) 1941

Leave It to Me (f Mukherjee) 1997

Leaves from Margaret Smith's Journal (f Whittier) 1849

Leaves from the Diary of an Impressionist: Early Writings (o Hearn) 1911

Leaves of Grass (po Whitman) 1855

Leaves of the Tree (pl Masters) 1909

Leaves, The Lion-Fish and the Bear (f Cheever) 1980

Leaving Another Kingdom: Selected Poems (po Stern) 1990

Leaving Cheyenne (f McMurtry) 1963

Leavings (pl Bullins) 1980

Lecherous Limericks (po Asimov) 1975

Lechery (pl Oates) 1985

Lectures (o Harte) 1909

Lectures in America (o Stein) 1935

Lectures in the Philosophy of Education 1899 (o Dewey) 1966

Lectures on Diseases of the Nervous System, Especially in Women (o S. Mitchell) 1881

Lectures on English Poets (o J. Lowell) 1897

Lectures on Fashion (o Willis) 1844

Lee in the Mountains and Other Poems (po Davidson) 1938

Lee: A Dramatic Poem (pl Masters) 1926

LeFou (po Creeley) 1952

Left Bank (pl Rice) 1931

Left Hand of the Electron (o Asimov) 1972

Left Heresy in Literature and Life (o Riding) 1939

Left out in the Rain: Poems 1947-1984 (po Snyder) 1986

Leftovers, A Care Package: Two Lectures (o W. Stafford) 1973

Legal Aspects of the Negro Problem (o J. Johnson)

Legal Wreck (f Gillette) 1888

Legend (pl Dell) 1915

Legend of "Norwood" (pl Daly) 1867

Legend of Ermengarde (po Guthrie) 1929

Legend of La Llorona (f Anaya) 1984

Legend of Silent Night (tv Isherwood) 1969

Legend of the Lake (po Whittier) 1893

Legend of the Lost (scr Hecht) 1957

Legends (po A. Lowell) 1921
Legends and Lyrics (po Hayne) 1872
Legends and Lyrics (po Whittier) 1890
Legends of New England (o Whittier) 1831
Legends of the Fall (f Harrison) 1979
Legends of the Saints (f Petry) 1970
Leibniz's New Essays Concerning the Human Understanding: A Critical Exposition (o Dewey) 1888
Leicester (pl Dunlap) 1794
Leila: Further in the Destinies of Darcy Dancer, Gentleman (f Donleavy) 1983
Leisler (f Ingraham) 1846
Lemons (pl Daly) 1877
Len Lye and the Problem of Popular Films (o Riding) 1938
Leningrad (po Hejinian) 1991
Leon Gaspard (o Waters) 1964
Leonor de Guzman (pl Boker) 1853
LeRoi Jones-Amiri (po Baraka) 1991
Les Blancs (pl Hansberry
Les Sentences dans la Poésie Grecque d'Homere à Euripide (o Stickney) 1903
Lesser Evils: Ten Quartets (po Soto) 1988
Lesser Magoo (pl Wellman) 1997
Lesson before Dying (f Gaines) 1993
Lesson Number One (scr Benchley) 1929
Lesson of Life and Other Poems (po Boker) 1848
Lesson of the Master, The Marriages, The Pupil, Brooksmith, The Solution, Sir Edmund Orme (f H. James) 1892
Lesson of the Masters (o Cowley) 1971
Lessons and Complaints (f Purdy) 1978
Lessons in Life for All Who Will Read Them (f Arthur) 1851
Lessons in Living (o Angelou) 1993
Lester's Luck (f Alger) 1901
Let 'em Eat Cake (pl Kaufman) 1933
Let Evening Come (po Kenyon) 1990
Let Freedom Ring (Song of the West) (scr Hecht) 1939
Let It Come Down (f Bowles) 1952
Let Me Feel Your Pulse (f Henry) 1910
Let Me Hear the Melody (pl Behrman) 1951
Let Me Lie (o Cabell) 1947
Let the Band Play Dixie and Other Stories (f R. Bradford) 1934
Let Us Be Gay (pl Crothers) 1929
Let Us Remember Him (pl Hughes) 1963
Let Your Mind Alone! and Other More or Less Inspirational Pieces (f Thurber) 1937
Let's Go Out and Play (radio Fitzgerald) 1935
Let's Hear It for the Queen: A Play (pl Childress) 1976
Let's Laugh (f Nasby) 1924
Let's Make Music (scr N. West) 1940
Let's Play Poison (tv Bradbury) 1992
Letter about Good Management under the Distemper of Measles (o Mather) 1713
Letter about the Present State of Christianity among the Christianized Indians (o Mather) 1705
Letter for Melville 1951 (po Olson) 1951
Letter from a Fugitive Slave (o Jacobs) 1855
Letter from America (po Bulosan) 1942
Letter from Li Po and Other Poems (po Aiken) 1955
Letter from Peking (f Buck) 1957
Letter of Introduction (pl Howells) 1892
Letter to a Friend in the Country (o Franklin) 1735

Letter to American Teachers of History (o Adams) 1910
Letter to Gen. Lafayette (o Cooper) 1831
Letter to George Washington (o Paine) 1796
Letter to God (po Patchen) 1947
Letter to His Countrymen (o Cooper) 1834
Letter to Jackie (pl M. Anderson) 1944
Letter to the Author of the Pamphlet Called An Answer to the Hampshire Narrative (o Edwards) 1737
Letter to the National Convention of France (o Barlow) 1793(?)
Letter to the People of Piedmont (o Barlow) 1795
Letter to the People of France and the French Armies (o Paine) 1797
Letter Written to Joel Lewis Griffing in 1814 (o Halleck) 1921
Letter-Book (o Sewall) 1886-88
Letters (o S. Anderson) 1953
Letters (f Barth) 1979
Letters (o Bierce) 1921
Letters (o S. Crane) 1960
Letters (o Dickinson) 1894
Letters (o Faulkner) 1984
Letters (o Guiney) 1926
Letters (o Harte) 1926
Letters (o Jewett) 1911
Letters (o J. Lowell) 1894
Letters (o Melville) 1960
Letters (o Poe) 1948
Letters (o Santos) 1995
Letters (o Wharton) 1988
Letters and Papers of Franklin and Richard Jackson 1753-1785 (o Franklin) 1947
Letters and Personal Writings (o Edwards) 1998
Letters and Social Aims (o Emerson) 1876
Letters for Origin 1950-1956 (o Olson) 1969
Letters from Abroad to Kindred at Home (o Sedgwick) 1841
Letters from and to the Ford Motor Company (o Moore) 1958
Letters from Baltimore: The Mencken-Cleator Correspondence (o Mencken) 1982
Letters from China and Japan (o Dewey) 1920
Letters from Maine: New Poems (po Sarton) 1984
Letters from New York (o Child) 1843
Letters from New York. Second Series (o Child) 1845
Letters from Parkman to E. G. Squier (o Parkman) 1911
Letters from Ring (o Lardner) 1979
Letters from Shimane and Kyushu (o Hearn) 1935
Letters from the East (o Bryant) 1869
Letters from the Raven, Being the Correspondence of Hearn with Henry Watkin (o Hearn) 1907
Letters from the South (o Paulding) 1817
Letters from under a Bridge, and Poems (o Willis) 1840
Letters Home (f Howells) 1903
Letters Now in Colby College Library (o Jewett) 1947
Letters of a Traveller (o Bryant) 1850
Letters of an Altrurian Traveller (1893-1894) (f Howells) 1961
Letters of Artemus Ward to Charles E. Wilson 1858-1861 (o Ward) 1900
Letters of Ayn Rand (o Rand) 1995
Letters of Crane and His Family (o H. Crane) 1974
Letters of Denise Levertov and William Carlos Williams (o W. Williams) 1998
Letters of Franklin and Jane Mecom (o Franklin) 1950
Letters of Gertrude Stein and Thornton Wilder (o Stein) 1996

Letters of Gertrude Stein and Van Vechten 1913-1946 (o Van Vechten) 1986

Letters of James and Theodore Flournoy (o W. James) 1966

Letters of Jonathan Oldstyle, Gent (f W. Irving) 1824

Letters of Lafayette and Jefferson (o Jefferson) 1929

Letters of Lanier: Selections from His Correspondence 1866-1881 (o Lanier) 1899

Letters of Samuel Lee and Sewall Relating to New England and the Indians (o Sewall) 1912

Letters of Stein and Carl Van Vechten 1913-1946 (o Stein) 1986

Letters on Various Interesting and Important Subjects (o Freneau) 1799

Letters to a King (o Tourgée) 1888

Letters to a Niece and Prayer to the Virgin of Chartres (o Adams) 1920

Letters to a Pagan (o Hearn) 1933

Letters to A.C. Benson and Auguste Monod (pl H. James) 1930

Letters to A. Joseph Armstrong (o Lindsay) 1940

Letters to Bab: Anderson to Marietta D. Finley 1916-1933 (o S. Anderson) 1985

Letters to Edith Brower (o Robinson) 1968

Letters to Elizabeth: A Selection of Letters from Steinbeck to Elizabeth Otis (o Steinbeck) 1978

Letters to Howard George Schmitt (o Robinson) 1940

Letters to Joe C. Brown (o R. Wright) 1968

Letters to Lithopolis from O. Henry to Mabel Wagnalls (o Henry) 1922

Letters to Madame Helvetius and Madame La Frete (o Franklin) 1924

Letters to the Citizens of the United States (o Paine) 1803

Letters to the Press 1758-1775 (o Franklin) 1950

Letters to Various Persons (o Thoreau) 1865

Letters to Walter Berry (pl H. James) 1928

Letters to William D. Ticknor (o Hawthorne) 1910

Letters to Yesinin (po Harrison) 1973

Letters: Poems MCMLIII-MCMLVI (po Duncan) 1958

Letting Go (f P. Roth) 1962

Lettre adtessee aus habitans du Piemont (o Barlow) 1793

Leviathan 99 (pl Bradbury) 1972

Levitation: Five Fictions (f Ozick) 1982

Lew Archer, Private Investigator (f Macdonald) 1977

Lewis of Monte Blanco (pl Dunlap) 1804

Lex Mercatoria (o Mather) 1705

Lexington (pl S. Howard) 1924(?)

Liar (pl Fitch) 1896

Liberal Imagination: Essays on Literature and Society (o Trilling) 1950

Liberalism and Social Action (o Dewey) 1935

Liberties (po S. Howe) 1980

Liberty and Peace (po Wheatley) 1784

Liberty Jones (pl Barry) 1941

Liberty Tree, with the Last Words of Grandfather's Chair (o Hawthorne) 1841

Libra (f Delillo) 1988

Libretto for the Republic of Liberia (po Tolson) 1953

Libris (o Van Vechten) 1942

Lice (po Merwin) 1967

Lichee Nuts (po Masters) 1930

Lie (pl Vonnegut) 1992

Lie Down in Darkness (f Styron) 1951

Lie of the Mind (pl}f Shepard) 1985

Lieutenant 1967

Life (pl Daly) 1876

Life (f Morris) 1973

Life Adventurous and Other Stories (f Farrell) 1947

Life along the Passaic River (f W. Williams) 1938

Life among the Piutes: Their Wrongs and Claims (o Winnemucca) 1883

Life among the Savages (o S. Jackson) 1953

Life amongst the Modocs: Unwritten History (o J. Miller) 1873

Life and Adventures of Santa Claus (f Baum) 1902

Life and Adventures of Josh Billings (f Shaw) 1883

Life and Character of Edwards, with a Number of His Sermons (o Edwards) 1765

Life and Death (po Creeley) 1998

Life and Death of the Renowned Mr. John Eliot (o Mather) 1691

Life and Energy (o Asimov) 1962

Life and Gabriella (f Glasgow) 1916

Life and Letters (o B. Taylor) 1884

Life and Morals of Jesus of Nazareth (o Jefferson) 1902

Life and Selected Writings of Jefferson (o Jefferson) 1944

Life and Times of Douglass (o Douglass) 1881

Life Around Us: Selected Poems on Nature (po Levertov) 1997

Life at Happy Knoll (f Marquand) 1957

Life Being the Best and Other Stories (f Boyle) 1988

Life Class (o Bemelmans) 1938

Life Doesn't Frighten Me (po Angelou) 1993

Life for a Life (f Herrick) 1910

Life Here and There (f Willis) 1850

Life I Really Lived (f J. West) 1979

Life in America (f Simms) 1848

Life in New York (pl Brougham) 1856

Life in the Clouds (pl Brougham) 1840

Life in the Forest (po Levertov) 1978

Life in the Iron Mills (f Rebecca Davis, Olsen) 1972

Life in the Theatre (pl Mamet) 1977

Life in the War Zone (o Atherton) 1916

Life Is Dream (pl Fornés) 1981

Life Is My Song (o Fletcher) 1937

Life Is Real (pl Rice) 1937

Life, Law, and Letters: Essays and Sketches (o Auchincloss) 1979

Life of Albert Gallatin (o Adams) 1879

Life of Captain John Smith (o Simms) 1847

Life of Charles Brockden Brown (o Dunlap) 1815

Life of Chevalier Bayard (o Simms) 1848

Life of Cooke (o Dunlap) 1815

Life of Francis Marion (o Simms) 1844

Life of Franklin Pierce (o Hawthorne) 1852

Life of Gen. Robert E. Lee (o J. Cooke) 1871

Life of General Ben Harrison (o L. Wallace) 1888

Life of George Cabot Lodge (o Adams) 1911

Life of Goethe (o Mowatt) 1844

Life of Mary Baker G. Eddy, and the History of Christian Science (o Cather) 1909

Life of Nancy (f Jewett) 1895

Life of Reason (o Santayana) 1905-06

Life of Sir William Phips (o Mather) 1929

Life of Stonewall Jackson (o J. Cooke) 1863

Life of the Dead (po Riding) 1933

Life of the Most Noble Arthur, Marquis and Earl of Wellington (o Dunlap) 1814

Life of Washington (o Paulding) 1835(?)

Life Sentences (pl Nelson) 1993
Life Span (po Villanueva) 1984
Life Studies (po Lowell) 1959
Life with No Joy in It and Other Plays and Pieces (pl Mamet) 1994
Life Work (o Hall) 1993
Life Work of Juan Diaz (tv Bradbury) 1963
Life's Picture History of World War II (o Dos Passos) 1950
Lifeboat (scr Steinbeck) 1944
Lifeboat Drill (pl T. Williams) 1979
Lift Every Voice and Sing (o J. Johnson) 1993
Lifted Masks: Stories (f Glaspell) 1912
Lifting Belly (f Stein) 1989
Light around the Body (po Bly) 1967
Light Can Be Both Wave and Particle (f Gilchrist) 1989
Light Exists in Spring, and Other Poems (po Dickinson) 1996
Light Fantastic (tv Laurents) 1967
Light in August (f Faulkner) 1932
Light in the Forest (f Richter) 1953
Light in the Piazza (f Spencer) 1960
Light in the Window (f Rinehart) 1948
Light of Her Countenance (f Boyesen) 1889
Light of the Star (f Garland) 1904
Light of Western Stars (f Grey) 1914
Light Up the Sky (pl Hart) 1949
Light Woman (f Gale) 1937
Light: A Narrative Poem (po J. Miller) 1907
Light's Diamond Jubilee (tv Hecht) 1954
Light-Fingered Gentry (f D. Phillips) 1907
Lightnin' (scr Behrman) 1930
Lights and Shadows of Real Life (f Arthur) 1851
Lights in the Valley (po Bodenheim) 1942
Like a Bulwark (po Moore) 1956
...Like a Lover (f Wescott) 1926
Like One of the Family (pl Childress) 1956
Like You're Nobody: The Letters of Louis Gallo to Saul Bellow, 1961-62 (o Bellow) 1966
Lilacs Overgrown (f Lin Tai-yi) 1960
Liliane (f Shange) 1994
Liliom (scr Behrman) 1930
Lilli Barr (f Bromfield) 1926
Lily (pl Belasco) 1909
Lily and the Totem (f Simms) 1850
Lily Dafon (pl Saroyan) 1960
Lily of the Valley (pl Hecht) 1942
Li'l' Gal (po Dunbar) 1904
Lime Twig (f Hawkes) 1961
Limericks Too Gross (po Asimov, Ciardi) 1978
Limestone Tree (f Hergesheimer) 1931
Lin McLean (f Wister) 1897
Lin Yutang Chuan (o Lin Tai-yi) 1989
Lincoln (f Vidal) 1984
Lincoln and Other Poems (po Markham) 1901
Lincoln Relics (po Kunitz) 1978
Linda Condon (f Hergesheimer) 1919
Linden Hills (f Naylor) 1985
Line of Love (f Cabell) 1905
Line of the Sun (f Cofer) 1989
Lineage of Lichfield: An Essay in Eugenics (o Cabell) 1922
Lines Long and Short: Biographical Sketches in Various Rhythms (f Fuller) 1917

Lines of Vision (pl Fornés) 1976
Linotte: The Early Diary 1914-1920 (o Nin) 1978
Linwoods (f Sedgwick) 1835
Lion and the Archer (po Hayden) 1948
Lion and the Carpenter and Other Tales from the Arabian Nights Retold (o J. Stafford) 1962
Lion and the Rose (po Sarton) 1948
Lion and the Unicorn (f Richard Davis) 1899
Lion in the Garden: Interviews with Faulkner 1926-1962 (o Faulkner) 1968
Lion of the West (pl Paulding) 1831
Lion Tail and Eyes: Poems Written out of Laziness and Silence (po J. Wright, Bly) 1962
Lionel Lincoln (f Cooper) 1825
Lispings of the Muse (po Payne) 1815
Listen (pl Creeley) 1972
Listen to the Mocking Bird (o S. Perelman) 1949
Listen to the People: Independence Day 1941 (po S. Benét) 1941
Listening Deep (po W. Stafford) 1984
Listening to the River: Seasons in the American West (po W. Stafford) 1994
Listening Woman (f Hillerman) 1977
Listening: A Chamber Play (pl Albee) 1976
Litany of Washington Street (o Lindsay) 1929
Literally True (o Stein) 1947
Literary and Social Silhouettes (o Boyesen) 1894
Literary Bible of Jefferson: His Commonplace Book of Philosophers and Poets (o Jefferson) 1928
Literary Chronicle 1920-1950 (o E. Wilson) 1956
Literary Correspondence of Davidson and Allen Tate (o Davidson) 1974
Literary Criticism (o J. Lowell) 1969
Literary Criticism (o Poe) 1965
Literary Essays (o Hearn) 1939
Literary Essays 1954-1974 (o Farrell) 1976
Literary Love-Letters and Other Stories (f Herrick) 1897
Literary Notebook (o Thoreau) 1964
Literary Recreations and Miscellanies (o Whittier) 1854
Literary Reviews and Essays on American, English, and French Literature (pl H. James) 1957
Literary Situation (o Cowley) 1954
Literate Passion: Letters of Nin and Henry Miller 1932-1953 (o Nin) 1987
Literati: Some Honest Opinions about Authorial Merits and Demerits (f Poe) 1850
Literature and Morality (o Farrell) 1947
Literature of Exhaustion, and The Literature of Replenishment (o Barth) 1982
Litko (pl Mamet) 1981
Litter of Rose Leaves (f S. Benét) 1930
Little Accident (pl Dell) 1928
Little Birds: Erotica (f Nin) 1979
Little Black Dog (o Herrick) 1931
Little Blue Light (pl E. Wilson) 1950
Little Book in C Major (o Mencken) 1916
Little Book of a Thousand Eyes (po Hejinian) 1996
Little Book of Nonsense (po Field) 1901
Little Book of Profitable Tales (f Field) 1889
Little Book of Tribune Verse: A Number of Hitherto Uncollected Poems, Grave and Gay (po Field) 1901
Little Book of Western Verse (po Field) 1889

Little Book on the Human Shadow (po Bly) 1988
Little Breeches and Other Pieces (po Hay) 1871
Little Children (f Saroyan) 1937
Little City of Hope: A Christmas Story (f Crawford) 1907
Little David: An Unproduced Scene from "The Green Pastures" (pl Connelly) 1937 Little Disturbances of Man: Stories of Men and Women in Love (f Paley) 1959
Little Drummer (f Harte) 1872
Little Duchess (scr Connelly) 1934
Little English Gallery (o Guiney) 1894
Little Essays (o Santayana) 1920
Little Flocks Guarded against Grievous Wolves (o Mather) 1691
Little Foxes (pl Hellman) 1939
Little Foxes (scr Parker) 1941
Little Foxes (o Stowe) 1866
Little Fraud (pl Harrigan) 1871
Little Friend (scr Isherwood) 1934
Little Friend, Little Friend (po Jarrell) 1945
Little Gidding (po Eliot) 1942
Little Ham (pl Hughes) 1935
Little Hero (pl Goodman) 1957
Little Hunchback Zia (f Burnett) 1916
Little Johnny Jones (pl Cohan) 1904
Little Journey (pl Crothers) 1918
Little Journey in the World (f Warner) 1889
Little Lady of the Big House (f London) 1916
Little Lord Fauntleroy (f Burnett) 1886
Little Man, Little Man (o James Baldwin) 1976
Little Me (pl Simon), 1962
Little Men (f J. West) 1954
Little Men: Life at Plumfield with Jo's Boys (f Alcott) 1871
Little Millionaire (pl Cohan) 1911
Little Miracle (pl Akins) 1936
Little Miss Million (pl Daly) 1893
Little Mocassin (f Neal) 1866
Little Nelly Kelly (pl Cohan) 1922
Little Norsk (f Garland) 1892
Little Ocean (pl Shepard) 1974
Little Orvie (f Tarkington) 1934
Little Pilgrims: A Sequel to The Tailor's Apprentice (f Arthur) 1843
Little Princess (pl Burnett) 1902
Little Pussy Willow (o Stowe) 1870
Little Regiment and Other Episodes of the American Civil War (f S. Crane) 1896
Little Saint Elizabeth and Other Stories (f Burnett) 1890
Little Savoyard and Other Stories (f Arthur) 1891
Little Sister (f Chandler) 1949
Little Steel (f Sinclair) 1938
Little Stone: Stories (f Bowles) 1950
Little Store (o Welty) 1975
Little Stories (f S. Mitchell) 1903
Little That Is All (po Ciardi) 1974
Little Tour in France (pl H. James) 1884
Little Tricker the Squirrel Meets Big Double the Bear (f Kesey) 1988
Little Who's Zoo of Mild Animals (po Aiken) 1977
Little Wizard Series (f Baum) 1913
Little Women (f Alcott) 1868-69
Littlest Revue (pl Nash) 1956
Live and Let Live (f Sedgwick) 1837

Live Another Day (po Ciardi) 1949
Live from Golgotha (f Vidal) 1992
Live or Die (po Sexton) 1966
Live Time to Time (po Ciardi) 1951
Lively Lady (f Roberts) 1931
Lives and Deeds of Our Self-Made Men (o Stowe) 1872
Lives and Times of Archy and Mehitabel (po Marquis) 1940
Lives of Distinguished American Naval Officers (o Cooper) 1846
Lives of Robert Young Hayne and Hugh Swinton Legare (o Hayne) 1878
Lives of the Poets: Six Stories and a Novella (f Doctorow) 1984
Lives of the Twins (f Oates) 1987
Lives of Wives (f Riding) 1939
Lives of X (po Ciardi) 1971
Living (o Dillard) 1992
Living by the Word: Selected Writings 1973-1987 (o A. Walker) 1988
Living By Fiction (o Dillard) 1982
Living End (f Elkin) 1979
Living for Show (pl Daly) 1885
Living in the Future (o Asimov) 1984
Living My Life (o Goldman) 1931
Living Present (o Atherton) 1917
Living Reed (f Buck) 1963
Living River (o Asimov) 1959
Living Thoughts of Jefferson (o Jefferson) 1940
Lizard Woman (f Waters) 1984
Lizzie (f S. Jackson) 1957
Llana of Gathol (f E. Burroughs) 1948
Lloronas, Women Who Howel: Autohistorias-Teorias and the Production of Writing, Knowledge and Identity (o Anzaldúa) 1994
Lo (pl Henry) 1909
Loading Mercury with a Pitchfork (po Brautigan) 1976
Local Boy Makes Good (pl Kaufman) 1944
Local Color (o Capote) 1950
Local News (po Soto) 1993
Locations (po Harrison) 1968
Locket (pl Masters) 1910
Lockwood Concern (f J. O'Hara) 1965
Locomotive (radio Parks), 1991
Log from the Sea of Cortez (o Steinbeck) 1951
Logan: A Family History (f Neal) 1822
Logic: The Theory of Inquiry (o Dewey) 1938
Logical Conditions of a Scientific Treatment of Morality (o Dewey) 1903
Loiterings of Travel (f Willis) 1840
Lolita (f Nabokov) 1955
Lolita in the Garden (pl Fornés) 1977
London (In 10 Cities) (pl Wellman) 1996
London Embassy (f Theroux) 1982
London Life, The Patagonia, The Liar, Mrs. Temperly (f H. James) 1889
London Snow: A Christmas Story (o Theroux) 1979
London Suite: A Comedy (pl Simon) 1993
London Wall (pl Van Druten) 1931
London's Yukon Women (f London) 1982
Lone Canoe, or the Explorer (pl Mamet) 1979
Lone Star Ranger (f Grey) 1915
Lone Star: A Symphonic Drama of Sam Houston and the Winning of Texas Independence from Mexico (pl Green) 1977
Lone Striker (po Frost) 1933

Loneliest Girl in the World (f Fearing) 1951
Lonely Crusade (f Himes) 1947
Lonely for the Future (f Farrell) 1966
Lonely Guy (scr Simon), 1984
Lonely Heart (pl Sheldon) 1921
Lonely Men (f L'Amour) 1969
Lonely on the Mountain (f L'Amour) 1980
Lonely One (tv Bradbury) 1992
Lonesome Dove (f McMurtry) 1985
Lonesome Gods (f L'Amour) 1983
Lonesome Road (o Redding) 1958
Lonesome Road: Six Plays for the Negro Theatre (pl Green) 1926
Long after Ecclesiastes (po Bradbury) 1985
Long after Midnight (f Bradbury) 1976
Long Christmas Dinner (pl Wilder) 1931
Long Day in November (f Gaines) 1971
Long Day's Journey into Night (pl O'Neill) 1956
Long Division: A Tribal History (po Rose) 1976
Long Dream (f R. Wright) 1958
Long Fatal Love Chase (f Alcott) 1995
Long Goodbye (f Chandler) 1953
Long Goodbye (pl T. Williams) 1940
Long Hot Summer (scr R Brown) 1985
Long Hot Summer (f Faulkner) 1958
Long Hunt (f Boyd) 1930
Long Live the King! (f Rinehart) 1917
Long Love (f Buck) 1949
Long March (f Styron) 1956
Long Night (scr Bambara) 1981
Long Night (pl Green) 1920
Long Night (f Lytle) 1936
Long Patrol: 25 Years of Writing (o Mailer) 1971
Long Pennant (f La Farge) 1933
Long Rain (tv Bradbury) 1992
Long Reach: New and Uncollected Poems 1948-1983 (po Eberhart) 1984
Long Ride Home (f L'Amour) 1989
Long Sigh the Wind Makes (po W. Stafford) 1991
Long Stay Cut Short (pl T. Williams) 1948
Long Street (po Davidson) 1961
Long Time Ago (pl Dell) 1917
Long Valley (f Steinbeck) 1938
Long Voyage Home (pl O'Neill) 1917
Long Walk (f King) 1979
Long Walk at San Francisco State and Other Essays (o Boyle) 1970
Long Walks and Intimate Talks (o Paley) 1991
Long Way from Home (o McKay) 1937
Long Years (tv Bradbury) 1990
Longest Day (scr J. Jones) 1962
Lonigan (f L'Amour) 1988
Look at the Harlequins! (f Nabokov) 1974
Look Homeward, Angel: A Story of the Buried Life (f Thomas Wolfe) 1929
Look How the Fish Live (f Powers) 1975
Look Who's Talking! (o S. Perelman) 1940
Looking 'em Over (f Farrell) 1960
Looking at Life (o Dell) 1924
Looking Back at Boyhood (o D. Mitchell) 1906
Looking Backward (o Lovecraft) 1920(?)
Looking Backward 2000-1887 (f Bellamy) 1888

Looking Beyond (f Lin Yutang) 1955
Loon (po Bly) 1977
Loon Lake (f Doctorow) 1980
Loose Canons: Notes on the Culture Wars (o Gates) 1992
Loose Lips (f R Brown) 1999
Loose Woman (po Cisneros) 1994
Lord Byron's Love Letter (pl T. Williams) 1946
Lord Chumley (pl Belasco) 1888
Lord Fairfax (f J. Cooke) 1888
Lord Mayor of Dublin (pl Harrigan) 1908
Lord of the Dawn: The Legend of Quetzacoatl (f Anaya) 1987
Lord Pengo: A Period Comedy (pl Behrman) 1963
Lord Timothy Dexter of Newburyport, Mass (o Marquand) 1925
Lord Weary's Castle (po Lowell) 1946
Lord's Will (pl Green) 1922
Lordly Hudson: Collected Poems (po Goodman) 1962
Lords of the Ghostland: A History of the Ideal (o Saltus) 1907
Lorenzo Bunch (f Tarkington) 1936
Lorgaire (pl Harrigan) 1878
Lorgnette (f D. Mitchell) 1850
Lorlie's Wedding (pl Daly) 1864
Los Cerritos: A Romance of the Modern Time (f Atherton) 1890
Lose with a Smile (o Lardner) 1933
Losing Battles (f Welty) 1970
Loss of Memory (pl Laurents) 1981
Loss of Roses (pl Inge) 1960
Losses (po Jarrell) 1948
Lost at Sea (f Alger) 1904
Lost Boy: A Novella (f Thomas Wolfe) 1992
Lost British Policy (o Tuchman) 1938
Lost Child's Fireflies (pl Saroyan) 1954
Lost Children (f Arthur) 1848
Lost Colony (pl Green) 1937
Lost Continent (f E. Burroughs) 1963
Lost Copper (po Rose) 1980
Lost Ecstasy (f Rinehart) 1927
Lost Face (f London) 1910
Lost Galleon and Other Tales (f Harte) 1867
Lost in the Bonewheel Factory (po Komunyakaa) 1979
Lost in the Cosmos: The Last Self-Help Book (o Percy) 1983
Lost in the Funhouse: Fiction for Print, Tape, Live Voice (f Barth) 1968
Lost in the Stars (pl M. Anderson) 1950
Lost in Yonkers (pl Simon) 1991
Lost Lady (f Cather) 1923
Lost Laysen (o M. Mitchell) 1996
Lost Look and Other Poems (po Van Doren) 1937
Lost on Venus (f E. Burroughs) 1935
Lost Pilot (po J. Tate) 1967
Lost Plays (pl Patchen) 1977
Lost Pleiad and Other Poems (po Chivers) 1845
Lost Prince (f Burnett) 1915
Lost Princess of Oz (f Baum) 1917
Lost Pueblo (f Grey) 1954
Lost Road (f Richard Davis) 1913
Lost Son and Other Poems (po Roethke) 1948
Lost State of Franklin (pl Reed) 1976
Lost Trail (f Grey) 1909
Lost Wagon Train (f Grey) 1936
Lost World: New Poems (po Jarrell) 1965
Lost Zoo (po Cullen) 1940

Lotos Leaves (pl Brougham) 1875
Lottery (f S. Jackson) 1949
Lottery of Love (pl Daly) 1889
Loudspeaker (pl Lawson) 1927
Louis Mitchell: A Sketch (o D. Mitchell) 1947
Louis Zukofsky: 16 Once Published (po Zukofsky) 1962
Louisa May Alcott Unmasked: Collected Thrillers (f Alcott) 1995
Louisa's Wonder Book: An Unknown Alcott Juvenile (f Alcott) 1975
Louisiana (f Burnett) 1880
Louisiana Cavalier: A Symphonic Drama of the 18th Century French and Spanish Struggle for the Settling of Louisiana (pl Green) 1976
Louisiana Territory (pl Kopit) 1975
Love (f Saroyan) 1959
Love (po R. Warren) 1981
Love Affair (f Bradbury) 1982
Love Affair: A Venetian Journal (o Morris) 1972
Love Affairs of a Bibliomaniac (o Field) 1896
Love Always (f Beattie) 1985
Love among the Cannibals (f Morris) 1957
Love among the Ruins (pl Rice) 1963
Love and Death in the American Novel (o Fiedler) 1966
Love and Death: The Complete Stories (f Fisher) 1959
Love and Fame (po Berryman) 1970
Love and How to Cure It (pl Wilder) 1931
Love and Its Derangements (po Oates) 1970
Love and Lore (o Saltus) 1890
Love and War, Art and God (po Shapiro) 1984
Love and War Poems (po Patchen) 1968
Love as Love, Death as Death (po Riding) 1928
Love Conquers All (o Benchley) 1922
Love, Death, and the Ladies' Drill Team (f J. West) 1955
Love Death Plays: Dialogue for Two Men, Midwestern Music, The Love Death, Venus and Adonis, The Wake, The Star (pl Inge) 1975
Love Duel (pl Akins) 1929
Love Factories (f Updike) 1993
Love, Here Is My Hat (f Saroyan) 1938
Love in a Cottage (f Arthur) 1848
Love in Greenwich Village (f Dell) 1926
Love in Harness (pl Daly) 1887
Love in High Life (f Arthur) 1849
Love in Humble Life (pl Payne) 1825
Love in Idleness (f Crawford) 1894
Love in Tandem (pl Daly) 1892
Love in the Backwoods (f L. Mitchell) 1897
Love in the Days of Rage (f Ferlinghetti) 1988
Love in the Machine Age: A Psychological Study of the Transition from Patriarchal Society (o Dell) 1930
Love in the Ruins: The Adventures of a Bad Catholic at a Time Near the End of the World (f Percy) 1971
Love in the United States, and The Big Shot (f Hergesheimer) 1932
Love Is Like That (pl Behrman) 1927
Love Is Not What You Think (o J. West) 1959
Love Letters (o Hawthorne) 1907
Love Letters (scr Rand) 1945
Love Letters to Eleanor Copenhauer Anderson (o S. Anderson) 1989
Love Medicine (f Erdrich) 1984
Love Nest (pl Sherwood) 1927
Love Nest and Other Stories (f Lardner) 1926

Love of Azalea (f Eaton) 1904
Love of Landry (f Dunbar) 1900
Love of Life and Other Stories (f London) 1907
Love of Parson Lord and Other Stories (f Freeman) 1900
Love on Crutches (pl Daly) 1885
Love Poems (po Giovanni) 1997
Love Poems (po Patchen) 1960
Love Poems (po Sexton) 1969
Love Poems: Tentative Title (po F. O'Hara) 1965
Love Revisited (pl R. Anderson) 1951
Love Scene (pl Coover) 1973
Love Songs (po Teasdale) 1917
Love Sonnets of a Cave Man and Other Verses (po Marquis) 1928
Love Space Demands (po Shange) 1991
Love Stories (f Rinehart) 1919
Love Story (pl Behrman) 1933
Love Suicide at Schofield Barracks (pl Linney) 1972
Love throughout the Ages (o Saltus) 1908
Love vs. Insurance (pl Harrigan) 1878
Love without Money (f Dell) 1931
Love Without Wings: Some Friendships in Literature and Politics (o Auchincloss) 1991
Love's Calendar, Lays of the Hudson, and Other Poems (po Hoffman) 1847
Love's Dilemmas (f Herrick) 1898
Love's Labor: An Eclogue (pl F. O'Hara) 1964
Love's Labour's Lost (pl Daly) 1891
Love's Lovely Counterfeit (f Cain) 1942
Love's Old Sweet Song (pl Saroyan) 1940
Love's Pilgrimage (f Sinclair) 1911
Love's Young Dream (pl Daly) 1879
Love-Lyrics (po Riley) 1899
Love-Songs of Childhood (po Field) 1894
Lovecraft at Last (o Lovecraft) 1975
Lovecraft Collectors Library (o Lovecraft) 1952-55
Loved One (scr Isherwood) 1965
Loveliest Afternoon of the Year, and Something I'll Tell You Tuesday (pl Guare) 1966
Lovely Leave (tv Parker) 1962
Lovely Shall Be Choosers (po Frost) 1929
Lovely Sunday for Creve Coeur (pl T. Williams) 1979
Lover's Revolt (f De Forest) 1898
Lovers and Husbands (f Arthur) 1845
Lovers and Keepers (pl Fornés) 1987
Lovers and Other Stories (f Buck) 1977
Lovers of Louisiana (f Cable) 1918
Lovers' Lane (pl Fitch) 1901
Lovers', Saint Ruth's, and Three Other Tales (f Guiney) 1895
Lovers' Vows (pl Dunlap) 1814
Lovers' Vows (pl Payne) 1809
Loves of Pelleas and Etarre (f Gale) 1907
Loves of Ricardo (po Sánchez) 1997
Lovesick (po Stern) 1987
Lovey Childs: A Philadelphian's Story (f J. O'Hara) 1969
Love's Livery (pl Brougham) 1840(?)
Loving a Woman in Two Worlds (po Bly) 1985
Loving Shepherdess (po Jeffers) 1956
Low-lands (f Pynchon) 1978
Low Life (pl Harrigan) 1897
Lowell Connector: Lines & Shots from Kerouac's Town (po Coolidge) 1993

Lucifer: A Theological Tragedy (pl Santayana) 1899
Luck (pl Steele) 1941
Luck and Pluck (f Alger) 1869
Luck of Roaring Camp and Other Sketches (f}f Harte) 1870
Lucky Darryl, 1977
Lucky Lady (scr Sherwood) 1926
Lucky Life (po Stern) 1977
Lucky Partners (scr Van Druten) 1940
Lucky Sam McCarver (pl S. Howard) 1926
Lucky Starr and the Pirates of the Asteroids (f Asimov) 1953
Lucky Starr and the Rings of Saturn (f Asimov) 1958
Lucky Starr and the Moons of Jupiter (f Asimov) 1957
Lucky Starr and the Oceans of Venus (f Asimov) 1954
Lucky Starr and the Big Sun of Mercury (f Asimov) 1956
Lucrece (pl Wilder) 1932
Lucretia Borgia (pl Stein) 1968
Lucy Church Amiably (f Stein) 1931
Lucy Gayheart (f Cather) 1935
Lucy Harding: A Second Series of Afloat and Ashore (f Cooper) 1844
Lucy Sanford: A Story of the Heart (f Arthur) 1848
Lucy Temple: One of the Three Orphans (f Rowson) 1842(?)
Lucy's Christmas (o Hall) 1994
Lucy's Summer (o Hall) 1995
Luke Walton (f Alger) 1889
Lullaby (pl Chin, Silko) 1976
Lulu Belle (scr MacArthur) 1948
Lulu Belle (pl Sheldon) 1926
Lulu's Library (f Alcott) 1886-89
Lume Spento (po Pound) 1908
Luminous Dreams (po Ginsberg) 1997
Lunar Landscapes: Stories and Short Novels 1949-1963 (f Hawkes) 1969
Lunatics and Lovers (pl Kingsley) 1954
Lunch Poems (po F. O'Hara) 1964
Lund des Frühlings (o Traven) 1928
Lurker at the Threshold (o Lovecraft) 1945
Lurking Fear and Other Stories (f Lovecraft) 1947
Lust and Lost Poems (po Schwartz) 1979
Lust Poems (po J. Lowell) 1895
Lust Poems (po Wylie) 1943
Lustra (po Pound) 1916
Lute Song (pl S. Howard) 1930
Luxury of Sin (po Oates) 1984
Lydia (scr Hecht) 1941
Lydia Bailey (f Roberts) 1947
Lydie Breeze (pl Guare) 1982
Lynchers (f Wideman) 1973
Lynching: America's National Disgrace (o J. Johnson) 1924
Lyonnesse: Hitherto Uncollected Poems (po Plath) 1971
Lyrical and Other Poems (po Simms) 1827
Lyrics of Love and Laughter (po Dunbar) 1903
Lyrics of Lowly Life (po Dunbar) 1896
Lyrics of Sunshine and Shadow (po Dunbar) 1905
Lyrics of the Hearthside (po Dunbar) 1899
Lytle-Tate Letters (o Lytle) 1987

Ma Rainey's Black Bottom (pl A. Wilson) 1981
Mabel: A Story, and Other Prose (o Creeley) 1976
Mabel Martin: A Harvest Idyl (po Whittier) 1876
Macario (f Traven) 1950

MacGuffin (f Elkin) 1991
Machine Dreams (f J. Phillips) 1984
Machineries of Joy (f Bradbury) 1964
Mad Dog Blues (pl Shepard) 1971
Mad Heiress (f Alger) 1981
Mad King (f E. Burroughs) 1926
Mad Man (f S. Delany) 1994
Mad Musician (pl Eberhart) 1962
Madam Sapphira: A Fifth Avenue Story (f Saltus) 1893
Madam, Will You Walk? (pl S. Howard) 1955
M. Butterfly (pl Hwang) 1988
Madame Butterfly (pl Belasco) 1900
Madame de Treymes (f Wharton) 1907
Madame Delphine (f Cable) 1881
Madame Delphine, Carancro, Grande Pointe (f Cable) 1887
Madeira Party (f S. Mitchell) 1895
Madelaine Morel (pl Daly) 1884
Madeleine and the Movies (pl Cohan) 1922
Madeline (f Arthur) 1843
Madeline, The Temptress (f Alger) 1981
Madelon (f Freeman) 1896
Madheart (pl Baraka) 1967
Madness in the Family (f Saroyan) 1988
Madonna of Carthagena (po A. Lowell) 1927
Madonna of the Future and Other Tales (f H. James) 1879
Madwoman in the Attic: A Study of Women and the Nineteenth-Century Literary Imagination (o Gilbert and Gubar) 1979
Madwoman of Central Park West (pl Laurents) 1979
Magda Goebbels (po Snodgrass) 1983
Maggie, a Girl of the Streets (f S. Crane) 1893
Maggie Cassidy (f Kerouac) 1959
Maggie the Magnificent (pl Kelly) 1929
Maggie—Now (f B. Smith) 1958
Maggy's Baby and Other Stories (f Arthur) 1852
Magic Barrel (f Malamud) 1958
Magic Brush (pl Lim) 1990
Magic City (po Komunyakaa) 1992
Magic Cloak of Oz (scr Baum) 1914
Magic Flute 1962
Magic Mirror: Selected Writings on the Theatre (o Nathan) 1960
Magic of Oz (f Baum) 1919
Magic Shell (f Mohr) 1995
Magic Tower (pl T. Williams) 1936
Magical City (pl Akins) 1915
Magician of Lublin (f Singer) 1960
Magician's Wife (f Cain) 1965
Magna (f Gale) 1939
Magnalia Christi Americana (o Mather) 1702
Magnificent Ambersons (f Tarkington) 1918
Magnificent Spinster (f Sarton) 1985
Magnolia (pl Tarkington) 1923
Magpie or the Maid? (pl Payne) 1815
Magpie's Shadow (po Winters) 1922
Maid of Arran (pl Baum)
Maiden (f Arthur) 1845
Maidstone (scr Mailer) 1971
Maidstone: A Mystery (pl Mailer) 1971
Main Street (f Lewis) 1920
Main Street to Broadway (scr Sherwood) 1953
Maine Poems (po Eberhart) 1988
Maine Question (pl Bannister) 1839

Maine Woods (o Thoreau) 1864

Maintains (po Coolidge) 1974

Main-Travelled Roads: Six Mississippi Valley Stories (f Garland) 1891

Majesty's Rancho (f Grey) 1938

Major (pl Harrigan) 1881

Major Andre (pl Fitch) 1903

Major Pendennis (pl L. Mitchell) 1916

Majors and Minors (po Dunbar) 1895

Majors and Their Marriages (o Cabell) 1915

Make Bright the Arrows: 1940 Notebook (po Millay) 1940

Make Light of It: Collected Stories (f W. Williams) 1950

Make Way for Lucia (pl Van Druten) 1949

Making a President: A Footnote to the Saga of Democracy (o Mencken) 1932

Making a Sensation and Other Tales (f Arthur) 1843

Making Do (f Goodman) 1963

Making Haste to Be Rich (f Arthur) 1848

Making His Mark (f Alger) 1901

Making It Up: Poetry Composed at St. Marks Church on May 9, 1979 (po Ginsberg) 1994

Making Money and Thirteen Other Very Short Plays (tv Saroyan) 1970

Making of a Marchioness (f Burnett) 1901

Making of Americans, Being a History of a Family's Progress (f Stein) 1925

Making of Ashenden (f Elkin) 1972

Malabar Farm (o Bromfield) 1948

Malachi (o Mather) 1717

Malamud Reader (o Malamud) 1967

Malcolm (pl Albee) 1966

Malcolm (f Purdy) 1959

Male Animal (pl Thurber) 1940

Malefactors (f Gordon) 1956

Malone's Night (pl Harrigan) 1876

Maltese Falcon (f Hammett) 1930

Mama (f McMillan) 1987

Mama Day (f Naylor) 1988

Mama I Love You (f Saroyan) 1956

Mambo Kings Play Songs of Love (f Hijuelos) 1989

Mamie Mason; ou, Un Exercise de la bonne volonte (f Himes) 1963

Mammary Plays (pl Vogel) 1998

Mammon of Unrighteousness (f Boyesen) 1891

Mammy Tittleback and Family: A True Story of Seventeen Cats (o H. Jackson) 1881

Man Against the Sky (po Robinson) 1916

Man and Boy (f Morris) 1951

Man and Wife (pl Daly) 1885

Man Bearing a Pitcher (pl Childress) 1969

Man Behind a Book (o Auchincloss) 1996

Man Called Noon (f L'Amour) 1970

Man Called Spade (f Hammett) 1945

Man Crazy: A Novel (f Oates) 1997

Man Eating Tiger (pl Hecht) 1927

Man Farthest Down: A Record of Observation and Study in Europe (o Washington) 1912

Man from Home (pl Tarkington) 1908

Man from Skibbereen (f L'Amour) 1973

Man from the Broken Hills (f L'Amour) 1975

Man from the USSR and Other Plays (pl Nabokov) 1984

Man in Full (f Tom Wolfe) 1998

Man in Lower Ten (f Rinehart) 1909

Man in the Black Coat Turns (po Bly) 1981

Man Named Thin and Other Stories (f Hammett) 1962

Man of Fortitude (pl Dunlap) 1807

Man of Letters in the Nineteenth-Century South: Selected Letters of Hayne (o Hayne) 1982

Man of the Forest (f Grey) 1920

Man on a Tightrope (scr Sherwood) 1953

Man on Fire: Luis Jimenez=EL hombre en llamas (o Anaya) 1994

Man on Horseback (pl Tarkington) 1912

Man on the Beach (f Harte) 1878

Man Overboard! (f Crawford) 1903

Man Possessed: Selected Poems (po W. Benét) 1927

Man Story (f E. Howe) 1889

Man That Corrupted Hadleyburg and Other Stories and Essays (f Twain) 1900

Man Upstairs (tv Bradbury) 1988

Man Who Came to Dinner (pl Hart; Kaufman) 1939

Man Who Could Not Lose (f Richard Davis) 1911

Man Who Cried I Am (f J. Williams) 1967

Man Who Died at Twelve O'Clock (pl Green) 1925

Man Who Died Twice (po Robinson) 1924

Man Who Dug Fish (pl Bullins) 1969

Man Who Forgot (pl Behrman) 1926

Man Who Found Himself (scr Tarkington) 1925

Man Who Had All the Luck (pl A. Miller) 1944

Man Who Had Everything (f Bromfield) 1935

Man Who Had Three Arms (pl Albee) 1982

Man Who Killed the Deer (f Waters) 1942

Man Who Knew Coolidge (f Lewis) 1928

Man Who Lived Alone (o Hall) 1984

Man Who Lived Underground (f R. Wright) 1971

Man Who Made Friends with Himself (f Morley) 1949

Man Who Outlived Himself (f Tourgée) 1898

Man Who Owns Broadway (pl Cohan) 1909

Man Who Sang the Sillies (po Ciardi) 1961

Man Who Saw through Heaven and Other Stories (f Steele) 1927

Man Who (Thought He) Looked Like Robert Taylor (f Santos) 1983

Man Who Was There (f Morris) 1945

Man Who Went to War (radio Hughes) 1944

Man Who Wins (f Herrick) 1897

Man with the Blue Guitar and Other Poems (po Stevens) 1937

Man with the Calabash Pipe: Some Observations (o La Farge) 1966

Man with the Golden Arm (f Algren) 1949

Man with the Heart in the Highlands (pl Saroyan) 1938

Man with the Hoe and Other Poems (po Markham) 1899

Man Without a Country and Other Tales (f S. Crane) 1995

Management of the Sick Room (o Mowatt) 1844

Manassas (f Sinclair) 1904

Mandala (f Buck) 1970

Mandarin in Manhattan (po Morley) 1933

Mandolin (po Dove) 1982

Mandy Oxendine: A Novel (f Chesnutt) 1997

Man-Eater (f E. Burroughs) 1955

Mango Tango (pl Hagedorn) 1978

Manhattan Transfer (f Dos Passos) 1925

Mankind (pl Daly) 1882

Man-Made World (o Gilman) 1911

Mannequin's Maid (pl B. Smith) 1939
Mannerhouse (pl Thomas [Clayton] Wolfe) 1948
Manor (f Singer) 1967
Man's Woman (f Norris) 1900
Man's World (pl Crothers) 1915
Mansart Builds a School (f Du Bois) 1959
Mansion (f Faulkner) 1959
Manson, The Miser (f Alger) 1981
Mantices (radio Wellman) 1973
Mantrap (f Lewis) 1926
Manual: A Practical Guide to the Sunday-School Work (o
    Eggleston) 1869
Manual of Parliamentary Practice for Use in the Senate of the
    United States (o Jefferson) 1801
Manuductio ad Ministerium (o Mather) 1726
Many Closets (o Childress) 1987
Many Long Years Ago (po Nash) 1945
Many Loves (pl W. Williams) 1958
Many Marriages (f S. Anderson) 1923
Many Moons (f Thurber) 1943
Many Thousands Gone (f J.Bishop; Bishop) 1931
Many-Windowed House: Collected Essays on American Writers
    and American Writing (o Cowley) 1970
Manzanita (po Snyder) 1971
Mao II (f Delillo) 1991
Map of Misreading (o Bloom) 1975
Marble Faun (po Faulkner) 1924
Marble Faun (f Hawthorne) 1860
Marbled Paper (po Merrill) 1982
Marcabrun (f Guthrie) 1926
March Hares (f Frederic) 1896
March of Folly: From Troy to Vietnam (o Tuchman) 1984
March of the Millennia: A Key to Looking at History (o Asimov)
    1990
March to Caobaland (f Traven) 1961
March to the Monteria (f Traven) 1964
Marching Men (f S. Anderson) 1917
Marching On (f Boyd) 1927
Marching Song (pl Lawson) 1937
Marco Millions (pl O'Neill) 1927
Marco Polo Sings a Solo (pl Guare) 1976
Mardi, and a Voyage Thither (f Melville) 1849
Margaret Fleming (pl Herne) 1890
Marginalia (o Lovecraft) 1944
Marginalization of Poetry: Language Writing and Literary History
    (o B. Perelman) 1996
Margret Howth: A Story of Today (f Rebecca Davis) 1862
Marianne Moore: The Cage and the Animal (o Hall) 1970
Marie (f Ingraham) 1845
Marie and Her Lover (f Sinclair) 1948
Marie Antoinette (f Sinclair) 1939
Marie Bertrand (f Alger) 1981
Marie De Berniere (f Simms) 1853
Marietta, a Maid of Venice (f Crawford) 1901
Marigold from North Viet Nam (po Levertov) 1968
Marilee (f Spencer) 1981
Marilyn: A Novel Biography (o Mailer) 1973
Marilyn's Daughter (f Rechy) 1988
Marina (po Eliot) 1930
Marion Darche (f Crawford) 1893
Marionettes (pl Faulkner) 1975

Mark Antony De Wolfe Howe 1808-1895: A Brief Record of a
    Long Life (o E. Howe) 1897
Mark Manly (f Ingraham) 1843
Mark Manning's Mission (f Alger) 1905
Mark Mason's Victory: The Trials and Triumphs of a Telegraph
    Boy (f Alger) 1899
Mark Stanton (f Alger) 1890
Mark Twain and Cable: The Record of a Literary Friendship (o
    Cable) 1960
Marked for Murder (f Macdonald) 1953
Market-Place (f Frederic) 1899
Mark's Reef (f Cooper) 1847
Marlowe (f Chandler) 1969
Marmion (pl Barker) 1816
Marne (f Wharton) 1918
Maroon: A Legend of the Caribbees, and Other Tales (f Simms)
    1855
Marquis (pl Belasco) 1889
Marriage (pl Fitch) 1892
Marriage (po Moore) 1923
Marriage by Moonlight (pl Belasco; pl Herne) 1879
Marriage Game (pl Fitch) 1901
Marriage Lines: Notes of a Student Husband (po Nash) 1964
Marriage of Figaro (pl Nelson) 1982
Marriage of Venus (pl Santayana) 1953
Marriage Play (pl Albee) 1987
Marriage Playground (f Wharton) 1930
Marriages and Infidelities (f Oates) 1972
Married and Single (f Arthur) 1845
Married Life: Its Shadows and Sunshine (f Arthur) 1852
Married or Single? (f Sedgwick) 1857
Married People (f Rinehart) 1937
Marrow of Tradition (f Chesnutt) 1901
Marry Me: A Romance (f Updike) 1976
Marrying Man (scr Simon) 1991
Mars Is Heaven (tv Bradbury) 1990
Mars, the Red Planet (o Asimov) 1977
Marse Covington (pl Ade) 1918
Marseilles (pl S. Howard) 1930
Marsena and Other Stories of the Wartime (f Frederic) 1894
Marsh Island (f Jewett) 1885
Mart Haney's Mate (f Garland) 1922
Martian (tv Bradbury) 1992
Martian Chronicles (f Bradbury) 1950
Martian Way and Other Stories (f Asimov) 1955
Martin Arrowsmith (f Lewis) 1925
Martin Eden (f London) 1909
Martin Faber and Other Tales (f Simms) 1837
Martin Faber: The Story of a Criminal (f Simms) 1833
Martin Luther King at Montgomery, Alabama (pl Childress) 1969
Marty (tv Chayefsky) 1953
Marty Malone (pl Harrigan) 1896
Martyr of Alabama and Other Poems (po F. Harper) 1895
Martyr Wife (f Arthur) 1844
Martyred (f Kim) 1964
Martyrs' Idyl and Shorter Poems (po Guiney) 1899
Maruja (f Harte) 1885
Marvelous Arithmetics of Distance: Poems, 1987-1992 (po Lorde)
    1993
Marvelous Land of Oz (f Baum) 1904
Marvels of Science (o Asimov) 1963

Mary (f Nabokov) 1970

Mary Burns, Fugitive (scr Parker) 1935

Mary Ellis (f Arthur) 1850

Mary Hollis (f Sedgwick) 1822

Mary Louise [in the Country, Solves a Mystery, and the Liberty Girls, Adopts a Soldier] (f Baum) 1916-19

Mary Magdalen (f Saltus) 1891

Mary Moreton (f Arthur) 1849

Mary of Magdala (f Saltus) 1903

Mary of Scotland (pl M. Anderson) 1933

Mary the Third (pl Crothers) 1923

Mary Wilbur (f Ingraham) 1845

Marya: A Life (f Oates) 1986

Maryland Muse (po E. Cooke) 1731

Mary's Fancy (po Creeley) 1970

Mary's Neck (f Tarkington) 1932

Marzio's Crucifix (f Crawford) 1887

M*A*S*H* (scr Lardner)

Mask for Janus (po Merwin) 1952

Mask of Motion (po Hejinian) 1977

Mask of State: Watergate Portraits (o McCarthy) 1974

Masked Ball (pl Fitch) 1892

Masked Gods: Navajo and Pueblo Ceremonialism (o Waters) 1950

Mason and Dixon (f Pynchon) 1997

Masque and Other Poems (po S. Mitchell) 1888

Masque of Judgment: A Masque-Drama (pl Moody) 1900

Masque of Kings (pl M. Anderson) 1936

Masque of Labor (pl MacKaye) 1912

Masque of Mercy (po Frost) 1947

Masque of Pandora and Other Poems (po Longfellow) 1875

Masque of Pedagogues (pl M. Anderson) 1957

Masque of Reason (po Frost) 1945

Masque of the Gods (pl B. Taylor) 1872

Masque with Clowns (po Wheelwright) 1936

Massacre at Fall Creek (f J. West) 1975

Master Eustace (f H. James) 1920

Master Key: An Electrical Fairy Tale (f Baum) 1901

Master Mind of Mars (f E. Burroughs) 1928

Master of the Inn (f Herrick) 1908

Master of the Revels (pl Marquis) 1934

Master Poisoner (pl Hecht) 1918

Master William Mitten (f Longstreet) 1864

Masterpiece Theatre: An Academic Melodrama (o Gilbert and Gubar) 1995

Master-Rogue: The Confessions of a Croesus (f D. Phillips) 1903

Masters House: A Tale of Southern Life (f Thorpe) 1854

Mast-Ship (f Ingraham) 1845

Matagorda (f L'Amour) 1967

Match Boy (f Alger) 1869

Matches (pl Baum) 1882

Matchmaker (pl Wilder) 1954

Mate Burke (f Ingraham) 1846

Mate of the Daylight, and Friends Ashore (f Jewett) 1883

Mater: An American Study in Comedy (pl MacKaye) 1908

Materia Critica (o Nathan) 1924

Materialist Today (o Lovecraft) 1926

Matilda (f Simms) 1846

Matisse, Picasso, and Gertrude Stein (o Stein) 1933

Matrilineal Poems (po Shange) 1983

Matrimonial Ads (pl Harrigan) 1877

Matter of Colour (o Hansberry) 1965

Matter of Faith (pl Fornés) 1986

Matter of Pride and Other Stories (f Mohr) 1997

Matter of Time (f J. West) 1966

Matthew Arnold (o Trilling) 1939

Matthias at the Door (po Robinson) 1931

Maud Martha (f Brooks) 1953

Maule's Curse: Seven Studies in the History of American Obscurantism (o Winters) 1938

Maurice Mystery (f J. Cooke) 1885

Mauve Gloves and Madmen, Clutter and Vine (o Tom Wolfe) 1976

Maverick Queen (f Grey) 1950

Max Dugan Returns (scr Simon) 1983

Maximilian (pl Masters) 1902

Maximum Bob (f Leonard) 1991

Maximum Overdrive (scr King) 1986

Maximum Security Ward 1964-1970 (po Guthrie) 1970

Maximus, from Dogtown I (po Olson) 1961

Maximus Poems (po Olson) 1960

Maximus Poems 1-10 (po Olson) 1953

Maximus Poems 11-22 (po Olson) 1956

Maximus Poems, IV, V, VI (po Olson) 1968

Maximus, to Himself (po Olson) 1970

May Blossom (pl Belasco) 1884

May Day in Town (pl R. Tyler) 1787

May Sarton: A Self-Portrait (o Sarton) 1982

May Sarton: Selected Letters, 1916-1954 (o Sarton) 1997

May 20, 1959 (po Olson) 1970

Mayan Letters (o Olson) 1953

Mayday (o Faulkner) 1978

Mayfield Deer (po Van Doren) 1941

Mayflower (f Stowe) 1843

Mayor and the Manicure (pl Ade) 1923

Mayor Harold Washington (po Brooks) 1983

Mazatlan: Sea (po Creeley) 1969

Maze of Love (f Traven) 1967

Mazes (o Rukeyser) 1970

McAllister's Legacy (pl Harrigan) 1885

McKenzie's Hundred (f Yerby) 1985

McLeod's Folly (f Bromfield) 1948

McNooney's Visit (pl Harrigan) 1887

McSorley's Inflation (pl Harrigan) 1882

McTeague: A Story of San Francisco (f Norris) 1899

McVeys (f Kirkland) 1888

Me and My Baby View the Eclipse (f L. Smith) 1990

Me and My Brother (scr Shepard) 1969

Me and the Colonel (scr Behrman) 1958

Meadow (pl Bradbury) 1948

Meadow Blossoms (f Alcott) 1879

Meadowlands (po Glück) 1996

Meaning of Marx: A Symposium (o Dewey) 1934

Meaning of Truth: A Sequel to "Pragmatism" (o W. James) 1909

Means and Ends (o Sedgwick) 1839

Measure of the Universe (o Asimov) 1983

Meat (f Steele) 1928

Meat out of the Eater (po Wigglesworth) 1670

Mechanism in Thought and Morals (o Holmes) 1871

Medal for Benny (scr Steinbeck) 1945

Medea (pl Jeffers) 1946

Medea and Some Poems (po Cullen) 1935

Medea at Kolchis: The Maiden Head (pl Duncan) 1965

Medical Essays 1842-1882 (o Holmes) 1883

Medicine for Melancholy (f Bradbury) 1959
Medieval Scenes (po Duncan) 1950
Medina (o McCarthy) 1972
Meditation on Saviors (o Jeffers) 1994
Meditations in an Emergency (po F. O'Hara) 1956
Meditations on the Insatiable Soul (po Bly) 1994
Mediterranean and Other Poems (po A. Tate) 1936
Mediterranean Winter—1906: Journal and Letters (o Page) 1971
Medusa: A Portrait (o Lovecraft) 1975
Medusa in Gramercy Park (po Gregory) 1961
Meet Me at the Morgue (f Macdonald) 1953
Meet Me in the Green Glen (f R. Warren) 1971
Meet My Maker the Mad Molecule (f Donleavy) 1964
Meeting by the River (f Isherwood) 1967
Meg (pl Vogel) 1977
Melanie and Other Poems (po Willis) 1835
Mellichampe: A Legend of the Santee (f Simms) 1836
Melodrama in Three Acts: On the Frontier (pl Isherwood) 1938
Melodrama Play (pl Shepard) 1967
Melodramatists (f Nemerov) 1949
Melomaniacs (f Huneker) 1902
Melville Goodwin, USA (f Marquand) 1951
Member of the Third House (f Garland) 1892
Member of the Wedding (f McCullers) 1946
Members of the Family (f Wister) 1911
Memoir of Joseph Curtis, A Model Man (o Sedgwick) 1858
Memoirs (o S. Anderson) 1942
Memoirs of a Shy Pornographer: An Amusement (f Patchen) 1945
Memoirs of an American Citizen (f Herrick) 1905
Memoirs of an Inconsequential Scribbler (o Lovecraft) 1977
Memoirs of Arii (o Adams) 1901
Memoirs of Charles Brockden Brown (o Dunlap) 1822
Memoirs of Hecate County (f E. Wilson) 1946
Memoirs of Madame d'Arblay (o Mowatt) 1844
Memoirs of Marau, Last Queen of Tahiti (o Adams) 1893
Memoirs of Stephen Calvert (f Brown) 1978
Memoirs of the Life of George Frederick Cooke (o Dunlap) 1813
Memoirs of the Life of William Wirt, Attorney General of the United States (o Kennedy) 1849
Memoirs: Parallel Text Edition (o Franklin) 1949
Memorable Providences, Relating to Witchcrafts and Possessions (o Mather) 1689
Memoralia (po Chivers) 1853
Memoranda during the War (o Whitman) 1876
Memoranda of the Life of Jenny Lind (o Willis) 1853
Memorial of the Present Deplorable State of New England (o Mather) 1707
Memorial: Portrait of a Family (f Isherwood) 1932
Memorie and Rime (o J. Miller) 1884
Memories (po Creeley) 1984
Memories and Studies (o W. James) 1911
Memories of Catholic Girlhood (o McCarthy) 1957
Memories of the Ford Administration (f Updike) 1992
Memory (f Lovecraft) 1970
Memory Gardens (po Creeley) 1986
Memory of Murder (f Bradbury) 1984
Memory of Roswell Smith (o Cable) 1892
Memory of Two Mondays (pl A. Miller) 1955
Memory Theatre of Giordano Bruno (radio Wellman) 1976
Memory Theatre of Giordano Bruno (pl Wellman) 1976
Memory's Fictions (o Santos) 1993

Men Against the Sky (scr N. West) 1940
Men and Brethren (f Cozzens) 1936
Men and Women (pl Belasco) 1890
Men I'm Not Married To (o Parker) 1922
Men in White (pl Kingsley) 1933
Men of Our Times (o Stowe) 1868
Men Versus the Man: A Conversation Between Robert Rives La Monte, Socialist, and Mencken, Individualist (o Mencken) 1910
Men Who Made the Nation (o Dos Passos) 1957
Men without Women (f Hemingway) 1927
Men, Women, and Dogs: A Book of Drawings (f Thurber) 1943
Men, Women, and Ghosts (po A. Lowell) 1916
Menaced World (po Levertov) 1984
Mencken Chrestomathy (o Mencken) 1949
Mencken on Music (o Mencken) 1961
Mencken's Last Campaign: Mencken on the 1948 Election (o Mencken) 1976
Mentone, Cairo, and Cob (o Woolson) 1895
Mentoria (f Rowson) 1791
Mercedes of Castile (f Cooper) 1840
Merchant of Venice (pl Belasco) 1922
Merchant of Venice (pl Daly) 1898
Merchant of Yonkers (pl Wilder) 1939
Merchant's Crime (f Alger) 1888
Merchants from Cathay (po W. Benét) 1913
Mercy (f Howells) 1892
Mercy of a Rude Stream (f H. Roth) 1994
Mercy Philbrick's Choice (f H. Jackson) 1876
Meridian (f A. Walker) 1976
Merle: A Novella and Other Stories (f Marshall) 1985
Merlin (po Robinson) 1917
Mermaids Singing (pl Van Druten) 1946
Merrily We Roll Along (pl Hart; Kaufman) 1934
Merry Dale (f Hergesheimer) 1924
Merry Gardener (pl Dunlap) 1802
Merry Malones (pl Cohan) 1927
Merry Month of May (f J. Jones) 1971
Merry Tales (f Twain) 1892
Merry Tales of the Three Wise Men of Gotham (f Paulding) 1826
Merry Wives of Windsor (pl Daly) 1886
Merry-Go-Round (pl Fitch) 1898
Merry-Go-Round (o Van Vechten) 1918
Merton of the Movies (pl Connelly; Kaufman) 1922
Mesh (po Coolidge) 1988
Message II (po Ginsberg) 1968
Message in the Bottle: How Queer Man Is, How Queer Language Is, and What One Has to Do with the Other (o Percy) 1975
Message of Auschwitz (o Styron) 1979
Messengers Will Come No More (o Fiedler) 1974
Messiah (f Vidal) 1954
Messiah of Stockholm (f Ozick) 1987
Met by Chance (pl B. Howard) 1887
Metamorphosis of 741 (po Merrill) 1977
Metaphor and Memory (o Ozick) 1989
Metaphor as Pure Adventure (o Dickey) 1968
Meteor (pl Behrman) 1930
Methods of Lady Walderhurst (f Burnett) 1901
Methow River Poems (po W. Stafford) 1995
Methuselah's Children (f Heinlein) 1958
Metrical History of Christianity (po E. Taylor) 1962
Metropolis (f Sinclair) 1908

Mettle of the Pasture (f J. Allen) 1903
Mexican Night (po Ferlinghetti) 1970
Mexican Prince (o Eggleston) 1881
Mexico City Blues (po Kerouac) 1959
Mexico Mystique: The Coming Sixth World of Consciousness (o Waters) 1975
Mexico's Magic Square (o E. Gardner) 1968
Mezzotints in Modern Music (o Huneker) 1899
M'Fingal: A Modern Epic Poem, Canto First (po Trumbull) 1775(?)
Mhil'daim (pl Kopit) 1963
Miami (o Didion) 1987
Miami and the Siege of Chicago: An Informal History of the Republican and Democratic Conventions of 1968 (o Mailer) 1968
Michael (pl Bullins) 1978
Michael Angelo (po Longfellow) 1884
Michael Bonham (pl Simms) 1852
Michael, Brother of Jerry (f London) 1917
Michael Scarlett: A History (f Cozzens) 1925
Michel Auclair (pl S. Howard) 1925
Mickelsson's Ghosts (f J. Gardner) 1982
Mid-American Chants (o S. Anderson) 1918
Midas Coffin (f M. Smith) 1975
Midas of the Rockies: The Story of Stratton and Cripple Creek (o Waters) 1937
Midcentury: A Contemporary Chronicle (f Dos Passos) 1961
Middle Kingdom: Poems 1929-1944 (po Morley) 1944
Middle of the Air (pl Rukeyser) 1945
Middle of the Journey (f Trilling) 1947
Middle of the Night (pl Chayefsky) 1954
Middle Passage (f C. Johnson) 1990
Middle Span (o Santayana) 1945
Middle Years (pl H. James) 1917
Middle-Aged Man on the Flying Trapeze: A Collection of Short Pieces (f Thurber) 1935
Middle-Class Education (f Oates) 1980
Middleman and Other Stories (f Mukherjee) 1988
Midlander (f Tarkington) 1923
Midnight Carnival (po Snodgrass) 1988
Midnight Chandler (f Chandler) 1971
Midnight Cry (o Mather) 1692
Midnight Mass (f Bowles) 1981
Midnight Salvage: Poems, 1995-1998 (po Rich) 1999
Midpoint and Other Poems (po Updike) 1969
Midshipman (f Ingraham) 1844
Midsummer Night's Dream (pl Daly) 1888
Midwestern Manic (pl Inge) 1969
Might as Well Be Dead (f Stout) 1956
Mignon (f Cain) 1962
Mildred Pierce (f Cain) 1941
Milhuas Blues and Gritos Norteños (po Sánchez) 1980
Military Duties Recommended to an Artillery Company (o Mather) 1687
Milk Train Doesn't Stop Here Anymore (pl T. Williams) 1962
Milk White Flag (pl Hoyt) 1893
Milkman's Boy (o Hall) 1997
Mill and the Tavern (f Arthur) 1878
Millennium: A Comedy of the Year 2000 (f Sinclair) 1924
Miller of New Jersey (pl Brougham) 1858
Miller of Old Church (f Glasgow) 1911
Million Dollar Month (po Plath) 1971

Millionaire of Rough-and-Ready, and Devil's Ford (f Harte) 1887
Millionaire's Daughter (pl Belasco) 1879
Millroy the Magician (f Theroux) 1994
Mills of the Kavanaughs (po Lowell) 1951
Milo Talon (f L'Amour) 1981
Mima (pl Belasco) 1928
Mimic Life (f Mowatt) 1856
Mind: A Reconstructed Text (o Edwards) 1963
Mind Breaths: Poems 1972-1977 (po Ginsberg) 1978
Mind in the Modern World (o Trilling) 1973
Mind-Reader: New Poems (po Wilbur) 1976
Mindwheel (f Pinsky) 1985
Mine the Harvest: A Collection of New Poems (po Millay) 1954
Mine: the One that Enters the Stories (po Coolidge) 1982
Mineola Twins (pl Vogel) 1997
Ming Yellow (f Marquand) 1935
Minick (pl Kaufman) 1924
Minister's Charge (f Howells) 1886
Minister's Wooing (f Stowe) 1859
Minna and Myself (po Bodenheim) 1918
Minor Dramas (pl Howells) 1907
Minor Scene (pl Bullins) 1966
Minorities in the City (o J. Williams) 1975
Minority Report: Mencken's Notebooks (o Mencken) 1956
Minute Men of 1774-1775 (pl Herne) 1886
Minute Particulars (po J.Bishop; Bishop) 1935
Mirabell: Books of Number (po Merrill) 1978
Mirabilia Dei (o Mather) 1719
Miracle in the Rain (f Hecht) 1943
Miracle Man (pl Cohan) 1914
Miracle Man (scr S. Perelman, Perelman) 1932
Miracle of a Bum (radio Hecht) 1945
Miracle of Rare Device (tv Bradbury) 1989
Miracle of the Bells (scr Hecht) 1948
Miracle of the Danube (pl M. Anderson) 1941
Miracle on the Pullman (pl Hecht) 1944
Miracle Play (pl Oates) 1973
Miracles of Perception: The Art of Willa Cather (o Welty) 1980
Miraculous Day of Amalia Gomez (f Rechy) 1991
Mirage (f Masters) 1924
Miriam and Other Poems (po Whittier) 1871
Mirror (pl Singer) 1973
Mirrors (po Creeley) 1983
Mirrors and Windows (po Nemerov) 1958
Mirrors of Chartres Street (o Faulkner) 1953
Mirrors of Venus: A Novel in Sonnets 1914-1938 (po Wheelwright) 1938
Mirthful Haven (f Tarkington) 1930
Misanthrope (pl Wilbur) 1955
Miscellaneous Observations (o Edwards) 1793
Miscellanies (o Hearn) 1924
Miscellanies (o Thoreau) 1894
Miseries of New York; or The Burglar and Counsellor (f Ingraham) 1844
Miser's Wedding (pl Dunlap) 1793
Misery (f King) 1987
Misfits (scr A. Miller) 1961
Misha's Party (pl Nelson) 1993
Misrepresentations Corrected and Truth Vindicated (o Edwards) 1752
Miss Bellard's Inspiration (f Howells) 1905
Miss Bonnybel (f J. Cooke) 1892

Miss Civilization (pl Richard Davis) 1905
Miss Crespigny: A Love Story (f Burnett) 1878
Miss Helyett (pl Belasco) 1891
Miss Hoyden's Husband (pl Daly) 1890
Miss Liberty (pl Sherwood) 1949
Miss Lonelyhearts (f N. West) 1933
Miss Ludington's Sister: A Romance of Immortality (f Bellamy) 1884
Miss Lulu Bett (f Gale) 1920
Miss McCobb, Manicurist (pl Fitch) 1907
Miss Muriel and Other Stories (f Petry) 1971
Miss Numè of Japan; a Japanese-American Romance (f Eaton) 1899
Miss Pinkerton (f Rinehart) 1932
Miss Ravenel's Conversion from Secession to Loyalty (f De Forest) 1867
Miss Temptation (pl Vonnegut) 1993
Miss Tu (f Lin Yutang) 1950
Miss Zilphia Gant (f Faulkner) 1932
Mississippi Gambler (scr Eaton) 1929
Mississippi Poems (po Faulkner) 1979
Mr. Ambrose's Letters on the Rebellion (o Kennedy) 1865
Mr. and Mrs. Baby and Other Stories (f Strand) 1985
Mister Antonio (pl Tarkington) 1916
Mr. Arcularis (pl Aiken) 1949
Mister Blue (f Creeley) 1964
Mr. Cough and the Phantom Sex (pl Purdy) 1960
Mr. Crewe's Career (f Churchill) 1908
Mr. Blake's Walking-Stick: A Christmas Story for Boys and Girls (f Eggleston) 1870
Mr. Cinderella (f Stout) 1938
Mr. Cohen Takes a Walk (f Rinehart) 1934
Mr. Dooley at His Best (o Dunne) 1938
Mr. Dooley in Peace and in War (o Dunne) 1898
Mr. Dooley in the Hearts of His Countrymen (o Dunne) 1899
Mr. Dooley on Making a Will and Other Necessary Evils (o Dunne) 1919
Mr. Dooley Remembers: The Informal Memoirs of Dunne (o Dunne) 1963
Mr. Dooley Says (o Dunne) 1910
Mr. Dooley's Opinions (o Dunne) 1901
Mr. Dooley's Philosophy (o Dunne) 1900
Mr. Evening: A Story and Nine Poems (f Purdy) 1968
Mr. Franklin: A Selection from His Personal Letters (o Franklin) 1956
Mr. Grantley's Idea (f J. Cooke) 1879
Mr. Hodge and Mr. Hazard (f Wylie) 1928
Mr. Hugh David MacWhirr Looks after His $1.00 Investment in the Pilot Newspaper (o Boyd) 1943
Mr. Incoul's Misadventure (f Saltus) 1887
Mr. Isaacs: A Tale of Modern India (f Crawford) 1882
Mr. Ives' Christmas (f Hijuelos) 1995
Mr. Jack Hamlin's Mediation and Other Stories (f Harte) 1899
Mr. Keegan's Elopement (f Churchill) 1903
Mr. Kris Kringle: A Christmas Tale (f S. Mitchell) 1893
Mr. Majestyk (f Leonard) 1974
Mr. Moto Is So Sorry (f Marquand) 1938
Mr. Moto Takes a Hand (f Marquand) 1940
Mr. Moto's Three Aces (f Marquand) 1956
Mr. Norris Changes Trains (f Isherwood) 1935
Mr. Peters' Connections (pl A. Miller) 1999

Mister Pitt (pl Gale) 1925
Mr. Pope and Other Poems (po A. Tate) 1928
Mr. Sammler's Planet (f Bellow) 1970
Mr. Smith (f Bromfield) 1951
Mr. Tommy Dove and Other Stories (f Deland) 1893
Mr. White, The Red Barn, Hell, and Bridewater (f Tarkington) 1935
Mr. Wilkinson's Widows (pl Gillette) 1891
Mr. Wilson's War (o Dos Passos) 1962
Mrs. Albert Grundy: Observations in Philistia (f Frederic) 1896
Mrs. Balfame (f Atherton) 1916
Mrs. Farrell (f Howells) 1921
Mrs. Flowers: A Moment of Friendship (o Angelou) 1986
Mrs. Grundy, Jr. (pl Fitch) 1893
Mrs. January and Mr. Ex (pl Akins) 1948
Mrs. John Hobbs (pl Crothers) 1899
Mrs. Parkington (f Bromfield) 1943
Mrs. Peckham Carouse (pl Ade) 1908
Mrs. Pendleton's Four-in-Hand (f Atherton) 1903
Mrs. Pickthorn and Mr. Hare (f Sarton) 1966
Mrs. Reynolds, and Five Earlier Novelettes (f Stein) 1952
Mrs. Ritter Appears (pl Kelly) 1917
Mrs. Skaggs's Husbands and Other Sketches (f Harte) 1873
Mrs. Stevens Hears the Mermaids Singing (f Sarton) 1965
Mrs. Ted Bliss (f Elkin) 1995
Mrs. Wellington's Surprise (pl Kelly) 1922
Mistress Betty (pl Fitch) 1895
Misunderstanding (f Farrell) 1949
Mitch Miller (f Masters) 1920
Mitchell, A Dynamo Going to Waste: Letters to Allen Edee 1919-1921 (o M. Mitchell) 1985
Mitchell's "Gone with the Wind" Letters 1936-1949 (o M. Mitchell) 1976
Mixed Couple (pl Harrigan) 1873
Moby Dick (f Melville) 1851
Moby-Dick (scr Bradbury) 1956
Moccasin Ranch (f Garland) 1909
Model and Other Stories (f Nin) 1995
Model Primer (o Field) 1882
Modern Century (o Frye) 1967
Modern Chivalry (f Brackenridge) 1792-1805
Modern Chronicle (f Churchill) 1910
Modern French Plays (pl Simpson) 1965
Modern Hero (f Bromfield) 1932
Modern Instance (f Howells) 1882
Modern Match (pl Fitch) 1892
Modern Mephistopheles (f Alcott) 1877
Modern Poets and Christian Teaching (o Markham) 1906
Modern Tales of Horror (o Hammett) 1932
Modern Vikings: Stories of Life and Sport in the Norseland (o Boyesen) 1887
Modern Writer (o S. Anderson) 1925
Modest Enquiry into the Nature and Necessity of a Paper-Currency (o Franklin) 1729
Modred: A Fragment (po Robinson) 1929
Modulations for Solo Voice (po Levertov) 1977
Mogg Megone (po Whittier) 1836
Mohun (f J. Cooke) 1869
Moise and the World of Reason (f T. Williams) 1975
Mojave Crossing (f L'Amour) 1964
Mojo: A Black Love Story (pl Childress) 1970

Mole on Lincoln's Cheek (pl Connelly) 1941

Moll Pitcher (po Whittier) 1831

Moll Pitcher, and The Minstrel Girl (po Whittier) 1840

Molly's Dream (pl Fornés) 1968

Moment in Peking: A Novel of Contemporary Chinese Life (f Lin Yutang) 1939

Moments en Voyage: Nine Poems for the Harvard Class of 1897 (po MacKaye) 1932

Moments of the Italian Summer (po J. Wright) 1976

Moments Return (po Ginsberg) 1970

Momma as She Became—Not as She Was (pl Rechy) 1978

Moms: A Praise Play for a Black Comedienne (pl Childress) 1986

Monday Night (f Boyle) 1938

Money (o Stein) 1973

Money: A Jazz Opera (pl Baraka) 1982

Money from Home (f Runyon) 1935

Money Magic (f Garland) 1907

Moneychangers (f Sinclair) 1908

Mongrel (pl Rice) 1924

Monikins: A Tale (f Cooper) 1835

Monitory and Hortatory Letter to Those English Who Debauch the Indians by Selling Strong Drink unto Them (o Mather) 1700

Monk and the Hangman's Daughter (f Bierce) 1892

Monkey Business (scr Hecht) 1952

Monkey Business (scr S. Perelman) 1931

Monks Are Monks: A Diagnostic Scherzo (o Nathan) 1929

Monody on the Death of Gen. Charles Cotesworth Pinckney (po Simms) 1825

Monroe's Embassy (o Brown) 1803

Monsieur Alphonse (pl Daly) 1886

Monsieur Beaucaire (f Tarkington) 1900

Monsieur Henri: A Foot-Note to French History (o Guiney) 1892

Monster (f Saltus) 1913

Monster and Other Stories (f S. Crane) 1899

Monster Den (po Ciardi) 1966

Monster Men (f E. Burroughs) 1929

Montage of a Dream Deferred (po Hughes) 1951

Montcalm and Wolfe (o Parkman) 1884

Montezuma and the Conquest of Mexico (o Eggleston) 1880

Montezuma, The Serf (f Ingraham) 1845

Month of Saturdays (o Parker) 1971

Month of Sundays (f Updike) 1975

Mont-Saint-Michel and Chartres (o Adams) 1904

Montserrat (pl Hellman) 1949

Monument (po Strand) 1991

Monuments to Interruption (o Welty) 1994

Moods (f Alcott) 1865

Moods, Cadenced and Declaimed (po Dreiser) 1926

Moods Philosophic and Emotional, Cadenced and Declaimed (po Dreiser) 1935

Moon (o Thoreau) 1927

Moon for the Misbegotten (pl O'Neill) 1947

Moon Is a Gong (pl Dos Passos) 1925

Moon Is a Harsh Mistress (f Heinlein) 1966

Moon Is Down (pl Steinbeck) 1942

Moon Lady (o Tan) 1992

Moon Lake and Other Stories (f Welty) 1980

Moon Maid (f E. Burroughs) 1926

Moon Men (f E. Burroughs) 1962

Moon of the Caribbees (pl O'Neill) 1918

Moon on a Fencepost (po Bly) 1988

Moon over Miami (pl Guare) 1989

Moon-Calf (f Dell) 1920

Moon-Face and Other Stories (f London) 1906

Moon-Flower (pl Akins) 1924

Moonlight Boy (f E. Howe) 1886

Moonlit Road and Other Ghost and Horror Stories (f Bierce) 1998

Moons of Grandeur (po W. Benét) 1920

Moon's Our Home (scr Parker) 1936

Moonshine War (f Leonard) 1969

Moontide (scr J. O'Hara) 1942

Moony's Kid Don't Cry (pl T. Williams) 1946

Moorcroft (pl B. Howard) 1874

Moore Reader (o Moore) 1961

Moose-Hunter (f Neal) 1864

Moral Equivalent of War and Other Essays, and Selections from Some Problems of Philosophy (o W. James) 1971

Moral Philosophy of James (o W. James) 1971

Moral Principles in Education (o Dewey) 1909

Moral Writings (o Dewey) 1976

Morality Play (pl Portillo Trambley) 1974

Morals (pl S. Howard) 1925

Morals of Abou Ben Adhem (f Nasby) 1875

Morals of Manners (o Sedgwick) 1846

Moran of the Lady Letty: A Story of Adventure off the California Coast (f Norris) 1898

Mordecai Lyons (pl Harrigan) 1882

More Adventures of Ellery Queen (f Queen) 1940

More Conversations with Eudora Welty (o Welty) 1996

More Conversations with Walker Percy (o Percy) 1993

More Deaths Than One (f Stout) 1949

More Die of Heartbreak (f Bellow) 1987

More Eggs of Things (o Sexton) 1964

More Fables (f Ade) 1900

More Fellow Countrymen (f Farrell) 1946

More Lecherous Limericks (po Asimov) 1976

More Matter (o Updike) 1999

More Night (o Rukeyser) 1981

More O. Henry (f Henry) 1933

More People (po Masters) 1939

More Songs (po Hovey) 1896

More Stately Mansions (pl O'Neill) 1962

More Tales of the Black Widowers (f Asimov) 1976

More than Somewhat (f Runyon) 1937

More Tish (f Rinehart) 1921

More Words of Science (o Asimov) 1972

Morgana: Two Stories from 'The Golden Apples.' (f Welty) 1988

Morgan's Passing (f A. Tyler) 1980

Morning (po Riley) 1907

Morning after the First Night (o Nathan) 1938

Morning Child (f Dorris) 1992

Morning Glory: Another Thing That Will Never Be My Friend: Twelve Prose Poems (po Bly) 1969

Morning in Antibes (f Knowles) 1962

Morning Is near Us (f Glaspell) 1940

Morning Noon and Night (f Cozzens) 1968

Morning Poems (po Bly) 1997

Morning Song of Lord Zero: Poems Old and New (po Aiken) 1963

Morning Star: Poems and Translations (po Rexroth) 1979

Morning Watch (f Agee) 1951

Morning, Winter, and Night (f M. Anderson) 1952

Morning Worship (po Van Doren) 1960

Morning-Glories and Other Stories (f Alcott) 1867

Moroccan Variations (po Coolidge) 1971

Morocco (o Bowles) 1993

Morris (o Morris) 1981

Morris: A Reader (o Morris) 1970

Morris Graeme (f Ingraham) 1843

Mortal Acts, Mortal Words (po Kinnell) 1980

Mortal Antipathy: First Opening of the New Portfolio (f Holmes) 1885

Mortal Image (f Wylie) 1927

Mortal Summer (po Van Doren) 1953

Mortality and Mercy in Vienna (f Pynchon) 1976

Morte d'Urban (f Powers) 1962

Mortgage on the Hip-Roof House (f Tourgée) 1896

Mortgaged Heart (o McCullers) 1971

Mortimer (f Ingraham) 1865

Mosby's Memoirs and Other Stories (f Bellow) 1968

Moses: A Story of the Nile (po F. Harper) 1869

Moses, Man of the Mountain (f Hurston) 1939

Mosquito Coast (f Theroux) 1982

Mosquitoes (f Faulkner) 1927

Mosses from an Old Manse (f Hawthorne) 1846

Most Likely to Succeed (f Dos Passos) 1954

Most Native of Sons (o J. Williams) 1970

Most of Perelman (o S. Perelman; Perelman) 1958

Most of the Game (pl Van Druten) 1936

Most Unholy Trade, Being Letters on the Drama (pl H. James) 1923

Mostly Sitting Haiku (po Ginsberg) 1978

Moth (f Cain) 1948

Moth and the Flame (pl Fitch) 1898

Mother (pl S. Anderson) 1937

Mother (f Arthur) 1846

Mother (f Buck) 1934

Mother (tv Chayefsky) 1954

Mother (po S. Mitchell) 1891

Mother (f Wister) 1907

Mother and the Father (pl Howells) 1909

Mother Carey's Chickens (pl Crothers) 1917

Mother Ditch (o La Farge) 1954

Mother Goose in Prose (o Baum) 1897

Mother Hunt (f Stout) 1963

Mother in History (o J. Stafford) 1966

Mother Knows Best (f Ferber) 1927

Mother Love (po Dove) 1996

Mother, May I? (po Villanueva) 1978

Mother Night (f Vonnegut) 1962

Mother of Us All (pl Stein) 1947

Mother-Light (f D. Phillips) 1905

Mothers (f Fisher) 1943

Mothers (pl Fornés) 1986

Mothers and Daughters: That Special Quality: An Exploration in Photographs (o Olsen) 1987

Mother's Book (o Child) 1831

Mother's Recompense (f Wharton) 1925

Mothers to Men (f Gale) 1911

Mothersill and the Foxes (f J. Williams) 1975

Mothersongs: Poems For, By, and about Mothers (o Gilbert and Gubar) 1995

Motion of History (pl Baraka) 1977

Motiveless Malignity (o Auchincloss) 1969

Motor-Flight through France (o Wharton) 1908

Mount Savage (pl Payne) 1822

Mount Vernon and Its Preservation (o Page) 1910

Mountain Blood (f Hergesheimer) 1915

Mountain Cat (f Stout) 1939

Mountain Cat Murders (f Stout) 1943

Mountain City (f Sinclair) 1929

Mountain Dialogues (o Waters) 1981

Mountain Interval (po Frost) 1916

Mountain Lion (f J. Stafford) 1947

Mountain Man (f Fisher) 1965

Mountain of the Lovers (po Hayne) 1875

Mountain Valley War (f L'Amour) 1978

Mountains (pl Thomas [Clayton] Wolfe) 1921

Mountains and Rivers without End (po Shapiro; Snyder) 1996

Mourners Below (f Purdy) 1981

Mourner's Vision (po Donnelly) 1850

Mourning Becomes Electra: A Trilogy (pl O'Neill) 1931

Mouse-Trap (pl Howells) 1889

Moveable Feast (o Hemingway) 1964

Movement: Documentary of a Struggle for Equality (o Hansberry) 1964

Moviegoer (f Percy) 1961

Moving On (f McMurtry) 1970

Moving Target (f Macdonald) 1949

Moving Target (po Merwin) 1963

Moving the Mountain (f Gilman) 1911

Mozart Myths: A Critical Reassessment (o W. Stafford) 1993

Much Ado about a Merchant of Venice (pl Brougham) 1858

Much Ado about Nothing (pl Daly) 1897

Mucker (f E. Burroughs) 1921

Mud (pl Fornés) 1983

Muddy Day (pl Harrigan) 1883

Mudhead Kiva (f Hillerman) 1992

Mulatto (pl Hughes) 1935

Mulberries in Pay's Garden (po Howells) 1907

Mulcahey Twins (pl Harrigan) 1870

Mulching of America (f Crews) 1995

Muldoon, The Solid Man (pl Harrigan) 1874

Mules and Men (o Hurston) 1935

Mulligan Guard (pl Harrigan) 1873

Mulligan Guard Ball (pl Harrigan) 1879

Mulligan Guard Chowder (pl Harrigan) 1879

Mulligan Guard Nominee (pl Harrigan) 1880

Mulligan Guard Picnic (pl Harrigan) 1878

Mulligan Guards' Christmas (pl Harrigan) 1879

Mulligan Guards' Surprise (pl Harrigan) 1880

Mulligans (f Harrigan) 1901

Mulligans' Silver Wedding (pl Harrigan) 1881

Mumbo Jumbo (f Reed) 1972

Mummy Took Cooking Lessons (po Ciardi) 1990

Murder, A Mystery, and a Marriage (f Twain) 1945

Murder at Monticello, or Old Sins (f R Brown) 1994

Murder at the ABA (f Asimov) 1976

Murder by Death (scr Simon) 1976

Murder by the Book (f Stout) 1951

Murder in Mount Holly (f Theroux) 1969

Murder in Style (f Stout) 1960

Murder in the Cathedral (pl Eliot) 1935

Murder in the Snow (pl B. Smith) 1938

Murder of Crows (pl Wellman) 1991

Murder of Lidice (po Millay) 1942

Murder on a Honeymoon (scr Benchley) 1935

Murder on the Prowl (f R Brown) 1998

Murder, She Meowed (f R Brown) 1996

Murder up My Sleeve (f E. Gardner) 1937

Murderer (tv Bradbury) 1990

Murderer Is a Fox (f Queen) 1945

Murmur in the Trees (po Dickinson) 1998

Murvale Eastmas, Christian Socialist (f Tourgée) 1890

Musard Ball (pl Brougham) 1858

Muses Are Heard: An Account of the Porgy and Bess Tour to Leningrad (o Capote) 1956

Museum (po Dove) 1983

Museum of Clear Ideas (po Hall) 1993

Museums and Women and Other Stories (f Updike) 1972

Music after the Great War and Other Studies (o Van Vechten) 1915

Music and Bad Manners (o Van Vechten) 1916

Music and Poetry: Essays upon Some Aspects and Inter-Relations of the Two Arts (o Lanier) 1898

Music for Chameleons (o Capote) 1980

Music from Behind the Moon (f Cabell) 1926

Music from Spain (f Welty) 1948

Music of Spain (o Van Vechten) 1918

Music School (f Updike) 1966

Music: Reflections on Jazz and Blues (o Baraka) 1987

Musk-Ox, Bison, Sheep, and Goat (o Wister) 1904

Mustang Man (f L'Amour) 1966

Mute Singer (f Mowatt) 1866

Muthologos: The Collected Lectures and Interviews of Olson (o Olson) 1976-79

Mutiny of the Elsinore (f London) 1914

Muzeeka (pl Guare) 1967

My American Son (tv Hwang) 1987

My Ántonia (f Cather) 1918

My Autobiography (o Cather) 1914

My Baseball Diary: A Famed Author Recalls the Wonderful World of Baseball, Yesterday and Today (o Farrell) 1957

My Bondage and My Freedom (o Douglass) 1855

My Christmas Dinner (pl F. O'Brien) 1852

My Colleen (pl Herne) 1892

My Days of Anger (f Farrell) 1943

My Dear Girl: The Correspondence of Franklin with Polly Stevenson, Georgiana and Catherine Shipley (o Franklin) 1927

My Dear Wister: The Frederic Remington-Wister Letters (o Wister) 1972

My Disillusionment in Russia (o Goldman) 1925

My Emily Dickinson (o S. Howe) 1985

My Farm of Edgewood: A Country Book (o D. Mitchell) 1863

My Father, Owen Wister, and Ten Letters . . . to His Mother during His First Trip to Wyoming in 1885 (o Wister) 1952

My Four Weeks in France (o Lardner) 1918

My Friend, The Tramp (f Harte) 1877

My Good Name (pl Laurents) 1997

My Heart and My Flesh (f Roberts) 1927

My Heart Laid Bare (f Oates) 1998

My Heart's in the Highlands (pl Saroyan) 1939

My Holy Satan: A Novel of Christian Twilight (f Fisher) 1958

My Host the World (o Santayana) 1953

My House (po Giovanni) 1972

My Kind of Crazy Wonderful People: 17 Stories and a Play (f Saroyan) 1966

My Lady (pl Dunbar) 1914

My Lady Dear, Arise! Songs and Sonnets in Remembrance of Marion Morse MacKaye (po MacKaye) 1940

My Lady Pokahontas: A True Relation of Virginia (f J. Cooke) 1885

My Larger Education, Being Chapters from My Experience (o Washington) 1911

My Life (po Hejinian) 1980

My Life and Hard Times (f Thurber) 1933

My Life and Loves in Greenwich Village (o Bodenheim) 1954

My Life as a Man (f P. Roth) 1974

My Life in Art (o Bemelmans) 1958

My Life, Starring Dara Falcon (f Beattie) 1997

My Life with Caroline (scr Van Druten) 1941

My Lips Betray (scr Behrman) 1933

My Lives and How I Lost Them (f Cullen) 1942

My Lulu Belle (pl MacArthur) 1925

My Mortal Enemy (f Cather) 1926

My Mother, My Father, and Me (pl Hellman) 1963

My Mother Would Be a Falconess (po Duncan) 1968

My Name Is Aquilon (pl Barry) 1949

My Name Is Aram (f Saroyan) 1940

My Name Is William Tell (po W. Stafford) 1992

My Next Bride (f Boyle) 1934

My Old Habit of Returning to Places (pl Wellman) 1997

My Old Man (f Runyon) 1939

My Other Life (f Theroux) 1996

My Other Loneliness: Letters of Wolfe and Aline Bernstein (o Thomas [Clayton] Wolfe) 1983

My Own Story (o J. Miller) 1890

My Pedagogic Creed (o Dewey) 1897

My Penitente Land: Reflections on Spanish New Mexico (o Chávez) 1974

My Pretty Pony (f King) 1989

My Robin (f Burnett) 1912

My San Francisco: A Wayward Biography (o Atherton) 1946

My Secret History (f Theroux) 1989

My Son Dan (pl Harrigan) 1896

My Son Is a Splendid Driver (f Inge) 1972

My Southern Home (o W. Brown) 1880

My Story (o Rinehart) 1931

My Study Windows (o J. Lowell) 1871

My Summer in a Garden (o Warner) 1871

My Ten Years in a Quandary and How They Grew (o Benchley) 1936

My Two Loves (scr R Brown) 1986

My Uncle Dudley (f Morris) 1942

My War with the United States (o Bemelmans) 1937

My Wicked, Wicked Ways (po Cisneros) 1987

My Wife and I (f Stowe) 1871

My Wife Ethel (f Runyon) 1939

My Wife's Mother (pl Harrigan) 1877

My Winter on the Nile, Among the Mummies and Moslems (o Warner) 1876

My World—and Welcome to It (f Thurber) 1942

Myra Breckenridge (f Vidal) 1968

Myron (f Vidal) 1974

Myself (po Creeley) 1977

Myself, Bettina (pl Crothers) 1908

Mysteries of Motion (f Calisher) 1983

Mysteries of the Backwoods; or Sketches of the Southwest (f Thorpe) 1845

Mysteries of Winterthurn (f Oates) 1984
Mysterious Key and What It Opened (f Alcott) 1867
Mysterious Ouphe (po Nash) 1965
Mysterious Rider (f Grey) 1921
Mysterious State-Room: A Tale of the Mississippi (f Ingraham) 1846
Mysterious Story-Book (f Sedgwick) 1856
Mysterious Stranger: A Romance (f Twain) 1916
Mystery and Manners: Occasional Prose (o O'Connor) 1969
Mystery Lamp (f Rinehart) 1925
Mystery of Hamlet, Prince of Denmark (pl MacKaye) 1950
Mystery of Metropolisville (f Eggleston) 1873
Mystery of the Raymond Mortgage (f Fitzgerald) 1960
Mystery of The Locks (f E. Howe) 1885
Mystery of Witch-Face Mountain and Other Stories (f Murfree) 1895
Mystic of Sex and Other Writings (o Nin) 1995
Mystical Marriage (o Mather) 1728
Mystics in Chicago (po J. Tate) 1968
Myth and Symbol: Critical Approaches and Applications (o Frye) 1963
Myths and Texts (po Snyder) 1960

Nabokov's Garden: A Guide to Ada (o Mason) 1974
Nacoochee (po Chivers) 1837
Nadir (po Wylie) 1937
Nain Rouge (pl Wellman) 1986
Naked and the Dead (f Mailer) 1948
Naked Angel (pl B. Smith) 1937
Naked in Garden Hills (f Crews) 1969
Naked in the Wind (po Ortiz) 1971
Naked Ladies (f Villanueva) 1994
Naked Lunch (f W. Burroughs) 1959
Naked on Roller Skates (f Bodenheim) 1931
Naked Sun (f Asimov) 1957
Name for Evil (f Lytle) 1947
Name Is Archer (f Macdonald) 1955
Name Is Fogarty: Private Papers on Public Matters (o Farrell) 1950
Names (po Coolidge) 1997
Names (f Delillo) 1982
Names of People (po Duncan) 1968
Naming of Beasts and Other Poems (po Stern) 1973
Nanao Knows (po Snyder) 1964
Nancy and Company (pl Daly) 1884
Nappy Edges (po Shange) 1972
Narcissa and Other Fables (f Auchincloss) 1983
Narration: Four Lectures (o Stein) 1935
Narrative and Legendary Poems (po Whittier) 1888
Narrative of Arthur Gordon Pym of Nantucket (f Poe) 1838
Narrative of Brown, A Fugitive Slave (o W. Brown) 1847
Narrative of Four Months' Residence among the Natives of a Valley in the Marquesas Islands (f Melville) 1846
Narrative of James Williams, An American Slave (o Whittier) 1838
Narrative of the Events Which Followed Bonaparte's Campaign in Russia (o Dunlap) 1814
Narrative of the Life of Douglass, An American Slave (o Douglass) 1845
Narrow Rooms (f Purdy) 1978
Narrows (f Petry) 1953
Nasby in Exile (f Nasby) 1882

Nasby Letters (f Nasby) 1893
Nasby Papers (f Nasby) 1864
Nash Omnibook (po Nash) 1967
Nash Pocket Book (po Nash) 1944
Nash's Musical Zoo (po Nash) 1947
Natalie and Other Stories (f Burnett) 1879
Natasqua (f Rebecca Davis) 1886
Nathan Hale (pl Fitch) 1899
Nathaniel Hawthorne: The Selected Works (o Cowley) 1971
National Liberation and Politics (o Baraka) 1974
National Lyrics (po Whittier) 1865
National Ode (po B. Taylor) 1877
Nationchild Plumaroja 1969-1972 (po Alurista) 1972
Native African Races and Culture (o J. Johnson) 1927
Native American (f Saroyan) 1938
Native American Tribalism: Indian Survivals and Renewals (o McNickle) 1962
Native Americans: Five Hundred Years After (o Dorris) 1975
Native Dancer (po Cofer) 1981
Native of Rock: Poems 1921-1922 (po Wescott) 1925
Native of Winby and Other Tales (f Jewett) 1893
Native Son (f R. Wright) 1940
Natural (f Malamud) 1952
Natural Affection (pl Inge) 1963
Natural Daughter (pl Dunlap) 1799
Natural History of Virginia (o Byrd) 1737 German version) by Richmond Croom Beatty and William J. Mulloy 1940
Natural Man (po Soto) 1985
Natural Numbers: New and Selected Poems (po Rexroth) 1963
Natural Perspective: The Development of Shakespearean Comedy and Romance (o Frye) 1965
Nature (o Emerson) 1836
Nature: Addresses and Lectures (o Emerson) 1849
Nature: An Essay, and Lectures of the Times (o Emerson) 1844
Nature's First Green (o H. Roth) 1979
Naughty Anthony (pl Belasco) 1899
Navy Alphabet (po Baum) 1900
Ne nous enervons pas! (f Himes) 1961
Neal Nelson (f Ingraham) 1845
Near Closing Time (pl B. Smith) 1939
Near East: Ten Thousand Years of History (o Asimov) 1968
Near Home (po Channing) 1858
Near Johannesburg Boy (po Brooks) 1986
Near Klamath (po Carver) 1968
Near the Ocean (po Lowell) 1967
Nearer the Grass Roots (o S. Anderson) 1929
Necessary Angel: Essays on Reality and the Imagination (o Stevens) 1951
Necessities of Life (po Rich) 1966
Ned McCobb's Daughter (pl S. Howard) 1926
Ned Myers (o Cooper) 1843
Ned Newton (f Alger) 1890
Need for an African Education (o Madhubuti) 1972
Needful Things (f King) 1991
Needles and Pins (pl Daly) 1884
Negro (o Du Bois) 1915
Negro (o Redding) 1967
Negro Americans, What Now? (o J. Johnson) 1934
Negro and His Music (o Locke) 1936
Negro and Parkway Community House (o R. Wright) 1941
Negro Art: Past and Present (o Locke) 1936

Negro Artist Comes of Age (o Locke) 1945

Negro Christianized (o Mather) 1706

Negro in America (o Locke) 1933

Negro in American Culture (o Locke) 1956

Negro in American Fiction (o S. Brown) 1937

Negro in Art (o Locke) 1940

Negro in Business (o Washington) 1907

Negro in the American Rebellion: His Heroism and His Fidelity (o W. Brown) 1867

Negro in the South: His Economic Progress in Relation to His Moral and Religious Development (o Du Bois; Washington) 1907

Negro in Washington (o S. Brown) 1969

Negro Mother and Other Dramatic Recitations (po Hughes) 1931

Negro Poetry and Drama (o S. Brown) 1937

Negro Question (o Cable) 1890

Negro South and North (o Du Bois) 1905

Negro: The Southerner's Problem (o Page) 1904

Negro Writing and the Political Climate (o Redding) 1970

Negry v Amerike (o McKay) 1923

Nehemiah: A Brief Essay on Divine Consolations (o Mather) 1710

Neighborhood Frontiers (o E. Gardner) 1954

Neighborhood Odes (po Soto) 1992

Neighborhood Stories (f Gale) 1914

Neighborly Poems (po Riley) 1891

Neighbors Henceforth (o Wister) 1922

Neighbours (pl Gale) 1926

Nelly's Silver Mine: A Story of Colorado Life (f H. Jackson) 1878

Nelson the Newsboy (f Alger) 1901

Nemesis (f Asimov) 1989

Neon Vernacular (po Komunyakaa) 1994

Neon Wilderness (f Algren) 1946

Nephew (f Purdy) 1960

Neptune's Defeat (pl Brougham) 1858

Nerdlandia (pl Soto) 1999

Nero Wolfe Cook Book (o Stout) 1973

Nerves (pl S. Benét) 1924

Nest of Ninnies (f Ashbery) 1969

Net of Jewels (f Gilchrist) 1992

Nets to Catch the Wind (po Wylie) 1921

Nettie (pl Ade) 1923

Network (scr Chayefsky) 1975

Neurotic Nightingale (o Fisher) 1935

Neutrino: Ghost Particle of the Atom (o Asimov) 1966

Nevada (f Grey) 1928

Never Come Morning (f Algren) 1942

Never Despair! (f Alger) 1887

Never, Never Ask His Name (pl Van Doren) 1965

Nevertheless (po Moore) 1944

Neveryona; or The Tale of Signs and Cities (f S. Delany) 1983

New & Selected Poems, 1940-1986 (po Shapiro) 1987

New Adventures of Ellery Queen (f Queen) 1940

New Adventures of Get-Rich-Quick Wallingford (scr MacArthur) 1931

New American Credo: A Contribution toward the Interpretation of the National Mind (o Nathan) 1927

New and Collected Poems (po Paley) 1992

New and Collected Poems (po Reed) 1990

New and Selected Poems (po Fearing) 1956

New and Selected Poems (po Nemerov) 1960

New Approach to Shakespeare's Early Comedies: Theoretical Foundations (o Burke) 1998

New Ark's a Moverin (pl Baraka) 1974

New Century History of the United States (o Eggleston) 1904

New Citizenship: A Civic Ritual (pl MacKaye) 1915

New Cosmopolis: A Book of Images (o Huneker) 1915

New Criticism (o Ransom) 1941

New Dooley Book (o Dunne) 1911

New England (pl Nelson) 1995

New England Nun and Other Stories (f Freeman) 1891

New England Tale, and Miscellanies (f Sedgwick) 1852

New England Tragedies (po Longfellow) 1868

New England Writers and Writing (o Cowley) 1996

New Exodus: A Study of Israel in Russia (o Frederic) 1892

New Flag: Satires (f Fuller) 1899

New Found Land: Fourteen Poems (po MacLeish) 1930

New Friends in Old Chester (f Deland) 1924

New Geography for Children (o Stowe) 1855

New Hampshire: A Poem with Notes and Grace Notes (po Frost) 1923

New Hampshire: Nine Poems (po Eberhart) 1980

New Hope (f Suckow) 1942

New Housekeeper's Manual (o Stowe) 1873

New Intelligent Man's Guide to Science (o Asimov) 1965

New Journalism (o Tom Wolfe) 1973

New Klondike (scr Lardner) 1926

New Leaf Mills: A Chronicle (f Howells) 1913

New Left: The Anti-Industrial Revolution (o Rand) 1971

New Letters (o J. Lowell) 1932

New Life (f Malamud) 1961

New Life (pl Rice) 1943

New Man and Woman (po Olson) 1970

New Marriage (pl L. Mitchell) 1911

New Mencken Letters (o Mencken) 1977

New Mexico, Rio Grande, and Other Essays (o Hillerman) 1992

New Mexico Triptych (f Chávez) 1940

New Mirror for Travellers, and Guide to the Springs (o Paulding) 1828

New Negro for a New Century (o Washington) 1900

New Negro: An Interpretation (o Locke) 1925

New Orleans Sketches (o Faulkner) 1955

New Path to the Waterfall (po Carver) 1989

New Pattern for a Tired World (o Bromfield) 1954

New Play (pl Saroyan) 1970

New Poems (po Levertov) 1996

New Poems: Eighty Songs at Eighty (po Markham) 1932

New Radiance and Other Scientific Sketches (o Hearn) 1939

New Samaria, and The Summer of St. Martin (f S. Mitchell) 1904

New Schoolma'am (f Alger) 1877

New Short Novels (f J. Stafford) 1954

New Short Novels 2 (f Mailer) 1956

New Sing Sing (o Richard Davis) 1915

New Song (po Hughes) 1938

New Spirit (po Ashbery) 1970

New Spoon River (po Masters) 1924

New Swiss Family Robinson (f Wister) 1882

New Testament (o S. Anderson) 1927

New Wizard of Oz (f Baum) 1903

New Wonderland (f Baum) 1900

New World (po Masters) 1937

New Year (f Buck) 1968

New Year Blues (po Ginsberg) 1972

New Year's Eve (pl Frank) 1929

New Year's Eve/1929 (f Farrell) 1967

New Years Garland for My Students, MIT 1969-1970 (po Levertov) 1970

New York (o Cooper) 1930

New York (po MacLeish) 1958

New York Boy (f Alger) 1890

New York City Sketches and Related Pieces (o S. Crane) 1966

New York Dissected (o Whitman) 1936

New York Head Shop and Museum (po Lorde) 1974

New York Idea (pl L. Mitchell) 1908

New York Madness (f Bodenheim) 1933

New Yorkers (f Calisher) 1966

New: Bone Dance (po Rose) 1994

New-England Tale (f Sedgwick) 1822

News from Robinson Cruso's Island (o Mather) 1720

News of the Night (pl Bird) 1929

News of the Spirit (f L. Smith) 1997

Newspaper Days 1899-1906 (o Mencken) 1941

Next Room of the Dream: Poems and Two Plays (po Nemerov) 1962

Next Time (pl Bullins) 1972

Next-to-Last Things (po Kunitz) 1985

Next to Nothing (po Bowles) 1976

Next to Nothing: Collected Poems 1926-1977 (po Bowles) 1981

Nexus (f H. Miller) 1960

Nice People (pl Crothers) 1921

Nick Adams Stories (f Hemingway) 1972

Nick and Nora (pl Laurents) 1991

Nick of the Woods (f Bird) 1837

Nickel Mountain: A Pastoral Novel (f J. Gardner) 1973

Nicodemus (po Robinson) 1932

Nigger (pl Sheldon) 1910

Nigger Heaven (f Van Vechten) 1926

Night among the Horses (f Barnes) 1929

Night and Morning (pl Brougham) 1846

Night at the Movies (f Coover) 1987

Night at the Opera (scr Kaufman) 1935

Night before Christmas (pl S. Perelman) 1942

Night Before Christmas, and Self-Sacrifice (pl Howells) 1916

Night Clerk's Troubles (pl Harrigan) 1875

Night Hurdling (po Dickey) 1983

Night Hurdling: Poems, Essays, Conversations, Commencements, and Afterwords (o Dickey) 1983

Night in Acadie (f Chopin) 1897

Night in Bombay (f Bromfield) 1940

Night in Question: Stories (f Wolff) 1996

Night in the Country (pl B. Smith) 1939

Night Life (pl Kingsley) 1962

Night Music (pl Odets) 1940

Night Must Fall (scr Van Druten) 1937

Night of January 16th (pl Rand) 1934

Night of the Beast (scr Bullins) 1971

Night of the Fourth (pl Ade) 1901

Night of the Hunter (pl Agee) 1960

Night of the Iguana (pl T. Williams) 1959

Night Off or, A Page from Balzac (pl Daly) 1885

Night over Taos (pl M. Anderson) 1932

Night over the Solomons (f L'Amour) 1986

Night Rider (f R. Warren) 1939

Night Shift (f King) 1978

Night-Side (f Oates) 1977

Night Song (f J. Williams) 1961

Night Thoughts (po E. Wilson) 1961

Night Train (f Macdonald) 1955

Night Travellers (f Spencer) 1991

Night Visitor and Other Stories (f Traven) 1966

Night's Work (pl Behrman) 1926

Night-Blooming Cereus (po Hayden) 1972

Night-Born . . . (f London) 1913

Nightfall (f Asimov) 1990

Nightfall and Other Stories (f Asimov) 1969

Nightless Nights: Nine Poems (po Oates) 1981

Nightmare at Noon (po S. Benét) 1940

Nightmare Begins Responsibility (po M. Harper) 1974

Nightmare Has Triplets: An Author's Note on Smire (o Cabell) 1937

Nightmare Town (f Hammett) 1948

Nightmares and Dreamscapes (f King) 1993

Nightmares in the Sky: Gargoyles and Grotesques (o King) 1988

Nights (f Doolittle) 1935

Nights and Days (po Merrill) 1966

Nights of Love and Laughter (f H. Miller) 1955

Nightwalk (pl Shepard) 1973

Nightwing (f M. Smith) 1977

Nightwood (f Barnes) 1936

Nilda (f Mohr) 1973

Nin Reader (o Nin) 1973

Nina (pl Dunlap) 1804

Nina Gordon (f Stowe) 1866

Nine (pl Kopit) 1981

9 Magic Wishes (o S. Jackson) 1963

Nine Tomorrows (f Asimov) 1959

1951 (pl Wellman) 1986

1919 (f Dos Passos) 1932

1939 (f Boyle) 1948

Ninety Days (pl Gillette) 1893

Nininger City (o Donnelly) 1856

Ninth Avenue (f Bodenheim) 1926

Ninth World (pl Wellman) 1989

Nirvana (pl Lawson) 1926

Nisei Bar and Grill (pl Hongo) 1976

Nixie (pl Burnett) 1890

No 'Count Boy (pl Green) 1925

No Day of Triumph (o Redding) 1942

No Decency Left (f Riding) 1932

No Evil Star: Selected Essays, Interviews, and Poems (o Sexton) 1985

No Hero (f Marquand) 1935

No Heroics Please: Uncollected Writings (o Carver) 1992

No Irish Wanted Here (pl Harrigan) 1875

No Laughing Matter (o Heller) 1986

No Love Lost: A Romance of Travel (po Howells) 1869

No Man's Land: the Place of the Women Writer in the Twentieth Century (o Gilbert and Gubar) 1988-1994

No Name (pl Daly) 1871

No Name in the Street (o James Baldwin) 1972

No Nature: New and Selected Poems (po Snyder) 1992

No News Is Good News (scr Benchley) 1943

No Place for an Angel (f Spencer) 1967

No Poems (o Benchley) 1932

No Retreat (po Gregory) 1933

No Retreat (pl Hart) 1930

No Room at the Inn (f Ferber) 1941

No, Sirree! (pl Connelly; Kaufman) 1922

No Star Is Lost (f Farrell) 1938

No Swank (o S. Anderson) 1934

No T.O. for Love, music by Jimmy Livingston (pl Chayefsky) 1945

No Thanks (po Cummings) 1935

No Third Path (o Kosinski) 1962

No Time for Comedy (pl Behrman) 1939

No Villain Need Be (f Fisher) 1936

No Villains (They Too Arise) (pl A. Miller) 1937

No. 1. Authentic Anecdotes of American Slavery . . . Aged Slaves (o Child) 1835

No. 2. Authentic Anecdotes of American Slavery (o Child) 1835

No. 3. Authentic Anecdotes of American Slavery (o Child) 1837

No! In Thunder: Essays on Myth and Literature (o Fiedler) 1960

Noa Noa (pl Agee) 1960

Noah an' Jonah an' Cap'n John Smith (po Marquis) 1921

Nobel Lecture (o Bellow) 1977

Noble Gases (o Asimov) 1966

Nobodaddy (pl MacLeish) 1926

Nobody (radio Wellman) 1972

Nobody Goes to Visit the Insane Anymore (po J. Tate) 1971

Nobody Knows My Name: More Notes of a Native Son (o James Baldwin) 1961

Nobody Say a Word and Other Stories (f Van Doren) 1953

Nobody's in Town (f Ferber) 1938

Nobody's Son (f Ingraham) 1851

Nocturne of Remembered Spring and Other Poems (po Aiken) 1917

Noel (po Longfellow) 1864

Nomad's Land (f Rinehart) 1926

Nonconformist's Memorial: Poems by Susan Howe (po S. Howe) 1993

Nonconformity: Writing on Writing (o Algren) 1996

None But the Lonely Heart (scr Odets) 1944

None Shall Look Back (f Gordon) 1937

Noon Wine (f Porter) 1937

Nora (pl Crothers) 1903

Norby and the Court Jester (f Asimov) 1991

Norby and the Invaders (f Asimov) 1984

Norby and the Lost Princess (f Asimov) 1985

Norby and the Oldest Dragon (f Asimov) 1990

Norby and the Queen's Necklace (f Asimov) 1986

Norby and Yobo's Great Adventure (f Asimov) 1989

Norby Chronicles (f Asimov) 1988

Norby Down to Earth (f Asimov) 1988

Norby Finds a Villain (f Asimov) 1987

Norby, the Mixed-up Robot (f Asimov) 1983

Norby: Robot for Hire (f Asimov) 1987

Norby's Other Secret (f Asimov) 1983

Norma Ashe (f Glaspell) 1942

Norman (f Ingraham) 1845

Norman Maurice (pl Simms) 1851

Norseland Tales (o Boyesen) 1894

Norseman's Pilgrimage (f Boyesen) 1875

North and South (po E.Bishop) 1946

North Atlantic Passage (po Wheelwright) 1925

North by West (po W. Stafford) 1975

North Carolina Poems (po Ammons) 1994

North of Boston (po Frost) 1914

North of Grand Central (f Marquand) 1956

North of Jamaica (o Simpson) 1972

North Percy (po Goodman) 1968

North Star (scr Hellman) 1943

North Star: A Motion Picture about Some Russian People (pl Hellman) 1943

North to Dakota (f M. Smith) 1976

North to the Rails (f L'Amour) 1971

Northern Lights (f T. O'Brien) 1975

Northern Travel (o B. Taylor) 1857

Northfield Poems (po Ammons) 1966

Northland Stories (f London) 1997

Northwest Cantos, Part 1 (o Sánchez) 1992

Northwest Ecolog (po Ferlinghetti) 1978

Northwest Passage (f Roberts) 1937

Not "A Fool's Errand," (f Ingraham) 1880

Not by Strange Gods: Stories (f Roberts) 1941

Not Everyday an Aurora Borealis for Your Birthday: A Love Poem (o Sandburg) 1998

Not for Children (pl Rice) 1935

Not Guilty: Report of the Commission of Inquiry into the Charges Made against Leon Trotsky in the Moscow Trials (o Dewey) 1938

Not Heaven (f Frank) 1953

Not Much Fun: The Lost Poems of Dorothy Parker (po Parker) 1996

Not on the Screen (f Fuller) 1930

Not Quite Dead Enough (f Stout) 1944

Not Smart (pl Steele) 1916

Not Under Forty (o Cather) 1936

Not Without Laughter (f Hughes) 1930

Not-Knowing: The Essays and Interviews of Donald Barthelme (o Barthelme) 1997

Note on Experts: Dexter Vespasian Joyner (o Thomas [Clayton] Wolfe) 1939

Note on Literary Criticism (o Farrell) 1936

Note-Books of Night (po E. Wilson) 1942

Notebook (o S. Anderson) 1926

Notebook (o S. Crane) 1969

Notebook (o Creeley) 1972

Notebook (po Lowell) 1970

Notebook 1967-1968 (po Lowell) 1969

Notebooks (pl H. James) 1947

Notebooks of Chandler, and English Summer: A Gothic Romance (o Chandler) 1976

Notebooks of Lazarus Long (f Heinlein) 1978

Notes after an Evening with William Carlos Williams (po Ginsberg) 1970

Notes and Commonplace Book (o Lovecraft) 1938

Notes and Fragments (o Whitman) 1899

Notes for My Biographer: Terse Paragraphs on Life and Letters (o E. Howe) 1926

Notes from a Sea-Diary: Hemingway All the Way (o Algren) 1965

Notes from China (o Tuchman) 1972

Notes of a Native Son (o James Baldwin) 1955

Notes of a Son and Brother (pl H. James) 1914

Notes of a War Correspondent (o Richard Davis) 1910

Notes of the Author on The Painted Bird 1965 (o Kosinski) 1965

Notes of Woe (po J. Tate) 1968

Notes on a Collection of Drawings by George du Maurier (pl H. James) 1884

Notes on a Dream (po M. Anderson) 1971
Notes on a Horsethief (f Faulkner) 1950
Notes on Democracy (o Mencken) 1926
Notes on Novelists and Some Other Notes (pl H. James) 1914
Notes on the History of American Free Enterprise (o Rand) 1959
Notes on the State of Virginia (o Jefferson) 1785
Notes on Thought and Vision, and The Wise Sappho (o Doolittle) 1982
Notes Toward a Supreme Fiction (po Stevens) 1942
Nothing Ever Breaks Except the Heart (f Boyle) 1966
Nothing Is Lost Save Honor: Two Essays (o Vonnegut) 1984
Nothing Personal (o James Baldwin) 1964
Nothing Sacred (scr Hecht) 1937
Nothing to Do: A Tilt at Our Best Society (po Alger) 1857
Notions of the Americans, Picked Up by a Travelling Bachelor (o Cooper) 1828
Notoriety (pl Harrigan) 1894
Notorious (scr Hecht) 1946
Nova (f S. Delany) 1968
Nova Express (f W. Burroughs) 1964
Novel, a Novella and Four Stories (f Lytle) 1958
Novel of Thank You (f Stein) 1958
Novel of the Future (o Nin) 1968
Novel: What It Is (o Crawford) 1893
Novel-Writing in an Apocalyptic Time (o Percy) 1984
Novelette and Other Prose 1921-1931 (f W. Williams) 1932
Novels and Stories (f Cather) 13 vols., 1937-41
Novels and Stories (f Richard Davis) 12 vols., 1916
Novels and Tales (f H. James) 14 vols., 1883
Novels and Tales (f H. James) 1907-17
Novels, Stories, Sketches, and Poems (o Page) 18 vols., 1906-12
November Boughs (po Whitman) 1888
Novio Boy (pl Soto) 1997
Novotny's Pain (f P. Roth) 1980
Now and Then: From Coney Island to Here (o Heller) 1998
Now and Then: Poems 1976-1978 (po R. Warren) 1978
Now I Lay Me Down to Sleep (f Bemelmans) 1943
Now Playing Tomorrow (pl Laurents) 1939
Now Poof She Is Gone (po Rose) 1994
Now Sheba Sings the Song (po Angelou) 1987
Now the Sky and Other Poems (po Van Doren) 1928
Now with His Love (po J.Bishop; Bishop) 1933
Now You See It (pl Patchen) 1966
Nuances (o Nin) 1970
Nude Croquet and Other Stories (f Fiedler) 1969
Nugget Finders (f Alger) 1894
Nuggets and Dust Panned Out in California (f Bierce) 1873
Number 91 (f Alger) 1887
Number Nine (pl Daly) 1897
Number of the Beast (f Heinlein) 1980
Number One (f Dos Passos) 1943
Numbers (po Creeley) 1968
Numbers (f Rechy) 1967
Nun's Story (scr R. Anderson) 1959
Nun's Story (tv Hagedorn) 1988
Nuplex Red (f M. Smith) 1974
Nuptial Flight (f Masters) 1923
Nyarlathotep (f Lovecraft) 1970
Nydia (pl Boker) 1929
Nye and Riley's Railway Guide (po Riley) 1888
Nye and Riley's Wit and Humor (po Riley) 1902

O Canada: An American's Notes on Canadian Culture (o E. Wilson) 1965
O Careless Love! (f Stout) 1935
O Evening Star! (pl Akins) 1936
O My Land, My Friends: The Selected Letters of Hart Crane (o H. Crane) 1997
O Pioneers! (f Cather) 1913
O Shepherd, Speak! (f Sinclair) 1949
O Taste and See: New Poems (po Levertov) 1964
O, That Way Madness Lies: A Play for Marionettes (pl Fuller) 1895
O to Be a Dragon (po Moore) 1959
O Ye Tongues (po Sexton) 1973
O. Henry Westerns (f Henry) 1961
O. Henryana: Seven Odds and Ends: Poetry and Short Stories (o Henry) 1920
Oak and Ivy (po Dunbar) 1893
Oak in the Acorn: On Remembrance of Things Past, and on Teaching Proust, Who Will Never Learn (o Nemerov) 1987
Oak Openings (f Cooper) 1848
Oak: A Poem (po Eberhart) 1957
Oakdale Affair; The Rider (f E. Burroughs) 1937
Oasis (f McCarthy) 1949
Obiter Scripta: Lectures, Essays, and Reviews (o Santayana) 1936
Objectivist Ethics (o Rand) 1961
Oblique Prayers: New Poems with 14 Translations from Jean Joubert (po Levertov) 1984
Oblivion Ha-Ha (po J. Tate) 1970
Obras (o Sánchez) 1971
O'Brien, Counselor-at-Low (pl Harrigan) 1879
Obscure Destinies (f Cather) 1932
Observations (o Capote) 1959
Observations (po Moore) 1924
Observations by Mr. Dooley (o Dunne) 1902
Observations Concerning the Scripture Economy of the Trinity and Covenant of Redemption (o Edwards) 1880
Observations on the Causes and Cure of Smoky Chimneys (o Franklin) 1787
Observations on the New Constitution (o M. Warren) 1788
Occasional Prose: Essays (o McCarthy) 1985
Occasions and Protests: Essays 1936-1964 (o Dos Passos) 1964
Occidental Gleanings: Sketches and Essays Now First Collected (o Hearn) 1925
Occult Lovecraft (o Lovecraft) 1975
Occurrence at Owl Creek Bridge and Other Stories (f Bierce) 1995
October (po Bradbury) 1983
October Country (f Bradbury) 1955
October Journey (po M. Walker) 1973
October Light (f J. Gardner) 1976
Octopus Frontier (po Brautigan) 1960
Odd Couple (pl Simon) 1965
Odd Fellow (f Ingraham) 1846
Odd Jobs: Essays and Criticism (o Updike) 1991
Oddest of Courtships (f De Forest) 1882
Oddly Lovely Day Alone (po Updike) 1979
Odds Against Him (f Alger) 1890
Ode (po Hopkinson) 1788
Ode and Arcadia (po Duncan) 1974
Ode from Ossian's Poems (po Hopkinson) 1794
Ode on a Lycian Tomb (po S. Mitchell) 1899
Ode on the Centenary of Abraham Lincoln (po MacKaye) 1909

Ode Recited at the Commemoration of the Living and Dead Soldiers of Harvard University (po J. Lowell) 1865

Ode to Hollywood (po Marquis) 1929

Ode to Liberty (pl S. Howard) 1934

Ode to the Confederate Dead (po A. Tate) 1930

Odes (po F. O'Hara) 1960

Odes to Roba (po Coolidge) 1991

Odette (pl Daly) 1882

Odor of Sanctity (f Yerby) 1965

Odyssey of a Hero (f Fisher) 1937

Odyssey of a Nice Girl (f Suckow) 1925

Odyssey of the North (f London) 1915

Oeuvres (o Franklin) 1773

Of a Fire on the Moon (o Mailer) 1971

Of All Things! (o Benchley) 1921

Of Love and Dust (f Gaines) 1967

Of Matters Great and Small (o Asimov) 1975

Of Men and the Writing of Books (o Redding) 1969

Of Mice and Men (f Steinbeck) 1937

Of Plymouth Plantation (o W. Bradford) 1896

Of Prisons and Ideas (po Dickey) 1987

Of the Causes of Yellow Fever, and the Means of Preventing It (o Paine) 1807

Of the Farm (f Updike) 1965

Of the War: Passages 22-27 (po Duncan) 1966

Of the Wings of Atlanta (o Du Bois) 1904

Of Thee I Sing (pl Kaufman) 1932

Of This Time, Of That Place and Other Stories (f Trilling) 1979

Of Time and Change: A Memoir (o Waters) 1998

Of Time and Space and Other Things (o Asimov) 1965

Of Time and the River: A Legend of Man Hunger in His Youth (f Thomas [Clayton] Wolfe) 1935

Of Wolves and Men (o Lopez) 1978

Of Woman Born: Motherhood As Experience and Institution (o Rich) 1976

Of Women and Their Elegance (o Mailer) 1980

Off Broadway: Essays about the Theatre (o M. Anderson) 1947

Off the Arm (f Marquis) 1930

Off the Beaten Track in Baja (o E. Gardner) 1967

Off-Hand Sketches (f Arthur) 1851

Office (pl Fornés) 1966

Official Guide of the Tarzan Clans of America (o E. Burroughs) 1939

Oh Dad, Poor Dad, Mamma's Hung You in the Closet and I'm Feelin' So Sad (pl Kopit) 1960

Oh Pray My Wings Are Gonna Fit Me Well (po Angelou) 1975

Oh, What a Paradise It Seems (f Cheever) 1982

O'Halloran's Luck and Other Short Stories (f S. Benét) 1944

O'Hara Generation (f J. O'Hara) 1969

Ohio Lady (pl Tarkington) 1916

Oil! (f Sinclair) 1927

Ol' King David and the Philistine Boys (f R. Bradford) 1930

Ol' Man Adam an' His Chillun (f R. Bradford) 1928

Olaf Stapledon (o Fiedler) 1982

Old Acquaintance (pl Van Druten) 1941

Old Ahab's Friend, and Friend to Noah, Speaks His Piece: A Celebration (po Bradbury) 1971

Old and New Poems (po Hall) 1990

Old Beauty and Others (f Cather) 1948

Old Booksellers and Other Poems (po J. Wright) 1976

Old Chester Days (f Deland) 1937

Old Chester Secret (f Deland) 1920

Old Chester Tales (f Deland) 1898

Old Christmas (pl Green) 1928

Old Continental (f Paulding) 1846

Old Creole Days (f Cable) 1879

Old Dog Barks Backwards (po Nash) 1972

Old Dominion: Her Making and Her Manners (o Page) 1908

Old Farm and the New Farm: A Political Allegory (f Hopkinson) 1857

Old Fogy: His Musical Opinions and Grotesques (o Huneker) 1913

Old Friends and New (f Jewett) 1879

Old Garden and Other Verses (po Deland) 1886

Old Gentleman of the Black Stock (f Page) 1897

Old Glory (pl Lowell) 1964

Old Gods Laugh: A Modern Romance (f Yerby) 1964

Old Home Day (o Hall) 1994

Old Horsefly (po Shapiro) 1992

Old Hutch (scr Kelly) 1936

Old Lady 31 (pl Crothers) 1916

Old Lavender (pl Harrigan) 1877

Old Letivia and the Mountain of Sorrows/La vieja Letivia y el monte de los pesares (f Mohr) 1996

Old Life (po Hall) 1996

Old Love (f Singer) 1979

Old Love and the New (pl B. Howard) 1878

Old Love Letters (pl B. Howard) 1897

Old Man and the Sea (f Hemingway) 1952

Old Man Joseph and His Family (pl Linney) 1977

Old Man of Edenton (pl Green) 1921

Old Man Rubbing His Eyes (po Bly) 1975

Old Man's Folly (f Dell) 1926

Old Mandarin: More Translations from the Chinese (po Morley) 1947

Old Mercy (po Stern) 1995

Old Neighborhood (pl Mamet) 1998

Old New York (f Wharton) 1924

Old New Yorker (pl Harrigan) 1899

Old Order: Stories of the South (f Porter) 1955

Old Pantagonian Express: By Train through the Americas (o Theroux) 1979

Old Pines and Other Stories (f Boyd) 1952

Old Portraits and Modern Sketches (o Whittier) 1850

Old Possum's Book of Practical Cats (po Eliot) 1939

Old Probability: Perhaps Rain—Perhaps Not (f Shaw) 1879

Old Ragpicker (pl Dreiser) 1916

Old Red and Other Stories (f Gordon) 1963

Old Regime in Canada (o Parkman) 1874

Old Religion: A Novel (f Mamet) 1997

Old Soak (pl Marquis) 1926

Old Soldier's Story: Poems and Prose Sketches (po Riley) 1915

Old South: Essays Social and Political (o Page) 1892

Old Swimmin'-Hole and 'leven More Poems (po Riley) 1883

Old Town (pl Ade) 1910

Old Wash Lucas (The Miser) (pl Green) 1921

Old Ways: Six Essays (o Snyder) 1977

Old Wives for New (f D. Phillips) 1908

Old-Fashioned Girl (f Alcott) 1870

Old-fashioned Thanksgiving and Other Stories (f Alcott) 1995

Old-Fashioned Roses (po Riley) 1888

Old-Fashioned Tales (f Gale) 1933

Old-Time Saloon (o Ade) 1931
Oldest Profession (pl Vogel) 1981
Oldtown Folks (f Stowe) 1869
Oleana (pl Mamet) 1993
Olinger Stories: A Selection (f Updike) 1964
Olive and Mary Anne (f Farrell) 1978
Olive of Minerva (f Dahlberg) 1976
Oliver Wiswell (f Roberts) 1940
Olivia (pl Belasco) 1878
Olly Olly Oxen Free (pl C. Johnson) 1988
Olson and Ezra Pound: An Encounter at St. Elizabeths (o Olson) 1975
Olson and Robert Creeley: The Complete Correspondence (o Olson) 1980-83
Olson/Den Boer: A Letter (o Olson) 1979
Olson in Connecticut: Last Lectures As Heard by John Cech, Oliver Ford, Peter Rittner (o Olson) 1975
Olson Reading at Berkeley (po Olson) 1966
Olympia (pl S. Howard) 1928
Omens of Millennium: The Gnosis of Angels, Dreams, and Resurrection (o Bloom) 1996
Omensetter's Luck (f Gass) 1966
Ommateum, with Doxology (po Ammons) 1955
Omnibus of Short Stories (f Farrell) 1956
Omoo: A Narrative of Adventures in the South Seas (f Melville) 1847
On a Darkling Plain (f Stegner) 1940
On Being Blue (o Gass) 1975
On Being Negro in America (o Redding) 1951
On Board Noah's Ark (o Bemelmans) 1962
On Bread and Poetry (o Snyder) 1977
On Common Ground (tv Vogel) 1999
On Crime Writing (o Macdonald) 1973
On Ellen Glasgow (o Cabell) 1938
On Experience, Nature, and Freedom: Representative Selections (o Dewey) 1960
On Flower Wreath Hill (po Rexroth) 1976
On Glory's Course (f Purdy) 1984
On Horseback: A Tour of Virginia, North Carolina, and Tennessee (o Warner) 1888
On Irish Themes (o Farrell) 1982
On Keeping Women (f Calisher) 1977
On Lies, Secrets, and Silence: Selected Prose, 1966-1978 (o Rich) 1979
On Meeting Authors (o Updike) 1968
On Messrs. Hussey and Coffin (po Wheatley) 1767
On Modern Poets (o Winters) 1959
On Newfound River (f Page) 1891
On Our Way (o Stein) 1959
On Picket Duty and Other Tales (f Alcott) 1864
On Politics (o Mencken) 1960
On Some of Life's Ideals (o W. James) 1912
On Symbols and Society (o Burke) 1989
On the Beaches of the Moon (po MacLeish) 1978
On the Bus with Rosa Parks (po Dove) 1999
On the Contrary (o McCarthy) 1961
On the Frontier (f Harte) 1884
On the Frontier: A Melodrama in Three Acts (pl Isherwood) 1939
On the Gulf (f Spencer) 1991
On the Makaloa Mat (f London) 1919
On the March to the Sea: A Southron Comedy (pl Vidal) 1961

On the Occasion of My Last Afternoon (f Gibbons) 1998
On the Old Trail (f Harte) 1902
On the Orient, North (tv Bradbury) 1988
On the Origins of Free-masonry (o Paine) 1810
On the Pulse of Morning (po Angelou) 1993
On the Rebound: A Story and Nine Poems (f Purdy) 1970
On the Reservation: Reflections on Boundary-Busting Border-Crossing Loose Canons (o P. Allen) 1998
On the Road (f Kerouac) 1957
On the Runway of Life, You Never Know What's Coming Off Next (pl Kopit) 1958
On the Slates (po Coolidge) 1992
On the Stairs (f Fuller) 1918
On Trial (pl Rice) 1914
On With the Story (f Barth) 1997
On Writing (o Nin) 1947
On Writing: Critical Studies on Writing as an Art (o Cather) 1949
Once (po A. Walker) 1968
Once a Lady (scr Akins) 1931
Once around the Block (pl Saroyan) 1956
Once in a Blue Moon (scr Hecht; MacArthur) 1935
Once in a Lifetime (pl Hart; Kaufman) 1930
Once There Was a War (o Steinbeck) 1958
Once upon a Time (f Barth) 1994
Once upon a Time (pl Crothers) 1918
Once upon a Time (f Richard Davis) 1910
Once Upon a Time and Other Child-Verses (o Freeman) 1897
One Afternoon with Mark Twain (o Ade) 1939
One Answer to a Question (o Berryman) 1981
One Arm and Other Stories (f T. Williams) 1948
One Basket: Thirty-One Stories (f Ferber) 1947
1 x 1 (po Cummings) 1944
One Christmas (o Capote) 1983
One Clear Call (f Sinclair) 1948
One Day (f Morris) 1965
One Day after Another (po Creeley) 1972
One Day and Poems (po Hall) 1991
One Day in the Afternoon of the World (f Saroyan) 1964
One Day, When I Was Lost: A Scenario Based on "The Autobiography of Malcolm X." (pl James Baldwin) 1972
One Day: A Poem in Three Parts (po Hall) 1988
One Fair Woman (f J. Miller) 1876
One Favored Acorn (po Frost) 1969
One Flea Spare (pl N. Wallace) 1997
One Flew Over the Cuckoo's Nest (f Kesey) 1962
One for New York (f J. Williams) 1975
One Heavenly Night (scr Bromfield) 1930
One Heavenly Night (scr S. Howard) 1930
One Hour Late (scr Parker) 1935
158-Pound Marriage (f J. Irving) 1974
100%: The Story of a Patriot (f Sinclair) 1920
$106,000 Blood Money (f Hammett) 1943
One I Knew Best of All: A Memory of the Mind of a Child (o Burnett) 1893
One Man in His Time (f Glasgow) 1922
One Man's Initiation—1917 (f Dos Passos) 1920
One Man's Meat (o White) 1942
£1,000,000 Bank-Note and Other New Stories (f Twain) 1893
One Minute Please (o Benchley) 1945
One More Free Man (pl Boyd) 1941
One of Our Girls (pl B. Howard) 1885

One of Ours (f Cather) 1922
One of Those Things (pl Kelly) 1913
One Sided Shoot-out (po Madhubuti) 1969
1000 Airplanes on the Roof (pl Hwang) 1989
$1000 a Week and Other Stories (f Farrell) 1942
One Thousand Fearful Words for Fidel Castro (po Ferlinghetti) 1961
1001 Afternoons in New York (f Hecht) 1941
One Time, One Place: Mississippi in the Depression: A Snapshot Album (o Welty) 1971
One Touch of Venus (pl Nash; S. Perelman; Perelman) 1944
1/20 (po Cummings) 1936
1.2.3.4.5.6.7.8.9.0 (po Creeley) 1971
One-Way Ticket (po Hughes) 1949
One Way to Heaven (f Cullen) 1932
One Woman's Life (f Herrick) 1913
One Word More: Intended for the Reasoning and Thoughtful among Unbelievers (o Neal) 1854
One Writer's Beginnings (o Welty) 1984
Onion Eaters (f Donleavy) 1971
Only a Trillion (o Asimov) 1957
Only a Woman (pl Daly) 1882
Only an Irish Boy (f Alger) 1894
Only Dark Spot in the Sky (po Dove) 1980
Only Thing That Counts: The Ernest Hemingway/Maxwell Perkins Correspondence, 1925-1947 (o Hemingway) 1996
Only When I Laugh (scr Simon) 1982
Ontological Proof of My Existence (pl Oates) 1972
Open Boat and Other Tales of Adventure (f S. Crane) 1898
Open Eye (po Ginsberg) 1972
Open Eye, Open Heart (po Ferlinghetti) 1973
Open Head (po Ginsberg) 1972
Open House (po Roethke) 1941
Open Me Carefully: Emily Dickinson's Intimate Letters to Susan Huntington Dickinson (o Dickinson) 1998
Open Sea (po Masters) 1921
Open-Eyed Conspiracy: An Idyl of Saratoga (f Howells) 1897
Opening of the Field (po Duncan) 1960
Opening the Hand (po Merwin) 1983
Openings in the Old Trail (f Harte) 1902
Opera Brevis (pl Wellman) 1977
Opera Goer (f D. Mitchell) 1852
Opera, Opera (pl Saroyan) 1955
Operas and Plays (pl Stein) 1932
Operation Shylock: A Confession (f P. Roth) 1993
Operation Sidewinder (pl Shepard) 1970
Opposing Self: Nine Essays in Criticism (o Trilling) 1955
Optimism (pl Guare) 1973
Optimist's Daughter (f Welty) 1972
Options (f Henry) 1909
Opus 100 (o Asimov) 1969
Opus 200 (o Asimov) 1979
Opus pistorum (f H. Miller) 1983
Opus Posthumous (o Stevens) 1957
Or Else: Poem/Poems 1968-1974 (po R. Warren) 1974
Oral History (f L. Smith) 1983
Oralloossa (pl Bird) 1832
Orange Christmas (o Hearn) 1941
Oranges (po F. O'Hara) 1953
Orations, Lectures, and Addresses (o Emerson) 1844
Orchards, Thrones and Caravans (po Patchen) 1955

Ordeal: A Mountain Romance of Tennessee (f Murfree) 1912
Ordeal in Space (f Heinlein) 1990
O'Reagans (pl Harrigan) 1886
Oregon Idyll (pl J. Miller) 1910
Oregon Message (po W. Stafford) 1987
Oregon Trail (o Parkman) 1872
Oresteia of Aeschylus (pl Lowell) 1978
Organizer (pl Hughes) 1939
Orgy (f Rukeyser) 1965
Orient Express (pl Daly) 1895
Orient Express (o Dos Passos) 1927
Oriental Articles (o Hearn) 1939
Origin of Evil (f Queen) 1951
Origin of Evil (po R. Tyler) 1793
Origin of Sadness (f Morris) 1984
Origin of the Brunists (f Coover) 1966
Origins of New Mexico Families in the Spanish Colonial Period (o Chávez) 1954
Ormond; or The Secret Witness (f Brown) 1799
Ornaments for the Daughters of Zion (o Mather) 1692
Orphan Angel (f Wylie) 1926
Orphan Children (f Arthur) 1850
Orphan Factory: Essays and Memoirs (o Simic) 1997
Orphanotrophium (o Mather) 1711
Orphans in Gethsemane (f Fisher) 1960
Orpheus (po Rukeyser) 1949
Orpheus Descending (pl T. Williams) 1957
Orpheus Road Company (pl Baum) 1917
O'Ruddy: A Romance (f S. Crane) 1903
O'Ryan 12345678910 (po Olson) 1965
O'Ryan 2 4 6 8 10 (po Olson) 1958
Oscar and Bertha (pl Fornés) 1991
Oscar over Here (pl Linney) 1995
Oscar Wilde: An Idler's Impression (o Saltus) 1917
Oswald's Tale: An American Mystery (o Mailer) 1996
Oswali at Athens (pl Payne) 1831
Other Foot (f Bradbury) 1987
Other Gods: An American Legend (f Buck) 1940
Other House (f H. James) 1896
Other Poe: Comedies and Satires (o Poe) 1983
Other Side of the House (po Dove) 1988
Other Side of the Street (f S. Jackson) 1956
Other Skies (po Ciardi) 1947
Other Universes of Isaac Asimov (f Asimov) 1987
Other Voices, Other Rooms (f Capote) 1948
Other Woman (pl Richard Davis) 1893
Otho (pl Neal) 1819
Our Angry Earth (o Asimov) 1991
Our Army at Monterey (o Thorpe) 1847
Our Army on the Rio Grande (o Thorpe) 1846
Our Blushing Brides (scr Lawson) 1930
Our Century (pl Wilder) 1947
Our Charley and What to Do with Him (o Stowe) 1858
Our Children: How Shall We Save Them? (f Arthur) 1849
Our Common Schools (o Parkman) 1890
Our Cranks (pl Harrigan) 1881
Our Dead behind Us (po Lorde) 1986
Our English Cousins (o Richard Davis) 1894
Our English Friend (pl Daly) 1884
Our Family (o Lin Tai-yi) 1939
Our Famous Women (o Stowe) 1884

Our Federal Union: The United States from 1816 to 1865 (o Asimov) 1975

Our Gang (f P. Roth) 1971

Our Government (o Cain) 1930

Our Heroic Themes (po Boker) 1865

Our House in the Last World (f Hijuelos) 1983

Our Hundred Days in Europe (o Holmes) 1887

Our Irish Cousins (pl Harrigan) 1877

Our Italy (o Warner) 1891

Our Lady (f Sinclair) 1938

Our Lady of Babylon (f Rechy) 1996

Our Lady of the Conquest (o Chávez) 1948

Our Lady Peace and Other War Poems (po Van Doren) 1942

Our Landlady (o Baum) 1941

Our Lives, Our Fortunes, and Our Sacred Honor (pl MacLeish) 1961

Our Low Makers (pl Harrigan) 1878

Our Mr. Wrenn (f Lewis) 1914

Our Mrs. McChesney (pl Ferber) 1915

Our Neighbour Opposite (f Burnett) 1878

Our Old Home (o Hawthorne) 1863

Our Silver (o Crawford) 1881

Our Town (pl Wilder) 1938

Our Visit to Niagara (f Goodman) 1960

Our World in Space (o Asimov) 1974

Ourselves (pl Crothers) 1913

Ourselves to Know (f J. O'Hara) 1960

Out Cry (pl T. Williams) 1971

Out for Business (f Alger) 1900

Out Goes She (f Stout) 1953

Out of Old Aunt Mary's (po Riley) 1904

Out of Sight (f Leonard) 1996

Out of the Earth (o Bromfield) 1950

Out of the East: Reveries and Studies in New Japan (o Hearn) 1895

Out of the Everywhere (o Asimov) 1990

Out of the Foam (f J. Cooke) 1871

Out of the Question (pl Howells) 1877

Out of the Rolling Ocean and Other Love Poems (po Bly) 1984

Out of the Sea (pl Marquis) 1927

Out of the South (pl Green) 1939

Out of the Sunset Sea (f Tourgée) 1893

Out on the Outskirts of Town (tv Inge) 1964

Out Trail (f Rinehart) 1923

Out with the Stars (f Purdy) 1993

Out-Doors at Idlewild (o Willis) 1855

Out-of-Town Places (o D. Mitchell) 1884

Out-of-Towners (scr Simon) 1970

Outcast Lady (scr Akins) 1934

Outcry (f H. James) 1911

Outer Banks (po Rukeyser) 1967

Outing with the Queen of Hearts (f Tourgée) 1894

Outland Piper (po Davidson) 1924

Outlaw of the Lowest Planet (po Patchen) 1946

Outlaw of Torn (f E. Burroughs) 1927

Outlaws of Mesquite (f L'Amour) 1990

Outline of Marriage (o Dell) 1926

Outlines from the Outpost (o J. Cooke) 1961

Outlines of a Critical Theory of Ethics (o Dewey) 1891

Outlyer and Ghazals (po Harrison) 1971

Outside (pl Glaspell) 1917

Outside Looking In (pl M. Anderson) 1925

Outsider (f R. Wright) 1953

Outsider and Others (f Lovecraft) 1939

Over All the Obscene Boundaries: European Poems and Translations (po Ferlinghetti) 1984

Over My Dead Body (f Stout) 1940

Over on the Dry Side (f L'Amour) 1975

Over the Hump (f E. Gardner) 1945

Over the Moon (scr Sherwood) 1937

Over the Teacups (o Holmes) 1890

Over Thoreau's Desk: New Correspondence 1838-1861 (o Thoreau) 1965

Overland (f De Forest) 1871

Overland in a Covered Wagon: An Autobiography (o J. Miller) 1930

Overland to the Islands (po Levertov) 1958

Overnight (pl Inge) 1969

Overnight to Many Distant Cities (f Barthelme) 1983

Overtones: A Book of Temperaments (o Huneker) 1904

Owl in the Attic and Other Perplexities (f Thurber) 1931

Owl King (po Dickey) 1977

Owl's Clover (po Stevens) 1936

Owls Don't Blink (f E. Gardner) 1942

Own Face (po Coolidge) 1978

Own Your Own Home (f Lardner) 1919

Ox-Cart Man (o Hall) 1979

Ox-Bow Incident (f Clark) 1940

Oxherding Tale (f C. Johnson) 1982

Oxota: A Short Russian Novel (po Hejinian) 1991

Oyster and the Pearl (pl Saroyan) 1953

Oyster Is a Wealthy Beast (f Purdy) 1967

Ozma of Oz (f Baum) 1907

Oz-Man Tales (f Baum) 6 vols., 1920

O-Zone (f Theroux) 1986

Pace That Kills (f Saltus) 1889

Pachuco Art, A Historical Perspective (o Montoya) 1977

Pacific Crossing (po Soto) 1992

Pacific Poems (po J. Miller) 1871

Package for Ponsonby (pl B. Smith) 1939

Pactolus Prime (f Tourgée) 1890

Paddle Your Own Canoe (f Alger) 1887

Paddy McGann (f Simms) 1972

Padre Ignacio (f Wister) 1911

Pagan (scr Lawson) 1929

Pagan Rabbi and Other Stories (f Ozick) 1971

Pagan Spain (o R. Wright) 1957

Pageant (pl Linney) 1988

Pageant in Seven Decades 1868-1938 (o Du Bois) 1938

Pageant of Birds (o Welty) 1975

Pages from an Old Volume of Life: A Collection of Essays 1857-1881 (o Holmes) 1883

Pages from Cold Point and Other Stories (f Bowles) 1968

Paid (scr MacArthur) 1931

Painful Predicament of Sherlock Holmes (pl Gillette) 1905

Paint Your Wagon (scr Chayefsky) 1969

Painted Bird (f Kosinski) 1965

Painted Lace and Other Pieces (1914-1937) (o Stein) 1955

Painted Veils (f Huneker) 1920

Painted Word (o Tom Wolfe) 1975

Painter Dreaming in the Scholar's House (po Nemerov) 1968

Painter's Eye: Notes and Essays on the Pictorial Arts (pl H. James) 1956

Pair of Patient Lovers (f Howells) 1901

Pal Joey (f J. O'Hara) 1940

Pale Fire (f Nabokov) 1962

Pale Horse, Pale Rider: Three Short Novels (f Porter)

Palestina (o Cahan) 1934

Palimpsest (f Doolittle) 1926

Paliser Case (f Saltus) 1919

Palm Sunday: An Autobiographical Collage (o Vonnegut) 1981

Palm-Bearers (o Mather) 1725

Palmetto-Leaves (o Stowe) 1873

Palo Duro: A Sound and Light Drama (pl Green) 1979

Pamela's Prodigy (pl Fitch) 1893

Pamphlet against Anthologies (o Riding) 1928

Pamphlets for the People, in Illustration of the Claims of the Church and Methodism (o Ingraham) 1854

Panama: Union of the Oceans (po J. Miller) 1912

Panatella (pl Roberts) 1907

Pandora Lifts the Lid (f Marquis; Morley) 1924

Pandora's Box (scr Maso) 1993

Panels for the Walls of Heaven (po Patchen) 1947

Pangolin and Other Verse (po Moore) 1936

Panic: A Play in Verse (pl MacLeish) 1935

Panic In Needle Park (scr Didion) 1971

Panorama and Other Poems (po Whittier) 1856

Pansie: A Fragment (f Hawthorne) 1864

Pansies and Orchids (po H. Jackson) 1884

Pansy Billings and Popsy: Two Stories of Girl Life (f H. Jackson) 1898

Pantagonia Revisited (o Theroux) 1986

Panther and the Lash: Poems of Our Times (po Hughes) 1967

Papa (pl Akins) 1913

Papa La Fleur (f Gale) 1933

Papa You're Crazy (f Saroyan) 1957

Paper Angels (pl Lim) 1980

Paper City (f Nasby) 1879

Paper Trail (o Dorris) 1994

Papers of Thomas Jefferson (o Jefferson) 1997

Paquita, The Indian Heroine (o J. Miller) 1881

Parables (po Fletcher) 1925

Parachute (f Guthrie) 1928

Paradise (f Barthelme) 1986

Paradise (f Morrison) 1997

Paradise Lost (pl Odets) 1936

Paradise Poems (po Stern) 1984

Paragon (f Knowles) 1971

Parentator (o Mather) 1724

Parents Day (f Goodman) 1951

Paris Bound (pl Barry) 1929

Paris France (o Stein) 1940

Paris in Spring (scr Parker) 1935

Paris Revisited (o Nin) 1972

Paris, Texas (scr Shepard) 1984

Parisian Sketches: Letters to the New York Tribune 1875-1876 (pl H. James) 1957

Park Avenue (pl Kaufman) 1946

Park City: New and Selected Stories (f Beattie) 1998

Parlor, Bedlam and Bath (o S. Perelman) 1930

Parlor Car (pl Howells) 1876

Parlor Magic (pl Lawson) 1963

Parnassians Personally Encountered (o Saltus) 1923

Parnassus on Wheels (f Morley) 1917

Parnell (scr Behrman; Van Druten) 1937

Parricide (pl Daly) 1873

Parsons' Pleasure (po Morley) 1923

Partial Portraits (pl H. James) 1888

Parties: Scenes from Contemporary New York Life (f Van Vechten) 1930

Parting and a Meeting (f Howells) 1896

Parting Friends (pl Howells) 1911

Partisan: A Tale of the Revolution (f Simms) 1835

Partners (f Auchincloss) 1974

Partners (f Deland) 1913

Partners in Crime (f Hinojosa) 1985

Parts of a World (po Stevens) 1942

Party at the Zoo (o Roethke) 1963

Party Dress (f Hergesheimer) 1930

Party Leaders: Sketches of Jefferson, Hamilton, Jackson, Clay, Randolph of Roanoke (o Joseph G. Baldwin) 1854

Pass the Gravy (f E. Gardner) 1959

Passage through India (o Snyder) 1984

Passage to India (po Whitman) 1871

Passages from the American Note-Books (o Hawthorne) 1868

Passages from the English Note-Books (o Hawthorne) 1870

Passages from the French and Italian Note-Books (o Hawthorne) 1871

Passin' Through (f L'Amour) 1985

Passing a Creche (po W. Stafford) 1978

Passing By: Selected Essays (o Kosinski) 1992

Passing Judgements (o Nathan) 1935

Passing of Chow-Chow (pl Rice) 1934

Passing Regiment (pl Daly) 1884

Passing Through: The Later Poems, New and Selected (po Kunitz) 1995

Passing: Perspectives of Rural America (o Harrison) 1988

Passion Artist (f Hawkes) 1979

Passion of Josef D (pl Chayefsky) 1964

Passion Play (f Kosinski) 1979

Passion Within (f Fisher) 1960

Passionate Pilgrim and Other Tales (f H. James) 1875

Passions and Other Stories (f Singer) 1975

Passions Spin the Plot (f Fisher) 1934

Passport to the War: A Selection of Poems (po Kunitz) 1944

Passwords (po W. Stafford) 1991

Past (po Kinnell) 1985

Past All Dishonor (f Cain) 1946

Pastime Stories (f Page) 1894

Pastimes of Aleck Maury: The Life of a True Sportsman (f Gordon) 1935

Pastures of Heaven (f Steinbeck) 1932

Pat Hobby Stories (f Fitzgerald) 1962

Patchen Drawing-Poem (po Patchen) 1962

Patchwork Girl of Oz (f Baum) 1913

Patchwork Planet (f A. Tyler) 1998

Paterna: The Autobiography (o Mather) 1976

Paterson, Book One (po W. Williams) 1946

Path of Sorrow (po Chivers) 1832

Pathfinder (f Cooper) 1840

Pathos of Distance: A Book of a Thousand and One Moments (o Huneker) 1913

Paths of Glory (pl S. Howard) 1935

Pathways to a Southern Coast (o Harrison) 1986
Patience Sparhawk and Her Times (f Atherton) 1897
Patricia Neal Story (tv R. Anderson) 1980
Patrins, To Which Is Added an Inquirendo into the Wit and Other Good Parts of His Late Majesty King Charles the Second (o Guiney) 1897
Patriot (f Buck) 1939
Patriotic Gore: Studies in the Literature of the American Civil War (o E. Wilson) 1962
Patriots (pl Kingsley) 1943
Paul Arniff (pl Belasco) 1880
Paul Bowles Photographs: "How Could I Send a Picture into the Desert?" (o Bowles) 1994
Paul Deverell (f Ingraham) 1845
Paul Fane (f Willis) 1857
Paul Gauguin: His Life and Art (o Fletcher) 1921
Paul Merchand, F.M.C (f Chesnutt) 1998
Paul Patoff (f Crawford) 1887
Paul Prescott the Runaway (f Alger) 1867
Paul Prescott's Charge (f Alger) 1865
Paul the Peddler (f Alger) 1871
Paul's Case and Other Stories (f Cather) 1996
Pause in the Desert (f La Farge) 1957
Pavilion of Women (f Buck) 1946
Pawn Ticket 210 (pl Belasco) 1887
Pawnbroker (f Wallant) 1961
Pay Dirt and Other Whispering Sands Stories (f E. Gardner) 1983
Pay Dirt, or Adventures at Ash Lawn (f R Brown) 1996
Payne to His Countrymen (o Payne) 1961
Peace Breaks Out (f Knowles) 1981
Peace in Friendship Village (f Gale) 1919
Peace, It's Wonderful (f Saroyan) 1939
Peace Like a River (f Fisher) 1957
Peace Manoeuvres (pl Richard Davis) 1914
Peace Plays Two (pl Kopit) 1990
Peach Bottom Nuclear Reactor Full of Sleepers (pl Wellman) 1988
Pear Like a Potato (po Updike) 1986
Pearl (f Steinbeck) 1947
Pearl of Orr's Island: A Story of the Coast of Maine (f Stowe) 1862
Pearl, Rendered into Modern English Verse (po S. Mitchell) 1906
Pearls Are a Nuisance (f Chandler) 1953
Pebble in the Sky (f Asimov) 1950
Peculiar Treasure (o Ferber) 1939
Peder Victorious (f Rølvaag) 1929
Pedestrian (f Bradbury) 1962
Pedestrian Accident (pl Coover) 1998
Peer Gynt (pl Green) 1951
Peer Gynt (pl Hwang) 1998
Peggy from Paris (pl Ade) 1903
Pelayo (po Mowatt) 1836
Pelayo: A Story of the Goth (f Simms) 1838
Pelican from a Bestiary of 1120 (po Wilbur) 1963
Pellucidar (f E. Burroughs) 1923
Pembroke (f Freeman) 1894
Pemmican: A Novel of the Hudson's Bay Company (f Fisher) 1956
Pencillings by the Way (o Willis) 1835
Penelope (pl Vonnegut) 1960
Penguin Modern Poets 19 (po Ashbery) 1971
Penguin Modern Poets 5 (po Ginsberg) 1963

Penguin Modern Poets 9 (po Levertov) 1967
Penguin Modern Poets 9 (po W. Williams) 1967
Penguin Modern Stories 2 (f Updike) 1969
Penhally (f Gordon) 1931
Penitent (f Singer) 1983
Pennsylvania Pilgrim and Other Poems (po Whittier) 1872
Penrod (f Tarkington) 1914
Penrod and Sam (f Tarkington) 1916
Penrod Jashber (f Tarkington) 1929
Pentecost of Calamity (o Wister) 1915
Penthouse Legend (pl Rand) 1973
Peony (f Buck) 1948
People (pl Glaspell) 1918
People and Houses (f Suckow) 1927
People, and Uncollected Short Stories (f Malamud) 1990
People for Whom Shakespeare Wrote (o Warner) 1897
People I Have Met (f Willis) 1850
People in a Diary: A Memoir (o Behrman) 1972
People Live Here: Selected Poems 1949-1983 (po Simpson) 1983
People of Darkness (f Hillerman) 1978
People of Our Neighborhood (f Freeman) 1898
People of the Valley (f Waters) 1941
People One Knows: Interviews with Insufficiently Famous Americans (o Updike) 1980
People with Light Coming Out of Them (pl Saroyan) 1941
People You Know (f Ade) 1903
Perch of the Devil (f Atherton) 1914
Perdido: A Barrio Story (o Sánchez) 1985
Peregrina (po Cofer) 1986
Perfect Analysis Given by a Parrot (pl T. Williams) 1958
Perfume of Eros: A Fifth Avenue Incident (f Saltus) 1905
Perhaps Women (o S. Anderson) 1931
Period of Adjustment: High Point over a Cavern: A Serious Comedy (pl T. Williams) 1958
Permanence and Change: An Anatomy of Purpose (o Burke) 1935
Permit Me Voyage (po Agee) 1934
Perpetual Light: A Memorial (po W. Benét) 1919
Persecuted Wife (pl Ade) 1925
Person, Place and Thing (po Shapiro) 1942
Person to Person (po Ciardi) 1965
Personae (po Pound) 1909
Personal Recollections of Joan of Arc (f Twain) 1896
Personality Plus: Some Experiences of Emma McChesney and Her Son, Jock (f Ferber) 1914
Persons and Places (o Santayana) 1963
Persons of Consequence: Queen Victoria and Her Circle (o Auchincloss) 1979
Perspectives by Incongruity (o Burke) 1964
Persuasions from the Terror of the Lord (o Mather) 1711
Pet Sematary (f King) 1983
Pete (pl Harrigan) 1887
Pete Raphael (f Cable) 1901
Peter (po Merrill) 1982
Peter Gudge Becomes a Secret Agent (f Sinclair) 1930
Peter Parley's Common School History (o Hawthorne) 1838
Peter Pilgrim (f Bird) 1838
Peter Smink (pl Payne) 1822
Peter Stuyvesant (pl B. Howard) 1899
Peter the Great (pl Dunlap) 1814
Peter Whiffle, His Life and Works (f Van Vechten) 1922
Petits poèmes pour un livre de lecture (o Stein) 1944

Petrified Forest (pl Sherwood) 1935

Petty Crimes (po Soto) 1998

Phaedra (pl Lowell) 1961

Phaedre (pl Wilbur) 1990

Phaenomena quaedam Apocalyptica (o Sewall) 1697

Phantom (pl Kopit) 1992

Phantomnation (pl Wellman) 1983

Phantoms of the Foot-Bridge and Other Stories (f Murfree) 1895

Phases of an Inferior Planet (f Glasgow) 1898

Pheasant (f Carver) 1982

Phenomenal Woman: Four Poems Celebrating Women (po Angelou) 1994

Phil, The Fiddler (f Alger) 1872

Philadelphia Fire (f Wideman) 1990

Philadelphia Story (pl Barry) 1939

Philip and His Wife (f Deland) 1894

Philip Goes Forth (pl Kelly) 1931

Philip Stanley (f Brown) 1807

Philip Vernon: A Tale in Prose and Verse (f S. Mitchell) 1895

Philippines Is in the Heart: A Collection of Short Stories (f Bulosan) 1979

Phillis's Reply to the Answer in Our Last by the Gentleman in the Navy (po Wheatley) 1775

Philosopher (pl Ashbery) 1982

Philosophers at Court (pl Santayana) 1953

Philosophical and Miscellaneous Papers (o Franklin) 1787

Philosophy 4: A Story of Harvard University (f Wister) 1903

Philosophy and Civilization (o Dewey) 1931

Philosophy of Dewey (o Dewey) 1928

Philosophy of Disenchantment (o Saltus) 1885

Philosophy of Edwards from His Private Notebooks (o Edwards) 1955

Philosophy of Friedrich Nietzsche (o Mencken) 1908

Philosophy of James (o W. James) 1925

Philosophy of Literary Form: Studies in Symbolic Action (o Burke) 1941

Philosophy of Santayana (o Santayana) 1936

Philosophy, Psychology, and Social Practice: Essays (o Dewey) 1963

Philosophy: Who Needs It? (o Rand) 1982

Philothea. A Romance (f Child) 1836

Phineas: Six Stories (f Knowles) 1968

Phoebe Daring (f Baum) 1912

Phoenix and the Tortoise (po Rexroth) 1944

Photographs (o Welty) 1989

Photographs and Words (o Morris) 1982

Photographs: Negatives: History as Apple Tree (po M. Harper) 1972

Photosynthesis (o Asimov) 1969

Phyllis of the Sierras, and A Drift from Redwood Camp (f Harte) 1888

Physical and Meteorological Observations and Suppositions (o Franklin) 1766

Physical Order and Moral Liberty: Previously Unpublished Essays (o Santayana) 1969

Piano Lesson (pl A. Wilson) 1990

Piazza Tales (f Melville) 1856

Pic (f Kerouac) 1971

Picasso (o Stein) 1938

Picasso Summer (scr Bradbury) 1972

Piccino and Other Child Stories (f Burnett) 1894

Picked-Up Pieces (o Updike) 1975

Pickling (radio Parks) 1990

Pickwick Papers (pl Daly) 1868

Picnic: A Summer Romance (pl Inge) 1953

Pictorial History of the Negro in America (o Hughes) 1956

Pictorial History of the American Indian (o La Farge) 1956

Picture America (o Morris) 1982

Picture and Text (pl H. James) 1893

Picture of St. John (po B. Taylor) 1866

Picture Palace (f Theroux) 1978

Picture Poems (po Patchen) 1962

Picture This (f Heller) 1988

Pictures (o Riding) 1933

Pictures: An Unpublished Poem (po Whitman) 1927

Pictures from an Institution: A Comedy (f Jarrell) 1954

Pictures from Brueghel and Other Poems (po W. Williams) 1962

Pictures of a Gone World (po Ferlinghetti) 1955

Pictures of Edgewood (o D. Mitchell) 1868

Pictures of Fidelman: An Exhibition (f Malamud) 1969

Pictures of Life and Death (po Patchen) 1947

Pictures of the Floating World (po A. Lowell) 1919

Picturesque Souvenir (o Bryant) 1851

Picturing Will (f Beattie) 1990

Piece of My Heart (f Ford) 1976

Piece of My Mind: Reflections at Sixty (o E. Wilson) 1956

Pieces (po Creeley) 1968

Pieces (po Rich) 1977

Pieces and Pontifications (o Mailer) 1982

Pieces of Soap: Essays by Stanley Elkin (o Elkin) 1992

Pieces of Three (po Goodman) 1942

Pied Piper Malone (scr Tarkington) 1924

Pierce Fenning (f Ingraham) 1846

Pierce-Arrow (po S. Howe) 1999

Pierre (f Melville) 1852

Pierre the Organ-Boy and Other Stories (f Arthur) 1852

Pietas in Patriam: The Life of His Excellency Sir William Phips (o Mather) 1697

Pietro Ghisleri (f Crawford) 1893

Pig Dreams: Scenes from the Life of Sylvia (po Levertov) 1981

Pigeon Feathers and Other Stories (f Updike) 1962

Pigeons (pl Lim) 1983

Pigeons and People (pl Cohan) 1941

Pigs in Heaven (f Kingsolver) 1993

Pike County Ballads and Other Pieces (po Hay) 1871

Pike's Peak: A Mining Saga (f Waters) 1971

Pilgrim and the Book (pl MacKaye) 1920

Pilgrim at Tinker Creek (o Dillard) 1974

Pilgrim Hawk: A Love Story (f Wescott) 1940

Pilgrim of the Apocalypse: A Critical Study of D. H. Lawrence (o Gregory) 1933

Pilgrimage of Festus (po Aiken) 1923

Pilgrims in Aztlán (f Méndez M.) 1993

Pill Versus the Springhill Mine Disaster (po Brautigan) 1968

Pillar of Fire (f Ingraham) 1859

Pillar of Fire and Other Plays (pl Bradbury) 1975

Pillar of Gratitude (o Mather) 1700

Pillars of Hercules: A Grand Tour of the Mediterranean (o Theroux) 1995

Pillars of Salt: An History of Some Criminals Executed in This Land for Capital Crimes (o Mather) 1699

Pillsbury Muddle (pl Harrigan) 1877

Pilot: A Tale of the Sea (f Cooper) 1823
Pinball (f Kosinski) 1982
Ping Pong Players (pl Saroyan) 1942
Ping-Pong Game (pl Saroyan) 1940
Pink and White Tyranny: A Society Novel (f Stowe) 1871
Pink Church (po W. Williams) 1949
Pink Marsh (f Ade) 1897
Pinktoes (f Himes) 1961
Pinky in Persia (o Boyle) 1968
Pinky, The Cat Who Liked to Sleep (o Boyle) 1966
Pinocchio in Venice (f Coover) 1991
Pins and Noodles (pl Lim) 1993
Pioneer (o J. Lowell) 1947
Pioneers (f Cooper) 1823
Pioneers and Caretakers: A Study of 9 American Women Novel-
    ists (o Auchincloss) 1985
Pioneers of France in the New World (o Parkman) 1865
Pioneers of New-York (o Hoffman) 1848
Pipe Night (f J. O'Hara) 1945
Pipes o' Pan at Zekesbury (po Riley) 1888
Pique (pl Daly) 1875
Pirate (pl Behrman) 1943
Pirate (f Ingraham) 1839
Pirate Blood (f E. Burroughs) 1970
Pirate Schooner (f Ingraham) 1877
Pirates of Venus (f E. Burroughs) 1934
Pisan Cantos (po Pound) 1948
Piscator Evangelicus (o Mather) 1695
Pistol (f J. Jones) 1959
Pistols for Two (o Mencken; Nathan) 1917
Pit: A Story of Chicago (f Norris) 1903
Pizarro in Peru (pl Dunlap) 1800
Place for Myself (tv C. Johnson) 1982
Place in Fiction (o Welty) 1957
Place in Space: Ethics, Aesthetics, and Watersheds: New and Se-
    lected Prose (o Shapiro; Snyder) 1995
Place of Dead Roads (f W. Burroughs) 1983
Place of Love (po Shapiro) 1942
Place of Minor Parties in the American Scene (o Dewey) 1932
Place to Come To (f R. Warren) 1977
Places (po Creeley) 1990
Plagiarized Material (f Oates) 1974
Plagued by the Nightingale (f Boyle) 1931
Plain Brown Rapper (o R Brown) 1976
Plain People (o E. Howe) 1929
Plain Song (po Harrison) 1965
Plain Truth (o Franklin) 1747
Plains Song: For Female Voices (f Morris) 1980
Plan B (f Himes) 1983
Planet (po Villanueva) 1993
Planet News 1961-1967 (po Ginsberg) 1968
Planet That Wasn't (o Asimov) 1976
Planets for Man (o Asimov) 1964
Plant (o King) 1982
Plant Dreaming Deep (o Sarton) 1968
Plantation Melodies, Old and New (pl Dunbar) 1901
Platonism and the Spiritual Life (o Santayana) 1927
Platonism in the Italian Poets (o Santayana) 1896
Play Days: A Book of Stories for Children (o Jewett) 1878
Play Ebony, Play Ivory (po Dumas) 1974
Play It As It Lays (f Didion) 1970

Play of Herod (pl MacLeish) 1968
Play Things (pl Saroyan) 1980
Play Time, Pseudo Stein (po Duncan) 1969
Playback (f Chandler) 1958
Player on the Other Side (f Queen) 1963
Player Piano (f Vonnegut) 1952
Players (f Delillo) 1977
Playing Around: The Million-Dollar Infield Goes to Florida (o
    Hall) 1974
Playing for Time (pl A. Miller) 1980
Playing in the Dark: Whiteness and the Literary Imagination (o
    Morrison) 1992
Playing the Mischief (f De Forest) 1875
Playing with Fire (pl Brougham) 1860
Plays (pl Fornés) 1986
Plays (pl Glaspell) 1920
Plays and Poems (o Boker) 1856
Plays by Richard Nelson: Early Plays (pl Nelson) 1998
Plays for Bleecker Street (pl Wilder) 1962
Plays of J.P. Donleavy; with a Preface by the Author (pl
    Donleavy) 1973
Plays of Negro Life (o Locke) 1927
Plays of the Natural and the Supernatural (pl Dreiser) 1916
Playwright at Work (o Van Druten) 1953
Plaza Suite (pl Simon) 1969
Pleasant Valley (o Bromfield) 1945
Please Explain (o Asimov) 1973
Please Pass the Guilt (f Stout) 1973
Please Plant This Book (po Brautigan) 1968
Pleased to Meet You (f Morley) 1927
Pleistocene Man: Letters from Olson to John Clarke during Octo-
    ber 1965 (o Olson) 1968
Plexus (f H. Miller) 1953
Plot It Yourself (f Stout) 1959
Plots and Counterplots: More Unknown Thrillers (f Alcott) 1976
Pluck and Luck (o Benchley) 1925
Plucky Paul (f Alger) 1888
Plum Tree (f D. Phillips) 1905
Pluralistic Universe: Hibbert Lectures at Manchester College on
    the Present Situation in Philosophy (o W. James) 1909
Plus Oedipus-Schmoedipus, The Story That Started It All (o Bel-
    low) 1966
Plute Creek (po Snyder) 1971
Plutocrat (f Tarkington) 1927
Plutonian Ode: Poems 1977-1980 (po Ginsberg) 1982
Po-ca-hon-tas (pl Brougham) 1855
Pocahontas (pl Barker) 1820
Pocahontas (o Eggleston) 1879
Pocho (f Villarreal) 1959
Pocket Book of O. Henry (f Henry) 1948
Podesta's Daughter and Other Miscellaneous Poems (po Boker)
    1852
Podkayne of Mars (f Heinlein) 1963
Poe as a Literary Critic (o J. Cooke) 1946
Poem Begun on Thursday, October 14, 1993, at O'Hare Airport,
    Terminal 3, around Six o'clock P.M (po Updike) 1994
Poem Dedicated to the Memory of Urian Oakes (o Mather) 1682
Poem Delivered before the Society of the United Brothers (po
    Willis) 1831
Poem for Black Hearts (po Baraka) 1967
Poem for Brother/Man (po Knight) 1972

Poem for Christmas (po Patchen) 1960

Poem Is a Journey (po Ortiz) 1981

Poem of Angela Yvonne Davis (po Giovanni) 1970

Poem on Divine Revelation (po Brackenridge) 1774

Poem on the Rising Glory of America (po Brackenridge; Freneau) 1772

Poem Outlines (po Lanier) 1908

Poem, Spoken at the Public Commencement at Yale College (po Barlow) 1781

Poem-Leaflets in Remembrance of Marion Morse Mackaye (po MacKaye) 1939

Poems: A Joking Word (po Riding) 1930

Poems about God (po Ransom) 1919

Poems All Over the Place: Mostly Seventies (po Ginsberg) 1978

Poems and Problems (po Nabokov) 1971

Poems: Areytos; or Songs and Ballads of the South (po Simms) 1860

Poems for Men (po Runyon) 1947

Poems for Tennessee (po Bly; W. Stafford) 1971

Poems from Prison (po Knight) 1968

Poems from the Margins of Thom Gunn's Moly (po Duncan) 1972

Poems Here at Home (po Riley) 1893

Poems, Lyrical and Dramatic (po Longfellow) 1848

Poems: Medley and Palestina (po De Forest) 1902

Poems: North and South—A Cold Spring (po E.Bishop) 1955

Poems of a Jew (po Shapiro) 1958

Poems of Ambrose Bierce (po Bierce) 1995

Poems of Cabin and Field (po Dunbar) 1899

Poems of Early and after Years (po Willis) 1848

Poems of Home and Travel (po B. Taylor) 1855

Poems of Humor and Protest (po Patchen) 1954

Poems of Love and Marriage (po Ciardi) 1988

Poems of Nature (po Whittier) 1886

Poems of Night (po Kinnell) 1968

Poems of Passion (po Willis) 1843

Poems of People (po Masters) 1936

Poems of Stanley Kunitz 1928-1978 (po Kunitz) 1979

Poems of the Orient (po B. Taylor) 1854

Poems of the War (po Boker) 1864

Poems of Two Friends (po Howells) 1860

Poems on Miscellaneous Subjects (po F. Harper) 1854

Poems on Slavery (po Longfellow) 1842

Poems Sacred, Passionate, and Humorous (po Willis) 1845

Poems to Poets (po Eberhart) 1976

Poems, Written and Published during the American Revolutionary War (po Freneau) 1809

Poems Written between the Years 1768 and 1794 (po Freneau) 1795

Poems Written during the Progress of the Abolition Question, 1830-1838 (po Whittier) 1837

Poem-scapes (po Patchen) 1958

Poet: A Lying Word (po Riding) 1933

Poet and the Dancer (po Doolittle) 1975

Poet and the Donkey (f Sarton) 1969

Poet and the Rent: A Play for Kids from Seven to 8:15 (pl Mamet) 1984

Poet at the Breakfast-Table: His Talks with His Fellow-Boarders and the Reader (o Holmes) 1872

Poet at Work: Recovered Notebooks from the Thomas Biggs Harned Walt Whitman Collection (o Whitman) 1998

Poet of the People: An Evaluation of James Whitcomb Riley (o Farrell; Gregory) 1951

Poet Turns on Himself (o Dickey) 1982

Poetic Disturbances (po Duncan) 1970

Poetic Equation: Conversations between Nikki Giovanni and Margaret Walker (o Giovanni; M. Walker) 1974

Poetics of Influence (o Bloom) 1989

Poetics of the Physical World (o Kinnell) 1969

Poetry and Ambition: Essays 1982-1988 (o Hall) 1988

Poetry and Repression: Revisionism from Blake to Stevens (o Bloom) 1976

Poetry and the Practical (o Simms) 1996

Poetry and the World (o Pinsky) 1988

Poetry and Truth: The Beloit Lectures and Poems (o Olson) 1971

Poetry for My People (po Dumas) 1970

Poetry, Gongorism, and a Thousand Years (o Jeffers) 1949

Poetry Package (po Morley) 1950

Poetry Wreck: Selected Essays 1950-1970 (o Shapiro) 1975

Poetry: A Closer Look (o Ciardi) 1963

Poets at Work (o Shapiro) 1948

Poet's Choice: Poems for Everyday Life (o Hass) 1998

Poets, Farewell! (po E. Wilson) 1929

Poets Journal (po B. Taylor) 1862

Poet's Testament: Poems and Two Plays (po Santayana) 1953

Poganuc People: Their Loves and Lives (f Stowe) 1878

Point of No Return (f Marquand) 1949

Point of View (pl Crothers) 1904

Point Reyes Poems (po Bly) 1974

Points in Time (o Bowles) 1982

Points of My Compass: Letters from the East, the West, the North, the South (o White) 1962

Poisoned Kiss and Other Stories from the Portuguese (f Oates) 1975

Poisonwood Bible (f Kingsolver) 1998

Polar Star (f M. Smith) 1989

Polaroid (po Coolidge) 1975

Poldekin (pl Tarkington) 1920

Police (pl Baraka) 1968

Policeman Bluejay (f Baum) 1907

Policewoman's Love-Hungry Daughter and Other Stories of Chicago Life (f Hecht) 1927

Politian: An Unfinished Tragedy (pl Poe) 1923

Political Culture and Leadership in India (o Mukherjee) 1991

Political Essays (o J. Lowell) 1888

Political Fable (f Coover) 1980

Political, Miscellaneous, and Philosophical Pieces (o Franklin) 1779

Political Self-Portrait (po Wheelwright) 1940

Political Thought of Franklin (o Franklin) 1965

Political Writings (o Barlow) 1796

Political Writings: Representative Selections (o Jefferson) 1955

Polly Fulton (f Marquand) 1947

Pomes Penyeach (po Patchen) 1959

Pomps and Vanities (f Frederic) 1913

Pomps of Satan (o Saltus) 1904

Ponder Heart (f Welty) 1954

Pool (f Rinehart) 1952

Poor Aubrey (pl Kelly) 1922

Poor Harold! (pl Dell) 1920

Poor Rich Man, and the Rich Poor Man (f Sedgwick) 1836

Poor Richard: An Almanack 1733 (o Franklin) 1732-46

Poor Richard Improved 1748 (o Franklin) 1747-64

Poor White (f S. Anderson) 1920

Poor Wise Man (f Rinehart) 1920
Poor Wood-Cutter and Other Stories (f Arthur) 1852
Poorhouse Fair (f Updike) 1959
Popecastle Inn (pl B. Smith) 1937
Poppies and Mandragora (po Saltus) 1926
Pops (pl Linney) 1986
Popular Theatre (o Nathan) 1918
Popularity (pl Cohan) 1906
Populist Manifestos (po Ferlinghetti) 1983
Porch Talk with Ernest Gaines (o Gaines) 1990
Porcupine (pl Robinson) 1915
Porcupine Man (pl Wellman) 1998
Port of Saints (f W. Burroughs) 1979
Port Town (pl Hughes) 1960
Portable Hemingway (f Hemingway) 1944
Portable Parker (o Parker) 1944
Portable Saul Bellow (o Bellow) 1974
Portable Steinbeck (o Steinbeck) 1946, 1958
Portable Yenberry (pl Connelly) 1962
Portion of Labor (f Freeman) 1901
Portion of That Field (o Brooks) 1967
Portland Illustrated (o Neal) 1874
Portnoy's Complaint (f P. Roth) 1969
Portrait in Brownstone (f Auchincloss) 1962
Portrait of a Ballerina (tv Vidal) 1956
Portrait of a Lady (f H. James) 1881
Portrait of a Madonna (pl T. Williams) 1946
Portrait of a Marriage (f Buck) 1945
Portrait of Delmore: Journals and Notes 1939-1959 (o Schwartz) 1986
Portrait of Mabel Dodge (o Stein) 1912
Portrait of Max: An Intimate Memoir of Sir Max Beerbohm (o Behrman) 1960
Portrait of Picasso As a Young Man (o Mailer) 1996
Portraits (o Van Vechten) 1978
Portraits and Prayers (o Stein) 1934
Portraits of Places (pl H. James) 1883
Portraits: Short Stories (f Chopin) 1979
Portugal Story: Three Centuries of Exploration and Discovery (o Dos Passos) 1969
Positronic Man (f Asimov) 1993
Possessing the Secret of Joy (f A. Walker) 1992
Possession (f Bromfield) 1925
Possibilities of the Negro: The Advance Guard of Race (o Du Bois) 1903
Post Office: A Memoir of His Father (o Olson) 1974
Post Road (pl Steele) 1935
Posthumous Sketch (f Oates) 1973
Postman Always Rings Twice (f Cain) 1934
Postman Always Rings Twice (scr Mamet) 1981
Postscript to a Saintly Life (o Santos) 1994
Pot Boiler (pl Sinclair) 1924
Pot of Earth (po MacLeish) 1925
Pot of Gold and Other Stories (o Freeman) 1892
Potato Face (o Sandburg) 1930
Potter's Field (pl Green) 1931
Potter's House (f Stegner) 1938
Pound/Williams: Selected Letters of Ezra Pound and William Carlos Williams (o W. Williams) 1996
Powers of Attorney (f Auchincloss) 1963
Practical Possum (po Eliot) 1947

Practical Sermons (o Edwards) 1788
Practice of the Wild (o Snyder) 1990
Pragmatism: A New Name for Some Old Ways of Thinking (o W. James) 1907
Prague Orgy (f P. Roth) 1985
Prairie Folks (f Garland) 1893
Prairie Songs (po Garland) 1893
Prairie: A Tale (f Cooper) 1827
Praise (po Hass) 1981
Praise to the End! (po Roethke) 1951
Praisesong for the Widow (f Marshall) 1983
Prater Violet (f Isherwood) 1945
Prayer for Owen Meany (f J. Irving) 1989
Praying Man (f Santos) 1982
Preacher (o Emerson) 1880
Preacher and the Rapper (pl Reed) 1997
Preacher and the Slave (f Stegner) 1950
Preaching from the Audience: Candid Comments on Life (o E. Howe) 1926
Precaution (f Cooper) 1820
Precious Memories (pl Linney) 1989
Predilections (o Moore) 1955
Preface to a Life (f Gale) 1926
Preface to a Twenty Volume Suicide Note (po Baraka) 1961
Preface to the Past (o Cabell) 1936
Prefaces to The Experience of Literature (o Trilling) 1979
Prejudices (o Mencken) 1919-27
Prelude (po Aiken) 1929
Prelude to Foundation (f Asimov) 1988
Prelude: Landscapes, Characters, and Conversations from the Earlier Years of My Life (o E. Wilson) 1967
Preludes (po Aiken) 1966
Preludes and Symphonies (po Fletcher) 1922
Preludes for Memnon (po Aiken) 1931
Preparatory Meditations upon the Day of Judgment (o Mather) 1692
Presence of Grace (f Powers) 1956
Presences: A Text for Marisol (o Creeley) 1976
Present Hour (po MacKaye) 1914
Present State of New-England (o Mather) 1690
Presenting Lily Mars (f Tarkington) 1933
Presents (f Barthelme) 1980
President (pl S. Howard) 1930
President Vanishes (scr MacArthur) 1934
President Vanishes (f Stout) 1934
President's Policy (f Nasby) 1877
Presidential Agent (f Sinclair) 1944
Presidential Mission (f Sinclair) 1947
Presidential Papers (o Mailer) 1963
Presidents Mystery (scr N. West) 1936
Presque Isle (pl Oates) 1982
Pressing into the Kingdom: On Seeking Salvation (o Edwards) 1998
Pretty Boy Floyd (f McMurtry) 1996
Pretty Mrs. Gaston and Other Stories (f J. Cooke) 1874
Pretty Polly Pemberton: A Love Story (f Burnett) 1877
Pretty Sister of Jose (f Burnett) 1889
Pretty Story, Written in the Year of Our Lord 2774 (f Hopkinson) 1774
Previous Engagement (pl Howells) 1897
Priapus and the Pool and Other Poems (po Aiken) 1925
Price (pl A. Miller) 1968

Price of a Ticket: Collected Nonfiction 1948-1985 (o James Baldwin) 1985

Price She Paid (f D. Phillips) 1912

Price Was High: The Last Uncollected Stories of Fitzgerald (f Fitzgerald) 1979

Pricksongs and Descants (f Coover) 1969

Pride and Prudence (f Arthur) 1850

Pride of Sonnets (po Morley) 1951

Pride or Principle—Which Makes the Lady? (f Arthur) 1844

Pride's Castle (f Yerby) 1949

Priest, and A Dead Priestess Speaks (po Doolittle) 1983

Prietita and the Ghost Woman (o Anzaldúa) 1995

Prietita Has a Friend—Prietita Tiene un Amigo (o Anzaldúa) 1991

Prima Donna: A Passage from City Life (f Simms) 1844

Primadonna: A Sequel to Soprano (f Crawford) 1908

Primary Geography for Children (o Stowe) 1833

Primer (po B. Perelman) 1981

Primer for Blacks (po Brooks) 1991

Primer for Combat (f Boyle) 1942

Primer for Poets (o Shapiro) 1965

Primer for the Gradual Understanding of Stein (o Stein) 1971

Primitive (f Himes) 1955

Primitive Like an Orb (po Stevens) 1948

Primitive World (pl Baraka) 1984

Primitivism and Decadence: A Study of American Experimental Poetry (o Winters) 1937

Primrose Path (po Nash) 1935

Prince and Boatswain: Sea Tales from the Recollections of Rear-Admiral Charles E. Clark (o Marquand) 1915

Prince and the Pauper (f Twain) 1881

Prince Deukalion: A Lyrical Drama (pl B. Taylor) 1878

Prince Hagen (f Sinclair) 1903

Prince Little Boy and Other Tales out of Fairy-Land (f S. Mitchell) 1888

Prince of Darkness and Other Stories (f Powers) 1947

Prince of India (f L. Wallace) 1893

Prince of Players (scr Hart) 1954

Prince of the House of David (f Ingraham) 1855

Prince Souvanna Phouma: An Exchange Between Wilbur and William Jay Smith (po Wilbur) 1963

Prince There Was (pl Cohan) 1927

Princess Aline (pl Richard Davis) 1895

Princess Casamassima (f H. James) 1886

Princess Marries the Page (pl Millay) 1932

Princess of Mars (f E. Burroughs) 1917

Princess Ozma of Oz (f Baum) 1942

Princess Royal (pl Daly) 1877

Princess Zim-Zam (pl Sheldon) 1911

Principal Products of Portugal (o Hall) 1995

Principia Scriptoriae (pl Nelson) 1986

Printer's Measure (tv Chayefsky) 1953

Prisoner of Second Avenue (pl Simon) 1971

Prisoner of Sex (o Mailer) 1971

Prisoners Base (f Stout) 1952

Private Brinksmanship (o Dickey) 1965

Private Correspondence (o Franklin) 1817

Private Dining Room and Other New Verses (po Nash) 1953

Pvt. Jim Crow (pl Hughes) 1945

Private Life of Axie Reed (f Knowles) 1986

Private Life, The Wheel of Time, Lord Beaupré, The Visits, Collaboration, Owen Wingrave (f H. James) 1893

Private Mythology (po Sarton) 1966

Private Secretary (pl Gillette) 1884

Prize Tale: A New England Sketch (f Stowe) 1834

Pro Aris et Focis: A Plea for Our Altars and Hearths (o Rebecca Davis) 1870

Problems and Other Stories (f Updike) 1979

Problems of Men (o Dewey) 1946

Processional: A Jazz Symphony of American Life (pl Lawson) 1925

Procrastination (pl Payne) 1829

Prodigal Giver (f Glaspell) 1946

Prodigal Parents (f Lewis) 1938

Prodigal Son (pl Daly) 1891

Prodigal Son (pl Hughes) 1965

Prodigal Son (po Robinson) 1929

Professional Frenchman (pl Wellman) 1984

Professional Patriots (o S. Howard) 1927

Professor (pl Gillette) 1881

Professor at the Breakfast-Table, with the Story of Iris (o Holmes) 1860

Professor of Desire (f P. Roth) 1977

Professor Pressensee, Materialist and Inventor (f J. Cooke) 1878

Professor Roars (pl B. Smith) 1938

Professor's House (f Cather) 1925

Professor's Wooing (pl Gillette) 1881

Program rewolucji ludowej Jakoba Jaworskiego (o Kosinski) 1955

Progress and Poetry of the Movies: A Second Book of Film Criticism (o Lindsay) 1995

Progress of Dulness (po Trumbull) 1772-73

Progress of Religious Ideas, through Successive Ages (o Child) 1855

Progress of Stories (f Riding) 1936

Progressive Education and the Science of Education (o Dewey) 1928

Prohibition (o Nasby) 1886

Project Moonbase (scr Heinlein) 1953

Projective Verse (o Olson) 1959

Prologue to America (f Thomas [Clayton] Wolfe) 1978

Promenade (pl Fornés) 1965

Promenades of an Impressionist (o Huneker) 1910

Prometheus Bound (pl Lowell) 1969

Promise (f Buck) 1943

Promised Lands (scr Sontag) 1974

Promises of Alice (f Deland) 1919

Promises, Promises (pl Simon) 1969

Promises: Poems 1954-1956 (po R. Warren) 1957

Promontory Point Revisited (tv Kopit) 1969

Pronto (f Leonard) 1993

Proof (po Winters) 1930

Proof Positive (pl Belasco) 1878

Prophet of the Great Smoky Mountains (f Murfree) 1885

Prophet: A Tragedy (pl B. Taylor) 1874

Prophets for a New Day (po M. Walker) 1970

Proposal for an Evangelical Treasury (o Mather) 1725

Proposals (pl Simon) 1997

Proposals for the Preservation of Religion in the Churches (o Mather) 1702

Proposals Touching the Accomplishment of Prophecies (o Sewall) 1713

Proprioception (o Olson) 1965

Prose and Poetry (o Harte) 1872

Prose and Poetry of Elinor Wylie (o W. Benét) 1934

Prose Contribution to Cuban Revolution (po Ginsberg) 1966

Prose Fictions Written for the Illustration of True Principles (f Arthur) 1844

Prose Romances 1: The Murders in the Rue Morgue, and The Man That Was Used Up (f Poe) 1843

Prose Works (o Whittier) 1866

Prose Works (o Willis) 1849

Prosody Handbook (o Shapiro) 1965

Prospect Before Us (o Dos Passos) 1950

Prospect of Peace (po Barlow) 1778

Prospects of a Golden Age (o Dos Passos) 1959

Prospects on the Rubicon (o Paine) 1787

Prospects on the War and Paper Currency (o Paine) 1793

Protectors (o J. Williams) 1964

Protegee of Jack Hamlin's and Other Stories (f Harte) 1894

Prothalamium (o Stein) 1939

Proud Flesh (pl R. Warren) 1947

Proud Flesh: Four Short Plays (pl Purdy) 1981

Proud Tower (o Tuchman) 1966

Provenca: Poems Selected from Personae, Exultations, and Canzoniere (po Pound) 1910

Proverb (pl Dunlap) 1804

Proverb Stories (f Alcott) 1868

Proving Trail (f L'Amour) 1979

Prufrock and Other Observations (po Eliot) 1917

Psalm Concerning the Castle (po Levertov) 1966

Psalm of Deaths and Other Poems (po S. Mitchell) 1891

Psalm of Thanksgiving (po Hopkinson) 1766

Psalms of David (po Dwight) 1801

Psalms of David in Metre (po Hopkinson) 1767

Psalterium Americanum (o Mather) 1718

Psyche's Art (f Alcott) 1868

Psychic Pretenders (pl Bullins) 1972

Psychology (o Dewey) 1887

Psychology and Philosophic Method (o Dewey) 1899

Psychology and Social Practice (o Dewey) 1901

Psychology of Number and Its Applications to Methods of Teaching Arithmetic (o Dewey) 1895

Public and Its Problems (o Dewey) 1927

Public Burning (f Coover) 1977

Public Good (o Paine) 1780

Public Outcry (po Oates) 1976

Public Speech (po MacLeish) 1936

Pudd'nhead Wilson (f Twain) 1894

Puella (po Dickey) 1982

Puella Mea (po Cummings) 1923

Puente Negro (pl Portillo Trambley) 1984

Pull Down Vanity and Other Stories (f Fiedler) 1962

Pull My Daisy (scr Kerouac) 1959

Pullman Car Hiawatha (pl Wilder) 1931

Pump House Gang (o Tom Wolfe) 1968

Pumpkin Girl (pl Lim) 1987

Pumpkin Seed Point (o Waters) 1969

Pun for Al Gelpi (po Kerouac) 1966

Punch for Judy (pl Barry) 1922

Punch: The Immortal Liar (po Aiken) 1921

Punch's Secret (f Sarton) 1974

Punishment that Educates (o Gilman) 1907

Punishment without Crime (tv Bradbury) 1988

Puppet Masters (f Heinlein) 1951

Puppet-Booth: Twelve Plays (pl Fuller) 1896

Pure Gold (f Rølvaag) 1930

Pure in Heart (pl Lawson) 1934

Purification (pl T. Williams) 1946

Puritan and His Daughter (f Paulding) 1849

Puritan Sage: Collected Writings (o Edwards) 1953

Purple and Fine Women (f Saltus) 1903

Purple Dragon and Other Fantasies (f Baum) 1976

Pursuit (po Plath) 1973

Pursuit of the Prodigal (f Auchincloss) 1959

Pushcart at the Curb (po Dos Passos) 1922

Pussycat and the Expert Plumber Who Was a Man (pl A. Miller) 1941

Put Yourself in My Shoes (f Carver) 1974

Putnam, the Iron Son of '76 (pl Bannister) 1844

Puttermesser Papers (f Ozick) 1997

Putting the Most into Life (o Washington) 1906

Puzzled America (o S. Anderson) 1935

Puzzles of the Black Widowers (f Asimov) 1990

Pylon (f Faulkner) 1935

Pythagorean Silence (po S. Howe) 1982

Q.B.I.: Queen's Bureau of Investigation (f Queen) 1954

QED: Queen's Experiments in Detection (f Queen) 1968

Quadroone (f Ingraham) 1840

Quaker City Holy Land Excursion: An Unfinished Play (pl Twain) 1927

Quality of Mercy (f Howells) 1892

Quare Medicine (pl Green) 1925

Quarry: New Poems (po Eberhart) 1964

Quartz Hearts (po Coolidge) 1978

Quasar, Quasar, Burning Bright (o Asimov) 1978

Quebec and New York (f Ingraham) 1839

Queen Christina (scr Behrman) 1933

Queen of Outer Space (scr Hecht) 1958

Queen of the Pirate Isle (f Harte) 1886

Queen Silver-Bell (f Burnett) 1906

Queen Titania (f Boyesen) 1881

Queen Zixi of Ix (f Baum) 1905

Queen's Husband (pl Sherwood) 1928

Queen's Twin and Other Stories (f Jewett) 1899

Queenie (f Calisher) 1971

Queens Full (f Queen) 1965

Queens of France (pl Wilder) 1932

Queer (f W. Burroughs) 1985

Queer Little Folks (f Stowe) 1886

Queer Little People (f Stowe) 1867

Queer Stories for Boys and Girls (f Eggleston) 1884

Query (po Updike) 1974

Quest for Certainty: A Study of the Relation of Knowledge and Action (o Dewey) 1929

Quest of Merlin and The Marriage of Guenevere (pl Hovey) 1891

Quest of the Silver Fleece (f Du Bois) 1911

Question of Our Speech, The Lesson of Balzac: Two Lectures (pl H. James) 1905

Question of Time (f Atherton) 1891

Questionable Shapes (f Howells) 1903

Questioning of Nick (pl Kopit) 1957

Questions (pl Hawkes) 1966

Questions of Travel (po E.Bishop) 1965

Quia Pauper Amavi (po Pound) 1919

Quick and Easy Math (o Asimov) 1964
Quick and the Dead (f L'Amour) 1974
Quick and the Dead (f Queen) 1956
Quick Graph: Collected Notes and Essays (o Creeley) 1970
Quiet Cities (f Hergesheimer) 1928
Quiet Days in Clichy (f H. Miller) 1956
Quiet Life, and The Tide on the Moaning Bar (f Burnett) 1878
Quiet of the Land (po W. Stafford) 1979
Quiet, Please (o Cabell) 1952
Quinzaine for This Yule (po Pound) 1908
Quits (pl Daly) 1881
Quo Vadimus?, or The Case for the Bicycle (o White) 1939
Quo Vadis (scr Behrman) 1951
Quodlibet, Containing Some Annals Thereof (f Kennedy) 1840
Quotations (o Washington) 1938
Quotations from Chairman Mao Tse-Tung (pl Albee) 1968

R.J.'s Mother and Some Other People (f Deland) 1908
Rabbi of Lud (f Elkin) 1987
Rabbit at Rest (f Updike) 1990
Rabbit Is Rich (f Updike) 1981
Rabbit Redux (f Updike) 1971
Rabbit, Run (f Updike) 1960
Rabble in Arms (f Roberts) 1933
Race Changes: White Skin, Black Face in American Culture (o Gilbert and Gubar) 1997
Race Contacts and Interracial Relations (o Locke) 1916
Race Problem and Peace (o J. Johnson) 1924
Races and People (o Asimov) 1955
Rachel Dyer: A North American Story (f Neal) 1828
Racine (o Cowley) 1923
Racketty-Packetty House (f Burnett) 1906
Radical Chic and Mau-Mauing the Flak Catchers (o Tom Wolfe) 1970
Radical Mystique (pl Laurents) 1995
Radigan (f L'Amour) 1958
Radio Play (pl Saroyan) 1940
Rafael (f Ingraham) 1845
Rafael Naarizokh (f Cahan) 1907
Raffle for Mrs. Hennessey's Clock (pl Harrigan) 1874
Raffles (scr S. Howard) 1930
Raffles (scr Van Druten) 1940
Rag Baby (pl Hoyt) 1884
Rag-Bag: A Collection of Ephemera (o Willis) 1855
Rag Doll Plagues (f Morales) 1992
Rage (f King) 1977
Rage in Heaven (scr Isherwood) 1941
Rage to Live (f J. O'Hara) 1949
Ragged Dick (f Alger) 1868
Ragged Lady (f Howells) 1899
Ragged Mountain Elegies (pl Hall) 1983
Ragnarok: The Age of Fire and Gravel (o Donnelly) 1883
Rag-Picker of Paris (pl Morley) 1937
Ragtime (f Doctorow) 1975
Rahab (f Frank) 1922
Raid of the Guerilla and Other Stories (f Murfree) 1912
Raiders of the Spanish Peaks (f Grey) 1938
Railroad of Love (pl Daly) 1887
Railroad: Trains and Train People in American Culture (o McPherson) 1976
Railway Police and The Last Trolley Ride (f Calisher) 1966

Rain (scr M. Anderson) 1932
Rain Five Days and I Love It (po Hugo) 1975
Rain from Heaven (pl Behrman) 1935
Rain in the Trees (po Merwin) 1988
Rain of Scorpions and Other Writings (f Portillo Trambley) 1976
Rainbow (f Buck) 1974
Rainbow Jordan (f Childress) 1981
Rainbow Trail (f Grey) 1915
Rainbow's End (f Cain) 1975
Rains Came: A Novel of Modern India (f Bromfield) 1937
Raintree County (f Lockridge) 1948
Raise High the Roof Beam, Carpenters, and Seymour: An Introduction (f Salinger) 1963
Raisin in the Sun (pl Hansberry) 1959
Raising Demons (o S. Jackson) 1957
Ralph Raymond's Heir (f Alger) 1892
Ralph Waldo Emerson (o Holmes) 1884
Ralstons (f Crawford) 1895
Ramero (f Ingraham) 1846
Ramona (f H. Jackson) 1884
Ramsey Milholland (f Tarkington) 1919
Randall Jarrell (o Shapiro) 1967
Randolph (f Neal) 1823
Random Recollections of an Old Doctor (f Arthur) 1846
Randy of the River (f Alger) 1906
Range of Poems (po Snyder) 1966
Rangle River (scr Grey) 1936
Ranson's Folly (f Richard Davis) 1902
Raoul Duffy: A Note (o Stevens) 1953
Rap on Race (o James Baldwin) 1971
Rapture of the Athlete Assumed into Heaven (pl Delillo) 1990
Rashel: A Biografia (o Cahan) 1938
Rasputin and the Empress (scr MacArthur) 1932
Ratio Disciplinae Fratrum Nov Anglorum: A Faithful Account of the Discipline Professed and Practiced in the Churches of New-England (o Mather) 1726
Rational Meaning: A New Foundation for the Definition of Words, and Supplementary Essays (o Riding) 1997
Ratner's Star (f Delillo) 1976
Ravages of a Carpet (o Stowe) 1865
Raven and Other Poems (po Poe) 1845
Raven's Wing (f Oates) 1986
Ravensnest (f Cooper) 1846
Raw Material (o La Farge) 1945
Rawhide Knot and Other Short Stories (f Richter) 1978
Rawlings Cookbook (o Rawlings) 1961
Raymond's Run (scr Bambara) 1985
Razzle Dazzle (pl Saroyan) 1942
Re: Creation (po Giovanni) 1970
Reaches of Heaven (f Singer) 1980
Reaching for the Mainland (po Cofer) 1987
Reading about My World (po Olson) 1968
Reading Henry James (o Auchincloss) 1975
Reading Public (o J. West) 1952
Reading Rilke: Reflections on the Problems of Translation (o Gass) 1999
Reading the Spirit (po Eberhart) 1936
Real Cool Killers (f Himes) 1959
Real Dope (f Lardner) 1919
Real Life of Sebastian Knight (f Nabokov) 1941
Real Little Lord Fauntleroy (pl Burnett) 1888

Real Losses, Imaginary Gains (f Morris) 1976
Real Soldiers of Fortune (f Richard Davis) 1906
Real Thing and Other Tales (f H. James) 1893
Real West Marginal Way: A Poet's Autobiography (o Hugo) 1986
Real Work: Interviews and Talks 1964-1979 (o Snyder) 1980
Real World (f Herrick) 1901
Realism and Reality (o Nin) 1946
Reality Sandwiches 1953-60 (po Ginsberg) 1963
Really, My Dear. . . (pl Morley) 1928
Really Short Poems of A. R. Ammons (po Ammons) 1990
Realm of Algebra (o Asimov) 1961
Realm of Essence (o Santayana) 1927
Realm of Matter (o Santayana) 1930
Realm of Numbers (o Asimov) 1959
Realm of Spirit (o Santayana) 1940
Realm of Truth (o Santayana) 1937
Realms of Being (o Santayana) 1942
Reason for the Pelican (po Ciardi) 1959
Reason Why (pl A. Miller) 1970
Reasonable Religion (o Mather) 1700
Reasons for Moving (po Strand) 1968
Reasons for Wishing to Preserve the Life of Louis Capet (o Paine) 1793
Reasons of the Heart: Maxims (o Dahlberg) 1965
Rebecca (f Rowson) 1814
Rebecca (scr Sherwood) 1940
Rebecca of Sunnybrook Farm (scr Behrman) 1932
Rebel Coaster (f Ingraham) 1867
Rebellion of the Hanged (f Traven) 1952
Rebels, or Boston before the Revolution (f Child) 1825
Rebirth Celebration of the Human Race at Artie Zabala's Off-Broadway Theatre (pl Saroyan) 1975
Recapitulation (f Stegner) 1979
Recent American Fiction: A Lecture (o Bellow) 1963
Recent Killing (pl Baraka) 1973
Recent Poems, 1986-1990 (po Updike) 1990
Recitative (o Merrill) 1986
Reckless Eyeballing (f Reed) 1986
Reckoner (po J. Tate) 1986
Reckoning (f Sarton) 1978
Reckoning and Other Stories (f Wharton) 1999
Recognition of Cuban Independence (o Adams) 1896
Recognitions (f Gaddis) 1955
Recognizable Image: Williams on Art and Artists (o W. Williams) 1978
Recollections of Europe (o Cooper) 1837
Reconstruction in Philosophy (o Dewey) 1920
Record, Literary and Political, of Five Months in the Year 1813 (o Dunlap) 1813
Recorder with Other Poems (po Halleck) 1833
Recovering: A Journal (o Sarton) 1980
Recovery (f Berryman) 1973
Recruiting Officer (pl Daly) 1885
Rector (pl Crothers) 1905
Rector of Justin (f Auchincloss) 1964
Red Badge of Courage: An Episode of the American Civil War (f S. Crane) 1895
Red, Black, Blond, and Olive: Studies in Four Civilizations: Zuni, Haiti, Soviet Russia, Israel (o E. Wilson) 1956
Red Book (o Kennedy) 1820-21
Red Box (f Stout) 1937

Red Brain (o Hammett) 1961
Red Bull (f Stout) 1945
Red Burning Light (pl Fornés) 1968
Red Carpet (pl Fuller) 1939
Red City: A Novel of the Second Administration of President Washington (f S. Mitchell) 1908
Red Coal (po Stern) 1981
Red Cross (pl Shepard) 1966
Red Cross Girl (f Richard Davis) 1912
Red Devil Battery Sign (pl T. Williams) 1975
Red Harvest (f Hammett) 1929
Red Jacket (po Goodman) 1955
Red Lamp (f Rinehart) 1925
Red Letter Nights (pl Daly) 1884
Red Mask (pl Brougham) 1856
Red Men and White (f Wister) 1896
Red One (f London) 1918
Red Owl (pl Gillette) 1909
Red Peony (f Lin Yutang) 1961
Red Planet (f Heinlein) 1949
Red Pony (f Steinbeck) 1937
Red Ribbon (pl Daly) 1870
Red Ribbon on a White Horse (f Yezierska) 1950
Red Riders (f Page) 1924
Red Rock: A Chronicle of Reconstruction (f Page) 1898
Red Roses for Bronze (po Doolittle) 1931
Red Rover: A Tale (f Cooper) 1827
Red Sand (f Stribling) 1924
Red Scarf (pl Daly) 1868
Red Shoes Run Faster (scr Green) 1949
Red Square (f M. Smith) 1992
Red Threads (f Stout) 1939
Red Wind (f Chandler) 1946
Red Wine and Yellow Hair (po Patchen) 1949
Red: Papers on Musical Subjects (o Van Vechten) 1925
Redburn, His First Voyage (f Melville) 1849
Rediscovery of North America (o Lopez) 1991
Redo (po Hejinian) 1984
Redskins; or Indian and Injin, Being the Conclusion of the Littlepage Manuscripts (f Cooper) 1846
Redwood (f Sedgwick) 1824
Reef (f Wharton) 1912
Reef Girl (f Grey) 1977
Reena and Other Stories (f Marshall) 1983
Reflected Glory (pl Kelly) 1937
Reflection on the Atomic Bomb (o Stein) 1973
Reflections (po H. Miller) 1981
Reflections at Fifty and Other Essays (o Farrell) 1954
Reflections in a Golden Eye (f McCullers) 1941
Reflections of a Jacobite (o Auchincloss) 1961
Reflections on Courtship and Marriage (o Franklin) 1746
Reflexions on Poetry and Poetics (o Nemerov) 1972
Regarding Wave (po Snyder) 1969
Reggae or Not! (po Baraka) 1982
Regierung (f Traven) 1931
Regina (pl Hellman) 1949
Regionalism in Indian Perspective (o Mukherjee) 1992
Register (pl Howells) 1884
Registers (po Coolidge) 1994
Regular Army, O! (pl Harrigan) 1874
Regular Fellows I Have Met (o Lardner) 1919

Regulators (po Duncan) 1985
Regulators (f King) 1996
Rehearsal (pl Morley) 1922
Rehearsing the Tragedy (pl Daly) 1888
Reign of Gilt (o D. Phillips) 1905
Reign of Law: A Tale of the Kentucky Hemp Fields (f J. Allen) 1900
Reilly and the Four Hundred (pl Harrigan) 1890
Reilly's Luck (f L'Amour) 1970
Reivers: A Reminiscence (f Faulkner) 1962
Rejoicings (po Stern) 1973
Relation of Literature to Life (o Warner) 1896
Relation or Journal of the Beginning and Proceedings of the English Plantation Settled at Plymouth (o W. Bradford) 1622
Relations Between Poetry and Painting (o Stevens) 1951
Relativity of Wrong: Essays on the Solar System and Beyond (o Asimov) 1988
Relearning the Alphabet (po Levertov) 1970
Religion of Solidarity (o Bellamy) 1940
Religious Mariner (o Mather) 1700
Religious Poems (po Stowe) 1867
Reluctant Citizen (tv Chayefsky) 1952
Reluctant Rapist (f Bullins) 1973
Remains (po Snodgrass) 1970
Remarks Concerning the Savages of North America (o Franklin) 1784
Remarks on Accepting the American Book Award (o Kinnell) 1984
Remarks on Important Theological Controversies (o Edwards) 1796
Rembrandt's Hat (f Malamud) 1973
Remembering Laughter (f Stegner) 1937
Remembering Poets: Reminiscences and Opinions–Dylan Thomas, Robert Frost, T.S. Eliot, Ezra Pound (o Hall) 1978
Rememberings 1895-1945: Four Poems (po MacKaye) 1945
Reminiscences of The Evening Post (o Bryant) 1851
Renascence and Other Poems (po Millay) 1917
Rendezvous with America (po Tolson) 1944
Rent Free (scr Rice) 1922
Repent in Haste (f Marquand) 1945
Replenishing Jessica (f Bodenheim) 1925
Reply in Behalf of the Women of America (o Stowe) 1863
Report from Paradise (f Twain) 1952
Report from Part One: An Autobiography (o Brooks) 1972
Report on the Condition and Needs of the Mission Indians of California (o H. Jackson) 1883
Report to the Commissioners on Lay-Out of East Rock Park (o D. Mitchell) 1882
Reports of My Death: An Autobiography (o Shapiro) 1990
Representative Men: Seven Lectures (o Emerson) 1850
Representative Selections (o J. Lowell) 1947
Representative Selections (o Parkman) 1938
Reprobate (pl H. James) 1894
Republic of Letters in America: The Correspondence of Bishop and Allen Tate (o J. Bishop) 1981
Republic of Letters: The Correspondence between Thomas Jefferson and James Madison, 1776-1826 (o Jefferson) 1995
Requiem for a Nun (pl Faulkner) 1951
Requiem for Harlem (f H. Roth) 1998
Rescued Year (po W. Stafford) 1966
Research (po Coolidge) 1982
Researches upon the Venom of Poisonous Serpents (o S. Mitchell) 1886

Researches upon the Venom of the Rattlesnake (o S. Mitchell) 1861
Residence in France with a Second Visit to Switzerland (o Cooper) 1836
Resort and Remedy of Those That Are Bereaved by the Death of an Eminent Minister (o Edwards) 1741
Rest in Pieces (f R Brown) 1992
Rest of the Robots (f Asimov) 1964
Resurrection (f J. Gardner) 1966
Retiring from Business (f Arthur) 1848
Reto en el paraíso (f Morales) 1983
Retour en Afrigue (f Himes) 1964
Retreat (f Welty) 1981
Retrospect (pl Dunlap) 1802
Retrospects and Prospects: Descriptive and Historical Essays (o Lanier) 1899
Return (po Jeffers) 1934
Return Half (pl Van Druten) 1924
Return of Buck Gavin (pl Thomas [Clayton] Wolfe) 1919
Return of Eden: Five Essays on Milton's Epics (o Frye) 1965
Return of Lanny Budd (f Sinclair) 1953
Return of Peter Grimm (pl Belasco) 1911
Return of Pinocchio (pl Nelson) 1983
Return of Several Ministers (o Mather) 1692
Return of Simple (f Hughes) 1994
Return of Tarzan (f E. Burroughs) 1915
Return of the Continental Op (f Hammett) 1945
Return of the O'Mahony (f Frederic) 1892
Return of the Rivers (po Brautigan) 1957
Return of the Soldier (pl Van Druten) 1928
Return of the Vagabond (pl Cohan) 1940
Return of the Vanishing America (o Fiedler) 1968
Return to a Place Lit by a Glass of Milk (po Simic) 1974
Return to Winesburg: Selections from Four Years of Writing for a Country Newspaper (o S. Anderson) 1967
Return: Poems Collected and New (po Alurista) 1982
Returning to Earth (po Harrison) 1977
Returning to Emotion (po Bodenheim) 1927
Reuben (f Wideman) 1987
Reuben and Rachel (f Rowson) 1798
Reunion (scr Connelly) 1942
Reunion (pl Mamet) 1976
Reunion in Vienna (pl Sherwood) 1931
Revelation of Saint Orgne, The Damned (o Du Bois) 1939
Revenge of the Lawn: Stories 1962-1970 (f Brautigan) 1971
Revenge of the Space Pandas, or Binky Rudich and the Two-Speed Clock (pl Mamet) 1977
Reverberator (f H. James) 1888
Reverend Griffith Davenport (pl Herne) 1899
Reveries of a Bachelor (f D. Mitchell) 1850
Reviewers Reviewed: A Satire (po Mowatt) 1837
Revived Remarks on Mark Twain (o Ade) 1936
Revolt in 2100 (f Heinlein) 1953
Revolution in Taste: Studies of Dylan Thomas, Allen Ginsberg, Sylvia Plath, and Robert Lowell (o Simpson) 1978
Revolutionary Petunias and Other Poems (po A. Walker) 1973
Rezanov (f Atherton) 1906
Rezanov and Dona Concha (f Atherton) 1937
Rhapsodist and Other Uncollected Writings (o Brown) 1943
Rhetoric of Motives (o Burke) 1950
Rhetoric of Religion: Studies in Logology (o Burke) 1961

Rhoda: A Life in Stories (f Gilchrist) 1995

Rhode Island: Eight Poems (po M. Harper) 1981

Rhymes of Childhood (po Riley) 1890

Rhymes of the Firing Line (po Runyon) 1912

Rhymes of Travel, Ballads, and Poems (po B. Taylor) 1848

Rhymes to Be Traded for Bread (po Lindsay) 1912

Rhythm in the Clouds (scr N. West) 1937

Ribbemont (pl Dunlap) 1803

Rich and Famous (pl Guare) 1974

Rich Boy and Other Stories (f Fitzgerald) 1998

Rich Relations (pl Hwang) 1986

Richard and Anne: A Play in Two Acts (scr M. Anderson) 1995

Richard Carvel (f Churchill) 1899

Richard Hurdis (f Simms) 1838

Richard Wright: Daemonic Genius (o M. Walker) 1988

Richelieu (o Auchincloss) 1972

Richelieu: A Domestic Tragedy (pl W. Irving; Payne) 1826

Riches Have Wings (f Arthur) 1847

Richmond: A Dramatic Poem (pl Masters) 1934

Riddle Rat (o Hall) 1977

Riddles Unriddled (po Wigglesworth) 1689

Ride down Mount Morgan (pl A. Miller) 1991

Ride for Revenge (f M. Smith) 1977

Ride the Dark Trail (f L'Amour) 1972

Ride the Pink Horse (scr Hecht) 1947

Ride the River (f L'Amour) 1983

Ride with Old Kit Kuncker and Other Sketches and Scenes of Alabama (f Hooper) 1849

Rider of Lost Creek (f L'Amour) 1976

Rider of the Ruby Hills (f L'Amour) 1986

Riders of the Purple Sage (f Grey) 1912

Ridin' the Moon in Texas: Word Paintings (po Shange) 1987

Riding for the Brand (f L'Amour) 1986

Riding Out the Tropical Depression (po Gilchrist) 1986

Riding Shotgun (f R Brown) 1997

Riding the Earthboy 40 (po Welch) 1971

Riding the Iron Rooster: By Train through China (o Theroux) 1989

Riding the Rap (f Leonard) 1995

Right Madness on Skye (po Hugo) 1980

Right Stuff (o Tom Wolfe) 1979

Right to Die (f Stout) 1964

Right to Love (scr Akins) 1930

Right to Love (f Glaspell) 1930

Right Way the Safe Way, Proved by Emancipation in the British West Indies, and Elsewhere (o Child) 1860

Right You Are, Mr. Moto (f Marquand) 1977

Rights of Man (o Paine) 1791-92

Riley Baby Book (po Riley) 1913

Rim of the World (pl Dell) 1915

Rimbaud (po Kerouac) 1960

Ring (o Updike) 1964

Ring Around Max: The Correspondence of Lardner and Max Perkins (o Lardner) 1973

Ringaleevio (scr Shepard) 1971

Ringers in the Tower: Studies in Romantic Tradition (o Bloom) 1971

Ringold Griffitt (f Ingraham) 1847

Rinkitink in Oz (f Baum) 1916

Rio Grande Fall (f Anaya) 1996

Riot (po Brooks) 1970

Rip Awake (pl Coover) 1972

Rip Tide: A Novel in Verse (po W. Benét) 1932

Rip Van Winkle (pl MacKaye) 1919

Rip Van Winkle (pl Nelson) 1981

Ripostes (po Pound) 1912

Riprap (po Snyder) 1959

Riprap, and Cold Mountain Poems (po Snyder) 1965

Rise of David Levinsky (f Cahan) 1917

Rise of Life on Earth (f Oates) 1991

Rise of Rosie O'Reilly (pl Cohan) 1923

Rise of Silas Lapham (f Howells) 1885

Risen from the Ranks (f Alger) 1874

Rising Gorge (o S. Perelman) 1961

Rising in the World (f Arthur) 1848

Rising Son (o W. Brown) 1874

Rising Star (pl Harrigan) 1877

Rising Tide (f Deland) 1916

Rita Will: Memoir of a Literary Rabble-Rouser (o R Brown) 1997

Rites and Witnesses (f Hinojosa) 1982

Ritual Masters (scr Bullins) 1972

Ritual To Raise the Dead and Foretell the Future (pl Bullins) 1970

Rival Warriors, Chiefs of the Five Nations (o Eggleston) 1881

Riven Doggeries (po J. Tate) 1979

River Lady (f Waters) 1942

River Notes: The Dance of Herons (o Lopez) 1979

River of Heaven (po Hongo) 1988

River to Pickle Beach (f Betts) 1972

Rivers and Mountains (po Ashbery) 1966

Rivers to the Sea (po Teasdale) 1915

Rivers West (f L'Amour) 1975

Riverside Drive (f Simpson) 1962

Rivet in Grandfather's Neck (f Cabell) 1915

Rivingstone (f Ingraham) 1855

Rivulets of Prose: Critical Essays (o Whitman) 1928

RJ on RJ: Robinson Jeffers and The Subtle Passion (o Jeffers) 1996

Road (f London) 1907

Road Between (f Farrell) 1949

Road Not Taken (po Frost) 1951

Road Through the Wall (f S. Jackson) 1948

Road to Glory (scr Faulkner) 1936

Road to Infinity (o Asimov) 1979

Road to Miltown (o S. Perelman) 1957

Road to Nirvana (pl Kopit) 1989

Road to Oz (f Baum) 1909

Road to Rome (pl Sherwood) 1927

Road to the Temple (o Glaspell) 1926

Roadhouse Nights (The River Inn) (scr Hecht) 1930

Roads of Destiny (f Henry) 1909

Roadside Harp (po Guiney) 1893

Roadwork (f King) 1981

Roan Stallion, Tamar, and Other Poems (po Jeffers) 1925

Roaring U.P. Trail (f Grey) 1918

Roast Beef Medium: The Business Adventures of Emma McChesney and Her Son, Jock (f Ferber) 1913

Rob of the Bowl: A Legend of St. Inigoe's (f Kennedy) 1838

Robber Bridegroom (f Welty) 1942

Robber Rocks: Letters and Memories of Crane 1923-1932 (o H. Crane) 1969

Robbers' Roost (f Grey) 1932

Robbery (pl Dunlap) 1799

Robbie (f Asimov) 1989

Robert Coverdale's Struggle (f Alger) 1910

Robert Creeley and the Genius of the American Commonplace: Together with the Poet's Own Autobiography (o Creeley) 1993

Robert E. Lee: Man and Soldier (o Page) 1911

Robert E. Lee: The Southerner (o Page) 1908

Robert Elsmere (pl Gillette) 1889

Robert Emmet: A Survey of His Rebellion and of His Romance (o Guiney) 1904

Roberts Reader (o Roberts) 1945

Robin (f Burnett) 1922

Robot Dreams (f Asimov) 1986

Robot Visions (o Asimov) 1990

Robots and Empire (f Asimov) 1985

Robots of Dawn (f Asimov) 1983

Robots: Machines in Man's Image (o Asimov) 1985

Rock and Shell: Poems 1923-1933 (po Wheelwright) 1933

Rock Garden (pl Shepard) 1964

Rock Springs (f Ford) 1987

Rock Wagram (f Saroyan) 1951

Rock: A Pageant Play (pl Eliot) 1934

Rocket Ship Galileo (f Heinlein) 1947

Rocket to the Moon (pl Odets) 1939

Rocking Chair (pl Shepard) 1965

Rocking Horse (po Morley) 1919

Roderick Hudson (f H. James) 1875

Rodolphe in Boston! (f Ingraham) 1844

Rodrigo Poems (po Cisneros) 1985

Roger Bloomer (pl Lawson) 1923

Roger la Honte (pl Daly) 1889

Roger's Version (f Updike) 1986

Rogue River Feud (f Grey) 1948

Roland Blake (f S. Mitchell) 1886

Roll Call: A Masque of the Red Cross (pl MacKaye) 1918

Roll River (f Boyd) 1935

Roll Sweet Chariot: A Symphonic Play of the Negro People (pl Green) 1934

Rolling Stone (f Alger) 1902

Rolling Stones (f Heinlein) 1952

Rolling Stones (f Henry) 1912

Rollo Johnson (f Ade) 1904

Roman Bartholow (po Robinson) 1923

Roman Empire (o Asimov) 1967

Roman Fever and Other Stories (f Wharton) 1997

Roman Hat Mystery (f Queen) 1929

Roman Holiday (f Sinclair) 1931

Roman Republic (o Asimov) 1966

Roman Scandals (scr Kaufman; Sherwood) 1933

Roman Singer (f Crawford) 1884

Roman Spring of Mrs (f T. Williams) 1950

Romance (pl Sheldon) 1914

Romance in the Roaring Forties and Other Stories (f Runyon) 1986

Romance Island (f Gale) 1906

Romance of Plain Man (f Glasgow) 1909

Romance of the Milky Way and Other Studies and Stories (o Hearn) 1905

Romance of the Republic (f Child) 1867

Romance of the Sunny South (f Ingraham) 1845

Romance of Travel (f Willis) 1840

Romantic Comedians (f Glasgow) 1926

Romantic Egoists: A Reflection in Eight Minutes (f Auchincloss) 1954

Romantic Life amongst the Red Indians: An Autobiography (o J. Miller) 1890

Romantic Manifesto: A Philosophy of Literature (o Rand) 1970

Romanticism and Consciousness: Essays in Criticism (o Bloom) 1970

Romantics (f Rinehart) 1929

Rommel Drives on Deep into Egypt (po Brautigan) 1970

Romulus: A New Comedy (pl Vidal) 1962

Roof of Tiger Lilies (po Hall) 1964

Room for a King (pl B. Smith) 1940

Room Forty-Five (pl Howells) 1900

Rooming House (po Gregory) 1932

Rooms in the House of Stone (o Dorris) 1993

Roosevelt: The Story of a Friendship 1880-1919 (o Wister) 1930

Root of His Evil (f Cain) 1952

Rootabaga Country (o Sandburg) 1929

Rootabaga Pigeons (o Sandburg) 1923

Rootabaga Stories (o Sandburg) 1922

Roots and Branches (po Duncan) 1964

Roots in Water (radio Nelson) 1989

Rope (scr Laurents) 1948

Rope (pl O'Neill) 1918

Rope (pl Stribling) 1928

Rope for Dr. Webster (o Cozzens) 1976

Rope of Wind and Other Stories (f Dumas) 1979

Ropes (pl Steele) 1925

Roping Lions in the Grand Canyon (f Grey) 1924

Rosary (scr Green) 1933

Rosary Murders (scr Leonard) 1987

Rose (f M. Smith) 1996

Rose Briar (pl Tarkington) 1922

Rose Family: A Fairy Tale (f Alcott) 1864

Rose for Ana Maria (f Yerby) 1976

Rose in Bloom: A Sequel to "Eight Cousins" (f Alcott) 1876

Rose Madder (f King) 1994

Rose of Dutcher's Coolly (f Garland) 1895

Rose of the Rancho (pl Belasco) 1906

Rose of Yesterday (f Crawford) 1897

Rose Tattoo (pl T. Williams) 1951

Roseanna McCoy (scr Green) 1949

Rosinante to the Road Again (o Dos Passos) 1922

Roswell (pl Kopit) 1993

Rosy Crucifixion: (f H. Miller) 1949

Rough and Ready; or Life Among the New York Newsboys (f Alger) 1869

Roughing It! (pl Daly) 1873

Round Table (o J. Lowell) 1913

Round the Clock (pl Daly) 1872

Round the Town (pl Parker) 1924

Round Up: The Stories (f Lardner) 1929

Roundabout Journey (o Warner) 1883

Route As Briefed (o J. Tate) 1999

Route Two (o Dorris) 1990

Routine (f W. Burroughs) 1987

Routines (pl Ferlinghetti) 1964

ROVA Improvisations (po Coolidge) 1994

Roving across Fields: A Conversation and Uncollected Poems 1942-1982 (po W. Stafford) 1983

Roving Mind (o Asimov) 1983

Row with Your Hair (po J. Tate) 1969

Roxy (f Eggleston) 1878

Royal Family (pl Ferber) 1927
Royal Family (pl Kaufman) 1928
Royal Fandango (pl Akins) 1923
Royal Gentleman (f Tourgée) 1881
Royal Middy (pl Daly) 1880
Royal Vagabond (pl Cohan) 1919
Royal Youth (pl Daly) 1881
Rubaiyat of Doc Sifers (po Riley) 1897
Rubber Band (f Stout) 1936
Rubyfruit Jungle (f R Brown) 1973
Rudolph and Amina (f Morley) 1930
Rugged Path (pl Sherwood) 1945
Ruin the Sacred Truths: Poetry and Belief from the Bible to the
    Present (o Bloom) 1989
Ruined Family and Other Tales (f Arthur) 1843
Ruined Gamester (f Arthur) 1844
Rujus and Rose (f Alger) 1870
Rulers of Kings (f Atherton) 1904
Rulers of the Mediterranean (o Richard Davis) 1894
Rulers of the South, Sicily, Calabria, Malta (o Crawford) 1900
Rules for Reducing a Great Empire to a Small One (o Franklin)
    1793
Rum Punch (f Leonard) 1992
Rumbin Galleries (f Tarkington) 1937
Rumination (po Eberhart) 1947
Rumor Verified: Poems 1979-1980 (po R. Warren) 1981
Rumors (pl Simon) 1988
Run Man, Run (f Himes) 1966
Run of Jacks (po Hugo) 1961
Run River (f Didion) 1963
Run, Sheep, Run (f Bodenheim) 1932
Runaway (f Dell) 1925
Runaway Colt (pl Hoyt) 1895
Runner in the Sun: A Story of Indian Maize (f McNickle) 1954
Running Dog (f Delillo) 1978
Running for Office (pl Cohan) 1903
Running Man (f King) 1982
Running Sun (po Purdy) 1971
Runyon a la Carte (f Runyon) 1944
Runyon Favorites (f Runyon) 1942
Runyon First and Last (f Runyon) 1949
Runyon from First to Last (f Runyon) 1954
Runyon on Broadway (f Runyon) 1950
Rupert's Ambition (f Alger) 1899
Rural Letters and Other Records of Thought at Leisure (o Willis)
    1849
Rural Studies, with Hints for Country Places (o D. Mitchell) 1867
Rushes (f Rechy) 1979
Russian Beauty and Other Stories (f Nabokov) 1973
Russian Journal (o Steinbeck) 1948
Russian People (pl Odets)
Rustlers of Pecos County (f Grey) 1914
Ruth Underwood (pl L. Mitchell) 1892
Ryder (f Barnes) 1928

S (f Updike) 1988
S-1 (pl Baraka) 1976
S. S. Glencairn: Four Plays of the Sea (pl O'Neill) 1926
S.O.T (Sons of Temperance) (pl Harrigan) 1876
S.S. San Pedro: A Tale of the Sea (f Cozzens) 1931
S.S. Tenacity (pl S. Howard) 1922

Sabbath Lyrics (po Simms) 1849
Sabbath Scene (po Whittier) 1854
Sabbath's Theater (f P. Roth) 1995
Sabbatical: A Romance (f Barth) 1982
Saboteur (scr Parker) 1942
Sack and Destruction of the City of Columbia, S.C (o Simms)
    1865
Sack of Rome (pl M. Warren) 1790
Sackett (f L'Amour) 1961
Sackett Brand (f L'Amour) 1965
Sackett's Land (f L'Amour) 1974
Sacred and Profane Memories (o Van Vechten) 1932
Sacred Clowns (f Hillerman) 1993
Sacred Cows . . . And Other Edibles (o Giovanni) 1988
Sacred Fount (f H. James) 1901
Sacred Hoop: Recovering the Feminine in American Indian Tradi-
    tions (o P. Allen) 1986
Sacred Poems (po Willis) 1843
Sad Dust Glories (po Ginsberg) 1975
Sad Lament of Pecos Bill on the Eve of Killing His Wife (pl
    Shepard) 1976
Saddest Summer of Samuel S (f Donleavy) 1966
Sadness (f Barthelme) 1972
Sadness and Happiness (po Pinsky) 1975
Safari West (po J. Williams) 1998
Safety First (pl Fitzgerald) 1916
Sag Harbor (pl Herne) 1900
Sagacity (po W. Benét) 1929
Sahara (scr Lawson) 1943
Sailing through China (o Theroux) 1984
Sailor from Gibraltar (scr Isherwood) 1967
Sailor Song (f Kesey) 1992
Sailor's Companion (o Mather) 1709
Saint Gregory's Guest and Recent Poems (po Whittier) 1886
Saint Jack (f Theroux) 1973
Saint Judas (po J. Wright) 1959
Saint Katy the Virgin (f Steinbeck) 1936
Saint Maybe (f A. Tyler) 1991
Saint Peter Relates an Incident of the Resurrection Day (po J.
    Johnson) 1930
Saints Get Together (pl B. Smith) 1937
Saipan: The War Diary of John Ciardi (o Ciardi) 1988
Salem's Lot (f King) 1975
Sally (f Asimov) 1989
Sally Bowles (f Isherwood) 1937
Sally Dows, Etc (f Harte) 1893
Salmagundi (po Faulkner) 1932
Salmagundi (f W. Irving; Paulding) 1807-08
Salome of the Tenements (f Yezierska) 1923
Saloon (pl H. James) 1911
Salt Eaters (f Bambara) 1980
Salt Garden (po Nemerov) 1955
Salt Line (f Spencer) 1984
Salvador (o Didion) 1983
Salvage (pl Belasco) 1925
Salvation (pl MacArthur) 1928
Salvation Gap and Other Western Classics (f Wister) 1999
Salvation Nell (pl Sheldon) 1908
Salvation on a String (pl Green) 1954
Salvation with Charles MacArthur (pl S. Howard) 1928
Salve Venetia: Gleanings from Venetian History (o Crawford) 1905

Sam Average (pl MacKaye) 1912
Sam Ego's House (pl Saroyan) 1947
Sam Holman (f Farrell) 1983
Sam Lawson's Oldtown Fireside Stories (f Stowe) 1872
Sam Steele's Adventures in Panama (f Baum) 1907
Sam Steele's Adventures on Land and Sea (f Baum) 1906
Sam, The Highest Jumper of Them All (pl Saroyan) 1960
Sam Tucker (pl Green) 1923
Same Door (f Updike) 1959
Sam's Bar (f Barthelme) 1987
Sam's Chance, and How He Improved It (f Alger) 1876
Samson (pl Howells) 1889
Samson and Delilah (pl Daly) 1889
Samuel the Seeker (f Sinclair) 1910
San Francisco in 1866, Being Letters to the Springfield Republi-
    can (o Harte) 1951
San Francisco Weather Report (po Brautigan) 1969
Sancho Panza (pl S. Howard) 1923
Sanctified Church (f Hurston) 1981
Sanctity of Marriage (pl Mamet) 1979
Sanctuary (f Faulkner) 1931
Sanctuary (f Wharton) 1903
Sanctuary: A Bird Masque (pl MacKaye) 1913
Sand Mountain (pl Linney) 1985
Sand Pebbles (scr R. Anderson) 1966
Sandalwood Box (pl Wellman) 1994
Sandbox (pl Albee) 1960
Sands of the Well (po Levertov) 1996
Santa Claus (f Ingraham) 1844
Santa Claus: A Morality (pl Cummings) 1946
Santa Claus's Partner (f Page) 1899
Santa Eulalia: The Religion of a Cuchumatan Indian Town (o La
    Farge) 1947
Santa Fe: The Autobiography of a Southwestern Town (o La
    Farge) 1959
Santa Go Home: A Case History for Parents (po Nash) 1967
Santayana on America (o Santayana) 1968
Santayana's America: Essays on Literature and Culture (o
    Santayana) 1967
Sant'Ilario (f Crawford) 1889
Santorini: Stopping the Leak (po Merrill) 1982
Sapphira and the Slave Girl (f Cather) 1940
Sappho (pl Fitch) 1899
Sappho and Phaon (pl MacKaye) 1907
Sappho of Green Springs and Other Tales (f Harte) 1891
Sara Crewe (f Burnett) 1887
Saracen Blade (f Yerby) 1952
Saracinesca (f Crawford) 1887
Sarah (f Rowson) 1813
Sarah and Son (scr Akins) 1930
Sarah Conley: A Novel (f Gilchrist) 1997
Saratoga (pl B. Howard) 1870
Saratoga, Hot (f Calisher) 1985
Saratoga Trunk (f Ferber) 1941
Sardonic Arm (po Bodenheim) 1923
Sargentville Notebook (po Strand) 1974
Sarita (pl Fornés) 1984
Saroyan Special: Selected Short Stories (f Saroyan) 1948
Saroyan's Fables (f Saroyan) 1941
Sartoris (f Faulkner) 1929
Sassafrass (f Shange) 1976

Sassafrass, Cypress & Indigo (f Shange) 1982
Satan in Goray (f Singer) 1955
Satan Never Sleeps (f Buck) 1952
Satanic Reader: Selections from the Invective Journalism (o Bierce)
    1968
Satanstoe (f Cooper) 1845
Satires (po Wellman) 1985
Satires and Bagatelles (o Franklin) 1937
Satires and Burlesques (f Twain) 1967
Satori in Paris (f Kerouac) 1966
Saturday Night and Other Stories (f Farrell) 1958
Saturday Papers (o W. Benét) 1921
Saturday's Children (pl M. Anderson) 1927
Saturn and Beyond (o Asimov) 1979
Saunterings (o Warner) 1872
Savage Holiday (f R. Wright) 1954
Savage Kingdom (f Grey) 1979
Savage Pellucidar (f E. Burroughs) 1963
Savage Wilds (pl Reed) 1997
Savage/Love (pl Shepard) 1979
Saved as by Fire (f Arthur) 1881
Saving Grace (f L. Smith) 1995
Saxe Holm's Stories (f H. Jackson) 1874-78
Say It with Oil: A Few Remarks about Wives (o Lardner) 1923
Scapegoat (scr Vidal) 1959
Scar Lover (f Crews) 1992
Scarecrow (pl MacKaye) 1908
Scarecrow of Oz (f Baum) 1915
Scarface, The Shame of the Nation (scr Hecht) 1932
Scarlet Car (f Richard Davis) 1907
Scarlet Feather (f Ingraham) 1845
Scarlet Letter: A Romance (f Hawthorne) 1850
Scarlet Letters (f Queen) 1953
Scarlet Pimpernel (scr Behrman; Sherwood) 1934
Scarlet Plague (f London) 1915
Scarlet Thread (f Betts) 1965
Scattered Poems (po Kerouac) 1971
Scattering of Salts (po Merrill) 1995
Scenario: A Film with Sound (pl H. Miller) 1937
Scenery and Antiquities of Ireland (o Willis) 1842
Scenes (po Bowles) 1968
Scenes from Humanitas (pl Bellow) 1962
Scenes from the Fifties (f Updike) 1995
Scenic Art: Notes on Acting and the Drama 1872-1901 (pl H.
    James) 1948
Scepticism and Animal Faith (o Santayana) 1923
Scherzo, From a Poem to be Entitled "The Proud City." (po
    Guthrie) 1933
Scholar's Caution and the Scholar's Courage (o Trilling) 1962
Scholar-Friends: Letters of Francis James Child and Lowell (o J.
    Lowell) 1952
School and Society (o Dewey) 1899
School and the Child, Being Selections from the Educational Es-
    says of Dewey (o Dewey) 1907
School for Dark Thoughts (po Simic) 1978
School for Husbands (pl Nelson) 1995
School for Husbands (pl Wilbur) 1990
School for Scandal (pl Daly) 1891
School for Soldiers (pl Dunlap) 1799
School for Wives (pl Wilbur) 1971
School History of Germany (o B. Taylor) 1874

School-Boy (o Holmes) 1879
Schoolmaster's Stories for Boys and Girls (f Eggleston) 1874
Schools of To-morrow (o Dewey) 1915
Schultz (f Donleavy) 1979
Science (po Hopkinson) 1762
Science and Creationism (o Asimov) 1984
Science Fiction by Asimov (f Asimov) 1986
Science Fiction of London (f London) 1975
Science, Numbers and I (o Asimov) 1968
Science of English Verse (o Lanier) 1880
Science Past, Science Future (o Asimov) 1975
Science versus Charlatanry: Essays on Astrology (o Lovecraft) 1979
Scion (o Dickey) 1980
Scooping (pl Nelson) 1977
Scorn of Women (pl London) 1906
Scottsboro Limited: Four Poems and a Play in Verse (po Hughes) 1932
Scoundrel (scr Hecht; MacArthur) 1935
Scout (f Simms) 1854
Scrap Leaves, Hasty Scribbles (po Ginsberg) 1968
Scrap of Paper [and] The Berrypicker (pl Purdy) 1981
Scrappy the Pup (po Ciardi) 1960
Scratch (pl MacLeish) 1971
Scream (pl Laurents) 1978
Screenplay for Three Comrades (pl Fitzgerald) 1978
Scripts for the Pageant (po Merrill) 1980
Scripture of Leaves (po W. Stafford) 1989
Scripture of the Golden Eternity (po Kerouac) 1960
Scrolls from the Dead Sea (o E. Wilson) 1955
Scrooge Rides Again (po Nash) 1960
Scum (f Singer) 1991
Sea (po Creeley) 1971
Sea Bat (scr Lawson) 1930
Sea Fairies (f Baum) 1911
Sea Fever (pl Van Druten) 1931
Sea Garden (po Doolittle) 1916
Sea Island Song (pl Childress) 1977
Sea Lion (f Kesey) 1991
Sea Lions (f Cooper) 1849
Sea of Cortez: A Leisurely Journal of Travel and Research (o Steinbeck) 1941
Sea of Grass (f Richter) 1937
Sea Wolf (scr Behrman) 1930
Seabirds Are Still Alive: Collected Stories (f Bambara) 1977
Sea-Change (pl Howells) 1888
Seacliff (f De Forest) 1859
Seagull on the Step (f Boyle) 1955
Seal in the Bedroom and Other Predicaments (f Thurber) 1932
Seaman's Friend (o Dana) 1841
Seaman's Manual (o Dana) 1841
Seamstress (f Arthur) 1843
Séance and Other Stories (f Singer) 1968
Search for the Elements (o Asimov) 1962
Search for the King: A Twelfth Century Legend (f Vidal) 1950
Searches and Seizures (f Elkin) 1973
Searching for Caleb (f A. Tyler) 1976
Searching for the Ox (po Simpson) 1976
Searching Wind (pl Hellman) 1944
Seascape (pl Albee) 1975
Seaside and the Fireside (po Longfellow) 1849

Season of Comfort (f Vidal) 1949
Season of Llorona (pl Anaya) 1979
Season of Peril (po Oates) 1977
Seasons at Eagle Pond (o Hall) 1987
Seasons of Light (po Levertov) 1988
Seaward: An Elegy on the Death of Thomas William Parsons (po Hovey) 1893
Sea-Wife (pl M. Anderson) 1932
Sea-Wolf (f London) 1904
Second April (po Millay) 1921
Second Avenue (po F. O'Hara) 1960
Second Book of Tales (f Field) 1896
Second Book of Verse (po Field) 1892
Second Browser's Dictionary and Native's Guide to the Unknown American Language (o Ciardi) 1983
Second Chance (f Auchincloss) 1970
Second Coming (f Percy) 1980
Second Confession (f Stout) 1949
Second Ewings (f J. O'Hara) 1977
Second Flowering: Works and Days of the Lost Generation (o Cowley) 1973
Second Foundation (f Asimov) 1953
Second Four Books of Poems (po Merwin) 1993
Second Generation (f D. Phillips) 1907
Second Growth (f Stegner) 1947
Second Leaf (po Riding) 1935
Second Man (pl Behrman) 1927
Second Overture (pl M. Anderson) 1940
Second Skin (f Hawkes) 1964
Second Stone: A Love Story (f Fiedler) 1963
Second Threshold (pl Barry; Sherwood) 1951
Second Tree from the Corner (o White) 1954
Second-Hand Smoke (pl Wellman) 1996
Secret (pl Belasco) 1913
Secret Agent X-9 (o Hammett) 1934
Secret Diary 1709-1712 (o Byrd) 1941
Secret Drawer (f Alger) 1981
Secret Garden (f Burnett) 1911
Secret History of the Dividing Line (po S. Howe) 1979
Secret Integration (f Pynchon) 1980
Secret Look (po J. West) 1974
Secret Love Letters; for Eleanor, a Letter a Day (o S. Anderson) 1991
Secret Meaning of Things (po Ferlinghetti) 1969
Secret of Freedom (pl MacLeish) 1959
Secret of the Universe (o Asimov) 1989
Secret River (o Rawlings) 1955
Secret Service (pl Gillette) 1895
Secret Story (f Saroyan) 1954
Secret Way (po Gale) 1921
Secretary to the Spirits (po Reed) 1977
Secrets and Surprises (f Beattie) 1978
Secrets from the Center of the World (o Harjo) 1989
Secrets of the Heart (f Buck) 1976
Secrets of the Rich (pl Kopit) 1976
Section: Rock-Drill: 86-95 de los cantares (po Pound) 1955
Seduced (pl Shepard) 1978
See Naples and Die (pl Rice) 1929
See No Evil: Prefaces, Essays & Accounts (o Shange) 1984
See You in the Morning (f Patchen) 1948
Seed Leaves: Homage to R.F (po Wilbur) 1974

Seed on the Wind (f Stout) 1930
Seed-Time and Harvest (f Arthur) 1851
Seems Like Old Times (scr Simon) 1980
Sees Behind Trees (f Dorris) 1996
Segues: A Correspondence in Poetry (po W. Stafford) 1983
Seize the Day (f Bellow) 1956
Seizure of Limericks (po Aiken) 1964
Self-Begotten (pl Wellman) 1982
Self-Consciousness: Memoirs (o Updike) 1989
Self-Development (o Simms) 1847
Self-Interviews (o Dickey) 1970
Self-Portrait: Ceaselessly into the Past (o Macdonald) 1981
Self-Portrait in a Convex Mirror (po Ashbery) 1975
Self-portrait in Tyvek Windbreaker (po Merrill) 1995
Selling of Joseph (o Sewall) 1700
Senator North (f Atherton) 1900
Senator Was Indiscreet (scr MacArthur) 1947
Senator's Wife (pl Belasco) 1887
Sense of Beauty, Being the Outlines of Aesthetic Theory (o Santayana) 1896
Sense of Justice (tv Vidal) 1955
Sense of Measure (o Creeley) 1972
Sense of the Beautiful (o Simms) 1870
Sense of the Past (f H. James) 1917
Senses and the Soul, and Moral Sentiment in Religion: Two Essays (o Emerson) 1884
SenseUs: The Rainbow Anthems (o Lim) 1990
Sensibility and Sense (pl Nelson) 1989
Senso (pl Bowles; T. Williams) 1970
Sensualists (f Hecht) 1959
Sensuous Dirty Old Man (o Asimov) 1971
Sent for You Yesterday (f Wideman) 1983
Sentences (po Nemerov) 1980
Sentimental Education (f Oates) 1978
Separate Flights (f Dubus) 1975
Separate Peace (f Knowles) 1959
Sepia Star (pl Bullins) 1977
Septimius Felton (f Hawthorne) 1872
Septimius: A Romance (f Hawthorne) 1872
Sequence of Seven (po Nemerov) 1967
Sequence, Sometimes Metaphysical (po Roethke) 1963
Sequestered Shrine (po MacKaye) 1950
Seraglio (f Merrill) 1957
Seraph on the Suwanee (f Hurston) 1948
Seraphic Days (o Chávez) 1940
Serena Blandish (pl Behrman) 1929
Serenade (f Cain) 1937
Serenata (pl Green) 1953
Serge Panine (pl Daly) 1883
Sergeant Hickey (pl Harrigan) 1891
Serious Doll (po Ashbery) 1975
Sermon (pl Mamet) 1981
Sermon Outlines (o Edwards) 1958
Sermons (o Edwards) 1780
Sermons and Soda Water (f J. O'Hara) 1960
Serpent and the Staff (f Yerby) 1958
Serpent in the Wilderness (po Masters) 1933
Servant-Master-Lover (pl Lawson) 1916
Service (o Thoreau) 1902
Set in Motion: Essays and Interviews (o Ammons) 1996
Set of Eight Songs (po Hopkinson) 1788

Set This House on Fire (f Styron) 1960
Seth's Brother's Wife: A Study of Life in the Greater New York (f Frederic) 1887
Setting Free the Bears (f J. Irving) 1969
Settled Out of Court (pl Gillette) 1892
Settled Out of Court (pl Saroyan) 1960
Seven (f McCullers) 1954
Seven Ages of Washington: A Biography (o Wister) 1907
7 & 6 (po Creeley) 1988
7 Blowjobs (pl Wellman) 1991
Seven Days (pl Rinehart) 1931
Seven Descents of Myrtle (pl T. Williams) 1968
Seven Guitars (pl A. Wilson) 1996
Seven Keys to Baldpate (pl Cohan) 1914
Seven Knights (f Ingraham) 1845
Seven Lyrics (po H. Crane) 1966
7 P.M. and Other Poems (po Van Doren) 1926
Seven Sleepers and Other Poems (po Van Doren) 1944
Seven Works (po B. Perelman) 1978
Seven-League Crutches (po Jarrell) 1951
Seventeen (f Tarkington) 1916
Seventeenth Century Suite in Homage to the Metaphysical Genius in English Poetry (1590-1690) (po Duncan) 1973
Seventeenth Degree (o McCarthy) 1974
Seventeenth Star (pl Green) 1953
Seventh Daughter (pl Richard Davis) 1910
Seventh Sense (o Roberts) 1953
7-20-8 (pl Daly) 1886
Seventy Cantos (po Pound) 1950
77 Dream Songs (po Berryman) 1964
Seventy-Six (f Neal) 1823
Sex and the Single Girl (scr Heller) 1964
Sex Life of the Polyp (scr Benchley) 1928
Sexton: A Self-Portrait in Letters (o Sexton) 1977
Sexual Outlaw: A Documentary (o Rechy) 1977
Sexual Perversity in Chicago (pl Mamet) 1974
Shackles of Power 1801-1826: Three Jeffersonian Decades (o Dos Passos) 1966
Shadow and Act (o Ellison) 1964
Shadow Country (po P. Allen) 1982
Shadow of a Doubt (scr Wilder) 1943
Shadow of a Dream (f Howells) 1890
Shadow of a Man (f Sarton) 1950
Shadow of the Trail (f Grey) 1946
Shadow on the Dial and Other Essays (o Bierce) 1909
Shadow Out of Time and Other Tales of Horror (f Lovecraft) 1968
Shadow over Innsmouth (f Lovecraft) 1936
Shadow over Innsmouth and Other Tales of Horror (f Lovecraft) 1971
Shadow Riders (f L'Amour) 1982
Shadow Train (po Ashbery) 1981
Shadowings (o Hearn) 1900
Shadows of Shasta (f J. Miller) 1881
Shadows on the Rock (f Cather) 1931
Shadowy Third and Other Stories (f Glasgow) 1923
Shadrach (f Styron) 1979
Shady Hill Kidnapping (tv Cheever) 1982
Shaker, Why Don't You Sing (po Angelou) 1983
Shakespeare in Harlem (po Hughes) 1942
Shakespeare in Harlem (pl Hughes; J. Johnson) 1959
Shakespeare: The Invention of the Human (o Bloom) 1998

Shakespeare's Twelfth Night (o Gilbert and Gubar) 1964
Shalako (f L'Amour) 1962
Shall We Complete the Trade? A Proposal for the Settlement of Foreign Debts to the United States (o Ransom) 1933
Shall We Gather at the River (po J. Wright) 1968
Shame Dance and Other Stories (f Steele) 1923
Shameless (f Cain) 1958
Shamus O'Brien at Home (pl Harrigan) 1872
Shanghai Lady (scr Eaton) 1929
Shanghaied (f Norris) 1899
Shapes of Clay (po Bierce) 1903
Shaping of England (o Asimov) 1969
Shaping of France (o Asimov) 1972
Shaping of North America from Earliest Times to 1763 (o Asimov) 1973
Shark! Tales of Man-Eating Sharks (f Grey) 1976
Sharp Teeth of Love (f Betts) 1997
Sharps and Flats (o Field) 1900
Shattered Idol (pl Fitch) 1893
Shaved Splits (pl Shepard) 1970
Shaving at Night (po Simic) 1982
Shawl: A Story and a Novella (f Ozick) 1989
Shawnee Prophet (o Eggleston) 1880
Shawshank Redemption (scr King) 1996
She (pl Gillette) 1887
She Had Some Horses (po Harjo) 1983
She Tells Her Daughter (pl Barnes) 1923
She Would and She Would Not (pl Daly) 1884
Sheepfold Hill: Fifteen Poems (po Aiken) 1958
Shelf in Woop's Clothing (po Wellman) 1990
Shelley's Mythmaking (o Bloom) 1959
Shelter (f J. Phillips) 1994
Sheltered Life (f Glasgow) 1932
Sheltering Plaid (pl Green) 1965
Sheltering Sky (f Bowles) 1949
Shelty's Travels (pl Dunlap) 1794
Shenandoah (pl B. Howard) 1897
Shenandoah (pl Schwartz) 1941
Shepherd of Guadaloupe (f Grey) 1930
Shepherds of the Mist (po J. Tate) 1969
Sheppard Lee (f Bird) 1836
Sherlock Holmes (pl Gillette) 1899
Sherlock Holmes Versus Jack the Ripper (f Queen) 1967
Sherwood Anderson and Other Famous Creoles (o Faulkner) 1986
Sherwood Anderson/Stein: Correspondence and Personal Essays (o Stein) 1972
Shetland Poems (po Berryman) 1994
Shield of Achilles: Essays on Beliefs in Poetry (o Gregory) 1944
Shifting for Himself, or, Gilbert Greyson's Fortunes (f Alger) 1876
Shifting Landscape: A Composite, 1925-1987 (o H. Roth) 1987
Shifts of Being (po Eberhart) 1968
Shills Can't Cash Chips (f E. Gardner) 1961
Shining (f King) 1977
Shining Hour (scr Nash) 1938
Shining Life (o J. Johnson) 1932
Ship from Shanghai (scr Lawson) 1930
Ship in the Desert (po J. Miller) 1875
Ship Island and Other Stories (f Spencer) 1968
Ship of Fools (f Porter) 1962
Ships Going into the Blue (o Simpson) 1994
Shipwreck (pl Dunlap) 1805

Shlemiel the First (pl Singer) 1974
Sho-Gun (pl Ade) 1904
Shoe Bird (o Welty) 1964
Shoes of Happiness and Other Poems (po Markham) 1915
Shoes of Wandering (po Kinnell) 1971
Shoeshine (pl Mamet) 1979
Shooting Star (f Stegner) 1961
Shopping for Death (tv Bradbury) 1956
Shore Acres (pl Herne) 1893
Shores of Light: A Literary Chronicle of the Twenties and Thirties (o E. Wilson) 1952
Short Essay to Do Good (o Sedgwick) 1828
Short Fiction (f Mailer) 1967
Short Friday and Other Stories (f Singer) 1964
Short History of Biology (o Asimov) 1964
Short History of Chemistry (o Asimov) 1965
Short History of New-England (o Mather) 1694
Short Novels (f W. Burroughs) 1978
Short Novels (f Steinbeck) 1953
Short Novels (f Thomas [Clayton] Wolfe) 1961
Short Poems (po Berryman) 1967
Short Reign of Pippin IV: A Fabrication (f Steinbeck) 1957
Short Stories (f Boyle) 1929
Short Stories (f Farrell) 1937
Short Stories (po Merrill) 1954
Short Stories (o Welty) 1949
Short Stories: A Selection (f S. Benét) 1942
Short Takes (f Runyon) 1946
Short Walk (f Childress) 1979
Shorter Novels and Stories of McCullers (f McCullers) 1972
Shosha (f Singer) 1978
Shotgun (pl Linney) 1995
Shoulders of Atlas (f Freeman) 1908
Show Boat (f Ferber) 1926
Show Is On (pl Hart) 1936
Show Must Go On (f Rice) 1949
Show Piece (f Tarkington) 1947
Show-Off: A Transcript of Life (pl Kelly) 1924
Showdown at Yellow Butte (f L'Amour) 1953
Shower of Summer Days (f Sarton) 1952
Showman's Daughter (pl Burnett) 1891
Shroud My Body Down (pl Green) 1934
Shrovetide in Old New Orleans (o Reed) 1978
Shunned House (f Lovecraft) 1928
Shut Up, He Explained (o Lardner) 1962
Shuttered Room and Other Tales of Horror (f Lovecraft) 1970
Shuttered Room and Other Pieces (o Lovecraft) 1959
Shuttle (f Burnett) 1907
Shy's Wise, Y's: The Griot's Tale (o Baraka) 1994
Siamese Twin Mystery (f Queen) 1933
Siberian Village (pl Dove) 1991
Sicilan (scr Vidal) 1970
Sicilian (f Puzo) 1984
Side Street and Other Stories (f Farrell) 1961
Sidnee Poet Heroical (pl Baraka) 1975
Sidney (f Deland) 1890
Sidonie, The Married Flirt (pl Kirkland) 1877
Siege of London, The Pension Beaurepas, and The Point of View (f H. James) 1883
Siesta in Xbalba and Return to the States (po Ginsberg) 1956
Sight (po Creeley) 1967

Sight (po Hejinian) 1999

Sight Unseen, and The Confession (f Rinehart) 1921

Sights and Spectacles 1937-1956 (o McCarthy) 1956

Sights and Spectacles: Theatre Chronicles 1937-1958 (o McCarthy) 1959

Sights Unseen (f Gibbons) 1995

Sign in Sidney Brustein's Window (pl Hansberry) 1965

Signature of All Things (po Rexroth) 1950

Signature to Petition on Ten Pound Island Asked of Me by Mr. Vincent Ferrini (po Olson) 1964

Signatus (o Mather) 1727

Significance of the Problem of Knowledge (o Dewey) 1897

Signifying Monkey: Towards a Theory of Afro-American Literary Criticism (o Gates) 1988

Signposts in a Strange Land (o Percy) 1991

Signs: A Poem (po Merwin) 1971

Silas Snobden's Office Boy (f Alger) 1973

Silence and Other Stories (f Freeman) 1898

Silence in the Snowy Fields (po Bly) 1962

Silence Now: New and Uncollected Earlier Poems (po Sarton) 1988

Silence of History (f Farrell) 1963

Silence of the Llano (f Anaya) 1982

Silences (o Olsen) 1978

Silent Dancing: A Partial Remembrance of a Puerto Rican Childhood (o Cofer) 1990

Silent Man (pl J. Miller) 1883

Silent Night, Lonely Night (pl R. Anderson) 1959

Silent Partner (pl Odets) 1972

Silent South (o Cable) 1885

Silent Speaker (f Stout) 1946

Silentiarius (o Mather) 1721

Silhouettes of American Life (f Rebecca Davis) 1892

Silk Stockings (pl Kaufman) 1955

Silver Bottle (f Ingraham) 1844

Silver Bullet (scr King) 1985

Silver Canyon (f L'Amour) 1956

Silver Cord (pl S. Howard) 1927

Silver Locusts (f Bradbury) 1951

Silver Pitchers, and Independence: A Centennial Love Story (f Alcott) 1876

Silver River (pl Hwang) 1997

Silver Ship of Mexico (f Ingraham) 1846

Silver Stallion (f Cabell) 1926

Silver Swan: Poems Written in Kyoto 1974-75 (po Rexroth) 1976

Silvered Rope (pl B. Smith) 1938

Simon (pl Hecht) 1962

Simon Wheeler, Detective (f Twain) 1963

Simpatico: A Play in Three Acts (pl Shepard) 1995

Simple Art of Murder (f Chandler) 1950

Simple Honorable Man (f Richter) 1962

Simple Life (pl Harrigan) 1905

Simple Speaks His Mind (f Hughes) 1950

Simple Stakes a Claim (f Hughes) 1957

Simple Takes a Wife (f Hughes) 1953

Simple's Uncle Sam (f Hughes) 1965

Simply Heavenly (pl Hughes) 1957

Sin of Madelon Claudet (The Lullaby) (scr MacArthur) 1931

Sinbad the Sailor (pl MacKaye) 1917

Since Ibsen: A Statistical Historical Outline of the Popular Theatre Since 1900 (o Nathan) 1933

Sincerely, Willis Wayde (f Marquand) 1955

Sincerity and Authenticity (o Trilling) 1972

Sincerity Forever (pl Wellman) 1990

Sinful Woman (f Cain) 1947

Sing All a Green Willow (pl Green) 1969

Sing, O Barren (o Dahlberg) 1947

Sing Sing (pl Harrigan) 1872

Sing to Me through Open Windows (pl Kopit) 1959

Singin' and Swingin' and Gettin' Merry Like Christmas (o Angelou) 1976

Singin' Billy (pl Davidson) 1952

Singing Jailbirds (pl Sinclair) 1924

Singing Steel (pl Hurston) 1934

Single Blessedness and Other Observations (f Ade) 1922

Single Hound (f Sarton) 1938

Single Man (f Isherwood) 1964

Single Rose: the Rose Unica and Commentary of Fray Manuel de Santa Clara (po Chávez) 1948

Singular Country (f Donleavy) 1990

Singular Man (f Donleavy) 1963

Singularities (po S. Howe) 1990

Sinister Sex and Other Stories of Marriage (f Hecht) 1927

Sink or Swim (f Alger) 1870

Sinner Sermons: A Selection of the Best Paragraphs of Howe (o E. Howe) 1926

Sinner's Place (pl Parks) 1984

Sinners in the Hands of an Angry God (o Edwards) 1741

Sinning with Annie and Other Stories (f Theroux) 1972

Sir Brasil's Falcon (po F. O'Brien) 1853

Sir Vidia's Shadow (o Theroux) 1998

Sir Walter Raleigh (o Thoreau) 1905

Sirens of Titan (f Vonnegut) 1959

Sissie (f J. Williams) 1963

Sister Carrie (f Dreiser) 1900

Sister Outsider: Essays and Speeches (o Lorde) 1984

Sister, Sister (tv Angelou) 1982

Sister's Sacrfice (pl Daly) 1891

Sisters (pl F. O'Brien) 1854

Sisters-in-Law: A Novel of Our Time (f Atherton) 1921

Sistine Eve and Other Poems (po MacKaye) 1915

Sitka (f L'Amour) 1957

Sitting Here (po Creeley) 1974

Sitting Pretty (scr S. Perelman) 1933

Situation of Poetry: Contemporary Poetry and Its Traditions (o Pinsky) 1977

6 A. M. (f Bodenheim) 1932

Six Degrees of Separation (pl Guare) 1990

Six Nights with the Washingtonians (f Arthur) 1842

Six Of One (f R Brown) 1978

Six-Piece Suite (po Ammons) 1979

Six Political Discourses Founded on the Scriptures (o Brackenridge) 1778

Six Sections from Mountains and Rivers without End (po Snyder) 1965

Six to One: A Nantucket Idyl (f Bellamy) 1878

Six Trees (f Freeman) 1903

Sixes and Sevens (f Henry) 1911

1601 (f Twain) 1939

Sixth Column (f Heinlein) 1949

Sixth Year (tv Chayefsky) 1953

Sixty Seconds (f Bodenheim) 1929

Sixty Years of Journalism (o Cain) 1986

63: Dream Palace (f Purdy) 1956
Skeeters Kirby (f Masters) 1923
Skeleton (tv Bradbury) 1988
Skeleton Crew (f King) 1985
Skepticism and Dissent: Selected Journalism, 1898-1901 (o Bierce) 1986
Sketch Book of Geoffrey Crayon, Gent (f W. Irving) 1819-20
Sketch of Old England by a New England Man (o Paulding) 1822
Sketch of the Early Life of Joseph Wood, Artist (o Paulding) 1834
Sketches (po Willis) 1827
Sketches from Real Life. I. The Power of Kindness. II. Home and Politics (f Child) 1850
Sketches in Prose and Occasional Verses (f Riley) 1891
Sketches of Life and Character (f Arthur) 1849
Sketches of Southern Life (po F. Harper) 1872
Sketches of Switzerland (o Cooper) 1836
Sketches of Switzerland, Part Second (o Cooper) 1836
Sketches of the Primitive Settlements on the River Delaware (o Barker) 1827
Sketches of the Sixties by Harte and Mark Twain from "The Californian" 1864-67 (o Harte) 1926
Sketches of the Valley and Other Works (f Hinojosa) 1980
Skidmores (pl Harrigan) 1874
Skin (o Allison) 1993
Skin and Bones (po P. Allen) 1988
Skin of Our Teeth (pl Wilder) 1942
Skin: Talking About Sex, Class, and Literature (o Allison) 1994
Skinny Island: More Tales of Manhattan (f Auchincloss) 1987
Skinwalkers (f Hillerman) 1986
Skippers of Nancy Gloucester (po MacKaye) 1924
Skippy (scr Marquis) 1931
Sky Devils (scr Benchley) 1932
Sky Is Gray (f Gaines) 1993
Sky Island (f Baum) 1912
Sky Sea Birds Trees Earth House Beasts Flowers (po Rexroth) 1970
Sky-Liners (f L'Amour) 1967
Skylight One: Fifteen Poems (po Aiken) 1949
Slabs of the Sunburnt West (po Sandburg) 1922
Slapstick (f Vonnegut) 1973
Slapstick Tragedy (pl T. Williams) 1966
Slaughter City (pl N. Wallace) 1996
Slaughter of the Innocents (pl Saroyan) 1957
Slaughterhouse-Five (f Vonnegut) 1969
Slave (pl Baraka) 1964
Slave (f Singer) 1962
Slave Girl (pl L. Mitchell) 1893
Slave King (f Ingraham) 1846
Slave Ship (scr Faulkner) 1937
Slave Ship: A Historical Pageant (pl Baraka) 1967
Slavery Days (pl Harrigan) 1875
Slavery in America, Being a Brief Review of Miss Martineau on That Subject (o Simms) 1838
Slavery in the United States (o Paulding) 1836
Slaves in Algiers (pl Rowson) 1794
Sleep Tight (f Purdy) 1979
Sleepers Awake (f Patchen) 1946
Sleepers Joining Hands (po Bly) 1973
Sleeping Beauty (f Macdonald) 1973
Sleeping Fires (f Atherton) 1922
Sleeping Fury (po Bogan) 1937
Sleeping with One Eye Open (po Strand) 1964

Sleeping-Car (pl Howells) 1883
Sleepwalkers (scr King) 1992
Slight Case of Murder (pl Runyon) 1940
Slightly Irregular Fire Engine (o Barthelme) 1971
Slim Princess (f Ade) 1907
Slipping-Down Life (f A. Tyler) 1970
Slouching towards Bethlehem (o Didion) 1968
Slow and Sure (f Alger) 1872
Slow Learner: Early Stories (f Pynchon) 1984
Slow Vision (f Bodenheim) 1934
Slowly, By Thy Hand Unfurled (f Linney) 1965
Slugger's Wife (scr Simon) 1985
Small Assassin (f Bradbury) 1962
Small Beer (o Bemelmans) 1939
Small Boy and Others (pl H. James) 1913
Small Craft Warnings (pl T. Williams) 1972
Small Faces (po Soto) 1986
Small Hours (pl Kaufman) 1951
Small Moment (po Nemerov) 1957
Small Room (f Sarton) 1961
Small Things (o Deland) 1919
Small War on Murray Hill (pl Sherwood) 1957
Smart Aleck Kill (f Chandler) 1953
Smart Set Criticism (o Mencken) 1968
Smart Set: Correspondence and Conversations (o Fitch) 1897
Smarty's Party (pl Kelly) 1923
Smash-Up—The Story of a Woman (scr Lawson; Parker) 1947
Smell of Fear (f Chandler) 1965
Smile (f Bradbury) 1991
Smile at the Foot of the Ladder (f H. Miller) 1948
Smire: An Acceptance in the Third Person (f Cabell) 1937
Smirt: An Urbane Nightmare (f Cabell) 1934
Smith: A Sylvan Interlude (f Cabell) 1935
Smithsonian Depositions, and Subject to a Film (po Coolidge) 1980
Smithsonian Institute (f Vidal) 1998
Smoke (tv Vidal) 1954
Smoke and Shorty (f London) 1920
Smoke and Steel (po Sandburg) 1920
Smoke Bellew (f London) 1912
Smoke from This Altar (po L'Amour) 1939
Smoke over the Prairie and Other Stories (f Richter) 1947
Smoke, Sound, and Fury: The Civil War Memoirs of Major-General Lew Wallace, U.S. Volunteers (o L. Wallace) 1998
Smoke's Way: Poems from Limited Editions (po W. Stafford) 1983
Smoking Car (pl Howells) 1900
Smoking Mountain: Stories of Postwar Germany (f Boyle) 1951
Smouldering Fires (scr Deland) 1925
Snake Pit (scr Laurents) 1948
Snapshots of a Daughter-in-Law: Poems, 1954-1962 (po Rich) 1963
Snare (f Spencer) 1972
Snarling Garland of Xmas Verses (po Creeley) 1954
Sniper (pl O'Neill) 1917
Snow Mountain (f Bemelmans) 1950
Snow Poems (po Ammons) 1977
Snow White (f Barthelme) 1967
Snow-Bound at Eagle's (f Harte) 1886
Snow-Bound: A Winter Idyl (po Whittier) 1866
Snow-Image and Other Twice-Told Tales (f Hawthorne) 1851
Snowfall (po Oates) 1978
Snowy Owl (po Eberhart) 1984

Snuggle Tales (f Baum) 1916-17
So (po Coolidge) 1971
So Big (f Ferber) 1924
So Little Time (f Marquand) 1943
So Red the Rose (scr M. Anderson) 1935
So the Wind Won't Blow It All Away (f Brautigan) 1982
So There, Poems 1976-1983 (po Creeley) 1998
Soak the Rich (scr Hecht; MacArthur) 1936
Social Evolution of the Black South (o Du Bois) 1911
Social Life in Old Virginia before the War (o Page) 1897
Social Principle: The True Source of National Permanence (o Simms) 1843
Social Remedies (o Cahan) 1889
Social Secretary (f D. Phillips) 1905
Social Significance of Modern Drama (o Goldman) 1914
Social Strugglers (f Boyesen) 1893
Social Swim (pl Fitch) 1893
Society and Solitude (o Emerson) 1870
Soft Machine (f W. Burroughs) 1961
Soft Machine, Nova Express, The Wild Boys (f W. Burroughs) 1980
Soft Shoulders (pl Morley) 1940
Soft Side (f H. James) 1900
Sojourner (tv McCullers) 1964
Sojourner (f Rawlings) 1953
Solar Barque (f Nin) 1958
Solar System and Back (o Asimov) 1970
Soldier (po Aiken) 1944
Soldier of '76 (pl Dunlap) 1801
Soldier Told What He Shall Do (o Mather) 1707
Soldiers of Fortune (f Richard Davis) 1897
Soldiers Tale (pl Shapiro) 1968
Soldiers' Pay (f Faulkner) 1926
Solid Gold Cadillac (pl Kaufman) 1954
Soliloquies in England and Later Soliloquies (o Santayana) 1922
Solitaire (pl Van Druten) 1942
Solitaire/Double Solitaire (pl R. Anderson) 1971
Solo: An American Dreamer in Europe 1933-34 (o Morris) 1983
Solstice (f Oates) 1985
Solution Passage: Poems, 1978-1981 (po Coolidge) 1986
Sombrero Fallout: A Japanese Novel (f Brautigan) 1976
Some Account of Inoculating the Small Pox (o Mather) 1721
Some Account of the Capture of the Ship Aurora (po Freneau) 1899
Some Adventures of Captain Simon Suggs (f Hooper) 1845
Some Americans Abroad (pl Nelson) 1989
Some Buried Caesar (f Stout) 1939
Some Came Running (f J. Jones) 1957
Some Can Whistle (f McMurtry) 1989
Some Champions: Sketches and Fiction (f Lardner) 1976
Some Chinese Ghosts (o Hearn) 1887
Some Communications of Broad Reference (o Riding) 1983
Some Considerations on the Bills of Credit (o Mather) 1691
Some Contemporary American Poets (o Fletcher) 1920
Some Correspondence and Six Conversations (o Fitch) 1896
Some Dangers in the Present Movement for Industrial Education (o Dewey) 1913
Some Day I'll Be a Millionaire: 34 More Great Stories (f Saroyan) 1943
Some Early Poems (po Olson) 1978
Some European Observations and Experiences (o Washington) 1900

Some Highways and Byways of American Travel (o Lanier) 1878
Some Honorable Men: Political Conventions 1960-1972 (o Mailer) 1976
Some Later Verses (po Harte) 1898
Some Live like Lazarus (tv Bradbury) 1992
Some Men (po Shange) 1981
Some New Letters and Writings (o Hearn) 1925
Some Notices of the Life and Writings of Fitz-Greene Halleck (o Bryant) 1869
Some of Our Neighbours (f Freeman) 1898
Some of the Reasons against Woman's Suffrage (o Parkman) 1883
Some of Us: An Essay in Epitaphs (o Cabell) 1930
Some Others and Myself: Seven Stories and a Memoir (f Suckow) 1952
Some People, Places, and Things That Will Not Appear in My Next Novel (f Cheever) 1961
Some Problems of Philosophy: A Beginning of an Introduction to Philosophy (o W. James) 1911
Some Putative Facts of Hard Record (o Cozzens) 1978
Some Seasonable Advice unto the Poor (o Mather) 1726
Some Slips Don't Show (f E. Gardner) 1957
Some Thoughts Concerning the Present Revival of Religion in New England (o Edwards) 1742
Some Time: Short Poems (po Zukofsky) 1956
Some Trees (po Ashbery) 1956
Some Turns of Thought in Modern Philosophy: Five Essays (o Santayana) 1933
Some Women Won't Wait (f E. Gardner) 1953
Somebody in Boots (f Algren) 1935
Somebody Knows (pl Van Druten) 1932
Somebody's Darling (f McMurtry) 1978
Someday, Maybe (po W. Stafford) 1973
Someday You'll Be Lying (po Kerouac) 1968
Someone Could Win a Polar Bear (po Ciardi) 1970
Someone in the House (pl Kaufman) 1918
Something about a Soldier (pl Saroyan) 1940
Something about Cats and Other Pieces (o Lovecraft) 1949
Something about Eve (f Cabell) 1927
Something Cloudy, Something Clear (pl T. Williams) 1981
Something Happened (f Heller) 1974
Something in Common and Other Stories (f Hughes) 1963
Something in the Wind (f L. Smith) 1971
Something to Say: Williams on Younger Poets (o W. Williams) 1985
Something To Remember Me By: Three Tales (f Bellow) 1992
Something Unspoken (pl T. Williams) 1953
Something Wicked This Way Comes (f Bradbury) 1962
Sometime (f Herrick) 1933
Sometimes a Great Notion (f Kesey) 1964
Sometimes Like a Legend (po W. Stafford) 1981
Somewhere among Us a Stone Is Taking Notes (po Simic) 1969
Somewhere in France (f Richard Davis) 1915
Son (pl Saroyan) 1950
Son at the Front (f Wharton) 1923
Son, Come Home (pl Bullins) 1968
Son of a Wanted Man (f L'Amour) 1984
Son of Man (radio MacLeish) 1947
Son of Old Harry (f Tourgée) 1892
Son of Perdition (f Cozzens) 1929
Son of Royal Langbrith (f Howells) 1904
Son of Tarzan (f E. Burroughs) 1917

Son of the Circus (f J. Irving) 1994
Son of the Gods, and A Horseman in the Sky (f Bierce) 1907
Son of the Morning (f Oates) 1978
Son of the Sun (f London) 1912
Son of the Wolf: Tales of the Far North (f London) 1900
Son-Daughter (pl Belasco) 1919
Song and Dance Man (pl Cohan) 1923
Song and Idea (po Eberhart) 1940
Song for Anninho (f G. Jones) 1981
Song for Gaia (po Snyder) 1979
Song for Simeon (po Eliot) 1928
Song in the Meadow (po Roberts) 1940
Song in the Wilderness (po Green) 1947
Song of El Coquí and Other Tales of Puerto Rico (f Mohr) 1995
Song of Francis (o Chávez) 1973
Song of Hiawatha (po Longfellow) 1855
Song of Solomon (f Morrison) 1977
Song of Songs (pl Sheldon) 1914
Song of the Border-Guard (po Duncan) 1952
Song of the Lark (f Cather) 1915
Song of the Vermonters (po Whittier) 1843
Song: A One Act Play about the Relationship of Art to Real Life
    (pl Baraka) 1983
Song: I Want a Witness (po M. Harper) 1972
Songs (po Harrigan) 1893
Songs and Other Poems (po Hoffman) 1846
Songs and Other Verse (po Field) 1896
Songs and Poems of the Class of 1829 (po Holmes) 1859
Songs and Satires (po Masters) 1916
Songs and Sonnets (po Masters) 1910-12
Songs at the Start (po Guiney) 1884
Songs for a Little House (po Morley) 1917
Songs for a Summer's Day (po MacLeish) 1915
Songs for Eve (po MacLeish) 1954
Songs for the Banjo (po Harrigan) 1888
Songs from Vagabondia (po Hovey) 1894
Songs o' Cheer (po Riley) 1905
Songs of a Day (po MacKaye) 1929
Songs of Far-Away Lands (po J. Miller) 1878
Songs of Father Goose (po Baum) 1900
Songs of Friendship (po Riley) 1915
Songs of Italy (po J. Miller) 1878
Songs of Jamaica (po McKay) 1912
Songs of Labor and Other Poems (po Whittier) 1850
Songs of Many Seasons (po Holmes) 1861
Songs of Our Nation (po Sinclair) 1941
Songs of the Mexican Seas (po J. Miller) 1887
Songs of the Redeemed: A Book of Hymns (o Mather) 1697
Songs of the Sierras (po J. Miller) 1871
Songs of the Soul (po J. Miller) 1896
Songs of the Sun-Lands (po J. Miller) 1873
Songs of Yesteryear (po Cohan) 1924
Songs to a Handsome Woman (po R Brown) 1973
Sonnen-Schöpfung: Indianische Legende (o Traven) 1936
Sonnet (po Lovecraft) 1936
Sonnets and Lyrics (po H. Jackson) 1886
Sonnets and Other Poems (po Hayne) 1857
Sonnets and Other Verses (po Santayana) 1894-96
Sonnets at Christmas (po A. Tate) 1941
Sonnets from Antan (po Cabell) 1929
Sonnets of Shakespeare: An Essay (o Donnelly) 1859

Sonnets to a Red-Haired Lady (from a Gentleman with a Blue
    Beard) and Famous Love Affairs (po Marquis) 1922
Sonnets to an Imaginary Madonna (po Fisher) 1927
Sonnets to Duse and Other Poems (po Teasdale) 1907
Sonnets: A Sequence of Profane Love (po Boker) 1929
Sons (f Buck) 1932
Sons of Darkness, Sons of Light: A Novel of Some Probability (f
    J. Williams) 1969
Sons of Liberty (f Ingraham) 1887
Sons of Spain (pl S. Howard) 1914
Sons of the Puritans (f Marquis) 1939
Sons of Usna: A Tragi-Apotheosis (pl Chivers) 1858
Son's Return: Selected Essays of Sterling A. Brown (o S. Brown)
    1996
Sophie's Choice (f Styron) 1979
Sophisticates (f Atherton) 1931
Soprano: A Portrait (f Crawford) 1905
Sor Juana and Other Plays (pl Portillo Trambley) 1983
Sorcerer's Apprentice: Tales and Conjuration (f C. Johnson) 1988
Sorceress (pl Daly) 1864
Sorrow and the Terror (o Mukherjee) 1987
Sorrow Dance (po Levertov) 1967
Sorrows of Frederick (pl Linney) 1966
Sorrows of Priapus (o Dahlberg) 1957
Sorties (o Dickey) 1971
Sot-Weed Factor (f Barth) 1960
Sot-Weed Factor (po E. Cooke) 1708
Sotweed Redivivus (po E. Cooke) 1730
Soul and Body of John Brown (po Rukeyser) 1940
Soul Clap Hands and Sing (f Marshall) 1961
Soul Looks Back in Wonder (po Angelou) 1994
Soul-Mate (f Oates) 1989
Soul of Melicent (f Cabell) 1913
Soul Survivor: Bits of Autobiography (o Bierce) 1998
Souls of Black Folk: Essays and Sketches (o Du Bois) 1903
Souls of Black Folk: Authoritative Text, Contexts, Criticism (o
    Gates) 1999
Souls Raised from the Dead (f Betts) 1994
Sound and the Fury (f Faulkner) 1929
Sound of a City (f Farrell) 1962
Sound of a Voice (pl Hwang) 1984
Sound of Falling Light: Letters in Exile (o Bulosan) 1960
Sound of Murder (f Fearing) 1952
Sound of Murder (f Stout) 1965
Sound of Rowlocks (f Steele) 1938
Sound of Thunder (tv Bradbury) 1989
Sound Wagon (f Stribling) 1935
Soundings from the Atlantic (o Holmes) 1863
Sounds of Poetry (o Pinsky) 1998
Sour Grapes (po W. Williams) 1921
Source of Embarrassment (f McCarthy) 1950
Sources (po Rich) 1983
Sources of a Science of Education (o Dewey) 1929
Sources of American Independence (o Simms) 1844
Sours of the Hills (po Snyder) 1969
South Moon Under (f Rawlings) 1933
South of the Angels (f J. West) 1960
South Sea Tales (f London) 1911
South Star (po Fletcher) 1941
South-Carolina in the Revolutionary War (o Simms) 1853
South-West (o Ingraham) 1835

Southern Cross (pl Green) 1936
Southern Discomfort (f R Brown) 1982
Southern Light (o Dickey) 1991
Southern Passages and Pictures (po Simms) 1839
Southern Road (po S. Brown) 1932
Southern Writers in the Modern World (o Davidson) 1958
Southerner Looks at Negro Discrimination: Selected Writings (o Cable) 1946
Southerners and Europeans: Essays in a Time of Disorder (o Lytle) 1988
Southward Ho! A Spell of Sunshine (f Simms) 1854
Souvenir (f Dell) 1929
Souvenir (pl Green) 1919
Souvenir from Qam (f Connelly) 1965
Souvenirs (po Merrill) 1984
Soveraignty and Goodness of God, Together with the Faithfulness of His Promises Displayed; Being a Narrative of the Captivity and Restauration of Mrs. Mary Rowlandson (o Rowlandson) 1682
Sowing and Reaping (o Washington) 1900
Space (po Coolidge) 1970
Space Cadet (f Heinlein) 1948
Space Family Stone (f Heinlein) 1969
Spain (pl Linney) 1993
Spain and Her Colonies (o Saltus) 1898
Spain in Flames (scr Hemingway) 1937
Spanish Bayonet (f S. Benét) 1926
Spanish Blood (f Chandler) 1946
Spanish Cape Mystery (f Queen) 1935
Spanish Earth (scr Hemingway) 1937
Spanish Galleon (f Ingraham) 1844
Spanish Husband (pl Payne) 1830
Spanish Love (pl Rinehart) 1920
Spanish Prisoner (pl Mamet) 1985
Spanish Student (pl Longfellow) 1843
Spanking the Maid (f Coover) 1982
Spark in the Tinder of Knowing (po Rexroth) 1968
Sparks Fly Upward (f La Farge) 1931
Sparrow's Fall and Other Poems (po F. Harper) 1894
Spartanburg Female College (o Simms) 1855
Speak Now (f Yerby) 1969
Speakin' o' Christmas and Other Christmas and Special Poems (po Dunbar) 1914
Speaking of Literature and Society (o Trilling) 1980
Speaking of Race: Hate Speech, Civil Rights, and Civil Liberties (o Gates) 1995
Speaking to Father (pl Ade) 1923
Spearmint and Rosemary (po Olson) 1979
Special Announcement (pl Saroyan) 1940
Special Delivery (tv Bradbury) 1959
Special Delivery: A Packet of Replies (o Cabell) 1933
Special Delivery: A Useful Book for Brand-New Mothers (o S. Jackson) 1960
Special View of History (o Olson) 1970
Specimen Days and Collect (o Whitman) 1882
Specimen Days in America (o Whitman) 1887
Specimens (po J. Miller) 1868
Spectacles (o Beattie) 1985
Spectator Bird (f Stegner) 1976
Specter of the Rose (scr Hecht) 1946
Spectre of Power (f Murfree) 1903

Spectre Steamer and Other Tales (f Ingraham) 1846
Speeches in Stirring Times, and Letters to a Son (o Dana) 1910
Speed of Darkness (po Rukeyser) 1968
Speed-the-Plow (pl Mamet) 1988
Spellbinder (scr Benchley) 1928
Spellbound (scr Hecht) 1945
Spence + Lila (f Mason) 1988
Sphere: The Form of a Motion (po Ammons) 1974
Sphinx (pl MacKaye) 1929
Spider Boy: A Scenario for a Moving Picture (f Van Vechten) 1928
Spider's House (f Bowles) 1955
Spik in Glyph? (po Alurista) 1981
Spill the Jackpot! (f E. Gardner) 1941
Spillway (f Barnes) 1962
Spin a Soft Black Song: Poems for Children (po Giovanni) 1971
Spinning the Crystal Ball: Some Guesses at the Future of American Poetry (o Dickey) 1967
Spinning-Wheel Stories (f Alcott) 1884
Spinoza of Market Street and Other Stories (f Singer) 1961
Spiral of Memory: Interviews (o Harjo) 1996
Spirit Level and Other Poems (po Morley) 1946
Spirit of Culver (scr N. West) 1939
Spirit of Sweetwater (f Garland) 1898
Spirit of the Border (f Grey) 1906
Spirit of the Scene (po W. Benét) 1951
Spirit Photography (o Hearn) 1933
Spirit Reach (po Baraka) 1972
Splendid Idle Forties: Stories of Old California (f Atherton) 1902
Splendor (scr Crothers) 1935
Splendor in the Grass (scr Inge) 1961
Split Images (f Leonard) 1981
Spoil of Office (f Garland) 1892
Spoils of Poynton (f H. James) 1897
Spoon River Anthology (po Masters) 1915
Sport of the Gods (f Dunbar) 1902
Sport Parade (scr Benchley) 1932
Sportswriter (f Ford) 1986
Spreading Fires (f Knowles) 1974
Spring and All (po W. Williams) 1923
Spring and So forth (po Baraka) 1960
Spring Birth and Other Poems (po Van Doren) 1953
Spring Cleaning, as Told by Queen Crosspatch (f Burnett) 1908
Spring Concert (f Tarkington) 1916
Spring Dance (pl Barry) 1936
Spring Drawing (po Hass) 1988
Spring in New Hampshire and Other Poems (po McKay) 1920
Spring Song (o Baraka) 1979
Spring Song (pl T. Williams) 1938
Spring Thunder and Other Poems (po Van Doren) 1924
Spring Trio (po Updike) 1982
Springtime (pl Tarkington) 1909
Springtime and Harvest: A Romance (f Sinclair) 1901
Spy (f Sinclair) 1919
Spy in the House of Love (f Nin) 1954
Spy: A Tale of the Neutral Ground (f Cooper) 1821
Spyglass: Views and Reviews 1924-1930 (o Davidson) 1963
Square Root of Wonderful (pl McCullers) 1958
Squatter Sovereignty (pl Harrigan) 1881
Squirrels (pl Mamet) 1974
St. Gaudens Masque-Prologue (pl MacKaye) 1905
St. George and the Godfather (o Mailer) 1972

St. Johns: A Parade of Diversities, H. L (o Cabell) 1943
St. Louis Woman (pl Cullen) 1946
St. Louis: A Civic Pageant (pl MacKaye) 1914
St. Martin's (po Creeley) 1971
St. Patrick's Day Parade (pl Harrigan) 1873
Stag at Bay (pl MacArthur) 1976
Stage Door (pl Ferber; Kaufman) 1936
Stage Door (tv Vidal) 1955
Stagecraft: The Adventures of a Strictly Moral Man (pl Baum) 1914
Stairs of Sand (f Grey) 1943
Stairs to the Roof (pl T. Williams) 1947
Stairway of Surprise (po W. Benét) 1947
Stallion Gate (f M. Smith) 1986
Stallion Road: A Screenplay (pl Faulkner) 1989
Stand (f King) 1978
Stand Up and Fight (scr Cain) 1939
Standard Dreaming (f Calisher) 1972
Standard of Liberty (o Brackenridge) 1802
Standard of Liberty: A Poetical Address (po Rowson) 1795
Standards (pl Lawson) 1916
Standing Still and Walking in New York (o F. O'Hara) 1975
Stanley Elkin's Magic Kingdom (f Elkin) 1985
Star Beast (f Heinlein) 1954
Star Is Born (scr Didion) 1976
Star Is Born (scr Hart) 1954
Star Is Born (scr Parker) 1937
Star of Araby (po Markham) 1937
Star of Ethiopia (pl Du Bois) 1913
Star Pit (radio S. Delany) 1972
Star Pit (f S. Delany) 1989
Star Rover (f London) 1915
Star Spangled Rhythm (scr Kaufman) 1942
Star-Spangled Girl (pl Simon) 1966
Star-Wagon (pl M. Anderson) 1937
Starcarbon: A Meditation on Love (f Gilchrist) 1994
Starluster (pl Wellman) 1979
Starman Jones (f Heinlein) 1953
Starry Harness (po W. Benét) 1933
Starry Place between the Antlers: Why I Live in South Carolina (o Dickey) 1981
Stars (po Jeffers) 1930
Stars in My Pocket Like Grains of Sand (f S. Delany) 1984
Stars in Their Courses (o Asimov) 1971
Stars, Like Dust— (f Asimov) 1951
Stars To-Night: Verses New and Old for Boys and Girls (po Teasdale) 1930
Stars: A Slumber Story (f Field) 1901
Starship Troopers (f Heinlein) 1959
Start in Life (pl Green) 1941
Start with the Sun: Studies in Cosmic Poetry (o Shapiro) 1960
Starting from San Francisco (po Ferlinghetti) 1961
Starting From Scratch: A Different Kind of Writers' Manual (o R Brown) 1988
Starved Rock (po Masters) 1919
State Fair (scr Green) 1933
State of Nature (f Goodman) 1946
State of Stony Lonesome (f J. West) 1984
State of the Nation (o Dos Passos) 1944
State of the Novel: Dying Art or New Science (o Percy) 1988
State Versus Elinor Norton (f Rinehart) 1934

Statement (po Boyle) 1932
States of Shock (pl Shepard) 1991
States of Shock, Far North, Silent Tongue (scr Shepard) 1993
States Talking (pl MacLeish) 1941
Station YYYY (pl Tarkington) 1927
Stations of the Air (po Ciardi) 1993
Stay with Me Flagons (f Ade) 1922
Steel Belt (f Ingraham) 1844
Steeple Bush (po Frost) 1947
Steeplejack (o Huneker) 1920
Stein on Picasso (o Stein) 1970
Steinbeck Pocket Book (o Steinbeck) 1943
Steinbeck Replies (o Steinbeck) 1940
Steinbeck: A Life in Letters (o Steinbeck) 1975
Steinway Collection of Paintings by American Artists (o Huneker) 1919
Stella (pl Kushner) 1987
Step-Father (f Oates) 1978
Stephen Crane (o Berryman) 1950
Stephen Crane: The Red Badge of Courage (o Berryman) 1981
Stephen Foster Story: A Symphonic Drama Based on the Life and Music of the Composer (pl Green) 1960
Stephen King's Creep Show (scr King) 1982
Stephen Vincent Benét: My Brother Steve (o W. Benét) 1943
Steps (f Kosinski) 1968
Sterne's Maria (pl Dunlap) 1799
Steve and Velma (pl Bullins) 1980
Stewed, Fried and Boiled (scr Benchley) 1929
Stick (f Leonard) 1983
Still Alarm (pl Kaufman) 1929
Still Another Pelican in the Breadbox (po Patchen) 1980
Still Life with Watermelon (f Mason) 1998
Still More Lecherous Limericks (po Asimov) 1977
Still Rebels, Still Yankees, and Other Essays (o Davidson) 1957
Stillness, and Shadows (f J. Gardner) 1986
Stillwell and the American Experience in China, 1911-1945 (o Tuchman) 1971
Stitch in Time (pl Connelly) 1981
Stocking Cap: A Story (f Olson) 1966
Stoic (f Dreiser) 1947
Stolen Past (f Knowles) 1983
Stolen White Elephant (f Twain) 1882
Stolen Wife (f Arthur) 1843
Stone, A Leaf, A Door (po Thomas [Clayton] Wolfe) 1945
Stone Cut Out from the Mountain/Lapis e Monte Excisus (o Mather) 1716
Stone Orchard (po Oates) 1980
Stones of Florence (o McCarthy) 1959
Stonewall Jackson and the Old Stonewall Brigade (o J. Cooke) 1954
Stonewall Jackson: A Military Biography (o J. Cooke) 1866
Stop at the Red Light (f E. Gardner) 1962
Stop-Light: 5 Dance Poems (pl Goodman) 1941
Stopover: Tokyo (f Marquand) 1957
Stopped Rocking (tv T. Williams) 1975
Stops of Various Quills (po Howells) 1895
Store (f Stribling) 1932
Store Boy (f Alger) 1887
Stories (f Cheever) 1956
Stories (f Fitzgerald) 1951
Stories (f Malamud) 1983

Stories (f J. Stafford) 1956

Stories about Our Dogs (o Stowe) 1865

Stories by the Man Nobody Knows: Nine Tales (f Traven) 1961

Stories for Boys (f Richard Davis) 1891

Stories for My Young Friends (f Arthur) 1848-51

Stories for Young Persons (f Sedgwick) 1840

Stories from History (f Ade) 1896

Stories in Light and Shadow (f Harte) 1898

Stories of American Life and Adventures: Third Reader Grade (o Eggleston) 1895

Stories of Bradbury (f Bradbury) 1980

Stories of China (f Buck) 1964

Stories of Elizabeth Spencer (f Spencer) 1981

Stories of Great Americans for Little Americans: Second Reader Grade (o Eggleston) 1895

Stories of Hawaii (f London) 1965

Stories of Love (f Nin) 1996

Stories of the Old Dominion from the Settlement to the End of the Revolution (f J. Cooke) 1879

Stories of the Sierras and Other Sketches (f Harte) 1872

Stories of the Street and of the Town (f Ade) 1894-1900

Stories Revived (f H. James) 1885

Stories, Storms, and Strangers (po W. Stafford) 1984

Stories That Could Be True: New and Collected Poems (po W. Stafford) 1977

Stories with a Moral, Humorous and Descriptive of Southern Life a Century Ago (f Longstreet) 1912

Stories: Alchemy and Others (f Lytle) 1984

Stork (pl Hecht) 1925

Storm (f Steele) 1914

Storm Centre (f Murfree) 1905

Storm in the West (pl Lewis) 1963

Storm Operation (pl M. Anderson) 1944

Story Book (f Arthur) 1843

Story for Strangers (pl Connelly) 1948

Story of a Child (f Deland) 1892

Story of a Country Town (f E. Howe) 1883

Story of a Mine (f Harte) 1877

Story of a Novel (o Thomas [Clayton] Wolfe) 1936

Story of a Play (f Howells) 1898

Story of a Story & Three Stories (f J. West) 1982

Story of a Thousand, Being a History of the 105th Volunteer Infantry, 1862 to 1865 (o Tourgée) 1896

Story of a Wonder Man (o Lardner) 1927

Story of Benjamin Franklin (o Du Bois) 1956

Story of Boon (f H. Jackson) 1874

Story of Chicago (o Kirkland) 1892-94

Story of Duciehurst: A Tale of the Mississippi (f Murfree) 1914

Story of Gus (pl A. Miller) 1947

Story of Keedon Bluffs (f Murfree) 1887

Story of Kennett (f B. Taylor) 1866

Story of My Life and Work (o Washington) 1900

Story of Norway (o Boyesen) 1886

Story of Old Fort Loudon (f Murfree) 1899

Story of Our Lives (po Strand) 1973

Story of Ruth (o Asimov) 1972

Story of Slavery (o Washington) 1913

Story of the Negro (o Washington) 1909

Story of the Normans (o Jewett) 1887

Story on Page One (scr Odets) 1960

Story Teller's Story (o S. Anderson) 1924

Storyteller (f Silko) 1981

Storyville (pl Bullins) 1977

Stowaway in the Sky (scr Behrman) 1962

Stradella: An Old Italian Love Tale (f Crawford) 1909

Straight Ahead (f Alger) 1891

Straight Deal (o Wister) 1920

Straight Hearts' Delight: Love Poems and Selected Letters 1947-1980 (po Ginsberg) 1980

Straight Road (pl Fitch) 1907

Strange Case of Miss Annie Spragg (f Bromfield) 1928

Strange Children (f Gordon) 1951

Strange Feet (pl Wellman) 1993

Strange Interlude (pl O'Neill) 1928

Strange Moon (f Stribling) 1929

Strange New Cottage in Berkeley (po Ginsberg) 1963

Strange True Stories of Louisiana (f Cable) 1889

Strange Victory (po Teasdale) 1933

Stranger (pl Dunlap) 1798

Stranger and Alone (o Redding) 1950

Stranger at Coney Island and Other Poems (po Fearing) 1948

Stranger from the Tonto (f Grey) 1956

Stranger in a Strange Land (f Heinlein) 1961

Stranger in Lowell (po Whittier) 1845

Stranger in Shakespeare (o Fiedler) 1972

Stranger on Horseback (scr L'Amour) 1955

Stranger's Birthday (pl Dunlap) 1800

Stranger's Pew (f Page) 1914

Strangers and Wayfarers (f Jewett) 1890

Strangers on a Train (scr Chandler) 1951

Strangest Kind of Romance (pl T. Williams) 1946

Stranglers of Paris (pl Belasco) 1881

Strategy and Tactics of a Pan African Nationalist Party (o Baraka) 1971

Straw (pl O'Neill) 1921

Straw for the Fire: From the Notebooks 1943-1963 (o Roethke) 1972

Straws and Prayer-Books (o Cabell) 1924

Stray Leaves from Strange Literature (o Hearn) 1884

Stream and the Sapphire: Selected Poems on Religious Themes (po Levertov) 1997

Street (f Petry) 1946

Street in Bronzeville (po Brooks) 1945

Street of Seven Stars (f Rinehart) 1914

Street Scene (pl Hughes) 1947

Street Scene (pl Rice) 1929

Street Scene (scr Rice) 1931

Street Sounds (pl Bullins) 1970

Street Where the Heart Lies (f Bemelmans) 1963

Streetcar Named Desire (pl T. Williams) 1947

Streets in the Moon (po MacLeish) 1926

Streets of Chance (f W. Burroughs) 1981

Streets of Durham (pl Thomas [Clayton] Wolfe) 1982

Streets of Laredo (f McMurtry) 1993

Streets of Night (f Dos Passos) 1923

Street's Kiss (po Ferlinghetti) 1998

Strength of Fields (po Dickey) 1977

Strength of Gideon and Other Stories (f Dunbar) 1900

Strength of the Strong (f London) 1911

Strictly Business: More Stories of the Four Million (f Henry) 1910

Strictly from Hunger (o S. Perelman) 1937

Strike at Tivoh Mills and What Came of It (f Arthur) 1879

Strike Up the Band (pl Kaufman) 1930

Striking In: The Early Notebooks of James Dickey (o Dickey) 1996

String (pl Childress) 1969

String Too Short to Be Saved (o Hall) 1961

Strive and Succeed (f Alger) 1872

Striving for Fortune (f Alger) 1901

Strollin' Twenties (tv Hughes) 1966

Strong and Steady (f Alger) 1871

Strong Hearts (f Cable) 1899

Strong Light of the Canonical: Kafka, Freud, and Scholem as Revisionists of Jewish Culture and Thought (o Bloom) 1987

Strong Rod Broken and Withered (o Edwards) 1748

Strong Shall Live (f L'Amour) 1980

Structure and Artifacts: Photographs 1933-1954 (o Morris) 1975

Structure of Rime XXVIII: In Memoriam Wallace Stevens (po Duncan) 1972

Struggles (Social, Financial and Political) of Petroleum V. Nasby (f Nasby) 1872

Struggling Upward (f Alger) 1890

Stuart Little (f White) 1945

Stubbornness of Geraldine (pl Fitch) 1906

Studies in German Literature (o B. Taylor) 1879

Studies in Logical Theory (o Dewey) 1903

Studies in the South and West (o Warner) 1889

Studies of Dylan Thomas, Allen Ginsberg, Sylvia Plath, and Robert Lowell (o Simpson) 1979

Studs Lonigan (f Farrell) 1935

Study in Dissent: The Warren-Gerry Correspondence (o M. Warren) 1968

Study in Terror (f Queen) 1966

Study of Ethics: A Syllabus (o Dewey) 1894

Study of Prison Reform (o Warner) 1886

Style's a Man (o Auchincloss) 1994

Subatomic Monster (o Asimov) 1985

Subterraneans (f Kerouac) 1958

Subway (pl Rice) 1929

Subway Circus (pl Saroyan) 1940

Success at Any Price (scr Lawson) 1934

Success Easier Than Failure (o E. Howe) 1917

Success Story (pl Lawson) 1932

Successful Life of Three: A Skit for Vaudeville (pl Fornés) 1965

Successful Love and Other Stories (f Schwartz) 1961

Such a Charming Young Man: Comedy in One Act (pl Akins) 1924

Such Counsels You Gave to Me and Other Poems (po Jeffers) 1937

Such Things Only Happen in Books (pl Wilder) 1931

Sud Linchom (f McKay) 1925

Sudden Death (f R Brown) 1983

Sudden Shower (pl Daly) 1886

Suddenly Last Summer (scr Vidal; T. Williams) 1959

Sue (pl Harte) 1902

Suffrage Songs and Verses (po Gilman) 1911

Suicide (pl Nelson) 1980

Suicide in B Flat (pl Shepard) 1976

Suicide or Murder? The Strange Death of Governor Meriwether Lewis (o Fisher) 1962

Suite V (po Coolidge) 1973

Sula (f Morrison) 1973

Sullivan County Sketches (f S. Crane) 1949

Sullivan's Christmas (pl Harrigan) 1877

Sultan of Sulu (pl Ade) 1903

Sumerian Vistas (po Ammons) 1987

Summary View of the Rights of British America (o Jefferson) 1774

Summer (f Wharton) 1917

Summer and Smoke (pl T. Williams) 1947

Summer Brave (pl Inge) 1962

Summer Comes to the Diamond O (pl B. Smith) 1940

Summer Day (f Deland) 1889

Summer in Arcady: A Tale of Nature (f J. Allen) 1896

Summer Kitchen: Poems (o Gilbert and Gubar) 1983

Summer Knowledge: New and Selected Poems 1938-1958 (po Schwartz) 1959

Summer Life (po Soto) 1990

Summer Never Ends (f Frank) 1941

Summer Pavilion (tv Vidal) 1955

Summer Poems 1969 (po Levertov) 1970

Summons (po Dickey) 1988

Sun Also Rises (f Hemingway) 1926

Sun and Shadow (f Bradbury) 1957

Sun Dial Time (f Marquis) 1936

Sun Do Move (pl Hughes) 1942

Sun Hunting: Adventures and Observations among the Native and Migratory Tribes of Florida (o Roberts) 1922

Sun Images (pl Portillo Trambley) 1976

Sun Is So Quiet (po Giovanni) 1996

Sun Moon Star (o Vonnegut) 1980

Sun Shines Bright (o Asimov) 1980

Sun under Wood: New Poems (po Hass) 1996

Sunday Dinner (pl Oates) 1970

Sunday School Conventions and Institutes (o Eggleston) 1867

Sundial (f S. Jackson) 1958

Sundog: The Story of an American Foreman, Robert Corvus Strang (f Harrison) 1984

Sunlight Dialogues (f J. Gardner) 1972

Sunny Memories of Foreign Lands (o Stowe) 1854

Sunny South (f Ingraham) 1860

Sunny-San (f Eaton) 1922

Sunpapers of Baltimore 1837-1937 (o Mencken) 1937

Sunrise in Suburbia (po Ashbery) 1968

Sunrise with Seamonsters: Travels and Discoveries 1964-1984 (o Theroux) 1985

Sunset Gun (po Parker) 1928

Sunset Pass (f Grey) 1931

Sunshine Boys (pl Simon) 1972

Sunshine Is an Only Child (po Purdy) 1973

Supercoon (scr Baraka) 1971

Superfluous Husband (pl Fitch) 1897

Superman (scr Puzo) 1978

Superman II (scr Puzo) 1981

Supernatural Horror in Literature (o Lovecraft) 1945

Supernaturalism of New England (o Whittier) 1847

Supernumerary Crisis (o Paine) 1783

Superstition (pl Barker) 1826

Superstitions (pl Shepard) 1983

Supper for the Dead (pl Green) 1928

Suppressed Desires (pl Glaspell) 1915

Suppression of African Slave-Trade to the United States of America 1638-1870 (o Du Bois) 1896

Surf Skiff or, The Heroines of the Kennebec (f Ingraham) 1847

Surly Tim and Other Stories (f Burnett) 1877

Surprise for the Bagpipe Player (po Patchen) 1956

Surprising Adventures of the Magical Monarch of Mo (f Baum) 1903

Surprising J.A. (pl F. O'Hara) 1974

Surrender (scr Behrman) 1931

Surrender to the Enemy (pl Green) 1917

Surrounded (f McNickle) 1936

Surry of Eagle's-Nest (f J. Cooke) 1866

Survey of Modernist Poetry (o Riding) 1927

Survivor and Others (f Lovecraft) 1957

Survivors (po Eberhart) 1979

Susan and God (pl Crothers) 1937

Susan Lenox: Her Fall and Rise (f D. Phillips) 1917

Suspect in Poetry (o Dickey) 1964

Suspended Drawing Room (o Behrman) 1965

Suspiria Vinctorum (o Mather) 1726

Susy: A Story of the Plains (f Harte) 1893

Sut Lovingood: Travels with Old Abe Lincoln (o Harris) 1937

Sut Lovingood: Yarns Spun by a "Nat'ral Born Durn'd Fool: Warped and Wove for Public Wear." (o Harris) 1867

Suzy (scr Parker) 1936

Swag (f Leonard) 1976

Swallow Barn (f Kennedy) 1832

Swan Song (pl Hecht; MacArthur) 1946

Swearing Off and Other Tales (f Arthur) 1843

Sweat (f Hurston) 1997

Sweeney Agonistes: Fragments of an Aristophanic Melodrama (pl Eliot) 1933

Sweeney in the Trees (pl Saroyan) 1940

Sweet and Twenty (pl Dell) 1921

Sweet as a Pickle and Clean as a Pig (po McCullers) 1964

Sweet Bird of Youth (pl T. Williams) 1956

Sweet Bye and Bye (pl Nash; S. Perelman) 1946

Sweet Charity (pl Simon) 1966

Sweet Devouring (o Welty) 1969

Sweet Enemy (pl Oates) 1965

Sweet Flypaper of Life (o Hughes) 1955

Sweet Kitty Bellairs (pl Belasco) 1903

Sweet Smell of Success (scr Odets) 1957

Sweet Thursday (f Steinbeck) 1954

Sweet William: A Memoir of Old Horse (f Hawkes) 1993

Sweethearts (scr Parker) 1938

Sweethearts (f J. Phillips) 1976

Sweethearts and Wives (f Arthur) 1843

Swimmers and Other Selected Poems (po A. Tate) 1970

Swimming Pool (f Rinehart) 1952

Swing Time at the Savoy (radio Hughes) 1949

Swingin' round the Cirkle (f Nasby) 1867

Swiss Family Manhattan (f Morley) 1932

Swiss Family Perelman (o S. Perelman) 1950

Switch (f Leonard) 1978

Swoop (pl Wellman) 1994

Sword and the Distaff, or, "Fair, Fat and Forty (f Simms) 1852

Sword Blades and Poppy Seed (po A. Lowell) 1914

Sword of Youth (f J. Allen) 1915

Swords (pl S. Howard) 1921

Swords of Mars (f E. Burroughs) 1936

Sybil (f Auchincloss) 1952

Sycamores (po Whittier) 1857

Sylvia (f Sinclair) 1913

Sylvia's Lovers (pl Belasco) 1875(?)

Sylvia's Marriage (f Sinclair) 1914

Sylvian: A Tragedy, and Poems (po L. Mitchell) 1885

Symptoms of Being 35 (o Lardner) 1921

Synthetic Men of Mars (f E. Burroughs) 1940

T. Tembarom (f Burnett) 1913

Tabloid News (f Bromfield) 1930

Taboo (f Steele) 1925

Taboo: A Legend Retold from the Dirghic of Saevius Nicanor (o Cabell) 1921

Tacey Cromwell (f Richter) 1942

Taggart (f L'Amour) 1959

Tahiti: Memoirs of Arii Taimai (o Adams) 1947

Tailor's Apprentice: A Story of Cruelty and Oppression (f Arthur) 1843

Take a Dream (pl Guare) 1978

Take It Easy (f Runyon) 1938

Taking of Miss Janie (pl Bullins) 1975

Taking Off (pl Guare) 1971

Taking Sides (po Soto) 1991

Tale for the Mirror: A Novella and Other Stories (f Calisher) 1962

Tale of a Lonely Parish (f Crawford) 1886

Tale of Sunlight (po Soto) 1978

Tale of Two Cities (scr Behrman) 1935

Tale of Valor: A Novel of the Lewis and Clark Expedition (f Fisher) 1958

Tales (f Poe) 1845

Tales and Sketches (f Sedgwick) 1835-44

Tales Before Midnight (f S. Benét) 1939

Tales for Fifteen (f Cooper) 1823

Tales from a Rolltop Desk (f Morley) 1921

Tales from Balzac (o Saltus) 1909

Tales from Real Life (f Arthur) 1845

Tales from Two Hemispheres (f Boyesen) 1876

Tales of a Traveller (f W. Irving) 1824

Tales of a Wayside Inn (po Longfellow) 1863

Tales of Adventure (f London) 1956

Tales of Burning Love (f Erdrich) 1996

Tales of Chicago Streets (f Hecht) 1924

Tales of City Life (f Sedgwick) 1850

Tales of Domestic Life (f Arthur) 1850

Tales of Manhattan (f Auchincloss) 1967

Tales of Manhattan (scr Hecht) 1942

Tales of Men and Ghosts (f Wharton) 1910

Tales of Neveryon (f S. Delany) 1979

Tales of New England (f Jewett) 1890

Tales of Soldiers and Civilians (f Bierce) 1891

Tales of the Argonauts and Other Sketches (f Harte) 1875

Tales of the Black Widowers (f Asimov) 1974

Tales of the Fish Patrol (f London) 1905

Tales of the Good Woman (f Paulding) 1829

Tales of the Grotesque and Arabesque (f Poe) 1840

Tales of the Jazz Age (f Fitzgerald) 1922

Tales of Three Cities (f H. James) 1884

Tales of Three Planets (f E. Burroughs) 1964

Tales of Trail and Town (f Harte) 1898

Tales of Yesteryear (f Auchincloss) 1994

Tales Out of School, Selected Interviews (o Creeley) 1993

Taliesin: A Masque (pl Hovey) 1899

Talifer (po Robinson) 1933

Talisman (f King) 1984

Talk from the Fifties (o Updike) 1979

Talk of New York (pl Cohan) 1907

Talk to Me Like the Rain and Let Me Listen (pl T. Williams) 1953

Talking Dog (pl Guare) 1985

Talking God (f Hillerman) 1989

Talking Horse: Bernard Malamud on Life and Work (o Malamud) 1996

Talking to You (pl Saroyan) 1942

Talks on Nationalism (o Bellamy) 1938

Talks to Teachers on Psychology, and to Students on Some of Life's Ideals (o W. James) 1899

Tall Houses in Winter (f Betts) 1958

Tall Men (po Davidson) 1927

Tall Story (pl Nemerov) 1990

Tall Stranger (f L'Amour) 1957

Tall Tales of the Kentucky Mountains (f MacKaye) 1926

Tallahassee (pl Wellman) 1991

Talley Method (pl Behrman) 1941

Tally-Ho! (pl J. Miller) 1883

Tama (f Eaton) 1910

Tamar and Other Poems (po Jeffers) 1924

Tamawaca Folks (f Baum) 1907

Tambourines to Glory (pl Hughes) 1963

Tamerlane and Other Poems (po Poe) 1827

Taming a Butterfly (pl Daly) 1867

Taming of Helen (pl Richard Davis) 1903

Taming of the Shrew (pl Daly) 1887

Tampico (f Hergesheimer) 1926

Tanar of Pellucidar (f E. Burroughs) 1930

Tanglewood Tales for Girls and Boys, Being a Second Wonder Book (o Hawthorne) 1853

Tango Palace (pl Fornés) 1963

Tape for the Turn of the Year (po Ammons) 1965

Taps at Reveille (f Fitzgerald) 1935

Taquisara (f Crawford) 1896

Tar Baby (scr Bambara) 1984

Tar Baby (f Morrison) 1981

Tar: A Midwest Childhood (o S. Anderson) 1926

Tartuffe (pl Wilbur) 1963

Tarzan and the Ant Men (f E. Burroughs) 1924

Tarzan and the Castaways (f E. Burroughs) 1964

Tarzan and the City of Gold (f E. Burroughs) 1933

Tarzan and the Forbidden City (f E. Burroughs) 1938

Tarzan and the Foreign Legion (f E. Burroughs) 1947

Tarzan and the Golden Lion (f E. Burroughs) 1923

Tarzan and the Jewels of Opar (f E. Burroughs) 1918

Tarzan and the Leopard Men (f E. Burroughs) 1935

Tarzan and the Lion-Man (f E. Burroughs) 1934

Tarzan and the Lost Empire (f E. Burroughs) 1929

Tarzan and the Madman (f E. Burroughs) 1964

Tarzan and the Tarzan Twins, with Jad-Bal-Ja, The Golden Lion (f E. Burroughs) 1936

Tarzan at the Earth's Core (f E. Burroughs) 1930

Tarzan, Lord of the Jungle (f E. Burroughs) 1928

Tarzan of the Apes (f E. Burroughs) 1914

Tarzan the Invincible (f E. Burroughs) 1931

Tarzan the Magnificent (f E. Burroughs) 1939

Tarzan the Terrible (f E. Burroughs) 1921

Tarzan the Untamed (f E. Burroughs) 1920

Tarzan Triumphant (f E. Burroughs) 1932

Tarzan Twins (f E. Burroughs) 1927

Tarzan's Quest (f E. Burroughs) 1936

Tattered Tom (f Alger) 1871

Tattooed Countess (f Van Vechten) 1924

Tavern-Keeper's Victims (f Arthur) 1860

Taylor Anecdote Book: Anecdotes and Letters of Zachary Taylor (o Thorpe) 1848

Tea and Sympathy (pl R. Anderson) 1953

Teacher and Society (o Dewey) 1937

Teaching a Stone to Talk (o Dillard) 1982

Teaching English (o Herrick) 1899

Teachings; The Satires, Parodies, Fables, Illustrated Stories, and Plays (o Barthelme) 1992

Tears and Smiles (pl Barker) 1808

Technology and the Frontiers of Knowledge (o Bellow) 1973

Tecumseh and the Shawnee Prophet (o Eggleston) 1878

Teeftallow (f Stribling) 1926

Teenytown (pl Hagedorn) 1988

Teeth Mother Naked at Last (po Bly) 1970

Teeth of the Lion (po Patchen) 1942

Teibele and Her Demon (pl Singer) 1978

Telegraph Boy (f Alger) 1879

Telephone (pl Harrigan) 1877

Telephone Poles and Other Poems (po Updike) 1963

T.V. Baby Poems (po Ginsberg) 1967

Tell Me a Riddle: A Collection (f Olsen) 1961

Tell Me How Long the Train's Been Gone (f James Baldwin) 1968

Tell Me, Tell Me: Granite, Steele, and Other Topics (po Moore) 1966

Tell My Horse (o Hurston) 1938

Tell Truth and Shame the Devil (pl Dunlap) 1797

Telling (o Riding) 1972

Telling Stories (o Didion) 1978

Temperamental People (f Rinehart) 1924

Temperance Tales (f Arthur) 1843

Temperence Town (pl Hoyt) 1893

Tempers (po W. Williams) 1913

Tempest (pl Daly) 1897

Temple in Nimes (po J. Wright) 1982

Temple of Independence (pl Dunlap) 1799

Temple of Minerva (pl Hopkinson) 1781

Temple of My Familiar (f A. Walker) 1989

Temple of Texts (o Gass) 1990

Temple of the Sun (o Doolittle) 1972

Temporary Facts (po W. Stafford) 1970

Temptation (pl Brougham) 1856

Temptation of Friar Goncol (f Field) 1900

Temptations (f Arthur) 1848

Ten Blocks on the Camino Real (pl T. Williams) 1948

Ten Days' Wonder (f Queen) 1948

Ten Letters and a Foreword (o Santayana) 1960

Ten Million Ghosts (pl Kingsley) 1936

Ten North Frederick (f J. O'Hara) 1955

Ten to One: Selected Poems (po B. Perelman) 1999

Ten Women in Gale's House and Shorter Poems (po Clark) 1932

Tenants (pl H. James) 1894

Tenants (f Malamud) 1971

Tenants of Moonbloom (f Wallant) 1963

Tender Buttons: Objects, Food, Rooms (po Stein) 1914

Tender Is the Night: A Romance (f Fitzgerald) 1934

Tenderness (f Oates) 1996

Tenement Lover (tv Hagedorn) 1981

There Was That Roman Poet Who Fell in Love at Fifty-Odd (po Shapiro) 1968

There Were Two Pirates (f Cabell) 1946

There Will Come Soft Rains (f Bradbury) 1989

There You Are (po Simpson) 1995

There's Always Another Windmill (po Nash) 1968

There's Always Juliet (pl Van Druten) 1931

There's Love All Day (po Patchen) 1970

There's Something I Got To Tell You (pl Saroyan) 1941

Therese, The Orphan of Geneva (pl Payne) 1821

These 13: Stories (f Faulkner) 1931

These Are My Rivers: New & Selected Poems, 1955-1993 (po Ferlinghetti) 1993

These Bars of Flesh (f Stribling) 1938

These Restless Heads: A Trilogy of Romantics (o Cabell) 1932

These Three (scr Hellman) 1936

They Brought Their Women (f Ferber) 1933

They Burned the Books (pl S. Benét) 1942

They Call Me Carpenter (f Sinclair) 1922

They Came Here First: The Epic of the American Indian (o McNickle) 1949

They Came in Chains (o Redding) 1950

They Can Only Hang You Once (f Hammett) 1949

They Fly at Ciron (f S. Delany) 1993

They Keep Riding down All the Time (po Patchen) 1947

They Knew What They Wanted (pl S. Howard) 1925

They of the High Trails (f Garland) 1916

They Released Barabbas (pl B. Smith) 1939

They Shall Have Music (scr Lawson) 1939

They Stooped to Folly: A Comedy of Morals (f Glasgow) 1929

They're Playing Our Song (pl Simon) 1978

Thicket of Spring: Poems 1926-1969 (po Bowles) 1972

Thief of Peirce: The Letters of Kenneth Laine Ketner and Walker Percy (o Percy) 1995

Thief of Time (f Hillerman) 1985

Thieves of Paradise (po Komunyakaa) 1998

Thieves' Canyon (f Grey) 1965

Thin Man (f Hammett) 1934

Thin Red Line (f J. Jones) 1962

Things as They Are: A Novel in Three Parts (f Stein) 1950

Things Change (scr Mamet) 1988

Things for a Distressed People to Think Upon (o Mather) 1696

Things Gone and Things Still Here (f Bowles) 1977

Things of This World (po Wilbur) 1956

Things That Happen When There Aren't Any People (po W. Stafford) 1980

Things They Carried (f T. O'Brien) 1990

Think Back on Us: A Contemporary Chronicle of the 1930s (o Cowley) 1969

Think Black (po Madhubuti) 1967

Think Fast, Mr. Moto (f Marquand) 1937

Thinking about the Longstanding Problems of Virtue and Happiness (o Kushner) 1995

Thinking of Home (o Faulkner) 1992

Thinner (f King) 1984

Third Circle (f Norris) 1909

Third Commandment (tv Hecht) 1959

Third Fourth of July (pl Cullen) 1946

Third Generation (f Himes) 1954

Third Generation (f Steele) 1929

Third Kingdom (radio Parks) 1990

Third Life of Grange Copeland (f A. Walker) 1970

Third Life of Per Smevik (f Rølvaag) 1971

Third Night (pl Thomas [Clayton] Wolfe) 1919

Third Violet (f S. Crane) 1897

Thirst (pl O'Neill) 1914

Thirsting Heart (pl Green) 1971

Thirsty Evil: Seven Short Stories (f Vidal) 1956

13 Clocks (f Thurber) 1950

Thirteen O'Clock: Stories of Several Worlds (f S. Benét) 1937

Thirteen Stories (f Welty) 1965

Thirteen Uncollected Stories (f Cheever) 1994

Thirteen Ways of Looking at a Black Man (o Gates) 1997

Thirty One Sonnets (po Eberhart) 1967

Thirty Poems (po Bryant) 1864

Thirty Stories (f Boyle) 1946

Thirty Things (po Creeley) 1974

$30,000 Bequest and Other Stories (f Twain) 1906

30,000 on the Hoof (f Grey) 1940

Thirty Years (pl Dunlap) 1828

Thirty Years (o Marquand) 1954

Thirty Years Ago (o Dunlap) 1836

34th Star (tv Linney), 1976

39 East (pl Crothers) 1919

31 Letters and 13 Dreams (po Hugo) 1977

This (po Olson) 1952

This Body Is Made of Camphor and Gopherwood: Prose Poems (po Bly) 1977

This Body the Earth (f Green) 1935

This Boy's Life: A Memoir (o Wolff) 1989

This Crooked Way (f Spencer) 1952

This Day's Death (f Rechy) 1969

This Declaration (pl Green) 1954

This Earth (po Faulkner) 1932

This Fine-Pretty World (pl MacKaye) 1923

This Great Unknowing: Last Poems (po Levertov) 1999

This Hunger (f Nin) 1945

This Is an Entertainment (pl T. Williams) 1976

This Is Murder (f E. Gardner) 1935

This Is My Century: New and Collected Poems (po M. Walker) 1988

This Is My Country Too (o J. Williams) 1964

This Is New York (pl Sherwood) 1930

This Is Not a Letter and Other Poems (po Boyle) 1985

This Journey (po J. Wright) 1982

This Mad Ideal (f Dell) 1925

This Man and This Woman (f Farrell) 1951

This Migrant Earth (f Rivera) 1985

This Music Crept by Me upon the Waters (pl MacLeish) 1953

This Poetry Thang: Voices from the Next Generation (pl Lim) 1997

This Property Is Condemned (pl T. Williams) 1942

This Proud Heart (f Buck) 1938

This Quiet Dust and Other Writings (o Styron) 1982

This Room and This Gin and These Sandwiches (pl E. Wilson) 1937

This Side of Jordan (f R. Bradford) 1929

This Side of Paradise (f Fitzgerald) 1920

This Strange Adventure (f Rinehart) 1929

This Strangest Everything (po Ciardi) 1966

This Thing Don't Lead to Heaven (f Crews) 1970

This Time: New and Selected Poems (po Stern) 1998

This Tree Will Be Here for a Thousand Years (po Bly) 1979

Thomas and Beulah (po Dove) 1986

Thomas Jefferson: The Making of a President (o Dos Passos) 1964

Thomas Wolfe as I Knew Him and Other Essays (o Fisher) 1963

Thoreau, The Poet-Naturalist (o Channing) 1873

Thoreau's Minnesota Journey: Two Documents (o Thoreau) 1962

Thornton Dial: Images of the Tiger (o Baraka) 1993

Thorofare (f Morley) 1942

Those Days: Early Writings by Raymond Carver: Eleven Poems and a Story (o Carver) 1987

Those Other People (o Childress) 1989

Those Who Perish (f Dahlberg) 1934

Those Who Ride the Night Winds (po Giovanni) 1983

Though Gently (po Riding) 1930

Thought in the Bride of What Thinking (po Hejinian) 1976

Thoughts for You! (po Baraka) 1984

Thoughts Occasioned by the Most Insignificant of all Human Events (o Kinnell) 1982

Thoughts on la Cultura, the Media, Con Safos and Survival (o Montoya) 1979

Thousand and One Afternoons in Chicago (f Hecht) 1922

Thousand and Second Night (po Merrill) 1963

Thousand Days for Mokhtar, and Other Stories (f Bowles) 1989

Thousand Years Ago: A Romance of the Orient (pl MacKaye) 1913

Three Americanisms (pl Wellman) 1993

Three at Wolfe's Door (f Stout) 1960

Three Black Pennys (f Hergesheimer) 1917

Three Comrades (scr Fitzgerald) 1938

Three Daughters of Madame Liang (f Buck) 1969

Three Doors to Death (f Stout) 1950

Three Easy Pieces (f Morris) 1993

Three Exposures (pl Guare) 1982

Three Fates (f Crawford) 1892

Three Flights Up (f S. Howard) 1924

Three for the Chair (f Stout) 1957

Three from the Earth (pl Barnes) 1919

Three Gringos in Venezuela and Central America (o Richard Davis) 1896

Three Heroines in New England Romance: Their True Stories (o Guiney) 1894

CCCLXXIV Poems (po Patchen) 1948

365 Reasons Not to Have Another War (o Paley) 1989

Three Illuminations in the Life of an American Author (f Updike) 1979

Three Lectures (o Frye) 1958

Three Letters to Joseph Conrad (pl H. James) 1926

Three Lives (f Auchincloss) 1993

Three Lives: Stories of the Good Anna, Melanctha, and the Gentle Lena (f Stein) 1909

Three Madrigals (po Ashbery) 1968

Three Married Men (scr Parker) 1936

Three Memorial Poems (po J. Lowell) 1877

Three Men Out (f Stout) 1954

Three of a Kind: Career in C Major, The Embezzler, Double Indemnity (f Cain) 1944

Three of Hearts (f Cain) 1949

Three of Us (pl Crothers) 1916

Three on Community (o Shapiro) 1996

Three on the Tower: The Lives and Works of Ezra Pound, T. S. Eliot, and William Carlos Williams (o Simpson) 1975

Three Papers on Fiction (o Welty) 1962

Three Partners (f Harte) 1897

Three Philosophical Poets: Lucretius, Dante, and Goethe (o Santayana) 1910

Three Pieces: spell #7; a photograph: lovers in motion; boogie woogie landscapes (pl Shange) 1981

Three Players of a Summer Game (pl T. Williams) 1955

Three Reliques of Ancient Western Poetry Collected by Wilson from the Ruins of the Twentieth Century (po E. Wilson) 1951

Three Roads (f Macdonald) 1948

Three Short Novels (f Boyle) 1958

Three Sisters (pl Jarrell) 1964

Three Sisters (pl Mamet) 1992

Three Sisters (pl Nelson) 1984

Three Soldiers (f Dos Passos) 1921

Three Stories and Ten Poems (f Hemingway) 1923

Three Tales (f Bowles) 1975

Three Tall Women (pl Albee) 1991

Three Taverns (po Robinson) 1920

Three Texts from Early Ipswich: A Pageant (pl Updike) 1968

Three Times Three (f Saroyan) 1936

Three Travelers Watch a Sunrise (pl Stevens) 1920

Three Views of Mt. Fuji: A Play (pl Shange) 1987

Three West: Conversations with Fisher, Max Evans, Michael Straight (o Fisher) 1970

Three Wise Guys and Other Stories (f Runyon) 1946

Three Witnesses (f Stout) 1956

Three Women: A Monologue for Three Voices (pl Plath) 1962

Three Worlds, Three Realms, Six Roads (po Snyder) 1966

Three Years in Europe (o W. Brown) 1852

Three-Headed Angel (f R. Bradford) 1937

Threefold Paradise of Cotton Mather: An Edition of Triparadisus (o Mather) 1995

Throne of David: From the Consecration of the Shepherd of Bethlehem to the Rebellion of Prince Absalom (f Ingraham) 1860

Thrones: 96-109 de los cantares (po Pound) 1959

Through a Glass, Clearly (f Asimov) 1967

Through Glacier Park: Seeing America First (o Rinehart) 1916

Through One Administration (f Burnett) 1883

Through the Eye of the Needle (f Howells) 1907

Through the Ivory Gate: A Novel (f Dove) 1992

Throwing Yourself Away (po Eberhart) 1984

Thunder in the City (scr Sherwood) 1937

Thunder Mountain (f Grey) 1935

Thunder on the Left (f Morley) 1925

Thundering Herd (f Grey) 1925

Thurber Album: A New Collection of Pieces about People (f Thurber) 1952

Thurber and Company (f Thurber) 1966

Thurber Carnival (f Thurber) 1945

Thurber Country: A New Collection of Pieces about Males and Females, Mainly of Our Own Species (f Thurber) 1953

Thurber Garland (f Thurber) 1955

Thurber's Dogs: A Collection of the Master's Dogs, Written and Drawn, Real and Imaginary, Living and Long Ago (f Thurber) 1955

Thursday Evening (pl Morley) 1921

Thurso's Landing and Other Poems (po Jeffers) 1932

Thuvia, Maid of Mars (f E. Burroughs) 1920

Ticey (pl Gillette) 1908

Ticket That Exploded (f W. Burroughs) 1962

Ticket to Paradise (scr N. West) 1936
Tickets for a Prayer Wheel (po Dillard) 1974
Tickless Time (pl Glaspell) 1918
Tide of Time (f Masters) 1937
Tides of Lust (f S. Delany) 1973
Tidewater Morning (f Styron) 1993
Tidewater Tales: A Novel (f Barth) 1987
Tiger in the House (o Van Vechten) 1920
Tiger Joy (po S. Benét) 1925
Tiger Tail (pl T. Williams) 1978
Tiger-Lilies (f Lanier) 1867 Tiger's Daughter (f Mukherjee) 1972
Tigers Wild; (pl Rechy) 1986
tigertiger (pl Wellman) 1995
Tik-Tok Man of Oz (pl Baum) 1913
Tilda (f Van Doren) 1943
Till the Day I Die (pl Odets) 1935
Tim Hazard (f Clark) 1951
Time Element and Other Stories (f J. O'Hara) 1972
Time Enough for Love (f Heinlein) 1973
Time for the Stars (f Heinlein) 1956
Time in the Rock: Preludes to Definition (po Aiken) 1936
Time Is Noon (f Buck) 1967
Time of Friendship (f Bowles) 1967
Time of Man (f Roberts) 1926
Time of Our Time (o Mailer) 1998
Time of the Cuckoo (pl Laurents) 1952
Time of War: Air Force Diaries and Pentagon Memos 1943-45 (o
    Cozzens) 1984
Time of Your Life (pl Saroyan) 1939
Time Out of Mind (scr Green) 1947
Time Pieces: The Photographs and Words of Morris (o Morris)
    1983
Time to Reap (radio S. Benét) 1942
Time Traveller: Poems 1983-1989 (po Oates) 1989
Time's Power: Poems, 1985-1988 (po Rich) 1989
Timequake (f Vonnegut) 1993
Times Are Never So Bad (f Dubus) 1983
Times Have Changed (pl Bromfield) 1935
Timespace Huracan: Poems, 1972-1975 (po Alurista) 1976
Timesteps (pl Vonnegut) 1979
Timoleon Etc (po Melville) 1891
Timothy Crump's Ward (f Alger) 1866
Timothy Dexter Revisited (o Marquand) 1960
Timothy Shaft (pl Belasco) 1921
Timothy's Angels (po W. Benét) 1947
Tin Can Tree (f A. Tyler) 1965
Tin Woodman of Oz (f Baum) 1918
Tinkle of Bells and Other Poems (po Riley) 1895
Tiny Alice (pl Albee) 1965
Tiny Closet (pl Inge) 1959
Tiote (pl Daly) 1880
Tired of Housekeeping (f Arthur) 1842
Tish (f Rinehart) 1916
Tish Marches On (f Rinehart) 1937
Tish Plays the Game (f Rinehart) 1926
Titan (f Dreiser) 1914
Title-Mart (pl Churchill) 1905
Tituba of Salem Village (f Petry) 1964
To a Blossoming Pear Tree (po J. Wright) 1977
To a God Unknown (f Steinbeck) 1933

To a Little Girl, One Year Old, in a Ruined Fortress (po R. War-
    ren) 1956
To Abolish Children and Other Essays (o Shapiro) 1968
To Be an Author: Letters of Charles W. Chesnutt, 1889-1905 (o
    Chesnutt) 1997
To Be Young, Gifted, and Black: A Portrait of Hansberry in Her
    Own Words (o Hansberry) 1969
To Bedlam and Part Way Back (po Sexton) 1960
To Bobchen Haas (o Stein) 1957
To Build a Fire and Other Stories (f London) 1995
To Cuba and Back: A Vacation Voyage (o Dana) 1859
To Dance a Stony Field (po N. Wallace) 1995
To Disembark (po Brooks) 1981
To Dwell in a Place of Strangers (pl Kopit) 1958
To Have and Have Not (scr Faulkner) 1945
To Have and Have Not (f Hemingway) 1937
To Heaven in a Golden Coach (pl T. Williams) 1961
To Hell with Dying (o A. Walker) 1988
To His Fellow Citizens (o Barlow) 1799-1800
To Jenny with Love (pl B. Smith) 1941
To Jerusalem and Back: A Personal Account (o Bellow) 1976
To Keep Moving, Essays 1959-1969 (o Hall) 1980
To Kill Again (f Stout) 1960
To Leeward (f Crawford) 1883
To Make a Poet Black (o Redding) 1939
To Mrs. Leonard (po Wheatley) 1771
To Mr. and Mrs.—-, on the Death of Their Infant Son (po
    Wheatley) 1784
To Obtain the Value of the Cake Measure from Zero (pl Coolidge)
    1970
To Possess the Land: A Biography of Arthur Rochford Manby
    (o Waters) 1973
To Quebec and the Stars (o Lovecraft) 1976
To Quito and Back (pl Hecht) 1937
To Raise the Dead and Foretell the Future (po Bullins) 1971
To Read Literature: Fiction, Poetry, Drama (o Hall) 1981
To Sail Beyond the Sunset (f Heinlein) 1987
To Say If You Love Someone and Other Selected Love Poems (po
    Patchen) 1948
To See the Dream (o J. West) 1957
To Sing Strange Songs (f Bradbury) 1979
To Stay Alive (po Levertov) 1971
To Tame a Land (f L'Amour) 1955
To the Chicago Abyss (tv Bradbury) 1989
To the Citizens of Pennsylvania, on the Proposal for Calling a
    Convention (o Paine) 1805
To the Dogs (pl Barnes) 1923
To the End of the Trail (po Hovey) 1908
To the Ends of the Universe (o Asimov) 1967
To the Far Blue Mountains (f L'Amour) 1976
To the Finland Station: A Study in the Writing and Acting of His-
    tory (o E. Wilson) 1940
To the Girls and Boys (o Jefferson) 1964
To the Holy Spirit: A Poem (po Winters) 1947
To the Honourable Miss S— and Other Stories (f Traven) 1981
To the ladies! (pl Connelly; Kaufman) 1923
To the Lost Man (f Grey) 1922
To the Loud Wind and Other Poems (po Hall) 1955
To the One I Love the Best (o Bemelmans) 1955
To the Reader (po B. Perelman) 1984
To the Rev. Mr. Pitkin (po Wheatley) 1772

To the White Sea (f Dickey) 1993

To Thomas Hubbard (po Wheatley) 1773

To Wally Pantoni, We Leave a Credenza (pl Guare) 1965

To Whom It May Concern and Other Stories (f Farrell) 1944

Toadstool Boy (pl Guare) 1960

Toast of the Town (pl Fitch) 1905

Tobias and the Angel (f Yerby) 1975

Today and Forever: Stories of China (f Buck) 1941

Today and Tomorrow and. . . (o Asimov) 1973

Today Is Friday (pl Hemingway) 1926

Today We Live (scr Faulkner) 1933

Todd Andrews to the Author (f Barth) 1979

Toddles (pl Fitch) 1906

Together (f Herrick) 1908

Toilers of the Hills (f Fisher) 1928

Toilet (pl Baraka) 1962

Toinette (f Tourgée) 1874

Tokyo-Montana Express (f Brautigan) 1980

Tol'able David (f Hergesheimer) 1923

Tom Brace: Who He Was and How He Fared (f Alger) 1901

Tom Sawyer Abroad (f Twain) 1894

Tom Sawyer, Detective, as Told by Huck Finn, and Other Tales (f Twain) 1896

Tom Temple's Career (f Alger) 1888

Tom Thatcher's Fortune (f Alger) 1888

Tom, The Bootblack (f Alger) 1880

Tom Tracy (f Alger) 1888

Tom Turner's Legacy: The Story of How He Secured It (f Alger) 1902

Tom: A Ballet (pl Cummings) 1935

Tomb and Other Tales (f Lovecraft) 1969

Tomcat in Love (f T. O'Brien) 1998

Tommy Gallagher's Crusade (f Farrell) 1939

Tommy Trot's Visit to Santa Claus (f Page) 1908

Tommyknockers (f King) 1987

Tomorrow (pl MacKaye) 1912

Tomorrow and Tomorrow (pl Barry) 1931

Tomorrow Midnight (f Bradbury) 1966

Tomorrow Will Be Better (f B. Smith) 1948

Tongues (pl Shepard) 1978

Tonto Woman and Other Western Stories (f Leonard) 1998

Tony, The Hero (f Alger) 1880

Too Far From Home: The Selected Writings of Paul Bowles (o Bowles) 1993

Too Far to Go: The Maples Stories (f Updike) 1979

Too Many Clients (f Stout) 1960

Too Many Cooks (f Stout) 1938

Too Many Women (f Stout) 1947

Too Much Johnson (pl Gillette) 1894

Tooth of Crime (pl Shepard) 1972

Top of the Heap (f E. Gardner) 1952

Torchbearers: A Satirical Comedy (pl Kelly) 1923

Torches (po J. Tate) 1968

Tornado Alley (f W. Burroughs) 1989

Torrent and the Night Before (po Robinson) 1896

Torrents of Spring: A Romantic Novel in Honor of the Passing of a Great Race (f Hemingway) 1926

Tortesa (pl Willis) 1839

Tortilla Flat (f Steinbeck) 1935

Tortuga (f Anaya) 1979

Tory Lover (f Jewett) 1901

Toscanini: The Hymn of Nations (scr Sarton) 1944

Tossing and Turning (po Updike) 1977

Touch (f Leonard) 1987

Touch of Danger (f J. Jones) 1973

Touch of Petulance (tv Bradbury) 1990

Touch of the Poet (pl O'Neill) 1957

Touched with Fire (tv Bradbury) 1990

Touchstone (f Wharton) 1900

Tough Guys Don't Dance (f Mailer) 1984

Toulemonde (po Morley) 1928

Tour of Duty (o Dos Passos) 1946

Tout pour plaire (f Himes) 1959

Tovarich (pl Sherwood) 1936

Toward a Better Life: Being a Series of Epistles or Declamations (f Burke) 1932

Toward Ideological Clarity (o Baraka) 1974

Toward the Century of Modern Man (radio S. Benét) 1942

Toward the End of Time (f Updike) 1997

Toward the Gulf (po Masters) 1918

Tower of Babel (pl Goodman) 1940

Tower of Ivory (f Atherton) 1910

Tower of Ivory (po MacLeish) 1917

Tower of Sand and Other Stories (f Steele) 1929

Towers of Toron (f S. Delany) 1964

Towers Open Fire (scr W. Burroughs) 1963

Town (f Faulkner) 1957

Town (f Richter) 1950

Town and the City (f Kerouac) 1950

Town Down the River (po Robinson) 1910

Town of Hill (po Hall) 1975

Townsend of Lichfield (o Cabell) 1930

Townsman (f Buck) 1945

Toxic Shock (f Paretsky) 1988

Toy Bone (po Hall) 1979

Toy Wife (scr Akins) 1938

Toynbee Convector (f Bradbury) 1988

Toys in a Field (po Komunyakaa) 1986

Toys in the Attic (pl Hellman) 1960

Track of the Cat (f Clark) 1949

Tracks (f Erdrich) 1988

Tracy's Tiger (f Saroyan) 1951

Trade Winds (scr Parker) 1938

Traffic in Women and Other Essays on Feminism (o Goldman) 1970

Tragedy and Comedy: Four Cubist Plays (pl Goodman) 1970

Tragedy Has Obligations (o Jeffers) 1973

Tragedy of Pudd'nhead Wilson, and The Comedy of Those Extraordinary Twins (f Twain) 1894

Tragedy of the Moon (o Asimov) 1973

Tragedy of X: A Drury Lane Mystery (f Queen) 1932

Tragedy of Y: A Drury Lane Mystery (f Queen) 1932

Tragedy of Z: A Drury Lane Mystery (f Queen) 1933

Tragic Muse (f H. James) 1890

Trail Driver (f Grey) 1936

Trail of the Hawk (f Lewis) 1915

Trail to Crazy Man (f L'Amour) 1986

Train and the City (f Thomas [Clayton] Wolfe) 1984

Train Boy (f Alger) 1883

Training of Children (o H. Jackson) 1882

Tramp Abroad (f Twain) 1880

Tramp's Excuse and Other Poems (po Lindsay) 1909

Transaction in Hearts (f Saltus) 1889

Transactions (scr Bambara) 1979

Transbluency: The Selected Poems of Amiri Baraka/LeRoi Jones (po Baraka) 1995

Transformation (f Hawthorne) 1860

Transformations (po Sexton) 1971

Transient Guest and Other Episodes (f Saltus) 1889

Transients (f Van Doren) 1935

Transit of Civilization from England to America in the Seventeenth Century (o Eggleston) 1901

Transit of Leo (pl Daly) 1895

Transit to Narcissus (f Mailer) 1978

Translations from the Chinese (po Morley) 1922

Transparent Things (f Nabokov) 1972

Transplanted (f Atherton) 1919

Transport to Summer (po Stevens) 1947

Trap (pl Richard Davis) 1914

Traps Need New Bait (f E. Gardner) 1967

Trash (f Allison) 1988

Travel Letters from New Zealand, Australia, and Africa (o E. Howe) 1913

Traveler (pl Connelly) 1939

Traveler and the Hill and the Hill (po Hejinian) 1998

Traveler from Altruria (f Howells) 1894

Travelers (pl Tarkington) 1927

Traveling through the Dark (po W. Stafford) 1962

Travellers (pl Barker) 1808

Travellers (f Sedgwick) 1825

Travelling Companions (f H. James) 1919

Travelling the World (o Theroux) 1990

Travelling Thirds (f Atherton) 1905

Travels (po Merwin) 1992

Travels in Greece and Russia (o B. Taylor) 1859

Travels in Two Democracies (o E. Wilson) 1936

Travels with Charley in Search of America (o Steinbeck) 1962

Travesty (f Hawkes) 1976

Tread the Green Grass (pl Green) 1931

Treason of Arnold (f Ingraham) 1847

Treason of the Senate (o D. Phillips) 1953

Treasure Mountain (f L'Amour) 1972

Treasure of Pleasant Valley (f Yerby) 1955

Treasure of the Ruby Hills (scr L'Amour) 1955

Treasure of the Sierra Madre (f Traven) 1934

Treasurer's Report (scr Benchley) 1928

Treasurer's Report and Other Aspects of Community Singing (o Benchley) 1930

Treat 'em Rough: Letters from Jack the Kaiser Killer (o Lardner) 1918

Treatise Concerning Religious Affections (o Edwards) 1746

Treatise Concerning the Lords Supper (o E. Taylor) 1966

Treatise on Grace and Other Posthumously Published Writings (o Edwards) 1971

Treatise on Right and Wrong (o Mencken) 1934

Treatise on the Gods (o Mencken) 1930

Tree Grows in Brooklyn (f B. Smith) 1943

Tree of Life (po Fletcher) 1918

Tree of Night and Other Stories (f Capote) 1949

Tree Telling of Orpheus (po Levertov) 1968

Trees (f Richter) 1940

Trees Die at the Top (f Ferber) 1938

Trees of His Father (pl B. Smith) 1937

Trelawney with Shelley and Byron (o J. Miller) 1922

Tremble Purple: Seven Poems (po Alurista) 1986

Trending into Maine (o Roberts) 1938

Trent's Trust and Other Stories (f Harte) 1903

Tres Macho—He Said (o Chávez) 1985

Tri-Color (po Simms) 1830

Trial of a Poet and Other Poems (po Shapiro) 1947

Trial of Joan of Arc on a Matter of Faith (pl Fornés) 1986

Trial without Jury (pl Payne) 1940

Triall by Armes (f Hergesheimer) 1929

Trials and Adventures of Herbert Mason (f Alger) 1887

Trials and Confessions of an American Housekeeper (f Arthur) 1854

Trials and Other Tribulations (f Runyon) 1948

Trials of a Needlewoman (f Arthur) 1853

Trials of the Human Heart (f Rowson) 1795

Tribes and Temples: A Record of the Expedition to Middle America Conducted by the Tulane University of Louisiana in 1925 (o La Farge) 1926-27

Tribulations and Laughter: A Memoir (o Behrman) 1972

Tribunals: Passages 31-35 (po Duncan) 1970

Tribune Primer (o Field) 1881

Tribute, and Circe: Two Poems (po Doolittle) 1917

Tribute to Freud, with Unpublished Letters by Freud to the Author (o Doolittle) 1956

Tribute to Gallantry (pl Hecht) 1943

Tribute to the Angels (po Doolittle) 1945

Tried and the Tempted (f Arthur) 1852

Trifler (pl Masters) 1908

Trifles (pl Glaspell) 1916

Trifles of Thought (po Green) 1917

Triggering Town: Lectures and Essays on Poetry and Writing (o Hugo) 1979

Trilogy (pl Capote) 1969

Trilogy (po Doolittle) 1973

Trilogy: An Experiment in Multimedia (o Capote) 1969

Trimmed Lamp and Other Stories of the Four Million (f Henry) 1907

Trini (f Portillo Trambley) 1986

Trio for Blunt Instruments (f Stout) 1964

Trip to Chinatown (pl Hoyt) 1891

Trip to Italy and France (po Ferlinghetti) 1980

Trip to Niagara; or Travellers in America (pl Dunlap) 1830

Trip to Parnassus (po Rowson) 1788

Trip to the West Indies (o E. Howe) 1910

Trip Trap: Haiku along the Road from San Francisco to New York 1959 (po Kerouac) 1973

Triple Jeopardy (f Stout) 1951

Triple Thinkers: Ten Essays on Literature (o E. Wilson) 1938

Triple Thinkers: Twelve Essays on Literary Subjects (o E. Wilson) 1948

Tripmaster Monkey: His Fake Book (f Kingston) 1987

Triptych (pl Eberhart) 1955

Tristessa (f Kerouac) 1960

Tristram (po Robinson) 1927

Triton (f S. Delany) 1976

Triumph of Achilles (po Glück) 1985

Triumph of Infidelity (po Dwight) 1788

Triumph of the Egg (pl S. Anderson) 1937

Triumph of the Spider Monkey (f Oates) 1976

Triumphal March (po Eliot) 1931

Triumphs of the Reformed Religion in America (o Mather) 1691
Trobar Clus (po Guthrie) 1923
Trojan Ending (f Riding) 1937
Trojan Horse (pl MacLeish) 1952
Trojan Horse (f Morley) 1937
Troll Garden (f Cather) 1905
Tropic of Cancer (f H. Miller) 1934
Tropic of Capricorn (f H. Miller) 1939
Tropical Winter (f Hergesheimer) 1933
Trouble Follows Me (f Macdonald) 1946
Trouble in Mind (pl Childress) 1955
Trouble in Triplicate (f Stout) 1949
Trouble Is My Business (f Chandler) 1951-53
Trouble on Triton: An Ambiguous Heterotopia (f S. Delany) 1996
Trouble with Genius: Reading Pound, Joyce, Stein, and Zukofsky
    (o B. Perelman) 1994
Trouble with Tigers (f Saroyan) 1938
Troubled Island (pl Hughes) 1935
Troubles of Queen Silver Bell (f Burnett) 1907
Trout Fishing in America (f Brautigan) 1967
Truce (f Ingraham) 1847
Truce of God (f Rinehart) 1920
Truckline Cafe (pl M. Anderson) 1946
True at First Light: A Fictional Memoir (f Hemingway) 1999
True Bear Stories (o J. Miller) 1900
True Bills (f Ade) 1904
True Confessions (scr Didion) 1981
True Crimes (pl Linney) 1996
True Excellency of a Minister of the Gospel (o Edwards) 1744
True Grace Distinguished from the Experience of Devils (o
    Edwards) 1753
True Night (po Snyder) 1980
True Riches and Other Tales (f Arthur) 1850
True Saints, When Absent from the Body, Are Present with the
    Lord (o Edwards) 1747
True Stories from History and Biography (o Hawthorne) 1851
True Story and the Recent Carnival of Crime (f Twain) 1877
True to the Core (pl Belasco) 1880
True West (pl Shepard) 1980
True Womanhood: A Tale (f Neal) 1859
Trumpet in the Land (pl Green) 1972
Trumpet of the Swan (f White) 1970
Trumpet Shall Sound (pl Wilder) 1926
Trust (f Ozick) 1966
Trust Me (f Updike) 1987
Truth (pl Fitch) 1907
Truth (pl B. Howard) 1878
Truth about Tristrem Varick (f Saltus) 1888
Truth Is More Sacred: A Critical Exchange on Modern Literature
    (o Dahlberg) 1961
Try and Trust (f Alger) 1873
Try Anything Once (f E. Gardner) 1962
Try! Try! (pl F. O'Hara) 1951
Trying Conclusions: New and Selected Poems, 1961-1991 (po
    Nemerov) 1991
Trying to Find Chinatown (pl Hwang) 1996
Trysting Place (pl Tarkington) 1923
T.S. Eliot (o Frye) 1963
Tucker (f L'Amour) 1971
Tucky the Hunter (o Dickey) 1978
Tuft by Puff (po W. Stafford) 1978

Tulips and Chimneys (po Cummings) 1923
Tumble Tower (f A. Tyler) 1993
Tunnel (f Gass) 1994
Tunnel in the Sky (f Heinlein) 1955
Tunnel Vision (f Paretsky) 1994
Turandot and Other Poems (po Ashbery) 1953
Turcaret (pl Merwin) 1961
Turmoil (f Tarkington) 1915
Turn Back the Clock (scr Hecht) 1933
Turn of the Screw (tv Vidal) 1955
Turn on the Heat (f E. Gardner) 1940
Turning Point (f Laurents) 1977
Turning Wind (po Rukeyser) 1939
Turns and Movies and Other Tales in Verse (po Aiken) 1916
Turps (f Runyon) 1951
Turtle Island (po Snyder) 1974
Turtles of Tasman (f London) 1916
Twain's Hannibal, Huck, and Tom (f Twain) 1969
Twain's Quarrel with Heaven: Captain Stormfield's Visit to Heaven
    and Other Sketches (f Twain) 1970
'Twas I (pl Payne) 1827
Tweedles (pl Tarkington) 1924
Twelfth Night (pl Daly) 1893
$1200 a Year (pl Ferber) 1920
Twelve Men (f Dreiser) 1919
Twelve Million Black Voices: A Folk History of the Negro in the
    United States (o R. Wright) 1941
Twelve Poems (po Wharton) 1926
Twelve Seasons (po Hall) 1983
Twelve Terrors of Christmas (o Updike) 1993
Twentieth Century (pl Hecht; MacArthur) 1932
Twentieth Century Discovery (o Asimov) 1969
Twentieth Century Pleasures: Prose on Poetry (o Hass) 1984
Twenty Days with Julian and Little Bunny: A Diary (o
    Hawthorne) 1904
Twenty Lessons in Reading and Writing Prose (o Davidson) 1955
Twenty Poems Less (po Riding) 1930
20,000 Leagues under the Sea (o Benchley) 1928
Twenty Years on Broadway, and the Years It Took to Get There
    (o Cohan) 1925
XXIV Elegies (po Fletcher) 1935
Twenty-Four Hours (f Bromfield) 1930
Twenty-One Letters (o Bierce) 1922
Twenty-One Letters to George Bryan (o H. Crane) 1968
Twenty-one Love Poems (po Rich) 1977
27 Wagons Full of Cotton (pl T. Williams) 1947
Twenty-Three and a Half Hours' Leave (f Rinehart) 1918
Twice Twenty Two (f Bradbury) 1966
Twice-Told Tales (f Hawthorne) 1837
Twilight (po Frost) 1894
Twilight Sleep (f Wharton) 1927
Twin Adventures: The Adventures of Saroyan: A Diary; The Ad-
    ventures of Wesley Jackson: A Novel (f Saroyan) 1950
Twin Hieroglyphs That Swim the River Dust (po Bradbury) 1978
Twin Roses (f Mowatt) 1857
Twin Sombreros (f Grey) 1941
Twinkle and Chubbins (f Baum) 1911
Twinkle Tales (f Baum) 1906
Twinkle, Twinkle (f T. O'Brien) 1994
Twins of Genius: Letters of Mark Twain, Cable, and Others (o
    Cable) 1953

Twins of Table Mountain (f Harte) 1879
Twisted Trinity (po McCullers) 1946
Two (f Crews) 1984
Two about Music (po W. Stafford) 1978
Two Admirals: A Tale of the Sea (f Cooper) 1842
Two Altars (o Stowe) 1855
Two Appreciations of John Jay Chapman (o Wister) 1934
Two Awfuls (pl Harrigan) 1875
Two Boys and a Girl (o Wolff) 1996
Two Brides (f Arthur) 1850
Two Cities (f Wideman) 1998
Two Citizens (po J. Wright) 1974
Two Clues: The Clue of the Runaway Blonde, The Clue of the
   Hungry Horse (f E. Gardner) 1947
Two Conceits for the Eye to Sing, If Possible (po A. Tate) 1950
Two Consolations (po Jeffers) 1940
Two Dead Girls (f King) 1996
Two Dissertations: Concerning the End of Which God Created
   the World; The Nature of True Virtue (o Edwards) 1765
$2.50 (pl Connelly) 1913
Two Dream Songs (po Berryman) 1965
Two Faced Woman (scr Behrman) 1941
Two Flights Up (f Rinehart) 1928
Two Frontiers: A Study in Historical Psychology (o Fletcher)
   1930
Two Galley Slaves (pl Payne) 1825
Two Gentlemen in Bonds (po Ransom) 1927
Two Gentlemen of Verona (pl Daly) 1895
Two Gentlemen of Verona (pl Guare) 1971
Two Husbands and Other Tales (f Arthur) 1845
Two Lectures on the Conduct of the Medical Life (o S. Mitchell)
   1893
Two Little Confederates (f Page) 1888
Two Little Girls and What They Did (f Arthur) 1899
Two Little Pilgrims' Progress: A Story of the City Beautiful (f
   Burnett) 1895
Two Long Poems (po Stern) 1990
Two Magics: The Turn of the Screw, Covering End (f H. James)
   1898
Two Men of Sandy Bar (pl Harte) 1876
Two Merchants (f Arthur) 1843
Two Natural Drummers (radio Wellman) 1973
2 Noh Plays (pl Goodman) 1941
Two of Us (pl Cohan) 1928
Two on an Island (pl Rice) 1940
Two or Three Ideas (o Stevens) 1951
Two or Three Things I Know for Sure (o Allison) 1995
Two Poems for Christmas (po Patchen) 1958
Two Poems of the Air (po Dickey) 1964
Two Prisoners (f Page) 1898
Two Sentences (po Goodman) 1970
Two Shakespearean Actors (pl Nelson) 1990
Two Short Paris Summertime Plays of 1974 (pl Saroyan) 1979
Two Short Plays: The Call, and A Murder (pl Inge) 1968
Two Sisters (f Arthur) 1844
Two Sisters: A Novel in the Form of a Memoir (f Vidal) 1970
Two Slatterns and a King: A Moral Interlude (pl Millay) 1921
Two Sonnets (po Updike) 1987
Two Stein Talks (po Hejinian) 1996
Two Stories: "Some Blue Hills at Sundown" and "The Man Who
   Kicked Cancer's Ass" (f Gilchrist) 1988

Two Trains Running (pl A. Wilson) 1990
Two Uncollected Poems (po Plath) 1980
Two Vanrevels (f Tarkington) 1902
Two Widows (pl Daly) 1874
Two Wives (f Arthur) 1851
Two Women (f Henry) 1910
Two Women: 1862 (po Woolson) 1877
Two Years before the Mast: A Personal Narrative of Life at Sea
   (o Dana) 1840
Two Years in the French West Indies (o Hearn) 1890
Two Young Fellows and Her Majesty's Marines (pl Harrigan) 1877
Two-Character Play (pl T. Williams) 1967
Two's Company (pl Nash) 1952
Two-Way Mirror (pl A. Miller) 1982
Tycoon (pl F. O'Brien) 1860
Typee (f Melville) 1846
Tyrannosaurous Rex (tv Bradbury) 1988
Tyrannosaurus Prescription and One Hundred Other Essays (o
   Asimov) 1989
Tyrannus Rex (po Ferlinghetti) 1969
Tyranny of the Dark (f Garland) 1905
Tyranny of the Normal (o Fiedler) 1996
Tyrants Destroyed and Other Stories (f Nabokov) 1975

Ugly Little Boy (f Asimov) 1992
Ugly Rumours (o Wolff) 1975
Ulisse (Ulysses) (scr Hecht) 1955
Ultima Thule (po Longfellow) 1880
Ultimate Good Luck (f Ford) 1981
Ultramarine (po Carver) 1986
Ultraviolet Sky (f Villanueva) 1993
Ulysses S. Grant (o Wister) 1900
Umbra: The Early Poems (po Pound) 1920
Unabridged London (f London) 1981
Unc' Edinburg: A Plantation Echo (f Page) 1895
Uncalled (f Dunbar) 1898
Uncanny Tales (f Crawford) 1911
Uncertain Certainty: Interviews, Essays, and Notes on Poetry (o
   Simic) 1985
Unchanging Love (pl Linney) 1991
Uncle Ben's New-Year's Gift (f Arthur) 1852
Uncle Eph's Christmas (pl Dunbar) 1900
Uncle Jacob's Secret (f Alger) 1890
Uncle Jimmy (pl Gale) 1922
Uncle Sam (pl Daly) 1873
Uncle Sam's Emancipation (f Stowe) 1853
Uncle Tom's Children: Four Novellas (f R. Wright) 1938
Uncle Tom's Cabin (f Stowe) 1852
Uncle Valentine and Other Stories: Uncollected Fiction 1915-1929
   (f Cather) 1973
Uncle Vanya (pl Fornés) 1987
Uncle Vanya (pl Mamet) 1989
Uncle Willy and Other Stories (f Faulkner) 1958
Uncommon Learning: Thoreau on Education (o Thoreau) 1999
Unconquered (pl Rand) 1940
Undefended Border (radio S. Benét) 1940
Under a Glass Bell (f Nin) 1944
Under Cover (pl Harrigan) 1903
Under the Andes (f Stout) 1985
Under the Crust (f Page) 1907
Under the Gaslight (pl Daly) 1867

Under the Lilacs (f Alcott) 1877
Under the Old Elm and Other Poems (po J. Lowell) 1885
Under the Polar Star (pl Belasco) 1896
Under the Redwoods (f Harte) 1901
Under the Roofs of Paris (f H. Miller) 1985
Under the Skylights (f Fuller) 1901
Under the Sweetwater Rim (f L'Amour) 1971
Under the Tonto Rim (f Grey) 1926
Under the Tree (po Roberts) 1922
Under the Weather (pl Bellow) 1966
Under the Wheel (pl Garland) 1890
Under the Willows and Other Poems (po J. Lowell) 1869
Under Water with Ogden Nash (po Nash) 1997
Undercliff: Poems 1946-1953 (po Eberhart) 1953
Undercurrent (pl Daly) 1888
Undergraduate Poems (po Eliot) 1949
Undergraduate Verses: Rhymed Minutes of the Hasty Pudding
    Club (po J. Lowell) 1956
Underground Man (f Macdonald) 1971
Underground River (pl Sarton) 1947
Underground Woman (f Boyle) 1975
Understanding America (o L. Mitchell) 1927
Understanding Physics (o Asimov) 1966
Understudies (f Freeman) 1901
Undertaker (pl Hawkes) 1967
Undertaker's Garland (po J.Bishop; E. Wilson) 1922
Undertow (scr Eaton) 1930
Undertow (f Steele) 1930
Underworld (f Delillo) 1997
Underworld (Paying the Penalty) (scr Hecht) 1927
Undesirable Governess (f Crawford) 1910
Undiscovered Country (f Howells) 1880
Undiscovered Fishing Stories (f Grey) 1983
Une Affaire de viol (f Himes) 1963
Une Grande Voix du Ciel a la France (o Mather) 1725
Unearthing (po Zukofsky) 1965
Unemployed Fortune Teller (o Simic) 1994
Unemployed Ghost (scr Connelly) 1931
Unending Blues (po Simic) 1986
Unending Crusade (f Sherwood) 1932
Unexpected Guests (pl Howells) 1893
Unfair Arguments with Existence: Seven Plays for a New Theatre
    (pl Ferlinghetti) 1963
Unfinished Cathedral (f Stribling) 1934
Unfinished Poems (po Moore) 1972
Unguided Tour (scr Sontag) 1983
Unholy Garden (scr Hecht; MacArthur) 1931
Unholy Loves (f Oates) 1979
Unholy Night (scr Hecht) 1929
Unhurried View of Erotica (o Nathan) 1958
Unicorns (o Huneker) 1917
U.S. Minister Bedloe (pl Ade) 1910
U.S.A (f Dos Passos) 1938
US. 1 (po Rukeyser) 1938
Union Club Mysteries (f Asimov) 1983
United States and England (o Paulding) 1815
Universal Baseball Association, Inc., J. Henry Waugh, Prop (f
    Coover) 1968
Universal Fears (f Hawkes) 1978
Universe: From Flat Earth to Black Holes—and Beyond (o
    Asimov) 1980

Universe: From Flat Earth to Quasar (o Asimov) 1966
University Pieces (o Faulkner) 1962
Unknowable (o Santayana) 1923
Unknown Man (f Leonard) 1977
Unknown Poe: An Anthology of Fugitive Writings (o Poe) 1980
Unlovely Sin and Other Stories of Desire's Pawns (f Hecht) 1927
Unmarried Father (f Dell) 1927
Unmasking of O (scr Vogel) 1997
Unpublished Essay on the Trinity (o Edwards) 1903
Unpublished Freneauana (o Freneau) 1918
Unpublished Letters in the Huntington Library (o B. Taylor) 1937
Unpublished Limericks and Cartoons (po Harte) 1933
Unpublished Poems (po Dickinson) 1935
Unpublished Selections from the Diary (o Nin) 1968
Unpunished: A Mystery (f Gilman) 1997
Unseen (scr Chandler) 1945
Unseen Hand (pl Shepard) 1969
Unseen Versailles (o Auchincloss) 1981
Unshaken Friend: Profile of Maxwell Perkins (o Cowley) 1986
Unspeakable Gentleman (f Marquand) 1922
Unspeakable Practices, Unnatural Acts (f Barthelme) 1968
Unstoppable Gray Fox (tv Saroyan) 1962
Until the Day Break (f Bromfield) 1942
Until They Sail (scr R. Anderson) 1957
Unto Such Glory (pl Green) 1928
Untouchables (scr Mamet) 1987
Untriangulated Stars: Letters to Harry de Forest Smith 1890-1905
    (o Robinson) 1947
Unvanquished (f Faulkner) 1938
Unwelcome Man (f Frank) 1917
Unwelcome Words: Seven Stories (f Bowles) 1987
Unwritten History (o J. Miller) 1972
Unwritten Play of Lord Byron (pl W. Irving) 1925
Up above the World (f Bowles) 1966
Up Close and Personal (scr Didion) 1996
Up for Grabs (f E. Gardner) 1964
Up from Nowhere (pl Tarkington) 1919
Up from Paradise (pl A. Miller) 1974
Up from Slavery: An Autobiography (o Washington) 1901
Up to Thursday (pl Shepard) 1965
U.P. Trail (f Grey) 1918
Uplands (po Ammons) 1970
Uplands of Dream (o Saltus) 1925
Uplift of Lucifer (pl Baum) 1915
Uplifters' Minstrels (pl Baum) 1916
Upon the Sweeping Flood and Other Stories (f Oates) 1966
Upper Berth (f Crawford) 1894
Upperworld (scr Hecht) 1934
Uprising (po Duncan) 1965
Ups and Downs (f Arthur) 1857
Upstate: Records and Recollections of Northern New York (o E.
    Wilson) 1971
Upton Sinclair: A Study in Social Protest (o Dell) 1927
Urania: A Rhymed Lesson (po Holmes) 1846
Uriel and Other Poems (po MacKaye) 1912
Urkey Island (f Steele) 1926
Urn (po Cowley) 1986
USA: A Dramatic Review (pl Dos Passos) 1963
Useful Knowledge (o Stein) 1928
Useless Servants (f Hinojosa) 1993
Uses of the Erotic: The Erotic as Power (o Lorde) 1978

Usher II (tv Bradbury) 1990
Usual Star (po Doolittle) 1934
Utah Blaine (f L'Amour) 1954
Utopia 14 (f Vonnegut) 1954
Utterly Perfect Murder (tv Bradbury) 1992

V (f Pynchon) 1963
Vacation of the Kelwyns: An Idyl of the Middle Eighteen-Seventies (f Howells) 1920
Vacation Song (po Millay) 1936
Vacation Time: Poems for Children (po Giovanni) 1980
Vagabond Scholar (o Santayana) 1962
Vagabond Tales (f Boyesen) 1889
Vagabondia (f Burnett) 1883
Vagaries Malicieux: Two Stories (f Barnes) 1974
Vain (pl Wister) 1958
Valdez Is Coming (f Leonard) 1970
Valerie (pl Belasco) 1886
Valiant One (pl Crothers) 1937
Valiant Runaways (f Atherton) 1898
Valley Forge (pl M. Anderson) 1934
Valley of Decision (f Wharton) 1902
Valley of the Moon (f London) 1913
Valley of the Tennessee (scr Sarton) 1944
Valley of Vision (f Fisher) 1951
Valley of Wild Horses (f Grey) 1947
Valparaiso (pl Delillo) 1999
Vampires (f Rechy) 1971
Van Bibber and Others (f Richard Davis) 1892
Van Der Decken: A Legendary Play of the Sea (pl Belasco) 1915
Van Gogh's Room at Arles: Three Novellas (f Elkin) 1993
Van Wyck Brooks (o Cowley) 1963
Van Zorn (pl Robinson) 1914
Vanderbilt Clinic (o Steinbeck) 1947
Vanderbilt Era: Profiles of a Gilded Age (o Auchincloss) 1989
Vandover and the Brute (f Norris) 1914
Vanishing American (f Grey) 1925
Vanishing Indian (f Grey) 1926
Vanishing Pioneer (scr Grey) 1928
Vanity of Duluoz: An Adventurous Education 1935-46 (f Kerouac) 1968
Vanity Square: A Story of Fifth Avenue Life (f Saltus) 1906
Vanqui (pl J. Williams) 1998
Vanya on 42nd Street (scr Mamet) 1994
Variations (o Huneker) 1921
Varieties of Religious Experience: A Study in Human Nature (o W. James) 1902
Variety of People (f Marquis) 1929
Varying Shore (pl Akins) 1921
Vasconselos: A Romance of the New World (f Simms) 1853
Vassall Morton (f Parkman) 1856
Vassar Viewed Voraciously: 16 Pencil Sketches (o Stevens) 1995
Vastness and Indifference of the World (po Eberhart) 1965
Vaudeville for a Princess and Other Poems (po Schwartz) 1950
Vegetable (pl Fitzgerald) 1923
Vehement Flame (f Deland) 1922
Veil, Turbine, Cord, and Bird (po Duncan) 1979
Vein of Iron (f Glasgow) 1935
Vein of Riches (f Knowles) 1978
Veldt (f Bradbury) 1987
Velvet Horn (f Lytle) 1957

Venetian Glass Nephew (f Wylie) 1925
Vengeful Gods (f Atherton) 1928
Venice Observed: Comments on Venetian Civilization (o McCarthy) 1956
Venice Poem (po Duncan) 1978
Venice, The Place and the People (o Crawford) 1909
Venture in 1777 (f S. Mitchell) 1908
Ventures in Common Sense (o E. Howe) 1919
Ventures into Verse (po Mencken) 1903
Venus (pl Crothers) 1927
Venus Envy (f R Brown) 1993
Venus in Sparta (f Auchincloss) 1958
Venus, Near Neighbor of the Sun (o Asimov) 1980
Venus: A Play (pl Parks) 1998
Vera the Medium (f Richard Davis) 1908
Verdict (scr Mamet) 1982
Verge (pl Glaspell) 1922
Vermilion Gate (f Lin Yutang) 1953
Vermont Notebook (po Ashbery) 1975
Vermont Sketches (pl Mamet) 1984
Verse (po Updike) 1965
Verse and Prose from the George H. Yenowine Collection (o Field) 1917
Verses (po H. Jackson) 1870
Verses (po Jewett) 1916
Verses (po Wharton) 1878
Verses and Jingles (po Ade) 1911
Verses from 1929 On (po Nash) 1959
Verses on the Times (po Wilbur) 1978
Versi prosaici (po Pound) 1959
Versus (po Nash) 1949
Very First Christmas Morning (pl Vonnegut) 1962
Very Young Poets (o Brooks) 1983
Vesta (pl Daly) 1877
Veteran and His Pipe (o Tourgée) 1886
Veteran Birth: The Gadfly Poems 1947-1949 (po Dickey) 1978
Via Crucis: A Romance of the Second Crusade (f Crawford) 1899
Vial Poured Out upon the Sea: A Remarkable Relation of Certain Pirates (o Mather) 1726
Vicarious Years (f Van Druten) 1955
Victim (f Bellow) 1947
Victor Hugo, and Golgotha: Two Essays (o Saltus) 1925
Victor Ollnee's Discipline (f Garland) 1911
Victor Vane, The Young Secretary (f Alger) 1894
Victoria (f Rowson) 1786
Victorina (o Mather) 1717
Victors (pl Wilder) 1949
Victory Gardens (scr Bambara) 1977
Victory over Japan (f Gilchrist) 1984
Vienna Notes (pl Nelson) 1978
Vietnam (o McCarthy) 1967
Vietnamese Wedding (pl Fornés) 1967
Vieux Carre (pl T. Williams) 1977
View and Reviews (pl H. James) 1908
View from a Height (o Asimov) 1963
View from Eighty (o Cowley) 1980
View from the Bridge (pl A. Miller) 1955
Views A-Foot (o B. Taylor) 1846
Views and Reviews in American Literature, History and Fiction (o Simms) 1846-1847
Vigil of a Nation (f Lin Yutang) 1944

Vigil of Faith and Other Poems (po Hoffman) 1842

Vignettes of Italy: A Cycle of Nine Songs for High Voice (po Teasdale) 1919

Viking Portable Library Steinbeck (o Steinbeck) 1943

Villa Magdalena (f Santos) 1965

Village (f Mamet) 1994

Village Doctors and Other Tales (f Arthur) 1843

Village Magazine (o Lindsay) 1910

Village Merchant (po Freneau) 1794

Village: Are You Ready Yet Not Yet (pl Stein) 1928

Villages Are the Heart of Spain (o Dos Passos) 1937

Vine Leaves (pl B. Smith) 1937

Vinegar Puss (o S. Perelman) 1975

Vineland (f Pynchon) 1990

Vintage Bradbury (f Bradbury) 1965

Vintage Mencken (o Mencken) 1955

Violent Bear It Away (f O'Connor) 1960

Violent Pastoral (po Merrill) 1965

Viper Jazz (po J. Tate) 1976

Virgilius (o Mather) 1719

Virgin Heiresses (f Queen) 1954

Virgin of Port Lligat (po Chávez) 1959

Virgin of the Sun (pl Dunlap) 1800

Virginalia (po Chivers) 1853

Virginia (f Glasgow) 1913

Virginia (pl Payne) 1834

Virginia Comedians (f J. Cooke) 1854

Virginia: A History of the People (o J. Cooke) 1883

Virginian: A Horseman of the Plains (f Wister) 1902

Virginie: Her Two Lives (f Hawkes) 1982

Virtual Reality (po B. Perelman) 1993

Virtue of Selfishness: A New Concept of Egoism (o Rand) 1964

Virtuous Girl (f Bodenheim) 1930

Virtuous Knight (f Sherwood) 1931

Virtuous Woman (f Gibbons) 1989

Vision in Spring (po Faulkner) 1984

Vision of Columbus (po Barlow) 1787

Vision of Cortes, Cain, and Other Poems (po Simms) 1829

Vision of Echard and Other Poems (po Whittier) 1878

Vision of Sir Launfal (po J. Lowell) 1848

Visionaries (f Huneker) 1905

Visionary Company: A Reading of English Romantic Poetry (o Bloom) 1961

Visionary Farms (pl Eberhart) 1951

Visioning (f Glaspell) 1911

Visions of Cody (f Kerouac) 1973

Visions of Gerard (f Kerouac) 1963

Visions of the Evening (po Fletcher) 1913

Visions of the Universe (o Asimov) 1981

Visit (pl Fornés) 1981

Visit to a Small Planet (tv Vidal) 1955

Visit to a Small Planet: A Comedy Akin to a Vaudeville (pl Vidal) 1957

Visit to India, China, and Japan in the Year 1853 (o B. Taylor) 1855

Visiting Emily Dickinson's Grave and Other Poems (po Bly) 1979

Vita Nova (po Glück) 1999

Vital Christianity (o Mather) 1725

Viva Villa! (scr Hecht) 1934

Viva Zapata! (scr Steinbeck) 1952

Vixen: Poems (po Merwin) 1997

Vixens (f Yerby) 1947

Vlemk, The Box-Painter (f J. Gardner) 1979

V-Letter and Other Poems (po Shapiro) 1944

Vocational Education in the Light of the World War (o Dewey) 1918

Voice (f Deland) 1912

Voice at the Back Door (f Spencer) 1956

Voice from Heaven (o Mather) 1719

Voice from the South (o Longstreet) 1847

Voice of Bataan (po Bulosan) 1943

Voice of God in a Tempest (o Mather) 1723

Voice of McConnell (pl Cohan) 1918

Voice of Nature (pl Dunlap) 1803

Voice of Reason: Essays in Objectivist Thought (o Rand) 1989

Voice of the City: Further Stories of the Four Million (f Henry) 1908

Voice of the People (f Glasgow) 1900

Voice of the Turtle (pl Van Druten) 1944

Voiced Connections of James Dickey: Interview and Conversations (o Dickey) 1989

Voices from the Moon (f Dubus) 1984

Voices in the House (f Buck) 1953

Voices of Freedom (po Whittier) 1846

Voices of the Night (po Longfellow) 1839

Volcano (f Santos) 1965

Volcano Journal (o Hongo) 1995

Volcano Lover (f Sontag) 1992

Voltaire (scr Green) 1933

Voltaire: A Biographical Fantasy (po Riding) 1927

Voltmeier (f Simms) 1969

Volunteers: A Musical Entertainment (pl Rowson) 1795

Voodoo Gods: An Inquiry into Native Myths and Magic in Jamaica and Haiti (o Hurston) 1939

Voyage (pl Hwang) 1992

Voyage and Other Versions of Poems by Baudelaire (po Lowell) 1968

Voyage to Boston (po Freneau) 1775

Voyage to Pagany (f W. Williams) 1928

Voyage to Purilia (f Rice) 1930

Voyage Unplanned (f Yerby) 1974

V.S. Naipaul: An Introduction to His Works (o Theroux) 1972

VV (f Alcott) 1870

VV (po Cummings) 1931

Waddy Googan (pl Harrigan) 1888

Wag the Dog (scr Mamet) 1997

Wager and Other Poems (po S. Mitchell) 1900

Waif of the Plains (f Harte) 1890

Waifs and Strays (f Henry) 1917

Wait and Hope (f Alger) 1877

Wait and Win: The Story of Jack Drummond's Pluck (f Alger) 1908

Wait Till the Clouds Roll By (f Alger) 1890

Waiting for Lefty (pl Odets) 1935

Waiting for the End (o Fiedler) 1964

Waiting for the Verdict (f Rebecca Davis) 1868

Waiting for Winter (f J. O'Hara) 1966

Waiting to Exhale (f McMillan) 1992

Wake for the Living: A Family Chronicle (o Lytle) 1975

Wake Island (po Rukeyser) 1942

Wake Up, Jonathan (pl Rice) 1921

Wakefield: A Folk-Masque of America (pl MacKaye) 1932
Wakefulness: Poems (po Ashbery) 1998
Waking: Poems 1933-1953 (po Roethke) 1953
Walden (o Thoreau) 1854
Waldo (f Theroux) 1967
Waldo and Magic, Inc (f Heinlein) 1950
Waldo Trench and Others: Stories of Americans in Italy (f Fuller) 1908
Waldo: Genius in Orbit (f Heinlein) 1958
Wales—A Visitation, July 29, 1967 (po Ginsberg) 1968
Walk on the Wild Side (f Algren) 1956
Walk through the Woods (f Sarton) 1976
Walkin' for Dat Cake (pl Harrigan) 1877
Walking (po Harrison) 1969
Walking Down the Stairs: Selections from Interviews (o Kinnell) 1977
Walking Drum (f L'Amour) 1984
Walking the Black Cat (po Simic) 1996
Walking to Sleep: New Poems and Translations (po Wilbur) 1969
Wall (po Creeley) 1969
Wall (f Rinehart) 1938
Wallace Stevens: The Poems of Our Climate (o Bloom) 1977
Walls Do Not Fall (po Doolittle) 1944
Wally for Queen! The Private Life of Royalty (pl Sinclair) 1936
Walter Griffith (f Alger) 1901
Walter Sherwood's Probation (f Alger) 1897
Wampeters, Foma, and Granfalloons: Opinions (o Vonnegut) 1974
Wan Lee, The Pagan and Other Sketches (f Harte) 1876
Wanderer (f Richter) 1966
Wanderer of the Wasteland (f Grey) 1923
Wanderer: A Colloquial Poem (po Channing) 1871
Wanderer's Daysong (po Levertov) 1981
Wandering Ghosts (f Crawford) 1911
Wandering Knife (f Rinehart) 1952
Wandering Recollections of a Somewhat Busy Life: An Autobiography (o Neal) 1869
Wanderings (f Herrick) 1925
Want Bone (po Pinsky) 1990
Wanton Mally (f Tarkington) 1932
Wapping Alice (f Twain) 1981
Wapshot Chronicle (f Cheever) 1957
Wapshot Scandal (f Cheever) 1964
War against the Kitchen Sink (pl Guare) 1996
War below Zero: The Battle for Greenland (o La Farge) 1944
War Boys (pl N. Wallace) 1993
War Bugs (o MacArthur) 1929
War Chief (f E. Burroughs) 1927
War Despatches (o S. Crane) 1964
War Games (f Morris) 1972
War in Heaven (f Barry) 1938
War in Heaven (pl Shepard) 1985
War Is Kind (po S. Crane) 1899
War of the Standards: Coin and Credit Versus Coin Without Credit (o Tourgée) 1896
War Party (f L'Amour) 1975
War Stories: Poems about Long Ago and Now (po Nemerov) 1987
War Tide (f Lin Tai-yi) 1943
Ward of the Golden Gate (f Harte) 1890
Warlock (f Harrison) 1981
Warm Wine: An Idyll (f Updike) 1973

Warning at My Leisure (po Goodman) 1939
Warning Hill (f Marquand) 1930
Warning to the Flocks (o Mather) 1700
Warnings (pl O'Neill) 1914
Warrior Marks: Female Genital Mutilation and the Sexual Blinding of Women (o A. Walker) 1993
Warrior's Path (f L'Amour) 1980
Wars I Have Seen (o Stein) 1945
Was That a Real Poem and Other Essays (o Creeley) 1979
Was That a Real Poem or Did You Just Make It Up Yourself (o Creeley) 1976
Washing (pl Fornés) 1976
Washington and Its Romance (o Page) 1923
Washington, D.C (f Vidal) 1967
Washington Irving (o Warner) 1881
Washington Square (f H. James) 1881
Washington, The Man Who Made Us (pl MacKaye) 1919
Waste (f Herrick) 1924
Waste Land (po Eliot) 1922
Waste of Timelessness and Other Early Stories (f Nin) 1977
Watch and Ward (f H. James) 1878
Watch on the Rhine (pl Hammett; Hellman) 1941
Watch on the Rhine (scr Hammett; Hellman) 1943
Watch Your Thirst: A Dry Opera (pl Wister) 1923
Watchers Out of Time and Others (f Lovecraft) 1974
Watchfires (f Auchincloss) 1982
Watchful Gods and Other Stories (f Clark) 1950
Watching My Name Go By (o Mailer) 1975
Watchtower over Tomorrow (scr Hecht) 1945
Water Engine (scr Mamet) 1992
Water Engine: An American Fable and Mr. Happiness (pl Mamet) 1977
Water Street (po Merrill) 1962
Water under the Earth (po Bly) 1972
Water Unlimited (o Roberts) 1957
Water Witch (f Cooper) 1830
Water-Bug's Mittens: Ezra Pound, What We Can Use (o Dickey) 1980
Water-Cresses (f Alcott) 1879
Water-Method Man (f J. Irving) 1972
Waterlily Fire: Poems 1932-62 (po Rukeyser) 1962
Waterloo Bridge (scr Behrman) 1940
Waterloo Bridge (pl Sherwood) 1930
Waters of Kronos (f Richter) 1960
Waterworks (f Doctorow) 1994
Wave (po Ashbery) 1984
Wave of Life (f Fitch) 1909
Wax Museum (pl Hawkes) 1966
Way Back (pl Laurents) 1946
Way Down South (scr Hughes) 1939
Way for a Sailor (scr MacArthur) 1930
Way of Ecben (f Cabell) 1929
Way of the World (pl Fitch) 1901
Way Out (pl Frost) 1929
Way Out of Educational Confusion (o Dewey) 1931
Way Some People Die (f Macdonald) 1951
Way Some People Live: A Book of Stories (f Cheever) 1943
Way to Peace (f Deland) 1910
Way to Prosper (f Arthur) 1851
Way to Prosperity (o Mather) 1690
Way to Rainy Mountain (po Momaday) 1969

Way to the Gold (f Steele) 1955

Way to the House of Santa Claus: A Christmas Story (f Burnett) 1916

Way to the Present: A Personal Record (o Van Druten) 1938

Way to Wealth (o Franklin) 1774

Way We Live (pl Daly) 1880

Way We Were (scr Laurents) 1973

Way We Were (f Laurents) 1972

Wayfarer: A Voice from the Southern Mountains (o Dickey) 1988

Ways of Light: Poems 1972-1980 (po Eberhart) 1980

Ways of Providence (f Arthur) 1852

Ways of the Hour: A Tale (f Cooper) 1850

Ways of White Folks (f Hughes) 1934

Wayside Courtships (f Garland) 1897

Wayward Bus (f Steinbeck) 1947

We and Our Neighbors (f Stowe) 1875

We Are Betrayed (f Fisher) 1935

We Are Chicano (pl Portillo Trambley) 1974

We Bombed in New Haven (pl Heller) 1968

We Don't Live Here Anymore (f Dubus) 1984

We Don't Live Here Anymore: The Novellas of Andre Dubus (f Dubus) 1984

We Don't Love with Our Teeth (f L. Smith) 1994

We Have Always Lived in the Castle (f S. Jackson) 1962

We Live Again (scr M. Anderson; Wilder) 1934

We Righteous Bombers (pl Bullins) 1969

We Stand United (radio S. Benét) 1940

We Stand United and Other Radio Scripts (pl S. Benét) 1945

We, the Dangerous: New and Selected Poems (po Mirikitani) 1995

We the Living (f Rand) 1936

We the People: A Symphonic Drama of George Washington and the Establishment of the United States Government (pl Green) 1976

We, The People (pl Rice) 1933

We Walk the Way of the New World (po Madhubuti) 1970

We Were the Mulvaneys (f Oates) 1997

We Will Never Die (pl Hecht) 1943

Weak Spot (pl Kelly) 1922

Wealth of the Soil (o Bromfield) 1952

Wear and Tear (o S. Mitchell) 1871

Wearing of the Gray. Being Personal Portraits, Scenes, and Adventures of the War (o J. Cooke) 1867

Weary Blues (po Hughes) 1926

Weather (po W. Stafford) 1969

Weather for Poetry: Essays, Reviews, and Notes on Poetry 1977-81 (o Hall) 1982

Weather Forecast for Utopia and Vicinity: Poems 1967-82 (po Simic) 1983

Weathergoose Woo! (f MacKaye) 1929

Web (pl O'Neill) 1914

Web and the Rock (f Thomas [Clayton] Wolfe) 1939

Web of Life (f Herrick) 1900

Wedding (pl Nelson) 1980

Wedding Band: A Love/Hate Story in Black and White (pl Childress) 1966

Wedding Bouquet: Ballet (pl Stein) 1936

Wedding Day and Other Stories (f Boyle) 1930

Wedding Finger (pl Purdy) 1973

Wedding in Hell (po Simic) 1994

Wedge (po W. Williams) 1944

Week on the Concord and Merrimack Rivers (o Thoreau) 1849

Weekend for Three (scr Parker) 1941

Weekend: A Comedy in Two Acts (pl Vidal) 1968

Weeping Pierrot and Laughing Pierrot (pl A. Lowell) 1914

Weimar 2 (pl Baraka) 1981

Weird Shadow over Innsmouth and Other Stories of the Supernatural (f Lovecraft) 1944

Welcome to Hard Times (f Doctorow) 1960

Welcome to Our City (pl Thomas [Clayton] Wolfe) 1923

Welcome to the Monkey House: A Collection of Short Works (f Vonnegut) 1968

Welded (pl O'Neill) 1924

We'll Have Fun (f J. O'Hara) 1996

Well of Bethlehem (po Goodman) 1957

Wellfleet Whale and Companion Poems (po Kunitz) 1983

Wellsprings of Life (o Asimov) 1960

Well-tempered Critic (o Frye) 1963

Wept of Wish Ton-Tish (f Cooper) 1829

We're No Angels (scr Mamet) 1989

Were You Ever a Child? (o Dell) 1919

West (po Olson) 1966

West from a Car-Window (o Richard Davis) 1892

West from Singapore (f L'Amour) 1987

West of Pittsburgh (pl Connelly; Kaufman) 1922

West of the Pecos (f Grey) 1937

West of Your City (po W. Stafford) 1960

West Side Story (pl Laurents) 1957

Westbrooke Hall (f J. Cooke) 1891

Western: A Saga of the Great Plains (f Yerby) 1982

Western Approaches: Poems 1973-1975 (po Nemerov) 1975

Western Borders (po S. Howe) 1976

Western Boy (f Alger) 1878

Western Canon: The Books and School of the Ages (o Bloom) 1994

Western Electric Communicade (pl Laurents) 1944

Western Ghost Town (pl B. Smith) 1939

Western Journal: A Daily Log of the Great Parks Trip, June 20-July 2, 1938 (o Thomas [Clayton] Wolfe) 1951

Western Lands (f W. Burroughs) 1987

Western Night (pl B. Smith) 1938

Western Star (po S. Benét) 1943

Western Union (f Grey) 1939

Western Writings (o S. Crane) 1979

Westerner (f Grey) 1977

West-Running Brook (po Frost) 1928

Westward Ha! or, Around the World in Eighty Cliches (o S. Perelman) 1948

Westward Ho! (f Paulding) 1832

Westward the Tide (f L'Amour) 1950

Westward to a High Mountain: The Colorado Writings of Helen Hunt Jackson (o H. Jackson) 1994

Westways: A Village Chronicle (f S. Mitchell) 1913

Wet Blanket (pl Daly) 1886

Wet Days at Edgewood, with Old Farmers, Old Gardeners, and Old Pastorals (o D. Mitchell) 1865

Wet Parade (f Sinclair) 1931

Wetherel Affair (f De Forest) 1873

Whale (f Melville) 1851

Wharton's War Charities in France (o Wharton) 1918

What a Kingdom It Was (po Kinnell) 1960

What a Man Sees Who Goes Away from Home (f Ade) 1896

What a Way to Go (f Morris) 1962

What Advertising Brings (pl Cohan) 1915
What Are Masterpieces (o Stein) 1940
What Are Years (po Moore) 1941
What Became of Anna Bolton (f Bromfield) 1944
What Diantha Did (f Gilman) 1912
What Didymus Did (f Sinclair) 1954
What Dooley Says (o Dunne) 1899
What Dreams May Come (f Atherton) 1888
What Happened When the Hopi Hit New York (po Rose) 1981
What Have I Ever Lost by Dying?: Collected Prose Poems (po Bly) 1992
What Henry James Knew and Other Essays on Writers (o Ozick) 1993
What I Lived For (f Oates) 1994
What Is Democracy? (o Dewey) 1939
What Is Found There: Notebooks on Poetry and Politics (o Rich) 1995
What Is She? A Sonnet of Sonnets to Marion Morse (po MacKaye) 1943
What Maisie Knew (f H. James) 1897
What Moon Drove Me to This? (po Harjo) 1980
What Novels Are (o Calisher) 1969
What Odd Expedients and Other Poems (po Jeffers) 1981
What of It? (o Lardner) 1925
What Price Glory? (pl M. Anderson) 1924
What Should She Do? or, Jealousy (pl Daly) 1874
What the Grass Says (po Simic) 1967
What the Hell for You Left Your Heart in San Francisco (f Santos) 1987
What the Moon Brings (f Lovecraft) 1970
What Thou Lovest Well, Remains American (po Hugo) 1975
What Time Collects (f Farrell) 1964
What Was Literature? (o Fiedler) 1982
What Was Mine and Other Stories (f Beattie) 1991
What Was the Relationship of the Lone Ranger to the Means of Production? (pl Baraka) 1979
What We Talk About When We Talk About Love (f Carver) 1981
What You Ought to Know about Your Baby (o Mencken) 1910
Whatever Happened to Gloomy Gus of the Chicago Bears? (f Coover) 1987
What's Happened to the Thorne's House? (pl Kopit) 1972
What's O'Clock (po A. Lowell) 1925
Wheat That Springeth Green (f Powers) 1988
Wheel of Life (f Glasgow) 1906
Wheel of Love and Other Stories (f Oates) 1970
When a Man Marries (f Rinehart) 1909
When a Woman Enjoys Herself and Other Tales of a Small Town (f E. Howe) 1928
When All the Woods Are Green (f S. Mitchell) 1894
When Boyhood Dreams Come True (f Farrell) 1946
When Elephants Last in the Dooryard Bloomed: Celebrations for Almost Any Day in the Year (po Bradbury) 1973
When God Laughs and Other Stories (f London) 1911
When I Look at Pictures (po Ferlinghetti) 1990
When Ladies Meet (pl Crothers) 1932
When Malindy Sings (po Dunbar) 1903
When One Has Lived a Long Time Alone (po Kinnell) 1990
When Peoples Meet (o Locke) 1942
When She Was Good (f P. Roth) 1967
When the Jack Hollers (pl Hughes) 1936
When the Rattlesnake Sounds: A Play (pl Childress) 1975

When the Santos Talked: A Retablo of New Mexico Tales (f Chávez) 1977
When the Turtles Sing and Other Unusual Tales (f Marquis) 1928
When the Whippoorwill— (f Rawlings) 1940
When Time Was Born (f Farrell) 1966
When Tomorrow Comes (scr Cain) 1939
When We Were Here Together (po Patchen) 1957
When West Was West (f Wister) 1928
Where Are the Other Rowboats? (po Patchen) 1966
Where Are You Going, Where Have You Been?: Selected Early Stories (f Oates) 1993
Where Are You Going, Where Have You Been? Stories of Young America (f Oates) 1974
Where Does One Go When There's No Place Left to Go? (o Crews) 1998
Where Is He? (pl Dunlap) 1801
Where Is Here? (f Oates) 1992
Where Robot Mice and Robot Men Run Round in Robot Towns: New Poems, Both Light and Dark (po Bradbury) 1977
Where Sparrows Work Hard (po Soto) 1981
Where the Battle Was Fought (f Murfree) 1884
Where the Blue Begins (f Morley) 1922
Where the Long Grass Blows (f L'Amour) 1976
Where the Mississippi Meets the Amazon (pl Hagedorn) 1978
Where the Sidewalk Ends (scr Hecht) 1950
Where The Cross Is Made (pl O'Neill) 1918
Where There's a Will (f Rinehart) 1912
Where There's a Will (f Stout) 1940
Where Water Comes Together with Other Water (po Carver) 1985
Where Were You When It Went Down? (pl Mamet) 1988
Where You'll Find Me and Other Stories (f Beattie) 1986
Where's Daddy? (pl Inge) 1965
Whiff of Death (f Asimov) 1968
While the Heart Beats Young (po Riley) 1906
Whilomville Stories (f S. Crane) 1900
Whip (po Creeley) 1957
Whirl Asunder (f Atherton) 1895
Whirligig (pl Wellman) 1989
Whirligigs (f Henry) 1910
Whirlpool (scr Hecht) 1950
Whispering Friends (pl Cohan) 1928
Whispering Sands: Stories of Gold Fever and the Western Desert (f E. Gardner) 1981
Whispers (scr Connelly) 1920
Whistle (f J. Jones) 1978
Whistle: A Work-in-Progress (f J. Jones) 1974
Whistlejacket (f Hawkes) 1988
White (po Simic) 1972
White Album (o Didion) 1979
White Blackbird and Other Writings (f Nin) 1985
White Buildings (po H. Crane) 1926
White Center (po Hugo) 1980
White Deer (f Thurber) 1945
White Desert (pl M. Anderson) 1923
White Dresses (pl Green) 1923
White Elephant (pl Sherwood) 1916
White Fang (f London) 1906
White Heron and Other Stories (f Jewett) 1886
White Horses of Vienna and Other Stories (f Boyle) 1936
White Jacket (f Melville) 1850
White Magic (f D. Phillips) 1910

White Maid (pl Payne) 1827
White Man, Listen! (o R. Wright) 1957
White Man's Burden (pl Theroux) 1987
White Mice (f Richard Davis) 1909
White Morning: A Novel of the Power of the German Women in Wartime (f Atherton) 1918
White Mule (f W. Williams) 1937
White Negro (o Mailer) 1957
White Noise (f Delillo) 1985
White Oxen and Other Stories (f Burke) 1924
White People (f Burnett) 1917
White Rat and Other Short Stories (f G. Jones) 1977
White Reader (o White) 1966
White Robe (f Cabell) 1928
White Rose (f Traven) 1965
White Sail and Other Poems (po Guiney) 1887
White Sand (po E. Wilson) 1950
White Shroud: Poems 1980-1985 (po Ginsberg) 1986
White Sister (f Crawford) 1909
White Terror and the Red: A Novel of Revolutionary Russia (f Cahan) 1905
White Wings (pl Barry) 1927
White-Faced Pacer (f Neal) 1863
White-Footed Deer and Other Poems (po Bryant) 1844
White-Haired Lover (po Shapiro) 1968
White-Jacket (f Melville) 1850
Whitewash (o Shange) 1997
Whitman and the Civil War: A Collection of Original Articles and Manuscripts (o Whitman) 1933
Whitman Looks at the Schools (o Whitman) 1950
Whitman of the New York Aurora (o Whitman) 1950
Whitman's Civil War (o Whitman) 1960
Whitman's New York: From Manhattan to Montauk (o Whitman) 1963
Whitman's Workshop (o Whitman) 1928
Whittier on Writers and Writing: The Uncollected Critical Writings (o Whittier) 1950
Who Are Happiest? and Other Stories (f Arthur) 1852
Who Are We Now? (po Ferlinghetti) 1976
Who Are You Really, Wanderer: Pages in the Language of Respect and Conciliation (o W. Stafford) 1993
Who Is Greatest? and Other Stories (f Arthur) 1852
Who Killed Don José (pl Anaya) 1987
Who Lost an American? Being a Guide to the Seamier Sides of New York City, Inner London, Paris, Dublin, Barcelona, Seville, Almería, Istanbul, Crete and Chicago, Illinois (o Algren) 1963
Who Owns America? A New Declaration of Independence (o Davidson; Lytle; Ransom) 1936
Who Stole the Monkey? (pl Harrigan) 1874
Who Will Know Us? (po Soto) 1990
Who's Afraid of Virginia Woolf? (pl Albee) 1962
Who's Who (pl Richard Davis) 1913
Whole Motion: Collected Poems, 1945-1992 (po Dickey) 1992
Whole Voyald and Other Stories (f Saroyan) 1956
Wholly Absorbed into My Own Conduits (po Olson) 1968
Whosoever Shall Offend (f Crawford) 1904
Why Are We in Vietnam? (f Mailer) 1967
Why, Daddy? (scr Benchley) 1944
Why Does Nobody Collect Me? (o Benchley) 1935
Why Europe Leaves Home (o Roberts) 1922
Why I Live at the P.O. and Other Stories (f Welty) 1995

Why the Y? (In Ybor) (pl Wellman) 1994
Wichita Vortex Sutra (po Ginsberg) 1966
Wicker (po Hejinian) 1996
Wickford Point (f Marquand) 1939
Wide Fields (f Green) 1928
Wide Is the Gate (f Sinclair) 1943
Wide Net and Other Stories (f Welty) 1943
Widening Circle (o Van Druten) 1957
Widow (pl Fornés) 1961
Widow Bedott (pl Nasby) 1879
Widow Chuan (f Lin Yutang) 1952
Widow for One Year (f J. Irving) 1998
Widow Morrison (f Arthur) 1841
Widow Rugby's Husband, A Night at the Ugly Man's, and Other Tales of Alabama (f Hooper) 1851
Widows (pl Kushner) 1991
Widow's Marriage (pl Boker) 1852
Widows Wear Weeds (f E. Gardner) 1966
Wieland (f Brown) 1798
Wife (f Arthur) 1845
Wife (f Mukherjee) 1975
Wife of His Youth and Other Stories of the Color Line (f Chesnutt) 1899
Wife of Two Husbands (pl Dunlap) 1804
Wigwam and the Cabin (f Simms) 1845-46
Wilbur Daniel Steele: Stories (f Steele) 1996
Wild Boys: A Book of the Dead (f W. Burroughs) 1971
Wild Card: Selected Poems, Early and Late (po Shapiro) 1998
Wild Country (f Bromfield) 1948
Wild Drams of a New Beginning (po Ferlinghetti) 1988
Wild Earth's Nobility: A Novel of the Old West (f Waters) 1935
Wild Flag: Editorials from the New Yorker on Federal World Government and Other Matters (o White) 1946
Wild Goslings: A Selection of Fugitive Pieces (o W. Benét) 1927
Wild Horse Mesa (f Grey) 1928
Wild Huntsman (pl W. Irving) 1924
Wild in the Country (scr Odets) 1961
Wild Iris (po Glück) 1992
Wild Is the River (f Bromfield) 1941
Wild Man of Borneo (pl Connelly) 1927
Wild Nights (f Oates) 1985
Wild 90 (scr Mailer) 1968
Wild Old Wicked Man and Other Poems (po MacLeish) 1968
Wild Ones (f Fisher) 1952
Wild Palms (f Faulkner) 1939
Wild Patience Has Taken Me This Far: Poems, 1978-1981 (po Rich) 1981
Wild Saturday and Other Stories (f Oates) 1984
Wild Scenes in the Forest and Prairie (f Hoffman) 1839
Wildash (f Ingraham) 1847
Wildbird (f Ingraham) 1869
Wilderness Road: A Symphonic Outdoor Drama (pl Green) 1955
Wilderness Trek (f Grey) 1944
Wilderness: A Tale of the Civil War (f R. Warren) 1961
Wildfire (f Grey) 1917
Wild-Goose Chase (pl Dunlap) 1800
Wildlife (f Ford) 1990
Will Mr. Merriwether Return from Memphis? (pl T. Williams) 1980
Will of Franklin 1757 (o Franklin) 1949
Will of Song: A Dramatic Service of Community Singing (pl MacKaye) 1919

Will Terril (f Ingraham) 1845
Will This Earth Hold? (pl Buck) 1945
Will to Believe, and Other Essays in Popular Philosophy (o W. James) 1897
Will to Change: Poems, 1968-1970 (po Rich) 1971
Will You Always Love Me? And Other Stories (f Oates) 1996
Will You Please Be Quiet, Please? (f Carver) 1976
Willard and His Bowling Trophies: A Perverse Mystery (f Brautigan) 1975
William Carlos Williams (o Burke) 1974
William Carlos Williams and Charles Tomlinson: A Transatlantic Connection (o W. Williams) 1998
William Ireland's Confession (pl A. Miller) 1941
William Vaughn Moody, Twenty Years After (po MacKaye) 1930
William Wetmore Story and His Friends (pl H. James) 1903
William Wilson (pl J. Gardner) 1978
Williams and James Laughlin: Selected Letters (o W. Williams) 1990
Williams' Poetry Talked About (o W. Williams) 1952
Williams-Siegel Documentary (o W. Williams) 1970
Willie Masters' Lonesome Wife (f Gass) 1968
Willing Performer (pl Ade) 1928
Williwaw (f Vidal) 1946
Will's Boy: A Memoir (o Morris) 1981
Will's Wonder Book (f Alcott) 1870
Wilson's Christmas Stocking: Fun for Young and Old (po E. Wilson) 1953
Wind (tv Bradbury) 1989
Wind from an Enemy Sky (f McNickle) 1978
Wind in the Rose-Bush and Other Stories of the Supernatural (f Freeman) 1903
Wind Song (o Sandburg) 1960
Windfall (f Murfree) 1907
Windless Cabins (f Van Doren) 1940
Window (f Dorris) 1997
Window at the White Cat (f Rinehart) 1910
Window Curtains (f Arthur) 1880
Window on Russia for the Use of Foreign Readers (o E. Wilson) 1972
Windows (po Creeley) 1990
Winds of Change and Other Stories (f Asimov) 1983
Winds of Doctrine: Studies in Contemporary Opinion (o Santayana) 1913
Windy City Blues (f Paretsky) 1995
Windy McPherson's Son (f S. Anderson) 1916
Wine (po Duncan) 1964
Wine from These Grapes (po Millay) 1934
Wine in the Wilderness: (scr Childress) 1969
Wine of Choice (pl Behrman) 1938
Winesburg, Ohio: A Group of Tales of Ohio Small Town Life (f S. Anderson) 1919
Wing of the Wind (f Ingraham) 1845
Wing-and-Wing (f Cooper) 1842
Winged Life: The Poetic Voice of Thoreau (o Thoreau) 1986
Winged Victory (pl Hart) 1943
Winged Victory (po MacKaye) 1927
Wingless Victory (pl M. Anderson) 1936
Wings (pl Kopit) 1978
Wings for Lai Ho (o Lim) 1982
Wings for to Fly: Three Plays of Negro Life, Mostly for the Ear but Also for the Eye (pl Green) 1959
Wings of the Dove (f H. James) 1902

Winkelberg (pl Hecht) 1958
Winner (pl Rice) 1954
Winner Take Nothing (f Hemingway) 1933
Winnie (o Brooks) 1991
Winnie and the Wolves (pl Gillette) 1923
Winning Lady and Others (f Freeman) 1909
Winter Count (o Lopez) 1981
Winter Diary and Other Poems (po Van Doren) 1935
Winter in the Blood (f Welch) 1974
Winter in the West (o Hoffman) 1835
Winter Insomnia (po Carver) 1970
Winter Journey (pl Odets) 1952
Winter Lightning: Selected Poems (po Nemerov) 1968
Winter Morning in Charlottesville (po Hass) 1977
Winter of Artifice (f Nin) 1939
Winter of Our Discontent (f Steinbeck) 1961
Winter Place (po Lim) 1989
Winter Sea: A Book of Poems (po A. Tate) 1944
Winter Ship (po Plath) 1960
Winter Trees (po Plath) 1971
Winter Wish (po Lovecraft) 1977
Winter-Meditations (o Mather) 1693
Winterset (pl M. Anderson) 1935
Winthrop Covenant (f Auchincloss) 1976
Winthropi Justa (o Mather) 1708
Wisdom of Fools (f Deland) 1897
Wisdom of Jefferson (o Jefferson) 1941
Wisdom of Santayana (o Santayana) 1964
Wisdom Tooth: A Fantastic Comedy (pl Connelly) 1927
Wise Blood (f O'Connor) 1952
Wise, Why's, Y's (po Baraka) 1995
Wish Tree (po Ciardi) 1962
Wish You Were Here (f R Brown) 1990
Wishing Tree (o Faulkner) 1967
Wister out West: His Journals and Letters (o Wister) 1958
Wit and Wisdom from Saltus (o Saltus) 1903
Wit and Wisdom of Dewey (o Dewey) 1949
Witch Diggers (f J. West) 1951
Witch of Prague (f Crawford) 1891
Witch of Ramoth and Other Tales (f Van Doren) 1950
Witchcraft of Salem Village (o S. Jackson) 1956
Witches of Eastwick (f Updike) 1984
Witches of Salem (scr A. Miller) 1958
Witching Times (f De Forest) 1967
Witch's Gold (f Garland) 1906
Witch-Woman (f Cabell) 1948
With a Delicate Air and Other Stories (f Buck) 1962
With a Reckless Preface: Two Plays (pl Lawson) 1934
With Both Armies in South Africa (o Richard Davis) 1900
With Eyes at the Back of Our Heads (po Levertov) 1960
With Formality and Elegance (o Van Vechten) 1977
With Gauge and Swallow, Attorneys (f Tourgée) 1889
With Her in Ourland: A Sequel to Herland (f Gilman) 1997
With Jazz (f Mason) 1996
With Shuddering Fall (f Oates) 1964
With the Allies (o Richard Davis) 1914
With the French in France and Salonika (o Richard Davis) 1916
With the Immortals (f Crawford) 1888
With the Procession (f Fuller) 1895
With Trumpet and Drum (o Field) 1892
With Wings as Eagles: Poems and Ballads of the Air (po W. Benét) 1940

Within an Inch of His Life (pl Belasco; Herne) 1879
Within the Rim and Other Essays 1914-1915 (pl H. James) 1919
Without (po Hall) 1998
Without Colors (pl Wellman) 1989
Without Love (pl Barry) 1943
Without Stopping: An Autobiography (o Bowles) 1972
Witness Tree (po Frost) 1942
Wives (pl B. Howard) 1879
Wizard of Oz (pl Baum) 1902
Wizard of Venus (f E. Burroughs) 1970
Wizard's Tears (o Sexton) 1975
Woffington: A Tribute to the Actress and the Woman (o Daly) 1888
Woggle-Bug (pl Baum) 1905
Woggle-Bug Book (f Baum) 1905
Wolf (scr Harrison) 1994
Wolf: A False Memoir (f Harrison) 1971
Wolfville (pl Fitch) 1905
Woman at Otowi Crossing (f Waters) 1966
Woman at the Washington Zoo: Poems and Translations (po Jarrell) 1960
Woman Called Fancy (f Yerby) 1951
Woman Hollering Creek and Other Stories (f Cisneros) 1991
Woman in Sacred History (o Stowe) 1873
Woman in the Case (pl Fitch) 1905
Woman in the Dark (scr Hammett) 1934
Woman Is the Death of the Soul (po Oates) 1970
Woman Lit by Fireflies (f Harrison) 1990
Woman of Andros (f Wilder) 1930
Woman of My Life (f Bemelmans) 1957
Woman on Her Way (f Van Druten) 1930
Woman Said Yes: Encounters with Life and Death (o J. West) 1976
Woman Speaks: The Lectures, Seminars, and Interviews of Nin (o Nin) 1975
Woman Ventures (f D. Phillips) 1902
Woman Warrior: Memoirs of a Girlhood among Ghosts (f Kingston) 1975
Woman Who Fell from the Sky (po Harjo) 1996
Woman Who Owned the Shadows (f P. Allen) 1986
Woman Who Was Changed and Other Stories (f Buck) 1979
Woman Within (o Glasgow) 1954
Woman Without a Name (pl Linney) 1986
Woman Won't (pl Daly) 1884
Woman's Face (scr Isherwood) 1941
Woman's Honor (pl Glaspell) 1918
Woman's Reason (f Howells) 1883
Woman's Revenge (pl Payne) 1832
Woman's Trials (f Arthur) 1851
Woman's Will (f Burnett) 1887
Women (f Tarkington) 1925
Women and Economics (o Gilman) 1898
Women and Honor: Some Notes on Lying (o Rich) 1977
Women and the Men (po Giovanni) 1975
Women and Thomas Harrow (f Marquand) 1958
Women and Water (pl Guare) 1984
Women as World Builders: Studies in Modern Feminism (o Dell) 1913
Women at Point Sur (po Jeffers) 1927
Women I'm Not Married To (o Parker) 1922
Women in American Labor History, 1825-1935: An Annotated Bibliography (o Forché) 1972

Women in Love and Other Poems (po Oates) 1968
Women Love Once (scr Akins) 1931
Women of Brewster Place (f Naylor) 1982
Women on the Porch (f Gordon) 1944
Women on the Wall (f Stegner) 1950
Women Who Got Away (f Updike) 1999
Women Who Hate Me (po Allison) 1983
Women Whose Lives Are Food, Men Whose Lives Are Money (po Oates) 1978
Women with Men (f Ford) 1997
Wonder (pl Daly) 1893
Wonder! A Woman Keeps a Secret (pl Daly) 1897
Wonder Hat: A Harlequinade (pl Hecht) 1920
Wonder-Book for Girls and Boys (o Hawthorne) 1851
Wonderful Death of Dudley Stone (tv Bradbury) 1989
Wonderful Ice-Cream Suit (pl Bradbury) 1965
Wonderful O (f Thurber) 1955
Wonderful Stories of Fuz-Buz and Mother Grabem the Spider (f S. Mitchell) 1867
Wonderful Wizard of Oz (f Baum) 1900
Wonderful Words, Silent Truth (o Simic) 1990
Wonderful Works of God Commemorated (o Mather) 1690
Wonderings (po Patchen) 1971
Wonderland (f Oates) 1971
Wonders of the African World (o Gates) 1999
Wonders of the Invisible World (o Mather) 1692
Woodcraft (f Simms) 1854
Wooded Forms (po Oates) 1972
Wooden Spoon (pl Daly) 1884
Woodman and Other Poems (po Channing) 1849
Woods (pl Mamet) 1977
Wooing of Malkatoon, Commodus (po L. Wallace) 1898
Wooing of Wistaria (f Eaton) 1902
Woollen Stocking (pl Harrigan) 1893
Worcester Account (o Behrman) 1954
Word "Woman" and Other Related Writings (o Riding) 1993
Words (po Creeley) 1965
Words About the Nature of Things (o Gass) 1985
Words and Thoughts (pl Marquis) 1924
Words and Ways: Stories and Incidents from My Cape Fear Valley Folklore Collection (f Green) 1968
Words for Dr. Y: Uncollected Poems with Three Stories (po Sexton) 1978
Words for Music (po Eliot) 1935
Words for the Wind: The Collected Verse (po Roethke) 1957
Words for the Wise (f Arthur) 1851
Words from History (o Asimov) 1968
Words from the Exodus (o Asimov) 1963
Words from the Myths (o Asimov) 1961
Words in Genesis (o Asimov) 1962
Words in the Mourning Time (po Hayden) 1970
Words of Love (po Buck) 1974
Words of Science and the History Behind Them (o Asimov) 1959
Words of Understanding (o Mather) 1724
Words on the Map (o Asimov) 1962
Words That Must Somehow Be Said: Selected Essays 1927-1984 (o Boyle) 1985
Words, Weather, and Wolfmen: Conversations with Tony Hillerman (o Hillerman) 1989
Work: A Story of Experience (f Alcott) 1873
Work of Art (f Lewis) 1934

Wrong Songs (po J. Tate) 1970
Wrongful Death: A Medical Tragedy (o Gilbert and Gubar) 1995
Wuthering Heights (scr Hecht; MacArthur) 1939
Wyandotte (f Cooper) 1843
Wycherly Woman (f Macdonald) 1961
Wynema, A Child of the Forest (f Callahan) 1891
Wynken, Blynken, and Nod: A Poem (po Field) 1998
Wyoming (f Grey) 1953
Wyrds (po P. Allen) 1967

X Stands for Unknown (o Asimov) 1984
Xaipe (po Cummings) 1950
Xargue and Other Poems (po G. Jones) 1985
Ximena (po B. Taylor) 1844
Xingu and Other Stories (f Wharton) 1916
XX (o Lim) 1987

Y & X (po Olson) 1948
Yallah (o Bowles) 1956
Yancey (pl Linney) 1988
Yankee at the Court of King Arthur (f Twain) 1889
Yankee Blue-Jacket (f Ingraham) 1888
Yankee Chronology (pl Dunlap) 1812
Yankee Fantasies (pl MacKaye) 1912
Yankee in Canada, with Anti-Slavery and Reform Papers (o Thoreau) 1866
Yankee Prince (pl Cohan) 1908
Yankee Tourist (pl Richard Davis) 1907
Yannina (po Merrill) 1973
Yaqui and Other Great Indian Stories (f Grey) 1976
Yates Pride (f Freeman) 1912
Year Bearers People (o La Farge) 1931
Year before Last (f Boyle) 1932
Year from a Correspondent's Note-Book (o Richard Davis) 1897
Year from a Reporter's Note-Book (o Richard Davis) 1897
Year of the Dragon (pl Chin) 1981
Yearling (f Rawlings) 1938
Years as Catches: First Poems (po Duncan) 1966
Years Life and Other Poems (po J. Lowell) 1841
Years of Wandering in Many Lands and Cities (o Thomas [Clayton] Wolfe) 1949
Yeats (o Bloom) 1970
Yekl and the Imported Bridegroom and Other Stories of the New York Ghetto (f Cahan) 1970
Yekl: A Tale of New York Ghetto (f Cahan) 1896
Yellow Back Radio Broke-Down (f Reed) 1969
Yellow Gentians and Blue (f Gale) 1927
Yellow House on the Corner (po Dove) 1980
Yellow Jack (pl S. Howard) 1934
Yellow Light (po Hongo) 1982
Yellow Pages: 59 Poems (po Merrill) 1974
Yellow Raft in Blue Water (f Dorris) 1987
Yellow Room (f Rinehart) 1945
Yellow Room: Love Poems (po Hall) 1971
Yellow Wallpaper (f Gilman) 1899
Yemassee: A Romance of Carolina (f Simms) 1835
Yentl, The Yeshiva Boy (pl Singer) 1974
Yerma (pl Merwin) 1966
Yes, Mrs. Williams: A Personal Record of My Mother (o W. Williams) 1959
Yes, Yes, No, No (pl Kushner) 1985

Yesterday's Love and Eleven Other Stories (f Farrell) 1948
Yet Other Waters (f Farrell) 1952
Yogi of Cockroach Court (f Waters) 1947
Yondering (f L'Amour) 1980
Yonnondio: From the Thirties (f Olsen) 1974
Yorick (pl Daly) 1874
Yorick's Love (pl Howells) 1878
You 'spute Me (pl Harrigan) 1871
You and I (pl Barry) 1923
You and Some Other Characters (po W. Stafford) 1987
You Came Along (scr Rand) 1945
You Can Die Laughing (f E. Gardner) 1957
You Can't Get There from Here (po Nash) 1957
You Can't Go Home Again (f Thomas [Clayton] Wolfe) 1940
You Can't Keep a Good Woman Down (f A. Walker) 1981
You Can't Take It with You (pl Hart; Kaufman) 1937
You, Emperors, and Others: Poems 1957-1960 (po R. Warren) 1960
You Get What You Give (f Bromfield) 1951
You Gonna Let Me Take You Out Tonight, Baby (pl Bullins) 1972
You Know I Can't Hear You When the Water's Running (pl R. Anderson) 1967
You Know Me Al: A Busher's Letters (f Lardner) 1916
You Know Who (po Ciardi) 1964
You Lovely People (f Santos) 1955
You Must Remember This (f Oates) 1987
You Must Revise Your Life (o W. Stafford) 1987
You Read to Me, I'll Read to You (po Ciardi) 1962
You Touched Me! (pl T. Williams) 1943
You Who Have Dreams (po M. Anderson) 1925
You Will Remember (scr Morley) 1941
Youma: The Story of a West-Indian Slave (f Hearn) 1890
Young Acrobat of the Great North American Circus (f Alger) 1888
Young Adventure (po S. Benét) 1918
Young Adventurer (f Alger) 1878
Young America (po Halleck) 1865
Young American (o Emerson) 1844
Young Artist (f Arthur) 1850
Young Artist, and The Bold Insurgent (f Ingraham) 1846
Young Bank Messenger (f Alger) 1898
Young Boatman of Pine Point (f Alger) 1892
Young Book Agent (f Alger) 1905
Young Captain Jack (f Alger) 1901
Young Circus Rider (f Alger) 1883
Young Desire (scr Eaton) 1930
Young Disciple (pl Goodman) 1955
Young Emperor William II of Germany: A Study in Character Development on a Throne (o Frederic) 1891
Young Explorer (f Alger) 1880
Young Folks' Ways (pl Burnett; Gillette) 1881
Young Genius (f Ingraham) 1843
Young Immigrunts (o Lardner) 1920
Young Lady at Home (f Arthur) 1847
Young Lincoln (pl B. Smith) 1944
Young Lonigan: A Boyhood in Chicago Streets (f Farrell) 1932
Young Lucretia and Other Stories (o Freeman) 1892
Young Manhood of Studs Lonigan (f Farrell) 1934
Young Mencken: The Best of His Work (o Mencken) 1973
Young Miner (f Alger) 1879
Young Mrs. Greeley (f Tarkington) 1929
Young Mrs. Winthrop (pl B. Howard) 1899

Young Mountaineers: Short Stories (f Murfree) 1897
Young Music Teacher and Other Tales (f Arthur) 1847
Young Musician (f Alger) 1906
Young Outlaw (f Alger) 1875
Young People's Pride (f S. Benét) 1922
Young Poets' Primer (o Brooks) 1981
Young Ranchman of the Missouri (f Alger) 1888
Young Salesman (f Alger) 1896
Young Wisdom (pl Crothers) 1914
Young Wolf: The Early Adventure Stories (f London) 1984
Young Woodley (scr Van Druten) 1930
Young Woodley (pl Van Druten) 1926
Younger Son (pl Belasco) 1893
Younger Son: Poet: An Autobiography in Three Parts (o Shapiro) 1988
Youngest (pl Barry) 1925
Youngest Camel (o Boyle) 1939
Your Army (pl S. Benét) 1944
Your Fiery Furnace (pl Green) 1926
Your Humble Servant (pl Tarkington) 1909
Your Lover Just Called: Stories of Joan and Richard Maple (f Updike) 1980
Your Native Land, Your Life (po Rich) 1986
Your Navy, in This Is War! (pl M. Anderson) 1942
Your Technocracy and Mine (scr Benchley) 1933
Your Turn, Mr. Moto (f Marquand) 1963
Yours, Isaac Asimov: A Lifetime of Letters (o Asimov) 1995
Youth and the Bright Medusa (f Cather) 1920
Youth of Jefferson (o J. Cooke) 1854

Youth of Washington, Told in the Form of an Autobiography (f S. Mitchell) 1904
Youth Takes Over (pl B. Smith) 1939
Yvernelle: A Legend of Feudal France (po Norris) 1891

Zabriskie Point (scr Shepard) 1970
Zalmonah (o Mather) 1725
Zami: A New Spelling of My Name (o Lorde) 1982
Zanina (pl Daly) 1880
Zanzibar (pl Lardner) 1903
Zaza (scr Akins) 1938
Zaza (pl Belasco) 1898
Zebra-Striped Hearse (f Macdonald) 1962
Zeke and Ned (f McMurtry) 1998
Zeph: A Posthumous Story (f H. Jackson) 1885
Zero Hour (tv Bradbury) 1992
Zia Summer (f Anaya) 1995
Zimmermann Telegram (o Tuchman) 1958
Zodiac (po Dickey) 1976
Zombie (f Oates) 1996
Zone Police (pl Richard Davis) 1914
Zoo Story (pl Albee) 1959
Zora (scr Bambara) 1971
Zoroaster (f Crawford) 1885
'Zouri's Christmas (f Tourgée) 1881
Zuckerman Bound: A Trilogy and Epilogue (f P. Roth) 1985
Zuckerman Unbound (f P. Roth) 1981
Zury, The Meanest Man in Spring County: A Novel of Western Life (f Kirkland) 1887

NOTES ON
ADVISERS AND
CONTRIBUTORS

ADISA, Opal Palmer. Writer and Caribbean critic. Professor, California College of Arts and Crafts, Oakland. Author of *Pina, The Many-Eyed Fruit* (for children), 1985, *Bake-Face and Other Guava Stories* (stories), 1986, *Travelling Women* (poetry collaborative with devorah major), 1989, *Fierce Love* (recording with devorah major), 1991, *Tamarind and Mango Women* (poetry), 1992, and *It Begins with Tears* (novel), 1997. **Essay:** John Edgar Wideman.

ADLER, Thomas P. Professor and head of English department, Purdue University. Author of *Robert Anderson* (1978), *Mirror on the Stage: The Pulitzer Plays as an Approach to American Drama* (1987), *"A Streetcar Named Desire: The Moth and the Lantern* (1990), and *American Drama: 1940-1960: A Critical History* (1994). **Essay:** Robert Anderson.

AIMONE, Joseph O. Member, English department, University of California at Davis. **Essays:** James Merrill; W.D. Snodgrass; Richard Wilbur.

ALEXANDER, M.J. Berry Professor of English Literature, University of St. Andrews, Scotland. Author of *The Earliest English Poems*, 1966, *Beowulf*, 1973, *Twelve Poems*, 1978, *The Poetic Achievement of Ezra Pound*, 1979, *Old English Riddles from the Exeter Book*, 1980, and *History of Old English Literature*, 1983. **Essays:** Marianne Moore; *The Cantos*.

ALEXANDER, Sandra Carlton. Fiction writer and professor of English, North Carolina Agricultural and Technical State University, Greensboro. Author of *Black Butterflies: Stories of the South in Transition* and of articles on Arna Bontemps and Ralph Ellison. Contributor of short stories to *Key West Review, The Griot, AIM Quarterly,* and *Obsidian II: Black Literature in Review.* Contributor of articles to *Black Books Bulletin* and *CLA Journal.* **Essay:** Anne Petry.

ALLEN, Walter. Novelist and literary critic. Author of seven novels, including *Get Out Early;* several critical works, including *Arnold Bennett*, 1948, *Reading a Novel*, 1949 (revised 1956, 1963), *Joyce Cary*, 1953 (revised 1963, 1971), *The English Novel*, 1954, *Six Great Novelists*, 1955, *The Novel Today*, 1955 (revised 1960), *George Eliot*, 1964, *The Modern Novel in Britain and the United States* (British edition: *Tradition and Dream*), 1964, *Some Aspects of the American Short Story*, 1973, and *The Short Story in English*, 1981. Also author of social history, including *The Urgent West: The American Dream and Modern Man*, 1969; and the memoirs *As I Walked Down New Grub Street*, 1981. Has taught at several universities in Britain, United States, and Canada. **Essay:** Ring Lardner.

ANDERSON, David D. Professor of American thought, Michigan State University, East Lansing. Author of *Louis Bromfield*, 1964, *Critical Studies in American Literature*, 1964, *Sherwood Anderson*, 1967, *Anderson's "Winesburg, Ohio,"* 1967, *Brand Whitlock*, 1968, *Abraham Lincoln*, 1970, *Robert Ingersoll*, 1972, *Woodrow Wilson*, 1975, and *Ignatius Donnelly*, 1980. Editor or coeditor of *The Black Experience*, 1969, *The Literary Works of Lincoln*, 1970, *The Dark and Tangled Path*, 1971, and *Sunshine and Smoke*, 1971. **Essay:** Louis Bromfield.

ANGLE, James. Professor of English, Eastern Michigan University, Ypsilanti. Author of poetry and fiction in periodicals, and an article on Edward Lewis Wallant in *Kansas Quarterly*, fall 1975. **Essay:** Edward Lewis Wallant.

ARNER, Robert D. Professor of English and comparative literature, University of Cincinnati. Author of monographs on Kate Chopin, James Thurber, and the legend of the lost colony in American literature; of numerous articles on early American writers, including Nathaniel Ward, Ebenezer Cooke, Edward Taylor, Anne Bradstreet, Joel Barlow, William Byrd II, Philip Freneau, Nathaniel Hawthorne, and Henry David Thoreau; and of introductions to works by Charles Brockden Brown. **Essays:** *The Damnation of Theron Ware; The Secret Life of Walter Mitty; The Tenth Muse.*

ASHLEY, Leonard R.N. Professor of English, Brooklyn College, City University of New York. Author of *Colley Cibber*, 1965, *Nineteenth-Century British Drama*, 1967, *Authorship and Evidence: A Study of Attribution and the Renaissance Drama*, 1968, *History of the Short Story*, 1968, *George Peele: The Man and His Work*, 1970, *The Wonderful World of Superstition, Prophecy, and Luck*, 1984, *The Wonderful World of Magic and Witchcraft*, 1986, and *The Dictionary of Sex Slang*, 1987. Editor of the Enriched Classics series, several anthologies of fiction and drama, and a number of facsimile editions. **Essays:** S.N. Behrman; Ludwig Bemelmans; George M. Cohan; Moss Hart; George S. Kaufman; George Kelly; Sidney Kingsley; Arthur Laurents; John Howard Lawson; Charles MacArthur; Henry Wheeler Shaw; *The Call of the Wild; Gravity's Rainbow; The Grapes of Wrath; Murder in the Cathedral.*

AUBERT, Alvin. Professor of English, Wayne State University, Detroit. Founding editor and publisher of *Obsidian: Black Literature in Review.* Author of three books of poetry: *Against the Blues*, 1972, *Feeling Through*, 1975, and *South Louisiana: New and Selected Poems*, 1985. **Essay:** James Weldon Johnson.

AUSTIN, James C. Professor emeritus of English language and literature, Southern Illinois University, Edwardsville. Author of *Fields of the Atlantic Monthly*, 1953, *Artemus Ward*, 1964, *Petroleum V. Nasby*, 1965, *Bill Arp*, 1970, *Popular Literature in America*, 1972, and *American Humor in France*, 1978; many articles on American literature, humor, and dialect; and the words and lyrics for four musical shows. **Essays:** Petroleum V. Nasby; *Margaret Howth; Modern Chivalry; The Scarlet Letter.*

BACHMAN, Linda P. Ph.D. candidate, Department of English, University of Michigan, Ann Arbor. Special assistant to director and staff writer, Development and Alumni Relations, University of Michigan Law School. **Essays:** Ellen Gilchrist; Tony Hillerman.

BAIN, Terry. Freelance writer. Author of articles and short stories in many publications, including *Prize Stories 1994: The O'Henry Awards.* **Essay:** Henry Louis Gates, Jr.

BARKER, Jonathan. Poetry librarian, Arts Council Poetry Library, London. Author of articles and reviews in *Agenda, PN Review, Times Literary Supplement,* and other periodicals. Editor of *The Arts Council Poetry Library Catalogue,* 6th edition, 1981, and *Selected Poems of W. H. Davies,* 1985. **Essay:** James Wright.

BASCARA, Victor D.C. Instructor of Asian-American studies and English, University of California at Berkeley. Author of articles on Asian-American cultural politics and cultural theory published in *Critical Mass: A Journal of Asian American Literary and Cultural Criticism* and *Amerasia Journal.* **Essay:** Bienvenido N. Santo.

BATTENBURG, John. Assistant professor of English, California Polytechnic State University, San Luis Obispo. Author of *English Monolingual Learners' Dictionaries: A User-Oriented Study* and of an article about Michael West. **Essay:** *Personal Narrative.*

BEATTY, Brian. Writer and reviewer, contributor to *Publisher's Weekly, Seventeen, Chattahoochee Review, Mid-American Review, New Mexico Humanities Review, THIS,* and *Sycamore Review.* Author of reviews of books by Rick Bass, Jean McGarry, David Wojahn, and Dennis Johnson. **Essay:** *Black Elk Speaks.*

BEIDLER, Peter G. Lucy G. Moses Professor of English, Lehigh University, Bethlehem, Pennsylvania. Author of seven books and more than a hundred articles on Native American literature, medieval British literature, modern American literature, and pedagogy, with titles including *Fig Tree John: An Indian in Fact and Fiction,* 1977, and *Ghosts, Demons, and Henry James: The Turn of the Screw at the Turn of the Century,* 1989. **Essays:** Louise Erdrich; *Love Medicine.*

BEJEL, Emilio. Professor of Spanish-American literature, University of Colorado, Boulder. Writer and poet. Author of *Buero Vallejo: lo moral, lo social y lo metafísico,* 1972, *Direcciones y Paraísos,* 1977, *Literatura de Nuestra América,* 1982, *José Lezama Lima, Poet of the Image,* 1990, *Escribir en Cuba,* 1991, (with Ramiro Fernández) *La subversión de la semiótica,* 1988, and *El Libro regalado,* 1994. Author of essays on homosexuality and nationalism in Latin American literature. **Essay:** *The Mambo Kings Play Songs of Love.*

BELLMAN, Samuel Irving. Professor emeritus of English, California State Polytechnic University, Pomona. Author of *Marjorie Kinnan Rawlings,* 1974, and *Constance Mayfield Rourke,* 1981; the short stories "Mars and Venus in the Groves of Academe," "School for Courtship," and "Man Woman Man Airplane"; and articles on John Steinbeck, Nathaniel Hawthorne, Mark Twain, J. D. Salinger, Barbara Pym, and others. **Essays:** Kenneth Burke; E.L. Doctorow; Edwin Markham; *Gifts of the Magi; The Legend of Sleepy Hollow; The Wonderful Wizard of Oz.*

BENNETT, George N. Late professor of English, Vanderbilt University, Nashville. Author of *William Dean Howells: The Development of a Novelist,* 1959, and *The Realism of William Dean Howells 1889-1920,* 1973. **Essay:** William Dean Howells.

BENSEN, Alice R. Professor of English, Eastern Michigan University, Ypsilanti. Author of *Rose Macaulay,* 1969. **Essays:** Elinor Wylie; *The Octopus.*

BISIGNANO, Dominic J. Associate professor of English, Indiana University-Purdue University, Indianapolis. **Essay:** Hannah Foster.

BLACKALL, Jean Frantz. Professor of English, Cornell University, Ithaca, New York. Member of board of editors, *Henry James Review.* Author of *Jamesian Ambiguity and the Sacred Fount* and of articles on Harold Frederic, Henry James, Charlotte Brontë, and Edith Wharton. **Essays:** Harold Frederic; *The Ambassadors; The House of Mirth; The Portrait of a Lady; Winesburg.*

BLOOM, Lynn Z. Professor of English, Virginia Commonwealth University, Richmond. Author or coauthor of *Doctor Spock: Biography of a Conservative Radical,* 1972, *American Autobiography 1945-1980: A Bibliography,* 1982, *Strategic Writing,* 1983, *Fact and Artifact: Writing Nonfiction,* 1985, and articles, reviews, and poetry in periodicals. Coeditor of *Bear, Man, andGod: Approaches to Faulkner's The Bear,* 1964 (revised 1971), *Forbidden Diary: A Record of Wartime Internment 1941-1945* by Natalie Crouter, 1980, *The Essay Connection,* 1983, and *The Lexington Reader,* 1987. **Essay:** Dorothy Parker.

BLOTNER, Joseph. Professor of English, University of Michigan, Ann Arbor. Author of *The Political Novel,* 1955, (with Frederick L. Gwynn) *The Fiction of J. D. Salinger,* 1958, *The Modern American Political Novel 1900-1966,* 1966, and *Faulkner: A Biography,* 2 vols., 1974 (revised and condensed edition, 1 vol., 1984). Editor or coeditor of *Faulkner in the University,* 1959, *Faulkner's Library: A Catalogue,* 1964, and *Selected Letters,* 1977, *Uncollected Stories,* 1979, and *Novels 1930-35* (Library of America series), 1985, by Faulkner. **Essay:** William Faulkner.

BODE, Walter. Editor, Grove Press, New York. Editor of *Audition Pieces: Monologues for Student Actors.* **Essays:** Roark Bradford; Ogden Nash; S.J. Perelman.

BOLDEN, B.J. Member, Department of English, University of Illinois, Urbana. **Essays:** Haki R. Madhubuti; Terry McMillan.

BOWDEN, Mary Weatherspoon. Member of the board of review, National Endowment for the Humanities Public Programs Division; coordinator of a scholarly edition of Philip Freneau's works. Author of *Philip Freneau,* 1976, and *Washington Irving,* 1981. **Essay:** Philip Freneau.

BRANTLEY, Jennifer. Assistant professor, English Department, University of Wisconsin-River Falls. Author of scholarly articles on Gloria Naylor and other topics, as well as poems published in *13th Moon, Hurricane Alice, Women and Language, genre, Kaleidoscope,* and other magazines. Reviewer for *Literary Magazine Review.* **Essay:** Lee Smith.

BRAYBROOKE, Neville. Writer and editor; contributor to the London *Times, Times Literary Supplement, Guardian, New Yorker, Saturday Review, Sunday Telegraph,* and *Tablet.* Author of three books about London and of *The Idler* (novel), 1961, *The Delicate Investigation* (play), 1969, and *Four Poems for Christmas,* 1986. Editor of *T. S. Eliot: A Symposium,* 1958, *A Partridge in a Pear Tree: A Celebration for Christmas,* 1960, *Pilgrim of the Future: A Teilhard de Chardin Symposium,* 1966, and *The Letters of J.R. Ackerley,* 1975. **Essays:** Djuna Barner; B. Traven.

BRIGHT, Jean. Associate professor of English, North Carolina Agricultural and Technical State University, Greensboro. Coeditor of *Images of the Negro in American*, 1965, and *Voices from the Black Experience*, 1972. Contributor to *Dictionary of Literary Biography*, vol. 33. **Essay:** Saunders Redding.

BROER, Lawrence R. Associate professor of English, University of South Florida, Tampa. Author of *Hemingway's Spanish Tragedy*, 1973, and many essays and reviews in periodicals. Editor of *Counter Currents*, 1973, and *The Great Escape of the '20's*, 1977, and coeditor of *The First Time: Initial Sexual Experiences in Literature*, 1974. **Essays:** Stephen Vincent Benét; William Rose Benét; Gore Vidal.

BROWN, Ashley. Professor of English, University of South Carolina, Columbia. Author of articles in *Sewanee Review, Southern Review, Spectator, Virginia Quarterly Review*, and other periodicals. Coeditor of *The Achievement of Wallace Stevens*, 1962, *Modes of Literature*, 1968, *Satire: An Anthology*, 1977, and *The Poetry Reviews of Allen Tate 1924-1944*, 1983. **Essays:** John Peale Bishop; Andrew Lytle; Allen Tate.

BROWN, Sharon. Instructor in American literature, School of Professional Development, State University of New York at Stoney Brook. Author of *American Travel Narratives as a Literary Genre from 1542-1832: The Art of a Perpetual Journey* (1993). **Essay:** Annie Dillard.

BROWNE, Terry. Professor of theater, State University of New York at Geneseo, and Fulbright Senior Scholar. Author of *Playwrights' Theatre: The English State Comany at the Royal Court Theatre* and *Off Off Broadway: Art and Economics,* as well as articles in various publications, including *Drama for Students, British Drama since World War II,* and *Twentieth Century American Playwrights.* **Essay:** *Margaret Fleming.*

BRUCE-NOVOA, Juan. Professor, Department of Spanish and Portuguese, University of California at Irvine. Contributor of articles, poems, and stories to *Mango, Riversedge, Puerto del Sol, Xalman,* and other periodicals. Author of *Inocencia perversa/Perverse Innocence* (poetry), 1976, *Chicano Authors: Inquiry by Interviews*, 1980, *Chicano Poetry: A Response to Chaos*, 1982, and *La literatura chicana a través de sus autores*, 1983. **Essays:** Alurista; John Rechy.

BRYSON, Craig. Freelance writer. **Essays:** Paul Bowles; William Gaddis; Andrew Lytle; Wright Morris; Frank Yerby.

BUCCO, Martin. Professor of English, Colorado State University, Fort Collins; executive secretary, Western Literature Association. Author of *The Voluntary Tongue* (poetry), 1957, *Frank Waters*, 1969, *Wilbur Daniel Steele*, 1972, *An American Tragedy Notes*, 1974, *E. W. Howe*, 1977, *René Wellek*, 1981, *Western American Literary Criticism*, 1984, and articles in *American Literature, Dictionary of Literary Biography, Western American Literature,* and *Western Humanities Review.* Editor of *Critical Essays on Sinclair Lewis*, 1986. **Essays:** Wilbur Daniel Steele; *Main Street; Main-Travelled Roads; Sister Carrie.*

BUNN, Susan Alice. Member, English Department, University of South Carolina, Columbia. **Essays:** Joan Didion; Cynthia Ozick.

BURCHELL, R.A. Senior lecturer in American history and institutions, University of Manchester, England. Author of *Westward Expansion*, 1974, and *The San Francisco Irish 1848-80*, 1980; essays in *History of the United States*, 1977, and *Introduction to American Studies*, 1981; and articles in *Journal of American Studies, California Historical Quarterly,* and *Immigrants and Minorities.* **Essays:** Helen Hunt Jackson; Francis Parkman; *The Education of Henry Adams: An Autiobiography.*

BYERMAN, Keith. Professor of English, Indiana State University, Terre Haute. Managing editor of *African American Review;* coauthor of *Alice Walker: An Annotated Bibliography*, 1989; author of *Fingering the Jagged Grain: Tradition and Form in Recent Black Fiction*, 1986, *Seizing the Word: Art, History, and Self in the Work of W. E. B. Du Bois*, 1994, and articles on James Baldwin, slave narratives, and various contemporary African American and Afro-Caribbean writers of fiction. **Essay:** Ernest J. Gaines.

CALHOUN, Richard J. Alumni distinguished professor of English, Clemson University, South Carolina. Executive editor of *South Carolina Review* and a member of the board of editors of *South Atlantic Review, James Dickey Newsletter,* and *American Literary Scholarship.* Author of *Galway Kinnell;* coauthor of *James Dickey;* editor of *Witness to Sorrow: The Autobiography of William J. Grayson* and of *James Dickey: The Expansive Imagination;* and coeditor of *The Tricentennial Anthology of South Carolina Literature; The South since Desegregation.* **Essays:** James Dickey; Galway Kinnell; *Life Studies.*

CANFIELD, Rob. Assistant professor of English, Rhodes College, Memphis, Tennessee. **Essay:** Suzan-Lori Parks.

CARDWELL, Guy A. Professor emeritus of English, Washington University, St. Louis. Author of *Der Amerikanische Roman*, 1954, *Charleston Periodicals*, 1960, and articles, poems, and stories in periodicals. Editor of *The Uncollected Poems of Henry Timrod*, 1942, *Readings from the Americas*, 1947, *Twins of Genius: Letters of Mark Twain, George Washington Cable, and Others*, 1953, *Discussions of Mark Twain*, 1963, and *Mississippi Writings* (Library of America series), 1982, and *The Innocents Abroad and Roughing It* (Library of America series), 1984, by Mark Twain. **Essays:** Henry Timrod; *The Adventures of Huckleberry Finn.*

CAREW-MILLER, Anna. Graduate student in English, University of New Mexico, Albuquerque. Author of articles on nineteenth-century American literature, the Native American oral tradition, and critical theory. **Essay:** Sarah Winnemucca.

CARPENTER, Brian. Teaching fellow, University of North Carolina at Chapel Hill. Editor of *The Carolina Quarterly* and author of essays on bourbon, pirates, and architecture in Southern literature. **Essay:** Elizabeth Spencer.

CARPENTER, Frederic I. Author of *Emerson and Asia*, 1920, *Emerson Handbook*, 1953, *American Literature and the Dream*, 1955, *Robinson Jeffers*, 1962, *Eugene O'Neill*, 1964 (revised 1979), and *Laurens van der Post*, 1969. Has taught at the University of Chicago, Harvard University, and the University of California at Berkeley. **Essays:** Robinson Jeffers; Conrad Richter.

CARPENTER, Humphrey. Freelance writer. Author of *J. R. R. Tolkien: A Biography*, 1977, *The Inklings*, 1978, *Jesus*, 1980, *W. H. Auden: A Biography*, 1981, the Mr. Majeika series for children, from 1984, *OUDS: A Centenary History of the Oxford University Dramatic Society*, 1985, *Secret Gardens: The Golden Age of Children's Literature*, 1985, and a biography of Ezra Pound. Editor of *The Letters of J. R. R. Tolkien*, 1981, and (with Mari Prichard) *The Oxford Companion to Children's Literature*, 1984. **Essay:** Ezra Pound.

CASSIDY, Thomas. Assistant professor of English, South Carolina State University, Orangeburg. Author of short stories and essays on Zora Neale Hurston, Toni Morrison, Edward Kamau Brathwaite, Jamaica Kincaid, and Arna Bontemps. **Essays:** Martin Robinson Delany; Henry L. Dumas; Toni Morrison.

CASTRONOVO, Russ. Assistant professor of English, University of Miami, Coral Gables. **Essay:** Harriet Ann Jacobs.

CHARTERS, Ann. Professor of English, University of Connecticut, Storrs. Author of *Kerouac: A Biography*, 1973, and editor of *The Beats: Literary Bohemians in Postwar America*, 1983, *The Viking Portable Beat Reader*, 1981, *The Story and Its Writer*, 1983, 4th edition, 1994, and *Major Writers of Short Fiction*, 1991. **Essay:** Ken Kesey.

CHOW, Balance T.P. Assistant professor of English, San Jose State University, California. Member of the editorial board of *MIFLC Review*. Contributor to *Masterplots II* and *Critical Survey of Poetry*. Author of articles on African American poets and on Asian-American, Chinese, and Native-American literature. **Essay:** Michael S. Harper.

CHOW, Karen. Graduate student in English, University of California at Santa Barbara. Coeditorial assistant, *Asian America: Journal of Culture and the Arts;* member of the Association of Asian American Studies. Author of articles on Shawn Wong's *Homebase* and on Americans of Hong Kong descent. **Essays:** Maxine Hong Kingston; *The Woman Warrior: Memories of a Girlhood Among Ghosts*.

CHRISTENSEN, Paul. Professor of modern literature, Texas A & M University, College Station. Author of several books of poetry and of *Charles Olson: Call Him Ishmael*, 1979. **Essays:** A.R. Ammons; John Berryman; Robert Bly; Louise Bogan; Robert Creeley; E.E. Cummings; Stanley Kunitz; Denise Levertov; James Merrill; W.S. Merwin; Frank O'Hara; Charles Olson; Kenneth Rexroth; W.D. Snodgrass; Gary Snyder; John Wheelwright; *Paterson*.

CIFELLI, Ed. Professor of English, County College of Morris, Randolph, New Jersey. Author of *David Humphreys*, editor of *The Selected Letters of John Ciardi*, coeditor of three volumes of the *Index of American Periodical Verse*. Author of articles on Cotton Mather, F. Scott Fitzgerald, Nathaniel Hawthorne, and Herman Melville. **Essay:** John Ciardi.

CLAIRE, William. President, Washington Resources Inc., Washington, D.C. Author of two books of poetry, *Strange Coherence of Our Dreams*, 1973, and *From a Southern France Notebook*, 1974; of *Publishing in the West: Alan Swallow*, 1975; and of articles in *Antioch Review, American Scholar, Nation, New Republic, New York Times,* and other periodicals. Editor of *The Essays of Mark Van Doren*, 1984. Founding editor and publisher of *Voyages: A National Literary Magazine*, 1967-73. **Essay:** Mark Van Doren.

CLANCY, Laurie. Melbourne-based novelist and freelance writer. Formerly associate professor, La Trobe University, Bundoora, Victoria. His most recent novel is *Night Parking*. **Essays:** Elmore Leonard; Henry Roth; Paul Theroux.

COHEN, Hennig. John Welsh Centennial Professor of History and Literature, University of Pennsylvania, Philadelphia. Author of *The South Carolina Gazette*, 1953, *Articles in American Studies 1954-1968*, 1972, and (with Tristram Potter Coffin) *The Parade of Heroes: Legendary Figures in American Lore*, 1978. Editor or coeditor of *Battle Pieces*, 1963, *Selected Poems*, 1964, and *White Jacket*, 1967, all by Herman Melville, and of *Humor of the Old Southwest*, 1964, *Folklore in America*, 1966, *The American Culture*, 1968, *Landmarks in American Writing*, 1969, *Folklore from the Working Folk of America*, 1973, *The Indians and Their Captives*, 1977, and *Herman Melville's Malcolm Letter*, 1987. Former editor of *American Quarterly* and president of the Melville Society. **Essay:** Herman Melville.

COHN, Ruby. Professor of comparative drama, University of California at Davis. Coeditor of *Modern Drama, Theatre Journal,* and *Cambridge Guide to World Drama*. Author of *Samuel Beckett: The Comic Gamut*, 1962, *Currents in Contemporary Drama*, 1969,*Edward Albee*, 1969, *Dialogue in American Drama*, 1971, *Back to Beckett*, 1974, *Modern Shakespeare Offshoots*, 1976, *Just Play: Beckett's Theatre*, 1980, *New American Dramatists 1960-1980*, 1982, *From Desire to Godot*, 1987 (reprinted 1999), *Retreats from Realism in Recent English Drama*, 1991, and *American Interplay in Recent Drama* (1995). **Essays:** Edward Albee; Ed Bullins; Eugene O'Neill.

COLAHAN, Clark. Associate professor of foreign languages and literatures, Whitman College, Walla Walla, Washington. Translator of *Persiles and Sigismunda: A Northern Story*, by Miguel de Cervantes, 1989, and *Knowledge, Writing and Power: The Visions of Sor María de Agreda*, 1994. Author of articles about Renaissance Spanish literature, Cervantes, and colonial New Mexican literature in *Bulletin of Hispanic Studies, Journal of Hispanic Philology,* and *Journal of Medieval and Renaissance Studies*. **Essay:** Fray Angélico Chávez.

COLLINS, William J. Freelance writer and music critic. **Essay:** Stephen Collins Foster.

CONDÉ, Mary. Lecturer in English and American literature, Queen Mary and Westfield College, University of London. Editor (with Thorunn Lonsdale) of *Caribbean Women Writers: Fiction in English*, 1999. **Essays:** Gayl Jones; Alice Walker.

CORBETT, William. Writer in residence at Massachusetts Institute of Technology. Author of several books of poems, including *Boston Vermont*, 1999. **Essay:** Charles Simic.

CORCORAN, Neil. Lecturer in English, University of Sheffield, England. Author of *The Song of Deeds: A Study of "The*

Anathemata" of David Jones, 1982, and of reviews in *PN Review* and *Times Literary Supplement.* **Essays:** Conrad Aiken; Robert Lowell; Demore Schwartz.

COX, Jay Ann. Adjunct lecturer in composition, folklore, and literature, University of Arizona, Tucson. Member of the American Folklore Society, Modern Language Association, and Western Literature Association. Author of articles on the Native American trickster, trickster and gender in contemporary literature, Chicano literature, Native American women, Larry McMurtry, and Mexican food. **Essays:** Roland Hinojosa; Louis L'Amour; Larry McMurtry; N. Scott Momaday; *The Road to Tamazunchale.*

COX, Martha Heasley. Professor of English and director of the Steinbeck Research Center, San Jose State University, California. Author of *Maxwell Anderson Bibliography,* 1958, *A Reading Approach to College Writing,* 1959 (and later editions), *Writing: Form, Process, Purpose,* 1962, *Image and Value: An Invitation to Literature,* 1966, (with Wayne Chatterton) *Nelson Algren,* 1975, and articles on Algren, Anderson, and John Steinbeck. Editor of *Classic American Short Stories,* 1969. **Essay:** Nelson Algren.

CROWDER, Richard H. Professor emeritus of English, Purdue University, West Lafayette, Indiana. Author of *Those Innocent Years* (on James Whitcomb Riley), 1957, *No Featherbed to Heaven: A Biography of Michael Wigglesworth,* 1962, and *Carl Sandburg,* 1964. Joint editor of *Frontiers of American Culture,* 1968. **Essays:** Carl Sandbury; Michael Wigglesworth.

CURRENT-GARCIA, Eugene. Hargis Professor Emeritus of American Literature, Auburn University, Alabama. Editor of *Southern Humanities Review,* 1967-79. Author of *O. Henry (W. S.Porter): A Critical Study,* 1965, and *The American Short Story Before 1850,* 1985. Editor (with Walton R. Patrick) of *American Short Stories,* 1952 (4th edition 1982), *What Is the Short Story?,* 1961, *Realism and Romanticism in Fiction,* 1962, *Short Stories of the Western World,* 1969, and *Shem, Ham, and Japeth: The Papers of W. O. Tuggle,* 1973. **Essays:** Anna Cora Mowatt; *Our Town; The Swimmer.*

DACE, Tish. Professor of English, Southeastern Massachusetts University, North Darmouth. Theater critic for *Plays International, Stages, Village Voice, Plays and Players, New York Times, New York Magazine, American Theatre, Playbill,* and other publications. Author of *LeRoi Jones (Imamu Amiri Baraka): A Checklist of Works by and about Him,* 1971, and *The Theatre Student: Modern Theatre and Drama,* 1973. **Essays:** Amiri Baraka; Sam Shepard; *Picnic; Streetcar Named Desire; The Weary Blues; Who's Afraid of Virginia Woolf?*

DAHL, Curtis. Samuel Valentine Cole Professor of English, Wheaton College, Norton, Massachusetts. Author of *Robert Montgomery Bird,* 1963, and articles on Bryant, Bulwer-Lytton, and Disraeli. Editor of *There She Blows: A Narrative of a Whaling Voyage,* by Ben-Ezra Ely. **Essay:** William Cullen Bryant.

DAY, Frank. Professor of English, Clemson University, South Carolina. Coeditor of the *South Carolina Review,* and editor of Twayne's United States Authors series. Author of *Sir William Empson: An Annotated Bibliography* and *Arthur Koestler: A Guide to Research.* **Essay:** Don Delillo.

DECK, Alice. Associate professor of English and African American studies, University of Illinois, Urbana. Author of articles on Harriet Jacobs, Zora Neale Hurston, and Noni Jabavu. **Essay:** *Beloved.*

DETERS, Joseph. Assistant professor, Department of Foreign Languages and Literature, University of Puget Sound, Tacoma, Washington. Author of articles on contemporary Spanish poets and the Chicano writer Alberto Rios. **Essay:** Rudolfo A. Anaya.

DEUTSCH, Leonard J. Dean of the Graduate School and professor of English, Marshall University, Huntington, West Virginia. Author of articles on Ralph Ellison, T. S. Eliot, Edgar Alan Poe, Rudolf Fisher, Kathryn Flagg, Carter G. Woodson, and Henry Louis Gates in *CLA Journal, Phylon, Bulletin of Bibliography, Negro American Literature Forum, Obsidian, MELUS Journal,* and *Dictionary of Literary Biography.* **Essay:** *The Sky Is Gray.*

DEWEY, Janice L. Lecturer in humanities, University of Arizona, Tucson. Author of articles in both Spanish and English on Jorge Luís Borges, the indigenous literatures of Mesoamerica and Amazonia, and Chicana literature. **Essay:** Estela Portillo Trambley.

DIAN, Li. Ph.D. candidate in Chinese literature, University of Michigan, Ann Arbor. Contributing translator of *The Anthology of Chinese Famous Writers' Self-Collected Works,* 1992, and translator of contemporary Chinese poetry in *Green Mountain Review,* summer/fall, 1993. **Essay:** Lin Yutang.

DICKINSON, Gloria Harper. Chairperson and associate professor of African American studies, Trenton State College, New Jersey. Member of the editorial advisory board of *Journal of Negro History.* Author of biographies of Margaret C. Hiawatha, Rev.Elizabeth Randolph, and Helen Jackson Lee in *Past and Promise: Lives of New Jersey Women.* **Essay:** John A. Williams.

DRAYTON, James M. Lecturer, California State University, Sacramento. **Essay:** John Dewey.

DUUS, Louise. Associate dean and lecturer in American studies, Douglass College, Rutgers University, New Brunswick, New Jersey. **Essay:** Rebecca Harding Davis.

EICHELBERGER, Clayton L. Professor of American literature, University of Texas at Arlington. Author of *A Guide to Critical Reviews of United States Fiction 1870-1910,* 2 vols., 1971-73, and *Published Comments on William Dean Howells through 1920: A Research Bibliography,* 1976. Editor of *Harper's Lost Reviews: The Literary Notes by Laurence Hutton, John Kendrick Bangs, and Others,* 1976. Editor of the journal *American Literary Realism,* 1967-77. **Essays:** Richard Harding Davis; Samuel Sewall; *The Awakening.*

EISINGER, Chester E. Professor emeritus of English, Purdue University, West Lafayette, Indiana. Author of *Fiction of the Forties,* 1963, and of articles in *Proletarian Writers of the Thirties,* 1968, and *Saturday Review.* Editor of *The 1940's: Profile of a Nation in Crisis,* 1969. **Essays:** Louis Auchincloss; William Styron; *Go Tell It on the Mountain; Herzog; Lolita; The Naked and the Dead.*

ELIAS, Eduardo F. Associate professor of Spanish and Chicano studies, University of Utah, Salt Lake City. Member of the board of editors of *The Bilingual Review/La revista bilingue.* **Essays:** Sandra Cisneros; *The House on Mango Street.*

EVANS, Patrick. Senior lecturer in English and American studies, University of Canterbury, Christchurch, New Zealand. **Essays:** Paul Bowles; Jean Stafford.

FANNING, Charles. Professor of English, Bridgewater State College, Massachusetts. Author of *Finley Peter Dunne and Mr. Dooley: The Chicago Years,* 1978, and of articles on Dunne, the Chicago Irish, James T. Farrell, and Irish-American literature. Editor of *Mr. Dooley and the Chicago Irish* (anthology), 1976, and *The Exiles of Erin: Nineteenth-Century Irish American Fiction,* 1987. **Essays:** George Ade; Finley Peter Dunne; James T. Farrell.

FARMER, Ann Dahlstrom. Assistant professor of English, Whittier College, California, and director of the Paper-in-the-Major Writing Program. Author of *Jessamyn West* (Western Writers series, no. 53), 1982, coauthor of *Creative Analysis,* revised edition, 1978, and *The Liberal Arts: Reading, Thinking, and Writing,* 1988, and contributor of Jessamyn West character descriptions to *Dictionary of American Literary Characters,* 1990. **Essay:** Jessamyn West.

FARMER, Philip José. Freelance writer. Author of more than 45 novels, including *Dayworld,* 1985, and of *Tarzan Alive: A Definitive Biography of Lord Greystoke,* 1972. **Essays:** L. Frank Baum; Edgar Rice Burroughs.

FENG, Pin-Chia. Ph.D. candidate, University of Wisconsin-Madison. Author of *Rethinking the Bildungsroman: Return of the Repressed in the Bluest Eye, Sula, The Woman Warrior, and China Men,* 1994. **Essays:** Amy Tan; *The Joy Luck Club.*

FERGUSON, Sallyann. Adviser. Professor of English, University of North Carolina at Greensboro. Former president of the Society for the Study of the Multi-Ethnic Literature of the United States (MELUS).

FERRARO, Thomas Joseph. Andrew W. Mellon Assistant Professor of English, Duke University, Durham, North Carolina. Author of *Ethnic Essays: Literary Immigrants in Twentieth-Century America,* 1993. **Essay:** Mario Puzo.

FITZGERALD, M.J. Freelance writer. Author of fictional works *Rope-Dancer,* 1986, and *Concertina,* 1987. **Essay:** *Wise Blood.*

FLETCHER, Ian. Professor of English, Arizona State University, Tempe; professor emeritus, University of Reading, England. Author of poetry and plays and of *Walter Pater,* 1959 (revised 1971), *Beaumont and Fletcher,* 1967, and *Swinburne,* 1973. Editor of anthologies of poetry and drama, works by Victor Plarr and John Gray, and *The Collected Poems of Lionel Johnson,* 1982. **Essays:** Fitz-James O'Brien; Edgar Saltus.

FLORA, Joseph M. Professor of English, University of North Carolina at Chapel Hill. Author of *Vardis Fisher,* 1965, *William Ernest Henley,* 1974, *Frederick Manfred,* 1974, and *Hemingway's Nick Adams,* 1982. Editor of *Southern Writers: A Biographical Dictionary* (with Robert Bain and Louis D. Rubin, Jr.), 1979, and of *The English Short Story 1880-1945,* 1985. **Essays:** Doris Waugh Betts; James Branch Cabell; Marc Connelly; Vardis Fisher; Zane Grey; Owen Wister; *Big Two-Hearted River.*

FOSTER, Edward Halsey. Professor and director of the American studies program, Stevens Institute of Technology, Hoboken, New Jersey. Author of *Catharine Maria Sedgwick,* 1974, *The Civilized Wilderness,* 1975, *Josiah Gregg and Lewis Hector Garrard,* 1977, *Susan and Anna Warner,* 1978, *Richard Brautigan,* 1983, and *William Saroyan,* 1984. Editor of *Hoboken: A Collection of Essays* (with Geoffrey W. Clark), 1976, and *Cummington Poems,* 1982. **Essays:** Fitz-Greene Halleck; Donald Grant Mitchell; Catharine Maria Sedgwick; Kurt Vonnegut, Jr.; Nathaniel Parker Willis; *The Bridge; The Dream Songs; The Maximus Poems.*

FRASER, G.S. Late reader in modern English literature, University of Leicester, England. Author of several books of poetry (collected as *Poems,* 1981); travel books; critical studies of Yeats, Dylan Thomas, Pound, Durrell, and Pope; and *The Modern Writer and His World,* 1953, *Vision and Rhetoric,* 1959, *Metre, Rhythm and Free Verse,* 1970, and *A Stranger and Afraid: The Autobiography of an Intellectual,* 1983. Editor of works by Keith Douglas and Robert Burns and of poetry anthologies. Died 1980. **Essays:** Katherine Anne Porter; Mary Roberts Rinehart; George Santayana.

FRENCH, Warren. Adviser. Honorary professor of American studies, University of Wales, Swansea. Member of the editorial boards of *Twentieth Century Literature* and *Western American Literature,* Institute of North American Studies. Author of *A Film Guide to "The Grapes of Wrath,"* 1973, *The South in Film,* 1981, *Jack Kerouac,* 1986, *J. D. Salinger Revisited,* 1988, *The San Francisco Poetry Renaissance, 1955-1960,* 1991, and *John Steinbeck Revisited,* 1994. **Essays:** Timothy Shay Arthur; Joseph Holt Ingraham; H.P. Lovecraft; J.D. Salinger; John Steinbeck; Thornton Wilder; *Howl; Invisible Man; On the Road.*

GABIN, Jane S. Independent scholar and instructor, Office ofContinuing Education, Duke University, Durham, North Carolina. Author of *A Living Minstrelsy: The Poetry and Music of Sidney Lanier,* 1985, and numerous articles in American studies. **Essays:** John Gould Fletcher; Richard Hovey; Sidney Lanier; *Little Women.*

GAINEY, Karen Wilkes. Associate professor of English and chair of Division of Arts and Letters, Limestone College, Gaffney, South Carolina. Author of articles on Jayne Anne Phillips, Rosellen Brown, and Barbara Pym. **Essay:** Anne Tyler.

GALL, Sally M. Writer and editor; editor of journal *EIDOS: The International Prosody Bulletin.* Author of *The Modern Poetic Sequence* (with M. L. Rosenthal), 1983, *Ramon Guthrie's Maximum Security Ward: An American Classic,* 1984, and more than 40 articles in collections and journals. Editor of *Maximum Security Ward and Other Poems* by Guthrie, 1984. **Essay:** Ramon Guthrie.

GARRETT, Kathleen Grimm. Freelance writer specializing in American labor literature. Contributor to *Book of Days* published by Pierian Press. **Essays:** Emma Goldman; Tillie Olsen.

GASPAR, Robert. Ph.D. from University of Connecticut, Storrs. Author of *Everyone and I Stopped Breathing: Jazz in American Poetry* and articles on jazz. **Essay:** *Their Eyes Were Watching God.*

GERBER, John C. Professor of English, State University of New York at Albany; general editor of the Iowa-California edition of the works of Mark Twain; member of the editorial board of *Resources for American Literary Study.* Author of *Factual Prose* (with Walter Blair), 1945, *Literature,* 1948, *Writers Resource Book,* 1953, and other books on writing and speaking. Editor of *Twentieth-Century Interpretations of The Scarlet Letter,* 1968, and *Studies in Huckleberry Finn,* 1971. **Essays:** Ralph Waldo Emerson; Mark Twain.

GIBSON, Donald B. Professor of English, Rutgers University, New Brunswick, New Jersey. Author of *The Fiction of Stephen Crane,* 1968, and *The Politics of Literary Expression: A Study of Major Black Writers,* 1981. Editor of *Five Black Writers,* 1970, *Black and White: Stories of American Life,* 1971, and *Modern Black Poets,* 1973. **Essay:** Melvin B. Tolson.

GITENSTEIN, R. Barbara. Associate professor of English, State University of New York at Oswego. Author of articles on Hawthorne, Singer, Bellow, and Ozick in *The Comparatist, Yiddish, Contemporary Jewish-American Poetry,* and other periodicals. **Essays:** Abraham Cahan; Saul Bellow; Bernard Malamud; Isaac Bashevis Singer.

GLASRUD, Clarence A. Professor emeritus of English, Moorhead State University, Minnesota; advisory editor, *Studies in American Fiction;* member of the board of publications of Norwegian-American Historical Association. Author of *Hjalmar Hjorth Boyesen: A Biographical and Critical Study,* 1963. Editor of *The Age of Anxiety,* 1960. **Essays:** H.H. Boyesen; F. Marion Crawford; Oliver Wendell Holmes; Wright Morris; John O'Hara; J.F. Powers; O.E. Rølvaag; Ruth Suckow; Charles Dudley Warner; Glenway Wescott.

GOODMAN, Charlotte Margolis. Professor of English, Skidmore College, Saratoga Springs, New York. Author of *Jean Stafford: The Savage Heart* and of articles on Anzia Yezierska, Edith Summers Kelley, Harriette Arnow, Henry James, Harvey Swados, and William Faulkner and on the bildungsroman. **Essay:** Anzia Yezierska.

GORDON, Lois. Professor and chair, Department of English and Comparative Literature, Fairleigh Dickinson University, Teaneck and Rutherford, New Jersey. Author of *Stratagems to Uncover Nakedness: The Dramas of Harold Pinter,* 1969, *Donald Barthelme,* 1981, *Robert Coover: The Universal Fictionmaking Process,* 1983, *American Chronicle 1920-1980,* 1987, and articles on Arthur Miller, Tennessee Williams, Samuel Beckett, T. S. Eliot, William Faulkner, Randall Jarrell, Philip Roth, Elizabeth Bishop, William Gaddis, and other modern writers. **Essays:** Richard Eberhart; Jonathan Edwards; Benjamin Franklin; Randall Jarrell; James Purdy; *Moby-Dick.*

GOULD, Janice. Writer and graduate student in English, University of New Mexico, Albuquerque. Author of poetry collection *Beneath My Heart* and of articles on American Indian literature. **Essay:** Simon J. Ortiz.

GOVAN, Sandra Y. Associate professor, Department of English, and coordinator, Ronald E. McNair Post-Baccalaureate Achievement Program, University of North Carolina at Charlotte; member, Wintergreen Writers' Collective; guest editor of the *Langston Hughes Review.* Author of essays on Samuel Delany, Octavia Butler, Gwendolyn Bennett, Alice Childress, black women as cultural conservators, and erotica in African American popular literature. Contributor to *Notable Black American Women, Erotique Noire, Sexual Politics in Popular Culture,* and *The Dictionary of Literary Biography.* **Essay:** Samuel R. Delany.

GRELLA, George. Associate professor of English, Rochester University, New York. Author of studies on Ian Fleming, Ross Macdonald, and John le Carré in *New Republic* and of articles on the detective novel, film, and popular culture. **Essay:** Ross Macdonald.

HADELLA, Paul. Writer, editor, and lecturer in English, South Oregon University, Ashland; member, Poets and Writers and of Western Literature Association. Contributor to *American Literary Realism, Steinbeck Newsletter,* and *Western American Literature.* Editor of poetry chapbook series published by Talent House Press. **Essay:** Michael Anthony Dorris.

HAEDICKE, Janet V. Professor of English, Northeast Louisiana University, Monroe. Chair, American Theatre and Drama Society program for 1999 Modern Language Associate Convention. Author of numerous articles on Beth Henley, David Mamet, Sam Shepard, and other American dramatists. **Essay:** David Henry Hwang.

HALL, Donald. Adviser. See his own entry.

HANS, Birgit. Assistant professor, Department of Indian Studies, University of North Dakota, Grand Forks. **Essay:** D'Arcy McNickle.

HARPER, Lisa C. Writer and graduate student at University of California, Davis. **Essays:** A.R. Ammons; Louis Auchincloss; Robert Creeley; Arthur Miller; Ellery Queen; William Styron.

HATTORI, Tomo. Assistant professor of Asian-American and English literature, University of Utah, Salt Lake City. **Essays:** Richard E. Kim.

HEATH-STUBBS, John. Writer and lecturer. Author of several books of poetry, including *The Immolation of Aleph,* 1985, a book of plays, *The Darkling Plain: A Study of the Later Fortunes of Romanticism,* 1950, *Charles Williams,* 1955, and studies of the verse satire, the ode, and the pastoral. Editor of anthologies and works by Shelley, Tennyson, Swift, Pope, and Thomas Gray. Translator of *The Ruba'iyat of Omar Khayyam* and of works by Giacomo Leopardi, Alfred de Vigny, and others. **Essay:** Hart Crane.

HEIM, William J. Associate professor of English and associate dean of Arts and Letters, University of South Florida, Tampa. Author of articles on Theodore Dreiser, Leigh Hunt, and Sheridan Le Fanu. **Essays:** Cotton Mather; Upton Sinclair; *The Fall of the House of Usher.*

HERSH, Allison. Lecturer in English, University of Michigan, Ann Arbor. Author of articles on Kathy Acker, Caroline Gordon, Caryl Churchill, and Robert Penn Warren. **Essays:** Gwendolyn Brooks; Hortense Calisher; Denise Levertov; Mary McCarthy; Laura Riding; Eudora Welty.

HEWITT, Geof. Freelance writer; founding editor of Kumquat Press. Author of five books of poetry. Editor of the poems of Alfred Starr Hamilton and of anthologies of poetry. **Essay:** Muriel Rukeyser.

HICKS, Jack. Teacher and freelance writer; has taught at University of California, Davis, and University of Paris. Author of *Cutting Edges: Young American Fiction for the 1970's,* 1973, and *In The Singer's Temple: Prose Fictions of Barthelme, Gaines, Brautigan, Piercy, Kesey, and Kosinski,* 1981. **Essays:** Donald Barthelme; William S. Burroughs; Jack Kerouac.

HIGGINS, William. Member of Department of English, Western Carolina University, Cullowhee, North Carolina. **Essays:** Winston Churchill; Robert Herrick; Joseph Kirkland; David Graham Phillips.

HITCHCOCK, Bert. Professor and head of the Department of English, Auburn University, Alabama; member of the bibliography committee, Society for the Study of Southern Literature. Author of *Richard Malcolm Johnston,* 1978. **Essays:** S. Weir Mitchell; *Cathedral.*

HOCKERSMITH, Thomas E. Member of the Department of English, Emory University, Atlanta. **Essays:** *The Man That Corrupted Hadleyburg.*

HOEFER, Jacqueline. Freelance writer. Author of articles on Samuel Beckett and other modern writers. **Essay:** Kay Boyle.

HOFFMAN, Daniel. Poet in residence and Felix E. Schelling Professor of English, University of Pennsylvania, Philadelphia. Author of several books of poetry, including *Brotherly Love,* 1981, and of critical works that include *The Poetry of Stephen Crane,* 1957, *Form and Fable in American Fiction,* 1961, *Barbarous Knowledge: Myth in the Poetry of Yeats, Graves, and Muir,* 1967, and *Poe Poe Poe Poe Poe Poe Poe,* 1972. Editor of the *Harvard Guide to Contemporary American Writing,* 1979, and of anthologies and works by Crane. **Essays:** Stephen Crane; Washington Irving; Edgar Allan Poe.

HOGAN, Robert. Freelance writer; former professor of English, University of Delaware, Newark. Author or coauthor of *The Experiments of Sean O'Casey,* 1960, *Arthur Miller,* 1964, *The Independence of Elmer Rice,* 1965, *The Plain Style,* 1967, *After theIrish Renaissance,* 1967, *Dion Boucicault,* 1969, *The Fan Club,* 1969, *Lost Plays of the Irish Renaissance,* 1970, *Eimar O'Duffy,* 1972, *Mervyn Wall,* 1972, *Conor Cruise O'Brien,* 1974, *The Modern Irish Drama,* 6 vols., 1975-86, and *Since O'Casey,* 1984. **Essay:** Elmer Rice.

HOKENSON, Jan. Associate professor of languages and linguistics, Florida Atlantic University, Boca Raton. Author of articles on Beckett, Celine, and Proust in *James Joyce Quarterly, L'Esprit Createur, Far-Western Forum,* and *Samuel Beckett: An Anthology of Criticism,* edited by Ruby Cohn, 1975. **Essay:** Ross Lockridge.

HOLDEN, Jonathan. University Distinguished Professor of English, Kansas State University, Manhattan. Author of *The Mark to Turn: A Reading of William Stafford's Poetry,* 1976, *The Rhetoric of the Contemporary Lyric,* 1980, *Style and Authenticity on Postmodern Poetry,* 1986, *The Fate of American Poetry,* 1992, *Guns and Boyhood in America: A Memoir of Growing Up in the 50s,* 1997, and seven collections of poetry. **Essay:** William Stafford.

HOLM, Janice Butler. Writer and teacher in Athens, Ohio. Contributing editor to the film journal *Wide Angle.* **Essay:** *Angels in America.*

HOLMAN, C. Hugh. Late William Rand Kenan Professor of English, chairman of the Division of Humanities, and special assistant to the chancellor, University of North Carolina at Chapel Hill; former editor of *Southern Literary Journal.* Author of five detective novels and of several critical books, including *The Development of American Criticism,* 1955, *The Southerner as American,* 1960, *Thomas Wolfe,* 1960, *Seven Modern American Novelists,* 1964, *John P. Marquand,* 1965, *The American Novel through Henry James: A Bibliography,* 1966 (revised 1979), *Three Modes of Modern Southern Fiction,* 1966, *The Roots of Southern Writing,* 1972, *The Loneliness at the Core: Studies in Thomas Wolfe,* 1975, *The Immoderate Past: The Southern Writer and History,* 1977, and *Windows on the World: Essays on American Social Fiction,* 1979. Editor of works by Wolfe, William Gilmore Simms, and others. Died 1981. **Essays:** Ellen Glasgow; Sinclair Lewis; John P. Marquand; Flannery O'Connor; Robert Penn Warren.

HOROWITZ, Arthur. Adjunct member of theater arts faculty, Marymount Manhattan College, New York. Author of articles and reviews in *Western European Stages* and *Journal of Beckett Studies.* **Essays:** John Guare; Paula Vogel; *American Buffalo.*

HUDOCK, Amy E. Visiting assistant professor of English, University of South Carolina, Columbia. **Essay:** Bharati Mukherjee.

HUDSPETH, Robert N. Associate professor of English, Pennsylvania State University, University Park. Author of *Ellery Channing,* 1973. Editor of *The Letters of Margaret Fuller,* 4 vols., 1983-87. **Essay:** William Ellery Channing.

HYNES, Jennifer A. Member, Department of English, University of South Carolina, Columbia. **Essay:** *The Age of Innocence.*

INGE, M. Thomas. Robert Emory Blackwell Professor of the Humanities, Randolph-Macon College, Ashland, Virginia. Author of studies of Southern literature and culture, American humor, ethnic American literature, modern fiction, popular culture, andcomic art. Editor of works by George Washington Harris and William Faulkner and of numerous collections, including *Agrarianism in American Literature,* 1969, *The Frontier Humorists,* 1975, *Ellen Glasgow: Centennial Essays,* 1976, *Black American Writers,* 2 vols., 1978, *Handbook of American Popular Culture,* 3 vols., 1979-81, *American Women Writers,* 1983, *James Branch Cabell: Centennial Essays,* 1983, *Huck Finn among the Critics,* 1985, and *Truman Capote: Conversations,* 1987. **Essays:** William Byrd; F. Scott Fitzgerald; George Washington Harris.

ISTEL, John. Adviser. Editor in chief, *Stagebill.* Former contributing editor of *American Theatre* magazine and associate editor for Back Stage Books. Author of articles and reviews in *Atlantic Monthly, Newsday, New York, Village Voice, American Theatre,* and *Mother Jones.* **Essays:** María Irene Fornés; Tony Kushner; Naomi Wallace; Mac Wellman.

JAMES, Theresa A. Writer. **Essay:** Robert Penn Warren.

JASKOSKI, Helen. Professor of English and comparative literature, California State University, Fullerton. Editor emeritus of *Studies in American Indian Literature.* Author of *The Tar Pit Murders, Poetry/Mind/Body,* and *Leslie Marmon Silko: A Study of the Short Form.* Editor of *Early Native American Writing: New Critical Essays.* **Essays:** Martin Cruz Smith; *Civil Disobedience; House Made of Dawn.*

JELINEK, Estelle C. Writer and editor. Author of *The Tradition of Women's Autobiography: From Antiquity to the Present,* 1986, and articles and reviews in *College English, Feminist Criticism, Women's Review of Books,* and *Women's Studies International.* Editor of *Women's Autobiography: Essays in Criticism,* 1980. **Essay:** Anaïs Nin.

JOHNSON, Alisa. Assistant professor of African American literature, Meredith College, Raleigh, North Carolina. **Essays:** Sandra M. Gilbert and Susan Gubar; Toni Cade Bambara.

JOHNSON, Robert K. Professor of English, Suffolk University, Boston. Author of *Neil Simon,* 1983, and articles on Richard Wilbur, Wallace Stevens, T.S. Eliot, and William Carlos Williams. **Essays:** Robert Frost; Archibald MacLeish; Howard Nemerov; Frederick Goddard Tuckerman; *The Death of the Hired Man; Snow-Bound; Somewhere I Have Never Travelled, Gladly Beyond.*

JONES, Andrew O. Associate in English, University of California, Davis. **Essays:** Amiri Baraka; Richard Eberhart; Stanley Kunitz; Howard Nemerov; Karl Shapiro; Gary Snyder.

JONES, J. Sydney. Writer; instructor in English, Cabrillo College, Aptos, California. Author of *Bike and Hike,* 1977, *Vienna Inside-Out,* 1979, *Hitler in Vienna,* 1980 and 1983, *Tramping in Europe,* 1984, *Viennawalks,* 1985 and 1994, *Time of the Wolf,* 1990, and *The Hero Game,* 1992. **Essays:** John Knowles; Betty Smith.

JONES, Lillie. Assistant professor of English, Alcorn State University, Lorman, Mississippi. **Essay:** Frances Ellen Watkins Harper.

JOYNER, Nancy Carol. Member of Department of English, Western Carolina University, Cullowhee, North Carolina. Author of *Edwin Arlington Robinson: A Reference Guide,* 1978. **Essays:** William Vaughn Moody; Laura Riding; Edwin Arlington Robinson; Susanna Rowson; *Because I could not stop for death; Look Homeward, Angel; Poetry.*

JUDD, Catherine. Assistant professor of English, University of Miami, Coral Gables. Author of articles on Florence Nightingale, George Eliot, Charlotte Brontë, and Charles Dickens's *Hard Times.* **Essays:** Susan Sontag.

KAPLAN, Zoë Coralnik. Adjunct assistant professor of speech and theater, John Jay College of Criminal Justice, City University of New York. **Essay:** Rachel Crothers.

KELLNER, Bruce. Professor of English, Millersville University, Pennsylvania. Author of *Carl Van Vechten and the Irreverent Decades,* 1968, and *Bibliography of the Work of Carl Van Vechten,* 1980. Editor of *Keep a-Inchin' Along: Selected Writings about Black Art and Letters by Van Vechten,* 1979, and *The Harlem Renaissance: A Historical Dictionary,* 1980. **Essays:** Hortense Calisher; Henry Blake Fuller; Joseph Hergesheimer; Henry Wadsworth Longfellow; Can Van Vechten

KING, Bruce. Adviser. Author of *Dryden's Major Plays,* 1966, *Marvell's Allegorical Poetry,* 1977, *New English Literatures: Cultural Nationalism in a Changing World,* 1980, *A History of Seventeenth-Century English Literature,* 1982, *Modern Indian Poetry in English,* 1987, *Three Indian Poets: Ezekiel, Ramanujan and Moraes,* 1991, *V. S. Naipaul,* 1993, and *Derek Walcott and West Indian Drama,* 1995. Editor of *Introduction to Nigerian Literature,* 1971, *Literatures of the World in English,* 1974, *A Celebration of Black and African Writing,* 1976, *West Indian Literature,* 1979, *Contemporary American Theatre,* 1991, *The Commonwealth Novel since 1960,* 1991, *Post-Colonial English Drama: Commonwealth Drama since 1960,* 1992, *The Later Fiction of Nadine Gordimer,* 1993, *West Indian Literature,* 1995, and *New National and Post-Colonial Literatures: An Introduction,* 1996. Series editor of *Modern Dramatists,* 1982-92, and *English Dramatists,* since 1990.

KING, Kimball. Member of Department of English, University of North Carolina at Chapel Hill; managing editor of *Southern Literary Journal.* Author of the bibliographies *Ten Modern Irish Playwrights,* 1979, and *Ten Modern American Playwrights,* 1982, and of *Augustus Baldwin Longstreet,* 1984. **Essays:** George Washington Cable; Lillian Hellman; Augustus Baldin Longstreet; Thomas Nelson Page.

KINNAMON, Keneth. Ethel Pumphrey Stephens Professor of English and chairman of department, University of Arkansas, Fayetteville. Author of *The Emergence of Richard Wright,* 1972. Editor of *Black Writers of America: A Comprehensive Anthology* (with Richard K. Barksdale), 1972, and *James Baldwin: A Collection of Critical Essays,* 1974. **Essays:** James Baldwin; Ralph Ellison; Langston Hughes.

KLINKOWITZ, Jerome. Professor of English and University Distinguished Scholar, University of Northern Iowa, Cedar Falls. Author of *Kurt Vonnegut,* 1982, *Listen: Gerry Mulligan/An Aural Narrative in Jazz,* 1991, *Donald Barthelme: An Exhibition,* 1991, *Writing under Fire: Stories of the Vietnam War,* 1977, *Nathaniel Hawthorne,* 1984, and many other books on contemporary culture. **Essay:** Robert Coover.

KUHN, John G. Professor of English and theater and chairman of the Division of English, Theater, and Classics, Rosemont College, Pennsylvania. **Essays:** James Nelson Barker; William Dunlap.

KULSHRESTHA, Chirantan. Teacher and freelance writer. Author of *The Saul Bellow Estate,* 1976, *Bellow: The Problem of Af-*

firmation, 1977, chapters in *Considerations*, 1977, and in *Through the Eyes of the World: International Essays in American Literature*, 1978, and articles in *Chicago Review, American Review, Quest, Indian Literature*, and other periodicals. Coeditor of *Not by Politics Alone!*, 1978, and editor of *Contemporary Indian English Verse: An Evaluation*, 1982. **Essays:** Robert E. Sherwood; Albion W. Tourgée.

LEAL, Luis. Professor emeritus, University of Illinois, Urbana, and Distinguished Lecturer, University of California, Santa Barbara. Winner of National Humanities Medal, 1997. Author of *Breve historia de la literatura hispanoamericana*, 1971, *Juan Rulfo*, 1983, *Aztlán y México*, 1985, *No Longer Voiceless*, 1995, and articles on Mariano Azuela, Tomás Rivera, José Montoya, Octavio Paz, and Carlos Fuentes. **Essays:** José Montoya; Tomás Rivera.

LEARY, Lewis. William Rand Kenan Professor of English Emeritus, University of North Carolina at Chapel Hill. Author of *Idiomatic Mistakes in English*, 1932, *That Rascal Freneau: A Study in Literary Failure*, 1941, *The Literary Career of Nathaniel Tucker*, 1951, *Articles on American Literature 1900-1975*, 3 vols., 1954-79, *Mark Twain*, 1960, *John Greenleaf Whittier*, 1961, *Washington Irving*, 1963, *Norman Douglas*, 1967, *Southern Excursions*, 1971, *Faulkner of Yoknapatawpha County*, 1973, and *American Literature: A Study and Research Guide*, 1976. Editor of works by Philip Freneau, Henry Wadsworth Longfellow, and Twain and of several collections of essays. **Essay:** Henry David Thoreau.

LEE, Hsiu-chuan. Ph.D. candidate in comparative literature, University of Michigan, Ann Arbor. **Essay:** Lin Tai-yi.

LESTER, Neil Andre. Assistant professor of English, University of Alabama, Tuscaloosa. Author of *Ntozake Shange: A Critical Study of the Plays*, 1994, and of articles and reviews for *Alabama Literary Review, African American Review, The Oxford Companion to Women's Writing in the United States*, and *The Lion and the Unicorn: A Critical Journal of Children's Literature*. **Essay:** Ntozake Shange.

LEVERNIER, James A. Associate professor of English and director of American studies, University of Arkansas at Little Rock. Coauthor of *Structuring Paragraphs: A Guide to Effective Writing*, 2nd edition 1986, and articles in *ESQ: A Journal of the American Renaissance, Research Studies, Markham Review, Explicator*, and other periodicals. Editor or coeditor of *An Essay for the Recording of Illustrious Providences* by Increase Mather, 1977, *The Indians and Their Captives*, 1977, *Souldiery Spiritualized: Seven Sermons Preached before the Artillery Companies of New England 1674-1774*, 1979, and *Sermons and Cannonballs*, 1982. **Essays:** Ebenezer Cooke; Frederick Douglass; Kenneth Fearing; Louise Imogen Guiney; Charles Fenno Hoffman; Francis Hopkinson; Joaquin Miller; Thomas Paine; Mary Rowlandson; Bayard Taylor; John Trumbull; *The Last of the Mohicans; Man That Corrupted Hadleyburg; Thanatopsis; The Federalist; Uncle Tom's Cabin*.

LEWIS, Naomi. Writer, critic, and broadcaster. Author of *A Visit to Mrs. Wilcox*, 1957, *Fantasy Books for Children*, 1975 (revised 1977), books for children, including *Once upon a Rainbow*, 1981, and *Come with Us*, 1982, and introductory essays to works on or by Hans Christian Andersen, E. Nesbit, Christina Rossetti, ArthurWaley, and others; contributor to the London *Observer, New Statesman, Times Literary Supplement, Listener*, and other periodicals. Editor of *A Peculiar Music: Poems for Young Readers* by Emily Brontë, 1971, and the anthologies *A Footprint on the Air*, 1983, and *Messages*, 1985. **Essay:** *The Country of the Pointed Firs*.

LING, Amy. Adviser. Professor of English and director of Asian-American studies, University of Wisconsin-Madison. Member of the advisory board for the Society for the Study of the Multi-Ethnic Literature of the United States (MELUS) and of the advisory council of the American Literature Section of the Modern Language Association. Author of *Between Worlds: Women Writers of Chinese Ancestry*, 1991. Coeditor of *Reading the Literatures of Asian America*, 1992, *The Spring of Asian American Literature: Collected Writings of Sui Sin Far*, 1994, and *The Oxford Companion to Women's Writing in the U.S.*

LOHOF, Bruce A. Director of U.S. Educational (Fulbright) Foundation in Pakistan, Islamabad. Author of *American Commonplace: Essays on Popular Culture in the United States*, 1983, and articles in *American Quarterly, Centennial Review, Journal of Popular Culture*, and other periodicals. Former director of American Studies Research Centre, Hyderabad, India. Has taught at the University of Miami and Heidelberg College, Tiffin, Ohio. **Essays:** James Agee; Horatio Alger; George Henry Boker; Margaret Deland; Timothy Dwight; Edward Eggleston; Zona Gale; H.L. Mencken.

LOMELI, Francisco A. Professor, University of California, Santa Barbara; member of editorial board of *Americas Review, Discurso Literario, Latino Studies Journal*, and *Revista Bilingüe/Bilingual Review*. Author of *La novelística de Carlos Droguett*, 1983, and of articles on Rudolfo Usigli, Alejandro Morales, Isabella Ríos, Tomás Rivera, and Eusebio Chacón. Coeditor of *Chicano Literature: A Reference Guide*, 1985, and *Dictionary of Literary Biography: Chicano Writers*, 1989 and 1992. **Essays:** Alejandro Morales; Ricardo Sánchez.

LONGEST, George C. Associate professor of English, Virginia Commonwealth University, Richmond. Author of *Three Virginia Writers: A Reference Guide*, 1978. **Essays:** James Lane Allen; Joseph G. Baldwin; Erskine Caldwell; Truman Capote; Bret Harte; Johnson Jones Hooper.

LOOSE, Margaret A. Graduate student at University of South Carolina, Columbia. **Essay:** *Ship of Fools*.

LOUIS, Deborah. Adviser. Director of instruction, curriculum and publications, Baltimore Community School, Maryland, and adjunct associate professor of political science and women's studies, University of Maryland-Baltimore County. Former director of National Women's Studies Association. Author of *And We Are Not Saved: A History of the Movement as People*, 1970.

LUCAS, John. Professor and head of Department of English and drama, Loughborough University, Leicestershire, England; advisory editor of *Victorian Studies, Literature and History*, and *Journal of European Studies*. Author of *Tradition and Tolerance in 19th-Century Fiction*, 1966, *The Melancholy Man: A Study of Dickens*, 1970, *Arnold Bennett*, 1975, *Egilssaga: The Poems*, 1975, *The Lit-*

erature of Change, 1977, *The 1930's: Challenge to Orthodoxy,* 1978, *Romantic to Modern,* 1982, and *Moderns and Contemporaries,* 1985. Editor of *Literature and Politics in the 19th Century,* 1971, and of works by George Crabbe and Jane Austen. **Essays:** Paul Goodman; Kenneth Patchen; Damon Runyon; Louis Simpson.

LUDINGTON, Townsend. Boshamer Professor of English and American Studies and chair of American studies, University of North Carolina at Chapel Hill. Author of *John Dos Passos: A Twentieth Century Odyssey,* 1980. Editor of *The Fourteenth Chronicle: Letters and Diaries of John Dos Passos,* 1973. **Essays:** John Dos Passos; Jack London.

MA, Sheng-mei. Assistant professor of English, James Madison University, Harrisonburg, Virginia. Author of collection of Chinese poems *Thirty, Left and Right,* 1989, and of articles on Asian-American literature, Orientalism, postcolonialism, and genocide literature. **Essay:** Carlos Bulosan.

MacLAINE, Brent. Freelance writer. **Essay:** Vladimir Nabokov.

MacSHANE, Frank. Professor, School of the Arts, and director of the Translation Center, Columbia University, New York. Author of *Many Golden Ages,* 1963, *The Life and Work of Ford Madox Ford,* 1965, *The Life of Raymond Chandler,* 1976, *The Life of John O'Hara,* 1980, and *Into Eternity: James Jones: The Life of an American Writer,* 1985. Editor of works by Chandler, Ford, O'Hara, and Jorge Luis Borges and translator of several books by Miguel Serrano. **Essays:** Raymond Chandler; Edward Dahlberg.

MADDEN, David. Writer in residence, Louisiana State University, Baton Rouge. Author of novels *(Bijou, The Suicide's Wife),* short stories *(The Shadow Knows, The New Orleans of Possibilities),* plays, poems, and critical works, including *James M. Cain,* 1970, *A Primer of the Novel,* 1980, and *Cain's Craft,* 1985. Editor of *Tough Guy Writers of the Thirties,* 1968, *Proletarian Writers of the Thirties,* 1968, *American Dreams, American Nightmares,* 1970, *Rediscoveries,* 1971, collections of essays on James Agee and Nathanael West, and other works. **Essay:** James M. Cain.

MAGISTRALE, Tony. Associate professor of English, University of Vermont, Burlington. Author of several books on Stephen King, including *Stephen King: The Second Decade,* articles on Flannery O'Connor, Richard Wright, and Wanda Coleman, and *Understanding Contemporary American Gothicism.* **Essay:** Stephen King.

MARIE, Jacquelyn. Reference librarian, women's studies, University of California, Santa Cruz. Contributor to *Feminist Writers* and *Gay and Lesbian Literature.* **Essay:** Gloria Anzaldúa; *Annie Allen.*

MARRS, Suzanne. Associate professor of English, State University of New York at Oswego. Author of articles in *American Literature, Southern Review, Mississippi Quarterly,* and other periodicals. **Essays:** Thomas Bangs Thorpe; *Losing Battles.*

MARSHALL, Tod. Assistant professor, Gonzaga University, Spokane, Washington. Author of articles and essays in *Paideuma,*

Cream City Review, and *Boston Review.* **Essays:** John Ashbery; Jim Harrison; Rovert Hass; Yusef Komunyakaa.

MATSUKAWA, Yuko. Assistant professor of English, Rhode Island College, Providence. Author of articles on Winnifred Eaton. **Essay:** Winnifred Eaton.

MATTSON, Francis O. Adviser. Curator, Berg Collection of English and American Literature, New York Public Library. Member of the advisory board for *Biblion.* Author of *Walt Whitman: In Life or Death Forever,* 1992, *Edna St. Vincent Millay, 1892-1950,* 1992, *Dandies and Doughties: Writers in Britain, 1890-1900,* 1993, and *Virginia Woolf and Her Circle,* 1993.

MAY, Charles E. Adviser. Professor of English, California State University, Long Beach. Author of *Short Story Theories,* 1977 (2nd edition 1994), *Twentieth Century European Short Story,* 1989, *Edgar Allan Poe: A Study of the Short Fiction,* 1991, *Fiction's Many Worlds,* 1992, *The Short Story: A Study of the Genre,* 1994, and more than a hundred articles on short fiction in numerous books and journals. **Essays:** Ann Beattie; Richard Ford; Northrop Frye; William H. Gass; Jayne Anne Phillips; Tobias Wolff; *Anatomy of Criticism; Cathedral; The Tunnel.*

McCAY, Mary A. Professor of English and chair of English Department, Loyola University, New Orleans. Author of books on Rachel Carson and Ellen Gilchrist and of numerous articles on contemporary American writers. **Essay:** Tim O'Brien.

McDOWELL, Margaret B. Professor of rhetoric and women's studies, University of Iowa, Iowa City. Author of *Edith Wharton,* 1976, and *Carson McCullers,* 1980. **Essay:** Carson McCullers.

McDOWELL, Robert. Founding publisher and editor of Story Line Press. Author of *Quiet Money,* a book of poems, and *The Diviners,* a book-length poem. Coauthor with Harvey Gross of *Sound and Form in Modern Poetry* and with Mark Jarman of *The Reaper Essays.* Editor of *Poetry after Modernism.* **Essays:** Malcolm Cowley; Donald Hall; Jane Kenyon; Etheridge Knight; Mark Strand; James Tate; *The Lost Son.*

McNAUGHTON, Howard. Reader, English University of Canterbury, Christchurch, New Zealand. Author of *Bruce Mason,* 1976, and *New Zealand Drama,* 1981. Editor of *Contemporary New Zealand Plays,* 1976, and *James K. Baxter: Collected Plays,* 1982. **Essays:** Ben Hecht; *Awake and Sing!; Strange Interlude.*

MESERVE, Walter J. Adviser. Distinguished professor emeritus in the Ph.D. programs in theater and English, City University of New York. Recipient of fellowships from the Rockefeller and Guggenheim foundations and of three Senior fellowships from National Endowment for the Humanities. Author and editor of sixteen books on theater and literature, including *An Outline History of American Drama,* 1965, *Robert Sherwood: Reluctant Moralist,* 1970, *An Emerging Entertainment: The Drama of the American People to 1828,* 1977, *American Drama* (with others), 1977, *American Drama to 1900: A Guide to Reference Sources,* 1980, and *Heralds of Promise: The Dramas of the American People during the Age of Jackson 1829-1849,* 1986. **Essays:** Zoë Akins; Nathaniel Bannister; Robert Montgomery Bird; John Brougham; Paddy Chayefsky; Augustin Daly; Clyde Fitch; Susan Glaspell;

Edward Harrigan; Bronson Howard; Sidney Howard; Charles Hoyt; Percy MacKaye; Langdon Mitchell; George Jean Nathan; John Howary Payne; Edward Sheldon; Neil Simon; Royall Tyler; *The Contast.*

MILLER, Jordan Y. Retired professor of English, University of Rhode Island, Kingston. Author of *Playwright's Progress: Eugene O'Neill and the Critics,* 1965, *The War Play Comes of Age,* 1969,and *Eugene O'Neill and the American Critic* (a bibliography), 1973. Editor of *American Dramatic Literature,* 1961, and *Twentieth-Century Interpretations of A Streetcar Named Desire,* 1971. **Essays:** Lorraine Hansberry; Janes A. Herne; William Inge.

MILLER, Tyrus. Associate professor of comparative literature and English, Yale University, New Haven, Connecticut. Author of *Late Modernism: Politics, Fiction, and The Arts between the World Wars,* 1999. **Essays:** Clark Coolidge; Lyn Hejinian; Susan Howe; Bob Perelman.

MILLS, Bruce. Assistant professor, Kalamazoo College, Michigan. Author of *Cultural Reformations: Lydia Maria Child and the Literature of Reform,* 1993, and of articles on Harriet Jacobs. **Essay:** Lydia Maria Child.

MITCHELL, Mozella. Professor of religion, University of South Florida, Tampa. Author of *Spiritual Dynamics of Howard Thurman's Theology 1992-1996,* 1985, *African American Religious History in Tampa Bay,* 1993, and *New Africa in America: The Blending of African and American Social and Religious Elements among Black People in Meridian, Mississippi, and Surrounding Counties,* 1994. Editor of *The Human Search: Howard Thurman and the Quest for Freedom,* 1993. **Essay:** Nikki Giovanni.

MOE, Christian H. Professor of theater, Southern Illinois University, Carbondale; member of advisory board, Institute of Outdoor Drama; bibliographer for the American Theatre Association. Author or coauthor of *Creating Historical Drama,* 1965, an essay on D. H. Lawrence, and several plays for children. Joint editor of *The William and Mary Theatre: A Chronicle,* 1968, and *Six New Plays for Children,* 1971. **Essays:** Romulus Linney; Marjorie Kinnan Rawlings; *The Glass Menagerie; The Member of the Wedding.*

MONTEIRO, George. Professor of English, Brown University, Providence, Rhode Island. Editor or coeditor of *Henry James and John Hay: The Record of a Friendship,* 1965, *Poems* by Emily Dickinson, 1967, *The Scarlet Letter* by Nathaniel Hawthorne, 1968, *The Poetical Works of Longfellow* (introduction), 1975, *The John Hay-Howells Letters: The Correspondence of John Milton Hay and William Dean Howells,* 1980, and *A Guide to the Atlantic Monthly's Contributors' Club,* 1983. **Essay:** John Hay.

MOORE, Jack B. Professor of English and chair of American studies, University of South Florida, Tampa. Author of *The Literature of Early America,* 1968, *The Literature of the American Renaissance,* 1969, *Guide to "Idylls of the King,"* 1969, *Maxwell Bodenheim,* 1970, *The Literature of the American Realistic Period,* 1971, *Cooper: The Last of the Mohicans* (study guide), 1971, *W. E. B. Du Bois,* 1981, and *Joe DeMaggio,* 1986. **Essays:** Maxwell Bodenheim; Ignatius Donnelly; Frank Yerby; *Looking Backward 2000-1887; Native Son.*

MOORE, Rayburn S. Professor of English and chair, Division of Language and Literature, Franklin College of Arts and Sciences, University of Georgia, Athens. Author of *Constance Fenimore Woolson,* 1963, *Paul Hamilton Hayne,* 1972, and numerous articles and reviews. Editor of *For the Major and Selected Short Stories of Constance Fenimore Woolson,* 1967, *A Man of Letters in the Nineteenth-Century South: Selected Letters of Paul Hamilton Hayne,* 1982, and *The History of Southern Literature* (with others), 1985. **Essays:** Thomas Holley Chivers; John Esten Cooke; Paul Hamilton Hayne; William Gilmore Simms; Constance Fenimore Woolson.

MORACE, Robert A. Professor of English, Daemen College, Amherst, New York. Author of *The Dialogic Novels of Malcolm Bradbury and David Lodge* and *John Gardner: An Annotated Secondary Bibliography,* as well as of numerous articles on contemporary and American fiction. Coeditor with Kathryn Van Spanckeren of *John Gardner: Critical Perspectives.* **Essay:** Carole Maso.

MORGAN, Bridget M. Independent scholar in medieval Spanish and modern Spanish-American literature. **Essay:** Oscar Hijuelos.

MORSBERGER, Katharine M. Feature writer, Pitzer College, Claremont, California. Author of *Lew Wallace: Militant Romantic* (with Robert E. Morsberger), 1980, and articles on Hawthorne and Steinbeck. **Essay:** Lew Wallace.

MORSBERGER, Robert E. Professor of English, California State Polytechnic, Pomona. Author of *James Thurber,* 1964, *Commonsense Grammar and Style,* 1965, *Swordplay and the Elizabethan and Jacobean Stage,* 1974, and *Lew Wallace: Militant Romantic* (with Katharine M. Morsberger), 1980. Editor of *Viva Zapata!* by John Steinbeck, 1975. **Essays:** Lew Wallace; *Ethan Brand.*

NADEL, I.B. Professor of English, University of British Columbia, Vancouver. Author of *Biography: Fiction, Fact and Form,* 1984, and articles on Victorian writing and Jewish fiction in *University of Toronto Quarterly, Criticism, Mosaic, Midstream, Prose Studies,* and other periodicals. **Essay:** *The Day of the Locust.*

NEVINS, Francis M., Jr. Professor of law, St. Louis University School of Law, Missouri. Author of three crime novels and numerous crime short stories, *Royal Bloodline: Ellery Queen, Author and Detective,* 1974, and articles in *Detectionary, Journal of Popular Culture, Armchair Detective,* and other collections and periodicals. Editor of *The Mystery Writer's Art,* 1971, works by Ellery Queen, Cornell Woolrich, Anthony Boucher, and Christianna Brand, and anthologies. **Essays:** Erle Stanley Gardner; Ellery Queen.

NORDGREN, Joe. Assistant professor of English, Lamar University, Beaumont, Texas; codirector of the Texas Reading Circuit. Author of entries for Denis Johnson, Raymond Carver, and Robert Olen Butler for the *Dictionary of Literary Biography* and of articles on D. H. Lawrence, Malcolm Lowry, Graham Greene, and Jean Rhys. **Essays:** Raymond Carver; *The Love Song of J. Alfred Prufrock.*

NORLAND, Brady. Freelance writer. **Essay:** Mary McCarthy.

NOVAK, Robert Lee. Associate professor of English, Indiana University at Fort Wayne. Author of *Sleeping with Sylvia Plath, Hemingway Poems,* short stories (including "Why the Salinger Kids Smoke," "Noise," and "Solipsism"), and the column "The Prufrock Corner." Editor of *The Windless Orchard.* Producer of television videos *Backyard Gardens.* **Essay:** Richard Brautigan.

OCASIO, Rafael. Assistant professor of Spanish and adviser in the Latin American studies program at Agnes Scott College, Decatur, Georgia. Author of articles on children's literature in Cuba, Cuban Santeria, and Reinaldo Arevas in *The Lion and the Unicorn, Journal of Caribbean Studies,* and *Romance Quarterly.* **Essay:** Judith Ortiz Cofer.

O'DONNELL, Thomas F. Late professor of English, State University of New York at Brockport. Author or coauthor of *Harold Frederic,* 1961, *A Bibliography of Harold Frederic,* 1975, and of articles on American writers, especially those of New York State, for *American Transcendental Quarterly* and other periodicals. Editor of works by Frederic, James Kirke Paulding, and Adriaen Van Der Donck. Died 1980. **Essays:** Anne Bradstreet; Joseph Rodman Drake; James Kirke Paulding.

OSTROM, Hans. Professor of English and codirector of African American studies, University of Puget Sound, Tacoma, Washington. Fulbright Senior Lecturer, Uppsala University, Sweden, 1994. Author and editor of ten books, including *Langston Hughes: A Study of the Short Fiction, Three to Get Ready* (novel), and *Genes of Writing.* **Essay:** The Fish.

PAOLINI, Shirley J. Professor of literature and dean of School of Human Sciences and Humanities, University of Houston, Clear Lake, Texas. Author of *Creativity, Culture and Values: Comparative Essays in Literary Aesthetics,* 1990, as well as essays in *Sino-American Relations since 1900,* 1991, *Language and Literature Today,* 1996, *Humanities and the Good Life,* 1997, and other books. General editor of *New Connections: Studies in Interdisciplinarity.* **Essay:** Louise Glück; Robert Pinsky.

PATROUCH, Joseph Francis. Professor of English, University of Dayton, Ohio. Member of Science Fiction and Fantasy Writers of America (SFWA) and Science Fiction Research Association (SFRA). Author of *Reginald Pecock,* 1970, *The Science Fiction of Isaac Asimov,* 1973, science fiction short stories, and articles on Robert A. Heinlein and Harlan Ellison and on teaching science fiction. **Essay:** Roberty Anson Heinlein.

PEDEN, William. Professor of English, University of Missouri, Columbia. Author of *Night in Funland and Other Stories,* 1968, *Twilight at Monticello* (novel), 1973, and *The American Short Story: Continuity and Change 1940-1975,* 1975. Coeditor of works by Thomas Jefferson, John Adams, and John Quincy Adams and of *New Writing in South Carolina,* 1971. **Essay:** O. Henry.

PENDERGAST, Tom. Graduate student in American studies at Purdue University, West Lafayette, Indiana. **Essays:** Robert Bly; James Dickey; John Hawkes; Arthur Kopit.

PEREIRA, Kim. Assistant professor of theater, Illinois State University, Normal. Actor, director, and author of *An African American Odyssey: Self-Authentification in the Plays of August Wilson,*

1994, and of articles on Shakespeare, George Bernard Shaw, and Wilson. **Essay:** August Wilson.

PERKINS, Barbara M. Managing editor of *Journal of Narrative Technique,* Eastern Michigan University, Ypsilanti. Author of articles in *Harper Handbook to Literature, American Literary Magazines: The Eighteenth and Nineteenth Centuries,* and other books and periodicals. **Essays:** Maxwell Anderson; John William De Forest.

PERKINS, George. Professor of English, Eastern Michigan University, Ypsilanti. Author or editor of *Writing Clear Prose,* 1964, *Varieties of Prose,* 1966, *The Theory of the American Novel,* 1970, *Realistic American Short Fiction,* 1972, *American Poetic Theory,* 1972, *The Practical Imagination* (with others), 1980, *The Harper Handbook to Literature* (with others), 1985, and *The American Tradition in Literature* (with others), 6th edition, 1985. **Essays:** Nathaniel Hawthorne; Henry James.

PERLOFF, Marjorie. Adviser. Sadie Dernham Patek Professor of Humanities, Stanford University, California. Author of *Rhyme and Meaning in the Poetry of Yeats,* 1970, *The Poetic Art of Robert Lowell,* 1973, *Frank O'Hara: Poet among Painters,* 1977, *The Poetics of Indeterminacy: Rimbaud to Cage,* 1981, *The Dance of the Intellect: Studies in the Poetry of the Pound Tradition,* 1985, *The Futurist Moment: Avant-Garde, Avant-Guerre, and the Language of Rupture,* 1986, *Poetic License: Studies in Modern and Postmodern Poetics,* 1989, *Radical Artifice: Writing Poetry in the Age of Media,* 1991, *Wittgenstein's Ladder: Poetic Language and the Strangeness of the Ordinary,* 1996, and *Poetry on & off the Page: Essays for Emergent Occasions,* 1998. Editor of *Postmodern Genres,* 1989, and *John Cage: Composed in America* (with Charles Junkerman), 1994.

PERRY, Margaret. Director of Libraries, Valparaiso University, Indiana. Author of *A Bio-Bibliography of Countée O. Cullen,* 1971, *Silence to the Drums: A Survey of the Literature of the Harlem Renaissance,* 1976, *The Harlem Renaissance: An Annotated Bibliography and Commentary,* 1982, and several short stories. **Essays:** Countee Cullen; Phillis Wheatley.

PERRY, Patsy B. Professor of English, North Carolina Central University, Durham. Author of articles on Frederick Douglass, James Baldwin, Benjamin Brawley, Leslie Pinckney Hill, and Chester Himes. Coeditor of *Poetry, Childhood and Spring: A Collection of Poems Written by Children and Young People,* 1979. **Essay:** James Alan McPherson.

PETTIS, Joyce. Professor of English, North Carolina State University at Raleigh; teacher of African American literature courses. Author of the critical study *Toward Wholeness in Paule Marshall's Fiction* and of numerous essays on women writers. **Essay:** Margaret Walker.

PICKARD, John B. Associate professor of English, University of Florida, Gainesville. Author of *Whittier: An Introduction and Interpretation,* 1961, introduction to *Legends of New England* by John Greenleaf Whittier, 1965, and *Emily Dickinson: An Introduction and Interpretation,* 1967. Editor of *Memorabilia of Whittier,* 1968, and *The Letters of Whittier,* 3 vols., 1975. **Essays:** James Russell Lowell; John Greenleaf Whittier.

PILDITCH, Jan. Lecturer, University of Waikato, Hamilton, New Zealand. **Essays:** John Gardner; William James.

PINSKER, Sanford. Shadek Professor of Humanities, Franklin and Marshall College, Lancaster, Pennsylvania. Member of editorial board for *Studies in American Jewish Literature* and contributing editor of the *Georgia Review.* Author of *Between Two Worlds: The American Novel in the 1960s,* 1978, and *Jewish-American Fiction, 1917-1987,* 1992. Coeditor of *Jewish-American History and Culture: An Encyclopedia,* 1992. **Essays:** Stanley L. Elkin; Joseph Heller; Norman Mailer.

POPOVICH, Helen Houser. President, Florida Atlantic University, Boca Raton. Author of articles on Samuel Beckett and on writing. **Essay:** John Van Druten.

PORTALES, Marco. Adviser. Professor of English, Texas A & M University, College Station. President of the Society for the Study of the Multi-Ethnic Literature of the United States (MELUS).

PRINCE, Valerie Sweeney. Author of essays on FrederickDouglass, Ernest Gaines, and the discourse of African American males. **Essays:** Alice Childress; Alain Locke.

PUDALOFF, Ross J. Associate professor of English, Wayne State University, Detroit. Associate editor of *Criticism: A Quarterly for Literature and the Arts.* Author of articles on Richard Wright, Henry David Thoreau, James Fenimore Cooper, and the Salem witch trials. **Essay:** Charlotte Perkins Gilman.

QUARTERMAIN, Peter. Associate professor of English, University of British Columbia, Vancouver. Author of articles on Louis Zukofsky, Robert Creeley, Ezra Pound, Basil Bunting, Guy Davenport, Charles Reznikoff, and other writers. Editor of *American Poets 1880-1945* for the *Dictionary of Literary Biography,* 1986. **Essays:** Robert Duncan; Allen Ginsberg; Gertrude Stein.

RAMEY, Deanna E. Ph.D. candidate at the University of South Carolina, Columbia. Author of articles on Toni Morrison and Alice Walker. **Essay:** Bobbie Ann Mason.

RAY, David. Professor of English, University of Missouri at Kansas City; editor of *New Letters.* Author of several books of poems, including *The Touched Life,* 1982, and a book of short stories. Editor or coeditor of *The Chicago Review Anthology,* 1959, *Richard Wright: Impressions and Perspectives,* 1973, *New Letters Reader,* 2 vols., 1984, and several anthologies of poetry. **Essay:** Horace Gregory.

RECKLEY, Ralph, Sr. Professor of English, Morgan State University, Baltimore. Founding member and former president of the Middle Atlantic Writers Association. Author of *21st Century Black American Women in Print* and of articles on Chester Himes, Toni Morrison, John A. Williams, Lola Jones, and James Baldwin. Editor of *James Baldwin: In Memoriam.* **Essay:** Chester Himes.

REED, John Q. Late chairman of the Department of English, Pittsburg State University, Kansas. Author of *Benjamin Penhallow Shillaber,* 1972, and of articles on Artemus Ward, Henry James, William Faulkner, and Mark Twain in *American Litera-*

ture, Midcontinent American Studies Journal, Encyclopaedia Britannica, Civil War History, and *Midwest Quarterly.* Died 1978. **Essay:** Artemus Ward.

REEVES, James. Author of more than fifty books, including poetry (*Collected Poems,* 1974), plays, works for children, and critical works such as *The Critical Sense,* 1956, *Understanding Poetry,* 1965, *Commitment to Poetry,* 1969, *Inside Poetry* (with Martin Seymour-Smith), 1970, and *The Reputation and Writings of Alexander Pope,* 1976. Editor of many collections and anthologies and of works by D. H. Lawrence, Robert Browning, Dickinson, Coleridge, Graves, Swift, and others. Translator of fairy tales. Died 1978. **Essay:** Emily Dickinson.

REILLY, Edward C. Associate professor of English, Arkansas State University, State University. Author of *William Kennedy,* 1991, *Understanding John Irving,* 1991, and articles about John Cheever, Shelby Foote, Jim Harrison, and Larry McMurtry. **Essay:** John Irving.

REILLY, John M. Professor of English, State University of New York at Albany. Author of many articles on African American literature, popular crime writing and social fiction, and bibliographical essays in *Black American Writers,* 1978, and *American Literary Scholarship.* Editor of *Twentieth-CenturyInterpretations of Invisible Man,* 1970, *Richard Wright: The Critical Reception,* 1978, and the reference book *Twentieth-Century Crime and Mystery Writers,* 1980 (2nd edition 1985). **Essays:** William Wells Brown, W.E.B. Du Bois; Dashiell Hammett; Zora Neale Hurston; Rex Stout; Jean Toomer; Richard Wright.

REILLY, Terry. Assistant professor of English, University of Alaska, Fairbanks. Author of essays on Shakespeare, Goethe, Pynchon, Arthur Young, and trauma theory. **Essay:** *The Crying of Lot 49.*

RENDER, Sylvia Lyons. Specialist in African American history and culture, Manuscript Division, Library of Congress, Washington, D.C. Author of *Charles W. Chesnutt,* 1980, the introduction articles in *Encyclopaedia Britannica, CLA Journal, North Carolina Folklore,* and *Tennessee Folklore Society Bulletin.* Editor of *The Short Fiction of Chesnutt,* 1974. **Essay:** Charles Waddell Chesnutt.

RICHARDS, Robert F. Associate professor of English, University of Denver. Author of articles on aesthetics, politics and literature, Ernest Hemingway, F. Scott Fitzgerald, Ralph Hodgson, and Thomas Hornsby Ferril and of the introduction to Ferril's *Words for Denver and Other Poems,* 1966. Editor of *Concise Dictionary of American Literature,* 1969. **Essays:** Waldo Frank; Oliver La Farge; Don Marquis.

RIDINGER, Robert B. Marks. Associate professor, University Libraries, Northern Illinois University, De Kalb. Compiler of *An Index to "The Advocate," the National Gay Newsmagazine, 1967-1982,* 1983, and *The Homosexual and Society: An Annotated Bibliography,* 1990. **Essay:** Audre Lorde.

RINGE, Donald A. Professor of English, University of Kentucky, Lexington. Author of *James Fenimore Cooper,* 1962, *Charles Brockden Brown,* 1966, *The Pictorial Mode: Space and Time in* *the Art of Bryant, Irving, and Cooper,* 1971, and *American Gothic Imagination and Reason in Nineteenth-Century Fiction,* 1982. Member of editorial board, *The Writings of James Fenimore Cooper.* **Essays:** Hugh Henry Brackenridge; Charles Brockden Brown; James Fenimore Cooper; John Pendleton Kennedy; John Neal.

RODRIGUEZ del PINO, Salvador. Associate professor of Chicano studies, Center for the Study of Ethnicity and Race in the Americas, University of Colorado, Boulder. Author of *La novela chicana escrita in español: cinco autores comprometidos* and of articles on Rolando Hinojosa, Miguel Méndez, Aristo Brito, and Tomás Rivera. **Essays:** Meguel Méndez M.; *Peregrinos de Aztlán.*

ROGERS, Gary W. Freelance writer. Author of articles on William Faulkner, Elmer Kelton, and Frank Waters. **Essay:** Frank Waters.

ROVIT, Earl. Professor of English, City College of New York. Author of *Herald to Chaos: The Novels of Elizabeth Madox Roberts,* 1960, *Ernest Hemingway,* 1963, *Saul Bellow,* 1967, and three novels, *The Player King,* 1965, *A Far Cry,* 1967, and *Crossings,* 1973. Editor of *Saul Bellow: A Collection of Critical Essays,* 1975. **Essays:** Henry Adams; John Barth; Theodore Dreiser; John Hawkes; James Jones; Elizabeth Madox Roberts; Trumbull Stickney; Jones Very; Nathanael West.

RUOFF, A. LaVonne Brown. Adviser. Professor of English, University of Illinois at Chicago. Editor of American Indian Lives series, University of Nebraska Press. Author of *American Indian Literatures,* 1990, and *Literatures of the American Indian,* 1990, and of articles on Samson Occom, William Apess, George Copway, Charles Eastman, Sarah Winnemucca, Leslie Silko, and Gerald Vizenor. Coeditor of *Redefining American Literary History,* 1990, and editor of E. Pauline Johnson's *The Moccasin Maker,* 1987.

RUPPERT, James. Professor of English and of Alaska Native studies, University of Alaska, Fairbanks. Former president of the Association for the Study of American Indian Literature. Author of *Guide to Poetry Explication: Volume 1, Colonial and Nineteenth-Century,* 1989, and *Mediation in Contemporary Native American Fiction,* 1995, and of articles on Leslie Silko, Louise Erdrich, and Henry Rowe Schoolcraft and on Native American oral narratives. **Essays:** Leslie Marmon Silko; *Ceremony.*

RUTHLEY, Glenn Richard. Member of Department of English, Eastern Michigan University, Ypsilanti. Author of *The Thorn of a Rose: Amy Lowell Reconsidered,* 1975. Editor of *A Shard of Silence: Selected Poems* by Lowell, 1957. **Essays:** Amy Lowell; Edgar Lee Masters; Edna St. Vincent Millay.

SADLER, Geoff. Assistant librarian, local studies, Chesterfield, Derbyshire, England. Author of Western novels (as Jeff Sadler), including *Throw of a Rope,* 1984, and *Manhunt in Chihuahua,* 1984, and of the *Justus* trilogy of plantation novels (as Geoffrey Sadler), 1982. **Essays:** Booker T. Washington; *Souls of Black Folk.*

SAFFIOTTI, Carol Lee. Associate professor of English, University of Wisconsin-Parkside, Kenosha. **Essay:** Sterling A. Brown.

SANDERSON, Stewart F. Honorary Harold Orton Fellow, University of Leeds, England; chairman of the Literature Committee, Scottish Arts Council. Author of *Hemingway,* 1961, and of many articles on British and comparative folklore and ethnology and on modern literature. Editor of *The Secret Common-Wealth* by Robert Kirk, 1970, *The Linguistic Atlas of England* (with others), 1978, and *Studies in Linguistic Geography,* 1985. **Essay:** Ernest Hemingway.

SANDOCK, Mollie. Assistant professor of English, Valparaiso University, Indiana. Author of articles on nineteenth-century literature and on librarianship in *Modern Philology, Library Quarterly, Nineteenth-Century Literature,* and other periodicals. **Essays:** *The Adventures of Tom Sawyer; The Catcher in the Rye; The Turn of the Screw.*

SAUCERMAN, James R. Professor and chair of Department of English, Northwest Missouri State University, Maryville. Former chair of the Missouri Humanities Council. Author of articles on Mark Twain, Ralph Waldo Emerson, Western American poetry, Wendy Rose, and Thomas Hornsby Ferril. **Essay:** Wendy Rose.

SAUL, George Brandon. Professor emeritus of English, University of Connecticut, Storrs; contributing editor, *Journal of Irish Literature.* Author of fiction (*The Wild Queen,* 1967), poetry (*Hound and Unicorn,* 1969, and *Adam Unregenerate,* 1977), and critical works, including *Prolegomena to the Study of Yeats' Poems* (1957) and *Plays* (1958), *Traditional Irish Literature and Its Backgrounds,* 1970, and *In Praise of the Half-Forgotten: Essays,* 1976. Also a composer. **Essay:** Sara Teasdale.

SCARRY, John. Professor of English, Hostos Community College, City University of New York; member of the board of editors of *Journal of Basic Writing.* Editor and author of books and articles on singers and the history of musical performance and on James Joyce and Joy Harjo. Coauthor of college composition textbooks, including *The Writer's Workplace.* **Essay:** Joy Harjo.

SCHWAB, Arnold T. Professor of English, California State University, Long Beach. Author of *James Gibbons Huneker: Critic of the Seven Arts,* 1963, and of articles on Huneker, George Moore, and Joseph Conrad in *American Literature, Nineteenth-Century Fiction,* and *Modern Philology.* Editor of *Americans in the Arts: Critiques by James Gibbons Huneker,* 1985. **Essay:** James Huneker.

SEELYE, Catherine. Freelance writer. Editor of *Charles Olson and Ezra Pound: An Encounter at St. Elizabeths,* 1975. **Essays:** Eugene Field; Vachel Lindsay.

SEYERSTED, Per. Professor of American literature, University of Oslo, Norway; vice president of the Nordic Association for Canadian Studies. Author of *Gilgamesj,* 1967, *Kate Chopin: A Critical Biography,* 1969, *Leslie Marmon Silko,* 1980, and *From Norwegian Romantic to American Realist: Studies in the Life and Writings of H. H. Boyesen,* 1984. Editor of *The Complete Works of Kate Chopin,* 1969, and *A Kate Chopin Miscellany* (with Emily Toth), 1979. **Essay:** Kate Chopin.

SHARMA, J.N. Professor and head of the Department of English, University of Jodhpur, India. **Essays:** Ambrose Bierce; William Saroyan.

SHEPHERD, Allen. Professor of English, University of Vermont, Burlington. Author of fiction and poetry in the *New Yorker, Colorado Quarterly,* and *Mississippi Review* and of articles on nineteenth- and twentieth-century American authors in *Modern Fiction Studies, Novel,* and *Southern Literary Journal.* Editor of *About These Stories,* 1994. **Essay:** Harry Crews.

SHEVIN, David A. Associate professor of English, Tiffin University, Ohio. Author of *The Discovery of Fire,* 1988, *Growl,* 1990, *Needles and Needs,* 1994, and other books. Coeditor of the literary anthologies *Red Shadow of Steel Mills,* 1991, and *Getting By: Stories of Working Lives,* 1996. **Essays:** Grace Paley; Ishmael Reed.

SHIH, David. Ph.D. candidate in English language and literature, University of Michigan, Ann Arbor. **Essay:** Wallace Stegner.

SHIRLEY, Carl R. Professor of Spanish and comparative literature, University of South Carolina, Columbia. Author of articles on Chicano history and literature, John Nichols, Edwin Corle, and Wilberto Canton, and coauthor (with Paula W. Shirley) of *Understanding Chicano Literature,* 1988. Coeditor of *Chicano Writers, First Series,* and *Chicano Writers, Second Series.* **Essay:** Alma Luz Villanueva.

SHOSTAK, Elizabeth. Contributing editor of *Boston Book Review.* Author of essays and reviews in *Women's Review of Books, Boston Globe, Newsday, Village Voice,* and other publications. **Essays:** Andre Dubus; Leslie A. Fiedler; John Irving; Denise Levertov; Barry Holstun Lopez; Bharati Mukherjee.

SHUCARD, Alan R. Professor of English, University of Wisconsin-Parkside, Kenosha. Author of three books of poetry and of *Countée Cullen,* 1984. **Essays:** Gwendolyn Brooks; Walter Van Tilburg Clark; Paul Laurence Dunbar; Robert Hayden.

SIMMONS, James R., Jr. Ph.D. candidate at University of South Carolina, Columbia. Author of article on Stanley J. Weyman for *Dictionary of Literary Biography: British Short Story Writers, 1880-1914: The Romantic Tradition.* **Essays:** Barbara W. Tuchman; *The Autobiography of Alice B. Toklas.*

SINGH, Amritjit. Teacher and freelance writer. Author of *The Novels of the Harlem Renaissance: Twelve Black Writers,* 1976, and of articles in *Indian Journal of American Studies* and other Indian and American periodicals. Coeditor of the bibliographies *Indian Literature in English,* 1977, and *Afro-American Poetry and Dramas,* 1977, and of *India: An Anthology of Contemporary Writing,* 1983. **Essay:** Claude McKay.

SMITH, Esther Marian Greenwell. Retired professor of language arts. Author of *William Godwin* (with Elton E. Smith), 1965, and *Mrs. Humphry Ward,* 1980; articles on Herman Melville, Nathaniel Hawthorne, Mrs. Humphry Ward, and Olivia Manning; two novels (*The Last Eight Days,* 1985, and *The Cascade Empire,* 1986); and fiction for youth for religious publishers. **Essays:** Pearl S. Buck; *Billy Budd.*

SMITH, Larry. Professor of English, Bowling Green State University at Firelands College, Huron, Ohio. Director of Bottom

Dog Press, Inc., and of the Firelands Writing Center. Author of *Kenneth Patchen,* 1978, and *Lawrence Ferlinghetti: Poet-at-Large,* 1982, and of articles on Edward Dahlberg, Kenneth Rexroth, Kenneth Patchen, Lawrence Ferlinghetti, and Sherwood Anderson. Wrote the scripts for and produced the documentaries *James Wright's Ohio,* 1987, and *Kenneth Patchen: An Art of Engagement,* 1988. **Essays:** Rita Dove; Lawrence Ferlinghetti; Barbara Kingsolver.

SMITH, Stan. Senior lecturer in English, University of Dundee, Scotland. Author of *A Sadly Contracted Hero: The Comic Self in Post-War American Fiction,* 1981, *Inviolable Voice: History and Twentieth-Century Poetry,* 1982, *W. H. Auden,* 1986, *Edward Thomas,* 1986, the introduction to *Twentieth-Century Poetry,* 1983, and essays in collections and journals. **Essays:** Lafeadio Hearn; Sylvia Plath; Theodore Roethke; Philip Roth; *The Assistant.*

SMITH-McCOY, Sheila. Professor, North Carolina State University at Raleigh. **Essay:** Gloria Naylor.

SOLOMON, Eric. Professor of English, San Francisco State University. Author of *Stephen Crane in England,* 1963, and *Stephen Crane: From Parody to Realism,* 1966, and of articles on nineteenth- and twentieth-century British and American fiction. Editor of *The Faded Banners,* 1960, and *The Critic Agonistes,* 1985. **Essays:** F. Scott Fitzgerald; Edmund Wilson; *Catch-22.*

STAGG, Louis Charles. Professor of English and director of graduate studies, Memphis State University, Tennessee. Author or coauthor of *Index to Poe's Critical Vocabulary,* 1966, *The Figurative Language of Shakespeare's Chief 17th-Century Contemporaries: An Index,* revised 3rd edition, 1982, *The Figurative Language of the Tragedies of Shakespeare's Chief 16th-Century Contemporaries: An Index,* 1984, and numerous articles and reviews. **Essays:** William Gillette; *The Death of a Salesman; Long Day's Journey into Night.*

STANFORD, Donald E. Alumni Professor of English Emeritus, Louisiana State University, Baton Rouge; editor emeritus of *Southern Review.* Author of two books of poems (*New EnglandEarth,* 1941, and *The Traveler,* 1955), *Edward Taylor,* 1965, *In the Classic Mode: The Achievement of Robert Bridges,* 1978, and *Revolution and Convention in Modern Poetry: Studies in Ezra Pound, T. S. Eliot, Wallace Stevens, Edwin Arlington Robinson, and Yvor Winters,* 1983. Editor of *The Poems of Edward Taylor,* 1960, *Metrical History of Christianity* by Taylor, 1962, *Nine Essays in Modern Literature,* 1965, *Selected Poems of Robert Bridges,* 1974, *Selected Poems of S. Foster Damon,* 1974, *Selected Letters of Robert Bridges,* 2 vols., 1983-84, *Selected Poems of John Masefield,* 1984, and *The Letters of John Masefield to Margaret Bridges 1915-1919,* 1984. **Essays:** Edward Taylor; Yvor Winters; *Gods Determinations; Sunday Morning.*

STANTON, Michael N. Associate professor of English, University of Vermont, Burlington. Author of *English Literary Journals 1900-1950,* 1982, and of articles on Robert Southey, Charles Dickens, and Stephen King. **Essays:** Isaac Asimov; Ray Bradbury.

STAVANS, Ilan. Novelist and critic; professor of Spanish at Amherst College, Massachusetts. Contributor to the *New York Times, Miami Herald, Nation,* and other periodicals. Author of

Imagining Columbus: The Literary Voyage, 1993, *The Hispanic Condition,* 1995, *Art and Anger,* 1996, and *The Riddle of Cantinflas: Essays on Hispanic Popular Culture,* 1998. Editor of *Growing Up Latino: Memoirs and Stories,* 1993, *Tropical Synagogues: Short Stories by Jewish Latin American Writers,* 1994, and *The Oxford Book of Latin American Essays,* 1997. Author of essays on Octavio Paz, Mario Vargas Llosa, and Gabriel García Márquez. **Essays:** Harold Bloom; José Antonio Villarreal.

STEDMAN, Jane W. Professor of English, Roosevelt University, Chicago. Author of articles and reviews in anthologies of Victorian studies, scholarly journals, and *Opera News.* Editor of *Gilbert Before Sullivan: Six Comic Plays,* 1967. **Essays:** David Belasco; *John Brown's Body.*

STERN, Madeleine B. Freelance writer; partner in Leona Rostenberg-Madeleine Stern Rare Books, New York. Author of *Louisa May Alcott,* 1950, *Imprints on History: Book Publishers and American Frontiers,* 1956, *We the Women: Career First of 19th-Century America,* 1963, *Heads and Headlines: The Phrenological Fowlers,* 1971, *Old and Rare: Thirty Years in the Book Business* (with Leona Rostenberg), 1975, *Books and Book People in 19th-Century America,* 1978, *Antiquarian Bookselling in the United States: A History from the Origins to the 1940's,* 1985, and several biographies for adults and children. Editor of *Women on the Move,* 1972, *The Victoria Woodhill Reader,* 1974, *Phrenological Dictionary of 19th-Century Americans,* 1982, and three works by Louis May Alcott, *Louisa's Wonder Book,* 1975, *Behind a Mask,* 1975, and *Plots and Counterplots,* 1976. **Essays:** Louisa May Alcott; Mary Noailles Murfree; Harriet Beecher Stowe.

STETCO, Dayana. Graduate assistant in English, Wayne State University, Detroit. Editor of and contributor to *Echinox* and *Poesis.* Author of articles on Harold Pinter, Henry David Thoreau, and modern Romantic literature and of the play *The Old Curiosity Shop,* 1985. **Essays:** Sterling A. Brown; Kenneth Burke; Ed Bullins; Augustin Daly; J.P. Donleavy; Arthur Laurents; David Mamet; Sidney Kingsley; J.F. Powers; Ayn Rand.

STOUCK, David. Professor of English, Simon Fraser University, Burnaby, British Columbia. Author of *Willa Cather's Imagination,* 1975, *Major Canadian Authors,* 1984, and *The Wardells and theVosburghs: Records of a Loyalist Family,* 1986. **Essay:** Sherwood Anderson.

STUCKEY, W.J. Professor of English, Purdue University, West Lafayette, Indiana; associate editor of *Journal of Narrative Technique.* Author of *Pulitzer Prize Novels,* 1966 (revised 1981), and *Caroline Gordon,* 1972. **Essays:** Edna Ferber; Caroline Gordon; Margaret Mitchell; Walker Percy; T.S. Stribling; Edith Wharton; *Old Mortality.*

STULL, James N. Freelance writer. Author of *Literary Selves: Autobiography and Contemporary American Nonfiction* and of articles on John McPhee, Tom Wolfe, Hunter S. Thompson, and American advertising. **Essay:** Tom Wolfe.

SUMMERS, Claude. William E. Stirton Professor in the Humanities and professor of English, University of Michigan-Dearborn. Author of *Christopher Isherwood,* 1980, *E. M. Forster,* 1983, *Gay Fictions, Wilde to Stonewall,* 1990. **Essay:** Elizabeth Bishop; Christopher Isherwood; Richard Wilbur.

SUMMERS, Joseph H. Roswell S. Burrows Professor Emeritus of English, University of Rochester, New York. Author of *George Herbert: Religion and Art,* 1954, *The Muse's Method: An Introduction to Paradise Lost,* 1962, and *The Heirs of Donne and Jonson,* 1970. Editor of *Selected Poems* by Andrew Marvell, 1961, *The Lyric and Dramatic Milton,* 1965, and *Selected Poetry* by George Herbert, 1967. **Essays:** Elizabeth Bishop; Richard Wilber.

SUTRO, Martha. Visiting professor, English Department, University of Montana, Missoula. **Essays:** John Barth; Saul Bellow; Harry Crews; Joy Harjo; Ellen Gilchrist; David Mamet; Joyce Carol Oates; Cynthia Ozick; Thomas Pynchon; Adrienne Rich; Philip Roth; Sam Shepard; Amy Tan; John Updike; Gore Vida; Tom Wolfe; *Darker.*

SWARTZLANDER, Susan. Associate professor of English, Grand Valley State University, Allendale, Michigan. Coeditor of *That Great Sanity: Critical Essays on May Sarton.* Author of essays on May Sarton, James Joyce, George Bernard Shaw, William Faulkner, Thomas Pynchon, and Nathaniel Hawthorne. **Essay:** May Sarton.

TANSELLE, G. Thomas. Vice president, John Simon Guggenheim Foundation, New York; adjunct professor of English, Columbia University, New York; bibliographical editor of *The Writings of Herman Melville* since 1968. Author of *Royall Tyler,* 1967, *Guide to the Study of United States Imprints,* 2 vols., 1971, *The Editing of Historical Documents,* 1978, *Selected Studies in Bibliography,* 1979, *The History of Books as a Field of Study,* 1981, and articles on descriptive bibliography and scholarly editing. **Essay:** Floyd Dell.

THWAITE, Ann. Freelance writer; member of editorial board of *Cricket* magazine. Author of twenty books for children and of two biographies, including *Waiting for the Party: The Life of Frances Hodgson Burnett,* 1974, and *Edmund Gosse: A Literary Landscape,* 1984. Editor of the *Allsorts* series for children, 1969-75, and of *My Oxford,* 1977. **Essay:** Frances Hodgson Burnett.

TOMANENG, Rowena. Graduate student, University of California, Santa Barbara. **Essays:** Janice Mirikitani.

TORRES, Hector Avalos. Associate professor of English andlinguistics, University of New Mexico, Albuquerque. Author of articles on Chicano/Chicana narrative and of *Storytelling Voices: Syntax, Style, and Authority in Contemporary Chicano/A Narrative.* **Essay:** Gary Soto.

TRAVERSI, Derek A. Professor emeritus of English literature, Swarthmore College, Pennsylvania. Author of *An Approach to Shakespeare,* 1938 (revised 1968), *Shakespeare: The Last Phase,* 1954, *Shakespeare: From Richard II to Henry V,* 1957, *Shakespeare: The Roman Plays,* 1963, *T. S. Eliot: The Longer Poems,* 1976, *The Literary Imagination: Studies in Dante, Chaucer, and Shakespeare,* 1982, and *The Canterbury Tales: A Reading,* 1983. **Essays:** T.S. Eliot; *The Waste Land.*

TURNER, Richard C. Professor and chair of English, Indiana University-Purdue University at Indianapolis. **Essays:** Richard Hugo; Adrienne Rich.

UBA, George. Professor of English and chair of Asian-American studies, California State University, Northridge. Former chair of Asian American Literature Discussion Group of the Modern Language Association. Member of the Society for the Study of the Multi-Ethnic Literature of the United States (MELUS), Association for Asian American Studies, and Tian Thi Nga. Author of articles on the poets Marilyn Chin, David Mura, and John Yau and author of poetry published in *Ploughshares, Carolina Quarterly,* and *The Journal of Ethnic Studies.* **Essays:** Jessica Tarahata Hagedorn; Garrett Kaoru Hongo.

VAN DYKE, Annette. Associate professor of interdisciplinary studies and of women's studies, University of Illinois at Springfield. Author of *The Search for a Woman-Centered Spirituality,* 1992, and of articles on Paula Gunn Allen, Louise Erdich, Leslie Marmon Silko, and S. Alice Callahan. **Essays:** Paula Guinn Allen; S. Alice Callahan.

WAGNER-MARTIN, Linda. Adviser. Haines Professor of English, University of North Carolina at Chapel Hill. Author of numerous books, including *The Poems of William Carlos Williams,* 1964, *Denise Levertov,* 1967, *The Prose of William Carlos Williams,* 1970, *Hemingway and Faulkner: Inventors/Masters,* 1975, *Introducing Poems,* 1976, *Hemingway: A Reference Guide,* 1977, *William Carlos Williams: A Reference Guide,* 1978, *John Dos Passos: Artist as American,* 1979, *Ellen Glasgow: Beyond Convention,* 1982, *Sylvia Plath: A Literary Biography,* 1987, *Anne Sexton: Critical Essays,* 1989, *The Modern American Novel,* 1989, *Telling Women's Lines: The New Biography,* 1994, *"Favored Strangers": Gertrude Stein and Her Family,* 1995, and *The Mid-Century American Novel,* 1997. Editor of *Heath Anthology of American Literature* and coeditor of *The Oxford Companion to Women's Writing in the United States.* Editor of works by or about William Faulkner, T. S. Eliot, Ernest Hemingway, William Carlos Williams, Robert Frost, Edith Wharton, and Sylvia Plath. **Essays:** Carolyn Forché; Kaye Gibbons; Anne Sexton; William Carlos Williams; *Ariel; The Sound and the Fury; The Sun Also Rises; Three Lives.*

WALKER, Marshall. Professor of English, University of Waikato, Hamilton, New Zealand. Author of *Robert Penn Warren: A Vision Earned,* 1979, *The Portrait of a Lady: Notes,* 1981, and *The Literature of the United States,* 1983. **Essay:** Chronology.

WALLACH, Mark I. Partner at Calfee, Halter and Geiswold, Cleveland. Author of *Christopher Morley* (with Jon Bracker), 1976, articles on Morley in *Markham Review* and *Dictionary of Literary Biography,* and articles in *Case Western Reserve Law Review* and other periodicals. **Essay:** Christopher Morley.

WALSER, Richard. Professor emeritus of English, North Carolina State University at Raleigh. Author of *Thomas Wolfe: An Introduction and Interpretation,* 1961, *Literary North Carolina,* 1970, *Thomas Wolfe, Undergraduate,* 1977, and *North Carolina Legends,* 1981. Editor or coeditor of *The Enigma of Thomas Wolfe,* 1953, *The Streets of Durham* by Wolfe, 1982, and *Thomas Wolfe Interviewed,* 1985. **Essays:** James Boyd; Paul Green; Thomas Wolfe.

WANG, Qun. Professor of English, California State University, Monterey Bay. Member of the Study of the Multi-Ethnic Literature of the United States (MELUS). Author of two books, *Race, Gender, and Class: Asian American Voices* and *On the Dramatization of the Illusory World in Tennessee Williams, Arthur Miller and Edward Albee's Major Plays,* and of numerous articles on American and American ethnic literature and culture. **Essays:** Charles Johnson; *The Color Purple; Raisin in the Sun.*

WARD, Carol M. Associate professor of English, Clemson University, South Carolina. Author of *Mae West: A Bio-Bibliography,* 1989, and *Rita Mae Brown,* 1993, and of articles about contemporary popular film. **Essay:** Rita Mae Brown.

WARNER, Val. Freelance writer. Author of two books of poems (*Under the Penthouse,* 1973, and *Before Lunch,* 1986) and of articles and reviews. Editor of *Collected Poems and Prose of Charlotte Mew,* 1981, and translator of *Centenary Corbière,* 1974. **Essay:** Shirley Jackson.

WATT, R.J.C. Lecturer in English, University of Dundee, Scotland. Author of articles on contemporary poetry and on textual problems in Shakespeare and of a book on Gerard Manley Hopkins. **Essays:** *The Big Sleep; The Murders in the Rue Morgue.*

WATTS, Harold H. Professor emeritus of English, Purdue University, West Lafayette, Indiana. Author of *The Modern Reader's Guide to the Bible,* 1949, *Ezra Pound and the Cantos,* 1952, *Hound and Quarry,* 1953, *The Modern Reader's Guide to Religions,* 1964, and *Aldous Huxley,* 1969. **Essays:** John Cheever; James Gould Cozzens; Hilda Doolittle; William Gaddis; Jerzy Kosinski; Thomas Pynchon; Wallace Stevens; John Updike; Eudora Welty; *All the King's Men.*

WEALES, Gerald. Professor of English, University of Pennsylvania, Philadelphia; drama critic for the *Reporter* and *Commonweal.* Author of *Religion in Modern English Drama,* 1961, *American Drama since World War II,* 1962, *A Play and Its Parts,* 1964, *Tennessee Williams,* 1965, *The Jumping-Off Place: American Drama in the 1960's,* 1969, *Clifford Odets,* 1971 (revised 1985), and *Canned Goods as Caviar: American Film Comedy in the 1930's,* 1985. Editor of several collections of plays and essays and of *The Complete Plays of William Wycherley,* 1966. **Essays:** Philip Barry; Robert Benchley; Arthur Kopit; Arthur Miller; Clifford Odets; James Whitcomb Riley; James Thurber; Mercy Warren; E.B. White; Tennessee Williams.

WEIR, Sybil B. Professor of English and American studies, San Jose State University, California. Author of articles on Theodore Dreiser, Gertrude Atherton, Constance Fenimore Woolson, and Elizabeth Drew Stoddard. **Essay:** Gertrude Atherton.

WESLEY, Marilyn C. Assistant professor of English, Hartwick College, Oneonta, New York. Author of *Refusal and Transgression in Joyce Carol Oates' Fiction,* 1993, and of articles on Tobias Wolff, Anne Hebert, and Emma Tennant. **Essay:** Joyce Carol Oates.

WESTBROOK, Perry D. Professor emeritus of English, State University of New York at Albany. Author of *Acres of Flint: Writers of New England,* 1951 (revised 1981), *Biography of an Island,* 1958, *The Greatness of Man: An Essay on Dostoevsky and Whitman,* 1961, *Mary Ellen Chase,* 1966, *Mary Wilkins Free-*

man, 1967, *John Burroughs*, 1974, *William Bradford*, 1978, and *Free Will and Determinism in American Literature*, 1979. Coeditor of *The Writing Women of New England*, 1982, and *The New England Town in Fact and Fiction*, 1982. **Essays:** Edward Bellamy; William Bradford; Mary E. Wilkins Freeman; Sarah Orne Jewett; *Leaves of Grass; Nature; The Rise of Silas Lapham; U.S.A.; Walden.*

WILD, Peter. Professor of English, University of Arizona, Tucson. Author of *The Afternoon in Dismay*, 1968, *New and Selected Poems*, 1973, *The Cloning*, 1974, *Chihuahua*, 1976, *Pioneer Conservations of Western America*, 1979, *Wilderness*, 1980, *James Welch*, 1983, *The Saguaro Forest*, 1986, and *The Brides of Christ*, 1991. Editor of *The Desert Reader*, 1991, and *The Autobiography of John C. Van Dyke*, 1993. **Essays:** James Welch; *Winter in the Blood.*

WILLIAMS, Wade. Assistant professor, Department of English, University of Puget Sound, Tacoma, Washington. **Essay:** Rudolfo A. Anaya.

WILOCH, Denise. Freelance writer. **Essays:** Maya Angelou; Joseph Heller; Jerzy Kosinski; Norman Mailer; W.S. Merwin; Walker Percy; Thomas Pynchon; Sam Shepard.

WINNIFRITH, T.J. Senior lecturer in English, University of Warwick, Coventry, England. Author or coauthor of *The Brontës and Their Background: Romance and Reality*, 1973, *The Brontës*, 1977, *Brontë Facts and Brontë Problems*, 1983, and *1984 and All's Well?*, 1984. Coeditor of *Aspects of the Epic*, 1983, *Greece Old and New*, 1983, *Selected Brontë Poems*, 1983, and works by Charlotte and Branwell Brontë. **Essay:** Lionel Trilling.

WONG, Shelley Sunn. Assistant professor of English and of Asian-American studies, Cornell University, Ithaca, New York. Author of articles on Charles Olson, Mina Loy, and Theresa Hak Kyung Cha. **Essay:** Frank Chin.

WOO, Miseong. Ph.D. candidate in theater and drama at University of Wisconsin-Madison. **Essay:** Genny Lim.

WOODRESS, James. Professor of English, University of California, Davis. Author of *Howells and Italy*, 1952, *Booth Tarkington*, 1955, *A Yankee's Odyssey: The Life of Joel Barlow*, 1958, *Dissertations in American Literature*, 1962, *Willa Cather:*

Her Life and Art, 1970, *American Fiction 1900-1950: A Guide to Information Sources*, 1975, and *Willa Cather: A Literary Life*, 1987. Editor or coeditor of *Voices from America's Past*, 1961, *Eight American Authors*, 1971, *The Troll Garden* by Cather, 1983, and *Critical Essays on Whitman*, 1983. **Essays:** Henry Adams; Joel Barlow; Willa Cather; Hamlin Garland; E.W. Howe; Thomas Jefferson; Frank Norris; Kenneth Roberts; Karl Shapiro; Booth Tarkington; Walt Whitman; *Common Sense; The Jungle; The Red Badge of Courage.*

WYRICK, Laura. Ph.D. candidate at Wayne State University, Detroit. **Essay:** Sara Paretsky.

YOUNG, Kenneth. Late literary and political adviser to Beaverbrook Newspapers, London; former editor of the *Yorkshire Post*, England. Author of *D. H. Lawrence*, 1952, *John Dryden*, 1954, *Ford Madox Ford*, 1958, *A. J. Balfour*, 1963, *Churchill and Beaverbrook*, 1966, *The Greek Passion: A Study in People and Politics*, 1969, *Sir Alec Douglas-Home*, 1970, *Stanley Baldwin*, 1976, *A Neighbourhood of Writers*, 1981, and other biographies, literary studies, and political and social histories. Editor of *Diaries of Sir Robert Bruce Lockhart*, 2 vols., 1973-80. Died 1985. **Essay:** Henry Miller.

YOUNG, Thomas Daniel. Gertrude Conway Vanderbilt Professor of English, Vanderbilt University, Nashville. Author or coauthor of *The Literature of the South*, 1952, *Donald Davidson: An Essay and a Bibliography*, 1965, *American Literature: A Critical Survey*, 1968, *John Crowe Ransom: Critical Essays and a Bibliography*, 1968, *Ransome*, 1971, *Davidson*, 1971, *Gentleman in a Dustcoat: A Biography of John Crowe Ransom*, 1976, *Tennessee Writers*, 1977, *The Vocation of Letters in America*, 1981, *The Past in the Present*, 1981, *Waking Their Neighbors Up: The Nashville Agrarians Rediscovered*, 1982, and *Ransom: An Annotated Bibliography*, 1982. Editor or coeditor of *The Literary Correspondence of Donald Davidson and Allen Tate*, 1971, *The New Criticism and After*, 1976, *Conversations with Malcolm Cowley*, 1986, and selected essays and letters of Ransom. **Essays:** Donald Davidson; John Crowe Ransom; *Absalom, Absalom!; The Great Gatsby.*

ZLOGAR, Laura Weiss. Professor of English, University of Wisconsin-River Falls. Author of articles on Amiri Baraka and Amy Tan, as well as on the works *Beloved, The Bluest Eye, Ceremony, Daughters, Jazz,* and *Praisesong for the Widow.* **Essay:** Paule Marshall; *I Know Why the Caged Bird Sings.*

ISBN 1-55862-417-1

90000

9 781558 624177